MAGAZINES
FOR
LIBRARIES™

This edition of
Magazines for Libraries 22nd edition
was prepared by ProQuest's Serials Editorial Department

Editorial
Laurie Kaplan, Director, Serials
Ewa Kowalska and Valerie Mahon, Managers, Metadata Services
Martha David, Metadata QA Analyst
Christopher King, Metadata Librarian Lead
Shawn Chen and Pappaparvathi Patham, Senior Metadata Librarians
Halyna Testerman, Filippo Valli, and Michael Weingardner, Metadata Librarians
O'Sheila Delgado, Provider Relations Specialist
Enrique Diaz and Christine Oka, Assistant Editors, Content and Development

MAGAZINES
FOR
LIBRARIES ™

TWENTY-SECOND EDITION

Edited by Cheryl LaGuardia

created by

Bill Katz

For the general reader and
school, junior college, college, university
and public libraries

Reviewing the best publications
for all serials collections
since 1969

ProQuest®

Start here.

Published by ProQuest LLC
Copyright © 2013 by ProQuest LLC
All rights reserved
Printed and bound in the United States of America

International Standard Book Numbers
ISBN 13: 978-1-60030-645-7
International Standard Serial Number 0000-0914
Library of Congress Catalog Card Number 86-640971

ISBN 978-1-60030-645-7

9 781600 306457

90000

CONTENTS

CONTENTS

PREFACE

DORA is Big News in Science

The San Francisco Declaration on Research Assessment (DORA) was developed by a number of scholarly journal editors and publishers during the Annual Meeting of the American Society for Cell Biology (ASCB) in San Francisco, CA, on December 16, 2012. Their goal was to improve the ways in which scientific research is evaluated by funding agencies, academic institutions, and others, particularly with respect to the Journal Impact Factor. In their declaration, the group reminds us that "the Journal Impact Factor, as calculated by Thomson Reuters, was originally created as a tool to help librarians identify journals to purchase, not as a measure of the scientific quality of research in an article." I'm wondering just how many of us now in the library profession are aware of that fact. The group went on to note that "the Journal Impact Factor has a number of well-documented deficiencies as a tool for research assessment. These limitations include: A) citation distributions within journals are highly skewed ; B) the properties of the Journal Impact Factor are field-specific: it is a composite of multiple, highly diverse article types, including primary research papers and reviews ; C) Journal Impact Factors can be manipulated (or "gamed") by editorial policy ; and D) data used to calculate the Journal Impact Factors are neither transparent nor openly available to the public ." The declaration includes recommendations for "improving the way in which the quality of research output is evaluated." You will find the Declaration at http://am.ascb.org/dora/, where you can read it, download it, sign it, and see just who else has signed it. SPARC gave their July 2013 Innovator award to the creators of DORA; read about it at http://sparc.arl.org/initiatives/innovator.

Open Access: on a Faster Track?

Numbers alone do not tell the full tale of what's been happening with Open Access over the past year. Going to the *Directory of Open Access Journals* (in this, its 10th year of existence), you'll find 9,904 journals listed as of September 15, 2013. That's a 22% increase in the number of titles listed since last year at this time, when *DOAJ* listed 8,148 journals. Compared to the increase from 2011 to 2012 (+16%) it's a modest climb in numbers, especially compared to the two previous years' increases (from 2010 to 2011 the increase was 29%; from 2009 to 2010 the increase was 24%).

Policy changes may actually reveal Open Access'] most recent progress. For example, on July 24, 2013, the University of California Academic Senate passed an Open Access

Policy, "ensuring that future research articles authored by faculty at all 10 campuses of UC will be made available to the public at no charge" with the Council's stated intent "to make these articles widely — and freely — available in order to advance research everywhere." This green, self-archiving OA policy covers over 8,000 UC faculty and about 40,000 publications a year from "the largest public research university in the world." Of especial note is the fact that UC's faculty members "receive roughly 8%of all research funding in the U.S." and that "the ten UC campuses generate around 2-3% of all the peer-reviewed articles published in the world every year." [from the UC press release, http://senate.universityofcalifornia.edu/open_access_press_release_2013.pdf]

That press release went on to state, "The adoption of this policy across the UC system also signals to scholarly publishers that open access, in terms defined by faculty and not by publishers, must be part of any future scholarly publishing system. The faculty remains committed to working with publishers to transform the publishing landscape in ways that are sustainable and beneficial to both the University and the public."

As clear as this may sound, some confusion appears to be arising about just what the policy actually means. There's an interesting post by David Wojick -- "Some University of California Open Access Policy Confusions" (http://scholarlykitchen.sspnet.org/2013/08/22/some-university-of-california-oa-policy-confusions/) -- with just as interesting comments, to be found on *The Scholarly Kitchen* blog. The post, along with the comments, highlights important points in the publication process that can impede or advance the applicability of true Open Access.

If you'd like to get some contextual help in understanding the choices that authors can make for Open Access, you might want to take a look at the University of Cambridge's "My Options" page for Open Access, https://www.openaccess.cam.ac.uk/. Just input the title of a journal and go through the menus to see what kinds of actual considerations, and options, may be available to paper authors.

Altmetrics: the Thick Plottens

Citation analysis and journal impact factors have continued to be the gold standards for measuring scholarly impact, but given the creation of DORA, along with the growing perception that citations alone don't reveal the quality of research, other methods of assessing the quality of journal articles are coming into play more strongly than in the past. Altmetrics have become much more than just a buzzword in the field, so much so that some folks have figured out ways to game them – thus compromising the integrity of the data and undoing the information to be gained from them. That has led to some other folks developing ways of thwarting the gamers, while others try to prove a correlation between altmetrics and citation analysis.

The fact that uses of social media and other alternative metric sources are proliferating at a great rate, especially among newer scholars, means that altmetrics are probably going to be around, and used, for quite a while. Here are a few articles and papers that can fill you in quickly on some of the issues being confronted within the academy in considering the use of altmetrics, both their promises and pitfalls. These are issues with which every librarian will want to be conversant, especially those of us working closely with journals:

- Delgado Lopez-Cozar, Emilio; Nicolas Robinson-Garcia; Daniel Torres Salinas, *Manipulating Google Scholar Citations and Google Scholar Metrics: simple, easy and tempting*, EC3 Working Papers 6, May 29, 2012, http://arxiv.org/abs/1212.0638.
- Howard, Jennifer, "Rise of 'Altmetrics' Revives Questions about How to Measure Impact of Research," *Chronicle of Higher Education*, June 3, 2013, http://chronicle.com/article/Rise-of-Altmetrics-Revives/139557/.
- Konkiel, Stacey, "Altmetrics: A 21st-Century Solution to Determining Research Quality," *ONLINE SEARCHER*, July/August 2013 Issue, http://tinyurl.com/lrvlu6g.
- Lin, Jennifer, "A Case Study in Anti-Gaming Mechanisms for Altmetrics: PLoS ALMs and DataTrust," *ACM Web Science Conference 2012 Workshop*, Evanston, IL, 21 June 2012, http://altmetrics.org/altmetrics12/lin/.
- Piwowar, Heather, Guest Editor, "Altmetrics: What, Why and Where?," *ASIS&T Bulletin*, April/May 2013, http://www.asis.org/Bulletin/Apr-13/AprMay13_Piwowar.html.
  m_bulThelwall, Mike; Stefanie Haustein; Vincent Larivière; Cassidy R. Sugimoto, "Do Altmetrics Work? Twitter and Ten Other Social Web Services," *PLOS ONE*, May 28, 2013, http://tinyurl.com/kn8cuo3.

Another source that may be particularly helpful is SPARC's *Article-Level Metrics Primer*, published in April 2013, the PDF of which is located at http://sparc.arl.org/sites/default/files/sparc-alm-primer.pdf. It describes how ALMs "pull from two distinct data streams: scholarly visibility and social visibility," combining altmetrics with more traditional citation metrics rather than relying solely on social media.

Pricing Increases: Just How Much?

Just how much have journal prices increased in recent years? Well, that depends upon a number of factors and upon which data you rely. According to Paula Gantz in her recently published report: "Digital Licenses Replace Print Prices as Accurate Reflection of Real Journal Costs," *Professional / Scholarly Publishing (PSP) Bulletin*, Volume 11, No. 3, Summer / Fall 2012, http://publishers.org/_attachments/docs/library/2012%20bulletin.pdf, "the effective price of an average journal in 2010 only 9% higher than in 1990." Ms. Gantz notes in that report that, "...using list prices of print subscriptions to calculate the real increase in serials expenditures is a misleading and inaccurate method for tracking how libraries are spending their serials budgets and fails to recognize the increased value they are receiving from the print-to-digital transition."

In their *Library Journal*, April 25, 2013 report, "Winds of Change / Periodicals Price Survey 2013," http://lj.libraryjournal.com/2013/04/publishing/the-winds-of-change-periodicals-price-survey-2013/, Stephen Bosch & Kittie Henderson note that, "in article, directly questions the validity of this study (the LJ Periodicals Price Survey) by suggesting that the "effective" price increase for an average journal was only 9% higher in 2010 as compared to 1990, not the six-fold increase documented over the years in this price study. There are good points raised by Gantz concerning the increased value derived from digital licenses and how the increase in research has resulted in increased content. There do need to be more substantive discussions concerning these issues and the failure of libraries to secure their piece of the research funding pie. However, the contention that the effective price of the average journal has only increased 9% and that the price of journals accessed in the UK has actually gone down 11% since 2004 cannot be accepted without much more data substantiating those claims. After searching the reports cited in the UK study, no reference to the cited data could be found. If this is derived data then the source for the primary data and the methodology used to derive the figure need to be documented."

Bosch and Henderson go on to note, "Those who have been involved with purchasing serials in the last 20 years know that serial prices have increased significantly and represent the largest inflationary factor for library budgets. To suggest that the real increase in serial prices is only 9% flies in the face of reality. The author derived the figure by using data from ARL that reported changes in the number of purchased serials and serial expenditures for the period 1990–2010. While the data does show that the numerical value resulting from dividing expenditures by the number of purchased serials did increase 9% over that period, to conclude that prices only increased 9% is incorrect. Between 1990 and 2010, ARL changed the definition of purchased serials. In 1990, the definition was based on subscribed titles. In 2010, the definition used by ARL had changed considerably: "Report the total number of unique serial titles, NOT SUBSCRIPTIONS, that you currently acquire and to which you provide access.... Report each title once, regardless of how many subscriptions or means of access you provide for that title" (definitions for 2010 and 2011 are essentially unchanged)."

Whatever the exact increase is, it can be generally acknowledged that library budgets have not kept up at the rate of increase in journal title costs, and that makes journal cuts inevitable for most every library. I've been hearing more and more of late from librarians around the country and around the world that they are finding *Magazines for Libraries* to be the source they rely on not just in terms of making those cuts, but also in justifying them when combined with data about local factors specific to their situations. That's a responsibility all of us who create *MFL* take very seriously as we continue to select core serial publications for libraries.

Thank you!

My thanks for this edition go to a number of folks, including the librarians who get in touch about ideas for MFL; the many authors who create the superb chapters within the book; Chris Oka and Enrique Diaz, the *MFL* associate editors who help with all the "heavy lifting" involved in each edition; and to Mike Weingardner and Laurie Kaplan from the Serials Solutions unit of ProQuest, who make this work possible.

Cheryl LaGuardia, Cambridge, Massachusetts, September 2013

STATISTICS FROM THE TWENTY-SECOND EDITION

Statistical information on the content of *Magazines for Libraries* continues a feature first introduced in the twelfth edition. The presentation of this information on recommended titles and their publishers is provided as the basis for further analysis-not only of the titles included in or excluded from the current edition of *Magazines for Libraries*, but of trends in the serials publishing industry.

All data in the charts and tables should be evaluated by the individual reader within the context of his or her own collection decision-making.

A Closer Look at Publishers and Their Titles

This twenty-second edition includes 5,341 titles produced by publishers of all types and sizes - from large commercial publishers, society and association publishers and university presses, to publishing startups and newsletter self-publishers. Overall, 2,393 publishers and imprints are represented. While the vast majority of publishers are those with 4 or fewer titles in *MFL*, there are 117 publishers with 5 or more titles selected for this edition.

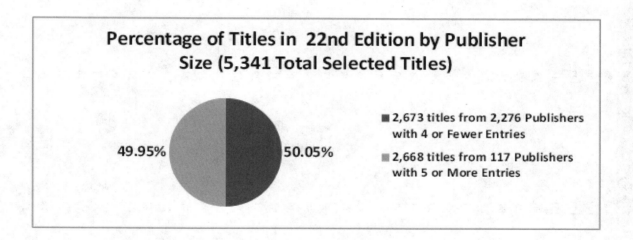

Percentage of Titles in 22nd Edition by Publisher Size (5,341 Total Selected Titles)

49.95%   50.05%

■ 2,673 titles from 2,276 Publishers with 4 or Fewer Entries

■ 2,668 titles from 117 Publishers with 5 or More Entries

A focused analysis of the 117 publishers with 5 or more entries is provided in **Table 1**, which includes the number of selected titles by feature and format availability. **Table 1** also includes aggregate information on the titles from publishers with 4 or fewer entries.

Table 2 includes a report on the number of publishers in each *MFL* subject chapter. As a benchmark of journal availability and the specific recommendations of the subject section contributors, **Table 3** and **Table 4** contain lists of each of the titles deleted since the last edition of *MFL*, sorted by publisher and by *MFL* subject. The prior edition's record sequence number is provided in both tables to allow the reader to reference the complete listing for a specific title in the older edition.

Commercial Publishers of Scholarly Journals

It is not surprising to see the names and imprints of prominent commercial publishers included in the list of companies with 5 or more entries in *Magazines for Libraries* (*see* **Table 1**). These names represent publishers in the professional publishing market with large portfolios of titles available for consideration. Their titles include scientific/technical, legal, business, and medical journals utilized by university and college students, professionals in specific research disciplines, and consumers seeking authoritative sources of scholarly information. Many of these companies and their imprints are among the top journal publishers overall.

Table 1 / Publishers with 5 or More Titles in This Edition

Publisher	Number of Titles	Number of Refereed Titles	Percentage Refereed	Number of Online Titles	Percentage Online
Routledge	300	284	95%	300	100%
Wiley-Blackwell Publishing, Inc.	148	136	92%	148	100%
Sage Publications, Inc.	125	123	98%	125	100%
Wiley-Blackwell Publishing Ltd.	121	114	94%	121	100%
Oxford University Press	96	93	97%	95	99%
Pergamon	95	92	97%	94	99%
Cambridge University Press	89	76	85%	89	100%
Springer New York LLC	87	82	94%	87	100%
Sage Publications Ltd.	84	81	96%	84	100%
Elsevier BV	80	76	95%	80	100%
Springer Netherlands	69	66	96%	69	100%
Taylor & Francis Inc.	43	38	88%	43	100%
Springer	42	40	95%	42	100%
Institute of Electrical and Electronics Engineers	41	22	54%	41	100%
John Wiley & Sons, Inc.	40	35	88%	40	100%
University of Chicago Press	38	38	100%	38	100%
Academic Press	37	37	100%	37	100%
The Johns Hopkins University Press	37	34	92%	37	100%
Emerald Group Publishing Ltd.	36	35	97%	36	100%
John Wiley & Sons Ltd.	33	31	94%	33	100%
Elsevier Ltd	32	29	91%	32	100%
Taylor & Francis	32	27	84%	32	100%
Duke University Press	29	24	83%	29	100%
American Psychological Association	27	24	89%	27	100%
Elsevier Inc.	27	24	89%	27	100%
American Chemical Society	25	24	96%	25	100%
Elsevier BV, North-Holland	23	23	100%	23	100%
Lippincott Williams & Wilkins	23	20	87%	23	100%
Source Interlink Companies	22	0	0%	20	91%
University of California Press, Journals Division	22	21	95%	22	100%
University of Illinois Press	19	19	100%	19	100%
Indiana University Press	18	14	78%	18	100%
University of Toronto Press, Journals Division	18	18	100%	18	100%
BioMed Central Ltd.	17	17	100%	17	100%
Hearst Magazines	17	0	0%	17	100%
Institute of Physics Publishing Ltd.	17	16	94%	17	100%
Scholastic Inc.	17	0	0%	17	100%

Publisher					
American Library Association	16	6	38%	16	100%
Bonnier Corp.	16	0	0%	16	100%
M.E. Sharpe, Inc.	16	16	100%	16	100%
Nature Publishing Group	15	14	93%	15	100%
M I T Press	14	11	79%	14	100%
Maney Publishing	14	13	93%	14	100%
Penton Media, Inc.	14	0	0%	14	100%
American Institute of Physics	13	12	92%	13	100%
Brill	13	12	92%	13	100%
Conde Nast Publications, Inc.	13	0	0%	13	100%
American Accounting Association	12	6	50%	12	100%
Annual Reviews	12	12	100%	12	100%
Association for Computing Machinery, Inc.	12	7	58%	11	92%
ePals Publishing Company	12	0	0%	11	92%
F + W Media Inc.	12	0	0%	12	100%
American Physical Society	11	11	100%	11	100%
B N P Media	11	0	0%	11	100%
Meredith Corporation	11	0	0%	8	73%
Time Inc.	11	0	0%	11	100%
American Meteorological Society	10	9	90%	10	100%
BowTie, Inc.	10	0	0%	4	40%
Human Kinetics, Inc.	10	10	100%	10	100%
Kalmbach Publishing Co.	10	0	0%	8	80%
Interweave Press, LLC.	9	0	0%	9	100%
N R C Research Press	9	9	100%	9	100%
American Institute of Aeronautics and Astronautics, Inc.	8	7	88%	8	100%
Baywood Publishing Co., Inc.	8	8	100%	8	100%
Hanley Wood, LLC	8	0	0%	7	88%
Palgrave Macmillan Ltd.	8	8	100%	8	100%
R S C Publications	8	8	100%	8	100%
Walter de Gruyter GmbH & Co. KG	8	6	75%	8	100%
Weider History Group	8	0	0%	8	100%
Wiley - V C H Verlag GmbH & Co. KGaA	8	8	100%	8	100%
Wiley-Blackwell Publishing Asia	8	7	88%	8	100%
American Society of Civil Engineers	7	7	100%	7	100%
C C H Inc.	7	0	0%	7	100%
Crain Communications, Inc.	7	0	0%	7	100%
Cygnus Business Media, Inc.	7	0	0%	7	100%
De Gruyter Mouton	7	7	100%	7	100%

Table 1 / Publishers with 5 or More Titles in This Edition

Publisher	Number of Titles	Number of Refereed Titles	Percentage Refereed	Number of Online Titles	Percentage Online
Hindawi Publishing Corporation	7	7	100%	7	100%
Mary Ann Liebert, Inc. Publishers	7	7	100%	7	100%
National Council of Teachers of English	7	7	100%	7	100%
Optical Society of America	7	6	86%	7	100%
University of Wisconsin Press, Journal Division	7	7	100%	7	100%
W.B. Saunders Co.	7	7	100%	7	100%
B M J Group	6	6	100%	6	100%
Belvoir Media Group, LLC	6	0	0%	6	100%
Edinburgh University Press Ltd.	6	6	100%	6	100%
Georgetown University Law Center	6	5	83%	5	83%
Haymarket Publishing Ltd.	6	0	0%	5	83%
Informa Healthcare	6	6	100%	6	100%
Institute for Operations Research and the Management Sciences (I N F O R M S)	6	6	100%	6	100%
Pennsylvania State University Press	6	5	83%	6	100%
PennWell Corporation	6	0	0%	6	100%
Rodale, Inc.	6	0	0%	5	83%
University of Nebraska Press	6	6	100%	6	100%
University of Texas Press, Journals Division	6	5	83%	6	100%
A S M E International	5	4	80%	5	100%
American Fisheries Society	5	5	100%	5	100%
American Real Estate Society	5	4	80%	5	100%
American Society for Microbiology	5	5	100%	5	100%
Cell Press	5	5	100%	5	100%
Copernicus GmbH	5	5	100%	5	100%
DanceMedia, LLC.	5	0	0%	5	100%
Elsevier Ltd., Trends Journals	5	5	100%	5	100%
Geological Society of America	5	4	80%	5	100%
Inderscience Publishers	5	5	100%	5	100%
Institute of Mathematical Statistics	5	5	100%	5	100%
Institutional Investor, Inc.	5	0	0%	5	100%
M A I K Nauka - Interperiodica	5	4	80%	5	100%
Multi-Science Publishing Co. Ltd.	5	5	100%	5	100%
National Geographic Society	5	0	0%	4	80%
Philosophy Documentation Center	5	5	100%	5	100%
Society of American Foresters	5	4	80%	5	100%
The Taunton Press, Inc.	5	0	0%	3	60%

TransWorld Media	5	0	0%	4	80%
University of California, Berkeley, School of Law	5	5	100%	5	100%
University of Hawaii Press	5	5	100%	5	100%
University of North Carolina Press	5	5	100%	5	100%
W G & L Financial Reporting & Management Research	5	0	0%	5	100%
Publishers (117) with 5 or more titles	**2668**	**2213**	**83%**	**2643**	**99%**
Publishers (2276) with 4 or fewer titles	**2673**	**910**	**34%**	**2108**	**79%**
All publishers	**5341**	**3123**	**58%**	**4751**	**89%**

Table 2 / No. of Publishers by MFL Subject

Section	No. of Publishers
ACCOUNTING AND TAXATION	36
ADVERTISING, MARKETING, AND PUBLIC RELATIONS	22
AERONAUTICS AND SPACE SCIENCE	39
AFRICA	43
AFRICAN AMERICAN	58
AGRICULTURE	30
ANIMAL RIGHTS/ANIMAL WELFARE	7
ANIME, COMICS, GRAPHIC NOVELS, AND MANGA	10
ANTHROPOLOGY	18
ANTIQUES	19
ARCHAEOLOGY	29
ARCHITECTURE	49
ARCHIVES AND MANUSCRIPTS	14
ART	65
ASIA AND THE PACIFIC	13
ASIAN AMERICAN	9
ASTROLOGY	5
ASTRONOMY	50
ATMOSPHERIC SCIENCES	22
AUTOMOBILES AND MOTORCYCLES	25
BEER, WINE, AND SPIRITS	15
BIBLIOGRAPHY	19
BIOLOGY	29
BIOTECHNOLOGY	16
BIRDS	20
BLIND AND VISUALLY IMPAIRED	15
BOATS AND BOATING	20
BOOKS AND BOOK REVIEWS	22
BOTANY	13
BUILDING AND CONSTRUCTION	11
BUSINESS AND FINANCE	88
CANADA	37
CARTOGRAPHY, GIS, AND IMAGERY	15
CHEMISTRY	14
CHILDREN	39
CIVIL LIBERTIES	22
CLASSICAL STUDIES	12
CLASSROOM MAGAZINES	14
COMMUNICATION	19
COMPUTERS AND INFORMATION TECHNOLOGY	25
COOKING AND COOKERY	14
CRAFT	20
CRIMINOLOGY AND LAW ENFORCEMENT	23
CULTURAL STUDIES	35
DANCE	12
DEATH AND DYING	16
DISABILITIES	12
DO-IT-YOURSELF	8
EARTH SCIENCES AND GEOLOGY	45

Table 2 / No. of Publishers by MFL Subject (cont.)

Section	No. of Publishers
ECOLOGY	14
ECONOMICS	22
EDUCATION	83
ELECTRONICS	28
ENERGY	32
ENGINEERING AND TECHNOLOGY	42
ENVIRONMENT AND CONSERVATION	23
EUROPE	26
FAMILY	11
FAMILY PLANNING	5
FASHION AND LIFESTYLE	12
FICTION: GENERAL/MYSTERY AND DETECTIVE	20
FICTION: SCIENCE FICTION, FANTASY, AND HORROR	42
FILMS	35
FIRE PROTECTION	7
FISH, FISHERIES, AND AQUACULTURE	17
FISHING	10
FOLKLORE	21
FOOD AND NUTRITION	8
FOOD INDUSTRY	8
FORENSICS	6
FORESTRY	28
GAMES AND GAMING	14
GARDENING	17
GAY, LESBIAN, BISEXUAL, AND TRANSGENDER	8
GENDER STUDIES	44
GENEALOGY	11
GENERAL INTEREST	21
GEOGRAPHY	24
GERIATRICS AND GERONTOLOGICAL STUDIES	22
GLOBALIZATION	12
GOVERNMENT PERIODICALS;b1FEDERAL	14
GOVERNMENT PERIODICALS;b1STATE AND LOCAL	56
HEALTH AND FITNESS	16
HEALTH CARE ADMINISTRATION	11
HEALTH PROFESSIONS	9
HIKING, CLIMBING, AND OUTDOOR RECREATION	9
HISTORY	19
HOME	10
HORSES	22
HOSPITALITY/RESTAURANT	13
HUMAN RESOURCES	5
HUMOR	7
HUNTING AND GUNS	8
INFORMATICS	8
INTERDISCIPLINARY STUDIES	7
INTERIOR DESIGN AND DECORATION	10
INTERNATIONAL MAGAZINES	24
JOURNALISM AND WRITING	25

Table 2 / No. of Publishers by MFL Subject (cont.)

Section	No. of Publishers
LABOR AND INDUSTRIAL RELATIONS	34
LANDSCAPE ARCHITECTURE	12
LATIN AMERICA AND SPAIN	41
LATINO STUDIES	16
LAW	76
LIBRARY AND INFORMATION SCIENCE	37
LINGUISTICS	22
LITERARY REVIEWS	52
LITERATURE	54
LITTLE MAGAZINES	25
MANAGEMENT AND ADMINISTRATION	25
MARINE SCIENCE AND TECHNOLOGY	47
MARRIAGE AND DIVORCE	6
MATHEMATICS	20
MEDIA AND AV	10
MEDICINE	20
MENOPAUSE/ANDROPAUSE	4
MIDDLE EAST	13
MILITARY	45
MODEL MAKING	10
MULTICULTURAL STUDIES	9
MUSIC	42
MUSIC REVIEWS	6
NATIVE AMERICANS	12
NEWS AND OPINION	26
NEWSPAPERS	14
NUMISMATICS	7
NURSING	7
OCCUPATIONS AND CAREERS	8
PALEONTOLOGY	7
PARANORMAL	7
PARENTING	15
PEACE AND CONFLICT STUDIES	15
PETS	21
PHILATELY	8
PHILOSOPHY	41
PHOTOGRAPHY	10
PHYSICS	20
PHYSIOLOGY	4
POLITICAL SCIENCE	18
POPULATION STUDIES	7
PREGNANCY	7
PRINTING AND GRAPHIC ARTS	24
PSYCHOLOGY	32
PUBLIC HEALTH	17
REAL ESTATE	16
RELIGION	54
ROBOTICS	23
SAFETY	6

Table 2 / No. of Publishers by MFL Subject (cont.)

Section	No. of Publishers
SCIENCE AND TECHNOLOGY	27
SEXUALITY	19
SLAVIC STUDIES	26
SOCIAL MEDIA	3
SOCIOLOGY AND SOCIAL WORK	42
SPIRITUALITY AND WELL-BEING	9
SPORTS	59
STATISTICS	21
TEENAGERS	10
TELEVISION, VIDEO, AND RADIO	12
THEATER	16
TRANSPORTATION	63
TRAVEL AND TOURISM	12
URBAN STUDIES	22
VETERINARY SCIENCE	19
WEDDINGS	7
WORLD WIDE WEB	11
ZOOLOGY	20

Table 3 / Titles Deleted Since the Last Edition, by Publishers

Publisher	Title	ISSN	21st Edition Sequence No.
A N S I Network	International Journal of Applied Economics and Finance	1991-0886	1131
A S M E International	Journal of Biomechanical Engineering	0148-0731	2170
Academic Press	Developmental Review	0273-2297	4653
Academic Press	Journal of Vocational Behavior	0001-8791	4702
Academy Science Publishers	Discovery and Innovation	1015-079X	196
Acadian Genealogy Exchange	Acadian Genealogy Exchange	0199-9591	2735
Access Intelligence, LLC	Studio/Monthly	1554-3412	3940
Acoustical Society of America	J A S A Express Letters		4464
Aero - News Network	Aero - News network	1530-9339	110
Alabama Genealogical Society	Alabama Genealogical Society Magazine	0568-806X	2763
American Association for State and Local History	History News	0363-7492	3119
American College of Forensic Psychiatry	American Journal of Forensic Psychology	0733-1290	4613
American Institute of Aeronautics and Astronautics, Inc.	Journal of Aerospace Computing, Information, and Communication	1542-9423	141
American Institute of Physics	Virtual Journal of Applications of Superconductivity	1553-9636	4513
American Institute of Physics	Virtual Journal of Atomic Quantum Fluids	1935-4061	4514
American Institute of Physics	Virtual Journal of Ultrafast Science	1553-9601	4518
American Mathematical Society	American Mathematical Society. Journal	0894-0347	3913
American Mathematical Society	American Mathematical Society. Transactions	0002-9947	3914
American Orff-Schulwerk Association	Orff Echo	0095-2613	4125
American Physical Society	Virtual Journal of Biological Physics Research	1553-9628	4515
American Physical Society	Virtual Journal of Nanoscale Science & Technology	1553-9644	4516
American Physical Society	Virtual Journal of Quantum Information	1553-961X	4517
American Psychological Association	Consulting psychology journal	1065-9293	4647
American Psychological Association	Psychoanalytic Psychology	0736-9735	4715
American Psychological Association	Psychological Methods	1082-989X	4720
American Psychological Association	Psychology, Public Policy, and Law	1076-8971	4727
American Psychological Association	Rehabilitation Psychology	0090-5550	4733
American Psychological Association	School Psychology Quarterly	1045-3830	4734
American Society of Appraisers, Business Valuation Committee	Business Valuation Review	0897-1781	7
Ammons Scientific Ltd.	Psychological Reports	0033-2941	4721
Arkansas Genealogical Society, Inc.	Arkansas Family Historian	0571-0472	2764
Art of Eating	Art of Eating	0895-6200	1507
Art U S	Art U S	1546-7082	522
Association for Computing Machinery, Inc.	Ubiquity	1530-2180	2209
Association for the Advancement of Computing in Education	Journal of Educational Multimedia and Hypermedia	1055-8896	3936
Association for Transpersonal Psychology	Journal of Transpersonal Psychology	0022-524X	4701
At-Home Dad	At-Home Dad	1081-5767	4261
Australian Institute of Genealogical Studies, Inc.	Genealogist	0311-1776	2741
AVWeb	AVWeb		124
B B C, African Service	Focus on Africa	0959-9576	200
Badgerdog Literary Publishing, Inc.	American Short Fiction	1051-4813	2374

Publisher	Publication	ISSN	No.
Baywood Publishing Co., Inc.	Journal of Recreational Mathematics	0022-412X	3898
Behaviorists for Social Responsibility	Behavior and Social Issues	1064-9506	4626
Black Raven Press	Mystery News	0734-9076	2392
Bongo Productions	Beat (Los Angeles)	1063-5319	4136
Boston Common Press	Cook's Country	1552-1990	1510
BowTie, Inc.	Aquarium Fish International	1942-5678	4302
Brent H. Holcomb, Ed. & Pub.	South Carolina Magazine of Ancestral Research	0190-826X	2796
Brigham Young University, College of Humanities	Literature and Belief	0732-1929	3711
Business Information Group	Food in Canada	1188-9187	2576
California State University, Los Angeles, College of Business & Economics	Business Forum (Los Angeles)	0733-2408	1017
Cambridge University Press	Cambridge Opera Journal	0954-5867	4080
Cambridge University Press	Journal of Ecclesiastical History	0022-0469	4831
Cambridge University Press	Modern Asian Studies	0026-749X	588
Cambridge University Press	Psychological Medicine	0033-2917	4719
Cambridge University Press	Society for American Music Journal	1752-1963	4129
Cambridge University Press	Twentieth Century Music	1478-5722	4133
Canadian Institute of Metallurgy	Exploration & Mining Geology	0964-1823	1747
Canadian Research & Development Center of Sciences and Cultures	Studies in Sociology of Science	1923-0176	5087
Canon Communications LLC	E D N	0012-7515	2056
Catholic University of America Press	Catholic Historical Review	0008-8080	3103
Center for Defense Information	Defense Monitor	0195-6450	4004
Chamber Music America	Chamber Music	1071-1791	4081
Clark County Nevada Genealogical Society (CCNGS)	Prospector	1085-3707	2785
Colorado Genealogical Society	Colorado Genealogist	0010-1613	2765
Columbia University, Department of Music	Current Musicology	0011-3735	4087
Commonwealth Business Media, Inc.	Musical America Worldwide	1933-3250	4119
Connecticut Society of Genealogists Inc.	Connecticut Nutmegger	0045-8120	2766
Contemporary Review Co. Ltd.	Contemporary Review	0010-7565	4167
Country Music Foundation, Inc.	Journal of Country Music (Online)		4140
Crain Communications, Inc.	Business Insurance	0007-6864	1104
Crain Communications, Inc.	Crain's Chicago Business	0149-6956	1070
Crain Communications, Inc.	Crain's New York Business	8756-789X	1071
Cybersocket Inc.	Cybersocket Web Magazine		4943
Czechoslovak Genealogical Society, Intl.	Nase Rodina	1045-8190	2744
Delaware Genealogical Society	Delaware Genealogical Society. Journal	0731-3896	2767
Delta Publishing Company	Authentik en Francaise	0791-3729	1392
Detroit Society for Genealogical Research, Inc.	Detroit Society for Genealogical Research. Magazine	0011-9687	2778
Directors Guild of America	D G A Magazine	1083-5253	2458
Drawn & Quarterly Publications	Drawn & Quarterly Showcase		339
Duke University Press	Eighteenth-Century Life	0098-2601	3106
Duke University Press	Journal of Medieval and Early Modern Studies	1082-9636	3097
E Q E S, Inc.	Nuclear Plant Journal	0892-2055	4903
e.Republic, Inc.	Government Technology	1043-9668	1034

Table 3 / Titles Deleted Since the Last Edition, by Publishers (cont.)

Publisher	Title	ISSN	21st Edition Sequence No.
East Tennessee Historical Society	Tennessee Ancestors	0882-0635	2797
Edinburgh University Press Ltd.	Scottish Historical Review	0036-9241	3101
Elsevier BV	Journal of Men's Health	1875-6867	2707
Elsevier BV	Journal of Wind Engineering and Industrial Aerodynamics	0167-6105	2139
Elsevier BV	Meat Science	0309-1740	2581
Elsevier Inc.	Behavior Therapy	0005-7894	4629
Elsevier Inc.	Evolution and Human Behavior	1090-5138	4658
Elsevier Inc.	Technological Forecasting and Social Change	0040-1625	1040
Elsevier Ltd	New Scientist	0262-4079	4915
Erotic Review Books	Erotic Review	1477-1594	4944
Essential Information	Multinational Monitor (Online)	2163-5285	1046
European Commission, Office for Official Publications of the European Union	European Commission. European Union. Bulletin		2297
F + W Media Inc.	Family Tree Magazine	1529-0298	2755
Fantagraphics Books, Inc.	Mome	1933-5652	345
Federation of Genealogical Societies	Federation of Genealogical Societies Forum	1531-720X	2756
Fernand Braudel Center for the Study of Economies, Historical Systems, and Civilizations	Fernand Braudel Center for the Study of Economies, Historical Systems, and Civilizations. Review	0147-9032	3107
Financial Executives International	Financial Executive	0895-4186	1155
Florida State Genealogical Society, Inc.	Florida Genealogist	0161-4932	2768
G A M A International	G A M A International Journal	1095-7367	1105
Genealogical Society of New Jersey	Genealogical Magazine of New Jersey	0016-6367	2787
Genealogical Society of Pennsylvania	Pennsylvania Genealogical Magazine	0882-3685	2794
Genealogical Society of Vermont	Vermont Genealogy	1086-2439	2801
Georgia Genealogical Society, Inc.	Georgia Genealogical Society Quarterly	0435-5393	2769
Global Finance Media, Inc.	Global Finance	0896-4181	1156
Great Falls Genealogy Society	Treasure State Lines	1060-0337	2782
Great Valley Publishing Company, Inc.	Today's Diet & Nutrition (Online)		2999
Greenleaf Publishing	Journal of Corporate Citizenship	1470-5001	1045
Greenspring Media Group Inc.	Drinks		748
Grove Enterprises, Inc.	Monitoring Times	0889-5341	5278
Gryphon Books	Hardboiled		2391
Hart Energy Publishing, LP	Midstream Business	2329-0692	5352
Harvard Health Publications Group	Harvard Mental Health Letter	1057-5022	3007
Health Ink & Vitality Communications	Vitality	1074-5831	3000
Historians Film Committee	Film & History	0360-3695	2461
Hmong American Partnership	Hmoob teen	1935-1542	5262
Hoffman Media, LLC	Cooking with Paula Deen	1558-1853	1509
Hogrefe Publishing	European psychologist	1016-9040	4657
Hogrefe Publishing	Methodology	1614-1881	4706
I C E Publishing	Geotechnique	0016-8505	2194

Table 3 / Titles Deleted Since the Last Edition, by Publishers (cont.)

Publisher	Title	ISSN	21st Edition Sequence No.
Maney Publishing	Institute of Energy. Journal	1743-9671	2112
Martha Stewart Living Ommimedia LLC	Everyday Food: a Martha Stewart magazine	1544-6395	1516
Martha Stewart Living Ommimedia LLC	Whole Living	2155-2371	3001
Maryland Genealogical Society	Maryland Genealogical Society. Journal	1948-0962	2777
Massachusetts Society of Mayflower Descendants	Mayflower Descendant	8756-3959	2759
Masthof Press	Mennonite Family History	0730-5214	2743
Mathematical Association of America	College Mathematics Journal	0746-8342	3918
Mathematical Association of America	Math Horizons	1072-4117	3899
Men's Defense Association	Liberator (Forest Lake)	1040-3760	2711
Mining Media International	Coal Age	1091-0646	1077
Minnesota Genealogical Society	Minnesota Genealogist	0581-0086	2780
Missouri State Genealogical Association	Missouri State Genealogical Association Journal	0747-5667	2781
Mystery Readers International	Mystery Readers Journal	1043-3473	2393
National Association of Insurance and Financial Advisors	Advisor Today	1529-823X	1102
National Council of Teachers of Mathematics	Mathematics Teaching in the Middle School	1072-0839	3905
National Council of Teachers of Mathematics	Teaching Children Mathematics	1073-5836	3907
National Genealogical Society	National Genealogical Society Quarterly	0027-934X	2760
National Safety Council	Safety & Health	0891-1797	4905
Nebraska State Genealogical Society	Nebraska Ancestree	0270-4463	2783
Nevada State Genealogical Society	Nevada Desert	1536-9579	2784
New Mexico Genealogical Society	New Mexico Genealogist	0545-3186	2788
New Netherland Connections	New Netherland Connections	1087-4542	2745
New York Genealogical and Biographical Society	New York Genealogical and Biographical Record	0028-7237	2789
North American Saxophone Alliance	Saxophone Symposium	0271-3705	4128
North Carolina Genealogical Society	North Carolina Genealogical Society Journal	0360-1056	2790
North Carolina State University	Meridian (Raleigh)	1097-9778	2050
OfficeVision, Inc.	Office Solutions	1529-1804	3803
Ohio Genealogical Society	Ohio Records & Pioneer Families	1063-4649	2791
Oklahoma Genealogical Society	Oklahoma Genealogical Society Quarterly	0474-0742	2792
Oregon Genealogical Society	Oregon Genealogical Society Quarterly	0738-1891	2793
Organization of American Kodaly Educators	Kodaly Envoy	1084-1776	4109
Oxford University Press	Oral History Review	0094-0798	3128
Paleontological Research Institution	American Paleontologist	1066-8772	4243
Palgrave Macmillan Ltd.	Journal of Public Health Policy	0197-5897	4758
Park Genealogical Books	Minnesota Genealogical. Journal	0741-3599	2779
Pediatrics for Parents, Inc.	Pediatrics for Parents	0730-6725	4275
Polish Genealogical Society of America, Inc.	Rodziny	1544-726X	2747
Pontifical Institute of Mediaeval Studies	Mediaeval Studies	0076-5872	3099
Post Script, Inc.	Post Script	0277-9897	2478
Psychology Press	Developmental Neuropsychology	8756-5641	4651

Publisher	Title	ISSN	No.
Purdue University Calumet, Department of Communication and Creative Arts	Global Media Journal	1550-7521	2907
Quick Fiction	Quick Fiction	1543-8376	2381
R S C Publications	Lab on a Chip	1473-0197	1253
Reiman Media Group, Inc.	Taste of Home: cooking, caring & sharing	1071-5878	1520
Rhinegold Publishing Ltd.	International Piano	2042-0773	4100
Rhode Island Genealogical Society	Rhode Island Roots	0730-1235	2795
Routledge	American Journal of Clinical Hypnosis	0002-9157	4611
Routledge	Asian Studies Review	1035-7823	577
Routledge	China Journal of Social Work	1752-5098	5102
Routledge	Historical Methods	0161-5440	3117
Routledge	International Journal of Clinical and Experimental Hypnosis	0020-7144	4663
Routledge	Journal of Feminist Family Therapy	0895-2833	4688
Routledge	Journal of Imperial and Commonwealth History	0308-6534	3123
Routledge	Neuropsychology, Development and Cognition. Section A	1744-411X	4708
Routledge	Social History	0307-1022	3114
Sage Publications Ltd.	Feminism & Psychology	0959-3535	4659
Sage Publications Ltd.	International Journal of Music Education	0255-7614	4098
Sage Publications Ltd.	International Small Business Journal	0266-2426	1063
Sage Publications, Inc.	American Psychoanalytic Association. Journal	0003-0651	4617
Sage Publications, Inc.	Current Directions in Psychological Science	0963-7214	4649
Sage Publications, Inc.	Health Education & Behavior	1090-1981	4751
Sage Publications, Inc.	Journal of Black Psychology	0095-7984	4672
Sage Publications, Inc.	Psychological Science in the Public Interest	1529-1006	4724
Sage Publications, Inc.	Teaching of Psychology	0098-6283	4737
Sanoma Independent Media	Russia Profile (Online)		4993
Scarlet Letters	Scarlet Letters		4954
Scottish Genealogy Society	Scottish Genealogist	0300-337X	2748
Seattle Genealogical Society	Seattle Genealogical Society. Bulletin	0559-2526	2802
Simple Cooking	Simple Cooking	0749-176X	1519
Society for Industrial and Applied Mathematics	S I A M Journal on Applied Mathematics	0036-1399	3927
Society for Seventeenth - Century Music	Journal of Seventeenth Century Music	1089-747X	4107
Society of Genealogists	Genealogists' Magazine	0016-6391	2742
SourceMedia, Inc.	Investment Dealers' Digest	0021-0080	1115
Spin Music	Spin	0886-3032	4144
Springer Netherlands	Instructional Science	0020-4277	3934
Springer New York LLC	Behavior Research Methods (Online)	1554-3528	4628
Springer New York LLC	Employee Responsibilities and Rights Journal	0892-7545	3789
Springer New York LLC	Machine Learning	0885-6125	2207
Springer New York LLC	Psychometrika	0033-3123	4729
Springer New York LLC	Psychonomic Bulletin & Review	1531-5320	4730
State University of New York at Stony Brook, Department of Art	Art Criticism	0195-4148	508
Swenson Swedish Immigration Research Center	Swedish American Genealogist	0275-9314	2749
T.E. Smith, Ed. & Pub.	Wine News	1065-4895	755

Table 3 / Titles Deleted Since the Last Edition, by Publishers (cont.)

Publisher	Title	ISSN	21st Edition Sequence No.
Taylor & Francis	Behaviour and Information Technology	0144-929X	4632
Taylor & Francis	International Journal of Control	0020-7179	2204
Technology Marketing Corp.	Customer Interaction Solutions	1533-3078	1078
Tennessee Genealogical Society	Tennessee Genealogical Magazine		2798
TES Association	Prometheus (New York)		4953
Texas State Genealogical Society	Stirpes	0039-1522	2799
The Beltane Papers	Beltane Papers	1074-3634	5130
The Johns Hopkins University Press	American Jewish History	0164-0178	3082
The Mathematical Association	Mathematics in School	0305-7259	3901
The Palatines to America Society	Palatine Immigrant	0884-5735	2746
The Taunton Press, Inc.	Sew Stylish	1935-8482	1528
U.S. Department of the Interior, National Parks Service	C R M (Washington)	1068-4999	2917
University of Auckland, Department of History	Graduate Journal of Asia-Pacific Studies	1176-2152	582
University of British Columbia, Pacific Affairs	Pacific Affairs	0030-851X	590
University of Chicago Press	China Journal	1324-9347	579
University of Hawaii Press	Biography: an interdisciplinary quarterly	0162-4962	3102
University of Illinois Press	Black Women, Gender & Families (Online)	1944-6462	241
University of Illinois Press	Music and the Moving Image	1940-7610	4112
University of London, Royal Holloway, Department of Politics and International Relations	Journal of Critical Globalisation Studies	2040-8498	2912
University of Michigan, Women's Studies Department	Michigan Feminist Studies	1055-856X	2715
University of Oklahoma, School of Music	Journal of Music Theory Pedagogy	0891-7639	4103
University of Pennsylvania Press	Journal of the Early Republic	0275-1275	3086
University of Saskatchewan, College of Arts and Science, Department of History	Canadian Journal of History	0008-4107	3090
University of Texas, Austin, McDonald Observatory	Universo Online		665
Utah Genealogical Association	Crossroads	1935-2328	2800
Vegetarian Resource Group	Vegetarian Journal	0885-7636	1521
VIZ Media, Llc	Shojo Beat	1932-1600	347
Warren Communications News, Inc.	Public Broadcasting Report	0193-3663	3939
Weekly Reader Corporation	Current Events	0011-3492	1411
Weekly Reader Corporation	Current Science	0011-3905	1405
Weekly Reader Corporation	Read Magazine	0034-0359	1395
Weekly Reader Corporation	Weekly Reader. Grade 1 Edition	1525-4984	1416
Wiley-Blackwell Publishing Ltd.	Art Book	1368-6267	506
Wiley-Blackwell Publishing Ltd.	International Journal of Psychoanalysis	0020-7578	4666
Wiley-Blackwell Publishing, Inc.	Political psychology	0162-895X	4712
Wine Enthusiast	Wine Enthusiast	1078-3318	754
Wisconsin State Genealogical Society, Inc.	Wisconsin State Genealogical Society Newsletter	1094-9445	2803
Women Express, Inc.	Teen Voices	1074-7494	5269
Word Results, Co.	Main Street Mom		4272

Table 4 / Titles Deleted Since the Last Edition by MFL Subject

Section	Title	ISSN	Publisher	21st Ed. Sequence
ACCOUNTING & TAXATION	Business Valuation Review	0897-1781	American Society of Appraisers, Business Valuation Committee	7
ACCOUNTING & TAXATION	Internal Auditing	1757-0999	Institute of Internal Auditors (UK and Ireland)	12
AERONAUTICS	Aero - News network	1530-9339	Aero - News Network	110
AERONAUTICS	AVWeb		AVWeb	124
AERONAUTICS	Journal of Aerospace Computing, Information, and Communication	1542-9423	American Institute of Aeronautics and Astronautics, Inc.	141
AFRICA	Discovery and Innovation	1015-079X	Academy Science Publishers	196
AFRICA	Focus on Africa	0959-9576	B B C, African Service	200
AFRICAN AMERICAN	Black Women, Gender & Families (Online)	1944-6462	University of Illinois Press	241
ANIME, COMICS, GRAPHIC NOVELS, AND MANGA	Mome	1933-5652	Fantagraphics Books, Inc.	345
ANIME, COMICS, GRAPHIC NOVELS, AND MANGA	Drawn & Quarterly Showcase		Drawn & Quarterly Publications	339
ANIME, COMICS, GRAPHIC NOVELS, AND MANGA	Shojo Beat	1932-1600	VIZ Media, Llc	347
ANTIQUES AND COLLECTING	Doll Reader	0744-0901	Madavor Media, Llc.	396
ANTIQUES AND COLLECTING	Teddy Bear Review	0890-4162	Jones Publishing, Inc.	389
ART	American Artist	0002-7375	Interweave Press, LLC.	502
ART	Art Book	1368-6267	Wiley-Blackwell Publishing Ltd.	506
ART	Art Criticism	0195-4148	State University of New York at Stony Brook, Department of Art	508
ART	Art U S	1546-7082	Art U S	522
ASIA & THE PACIFIC	Asian Studies Review	1035-7823	Routledge	577
ASIA & THE PACIFIC	China Journal	1324-9347	University of Chicago Press	579
ASIA & THE PACIFIC	Graduate Journal of Asia-Pacific Studies	1176-2152	University of Auckland, Department of History	582
ASIA & THE PACIFIC	Modern Asian Studies	0026-749X	Cambridge University Press	588
ASIA & THE PACIFIC	Nichibunken Japan Review	0915-0986	International Research Center for Japanese Studies (Nichibunken)	589
ASIA & THE PACIFIC	Pacific Affairs	0030-851X	University of British Columbia, Pacific Affairs	590
ASTRONOMY	Universo Online		University of Texas, Austin, McDonald Observatory	665
BEER, WINE, AND SPIRITS	Drinks		Greenspring Media Group Inc.	748
BEER, WINE, AND SPIRITS	Wine Enthusiast	1078-3318	Wine Enthusiast	754
BEER, WINE, AND SPIRITS	Wine News	1065-4895	T.E. Smith, Ed. & Pub.	755
BUSINESS AND FINANCE	Advisor Today	1529-823X	National Association of Insurance and Financial Advisors	1102
BUSINESS AND FINANCE	Business Forum (Los Angeles)	0733-2408	California State University, Los Angeles, College of Business & Economics	1017
BUSINESS AND FINANCE	Business Insurance	0007-6864	Crain Communications, Inc.	1104
BUSINESS AND FINANCE	Coal Age	1091-0646	Mining Media International	1077
BUSINESS AND FINANCE	Crain's Chicago Business	0149-6956	Crain Communications, Inc.	1070
BUSINESS AND FINANCE	Crain's New York Business	8756-789X	Crain Communications, Inc.	1071
BUSINESS AND FINANCE	Customer Interaction Solutions	1533-3078	Technology Marketing Corp.	1078

Table 4 / Titles Deleted Since the Last Edition by MFL Subject (cont.)

Section	Title	ISSN	Publisher	21st Ed. Sequence
ENGINEERING AND TECHNOLOGY	International Journal of Intelligent Control and Systems	0218-7965	World Scientific Publishing Co. Pte. Ltd.	2216
ENGINEERING AND TECHNOLOGY	Journal of Biomechanical Engineering	0148-0731	A S M E International	2170
ENGINEERING AND TECHNOLOGY	Machine Learning	0885-6125	Springer New York LLC	2207
ENGINEERING AND TECHNOLOGY	Ubiquity	1530-2180	Association for Computing Machinery, Inc.	2209
EUROPE	European Commission. European Union. Bulletin		European Commission, Office for Official Publications of the European Union	2297
FICTION: GENERAL/MYSTERY & DE-TECTIVE	American Short Fiction	1051-4813	Badgerdog Literary Publishing, Inc.	2374
FICTION: GENERAL/MYSTERY & DE-TECTIVE	Hardboiled		Gryphon Books	2391
FICTION: GENERAL/MYSTERY & DE-TECTIVE	Mystery News	0734-9076	Black Raven Press	2392
FICTION: GENERAL/MYSTERY & DE-TECTIVE	Mystery Readers Journal	1043-3473	Mystery Readers International	2393
FICTION: GENERAL/MYSTERY & DE-TECTIVE	Quick Fiction	1543-8376	Quick Fiction	2381
FILMS	Creative Screenwriting	1084-8665	Inside Information Group	2457
FILMS	D G A Magazine	1083-5253	Directors Guild of America	2458
FILMS	Film & History	0360-3695	Historians Film Committee	2461
FILMS	Hollywood Life	1557-7228	Line Publications LLC	2471
FILMS	Post Script	0277-9897	Post Script, Inc.	2478
FOOD INDUSTRY	Food in Canada	1188-9187	Business Information Group	2576
FOOD INDUSTRY	Meat Science	0309-1740	Elsevier BV	2581
GENDER STUDIES	Bridges: a Jewish feminist journal	1046-8358	Indiana University Press	2678
GENDER STUDIES	Journal of Men's Health	1875-6867	Elsevier BV	2707
GENDER STUDIES	Liberator (Forest Lake)	1040-3760	Men's Defense Association	2711
GENDER STUDIES	Michigan Feminist Studies	1055-856X	University of Michigan, Women's Studies Department	2715
GENEALOGY	Acadian Genealogy Exchange	0199-9591	Acadian Genealogical Exchange	2735
GENEALOGY	Alabama Genealogical Society Magazine	0568-806X	Alabama Genealogical Society	2763
GENEALOGY	American Ancestors	2154-6533	New England Historic Genealogical Society	2750
GENEALOGY	Arkansas Family Historian	0571-0472	Arkansas Genealogical Society, Inc.	2764
GENEALOGY	Colorado Genealogist	0010-1613	Colorado Genealogical Society	2765
GENEALOGY	Connecticut Nutmegger	0045-8120	Connecticut Society of Genealogists Inc.	2766
GENEALOGY	Crossroads	1935-2328	Utah Genealogical Association	2800
GENEALOGY	Delaware Genealogical Society. Journal	0731-3896	Delaware Genealogical Society	2767
GENEALOGY	Detroit Society for Genealogical Research. Magazine	0011-9687	Detroit Society for Genealogical Research, Inc.	2778
GENEALOGY	Family History	0014-7265	Institute of Heraldic and Genealogical Studies	2740
GENEALOGY	Family Tree Magazine	1529-0298	F + W Media Inc.	2755
GENEALOGY	Federation of Genealogical Societies Forum	1531-720X	Federation of Genealogical Societies	2756
GENEALOGY	Florida Genealogist	0161-4932	Florida State Genealogical Society, Inc.	2768
GENEALOGY	Genealogical Magazine of New Jersey	0016-6367	Genealogical Society of New Jersey	2787

	Title	Publisher	ISSN	
GENEALOGY	Genealogist	Australian Institute of Genealogical Studies, Inc.	0311-1776	2741
GENEALOGY	Genealogists' Magazine	Society of Genealogists	0016-6391	2742
GENEALOGY	Georgia Genealogical Society Quarterly	Georgia Genealogical Society, Inc.	0435-5393	2769
GENEALOGY	Great Migration Newsletter	New England Historic Genealogical Society	1049-8087	2758
GENEALOGY	Hawkeye Heritage	Iowa Genealogical Society	0440-5234	2772
GENEALOGY	Hoosier Genealogist	Indiana Historical Society	1054-2175	2771
GENEALOGY	Illinois State Genealogical Society Quarterly	Illinois State Genealogical Society	0046-8622	2770
GENEALOGY	Kentucky Ancestors	Kentucky Historical Society	0023-0103	2774
GENEALOGY	Louisiana Genealogical Register	Louisiana Genealogical and Historical Society	0148-7655	2775
GENEALOGY	Maine Genealogist	Maine Genealogical Society	1064-6086	2776
GENEALOGY	Maryland Genealogical Society. Journal	Maryland Genealogical Society	1948-0962	2777
GENEALOGY	Mayflower Descendant	Massachusetts Society of Mayflower Descendants	8756-3959	2759
GENEALOGY	Memnonite Family History	Masthof Press	0730-5214	2743
GENEALOGY	Minnesota Genealogical. Journal	Park Genealogical Books	0741-3599	2779
GENEALOGY	Minnesota Genealogist	Minnesota Genealogical Society	0581-0086	2780
GENEALOGY	Missouri State Genealogical Association Journal	Missouri State Genealogical Association	0747-5667	2781
GENEALOGY	Nase Rodina	Czechoslovak Genealogical Society, Intl.	1045-8190	2744
GENEALOGY	National Genealogical Society Quarterly	National Genealogical Society	0027-934X	2760
GENEALOGY	Nebraska Ancestree	Nebraska State Genealogical Society	0270-4463	2783
GENEALOGY	Nevada Desert	Nevada State Genealogical Society	1536-9579	2784
GENEALOGY	New Hampshire Genealogical Record	Indian Council for Cultural Relations	1055-0763	2786
GENEALOGY	New Mexico Genealogist	New Mexico Genealogical Society	0545-3186	2788
GENEALOGY	New Netherland Connections	New Netherland Connections	1087-4542	2745
GENEALOGY	New York Genealogical and Biographical Record	New York Genealogical and Biographical Society	0028-7237	2789
GENEALOGY	North Carolina Genealogical Society Journal	North Carolina Genealogical Society	0360-1056	2790
GENEALOGY	Ohio Records & Pioneer Families	Ohio Genealogical Society	1063-4649	2791
GENEALOGY	Oklahoma Genealogical Society Quarterly	Oklahoma Genealogical Society	0474-0742	2792
GENEALOGY	Oregon Genealogical Society Quarterly	Oregon Genealogical Society	0738-1891	2793
GENEALOGY	Palatine Immigrant	The Palatines to America Society	0884-5735	2746
GENEALOGY	Pennsylvania Genealogical Magazine	Genealogical Society of Pennsylvania	0882-3685	2794
GENEALOGY	Prospector	Clark County Nevada Genealogical Society (CCNGS)	1085-3707	2785
GENEALOGY	Rhode Island Roots	Rhode Island Genealogical Society	0730-1235	2795
GENEALOGY	Rodziny	Polish Genealogical Society of America, Inc.	1544-726X	2747
GENEALOGY	Scottish Genealogist	Scottish Genealogy Society	0300-337X	2748
GENEALOGY	Seattle Genealogical Society. Bulletin	Seattle Genealogical Society	0559-2526	2802
GENEALOGY	South Carolina Magazine of Ancestral Research	Brent H. Holcomb, Ed. & Pub.	0190-826X	2796
GENEALOGY	Stirpes	Texas State Genealogical Society	0039-1522	2799
GENEALOGY	Swedish American Genealogist	Swenson Swedish Immigration Research Center	0275-9314	2749
GENEALOGY	Tennessee Ancestors	East Tennessee Historical Society	0882-0635	2797
GENEALOGY	Tennessee Genealogical Magazine	Tennessee Genealogical Society		2798
GENEALOGY	Treasure State Lines	Great Falls Genealogy Society	1060-0337	2782

Table 4 / Titles Deleted Since the Last Edition by MFL Subject (cont.)

Section	Title	ISSN	Publisher	21st Ed. Sequence
GENEALOGY	Treesearcher	0564-1845	Kansas Genealogical Society, Inc.	2773
GENEALOGY	Vermont Genealogy	1086-2439	Genealogical Society of Vermont	2801
GENEALOGY	Wisconsin State Genealogical Society Newsletter	1094-9445	Wisconsin State Genealogical Society, Inc.	2803
GLOBALIZATION	Global Media Journal	1550-7521	Purdue University Calumet, Department of Communication and Creative Arts	2907
GLOBALIZATION	Journal of Critical Globalisation Studies	2040-8498	University of London, Royal Holloway, Department of Politics and International Relations	2912
GLOBALIZATION	Yale Global Online		Yale University, Center for the Study of Globalization	2915
GOVERNMENT PERIODICAL FEDERAL	C R M (Washington)	1068-4999	U.S. Department of the Interior, National Parks Service	2917
HEALTH AND FITNESS	Harvard Mental Health Letter	1057-5022	Harvard Health Publications Group	3007
HEALTH AND FITNESS	Today's Diet & Nutrition (Online)		Great Valley Publishing Company, Inc.	2999
HEALTH AND FITNESS	Vitality	1074-5831	Health Ink & Vitality Communications	3000
HEALTH AND FITNESS	Whole Living	2155-2371	Martha Stewart Living Omnimedia LLC	3001
HEALTH CARE ADMINISTRATION	Joint Commission Journal on Quality and Patient Safety	1553-7250	Joint Commission Resources, Inc.	3019
HISTORY	American Jewish History	0164-0178	The Johns Hopkins University Press	3082
HISTORY	Biography: an interdisciplinary quarterly	0162-4962	University of Hawaii Press	3102
HISTORY	Canadian Journal of History	0008-4107	University of Saskatchewan, College of Arts and Science, Department of History	3090
HISTORY	Catholic Historical Review	0008-8080	Catholic University of America Press	3103
HISTORY	Clio (Ft. Wayne)	0884-2043	Indiana University, Department of English and Linguistics	3104
HISTORY	Eighteenth-Century Life	0098-2601	Duke University Press	3106
HISTORY	Fernand Braudel Center for the Study of Economies, Historical Systems, and Civilizations. Review	0147-9032	Fernand Braudel Center for the Study of Economies, Historical Systems, and Civilizations	3107
HISTORY	Historical Methods	0161-5440	Routledge	3117
HISTORY	History News	0363-7492	American Association for State and Local History	3119
HISTORY	Irish Historical Studies	0021-1214	Irish Historical Society	3095
HISTORY	Journal of Ecclesiastical History	0022-0469	Cambridge University Press	4831
HISTORY	Journal of Imperial and Commonwealth History	0308-6534	Routledge	3123
HISTORY	Journal of Medieval and Early Modern Studies	1082-9636	Duke University Press	3097
HISTORY	Journal of the Early Republic	0275-1275	University of Pennsylvania Press	3086
HISTORY	Literature & History	0306-1973	Manchester University Press	3112
HISTORY	Mediaeval Studies	0076-5872	Pontifical Institute of Mediaeval Studies	3099
HISTORY	Oral History Review	0094-0798	Oxford University Press	3128
HISTORY	Scottish Historical Review	0036-9241	Edinburgh University Press Ltd.	3101
HISTORY	Social History	0307-1022	Routledge	3114
LITERATURE	Ciberletras	1523-1720	Lehman College, City University of New York, Department of Languages and Literatures	3684
LITERATURE	Literature and Belief	0732-1929	Brigham Young University, College of Humanities	3711

Category	Title	Publisher	ISSN	Page
MANAGEMENT AND ADMINISTRATION	Employee Responsibilities and Rights Journal	Springer New York LLC	0892-7545	3789
MANAGEMENT AND ADMINISTRATION	Office Solutions	OfficeVision, Inc.	1529-1804	3803
MATHEMATICS	American Mathematical Society. Journal	American Mathematical Society	0894-0347	3913
MATHEMATICS	American Mathematical Society. Transactions	American Mathematical Society	0002-9947	3914
MATHEMATICS	College Mathematics Journal	Mathematical Association of America	0746-8342	3918
MATHEMATICS	Journal of Recreational Mathematics	Baywood Publishing Co., Inc.	0022-412X	3898
MATHEMATICS	Math Horizons	Mathematical Association of America	1072-4117	3899
MATHEMATICS	Mathematics in School	The Mathematical Association	0305-7259	3901
MATHEMATICS	Mathematics Teaching in the Middle School	National Council of Teachers of Mathematics	1072-0839	3905
MATHEMATICS	S I A M Journal on Applied Mathematics	Society for Industrial and Applied Mathematics	0036-1399	3927
MATHEMATICS	Teaching Children Mathematics	National Council of Teachers of Mathematics	1073-5836	3907
MEDIA & AV	Instructional Science	Springer Netherlands	0020-4277	3934
MEDIA & AV	Journal of Educational Multimedia and Hypermedia	Association for the Advancement of Computing in Education	1055-8896	3936
MEDIA & AV	Public Broadcasting Report	Warren Communications News, Inc.	0193-3663	3939
MEDIA & AV	Studio/Monthly	Access Intelligence, LLC	1554-3412	3940
MILITARY	Defense Monitor	Center for Defense Information	0195-6450	4004
MUSIC - GENERAL	Cambridge Opera Journal	Cambridge University Press	0954-5867	4080
MUSIC - GENERAL	Chamber Music	Chamber Music America	1071-1791	4081
MUSIC - GENERAL	Current Musicology	Columbia University, Department of Music	0011-3735	4087
MUSIC - GENERAL	Double Reed	International Double Reed Society	0741-7659	4088
MUSIC - GENERAL	Fontes Artis Musicae	International Association of Music Libraries, Archives and Documentation Centres (U.S. Branch)	0015-6191	4094
MUSIC - GENERAL	Horn Call	International Horn Society	0046-7928	4095
MUSIC - GENERAL	International Journal of Music Education	Sage Publications Ltd.	0255-7614	4098
MUSIC - GENERAL	International Piano	Rhinegold Publishing Ltd.	2042-0773	4100
MUSIC - GENERAL	ITG Journal	International Trumpet Guild		4096
MUSIC - GENERAL	Journal of Music Theory Pedagogy	University of Oklahoma, School of Music	0891-7639	4103
MUSIC - GENERAL	Journal of Seventeenth Century Music	Society for Seventeenth - Century Music	1089-747X	4107
MUSIC - GENERAL	Kodaly Envoy	Organization of American Kodaly Educators	1084-1776	4109
MUSIC - GENERAL	Music and the Moving Image	University of Illinois Press	1940-7610	4112
MUSIC - GENERAL	Musical America Worldwide	Commonwealth Business Media, Inc.	1933-3250	4119
MUSIC - GENERAL	Orff Echo	American Orff-Schulwerk Association	0095-2613	4125
MUSIC - GENERAL	Saxophone Symposium	North American Saxophone Alliance	0271-3705	4128
MUSIC - GENERAL	Society for American Music Journal	Cambridge University Press	1752-1963	4129
MUSIC - GENERAL	Twentieth Century Music	Cambridge University Press	1478-5722	4133
MUSIC - POPULAR	Beat (Los Angeles)	Bongo Productions	1063-5319	4136
MUSIC - POPULAR	Journal of Country Music (Online)	Country Music Foundation, Inc.		4140
MUSIC - POPULAR	Spin	Spin Music	0886-3032	4144
MUSIC REVIEWS	In Music We Trust	In Music We Trust, Inc.		4150
NEWS & OPINION	Contemporary Review	Contemporary Review Co. Ltd.	0010-7565	4167
PALEONTOLOGY	American Paleontologist	Paleontological Research Institution	1066-8772	4243
PARENTING	At-Home Dad	At-Home Dad	1081-5767	4261
PARENTING	Family Matters!	Kokopellis Treasures	1529-2673	4264

Table 4 / Titles Deleted Since the Last Edition by MFL Subject (cont.)

Section	Title	ISSN	Publisher	21st Ed. Sequence
PARENTING	Main Street Mom		Word Results, Co.	4272
PARENTING	Pediatrics for Parents	0730-6725	Pediatrics for Parents, Inc.	4275
PETS	Aquarium Fish International	1942-5678	BowTie, Inc.	4302
PHYSICS	J A S A Express Letters		Acoustical Society of America	4464
PHYSICS	Virtual Journal of Applications of Superconductivity	1553-9636	American Institute of Physics	4513
PHYSICS	Virtual Journal of Atomic Quantum Fluids	1935-4061	American Institute of Physics	4514
PHYSICS	Virtual Journal of Biological Physics Research	1553-9628	American Physical Society	4515
PHYSICS	Virtual Journal of Nanoscale Science & Technology	1553-9644	American Physical Society	4516
PHYSICS	Virtual Journal of Quantum Information	1553-961X	American Physical Society	4517
PHYSICS	Virtual Journal of Ultrafast Science	1553-9601	American Institute of Physics	4518
PSYCHOLOGY	American Journal of Clinical Hypnosis	0002-9157	Routledge	4611
PSYCHOLOGY	American Journal of Forensic Psychology	0733-1290	American College of Forensic Psychiatry	4613
PSYCHOLOGY	American Psychoanalytic Association. Journal	0003-0651	Sage Publications, Inc.	4617
PSYCHOLOGY	Behavior and Social Issues	1064-9506	Behaviorists for Social Responsibility	4626
PSYCHOLOGY	Behavior Research Methods (Online)	1554-3528	Springer New York LLC	4628
PSYCHOLOGY	Behavior Therapy	0005-7894	Elsevier Inc.	4629
PSYCHOLOGY	Behaviour and Information Technology	0144-929X	Taylor & Francis	4632
PSYCHOLOGY	Consulting psychology journal	1065-9293	American Psychological Association	4647
PSYCHOLOGY	Current Directions in Psychological Science	0963-7214	Sage Publications, Inc.	4649
PSYCHOLOGY	Developmental Neuropsychology	8756-5641	Psychology Press	4651
PSYCHOLOGY	Developmental Review	0273-2297	Academic Press	4653
PSYCHOLOGY	European psychologist	1016-9040	Hogrefe Publishing	4657
PSYCHOLOGY	Evolution and Human Behavior	1090-5138	Elsevier Inc.	4658
PSYCHOLOGY	Feminism & Psychology	0959-3535	Sage Publications Ltd.	4659
PSYCHOLOGY	International Journal of Clinical and Experimental Hypnosis	0020-7144	Routledge	4663
PSYCHOLOGY	International Journal of Psychoanalysis	0020-7578	Wiley-Blackwell Publishing Ltd.	4666
PSYCHOLOGY	Journal of Black Psychology	0095-7984	Sage Publications, Inc.	4672
PSYCHOLOGY	Journal of Feminist Family Therapy	0895-2833	Routledge	4688
PSYCHOLOGY	Journal of the History of the Behavioral Sciences	0022-5061	John Wiley & Sons, Inc.	4700
PSYCHOLOGY	Journal of Transpersonal Psychology	0022-524X	Association for Transpersonal Psychology	4701
PSYCHOLOGY	Journal of Vocational Behavior	0001-8791	Academic Press	4702
PSYCHOLOGY	Methodology	1614-1881	Hogrefe Publishing	4706
PSYCHOLOGY	Neuropsychology, Development and Cognition. Section A	1744-411X	Routledge	4708
PSYCHOLOGY	Political psychology	0162-895X	Wiley-Blackwell Publishing, Inc.	4712
PSYCHOLOGY	Psychoanalytic Psychology	0736-9735	American Psychological Association	4715
PSYCHOLOGY	Psychological Medicine	0033-2917	Cambridge University Press	4719
PSYCHOLOGY	Psychological Methods	1082-989X	American Psychological Association	4720
PSYCHOLOGY	Psychological Reports	0033-2941	Ammons Scientific Ltd.	4721

HOW TO USE THIS BOOK

*Title. *ISSN. Date Founded. *Frequency. *Price. Editor. Publisher and Address, * Internet-WWW. lllustrations, Index, Advertising. *Sample. *Refereed. Circulation. *Date Volume Ends. *CD-ROM. Microform. Reprint. *Online. *Indexed. *Book Reviews. * Audience. * Annotation

The bibliographic data in the entries contain the items shown in the box above. Items preceded by an asterisk are fully explained in the paragraphs that follow. The Abbreviations section lists the general abbreviations found in the bibliographic information in the numbered entries.

The detailed Subject Index enables the user to access the enormous amount of information that may not be readily retrievable from the alphabetically arranged Title Index. All subject classifications used, as well as variations in wording of subject headings, are listed in the Subject Index. The numbers that appear in the indexes refer to the magazine entry numbers, not page numbers.

Title

The periodicals in this book are listed alphabetically, by title, under the subjects given in the Contents. They are numbered sequentially, beginning with 1 on page 1 and ending with 5,603, the last magazine entry in the book, on page 848.

ISSN Numbers

This international standard, which is used all over the world by serial publishers to distinguish similar titles from each other, directly follows the title. *Ulrich's Periodicals Directory* was used to verify this information.

Frequency and Price

The frequency is given immediately after the founding date, and the symbols used are explained in the General Abbreviations section. The price quoted is the annual subscription rate given by the publisher, usually as of 2010. A large number are prices for 2011. Prices are relative and, of course, subject to change-probably upward. Furthermore, the fluctuation of the dollar makes the prices of foreign magazines even more relative. The phrase "Controlled Circ." is found after some titles. This means the magazine has a controlled circulation and is sent free to certain individuals whom the advertisers are trying to reach. Such a magazine is financed solely by advertisements, and the controlled circulation indicates the publisher has targeted a certain audience or audiences for the advertisers. For a listing of controlled circulation serials, with full addresses, see the index volume of *Ulrich's Periodicals Directory*. "Others" means those who are outside that select audience and must pay for the title. Often the publisher is willing to send the magazine free to libraries, but in any case an inquiry should be made.

World Wide Web

The web address (URL) represents the address at the time of the compilation. As anyone knows who uses the Internet, the address may change frequently. In a case where the address does not prove correct, try shortening the address back to the "root" or entering the name of the magazine in the search engine box. Normally this works.

Sample

Publishers were asked whether or not they would send a free copy of the magazine to a library if requested. Those who replied favorably are indicated by the single word "sample". The request should be made by the head of the library, or by the head of the serials department, and written on official stationery. The indication that publishers are willing to send samples to institutions does not mean they are necessarily interested in sending them to individual subscribers. And one additional note: Several publishers would not supply review copies of their publications. So, if there are a few titles not in the list that you might otherwise expect to see here, that is why. *MFL* does depend on publisher cooperation to be able to access and examine titles for possible inclusion.

Refereed

This term is used to indicate that manuscripts published in the journal have been reviewed by experts and specialists in the field before being accepted for publication. Sometimes refereed journals are characterized as "peer-reviewed." This process tends to make scholars trust the reliability of the content of an article more than a non-refereed article.

Date Volume Ends

Librarians find it helpful to know when a publisher ends a volume-obviously for purposes of binding. The information provided is from the publisher.

Online

This includes the basic sources of online access to a particular title. This may be in reference to an index, or it may be in reference to the full-text of articles in the journal.

Indexed

Information on where titles are indexed or abstracted is given-in abbreviated format-following the bibliographic data. Also indicated are major subject indexes in which the periodicals are indexed. Major must be emphasized. The list of the A&Is recommended by *MFL* subject specialist, can be found on page xliii. The term index in the bibliographic description indicates that the publisher has an index to the periodical.

Book Reviews

Information given refers to the approximate number of reviews that appear in a typical issue of the periodical and the average length.

Audience

Ems (elementary and middle school students); Hs (high school students); Ga (General Adult); Ac (Academic audience); Sa (Special Adult). Each magazine has an indication of audience or type of library for which it is suited. The scale is specific, but as most magazines are for more than one audience, several audience levels are usually given for each title. Periodicals for elementary and middle school students (Ems) are not separated because it is often difficult to draw the line between these two age groups. The titles and descriptive annotations leave little doubt as to the level of maturity for which the magazine is intended. Generally, elementary and middle school means the age group from 4 to 14 years and/or those in elementary or middle school. The high school level (Hs) overlaps and may include middle school, but for the most part, these are titles suitable for those from 14 years up to 18 years and/or in high school. Magazines suitable for public libraries and college and university library reading rooms are rated General Adult (Ga). Publications designated Academic audience (Ac) should be considered for junior colleges, colleges, and universities. Magazines rated Special Adult (Sa) are for specialized audiences and will be read by few people other than professionals or students of a particular subject. It is assumed that the audience symbols are only guides, not designations for type of library-which is to say that the symbol Ga does not mean the magazine is only limited to public libraries any more than Ac means a magazine is only for academic libraries. Obviously the choice should be made by the librarian, and this will depend on his or her assessment of the audience to be served. Public libraries will often include many of the same magazines found in all other libraries

Annotation

The annotations are generally short summaries describing the scope, purpose, and intent of each magazine, bias (if any), and target audience as described above. In making their recommendations chapter authors are assessing the usefulness and readability of articles in each journal for various audiences. The fact that a journal is listed in *Magazines/or Libraries* indicates that it is considered to be a core title for the listed audience and recommended to the libraries serving them.

ABBREVIATIONS

■ GENERAL ABBREVIATIONS

a.	Annual	Irreg.	Irregular
Ac	Academic (Junior Colleges, Colleges, Universities)	ISSN	International Standard Serial Number
adv.	advertising	ITL	Italian Lira
Aud.	Audience	m.	Monthly
bi-m.	Every two months	N.S.	New Series
bi-w.	Every two weeks	NLG	Dutch Guilder
Bk. rev	Book reviews	no., #, nos.	number(s)
Circ.	circulation	q.	Quarterly
CND	Canadian Dollar	rev.	revIews
d.	Daily	Sa	Special Adult
DEM	Deutsche Mark	s-a.	Twice annually
Ed., Eds.	Editor(s)	s-m.	Twice monthly
Ems	Elementary and Middle School	s-w.	Twice weekly
EUR	Euro	31m.	Three times a month
fortn.	Fortnightly	3/w	Three times a week
FRF	French Franc	3/yr.	Three times per year
Ga	General Adult	USD	U.S. Dollars
GPB	British Pound	vol., vols.	volume(s)
Hs	High School	w.	Weekly
illus.	illustrations	yr., yrs.	year(s)

Controlled Circ. Controlled circulation (free to certain groups)

ABSTRACTS AND INDEXES

This is a list of the abstracting and indexing tools recommended by MFL chapter authors in this edition. For the most current and accurate information on each simply Google the title to locate full product content at the publishers'/ providers' web sites.

AATA Online: Abstracts of International Conservation Literature

ABI/INFORM

ABI/Inform Global

Abstract Bulletin of Paper Science and Technology

Abstracts in Anthropology

Abstracts in Social Gerontology

Academic OneFile

Academic Search Complete

Academic Search Premier

Accounting and Tax Index

Aerospace and High Technology Database

African Studies

African Studies Abstracts

AgeLine

AGRICOLA

Air University Library Index to Military Periodicals

Alternative Press Index

Alt-HealthWatch

Alt-PressWatch

America: History and Life

American Bibliography of Slavic and Eastern European Studies (ABSEES)

Annee Philologique, L'

Annual Bibliography of English Language Literature (ABELL)

Anthropological Index Online

Anthropological Literature Online

AnthroSource

Applied Science and Technology Abstracts

Applied Science and Technology Index

Aquatic Sciences and Fisheries Abstracts

Architectural Index

Architectural Publications Index

Art Abstracts

Art and Architecture Complete

Art Index

ARTbibliographies Modern

Arts & Humanities Citation Index

ASFA Aquaculture Abstracts

ASSIA

ATLA Religion Index

Avery Index to Architectural Periodicals

Berg Fashion Library

BHA Bibliography of the History of Art

ABSTRACTS AND INDEXES

Education Index

Education Research Complete

Ekistic Index of Periodicals

Electronics and Communications Abstracts

Elsevier BV

EMBASE

Engineering Index

Engineering Index Monthly

Environment Index

Environmental Sciences and Pollution Management

ERIC

Ethnic NewsWatch

Expanded Academic ASAP

Factiva

Family and Society Studies Worldwide

Family Index

Family Studies Abstracts

Feminist Periodicals

Film & Television Literature Index

Food Science and Technology Abstracts

Forest Science Database

Forestry Abstracts

FRANCIS

Gale Educator's Reference Complete

Garden, Landscape and Horticulture Index

GenderWatch

General Business File ASAP

General OneFile

General Reference Center Gold

GEOBASE

Geographical Abstracts

Geographical Abstracts B: Biogeography and Climatology

GeoRef

Google Scholar

Health & Safety Science Abstracts

Health Source: Consumer Edition

Health Source: Nursing/Academic

Hispanic American Periodicals Index (HAPI)

Historical Abstracts

Horticultural Science Abstracts

Hospitality and Tourism Complete

Hospitality and Tourism Index

Humanities Index

Humanities International Complete

Humanities International Index

IBZ

ICONDA

IEEE Computer Society Digital Library

Index Islamicus

Index to Current Urban Documents

Index to Foreign Legal Periodicals

Index to How to Do It Information

Index to Jewish Periodicals

Index to Legal Periodicals and Books

Index to Legal Periodicals and Books Retrospective

ABSTRACTS AND INDEXES

Index Veterinarius

Information Science and Technology Abstracts

InfoTrac

IngentaConnect

INSPEC

International Aerospace Abstracts

International African Bibliography

International Bibliography of the Social Sciences

International Bibliography of Theatre & Dance with Full Text

International Index to Black Periodicals

International Index to Black Periodicals Full Text

International Index to Film Periodicals

International Index to Music Periodicals

International Index to the Performing Arts

International Philosophical Bibliography = Repertoire Bibliographique de la Philosophie

International Political Science Abstracts

Internet and Personal Computing Abstracts

Language Teaching

LegalTrac

Leisure, Recreation and Tourism Abstracts

Leisure Tourism Database

LexisNexis

LGBT Life

Library Information Science and Technology Abstracts (LISTA)

Library Literature

Library Literature and Information Science

Linguistics Abstracts

Linguistics and Language Behavior Abstracts

LISA: Library and Information Science Abstracts

MAS Ultra – School Edition

MasterFILE Premier

MathSciNet

MEDLINE

Metals Abstracts

Meteorological and Geoastrophysical Abstracts

Middle Search

MLA International Bibliography

Music Index

Mystery Short Fiction

National Sea Grant Library Database

New Testament Abstracts

Numismatic Literature

Nursing Resource Center

Nutrition Abstracts and Reviews

Old Testament Abstracts

OmniFile Full Text

PAIS International

Peace Research Abstracts

Periodicals Abstreacts

Philosopher's Index

Physical Education Index

Physics Abstracts

PIO-Periodicals Index Online

Pirabase

Pollution Abstracts

Press

Primary Search

PrimateLit

Project MUSE

ProQuest 5000

ProQuest Central

ProQuest eLibrary

ProQuest Nursing and Allied Health Source

ProQuest Research Library

PsycArticles

PsycINFO

PubMed

Quarterly Index to Africana Periodical Literature

Race Relations Abstracts

Reader's Guide to Periodical Literature

Resources in Education

RILM Abstracts of Music Literature

Risk Abstracts Online

SAO/NASA Astrophysics Data System (ADS)

Science Citation Index

ScienceDirect

Scopus

Social Sciences Abstracts

Social Sciences Citation Index

Social Sciences Index

Social Services Abstracts

Social Work Abstracts

SocINDEX

Sociological Abstracts

SPORTDiscus

Studies on Women and Gender Abstracts

TOCS-IN

Transport

TRANweb

TreeSearch

TRIS Electronic Bibliographic Data Base

Urban Studies Abstracts

Vertical File Index

Violence and Abuse Abstracts

Water Resources Abstracts

Web of Science

Wilson OmniFile

Women Studies Abstracts

Women's Studies International

World Agricultural Economics and Rural Sociological Abstracts

Worldwide Political Science Abstracts

Zeitungs – Index

Zentralblatt MATH

Zoological Record

CONSULTANTS

Full names and addresses are given for the consultants at the head of each section.

Adams, Christine (Accounting & Taxation)

Anderson, Serin (Family Planning)

Arendt, Julie (Animal Welfare)

Ashmun, Julia D. (Boats & Boating)

Avery, Bonnie E. (Forestry)

Baker, Pam (Books & Book Reviews)

Bales, Stephen (Religion)

Bartley, Drew (Genealogy)

Baughman, Pauline (Automobiles & Motorcycles)

Bell, Emily (Health Care Administration; Public Health)

Bennett, Elizabeth Z. (History)

Bernnard, Deborah F. (Bibliography)

Bishop, Sasha (World Wide Web)

Blake, Michael J. (Fishing)

Boyd, C. Trenton (Veterinary Science)

Braxton, Susan (Science & Technology)

Bruno, Tom (Anime, Comics, Graphic Novels, & Manga; Archaeology; Classical Studies)

Buchanan, Heidi (Literature)

Burchsted, Fred (Geography)

Burton, Jean Piper (Folklore)

Butler, Barbara A. (Marine Science & Technology)

Calgano, Theresa (Engineering & Technology)

Campbell, Nancy F. (Communications)

Carter, David (Games and Gaming)

Casper, Christianne (Astrology; Paranormal)

Clymer, Joanne (International Magazines)

Coe, Erica L. (Music Reviews)

Collins, Linda (Horses)

Cronin, Jeff (Real Estate)

Crowley, Gwyneth (Economics)

Dankert, Holly Stec (Art; Interior Design & Decoration)

Deards, Kiyomi (Physics)

Dotson, Danny (Statistics)

Duhon, Lucy (Children)

Duong, Khue (Informatics)

Ehrenhart, David (Fire Protection)

Elwood, Caitlin (Law)

Escobar, Hector (Model Making)

Fagan, Sarah (Home)

Feind, Rebecca (Social Media)

Gao, Wenli (Fish, Fisheries, & Aquaculture)

Garson, Deborah S. (Education)

Gardinier, Lisa (Latino Studies)

Geary, Mary Kathleen (Transportation)

Georgas, Helen (Little Magazines)

Grallo, Jacqui (Books & Book Reviews)

Groves, Adam (Fire Protection)

Hendricks, Leta (Fashion & Lifestyle)

Hodgson, Jim (Forensics; Physiology)

Hussein, Nada (Middle East)

Huwe, Terence K. (Labor & Industrial Relations)

Imre, Andrea (Multicultural Studies)

Irwin-Smiler, Kate (Occupations & Careers)

Jackson, Amy (Library & Information Science)

Johns-Masten, Kathryn (Birds)

Junghahn, Lisa (Business & Finance)

Kale, Esmeralda (Africa)

Kasperek, Sheila (Travel & Tourism)

Kendall, Susan (Biotechnology)

Kent, Caroline M. (Films; Journalism & Writing; Parenting)

Kline, Hilary (Gay, Lesbian, Bisexual, & Transgender; Paleontology)

Klink, Sara (Biology)

Krajewski, Rex (Gardening)

Krug, Emily (News & Opinion)

Kumar, Suhasini (Peace & Conflict Studies)

Kunkel, Lilith (Gender Studies)

Kvinnesland, Lynne (Literary Reviews)

LaBonte, Kristen (Ecology)

LaGuardia, Cheryl (Abstracts & Indexes; Chemistry; Craft; Economics; Europe; Fashion & Lifestyle)

Lamb, Bill (Music – Popular)

Lange, Jessica (Canada)

Larsen, Alison (Urban Studies)

Leigh, Miriam (Civil Liberties; Menopause/Andropause)

Lener, Edward F. (Earth Sciences & Geology)

Lincove, David (Political Science)

Loa, Berlin (Native Americans; Photography)

Long, Ann (Marriage & Divorce)

Lopez, Caroline Mandler (Cooking & Cookery)

Lowrie, Reed (Zoology)

Lundstrom, Kacy (Classroom Magazines)

Macfarlane, Carrie M. (Do-It-Yourself)

Markley, Patricia (Geriatrics & Gerontological Studies)

Martin, Heath (Literature)

McCaffrey, Erin K. (Family)

McClusky, Duncan (Agriculture)

McCutcheon, Camille (Blind & Visually-Impaired; Pets)

McDonough, Beth (Disabilities)

McGuire, Nancy (Human Resources)

McKeigue, Elizabeth (International Magazines; Theater)

McKinnon, Dawn (Canada)

McMain, Lynn (Nursing; Pregnancy)

McMinn, Howard Stephen (Aeronautics & Space Science)

Mealey, Nathan (Computers & Information Technology)

Meier, John J. (Mathematics)

Meszaros, Rosemary (Government Periodicals, Federal; Government Periodicals, State & Local)

Metcalf, Susan (Criminology & Law Enforcement)

Moore, Susan (Atmospheric Sciences)

Morgan, Marilyn (Spirituality & Well-Being)

Murray, Tara (Philately)

Newland, Patricia (Death & Dying)

CONSULTANTS

Oka, Christine (Asia & the Pacific; Asian American; Chemistry; Genealogy; Humor; Hunting & Guns; Safety)

Pannone, Jason (Philosophy)

Paranick, Amber (General Interest)

Park, Betsey (Sports)

Parker, Joshua (Middle East – Judaica Section)

Pearse, Michelle (Law)

Phelps, Devin (News & Opinion)

Providenti, Michael J. (Communication)

Randall, Eleanor (Health Professions)

Reed, Andrea (Media & A/V)

Regan, Alexandra (Craft)

Richardson, Diane (Fire Protection)

Rickert, Kathi (Sociology & Social Work)

Roberts, Sarah (Europe)

Robinson, Margaret E. (Food Industry)

Rogers, Kandace (Beer, Wine, & Spirits)

Rojeski, Mara (Population Studies)

Ronningen, Jim (Newspapers)

Ruan, Lian (Fire Protection)

Rudisell, Carol (African American)

Saloiye, Laura A. (Fiction: Science Fiction, Fantasy, & Horror)

Sands, Diane T. (Environment & Conservation; Food & Nutrition)

Scanlon, Donna (General Interest)

Schmidt, Krista (Health & Fitness)

Schwartz, Vanette M. (Cultural Studies)

Scott, Michael (Latin America & Spain)

Seaman, Priscilla (Anthropology)

Shelton, Mark (Education)

Shrode, Flora G. (Earth Sciences & Geology)

Siegler, Sharon L. (Energy; Robotics)

Smith, Donna B. (Printing & Graphic Arts)

Sobinski-Smith, Mary Jane (Management & Administration)

Sprung, Amy (Teenagers)

Staiger, Jeff (Linguistics)

Storm, Paula M. (Electronics)

Stormes, Sheridan (Music - General)

Straw, Joe (Military)

Sugrue, Edward Creighton (Astronomy)

Sullivan, Laura A. (Communication)

Sundheim, Jennifer (Hiking, Climbing, & Outdoor Recreation)

Tadman, Andrew (Antiques)

Thomas, Mary Augusta (Dance)

Tidwell, Judith (Globalization)

Tomlin, Patrick (Landscape Architecture)

Trendler, Amy (Architecture)

Truslow, Hugh (Slavic Studies)

Tsang, Daniel (Sexuality)

Van de Streek, David (Numismatics)

Vaughn, Cynthia (Medicine)

Watson, Amy (Hospitality/Restaurant)

Webster, Janet (Marine Science & Technology)

Weimer, Kathy (Cartography, GIS, & Imagery)

Weiss, Deborah (Weddings)

Wharton, Nick (Building & Construction)

White, Darla (Home)

Williams, Clay (Advertising, Marketing & Public Relations)

Williams, Stacie (Archives & Manuscripts)

Wingfield, Rebecca (Fiction: General/Mystery & Detective)

Wolfe, Mark (Bibliography)

Wood, Wendy (Printing & Graphic Arts)

Woolums, Jill (Psychology)

Worster, Paul (Television, Video & Radio)

Young, Courtney L. (Interdisciplinary Studies)

Zhe-Heimerman, Kari (Botany)

MAGAZINES FOR LIBRARIES

■ ACCOUNTING AND TAXATION

Professional/Scholarly/Taxation

Christine Adams, Business & Economics Librarian, William F. Maag, Jr. Library, Youngstown State University, One University Plaza, Youngstown, OH 44555; cmadams02@ysu.edu

Introduction

During the past several years, numerous events have occurred to significantly impact the accounting and tax professions. In order to address the debt-ceiling crisis, the Budget Control Act of 2011 was signed into law. One of the stipulations of the Act required Congress to formulate a plan to decrease the deficit by $1.2 trillion. If Congress failed to act by November 2012, automatic cuts or "sequestrations" would go into effect beginning January 2013. These impending cuts in government spending occasioned by the Budget Control Act and the simultaneous expiration of the Bush tax cuts became known as the "fiscal cliff." To contend with the looming fiscal-cliff crisis, the American Taxpayer Relief Act (ATRA) of 2012 was passed in the Senate. This Act made permanent much of the lower rates of the Bush tax cuts, while sustaining higher tax rates and caps on tax deductions and credits for upper income levels. The ATRA of 2012 addressed the tax aspects of the fiscal cliff crisis, but deferred for two months the issue of sequestration. The two-month deadline lapsed without the formulation of a resolution, triggering across-the-board government spending cuts. These events prompted so many tax issues and changes that the Internal Revenue Service delayed the beginning of tax season in 2013, as many tax forms required updating due to changes legislated in the fiscal-cliff deal.

The next year promises to be another interesting one for the IRS. A federal court ruled that the IRS does not have the statutory authority to enforce its Registered Tax Return Preparer program; meanwhile, a document was released by the American Civil Liberties Union indicating that the criminal division of the IRS may be accessing taxpayer e-mails without search warrants; and information surfaced that the IRS had unfairly scrutinized Tea Party groups applying for tax exempt status. These issues will undoubtedly result in countless changes affecting accounting and tax professionals, well into the next tax year and beyond.

The incessant changes in our government and economy justify the need for high-quality accounting and tax publications. Professionals and academics are required to stay current regarding new standards and developments, and therefore rely heavily upon the literature of their profession. Titles in this list are presented in three major sections: (1) "Professional" titles that provide practical information to CPAs and accounting professionals; (2) "Scholarly" titles that publish the results of academic research relevant to the profession; and (3) "Taxation" titles that provide information specific to those preparing tax returns and providing tax advice. A balanced blend of information from all three categories is of value to accounting and tax professionals.

Practical information supplied by professional journals is vital for daily practice, while theoretical academic research is of the utmost importance in order to analyze and improve the profession. This list attempts to strike a balance between the practical and the theoretical to help libraries build a solid accounting and taxation collection, especially academic libraries that support accounting research and post-graduate programs. With the shift toward International Financial Reporting Standards, journals espousing global perspectives continue to grow in importance. This list attempts to provide sources of information and research not only from the United States, but from other parts of the world as well.

The formats in which titles are available are continuously transforming. Of course, most journals are still available in print format, but all provide for electronic access in some form. Many titles are published by major content providers and are available through database subscriptions, while some are published by associations that provide electronic access at their web sites through membership or subscription. The association web sites are especially useful for professionals because of the enhanced features, such as daily updates, blogs, RSS feeds, e-newsletters, searchable archives, professional development opportunities, and more. Many content providers, journals, and associations now have social media presences and mobile applications available for various devices.

The resources suggested in this list should assist in forming a well-rounded core collection for accounting researchers and professionals. Because accounting and taxation intersect with so many other subject areas, librarians may also wish to consider sources listed in other sections of this volume, such as Business and Finance, Economics, and Law.

Basic Periodicals

Ac: *Accounting, Organizations & Society, Accounting Review, Accounting Today, The CPA Journal, Contemporary Accounting Research, Journal of Accountancy, Journal of Accounting Research, Journal of Accounting & Economics, Journal of Accounting Research.*

Basic Abstracts and Indexes

ABI/INFORM, Accounting and Tax Database, Business & Company ProFile ASAP, Business Periodicals Index, Business Source Complete.

Professional

1. *Accountancy.* Formerly (until 1938): *Incorporated Accountants' Journal.* [ISSN: 0001-4664] 1889. m. Free to members; Non-members, GBP 79. Ed(s): Penny Sukhraj, Sara White. Wolters Kluwer UK Ltd., 145 London Rd, Kingston upon Thames, KT2 6SR, United Kingdom; info@wolterskluwer.com; http://www.cch.co.uk. Illus., index, adv. Vol. ends: Jun/Dec. Microform: PQC. *Indexed:* A22, ABIn, ATI, B01, B02, BRI. *Aud.:* Sa.

In publication for over 123 years, *Accountancy* is a monthly professional journal whose focus is on major issues, current news, and technical developments affecting the United Kingdom accounting professions. Published by CCH, each issue provides in-depth insight, topical comment, and authoritative analysis from leading industry professionals, including technical tax specialists, auditors, forensic experts, tax lawyers, and more. The magazine presents technical and authoritative analysis on complex tax, accounting, and audit issues. The publication is divided into four core categories—"Tax," "Accounting," "Audit," and "Development"—and is color-coded for easy access. The companion web site, *Accountancy Live,* provides electronic access to the publication by subscription.

2. *The Accountant.* Incorporates (1989-1996): *Corporate Accounting International.* [ISSN: 0001-4710] 1874. m. V R L Financial News, 40-42 Hatton Garden, London, EC1 N8EB, United Kingdom; info@vrlfinancialnews.com; http://vrl.trimetric.com. Illus., index, adv. *Indexed:* A22, ATI, B02, B03, BRI, C42. *Aud.:* Sa.

Established in 1874, *The Accountant* is one of the oldest and most highly regarded trade magazines in the world. This journal is published monthly for those involved in the accounting profession, and each issue reports global news, surveys worldwide accounting bodies, provides commentary from industry figures, and profiles business and industry leaders. Regular coverage is provided for products and product innovation, country surveys, technological developments, trends and industry developments, opinions of key players, market-sizing and global perspective, etc. Members of The Association of Chartered Certified Accountants may include reading of *The Accountant* toward Continuing Professional Development qualification, if it has helped them to acquire knowledge and skills relevant to their position. Electronic access to recent editions is provided at the magazine's web site by subscription.

3. *Accounting & Business.* Former titles (until 1998): *Certified Accountant;* (until 1972): *Certified Accountants' Journal;* (until 1966): *Accountants Journal.* [ISSN: 1460-406X] 19??. 10x/yr. Free to members. Ed(s): Chris Quick, Rosana Mirkovic. Association of Chartered Certified Accountants, 29 Lincoln's Inn Fields, London, WC2A 3EE, United Kingdom; info@accaglobal.com; http://www.accaglobal.com. Illus. *Indexed:* A22, ATI. *Bk. rev.:* 3, 150-400 words, signed. *Aud.:* Sa.

Accounting & Business is a professional magazine for members of the Association of Chartered Certified Accountants, a global body for professional accountants. It is published ten times per year in six separate editions—International, China, Malaysia, Singapore, Ireland, and the U.K.—with essential information for accountants and business professionals around the world. Each issue features news in pictures, news in graphics, news round-up, and analysis. Business and accounting-related articles are featured in various sections, including "Viewpoint," "Technical," "Corporate," and "Practice." If an article is relevant to professional development needs, it can count toward verifiable Continuing Professional Development. A full text archive of the various editions from recent years is freely available at the ACCA web site.

4. *Accounting Horizons.* [ISSN: 0888-7993] 1987. q. USD 370. Ed(s): Dana R Hermanson. American Accounting Association, 5717 Bessie Dr, Sarasota, FL 34233; info@aaahq.org; http://aaahq.org. Illus., index, adv. Refereed. Circ: 5500. Vol. ends: Dec. Reprint: PSC. *Indexed:* A22, ABIn, ATI, B01, B02, IBSS. *Aud.:* Ac, Sa.

Accounting Horizons is a refereed scholarly journal published by the American Accounting Association. One of the main objectives of the publication is "to establish a dialogue—a bridge of ideas—between accounting academics and the business community." The content is written for academics and professionals, including researchers, educators, practitioners, regulators, and students of accounting. Articles focus on a wide variety of accounting topics and provide insight into the accounting profession as a whole, from ethics to financial reporting, to regulation of the profession. Topics are relevant to current accounting issues and the future of the accounting profession. Also presented are reviews of professional literature, commentaries on practice, and reports of current events. *Accounting Horizons* is published quarterly and is an ISI-listed journal.

5. *Accounting Perspectives.* Formerly (until 2006): *Canadian Accounting Perspectives.* [ISSN: 1911-382X] 2001. s-a. Ed(s): Amin Mawani. Canadian Academic Accounting Association, 245 Fairview Mall Dr, Ste 410, Toronto, ON M2J 4T1, Canada; admin@caaa.ca; http://www.caaa.ca. Refereed. Reprint: PSC. *Indexed:* A22, ABIn, ATI, B01, E01. *Aud.:* Ac, Sa.

Accounting Perspectives is a refereed scholarly journal published semi-annually by Wiley-Blackwell on behalf of the Canadian Academic Accounting Association, an organization for those involved in research and education related to accounting. The publication provides a forum for scholarly research conducted by academics and practitioners that addresses current issues in the field of accounting. Topics discussed include financial accounting and reporting, auditing and other assurance services, management accounting and performance measurement, corporate governance, information systems and related technologies, tax policy and practice, professional ethics, accounting education, and more. The journal presents applied research, analysis, and commentary of interest to academics, practitioners, financial analysts, financial executives, regulators, accounting policy makers, and students. Content also includes field studies, case histories, essays, discussion forums, instructional cases, and education articles. Although published in Canada, the journal seeks a global readership, as well as global submissions. All theoretical and methodological perspectives are welcome.

6. *Accounting Today: the business newspaper for the tax and accounting community.* [ISSN: 1044-5714] 1987. bi-w. USD 139. Ed(s): Daniel Hood. SourceMedia, Inc., One State St Plz, 27th Fl, New York, NY 10004; custserv@sourcemedia.com; http://www.sourcemedia.com. Illus. *Indexed:* A22, ATI, B01, B02, B03, BRI, C42, CompLI, I15. *Aud.:* Sa.

Accounting Today provides relevant business news and practical information for the tax and accounting community. The biweekly newspaper aids CPAs in public practice in making informed decisions concerning their businesses. Coverage includes mergers and acquisitions, Sarbanes-Oxley compliance and legislative updates, critical changes in tax laws, growth strategies and rapidly expanding client services, technology and financial planning, etc. Each issue features sections dedicated to "Top of the News," "Opinion," "Tax Practice," "Assurance," "Financial Planning," "Technology," "Practice Resources," and "Accounting Tomorrow." Their annual rankings, especially the Top 100 Firms and the Top 100 Most Influential People in Accounting, are of widespread note in the accounting profession. The companion web site includes electronic access to current and recent issues.

7. *C A Magazine.* Incorporates (1969-1996): *C I C A Dialogue;* Former titles (until 1974): *Chartered Accountant;* (until 1971): *Canadian Chartered Accountant;* Which incorporated (1949-1953): *Canadian Chartered Accountant Tax Review.* [ISSN: 0317-6878] 1911. 10x/yr. USD 28 domestic (Students, USD 25). Ed(s): Okey Chigbo. Canadian Institute of Chartered Accountants, 277 Wellington St W, Toronto, ON M5V 3H2, Canada; http://www.cica.ca. Illus., adv. Microform: PQC. *Indexed:* A22, ABIn, ATI, B01, B02, BRI, C37. *Aud.:* Sa.

CA Magazine is published ten times per year, in French and English, by the Canadian Institute of Chartered Accountants for the benefit of CAs and CA students. The magazine provides a forum for analysis, discussion, and debate on existing practices and emerging issues. It informs CAs about developments that affect the profession, whether public practice, industry, government, or academia. Feature articles cover a wide range of topics, including technological advances, business trends that affect members of the profession and their clients, and growing opportunities for CAs in the global marketplace. The publication is divided into an "Upfront" section (short profiles, news of interest, general business items), "Features," "Regulars" (Assurance, Fraud, People Management, Taxation, Standards, etc.), "From the Profession" (news and recently issued pronouncements), and "Columns" (editorial). A full-text archive going back to 1997 is available at the magazine web site.

8. *The C P A Journal.* Former titles (until Dec.1975): *The C P A;* (until Jun.1975): *C.P.A. Journal;* (until 1972): *Certified Public Accountant;* (until 1971): *New York Certified Public Accountant: C P A;* (until 1935): *New York State Society of Certified Public Accountants. Bulletin.* [ISSN: 0732-8435] 1930. m. Ed(s): Anthony H Sarmiento. New York State Society of Certified Public Accountants, 3 Park Ave, 18th Fl, New York, NY 10016; http://www.cpaj.com. Illus., adv. Vol. ends: Dec. *Indexed:* A22, ABIn, ATI, B01, B02, BRI. *Bk. rev.:* 0-1, 250-350 words, signed. *Aud.:* Sa.

The CPA Journal is a monthly publication of the New York State Society of CPAs and has been one of the leading national accounting publications for nearly 80 years. It is "[e]dited by CPAs for CPAs," and its goal is to provide accounting practitioners, educators, and other financial professionals with analysis, perspective, and debate on developments in the areas of accounting, auditing, taxation, finance, management, technology, and professional ethics. Content includes the latest news and developments for auditing standards, technology, IRS tax issues, legislation and regulation, taxation, e-commerce, budgeting, trends, and more. The focus is on practical information and thoughtful analysis of relevant issues. Article formats include general interest, technical interest, and those that express an opinion, perspective, or viewpoint. The journal's double-blind review process ensures the highest technical quality. The full text of *The CPA Journal* is available online going back to 1989, as well as article indexes from 2001 to the present.

9. *C P A Practice Advisor: today's technology for tomorrow's firm.* Former titles (until 2011): *The C P A Technology Advisor;* (until 2004): *The C P A Software News;* (until 1991): *N S P A Software News.* [ISSN: 2160-8725] 1991. 8x/yr. Free to qualified personnel. Ed(s): Darren Root, Isaac M O'Bannon. Cygnus Business Media, Inc., 1233 Janesville Ave, PO Box 803, Fort Atkinson, WI 53538; http://www.cygnus.com. Adv. *Indexed:* ABIn, ATI, B01, B02. *Aud.:* Sa.

CPA Practice Advisor is published eight times per year by Cygnus Business Media. The publication's mission is to serve, inform, educate, and lead tax and accounting professionals in the areas of technology, workflow systems, and best practices so that their firms can become more efficient, productive, and profitable. Through in-depth reviews, interactive tools, insightful columns, timely features, and examinations of best practices and strategies, the goal is to help identify the most beneficial combination of technology and processes. *CPA Practice Advisor* is the only profession-focused workflow technology resource that assists public accountants in advising small business clients regarding business management strategies that can help increase productivity. Content includes technology and software reviews, columns from industry leaders, and user-oriented features. This publication is widely respected for its editorial independence, objectivity, and integrity. Recent digital issues are accessible from the magazine's web site with free registration.

10. *C P A Practice Management Forum.* [ISSN: 1556-0899] 2005. m. USD 510 combined subscription (print & online eds.). Ed(s): Sandra Lim, Terry Vaughan. C C H Inc., 2700 Lake Cook Rd, Riverwoods, IL 60015; cust_serv@cch.com; http://www.cchgroup.com/. *Indexed:* ABIn, ATI, B01. *Aud.:* Sa.

CPA Practice Management Forum from CCH is a monthly magazine that provides news, commentary, and features that focus on key topics of importance to CPA firm managers and partners. The focus of the publication is on helping accounting firm leaders deal effectively with critical challenges. Successful accounting firms and their strategies are examined, and practical advice is provided from knowledgeable managing partners, human resource directors, marketing managers, etc. Each issue provides practitioner advice on firm growth and management; techniques to improve employee retention, productivity, and profitability; methods for recruiting prospects and cultivating leaders; strategies for creating a positive and productive firm culture; profiles of unique and successful accounting firms; tips on successful practice development approaches, marketing, and strategic development; etc. A list of relevant conferences, seminars, and workshops is provided at the end of each issue.

11. *Cost Management.* Formerly (until 1992): *Journal of Cost Management for the Manufacturing Industry.* [ISSN: 1092-8057] 1987. 1 Base Vol(s) bi-m. Ed(s): Paul Sharman, Jack Nestor. W G & L Financial Reporting & Management Research, 395 Hudson St, New York, NY 10014; ria.customerservices@thomson.com; http://ria.thomson.com. Adv. Reprint: PSC. *Indexed:* A22, ABIn, ATI. *Aud.:* Sa.

Cost Management is a bimonthly trade publication that features articles, experience-based columns, and case studies on topics related to cost management. The goal of the publication is to aid readers in developing and improving the financial and nonfinancial performance of business using cost-management techniques and systems. Topics addressed include cost-management systems, methods and techniques, performance measurement, investment justification criteria, etc. Articles are written for a diverse audience with varying degrees of knowledge and are concise and to the point.

12. *Financial Management.* Former titles (until 2000): *Management Accounting;* (until 1965): *Cost Accountant.* [ISSN: 1471-9185] 1921. m. Free to members. Ed(s): Lawrie Holmes. Chartered Institute of Management Accountants, 26 Chapter St, London, SW1P 4NP, United Kingdom; cima.contact@cimaglobal.com; http://www.cimaglobal.com. Illus., index, adv. Reprint: SCH. *Indexed:* A22, ABIn, ATI, B01, B02, BRI, JEL. *Aud.:* Sa.

Financial Management is the official magazine of the Chartered Institute of Management Accountants, a professional body with a focus on management accounting careers in public and private-sector business. It is the largest accountancy title and the fifth-largest business-to-business publication in the United Kingdom. Each issue covers essential matters for CIMA members and

provides information, technical updates, analysis, and current news. Primary readers include business leaders and key decision-makers from leading companies and commercial organizations around the world. Recent digital editions are available at the magazine's web site.

13. *Internal Auditing.* [ISSN: 0897-0378] 1986. 1 Base Vol(s) bi-m. Ed(s): Susan Weisenfeld, Jack Nestor. W G & L Financial Reporting & Management Research, 395 Hudson St, New York, NY 10014; ria.customerservices@thomson.com; http://ria.thomson.com. Adv. *Indexed:* A22, ABIn, ATI, B02, BRI. *Aud.:* Ac, Sa.

Internal Auditing is a bimonthly publication that features practice-oriented content on critical issues facing internal auditors. The goal of the publication is to aid internal auditors in pinpointing and solving audit problems, understanding information technology, conducting effective and efficient audits, managing internal-auditing departments, and staying current in audit trends and developments. Articles are primarily practice-oriented and are of interest to those in the internal-auditing profession. Issues feature practical advice, study results and summaries of current audit research, analysis of current developments and trends, best practices, case studies, professional standards and issues, and feedback on new initiatives and standards from COSO, the Institute of Internal Auditors, and other organizations. Sample topics include compliance issues, risk assessment, fraud prevention, corporate governance, and IT auditing.

14. *Internal Auditor: global perspectives on risk, control and governance.* Formerly (until 19??): *I I A Research Reports.* [ISSN: 0020-5745] 1944. bi-m. USD 60 combined subscription in North America (print & online eds.); USD 84 combined subscription elsewhere (print & online eds.). Ed(s): Anne Millage, David Salierno. Institute of Internal Auditors, Inc., 247 Maitland Ave, Altamonte Springs, FL 32701; custserv@theiia.org; http://www.theiia.org. Illus., index. Refereed. Vol. ends: Dec. Microform: PQC. Reprint: SCH. *Indexed:* A22, ABIn, ATI, B01, B02, BRI, C42. *Bk. rev.:* 1-2, 500-1,000 words, signed. *Aud.:* Ac, Sa.

Internal Auditor is a bimonthly publication from the Institute of Internal Auditors and features global content relevant to the internal auditing profession. The goal of the publication is to provide practitioners with essential information and practices needed for day-to-day operations. Content includes articles that focus on practical application of topics discussed, case studies describing procedures or methodology including actual or hypothetical examples, and analysis of studies and surveys that draw conclusions from research and analyze the impact on the internal-auditing profession. Content of the magazine is divided between in-depth feature articles and departments, which present a more narrow focus or an opinionated tone. Regular features include "Reader Feedback," "Fraud Findings," "In My Opinion," "ITAudit," "Back to Basics," "Risk Watch," and "Governance Perspectives." Topics are timely and offer practical insight and expert advice to readers.

15. *Journal of Accountancy.* [ISSN: 0021-8448] 1905. m. Ed(s): Kim Nilsen, Rocky S Rosen. American Institute of Certified Public Accountants, 1211 Ave of the Americas, New York, NY 10036; journal@aicpa.org; http://www.aicpa.org. Illus., index, adv. Sample. Vol. ends: Jun/Dec. *Indexed:* A22, ABIn, ATI, B01, B02, BRI, CBRI, CLI, L14, P02. *Aud.:* Ac, Sa.

In publication for over 100 years, the *Journal of Accountancy* is the flagship publication of the American Institute of Certified Public Accountants, whose members include finance and accounting professionals from public accounting firms, corporations, government agencies, and nonprofit organizations. Each issue contains feature articles on subjects such as accounting, financial reporting, auditing, taxation, personal financial planning, technology, business valuation, professional development, ethics, liability issues, consulting, practice management, education, and more. Articles are presented relating to the following categories: "Practical," "Corporate," "Technical," "Professional Issues," and "Future." "Practical" articles discuss business problems and offer actual or hypothetical solutions. "Corporate" articles explore aspects of corporate finance. "Technical" articles cover new standards or best practices, including regulatory actions. "Professional Issue" articles address issues that face the accounting profession and provide guidance. "Future" articles are based on academic research or fast-moving trends that have an immediate or near-future impact on the accounting profession. Regular columns are also featured in each issue.

16. ***The Journal of Government Financial Management.*** Former titles (until 2001): *The Government Accountants Journal;* (until 1976): *The Federal Accountant.* [ISSN: 1533-1385] 1950. q. Free to members; Non-members, USD 95. Ed(s): Marie S. Force. Association of Government Accountants, 2208 Mount Vernon Ave, Alexandria, VA 22301; http://www.agacgfm.org. Illus., index, adv. Refereed. Circ: 14769. Vol. ends: Winter. Microform: PQC. *Indexed:* A22, ABIn, ATI, B01, BRI. *Aud.:* Ac, Sa.

The Journal of Government Financial Management is a refereed journal that is published quarterly by the Association of Government Accountants, a member organization for financial professionals in government. The purpose of the journal is to contribute to the literature of the government financial management profession. The publication provides in-depth information to government financial managers in federal, state, and local government, as well as the private sector and academia. It is read by accountants, auditors, budget analysts, electronic data processors, finance directors, information resource managers, chief financial officers, inspectors general, consultants, and systems designers. Areas of interest include hardware/software products, business supplies, office equipment, management and IT consulting services, education and training, products and services, professional development resources, research tools, temporary services, and more.

17. ***Main Street Practitioner.*** Incorporates (1956-2009): *Tax Magazine;* Formerly (unitl 2004): *The N S A Practitioner.* 19??. bi-m. Free to members. Ed(s): Julene Joy. National Society of Accountants, 1010 N. Fairfax St., Alexandria, VA 22314-1574; http://www.nsacct.org/. *Aud.:* Sa.

Main Street Practitioner is a publication of the National Society of Accountants, an association for "Main Street" tax and accounting professionals. The publication is aimed at all levels of tax professionals, with an emphasis on those who manage or own their own tax and accounting businesses. Articles discuss and analyze cutting-edge information, current trends, and best practices. Subject areas include bankruptcy, corporations, estate planning, IRS negotiation, new tax regulations, partnerships, professional development, Social Security benefits, tax season preparation, and more. Each issue focuses on a particular theme and includes special features, case studies, tax tips, and best-practice advice from experts. The magazine is published six times per year in digital format and in a short-run full-color printed version.

18. ***Public Accounting Report.*** Incorporates (2000-2004): *C P A Financial Services Advisor.* [ISSN: 0161-309X] 1978. m. Ed(s): Julie Lindy. C C H Inc., 2700 Lake Cook Rd, Riverwoods, IL 60015; cust_serv@cch.com; http://www.cchgroup.com/. *Indexed:* ATI, B01, B02. *Aud.:* Sa.

CCH's *Public Accounting Report* is a monthly newsletter that provides competitive intelligence for public accounting firms as well as the entire accounting profession. The publication is "renowned for its straight reporting and analysis of the news, developments, and trends that have defined the profession for more than 20 years." The primary audience includes public accounting firm partners and professionals, opinion leaders, and industry observers. Content features current news, in-depth firm profiles, mergers and acquisitions, office closings, key personnel moves, legal and regulatory issues, competitive intelligence, niche practices, product launches, and more. A subscription includes special reports and extras, including the "PAR Top 100," an annual ranking of the 100 largest accounting firms in the U.S., and the "PAR Professors Survey," an annual ranking of the best accounting programs in the U.S. based on the opinions of accounting professors from American universities.

19. ***S E C Accounting Report.*** [ISSN: 0146-485X] 1974. 1 Base Vol(s) m. Ed(s): Paul J Wendell. W G & L Financial Reporting & Management Research, 195 Broadway, New York, NY 10007; ria.customerservices@thomson.com; http://ria.thomson.com. Illus., index. Vol. ends: Nov. *Indexed:* ATI. *Aud.:* Sa.

The *SEC Accounting Report* is a monthly newsletter that reports on rulings and official releases of the Securities and Exchange Commission. The focus of the publication is on changes and new rulings, as well as the effects of those changes. Each issue provides readers with analysis of promulgations from the SEC, Financial Accounting Standards Board, International Accounting Standards Board, and Public Company Accounting Oversight Board, and the resulting compliance requirements. This publication specializes in: alerting readers to new SEC developments and federal regulations; explaining key issues and analyzing implications; providing guidance for complex compliance issues; forecasting changes and new rulings from federal agencies; reporting important court actions and proceedings; and outlining techniques and approaches successfully used by others.

20. ***Strategic Finance.*** Former titles (until 1999): *Management Accounting;* (until 1968): *N A A Management Accounting;* (until 1965): *N A A Bulletin;* (until 1957): *N A C A Bulletin;* (until 1925): *National Association of Cost Accountants. Official Publications.* [ISSN: 1524-833X] 1919. m. USD 195. Ed(s): Kathy Williams. Institute of Management Accountants, 10 Paragon Dr, Ste 1, Montvale, NJ 07645; ima@imanet.org; http://www.imanet.org. Illus., index, adv. Vol. ends: Jun. Microform: PQC. Reprint: SCH. *Indexed:* A22, ABIn, ATI, B01, B02, BRI, EconLit, JEL. *Aud.:* Sa.

Strategic Finance is a monthly publication of the Institute of Management Accountants, a worldwide professional association for accountants and finance professionals working in business. The magazine provides timely and relevant information about practices and trends in finance, accounting, and information management. Articles offer advice to help readers perform their jobs more effectively, advance their careers, grow personally and professionally, and make their organizations more profitable. A notable feature is the "Annual Career Issue and Salary Survey," where IMA members' salaries are evaluated. Access to select articles is available at the IMA web site, and back issues are available for purchase.

Scholarly

21. ***Abacus: a journal of accounting, finance and business studies.*** [ISSN: 0001-3072] 1965. q. GBP 440. Ed(s): Stewart Jones, C Harrison-Ford. Wiley-Blackwell Publishing Asia, 155 Cremorne St, Richmond, VIC 3121, Australia; melbourne@wiley.com; http://www.wiley.com/. Illus., adv. Sample. Refereed. Reprint: PSC. *Indexed:* A22, ABIn, ATI, AmHI, B01, E01, IBSS, RiskAb. *Aud.:* Ac.

In publication since 1965, *Abacus* is a refereed scholarly journal published on behalf of the Accounting Foundation, The University of Sydney. The publication provides a forum for the expression of independent and critical thought on matters of current academic and professional interest in accounting, finance, and business. Articles feature current research, critical evaluation of current developments in theory and practice, analysis of the effects of regulatory framework, and exploration of alternatives to, and explanations of, past and current practices. The content is international in scope, with emphasis on international accounting and accounting history. *Abacus* is published quarterly and is an ISI-listed journal.

22. ***Accounting and Business Research.*** Formerly (until 1970): *Accounting Research.* [ISSN: 0001-4788] 19??. 5x/yr. GBP 392 (print & online eds.). Ed(s): Vivien Beattie. Routledge, 4 Park Sq, Milton Park, Abingdon, OX14 4RN, United Kingdom; subscriptions@tandf.co.uk; http://www.tandfonline.com. Illus., index, adv. Sample. Refereed. Microform: PQC; WMP. Reprint: PSC. *Indexed:* A22, ABIn, ATI, B01, B02, BRI, H&TI, IBSS. *Bk. rev.:* 0-4, 750-1,250 words, signed. *Aud.:* Ac.

Accounting and Business Research is a refereed scholarly journal that publishes papers that present a substantial and original contribution to knowledge in accounting, finance, and business research. The goal of the publication is to contribute to developing and understanding the role of accounting in business. Authors take a theoretical or empirical approach, using either quantitative or qualitative methods. Research articles cover all areas of accounting, including corporate governance, auditing, and taxation. While primarily directed to academics, this journal is also of value to practitioners and others who are concerned with the latest developments and new ideas in the field. ABR is published five times per year and is an ISI-listed journal.

23. Accounting and Finance. Former titles (until 1979): *Accounting Education;* (until 1973): *Australasian Association of University Teachers of Accounting. News Bulletin.* [ISSN: 0810-5391] 1960. q. GBP 406. Ed(s): Steven Cahan. Wiley-Blackwell Publishing Asia, 155 Cremorne St, Richmond, VIC 3121, Australia; subs@blackwellpublishingasia.com; http://www.wiley.com/. Adv. Sample. Refereed. Microform: PQC. Reprint: PSC. *Indexed:* A22, ABIn, ATI, B01, B02, BRI, E01. *Aud.:* Ac.

Accounting and Finance is a refereed scholarly journal published on behalf of the Accounting and Finance Association of Australia and New Zealand. The journal publishes theoretical, empirical, and experimental papers that significantly contribute to the disciplines of accounting, finance, business information systems, and related disciplines. The publication applies economic, organizational, and other theories to accounting and finance phenomena and presents periodic special issues with themes such as research methods in management accounting. Authors employ a wide range of research methods, including statistical analysis, analytical work, case studies, field research, and historical analysis, to examine relevant research questions from a wide range of perspectives. Readership includes academics, graduate students, and all those interested in accounting and finance research, including practitioners in accounting, corporate finance, investments, and merchant and investment banking. *Accounting and Finance* is published quarterly and is an ISI-listed journal.

24. Accounting and the Public Interest. [ISSN: 1530-9320] 2001. a. USD 135 Free to members. American Accounting Association, 5717 Bessie Dr, Sarasota, FL 34233; info@aaahq.org; http://aaahq.org. Adv. *Indexed:* ABIn, ATI, B01. *Aud.:* Ac.

Accounting and the Public Interest is an academic journal published annually by the Public Interest Section of the American Accounting Association. The goal of the publication is to provide a forum for academic accounting research that addresses the public interest and takes a socially responsive, and responsible, perspective. Alternative theories and methodologies are considered, as well as more traditional ones. Studies and findings are required to be linked to the public interest by situating them within a historical, social, and political context, as well as providing guidance for responsible action. Research articles cover topics in all areas of accounting, such as financial accounting and auditing, accounting in organizations, social and environmental accounting, government and professional regulation, taxation, gender and diversity issues, professional and business ethics, information technology, accounting and business education, governance of accounting organizations, and more.

25. Accounting, Auditing and Accountability Journal. Formerly (until 1989): *Accounting Auditing and Accountability.* [ISSN: 1368-0668] 1988. 8x/yr. EUR 7949 combined subscription in Europe (print & online eds.); USD 8349 combined subscription in the Americas (print & online eds.); GBP 5619 combined subscription in the UK & elsewhere (print & online eds.). Ed(s): Lee Parker, James Guthrie. Emerald Group Publishing Ltd., Howard House, Wagon Ln, Bingley, BD16 1WA, United Kingdom; emerald@emeraldinsight.com; http://www.emeraldinsight.com. Illus. Sample. Refereed. Vol. ends: No. 5. Reprint: PSC. *Indexed:* A22, ABIn, ATI, B01, B02, BRI, E01, IBSS, MLA-IB, RiskAb. *Bk. rev.:* 1-2, 500-1,500 words, signed. *Aud.:* Ac.

Accounting, Auditing and Accountability Journal is a refereed scholarly journal that is dedicated to the advancement of accounting knowledge and provides a forum for research on the interaction between accounting and auditing and the impact on socioeconomic and political environments. The goal of this publication is to present detailed analysis and critical assessment of current practice, discuss the implications of new policy alternatives, and explore the impact of accounting on the socioeconomic and political environment. Research and analysis may be international, national, or organization-specific in its approach. Coverage includes such topics as alternative explanations for observed practice, critical and historical perspectives on current issues and problems, political influences on policy making, social and political aspects of accounting standards, etc. Readership includes accounting and management

researchers, accountants, administrators, managers, accounting and auditing policy makers, and accounting students. The journal is published eight times per year and has been accepted for inclusion in ISI.

26. Accounting Education: an international journal. [ISSN: 0963-9284] 1992. 6x/yr. GBP 1027 (print & online eds.). Ed(s): Richard M S Wilson. Routledge, 4 Park Sq, Milton Park, Abingdon, OX14 4RN, United Kingdom; subscriptions@tandf.co.uk; http://www.tandfonline.com. Illus., index, adv. Sample. Refereed. Vol. ends: Dec. Reprint: PSC. *Indexed:* A22, ABIn, ATI, B01, E01, PsycInfo. *Bk. rev.:* 0-2, 500-750 words, signed. *Aud.:* Ac.

Accounting Education is a refereed scholarly journal that is dedicated to publishing research-based papers and other information on key aspects of accounting education and training relevant to practitioners, academics, trainers, students, and professional bodies. The primary goal of the journal is to enhance the educational base of accounting practice and thereby produce effective accounting practitioners, who in turn improve the quality of accounting practice. The publication is a forum for the exchange of ideas, experiences, opinions, and research results examining the preparation of students for careers in public accounting, managerial accounting, financial management, corporate accounting, controllership, treasury management, financial analysis, internal auditing, and accounting in government and other non-commercial organizations, as well as continuing professional development for accounting practitioners. Topics are international in scope, and coverage includes curriculum issues, computing matters, teaching methods, and research pertinent to accounting education.

27. Accounting Forum. [ISSN: 0155-9982] 1978. q. EUR 453. Ed(s): Glen Lehman. Elsevier Ltd, 32 Jamestown Rd, Camden, London, NW1 7BY, United Kingdom; corporate.sales@elsevier.com. Adv. Sample. Refereed. *Indexed:* A22, ABIn, B01, BRI, C&ISA, CerAb, E01. *Bk. rev.:* Number and length vary. *Aud.:* Ac.

Accounting Forum is a refereed scholarly journal, published quarterly, whose goal is to advance the knowledge of theory and practice in all areas of accounting, business finance, and related subjects. The publication promotes a greater understanding of the role of business in the global environment and provides a forum for the intellectual exchange of academic research in business fields, particularly within the accounting profession. Coverage includes accounting theory, auditing, financial accounting, finance and accounting education, management accounting, small business, social and environmental accounting, and taxation. The journal is published for the benefit of practitioners, academics, and students. Each issue presents peer-reviewed articles, notes and comments, and a book review section.

28. Accounting Historians Journal. Formerly (until 1977): *Accounting Historian.* [ISSN: 0148-4184] 1974. s-a. Free to members. Ed(s): Christopher Napier, Dr. Richard Fleischman. Academy of Accounting Historians, Case Western Reserve University, Weatherhead School of Management, Cleveland, OH 44106; acchistory@case.edu; http://www.aahhq.org/. Illus. Refereed. Vol. ends: Dec. *Indexed:* A22, ATI, B01, B02, BRI. *Bk. rev.:* 4-5, 750-1,500 words, signed. *Aud.:* Ac, Sa.

Accounting Historians Journal is a refereed scholarly journal published twice per year by the Academy of Accounting Historians, a nonprofit organization that researches how accounting principles and rules have changed over time. The publication explores different topics relating to the history of accounting, such as auditing challenges during the Great Depression and changes in auditing techniques during a particular period of time. Content is international in scope and addresses the evolution of accounting thought and practice. Topics are related to accounting history, including but not limited to research that provides an historical perspective on contemporary accounting issues. Past issues of the journal are available electronically at the University of Mississippi Libraries' Digital Accounting Collection.

29. Accounting History. Formerly (until 1989): *Accounting History Newsletter.* [ISSN: 1032-3732] 1980. q. USD 859. Ed(s): Garry Carnegie, Brian West. Sage Publications Ltd., 1 Oliver's Yard, 55 City Rd, London, EC1Y 1SP, United Kingdom; info@sagepub.co.uk; http://www.uk.sagepub.com. Illus., adv. Sample. Refereed. Reprint: PSC. *Indexed:* A22, ATI, E01. *Aud.:* Ac.

Accounting History is a refereed scholarly journal published quarterly in association with The Accounting and Finance Association of Australia and New Zealand. The publication provides an international perspective and a forum for the publication of high-quality manuscripts on the historical development of accounting. It seeks to advance an understanding of the interaction of accounting and its socioeconomic and political environments within historical contexts. Research articles address a wide range of topics and periods and a variety of methodological approaches including biography, prosopography, institutional history, public-sector accounting history, business history through accounting records, and comparative international accounting history. It is a premier journal in its field and is a valuable resource for academics, practitioners, and students who seek to understand accounting's past and present.

30. *Accounting, Organizations and Society: an international journal devoted to the behavioural, organizational & social aspects of accounting.* [ISSN: 0361-3682] 1976. 8x/yr. EUR 2518. Ed(s): Christopher Chapman. Pergamon, The Blvd, Langford Ln, E Park, Kidlington, OX5 1GB, United Kingdom; JournalsCustomerServiceEMEA@elsevier.com; http://www.elsevier.com. Illus., adv. Sample. Refereed. Microform: PQC. *Indexed:* A22, ABIn, ATI, B01, B02, C&ISA, CerAb, IBSS, MLA-IB. *Aud.:* Ac.

Accounting, Organizations and Society is a refereed scholarly journal published eight times per year. The publication is international in scope and focuses on aspects of the relationship between accounting and human behavior, organizational structures and processes, and the changing social and political environment of the enterprise. Topics addressed include the social role of accounting; social audit and accounting for scarce resources; the provision of accounting information to employees and trade unions and the development of participative information systems; processes that influence accounting innovations and the social and political aspects of the setting of accounting standards; behavioral studies of the users of accounting information; information-processing views of organizations; human resource accounting; cognitive aspects of accounting and decision-making processes; and more. It is an ISI-listed journal and one of *Financial Times'* top 45 journals used in business school research rankings.

31. *Accounting Research Journal.* [ISSN: 1030-9616] 1988. s-a. EUR 169 combined subscription in Europe (print & online eds.); USD 249 combined subscription in the Americas (print & online eds.); GBP 139 combined subscription in the UK & elsewhere (print & online eds.). Ed(s): Stuart Tooley, Ellie Chapple. Emerald Group Publishing Ltd., Howard House, Wagon Ln, Bingley, BD16 1WA, United Kingdom; information@emeraldinsight.com; http://www.emeraldinsight.com. Adv. Sample. Refereed. Reprint: PSC. *Indexed:* ATI, B01. *Aud.:* Ac, Sa.

The *Accounting Research Journal* is a refereed scholarly journal, published semiannually, that provides an international forum for communication between the profession and academics on emerging areas in contemporary accounting research and practice in all areas of accounting, finance, and related disciplines. The focus of the journal is on interdisciplinary studies and research on contemporary accounting issues arising in specific countries and regions and of relevance to the private sector, public sector, or not-for-profit sector. Topics addressed include reporting for the future, climate change and sustainability, accounting education, taxation policy and outcomes, forensic accounting, fraud, corporate and behavioral governance, reporting on the Internet, alternative reporting formats, integrated reporting, accounting and e-business, non-financial performance measurement and reporting, and more. The audience for this publication includes accounting, finance and management researchers, educators, practitioners, and policy makers interested in the role of accounting in organizations.

32. *The Accounting Review.* [ISSN: 0001-4826] 1926. bi-m. USD 450 United States. Ed(s): John Harry Evans, III. American Accounting Association, 5717 Bessie Dr, Sarasota, FL 34233; info@aaahq.org; http://aaahq.org. Illus., index, adv. Refereed. Circ: 8000. Vol. ends: Oct. Microform: PQC. Reprint: PSC. *Indexed:* A22, ABIn, ATI, B01, B02, BRI, CBRI, EconLit, IBSS, JEL. *Bk. rev.:* 2-3, 350-1,500 words, signed. *Aud.:* Ac.

In publication since 1926, *The Accounting Review* is a refereed scholarly journal published bimonthly by the American Accounting Association. The AAA promotes worldwide excellence in accounting education, research, and practice, and their policies state that *The Accounting Review* "should be viewed as the premier journal for publishing articles reporting the results of accounting research and explaining and illustrating related research methodology." Areas of coverage include accounting information systems, auditing and assurance services, financial accounting, management accounting, taxation, and all other areas of accounting, broadly defined. The primary audience for this publication is academicians, graduate students, and others interested in accounting research. It is an ISI-listed journal and one of *Financial Times'* top 45 journals used in business school research rankings.

33. *Asia - Pacific Journal of Accounting & Economics.* Formerly (until 2000): *Asia - Pacific Journal of Accounting.* [ISSN: 1608-1625] 1993. s-a. GBP 220 (print & online eds.). Routledge, 4 Park Sq, Milton Park, Abingdon, OX14 4RN, United Kingdom; subscriptions@tandf.co.uk; http://www.tandfonline.com. Refereed. Reprint: PSC. *Indexed:* ABIn, ATI, EconLit, JEL. *Aud.:* Ac.

The *Asia-Pacific Journal of Accounting & Economics* is a refereed scholarly journal published on behalf of the City University of Hong Kong and National Taiwan University. The publication provides an international forum for theoretical and empirical research in all areas of economics and accounting. Although most articles relate to the Asia-Pacific region, research from scholars that relates to other regions is also included. Coverage is focused on areas including auditing, financial reporting, earnings management, financial analysts, the role of accounting information, international trade and finance, industrial organization, strategic behavior, market structure, financial contracts, corporate governance, capital markets, and financial institutions. *APJAE* is published three times per year and is an ISI-listed journal.

34. *Auditing: a journal of practice and theory.* [ISSN: 0278-0380] 1981. q. USD 120. Ed(s): Robert Knechel. American Accounting Association, 5717 Bessie Dr, Sarasota, FL 34233; info@aaahq.org; http://aaahq.org. Illus., adv. Refereed. Circ: 2000. Reprint: PSC. *Indexed:* A22, ABIn, ATI, B01, B02. *Aud.:* Ac, Sa.

Auditing: A Journal of Practice & Theory is a refereed scholarly journal published by the American Accounting Association. The goal of the publication is to improve the practice and theory of internal and external auditing and to promote communication between research and practice that influences present and future developments in auditing education, as well as auditing research and practice. Articles report the results of original research that put forth improvements in auditing theory or auditing methodology. Also included are discussion and analysis of current issues that affect prospects for developments in auditing practice and in auditing research; practices and developments in auditing in different countries; and uses of auditing in new ways and for different purposes. *Auditing* is published quarterly and is an ISI-listed journal.

35. *Behavioral Research in Accounting.* [ISSN: 1050-4753] 1989. s-a. USD 150. Ed(s): Vicky Arnold. American Accounting Association, 5717 Bessie Dr, Sarasota, FL 34233; info@aaahq.org; http://aaahq.org. Adv. Circ: 1400. Microform: PQC. Reprint: PSC. *Indexed:* A22, ABIn, ATI, B01, B02, EconLit, JEL. *Aud.:* Ac, Sa.

Behavioral Research in Accounting is an academic journal published by the Accounting, Behavior and Organizations Section of the American Accounting Association. The mission of the ABO Section is to encourage excellence in research and education regarding the interface between behavioral and organizational sciences and accounting. *BRIA* promotes wide dissemination of the results of systematic scholarly inquiries into the broad field of accounting. The focus of the publication is on original research that relates to accounting and how it affects and is affected by individuals and organizations. Content includes theoretical papers and papers based upon empirical research, mainly field, survey, and experimental. The journal is published semi-annually, and is directed primarily to members of the AAA, particularly the ABO Section.

36. *The British Accounting Review.* [ISSN: 0890-8389] 1969. q. EUR 914. Ed(s): Alan Lowe, Nathan Joseph. Academic Press, 32 Jamestown Rd, Camden, London, NW1 7BY, United Kingdom; corporate.sales@elsevier.com; http://www.elsevier.com/. Adv. Sample. Refereed. Reprint: PSC. *Indexed:* A22, ABIn, ATI, B01, E01, IBSS. *Aud.:* Ac.

The British Accounting Review is a refereed scholarly journal published quarterly by the British Accounting & Finance Association. The journal features original and scholarly research papers relating to the broad fields of accounting and finance. Papers may be theoretical, supported with analytical applications of the theory, or empirical, demonstrating the use of appropriate data collection methods and motivated by appropriate theory. Research methods may be analytical, archival, experimental, or qualitative, as well as statistical or econometric in nature. Topics include financial reporting and corporate disclosure, management accounting, accounting information systems, public sector accounting, social and environmental accounting, accounting education, accounting history, taxation, financial regulation, auditing and auditing risk, corporate finance, financial markets and institutions, asset pricing, behavioral finance and risk management, and more. The audience for this journal includes academics, accountants, auditors, students, finance managers and directors, corporate treasurers, accounting and auditing standards bodies, government departments, and financial regulators.

37. Contemporary Accounting Research. [ISSN: 0823-9150] 1984. q. Ed(s): Patricia O'Brien. Canadian Academic Accounting Association, 245 Fairview Mall Dr, Ste 410, Toronto, ON M2J 4T1, Canada; admin@caaa.ca; http://www.caaa.ca. Illus., adv. Refereed. Vol. ends: Winter. Microform: PQC. Reprint: PSC. *Indexed:* A22, ABIn, ATI, B01, E01, EconLit, IBSS, JEL. *Aud.:* Ac.

Contemporary Accounting Research is a refereed scholarly journal published quarterly on behalf of the Canadian Academic Accounting Association. *CAR* provides a forum for high-quality research that contributes to the understanding of all aspects of accounting's role within organizations, markets, or society. The journal is international in scope, and its goal is to reflect the geographical and intellectual diversity in accounting research. Coverage includes all aspects of accounting, including audit, financial, information systems, managerial, and tax. Research methods may be analytical, archival, case study, empirical, field, or experimental in nature. Topics often cross disciplines to include economics, finance, history, psychology, sociology, or any that help to examine the role of accounting within organizations, markets, or society. Articles may be written in either English or French. CAR is an ISI-listed journal and one of *Financial Times'* top 45 journals used in business school research rankings.

38. Critical Perspectives on Accounting. [ISSN: 1045-2354] 1990. 8x/yr. EUR 1018. Ed(s): M Annisette, D Neu. Academic Press, 32 Jamestown Rd, Camden, London, NW1 7BY, United Kingdom; corporate.sales@elsevier.com; http://www.elsevier.com/. Illus., adv. Sample. Refereed. Vol. ends: Dec. Reprint: PSC. *Indexed:* A22, ABIn, ATI, B01, E01, IBSS. *Aud.:* Ac.

Critical Perspectives on Accounting is a refereed academic forum for scholars worldwide who are interested in the broader social, economic, and political issues raised by accounting technologies and corporate behavior. Contributors to this publication subscribe to the belief that conventional theory and practice are not suited to the challenges of the modern era, and that accounting practices and corporate behavior are connected with many of today's allocative, distributive, social, and ecological problems. Many of the research articles presented seek to reformulate corporate, social, and political activity, and suggest the theoretical and practical means by which to do so. Research topics include accounting's involvement in gender and class conflicts in the workplace; management accounting's role in organizing the labor process; the political economy of accounting; and financial accounting's role in the processes of international capital formation, and its impact on stock market stability and international banking activities, etc.

39. Current Issues in Auditing. [ISSN: 1936-1270] 2007. s-a. Free. Ed(s): Dorsey Baskin, Richard W Houston. American Accounting Association, 5717 Bessie Dr, Sarasota, FL 34233; info@aaahq.org; http://aaahq.org. Adv. *Indexed:* ATI, B01. *Aud.:* Ac, Sa.

Current Issues in Auditing is an academic journal published semiannually by the Auditing Section of the American Accounting Association. The goal of the publication is to promote the widespread dissemination of ideas to auditing academics and practitioners and to advance the dialogue between them on current issues facing the auditing practice community. Coverage includes all aspects of auditing, including practice-related issues in external auditing, internal auditing, government auditing, IT auditing, and assurance services.

Topics include new opportunities and challenges, emerging areas, global developments, effects of new regulations or pronouncements, effects of technological or market developments on audit processes, and more. The journal presents papers authored by academics, practitioners, and regulators that are comprehensible and contain a substantive, relevant message for those interested in auditing practice. Published in electronic format only, it is freely available at the AAA web site.

40. European Accounting Review. Supersedes (1989-1992): *European Accounting Association. Newsletter.* [ISSN: 0963-8180] 1992. q. GBP 494 (print & online eds.). Ed(s): Laurence Van Lent. Routledge, 4 Park Sq, Milton Park, Abingdon, OX14 4RN, United Kingdom; subscriptions@tandf.co.uk; http://www.tandfonline.com. Adv. Sample. Refereed. Reprint: PSC. *Indexed:* A22, ABIn, ATI, B01, E01, IBSS. *Bk. rev.:* Number and length vary. *Aud.:* Ac.

The *European Accounting Review* is a refereed scholarly journal published on behalf of the European Accounting Association, an organization whose aim is to link together the Europe-wide community of accounting scholars and researchers. As the only accounting journal to provide a European forum for the reporting of accounting research, *EAR* is dedicated to the advancement of accounting knowledge and the publication of high-quality accounting research. The international journal emphasizes openness and flexibility, not only regarding the substantive issues of accounting research, but also with respect to paradigms, methodologies, and styles of conducting that research. With the advent of the single European market and the resulting harmonization of accounting standards and regulations, *EAR* is viewed as an increasingly important forum for the development of accounting theory and practice. The journal is published quarterly and is an ISI-listed journal.

Financial Accountability & Management. See Business and Finance/Scholarly section.

Government Finance Review. See Business and Finance/Scholarly section.

41. The International Journal of Accounting. Formerly (until 1989): *The International Journal of Accounting Education and Research.* [ISSN: 1094-4060] 1965. q. EUR 513. Ed(s): R Abdel-Khalik. Pergamon, The Blvd, Langford Ln, E Park, Kidlington, OX5 1GB, United Kingdom; JournalsCustomerServiceEMEA@elsevier.com; http://www.elsevier.com. Illus., adv. Sample. Refereed. Reprint: PSC. *Indexed:* A22, ABIn, ATI, B01, IBSS. *Bk. rev.:* 5-6, 1,000-1,500 words, signed. *Aud.:* Ac.

The International Journal of Accounting is a refereed scholarly journal whose goal is to advance the academic and professional understanding of accounting theory, policies, and practice from an international perspective and viewpoint. Research articles relate the present and potential ability of accounting to aid in analyzing and interpreting international economic transactions and the economic consequences of such reporting, both in profit and nonprofit environments. The journal takes a broad view of the origins and development of accounting, with emphasis on its functions in an increasingly interdependent global economy. Another area of focus is research that helps to explain current international accounting practices, with related theoretical justifications, and to identify criticisms of current policies and practice. The journal is published quarterly and each issue contains articles, book reviews, and announcements.

42. International Journal of Accounting Information Systems. [ISSN: 1467-0895] 2000. q. EUR 555. Ed(s): A I Nicolaou. Pergamon, The Blvd, Langford Ln, E Park, Kidlington, OX5 1GB, United Kingdom; JournalsCustomerServiceEMEA@elsevier.com; http://www.elsevier.com. Adv. Sample. Reprint: PSC. *Indexed:* ATI, B01, CompLI. *Aud.:* Ac.

The *International Journal of Accounting Information Systems* is an academic journal, published quarterly, whose goal is to examine the evolving relationship between accounting and information technology, and to publish research that advances basic theory and provides guidance to practice. Articles written by practitioners and academicians range from empirical to analytical, and from practice-based to the development of new techniques, but they primarily relate to problems facing the integration of accounting and information technology. Issues addressed include information systems assurance, electronic dissemination of accounting information, control and auditability of information systems, management of information technology, artificial intelligence research in accounting, development issues in accounting and information systems, human factors issues related to information technology, development of theories related to information technology, methodological issues in information technology research, information systems validation, human–computer interaction research in accounting information systems, and more.

43. International Journal of Auditing. [ISSN: 1090-6738] 1997. 3x/yr. GBP 552. Ed(s): Jenny Stewart. Wiley-Blackwell Publishing Ltd., The Atrium, Southern Gate, Chichester, PO19 8SQ, United Kingdom; customer@wiley.com; http://www.wiley.com/. Adv. Sample. Refereed. Reprint: PSC. *Indexed:* A22, ABIn, ATI, B01, E01, IBSS, RiskAb. *Aud.:* Ac.

The *International Journal of Auditing* is a refereed scholarly journal, published three times per year, whose goal is to publish the results of original auditing research conducted in research institutions and in practice. The publication also aims to advance knowledge in auditing by publishing critiques, thought leadership papers, and literature reviews on various aspects of auditing. Articles are presented that have international appeal and address the audit challenges of the present and the future. Research may have an analytical and statistical, behavioral, economic and financial, sociological, critical, or historical basis. Topics include financial statement audits, public sector/governmental auditing, internal auditing, audit education including case studies, audit aspects of corporate governance, audit quality, audit fees, audit-related ethical issues, audit regulation, independence issues, legal liability, auditing history, new and emerging audit and assurance issues, and more. Content is accessible and relevant to auditing practitioners and researchers around the world.

44. Issues in Accounting Education. [ISSN: 0739-3172] 1983. q. USD 375. Ed(s): Lori Holder-Webb. American Accounting Association, 5717 Bessie Dr, Sarasota, FL 34233; info@aaahq.org; http://aaahq.org. Illus., adv. Refereed. Circ: 6000. Vol. ends: No. 4. Reprint: PSC. *Indexed:* A22, ABIn, ATI, B01, B02, BRI. *Bk. rev.:* 2-20, 500-1,500 words, signed. *Aud.:* Ac.

Issues in Accounting Education is a refereed scholarly journal that is published quarterly by the American Accounting Association. The goal of the publication is to publish research, commentaries, instructional resources, and book reviews that assist accounting faculty in teaching and that address important issues in accounting education. The journal is divided into the following sections: "Educational Research" (mainly empirically derived and statistically analyzed studies), "Instructional Resources" (cases derived from actual or simulated business activities, including learning objectives, implementation guidance, and teaching notes), "Learning Strategies" (descriptions and suggestions of how to implement learning and evaluation techniques), "Commentaries" (observations on issues affecting the education of those entering the accounting profession), and "Textbook and Software Reviews." Research topics include the learning process, curriculum development, professional certification, assessment, career training, employment, instruction, and more. Content is of interest to an international readership.

45. Journal of Accounting and Economics. [ISSN: 0165-4101] 1979. 6x/yr. EUR 1713. Ed(s): S P Kothari, Jerold L Zimmerman. Elsevier BV, North-Holland, Postbus 211, Amsterdam, 1000 AE, Netherlands; JournalsCustomerServiceEMEA@elsevier.com; http://www.elsevier.com. Illus., index, adv. Refereed. Vol. ends: Jun/Dec. Microform: PQC. *Indexed:* A22, ABIn, ATI, B01, EconLit, IBSS, JEL. *Aud.:* Ac.

The *Journal of Accounting and Economics* is a refereed scholarly journal that encourages economics-based research that advances accounting knowledge. The publication provides a forum for the publication of high-quality manuscripts that employ economic analyses of accounting problems. A wide range of research methodologies are accepted. Topics include the role of accounting within the firm, the information content and role of accounting numbers in capital markets, the role of accounting in financial contracts and in monitoring agency relationships, the determination of accounting standards, government regulation of corporate disclosure and/or the accounting profession, the theory of the accounting firm, and more. This journal encourages

researchers to address unexplored accounting-related topics and to challenge conventional wisdom using rigorous economic analysis. *JAE* is an ISI-listed journal and one of *Financial Times*' top 45 journals used in business school research rankings.

46. Journal of Accounting & Organizational Change. [ISSN: 1832-5912] 2005. s-a. EUR 679 combined subscription in Europe (print & online eds.); USD 939 combined subscription in the Americas (print & online eds.); GBP 489 combined subscription in the UK & elsewhere (print & online eds.). Ed(s): Zahirul Hoque. Emerald Group Publishing Ltd., Howard House, Wagon Ln, Bingley, BD16 1WA, United Kingdom; emerald@emeraldinsight.com; http://www.emeraldinsight.com. Sample. Refereed. Reprint: PSC. *Indexed:* A22, ABIn, ATI, E01, RiskAb. *Aud.:* Ac, Sa.

The *Journal of Accounting & Organizational Change* is a refereed scholarly journal whose goal is to publish multi-discipline research that relates to organizational and accounting systems changes in the global business environment. Emphasis is placed on exploring how organizations change and how the change process affects internal-organizational processes. The publication seeks to explain new techniques, processes, and philosophies associated with the rise of strategy-oriented accounting and information systems. Content includes empirical and case study articles, replications of previously published studies, and review articles on advances in accounting and organizational change research. Topics include accounting and management control systems in change management; changes in social and environmental accounting reporting; accountability and performance in the public and private sectors; triple bottom-line reporting and social accountability issues; accounting change in transitional and developing economies; public sector reform and accounting change; corporate failure and auditing change; multinational organizational change; and more. Content of this journal is useful to accountants and organizational experts from industry, the public sector, consulting, and academia.

47. Journal of Accounting and Public Policy. [ISSN: 0278-4254] 1982. 6x/yr. EUR 886. Ed(s): Lawrence A Gordon, Martin Loeb. Elsevier Inc., 360 Park Ave S, New York, NY 10010; usinfo-f@elsevier.com; http://www.elsevier.com. Illus., index, adv. Sample. Refereed. Vol. ends: Winter. Microform: PQC. *Indexed:* A22, ABIn, ATI, B01, BRI, IBSS, P61, RiskAb, SSA. *Aud.:* Ac, Sa.

The *Journal of Accounting and Public Policy* is a refereed scholarly journal whose goal is to publish research papers that focus on the relationship between accounting and public policy. Articles are presented that address, through theoretical or empirical analysis, the effect of accounting on public policy and vice versa. Research articles concentrate on the interrelationship between accounting and various disciplines, including economics, public administration, political science, policy science, social psychology, sociology, and law. A feature of the publication is the "Accounting Letters" section, which publishes short research articles that facilitate the rapid dissemination of important accounting research. The journal is published six times per year and is ISI-listed.

Journal of Accounting, Auditing and Finance. See Business and Finance/Scholarly section.

48. Journal of Accounting Education. [ISSN: 0748-5751] 1983. q. EUR 802. Ed(s): David E Stout. Pergamon, The Blvd, Langford Ln, E Park, Kidlington, OX5 1GB, United Kingdom; JournalsCustomerServiceEMEA@elsevier.com; http://www.elsevier.com. Illus., adv. Sample. Refereed. Microform: PQC. *Indexed:* A22, ABIn, ATI, B01. *Aud.:* Ac.

The *Journal of Accounting Education* is a refereed scholarly journal, published quarterly, whose goal is to promote and publish research on accounting education issues and contribute to the improvement of the quality of accounting education worldwide. Articles are included that present the results of empirical studies that are useful to accounting educators in the exchange of ideas and relevant instructional resources. The instructional resources featured in *JAEd* meet relevant educational objectives and are available for general use. Topics addressed are relevant to accounting education, including uses of technology, learning styles, assessment, curriculum, and faculty issues. The journal is divided into three separate sections: "Main Articles" (mostly results of empirical studies), "Educational Cases" (case studies), and "Teaching and Educational Notes" (instructional resources and short papers on topics of interest).

49. *Journal of Accounting Literature.* [ISSN: 0737-4607] 1982. a. EUR 265. Ed(s): W R Knechel, Stephen Kwaka Asare. Elsevier Inc., 360 Park Ave S, New York, NY 10010; http://www.elsevier.com. Illus. Refereed. Reprint: PSC. *Indexed:* A22, ABIn, ATI, B01. *Bk. rev.:* Number and length vary. *Aud.:* Ac.

The *Journal of Accounting Literature* is a refereed scholarly journal, published annually, whose goal is to publish synthesis and original research that makes a fundamental and substantial contribution to the understanding of accounting phenomena, specifically papers that synthesize an area of research in a concise and rigorous manner to assist academics and others to gain knowledge and appreciation of diverse research areas or that present high-quality, multi-method, original research on a broad range of topics relevant to accounting, auditing, and taxation. The lead article of each issue is consistently a synthesis article on an important research topic, with the remaining articles as a mix of synthesis and original research papers. In addition to traditional research topics and methods, the publication includes meta-analyses, field studies, critiques of papers published in other journals, emerging developments in accounting theory, commentaries on current issues, innovative experimental research, book reviews, and more.

50. *Journal of Accounting Research.* [ISSN: 0021-8456] 1963. 5x/yr. GBP 666. Ed(s): Lisa Johnson. Wiley-Blackwell Publishing, Inc., 111 River St, Hoboken, NJ 07030; info@wiley.com; http://onlinelibrary.wiley.com/. Illus. Sample. Refereed. Microform: MIM; PQC. Reprint: PSC. *Indexed:* A22, ABIn, ATI, B01, B02, E01, EconLit, IBSS, JEL, RiskAb. *Aud.:* Ac.

In publication since 1963, the *Journal of Accounting Research* is a refereed scholarly journal that is published on behalf of the Accounting Research Center at the University of Chicago Booth School of Business. *JAR* is the oldest private research journal in the field and is ranked as one of the top accounting research journals in the world. The journal publishes original research using analytical, empirical, experimental, and field-study methods in all areas of accounting. Four regular issues are published per year as well as one conference issue, which contains papers and discussions from the annual accounting research conference that takes place at the University of Chicago. *JAR* is published five times per year, is an ISI-listed journal, and is one of *Financial Times'* top 45 journals used in business school research rankings.

Journal of Business Finance & Accounting. See Business and Finance/Trade Journals section.

51. *Journal of Emerging Technologies in Accounting.* [ISSN: 1554-1908] 2004. a. USD 125 per issue. Ed(s): Alex Kogan. American Accounting Association, 5717 Bessie Dr, Sarasota, FL 34233; info@aaahq.org; http://aaahq.org. Adv. Refereed. Circ: 300. *Indexed:* ATI, B01. *Aud.:* Ac, Sa.

The *Journal of Emerging Technologies in Accounting* is an academic journal that is published annually by the Artificial Intelligence/Emerging Technologies Section of the American Accounting Association. The purpose of this AAA section is to improve and facilitate the research, education, and practice of advanced information systems, cutting-edge technologies, and artificial intelligence in the fields of accounting, information technology, and management advisory systems. The goal of *JETA* is to encourage, support, and disseminate high-quality research focused on emerging technologies and artificial-intelligence issues related to accounting. The journal focuses on studies that include research on strategic and emerging technologies and the impact on accounting and business environments; discovery and exploratory research about technological environments; conceptual research about the technological environment; field research of emerging and new technologies; studies on previously emerging technologies in an historical perspective; integrative plans for emerging technologies in all areas of accounting; and more.

52. *Journal of International Accounting, Auditing and Taxation.* [ISSN: 1061-9518] 1992. s-a. EUR 499. Ed(s): S C Rhoades-Catanach, A H Catanach. Pergamon, The Blvd, Langford Ln, E Park, Kidlington, OX5 1GB, United Kingdom; JournalsCustomerServiceEMEA@elsevier.com; http://www.elsevier.com. Illus., adv. Sample. Refereed. Microform: PQC. Reprint: PSC. *Indexed:* A22, ABIn, ATI, B01, IBSS. *Aud.:* Ac, Sa.

The *Journal of International Accounting, Auditing and Taxation* is a refereed scholarly journal, published twice per year, that presents research in all areas of international accounting, including auditing, taxation, and management advisory services. The goal of the publication is to bridge the gap between academic researchers and practitioners by publishing papers that are relevant to the development of the field of accounting. Content includes applied research findings; critiques of current accounting practices and the measurement of their effects on business decisions; general-purpose solutions to problems through models; and essays on world affairs that affect accounting practice.

53. *Journal of International Accounting Research.* [ISSN: 1542-6297] 2002. s-a. USD 120. Ed(s): Mike Welker. American Accounting Association, 5717 Bessie Dr, Sarasota, FL 34233; info@aaahq.org; http://aaahq.org. Adv. Circ: 1300. Reprint: PSC. *Indexed:* ABIn, ATI, B01, BRI. *Bk. rev.:* Number and length vary. *Aud.:* Ac, Sa.

The *Journal of International Accounting Research* is an academic journal published twice per year by the International Accounting Section of the American Accounting Association. The goal of the publication is to increase understanding of the development and use of international accounting and reporting practices and thereby improve those practices. A wide variety of research methods are accepted, including empirical-archival, experimental, field studies, and theoretical. The journal is directed toward a diverse audience and focuses on articles relating to auditing, financial accounting, managerial accounting, tax, and other specialties within the field of accounting. International coverage areas include the reporting of international economic transactions; the study of differences among practices across countries; the study of institutional and cultural factors that shape practices in a single country but have international implications; the effect of international accounting practices on users; etc. *JIAR* includes sections for "Notes," "Commentaries," and "Book Reviews."

Journal of International Financial Management and Accounting. See Business and Finance/Scholarly section.

54. *Journal of Islamic Accounting and Business Research.* [ISSN: 1759-0817] 2010. s-a. EUR 419 combined subscription in Europe (print & online eds.); USD 579 combined subscription in the Americas (print & online eds.); GBP 369 combined subscription in the UK & elsewhere (print & online eds.). Ed(s): Dr. Mohammad Hudaib, Roszaini Haniffa. Emerald Group Publishing Ltd., Howard House, Wagon Ln, Bingley, BD16 1WA, United Kingdom; emerald@emeraldinsight.com; http://www.emeraldinsight.com. Refereed. Reprint: PSC. *Indexed:* ATI. *Aud.:* Ac, Sa.

The *Journal of Islamic Accounting and Business Research* is a refereed scholarly journal, published twice per year, whose objectives are to provide a forum for the advancement of accounting and business knowledge based on Shari'ah and to publish articles on the interplay between Islamic business ethics, accounting, auditing, and governance in promoting accountability, socioeconomic justice (adl), and everlasting success (al-falah). The publication presents current theoretical and empirical research and practice in Islamic accounting, auditing, and corporate governance; management of Islamic organizations; accounting regulation and policy for Islamic institutions; Shari'ah auditing and corporate governance; and financial and non-financial performance measurement and disclosure in Islamic institutions. *JIABR* is the only journal that offers a platform for publishing both theory and practice of Islamic accounting, auditing, and business research beyond Islamic banking, finance, and economics. The audience for this publication includes scholars and researchers, professionals, and managers involved in Islamic business organizations, and students pursuing studies related to Islamic business.

55. *Journal of Management Accounting Research.* [ISSN: 1049-2127] 1989. a. USD 125 per issue. Ed(s): Ramji Balakrishnan. American Accounting Association, 5717 Bessie Dr, Sarasota, FL 34233; info@aaahq.org; http://aaahq.org. Illus., adv. Refereed. Circ: 2000. Reprint: PSC. *Indexed:* A22, ABIn, ATI, B01, B02, EconLit, JEL. *Aud.:* Ac, Sa.

The *Journal of Management Accounting Research* is a refereed scholarly journal that is published annually by the Management Accounting Section of the American Accounting Association. The goal of *JMAR* is to contribute to the expansion of knowledge related to the theory and practice of management accounting by promoting the dissemination of high-quality applied and theoretical research throughout the world. Coverage includes all areas of management accounting, including budgeting, internal reporting, incentives, performance evaluation, the interface between internal and external reporting, etc. Research articles discuss internal reporting and decision making; profit and nonprofit organizations; service and manufacturing organizations and domestic, foreign, and multinational organizations; etc. The publication accepts all types of research methods, including analytical, empirical, archival, case study, conceptual, experimental, and survey. The audience for this journal is the membership of the Management Accounting Section of the AAA and all others interested in management accounting.

56. *Management Accounting Research.* Former titles (until 1990): *Chartered Institute of Management Accountants Abstracts Bulletin;* (until 1987): *Institute of Cost and Management Accountants. Abstracts Bulletin.* [ISSN: 1044-5005] 1983. q. EUR 721. Ed(s): R W Scapens. Academic Press, 32 Jamestown Rd, Camden, London, NW1 7BY, United Kingdom; corporate.sales@elsevier.com; http://www.elsevier.com/. Illus., adv. Sample. Refereed. Vol. ends: Dec. Reprint: PSC. *Indexed:* A22, ABIn, ATI, B01, E01, IBSS. *Aud.:* Ac.

Management Accounting Research is a refereed scholarly journal whose goal is to publish original research in the field of management accounting. The publication provides an international forum for the dissemination of research, with papers written by prestigious international authors who discuss and analyze management accounting in many different parts of the world. Content includes case studies, field work, and other empirical research, analytical modeling, scholarly papers, distinguished review articles, comments and notes. *MAR* is published quarterly and is an ISI-listed journal.

57. *Managerial Auditing Journal.* [ISSN: 0268-6902] 1986. 9x/yr. EUR 11719 combined subscription in Europe (print & online eds.); USD 13849 combined subscription in the Americas (print & online eds.); GBP 7879 combined subscription in the UK & elsewhere (print & online eds.). Ed(s): Philomena Leung, Barry J Cooper. Emerald Group Publishing Ltd., Howard House, Wagon Ln, Bingley, BD16 1WA, United Kingdom; emerald@emeraldinsight.com; http://www.emeraldinsight.com. Sample. Refereed. Reprint: PSC. *Indexed:* A22, ABIn, ATI, B01, E01, RiskAb. *Aud.:* Ac.

Managerial Auditing Journal is a refereed scholarly publication that provides a global forum for the examination of current research and practice in auditing and assurance. The journal reflects a contemporary approach by taking readers beyond traditional conventions and discussing ways that today's auditors and assurance providers are analyzing governance, risk management, and performance matters. *MAJ* addresses the relationship between theory and practice by exploring trends, paradigms, and perspectives including the ethical, social, environmental, and economic aspects of contemporary assurance, management performance, and governance issues. Research areas include the regulatory and professional frameworks of corporate and public-sector governance, ethics, risk, and management performance from multi-disciplinary perspectives. Studies may have an analytical, theoretical, or methodological focus and may employ a wide range of research methods, including empirical, experimental, explanatory, case-based analysis, surveys, field studies, conceptual, archival, or critical. The audience for this journal includes academics and researchers, internal and external audit and assurance providers, management and directors, regulators and standard setters, risk managers, and audit committees.

58. *Review of Accounting Studies.* [ISSN: 1380-6653] 1996. 3x/yr. EUR 764 (print & online eds.). Ed(s): Russell Lundholm. Springer New York LLC, 233 Spring St, New York, NY 10013; service-ny@springer.com; http://www.springer.com/. Illus., adv. Sample. Refereed. Vol. ends: No. 4. Reprint: PSC. *Indexed:* A22, ABIn, ATI, B01, E01, EconLit, JEL, RiskAb. *Aud.:* Ac.

Review of Accounting Studies is a refereed scholarly journal whose objective is to provide an outlet for significant academic research in accounting, including theoretical, empirical, and experimental work. The publication is committed to the principle that distinctive scholarship is rigorous, so research must contribute to the discipline of accounting. All research methods are accepted. The audience for this publication includes all who take an active interest in accounting research. *RAS* is published quarterly, is an ISI-listed journal, and is one of *Financial Times'* top 45 journals used in business school research rankings.

Review of Quantitative Finance and Accounting. See Business and Finance/Scholarly section.

Taxation

59. *A T A Journal of Legal Tax Research.* [ISSN: 1543-866X] 2003. a. USD 135 Free to members. Ed(s): Anthony P Curatola. American Accounting Association, 5717 Bessie Dr, Sarasota, FL 34233; info@aaahq.org; http://aaahq.org. Adv. *Indexed:* ATI, B01. *Aud.:* Ac, Sa.

The *ATA Journal of Legal Tax Research* is an online academic journal published by the American Taxation Association, the Tax Section of the American Accounting Association. The journal publishes original research studies that employ legal research methodologies. Content addresses important current tax issues including the history, development, and congressional intent of specific provisions. Research articles propose improvements in tax systems and unique solutions to problems. Proposed or recent tax rule changes are critically analyzed from both technical and policy perspectives. The journal is of value to ATA members and all persons with an interest in tax education and research.

60. *American Taxation Association. Journal.* [ISSN: 0198-9073] 1979. s-a. USD 120. Ed(s): John Phillips. American Accounting Association, 5717 Bessie Dr, Sarasota, FL 34233; info@aaahq.org; http://aaahq.org. Illus., adv. Circ: 1100. Reprint: PSC. *Indexed:* A22, ABIn, ATI, B01, B02, BRI. *Bk. rev.:* 5-10, 500-1,000 words, signed. *Aud.:* Ac, Sa.

The *Journal of the American Taxation Association* is an academic journal published twice per year by the American Taxation Association, the Tax Section of the American Accounting Association. The ATA promotes the study of, and the acquisition of knowledge about, taxation. The publication is dedicated to disseminating a wide variety of tax knowledge, and to fulfill this responsibility, tax research is accepted that employs quantitative, analytical, experimental, and descriptive methods. Feature articles are followed by discussion submitted by other contributors and a summary of all papers included in the issue. The *JATA* also publishes reviews of textbooks and other books of interest to tax scholars. Readership of the journal includes members of the ATA and other persons with an interest in tax education and research.

61. *Corporate Taxation.* Formerly (until Jan. 2001): *Journal of Corporate Taxation.* [ISSN: 1534-715X] 1973. 1 Base Vol(s) bi-m. Ed(s): Sandra K Lewis. R I A, PO Box 6159, Carol Stream, IL 60197; ria.customerservices@thomson.com; http://ria.thomsonreuters.com. Illus., adv. Vol. ends: Winter. Microform: MIM; PQC. *Indexed:* A22, ABIn, ATI, B01, B02, BLI, BRI, CLI, L14. *Aud.:* Sa.

Corporate Taxation is a bimonthly publication written *by* corporate tax professionals *for* corporate tax professionals. The magazine provides authoritative analysis and guidance from the leading experts in corporate taxation. Each issue delivers timely, in-depth coverage of such topics as corporate organizations and reorganizations, compensation and fringe benefits, international developments, consolidated returns, etc. Articles are presented that address topics of importance to practitioners and provide guidance on structuring transactions to produce optimal tax consequences and satisfying compliance mandates with maximum efficiency. This publication does not discuss theoretical matters or how the law could or should be changed.

62. *International Tax Journal.* [ISSN: 0097-7314] 1974. bi-m. USD 329. Ed(s): Lowell D Yoder. C C H Inc., 2700 Lake Cook Rd, Riverwoods, IL 60015; cust_serv@cch.com; http://www.cchgroup.com/. Illus., adv. Microform: WSH; PQC. *Indexed:* A22, ABIn, ATI, B01, B02, BRI, CLI, L14. *Aud.:* Sa.

The *International Tax Journal* is a bimonthly publication from CCH that presents articles on international tax topics for the benefit of tax professionals and multinational businesses. Written by a team of international tax experts, the magazine focuses on U.S. tax on domestic and international business income as well as the interaction of international tax regimes with U.S. tax law. Also presented are feature articles and columns on specific foreign tax regimes that may be of interest to tax practitioners who advise companies on doing business internationally. Topics addressed include anti-deferral and anti-tax avoidance; international partnerships; foreign tax credits; international tax controversies; technology and telecommunications; transfer pricing; financing international operations; treaties, subpart F, economic developments, tax rules of foreign countries; pending legislation; international tax opportunities and pitfalls; etc. The readership of this publication is primarily tax attorneys who advise international businesses.

63. *Journal of International Taxation.* [ISSN: 1049-6378] 1990. 1 Base Vol(s) m. USD 420; USD 645 combined subscription (print & online eds.). Ed(s): Peter M Daub. W G & L Financial Reporting & Management Research, 395 Hudson St, New York, NY 10014; ria.customerservices@thomson.com; http://ria.thomson.com. Adv. Circ: 2500. *Indexed:* A22, ABIn, ABS&EES, ATI. *Aud.:* Sa.

The *Journal of International Taxation* is a monthly publication that provides an authoritative, in-depth, and practical analysis of the laws, regulations, treaties, and decisions governing international taxation. The focus is on developing practical strategies to limit tax liability and avoid unnecessary tax penalties. It presents news on the latest major tax developments in the U.S. and around the world, with a focus on transactions both inbound (foreign businesses in the U.S.) and outbound (U.S. businesses abroad). Topics include expatriation and inversion; transfer pricing policies and developments; treaties and treaty shopping; financial products and current strategies; tax issues among major U.S. trading partners; international tax developments; tax shelters; etc. Regular columns include: "Global Reach" (examines major U.S. court decisions, Treasury regulations, and IRS pronouncements); "Dateline" (correspondents from 25 countries describe developments affecting multi-nationals and international investors); and "Ernst & Young's Foreign Desk Report" (updates and analysis by E&Y tax experts). Articles are practical and include specific planning advice and strategies.

64. *Journal of State Taxation.* [ISSN: 0744-6713] 1982. bi-m. USD 470 combined subscription (print & online eds.). Ed(s): James T Collins. C C H Inc., 2700 Lake Cook Rd, Riverwoods, IL 60015; cust_serv@cch.com; http://www.cchgroup.com/. Microform: WSH; PQC. *Indexed:* ABIn, ATI, B01, B02, BRI, CLI, L14. *Aud.:* Sa.

The *Journal of State Taxation* is a bimonthly publication from CCH whose goal is to help practitioners meet, master, and stay ahead of today's complex state tax challenges. Articles provide guidance and insight from leading practitioners in state taxation. The magazine offers many unique features, such as the "Multistate Tax Charts" and "Frequently Asked Multistate Tax Questions." It includes four regular columns by top names in state taxation: "Apportionment News," "Nexus News," "Sales Tax Corner," and "State of the States." Regular alerts are provided to keep practitioners up-to-date on current topics, such as state tax incentives; sales tax exemptions; refund opportunities; and proposed, pending, or recently enacted legislation. Coverage of important cases is reported, along with assessments of the impact. *JST* publishes easy-to-read and easy-to-understand tips and suggestions on how to reduce state and local tax liabilities.

65. *Journal of Taxation: a national journal of current developments, analysis, and commentary for tax professionals.* [ISSN: 0022-4863] 1954. 1 Base Vol(s) m. USD 335; USD 495 combined subscription (print & online eds.). Ed(s): Joseph I Graf, Sheldon I Banoff. R I A, PO Box 6159, Carol Stream, IL 60197; ria@thomson.com; http://ria.thomsonreuters.com. Illus., index, adv. Circ: 14000. Microform: PQC. *Indexed:* A22, ABIn, ATI, B01, B02, BLI, BRI, CLI, JEL, L14, P02. *Aud.:* Sa.

The *Journal of Taxation* is published monthly and is dedicated to the needs of tax practitioners. The focus is on practical information and tax-planning ideas. In-depth articles from leading practitioners are presented that examine the problems that tax lawyers and CPAs regularly face in practice. The publication

also provides current tax news, the latest tax law changes, court decisions, revenue rulings, and administrative actions. Topics addressed do not include theoretical matters or policy discussion of how the law should be changed; however, constructive criticism of administrative or judicial interpretations of the law is included.

66. *Journal of Taxation of Financial Products.* [ISSN: 1529-9287] 2000. q. Ed(s): Mark H Price. C C H Inc., 2700 Lake Cook Rd, Riverwoods, IL 60015; cust_serv@cch.com; http://www.cchgroup.com/. *Indexed:* ATI, B01, B02. *Aud.:* Sa.

The *Journal of Taxation of Financial Products* is published quarterly by CCH and is devoted exclusively to the analysis of tax ramifications of derivatives and other financial products. It emphasizes the tax treatment of hedges; identifying strategies to maximize the tax-inclusive return for investment vehicles and cross-border derivative transactions; and examining the tax uncertainty from new derivative products. The publication includes complete tax coverage, including strategies and insights into regulatory developments, state and local tax, and international tax issues. Comprehensive, in-depth articles are presented, as well as advice and strategies from practicing professionals. Current tax developments on the federal, international, and state and local levels are regularly reported. Perspective columns are featured relating to high-net-worth investors, investments and hedge funds, capital markets, insurance, international taxation, regulatory issues, and state and local developments. The readership for *JTFP* includes tax practitioners, corporate finance managers, and financial services firm professionals.

67. *Journal of Taxation of Investments.* [ISSN: 0747-9115] 1983. q. Ed(s): Erik M Jensen. Civic Research Insitute, 4478 US Rte 27, PO Box 585, Kingston, NJ 08528; order@civicresearchinstitute.com; http://www.civicresearchinstitute.com. *Indexed:* A22, ABIn, ATI, B02, CLI, L14. *Aud.:* Sa.

The *Journal of Taxation of Investments* is published quarterly by the Civic Research Institute. The publication focuses on developments and trends that affect the tax aspects of corporate investing. It helps to evaluate financial instruments, to choose the best products and structures for clients, and to limit the tax impact on investment portfolios. Investments surveyed include: equity and debt securities; real estate, REITs and REMICs; derivatives; domestic and global markets; hedge funds and mutual funds; equity swaps; and more. Topics addressed are of interest to corporate, institutional, or individual investors; to those who offer investments; and to relevant legal and accounting advisors. While the focus of *JTI* is on tax issues, non-tax issues, such as regulatory restrictions on investors and investments, are also covered. Articles are generally practical, but theoretical discussions are sometimes included. Although most of the content covers U.S. tax and regulatory law, issues related to investing in non-U.S. countries are also examined.

68. *National Tax Journal.* Formerly (until 1948): *National Tax Association. Bulletin.* [ISSN: 0028-0283] 1916. q. USD 110 (Individuals, USD 100; Free to members). Ed(s): George R Zodrow, William M Gentry. National Tax Association, 725 15th St, N W, Ste 600, Washington, DC 20005; natltax@aol.com; http://www.ntanet.org. Illus., index. Refereed. Vol. ends: Dec. Microform: WSH; PQC. *Indexed:* A22, ABIn, ATI, B01, B02, BLI, BRI, CLI, EconLit, IBSS, JEL, L14, P02. *Aud.:* Ac, Sa.

The *National Tax Journal* is a refereed scholarly journal that is published quarterly by the National Tax Association, an organization dedicated to advancing the understanding of the theory and practice of public finance. The goal of the publication is to encourage and disseminate high-quality original research on governmental tax and expenditure policies. The focus is on economic, theoretical, and empirical analysis of tax and expenditure issues, with an emphasis on policy implications. Most regular issues include an "NTJ Forum," which features invited papers by leading scholars that examine a current tax or expenditure policy issue. The December issue is devoted to papers presented at the NTA's annual spring symposium. Forum papers and articles in the December issue are not subject to peer review. The readership for *NTJ* is diverse, including academics, private-sector and government economists, accountants, and attorneys, as well as business and government tax practitioners. While the full text for articles going back to 1988 is freely available at the NTA web site, the most recent two years are only available to NTA members.

69. *Practical Tax Strategies.* Formed by the merger of (1966-1998): *Taxation for Accountants;* (1972-1998): *Taxation for Lawyers.* [ISSN: 1523-6250] 1998. 1 Base Vol(s) m. Ed(s): Brian M O'Neil. W G & L Financial Reporting & Management Research, 395 Hudson St, New York, NY 10014; ria.customerservices@thomson.com; http://ria.thomson.com. Illus., index, adv. *Indexed:* A22, ABIn, ATI, B02, CLI, L14. *Aud.:* Sa.

Practical Tax Strategies is a monthly publication that provides tax professionals with strategies to reduce client taxes and satisfy statutory and regulatory compliance mandates. It offers practical information and analysis on recent tax developments, as well as planning strategies related to federal income, estate, and gift taxes. Advice is given on how to maximize savings and minimize risk in every major tax area, including corporations, partnerships, S corporations, LLCs, real estate, accounting, estate planning, personal transactions, compensation, etc. Articles are written by tax practitioners who understand the issues that arise when servicing clients. Insight is provided by columnists who describe new developments in practicing before the IRS and help readers assess their own knowledge of critical tax concepts. Content focuses on practical information, thus theoretical matters or how the law could or should be changed are not discussed.

70. *The Tax Adviser: a magazine of tax planning, trends and techniques.* [ISSN: 0039-9957] 1970. m. Free to members. Ed(s): Rocky S Rosen. CPA2Biz, Inc., 100 Broadway 6th Fl, New York, NY 10005; service@cpa2biz.com; https://www.cpa2biz.com. Illus., index, adv. Microform: WSH; PQC. *Indexed:* A22, ABIn, ATI, B01, B02, BRI, CLI, L14. *Aud.:* Sa.

The Tax Adviser is a monthly publication from the American Institute of Certified Public Accountants. It is an authoritative source for news, analysis, and guidance on federal and state taxation, with a focus on reporting and explaining federal tax issues to tax practitioners. Through articles and regular columns, *TTA* deals primarily with the technical aspects of federal (and some state) taxation, providing practical, administrative, and technical commentary. Readers are kept informed about the latest plans and actions by the IRS, how to take advantage of the latest tax developments, lessons learned from practitioners, updates on laws and regulations, major annual updates, etc. Articles are authored by CPAs, lawyers, tax executives, and professors. The publication is of interest to anyone who must stay informed on federal tax matters. Select articles are available full-text at the AICPA web site.

71. *The Tax Executive.* [ISSN: 0040-0025] 1944. bi-m. USD 120 in US & Canada; USD 145 elsewhere; USD 22 per issue. Ed(s): Timothy J McCormally. Tax Executives Institute, Inc., 1200 G St N W, Ste 300, Washington, DC 20005; http://www.tei.org/. Illus., adv. Vol. ends: Nov/Dec. Microform: PQC. Reprint: WSH. *Indexed:* A22, ABIn, ATI, B01, B02, BRI, CLI, L14. *Aud.:* Sa.

The Tax Executive is a professional journal published bimonthly by Tax Executives Institute, a worldwide association for in-house tax professionals. *TEI* is dedicated to the development of sound tax policy, compliance with and uniform enforcement of tax laws, and minimization of administration and compliance costs to the benefit of both government and taxpayers. The publication covers current issues of tax policy, administration and management, TEI advocacy initiatives, and more. Each issue features original articles by top law and accounting practitioners, as well as the insights and real-world experiences of TEI members. Readership includes accountants, lawyers, and corporate and business employees who are responsible for the tax affairs of their employers in an executive, administrative, or managerial capacity. Select articles are freely available at the TEI web site.

Tax Law Review. See Law section.

The Tax Lawyer. See Law section.

72. *Tax Notes: the weekly tax service.* Former titles (until 1996): *Tax Notes Microfiche Data Base;* (until 1981): *Tax Notes.* [ISSN: 0270-5494] 1972. w. Ed(s): Meredith Stevenson Fath, Patrick Sullivan. Tax Analysts, 400 S Maple Ave, Ste 400, Falls Church, VA 22046; cservice@tax.org; http://www.taxanalysts.com/. Sample. *Indexed:* A22, ATI, B02, B03, BRI, CLI, L14. *Aud.:* Sa.

Published by Tax Analysts, *Tax Notes* provides a weekly summary of federal tax news. The publication updates readers with news and commentary that cover all federal tax laws, regulations, and policy developments. Content includes special reports, in-depth analytical articles, investigative reports, and commentary from leading practitioners, scholars, government officials, and Tax Analysts staff. Topics addressed include coverage of the latest congressional action and comments from Treasury and IRS officials; just-released IRS regulations, revenue rulings, revenue procedures, announcements, and chief counsel advice; White House budget proposals, tax bills introduced by Congress, and cost estimates of those proposals; and more. Readership includes tax professionals in law and accounting firms, corporations, and government agencies. A searchable web archive going back to 1972 is available to subscribers at the Tax Analysts web site.

73. *Taxes - The Tax Magazine.* Former titles (until 19??): *Taxes;* (until 1939): *Tax Magazine;* (until 1931): *The National Tax Magazine;* (until 1930): *The National Income Tax Magazine.* 1923. m. USD 349. Ed(s): Kurt Diefenbach, Shannon Fischer. C C H Inc., 2700 Lake Cook Rd, Riverwoods, IL 60015; cust_serv@cch.com; http://www.cchgroup.com/. Illus. Vol. ends: Dec. Microform: PQC. *Indexed:* A22, ATI, B02, CLI, L14. *Aud.:* Sa.

Taxes - The Tax Magazine is a monthly publication from CCH Tax and Accounting that provides readers with practice-oriented analysis of federal, state, and international tax issues. Written by tax experts, articles provide guidance for navigating tax rules and regulations and analysis of current tax issues, trends, and legislative developments. Regular columns include: "Corporate Tax Watch," "Employee Benefits Column," "Federal Tax Practice Standards," "The Estate Planner," "Family Tax Planning Forum," "International Tax Watch," "Tax Practice," "Tackling Taxes," "Tax Meetings," and "Tax Trends." Special conference issues, published in March and June, present papers and panel discussions presented at the University of Chicago Law School's Annual Federal Tax Conference and the Tax Council Policy Institute's Annual Symposium.

■ ADVERTISING, MARKETING, AND PUBLIC RELATIONS

See also Business; Communication; and Journalism and Writing sections.

Clay Williams, Deputy Chief Librarian, Hunter College Libraries, Hunter College, New York, NY 10065

Introduction

In choosing the journals for inclusion here, one must recognize the profound influences that the online environment has upon both scholarship and business. As predicted, the Internet as the medium of the journals themselves has become the medium and the message. The web as a topic of intellectual discussion is not up for discussion, but the online world has become more transparent and a part of everyone's day-to-day life and is now taken for granted by all. The journals directed at practitioners describe uses of the web in the various manifestations of advertising, while the academic journals explore the effects that the Internet is having on advertising, marketing, and public relations, and what effects the authors think it could or should have.

Practitioners continue to discover ways to use the media to succeed, and the Internet is certainly the major game in town. However, comprehending the online world in its many manifestations and sometimes hidden agendas, if you will, makes things difficult to pin down for more than a moment. Many articles appear on these topics in journals that focus ostensibly on business and marketing. No one questions the importance of advertising, and certainly no one can avoid the role that spin doctors or public relations practitioners are playing in the world today in business.

The inherent pitfalls of the Internet become problematic for a work such as *Magazines for Libraries* because some electronic journals (not to mention companies) do not stay around long enough for their importance to even register, particularly in the academic world. Where are these journals archived and for how long, and in what format? Will they be archived somewhere? If not by the vendors, then where? Consider, as well, that the full-text versions of some journals are best reached via such databases as Lexis-Nexis and EBSCO's various databases, which are now ubiquitous in colleges and public libraries and available at home to subscribers. However, occasional lags in the promptness of recent articles in the promised full-text format speak of other forces at work. The inconsistency only frustrates users, as they see excellent articles abstracted and unavailable because of costs.

The variety of formats we see is representative of the transitional period we are in, and the scholarship reflects that as well. Open access does appear more often, and this battle will now take place in plain view. Does the emperor have any clothes? The profound influence the vendors have in bundling the various journals and magazines has a greater impact in the world of adademe than in the professional world, where a company would subscribe to an individual title. This is not the case for the college in which a journal is a part of a package and so are the years subscribed to as well.

Basic Periodicals

Ga: *Advertising Age, Adweek, B to B, Brandweek, Public Relations Quarterly;* Ac: *Advertising Age, B to B, Journal of Advertising, Journal of Advertising Research, The Journal of Consumer Marketing, Journal of Consumer Research, Journal of Macromarketing, Journal of Marketing, Journal of Marketing Research, Marketing News, Marketing Research, O'Dwyer's P R Report, Public Relations Review, Sales & Marketing Management.*

Basic Abstracts and Indexes

ABI/INFORM, Business Periodicals Index, Business Source Elite, Expanded Academic ASAP.

74. *Academy of Marketing Science. Journal.* [ISSN: 0092-0703] 1973. q. EUR 646 (print & online eds.). Ed(s): Tomas Hult. Springer New York LLC, 233 Spring St, New York, NY 10013; journals-ny@springer.com; http://www.springer.com. Illus., adv. Refereed. Circ: 3000. Vol. ends: Oct (No. 4). Reprint: PSC. *Indexed:* A22, ABIn, B01, B02, BRI, E01, P02, PsycInfo. *Bk. rev.:* 2-6, 300-1,000 words. *Aud.:* Ac.

This is the official journal of the Academy of Marketing Science. Articles intended for theoreticians disseminate research results related to the international impact of economics, ethics, and social forces. A regular section concerns marketing and the law. Recent issues contain articles that include a study that examines the effects of downsizing on organizational buying behavior, the concept of culture, the definition of organizational memory, and the dimensions of decision-making context. A reasonable price for an important journal that deals largely with theory.

75. *Advertising Age.* Incorporates (1979-2004): *American Demographics;* (198?-200?): *Focus;* Which was formerly (1982-198?): *Advertising Age's Focus;* (1953-1974): *Promotion;* Which was formerly: *Advertising & Sales Promotion;* (until 1961): *Advertising Requirements;* (in 1958): *Advertising Agency.* [ISSN: 0001-8899] 1930. w. Students, USD 79 (print & online eds.); USD 99 combined subscription domestic (print & online eds.). Ed(s): Rance Crain. Crain Communications, Inc., 711 Third Ave, New York, NY 10017; info@crain.com; http://www.crain.com. Illus., adv. Vol. ends: Dec. Microform: CIS; PQC. *Indexed:* A01, A22, ABIn, B01, B02, B03, BLI, BRI, C37, C42, Chicano, F01, MASUSE, P02. *Aud.:* Ga, Ac, Sa.

For the student and the practitioner, this tabloid contains enormous amounts of fascinating and useful data. The coverage is thorough yet succinct, and touches on all aspects of advertising. Because it is a weekly, the information is current and topical. It covers important campaigns with text and graphics. The "Annual Agency Report" is a statistical issue that covers the top agencies worldwide. The publication has feature articles on people, on issues such as tobacco and alcohol advertising, and on forthcoming campaigns and spots to watch for, such as those during the Super Bowl. Advertising on the web is not ignored. The title is one of the best for the price in this field. Highly recommended for college, public, and special collections.

76. *Advertising & Society Review.* [ISSN: 1534-7311] 2000. q. USD 100. Ed(s): Linda Scott. Advertising Educational Foundation, 220 E 42nd St, Ste 3300, New York, NY 10017; sk@aef.com; http://www.aef.com. Adv. Refereed. *Indexed:* A22, E01. *Aud.:* Ac.

This twenty-first-century addition to scholarship attempts to approach advertising as a cultural phenomenon and to look at it as an academic pursuit. The articles are extensive, and the topics covered are far from narrow. Recent articles discuss "Spirituality that Sells: Religious Imagery in Magazine Advertising," while others concern advertising during World War I. These are not just historical treatises or opinion pieces, but are empirical studies as well.

77. *B to B: the magazine for marketing and e-commerce strategists.* Former titles (until 2000): *Advertising Age's Business Marketing;* (until 1994): *Business Marketing;* (until 1983): *Industrial Marketing;* (until 1935): *Class & Industrial Marketing;* Which was formed by the merger of (19??-1927): *Class;* (19??-1927): *Industrial Marketing.* [ISSN: 1530-2369] 1935. m. USD 59 combined subscription domestic (print & online eds.); USD 69 combined subscription Canada (print & online eds.); USD 89 combined subscription elsewhere (print & online eds.). Ed(s): John Obrecht, Ellis Booker. Crain Communications, Inc., 711 Third Ave, New York, NY 10017; info@crain.com; http://www.crain.com. Illus., index, adv. Circ: 41344. Vol. ends: Dec. Microform: MIM; PQC. *Indexed:* A22, ABIn, B01, B02, B03, BLI, BRI, C37, C42, I15. *Aud.:* Ga, Ac, Sa.

Also known as *Advertising Age's B to B,* this Crain publication contains articles that discuss e-commerce, publishing, business-to-business marketing, and a variety of face-to-face encounters including trade shows. Case studies provide the foundation for suggestions on creating and expanding a presence in existing and emerging international markets. News, statistics, software reviews, technology reports, analysis of research aids, and company market-share information are regularly included. The magazine's web presence is less extensive since the dot-com meltdown. There is certainly an effort to consider that the best customers will want their data quickly, and the web site provides e-mail updates to subscribers. Topics reflect changes in the information industry of interest to many librarians, and this title should be available in public, academic, and special libraries.

78. *Campaign (London, 1968).* Former titles (until 1968): *W P N Advertisers' Review;* (until 1964): *World's Press News and Advertisers' Review.* [ISSN: 0008-2309] 1929. w. GBP 199. Ed(s): Michael Porter, Claire Beale. Haymarket Publishing Ltd., 174 Hammersmith Rd, London, W6 7JP, United Kingdom; info@haymarket.com; http://www.haymarket.com. Illus., adv. *Indexed:* ABIn, B01, B02, B03, BRI, PhotoAb. *Aud.:* Sa.

This title is included because of its prominence in Britain and the European Union. Political articles that affect American companies are available in the online version, *Campaignlive,* which also provides regular international news feeds. Full text is available in mainstream databases as well, which certainly raises the publication's profile. The articles are generally short, 150–500 words.

79. *Direct Marketing (Online): we cover it all.* Former titles (until 2004): *Direct Marketing (Print);* (until 1968): *Reporter of Direct Mail Advertising.* 1938. m. Free. Ed(s): Joseph Gatti. Hoke Communications, Inc., 224 Seventh St, Garden City, NY 11530. Illus., index, adv. Vol. ends: Apr. Microform: PQC. *Indexed:* A22, ABIn, B01, B02, B03, BLI, BRI, P02. *Aud.:* Ga, Sa.

This title is an up-to-date, easy-to-read online magazine dealing with all the major media and their needs regarding direct marketing. A recent article investigates the problems with rising postal costs; another discusses web-based marketing research, but the magazine certainly does not ignore catalog marketing. It has inclusive columns and a calendar of events. Essential for large public libraries, special libraries, and academic libraries.

80. *Industrial Marketing Management.* [ISSN: 0019-8501] 1971. 8x/yr. EUR 1424. Ed(s): Peter J LaPlaca. Elsevier Inc., 360 Park Ave S, New York, NY 10010; usinfo-f@elsevier.com; http://www.elsevier.com. Illus., adv. Sample. Refereed. Circ: 1060 Paid and free. Vol. ends: Nov. Microform: PQC. *Indexed:* A22, ABIn, B01, IBSS, PsycInfo. *Aud.:* Ac.

This very important scholarly journal provides eight to ten clear, well-written articles on topics such as product development, production presentation, advertising, sales, and pricing. Articles often focus on statistical analysis techniques, such as a recent one titled "A Conceptual Model for Building and Maintaining Relationships between Manufacturers' Representatives and their Principals." There is diversity, however; for example, other recent topics include modeling of business-to-business partnerships and the impact of antitrust guidelines on competition.

81. International Journal of Advertising. Formerly: *Journal of Advertising;* Which superseded (1978-1980): *Advertising Magazine;* Which was formerly: *Advertising;* (1964-1978): *Advertising Quarterly.* [ISSN: 0265-0487] 1982. q. GBP 284 combined subscription (print & online eds.); EUR 484 combined subscription (print & online eds.); USD 456 combined subscription (print & online eds.). Ed(s): Charles R Taylor. World Advertising Research Center Ltd., Farm Rd, Henley-on-Thames, RG9 1EJ, United Kingdom; enquiries@warc.com; http://www.warc.com/. Illus., index, adv. Sample. Refereed. Circ: 800. *Indexed:* A22, ABIn, B01, B02, BAS, BRI, P02, PsycInfo, RiskAb. *Aud.:* Ac.

This refereed scholarly journal is devoted to publishing authoritative studies for practitioners and academics in the fields of marketing, advertising, and public relations. Articles average about ten pages each. Recent articles include such topics as beer brand advertising and market share in the United States between 1977 and 1998, and a study of the response to banner ads on the web. This title is imperative for research libraries that support programs in advertising and marketing.

82. International Journal of Design. [ISSN: 1991-3761] 2007. 3x/yr. Ed(s): Lin-Lin Chen, Yaliang Chuang. National Taiwan University of Science and Technology, Graduate Institute of Design, 43, Sec. 4, Keelung Rd., Taipei, Taiwan, Republic of China. Refereed. *Indexed:* A07, ABIn, ArtHuCI, ErgAb. *Aud.:* Sa.

This new journal is open access and thus can be difficult to judge for libraries. That being said, open-access journals are marketed by librarians via lists and word of mouth. Recent articles include "Creating Economic Value by Design" and "Cross-Functional Cooperation with Design Teams in New Product Development." Articles such as these will allow the journal to spread far beyond its Asian roots. In fact, the articles are written by Europeans as well as Asian, and English is the lingua franca.

83. International Journal of Internet Marketing and Advertising. [ISSN: 1477-5212] 2003. 4x/yr. EUR 494 (print or online eds.)). Ed(s): Dr. HsiuJu Rebecca Yen. Inderscience Publishers, PO Box 735, Olney, MK46 5WB, United Kingdom; editorial@inderscience.com; http://www.inderscience.com. Refereed. *Indexed:* ABIn, B02, C&ISA, CerAb, RiskAb. *Aud.:* Ac, Sa.

The quarterly focuses on the emerging changes in theories, strategies, and management methods of marketing and advertising, brought about by the Internet and information technology applications, and their implications for the associated processes, products, and services. Emphasis is on the related social, political, and economic issues, as well as emerging issues of interest to professionals and academics. A recent issue included an article entitled "The role of product reviews on mobile devices for in-store purchases: consumers' usage intentions, costs[,] and store preferences."

84. International Journal of Research in Marketing. [ISSN: 0167-8116] 1984. 4x/yr. EUR 907. Ed(s): S Stremersch, A Buitez. Elsevier BV, Radarweg 29, PO Box 211, Amsterdam, 1000 AE, Netherlands; JournalsCustomerServiceEMEA@elsevier.com; http://www.elsevier.com. Illus., index, adv. Refereed. Vol. ends: Nov. Microform: PQC. *Indexed:* A22, ABIn, B01, BRI, PsycInfo. *Bk. rev.:* 0-1. *Aud.:* Ac, Sa.

This title is designed to communicate developments in marketing theory and results of empirical research from any country and from a variety of disciplinary approaches. Coverage includes for-profit as well as nonprofit marketing, consumer behavior, products, pricing, marketing communication, marketing channels, strategic marketing planning, industrial marketing, and international marketing. Recent issues include five or six articles on such topics as consumer-

choice behavior in online and traditional supermarkets, and the effects of brand name, price, and other search attributes. Another article topic is homeostasis and consumer behavior across cultures. Although expensive for a quarterly, it does cover areas that other journals do not.

85. International Marketing Review. Incorporates (1986-1988): *Industrial Marketing and Purchasing.* [ISSN: 0265-1335] 1983. bi-m. EUR 12069 combined subscription in Europe (print & online eds.); USD 14099 combined subscription in the Americas (print & online eds.); GBP 8109 combined subscription in the UK & elsewhere (print & online eds.). Ed(s): Jeryl Whitelock, John W Cadogan. Emerald Group Publishing Ltd., Howard House, Wagon Ln, Bingley, BD16 1WA, United Kingdom; emerald@emeraldinsight.com; http://www.emeraldinsight.com. Illus., index. Sample. Refereed. Vol. ends: No. 5. Reprint: PSC. *Indexed:* A22, ABIn, B01, B02, BRI, C42, E01, PsycInfo, RiskAb. *Bk. rev.:* 2, 1,000 words. *Aud.:* Ac.

International marketing management is a complex and interesting area of marketing research. This expensive journal is part of an expensive group of marketing journals from MCB. Despite its small subscriber base and high cost, it does have an international readership among academicians because of its excellent articles, research reports, literature reviews, and occasional book reviews. Issues are often devoted to a single topic—recently, for example, retailing. Despite its being indexed prominently, the subscription price makes this journal impossible for many libraries. Naturally, this makes document delivery problematic.

86. Journal of Advertising. [ISSN: 0091-3367] 1972. q. GBP 213 (print & online eds.). Ed(s): Wei-Na Lee. Routledge, 325 Chestnut St, Ste 800, Philadelphia, PA 19106; customerservice@taylorandfrancis.com; http://www.tandfonline.com. Illus., index, adv. Sample. Refereed. Vol. ends: Dec. Microform: PQC. Reprint: PSC. *Indexed:* A22, ABIn, B01, B02, BLI, BRI, C42, E01, IBSS, P02, PsycInfo, RILM. *Bk. rev.:* 0-1, 1,000-2,000 words. *Aud.:* Ac.

This journal cleaves closely to the classic academic model: the articles are all well footnoted and abstracted. They are very theoretical, with extensive use of statistics and well-defined methodologies. A recent issue includes an article titled "The Role of Myth in Creative Advertising Design," and another article explores managers' perceptions of the impact of sponsorship on brand equity. The review process is a blind one, but unfortunately, a call for papers does not come through when the journal is reached only through the indexes.

87. Journal of Advertising Research. [ISSN: 0021-8499] 1960. q. GBP 212; EUR 314; USD 315. Ed(s): Geoffrey Precourt. World Advertising Research Center, 432 Park Ave S, 6th F, New York, NY 10016; enquiries@warc.com; http://www.warc.com/. Illus., index. Sample. Microform: PQC. *Indexed:* A22, ABIn, B01, B02, BRI, Chicano, E01, P02, PsycInfo. *Aud.:* Ac, Sa.

This trade periodical, published by the Advertising Research Foundation, consists of well-researched and footnoted articles that are easier to read than those found in most academic journals. The charts and illustrations will not intimidate undergraduates with complicated explanations of methodology. A recent issue presents an article titled "Brain-Imaging Detection of Visual Scene Encoding in Long-Term Memory for TV Commercials." The editorial board is a blend of academics and professionals in the field. There is a calendar of foundation events in each issue.

88. Journal of Business & Industrial Marketing. Incorporates (1993-1994): *Journal of International Marketing.* [ISSN: 0885-8624] 1986. 8x/yr. EUR 10639 combined subscription in Europe (print & online eds.); USD 4509 combined subscription in the Americas (print & online eds.); GBP 7159 combined subscription in the UK & elsewhere (print & online eds.). Ed(s): Wesley J Johnston. Emerald Group Publishing Ltd., Howard House, Wagon Ln, Bingley, BD16 1WA, United Kingdom; emerald@emeraldinsight.com; http://www.emeraldinsight.com. Illus., index. Sample. Refereed. Vol. ends: No. 4. Reprint: PSC. *Indexed:* A22, ABIn, B01, B02, BRI, E01, FS&TA, RiskAb. *Bk. rev.:* 1-4, 750-1,000 words. *Aud.:* Sa.

Academicians provide practical applications and new ideas based on marketing research to demonstrate the relationship of research to practice in each issue. This is another of MCB University Press's (Emerald Group) products. Recent articles explore sales-force automation usage, effectiveness, and cost-benefit in Germany, England, and the United Kingdom; and studying distance learning for Malaysian sales forces. Marketing educators and practitioners are the intended audience.

89. *Journal of Consumer Marketing.* Incorporates (1996-1997): *Franchising Research.* [ISSN: 0736-3761] 1983. 7x/yr. EUR 10639 combined subscription in Europe (print & online eds.); USD 4749 combined subscription in the Americas (print & online eds.); GBP 7159 combined subscription in the UK & elsewhere (print & online eds.). Ed(s): Richard C Leventhal. Emerald Group Publishing Ltd., Howard House, Wagon Ln, Bingley, BD16 1WA, United Kingdom; emerald@emeraldinsight.com; http://www.emeraldinsight.com. Illus., index. Sample. Refereed. Vol. ends: Nov. Microform: PQC. Reprint: PSC. *Indexed:* A22, ABIn, B01, B02, BLI, BRI, E01, H&TI, PsycInfo, RiskAb. *Bk. rev.:* 2, 500-1,000 words. *Aud.:* Ac, Sa.

Articles in this expensive title report on a wide range of research related to all aspects of consumer marketing. Book reviews are extensive and well written. This journal is indexed in mainstream databases, and students will appreciate that the articles are on current topics of interest. For example, a recent article reports on "Baby Boomers and Busters: An Exploratory Investigation of Attitudes toward Marketing, Advertising and Consumerism." A regular feature on franchising adds to the mix.

90. *Journal of Consumer Psychology.* [ISSN: 1057-7408] 1992. 4x/yr. EUR 664. Ed(s): C W Park. Elsevier Inc., 360 Park Ave S, New York, NY 10010; usinfo-f@elsevier.com; http://www.elsevier.com. Adv. Sample. Refereed. Reprint: PSC. *Indexed:* A01, A22, ABIn, ASSIA, B01, E01, H&TI, PsycInfo, RILM. *Aud.:* Ac, Sa.

This title is very much directed toward academics in the field. Articles can include collaborations between faculty in management and psychology. There are peer-reviewed articles in the field of consumer psychology that include topics such as the role of advertising, consumer attitudes, decision-making processes, and direct brand experience. Other topics covered include the development and change of consumer attitudes; judgment, choice, and decision processes; and social cognition research. A recent article is titled "Consumers' Responses to Negative Word-of-Mouth Communication: An Attribution Theory Perspective."

91. *Journal of Consumer Research.* [ISSN: 0093-5301] 1974. bi-m. USD 437 (print & online eds.). Ed(s): Mary F Luce, Ann L McGill. University of Chicago Press, 1427 E 60th St, Chicago, IL 60637; subscriptions@press.uchicago.edu; http://www.journals.uchicago.edu. Illus., index, adv. Sample. Refereed. Vol. ends: Apr. Microform: PQC. Reprint: PSC. *Indexed:* A01, A22, ABIn, Agr, B01, B02, Chicano, EconLit, ErgAb, FS&TA, H&TI, JEL, PsycInfo, RILM. *Aud.:* Ac, Sa.

A dozen associations co-sponsor this journal, which reports on the research results from numerous disciplines in a dozen articles in each issue. Culture swapping, price perception, consumer-choice deferral, and the role of gifts in the reformulation of interpersonal relationships serve to represent the diversity of the contents. This title covers the latest hot topics in consumer research, and it is a good choice for both large public and academic libraries.

92. *Journal of Global Marketing.* Incorporates (1991-2009): *Journal of Euro-Marketing.* [ISSN: 0891-1762] 1987. 5x/yr. GBP 809 (print & online eds.). Ed(s): Patricia Todd. Routledge, 325 Chestnut St, Ste 800, Philadelphia, PA 19106; customerservice@taylorandfrancis.com; http://www.tandfonline.com. Illus., adv. Sample. Refereed. Vol. ends: Winter (No. 4). Microform: PQC. Reprint: PSC. *Indexed:* A01, A22, ABIn, B01, E01, H&TI, PsycInfo, RiskAb. *Bk. rev.:* 3-4, 500-1,000 words. *Aud.:* Ac, Sa.

Under the auspices of the International Business Press, this journal provides relatively inexpensive access to practical, and sometimes comparative, information on specific aspects of marketing in various countries and geographic regions. Topics address transborder information flow, intellectual property issues, counterfeit goods, market penetration strategies, and personal communication. Recent articles include "The Relationship Between Consumer Ethnocentrism and Human Values, On the Marketing of Nations: A Gap Analysis of Managers' Perceptions, Linking Product Evaluations and Purchase Intention for Country-of-Origin Effects" and "Increasing the Effectiveness of Export Assistance Programs: The Case of the California Environmental Technology Industry." This is a highly selective journal, with about half international subscribers. Only information of interest to nonspecialists is considered for inclusion in this title.

Journal of Hospitality Marketing and Management. See Hospitality/Restaurant section.

93. *Journal of Interactive Advertising.* [ISSN: 1525-2019] 2000. s-a. GBP 79. Ed(s): Steve Edwards. Routledge, 325 Chestnut St, Ste 800, Philadelphia, PA 19106; customerservice@taylorandfrancis.com; http://www.tandfonline.com. Refereed. *Indexed:* B01. *Aud.:* Ac, Sa.

This publication, as an open-access journal, appears to focus on the leveling aspects of technology. The use of the social web plays a large part in the choice of articles, as does the use of computers by all the family, so to speak. Recent articles have included "Facebook Me: Collective Self-Esteem, Need to Belong, and Internet Self-Efficacy as Predictors of the iGeneration's Attitudes toward Social Networking Sites," which goes far in defining the focus of this journal. Another article is about "The Effectiveness of Product Placement in Video Games." There does, nonetheless, appear to be an effort to present case studies to the users, and these case studies are from both the academic world and the marketplace.

94. *Journal of Macromarketing.* [ISSN: 0276-1467] 1981. q. USD 538. Ed(s): Terrence H Witkowski. Sage Publications, Inc., 2455 Teller Rd, Thousand Oaks, CA 91320; info@sagepub.com; http://www.sagepub.com. Illus., adv. Sample. Refereed. Vol. ends: Fall (No. 2). Reprint: PSC. *Indexed:* A22, ABIn, B01, E01. *Bk. rev.:* 2-6, 1,000-3,000 words. *Aud.:* Ac.

The scholarly articles in this journal address a wide range of social issues, international and domestic, and the impact of marketing upon them. The authors approach topics from many perspectives: historical, analytical, theoretical, and general. Articles in recent issues discuss marketing and the natural environment and the role for morality, and there is a study that examines the marketing literature within the publications of the American Economic Association. Each issue has several extensive, signed book reviews. This work is worth the price for a program concerned with business ethics.

95. *Journal of Marketing.* Formed by the merger of (1934-1936): *The American Marketing Journal;* (1935-1936): *The National Marketing Review.* [ISSN: 0022-2429] 1936. bi-m. USD 350 (print or online ed.) Individuals, USD 120 (print or online ed.); Free to members). Ed(s): Francesca V Cooley, Ajay K Kohli. American Marketing Association, 311 S Wacker Dr, Ste 5800, Chicago, IL 60606; info@ama.org; http://www.marketingpower.com. Illus., index, adv. Refereed. Circ: 8900 Paid. Vol. ends: No. 4. Microform: PQC. Reprint: PSC. *Indexed:* A22, ABIn, B01, B02, BAS, BLI, BRI, CBRI, H&TI, JEL, P02, PsycInfo, RILM. *Bk. rev.:* 3, 1,000-4,000 words. *Aud.:* Ac.

This official publication of the American Marketing Association includes research articles that must provide a practical link to an application. Articles must be theoretically sound, provide new information or a fresh insight into an unsolved problem, and benefit both practitioners and academicians. Articles tend to be thoughtful, well researched, and interesting. This is a core title for any academic library that supports business programs, especially marketing education programs. There are regular, lengthy book reviews. Recent articles discuss the acquisition and utilization of information in new product alliances and two aspects of brand loyalty: purchase loyalty and attitudinal loyalty. Online subscriptions are available directly from the publisher.

96. *Journal of Marketing Education.* [ISSN: 0273-4753] 1979. 3x/yr. USD 624. Ed(s): Douglas J Lincoln. Sage Publications, Inc., 2455 Teller Rd, Thousand Oaks, CA 91320; info@sagepub.com; http://www.sagepub.com. Illus., index, adv. Sample. Refereed. Vol. ends: Fall (No. 3). Reprint: PSC. *Indexed:* A22, ABIn, B01, E01, ERIC, PsycInfo. *Aud.:* Ac.

This journal is cosponsored by the Western Marketing Educators Association and the publisher. Each issue includes several papers of about ten pages in length on various aspects of marketing education. Recent articles discuss analyzing the perceptions and preferences of master's of business administration (MBA) students regarding face-to-face versus distance-education methods for delivering a course in marketing management; and familiarizing marketing educators with the process of creative problem-solving. A wise investment as the makeup of marketing departments evolves.

97. *Journal of Marketing Research.* [ISSN: 0022-2437] 1964. bi-m. USD 350 (print or online ed.) Individuals, USD 120 (print or online ed.); Free to members). Ed(s): Francesca Cooley, Tulin Erdem. American Marketing Association, 311 S Wacker Dr, Ste 5800, Chicago, IL 60606; info@ama.org; http://www.marketingpower.com. Illus., index, adv. Refereed. Circ: 4900 Paid. Vol. ends: Nov. Microform: PQC. Reprint: PSC. *Indexed:* A22, ABIn, B01, B02, BRI, EconLit, FS&TA, JEL, PsycInfo. *Bk. rev.:* Number and length vary. *Aud.:* Ac.

This core journal presents the results of scholarly and empirical research without the restriction (which accompanies the *Journal of Marketing*) of linking it to practical applications. Mathematical marketing research included in this journal requires that readers possess a strong background in quantitative methods. Papers in recent issues examine negative customer feedback and consumer reactions to corporate social responsibility. Each issue includes a section of research notes on topics such as an empirical analysis of the growth stage of the product life cycle, or the design of research studies for maximum impact; and a section of book reviews.

98. *Journal of Public Relations Research.* Former titles (until 1992): *Public Relations Research Annual;* (until 1989): *Public Relations Research & Education.* [ISSN: 1062-726X] 1984. q. GBP 560 (print & online eds.). Ed(s): Karen Russell. Routledge, 325 Chestnut St, Ste 800, Philadelphia, PA 19106; customerservice@taylorandfrancis.com; http://www.tandfonline.com. Adv. Sample. Refereed. Reprint: PSC. *Indexed:* A22, ABIn, B01, E01, PsycInfo. *Bk. rev.:* Number and length vary. *Aud.:* Ac, Sa.

This academic journal contains long articles aimed at the advanced student or scholar. A recent article is on "Expansion of Ethics as the Tenth Generic Principle of Public Relations Excellence: A Kantian Theory and Model for Managing Ethical Issues," which demonstrates the journal's focus.

99. *Journal of Services Marketing.* [ISSN: 0887-6045] 1987. 7x/yr. EUR 10639 combined subscription in Europe (print & online eds.); USD 4749 combined subscription in the Americas (print & online eds.); GBP 7159 combined subscription in the UK & elsewhere (print & online eds.). Ed(s): Charles Martin. Emerald Group Publishing Ltd., Howard House, Wagon Ln, Bingley, BD16 1WA, United Kingdom; emerald@emeraldinsight.com; http://www.emeraldinsight.com. Illus. Sample. Refereed. Vol. ends: Nov (No. 4). Reprint: PSC. *Indexed:* A22, ABIn, B01, B02, BRI, E01, P02. *Bk. rev.:* Number and length vary. *Aud.:* Ac, Sa.

This international marketing journal for practitioners provides research reports on a variety of topics related to all aspects of the service economy, including benchmarking, customer perception, customer satisfaction, quality and performance, marketing operations, and marketing management. A recent article concerns perceived managerial sincerity, feedback-seeking orientation, and motivation among front-line employees of a service organization. Each issue contains five to seven articles, 10–15 pages in length; abstracts of current research literature; and book reviews. This important journal is overpriced for many academic programs that could benefit from a subscription.

100. *Marketing.* Formerly (until 19??): *I S M A.* [ISSN: 0025-3650] 1931. w. GBP 199. Ed(s): Noelle McElhatton. Haymarket Publishing Ltd., 174 Hammersmith Rd, London, W6 7JP, United Kingdom; info@haymarket.com; http://www.haymarket.com. Illus., adv. Circ: 40000. Vol. ends: Dec. Microform: PQC. *Indexed:* A22, ABIn, B01, B02, BRI, C37. *Aud.:* Ga, Sa.

This publication is the newspaper of marketing. Functioning much like a trade magazine, it focuses on international marketing news regarding companies, individuals, brands, legal wrangles, technology, and general areas of market research, advertising, use of emerging technologies, image, and market positioning through dozens of short articles. Survey results and awards are reported, such as a recent report on awards for the best direct-marketing campaigns.

101. *Marketing News: reporting on marketing and its association.* [ISSN: 0025-3790] 1967. bi-w. Free to members. Ed(s): Allison Enright. American Marketing Association, 311 S Wacker Dr, Ste 5800, Chicago, IL 60606; info@ama.org; http://www.marketingpower.com. Illus., adv. Circ: 38000. Vol. ends: No. 26. Microform: MIM; PQC. *Indexed:* A22, ABIn, B01, B02, B03, BRI, Chicano. *Aud.:* Ac, Sa.

The American Marketing Association produces this core trade and industry newspaper to provide timely information to practitioners about the most recent innovations and practices of today's leading companies. A calendar of events, association activities, and a variety of methods and techniques for achieving marketing goals in a company, for a product, or within the industry as a whole are presented in short articles. An annual directory of consultants is published each June. Sample articles include one on digital yellow pages, and another on the actual profile of baby boomers in marketing terms and marketing to them since the dot-com crash.

102. *Marketing Research: a magazine of management and applications.* [ISSN: 1040-8460] 1989. q. USD 125 (Individuals, USD 90; Free to members). Ed(s): Michael Fielding, Chuck Chakrapani. American Marketing Association, 311 S Wacker Dr, Ste 5800, Chicago, IL 60606; info@ama.org; http://www.marketingpower.com. Illus., index, adv. Sample. Refereed. Circ: 5000 Paid. Vol. ends: No. 4. Reprint: PSC. *Indexed:* A22, ABIn, B01, B02, BLI, BRI. *Aud.:* Ac, Sa.

In this core title, the American Marketing Association seeks to emphasize the advancement of the theoretical base of marketing science. It is aimed at market research academicians and practitioners, and each issue contains several well-written articles on the practical aspects of marketing research. Feature articles often examine cyber-research, including techniques, software, methods, and models for data collecting. Regular departments focus on software reviews, legislative and regulatory issues, secondary research, research methods, and data collections. A recent article is titled "Safe Harbor Principles for the European Privacy Directive Are Finalized." The editorial board includes representatives of research firms and academicians.

103. *Marketing Science: the marketing journal of INFORMS.* [ISSN: 0732-2399] 1982. bi-m. USD 505 (print & online eds.). Ed(s): Preyas Desai. Institute for Operations Research and the Management Sciences (I N F O R M S), 7240 Pky Dr, Ste 300, Hanover, MD 21076; informs@informs.org; http://www.informs.org. Illus., index. Refereed. Circ: 1800. *Indexed:* A22, ABIn, B01, B02, EconLit, IBSS, JEL, PsycInfo. *Aud.:* Ac, Sa.

The Operational Research Society of America and the Institute of Marketing Science produce this journal, in which authors use mathematics and statistics to evaluate marketing science. It presents papers that offer significant new marketing insights and implications for academics and quantitatively oriented practitioners. One example is a paper on "Direct Competitive Pricing Behavior in the Auto Market: A Structural Analysis." The wide variety of methodologies provides researchers with ideas for approaching research, as well as reports on current concerns. Recent topics include "Patterns in Parameters of Buyer Behavior Models: Generalizing from Sparse Replication. A Model for the Analysis of Asymmetric Data in Marketing Research"; "Application, Predictive Test, and Strategy Implications for a Dynamic Model of Consumer Response"; and "Modeling Retail Customer Behavior at Merrill Lynch."

104. *Media Industry Newsletter.* Incorporates in part (in 2002): *m i n's New Media Report;* Which incorporated (1994-1997): *Interactive Video News;* Which was formed by the merger of (1993-1994): *Video Services News;* (1990-1994): *Video Marketing Newsletter;* Formerly: *Magazine Industry Newsletter.* [ISSN: 0024-9793] 1948. w. USD 995 combined subscription (print & online eds.). Ed(s): Steven Cohn, Greer Jonas. Access Intelligence, LLC, 4 Choke Cherry Rd, 2nd Fl, Rockville, MD 20850; clientservices@accessintel.com; http://www.accessintel.com. Illus., index. Vol. ends: Dec. *Indexed:* ABIn, B01, B03, BRI. *Aud.:* Sa.

This loose-leaf title is devoted to the media industry, especially magazine and newspaper publications. Its eight to ten pages are filled with statistics regarding advertising in the consumer-magazine publishing industry. There is an opinion article in each issue, and many short pieces on the various industries. This title describes itself as "the first source for magazine advertising data (boxscores)," and it does keep its readers up-to-date on what is happening in the field. Despite the importance of the data, it is a bit pricey for what it might bring to an academic library, but fortunately it is indexed in Lexis-Nexis Academic Universe.

105. *O'Dwyer's.* Former titles (until Dec.2009): *O'Dwyer's P R Report;* (until 2006): *O'Dwyer's P R Services Report.* [ISSN: 2153-3148] 1987. m. USD 60 domestic; USD 90 Canada; USD 125 elsewhere. Ed(s): Jack O'Dwyer, Jon Gingerich. J.R. O'Dwyer Co., Inc., 271 Madison Ave, Ste 600, New York, NY 10016; http://www.odwyerpr.com. Adv. Circ: 2000 Paid and controlled. *Indexed:* BRI. *Aud.:* Sa.

This newsletter publishes articles on current topics and trends of interest to PR professionals, including profiles of firms and discussions of legal and financial issues. It includes such columns as "Web Sitings," which reports on recent developments in the field on the web. This work differs from *O'Dwyer's PR Newsletter* in that it contains more news and less opinion. The columns are informational in intent without any particular political slant. Issues include a PR job market section, and are still considered the gold standard by many in the field.

106. *O'Dwyer's P R Newsletter.* Former titles: *Jack O'Dwyer's Newsletter; Jack O'Dwyer's P R Newsletter.* 1968. w. USD 295 domestic; USD 320 foreign. Ed(s): Jack O'Dwyer, Kevin McCauley. J.R. O'Dwyer Co., Inc., 271 Madison Ave, Ste 600, New York, NY 10016; john@odwyerpr.com; http://www.odwyerpr.com. Circ: 20000 Paid. *Aud.:* Sa.

This indispensable weekly provides the latest news and information on public relations firms and professionals. It subdivides the news rather casually in the "PR Opinion/Items" and "Media News" sections. Under each are several stories that the editors have deemed important for professionals to read. The former gives editorial opinions on politics as they affect this field. In the latter, recently, CCNY Communications Hall of Fame inductees are found next to the announcement of the winner of the McDonald's account. Recommended for all professionals and large public libraries.

107. *Psychology & Marketing.* [ISSN: 0742-6046] 1984. m. GBP 1218. Ed(s): Dr. Ronald Jay Cohen, Rajan Nataraajan. John Wiley & Sons, Inc., 111 River St, MS 4-02, Hoboken, NJ 07030; info@wiley.com; http://www.wiley.com/WileyCDA/. Illus., index, adv. Refereed. Vol. ends: No. 6. Microform: PQC. Reprint: PSC. *Indexed:* A22, ABIn, B01, PsycInfo. *Aud.:* Ac, Sa.

This title presents research that bridges academic and practical interests in marketing and advertising through the application of psychological principles to marketing strategy. Research reports are based on "fundamental factors that affect buying, social and cultural trends, psychological profiles of potential customers, and changes in customer behavior." Recent papers discuss the dangers of using deceptive practices in the mail-order business; using deception to measure service performance; and "Romancing the Past: Heritage Visiting and the Nostalgic Consumer." The journal is widely indexed, and the in-depth articles are well written. An important, although expensive, addition for academic and special libraries.

108. *Public Relations Review: a global journal of research and comment.* [ISSN: 0363-8111] 1975. 5x/yr. EUR 684. Ed(s): Ray E Hiebert. Elsevier Ltd, 32 Jamestown Rd, Camden, London, NW1 7BY, United Kingdom; corporate.sales@elsevier.com; http://www.elsevier.com. Illus., adv. Sample. Vol. ends: Dec. Microform: PQC. Reprint: PSC. *Indexed:* A01, A22, ABIn, B01, B02, BRI, P02, P61, SSA. *Bk. rev.:* 5-6, 500-1,000 words. *Aud.:* Ga, Ac, Sa.

This journal considers its title an important guide to its content: there are pieces that could be called research, although some might question the format of the methodology section in the articles. There are pieces that comment on how government policy directly affects aspects of a public relations officer's life. The book reviews alone are worth the cover price. They are extensive and could be considered articles in themselves, perhaps thus fulfilling the "review" promise in the title. A fifth issue published midyear is an extensive bibliography that will interest librarians.

109. *Public Relations Strategist.* [ISSN: 1082-9113] 1995. q. USD 150 domestic; USD 160 Canada; USD 170 elsewhere. Ed(s): Donald K Wright. The Public Relations Society of America, Inc., 33 Maiden Ln, 11th Fl, New York, NY 10038; prssa@prsa.org; http://www.prsa.org. Adv. *Indexed:* A22, B01. *Aud.:* Sa.

This journal is included in the price of Public Relations Society membership dues. It contains about ten articles of interest to the trade. The editors wish to emphasize the regular interviews with CEOs of the leading firms in the field. Recent articles include one on the "Ethical Challenge of Global Public Relations."

110. *Public Relations Tactics.* [ISSN: 1080-6792] 1994. m. USD 100 domestic; USD 110 Canada; USD 120 elsewhere. Ed(s): John Elsasser. The Public Relations Society of America, Inc., 33 Maiden Ln, 11th Fl, New York, NY 10038; prssa@prsa.org; http://www.prsa.org. *Indexed:* B01. *Aud.:* Sa.

This tabloid directs its articles toward professionals, and they are written by their peers. The articles can concern independent practitioners or employees of big firms. Each issue has a listing of upcoming events such as trade shows. Polls are included that are of interest and importance to the audience, but with little analysis. The articles also keep readers abreast of recent court rulings that have an impact upon the field. This publication is an important mouthpiece for the profession.

■ AERONAUTICS AND SPACE SCIENCE

Howard Stephen McMinn, Director of Collections and Scholarly Communication, Brookens Library, Room 234, University of Illinois at Springfield, One University Plaza, Springfield, IL 62703-5407; stephen.mcminn@uis.edu

Introduction

The terms *aeronautics, astronautics,* and *space science* do not conjure up the romantic images of early aviators and aviation pioneers or the excitement of space exploration, but they are the basic elements of these inspiring endeavors. This romantic concept of flying and space exploration is communicated through the popular journals that capture the adventure, excitement, and sport of all types of aviation and aircraft from ballooning to spaceflight. The science and technology that support aviation and spaceflight—i.e., aeronautics, astronautics, and space science—are highly technical fields that require very specialized, technical information created by experts in their fields. This section tries to balance these different perspectives by presenting the best aviation and spaceflight magazines, along with the most significant technical journals in these fields.

Some aspects of these fields, those connected with military aviation or the commercial aspects of aviation industry—that is, those dealing with airlines, airports, manufacturing, maintenance, and travel—can be found in the "Military" and "Transportation" sections. This section is composed of the important scientific and technical journals required by researchers, scientists, and engineers along with the leading general-interest publications that cover the various areas of aviation and flight.

From a library perspective, the fields of aeronautics, astronautics, and space science have not seen the explosive growth in new technical journals that some disciplines have experienced in the past few years, but there are a number of new technical journals that have either recently published their first issue or are on the launch pad, but are too new to be included among the leading journals in the field.

Overall, the section has been realigned to focus on journals that cover the key areas rather than the legal, medical, or policy aspects of these disciplines. As the focus of the research journals in the space sciences tends to overlap with the field of astronomy, those interested in space sciences should consult the "Astronomy" section for additional relevant titles.

Similarly, there hasn't been much change in terms of the number of general-interest flight and aviation magazines published. Most of the popular aviation and business focused journal have web and electronic reader versions for iPad, Kindle, smart phones, or other devices. The journals and magazines that follow should provide ample information to aid in the development of a core collection for the researcher in aeronautics and space sciences, or for those interested in the best general aviation and flying publications.

Basic Periodicals

Hs: *Air & Space–Smithsonian, Aviation Week & Space Technology, Flying;* Ga: *Air & Space–Smithsonian, A O P A Pilot, Aviation Week & Space Technology, Flying, FlyPast, Plane and Pilot, Soaring;* Ac (Nontechnical): *Aerospace America, Aviation Week & Space Technology, Flight International, Space Policy, Vertiflite;* Ac (Technical): *Acta Astronautica, The Aeronautical Journal, A I A A Journal, Journal of Aircraft, Journal of Spacecraft and Rockets, Journal of the Astronautical Sciences, Progress in Aerospace Sciences.*

Basic Abstracts and Indexes

Aerospace & High Technology Database, The Engineering Index Monthly, International Aerospace Abstracts, Scopus.

111. *A A H S Journal.* Formerly (until 1980): *American Aviation Historical Society Journal.* [ISSN: 0882-9365] 1956. q. Free to members. Ed(s): Hayden Hamilton, Albert Hansen. American Aviation Historical Society, 2333 Otis St, Santa Ana, CA 92704. Illus., adv. Vol. ends: No. 4. *Aud.:* Ac, Sa.

This journal, produced by the American Aviation Historical Society (AAHS), consists of well-researched scholarly articles on all areas of aviation history. The primary emphasis is on the history of general aviation and commercial flight technology, not on military or space history and events, as is the case with other aviation history magazines. All areas of aviation history are included, from famous aviators and engineers to aircraft design and manufacture, to the history of aerospace advancements and technical achievements. The journal contains primarily black-and-white photographs (appropriate for the time periods covered) and illustrations. Articles are written by historians, military personnel, and scholars, and are produced by society members; and most have an American flavor. Ongoing departments include "Remember When?" (highlighting an historical aircraft), "Forum of Flight" (consisting of interesting or unusual black-and-white photographs of aircraft submitted by members), and "News and Comments from our Readers" (including items of interest, news, and conference activities). AAHS also publishes an electronic newsletter, *AAHS Flightline,* that provides interesting articles along with information of interest to the society's membership. This scholarly and informative journal is appropriate for academic and public libraries with strong history or aviation collections.

112. *A I A A Journal: devoted to aerospace research and development.* Formed by the merger of (1958-1963): *Journal of the Aerospace Sciences;* Which was formerly (1934-1958): *Journal of the Aeronautical Sciences;* (1959-1963): *A R S Journal;* Which was formerly (until 1959): *Jet Propulsion;* (until 1954): *American Rocket Society. Journal;* (until 1945): *Astronautics;* (1930-1932): *American Interplanetary Society. Bulletin.* [ISSN: 0001-1452] 1963. m. Members, USD 80 (print & online eds.); Non-members, USD 1560. Ed(s): Peretz P Friedmann, Michael Baden-Campbell. American Institute of Aeronautics and Astronautics, Inc., 1801 Alexander Bell Dr, Ste 500, Reston, VA 20191; custserv@aiaa.org; http://www.aiaa.org. Illus., index. Sample. Refereed. Vol. ends: No. 12. Microform: PMC; PQC. Reprint: PSC. *Indexed:* A01, A22, ApMecR, BRI, C&ISA, CerAb, EngInd, H24, MathR, P02. *Bk. rev.:* 1-2, 300-500 words. *Aud.:* Ac.

This is the leading overarching research-oriented journal of the American Institute of Aeronautics and Astronautics (AIAA), and it covers all topics of broad interest to the membership, as opposed to the more narrowly focused

scope of the organization's other journals. This journal is designed to disseminate original research papers that discuss new theoretical developments or experimental results for the advancement of astronautics and aeronautics. The areas covered include aerodynamics, aeroacoustics, fluid mechanics, reacting flows, hydrodynamics, research instrumentation and facilities, structural mechanics and materials, propulsion, aircraft technology, STOL/VTOL, fluid dynamics, thermophysics and thermochemistry, and interdisciplinary topics. The journal is divided into sections arranged by broad subject classification: "Aircraft Technology, Conventional, STOL/VTOL," "Fluid Dynamics," "Interdisciplinary Topics," and "Structural Mechanics and Materials." Additional sections are occasionally added when appropriate, such as "Propulsion" and "Thermophysics and Heat Transfer." Periodically, special sections or issues devoted to a specific topic are published. The journal also has a letters section, "Aerospace Letters," to facilitate the rapid communication of new and potentially important results. Other sections are occasionally added, such as lecture articles and survey papers to provide comprehensive overviews of subjects of interest to the journal's readership. Appropriate for all academic, technical, and larger public libraries.

113. *A O P A Pilot.* [ISSN: 0001-2084] 1958. m. Free to members. Ed(s): Thomas B Haines. Aircraft Owners and Pilots Association (A O P A), 421 Aviation Way, Frederick, MD 21701; aopahq@aopa.org; http://www.aopa.org. Illus., index, adv. Circ: 367882 Paid and controlled. Vol. ends: Dec. *Bk. rev.:* 1-2, 300-500 words. *Aud.:* Ga, Sa.

This journal is the primary vehicle of the Aircraft Owners and Pilots Association, which is the world's largest aviation organization that meets the needs of all pilots—from student pilots to space shuttle pilots—for over 70 years. However, the journal is geared toward the private pilot and aircraft owner with emphasis on ownership related issues and flight safety. Articles include information on safety; flying tips and techniques; airports, nearby accommodations, and attractions; newly certified aircraft, along with specifications; and, of course, general-interest pieces on aircraft and flying. There are numerous departments that contain general information pertinent to association members and pilots, such as regulatory news, safety-related information, a calendar of events, and information on new aircraft and equipment, along with meeting and organizational notes. The journal provides many photographs, as well as illustrations for aviation buffs that highlight the text. The magazine contains a large commentary section that is usually geared at members but also contains information on safety, along with other issues and concerns with piloting aircraft. AOPA produces two companion publications, *AOPA Flight Training,* which provides in-depth information for pilots and pilots-in-training, and *AOPA Pilot Magazine—Turbine Edition,* which includes all the articles in the magazine with additional articles for turbine-powered aircraft. One of the best general-interest aviation publications, and an excellent addition to general-aviation collections.

114. *Acta Astronautica.* Formerly (until 1974): *Astronautica Acta.* [ISSN: 0094-5765] 1955. s-m. EUR 5256. Ed(s): Rock Jeng-Shing Chern. Pergamon, The Blvd, Langford Ln, E Park, Kidlington, OX5 1GB, United Kingdom; JournalsCustomerServiceEMEA@elsevier.com; http://www.elsevier.com. Illus., adv. Sample. Refereed. Microform: PQC. *Indexed:* A01, A22, AbAn, ApMecR, C&ISA, CerAb, EngInd, H24, M&GPA. *Aud.:* Ac.

This research-level publication covering the field of astronautics and space sciences, with contributions and readership on a global scale, is produced by the International Academy of Astronautics (IAA). Each issue presents peer-reviewed papers in the areas of life sciences, astronautics, space sciences, and space technology, to promote the peaceful scientific exploration of space to aid humanity. In addition, it covers the design, development, research, and technological advances necessary to accomplish this goal. Articles cover microgravity, space station technology, spacecraft, interplanetary flight, satellites, power and propulsion, geomagnetism, GPS, and space economics, along with traditional areas of research such as materials science, guidance and control, etc. The journal often devotes part of an issue, or publishes an entire special issue, to a specific topic or a collection of selected papers from conferences sponsored by the International Academy of Astronautics or the International Astronautical Federation, such as the recent issue on searching for life signatures and the Humans in Space Symposium. The journal also publishes

"Academy Transaction Notes" and other items of interest to academy members when appropriate. Overall, the journal's broad-coverage with its international scope is appropriate for academic and research libraries.

Ad Astra. See Astronomy section.

115. *Advances in Space Research.* Formed by the merger of (1978-1981): *Advances in Space Exploration;* (1963-1981): *Life Sciences and Space Research;* (1960-1980): *Space Research.* [ISSN: 0273-1177] 1981. s-m. EUR 4956. Ed(s): J Lastovicka. Pergamon, The Blvd, Langford Ln, E Park, Kidlington, OX5 1GB, United Kingdom; JournalsCustomerServiceEMEA@elsevier.com; http://www.elsevier.com. Illus., adv. Sample. Refereed. Vol. ends: No. 24. Microform: PQC. *Indexed:* A01, A22, C&ISA, CerAb, EngInd, M&GPA. *Aud.:* Ac, Sa.

This journal presents information on fundamental research obtained by utilizing aerospace vehicles, and is primarily of interest to physicists, astronomers, and the general field of space science. As the official journal of the Committee on Space Research (COSPAR), a scientific committee of the International Council of Scientific Unions, *Advances in Space Research* covers all areas of fundamental research obtained with the use of all types of space vehicles including balloons, rockets, rocket-propelled vehicles, and other aerospace vehicles, regardless of political considerations. A sampling of the topics covered includes planets and small bodies of the solar system, the ionosphere, solar energy, geomagnetism, cosmic rays, solar radiation, astrophysics, studies of the upper atmosphere, materials sciences research, life sciences as related to space, and space studies of Earth's surface. Much of the information contained in the journal has been taken from various meetings and symposia sponsored by COSPAR. Therefore, most issues contain papers on similar topics or in a single area of interest. Even though papers are taken from various conferences, they are thoroughly reviewed before inclusion in the journal. Also, special issues can be purchased individually. Most of the items of interest to the organization's membership are in the sister publication, *Space Research Today.*

116. *The Aeronautical Journal.* Incorporates (1949-1983): *Aeronautical Quarterly;* Former titles (until 1968): *Royal Aeronautical Society. Journal;* Which incorporated (1947-1959): *Helicopter Association of Great Britain. Journal;* (until 1923): *Aeronautical Journal;* (until 1987): *Aeronautical Society of Great Britain. Annual Report.* [ISSN: 0001-9240] 1897. m. Free to membership. Ed(s): Peter Bearman. Royal Aeronautical Society, 4 Hamilton Pl, London, W1J 7BQ, United Kingdom; publications@aerosociety.com; http://www.aerosociety.com. Illus., index, adv. Refereed. Vol. ends: Dec. *Indexed:* A22, ApMecR, EngInd, MathR. *Bk. rev.:* 2-3, 300-500 words. *Aud.:* Ac.

The purpose of this long-standing monthly aeronautical engineering research journal, produced by the Royal Aeronautical Society, is to foster the advancement of all aspects of aeronautical, aerospace, and space sciences. The journal publishes five to eight articles per issue related to the research, design, development, construction, and operation of aircraft and space vehicles. Topics of the papers include fluid mechanics and aerodynamics, propulsion, structures and materials, rotocraft, astronautics, dynamics and control, noise and vibration, guided flight, air transport, and test flying and flight simulation. Also included are the "Technical Notes" sections to encourage rapid dissemination of information and to foster discussion on current research and "Survey Papers," which focus on a specific aspect of aeronautics and astronautics. The journal has moved away from information that is geared solely to society members to providing strictly technical articles, although it does provide two or three book reviews per issue. Occasional special issues are published that are focused on a single topic or theme, or comprised of selected technical papers presented at major U.K. aeronautical conferences. Membership and related society information is available in the society's companion publication, *Aerospace.*

117. *AeroSafety World.* Formerly (until 2007): *Aviation Safety World;* Formed by the merger of (1987-2006): *Accident Prevention;* Which was formerly (until 1987): *F S F Accident Prevention Bulletin;* (1987-2006): *Airport Operations;* Which was formerly (until 1987): *F S F Airport Operations Safety Bulletin;* (1954-2006): *Aviation Mechanics Bulletin;* (1987-2006): *Cabin Crew Safety;* Which was formerly (until 1987): *F S F Cabin Crew Safety Bulletin;* (until 1975): *Cabin Crew Safety Exchange;* (1988-2006): *Flight Safety Digest;* Which was formerly (until

1988): *F S F Flight Safety Digest;* (until 1984): *Flight Safety Digest;* (until 1982): *Flight Safety Facts and Reports;* (until 1974): *Flight Safety Facts and Analysis;* (1987-2006): *Helicopter Safety;* Which was formerly (until 1987): *F S F Helicopter Safety Bulletin;* (until 1985): *Helicopter Safety Bulletin;* (1988-2006): *Human Factors & Aviation Medicine;* Which was formerly (until 1988): *F S F Human Factors Bulletin & Aviation Medicine.* [ISSN: 1934-4015] 2006. m. Free to members. Ed(s): Frank Jackman. Flight Safety Foundation, Inc., 601 Madison St, Ste 300, Alexandria, VA 22314; http://www.flightsafety.org. Adv. *Bk. rev.:* Number and length vary. *Aud.:* Ga, Ac, Sa.

This journal, published by the Flight Safety Foundation, provides articles and in-depth analysis of important safety issues that face the industry, along with numerous standard departments. The feature articles deal with all areas of safety within all sectors of the aviation industry. Expanded versions of feature articles are occasionally available on the foundation's web site. The departments contain news items, editorials, letters to the editor, a calendar of events, and information on the foundation and its members. The "DataLink" section provides articles that include data and analysis on topics specific to aviation and safety. The "InfoScan" section provides in-depth coverage of selected reports, reviews of books, and web sites of interest to those involved with safety. The "OnRecord" section covers important information taken from the final reports in investigations, which provide awareness of problems so that others would avoid them in the future. This journal was created through the merging of seven newsletters produced by the foundation. These newsletters are listed primarily to provide a glimpse at the subjects covered by this journal: *Accident Prevention, Airport Operations, Aviation Mechanics Bulletin, Cabin Crew Safety, Flight Safety Digest, Helicopter Safety,* and *Human Factors & Aviation Medicine.* The journal is an important, timely publication for those working in the industry or interested in aviation safety. It is now published in three languages: English, Chinese, and Spanish.

118. *Aerospace America.* Former titles (until 1984): *Astronautics and Aeronautics;* (until 1964): *Astronautics and Aerospace Engineering;* Which was formed by the merger of (1957-1963): *Astronautics;* (1958-1963): *Aesrospace Engineering;* Which was formerly (1942-1958): *Aeronautical Engineering Review;* Astronautics and Aeronautics superseded in part (1964-1975): *A I A A Bulletin.* [ISSN: 0740-722X] 1932. m. Free to members; Non-members, USD 163. Ed(s): Elaine J Camhi. American Institute of Aeronautics and Astronautics, Inc., 1801 Alexander Bell Dr, Ste 500, Reston, VA 20191; custserv@aiaa.org; http://www.aiaa.org. Illus., index, adv. Sample. Refereed. Vol. ends: No. 12. Microform: PQC. *Indexed:* A01, A22, ABS&EES, ApMecR, BRI, C&ISA, CerAb, EngInd, M&GPA, P02. *Aud.:* Hs, Ga, Ac.

Aerospace America is the membership general-interest publication of the American Institute of Aeronautics and Astronautics (AIAA). The two or three feature articles are published in each issue covering all aspects of the industry—economic issues, government rules and financing, aircraft, materials, space transportation, spacecraft, and defense. The articles usually provide more of an overview on the topic and primarily interpret or review new research, engineering issues, program developments, and future trends in aeronautics or space sciences. The articles are still quite sophisticated and comprehensive, utilizing many color photographs and illustrations. The journal is devoted to keeping AIAA members up-to-date on major events and issues in their field, and serves as the prime vehicle for relaying information on the institute's activities. It contains valuable news of upcoming conferences and events, along with sections such as "International Beat" and "Washington Watch," with recent industry news, and "Conversations," composed of interviews with important people in the industry or people who impact the industry (such as lawmakers). Other sections provide information on new systems, software, materials, or products of note; an almanac of past aerospace milestones of interest; and career-related information. New sections include green engineering, as well as aircraft and electronics updates. The December issue is a special one devoted to reviewing the highlights, accomplishments, and news of note for previous year in aerospace. Overall, this journal is a valuable addition for all types of libraries.

119. *Aerospace Engineering.* Former titles (until 2011): *Aerospace Engineering & Manufacturing;* (until 2008): *Aerospace Engineering;* (until 1983): *S A E in Aerospace Engineering.* [ISSN: 2156-7743] 1981. q. Free to members; Non-members, USD 65. Ed(s): Jean Broge. S A E

Inc., 400 Commonwealth Dr, Warrendale, PA 15096; CustomerService@sae.org; http://www.sae.org. Illus., index, adv. Vol. ends: Dec. *Indexed:* A22, B02, B03, C&ISA, CerAb, H24. *Bk. rev.:* 1-2. *Aud.:* Ac, Sa.

This journal, produced by the Society of Automotive Engineers (SAE), is designed to provide technical assistance and state-of-the-art technical information of interest to designers, manufacturers, and project managers of aerospace systems and components. Its emphasis is more on applications, testing, and reliability of aerospace components than on theoretical or experimental results. Unlike most trade-oriented magazines, there is very little information on people, events, or the business side of the industry. The journal covers all areas of interest to aerospace engineers, including avionics, new materials, system and component design, propulsion systems, system maintainability, structural design, and related engineering topics. It is an important vehicle for new-product information, product literature, computer products, and other technical information. Its focus is on conveying practical timely information to those working in the field. The more theoretical and technical research are presented as papers at SAE conferences and symposia and published in the *SAE Transactions, Aerospace Engineering.* Appropriate for technical and academic libraries.

120. *Aerospace Manufacturing and Design.* 2007. 7x/yr. USD 45 in Canada & Mexico (Free to qualified personnel). Ed(s): Tom Grasson, Elizabeth Modic. G I E Media Inc., 4020 Kinross Lakes Pky, Richfield, OH 44286; http://www.giemedia.com/pages/home/default.aspx. Adv. Circ: 15000. *Aud.:* Ac, Sa.

Aerospace Manufacturing and Design is one of the most technically-oriented trade journals in the field. The articles are highly technical and focused on all aspects of manufacturing and design in the aerospace industry. The orientation is also slightly different, with each issue's having a top feature or single cover article along with four or five other articles. Then there are the standard departments that accompany most trade journals, which focus on industry news, opinions, and the outlook. There is little focus on people in the industry, with most of the departments focused on new products or services, including a "Reference Guide" in each issue. There are two departments of note: the first is "Expert Opinion," providing information from an expert in the field on a design or manufacturing topics; and the other is the "Aviation Appreciation" department, where readers can enter a "name that plane" contest. All of the typical aviation subjects are covered, including safety issues, government regulation, and financial outlooks. The primary focus is on manufacturing and design, with articles on precision manufacturing, thermal management, composite repair, inspection issues, lean manufacturing, and productivity and leadership, among others. There are periodic special features such as more than one *Buyers Guide.* This is a valuable new trade journal that recognizes and fills its claimed niche for the aerospace industry.

121. *Aerospace Science and Technology.* Formed by the merger of (1963-1997): *Recherche Aerospaciale;* Which was formerly (1948-1963): *La Recherche Aeronautique;* (1974-1997): *Recherche Aerospatiale (English Edition);* (1977-1997): *Zeitschrift fuer Flugwissenschaften und Weltraumforschung;* Which was formed by the merger of (1953-1977): *Zeitschrift fuer Flugwissenschaften;* (1964-1977): *Raumfahrtforschung;* Which was formerly (1957-1964): *Raketentechnik und Raumfahrtforschung.* [ISSN: 1270-9638] 1997. 8x/yr. EUR 514. Ed(s): J.A. Ekaterinaris. Elsevier Masson, 62 Rue Camille Desmoulins, Issy les Moulineaux, Cedex 92442, France; infos@elsevier-masson.fr; http://www.elsevier-masson.fr. Illus., index. Sample. Refereed. Vol. ends: No. 8. *Indexed:* A01, A22, ApMecR, C&ISA, CerAb, EngInd, MathR. *Aud.:* Ac, Sa.

This journal is international in scope, presenting articles from original research, review articles, and condensed versions of recently completed doctoral theses in all areas of aerospace science and technology. Topics covered include all issues related to aerospace research, from fundamental research to industrial applications for the design and manufacture of aircraft, helicopters, missiles, launch vehicles, and satellites. Included are articles on aerodynamics, computational fluid dynamics (CFD), computer simulation, materials and structures, flight mechanics, guidance and control, automatic systems, propulsion systems, and analysis of experimental data. The journal originated by combining two of the leading aerospace journals from France and Germany.

Aerospace Science and Technology boasts an international editorial team that consists of important members of the European aerospace community. The addition of research organizations from Italy, Spain, the Netherlands, and Sweden has solidified its position as one of the leading European journals in the discipline. Occasionally, special issues are published that comprise selected papers from European aerospace conferences or focused on a specific topic, such as the recent issues on rotocraft research and vortex flow experiment 2 (VFE-2). Recommended for research-level collections.

122. *Aerospace Testing International.* [ISSN: 1478-2774] 2002. q. Free. Ed(s): Christopher Hounsfield. U K & International Press, Abinger House, Church St, Dorking, RH4 1DF, United Kingdom; info@ukintpress.com; http://www.ukipme.com. Adv. Circ: 11000. *Aud.:* Ac, Sa.

This trade journal is specifically focused on the testing of aerospace systems and components, providing a wealth of information for professionals who are concerned with aerospace testing, evaluation, and inspection. All areas of aviation and aerospace manufacturing are covered, including civil and military aerospace, defense systems, launch vehicles, satellites, and space systems. The journal contains most of the elements of a typical trade publication—that is, news, feature articles, industry interviews, and information on services available for the aerospace testing industry. There is an entire section on products and services with technical profiles of new equipment and services. The journal has regular columns that present news, current information on the people and companies in the industry, and announcements and newsworthy events. As the journal is published quarterly, its focus is not on breaking news and day-to-day activities, but on providing in-depth analysis of issues and trends within this segment of the aerospace industry. The journal also produces a review or showcase issues aimed at experts in the field, which provides greater scientific focus as it describes in detail the latest research, developments, methods, and science behind the technologies. Given the importance that safety plays in the industry, this is an important publication to address not only basic safety issues but performance issues, reliability issues, and quality issues that are critical to the aerospace community.

The Air & Space Power Journal. See Military section.

123. *Air & Space - Smithsonian.* Formerly (until 1986): *Air & Space.* [ISSN: 0886-2257] 1978. bi-m. USD 26 domestic; USD 32 foreign; USD 4.99 newsstand/cover. Ed(s): Paul Hoversten, Linda Musser Shiner. Smithsonian Institution, Air & Space Magazine, MRC 513, PO Box 37012, Washington, DC 20013; airspace@emailcustomerservice.com. Illus., adv. Vol. ends: No. 6. *Indexed:* A01, A22, ASIP, BRI, C&ISA, CBRI, CerAb, MASUSE, P02. *Bk. rev.:* 4-5, 800-1,000 words. *Aud.:* Ems, Hs, Ga, Ac.

Air & Space/Smithsonian is the best overall journal for general-aviation and space enthusiasts, as every aspect of aerospace and aviation is covered in a comprehensive and entertaining fashion, with outstanding photographs and illustrations. It provides current topical articles on current aviation, space, aeronautics, and astronautical topics, historical information, future trends, and scientific advancements in all areas of aviation. The coverage is broad, from military, general, and commercial aviation to articles on space flight and exploration. It profiles people—both aviation pioneers and present-day decision-makers and innovators—as well as highlighting technological and scientific advancements. The strength of this publication is that its articles provide in-depth scientific and technical information in an informative, educational, and entertaining format. The range of topics is so broad that only mentioning a few of them would be a disservice. This magazine is the closest thing to actually visiting the Air and Space Museum in Washington, D.C., and marveling at the history of aviation while imagining its future possibilities. Departments are "In the Museum," "Above and Beyond," "Oldies and Oddities," "One More and Higher," and "Sightings." This is one of those rare magazines that should be mandatory for any type of library.

124. *Air Power History.* Former titles (until 1989): *Aerospace Historian;* (until 1965): *Airpower History.* [ISSN: 1044-016X] 1954. q. Free to members. Air Force Historical Foundation, PO Box 790, Clinton, MD 20735; execdir@afhistoricalfoundation.org; http://www.afhistoricalfoundation.org/. Illus., adv. Refereed. Vol. ends: Dec. Microform: PQC. *Indexed:* A01, B02, BAS, BRI, CBRI, P02. *Bk. rev.:* 5-10, 500-750 words. *Aud.:* Ac, Sa.

This journal is the premier scholarly journal for research into the history of aerospace, aviation, and space science. The journal chronicles historic events in all fields of aviation, including general aviation and space missions—with the majority of articles concerned with military aviation, as it is published by the Air Force Historical Foundation. All time periods are covered, from the earliest use of aviation to more current topics such as Desert Storm. Articles are interesting reading as well as solid history, with extensive bibliographies. The majority of articles are written by historians, military personnel, museum curators, and others who possess both a strong academic foundation in history and a background in aviation. Numerous photographs and illustrations bring the text alive, but most are in black-and-white due to the time periods covered by the majority of articles. The magazine also includes Air Force Historical Foundation symposium notices, numerous book reviews, letters, news, notices, calendar, obituaries, and reunions. The journal started publishing issues online only in the fall of 2012 with alternating print and electronic versions. This journal is highly recommended for aviation buffs, military history enthusiasts, and a general readership. It would be appropriate for all types of libraries based on its content, but its limited focus will not appeal to more specialized libraries.

125. Air Transport World. [ISSN: 0002-2543] 1964. m. USD 75 domestic (Free to qualified personnel). Ed(s): Perry Flint, Kathryn Young. A T W Media Group, 8380 Colesville Rd, Ste 700, Silver Spring, MD 20910. Illus., index, adv. Circ: 1611 Paid. Microform: PQC. *Indexed:* A22, ABIn, ABS&EES, B01, B02, B03, BRI, C&ISA, C42, CerAb, H24. *Aud.:* Sa.

This business-oriented journal covers the area of world airline management, embracing all aspects of commercial aviation and the surrounding industries. The primary focus is on the airline industry, airport management, and related issues. The industry aspects of commercial aviation are another area of focus, with several informative segments that include data and statistics on commuter traffic, airport usage, fuel prices, and foreign exchange rates. Broad article categories include technology, airways, airlines, safety, marketing, maintenance, cargo, and passenger service. Articles on the people involved in this side of the aviation spectrum are informative and enlightening. The "Trends" section provides industry snapshots that are presented simply in graphical format and impart important industry data quickly. Another important section is "Analysis," which provides analysis of the industry beyond the simple facts and figures. Periodically, the journal includes directory information on specific topics—that is, practical, factual information for industry insiders—such as a maintenance directory, airline of the year, etc. The journal also publishes topically-focused issues that provide valuable information to those within the industry, such as an industry forecast issue. Although the journal is primarily a trade publication for the commercial aviation segment of the industry, it provides valuable information on all aspects of aviation.

126. Aircraft Engineering and Aerospace Technology: an international journal. Formerly (until 1986): *Aircraft Engineering.* [ISSN: 1748-8842] 1929. bi-m. EUR 5489 combined subscription in Europe (print & online eds.); USD 6329 combined subscription in the Americas (print & online eds.); GBP 3949 combined subscription in the UK & elsewhere (print & online eds.). Ed(s): Askin Isikveren. Emerald Group Publishing Ltd., Howard House, Wagon Ln, Bingley, BD16 1WA, United Kingdom; emerald@emeraldinsight.com; http://www.emeraldinsight.com. Illus. Sample. Refereed. Vol. ends: No. 6. Reprint: PSC. *Indexed:* A01, A22, ABIn, BrTechI, C&ISA, CerAb, E01, EngInd, H24. *Bk. rev.:* 1-3, 100-250 words. *Aud.:* Ac, Sa.

This journal recently shifted from a hybrid trade journal and research journal format to one devoted primarily to disseminating innovative scientific methods, and research and technology ideas. It is primarily composed of six to eight articles that are designed to benefit the design, development, project management, manufacture, or operation of current or future aerospace vehicle systems. The journal's strength is still in getting leading practitioners in the field to contribute articles of interest to both researchers and fellow practitioners. The research articles are categorized as to their content, with most being either research papers or technical papers, but there are also other categories, including literature reviews, case studies, conceptual papers, and general reviews. Along with this change, the journal is starting to include special issues on a single topic, such as the recent issues on aircraft design education or important conference papers such as those from the International Conference on Intelligent Unmanned Systems. Appropriate for both academic and larger public libraries.

127. American Helicopter Society. Journal. [ISSN: 0002-8711] 1956. q. USD 300 (Members, USD 45; Non-members, USD 170). Ed(s): J V R Prasad. American Helicopter Society, Inc., 217 N Washington St, Alexandria, VA 22314; staff@vtol.org; http://www.vtol.org. Illus. Sample. Refereed. Vol. ends: No. 4. *Indexed:* A01, A22, ApMecR, C&ISA, CerAb, EngInd. *Aud.:* Ac.

This journal is composed of original technical papers that deal with all aspects of the design, theory, and practice of vertical flight. It is published by the American Helicopter Society, and the papers cover three main areas: research and engineering; design and manufacturing; and operations. They are designed to foster the exchange of significant new ideas, information, and research about helicopters and V/STOL aircraft. The emphasis is on computational fluid dynamics (CFD), structures, aerodynamics (both basic and applied), handling qualities, and acoustics. Additional areas include vehicle and component design, manufacture, and testing; operational aspects, including support, noise and vibration, control and control failure, safety and reliability, materials, and design criteria; and historical information. In addition to full articles, the occasional "Technical Notes" section provides a forum for brief, timely updates on current research topics. The articles fall into several categories, including invited papers, full papers, review articles, and historical articles. This journal focuses on the more technical aspects of vertical flight, with the general-interest and membership information included in the organization's companion publication, *Vertiflite.* The value of this publication to academic collections that supports aeronautics and engineering has been enhanced, now that the journal provides online access and expanded its indexing sources.

Aviation History. See Military section.

128. Aviation Week & Space Technology. Former titles (until 1960): *Aviation Week, Including Space Technology;* (until 1958): *Aviation Week;* Which was formed by the merger of (1943-1947): *Aviation News;* (1922-1947): *Aviation;* Which incorporated (in 1948): *Air Transport.* [ISSN: 0005-2175] 1916. w. USD 103 domestic; USD 109 in Canada & Mexico; USD 160 in Europe. Ed(s): Anthony L Velocci. Aviation Week Group, 2 Penn Plz, 25th Fl, New York, NY 10121; buccustserv@cdsfulfillment.com; http://www.aviationweek.com. Illus., adv. Circ: 93190 Paid. Vol. ends: No. 26. Microform: PQC. *Indexed:* A01, A22, ABIn, ABS&EES, ApMecR, B01, B02, B03, BRI, BrTechI, C&ISA, C37, CerAb, EngInd, H24, MASUSE, P02. *Aud.:* Ga, Ac.

This is the premier trade magazine covering aviation, aerospace, and aeronautics. All segments of the aerospace industry are featured and detailed, along with many short but insightful articles. The regular sections such as "Commercial Programs" and "The World" provide news items of note and other industry happenings; also included is "Air Transport," which covers commercial and general aviation. The magazine then segments the rest of its articles into topical sections such as "Repair and Overhaul," "Aerospace Business," "Space," "Rotorcraft," "Propulsion," and "Defense." Also provided is valuable, up-to-date information on the respective subject area. Special reports on important topics or issues, such as innovation and privatization, are included when appropriate. In addition, the magazine contains industry outlooks and profiles, features on people within the industry such as the person of the year, a calendar of events, and news and information from government and other regulatory agencies. A special issue is usually published in early January, which provides outlook/specification tables for all areas of the aerospace industry. Other major sections include a world military aircraft inventory; prime contractor and major manufacturer profiles; major airline profiles; and commercial satellite operators. Other special issues include art and photography and coverage of the major air shows, Farnborough and Paris. The combination of industry publication and general-interest articles makes this a valuable resource for all types of libraries, from high school to academic.

129. Ballooning. [ISSN: 0194-6854] 1977. bi-m. Free to members. Ed(s): Glen Moyer. Balloon Federation of America, 1601 N Jefferson, PO Box 400, Indianola, IA 50125; bfaoffice@bfa.net; http://www.bfa.net. Illus., adv. Sample. Vol. ends: No. 6. *Indexed:* SD. *Bk. rev.:* 1-4, 300-500 words. *Aud.:* Ga, Sa.

This is the best of the limited number of general-interest magazines for the ballooning enthusiast. The journal is produced by the Balloon Federation of America and covers the sport both in the U.S. and from an international perspective. Articles cover the full range of topics of interest to ballooning enthusiasts, including but not limited to safety issues, equipment, profiles of members, descriptions of balloon trips, noteworthy events in ballooning, and information on competitions. The magazine includes excellent color and black-and-white photographs, results from rallies, information on new products, reviews of products and literature, and a directory of the federation's officers. The federation's web site has been enhanced with content from the journal, and provides news, events, and competitions of interest to members. It provides quality content with a good layout and organization scheme, and is suitable for all ages.

130. *British Interplanetary Society Journal.* Incorporates (1946-1947): *British Interplanetary Society. Bulletin;* Which was formerly (until 1946): *Combined British Astronautical Societies. Official Bulletin.* [ISSN: 0007-084X] 1934. m. Members, GBP 15; Non-members, GBP 40. Ed(s): Kelvin Long. British Interplanetary Society, 27-29 S Lambeth Rd, London, SW8 1SZ, United Kingdom; mail@bis-spaceflight.com; http://www.bis-space.com/. Illus., index. Refereed. Vol. ends: No. 12. Microform: PQC. Reprint: PSC. *Indexed:* A22. *Aud.:* Ac, Sa.

This monthly publication of the British Interplanetary Society contains articles that cover all aspects of space exploration, with each issue dedicated to one or two specific subjects, topics, or themes. Emphasis is solely on space and space-based applications. Sample topics include the history of rocket development, solar cells, stellar wind, orbital mechanics, solar sails, robotic exploration, space colonization, space debris, space commerce, and related areas of aeronautics, astronautics, and space sciences. Examples of current issue themes or conference topics that are included in the publication are interstellar travel, project Icarus and project Daedalus, SETI, fusion propulsion; science in the cosmos; SKYLON, and the international space station; economic, legal, educational, and social aspects of developing an interstellar space program; and time-distance solutions. Most issues contain four to eight articles per issue, with some articles taken from IAA's International Astronautical Conference or other conferences, such as the recent 100 Year Starship conference. Recently, the journal has been producing a number of double issues. The journal also contains brief information on the society's activities and announcements. Their companion publication, *Spaceflight,* provides more news and membership information, as well as book reviews and articles written by those directly involved with particular projects or missions. Appropriate for major research libraries.

Business and Commercial Aviation. See Transportation section.

131. *Canadian Aeronautics and Space Journal (Online).* Former titles (until 2005): *Canadian Aeronautics and Space Journal (Print);* Which incorporated (1968-1975): *C.A.S.I. Transactions;* (until 1962): *Canadian Aeronautical Journal;* Which incorporated (1954-1955): *C.A.I. Log.* [ISSN: 1712-7998] 1955. q. CAD 97.75 combined subscription domestic (online & CD-ROM eds.); CAD 88 combined subscription Canada (online & CD-ROM eds.); CAD 92 combined subscription elsewhere (online & CD-ROM eds.)). Ed(s): Steve Zan. Canadian Aeronautics and Space Institute, 350 Terry Fox Dr, Ste 104, Kanata, ON K2K 2W5, Canada; casi@casi.ca; http://www.casi.ca. Illus., index. Refereed. Vol. ends: No. 4. Microform: MML; PQC. *Indexed:* A22, ApMecR, C&ISA, CBCARef, CerAb, EngInd. *Bk. rev.:* 2-3, 300-400 words. *Aud.:* Ac.

This official publication of the Canadian Aeronautics and Space Institute (CASI) disseminates technical and research information in the areas of aeronautical and aerospace sciences to the international community. The journal includes articles on recent research and technical discoveries in all areas of aeronautics, including aerospace materials, spacecraft thermal design, aerodynamics, aircraft design and analysis, aircraft component design, and wind tunnel investigations. Original articles cover such topics as flight testing, astronautics, structures and materials, simulation and training, aerospace operations, and aircraft design and development. The journal recently began to publish occasional special issues in which all articles are focused on a single topic or issues composed of papers from selected conferences. Although the quality of articles remains strong, there is some concern regarding the variations in the number of articles published per issue over the past few years, ranging from one to eight articles in the three issues per year. The journal periodically

includes book reviews and abstracts of recent reports from CASI. As this title is Canadian, articles are published in either English or French, with abstracts in both languages. This research-oriented magazine is appropriate for academic, technical, and research libraries.

132. *E S A Bulletin.* Formerly (1968-1975): *E S R O - E L D O Bulletin.* [ISSN: 0376-4265] 1966. q. Free. Ed(s): Carl Walker. European Space Agency, Communication Production Office, ESRIN, Casella Postale 64, Frascati, I-00044, Italy; esapub@esa.int. Illus. Circ: 25000. *Indexed:* C&ISA, CerAb, EngInd. *Aud.:* Hs, Ga, Ac.

ESA Bulletin is the flagship magazine of the European Space Agency, and is similar to what *Science @ NASA* would be if it was a print journal as opposed to online only. The majority of the journal is composed of feature articles of interest to the space-focused public, such as recent articles on the history of women in space and ensuring a sustainable space environment, or plans on dealing with space debris. The journal has added a yearly feature that highlights the most fascinating space images from the year. Occasionally, an issue is devoted primarily to a single topic, such as the issue celebrating the 150th edition of the journal. The magazine is highly illustrated and interesting to read. The ability to get the full magazine-reading experience online makes this the perfect blend of online and print journal. This quarterly journal highlights the major space projects of the ESA and recent news of interest to the agency in the "News in Brief" and the "Programmes in Progress" sections. It should be noted that the "Programmes in Progress" section, concerning the status of ESA's major space projects, is quite extensive, given the numerous projects currently undertaken by the agency, along with timelines, photographs, and illustrations. This information is highly illustrated and informative, and would be of interest to anyone interested in the exportation of space.

133. *F A A Safety Briefing: your source for general aviation news and information.* Former titles (until 2010): *F A A Aviation News;* (until 1987): *F A A General Aviation News;* (until 1976): *F A A Aviation News;* (until 196?): *United States. Federal Aviation Agency. Aviation News.* 1961. bi-m. USD 21 domestic; USD 29.40 foreign; USD 8 per issue domestic. Ed(s): Lynn McCloud, Susan Parson. U.S. Federal Aviation Administration, 800 Independence Ave, SW, Washington, DC 20591; http://www.faa.gov. Illus. Microform: MIM; PQC. *Aud.:* Ga.

This journal produced by the Federal Aviation Administration (FAA) and it is designed to promote all areas of aviation safety with safety-related news and articles. Although this title is produced by the FAA and all areas of flight safety are covered, much of the information is on safety issues faced by pilots. Articles cover regulations, people within the aviation safety arena, FAA facilities, weather, night flying, and any aspect of aircraft, pilots, or equipment relating to safety. The journal is available both in print and electronically (in pdf as well as formats for iPad, Nook, Kindle, and Android devices). Major departments include "Flight Forum," a feedback section with responses from the FAA; and "Aeromedical Advisory" and "Ask Medical Certification," the latest information on aviation medicine, with more of an emphasis on healthy flying. Regular departments include "Checklists," "Nuts, Bolts, and Electrons," and "Angle of Attack," which are provided to provide news, maintenance alerts, safety reminders, and other timely information designed to protect pilots and aircraft. Other departments, "Jumpseat" and "Postflight," include editorials, runway safety issues, and profiles of FAA employees. The archive of back issues extends back to 2001. Appropriate for research and technical libraries or people interested in flight safety and training. URL: www.faa.gov/news/safety_briefing

134. *Flight International.* Formerly (until 1962): *Flight;* Incorporates (1966-1968): *Aeroplane;* Which was formerly (until 1966): *Aeroplane and Commercial Aviation News;* (until 1962): *Aeroplane and Astronautics;* (until 1959): *Aeroplane.* [ISSN: 0015-3710] 1909. w. Ed(s): Murdo Morrison. Reed Business Information Ltd., Quadrant House, The Quadrant, Sutton, SM2 5AS, United Kingdom; rbi.subscriptions@qss-uk.com; http://www.reedbusiness.co.uk/. Illus., index, adv. Vol. ends: Dec. Microform: PQC. *Indexed:* A22, ABIn, B02, B03, BRI, BrTechI, C&ISA, CerAb, H24. *Aud.:* Ga, Ac.

This international trade publication provides a global perspective on the aerospace industry and covers every aspect—airframe systems and components, support equipment, air transport, general aviation, defense, spaceflight, and regulatory agencies and authorities worldwide. The news section contains subsections such as "News Analysis," "Technology," "Business Aviation," "Defense," "General Aviation," and "Spaceflight." The articles section usually contains two or three feature articles on topics of interest, such as industry forecasts for the upcoming year, market trends, military aircraft, new aircraft, and safety. The "Regulars" section contains letters, jobs, classifieds, commentary, aerospace awards, newsmakers, and similar items. Occasionally, there are directories of world aircraft, maintenance facilities, turbine engine manufacturers, and world airlines, as well as useful ranking information such as the top 100 aerospace companies, airline safety statistics, and space launch calendars. There are also occasional supplements or special issues on hot topics or industry trends. The magazine is one of the few that still provide cutaway schematics of new aircraft. This magazine is similar to *Aviation Week & Space Technology,* but with a greater international flavor. Recommended for both academic libraries and larger public libraries.

135. Flying. Formerly: *Flying Including Industrial Aviation.* [ISSN: 0015-4806] 1927. m. USD 14 domestic; USD 22 foreign. Ed(s): Mac J McClellan, Lane Wallace. Hachette Filipacchi Media U.S., Inc., 1633 Broadway, New York, NY 10019; flyedit@hfmus.com; http://www.hfmus.com. Illus., index, adv. Sample. Circ: 226000. Vol. ends: No. 12. *Indexed:* A22, BRI, C37, CBRI, P02. *Aud.:* Hs, Ga, Ac, Sa.

Flying has the broadest scope of the numerous magazines geared toward the private pilot and flying enthusiast. The major articles fall into the "Features" section, with most articles covering the various aspects of flying such as safety issues, historical topics, airports, rules and regulations, aircraft, and aircraft instrumentation. Every aspect of general aviation is covered; however, the emphasis is on flying, safety or safe flying topics, and contemporary aircraft. The feature articles are written primarily to excite the reader and instill or convey the love of flying. Other articles are designed to impart practical advice and cover items of interest to the flying public. The magazine includes the sections "Flying News and Notes," which provides news for pilots, letters to the editor, a calendar of flying rallies and events, and other aviation news along with new product information; "Flying Safely," which offers safety information ranging from flight schools to human factors, to accident reports; "Flying Opinion," which informs and aids readers with information imparted in a personal manner through anecdotes and stories; and "I learned about flying from that," which provides cautionary tales of what not to do. Overall, the magazine is informative and interesting, with excellent photography. It deserves a place in most libraries.

136. FlyPast: the UK's top selling aviation monthly. [ISSN: 0262-6950] 1980. m. GBP 41 includes domestic & USA; GBP 51 elsewhere; GBP 4.10 per issue. Ed(s): Ken Ellis. Key Publishing Ltd., PO Box 300, Stamford, PE9 1NA, United Kingdom; info@keypublishing.com; http://www.keypublishing.com. Illus., index, adv. Vol. ends: No. 12. *Bk. rev.:* Number and length vary. *Aud.:* Ga, Sa.

This publication is advertised as Britain's top-selling aviation monthly and is essentially a general-interest, history-focused aviation journal. Although the primary focus is historical, with a particular emphasis on military history, there is an additional focus on restoration and preservation of aircraft. Unlike academic historical aviation magazines, this journal is geared toward a general readership. The magazine is heavily illustrated with numerous photographs (in both color and in black-and-white), which is expected given the historical focus of the journal. The articles are informative and interesting and cover many of the same topics as the general-interest aviation magazines, including events and news with additional departments focused on restoration and preservation. There are occasionally special sections that highlight particular topics, such as the recent one covering the history of the development of jet power, or the helpful air show guide. The journal also produces special issues such as the one recently released, "Battle of the Ruhr." The product review sections include memorabilia, books, videos, and art prints. Numerous advertisements for memorabilia and related items are found throughout. This magazine appeals to military-history enthusiasts, and to those interested in military aviation and/or aviation history, as well as aircraft restoration and preservation.

137. I C A O Journal. Former titles (until 1990): *I C A O Bulletin;* (until 1953): *I C A O Monthly Bulletin;* (until 1947): *P I C A O Monthly Bulletin.* [ISSN: 1014-8876] 1946. bi-m. USD 40. International Civil

Aviation Organization (I C A O), 999 University St, Montreal, PQ H3C 5H7, Canada; icaohq@icao.int; http://www.icao.int. Illus., adv. Vol. ends: Dec. Microform: CIS. *Indexed:* C&ISA, CerAb, H24, M&GPA, RiskAb. *Aud.:* Ac, Sa.

The primary mission of this journal is the dissemination of the accounts, activities, and progress of the International Civil Aviation Organization (ICAO) to its membership and the global aerospace community, especially those interested in civil aviation. Although the stated mission of the magazine is to relate the organization's activities to its members, it provides articles that would be of interest to anyone involved with civil aviation and air transport; it also puts an emphasis on political and regulatory information, but it includes some science and technical information as well. Articles include such topics as airports and airport management; regulations; air traffic control and air traffic management; environmental issues; airport and aircraft safety issues and methodologies; security, guidance, control, and monitoring equipment; aerodynamics and vehicle control; and related civil aviation issues. The "News in Brief" section contains news of interest to members and a calendar of IACO events. The ICAO also publishes a number of regional reports, along with two recent publications, including *MRTD Report,* started in 2013, where "MRTD" stands for machine-readable travel documents; and *Training Report,* started in 2011. This journal provides valuable insight into and information on the civil and commercial aviation industry, and is appropriate for research and government libraries.

138. I E E E Aerospace and Electronic Systems Magazine. Formerly (until 1986): *I E E E Aerospace and Electronic Systems Society Newsletter.* [ISSN: 0885-8985] 1961. m. USD 575; USD 690 combined subscription (print & online eds.). Institute of Electrical and Electronics Engineers, 445 Hoes Ln, Piscataway, NJ 08854; contactcenter@ieee.org; http://www.ieee.org. Illus., index, adv. Refereed. Vol. ends: No. 12. *Indexed:* A22, C&ISA, CerAb, EngInd. *Bk. rev.:* 1, 500-1,500 words. *Aud.:* Ac, Sa.

This publication is the main avenue for the dissemination of information to the members of the society, which latter consists of those members of Institute of Electrical and Electronics Engineers (IEEE) who are interested in the fields of navigation, avionics, spacecraft, aerospace power, radar, sonar, telemetry, defense, transportation, automated testing, and command and control. The three to six feature articles in each issue cover those areas in which the fields of computer and electrical engineering overlap with the areas of aeronautical and astronautical engineering. The articles deal primarily with the organization, design, development, integration, and operation of complex systems for air, space, and ground environments in the above areas. The journal's objective is to provide timely, useful, and readable systems information for engineers. The more technically focused articles of interest to the membership are published in the society's sister publication, *IEEE Transactions on Aerospace and Electronic Systems.* The journal also includes information of interest to the membership, such as conference reports, columns (editorials), notices of upcoming meetings and conferences, book reviews, and other membership-related information. The journal has recently revamped its format, making it more professionally organized and readable, as well as adding student research. The journal also publishes one or two special issues devoted to a specific topic, such as the upcoming issue on "Wide Area and Staring Synthetic Aperture Radar." Primarily of importance to academic and technical libraries and members.

139. I E E E Transactions on Aerospace and Electronic Systems. Formed by the merger of (1963-1965): *I E E E Transactions on Aerospace;* (1963-1965): *I E E E Transactions on Aerospace and Navigational Electronics;* (1963-1965): *I E E E Transactions on Military Electronics;* (1963-1965): *I E E E Transactions on Space Electronics and Telemetry;* Which was formerly (until 1963): *I R E Transactions on Space Electronics and Telemetry;* (until 1959): *I R E Transactions on Telemetry and Remote Control;* I E E E Transactions on Aerospace and Navigational Electronics was formerly (until 1963): *I R E Transactions on Aerospace and Navigational Electronics;* (until 1961): *I R E Transactions on Aeronautical and Navigational Electronics;* (until 1955): *I R E Professional Group on Aeronautical and Navigational Electronics. Transactions;* (until 1953): *I R E Professional Group on Airborne Electronics. Transactions;* I E E E Transactions on Military Electronics was formerly (until 1963): *I R E Transactions on Military Electronics.*

[ISSN: 0018-9251] 1965. q. Ed(s): Peter K Willett. Institute of Electrical and Electronics Engineers, 445 Hoes Ln, Piscataway, NJ 08854; customer.service@ieee.org; http://www.ieee.org. Illus., index, adv. Refereed. Vol. ends: No. 4. *Indexed:* A01, A22, ApMecR, B01, BRI, C&ISA, CerAb, EngInd, MathR. *Aud.:* Ac.

This journal published by IEEE is primarily geared toward those individuals working or studying in the areas of aerospace electronic systems, which includes command, control, and communications systems; avionics; systems engineering; aircraft control; aircraft navigation; missile guidance; satellites; multisensor systems; electronic warfare systems; navigation, target tracking, and global positioning systems; energy conversion systems; intelligent systems; radar systems; robotics systems; space systems; and support systems. The more-than-30 research articles per issue range from specific papers on individual systems to those that cover general research, design, and testing of systems and subsystems. The journal prides itself on being one of the top five most-cited scholarly journals in the area of aerospace engineering, which demonstrates the importance that computers, communications, and electronics play in the field. Included with the full papers is a correspondence section for brief discussions of new research. Essentially, this is the systems magazine for aerospace engineering. This research publication provides a correspondence section and a letters section, and it has been upgraded with color images and illustrations when appropriate. Some of this journal's articles may be available under IEEE's newly adopted open-access policy. Membership and related information is provided by the society's sister publication, *IEEE Aerospace and Electronic Systems Magazine.* Recommended for all types of academic and technical libraries.

140. ***Institution of Mechanical Engineers. Proceedings. Part G: Journal of Aerospace Engineering.*** Supersedes in part (in 1989): *Institution of Mechanical Engineers. Proceedings. Part D: Transport Engineering;* Which superseded in part (1847-1982): *Institution of Mechanical Engineers. Proceedings.* [ISSN: 0954-4100] 1984. m. USD 4533. Sage Publications Ltd., 1 Oliver's Yard, 55 City Rd, London, EC1Y 1SP, United Kingdom; info@sagepub.co.uk; http://www.uk.sagepub.com. Illus. Sample. Refereed. Vol. ends: No. 6. Reprint: PSC. *Indexed:* A01, A22, ApMecR, B01, BrTechI, C&ISA, CerAb, E01, EngInd, H24. *Bk. rev.:* 1-2, 500-750 words. *Aud.:* Ac.

The *Journal of Aerospace Engineering,* produced by the United Kingdom's mechanical engineering society (IMechE), publishes papers in the field of aeronautical engineering that are of interest to mechanical engineers and vice versa. The publication provides peer-reviewed articles that are designed to further the advancement of the field of aeronautical engineering, especially in the areas of civil and military aircraft, space systems, and their components. Topics cover research, design, development, testing, operation, and service and repair of vehicles and their components. Fields covered include aerodynamics, fluid mechanics, propulsion and fuel systems, avionics and flight control systems, structural and mechanical design, materials science, testing and performance, and airports and spaceports. The journal is published monthly with 10–12 articles per issue that focus on aerospace engineering topics that are closely aligned with those of mechanical engineering. Occasionally, a volume may be devoted to a special topic or theme, such as recent issues on electrification of aircraft systems: power and control. Often these special issues are papers taken from recent conferences or symposia on the topic. Appropriate for academic and technical libraries.

141. ***The International Journal of Aeroacoustics.*** [ISSN: 1475-472X] 2002. 8x/yr. GBP 498; GBP 514 combined subscription (print & online eds.). Ed(s): Ganesh Raman. Multi-Science Publishing Co. Ltd., 5 Wates Way, Brentwood, CM15 9TB, United Kingdom; info@multi-science.co.uk; http://www.multi-science.co.uk. Sample. Refereed. *Indexed:* A01, C&ISA, CerAb. *Aud.:* Ac, Sa.

The subject of aeroacoustics has increased in importance within the aerospace and aeronautical engineering field recently, due to advances in air, space, and high-speed ground transportation and their effects on people and the environment. The issue of noise and its impact on people, structures (both vehicle- and ground-based support structures), vehicle components, and the overall environment comprise much of the focus of this research journal. The journal focuses on all areas of aeroacoustics, publishing four to six research articles per issue, along with occasional survey or review articles on

fundamental and applied aeroacoustics topics. A sampling of the topics covered includes fluid flow, jet noise, computational fluid mechanics and aerodynamics, instability of high speed jets, turbulence, and shock. The articles associate these topics with all aspects of civil and military aircraft, automobile, and high-speed train aeroacoustics and related phenomena. The journal makes exceptional use of illustrations (in color and black-and-white) to enhance the technical information. Some issues are composed of selected papers from workshops and conferences related to aeroacoustics or special topical issues. Recommended for academic and research libraries.

142. ***International Journal of Aerospace Engineering.*** [ISSN: 1687-5966] 2007. USD 295. Ed(s): Ramesh Talreja. Hindawi Publishing Corporation, 410 Park Ave, 15th Fl, PMB 287, New York, NY 10022; hindawi@hindawi.com; http://www.hindawi.com. Refereed. *Indexed:* A01, H24. *Aud.:* Ac, Sa.

This international, open-access journal from Hindawi Publishing Corporation covers all aspects of aerospace engineering, including aerodynamics and fluid mechanics, structures, mechanics of materials, dynamics and control, aeroacoustics, flight mechanics, aeroelasticity, propulsion, avionics, and flight control systems. The purpose is to provide an outlet for scholarly research along with practical engineering solutions, and design methodologies for aircraft, space vehicles, and unmanned air vehicles (UAVs). The journal currently publishes more than three times the number of articles from its inception in 2008. This open-access journal is supported via article process charges paid by the authors, their funding agency, or their supporting institution. The journal occasionally publishes focused issues and special issues; these are articles on selected or focused topics that have high interest within the community within the scope of the journal. Some examples of focused and special issues include those recently published on aircraft flight control systems; spacecraft propulsion; and formation flight control. All articles, including those in focused and special issues, are peer-reviewed and of the highest quality, and this journal would be of interest to those within the aerospace engineering community.

143. ***International Journal of Micro Air Vehicles.*** [ISSN: 1756-8293] 2009. q. GBP 288; GBP 299 combined subscription (print & online eds.). Ed(s): Mark Reeder. Multi-Science Publishing Co. Ltd., 5 Wates Way, Brentwood, CM15 9TB, United Kingdom; info@multi-science.co.uk; http://www.multi-science.co.uk. Sample. Refereed. *Indexed:* A01. *Aud.:* Ac, Sa.

This journal, started in 2009, specifically covers the emerging field of unmanned aerial vehicles (UAVs), specifically micro air vehicles (MAVs), which have unique design, manufacturing, and piloting or flying issues. This journal is designed to provide a forum for the multidisciplinary research being conducted in this new and rapidly emerging specialty in the aerospace field. The articles cover many of the same aspects of other aerospace vehicles, including aerodynamics, propulsion systems, control, avionics, structures, etc. The main differences are the result of the size, mission, and challenges of these unpiloted aircraft, leading to different perspectives on these traditional areas such as nano-structures, micro-propulsion systems, flexible structures, low Reynolds aerodynamics, flapping wing flight, and target search and tracking. This quarterly journal publishes four to five peer-reviewed articles per issue that cover the applied research and fundamental science in this specialized area. This new and emerging area of interest has also spawned a new trade journal, *Unmanned Systems Magazine,* which might also be of interest to people working in this area.

144. ***Jonathan's Space Report.*** 1989. w. Free. Ed(s): Jonathan McDowell. Harvard - Smithsonian Center for Astrophysics, 60 Garden St, Cambridge, MA 02138; http://www.cfa.harvard.edu/. *Aud.:* Ac.

This electronic newsletter is designed to provide information on all space launches, including manned missions and automated satellites. Users interested in this information can receive the newsletter via e-mail. A recent issue contains information about the international space station as well as all international launches, including suborbital launches. The newsletter is organized into sections organized by mission or launch vehicle, often with tables such as recent orbital launches and suborbital launches. A new feature is translations into Italian, German, and Portuguese. Along with the newsletter, there is a link to "Jonathan's Space Home Page," which provides links to image files, historical articles, and other information and sites related to space exploration. Also included are links to a geostationary satellite log, a launch log, and a satellite catalog. The newsletter is fully archived and available, back to its original issue in January 1989. Overall, the newsletter is not very fancy, but if you are looking for space-vehicle launch information from a reliable source, this is the place. URL: www.planet4589.org/space/jsr/jsr.html

145. *Journal of Aerospace Engineering.* [ISSN: 0893-1321] 1988. q. USD 509. Ed(s): Wieslaw Binienda. American Society of Civil Engineers, 1801 Alexander Bell Dr, Reston, VA 20191; http://www.asce.org. Illus., index, adv. Refereed. Vol. ends: No. 4. Microform: PQC. *Indexed:* A01, A22, ApMecR, BRI, C&ISA, CerAb, EngInd, H24, M&GPA. *Aud.:* Ac.

The main emphasis of this journal, produced by the American Society of Civil Engineers (ASCE), is on the practical application and development of civil engineering concepts, designs, and methodologies for aeronautics and space applications and the transfer of these technologies to other civil engineering applications. This international publication provides information related to the civil engineering aspects of aerospace engineering, primarily structural aspects of space engineering, applied mechanics, aeronautics, and astronautics. Sample topics include flight control systems, autopilot, MEMS, smart composite structures, lunar soil mechanics, environmental factors in inhabited space facilities, aerodynamics of structures, extraterrestrial construction, aerospace materials, polymers and laminates, remote sensing, and robotics as related to aeronautics and aerospace engineering. Both full papers (10–20 per issue), case studies, and technical notes are included, with the emphasis being on fully refereed papers that are designed to share information between civil engineers and related engineering disciplines. Special topical issues or special sections are occasionally published, such as the recent section on intelligent unmanned systems, or the special issues on "In Situ Resource Utilization" (ISRU). A valuable addition to academic and technical libraries.

146. *Journal of Aerospace Information Systems.* Formerly (until 2013): *Journal of Aerospace Computing, Information, and Communication.* [ISSN: 2327-3097] 2004. m. Members, USD 40; Non-members, USD 445. Ed(s): Ashok N Srivastava. American Institute of Aeronautics and Astronautics, Inc., 1801 Alexander Bell Dr, Ste 500, Reston, VA 20191; custserv@aiaa.org; http://www.aiaa.org. Sample. *Indexed:* C&ISA, CerAb, EngInd. *Aud.:* Ac, Sa.

This electronic-only journal from AIA—formerly titled *Journal of Aerospace Computing, Information, and Communication*—is primarily geared toward those individuals who work or study in the areas of aerospace computing, information, and communication systems. The scope of coverage includes such topics as aerospace systems and software engineering, information technology, knowledge management, computational techniques, remotely operated vehicles, UAVs (unmanned aerial vehicles), real-time systems, embedded systems, software engineering and reliability, systems engineering and integration, communication systems, signal processing, data fusion, high-performance computing systems and software, expert systems, robotics, intelligent and autonomous systems, and human–computer interfaces. The articles are designed to highlight current research in three main areas—computing, information, and communications—and this research concerns the design of aerospace components, systems, and vehicles. Along with the full papers, the journal includes summary papers along with technical notes and letters for the brief discussion of new research. The journal periodically publishes an issue devoted to a specific topic or theme. There is an increasingly greater role that electronics, communication, control, autonomic software systems, and information systems have in the design and operation of aerospace systems and vehicles. Thus, this journal fills an important niche in the transfer of information and technology, both from aerospace engineering to other engineering disciplines, and vice versa. Recommended for academic and technical libraries. URL: http://arc.aiaa.org/loi/jais

147. *Journal of Aircraft: devoted to aeronautical science and technology.* [ISSN: 0021-8669] 1963. bi-m. Members, USD 65 (print & online eds.); Non-members, USD 855). Ed(s): Thomas M Weeks, Michael Baden-Campbell. American Institute of Aeronautics and Astronautics, Inc., 1801 Alexander Bell Dr, Ste 500, Reston, VA 20191; custserv@aiaa.org; http://www.aiaa.org. Illus., index. Sample. Refereed. Vol. ends: No. 6. Microform: PQC. *Indexed:* A01, A22, ApMecR, C&ISA, CerAb, EngInd, H24, M&GPA, P02. *Aud.:* Ac.

This journal, published by AIAA, is devoted primarily to the dissemination of original papers for the advancement of airborne flight. The focus is on the promotion of applied science and technology related to airborne flight, including articles on significant advances in the operation of aircraft, advances in aircraft themselves, and the application of aircraft technologies to other disciplines. All types of vehicles related to airborne flight are covered, including commercial and military aircraft, STOL and V/STOL aircraft, and subsonic, supersonic, transsonic, and hypersonic aircraft. Areas covered include aircraft and aircraft systems design and operation, flight mechanics, flight and ground testing, computational fluid dynamics (CFD), aerodynamics, and structural dynamics. Related areas—such as application of computer technology to aircraft and aircraft systems, air traffic management, artificial intelligence, production methods, engineering economic analysis, and logistics support—are also covered. Accompanying the full-length papers (30–40 per issue) are "Technical Comments" and "Engineering Notes," designed to further communication within the field. The journal also publishes "Design Forum" papers, which range from design case studies to presentations of new methodologies and emerging design trends, survey papers, and lectures, such as Wright Brothers Lecture. This highly technical journal is recommended for academic, technical, and research libraries.

148. *Journal of Guidance, Control, and Dynamics: devoted to the technology of dynamics and control.* Formerly (until 1982): *Journal of Guidance and Control.* [ISSN: 0731-5090] 1978. bi-m. Members, USD 70 (print & online eds.); Non-members, USD 870). Ed(s): George T Schmidt, Becky Rivard. American Institute of Aeronautics and Astronautics, Inc., 1801 Alexander Bell Dr, Ste 500, Reston, VA 20191; custserv@aiaa.org; http://www.aiaa.org. Illus., index. Sample. Refereed. Vol. ends: No. 6. *Indexed:* A22, ApMecR, C&ISA, CerAb, EngInd, H24. *Bk. rev.:* 1, 750-1,000 words. *Aud.:* Ac.

This journal's primary focus is the advancement of guidance, control, and dynamics through the publishing of original, peer-reviewed papers that highlight the development, design, and application of new technology in aeronautics, astronautics, celestial mechanics, and related fields. Topics of articles include astrodynamics, control systems design, control theory, dynamics, stability, guidance, control, navigation, systems optimization, avionics, and information processing. There are also articles that highlight advances in the guidance and control of new aircraft, spacecraft, and related systems. In addition to approximately 30 full-length papers per issue, the journal includes engineering notes, technical comments, and book reviews. It occasionally publishes special issues on a single topic. Although the journal is published by AIAA, the various topics covered by the fields of guidance, control, and dynamics are important to other engineering fields than aeronautics, making this journal a valuable addition to research collections in engineering.

149. *Journal of Propulsion and Power: devoted to aerospace propulsion and power.* [ISSN: 0748-4658] 1985. bi-m. Members, USD 60 (print & online eds.); Non-members, USD 945). Ed(s): Vigor Yang, Becky Rivard. American Institute of Aeronautics and Astronautics, Inc., 1801 Alexander Bell Dr, Ste 500, Reston, VA 20191; custserv@aiaa.org; http://www.aiaa.org. Illus., index. Sample. Refereed. Vol. ends: No. 6. *Indexed:* A22, ApMecR, C&ISA, CerAb, EngInd. *Aud.:* Ac.

This journal focuses specifically on aerospace propulsion and power systems. It is the primary journal that covers combustion, power generation and use, and overall propulsion systems and/or individual propulsion system components as they relate to the fields of aeronautics, astronautics, and space sciences. Topics include air-breathing propulsion systems (from turbine engines to scramjets), electric propulsion systems, solid and liquid rocket systems, hybrid propulsion systems, advanced propulsion systems, and all propulsion system components. Original papers are presented to highlight recent advances in the areas of research, development, design, and applications. Subjects include fuel and propellants, power generation and transmission in aerospace systems, jet pumps, combustors and combustion chambers, combustion of fuels, computational fluid dynamics (CFD), fluid mechanics, and solid mechanics. Accompanying the full-length technical papers (20–25 per issue) are "Technical Notes" and "Technical Comments." These sections are designed for rapid dissemination of research results. The journal recently started publishing occasional special issues that are devoted to a single topic. An excellent addition to any research-oriented engineering library.

150. *Journal of Spacecraft and Rockets: devoted to astronautical science and technology.* [ISSN: 0022-4650] 1964. bi-m. Members, USD 60 (print & online eds.); Non-members, USD 810 (print or online ed.). Ed(s): E Vincent Zoby, Becky Rivard. American Institute of Aeronautics and Astronautics, Inc., 1801 Alexander Bell Dr, Ste 500, Reston, VA 20191; custserv@aiaa.org; http://www.aiaa.org. Illus., index. Sample. Refereed. Vol. ends: No. 6. Microform: PQC. *Indexed:* A01, A22, ApMecR, C&ISA, CerAb, EngInd. *Aud.:* Ac.

This journal from AIAA covers recent research, design, and current developments in the broad area of spacecraft and rockets and their accompanying systems, subsystems, and components. The 20–25 articles per issue focus on space sciences, including spacecraft, space vehicles, tactical and strategic missile systems and subsystems, applications, missions, and environmental interactions. Information is given on spacecraft and missile systems configurations, launch and reentry vehicles, transatmospheric vehicles, system and subsystem design, application and testing, mission design and analysis, applied and computational fluid dynamics, applied aerothermodynamics, and structures and materials as related to vehicle design and analysis. In addition, the journal covers such topics as space processing and manufacturing, operations in space, interactions between space vehicles, design of sensors, ground-support systems design, and the transfer of space technologies to other fields. All areas of aeronautics are covered, including propulsion, guidance and control, aircraft technology (conventional and STOL/VTOL), structural systems of spacecraft and missiles, missile design, and performance of space vehicles. Occasionally, issues include engineering notes, technical comments, and survey papers. Special issues on specific topics are also occasionally published. Recommended for all types of research libraries or engineering collections.

151. *Journal of the Astronautical Sciences.* Supersedes in part (in 1962): *Astronautical Sciences Review;* Which was formerly (until 1958): *Journal of Astronautics;* (until 1955): *Astronautics.* [ISSN: 0021-9142] 1954. q. EUR 146 (print & online eds.). Ed(s): Kathleen Howell, Henry J Pernicka. Springer, Tiergartenstr 17, Heidelberg, 69121, Germany; subscriptions@springer.com; http://www.springer.com. Illus., index. Refereed. Vol. ends: No. 4. *Indexed:* A22, C&ISA, CCMJ, CerAb, EngInd, H24, M&GPA, MSN, MathR. *Aud.:* Ac.

This journal provides topical information, research, and reviews on state-of-the-art technologies in all areas of astronautics, including astrodynamics, celestial mechanics, flight mechanics, navigation and guidance, and space sciences. Topics of articles include such areas as altitude dynamics, orbit determination, altitude stability, orbital mechanics/dynamics, propulsion systems (both conventional and electric), trajectory optimization, space mission analysis, numerical methods, maneuvering of flight vehicles, dynamics and control, and new astronautical systems and their applications. The journal occasionally includes technical notes to speed up communication of new technological and scientific advances. Likewise, the journal occasionally publishes papers taken from important conferences or symposia sponsored by the American Astronautical Society (AAS), such as papers taken from the recent George H. Born Astronautics Symposium. The general-interest articles and membership-related information, including news, events, a calendar, new books, and conference reports, are provided in the society's magazine, *Space Times.* Most appropriate for academic and technical libraries.

152. *Journal of Thermophysics and Heat Transfer: devoted to thermophysics and heat transfer.* [ISSN: 0887-8722] 1987. q. Members, USD 55 (print & online eds.); Non-members, USD 685 (print or online ed.). Ed(s): Alfred L Crosbie, Becky Rivard. American Institute of Aeronautics and Astronautics, Inc., 1801 Alexander Bell Dr, Ste 500, Reston, VA 20191; custserv@aiaa.org; http://www.aiaa.org. Illus., index, adv. Sample. Refereed. Vol. ends: No. 4. *Indexed:* A22, ApMecR, C&ISA, CerAb, EngInd. *Aud.:* Ac.

This AIAA publication provides a forum for communicating original research in areas utilized by designers of aerospace systems and components, including all methods of heat transfer—radiative, conductive, and convective, and combinations of these methods. In addition, the effects of these heat-transfer methods are also included. Topics of interest in the corresponding area of thermophysics include mechanisms and properties involved with thermal energy transfer and storage in liquids, gases, solids, and systems that compose one or more of the physical states. Articles cover such topics as aerothermodynamics, conduction, phase change, radiative heat transfer, thermophysical properties, numerical heat transfer, nonintrusive diagnostics, vibrational kinetics, thermal control systems, convective heat transfer, and other areas of thermophysics, thermodynamics, and heat transfer. These issues are of primary importance to many aerospace-related areas of study, from the propulsion and space vehicle design to the impact on computational fluid dynamics due to extreme temperatures and energy transfer. The journal also includes comments and technical notes. The use of color illustrations and photographs greatly aids in enhancing the technical information provided by this publication. Recommended for major research collections, whether academic or technical.

153. *Kitplanes: your homebuilt aircraft authority.* Formerly (until 198?): *Guide to kitplanes.* [ISSN: 0891-1851] 1984. m. USD 29.95 combined subscription domestic (print & online eds.); USD 41.95 combined subscription foreign (print & online eds.). Ed(s): Paul Dye, Mark Schrimmer. Belvoir Media Group, LLC, PO Box 5656, Norwalk, CT 06856; customer_service@belvoir.com; http://www.belvoir.com. Illus., adv. Vol. ends: No. 12. *Indexed:* IHTDI. *Aud.:* Ga, Sa.

This magazine covers the specialized areas of hobbyists and enthusiasts who wish to design, build, and fly their own aircraft. Articles cover all aspects of traditional pilot-focused aviation magazines, such as flying, training, safety, and maintenance, with emphasis on home-built aircraft. This journal also covers the theory and other technical issues related to aircraft design, construction, and flying, with most articles focused on the construction and flying of personal aircraft. Along with feature articles dubbed "Flight Reports," the magazine includes articles in such areas as "Builder Spotlight," "Shop Talk," and "Designers Notebook." The other departments such as "Exploring," "Kit Bits," and remaining sections provide information on new products and tools, a calendar of events, editorial and readers' comments, classifieds, and information on competitions. There are many color and black-and-white photographs and illustrations, plus information on products and services, in-flight reports, and information on new aircraft. Emphasis is placed on providing useful how-to tips and other practical advice and information. Geared to the flying public, hobbyists, and enthusiasts and the ultimate "do it yourself" crowd.

154. *Light Sport and Ultralight Flying!: the magazine for sport pilots.* Former titles (until 2009): *Ultralight Flying;* (until 1985): *Glider Rider.* 1976. m. USD 29.95 domestic; USD 44.95 in Canada & Mexico; USD 59.95 elsewhere. Glider Rider, Inc., 1085 Bailey Ave, Chattanooga, TN 37404. Illus., adv. Sample. Vol. ends: Dec. *Aud.:* Ga, Sa.

This magazine is focused on light sport and ultralight aircraft, but in general it is similar to the other general aviation magazines. Its unique coverage is presented through feature articles, columns, and departments. The feature articles cover the unique issues related to owning and flying ultralight and light sport aircraft. These articles cover the same topics as other general aviation magazines, including articles on new aircraft, flying, safety, and training. Reports from rallies and contests for ultralight and light sport aircraft are also featured. There are also numerous advertisements and photographs. The standard departments and columns contain news, reports from events, information on competitions, new-product announcements and reviews, safety items, and a calendar of events. The journal provides an abundance of information on products, equipment, and safety. The articles are well written, and the magazine provides excellent practical information for ultralight and sport aircraft enthusiasts. A special issue devoted to products and equipment, or a "Buyer's Guide" issue, is usually published in January. Appropriate for general aviation–focused libraries.

155. *Plane and Pilot.* Incorporates (in 1987): *Homebuilt Aircraft; Airways.* [ISSN: 0032-0617] 1965. 7x/yr. USD 14.97 domestic; USD 29.97 foreign; USD 7 per issue. Werner Publishing Corporation, 12121 Wilshire Blvd, 12th Fl, Los Angeles, CA 90025; http://www.wernerpublishing.com. Illus., adv. Microform: PQC. *Indexed:* A22, IHTDI. *Aud.:* Hs, Ga, Sa.

This journal with the subtitle "the excitement of personal aviation & private ownership" is devoted primarily to the interests of recreational flyers or pilots. It includes articles on flying, aircraft, new products and aircraft, pilot aids, safety information, flying events, information on rules and regulations, and other general-interest items for pilots and aviation buffs. Almost every issue provides a review of new aircraft. There are classifieds, editorials, and letters to the editor. Regular columns and departments include sections on aircraft, safety, and training, along with such columns as "Pilot Reports," which highlights and evaluates new aircraft, and "NTSB Debriefer," which covers safety issues. Most other columns provide practical advice and tips for pilots such as "Ask P&P" and "Grassroots." One of the distinctive features of this journal that makes it more attractive for libraries is the recent buyers' guide and the journal's emphasis on learning to fly, training, and safety. There are usually features on topics of interest for general aviation enthusiasts, from purchasing aircraft to tips on better piloting, as well as new planes and equipment.

156. *Progress in Aerospace Sciences: an international review journal.* Formerly (until 1970): *Progress in Aeronautical Sciences.* [ISSN: 0376-0421] 1961. 8x/yr. EUR 2351. Pergamon, The Blvd, Langford Ln, E Park, Kidlington, OX5 1GB, United Kingdom; JournalsCustomerServiceEMEA@elsevier.com; http://www.elsevier.com. Illus., adv. Sample. Refereed. Microform: PQC. *Indexed:* A01, A22, ApMecR, C&ISA, CerAb, EngInd. *Aud.:* Ac.

This review journal is designed to bring together current advances in the field of aerospace sciences for those involved with research and development, and for other researchers who need technical information. The review articles, which contain extensive bibliographies, provide a concise and orderly summary of topics with enough detail that academics in all related fields can gain insight into the most recent and advanced research available. All aspects of aeronautical engineering are covered, including aerodynamics and fluid dynamics; aircraft design and performance; avionics; vehicle dynamics; guidance and control; fracture mechanics; combustion and propulsion systems; composite materials; wind tunnel design and testing; wind shear; and flight safety. Each issue usually contains two to six in-depth articles that are usually broken down into the typical sections of review articles: extensive background of the subject, a state-of-the-art review, and recommendations for further research. Color illustrations add to the clarity and understanding of the research presented. The journal has recently begun to occasionally publish a special-themed issue focused on a specific topic or papers originating from important aerospace conferences such as the recent issue devoted to Theodore von Karman. The journal also attempts to take the full advantage of electronic publishing with color illustrations, animated illustrations and video options available to authors. Highly recommended for research collections, whether in the research sector or in academe.

157. *Science at N A S A.* 19??. d. Free. Ed(s): Kathy Watkins. N A S A Headquarters, Public Communications Office, Ste 5K39, Washington, DC 20546; public-inquiries@hq.nasa.gov; http://www.nasa.gov. *Aud.:* Hs, Ga, Ac.

Science@NASA is a source for informative articles based on the research activities of the National Aeronautics and Space Administration (NASA). It serves as a gathering place for all NASA scientific and technical information and news releases. Most of the articles are listed under the "Science News" section or organized under categories such as "Earth," "Heliophysics," "Planets," and "Astrophysics." In addition, information is provided on missions and technology. The articles are usually presented with at least one graphic (photograph, illustration, or video) and links to the author. Topics covered include space weather, planetary science, microgravity, science highlights, and technology transfer. Under the broad categories, there is a further listing of missions and articles by focus areas, such as water and energy cycles, weather, space environment, magnetospheres, small bodies of the solar system, dark energy, dark matter, and black holes, etc. All of these sections provide additional stories that highlight NASA activities and discoveries. The site provides a wealth of information in all areas of science in a readable, concise format, and highlighted with illustrations, color photographs, and videos. This is a good starting point for scientific information from NASA for all educational levels. There is a pull-down menu that leads users to NASA information for educators, teens, kids, citizen scientists, and researchers. For an alternative look at NASA's activities, check out the NASA Watch site (www.nasawatch.com). Suitable for almost any age, and recommended for anyone interested in the space program. URL: http://science.nasa.gov

158. *Soaring.* Supersedes (in 1937): *The Gliding and Soaring Bulletin.* [ISSN: 0037-7503] 1932. m. Free to members. Soaring Society of America, Inc, PO Box 2100, Hobbs, NM 88241; info@ssa.org; http://www.ssa.org. Illus., adv. Vol. ends: No. 12. *Indexed:* A22, BAS, BRI, SD. *Bk. rev.:* Number and length vary. *Aud.:* Ga, Sa.

This journal is analogous to *Ballooning* and *Light Sport and Ultralight Flying* except that its primary emphasis is on propulsionless-aircraft flight or glided flight. The publication is the main communication vehicle for the Soaring Society of America, and it includes articles, photographs, news, and other items of interest for enthusiasts of gliding or soaring. The journal's feature articles include contest reports, information on safety issues, fly-in reports, and in-depth product reviews of new aircraft and systems. Topics of the general-interest articles include historical perspectives on gliding, safety issues, pioneers in the sport of gliding, aerial photography, information on towing, and articles on new equipment and tools such as the use of Google Maps. There are additional regular features on soaring and gliding events, conferences and competitions, general news of the society, book reviews, tips on safety, reader mail, and classified ads. Soaring enthusiasts will also enjoy the online soaring magazine, the *Soaring Cafe* (http://soaringcafe.com). This is a good general-interest magazine for hobbyists and other interested readers, and appropriate for all types of libraries.

159. *Space Policy.* [ISSN: 0265-9646] 1985. q. EUR 1610. Ed(s): Frances Brown. Pergamon, The Blvd, Langford Ln, E Park, Kidlington, OX5 1GB, United Kingdom; JournalsCustomerServiceEMEA@elsevier.com; http://www.elsevier.com. Illus., adv. Sample. Refereed. Microform: PQC. *Indexed:* A01, A22, BRI, C&ISA, CerAb, P61, SSA. *Bk. rev.:* 4-5, 500-1,000 words. *Aud.:* Ac, Sa.

This journal is one of the few interdisciplinary journals in the field of aeronautics and space science, and is designed to provide a forum for the discussion of how space policies will shape the future of space exploration, utilization, and related issues. The issues discussed include the impact of scientific discoveries obtained through space applications and research, space activities and discoveries that impact industry and society, and the resulting economic, political, social, legal, and moral issues raised. The exchange of ideas and opinions is as much a part of this journal as is the exchange of scientific and technical information on space activities and developments. Many of the six to ten articles per issue center on the topics associated with the use of space and the overall implications of this use. Topics range from space law and space commercialization to the history and current status of space programs, to space exploration and lunar development, to satellite systems and global positioning systems. The journal also provides position papers, editorials and comments, and reports along with information on new international developments in space, book reviews, and news of upcoming conferences and meetings. This unique approach that blends political, philosophical, business, and societal issues with scientific and engineering issues makes this journal more appropriate for academic libraries.

160. *Space Science Reviews.* [ISSN: 0038-6308] 1962. 32x/yr. EUR 3240 (print & online eds.). Ed(s): Hans Bloemen. Springer Netherlands, Van Godewijckstraat 30, Dordrecht, 3311 GX, Netherlands; http://www.springer.com. Illus., adv. Sample. Refereed. Vol. ends: No. 4. Microform: PMC; PQC. Reprint: PSC. *Indexed:* A01, A22, BRI, C&ISA, CerAb, E01, EngInd, M&GPA. *Bk. rev.:* 10-12, 100-300 words. *Aud.:* Ac.

This international review journal is composed of papers on the various topics related directly to space sciences. The magazine defines space science as scientific research carried out by means of rockets, rocket-propelled vehicles, stratospheric balloons, and observatories on the Earth and the Moon. The journal is primarily oriented toward the advancement of pure science, leaning more toward astronomy, with limited coverage of the technical aspects of space science. The papers, some of which comprise an entire volume, provide a synthesis of the current research and developments in the numerous branches of space science. The journal covers all areas of space science, including, but not limited to, the Big Bang theory, supernovae, cosmic rays, solar variability and climate, infrared space observation, airborne observatories, solar-wind phenomena, and characteristics of interstellar matter. The number of special or topical issues published by the journal has recently increased, with issues focused on such topics as cosmic rays in the heliosphere. In addition, the journal includes book reviews and short communications. This is one of the few traditional journals in the field that provides a large number of open-access articles. Appropriate for academic libraries.

Spaceflight. See Astronomy section.

161. *Sport Aviation.* Former titles (until 1961): *Sport Aviation and the Experimenter;* (until 1958): *Experimenter.* [ISSN: 0038-7835] 19??. m. Free to members. Experimental Aircraft Association, Inc., 3000 Poberezny Rd, Oshgosh, WI 54902; info@eaa.org; http://www.eaa.org/. Illus., adv. Sample. Vol. ends: Dec. *Indexed:* IHTDI. *Aud.:* Ga, Sa.

Sport Aviation is the main publication of the EAA (Experimental Aircraft Association). It is a cross between magazines geared for pilots and aviation enthusiasts and those aimed at specific areas of aviation, such as ultralights and ballooning. The magazine promotes general aviation and covers all types of aircraft, from military and private aircraft to helicopters and rotocraft, with the primary emphasis on the sport of aviation and sport aircraft. There are numerous feature articles and other information for anyone interested in general aviation and aircraft. The unique aspect of the magazine are the articles on the technical aspects of customizing aircraft, and building and restoring aircraft, as well as articles on classic aircraft, whether military or commercial, or seaplanes. In addition, the magazine contains the major sections that provide the bulk of the information of interest to the members of the journal's parent organization, the Experimental Aircraft Association (EAA). "Commentary" consists of columns and editorials. "Members Central" provides information and news of interest to members of EAA, such as a calendar of events, association news, a memorial section, and member services. The other sections, such as the "Hands-on" section, provide practical information for those building and restoring aircraft, and "Better Pilot," which focuses on safety. The updated format has resulted in a more appealing look and feel, while the content remains as good as ever. There are periodic special sections included that are primarily focused on EAA's educational, preservation, and legacy-building activities and youth initiatives. A worthwhile addition to general-interest collections and public libraries.

162. *Vertiflite.* Incorporates (in 19??): *American Helicopter Society. Directory of Members;* Former titles (until 1963): *Verti-flite Newsletter;* (until Apr.1963): *American Helicopter Society. Newsletter.* [ISSN: 0042-4455] 1953. bi-m. Members, USD 40; Non-members, USD 135. Ed(s): Kim Smith. American Helicopter Society, Inc., 217 N Washington St, Alexandria, VA 22314; staff@vtol.org; http://www.vtol.org. Illus., index, adv. Vol. ends: No. 5. *Indexed:* A22, C&ISA, CerAb, EngInd. *Bk. rev.:* 1-2, 700-1,000 words. *Aud.:* Ga, Ac.

This is the membership-focused publication of the American Helicopter Society (AHS), which aims at providing information on the advances being made in the areas of vertical flight and promoting the wider use of helicopters and other vertical-flight aircraft. Research articles on rotocraft technology can be found in the society's companion publication, the *Journal of the American Helicopter Society. Vertiflite* provides feature articles on helicopters and rotocraft technology and other broad issues relevant to the entire membership, such as new aircraft, new technologies, safety issues, and military technology. Along with these feature articles are book reviews, a calendar of events, information on conference activities, industry briefs, a member-update section, and related news items. The topics or types of articles include the military procurement of helicopters; reviews of new helicopters; the world rotocraft marketplace; and studies on rotoheads in wake fields. Recommended for academic and technical libraries.

■ AFRICA

Esmeralda Kale, Bibliographer of Africana, Herskovits Library of African Studies, Northwestern University, 1970 Campus Drive, Evanston, IL 60077; 847-491-3941; ekale@northwestern.edu

Introduction

The journals and magazines selected in this section are presented in alphabetical order by title. It would have been challenging to attempt to categorize them, and so emphasis was placed on the inclusion of titles that represent a breadth of subjects. Highly specialized titles have been excluded. The titles included have been selected to guide the user in the identification of a core list of titles for this subject area.

Basic Periodicals

Hs: *Focus on Africa;* Ga: *Africa Research Bulletin. Economic, Financial and Technical Series; Africa Research Bulletin. Political, Social and Cultural Series; African Business; Journal of Modern African Studies; New African; Transition;* Ac: *Africa; Africa Confidential; Africa Today; African Affairs; African Studies Review; History in Africa; Presence Africaine; Research in African Literatures.*

Basic Abstracts and Indexes

African Studies, African Studies Abstracts, Current Bibliography on African Affairs, International African Bibliography, PAIS International, Quarterly Index to Africana Periodical Literature.

163. *Africa.* [ISSN: 0001-9720] 1928. q. plus a. bibliography. GBP 300 Africa Bibliography only (print & online eds.) Individuals, GBP 81 includes Africa Bibliography (print & online eds.). Ed(s): Karin Barber. Cambridge University Press, The Edinburgh Bldg, Shaftesbury Rd, Cambridge, CB2 8RU, United Kingdom; information@cambridge.org; http://journals.cambridge.org. Illus., index, adv. Sample. Refereed. Circ: 1250. Vol. ends: No. 4. Reprint: PSC. *Indexed:* A01, A22, A47, AbAn, AmHI, BRI, E01, FR, IBSS, IIBP, MLA-IB, P02, RILM. *Bk. rev.:* 10-15, 750-2,500 words. *Aud.:* Ac, Sa.

Africa is one of the oldest scholarly journals focusing on the continent, in publication for more than 80 years. It is the journal of the International African Institute in London, which has played a seminal role in the development of the field of African Studies. It is interdisciplinary in approach, and subject coverage includes the social sciences, history, the environment, and life sciences, with strong emphasis on issues of development, links between local and national levels of society, and cultural studies. Each issue usually contains articles with extensive bibliographies. Articles are accompanied by abstracts in English and French. Book reviews and review essays are substantial. *Africa Bibliography* (see below in this section), a comprehensive, categorized, and indexed annual listing of published work in African Studies from the previous year, is included with the full subscription, or it can be purchased separately. *Africa* is a African Studies periodical that is highly recommended for all academic collections and large general collections.

164. *Africa Bibliography.* [ISSN: 0266-6731] 1985. a. GBP 324 (print & online eds.). Ed(s): Dr. Terrry A BArringer. Cambridge University Press, The Edinburgh Bldg, Shaftesbury Rd, Cambridge, CB2 8RU, United Kingdom; http://journals.cambridge.org. Illus. *Indexed:* A01, A22, FR. *Aud.:* Ga, Ac, Sa.

Begun anew in 1984 in conjunction with the International African Institute's journal *Africa,* this annual review reports on African publications (books, periodical articles, pamphlets, book chapters) that are primarily in the social sciences, humanities, and arts, with selected coverage of the medical, biological, and physical sciences as they are relevant to readers from a social sciences/arts background. Coverage is of the entire continent and its associated islands. The introduction is always worth reading; it is usually an essay on some aspect of librarianship. Recent themes have included ways of seeing Africa; the three stages of African Studies reference works; and facilitating scholarly communication in African Studies. *Africa Bibliography* is arranged by region and country and preceded by a section for the continent as a whole. The sections are divided by subject classes with author and subject indexes. The consolidated searchable online resource brings all the articles together since the inception of the bibliography. This recommended reference is an easy-to-use resource for locating current, popular, and scholarly African materials. It is useful both for those developing comprehensive collections and for libraries that can only afford to select a few items for geographic coverage of current literature. Some libraries may opt to acquire the *Bibliography* with a subscription to *Africa* (above in this section).

165. *Africa Confidential.* Formerly (until 1967): *Africa.* [ISSN: 0044-6483] 1960. fortn. GBP 798 combined subscription (print & online eds.); USD 1317 combined subscription (print & online eds.). Ed(s): Clare Tauben, Patrick Smith. Asempa Ltd., 73 Farringdon Rd, London, EC1M 3JQ, United Kingdom; info@africa-confidential.com. Illus., adv. Vol. ends: Dec. *Indexed:* A01, A22, E01. *Aud.:* Ga, Ac, Sa.

For more than 50 years, *Africa Confidential* has been a source of current political, military, and economic intelligence reporting and analysis. A wealth of information can be found in this eight-page newsletter. Online subscriptions are also available at the journal's web site. Biweekly issues provide "inside track" information on African leaders and analysis of general trends and specific events in Africa, written by a network of correspondents throughout Africa. The articles have no bylines—the contributors write on the basis of anonymity. This widely read newsletter remains in heavy demand, and is highly recommended for both general and academic collections. URL: www.africa-confidential.com

166. *Africa Development.* [ISSN: 0850-3907] 1976. q. USD 32 (Individuals, USD 30). Ed(s): Felicia Oyekanmi. Council for the Development of Social Science Research in Africa, Avenue Cheikh, Anta Diop x Canal IV, BP 3304, Dakar, Senegal; codesria@sentoo.sn; http://www.codesria.org. Illus., adv. Refereed. Circ: 600. *Indexed:* AbAn, C45, IBSS, IIBP, RRTA. *Bk. rev.:* 2-5, 1,000-1,500 words. *Aud.:* Ac, Sa.

This quarterly bilingual journal (parallel title: *Afrique et Developpement*) is published by the Council for the Development of Social Science Research in Africa (CODESRIA). It supports CODESRIA's principal objective of "exchange of ideas among African scholars from a variety of intellectual persuasions and various disciplines." African authors contribute articles on cultural, social, political, and economic issues of society in Africa. This title is slightly behind in publication; but the focus may be on an issue in a specific country, or on continent-wide issues. Preceded by abstracts in English and French, the articles tend to cut across disciplinary boundaries. The articles may be in either French or English, although English predominates. *Africa Development* is the oldest regularly published social science journal in Africa, and is highly recommended for academic and special audiences and institutions interested in including social science analysis from African scholars. CODESRIA publications participate in the Africa Journals Online project (www.ajol.info), but tables of contents and the full text of articles are also posted on the CODESRIA web site (www.codesria.org/Publications.htm), along with other organization journals, including (see below) *African Sociological Review, CODESRIA Bulletin,* and *Afrika Zamani.*

167. *Africa Insight.* Formerly (until 1979): *South African Journal of African Affairs.* [ISSN: 0256-2804] 1971. q. ZAR 500 (Individuals, ZAR 250). Ed(s): Elizabeth Le Roux. Africa Institute of South Africa, PO Box 630, Pretoria, 0001, South Africa; ai@ai.org.za. Illus., index, adv. Sample. Refereed. Circ: 5000. Microform: PQC. *Indexed:* A22, C45, IBSS, IIBP, MLA-IB, P61, RILM, RRTA, SSA. *Bk. rev.:* 3-5, 500-700 words. *Aud.:* Ga, Ac, Sa.

Africa Insight is a publication of the Africa Institute of South Africa, a think tank devoted to production of knowledge on Africa. The journal is a forum for diverse topics that focuses on the process of change in Africa. Topics are wide-ranging: political trends and events, democratization, economic issues, regional cooperation, international relations, conflict resolution, aspects of education and training, health, community development, food security, and institutional capacity building. While many articles focus on southern Africa, the scope of the journal is the entire continent. Recent issues contain essays on South Africa's participation in BRIC; regional initiative in peace-support operations; and the contribution of environmental factors to the professional success of women challenges. The articles are scholarly, researched, and frequently illustrated. This title is of interest to educators, institutions, and decision makers in business and the public sector, but also to a wider audience interested in Africa. Recommended and suitable for academic and large public libraries, as well as special audiences.

168. *Africa Quarterly: a journal of African affairs.* [ISSN: 0001-9828] 1961. q. Indian Council for Cultural Relations, Azad Bhavan, Indraprastha Estate, New Delhi, 110 002, India; pdpub@iccrindia.org; http://www.iccrindia.net. Illus., index, adv. Vol. ends: Oct. Microform: PQC. *Indexed:* A22, IBSS, MLA-IB. *Bk. rev.:* Number and length vary. *Aud.:* Ac, Sa.

This publication of the Indian Council for Cultural Relations promotes understanding between India and Africa, and features articles that examine important themes that affect both areas, e.g., global warming, Asian–African relations, postwar stress victims in Nigeria, globalization, etc. Scholars around the world contribute to the six to eight thoroughly researched and accessible articles in each issue. There are also three or four substantive book reviews. Africa-related activities in India and conference notes are often included. Significant in the context of globalization and the growing importance of non-Western inter-regional, BRIC cooperation, *Africa Quarterly* is a good addition to larger Africana collections.

169. *Africa Renewal.* Former titles (until vol.18,no.3, 2004): *Africa Recovery;* (until 1987): *Africa Emergency Report.* [ISSN: 1816-9627] 1985. q. Ed(s): Julie Thompson. United Nations, Department of Public Information, United Nations Bldg, L-172, New York, NY 10017. *Aud.:* Hs, Ga, Ac, Sa.

Africa Renewal is an illustrated United Nations publication that examines the many issues that confront the people of Africa, its leaders, and its international partners. Coverage includes economic reform, debt, education, health, women's advancement, conflict and civil strife, climate change, democratization, development, aid, investment, trade, and many other topics. Reporting tracks policy debates and shows the effect of policies on the people. It also reports on and examines the many different aspects of the U.N.'s involvement in Africa, especially within the framework of the New Partnership for Africa's Development (NEPAD). The modest price, the focus on contemporary issues, and the accessible writing make this a suitable choice for most libraries interested in Africa. Each issue is freely available on the U.N. web site. URL: www.un.org/africarenewal/magazine

170. *Africa Research Bulletin. Economic, Financial and Technical Series.* Former titles (until 1992): *Africa Research Bulletin. Economic Series;* (until 1985): *Africa Research Bulletin. Economic, Financial and Technical Series;* (until Apr.1965): *Africa Research Bulletin. Africa: Economic, Financial and Technical Series;* (until Feb.1965): *Africa Research Bulletin. Africa: Economic, Financial and Technical.* [ISSN: 0001-9852] 1964. m. GBP 1026. Ed(s): Virginia Baily, Veronica Hoskins. Wiley-Blackwell Publishing Ltd., The Atrium, Southern Gate, Chichester, PO19 8SQ, United Kingdom; customer@wiley.com; http://www.wiley.com/. Illus., index, adv. Sample. *Indexed:* A22, ABIn, B01, E01, RiskAb. *Aud.:* Ac, Sa.

Providing in-depth coverage and analysis drawn from Africa and around the world, this monthly economic news digest extracts text and summaries from media sources, including African newspapers, news agencies, radio broadcasts, and United Nations agency publications, as well as information from government gazettes, international organizations, and selected European newspapers and journals. After a lead article, six sections cover issues related to cooperation, trade, economic policies, infrastructure, commodities, industry, and economic aid. Charts, graphs, and maps accompany articles. It is available online to subscribers. The publisher issues a companion series, *Africa Research Bulletin. Political, Social, and Cultural Series.* Both are highly recommended for specialized and large public and academic libraries for the extensive (but expensive) coverage.

171. *Africa Research Bulletin. Political, Social and Cultural Series.* Former titles (until 1992): *Africa Research Bulletin. Political Series;* (until 1985): *Africa Research Bulletin. Political, Social, and Cultural Series;* (until Mar.1965): *Africa Research Bulletin. Africa, Political, Social, and Cultural Series;* (until Feb.1965): *Africa Research Bulletin. Africa, Political, Social, and Cultural.* [ISSN: 0001-9844] 1964. m. GBP 1026. Ed(s): Veronica Hoskins, Virginia Baily. Wiley-Blackwell Publishing Ltd., The Atrium, Southern Gate, Chichester, PO19 8SQ, United Kingdom; customer@wiley.com; http://www.wiley.com/. Illus., index, adv. Sample. *Indexed:* A01, A22, E01, P02. *Aud.:* Ga, Ac, Sa.

In this, a companion journal to the *African Research Bulletin. Economic, Financial and Technical Series* (see above), information is drawn from hundreds of acknowledged sources including local press, web sites, and radio to provide news and commentary on politics and society. Sources from Africa are complemented by information from government gazettes, international agencies, and the European and American press. Coverage includes major conference reports; government changes, and lists of new officials; internal security; the military; international relations; and cultural and social information. A lead article is followed by principal content sections that are geographically arranged by country. Major political/military events often appear in chronological order; and charts, graphs, and maps illustrate the articles. The online format follows that of the print. In addition to providing a detailed index, the web allows full-text searching. Expensive, but like the economic series, essential for specialized and academic libraries, especially large research institutions.

172. *Africa Today.* [ISSN: 0001-9887] 1954. q. USD 199.50 (print & online eds.). Ed(s): Maria Grosz-Ngate, Samuel Obeng. Indiana University Press, 601 N Morton St, Bloomington, IN 47404; journals@indiana.edu; http://iupjournals.org. Illus., index, adv. Sample. Refereed. Circ: 1300 Paid. Vol. ends: Fall. Microform: PQC. Reprint: PSC. *Indexed:* A01, A22, AbAn, BRI, C45, CBRI, E01, IBSS, IIBP, MLA-IB, P02, P61, RILM, RRTA, SSA. *Bk. rev.:* 5-15, 750 words. *Aud.:* Ga, Ac, Sa.

Articles in *Africa Today* examine a wide variety of current social, political, and economic issues. Originally the bulletin of the anti-apartheid American Committee on Africa, *Africa Today* is now an academic journal published by Indiana University. An interdisciplinary publication, it includes occasional articles in the arts and humanities, as well as research in the social sciences. Many issues are on specific themes. The range of the journal can be seen in recent issues that feature articles on alleviating poverty in Ghana; appropriating the American dream in Kogelo; and resources for adjusting well to work migration. There are several interesting and incisive book reviews included in each issue. A list of books received at the end of each issue. This is an affordable, recommended publication for both general audiences and academic collections.

173. *Africa Today: voice of the continent.* [ISSN: 1357-311X] 1995. m. Free to members. Africa Today, Ste 6, Third Fl, AMC House, 12 Cumberland Ave, London, NW10 7QL, United Kingdom; publisher@africatoday.com. Adv. *Indexed:* AbAn. *Aud.:* Ga.

Not to be confused with the academic journal of the same title published by Indiana University, *Africa Today, Voice of the Continent* is a monthly consumer newsmagazine published, like many others, with a Nigerian editorial staff and a publication address in London. It aims to be a market leader in newsmagazine format for Pan-Africa news and current affairs, and its cover stories range from such topics as "Man of the Year" Yar'adua, an uncommon African leader, to President Gbagbo's dangerous game. Features on business, sport, tourism, etc., complement regular coverage of developments in countries around the continent. Selected stories from current and back issues are featured on the journal web site. The editors pride themselves on the consistency of publication; it has not missed an issue in its decade-plus existence. Libraries with an African Studies or international focus may consider this title, as may public libraries that serve an African Diaspora community. URL: http://africatoday.com

174. *African Affairs.* Former titles (until 1944): *Royal African Society. Journal;* (until 1935): *African Society. Journal.* [ISSN: 0001-9909] 1901. q. EUR 460. Oxford University Press, Great Clarendon St, Oxford, OX2 6DP, United Kingdom; enquiry@oup.co.uk; http://www.oxfordjournals.org/. Illus., adv. Sample. Refereed. Reprint: PSC. *Indexed:* A01, A22, A47, AbAn, AmHI, BRI, C45, E01, IBSS, IIBP, MLA-IB, P02, P61, RILM, RRTA, SSA. *Bk. rev.:* 5-15, 500-1,500 words. *Aud.:* Ac, Sa.

Published on behalf of the Royal African Society (United Kingdom), this highly ranked scholarly journal has a long tradition—over 100 years—of covering Africa from a broad range of social science and cultural perspectives. Each issue includes several scholarly articles that focus on recent political, social, and economic developments in sub-Saharan countries. Historical studies relevant to current events on the continent are also featured. The journal regularly posts news of meetings of the Royal African Society and includes the society's annual meeting minutes, announcements, and annual report. Very useful to scholars, students, and librarians is the large bibliographic section with its book reviews, a bibliography of current publications by region, and a bibliography of Africa-related articles. Oxford University Press provides abstracts of major articles online and a facility to search the online tables of contents and abstracts. A

valuable resource for a wide audience including students, scholars, librarians, and anyone interested in recent and historical literature on sub-Saharan Africa, *African Affairs* remains a basic choice for all collections. URL: http://afraf.oupjournals.org

175. *African and Black Diaspora: an international journal.* [ISSN: 1752-8631] 2008. s-a. GBP 207 (print & online eds.). Ed(s): Dr. Sandra Jackson, Dr. Fassil Demissie. Routledge, 325 Chestnut St, Ste 800, Philadelphia, PA 19106; customerservice@taylorandfrancis.com; http://www.tandfonline.com. Sample. Refereed. Reprint: PSC. *Indexed:* A22, E01, IBSS, IIBP. *Bk. rev.:* Number and length vary. *Aud.:* Ga, Ac, Sa.

This new peer-reviewed journal publishes articles, commentaries, and book reviews on the interdisciplinary field of African Diaspora Studies. From a global perspective, it considers the geographical, cultural, social, political, and psychological movements of peoples of African descent. Recent articles and themes have included the African diaspora in Brazil; and the African Renaissance. This journal should prove useful to libraries that support both African Studies and African American collections. Tables of contents are available online. URL: www.tandf.co.uk/journals/titles/17528631.asp

176. *African Archaeological Review.* [ISSN: 0263-0338] 1983. s-a. EUR 455 (print & online eds.). Ed(s): Adria LaViolette. Springer New York LLC, 233 Spring St, New York, NY 10013; service-ny@springer.com; http://www.springer.com/. Illus., adv. Sample. Refereed. Microform: PQC. Reprint: PSC. *Indexed:* A01, A07, A22, A47, AbAn, AmHI, ArtHuCI, BRI, E01, FR, IIBP. *Bk. rev.:* 1-2, 1,000-1,500 words. *Aud.:* Ac, Sa.

This journal features international scholarship on aspects of African archaeology. Each issue contains one or two authoritative, and substantial, articles on archaeological research and activities in Africa. Recent focus has been on the origins of African sheep, and domestic pigs in Africa. Emphasis is given to issues dealing with cultural continuities or discontinuities; inter-regional processes; bio-cultural evolution; the role of cultural materials in politics and ideology; and the application of ethno-historical techniques. Field data from sites or localities are often reported. The journal usually includes one or two substantive book reviews. It is of importance in the field and is recommended for institutions with an interest in anthropology and archaeology. Available in print and online. The Springer web site features an Online First preview of proofed papers scheduled for publication. URL: www.springerlink.com/content/0263-0338

177. *African Arts.* [ISSN: 0001-9933] 1967. q. USD 199 (print & online eds.). Ed(s): Leslie Ellen Jones. M I T Press, 55 Hayward St, Cambridge, MA 02142; journals-cs@mit.edu; http://mitpress.mit.edu. Illus., adv. Refereed. Microform: PQC. *Indexed:* A01, A06, A07, A22, A47, A51, AmHI, ArtHuCI, BRI, C37, E01, FR, IIBP, MASUSE, MLA-IB, P02, RILM. *Bk. rev.:* 3-4, 200-700 words. *Aud.:* Hs, Ga, Ac, Sa.

This visually appealing, glossy journal is devoted to the plastic and graphic arts of Africa and its Diaspora. Architecture, arts of personal adornment, and contemporary and popular arts are featured, as well as music, film, theater, and other forms of expressive culture. Each issue usually includes four to eight articles with beautiful black-and-white and color illustrations and photos. Entire issues are often devoted to topical concerns and discussions. Exhibit announcements; descriptive reviews of major exhibits; and book, video, and/or theater reviews appear in each issue. The presentation, subject matter, and accessible writing make this a good choice for all audiences. Distributed by MIT Press for the African Studies program at UCLA, it is available in print or online.

178. *The African Book Publishing Record.* [ISSN: 0306-0322] 1975. q. EUR 455. Ed(s): Cecile Lomer. De Gruyter Saur, Mies-van-der-Rohe-Str 1, Munich, 80807, Germany; wdg-info@degruyter.com; http://www.degruyter.com/browse?publisher=KGS. Illus., adv. Circ: 500 Controlled. Vol. ends: No. 4. Reprint: PSC. *Indexed:* A22, E01, IIBP, MLA-IB. *Bk. rev.:* 35-55, 200-400 words. *Aud.:* Ac, Sa.

ABPR provides comprehensive bibliographic and acquisitions data on new and forthcoming publications from the African continent. It includes books published in English or French, and also lists significant titles in African languages. Bibliographic lists arranged by subject, author, and country supplement large book review sections. Features include reviews of new periodicals, an annual annotated review of African reference books, articles, news relating to the African book trade or African publishing, and listings of book awards and prizes. *ABPR* is highly recommended for academic, large public, and special libraries interested in acquiring specialized African materials.

179. *African Business.* [ISSN: 0141-3929] 1966. 11x/yr. GBP 40 domestic; EUR 80 foreign. Ed(s): Anver Versi. I C Publications Ltd., 7 Coldbath Sq, London, EC1R 4LQ, United Kingdom; icpubs@africasia.com; http://www.africasia.com/. Illus., index, adv. Sample. Microform: PQC. *Indexed:* A22, ABIn, B01, B02, BRI, IIBP. *Bk. rev.:* 1-5, 100-500 words. *Aud.:* Hs, Ga, Ac, Sa.

With a pan-African focus, *African Business* provides information on business trends, risks, and opportunities in Africa in a familiar newsmagazine format. Each issue usually consists of several sections. The "cover story section" has three, or sometimes four or more, substantial articles on current business and economic issues. The "Special reports" section includes shorter articles that might be on a particular theme. Usually pieces on African telecoms, ports, and mining appear in each issue. The sections about "Aviation," "Shipping," and the "Development" are shorter, with possibly a single article per section. The "Countryfile" section features several specific-country analyses of economic developments and trends. News of conferences, trade exhibition dates, African currency tables, book reviews, and columnists with opinions and advice are included. *AB* has won awards for business reporting in Africa. With content presented in a colorful, lively, and readable manner, it is recommended for general, academic, and special library collections. It is current and relevant to anyone seeking to understand business in Africa. It also forms part of a number of titles published by IC Publications in London such as *New African,* listed below. For in-depth country analysis, see *Country Reports* (below in this section). The *AB* web site includes some sections of current and past issues. URL: www.africasia.com/africanbusiness

180. *African Development Review.* [ISSN: 1017-6772] 1989. q. GBP 211. Ed(s): Hassan Aly, Kupukile Mlambo. Wiley-Blackwell Publishing Ltd., The Atrium, Southern Gate, Chichester, PO19 8SQ, United Kingdom; customer@wiley.com; http://www.wiley.com/. Illus., adv. Sample. Refereed. *Indexed:* A01, A22, ABIn, ASSIA, B01, C45, E01, EconLit, IBSS, JEL, P61, RiskAb, SSA. *Bk. rev.:* Number and length vary. *Aud.:* Ac, Sa.

The African Development Bank is a regional, multilateral development-finance institution that finances projects that contribute to the growth and development of African economies. The *Review*, published by Wiley–Blackwell on behalf of the bank, is a "professional journal devoted to the study and analysis of development policy in Africa." Emphasis is on the relevance of research findings to policy rather than on purely theoretical or quantitative contributions. It is published four times a year, and each issue includes about six scholarly, technical articles on developmental economics, policy, and planning issues, such as macroeconomic policies, private-sector development, and income distribution and poverty alleviation. The focus may be on recent critical issues or empirical analyses and case studies, either comparative or of single countries. Articles are generally in English, and occasionally in French. All articles have both English and French abstracts. There are book reviews, conference reports, and comments on reviewed articles. Online access is provided for subscribers, and individual articles may be purchased on the publisher's web site. Free online access to institutions in the developing world is provided through United Nations initiatives (AGORA and OARE). More technical and more focused on economics than *Africa Development* (above in this section), this journal is recommended for academic and special audiences.

181. *African Economic History.* Formerly (until 1976): *African Economic History Review.* [ISSN: 0145-2258] 1974. a. USD 58.80 (print & online eds.). Ed(s): Paul E Lovejoy, Jose C Curto. University of Wisconsin at Madison, African Studies Program, 4141 Helen C. White Hall, 600 N. Park St, Madison, WI 53706; saadell@wisc.edu; http://afroamericanstudies.wisc.edu. Illus., adv. Sample. Refereed. Reprint: PSC. *Indexed:* ABIn, AbAn, ArtHuCI, EconLit, IBSS, IIBP, JEL. *Bk. rev.:* 8-10, 600-1,000 words. *Aud.:* Ga, Ac, Sa.

African Economic History covers economic history from the pre-colonial era to the twentieth century, and articles in this annual journal aim to contribute to historical knowledge and provide insights into contemporary economic and political issues on the continent. This journal is an important addition to collections with an interest in both African history and economics. The book review section is substantial. Usually behind in publication, this journal is recommended for specialized collections, academic libraries, and large public libraries.

182. *African Geographical Review.* Formerly (until 2001): *East African Geographical Review.* [ISSN: 1937-6812] 1963. s-a. GBP 142 (print & online eds.). Ed(s): Isaac Luginaah. Routledge, 2 Park Sq, Milton Park, Abingdon, OX14 4RN, United Kingdom; http://www.routledge.com. Adv. Sample. Refereed. Reprint: PSC. *Indexed:* A01. *Bk. rev.:* Number and length vary. *Aud.:* Ac, Sa.

The African Specialty Group of the Association of American Geographers publishes this journal, originally founded in 1963 at Makerere University in Uganda. The aim of this annual publication is to enhance the standing of African regional geography and to promote a better representation of African scholarship. Articles are contributed by scholars throughout the world. Articles may be from any subfield of geography, as well as those that are theoretical, empirical, or applied in nature. The journal features short commentaries on contemporary issues in Africa, research articles, methodological or field notes, editorials, and a few short book reviews. This title is slightly behind in publication. Some articles are specialized, while many are of broader social-science interest. For academic and specialized collections.

183. *African Historical Review.* Formerly (until 2008): *Kleio.* [ISSN: 1753-2523] 1969. s-a. GBP 170 (print & online eds.). Ed(s): Muchaparara Musemwa. UniSA Press, PO Box 392, Pretoria, 0003, South Africa; unisa-press@unisa.ac.za; http://www.unisa.ac.za/press. Illus., adv. Refereed. Circ: 3200. Reprint: PSC. *Indexed:* A22, E01, IBSS, IIBP. *Bk. rev.:* Number and length vary. *Aud.:* Ac.

Published in South Africa for about 35 years as *Kleio: A Journal of Historical Studies from Africa,* this journal was originally a research and teaching forum for the History Department of the University of South Africa, and evolved into an internationally recognized academic journal. Relaunched in 2008 as *African Historical Review* and now one of the journals co-published by the university and Routledge, it aims for a wider audience with contributors from Africa. It includes three to five research articles, review articles, and an often lengthy book review section in each issue. While regional scholarship is still featured, the intent is to include writing and research on an array of historical topics regarding Africa with diverse theoretical frameworks and methodologies. Suitable for collections that support African Studies, and valuable for bringing African scholarship to readers internationally.

184. *African Identities: journal of economics, culture and society.* [ISSN: 1472-5843] 2003. q. GBP 417 (print & online eds.). Ed(s): Hannah Soong, Pal Ahluwalia. Routledge, 4 Park Sq, Milton Park, Abingdon, OX14 4RN, United Kingdom; subscriptions@tandf.co.uk; http://www.tandfonline.com. Adv. Sample. Refereed. Reprint: PSC. *Indexed:* A01, A22, E01, IBSS, IIBP. *Bk. rev.:* Number and length vary. *Aud.:* Ga, Ac, Sa.

Serving as an interdisciplinary forum for critical examinations of African and diasporic cultural production, including popular culture, this title is available in print and online. Five to eight articles in each issue examine film, drama, literature, popular music, and culture in the context of African identity. Recent articles have discussed the Mali crisis; analysis of race and gender in advertisements in a South African in-flight magazine; and the Igbo quest for self-determination in Nigeria. The cultural studies approach and theoretical language of the articles mean that this journal will be most useful in academic settings, but it is of high value for collections that support cultural studies of Africa and its diaspora.

185. *African Journal of Ecology.* Former titles (until 1979): *East African Wildlife Journal;* (until 1963): *Wild Life.* [ISSN: 0141-6707] 1959. q. GBP 866. Ed(s): Frederick I B Kayanja. Wiley-Blackwell Publishing Ltd., The Atrium, Southern Gate, Chichester, PO19 8SQ, United

Kingdom; customer@wiley.com; http://www.wiley.com/. Illus., index, adv. Sample. Refereed. Vol. ends: Dec. Microform: PQC. Reprint: PSC. *Indexed:* A01, A22, AbAn, Agr, C45, E01, IndVet, P02, RRTA, S25. *Bk. rev.:* 1-3, 250-800 words. *Aud.:* Ga, Ac, Sa.

Published in Nairobi on behalf of the East African Wild Life Society, this important journal, formerly called *East African Wildlife Journal,* includes original research on the plant and animal ecology of Africa. Six to eight scholarly scientific articles are included in each issue. Graphs, tables, and high-quality illustrations accompany the articles on wildlife and plant ecology. Although articles are in English, a brief summary in French is included for each article. Book reviews are included and brief communications often round out some of the issues. Comprehensive reviews on topical subjects are also sometimes featured. The editors see the readership as wildlife biologists, academics in biological sciences, undergraduates, and schoolteachers. Tables of contents and reprint services are available at www.blackwellpublishing.com. The journal itself is also online through Blackwell's Synergy journals service for subscribers. Highly recommended for general science, biology, and botany collections, and for research and academic libraries with an environment or ecology program.

186. *African Research and Documentation.* Formed by the merger of (1964-1972): *African Studies Association of the United Kingdom. Bulletin;* (1962-1972): *Library Materials on Africa.* [ISSN: 0305-862X] 1973. 3x/yr. Free to members. Ed(s): Terry Barringer. Standing Conference on Library Materials on Africa, Social Science Collections & Research, British Library St Pancras, London, NW1 2DB, United Kingdom; scolma@hotmail.com; http://scolma.org. Illus., index, adv. *Indexed:* A22, BAS, IIBP, MLA-IB. *Bk. rev.:* 4-6, 250-1,000 words. *Aud.:* Ac, Sa.

Publishing articles on all aspects of libraries, archives, and bibliographical matters relating to Africa and African Studies, this journal is a good collection-development tool. It provides current information on publishing trends, bibliographic research projects, reference sources, book reviews, major scholarly writings, and announcements relating to African research sources. Articles focus on current topics or research resources. Issues also include information on Africa-related conferences and meetings, especially those taking place in Great Britain. Papers presented at conferences are often included. Periodically, the journal provides an updated listing of African Studies resources on the Internet. In "Notes and News," one can find a summary of activities in various institutions with Africana collections. Book reviews by librarians cover a wide variety of scholarly works, including some very specialized items. Tables of contents for recent issues are available online. Recommended as a very useful tool for Africana librarians and scholars. URL: www.lse.ac.uk/library/scolma/ardmain.htm

187. *African Sociological Review.* Incorporates (in 1995): *South African Sociological Review;* Which was formerly (until 1988): *A S S A Proceedings (Association for Sociology in South Africa).* [ISSN: 1027-4332] 1973. s-a. ZAR 70 (Individuals, ZAR 40). Ed(s): Fred Hendricks. Council for the Development of Social Science Research in Africa, Avenue Cheikh, Anta Diop x Canal IV, BP 3304, Dakar, Senegal; codesria@ssonatel.senet.net; http://www.codesria.org. Illus., adv. Refereed. Circ: 600. *Indexed:* IBSS, IIBP, P61, SSA. *Bk. rev.:* 1,200-1,500 words. *Aud.:* Ac, Sa.

African Sociological Review is also known as a forum for research-based publishing by African scholars to promote sociological and anthropological thought. It is sponsored by CODESRIA (Council for the Development of Social Science Research in Africa), and each issue generally contains four or five articles, usually in English but with occasional French-language essays. Recent articles include sociology and social work in Nigeria; theater for development; and private returns on education in Gahana. Research reports, important addresses or speeches, review essays, or argument pieces ("Debates") are selectively included. This journal is important to academic institutions with advanced degrees in sociology, as well as Africana collections. The table of contents is available through African Journals Online (www.ajol.info), and the journal is freely available online. Although the publication schedule is semi-annual, there are often delays.

188. *African Studies.* Formerly (until 1942): *Bantu Studies.* [ISSN: 0002-0184] 1921. 3x/yr. GBP 420 (print & online eds.). Ed(s): Elizabeth Gunner, Bridget Kenny. Routledge, 4 Park Sq, Milton Park, Abingdon, OX14 4RN, United Kingdom; subscriptions@tandf.co.uk; http://www.tandfonline.com. Illus., adv. Sample. Refereed. Reprint: PSC. *Indexed:* A01, A22, A47, AbAn, AmHI, C45, E01, IBSS, IIBP, MLA-IB, P61, RRTA, SSA. *Aud.:* Ac, Sa.

Published three times a year, this scholarly South African journal is editorially based at the University of the Witwatersrand. The journal encourages dialogue between scholars writing about various nations in Africa, especially southern countries. Each issue includes six to nine articles. This journal was originally focused on anthropology and linguistics, but its scope is now much broader—encompasssing history, sociology, politics, geography, literary, and cultural studies. A recent issue has articles on the nature of democracy in Kwasi Wiredu's democracy by consensus, and regional environmental governance in the Lake Victoria region. There are frequent issues devoted to specific themes. This journal is published on behalf of the university by Routledge, part of the Taylor & Francis Group; and at the publisher's web site (www.tandf.co.uk/journals), one can browse the contents pages of the issues, with full text available to subscribers and with individual issues and articles for purchase. Recommended for larger collections.

189. *African Studies Quarterly: the online journal of African studies.* [ISSN: 2152-2448] 1997. q. Free. Ed(s): R Hunt Davis, Shylock Muyengwa. University of Florida, Center for African Studies, 427 Grinter Hall, PO Box 115560, Gainesville, FL 32611; www@africa.ufl.edu; http://www.africa.ufl.edu/. Illus., adv. Refereed. *Indexed:* A01, AmHI, BRI, IIBP. *Bk. rev.:* 5-15, 500-1,000 words. *Aud.:* Ac.

Only available online, this interdisciplinary, refereed academic journal is published by the Center for African Studies at the University of Florida. Focused on contemporary Africa, it includes both research and opinion in all disciplines. Each issue features approximately three to five articles, extensive book reviews, and frequent review essays. Thematic issues are published frequently. This journal is freely available on the web. URL: http://web.africa.ufl.edu/asq

190. *African Studies Review.* Incorporates (1975-1980): *A S A Review of Books;* Formerly (until 1970): *African Studies Bulletin;* Which incorporated (1962-1964): *Africana Newsletter.* [ISSN: 0002-0206] 1958. 3x/yr. GBP 243 (print & online eds.). Ed(s): Ralph Faulkingham, Mitzi Goheen. Cambridge University Press, The Edinburgh Bldg, Shaftesbury Rd, Cambridge, CB2 8RU, United Kingdom; http://journals.cambridge.org. Illus., adv. Refereed. Vol. ends: Dec (No. 3). *Indexed:* A01, A22, A47, AbAn, BRI, E01, FR, IBSS, IIBP, MLA-IB, P02, RILM. *Bk. rev.:* Number and length vary. *Aud.:* Ga, Ac.

A multidisciplinary journal published by the African Studies Association, *ASR* aims to encourage scholarly debates across disciplines. It includes peer-reviewed articles by international scholars. The concerns of Africa and its diaspora are exposed from a discussion of sociological, political, and historical viewpoints. Each issue contains extensive book reviews and film reviews, commentaries, and a list of books received. A good resource for collection development, and a must-have for Africana collections, and academic and research libraries.

191. *African Vibes: where the world meets Africa.* [ISSN: 1932-1198] 2006. bi-m. USD 19.95; USD 25.95 combined subscription (print & online eds.); USD 3.95 newsstand/cover. African Vibes, PO Box 10203, Canooga Park, CA 91309. Adv. *Aud.:* Ga.

From fashion to sports, from physiological problems to arts and artistry, this magazine is a potpourri of everything, and aims to "enlighten the world about the African." Many articles focus on Africans in the United States and provide advice on such matters as medical, life, and disability insurance; homeownership; personal relationships; and health matters. Interviews with famous African personalities are also included. Recommended for public libraries. Available in print and online. URL: www.africanvibes.com

192. *Afrique Contemporaine: Afrique et developpement.* [ISSN: 0002-0478] 1962. q. EUR 65 domestic; EUR 65 Belgium; EUR 75 elsewhere. Agence Francaise de Developpement, 5 Rue Roland-Barthes, Paris, 75598 cedex 12, France. Illus., index, adv. Circ: 2000. *Indexed:* A22, IBSS, MLA-IB, PdeR. *Bk. rev.:* 95, 50-100 words. *Aud.:* Ac, Sa.

This French-language journal focuses on development, trends, and issues in politics and economics, and country-to-country matters, as well as international relations in contemporary Africa. It aims to communicate the analysis and opinions of researchers and various French and foreign specialists involved in the development of the African continent as a whole, with a view amounting to that of achieving sustainable development. Recently, each number has centered on various themes such as agricultural cooperation, and China and Brazil in Africa. Brief biographies and interviews are included. *Afrique Contemporaine* includes brief book annotations classed by country and topic. Recommended for academic and research collections.

193. *Afrique Magazine.* Former titles (until 1989): *Jeune Afrique Magazine;* (until 1986): *J A Magazine;* (until 1985): *Jeune Afrique Magazine.* [ISSN: 0998-9307] 1981. m. 10/yr. EUR 29. Afrique et Mediterranee International, 31 Rue Poussin, Paris, 75016, France; http://www.afriquemagazine.com/. Adv. Circ: 55000. *Bk. rev.:* Occasional. *Aud.:* Hs, Ga, Ac.

One of several glossy publications from Le Groupe Jeune Afrique, this is a French-language consumer magazine that is aimed at youthful, upwardly-mobile Africans and diasporic Africans. Coverage ranges from lifestyle articles and features on international figures to food, health, sports, fashion, travel, and music. This journal is mostly informational, but more serious subjects are treated. It is recommended for French and African Studies collections. Summaries of contents of the current issue are available on the magazine's web site.

194. *Azania: archaeological research in Africa.* [ISSN: 0067-270X] 1966. q. GBP 187 (print & online eds.). Ed(s): Peter Robertshaw, Kevin MacDonald. Taylor & Francis, 4 Park Sq, Milton Park, Abingdon, OX14 4RN, United Kingdom; subscriptions@tandf.co.uk; http://www.tandfonline.com. Illus., index, adv. Refereed. Reprint: PSC. *Indexed:* A01, A22, A47, ArtHuCI, E01, FR, IBSS. *Bk. rev.:* 10-12. *Aud.:* Ac, Sa.

"Azania" is an ancient name for East Africa. This journal of the British Institute in Eastern Africa has expanded its scope from pre-colonial history and archaeology of Eastern Africa to the exclusive focus of the archaeology of Africa past. Now called *Azania: Archaeological Research in Africa,* this title publishes articles on all aspects of archaeological research on the continent, regardless of period or area. It is published quarterly, and its peer-reviewed articles or briefer reports address fieldwork, new methodologies, and/or theoretical concerns, or provide a synthesis of key ideas. Articles are technical and accompanied by photos, graphs, and data. Papers may be in English or French, with abstracts in both languages. *Azania* is recommended for libraries with an interest in archaeology and Africana collections.

195. *C O D E S R I A Bulletin.* Formerly: *Africana Newsletter.* [ISSN: 0850-8712] 1987. q. Free to qualified personnel. Ed(s): Francis B Nyamnjoh. Council for the Development of Social Science Research in Africa, Avenue Cheikh, Anta Diop x Canal IV, BP 3304, Dakar, Senegal; codesria@ssonatel.senet.net. *Indexed:* IIBP. *Aud.:* Ac, Sa.

Based in Senegal, CODESRIA is an important pan-African research organization with a primary focus on the social sciences. The *Bulletin* aims to stimulate discussion, encourage cooperation among African researchers, facilitate an exchange of information on projects, and report on conferences and seminars. Short, accessible articles are grouped as "Debates" on a theme or topical issue, or alternatively as "Perspectives" on current concerns. The organization publishes several other journals including *Africa Development* (see above), the longest-standing Africa-based social science journal; *Afrika Zamani,* a journal of history; the *African Sociological Review* (see above); and the *African Journal of International Affairs.* Tables of contents, abstracts, and often the full text of articles are available at the CODESRIA web site. CODESRIA journals are part of the African Journals Online project.

196. *Cahiers d'Etudes Africaines.* [ISSN: 0008-0055] 1960. q. EUR 83 (Individuals, EUR 50). Ed(s): J L Amselle. College de France, Ecole des Hautes Etudes en Sciences Sociales (E H E S S), 131 Bd Saint-Michel, Paris, 75005, France; editions@ehess.fr; http://www.ehess.fr. Illus., adv. Sample. Microform: IDC. *Indexed:* A22, A47, FR, IBSS, IIBP, MLA-IB, P61, SSA. *Bk. rev.:* 9-14, 100-1,400 words. *Aud.:* Sa.

International and interdisciplinary, this important bilingual (French and English) journal publishes scholarly articles on Africa and its diaspora (the Caribbean, the Americas, and Europe). Over 50 years old, this journal focuses primarily on the social sciences, but it also features scholarship in history, popular culture, archaeology, communication, and literature. Possibly one or two articles of the five or six in each issue are in English. Each article has an abstract in either French or English. There are frequent thematic volumes with essays on a region or a problem or issue. Review essays, critical book reviews, and a list of publications received are included. For specialized audiences, larger academic collections, and those with an interest in Francophone Africa.

197. *Canadian Journal of African Studies.* Formerly (until 1967): *Bulletin of African Studies in Canada.* [ISSN: 0008-3968] 1963. 3x/yr. GBP 229 (print & online eds.). Ed(s): Roger Riendeau, Roger Riendeau. Routledge, 325 Chestnut St, Ste 800, Philadelphia, PA 19106; customerservice@taylorandfrancis.com; http://www.tandfonline.com. Illus. Sample. Refereed. *Indexed:* A22, AbAn, C45, CBCARef, IIBP, MLA-IB, PdeR, RILM, RRTA. *Bk. rev.:* 30-40, 500-1,000 words. *Aud.:* Ac, Sa.

Most articles in the bilingual journal of the Canadian Association of African Studies appear in English, unless the theme of an issue is a Francophone country. Articles include an abstract in French if the article is in English, and vice versa. Committed to the study and promotion of Africa in Canada, this journal is focused on anthropology, political economy, history, geography, and development, especially assessment of development strategies, all of which reflect a broad coverage of the social sciences and humanities. Articles, research notes, and book review essays are included in each issue. The extensive reviews and essays serve as a valuable resource for scholars and librarians to stay abreast of research, debates, and publications in the field of African Studies. Suitable for large academic libraries or collections with a regional interest.

198. *Country Reports.* 1971. q. Economist Intelligence Unit Ltd., 111 W 57th St, New York, NY 10019; newyork@eiu.com; http://www.eiu.com. Sample. Circ: 40000. *Aud.:* Ga, Ac, Sa.

Published by the Economist Intelligence Unit, this series of analytical reports aims to assist executive business decisions by providing timely and impartial analysis on worldwide market trends and business strategies for close to 200 countries. The quarterly reports monitor and analyze developments and trends in politics, policy, and economy. Placing recent events in context, the reports provide a two-year outlook for each country. Graphs and charts illustrate the economic trends and data. Subscriptions per country for print or web access include quarterly main reports and a country profile—an annual reference tool that analyzes political, infrastructural, and economic trends over the longer term. From the same group that publishes *The Economist* and *EIU ViewsWire, Country Reports* is a reliable, long-standing source of data and country intelligence. Formats are accessible, and information is timely, especially with the Internet access and updates. This is an expensive publication; however, specialized collections may want to consider reports on particular countries of interest rather than the entire set.

199. *Current Writing: text and reception in southern Africa.* [ISSN: 1013-929X] 1989. s-a. GBP 152 (print & online eds.). Ed(s): J U Jacobs. Routledge, 4 Park Sq, Milton Park, Abingdon, OX14 4RN, United Kingdom; subscriptions@tandf.co.uk; http://www.tandfonline.com. Illus., index. Refereed. Vol. ends: Oct. Reprint: PSC. *Indexed:* BRI, MLA-IB. *Bk. rev.:* 15-20, 300-1,200 words. *Aud.:* Ac, Sa.

Current Writing is the official journal of the Southern African Association for Commonwealth Literature and Languages. It includes essays on contemporary and republished texts in southern Africa and on the interpretation of world texts from a southern African perspective. Scholars from southern Africa are the primary contributors. The review section is an important part of the journal, in which new publications are evaluated. The journal is of interest to those studying the development in writing and literature in southern Africa. Writing style and content were greatly influenced by political and social changes in the region. This journal is suitable for comprehensive academic and special collections. Abstracts are available on the journal's web site. URL: http://currentwriting.ukzn.ac.za

200. *Drum: Africa's leading magazine beating to the pulse of the times.* [ISSN: 0419-7674] 1951. m. ZAR 349.13 domestic; ZAR 725.29 Namibia; ZAR 1219.61 Zimbabwe. Ed(s): Esmare Weideman. Media24 Ltd., Naspers Centre, 40 Heerengracht St, PO Box 1802, Cape Town, 8000, South Africa; http://www.media24.com. Illus., adv. Circ: 59664. *Indexed:* MLA-IB. *Bk. rev.:* Number and length vary. *Aud.:* Hs, Ga, Ac.

Drum (South Africa) is a long-running, popular, consumer-oriented magazine. It has been a unique vehicle for Black expression in South Africa since the 1950s. Sports heroes, models, political figures, and celebrities are featured on the cover of each weekly issue. Sections on children, women, and entertainment appear in most issues, in addition to regular columns that offer advice, horoscopes, puzzles, etc. It can be compared to both *People* and *The National Enquirer. Drum* reflects the multicultural, middle-class, youth-oriented "new" country that is South Africa. Highly recommended as a colorful and appealing popular source, which offers insight on the values and aspirations of South Africans.

201. *Eastern Africa Social Science Research Review.* [ISSN: 1027-1775] 1985. 2x/yr. USD 23 in Africa; USD 35 elsewhere. Ed(s): Mohamed Salih, Bahru Zewde. Organization for Social Science Research in Eastern Africa, PO Box 31971, Addis Ababa, Ethiopia; pub.ossrea@telecom.net.et; http://www.ossrea.net. Refereed. Circ: 500. *Indexed:* A22, C45, E01, IIBP, P61, SSA. *Bk. rev.:* Number and length vary. *Aud.:* Ac, Sa.

The Organization for Social Science Research in Eastern Africa (OSSREA), based in Ethiopia, publishes this biannual forum of articles on economic, political, social, and development issues of the countries and sub-regions within eastern and southern Africa. It is one of the major African-published journals. This title is focused on the social sciences, and its coverage includes discussion of policies, scholarly articles, book reviews, and shorter communications that are presumed to be of interest to development planners and policymakers, as well as academics. Recent issues contain substantial essays on such topics as children's, and feminism and gender budgeting. A consistent venue for African scholars, it is a good addition to libraries that support African Studies. There is online access to tables of contents through the African Journals OnLine program.

202. *English in Africa.* [ISSN: 0376-8902] 1974. 3x/yr. ZAR 270 (Individuals, ZAR 245; USD 74 foreign). Ed(s): Gareth Cornwell. Rhodes University, Institute for the Study of English in Africa, PO Box 94, Grahamstown, 6140, South Africa; isea@ru.ac.za; http://www.ru.ac.za/isea. Illus., index, adv. Refereed. Vol. ends: May/Oct (No. 2). *Indexed:* A01, A22, AmHI, BEL&L, BRI, IBSS, IIBP, MLA-IB. *Bk. rev.:* Number and length vary. *Aud.:* Ac, Sa.

A scholarly journal devoted to the study of African literature and English as a language of Africa, *English in Africa* is published by the Institute for the Study of English in Africa, a research institute within Rhodes University. Contributors are generally established writers or academics from South Africa, the United Kingdom, and the United States. *English in Africa* specializes in publishing previously unpublished or out-of-print primary material, including articles and letters by writers of Africa, as well as scholarly articles on African writing in English, especially African literature. The former editor described its range as: "Archival research; bibliographical work; charting emerging talent; looking afresh at well-known works; exploring the potential in exciting new writing." Most articles are historical or cultural studies rather than theoretical inquiries. Reviews, review articles, or discussions between writers regularly conclude each issue. More literary and broader in scope than *Current Writing* (see above), *English in Africa* is suitable for academic institutions with a strong emphasis in English, cultural studies, or African Studies. There are often thematic issues. Full-text articles are now available through several databases, so readers outside South Africa will become more familiar with this publication.

203. *History in Africa: an annual journal of method.* [ISSN: 0361-5413] 1974. a. GBP 128 (print & online eds.). Cambridge University Press, 32 Ave of the Americas, New York, NY 10013; information@cambridge.org; http://www.cambridge.org/us/. Illus., adv. Refereed. *Indexed:* A22, A47, E01, IBSS, IIBP, MLA-IB, RILM. *Aud.:* Ac, Sa.

One of two publications by the African Studies Association, this annual publication contains articles in all aspects of African history and culture. Historiography, historical methodology, and archival research and reports from within Africa make this a valuable resource for historians, researchers, and advanced graduate students. It is an important resource for history-teaching programs, and the essays often reflect new trends in African historical research. This is an essential journal for institutions that support African history programs, and is highly recommended as a basic journal for academic and Africana libraries.

204. *International Journal of African Historical Studies.* Formerly (until 1972): *African Historical Studies.* [ISSN: 0361-7882] 1968. 3x/yr. USD 145 (Individuals, USD 65). Ed(s): Michael DiBlasi. Boston University, African Studies Center, 270 Bay State Rd, Boston, MA 02215; ascpub@bu.edu; http://www.bu.edu/africa. Illus., index. Vol. ends: No. 3. *Indexed:* A01, A22, A47, ABS&EES, AbAn, AmHI, ArtHuCI, BRI, FR, IBSS, IIBP, MLA-IB, P02. *Bk. rev.:* 65-80, 500-800 words. *Aud.:* Ac, Sa.

Published at the African Studies Center at Boston University, this scholarly periodical covers all aspects of African history with a "focus on the study of the African past" in Africa and the African diaspora. Each issue contains several substantial articles. Recent topics covered are human rights and the African airwaves; the changing function of traditional dance in Zulu society; and Africans and the growing uranium trade. The extensive book review section in each issue and the frequent review essays make this journal a significant collection-development tool. Recommended for academic collections and large public libraries. URL: www.bu.edu/africa/publications/ijahs/current/index.html

205. *Islamic Africa Journal.* Formerly (until 2010): *Sudanic Africa.* [ISSN: 2154-0993] 1995. q. USD 125. Northwestern University Press, 629 Noyes St, Evanston, IL 60208; nupress@northwestern.edu; http://www.nupress.northwestern.edu. Index. Refereed. Circ: 250. *Aud.:* Ac, Sa.

This online journal promotes the interaction between scholars of Islam and Africa across historical periods. Published twice a year, it incorporates its previous title *Sudanic Africa.* Focused on the social sciences and the humanities, it welcomes discourse on Islam and Muslim life in Africa. Recommended for academic libraries with an interest in Islam.

206. *Jeune Afrique.* Former titles (until 2006): *L' Intelligent;* (until 2000): *Jeune Afrique.* [ISSN: 1950-1285] 1960. w. 44/yr. EUR 124 domestic; EUR 154 in Europe; EUR 174 in North Africa. Ed(s): Bechir Ben Yahmed. Groupe Jeune Afrique, 57 bis, Rue d'Auteuil, Paris, 75016, France; redaction@jeuneafrique.com; http://www.groupeja.com. Illus., adv. Circ: 100000. Microform: PQC. *Indexed:* A22, MLA-IB, PdeR. *Aud.:* Ga, Ac, Sa.

Jeune Afrique is the principal French-language newsweekly on Africa. Glossy, colorful, and published in Paris with a format similar to U.S. weekly newsmagazines, it has very good coverage of North Africa and former Francophone sub-Saharan African countries. It reports on on all the countries of the continent and discusses Africa's relationship with other parts of the world. Each issue has news and interpretative and editorial commentary on Africa. It includes feature articles on international, political, cultural, and economic developments. Recommended for collections with Francophone-area interest, and for general academic collections. URL: www.jeuneafrique.com

207. *Journal of African Cultural Studies.* Formerly (until 1998): *African Languages and Cultures.* [ISSN: 1369-6815] 1988. s-a. GBP 260 (print & online eds.). Ed(s): Carli Coetzee. Routledge, 4 Park Sq, Milton Park, Abingdon, OX14 4RN, United Kingdom; subscriptions@tandf.co.uk; http://www.tandfonline.com. Illus., index, adv. Sample. Refereed. Vol. ends: Dec. Reprint: PSC. *Indexed:* A01, A22, A47, AbAn, AmHI, ArtHuCI, E01, IBSS, IIBP, MLA-IB, P61, RILM, SSA. *Aud.:* Ac, Sa.

Editorially based at the School of Oriental and African Studies, London, *JACS* has a special commitment to African scholarship. With a focus on African culture, articles address literature (particularly African-language literature), performance, art, music, and media studies. Meanwhile, the articles still have a continuing interest in languages of Africa as channels for the expression of culture. A recent thematic issue was entitled "New Media entrepreneurs and the changing styles of public communication in Africa." International contributors provide scholarly content. Recommended for academic and general libraries with an interest in Africana, cultural studies, literature, and linguistics.

208. *Journal of African Economies.* [ISSN: 0963-8024] 1992. 5x/yr. EUR 645. Ed(s): Marcel Fafchamps. Oxford University Press, Great Clarendon St, Oxford, OX2 6DP, United Kingdom; enquiry@oup.co.uk; http://www.oxfordjournals.org/. Illus., adv. Sample. Refereed. Reprint: PSC. *Indexed:* A22, ABIn, C45, E01, EconLit, IBSS, IIBP, JEL, RRTA. *Bk. rev.:* 1-5, 800-1,200 words. *Aud.:* Ac, Sa.

This title is focused on an audience beyond academia. Valuable to consultants, policymakers, traders, financiers, development agents, and aid workers, this scholarly journal offers "rigorous economic analysis, focused entirely on Africa, for Africans and anyone interested in the continent." Tables, graphs, and data often accompany articles that cover theories on African fiscal and monetary policies, trade, agricultural labor, and production. Just a sample of the topics that recent issues offer are: the impact of European settlement within French west Africa; the determinants and macroeconomic impact of remittances in sub-Saharan Africa; and income shocks and corruption in Africa. Book reviews and annotated listings of recent working papers in developmental economics are featured in some issues. Online access is available to subscribers, and the site also offers the option to purchase individual articles for a fee. Free or reduced-cost online access is offered to institutions in developing countries. Highly recommended for academic libraries and economics collections. URL: http://jae.oxfordjournals.org

209. *The Journal of African History.* [ISSN: 0021-8537] 1960. 3x/yr. GBP 255. Ed(s): Justin Willis, Cheikh A Babou. Cambridge University Press, The Edinburgh Bldg, Shaftesbury Rd, Cambridge, CB2 8RU, United Kingdom; journals@cambridge.org; http://www.cambridge.org/uk. Illus., index, adv. Sample. Refereed. Circ: 2000. Microform: PQC. Reprint: PSC. *Indexed:* A01, A22, A47, AbAn, AmHI, ArtHuCI, BRI, E01, FR, IBSS, IIBP, MLA-IB, NumL, P02, P61, RILM, SSA. *Bk. rev.:* 20-35, 500-1,400 words. *Aud.:* Ac, Sa.

With an increasing emphasis on economic, cultural, and social history, articles in this excellent journal cover all aspects and periods of African history, from the late Stone Age to the present. This journal is published three times a year, and each issue includes five or six long scholarly research articles. Essay topics include: "Korle and the mosquito: histories and memories of the anti-malaria campaign in Accra, 1942–45"; and "A chronicle of a coup foretold: Valentine Musakanya and the 1980 coup attempt in Zambia." The book review section serves as a good resource for collection development. Online access is available to subscribers. A searchable digital archive with all the articles published from 1960 to 1996 has recently become available from the publishers. Tables of contents and abstracts are available free on this journal's web site. Highly recommended for collections that support the study of African history. For a similar journal in quality and scope, see *International Journal of African Historical Studies* (above in this section).

210. *Journal of African Law.* [ISSN: 0021-8553] 1956. s-a. GBP 156. Ed(s): Fareda Banda, Chaloka Beyani. Cambridge University Press, The Edinburgh Bldg, Shaftesbury Rd, Cambridge, CB2 8RU, United Kingdom; journals@cambridge.org; http://www.cambridge.org/uk. Adv. Circ: 500. Microform: WSH; PMC. Reprint: PSC; WSH. *Indexed:* A01, A22, A47, BRI, CLI, E01, IBSS, IIBP, L14, MLA-IB, RiskAb. *Bk. rev.:* Number and length vary. *Aud.:* Ga, Ac, Sa.

For more than 50 years, the *Journal of African Law* has addressed the laws and legal issues of the entire sub-Saharan continent. Published by Cambridge University Press for the School of Oriental and African Studies, University of London, this journal highlights comparative legal issues and those of international significance. A separate section covers recent legislation, case law, law reform proposals, and international developments that affect Africa. The scope includes criminal law, family law, human rights, and nationality and constitutional law. Articles are on such topics as law and development in Nigeria; corporate criminal liability in South Africa; and the African law of coups and the situation in Eritrea. This journal is geared toward development workers and policymakers, as well as academics and professional lawyers, with

a focus on African institutions—laws, enforcement mechanisms, and organizations—so the better understanding of the institutions and their histories will promote development on the continent. An good choice for law and Africana collections.

211. *Journal of Asian and African Studies.* [ISSN: 0021-9096] 1965. bi-m. USD 1000. Ed(s): Nigel C Gibson. Sage Publications Ltd., 1 Oliver's Yard, 55 City Rd, London, EC1Y 1SP, United Kingdom; info@sagepub.co.uk; http://www.uk.sagepub.com. Sample. Refereed. Reprint: PSC. *Indexed:* A01, A22, A47, AbAn, BAS, BRI, E01, FR, IBSS, IIBP, MLA-IB, P02, P61, RILM, RiskAb, SSA. *Bk. rev.:* 2-3. *Aud.:* Ac, Sa.

This peer-reviewed journal looks at new nations of Asia and Africa in the context of such topics as development and change, technology and communication, globalization, economics, and a host of other topics. Recent issues reflect the diversity of coverage, such as perceptions of social change in Nepal; colonial hangover in the case of the CFA; and "Is there a distinct style of Asian democracy?" Each issue usually includes book reviews; special issues are often published around certain themes. The journal aims to present "cutting-edge issues and debates" around the dynamics of global change and development in Asia and Africa. Available online to subscribers, this journal is suitable for academic collections.

212. *Journal of Contemporary African Studies.* [ISSN: 0258-9001] 1981. q. GBP 750 (print & online eds.). Ed(s): Fred Hendricks. Routledge, 4 Park Sq, Milton Park, Abingdon, OX14 4RN, United Kingdom; subscriptions@tandf.co.uk; http://www.tandfonline.com. Illus., adv. Sample. Refereed. Vol. ends: No. 2. Reprint: PSC. *Indexed:* A01, A22, ASSIA, C45, E01, IBSS, IIBP, MLA-IB, P61, SSA. *Bk. rev.:* 5-15, 500-1,000 words. *Aud.:* Ac, Sa.

Interdisciplinary, with a focus on developments and change in Africa, this South African journal (now published by Routledge) aims to provide a scholarly understanding of contemporary Africa through research and writing in the social sciences and humanities. The journal includes sociology, urban studies, modern history, education, literature, and development studies; and there is wide scope to its research. While the editors are based in South Africa, primarily at Rhodes University, the scope is the whole sub-Saharan continent, and the contributors are wide-ranging. Special thematic issues are often published; the most recent one focused on China's rise in Africa. Recent essays have covered more women in the Tanzanian legislature, and the southern Cameroons and minority rights. Book reviews appear in each issue. This is an important selection for contemporary African Studies, and recommended for academic collections and those with strong interest in Africa.

213. *Journal of Eastern African Studies.* [ISSN: 1753-1055] 2007. q. GBP 617 (print & online eds.). Ed(s): Jason Mosley. Routledge, 4 Park Sq, Milton Park, Abingdon, OX14 4RN, United Kingdom; subscriptions@tandf.co.uk; http://www.tandfonline.com. Adv. Sample. Reprint: PSC. *Indexed:* A22, C45, E01, IBSS, IIBP, P61, RRTA, SSA. *Aud.:* Ac, Sa.

Based in Kenya, The British Institute in Eastern Africa exists to "promote research into the archaeology, history, linguistics[,] and anthropology of Eastern Africa." This scholarly new publication from the Institute is published by Routledge. It features broad coverage in the humanities and the social sciences, and especially encourages interdisciplinary analysis and comparative perspectives, as well as research with significant theoretical or methodological approaches. The Institute also produces the annual journal *Azania* (see above), which is focused more specifically on the archaeology and history of East Africa. Recommended for academic libraries.

214. *Journal of Modern African Studies.* [ISSN: 0022-278X] 1963. q. GBP 288. Ed(s): Paul Nugent, Leonardo A Villalon. Cambridge University Press, The Edinburgh Bldg, Shaftesbury Rd, Cambridge, CB2 8RU, United Kingdom; journals@cambridge.org; http://www.cambridge.org/uk. Illus., index, adv. Sample. Refereed. Circ: 1600. Vol. ends: Dec. Microform: PQC. Reprint: PSC. *Indexed:* A01, A22, ABIn, AbAn, AmHI, BAS, BRI, C45, E01, IBSS, IIBP, MLA-IB, NumL, P02, P61, RRTA, RiskAb, SSA. *Bk. rev.:* 0-25, 500-2,000 words. *Aud.:* Ac, Sa.

Intended for academics, students, and practitioners as well as general readers, this scholarly but accessible journal aims to present fair and balanced views of "controversial issues." It largely focuses on contemporary Africa, with an emphasis on politics, economics, societies, and international relations. Articles are written by specialists and scholars in the field. Recent articles include such topics as the moral debates over economy, war, and state in the Sudan; local election observers in Tanzania; and herding contracts in the far northern region of Cameroon. Shorter pieces on literature, culture, and aspects of social history also appear. Critical book reviews are also included. Available electronically to subscribers at the web site; here, guests can view abstracts of articles. Intended and suitable for students, academics, and general readers, it is highly recommended for academic libraries and general collections.

215. The Journal of North African Studies. Formerly (until 19??): *Morocco.* [ISSN: 1362-9387] 1996. 5x/yr. GBP 424 (print & online eds.). Ed(s): George Joffe, John P Entelis. Routledge, 4 Park Sq, Milton Park, Abingdon, OX14 4RN, United Kingdom; subscriptions@tandf.co.uk; http://www.tandfonline.com. Adv. Sample. Refereed. Reprint: PSC. *Indexed:* A22, AmHI, E01, IBSS, IIBP, MLA-IB, P61, SSA. *Bk. rev.:* Number and length vary. *Aud.:* Ac, Sa.

This journal is one of a handful that attempt to link sub-Saharan Africa and the Middle East, a region rarely treated as coherent. It serves as a forum for scholars of and from North Africa. The peer-reviewed articles cover country-based and regional themes in historical topics and in the social sciences. There are five to eight articles per issue, featuring both contemporary analysis and historical treatments, as well as book reviews. The book reviews serve as a useful collection development tool. Special issues (usually available as books) appear regularly. This journal is a valuable addition to scholarship of Africa. Recommended for academic and special libraries. Members of the American Institute of Maghrib Studies receive a subscription as part of their membership.

216. Journal of Religion in Africa. Incorporates (1971-1975): *African Religious Research.* [ISSN: 0022-4200] 1967. q. EUR 317. Ed(s): Adeline Masquelier. Brill, PO Box 9000, Leiden, 2300 PA, Netherlands; cs@brill.nl; http://www.brill.nl. Illus., adv. Refereed. Vol. ends: No. 4. Reprint: PSC. *Indexed:* A01, A22, A47, AmHI, ArtHuCI, E01, FR, IBSS, IIBP, MLA-IB, R&TA, RILM. *Bk. rev.:* 4-6, 750+ words. *Aud.:* Ac, Sa.

This journal is one of the leading international journals in religious studies. It focuses on religious traditions in all forms and on the history of religion and ritual within the African continent, particularly in sub-Saharan Africa. It is open to every methodology, and scholars from a variety of disciplines and countries contribute to each issue, which is frequently on a particular topic introduced by editorial comment. The journal occasionally publishes religious texts in their original African language. Book reviews and longer review articles are also included. As one of the few English-language journals with a focus on religion in Africa, it is important for religious studies, but is also of interest to a humanities and social science readership. For academic and larger collections.

217. Journal of Southern African Studies. [ISSN: 0305-7070] 1974. q. GBP 635 (print & online eds.). Routledge, 4 Park Sq, Milton Park, Abingdon, OX14 4RN, United Kingdom; subscriptions@tandf.co.uk; http://www.tandfonline.com. Illus., adv. Sample. Refereed. Microform: PQC. Reprint: PSC. *Indexed:* A01, A22, A47, AbAn, AmHI, C45, E01, IBSS, IIBP, IndVet, MLA-IB, P02, P61, RILM, RRTA, SSA. *Bk. rev.:* 4-6, 200-1,000 words. *Aud.:* Ac, Sa.

This international journal features academic scholarship that presents new perspectives from various disciplines in the social sciences and humanities. New theoretical approaches and scholarly inquiry are applied to issues and social problems in the region of southern Africa. Issues often include six to ten extensive articles, review essays, and book reviews. The range of topics is broad: recent issues contain articles on Angola's citizenship island and colonialism in Mozambique; and why the university of Botswana, Lesotho, and Swaziland failed. One or two of each year's four issues are devoted to broad themes such as "Religious biography." Highly recommended for academic and specialized collections.

218. Journal of Sustainable Development in Africa. [ISSN: 1520-5509] 1999. q. Free. Ed(s): Valentine Udoh James. Clarion University, 840 Wood St, Clarion, PA 16214; info@clarion.edu; http://www.clarion.edu. *Indexed:* C45. *Bk. rev.:* 2 per issue. *Aud.:* Ac, Sa.

The sustainability in African development is the focus of this online refereed journal. Four to five articles and a book review in each issue bring a multidisciplinary perspective to the economic, sociopolitical, cultural, and environmental issues that surround sustainable development and governance on the continent. It is one of the few journals that aim to "address Africa's sustainability issues from multidisciplinary and interdisciplinary perspectives." Articles cover both broad and local topics. Slightly behind in publication, this journal is recommended for larger collections. URL: www.jsd-africa.com

219. The Journal of the Middle East and Africa. [ISSN: 2152-0844] 2010. s-a. GBP 150 (print & online eds.). Ed(s): J Peter Pham. Taylor & Francis Inc., 325 Chestnut St, Ste 800, Philadelphia, PA 19106; customerservice@taylorandfrancis.com; http://www.tandfonline.com. Adv. Sample. *Indexed:* A01. *Aud.:* Ga, Ac, Sa.

Serving as the official journal of the Association for the Study of the Middle East and Africa, this journal aims at "exploring the historic social, economic, and political links between these two regions, as well as the modern challenges they face." Interdisciplinary in nature, it is one of the few journals that provide combined inclusion of these regions. This title has approximately six to eight articles per issue; and commentaries and book reviews are included. A most recent special issue focused on "North African revolutions." Still a relatively new publication, it is a journal that should not be overlooked. Of interest to academic libraries with an interest in this region.

220. The Maghreb Review. [ISSN: 0309-457X] 1976. q. GBP 295. Ed(s): Mohamed Ben Madani. Maghreb Review, 45 Burton St, London, WC1H 9AL, United Kingdom. Illus. Refereed. *Indexed:* A22, IBSS, MLA-IB. *Bk. rev.:* 4-6, 2,000-4,000 words. *Aud.:* Ac, Sa.

Independent, interdisciplinary, and bilingual, this journal is one of the oldest English/French publications that are devoted to the study of North Africa and Islamic culture and religion. Its specific focus is the region of the Maghreb: Algeria, Tunisia, Libya, Morocco, and Mauritania. International scholars contribute articles on archaeology, anthropology, politics, history, religion, and literature—the spectrum of the social sciences and humanities—as they relate to the Berber, Arab, and Islamic heritage of this crossroads region and its interaction with sub-Saharan Africa, the Mediterranean, and the Middle East. Six to eight articles appear in each issue, some in both languages and some with translated abstracts. There are frequent special issues on topics such as health in the Maghreb, or the Middle East and North Africa. Abstracts of relevant theses or dissertations and conference papers are featured. It is available online via subscription. Recommended for larger collections with an interest in North Africa.

221. Matatu: journal for African culture and society. [ISSN: 0932-9714] 1987. s-a. Ed(s): Holger G Ehling. Editions Rodopi B.V., Tijnmuiden 7, Amsterdam, 1046 AK, Netherlands; orders-queries@rodopi.nl; http://www.rodopi.nl. Illus., adv. Refereed. *Indexed:* A01, A22, IIBP, MLA-IB, P61. *Aud.:* Ga, Ac, Sa.

Matatu, named for the crowded mini-buses used as public transport in East Africa, is a semi-annual refereed journal that is devoted to African literatures and societies that "promote interdisciplinary dialogue between literary and cultural studies, historiography, the social sciences[,] and cultural anthropology." The focus is on African (including Afro-Caribbean) culture and literature, providing a forum for critical debates and exploration of African modernities. While *Matatu* is a journal, each volume is on a specific theme and is priced to be purchased separately. Articles, interviews, and autobiographical vignettes are just a few of the materials included in this journal. Recent issues have dealt with African culture and literature; Nigerian literature and culture; and spheres public and private, reflective of western genres in African literature. Considering Africa in the global context, this journal is a excellent addition to the arts and cultural studies in academic libraries.

222. New African. Former titles (until 1978): *New African Development;* (until 1977): *African Development.* [ISSN: 0142-9345] 1966. 11x/yr. GBP 40 domestic; EUR 80 foreign. Ed(s): Baffour Ankomah. I C Publications Ltd., 7 Coldbath Sq, London, EC1R 4LQ, United Kingdom; icpubs@africasia.com; http://www.africasia.com/. Illus., adv. Sample. Microform: PQC. *Indexed:* A01, A22, B02, BRI, IIBP, MLA-IB. *Aud.:* Hs, Ga, Ac.

A glossy consumer newsmagazine from the same publisher as that of *African Business* (see above), *New African* covers the entire spectrum of contemporary African life: political reporting, economic and financial analysis, and articles on culture and social affairs. Each issue includes more than one cover story that deals with a major social or political issue or personality. Many of the articles are on issues that are scandalous in nature. The scope is pan-African and related to the diaspora, although most features focus on sub-Saharan Africa. Each issue has a section called "Around Africa," which reports on news from specific countries and presents longer special reports on a featured country. The online version offers summaries of the cover stories and the table of contents of issues, as well as text of major special reports. The same publisher releases the *New African Yearbook* with facts and figures on each of the 53 countries. As one of the oldest monthly magazines, *New African* is recommended for collections with an interest in Africa.

223. *Newswatch: Nigeria's weekly newsmagazine.* [ISSN: 0189-8892] 1985. w. NGN 70 per issue. Ed(s): Dan Ochima Agbese. Newswatch Communications Ltd., Oregun, 3 Billingsway, PMB 21499, Ikeja, Nigeria. Illus., index, adv. Circ: 150084. *Aud.:* Hs, Ga, Ac.

This Nigerian newsmagazine is Africa's largest-selling weekly outside of South Africa. It includes politically-oriented news, primarily about Nigeria, but also African and international news. Regular articles cover science, technology, politics, business and finance, the stock market, arts and society, and environmental reports. Cheeky, scandalous, and critical of the government, it has at times been banned in Nigeria. This important, critical, risk-taking newsmagazine is recommended for all audiences.

224. *Nka: journal of contemporary African art.* [ISSN: 1075-7163] 1994. s-a. USD 160. Duke University Press, 905 W Main St, Ste 18 B, PO Box 90660, Durham, NC 27701; dukepress@duke.edu; http://www.dukeupress.edu. Illus. Refereed. Reprint: PSC. *Indexed:* A07, A51, IIBP. *Bk. rev.:* Number and length vary. *Aud.:* Ga, Ac, Sa.

Published in conjunction with the Africana Studies and Research Center at Cornell, this beautifully produced tri-annual journal covers the diaspora as well as the arts from film to poetry to sculpture. The editors are art critics and curators who aim to make "significant contributions to the intellectual dialogue on world art and [to] the discourse on internationalism and multiculturalism in the arts." They also aim to bring an awareness of contemporary African and diasporic art and culture to the world. A good choice for both public and academic libraries. Tables of contents are available at www.nkajournal.org. Slightly delayed in publication.

225. *Philosophia Africana: analysis of philosophy and issues in Africa and the Black Diaspora.* Former titles (until 2001): *African Philosophy;* (until 1998): *S A P I N A Newsletter (Society for African Philosophy in North America).* [ISSN: 1539-8250] s-a. USD 590 (Individuals, USD 205). Ed(s): Kibujjo m Kalumba. Ball State University, Department of Philosophy and Religious Studies, 2000 W University Ave, NQ 211, Muncie, IN 47306; http://www.bsu.edu/philosophy/. Index, adv. Refereed. *Indexed:* A01, A22, AmHI, ArtHuCI, BRI, E01, IIBP, IPB, MLA-IB. *Bk. rev.:* Number and length vary. *Aud.:* Ac, Sa.

This academic journal publishes "philosophical or philosophically interdisciplinary works that explore pluralistic experiences of Africa and the Black Diaspora[,] from both universal and comparative points of view." Articles also may represent original or critical interpretations of creative and artistic works that are relevant to Africa and its diaspora. Book reviews and occasional conference reports are included. Of interest to academic libraries that support philosophy programs, and also to those with African Studies collections. Slightly behind in publication.

226. *Politique Africaine.* [ISSN: 0244-7827] 1981. q. EUR 75 domestic; EUR 85 in Europe; EUR 85 in Africa. Ed(s): Richard Banegas. Editions Karthala, 22-24 Boulevard Arago, Paris, 75013, France; karthala@orange.fr; http://www.karthala.com. Illus., adv. Refereed. Circ: 3500. *Indexed:* A22, FR, IBSS, MLA-IB, RILM. *Bk. rev.:* 20-25, 50-200 words. *Aud.:* Ac, Sa.

Published in France, this quarterly political science journal includes articles that usually relate to a specific theme, or focus on a particular country. The scope is really the entire African continent, especially sub-Saharan Africa. Apart from the thematic articles, the remainder of each issue includes briefer articles, speeches, and recent political developments. It also includes major meeting and conference announcements, book reviews, and lists of books received. Tables of contents and abstracts in English are available online. Older issues, generally after five years, have the full text of the articles available for free in pdf format, while newer issues have abstracts only for major articles. Recommended for larger collections and those with Francophonic interests. URL: www.politique-africaine.com

227. *Presence Africaine: revue culturelle du monde noir.* [ISSN: 0032-7638] 1947. s-a. EUR 58. Societe Africaine de Culture, 25 bis rue des Ecoles, Paris, 75005, France. Illus. Refereed. Circ: 3000 Controlled. *Indexed:* A22, AmHI, IBSS, MLA-IB, RILM. *Bk. rev.:* Number and length vary. *Aud.:* Ga, Ac, Sa.

Presence Africaine has a long, illustrious history, and remains the most influential French-language journal on Africa. It was founded in 1947 by Alioune Diop, a Senegalese intellectual and seminal figure in the discourse on Africa. Its early years coincided with the struggles against colonialism as well as the development of the "Negritude" movement. *PA* was the leading journal of anticolonial intellectuals in France and Africa, and a major publisher of African writers. Now bilingual (in French and English), *PA* remains a leading cultural journal of the African diaspora, and is indispensable for academic collections, especially those that support African Studies and literature. Issues feature critical and historical articles, book reviews and discussions, and creative writing. This journal remains important for all libraries with serious interest in Africa.

228. *Research in African Literatures.* [ISSN: 0034-5210] 1970. q. USD 199.50 (print & online eds.). Ed(s): Ruthmarie H Mitsch, Kwaku Larbi Korang. Indiana University Press, 601 N Morton St, Bloomington, IN 47404; journals@indiana.edu; http://iupress.indiana.edu. Illus., index, adv. Sample. Refereed. Circ: 650. Microform: PQC. Reprint: PSC. *Indexed:* A01, A22, AbAn, AmHI, ArtHuCI, BEL&L, BRI, E01, ENW, F01, FR, IBSS, IIBP, MLA-IB, P02, RILM. *Bk. rev.:* 5-21, 1,000-2,000 words. *Aud.:* Ac, Sa.

An essential source for scholarly study of the literatures of Africa, *RAL* includes scholarly essays; extensive bibliographies; and long reviews on all aspects of oral and written literatures, music, film, and theater of Africa. Articles are in English; but literatures in English, French, or African languages are included. The scope extends to the literature and arts of the Black diaspora as well. Each issue contains up to 20 contributions, including discussions of short and long fiction, poetry, drama, important new writers, music, film, and theater, as well as literary developments. Book reviews, and often review essays, are featured. Information is included on African publishing, and there are announcements of importance to Africanists. Each year, one to two special issues or groupings of articles explore themes. This journal is a standard and highly recommended source for academic and large public libraries, and for anyone interested in African literature and literary criticism.

229. *Review of African Political Economy.* [ISSN: 0305-6244] 1974. q. GBP 535 (print & online eds.). Routledge, 4 Park Sq, Milton Park, Abingdon, OX14 4RN, United Kingdom; subscriptions@tandf.co.uk; http://www.tandfonline.com. Illus., adv. Sample. Refereed. Reprint: PSC. *Indexed:* A22, ABIn, AbAn, B01, C45, E01, EconLit, IBSS, IIBP, JEL, MLA-IB, P61, RiskAb, SSA. *Bk. rev.:* 4-7, 900-3,000 words. *Aud.:* Ac, Sa.

This long-established refereed journal has a particular focus on inequality, exploitation, and oppression. The editorial policy of *ROAPE* proudly reaffirms its definite political stance and an agenda that includes addressing globalized capitalism; U.S. militarism; patterns of social reproduction; state failures and conflict; and resistance and solidarity. In short, the journal provides a leftist analysis of political economy in Africa. Each themed issue begins with an editorial, and contains five to nine articles. Shorter "Briefings" on news and informative topical articles are also included. Authors are also solicited for "Debates," which are short articles with a position on a controversial topic, and which engage with a previous piece or invite response. Book reviews and announcements are also featured. The web site provides announcements and abstracts of articles from current and past issues. Highly recommended for academic and special audiences.

230. *Transition: an international review.* Former titles (until 1977): *Ch'indaba;* (until no.50, 1975): *Transition.* [ISSN: 0041-1191] 1961. 3x/yr. USD 156.50 (print & online eds.). Ed(s): Tommie Shelby. Indiana University Press, 601 N Morton St, Bloomington, IN 47404; iupress@indiana.edu; http://iupress.indiana.edu. Illus., adv. Sample. Circ: 1100 Paid and controlled. Vol. ends: Aug. *Indexed:* A22, ABS&EES, AmHI, BRI, E01, IIBP, MLA-IB. *Bk. rev.:* 2-3. *Aud.:* Ga, Ac, Sa.

Originally published in Uganda, *Transition* served as a forum for intellectual debate from the time of decolonization until 1976. Brought back as a new series by Henry Louis Gates in 1991, this journal takes a critical look at culture, cultural icons, literature, visual imagery, and the arts. In Gates's words, it aims to be a "clearing house for the freshest, most compelling, most curious ideas about race—indeed, about what it means to be human—today." After some interruptions in recent years, the publication is back on track. The scope of *Transition* is not just Africa but the entire post-colonial world, with a multicultural perspective; it bills itself as "an international review of politics, culture, and ethnicity from Beijing to Bujumbura." It is led by highly respected scholars. Leading intellectuals and literati serve as board members and as contributors. The essays are clearly written, provocative, and engaging. Worthy of notice are the striking illustrations and photographs. A venue for cultural criticism, this journal is very highly recommended for both general and academic institutions.

231. *Ufahamu (Online): journal of African studies.* Formerly (until 2009): *Ufahamu (Print).* [ISSN: 2150-5802] 1970. s-a. Free. Ed(s): Kim Foulds, Amy Pojar. University of California, Digital Library - eScholarship, http://www.escholarship.org. Illus., adv. Sample. *Indexed:* A22, IBSS, IIBP, MLA-IB. *Bk. rev.:* 1-2, 1,000-2,500 words. *Aud.:* Ga, Ac.

From the Swahili word meaning "understanding, comprehension[,] or being and remaining aware," *Ufahamu* is published by the African Activist Association, a graduate student organization at the University of California at Los Angeles. *Ufahamu* presents articles from established writers and academics as well as graduate students and nonacademic researchers. Founded as a journal of opinion on social issues, it continues to provide an interdisciplinary forum for those whose approach is both scholarly and activist. It includes articles on history, politics, economics, sociology, anthropology, law, and planning and development, as well as literature and the arts in the African continent and diaspora. Creative writing is occasionally included. Addressing an audience of both scholars and general readers, it is recommended for academic institutions and larger general libraries. Today, *Ufahamu* is freely available online. URL: http://repositories.cdlib.org/international/asc/ufahamu

■ AFRICAN AMERICAN

See also Africa; and Ethnic Interests sections.

Carol A. Rudisell, Librarian, Reference Dept., University of Delaware Library, Newark, DE 19717-5267; rudisell@udel.edu

Introduction

African American periodicals have a long history, dating back to 1827 when Russwurm and Cornish issued *Freedom's Journal,* the first weekly edited by and for African Americans. "We wish to plead our own cause . . . [T]oo long have others spoken for us," the publishers stated in their first editorial. The desire to set the record straight, to provide an authentic voice, and to define and interpret one's own reality remains a goal of contemporary African American publications.

Titles in this section fall primarily into two categories: popular magazines that target African American audiences, and scholarly journals in the interdisciplinary field of African American Studies. Scholars and laypersons alike use both types of publications. For example, university professors have introduced the scholarly analysis of hip-hop culture into the curriculum, so hip-hop magazines have become valuable source material. When selecting periodicals, librarians should consider the interconnectedness of scholarly and popular publications and analyze the informational content that each provides.

POPULAR MAGAZINES.

Just as nineteenth-century journals reflected a multiplicity of concerns ranging from literacy, to spiritual growth, to abolition, contemporary magazines also convey the diverse interests of today's African American "community," which is anything but a monolithic bloc. African American popular magazines cover news and opinion, fashion, lifestyle, personal finance and business management, popular history and culture, religion, and music. There are "aspirational" or lifestyle magazines targeted to middle-class and upper-middle-class readers; there are also hip-hop magazines designed for urban youth, gospel magazines directed at African American Christians, and many more general publications.

Despite the diversity of the publications, readers will find similar storylines appearing in many of them. Writings reflect a continued concern for social justice in black communities throughout the world. Most recently there has been much written on the murder of Trayvon Martin, an unarmed African American Florida teen who was killed by a neighborhood watch captain. Perhaps the most prevalent storyline encountered in recent years concerns the presidency of Barack Obama and the significance of his election to the African American community. The continued excitement, joy, and pride brought on by the election of America's first black president have been chronicled in each African American magazine, regardless of the publication's scope. In fact, stories about the Obamas have driven the sales of mainstream magazines as well, and, in the words of Janice Min, editor of *Us Weekly,* led to "the rise of politics as an entertainment theme." Academic publications have analyzed the economic and social impact of Obama Administration policies on African American populations, and scholars have interrogated the concept of a "postracial America."

Recent surveys show that African American and ethnic communities seek out media that cover their cultural and political concerns. As mainstream media have struggled to retain their audiences, ethnic media have continued to pick up new readers and viewers. Despite this strong interest, the downturn in the economy, along with declining advertising revenues, has made it difficult for both popular magazines and scholarly journals to stay afloat. *Vibe,* a leading popular African American magazine, had ceased publication for about a year until it and its sister publication *Uptown* were purchased by a media group that is now headed by basketball giant and business entrepreneur Earvin "Magic" Johnson. To strengthen their brand, publishers have expanded their presence on the web and developed apps for mobile phones, tablets, and e-readers, technologies that are being enthusiastically adopted by African American readers. Some publishers have permitted Google to digitize their back files. *Black Enterprise, Crisis, Ebony, Jet,* and *Vibe* back files are now accessible at books.google.com, as are Johnson Publishing Company's older titles, *Black World* and *Negro Digest.* African American magazines have also embraced social media, especially Facebook, Twitter, and YouTube, as a way of strengthening their brand. Publishers have adopted various cost-cutting measures, so readers may experience fewer issues per volume, smaller page counts, less expensive paper, online access only, or increased subscription prices. Several publishers are seriously behind in their publication schedules, such as *African American Legacy. Homes of Color* appears to have ceased, and the *Black Collegian,* while electing to retain its web site, changed the title of its print publication to *Diversity Employers.* New to this section is *Black EOE Journal,* a career and business magazine. Magazines that are local or regional in scope have not been included unless they have attained a national readership. Librarians seeking to learn of local or regional titles should consult *Ulrich's Periodicals Directory.* Also, local bookstores are a good source of new local publications.

SCHOLARLY JOURNALS.

The journals reviewed in this section are primarily interdisciplinary in scope. Cross-references are included for those journals that focus on a single discipline—for example, the *Journal of Black Psychology.* Disciplines represented within the interdisciplinary publications include anthropology, art, art history, communications, creative writing, economics, education, gender studies, history, law, literature, music, political science, psychology, public policy, religion, sociology, and theater and the performing arts.

A growing trend in academia to examine African American issues within a broader international context is evident in many of the journals. The scholarly publications reviewed have significant African American content, although some have broadened their scope to include "Africana Studies," "Black Studies," "Pan-African Studies," or "the African diaspora." The first three terms are applied interchangeably to the study of people of African descent, regardless of where they live, whereas "the African diaspora" refers to people of African descent living outside of Africa. Other journals have adopted a multicultural or "ethnic" approach and cover other peoples of color.

The maturation of the critical race theory movement within the legal profession and beyond has resulted in the publication of several law reviews that focus on race. While some of the reviews examine the full range of issues pertaining to race, others take a narrower focus on topics such as race and poverty, or race and gender. Together these journals provide several avenues for critical race theorists to further explore ideas that have shaped the movement—ideas pertaining to interest convergence, the social construction of race, the critique of color-blindness, differential racialization, and intersectionality, to name but a few. Law reviews newly added to this section are the *Columbia Journal of Race and Law* and the *Georgetown Journal of Law & Modern Critical Race Perspectives*.

In addition to the race-related law reviews added to this section, several other new scholarly titles have been added, including: *Journal of African American Males in Education, Journal of Black Masculinity, Journal of Race, Ethnicity and Religion, Race and Justice,* and *Race and Social Problems.* Also added are three older titles: *Journal of the National Black Nurses Association,* the *National Political Science Review,* and the *Publication of the Afro-Latin/ American Research Association (PALARA).* Title changes, cessations, and other changes have been minimal; however, several publishers have been unable to maintain their publishing schedules. Following the retirement of its founder Eugene Redmond, *Drumvoices Revue* is now an occasional publication only. *The Journal of Blacks in Higher Education* has moved to a reduced, online-only format following the death of its founder, James Cross. *Vital Issues: The Journal of African American Speeches* appears to have ceased publication.

Basic Periodicals

Ems: *Black History Bulletin, The Crisis;* Hs: *American Legacy, Black Enterprise, Black History Bulletin, Black Scholar, The Crisis, Ebony, Journal of African American History, Vibe;* Ga: *African American Review, Black Enterprise, Black History Bulletin, Black Scholar, Callaloo, The Crisis, Ebony, Essence (New York), Jet, Journal of Black Studies, Journal of African American History, Souls, Vibe;* Ac: *African American Review, Black Enterprise, Black History Bulletin, Black Music Research Journal, Black Scholar, Callaloo, The Crisis, Diverse Issues in Higher Education, Du Bois Review, Ebony, Essence, International Review of African American Art, Jet, Journal of African American History, Journal of Black Psychology, Journal of Black Studies, Journal of Negro Education, National Black Law Journal, Race & Class, The Review of Black Political Economy, Souls, Transforming Anthropology, Transition, Vibe.*

Basic Abstracts and Indexes

Academic OneFile, America: History and Life, Ethnic NewsWatch, Humanities International Index, International Index to Black Periodicals Full Text, Masterfile Premier, MLA International Bibliography, Sociological Abstracts, Web of Science.

232. *About Time.* [ISSN: 1060-3905] 1972. m. USD 14; USD 3 per issue. About...Time Magazine Inc., 283 Genesee St, Rochester, NY 14611. Illus., adv. Sample. Circ: 28000. Vol. ends: Dec. *Indexed:* ENW. *Bk. rev.:* 1-2, 500-1,500 words. *Aud.:* Hs, Ga, Ac.

This magazine is an independent publication based in Rochester, New York, that has continuously published stories of interest to African Americans since 1972. Although it has a strong focus on the local Rochester area, it also provides excellent coverage of issues of national or international significance. Through personal stories, reports, and analysis, the magazine presents a critical perspective that differs from that of more mainstream magazines. Its feature stories cover a wide variety of topics including history, politics, literature, education, and family issues. Insightful commentary from political analysts such as journalist Earl Ofari Hutchinson frequently appears. The magazine

includes poetry and reviews of books, music, theatrical productions, feature films, and television documentaries. Recommended for all public libraries and high school libraries that serve African American communities. A highly recommended title for public, academic, and high school libraries in the New York State area.

African-American Career World: the diversity employment magazine. See Occupations and Careers section.

233. *African American Review.* Former titles (until 1992): *Black American Literature Forum;* (until 1976): *Negro American Literature Forum.* [ISSN: 1062-4783] 1967. q. USD 80. Ed(s): Nathan Grant. African American Review, Saint Louis University, Adorjan Hall 317, 3800 Lindell Blvd, St Louis, MO 63108; http://aar.slu.edu/. Illus., index, adv. Sample. Refereed. Microform: PQC. Reprint: PSC. *Indexed:* A01, A22, ABS&EES, AmHI, ArtHuCI, BEL&L, BRI, CBRI, E01, F01, IIBP, MASUSE, MLA-IB, P02, RILM. *Bk. rev.:* Number and length vary. *Aud.:* Ga, Ac.

Published quarterly, *African American Review* is a peer-reviewed journal that features literary and cultural criticism, interviews, poetry, short fiction, and book reviews. As the official publication of the Modern Language Association's Division of Black American Literature and Culture, this well-established journal provides a venue for scholars and practitioners of the arts and humanities to engage in intellectual discourse. The topics and time periods covered are wide-ranging and include the works of lesser-known writers in addition to the works of literary giants such as Toni Morrison and James Baldwin. While the primary focus is on the work of African American writers, the journal also includes pieces on African and Caribbean literature. "Forgotten Manuscripts" features fascinating stories of recently uncovered literary works. This is an important publication for libraries that support undergraduate or graduate programs in American literature, creative writing, or dramatic arts. General readers will also appreciate the literary and cultural analysis that the journal provides, so libraries that serve African American communities will also want to have this in their collections.

African and Black Diaspora. See Africa section.

Afro-American Historical and Genealogical Society. Journal. See Genealogy/International and Ethnic-Interest Studies section.

Afro-Hispanic Review. See Multicultural Studies section.

234. *Afro-Latin/American Research Association. Publication.* [ISSN: 1093-5398] 1997. a. USD 25 (Individuals, USD 15). Ed(s): Antonio D Tillis. Dartmouth College, African and African-American Studies, HB 6134, 34 N Main St, Hanover, NH 03755; info@alarascholars.org; http://www.alarascholars.org/. *Indexed:* IIBP, MLA-IB. *Bk. rev.:* Number and length vary. *Aud.:* Ac.

PALARA, the Publication of the Afro-Latin/American Research Association, is an annual journal that publishes research articles, creative writing, and book reviews pertaining to African diaspora studies in the Americas. While pieces written in English, Spanish, French, and Portuguese are welcome, Spanish and English appear to be the predominant languages. The journal is multidisciplinary and solicits works in literature, history, linguistics, and the social sciences; however, the majority of the published work is either literary or historical. Each issue carries approximately five to ten articles and three to five book reviews; poetry and other creative work are also featured. While the journal is international in scope and has an impressive editorial board drawn from nations throughout the world, readers can find in this journal criticism of familiar American authors such as Julia Alvarez and Junot Diaz. Recommended for academic libraries that support Africana Studies, Ethnic Studies, or Latin American Studies.

235. *American Legacy: celebrating African-American history and culture.* Formerly (until 1996): *Legacy (New York).* [ISSN: 1086-7201] 1995. q. USD 9.95 domestic; USD 15.95 foreign; USD 2.95 newsstand/cover. R J R Communications Inc., 7 W Broadway St, Ste 201, Mt Vernon, NY 10552. Illus., adv. Sample. Circ: 86180 Paid. Vol. ends: Winter. *Indexed:* A01, IIBP, RILM. *Aud.:* Ems, Hs, Ga, Ac.

American Legacy is an attractive, nicely illustrated quarterly devoted to African American history and culture. It offers photographs, artwork, historical essays, stories, and folklore about black life and culture in the United States. Although the magazine's strengths lie in its coverage of African American history at national, regional, and local levels, it also looks beyond American borders at black societies in other parts of the world. This magazine is a suitable title for all school and public libraries, and all African American collections. Unfortunately its publication schedule is seriously delayed and its future is uncertain.

Black Camera See Films section.

236. *The Black E O E Journal: the employment & entrepreneur magazine.* 1991. q. USD 16. Ed(s): Christine Stossel. DiversityComm, Inc., 18 Technology Dr., Ste 170, Irvine, CA 92618; aortega@hnmagazine.com; http://diversitycomm.net/. Adv. *Bk. rev.:* Number and length vary. *Aud.:* Ga.

The *Black EOE Journal* is a career magazine that provides information for African Americans who seek employment and business opportunities within corporate America. The glossy, heavily illustrated magazine with an abundance of corporate advertising seeks to "connect, educate[,] and promote equal opportunity[,] thus creating a more diverse environment." The quarterly magazine publishes about four feature articles, many of which profile accomplished professionals, along with regular columns on topics such as workforce diversity, business-to-business, STEM, finance, money and insurance, and government. The magazine also publishes book reviews and a calendar of career fairs and events. A companion web site features more up-to-date news and events, and features a searchable job bank. The magazine is available in print and electronic formats. Recommended for public libraries. URL: www.blackeoejournal.com

237. *Black Enterprise.* [ISSN: 0006-4165] 1970. m. USD 12.95 domestic; USD 3.99 foreign. Ed(s): Derek Dingle, Alisa Gumbs. Earl G. Graves Publishing Co., Inc., 130 Fifth Ave, 10th Fl, New York, NY 10011-4399; hanks@blackenterprise.com. Illus., adv. Sample. Circ: 500000 Paid. Vol. ends: Jul. Microform: PQC. Indexed: A01, A22, ABIn, B01, B02, B03, BLI, BRI, C37, C42, CBRI, ENW, F01, IIBP, MASUSE, P02. *Bk. rev.:* 2-3, 250-500 words. *Aud.:* Hs, Ga, Ac.

A magazine "whose mission has always centered on closing the black wealth gap and financially empowering African Americans," *Black Enterprise* was established in 1970. A glossy magazine with abundant corporate advertising, it addresses the financial and business concerns of the African American community, especially consumers, employees, professionals, and entrepreneurs. Each issue includes several feature articles that fall into recurring categories, some of which are "Wealth for Life," which presents a biographical profile; "Personal Finance"; "Small Business"; "BE 100s," which profiles one of the nation's top 100 black-owned companies; and "Power Player," which provides an interview. The magazine also offers shorter columns on news, health, technology, popular psychology, and travel and leisure. While *BE* is rich with information on personal finance and corporate success, you won't find much critical analysis of capitalism or discussion of alternative economic systems. The magazine's annual polls, surveys, interviews, and company profiles will interest high school and academic audiences. Highly recommended for public and academic libraries. High school libraries that serve African American students will also want to consider this title.

238. *Black History Bulletin: a publication of the Association for the Study of African-American Life and History.* Formerly (until 2002): *Negro History Bulletin.* [ISSN: 1938-6656] 1937. s-a. USD 50. Ed(s): LaVonne I Neal, Alicia L Moore. The Association for the Study of African-American Life and History, Inc., C.B. Powell Bldg, Ste C-142, 525 Bryant St, NW, Washington, DC 20059; info@asalh.net; http://www.asalh.org. Illus., index. Sample. Refereed. Microform: PMC; PQC. Indexed: A01, A06, A22, BRI, CBRI, IIBP, MASUSE, MLA-IB, NumL, RILM. *Bk. rev.:* 2-3, 250-500 words. *Aud.:* Ems, Hs, Ga, Ac.

Established in 1937 at the urging of Mary McLeod Bethune, *Black History Bulletin* (formerly *Negro History Bulletin*) is published by the Association for the Study of African American Life and History. The *Bulletin* is a semi-annual, peer-reviewed journal that aims to publish "information about African Americans in U.S. history, the African diaspora generally, and the peoples of Africa." Targeting primarily secondary school educators, the *Bulletin* places emphasis on articles that focus on middle and high school U.S. history, or social studies methods for teachers. The magazine offers lesson plans that address national social studies standards, quizzes, and classroom activities, as well as reproductions of primary documents that may be incorporated into the curriculum. Recent issues have been thematic and have focused on topics such as literacy scholarship and black women. Educators seeking to create Black History Month lessons and activities will find the practical applications within this publication especially helpful. Recommended for school libraries of all levels, but a must for middle and high school libraries that serve African American youth. Also recommended for libraries that support college and university teacher training programs, and public libraries that serve African American communities.

239. *Black Masks.* [ISSN: 0887-7580] 1984. bi-m. USD 25; USD 4 per issue. Ed(s): Beth Turner. Black Masks, PO Box 7334, Athens, GA 30604. Illus., adv. Vol. ends: May/Jun. Indexed: ENW, IIBP. *Bk. rev.:* Number and length vary. *Aud.:* Ga, Ac.

For more than 25 years, *Black Masks* has celebrated black theater by publishing "articles and papers on performing, literary or visual arts[,] and artists of African descent." Initially this slender magazine of 16 pages focused primarily on the performing arts in the New York area, but throughout the years its coverage has extended to other states as well. Each issue includes several feature articles and an "Arts Hotline" section that contains notices of new books, televised events, and upcoming performances and exhibitions throughout the United States. The "Arts Hotline" is also available on the magazine's web site and is searchable by geographic location. Recommended for libraries with strong theater and/or African American Studies collections. URL: www.blackmasks.com

240. *Black Music Research Journal.* [ISSN: 0276-3605] 1980. s-a. USD 110 (print & online eds.). Ed(s): Horace Maxile. University of Illinois Press, 1325 S Oak St, Champaign, IL 61820; journals@uillinois.edu; http://www.press.uillinois.edu. Illus., index, adv. Sample. Refereed. Indexed: A22, AmHI, ArtHuCI, E01, IIBP, IIMP, RILM. *Aud.:* Ga, Ac.

This journal began in 1980 at Fisk University's Institute for Research in Black American Music. Since 1983, the journal has formed part of the Center for Black Music Research at Columbia College in Chicago. A scholarly journal published semi-annually, it includes articles about the philosophy, aesthetics, history, and criticism of black music. The journal seeks to promote an understanding of "the common roots of the music, musicians, and composers of the global African diaspora," and supports interdisciplinary scholarship on all genres of black music. In addition to articles on blues, jazz, gospel, rhythm and blues, and hip-hop, there are also pieces on opera and concert music, ring shouts, reggae, meringue, salsa, and other forms of traditional and contemporary Caribbean and African music. Many issues are devoted to a single theme, such as Music of Black Los Angeles. A required journal for college and research library collections that support music or African American Studies programs. Public libraries that serve black communities will also want to consider this title.

241. *Black Renaissance.* [ISSN: 1089-3148] 1996. 3x/yr. USD 35 domestic; USD 42 foreign. Ed(s): Quincy Troupe. New York University, Institute of African American Affairs, 41 E 11th St, 7th Fl, New York, NY 10003; http://africanastudies.as.nyu.edu/page/home. Illus. Vol. ends: Spring. Indexed: AmHI, BRI, ENW, IIBP, MLA-IB, RILM. *Bk. rev.:* Number and length vary. *Aud.:* Ga, Ac.

Edited by the accomplished writer Quincy Troupe, *Black Renaissance/ Renaissance Noire* "invites Black genius to apply itself to the realities of the twenty-first century with uncompromised thought, generous and readable analysis, and commentary." It publishes essays, poetry, fiction, interviews, letters, book reviews, photography, and art that critically address contemporary issues facing black people throughout the world. Its large format is well suited for the photographs and other pieces of visual art that contribute to the richness of this fine publication. It has published some of the most important black thinkers, writers, and artists, including Chinua Achebe, Amiri Baraka, Maryse Conde, Jean-Michel Basquiat, Edouard Glissant, Ngugi wa Thiong'o, Ishmael Reed, Derek Walcott, and John Edgar Wideman. Highly recommended for academic collections and larger public libraries.

242. *The Black Scholar: journal of black studies and research.* [ISSN: 0006-4246] 1969. q. USD 265 (print & online eds.). Ed(s): Laura Chrisman, Maize Woodforde. Black World Foundation, PO Box 2869, Oakland, CA 94609. Illus., adv. Sample. Refereed. Microform: MIM; PQC. *Indexed:* A01, A22, AmHI, BRI, CBRI, IIBP, MASUSE, MLA-IB, P02, RILM, SWR&A. *Bk. rev.:* 2-3, 500-1,000 words. *Aud.:* Hs, Ga, Ac.

Founded in 1969 during the Black Studies movement, *Black Scholar* continues to serve as a place where "college intellectuals, street academicians, and movement leaders come to grips with the basic issues of black America." Each issue is thematic, and although African American concerns feature prominently, *Black Scholar* regularly publishes articles on black culture outside the United States. The breadth of the journal's coverage can be illustrated by past issue topics that have included the struggle in Zimbabwe, facets of black masculinity, and rethinking pan-Africanism for the twenty-first century. While it regularly publishes the works of senior scholars and well-known activists, *Black Scholar* also encourages "young, newly developing black writers and black students" to submit their work. Each issue includes several feature articles, book reviews, current book announcements, and a classified ad section that lists employment opportunities in higher education. Following the retirement of founder and long-time editor Robert Chrisman, the journal was relaunched under the editorship of Laura Chrisman, with an expanded board that incorporated a new generation of scholars and activists. With changes in its editorial staff and focus, *The Black Scholar* seeks to "strengthen its position as the primary space for interdisciplinary, cross-cultural black reflection and conversation." The journal is available in print and electronic format. Recommended for academic and public library collections. High schools with a sizable African American student body will also want to consider this title. URL: www.theblackscholar.org

243. *C L A Journal.* [ISSN: 0007-8549] 1957. q. Free to members; Non-members, USD 80. Ed(s): Cason L Hill. College Language Association, c/o Yakini B. Kemp, PO Box 38515, Tallahassee, FL 32315; yakini.kemp@famu.edu; http://www.clascholars.org. Illus., index. Sample. Refereed. *Indexed:* A01, A22, ABS&EES, AmHI, ArtHuCI, BRI, IIBP, MLA-IB, P02. *Bk. rev.:* 3-6, 500-1,500 words. *Aud.:* Ac.

The College Language Association (CLA), founded in 1937 by a group of black scholars and educators, is an organization of college teachers of English and foreign languages. Since 1957, the association has published the *CLA Journal*, featuring scholarly research and reviews of books in the areas of language, literature, literary criticism, linguistics, and pedagogy. Since only those articles written by CLA members and subscribers are considered for publication, the journal reflects the research interests of the association. While most articles focus on African American literature, West Indian, Afro-Hispanic, and African literatures are also covered. Criticism of black francophone literature is also represented in *CLA Journal*. Although English is the predominant language, articles written in other languages have been published. The journal also includes association news, such as membership lists, publications by members, committee rosters, and conference announcements. Additionally, the journal includes job announcements. Recommended for academic library collections.

244. *Callaloo.* [ISSN: 0161-2492] 1976. q. USD 165. Ed(s): Charles Henry Rowell. The Johns Hopkins University Press, 2715 N Charles St, Baltimore, MD 21218; http://www.press.jhu.edu. Illus., index, adv. Sample. Refereed. Circ: 600. Vol. ends: Fall. Reprint: PSC. *Indexed:* A01, A22, AmHI, ArtHuCI, BRI, CBRI, E01, IIBP, MLA-IB, P02, RILM. *Bk. rev.:* Number and length vary. *Aud.:* Ga, Ac.

Although it began in 1976 as a venue for Southern African American writers lacking publishing outlets, *Callaloo* now publishes internationally renowned authors, and it ranks among the premier black literary journals. In keeping with its name—callaloo is a stew served in Louisiana, Brazil, and the Caribbean—it offers an array of cultures and genres; issues include fiction, poetry, plays, critical essays, cultural studies, interviews, annotated bibliographies, visual art, and photography. The journal regularly features new and emerging writers, including participants of the Callaloo Creative Writing Workshops, a national retreat of fiction writers and poets. Operating on the principle that there is "infinite variety in Black Art," the journal is international in scope and publishes in French and Spanish in addition to English. Special thematic issues that focus on individual authors, regions, or genres, such as the one on "Jazz Poetics," have

earned awards from major publishing associations, and the journal was recently ranked among the top 15 literary magazines in the U.S. by *Every Writer's Resource.* Required for academic libraries and recommended for public libraries.

245. *Challenge (Atlanta): a journal of research on African American men.* [ISSN: 1077-193X] 1990. s-a. USD 25 (Individuals, USD 10). Ed(s): Ida Rousseau Mukenge. Morehouse Research Institute, 830 Westview Dr, SW, Atlanta, GA 30314; http://www.morehouse.edu/. Illus. Sample. Refereed. Vol. ends: Dec. *Indexed:* A01, ERIC, IIBP, P61, SSA. *Aud.:* Ga, Ac.

An official publication of the Morehouse Research Institute at Morehouse College, the only all-male historically black college in the United States, *Challenge* publishes scholarly articles "on any aspect of issues germane to African American life with particular emphasis on African American men, their families, and their communities." The interdisciplinary journal publishes thematic issues that are devoted to a social, health, or political issue that disproportionately affects African American men. All articles, solicited and unsolicited, are subjected to a blind review process. A past issue devoted to men's health included articles on health care disparities in the United States, quality-of-life issues in urban HIV-infected African American males, and access to mental health care and substance abuse treatment for men of color in the United States. Although the publisher does not offer subscriptions in electronic format, the full text of the journal can be found in aggregated databases such as *Black Studies Center* and *Academic OneFile*. Recommended for academic libraries that support African American and/or public policy collections. Large urban public libraries may also want to acquire this title.

246. *Columbia Journal of Race and Law.* [ISSN: 2155-2401] 2011. s-a. Ed(s): Chade Severin, Austin Leach. Columbia University, School of Law, 435 W 116th St, New York, NY 10027; cblr@law.columbia.edu; http://www.law.columbia.edu. *Indexed:* L14. *Bk. rev.:* Number and length vary. *Aud.:* Ac.

The *Columbia Journal of Race and Law* (*CJRL*), a publication of the Columbia Law School, sets out "to establish a dialogue on historic and contemporary notions of socio-political and legal challenges facing racial and ethnic minorities." *CJRL,* which began in 2011, publishes research articles, notes, essays, and book reviews on issues such as affirmative action, immigration, employment law, community development, criminal law, environmental justice, voting rights, and education. The journal is issued twice per year and encourages work from scholars, practitioners, policymakers, and students. Recommended for academic libraries, especially those with legal studies programs, and law school libraries. Early volumes are available on the web with open access. URL: http://cjrl.columbia.edu

247. *The Crisis.* Former titles (until 2003): *New Crisis;* (until 1997): *The Crisis.* [ISSN: 1559-1573] 1910. q. USD 12; USD 20 combined subscription (print & online eds.). Ed(s): Jabari Asim. The Crisis Publishing Company, Inc., 4805 Mt Hope Dr, Baltimore, MD 21215. Illus., adv. Sample. Microform: BHP; PQC. *Indexed:* A01, A22, AbAn, AmHI, BRI, IIBP, MASUSE, MLA-IB, P02, RILM. *Bk. rev.:* 2-3, 200-500 words. *Aud.:* Ems, Hs, Ga, Ac.

Founded in 1910 by W.E.B. Du Bois, the eminent scholar and founding father of the National Association for the Advancement of Colored People (NAACP), *The Crisis* is one of the oldest continuously published African American periodicals in print. Through the years it has been a "crusading voice for civil rights" and a respected source of thought, opinion, and analysis on issues pertaining to African Americans. Although the magazine is legally a separate entity, it serves as the official publication of the NAACP; news of the organization, both national and local, can be found in the "NAACP Today" section. All other sections of the magazine, including feature stories, current news, music reviews, theater reviews, book reviews, and interviews, reflect the opinion of the individual authors and not the NAACP. Although its issues are slender (each issue is about 50 pages), the magazine's sparse advertising and concentrated focus on the educational, economic, political, and social aspects of race make it a very substantial publication. The magazine states that it is committed to "battle tirelessly for the rights of humanity and the highest ideals of democracy" and also seeks to "serve as a trustworthy record of the darker races." Back issues are freely available via Google Books, and current subscriptions are available for print and/or digital formats. *The Crisis* is highly recommended for academic, school, and public libraries. URL: http://thecrisismagazine.com

248. *Diverse: Issues in Higher Education.* Formerly (until Aug.2005): *Black Issues in Higher Education.* [ISSN: 1557-5411] 1984. bi-w. USD 26 combined subscription domestic (print & online eds.); USD 50 combined subscription Canada (print & online eds.); USD 60 combined subscription elsewhere (print & online eds.). Ed(s): Toni Coleman. Cox, Matthews & Associates, Inc., 10520 Warwick Ave, Ste B 8, Fairfax, VA 22030. Illus., adv. Vol. ends: Feb. *Indexed:* A01, A22, BRI, Chicano, ENW, ERIC, HEA, IIBP, MLA-IB. *Aud.:* Ac.

Since its founding in 1984 as *Black Issues in Higher Education, Diverse* has been the premier newsmagazine that covers issues concerning people of color in higher education. As its earlier title suggests, initially its focus was primarily on African Americans, but in recent years it has expanded its scope to include Latino, Asian American, Native American, and other interests. Its coverage of African American concerns remains quite strong, however. Its attractive design, liberal use of color photographs, and clear writing make it a very readable publication. Each issue includes feature stories that run the gamut from general educational trends (e.g., emergency notification technologies) to issues affecting people of color, such as efforts to create pipelines to college presidencies for Asian American administrators. The magazine also carries news of recent appointments, grant awards, upcoming conferences, and a very substantial section devoted to academic employment opportunities. It publishes many special, thematic editions (e.g., technology, state of education in a particular state), and its special report on the top 100 institutions that graduate the most students of color is a welcome annual feature. The magazine supports a robust companion web site that provides news, special reports, blogs, opinion, searchable job announcements, and a wide array of multimedia, including slides and videos. Data from the top 100 annual survey is also presented at the site. This is a required title for academic libraries and is recommended for public and secondary school libraries that serve diverse communities. URL: http://diverseeducation.com

249. *Diversity Employers.* Formerly (until 2011): *The Black Collegian.* [ISSN: 2159-8835] 1970. a. Free to qualified personnel. Ed(s): Preston J Edwards, Jr. IMDiversity, Inc., 140 Carondolet St, New Orleans, LA 70130. Illus., adv. Microform: PQC. *Indexed:* A01, A22, BRI, C37, ENW, IIBP, MASUSE, P02. *Aud.:* Hs, Ga, Ac.

Diversity Employers is a career magazine targeted to both recent college graduates and more experienced professionals seeking information on career planning, job opportunities, postgraduate education, internships, study abroad programs, and other career advancement opportunities. The magazine is an expansion of *The Black Collegian,* a publication founded in 1970 to provide black college students with similar types of career information. The magazine has developed a reputation for providing quality information on overseas study, graduate and professional schools, resume writing, career overviews, employer profiles, and other topics designed to assist students with their transition from college to work life. While the magazine provides quality articles on all aspects of diversity, it continues its tradition of featuring brief articles on African American historical topics. Popular features of the magazine are its "Job Outlook" and "Top 100 Employers" articles. Although the magazine has an expanded scope, it has reduced its number of issues and is now an annual publication. The magazine maintains a companion web site that provides access to articles and other content from the magazine, as well as a searchable job bank that jobseekers will appreciate. An archive of articles published under the magazine's former name, along with some new content, is available at www.blackcollegian.com; many of the tools at this site direct the reader to new site. Recommended for college libraries. High school and public libraries that serve African American and ethnic communities might also consider purchasing this title. URL: www.diversityemployers.com

250. *Du Bois Review: social science research on race.* [ISSN: 1742-058X] 2003. s-a. GBP 156 (print & online eds.). Ed(s): Michael Dawson, Lawrence Bobo. Cambridge University Press, The Edinburgh Bldg, Shaftesbury Rd, Cambridge, CB2 8RU, United Kingdom; journals@cambridge.org; http://www.cambridge.org/uk. Adv. Refereed. Reprint: PSC. *Indexed:* A22, E01, IIBP, P61, SSA. *Bk. rev.:* Number and length vary. *Aud.:* Ga, Ac.

Bearing the name of the gifted scholar W.E.B. Du Bois, this journal seeks to present "the best cutting-edge research on race" from the social sciences. The journal is edited by professors Lawrence D. Bobo (Harvard University) and Michael C. Dawson (University of Chicago) and is published by Cambridge University Press for the W.E.B. Du Bois Institute for African and African American Research at Harvard University. Its editorial board is comprised of eminent scholars drawn from many disciplines. *DBR* also provides a forum for discussion of race issues from a range of disciplines, including economics, political science, sociology, anthropology, law, communications, public policy, psychology, and history. Each issue of *DBR* opens with introductory remarks from the editors that set the stage for three subsequent sections: "State of the Discipline," where invited essays and provocative think-pieces appear; "State of the Art," which features articles based on empirical research; and "State of the Discourse," which includes review essays on current scholarly books, controversies, and research threads. Journal subscriptions are available for print or electronic copy. The journal's web site previews articles of upcoming issues in its "FirstView" section, has some interactive features and supports easy downloading to select e-readers. With exceptionally well-written articles, the *Du Bois Review* is highly recommended for academic and large public libraries. URL: http://journals.cambridge.org/action/displayJournal?jid=DBR

251. *Ebony.* Incorporates (1985-1998): *E M: Ebony Man;* (1970-1976): *Black World;* Which superseded (1950-1970): *Negro Digest.* [ISSN: 0012-9011] 1945. m. USD 14.97 domestic; USD 14.97 Canada; USD 44.97 elsewhere. Ed(s): Amy DuBois Barnett. Johnson Publishing Co., Inc., 820 S Michigan Ave, Chicago, IL 60605. Illus., adv. Sample. Circ: 1937000 Paid. Vol. ends: Oct. Microform: NBI; PQC. *Indexed:* A01, A22, AmHI, BRI, C37, MASUSE, MLA-IB, P02, RILM. *Bk. rev.:* 9-12, 25-50 words. *Aud.:* Ems, Hs, Ga, Ac.

Founded by John H. Johnson in 1945, *Ebony* continues to be the most widely circulated magazine targeted to African American readers. Committed to publishing positive, uplifting images of black people, the magazine includes articles on successful individuals in entertainment, sports, politics, and religion. It also has regular features on relationships, parenting, personal finance, fashion, beauty, travel, cooking, and medical advice. *Ebony* also has a section on new books and memorable photographs drawn from its extensive photo archives. In recent years, *Ebony* has suffered financially and therefore has made an effort to boost its appeal to younger readers who might be drawn to *Vibe, Upscale,* or one of the other relatively recent entries in the magazine market. To remain competitive, the magazine adopted a fresh logo and look, and its publisher relaunched its web site, which features international politics, arts, and culture, is updated daily, and is highly interactive. Back issues of *Ebony* are are freely available via its web site and also at Google Books; however, current subscriptions are available for print only. A popular title that has been credited with "helping promote and record African-American culture and providing important outlets for a community that for too long was neglected by the mainstream media," *Ebony* is highly recommended for all high school, academic, and public libraries. URL: http://ebony.com

Essence. See Fashion and Lifestyle section.

Ethnic and Racial Studies. See Multicultural Studies section.

252. *Georgetown Journal of Law & Modern Critical Race Perspectives.* [ISSN: 1946-3154] 2008. s-a. USD 30. Ed(s): Noah Rich. Georgetown University Law Center, 600 New Jersey Ave, NW, Washington, DC 20001; http://www.law.georgetown.edu. *Indexed:* L14. *Bk. rev.:* Number and length vary. *Aud.:* Ac.

Founded in 2007 by law students who were inspired by their experiences with critical race theorists, the *Georgetown Journal of Law & Modern Critical Race Perspectives* (*MCRP*) seeks to "bridge the gap between scholarship and activism by promoting dialogue that extends beyond the normal academic realm." The journal, one of a few journals devoted to legal scholarship on race and identity, is grounded in critical race theory and seeks to address and transform "the subordinated relationships that have historically defined race around the world." To further encourage dialogue, *MCRP* often includes reaction papers along with the four to five research articles that it publishes. The journal also includes notes and book reviews. Published twice per year in print format only, *MCRP* publishes work from faculty, law students, and practitioners from throughout the nation who are dedicated to advancing social justice. Recent articles have included "Racial Discrimination in Medicine versus Race-Based Medicine" and "Black Strikes: The Focus of Controversy and the Effect of Race-Based Peremptory Challenges on the American Jury System." Although not available online, print-on-demand copies may be obtained at: https://articleworks.cadmus.com/geolaw/mcr.html. Highly recommended for academic libraries that support legal studies programs and law schools.

253. Gospel Today Magazine: America's leading Christian lifestyle magazine. Formerly (until 1995): *Score.* [ISSN: 1081-8162] 1989. bi-m. USD 19.97. Horizon Concepts, Inc., PO Box 1009, Hendersonville, TN 37077; sales@horizonconcepts.net; http://www.horizonconcepts.com/. Illus., adv. *Bk. rev.:* Number and length vary. *Aud.:* Ga.

Gospel Today began in 1989 as a newsletter devoted to the gospel music industry. It has since changed titles, expanded its content, and broadened its scope to include all Christian lifestyle issues, especially those pertaining to African Americans. Each issue has several feature articles that include interviews with gospel music celebrities, prominent ministers, and other African American personalities. It also provides lively articles on topics such as dating and celibacy, innovative church programming and ministries, and the state of finances in today's "megachurch." The magazine also looks at issues in the general news such as presidential elections, but provides a Christian perspective. Much like other general-interest magazines, *Gospel Today* also has regular columns on beauty, health and fitness, personal finance, and personal relationships, as well as a section for teens. The magazine also provides gospel industry news, CD reviews, book reviews, a crossword puzzle based on biblical scripture, and inspirational words written by various ministers. Although digital subscriptions are not available, blog posts at wwww.mygospeltoday.com discuss the magazine's feature articles. Recommended for public libraries that serve African American populations.

254. The Griot. [ISSN: 0737-0873] 1981. s-a. Free to members. Ed(s): Andrew Baskin. Southern Conference on African-American Studies, Inc., c/o Howard Jones, PO Box 330163, Houston, TX 77233; scaasi6@aol.com; http://www.scaasi.org. Illus., adv. *Indexed:* IIBP, MLA-IB, RILM. *Bk. rev.:* 1-4, 500-1,000 words. *Aud.:* Ac.

The Griot is the official journal of the Southern Conference on African American Studies, an organization that, in 1979, brought together "all interested minds, regardless of color or creed, who were interested in interpreting and preserving African American history and culture, especially that which had originated in and/or affected the south." While the journal primarily publishes articles in the humanities that "further enhance knowledge of the African's (African, African-American, Caribbean) experience," it occasionally includes work written by social scientists. Essays, criticism, poetry, and book reviews are also featured in the journal. Although the publisher does not offer online subscription, the full text of *The Griot* can be found in the *Black Studies Center.* Recommended for academic libraries that seek to build comprehensive Africana collections.

255. Harvard Journal of African American Public Policy. [ISSN: 1081-0463] 1989. a. USD 40. Ed(s): Timothy Cunningham, Christopher Arlene. Harvard University, John F. Kennedy School of Government, 79 John F Kennedy St, PO Box 142, Cambridge, MA 02138; http://www.hks.harvard.edu/. Adv. Refereed. *Indexed:* A01, BRI, IIBP. *Bk. rev.:* Number and length vary. *Aud.:* Ac, Sa.

Published by graduate students at the John F. Kennedy School of Government at Harvard University, this journal examines the relationship between policy making and the African American experience. Founded in 1989, this scholarly journal aims to "educate and provide leadership that improves the quality of public policies affecting the African American community." The journal, which has published works by leading policy makers, scholars and political analysts, includes research articles, interviews, essays, and an occasional book review. Published annually, it is available both in print for a modest subscription fee and also online as an open-access journal. This excellent title is highly recommended for academic libraries and public policy collections. URL: http://isites.harvard.edu/icb/icb.do?keyword=k74757&pageid=icb.page375026

256. Hip Hop Weekly: covering the entire hip hop culture. [ISSN: 1932-5177] 2007. w. USD 49.95. Ed(s): Cynthia Horner. Z & M Media, LLC, 401 E Las Olas Blvd, Ste 130-56, Ft. Lauderdale, FL 33301. Illus., adv. Circ: 100000 Paid. *Aud.:* Ga.

Published by David Mays and Ray "Benzino" Scott, founders of the pioneering hip-hop magazine *The Source, Hip Hop Weekly* is a glossy celebrity magazine that seeks to be "a more timely and more engaging way to serve today's hip-hop consumer." Voted Best Magazine at the 2009 Urban Music Awards, *Hip Hop Weekly* records the movements of hip-hop icons through feature articles, interviews, and a liberal use of photography. While most articles focus on the personal lives and musical developments of hip-hop celebrities, artists often weigh in on current news topics unrelated to music. The magazine has regular features on fashion and beauty, and also includes reviews of new albums, mixtapes, DVDs, films, games, and web sites. Columns by "shock-jocktress" Wendy Williams and other media personalities have contributed to the popularity of this publication. Similar in style to *People,* articles are short and easy to read. Strong language used by musicians during interviews has been redacted. Recommended for urban public libraries that serve young adults and older teens. Academic libraries that seek to build comprehensive collections on African American popular culture may also consider this title.

257. Howard Journal of Communications. [ISSN: 1064-6175] 1988. q. GBP 268 (print & online eds.). Ed(s): Carolyn A. Stroman. Taylor & Francis Inc., 325 Chestnut St, Ste 800, Philadelphia, PA 19106; customerservice@taylorandfrancis.com; http://www.tandfonline.com. Illus., index, adv. Sample. Refereed. Vol. ends: Dec. Reprint: PSC. *Indexed:* A01, A22, ABS&EES, B01, BAS, E01, H24, IIBP, MLA-IB, P61, PsycInfo, RiskAb, SSA. *Bk. rev.:* Number and length vary. *Aud.:* Ac.

The *Howard Journal of Communications* is a scholarly journal that examines the influence of ethnicity, gender, and culture on communication issues. The majority of the editorial staff is located at Howard University, a historically black college; the editorial board is highly diverse and located at major research institutions in the United States and abroad. While many of the articles focus on African Americans, the scope of this quarterly is highly multicultural. Past articles have included "The Effects of Involvement in Sports on Attitudes toward Native American Sport Mascots," "Hispanic/Latino Identity Labels: An Examination of Cultural Values and Personal Experiences," and "Change and the Illusion of Change: Evolving Portrayals of Crime News and Blacks in a Major Market." In addition to the four to six peer-reviewed articles that appear in each issue, the journal includes an occasional book review. Some issues have a special theme, for example, "Health Communication and Health Disparities." Available in both print and electronic formats, this title is highly recommended for academic libraries that support programs in communications, journalism, social psychology, speech, gender studies, and multicultural studies. URL: www.tandfonline.com/loi/uhjc20

Howard Law Journal. See Law section.

International Review of African American Art. See Art/Museum Publications section.

258. Jet. [ISSN: 0021-5996] 1951. w. USD 20 domestic; USD 50 Canada; USD 70 elsewhere. Ed(s): Mitzi Miller. Johnson Publishing Co., Inc., 820 S Michigan Ave, Chicago, IL 60605; http://www.johnsonpublishing.com. Illus., adv. Microform: NBI; PQC. *Indexed:* BRI, C37, MASUSE, P02. *Aud.:* Hs, Ga, Ac.

Founded in 1951 by the legendary African American publisher John H. Johnson, *Jet* remains the leading weekly African American newsmagazine. A sister publication to *Ebony, Jet* provides a cover story; national and international news items pertaining to black people living in the United States, Africa, and the Caribbean; sports and entertainment news; regular columns on health, education, labor, parenting, and fashion; "This Week in Black History"; the "Week's Best Photos"; obituaries and wedding announcements; and the "Jet Beauty of the Week." It also includes film and music reviews, top music sales, and a television schedule. Its small, portable format and short items make *Jet* a quick, easy way to keep up with what's happening in "the Black community." It is supplemented by a daily online magazine, http://jetmag.com, which features news updates, videos, a Twitter feed, and a blog. Despite its crisp, new look and updated logo, *Jet* continues to battle lagging sales and stiff competition from web sites such as http://thegrio.com, http://theroot.com, and http://blackamericaweb.com. *Jet* continues to be a required title for all libraries that serve African Americans.

259. *Journal of African American History.* Formerly (until 2002): *Journal of Negro History.* [ISSN: 1548-1867] 1916. q. USD 375 (print & online eds.). Ed(s): Sylvia Y Cyrus, V P Franklin. The Association for the Study of African-American Life and History, Inc., C.B. Powell Bldg, Ste C-142, 525 Bryant St, NW, Washington, DC 20059; info@asalh.net; http://www.asalh.org. Illus., adv. Refereed. Microform: PQC. *Indexed:* A01, A06, A22, AmHI, BRI, CBRI, IIBP, MLA-IB, NumL. *Bk. rev.:* Number and length vary. *Aud.:* Hs, Ac, Sa.

Founded in 1916 as the *Journal of Negro History* by Carter G. Woodson, this is the premier journal in the field of African American history. Published by the Association for the Study of African American Life and History, the founders of Black History Month, this peer-reviewed quarterly includes scholarly articles on all aspects of African American history. The journal often releases special thematic issues; recent ones include "African American and the History of Sport" and "To Be Heard in Black and White: Historical Perspectives on Black Print Culture." Also included are book reviews, memorial tributes, announcements, and publishers' advertisements. Print and digital formats are available. This is an essential title for libraries that support black history programs, and is highly recommended for all academic and research libraries. URL: www.jstor.org/action/showPublication?journalCode=jafriamerhist

260. *Journal of African American Males in Education.* [ISSN: 2153-9065] 2010. q. Free. Journal of African American Males in Education, 2689 E Oakleaf Dr, Tempe, AZ 85281; jlukewood@asu.edu. Refereed. *Bk. rev.:* Number and length vary. *Aud.:* Ga, Ac.

The *Journal of African American Males in Education* (*JAAME*) is a peer-reviewed journal devoted to scholarship on African American males in education. It publishes research on African American males at all educational levels, from pre-school to graduate school, and in multiple roles (e.g., students, teachers, faculty, staff, administrators). While *JAAME* authors examine black male underachievement and gaps in educational attainment, they go far beyond this by also looking at factors that have contributed to academic excellence within black male populations. Most articles, about four or five per issue, are based on original research using both quantitative and qualitative methods; some articles are based on literature reviews and conceptual analysis. An occasional book review is included. *JAAME* is published online only and is open access. Recommended for academic libraries, and public and school libraries that serve African American communities. URL: http://journalofafricanamericanmales.com

261. *Journal of African American Studies.* Former titles (until 2003): *Journal of African American Men;* (until 1995): *Journal of African American Male Studies.* [ISSN: 1559-1646] 1993. q. EUR 411 (print & online eds.). Ed(s): Anthony J Lemelle. Springer New York LLC, 233 Spring St, New York, NY 10013; journals@springer-ny.com; http://www.springer.com. Illus. Refereed. Vol. ends: Aug. Reprint: PSC. *Indexed:* A01, A22, AmHI, BRI, E01, HEA, IIBP, MLA-IB, P61, SSA. *Bk. rev.:* Number and length vary. *Aud.:* Ac.

Formerly the *Journal of African American Men,* the *Journal of African American Studies* is a peer-reviewed quarterly that publishes theoretical and empirical articles on issues affecting persons, both male and female, of African descent. Although the journal is multidisciplinary in scope, its content is largely sociological, and research dealing with gender or identity is especially strong. Recent issues have covered topics such as gendered racial microaggressions among black women college students; negotiating the impact of racism on the career development of African American professional men; and an interdisciplinary analysis of black girls' and women's resistance strategies. Edited by Anthony Lemelle, Jr., at the John Jay College of Criminal Justice, CUNY, the journal also includes scholarly book reviews. Print and digital formats are available. An important title for academic libraries, especially those that support strong sociology and gender studies programs. URL: www.springerlink.com/content/112866/?MUD=MP

262. *Journal of Black Masculinity.* [ISSN: 2155-1189] 2010. q. USD 13.95 per issue. Ed(s): Dr. C P Gause. University of North Carolina at Greensboro, PO Box 26170, Greensboro, NC 27402; cpgause@uncg.edu; http://www.uncg.edu. Refereed. *Bk. rev.:* Number and length vary. *Aud.:* Ga, Ac.

The *Journal of Black Masculinity,* a scholarly journal that is issued three times per year, publishes "analyses of Black and Multi-racial Masculinities across the Diaspora." With an editorial staff based at University of North Carolina, Greensboro, and a largely Southern editorial staff, the journal seeks to publish articles from all disciplines and to also include poetry, art, and other media. The journal's inaugural issue characterized media representation of the black male as "a sadistic and masochistic heterosexist black masculine cyborg," an image the editor set out to debunk by bringing together "scholars, dancers, teachers, poets, educators, Hip Hop artists, policymakers, spoken-word performers, politicians, and researchers to celebrate and affirm our black masculinities." Thus far, issues have consisted of five to eight articles, with some poetry and an occasional book review. Some issues have been thematic and have addressed topics such as "African Americans and Public Health" and "The Philosophical Underpinnings of Gender Identity." While many of its articles focus on black men, there are several outliers that address the black community in general or focus specifically on women. Given the availability of well-established journals that address the general African American population, the *Journal of Black Masculinity* would do well to stick to its stated focus, while at the same time developing an identity that distinguishes it from *Challenge: A Journal of Research on African American Men.* Print and electronic copies of single issues may be purchased from its web site or through Amazon.com. The cost of an ongoing subscription seems high in comparison to the price of single issues. Recommended for large academic and public libraries that seek to develop comprehensive African American collections. URL: www.blackmasculinity.com

Journal of Black Psychology. See Psychology section.

263. *Journal of Black Studies.* [ISSN: 0021-9347] 1970. 8x/yr. USD 1237. Ed(s): Molefi Kete Asante. Sage Publications, Inc., 2455 Teller Rd, Thousand Oaks, CA 91320; info@sagepub.com; http://www.sagepub.com. Illus., index, adv. Sample. Refereed. Vol. ends: Jul. Microform: PQC. Reprint: PSC. *Indexed:* A01, A22, ASSIA, AmHI, BRI, BrArAb, CBRI, E01, HEA, IBSS, IIBP, MLA-IB, P02, P61, PsycInfo, RILM, RiskAb, SSA, SWR&A. *Bk. rev.:* Number and length vary. *Aud.:* Ga, Ac.

One of the top-tier African American Studies academic journals, the *Journal of Black Studies* began in 1970 during the height of the Black Studies movement. Its current editor, Dr. Molefi Asante, founded the journal, then subsequently headed the nation's first doctoral program in Africana Studies. Published eight times per year, the journal explores all aspects of the black experience, focusing not only on African Americans, but also on Africa, the Caribbean region, and the African diaspora throughout the world. Issues include five to ten articles, review essays, and an occasional book review. The scholarship inside *JBS* covers a wide range of subject areas, including: contemporary political and social issues, history, economics, literature, art, and more. While the editor is closely affiliated with Afrocentricity, a concept that is well-represented in the journal, articles reflect a variety of philosophical perspectives and research methodologies. Available in print and digital formats. Highly recommended for academic libraries and large public libraries that serve black communities. URL: www.sagepub.com/journal.aspx?pid=129

264. *Journal of Blacks in Higher Education (Online).* 1993. w. Free. The J B H E Foundation, Inc., 200 W 57th St, Ste 1304, New York, NY 10019; info@jbhe.com. Adv. *Indexed:* IIBP. *Bk. rev.:* Number and length vary. *Aud.:* Ac.

The *Journal of Blacks in Higher Education* was founded in 1993 as a scholarly publication whose purpose was "simply to show major racial imbalances and leave competitive markets and other nonlegislative forces to operate on the information provided." Estimating that African American families spend about $3 billion a year on tuition, room, board, and books, *JBHE* editors conclude that "surely, for this sum of money[,] [black parents] are entitled to have clear and detailed information about which institutions have successfully integrated their campuses and provide a hospitable educational and social environment for black students." Following the death of *JBHE* founder Ted Cross in 2010, the journal ceased as a print publication and moved to an online-only format consisting of a weekly publication, *JBHE Weekly Bulletin*, that is delivered via e-mail, along with a very robust web site. Like the print journal that preceded it, the web site features news articles that address the history and current state of African Americans in higher education, but its real strength lies in the wealth of statistical data that it presents. Data from myriad sources—federal and state governments, colleges and universities, and other private institutions—are prominently featured throughout the site's categories, which include: breaking news, HBCU news, research and studies, enrollments, racial gaps, and campus racial incidents. Rankings, charts, and graphs that cover everything from enrollments and education attainment, to academic success in the professions, to most-frequently cited authors can be found here. Its "Statistic of the Week" section reports data on the relative standing of blacks to whites in American society. The site also regularly includes notices of new books and articles, abstracts of new research reports with links to downloadable content when available, appointments, tenure decisions and promotions, minority-related grants, job and fellowship opportunities, and notable honors and awards. The weekly bulletin and web site are both open access. Highly recommended for academic libraries. URL: www.jbhe.com

265. *Journal of Multicultural Counseling and Development.* Formerly (until 1985): *Journal of Non-White Concerns in Personnel and Guidance.* [ISSN: 0883-8534] 1972. q. GBP 141. Ed(s): Gargi Roysircar-Sodowsky. Wiley-Blackwell Publishing, Inc., 111 River St, Hoboken, NJ 07030; info@wiley.com; http://www.wiley.com/. Illus., adv. Refereed. Circ: 2000. Vol. ends: Oct. Microform: PQC. Reprint: PSC. *Indexed:* A01, A22, BRI, Chicano, ENW, ERIC, HEA, IIBP, PsycInfo, SWR&A. *Bk. rev.:* Occasional. *Aud.:* Ac.

This journal is published by the Association for Multicultural Counseling and Development, a member association of the American Counseling Association. Each issue includes four or five articles and an occasional book review that pertains to multicultural or ethnic interests in all areas of counseling and human development. While articles are published in English, author abstracts are provided in both English and Spanish. With a special focus on racial and ethnic issues in the United States, the journal accepts articles based on research, theoretical works, and reports on practical applications. Native American, Latino/a, Asian American, and African American concerns seem to get equal attention in this publication. Articles pertaining to immigrant populations and whiteness studies are also included. Academic libraries that support counseling, human resource management, psychology, social work, or ethnic studies programs will want to consider acquiring this title. Subscriptions are available for print and electronic editions, and the title is also included in several aggregated databases. URL: http://onlinelibrary.wiley.com/journal/10.1002/%28ISSN%292161-1912

266. *Journal of Negro Education: a Howard University quarterly review of issues incident to the education of black people.* [ISSN: 0022-2984] 1932. q. USD 300 (print & online eds.). Ed(s): Ivory A Toldson. Howard University, School of Education, 2900 Van Ness St, NW, Washington, DC 20008; jelbedour@howard.edu; http://www.howard.edu/schooleducation/. Illus., index, adv. Sample. Refereed. Vol. ends: Fall. *Indexed:* A01, A22, BRI, CBRI, Chicano, ERIC, HEA, IIBP, MLA-IB, P02, P61, PsycInfo, RILM, SSA, SWR&A. *Bk. rev.:* 4-6, 1,000-2,500 words. *Aud.:* Ac.

Throughout 80 consecutive years of publication, the *Journal of Negro Education* has been a major source of scholarship on every aspect of black education. In addition to publishing on professional education, this peer-reviewed journal also encompasses the social sciences, the physical and natural sciences, the arts, and technology. *JNE* has published an interesting array of special issues on topics as diverse as "Looking beyond the Digital Divide: Computers and Technology in Education," "Early Education and One-Room Schoolhouses," and "Hip Hop, Rap, and Oppositional Culture in Education." Although the journal aims to address educational issues that pertain to black people throughout the world, its contents focus primarily on African Americans. Special features include book and media reviews, news, and announcements. Current subscriptions are available for print only, although back issues are available digitally to JSTOR subscribers at www.jstor.org. A core title for academic libraries, especially those that support education programs.

267. *Journal of Pan African Studies.* [ISSN: 1942-6569] q. Free. Ed(s): Tristan Allen, Nura Sediqe. Journal of Pan African Studies, PO Box 20151, Phoenix, AZ 85036-0151. Refereed. *Indexed:* IIBP. *Bk. rev.:* Number and length vary. *Aud.:* Ga, Ac.

This online, open-access, scholarly journal publishes interdisciplinary, peer-reviewed articles and creative work on a wide range of topics pertaining to African peoples living in Africa and throughout the world. It aims to include works that "ask questions and seek answers to critical contemporary issues, based on an affirmative African centered logic and language of liberation." Sporting an attractively designed interface and strong academic content, the journal has an impressive editorial board comprised of librarians, university faculty, independent scholars, activists, and publishers. Recommended for academic libraries that support African Studies or Africana programs and public libraries that serve black communities. URL: www.jpanafrican.com

268. *The Journal of Race and Policy.* [ISSN: 1540-8450] 2005. a. Ed(s): Michael L. Clemons. Old Dominion University, Department of Political Science and Geography, 5115 Hampton Boulevard, Norfolk, VA 23529; http://odu.edu. *Indexed:* IIBP. *Aud.:* Ac, Sa.

Founded in 2005 by the Institute for the Study of Race and Ethnicity at Old Dominion University, the *Journal of Race and Policy* is an interdisciplinary journal published annually that includes research focusing on the interplay of race, ethnicity, and public policy. *JRP* also publishes articles that pertain to race in the Commonwealth of Virginia, especially the Hampton Roads region. The journal offers a variety of disciplines, approaches, and methodologies, and aims "to achieve both practicality and theoretical relevance among the ranks of national interdisciplinary peer-reviewed journals concerned with race, ethnicity, culture, class and diversity in American society and globally." A recent special issue presents the proceedings of the University of Virginia in St. Kitts and Nevis Program and includes articles that focus on public health, health policy, and disaster management in St. Kitts and Nevis. Recommended for academic libraries that support African American studies, ethnic studies, and public policy programs. Collections that document the South will also want to consider this title.

269. *Journal of Race, Ethnicity, and Religion.* [ISSN: 2153-2370] 2010. m. Free. Ed(s): Miguel A De La Torre. Sopher Press, c/o Miguel A De La Torre, Iliff School of Theology, Denver, CO 80210; info@sopherpress.com; http://www.sopherpress.com. *Bk. rev.:* Number and length vary. *Aud.:* Ac.

Founded in 2010 at the Iliff School of Theology as an open-access journal, *JRER* intends to create a space where religion scholars of color "can study the oppression of our communities and ourselves as a network of interdependent histories." The journal seeks to look within communities of color, with their myriad traditions and cultures, for answers to the religious questions that face scholars and society. *JRER,* whose issue numbering is a bit erratic, includes scholarly essays and book reviews. Topics pertaining to African Americans have included the genesis of African American religious scholarship, and African American children's influence on Mennonite religious practice. These articles have been presented alongside those pertaining to Asian American, Arab American, Native American, and Latino populations. Recommended for academic libraries, especially those that support religious studies or theological schools. URL: www.raceandreligion.com

270. *The Journal of Religious Thought.* [ISSN: 0022-4235] 1943. s-a. Howard University, School of Divinity, 1400 Shepherd St, NE, Washington, DC 20017; http://divinity.howard.edu/. Illus. Refereed. Microform: PQC. *Indexed:* A01, A22, AmHI, BAS, BRI, FR, IIBP, MLA-IB, P02, R&TA, RILM. *Bk. rev.:* 2-3, 250-1,500 words. *Aud.:* Ac, Sa.

The Journal of Religious Thought was established in 1943 by the faculty of the Howard University School of Divinity. This academic journal's mission is to "advance knowledge and share the results of scholarship in the field of religion generally, with special attention to the issues that variously pertain to ministry of the black church and related aspects of the black religious experience." In addition to feature articles, the journal includes book reviews, review essays, and a listing of books received for review. A special feature of the journal is its "Pastor's Corner," which is comprised of shorter pieces—poems, speeches, sermons, and other inspirational writings—that are aimed at people working in local religious settings. Initially a quarterly publication, the journal is seriously delayed and its future is uncertain. Libraries that support seminaries, religious studies, African Studies, and Africana Studies programs will want to consider this title, as will black church libraries.

Living Blues. See Music/Popular section.

Meridians. See Gender Studies section.

The National Black Law Journal. See Law section.

271. National Black Nurses' Association. Journal. [ISSN: 0885-6028] 1986. s-a. Free to members; Non-members, USD 150. Ed(s): Joyce Newman Giger. National Black Nurses' Association, 8630 Fenton St, Ste 330, Silver Spring, MD 20910; contact@nbna.org; http://www.nbna.org. Adv. Refereed. *Indexed:* A22, Agr, SWR&A. *Aud.:* Ac.

The *Journal of the National Black Nurses Association* (*JNBNA*), published twice a year, includes scholarship on issues related to health care in black communities. Written primarily by nursing and health-care faculty from institutions located throughout the U.S., articles may include discussions of educational, social, economic, and legislative topics. Articles, about ten per issue, are subjected to blind review. A recent issue covered topics such as: psychosocial barriers to breast cancer treatment experienced by African American women; employment and breastfeeding outcomes among a sample of African American women; and the personal characteristics and cognition in older African Americans with hypertension. While the journal provides an avenue for black nurses to share their scholarly work regarding clinical practice or research that affects the black community, it is open to scholars of other ethnicities as well. Highly recommended for academic libraries with nursing or public health programs.

National Medical Association. Journal. See Medicine section.

272. National Political Science Review. [ISSN: 0896-629X] 1989. a. Ed(s): David Covin, Michael Mitchell. Transaction Publishers, 35 Berrue Cir, Piscataway, NJ 08854; trans@transactionpub.com; http://www.transactionpub.com. Refereed. *Indexed:* IIBP. *Bk. rev.:* Number and length vary. *Aud.:* Ac.

The *National Political Science Review* (*NPSR*) is an annual refereed publication of the National Conference of Black Political Scientists (NCOBPS). It seeks to provide lively scholarly discourse on domestic and global politics and policies that "advantage or disadvantage groups by reason of race, ethnicity, gender[,] and/or other such factors." Since the journal serves a broad audience of social scientists, including historians, sociologists, anthropologists, theologians, economists, ethicists, and others, it also considers contributions on any subject that has "significant political and social dimensions." It publishes about four blind-reviewed articles based on theoretical and empirical research, as well as several papers that were presented at the most recent NCOBPS meeting. Collaborative efforts by two or more contributors are encouraged, although works by single authors are also included. *NPSR* has recently introduced a "Works in Progress" section that consists of essays that showcase the works of senior political scientists and bring their research agendas to the attention of the political science profession. The personal essays show how the senior scholars craft their research—how they choose their topics and research methodologies—and are intended to help younger scholars design their own research agendas. The journal is available online as part of the Black Studies Center database. The journal publishes about ten critical book reviews per issue. Highly recommended for academic libraries.

273. Negro Educational Review. [ISSN: 0548-1457] 1950. q. USD 30. Ed(s): Alice M Scales. Negro Educational Review, Inc., NER Editorial Office, School of Journalism and Graphic Communication, Tallahasse, FL 32307. Illus., index. Sample. Refereed. Vol. ends: Oct. *Indexed:* A01, A22, ERIC, HEA, IIBP, MLA-IB, P02. *Bk. rev.:* 1-2, 500-1,500 words. *Aud.:* Ac.

The *Negro Educational Review* began as a publishing outlet for faculty at historically black colleges and universities; however, current contributors come from all types of educational institutions. This refereed journal aims to publish

quarterly issues; however, recent economic conditions have constrained its releases to one or two combined issues per year. *NER* publishes articles on issues related to "Black experiences throughout the African Diaspora." While the journal's title suggests that its focus is solely on education, it actually covers the full spectrum of scholarship and includes articles on the social and behavioral sciences, the biological and physical sciences, and the humanities, as well as on professional education. For example, past issues have included articles on "Middle Passage in the Triangular Slave Trade: The West Indies," "Government Acquisition of Private Property for Public Use: An Analysis of United States Supreme Court Decisions," and "The Socioeconomic Impact of Lymphatic Filariasis in Tropical Countries." The journal also publishes thematic issues such as a recent one that examined underrepresented women in academe. In addition to scholarly articles, the journal also features book reviews, news reports, and announcements. Subscriptions are available for print copies only; however, back issues can be found in the ProQuest *Black Studies Center* database at http://bsc.chadwyck.com. Recommended for academic libraries and large public libraries that serve black communities.

274. The Network Journal: black professional and small business magazine. [ISSN: 1094-1908] 1993. 10x/yr. USD 15 domestic; USD 21 Canada; USD 40 elsewhere. Ed(s): Rosalind McLymont. Network Journal, 39 Broadway, Ste 2120, New York, NY 10006. Illus., adv. Sample. *Indexed:* ENW. *Bk. rev.:* Number and length vary. *Aud.:* Ga, Sa.

Beginning as a black-and-white tabloid newspaper in 1993, *The Network Journal* is now a full-color, glossy trade magazine with a robust readership. Targeted to black professionals, business owners, and "upwardly mobile individuals," the monthly magazine presents feature articles designed to provide readers with innovative business ideas and techniques, inspirational stories, and information regarding legal matters, marketing, office technology, and taxation. While *The Network Journal* occasionally prints items regarding personal finance and consumer news, this type of information is far more abundant in *Black Enterprise*. Other features include brief interviews, book reviews, and announcements of upcoming seminars and events. The magazine also sponsors the annual "40-Under-Forty Awards," which highlights 40 people for career excellence, and the "25 Influential Black Women in Business Awards." Print and digital subscriptions are available, and the journal is also available in select databases. Articles from back issues of the magazine are available at the journal's companion web site, which also hosts current news, feature articles, an events calendar, photos, and videos. A useful publication for most public libraries and business collections. URL: www.tnj.com/

275. The North Star (Rochester): a journal of African American religious history. [ISSN: 1094-902X] 1997. s-a. Free. North Star (Rochester), c/o Frederick Douglass Institute for African-American Studies, University of Rochester, Rochester, NY 14627. Illus. Refereed. *Bk. rev.:* Number and length vary. *Aud.:* Ga, Ac.

Published exclusively online, *The North Star* is supported by the University of Rochester in association with the Afro-American Religious History group of the American Academy of Religion. The journal publishes peer-reviewed articles, based on historical research, that explore the religious cultures of African Americans, although work from other disciplines is also considered. *North Star* also includes comparative studies of religious cultures in Africa and elsewhere in the African diaspora. Work from junior scholars and graduate students is encouraged. In addition to featured articles, each issue includes book reviews, events, and new publications, research collections, and Internet resources. The journal has been on hiatus; however, its editor indicates it will resume publication. URL: http://northstarjournal.org

276. Obsidian: Literature in the African Diaspora. Former titles (until 2006): *Obsidian 3: Literature in the African Diaspora;* (until 1999): *Obsidian 2: Black Literature in Review;* (until 1986): *Obsidian: Black Literature in Review.* [ISSN: 2161-6140] 1975. s-a. USD 28 (Individuals, USD 22). North Carolina State University, English Department, 221 Tompkins Hall, PO Box 8105, Raleigh, NC 27695; http://english.chass.ncsu.edu. Illus. Refereed. Microform: PQC. *Indexed:* A22, AmHI, BRI, IIBP, MLA-IB, P02. *Bk. rev.:* Number and length vary. *Aud.:* Ga, Ac.

This literary review publishes contemporary poetry, fiction, drama, and nonfiction prose "from within and concerning the African Diaspora." Recent issues have also included color reproductions of a featured visual artist. Hosted for many years by the English Department of North Carolina State University, *Obsidian* (previously *Obsidian 3*) is currently being edited by Sheila Smith McKoy. The journal seeks to support both new and established writers and displays an appreciation for the range and quality of writing by black authors. Scholarly critical studies have been added to the journal and often contribute to an issue's special theme, e.g., the centennial celebration of Richard Wright, a tribute to Carolina African American Writers' Collective. Book reviews are also included. *Obsidian* is recommended for academic libraries, especially those that support creative writing and Black Studies programs. Large public libraries will also want to consider acquiring this excellent literary journal.

Philosophia Africana See Africa section.

277. *Pluck!: the journal of Affrilachian art & culture.* [ISSN: 1935-0163] 2007. 3x/yr. USD 30. Ed(s): Frank X Walker. Duncan Hill Press, PO Box 14057, Cincinnati, OH 45250-0057. Circ: 5000. *Bk. rev.:* Number and length vary. *Aud.:* Ga, Ac.

A journal with a unique mission, *Pluck!* seeks to "celebrate the rich artistic and cultural heritage of the Appalachian region and the urban centers that are home to its many migrants." It features works that "celebrate outstanding contemporary literature from throughout the [African] Diaspora." Through poetry, fiction, creative nonfiction, images, and essays, *Pluck!* offers an "Affrilachian" aesthetic—work that "unites the broad spectrum of the African and African American ethos and aesthetic to the Appalachian region." The journal is edited and published by Frank X. Walker, a founding member of the Affrilachian Poets and a Cave Canem fellow, who has attracted literary submissions from outstanding writers such as Marilyn Nelson, Lamont B. Steptoe, and Sonia Sanchez. Initially the journal was published three times per year; however, its publication schedule is seriously delayed. Highly recommended for academic libraries that support Appalachian Studies. It is recommended for academic libraries that seek to build comprehensive Southern literature or African American literature collections. Public libraries that serve African American residents of the Appalachian region will also be interested in acquiring this title.

278. *Race & Class: a journal on racism, empire and globalisation.* Formerly (until 1974): *Race*. [ISSN: 0306-3968] 1959. q. USD 527. Ed(s): Arun Kundnan, Hazel Waters. Sage Publications Ltd., 1 Oliver's Yard, 55 City Rd, London, EC1Y 1SP, United Kingdom; info@sagepub.co.uk; http://www.uk.sagepub.com. Adv. Sample. Refereed. Reprint: PSC. *Indexed:* A01, A22, AbAn, AmHI, BAS, BRI, E01, FR, IBSS, IIBP, MLA-IB, P02, P61, RiskAb, SSA. *Bk. rev.:* Number and length vary. *Aud.:* Ac.

Race & Class is a quarterly British journal that is international in scope and examines racism, class bias, and imperialism in contemporary society and historically. Formerly titled *Race,* the journal was established in 1959 by the Institute of Race Relations, a nonprofit organization known for cutting-edge "research and analysis that informs the struggle for racial justice in Britain and internationally." It has an international editorial board that includes African American scholars, and it regularly publishes articles about African American history and life. Its peer-reviewed research articles, commentaries, and book reviews are scholarly, incisive, and usually far left-of-center. Contributors include academics, scientists, artists, novelists, journalists, and politicians. A good example of the journal's interest in American race relations is its special issue titled "Cedric Robinson and the Philosophy of Black Resistance," which focused on Robinson's studies of black Marxism. The journal is available in print and electronic formats. Highly recommended for academic libraries. URL: http://rac.sagepub.com/

279. *Race and Justice: an international journal.* [ISSN: 2153-3687] 2011. q. USD 581. Ed(s): Shaun L. Gabbidon. Sage Publications, Inc., 2455 Teller Rd, Thousand Oaks, CA 91320; info@sagepub.com; http://www.sagepub.com. Refereed. *Bk. rev.:* Number and length vary. *Aud.:* Ac.

Race and Justice, a peer-reviewed quarterly, is the official journal of the American Society of Criminology, Division on People of Color and Crime. A forum for scholarship on race, ethnicity, and justice, the journal is especially interested in publishing policy-oriented papers that examine how race/ethnicity intersects with justice system outcomes across the globe. Journal articles emanate from varied disciplines and employ methodological approaches that are qualitative and/or quantitative. Recent topics have included: "Racial Disparity in Iowa Prisons," "Race, Geography, and Juvenile Justice: An Exploration of the Liberation Hypothesis," and "Assessments of Crime Seriousness on an American Indian Reservation." Each issue usually presents four articles and a book review. The journal is available in print and electronic formats. Recommended for academic libraries that support criminal justice programs. URL: http://raj.sagepub.com

280. *Race and Social Problems.* [ISSN: 1867-1748] 2009. q. EUR 283 (print & online eds.). Ed(s): Gary F Koeske. Springer New York LLC, 233 Spring St, New York, NY 10013; service-ny@springer.com; http://www.springer.com. Sample. Refereed. Reprint: PSC. *Indexed:* A22, ABIn, E01, P61, PsycInfo, SSA. *Aud.:* Ac.

Race and Social Problems, a quarterly journal that is multiracial and multidisciplinary, provides a forum for the publication of articles that address race and its "enduring relationship to psychological, socioeconomic, political, and cultural problems facing present day society." The journal, with an international editorial board, explores topics such as criminal justice, economic conditions, education, elderly, families, health disparities, mental health, race relations, and youth. Nearly all articles pertain to race in the United States, although some offer an international perspective. Black, Asian, and Latino populations are frequently addressed. The journal publishes mostly original empirical articles, about four per issue, which use a variety of methodologies, including quantitative and qualitative. Articles are subjected to a double-blind peer-review process. Occasionally the journal publishes non-empirical articles such as policy proposals, critical analyses, and historical analyses. Issues are occasionally edited by a guest editor who focuses on a single social problem, e.g., "Race and Mental Health." The journal operates on the premise that "virtually every race-related social problem impacts on every other race-related social problem that we are attempting to understand and ameliorate," and its hope is that each issue will be of relevance to "race-focused scholars." The journal is available in print and electronic editions. Recommended for all academic libraries, especially those that support social work programs. URL: www.springerlink.com/content/1867-1748

Race, Gender & Class. See Interdisciplinary Studies section.

The Review of Black Political Economy. See Labor and Industrial Relations section.

281. *Savoy: power. substance. style.* Formerly (until 2000): *Emerge*. [ISSN: 1532-3692] 1989. q. USD 15.95 domestic; USD 25.95 Canada; USD 35.95 elsewhere. L P Green & Partners, Inc., 3379 Peachtree Rd, NE, Ste 230, Atlanta, GA 30326. Adv. *Indexed:* BRI, ENW, IIBP, MLA-IB, P02. *Bk. rev.:* Number and length vary. *Aud.:* Ga, Ac.

Savoy is an attractive, glossy magazine that seeks "to celebrate the true African American experience" by highlighting the "achievements, style[,] and culture of the African American and urban community." Named for Harlem's historic ballroom, *Savoy* began publication in 1999, but folded on two separate occasions. Now based in Atlanta under new ownership, *Savoy* targets its publication to affluent African American urban professionals. This stylish lifestyle magazine provides a mix of news and hot topics, entertainment, sports, business, technology, fashion, travel, and health. Especially popular is the "Savoy 2010 Top 100 Most Influential Blacks in Corporate America," an annual feature that showcases business leaders who are influential not just within their companies, but also in their surrounding communities. Profiles of the top 100 are featured on the magazine's companion web site, which also carries a few select news stories on culture, sports, technology, and business. Recommended for public libraries that serve African American populations, especially those located in urban and suburban areas. URL: http://savoynetwork.com/

282. *Sister 2 Sister.* [ISSN: 1071-5053] 1988. m. Ed(s): Lorenzo Brown. Sister 2 Sister, Inc., PO Box 41148, Washington, DC 20018-0548. Illus., adv. Sample. Vol. ends: Dec. *Bk. rev.:* 1, 250 words. *Aud.:* Ga.

Begun in 1988 as an eight-page newsletter targeted at prominent black women in the entertainment and music industries, *Sister 2 Sister* has become a popular source of black celebrity news. Jamie Foster Brown, the magazine's founder and publisher, begins each issue with "Meow," a lengthy log of her latest findings written in a breezy, conversational style. In addition to the hottest news on African American stars in movies, music, sports, and entertainment, the magazine also has regular columns on health and fitness, fashion and beauty, popular psychology, home improvement, and automobiles. Readers will also appreciate the biographical profiles of successful women in the entertainment industry, as well as the lengthy interviews published in each issue. The magazine also includes music, television, and film reviews. Although the magazine is available in print only, a complementary web site at www.s2smagazine.com features recent news, videos, and several discussion forums. Recommended for public libraries that serve African American communities.

283. *Slavery and Abolition: a journal of slave and post-slave studies.* [ISSN: 0144-039X] 1980. q. GBP 486 (print & online eds.). Ed(s): Gad Heuman. Routledge, 4 Park Sq, Milton Park, Abingdon, OX14 4RN, United Kingdom; subscriptions@tandf.co.uk; http://www.tandfonline.com. Illus., index, adv. Sample. Refereed. Vol. ends: Dec. Microform: PQC. Reprint: PSC. *Indexed:* A01, A22, AmHI, ArtHuCI, E01, IIBP, P61. *Bk. rev.:* 9-15+, 500-1,000 words. *Aud.:* Ac.

Slavery and Abolition is a refereed journal devoted to the study of slavery from the ancient period to the present; it also examines issues relating to the dismantling of slavery and to slavery's legacy. The journal provides perspectives on this sensitive and often controversial topic from a variety of disciplines including history, anthropology, sociology, and literature. Although readers will encounter articles on bondage in ancient Greece or in early Asian history, the bulk of the scholarship focuses on the trans-Atlantic slave trade that brought enslaved Africans to Latin America, the Caribbean, and North America. In addition to special thematic issues, the journal provides an important bibliographical supplement on slavery compiled by Thomas Thurston that updates Joseph C. Miller's published bibliography, "Slavery and Slaving in World History." (The bibliography is searchable online at www.vcdh.virginia.edu/bibliographyofslavery/search.php.) Book reviews and review articles are also included. The journal is available in print and online. Highly recommended for academic libraries. URL: www.tandfonline.com/loi/fsla20

284. *Souls: a critical journal of Black politics, culture, and society.* [ISSN: 1099-9949] 1999. q. GBP 184 (print & online eds.). Ed(s): Elizabeth Hinton. Taylor & Francis Inc., 325 Chestnut St, Ste 800, Philadelphia, PA 19106; customerservice@taylorandfrancis.com; http://www.tandfonline.com. Sample. Reprint: PSC. *Indexed:* A22, E01, IIBP, P61. *Bk. rev.:* 1, 1,000-2,000 words. *Aud.:* Ga, Ac.

Souls is an interdisciplinary quarterly journal that is "produced in the spirit of the intellectual activism of W. E. B. Du Bois" and seeks to present "creative and challenging interpretations of the key issues now being confronted by scholars of modern Black America, Africa, and the Caribbean." The journal was established in 1999 with the sponsorship of the Center for Contemporary Black History, the research unit of the Institute for Research in African-American Studies at Columbia University, and was for many years edited by activist scholar Manning Marable. *Souls* brings together intellectual thought from within and without academe to critically examine black history, politics, socioeconomic research, social theory, and culture. It concentrates on the post-1945 period that witnessed anti-colonial movements throughout Africa and the Caribbean, and the civil rights and Black Power movements within the United States. Beginning with a substantive quotation from Du Bois that sets the stage for the following pages, each issue focuses on a central theme that links the six or more feature articles. Most issues also include a "First Person" section, which consists of an in-depth interview. Readers will appreciate both the attractive presentation and the hard-hitting analysis provided by this journal. The journal is available in print and online. Highly recommended for academic libraries and for large public libraries, especially those with Black Studies collections. URL: www.tandfonline.com/loi/usou20

285. *The Source (New York, 1988): the magazine of hip-hop music, culture & politics.* [ISSN: 1063-2085] 1988. m. USD 25 domestic; USD 40.95 Canada; USD 65.95 foreign. Ed(s): Amy Andrieux. Northstar Group Publishers, 11 Broadway, 3d Fl, New York, NY 10004. Illus. Circ: 370700 Paid. *Indexed:* IIMP, IIPA. *Aud.:* Ga, Ac.

Founded initially as a newsletter in 1988 by two Harvard University students, *The Source* is now one of the leading hip-hop magazines on the market. Once considered the "hip-hop bible," the magazine covers all aspects of the hip-hop music industry and includes musician interviews, feature stories, and concert and recording reviews. Although music is its heart, this publication also includes some general news and current events, political commentary, and sports items. Its companion web site offers sections on the same categories, but also provides a music channel, videos, and live streaming of music events and artist interviews. *The Source* has embraced mobile technologies and social media, so fans may purchase apps, subscribe to its YouTube channel, or follow it on Twitter. Recommended for urban public libraries that serve 18- to 24-year-old populations. Also recommended for libraries with strong popular music collections. URL: www.thesource.com

286. *Transforming Anthropology.* [ISSN: 1051-0559] 1990. s-a. GBP 37 (print & online eds.). Ed(s): John L. Jackson, Jr., Deborah A. Thomas. American Anthropological Association, 2200 Wilson Blvd, Ste 600, Arlington, VA 22201; http://www.aaanet.org. Adv. Sample. Refereed. Reprint: PSC. *Indexed:* A22, ASSIA, E01, IIBP, P61, SSA. *Bk. rev.:* Number and length vary. *Aud.:* Ac.

Transforming Anthropology is the official journal of the Association of Black Anthropologists and is published by the American Anthropological Association. The journal explores "the contemporary and historical construction of social inequities based on race, ethnicity, class, gender, sexuality, nationality and other invidious distinctions." *Transforming Anthropology* features peer-reviewed research articles, research reports, discussions, briefs on works-in-progress, and interviews. It also publishes book, film, and video reviews. The topics covered are international in scope, although the United States, the Caribbean, and Africa are highly represented. The journal is available in print and electronic formats. This title is highly recommended for university and research libraries. URL: http://onlinelibrary.wiley.com/journal/10.1111/%28ISSN%291548-7466

Transition. See Africa section.

287. *Trotter Review.* Formerly (until 1992): *Trotter Institute Review.* [ISSN: 1070-695X] 1987. a. Ed(s): Kenneth Cooper. William Monroe Trotter Institute, 100 Morrissey Blvd, Boston, MA 02125; trotterinstitute@umb.edu; http://www.trotter.umb.edu/. Adv. *Indexed:* IIBP. *Aud.:* Ac, Sa.

An annual publication of the William Monroe Trotter Institute of the University of Massachusetts–Boston, the *Trotter Review* historically published articles addressing race and race relations in the United States and abroad. The journal's strong public policy content reflected the service orientation of its parent institution, the Trotter Institute, which was founded in 1984 to provide research, technical assistance, and public service to the black community and other communities of color in Boston and Massachusetts. In recent years, the journal modified its focus and now has "one hand in the academic and the other hand in the journalistic" as it "tracks the issues that matter most to blacks (broadly defined and inclusive of the diaspora)." Further, it seeks to encourage scholars, students, members of the public, and elected officials to address key issues, to increase dialogue about social problems, and to contribute to solutions. Published since 1987, the journal covers education, economic development, immigration, religion, politics, and race relations. It takes a thematic approach and has published special issues on "Literacy, Expression and the Language of Resistance," "Religion and Civil Society," and "Homosexuality and the Black Community." *Trotter Review* is available in print and online as an open-access publication. Academic libraries that support urban affairs, public policy, and African American Studies programs will want to consider this title. URL: http://scholarworks.umb.edu/trotter_review

288. *Upscale: for the affluent lifestyle.* [ISSN: 1047-2592] 1989. 9x/yr. USD 19.95. Upscale Communications, Inc., 2141 Powers Ferry Rd, Marietta, GA 30067. Illus., adv. Sample. Circ: 182305. *Bk. rev.:* Number and length vary. *Aud.:* Ga, Ac.

Upscale, a glossy, full-color publication, describes itself as "the ultimate lifestyle magazine that addresses the needs of the most stylish and educated African-American." It aims to keep "savvy, trendy and successful African-Americans" informed and entertained as well as enlightened and encouraged. Somewhat similar in scope to *Ebony,* the magazine regularly presents feature articles on up-and-coming people in entertainment and business; current events; fashion, beauty, and style; relationships; health and fitness; interior design and the arts; and travel. *Upscale* also includes brief reviews of books, films, music, and restaurants. Although it reflects a Southern orientation, the magazine clearly has a national reach. Recommended for public libraries that serve African American communities, especially those located in urban and suburban areas.

289. Uptown (Harlem). 2004. bi-m. USD 11.95. Ed(s): Jeija Minor. Uptown Media Group, 113 E 125th St, 2nd Fl, Harlem, NY 10035. *Bk. rev.:* Number and length vary. *Aud.:* Ga.

Uptown is a beautifully designed magazine with a clean layout, and is lavishly illustrated. It indeed reflects "a new renaissance of luxury, lifestyle and living." Targeting affluent African Americans who reside in urban areas, the magazine initially had a strong focus on New York City and was inspired by the revitalization of Harlem, Black America's cultural Mecca. But while New York cultural events are core to the magazine, readers will also find much to read about other major metropolitan areas. *Uptown* publishes regional editions for Atlanta, Chicago, Washington, D.C., and Charlotte. Feature articles cover a wide array of topics such as politics, business and industry, travel, and biographical profiles of successful African Americans. Briefer articles highlight luxurious goods and services such as real estate, automobiles, wines and spirits, beauty products and spas, restaurants, and electronic gadgetry. Fashion photography, when available, is exceptionally well done, as is all of the magazine's photography. *Uptown* also provides reviews of artists' shows, films, theater, music, and books. Its companion web site features a video channel dubbed UPTOWN TV, as well as news, product recommendations, and city guides to fine dining, hotels, and hot night spots. The web site shares content from partner web sites, including its sister publication *Vibe.* Recommended for urban public libraries, especially in those metropolitan areas mentioned above. Suburban public libraries that serve more affluent African American populations will also be interested in this title. URL: http://uptownmagazine.com

290. Urban Influence Magazine. 2004. bi-m. Ed(s): Tamara M Brown. T. Brown Publishing, Inc., 1312 A South Federal, Chicago, IL 60605; http://www.tbrownpublishing.com. *Aud.:* Ga, Ac.

This glossy, attractively designed magazine began in 2004 as an association publication that was disseminated to members of its parent organization, the National Urban League, but it has recently expanded its distribution to national newsstands and individual subscribers. Founded in 1910 as an organization seeking to assist Southern blacks adapt to life in Northern urban areas, the National Urban League, through more than 100 local affiliates, seeks to "enable African Americans to secure economic self-reliance, parity, power and civil rights." *Urban Influence Magazine* serves as a vehicle of providing information on the league's five-step agenda of empowering African Americans in the areas of economics, education, health and quality of life, civil rights, and civic engagement. Targeting young, urban, African American professionals, the bimonthly magazine provides three or four well-written feature articles that focus on community, business, or urban lifestyle. It also has regular columns on wellness, business tips, technology, "urban influencer profiles," entertainment, and league news. The magazine is on hiatus and its future is uncertain. Recommended for academic libraries and public libraries that serve urban African American populations.

291. Vibe (Online). . Spin Music, 276 Fifth Ave, 7th Fl., New York, NY 10001; http://www.spinmedia.com/. *Aud.:* Ga, Ac.

Founded in 1993 by famed record producer Quincy Jones, *Vibe* is one of the most popular African American magazines currently on the market. Despite its popularity, financial woes caused it to briefly suspend publication. It was purchased by a new owner and was back on the newsstands, albeit without its glossy presentation. A lifestyle magazine that conveys the contemporary urban scene, *Vibe* highlights hip-hop culture, including not only the music and musicians but also the fashion industry that has grown up around rap and hip-hop. Each issue has three to four feature articles that usually focus on an artist,

but that often cover historical aspects of hip-hop culture. The magazine features celebrity interviews, and it covers *and creates* trends and events in music, fashion, and art. While its articles are well written, it has a busy layout and a large number of advertisements. *Vibe Vixen,* previously a separate publication targeting urban women, is issued as an occasional supplement to *Vibe.* The magazine supports a lively companion web site that features news, music, videos, and select articles from a print archive. Urban public libraries that serve an 18- to 24-year-old population will want to have this title. Also, libraries with strong fashion and/or popular music collections should consider it. URL: www.vibe.com

292. Wax Poetics. [ISSN: 1537-8241] 2002. q. USD 38 domestic; USD 75 Canada; USD 95 elsewhere. Ed(s): Andre Torres. Wax Poetics Inc., 45 Main St, Ste 224, Brooklyn, NY 11201. Illus., adv. *Aud.:* Ga, Ac, Sa.

Edited by music aficionado Andre Torres, *Wax Poetics* is a small Brooklyn-based magazine that focuses on the history and culture of American popular music, especially funk, soul, hip-hop, and jazz. It aims to educate "the masses about the origins of their musical interests." It is avant-garde in style and regularly features insightful essays, interviews, and high-quality vintage photographs. Music collectors will appreciate the reviews of recordings that were originally released as vinyl LPs, along with reproductions of album labels and cover art. While music is at the core of this magazine, it also covers writers, artists, and themes associated with the music being featured. For example, one issue focusing on soundtracks of blaxploitation films also included a fascinating essay on ex-pimp and writer Robert Beck (a.k.a. Iceberg Slim) and his influence on urban literature. *Wax Poetics* has developed a significant following over the years, and demand for its early issues resulted in the publishing of an edited anthology. The magazine maintains a fresh web site that provides access to select articles from the magazine, along with photos, videos, music, and a blog. Recommended for college and university libraries that support popular culture programs. Also recommended for urban public libraries. URL: www.waxpoetics.com/

293. The Western Journal of Black Studies. [ISSN: 0197-4327] 1977. q. USD 90 (Individuals, USD 30). Ed(s): E Lincoln James. Washington State University Press, 700 Cleveland Hall, Pullman, WA 99164; http://wsupress.wsu.edu. Illus., index, adv. Refereed. Vol. ends: Winter. *Indexed:* A01, A22, AmHI, BRI, IIBP, MLA-IB, P02, P61, RILM, SSA, SWR&A. *Bk. rev.:* Number and length vary. *Aud.:* Ac.

Founded in 1977, *The Western Journal of Black Studies* is an interdisciplinary journal that publishes scholarly articles on "issues related to the African Diaspora and experiences of African/African Americans in the United States." Sponsored by Washington State University, the journal has an editorial board composed of distinguished scholars from throughout the United States who are working primarily in the social sciences and humanities. All articles are subjected to blind peer review. Each issue includes about five feature articles and several scholarly book reviews. The journal has received the C.L.R. James Award for scholarly publication in the field of Black Studies. Subscriptions are available for print only, although the journal is represented in several aggregated databases. The journal maintains a web page where readers can browse the tables of contents for current and back issues. The web page also lists books that are available for review. Recommended for academic libraries and large public libraries that serve African American populations. URL: http://public.wsu.edu/~wjbs/index.html

294. X X L: hip-hop on a higher level. [ISSN: 1093-0647] 1997. 9x/yr. USD 19.97 domestic. Harris Publications, Inc., 1115 Broadway, New York, NY 10010; subscriptions@harris-pub.com; http://www.harris-pub.com. Illus., adv. *Aud.:* Ga.

XXL, an urban lifestyle magazine, is regarded as one of the best hip-hop insider magazines. Somewhat similar to its rival *The Source,* it covers all aspects of hip-hop music and culture, including the business side of the music industry. Published since 1997, the magazine includes feature articles, interviews, commentaries, and reviews. While its primary focus is on musicians, producers, and others affiliated with the industry, the magazine also features actors, filmmakers, comedians, and other entertainment industry personalities, as well as athletes. *XXL* also includes news, current events, upcoming music releases, and the "Eye Candy" section, which consists of photographs of scantily clad women. As with the music that it covers, the language of the magazine is "adult" in nature, and although its title suggests otherwise, this is a magazine that's all about music. The magazine is available in print and digital formats. Its companion web site is highly interactive, with frequently updated news, music reviews, photos, and videos. The magazine is fully engaged with all the major social media outlets. Recommended for urban public libraries that serve older teens and adults. URL: www.xxlmag.com

■ AGRICULTURE

Duncan McClusky, Branch Librarian, College of Agricultural and Environmental Sciences, Tifton Campus, University of Georgia, Tifton, GA 31793

Introduction

Agriculture continues to be one of America's largest industries. Millions of people are either farming or working in a related field. Farmers have to contend with natural disasters such as tornadoes, hurricanes, or droughts; financial costs of what they need to supply in order to produce a crop or what they will be paid for their crop, as well as government budget reductions; and the numerous diseases, weeds, or parasites that can destroy a crop quickly. Farmers face many challenges and they continue to feed the world. Google Scholar is frequently used by patrons, but it should be considered only one database. The EBSCO Discovery Service is useful in searching multiple databases that the library subscribes to at one time. Agris, Agricola, and CAB Direct continue to be the main agricultural databases.

Basic Periodicals

Hs, Ga: *Amber Waves, Farm Journal, Progressive Farmer (Southwest), Successful Farming;* Ac: *Crop Science, Journal of Animal Science, Journal of Dairy Science, Poultry Science.*

Basic Abstracts and Indexes

AGRICOLA, Biological and Agricultural Index, CAB Direct.

295. *Acres U S A: the voice of eco-agriculture.* [ISSN: 1076-4968] 1971. m. USD 27 domestic; USD 37 foreign. Ed(s): Fred C Walters, Samuel Bruce. Acres U S A, PO Box 91299, Austin, TX 78709-1299; info@acresusa.com; http://www.acresusa.com. Illus., adv. Circ: 11000 Paid. *Aud.:* Hs, Ga.

This trade publication is a valuable source of information for those interested in organic and sustainable farming. There are six to ten feature articles and one interview in each issue. Six issues a year are centered on a particular focus (seeds, poultry, soils, cattle and grazing, dairy, and compost). The publication contains a number of regular columns such as "Eco-Gardener," "In the Spotlight," "Health and Healing," and "The Natural Vet." A good source of information on ecological meetings and pertinent books.

296. *Agri-Pulse Newsletter.* Incorporates (1981-2007): *The Webster Agricultural Letter.* 2005. w. USD 397. Ed(s): Sara Wyant. Agri-Pulse Communications Inc., 5 N 985 Rt #31, St. Charles, IL 60175. *Aud.:* Hs, Ga.

The editor provides subscribers with 48 electronic issues a year on the agricultural developments in Washington, D.C. The articles and reports are usually short and easy to read. The web site contains a weekly audio and video section. The "Agri-Pulse Open Mic" provides a verbal interview with people in agriculture. An invaluable resource for those monitoring federal agricultural issues.

297. *The Agricultural Education Magazine.* Former titles (until 1980): *Agricultural Education;* (until 1962): *Agricultural Education Magazine;* (until 1937): *Agricultural Education.* [ISSN: 0732-4677] 1929. bi-m. USD 12 domestic; USD 25 foreign. Ed(s): Harry Boone, Jr. Agricultural Education Magazine, Inc., 300 Garrigus Bldg, The University of Kentucky, Lexington, KY 40546; jjackman.naae@uky.edu. Illus., index. Sample. Vol. ends: No. 6. Microform: PQC. *Indexed:* A22, Agr. *Aud.:* Hs, Ac.

Agricultural teachers would find this journal valuable. Articles center on a theme, and there are about nine articles on the theme. Some of the themes covered are "Going Green with Agricultural Education," "Serving Students with Special Needs in Agricultural Education," and "Using Interactive Technologies in Agricultural Education."

298. *Agricultural History.* Formerly (until 1927): *Agricultural History Society. Papers.* [ISSN: 0002-1482] 1921. q. USD 175 (print & online eds.). Ed(s): Claire Strom. Agricultural History Society, Department of History, UALR, 2801 S University Ave, Little Rock, AR 72324-1099; JGiesen@history.msstate.edu; http://www.aghistorysociety.org. Illus., index, adv. Sample. Refereed. Vol. ends: Fall. Microform: PQC. *Indexed:* A01, A22, ABS&EES, Agr, AmHI, ArtHuCI, BAS, BRI, BrArAb, C45, E01, FR, GardL, IBSS, IndVet, MLA-IB, NumL, P02, RILM, RRTA. *Bk. rev.:* 15-30, 150-600 words. *Aud.:* Ac, Sa.

This journal focuses on all aspects of international agricultural history, and there are usually five to six articles per issue, in addition to several book reviews. Issues may also contain announcements, society news, and a call for papers. This journal would be of interest to agricultural and historical researchers.

299. *Agricultural Research (Online).* [ISSN: 2169-8244] 1953. 10x/yr. Free. Ed(s): Robert Sowers. U.S. Department of Agriculture, Agricultural Research Service, Jamie L Whitten Bldg, Room 302A, 1400 Independence Ave, SW, Washington, DC 20250; http://www.ars.usda.gov. *Aud.:* Hs, Ga, Ac.

This Agricultural Research Service (ARS) publication reports on research by United States Department of Agriculture (USDA) scientists that benefits farmers or prevents an outbreak of disease. Most articles are less than two pages long and written so that a non-scientist can understand them. The journal is available online back to 1996, and there is an online index by title back to 1978. This publication is useful for those wanting to monitor current USDA research. It states, "Complimentary one-year subscriptions are available directly from ARS to public libraries, schools, USDA employees[,] and the news media. Call (301) 504-1660 or e-mail armag@ars.usda.gov."

300. *Agronomy Journal: an international journal of agriculture and natural resource sciences.* Incorporates (1988-1999): *Journal of Production Agriculture;* Formerly: *American Society of Agronomy. Journal.* [ISSN: 0002-1962] 1907. bi-m. USD 635. Ed(s): D Bullock. American Society of Agronomy, Inc., 677 S Segoe Rd, Madison, WI 53711; journals@agronomy.org; https://www.agronomy.org. Illus., index, adv. Sample. Refereed. Circ: 3200 Paid. Vol. ends: Nov/Dec. Microform: PMC. *Indexed:* A22, Agr, C45, EngInd, FS&TA, M&GPA, RRTA, S25. *Aud.:* Ac, Sa.

A society periodical that "publishes articles reporting research findings in soil-plant relationships; crop science; soil science; biometry; crop, soil, pasture, and range management; crop, forage, and pasture production and utilization; turfgrass; agroclimatology; agronomic models; integrated pest management; integrated agricultural systems; and various aspects of entomology, weed science, animal science, plant pathology, and agricultural economics as applied to production agriculture." Other publications that are accepted include notes, observations, review and interpretation papers, and a forum section. This journal would be useful to an academic or research facility working in agronomy.

301. *Amber Waves (Online).* bi-m. U.S. Department of Agriculture, Economic Research Service, 1800 M St NW, Washington, DC 20036; ersinfo@ers.usda.gov; http://www.ers.usda.gov. *Aud.:* Hs, Ga.

Three former USDA Economic Research Service journals were merged into this title to report on research and activities in the department. Graphs and tables are frequently used in this publication. This journal would be valuable to those interested in agricultural economics.

302. American Journal of Experimental Agriculture. [ISSN: 2231-0606] 2011. q. Free. Ed(s): Mintesinot Jiru. Sciencedomain International, U GF, DLF City Phase-III, Delhi NCR, Gurgaon, 122 001, India; contact@sciencedomain.org; http://www.sciencedomain.org. Adv. *Indexed:* A01, C45. *Aud.:* Ac, Sa.

This international publication covers all fields of agriculture and biology, and articles are made available online immediately. There are nine or ten research articles and possibly a review article in each issue. This journal is available for free on the web.

303. American Society of Agricultural and Biological Engineers. Transactions. Former titles (until 2006): *American Society of Agricultural Engineers. Transactions;* (until 1958): *American Society of Agricultural Engineers. Transactions.* [ISSN: 2151-0032] 1907. bi-m. Members, USD 190; Non-members, USD 584. Ed(s): Glenn Laing. American Society of Agricultural and Biological Engineers, 2950 Niles Rd, St Joseph, MI 49085; hq@asabe.org; http://www.asabe.org. Illus., index. Sample. Refereed. Vol. ends: Nov/Dec. *Indexed:* A01, A22, Agr, C&ISA, C45, CerAb, EngInd, FS&TA, IndVet, M&GPA, RRTA, S25. *Aud.:* Ac, Sa.

This journal is contains approximately 2,000 pages of peer-reviewed articles separated into sections such as "Power and Machinery," "Soil and Water," "Food and Process Engineering Institute," "Structures and Environment," "Information and Electrical Technologies," and "Education." This journal should be in any academic library that provides support for agricultural and engineering programs.

304. Animal Frontiers: the review magazine of animal agriculture. [ISSN: 2160-6056] 2011. q. Free to members. American Society of Animal Science, PO Box 7410, Champaign, IL 61826; asas@assochq.org; http://www.asas.org. *Indexed:* C45. *Aud.:* Ac, Sa.

Three cooperating societies are working together to produce a journal in a format that no one was familiar with beforehand. Each issue contains five or six invited articles on international animal agricultural issues that follow a particular theme. Online access is free, and the print subscription is relatively inexpensive.

305. Computers and Electronics in Agriculture. Incorporates (in 1998): *A I Applications;* Which superseded (1987-1990): *A I Applications in Natural Resource Management.* [ISSN: 0168-1699] 1985. 10x/yr. EUR 1958. Ed(s): N. H. Hancock, G van Straten. Elsevier BV, Radarweg 29, PO Box 211, Amsterdam, 1000 AE, Netherlands; JournalsCustomerServiceEMEA@elsevier.com; http://www.elsevier.nl. Illus. Sample. Refereed. Vol. ends: Dec. Microform: PQC. *Indexed:* A01, A22, Agr, C&ISA, C45, CerAb, CompLI, EngInd, FS&TA, IndVet, S25. *Aud.:* Ac, Sa.

This international journal contains between 15 and 20 articles per issue that cover technological advances in computer utilization, electronic instrumentation, and control systems in agriculture and related industries. Online a researcher can access journal issues in progress, as well as other articles that have been accepted. This journal would be valuable in any agricultural collection, especially where precision agricultural research is being done.

306. Crop Management. [ISSN: 1543-7833] 2002. irreg. USD 45. Ed(s): Dan Sweeney. Plant Management Network, 3340 Pilot Knob Rd, St Paul, MN 55121; http://www.plantmanagementnetwork.org. Refereed. *Indexed:* Agr, C45. *Aud.:* Ac, Sa.

The Plant Management Network provides access to four journals, including this one, as well as image collections, proceedings and symposiums, extension service material, plant disease management reports, arthropod management tests, and a newsletter. *Crop Management* is an "applied journal covering crop management practices, crop nutrients, and production agriculture." The journal contains peer-reviewed articles as well as numerous "News and Opinions" articles. Academic facilities and scientists will be interested in these Plant Management publications.

307. Crop Science: a journal serving the international community of crop scientists. [ISSN: 0011-183X] 1961. bi-m. Members, USD 50 (print or online ed.). Ed(s): E Charles Bummer, Elizabeth Gebhardt. Crop Science Society of America, 5585 Guilford Rd, Madison, WI 53711; cca@agronomy.org; https://www.crops.org. Illus., index, adv. Refereed. Vol. ends: Nov/Dec. *Indexed:* A01, A22, Agr, BRI, C45, FS&TA, IndVet, P02, RRTA, S25. *Bk. rev.:* Number and length vary. *Aud.:* Ac.

Papers are separated into the broad subject areas of: crop breeding and genetics; plant genetic resources; genomics, molecular genetics, and biotechnology; crop physiology and metabolism; seed physiology, production, and technology; crop ecology, production, and management; pest management; forage and grazing lands; biomedical, health-beneficial, and nutritionally enhanced plants; and turf grass science. Occasionally there is a book review. This journal would be useful to a scientist or university student in crop science.

308. Experimental Agriculture. Formerly (until 1965): *Empire Journal of Experimental Agriculture.* [ISSN: 0014-4797] 1933. q. GBP 545. Ed(s): Dave Harris. Cambridge University Press, The Edinburgh Bldg, Shaftesbury Rd, Cambridge, CB2 8RU, United Kingdom; information@cambridge.org; http://www.cambridge.org/uk. Illus., adv. Sample. Refereed. Circ: 1700. Microform: PQC. Reprint: PSC. *Indexed:* A22, Agr, C45, E01, FS&TA, IndVet, P02, S25. *Bk. rev.:* 5-10, 200 words. *Aud.:* Ac, Sa.

This scientific publication concentrates on crop field research projects in tropical or warm world regions. The journal publishes reports on new experimental techniques and methods. Recent articles cover research such as the effect of saline irrigation on mustard, and germination of rapeseed. There are numerous book reviews in each issue. A valuable journal for libraries that serve tropical agronomy research.

309. Farm Bureau News. Formerly: *American Farm Bureau Federations Official News Letter.* [ISSN: 0197-5617] 1921. 22x/yr. USD 10. Ed(s): Lynne Finnerty. American Farm Bureau Federation, 600 Maryland Ave, S W, Ste 800, Washington, DC 20024; fbnews@fb.com; http://www.fb.com/ . Illus. Circ: 50000 Paid. *Aud.:* Ga.

This electronic publication from the American Farm Bureau Federation, with 22 issues per year, covers political and economic issues related to farming. The regular sections include "Capital View," "State Focus," "Grassroots," "For the Record," and "Corner Post." This publication is easy to read and would be useful to anyone interested in a fast review of farming issues.

310. Farm Journal: the magazine of American agriculture. Formerly (until 1956): *Farm Journal and Country Gentleman;* Which was formed by the merger of (1945-1955): *Farm Journal;* Which was formerly (until 1945): *Farm Journal and Farmer's Wife;* (1898-1955): *The Country Gentleman;* Which was formerly (until 1898): *The Cultivator & Country Gentleman.* [ISSN: 0014-8008] 1877. m. Ed(s): Katie Humphreys, Karen Freiberg. Farm Journal Media, PO Box 958, Mexico, MO 65265; http://www.agweb.com. Illus., adv. Circ: 44281 Paid. Vol. ends: Dec. Microform: PQC. *Indexed:* A22, B02, B03, BRI, P02. *Aud.:* Hs, Ga.

This journal covers business information for people who own farms or ranches with seven or eight articles in each issue. Regular features include "Machinery Journal," "$100 Ideas," "Production Journal," "Outlook," and "Tailgate Talk." A subscriber can receive *AgWeb Daily, AgWeb Weekly, Farm Journal Legacy Moment,* or other e-mails from other related journals. There are radio broadcasts that can be accessed from the webpage.

311. Farmer's Market Online. [ISSN: 1521-6802] 1995. w. Free. Hofferber, PO Box 1003, Sun Valley, ID 83353. *Aud.:* Ga.

This electronic shopping site is set up "to resemble an open-air market" where producers can sell directly to the consumer. There are also helpful "booths" set up to provide advice for web surfers. Subscribers can sign up to receive a weekly newsletter that may include information on dates for a farmer's market, recipes, notes from readers, or information about people on the site. An interesting site for those wanting to explore available products.

312. *Feedstuffs: the weekly newspaper for agribusiness.* [ISSN: 0014-9624] 1929. w. USD 144 domestic; USD 150 Canada; USD 210 in the Americas. Ed(s): Sarah Muirhead. Miller Publishing Co., 12400 Whitewater Dr, Ste 160, Minnetonka, MN 55343. Illus., adv. Sample. Circ: 15650. Vol. ends: Dec. Microform: PQC. *Indexed:* A22, Agr, B02, B03, BRI, C45, IndVet. *Aud.:* Ga, Ac, Sa.

This tabloid-format publication rotates the focus of the bottom line and insider sections from beef, dairy, poultry, and swine. There is an emphasis placed on the "FoodLink" section of the newspaper. Each issue has opinion, "Mill Market," "Ingredient Market," and "MarketWatch" sections. Each year there is a *Feedstuffs Reference Issue and Buyers Guide*. Many articles are short, and the publication would be useful to anyone interested in agricultural business.

313. *Food Outlook: global market analysis.* [ISSN: 0251-1959] 1975. s-a. Food and Agriculture Organization of the United Nations (F A O), Viale delle Terme di Caracalla, Rome, 00153, Italy; publications-sales@fao.org; http://www.fao.org. Illus. *Indexed:* C45. *Aud.:* Ga, Ac.

This electronic journal is published in English, French, and Spanish and is available in print to 4,600 institutions and individuals. Market summaries provide a paragraph report with a table of information. The "Assessment" section provides more detailed reports on crops such as cereals, wheat, coarse grains, rice, oilseed, sugar, meat, milk, and fish. A recent issue covers cassava. This publication would be useful to those interested in agricultural economics and to those concerned with food shortages.

314. *Hoard's Dairyman: the national dairy farm magazine.* [ISSN: 0018-2885] 1885. s-m. 20/yr. USD 18 domestic; USD 45 foreign. Ed(s): Steven A Larson. W.D. Hoard and Sons Co., PO Box 801, Fort Atkinson, WI 53538; hoards@hoards.com; http://www.hoards.com/. Illus., index, adv. Vol. ends: Dec. Microform: PQC. *Indexed:* A22, FS&TA. *Aud.:* Ga, Ac, Sa.

This folio-sized publication provides brief articles on subjects of interest to dairy farmers. Regular sections include business; feeding, breeding, and herd health; and crops, soils, and fertilizers. Departments include "around the kitchen table"; artificial breeding; cowside practice; farm flashes; handy hints; and "Washington Dairy Grams." This journal would be valuable for a library near dairy cattle operations.

315. *Horticulture and Home Pest News.* Formerly (until 199?): *Horticulture and Home Pest Newsletter.* 1987. w. Free. Iowa State University Entomology Extension Service, Department of Entomology, Insectary Building, Ames, IA 50011; contact@iastate.edu; http://www.iastate.edu. *Aud.:* Ga, Ac, Sa.

This publication contains two to six brief, timely articles from Iowa State University extension agents from the entomology, horticulture, and plant pathology departments. Recent articles report on starting seeds indoors, vegetable seed selection, home garden tomatoes, and the effect of the weather on insects.

316. *Journal of Agricultural and Food Chemistry.* [ISSN: 0021-8561] 1953. bi-w. USD 2520. Ed(s): Matt Hotze, James N Seiber. American Chemical Society, 1155 16th St N W, Washington, DC 20036; help@acs.org; http://pubs.acs.org. Illus., adv. Sample. Refereed. Circ: 71104. *Indexed:* A22, AbAn, Agr, C45, FS&TA, H24, IndVet, OceAb, RRTA. *Aud.:* Ac, Sa.

This journal publishes over 1,700 articles in a year, and the articles are frequently cited in other articles. The subject divisions include agricultural and environmental chemistry; analysis and chemosensory perception of flavor; analytical methods; bioactive constituents and functions; biofuels and biobased products; chemical aspects of biotechnology and molecular biology; food and beverage chemistry/biochemistry; and food safety and toxicology. This journal is important for any food science or agricultural research library.

317. *Journal of Agricultural Safety and Health.* [ISSN: 1074-7583] 1995. q. Members, USD 96; Non-members, USD 191. Ed(s): David L Hard. American Society of Agricultural and Biological Engineers, 2950 Niles Rd, St Joseph, MI 49085; hq@asabe.org; http://www.asabe.org. Illus., index. Refereed. Vol. ends: Nov. *Indexed:* Agr, C45, ErgAb, H24, IndVet, RRTA, RiskAb. *Aud.:* Ga, Ac.

This international journal covers all areas related to agricultural safety and health with approximately five articles in each issue. Recent articles have been on the cost of farm fatalities or accidents on farms in Australia and Finland and age-appropriate farm safety curriculum. This journal would be valuable in any rural library.

318. *Journal of Agricultural Science.* [ISSN: 1916-9752] 2009. s-a. Free. Ed(s): Tunde Akim Omokanye, Anne Brown. Canadian Center of Science and Education, 4915 Bathurst St, Unit 209-309, Toronto, ON M2R 1X9, Canada; info@ccsenet.org; http://www.ccsenet.org. Sample. Refereed. Circ: 200. *Indexed:* A01, C37, C45, P02. *Aud.:* Ac, Sa.

All areas of agricultural science are covered in this open-access journal from the Canadian Center of Science and Education. Electronic articles that have been accepted can be accessed before the publishing in a printed journal. There are about 30 articles in each published issue that cover topics such as management of cauliflower pests, chlorophyll content in avocados, and yield predictions for sugar beets.

319. *Journal of Animal Science: leading source of new knowledge and perspectives in animal science.* Supersedes in part: *American Society of Animal Production. Record of Proceedings of the Annual Meeting;* Which was formerly (until 1913): *American Society of Animal Nutrition. Record of Proceedings of Annual Meeting.* [ISSN: 0021-8812] 1942. 12x/yr. Members, USD 235; Non-members, USD 525. Ed(s): Steven A Zinn. American Society of Animal Science, 1111 N Dunlap Ave, Savoy, IL 61874; johne@assochq.org; http://www.asas.org. Illus., index. Refereed. Circ: 5000. Vol. ends: Dec. Microform: PMC; PQC. *Indexed:* A01, A22, AbAn, Agr, BRI, C45, FS&TA, IndVet, P02. *Bk. rev.:* 1-5, 35-100 words. *Aud.:* Ac, Sa.

This journal of the American Society of Animal Science covers all aspects of the subject, including molecular genetics; quantitative genetics; physiology, endocrinology, and reproduction; growth and developmental biology; meat science and muscle biology; nonruminant nutrition; behavior; pharmacology and toxicology; ruminant nutrition; health and well-being; management; contemporary issues; and pre- and post-harvest product safety. Some society news is included in the issues. This journal should be in any collection that provides support to animal researchers.

320. *Journal of Dairy Science.* [ISSN: 0022-0302] 1917. m. USD 949. Elsevier Inc., 360 Park Ave S, New York, NY 10010; JournalCustomerService-usa@elsevier.com; http://www.elsevier.com. Illus., index, adv. Refereed. Vol. ends: Dec. Microform: PMC; PQC. *Indexed:* A01, A22, AbAn, Agr, B01, C45, FS&TA, IndVet, RRTA. *Aud.:* Ac, Sa.

The American Dairy Science Association publishes approximately 4,400 pages per year in this journal, covering all aspects of dairy cattle research, including dairy foods; genetics and breeding; nutrition, feeding, and calves; physiology and management; and "our industry today." The announcements section may contain employment information. A must for any library that supports a cattle research program.

321. *Journal of Plant Registrations.* [ISSN: 1936-5209] 2007. 3x/yr. USD 615. Ed(s): E Charles Bummer, Elizabeth Gebhardt. Crop Science Society of America, 677 S Segoe Rd, Madison, WI 53711; cca@agronomy.org; https://www.crops.org. Adv. Refereed. *Indexed:* Agr, C45. *Aud.:* Ga, Ac, Sa.

Researchers are developing new cultivars, parental lines, germplasms, and genetic stock of plants for various reasons, such as disease prevention, or drought tolerance, or producing a different-color leaf or flower. Knowledge of these new plants can be financially beneficial to farmers, and can be the basis for interesting commentary to the home gardener.

322. *Poultry Science.* [ISSN: 0032-5791] 1908. m. USD 575 (print & online eds.) Members, USD 200 (print & online eds.). Ed(s): Colin Scanes. Poultry Science Association Inc., 1111 N Dunlap Ave, Savoy, IL 61874; psa@assochq.org; http://www.poultryscience.org. Illus., index, adv. Refereed. Circ: 3500 Paid. Vol. ends: Dec. Microform: PQC. *Indexed:* A01, A22, Agr, C45, FS&TA, IndVet. *Bk. rev.:* 2-4, 200-500 words. *Aud.:* Ac, Sa.

This professional association journal separates papers into the sections "Environment, Well-Being, and Behavior"; "Genetics, Immunology, Health, and Disease"; "Molecular, Cellular, and Developmental Biology"; "Metabolism and Nutrition"; "Physiology"; "Endocrinology and Reproduction"; "Processing, Products, and Food Safety"; and "Production, Modeling, and Education." The journal would be valuable in any collection that provides support to poultry farmers or researchers.

323. *Progressive Farmer (Southwest).* Formed by the merger of (1886-19??): *Progressive Farmer for Oklahoma; Progressive Farmer for Texas East; Progressive Farmer for the West;* All of which superseded in part (in 19??): *Progressive Farmer. Texas - Oklahoma - New Mexico - Arizona.* [ISSN: 0033-0760] 12x/yr. USD 24 domestic. Ed(s): Jack Odle, Gregg Hillyer. Progressive Farmer, Inc., 2204 Lakeshore Dr, Ste 415, Birmingham, AL 35209; classifieds@progressivefarmer.com; http://www.progressivefarmer.com. Illus., adv. Vol. ends: Dec. Microform: PQC. *Indexed:* A22, ABIn. *Aud.:* Hs, Ga, Ac.

This journal is written for those living on farms or involved in agriculture. There are usually four feature articles in each issue. Other articles are grouped into sections entitled "Your Land," "Your Farm," "Your Life," and "First Look." Recent feature articles have been on women's roles increasing on the farm; growth in the farmland market; and farm hunts. The last page contains a number of quotes. A library in a farming area would find this journal valuable.

324. *Renewable Agriculture and Food Systems.* Formerly (until 2004): *American Journal of Alternative Agriculture.* [ISSN: 1742-1705] 1986. q. GBP 288. Ed(s): Rick Welsh, Lydia Oberholtzer. Cambridge University Press, The Edinburgh Bldg, Shaftesbury Rd, Cambridge, CB2 8RU, United Kingdom; information@cambridge.org; http://www.cambridge.org/uk. Illus., adv. Sample. Refereed. Reprint: PSC. *Indexed:* A01, A22, Agr, BRI, C45, E01, FS&TA, GardL, IndVet, P02, RRTA. *Bk. rev.:* 2-4, 400-600 words. *Aud.:* Ga, Ac.

This journal publishes articles intended for a multidisciplinary audience on "biological, physical, or social science aspects of alternative and renewable agriculture and food systems." Articles can be research, review, or preliminary reports. A recent special issue focused on conservation tillage. Recent articles have been on the effect of mint vermicompost on a rotation of mint, rice, and wheat; and the management of sulfur in wine grapes. This journal would be easily understood by a wide range of readers and would be useful in any agricultural library.

325. *Resource (Niles): engineering & technology for a sustainable world.* Formed by the merger of (1920-1994): *Agricultural Engineering;* (1983-1994): *Within A S A E.* [ISSN: 1076-3333] 1994. bi-m. Members, USD 24; Non-members, USD 90. Ed(s): Sue Mitrovich. American Society of Agricultural and Biological Engineers, 2950 Niles Rd, St Joseph, MI 49085; hq@asabe.org; http://www.asabe.org. Illus., adv. Vol. ends: Dec. Microform: PQC. *Indexed:* A22, B02, BRI, C45, EngInd, IndVet, P02. *Aud.:* Ac.

This society publication contains four feature articles and regular department reports. The articles are relatively short and easy to read. Professional employment opportunities are listed. One issue annually highlights AE50 awards for new advances in agricultural systems. Most appropriate for agricultural and engineering libraries.

326. *Soil Science Society of America. Journal.* Formerly (until 1976): *Soil Science Society of America. Proceedings.* [ISSN: 0361-5995] 1936. bi-m. USD 635 domestic; USD 683 foreign. Ed(s): D D Myroid, Sally D Logsdon. Soil Science Society of America, 5585 Guilford Rd, Madison, WI 53711; http://www.soils.org/. Illus., index, adv. Refereed. Vol. ends: Nov/Dec. Microform: PMC. *Indexed:* A01, A22, Agr, BRI, C&ISA, C45, CerAb, EngInd, P02, RRTA, S25. *Aud.:* Ac, Sa.

Articles are grouped by the various sections within the Soil Science Society of America. Sections utilized include soil science issues; soil physics; soil chemistry; soil biology and biochemistry; soil fertility and plant nutrition; pedology; soil and water management and conservation; forest, range, and wildland soils; wetland soils; and nutrient management and plant analysis. Articles present original research for scientists or researchers in the field.

327. *Successful Farming: for families that make farming their business.* Incorporates (in 1989): *Successful Farming in the South;* (in 1929): *Dairy Farmer;* Which was formerly (until 1919): *Kimball's Dairy Farmer.* [ISSN: 0039-4432] 1902. m. USD 15.95 domestic; USD 27.95 foreign; USD 2.95 per issue. Ed(s): Loren Kruse, John Walter. Meredith Corporation, 1716 Locust St, Des Moines, IA 50309; patrick.taylor@meredith.com; http://www.meredith.com. Illus., adv. Sample. Circ: 440000. *Indexed:* A22, ABIn, B02, BRI, P02. *Aud.:* Hs, Ga.

This trade publication covers farms and farm life with many advertisements in each issue. The print version has a cover story, and sections such as "your profit"; "Can their problem be solved?"; "Machinery Pete"; "business partners"; "healthy manager"; "farmers for the future"; "family"; and a recipe. Online there are articles from the journal at www.agriculture.com. This journal would be nice to have for any library in an agricultural area.

328. *U.S. Department of Agriculture. National Agricultural Statistics Service. Agricultural Prices.* Former titles (until 1942): *United States. Bureau of Agricultural Economics. Farm Product Prices;* (until 19??): *Average Prices Received by Farmers for Farm Produce.* [ISSN: 0002-1601] 19??. m. U.S. Department of Agriculture, National Agricultural Statistics Service, Rm 5805 S, Washington, DC 20250; nass@nass.usda.gov; http://www.nass.usda.gov/. *Indexed:* AmStI. *Aud.:* Hs, Ga, Ac.

This is an example of the USDA National Agricultural Statistics Service's many serial reports that are available on the USDA web site. This monthly publication provides "prices received by farmers for principal crops, livestock[,] and livestock products; indexes of prices received by farmers; feed price ratios; and indexes of prices paid by farmers." Anyone interested in tracking agricultural production, trade, prices, and the effects of weather on crops will enjoy these newsletters.

329. *Weekly Weather and Crop Bulletin.* Incorporates (1899-1932): *Snow and Ice Bulletin;* Which was formerly (until 1899): *Snow and Ice Chart.* [ISSN: 0043-1974] 1872. w. Free. Ed(s): Brad Rippey. The Joint Agricultural Weather Facility, NOAA/USDA, Joint Agricultural Weather Facility, USDA South Bldg, RM 4443, Washington, DC 20250; http://www.usda.gov/oce/weather/. Illus., index. Vol. ends: Dec. *Indexed:* A22, AmStI. *Aud.:* Ga, Ac.

This electronic weekly is posted by 5:00 p.m. on Wednesday, unless there has been a federal holiday earlier in the work week. It provides meteorological information for farmers and information on the status of various crops. Many charts of the United States are used to illustrate information such as temperature and precipitation data. International weather and crop information is also provided. This is a valuable resource for libraries that serve patrons interested in meteorology and its relationship to agriculture.

■ ANIMAL RIGHTS/ANIMAL WELFARE

See also Birds; Horses; Pets; and Veterinary Science sections.

Julie Arendt, Science and Engineering Librarian; Library Affairs, Morris Library; Mail code 6632; Southern Illinois University, Carbondale; Carbondale, IL 62901-6632; jarendt@lib.siu.edu; FAX: 618-453-3440.

Cheryl LaGuardia, Research Librarian, Widener Library, Harvard University

Introduction

Animal welfare magazines include many publications promoting humane treatment of animals. They include pet-related topics such as the appropriate care for a specific species or the importance of neutering and spaying. The animal welfare heading also encompasses animal rights publications. Animal rights magazines go beyond promoting better treatment of animals to advocating an end to activities that harm animals. This advocacy can include an end to eating meat, an end to animal products, an end to laboratory testing on animals, and an end to many uses of animals in entertainment.

Many animal welfare and animal rights publications are produced by nonprofit animal welfare and animal rights organizations. Often these publications emphasize the work of the nonprofit. Nonprofit groups produce these magazines partly as a way to publicize animal welfare and animal rights issues and partly as a benefit for donors. Many of these titles are available online at no charge.

From children's newsletters to specialized academic journals, from mild animal shelter magazines to animal rights tracts, animal welfare magazines cover a range of perspectives. The following magazines provide a glimpse of this range.

Basic Periodicals

Ems: *Grrr!: kids bite back*; Hs: *AllAnimals, P E T A's Animal Times (English Edition)*; Ga: *AllAnimals, The Å V Magazine, P E T A's Animal Times (English Edition)*; Ac: *Animal Welfare; ro; Sa: Animal Sheltering*.

Basic Abstracts and Indexes

Academic Search Premier, AGRICOLA, IngentaConnect.

330. A S P C A Action. [ISSN: 1554-6624] 2005. q. Free to members. American Society for the Prevention of Cruelty to Animals, 424 E 92nd St, New York, NY 10128; information@aspca.org; http://www.aspca.org. *Aud.:* Hs, Ga.

ASPCA Action is the member newsletter for supporters of the American Society for the Prevention of Cruelty to Animals (ASPCA). This full-color magazine typically has about 18 pages per issue. Feature articles highlight cruelty prevention and cruelty remediation, with an emphasis on companion animals. *ASPCA Action* also includes short articles on pet care. News briefs, legislative victories, and animal rescue sections highlight the results of the ASPCA's activities.

331. The A V Magazine. Former titles (until 1977): *The A-V;* (until 1939): *Starry Cross;* (until 1919): *Journal of Zoophily.* [ISSN: 0274-7774] 1892. m. Free to qualified personnel. Ed(s): Crystal Schaeffer. American Anti-Vivisection Society, 801 Old York Rd, Ste 204, Jenkintown, PA 19046; aavs@aavs.org; http://www.aavs.org/. Illus. Sample. *Aud.:* Hs, Ga.

Published by the American Anti-Vivisection Society, *The AV Magazine* opposes the use of animals in laboratory research. Many articles address one of three goals: to develop alternatives to animal testing, to persuade government regulators to recognize and accept the alternatives, and to persuade industry and universities to use the alternatives. Although it is a glossy full-color magazine, its articles are detailed and several pages long. Articles often provide complete citations for their sources. Online copies of articles are available for free on *The AV Magazine* website.

332. Act'ionLine. Former titles: *Friends of Animals Reports; Animals (New York); Actionline.* [ISSN: 1072-2068] 1977. q. Friends of Animals, Inc., 777 Post Rd, Ste 205, Darien, CT 06820-4721; http://www.friendsofanimals.org. Illus., index, adv. Sample. Vol. ends: Winter. *Bk. rev.:* Occasional. *Aud.:* Hs, Ga.

Act'ionLine is published by Friends of Animals, an organization that "advocates for the right of animals to live free according to their own terms." It sometimes disputes measures proposed by mainstream animal welfare organizations. For example, where an animal welfare organization would advocate for humane farming practices, *Act'ionLine* advocates for an end to animal agribusiness. *Act'ionLine* provides articles about a variety of animals and has a special emphasis on vegan eating. Shorter articles include a "Cheers and Jeers" page in

every issue and frequent articles on vegan food and cooking. Longer articles often have footnotes that cite their sources and provide places for readers to obtain further information. Issues of *Act'ionLine* are available for free at the Friends of Animals website.

333. AllAnimals. Former titles (until 1999): *H S U S News; Humane Society News;* (until 1989): *Humane Society of the United States. News.* 1954. q. USD 25 membership. Humane Society of the United States, 2100 L St, N W, Washington, DC 20037; corprelations@humanesociety.org; http://www.hsus.org. Illus., adv. Circ: 416953 Paid. *Aud.:* Hs, Ga.

AllAnimals is published for members of the Humane Society of the United States. Coverage emphasizes companion animals, but it includes some articles about issues affecting wildlife and farm animals. Attractive photographs accompany short articles about the welfare of both wild and domesticated animals. Many of the articles will appeal to a broad audience. For example, recent issues include detailed articles about pet care and about the humane removal of wildlife from garages or attics.

334. Alternatives to Laboratory Animals. Former titles (until 1981): *A T L A Abstracts;* (until 1974): *Alternatives to Laboratory Animals. Abstracts.* [ISSN: 0261-1929] 1973. bi-m. GBP 140; USD 294; GBP 194 combined subscription (print & online eds.). Ed(s): Susan Trigwell, Michael Balls. Fund for the Replacement of Animals in Medical Experiments, Russell & Burch House, 96-98 N Sherwood St, Nottingham, NG1 4EE, United Kingdom; frame@frame.org.uk; http://www.frame.org.uk. Illus., index, adv. Sample. Refereed. Vol. ends: Dec. *Indexed:* A22, Agr, C45, ExcerpMed, IndVet. *Bk. rev.:* 4, 575 words. *Aud.:* Ac, Sa.

This journal covers the development, validation, introduction, and use of alternatives to laboratory animals. Many articles describe research to validate and evaluate non-animal research techniques. These techniques range from computer models to media for growing cell lines. Articles are often specialized and technical. *Alternatives to Laboratory Animals* also includes a conference reports section and a large comments section. This journal is appropriate for larger academic libraries or special libraries in organizations where laboratory animals might be used.

335. Animal Sheltering: animal services / rescues / shelter. Formerly (until 1996): *Shelter Sense.* 1978. bi-m. USD 20 domestic; USD 25 foreign. Ed(s): Nancy Lawson. Humane Society of the United States, 2100 L St, N W, Washington, DC 20037; http://www.hsus.org. Illus., adv. Sample. Circ: 5512 Paid. Vol. ends: Nov/Dec. *Bk. rev.:* Number and length vary. *Aud.:* Sa.

Shelter managers can find ideas and advice in *Animal Sheltering*. Articles cover practical aspects of managing a shelter. Beyond just discussing animal care, this trade magazine discusses many areas of shelter management. It includes advice on topics such as how to testify in court during cruelty investigations and how to establish a humane education program for children. *Animal Sheltering* also includes useful information for veterinarians who work with animal shelters, so this magazine would be useful both in shelters and in veterinary libraries. Back issues are available for free online.

Anthrozoos. See Pets section.

Best Friends. See Pets section.

336. K I N D News. 1983. m. 9/yr. USD 30 domestic; USD 50 foreign. Ed(s): Catherine Vincenti. National Association for Humane and Environmental Education (N A H E E), 67 Norwich Essex Turnpike, East Haddam, CT 06423; youth@humanesocietyyouth.org; http://www.humanesocietyyouth.org. Circ: 1120000 Paid. *Aud.:* Ems.

KIND News is a short children's publication produced by the Humane Society of The United States. It has three editions: Primary for kindergarten to grade two, Junior for grades three and four, and Senior for grades five and six. An "Ask Dr. Kind" column answering children's questions about pets is a regular feature in all three versions. All three versions have short articles about wild animals and pet care. The Junior and Senior editions include the "Mutts" comic strip, a "KIND Club Zone" featuring activities that student groups have done to help animals, and "KIND Quiz" questions about that issue. Classroom activities and materials are available for teachers to use with *KIND News*.

Our Animals. See Pets section.

337. *P E T A's Animal Times (English Edition).* Formerly (until 1994): *P E T A News.* 1980. q. Membership, USD 16. Ed(s): Ingrid Newkirk. People for the Ethical Treatment of Animals, Inc., 501 Front St, Norfolk, VA 23510; peta@peta.org; http://www.peta.org. Illus. Sample. Circ: 350000 Paid and controlled. Vol. ends: Winter. *Aud.:* Hs, Ga.

PETA's Animal Times is a colorful publication from the animal rights organization People for the Ethical Treatment of Animals (PETA). Short articles present PETA's activism, vegan recipes, and celebrities who are active in animal rights issues. Longer exposes address topics such as animal testing at universities, practices in a turkey slaughterhouse, and egg production in factory farms. Articles regularly encourage readers to go vegan, to avoid fur, and to get involved in protecting animals.

■ ANIME, COMICS, GRAPHIC NOVELS, AND MANGA

Tom Bruno, Associate Director of Resource Sharing and Reserves, Sterling Memorial Library, Yale University, New Haven, CT 06511

Introduction

There may have been a time when anime, comics, graphic novels, and manga were unfamiliar subjects to a librarian, but in recent years the market in North America for all of these has exploded dramatically. Bookstores and public libraries now stock entire sections with the latest manga series, while anime films have moved from special screenings at college fan clubs and art house theaters to the suburban multiplex, and comic artists and graphic novelists have been National Book Award finalists and even won the Pulitzer Prize. Having long been relegated to the stuff of juvenile fiction or esoteric enthusiasts, these art forms are beginning to gain mainstream respect among critics and the general public alike.

Over the past few years, manga and anime have experienced a surge in popularity in the United States and Canada, driven by a youth market enamored with Japanese popular culture ("J-pop") and adults who grew up reading comic books and watching early "Japanimation" exports such as *Astro Boy, Star Blazers,* and *Speed Racer* on television. Although this J-pop invasion was accompanied by a host of glossy consumer magazines, such as *Newtype USA, Protoculture Addicts,* and *Wizard,* many of these publications have folded in the past few years in the face of market consolidation and high production costs, though the popular "tankobon" anthologies of popular manga series are still available through publications such as *Weekly Shonen Jump.*

Comics and graphic novels, on the other hand, have finally come into their own with a series of new scholarly publications, as an increasing number of colleges and universities turn to more serious consideration of the medium. Although this section will mostly restrict itself to magazines and periodicals about comics and graphic novels, the graphical orientation of this genre makes it hard to ignore "tankobon"-style anthology publications, which are as much reviews of their medium as are traditional print journals.

Clearly, anime, comics, graphic novels, and manga are art forms that resist easy categorization, and as these modes of expression gain a more secure foothold in popular culture, the more they are blurred into one all-encompassing genre. A fantastic example of this is the work of Bryan Lee O'Malley, a Canadian cartoonist whose award-winning *Scott Pilgrim* series of graphic novels is directly inspired by the manga tradition. At the same time, anime and manga are borrowing increasingly from North American comic books, graphic novels, feature films, and even literature. The recent release of director Guillermo del Toro's giant robot/monster blockbuster film *Pacific Rim* is an excellent example of the rich cross-fertilization that occurs back and forth between Japan and Hollywood.

It is perhaps not surprising, then, that such a fluid and dynamic body of multimedia does not yet have many periodicals that cover it exclusively. With the notable exception of *Mechademia,* it is still particularly difficult to find academic or scholarly journals whose sole focus is anime and manga, although critical reception and interpretation of the genre can be found in many periodicals about film animation or contemporary East Asia culture. While it is true that comics and graphic novels have seen the emergence of a body of scholarly literature, the selection of general-interest magazines about anime, manga, comics, and graphic novels has contracted significantly in recent years, as fandom has migrated to blogs and social media for their previews, news, and reviews, or folded entirely into mainstream entertainment publications. This latter transformation of popular culture is perhaps the surest sign that anime, comics, graphics novels, and manga have been successfully assimilated and finally come into their own.

Basic Periodicals

See above.

Basic Abstracts and Indexes

MLA International Bibliography.

338. *The Best American Comics.* [ISSN: 1941-6385] 2006. a. USD 20 per issue 2011 edition. Ed(s): Lynda Barry, Matt Madden. Houghton Mifflin Harcourt Publishing Company, 222 Berkeley St, Boston, MA 02116; trade_publicity@hmco.com; http://www.hmco.com/. *Aud.:* Ga, Ac, Sa.

While some special pleading may be in order to include this publication as a magazine, *The Best American Comics* is the definitive annual sampling of America's emerging talents in the field of comic art. Each volume is 352 pages and is edited by a new guest editor chosen every year by series editors Jessica Abel and Matt Madden, both of them comic book writers and artists themselves (as well as wife and husband). This publication features more than two dozen excerpts that cull "the best stories from graphic novels, pamphlet comics, newspapers, magazines, mini-comics, and the Internet." The guest editor for 2012 was Francoise Mouly—designer, artist, colorist, and art editor of *The New Yorker.* In a field that is as visual as it is textual, there is no better introduction to the medium of comic art than a selection of cutting-edge authors, and *The Best American Comics* has delivered just that since its launch in 2006. Also noteworthy are the guest editors' forwards and the inclusion of "expanded selection lists" of artists/authors who did not make the cut. This series is an absolutely indispensable resource for any library, and may be of great assistance to collection development librarians who are eager to keep up with comics and graphic novels.

339. *The Comics Journal: the magazine of comics news & criticism.* Formerly (until 1977): *Nostalgia Journal.* [ISSN: 0194-7869] 1974. 3x/yr. USD 75 domestic; USD 90 Canada; USD 120 elsewhere. Ed(s): Timothy Hodler, Dan Nadel. Fantagraphics Books, Inc., 7563 Lake City Way NE, Seattle, WA 98115; http://www.fantagraphics.com. Illus., adv. *Bk. rev.:* 2-4 pages of reviews. *Aud.:* Ga, Ac, Sa.

Fantagraphics' *Comics Journal* is "a magazine that covers the comics medium from an arts-first perspective." Each 200-page issue contains an eclectic mix of comics news and reviews, as well as interviews with artists and writers from the whole spectrum of the field—from mainstream to indie comics, from newsstand superhero monthlies to more adult-themed graphic novels and underground publications. Recent issues have covered such topics as interviews with Kevin Eastman (creator of *Teenage Mutant Ninja Turtles*), *Mad Magazine* illustrator Will Elder, and the response to James Kochalka's infamous 1996 letter/essay "Craft Is The Enemy." Although all of its contributors are clearly fans of comics and graphic novels, *Comics Journal* revels in its contentious relationship with the industry, applying a level of literary criticism and investigative journalism that is unusual for a medium whose major periodicals smack of unqualified mutual appreciation and boosterism. Issues are generously illustrated mostly in black-and-white, with some color prints, and feature artwork from some of the finest comics talent from around the world. *Comics Journal* also maintains a first-rate web presence, with selected excerpts available free to the public and full online content for print subscribers. This is an essential resource for both general and specialized library collections.

340. *European Comic Art.* [ISSN: 1754-3797] 2008. s-a. GBP 102 (print & online eds.). Ed(s): Laurence Grove, Ann Miller. Berghahn Books Ltd., 3 Newtec Pl, Magdalen Rd, Oxford, OX4 1RE, United Kingdom; journals@berghahnbooks.com; http://www.berghahnbooks.com. Adv. Refereed. *Indexed:* A07, A51, BRI, MLA-IB. *Aud.:* Ac, Sa.

A joint publication of American Bande Dessinee Society and the International Bande Dessinee Society from Berghahn Books Ltd., *European Comic Art* is "the first English-language scholarly publication devoted to the study of European-language graphic novels, comic strips, comic books and caricature." Each issue contains four to six articles and several reviews of recent European comics, covering publications in all European languages, with special emphasis on works French and English, and accompanied by illustrations in black-and-white. Recent topics addressed include a study of names and wordplay in Herge's *Tintin*, the impact of Louis Napoleon Bonaparte on European comic art, and comic adaptations of literary works. While this journal is not intended for general audiences, *European Comic Art* is a welcome addition to academic and special library collections and provides an important avenue of access to contemporary European scholarship in the field of comics and graphic novels.

341. *ImageTexT: interdisciplinary comics studies.* [ISSN: 1549-6732] 2004. 3x/yr. Free. Ed(s): Donald Ault. University of Florida, Department of English, 4008 Turlington Hall, PO Box 117310, Gainesville, FL 32611; http://www.english.ufl.edu/. Refereed. *Indexed:* MLA-IB. *Bk. rev.:* 1-4, signed. *Aud.:* Ac, Sa.

Given the decidedly postmodern and multimedia nature of the comics/graphic novel genre, it is perhaps surprising that there aren't more open-access online journals covering the field. *ImageTexT,* published by the University of Florida's English Department, makes up for this relative scarcity, however, by offering an academic review of the medium that is as in-depth as it is comprehensive. *ImageTexT* is a free, open-access, peer-reviewed online publication, and each issue features 8–12 articles (including one to four book reviews) written by an international body of contributors including graduate students, professors, and educated laypersons. Articles are formatted specifically for online reading, contain lavish color illustrations, and permit easy browsing and navigation. Recent issues address such topics as "Shakespeare and Visual Rhetoric"; narrative continuity and historiography in DC Comics' 1985 *Crisis on Infinite Earths*; and visions of utopia in Japanese anime. *ImageTexT* should be on every librarian's short list of comics journals, not just because it's open-access and free, but because it's quite simply one of the best periodicals out there representing the intersection of comics and serious scholarship.

342. *International Journal of Comic Art.* [ISSN: 1531-6793] 1999. s-a. USD 60 (Individuals, USD 45). John A. Lent, Ed & Pub, 669 Ferne Blvd, Drexel Hill, PA 19026. Illus., adv. *Indexed:* A07, MLA-IB. *Bk. rev.:* 5-10, signed. *Aud.:* Ac, Sa.

The brainchild of John A. Lent, Professor of Mass Media and Communication at Temple University, the *International Journal of Comic Art* (*IJOCA*) is a scholarly publication of truly international scope that brings together the study of the related genres of anime, comics, graphic novels, and manga all under the same masthead. Each issue ranges between 300 and 800-plus pages and contains a dizzying array of academic articles that cover aspects of comics from over 50 different countries, with equal emphasis on manga and anime and on the comic art forms of the West. The most recent issue addresses topics as diverse as comics in Israel, metafiction in Charles Schulz's "Peanuts," and the relationship of Alan Moore's *V for Vendetta* to the Occupy Movement. Each issue includes black-and-white illustrations and several book reviews of recent international publications in the field. While such a journal might not appeal to a more general audience, for academic and special libraries the *International Journal of Comic Art* is unparalleled in its global scope and scholarly treatment of the anime and manga genres.

343. *Journal of Graphic Novels & Comics.* [ISSN: 2150-4857] 2010. s-a. GBP 217 (print & online eds.). Ed(s): Joan Ormrod, David Huxley. Routledge, 4 Park Sq, Milton Park, Abingdon, OX14 4RN, United Kingdom; subscriptions@tandf.co.uk; http://www.tandfonline.com. Refereed. *Indexed:* A51. *Bk. rev.:* 6-10 per issue, 1-2 pages each, signed. *Aud.:* Ac, Sa.

The *Journal of Graphic Novels and Comics* is a semi-annual publication from editors David Huxley and Joan Ormrod, both members of the Faculty of Art & Design at Manchester Metropolitan University. Although published in the United Kingdom, this journal professes an international scope, with the goal to "establish a dialogue between academics, historians, theoreticians[,] and practitioners of comics." Each issue is between 80 and 110 pages and contains several articles with color illustrations, as well as six to ten reviews of books recently published in the field. The journal covers various aspects of worldwide culture such as George Benjamin Luks and the comic weeklies of the nineteenth century, the construction of comic bookstores as social spaces, and gender and sexuality in "Boys' Love" manga. As comics and graphic novels continue to gain mainstream acceptance both in society and in academia, it is encouraging to see the launch of new scholarly periodicals such as the *Journal of Graphic Novels and Comics,* which is a welcome addition to any research collection that focuses on the field of comic studies.

344. *Mechademia: an annual forum for anime, manga and the fan arts.* [ISSN: 1934-2489] 2006. a. USD 112.50 (print & online eds.). Ed(s): Frenchy Lunning. University of Minnesota Press, Ste 290, 111 Third Ave S, Minneapolis, MN 55401; ump@umn.edu; http://www.upress.umn.edu. Illus. *Indexed:* A07, A22, E01, MLA-IB. *Bk. rev.:* 5-10 reviews, signed. *Aud.:* Ga, Ac.

A publication of the University of Minnesota Press, *Mechademia* is the only academic journal dedicated exclusively to the study of anime and manga in the United States. "[W]e see these not as objects but as arts whose production, distribution, and reception generate networks of connections. Thus our subject area extends from manga and anime to game design, fashion, graphics, packaging, and toy industries[,] as well as a broad range of fan practices related to popular culture in Japan, including gaming, cosplay, fan artwork, anime music videos, anime improvisations, etc." In acknowledgment of this broad spectrum of interconnected content, criticism, and cultural reception, the editors of *Mechademia* have cast their net wide, soliciting submissions from not only traditional academics but from filmmakers, writers, artists, and critics at large. The senior advisory board is similarly diverse, with professors of Eastern Asian languages and literature, communications, film studies, and fine arts and design, as well as independent scholars and writers. Each illustrated issue is 184 pages and contains 10–15 scholarly essays and five to ten signed reviews of books, films, and other related media organized around a central theme. Recent themes have included the works of Tezuka Osamu and the impact of anime and manga on depictions of lines of sight and perspective. *Mechademia* is ambitious in scope, a delightful exploration of what its editors have dubbed the "Art Mecho" movement that embraces the global J-pop phenomenon from a critical distance. This journal would make a fine addition to both public and academic library collections that treat the subjects of contemporary Japanese culture and its reception abroad.

345. *Otaku U S A.* [ISSN: 1939-3318] 2007. bi-m. USD 19.95 domestic; USD 31.95 foreign. Ed(s): Patrick Macias. Sovereign Media Co., 6731 Whittier Ave, McLean, VA 22101; laura@sovhomestead.com; http://sovmedia.sovhomestead.com/. Illus., adv. *Bk. rev.:* 20-25 manga reviews, 5-10 anime reviews, 5-10 video game reviews, 3-5 music CD reviews. *Aud.:* Hs, Ga.

A relatively new arrival to the field of anime and manga magazines, *Otaku USA* takes its name from the Japanese word *otaku,* which translates roughly as "nerd" or "geek" or, better yet, the more colloquial slang word "fanboy." *Otaku USA* offers a distinctly American fanboy take on the phenomenon of Japanese pop culture, positioning itself as an "independent" alternative to the other glossy, mass-media anime and manga magazines published by the Japanese entertainment industry jointly in North America and Japan. The magazine offers not only the standard fare of anime/magna previews and reviews, and coverage of the latest video games, toy releases, anime television reviews, Japanese and J-pop–inspired music, and anime and manga conventions. But *Otaku USA* also devotes a significant amount of attention to toys—including the emerging subgenres of "gunpla" (based on the Gundam plastic models kits sold worldwide by Bandai) and "cosplay" (dressing in costume as your favorite anime/manga characters—a convention favorite). Recent issues have also featured 3D printing and its growing popularity among anime and manga enthusiastics. Each issue is also accompanied by a manga preview insert, color centerfold posters, and a DVD containing anime short features, trailers of upcoming releases, and playable demos of the latest video games. Although it is hard for a newcomer to compete with the established anime and manga magazine titles, *Otaku USA* carves out a niche for itself by emphasizing the American perspective on the genre and the reaction in the United States to the J-pop invasion. Articles may not be as lavishly illustrated as the established competition, but the editors of *Otaku USA* compensate with feature articles that are specifically geared toward the American reader and that are written with a fan's enthusiasm for the genre, tempered with a broader introspection as to the deeper meanings of Japanese pop culture and its two-way creative relationship with the United States and the West. As such a hybrid creation itself, *Otaku USA* is a worthwhile addition to any library collection and a great resource for both young and old would-be American *otaku*. Following the demise of the popular title of *Protoculture Addicts* (which has not folded, but has not released a new issue since 2008), *Otaku USA* is now the only regular publication covering anime news in North America.

346. *Studies in Comics.* [ISSN: 2040-3232] 2010. s-a. GBP 150 (Individuals, GBP 36). Ed(s): Chris Murray, Julia Round. Intellect Ltd., The Mill, Parnall Rd, Fishponds, Bristol, BS16 3JG, United Kingdom; info@intellectbooks.com; http://www.intellectbooks.co.uk/. Adv. Sample. *Indexed:* A51. *Bk. rev.:* 1-10 per issue, 3-6 pages each, signed. *Aud.:* Ac, Sa.

Another recently-launched scholarly periodical from the United Kingdom, *Studies in Comics* is a peer-reviewed journal edited by Julia Round of Bournemouth University and Chris Murray of the University of Dundee. Their aim is "to make available articles of an exceptional academic standard with a strong theoretical focus." Each issue contains between six and 20 articles, interviews with current artists/authors, and several reviews of current monographs in the field of comics studies. Topics covered include the semiotic resources of comics in movie adaptation, transmedia and the comic publishing industry, and the reception of Japanese theories of postmodern cultural consumption in comics studies; the third issue (volume 2, issue 1) is a thematic one devoted to the works of comics giant Alan Moore. *Studies in Comics* is an ambitious journal, bringing serious literary criticism to bear on the comic art medium, and it would make an excellent addition to any college or university library collection.

347. *Weekly Shonen Jump.* Former titles (until 2013): *Weekly Shonen Jump Alpha;* (until 2012): *Shonen Jump.* 2003. w. Viz Media, LLC, PO Box 77010, San Francisco, CA 94107; media@viz.com; http://www.viz.com/. Illus. *Bk. rev.:* 10-15 manga chapter previews. *Aud.:* Hs, Ga.

From the Japanese word *shonen*, meaning boy, *Weekly Shonen Jump* (formerly *Shonen Jump*, then *Weekly Shonen Jump Alpha*) is a monthly American counterpart to Shueisha's Japanese publication of the same name, published in partnership with VIZ Media since 2003. "Made of the characters meaning few and years," reads the editorial statement, "shonen is Japanese for boy but can also mean pure of heart. Manga and anime created for shonen are among the most popular in the world[,] with fans of all ages and genders." Each 384-page issue contains 10–15 serialized manga chapters printed in black-and-white, with several color and a few glossy pages at both the beginning and the end of each book. It contains manga news and reviews of anime, videogames, toys, and collectible card games. *Weekly Shonen Jump* also contains extensive coverage of videogame and collective card–gaming strategy, as well as interviews with developers and previews of new gaming products (some issues also contain free collectible trading cards from such popular lines as Yu-Gi-Oh). Each serial chapter installment includes a useful introduction for first-time readers, including a summary of plot elements and a description of the major characters. Like its Japanese counterpart, *Weekly Shonen Jump* is printed right-to-left to preserve the aesthetics of the original manga. *Weekly Shonen Jump* is also an excellent overview of the field of available manga publications, and is a good indicator of what is currently popular among younger readers. As such, it is an important part of any library manga collection. URL: http://shonenjump.viz.com/

■ ANTHROPOLOGY

Priscilla Seaman, Reference and Instruction Librarian, Lupton Library, University of Tennessee at Chattanooga, TN 37403; FAX: 423-425-4775; priscilla-seaman@utc.edu

Introduction

In the broadest sense, anthropology is the science and study of humankind. More specifically, the discipline studies human beings in their biological, cultural, and social aspects. Four major subdisciplines constitute the field: archaeology, biological/physical anthropology, cultural/social anthropology, and linguistics. Archaeologists, cultural anthropologists, and linguists examine the material, social, and symbolic lives of humans past and present. Physical anthropologists examine humanity as a biological phenomenon, including studying evolutionary history.

Due to the broad scope of anthropological examinations of humankind, and the proliferation of subdisciplines, the number of available journals is extensive. The titles included in this section were chosen for breadth of subject matter and represent the four branches of anthropology.

The American Anthropological Association (AAA) is the largest professional society of anthropology in the U.S. A library's core collection should contain some of the association's 20-plus serials, including its flagship publication, *The American Anthropologist*. The following selection of anthropological journals provides guidance for building a core periodical collection.

Basic Periodicals

Ga: *American Anthropologist, Annual Review of Anthropology, Current Anthropology, Reviews in Anthropology;* Ac: *American Anthropologist, American Ethnologist, American Journal of Physical Anthropology, Current Anthropology, Royal Anthropological Institute. Journal.*

Basic Abstracts and Indexes

Abstracts in Anthropology, Anthropological Index, Anthropological Literature.

348. *American Anthropologist.* Supersedes (in 1988): *Transactions of the Anthropological Society of Washington.* [ISSN: 0002-7294] 1888. q. GBP 277 (print & online eds.). Ed(s): Tom Boellstorff. Wiley-Blackwell Publishing, Inc., 111 River St, Hoboken, NJ 07030; info@wiley.com; http://onlinelibrary.wiley.com/. Illus., index. Refereed. Vol. ends: Dec. Microform: PQC. Reprint: PSC. *Indexed:* A01, A06, A22, A47, ABS&EES, AbAn, B01, BAS, BEL&L, BRI, BrArAb, C45, CBRI, Chicano, E01, F01, FR, IBSS, MLA-IB, NumL, P02, P61, PsycInfo, RILM, RRTA, SSA. *Bk. rev.:* 50-60, 250-300 words. *Aud.:* Ga, Ac.

In publication since 1888, this flagship journal of the American Anthropological Association furthers the association's mission by publishing articles, commentaries, and essays on all facets of anthropological knowledge. The journal content is approximately arranged into the following sections: research articles; public anthropology; visual anthropology including film, television, and the occasional YouTube review; distinguished lectures; and an extensive book review section. *American Anthropologist* is a vital resource for anthropologists and most academic libraries.

349. *American Ethnologist.* [ISSN: 0094-0496] 1974. q. GBP 217 (print & online eds.). Ed(s): Angelique Haugerud. Wiley-Blackwell Publishing, Inc., 111 River St, Hoboken, NJ 07030; info@wiley.com; http://onlinelibrary.wiley.com/. Illus., index. Refereed. Circ: 3500. Vol. ends: Nov. Microform: PQC. Reprint: PSC. *Indexed:* A01, A22, A47, ABS&EES, AmHI, BAS, BRI, C45, CBRI, Chicano, E01, FR, IBSS, MLA-IB, P02, P61, PsycInfo, RILM, RRTA, SSA. *Bk. rev.:* Number and length vary. *Aud.:* Ac.

In its own description, *American Ethnologist* conveys "the ongoing relevance of the ethnographic imagination to the contemporary world." The journal lives up to its mission by featuring original research on topical cultural events and concerns. Recent issues include articles on the Occupy Movement and the Arab Spring uprising. International in scope, this journal presents a broad overview of ethnology and ethnographic research. A core title for most academic libraries.

350. *American Journal of Physical Anthropology.* [ISSN: 0002-9483] 1918. 14x/yr. GBP 1859. Ed(s): Christopher Ruff. John Wiley & Sons, Inc., 111 River St, MS 4-02, Hoboken, NJ 07030; info@wiley.com; http://www.wiley.com/WileyCDA/. Illus., index, adv. Refereed. Vol. ends: Dec. Microform: PQC. Reprint: PSC. *Indexed:* A01, A22, A47, AbAn, BAS, BRI, C45, Chicano, ExcerpMed, FR, IBSS, IndVet, MLA-IB, P02. *Bk. rev.:* 5-10, 1,200 words. *Aud.:* Ac.

The *American Journal of Physical Anthropology* is the official journal of the the American Association of Physical Anthropologists. As measured by impact factor, it ranks among the top journals listed in the anthropology category of the Social Science Citation Index. Articles encompass the evolution of primates, with an emphasis on human variation and evolution. This journal is published monthly and includes two supplements: the *Annual Meeting Issue* and *The Yearbook of Physical Anthropology*.

351. *Annual Review of Anthropology.* Formerly (until 1972): *Biennial Review of Anthropology.* [ISSN: 0084-6570] 1959. a. USD 226 (print or online ed.). Ed(s): Samuel Gubins, Donald Brenneis. Annual Reviews, PO Box 10139, Palo Alto, CA 94303; service@annualreviews.org; http://www.annualreviews.org. Illus. Refereed. Microform: PQC. Reprint: PSC. *Indexed:* A01, A22, A47, BAS, BrArAb, C45, FR, IBSS, MLA-IB, NumL, P02, P61, PsycInfo, RILM, SSA. *Aud.:* Ga, Ac.

The *Annual Review of Anthropology* keeps readers current with recent trends and research in the discipline. The *Annual Review* series publishes reviews in 40 different scientific fields. "The comprehensive critical review not only summarizes a topic but also roots out errors of fact or concept and provokes discussion that will lead to new research activity." This title covers significant developments in each of the subfields of anthropology, and includes a section for international anthropology and regional studies. Each volume offers several special themes. Volume 39 of the *Review* features a theme entitled "Modalities of Capitalism" and, among the thematic articles, one entitled "The Anthropology of Credit Card Debt."

Anthropological Linguistics. See Linguistics section.

352. *Anthropological Quarterly.* Formerly (until 1953): *Primitive Man.* [ISSN: 0003-5491] 1928. q. USD 178. Ed(s): Roy Richard Grinker. George Washington University, Institute for Ethnographic Research, 2110 G St, NW, Washington, DC 20052; rgrink@gwu.edu; http://departments.columbian.gwu.edu/anthropology/research/ier/. Illus., index, adv. Refereed. Vol. ends: Oct. Microform: MIM; PQC. *Indexed:* A01, A22, A47, ABS&EES, AbAn, BAS, BRI, Chicano, E01, EIP, FR, IBSS, MLA-IB, P02, P61, RILM, SSA. *Bk. rev.:* Number and length vary. *Aud.:* Ga, Ac.

A publication of the The George Washington University Institute for Ethnographic Research, *Anthropological Quarterly* offers peer-reviewed articles on social and cultural anthropology. In addition to the goal of "the rapid dissemination of articles that blend precision with humanism," this journal contains a section of "Social Thought and Commentary," which is "a forum for scholars within and outside the discipline of anthropology to add their voices to contemporary public debates." The book reviews, including new-book releases, are often in-depth and extensive.

353. *Anthropology & Education Quarterly.* Former titles (until 1976): *Council on Anthropology and Education Quarterly;* (until 1974): *Council on Anthropology and Education Newsletter.* [ISSN: 0161-7761] 1970. q. GBP 69 (print & online eds.). Ed(s): Katherine S Mortimer, Nancy H Hornberger. American Anthropological Association, 2200 Wilson Blvd, Ste 600, Arlington, VA 22201; http://www.aaanet.org. Illus., index, adv. Refereed. Circ: 1500. Vol. ends: Dec. Microform: PQC. Reprint: PSC. *Indexed:* A22, A47, ABS&EES, BRI, Chicano, E01, ERIC, FR, IBSS, MLA-IB, P61, PsycInfo, RILM. *Bk. rev.:* Number and length vary. *Aud.:* Ga, Ac.

This journal, the official publication of the Council on Anthropology and Education, publishes anthropological research in education, in the U.S. and internationally, and discusses educational development and the teaching of anthropology. Its peer-reviewed articles use ethnographic research to address problems of practice in addition to addressing broad theoretical questions. Articles would interest educators, sociologists, and social workers in addition to anthropologists. The titles of books reviewed are listed in each issue, but the full reviews are found only online. URL: www.aanet.org/cae/aeq.html

354. *Anthropology and Humanism.* Formerly (until 1993): *Anthropology and Humanism Quarterly.* [ISSN: 1559-9167] 1974. s-a. GBP 42 (print & online eds.). Ed(s): Edith Turner. Wiley-Blackwell Publishing, Inc., Commerce Pl, 350 Main St, Malden, MA 02148; info@wiley.com; http://onlinelibrary.wiley.com/. Illus., adv. Vol. ends: Dec. Reprint: PSC. *Indexed:* A01, A22, A47, AmHI, E01, IBSS, MLA-IB, RILM. *Bk. rev.:* 3-5, 1,200 words. *Aud.:* Ga, Ac.

This scholarly journal accepts contributions from the four subdisciplines of anthropology and from scholars in the humanities and other social science disciplines. *Anthropology and Humanism* sets itself apart by publishing work in a variety of genres: poetry, fiction, creative nonfiction, photo essays, and drama. *AH* focuses its content on the core question of the discipline: what is it to be human? Because of its cross-disciplinary nature and its mission of pushing the boundaries of scholarly inquiry and creativity, this journal makes a unique addition to a core anthropology journal collection.

355. *Anthropology Today.* Formerly (until 1985): *R A I N (Royal Anthropological Institute News).* [ISSN: 0268-540X] 1974. bi-m. GBP 98. Ed(s): Gustaaf Houtman. Wiley-Blackwell Publishing Ltd., The Atrium, Southern Gate, Chichester, PO19 8SQ, United Kingdom; customer@wiley.com; http://www.wiley.com/. Illus., adv. Sample. Refereed. Microform: PQC. Reprint: PSC. *Indexed:* A01, A22, A47, BrArAb, C37, E01, FR, IBSS, MASUSE, MLA-IB, NumL, P02, RILM. *Aud.:* Ga, Ac.

A non-refereed publication, *Anthropology Today* publishes articles that apply anthropological analysis to public and current issues. The journal is international in scope and sources, and provides an interface between the discipline of anthropology and applied fields such as medicine and education. Articles are shorter in length than the research articles of many peer-reviewed journals, but the breadth of the discipline is reflected in the array of topics addressed. Journal sections include narratives, comments, news, and conferences, in addition to original articles.

356. *Anthropos: revue internationale d'ethnologie et de linguistique.* [ISSN: 0257-9774] 1906. 2x/yr. CHF 190; EUR 125. Ed(s): Othmar Gaechter. Editions Saint-Paul Fribourg, Perolles 42, Fribourg, 1700, Switzerland; info@paulusedition.ch; http://www.paulusedition.ch. Illus., index. Refereed. Circ: 1000. *Indexed:* A22, A47, AbAn, BAS, IBSS, MLA-IB, P61, RILM, SSA. *Bk. rev.:* 30, length varies. *Aud.:* Ac.

Anthropos is a publication of the Anthropos Institute, an organization located in Germany, whose original statutes are grounded in theological discourse and "the restless searching of the human spirit in the history of peoples and cultures." Articles are in English, French, and German and delve into matters of anthropology, ethnology, linguistics, and religious studies. Issues are lengthy, containing over ten articles of 15–20 pages, as well as reports and comments, and about half of each issue is devoted to an extensive book reviews section, sometimes reviewing over 50 new titles.

357. *Arctic Anthropology.* [ISSN: 0066-6939] 1962. s-a. USD 230 (print & online eds.). Ed(s): Susan A Kaplan. University of Wisconsin Press, Journal Division, 1930 Monroe St, 3rd Fl, Madison, WI 53711; journals@uwpress.wisc.edu; http://www.uwpress.org. Illus., index, adv. Refereed. Circ: 1500. Microform: PQC. Reprint: PSC. *Indexed:* A01, A22, A47, ABS&EES, AbAn, BAS, E01, FR, IBSS, MLA-IB, RILM. *Bk. rev.:* Number and length vary. *Aud.:* Ga, Ac.

Articles in the journal *Arctic Anthropology* concentrate on the the study of Old and New World Northern cultures and people. The subdisciplines of anthropology are represented in the journal content with an emphasis on arctic, subarctic, and contiguous regions. Articles explore topics such as the peopling of the New World, as well as topics of contemporary cultures of northern peoples. Recent articles entitled "The Distribution of Alcohol among the Natives of Russian America" and "Two Chiefs' Houses from the Western Aleutian Islands" provide a view into the scholarly focus of this journal.

358. The Australian Journal of Anthropology. Formerly (until 1990): *Mankind.* [ISSN: 1035-8811] 1931. 3x/yr. GBP 172. Ed(s): Martha Macintyre. Wiley-Blackwell Publishing Asia, 155 Cremorne St, Richmond, VIC 3121, Australia; melbourne@wiley.com; http://www.wiley.com/. Illus., index, adv. Refereed. Reprint: PSC. *Indexed:* A01, A22, A47, BAS, BRI, BrArAb, E01, FR, IBSS, MLA-IB, P02, P61, RILM, SSA. *Bk. rev.:* Number varies, 800-1,000 words. *Aud.:* Ga, Ac.

Formerly entitled *Mankind,* this refereed journal publishes papers and book reviews in anthropology and related disciplines. A publication of the Australian Anthropological Society, this journal places a special emphasis on anthropological research based in Australia and neighboring countries in the Pacific and Asian regions. One of three annual issues is devoted to a special topic. Articles are 10–20 pages in length, and each issue contains approximately 125 pages.

359. Cultural Anthropology. [ISSN: 0886-7356] 1986. q. GBP 66 (print & online eds.). Ed(s): Mike Fortun, Kim Fortun. Wiley-Blackwell Publishing, Inc., 111 River St, Hoboken, NJ 07030; info@wiley.com; http://onlinelibrary.wiley.com/. Illus. Sample. Refereed. Vol. ends: Nov. Reprint: PSC. *Indexed:* A01, A22, A47, ABS&EES, AbAn, AmHI, BAS, BRI, C45, E01, IBSS, MLA-IB, P02, P61, RILM, RRTA, SSA. *Bk. rev.:* Number and length vary. *Aud.:* Ac.

One of the highest-ranked anthropology journals of the ISI Journal Citation system, *Cultural Anthropology* promotes scholarship in cultural studies and the theory of culture. The Society of Cultural Anthropology, which publishes this journal, has as its mission to connect anthropology with other disciplines: history, literature, philosophy, and the social sciences. To that end, articles often focus on topics of interest to these disciplines, and include literary criticism and theory. Issues include original articles, special and thematic features (e.g., "The Future of Neoliberalism"), and a smattering of book reviews. A core title for academic collections.

360. Current Anthropology. Formerly (until 1955): *Yearbook of Anthropology.* [ISSN: 0011-3204] 1955. bi-m. USD 362 (print & online eds.). Ed(s): Lisa McKamy, Mark Aldenderfer. University of Chicago Press, 1427 E 60th St, Chicago, IL 60637; subscriptions@press.uchicago.edu; http://www.journals.uchicago.edu. Illus., index, adv. Sample. Refereed. Microform: PQC. Reprint: PSC. *Indexed:* A01, A22, A47, ABS&EES, AbAn, BAS, BRI, BrArAb, FR, IBSS, MASUSE, MLA-IB, NumL, P02, P61, PsycInfo, RILM, SSA. *Bk. rev.:* 3-5, 2,000 words. *Aud.:* Ga, Ac.

Current Anthropology is a transnational journal devoted to research on humankind, including social, cultural, and physical anthropology, as well as ethnology, archaeology, folklore, and linguistics. Issues include articles, discussions, forums, reports, and book and film reviews. *Anthropological Currents* summarizes empirical research in other anthropology publications. For professional and general readership.

361. Dialectical Anthropology: an independent international journal in the critical tradition committed to the transformation of our society and the humane union of theory and practice. [ISSN: 0304-4092] 1975. q. EUR 571 (print & online eds.). Ed(s): Anthony Marcus, Kirk Dombrowski. Springer Netherlands, Van Godewijckstraat 30, Dordrecht, 3311 GX, Netherlands; http://www.springer.com. Illus., index, adv. Vol. ends: Dec. Microform: PQC. Reprint: PSC. *Indexed:* A01, A22, A47, AbAn, AmHI, BAS, BRI, E01, FR, IBSS, MLA-IB, P61, SSA. *Aud.:* Ac.

Dialectical Anthropology provides a "forum for a dialectical approach to social theory and political practice" and "seeks to invigorate discussion among left intellectuals...scholars and activists working in Marxist and broadly political-economic traditions." This journal publishes social critiques of contemporary civilization in the form of peer-reviewed articles, essays, reviews, poetry, memoirs, and more. Occasional issues are thematic. *Dialectical Anthropology* is self-described as "a major contributor to the radical literature of our time."

362. Ethnography. [ISSN: 1466-1381] 2000. q. USD 941. Ed(s): Peter Geschiere, Paul Willis. Sage Publications Ltd., 1 Oliver's Yard, 55 City Rd, London, EC1Y 1SP, United Kingdom; info@sagepub.co.uk; http://www.uk.sagepub.com. Adv. Sample. Refereed. Reprint: PSC. *Indexed:* A22, A47, E01, IBSS, MLA-IB, P61, SSA. *Aud.:* Ac.

An international and interdisciplinary peer-reviewed journal, *Ethnography* "provides a forum for the study of social and cultural change." Of special note, this journal endeavors to "bridge the chasm between sociology and anthropology." Each issue is composed of four to five articles averaging 25–30 pages in length. In addition to the journal's emphasis on sociology and anthropology, authors from other disciplines are represented, such as geography, social work, and economics.

Ethnohistory. See Multicultural Studies section.

363. Ethnology: an international journal of cultural and social anthropology. [ISSN: 0014-1828] 1962. q. USD 50 (print or online ed.) Individuals, USD 28 (print or online ed.). Ed(s): Leonard Plotnicov, Katherine A Lancaster. University of Pittsburgh, Department of Anthropology, 3310 Posvar Hall, 230 S Bouquet St, Pittsburgh, PA 15260; jsalter@pitt.edu; http://www.anthropology.pitt.edu/. Illus., index. Refereed. Vol. ends: Oct. Microform: PQC. *Indexed:* A01, A22, A47, ABS&EES, BAS, BrArAb, Chicano, FR, IBSS, MLA-IB, P02, P61, RILM, SSA, SWR&A. *Aud.:* Ga, Ac.

A publication of the University of Pittsburgh Anthropology Department, *Ethnology* publishes original articles that analyze culture and society. This journal includes international and interdisciplinary research, and combines field-based research with theory. Although they are peer-reviewed, many articles could appeal to the general public as well as to scholars. Articles average five per issue, and each are about 15–20 pages in length and deal with topics such as identity, fertility, religion, work, and marriage.

364. Ethnos: journal of anthropology. [ISSN: 0014-1844] 1936. q. GBP 401 (print & online eds.). Ed(s): Mark Graham, Nils Bubandt. Routledge, 4 Park Sq, Milton Park, Abingdon, OX14 4RN, United Kingdom; subscriptions@tandf.co.uk; http://www.tandfonline.com. Illus., index, adv. Sample. Refereed. Reprint: PSC. *Indexed:* A01, A22, A47, AbAn, BAS, E01, FR, IBSS, MLA-IB, P61, RILM, SSA. *Bk. rev.:* Number varies, 1,000 words. *Aud.:* Ac.

Original papers on theoretical, methodological, and empirical developments in the discipline of sociocultural anthropology are featured in this publication. Each issue averages five articles of about 25 pages, and an occasional issue publishes approximately six book reviews several pages in length. Articles and contributors are international. As an example of the global scope of *Ethnos,* a recent issue features articles that focus on anthropological topics in Kazakhstan, China, rural France, Cape Verde, and Bengal, India.

365. Ethos (Malden). [ISSN: 0091-2131] 1973. q. GBP 56 (print & online eds.). Wiley-Blackwell Publishing, Inc., 111 River St, Hoboken, NJ 07030; info@wiley.com; http://onlinelibrary.wiley.com/. Illus. Refereed. Vol. ends: Dec. Microform: PQC. Reprint: PSC. *Indexed:* A22, A47, ASSIA, E01, IBSS, MLA-IB, PsycInfo. *Bk. rev.:* Number and length vary. *Aud.:* Ac.

Published by the Society of Psychology Anthropology, *Ethos* concentrates its scholarly content on issues of psychology and anthropology. Articles include a variety of psychocultural topics, such as cultural cognition, transcultural psychiatry, ethnopsychiatry, socialization, and psychoanalytic anthropology. Content includes original articles, essays, commentaries, and book and film reviews, as well as many "special topics" issues. "Psychological Anthropology and Adolescent Well-Being" provides an example of a recent special topics issue.

366. Evolutionary Anthropology: issues, news, and reviews. [ISSN: 1060-1538] 1992. bi-m. GBP 487. Ed(s): John G Fleagle. John Wiley & Sons, Inc., 111 River St, MS 4-02, Hoboken, NJ 07030; info@wiley.com; http://www.wiley.com/WileyCDA/. Illus., adv. Refereed. Microform: PQC. Reprint: PSC. *Indexed:* A22, A47, AbAn, IBSS. *Bk. rev.:* Number and length vary. *Aud.:* Ac.

ANTHROPOLOGY

The top-ranked journal in the ISI Journal Citation Reports, *Evolutionary Anthropology* focuses on all aspects of biological anthropology, paleoanthropology, and archaeology, as well as social biology, genetics, and ecology. This journal also publishes general news of relevant developments in the scientific, social, or political arenas. Book reviews, professional news, letters to the editor, and a calendar are included. Most issues feature an editorial column entitled "Crotchets & Quiddities," which addresses evolutionary concepts and questions that are intended to stimulate thought on various evolutionary anthropology topics.

367. Field Methods. Former titles (until 1999): *Cultural Anthropology Methods Journal;* (until 1995): *C A M: Cultural Anthropology Methods;* (until 1993): *C A M Newsletter.* [ISSN: 1525-822X] 1989. q. Ed(s): H Russell Bernard. Sage Publications, Inc., 2455 Teller Rd, Thousand Oaks, CA 91320; info@sagepub.com; http://www.sagepub.com. Adv. Sample. Refereed. Reprint: PSC. *Indexed:* A01, A22, A47, E01, IBSS, P61, PsycInfo, SSA. *Aud.:* Ac.

Formerly entitled *Cultural Anthropology Methods,* this peer-reviewed journal publishes articles about the methods used by field workers in the social and behavioral sciences and the humanities. Articles focus on issues in the methods used and innovations in the collection, management, and analysis data about human thought and behavior. Most issues publish five to six articles in the 10- to 20-page range. This journal, which operates under the motto "methods belong to all of us," aims to reach scholars, students, and professionals who do fieldwork.

Human Ecology. See Environment and Conservation section.

368. Human Organization. Formerly (until 1949): *Applied Anthropology.* [ISSN: 0018-7259] 1941. q. USD 95 (print & online eds.); Free to members. Ed(s): Jeffrey C Johnson, David Griffith. Society for Applied Anthropology, PO Box 2436, Oklahoma City, OK 73101; info@sfaa.net; http://www.sfaa.net. Illus., index, adv. Refereed. Circ: 3500. Vol. ends: Winter. *Indexed:* A22, A47, ABIn, AbAn, B01, BAS, C45, Chicano, FR, IBSS, MCR, MLA-IB, P02, P61, PsycInfo, RILM, RRTA, SSA, SWR&A. *Aud.:* Ac.

This refereed journal is published by the Society for Applied Anthropology. *Human Organization* features articles on the scientific investigations of how human beings relate to one another and how these principles are applied to practical problems. Included in the journal are sections on government, industry, health care, and international affairs. Research in this journal spans the globe. A recent issue features research conducted in fertility clinics in Germany, fishing communities in the Amazon, and dengue fever in Brazil.

369. Journal of Anthropological Archaeology. [ISSN: 0278-4165] 1982. q. EUR 711. Ed(s): John M O'Shea. Academic Press, 3251 Riverport Ln, Maryland Heights, MO 63043; JournalCustomerService-usa@elsevier.com; http://www.elsevierdirect.com/brochures/academicpress/index.html. Illus., adv. Refereed. Vol. ends: Dec. *Indexed:* A01, A22, A47, AbAn, AmHI, ArtHuCI, BAS, BrArAb, E01, FR, IBSS, NumL. *Aud.:* Ac.

This refereed, international journal publishes articles on the theory and methodology of archaeology. Articles center on archaeological topics spanning a time frame from the emergence of human culture to contemporary investigations and observations. In addition to the journal's focus on archaeology, occasional contributions come from ethnographers, sociologists, and geographers. Issues typically contain approximately six scholarly articles that range in length from 15 to 40 pages. An occasional special-topic issue will have shorter contributions.

370. Journal of Anthropological Research. Former titles (until 1973): *Southwestern Journal of Anthropology;* (until 1945): *New Mexico Anthropologist.* [ISSN: 0091-7710] 1937. q. USD 60 (Individuals, USD 35). Ed(s): Lawrence G Straus. University of New Mexico, Department of Anthropology, MSC01 1040, Anthropology 1, University of New Mexico, Albuquerque, NM 87131; anthro@unm.edu; http://

www.anthropologyunm.org/. Illus., index. Refereed. Vol. ends: Winter. Microform: PQC. *Indexed:* A01, A22, A47, ABS&EES, AbAn, BAS, BRI, BrArAb, FR, IBSS, MLA-IB, NumL, P02, P61, RILM, SSA. *Bk. rev.:* Number and length vary. *Aud.:* Ga, Ac.

The *Journal of Anthropological Research* publishes peer-reviewed research articles and book reviews in all subfields of anthropology. Formerly the *Southwestern Journal of Anthropology,* this publication gives some weight to articles relating to the American Southwest and northern Mexico. Most issues have four articles, 20 pages in length, and current, critical book reviews averaging one page in length. Book reviews comprise a large portion of the journal's content, featuring up to 20 or more book reviews per issue.

371. Journal of Human Evolution. [ISSN: 0047-2484] 1972. m. EUR 2399. Ed(s): Mark Teaford, David Begun. Academic Press, 32 Jamestown Rd, Camden, London, NW1 7BY, United Kingdom; corporate.sales@elsevier.com; http://www.elsevier.com/. Illus., index, adv. Refereed. Vol. ends: Dec. Reprint: PSC. *Indexed:* A01, A22, A47, AbAn, AnBeAb, BrArAb, E01, FR, IBSS. *Bk. rev.:* Number and length vary. *Aud.:* Ac.

The central focus of this journal is to publish scholarly articles on all aspects of human evolution. Articles cover both paleoanthropological work, including human and primate fossils, and comparative studies of living species. It is a reputed journal in the field of anthropology and highly ranked in its Impact Factor, and its contents include original research, review articles, news, communication of new discoveries, and forthcoming papers. Occasional issues link to book reviews published on the Elsevier blog: www.elsevierblogs.com/jhevReviews.

372. The Journal of Latin American and Caribbean Anthropology. Former titles (until 2007): *Journal of Latin American Anthropology;* (until 1995): *The Latin American Anthropology Review.* [ISSN: 1935-4932] 1989. 3x/yr. GBP 43 (print & online eds.). Ed(s): Andrew Canessa. American Anthropological Association, 2200 Wilson Blvd, Ste 600, Arlington, VA 22201; http://www.aaanet.org. Adv. Sample. Refereed. Reprint: PSC. *Indexed:* A22, A47, BRI, E01, IBSS, MLA-IB, P61, SSA. *Bk. rev.:* Number and length vary. *Aud.:* Ac.

The official publication of the Latin American Anthropology Section of the American Anthropological Association, this journal is devoted to publishing articles on research in Mexico, Central and South America, and the Caribbean. Articles may be published in Spanish or English. Each issue has five to seven articles, and theme issues are common. Issues often include films and numerous book reviews.

373. Medical Anthropology Quarterly: international journal for the cultural and social analysis of health. Former titles (until 1983): *Medical Anthropology Newsletter;* (until 1968): *Medical Anthropology.* [ISSN: 0745-5194] 19??. q. GBP 72 (print & online eds.). Ed(s): Ellen McCarthy, Mark Luborsky. Wiley-Blackwell Publishing, Inc., 111 River St, Hoboken, NJ 07030; info@wiley.com; http://onlinelibrary.wiley.com/. Illus. Sample. Refereed. Vol. ends: Dec. Reprint: PSC. *Indexed:* A22, A47, ABS&EES, AbAn, BRI, C45, E01, IBSS, MLA-IB, P61, SSA. *Bk. rev.:* Number and length vary. *Aud.:* Ac.

As the title suggests, this journal publishes research and theory in the field of medical anthropology. It is produced by the Society for Medical Anthropology, and the journal's "broad field views all inquiries into health and disease in individuals from the holistic and cross-cultural perspective distinctive of anthropology." Contents include original articles, book reviews, and an occasional special focus section. A recent issue of special focus was "devoted to the ways that military servicemembers' bodies are figured, deployed, symbolized, and represented."

374. Oceania. [ISSN: 0029-8077] 1930. 3x/yr. GBP 151. Ed(s): Nancy Williams, Jadran Mimica. Wiley-Blackwell Publishing Asia, 155 Cremorne St, Richmond, VIC 3121, Australia; melbourne@wiley.com; http://www.wiley.com/. Illus., index. Refereed. Microform: PQC. *Indexed:* A01, A22, A47, ASSIA, AbAn, AmHI, BAS, BRI, FR, IBSS, MLA-IB, P02, RILM. *Bk. rev.:* 7, length varies. *Aud.:* Ac.

Oceania publishes peer-reviewed research and review articles in the field of social and cultural anthropology in Australia, Melanesia, Polynesia, Micronesia, and Southeast Asia. An important source for Australian and Pacific Studies, it covers past and present customs, ceremonies, folklore, and belief systems of the region. Included are guest-edited thematic issues, maps, graphs, and some illustrations. This journal is recommended for academic libraries that serve anthropology programs or Asian, Pacific, or Australian Studies programs.

375. *Royal Anthropological Institute. Journal.* Formerly (until 1995): *Man;* Incorporates (1907-1965): *Royal Anthropological Institute of Great Britain and Ireland. Journal;* Which was formerly (until 1907): *Anthropological Institute of Great Britain and Ireland. Journal;* Which was formed by the merger of (1869-1872): *Ethnological Society of London. Journal;* Which was formerly (until 1869): *Ethnological Society of London. Transactions;* (until 1861): *Ethnological Society of London. Journal;* (1870-1872): *Journal of Anthropology;* Which was formerly (until 1870): *Anthropological Review.* [ISSN: 1359-0987] 1901. q. GBP 422 (print or online ed.). Ed(s): Simon Coleman. Wiley-Blackwell Publishing Ltd., 9600 Garsington Rd, Oxford, OX4 2DQ, United Kingdom; customer@wiley.co.uk; http://www.wiley.com/. Illus., index, adv. Refereed. Vol. ends: Dec. Microform: BHP; PQC. Reprint: PSC. *Indexed:* A01, A22, A47, BAS, BRI, BrArAb, E01, FR, IBSS, MLA-IB, P02, P61, RILM, SSA. *Bk. rev.:* 40, 350 words. *Aud.:* Ac.

Formerly entitled *Man,* the *Journal of the Royal Anthropological Institute* is the principal journal of the long-standing anthropological organization of the same name. Articles are international in scope and cover all branches of anthropology. This journal is known for its extensive book review section; over 40 reviews are published per issue. In addition to comments, review articles, and original research, most issues contain a lively and readable essay entitled "What I'm Reading."

376. *Visual Anthropology Review.* Former titles (until 1991): *Society for Visual Anthropology Review;* (until 1990): *S V A Review; S V A Newsletter;* (until 1985): *Society for the Anthropology of Visual Communication. Newsletter;* (until 1973): *P I E F Newsletter.* [ISSN: 1058-7187] 1970. s-a. GBP 26 (print & online eds.). Ed(s): Laura Lewis, Liam Buckley. Wiley-Blackwell Publishing, Inc., 111 River St, Hoboken, NJ 07030; info@wiley.com; http://www.wiley.com/. Adv. Sample. Reprint: PSC. *Indexed:* A01, A22, A47, BrArAb, E01, IBSS, MLA-IB, P61, SSA. *Aud.:* Ac.

The content of this journal focuses on the study of visual aspects of human behavior and the use of visual media in anthropology research and teaching. *Visual Anthropology Review* has been in publication since the 1970s. Its specialized scope may draw a narrower audience; however, the use of and emphasis on visual media in teaching and learning have increased in recent times. Examples of articles, reviews, and commentary featured in this journal include indigenous media, applied visual anthropology, photography, film, video, art, dance, design, and architecture. Given the breadth of visual representation, *Visual Anthropology Review* has cross-disciplinary appeal.

■ ANTIQUES

General/Doll Collecting

Andrew Tadman, Reference Librarian, East Baton Rouge Parish Library, 7711 Goodwood Blvd., Baton Rouge, LA 70806; atadman@ebrpl.com

Introduction

The antiques industry is inextricably tied to online auctions and e-business. However, while the trade continues to diversify into new technologies, it still holds onto some more traditional methods. Antique shops, fairs, auctions, flea markets, and printed classifieds are still primary sources for those on the hunt for that perfect something. The traditional antiques industry is thriving despite increased competition from online auction sites like eBay that lack the personal touch, sense of trust, and interaction that the shopper in a small crafts fair would get.

The increase in the number and accessibility of antiques resources has popularized the buying and selling of antiques and collectibles to a wide variety of populations. Antiques aren't just for the grandparent set anymore. Younger generations feel the lure of vintage and retro items. While these may not be true antiques in the official sense of the word, the markets are similar enough to overlap.

In a tough economy, every patron with an attic is looking to find a way to turn those hidden treasures and antique heirlooms into money. Public library reference desks are getting increasing numbers of questions about antiques. Library programs about antiques are drawing large responses. Not only is the classic *Antiques Roadshow* extremely popular, but a quick online search for television shows related to antiques, auctions, or collectors turns up no less than 37 other programs. The thrill of the hunt at garage sales, fairs, and auctions captivates not only avid antique collectors, but even those who just watched *Cash in the Attic* for the first time.

To accommodate the growing interest in online antique shopping, some traditional antiques magazines have started or significantly beefed up their web presences. To entice visitors, these sites now offer free additional articles, videos, photo galleries, digital editions, and increased access to the content of the print magazine. While there are many general antiques resources online, few can match the level of specialization, expertise, and depth of coverage that the publications listed in this section reach.

The best antiques and collectibles magazines bridge the gap between the Internet-savvy hunter and someone who would rather see a printed calendar of the local antiques events. The main audience for these magazines and newspapers would be public library patrons. The specific publications required for each library will vary based on the needs and interests of the local community.

Basic Periodicals

FINE ANTIQUES/OBJETS D'ART. Ga: *Antique Collecting, The Magazine Antiques.*

POPULAR ANTIQUES/COLLECTIBLES. Ga: *Antique Trader, Collector Editions, Maine Antique Digest.*

DOLL COLLECTING. Ga: *Contemporary Doll Collector, Doll Reader, Dolls: the collector's magazine.*

Basic Abstracts and Indexes

Readers' Guide to Periodical Literature.

General

377. *Antique Bottle and Glass Collector.* [ISSN: 8750-1481] 1984. m. USD 25 domestic; USD 28 Canada; USD 31 elsewhere. Ed(s): James Hagenbuch. Boyertown Publishing, 102 Jefferson St, PO Box 180, East Greenville, PA 18041; glswrk@enter.net; http://www.glswrk-auction.com. Illus., adv. Circ: 4100 Paid. *Aud.:* Ga.

This glossy magazine is the major publication that covers the specific area of antique bottles and glass. One of the highlights of the publication is the use of large, full-color, high-quality pictures featured in the majority of articles, although there are also black-and-white photos. Entertaining articles cover the wide spectrum of collectible glasses and bottles. They really bring the pieces featured to life. As well as the latest news, there are sections such as letters to the editor, young collectors' corner, and collector and expert interviews, which highlight the sense of the publication's serving the wider antique glass community. The magazine is accessible and readable even without prior knowledge of the subject. There is a classifieds section that is valuable to collectors, as well as listings of upcoming auctions and related web sites. The *Antique Bottle and Glass Collector* web site also contains classifieds and a glass show calendar. Recommended for both serious collectors and those with a more casual interest. URL: www.glswrk-auction.com/

378. *Antique Collecting: the magazine for collectors and enthusiasts.*
Incorporates (1946-2006): *Antique Dealer & Collectors Guide;* Which incorporated (1981-1982): *Art & Antiques;* Which was formerly (until 1981): *Art & Antiques Weekly;* Antique Dealer & Collectors Guide was formerly (until 1946): *Antique Dealers' Weekly and Collectors' Guide.* [ISSN: 0003-584X] 1966. 10x/yr. GBP 32 domestic; GBP 48 in Europe; GBP 64 elsewhere. Antique Collectors Club, Sandy Ln, Old Martlesham, Woodbridge, IP12 4SD, United Kingdom; info@antique-acc.com; http://www.antiquecollectorsclub.com. Illus., adv. Sample. *Indexed:* RILM. *Bk. rev.:* 2-6, 100-500 words. *Aud.:* Ga, Sa.

Antique Collecting is a British publication with a wide coverage of different antiques from ceramics to furniture and everything in between. This glossy, full-color publication has a long history. Its latest iteration has been published by the Antiques Collector's Club since 1966. From the issues I have covered, the articles have all been very strong and of a high standard, accompanied by superbly detailed photographs. The quality of the publication shines throughout. Regular features include news, an editorial, and discussion of a featured recent auction. The British fair and auction calendars take up quite a few pages and serve as a valuable resource. The back of each issue contains a directory of antiques clubs, which could be a good source for contacts. Although the articles are outstanding, the fact that this is a British publication may make it slightly less useful to American readers. The classifieds, auction reviews, and listings are, of course, for Britain. The accompanying web site includes editorials and other features taken from issues, as well as an excellently presented sample digital issue that you can read online. This is a great feature for getting to know more about the magazine before making a decision on subscribing. Recommended for patrons with an interest in European antiques. URL: www.antique-collecting.co.uk/

379. *Antique Trader.* Former titles (until 2000): *The Antique Trader Weekly;* (until 19??): *Antique Trader.* 1957. 26x/yr. USD 59.98; USD 2.99 newsstand/cover. Ed(s): Karen Knapstein. F + W Media Inc., 700 E State St, Iola, WI 54990; contact_us@fwmedia.com; http://www.fwmedia.com/. Illus., adv. Circ: 24367 Paid. *Bk. rev.:* 30, length varies. *Aud.:* Ga.

Since it debuted in 1957, *Antique Trader* has been a leader in the field of antiques and collectibles. It is a respected name that is also behind the popular annual *Antique Trader Antiques & Collectibles Price Guide,* a key antiques reference book. *Antique Trader* is newsprint, and mostly black-and-white with some color pages. The focus is very much on auctions, buying, and selling. There is coverage of all varieties of antiques and collectibles. The detailed auction previews and highlights of recent auctions and shows are the backbone of the newspaper. The frequency of its publication means very timely news coverage and the latest sale prices. There are regular features including readers' letters and articles on collecting and selling. They are well written and offer expert advice. The events and convention calendars are extensive and a valuable resource. As a trade publication with a focus on the trade part, there is a lot of advertising, but the advertisements don't feel out of place. It also offers a directory of merchants' web sites and classified ads. The web site is rich in content and offers many of the regular features. A large selection of past articles can be browsed by category. There are also features, free classifieds, events, and a frequently updated blog. There is an additional free weekly "eNewsletter" available for subscription. *Antique Trader* is highly recommended for public libraries due to its broad coverage, trade resources, quality content, and frequency. URL: www.antiquetrader.com/

380. *Antiques & Auction News.* Formerly: *Joel Sater's Antiques and Auction News.* 1969. w. Fri. USD 80. Ed(s): Denise M Sater. Engle Printing & Publishing Co., Inc., 1425 W Main St, PO Box 500, Mt. Joy, PA 17552; http://www.engleonline.com. *Aud.:* Ga.

The geographic focus of this newspaper is the East Coast. It is available at shows all over the area, and billed as the "The most widely read collectors' newspaper in the East." The publication has been around since 1969 and has a respected tradition and reputation. It's a short weekly publication, mostly listing shows and auctions with articles covering news, recent events, and prices, as well as articles on collecting. The auction and show coverage is good and is the backbone of the newspaper. There are also store and auction directories, classifieds, and lots of advertising. It is mostly black-and-white with occasional sections in color. All of the content in the newspaper is available on the web site, with complete e-editions on the site available to read or download. The main part of the web site is frequently updated with articles, auction results, and the events calendar. Recommended as a must for libraries on the East Coast within the newspaper's area of coverage. URL: www.antiquesandauctionnews.net/

381. *Antiques Roadshow Insider: news, trends, and analysis from the world of antiques and collectibles.* [ISSN: 1544-2659] 2001. m. USD 45 domestic; USD 55 Canada. Belvoir Media Group, LLC, PO Box 5656, Norwalk, CT 06856; customer_service@belvoir.com; http://www.belvoir.com. *Indexed:* BRI. *Aud.:* Ga.

There are few names as synonymous with antiques as *Antiques Roadshow,* the continually popular television show on both sides of the Atlantic that creates huge excitement whenever it comes to a town. The *Antiques Roadshow Insider* is a newsletter-format publication, all color, which supplements the television show. It takes readers behind the scenes of the show, with interviews with dealers, appraisers, auctioneers, and other experts. The publication provides news, what items are in demand, and vital tips to collecting and looking for hidden bargains. Each issue explores a variety of particular antiques and collectibles. "On the Road" is a regular feature that offers highlights from previous stops of the *Antiques Roadshow* and details of the most interesting finds, complete with pictures. It's a fairly short publication, but full of concise and worthy articles. Highly recommended for public library collections, and likely always to be in demand from patrons for its general appeal and varied coverage of different antiques and collectibles. The web site of the *Antiques Roadshow Insider* is fairly sparse, with a selection of older articles available, and subscription information. URL: www.antiquesroadshowinsider.com/

382. *AntiqueWeek: weekly antique, auction and collectors' newspaper.* Former titles (until 1986): *Antique Week - Tri-State Trader;* (until 1983): *Tri-State Trader.* [ISSN: 0888-5451] 1968. w. Mon. USD 41 in state; USD 47.25 out of state. Ed(s): Connie Swaim. MidCountry Media USA, 27 N Jefferson St, PO Box 90, Knightstown, IN 46148. Illus., adv. Sample. Circ: 40000. Vol. ends: Mar. *Bk. rev.:* 16, length varies. *Aud.:* Ga.

This partial-color weekly newspaper contains up-to-date, concise news and commentary from the antiques world. In addition to sales news, some of the articles offer a human-interest slant. Regular features include a show and auction calendar, antique web site listings, a mall and shop directory, and classifieds. The short articles are interesting and well written, but the focus is more on the listings. It is very heavy on advertising. There are different editions for central and eastern parts of the United States to go along with the national coverage. It's very accessible to all readers, including the most casual collectors. The photographs suffer somewhat because of the newsprint format. This publication is not groundbreaking, but it does provide timely coverage. Not essential, but worth considering for public libraries covered by the "Eastern" and "Central" editions. The web site contains newspaper cover stories, the calendars, and classifieds. A nice feature is that they have an "Antique Week Community" section that includes a discussion board. URL: www.antiqueweek.com/

383. *Art & Antiques: for collectors of the fine and decorative arts.* Incorporates (1967-Jan.1994): *Antique Monthly;* Former titles (until 1984): *Art & Antiques;* (until 1980): *American Art and Antiques.* [ISSN: 0195-8208] 1978. m. USD 80 domestic; USD 105 Canada; USD 120 elsewhere. Ed(s): Christy Grosz, John Dorfman. CurtCo Robb Media LLC., 29160 Heathercliff Rd, Ste 200, Malibu, CA 90265; support@robbreport.com; http://www.curtco.com. Illus., adv. Sample. Circ: 66000 Paid. *Indexed:* A01, A07, A22, A51, ABS&EES, ASIP, AmHI, RILM. *Bk. rev.:* 6, length varies. *Aud.:* Ga.

When browsing issues of *Art & Antiques,* it is immediately clear that this is a high-end publication. The first thing to notice is the incredible presentation. It has a spacious layout, with plenty of white space that highlights the quality photographs inside. It is a joy to look at, with very minimal advertising. One feature of note is "City Focus," which describes the art and antique offerings from a different city in each issue. The featured articles are in-depth and often accompanied by striking visuals. Regular sections include "In Perspective," which is news and market reports; "Objects of Desire," a look at a particular work; and exhibition coverage. The detailed exhibition coverage is a true highlight and strength of the publication. There are also book reviews, essays, and a collecting section focused on a specific area. The majority of the art and antiques featured are not everyday pieces, but in no way does this detract from the quality and the appeal. This publication is highly recommended for all collections. The *Art & Antiques* web site contains a great deal of content, such as dozens of articles from past issues, which include the pictures in higher definition than on the printed page. There is a free supplemental "eNewsletter" with exclusive content to accompany the magazine. URL: www.artandantiquesmag.com/

384. ***Kovels on Antiques and Collectibles: the newsletter for collectors, dealers and investors.*** Former titles (until 1981): *Kovels on Antiques and Collectables;* (until 1977): *Ralph and Terry Kovel on Antiques.* 1974. m. USD 27 in US & Canada; USD 42 elsewhere. Antiques, Inc., PO Box 22192, Beachwood, OH 44122; http://www.kovels.com. Illus. Sample. *Bk. rev.:* Number and length vary. *Aud.:* Hs, Ga.

This newsletter is published by one of the most trusted names in the industry, Kovels. The quality and reliability of the information is immediately apparent. As expected, the focus is very much on pricing and consumer interest. It's a short publication full of concise snippets of information, printed in full color, on newsletter paper with plentiful pictures, and is advertisement-free. Regular features include sales reports, which cover a variety of collectibles in each issue, and a brief overview of a recent featured sale. Other regular features include a "Dictionary of Marks," which gives information on specific artist or company markings found on antiques. There is also a "Buyer's Price Guide," which highlights the prices recent sales have fetched, and a "Collector's Gallery." The newsletter has a very specific scope of disseminating pricing information and acting as a visual resource to help readers identify items of value. This is recommended for all libraries and is an excellent supplemental addition to the annual *Kovels' Price Guide.* As expected, with the backing of this publication, the Kovels web site is in-depth and includes price guides, an events calendar, and a collector services directory. A good portion of the content is freely accessible, and subscribers to this newsletter get access to an annual index. There is also premium online content that requires an additional subscription. URL: www.kovels.com

385. ***The Magazine Antiques.*** Former titles (until 1971): *Antiques;* (until 1952): *Magazine Antiques;* (until 1928): *Antiques.* [ISSN: 0161-9284] 1922. m. USD 29.95 domestic; USD 79.95 Canada; USD 95 elsewhere. Brant Publications, Inc., 575 Broadway, 5th Fl, New York, NY 10012. Illus., index. Vol. ends: Dec. Microform: PQC. *Indexed:* A06, A07, A22, A51, ArtHuCI, BAS, BRI, CBRI, MLA-IB, P02, RILM. *Bk. rev.:* 1-9, length varies. *Aud.:* Ga, Ac, Sa.

Founded in 1922, *The Magazine Antiques* is a leading publication in the field, focused primarily on furniture and fine and decorative arts. This glossy, all-color publication boasts beautiful photographs and a wealth of articles and features. It is a thick magazine with more content than most, although it does have a fair amount of appropriate, low-key advertising. Regular features include "Current and Coming," listing shows, fairs, and events, and "Farther Afield," which looks at exhibitions and events outside of the United States. Other prominent features include dealer profiles; book reviews; "On the Money," a look at specific valuable pieces; and "Talking Antiques," which provides short interviews with experts. One of the sections that is particularly interesting is called "New Collector," which focuses on a different collectible each month and offers background information, advice, and further reading. The quality of the expertly written articles really sets this publication apart. This is a publication with a rich history; the web site features a wonderful magazine cover archive section going all the way back to 1922. There is a calendar of exhibitions and a large directory of auction houses, dealers, museums, and services with over 750 listings. This directory is a valuable additional resource. There are also selected articles and features taken from the magazine. This publication gets the highest recommendation and is a must for most collections, but especially for public libraries. URL: www.themagazineantiques.com/

386. ***Maine Antique Digest.*** [ISSN: 0147-0639] 1973. m. USD 43 domestic; USD 67 foreign. Ed(s): S Clayton Pennington. Maine Antique Digest, Inc., 911 Main St, PO Box 1429, Waldoboro, ME 04572. Illus., adv. Sample. Vol. ends: Dec. Microform: PQC. *Indexed:* A22. *Bk. rev.:* 2-3, 500-2,000 words. *Aud.:* Ga, Sa.

Billed as the "Marketplace for Americana," this journal covers a wealth of antiques and collectibles, and is mainly focused on providing information for dealers. Despite the title, the coverage is national. This publication is a hefty newspaper made up of multiple separate sections. It is primarily black-and-white with some color images. Regular features include readers' letters, obituaries, "In the Meeting Place," and a great news section called "Fragments." The real strength is the depth of coverage of auctions and shows, highlighting pieces sold and prices. This coverage is unrivaled. Featured articles are well written and contain valuable information for collectors and sellers. There are frequent articles on marketing, collecting, and antique hunting. Book reviews are also featured. Due to the newsprint format, the picture quality is somewhat reduced. The publication also features a heavy amount of advertising on nearly every page. The size of the publication and the amount of content make this a valuable resource for those in the antiques and collectibles trade. The publisher also produces an annual *Antique Trade Directory*, which lists dealers, organizations, auctioneers, and show promoters. The companion web site contains a few sample articles and an events calendar, but the majority of content is limited to subscribers. These resources include a digital edition, a price database, and article archives. This publication is recommended if it fits the user need, but is intended more for the serious collector than those with a casual interest. URL: www.maineantiquedigest.com

387. ***Teddy Bear and Friends.*** Incorporates (1986-2012): *Teddy Bear Review.* [ISSN: 0745-7189] 1983. bi-m. USD 29.95 combined subscription domestic (print & online eds.); USD 49.95 combined subscription Canada (print & online eds.); USD 59.95 combined subscription elsewhere (print & online eds.). Jones Publishing, Inc., PO Box 5000, Iola, WI 54945; http://www.jonespublishing.com. Adv. *Indexed:* BRI. *Aud.:* Ga.

After merging with *Teddy Bear Review* in 2012, this publication is the leading magazine covering teddy bear collecting. This glossy, all-color magazine features lots of photography of bears and plush toys. The focus is shared between modern and antique bears. The magazine sponsors an industry-wide competition called the "Teddy Bear of the Year Awards" (TOBY), which covers multiple aspects of teddy bear design and creation. In addition to featured articles, each issue offers regular sections including teddy bear reviews, teddy bear restoration, artist interviews, news, coverage of conventions and shows, and a look at upcoming events. An interesting feature of each issue is the "Paw-Terns Plus" craft, which provides patterns and instructions for creating your own stuffed animal. While the crafts are a bit beyond this reviewer's skill level, they comprise a valuable addition to the magazine. *Teddy Bear* is fairly short, running at 50 pages, and contains quite a bit of advertising. Recommended for public libraries, and useful and suitable for all ages. The accompanying web site contains some good information, including numerous sample articles and a blog. URL: www.teddybearandfriends.com

388. ***Treasures (Des Moines): antique to modern collecting.*** Formed by the merger of (1959-2011): *Collectors News;* (1993-2011): *Antiques & Collecting Magazine;* Which was formerly (until Oct.1993): *Antiques and Collecting Hobbies;* (until 1985): *Hobbies: The Magazine for Collectors;* Which was formed by the 1931 merger of: *Sports and Hobbies;* (1901-1931): *Philatelic West; Hobby News; Collector's Work; Eastern Philatelist; Hobbies: The Magazine for Collectors* incorporated: *Shipmodeler.* [ISSN: 2162-3147] 1931. m. Lightner Publishing Corporation, 1006 S Michigan Ave, Ste 500, Chicago, IL 60605. Illus. Sample. Vol. ends: Feb. Microform: PQC. *Indexed:* A22, BRI, C37, CBRI, MLA-IB, P02. *Bk. rev.:* 4-6, 30-100 words. *Aud.:* Ga.

Treasures is an umbrella publication that took in *Antiques and Collectibles Magazine, Collectors News, Collectors' Information Bureau,* and *Collector Editions.* "Umbrella" is a good term for this publication, because it covers a wide range of antique forms and looks at modern collectibles as well as traditional antiques. This is a glossy, all-color publication. Regular features include editorials and advice from respected experts, antiques news, auction news, and current prices from Kovels. The news section, "Ken's Korner," is a highlight, featuring interesting and entertaining tidbits pulled together each month. The regularly featured collector and artist profiles are also strong sections. There is quite a bit of advertising, but it is grouped toward the rear of the magazine with the monthly events calendar, and so it avoids being overly intrusive. The magazine's accompanying web site has a very useful section on

"Care and Repair" of antiques, which answers some important questions that collectors may have, as well as a directory of service providers. There is also a preview digital edition of the magazine available to read online. The wide scope, entertaining features, current reference information, and accessibility of this magazine all make it a must for public libraries. URL: www.treasuresmagazine.com/

389. Yesteryear: your monthly guide to antiques and collectibles. Former titles (until 1979): *Yester-Year;* (until 1977): *Yester-Year Antique Marketplace.* [ISSN: 0194-9349] 1975. m. USD 19. Ed(s): Michael Jacobi. Yesteryear Publications, Inc., PO Box 2, Princeton, WI 54968; yesteryearantiques@centurytel.net; http://www.antiqueswisconsin.com/. Illus. *Bk. rev.:* 2-10, 200-300 words. *Aud.:* Ga.

This newspaper features antiques and collectibles, with more of a focus on the collectibles side. The strongest aspect, and the backbone of the publication, is the amount of readers' questions answered. There are four "Question & Answer" sections: "Know Your Antiques," with answers from expert Terry Kovel; "Common Sense Antiques" by Fred Taylor, which specifically covers furniture; "Rinker on Collectibles" by Harry Rinker; and "Antique or Junque" by Anne McCollam. In addition to featured articles, the publication offers a detailed calendar of events, sales, and flea markets around Wisconsin and the surrounding North Central states. There is also an antique shop directory and plenty of advertising. The accompanying web site contains a sample issue and subscription information, but not much else. This is a useful regional publication and would be recommended for public libraries in the geographic area covered. URL: http://yesteryearpublications.com

Doll Collecting

When you think about doll collecting, the first thing that may pop into your mind is Barbie or G.I. Joe, but there is a world of dolls beyond these popular collectible franchises. The world of doll collecting and crafting is diverse, and this is reflected in the variety and focus of doll magazines. There are publications focused on art dolls, antique dolls, fashion dolls, accessories, doll houses, and more. There is a strong support base for these titles both in the United States and across the Atlantic. The industry has not been able to escape the general decline in popularity of printed periodicals, as this past year saw another merger of major publications, with *Doll Reader* joining with *Dolls: The Collector's Magazine.* Most of the publications have embraced the shifting media to provide more online content, as well as additional content that supplements and adds value to the print publications.

For many collectors, dolls are much more than just an investment. They can be a very expensive labor of love. The struggling economy has impacted doll collectors, as it has everyone who has had to cut back, but the future looks brighter. Examining and reviewing these magazines has been a fascinating experience. The quality of content is generally outstanding, and the passion of the publishers, writers, and collectors bodes well for the future strength of this area of publishing.

390. Antique Doll Collector. Formerly (until 1997): *Antique Doll World.* [ISSN: 1096-8474] 1993. m. USD 42.95. Puffin Co., LLC, PO Box 239, Northport, NY 11768. Adv. *Bk. rev.:* Number and length vary. *Aud.:* Ga.

This publication is styled as the complete guide to antique, vintage, and collectible dolls. This is a colorful glossy publication with an emphasis on presentation. Every page is bright and vibrant with plentiful high-quality pictures and galleries of the dolls. The focus, as the titles suggests, is on antique dolls, and the coverage is unrivaled and splendid. The articles are informative and varied, covering artists, particular dolls, fashions, and more from experts on the subjects. Articles are accessible and interesting even to the layperson, and a real strength of the magazine. Regular features include news, doll show reviews, classifieds, and events calendars. The convention coverage is especially significant. The only major downside to the publication is that there is quite a bit of advertising, although the fact that the magazine is longer than most compensates somewhat. Overall, this is strongly recommended for public library collections. The web site does not offer much additional content or

complementary features, but there is an events calendar with web addresses and other contact information for upcoming shows. You can also find the table of contents for the current issue and a full digital edition sample issue. URL: www.antiquedollcollector.com/

391. Art Doll Quarterly. [ISSN: 1939-5027] 2003. q. USD 34.99 domestic; USD 44.99 Canada; USD 59.99 elsewhere. Stampington & Company, LLC., 22992 Mill Creek, Ste B, Laguna Hills, CA 92653; publisher@stampington.com; http://www.stampington.com. Adv. *Bk. rev.:* Number and length vary. *Aud.:* Ga.

This all-color publication covers every kind of art doll and sculpted figure. The presentation of the magazine is immediately striking, with its high-quality images that showcase even the smallest details of the dolls presented. The pictures are sumptuous, and this is especially true of the "Show and Tell" gallery section. Regular features include doll-artist profiles, readers' letters, news, and interviews. There is a strong emphasis on creation, crafting, and reader interaction. In each issue, there are detailed tutorials to craft specific dolls, along with tips for doll crafting and care. There are frequently patterns and creative challenges. The creative challenges ask readers to create a doll to match a theme, such as characters from books or brides. There are also articles about classes, techniques, and tools. The level of skill involved with many of the dolls featured may not make this magazine accessible to newcomers, but this is an unrivaled publication for experienced doll makers. The *Art Doll Quarterly* web site is a section of the publisher's site, and there is little content other than subscription and back-issue information. The quality of this publication and the creative resources it provides make this a must for public libraries where there is an interest. URL: www.artdollquarterly.com/

392. Doll Castle News: the doll collector's magazine. [ISSN: 0363-7972] 1961. bi-m. USD 19.95 domestic; USD 26 Canada; USD 50 elsewhere. Ed(s): Dorita M Mortenson. Castle Press Publications, Inc., PO Box 601, Broadway, NJ 08808. Illus. Vol. ends: Jan/Feb. *Bk. rev.:* 3-4, 100-150 words. *Aud.:* Ga, Sa.

For serious doll collectors, *Doll Castle News* is in both color and black-and-white, and features articles about dolls ranging from antique and vintage through contemporary. Here you will find many projects and patterns for dolls, and each issue includes a doll craft project. The instructions are very clear and well written. Feature articles are signed, well researched, and written in a familiar style, and the illustrations and photographs are excellent. Regular columns include useful information in "From the Antique Doll Cupboard," "Appraising Your Dolls," and "From the Scrapbook." Highly recommended for public libraries whose clientele has an interest in the subject. The web site offers a wealth of practical and fun information and an online newsletter. URL: www.dollcastlemagazine.com

393. Doll Collector: for the love of dolls. Former titles (until May 2010): *Contemporary Doll Collector;* (until 1994): *Contemporary Doll Magazine.* [ISSN: 2153-3458] 1990. bi-m. USD 23.95 domestic; USD 35.95 foreign. Ed(s): Ruth M Keessen, Laurel Bowen. Scott Publications, 30595 Eight Mile, Livonia, MI 48152; contactus@scottpublications.com; http://www.scottpublications.com. Illus., index, adv. Sample. Vol. ends: Oct/Nov. *Aud.:* Ga, Sa.

Doll Collector: For the Love of Dolls is a full-color glossy magazine that covers multiple aspects of doll collecting. Features include news, artist interviews, doll collector clubs, and show and auction reports. Each issue contains a showpiece gallery of high-quality doll pictures. Interestingly, the magazine has a recurring feature of patterns and instructions for making doll clothing and accessories. "Dolls We Love" is a particularly interesting section, which features in-depth coverage of a particular doll or doll line. Articles are useful and accessible to both casual and ardent collectors, with a focus on contemporary dolls, but good coverage of vintage dolls as well. There are also the usual collecting resources you would expect, with classifieds and an events calendar. *Doll Collector* is suitable for any reader interested in doll collecting. Highly recommended for a public library collection. URL: http://scottpublications.com/cdcmag/

394. Dolls: the collector's magazine. Incorporates (in 2003): *Doll World.* [ISSN: 0733-2238] 1982. 10x/yr. USD 34.95 (print or online ed.); USD 44.95 combined subscription (print & online eds.). Ed(s): Nadya Rondon. Jones Publishing, Inc., N 7450 Aanstad Rd, PO Box 5000, Iola, WI 54945; jonespub@jonespublishing.com; http://www.jonespublishing.com. Illus., adv. Circ: 95000 Paid. Vol. ends: Dec. *Bk. rev.:* 2-4, 100-150 words. *Aud.:* Ga, Sa.

Dolls magazine covers multiple facets of the collectible doll industry, from high-end artist works to popular manufacturer pieces, fashion dolls, and ball-jointed dolls. It is a full-color, glossy publication that features detailed, quality photographs. Popular title *Doll Reader* merged into this publication in 2012. The magazine includes a large number of short feature articles and regular sections such as news, doll show reviews, an events calendar, and classifieds. Semi-regular staples of the magazine include question-and-answer sections and portraits. There is a fairly heavy amount of advertising in this publication. Overall, the content seems somewhat superficial, with the articles lacking length or depth and the publication acting more as a showcase for the doll pictures and artists. The sense of community and the human touch found in other doll collector magazines seems to be missing here. The magazine has quite a significant online presence. Web site features include a blog, numerous articles, directories of doll hospitals and retailers, and an events calendar. Digital editions are available alongside a subscription that offers additional multimedia bonus content. Recommended if this publication fits a specific need; suitable for public libraries, but lacking depth. URL: www.dollsmagazine.com/

395. *Dolls House World.* Incorporates: *International Dolls House News.* [ISSN: 0961-0928] 1989. m. GBP 46 domestic; USD 110 United States; GBP 70 in Europe. Ed(s): Joyce Dean. Ashdown Publishing Ltd., The Digital Farm, Park Farm, Arundel, BN18 0AG, United Kingdom; support@ashdown.co.uk; http://www.ashdown.co.uk. Illus., adv. Sample. *Aud.:* Ga, Sa.

This is a British publication that has been in print for over 20 years. The focus of this publication is on miniature accessories for dolls and on doll houses. It's an accessible publication suitable for beginners and for experienced miniaturists. The color photography of the miniatures is excellent and allows the details to be clearly seen. *Dolls House World* is written by experts who are clearly passionate about the subject, which comes through in the enjoyable articles. One of the core components of the magazine is the projects, including miniature projects, knitting, and other crafts, with complete patterns and step-by-step instructions on how to create them. These crafts add a great deal of value and interaction to the publication. There are also interesting featured articles and interviews with artists and club news, along with reviews of recent doll house and miniature fairs, and an events calendar. The magazine has a large social media and multimedia presence, including a blog. In addition to the print edition, there are digital editions available through an app for all common devices. There is also a 24-hour TV channel, "dollshouse.TV." These are all available through subscription, either separately or bundled. However, there is little content available on the web site unless you are a subscriber. *Dolls House World* covers a specific area of the doll world, but what it covers, it covers well. Recommended for public libraries where there is a demand. URL: www.dollshouseworld.com/

396. *F D Q Fashion Doll Quarterly.* 2006. q. USD 36 domestic; USD 45 Canada; USD 72 elsewhere. Ed(s): Pat Henry. F D Q Media LLC, 299 Eastern Pky, Germantown, NY 12526. Adv. *Aud.:* Ga.

As the title suggests, this glossy magazine is focused on fashion dolls. This publication caters to a very specific interest, and is billed as the ultimate source for fashion doll collectors. One of the highlights of the magazine is the superb doll photography, which really sets it apart. The reader gets the feel of a couture magazine and the photography is fitting for that style. Some of the photographs are artfully revealing, as regular fashion magazines can be, and so it may not be suitable for younger readers. Although the pictures are a key aspect of this magazine, the articles are not just filler. Regular features include news, artist interviews, event coverage, and the latest fashion trends and dolls. Articles, especially the interviews, were interesting and informative, even to a layperson. There is also coverage of doll crafts, plus ideas for miniature accessories and scene decor that readers are encouraged to try. The focus of the dolls is mostly contemporary, with some retrospective features. Supplemental material is available between quarterly issues and is available as a digital download. This is a fairly unique publication. Due to its specific (but in no way limited) scope, this would be a worthy addition to a library collection. URL: www.fashiondollquarterly.net/

■ ARCHAEOLOGY

Tom Bruno, Associate Director of Resource Sharing and Reserves, Sterling Memorial Library, Yale University, New Haven, CT 06511

Introduction

Archaeology has seen a minor renaissance in scholarship and increased public interest in recent years. While some of this resurgence has been driven by popular speculation about the supposed "Mayan Apocalypse" of 2012, a great deal of this revival can be attributed to the application of archaeological findings to current topics such as environmental studies, sustainability, and the preservation and survival of cultural heritage from pre-Columbian folk traditions to local commemorations of World War II. Whether debunking pseudoscientific theories about the end of the world or enlightening readers to the very real problems of sustainable civilizations and endangered archaeological resources, archaeology has never seemed more relevant than it does today.

Publications about archaeology fall into three basic subdivisions: general, regional, and scientific. While most general and some regional magazines may be of interest to high school and public libraries, scientific archaeology journals tend to appeal primarily to an academic audience and can be quite esoteric in subject matter and scope.

For various historical reasons, regional archaeological journals have aligned themselves with related disciplines in a manner that is peculiar to each region. For example, the archaeology of ancient Greece and Rome is studied in close association with the fields of classical philology, the fine arts, and history; meanwhile, New World archaeology is strongly influenced by trends in anthropology, ethnology, and linguistics. As a result, many regional publications will not only be of interest to readers outside of the traditional sphere of archaeology but may also be considered indispensable parts of other scholarly collections.

Periodicals that are truly local in scope are not included in this section, but can be found among the listings of magazines for specific geographical regions.

Basic Periodicals

Hs: *American Archaeology, Archaeology, Expedition;* Ga: *American Archaeology, Archaeology, Biblical Archaeology Review, Egyptian Archaeology, Expedition;* Ac: *American Antiquity, American Journal of Archaeology, Antiquity, Archaeology, Archaeometry, Expedition, Journal of Roman Archaeology, Near Eastern Archaeology, North American Archaeologist, World Archaeology.*

Basic Abstracts and Indexes

AATA Online: abstracts of international conservation literature, Abstracts in Anthropology, Anthropological Index Online, British and Irish Archaeological Bibliography.

397. *Acta Archaeologica.* [ISSN: 0065-101X] 1930. a. GBP 111. Ed(s): Klavs Randsborg. Wiley-Blackwell Publishing, Inc., Commerce Pl, 350 Main St, Malden, MA 02148; info@wiley.com; http://onlinelibrary.wiley.com/. Illus., adv. Refereed. Reprint: PSC. *Indexed:* A01, A22, AbAn, AmHI, ArtHuCI, BrArAb, E01, FR, MLA-IB, NumL. *Aud.:* Ac.

This annual publication of the Institute of Archaeology in Copenhagen is a scholarly journal with editors and contributors of international renown. Although its primary focus is the archaeology of Scandinavia and the North Atlantic until 1500 A.D., *Acta Archaeologica* also explores the relationship of the Nordic world to that of Continental Europe, the Mediterranean, and beyond (contributions from Arctic and maritime archaeology are specifically solicited by the editorial board). Articles are written mostly in English, with occasional offerings in French, German, and Italian. Each volume is published in two issues: the first is often devoted to a single theme, such as Viking graves and ship burials; and the second issue contains a series of four to ten articles on various topics. Both issues of each volume contain numerous illustrations and line drawings. The rising prominence of "Atlantic Studies" and other such cross-disciplinary modes of research make this journal an indispensable part of any academic research collection.

African Archaeological Review. See Africa section.

398. *American Antiquity.* [ISSN: 0002-7316] 1935. q. Free to members. Society for American Archaeology, 900 Second St, NE #12, Washington, DC 20002-3560; publications@saa.org; http://www.saa.org/. Illus., index, adv. Refereed. Circ: 6600. Vol. ends: Oct. *Indexed:* A01, A06, A07, A22, A47, ABS&EES, AbAn, AmHI, ArtHuCI, BRI, BrArAb, CBRI, FR, MLA-IB, NumL, P02. *Bk. rev.:* Varies per issue, 500-700 words, signed. *Aud.:* Ac, Sa.

One of several journals published by the Society for American Archaeology, *American Antiquity* is a quarterly review of New World archaeology, with a focus on the prehistory of the United States and Canada (since 1990, articles on the archaeology of Latin America have appeared in *Latin American Antiquity*, also a publication of the Society for American Archaeology and reviewed in this section). Each issue features four to six original scholarly papers, field reports from archaeological sites throughout the Americas, and a varying number of book reviews, as well as a "Comments" section that permits society members to address at length and debate the merits of the work presented in previous issues. The primary focus of the journal is prehistoric, with recent issues covering such topics as Late Pleistocene Western Camel hunting in Southwestern Canada; the continuity of Native American culture in Colonial New England; and pine nut processing in Southern California. Special attention is also paid to scholarship in the fields of linguistics and anthropology. Articles are accompanied by high-quality illustrations and maps. *American Antiquity* is a free publication for members of the Society for American Archaeology.

399. *American Archaeology.* Formerly (until 1997): *Archaeological Conservancy Newsletter.* [ISSN: 1093-8400] 1980. q. Free to members; USD 3.95 newsstand/cover. Ed(s): Michael Bawaya. Archaeological Conservancy, 5301 Central Ave, NE, Ste 902, Albuquerque, NM 87108; tacinfo@nm.net; http://www.americanarchaeology.org. Illus. *Indexed:* AbAn. *Bk. rev.:* 2-4, 200-300 words, signed. *Aud.:* Ga.

A quarterly publication of The Archaeological Conservancy, located in Albuquerque, New Mexico, *American Archaeology* is "the only consumer magazine devoted to the excitement and mystery of archaeology in the United States, with additional coverage of Canada and Latin America." Each issue contains several articles with color photographs, maps, and other illustrative material that highlights recent developments in the field. Recent articles cover such topics as the evidence for Solutrean migrations to the New World from Iberia, and the controversy surrounding the new amateur relic-hunter reality show *American Diggers*. *American Archaeology* also contains information of interest to members of The Archaeological Conservancy and lists the acquisition of new sites under its aegis, field reports from current conservancy projects, and opportunities for field school and volunteer work. Book reviews are concise but informative, and include recently published multimedia offerings as well.

400. *American Journal of Archaeology.* Formerly (until 1897): *American Journal of Archaeology and of the History of the Fine Arts.* [ISSN: 0002-9114] 1885. q. USD 325 (print & online eds.). Ed(s): Madeleine J Donachie, Naomi Norman. Archaeological Institute of America (Boston), 656 Beacon St, Boston, MA 02215; aia@aia.bu.edu; http://www.archaeological.org. Illus., index, adv. Refereed. Vol. ends: Oct. Microform: PMC; PQC. *Indexed:* A01, A06, A07, A22, ABS&EES, AbAn, AmHI, ArtHuCI, BAS, BRI, BrArAb, CBRI, Chicano, FR, MLA-IB, NumL, P02. *Bk. rev.:* 15-25, 1-2 columns, signed. *Aud.:* Ac, Sa.

Published by The Archaeological Institute of America, located at Boston University, the *American Journal of Archaeology* is a quarterly review of current scholarship in the field of Mediterranean, Near Eastern, and Egyptian archaeology. Each issue includes articles, field reports, "necrologies" of recently deceased archaeologists of note, proceedings and awards of The Archaeological Institute, and museum and book reviews, as well as longer thematic review articles two or three pages in length. Recent issues cover such

topics as agricultural strategies and political economy in Ancient Anatolia; pottery repairs in antiquity; and health and social well-being in Late Roman Britain. The fourth issue contains a cumulative contents listing for the entire volume, arranged by section. The *American Journal of Archaeology* now offers a robust online portal, with links to current and past content, a preview of upcoming articles, a blog containing online reviews and a discussion forum, and social networking integration with Facebook.

401. *Ancient Mesoamerica.* [ISSN: 0956-5361] 1990. s-a. GBP 283. Ed(s): Geoffrey G McCafferty, William R Fowler, Jr. Cambridge University Press, The Edinburgh Bldg, Shaftesbury Rd, Cambridge, CB2 8RU, United Kingdom; journals@cambridge.org; http://www.cambridge.org/uk. Adv. Refereed. Circ: 800. Reprint: PSC. *Indexed:* A01, A22, A47, AbAn, ArtHuCI, E01, IBSS. *Aud.:* Ac, Sa.

An international publication, *Ancient Mesoamerica* is a scholarly journal that covers the study of pre-Columbian Mesoamerican archaeology and its intersection with the allied disciplines of art history, ethnohistory, linguistics, and cultural anthropology. Each issue contains approximately 8–12 articles written in English and (to a lesser extent) Spanish, accompanied by maps, line drawings, and other illustrative matter. The subject matter reflects the interdisciplinary ethos of the journal, with special attention paid to the historical linguistics of indigenous Mesoamerican languages. *Ancient Mesoamerica* also has a strong anthropological focus, reflecting the New World affinity between the fields of archaeology and anthropology. Recent issues explore such topics as sacred geography in the Nochixtlan Valley, Proto-Uto-Aztecan as a Mesoamerican language, and Ancient Maya mosaic mirrors. This is an excellent review of the state of Mesoamerican research that is as accessible to laypersons as it is useful to scholars.

402. *The Antiquaries Journal.* Formerly (until 1921): *Society of Antiquaries of London. Proceedings.* [ISSN: 0003-5815] 1843. a. GBP 133 (print & online eds.). Ed(s): Kate Owen. Society of Antiquaries of London, Burlington House, Piccadilly, London, W1J 0BE, United Kingdom; admin@sal.org.uk; http://www.sal.org.uk. Illus., index. Refereed. Microform: IDC; PQC. *Indexed:* A&ATA, A06, A22, API, AbAn, AmHI, BRI, BrArAb, FR, MLA-IB, NumL, RILM. *Bk. rev.:* 40-50, 1-2 columns, signed; 1-2 review articles. *Aud.:* Ac, Sa.

The Society of Antiquaries of London publishes this annual journal, an international review "concerned with all matters of interest to antiquarians—including all aspects of archaeology, architectural and art history, conservation, heraldry, anthropological, ecclesiastical, documentary, musical and linguistic study." Each volume offers five to ten submissions of 20–80 pages in length, a dozen or more "shorter" contributions that are as substantial as feature articles in other magazines, review articles, and 40–50 book reviews that offer a comprehensive survey of recent publications in the field. Articles are lavishly illustrated both in black-and-white and in color. While *The Antiquaries Journal* solicits original research from around the globe, the majority of work focuses on the United Kingdom and continental Europe. Recent volumes cover Roland and Crusade imagery in an English royal chapel; evidence for prehistoric salt extraction in Hungary; and the Jewish catacombs in Roman Melite. This is a first-rate publication that will appeal to scholars not only in archaeology but in many other related fields.

403. *Antiquity: a quarterly review of world archaeology.* [ISSN: 0003-598X] 1927. q. EUR 248. Ed(s): Chris Scarre. Antiquity Publications Ltd., King's Manor, York, YO1 7EP, United Kingdom; reviews@antiquity.ac.uk. Illus., index, adv. Sample. Refereed. Vol. ends: Dec. Microform: MIM; IDC; PQC. *Indexed:* A01, A06, A07, A22, A47, AbAn, AmHI, ArtHuCI, BAS, BRI, BrArAb, FR, IBSS, MLA-IB, NumL, P02, RILM. *Bk. rev.:* 12-15, 1-3 pages, signed; 4-6 book review articles, 3-5 pages, signed. *Aud.:* Ac, Sa.

A quarterly publication of the Antiquity Trust edited by the Department of Archaeology at the University of York in the United Kingdom, *Antiquity* is "an international peer-reviewed journal of archaeological research that aims to communicate the most significant new discoveries, theory, and method and cultural resource issues rapidly and in plain language to the academy and the profession." Each issue features 8–12 articles focused on research, three to six articles concerning method, several "debate" articles in which authors respond to each other's recent work, and book reviews as well as more substantial, thematic book-review articles. The scope of *Antiquity* is truly international and diachronic—recent topics include the prehistory of primates, animation in Paleolithic art, and the archaeology of civil war and dictatorship in Spain. Both color and black-and-white illustrations accompany each article, as well as maps, charts, and photographs. This journal is an indispensable part of any archaeological research collection.

404. *Archaeology: a magazine dealing with the antiquity of the world.* [ISSN: 0003-8113] 1948. bi-m. USD 21.95 domestic (Free to members). Ed(s): Peter Young, Eti Bonn-Muller. Archaeological Institute of America, 36-36 33d St, Long Island City, NY 11106; aia@aia.bu.edu; http://www.archaeological.org/. Illus., index, adv. Refereed. Circ: 225000. Vol. ends: Nov/Dec. Microform: PQC. *Indexed:* A01, A06, A07, A22, A47, ABS&EES, AbAn, AmHI, ArtHuCI, BAS, BRI, BrArAb, C37, CBRI, FR, MASUSE, MLA-IB, NumL, P02, RILM. *Bk. rev.:* 5-10, 1-2 columns, signed. *Aud.:* Hs, Ga, Ac, Sa.

While the Archaeological Institute of America, located at Boston University, also publishes the more scholarly *American Journal of Archaeology* for a professional archaeological audience, its bimonthly title *Archaeology* is a general-interest magazine intended for wider circulation. Each issue contains several feature articles with glossy color photos, a "World Roundup" of archaeology news, interviews with prominent archaeologists, and five to ten reviews of books, movies, multimedia products, and museums. The scope of *Archaeology* is global and ranges from prehistoric archaeology to the present, with a special emphasis on the growing role of science and technology in the field. Recent issues cover such topics as the investigation of a burial chamber of an ancient Egyptian singer; the search for a "lost" Roman aqueduct; and the archaeology of the *Titanic*. Like its more academically oriented sister publication, *Archaeology* boasts a dynamic web presence, including a weekly compilation of television programming dealing with the ancient world; links to archaeology-related travel, retail, and educational programs and events; and social networking integration. This informative and entertaining magazine is useful not only to general audiences but also to college and university libraries.

405. *Archaeology in Oceania.* Formerly (until 1981): *Archaeology and Physical Anthropology in Oceania.* [ISSN: 0003-8121] 1966. 3x/yr. GBP 104. Ed(s): J Peter White. Wiley-Blackwell Publishing Asia, 155 Cremorne St, Richmond, VIC 3121, Australia; melbourne@wiley.com; http://www.wiley.com/. Illus., index. Vol. ends: Oct. *Indexed:* A01, A22, A47, AbAn, ArtHuCI, BAS, BRI, FR, IBSS, MLA-IB. *Bk. rev.:* 1-10, 1-3 columns, signed. *Aud.:* Ac, Sa.

Oceania Publications, a department within the Faculty of Arts at the University of Sydney in Australia, produces this journal three times a year, covering the archaeology of "the lands of the western Pacific rim and all the islands of the Pacific Ocean, including Australia." Each issue contains one to three articles refereed by scholars in the field, research reports from the field, and several book reviews. Accompanying illustrations are in black-and-white and include maps, line drawings, and photographs. Recent issues feature articles about intrusion, integration, and innovation on small (and not-so-small) islands; Middle–late Holocene skin-working tools in Melanesia; and climate change in the occupation and abandonment of Palau's Rock Islands. *Archaeology in Oceania* also welcomes research in the field of human biological studies, with a strong emphasis on anthropology.

406. *Archaeology of Eastern North America.* Incorporates (1941-1977): *Eastern States Archaeological Federation. Bulletin.* [ISSN: 0360-1021] 1973. a. Free to members. Ed(s): Arthur E Spiess. Eastern States Archeological Federation, PO Box 386, Bethlehem, CT 06751; busmanager@esaf-archeology.org; http://www.esaf-archeology.org. Illus. *Indexed:* A47, AbAn. *Aud.:* Ac.

An annual publication of the Eastern States Archaeological Federation, *Archaeology of Eastern North America* is a forum for the latest fieldwork and research by archaeologists and state archaeological societies in the Eastern United States. Each issue contains five to ten articles ranging from site reports to ethnohistorical research and "applied archaeology." Recent articles cover such topics as Native American use of fossil shark teeth in the Chesapeake Bay Region; wampum and other seventeenth-century shell games; and colonization and cultural change during the Early Archaic Period in Northwestern Ohio.

Illustrations are in black-and-white, and include photographs, charts, maps, and line drawings. Subscription to this journal is a benefit of membership in the Eastern States Archaeological Federation.

407. *Archaeometry.* [ISSN: 0003-813X] 1958. bi-m. GBP 246. Ed(s): James Burton, E Pernicka. Wiley-Blackwell Publishing Ltd., The Atrium, Southern Gate, Chichester, PO19 8SQ, United Kingdom; customer@wiley.com; http://www.wiley.com/. Illus., adv. Sample. Refereed. Vol. ends: Aug. Reprint: PSC. *Indexed:* A&ATA, A01, A22, A47, AbAn, ArtHuCI, BAS, BrArAb, E01, FR, NumL. *Aud.:* Ac, Sa.

Published for the University of Oxford in association with the Gesellschaft fuer Naturwissenschaftliche Archaeologie, ARCHAEOMETRIE, the Society for Archaeological Sciences, and the Associazione Italiana di Archeometria, *Archaeometry* is "an international research journal covering the application of the physical and biological sciences to archaeology and the history of art." Each issue contains 8–12 articles from scholars in the fields of archaeology and intersecting scientific disciplines, with a strong emphasis on materials science research. High-quality color and black-and-white illustrations accompany each article. The geographical and temporal scope of *Archaeometry* is wide-ranging, and recent articles cover such topics as the inclusions in mortars of different historical periods from Greek monuments; the provenance of obsidian in the Eastern Yemen Plateau; and the comparative radiocarbon dating of shell and wood artifacts from pre-Columbian sites in Cuba.

408. *Before Farming: the archaeology and anthropology of hunter-gatherers.* [ISSN: 1476-4253] 2002. a. GBP 125 (print & online eds.) Individuals, GBP 40 (print & online eds.). Western Academic & Specialist Press, PO Box 191, Liverpool, L23 3WZ, United Kingdom; http://www.waspress.co.uk/. *Bk. rev.:* 1-4, signed. *Aud.:* Ac, Sa.

Published by the Western Academic and Specialist Press (WASP), *Before Farming* is an interesting "hybrid" online/print journal that features anthropological and archaeological research on hunter-gatherers. Although the electronic version of this periodical is quarterly, the print edition comes out annually and is a compilation of the previous year's online content. Each quarterly online issue features several articles containing maps, color images, and other illustrative materials, as well as a few book reviews. Due to the high-resolution and dynamic nature of some of *Before Farming*'s electronic content, not everything that appears in the online edition is found in the print annual. Past issues have explored a wide spectrum of subjects and themes, ranging from Mesolithic bone industry in Serbia; ceremonial centers in Late Natufian Nahal Oren; and evidence of Neanderthal symbolic behavior in France. Archaeologists and anthropologists are increasingly interested in the period of human prehistory before the advent of agriculture, and *Before Farming* is an impressive contribution to this important emerging field of study.

409. *Biblical Archaeology Review.* Incorporates (1998-2006): *Archaeology Odyssey;* (1992-2005): *B R;* Which was formerly (1985-1992): *Bible Review.* [ISSN: 0098-9444] 1975. bi-m. USD 13.97 domestic (Free to members). Ed(s): Dorothy D Resig, Hershel Shanks. Biblical Archaeology Society, 4710 41st St, NW, Washington, DC 20016; bas@bib-arch.org; http://www.bib-arch.org/. Illus., adv. Vol. ends: Nov/Dec. *Indexed:* A01, A07, A22, AbAn, AmHI, BRI, FR, IJP, MLA-IB, R&TA, RILM. *Bk. rev.:* 3-4, length 2-3 columns, signed. *Aud.:* Ga, Ac, Sa.

Biblical Archaeology Review, a bimonthly publication of the Biblical Archaeology Society, describes itself as "the only nonsectarian forum for the discussion of Biblical archaeology." Recently consolidated (as of January/February 2006) with the society's secular general-interest archaeology magazine *Archaeology Odyssey,* BAR promises an expanded periodical that will offer articles of interest both to biblical archaeology enthusiasts and to those with a broader interest in the field. Each glossy color issue offers several feature articles and regular departmental columns that present news, reviews, and editorials, as well as thoughtful and intelligent debate on current controversial subjects. Recent topics explored include unexcavated synagogues in Turkey; the historical evidence of Pharaoh Sheshonq's military campaign against Jerusalem; and the archaeological dating of the Psalms. *BAR* also has a fresh web portal for its content, including links to multimedia offerings such as audio interviews, video highlights from Biblical archaeology documentaries, and a lively "Debates" section that invites readers to comment on recent articles and other current topics in the field.

410. Cambridge Archaeological Journal. [ISSN: 0959-7743] 1991. 3x/yr. GBP 200 (print & online eds.). Ed(s): John Robb. Cambridge University Press, The Edinburgh Bldg, Shaftesbury Rd, Cambridge, CB2 8RU, United Kingdom; journals@cambridge.org; http://www.cambridge.org/uk. Illus., index, adv. Refereed. Circ: 1800. Vol. ends: Oct. Reprint: PSC. *Indexed:* A01, A07, A22, A47, AmHI, ArtHuCI, BrArAb, E01, NumL. *Bk. rev.:* 1-3 pages, signed. *Aud.:* Ac, Sa.

Although this journal, published by Cambridge University Press on behalf of the McDonald Institute for Archaeological Research, has recently undergone some minor changes in format, its new editor John Robb promises that "*CAJ* will continue to be defined by its core area, the archaeology of human symbolic capabilities and practices—whether in potlaches or pyramids, hand-axes or henges, rock carvings or castles—and as studies in all approaches from evolutionary archaeology to interpretive archaeology, from human evolution to hermeneutics." This formerly biannual publication now offers three issues per year, in February, June, and October, and adds to its combination of feature articles, research notes, and reviews of occasional "conversations" with members of the international archaeology community on various topics of current interest to the field. Recent issues in this new format offer scholarly articles on texting and moral narrative in the murals of Bonampak at Chiapas; Middle Stone Age bow-and-arrow technology; and the coin economy on the East African Swahili Coast.

411. Canadian Journal of Archaeology. Formerly (until 1977): *Canadian Archaeological Association. Bulletin.* [ISSN: 0705-2006] 1969. s-a. Free to members. Ed(s): Gerry Oetelaar. Canadian Archaeological Association, c/o Jack Brink, Royal Alberta Museum, Edmonton, AB T5N 0M6, Canada; president@canadianarchaeology.com; http://www.canadianarchaeology.com. Illus., adv. Refereed. *Indexed:* A01, A47, BrArAb, CBCARef, FR. *Bk. rev.:* 8-15, 3 pages, signed. *Aud.:* Ac, Sa.

A biannual publication of the Canadian Archaeological Association, this journal functions both as a comprehensive review of ongoing field projects and research in Canada and as a scholarly forum for the broader issues of theory and praxis in the archaeological discipline. Articles are in either English or French and are illustrated with black-and-white photographs, line drawings, maps, graphs, and charts. Each issue contains a feature article of approximately 20–30 pages in length, followed by several shorter research and field reports, and reviews of recent monographs in archaeology and anthropology from Canadian authors. Although the principal contributors to the *Canadian Journal of Archaeology* are college and university faculty in Canada, other cultural institutions from both the public and private sectors are also represented. Recent articles cover seasonal bird exploitation by recent Indian and Beothuk hunter-gatherers of Newfoundland; soilscapes and places inside Labrador Inuit dwellings; and relations between archaeologists and local governments in British Columbia.

412. Egyptian Archaeology. [ISSN: 0962-2837] 1991. a. Free to members; Non-members, GBP 5.95. Ed(s): Dr. Patricia Spencer, Rob Tamplin. Egypt Exploration Society, 3 Doughty Mews, London, WC1N 2PG, United Kingdom; http://www.ees.ac.uk. Illus., index, adv. Circ: 2500. *Bk. rev.:* 4-7, 1-2 columns, signed. *Aud.:* Ga, Ac.

The Egypt Exploration Society, founded in 1882, has published this semi-annual magazine for its membership since 1991. Each issue has approximately 12–14 articles of one to three pages in length on a variety of topics in ancient Egyptian archaeology, art, and papyrology, accompanied by glossy color photographs, drawings, and computer re-creations. The "Digging Diary" offers a roundup of field reports from ongoing excavations and highlights expeditions headed by the society, and a "Notice Board" details upcoming events for members in both Egypt and the United Kingdom. Recent issues feature conservation and site-management at the Luxor Temple, ancient Theban waterways, and a papyrus from the House of Life at Akhetaten. Although this periodical is chiefly targeted toward members of the Egypt Exploration Society, its accessible articles and rich visual content make it a fine resource for amateur archaeologists and Egyptophiles alike.

413. Expedition. Formerly (until 1958): *University Museum Bulletin;* Which superseded (in 1930): *University Museum Bulletin.* [ISSN: 0014-4738] 1930. 3x/yr. USD 35. Ed(s): Jane Hickman. University of Pennsylvania Museum, 3260 S St, Philadelphia, PA 19104; http://www.museum.upenn.edu. Illus., index. Refereed. Vol. ends: Winter. Microform: PQC. *Indexed:* A&ATA, A01, A06, A07, A22, A47, AbAn, BAS, BRI, FR, NumL, P02, RILM. *Bk. rev.:* 1-2 columns, signed. *Aud.:* Hs, Ga, Ac.

Published three times a year by the University of Pennsylvania's Museum of Archaeology and Anthropology, *Expedition* "offers direct access to the latest findings of archaeologists and anthropologists around the world." Each issue contains several feature articles, a special feature that often takes a closer look at the museum's own members and component academic departments, field and research notes, book reviews, and an "exhibit notes" section that details the latest traveling and permanent museum exhibitions of note. The glossy color format allows for ample and lavish illustrations, including photographs and topographical maps of featured archaeological sites. Recent issues of *Expedition* cover such topics as bulls and bull-leaping in the ancient Minoan world; Afghan war rugs and globalization; and the recent pop-culture fascination with the Mayans and apocalyptic predictions in 2012. This lively magazine is an interesting synthesis of scholarly topics with a more accessible general-interest format, and as such it is a useful resource for both academic and public libraries.

414. Geoarchaeology: an international journal. [ISSN: 0883-6353] 1986. bi-m. GBP 1247. Ed(s): Jamie C Woodward, Gary Huckleberry. John Wiley & Sons, Inc., 111 River St, MS 4-02, Hoboken, NJ 07030; info@wiley.com; http://www.wiley.com/WileyCDA/. Adv. Refereed. Microform: PQC. Reprint: PSC. *Indexed:* A22, ArtHuCI, BrArAb, NumL. *Bk. rev.:* 0-3, 1-2 pages, signed. *Aud.:* Ac, Sa.

This journal, published eight times a year, presents cutting-edge interdisciplinary scholarship between the fields of archaeology and the Earth sciences, "focusing on understanding archaeological sites, their natural context, and particularly the aspects of site formation processes." While the primary focus of *Geoarchaeology* is on the relationship of archaeology to dynamic physical processes, the editorial board also solicits articles concerning faunal and botanical remains, as well as the material analysis of manmade artifacts. Each issue contains several features of 20–40 pages in length, covering topics as diverse as palaeogeographic changes in the Ukraine during the Mid- to Late-Holocene; the exploitation of plant resources by early *Homo sapiens*; and the composition, technology of manufacture, and circulation of Hellenistic pottery from the Eastern Adriatic. Most issues also contain book reviews and "short contributions" that allow scholars to promulgate interim findings with fewer editorial restrictions. Black-and-white illustrations accompany each article in the form of photographs, charts and graphs, and line drawings. Although seemingly esoteric in its appeal, *Geoarchaeology* highlights the fundamental scientific processes that underlie all branches of archaeology. This journal is an invaluable asset to any research collection.

415. Heritage & Society. Formerly (until 2011): *Heritage Management.* [ISSN: 2159-032X] 2008. s-a. GBP 204 (print & online eds.). Ed(s): Neil A Silberman, Elizabeth S Chilton. Left Coast Press, Inc., 1630 N Main St, Ste 400, Walnut Creek, CA 94596; Explore@LCoastPress.com; http://www.lcoastpress.com. Refereed. Reprint: PSC. *Indexed:* C45. *Bk. rev.:* 2-3, signed. *Aud.:* Ga, Ac.

Launched in the spring of 2008 by Left Coast Press, *Heritage & Society* "is a global, peer-reviewed journal that provides a venue for using scholarly, professional, and indigenous knowledge to address broader societal concerns about managing cultural heritage." As its editors are both professors who are actively involved with various cultural preservation initiatives, *Heritage & Society* is an engaging mix of scholarly research and grass-roots activism. Each issue contains articles of interest not only to archaeologists but to those who work for indigenous communities, governmental agencies, and museums and other private or public cultural management organizations; and it highlights current policy and legislation affecting issues of heritage management. Recent issues address a wide range of topics, including the use of "Reverse Archaeology" in modern spatial planning; the challenges of sustaining intangible cultural heritage; and archaeology, identity, and demographic imbalance in the Arab Emirates. While this is a relatively new publication, *Heritage & Society* is a timely addition to any archaeological collection, and of special interest to any library with a focus on indigenous cultures.

416. *Hesperia.* [ISSN: 0018-098X] 1932. q. USD 185 (print & online eds.). Ed(s): Dr. Tracey Cullen. American School of Classical Studies at Athens, 54 Souidias St, Athens, 106 76, Greece; ascsa@ascsa.org; http://www.ascsa.edu.gr. Illus. Refereed. Circ: 1100. *Indexed:* A06, A07, A22, AbAn, AmHI, ArtHuCI, BRI, E01, FR, MLA-IB, NumL, P02. *Aud.:* Ac, Sa.

An impressive quarterly publication of the American School of Classical Studies at Athens, *Hesperia* "welcomes submissions from all scholars working in the fields of Greek archaeology, art, epigraphy, history, materials science, ethnography, and literature. Geographical boundaries are broadly defined as those of the entire Greek world, and no chronological restrictions are imposed." Each attractively composed issue contains several articles of substantial length (20–80 pages) and includes lavish illustrations both in color and in black-and-white, ample footnotes, and comprehensive scholarly bibliographies. Recent issues cover the first wheel-made pottery in the Aegean; Hellenistic freestanding sculpture from the Athenian Agora; and evidence of ancestor cult worship at Troy. This flagship journal of Greek archaeology is an indispensable part of any research collection, and by virtue of its diachronic and interdisciplinary approach, it will be of value to anyone interested in Greek history and culture in general.

417. *Historical Archaeology.* [ISSN: 0440-9213] 1967. q. Free to members. Ed(s): J W Joseph. Society for Historical Archaeology, 9707 Key W Ave, Ste 100, Rockville, MD 20850; hq@sha.org; http://www.sha.org. Illus., index. Sample. Refereed. Vol. ends: Dec. *Indexed:* A01, A07, A22, AbAn, AmHI, ArtHuCI, BRI, BrArAb, IBSS, MLA-IB, NumL. *Bk. rev.:* 20-40, 1-2 columns, signed. *Aud.:* Ac, Sa.

This quarterly publication of the Society for Historical Archaeology focuses on the archaeology of past societies that are also part of the historical record, a multidisciplinary field that draws upon the allied disciplines of anthropology, history, geography, and folklore to help reconstruct the past. Each issue contains several feature articles that are submitted primarily by members of the society (with occasional offerings from other scholars as well) and are illustrated with black-and-white photographs, maps, and line drawings. The articles cover an international range of topics such as French Colonial pottery; the sourcing of gunflints; and using geodatabases to generate "living documents" for archaeology in New Zealand. The journal also reviews a substantial number of recent publications (20–40 books) in the burgeoning field of historical archaeology. Subscription is free to society members.

418. *International Journal of Osteoarchaeology.* [ISSN: 1047-482X] 1991. bi-m. GBP 818. John Wiley & Sons Ltd., The Atrium, Southern Gate, Chichester, PO19 8SQ, United Kingdom; customer@wiley.com; http://www.wiley.com. Adv. Sample. Refereed. Microform: PQC. Reprint: PSC. *Indexed:* A22, ArtHuCI, BrArAb, NumL, P02. *Bk. rev.:* 2-4, 1-2 pages, signed. *Aud.:* Ac, Sa.

This bimonthly scholarly publication deals with "all aspects of the study of human and animal bones from archaeological contexts." As with most scientific archaeological journals, the *International Journal of Osteoarchaeology* is both global and diachronic in scope, including such diverse material as contrasting patterns of dental microtrauma in Inuit and European populations; a study of medieval dogs in Novgorod; and diet, nutritional status, and oral health among hunter-gatherers in Argentina. Each issue contains between five and ten research articles, occasional short reports, and two to four book reviews of recently published monographs in the field. Although this is a highly specialized journal, its subject matter is of critical importance to the modern archaeologist, and its usefulness to historians and other social scientists makes it a fascinating addition to any academic collection.

419. *Journal of Archaeological Method and Theory.* Former titles (until 1994): *Archaeological Method and Theory;* (until 1989): *Advances in Archaeological Method and Theory.* [ISSN: 1072-5369] 1978. q. EUR 611 (print & online eds.). Ed(s): James M Skibo, Catherine M Cameron. Springer New York LLC, 233 Spring St, New York, NY 10013; service-ny@springer.com; http://www.springer.com/. Adv. Refereed. Reprint: PSC. *Indexed:* A01, A22, A47, ArtHuCI, BrArAb, E01, IBSS, NumL, P02. *Aud.:* Ac, Sa.

The quarterly, international, scholarly *Journal of Archaeological Method and Theory* "furnishes timely and authoritative topical syntheses, substantial original articles that critically assess and integrate research on a specific subject in archaeological method or theory." Special attention is given to scholarship about archaeological method and theory, allowing practitioners of the field an interesting opportunity for self-criticism and a meta-critique of archaeology. Each issue contains two to six articles with black-and-white illustrations covering such topics as the origins of the concept of "Palaeolithic Art"; landscape phenomenology and GIS; and shipwreck identity and methodology in nautical archaeology.

420. *Journal of Archaeological Science.* [ISSN: 0305-4403] 1974. m. EUR 2116. Ed(s): C O Hunt, Richard G Klein. Academic Press, 32 Jamestown Rd, Camden, London, NW1 7BY, United Kingdom; corporate.sales@elsevier.com; http://www.elsevier.com/. Illus., index, adv. Sample. Refereed. Vol. ends: Nov. Reprint: PSC. *Indexed:* A&ATA, A01, A07, A22, A47, AbAn, ArtHuCI, BrArAb, E01, FR, FS&TA, NumL. *Bk. rev.:* Number and length vary, signed. *Aud.:* Ac, Sa.

Published monthly in association with the Society for Archaeological Sciences, the *Journal of Archaeological Science* is "aimed at archaeologists and scientists with particular interests in advances in the application of scientific techniques and methodologies to all areas of archaeology." Every issue includes approximately 12–15 articles from an international group of scholars, covering a truly interdisciplinary range of topics, including trace elements and gilding in Early Cambodian gold and silver; Western Mediterranean sand deposits as a raw material in Roman glass production; and GIS-based modeling of landscape changes in west-central Jordan. Review articles are also occasionally featured. Each article is amply illustrated in black-and-white, and includes substantial charts, graphs, and other ancillary materials, as well as an extensive bibliography.

421. *Journal of Field Archaeology.* [ISSN: 0093-4690] 1974. q. GBP 133 (print & online eds.). Ed(s): Curtis Runnels. Maney Publishing, Ste 1C, Joseph's Well, Hanover Walk, Leeds, LS3 1AB, United Kingdom; maney@maneypublishing.com; http://maneypublishing.com/. Illus., adv. Sample. Refereed. Circ: 1200 Paid. Vol. ends: Winter. Microform: PQC. Reprint: PSC. *Indexed:* A&ATA, A07, A22, A47, ABS&EES, AbAn, AmHI, ArtHuCI, BAS, BRI, BrArAb, FR, NumL, RILM. *Bk. rev.:* 3-12, 2-4 pages, signed. *Aud.:* Ac, Sa.

Boston University publishes the *Journal of Field Archaeology* four times a year, both as a global survey of current archaeological excavations and as a forum for methodological and theoretical discussion. Each issue contains field reports from around the world, "special studies" of selected topics or archaeological sites, review articles, and a varying amount of shorter book reviews that cover new publications in the field. Illustrations are in black-and-white and include photographs, maps, charts, and graphs, as well as line drawings. Recent special study topics examine zooarchaeological and funerary perspectives on Mochica culture in Peru; archaeological site disturbances by seals and sea lions on California's Northern Channel Islands; and a comparison of fluoride and radiocarbon dating of black bear bones from Lawson Cave, Missouri.

422. *Journal of Mediterranean Archaeology.* [ISSN: 0952-7648] 1988. s-a. USD 315 (print & online eds.). Ed(s): A Bernard Knapp, Peter van Dommelen. Equinox Publishing Ltd., Unit S3, Kelham House, Sheffield, S3 8AF, United Kingdom; journals@equinoxpub.com; http://www.equinoxpub.com/. Adv. Refereed. *Indexed:* A01, A22, ArtHuCI. *Aud.:* Ac.

A semi-annual publication with a truly regional focus, the *Journal of Mediterranean Archaeology* is "the only journal currently published that deals with the entire multicultural world of Mediterranean archaeology." Each issue presents several scholarly articles from a host of international contributors, with special emphasis on social interaction and change, as well as broader contemporary theoretical approaches to Mediterranean archaeology with respect to "gender, agency, identity and landscape." Recent issues feature Mycenaean long-distance exchange; archaeological heritage and spiritual protection in Palestine; and an examination of Sir Arthur Evans, Sir James George Frazer, and the Invention of Minoan Religion. Illustrations are in black-and-white, and include photographs, maps, and line drawings. As the archaeology of the Mediterranean has historically been attracted to somewhat insular modes of inquiry, the *Journal of Mediterranean Archaeology* brings a much-needed interdisciplinary philosophy and methodology, and thus it is a welcome addition to any academic research collection.

423. *Journal of Roman Archaeology.* [ISSN: 1047-7594] 1988. a. Individuals, USD 69.75. Ed(s): John H Humphrey. Journal of Roman Archaeology LLC., The Editor, JRA, 95 Peleg Rd, Portsmouth, RI 02871. Illus. Refereed. *Indexed:* A07, A22, BrArAb, NumL. *Bk. rev.:* 50-70, 4 pages, signed. *Aud.:* Ac, Sa.

This international journal, published annually in two fascicules, covers not only the latest developments in Roman archaeology but topics in ancient Roman art, history, classical philology, and Greco-Roman culture. The first fascicule of each volume contains 10–15 scholarly articles of varying lengths (5–30 pages), followed by 10–15 archaeological reports and notes from the field; the second fascicule contains either a "Review Discussions" or "Debates and Response" section, followed by 50–70 book reviews averaging four pages each. Occasionally, articles and book reviews will be centered on a particular theme: for example, a recent volume features five scholarly papers about Roman slavery. Other recent volumes feature articles about the Horologium of Augustus; animal husbandry and diet in the northwest provinces; and infant death and burial in Roman Italy. Although submissions are welcomed in English, Spanish, French, Italian, and German, the majority of material is written in English. Illustrations and photographs are mostly in black-and-white, with a rare color plate. Drawing submissions from the most respected academic institutions around the world, the *Journal of Roman Archaeology* is an indispensable resource for scholars of Greco-Roman civilization.

424. *Kiva: the journal of Southwestern anthropology and history.* [ISSN: 0023-1940] 1935. q. GBP 218 (print & online eds.). Ed(s): James E Snead. Left Coast Press, Inc., 1630 N Main St, Ste 400, Walnut Creek, CA 94596; journals@lcoastpress.com; http://www.lcoastpress.com. Illus., adv. Sample. Refereed. Circ: 500. Vol. ends: Jun. Reprint: PSC. *Indexed:* A22, A47, AbAn, MLA-IB, RILM. *Bk. rev.:* Number and length vary, signed. *Aud.:* Ac, Sa.

A quarterly publication of the Arizona Archaeological and Historical Society, *Kiva* covers the archaeology of the American Southwest, publishing "the best voices in southwest archaeology," while it incorporates the related fields of history, ethnology and anthropology, and linguistics. Each issue contains three to five feature articles and includes black-and-white illustrations, exploring such topics as climate change and cultural response in the prehistoric American Southwest; and the geoarchaeology of water storage in the Chupadera Basin of New Mexico. A special issue recently was dedicated entirely to the Hohokam of the Sonoran Desert. A recent theme issue also has focused on the archaeology of perishable goods. Each volume features several book reviews. Note: Beginning in September 2012, *Kiva* was expected to be published by Left Coast Press, Inc., in a partnership with the Arizona Archaeological and Historical Society.

425. *Latin American Antiquity.* [ISSN: 1045-6635] 1990. q. Free to members. Society for American Archaeology, 900 Second St, NE #12, Washington, DC 20002-3560; publications@saa.org; http://www.saa.org/. Illus., index, adv. Refereed. Circ: 1600. Vol. ends: Dec. *Indexed:* A01, A22, A47, AbAn, AmHI, ArtHuCI, BRI, CBRI. *Bk. rev.:* 4-5, 300-700 words, signed. *Aud.:* Ac, Sa.

A sister publication of *American Antiquity* (above in this section), this quarterly journal is the Society for American Archaeology's clearinghouse for scholarly research in "archaeology, prehistory, and ethnohistory in Mesoamerica, Central America, and South America, and culturally related areas." Each issue presents two to four feature articles written in either English or Spanish (with an English abstract), preliminary reports, comments, and book reviews. Illustrative matter is sparse and in black-and-white. Recent topics explored include the hydroarchaeological methods in Palenque; the domestication and early spread of manioc; and evidence for ritual engineering in the Late/Terminal Classic site plan of La Milpa, Belize. *Latin American Antiquity* regularly features some of the most preeminent scholars and archaeologists in the field today, and thus is an essential component to any New World archaeological research collection.

426. *Medieval Archaeology.* [ISSN: 0076-6097] 1957. a. GBP 145 (print & online eds.). Ed(s): Dr. Oliver M Creighton. Maney Publishing, Ste 1C, Joseph's Well, Hanover Walk, Leeds, LS3 1AB, United Kingdom; maney@maneypublishing.com; http://maneypublishing.com/. Illus., adv. Refereed. Reprint: PSC. *Indexed:* A&ATA, A01, A07, A22, AbAn, AmHI, ArtHuCI, BEL&L, BRI, BrArAb, NumL, RILM. *Bk. rev.:* 30-50, 500-1,000 words, signed. *Aud.:* Ac, Sa.

The Society for Medieval Archaeology publishes this annual scholarly journal of international standing. *Medieval Archaeology* primarily covers the archaeology of Britain and Ireland from the fifth to the sixteenth century A.D., although articles about contemporaneous developments in continental Europe and elsewhere are welcomed by the editors. Recent volumes have featured such topics as Anglo-Saxon immigration; the ecology of Crusading; and Viking-age mortuary drama and the origin of Norse mythology. More general articles focusing on theory and methodology are also featured, especially those concerned with the impact of new technologies on the discipline of archaeology. Each issue has approximately eight feature articles, notes and news, and 30–50 reviews of monographs in archaeology and related disciplines in the humanities and social sciences, as well as a directory of current archaeological fieldwork in Britain and Ireland. Illustrations are primarily black-and-white drawings, with the occasional photograph and color plate.

427. *Midcontinental Journal of Archaeology.* [ISSN: 0146-1109] 1976. 3x/yr. GBP 130 (print & online eds.). Ed(s): Thomas Emerson. Maney Publishing, Ste 1C, Joseph's Well, Hanover Walk, Leeds, LS3 1AB, United Kingdom; maney@maneypublishing.com; http:// maneypublishing.com/. Illus., index, adv. Sample. Refereed. *Indexed:* A07, A22, A47, AbAn, BRI, BrArAb, FR. *Aud.:* Ac, Sa.

Under new editorship as of 2006, *MCJA* is the semi-annual publication of the Midwest Archaeological Conference, whose purview encompasses "the region between the Appalachian Mountains and the Great Plains, from the Boreal Forests to the Gulf of Mexico, and on closely related subjects." Each issue contains five to eight articles on topics ranging from archaeology to anthropology, history, and linguistics, spanning from the prehistoric period to the nineteenth century. Illustrations are sparse and in black-and-white. *MCJA* will occasionally offer an issue dedicated to a single theme, such as the archaeology of the Potawatomi during the Removal Period or the Mississippian occupation of Cahokia. Recent issues feature Fort Ancient mortuary practices at Clark Rockshelter in Kentucky, and a retrospective of archaeological findings by the Ohio Historical Society at the Seip Earthworks from 1971 to 1977. This journal has widened its scope significantly in recent years to become the preeminent forum for archaeological research in the Midwestern United States and Canada, and is therefore an important component in any research collection that specializes in North American archaeology.

428. *Near Eastern Archaeology.* Formerly (until 1998): *Biblical Archaeologist.* [ISSN: 1094-2076] 1938. q. USD 200 (print & online eds.). Ed(s): Ann E Killebrew. American Schools of Oriental Research, 656 Beacon St, 5th Fl, Boston, MA 02215; asor@bu.edu; http:// www.asor.org. Illus., index, adv. Refereed. Circ: 3500. Vol. ends: Dec. Microform: PQC. *Indexed:* A&ATA, A01, A06, A07, A22, A47, AmHI, ArtHuCI, BRI, FR, IJP, MLA-IB, NumL, P02, R&TA, RILM. *Bk. rev.:* 1-4, 500-1,000 words, signed. *Aud.:* Ac, Sa.

This glossy, colorful magazine, published four times a year by the American Schools of Oriental Research, "brings to life the ancient world from Mesopotamia to the Mediterranean with vibrant images and authoritative analyses." Each issue offers four to six lavishly illustrated feature articles that detail recent archaeological research in the Middle East, with special emphasis on new and alternative approaches to traditional methodologies, while shorter "Arch-facts" provide a forum for preliminary findings and quick reports from the field. Several book reviews are also featured in each issue. Recent topics include ancient toilets and toilet habits; religious symbolism in Hittite representational art; and the Iron Age city of Gezer guarding the border of Jerusalem.

429. *North American Archaeologist.* [ISSN: 0197-6931] 1979. q. USD 430 (print & online eds.) Individuals, USD 117 (print & online eds.). Ed(s): Roger W Moeller. Baywood Publishing Co., Inc., 26 Austin Ave, PO Box 337, Amityville, NY 11701; info@baywood.com; http://

www.baywood.com. Illus. Sample. Refereed. Vol. ends: No. 4. *Indexed:* A22, A47, AbAn, AmHI, ArtHuCI, BrArAb, FR, MLA-IB. *Bk. rev.:* 2-6 per volume, 2 pages, signed. *Aud.:* Ac, Sa.

This quarterly publication describes itself as "the only general journal dedicated solely to North America—with total coverage of archaeological activity in the United States, Canada, and Northern Mexico (excluding Mesoamerica)," with particular interest in exploring archaeology from an evolutionary perspective and addressing issues in the growing fields of resource management and contract archaeology. Each issue offers several feature articles, with occasional book reviews. The fourth issue of each volume contains an annual directory of national, regional, state, and provincial archaeological associations in North America. Illustrations are sparse and in black-and-white. Recent topics include making and breaking pots in a Late Prehistoric village in the Midwest United States; architectural adaptation in Cherokee townhouses to European contact; and marine invertebrates and complex hunter-gatherers on Late Holocene San Miguel Island, California. With such offerings as special issues dedicated to "Ethics and the Hyperreality of the Archaeological Thought World," *North American Archaeologist* offers readers a thought-provoking mix of theory and methodology that makes it a welcome addition to an academic research library.

430. *Oxford Journal of Archaeology.* [ISSN: 0262-5253] 1982. q. GBP 540. Wiley-Blackwell Publishing Ltd., The Atrium, Southern Gate, Chichester, PO19 8SQ, United Kingdom; customer@wiley.com; http://www.wiley.com/. Illus., adv. Sample. Refereed. Reprint: PSC. *Indexed:* A&ATA, A01, A22, ArtHuCI, BrArAb, E01, FR, IBSS, NumL, P02. *Aud.:* Ac, Sa.

A quarterly journal published in association with the Institute of Archaeology at the University of Oxford, the *Oxford Journal of Archaeology* provides an unparalleled comprehensive review of the latest scholarship in European and Mediterranean archaeology. Each issue consists of four to eight articles solicited from some of the most respected scholars in the field, and feature such topics as Bronze Age metalwork deposition in Western Britain; ancient ceramic beehives; and commodities and values in Middle Bronze Cypro-Levantine exchanges. Special emphasis is also given to the latest technological developments in the field. Illustrations are in black-and-white, and include photographs, maps, charts and graphs, and fine line drawings. This journal is an essential part of any archaeological research collection, and required reading for any practitioner of European or Mediterranean archaeology.

431. *Post-Medieval Archaeology.* [ISSN: 0079-4236] 1967. s-a. GBP 248 (print & online eds.). Ed(s): Jacqui Pearce. Maney Publishing, Ste 1C, Joseph's Well, Hanover Walk, Leeds, LS3 1AB, United Kingdom; maney@maneypublishing.com; http://maneypublishing.com/. Adv. Refereed. Reprint: PSC. *Indexed:* A01, AbAn, ArtHuCI, BrArAb, NumL. *Bk. rev.:* 15-20, 1-2 pages, signed. *Aud.:* Ac, Sa.

This semi-annual publication of the Society for Post-Medieval Archaeology is "devoted to the study of the material evidence of European society wherever it is found in the world," documenting the archaeology and ethnohistory of the transition from the medieval era to modern industrial society. The first issue of each volume contains several scholarly articles on a diverse range of topics, such as the 400th anniversary of Bermuda in archaeology; a late/post-medieval foundry in Dubrovnik; and twentieth-century naval victualling finds in England. The second issue offers feature articles, society notes, a comprehensive roundup of archaeological fieldwork in Great Britain and Ireland, and a subject index to the volume. Articles are amply illustrated in black-and-white, and include photographs, maps, charts, graphs, and line drawings. While *Post-Medieval Archaeology* has traditionally focused on the archaeology of the British Isles and to a lesser extent that of Ireland and continental Europe, recent issues have broadened this scope to include the Western Hemisphere and elsewhere. The archaeology of this period is of critical importance not just to practitioners of the field but to anyone with an interest in modern history.

432. *World Archaeology.* [ISSN: 0043-8243] 1969. 5x/yr. GBP 509 (print & online eds.). Routledge, 4 Park Sq, Milton Park, Abingdon, OX14 4RN, United Kingdom; subscriptions@tandf.co.uk; http://www.tandfonline.com. Illus., index, adv. Sample. Refereed. Microform: PQC. Reprint: PSC. *Indexed:* A&ATA, A01, A07, A22, A47, AbAn, AmHI, ArtHuCI, BAS, BrArAb, E01, FR, IBSS, MLA-IB, NumL, P02. *Aud.:* Ac, Sa.

A quarterly scholarly publication, *World Archaeology* "is the only journal established specifically to deal with archaeology on a world-wide multi-period basis." Each issue contains six to ten articles organized around a particular theme by a different editor; articles are accompanied by photographs, maps, charts, graphs, and line drawings in black-and-white. Past themes include the archaeology of sport and pastimes, faunal extinctions and introductions, and postcolonial archaeologies. Each fourth issue of *World Archaeology* is published in a special format under the title "Debates in World Archaeology," as a forum for less formal scholarly debate on topics of interest to the archaeological community. Both the thematic emphasis and the dedicated space for regular discussion make this journal an indispensable resource for any archaeological collection.

■ ARCHITECTURE

See also Interior Design and Decoration; Landscape Architecture; and Urban Studies sections.

Amy Trendler, Architecture Librarian, Ball State University, Muncie, IN 47306; aetrendler@bsu.edu

Introduction

From popular magazines to academic journals and trade weeklies, the titles listed here cover the wide range of periodicals that cater to readers of architectural literature. There is at least one journal targeted to every segment of that audience, including professional architects, students, scholars, and the general public. All of the titles in this section would find a place on the shelves of an architecture library; many would also be at home in an academic or public library.

In terms of subject matter, there are periodicals devoted to broad and narrow topics in architecture including theory, history, education, popular culture, and general interest. Some focus on a particular geographic region, while others present buildings and designs from established and up-and-coming architects working around the world. Many "architecture" titles also feature articles on other aspects of art, design, or culture, and the contributors to most titles are not limited to practicing architects or architectural faculty.

A significant number of the titles listed here are well illustrated with large-format color photographs of newly completed buildings, drawings of proposed designs, and archival photographs. Some titles go a step farther and seek to more fully document works through plans, concept drawings, sections, elevations, and site plans. The text varies from news updates and simple descriptions to detailed analyses, thoughtful critiques of buildings, and essays exploring architectural theory.

Digital editions, including iPad editions, of magazines in architecture are on the rise, but the print issues of many titles in this section are still going strong. Often carefully designed compositions of images, text, plans, and details, sometimes large-format, and always visually interesting, the printed pages of an architectural magazine are a finely crafted means of communicating information about projects and topics in the field.

Basic Periodicals

Ga: *Architect, Architectural Record, Architecture Week, Azure, Fine Homebuilding, GreenSource, Metropolis, Preservation, Wallpaper;* Ac: *A & U, Architectural Design, Architectural Review, El Croquis, Domus, G A Document, Journal of Green Building, R I B A Journal, Society of Architectural Historians. Journal.*

Basic Abstracts and Indexes

Architectural Index, Architectural Publications Index, Art & Architecture Complete, Art Index, Avery Index to Architectural Periodicals.

433. *2 G: revista internacional de arquitectura.* 1997. q. EUR 150. Editorial Gustavo Gili, S.A., Rosello 87-89, Barcelona, 08029, Spain; info@ggili.com; http://www.ggili.com. Adv. Circ: 20000. *Aud.:* Ac, Sa.

Much as with *El Croquis,* issues of *2G* focus exclusively on the work of a single designer or firm. More than a dozen building studies are accompanied by color photographs, plans, site plans, section drawings, and other illustrations. The subjects are drawn from all over the world and most recently Argentina, Portugal, Belgium, Italy, and Chile. An introduction or critical essay or two preface the studies, and an opinion piece or other writing from the designer usually appears in the last pages of the issue. Text is in both English and Spanish. Tables of contents and small preview pages are available for free online. A digital edition is available for purchase; and beginning with issue no. 65, the magazine is no longer published in print. Recommended for architecture libraries.

434. *A A Files.* Former titles (until 1981): *A A Quarterly;* (until 1969): *Arena;* (until 19??): *Architectural Association Journal;* (until 195?): *A A Journal.* [ISSN: 0261-6823] 1981. s-a. Free to members; Non-members, GBP 32. Architectural Association Inc., 36 Bedford Sq, London, WC1B 3ES, United Kingdom; publications@aaschool.ac.uk; http://www.aaschool.ac.uk. Illus. *Indexed:* A06, A07, A22, API, MLA-IB. *Bk. rev.:* 6-8, 1,500 words. *Aud.:* Ac.

Wide-ranging articles on contemporary architects and their projects, essays on architectural history or theory, and thorough exhibition and book reviews can be found in the richly illustrated, advertisement-free pages of *AA Files.* Published twice a year by the Architectural Association School of Architecture in London, the journal grows out of the research of the school's faculty, the school's impressive lecture and exhibition program, and "a rich and eclectic mix of architectural scholarship from all over the world." Architects, architectural and art historians, academics, and the occasional poet or artist make up the list of contributors. The journal's web site offers full text of published volumes to members; full text from all but the most current year is available in JSTOR. Recommended for academic and architecture libraries.

435. *A & T.* [ISSN: 1132-6409] 1992. s-a. A + T Editiones, General Alava 15-2 A, Vitoria-Gasteiz, 01005, Spain; aplus@aplus.net; http://www.aplus.net/. Illus. *Aud.:* Ac, Sa.

An issue of this advertisement-free, semi-annual Spanish periodical analyzes several buildings or projects as part of an overall theme. Public space, landscape urbanism, and high-rise and low-rise mixed-use buildings were among the recent themes. The visual coverage of the selected buildings and projects is exhaustive and includes numerous photographs, plans (for every floor, even for the high-rise projects), sections, and details. In addition, *a + t* is unique in creating graphics that illustrate the analysis. For example, the mixed-use publications featured graphics detailing the percentage of individual uses (commercial, housing, office space, etc.), comparing floor space and site coverage, and situating the works in context. All text is in both Spanish and English. A preview of some content from the issues is available for free online, but the full text appears only in the printed or digital publication. Recommended for architecture libraries.

436. *A & U.* [ISSN: 0389-9160] 1971. m. JPY 30000 domestic. Ed(s): Nobuyuki Yoshida. Japan Architects Co., Ltd., 2-31-2 Yushima, Bunkyo-ku, Tokyo, 113-0034, Japan; ja-business@japan-architect.co.jp; http://www.japan-architect.co.jp/. Illus., index, adv. Circ: 25000. Vol. ends: Dec. *Indexed:* A07, A22, API, ArtHuCI. *Bk. rev.:* Number and length vary. *Aud.:* Ac, Sa.

This profusely illustrated Japanese periodical is one of several titles that are largely devoted to building studies (see also, for example, the GA publications such as *GA Document*). A selected theme or a pair of themes characterizes each issue, and recent subjects were architecture in Germany, 30 architects in Istanbul, architecture in post-crisis, and glass architecture. Essays and interviews appear on the pages of *A + U,* but most pages are filled with the building studies, which are international in scope and meticulous in detail. Each study is composed of several paragraphs of description and numerous illustrations, details, plans, elevations, and conceptual drawings. Brief biographies of the architects whose work appears in the issues are always found on the last few pages. Text is in both Japanese and English. Tables of contents for those issues that are still available for purchase (currently 2000–present) are online, along with selected text and the occasional page view. Recommended for architecture libraries.

437. *A R Q: Architectural Research Quarterly.* [ISSN: 1359-1355] 1995. q. GBP 256. Ed(s): Adam Sharr, Richard Weston. Cambridge University Press, The Edinburgh Bldg, Shaftesbury Rd, Cambridge, CB2 8RU, United Kingdom; journals@cambridge.org; http://www.cambridge.org/uk. Adv. Refereed. Reprint: PSC. *Indexed:* A07, A22, API, ArtHuCI, E01. *Bk. rev.:* Number and length vary. *Aud.:* Ac.

A quarterly published in Great Britain, *ARQ* is meant to act "as an international forum for practitioners and academics by publishing cutting-edge work covering all aspects of architectural endeavour." The lengthy, well-illustrated articles in an issue are grouped into the broad categories of design, theory, history, criticism, practice, or urbanism. Topics range from the historical to the contemporary. Detailed building studies, book reviews, interviews, or thought pieces complete an issue. Contributors are generally British, but the work of European, Australian, and American authors, educators, and architects also appears in the pages of *ARQ*. Abstracts for issues beginning with volume 1 (1995) are freely accessible online. For those who do not have a subscription, full text of the journal content may be purchased from Cambridge Journals on an article-by-article basis. Recommended for architecture libraries.

438. *A V Monografias.* [ISSN: 0213-487X] 1985. bi-m. 5 / yr. EUR 115 domestic; EUR 140 in Europe; EUR 160 elsewhere. Arquitectura Viva S.L., Aniceto Marinas 32, Madrid, 28008, Spain. Illus., adv. Circ: 9000. *Indexed:* API, RILM. *Aud.:* Ac, Sa.

A selected theme defines each number of *AV Monografias,* a bimonthly journal published in Madrid, Spain. The theme might be a building type (housing and schools are recent examples), individual designers and firms (such as Herzog & De Meuron, Eduardo Souto de Moura), a geographic area (Latin America, China), or the annual review of Spanish architecture. The work of contemporary Spanish designers figures prominently in the pages of the journal, but subjects and themes from farther afield make frequent appearances. An issue may contain a few essays, but most pages are devoted to anywhere from ten to 24 building studies accompanied by a wealth of illustrative matter (photographs, plans, sections, elevations, site plans, sketches, details, and diagrams). All text is in both Spanish and English. Available in print or digital editions; tables of contents may be viewed on the publisher's web site. Recommended for architecture libraries.

439. *A10: new European architecture.* [ISSN: 1573-3815] 2004. bi-m. EUR 59.50 in Europe; EUR 79.50 elsewhere. Ed(s): Indira van't Klooster. A10 Publishers bv, PO Box 51095, Amsterdam, 1007 EB, Netherlands; mail@a10.eu; http://www.a10.eu. Adv. *Aud.:* Ac, Sa.

European architecture is covered by many an architectural periodical, but the exclusive focus of *A10* means that it delves even deeper into this territory, covering all corners of the region in addition to the big names. Recent locales included Estonia, Lithuania, Slovenia, Ireland, and the Czech Republic as well as the more typical Italy, Spain, France, and Great Britain. Articles tend to be short and accompanied by only a handful of color photographs and plans, but each issue includes a dozen or more projects, as well as an interview with a designer or firm and short articles on building types, materials, or locales. In 2012, this magazine re-dedicated itself to representing the European architectural scene and the work of young designers and firms, adding several new features on changing locations (Barcelona, Germany, and Russia were recently featured), and details on the most important features of a newly-built work in "Section." A good choice for those wanting a fuller picture of the European architectural scene. Select articles are available for free online, but the complete contents are reserved for the print magazine. Recommended for architecture libraries.

440. *Abitare: home, town and environmental living.* Formerly (until 1962): *Casa Novita.* [ISSN: 0001-3218] 1961. 11x/yr. Ed(s): Stefano Boeri. R C S Periodici, Via San Marco 21, Milan, 20121, Italy; info@periodici.rcs.it. Illus. *Indexed:* A06, A07. *Bk. rev.:* Number and length vary. *Aud.:* Ga, Ac, Sa.

This Italian monthly covers the international architecture and design scene with, not surprisingly, a somewhat higher concentration of Italian subjects. This title is published ten times a year, and each issue contains a wealth of information in numerous topical articles, profiles of designers, exhibition reviews, design news, and project critiques. Every piece in the journal is well illustrated, and the architecture projects are meticulously documented with photographs, plans, sections, and elevations. Tables of contents are available free online and a digital edition of the magazine is available for purchase. All text is in both Italian and English. Recommended for architecture and large public libraries.

441. *Architect: the new face of architecture.* Former titles (until 2006): *Architecture;* (until 1983): *A I A Journal;* (until 1957): *American Institute of Architects. Journal;* Architecture Incorporated (1992-1995): *Building Renovation;* (1920-1995): *Progressive Architecture;* Which was formerly (until 1945): *Pencil Points (East Stroudsburg, 1944);* (until 1943): *New Pencil Points;* (until 1942): *Pencil Points (East Stroud, 1920);* Which incorporated: *Monograph Series (New York, 1929);* (1983-1986): *Architectural Technology.* [ISSN: 1935-7001] 2006. m. USD 59 domestic (Free to qualified personnel). Ed(s): Ned Cramer, Greig O'Brien. Hanley Wood, LLC, 1 Thomas Cir, NW, Ste 600, Washington, DC 20005; http://www.hanleywood.com. Adv. Circ: 3213 Paid. *Indexed:* A01, A07, AmHI, B01, MASUSE, P02. *Bk. rev.:* Number and length vary. *Aud.:* Ac, Sa.

In 2011, this monthly trade publication replaced *Architectural Record* as the official magazine of the American Institute of Architects (AIA), and it is now sent free to AIA members. *Architect* had already established itself as a great resource for information on architectural practice in the United States, and now it includes more news items on AIA events, programs, and awards. Feature articles and departments that focus on the business side of architecture will appeal to the professional; the well-illustrated case studies, news and events, architect interviews, and book, product, and exhibition reviews will also appeal to a wider audience. A salary survey and a ranking of top U.S. firms are published annually. The full text of articles and departments in each issue are available for free on the *Architect* web site, as well as additional images of projects that appeared in the print publication, current news, job postings, and blogs. Recommended for architecture libraries and large public libraries.

442. *The Architects' Journal: the home of british architecture.* Former titles (until 1919): *Architects' and Builders' Journal;* (until 1910): *Builders' Journal and Architectural Engineer.* [ISSN: 0003-8466] 1895. w. GBP 165 combined subscription domestic (print & online eds.); GBP 231 combined subscription foreign (print & online eds.). Ed(s): Christine Murray. E M A P Publishing Ltd., 69 - 77 Paul St, London, EC2A 4NQ, United Kingdom; reception.GLH@topright-group.com; http://www.emap.com. Illus., adv. Sample. Circ: 7415. *Indexed:* A06, A07, A22, API, AmHI, BRI, BrTechI, C&ISA. *Bk. rev.:* Number and length vary. *Aud.:* Ac, Sa.

An issue of this weekly British trade publication contains short news pieces, a detailed building study, a technical study devoted to noteworthy details or solutions from current projects, and an exhibition or book review. Recruitment notices, interviews, and a column on an aspect of architectural practice in Great Britain round out the issue. *The Architects' Journal* is an excellent resource for architects working or contemplating work in Great Britain, and the building studies and feature articles will appeal to anyone interested in contemporary British architecture. The *AJ* web site does not recreate the format of the magazine, but the complete contents from the print issues are available online to subscribers, as well as additional features only available online. An iPad edition is also available for purchase. Recommended for architecture libraries.

443. *The Architect's Newspaper (New York Edition).* [ISSN: 1552-8081] 2003. 20x/yr. Ed(s): William Menking. The Architect's Newspaper, Llc., 21 Murray St, 5th Fl, New York, NY 10007. Adv. Circ: 15000 Paid and controlled. *Aud.:* Sa.

As the title implies, this periodical is a glossy, tabloid-format publication filled with news items written for an audience of professional architects. The East edition is published 20 times per year; the West and Midwest editions are published nine or ten times a year. A longer feature article and 18–20 brief articles and short news pieces fill the pages of each issue. Very few articles are carried by all the editions. While the longer feature article may chronicle a historical subject, explore a building type, or report on architecture abroad, most articles describe newly completed works, projects under development, events, and exhibitions within the edition's geographic area. A critical review or commentary may also make an appearance. Befitting the newspaper format, the articles are illustrated by one or more color photographs, but these do not approach the scale or breadth of the average architecture magazine. Select content and images from an issue are available for free online and occasionally more images accompany the online article, but the full contents of a print issue are not available in a digital edition. A subscription to the *Architect's Newspaper* is free to registered architects in the states covered by each edition. Recommended for architecture libraries.

444. *Architectural Design.* Formerly (until 1947): *Architectural Design & Construction.* [ISSN: 0003-8504] 1930. bi-m. GBP 229. Ed(s): Helen Castle. John Wiley & Sons Ltd., The Atrium, Southern Gate, Chichester, PO19 8SQ, United Kingdom; customer@wiley.com; http://www.wiley.com. Illus., index, adv. Sample. Vol. ends: Nov/Dec. *Indexed:* A06, A07, A22, API, ArtHuCI, C&ISA, CerAb, EIP. *Bk. rev.:* 8, 250 words. *Aud.:* Ac, Sa.

Architectural Design is a bimonthly journal well-known for its timely, theme-based issues on topics in architecture, landscape architecture, interior design, and urban design. In each issue, an editorial from editor Helen Castle sets the scene, followed by profiles of the guest editor or editors who curated the issue and their introduction to the selected topic. Recent topics included "the new pastoralism: landscape into architecture" and "the innovation imperative: architectures of vitality." Numerous color illustrations accompany the 15 or more articles, essays, or interviews by architects, architectural historians, theorists, artists, and academics fill the journal. Beginning with issues published in 2005, pdf full text of this title is available through subscription to Wiley InterScience; individuals can purchase an iPad edition of the journal. Recommended for architecture and large academic libraries.

Architectural Digest. See Interior Design and Decoration section.

445. *Architectural Record.* Incorporates: *American Architect and Architecture; Western Architect and Engineer.* [ISSN: 0003-858X] 1891. m. USD 49. Ed(s): Robert Ivy, Elisabeth Broome. McGraw-Hill Construction Dodge, 148 Princeton-Hightstown Rd. N1, Hightstown, NJ 08520; http://construction.com. Illus., index, adv. Circ: 115155 Paid. Vol. ends: Dec. *Indexed:* A01, A06, A07, A22, ABS&EES, API, AmHI, ArchI, ArtHuCI, B01, B02, BRI, C37, F01, GardL, MASUSE, MLA-IB, P02, RILM. *Bk. rev.:* 6, 50-250 words. *Aud.:* Ga, Ac, Sa.

This long-running (the first issue appeared in 1891) glossy trade magazine is a great source of information on contemporary American architecture. The focus is on the United States and Canada, but issues often include information on projects and architects from all over the world. Sections devoted to selected building types, product information, architectural technology, interiors, lighting, and current projects are regularly published alongside feature articles, architect interviews, book reviews, and exhibition and lecture notices. All of the sections and articles are well illustrated. Much of the content from the print magazine, including images, is available online, but full content is reserved for those who subscribe to the print or digital versions of this title. Recommended for all library types.

446. *The Architectural Review.* Incorporates (in 1909): *Details.* [ISSN: 0003-861X] 1896. m. Individuals, GBP 88 (print & online eds.); Free to qualified personnel). Ed(s): Catherine Slessor. Emap Construct Ltd., 69-77 Paul St, London, EC2A 4NW, United Kingdom; http://www.emap.com. Illus., adv. Microform: IDC. *Indexed:* A&ATA, A01, A06, A07, A22, API, AmHI, ArchI, ArtHuCI, BAS, BRI, BrTechI, C&ISA, CerAb, GardL, P02. *Bk. rev.:* 4-6, 500 words. *Aud.:* Ga, Ac, Sa.

Covering some of the same ground as *Architectural Record*, this journal offers the British perspective and a focus on British, European, and world architecture, in that order. The five or six building studies of international projects featured in an issue are well-documented with color photographs, plans, sections, and details. Architecture news, interviews, editorials, a brief description of the state of architecture in a foreign locale, and an opinion piece preface the building studies; book and exhibition reviews, and series that consider architecture luminaries, current pedagogy, and a featured architectural drawing on the last page complete the issue. A good choice for British and European architecture, and a good companion to *Architectural Record*. The full text of articles, building studies, and other content from the print issue is available for free online if individuals register with the *Architectural Review* web site; a digital edition is available by subscription. Recommended for architecture and large public libraries.

447. Architecture Asia. [ISSN: 1675-6886] 2009. q. 0 membership. Architects Regional Council of Asia, 1603-55, Seocho 1-dong, Seocho-gu, Seoul, Korea, Republic of; http://www.arcasia.org/. *Bk. rev.*: Number and length vary. *Aud.*: Ac, Sa.

Architecture Asia is the quarterly journal of the Architects Regional Council of Asia (ARCASIA), which is composed of the national institutes of architects of 18 countries from China to India, the Philippines, Japan, Indonesia, and most everywhere in between. Issues are organized around a theme (emergent architecture and "a language of architecture" are recent examples), and present a dozen building studies of works spread across the region. Along with descriptions, the building studies include color photographs, plans, and often additional drawings, elevations, or sections. A feature article or two, book reviews, and reports on local design events round out the tables of contents. Interest in this part of the world remains strong, as evidenced by coverage in international design periodicals, and this title is an excellent English-language choice for its focus on both the area and native architects. Beginning with the 2011 issues, an online edition of the journal is available for free to individuals who register on the journal's web site. Recommended for architecture libraries.

448. L'Architecture d'Aujourd'hui. Formerly: *Architecture Francaise.* [ISSN: 0003-8695] 1930. bi-m. EUR 150. L'Architecture d'Aujourd'hui, http://www.larchitecturedaujourdhui.fr/en/. Illus., adv. *Indexed*: A06, A07, A22, API, BAS. *Bk. rev.*: Number and length vary. *Aud.*: Ac, Sa.

First published in the 1930s, this well-respected French journal folded in 2007, only to reappear in 2009 with a new editorial board that includes a number of international designers (Shigeru Ban, Frank Gehry, Philippe Starck, Winy Maas, and others) and a new abbreviation: 'A'A'. Rather than using a topical theme to organize each issue, the revived journal is pursuing a renewed focus on providing a forum for architectural discourse. The work and thoughts of five or more contemporary architects and firms are featured in an issue, alongside numerous short news pieces, profiles, and a review section covering exhibitions, books, and more. Largely free of ads, the pages of 'A'A' are packed with color photographs that illustrate most every article and notice, along with some drawings, plans, and models. All text appears in French and English. A digital edition of the journal is available to individual subscribers. Recommended for architecture libraries.

449. Architecture plus Design. [ISSN: 0970-2369] 1984. m. INR 1500. Media Tranasia (India) Pvt. Ltd., 323, Udyog Vihar Phase 4, Gurgaon, 122 016, India; http://www.mediatransasia.in. Illus. Refereed. *Indexed*: A07. *Aud.*: Ac, Sa.

This monthly publication, "an Indian journal of architecture," is directed toward architects working in India. Some articles cover current or historical topics in Europe and North America, but the real attraction is the coverage of Indian architecture. Typically, most of the building studies are of works in India or by Indian designers, accompanied by color photographs and plans. The image quality can be inferior to that of other architecture and design journals, but for those interested in the subject matter, this title is useful nonetheless. Content is currently not available online. Recommended for architecture libraries where there is interest.

450. Architecture Week: the new magazine of design and building. 2000. w. Free. Ed(s): Kevin Matthews. Artifice, Inc., PO Box 1588, Eugene, OR 97440; artifice@artifice.com; http://www.artifice.com. Adv. *Bk. rev.*: Number and length vary. *Aud.*: Ga, Ac, Sa.

Each issue of this online weekly publication features several new articles in the magazine's categories of design, people and places, context, culture, and technology. Some articles are excerpts from recently published books on architects, firms, or current topics, while others are written for *Architecture Week* on design industry award-winners, newly completed works, or issues in architecture. The intended audience is made up of practicing architects, students and faculty, and the general public. An e-mail newsletter and the text and thumbnail images of the magazine are available for free; paid subscribers have access to the full-size images. Recommended for architecture libraries and larger public libraries.

451. Azure: design architecture & art. Former titles (until 1985): *Village Gazette;* (until 1984): *WestClair Gazette.* [ISSN: 0829-982X] 1984. 6x/yr. CAD 34.95 domestic; USD 34.95 United States; USD 65 elsewhere.

Azure Publishing Inc., 460 Richmond St W, Ste 601, Toronto, ON M5V 1Y1, Canada; azure@azureonline.com. Illus., adv. Circ: 20000 Paid. *Indexed*: CBCARef. *Bk. rev.*: Number and length vary. *Aud.*: Ga, Ac, Sa.

Azure is a Canadian architecture and design magazine that covers both North American and European design in the eight issues published during the year. Several issues focus on recurring themes, including an annual houses issue, design trends, green design, and the *Azure* awards issue. An issue is composed of several feature articles, accompanied by shorter pieces on new buildings, news items, a designer or firm profile, products and materials sections, and book reviews. This title will appeal to the same design-conscious audience that reads *Metropolis* or *Wallpaper*. A few of the articles, some of the recurring departments, and select images are available for free online, but the full content of the magazine is reserved for subscribers to the print or digital issue. Recommended for architecture and public libraries.

452. Blueprint (Chelmsford): architecture, design & contemporary culture. [ISSN: 0268-4926] 1983. m. GBP 49 domestic; EUR 121 in Europe; USD 179 United States. Progressive Media Group, John Carpenter House, John Carpenter St, London, EC4Y 0AN, United Kingdom; pmg@progressivemediagroup.com; http://www.progressivemediagroup.com/. Adv. Sample. *Indexed*: A07, A22, A51. *Bk. rev.*: Number and length vary. *Aud.*: Ac, Sa.

This British monthly offers a critical view of architecture and design in Great Britain and farther afield. An issue is composed of an opinion column, brief notices of newly built works, a point-of-view piece from a contemporary designer, book or exhibition reviews, and a products section. Four longer feature articles on an architect or design firm, an event such as a design fair, or a significant project or building complete the issue. The architecture articles do not document the works as fully as do other magazines (see, for example, *Abitare, Casabella,* or *Architectural Review*) in that they do not always include a plan or elevation; but there are numerous color photographs and a sketch or detail spread across the large format pages. Subscribers may choose a print or digital subscription. Recommended for architecture libraries.

Built Environment. See Urban Studies section.

453. Canadian Architect. [ISSN: 0008-2872] 1956. m. CAD 52.95 domestic (Students, USD 32.50). Ed(s): Ian Chodikoff. Business Information Group, 12 Concorde Pl, Ste 800, Toronto, ON M3C 4J2, Canada; orders@businessinformationgroup.ca; http://www.businessinformationgroup.ca. Illus., adv. Microform: MML. *Indexed*: A01, A06, A07, A22, ABIn, API, B01, BRI, C37. *Aud.*: Ga, Sa.

The monthly magazine of the Royal Architectural Institute of Canada, *Canadian Architect* consists of building studies, architecture news, product reviews, and reports on exhibitions, conferences, and other events. Most of the content is related to the Canadian built environment or the practice of architecture in Canada. Though slim (at about 50 pages), each issue is well illustrated and contains a full array of plans, sections, and drawings for the building studies. This is a great resource for those interested in Canadian architecture or for architects working in the country. Full text and images from the print magazine, starting with the January 2001 issue, are available online; digital editions of the magazine are restricted to those with a subscription. Recommended for architecture and public libraries.

454. Casabella: rivista internazionale di architettura. Former titles (until 1964): *Casabella Continuita;* (until 1954): *Costruzioni Casabella;* (until 1939): *Casabella;* (until 1932): *La Casa Bella.* [ISSN: 0008-7181] 1928. m. 10/yr. EUR 81.90; EUR 12 newsstand/cover. Ed(s): Francesco Dal Co. Arnoldo Mondadori Editore SpA, Via Mondadori 1, Segrate, 20090, Italy; infolibri@mondadori.it; http://www.mondadori.com. Illus., index, adv. Circ: 45000 Paid. *Indexed*: A06, A07, A22, API. *Bk. rev.*: 8, 150 words. *Aud.*: Ac, Sa.

Casabella is a large-format Italian journal that covers international contemporary architecture and the occasional historical subject in issue published 11 times a year. An issue may consist of several building studies and a theoretical essay or article on a historical topic, or a mix of building studies and short articles on a specific theme (new Italian churches were recently featured; and an upcoming issue on architects under 30 will mark the 85th anniversary of the journal). An interview with an influential architect may also be included. The building studies offer numerous plans, details, sections, and color photographs spread across the expansive pages. In the Italian/English edition, English translations are printed in the captions for the illustrations, and English text for most, but not all, of the articles is printed in the back of the journal. Book and exhibition reviews, shorter articles, and the extensive product review section are in Italian only. A digital edition is available by subscription. Recommended for architecture libraries.

455. Crit: the value of value engineering. Formerly (until 1977): *Telesis;* Incorporates (1986-1995): *A I A S News;* Which was formerly (until 1986): *Newsflash;* (until 1984): *A S C / A I A News;* (until 1978): *American Institute of Architects. Association of Student Chapters. News.* [ISSN: 0277-6863] 1976. s-a. USD 25 Free to members. Ed(s): Zachary R Heineman. American Institute of Architecture Students, 1735 New York Ave, N W, Washington, DC 20006; mailbox@aias.org; http://www.aias.org. Illus., adv. *Aud.:* Ac.

The journal of the American Institute of Architecture Students (AIAS), *Crit* is a "celebration of student work" published twice a year. The feature articles, student projects, essays, opinion pieces, and interviews that make up each issue are contributed by student authors as well as architects and educators. Most pieces are two to four pages in length, and illustrated only by small black-and-white or monochrome photographs and drawings. Whereas other architecture publications draw the eye with glossy pages and gorgeous photographs, the attraction of this title is its function as a window onto student interests, projects, and competitions in the United States and Canada. Content is not currently available online. Recommended for architecture libraries.

456. El Croquis: de arquitectura y diseno. [ISSN: 0212-5633] 1982. bi-m. EUR 217 domestic; EUR 285 in Europe; EUR 326 in US & Canada. Ed(s): Paloma Poveda. El Croquis Editorial, Av. Reyes Catolicos 9, El Escorial, Madrid, 28280, Spain; elcroquis@elcroquis.es; http://www.elcroquis.es/. Adv. Circ: 30000. *Indexed:* A07, A22, API, RILM. *Aud.:* Ac, Sa.

An issue of *El Croquis* functions less like a journal and more like a monograph on an international architect, firm, or occasional theme. Recent issues featured architects Smiljan Radic, Sean Godsell, Glenn Murcutt. Essays, interviews, or biographies may be included, but the exhaustive documentation of built works and projects are the true subjects of this publication. Each work is accompanied by page after page of illustrations, plans, details, conceptual drawings, models, sections, and elevations. The illustrative matter far outweighs the textual descriptions, which are printed in both Spanish and English. An excellent source for visual documentation of the work of international architects. Subscribers also have access to the journal online; digital issues can be purchased individually as well. Recommended for architecture libraries.

457. Detail (German Edition): Zeitschrift fuer Architektur & Baudetail. [ISSN: 0011-9571] 1961. 10x/yr. Individuals, EUR 139.90; Students, EUR 74.70; EUR 15.50 newsstand/cover. Ed(s): Christian Schittich. Institut fuer Internationale Architektur-Dokumentation GmbH, Hackerbruecke 6, Munich, 80335, Germany. Illus., adv. Circ: 31346 Paid and controlled. *Indexed:* A22. *Bk. rev.:* Number and length vary. *Aud.:* Ac, Sa.

Like many other architecture journals, *Detail* is devoted to contemporary international architecture and features an impressive array of color photographs of recent works. What sets this journal apart is that each of the eight to ten articles on a building in the "documentation" section is accompanied by a large-scale section drawing of a detail that has been redrawn by *Detail* staff. Photographs, plans, and small-scale sections similar to those found in other journals also appear in the article. Buildings in the documentation section and the articles in the shorter "discussion" and "technology" sections focus on a selected theme (building for children, concrete, and "translucent, transparent" were recently featured). Brief news pieces, book and exhibition reviews, and a products section complete each issue. Eight issues of the English edition are published in a year: six themed issues and two supplemental issues, titled *Detail Green,* on sustainable architecture. The original German-language publication is published 12 times a year and is available in a bilingual German/English edition. Digital editions of these publications are also available by subscription. Photos and text for some projects are available online, but the details, plans, and other drawings only appear in the full journal. Recommended for architecture libraries. *Detail* readers will also be interested in *The Plan,* the Italian journal that publishes contemporary building details.

458. Domus: architettura arredamento arte. [ISSN: 0012-5377] 1928. m. 11/yr. Editoriale Domus, Via Gianni Mazzocchi 1/3, Rozzano, 20089, Italy; editorialedomus@edidomus.it; http://www.edidomus.it. Illus. *Indexed:* A06, A07, A22, API, RILM. *Bk. rev.:* 7, 750 words. *Aud.:* Ac, Sa.

An excellent source for information on contemporary design, *Domus* is a large-format Italian monthly magazine that focuses on architecture but also covers furniture, interiors, and art. All the text is in both English and Italian, from the extensive exhibition calendar to the feature articles, building studies, interviews, and book and product reviews. Color photographs often fill the pages and extend to double spreads, and the building studies contain many plans, sections, and details. The scope is truly international; articles in a single issue often range from Europe to North America, India to China, and everywhere in between. Local editions delve deeper into their geographic areas, which include Israel, India, China, and Central America. Individual subscribers may purchase online access to the most recent issues or the online archives for the journal, which begins with the first issue published in 1928. An iPad edition is also available for purchase or subscription. Recommended for architecture and large public libraries.

459. Eco-Structure: improving environmental performances of buildings and their surroundings. [ISSN: 1556-3596] 2003. bi-m. Hanley Wood, LLC, 1 Thomas Cir, NW, Ste 600, Washington, DC 20005; fanton@hanleywood.com; http://www.hanleywood.com. Adv. *Aud.:* Ac, Sa.

When the American Institute of Architects (AIA) chose *Architect* as the new official magazine of the AIA beginning in 2011 (replacing *Architectural Record*), Hanley Wood's sustainability title *Eco-structure* also became part of the AIA publications line-up (and it has replaced the function of *GreenSource*). A couple of AIA-related items joined the content that this bimonthly magazine had already been printing, including news items, products, and several recurring departments that profile buildings and technologies, as well as an interview with a figure in sustainability. Two or three feature articles in each issue take a slightly longer look at a building or profile a firm, organization, or business with a strong sustainable design component. In 2013, Hanley Wood launched a new online presence, http://ecobuildingpulse.com, to pull together several of its publications that focus on sustainability. Expected in the fall of 2013, two of the publisher's titles, *Eco-structure* and *EcoHome,* will be printed on flip sides of a single issue and will be distributed as one publication; subscriptions to this dual-title publication will continue as *Eco-structure.* Digital editions of issues of both titles starting with January/February 2009 are available free on http://ecobuildingpulse.com. Recommended for architecture and public libraries.

460. Evolo. [ISSN: 1946-634X] 2009. s-a. USD 39.95; USD 24.95 newsstand/cover per issue. Ed(s): Carlo Aiello, Noemie Deville. eVolo LLC, 570 W, 204th St 1B, New York, NY 10034; contact@evolo.us; http://www.evolo.us. Illus., adv. *Aud.:* Ac, Sa.

eVolo is a semi-annual publication that specializes in imaginative designs that highlight "technological advances, sustainability, [or] innovative design." A couple of articles might set the stage for an issue's theme by considering the historical aspect of such topics as skyscrapers, cities, or housing; the remainder of an issue is filled with pages of forward thinking, sometimes fantastical, projects. The designs are from architects in well-known firms with many completed works to their credit as well as more fanciful designers with few built works. Winners of *eVolo's* annual skyscraper competition are published in the spring issue, while the fall issue tackles a selected theme. A good choice for students and professional designers interested in current, speculative projects. Content is not currently available online. Recommended for architecture libraries.

461. G A Document. [ISSN: 0389-0066] q. A.D.A. Edita Tokyo Co. Ltd., 3-12-14 Sendagaya, Shibuya-ku, Tokyo, 151-0051, Japan. *Indexed:* A07. *Aud.:* Ac, Sa.

Issues of this large-format journal are focused solely on five or more recently completed buildings designed by a variety of architects and firms from all over the world. In a typical issue, a few paragraphs in both English and Japanese preface a rich collection of photographs, plans, elevations, sections, and details of the chosen works. Special issues may be devoted to the work of a single architect or firm, and an annual yearbook issue highlights international projects from two dozen or more architects. *GA Houses* is a similar title offered by the same Tokyo publisher, A.D.A. Edita. Both are great resources for visual documentation of recent, international architecture. Lists of the works that are included in issues of both publications are available online, but there are only a few small images of pages from the printed issues. Recommended for architecture libraries.

462. *GreenSource: magazine of sustainable design.* [ISSN: 1930-9848] 2006. bi-m. USD 19.95 in US & Canada; USD 40 elsewhere. Ed(s): Nadav Malin. McGraw-Hill Companies, Inc., 1221 Ave of the Americas, 43rd fl, New York, NY 10020; customer.service@mcgraw-hill.com; http://www.mcgraw-hill.com. Adv. Circ: 42000 Controlled. *Aud.:* Ga, Ac, Sa.

This title is published six times a year, and each issue of *GreenSource* offers five to seven case studies of green buildings, a couple of feature articles, several shorter pieces on news and people, and an extensive section of green product reviews. The case studies cover housing, public, and commercial architecture and are illustrated with photos, plans, and details that highlight the sustainable characteristics of the work, as well as charts or diagrams analyzing the annual precipitation and temperature at the site. A great source of information for architects and builders, *GreenSource* will also appeal to a wider audience interested in sustainable architecture. Digital editions of the issues are available for individual purchase or by subscription. Recommended for all library types.

463. *Grey Room.* [ISSN: 1526-3819] 2000. q. USD 300 (print & online eds.). Ed(s): Ben Young. M I T Press, 55 Hayward St, Cambridge, MA 02142; journals-cs@mit.edu; http://mitpress.mit.edu. Adv. Refereed. *Indexed:* A01, A07, A22, A51, ArtHuCI, E01. *Aud.:* Ac.

A handful of lengthy articles are the main focus of this quarterly, which seeks to "[bring] together scholarly and theoretical articles from the fields of architecture, art, media, and politics to forge a cross-disciplinary discourse uniquely relevant to contemporary concerns." Theory plays a significant role in most articles. For example, the theme of a recent issue was "Multiplying the Visual: Image and Object in the Nineteenth Century." Contributors are largely scholars from North America, but Great Britain, Australia, and Europe are also represented. Articles are available in JSTOR with a moving wall of five years; full text is available by subscription on the MIT Press Journals web site or for purchase on an article-by-article basis. Recommended for architecture and academic libraries.

464. *Harvard Design Magazine.* Former titles (until 1997): *G S D News;* (until 1983): *H G S D News.* [ISSN: 1093-4421] 1977. s-a. USD 56. Ed(s): William S Saunders. Harvard University, Graduate School of Design, 48 Quincy St, Gund Hall, Cambridge, MA 02138; http://www.gsd.harvard.edu/. Illus., adv. Refereed. *Indexed:* A07, A51. *Bk. rev.:* Number and length vary. *Aud.:* Ac.

The magazine of Harvard University's Graduate School of Design, this biannual publication covers current topics in architecture, landscape architecture, urban design, and planning with a critical eye. A theme serves as the touchstone for an issue; recent examples featured landscape architecture's core, architecture's core, and architectures of Latin America. Within the boundaries of the selected theme, articles focus on culture, theory, design, history, technology, and materials. Article authors are educators, practicing architects and designers, architectural historians and critics, and the occasional graduate student. Book reviews and several short articles on topics unrelated to the issue's theme round out each issue. Pdf copies of selected articles from the print issues are available for free on the magazine's web site. Recommended for architecture libraries.

465. *J A.* Formerly (until 1991): *Japan Architect.* [ISSN: 1342-6478] 1956. q. JPY 10000 domestic; USD 100 in North America. Ed(s): Yutaka Shikata. Shinkenchiku-sha Co. Ltd., 2-31-2 Yushima, Bunkyo-ku, Tokyo, 113-0034, Japan; http://www.japan-architect.co.jp. Illus., adv. Circ: 18000 Paid. *Indexed:* A06, A07, API, BAS. *Aud.:* Ac, Sa.

A year's worth of this Japanese quarterly is made up of a yearbook issue and three issues on either a single Japanese architect or firm, or a topical theme. This title is virtually advertisement-free, and the large-format pages of every issue are given over to the numerous color photographs, detailed drawings, plans, sections, and elevations that accompany a short description of each building. The emphasis is on works at home and abroad by world-renowned or up-and-coming Japanese architects; works in Japan by international architects are also featured. This is an essential resource for Japanese architecture. All text is in English and Japanese. Tables of contents and a few pages views from an issue are available online, but these represent only a fraction of the content from the printed issue. Recommended for architecture libraries.

Journal of Architectural and Planning Research. See Urban Studies section.

466. *Journal of Architectural Education.* Former titles (until 1984): *J A E;* (until 1975): *Journal of Architectural Education.* [ISSN: 1046-4883] 1947. s-a. GBP 334 (print & online eds.). Ed(s): George Dodds, Jerry Portwood. Wiley-Blackwell Publishing, Inc., 111 River St, Hoboken, NJ 07030; info@wiley.com; http://onlinelibrary.wiley.com/. Illus., index. Refereed. Vol. ends: Aug. Microform: PQC. Reprint: PSC. *Indexed:* A01, A06, A07, A22, API, AmHI, ArchI, ArtHuCI, E01, MLA-IB. *Bk. rev.:* 5-6, 1,500 words. *Aud.:* Ac.

This scholarly refereed journal is published biannually by Taylor and Francis for the Association of Collegiate Schools of Architecture (ACSA). Each issue is composed of a mix of essays and articles—sometimes developed from sessions at the ACSA conference—as well as architectural criticism, and book and exhibition reviews. This title is a good resource for discovering those topics of interest in North American architectural education and current scholarship in the field, which means it will be of interest almost exclusively to an academic audience. Full text of articles published from 1998 to the present is available via subscription; articles published from 1947 on are available in JSTOR, with a moving wall of seven years. Recommended for architecture libraries.

467. *The Journal of Architecture.* [ISSN: 1360-2365] 1996. bi-m. GBP 957 (print & online eds.). Ed(s): Peter Gibbs-Kennet, Murray Fraser. Routledge, 4 Park Sq, Milton Park, Abingdon, OX14 4RN, United Kingdom; subscriptions@tandf.co.uk; http://www.tandfonline.com. Illus., adv. Sample. Refereed. Reprint: PSC. *Indexed:* A01, A22, API, ArtHuCI, B01, C&ISA, CerAb, E01. *Bk. rev.:* Number and length vary. *Aud.:* Ac.

Jointly published six times a year by Routledge and the Royal Institute of British Architects, this scholarly peer-reviewed journal has an international scope and an editorial board made up of regional editors from 20 countries. Students, academics, and practitioners contribute articles on contemporary and historical topics in architectural theory, methodology, or the intersections between architecture and technology or architecture and culture. Several issues in a volume are devoted to special topics, and most issues contain book reviews and a detailed, critical review of a building or group of buildings. Institutions may choose an online-only or combined print-and-online subscription. Recommended for architecture and large academic libraries.

468. *Journal of Green Building.* [ISSN: 1552-6100] 2006. q. USD 489 (Individuals, USD 149). Ed(s): Steffen Lehmann. College Publishing, 12309 Lynwood Dr, Glen Allen, VA 23059; collegepub@mindspring.com; http://www.collegepublishing.us. Sample. Refereed. *Indexed:* ArtHuCI. *Aud.:* Ac, Sa.

Two sections, the "industry corner" and "research articles," make up each issue of this quarterly journal, which is devoted to design and construction topics in green building. The scholarly research articles are peer-reviewed, while the "industry corner" is written for an audience of practitioners by architects, engineers, and other professionals. Small photographs and diagrams accompany the articles, but the focus here is on the research and textual information instead of big, glossy images. Subjects covered include green building materials, techniques, case studies, and education. A strong mix of practical information, theory, and research, this title is a great resource on a timely topic. Subscriptions are available for print only or print and online; online subscribers have access to current issues and the previously printed issues. Recommended for architecture libraries.

Landscape Architecture. See Landscape Architecture section.

Landscape Journal. See Landscape Architecture section.

469. *Log (New York).* [ISSN: 1547-4690] 2003. 3x/yr. USD 36 domestic; USD 40 in Canada & Mexico; USD 60 elsewhere. Ed(s): Cynthia Davidson. Anyone Corporation, 41 W 25th St, 11th Fl, New York, NY 10010; any@anycorp.com; http://www.anycorp.com. Adv. *Aud.:* Ac.

Published three times a year, *Log* is "an independent journal on architecture and the contemporary city" that explores a different theme in each issue. Recent themes were architecture criticism, observations in architecture and the contemporary city, and "stocktaking," which investigates "the current conditions of architectural practice, pedagogy, theory, and criticism." Deliberately devoid of the glossy images that appear in architecture magazines, the 15 or more articles, essays, conversations, and opinion pieces in an issue are of a literary style. Authors tend to be scholars in architecture, architectural history, culture, and theory, or practicing architects who also teach. A postcard or print related to the theme is included with each issue. Previews of many articles are available online, but the full content is reserved for the printed journal. Recommended for architecture libraries.

470. *Lotus International: rivista trimestrale di architettura - quarterly architectural review.* Formerly (until 1970): *Lotus.* [ISSN: 1124-9064] 1963. 4x/yr. EUR 86. Editoriale Lotus, Via Santa Maria 19a, Milan, 20123, Italy; abbonamenti@editorialelotus.it. *Indexed:* A06, A07, ArtHuCI, BAS. *Aud.:* Ac, Sa.

Projects presented in the pages of *Lotus International* are by a roll call of world-renowned international architects. The critical essays, articles, and building studies center on a theme or building type in each issue of this Italian quarterly. Subjects that were recently covered include Italian theory and landscape urbanism. The building studies are accompanied by an array of high-quality photographs, plans, details, and sections, all with detailed captions. Text is in both Italian and English. Tables of contents and small images of the printed pages are available for free online; individuals can purchase pdf copies of issues beginning with no. 114 (2002). Recommended for architecture libraries.

471. *Mark: another architecture.* [ISSN: 1574-6453] 2005. bi-m. Mark Publishers, Laan der Hesperiden 68, Amsterdam, 1076 DX, Netherlands. Adv. *Aud.:* Ac, Sa.

Issues of this Dutch bimonthly present dozens of projects in Europe, North America, South America, and Asia by world-renowned designers and rising talents, making *Mark* a veritable catalog of what's new in architecture around the world. The "notice board" section posts a color photo and basic facts for 8–12 projects on paper, the "cross section" devotes two pages each to 12 newly built works, and the "long section" presents 10–12 more buildings in longer articles accompanied by many photographs, plans, and drawings, as well as interviews with designers or firms. Several feature articles and a products section complete the issue. A preview of the digital edition of the magazine is available for free online, while access to the complete digital edition must be purchased. Recommended for architecture libraries.

472. *Metropolis: architecture design.* [ISSN: 0279-4977] 1981. 11x/yr. USD 27.95 domestic; USD 42.95 Canada; USD 110 elsewhere. Ed(s): Susan S Szenasy, Martin C Pedersen. Bellerophon Publications, Inc., 61 W 23rd St, 4th Fl, New York, NY 10010; MetropolisMagazine@emailcustomerservice.com. Illus., adv. Circ: 61000. Vol. ends: Jun. *Indexed:* A07, A22, ASIP. *Bk. rev.:* 2. *Aud.:* Ga, Ac, Sa.

This suave design magazine covers the urban international scene in recent architecture, restorations, product and furniture design, and planning. Alongside news and events, interviews, book reviews, and short essays, the "Observed" section contains eight to ten short articles on topics such as architecture, planning, textiles, education, products and materials, and preservation. The somewhat longer feature articles may cover similar topics in greater detail, or focus on broader themes. Of interest to those working in design fields, *Metropolis* also makes for good reading for the design-conscious and the urban dweller. Subscribers can opt for a print or digital-only subscription. Recommended for architecture, academic, and large public libraries.

473. *Open House International: the journal of an association of institutes and individuals concerned with housing, design and development in the built environment.* Formerly (until 1983): *Open House.* [ISSN: 0168-2601] 1976. q. Free to members. Ed(s): Nicholas Wilkinson. Open House International Association, PO Box 74, Gateshead, NE9 5UZ, United Kingdom. Adv. Refereed. *Indexed:* A22, API, ArtHuCI. *Aud.:* Ac, Sa.

Most issues of this refereed quarterly are guest-edited and focused on a topical theme related to housing, neighborhoods, or urbanism. Articles are contributed by worldwide educators, scholars, and the occasional designer. Small black-and-white photographs, plans, charts, and maps illustrate the journal, but the main value here is the research and projects detailed by the authors. The journal and archives are available online for subscribers, and the archives may also be purchased on DVD or online. Recommended for architecture libraries.

474. *The Plan: architecture & technologies in detail.* [ISSN: 1720-6553] 2002. 3x/yr. Centauro SRL, Via del Pratello 8, Bologna, 40122, Italy; http://www.centauro.it. *Indexed:* A07. *Aud.:* Ac, Sa.

The Plan is an Italian journal that compares favorably with both *Detail,* for drawings of contemporary building details, and *GA Document,* for the wealth of visual documentation. The three to five building studies in each issue are accompanied by a section drawing of a detail and numerous color photographs, plans, site plans, sections, sketches, and diagrams. In addition to the international, contemporary buildings featured in the studies, issues include a section on "the city plan" that uses maps and other data to tell the story of a world city. Some issues include an "old & new" section, documenting an addition or intervention in a historic building, which is illustrated with as many images and detail drawings as the contemporary building studies. The "report" section in the last pages describes and illustrates eight or more new buildings, products, or firms in one or two pages each. All text is in both Italian and English. Limited content is available for free on *The Plan* web site, while full content can be purchased by subscription or in an iPad edition. Recommended for architecture libraries.

475. *Praxis (Columbus): a journal of writing and building.* [ISSN: 1526-2065] 1999. s-a. USD 96 (Individuals, USD 52). Ed(s): Ashley Schafer. Praxis, Inc., P O Box 380225, Cambridge, MA 02238-0225. *Indexed:* AmHI. *Aud.:* Ac.

Design, theory, and practice are explored in the articles published under the overarching themes of each issue of *Praxis,* the journal of writing and building. Issue 10 considered the dual meanings of "urban matters," and issue 11/12 offered readers "11 architects, 12 conversations," while issue 13 focused on "ecologics." An issue consists of a dozen or more thoughtful articles and thought-provoking essays along with color photos, plans, diagrams, and models. Contributors tend to be architects or educators in North America with some contributions from farther afield. *Praxis* is slated to be published approximately two times a year by its all-volunteer staff. Articles from this journal are not available online. Recommended for architecture libraries.

476. *Preservation.* Former titles (until vol.48, no.4, 1996): *Historic Preservation;* (until 1952): *National Council for Historic Sites and Buildings Quarterly Report;* Which incorporated (1990-1995): *Historic Preservation News;* Which was formerly (until 1990): *Preservation News.* [ISSN: 1090-9931] 1949. bi-m. Free to members. Ed(s): James H Schwartz, Arnold Berke. National Trust for Historic Preservation, 1785 Massachusetts Ave, NW, Washington, DC 20036. Illus., adv. Vol. ends: Nov. Microform: PQC. *Indexed:* A&ATA, A06, A07, A22, ABS&EES, API, ArtHuCI, GardL, RILM. *Bk. rev.:* 4, 300-500 words. *Aud.:* Ga, Ac, Sa.

A snapshot of preservation activities in the United States, *Preservation* is a glossy quarterly magazine that is sent to National Trust members. Buildings, towns, main streets, and the natural world are all candidates for preservation and subjects for the journal's articles and departments. Issues include book reviews and short pieces on news and events. A recurring travel section highlights historic buildings and sites in the United States and abroad and promotes National Trust tours. The "transitions" section keeps tabs on that which has been "lost, threatened, saved, [or] restored." Those in the historic preservation field should be aware of this title, but may be more interested in *Forum Journal,* which is also published by the National Trust; members of the general public interested in preservation will consider the magazine essential reading. The text of the printed *Preservation* magazine is available on the National Trust web site with selected images; *Forum Journal* articles are available online to members of the National Trust Forum who register with the site. Recommended for all library types.

477. R I B A Journal. Incorporates (1986-2003): *R I B A Interiors;* Former titles (until 1993): *Royal Institute of British Architects. Journal;* (until 1987): *Architect;* (until 1986): *R I B A Journal;* (until 1965): *Royal Institute of British Architects. Journal;* Which was formed by the merger of (1879-1893): *Royal Institute of British Architects. Transactions;* Which was formerly (until 1879): *Royal Institute of British Architects. Sessional Papers;* (until 1877): *Sessional Papers Read at the Royal Institute of British Architects;* (until 1854): *Royal Institute of British Architects. Transactions;* (1887-1893): *Royal Institute of British Architects. Journal of Proceedings;* Which was formerly (until 1887): *Royal Institute of British Architects. Journal of Proceedings;* (until 1885): *Royal Institute of British Architects. Proceedings.* [ISSN: 1463-9505] 1893. m. GBP 63 domestic; EUR 120 foreign. Atom Publishing, Clerkenwell House, 45/47 Clerkenwell Green, London, EC1R 0EB, United Kingdom; info@atompublishing.co.uk; http://www.atompublishing.co.uk/. Illus., index, adv. Sample. Circ: 29936. Vol. ends: Dec. Microform: PQC. *Indexed:* A06, A07, A22, API, AmHI, BAS, BrTechI, EIP. *Bk. rev.:* 3, 200 words. *Aud.:* Ac, Sa.

A rich source of information for architects practicing in Great Britain, the Royal Institute of British Architects' trade journal is also notable for its coverage of British architecture. This title is published ten times a year, and each issue is made up of one or more well-illustrated building studies, critiques, and firm profiles joined by news, opinion pieces, and reviews. The "intelligence" section is devoted to short pieces on the issues and concerns of British architectural practice, as well as product reviews and technical news. Classified and display advertisements and recruitment postings complete the issue. Along with *Architect's Journal,* this title is a good resource for those considering work in Great Britain. Subscribers may opt for the digital edition. Recommended for architecture libraries.

478. Society of Architectural Historians. Journal. Formerly (until 1946): *American Society of Architectural Historians. Journal.* [ISSN: 0037-9808] 1940. q. USD 493 (print & online eds.). Ed(s): Mary Christian, David Brownlee. University of California Press, Journals Division, 2000 Ctr St, Ste 303, Berkeley, CA 94704; customerservice@ucpressjournals.com; http://www.ucpressjournals.com. Illus., index, adv. Refereed. Circ: 4000. Vol. ends: Dec. Microform: PQC. *Indexed:* A06, A07, A22, ABS&EES, API, ArtHuCI, BAS, BrArAb, GardL, MLA-IB, NumL, RILM. *Bk. rev.:* 20, 1,500 words. *Aud.:* Ac.

The *Journal of the Society of Architectural Historians* (*JSAH*) is a scholarly refereed quarterly composed of lengthy essays and thoughtful, informative exhibition, book, and media reviews. From ancient to modern, and technical to theoretical, all aspects of the built environment, urbanism, and landscape studies fall under the purview of this journal. An indispensable resource for architectural history, this title is also of interest to those in fields such as urban studies, history, and cultural studies. In 2010, *JSAH* made news when it debuted its online version. Published by the University of California Press, the online version goes beyond the static treatment of most other journals that have migrated from print, and takes advantage of multimedia enhancements such as sound files, high-quality zoomable images, and interactive maps. *JSAH* is also now part of JSTOR's Current Scholarship Program, which means that current subscribers can access all issues from 1947 to the present in JSTOR. Recommended for architecture and academic libraries.

479. Taunton's Fine Homebuilding. Formerly (until 1991): *Fine Homebuilding.* [ISSN: 1096-360X] 1981. 8x/yr. USD 37.95 in US & Canada; USD 45.95 elsewhere; USD 7.99 per issue. Ed(s): Chris Ermides. The Taunton Press, Inc., 63 South Main St, PO Box 5506, Newtown, CT 06470; publicrelations@taunton.com; http://www.taunton.com. Illus., adv. Circ: 300000 Paid. *Indexed:* API, ASIP, BRI, CBRI, IHTDI. *Bk. rev.:* 3, 500 words. *Aud.:* Ga, Ac, Sa.

A popular magazine for the homebuilder, this journal also makes good reading for homeowners or students in design or construction fields. Departments and articles cover topics related to construction and home improvement projects, tools and methods, and materials and best practices. The focus is on houses that are average or small in size and on affordable building projects that a skilled do-it-yourselfer could successfully complete. More than simply a publication devoted to technique, *Fine Homebuilding* pays equal attention to the finished products. Many color photographs accompany the feature articles, and the annual houses and kitchen-and-bath special issues showcase stunning, well-crafted designs. Online members have access to full text of articles; excerpts and some images are available to all. A digital edition is also available for purchase. Recommended for public libraries and architecture libraries where there is interest.

480. Volume. Formed by the merger of (2001-2004): *Archis (English Edition);* (1986-2004): *Archis (Deventer);* Which was formerly (until 1985): *Wonen - T A - B K;* (1960-1972): *Tijdschrift voor Architectuur en Beeldende Kunsten.* [ISSN: 1574-9401] 2005. q. Ed(s): Arjen Oosterman, Christian Ernsten. Archis Foundation, PO Box 14702, Amsterdam, 1001 LE, Netherlands; info@archis.org; http://www.archis.org. Illus., adv. Circ: 6000. *Indexed:* A22, API, RILM. *Aud.:* Ac, Sa.

A project of the Archis foundation (an experimental think tank), AMO (the design and research arm of architectural firm OMA), and C-LAB (Columbia University's Laboratory for Architectural Broadcasting), *Volume* is billed as an "independent quarterly magazine that sets the agenda for architecture and design." To this end, the pages of an issue are filled with short essays, opinion pieces, critiques, and artists' projects that dissect, contextualize, or question the theme under consideration. Recent issues investigated interiors, building new cities, and biosynthetics in "everything under control: building with biology." Tables of contents and select articles for *Volume,* and its precursor *Archis,* are available online. Recommended for architecture libraries.

481. Wallpaper. [ISSN: 1364-4475] 1996. m. GBP 29.49 domestic; USD 55 in US & Canada; EUR 56.60 in Europe. Ed(s): Tony Chambers. I P C Media Ltd., The Blue Fin Bldg, 110 Southwark St, London, SE1 0SU, United Kingdom; http://www.ipcmedia.com/. Adv. Circ: 108050. *Bk. rev.:* Number and length vary. *Aud.:* Ga, Ac, Sa.

Published 11 times a year, *Wallpaper* is a British design and lifestyle magazine composed of both feature articles and sections on architecture, art, cars, design, fashion, interiors, and travel. In addition to its own section, architecture may appear in the feature articles, the book reviews, and elsewhere throughout the issue. Recently completed international buildings, future projects, materials, and well-known or up-and-coming architects are highlighted. This title is well-suited to architecture audiences and those interested in all forms of world design. The magazine's web site is its own entity, offering similar content to that of the print magazine as well as some additional photographs and videos, but it offers only brief summaries of the text from the magazine, which is available in print or an iPad edition. Recommended for architecture, academic, and large public libraries.

482. Werk - Bauen & Wohnen. Formed by the merger of (1946-1982): *Bauen und Wohnen;* (1914-1982): *Werk.* [ISSN: 0257-9332] 10x/yr. CHF 200 domestic (Students, CHF 140). Zollikofer AG, Fuerstenlandstr 122, St. Gallen, 9001, Switzerland; leserservice@zollikofer.ch; http://www.zollikofer.ch. Adv. Circ: 9000. *Indexed:* A06, A07, A22, API, BAS. *Bk. rev.:* Number and length vary. *Aud.:* Ac, Sa.

Issue 6 for the 2013 *Werk bauen und wohnen,* the German-language Swiss publication, debuted a redesign for the 100-year-old magazine. In addition to a new graphic design, some of the content organization has changed, although each issue will continue to be devoted to a theme like the recently featured "durable, sustainable"; the Limmat Valley in Switzerland; and pavilions. Switzerland has long been this title's primary focus, but international buildings and projects may also appear in the articles, news, or reviews. Feature articles are accompanied by an impressive collection of color photographs, plans, site plans, sections, and details, as well as English and French summaries. Profiles of new buildings and interiors, book and exhibition reviews, news and events, and shorter articles on architectural practice and other topical subjects are in German only. A synopsis of the content of each issue is available online, but the full articles appear only in the printed issue. Recommended for architecture libraries.

■ ARCHIVES AND MANUSCRIPTS

General/National, Regional, and State Newsletters/National, Regional, and State Newsletters—Canada/National, Regional, and State Newsletters—United States/Special-Interest Newsletters

See also Bibliography; History; and Library and Information Science sections.

Stacie Williams, Access and Reference, Countway Library of Medicine, Harvard University

Melanie Wisner, Technical Services—Manuscript Section, Houghton Library, Harvard University;

Cheryl LaGuardia, Research Librarian, Widener Library, Harvard University

Introduction

The archivist's mission is to establish and maintain control, both physical and intellectual, over records of enduring value. The definition of "record" is ever a subject of healthy debate, particularly as archivists, curators, records managers, librarians, museum professionals, historians, and students increasingly examine each other's priorities.

The question of "enduring value" goes to the heart of the archival profession: the role of the keeper in determining what histories will be created and preserved. Public debate is a feature of the cultural heritage scene in the twenty-first century. Medieval manuscript curators, audiofile metadata specialists, and pushers of the traditional document box each have their specialized practices, but the core question—what to acquire and keep—they all share, and their answers to the question are increasingly subject to public comment.

The periodical literature of the archival and allied professions is concerned with cultural heritage materials in all physical and electronic formats. A number of magazines, newsletters, and online communications review trends, practices, and innovative uses of archival materials; they discuss how, with insufficient resources, to deliver archival content to an impatient society; and they offer news and guidance to individual collectors and large research institutions alike.

While large and/or well-funded institutions have made their holdings available online to a greater or lesser extent, the provision of digital content and services to users is still a pipe dream for many smaller/unfunded archives. Even the best-funded institutions carry some backlog of undescribed holdings. Fortunately, there are more tools becoming available that may help, and more affordably. Many journal articles concern locally-grown software, creative and collaborative ways to produce digital collections, and workflow solutions that may help colleagues.

As of this writing, EAD (Encoded Archival Description) is nearly 20 years old, and a plethora of other metadata standards have emerged to serve the cultural heritage community. Archival repositories need to migrate their "legacy data"—descriptive and other information on paper or in obsolete electronic formats—into formats that meet the new standards in order to serve the global community of researchers. This work is often bundled into grant-funded projects, and project management with digitization is heavily covered in archival journals and newsletters.

Concerns about archival education and diversity in the profession are often expressed in the literature. Graduate programs need to attract the young and the multicultural; archival educators are frequent contributors to the major journals.

Manmade and natural disasters have awakened a broad awareness of the fragility of cultural heritage embodied in the world's libraries, archives, and museums. Professionals in all these settings continue to report in from the field, sometimes long after the public's eye has moved on. The experience of traumatic loss of cultural property has by ethical mandate led archival leaders into the global political realm on behalf of the cultural record. In the United

States, the Society of American Archivists (SAA), often in concert with the American Library Association and other professional bodies, also routinely takes stands on national legislative issues, often over access to governmental records. This is not a new but certainly is an amplified role, and developments may be followed in the larger journals.

The literature of archives and manuscripts is predominantly scholarly and often theoretical in the large national and regional journals, and most practical in the local and specialized newsletters. Taken as a body of work, it promotes best practices, builds community among the custodians and users of original cultural materials, and never fails to pose difficult questions about the work of preserving the raw material of history.

Basic Periodicals

Ga: *Archivist, Prologue (College Park);* Ac: *American Archivist, Archival Issues, Archivaria, Comma, The Information Management Journal.*

Basic Abstracts and Indexes

America: History and Life, Historical Abstracts, LISA: Library and Information Science Abstracts, Library Literature.

General

483. *American Archivist.* [ISSN: 0360-9081] 1938. s-a. USD 169 (print or online ed.) Individuals, USD 139 (print or online ed.); Free to members). Ed(s): Mar Jo Pugh. Society of American Archivists, 17 N State St, Ste 1425, Chicago, IL 60602; info@archivists.org; http://www.archivists.org. Illus., index, adv. Refereed. Vol. ends: Fall. *Indexed:* A22, ABS&EES, BRI, CBRI, FR, ISTA, MLA-IB. *Bk. rev.:* 9-11, 400-1,500 words. *Aud.:* Ac, Sa.

American Archivist is the semi-annual, refereed journal of the Society of American Archivists, a heavily relied-on collection of national archival practice, procedure, and theory. Its content strives to provide contextual analysis of collections, and the relationship of those collections to archivists, students of archival studies, users, and macro and micro communities. Recurring topics include cultural preservation, born-digital archives, and trends in records management. Literature review, case studies, commentaries, and resource lists also appear in every issue. The journal addresses the critical role that technology and copyright play in archives, whether through digital asset-management systems or as a preservation tool. Recent articles include an analysis on archives in the context of the Occupy movement, and using provenance to define third-party privacy. As of this writing, issues beginning in 1938 are available online with a subscription. The journal plays a key role in informing archival theory and policy in the United States, as it is the journal that represents the largest professional archives group in North America. Widely used in archives management programs and continues to offer strong analysis and resources.

484. *Archival Issues.* Formerly (until 1992): *Midwestern Archivist.* [ISSN: 1067-4993] 1976. s-a. Free to members. Midwest Archives Conference, c/o William J Maher, University Archivist, University of Illinois Archives, Urbana, IL 61801; w-maher@illinois.edu; http://www.midwestarchives.org. Illus., index, adv. Refereed. Vol. ends: No. 2. *Bk. rev.:* 6-8, 750-1,500 words. *Aud.:* Ac, Sa.

Archival Issues, a peer-reviewed journal published by the Midwest Archives Conference, purports to address contemporary issues in archives, which it does by publishing many case studies borne out of state and city archives, or local special collections. Recent issues discuss poetry archives in Washington, D.C.; building digital libraries out of small collections; and a discussion of Greene and Meissner's "More Product, Less Process" as applied to the Jim Wright papers at Texas Christian University. Some regional issues related to preservation and climate are also featured, but they would be relevant to any archives. The journal is published twice a year, and features archives professionals and instructors specializing in preservation of film and sound recordings, copyright, and innovative business concepts. Key archival analysis is being discussed, but a collection development department may find acquisition of this title superfluous.

485. *Archival Science: international journal on recorded information.*
Incorporates (in 2001): *Archives & Museum Informatics;* Which was formerly (1987-1989): *Archival Informatics Newsletter.* [ISSN: 1389-0166] 2000. q. EUR 398 (print & online eds.). Ed(s): Eric Ketelaar, Karen Anderson. Springer Netherlands, Van Godewijckstraat 30, Dordrecht, 3311 GX, Netherlands; http://www.springer.com. Adv. Refereed. Reprint: PSC. *Indexed:* A22, ABIn, BRI, E01, ISTA. *Aud.:* Ac, Sa.

Archival Science, which is published quarterly in the Netherlands, claims to cover "all aspects of archival science theory, methodology, and practice...around the world." However, these aspects seem to center around archives and cultural heritage as a record of history, and also to span the Americas, which is excellent for readers desiring a wider perspective. Issues are generally themed; the most recent issue includes articles such as "Local archives and community collecting in the digital age," "Indigenous human rights and knowledge in archives, museums, and libraries," and "Native America's twenty-first-century right to know." The journal, aimed at archives students and educators, is useful to readers pondering cultural self-determination, and more Derrida-type questions about the legitimacy of records and history. Abstracts of the journal articles are available online.

486. *Archivaria.* Formerly (until 1975): *Canadian Archivist.* [ISSN: 0318-6954] 1963. s-a. CAD 295 (print & online eds.) Individuals, CAD 125 (print & online eds.); Free to members). Ed(s): Michael M Dufresne, Carolyn Heald. Association of Canadian Archivists, PO Box 2596, Ottawa, ON K1P 5W6, Canada; aca@archivists.ca; http://www.archivists.ca. Illus., index, adv. Refereed. *Indexed:* A&ATA, A22, BRI, C37, CBCARef, CBRI. *Bk. rev.:* 10-20, 750-2,500 words. *Aud.:* Ac, Sa.

Archivaria functions as the Canadian twin of *American Archivist.* The journal, published twice a year by the Association of Canadian Archivists, centers on the "scholarly investigation" of archives in Canada and wider international circles, and is bilingual for its Quebecois readers. *Archivaria*'s international scope is robust, and its recent contributors, like Terry Cook and Mark Matienzo, are well known in American archives scholarship. Topics include archives as they relate to history, education and instruction around born-digital materials, and archival ethics. Recent book reviews discuss books on digital curation, metadata, and film preservation. The full scope of this journal's content is available electronically, and tables of contents are open to subscribers and non-subscribers. It provides a good complement to *American Archivist* or any other archives education journals.

487. *Archives.* [ISSN: 0003-9535] 1949. s-a. Free to members; Non-members, GBP 50. Ed(s): Ruth Paley. British Records Association, c/o Finsbury Library, 245 St John St, London, EC1V 4NB, United Kingdom; brrecass@btconnect.com; http://www.britishrecordsassociation.org.uk. Illus., index. Refereed. Circ: 1300. Vol. ends: Oct. *Indexed:* A22, AmHI, BrArAb, NumL. *Bk. rev.:* 25-30, 300-800 words. *Aud.:* Ac, Sa.

Archives, published by the British Records Association for the past 80 years, is a scholarly, peer-reviewed journal devoted to British history and records. European in its desire to ponder philosophical questions on archives and the nature of records, the journal ascribes to document and guide archives scholarship through book reviews, procedural analysis, and case studies. Recent articles in the journal include: a story on the Sheffield Park Archives; a piece on Parliamentary records; and a piece on re-dating the Cartum Baronum, or King Henry II's Charter of the Barons. Researchers, archivists, historians, and other scholars would find *Archives* extremely useful in their studies, especially if they are focusing exclusively on British collections.

488. *Archives and Manuscripts.* Formerly (until 1955): *Bulletin for Australian Archivists.* [ISSN: 0157-6895] 1954. 3x/yr. GBP 197 (print & online eds.). Ed(s): Sebastian Gurciullo. Australian Society of Archivists Inc., PO BOX A623, Sydney South, NSW 1235, Australia; office@archivists.org.au; http://www.archivists.org.au. Illus., adv. Refereed. Vol. ends: Nov. Reprint: PSC. *Bk. rev.:* 15-20, 500-2,000 words. *Aud.:* Ac, Sa.

The triannually published journal *Archives and Manuscripts,* which is peer-reviewed and published by the Australian Society of Archivists, Inc., aims to inform its national archives community about the "theory and practice of archives and record-keeping." The audience is primarily professionals, educators, researchers, and students. The country's diversity, along with occasional perspective from New Zealand and Fiji, is a basis for critical insight and analysis in articles about adoption records and archives and their use with child abuse victims; archival education and literacy around indigenous communities; and archival ethics related to such issues. The journal includes an "International Notes" section that describes regional archival practices, current projects of interest, and literature reviews. Article abstracts are available online. Professionals looking to explore nontraditional archives, or collections that pertain to indigenous groups, would find *Archives and Manuscripts* very useful.

489. *Archives and Records.* Former titles (until 2013): *Society of Archivists. Journal;* (until 1955): *Society of Local Archivists. Bulletin.* [ISSN: 2325-7962] 1947. s-a. GBP 289 (print & online eds.). Ed(s): Alexandrina Buchanan, Charlotte Harrison. Routledge, 4 Park Sq, Milton Park, Abingdon, OX14 4RN, United Kingdom; subscriptions@tandf.co.uk; http://www.tandfonline.com. Illus., index, adv. Sample. Refereed. Microform: PQC. Reprint: PSC. *Indexed:* A01, A22, AmHI, ArtHuCI, BrArAb, E01, FR, NumL, P02. *Bk. rev.:* 15-25, 600-1,400 words. *Aud.:* Ac, Sa.

The *Journal of the Society of Archivists,* which is published twice a year by the Archives and Records Association, covers archives "challenges and opportunities presented by new media and information technology" in the United Kingdom and Ireland. Though its focus is mostly on European archives, English-speaking countries would no doubt find the journal useful when comparing similar concerns around preservation, ethics, provenance, and technology. Some issues are themed, but all contain a mix of literature reviews, essays, case studies, and relevant cultural analysis. Recent articles include: "Community engagement and the Olympics," "West Yorkshire's Sporting Heroes," and "Many happy returns: Advocacy and the development of archives." This journal would likely be useful to researchers or archivists working on Western European collections, or those documenting colonialism and its influence on archives. It would also appeal to practicing professionals interested in changing archival theories. Issues are available online, in their entirety.

490. *The Information Management Magazine.* Former titles (until 1999): *Records Management Quarterly;* (until Jan.1986): *A R M A Records Management Quarterly;* (until 1976): *Records Management Quarterly;* (until 1967): *Records Review.* [ISSN: 1535-2897] 1960. bi-m. Free to members. Ed(s): Vicki Weiler, Amy Lanter. A R M A International, 11880 College Blvd, Ste 450, Overland Park, KS 66210; Sales.Dept@armaintl.org; http://www.arma.org. Illus., index, adv. Vol. ends: Dec. Microform: PQC. *Indexed:* A01, A22, ABIn, B01, B02, BRI, CompLI. *Bk. rev.:* 1-4, 1,000-2,500 words. *Aud.:* Ac, Sa.

Also referred to as ARMA International, the professional, nonprofit Association of Records Managers and Administrators International produces the peer-reviewed *Information Management Magazine.* The target audience for the journal is record and information managers, and its focus is "the application of management principles and appropriate technologies to the production, coordination, acquisition, organization, representation, control, dissemination, use, and ultimate disposition of information, whatever the format...leading to the more effective functioning of organizations of all kinds." Recent articles include questions on mobile technology in "Mobile usage raises information governance, data security concerns"; "EHRs: Now there's an app for that"; and "Ikea paid [a] firm to spy on customers, staff." The journal stays current on technology issues, which is critical given the influx of born-digital data that comprises the bulk of record-keeping in the twenty-first century. The journal publishes six times a year and is available electronically.

491. *Journal of Archival Organization.* [ISSN: 1533-2748] 2002. q. GBP 312 (print & online eds.). Ed(s): Thomas J Frusciano. Routledge, 325 Chestnut St, Ste 800, Philadelphia, PA 19106; customerservice@taylorandfrancis.com; http://www.tandfonline.com. Adv. Refereed. Circ: 42 Paid. Reprint: PSC. *Indexed:* A01, A22, E01, ERIC, ISTA, RILM. *Bk. rev.:* Number and length vary. *Aud.:* Ac, Sa.

The quarterly and peer-reviewed *Journal of Archival Organization* "places emphasis on emerging technologies, applications, and standards that range from Encoded Archival Description (EAD) and methods of organizing archival collections for access on the World Wide Web to issues connected with the digitization and display of archival materials." Which is to say that the journal covers all the usual bases in regard to archival scholarship. The publisher, which has frequently published journals and textbooks related to library science, knows its intended audience well, pulling together a series of articles about metadata, book reviews addressing digitization texts, and the fate of a historically black university's college archives. Regular web site, book reviews, and interviews with leading archives or history scholars are featured; however, because the journal covers similar ground as some other archives-related journals, libraries may not need to create priority space for the journal on its shelves. It is good work, but ultimately, more compelling scholarship is available. Tables of content and abstracts are available electronically.

492. *Manuscripta: a journal devoted to manuscript studies.* Incorporates in part (in 1956): *Historical Bulletin.* [ISSN: 0025-2603] 1957. 2x/yr. EUR 137 combined subscription (print & online eds.). Brepols Publishers, Begijnhof 67, Turnhout, 2300, Belgium; periodicals@brepols.net; http://www.brepols.net. Illus., adv. *Indexed:* ABS&EES, AmHI, BEL&L, IPB, MLA-IB, RILM. *Bk. rev.:* Number and length vary. *Aud.:* Ac, Sa.

Manuscripta, a biannual journal published by Brepols Publishers, specifically focuses on Renaissance studies and manuscripts, including the study of paleography, codicology, illumination, and book production/preservation. Such a specialized journal would do well at a university or library with a broad Renaissance or medieval studies program or collection, but more general liberal arts programs may not need something with such a narrow focus. Recent articles include: "Signs on the edge: Space, text, and margin in medieval manuscripts"; abstracts from the 38th annual Saint Louis Conference on Manuscript Studies; and cathedral rituals in medieval Florence, Italy. Brepols publishes the journal for the Knights of Columbus Vatican Film Library at Saint Louis University. Issues are available online.

493. *Manuscripts.* Formerly (until 1953): *Autograph collectors' Journal.* [ISSN: 0025-262X] 1948. q. Free to members. Ed(s): David R Chesnutt. Manuscript Society, 14003 Rampart Ct, Baton Rouge, LA 70810; sands@manuscript.org; http://www.manuscript.org. Illus., index, adv. Circ: 1500. Vol. ends: No. 4. Microform: PQC. *Indexed:* A22, AmHI, MLA-IB. *Bk. rev.:* Number and length vary. *Aud.:* Ga.

The quarterly journal *Manuscripts* was started in 1948 by the nonprofit Manuscript Society, which was known previously as the National Society of Autograph Collectors. The group's aim is scholarly documentation of historical manuscripts for historians, private collectors, and antiquarians. On the surface, this slim journal is highly specialized, but it is actually an excellent asset for museum curators, archivists, and special-collections librarians who are looking for analysis on authentication and provenance. Issues include book reviews and resource guides for collectors, along with essays on recent trends, particularly in auctions and collecting. A recent issue featured articles on "First Lady Manuscripts," "The Pierpoint Telegram Series," and papal pronouncements. Because the journal is for collectors, news items concerning the marketplace are also included. Issues are available in print or by becoming a member of the Manuscript Society.

494. *Prologue (Washington).* Formerly (until 1969): *National Archives Accessions.* [ISSN: 0033-1031] 1940. q. USD 24 domestic; USD 30 per issue foreign; USD 6 per issue. National Archives and Records Administration, 8601 Adelphi Rd, College Park, MD 20740; http://www.archives.gov. Illus., index. Vol. ends: Winter. *Indexed:* A07, A22, ABS&EES, AmHI, ArtHuCI. *Aud.:* Ga.

Prologue is a quarterly journal that highlights collections of the National and Archives and Records Administration (NARA), including presidential libraries. The journal is published by the National Archives Trust Fund Board to a target audience of researchers, educators, historians, genealogists, and other information management professionals. Because many of the articles are written in a news feature format, the journal is great complement to more scholarly resources, and it humanizes many of the collections, in addition to discussing archival theory and procedure. Recent articles include documents

found after the *Titanic* sunk; "A terrorist cell's final days"; and commentary about "More Product, Less Process" by current National Archivist David Ferriero. Selected articles from current and back issues are available online.

495. *Provenance.* Formerly (until 1983): *Georgia Archive.* [ISSN: 0739-4241] 1972. a. USD 40 Free to members. Ed(s): Susan Dick Hoffius, Brian Wilson. Society of Georgia Archivists, PO Box 133085, Atlanta, GA 30333; subscriptions@soga.org; http://www.soga.org. Illus., index. Refereed. Vol. ends: No. 1. *Bk. rev.:* 3-4, 750-1,250 words. *Aud.:* Ac, Sa.

The Society of Georgia Archivists created the journal *Provenance* in 1972, and it was the first journal ever published by a state or regional organization. Since then, the journal has continued to "focus on the archival profession in the theory and practice of archival management" with a much wider audience, as it is currently circulated nationally and internationally. The journal is published annually, and thus it tends to offer more thoughtful perspective on current archives-related events, since enough time has usually passed before any issues are published. Nuanced articles and book reviews from a recent issue include, respectively, "Preservation of the video game" and "Archival Anxiety and the Vocational Calling." Also, because the journal tends to encourage first-time writers, many of the articles bring a fresh voice and insight, as the journal is not weighted down by articles from the more well-known names in the archives field. The journal seems geared toward students in archival studies or library science programs, and is available in print; also, back issues can be ordered from the Society of Georgia Archivists. *Provenance* is an excellent resource to include among archives studies texts, especially for younger professionals and students.

496. *The Public Historian.* [ISSN: 0272-3433] 1978. q. USD 239 (print & online eds.). Ed(s): Lindsey Reed, Randolph Bergstrom. University of California Press, Journals Division, 2000 Ctr St, Ste 303, Berkeley, CA 94704; customerservice@ucpressjournals.com; http://www.ucpressjournals.com. Illus., index, adv. Refereed. Circ: 1615. Microform: PQC. Reprint: PSC. *Indexed:* A01, A22, AmHI, ArtHuCI, BRI, CBRI, E01, P61, SSA. *Bk. rev.:* 30-60, 1,000-2,800 words. *Aud.:* Ac, Sa.

The Public Historian is a quarterly journal published by the University of California Press for the National Council on Public History, and it refers to itself as the "voice of the public history movement" locally. But it is not afraid to tackle historical movement in a regional or national sense. Issues are generally themed; recent issues include articles on "Mythologizing memories: A critique of the Utah Korean War Memorial"; a book review on the Women's Rights National Historical Park; and a special Civil War review section. Strong analysis is provided on topics related to grassroots movements, museum exhibits, ethics, and oral histories. The journal would be a particularly good addition to a university or library with a focus on grassroots movements, ethnic studies, and regional history.

497. *R B M: A Journal of Rare Books, Manuscripts and Cultural Heritage.* Formerly (until 2000): *Rare Books and Manuscripts Librarianship.* [ISSN: 1529-6407] 1986. s-a. Free to members; Non-members, USD 42; USD 21 per issue. Ed(s): Beth M Whittaker. American Library Association, 50 E Huron, Chicago, IL 60611; customerservice@ala.org; http://www.ala.org. Illus., index, adv. Sample. Refereed. Vol. ends: No. 2. *Indexed:* A22, MLA-IB. *Bk. rev.:* Number and length vary. *Aud.:* Ac, Sa.

A Journal of Rare Books, Manuscripts, and Cultural Heritage is published biannually by the Association of College and Research Libraries (ACRL). The journal's special focus on rare books, preservation, and cultural heritage is essential reading for scholars of history, library science, book dealers, and archivists. Recent articles include "Maps as special collections: Bibliographic control of hidden material at Yale University," "Early printed books and material objects," and "The embedded curator: Reexamining the documentation strategy of archival acquisitions in a Web 2.0 environment." These articles provide compelling analysis of the theory and practice of preserving these resources, provenance, and best practices by institutions that are caring for items that define our cultural heritage. Book reviews and annotated catalogues are also included in most issues. Issues are available electronically.

National, Regional, and State Newsletters

The newsletters of state, provincial, and regional associations provide archivists in the field with current awareness of challenges and opportunities, a sense of community, and a forum for professional development. They track state and provincial legal trends, list professional and public workshops, announce and report on local meetings, describe funding opportunities, publish job announcements, and gather news from member repositories. The larger or most active associations may publish articles on a par with the national journals, but they generally focus on shorter-range issues and resources to support the daily work of their members. Most organizations publish issues in pdf format that are available online, some restricting recent issues to members only; a few still print newsletters that are a benefit of membership. The following publications of national, regional, state, and provincial archival associations are arranged geographically.

National, Regional, and State Newsletters—Canada

ACA Bulletin. [ISSN: 0709-4604] 6/yr. Larry Dohey. ACA Bulletin, Roman Catholic Archdiocese, P.O. Box 1363, St. John's, NL Canada A1C 5M3 (http://archivists.ca/publications/bulletin.aspx).

ALBERTA

ASA Newsletter. q. Archives Society of Alberta, P.O. Box 4067, South Edmonton Post Office, Edmonton, AB T6E 4S8 (http://www.archivesalberta.org/default.asp?V_ITEM_ID=69).

BRITISH COLUMBIA

AABC Newsletter. [ISSN: 1183-3165] q. Archives Association of British Columbia, 34A - 2755 Lougheed Highway, Suite #249, Port Coquitlam, BC V3B 5Y9 (http://aabc.bc.ca/aabc/newsletter/default.htm).

MANITOBA

ArchiNews/ArchiNouvelles. [ISSN: 1193-9958] q. Association for Manitoba Archives, Box 26005 Maryland P.O., Winnipeg, MB R3G 3R3 (http://www.mbarchives.mb.ca/communique.htm).

NEWFOUNDLAND AND LABRADOR

ANLA Bulletin. [ISSN: 0821-7157] q. Association of Newfoundland and Labrador Archives, P.O. Box 23155, St. John's, NL A1B 4J9 (http://www.anla.nf.ca/).

ONTARIO

Off the Record. q. Archives Association of Ontario, 1444 Queen Street East, Suite #205, Toronto, ON M4L 1E1 (http://aao.fis.utoronto.ca/aa/otr.html).

QUEBEC

La Chronique. 10/yr. L'Association des archivistes du Quebec, C.P. 9768, succ. Sainte-Foy, Quebec G1V 4C3 (http://www.archivistes.qc.ca/publication/chronique.html).

SASKATCHEWAN

SCAA Newsletter. Saskatchewan Council for Archives and Archivists, Kathlyn Szalasznyj, Outreach, 2506 Woodward Avenue, Saskatoon, SK S7J 2E5 (http://scaa.usask.ca/newsletter.html).

YUKON

YCA Newsletter. Yukon Council of Archives, Publications Committee, Box 31089, Whitehorse, Yukon Y1A 5P7 (http://www.yukoncouncilofarchives.ca/sections/newsletter/newsletter.html).

National, Regional, and State Newsletters—United States

Archival Outlook. [ISSN: 1520-3379] 6/yr. Teresa M. Brinati. SAA, 17 North State St., Suite 1425, Chicago, IL 60602-3315 (www.archivists.org/periodicals/ao.asp).

ALABAMA

The Alabama Archivist. s-a. $10. Carol Ellis. Society of Alabama Archivists, P.O. Box 300100, Montgomery, AL 36130-0100 (http://www.alarchivists.org/publications.html).

CALIFORNIA

SCA Newsletter. q. $45. Society of California Archivists, Long Beach Public Library, Collection Services Department, 101 Pacific Ave., Long Beach, CA 90822 (http://www.calarchivists.org/SCANewsletter).

DELAWARE VALLEY

Archival Arranger. 3/yr. $12. Joanne McKinley. Delaware Valley Archivists Group, New Jersey Division of Archives and Records Management, 2300 Stuyvesant Ave., P.O. Box 307, Trenton, NJ 08625 (http://www.dvarchivists.org/).

FLORIDA

The Florida Archivist. q. $20. Michael Zaidman. Society of Florida Archivists, P.O. Box 2746, Lakeland, FL 33806-2746 (http://www.florida-archivists.org/newsletter.htm).

GEORGIA

SGA Newsletter. q. $25. Renna Tuten. Society of Georgia Archivists, P.O. Box 133085, Atlanta, GA 30333 (http://www.soga.org/pubs/nltr/issues.php).

HAWAII

AHA Newsletter. q. $15. Association of Hawai'i Archivists, P.O. Box 1751, Honolulu, HI 96806 (http://www2.hawaii.edu/~wertheim/AHA.html).

INTERMOUNTAIN

CIMA Newsletter. q. $15. Roy Webb. Conference of Inter-Mountain Archivists, J. Willard Marriott Library, 295 South 1500 E., University of Utah, Salt Lake City, UT 84112 (http://www.lib.utah.edu/cima/news.html).

KENTUCKY

The Kentucky Archivist. s-a. $10. Jim Cundy. Kentucky Department for Libraries and Archives, 300 Coffee Tree Road, P.O. Box 537, Frankfort, KY 40602-0537 (http://kyarchivists.org/kyarch.htm).

LOUISIANA

LAMA Newsletter. [ISSN: 1073-1008] s-a. $15. Phyllis Kinnison, Louisiana State University, Special Collections, Hill Memorial Library, Baton Rouge, LA 70803 (http://www.nutrias.org/lama/lama.htm).

LOUISIANA, NEW ORLEANS

Greater New Orleans Archivists Newsletter. 3/yr. $10. Lester Sullivan, Archives & Special Collections, Xavier University Library, 7325 Palmetto St., New Orleans, LA 70125 (http://nutrias.org/gnoa/gnoa.htm).

MICHIGAN

Open Entry. s-a. $20. Bob Garrett, Archives of Michigan: garrettr1@michigan.gov (http://www.maasn.org/).

MID-ATLANTIC

Mid-Atlantic Archivist. [ISSN: 0738-9396] q. $35. Michael P. Martin. Mid-Atlantic Regional Archives Conference, P.O. Box 710215, Oak Hill, VA 20171 (http://www.lib.umd.edu/MARAC/committees/marac-pubs.html).

MIDWEST

MAC Newsletter. [ISSN: 0741-0379] q. $30. Kathy Koch. Midwest Archives Conference, 4440 PGA Boulevard, Suite 600, Palm Beach Gardens, FL 33410 (http://www.midwestarchives.org/macnewsletter.asp).

MINNESOTA, MINNEAPOLIS-ST. PAUL

TCART Newsletter. s-a. Candy Hart. Twin Cities Archives Round Table, Archives MS-C1919, Hamline University, 1536 Hewitt Ave., St. Paul, MN 55104 (http://www.tcartmn.org/).

MISSISSIPPI

The Primary Source. [ISSN: 0741-6563] s-a. Peggy Price. Society of Mississippi Archivists, P.O. Box 1151, Jackson, MS 39215-1151 (http://www.msarchivists.org/theprimarysource/).

MISSOURI, KANSAS CITY

The Dusty Shelf. q. $15. Kathi Whitman. Kansas City Area Archivists, c/o Western Historical Manuscripts Collection, University of Missouri-Kansas City, 320 Newcomb Hall, 5100 Rockhill Road, Kansas City, MO 64110-2499 (http://www.umkc.edu/KCAA/DUSTYSHELF/DUSTY.HTM).

MISSOURI, ST. LOUIS

The Acid Free Press. $7.50. Mike Everman. Association of St. Louis Area Archivists, Saint Louis University Archives Pius Library 307, 3650 Lindell Blvd., St. Louis, MO 63108 (http://www.stlarchivists.org/index.php?pr=Home_Page).

NEW ENGLAND

NEA Newsletter. q. $30. New England Archivists, George C. Gordon Library, Worcester Polytechnic Institute, 100 Institute Road, Worcester, MA 01609 (http://www.newenglandarchivists.org/newsletter/index.html).

NEW YORK, NEW YORK

Metropolitan Archivist. s-a. $25. Rachel Chatalbash. Archivists Round Table of Metropolitan New York, Inc., P.O. Box 151, New York, NY 10274-0154 (http://www.nycarchivists.org/pubMetro.html).

NORTH CAROLINA

North Carolina Archivist. s-a. $25. Cat Saleeby McDowell. Society of North Carolina Archivists, P.O. Box 20448, Raleigh, NC 27619 (http://www.ncarchivists.org/pubs/newslet.html).

NORTHWEST

Easy Access. q. $15. John Bolcer. Northwest Archivists, Inc., Univ. of Washington, UW Libraries, Box 352900, Seattle, WA 98195-2900 (http://www.lib.washington.edu/nwa/EasyAccess.html).

OHIO

The Ohio Archivist. [ISSN: 1047-5400] s-a. $15. Beth Kattelman. Society of Ohio Archivists, Jerome Lawrence and Robert E. Lee Theatre Research Institute, The Ohio State University, 1430 Lincoln Tower, 1800 Cannon Dr., Columbus, OH 43210 (http://www.ohioarchivists.org/newsletter.html).

ROCKY MOUNTAINS

The Rocky Mountain Archivist. [ISSN: 1098-7711] q. $15. Ashley Large. Society of Rocky Mountain Archivists, Colorado State University, 1019 Morgan Library, Fort Collins, CO 80523 (http://www.srmarchivists.org/newsletter/default.htm).

SOUTHWEST

The Southwestern Archivist. [ISSN: 1056-1021] q. $10. Katie Salzmann, Kris Toma. Society of Southwest Archivists, P.O. Box 225, Gaithersburg, MD 20884 (http://southwestarchivists.org/HTML/Publications.htm).

TENNESSEE

Tennessee Archivist. q. $20. Jay Richiuso. Society of Tennessee Archivists, Tennessee State Library and Archives, 403 Seventh Ave. N., Nashville, TN 37243 (http://www.tennesseearchivists.org/newsletter.html).

WASHINGTON, SEATTLE

SAA Newsletter. 3/yr. $15. Seattle Area Archivists, P.O. Box 95321, Seattle, WA 98145-2321 (http://www.historylink.org/saa/Newsletters.htm).

Special-Interest Newsletters

Archivists caring for the same types of records, performing the same functions, working in similar specialized institutions, or collecting in the same areas benefit from sharing knowledge and news in special-interest newsletters. Many relevant newsletters are published by sections and roundtables of the Society of American Archivists. These groups meet at the SAA annual conference, and many post meeting notes as well as periodic news, reviews, and outside resources; some also publish fuller articles. The list below offers all the special-interest publications (and a couple of newsletters/web sites or blogs) emanating from SAA groups, with selected others, most of which are available online and many of which, published as pdf documents, require Adobe Reader. Newsletters from the allied fields of preservation and conservation are included; individual repositories' publications are not included. Editors of newsletters and web content change frequently, so readers are advised to contact the group directly for current information or SAA where relevant: Society of American Archivists, 17 North State St., Suite 1425, Chicago, IL 60602-3315 (http://archivists.org).

ACQUISITION AND APPRAISAL

Acquisition and Appraisal Section Newsletter, SAA (http://www.archivists.org/saagroups/acq-app/newsletter.asp).

BUSINESS

Business Archives Section web site, SAA (http://www.archivists.org/saagroups/bas/welcome.asp).

COLLEGE AND UNIVERSITY ARCHIVES

The Academic Archivist. College and University Archives Section, SAA (http://www.archivists.org/saagroups/cnu/index.asp).

CONGRESSIONAL PAPERS

Congressional Papers Roundtable Newsletter, SAA (http://www.archivists.org/saagroups/cpr/newsletters.asp).

DESCRIPTION

Descriptive Notes. Description Section, SAA (http://www.archivists.org/saagroups/descr/index.asp).

EAD (ENCODED ARCHIVAL DESCRIPTION)

EAD Roundtable web site, SAA (http://www.archivists.org/saagroups/ead/).

ELECTRONIC RECORDS

Electronic Records Section Newsletter, SAA (http://www.archivists.org/saagroups/ers/news.asp).

Crossroads: developments in electronic records management and information technology. Committee on Electronic Records and Information Systems (CERIS), NAGARA. 4/yr. $75. Membership benefit; two years past and earlier available online to non-members. National Association of Government Archives and Records Administrators, 90 State St., Suite 1009, Albany, NY 12207 (http://www.nagara.org/displaycommon.cfm?an=1&subarticlenbr=79).

FILM

AMIA Newsletter. [ISSN 1075-6477] q. $50. David Lemieux. Association of Moving Image Archivists, 1313 North Vine St., Hollywood, CA 90028 (http://www.amianet.org/resources/newsletter.php).

GOVERNMENT RECORDS

Official Word: The Government Records Section Newsletter. Government Records Section, SAA (http://www.archivists.org/saagroups/gov/newsletters/index.asp).

NAGARA Clearinghouse: news and reports on government records. 4/yr. $75. Membership benefit. National Association of Government Archives and Records Administrators, 90 State St., Suite 1009, Albany, NY 12207 (http://www.nagara.org/displaycommon.cfm?an=1&subarticlenbr=78).

LESBIAN AND GAY

Archival InQueeries. Lesbian and Gay Archives Roundtable, SAA (http://www.archivists.org/saagroups/lagar/newsletters/index.html).

MANAGEMENT

Archives Management Roundtable Newsletter, SAA (http://www.archivists.org/saagroups/archmgmt/newsletters.asp).

MANUSCRIPTS

Manuscript Repositories Section Newsletter, SAA (http://www.archivists.org/saagroups/mss/newsletter.asp).

The Manuscript Society News. 4/yr. $60. The Manuscript Society, 1960 East Fairmont Dr., Tempe, AZ 85282-2844 (http://manuscript.org/publications.html).

RBMS Newsletter. 2/yr. Association of College and Research Libraries, ALA, 50 E. Huron St., Chicago, IL 60611 (http://www.rbms.info/publications/index.shtml#newsletter).

MULTICULTURAL

Archivists and Archives of Color Roundtable Newsletter, SAA (http://www.archivists.org/saagroups/aac/Activities.htm).

Native American Archives Roundtable Newsletter, SAA (http://www.archivists.org/saagroups/nat-amer/index_files/Page435.htm).

MUSEUMS

Museum Archives Section blog, SAA (http://saa-museum.blogspot.com/).

ORAL HISTORY

Oral History Section Newsletter, SAA (http://www.archivists.org/saagroups/oralhist/newsletters.asp).

PERFORMING ARTS

Performance!. Performing Arts Roundtable, SAA (http://www.archivists.org/saagroups/performart/newsletter/index.html).

PRESERVATION AND CONSERVATION

AIC News. [ISSN: 0887-705X] 6/yr. $105. American Institute for Conservation of Historic and Artistic Works, 1156 15th St., NW, Suite 320, Washington, DC 20005-1714 (http://aic.stanford.edu/library/aicnews_archive.html).

Conservation, The GCI Newsletter. [ISSN: 0898-4808] 3/yr. Free. Jeffrey Levin. The Getty Conservation Institute, 1200 Getty Center Dr., Suite 700, Los Angeles, CA 90049-1684 (http://www.getty.edu/conservation/publications/newsletters/).

Guild of Book Workers Newsletter. [ISSN: 0730-3203] 6/yr. $75. Jody Beenk. Guild of Book Workers, 521 Fifth Ave., New York, NY 10175 (http://palimpsest.stanford.edu/byorg/gbw/news.shtml).

Infinity. Preservation Section, SAA (http://www.archivists.org/saagroups/preserv/text/news.htm).

International Preservation News: a newsletter of the IFLA Core Activity for Preservation and Conservation. 3/yr. Library of Congress, 101 Independence Ave., SE, Washington, DC 20540-4500 (http://www.ifla.org/VI/4/ipn.html).

WAAC Newsletter. [ISSN: 1052-0066] 3/yr. $35. Western Association for Art Conservation, 5905 Wilshire Blvd., Los Angeles, CA 90036 (http://palimpsest.stanford.edu/waac/wn/).

RECORDED SOUND

Recorded Sound Roundtable Newsletter, SAA (http://www.archivists.org/saagroups/recsound/newsletters.asp).

RECORDS MANAGEMENT

The Records Manager. Records Management Roundtable, SAA (http://www.archivists.org/saagroups/recmgmt/newsletters.asp).

REFERENCE

RAO News. Reference, Access, and Outreach Section, SAA (http://www.archivists.org/saagroups/rao/index.asp).

RELIGIOUS

The Archival Spirit. Archivists of Religious Collections Section, SAA (http://www.saa-arcs.org/).

NEARI Newsletter. $10. New England Archivists of Religious Institutions, Boston CSJ Archives, 637 Cambridge St., Brighton, MA 02135-2801 (http://www.csjboston.org/neari.htm).

SCIENCE, TECHNOLOGY, AND HEALTH CARE

Archival Elements. Science, Technology, and Health Care Roundtable, SAA (http://www.archivists.org/saagroups/sthc/publications.html).

VISUAL MATERIALS

VIEWS: The Newsletter of the Visual Materials Section. Visual Materials Section, SAA (http://www.lib.lsu.edu/SAA/views.html).

■ ART

General/Museum Publications

See also Craft section.

Holly Stec Dankert, Head of Readers' Services, The School of the Art Institute of Chicago, John M. Flaxman Library, 37 S. Wabash, Chicago, IL 60603; FAX: 312-899-1851; hdankert@saic.edu.

Nathaniel Feis, Serials-Cataloging Librarian, John M. Flaxman Library, The School of the Art Institute of Chicago, 37 S. Wabash, Chicago, IL 60603; FAX: 312-899-1851; nfeis@saic.edu

Introduction

Although the primary readers of art publications continue to be artists, art dealers, art collectors, museum curators, art historians, and scholars, many of the titles in this section will be of interest to members of the general public, and especially students. The terms *art* and *arts* as used in this section can be defined as two- or three-dimensional visual arts of all media including, but not limited to, paint, pencil, ink, found objects, clay, bronze, other metals, video, film, new media, photography, decorative arts, and performance art. However, as museums, scholars, and the artists themselves continue to redefine what art is, many other types of work are up for discussion in these publications, including sound art. Who can say which of the senses an artist might attempt to reach next?

The "General" subsection below features core titles for art collections or libraries where there is an interest in artistic work and culture, including general-interest magazines, scholarly and professional journals, and instructional magazines for artists. Also, attempts have been made to include journals that focus on art from various parts of the globe and on specific areas in the art world. Bulletins from major museums highlighting their own collections are divided into a separate category following the "General" subsection.

Most titles exist in some online version; but, partially due to the fact that full-color imagery is still largely dependent on print media for the best-quality reproduction, the print journals are still the primary venue for art scholarship and information. Many of these magazine web sites provide only subscription and general information. Core titles with additional web content are indicated usually within the description of the apropos titles; however, due to the ever-changing nature of the web, a title that lacks a noteworthy web site at the time of publication may, in fact, have a significant Internet presence by the time one is consulting this resource. The present contributors hope that the entries in this section will give librarians a reasonable perspective on the sorts of journals that are available concerning art in all its diverse forms.

Basic Periodicals

GENERAL. Ems: *The Artist's Magazine;* Hs: *American Artist, Art in America, The Artist's Magazine;* Ga: *American Artist, Art & Antiques, Art in America, Artforum International, The Artist's Magazine;* Ac: *Art Bulletin, Art History, Art in America, Art Journal, Artforum International, Artnews.*

MUSEUM PUBLICATIONS. The *Metropolitan Museum of Art Bulletin* is the best multipurpose museum publication for all ages. A local museum publication should also be chosen for regional representation.

Basic Abstracts and Indexes

Art Index, ARTbibliographies Modern; the *BHA: Bibliography of the History of Art.*

General

African Arts. See Africa section.

498. *Afterall: a journal of art, context and enquiry.* [ISSN: 1465-4253] 1998. 3x/yr. USD 146 (print & online eds.). Ed(s): Pablo Lafuente, Nuria Enguita Mayo. University of Chicago Press, 1427 E 60th St, Chicago, IL 60637; custserv@press.uchicago.edu; http://www.journals.uchicago.edu. Adv. Refereed. *Indexed:* A07, A51. *Aud.:* Ga, Ac, Sa.

Afterall is a European-based contemporary arts magazine founded by college of art and design professionals. The editorial staff—now including museum, academic press, and higher education oversight—continues to offers "in-depth analysis of artists' work, along with essays that broaden the context in which to understand it." Each issue provides the reader with lengthy, well-researched articles—including notes and bibliographies—about a few selected contemporary artists; and it often includes several different writers discussing the same artists' work from varying perspectives. Adding to the information in the print journal, the web site includes many other articles not included in the print version, among other information.

Afterimage. See Photography section.

499. *American Art.* Formerly (until 1991): *Smithsonian Studies in American Art.* [ISSN: 1073-9300] 1987. 3x/yr. USD 233 (print & online eds.). Ed(s): Emily D. Shapiro. University of Chicago Press, 1427 E 60th St, Chicago, IL 60637; subscriptions@press.uchicago.edu; http://www.journals.uchicago.edu. Illus., adv. Sample. Refereed. Vol. ends: Fall. *Indexed:* A01, A07, A22, A51, AmHI, ArtHuCI, MASUSE, MLA-IB, P02, RILM. *Aud.:* Ga, Ac.

Produced by the Smithsonian American Art Museum, *American Art* encompasses the visual heritage of the United States from its beginning in the colonial era to the present. Interdisciplinary articles range from history to archaeology, anthropology, and cultural studies, all with a focus on visual arts. While the editorial statement indicates that the scope is primarily fine arts, *American Art* includes works of popular culture, public art, film, photography, electronic multimedia, and decorative arts and crafts. Each issue offers a mix of scholarly feature articles and a commentary that focuses on an issue or artist of importance to the Smithsonian or to the American art world at large. Articles are written in accessible language, and the mix of color and black-and-white photographs makes this well suited to public libraries and colleges and universities.

500. *Apollo.* [ISSN: 0003-6536] 1925. m. GBP 52 domestic; GBP 54 in Europe; GBP 56 elsewhere. Ed(s): Oscar Humphries. Apollo Magazine Ltd., 22 Old Queen St, London, SW1H 9HP, United Kingdom; apollo@cisubs.co.uk. Illus., adv. Vol. ends: Dec. Microform: PQC. Reprint: PSC. *Indexed:* A06, A07, A22, A51, API, ArtHuCI, BAS, BRI, CBRI, MLA-IB, RILM. *Bk. rev.:* 6-7, 800-1,000 words. *Aud.:* Ga, Ac.

Tastefully illustrated and international in scope, *Apollo*'s issues target ancient through contemporary art, whatever the market is collecting, with six or seven articles aimed at an educated audience and written by curators, professors, and other art experts. The December issue reviews the year with feature articles on acquisitions, exhibitions, a personality of the year, and more. Each issue includes a diary of museum shows, book reviews, and loads of Paris, London, and New York gallery ads. It is geared toward collectors and curators but is also relevant to academicians. Appropriate for large public libraries and academic libraries that serve art programs.

501. *Archives of Asian Art.* Formerly (until 1967): *Chinese Art Society of America. Archives.* [ISSN: 0066-6637] 1946. a. USD 120. Ed(s): Naomi Noble Richard. University of Hawaii Press, 2840 Kolowalu St, Honolulu, HI 96822; uhpjourn@hawaii.edu; http://www.uhpress.hawaii.edu. Illus., index. Refereed. *Indexed:* A06, A07, A22, BAS, E01, FR, MLA-IB. *Aud.:* Ac, Sa.

Published annually to highlight research and acquisitions of Asian art in North American museums. *Archives of Asian Art* provides a forum for scholars with four to six lengthy articles that are generously illustrated. This publication serves as one of the few English-language resources for serious students and scholars. Highly recommended for research collections in academic libraries.

Art & Antiques. See Antiques section.

502. *Art Asia Pacific: contemporary visual culture.* [ISSN: 1039-3625] 1993. bi-m. USD 72. Ed(s): William Pym, Elaine W Ng. Art Asia Pacific Publishing, Llc., 245 Eighth Ave, Ste 247, New York, NY 10011. Illus., adv. *Indexed:* A07, A51, AmHI. *Aud.:* Ac, Sa.

Relaunched in 2003, *Art Asia Pacific* covers leading figures and trends in Asian contemporary art. Several feature-length articles cover artists from Korea, China, Japan, Taiwan, Thailand, and Pacific islands in this glossy and minimally stylized magazine. Full-color imagery predominates in both features and international gallery ads. Regular departments showcase happenings ("Events," "State of the Arts," "News," "Profile," "Hot Spots," "One-on-One") and exhibition reviews in Asia and major U.S. cities. Subscriber information and tables of contents for the current and the previous issue are available online. Written in straightforward language to appeal to a wide audience, *Art Asia Pacific* is recommended for academic and large public libraries. URL: http://artasiapacific.com/

503. *The Art Bulletin.* Former titles (until 1919): *College Art Association of America. Bulletin (Print);* (until 1917): *College Art Association. Bulletin (Print).* [ISSN: 0004-3079] 1913. q. Free to members. Ed(s): Richard J Powell. College Art Association, 275 Seventh Ave, 18th Fl, New York, NY 10001; nyoffice@collegeart.org; http://www.collegeart.org. Illus., index, adv. Refereed. Vol. ends: No. 4. Microform: IDC; PQC. *Indexed:* A01, A06, A07, A22, A51, ABS&EES, API, AmHI, ArtHuCI, BAS, BRI, BrArAb, CBRI, MASUSE, MLA-IB, NumL, P02, RILM. *Bk. rev.:* Numerous, essay length. *Aud.:* Ac.

Published quarterly by the College Art Association (CAA), *The Art Bulletin* serves as a forum for leading scholarship and debate in contemporary art-historical practice. Research articles cover all periods, many in Western art, and are usually accompanied by some color but mostly black-and-white photos. Abstracts of each article are provided in the table of contents. See CAA's online portal for table of contents archives back to 1996, plus job listings in the arts and other benefits to members. *The Art Bulletin* is considered essential for all research collections and academic libraries. URL: www.collegeart.org

Art Education. See Education/Specific Subjects and Teaching Methods/ The Arts section.

504. *Art History.* [ISSN: 0141-6790] 1978. 5x/yr. GBP 565. Ed(s): Genevieve Warwick. Wiley-Blackwell Publishing Ltd., The Atrium, Southern Gate, Chichester, PO19 8SQ, United Kingdom; customer@wiley.com; http://www.wiley.com/. Illus., index, adv. Sample. Refereed. Vol. ends: Dec. Microform: PQC. Reprint: PSC. *Indexed:* A01, A07, A22, A51, API, AmHI, ArtHuCI, BAS, BRI, E01, MLA-IB, P02, RILM. *Bk. rev.:* 9-11, essay length. *Aud.:* Ac.

The international Association of Art Historians publishes *Art History* to provide research in the historical and theoretical aspects of traditional visual arts—primarily two-dimensional works on paper and canvas, with occasional forays into three-dimensional art—from both Western and Eastern hemispheres. Articles that explore the arts in their interdisciplinary context are encouraged. Targeted to art and design professionals and others concerned with the advancement of the history of art, *Art History* seeks to consider related cultural, economic, and social issues as well. Illustrations are minimal and appropriate to the theses posited in the four papers that are presented in each issue. Librarians will especially appreciate the extensive scholarly book reviews written by experts in the field. Recommended for all academic libraries.

505. *Art in America.* Former titles (until 1939): *Art in America and Elsewhere;* (until 1921): *Art in America.* [ISSN: 0004-3214] 1913. m. USD 29.95 domestic; USD 79.95 Canada; USD 95 elsewhere. Ed(s): David Ebony. Brant Publications, Inc., 575 Broadway, 5th Fl, New York, NY 10012. Illus., adv. Microform: PQC. *Indexed:* A01, A06, A07, A22, A51, ABS&EES, AmHI, ArtHuCI, BRI, CBRI, Chicano, F01, MASUSE, MLA-IB, P02, RILM. *Bk. rev.:* 2-3, 1,000 words. *Aud.:* Ga, Ac.

A standard in the field, *Art in America* strives to bring renowned artists, exhibitions, and performances to the American art world. Brief articles cover both U.S. and international news items, issues, commentary, exhibitions, and occasional regional pieces. A handful of feature articles focus primarily on contemporary artists, while including one on past masters of the nineteenth and twentieth centuries. Written for an educated audience of art collectors, dealers, and curators, *Art in America* nevertheless is suitable for large public and academic libraries whose users will find the many gallery and exhibition advertisements and show listings useful.

506. *Art India: the art news magazine of India.* [ISSN: 0972-2947] 1996. q. INR 520 domestic; USD 34 foreign; GBP 19 foreign. Art India Publishing Co. Pvt. Ltd., Jindal Mansion, 5-A Dr G Deshmukh Marg, Mumbai, 400 026, India. Adv. *Indexed:* A51. *Bk. rev.:* Number and length vary. *Aud.:* Ac, Sa.

For over a decade, *Art India* has been showcasing the contemporary Indian art world and promoting a critical platform for exploring new media art, painting, sculpture, photography, and architecture. There is substantial reporting in English that covers cultural and societal issues in the visual arts, profiles and interviews of current visual artists, many reviews of Indian artists (local and international), and book reviews and gallery listings. Much current content and access to archives are available online. Appropriate for museum, academic, and public libraries that serve visual artists and collectors. URL: www.artindiamag.com

507. *Art Journal.* Formerly (until 1960): *College Art Journal;* Which superseded (in 1941): *Parnassus.* [ISSN: 0004-3249] 1941. q. Free to members. Ed(s): Katy Siegel. College Art Association, 275 Seventh Ave, 18th Fl, New York, NY 10001; nyoffice@collegeart.org; http://www.collegeart.org. Illus., adv. Refereed. Microform: PQC. *Indexed:* A&ATA, A01, A06, A07, A22, A51, ABS&EES, API, AmHI, ArtHuCI, BAS, BRI, CBRI, MASUSE, MLA-IB, P02. *Bk. rev.:* 6, length varies. *Aud.:* Ac.

Art Journal is an academic periodical published by the College Art Association. The editorial board seeks to create a dialogue among educators teaching art, design, criticism and theory, art history, and visual culture. Articles are of a scholarly nature and focus on cultural change reflected in the visual arts, selecting "vital, intellectually compelling, and visually engaging" subjects of the twentieth and twenty-first centuries. Contemporary works and artists are featured, with black-and-white and color illustrations. Highly recommended for all academic libraries.

508. *Art Monthly.* [ISSN: 0142-6702] 1976. 10x/yr. GBP 55 (Individuals, GBP 46; GBP 4.80 per issue domestic). Ed(s): Patricia Bickers. Britannia Art Publications Ltd., 28 Charing Cross Rd, London, WC2H 0DB, United Kingdom. Adv. Sample. *Indexed:* A01, A07, A22, A51, AmHI, BRI. *Bk. rev.:* 1-3, 1,000 words. *Aud.:* Ga, Ac.

This journal is primarily concerned with the contemporary art world as it manifests itself in the United Kingdom. Each issue of *Art Monthly* includes interviews with, and profiles of, leading figures in the art world, as well as up-and-coming artists and critics' explorations of germane trends in art and the art world. It also contains art news, book reviews, reports from other parts of the globe, and a lengthy section of exhibition listings and reviews from throughout the United Kingdom.

509. *Art New England: a resource for the visual arts.* [ISSN: 0274-7073] 1979. bi-m. USD 28 domestic; USD 33 Canada; USD 40 elsewhere. Ed(s): Debbie Hagan. Art New England, Inc., 332 Congress St, Ste 2, Boston, MA 02210; production@artnewengland.com. Illus., adv. Vol. ends: Dec. *Indexed:* A07. *Aud.:* Ga, Ac.

This tabloid-format magazine offers regional art news for the New England area, focusing on artists, exhibitions, performances, and installations from that region. Also useful to local artists are the guides to schools and artists' directories found in each issue, plus advertising for classes, workshops, degrees, and programs in the area. The journal web site offers additional content in blogs and some archived content. Recommended for public and academic libraries that serve studio arts programs in the Northeast. URL: http://artnewengland.com/

510. *The Art Newspaper (International Edition).* Incorporated (1988-1989): *Journal of Art.* [ISSN: 0960-6556] 1990. 11x/yr. EUR 110 in Europe; EUR 130 elsewhere. Umberto Allemandi & C., Via Mancini 8, Turin, 10131, Italy; http://www.allemandi.com. Adv. Sample. Circ: 14000 Paid. *Indexed:* A07, A22, A51. *Aud.:* Ga, Ac, Sa.

The Art Newspaper is a true newspaper in its format and content. Its focus is commentary and news of the international art world. It is divided into two sections. The first section is devoted to what's going on in private, national, and international museums; legislation/regulation in the arts; financial crises and funding issues; the effects of world events on art collections; and scandals from all areas. Columnists and op/ed writers turn a critical eye on governments around the world and the effects that their policies have on the arts; plus, there are other regular commentaries. The second section lists exhibitions around the globe, divided into New York, the rest of the United States, London, the rest of the United Kingdom, France, Germany, and the rest of the world. There is also an auction listing. The web site offers some free content and is worth bookmarking. An excellent source for keeping up with world art news and people. Highly recommended for all libraries.

511. *Art Nexus (Spanish Edition).* Formerly (until 1991): *Arte en Colombia Internacional.* [ISSN: 0121-5639] 1976. q. USD 32. Ed(s): Celia Sredni de Birbragher. Arte en Colombia Ltda., Apartado Aereo 90193, Bogota, Colombia; info@artnexus.com. Illus., adv. Refereed. Circ: 16000. *Indexed:* A22, RILM. *Bk. rev.:* 1-3, 1,000 words. *Aud.:* Ga, Ac, Sa.

Art Nexus offers an opportunity to explore many aspects of Latin American visual arts. Issues include interviews, profiles, discussion, and criticism that focuses on individual artists or groups of artists. These inspections of art at the individual level are augmented by features on international festivals, fairs and conferences, and reviews and discussions of exhibitions by Latin American artists or concentrating on Latin American art held all over the world. There are also book and catalogue reviews as well as an extensive gallery guide. Online, the reader is provided with further information about news, exhibitions, and events throughout the Latin American art world, visual galleries, and an astounding database of contemporary Latin American artists, along with other relevant information. URL: www.artnexus.com

512. *Art Now Gallery Guide: Collector's Edition.* Former titles: *Art Now Gallery Guide: International Edition; Art Now Gallery Guide: National Edition; Art Now: U S A - National Art Museum and Gallery Guide.* 1982. 10x/yr. USD 45 domestic; USD 52 foreign. Ed(s): Patricia Yannotta. Louise Blouin Media, 601 West 26th St, Ste 410, New York, NY 10001. Illus., adv. Circ: 6000. *Aud.:* Ga, Ac, Sa.

Art Now Gallery Guide informs readers about exhibitions at art galleries and museums across the United States, serving as a current-awareness directory in the contemporary art world. Divided into regional publications—New York/New England/Mid-Atlantic, Southeast, Midwest, and West editions—this pocket-size ten-issue reference book offers events, highlights, and listings of private art dealers and services in each region. Area maps provide a special feature in these regional editions. A great value for the price, this title is useful for all types of libraries.

513. *Art Papers Magazine.* Formerly (until 1999): *Art Papers;* Which was formed by the merger of (1977-1980): *Contemporary Art - Southeast;* (1980-1981): *Atlanta Art Papers;* Which was formerly (until 1980): *Atlanta Art Workers Coalition Newspaper;* (until 1978): *A A W C Ltd. Newsletter.* [ISSN: 1524-9581] 1981. bi-m. USD 45 in Canada & Mexico (Members, USD 30; Non-members, USD 35). Ed(s): Sylvie Fortin. Art Papers, Inc., PO Box 5748, Atlanta, GA 31107; creative@artpapers.org. Illus., adv. Vol. ends: Nov/Dec. Microform: PQC. *Indexed:* A07, A22, A51, ABS&EES. *Bk. rev.:* 1, 1,000 words. *Aud.:* Ga, Ac, Sa.

Art Papers defines itself as "the critical voice covering more regions of the U.S." and is dedicated to providing advocacy and a forum for the examination and expression of diverse and independent perspectives on the role of art. Controversial topics and criticism cover cultural, social, and philosophical issues related to all visual arts, including photography, mixed media, and film. The excellent web site, plus departments that feature studio visits, interviews, collecting and art resources, regional artists' gallery shows, and reviews make this resource valuable for artists and for all those who are interested in contemporary art. Appropriate for public, college, and university libraries. URL: www.artpapers.org

514. *Art Press: la revue de l'art contemporain.* [ISSN: 0245-5676] 1972. m. Individuals, EUR 6.50. Ed(s): Catherine Millet. ArtPublications, 8 rue Francois Villon, Paris, 75015, France. *Indexed:* A07, A22, A51. *Bk. rev.:* Number and length vary. *Aud.:* Ac, Sa.

Published bilingually, with French and English integrated side by side, this international monthly explores contemporary visual arts, literature, video, film, performance, electronic arts, music, theater, new media—a broad array of global cultural phenomena. Feature-length articles are sometimes thematic, covering important events, philosophies, and emerging trends in contemporary art and society. Editorials, interviews (with artists, curators, dealers), book and exhibition reviews, and thematic columns (art market, literature) complete each issue. Recommended for research collections in the arts.

515. *Art Review (London).* Former titles (until 1993): *Arts Review;* (until 1961): *Art News & Review.* [ISSN: 1745-9303] 1949. m. GBP 36 domestic; EUR 50 in Europe; USD 60 United States includes Canada. Art Review Ltd., 1 Sekforde St, London, EC1R 0BE, United Kingdom; info@art-review.co.uk. Illus., index, adv. Microform: PQC. *Indexed:* A07, A22, A51. *Bk. rev.:* Number and length vary. *Aud.:* Ga, Ac.

A consumer publication that reports on the current international contemporary art scene, *Art Review* features five articles on visual arts, photography, design, or the artists themselves. The United Kingdom is primarily covered, but there are also segments devoted to international art, style, objects, collectors, and critics. Regional reviews and exhibition guides attempt a more inclusive overview of contemporary art. The magazine's glitzy, insider presentation of art news will appeal to all audiences. Useful for research collections that are trying to provide comprehensive coverage of the art world.

516. *Art Therapy.* Supersedes in part: *American Journal of Art Therapy.* [ISSN: 0742-1656] 1983. q. GBP 191 (print & online eds.). Ed(s): Lynn Kaplan. American Art Therapy Association, Inc., 225 N Fairfax St, Alexandria, VA 22314; info@arttherapy.org; http://www.americanarttherapyassociation.org/. Adv. Refereed. Reprint: PSC. *Indexed:* A22, A51, ERIC, PsycInfo. *Bk. rev.:* 3-5, 1,000 words. *Aud.:* Ac, Sa.

This is the official journal of the American Art Therapy Association, and its stated purpose is to "advance the understanding of how visual art functions in the treatment, education, development, and enrichment of people." Each issue contains three articles written by art therapy professionals; viewpoints and commentary on issues of concern to the profession; and book reviews and news briefs in the field. One of the few scholarly publications devoted exclusively to this profession, *Art Therapy* is appropriate for academic or special libraries.

517. *Artes de Mexico.* [ISSN: 0300-4953] 1953. q. MXN 900 domestic; USD 90 foreign. Ed(s): Ana Maria Perez Rocha. Artes de Mexico y del Mundo S.A., Plaza Rio de Janeiro 52, Col Roma, Mexico City, 06700, Mexico; artesdemexico@artesdemexico.com; http://www.artesdemexico.com/. Illus., adv. Refereed. Circ: 20000 Paid. *Indexed:* A06, A07, A51, RILM. *Aud.:* Ac, Sa.

Artes de Mexico is reminiscent of coffee-table art books with its large format and lavishly illustrated blend of vibrantly photographed arts, crafts, and cultural phenomena of Mexico. Each thematic issue offers divergent viewpoints on a single subject, as seen most recently in "Art & Poetry of the Circus" and "The Jesuits & Science." This journal usually contains at least some feature-length articles, and the variety and length of essays, interviews, or poetry make each issue distinctive. All are written in Spanish with English translations at the back of the issue. Recommended for libraries with strong art and/or multicultural collections.

518. *Artforum International.* Formerly (until 1982): *Artforum.* [ISSN: 1086-7058] 1962. 10x/yr. USD 46 domestic; USD 65 Canada; USD 132 elsewhere. Ed(s): Tim Griffin. Artforum International Magazine, Inc., 350 Seventh Ave, New York, NY 10001; generalinfo@artforum.com; http://www.artforum.com. Illus., adv. Vol. ends: Sep/Jun. Microform: PQC. *Indexed:* A01, A06, A07, A22, A51, ABS&EES, AmHI, ArtHuCI, BAS, BRI, F01, MLA-IB, P02, RILM. *Bk. rev.:* 1, length varies. *Aud.:* Ga, Ac.

The primary magazine for reporting on international contemporary art, *ArtForum* is accessible to a wide audience. Critical articles on all media—sculpture, painting, installation, architecture, video and music art, mixed media, and popular culture—frequently include artist interviews. Glossy ads proliferate, featuring the latest shows at galleries around the world. Regular reviews cover individual artists, gallery exhibits, film, music, books, top-ten lists, and other art world events. Included three times a year are previews of 50 upcoming exhibitions. A calendar of international art events is provided in every issue. The magazine's web site offers worthwhile extras: an international museum finder, blogs, festivals/biennials, free art resources, art zines, news briefs, etc. Essential for all art libraries, collectors, and curators of contemporary art. Highly recommended for all academic and large public libraries. URL: www.artforum.com

519. *The Artist: inspiration, instruction & practical ideas for all artists.* Incorporates (1966-1986): *Art and Artists.* [ISSN: 0004-3877] 1931. m. GBP 32.50 domestic; USD 45 foreign. The Artists' Publishing Company Limited, Caxton House, 63-65 High St, Tenterden, TN30 6BD, United Kingdom. Illus., index, adv. Sample. *Indexed:* A06, A07, A22. *Bk. rev.:* Number and length vary. *Aud.:* Ga, Ac.

The British equivalent to *American Artist, The Artist* provides many instructional articles for professional and amateur artists. A dozen articles offer practical advice on technique, materials, and other helpful technical information, and are illustrated with lots of easy-to-follow color illustrations. The focus is generally representational art, landscapes, and figurative and still-life portrayals. Exhibition reviews, profiles of contemporary artists, interviews, and other current news in the United Kingdom make up the rest of the contents. Recommended for public libraries and schools with fine arts programs.

520. *The Artist's Magazine.* [ISSN: 0741-3351] 1984. 10x/yr. USD 22.96. Ed(s): Maureen Bloomfield. F + W Media Inc., 10151 Carver Rd, Ste 200, Blue Ash, OH 45242; contact_us@fwmedia.com; http://www.fwmedia.com/. Illus., adv. Circ: 76590 Paid. *Indexed:* A22, A51, ABIn, IHTDI. *Bk. rev.:* 50, 200 words. *Aud.:* Hs, Ga.

The Artist's Magazine is a monthly publication designed for artists of all levels of accomplishment from beginner to professional. Most of the articles instruct and present various working methods, materials, tools, and techniques. Marketing information is provided, plus announcements of study opportunities and art competitions. The accompanying web site is most useful to artists, providing business tips, technical questions and answers, clinics, and much more. This is an educational and instructive publication that would be most useful for school art programs or public libraries. URL: www.artistsmagazine.com

521. *Artlink: a contemporary art magazine in Australia.* [ISSN: 0727-1239] 1981. q. AUD 90 (Individuals, AUD 55; AUD 14 per issue domestic). Ed(s): Stephanie Radok. Artlink Australia, Station Arcade, PO Box 8141, Adelaide, SA 5000, Australia. Illus., adv. Refereed. *Indexed:* A51. *Aud.:* Ac, Sa.

An Australian contemporary art magazine, *Artlink* has a scope that includes diverse visual-culture expression by the artists of Australia and the Asia–Pacific region. Articles on new media, Internet art, video, electronic arts, performance pieces, photography, mixed media, and outsider and aboriginal art are presented. Each richly illustrated issue offers a wide range of viewpoints, examining broad themes such as "Beauty and Terror" that surveys current indigenous artists, or "Diaspora," which details the shifting cultures of Australia and diasporic artists. Also included are a dozen or more short articles; "Artrave," news for the region; and exhibition reviews. Recommended for libraries where there is an interest in contemporary art.

522. *Artnews.* Former titles (until 1923): *American Art News;* (until 1904): *Hyde's Weekly Art News.* [ISSN: 0004-3273] 1902. 11x/yr. USD 39.95 domestic; USD 59.95 Canada; USD 99.95 elsewhere. Ed(s): Robin Cembalest, Milton Esterow. Artnews LLC, 48 W 38th St, New York, NY 10018; http://www.artnews.com. Illus., adv. Circ: 81585 Paid. Vol. ends: Dec. Microform: MIM; PQC. *Indexed:* A&ATA, A01, A06, A07, A22, A51, ABS&EES, AmHI, ArtHuCI, BRI, CBRI, F01, IIPA, MASUSE, MLA-IB, P02, RILM. *Bk. rev.:* 3-4, 300-500 words. *Aud.:* Hs, Ga, Ac.

As the name implies, *ARTnews* is a primary news source for keeping current with American and international contemporary art. Many feature-length articles cover new genres, plus cover pieces for collectors and those who maintain collections. Regular departments explore personalities, national and international art news, new talent, the art market, book reviews, exhibition and competition listings, classifieds, and a smattering of regional, national, and international exhibition reviews. The web site mirrors the print edition and offers some free content, along with tables of content to back issues since 1996. A biweekly report on the art market, *ARTnewsletter* can be delivered via e-mail and is targeted toward art professionals and serious collectors who wish to follow art treads globally. This standard art magazine is highly recommended for all libraries. URL: www.artnews.com

523. *Beaux Arts Magazine.* [ISSN: 0757-2271] 1983. m. EUR 49. Beaux Arts Magazine, 101 Bd Murat, Paris, 75016, France; courrier@beauxartsmagazine.com; http://www.beauxartsmagazine.com/. Illus., index, adv. Sample. Circ: 49000. *Indexed:* A07, A22, A51, RILM. *Bk. rev.:* Number and length vary. *Aud.:* Ga.

Published in France, *Beaux Arts Magazine* is a beautifully illustrated periodical aimed at the art collector. Articles are written for a general audience, and the scope covers all of Europe. Included are auction news and sales, exhibition announcements, museum events, interviews, a calendar of events, book reviews, and occasional performance and movie reviews. Written in French, the American edition includes abstracts of the articles in English, which increases the utility of this attractive publication. Recommended for libraries with extensive art holdings.

524. *Bidoun: a quarterly forum for middle eastern talent.* [ISSN: 1551-4048] 2004. q. USD 42 domestic; USD 48 Canada; USD 58 in Europe. Ed(s): Lisa Farjam. Bidoun, Inc, 47 Orchard St, New York, NY 10002; subs@bidoun.com. Illus. *Bk. rev.:* 1-5, 1,000+ words. *Aud.:* Ga, Ac, Sa.

This journal is a forum for spreading information and creating a dialogue about contemporary arts and culture in the Middle East and its diaspora. Its cross-cultural and multidisciplinary approach allows it to cover any and all aspects of culture and art created by Middle Easterners, those of Middle Eastern descent, and/or those who relate to the Middle East as a region or as a concept. Issues are composed of artist interviews and profiles, and articles about specific arts, cultural ideas, or events. Subjects include art, music, literature, and architecture, among others. The web site includes selected full-text articles and general information. Recommended for public and academic libraries, especially those with an interest in the arts and/or Middle Eastern or cross-cultural studies. URL: www.bidoun.com

525. *Burlington Magazine.* Formerly (until 1948): *Burlington Magazine for Connoisseurs.* [ISSN: 0007-6287] 1903. m. GBP 862 (print & online eds.) Individuals, GBP 238 (print & online eds.). Ed(s): Richard Shone. Burlington Magazine Publications Ltd., 14-16 Dukes Rd, London, WC1H 9SZ, United Kingdom; burlington@burlington.org.uk. Illus., adv. Vol. ends: Dec. Microform: IDC. Reprint: PSC. *Indexed:* A&ATA, A06, A07, A22, A51, API, ArtHuCI, BAS, BEL&L, BRI, BrArAb, CBRI, MLA-IB, RILM. *Bk. rev.:* 10-15, 1,000 words. *Aud.:* Ac.

Begun in 1903 to lavishly illustrate, attribute, discover, and document western European art for connoisseurs, *Burlington Magazine* has long maintained a well-respected reputation among art historians and other scholars. Its aim and scope today cover all historical periods from prehistoric art to modern Western art, including works and artists outside of Europe. Its design is elegant and gracious, and it has lots of full-color images. Articles by experts in the field focus on new developments, historical documents, conservation practices, and the history of collecting art. Book reviews, shorter notices, obituaries, exhibition information, and a calendar of events round out this important journal. Recommended for all research collections in academic and special libraries.

526. *Canadian Art.* Formed by the merger of (1967-1984): *Arts Canada;* Which was formerly (until 1967): *Canadian Art;* (until 1943): *Maritime Art;* (1974-1984): *Artsmagazine;* Which was formerly (until 1974): *Art;* (until 1969): *Society of Canadian Artists. Journal.* [ISSN: 0825-3854] 1984. q. CAD 24 domestic; CAD 34 United States; CAD 42 elsewhere. Ed(s): Richard Rhodes. Canadian Art Foundation, 215 Spadina Ave, Ste 320, Toronto, ON M5T 2C7, Canada. Illus., adv. Vol. ends: Winter. Microform: MML. *Indexed:* A06, A07, A51, BRI, C37, CBCARef. *Bk. rev.:* 1-3, 500 words. *Aud.:* Ga, Ac, Sa.

Published in part by the Canadian government, Canada Council, and the Ontario Arts Council, *Canadian Art* is a quarterly that is devoted to the visual arts of that country. It is beautifully designed, with lots of full-color images, and the subject matter covers painting, sculpture, illustration, design, architecture, photography, and film. Articles are not limited to any particular time period; however, profiles of individual contemporary artists with reproductions of their works or group shows predominate, making this an invaluable resource for contemporary Canadian art. The magazine's web site is also worth bookmarking. This publication is aimed toward a general audience that includes art collectors and regular guests of art galleries. URL: www.canadianart.ca

527. *Contemporary.* Incorporates (1994-2002): *World Art;* Former titles (until 2002): *Contemporary Visual Arts;* (until 1997): *Contemporary Art;* (until 1992): *Green Book.* [ISSN: 1475-9853] 1979. m. GBP 69

(Individuals, GBP 59). Contemporary Magazine, Studio 56, 4 Montpelier St, Knightsbridge, London, SW7 1EE, United Kingdom; http://www.contemporary-magazine.com. Illus., adv. *Indexed:* A22, A51. *Bk. rev.:* 1-2, 1,000 words. *Aud.:* Ac, Sa.

Boasting a readership of 75,000, the international art journal *Contemporary* has contributors from the United Kingdom, North America, Africa, New Zealand, and Australia. Bimonthly issues are devoted to special themes. These special issues, titled *Contemporary 21,* offer critical analysis of broad categories, e.g., art and architecture, performance, digital art, and photography, including profiles of 21 artists in that field. The remaining issues throughout the year present regular observations on "visual arts, news, books, trivia, architecture, houses, design, fashion, film, music, new media, photography, dance, [and] sport," offering a very wide range of every media utilized by visual artists worldwide. Important for libraries with collections that address contemporary art.

Critical Inquiry. See Cultural Studies section.

528. Flash Art International. [ISSN: 0394-1493] 1979. bi-m. Ed(s): Helena Kontova, Giancarlo Politi. Giancarlo Politi Editore, Via Carlo Farini 68, Milan, 20159, Italy; http://www.flashartonline.it. Illus., adv. *Indexed:* A06, A07, A22, A51. *Bk. rev.:* 2-3, 600-900 words. *Aud.:* Ga, Ac.

This self-proclaimed world's leading art magazine is filled with glossy ads from galleries as widely disparate as McLean, Virginia, and Milan to the Netherlands and New York. *Flash Art* has long used its journalistic tone to bring the North American and European contemporary art world into its readership, and it continues as a strong voice in current news and criticism in the visual arts. Each issue contains news updates, gallery reviews, interviews, and feature articles on two- and three-dimensional and performance art, video, and mixed media works and their creators. Recommended as an important basic international source for all libraries with an interest in art and art criticism.

529. Frieze: contemporary art and culture. [ISSN: 0962-0672] 1991. 8x/yr. GBP 35 domestic; GBP 41 foreign; GBP 60 combined subscription (print & online eds.). Ed(s): Rosalind Furness, Jennifer Higgie. Frieze Publishing Ltd., 1 Montclare St, London, E2 7EU, United Kingdom; http://www.frieze.com/. Adv. Sample. Circ: 26520. *Indexed:* A22, A51. *Bk. rev.:* 3-4, 500-1,000 words. *Aud.:* Ac, Sa.

London-based *Frieze* is the self-proclaimed "leading contemporary art and culture publication" in Europe. This claim is supported not only by a half-dozen feature articles on the current European art scene and numerous gallery/exhibition reviews, but also by extensive coverage of film, performance, music, and all visual arts. The editors give exposure to established but also very new artists in reviews, feature articles, and hundreds of full-color gallery ads in each packed issue. *Frieze* sponsors the annual Frieze Art Fair in London every October, showcasing 150 galleries and their artists. The web site offers full-text magazine content, art world news, and Frieze Art Fair updates. Recommended for all libraries that wish to provide access to international contemporary art. URL: www.frieze.com

530. I F A R Journal. Formerly (until 1998): *I F A R Reports;* Which was formed by the merger of (1981-1985): *Art Research News;* (1980-1985): *Stolen Art Alert;* Which was formerly (until 1980): *Art Theft Archive Newsletter.* [ISSN: 1098-1195] 1984. q. Free to members; Non-members, USD 75. Ed(s): Sharon Flescher, Kathleen Ferguson. International Foundation for Art Research, Inc., 500 Fifth Ave, New York, NY 10110; http://www.ifar.org. Illus., index, adv. *Indexed:* A07, A51. *Aud.:* Sa.

IFAR Journal, the mouthpiece of the International Foundation for Art Research (IFAR), informs the art community about recent art theft, authentication, fraud, and art laws through feature articles. From its founding, IFAR has been a resource for scholarship in authentication research, maintaining a list of stolen art plus authenticating problematic works of art and providing a clearinghouse for legal issues. With its recent shift away from maintaining a stolen-art database (now the purview of the Art Loss Register), IFAR is able to publish new depths of scholarship in authentication research. Featured in each issue are four or five well-researched articles, plus brief discussions of art and the law, updates, and news items. Selections from the Art Loss Register, consisting of art theft reports and recent items stolen, plus a recovery list, are printed in each

issue. As an advocate for the entire art community, *IFAR Journal* provides important research about provenance and attribution not found in other art journals. Appropriate for research and municipal libraries.

Journal of Aesthetic Education. See Cultural Studies section.

Journal of Aesthetics and Art Criticism. See Cultural Studies section.

531. The Journal of Canadian Art History. [ISSN: 0315-4297] 1974. s-a. CAD 35 (Individuals, CAD 28). Ed(s): Sandra Paikowsky. Journal of Canadian Art History, Concordia University, 1455 boul. de Maisonneuve ouest, Montreal, PQ H3G 1M8, Canada. Illus., index, adv. Refereed. Vol. ends: No. 2. Microform: MML. *Indexed:* A06, A07, BRI, C37, CBCARef, MLA-IB, PdeR. *Bk. rev.:* 4-5, lengthy. *Aud.:* Ac, Sa.

The national art history journal in Canada, JCAH is a scholarly periodical devoted to the research of Canadian art, architecture, decorative arts, and photography. It includes all historical and contemporary periods, with articles that are sparingly illustrated in black-and-white. Both English- and French-language submissions are accepted, and three- or four-page summaries are translated into the other appropriate language. Also included on a regular basis are bibliographies, such as of individual artists and architects; theses and dissertations in Canadian art and architecture; and book reviews and reviews of exhibition catalogues specific to Canadian art. Appropriate for research collections in academic libraries.

532. Journal of Pre-Raphaelite Studies. Former titles (until 1992): *Journal of Pre-Raphaelite and Aesthetic Studies;* (until 1987): *Journal of Pre-Raphaelite Studies;* (until 1980): *Pre-Raphaelite Review.* [ISSN: 1060-149X] 1977. s-a. CAD 24; GBP 17. Ed(s): David Latham. Journal of Pre-Raphaelite Studies, c/o David Latham, 208 Stong College, York University, Toronto, ON M3J 1P3, Canada. Illus. Sample. Refereed. *Indexed:* A07, AmHI, ArtHuCI, BRI, C37, MLA-IB, RILM. *Aud.:* Ac.

Founded to create a forum for the study of Pre-Raphaelite, Aesthetic, and Decadent art, culture, and literature of the nineteenth century, JPRS publishes research on such renowned artists as Dante Gabriel Rosetti, Christina Rosetti, Edward Burne-Jones, William Morris, and the cult of Pre-Raphaelites worldwide and its interaction with Victorian literary figures (e.g., Edith Wharton, Oscar Wilde) and Victorian culture and mores. A dozen papers, sparsely illustrated with black-and-white images, are printed in this small-scale semi-annual journal. Articles include historical examinations and interdisciplinary studies on the creation of sexual knowledge, Victorian masculinities, and consumerism and industrial art. Although targeting a fairly narrow topic, JPRS is important for academic libraries with studies in nineteenth-century literary and art history programs.

533. Journal of the Warburg and Courtauld Institutes. Formerly (until 1940): *Warburg Institute. Journal.* [ISSN: 0075-4390] 1937. a. GBP 110. Ed(s): Paul Crossley, Elizabeth McGrath. Warburg Institute, University of London, Woburn Sq, London, WC1H 0AB, United Kingdom; warburg.books@sas.ac.uk; http://warburg.sas.ac.uk/home/. Illus., index. Refereed. Reprint: PSC. *Indexed:* A06, A07, A22, AmHI, ArtHuCI, BEL&L, CCMJ, FR, MLA-IB, MSN, MathR, RILM. *Aud.:* Ac.

Published in a single volume, JWCI provides an outlet for scholarly research in art history and classical studies, especially as reflected in European art and letters. It is the scholarly journal for the University of London, School of Advanced Study, The Warburg Institute, and the University of London's Courtauld Institute of Art. Although the journal is plagued by a lagging publication cycle, the half-dozen lengthy scholarly articles in each edition are important not only to art historians but to scholars in religion, science, literature, sociology, philosophy, and anthropology. Recommended for all academic libraries that support significant art history programs and other special research collections.

534. Journal of Visual Culture. [ISSN: 1470-4129] 2002. 3x/yr. USD 691. Ed(s): Marquard Smith. Sage Publications Ltd., 1 Oliver's Yard, 55 City Rd, London, EC1Y 1SP, United Kingdom; info@sagepub.co.uk; http://www.uk.sagepub.com. Sample. Refereed. Reprint: PSC. *Indexed:* A01, A07, A22, A47, A51, ArtHuCI, E01, F01, IBSS, MLA-IB. *Bk. rev.:* Number and length vary. *Aud.:* Ac, Sa.

This is an international and interdisciplinary scholarly journal, with editors from the United Kingdom, the United States, and France. The *Journal of Visual Culture* "promotes research, scholarship[,] and critical engagement with visual cultures." Authored by professors, scholars, and critics in the humanities and social sciences, six to eight thought-provoking articles that are featured in each issue examine ideas, concepts, metaphors, and philosophies in international visual and cultural practices. A variety of methodologies broaden the debate in topics that include blackness and whiteness, appearances, surfaces, voyeurism, the public sphere, image, imagination, censorship, copy, reproduction, aesthetics, mimesis, tropes, spectacle, simulation, and many other critical theories studied in academe today. Appropriate for academic libraries.

535. *Koreana: Korean art and culture.* [ISSN: 1016-0744] 1987. q. KRW 18000 domestic; USD 33 in Japan, Hong Kong, Taiwan & China; USD 37 elsewhere. Korea Foundation, 10th Fl, Diplomatic Center Bldg, 2558 Nambusunhwanno, Seocho-gu, PO Box 227, Seoul, 137-863, Korea, Republic of; http://www.kf.or.kr/. Adv. Circ: 9000. *Indexed:* A07, A51, AmHI, BAS, MLA-IB, RILM. *Aud.:* Ga, Ac, Sa.

This beautifully illustrated quarterly magazine in English is devoted to traditional and contemporary Korean art and culture. Four to six feature articles typically revolve around a theme such as weddings, traditional and contemporary; Korean perceptions of life and death; or national treasures such as the Gyujanggak archives. Regular departments include interviews with architects and artists, cuisine and arts of living, discovering Korea, a featured masterpiece, an art review, and a small section devoted to Korean literature. Much full-text content from current and archived issues can be found for free on the magazine's web site. Recommended for academic libraries and large public libraries. URL: www.koreana.or.kr

536. *Leonardo & Leonardo Music Journal.* Formerly: *Leonardo/Isast.* [ISSN: 0024-094X] 1968. 6x/yr. USD 698 (print & online eds.). Ed(s): Roger F Malina, Pamela Grant-Ryan. M I T Press, 55 Hayward St, Cambridge, MA 02142; journals-cs@mit.edu; http://mitpress.mit.edu. Illus., adv. Refereed. Microform: PQC. *Indexed:* A&ATA, A01, A06, A07, A22, A51, ABS&EES, ArtHuCI, E01, EIP, MLA-IB, RILM. *Bk. rev.:* 10-15, 2,000+ words. *Aud.:* Ac, Sa.

Leonardo focuses on the arts as they intersect with the scientific disciplines and developing technologies, within an international scope and from an academic perspective. This journal attempts to foster communication between technology-minded artists by providing information on current, emerging, and historical trends in the use of science in the arts. Issues contain artists' statements, interviews, general articles, and special sections all related to the journal's mission. The web site includes sample articles, cumulative indexing, and general information about the journal, the society, and relevant news and events. Recommended for academic libraries. URL: www.leonardo.info

537. *Master Drawings: devoted exclusively to the study and illustration of drawings.* [ISSN: 0025-5025] 1963. q. USD 105 domestic; USD 135 foreign. Ed(s): Jane Turner. Master Drawings Association, Inc., 225 Madison Ave, New York, NY 10016. Illus., index, adv. Refereed. Vol. ends: No. 4. *Indexed:* A06, A07, A22, ArtHuCI. *Bk. rev.:* Number varies, essay length. *Aud.:* Ac, Sa.

This journal is published by the Master Drawings Association of New York, and its audience is primarily art historians, collectors, and dealers. An academic quarterly, it provides a venue for the exclusive study of drawings and occasionally other works on paper, e.g., engraving and watercolor since the Renaissance. Thematic issues concentrate mainly on the old masters up to 1900 and are written for scholars. Authors tend to be art history fellows, professors, and museum curators, and they focus on new developments and reattributions of specific drawings. Appropriate for academic libraries that support art history programs.

538. *Modern Painters.* [ISSN: 0953-6698] 1988. 9x/yr. USD 50. Ed(s): Roger Tatley. L T B Media, 601 W 26th St, Ste 410, New York, NY 10001; http://www.louiseblouinmedia.com/. Adv. *Indexed:* A01, A07, A22, A51, RILM. *Bk. rev.:* 5-8, 500 words. *Aud.:* Ac, Sa.

Not devoted exclusively to painting as the title implies, *Modern Painters* brings together leading voices in visual arts criticism and analysis—academics, writers, and artists—to provide stimulating discussions of current practices in international art. Stating a mission to "not only report . . . but define and shape important events and trends in the art and cultural worlds," *Modern Painters* succeeds admirably. Feature articles are devoted to politics and art, reviews of current practices, introduction of new artists, and examination of important movements and media. Full-page color gallery and exhibition ads predominate in this oversize monthly. One artist's studio practice is featured in each issue, as well as book and exhibition reviews. An important international title for all comprehensive art collections in any library.

539. *New American Paintings.* [ISSN: 1066-2235] 1993. bi-m. USD 89 domestic; USD 139 in Canada & Mexico; USD 189 elsewhere. The Open Studios Press, 450 Harrison Ave., 47, Boston, MA 02118; info@newamericanpaintings.com. Illus. *Aud.:* Ga, Ac, Sa.

New American Paintings is a unique publication in the art world. Rather than including a number of interviews, critical essays, or artist profiles, each well-constructed, lushly illustrated issue features page after page of paintings (one per page), broken up only by a brief biography, artist statement, and contact information for each of the painters presented. The painters in each issue are usually culled from a specific regional juried exhibition, so a variety of lesser-known artists are brought to light in each issue.

540. *New Criterion.* [ISSN: 0734-0222] 1982. 10x/yr. USD 48 combined subscription domestic (print & online eds.); USD 62 combined subscription Canada (print & online eds.); USD 70 combined subscription elsewhere (print & online eds.). Ed(s): James Panero, Roger Kimball. Foundation for Cultural Review, 900 Broadway, Ste 602, New York, NY 10003. Illus., adv. Microform: PQC. *Indexed:* A01, A07, A22, A51, AmHI, BRI, MLA-IB, RILM. *Bk. rev.:* 3, lengthy. *Aud.:* Ga, Ac.

New Criterion is published by the Foundation for Cultural Review, which gives the magazine a much wider scope than strictly visual arts. Poets, authors, public policy scholars, humanities lecturers, and critics all contribute to create a vehicle for poetry, arts criticism, and commentary on cultural life in America. Departments in theater, art, music, and the media provide substantial reviews, and exhibition listings and book reviews make regular appearances in this periodical. Engaging and interesting to the informed reader, *New Criterion* is recommended for both public and academic libraries.

541. *n.paradoxa: international feminist art journal.* [ISSN: 1461-0434] 1998. s-a. GBP 32 (Individuals, GBP 18). Ed(s): Katy Deepwell. K T Press, 38 Bellot St, E Greenwich, London, SE10 OAQ, United Kingdom; ktpress@ktpress.co.uk; http://www.ktpress.co.uk. Refereed. *Indexed:* A07, A51. *Aud.:* Ga, Sa.

This international feminist journal focuses on the visual arts. It publishes in-depth analyses of contemporary women's art and interviews with women artists, as well as articles on feminist art theory. It also provides information on women's art organizations and exhibitions; chronicles the contemporary women's art movement; and includes reviews of publications about contemporary women artists. Some issues are thematic. It is a valuable resource for students, artists, and academics, and is available in online and print editions, which publish different and separate content. URL: http://web.ukonline.co.uk/n.paradoxa

542. *October.* [ISSN: 0162-2870] 1976. q. USD 257 (print & online eds.). Ed(s): Adam Lehner. M I T Press, 55 Hayward St, Cambridge, MA 02142; journals-cs@mit.edu; http://mitpress.mit.edu. Illus., adv. Refereed. Microform: PQC. *Indexed:* A01, A07, A22, A51, ABS&EES, AmHI, ArtHuCI, E01, MLA-IB, RILM. *Aud.:* Ac.

October is an important voice of art criticism and theory. Founded in New York by a group of theoreticians, it has focused on themes of postmodernism and poststructuralist discourse in America. Frequently monothematic, issues offer approximately a half-dozen lengthy scholarly discourses of the societal or cultural impact of the visual arts. Contributors are scholars, critics, and artists from a variety of academic disciplines, with the arts, film, and literature predominating. Intellectually rigorous, *October* will appeal to many scholars in the humanities. Recommended for academic research collections.

543. *Oriental Art: devoted to the study of all forms of Oriental art.* [ISSN: 0030-5278] 1948. 5x/yr. USD 80; GBP 60. Oriental Art Magazine, 47 Hill St, #06-06, Singapore, 179365, Singapore. Illus., index, adv. Vol. ends: Winter. *Indexed:* A&ATA, A06, A07, A22, ArtHuCI, FR, MLA-IB, RILM. *Bk. rev.:* 4-5, length varies. *Aud.:* Ac, Sa.

In the last few years, *Oriental Art* has suffered from significant delays and is continuing to be published irregularly. Lavishly illustrated with glossy, full-color reproductions, *Oriental Art* is an inclusive journal that extends coverage to art in India, the Islamic world, and all of Southeast Asia, beyond the traditional China and Japan focus. Five or six scholarly, in-depth articles written by international experts in the field are featured. Similarly, book reviews are quite lengthy and written for scholars. Focusing on historical Asian art, it is suited for research collections in academic and special libraries.

544. *Oxford Art Journal.* [ISSN: 0142-6540] 1978. 3x/yr. EUR 297. Oxford University Press, Great Clarendon St, Oxford, OX2 6DP, United Kingdom; enquiry@oup.co.uk; http://www.oxfordjournals.org/. Illus., adv. Sample. Vol. ends: No. 2. Reprint: PSC. *Indexed:* A07, A22, A51, ArtHuCI, E01. *Bk. rev.:* 8, essay length. *Aud.:* Ac.

A venue for critical analysis of the visual arts, primarily Western, the *Oxford Art Journal* has contributed to the reexamination of art history through social context and political interpretations. Seven to ten scholarly, peer-reviewed papers represent research in the visual arts and related historical and philosophical issues from antiquity to contemporary art practice. It is well illustrated with black-and-white photos. Six or seven signed book reviews and the focus on the historical, social commentary of art make this appropriate for college and university libraries.

545. *Print Quarterly.* [ISSN: 0265-8305] 1984. q. GBP 85 domestic; GBP 101 in US & Canada; GBP 92 elsewhere. Ed(s): Rhoda Eitel-Porter. Print Quarterly Publications, 10 Chester Row, London, SW1W 9JH, United Kingdom. Illus., adv. Refereed. Vol. ends: Dec. *Indexed:* A07, A22, A51, ArtHuCI. *Bk. rev.:* Number and length vary. *Aud.:* Ac, Sa.

Print Quarterly is the leading publication in its field. Devoted to the art of the printed image, whether engraving, intaglio, woodprint, lithograph, drypoint, or zincograph, it covers the history of printmaking from the fifteenth century to the present. Features include three to four peer-reviewed articles and in-depth book reviews. The publication is well illustrated, and the articles are written for academicians, although collectors would also find this a very useful source of information. It includes unique sections devoted to news items in the print and graphic arts world (new attributions, the latest serial publications, brief articles on societies) that go beyond the ordinary current events news. This journal is recommended for academic art libraries, museums, and other special collections.

546. *Public Art Review.* [ISSN: 1040-211X] 1989. s-a. USD 24 domestic; USD 31 in Canada & Mexico; USD 37 elsewhere. Forecast Public Art, 2324 University Ave W, Ste 104, St. Paul, MN 55114; http://www.forecastpublicart.org. Adv. Refereed. *Indexed:* A07, A22, A51. *Aud.:* Ga, Ac, Sa.

Public Art Review is produced by Forecast Public Artworks, a Minneapolis-based consulting group. The magazine's scope includes not only local public artworks but regional and national as well. Striving to encourage public art and artists, *PAR* features articles on maintaining and conserving public art; consulting and managing projects—often of city-wide plans; and exploring critically contemporary public art in America, whether smaller-scale individual pieces or large-scale, big-name projects. Occasional pieces cover international public art constructions. Recommended for art, architecture, and urban planning collections in large public and academic libraries.

547. *R A C A R.* [ISSN: 0315-9906] 1974. s-a. Free to members. Ed(s): Barbara Winters. Association d'Art des Universites du Canada, Department of History in Art, University of Victoria, Box 1700, Victoria, BC V8W 2Y2, Canada; bwinters@finearts.uvic.ca. Illus. Refereed. Circ: 900. Vol. ends: No. 2. *Indexed:* A07, A51, BRI, C37, CBCARef. *Bk. rev.:* 6, essay length. *Aud.:* Ac.

RACAR is published by the Universities Art Association of Canada with the assistance of the Social Sciences and Humanities Research Council of Canada, and it is the leading scholarly Canadian art journal. Peer-reviewed articles feature lengthy treatments of Western art history, written in either French or English and illustrated with black-and-white photos. The latest issues focus on art of nineteenth- and twentieth-century Europe. Appropriate for academic and research collections.

548. *Raw Vision.* [ISSN: 0955-1182] 1989. q. GBP 37 (Individuals, GBP 27). Ed(s): John Maizels. Raw Vision Ltd., PO Box 44, Watford, WD25 8LN, United Kingdom. Adv. *Indexed:* A07, A51. *Bk. rev.:* 5-10, 1,000+ words. *Aud.:* Ga, Ac.

Self-described as "the world's leading journal of outsider art, art brut and contemporary folk art," this journal covers art, artists, and art forms that are usually not included in traditional art histories or studied in art journals. Each heavily illustrated issue contains features on individual artists, movements within the above areas, and other "intuitive" and "marginal" arts. There are also news and reviews of contemporary exhibitions and events. The web site includes news, excerpts from current and past issues, links to associated galleries and museums, and other relevant information. Recommended for academic, museum, and public libraries where there is an interest in nontraditional arts and culture.

549. *Revue de l'Art.* [ISSN: 0035-1326] 1968. q. EUR 80 domestic; EUR 95 foreign. Ophrys, 25 Rue Ginoux, Paris, 75737, France; editions.ophrys@ophrys.fr; http://www.ophrys.fr. Illus. *Indexed:* A&ATA, A07, A22, ArtHuCI, RILM. *Bk. rev.:* 4-5, essay length. *Aud.:* Ac.

Emphasizing French art of the Neoclassic through Impressionist eras, this journal provides international scholarship. Abstracts occasionally summarize the contents of the French-language articles in English and German. Each issue includes book reviews, biographical essays, a calendar of museum exhibitions, and critical bibliographies. Appropriate for research collections in academic or special libraries in the arts.

550. *Sculpture.* Incorporates (1993-1995): *Maquette;* Which was formerly (until 1993): *Sculpture Maquette;* Former titles (until 1987): *International Sculpture;* (until 1985): *Sculptors International;* (until 1982): *International Sculpture Center. Bulletin;* (until 19??): *National Sculpture Center. Bulletin.* [ISSN: 0889-728X] 19??. 10x/yr. Free. International Sculpture Center, 1633 Connecticut Ave NW 4th fl, Washington, DC 20009; http://www.sculpture.org/. Illus., adv. Circ: 22000. Vol. ends: Dec. *Indexed:* A07, A22, A51. *Bk. rev.:* 10-12, 150 words. *Aud.:* Ga, Ac, Sa.

Published by the International Sculpture Center, this is the only international publication of its kind devoted exclusively to all forms of contemporary sculpture. Richly illustrated with full-color photography, the feature articles concentrate on traditional forms of three-dimensional arts. With gallery ads, news briefs, exhibition announcements, interviews with sculptors, a column devoted to commissions (a major source of revenue), and reviews of installations, this a useful title to artists, collectors, and scholars. Recommended for all academic libraries with significant art programs and for larger public libraries.

551. *Tribal Art.* Former titles (until 2006): *Tribal;* (until 2002): *The World of Tribal Arts.* 1994. q. Ed(s): Jonathan Fogel. Primedia Inc., 2261 Market St, Ste 644, San Francisco, CA 94114; jmfogel@pacbell.net. Illus., adv. Sample. Refereed. *Indexed:* A07, A47, A51, MLA-IB. *Bk. rev.:* 8-12, 1,000+ words. *Aud.:* Ga, Ac, Sa.

According to this journal's web site, *Tribal* is the "only magazine dedicated to fine and antique traditional art from the Americas, Africa, Asia, Indonesia, Polynesia, Melanesia[,] and Micronesia." Each extensively illustrated issue features articles and information on art and antiques from specific tribes, geographic areas, and time periods. It also includes features on collectors, collecting, and exhibitions and auctions. *Tribal Art* provides a unique perspective on some of the non-canonical histories of art. Recommended for museum, academic, and public libraries that have an interest in indigenous arts and antiques.

552. *Twice.* Formerly (until 1996): *Dance Ink.* 1997. s-a. USD 30 domestic; USD 40 foreign. Ed(s): Patsy Tarr, Jane Rosch. 2wice Arts Foundation, Inc., PO Box 980, East Hampton, NY 11937. Adv. *Aud.:* Ga, Ac, Sa.

2wice is a very special publication. Each issue has a unique theme, and all of the content within the issue, which is selected from all corners of the art world, is geared toward exemplifying that theme. Some themes are intangible, like "formal" or "glow," while others are more visceral, like "animal" or "car," and while still others are quite specific, like "Cunningham-Rauschenberg"—a retrospective of the two artists. The journal describes itself on its web site, which includes excerpts and images from the journal, as "popular and academic, serious and humorous." It is beautifully constructed and printed, and artfully made. Though the dimensions of the journal remain consistent (30 x 21 in.), each issue is structured in a different manner—sometimes horizontal; sometimes vertical; sometimes with extensive text; sometimes with almost no text at all; sometimes printed on very thin paper. And sometimes it is a collection of booklets inside a box that is the size of the other issues. Each issue is a bit of a surprise.

553. *West 86th: a journal of decorative arts, design history, and material culture.* Formerly (until Mar.2010): *Studies in the Decorative Arts.* [ISSN: 2153-5531] 1993. s-a. USD 132 (print & online eds.). Ed(s): Paul Stirton. University of Chicago Press, 1427 E 60th St, Chicago, IL 60637; subscriptions@press.uchicago.edu; http://www.journals.uchicago.edu. Illus., adv. Sample. Refereed. Reprint: PSC. *Indexed:* A07, A51, BRI, CBRI. *Bk. rev.:* Number varies, essay length. *Aud.:* Ga, Ac.

West 86th, formerly titled *Studies in the Decorative Arts,* emphasizes analytical and interpretative scholarly research of the decorative arts, regardless of media, culture, era, or geographic location. Recent issues highlight research from all time periods with most space given to Western European objects, although some articles occasionally focus on non-Western arts or influence. Focusing on the decorative arts as documents of material culture and placing them within their social and political contexts, the journal provides a forum for new research in the field. Four to six peer-reviewed articles are sparsely illustrated with black-and-white photographs. Each issue includes signed reviews of important new books, exhibitions, and discussions of developments in conservation and restoration. Recommended for larger public libraries and college and university libraries.

554. *Woman's Art Journal.* [ISSN: 0270-7993] 1980. s-a. USD 88 (print & online eds.) Individuals, USD 36). Ed(s): Joan Marter, Margaret Barlow. Old City Publishing, Inc., 628 N 2nd St, Philadelphia, PA 19123; info@oldcitypublishing.com; http://www.oldcitypublishing.com. Illus., index. Sample. Refereed. Vol. ends: No. 2. Microform: PQC. *Indexed:* A07, A22, A51, ABS&EES, ArtHuCI, BRI, FemPer, MLA-IB. *Bk. rev.:* 5-13, 400-3,500 words, signed. *Aud.:* Hs, Ga, Ac, Sa.

Intended to focus as a platform for re-examining feminist ideas, this publication covers women in the visual arts and related areas from antiquity to the present, although recent issues focus on the modern era through the present decade. Each issue is divided roughly into two sections: "Portraits, Issues and Insights," about individual women artists or genres, and "Reviews," which covers exhibitions and publications by and about women artists. Contributors include artists, critics, art professionals, and academics; all voices are welcome. Issues include high-quality black-and-white and color illustrations. Of interest for art and women's studies collections.

555. *Word & Image: a journal of verbal/visual enquiry.* [ISSN: 0266-6286] 1985. q. GBP 708 (print & online eds.). Routledge, 4 Park Sq, Milton Park, Abingdon, OX14 4RN, United Kingdom; subscriptions@tandf.co.uk; http://www.tandfonline.com. Illus., adv. Sample. Refereed. Reprint: PSC. *Indexed:* A01, A07, A22, A51, AmHI, ArtHuCI, B01, BEL&L, E01, FR, MLA-IB, RILM. *Bk. rev.:* Number varies, 1 page. *Aud.:* Ac, Sa.

Word & Image is an interdisciplinary journal that focuses on the "study of the encounters, dialogues[,] and mutual collaboration (or hostility) between verbal and visual languages," regardless of media. As such, it is important to literary critics, art historians, linguisticians, social historians, philosophers, and psychologists alike. Scholarly articles examine the many complicated relationships between words and images. Issues sometimes revolve around a central theme, with guest editors invited to participate, but most cover a variety

of subjects from discourse of aesthetics and ontology to Gilded Age political culture. Articles are primarily in English, but French and German occasionally appear. Strictly a scholar's resource, it is recommended for academic libraries. Universities that support programs in linguistics and literature, art history, and communications will find this journal indispensable.

556. *Zeitschrift fuer Kunstgeschichte.* Formed by the merger of (1876-1932): *Repertorium fuer Kunstwissenschaft;* (1866-1932): *Zeitschrift fuer Bildende Kunst;* (1923-1932): *Jahrbuch fuer Kunstwissenschaft;* Which was formerly (1908-1923): *Monatshefte fuer Kunstwissenschaft;* (1905-1908): *Monatshefte der Kunstwissenschaftlichen Literatur.* [ISSN: 0044-2992] 1932. 4x/yr. EUR 92; EUR 28.50 newsstand/cover. Ed(s): Andreas Toennesmann, Andreas Beyer. Deutscher Kunstverlag GmbH, Nymphenburger Str 90e, Munich, 80636, Germany; info@deutscherkunstverlag.de; http://www.deutscherkunstverlag.de. Illus., index, adv. Circ: 900. Vol. ends: No. 4. Reprint: PSC. *Indexed:* A06, A07, A22, A51, AmHI, ArtHuCI, MLA-IB, RILM. *Bk. rev.:* 3-4, lengthy. *Aud.:* Ac.

The focus is scholarly research in traditional Western visual arts, from the ancient Greeks through twentieth-century European artists, making this leading German publication a standard in the field of art history since the 1930s. Black-and-white and occasionally color photography illustrate the five or six peer-reviewed articles that represent international art history research. Articles appear in German, English, French, or Italian. Lengthy book reviews provide extensive treatment of three or four books in each issue. Appropriate for museum and academic libraries, especially those with art history programs.

Museum Publications

557. *Archives of American Art Journal.* Formerly (until 1964): *Archives of American Art. Quarterly Bulletin;* (until 1962): *Archives of American Art. Bulletin.* [ISSN: 0003-9853] 1960. s-a. USD 50 (Individuals, USD 65; Free to members). Ed(s): Darcy Tell. Smithsonian Institution, Archives of American Art, 1285 Ave of the Americas, Lobby Level, New York, NY 10019; weinerj@si.edu; http://www.aaa.si.edu. Illus. *Indexed:* A06, A07, A22, A51, ArtHuCI, MLA-IB. *Bk. rev.:* Number and length vary. *Aud.:* Ac, Sa.

This journal publishes cultural and social research about the permanent collections of the Archives of American Art. Housed in the Smithsonian Institution, the Archives of American Art provide researchers with access to the largest collection of documents on the history of the visual arts in the United States from the eighteenth century to the recent past. Three or four articles in each issue feature papers of artists, collectors, art historians, and other art world figures, and records of dealers, museums, and other institutions. Book reviews and regional reports that cover new acquisitions to the archives round out this important resource of historical documentation. Highly recommended for research collections.

558. *Art Institute of Chicago. Museum Studies.* [ISSN: 0069-3235] 1966. s-a. USD 60 (Individuals, USD 35; Members, USD 30). Ed(s): Greg Nosan. Art Institute of Chicago, 111 S Michigan Ave, Chicago, IL 60603; aic.publicaffairs@artic.edu; http://www.artic.edu/aic. Illus., index. Refereed. Vol. ends: No. 2. Microform: PQC. *Indexed:* A06, A07, A22, A51, ArtHuCI, RILM. *Aud.:* Ac, Sa.

Museum Studies is published semi-annually, and more often than not it is monothematic, covering such subjects as decorative arts, European painting, American art, architecture, or individual collectors. Anywhere from three to six articles, lavishly illustrated in color and black-and-white, feature the permanent collection and history of the Art Institute of Chicago. Presenting recent scholarship, contributors include museum curators, art historians, and lecturers, in addition to museum personnel. Recommended for all museum collections and academic libraries.

559. *International Review of African American Art.* Formerly (until 1984): *Black Art.* [ISSN: 1045-0920] 1976. q. USD 42 (Free to members). Hampton University Museum, Hampton University, Hampton, VA 23668; museum@hamptonu.edu; http://museum.hamptonu.edu. Illus. Refereed. Vol. ends: No. 4. *Indexed:* A01, A06, A07, A22, A51, AmHI, ArtHuCI, BRI, IIBP, MLA-IB, P02. *Bk. rev.:* Number and length vary. *Aud.:* Hs, Ga, Ac, Sa.

This monthly magazine published by the Hampton University Museum features interviews, biographical essays, and articles about visual and performing artists of African American heritage. While stating that it is "international," *IRAAA* primarily covers African American artists in the United States and occasionally Caribbean and South American artists as well. This full-color, well-illustrated journal frequently chooses one aspect of African American art for the subject of an issue. It includes a handful of book or exhibition reviews and noteworthy news on rising artists or new acquisitions. Cultural history and social themes related to the experience of the African American artist make this of interest to anyone conducting research in African American culture or American Studies. Recommended for all academic and large public libraries.

560. *Metropolitan Museum Journal.* [ISSN: 0077-8958] 1968. a. USD 91 (print & online eds.). Ed(s): Elizabeth L Block. University of Chicago Press, 1427 E 60th St, Chicago, IL 60637; custserv@press.uchicago.edu; http://www.press.uchicago.edu. Illus. Refereed. *Indexed:* A06, A07, A22, ArtHuCI, BAS, MLA-IB, RILM. *Aud.:* Ac, Sa.

This journal publishes new scholarly research that examines works of art in the permanent collection of the Metropolitan Museum of Art and related matters. Articles investigate the cultural context of these art objects and cover archival research and technical analyses. Contributors are usually specialists, researchers, or museum staff. Because the Metropolitan Museum is one of the premier museums in the United States, this publication is highly recommended for all research collections in academic, museum, and special libraries.

561. *Metropolitan Museum of Art Bulletin.* Incorporates (1986-1988): *Metropolitan Museum of Art. Recent Acquisitions;* Which was formerly (1979-1985): *Metropolitan Museum of Art. Notable Acquisitions.* [ISSN: 0026-1521] 1905. q. Free to members; Non-members, USD 30. Ed(s): John P O'Neill, Sue Potter. Metropolitan Museum of Art, 1000 Fifth Ave, New York, NY 10028; communications@metmuseum.org; http://www.metmuseum.org. Illus., index. Sample. Vol. ends: No. 4. *Indexed:* A&ATA, A01, A06, A07, A51, AmHI, ArtHuCI, BAS, FR, MLA-IB, NumL, RILM. *Aud.:* Ga, Ac, Sa.

One of the two Metropolitan Museum of Art publications, the *Bulletin* focuses on one artist, theme, historical period, or item from the permanent collection in one lengthy article. Most contributions are written by museum personnel, but occasionally outside scholars may compose an article. Recent acquisitions are noted in the fall issue. The primary audience for this publication is museum members and art historians, but it is highly recommended for all academic libraries.

562. *The Outsider.* 1996. 3x/yr. Free to members. Ed(s): Janet Franz. Intuit. The Center for Intuitive and Outsider Art, 756 N Milwaukee Ave, Chicago, IL 60622; intuit@art.org; http://www.art.org. *Bk. rev.:* 2-5, 1,000+ words. *Aud.:* Ga, Ac, Sa.

This journal from Intuit: the Center for Intuitive and Outsider Art focuses on outsider art, folk art, intuitive art, and art brut, which are all featured at this museum and are within the unique niche of the art world that it serves. *The Outsider* includes features on artists and surveys and studies of aspects of outsider art, among other articles. It also functions as a newsletter for the center that provides information on upcoming events, exhibitions, recent acquisitions, and other pertinent information. Recommended to museum and academic libraries with an interest in outsider art.

563. *La Revue des Musees de France.* Former titles (until 2008): *La Revue du Louvre et des Musees de France;* (until 1961): *La Revue des Arts;* (until 1951): *Musees de France;* (until 1948): *Bulletin des Musees de France;* (until 1915): *Les Musees de France;* (until 1911): *Bulletin des Musees de France;* (until 1908): *Musees et Monuments de France.* [ISSN: 1962-4271] 1951. bi-m. EUR 69. Ed(s): Danielle Gaborit Chopin, Jean Pierre Cuzin. Editions de la Reunion des Musees Nationaux, 49 Rue Etienne Marcel, Paris, Cedex 1 75039, France; http://www.rmn.fr. Illus., adv. Refereed. *Indexed:* A&ATA, A06, A07, ArtHuCI, BAS, FR, RILM. *Aud.:* Ac, Sa.

This beautiful publication with lavish illustrations provides coverage of the special collections and works of art in the Louvre and other national museums of France. Information on new acquisitions, temporary exhibitions, and restoration work is regularly featured. Exhibition reviews, subject bibliographies, and calendars of events are also included. Text is in French; abstracts are in English and German. Recommended for all academic and museum libraries.

564. *Studies in Modern Art.* [ISSN: 1058-997X] 1991. irreg. Members, USD 22.50; Non-members, USD 25. Museum of Modern Art, 11 W 53rd St, New York, NY 10019; http://www.moma.org. Illus. *Indexed:* A07. *Aud.:* Ga, Ac, Sa.

Issued by the Museum of Modern Art in New York, *Studies in Modern Art* might be more appropriately categorized as a monograph published serially. It showcases important collections, important works of art, and special programs at the museum. The journal maintains high standards of scholarship and makes a significant contribution to the serious study of contemporary art. Issues are frequently monothematic. This journal is published irregularly, and issues are appropriate for academic, museum, and large public libraries.

565. *Studies in the History of Art.* Supersedes in part (in 1972): *Report and Studies in the History of Art.* [ISSN: 0091-7338] 1967. irreg. National Gallery of Art, 2000B S Club Dr, Landover, MD 20785; pressinfo@nga.gov; http://www.nga.gov. Illus. *Indexed:* A06, A07, A22, ArtHuCI, MLA-IB. *Aud.:* Ga, Ac, Sa.

Designed to document scholarly symposia, this series-as-a-book is sponsored in part by the National Gallery of Art's Center for Advanced Study of the Visual Arts. Each monothematic volume presents a dozen or so research papers from a single symposium, and they foster study of the history, theory, and criticism of art, architecture, and urbanism. Recent topics cover Renaissance bronzes, paintings of Hans Holbein, and Olmec art and archaeology. An important resource for research art collections in all institutions.

566. *Tate Etc.* Formerly (until 2004): *Tate.* [ISSN: 1743-8853] 1993. 3x/yr. GBP 15 domestic; GBP 17 in Europe; EUR 21 in Europe. Ed(s): Simon Grant. Tate Etc., Millbank, London, SW1P 4RG, United Kingdom; subscriptions@tate.org.uk; http://www.tate.org.uk. Adv. *Indexed:* A07, A51. *Aud.:* Ga, Ac, Sa.

The Tate Gallery's contribution to museum literature is refreshing in the presentation of its collections in a contemporary art-magazine format. *Tate Etc.* features essays, artist interviews, briefs, artistic collaborations, and updates about the Tate's vast holdings that range from 1500 through contemporary art. A significant portion of the magazine is devoted to modern and contemporary international art in all media. Unlike with most publishers, every past issue is available free online, with many images, but not all. Recommended for large public libraries and academic and special collections. URL: http://tate.org.uk/tateetc

567. *Winterthur Portfolio: a journal of American material culture.* Incorporates: *Winterthur Conference Report.* [ISSN: 0084-0416] 1964. 3x/yr. USD 236 (print & online eds.). Ed(s): Elizabeth Milroy, Amy Earls. University of Chicago Press, 1427 E 60th St, Chicago, IL 60637; subscriptions@press.uchicago.edu; http://www.journals.uchicago.edu. Illus., index, adv. Sample. Refereed. Reprint: PSC. *Indexed:* A01, A06, A07, A22, A51, API, AmHI, ArtHuCI, BRI, MLA-IB. *Bk. rev.:* Number and length vary. *Aud.:* Ac.

Winterthur Portfolio is a strong academic press journal published on behalf of the Winterthur Museum. It covers the arts in America, including American Studies, technology and design, architecture, decorative arts, and material culture, as well as fine art. Three articles are featured, drawing scholarly expertise from diverse fields of cultural geography, ethnology, anthropology, archaeology, art history, folks studies, and literature, to name a few. Articles are often lavishly illustrated with both color and black-and-white photography. Approximately ten book reviews of academic note are offered in each issue. Important for special and academic libraries, especially those with American Studies programs.

568. *Women in the Arts.* Formerly (until 1991): *National Museum of Women in the Arts News.* [ISSN: 1058-7217] 1983. q. Free to members. National Museum of Women in the Arts, 1250 New York Ave, NW, Washington, DC 20005; member@nmwa.org; http://www.nmwa.org. Adv. *Aud.:* Ac, Sa.

Produced by the National Museum of Women in the Arts (NMWA), this glossy magazine recognizes the achievements of women artists, musicians, authors, and other contributors to world culture. The museum exists to promote women in all the visual arts, music, theater, film, and literature throughout the world. This broad mission allows for a wide variety of topics to be featured in each issue, contemporary and historical. *Women in the Arts* regularly reports on new acquisitions, regional updates, and other NMWA news, plus it contains a calendar of events and exhibitions. Available with an annual museum membership, *Women in the Arts* is recommended for museum, academic, and large public libraries.

■ ASIA AND THE PACIFIC

Christine K. Oka, Library Instruction Specialist, 270 Snell Library, Northeastern University, Boston, MA 02115; c.oka@neu.edu

Introduction

In this section, you will find a selection of publications that reflect the diversity of area studies, as well as the geographic areas of Asia and the Pacific. As libraries are faced with tighter budgets and reduced staffing, librarians are asked to take on additional collection/subject responsibilities, and required to be more selective in their collection decisions. This section aims to help by providing a core selection of titles needed in support of research at academic and special libraries and for public libraries that serve users with an interest in Asia and the Pacific.

Basic Periodicals

Asia Policy, Asian Studies Review, Harvard Journal of Asiatic Studies, Journal of Asian Studies.

Basic Abstracts and Indexes

America: History and Life, AnthroSource, Bibliography of Asian Studies (BAS), Historical Abstracts, PAIS International, Sociological Abstracts.

Archives of Asian Art. See Art/General section.

569. Asia Policy. [ISSN: 1559-0968] 2006. s-a. USD 95. Ed(s): Mark W Frazier, C. C Fair. National Bureau of Asian Research, 4518 University Way N E, Ste 300, Seattle, WA 98105-4530; nbr@nbr.org; http://www.nbr.org. Refereed. *Indexed:* A22, E01. *Bk. rev.:* Number and length vary. *Aud.:* Ga, Ac, Sa.

This is "a peer-reviewed scholarly journal presenting policy-relevant academic research on the Asia-Pacific that draws clear and concise conclusions useful to today's policymakers." The journal is a publication of NBAR, National Bureau of Asian Research. In the guidelines for submission, articles are to include social scientific research as it relates to "policy implications on issues of import to the region"; research notes of "new, important, and even exploratory conceptual frameworks or descriptive information of use to policymakers"; and policy analyses that present "research-based argumentation on crucial policy matters." Articles cover all parts of the Asian continent; recent issues include "Balancing Rivals: India's Tightrope between Iran and the United States" and "China's Participation in Global Governance from a Comparative Perspective." This latter article studies comparative data on emerging countries' participation in global governance to explain China's relatively low participation, and discusses the policy implications for the United States and the rest of the world. Two valuable features for readers studying Asia include the "Roundtables." In a recent issue, *Asia Policy* provided a "Roundtable" on the topic of "Regional Perspectives on U.S. Strategic Rebalancing," with essays from "experts in Australia, China, India, Japan, Singapore, South Korea, Taiwan, and Thailand." There also is a "Book Review Roundtable," a collection of reviews (and analyses) of specific books, along with the authors' responses. Both "Roundtables" showcase the multiple perspectives and interpretations of policy

and issues. All *Asia Policy* content is free for 60 days after publication at www.nbr.org. Highly recommended for all libraries, and in print format for institutions where computer access may be limited.

570. Asian Ethnicity. [ISSN: 1463-1369] 2000. q. GBP 342 (print & online eds.). Ed(s): Chih-yu Shih. Routledge, 4 Park Sq, Milton Park, Abingdon, OX14 4RN, United Kingdom; subscriptions@tandf.co.uk; http://www.tandfonline.com. Adv. Sample. Refereed. Reprint: PSC. *Indexed:* A01, A22, E01, IBSS, P61, SSA. *Bk. rev.:* Number and length vary. *Aud.:* Ga, Ac.

This cross-disciplinary journal addresses topics concerned with Asian ethnicity and identity. The peer-reviewed articles deal with ethnic minority groups and ethnic relations in Asia with its complex issues of identity and transnational migration. China, India, and Indonesia, as the most populous countries in the region, are more prominently discussed. Topics covered in recent issues include "Integration policy in Singapore: A transnational inclusion approach," and "Border Regions and India's neighborhood linkages: A Comparative Study of Indian Punjab and West Bengal." Each issue includes several book reviews of interest to an academic or general audience, such as "Personal Names in Asia; History, Culture and Identity," and "The Dragon and the Taniwha: Maori and Chinese in New Zealand." Recommended for academic and research libraries, and large public libraries that serve populations with an interest in Asia and ethnic studies.

571. Asian Survey: a bimonthly review of contemporary Asian affairs. Supersedes (in 1961): *Far Eastern Survey;* Which was formerly (until 1935): *Institute of Pacific Relations. American Council. Memorandum.* [ISSN: 0004-4687] 1932. bi-m. USD 454 (print & online eds.). Ed(s): David Fraser, Lowell Dittmer. University of California Press, Journals Division, 2000 Ctr St, Ste 303, Berkeley, CA 94704; customerservice@ucpressjournals.com; http://www.ucpressjournals.com. Illus., index, adv. Sample. Refereed. Vol. ends: Dec. Microform: PQC. Reprint: PSC. *Indexed:* A01, A22, ABS&EES, BAS, C45, E01, ENW, IBSS, MLA-IB, P02, P61, SSA. *Aud.:* Ac.

Self-described as the only bimonthly academic journal of contemporary Asian affairs published in the U.S., *Asian Survey* "consistently publishes articles by leading American and foreign scholars, whose views supplement and contest meanings disseminated by the media. Journal coverage ranges in scope from diplomacy, disarmament, missile defense, military, and modernization, to ethnicity, ethnic violence, economic nationalism, general elections, and global capitalism." The in-depth analysis and commentary on political, economic, and social developments in Asia are what have made it a valuable resource for "academics, government and security officials, business executives, and journalists" for over 40 years. "Scholarly analysis and commentary offer strategies for the future, and timely special issues focus on areas of crisis and change." A number of articles in a recent issue demonstrate the interest in China and U.S. relations and their positions as world powers: "China's Ambitions, America's Interests, Taiwan's Destiny, and Asia's Future," "China's Controversial Role in North Korea's Economic Transformation: The Dilemmas of Dependency," and "Repurposing Telecoms for Capital in China: System Development and Inequality." The February 2013 issue contained "A Survey of Asia in 2012," with overviews, such as "The United States and Asia in 2012: Domestic Politics Takes Charge," and by countries, including Indonesia, North Korea, Russia, Bangladesh, and Afghanistan. Recommended for academic and special libraries.

572. ASIANetwork Exchange: a journal for Asian studies in the liberal arts. Formerly (until 1993): *Asian Exchange.* [ISSN: 1943-9938] 1992. s-a. Free. Ed(s): Lisa Trivedi, Erin McCarthy. ASIANetwork, c/o Teddy O Amoloza, Illinois Wesleyan University, Bloomington, IL 61701; tamoloza@iwu.edu; http://www.asianetwork.org/. Refereed. *Indexed:* A01. *Aud.:* Ac, Sa.

The ASIANetwork began in 1992 and grew from a series of conferences to a consortium of over 170 North American colleges that were organized to encourage and strengthen Asian studies in undergraduate liberal arts education, and to offer resources and programs to support firsthand experience of Asian cultures. *ASIANetwork Exchange* is peer-reviewed, multidisciplinary in scope, and open-access. The goal is to disseminate "high-quality pedagogical essays" and "articles that are suitable for incorporation in the undergraduate classroom."

It is published on the Open Journal Systems platform, which provides Search and Browse (by issue, author, or title) features, links to information for readers, authors, and librarians as well as a notification system and font-size controls. Issues contain "Notes from the Editors," "Articles," and "Book and Media Reviews," with articles about Asia such as "Islam and Ecology: Southeast Asia, Adat, and the Essence of Keramat," examining Christian and Muslim views of nature and religion to "Between: Capital, Culture, and the Transformation of Hong Kong's Universities," which discusses practice and outcomes accompanying upcoming major educational reform at public universities in Hong Kong. Access at www.asianetworkexchange.org/index.php/ane. Issues published prior to fall 2011 may be accessed through the ASIANetwork web site at www.asianetwork.org/exchange.html.

The Australian Journal of Anthropology. See Anthropology section.

573. China Today. Formerly (until 1990): *China Reconstructs.* [ISSN: 1003-0905] 1990. m. USD 34.40. Ed(s): Tang Shubiao. Jinri Zhongguo Zazhishe, 24 Baiwanzhuang Rd., Beijing, 100037, China. Illus. Vol. ends: Dec. *Indexed:* A01, A22, BRI, F01. *Aud.:* Ga, Ac, Sa.

Consider the glossy magazine, *China Today* as THE magazine on everything about China. Each month, there are articles arranged under broad categories, such as "Economy," "Society/Life," and "Culture." The "Departments" section includes "Letters," "Opinion," and "Book Report," along with a food feature called "Pot Luck." There are also stories of Chinese art and cultural history in two categories, "Connoisseur" and "Cultural Custodians." Every issue is packed with beautiful color photographs and informative articles about life in China. Cover stories of recent issues looked at "Chinese Education Under Change," with special reports on early childhood education, reforms in teaching methods, and college examinations. Cover stories in other issues went from entertainment—"The Chinese film industry in depth: The power of the market and beyond *Kung Fu*"—to the more serious subject of global poverty, especially on China's poverty eradication efforts as reviewed by the World Bank. *China Today* is a core resource for academic and public libraries.

574. Contemporary Southeast Asia: a journal of international and strategic affairs. [ISSN: 0129-797X] 1979. 3x/yr. SGD 119 in Singapore, Malaysia & Brunei. Ed(s): Ian Storey. Institute of Southeast Asian Studies, 30 Heng Mui Keng Terrace, Pasir Panjang, Singapore, 119614, Singapore; publish@iseas.edu.sg; http://www.iseas.edu.sg/. Illus., index, adv. Refereed. Vol. ends: Dec. Microform: PQC. Reprint: SCH. *Indexed:* A01, A22, ABIn, BAS, BRI, E01, IBSS, P02, P61, SSA. *Bk. rev.:* 6-8, 600-1,000 words. *Aud.:* Ac, Sa.

Identified by members of the Bibliography of Asian Studies Advisory Committee as one of the most important journals in Asian Studies, *Contemporary Southeast Asia* is an international, refereed publication that is over 20 years old, and with a "new phase of specialization to reflect more directly the changing priorities of the Institute of Southeast Asian Studies (ISEAS)[,] as well as to cater to an increasing demand among our subscribers for a focus on issues related to domestic politics, international affairs, and regional security. This primary emphasis on political developments, socioeconomic change[,] and international relations is in keeping with the rapid advances in the field of strategic studies concerning not just Southeast Asia but, indeed, the larger Asia-Pacific environment." Recent issues live up to this new focus with articles about "Understanding Recent Political Changes in Myanmar." The environment and society, comprising another important issue, is explored in "Bauxite Mining in Vietnam's Central Highlands: An Arena for Expanding Civil Society?" The author's case study of a bauxite mining controversy found that "Between 2007 and 2010, civil society activists, bloggers, environmentalists, lawyers, and senior Communist Party officials, mobilized and coordinated opposition with an efficiency and strength that surprised both Vietnamese policy-makers and international scholars of Vietnamese society. Moreover, the extent of the news coverage, governmental reviews[,] and public petitions criticizing the bauxite mines, revealed a vibrant civil society in Vietnam." Articles are well written and provide historic background and context, making them also accessible for general readers. In addition to the articles, each issue contains thoughtful book reviews. Highly recommended for academic and special libraries, and also appropriate for public libraries that serve users with an interest in Asia and international relations.

575. Electronic Journal of Contemporary Japanese Studies. [ISSN: 1476-9158] 2001. irreg. Free. Ed(s): Peter Matanle. University of Sheffield, School of East Asian Studies, Shearwood Rd, Sheffield, S10 2TD, United Kingdom; seas@sheffield.ac.uk; http://www.sheffield.ac.uk/seas/. Index. Refereed. *Indexed:* IBSS. *Bk. rev.:* Number and length vary. *Aud.:* Ga, Ac, Sa.

Electronic Journal of Contemporary Japanese Studies, a.k.a. *ejcjs,* is an academic social sciences journal that is "dedicated to publishing research and scholarly writing on all issues related to Japan." It is published solely online, and its editorial policy for sustainable research is not to charge for access or any administrative fees to its contributors; the journal is funded by donations and "any other benefits that we can gain by [I]nternet publishing." Content includes articles, discussion papers, essays, creative writing, photography, and art, along with book and film reviews, notices, resource information, and web links. Research articles undergo double-blind peer review, with recent ones demonstrating the diversity of research topics, such as "New Challenges After Fukushima: Nuclear Energy, Critical Junctures and Regional Development Policies in Japan," an article asking "Is the use of kanji increasing in the Japanese writing system?" Could the use of word-processing technology actually increase the use of kanji, or Chinese characters in Japanese writing? The journal focus extends to the United States with "The Era of Dual Life: The Shin-Issei, the Japanese Contemporary Migrants to the U.S.," a look at the "new first generation" Japanese in the U.S. Although maintained by volunteers, the *ejcjs* web site is able to provide indexing to articles: by year of publication, or by choosing one of the broad categories by journal issue, and author. The necessity for keeping things simple has made this online journal user-friendly and easy to read. Appropriate for research and academic libraries, as well as public libraries. URL: www.japanesestudies.org.uk

Europe-Asia Studies. See Slavic Studies section.

576. Harvard Journal of Asiatic Studies. [ISSN: 0073-0548] 1936. s-a. USD 60 (Individuals, USD 36). Ed(s): Joanna Handlin Smith. Harvard-Yenching Institute, 2 Divinity Ave, Cambridge, MA 02138; http://www.harvard-yenching.org/. Illus., index. Sample. Refereed. Vol. ends: Dec. Microform: MIM; PQC. Reprint: SCH. *Indexed:* A01, A06, A22, AmHI, ArtHuCI, BAS, BRI, CBRI, E01, FR, IBSS, MLA-IB, P02, RILM. *Bk. rev.:* 12-15 reviews, 8-12 pages. *Aud.:* Ac, Sa.

This journal is published twice a year with support from the Harvard-Yenching Institute, and with the stated mission "to disseminate original, outstanding research and book reviews on the humanities in Asia, focusing at present on the areas of China, Japan, Korea, and Inner Asia." This semi-annual publication "has institutional and individual subscribers in roughly forty countries," and covers the art, literature, history, and philosophy of Asia. Each issue contains refereed articles and a dozen substantial, in-depth book reviews. Research in recent issues looked at the legacy of the Japanese historical figure, Taira no Kiyomori, from a new perspective—putting forth the theory of "ritual regimes" instead of focusing on the political and military outcome of the Genpei War in "Rites and Rule: Kiyomori at Itsukushima and Fukuhara." Another article examined the anomaly of the sixth-century epitaph of Prince Shedi Huiluo. At that time, it was believed the tomb was never to be damaged or opened, but the Prince's epitaph ends with, "My tomb will be opened in eight hundred years..."—which is the intriguing title of the article. The journal also includes review articles and book reviews, with a heavy concentration on Japan and China—such as reviews for *Coins, Trade, and the State: Economic Growth in Early Medieval Japan*; *Manufacturing Modern Japanese Literature: Publishing, Prizes, and the Ascription of Literary Value*; *Food, Sacrifice, and Sagehood in Early China*; and *Art by the Book: Painting Manuals and the Leisure Life in Late Ming China*. Recommended for special libraries and academic libraries.

577. India Today International. [ISSN: 0971-4537] 1981. fortn. GBP 73 United Kingdom; USD 78 United States; CAD 104 Canada. Ed(s): Aroon Purie. Living Media India Pvt. Ltd., F-14/15, Connaught Pl, New Delhi, 110 001, India; wecare@intoday.com; http://www.indiatoday.com. *Bk. rev.:* 1-2 per issue; varying length. *Aud.:* Hs, Ga.

India Today International is a general-interest magazine on India, covering almost everything about the country. This is not an official government publication, so the articles provide independent, sometimes critical, views of

India, with a special report on urban slums "Delhi's Ugly Underbelly," or a cover story on "Deadly Teens: Young and Dangerous," the Delhi gang rape illustrating a rise in crimes by minors. The content about the politics or social conditions are well written, but not dumbed down to make them easy for the outsider. But read a few issues and your interest will be rewarded with an appreciation and some understanding of uniquely Indian conventions and systems. Issues also include articles about sport, especially cricket, and leisure news covering celebrities, fashion, television and film, and books. Recommended for libraries that support Asian studies or serve South Asian populations, such as high school, academic, and public libraries. *India Today International* also has a web site with updated world-news and India-news links, including articles on movies, cricket, sports, and lifestyle, as well as videos. URL: http://indiatoday.intoday.in/

578. *International Journal of Asia - Pacific Studies.* [ISSN: 1823-6243] 2005. s-a. Free. Penerbit Universiti Sains Malaysia, Pulau Pinang, 11800, Malaysia; http://www.penerbit.usm.my. Refereed. *Bk. rev.:* 1,500-2,000 words. *Aud.:* Ac.

Published under the auspices of the Asian Pacific Research Unit (APRU) at Universiti Sains Malaysia, the *International Journal of Asia-Pacific Studies* is a "multidisciplinary, internationally refereed publication focusing primarily on Asia (West, South, Southeast[,] and East), Australasia[,] and the Pacific Rim regions of the Americas (North, Central[,] and South)." This e-journal carries out the mission of the APRU to disseminate original research in the disciplines of "politics, history, indigenous languages and literature, religion, man and the environment, ethno-history, anthropology, cultural heritage, social issues, economic development, war and conflict resolution, prehistory and archaeology, and the arts" to a global community. A recent thematic issue on music in Asia demonstrates this diversity with aim to draw "upon theories and approaches in media studies, gender and fan studies, as well as anthropology, history, political science, and ethnomusicology, these articles engage in a timely dialogue on how music impacts discourses of the nation state, identity formation and transnational flows of cultural production." The articles included Korean popular music and public protest and resistance, hip hop and street dance in the Philippines, and ritual village music in India. When available, book reviews are substantial, between 1,500 and 2,000 words. Recommended for academic libraries.

579. *Islands: an international magazine.* [ISSN: 0745-7847] 1981. 8x/yr. USD 14.97 domestic; USD 22.97 Canada; USD 30.97 elsewhere. Bonnier Corp., 460 N Orlando Ave, Ste 200, Orlando, FL 32789; http://www.bonniercorp.com. Illus., adv. Sample. Circ: 202736 Paid. Vol. ends: Nov/Dec (No. 6). *Indexed:* BRI. *Bk. rev.:* 0-2 reviews, 200 words. *Aud.:* Hs, Ga, Ac, Sa.

What is a popular, glossy travel magazine doing here? *Islands* is a publication that can be overlooked because of its scope—islands all over the world are visited, photographed, and described here. What makes this different from most travel magazines are the thoughtful and in-depth articles highlighting specific historical, cultural, or natural features about islands. Of course, islands in the Caribbean and the Mediterranean are covered, but where else would one find an article about the natural wonders of Hawaii, Tahiti, Papua New Guinea, and New Zealand wine country, along with articles about "Maui from the Ground Up," where "growing their own food is no passing fad in this Hawaiian island." It is a matter of survival, with a goal of making the island 100 percent food self-sufficient by 2050. A recent issue featured food, or travel by taste, with articles about street food carts on Hong Kong Island, and "lively bites" such as honey-glazed octopus lollipops in Japan or large land snails in garlic butter on the Isle of Pines in New Caledonia. Recommended for public libraries and a useful, perhaps unexpected, resource for academic libraries that support cultural anthropology, hospitality, and area studies, including Asian Studies.

Japanese Journal of Religious Studies. See Religion section.

Journal of Asian and African Studies. See Africa section.

Journal of Asian Martial Arts. See Sports/Specific Sports section.

580. *Journal of Asian Studies.* Former titles (until 1956): *The Far Eastern Quarterly;* (until 1941): *Bulletin of Far Eastern Bibliography.* [ISSN: 0021-9118] 1936. q. GBP 138 (print & online eds.). Ed(s): Jeffrey N Wasserstrom. Cambridge University Press, The Edinburgh Bldg, Shaftesbury Rd, Cambridge, CB2 8RU, United Kingdom; journals@cambridge.org; http://www.cambridge.org/uk. Illus., index, adv. Sample. Refereed. Circ: 8300. Vol. ends: Dec. Microform: PQC. Reprint: PSC. *Indexed:* A01, A06, A22, A47, ABIn, ABS&EES, AmHI, ArtHuCI, BAS, BRI, C45, CBRI, E01, FR, IBSS, JEL, MLA-IB, P02, P61, RILM, RRTA, SSA. *Bk. rev.:* 40-50. *Aud.:* Ac, Sa.

Essential for any library that supports Asian Studies, this is the publication of the Association for Asian Studies, "The Professional Association for Scholars and Students Interested in Asia." Established in 1936, *JAS* is committed to publishing "the very best empirical and multidisciplinary work on Asia, spanning the arts, history, literature, the social sciences, and cultural studies." Each issue contains an editorial foreword, articles, review essays, and substantial book reviews that cover "South and Southeast Asia to China, Inner Asia, and Northeast Asia." A recent issue introduced "Asia Beyond the Headlines," with an interactive twist: rather than a collection of essays on the headline topic, the journal published "an extended dialogue on an issue in the news, in which two specialists, in Japanese and Korean politics, respectively, responded to a series of questions put to them by David C. Kang, a scholar of international relations with a Northeast Asian focus." The research article, "Peter Hessler: Teacher, Archaeologist, Anthropologist, Travel Writer, Master Storyteller," was by China specialist Paul A. Cohen, whose aim was to assess Hessler's books for their contribution to and encouragement of a deeper understanding of Chinese life today. Another article about history's impact on the present was reviewed in "Ethnicity, Violence, and Khmer-Vietnamese Relations: The Significance of the Lower Mekong Delta, 1756-1954." In addition to discussions and research articles, there are extensive book reviews. Highly recommended for academic and special libraries.

Oceania. See Anthropology section.

Pacific Philosophical Quarterly. See Philosophy section.

Philosophy East and West. See Philosophy section.

581. *Positions: Asia critique.* [ISSN: 1067-9847] 1993. q. USD 302. Duke University Press, 905 W Main St, Ste 18 B, PO Box 90660, Durham, NC 27701; subscriptions@dukeupress.edu; http://www.dukepress.edu. Adv. Sample. Refereed. Reprint: PSC. *Indexed:* A01, A22, ArtHuCI, BAS, E01, MLA-IB, P61, SSA. *Bk. rev.:* Number and length vary. *Aud.:* Ga, Ac, Sa.

The stated purpose of *positions* is to offer "a fresh approach to East Asia and Asian American studies," and to create a forum of debate for all concerned with the social, intellectual, and political events unfolding in East Asia and within the Asian Diaspora. It accomplishes this with double-blind, peer-reviewed articles from faculty and researchers in the expected areas of specialties within Asian Studies, but it pushes the boundaries with contributors in anthropology, literature, history, philosophy, economics, film, and television studies. Recent "Special Issues" concentrated on Japan, but also showed the range of disciplines with issues titled *Collectivism in Twentieth Century Art* and *Imperial Japan and Colonial Sensibility.* Other issues of *positions* have reflected the diversity of articles with "The Suppressed in the Modern Urbanscape: Cultural Difference and Film in Singapore," "The Horrific and the Exemplary: Public Stories and Education Reform in Late Socialist China," and "The Modern Girl and the Vamp: Hollywood Film in Tanizaki Jun'ichiro's Early Novels." The articles discuss modernist architecture in Singapore, and range from a look at public housing (and its denizens) as presented in films, to what can be learned from news stories about young students committing murder or suicide. Coverage also ranges from policy planning for educational reform in China, to Tanizaki's creation of the "modern girl" as depicted in his novels. On the latter: "This article examines the actresses, including Mary Pickford, Gloria Swanson, Bebe Daniels, and others, that Tanizaki uses as models for the modern girl in these two novels. The existing narrative of the Hollywood vamp informs Tanizaki's description of the modern girl, even as that narrative is necessarily transformed in a Japanese context." Articles in *positions* are well written, and would be of interest to researchers, including undergraduate students. Recommended for academic libraries.

■ ASIAN AMERICAN

Christine K. Oka, Library Instruction Coordinator, 270 Snell Library, Northeastern University, Boston, MA 02115; c.oka@neu.edu

Introduction

Asian Americans are an incredibly diverse ethnic, religious, and socioeconomic group that defies (and sometimes denies) the single descriptor. This presents a challenge to libraries when it comes to providing Asian American magazines and journals for their users. The official U.S. Census description "Asian" refers to those having origins in any of the original peoples of the Far East, Southeast Asia, or the Indian subcontinent—including, for example, Cambodia, China, India, Japan, Korea, Malaysia, Pakistan, the Philippine Islands, Thailand, and Vietnam. "'Pacific Islander' refers to those having origins in any of the original peoples of Hawaii, Guam, Samoa, or other Pacific Islands" (Reeves, 2003). These "official" definitions are only the tip of the iceberg in describing how this population self-identifies. The situation is further complicated with library resources variously categorizing the group under "ethnic interests" or subsuming Asian American into Asia. The confusion is understandable. As Shawn Wong noted, "Sixty percent of the Asians in America are foreign born, which makes me the exception rather than rule in the country of my birth. People in Asia know I'm foreign and people in America assume that I am foreign born" (Wong, 1998).

Then there is the ubiquitous bottom line. While the Asian American market is perceived as a prosperous demographic for advertisers, magazines must move carefully to capture enough readers to justify the advertising investment. Jeff Yang, cofounder of the late *a.Magazine,* described the tightrope magazines have to walk in order to appeal to "Asians who want hard news and coverage of political and social issues, and . . . the ones who bought it because Lucy Liu was on the cover...." He hopes there will be another "independent, community-owned general-interest title that strives to reach a broad base of Asian Americans" (Chansanchai, 2003).

The recession hasn't made it easy for magazines; many promising titles have come in and out of existence since the last edition of *Magazines for Libraries.* For example, *Azine: Asian American Movement Ezine,* published with donations and the work of volunteers, recently announced on its web site (www.apimovement.com/) that "due to limitations in our resources, we are unable to continue one of the original intents[,] i.e.[,] to be a source of current news on Asian American activism. We will continue to archive documents from Asian American activist individuals and groups and be a resource to those interested in activism." Other publications have placed some of their content online to encourage subscriptions for the rest of the story in the print format.

In the interest of "truth in advertising," with *Magazines for Libraries,* I have identified magazines and online publications for many types of libraries that serve a variety of audiences. The titles that are likely to be longer-term, continuing publications that libraries can reasonably expect to obtain (or link to), and that are of interest to a broad spectrum of library readers throughout the country, are listed here. Libraries could meet some of the needs of Asian-born and Asian American users by exploring online news sources and newspapers such as *Asian Week* (www.asianweek.com), and open-access journals, available online at no charge. Also, full text for a variety of Asian American publications is available on the web by subscription; most notably, in *Ethnic NewsWatch,* a database published by ProQuest (www.proquest.com).

REFERENCES

Chansanchai, Athima. "Struggle to Survive on the Newsstands." *DateLine AAJA: Quarterly Newsletter of the Asian American Journalists Association.* Spring 2003; vol. 10, no. 1; pp. 1–4. Retrieved June 11, 2006, from www.aaja.org/resources/publications/dateline/dateline_spring_03.pdf.

Reeves, Terrance, and Claudette Bennett. *The Asian and Pacific Islander Population in the United States: March 2002.* Current Population Reports, pp. 20-540, U.S. Census Bureau, Washington, D.C., 2003. Retrieved June 13, 2006, from www.census.gov/prod/2003pubs/p20-540.pdf.

Wong, Shawn. "The Chinese Man Has My Ticket." In: Susan Richards Shreve and Porter Shreve, eds. *How We Want to Live: Narrative on Progress.* Boston: Beacon Press, 1998; pp. 142–149.

Basic Periodicals

Hs: *Audrey Magazine, Hyphen, KoreAm Journal;* Ga: *Amerasia Journal, Audrey Magazine, Hyphen, KoreAm Journal;* Ac: *Amerasia Journal, Journal of Asian American Studies.*

Basic Abstracts and Indexes

America: History and Life, Ethnic NewsWatch, Race Relations Abstracts, Sociological Abstracts.

582. ***Amerasia Journal: the national interdisciplinary journal of scholarship, criticism, and literature on Asian and Pacific American.*** [ISSN: 0044-7471] 1971. 3x/yr. USD 445 (Individuals, USD 99.99). Ed(s): Russell C Leong. University of California, Los Angeles, Asian American Studies Center, 3230 Campbell Hall, 405 Hilgard Ave, Los Angeles, CA 90095; aascpress@aasc.ucla.edu; http://www.aasc.ucla.edu/. Illus., index, adv. Sample. Refereed. Vol. ends: No. 3. Microform: PQC. *Indexed:* A01, A22, AmHI, ArtHuCI, BAS, BRI, CBRI, MLA-IB, P02, RILM. *Bk. rev.:* Number varies, 3-4 pages. *Aud.:* Ga, Ac.

Amerasia Journal is the oldest continuously published academic journal in the interdisciplinary field of Asian American Studies, and it appears three times a year—winter, spring, and fall. In addition to substantial book and film reviews, each thematic issue contains articles by writers of all ethnicities and disciplines. A recent issue, *Transoceanic Flows: Pacific Islander Interventions across the American Empire,* is the first *Amerasia Journal* devoted to Pacific Islander studies, and covers the persistent discussion of the complexities of identity, communities, and "diverse groups of people with different and even divergent interests, experiences, and social positions." Another recent issue, *Los Angeles Since 1992: Commemorating the 20th Anniversary of the Uprisings,* examined the aftereffects of these events, with the table of contents covering "Reflections," "Mediated Representations," "Community Interactions," and "Literature and Book Reviews." Additional discourse is available on the journal's blog at www.amerasiajournal.org/blog/. Thought-provoking articles and in-depth interviews and review articles make this journal essential for all academic libraries that support ethnic and multicultural studies, and highly recommended for large public libraries that serve Asian American and other ethnic communities.

583. ***Asian American Journal of Psychology.*** [ISSN: 1948-1985] 2010. q. USD 403. Ed(s): Frederick Leong. American Psychological Association, 750 First St, NE, Washington, DC 20002; journals@apa.org; http://www.apa.org. Adv. Circ: 800. *Indexed:* PsycInfo. *Aud.:* Ac, Sa.

The official publication of the Asian American Psychological Association, the *Asian American Journal of Psychology* is "dedicated to research, practice, advocacy, education, and policy within Asian American psychology." The goal of the *AAJP* is to be a resource of "empirical, theoretical, methodological, and practice[-]oriented articles and book reviews covering topics relevant to Asian American individuals and communities, including prevention, intervention, training, and social justice." The first issue of 2012, an inaugural thematic issue, is based on research and analysis related to the National Latino Asian American Study (NLAAS) Dataset—Part I. Some background information: the NLAAS, funded by the National Institute of Mental Health (NIMH), is described as "a nationally representative community household survey that estimates the prevalence of mental disorders and rate of mental health service utilization by Latinos and Asian Americans in the United States...." In the *Special Issue: Secondary Analysis of the National Latino Asian American Study (NLAAS) Dataset—Part I,* there are articles analyzing the NLAAS Dataset, including "Recursive Partitioning Analysis of Lifetime Suicidal Behaviors in Asian Americans," "The Physical and Mental Health Effects of Age of Immigration, Age, and Perceived Difference in Social Status among First Generation Asian

Americans," and "Asian Immigrants' Mental Health Service Use: An Application of the Life Course Perspective." Recommended for academic and special libraries that support psychology, counseling, human services, and multicultural studies.

584. *Asian American Literature Discourse and Pedagogies.* [ISSN: 2154-2171] 2010. a. Free. Ed(s): Noelle Brada-Williams. San Jose State University, One Washington Sq, San Jose, CA 95192; noelle.brada-williams@sjsu.edu; http://www.sjsu.edu/. Refereed. *Aud.:* Hs, Ga, Ac, Sa.

While polling local educators and students about Asian American literature, founding editor Noelle Brada-Williams was surprised to discover how only a few names were mentioned (Amy Tan and Pearl S. Buck), and "the tendency for both students and teachers to break apart the term 'Asian American' into separate and seemingly unrelated words...." *Asian American Literature Discourse and Pedagogies* was developed "to be a resource for teachers, students, and readers, even when they may not have access to the increasingly expensive journal databases subscribe to by most university libraries. We want to provide high quality peer-reviewed work even to those who may not have access to research beyond a simple internet search." Available through the Directory of Open Access Journals web site, www.doaj.org, this journal is published annually. The latest issue is thematic: "Teaching Food and Foodways in Asian American Literature and Popular Culture." The essays could be about a specific work, such as "Hybrid Veggies & Mixed Kids: Ecocriticism and Race in Ruth Ozeki's Pastoral Heartlands," or more generalized: "Feasting with 'the Other': Transforming the Self in Food Adventuring Programs." The latter essay is a fascinating critique of food travel television programs and how descriptions of "the Other" are handled. The text would be of interest to a teacher or a general reader, or could be used as a student reading assignment. Open access and linking recommended for academic (high school and college) and public library web pages.

585. *AsianWeek (Online): the voice of Asian America.* 2009. irreg. Ed(s): Ted Fang. Pan Asia Venture Capital Corporation, 809 Sacramento St, San Francisco, CA 94108; apang@asianweek.com; http://www.pavc.com. Adv. *Aud.:* Hs, Ga, Ac, Sa.

Based in San Francisco, *AsianWeek* is the oldest English-language newspaper serving the Asian American and Pacific Islander American community. Published since 1979 in tabloid format, *AsianWeek* ceased printing in 2009, becoming an online-only publication supported by advertising. *AsianWeek* has capitalized on the online environment and provides access to content through a calendar to browse the archive by date, subject boxes for links to "Recent Posts" and "Featured Stories," along with an extensive alphabetical listing of "Categories," such as "Art," "Bloggers," "Chinese Real Estate," "Discrimination," "Food," "Fukushima," "Sports," and "Terrorism." You can learn about Fukushima tuna (pulled in from the Fukushima NukeBlog Index); the article also appears under the "Global" category. The web site is enhanced with some video content, and the price is right; there is no charge for accessing *AsianWeek*. Libraries that serve Asian American and Pacific Islander American communities should link to it. URL: www.asianweek.com/

586. *Audrey Magazine: the Asian American women's lifestyle magazine.* [ISSN: 1936-3362] 2003. bi-m. USD 10 domestic; USD 40 Canada; USD 74 elsewhere. Ed(s): Anna M Park. Audrey Magazine, 17000 S Vermont Ave., Ste A, Gardena, CA 90247. Adv. Circ: 10000. *Aud.:* Hs, Ga.

Audrey Magazine describes itself as "the go-to publication for the modern Asian American woman intent on establishing and reinforcing her roots and getting in touch with the Asian American culture." It is celebrating its eighth year of publication, a noteworthy accomplishment in the transitory life of popular Asian American periodicals. In addition to the expected glossy fashion and beauty features in "Audrey Style" and "Beauty Kit," the magazine also has articles on current social issues in "Audrey Living," and profiles of prominent Asian Americans in the section "Happenings: The must-know Asian Americans on our radar, from breakout stars to groundbreaking artists." Recent issues featured interviews with Mindy Kaling from *The Office* and Hannah Simone from *The New Girl* television series. More serious topics have included binge drinking among Asian American women. As one reader wrote, "How often can Asian American girls flip through a magazine or through the channels on TV and see models and actresses who look like them? ... Asian American girls are left

without role models from their cultural background." *Audrey Magazine* comes out quarterly, but readers can check the web page at http://audreymagazine.com for updates and multimedia on events, news, opinions, and style. Recommended for school and public libraries that serve the Asian American community.

587. *Hyphen.* 2003. s-a. USD 25. Ed(s): Lisa Wong Macabasco. Hyphen, 17 Walter U. Lum Pl, San Francisco, CA 94108. Illus. Sample. *Aud.:* Hs, Ga, Ac, Sa.

Founded ten years ago, *Hyphen* has grown from "the little magazine that could" into a glossy magazine telling the stories of the many communities that make up Asian America. Funded by grants and with articles contributed by volunteers, *Hyphen* marks its tenth year with a "redesign to showcase augmented text, photos[,] and graphics." The magazine continues to cover culture, profiles of Asian American leaders, politics, health, art, and commentary. The magazine is complemented by a web site that not only provides access to a digital copy of the previous issue, but previews articles from the current one. There's also a blog, events calendar, and a store, with the proceeds supporting the magazine. Articles in the 25th issue include an interview with George Takei, and stories range from serious issues, such as Asian Pacific Islander caregivers, "an overlooked, neglected work force"; to food—e.g., "Above the Fold: Inside San Francisco's Gold Gate Fortune Cookie Factory"; to fun—e.g., "Hit List: the 25 best Asian and Asian American characters in pop culture." *Hyphen* has matured from an edgy publication for the young, hip Asian American to a magazine with multicultural and multigenerational appeal. Highly recommended for public libraries that serve Asian American communities, and special libraries and academic libraries that support ethnic or multicultural studies. URL: www.hyphenmagazine.com

588. *Journal of Asian American Studies.* [ISSN: 1097-2129] 1998. 3x/yr. USD 123. Ed(s): Min Hyoung Song. The Johns Hopkins University Press, 2715 N Charles St, Baltimore, MD 21218; http://www.press.jhu.edu. Illus., adv. Sample. Refereed. Circ: 670. Vol. ends: Oct. Reprint: PSC. *Indexed:* A22, BAS, E01, MLA-IB, P02, P61, RILM, SSA. *Bk. rev.:* Number varies, 2-3 pages. *Aud.:* Ga, Ac.

The Association for Asian American Studies was founded in 1979 with the mission of advancing excellence in teaching and research in the field and promoting closer ties and understanding among the various groups within it—Chinese, Japanese, Korean, Filipino, Hawaiian, Southeast Asian, South Asian, and Pacific Islander, among others. The association's official journal publishes articles that explore the historical, social, and cultural aspects of the Asian American community and the Asian diaspora. Articles document research in these areas, along with new theoretical developments, methodological innovations, public policy concerns, pedagogical issues, and book, media, and exhibition reviews. This diversity is reflected in recent issues, examining themes of transnational migration and citizenship. The article "New Geographies of Migration?: A Canada-U.S. Comparison of Highly Skilled Chinese and Indian Migration" looked at these migrants in Canada and the United States and "the impact of the changing geo-economic-political order to their migration." In "The Performance of Property: Suburban Homeownership as a Claim to Citizenship for Filipinos in Daly City," the research "suggests that the high rate of homeownership among Filipinos is a means of displaying their citizenship and belonging in the United States." Each issue also contains a collection of substantial book reviews. The online version of this journal is available in the Johns Hopkins University Project Muse collection. Essential for academic libraries that support Asian American and other ethnic studies programs.

589. *Journal of Southeast Asian American Education & Advancement.* [ISSN: 2153-8999] 2006. irreg. Free. National Association for the Education and Advancement of Cambodian, Laotian, and Vietnamese Americans, University of Hawai'i, Dept of IPLL, Spalding Hall 255, Honolulu, HI 96822; wayne.wright@utsa.edu; http://jsaaea.coehd.utsa.edu/index.php/JSAAEA/. Index, adv. Refereed. *Bk. rev.:* 3-5 per issue. *Aud.:* Ga, Ac, Sa.

Journal of Southeast Asian American Education and Advancement (*JSAAEA*) is an official publication of The National Association for the Education and Advancement of Cambodian, Laotian, and Vietnamese Americans (NAFEA), with support from the Department of Bicultural-Bilingual Studies and the College of Education and Human Development at the University of Texas, San

Antonio. It is also an online, open-access, peer-reviewed journal that provides a forum for researchers, teachers, and readers with a shared "interest in Southeast Asian Americans and their communities." The journal takes an interdisciplinary look at education and advancement, through public policy, social work, health, community development, and political advocacy. There are also book reviews. Less usual is the solicitation from the Author Guidelines web page: "submissions to the Creative and Literary Works section of the journal are especially encouraged from youth and young adult Southeast Asian American students in K-12 or college, as well as other community members, which focus on issues of identity and/or the Southeast Asian American experience." This journal is a product of the online environment, and each issue appears to be an annual; but in the policy statement to authors, articles published by *JSAAEA* will be added to the table of contents of the "current" volume as they become available. This journal is recommended for academic libraries, public libraries, and special libraries that serve researchers, educators, and professionals who serve Southeast Asian American communities.

590. *KoreAm Journal: the Korean American experience.* Incorporates (1980-2002): *Korean Culture;* Former titles (until Nov.2001): *KoreAm;* (until Feb.2001): *KoreAm Journal.* [ISSN: 1541-1931] 1990. m. USD 28 domestic. Ed(s): Y. Peter Kang, Julie Ha. Korean American Publications, 17000 S Vermont Ave, Ste A, Gardena, CA 90247; info@koreamjournal.com; http://www.iamkoream.com. Illus., adv. *Bk. rev.:* Number and length vary. *Aud.:* Hs, Ga, Ac, Sa.

Originally founded as a tabloid-format publication in 1990, *KoreAm Journal* burst onto the glossy magazine market "to provide a forum nationwide for English-speaking Korean Americans." It has come a long way, with articles covering a broad range of interests and achieving a balance between information and entertainment. An example of this diversity is reflected in recent articles in the "Features" section: the death of longtime North Korean dictator Kim Jong-il and the future of North Korea; the exploding popularity of Korean food in mainstream America; "I Am Zainichi" (Korean residents in Japan); and the personal struggle for identity of a Korean American woman who had long believed she was ethnically Japanese. In addition to the "Features," each issue looks at "Culture, Etc.," covering media, music, books, film, and food. There's the "Hot Pot" section on hot-button topics, such as how taboos prevent the Korean and Korean American community from discussing or seeking help for depression and other mental health issues. An inspiring story in this section was about "comfort women," Korean girls forced into sexual slavery for the Japanese army during World War II and their continuing protest for justice from the Japanese government; they began their protest in 1992 in front of the Japanese Embassy in Seoul. Selected articles are available on the journal web site, along with links to media, events, and a store. *KoreAm* is recommended for libraries that serve Korean American populations and for academic libraries that support Asian American and ethnic studies programs. URL: http://iamkoream.com

■ ASTROLOGY

Christianne Casper, Instruction Coordinator, Broward Community College, South Campus, 7200 Pines Blvd., Pembroke Pines, FL 33024; ccasper@broward.edu

Introduction

Astrology dates back to the Babylonians in the second millennium B.C. Since then, astrology has influenced language, literature, religion, science, philosophy, and psychology. It has evolved as the study of major planets, stars, and celestial bodies and their cyclical paths' influence on the rhythms of life. People from all cultures around the world have been and continue to be strongly interested in astrology. People turn to astrology as a way to gain greater insight into their past, present, and future lives.

The study of astrology involves observations, measurements, and calculations about the stars and planets to produce a framework for symbolic patterns according to their positions and aspects. Analyzing these patterns, astrologists attempt to explain and predict social, political, emotional, and other important aspects of life.

Some popular astrology journals include *Horoscope Guide, Dell Horoscope,* and *The Mountain Astrologer.* These journals provide information on personal horoscopes and guides to world events. Other journals, such as *Today's Astrologer,* focus on a more scholarly, research-oriented approach. The following list includes publications for all levels of interest.

Basic Periodicals

Hs: *Horoscope Guide;* Ga: *Dell Horoscope, The Mountain Astrologer;* Ac: *Today's Astrologer.*

Basic Abstracts and Indexes

Academic Search Premier, MasterFILE Premier.

591. *Dell Horoscope.* Formerly (until 199?): *Horoscope.* [ISSN: 1080-1421] 1935. m. USD 29.97 domestic; USD 54.97 foreign. Ed(s): Ronnie Grishman. Dell Magazines, 475 Park Ave S, 11 Fl, New York, NY 10016; delleditorial@pennypublications.com; http://www.pennydellpuzzles.com. Illus., adv. Circ: 240000 Paid. Vol. ends: Dec. *Indexed:* BRI, CBRI. *Bk. rev.:* 3, signed. *Aud.:* Hs, Ga.

Dell Horoscope is one of the most popular astrology magazines. The articles cover general-interest topics ranging from world and national affairs to personal problems. Also included are yearly, monthly, and daily guides. The regular features include letters to the editor, answers to readers' astrological questions, a monthly planetary data table, and book and product reviews. *Dell Horoscope* is written with both professional astrologers and amateurs in mind. The online version includes daily forecasts, a readers' forum, and links to other astrology web sites. Also of interest is "Cosmic Connections," which lists astrological activities in the United States and Canada.

592. *Horoscope Guide: the last word in astrology.* [ISSN: 8750-3042] 19??. m. USD 37.90. Kappa Publishing Group, Inc., 6198 Butler Pike, Ste 200, Blue Bell, PA 19422; http://www.kappapublishing.com. Illus., adv. *Bk. rev.:* 2-3. *Aud.:* Hs, Ga.

This magazine is designed for the astrology enthusiast. Each monthly issue includes a quick-reference section for daily forecasts regarding each sign for that month. There are three or four feature articles that address such diverse topics as family and personal issues, spiritual wellness, and current events as influenced by astrology. Monthly features include advice columns, zodiagram, a planning calendar, and a yearly forecast for the current sign. The online version provides the table of contents for the current issue, and allows access to an article from the current issue in "Read a Story."

593. *International Astrologer.* Formerly: *Kosmos.* 1968. 3x/yr. Free to members. Ed(s): Vickie Pelz. International Society for Astrological Research, Inc., PO Box 38613, Los Angeles, CA 90038; mmacycles@mail.msn.com; http://www.isarastrology.com. Illus., adv. Refereed. *Aud.:* Ac, Sa.

This journal is designed to advance the field of astrological research, intended for both students and professional astrologers. Feature articles offer diverse discussions of astrological interest, ranging from general community news to political/celebrity analysis, and including how-to columns on research, and financial astrology. The journal also contains conference information for the International Society for Astrological Research, including annual conference reports and evaluations.

594. *The Mountain Astrologer: your gateway to understanding the cosmos.* [ISSN: 1079-1345] 1987. bi-m. USD 39 in US & Canada; USD 59 in the Americas; USD 80 in Asia & the Pacific. Ed(s): Janette deProsse. Mountain Astrologer, PO Box 970, Cedar Ridge, CA 95924. Illus., adv. Sample. Vol. ends: Nov/Dec. *Bk. rev.:* 3-5. *Aud.:* Ga, Sa.

The Mountain Astrologer provides a wealth of information for professional and amateur astrologers alike. Standard features include a "Forecast Calendar," "Astrology News," "Current Lunations," letters to the editor, a professional directory, and signed book and astrological web site reviews. The web site reviews and the abundance of charts are extremely helpful. The online version lists the table of contents of the current issue and provides an index of articles from 1990 to 2010. Web site recommendations are also available. In addition, there is a "New to Astrology" section, which provides an overview of basic concepts of astrology.

595. *Today's Astrologer.* Former titles (until 199?): *American Federation of Astrologers Bulletin; A F A Bulletin;* (until 1945): *A F S A Bulletin.* [ISSN: 1067-1439] 1938. m. Free to members. American Federation of Astrologers, Inc., 6535 S Rural Rd, Tempe, AZ 85283; http://www.astrologers.com. Illus., index. Circ: 2700 Controlled. *Aud.:* Sa.

Today's Astrologer, the bulletin of the American Federation of Astrologers (AFA), was established as a forum to promote astrology through research and education. There is an average of five articles per issue. Regular departments include "Data Exchange," "The Question Box," and "The Communication Center." This last department is a calendar of activities of member organizations and other astrology affiliates. Finally, a "Lunation/Full Moon" chart is provided. URL: www.astrologers.com

■ ASTRONOMY

See also Aeronautics and Space Science; and Atmospheric Sciences sections.

Edward Creighton Sugrue, Jr., Wolbach Library, Harvard-Smithsonian Center for Astrophysics, 60 Garden St., Cambridge, MA 02138; edsugrue@hotmail.com

Introduction

The great widespread interest in the Transit of Venus, in June 2012, proved what many of us already know: astronomy is a beloved, popular, and universal subject, valued everywhere. The science of astronomy encompasses both the practical and the philosophical. It seeks to understand asteroids that could threaten us all, yet it also strives to understand how the universe began, and how it may one day end.

What astronomers do every day, today, would have been considered science fiction until very, very recently. They detect planets revolving around stars that are so faint that their professional forebears could not even have detected the stars, let alone the planets. The Kepler observatory satellite has already identified several hundred stars as likely candidates for harboring new planets. Astronomers also search for life on distant worlds in the sky. Mathematically inclined astronomers today are developing the conceptual apparatus to investigate the existence of other dimensions.

All of these astronomical activities can remind us of the original meaning of the word "awesome." Yet, as truly awesome as they are, none of these pursuits would be possible were it not for a network of timely, topical communication among astronomers, and between the astronomers and the public at large.

Modern astronomers' jobs are made vastly easier by staying well informed about recent developments in their field. One of the best ways to do this is by means of the journals discussed in this section. Similarly, the interested public is well served by being able to follow these astronomers as they work, as their research is published.

The selections put forward here include titles of interest to a diverse range of readers, ranging from Spanish-speaking children, to the average intelligent adult, to hobbyists with a specific astronomical interest, to professional astronomers.

There is a wide range of astronomical periodicals available, many of which are indeed quite democratic in spirit, and aim at a wider audience. However, librarians need to take extra care concerning which periodicals they select in this area of study for their institutions. Although many of the following periodicals are aimed at the general public, other periodicals are so esoteric that even undergraduate astronomy students have trouble wading through them.

Take care, also, not to assume that the periodicals listed under Basic Periodicals below are "basic" in the sense of being simple. Many of them are overflowing with high-level equations, and are only basic in that they are invaluable components of any serious academic astronomy library. Also note that "basic" periodicals are distinct from "core" periodicals. Core periodicals are chosen and agreed upon by specialized science libraries. They can be

identified by consulting PAMNET, which is described below in this introduction. In general, in determining a periodical's prospective value to your library, pay attention to the audience codes that periodicals have been assigned, and take time to examine their annotations and their web sites.

That said, a lot of these periodicals do provide terrific information to committed amateur astronomers, of whom there are many. Amateur astronomers, after all, make major contributions to the field on a regular basis. The general-audience periodicals serve a role that is at least as valuable as the specialized journals, because many thoughtful people, including children, harbor a great love of astronomy yet simply don't have the time to study it in any great depth. Many periodicals listed here fall somewhere between the abstruse journals and the nontechnical ones. Quite a few of these tend to specialize in a particular area of astronomical research, such as meteors, cosmology, or the planets of our solar system.

Most of these publications, although not all, can be found on the Internet. Several excellent periodicals are available free of charge on the web. This section includes a couple of journals that are designed entirely to translate research being done in Russia. For journals with a similar function, seek out *Ulrich's Periodicals Directory.*

A word to the wise: If you are new to this field, do not confuse *Astronomy and Astrophysics Abstracts* with *Astronomy and Astrophysics.* They sound like they should be connected somehow, but they are completely unrelated publications, and the similarity in their titles is merely an annoying coincidence.

Special mention in this category goes to a publication that is technically not a serial, but that needs to be mentioned in this context. A valuable, beautifully illustrated, eye-catching resource, *Astronomical Calendar* by Guy Ottewell, published by Furman University in Greenville, South Carolina, is generally considered to be the most beautiful, and one of the most treasured, of all the annual sky atlases.

Academic librarians who are new to the field also need to be aware of PAMNET. PAMNET is a valuable, professional online forum, useful for discussing astronomy periodicals and other information sources with fellow information professionals and librarians. PAMNET can easily be found online at http://pantheon.yale.edu/~dstern/astro.html. *Astronomy and Astrophysics Abstracts,* NASA's ADS (http://adswww.harvard.edu), and INSPEC are excellent indexing services.

Basic Periodicals

Ems: *Abrams Planetarium Sky Calendar, SkyWatch;* Hs, Ga: *Astronomy, Griffith Observer, Mercury, Sky & Telescope, SkyWatch;* Ac: *The Astronomical Journal, Astronomy, Astronomy & Astrophysics, Royal Astronomical Society. Monthly Notices.*

Basic Abstracts and Indexes

INSPEC, SAO/NASA Astrophysics Data System (ADS).

596. *A A V S O Journal.* [ISSN: 0271-9053] 1972. s-a. USD 50 Free to members. American Association of Variable Star Observers, 49 Bay State Rd, Cambridge, MA 02138; aavso@aavso.org; http://www.aavso.org. Illus., index. Refereed. Vol. ends: No. 2. *Bk. rev.:* 1-2, 400-600 words. *Aud.:* Ac, Sa.

The American Association of Variable Star Observers (AAVSO) has members in more than 40 countries and is the largest organization of variable-star observers in the world. Its members include both amateur and professional astronomers, and they first watch and track variable stars (those stars whose luminosity changes over time), then submit their observations to the AAVSO. Amateur astronomers play a very important role in the tracking of variable stars, as there are far too many for only professionals to follow. The AAVSO web site has such features as: a search engine designed to locate variable stars in the AAVSO charts; a variety of online tools to assist observers in processing their information; and even a "variable star of the month." The electronic, online version of this journal can be found on the web site, as well. This journal publishes refereed, scientific papers on variable-star research; observer observation totals; activities of AAVSO committees; letters to the editor; and the Annual Report of the Director. It is a valuable, respected source of information within the astronomical community. URL: www.aavso.org/publications/jaavso

597. *Abrams Planetarium Sky Calendar.* [ISSN: 0733-6314] 1969. q. USD 11 domestic; USD 14 foreign. Michigan State University, Talbert & Leota Abrams Planetarium, Michigan State University, East Lansing, MI 48824; http://www.pa.msu.edu/abrams/. Illus. *Aud.:* Ems, Hs, Ga, Ac.

Sky Calendar, as the name suggests, is laid out like a calendar, presenting a new page for each month. The reverse side of each page presents a simplified sky map for that month, printed for use at mid-evening, at a latitude selected because it is near the mean latitude of some of the most populous areas in the continental United States (approximately 40 degrees north latitude). Diagrams in the boxes for each day invite the reader to track the moon's rapid motion past the planets, and past the brighter stars. Similarly, readers can follow the (apparently) slower pace of the planets, in their conjunctions with bright stars, with other planets, and with the largest asteroids in their orbits. This is a very specialized publication that serves only the purpose described here. You will not find, for example, articles, book reviews, or evaluations of software; you will just find the charts. The highly illustrated format and easy-to-follow guide make the loose-leaf calendar popular. Information presented in the calendar can be used (with permission) as a teaching tool by members of astronomical societies and teachers. URL: www.pa.msu.edu/abrams/SkyCalendar

598. *Ad Astra: to the stars: the magazine of the National Space Society.* [ISSN: 1041-102X] 1989. 6x/yr. National Space Society, 1620 I St., N.W., Ste 615, Washington, DC 20003-4316; nsshq@nss.org; http://www.nss.org. Illus., adv. Circ: 26800 Paid and free. Vol. ends: No. 6. *Indexed:* A01, A22, ABS&EES, BRI, P02. *Bk. rev.:* Number and length vary. *Aud.:* Hs, Ga, Ac, Sa.

Ad Astra contains articles and news stories concerning U.S. and international space programs, federal space policy formation, commercial space endeavors, emerging space technologies, and recent scientific achievements pertinent to astronomy. It is the membership publication of the National Space Society, and its articles can be read both by space and astronomy enthusiasts and by those with extensive education in the field. Regular departments in the publication include "Launch Pad," "Mission Control," "Countdown," "Space Community," and "Lifting Off." The primary focus is, of course, the space program, but often there are articles dealing with broader astronomical issues such as cosmology, or, on occasion, wholly speculative articles about possible future space-related ventures. The journal sometimes includes reviews for outstanding space-related children's books on its web site. This popular journal has numerous beautiful illustrations and photographs, and has helped spark an early interest in space in many people. A valuable addition to any library, whether it specializes in astronomy or not. URL: www.nss.org/adastra

599. *Advances in Astronomy.* [ISSN: 1687-7969] 2008. USD 395. Hindawi Publishing Corporation, 410 Park Ave, 15th Fl, PMB 287, New York, NY 10022; orders@hindawi.com; http://www.hindawi.com. Refereed. *Indexed:* A01, M&GPA. *Aud.:* Ac, Sa.

Advances in Astronomy is a peer-reviewed, open-access journal, publishing original research articles, as well as review articles in all areas of astronomy and astrophysics. Intended for serious astronomers, physicists, and other scientists, it attracts authors from observatories and universities all over the world. Some recent articles discuss vacuum energy, cosmic microwave background radiation anisotropies, and techniques for exoplanet transit photometry. URL: www.hindawi.com/journals/aa

600. *American Astronomical Society. Bulletin.* Incorporates (1981-1986): *Mount Wilson and Las Campanas Observatories. Annual Report of the Director;* Which was formerly (until 1981): *Hale Observatories. Annual Report of the Director;* (until 1970): *Mount Wilson and Palomar Observatories. Annual Report of the Director;* (1918-1948): *Mount Wilson Observatory. Annual Report of the Director;* Supersedes in part (in 1969): *The Astronomical Journal.* [ISSN: 0002-7537] 1969. q. Members, USD 35. American Astronomical Society, 2000 Florida Ave, NW, Ste 400, Washington, DC 20009; aas@aas.org; http://aas.org/. Illus. Vol. ends: No. 4. *Indexed:* A22. *Aud.:* Ac, Sa.

The function of the *Bulletin* is to give the American Astronomical Society (AAS) a professional forum in which to present the abstracts of papers from conferences and meetings, and to present notices of the society that are likely to be of interest to the professional astronomical community. Annual observatory reports and reports of the society itself are also published here. The observatory reports are particularly useful to people wanting to determine the observational capabilities and major research programs of various observatories. The *Bulletin* sometimes includes such interesting papers as "The Most Frequently-Cited Astronomical Papers Published during the Past Decade," Alvin Toffler-esque discussions of likely cultural changes in the twenty-first century and their impact on astronomy, and the real value of a Ph.D. The AAS reserves its *Astronomical Journal* and *Astrophysical Journal* (both below in this section) for original research papers. URL: www.aas.org/publications/baas

601. *Annual Review of Astronomy and Astrophysics.* [ISSN: 0066-4146] 1963. a. USD 246 (print or online ed.). Ed(s): Samuel Gubins, Sandra M Faber. Annual Reviews, PO Box 10139, Palo Alto, CA 94303; service@annualreviews.org; http://www.annualreviews.org. Refereed. Microform: PQC. Reprint: PSC. *Indexed:* A01, A22, C&ISA, CerAb, M&GPA. *Aud.:* Ac, Sa.

This is a valuable synthesis of the current state of research in a wide range of topics of astronomical inquiry. It is thoroughly updated once each year. Each volume contains roughly 15–20 articles, each dealing with a currently "hot" topic in astronomy. The articles give the reader a detailed overview of what kind of research is being done, and on what specific problems and issues researchers are striving to focus still more resources. Each article is followed up by a selected bibliography of several dozen of the most important published papers in that particular area of inquiry, for the year. These bibliographies are chosen by some of the top people in the world in that particular subfield. Be aware that the articles assume a certain scientific sophistication and awareness on the part of the reader. *ARAA* is a tremendously useful volume for librarians and astronomers, and it is often kept behind the circulation desk in science libraries to keep it safe. URL: http://arjournals.annualreviews.org/loi/astro?cookieSet=1

602. *Association of Lunar and Planetary Observers. Journal.* [ISSN: 0039-2502] 1947. q. Free. Ed(s): Ken Poshedly. Association of Lunar and Planetary Observers, c/o Matthew L. Will, P O Box 13456, Springfield, IL 62791; will008@attglobal.net; http://www.alpo-astronomy.org. Illus., adv. Refereed. Vol. ends: No. 4. *Bk. rev.:* 1-2, 300-500 words. *Aud.:* Ac, Sa.

Not to be confused with the *Lunar and Planetary Information Bulletin.* Sometimes known by its alternate title, *The Strolling Astronomer,* this journal is a publication of the Association of Lunar and Planetary Observers (ALPO). It specializes in publishing astronomical studies and articles relating to the study of our own solar system. Cosmology, or the study of other star systems, is not covered here. The journal is regularly mailed to members of ALPO, an international organization of amateur and professional astronomers. Not an easy magazine to leaf through, it can be a learning experience for the novice astronomer who is not afraid of a challenge. Contents often include calls for papers, book reviews, and updates and surveys of specific organized observing programs. ALPO has many subdivisions, each with its own publication, and subscriptions to these other publications need to be handled directly with each division. The ALPO web site can help settle questions concerning which publications might be best for you. *The Strolling Astronomer* is considered to be the means of coordinating all the various areas of ALPO research under a single cover. Reports and observations from readers and staff are always welcome for all publications, provided they have not been published elsewhere. Useful for serious science libraries. URL: www.alpo-astronomy.org

603. *The Astronomical Almanac.* Supersedes (1960-1981): *Astronomical Ephemeris;* (1852-1980): *American Ephemeris and Nautical Almanac;* (1766-1852): *Nautical Almanac and Astronomical Ephemeris.* [ISSN: 0737-6421] 1766. a. USD 57. U.S. Naval Observatory, 3450 Massachusetts Ave, Washington, DC 20392; http://www.usno.navy.mil/. *Aud.:* Hs, Ga, Ac, Sa.

The Astronomical Almanac is one of the fruits of a long-standing collaboration between American and British nautical almanac services. It features invaluable, authoritative tables and charts, as opposed to discursive articles. It contains precise ephemerides of the Sun, Moon, planets, and satellites, data for eclipses, and information on other astronomical phenomena for a given year. Most data are tabulated at one-day intervals. This journal includes geocentric positions of the Sun, Moon, planets, and bright stars; heliocentric positions of the planets and their orbital elements; universal and sidereal times; daily polynomials for the Moon's position; physical ephemerides of the Sun, Moon, and planets;

elongation times and differential coordinates of selected satellites of the planets; rise, set, and transit times of the Sun and Moon; eclipse data and maps; tables of reference data for various celestial objects; useful formulae; and other information. Don't miss the "Explanatory Supplement" to this publication. The supplement is an authoritative source on astronomical phenomena and calendars, and offers detailed directions for performing practical astronomy. All in all, this is a very valuable, esteemed resource—generally given pride of place in any serious astronomy collection. URL: www.usno.navy.mil/USNO/astronomical-applications/publications/astro-almanac

604. *The Astronomical Journal.* [ISSN: 0004-6256] 1849. m. USD 915 combined subscription (print & online eds.). Ed(s): John S Gallagher, III, Anita H Makuluni. Institute of Physics Publishing, Inc., Space Astronomy Lab, Chamberlin Hall, University of Wisconsin, Madison, WI 53706; http://www.iop.org. Illus., index. Refereed. Vol. ends: No. 6. *Indexed:* A22, ApMecR, CCMJ, CompR, M&GPA, MSN, MathR. *Aud.:* Ac, Sa.

Considered to be one of the five or six "core" journals in any serious astronomy collection, *AJ* is essential for any academic institution with an astronomy program, and is indispensable to serious astronomers. A preferred vehicle for publishing original observations and research with a fairly short publication time, this journal publishes many seminal papers. Emphasis is placed on scientific results derived from observations, as opposed to concepts extrapolated from theory. Coverage includes the traditional areas of astronomy, and expanded topics, including all currently "hot" subjects, such as detection of new planets; large-scale structure of the universe; asteroids that are likely to strike the Earth; and every imaginable other topic pertaining to astronomy. This journal and *Astrophysical Journal* (below in this section) comprise the main U.S. publications of new research in the fields of astronomy and astrophysics, similar to the European *Astronomy and Astrophysics* (below in this section). URL: www.iop.org/EJ/journal/-page=scope/1538-3881

605. *Astronomical Society of the Pacific. Publications.* [ISSN: 0004-6280] 1889. m. USD 481 (print & online eds.). Ed(s): Jeff Mangum. University of Chicago Press, 1427 E 60th St, Chicago, IL 60637; subscriptions@press.uchicago.edu; http://www.journals.uchicago.edu. Illus., index, adv. Sample. Refereed. Reprint: PSC. *Indexed:* A22, M&GPA, MathR. *Aud.:* Ac, Sa.

The Astronomical Society of the Pacific (ASP) publishes several titles, among them *Universe in the Classroom* and *Mercury* (both below in this section), *Publications of the ASP,* and *Selectory,* a catalog of equipment for astronomy. The ASP's mission is "to advance the science of astronomy and disseminate astronomical information," and it uses some of its publications to this end. Be aware that *Publications* is an actual title—it does not simply refer to a group of publications, but rather constitutes an actual periodical in and of itself. *Publications* is the ASP's technical journal, which includes refereed reports on current research, Ph.D. thesis abstracts, and review articles on astronomy and astrophysics. It prides itself on giving equal coverage to "all wavelengths and distance scales" of astrometric data. URL: www.journals.uchicago.edu/page/pasp/brief.html

606. *Astronomy.* [ISSN: 0091-6358] 1973. m. USD 42.95 domestic; USD 50.95 Canada; USD 58.95 elsewhere. Ed(s): David J Eicher. Kalmbach Publishing Co., 21027 Crossroads Circle, Waukesha, WI 53187; http://www.kalmbach.com. Illus., adv. Vol. ends: Dec. *Indexed:* A01, A22, BRI, C37, CBRI, IHTDI, MASUSE, P02. *Bk. rev.:* 5-6, 50-500 words. *Aud.:* Hs, Ga, Ac.

As indicated by its circulation, this is one of the most popular astronomy publications among casual sky watchers. Insightful, well-written articles, aimed at a popular audience, are brought together here with some truly spectacular full-color photographs of some of the most "stellar" sights in the heavens. *Astronomy* provides readers with space news reports, monthly observing tips, reviews of telescope-related products, hobby information, and the latest news on space exploration. The web site includes extremely user-friendly podcasts, blogs, and an online Q&A readers forum. A very helpful sky chart, as well as observing tips for locating specific objects in the sky, are to be found in the periodical, in a visually appealing format that is both pleasant and stimulating to read. This would be a welcome addition to virtually any library. URL: www.astronomy.com

607. *Astronomy & Astrophysics.* Superseded in part (in 1968): *Zeitschrift fuer Astrophysik;* Incorporated (1947-1992): *Astronomical Institutes of Czechoslovakia. Bulletin;* (1966-2000): *Astronomy & Astrophysics. Supplement Series;* Which was formerly (until 1970): *Astronomical Institutes of the Netherlands. Bulletin. Supplement Series;* Which incorporated (1900-1960): *Kapteyn Astronomical Laboratory at Groningen. Publications;* Which was formerly (until 1924): *Astronomical Laboratory at Groningen. Publications.* [ISSN: 0004-6361] 1930. 24x/yr. EUR 4376 (print & online eds.) Individuals, EUR 4260 (print & online eds.). E D P Sciences, 17 Ave du Hoggar, Parc d'Activites de Courtaboeuf, Les Ulis, 91944, France; subscribers@edpsciences.org; http://www.edpsciences.org. Illus., index, adv. Sample. Refereed. Vol. ends: No. 3. Microform: PQC. *Indexed:* A22, ApMecR, C&ISA, CerAb, EngInd, M&GPA, MathR. *Aud.:* Ac, Sa.

Sponsored by the European Southern Observatory, this publication represents scientific organizations in 17 European countries. The journal is a cooperative effort that grew out of the merger of the publications of several of the represented organizations. It once had a supplement, published separately, but today the main journal and the supplement are published under a single cover. Or, the journal can be accessed through their website. Papers relate to all aspects of astronomy and astrophysics (theoretical, observational, and instrumental), regardless of the techniques used to obtain the results. Some items that will *not* be found in this journal include observatory reports, review papers, and conference proceedings. Especially since the merging of this title with its supplement, coverage includes all areas of astronomy and astrophysics, including connected fields. Therefore, for example, this journal might include articles on such subjects as computational techniques that might have applications in astronomy, atomic or molecular physics, or even statistical mathematics. The journal intends to review all important fields relevant to the study of astronomy and astrophysics from time to time, while frequency of review is dictated by the amount of activity in an area. This research publication is comparable to *The Astronomical Journal* and *The Astrophysical Journal.* Recently added features include the ability to view the most recent issue on the web site, for registered readers. These readers can also sign up for e-mail alerts concerning their favorite astronomical topics. URL: www.aanda.org

608. *Astronomy & Geophysics.* Formerly (until 1997): *Royal Astronomical Society. Quarterly Journal.* [ISSN: 1366-8781] 1960. bi-m. EUR 360. Ed(s): Sue Bowler. Oxford University Press, Great Clarendon St, Oxford, OX2 6DP, United Kingdom; jnl.orders@oup.co.uk; http://www.oxfordjournals.org. Illus., index, adv. Sample. Refereed. Circ: 3700. Vol. ends: No. 6. Microform: PQC. Reprint: PSC. *Indexed:* A01, A22, E01, M&GPA, MathR, P02. *Bk. rev.:* Number and length vary. *Aud.:* Ac, Sa.

After a redesign in 1996, *Astronomy & Geophysics* replaced the *Quarterly Journal of the Royal Astronomical Society* as its topical publication. One objective of the journal is to promote communication among general astronomers and planetary scientists. Therefore, it often has exceptionally strong coverage of planetary sciences, yet it also has excellent coverage of cosmology, black holes, astrophotography, etc. Articles are written in accessible language, without many equations or formulae, and include related topics such as interdisciplinary research, information about upcoming international conferences, science policy, the history of the fields of study of astronomy- or geophysics-related topics, social issues within the astronomical community, astronomy-related news, and topical book and software reviews. Many traditions from the *Quarterly Journal* remain, such as the journal being a forum for discussion of fundamental and controversial scientific issues. Among other new features, available for consideration on the web site, is the ability for readers to alert their librarian to any given article in case the librarian is engaged in creating new subject guides, etc. URL: www.blackwellpublishing.com/journal.asp?ref=1366-8781&site=1

609. *Astronomy Education Review: a lively electronic compendium of research, news, resources and opinion.* [ISSN: 1539-1515] 2002. q. Free. Ed(s): Thomas A Hockey, Judy Johnson. National Optical Astronomy Observatory, 950 N Cherry Ave, Tucson, AZ 85719; outreach@noao.edu; http://www.noao.edu/. *Indexed:* ERIC. *Bk. rev.:* Number and length vary. *Aud.:* Hs, Ac.

An innovative new online journal, this unassuming little venture can really be of great assistance to astronomy educators. The mission of this journal is shaped as much by the philosophy of education as it is by the spirit of astronomy. Subscribers will find articles on applying educational methodologies to astronomy; pointers on salient educational journals of which the educator may have been unaware; and postings concerning symposia, workshops, funding sources, and job openings. Furthermore, if you are, or know of, a science educator who wishes to share the fruits of their experiences in teaching astronomy, this is an avenue that you could explore. The web site also features book reviews, and the opportunity to participate in online discussions and informal forums on issues pertaining to astronomical education. URL: http://aer.noao.edu/cgi-bin/new.pl

610. *Astronomy Reports.* Former titles (until 1993): *Soviet Astronomy;* (until 1974): *Soviet Astronomy A.J.* [ISSN: 1063-7729] 1924. m. EUR 3972 (print & online eds.). Ed(s): Alexander A Boyarchuk. M A I K Nauka - Interperiodica, Profsoyuznaya ul 90, Moscow, 117997, Russian Federation; compmg@maik.ru; http://www.maik.ru. Illus., index. Sample. Refereed. Vol. ends: No. 6. Reprint: PSC. *Indexed:* A01, A22, E01, M&GPA, MathR. *Bk. rev.:* Number and length vary. *Aud.:* Ac, Sa.

This journal is displayed prominently at any serious astronomy library. *Astronomy Reports* is a cover-to-cover translation of the principal Russian astronomy journal *Astronomicheskii Zhurnal,* and is available simultaneously with the Russian edition from Maik Nauka/Interperiodica Publishing. Russia has a long and proud tradition of producing great astrophysicists, and a lot of cutting-edge science is first reported in the Russian journals. Issues consist of about 10–20 articles in many areas of astronomy, including radio astronomy, theoretical and observational astrophysics, physics of the sun, planetary science, stellar astronomy, celestial mechanics, astronomical methods and instrumentation, and issues having to do with cosmological large-scale structure. Proceedings of international conferences and book reviews are also included. URL: www.springer.com/astronomy/journal/11444

611. *The Astrophysical Journal: an international review of astronomy and astronomical physics.* Formerly (until 1985): *Astronomy and Astro-Physics.* [ISSN: 0004-637X] 18??. 18x/yr. USD 3105 (print & online eds.). Ed(s): Ethan T Vishniac. Institute of Physics Publishing, Inc., The Public Ledger Bldg, Ste 929, 150 S Independence Mall W, Philadelphia, PA 19106; info@ioppubusa.com; http://www.iop.org. Illus., index. Refereed. *Indexed:* A01, A22, M&GPA, MathR. *Aud.:* Ac, Sa.

This is widely deemed to be the most important research journal in the world for research related to astronomy and astrophysics. Many astronomical and astrophysical discoveries of the twentieth and twenty-first centuries were first reported in this peer-reviewed official publication of the American Astronomical Society. Any major astronomy library considers this to be part of its "core" collection. Be aware, the astrophysics presented here is extremely esoteric, with many elaborate equations and graphs in every single article. A supplement series accompanies the journal, its main purpose being to present substantial and extensive support for material found in the main journal. Access to a full-text electronic version is free with a paid print subscription. URL: http://iopscience.iop.org/0004-637X/

612. *Astrophysics.* [ISSN: 0571-7256] 1965. q. EUR 3551 (print & online eds.). Ed(s): David M Sedrakyan. Springer New York LLC, 233 Spring St, New York, NY 10013; service-ny@springer.com; http://www.springer.com. Illus., index, adv. Sample. Refereed. Vol. ends: No. 4. Microform: PQC. Reprint: PSC. *Indexed:* A01, A22, ApMecR, C&ISA, CerAb, E01, M&GPA, MathR. *Aud.:* Ac, Sa.

The Consultants Bureau, a subsidiary of Plenum Publishing, is responsible for publishing dozens of English translations of Russian journals, including *Astrophysics,* a cover-to-cover translation of the Russian *Astrofizika.* This journal presents data obtained at Sternberg Astronomical Institute and all principal observatories in Russia, along with recent theoretical and experimental advances in astrophysics. Like *Astronomy Reports,* this is full of cutting-edge Russian science and is geared toward a higher-level audience. Articles deal with the entire range of astronomical and astrophysical phenomena. Topics of papers include planetary atmospheres, interstellar matter, solar physics, and space astrophysics, along with a broad range of related topics. URL: www.springer.com/astronomy/practical+astronomy/journal/10511

613. *Astrophysics and Space Science: an international journal of astronomy, astrophysics and space science.* Incorporates (1970-1972): *Cosmic Electrodynamics;* (1975-1981): *Space Science Instrumentation.* [ISSN: 0004-640X] 1968. m. EUR 5453 (print & online eds.). Ed(s): Michael A Dopita. Springer Netherlands, Van Godewijckstraat 30, Dordrecht, 3311 GX, Netherlands; http://www.springer.com. Illus., index, adv. Sample. Refereed. Vol. ends: No. 2. Microform: PQC. Reprint: PSC. *Indexed:* A01, A22, C&ISA, CCMJ, CerAb, E01, M&GPA, MathR. *Aud.:* Ac, Sa.

This respected journal publishes original contributions, invited reviews, and conference proceedings over the entire range of astronomy and astrophysics. It includes observational and theoretical papers as well as those concerned with the techniques of instrumentation. Observational papers can include data from ground-based, space, and atmospheric facilities. *Astrophysics and Space Science* has published, and continues to publish, landmark papers in its field. It is widely considered an indispensable source of information for professional astronomers, astrophysicists, and space scientists. The supplemental publication *Experimental Astronomy* (below in this section) is included with the subscription at no extra cost. URL: www.springer.com/astronomy/journal/10509

614. *Astrophysics and Space Sciences Transactions (Online).* [ISSN: 1810-6536] 2004. irreg. Free. Copernicus GmbH, Bahnhofsallee 1e, Goettingen, 37081, Germany; info@copernicus.org; http://www.copernicus.org. Refereed. *Aud.:* Ac.

Published in Germany, and articles in English, this is an open-access, wide-ranging, international scientific publication dealing with all areas of astronomy. Papers dealing with the technology and instrumentation accompanying various areas of inquiry are also included. A (free) article alert system is included for enthusiasts with a particular research interest. Articles are double-blind peer-reviewed. Back issues of articles are available in print, if so desired. URL: www.astrophysics-and-space-sciences-transactions.net/home.html

615. *Astrum.* [ISSN: 0210-4105] 1960. bi-m. Membership, EUR 78. Agrupacio Astronomica de Sabadell, Apdo de Correos 50, Sabadell, Barcelona, 08200, Spain; secretaria@astrosabadell.org; http://www.astrosabadell.org. Illus., adv. Circ: 2000. *Aud.:* Hs, Ga.

Astrum is a colorful astronomy magazine in Spanish, aimed at a popular audience. ProQuest has chosen to survey some astronomy periodicals in Spanish, so that librarians serving constituencies with a growing Spanish-speaking population can accommodate the needs of those patrons. *Astrum* serves this role quite well. It is not a commercial magazine—it is mailed free to members of the Agrupacio Astronomica de Sabadell and to astronomical centers and libraries. However, if your library seeks to foster an interest in science in Hispanic children, you might consider e-mailing the publishing part of the Agrupacio. *Astrum* includes articles, sky charts, ephemerides, and even surveys of Spanish-language Internet resources having to do with astronomy. Furthermore, it is full of very colorful, high-resolution photographs of many of the more beautiful areas in the sky. URL: www.astrosabadell.org/html/ca/publicacions.htm

616. *British Astronomical Association. Journal.* [ISSN: 0007-0297] 1890. bi-m. GBP 44 Free to members. Ed(s): Hazel McGee. British Astronomical Association, Burlington House, Picadilly, London, W1J 0DU, United Kingdom; office@britastro.org; http://www.britastro.org. Illus., index, adv. Sample. Refereed. Vol. ends: No. 6. *Indexed:* A01, A22, BRI. *Bk. rev.:* 6-20, 500-1,000 words. *Aud.:* Ac, Sa.

Since its founding in 1890, this journal has published the observations and work of British Astronomical Association (BAA) members, and members receive the journal free. However, nonmembers are eligible to receive the journal if they contact the publisher. Many articles and items of interest to all amateur astronomers are published, along with the observations and work of BAA members. The letters to the editor are often lively and opinionated, with discussions on any subject having to do with astronomy, especially at the amateur level. Subscribers are offered special deals on astronomy-related products from time to time, such as CD-ROMs or software. Although this publication is geared to amateur astronomers and professionals who focus on observational techniques, it does not include the star charts and viewing guides that are published by equivalent American publications, such as *Astronomy* and *Sky & Telescope*. URL: www.britastro.org/jbaa

617. *Celestial Mechanics and Dynamical Astronomy: an international journal of space dynamics.* Formerly (until 1989): *Celestial Mechanics.* [ISSN: 0923-2958] 1969. m. EUR 2286 (print & online eds.). Ed(s): Sylvio Ferraz-Mello. Springer Netherlands, Van Godewijckstraat 30, Dordrecht, 3311 GX, Netherlands; http://www.springer.com. Illus., index, adv. Sample. Refereed. Vol. ends: No. 4. Microform: PQC. Reprint: PSC. *Indexed:* A01, A22, ApMecR, BRI, C&ISA, CCMJ, CerAb, E01, M&GPA, MSN, MathR. *Aud.:* Ac, Sa.

This international publication is concerned with the entire scope of dynamical astronomy and its applications, as well as with peripheral fields. It is heavily math- and physics-oriented, which can make reading difficult for those not well-versed in these fields. Articles cover all aspects of celestial mechanics: mathematical, physics-related, and computational, including computer languages for analytical developments. The majority of the articles are in English. This noteworthy publication is considered in the astronomical community to be the journal of record in its area, and it belongs in any complete astronomical library. URL: www.springer.com/astronomy/astrophysics+and+astroparticles/journal/10569

618. *The Classroom Astronomer.* [ISSN: 2151-0105] 2009. q. USD 29 domestic; USD 35 in Canada & Mexico; USD 45 elsewhere. Ed(s): Dr. Lawrence Krumenaker. Hermograph Press, PO Box 29023, Atlanta, GA 30359-0023; inquiries@hermograph.com; http://www.hermograph.com. Adv. *Aud.:* Ems, Hs, Ac.

The Classroom Astronomer is a quarterly pdf and printed publication designed as a practitioner journal for classroom teachers of astronomy. While aimed at the high school level, it also provides tips, techniques, and informative how-to articles for teachers of grades K–8 and undergraduate college "Astro 101" courses. The journal's mission is to increase the amount of astronomy in school systems and improve the skills of teachers. It has readers in 15 countries, is praised by scientists working with the Chandra observatory, and is notable for a truly infectious enthusiasm. Give this unpretentious little journal a chance. URL: http://classroomastronomer.toteachthestars.net/index.htm

619. *Communicating Astronomy with the Public Journal.* [ISSN: 1996-5621] 2007. q. International Astronomical Union, IAU-UAI Secretariat, 98bis Blvd Arago, Paris, 75014, France; iau@iap.fr; http://www.iau.org. Refereed. *Bk. rev.:* Number and length vary. *Aud.:* Ac, Sa.

CAP is designed to provide a forum for professionals in the area of astronomy education, at planetariums, and in astronomy-related public outreach, to share insights, methods, and viewpoints. It hopes to make it easier for people in these fields to share both the excitement of science and the actual new information about the universe that today's astronomers are coming to comprehend. Many people in the world today do not realize the awesome magnitude of the leaps forward that our knowledge of the universe is taking, due to advances in technology, in our lifetime. *CAP* seeks to help remedy this situation. This innovative journal is intended to be complementary to *Astronomy Education Review,* which is described earlier in this section. URL: www.capjournal.org/index.php

620. *Earth, Moon, and Planets: an international journal of solar system science.* Former titles (until 1984): *Moon and the Planets;* (until 1978): *Moon.* [ISSN: 0167-9295] 1969. 8x/yr. EUR 1241 (print & online eds.). Ed(s): M S Gudipati. Springer Netherlands, Van Godewijckstraat 30, Dordrecht, 3311 GX, Netherlands; http://www.springer.com. Illus., index, adv. Sample. Refereed. Vol. ends: Dec. Microform: PQC. Reprint: PSC. *Indexed:* A01, A22, BRI, C&ISA, CerAb, E01, M&GPA. *Bk. rev.:* Number and length vary. *Aud.:* Ac, Sa.

This international journal publishes original contributions on subjects ranging from star and planet formation and the origin and evolution of the solar and extra-solar planetary systems to asteroids, comets, meteoroids, and near-Earth objects. The research done in this journal on near-Earth objects (NEOs) includes studies on asteroids that are considered likely candidates to one day strike Earth. A point to bear in mind is that the planets covered in this journal include

exoplanets, native to star systems beyond our own. This is very quickly becoming a much more significant area of study than it was just a few years ago. This journal also publishes relevant special issues and topical conference proceedings, review articles on problems of current interest, and book reviews. For example, this journal published a special issue dealing with the Shoemaker-Levy comet striking Jupiter. The editor welcomes proposals from guest editors for special thematic issues. URL: www.springer.com/astronomy/journal/11038

621. *Experimental Astronomy: an international journal on astronomical instrumentation and data analysis.* [ISSN: 0922-6435] 1989. bi-m. EUR 811 (print & online eds.). Ed(s): Peter von Ballmoos. Springer Netherlands, Van Godewijckstraat 30, Dordrecht, 3311 GX, Netherlands; http://www.springer.com. Illus. Sample. Refereed. Vol. ends: No. 4. Microform: PQC. Reprint: PSC. *Indexed:* A01, A22, C&ISA, CerAb, E01, M&GPA. *Aud.:* Ac, Sa.

Experimental Astronomy acts as a medium for the publication of papers on the instrumentation and data handling necessary for the conduct of astronomy at all wavelength fields, including radio, X-rays, etc. *Experimental Astronomy* publishes full-length articles, research letters, and reviews on developments in detection techniques, instruments, data analysis, and image-processing techniques. These technical specializations are evolving so quickly that the coverage provided in this journal is of great importance to anyone with a professional interest in having truly current technical information. Occasionally, special issues are published to provide in-depth coverage on the instrumentation or analysis connected with a particular project, such as satellite experiments. Subscribers to *Astrophysics and Space Science* (above in this section) receive this publication as a supplement, but it can also be purchased alone. URL: www.springer.com/astronomy/journal/10686

622. *Griffith Observer.* [ISSN: 0195-3982] 1937. m. USD 30 in US & Canada; USD 31 Mexico; USD 35 elsewhere. Griffith Observatory, 2800 E Observatory Rd, Los Angeles, CA 90027; info@GriffithObs.org; http://www.griffithobs.org. Illus., index. Sample. Vol. ends: Dec. *Indexed:* MLA-IB. *Aud.:* Hs, Ga.

Published monthly by the observatory, this journal provides information about the activities at the Griffith Observatory and popular articles about astronomy. It is comparable in aims and scope to the Spanish-language journal *Astrum.* Sky charts, illustrations, guides to useful Internet links, and photographs enhance this publication, which strives to create a lifelong interest in science in its readers. For its efforts at popularizing astronomy, the *Griffith Observer* has been characterized as "the Carl Sagan of astronomy periodicals." URL: www.griffithobs.org/Observer.html

623. *Icarus.* [ISSN: 0019-1035] 1962. m. EUR 6472. Ed(s): P D Nicholson. Academic Press, 3251 Riverport Ln, Maryland Heights, MO 63043; JournalCustomerService-usa@elsevier.com; http://www.elsevierdirect.com/brochures/academicpress/index.html. Illus., index, adv. Refereed. Vol. ends: No. 2. *Indexed:* A01, A22, BRI, C&ISA, CerAb, E01, M&GPA. *Bk. rev.:* 2-3, 150-2,000 words. *Aud.:* Ac, Sa.

Devoted to publishing original contributions in planetary science and the study of solar systems (be they our own solar system, or other, recently discovered planetary systems orbiting more distant stars), this is another very prominent journal for academic libraries. Librarians should note that these fields are focused primarily on relatively local astronomy. Articles are generally about planets, moons, the Sun, or asteroids within our solar system. Coverage of cosmology, black holes, quasars, or theoretical physics is very rarely included. Articles concerning extrasolar planets, or "exoplanets"—i.e., planets revolving around stars other than the Sun—are included on the grounds that stars with exoplanets constitute solar systems in their own right. This field is quite new, but it is increasingly important. All aspects of planetary-system research are included, such as results of new research and observations. Special sections or issues are also a feature. All articles appear in English, but occasional abstracts are in German, French, or Russian. URL: www.elsevier.com/wps/find/journaldescription.cws_home/622843/bibliographic

624. *International Astronomical Union. Minor Planet Center. Minor Planet Circulars - Minor Planets and Comets.* Former titles (until 1979): *M P C;* (until 1978): *Minor Planet Circulars.* [ISSN: 0736-6884] 1947. m. International Astronomical Union, Minor Planet Center, 60 Garden St, PO Box 18, Cambridge, MA 02138; iausubs@cfa.harvard.edu; http://www.cfa.harvard.edu/iau/mpc.html. Illus. *Aud.:* Ac, Sa.

Generally published on the date of the full moon (hence, the approximately monthly frequency), *Minor Planet Circulars* are available both in print and electronically as the *Minor Planets Electronic Circulars*. Astrometric observations on comets and on particularly unusual minor planets are included, although some information is summarized in observatory code. For those who may not be aware of this, "minor planets" is another accepted term for "asteroids." These circulars are published by the agency in charge of keeping an eye out for asteroids that may one day strike Earth. The circulars were once sent out as telegrams, and even today they retain the pithiness of the telegram. No space is wasted, and there is seldom anything resembling actual articles. New numberings and namings of asteroids/minor planets are also announced in the *Circulars*. Please note: Paid subscriptions are no long accepted as of 2010. URL: www.minorplanetcenter.net/iau/services/MPCServices.html

625. International Comet Quarterly. Formerly (until 1979): *The Comet.* [ISSN: 0736-6922] 1973. q. plus a. handbook. USD 45. Ed(s): Daniel W E Green. International Comet Quarterly, Smithsonian Astrophysical Observatory, 60 Garden St, Cambridge, MA 02138. Illus., index. Refereed. Vol. ends: No. 4. *Aud.:* Ac, Sa.

The *International Comet Quarterly* (*ICQ*) is the primary location for information about comets and observing comets, and it serves as a link between professional and serious amateur astronomers. Observations, discoveries, and research related to comets can be found in this publication. Also published are announcements concerning international conferences that have to do with the extremely important work of detecting comets and asteroids that are likely someday to strike Earth. The annual subscription cost includes a copy of the annual *Comet Handbook,* which contains ephemerides and orbital elements for comets observable in the coming year. This journal is not geared to a general readership; only professionals and very serious amateur astronomers who focus on comets will need this publication for their research. The web site is deliberately kept at a low-tech, 1999-ish level with few graphics, so that people and libraries with slow modem connections can access the important information provided here. URL: http://cfa-www.harvard.edu/icq/icq.html

626. International Journal of Astrobiology. [ISSN: 1473-5504] 2002. q. Ed(s): Rocco Mancinelli. Cambridge University Press, The Edinburgh Bldg, Shaftesbury Rd, Cambridge, CB2 8RU, United Kingdom; journals@cambridge.org; http://www.cambridge.org/uk. Adv. Refereed. Circ: 450. Reprint: PSC. *Indexed:* A22, E01, M&GPA. *Bk. rev.:* Number and length vary. *Aud.:* Ga, Ac, Sa.

A relatively new publication, this fascinating journal provides an introduction to the burgeoning world of "astrobiology." This topic includes not only the search for intelligent extraterrestrial life, but also the study of interstellar chemical conditions conducive to the appearance of primitive lifeforms. The possibility of life on Mars is discussed, as are the relatively high chances of discovering life on Saturn's moon Titan, or in the seas of Jupiter's moon Europa. The history of the study of astrobiology is an intriguing topic in its own right, and it is not slighted in the contents of this journal. Related inquiries are made into such issues as adaptations made by terrestrial lifeforms to extreme environments on Earth. The journal includes peer-reviewed research papers, book reviews, and overviews of this fast-evolving discipline. This journal is intended primarily as a forum for biochemists, astronomers, and other professionals in allied fields, but the inherently fascinating nature of the topic could make some readers choose to put in the extra effort required to wade through an issue. URL: http://journals.cambridge.org/action/displayJournal?jid=IJA

627. Journal for the History of Astronomy. Incorporates (1979-2002): *Archaeoastronomy.* [ISSN: 0021-8286] 1970. q. USD 320 in the Americas & Japan (print & online eds.) Individuals, USD 98 in the Americas & Japan). Ed(s): Michael Hoskin. Science History Publications Ltd., 16 Rutherford Rd, Cambridge, CB2 8HH, United Kingdom; shp@shpltd.co.uk; http://www.shpltd.co.uk. Illus. Refereed. Vol. ends: No. 4. *Indexed:* A01, A22, A47, ArtHuCI, BRI, BrArAb, CCMJ, FR, MLA-IB, MathR, NumL. *Bk. rev.:* 6-16, 300-1,000 words. *Aud.:* Ac, Sa.

The only journal of its type, this covers the history of astronomy from its earliest times. The research presented is a pleasant, fascinating change of pace from the heavily math- and science-oriented publications so common (and so important) in astronomy. Few journals capture more successfully the spirit of astronomy, in the sense of the important role it has played throughout the historical struggle

between reason and superstition. This journal's subject matter is not rigidly restricted to the history of astronomy per se. For example, sometimes intellectual forays are made into relevant topics in the study of the history of mathematics, or of physics. A supplemental publication, *Archaeoastronomy,* is included with a subscription. This supplement is dedicated to investigating astronomical practice and celestial lore in ancient societies from all over the world. Sample articles might include, for example, discussion of ancient Mayan, Inca, Greek, or Egyptian astronomical traditions and edifices, by experts who are learned in these fields. URL: www.shpltd.co.uk/jha.html

628. Journal of Cosmology and Astroparticle Physics. [ISSN: 1475-7516] 2003. m. GBP 1251. Institute of Physics Publishing Ltd., Temple Circus, Temple Way, Bristol, BS1 6HG, United Kingdom; custserv@iop.org; http://ioppublishing.org. Sample. Refereed. *Indexed:* CCMJ, M&GPA, MSN, MathR. *Aud.:* Ac, Sa.

A fairly new journal, *JCAP* is an ambitious, selective online periodical that focuses on the interrelationships between the smallest of subatomic particles and the nature of the universe at its grandest scales, "in the large." Common topics include string theory, gravitational waves, "p-brane democracy," M-theory, brane cosmology, black holes, implications of subatomic particles upon the large-scale structure of the universe, and other cosmological issues. Criteria for article acceptance are "scientific quality, originality[,] and relevance." This journal is probably too advanced for most amateur hobbyists, but it has been placed on many "core" reading lists for academic science libraries, even in these financially strapped times. URL: www.iop.org/EJ/journal/JCAP

629. Living Reviews in Solar Physics. [ISSN: 1614-4961] 2004. irreg. Free. Ed(s): S K Solanki. Max-Planck-Institut fuer Sonnensystemforschung, Max-Planck-Str 2, Katlenburg-Lindau, 37191, Germany; presseinfo@mps.mpg.de; http://www.mps.mpg.de. Refereed. *Indexed:* A01. *Aud.:* Ac, Sa.

This is a peer-reviewed, online forum for cutting-edge research and discussion of solar and heliospheric physics. The word "living" is built into this journal's title because authors keep their articles "alive" by means of frequent online updates. *Living Reviews* also wishes to be known for its up-to-date, critical reviews of the particular subfield of solar research covered by a given article. Bibliographic subject guides to assist in further research are always appended. These guides are updated often by the authors, and include links to helpful web sites. This journal aims to become an online starting point for graduate students; and for professionals in the field, it aims to open the most significant doors of online research as they emerge. URL: http://solarphysics.livingreviews.org

630. Lunar and Planetary Information Bulletin. [ISSN: 1534-6587] 1978. q. Free. Ed(s): Paul Schenk. Lunar and Planetary Institute, 3600 Bay Area Blvd, Houston, TX 77058; order@lpi.usra.edu; http://www.lpi.usra.edu. Illus. *Bk. rev.:* Number and length vary. *Aud.:* Ga, Ac.

Not to be confused with the *Association of Lunar and Planetary Observers Journal.* This is a real treat for the layperson who has the background and command of vocabulary. The Lunar and Planetary Institute provides support services to NASA, and to planetary scientists. Their publication covers astronomical topics that are likely to be of interest to the average involved reader, such as potential fossils on Mars, or the adaptation of hydroponic plant cultures to possible long-term space missions for life-support purposes. A regular section titled "Spotlight on Education" focuses on events and programs that provide planetary scientists and astronomers with an opportunity to do outreach work to the community. There is a "New in Print" section that takes the reader on a tour of recently published books in the field. Often, one of these titles is singled out for an in-depth review, which sometimes includes an interview with the author. Also, the "News from Space" section is excellent, containing six or seven short articles about exciting goings-on in astronomy. Intelligent, well-written discussions can be found dealing with such questions as the origin of the solar system or of the asteroid belt. An objective and scientific approach, written in a delightfully accessible style. URL: www.lpi.usra.edu/publications/newsletters/lpib

631. Mercury (Online). Former titles (until 2008): *Mercury (Print);* (until 1972): *Astronomical Society of the Pacific. Leaflet.* 1925. q. USD 72 Free to members. Ed(s): Paul Deans. Astronomical Society of the Pacific, 390 Ashton Ave, San Francisco, CA 94112; astro@astrosociety.org; http://www.astrosociety.org. Illus., index, adv. Vol. ends: No. 6. *Indexed:* A01, A22, BRI, MASUSE, P02. *Bk. rev.:* 2-6, 50-200 words. *Aud.:* Hs, Ga, Sa.

Mercury is now entirely online, and its purpose is to provide the necessary perspective for understanding astronomy. This nonspecialist magazine is geared toward a broad public audience, and features articles on topics ranging from astronomy research and education, to archaeoastronomy, history, and public policy. It is the most widely read online publication of the Astronomical Society of the Pacific (ASP), a nonprofit organization whose goal is to promote public interest and awareness of astronomy through education and outreach programs. As the online membership magazine of the ASP, it has made a name for itself as *the* resource for teachers to follow innovations in astronomy education. Frequently, there are articles dealing with the role of education in science, and the role of science in society. The magazine includes sky calendars and sky maps for use in the Northern Hemisphere. Book reviews are included, as are regular sections on current observing prospects, "armchair astrophysics," and news highlights from the world of astronomy. URL: www.astrosociety.org/pubs/mercury/mercury.html

632. The Messenger. [ISSN: 0722-6691] 1974. q. Free. Ed(s): M H Ulrich. European Southern Observatory, Karl Schwarzschild Str 2, Garching, 85748, Germany; ips@eso.org; http://www.eso.org. Illus., index. Sample. *Aud.:* Ac, Sa.

Published by the European Southern Observatory (ESO) in La Silla, Chile, this magazine presents the activities of the ESO to the public. Subscription is free of charge. The periodical is roughly comparable to the *Griffith Observer,* in that it acts as a window into the activities of a major observatory, but it adds an international flavor. The primary significance of this journal is that it emphasizes the astronomy of the Southern Hemisphere, which is often given short shrift in many astronomy journals. As the audience codes indicate, many of the articles are quite high-level, full of equations, graphs, etc. However, the photographs of the ESO staff happily toiling away at their astro-projects make the reader feel like a guest in the home of an interesting extended family. The ESO observatory is supported by eight countries—Belgium, Denmark, France, Germany, Italy, Sweden, Switzerland, and the Netherlands—and it receives 800 proposals a year for research that would require use of the facility. URL: www.eso.org/sci/publications/messenger

633. Meteorite! [ISSN: 1173-2245] 1995. q. USD 35. Ed(s): Larry Lebovski, Nancy Lebovski. University of Arkansas, Center for Space and Planetary Sciences, 202 Old Museum Bldg, Fayetteville, AR 72701; metpub@uark.edu; http://meteoritemag.uark.edu/index.htm. Adv. *Aud.:* Ga, Ac, Sa.

Some past articles from this publication are available at the publisher's web site, but the only way to get the full articles and the photos is to subscribe. Published quarterly, *Meteorite!* is a forum for publishing information and research on collecting, new falls and finds, asteroids, craters, and historical and prehistoric meteorite events. Of the several journals described in this section that focus on meteors, this is perhaps the best suited for the amateur enthusiast. URL: www.meteoritemag.org/index.htm

634. Meteoritics and Planetary Science. Former titles (until 1996): *Meteoritics;* (until 1953): *Contributions of the Meteoritical Society;* (until 1947): *Contributions of the Society for Research on Meteorites.* [ISSN: 1086-9379] 1935. m. GBP 1005 (print & online eds.). Ed(s): Agnieszka P Baier. John Wiley & Sons, Inc., 111 River St, MS 4-02, Hoboken, NJ 07030; info@wiley.com; http://www.wiley.com/WileyCDA/. Illus., index, adv. Sample. Refereed. Vol. ends: No. 6. Microform: PQC. Reprint: PSC. *Indexed:* A01, A22, E01, M&GPA. *Aud.:* Ac, Sa.

This scholarly journal is published by the Meteoritical Society, an international organization that studies the smallest bodies in the solar system. It is free to society members. Articles are peer reviewed and are always original. Articles published here cannot be found elsewhere. *MaPS* provides a forum for discussing the study of extraterrestrial matter and history, including asteroids, comets, tektites, impact craters, and interplanetary dust—uniting professionals from a variety of backgrounds including geology, physics, astronomy, and chemistry. Planetary science is also given coverage. This means that articles can sometimes be found here that deal with the planets and moons of our solar system, including our own moon. Of the several journals dealing largely with meteors and asteroids, this is the one that deals most directly with what we can

learn from meteors, especially what we can learn about the origins of our solar system. This journal is different from, for example, the *Minor Planet Circulars,* in that it includes articles as well as raw data. URL: http://meteoritics.org

635. New Astronomy. [ISSN: 1384-1076] 1996. 8x/yr. EUR 940. Ed(s): G Brunetti, M Fukugita. Elsevier BV, Radarweg 29, PO Box 211, Amsterdam, 1000 AE, Netherlands; JournalsCustomerServiceEMEA@elsevier.com; http://www.elsevier.com. Illus. Sample. Refereed. Vol. ends: No. 8. *Indexed:* A01, A22, C&ISA, CerAb, EngInd, M&GPA. *Aud.:* Ac, Sa.

This journal includes full-length research articles and letter articles. In recent years, it has shifted its focus to emphasize computational astronomy, i.e., computer modelling, and mathematical methodology and applications, and *NA* hopes to become the leading journal in this area. It aims to have a very short publication time, which keeps it very close to the cutting edge of astronomy. It prides itself on sending personal e-mails to astronomers about upcoming articles in their specialties. It covers solar, planetary, stellar, galactic, and extragalactic astronomy and astrophysics, and reports on original research in all wavelength bands, ranging from radio to gamma-ray. Topics include all fields of astronomy and astrophysics: theoretical, observational, and instrumental. An institutional subscription provides web access for everyone at a subscribing institute, an archival paper edition, and an electronic copy for LAN distribution. Slightly lower prices for smaller institutions and for individuals are available upon request, and a two-month free trial is available for individuals. URL: www.elsevier.com/locate/newast

636. New Astronomy Reviews. Formerly (until 1998): *Vistas in Astronomy;* Incorporates (1977-1991): *Astronomy Quarterly.* [ISSN: 1387-6473] 1958. 12x/yr. EUR 1238. Ed(s): J Audouze, P A Charles. Elsevier BV, North-Holland, Postbus 211, Amsterdam, 1000 AE, Netherlands; JournalsCustomerServiceEMEA@elsevier.com; http://www.elsevier.com. Illus., index, adv. Sample. Refereed. Vol. ends: No. 45. Microform: PQC. *Indexed:* A01, A22, BAS, MathR. *Aud.:* Ac, Sa.

Although the name of this journal has changed, there has been no significant content change from years past. The journal still includes historical perspectives and in-depth reports, review articles, and surveys of findings on major activities in astronomical research. Contributions include reprints in specific areas and in-depth review articles that survey major areas of astronomy. The journal covers solar, planetary, stellar, galactic, and extragalactic astronomy and astrophysics. It reports on original research in all wavelength bands, ranging from radio to gamma-ray. This journal might be seen as taking the broad-based coverage of *Mercury* to a higher level, for reading by professional scientists. Written for astronomers, astrophysicists, and space scientists. URL: www.journals.elsevier.com/new-astronomy-reviews/#description

637. North American Skies (Online). Formerly: *North American Skies (Print).* 1996. m. Free. Ed(s): Larry Sessions. Final Copy, 6874 E Harvard Ave., Denver, CO 80224; starman@usa.net; http://webcom.com/safezone/NAS/. *Aud.:* Ems, Hs, Ga.

This is a layperson's guide to the stars and planets, suitable for both young people and adults. *North American Skies* provides information on stars, planets, eclipses, meteor showers, and other events visible in the sky. Times are given for the Mountain Time Zone, and some information, such as the Sun and moon rise-and-set tables, is specific to Denver. However, most information is applicable throughout North America, given the appropriate time-zone change. Each issue provides a feature article (with past articles also available online) and a sky chart and instructions for its use. Another regular feature is a monthly sky calendar that lists only events that can be seen in North America with the unaided eye. Other helpful features include links about sighting satellites or shuttlecraft, telescope-related questions, and forms to facilitate reporting meteor sightings. Be aware that the web site sometimes makes certain politically charged statements, so just be prepared for that. URL: http://home.comcast.net/~sternmann/index.htm

638. The Observatory: a review of astronomy. [ISSN: 0029-7704] 1877. bi-m. GBP 70 (Individuals, GBP 15). Ed(s): D J Stickland. Observatory, 16 Swan Close, Grove, OX12 0QE, United Kingdom. Illus., index, adv. Refereed. Vol. ends: No. 6. *Indexed:* A22, MathR. *Bk. rev.:* Number and length vary. *Aud.:* Ga.

This journal is sent free to members of the Royal Astronomical Society (RAS), and it is owned and managed by the editors. Meetings of the RAS are reported, but information does not generally overlap with what appears in the official RAS publications *Monthly Notices* and *Astronomy and Geophysics*. Those two are considered the most important publications of this society, while *The Observatory* is more of a supplement. Papers and correspondence tend to be short but scholarly, with few illustrations. *The Observatory* prides itself on publishing "the most comprehensive set of book reviews in astronomy." URL: www.ulo.ucl.ac.uk/obsmag

Odyssey. See Children section.

639. *The Open Astronomy Journal.* [ISSN: 1874-3811] 2008. irreg. Free. Bentham Open, PO Box 294, Bussum, AG 1400, Netherlands; subscriptions@benthamscience.org; http://www.benthamscience.com. Refereed. *Indexed:* A01, M&GPA. *Aud.:* Ga, Ac, Sa.

Bentham Open scientific journals went online in 2008. They aim to provide high-quality, scientific research articles, reviews, and letters in a free, open-access, online forum. *OAJ* is peer reviewed and seeks to be a complete and reliable source of information on current developments in all areas of astronomy and astrophysics. It emphasizes the publication of quality papers in a timely fashion, and making information and insights available to the global community of researchers. The format is comparable to *Living Reviews in Solar Physics*, and probably represents the wave of the future. URL: www.bentham.org/open/toaaj/index.htm

640. *Planetarian.* [ISSN: 0090-3213] 1972. q. Free to members. Ed(s): Sharon Shanks. International Planetarium Society, Griffith Observatory, 2800 E Observatory Rd, Los Angeles, CA 90027; http://www.griffithobservatory.org. Illus., index, adv. Refereed. Vol. ends: No. 4. Microform: PQC. *Indexed:* A01, A22. *Aud.:* Hs, Ac, Sa.

Planetarian is free with membership in the International Planetarium Society, but there is also the option for libraries to purchase the journal separately. The majority of the publication is devoted to astronomy education, with special emphasis on the role planetariums can play. For example, an article may discuss the value of planetariums as teaching aids to help students develop a three-dimensional vision of the structure of our galaxy. Another topic is planetariums acting as aids in helping students visualize actual or potential space voyages. This is a fairly specialized journal, but certainly a very interesting and very readable one. It includes much information of interest to astronomers, academic libraries, school libraries, and science teachers. URL: www.ips-planetarium.org/?plntrn

641. *Planetary and Space Science.* [ISSN: 0032-0633] 1959. 15x/yr. EUR 4234. Ed(s): R Schulz. Pergamon, The Blvd, Langford Ln, E Park, Kidlington, OX5 1GB, United Kingdom; JournalsCustomerServiceEMEA@elsevier.com; http://www.elsevier.com. Illus., adv. Sample. Refereed. Microform: PQC. *Indexed:* A01, A22, ApMecR, C&ISA, CerAb, EngInd, M&GPA. *Aud.:* Ac, Sa.

This is the official journal of the European Geophysical Society, Planetary and Solar Systems Sciences Section. It includes both articles, and "short communications" (letters). While this journal still focuses primarily upon coverage of planetary and solar system research, as in times past, its scope has now broadened to include extra-solar systems and astrobiology, comprehensive review articles, and meetings papers. Articles still tend to be focused upon planetary systems—but with recent advances in astronomy, some of the planets studied lie outside of our solar system. Articles dealing with such topics as cosmology, black holes, active galactic nuclei, or quasars will not be found, as they do not relate to planetary systems. Ground-based and space-borne instrumentation and laboratory simulation of solar system processes are included. This journal has a fairly similar mission and audience to *Icarus,* and libraries may want to compare these two excellent journals to consider which best meets their needs. The intended audience includes professional astronomers, astrophysicists, atmospheric physicists, geologists, and planetologists. URL: www.elsevier.com/wps/find/journaldescription.cws_home/200/description#description

642. *Popular Astronomy.* Formerly (until 1981): *Hermes;* Incorporates (in 1981): *S P A News Circular.* [ISSN: 0261-0892] 1953. q. Free to members. Society for Popular Astronomy, c/o Guy Fennimore, 36 Fairway, Nottingham, NG12 5DU, United Kingdom; secretary@popastro.com; http://www.popastro.com/. Illus. *Indexed:* MLA-IB. *Aud.:* Hs, Ga, Ac.

This highly readable British publication covers all aspects of astronomy. Each issue is packed with articles and photographs, many in color. Regular features include a review of developments in astronomy and space science; methods, advice, and ideas for the practical amateur astronomer; and a sky diary of what's upcoming in the next week. There is an unusual section called "Amateur Scene," which provides interviews and surveys dealing with the very active amateur astronomy scene—astronomy clubs, "open sky nights" at college observatories, and the like. The clear, readable style will appeal to beginners and more experienced amateurs alike. This journal is roughly comparable in scope and approach to *Astronomy* and *Sky & Telescope*. URL: www.popastro.com/spapop/home.htm

643. *Radio Physics and Radio Astronomy.* [ISSN: 2152-274X] 2010. q. USD 809. Ed(s): Leonid M Lytvynenko. Begell House, Inc., 50 Cross Hwy, Redding, CT 06896; orders@begellhouse.com; http://www.begellhouse.com. Sample. Refereed. *Aud.:* Ac, Sa.

Radio Physics and Radio Astronomy was founded in 1995 by the National Academy of Sciences of Ukraine (NASU), the Institute of Radio Astronomy of NASU, and the Ukrainian Committee URSI. Today, in its English-language incarnation, the journal publishes articles on investigations into radio physics and electronic engineering (electromagnetic wave generation, electromagnetic wave propagation in natural and artificial media, radio-frequency antennae and receivers, signal processing, and achievements of microwave technologies), radio astronomy (radio telescopes and radio-astronomy observation equipment; and technique, results, and analysis of radio-astronomy research efforts within the whole frequency range), and astrophysics. URL: www.begellhouse.com/journals/6fd1549c0e2c05da

644. *Royal Astronomical Society. Monthly Notices.* Formerly (until 1833): *Astronomical Society of London. Monthly Notices.* [ISSN: 0035-8711] 1827. 36x/yr. EUR 6327. Ed(s): D R Flower. Oxford University Press, Great Clarendon St, Oxford, OX2 6DP, United Kingdom; jnl.orders@oup.co.uk; http://www.oxfordjournals.org. Illus., adv. Sample. Refereed. Microform: PQC. Reprint: PSC. *Indexed:* A01, A22, C&ISA, CerAb, E01, M&GPA, MathR. *Aud.:* Ac, Sa.

This journal is considered to be a "core" publication for any high-level astronomy library. Since 1827, it has published timely articles, from contributors all over the world (not just from the U.K.), on all areas of astronomy, including positional and dynamical astronomy, astrophysics, radio astronomy, cosmology, space research, instrument design, and more. Replete with equations, this periodical is indispensable for the serious astronomer, but rather slow going for anyone but the most committed amateur. This journal includes some new keyword search features, so if you have perused this journal in the past, be ready for some pleasant surprises. Note that *The Observatory: A Review of Astronomy* (above in this section) is an optional companion to this journal. URL: www.blackwellpublishing.com/journal.asp?ref=0035-8711

645. *Royal Astronomical Society of Canada. Observer's Handbook.* Formerly (until 1911): *Canadian Astronomical Handbook.* [ISSN: 0080-4193] 1907. a. USD 25.95 per issue. Ed(s): Patrick Kelly. Royal Astronomical Society of Canada, 203-4920 Dundas St W, Toronto, ON M9A 1B7, Canada; nationaloffice10000@rasc.ca; http://www.rasc.ca/. Illus., index. Microform: PQC. *Aud.:* Ems, Hs, Ga, Ac, Sa.

The *Observer's Handbook* is a guide published annually since 1907 by The Royal Astronomical Society of Canada. Through its long tradition and the highly respected expertise of its contributors, it has come to be regarded as the standard North American reference for data concerning the sky. The material in it is of interest to professional and amateur astronomers, scientists, teachers at all levels, students, science writers, campers, scout and guide leaders, and others. The guide is an integral part of many astronomy courses at the secondary and university levels, and it is on the reference shelf of many libraries of various kinds. URL: www.rasc.ca/handbook

Science. See Science and Technology/General section.

646. The Science Teacher. Formerly (until 1937): *Illinois Chemistry Teacher.* [ISSN: 0036-8555] 1934. 9x/yr. Free to members. Ed(s): Stephanie Liberatore. National Science Teachers Association, 1840 Wilson Blvd, Arlington, VA 22201; pubinfo@nsta.org; http://www.nsta.org/. Illus., index, adv. Sample. Refereed. Circ: 28500. Vol. ends: May. Microform: PQC. *Indexed:* A01, A22, BRI, ERIC, P02. *Aud.:* Ems, Hs.

The Science Teacher is not exclusively an astronomy periodical, but it frequently devotes a lot of coverage to astronomy. This is one of the publications of the National Science Teachers Association (NSTA), and is aimed at secondary school teachers. *Science and Children* is a parallel journal published by the same association, directed at teachers of a younger age bracket. Both of these are highly respected journals that take a hands-on approach to education. They are each constantly brimming over with specific ideas for age-appropriate activities, as opposed to the jargon of educational theory. If your library includes teachers among its patrons, you should be aware of these journals for their utility in the communication of the wonder of astronomy to young minds. NSTA journals are a member benefit and are not available by subscription. URL: www.nsta.org/highschool

647. Sky & Telescope: the essential magazine of astronomy. Formed by the merger of (1936-1942): *The Sky;* Which superseded (in 1936): *Drama of the Skies;* (1933-1942): *The Telescope;* Which superseded (in 1933): *Telescope.* [ISSN: 0037-6604] 1941. m. USD 37.95 domestic; USD 49.95 Canada; USD 61.95 elsewhere. Ed(s): Robert Naeye. Sky Publishing Corp., 90 Sherman St, Cambridge, MA 02140; info@SkyandTelescope.com. Illus., index, adv. Vol. ends: Jun/Dec. Microform: PQC. *Indexed:* A01, A22, BRI, CBRI, IHTDI, MLA-IB, P02. *Bk. rev.:* 4-5, 350-1,000 words. *Aud.:* Hs, Ga, Ac.

Since it began publication in 1941, *Sky & Telescope* has been a leader in providing accurate and up-to-date information on astronomy and space science. The magazine chose its subtitle of "the essential magazine of astronomy" itself, but it is able to get away with it. It is written so that it appeals to all astronomy enthusiasts, from the youngest novice to the most seasoned professional. Its articles are painstakingly edited to be easily understood by both technically savvy readers and those who benefit from clear descriptive language and graphics. Regular features include book reviews, a sky calendar, news notes, and tips on imaging the sky. Annually, the journal prints a directory of organizations, institutions, and businesses related to astronomy. URL: www.skyandtelescope.com

648. SkyNews: the Canadian magazine of astronomy and stargazing. [ISSN: 0840-8939] 1988. bi-m. Free to members; Non-members, CAD 26; Students, CAD 15. Ed(s): Terence Dickinson. SkyNews Inc, PO Box 10, Yarker, ON K0K 3N0, Canada; skynews@on.aibn.com. Illus., adv. Vol. ends: No. 6. *Indexed:* BRI, C37, CBCARef. *Aud.:* Hs, Ga, Ac.

A useful, very popular publication for novice stargazers. Each colorful issue contains news, columns, features, an excellent sky chart, and equipment reviews. Articles are directed primarily, but not exclusively, to a Canadian audience. What this may mean to an American library is simply that some of the tables presented will have been calibrated with more northerly latitudes in mind. This may have a certain impact on the utility of *some* of the information provided, but the articles and equipment reviews, of course, will still be quite useful, enjoyable, and engrossing. URL: www.skynewsmagazine.com

649. SkyWatch: tour guide for stargazing and space exploration. [ISSN: 1089-4888] 1996. a. USD 6.99 per issue in US & Canada; USD 7.99 per issue elsewhere. Ed(s): Robert Naeye. Sky Publishing Corp., 90 Sherman St, Cambridge, MA 02140; info@SkyandTelescope.com; http://www.skyandtelescope.com. Adv. *Aud.:* Ems, Hs, Ga.

Published by the people who bring us *Sky & Telescope,* this annual listing of sky events is meant for beginners or serious amateurs. A portable, uncomplicated guide to the night sky, *SkyWatch* is a useful observing tool. Included are star charts from September of one year through December of the following year; a map of the lunar surface; a gallery of state-of-the-art astrophotography; and articles on choosing telescopes, binoculars, and other astronomy gear. Also

helpful is the featured how-to article on finding 16 of the most popular objects for viewing in the night sky. This publication can be compared to the *Observer's Handbook* (see *Royal Astronomical Society of Canada. Observer's Handbook,* above in this section). URL: www.shopatsky.com/product/sky-watch-2012/

650. Solar Physics: a journal for solar and solar-stellar research and the study of solar terrestrial physics. [ISSN: 0038-0938] 1967. 14x/yr. EUR 5630 (print & online eds.). Ed(s): John Leibacher, Lidia van Driel-Gesztelyi. Springer Netherlands, Van Godewijckstraat 30, Dordrecht, 3311 GX, Netherlands; http://www.springer.com. Illus., index, adv. Sample. Refereed. Vol. ends: No. 14. Microform: PQC. Reprint: PSC. *Indexed:* A01, A22, BRI, E01, M&GPA. *Aud.:* Ac, Sa.

Solar Physics was founded in 1967 and is the principal journal for the publication of the results of fundamental research on the Sun. It is meant to be read by serious scientists. The journal treats all aspects of solar physics, ranging from the internal structure of the Sun and its evolution, to the outer corona and solar wind in interplanetary space. Papers on solar-terrestrial physics and on stellar research are also published when their results have a direct bearing on our understanding of the Sun. URL: www.springer.com/astronomy/astrophysics/journal/11207

651. Solar System Research. [ISSN: 0038-0946] 1967. bi-m. EUR 4571 (print & online eds.). Ed(s): Mikhail Ya Marov. M A I K Nauka - Interperiodica, Profsoyuznaya ul 90, Moscow, 117997, Russian Federation; compmg@maik.ru; http://www.maik.ru. Illus. Sample. Refereed. Vol. ends: No. 6. Reprint: PSC. *Indexed:* A01, A22, BRI, E01, M&GPA. *Aud.:* Ac, Sa.

This journal is translated into English by MAIK Nauka/Interperiodica Publishing and is published simultaneously with the Russian edition. Review papers appear regularly, along with notes on observational results and communications on scientific meetings and colloquiums. *Solar System Research* is the only journal from Russia that deals with the topics of planetary exploration, including the results of original study obtained through ground-based and/or space-borne observations and theoretical/computer modeling. In recent years, the journal has significantly expanded the scope of its interest through the involvement of new research fields such as planetary geology and cosmophysics, planetary plasma physics and heliosphere, atmospheric sciences, and general problems in comparative planetology. Yet, as in the past, the journal's focus remains upon our own solar system, as opposed to exoplanets. URL: www.springer.com/astronomy/journal/11208

652. Spaceflight. [ISSN: 0038-6340] 1956. m. Free to members; Non-members, GBP 4.50. British Interplanetary Society, 27-29 S Lambeth Rd, London, SW8 1SZ, United Kingdom; mail@bis-space.com/; http://www.bis-space.com/. Illus., index, adv. Vol. ends: No. 12. Microform: PQC. *Indexed:* A22, ApMecR, B03, BrArAb, BrTechI, C&ISA, CerAb. *Aud.:* Hs, Ga, Ac, Sa.

Published since 1956, this is considered to be a core journal by most astronomy libraries. Regarded as an authoritative periodical, *Spaceflight* focuses primarily upon national, international, and commercial efforts to explore space. Articles cover such topics as ongoing space shuttle missions, details of space station life, and educational efforts aimed at popularizing these initiatives. In general, articles are aimed at a presumably intelligent audience that may or may not be professionally involved in space exploration. URL: www.bis-space.com/products-page/magazines-and-journals/spaceflight-magazine/

653. StarDate. Formerly (until 1986): *McDonald Observatory News.* [ISSN: 0889-3098] 1972. bi-m. USD 24 domestic; USD 29 in Canada & Mexico; USD 40 elsewhere. Ed(s): Damond Beeningfield, Gary Harrison. University of Texas, Austin, McDonald Observatory, 1 University Station A2100, Austin, TX 78712; reu@astro.as.utexas.edu; http://www.as.utexas.edu/reu/. Illus. Sample. *Aud.:* Ems, Hs, Ga.

StarDate is known to many as a radio show, but you can find the same information and more in the online edition or by purchasing a paper copy. The magazine is perfect for amateur astronomers and anyone interested in celestial events and space exploration. It is updated daily, and includes such helpful features as an astronomical "Tip of the Day," which concerns interesting things to observe in the sky; a section called "Today on Stardate," which presents articles on all kinds of topics from astronomy and the history of astronomy, including archaeo-astronomy; and daily astronomical questions to ponder. There are also Internet links about astronomy and an astronomical search engine for online research. URL: http://stardate.org

654. *The Universe in the Classroom: a newsletter on teaching astronomy.* [ISSN: 0890-6866] 1984. q. Free. Ed(s): Anna Hurst. Astronomical Society of the Pacific, 390 Ashton Ave, San Francisco, CA 94112; service@astrosociety.org; http://www.astrosociety.org. Illus., adv. *Aud.:* Ems, Hs.

This is an electronic educational newsletter for teachers. Published by our old friend, the Astronomical Society of the Pacific, *Universe in the Classroom* assumes no background in astronomy on the part of the teacher. It is designed to suggest activities and lesson plans that the teacher can employ for her or his students, to enhance their natural wonder at the night sky. Efforts are made to keep the content of each issue relevant, in some way, to astronomical topics that may currently be in the news. The web site strives to include updated links to resources and to assist the educator in developing her or his own understanding of various topics. URL: www.astrosociety.org/education/publications/tnl/about.html

■ ATMOSPHERIC SCIENCES

See also Marine Science and Technology section.

Susan Moore, Catalog Librarian and Bibliographer, Rod Library, University of Northern Iowa, Cedar Falls, IA 50613; susan.moore@uni.edu

Introduction

"Atmospheric sciences" include a number of specific disciplines such as meteorology, climatology, atmospheric chemistry, and weather forecasting. Other disciplines concerned with weather and the study of the atmosphere are also included. The weather events of 2012 with a warmer than usual winter in North America and a snowier than usual winter in Europe have increased interest in what is going on in the atmosphere.

The publications listed in this section include research journals and general-interest periodicals devoted to the study of weather and atmospheric sciences. The list provides information on titles for libraries in North America that primarily publish articles concerning meteorology, climatology, atmospheric chemistry, atmospheric physics, weather forecasting, and related areas.

Journals in languages other than English have not been included; however, some journals from regions outside North America that are published in English are included because researchers are interested in weather phenomena wherever they occur.

As the federal government moves increasingly to electronic publishing, many of the titles formerly printed are now available chiefly via the web. Government sites provide access to additional information. These sites include:

National Weather Service, Internet Weather Source. http://weather.noaa.gov/index.html. This is a very useful web site of weather and forecasting data from the National Weather Service and includes links to areas covered by watches and warnings. Other links included are *United States Weather, Radar Graphics, Weather Maps, International Weather Conditions, Aviation Weather,* and *Marine Weather.* Conditions at each National Weather Service observing station are available by following the *United States Weather* link. Specific conditions provided for each station are wind, visibility, sky conditions, temperature, dew point, relative humidity, and barometric pressure. Summaries of the previous 24 hours for each station are also included. Conditions for areas not covered by an NWS station are given in the section "Forecasts, Watches and Warnings," though the National Weather Service does indicate that the weather conditions given for non-official sites may not meet NWS quality-control standards.

National Climatic Data Center. www.ncdc.noaa.gov/oa/about/about.html. This is the web site of the National Climatic Data Center. Information about weather in the United States is available either for free or by subscription through this site. Free titles include *Monthly Precipitation Probabilities 1971–2000, Annual Degree Days to Selected Bases 1971–2000, Monthly*

Divisional Normals/Standard Deviations 1971–2000, Frost/Freeze Data 1951–1980, Snow Normals 1971–2000, Extreme Weather and Climate Events, and *State of the Climate,* as well as many other informative publications.

Weather and Climate. www.usda.gov/oce/weather/index.htm. This web site is a joint project of the World Agricultural Outlook Board of the U.S. Department of Agriculture and the National Oceanic and Atmospheric Administration, and it includes links to publications that provide important meteorological information to those engaged in agriculture and related fields. Titles included are *U.S. Agricultural Weather Highlights, Weekly Weather and Crop Bulletin,* and *Major World Crop Areas and Climatic Profiles.* These publications include specific information for farmers, such as current agricultural weather highlights and crop production reviews.

Basic Periodicals

Hs: *Weatherwise;* Ga: *American Meteorological Society. Bulletin; Weather; Weatherwise; WMO Bulletin;* Ac: *American Meteorological Society. Bulletin; Atmospheric Science Letters; Climate Dynamics; Journal of Applied Meteorology and Climatology; Journal of Climate; Journal of Geophysical Research: Atmospheres; Journal of the Atmospheric Sciences; Monthly Weather Review; Royal Meteorological Society. Quarterly Journal; Weather; Weather and Forecasting; Weather, Climate, and Society; Weatherwise; WMO Bulletin.*

Basic Abstracts and Indexes

Chemical Abstracts, Geographical Abstracts B: Biogeography and Climatology, INSPEC, Meteorological and Geoastrophysical Abstracts, Science Citation Index.

655. *Acta Meteorologica Sinica.* [ISSN: 0894-0525] 1987. bi-m. EUR 791 (print & online eds.). Ed(s): Zhou Xiuji. Chinese Meteorological Society, 46 Zhongguancun Nan Dajie, Haidian District, Beijing, 100081, China. Illus., index, adv. Refereed. Circ: 300 Paid. Microform: PQC. *Indexed:* M&GPA. *Aud.:* Ac, Sa.

This title publishes papers translated from the Chinese edition of this Chinese Meteorological Society journal, along with papers submitted in English from other countries. Areas of emphasis include climatology, pure and applied meteorology, atmospheric physics and chemistry, atmospheric sounding and remote sensing, and air pollution meteorology. Many of the articles cover Asia. Review articles, as well as original research, are accepted. Recommended for research collections.

656. *Advances in Atmospheric Sciences.* [ISSN: 0256-1530] 1984. bi-m. EUR 895 (print & online eds.). Ed(s): Guoxiong Wu, Da-Lin Zhang. Chinese Academy of Sciences, Institute of Atmospheric Physics, PO Box 9804, Beijing, 100029, China; http://www.iap.ac.cn/. Refereed. Circ: 1000. Reprint: PSC. *Indexed:* A22, C&ISA, C45, CerAb, E01, M&GPA, S25. *Aud.:* Ac.

Publishes original scholarly articles on the "dynamics, physics, and chemistry of the atmosphere and ocean." The geographic areas that most articles focus on are Asia and the Pacific Ocean, although other geographic areas are also covered. Meant for researchers in meteorology and atmospheric sciences, the articles are fairly technical.

Agricultural and Forest Meteorology. See Forestry section.

657. *American Meteorological Society. Bulletin.* [ISSN: 0003-0007] 1920. m. Free to members; Non-members, USD 130. Ed(s): Jeffrey Rosenfeld. American Meteorological Society, 45 Beacon St, Boston, MA 02108; amspubs@ametsoc.org; http://www.ametsoc.org. Illus., index, adv. Refereed. Vol. ends: Dec. Microform: PMC. *Indexed:* A01, A22, ABS&EES, ApMecR, BRI, C45, E01, EngInd, M&GPA, OceAb, P02, RRTA, S25. *Bk. rev.:* Occasional, 200-500 words. *Aud.:* Ga, Ac.

This publication is the official organ of the American Meteorological Society. It normally contains "editorials, topical reports to members, articles, professional and membership news, conference announcements, programs and summaries, book reviews, and coverage of society activities." Each issue includes a calendar of professional meetings. Particularly helpful for librarians is the regular supplement that lists current publications available from the society. The society's annual report is also a regular supplement. This title should be in the collection of any library in the United States that supports teaching and research in atmospheric science, meteorology, climatology, and related fields. It is also available to members through the society's web site.

658. *Atmosfera.* [ISSN: 0187-6236] 1988. q. USD 80 (Individuals, USD 60; MXN 300 domestic). Ed(s): Carlos Gay. Universidad Nacional Autonoma de Mexico, Centro de Ciencias de la Atmosfera, Circuito Exterior, Ciudad Universitaria, Mexico City, 04510, Mexico. Illus., index. Refereed. Vol. ends: Dec. *Indexed:* A22, M&GPA. *Aud.:* Ac.

This journal publishes theoretical, empirical, and applied research on topics related to the atmospheric sciences. Interdisciplinary articles are also published. Articles are in English, with abstracts in English and Spanish. Short contributions and correspondence are also occasionally published. While it publishes articles on atmospheric science in general, the journal's particular strength is its coverage of Latin America and neighboring oceans.

659. *Atmosphere - Ocean.* Supersedes (with vol.16, 1978): *Atmosphere.* [ISSN: 0705-5900] 1963. q. GBP 130 (print & online eds.). Routledge, 4 Park Sq, Milton Park, Abingdon, OX14 4RN, United Kingdom; subscriptions@tandf.co.uk; http://www.tandfonline.com. Illus., index. Refereed. Circ: 600 Paid. Reprint: PSC. *Indexed:* A22, ApMecR, C45, M&GPA, OceAb, S25. *Bk. rev.:* Occasional, 750-1,000 words. *Aud.:* Ac, Sa.

This journal is the principal scientific journal of the Canadian Meteorological and Oceanographic Society and is very good at covering studies that have a Canadian focus. Many of the researchers are Canadian, but foreign contributions are also published. Areas of particular interest are Arctic, coastal, and mid- to high-latitude regions. The journal publishes occasional special issues on topics of interest in meteorology and related fields. Articles may be in English or French, although most are in English. Abstracts are in both languages.

660. *Atmospheric Environment.* Formed by the merger of (1990-1994): *Atmospheric Environment. Part A, General Topics;* (1990-1994): *Atmospheric Environment. Part B, Urban Atmosphere;* Both of which superseded in part (in 1990): *Atmospheric Environment;* Which superseded in part (in 1967): *Air and Water Pollution;* Which was formerly (until 1963): *International Journal of Air and Water Pollution;* (until 1961): *International Journal of Air Pollution.* [ISSN: 1352-2310] 1967. 18x/yr. EUR 8186. Ed(s): P Brimblecombe, C K Chan. Pergamon, The Blvd, Langford Ln, E Park, Kidlington, OX5 1GB, United Kingdom; JournalsCustomerServiceEMEA@elsevier.com; http://www.elsevier.com. Illus., adv. Sample. Refereed. Microform: MIM; PQC. *Indexed:* A01, A22, ApMecR, C&ISA, C45, CEA, CerAb, EngInd, ExcerpMed, H24, IndVet, M&GPA, OceAb, RRTA, RiskAb, S25. *Aud.:* Ac.

Atmospheric Environment puts an emphasis on original research that covers "air pollution and its societal impacts." Of particular interest are papers concerning the impacts of natural and human-induced changes to the Earth's atmospheres. Some review articles are published. Some issues publish papers presented at specific conferences; there are also thematic issues.

661. *Atmospheric Research.* Formerly (until 1986): *Journal de Recherches Atmospheriques.* [ISSN: 0169-8095] 1963. 16x/yr. EUR 2636. Ed(s): A Flossmann. Elsevier BV, Radarweg 29, PO Box 211, Amsterdam, 1000 AE, Netherlands; JournalsCustomerServiceEMEA@elsevier.com; http://www.elsevier.nl. Illus., index. Refereed. *Indexed:* A01, A22, C&ISA, C45, CerAb, EngInd, M&GPA, OceAb, S25. *Aud.:* Ac.

This journal publishes research papers, review articles, letters, and notes concerning "the meteorological processes that occur in the part of the atmosphere where meteorological events occur." While all processes from the ground to the tropopause are covered, the physics of clouds and precipitation continues to be a topic of focus for the journal. Special issues are published occasionally. Articles are primarily in English. Recent topics covered include carbon aerosols in suburbia; a localized heavy rainfall event; and the effect of weather on ion emissions from high-voltage power lines.

662. *Atmospheric Science Letters.* [ISSN: 1530-261X] 2000. q. GBP 234. Ed(s): Alan Gadian. John Wiley & Sons Ltd., 1-7 Oldlands Way, PO Box 808, Bognor Regis, PO21 9FF, United Kingdom; cs-journals@wiley.com; http://eu.wiley.com/WileyCDA/. Adv. Refereed. *Indexed:* A22, E01, M&GPA. *Bk. rev.:* Number and length vary. *Aud.:* Ac, Sa.

This online journal of the Royal Meteorological Society seeks to provide shorter contributions to the atmospheric and related sciences a peer-reviewed path to publication. Topics of particular interest include dynamical meteorology, numerical weather prediction, physical processes of the atmosphere, and new or improved observations from instrumentation.

663. *Australian Meteorological and Oceanographic Journal.* Former titles (until 2009): *Australian Meteorological Magazine;* (until 1952): *Weather Development and Research Bulletin;* (until 1946): *Tropical Weather Research Bulletin;* (until 1944): *Tropical Research Bulletin.* [ISSN: 1836-716X] 1944. q. AUD 120 (Individuals, AUD 43). Ed(s): David Karoly, Blair Trewin. Bureau of Meteorology, Centre for Australian Weather and Climate Research, GPO Box 1289, Melbourne, VIC 3001, Australia; a.hollis@bom.gov.au; http://www.bom.gov.au. Illus., index. Refereed. *Indexed:* A22, M&GPA, OceAb, S25. *Aud.:* Ga.

This title is an official publication of the Australian Bureau of Meteorology and therefore features the meteorology of Australia and the southern hemisphere. Most of the contributors are Australian as well. This journal publishes research articles that deal with the meteorology of Australia, the South Pacific Ocean, and the Indian Ocean. These are areas not well served by other titles in the field. Reports of the scientific meetings of the Australian Meteorological and Oceanographic Society are also published.

664. *Boundary-Layer Meteorology: an international journal of physical and biological processes in the atmospheric boundary layer.* [ISSN: 0006-8314] 1970. m. EUR 3443 (print & online eds.). Ed(s): John R Garratt. Springer Netherlands, Van Godewijckstraat 30, Dordrecht, 3311 GX, Netherlands; http://www.springer.com. Illus., index, adv. Refereed. Vol. ends: Dec. Microform: PQC. Reprint: PSC. *Indexed:* A01, A22, Agr, ApMecR, C&ISA, C45, CerAb, E01, EngInd, M&GPA, OceAb, S25. *Bk. rev.:* Occasional, 350-500 words. *Aud.:* Ac.

This journal covers "the physical, chemical[,] and biological processes occurring in the lowest few kilometres of the Earth's atmosphere." It publishes "theoretical, numerical[,] and experimental studies of the atmospheric boundary layer over both land and sea surfaces." Articles are intended for professionals in atmospheric science. The subject areas included are agriculture and forestry, air pollution, hydrology, micrometeorology, the planetary boundary layer, air–sea interaction, surface boundary layer, numerical modeling of boundary layers, and urban meteorology. Special issues on particular topics are occasionally published.

665. *Climate Dynamics: observational, theoretical and computational research on the climate system.* [ISSN: 0930-7575] 1986. 16x/yr. EUR 5255 (print & online eds.). Ed(s): Dr. Jean-Claude Duplessy, Edwin K Schneider. Springer, Tiergartenstr 17, Heidelberg, 69121, Germany. Adv. Refereed. Reprint: PSC. *Indexed:* A01, A22, Agr, E01, M&GPA, OceAb, S25. *Aud.:* Ac.

This title covers all aspects of the dynamics of the global climate system. The articles and the editorial board are international in scope. The journal especially welcomes papers that cover "original paleoclimatic, diagnostic, analytical[,] and numerical modeling research on the structure and behavior of the atmosphere, oceans, cryosphere, biomass[,] and land surface as interacting components of the dynamics of global climate." Recent topics covered include tree ring analysis of precipitation in central China; circulation models applicable to the South Asian monsoon; and Indian megadroughts and megafloods. Recommended for academic libraries.

666. *Climatic Change: an interdisciplinary, international journal devoted to the description, causes and implications of climatic change.* [ISSN: 0165-0009] 1977. 24x/yr. EUR 3978 (print & online eds.). Springer Netherlands, Van Godewijckstraat 30, Dordrecht, 3311 GX, Netherlands; http://www.springer.com. Illus., index, adv. Refereed. Microform: PQC. Reprint: PSC. *Indexed:* A01, A22, ABIn, Agr, BRI, C45, E01, EngInd, IndVet, M&GPA, OceAb, P02, RRTA, S25. *Bk. rev.:* Number and length vary. *Aud.:* Ac.

This interdisciplinary journal is "dedicated to the totality of the problem of climatic variability and change." Articles are published from a variety of disciplines in the sciences, social sciences, and other fields interested in climatic variation. Occasional special issues focus on topics of particular interest. Given the wide range of disciplines covered and the increasing interest in interdisciplinary research, this journal should be of interest to academic libraries in general.

667. *Climatological Data (Online).* Formerly (until 19??): *Climatological Data (Print).* 1890. m. plus a. update. USD 4 per issue. U.S. National Climatic Data Center, Federal Bldg, 151 Patton Ave, Asheville, NC 28801; ncdc.info@noaa.gov; http://www.ncdc.noaa.gov. Illus. Sample. Circ: 23000. *Aud.:* Hs, Ga, Ac, Sa.

A compilation of monthly temperature and precipitation data for weather stations in each state. For some areas (New England, Maryland/Delaware/District of Columbia, Hawaii/Pacific Islands, and Virgin Islands/Puerto Rico), there are regional editions. Average maximum and minimum temperatures are given for each National Weather Service official station, along with temperature extremes. Total precipitation and deviation from normal are also provided. The July issue includes monthly heating degree days and snow data for the previous July through June. Maps showing current weather patterns and charts based on historic data are included.

668. *Dynamics of Atmospheres and Oceans.* [ISSN: 0377-0265] 1977. 6x/yr. EUR 1352. Ed(s): A Moore. Elsevier BV, Radarweg 29, PO Box 211, Amsterdam, 1000 AE, Netherlands; JournalsCustomerServiceEMEA@elsevier.com; http://www.elsevier.nl. Illus., index, adv. Sample. Refereed. Vol. ends: Jan. Microform: PQC. *Indexed:* A01, A22, ApMecR, C&ISA, CerAb, EngInd, M&GPA, OceAb, S25. *Aud.:* Ac, Sa.

This international journal focuses on research into atmospheres and oceans as fluid dynamic systems, especially the "processes governing atmospheres, oceans, and climate." Papers that explore the interactions of the air and sea and other components of the climate system are encouraged. Most articles are technical in nature and assume familiarity with mathematical modeling. Fields represented by the authors include meteorology, atmospheric science, environmental engineering, Earth sciences, and other fields. Occasionally, an issue will be devoted to a specific topic.

669. *Earth Interactions.* [ISSN: 1087-3562] 1996. d. Non-members, USD 145. Ed(s): Jon Foley, Roni Avissar. American Geophysical Union, 2000 Florida Ave, NW, Washington, DC 20009; http://www.agu.org. Illus. Refereed. *Indexed:* A01, A22, E01, M&GPA, S25. *Aud.:* Ac.

This journal publishes articles that deal with "the interactions between the lithosphere, hydrosphere, atmosphere[,] and biosphere in the context of global issues or global change." *Earth Interactions* is a joint publication of the American Geophysical Union, the American Meteorological Society, and the Association of American Geographers. The journal publishes articles that cover original research, review articles, and brief reports concerning data or models. A subscription is required to view the published articles. Since the journal is completely electronic, authors are encouraged but not required to use animations or other components. URL: http://earthinteractions.org

670. *Electronic Journal of Operational Meteorology.* 2001. irreg. National Weather Association, 228 W Millbrook Rd, Raleigh, NC 27609; president@nwas.org; http://www.nwas.org. *Indexed:* M&GPA. *Aud.:* Ga, Ac.

This electronic publication of the National Weather Association allows members and guests to publish their "procedures, research, and technical studies related to operational forecasting." It is intended to provide a venue for quick publication of studies and therefore complements the *National Weather Digest.* URL: www.nwas.org/ej/index.php

671. *International Journal of Biometeorology: the description, causes, and implications of climatic change.* [ISSN: 0020-7128] 1957. bi-m. EUR 910 (print & online eds.). Ed(s): Scott C Sheridan. Springer, Tiergartenstr 17, Heidelberg, 69121, Germany. Illus., index, adv. Refereed. Circ: 1300. Vol. ends: Mar. Reprint: PSC. *Indexed:* A01, A22, AbAn, Agr, C45, E01, FR, IndVet, M&GPA, RRTA, S25. *Aud.:* Ac.

This title publishes original research papers, review articles, and short communications on "the interactions between living organisms and factors of the natural and artificial atmospheric environment." Articles cover the impact that the environment has on humans, animals, and plants, down to single-cell organisms. Recent topics include the blooming of apple buds in western Europe; the effects of evaporative cooling on milk production of dairy cows in the tropics; and desert dust impacts on human health. This title is of interest to biologists and medical professionals as well as Earth and atmospheric scientists.

672. *International Journal of Climatology.* Formerly (until 1989): *Journal of Climatology.* [ISSN: 0899-8418] 1981. 15x/yr. GBP 1932. Ed(s): G R McGregor. John Wiley & Sons Ltd., The Atrium, Southern Gate, Chichester, PO19 8SQ, United Kingdom; customer@wiley.com; http://www.wiley.com. Illus., index, adv. Sample. Refereed. Vol. ends: Dec. Microform: PQC. Reprint: PSC. *Indexed:* A22, C45, EngInd, FR, M&GPA, OceAb, RRTA, S25. *Bk. rev.:* 300-500 words. *Aud.:* Ac, Sa.

The title "aims to span the well-established but rapidly growing field of climatology." Thus, it covers climate system science, climatic variability and climate change, local to global scale climate observations and modeling, the application of climatological knowledge to environmental assessment and economic production, and climate and society interactions as well as other topics. The journal is international in scope. Research papers, reviews of progress, and reports are all published here. Book reviews are also included.

673. *The International Journal of Meteorology.* Formerly (until Sep.2005): *Journal of Meteorology.* [ISSN: 1748-2992] 1975. 10x/yr. GBP 120 (Individuals, GBP 41.50). Ed(s): Samantha J A Hall. Artetech Publishing Co., 20 Massey Ave, Lymm, WA13 0PJ, United Kingdom. Illus., index, adv. Sample. Refereed. Vol. ends: Dec. *Indexed:* A22, C45, M&GPA. *Bk. rev.:* 750-1,000 words. *Aud.:* Ga, Ac.

Published by the Tornado and Storm Research Organisation, this title specializes in severe weather and meteorology. It also covers atmospheric phenomena in the United Kingdom, Ireland, and the European continent. Well-illustrated, the journal is of interest to meteorologists and weather enthusiasts. There are occasional special issues that usually cover notable weather events. The editorial board's membership is international, but half are from the United Kingdom and Ireland.

674. *Journal of Applied Meteorology and Climatology.* Formerly (until Jan.2006): *Journal of Applied Meteorology;* Which supersedes in part (in 1988): *Journal of Climate and Applied Meteorology;* Which was formerly (1962-1983): *Journal of Applied Meteorology.* [ISSN: 1558-8424] 1962. m. Non-members, USD 1075 (print & online eds.). Ed(s): Robert M Rauber. American Meteorological Society, 45 Beacon St, Boston, MA 02108; amspubs@ametsoc.org; http://www.ametsoc.org. Illus., index, adv. Refereed. Vol. ends: Dec. *Indexed:* A01, A22, ApMecR, C&ISA, CerAb, E01, EngInd, M&GPA, OceAb, P02, S25. *Aud.:* Ac, Sa.

A publication of the American Meteorological Society, this journal publishes applied research related to physical meteorology, weather modification, satellite meteorology, radar meteorology, boundary layer processes, air pollution meteorology, and applied meteorological numerical models, as well as other topics. The articles are scholarly in nature and can be very technical. There are occasional issues on a specific theme. Given its wide scope, this journal is of interest to more than just atmospheric scientists.

675. *Journal of Atmospheric and Oceanic Technology.* [ISSN: 0739-0572] 1984. m. Non-members, USD 530 (print & online eds.). Ed(s): V Chandrasekar, Julie Haggerty. American Meteorological Society, 45 Beacon St, Boston, MA 02108; amspubs@ametsoc.org; http://www.ametsoc.org. Illus., index, adv. Refereed. Vol. ends: Dec. *Indexed:* A01, A22, C&ISA, C45, CerAb, E01, EngInd, M&GPA, OceAb, S25. *Aud.:* Ac.

This journal from the American Meteorological Society covers descriptions of the instrumentation and methodology used in atmospheric and oceanic research. Given this focus, the articles are geared toward researchers and not practicing meteorologists. A section for brief articles on works in progress is occasionally included. Since 2006 there are separate sections for atmospheric and oceanic articles. This title is primarily of interest to those in the atmospheric sciences.

676. *Journal of Atmospheric Chemistry.* [ISSN: 0167-7764] 1983. 9x/yr. EUR 1142 (print & online eds.). Ed(s): Eliot L Atlas. Springer Netherlands, Van Godewijckstraat 30, Dordrecht, 3311 GX, Netherlands; http://www.springer.com. Illus., adv. Refereed. Microform: PQC. Reprint: PSC. *Indexed:* A01, A22, Agr, BRI, C45, E01, ExcerpMed, M&GPA, OceAb, S25. *Aud.:* Ac.

Publishes research on the chemistry of the Earth's atmosphere, especially the region below 100 kilometers. Recent articles cover aerosol chemistry over a tropical city; tracking the emission sources of sulfur and carbon in Hong Kong; and particulate matter concentrations in Dresden, Germany. As might be assumed from the topics covered, the articles are geared toward scientists and researchers.

677. *Journal of Climate.* Supersedes in part (in 1988): *Journal of Climate and Applied Meteorology;* Which was formerly (1962-1983): *Journal of Applied Meteorology.* [ISSN: 0894-8755] 1962. s-m. Members, USD 713 (print & online eds.); Non-members, USD 950 (print & online eds.). Ed(s): Andrew Weaver. American Meteorological Society, 45 Beacon St, Boston, MA 02108; amspubs@ametsoc.org; http://www.ametsoc.org. Illus., index, adv. Refereed. Vol. ends: Dec. *Indexed:* A01, A22, Agr, C45, E01, EngInd, M&GPA, OceAb. *Aud.:* Ac, Sa.

Focuses on articles concerned with research in such areas as large-scale variability of the atmosphere, oceans, and land surface; changes in the climate system (including those caused by human activities); and climate simulation and prediction. Brief reports and comments are also published. The journal will occasionally publish review articles, but they must be approved by the editor prior to submission. Recent articles cover tropical cyclone position, intensity, and intensity life cycle, the weakening of the Eurasian and North African monsoons in the 1960s, and East Antarctic landfast sea ice distribution and variability from 2000 to 2008.

678. *Journal of Geophysical Research: Atmospheres.* Supersedes in part: *Journal of Geophysical Research;* Which was formerly (until 1949): *Magnetism and Atmospheric Electricity;* (until 1899): *Terrestrial Magnetism.* [ISSN: 2169-897X] 1896. s-m. USD 9387. Ed(s): Steven J Ghan. Wiley-Blackwell Publishing, Inc., 111 River St, Hoboken, NJ 07030; info@wiley.com; http://onlinelibrary.wiley.com/. Illus. *Aud.:* Ac, Sa.

A publication of the American Geophysical Union, this journal publishes articles about the physics and chemistry of the atmosphere, including "the atmospheric-biospheric, lithospheric, or hydrospheric interface." Recent topics include ozone temperature in the upper stratosphere as a measure of chlorine content, air traffic scheduling and contrail cirrus forcing, and changes in the Antarctic ozone hole. Geared to professionals and graduate students.

679. *Journal of Hydrometeorology.* [ISSN: 1525-755X] 2000. bi-m. Non-members, USD 500 (print & online eds.). Ed(s): Guido Salvucci, William J Gutowski. American Meteorological Society, 45 Beacon St, Boston, MA 02108; amspubs@ametsoc.org; http://www.ametsoc.org. Refereed. *Indexed:* A01, A22, C45, E01, M&GPA, S25. *Aud.:* Ac, Sa.

This journal covers "research related to the modeling, observing, and forecasting of processes related to water and energy fluxes and storage terms, including interactions with the boundary layer and lower atmosphere, and including processes related to precipitation, radiation, and other meteorological inputs." As with most American Meteorological Society publications, it also publishes brief reports and comments. Recent topics include model-based seasonal prediction of droughts in the contiguous United States; estimating the impact of climate change on storm runoff in northern Australia; and soil moisture estimation using thermal inertia.

680. *Journal of the Atmospheric Sciences.* Formerly (until 1962): *Journal of Meteorology.* [ISSN: 0022-4928] 1944. m. Non-members, USD 1500 (print & online eds.). Ed(s): Dr. Ka-Kit Tung. American Meteorological Society, 45 Beacon St, Boston, MA 02108; amspubs@ametsoc.org; http://www.ametsoc.org. Illus., index, adv. Refereed. *Indexed:* A01, A22, ApMecR, C&ISA, CCMJ, CerAb, E01, EngInd, M&GPA, MSN, MathR, OceAb, P02, S25. *Aud.:* Ac, Sa.

This journal from the American Meteorological Society publishes "basic research related to the physics, dynamics, and chemistry of the atmosphere of Earth and other planets, with emphasis on the quantitative and deductive aspects of the subject." A few brief articles are published, but the majority are longer and quantitative in nature. Rarely, there is a section for notes and correspondence.

681. *Meteorological Applications.* [ISSN: 1350-4827] 1994. q. GBP 316. Ed(s): P J. A Burt. John Wiley & Sons Ltd., The Atrium, Southern Gate, Chichester, PO19 8SQ, United Kingdom; customer@wiley.com; http://www.wiley.com. Adv. Sample. Refereed. Reprint: PSC. *Indexed:* A22, C45, E01, M&GPA, RRTA, S25. *Aud.:* Ac.

Meant for applied meteorologists, forecasters, and other users of meteorological services, this journal of the Royal Meteorological Society covers a range of topics, including applications of meteorological and climatological data and their benefits, analysis and prediction of weather hazards, performance and verification of numerical models and forecasting aids, training techniques, and practical applications of ocean and climate models. Brief news items on applications of meteorology are also published. There are occasional special issues that deal with topics of current interest.

682. *Meteorological Society of Japan. Journal.* [ISSN: 0026-1165] 1882. bi-m. Meteorological Society of Japan, c/o Japan Meteorological Agency, 3-4 Ote-Machi 1-chome, Tokyo, 100-0004, Japan; http://www-cmpo.mit.edu/met_links/full/imsjap.full.html. Illus. Refereed. Vol. ends: Dec. *Indexed:* A22, C45, M&GPA. *Aud.:* Ac.

The journal publishes "research papers in the science of pure and applied meteorology." All articles are in English. Since this is the research journal of the Meteorological Society of Japan, East Asia and the western Pacific Ocean are well covered; but this journal also publishes articles that concern general meteorological topics as well as other parts of the world.

683. *Meteorology and Atmospheric Physics.* Formerly (until 1986): *Archives for Meteorology, Geophysics, and Bioclimatology. Series A: Meteorology and Geophysics - Archiv fuer Meteorologie, Geophysik und Bioklimatologie. Series A.* [ISSN: 0177-7971] 1948. m. EUR 3055 (print & online eds.). Ed(s): C Simmer. Springer Wien, Sachsenplatz 4-6, Vienna, 1201, Austria; journals@springer.at; http://www.springer.at. Illus., adv. Sample. Refereed. Circ: 500 Paid. Vol. ends: Dec. Microform: PQC. Reprint: PSC. *Indexed:* A22, Agr, BRI, C&ISA, C45, CerAb, E01, M&GPA, P02. *Bk. rev.:* 200-500 words. *Aud.:* Ac, Sa.

Publishes articles of original research in the areas of physical and chemical processes in the atmosphere, including radiation, optical effects, electricity, atmospheric turbulence, and transport processes. Atmospheric dynamics, general circulation in the atmosphere, synoptic meteorology, and analysis of weather systems in specific regions are also covered. The journal is international in scope, and authors and research are from around the world.

684. *Monthly Weather Review.* [ISSN: 0027-0644] 1872. m. Members, USD 1200 (print & online eds.); Non-members, USD 1600 (print & online eds.). Ed(s): David M Schultz. American Meteorological Society, 45 Beacon St, Boston, MA 02108; amspubs@ametsoc.org; http://www.ametsoc.org. Illus., index, adv. Refereed. Vol. ends: Dec. Microform: PMC. *Indexed:* A01, A22, ApMecR, C&ISA, C45, CerAb, E01, EngInd, M&GPA, S25. *Aud.:* Ac, Sa.

Focusing on phenomena that have seasonal or subseasonal time scales, this American Meteorological Society journal publishes research related to the analysis and prediction of observed atmospheric physics and circulations. Occasionally, the journal will publish review articles as well as articles on high-impact weather events. A recurring column is the "Picture of the Month" that features a photograph of interesting weather phenomena.

685. *National Weather Digest.* [ISSN: 0271-1052] 1976. s-a. Free to members; Non-members, USD 60. Ed(s): Gary Ellrod, Tony Lupo. National Weather Association, 228 W Millbrook Rd, Raleigh, NC 27609; natweaasoc@aol.com; http://www.nwas.org. Illus., index. Refereed. Vol. ends: Nov. *Indexed:* BRI, M&GPA. *Bk. rev.:* 1-2, 500-700 words. *Aud.:* Ga, Ac.

This official publication of the National Weather Association serves as a venue for association members and others to "share their experiences, procedures, ideas, research, [and] technical studies." Published at least semi-annually, it also includes correspondence and information for the members of the association. Technical papers published in the section labeled "Articles" are peer reviewed, while those published in "Technical Notes" are not.

686. Royal Meteorological Society. Quarterly Journal: a journal of the atmospheric sciences, applied meteorology, and physical oceanography. Incorporates (1922-1950): *Bibliography of Meteorological Literature.* [ISSN: 0035-9009] 1871. 8x/yr. GBP 599. Ed(s): John Thuburn, Mark P Baldwin. John Wiley & Sons Ltd., The Atrium, Southern Gate, Chichester, PO19 8SQ, United Kingdom; customer@wiley.com; http://www.wiley.com. Illus., index, adv. Sample. Refereed. Vol. ends: Oct. *Indexed:* A22, C&ISA, C45, CerAb, EngInd, M&GPA, OceAb. *Bk. rev.:* Number and length vary. *Aud.:* Ac, Sa.

This publication is considered one of the major research journals in meteorology. It covers research in atmospheric sciences, applied meteorology, and physical oceanography. The papers are scholarly and technical. Although the editorial board is primarily British, the journal publishes articles from scholars around the world. Book reviews appear in some issues. Also, some issues publish the papers from a particular scientific meeting or on a specific topic. Recommended for libraries that support atmospheric and Earth sciences programs.

687. Russian Academy of Sciences. Izvestiya. Atmospheric and Oceanic Physics. Formerly: *Academy of Sciences of the U S S R. Izvestiya. Atmospheric and Oceanic Physics;* Which superseded in part (in 1965): *Academy of Sciences of the U S S R. Bulletin. Geophysics Series.* [ISSN: 0001-4338] 1957. bi-m. EUR 1917 (print & online eds.). Ed(s): Georgii S Golitsyn. M A I K Nauka - Interperiodica, Profsoyuznaya ul 90, Moscow, 117997, Russian Federation; compmg@maik.ru; http://www.maik.ru. Reprint: PSC. *Indexed:* A22, C45, CCMJ, E01, M&GPA, MSN, MathR. *Aud.:* Ac, Sa.

This is the English translation of *Izvestiya Rossiiskoi Akademii Nauk—Fizika Atmosfery i Okeana,* and it "publishes original scientific research and review articles on vital issues in the physics of the Earth's atmosphere and hydrosphere and climate theory." Also it occasionally publishes papers on research techniques and brief communications. Articles are technical in nature and written primarily by scientists from Russia and the other former Soviet states.

688. Tellus. Series A: Dynamic Meteorology and Oceanography (Online). Supercedes in part: *Tellus (Online).* [ISSN: 1600-0870] 1990. 5x/yr. Free. Co-Action Publishing, Ripvaegen 7, Jaerfaella, 17564, Sweden; info@co-action.net; http://www.co-action.net. Refereed. *Aud.:* Ac, Sa.

This peer-reviewed journal of the International Meteorological Institute in Stockholm focuses on dynamic meteorology, climatology, and oceanography, which includes synoptic meteorology, weather forecasting, climate analysis, and numerical modeling. The journal publishes both original research and review articles. Occasional special issues on topics of current interest and conference proceedings are also published. Recommended for libraries that serve atmospheric scientists and oceanographers.

689. Tellus. Series B: Chemical and Physical Meteorology (Online). Supercedes in part: *Tellus (Online).* [ISSN: 1600-0889] 1990. 5x/yr. Free. Co-Action Publishing, Ripvaegen 7, Jaerfaella, 17564, Sweden; info@co-action.net; http://www.co-action.net. Refereed. *Aud.:* Ac, Sa.

This journal of the International Meteorological Institute in Stockholm focuses on biogeochemical cycles, surface exchange processes, aerosol science, air chemistry, long-range and global transport, and cloud physics. The journal publishes both original research and review articles. There are occasionally special issues that cover conference proceedings or topics of current interest. Recommended for libraries that serve those studying hydrology, geography, atmospheric sciences, and oceanography.

690. Theoretical and Applied Climatology. Formerly (until 1985): *Archives for Meteorology, Geophysics, and Bioclimatology. Series B: Climatology, Environmental Meteorology, Radiation Research - Archiv fuer Meteorologie, Geophysik und Bioklimatologie. Series B.* [ISSN: 0177-798X] 1948. m. EUR 4165 (print & online eds.). Ed(s): H Grassl. Springer Wien, Sachsenplatz 4-6, Vienna, 1201, Austria; journals@springer.at; http://www.springer.at. Adv. Sample. Refereed. Circ: 500 Paid. Microform: PQC. Reprint: PSC. *Indexed:* A01, A22, BRI, C45, E01, FR, M&GPA, P02, RRTA. *Aud.:* Ac, Sa.

This journal's focus includes "climate modeling, climate changes and climate forecasting, micro- to mesoclimate, applied meteorology as in agro- and forest meteorology, biometeorology, building meteorology and atmospheric radiation problems as they relate to the biosphere; effects of anthropogenic and natural aerosols or gaseous trace constituents; hardware and software elements of meteorological measurements, including techniques of remote sensing, among other topics of current interest." Articles are technical and scholarly in nature and are not limited to one geographic area. Recent articles cover East Asia, India, Iran, and the Baltics.

691. W M O Bulletin. [ISSN: 0042-9767] 1952. q. CHF 85. Ed(s): Hong Yan. World Meteorological Organization, 7 bis Avenue de la Paix, Case postale 2300, Geneva, 1211, Switzerland; pubsales@gateway.wmo.ch; http://www.wmo.int. Illus., index, adv. Circ: 6500. Vol. ends: Oct. *Indexed:* A22, C45, M&GPA, OceAb, RRTA, S25. *Bk. rev.:* 2-5, 300-500 words. *Aud.:* Ga, Ac.

The World Meteorological Organization is a specialized agency of the United Nations, and this is its official journal. Each issue has a theme. It publishes scholarly articles on meteorology, climatology, hydrology and the environment, and related fields. Each issue includes a calendar of coming events, and book reviews are also a standard feature. Recommended.

692. Weather. Incorporates (1965-2003): *Weather Log.* [ISSN: 0043-1656] 1946. m. GBP 64. Ed(s): Bob Prichard. John Wiley & Sons Ltd., The Atrium, Southern Gate, Chichester, PO19 8SQ, United Kingdom; customer@wiley.com; http://www.wiley.com. Illus., index, adv. Sample. Refereed. Vol. ends: Dec. Reprint: PSC. *Indexed:* A22, M&GPA, S25. *Aud.:* Hs, Ga, Ac.

This journal is meant for both the meteorological professional and the interested layman. The articles attempt to keep technical terminology and mathematical equations to a minimum. It covers weather around the world, but since it is a publication of the Royal Meteorological Society, there is a slight emphasis on the United Kingdom. As the house journal of the RMS, the journal includes news of the society including reports of meetings and conferences. There is a letters section, with most letters coming from the United Kingdom. Recommended for both academic and public libraries.

693. Weather and Forecasting. [ISSN: 0882-8156] 1986. bi-m. Non-members, USD 530 (print & online eds.). Ed(s): William A Gallus, Dr. Brian A Colle. American Meteorological Society, 45 Beacon St, Boston, MA 02108; amspubs@ametsoc.org; http://www.ametsoc.org. Illus., index, adv. Refereed. *Indexed:* A01, A22, E01, EngInd, M&GPA. *Aud.:* Ac.

Publishes research that can lead to "improvements in operational forecasting." The articles are technical in nature. Research covered includes deterministic and ensemble forecasting and analysis, case studies of significant weather events, and the capabilities of current physics, numerics, and data assimilation approaches in forecasting. Authors are from around the world, as is the geographic coverage of the articles. As with most American Meteorological Society publications, a section for brief reports and comments is part of many issues. Geared to forecasters, it may also be of interest to atmospheric scientists in general.

694. Weather, Climate, and Society. [ISSN: 1948-8327] 2009. q. Non-members, USD 355 (print & online eds.). American Meteorological Society, 45 Beacon St, Boston, MA 02108; amspubs@ametsoc.org; http://www.ametsoc.org. *Indexed:* A22, E01. *Bk. rev.:* Number and length vary. *Aud.:* Ga, Ac.

This quarterly journal of the American Meteorological Association covers research on and analysis of the interactions between weather and climate and society. Articles are published that focus on a broad range of topics concerning the interface between weather and/or climate, and society. Since the focus is interdisciplinary, articles that involve both natural/physical scientists and social scientists are encouraged. Recent articles cover topics such as air quality forecasting in the mid-Atlantic region; winter weather events and socioeconomic impacts across Oklahoma from 2000 to 2010; and gender and asset dimensions over water insecurity in cities in the Philippines.

695. *Weatherwise.* [ISSN: 0043-1672] 1948. bi-m. GBP 114. Taylor & Francis Inc., 325 Chestnut St, Ste 800, Philadelphia, PA 19106; customerservice@taylorandfrancis.com; http://www.tandfonline.com. Illus., index. Microform: PQC. Reprint: PSC. *Indexed:* A01, A22, BRI, C37, E01, M&GPA, MASUSE, P02. *Bk. rev.:* Number and length vary. *Aud.:* Ga, Ac, Sa.

This popular magazine has as its target audience the intelligent layperson interested in weather. It publishes general-interest articles on weather, particularly on weather anomalies. Regular features include responses to reader questions and a review of weather over North America during the preceding two months. Photographs are usually in color. The March/April issue includes a summary of weather events from the previous year. There is also an annual photo contest. Recommended for all libraries that serve users with an interest in weather.

Weekly Weather and Crop Bulletin. See Agriculture section.

■ AUTOMOBILES AND MOTORCYCLES

Pauline Baughman, Reference Librarian, Multnomah County Library, 801 SW 10th Ave., Portland, OR 97205; paulineb@multcolib.org

Introduction

The ever-tumultuous world of the automotive industry seems to be on the road to recovery after several years of highs and lows. The devastating 2011 earthquake and tsunami in Japan affected both automakers and the American public by disrupting the global supply chain and sales and production around the world, while electric vehicles gained widespread appeal, technology added new safety features to vehicles, and Saab filed for bankruptcy.

Even so, 2012 has seen both an incredible recovery in the Japanese auto industry and an increase in car sales in the U.S., thanks to low interest rates, pent-up demand, and lower gas prices. Not everyone is rushing out to buy a new vehicle, however. Increased vehicle reliability, despite the "Cash for Clunkers" program, has given rise to older vehicles being on the road longer than ever.

While automakers worry about import competition, new fuel economy requirements, stricter emissions standards, parts suppliers and manufacturers, and market share, the American public simply continues to love its motor vehicles. Auto racing, collector cars, motorcycles, and car shows appeal to a huge portion of the population, and there are plenty of magazines published to prove it.

Americans love the road. Whether the vehicle of choice is an aging wood-paneled station wagon, a Honda motorcycle, a shared vehicle, a Vespa, or a Ferrari, everyone has their favorite mode of getting around. Partial to BMWs? Drag racing? Green transportation? Mini-trucks? Whatever the interest, there is undoubtedly a specific magazine geared to the audience. Whether your patrons are classic car enthusiasts, race enthusiasts who spend most of their time enjoying races from the comfort of their recliner, automotive industry professionals, or just average Americans wanting to dream about the latest new cars, there is a title for everyone.

The selected list of titles below reflects only a small portion of the magazines published for car and motorcycle enthusiasts; if a particular autosport or auto lifestyle is popular locally, librarians may wish to seek out specialized titles to support that interest.

Basic Periodicals

Automobile, Car and Driver, Cycle World, Motor Trend, Motorcyclist.

Basic Abstracts and Indexes

Academic Search Premier, MasterFILE Premier, Readers' Guide to Periodical Literature.

696. *American Bagger: the original American v-twin performance touring and customizing authority.* [ISSN: 2159-2810] 2006. m. USD 21.95 domestic; USD 27.95 Canada; USD 57.95 elsewhere. Maverick Publications, 3105 W Fairgrounds Loop, Ste 200, Spearfish, SD 57783; info@maverickpub.com; http://www.maverickpub.com. Adv. *Aud.:* Ga.

American Bagger is a fine example of just one of the highly specialized titles available in the world of motorcycles. This magazine is aimed at the enthusiast who loves custom touring cycles with saddlebags—a.k.a. "Baggers"—and is packed with stunning color photos and information on one-of-a-kind, customized v-twin touring bikes. For larger public libraries.

697. *American Motorcyclist.* Former titles (until Sep.1977): *A M A News;* (until 19??): *American Motorcycling.* [ISSN: 0277-9358] 1947. m. Free to members. Ed(s): Grant Parsons. American Motorcyclist Association, 13515 Yarmouth Dr, Pickerington, OH 43147; http://www.ama-cycle.org/magazine/index.html. Illus., adv. Sample. Vol. ends: Dec. *Bk. rev.:* 1-5, 500-2,000 words. *Aud.:* Ga, Sa.

American Motorcyclist is distributed monthly to the more than 280,000 members of the American Motorcyclist Association (AMA). The AMA acts as a political lobby for motorcyclists, and reports on legislative issues that affect your right to ride are often included, along with feature stories and rider profiles. Activities, both state-by-state and national, are also included. Readers should expect to find photos of dirt bikes, road races, new bikes, and families on the glossy, full-color pages. Recommended for large public libraries.

698. *Antique Automobile.* Formerly (until 19??): *Antique Automobile Club of America. Bulletin.* [ISSN: 0003-5831] 1937. bi-m. Free to members. Ed(s): West Peterson. Antique Automobile Club of America, 501 W Governor Rd, PO Box 417, Hershey, PA 17033; general@aaca.org; http://www.aaca.org. Illus., adv. Microform: PQC. *Indexed:* A22. *Aud.:* Ga.

Published by the Antique Automobile Club of America (AACA), *Antique Automobile* is the first historical automotive society publication. The goal of the club is to perpetuate "the pioneer days of automobiling by furthering the interest in and preserving of antique automobiles," and this title will be of interest to all serious antique automobile enthusiasts. The AACA uses the term *automobile* to include all "self-propelled vehicles intended for passenger use," including cars, race vehicles, trucks, fire vehicles, and motorcycles. Approximately half of the magazine is in full color. Columns, news, a calendar of events, and a comprehensive list of all AACA regions and chapters are included in each issue.

699. *Automobile Magazine.* Former titles (until 1989): *Automobile;* (until 1987): *Automobile Magazine.* 1986. m. USD 10 domestic; USD 23 Canada; USD 25 elsewhere. Ed(s): Jean Jennings, Gavin Conway. Source Interlink Companies, 6420 Wilshire Blvd, 10th Fl, Los Angeles, CA 90048; dheine@sourceinterlink.com; http://www.sourceinterlinkmedia.com. Illus., adv. Sample. Circ: 561338 Paid. *Indexed:* A22, ASIP, BRI. *Aud.:* Hs, Ga, Ac.

Automobile is geared to the general car enthusiast, covering new vehicles, preview vehicles, and collector cars. Full-color photos of auto interiors and exteriors are excellent; car reviews are primarily subjective and lack the technical data included in other general-interest automobile magazines such as *Car and Driver* and *Road & Track.* Columns are well written and entertaining and occasionally irreverent; *Automobile* is a fun read. Although somewhat thin, this magazine will be popular in any public library. Its reasonable price makes it a must-have purchase.

700. *Automotive Engineering International.* Incorporates (1989-1998): *Truck Engineering;* Former titles (until 1998): *Automotive Engineering;* (until 1972): *S A E Journal of Automotive Engineering;* Which superseded in part (in 1970): *S A E Journal;* Which was formerly (until 1928): *Society of Automotive Engineers. Journal;* (until Jun.1917): *S A E Bulletin.* [ISSN: 1543-849X] 1917. m. Free to members; Non-members, USD 140. S A E Inc., 400 Commonwealth Dr, Warrendale, PA 15096; CustomerService@sae.org; http://www.sae.org/automag. Illus., adv. Circ: 85813. Vol. ends: Dec. Microform: PMC. *Indexed:* A22, B02, C&ISA, CerAb, P02. *Aud.:* Ac, Sa.

This publication of the Society for Automotive Engineers is the premier source for technology and product information for vehicle design, development, and manufacture. Features include editorials, sections on global vehicles, technology reports, insiders and insights, and regulations and standards. Very much aimed at the automotive professional, articles are technical and in depth, covering everything from aerodynamics to LEDs in instrument panels. Highly recommended for academic libraries and specialized collections.

701. *Automotive Industries.* Former titles (until 1994): *Chilton's Automotive Industries;* (until 1976): *Automotive Industries;* (until 1972): *Chilton's Automotive Industries;* (until 1970): *Automotive Industries;* (until 1947): *Automotive and Aviation Industries;* (until 1942): *Automotive Industries;* (until 1917): *Automobile and Automotive Industries;* Incorporated (1923-1934): *Automotive Abstracts;* and incorporated in part (in 1917): *The Horseless Age.* [ISSN: 1099-4130] 1895. m. Ed(s): Edward Richardson. Diesel & Gas Turbine Publications, 20855 Watertown Rd, Ste 220, Waukesha, WI 53186; http://www.dieselpub.com. Illus., adv. Circ: 25722. Microform: CIS; PMC; PQC. *Indexed:* A22, ABIn, B01, B02, B03, BRI, C&ISA, C42, CerAb, EngInd. *Aud.:* Ga, Ac, Sa.

Automotive Industries is "devoted to providing global coverage on all aspects of the automobile marketplace, with an emphasis on the people, products and processes that shape the industry." With in-depth news, information, insight, and analysis on the global events that affect the auto industry, this title is geared to automotive manufacturers and suppliers. Recent articles, for example, cover o-rings, breakthroughs in aluminum wheels, and algae biofuels. Highly recommended for all libraries that support the automotive industry, as well as academic libraries with automotive design programs.

702. *Automotive News: engineering, financial, manufacturing, sales, marketing, servicing.* Incorporates (1939-1942): *Automotive Service;* Formerly (until 1938): *Automotive Daily News.* [ISSN: 0005-1551] 1925. w. Mon. USD 159 domestic (print or online ed.); USD 239 Canada (print or online ed.); USD 395 elsewhere (print or online ed.). Ed(s): Richard Johnson, David Sedgwick. Crain Communications, Inc., 1155 Gratiot Ave, Detroit, MI 48207; info@crain.com; http://www.crain.com. Illus., adv. Circ: 80000 Paid. Vol. ends: Dec. Microform: CIS; PMC; PQC. *Indexed:* A22, ABIn, B01, B02, B03, BRI, C&ISA, C37, C42, CerAb, P02. *Aud.:* Ac, Sa.

Automotive News is the leading source of news information for the automotive industry, providing in-depth coverage of the industry from North America to Europe to Asia. All aspects of the industry are covered, from engineering, design, and production to marketing, sales, and service. Opinion articles, a calendar, sales figures, and classifieds are included in every issue. This title is required reading for the automotive professional and is recommended for larger collections.

703. *AutoWeek.* Former titles: *Autoweek and Competition Press;* (until 196?): *Competition Press.* [ISSN: 0192-9674] 1958. bi-w. w. until 2009. USD 29.95. Ed(s): Wes Raynal, Roger Hart. Crain Communications, Inc., 1155 Gratiot Ave, Detroit, MI 48207; http://www.crain.com. Illus., adv. Circ: 350000 Paid. Vol. ends: Dec. *Indexed:* A22, ABIn, B01, BRI, C37, MASUSE. *Aud.:* Ga.

AutoWeek is a weekly publication for auto enthusiasts. Thanks to its frequency, it is often the first to publish photographs of pre-production car models. Content includes car reviews, news, motorsports coverage (including rally, Le Mans, NASCAR, and Formula One), and automotive trends. Readers of *Automotive News* also tend to enjoy this title, which is highly recommended for all collections.

704. *Car and Driver.* Formerly: *Sports Cars Illustrated.* [ISSN: 0008-6002] 1956. m. USD 10; USD 4.99 newsstand/cover. Ed(s): Eddie Alterman. Hearst Magazines, 1585 Eisenhower Pl, Ann Arbor, MI 48108; HearstMagazines@hearst.com; http://www.hearst.com. Illus., adv. Sample. *Indexed:* A01, A22, BRI, C37, MASUSE, P02. *Aud.:* Hs, Ga.

Car and Driver is one of the most well-known and well-respected general-interest automobile magazines, and for good reason. Filled with well-written reviews, high-quality photography, car comparisons, road tests, and car previews, *Car and Driver* both educates and entertains car enthusiasts with authoritative information and a large dose of humor. The annual "10 Best Cars" issue is not to be missed. Highly recommended for all public libraries.

705. *Car Craft: do-it-yourself street performance.* Formerly: *Honk.* [ISSN: 0008-6010] 1953. m. USD 12 domestic; USD 24 Canada; USD 36 elsewhere. Ed(s): Douglas Glad. Source Interlink Companies, 6420 Wilshire Blvd, 10th Fl, Los Angeles, CA 90048; dheine@sourceinterlink.com; http://www.sourceinterlink.com. Illus., adv. Circ: 288524 Paid. *Indexed:* A22, BRI. *Aud.:* Hs, Ga.

Car Craft is aimed at the hands-on, do-it-yourself car enthusiast who is interested in rebuilding, maintaining, and customizing high-performance, American-made street cars built after 1955, primarily muscle cars. Articles include technical topics (such as an explanation of electronic fuel injection), how-to pieces (how to build a trick dashboard), and project cars. Columns are humorous and well written. For public libraries.

706. *Collectible Automobile.* Formerly: *Consumer Guide Elite Cars.* [ISSN: 0742-812X] 1984. bi-m. Ed(s): John Biel. Publications International Ltd., 7373 N Cicero Ave, Lincolnwood, IL 60712; customer_service@pubint.com; http://www.pubint.com. Illus., adv. Circ: 100000. *Bk. rev.:* 1-5, 500-2,000. *Aud.:* Ga, Sa.

Collectible Automobile is a vintage car lover's dream. Each issue features three or four automobiles, detailing their design and technical history, along with photo features, segments on collectible commercial vehicles, and personality profiles. Cars featured range from early models to models produced only 20 years ago. This title is full of high-quality, full-color photographs on glossy paper, many of which feature close-ups of unique car details. With little advertising and excellent writing, this magazine is the top choice for collectible car fanatics and the casual enthusiast looking for eye candy. Highly recommended for all public libraries and libraries with automotive collections.

707. *Cycle World.* Incorporates: *Cycle.* [ISSN: 0011-4286] 1961. m. USD 22 for 2 yrs. domestic; USD 4.99 per issue. Ed(s): Matthew Miles. Hachette Filipacchi Media U.S., Inc., 1633 Broadway, New York, NY 10019; flyedit@hfmus.com; http://www.hfmus.com. Illus., adv. Sample. *Indexed:* A22, BRI, C37, MASUSE, P02. *Bk. rev.:* Number and length vary. *Aud.:* Hs, Ga.

This high-quality magazine covers the entire spectrum of motorcycling, including sport bikes, dirt bikes, standards, and cruisers. Each issue contains plenty of color photographs, technical articles, road tests with detailed technical and performance data, race coverage, interviews, and special features, along with well-written columns. Recent articles cover everything from racing fuels to electric jacket linings. This well-liked, well-known publication is recommended for public libraries.

708. *Dirt Rider Magazine.* [ISSN: 0735-4355] 1982. m. Bonnier Corp., 2 Park Ave, 9th Fl, New York, NY 10016; http://www.bonniercorp.com. Illus., adv. Circ: 137379 Paid. *Indexed:* IHTDI. *Aud.:* Ga.

Dirt Rider focuses on off-road motorcycling for enthusiasts of all ages and abilities. Its features include stories about how and where to ride, new equipment, and motorcycles and prominent individuals in the sport. Regular articles include dirt bike tests and comparisons, technical how-to tips, race reports and upcoming races, and product information. Recommended for public libraries.

709. *F 1 Racing.* [ISSN: 1361-4487] 1996. m. GBP 38.70. Ed(s): Stewart Williams, Hans Seeberg. Haymarket Publishing Ltd., Teddington Studios, Broom Rd, Middlesex, TW11 9BE, United Kingdom; info@haymarket.com; http://www.haymarket.com. Adv. Circ: 58806. *Aud.:* Ga.

Formula 1, the world's most expensive sport, has been popular everywhere around the globe, with the exception of the United States, since 1950. Recent years, however, have shown an increase in the popularity of F1 racing in the United States, as evidenced by plans to build an F1 track in Austin, Texas, by 2012. Aimed at F1 enthusiasts, this magazine features high-quality photographs, comprehensive coverage of drivers, races, race tracks, and technical information on the cars and the teams, as well as F1 developments. The global popularity of F1 racing, coupled with the return of the U.S. Grand Prix to the 2012 F1 racing calendar, make this a title for serious consideration for public libraries.

710. *Four Wheeler Magazine: world's leading four wheel drive magazine.* [ISSN: 0015-9123] 1962. m. USD 10 domestic; USD 22 Canada; USD 34 elsewhere. Ed(s): Ken Brubaker, Douglas McColloch. Source Interlink Companies, 6420 Wilshire Blvd, 10th Fl, Los Angeles, CA 90048; dheine@sourceinterlink.com; http://www.sourceinterlink.com. Illus., adv. Circ: 235957. Vol. ends: Dec. *Aud.:* Ga.

Four Wheeler covers 4x4 trucks, SUVs, and off-road vehicles. It presents a wide range of articles including domestic trail rides, event coverage, new-vehicle testing and evaluation, and technical articles designed for four-wheelers of all abilities, as well as how-to installation articles, equipment guides, and comprehensive product testing. Feature issues include "Four Wheeler of the Year" and "Pickup Truck of the Year." Recommended for public libraries.

711. *Green Car Journal.* Incorporates: *Environmental Vehicles Review.* [ISSN: 1059-6143] 1992. q. Demand Media Inc., 1333 Second St, Ste 100, Santa Monica, CA 90401; http://www.demandmedia.com. *Aud.:* Ga, Ac, Sa.

Green Car Journal offers "a unique perspective that's largely absent from mainstream automotive magazines: consistent and thorough coverage of vehicles and technologies that takes environmental performance into account." This title contains information on electric, alternative-fuel, and low-emission vehicles, and features articles on issues such as green fleets, top fuel economy favorites, and auto trends. In addition, the magazine awards an annual "Green Car of the Year." Highly recommended for all collections.

712. *Hemmings Classic Car.* [ISSN: 1550-8730] 2004. m. USD 18.95 domestic; USD 29.48 Canada; USD 32.95 elsewhere. Hemmings Publishing, 222 Main St, PO Box 256, Bennington, VT 05201; hmnmail@hemmings.com; http://www.hemmings.com. *Aud.:* Ga, Sa.

Self-described as "the definitive all-American collector-car magazine," *Hemmings Classic Car* focuses on American-built collector cars, targeting enthusiasts, owners, collectors, dealers, restorers, and parts manufacturers. This title features all eras of autos, with a primary focus on post-war vehicles. Of particular interest is the buyers' guide in each issue, which focuses on a particular make and model for particular years, detailing technical aspects of the vehicle, parts prices, and what you can expect to pay. Recommended for large public libraries and automotive collections.

713. *Hemmings Motor News.* 1954. m. USD 31.95 domestic; USD 56.14 Canada; USD 98.95 Mexico. Hemmings Publishing, 222 Main St, Bennington, VT, 05201; Adv. Sample. *Aud.:* Ga.

Hemmings Motor News describes itself as the "world's largest collector car marketplace," and indeed it is. Each issue is over 500 pages long; approximately 80 pages are dedicated to features and articles, and the rest contain classifieds and other advertising. As with *Hemmings Classic Car,* each issue provides a buyers' guide, as well as interesting features that profile vehicles, car design, auto show coverage, and upcoming events. Recommended for public libraries and automotive collections.

714. *Hot Rod.* Formerly (until 1953): *Hot Rod Magazine.* [ISSN: 0018-6031] 1948. m. USD 14 domestic; USD 26 Canada; USD 38 elsewhere. Ed(s): Rob Kinnan. Source Interlink Companies, 6420 Wilshire Blvd, 10th Fl, Los Angeles, CA 90048; edisupport@sourceinterlink.com; http://www.sourceinterlink.com. Illus., adv. Sample. Circ: 675535. Vol. ends: Dec. Microform: PQC. *Indexed:* A22, BRI, C37, CBCARef, MASUSE, P02. *Bk. rev.:* 1-3, 200-500 words. *Aud.:* Hs, Ga.

Hot rodding, the art of modifying automobiles for performance and appearance, is hugely popular, and this magazine is filled with wonderful photos of heavily modified cars (ever seen a tricked-out two-door '64 Buick wagon?). Articles cover how-to information, people, races, and technical know-how, such as a recent article on how to get started with welding, and another on ethanol as a performance fuel. Each issue of *Hot Rod* is in full color, with lots of advertising. Recommended for all public libraries.

715. *Motocross Action.* [ISSN: 0146-3292] 1973. m. USD 19.99. Hi - Torque Publications, Inc., 25233 Amza Dr, Valencia, CA 91355; http://www.hi-torque.com. Adv. *Indexed:* SD. *Aud.:* Ga.

Aimed at the motocross racing enthusiast, this action-packed magazine features riding tips, race reports, bike tests, technical tips, interviews, and equipment reviews. This title will be of interest to both motocross racers and spectators. Recommended for public libraries.

716. *MOTOR: covering the world of automotive service.* [ISSN: 0027-1748] 1903. m. USD 48 domestic (Free to qualified personnel). Ed(s): John Lypen. Hearst Business Media, 1301 W. Long Lake Rd, Ste 300, Troy, MI 48098; http://www.hearst.com. Illus., index, adv. Sample. Microform: PQC. *Indexed:* A22, ABIn. *Aud.:* Sa.

MOTOR is a specialized magazine aimed at owners, managers, and technicians of retail automotive service and repair shops and car dealerships. Articles cover technical aspects, such as which model of car has windows that won't open, and business management aspects, such as how to turn your good shop into a great shop. Diagnostic techniques and service procedures, new product information, and industry news are also included. Recommended for vocational and technical schools, automotive collections, and collections that serve the small-business community.

717. *Motor Trend.* Incorporates (in 19??): *Car Life;* (in 1971): *Sports Car Graphic;* (in 1971): *Wheels Afield.* [ISSN: 0027-2094] 1949. m. USD 10 domestic. Ed(s): Angus MacKenzie. Source Interlink Companies, 6420 Wilshire Blvd, 10th Fl, Los Angeles, CA 90048; dheine@sourceinterlink.com; http://www.sourceinterlinkmedia.com. Illus., index, adv. Circ: 1112574 Paid. Vol. ends: Dec. *Indexed:* A01, A22, BRI, C37, CBCARef, MASUSE, P02. *Aud.:* Hs, Ga, Ac.

Motor Trend is one of the most well-known consumer automotive magazines, thanks in part to its highly coveted "Motor Trend Car of the Year Award." Chock-full of automobile reviews, interviews, and consumer information, the magazine covers a wide spectrum of vehicles. Reviews include first tests, long-term tests, and side-by-side car comparisons, and contain specs, test data, and consumer information. Inexpensive, informative, and entertaining at the same time (a recent feature highlights the cars driven by the presidential candidates), this magazine is highly recommended for all collections.

718. *Motorcycle Classics: ride 'em, don't hide 'em.* [ISSN: 1556-0880] 2005. bi-m. USD 29.95 domestic; USD 39.95 foreign. Ogden Publications, Inc., 1503 SW 42nd St, Topeka, KS 66609; http://www.ogdenpubs.com. Adv. *Aud.:* Ga.

Many motorcycle magazines focus on a particular type of motorcycle. *Motorcycle Classics* is dedicated to the classic and vintage motorcycles of yesteryear, whether made in the U.S. or overseas, whether cruisers, touring, or standard bikes, or whether BMW, Honda, or Harley. Each issue features articles on motorcycle and equipment reviews, restoration projects, and future collectibles. Recommended for large public libraries.

719. *Motorcycle Consumer News.* Former titles (until 1994): *Road Rider's Motorcycle Consumer News;* (until 1993): *Road Rider;* (until 1970): *Road Rider News.* [ISSN: 1073-9408] 1969. m. USD 22 domestic; USD 40 foreign. Ed(s): Dave Searle. BowTie, Inc., 2401 Beverly Blvd, PO Box 57900, Los Angeles, CA 90057; http://www.bowtieinc.com. Illus., adv. Sample. Circ: 60000 Paid. Vol. ends: Dec. *Aud.:* Ga.

Motorcycle Consumer News is often described as the *Consumer Reports* of the motorcycle world. Unlike the vast majority of motorcycle magazines, it accepts no advertising, is printed on glare-free paper, and is not sold at newsstands. Each issue features recalls, first impressions of bikes, extensive model evaluations, product comparisons, an events calendar, and feature articles—one recent article features crash survey results. This unbiased magazine deserves a place in every public library.

720. *Motorcyclist.* Incorporates (1970-1988): *Motorcycle Buyer's Guide.* [ISSN: 0027-2205] 1912. m. USD 10 domestic; USD 22 Canada; USD 34 elsewhere. Bonnier Corp., 2 Park Ave, 9th Fl, New York, NY 10016; http://www.bonniercorp.com. Illus., adv. Circ: 239388 Paid. *Indexed:* A22, BRI, IHTDI. *Aud.:* Hs, Ga.

Motorcyclist is the premier title for all-around, general motorcycle enthusiasts, covering racing, street motorcycling (including cruising, touring, and commuting), and the occasional historical race. International motorcycle shows are often covered, and each issue contains well-written, lengthy evaluations of new bikes that include superb color photographs and technical details. Regular sections include "First Rides," "Road Tests," "Flashback," "Gearbox," and "Motorcycle Escapes." Highly recommended for all public libraries.

721. *National Kart News.* 1986. m. Ed(s): Mike Burrell. National Kart News, 51535 Bitterweed Rd, Granger, IN 46530. Illus., adv. *Aud.:* Sa.

Karting is the sport of driving a small, open-wheel motor vehicle around a circuit, whether indoors or outdoors. *National Kart News* is the leading karting magazine in the United States, and each issue contains technical articles, such as engine tuning and clutch adjusting, event coverage and race reports, news, and product reviews. Annual special issues include the Chassis and Engine Buyers' Guides. Recommended for libraries where there is a strong karting community.

722. *Racer: racing news from the world over.* [ISSN: 1066-6060] 1992. m. USD 49.95 domestic; USD 74.95 Canada; USD 99.95 elsewhere. Haymarket Worldwide Inc., 16842 Von Karman Ave, Ste 125, Irvine, CA 92606; http://www.haymarketnetwork.com. Adv. Sample. *Aud.:* Ga.

Racer is the largest general-interest motorsports magazine in the United States. It covers all flavors of auto racing events—Formula 1, Indycar, NASCAR, NHRA, sports and GT cars, and World Rally. With in-depth features, interviews, and stunning full-color photography, *Racer* gives readers a behind-the-scenes look at the world of racing. Each issue includes a day-by-day listing of all live and taped television motorsports events for the month. Recommended for all public libraries.

723. *Rider: motorcycle touring & sport touring.* [ISSN: 1522-9726] 1974. m. USD 12 domestic. Ed(s): Donya Carlson, Mark Tuttle. Affinity Group Inc., 2575 Vista Del Mar, Ventura, CA 93001; info@affinitygroup.com; http://www.affinitygroup.com. Illus., index, adv. Circ: 122000. *Indexed:* BRI. *Aud.:* Ga.

Rider is a general-interest motorcycling magazine aimed at the road and street motorcycle enthusiast, focusing on touring, cruising, and sport bikes. Regular features include equipment reviews, ride reports, maintenance tips, and how-to articles on riding skills and gear. This title focuses more on the rides themselves, rather than the equipment, with a nod to those who use their bikes to commute. Recommended for public libraries.

724. *Road & Track.* [ISSN: 0035-7189] 1947. m. USD 10; USD 4.99 newsstand/cover. Ed(s): Larry Webster. Hearst Magazines, 1499 Monrovia Ave, Newport Beach, CA 92663; HearstMagazines@hearst.com; http://www.hearst.com. Illus., index, adv. Sample. Vol. ends: Dec. *Indexed:* A01, A22, BRI, C37, MASUSE, P02. *Bk. rev.:* 1-2, 2,000 words. *Aud.:* Hs, Ga.

Road & Track is one of the oldest automobile enthusiast magazines in the United States, founded in 1947. Its full-color, glossy pages feature everything from the latest concept cars from auto shows worldwide to production and sports cars. Regular features include road tests—both first looks and long-term—as well as technical and styling analysis, and trends. Each issue also includes coverage of at least one automobile race. *Road & Track* is recommended for all public libraries.

725. *Road Runner Motorcycle Touring & Travel.* Formerly (until 2007): *Road Runner Motorcycle Cruising & Touring.* [ISSN: 1939-7976] 2001. 6x/yr. USD 29.95. Ed(s): Andy Seiler. RoadRUNNER Publishing, 3601 Edgemoor Court, Clemmons, NC 27012; Christa@RRmotorcycling.com. Adv. *Aud.:* Ga.

RoadRUNNER magazine is "dedicated to serving active motorcycle enthusiasts by providing them with a comprehensive resource of national and international tours, exciting and picturesque new places to ride, and valuable information on new motorcycles and products that enhance their riding experience." Each issue lives up to this mission with the inclusion of six to seven touring articles from the U.S. and abroad, motorcycle and product reviews, and fantastic color photographs. For motorcyle enthusiasts who enjoy touring and those who just prefer to armchair travel. Recommended for public libraries.

726. *Scoot! Magazine.* Formerly (until 2007): *Scoot! Quarterly.* 199?. bi-m. Scoot!, PO Box 9605, San Jose, CA 95157; casey@scooter.com ; http://www.scooter.com. Adv. Sample. *Aud.:* Hs, Ga.

Scoot! is the only magazine dedicated to those who appreciate both vintage and modern motorscooters. Each issue is packed with full-color photographs that illustrate numerous articles on choosing and caring for your scooter, rally reviews, scooter and product reviews, and "Reader's Rides." Recommended for public libraries where scooter culture is popular.

727. *Specialty Car (Year): your source for kit and component cars.* Former titles (until 199?): *Kit Car;* (until 1993): *Specialty Car;* (until 199?): *Petersen's Kit Car;* Incorporates (1985-2001): *Kit Car Illustrated.* 1982. bi-m. USD 14.97 domestic; USD 20.97 Canada; USD 26.97 elsewhere. Ed(s): Brian Smith. Source Interlink Companies, 6420 Wilshire Blvd, 10th Fl, Los Angeles, CA 90048; dheine@sourceinterlink.com; http://www.sourceinterlinkmedia.com. Illus., adv. Circ: 53219. Microform: PQC. *Aud.:* Ga, Sa.

Specialty Car fills a niche in the large automotive magazine world with this specialized publication aimed at the car enthusiast who wants to purchase or build a drivable car from the ground up. Issues focus on replicas of classic and sports cars of the past and present, and include features on particular models, events, in-depth technical know-how (such as how to pinstripe a car), and a product showcase. For larger libraries.

728. *Stock Car Racing.* [ISSN: 0734-7340] 1964. m. USD 15 domestic; USD 27 Canada; USD 39 elsewhere. Ed(s): Larry Cothren. Source Interlink Companies, 5555 Concord Parkway South, Ste 326, Concord, NC 28027; dheine@sourceinterlink.com; http://www.sourceinterlinkmedia.com. Illus., adv. Circ: 257296 Paid. *Aud.:* Hs, Ga.

Stock Car Racing is for fans of the NASCAR competition to Grand National and sprint car racing. It covers all aspects of stock car racing, including behind-the-scenes race coverage, previews, and forecasts for stock car competitions throughout the United States. Driver profiles, interviews with racing teams and owners, and equipment reviews are also included. Recommended for public libraries where racing is popular.

729. *Truckin': world's leading sport truck publication.* [ISSN: 0277-5743] 1975. 13x/yr. USD 24.95 domestic; USD 37.95 Canada; USD 50.95 elsewhere. Ed(s): Steve Warner. Source Interlink Companies, 2400 E Katella Ave, Ste 700, Anaheim, CA 92806; dheine@sourceinterlink.com; http://www.sourceinterlinkmedia.com. Illus., adv. Circ: 133353 Paid. *Aud.:* Hs, Ga.

This title is dedicated to the truck enthusiast and covers trucks, SUVs, 4x4 lifted off-road vehicles, mini-trucks, and custom trucks. Customization, new model reviews, and technical tips (a recent article covers how to lower your suspension) are all regular features. The majority of the trucks in this magazine are recent vehicles, and readers are likely to encounter lots of color photos of trucks with painted flames. Recommended for large public libraries.

730. *Vintage Motorsport: the journal of motor racing history.* [ISSN: 1052-8067] 1982. bi-m. USD 45 domestic; USD 55 in Canada & Mexico; USD 80 in South America. Ed(s): Randy Riggs. Vintage Motorsport Inc., PO Box 7200, Lakeland, FL 33807. Adv. *Bk. rev.:* Number and length vary. *Aud.:* Hs, Ga, Ac.

This title provides a fascinating look into the history of auto racing. Filled with stunning old and new photos of vintage racecars, *Vintage Motorsport* also contains racer profiles and articles covering auto races, both current and historic. The magazine covers current vintage racing news, event schedules, and commentary. Recommended for comprehensive collections.

731. *Ward's AutoWorld.* Formerly: *Ward's Quarterly.* [ISSN: 0043-0315] 1964. m. USD 69 domestic (Free to qualified personnel). Ed(s): Barbara L McClellan. Ward's Automotive Group, 3000 Town Ctr, Ste 2750, Southfield, MI 48075; wards@wardsauto.com; http://www.wardsauto.com. Illus., index, adv. Circ: 68200 Controlled. *Indexed:* A22, ABIn, B01, B02, BRI, C&ISA, CerAb. *Aud.:* Ac, Sa.

Ward's Automotive Group has covered the auto industry for more than 80 years. This publication covers a wide spectrum of the industry, with articles on vehicle technology, global industry trends, labor and management issues, the latest in manufacturing and materials, and economic, political, and legal issues. Special issues include Ward's ten best engines, an annual suppliers issue, and a state-of-the-industry issue. Recommended for specialized academic collections and large public libraries.

■ BEER, WINE, AND SPIRITS

Kandace Rogers, Director, Library and Learning Resource Center, Sullivan University, Lexington, KY

Introduction

Improvements in economic conditions over the last year have created a shift in alcoholic beverage sales, with spirits taking the lead over beer and wine. Levels of consumer purchasing fluctuated from value-priced beverages to more premium and upscale selections, prompting a rise in items such as small-batch spirits and seasonal ales. The rising popularity of craft beer has influenced growth in brew pubs and local breweries, both emerging as strong players in bar and restaurant venues, as well as in home-brewer and winemaker communities.

Beer, wine, and spirit magazines continue to emphasize "drinks culture," with the majority tailoring content to the consumer. Content includes topics such as guidelines to pairing food and a spirit of choice; restaurant reviews; drinks history; brewing recipes; and buyer's guides and directories. Industry performance and outlook play a role in selecting titles, paired with analysis of current trends to appeal to readers of both amateur and professional expertise. Publications with ratings and rankings will appeal to the more serious reader as well as to students and beginners working to improve their knowledge of a particular brew or pour.

Social media continues to impact print content as each publisher refines its supplemental web site content with a variety of features that are only available online. Access to online content varies from free with print subscription, to additional fee with print or electronic-only access.

In addition to the beverage-centric titles, libraries with culinary arts programs may want to explore market analysis publications such as *Beer Marketer's Insights* for industry sales or titles such as the *Journal of Wine Economics* for scholarly content.

Basic Periodicals

All About Beer; Mutineer; Whisky Advocate; Wine Spectator.

Basic Abstracts and Indexes

Academic Search Premier; Hospitality and Tourism Index; MasterFILE Premier.

732. *All About Beer.* [ISSN: 0898-9001] 1980. bi-m. USD 19.99 domestic. Ed(s): John Holl. Chautauqua Press, 501 Washington St, Ste H, Durham, NC 27701; operations@allaboutbeer.com. Illus., adv. *Bk. rev.:* Occasional. *Aud.:* Ga, Sa.

Publishing six issues a year for over 30 years, *All About Beer* covers beer culture with a well-rounded mix of articles about home brewing, craft breweries, and lists of award-winning beers useful for both the consumer and restaurant professional. Recent changes have reduced the amount of coverage of big-beer America and large breweries in order to offer alternatives, giving a particular nod to the microbrewery/craft beer phenomenon. Each issue contains a feature article and an extensive buyer's guide on a particular style of beer, using a 100-point rating scale and analyses written by Beverage Testing Institute, an independent review service. Reviews and columns feature brewers and brewing around the world with a companion web site offering supportive content, particularly in beer travel and tourism. The magazine also sponsors the World Beer Festival event, hosted in various states throughout the year.

733. *The Beer Connoisseur Magazine.* [ISSN: 2151-4356] 2009. q. USD 21 domestic; USD 29 Canada; USD 49 elsewhere. On Tap Publishing, PO Box 420903, Atlanta, GA 30342; ldavis@ontappublishing.com. Adv. *Aud.:* Ga, Sa.

A more sophisticated publication about beer than some of its counterparts, *Beer Connoisseur* writes about beer as *Wine Spectator* does about wine. Articles promote beer as a cultured accompaniment to fine cuisine and dining with a global scope. This title offers scored beer reviews from blind taste tests that are conducted by industry experts, with extensive commentary and U.S. distribution information. Subscription offerings include tablet versions and a password-protected online library, each with special pricing comparable to print offerings.

734. *Beer West.* Formerly (until 2011): *Beer Northwest.* 2007. q. USD 20. Ed(s): Megan Flynn. Flynn Media, PO Box 12504, Portland, OR 97212; http://www.beernw.com/. *Aud.:* Ga, Sa.

Launched in 2007 as *Beer Northwest, Beer West* was re-launched in 2011 and oriented to the West Coast, a prolific brewing region. It advises on brew and food pairings in addition to beer events in the Pacific region. An annual food issue expands on ways to incorporate beer into both food preparation and consumption. While this magazine is regional, it offers an array of topics and site-visits nationally and internationally that should satisfy a broader audience. A great resource for brewers and beer enthusiasts alike, this should be a definite consideration for those in its geographic area.

735. *BeerAdvocate.* 2007. m. USD 29.99; USD 3.99 per issue. Ed(s): Jason Alstroem. BeerAdvocate, PO Box 534, Boston, MA 02128; sales@beeradvocate.com. Illus., adv. *Aud.:* Ga, Sa.

Since 1996, the *Beer Advocate* web site has been a popular place for finding information and learning about the craft beer revolution. Founded by two brothers with the motto to "respect beer," the magazine grew from the web site and began publishing in 2007. Still refining editorial content, the editors are working toward blending the printed version with online content, and they have set clear goals on their plan to grow the magazine and allow it to both complement the web site and find its own voice. Definitely one to watch as it matures with each additional issue.

736. *The Bourbon Review.* 2008. q. USD 14.99. Ed(s): Justin Thompson. The Bourbon Review, PO Box 24270, Lexington, KY 40524. *Aud.:* Ga, Sa.

Beginning publishing in 2008, *The Bourbon Review* is just beginning to find its editorial place among the spirited journals. Dedicated to exploring the trends and history of bourbon, the *Review* surveys bourbon appreciation in the South as well as across the United States, in locations such as Las Vegas or Austin. Articles take a critical examination of current techniques such as the distillery movement and craft bourbons, with editorials on topics such as blended bourbons as trends or true improvements to the craft. Issues include an events calendar, a distillery directory, and travel suggestions with maps to facilitate a tour of tasting rooms. Definitely a publication to watch as it matures with its topic over the next few years.

737. *Brew Your Own: the how-to homebrew beer magazine.* [ISSN: 1081-826X] 1995. 8x/yr. USD 28 domestic. Ed(s): Chris Colby. Brew Your Own, 5515 Main St, Manchester Center, VT 05255; byo@byo.com. Illus., adv. Sample. Circ: 40000 Paid. *Bk. rev.:* Number and length vary. *Aud.:* Ga, Sa.

Brew Your Own is the largest-circulating magazine dedicated to the homebrewer, beginning publishing in 1995. This title is written for brewers of various expertise levels, and all aspects of homebrewing are included. While much of this information may also be available in numerous introductory books on homebrewing, this magazine provides current information and recommendations to assist the homebrewer—including brewing recipes, supply recommendations, a supplier directory arranged by state, and book reviews. In addition to significant free content on the BYO web site, both print and digital subscriptions are available at separate prices.

738. *Imbibe.* [ISSN: 1557-7082] 2006. bi-m. USD 20 domestic; USD 40 foreign. Imbibe Media Inc, 1028 SE Water Ave, Ste 285, Portland, OR 97214. Illus., adv. *Aud.:* Ga, Sa.

Publishing since 2006, *Imbibe* offers a well-rounded exploration of the world of drinks and beverage appreciation. It describes itself as the ultimate guide to liquid culture, and issues provide articles and recommendations on homemade sodas, tea, and coffee as well as beer, wine, and cocktails. A companion web site has access to portions of the magazine archive as well as unique articles, additional drink recipes, and a news blog. Specific issues highlight topics such as the annual beer guide in the fall, a holiday issue, summer drinks, and other seasonal subjects. This title is a multiple award-winner, and each issue offers an extensive coverage of all aspects of drink consumption.

739. *Mutineer: fine beverage, refined.* 2008. bi-m. USD 14.99. Ed(s): Brian Kropf. Wine Mutineer LLC, 7510 Sunset Blvd, Los Angeles, CA 90046; general@mutineermagazine.com. Illus., adv. *Aud.:* Ga, Sa.

A relative newcomer, *Mutineer* magazine focuses on fine beverages with an emphasis on wine, beer, and spirits. Founded by sommelier Alan Kropf and beer expert J.J. Bagley in 2008, it has steadily improved its content over the years to appeal to a wide audience. Articles and writing are accessible to both the layman and the culinary professional. For example, articles on stocking a bar examine home bar contents as well as inventory advice for a successful restaurant bar. Columns incorporate beverage science and examine all things "beverage," including coffee and soda fountain preparations in addition to beer, wine, and liquors. Presenting a well-balanced overview of the fine beverage industry, *Mutineer* is an exceptional addition to spirited publishing.

740. *The New Brewer: the magazine for micro and pub brewers.* [ISSN: 0741-0506] 1983. bi-m. Membership, USD 155; USD 15 per issue. Ed(s): Jill Redding. BREWERS ASSOCIATION, PO Box 1679, Boulder, CO 80306; info@brewersassociation.org; http://www.brewersassociation.org. Adv. Circ: 13000 Paid. *Indexed:* H&TI. *Aud.:* Ga, Sa.

The New Brewer is the official journal of the Brewers Association. Established in 1983, it functions as support for professional brewers and breweries of all sizes, on all aspects of their craft and business. Issues include technical brewing information and advice for improving the production process. The title offers a substantial supplier directory with news and reviews of new products and analysis of trends in the industry. This journal is supplemented by web site content, and it covers current legislation and government action that affects breweries and gives guidance on business operations and management. Sharing its editor with *Zymurgy*, *The New Brewer* offers comprehensive coverage for breweries varying from "fewer than 500 barrels per year up to more than 800,000 barrels."

741. *Whisky Advocate: everything for the whisky enthusiast.* Former titles (until 2011): *Malt Advocate*; (until 1994): *On Tap*. 19??. q. USD 18 domestic; USD 24 Canada; USD 40 elsewhere. Ed(s): John Hansell. Whisky Advocate, 167 Main St, Emmaus, PA 18049. Illus. *Aud.:* Ga, Sa.

Renamed in the fall of 2011, *Whisky Advocate* (formerly *Malt Advocate*) has been the leading publication on all things whisky for the last 20 years. Though widely known for its coverage on whisky, the publication is dedicated to all malt beverages. It publishes four times a year, and each issue features extensive coverage of topics such as craft bourbons, how to build a collection, and shopping at bottle auctions. Regular columns include travel suggestions, interviews with master distillers, and drink recipes. Each issue has a buyer's guide that rates whiskies from around the world, including a few beer selections and a directory of craft distillers. This magazine is also the presenter of the annual Whisky Fest, a sampling and educational event hosted in major U.S. cities.

742. *Wine Advocate.* [ISSN: 0887-8463] 1978. bi-m. Ed(s): Robert M Parker. Wine Advocate, Inc., PO Box 311, Monkton, MD 21111-0311; info@erobertparker.com; https://www.erobertparker.com/. *Aud.:* Ga, Sa.

Publishing since 1978, the *Wine Advocate* is the creation of Robert M. Parker Jr., an internationally known oenophile. It contains no photographs or advertising, and its format is similar to that of a trade publication. Wine ratings use the Parker Points 50–100 scale and are intended for consumer use, not to promote a particular wine or winery. Mr. Parker is scheduled to step down as editor-in-chief of the print version at the end of 2013, to focus his efforts on the web site www.erobertparker.com, which is a separate subscription service with searchable archives of the *Advocate* back to 1992 and other supplemental analyses. While he will still be writing for the print version, it is unknown how editorial changes will affect content over the next few years.

743. *Wine & Spirits: the practical guide to wine.* Formerly (until 198?): *Wine & Spirits Buying Guide.* [ISSN: 0890-0299] 1981. 8x/yr. USD 29.95. Ed(s): Joshua Greene. Wine & Spirits Magazine, Inc., 2 W 32nd St, Ste 601, New York, NY 10001; subscription@wineandspiritsmagazine.com. Illus. *Indexed:* H&TI. *Aud.:* Ga, Sa.

Wine & Spirits is a more mainstream alternative to the more formal wine magazines. It utilizes polls and lists for many of its reviews and rankings, and this serves to make information more accessible and easy to understand for a broad audience of readers. This title publishes eight times a year, and offers print subscribers free access to supplemental content on the *Wine & Spirits* web page, in a capacity that allows searches for wines by winery, rating, or price range. While the magazine has received awards for its fine wine journalism, it is targeted to more than just the wine enthusiast, with extensive articles on premium distilled spirits. Its lower annual subscription rate make it worth consideration to reach a broad audience of readers.

744. *Wine Spectator.* [ISSN: 0193-497X] 1976. 15x/yr. USD 49.95 domestic; USD 80 Canada; USD 145 elsewhere. Ed(s): Kim Marcus, Marvin R Shanken. Marvin R. Shanken Communications, Inc., 387 Park Ave S, New York, NY 10016; mmorgenstern@mshanken.com; http://www.mshanken.com/. Illus., adv. *Indexed:* B01, BRI, H&TI, P02. *Aud.:* Ga, Sa.

Publishing since 1976, *Wine Spectator* has a glossy format and open design that make it the most recognized wine consumer magazine in the industry. The magazine covers current news, personalities in the industry, food and cooking, and selected upscale spirits, but it is best known for the scores and ratings section for wine guidance and recommendations. Recent editorial changes have prompted criticism for the journal's not retaining a steady panel of expert tasters that readers can follow for suggestion decisions and matching tastes, but these changes have not affected its popularity. Leading the industry, *WS* is the first publisher to offer multiple apps to put ratings in the hands of readers. Subscription options include print or print-plus-password access to WS.com content, which includes free access to the WS School for beginners. Online content also includes access to other Shanken publications, discussion forums, daily news updates, and job listings for jobs in the wine industry.

745. *WineMaker: creating your own great wines.* 2003. bi-m. USD 25 domestic; USD 28 Canada; USD 45 elsewhere. Ed(s): Betsy Parks. Battenkill Communications LLP, 5053 Main St., Ste. A, Manchester Center, VT 05255. Adv. Circ: 108500 Paid and controlled. *Aud.:* Ga, Sa.

The sister magazine of the publishing group behind the beer title *Brew Your Own*, *WineMaker* magazine is written for the amateur winemaker. Aimed at readers from beginner to expert, articles instruct on a variety of knowledge levels and experience. The title was launched in 1998, and issues provide tips on growing your own grapes, exploring wine kits, and developing a wine cellar, and include a supplier directory. The title publishes a print and an online edition, and the web site provides additional content such as recipes and the magazine archive. *WineMaker* also sponsors the world's largest wine competition devoted to hobby wines, as well as sponsors the WineMaker International Amateur Wine Competition and hosts the annual WineMaker Magazine Conference.

746. *Zymurgy.* [ISSN: 0196-5921] 1978. bi-m. Free to members. Ed(s): Jill Redding. American Homebrewers Association Inc., PO Bos 1679, Boulder, CO 80306; info@brewersassociation.org; http://www.homebrewersassociation.org. Illus., adv. Circ: 22000. *Indexed:* P02. *Aud.:* Ga, Sa.

The journal of the American Homebrewers Association (a division of the Brewers Association), *Zymurgy* provides recipes, comprehensive technical information, and the latest trends for the amateur brewer. Articles explore all aspects of brewing, from how to select and evaluate ingredients, to building brewing equipment. In addition, advertising from specialized manufacturers and distributors of homebrew products and supplies provides a great resource for the reader. Subscription includes membership in the AHA as well as access to significant content on the companion web site—which provides journal archives, instruction videos and articles, and access to the AHA community events and forums.

■ BIBLIOGRAPHY

See also Books and Book Reviews; Library and Information Science; and Printing and Graphic Arts sections.

Deborah F. Bernnard, Head, Dewey Graduate Library, University at Albany, Albany, NY 12222; dbernnard@albany.edu.

Mark Wolfe, Curator of Digital Collections, M. E. Grenander Department of Special Collections and Archives, Science Library, University at Albany, Albany, NY 12222; mwolfe@albany.edu

Introduction

Bibliography is the study of books as physical objects. While the term is often limited to the practice of *enumerative* bibliography, as in (for example) the process of making lists of books by author, the domain of knowledge is much broader and deeper. Bibliography, as it pertains to the magazines listed in this section, is predominantly concerned with the broader category of *analytical* bibliography.

In *Book Collecting: A Modern Guide* (Bowker, 1977), Terry Belanger divides *analytical* bibliography into several types: *historical* ("the history of books broadly speaking, and the persons, institutions, and machines producing them"), *textual* ("the relationship between the printed text as we have it before us and that text as conceived by its author"), and *descriptive* ("the close physical description of books"). The subject of bibliography is of interest to rare-book librarians, curators, bibliophiles, and scholars who are interested in medieval studies and the history of the book.

Journals that cover bibliography are often produced by bibliographical societies. These societies are not necessarily affiliated with an educational institution, and their membership consists of anyone who has an interest in bibliography. The Bibliographic Society of America is one example of a national society. Included here are publications by American, British, Australian, New Zealand, and Canadian Societies. Other important journals for the field are published by research universities whose collections are often the subject of the articles found in these journals. Also important for bibliography collections are journals that specialize in specific aspects of bibliography, such as *Gutenberg-Jahrbuch,* which is devoted to Johannes Gutenberg. Other journals may be specific to book history and book collecting.

Basic Periodicals

Ac, Sa: *Bibliographical Society of America. Papers; The Library; Studies in Bibliography.*

Basic Abstracts and Indexes

America: History and Life, Historical Abstracts, Library Literature & Information Science, MLA International Bibliography.

747. *La Bibliofilia: rivista di storia del libro e di bibliografia.* [ISSN: 0006-0941] 1899. 3x/yr. EUR 148 (print & online eds.). Ed(s): Edoardo Barbieri. Casa Editrice Leo S. Olschki, Viuzzo del Pozzetto 8, Florence, 50126, Italy; celso@olschki.it; http://www.olschki.it. Illus., adv. Vol. ends: Sep/Dec. *Indexed:* A22, MLA-IB, RILM. *Bk. rev.:* 6-10, 300-3,000 words. *Aud.:* Ac, Sa.

First published in 1899, *La Bibliofilia* is a venerable Italian publication that covers publishing, printing, and the book trade in Italy. Articles are written in German, English, French, and Italian, with English abstracts included at the end of each article. Research articles, book reviews, and a notes section are found in each issue. Most of the reviews are of books published in Italian, although some issues include an Americana section in which books published in the United States are reviewed in English. Recommended for special collections and academic libraries that support substantial Italian Studies programs.

748. *Bibliographical Society of America. Papers.* Incorporates (1907-1912): *Bibliographical Society of America. Bulletin;* Formerly (1905-1909): *Bibliographical Society of America. Proceedings and Papers.* [ISSN: 0006-128X] 1905. q. Free to members. Ed(s): Travis Gordon, T H Howard-Hill. Bibliographical Society of America, PO Box 1537, New York, NY 10021; bsa@bibsocamer.org; http://www.bibsocamer.org. Illus., index, adv. Refereed. Vol. ends: Dec. Reprint: PSC. *Indexed:* A01, A22, AmHI, ArtHuCI, BEL&L, BRI, CBRI, MLA-IB, P02, RILM. *Bk. rev.:* 7-10 of 500-2,500 words; plus 4-6 more of 200-500 words. *Aud.:* Ac, Sa.

Published since 1905, the *Papers of the Bibliographical Society of America* contains articles on book and manuscript printing, distribution, and collecting in all disciplines. Each issue contains three to four peer-review articles and a notably large selection of book reviews. Bibliographical notes and review essays may also be included in select issues. It is published quarterly; issue four contains an index to the whole volume. Recent article titles include "Two Gutenberg Bibles Used as Compositor's Exemplars"; "John Dicks's Illustrated Edition of 'Shakspere for the Millions'"; and "The Types of the French Renaissance". Recommended for Special Collections and large public and academic libraries.

749. *Bibliographical Society of Canada. Papers.* Supersedes: *Bibliographical Society of Canada. Newsletter.* [ISSN: 0067-6896] 1962. s-a. Ed(s): Dr. Jennifer Connor. Bibliographical Society of Canada, PO Box 575, Toronto, ON M5S 2T1, Canada; http://www.library.utoronto.ca/bsc. Refereed. *Indexed:* BRI, C37, CBCARef, MLA-IB, RILM. *Bk. rev.:* Number and length vary. *Aud.:* Ac, Sa.

The *Papers of the Bibliographical Society of Canada* is the official publication of the society, which is the premier journal in Canada on the study of bibliography. The journal features three regular sections, research articles, "Books in Review," and "Brief Notices." The journal averages one to three articles per issue, with about one quarter of them published in French, some of which are accompanied by illustrations. Articles range in topics from printing and publishing history to textual studies, many of which draw on Canadian history and its connections to bibliography. Recent issues include titles such as, "'Crying Over Spilled Milk': A Publishing History of Sam Steele's Forty Years in Canada" and "From Gleam of Light to Seedbed of a National Institute: The Canadian Free Library for the Blind, 1906-1918." Each issue includes numerous book reviews of scholarship printed in English and French. This is a high-quality publication and would be at home in any academic library, especially those wanting a Canadian perspective on the subject.

750. *Bodleian Library Record.* Formerly (until 1938): *Bodleian Quarterly Record.* [ISSN: 0067-9488] 1914. s-a. GBP 50 (Individuals, GBP 40). Bodleian Library, Broad St, Oxford, OX1 3BG, United Kingdom; fob@bodley.ox.ac.uk; http://www.ouls.ox.ac.uk. Illus., index. Refereed. Circ: 1500 Paid. Vol. ends: Oct. Microform: PQC. *Indexed:* A22, AmHI, MLA-IB. *Aud.:* Ac, Sa.

The *Bodleian Library Record,* published semiannually, contains articles by researchers who have used the Library's collections. Because the collections date back to 1602, there is no end to possible research topics. Each issue contains a "Notes and News" section, in which information is imparted about past and present library staff and events; reviews of monographs published by The Bodleian Library; notable accessions; and a "Notes and Documents" section, in which scholars describe selected manuscripts in the collection. There are also several feature articles in each issue that delve deeply into Bodleian collections. Recent titles include "Kafka's Writings: Private Confessions or Public Property?" and "Ragtime to Riches: The Remarkable Story of Walter Harding's Book and Music Collection." Color plates of items in the Bodleian collections contribute to the rich content in this publication. Recommended for special collections and larger academic libraries.

751. The Book Collector. Supersedes (in 1952): *Book Handbook.* [ISSN: 0006-7237] 1952. q. GBP 56 domestic; EUR 85 in Europe; USD 115 elsewhere. Ed(s): Nicolas Barker. Collector Ltd., PO Box 12426, London, W11 3GW, United Kingdom; editor@thebookcollector.co.uk. Illus., index, adv. Sample. Vol. ends: Winter. Microform: PQC. Reprint: PSC. *Indexed:* A22, AmHI, ArtHuCI, BEL&L, BRI, CBRI, MLA-IB, RILM. *Bk. rev.:* 4-8, 500-3,000 words. *Aud.:* Ac, Sa.

Created in 1952 by Ian Fleming of James Bond fame, *The Book Collector* contains scholarly essays, lists, catalogs, and news from the rare-book and antiquarian trade worlds in the United Kingdom, with some coverage of the United States. Nicolas Barker has been editor since 1965, and his point of view is evident throughout the publication, most notably in the "News and Comments" section, which opines on all things related to the printed book. The journal is published quarterly; recent articles have explored handwriting, an eighteenth-century private library, and book binding. Black-and-white reproductions of book pages, including marginalia, are found within each issue. Reviews of relevant publications are included at the end of each issue. Recommended for special collections and larger academic and public libraries.

752. Book History. [ISSN: 1098-7371] 1998. a. USD 70. Ed(s): Jonathan Rose, Ezra Greenspan. The Johns Hopkins University Press, 2715 N Charles St, Baltimore, MD 21218; http://www.press.jhu.edu. Illus., adv. Refereed. Circ: 900. Reprint: PSC. *Indexed:* A01, A22, AmHI, E01, MLA-IB. *Aud.:* Ac, Sa.

There is an immense variety and depth of scholarship to be gleaned from the history of the book. *Book History,* the official journal of the Society for the History of Authorship, Reading and Publishing, serves as the venue for publication of this scholarship. This annual, hardcover publication contains about a dozen well-researched articles on topics ranging from authorship to university presses. Illustration, censorship, and ebooks are also among the many topics scrutinized by scholars. A short biography of each contributor is listed at the end of each issue. The journal only publishes scholarly essays and articles. It does not include reviews or commentary. However, each issue contains a valuable literature review article on a specific print, publishing, or book history topic. Recommended for special collections and larger academic and public libraries.

753. Cambridge Bibliographical Society. Transactions. [ISSN: 0068-6611] 1949. a. Cambridge Bibliographical Society, c/o Cambridge University Library, W Rd, Cambridge, CB3 9DR, United Kingdom; cbs@lib.cam.ac.uk; http://www.lib.cam.ac.uk/cambibsoc. Illus. Refereed. *Indexed:* A22, MLA-IB. *Aud.:* Ac, Sa.

Published annually, the *Transactions of the Cambridge Bibliographical Society* focuses on University of Cambridge–related research. This may include articles on works found in Cambridge libraries, works written by Cambridge authors, or works published by Cambridge University establishments. Each slim volume contains three or four disparate articles. High-quality color reproductions of illustrations, pages, and photographs accompany many of the articles. Each volume also includes a short summary of the society's activities during the year. Recommended for larger academic and special collections libraries.

754. Gutenberg - Jahrbuch. [ISSN: 0072-9094] 1926. a. EUR 75 per issue. Ed(s): Stephan Fuessel. Harrassowitz Verlag, Kreuzberger Ring 7b-d, Wiesbaden, 65205, Germany; service@harrassowitz.de; http:// www.harrassowitz.de. Illus. Circ: 2200 Controlled. Reprint: PSC. *Indexed:* FR, MLA-IB, RILM. *Aud.:* Ac, Sa.

Gutenberg Jahrbuch is an annual devoted to scholarship on the life of Johannes Gutenberg, as well as the history of the book. Although it is published in Germany, its articles are written in German, English, Italian, Spanish, and French. Each volume is beautifully produced with both color and black-and-white reproductions. Selected recent titles of English language articles are "The Complex Genealogy of Hans Holbein the Younger's Illustrations of ;Moriae Encomium"; "Three Fifteenth Century Proof Sheets with Manuscript Corrections from Nuremberg Presses"; "The Social and Geographical Repositioning of a Minor Printer in Eighteenth Century Antwerp"; and "A Forgotten Gutenberg Bible from the Monastery of Santo Domingo de Silos." Recommended for academic libraries and special collections.

755. Harvard Library Bulletin. Former titles (until 1947): *Harvard University Library. Notes;* (until 1941): *Harvard Library Notes.* [ISSN: 0017-8136] 1920. q. USD 35 in North America; USD 41 elsewhere; USD 15 per issue. Ed(s): William P Stoneman. Harvard University Library, Wadsworth House, 1341 Massachusetts Ave, Cambridge, MA 02138; http://hul.harvard.edu. Illus. Refereed. Vol. ends: Winter. Microform: MIM; PQC. *Indexed:* A22, ABS&EES, ArtHuCI, BAS, MLA-IB, RILM. *Aud.:* Ac, Sa.

The *Harvard Library Bulletin* is broad in scope—articles may be about an exhibition at the library, a collection, a notable work, or a person with a Harvard connection such as Ralph Waldo Emerson (who attended Harvard at age 14). Most issues contain two or three disparate articles. However, themed issues are occasionally published. Recent titles of themed issues are "A Guide to Ukrainian Special Collections at Harvard University" and "The Edward Lear Collection at Harvard University: Essays, A Checklist of the Incomparable Collection and an Exhibition Catalog on the Occasion of the 200th Anniversary of Lear's Birth." The first title is a bibliography and inventory of Harvard's Ukrainian collections, and the second includes the catalog for a library exhibition on Edward Lear; Harvard's Houghton Library holds the world's most comprehensive collection of original Lear paintings. High-quality color reproductions of exhibit items are often included. Recommended for large academic and special collections.

756. Huntington Library Quarterly: studies in English and American history and literature. Formerly (until 1937): *The Huntington Library. Bulletin.* [ISSN: 0018-7895] 1931. q. USD 241 (print & online eds.). Ed(s): Jean Patterson, Susan Green. University of California Press, Journals Division, 2000 Ctr St, Ste 303, Berkeley, CA 94704; customerservice@ucpressjournals.com; http://www.ucpressjournals.com. Illus., index, adv. Sample. Refereed. Circ: 429. Microform: PQC. Reprint: PSC. *Indexed:* A01, A06, A07, A22, AmHI, ArtHuCI, BRI, E01, FR, MLA-IB, P02, RILM. *Bk. rev.:* 1-4, 2,000-7,500 words. *Aud.:* Ac, Sa.

The Huntington Library, a private library founded in 1919 by American philanthropist Henry E. Huntington, houses a large and rich collection of British and American history and literature rare books and manuscripts. However, articles in the *Huntington Library Quarterly* do not only cover items in the collection. Often, themed issues are interspersed throughout a volume. Recent titles of themed issues are "Sesquicentennial Impressions: A Celebration of *Leaves of Grass* (1860)" and "Reason, Evidence and Erudition in Early Modern Europe." Issues that are not themed may contain substantial review sections as well as a "Notes and Documents" feature, in which scholars provide bibliographical notes on selected rare items in the collection. "Intramuralia," a listing of Huntington Library acquisitions for a year, is included approximately two years after the actual acquisition. Black-and-white reproductions of manuscript pages, paintings, drawings, or photographs are included as appropriate. Recommended for academic libraries and special collections.

757. John Rylands University Library of Manchester. Bulletin. Formerly (until 1972): *John Rylands Library. Bulletin.* [ISSN: 0301-102X] 1903. s-a. GBP 150 (print & online eds.). Ed(s): Paul Fouracre. Manchester University Press, Coupland Bldg 3, Oxford Rd, Manchester, M13 9NR, United Kingdom; mup@manchester.ac.uk; http:// www.manchesteruniversitypress.co.uk/. Illus., index, adv. Refereed. Microform: IDC. *Indexed:* A22, AmHI, ArtHuCI, BAS, BEL&L, BrArAb, FR, MLA-IB, NumL, R&TA. *Aud.:* Ac, Sa.

The *Bulletin of the John Rylands University Library of Manchester* covers a wide range of subjects, and often publishes articles that have been researched at the John Rylands University Library. The library's collections are vast and boast a large collection of early Methodist papers. Its holdings include "12,500 books printed between 1475 and 1640, and 45,000 printed between 1641 and 1700." Themed issues are published at least once per volume. This journal has been published erratically in recent years; the latest issue is dated 2006 but was published in 2010. Publication is slated to resume in 2014 by the Manchester University Press. Recommended for large academic and special collections.

758. The Library: the transactions of the Bibliographical Society.
Incorporates (1893-1919): *Bibliographical Society. Transactions;* Formerly (until 1889): *Library Chronicle.* [ISSN: 0024-2160] 18??. q. EUR 281. Ed(s): Dr. Bill Bell. Oxford University Press, Great Clarendon St, Oxford, OX2 6DP, United Kingdom; enquiry@oup.co.uk; http://www.oxfordjournals.org/. Illus., index, adv. Sample. Refereed. Vol. ends: Dec. Microform: PQC. Reprint: PSC. *Indexed:* A22, AmHI, ArtHuCI, BRI, BrArAb, CBRI, E01, MLA-IB, NumL. *Bk. rev.:* 10-13, 1,000-2,000 words. *Aud.:* Ac, Sa.

The *Library* is a publication of the Bibliographical Society, and is the premier scholarly journal on the study of bibliography and book history in the U.K. "All aspects of descriptive, analytical, textual[,] and historical bibliography come within" the scope of *The Library*. The journal typically devotes each issue to two or three full-length scholarly articles, as well as extensive book reviews. Each issue devotes space to three regular sections: "Books Received" contains a listing of new monographs; "Recent Books" features an annotated listing relevant to the field of bibliography; and "Recent Periodicals" features published articles germane to bibliography that are categorized by language or place of publication. The journal is indexed yearly. This is an excellent journal that should be subscribed to by large research universities, and those libraries that support programs in the history of the book and rare-book librarianship.

759. Matrix (Herefordshire): a review for printers and bibliophiles. [ISSN: 0261-3093] 1981. a. GBP 90 per issue. Whittington Press, Lower Marston Farm, Leominster, HR6 0NJ, United Kingdom; rose@whittingtonpress.plus.com; http://www.whittingtonpress.com. Illus. *Indexed:* A51. *Bk. rev.:* 12-25, 100-2,500 words. *Aud.:* Ac, Sa.

The *Matrix* is a book-length journal that is published yearly and printed using a letterpress on handmade paper. The *Matrix* is an exquisite publication that is a collectible object itself. It features numerous tipped-in illustrations, pull-out posters printed with woodblock type, glossy color plates, and other expressive features typical of the book arts. The journal will inspire scholars of the book arts, typography, and book historians. This journal is truly unique and stands out among nearly all of the bibliography journals for the amount of care and quality of materials spent on each issue. While the articles are well written and engaging, one should not look to this journal for conventional academic research articles. Innovative uses of typeface accompany some articles, like "A century of futurist typography" or "'The Future is Now': The Golden Years of 'Architectural Design.'" This journal is appropriate for any large academic institution, and those that support programs in book arts, rare-book librarianship, and the history of the book, as well as bibliophiles.

760. Princeton University Library Chronicle. Incorporates: *Princeton University Library. Biblia.* [ISSN: 0032-8456] 1939. 3x/yr. USD 50 (Individuals, USD 25; Free to members). Ed(s): Gretchen M Oberfrane. Friends of Princeton University Library, 1 Washington Rd, Princeton, NJ 08544; principi@princeton.edu; http://www.fpul.org. Illus., index. Refereed. Vol. ends: Spring. *Indexed:* A22, AmHI, BAS, MLA-IB. *Aud.:* Ac, Sa.

The *Princeton University Library Chronicle* is a publication of the Friends of the Princeton University Library. The journal covers many aspects of bibliography—aiming to "publish articles of scholarly importance and general interest based on research in the rare book and manuscripts collection of the Princeton University Library." Each issue typically features three or four well-documented research articles that are generously illustrated, sometimes in color. Recent acquisitions of books, coins, manuscripts, and art that are new and notable to the library collections are described by curators and librarians of the collections. The *Chronicle* features meeting notes under the section "Friends of the Library." Also, there is a short "Cover Note" that describes the cover illustration (which can range 1–12 pages in length). There can be thematic issues, such as one themed around Irish writers and literature that included original submissions or extracts from works in progress. A comprehensive index of each volume is published yearly with the journal. This journal would be appropriate in any academic library that supports programs in the humanities or information studies programs.

Printing Historical Society. Journal. See Printing and Graphic Arts section.

Printing History. See Printing and Graphic Arts section.

761. The Private Library. Formerly (until 1958): *P L A Quarterly.* [ISSN: 0032-8898] 1957. q. Private Libraries Association, c/o Jim Maslen, 29 Eden Dr, Hull, HU8 8JQ, United Kingdom; http://www.plabooks.org/. Illus., index. Refereed. *Indexed:* MLA-IB. *Bk. rev.:* 1-3, 500-3,000 words. *Aud.:* Sa.

The *Private Library* is published quarterly by The Private Libraries Association. Each issue is slim but inviting and refreshing nonetheless. The journal features academic articles that will appeal to the scholar of bibliography as well as to book collectors. Each issue typically features two or three articles that include checklists of the books mentioned, typically illustrated, and sometimes in color. The journal focuses "on books that can be collected today" and features "printed essays by members' libraries, speciali[z]ed collections, the work of the private press, illustrators and, indeed, any aspect of the mania likely to appeal to collectors," many of which focus on book collection in the U.K. The *Private Library* presents one of the most enjoyable publications in the field of bibliography for the specialist and non-specialist, while it maintains academic rigor and excellence. It is appropriate for bibliophiles, academic libraries, and some larger public libraries.

Quaerendo: a quarterly journal from the Low Countries devoted to manuscripts and printed books. See Printing and Graphic Arts section.

RBM: A Journal of Rare Books, Manuscripts and Cultural Heritage. See Archives and Manuscripts section.

762. Script and Print: bulletin of the Bibliographical Society of Australia and New Zealand. Formerly (until 2004): *Bibliographical Society of Australia and New Zealand. Bulletin.* [ISSN: 1834-9013] 1970. q. Ed(s): Shef Rogers. Bibliographical Society of Australia & New Zealand, c/o Archives, Special Collections & Grainger Museum, 3rd Fl, Baillieu Library, Melbourne, VIC 3010, Australia; morrison@umimelb.edu.au. Illus. Sample. Refereed. *Indexed:* MLA-IB, RILM. *Bk. rev.:* 2-3, 800-1,400 words. *Aud.:* Ac, Sa.

Script and Print is a quarterly journal that has been in publication since 1970, and is the premier journal of its kind in Australia and New Zealand. *Script and Print* publishes on all aspects of bibliography, including "physical bibliography: the history of printing, publishing, bookselling, type founding, paper making, bookbinding; paleography and codicology; [and] writing, editing and textual bibliography." Each issue features four or five scholarly articles that are well referenced and occasionally illustrated, and there are typically three or four full-length book reviews. Recent issues have featured articles entitled "Charles Ackers Revisited: Biographical Details and Further Books" and "A Rediscovered Hazlitt Manuscript." *Script and Print* will appeal to an international audience, and is appropriate for any large academic library that seeks to support programs in rare-book librarianship and the history of the book.

763. Scriptorium: international review of manuscript studies and bulletin codicologique (book reviews). [ISSN: 0036-9772] 1947. s-a. Ed(s): O Legendre, P Cockshaw. Centre d'Etude des Manuscrits, Bd de l'Empereur 4, Brussels, 1000, Belgium. Illus., adv. Refereed. Circ: 900. Vol. ends: No. 2. *Indexed:* A22, ArtHuCI, BEL&L, FR, IPB, MLA-IB, RILM. *Bk. rev.:* 300-350, 50-1,500 words. *Aud.:* Ac, Sa.

Scriptorium is a biyearly multi-language international publication founded in 1946 on the study of medieval manuscript research. The book-length journal covers the subject of codicology, which is the "...material description of any aspect of manuscripts: supporting material, page-setting, binding, paleography, miniatures..." and the journal "inform[s] on cultural environment and offer[s] a bibliography regarding mediaeval manuscripts through Western, Eastern[,] and Central Europe." In addition, the *Scriptorium* devotes nearly half of each issue to the *Bulletin codicologique,* which features over 100 pages or as many as 300 book review entries per issue. It includes brief reviews of books and recent papers published by French, English, Spanish, German, and Italian scholars. Color plates are featured (on glossy paper at the back of the journal) that correspond to the research articles. The journal's editors write that the *Bulletin codicologique* "presents in fact a state of affairs regarding manuscript-related studies and serves as a thread for the scholar who risks losing his way amidst documentation that has become labyrinthine." *Scriptorium* is an essential resource for any serious research programs in medieval studies.

764. Studies in Bibliography. Formerly (until 1950): *University of Virginia. Papers of the Bibliographical Society.* [ISSN: 0081-7600] 1948. a. USD 70 per issue. Ed(s): David L Vander Meulen. University of Virginia Press, PO Box 400318, Charlottesville, VA 22904; upressva@virginia.edu; http://www.upress.virginia.edu. Illus. Refereed. *Indexed:* A22, E01, MLA-IB. *Aud.:* Ac, Sa.

Studies in Bibliography is a publication of the Bibliographical Society of the University of Virginia. The journal self-purports to being "one of the pre-eminent journals in the fields of analytical bibliography, textual criticism, manuscript study, and the history of printing and publishing." *Studies in Bibliography* was founded in 1948 by Fredson Bowers, who was one of the most important bibliography scholars of the twentieth century; the journal has continued its commitment to excellence under the editorship of David L. Vander Meulen. Many articles published in the journal have become part of the core curriculum in courses on bibliography. Recent issues have featured articles such as "The Textual Criticism of Visual and Aural Works," "Compositor B's Speech-Prefixes in the First Folio of Shakespeare and the Question of Copy for *2 Henry IV,*" and "Memorial Transmission, Shorthand, and *John of Bordeaux.*" The notable American scholar Thomas Tanselle is a regular contributor to the journal. *Studies in Bibliography* is published annually as one volume. Recent volumes feature seven to nine full-length articles, but generally lack illustration. This is a must for academic libraries that support or serve library science, rare-book librarianship, the history of the book, and private book collectors.

765. Textual Cultures: texts, contexts, interpretation. [ISSN: 1559-2936] 2006. s-a. USD 106.50 (print & online eds.). Ed(s): H Wayne Storey, Edward Burns. Indiana University Press, 601 N Morton St, Bloomington, IN 47404; journals@indiana.edu; http://iupress.indiana.edu. Adv. Refereed. Circ: 325. Reprint: PSC. *Indexed:* A01, A22, AmHI, BRI, E01, MLA-IB. *Bk. rev.:* 4-12, 800-2,400 words. *Aud.:* Ac, Sa.

Textual Cultures is a publication of the Society for Textual Scholarship. The journal is published twice a year in English, French, German, Spanish, and Italian, and each issue includes English abstracts for every article, although the majority of submissions are published in English. The journal features many topics that range from historical studies to theoretical issues that confront the field of bibliography. The journal's self-described focus deals with "textual editing, redefinitions of textuality, the history of the book, material culture, and the fusion of codicology with literary, musicological, and art historical interpretation and iconography." Recent issues have featured articles that explore the theoretical aspects of bibliography is such articles as "Bibliography and the Sociology of American Indian Texts" and "'Reportless Places': Facing the Modern Manuscript." Each issue contains five or six research articles under "Essays," and four to six substantial book reviews that are organized by language and origin under such headings such as "Anglo-American Reviews" and "Continental and Mediterranean Reviews." This is a rigorous academic journal that would be appropriate for any academic library that supports programs in literature, history of the book, and rare-book librarianship.

■ BIOLOGY

General/Biochemistry and Biophysics/Cell and Molecular Biology/ Developmental Biology/Genetics/Microbiology

See also Agriculture; Biotechnology; Birds; Environment, Conservation, and Outdoor Recreation; Marine Science and Technology; and Science and Technology sections.

Sara Klink, Assistant Library Director, Stark State College Digital Library, North Canton, OH 44720

Introduction

Biology is the science of life. It is concerned with the characteristics and behaviors of organisms, how species and individuals come into existence, and their interactions with each other and with their environment. Biology encompasses a broad spectrum of academic fields that are often viewed as independent disciplines. Since the field of biological science is so encompassing and covers so many disciplines, it becomes necessary to create a number of subsections to organize this section. These subsections include "General" biology, "Genetics," "Microbiology," "Developmental Biology," "Biochemistry and Biophysics," and "Cell and Molecular Biology," several of which have much crossover with the genetics, biochemistry, and molecular biology disciplines.

The majority of these titles are geared toward a very specific audience, such as subject-specific biologists, researchers, professors and educators, college-level students, and occasionally the general biologist. Since much of today's research involves timely access to information, it becomes imperative that journals within these disciplines maintain an online presence. Each of the journals selected for this section does have an easy-to-find, accessible web site or is an online journal. Many titles offer some level of access online for free to nonsubscribers, with many offering full open access.

Open access, which stands for unrestricted access and unrestricted reuse, has completely changed the way libraries and researchers access information within the sciences. In 2008, the National Institute of Public Health Access (NIH) began requiring any research funded by the NIH to submit an electronic version of the final, peer-reviewed manuscripts on acceptance for publication. The articles must be made publicly available no later than 12 months after the official date of publication, to the National Library of Medicine's PubMed Central. PubMed Central (PMC) is the NIH digital archive of full-text, peer-reviewed journal articles. This opened up the field to many new titles that are completely online journals or, for many preexisting titles, it moved all of their content to the open-access environment.

To take it a step further, there is a growing amount of content being published under the Creative Commons Attribution License. Under this agreement, authors will retain copyright ownership, but they are allowing anyone to download, use, reuse, distribute, or even modify the content, as long as the original author and source are cited. This license eliminates the need to contact the publisher or author directly.

The field of science has been leading the way and challenging much of what we have always known and done, in more ways than one.

Basic Periodicals

Ac: *Biochemistry; Cell; Genetics; Microbiology and Molecular Biology Reviews; National Academy of Sciences. Proceedings; The Quarterly Review of Biology.* Ga: *BMC Biology; Journal of Biology; Nature; Science.*

Basic Abstracts and Indexes

Biological Abstracts, Biological Abstracts/RRM, Biological and Agricultural Index, Biology Digest, Current Contents/Agriculture, Current Contents/Life Sciences.

General

The Auk. See Birds section.

766. *B M C Biology.* [ISSN: 1741-7007] 2004. irreg. Free. Ed(s): Miranda Robertson. BioMed Central Ltd., 236 Gray's Inn Rd, London, WC1X 8HB, United Kingdom; info@biomedcentral.com; http://www.biomedcentral.com. Adv. Refereed. *Indexed:* A01, AnBeAb, C45, IndVet. *Aud.:* Ga, Ac, Sa.

B M C Biology is the flagship biology journal of the B M C series published by BioMed Central. The journal publishes research and methodology articles of special importance and broad interest in any area of biology and biomedical sciences. Types of articles include research articles; database articles that describe either a new biomedical database or a database that has been substantially changed and improved since it was last described in a journal; methodology articles that present a new experimental or computational method, test, or procedure; and software articles in which authors of software applications, tools, or algorithm implementations publish descriptions of their code using the software article type. *B M C Biology* is a full-text online journal. All research articles are published after full peer review. All articles are published online at the journal's web site, without barriers to access, immediately upon acceptance. Full text is also available free through PubMed Central. Highly recommended for academic and special libraries that support a biology program. Also recommended for public libraries that support a science collection. URL: www.biomedcentral.com/bmcbiol

767. *Biochimica et Biophysica Acta. General Subjects.* Supersedes in part (in 1964): *Biochimica et Biophysica Acta.* [ISSN: 0304-4165] 1947. 12x/yr. EUR 3728. Ed(s): E Amer, S S Krag. Elsevier BV, Radarweg 29, PO Box 211, Amsterdam, 1000 AE, Netherlands; JournalsCustomerServiceEMEA@elsevier.com; http://www.elsevier.nl. Refereed. Microform: PQC. *Indexed:* A01, A22, C45, ExcerpMed, IndVet. *Aud.:* Ga, Ac.

Articles published in *General Subjects* can cover a wide variety of general biology topics. Examples include: medically important biochemistry/biophysics research, nanobiology, systems biology, chemical biology, structural biology, novel complexes, cellular signaling, glycobiology, redox biology, stem cells, imaging methodologies, and mechanistic characterization. This journal is one of the nine topical journals from *Biochimica et Biophysica Acta* (*BBA*). It contains "original, hypothesis-driven studies or reviews covering subjects in biochemistry and biophysics that are considered to have general interest for a wide audience." Online access is available from 1964 to present via the publisher's web site, ScienceDirect. Appropriate for academic and general libraries. URL: www.journals.elsevier.com/bba-general-subjects/#description

768. *Biological Reviews.* Former titles (until 1998): *Cambridge Philosophical Society. Biological Reviews;* (until 1936): *Cambridge Philosophical Society. Biological Reviews and Biological Proceedings;* (until 1926): *Cambridge Philosophical Society. Proceedings. Biological Sciences.* [ISSN: 1464-7931] 1923. q. GBP 286. Ed(s): William Foster. Wiley-Blackwell Publishing Ltd., The Atrium, Southern Gate, Chichester, PO19 8SQ, United Kingdom; customer@wiley.com; http://www.wiley.com/. Illus., index, adv. Sample. Refereed. Vol. ends: Nov. Microform: IDC; PQC. Reprint: PSC. *Indexed:* A01, A22, Agr, AnBeAb, C45, E01, IndVet, P02. *Aud.:* Ac, Sa.

Covering the entire range of the biological sciences, *Biological Reviews* presents review articles aimed at general biologists as well as specialists in the field. Each issue contains (on average) five articles, each having a detailed table of contents, an introduction, a summary, and a substantial bibliography. Online content (in full text) is provided through Wiley Online Library from 1923 to the present. Individuals interested in biology are likely to find at least one article of interest in every issue. This journal is appropriate for experts, researchers, and scholars. An excellent resource for general academic as well as research collections that support biology programs. URL: http://onlinelibrary.wiley.com/journal/10.1111/%28ISSN%291469-185X/issues

769. *BioScience: organisms from molecules to the environment.* Formerly (until 1964): *A I B S Bulletin.* [ISSN: 0006-3568] 1951. m. EUR 468. Ed(s): Timothy M Beardsley, James Verdier. Oxford University Press, 2001 Evans Rd, Cary, NC 27513; jnlorders@oup-usa.org; http://www.oxfordjournals.org. Illus., index, adv. Refereed. Circ: 7000. Vol. ends: Dec. Microform: PQC. Reprint: PSC. *Indexed:* A01, A22, Agr, AnBeAb, BRI, C45, CBRI, E01, ERIC, GardL, IndVet, MASUSE, MLA-IB, P02, RRTA, S25. *Bk. rev.:* 2-7, 600-2,000 words. *Aud.:* Ga, Ac, Sa.

BioScience is geared toward "a broad readership including professional biologists, biology teachers/professors, and advanced students." It is published by the American Institute of Biological Sciences (AIBS), and its content includes authoritative overviews of current research in biology, accompanied by essays and discussion sections on education, public policy, history, and basic concepts of the biological sciences. Also included are articles about research findings and techniques, advances in biology education, feature articles about the latest frontiers in biology, discussions of professional issues, book reviews, news about AIBS, a policy column ("Washington Watch"), and an education column ("Eye on Education"). Selected sections are available for free access online each month. Full text is available with a subscription. All AIBS members receive free subscriptions to print and online issues. Recommended for special, academic, and large public libraries.

Chickadee. See Children section.

770. *Current Biology.* [ISSN: 0960-9822] 1991. 24x/yr. EUR 2007. Ed(s): Geoffrey North. Cell Press, 600 Technology Sq, Cambridge, MA 02139. Illus., adv. Sample. Refereed. Vol. ends: Dec. *Indexed:* A01, A22, AbAn, AnBeAb, C45, E01, IndVet, RRTA. *Aud.:* Ga, Ac, Sa.

Current Biology's primary goal is to foster communication across fields of biology by publishing important findings of general interest from diverse fields and by providing highly accessible editorial articles that aim to inform non-specialists. The journal includes articles that present conceptual advances of unusual significance regarding a biological question of high interest, concise reports concerning findings of broad biological interest, and news. Non-subscribers have free online access to the featured article of the current issue as well as the "Primer," which is a highlighted article. Additionally, *Current Biology* publishes papers online ahead of the print issue each week. Appropriate for special and academic libraries, especially those that support biology programs, and large public libraries. All articles older than one year are available through the Cell Press web site archive. URL: www.current-biology.com

771. *Evolution: international journal of organic evolution.* [ISSN: 0014-3820] 1947. m. GBP 609 (print & online eds.). Ed(s): Mark D Rausher, Daphne Fairbairn. Wiley-Blackwell Publishing Ltd., 9600 Garsington Rd, Oxford, OX4 2DQ, United Kingdom; customer@wiley.co.uk; http://www.wiley.com/. Illus., index, adv. Sample. Refereed. Circ: 4500. Vol. ends: Dec. Microform: PQC. Reprint: PSC. *Indexed:* A01, A22, AbAn, Agr, AnBeAb, BRI, C45, E01, FS&TA, IndVet, OceAb, P02. *Bk. rev.:* 0-2, 1,000-3,000 words. *Aud.:* Ac, Sa.

The main objectives of this journal are the promotion of the study of organic evolution and the integration of the various fields of science concerned with evolution. Contents include regular papers, perspectives, brief communications, and comments, as well as book reviews. Online special features include "Online Accepted" and "Online Early" articles, which are available online before being included in print at an undecided date. Non-subscribers have limited access to sample issues in full text online. Highly recommended for all academic libraries and some special libraries. *Evolution*'s full-text content is online for subscribers via Wiley Online Library. URL: http://onlinelibrary.wiley.com/journal/10.1111/%28ISSN%291558-5646

772. *The F A S E B Journal.* Supersedes (in 1987): *Federation of American Societies for Experimental Biology. Federation Proceedings.* [ISSN: 0892-6638] 1987. m. Individuals, USD 260 (print & online eds.). Ed(s): Gerald Weissmann. Federation of American Societies for Experimental Biology, 9650 Rockville Pike, Bethesda, MD 20814; staff@faseb.org; http://www.faseb.org. Illus., index, adv. Refereed. Circ: 6000 Paid. *Indexed:* A01, A22, Agr, C45, FS&TA, IndVet. *Bk. rev.:* Number and length vary. *Aud.:* Ac, Sa.

The *FASEB Journal* (Federation of American Societies for Experimental Biology) publishes papers that have integrated one or more of the member disciplines. These member societies are the American Physiological Society, American Society for Biochemistry and Molecular Biology, American Society for Pharmacology and Experimental Therapeutics, American Society for Investigative Pathology, American Society for Nutritional Sciences, American Association of Immunologists, Biophysical Society, American Association of Anatomists, Protein Society, American Society for Bone and Mineral Research, American Society for Clinical Investigation, Endocrine Society, American Society of Human Genetics, Society for Developmental Biology, American Peptide Society, Association of Biomolecular Resource Facilities, Society for the Study of Reproduction, Teratology Society, Radiation Research Society, Society for Gynecologic Investigation, and Environmental Mutagen Society. Contents include editorials, essays, review articles, research communications, and book reviews. Online, full-text access is provided online from July 1987 to the present. Recommended for most biology collections in special and academic libraries. URL: www.fasebj.org

773. The Journal of Neuroscience. [ISSN: 0270-6474] 1981. w. Free to members; Non-members, USD 1155 (print & online eds.). Ed(s): John H R Maunsell. Society for Neuroscience, 1121 14th St, NW, Ste 1010, Washington, DC 20005; info@sfn.org; http://www.sfn.org. Illus., index. Refereed. Vol. ends: Dec. Microform: PQC. *Indexed:* A01, A22, AnBeAb, C45, ExcerpMed, IndVet, PsycInfo, RILM. *Aud.:* Ac, Sa.

This is the official journal of the Society for Neuroscience. It publishes papers on a broad range of topics for those working on the nervous system. Contents include brief communications intended for fast publication of exciting and timely findings and regular articles; these range from cellular and molecular research to developmental and behaviorial studies. Full text is available online with a subscription. Free access is provided to most of the content via the publisher's web site. Appropriate for academic and special libraries, and useful in biology and medical collections. URL: www.jneurosci.org/

774. National Academy of Sciences. Proceedings. [ISSN: 0027-8424] 1914. w. USD 785 (print & online eds.). Ed(s): Randy R Schekman. National Academy of Sciences, 500 Fifth St, NW, Washington, DC 20001; subspnas@nas.edu. Illus., index, adv. Sample. Refereed. Circ: 10132. Vol. ends: Dec. Microform: PQC. *Indexed:* A01, A22, Agr, AnBeAb, BRI, C45, ExcerpMed, FS&TA, IndVet, MathR, OceAb, P02, PsycInfo, RRTA. *Aud.:* Ac, Sa.

Covering the physical sciences, biological sciences, and social sciences, this journal includes papers in the categories of research reports, commentaries, reviews, colloquium papers, perspectives, and reports on the National Academy of Sciences. As one of the world's most-cited multidisciplinary scientific serials, it covers all areas of the biological sciences, with the heaviest focus on cell biology and biochemistry. It is published weekly in print and daily online. Full text is available online with a subscription. There is free access to tables of contents, abstracts, and the new early edition feature. All content older than six months is also made available online via the publisher's web site and PubMed. Individual and institutional subscriptions are available. Appropriate for academic and special libraries, and essential for most science collections. URL: www.pnas.org

Natural History. See Science and Technology/General section.

775. Nature: international weekly journal of science. Incorporates (1971-1973): *Nature. Physical Science;* (1971-1973): *Nature. New Biology;* Both of which superseded in part (in 1971): *Nature.* [ISSN: 0028-0836] 1869. w. EUR 3225 in Europe; USD 4055 in the Americas; GBP 2083 in the UK & elsewhere. Ed(s): Dr. Philip Campbell. Nature Publishing Group, The MacMillan Bldg, 4 Crinan St, London, N1 9XW, United Kingdom; feedback@nature.com; http://www.nature.com. Illus., index, adv. Sample. Refereed. Vol. ends: Dec. Microform: PMC; PQC. *Indexed:* A&ATA, A01, A22, A47, AbAn, Agr, AnBeAb, ApMecR, B03, BAS, BRI, BrArAb, BrTechI, C&ISA, C37, C45, CBRI, CerAb, EngInd, ExcerpMed, FS&TA, IndVet, M&GPA, MASUSE, MLA-IB, MSN, MathR, NumL, OceAb, P02, PsycInfo, RILM, RRTA, S25. *Aud.:* Ga, Ac, Sa.

Nature is the most cited weekly science journal, with over 390,000 cites. It publishes significant advances in any branch of science, and provides a forum for the reporting and discussion of scientific news and issues. It also provides rapid, authoritative, insightful, and arresting news and interpretation of topical and coming trends that affect science, scientists, and the wider public. Online content is available with a subscription. Free sample issues and trials are available. Archived content dating from 1869 to 1949 is available with a separate subscription. Online features include podcasts, videos, "Weekly Highlights," and select content in full text. Highly recommended for any library that supports the sciences. URL: www.nature.com/nature/index.html

Owl. See Children section.

776. Perspectives in Biology and Medicine. [ISSN: 0031-5982] 1957. q. USD 160. Ed(s): Solveig C Robinson, Alan N Schecter. The Johns Hopkins University Press, 2715 N Charles St, Baltimore, MD 21218; http://www.press.jhu.edu. Illus., index, adv. Sample. Refereed. Circ: 591. Vol. ends: Summer. Microform: PQC. Reprint: PSC. *Indexed:* A01, A22, AbAn, BRI, C45, E01, IndVet, MLA-IB, P02, PsycInfo, RRTA. *Bk. rev.:* 2-9, 300-1,200 words. *Aud.:* Ac, Sa.

Perspectives in Biology and Medicine is an "interdisciplinary journal that publishes articles on a wide range of biomedical topics such as neurobiology, biomedical ethics[,] and history to genetics, evolution, and ecology." Contents include "essays that place biological and medical topics in broader scientific, social, or humanistic contexts." Also included are book reviews, essay reviews, and letters to the editors. Most essays range from 4,000 to 7,000 words, in addition to an abstract. Although many essays are invited, voluntary contributions are welcomed. Authors are encouraged to adopt individualized writing styles. Print and online subscriptions are available for individuals and institutions. Full text is provided online by The Johns Hopkins University Press Project Muse, from 2000 to the present. Appropriate for academic, special, and medical libraries. URL: http://muse.jhu.edu/journals/perspectives_in_biology_and_medicine/

777. The Quarterly Review of Biology. [ISSN: 0033-5770] 1926. q. USD 396 (print & online eds.). Ed(s): Daniel E Dykhuizen, Gregory A Wray. University of Chicago Press, 1427 E 60th St, Chicago, IL 60637; subscriptions@press.uchicago.edu; http://www.journals.uchicago.edu. Illus., index, adv. Sample. Refereed. Vol. ends: Dec. Microform: PQC. Reprint: PSC. *Indexed:* A01, A22, AbAn, AnBeAb, BRI, C45, CBRI, IndVet, P02, S25. *Bk. rev.:* 100+, 200-1,500 words. *Aud.:* Ga, Ac, Sa.

The Quarterly Review of Biology publishes articles in all areas of biology, but with a traditional emphasis on evolution, ecology, and organismal biology. *QRB* papers offer important new ideas, concepts, and syntheses. Content includes concise, authoritative articles, theoretical papers, comprehensive book reviews arranged by subject, and timely assessments of the life sciences. Online full text is available from 1926 to the present, with a free sample issue via JSTOR. Individual and institutional subscriptions are available. Appropriate for general biology collections and special, academic, and large public libraries. URL: www.press.uchicago.edu/ucp/journals/journal/qrb.html

Ranger Rick. See Children section.

Science. See Science and Technology/General section.

778. Systematic Biology. Formerly (until 1992): *Systematic Zoology.* [ISSN: 1063-5157] 1952. bi-m. EUR 317. Ed(s): Ronald W DeBry. Oxford University Press, Great Clarendon St, Oxford, OX2 6DP, United Kingdom; enquiry@oup.co.uk; http://www.oxfordjournals.org/. Illus., index, adv. Sample. Refereed. Vol. ends: Dec. Microform: PQC. Reprint: PSC. *Indexed:* A01, A22, AbAn, Agr, C45, E01, OceAb. *Bk. rev.:* 0-2, 800-2,000 words. *Aud.:* Ac, Sa.

Systematic Biology is a bimonthly publication of the Society of Systematic Biologists. The goal of this journal is the "advancement of systematic biology in all its aspects of theory, principles, methodology, and practice, for both living and fossil organisms." Contents include original research papers on methods of systematics as well as phylogeny, evolution, morphology, biogeography, paleontology, genetics, and the classification of all living things. There is a viewpoint section that offers discussion, book reviews, and news. Full text from 1952 to the present is available online with a subscription. There are select Open Access articles within some issues. Recommended for special and academic libraries. URL: http://sysbio.oxfordjournals.org/

Biochemistry and Biophysics

779. *Analytical Biochemistry.* [ISSN: 0003-2697] 1960. 24x/yr. EUR 9257. Ed(s): William Jakoby. Elsevier Inc., 1600 John F Kennedy Blvd, Philadelphia, PA 19103; JournalCustomerService-usa@elsevier.com; http://www.elsevier.com. Illus., index, adv. Sample. Refereed. *Indexed:* A01, A22, AbAn, C45, E01, ExcerpMed, FS&TA, IndVet. *Bk. rev.:* 0-2, 240-500 words. *Aud.:* Ac, Sa.

Analytical Biochemistry places an emphasis on methods in the biological and biochemical sciences. More specifically, it publishes methods in analytical techniques, membranes and membrane proteins, molecular genetics, protein purification, immunological techniques applicable to biochemistry, immunoassays that introduce a unique approach, cell biology, general cell and organ culture, and pharmacological and toxicological research techniques. Contents include original research articles, review articles on methods for biological and biochemical sciences, and notes and tips, which include methods summarized in a short format. Full-text articles are available online for the entire run of the publication through Elsevier-ScienceDirect. This journal is geared specifically to biochemists and would be a useful resource for academic and research libraries.

780. *Biochemical and Biophysical Research Communications.* [ISSN: 0006-291X] 1959. 52x/yr. EUR 11874. Ed(s): W J Lennarz. Elsevier Inc., 1600 John F Kennedy Blvd, Philadelphia, PA 19103; JournalCustomerService-usa@elsevier.com; http://www.elsevier.com. Illus., index, adv. Sample. Refereed. *Indexed:* A01, A22, AbAn, Agr, C45, E01, ExcerpMed, FS&TA, IndVet. *Aud.:* Ac, Sa.

Biochemical and Biophysical Research Communications is known as the "premier international journal devoted to the very rapid dissemination of timely and significant experimental results in diverse fields of biological research." Contents include the "Breakthroughs" and "Views" sections, which contain mini-reviews and collections of special-interest manuscripts. The broad range of research areas includes biochemistry, biophysics, bioinformatics, cancer research, cell biology, developmental biology, immunology, molecular biology, neurology, plant biology, and proteomics. Print and online subscriptions are available to individuals and institutions. This is a Open Access journal. Full text is available online via Elsevier's ScienceDirect web site. Useful for biochemists and biophysicists as well as academic and research libraries.

781. *Biochemical Journal.* Formed by the merger of (1973-1984): *Biochemical Journal. Cellular Aspects;* (1973-1984): *Biochemical Journal. Molecular Aspects;* Both of which superseded in part (in 1973): *Biochemical Journal.* [ISSN: 0264-6021] 1984. s-m. EUR 4710 (print & online eds.). Portland Press Ltd., 3rd Fl, Charles Darwin House, 12 Roger St, London, WC1N 2JU, United Kingdom; editorial@portlandpress.com; http://www.portlandpress.com/. Illus., index, adv. Refereed. Microform: PMC; PQC. *Indexed:* A01, A22, AbAn, Agr, C45, EngInd, ExcerpMed, FS&TA, IndVet, RRTA. *Aud.:* Ac, Sa.

Biochemical Journal publishes research "papers on all aspects of biochemistry and cellular and molecular biology." Theoretical contributions will be considered equally with papers dealing with experimental work. Contents include research papers that make a significant contribution to biochemical knowledge, including new results obtained experimentally, descriptions of new experimental methods or new interpretations of existing results, research communications, and reviews. Published by Biochemical Society's Portland Press, the journal provides free online access to its entire archive in full text from 1906 minus the current year. Open access is also provided through PubMed Central. Recommended for special and academic libraries. URL: www.biochemj.org/bj/toc.htm?S=0

782. *Biochemistry.* [ISSN: 0006-2960] 1962. w. USD 5045. Ed(s): Richard N Armstrong. American Chemical Society, 1155 16th St N W, Washington, DC 20036; help@acs.org; http://pubs.acs.org. Illus., index, adv. Sample. Refereed. Vol. ends: Dec. *Indexed:* A01, A22, AbAn, Agr, BRI, C45, EngInd, ExcerpMed, FS&TA, IndVet. *Aud.:* Ac, Sa.

Published weekly by the American Chemical Society (ACS), *Biochemistry* "presents the latest discoveries from around the world, to deepen your understanding of biological phenomena." Contents include developments in which chemistry, biochemistry, and molecular and cell biology meet. Articles cover structure, functions, and regulation of biologically active molecules; gene structure and expression; biochemical mechanisms; protein biosynthesis; protein folding, and global protein analysis and function; membrane structure/function relationships; biochemical methods; bioenergetics; and bioinformatics and immunochemistry. "Rapid Reports," a new feature, is reserved for timely topics of unusual interest; it is posted online as "Articles ASAP" on an expedited schedule, and are also immediately indexed on the "Biochemistry Rapid Reports" web page. The ACS provides free online access to the full text of *Biochemistry.* Full text is also provided online with institutional subscriptions to ACS Web Editions, covering content from 1996 to the present; and ACS Legacy Archives contains articles from 1879 to 1995 in pdf format. Appropriate for special and academic libraries. URL: http://pubs.acs.org/journals/bichaw/index.html

783. *Biochemistry and Cell Biology.* Former titles (until 1986): *Canadian Journal of Biochemistry and Cell Biology/Revue Canadien de Biochimie et Biologie Cellulaire;* (until 1983): *Canadian Journal of Biochemistry;* Which supersedes in part (in 1963): *Canadian Journal of Biochemistry and Physiology;* Which was formerly (until 1954): *Canadian Journal of Medical Sciences;* (until 1950): *Canadian Journal of Research. Section E: Medical Sciences.* [ISSN: 0829-8211] 1929. bi-m. CAD 970. Ed(s): Dr. James R Davie. N R C Research Press, 1200 Montreal Rd, Bldg M-55, Ottawa, ON K1A 0R6, Canada; pubs@nrc-cnrc.gc.ca; http://pubs.nrc-cnrc.gc.ca. Illus., index, adv. Sample. Refereed. Circ: 913. Microform: MML; PMC; PQC. *Indexed:* A01, A22, Agr, C37, C45, CBCARef, E01, EngInd, ExcerpMed, FS&TA, IndVet. *Aud.:* Ac, Sa.

Biochemistry and Cell Biology "explores every aspect of general biochemistry, and includes up-to-date coverage of experimental research into cellular and molecular biology." Contents include review topics of current interest and notes contributed by international experts. Special issues are dedicated each year to expanding new areas of research in biochemistry and cell biology. First published in 1929, this Canadian journal presents papers in both French and English, although the majority are in English. Full-text online content is available from 1954 through the present by subscription only. There is a sample issue to review via the publisher's web site. Recommended for special and academic libraries. URL: http://pubs.nrc-cnrc.gc.ca/rp-ps/journalDetail.jsp?jcode=bcb&lang=eng

784. *Biochimica et Biophysica Acta. Proteins and Proteomics.* Former titles (until 2002): *B B A - Protein Structure and Molecular Enzymology;* (until 1982): *B B A - Protein Structure.* [ISSN: 1570-9639] 1967. 12x/yr. EUR 4387. Ed(s): Irene Lee, Yuji Goto. Elsevier BV, Radarweg 29, PO Box 211, Amsterdam, 1000 AE, Netherlands; JournalsCustomerServiceEMEA@elsevier.com; http://www.elsevier.nl. Refereed. Microform: PQC. *Indexed:* A01, A22, C45, ExcerpMed, FS&TA, IndVet. *Aud.:* Ac, Sa.

Articles published in *Proteins and Proteomics* covers "protein structure conformation and dynamics; protein folding; protein-ligand interactions; enzyme mechanisms, models and kinetics; protein physical properties and spectroscopy; and proteomics and bioinformatics analyses of protein structure, protein function, or protein regulation." This journal is one of the nine topical journals from *Biochimica et Biophysica Acta (BBA).* It contains regular papers, reviews, and mini-reviews on recent developments. Print and online subscriptions are available. Online access is available from 2002 to present via the publisher's web site, ScienceDirect. Appropriate for academic and special libraries. URL: www.journals.elsevier.com/bba-proteins-and-proteomics/#description

785. *Biochimica et Biophysica Acta. Reviews on Cancer.* Supersedes in part (in 1974): *Biochimica et Biophysica Acta: N. Nucleic Acids and Protein Synthesis;* Which was formerly (until 1965): *Biochimical et Biophysica Acta. Specialized Section on Nucleic Acids and Related*

Subjects. [ISSN: 0304-419X] 1963. 4x/yr. EUR 1504. Ed(s): William Hahn. Elsevier BV, Radarweg 29, PO Box 211, Amsterdam, 1000 AE, Netherlands; JournalsCustomerServiceEMEA@elsevier.com; http://www.elsevier.nl. Refereed. Microform: PQC. *Indexed:* A01, A22, ExcerpMed, FS&TA. *Aud.:* Ac, Sa.

Reviews published in *Cancer Reviews* focus on "the whole field of the biology and biochemistry of cancer, emphasizing oncogenes and tumor suppressor genes, growth-related cell cycle control signalling, carcinogenesis mechanisms, cell transformation, immunologic control mechanisms, genetics of human (mammalian) cancer, control of cell proliferation, genetic and molecular control of organismic development, rational anti-tumor drug design. In short, the journal presents critical invited reviews on new developments in cancer investigation at the molecular level." This journal is one of the nine topical journals from *Biochimica et Biophysica Acta (BBA)*. It contains reviews and mini-reviews. Print and online subscriptions are available. Online access is available from 1974 to present via the publisher's web site, ScienceDirect. Appropriate for academic and special libraries. URL: www.journals.elsevier.com/bba-reviews-on-cancer/#description

786. *Biophysical Journal.* Incorporates (1970-1973): *Biophysical Society. Program and Abstracts;* Which was formerly (until 1970): *Biophysical Society. Meeting. Abstracts;* (until 1959): *Biophysical Society. Meeting. Program and Abstracts.* [ISSN: 0006-3495] 1958. s-m. EUR 1239. Ed(s): Edward H Egelman. Cell Press, 11830 Westline Industrial Dr, St. Louis, MO 63146; feedback@cell.com; http://www.cell.com/cellpress. Illus., index, adv. Refereed. Microform: PQC. *Indexed:* A22, AbAn, Agr, ApMecR, C45, FS&TA, IndVet. *Aud.:* Ac, Sa.

Information published in *Biophysical Journal* includes "original articles, letters[,] and reviews on biophysical topics" that emphasize molecular and cellular aspects of biology. There are original research articles, biophysical letters for the rapid publication of short and important articles, comments to the editor, reviews of current interest in biophysics, and new and notable commentaries that highlight papers found in the same issue. The journal is edited by the Biophysical Society, and all programs and abstracts for annual meetings are included with a subscription. Full-text online content is available from 1960 to the present through PubMed Central. The journal has a 12-month embargo policy, after which the journal submits the final published article on behalf of the author to PubMed Central automatically.

787. *The F E B S Journal.* Former titles (until 2005): *European Journal of Biochemistry;* (until 1967): *Biochemische Zeitschrift;* Which incorporated (1901-1908): *Beitrage zur Chemischen Physiologie und Pathologie.* [ISSN: 1742-464X] 1906. fortn. GBP 3077. Ed(s): Richard Perham. Wiley-Blackwell Publishing Ltd., The Atrium, Southern Gate, Chichester, PO19 8SQ, United Kingdom; customer@wiley.com; http://www.wiley.com/. Illus., index, adv. Sample. Refereed. Microform: PQC. Reprint: PSC. *Indexed:* A01, A22, Agr, C45, E01, ExcerpMed, FS&TA, IndVet, P02. *Aud.:* Ac, Sa.

The FEBS Journal (Federation of European Biochemical Societies) is "devoted to the rapid publication of full-length papers describing original research in all areas of the molecular life sciences." Publishing preference is given to research that advances new concepts or develops new experimental techniques. Contents include research papers, reviews, mini-reviews, and meeting reports. Article topics cover a variety of subdisciplines, including but not limited to immunology, molecular genetics, nucleic acids, protein synthesis, developmental biology, bioenergetics, systems biology, and molecular evolution. There is free access to review articles published to date, as well as the archives from 1967. Online, full text is provided through Wiley Online Library. Recommended for special and academic libraries. URL: http://onlinelibrary.wiley.com/journal/10.1111/%28ISSN%291742-4658

788. *F E B S Letters.* [ISSN: 0014-5793] 1968. 30x/yr. EUR 6583. Ed(s): F Wieland. Elsevier BV, Radarweg 29, PO Box 211, Amsterdam, 1000 AE, Netherlands; JournalsCustomerServiceEMEA@elsevier.com; http://www.elsevier.nl. Illus., index, adv. Refereed. Microform: PQC. *Indexed:* A01, A22, C45, ExcerpMed, FS&TA, IndVet. *Aud.:* Ac, Sa.

FEBS Letters, published by the Federation of European Biochemical Societies, is an "international journal established for the rapid publication of essentially final short reports in the fields of molecular biosciences." Contents cover

biochemistry, structural biology, biophysics, computational biology, molecular genetics, molecular biology, and molecular cell biology. Studies may be on microbes, plants, or animals. Found within each issue are mini-reviews, hypotheses, and research letters, all on an international level. Online, full-text access is available through Elsevier's ScienceDirect with most of the archives available for free. Appropriate for special and academic libraries. URL: www.sciencedirect.com/science/journal/00145793

789. *Journal of Biochemistry.* [ISSN: 0021-924X] 1922. m. EUR 471. Ed(s): Kohei MIYAZONO, Kiyoko Fukami. Oxford University Press, Great Clarendon St, Oxford, OX2 6DP, United Kingdom; enquiry@oup.co.uk; http://www.oxfordjournals.org/. Illus., index, adv. Sample. Refereed. Microform: PMC. Reprint: PSC. *Indexed:* A01, A22, Agr, C45, E01, ExcerpMed, FS&TA, IndVet. *Aud.:* Ac, Sa.

This journal publishes articles on biochemistry, biotechnology, molecular biology, and cell biology. Contents include reviews, regular research articles, and brief communications in English. It is published by Oxford University Press on behalf of the Japanese Biochemical Society, and full text is available online with a subscription. Additional online features include e-mail alerts with CiteTrack. Recommended for special and academic libraries that support chemists, biologists, physicians, and physiologists. URL: http://jb.oxfordjournals.org/

790. *Journal of Biological Chemistry.* [ISSN: 0021-9258] 1905. w. USD 3490 (print & online eds.). Ed(s): Martha J Fedor. American Society for Biochemistry and Molecular Biology, Inc., 9650 Rockville Pike, Bethesda, MD 20814; asbmb@asbmb.faseb.org; http://www.asbmb.org. Illus., index, adv. Refereed. Circ: 3300 Paid. Vol. ends: Dec. Microform: PMC; PQC. *Indexed:* A01, A22, AbAn, Agr, C45, EngInd, ExcerpMed, FS&TA, IndVet. *Aud.:* Ac, Sa.

This weekly journal focuses on original research reports in biochemistry and molecular biology, and includes such topics as developmental biology, computational biology, metabolism, protein chemistry, and nucleic acids. Contents include original research papers that make novel and important contributions to the understanding of any area of biochemistry or molecular biology. Accelerated publication that presents new information of high importance and interest to the broad readership is by invitation only. Online features include "JBC Papers in Press," which comprises papers in manuscript form that have been accepted and published in *JBC Online* but that have not been copy edited nor yet appeared in a printed issue of the journal. Both print and online subscriptions are available. There is some online, full-text access available in pdf format from 1905 to the present. 2008 to the present is available in full text through PubMed Central. Highly recommended for special libraries and academic libraries that support biology programs. URL: www.jbc.org

791. *Molecular Genetics and Metabolism.* Former titles (until 1998): *Biochemical and Molecular Medicine;* (until 1995): *Biochemical Medicine and Metabolic Biology;* (until 1986): *Biochemical Medicine.* [ISSN: 1096-7192] 1967. m. EUR 2260. Ed(s): Dr. Edward R B McCabe, L L McCabe. Academic Press, 3251 Riverport Ln, Maryland Heights, MO 63043; JournalCustomerService-usa@elsevier.com; http://www.elsevierdirect.com/brochures/academicpress/index.html. Adv. Sample. Refereed. *Indexed:* A01, A22, AbAn, Agr, C45, E01, ExcerpMed, IndVet, RRTA. *Aud.:* Ac, Sa.

Molecular Genetics and Metabolism is the official journal of the Society for Inherited Metabolic Disorders. The journal is a contribution to the understanding of the metabolic basis of disease. The journal publishes articles that describe investigations that use the tools of biochemistry and molecular biology for studies of normal and diseased states. Research areas include inherited metabolic diseases, systems biology, intercellular and intracellular metabolic relationships, cellular catalysts, and disease pathogenesis and treatment. Full-text access is available online from ScienceDirect. Online features include a free sample issue. Recommended for special and academic libraries with a strong biological program. URL: www.journals.elsevier.com/molecular-genetics-and-metabolism/

Cell and Molecular Biology

792. *B M C Cell Biology.* [ISSN: 1471-2121] 2000. irreg. Free. Ed(s): Christopher Morrey. BioMed Central Ltd., 236 Gray's Inn Rd, London, WC1X 8HB, United Kingdom; info@biomedcentral.com; http://www.biomedcentral.com. Adv. Refereed. *Indexed:* A01, C45, ExcerpMed, IndVet. *Aud.:* Ac, Sa.

B M C Cell Biology is an open-access journal that publishes original peer-reviewed research articles in all aspects of cell biology, including cellular compartments, traffic, signaling, motility, adhesion, and division. Types of articles include research articles; database articles that describe either a new biomedical database or a database that has been substantially changed and improved since it was last described in a journal; methodology articles that present a new experimental or computational method, test, or procedure; and software articles in which authors of software applications, tools, or algorithm implementations publish descriptions of their code using the software article type. *B M C Cell Biology* is a full-text online journal. All research articles are published after full peer review. All articles are published without barriers to access, immediately upon acceptance. Full text is available free at PubMed Central from 2000 to the present, or via the publisher's site (below). Recommended for academic and special libraries that support a biology program. URL: www.biomedcentral.com/bmccellbiol

793. *Biochimica and Biophysica Acta. Molecular and Cell Biology of Lipids.* Former titles (until 1999): *B B A - Lipids and Lipid Metabolism;* (until 1965): *Biochimica et Biophysica Acta. Lipids and Related Subjects.* [ISSN: 1388-1981] 1963. 12x/yr. EUR 3870. Ed(s): Suzanne Jackowski. Elsevier BV, Radarweg 29, PO Box 211, Amsterdam, 1000 AE, Netherlands; JournalsCustomerServiceEMEA@elsevier.com; http://www.elsevier.nl. Refereed. Microform: PQC. *Indexed:* A01, A22, C45, ExcerpMed, FS&TA, IndVet. *Aud.:* Ac, Sa.

Articles published in *Molecular and Cell Biology of Lipids* focus on "original research dealing with novel aspects of molecular genetics related to the lipidome, the biosynthesis of lipids, the role of lipids in cells and whole organisms, the regulation of lipid metabolism and function, and lipidomics in all organisms." This journal is one of the nine topical journals from *Biochimica et Biophysica Acta (BBA).* It contains original research papers and papers that detail novel methodology with insight in the area of lipids. Print and online subscriptions are available. Online access is available from 1999 to present via the publisher's web site, ScienceDirect. Appropriate for academic and special libraries. URL: www.journals.elsevier.com/bba-molecular-and-cell-biology-of-lipids/#description

794. *Biochimica et Biophysica Acta. Bioenergetics.* Formed by the merger of (1965-1966): *Biochimica et Biophysica Acta. Biophysics including Photosynthesis;* Which was formerly (1963-1964): *Biochimica et Biophysica Acta. Specialized Section on Biophysical Subjects;* (1965-1966): *Biochimica et Biophysica Acta. Enzymology and Biological Oxidations;* Which was formerly (1963-1964): *Biochimica et Biophysica Acta. Specialized Section on Enzymological Subjects.* [ISSN: 0005-2728] 1963. 12x/yr. EUR 3391. Ed(s): Uli Brandt, Fabrice Rappaport. Elsevier BV, Radarweg 29, PO Box 211, Amsterdam, 1000 AE, Netherlands; JournalsCustomerServiceEMEA@elsevier.com; http://www.elsevier.nl. Refereed. Microform: PQC. *Indexed:* A01, A22, C45, ExcerpMed, FS&TA, IndVet. *Aud.:* Ac, Sa.

Articles published in *Bioenergetics* "focus on biological membranes involved in energy transfer and conversion. In particular, [this journal] focuses on the structures obtained by X-ray crystallography and other approaches, and molecular mechanisms of the components of photosynthesis, mitochondrial and bacterial respiration, oxidative phosphorylation, motility and transport. It spans applications of structural biology, molecular modeling, spectroscopy and biophysics in these systems, through bioenergetic aspects of mitochondrial biology including biomedicine aspects of energy metabolism in mitochondrial disorders, neurodegenerative diseases like Parkinson's and Alzheimer's, aging, diabetes and even cancer." This journal is one of the nine topical journals from *Biochimica et Biophysica Acta (BBA).* It contains full-length research articles and review papers. Print and online subscriptions are available. Online access

is available from 1967 to present via the publisher's web site, ScienceDirect. Appropriate for academic and special libraries. URL: www.journals.elsevier.com/bba-bioenergetics/#description

795. *Biochimica et Biophysica Acta. Biomembranes.* Incorporates (1972-2002): *B B A - Reviews on Biomembranes.* [ISSN: 0005-2736] 1947. 12x/yr. EUR 5828. Ed(s): Hans Vogel, Yechiel Shai. Elsevier BV, Radarweg 29, PO Box 211, Amsterdam, 1000 AE, Netherlands; JournalsCustomerServiceEMEA@elsevier.com; http://www.elsevier.nl. Refereed. Microform: PQC. *Indexed:* A01, A22, C45, ExcerpMed, FS&TA, IndVet. *Aud.:* Ac, Sa.

Articles published in *Biomembranes* "focus on membrane structure, function and biomolecular organization, membrane proteins, receptors, channels and anchors, fluidity and composition, model membranes and liposomes, membrane surface studies and ligand interactions, transport studies, and membrane dynamics." This journal is one of the nine topical journals from *Biochimica et Biophysica Acta (BBA).* It contains regular papers, reviews, and mini-reviews. Print and online subscriptions are available. Online access is available from 1967 to present via the publisher's web site, ScienceDirect. Appropriate for academic and special libraries. URL: www.journals.elsevier.com/bba-biomembranes/#description

796. *Biochimica et Biophysica Acta. Molecular Cell Research.* [ISSN: 0167-4889] 1982. 12x/yr. EUR 3390. Ed(s): Anita Corbett, Nikolaus Pfanner. Elsevier BV, Radarweg 29, PO Box 211, Amsterdam, 1000 AE, Netherlands; JournalsCustomerServiceEMEA@elsevier.com; http://www.elsevier.nl. Refereed. Microform: PQC. *Indexed:* A01, A22, C45, ExcerpMed, FS&TA, IndVet. *Aud.:* Ac, Sa.

Articles published in *Molecular Cell Research* focus on "understanding the mechanisms of cellular processes at the molecular level. These include aspects of cellular signaling, signal transduction, cell cycle, apoptosis, intracellular trafficking, secretory and endocytic pathways, biogenesis of cell organelles, cytoskeletal structures, cellular interactions, cell/tissuedifferentiation and cellular enzymology." This journal is one of the nine topical journals from *Biochimica et Biophysica Acta (BBA).* It contains studies at the interface between cell biology and biophysics, and reviews and mini-reviews on timely topics. Online access is available from 1982 to present via the publisher's web site, ScienceDirect. Appropriate for academic and special libraries. URL: www.journals.elsevier.com/bba-molecular-cell-research/#description

797. *BioEssays: advances in molecular, cellular and developmental biology.* [ISSN: 0265-9247] 1984. m. GBP 1082. Ed(s): Andrew Moore. John Wiley & Sons Ltd., The Atrium, Southern Gate, Chichester, PO19 8SQ, United Kingdom; customer@wiley.com; http://www.wiley.com. Adv. Sample. Refereed. Reprint: PSC. *Indexed:* A01, A22, AbAn, Agr, BRI, C45, ExcerpMed, IndVet, P02. *Bk. rev.:* 0-3, 500-600 words. *Aud.:* Ac, Sa.

As one of the leading review journals in biology, *BioEssays* "is a review-and-discussion journal publishing novel insights, forward-looking reviews[,] and commentaries in contemporary biology with a molecular, genetic, cellular, or physiological dimension. A further aim is to emphasise transdisciplinarity and integrative biology in the context of organismal studies, systems approaches, through to ecosystems where appropriate." Contents are divided into three main sections, "Insights & Perspectives" (for ideas, hypotheses, and commentaries), "Prospects & Overviews" (for review-style articles) and "Reports & Opinion" (for meeting reports, book reviews, and letters to the editor). The "Prospects & Overviews" section contains mini-reviews highlighting very recent research articles, and longer papers that present a field, its developments, and prospects for a broad readership. Online open access is available via Wiley Online Library. Subscriptions are also available. In addition, this journal has "Virtual Issues" that are online compilations of previously published articles that highlight a topical area of interest. Those collections are updated regularly, and the articles are freely available for a limited period of time. This is a good source for all biology collections as well as special and academic libraries. URL: http://onlinelibrary.wiley.com/journal/10.1002/%28ISSN%291521-1878

798. *Cell.* [ISSN: 0092-8674] 1974. bi-w. EUR 2181. Ed(s): Emilie Marcus. Cell Press, 600 Technology Sq, Cambridge, MA 02139; http://www.cell.com/cellpress. Illus., index, adv. Sample. Refereed. *Indexed:* A01, A22, AbAn, BRI, C45, ExcerpMed, FS&TA, IndVet. *Aud.:* Ac, Sa.

Launched in 1974, *Cell* publishes novel results within all areas of experimental biology, including human genetics, cancer, immunology, systems biology, neuroscience, signaling, and disease. Papers considered for publication must provide significant conceptual advances or raise provocative questions regarding an interesting biological issue. In December 2005, *Cell* was relaunched, and contents now include reviews and mini-reviews that provide in-depth analysis on scientific policy and economic, political, and social trends. There are also commentaries, viewpoints, essays, point–counterpoint discussions of controversial findings, and letters to the editor. Online features include podcasts; "PaperClips," which present short, five-minute conversations between the *Cell* editor and an author exploring the rationale and implications of the findings; and "SnapShots," which are handy reference guides. Online access to full text is available via ScienceDirect. At the web site are featured articles from the current issue of *Cell Online*; supplemental data (web-based material not available in the printed journal); and tables of contents for all archived issues of *Cell Online*. Recommended for academic and special libraries. URL: www.cell.com

799. The E M B O Journal. [ISSN: 0261-4189] 1982. s-m. EUR 3193 in Europe; USD 3369 in the Americas; JPY 546300 Japan. Ed(s): Bernd Pulverer. Nature Publishing Group, The MacMillan Bldg, 4 Crinan St, London, N1 9XW, United Kingdom; http://www.nature.com. Illus., index, adv. Sample. Refereed. Vol. ends: Dec. *Indexed:* A01, A22, Agr, C45, E01, ExcerpMed, FS&TA, IndVet. *Aud.:* Ac, Sa.

The EMBO Journal (European Molecular Biology Organization) provides "rapid publication of full-length papers describing original research of general rather than specialist interest in molecular biology and related areas." Articles report novel findings of wide biological significance in such areas as structural biology, immunology, plant biology, RNA, proteins, cellular metabolism, and molecular biology of disease. The journal is published 24 times a year by the Nature Publishing Group, and full text is available online with a subscription. Non-subscribers have a limited access to sample issues online. Open access is available through PubMed Central. This journal offers subject searching to browse online. Established as one of the most influential molecular biology journals, it is recommended for academic and research libraries. URL: www.nature.com/emboj/index.html

800. E M B O Molecular Medicine (Online). [ISSN: 1757-4684] 2008. m. Free. Ed(s): Stefanie Dimmeler, Anneke Funk. Wiley - V C H Verlag GmbH & Co. KGaA, Postfach 101161, Weinheim, 69451, Germany; info@wiley-vch.de; http://www.wiley-vch.de. Refereed. *Aud.:* Ac, Sa.

EMBO Molecular Medicine is a peer-reviewed online journal "dedicated to a new research discipline at the interface between clinical research and basic biology." Topics covered include: aging, angiogenesis, cancer biology, channelopathies, differentiation and development, endocrinology/metabolic disease, genetics/epigenetics, genomics, transcriptomics, proteomics, metabolomics of disease, systems medicine, gene therapy, immunology and inflammation, infectious diseases, neurodegeneration, neurological diseases and myopathies, sensory defects, stem cells and regenerative medicine, and vascular and cardiovascular biology. It contains research articles as full-length research papers and short reports. In addition, the journal publishes editorials and review articles in innovative formats that target a broad and non-specialized audience. All articles published in *EMBO Molecular Medicine* are fully open-access via Wiley Open Access Journals. Articles are immediately and freely available to read, download, and share. Online access is available from 2009 to present. Appropriate for academic and special libraries. URL: http://onlinelibrary.wiley.com/journal/10.1002/%28ISSN%291757-4684

801. Experimental Cell Research: emphasizing molecular approaches to cell biology. [ISSN: 0014-4827] 1950. 20x/yr. EUR 8168. Ed(s): U Lendahl. Academic Press, 3251 Riverport Ln, Maryland Heights, MO 63043; JournalCustomerService-usa@elsevier.com; http://www.elsevierdirect.com/brochures/academicpress/index.html. Illus., index, adv. Refereed. *Indexed:* A01, A22, Agr, C45, E01, ExcerpMed. *Aud.:* Ac, Sa.

Experimental Cell Research "promotes the understanding of cell biology by publishing experimental studies on the general organization and activity of cells." Research is published on all aspects of cell biology, from the molecular level to cell interaction and differentiation. Contents include papers that provide novel and significant insights into important problems within these areas. Specific topics include cancer research, developmental biology, meiosis and mitosis, RNA processing, and stem cell biology. Online full-text access is provided by Elsevier's ScienceDirect, and sample issues are available free. This journal is recommended for molecular and cell biologists and cancer researchers, and for academic and research libraries, especially those that support research in cell or molecular biology or cancer. URL: www.journals.elsevier.com/experimental-cell-research/

802. The Journal of Cell Biology. Formerly (until 1962): *Journal of Biophysical and Biochemical Cytology.* [ISSN: 0021-9525] 1955. bi-w. USD 4685 (print & online eds.). Ed(s): Tom Misteli. Rockefeller University Press, 1114 First Ave, New York, NY 10021; subs@rockefeller.edu; http://www.rupress.org. Illus., index, adv. Sample. Refereed. Circ: 1423 Paid. Microform: PQC. *Indexed:* A01, A22, Agr, BRI, C45, ExcerpMed, IndVet, P02. *Aud.:* Ac, Sa.

The Journal of Cell Biology publishes papers on all aspects of cellular structure and function. Articles must provide novel and significant mechanistic insight into a cellular function that will be of interest to a general readership. Published materials are limited in size but may include concise articles and reports that have the potential to open new avenues of research. The biweekly journal is published by The Rockefeller University Press with the assistance of Stanford University Libraries, a nonprofit organization. Editors are scientists who review articles only within their chosen field. All articles are available in full text online after six months in print. Open access is also available through PubMed Central from 1962 through 2009. In January 2001, in response to calls from the research community to provide free access to the results of publicly funded research, the *JCB* was one of the first journals to release its primary research content to the public six months after publication. In June 2003, all of the back content of the *JCB* starting from volume 1, issue 1, was posted on the *JCB* web site to the general public for free. This journal provides news and short reviews that are useful to students, researchers, and professionals. Appropriate for academic and special libraries. URL: http://jcb.rupress.org/

803. Journal of Cell Science. Formerly (until 1966): *Quarterly Journal of Microscopical Science.* [ISSN: 0021-9533] 1852. s-m. USD 3576. Ed(s): Michael Way. The Company of Biologists Ltd., 140 Cowley Rd, Cambridge, CB4 0DL, United Kingdom; sales@biologists.com; http://www.biologists.org. Illus., index. Sample. Refereed. Vol. ends: Dec. Microform: BHP. *Indexed:* A01, A22, Agr, C45, ExcerpMed, IndVet. *Aud.:* Ac, Sa.

Covering the complete range of topics in cell biology, *Journal of Cell Science* is also of key interest to developmental biologists, molecular biologists, and geneticists. Contents include research articles, review articles, brief syntheses of important areas, commentaries, "Cell Science at a Glance," and "Sticky Wickets," which provides controversial views of life-science research. The journal is published twice a month by the Company of Biologists, a nonprofit organization determined to promote research and knowledge in the study of biology. Full-text online content of all subsections and one open-access research article are provided for free for each issue. Some content is also available through PubMed Central. Recommended for special and academic libraries. URL: http://jcs.biologists.org

804. Journal of Molecular Biology. [ISSN: 0022-2836] 1959. 24x/yr. EUR 9575. Ed(s): Peter Wright. Academic Press, 32 Jamestown Rd, Camden, London, NW1 7BY, United Kingdom; corporate.sales@elsevier.com; http://www.elsevier.com/. Illus., index, adv. Sample. Refereed. *Indexed:* A01, A22, AbAn, Agr, C45, E01, ExcerpMed, FS&TA, IndVet. *Aud.:* Ac, Sa.

Published weekly, the *Journal of Molecular Biology* contains "original scientific research concerning studies of organisms or their components at the molecular level." Specific research areas include gene structure, expression, replication, and recombination in eukaryotic and prokaryotic organisms; the structure, function, and chemistry of proteins, nucleic acids, and other macromolecules; cellular and developmental biology; and the genetics, structure, and growth cycles of viruses and bacteriophages. Online, full-text access is provided by Elsevier's ScienceDirect from 1959 to the present, and includes one free sample issue. Appropriate for any academic library or research institution that supports biologists. URL: www.journals.elsevier.com/journal-of-molecular-biology/

805. Molecular and Cellular Biology. [ISSN: 0270-7306] 1981. s-m. USD 2254. Ed(s): Roger J Davis. American Society for Microbiology, 1752 N St, NW, Washington, DC 20036; journals@asmusa.org; http://www.asm.org. Illus., index, adv. Refereed. Vol. ends: Dec. Microform: PQC. *Indexed:* A01, A22, C45, ExcerpMed, IndVet. *Aud.:* Ac, Sa.

Molecular and Cellular Biology is an "authoritative source of fundamental knowledge and new developments in all aspects of the molecular biology of eukaryotic cells." Topics emphasized include gene expression, transcriptional regulation, cell growth and development, nucleocytoplasmic communication, cell and organelle structure and assembly, and mammalian genetic models. Full text is available through PubMed Central. Rated in the top 100 most influential research journals by the Special Libraries Association in the biochemistry and molecular biology field. Recommended for undergraduates and researchers in special and academic libraries. URL: http://mcb.asm.org/

806. Molecular Biology and Evolution. [ISSN: 0737-4038] 1983. m. EUR 782. Ed(s): Marcy Uyenoyama. Oxford University Press, 2001 Evans Rd, Cary, NC 27513; http://www.oxfordjournals.org. Illus., index. Refereed. Vol. ends: Nov. Microform: PMC; PQC. Reprint: PSC. *Indexed:* A22, AbAn, C45, E01, ExcerpMed, IndVet, P02. *Aud.:* Ac, Sa.

Presenting research at the interface between molecular and evolutionary biology, *Molecular Biology and Evolution* "publishes investigations of molecular evolutionary patterns and processes, tests of evolutionary hypotheses that use molecular data[,] and studies that use molecular evolutionary information to address questions about biological function at all levels of organization." Contents include two types of categories: research articles, which are conventional in form without strict length limitations; and letters, which are short communications that contain findings of outstanding interest to a broad readership. Full text is available online from 1983 to the present, with a number of open-access articles available in the archive. Open access is available at PubMed Central from 2008 to the present. Appropriate for academic and research libraries. URL: http://mbe.oxfordjournals.org/

807. Molecular Biology of the Cell (Online). [ISSN: 1939-4586] 1990. m. USD 556 Tier 1 (Free to members). Ed(s): David G Drubin. American Society for Cell Biology, 8120 Woodmont Ave, Ste 750, Bethesda, MD 20814; ascbinfo@ascb.org; http://www.ascb.org. Sample. Refereed. *Aud.:* Ac, Sa.

Molecular Biology of the Cell (*MBC*) is published monthly online by the American Society for Cell Biology. The journal publishes original and scholarly research reports that contribute significantly to the scientific understanding of the molecular basis of cell structure and function. *MBC* serves as a forum for presenting in full the significant advances that arise from a combination of experimental approaches (e.g., biochemical, genetic, morphological, and immunochemical). Articles include supplementary datasets, video data, and previously unpublished data and methods that support the conclusions drawn. Accepted articles are published rapidly after acceptance and ahead of a print version. *MBC* is an online journal with full-text content available from 1997 to the present with subscription. Non-subscribers have access to tables of contents, abstracts, and a full sample issue at no cost and without having to register. Unredacted accepted manuscripts are freely accessible immediately through MBoC In Press. Final published versions are freely accessible two months after publication at www.molbiolcell.org. *MBoC* is also available online through PubMed Central, which is sponsored by the U.S. National Library of Medicine. Access earlier than two months is available through subscription or membership in the ASCB. Recommended for academic and special libraries that support a biology program. URL: www.molbiolcell.org

808. Molecular Cell. [ISSN: 1097-2765] 1997. s-m. EUR 2117. Ed(s): Emilie Marcus, John Pham. Cell Press, 600 Technology Sq, Cambridge, MA 02139; celleditor@cell.com. Refereed. Circ: 1514. *Indexed:* A01, A22, AbAn, ExcerpMed. *Aud.:* Ac, Sa.

Molecular Cell publishes reports of unusual significance to researchers in the field. Topics focus on "analyses at the molecular level in any area of biology, particularly that of molecular biology (including replication, recombination, repair, gene expression, RNA processing, translation, and protein folding, modification and degradation)." Papers considered for publication must provide significant insights or raise provocative questions and hypotheses. The majority of each issue consists of research articles, and shorter papers make up a small section. Free online full text is available 12 months after publication. Additionally, "Online Now" is a Thursday feature where the journal publishes articles online prior to print publication. Appropriate for special and academic libraries. URL: www.molecule.org

809. Nucleic Acids Research. [ISSN: 0305-1048] 1974. 22x/yr. EUR 3699. Ed(s): Barry Stoddard, Keith Fox. Oxford University Press, Great Clarendon St, Oxford, OX2 6DP, United Kingdom; jnl.orders@oup.co.uk; http://www.oxfordjournals.org. Illus., index, adv. Sample. Refereed. Vol. ends: Dec. Reprint: PSC. *Indexed:* A22, AbAn, Agr, C45, E01, ExcerpMed, FS&TA, IndVet. *Aud.:* Ac, Sa.

Nucleic Acids Research is an open-access journal that provides for rapid publication of cutting-edge research into nucleic acids within chemistry, computational biology, genomics, molecular biology, nucleic acid enzymes, RNA, and structural biology. Print contents include standard papers, surveys, and summaries that present brief, formal reviews relevant to nucleic acid chemistry and biology. Online contents include all articles and methods papers that describe novel techniques or advances in existing techniques that are highly significant, and supplemental materials. This journal is published by Oxford University Press, and all issues, from 1974 to present, are freely available online under an open-access model. Content is also available through PubMed Central. Recommended for academic and research libraries with biology, medical, and chemistry collections. URL: http://nar.oxfordjournals.org/

Developmental Biology

810. B M C Developmental Biology. [ISSN: 1471-213X] 2000. irreg. Free. Ed(s): Philippa Harris. BioMed Central Ltd., 236 Gray's Inn Rd, London, WC1X 8HB, United Kingdom; info@biomedcentral.com; http://www.biomedcentral.com. Adv. Refereed. *Indexed:* A01, C45, IndVet. *Aud.:* Ac, Sa.

B M C Developmental Biology is an open-access journal that publishes original peer-reviewed research articles in all aspects of cellular, tissue-level, and organismal aspects of development. Types of articles include research articles; database articles that describe either a new biomedical database or a database that has been substantially changed and improved since it was last described in a journal; methodology articles that present a new experimental or computational method, test, or procedure; and software articles in which authors of software applications, tools, or algorithm implementations publish descriptions of their code using the software article type. *B M C Developmental Biology* is a full-text online journal. All research articles are published after full peer review. All articles are published, without barriers to access, immediately upon acceptance. Full text is available free online through PubMed Central from 2001 to the present, or via the publisher's web site (below). Recommended for academic and special libraries that support a biology program. URL: www.biomedcentral.com/bmcdevbiol

811. Development (Cambridge): for advances in developmental biology and stem cells. Formerly (until 1987): *Journal of Embryology and Experimental Morphology*. [ISSN: 0950-1991] 1953. s-m. USD 4193. Ed(s): Olivier Pourquie. The Company of Biologists Ltd., 140 Cowley Rd, Cambridge, CB4 0DL, United Kingdom; sales@biologists.com; http://www.biologists.org. Illus., index. Sample. Refereed. Vol. ends: Dec. *Indexed:* A01, A22, C45, ExcerpMed, IndVet. *Aud.:* Ac, Sa.

Known as a primary research journal, *Development* provides "insight into mechanisms of plant and animal development[,] covering all aspects from molecular and cellular to tissue levels." It acts as a forum for all research that offers genuine insight into developmental mechanisms, and experimental papers are given top priority. Studies can address any aspect of the developmental process, including evolutionary studies, stem cells and nuclear reprogramming, regional specification, morphogenesis, and organogenesis.

Published by the Company of Biologists, this journal includes research articles and meeting reviews. Full text is available online, from 1953 to the present. Additionally, *Development* also publishes articles online ahead of their being published in print their ePress site on a weekly basis. Recommended for academic and special libraries. URL: http://dev.biologists.org/content/by/year

812. *Developmental Biology.* [ISSN: 0012-1606] 1959. 24x/yr. EUR 10058. Ed(s): R Krumlauf. Academic Press, 3251 Riverport Ln, Maryland Heights, MO 63043; JournalCustomerService-usa@elsevier.com; http://www.elsevierdirect.com/brochures/academicpress/index.html. Illus., index, adv. Sample. Refereed. *Indexed:* A01, A22, AbAn, Agr, C45, E01, ExcerpMed, IndVet. *Aud.:* Ac, Sa.

Developmental Biology publishes "research on the mechanisms of development, differentiation, and growth in animals and plants at the molecular, cellular, and genetic levels." Research areas of particular interest include molecular genetics of development, control of gene expression, cell interactions and cell-matrix interactions, mechanisms of differentiation, growth factors and oncogenes, regulation of stem cell populations, gametogenesis and fertilization, developmental endocrinology, plant development, and the evolution of developmental control. Contents include original research papers that contribute new information to the understanding of developmental mechanisms, review articles intended to reach a broad readership, and a section called "Genomes and Developmental Control," dedicated to papers that address the analysis of developmental processes and systems involving animals and plants. Online, full-text access is provided through Elsevier's ScienceDirect. All articles published after 12 months have unrestricted access and will remain permanently free to read and download. This journal is considered the best in its field. Recommended for academic and special libraries. URL: www.journals.elsevier.com/developmental-biology/

813. *Genes & Development.* [ISSN: 0890-9369] 1987. s-m. USD 1420 (print & online eds.). Ed(s): T Grodzicker. Cold Spring Harbor Laboratory Press, 500 Sunnyside Blvd, Woodbury, NY 11797; cshpress@cshl.edu; http://www.cshlpress.com. Illus., index, adv. Sample. Refereed. Vol. ends: Dec. Reprint: PSC. *Indexed:* A01, A22, AbAn, C45, ExcerpMed, IndVet. *Aud.:* Ac, Sa.

Genes & Development publishes "high quality research papers of broad general interest and biological significance in the areas of molecular biology, molecular genetics[,] and related fields." Contents include two main formats: research papers that occupy up to 12 journal pages, and short research communications that provide compelling, novel, and important conclusions. Also included are review articles and perspectives. Online and print subscriptions are available separately. Free sample issues are found online, as well as access to tables of contents and abstracts. Open access is available from 1989 to the present. Recommended for special and academic libraries. URL: http://genesdev.cshlp.org/

Genetics

814. *American Journal of Human Genetics.* [ISSN: 0002-9297] 1948. m. EUR 1206. Ed(s): Emilie Marcus, Cynthia C Morton. Cell Press, 600 Technology Sq, Cambridge, MA 02139; celleditor@cell.com. Illus., index, adv. Refereed. Vol. ends: Dec. Microform: MIM; PQC. *Indexed:* A01, A22, AbAn, BAS, BRI, C45, Chicano, ExcerpMed, IndVet, P02. *Bk. rev.:* 0-3, 200-1,200 words. *Aud.:* Ac, Sa.

Published for The American Society of Human Genetics, which is the primary professional membership organization for human geneticists in the Americas, this journal is a "record of research and review relating to heredity in humans and to the application of genetic principles in medicine and public policy, as well as in related areas of molecular and cell biology." Papers appear on such topics as behavioral genetics, biochemical genetics, clinical genetics, cytogenetics, dysmorphology, gene therapy, genetic counseling, genetic epidemiology, genomics, immunogenetics, molecular genetics, neurogenetics, and population genetics. Also included are review articles, reports, conference announcements, employment notices, and letters to the editors. Online access is provided by through multiple full-text sources. All *AJHG* articles, from 1949 to the present, are freely available at PubMed Central starting six months after publication. A good source for special and academic libraries.

815. *B M C Genetics.* [ISSN: 1471-2156] 2000. irreg. Free. Ed(s): Simon Harold. BioMed Central Ltd., 236 Gray's Inn Rd, London, WC1X 8HB, United Kingdom; info@biomedcentral.com; http://www.biomedcentral.com. Adv. Refereed. *Indexed:* A01, C45, ExcerpMed, IndVet, RRTA. *Aud.:* Ac, Sa.

B M C Genetics is an open-access journal that publishes original peer-reviewed research articles in all aspects of inheritance and variation in individuals and among populations. Types of articles include research articles; database articles that describe either a new biomedical database or a database that has been substantially changed and improved since it was last described in a journal; methodology articles that present a new experimental or computational method, test, or procedure; and software articles in which authors of software applications, tools, or algorithm implementations publish descriptions of their code using the software article type. *B M C Genetics* is a full-text online journal. All research articles are published after full peer review. All articles are published, without barriers to access, immediately upon acceptance. Full text is available online through PubMed Central from 2000 to the present, or via the publisher's web site (below). Recommended for academic and special libraries that support a biology program. URL: www.biomedcentral.com/bmcgenet

816. *Biochimica et Biophysica Acta. Gene Regulatory Mechanisms.* Formerly (until 2008): *B B A - Gene Structure and Expression;* Which superseded in part (in 1982): *Biochimica et Biophysica Acta: N. Nucleic Acids and Protein Synthesis;* Which was formerly (until 1965): *Biochimica et Biophysica Acta. Specialized Section on Nucleic Acids and Related Subjects.* [ISSN: 1874-9399] 1962. 12x/yr. EUR 3369. Ed(s): Joseph Reese. Elsevier BV, Radarweg 29, PO Box 211, Amsterdam, 1000 AE, Netherlands; JournalsCustomerServiceEMEA@elsevier.com; http://www.elsevier.nl. Refereed. Microform: PQC. *Indexed:* A01, A22, C45, ExcerpMed, FS&TA, IndVet. *Aud.:* Ac, Sa.

Gene Regulatory Mechanisms includes "reports that describe novel insights into mechanisms of transcriptional, post-transcriptional[,] and translational gene regulation. Special emphasis is placed on papers that identify epigenetic mechanisms of gene regulation, including chromatin, modification, and remodeling. This section also encompasses mechanistic studies of regulatory proteins and protein complexes; regulatory or mechanistic aspects of RNA processing; regulation of expression by small RNAs; genomic analysis of gene expression patterns; and modeling of gene regulatory pathways." This journal is one of the nine topical journals from *Biochimica et Biophysica Acta* (*BBA*). It contains descriptive reports and research papers. Print and online subscriptions are available. Online access is available from 2008 to present via the publisher's web site, ScienceDirect. Appropriate for academic and special libraries. URL: www.journals.elsevier.com/bba-gene-regulatory-mechanisms/#description

817. *Biochimica et Biophysica Acta. Molecular Basis of Disease.* [ISSN: 0925-4439] 1990. m. EUR 2086. Ed(s): Ronald Oude Elferink, Jeffrey Keller. Elsevier BV, Radarweg 29, PO Box 211, Amsterdam, 1000 AE, Netherlands; JournalsCustomerServiceEMEA@elsevier.com; http://www.elsevier.nl. Refereed. Microform: PQC. *Indexed:* A01, A22, ExcerpMed, FS&TA. *Aud.:* Ac, Sa.

Articles published in *Molecular Basis of Disease* "covers the biochemistry and molecular genetics of disease processes and models of human disease specifically aspects of aging, cancer, metabolic-, neurological-, and immunological-based disease." This journal is one of the nine topical journals from *Biochimica et Biophysica Acta* (*BBA*). Articles emphasize the underlying mechanisms of disease pathways and provide novel contributions to the understanding and/or treatment of these disorders. Print and online subscriptions are available. Online access is available from 1990 to present via the publisher's web site, ScienceDirect. Appropriate for academic and special libraries. URL: www.journals.elsevier.com/bba-molecular-basis-of-disease/#description

818. *Genome Research.* Formerly (until 1995): *P C R Methods and Applications.* [ISSN: 1088-9051] 1991. m. Ed(s): Hillary E Sussman, Judy Cuddihy. Cold Spring Harbor Laboratory Press, 500 Sunnyside Blvd, Woodbury, NY 11797; cshpress@cshl.edu; http://www.cshlpress.com. Illus., adv. Sample. Refereed. Circ: 50000. Reprint: PSC. *Indexed:* A01, A22, AbAn, C45, ExcerpMed, FS&TA, IndVet. *Aud.:* Ac, Sa.

Articles published in *Genome Research* focus on gene discovery, comparative genome analysis, proteomics, evolution studies, informatics, genome structure and function, technological innovations and applications, statistical and mathematical methods, cutting-edge genetic and physical mapping, and DNA sequencing. This journal presents new data published in the form of articles and letters, review articles, perspectives, and insight/outlook articles that provide commentary on recent advances. Submitted articles selected by the editor are peer reviewed, and all accepted papers must present original research; researchers should be prepared to make available all materials needed to duplicate their work. *Genome Research* follows the guidelines for fair use of community resource data. Print and online subscriptions are available. Online access is available from 1997 to present via the publisher's web site. Appropriate for academic and special libraries. URL: http://genome.cshlp.org/

819. *Heredity.* [ISSN: 0018-067X] 1947. m. EUR 1000 in Europe; USD 1215 in the Americas; JPY 171000 Japan. Ed(s): Manfred J Muller. Nature Publishing Group, The MacMillan Bldg, 4 Crinan St, London, N1 9XW, United Kingdom; nature@nature.com; http://www.nature.com. Illus., index, adv. Sample. Refereed. Microform: PQC. *Indexed:* A01, A22, AbAn, Agr, BRI, C45, E01, FS&TA, IndVet. *Bk. rev.:* 4-5, 400-2,000 words. *Aud.:* Ac, Sa.

Heredity, published for The Genetics Society, presents "high-quality articles that describe original research and theoretical insights in all areas of genetics." Contents include original research articles, short reviews, book reviews, and news and commentaries that keep researchers and students updated about advances in the field. Online features include the monthly "Heredity Podcast" and a number of feature articles for free. Archived content is freely available after 12 months. Appropriate for special and academic libraries. URL: www.nature.com/hdy/index.html

820. *Human Biology (Detroit): the international journal of population genetics and anthropology.* [ISSN: 0018-7143] 1929. bi-m. USD 436 (print & online eds.). Ed(s): Evelyne Heyer. Wayne State University Press, The Leonard N Simons Bldg, 4809 Woodward Ave, Detroit, MI 48201; http://wsupress.wayne.edu/. Illus., index, adv. Refereed. Vol. ends: Dec. Microform: PQC. *Indexed:* A01, A22, A47, ABS&EES, BAS, BRI, C45, Chicano, E01, P02, RRTA. *Bk. rev.:* 1-3, 500-1,400 words. *Aud.:* Ac, Sa.

This journal publishes ideas, methods, and techniques in the human biology field. Topics include evolutionary and genetic demography, behavioral genetics, population genetics, quantitative genetics, genetic epidemiology, molecular genetics, and growth physiology focusing on genetic/environmental interactions. *Human Biology* is also available in electronic format through BioOne and Project Muse and is searchable via Medline. Subscriptions are available to individuals and institutions, and student/senior discounts are offered. Appropriate for academic and special libraries with collections in anthropology, biology, and medicine. URL: http://wsupress.wayne.edu/journals/humanbio

821. *Journal of Heredity.* Formerly (until 1914): *American Breeders' Magazine.* [ISSN: 0022-1503] 1903. bi-m. EUR 504. Ed(s): C Scott Baker, Anjanette Baker. Oxford University Press, Great Clarendon St, Oxford, OX2 6DP, United Kingdom; enquiry@oup.co.uk; http://www.oxfordjournals.org/. Illus., index, adv. Refereed. Circ: 900. Vol. ends: Nov/Dec. Microform: IDC; PMC; PQC. Reprint: PSC. *Indexed:* A01, A22, AbAn, Agr, AnBeAb, BRI, C45, E01, ExcerpMed, FS&TA, IndVet, MLA-IB, P02. *Bk. rev.:* 0-5, 300-900 words. *Aud.:* Ac, Sa.

This journal contains articles on organismic genetics such as "gene action, regulation, and transmission in both plant and animal species, including the genetic aspects of botany, cytogenetics and evolution, zoology, and molecular and developmental biology." Contents include research papers, brief communications, announcements, and review articles. Also included are papers on rapidly advancing fields such as genome organization, comparative gene mapping, animal models of human disease, and molecular genetics of resistance to infectious disease in plants and animals. Full text is available online from 1910 to the present with a subscription or open access via PubMed. Recommended for a wide range of biologists as well as special and academic libraries. URL: http://jhered.oxfordjournals.org/

822. *Molecular Genetics and Genomics: an international journal.* Former titles (until 2001): *Molecular and General Genetics;* (until 1966): *Zeitschrift fuer Vererbungslehre;* (until 1957): *Zeitschrift fuer Induktive Abstammungs- und Vererbungslehre.* [ISSN: 1617-4615] 1908. m. EUR 4679 (print & online eds.). Ed(s): Stefan Hohmann. Springer, Tiergartenstr 17, Heidelberg, 69121, Germany. Illus., index, adv. Sample. Refereed. Microform: PQC. Reprint: PSC. *Indexed:* A01, A22, AbAn, Agr, C45, E01, ExcerpMed, FS&TA, IndVet. *Aud.:* Ac, Sa.

Molecular Genetics and Genomics publishes research in all areas of genetics and genomics, as well as encompassing experimental and theoretical approaches in all organisms. The journal is intended for biologists, and contents include review articles and original research articles in areas that include mechanisms for extending longevity in a variety of organisms; screening of yeast metal homeostasis genes involved in mitochondrial functions; molecular mapping of cultivar-specific avirulence genes in the rice blast fungus; and more. Full text is available online from 1996 to the present. Many articles are offered free online through Springer Open Choice. Recommended for special and academic libraries. URL: www.springer.com/life+sciences/cell+biology/journal/438

823. *Nature Genetics.* [ISSN: 1061-4036] 1992. m. EUR 3936 in Europe; USD 4958 in the Americas; GBP 2544 in the UK & elsewhere. Ed(s): Myles Axton. Nature Publishing Group, 75 Varick St, 9th Fl, New York, NY 10013; nature@natureny.com; http://www.nature.com. Illus., index, adv. Sample. Refereed. *Indexed:* A01, A22, AbAn, Agr, BRI, C45, ExcerpMed, IndVet. *Bk. rev.:* 1, 700-1,000 words. *Aud.:* Ac, Sa.

Nature Genetics publishes genetic and functional genomic studies on human traits and other organisms, including the mouse, fly, nematode, and yeast. It focuses on the genetic basis for common and complex diseases as well as the mechanism, architecture, and evolution of gene networks. Contents include editorials, research articles, letters, news and views, and meeting reports. Online features include "Free Association" and the "Nature Genetics" blog, which contains links and editorial comments on research and news in genetics, as well as reader feedback. Online full text is available from 1997 to the present with a subscription. Sample issues are available. Appropriate for special and academic libraries that support biology programs. URL: www.nature.com/ng/index.html

824. *R N A.* [ISSN: 1355-8382] 1995. m. USD 1045 (print & online eds.). Ed(s): Dr. Timothy W Nilsen. Cold Spring Harbor Laboratory Press, 500 Sunnyside Blvd, Woodbury, NY 11797; cshpress@cshl.edu; http://www.cshlpress.com. Adv. Sample. Refereed. Circ: 40000. *Indexed:* A22, C45, E01, ExcerpMed, IndVet. *Aud.:* Ac, Sa.

RNA serves as an international forum. It is a monthly publication that "provides rapid publication of significant original research in all areas of RNA structure and function in eukaryotic, prokaryotic, and viral systems." Topics covered include structural analysis; rRNA, mRNA, and tRNA structure, function, and biogenesis; alternative processing; ribosome structure and function; translational control; RNA catalysis; RNA editing; RNA transport and localization; regulatory RNAs; large and small RNP structure, function, and biogenesis; viral RNA metabolism; RNA stability and turnover; in vitro evolution; and RNA chemistry. Contents include reports, articles, and bioinformatics that describe computer-based analysis of sequence data, hypotheses, methods, letters to the editor, perspectives, mini-reviews, and meeting summaries. Subscriptions to the print journal include full online access; online-only subscriptions are available to institutions. Full text from 1995 to the present is provided by PubMed Central, with some back content in full text via the publisher's web site. Appropriate for special and academic libraries. URL: http://rnajournal.cshlp.org/

Microbiology

Applied and Environmental Microbiology. See Biotechnology section.

825. *Canadian Journal of Microbiology.* [ISSN: 0008-4166] 1954. m. CAD 1150. Ed(s): Dr. Jim J Germida, H G Deneer. N R C Research Press, 1200 Montreal Rd, Bldg M-55, Ottawa, ON K1A 0R6, Canada; pubs@nrc-cnrc.gc.ca; http://pubs.nrc-cnrc.gc.ca. Illus., index, adv. Sample. Refereed. Circ: 1341. Vol. ends: Dec. Microform: MML; PMC; PQC. *Indexed:* A01, A22, Agr, C37, C45, CBCARef, E01, EngInd, ExcerpMed, FS&TA, IndVet, RRTA, S25. *Aud.:* Ac, Sa.

Published since 1954, *Canadian Journal of Microbiology* presents "contributions by recognized scientists worldwide." Topics include "applied microbiology and biotechnology; microbial structure and function; fungi and other eucaryotic protists; infection and immunity; microbial ecology; physiology, metabolism, and enzymology; and virology, genetics, and molecular biology." Contents include articles, notes, mini-reviews, reviews, and letters. Although papers in French are accepted, the majority of the journal is in English. Online content is available in full text from 1997 to the present with subscriptions. A recommended source for academic and special libraries. URL: http://pubs.nrc-cnrc.gc.ca/rp-ps/journalDetail.jsp?jcode=cjm&lang=eng

826. Current Microbiology. [ISSN: 0343-8651] 1978. m. EUR 1523 (print & online eds.). Ed(s): Erko Stackebrandt. Springer New York LLC, 233 Spring St, New York, NY 10013; service-ny@springer.com; http://www.springer.com/. Illus., adv. Refereed. Microform: PQC. Reprint: PSC. *Indexed:* A01, A22, AbAn, Agr, C45, E01, ExcerpMed, FS&TA, IndVet, P02. *Aud.:* Ac, Sa.

Current Microbiology offers rapid publication of new research on all aspects of microbial cells, including prokaryotes and eukaryotes and, where appropriate, viruses. The coverage spans general, medical, and applied microbiology and virology, drawing on physiology, biochemistry, genetics, biotechnology, morphology, taxonomy, diagnostic methods, and immunology as applied to microorganisms. The journal has an online version with content from 1978 to the present. Recommended for biology collections in special and academic libraries. URL: www.springerlink.com/content/0343-8651

827. International Journal of Systematic and Evolutionary Microbiology. Former titles (until 2000): *International Journal of Systematic Bacteriology;* (until 1966): *International Bulletin of Bacteriological Nomenclature and Taxonomy.* [ISSN: 1466-5026] 1951. m. USD 1171 combined subscription in North America (print & online eds.); GBP 709 combined subscription elsewhere (print & online eds.). Ed(s): Dr. Aharon Oren. Society for General Microbiology, Marlborough House, Basingstoke Rd, Spencers Wood, Reading, RG7 1AG, United Kingdom; admin@sgm.ac.uk; http://www.sgm.ac.uk. Illus., index, adv. Sample. Refereed. Vol. ends: Oct/Dec. Microform: PQC. *Indexed:* A22, AbAn, Agr, C45, ExcerpMed, FS&TA, IndVet. *Bk. rev.:* 1, 1,000-1,200 words. *Aud.:* Ac, Sa.

This journal publishes papers dealing with "all phases of the systematics of bacteria, including taxonomy, nomenclature, identification, characterization[,] and culture preservation," featuring descriptions of the majority of all new prokaryotic and yeast species. Online access is provided by Stanford's HighWire Press to print subscribers, and free sample issues starting from 1951 are available online. Some issues are also available through PubMed Central. This journal is a cornerstone in the field of microbial systematics. Appropriate for special and academic libraries. URL: http://ijs.sgmjournals.org/

828. Journal of Bacteriology. [ISSN: 0021-9193] 1916. s-m. USD 2080. Ed(s): Thomas j Silhavy. American Society for Microbiology, 1752 N St, NW, Washington, DC 20036; journals@asmusa.org; http://www.asm.org. Illus., index, adv. Refereed. Vol. ends: Dec. Microform: PQC. *Indexed:* A01, A22, AbAn, Agr, BRI, C45, ExcerpMed, FS&TA, IndVet, P02. *Aud.:* Ac, Sa.

This journal is ranked number 16 out of 88 journals in the microbiology category by ISI's Journal Citation Reports. It publishes new knowledge of bacteria and other microorganisms. Topics include structural biology, molecular biology and pathogens, microbial communities and interactions, gene replication, and plant microbiology, physiology, and metabolism. Contents include guest commentaries, mini-reviews, meeting reviews and presentations, and research articles on genetics and molecular biology. There is online access to articles from 1916 to the present, and access is free six months after an issue is published through PubMed Central. Highly recommended for biology collections in special and academic libraries. URL: http://jb.asm.org/

829. The Journal of Eukaryotic Microbiology. Former titles (until 1993): *Journal of Protozoology;* (until 1954): *Society of Protozoologists. Proceedings.* [ISSN: 1066-5234] 1950. bi-m. GBP 277. Ed(s): Denis H Lynn, Portia A Holt. Wiley-Blackwell Publishing, Inc., 111 River St, Hoboken, NJ 07030; info@wiley.com; http://www.wiley.com/. Illus., index, adv. Sample. Refereed. Vol. ends: Nov/Dec. Reprint: PSC. *Indexed:* A01, A22, AbAn, Agr, C45, E01, IndVet. *Aud.:* Ac, Sa.

The Journal of Eukaryotic Microbiology publishes "original research on protists, including lower algae and fungi." Topics cover all aspects of these organisms, including behavior, biochemistry, cell biology, chemotherapy, development, ecology, parasitology, and systematics. Journal contents include research articles, communications, and reviews by invitation only. Occasionally, special reports make up supplements. Online access from 1954 to the present is available with a subscription. Free access is available from 1997 to present via Wiley Online Library. Additional online features include free e-mail alerts and free sample issues. URL: http://onlinelibrary.wiley.com/journal/10.1111/%28ISSN%291550-7408

830. Journal of Virology. [ISSN: 0022-538X] 1967. s-m. USD 2698. Ed(s): Rozanne M Sandri-Goldin. American Society for Microbiology, 1752 N St, NW, Washington, DC 20036; journals@asmusa.org; http://www.asm.org. Illus., index, adv. Refereed. Microform: PQC. *Indexed:* A01, A22, AbAn, Agr, C45, ExcerpMed, FS&TA, IndVet. *Aud.:* Ac, Sa.

Known as a premier source concerning viruses, the *Journal of Virology* "provides fundamental new information obtained in studies using cross[-]disciplinary approaches." Topics included are structure and assembly, replication, recombination and evolution, virus–cell interaction, transformation and oncogenesis, gene therapy, vaccines and antiviral agents, and pathogenesis and immunity. Much content is focused on viruses that impact humans, through guest commentaries, mini-reviews, and spotlight features. There is online access from 1967 to the present. Online access to full text is provided for free four months after articles have been published in print. Content is also available through PubMed Central. This highly regarded title is recommended for academic and special libraries. URL: http://jvi.asm.org

831. Microbiology. Formerly (until 1994): *Journal of General Microbiology.* [ISSN: 1350-0872] 1947. m. USD 1659 combined subscription in North America (print & online eds.); GBP 950 combined subscription elsewhere (print & online eds.). Ed(s): Agnes Fouet. Society for General Microbiology, Marlborough House, Basingstoke Rd, Spencers Wood, Reading, RG7 1AG, United Kingdom; admin@sgm.ac.uk; http://www.sgm.ac.uk. Illus., index, adv. Sample. Refereed. Vol. ends: Dec. Microform: PMC. *Indexed:* A01, A22, AbAn, Agr, C45, ExcerpMed, FS&TA, IndVet. *Aud.:* Ac, Sa.

Microbiology is one of the world's leading microbiological journals, with more than 3,000 pages per issue. It is published by the Society for General Microbiology. Contents include research papers, reviews, mini-reviews, a microbiology comment section for readers' responses, and the occasional special issue. Sections include "biochemistry and molecular biology, biodiversity and evolution, cell and developmental biology, environmental microbiology, genes and genomes, pathogens and pathogenicity, physiology, plant-microbe interactions, and theoretical microbiology." Full text is available online from 1994 to the present with subscription via Stanford's HighWire Press. A free sample issue can be found online. Some content is also available through PubMed Central. Appropriate for academic and special libraries. URL: http://mic.sgmjournals.org

832. Microbiology and Molecular Biology Reviews. Former titles (until 1997): *Microbiological Reviews;* (until 1978): *Bacteriological Reviews.* [ISSN: 1092-2172] 1937. q. USD 1213. Ed(s): Diana Downs. American Society for Microbiology, 1752 N St, NW, Washington, DC 20036; journals@asmusa.org; http://www.asm.org. Illus., index, adv. Refereed. Vol. ends: Dec. Microform: PQC. *Indexed:* A01, A22, Agr, C45, ExcerpMed, FS&TA, IndVet, P02. *Aud.:* Ac, Sa.

This is recognized as the "definitive broad-based review journal in the disciplines of microbiology, immunology, and molecular and cellular biology." It is published by the American Society of Microbiology. Articles provide the latest findings on bacteria, viruses, parasites, fungi, and other eukaryotes. Contents include mostly review articles on the following topics: cellular biology, ecology, genetics, host–parasite relationships leading to disease, molecular biology, physiology and enzymology, and virology. Subscriptions are available as print and online. Online access is provided via Stanford's HighWire Press, with full text from 1937 to the present. Non-subscribers have free full-text access up to one year after an issue's publication. Open access is also available through PubMed Central. A good source for special libraries and academic biology collections. URL: http://mmbr.asm.org/

833. *MicrobiologyOpen.* [ISSN: 2045-8827] 2012. Free. Ed(s): Pierre Cornelis. John Wiley & Sons Ltd., 1-7 Oldlands Way, PO Box 808, Bognor Regis, PO21 9FF, United Kingdom; cs-journals@wiley.com; http://www.wiley.com. Refereed. *Indexed:* ExcerpMed. *Aud.:* Ac, Sa.

MicrobiologyOpen is a new peer-reviewed online journal that delivers rapid decisions and fast publication of microbial science on topics such as eukaryotic microorganisms, prokaryotes (bacteria and archaea), and viruses infecting or interacting with microorganisms, including genetic, biochemical, biophysical, bioinformatic, and structural analyses. It contains journal features, original research articles, reviews, and editorials. All articles published by *MicrobiologyOpen* are fully open-access via Wiley Open Access Journals. Articles are immediately and freely available to read, download, and share. Online access is available from 2012 to present. Appropriate for academic and special libraries. URL: http://onlinelibrary.wiley.com/journal/10.1002/%28ISSN%292045-8827

834. *Virology.* [ISSN: 0042-6822] 1955. 26x/yr. EUR 8857. Ed(s): Robert A Lamb. Academic Press, 3251 Riverport Ln, Maryland Heights, MO 63043; JournalCustomerService-usa@elsevier.com; http://www.elsevierdirect.com/brochures/academicpress/index.html. Illus., index, adv. Sample. Refereed. *Indexed:* A01, A22, AbAn, Agr, C45, E01, ExcerpMed, FS&TA, IndVet. *Aud.:* Ac, Sa.

Virology publishes results of basic research in all areas of virology, including the viruses of vertebrates and invertebrates such as plants, bacteria, yeasts, and fungi. Contents include regular articles that present results of basic research that break new ground; rapid communications, which are brief, definitive reports of high significance; and mini-reviews, which discuss cutting-edge developments and themes in virology. Topics include virus replication, virus structure and function, virus-cell biology, gene therapy, viral pathogenesis and immunity, and emerging viruses. Elsevier's ScienceDirect provides online access to full text. This journal is recognized as a leading resource for current information in this field. Recommended for academic and special libraries, and appropriate for undergraduates as well as researchers. URL: www.journals.elsevier.com/virology/

■ BIOTECHNOLOGY

See also Biology section.

Susan K. Kendall, Ph.D., Health Sciences Coordinator and Liaison and Bibliographer for the Basic Biomedical Sciences, Michigan State University Libraries, East Lansing, MI 48824-1048

Introduction

Biotechnology is a dynamic and growing field with exciting potential. It is an applied science, meaning knowledge from the basic biological sciences, particularly from biochemistry, genetics, molecular biology, or cell biology, is applied to practical purposes in medicine, agriculture, food science, or environmental studies and developed into commercial products. In some cases, biological sciences are combined with other areas of study like engineering, material science, computer science, or chemistry, in interdisciplinary ways.

Several specific areas of biotechnology have received a lot of attention in recent years. Stem cell research and regenerative medicine promise to heal diseases by creating new tissues or regenerating tissues that are damaged or diseased. Gene therapy promises to correct diseases by replacing faulty genes with good ones. Pharmacogenomics promises to make more effective, personalized medicines and drugs for individuals based on their genetic makeup. Genetic engineering of plants promises to create new and improved biofuels or food crops. Genetic engineering of microorganisms promises to give us environmentally sound ways to clean up the planet, such as biodegradation of pollutants. Not surprisingly, reality is more complex than some of the glowing promises. Environmentalists, bioethicists, and the public have viewed some of the advances of biotechnology with concern. Nevertheless, most people seem to believe that being able to translate biological findings into useful products to improve our lives is the main reason to support so much biological research.

Scientists doing biotechnology publish advances in their research in many different kinds of journals, ranging from basic biology to medical, chemical, or engineering journals, depending on their focus. There are a growing number of journals devoted specifically to biotechnology and all its subfields, such as drug discovery, regenerative medicine, nanomedicine, genomics and proteomics, agricultural biotechnology, gene therapy, bioinformatics, and the like. Some of the most highly-regarded specialized ones are listed in this section. However, none of the journals focusing solely on biotechnology quite reaches the importance of the most prestigious journals in biology or medicine. The librarian collecting in this area should be aware that, depending on the topic, the very best biotechnology papers may be published in journals such as *Nature, Science, Nature Genetics, Cell,* and *The New England Journal of Medicine.*

Like journals in the other sciences, biotechnology journals are all available in electronic format, and sometimes only in electronic format. Even the older issues of most journals have now been digitized back to the first volume. For current issues, the electronic version is usually now considered the version of record, and the print journals are becoming more stripped down. Frequently, printed issues contain only a subset of the total number of published articles, and, by the time the printed version of an article is published, that article may already have been available online for weeks. Some publishers have even discontinued using color photos in the printed versions. Furthermore, the electronic versions can also contain information (video or large data sets, for example) that was never possible to publish in the printed volumes. Mobile versions of journals (just like mobile versions of bibliographic databases) are starting to become more common as publishers seek to make them more user-friendly for people with smart phones and other devices. One challenge for this has been the problem of institutional authentication when users are not in the institution's network and are trying to access a library-subscribed journal rather than a personal subscription. Some publishers have not worked this problem out yet, and their mobile version relies on an individual password. Other publishers have created some procedures for users to authorize their devices while within their institution's network for later use outside the network. No doubt solutions to this technical problem will be worked out in the next few years.

The social side of science tends to get emphasized with electronic journals. Almost all of them now include capabilities for sharing and social bookmarking of articles by e-mail, Facebook, CiteULike, Del.icio.us, Connotea, Google+, Mendeley, and Twitter. Some publishers have created online communities around a single journal or set of journals to take advantage of the Internet beyond displaying their journal volumes, issues, and articles in a more traditional way that mimics print. These can take the form of subject-specific gateway web portals that provide access not only to the journal articles but also to news stories, blogs, discussion forums, events calendars, podcasts, announcements, advertisements, and other content, some of it available for free. No doubt the hope is that researchers will bookmark a favorite gateway site, and, when using the site, be drawn to read the publisher's journals. Forums and comments sections that encourage two-way communication between authors and readers rather than just the primarily one-way communication of a traditional journal (with occasional letters to the editor) have much potential, but still remain not widely embraced or used beyond the occasional short comments. Scientists have little time to pursue activities that do not directly lead to career rewards, and forums and blogs are not (yet) a part of that reward system. Some discussion forums may thrive, and others may not, as busy scientists prioritize which online communities are worth their limited time and provide the best networking possibilities. It will be interesting to follow this trend as younger scientists move up the ranks to see whether this has any impact on future publishing models.

Electronic journals and web portals have driven a trend toward the steady breakdown of the importance of volumes or issues of journals, even though predictions of the demise of journals themselves have not been borne out. The individual article is the important unit. This has always been somewhat true when users find articles by searching an index like Medline, but it seems even more to be the case now. Scientists still value the journal name and reputation to give them an idea of the trustworthiness of the content. Volumes and issues still exist, but, it seems, primarily to allow for efficient citation. Rapid publication of individual articles online as they are peer-reviewed and accepted, but perhaps not yet copy edited, is very common and now expected by scientists in a rapidly changing field like biotechnology. Where scientists used to subscribe to table of contents services and browse new issues of their favorite journals when they were published, perhaps monthly, they now must daily monitor what is new on the journal's web site, perhaps by using automatic RSS feeds or by following a journal on Twitter. Publishers' web gateways or portals further break up journal issues by listing "highlighted articles," "most downloaded articles," or groups of articles with a similar theme, pulling content from different issues or from different journals (by the same publisher, of course) to create a "virtual issue." Scientists clicking on these hyperlinks to individual articles and creating their own lists of favorites are like most users of any kind of information on the Internet. They have become used to following information and ideas from one place to the next without regard for hierarchy, and they enjoy customizing web sites to suit their own particular needs and interests.

Open-access publishing with the author-pays model is now widespread in the biological sciences, and biotechnology is no exception. The open-access philosophy says that information should be immediately freely available electronically to everyone, and the publishing costs of editing, peer review, or putting the papers online should be covered by something other than a personal or library subscription. The funding source could be a granting agency or the authors themselves. While the majority of important journals in biotechnology are still mostly subscription-based, many of the major publishers have a hybrid journal model for their journals, allowing both restricted and open-access articles to be included. Authors who wish to pay an extra fee to make their articles open access may choose to do that. These same publishers are also experimenting with creating new completely open-access journals. Free public access to taxpayer-funded research has been a hotly debated topic over the last several years. The driving force behind this is the idea that taxpayers fund research with the hope that results will be translated into useful information and practical cures and products. Making the information available to as many people as possible is a key part of the process of encouraging this translation. On April 2008, the National Institutes of Health Public Access Policy became law in the United States, requiring that all papers reporting on research funded by the National Institutes of Health be made available for free to the public on the PubMed Central site no later than 12 months after initial publication. In the United Kingdom, a major funder of biomedical research, the private Wellcome Trust charitable foundation, requires that publications based on research funded by it be made freely available on PubMed Central and U.K. PubMed Central within six months of publication. The trust also provides funding to cover any author-paid open-access fees. Both of these are compromises for open-access proponents who insist that immediate free access is the goal. Whether further laws or policies will extend the free access requirements to non-biomedical funded research remains to be seen. The publishers of all of the journals listed below advertise that they will work with authors to make sure they are in compliance with the current requirements of their funding agencies.

The number of serials in the biotechnology area is already quite large and continues to grow along with the field. The journals or magazines listed here were chosen from that large number based on several criteria, but the librarian should be aware that for any given subfield of biotechnology, many other quality journals should be considered. In choosing journals for the list below, impact factor was taken into account. A journal's impact factor is based primarily on citation data, with the assumption that journals containing highly cited articles tend to be of higher quality. Impact factors are calculated by Thomson Reuters' Scientific Division, which owns the former Institute for Scientific Information (ISI), which developed this measure, and are published in the database Journal Citation Reports. Journal Citation Reports tracks the impact factor of 160 journals that it classifies in the biotechnology subject area. The impact factor as a measure of quality is generally useful and important for the life sciences, so professional journals with higher impact factors were often picked for the list below. However, overdependence on impact factors for journal ranking has been criticized widely, so other criteria were also taken into consideration for this list.

Journals of different types and from different publishers were chosen to diversify the list. Well-known general biotechnology journals with original research or reviews were included, as were specialized journals representing the many different subfields of biotechnology. Both open-access and more traditional journals made the list. The newness and emerging quality of the field can be noted from some of the information about the journals listed. Many are less than 20 years old, and some have only been around for a few years. Still others have undergone name changes or expansions to reflect trends. Some of the journals publish only original primary research; others publish only review articles; and still others publish a combination of these, along with other types of articles commenting on the ethical, legal, or regulatory issues that surround biotechnology.

All of the journals listed are indexed in at least one major bibliographic database such as Medline, Web of Science, or Biological Abstracts. A good academic or corporate research and development library that serves scientists in biotechnology will have a mix of both the general and relevant subject-specific journals to include the range of primary research, review, and news or regulatory articles. A library serving non-scientists who are interested in biotechnology from a business or other angle will likely have only the journals that contain a news section or articles with a business, legal, or regulatory slant. These are the ones noted as appropriate for a general audience. Only a couple of the most general journals or magazines listed would be appropriate for a public library.

Basic Periodicals

Ga: *Scientific American;* Ac, Sa: *Nature Biotechnology, Trends in Biotechnology.*

Basic Abstracts and Indexes

Biological Abstracts, MEDLINE, Scopus, Web of Science.

835. *Applied and Environmental Microbiology.* Formerly (until 1976): *Applied Microbiology.* [ISSN: 0099-2240] 1953. s-m. USD 1820. Ed(s): Harold L Drake. American Society for Microbiology, 1752 N St, NW, Washington, DC 20036; journals@asmusa.org; http://www.asm.org. Illus., index, adv. Refereed. Vol. ends: Dec. *Indexed:* A01, A22, AbAn, Agr, BRI, C45, EngInd, FS&TA, H24, IndVet, OceAb, P02, RRTA, S25. *Aud.:* Ac, Sa.

Published by the American Society for Microbiology, this journal, while not solely focused on biotechnology, contains a significant number of articles devoted to research in biotechnology; industrial, environmental, and food microbiology; and applied areas where new products or practical benefits are the results of microbial research. Each issue is divided into anywhere from 12 to 15 subject sections, so researchers can easily skip to the sections that interest them the most, for instance, food microbiology or biodegradation, or physiology. Almost all of the articles are peer-reviewed research articles, but occasional issues will contain a minireview, guest commentary, or meeting review article at the beginning. A methods section publishes peer-reviewed articles on new methods that can demonstrate a practical application. Research scientists in many different applied microbiology fields would be interested in this journal.

836. *Applied Microbiology and Biotechnology.* Former titles (until 1984): *European Journal of Applied Microbiology and Biotechnology; European Journal of Applied Microbiology.* [ISSN: 0175-7598] 1975. 18x/yr. EUR 8465 (print & online eds.). Ed(s): Alexander Steinbuechel. Springer, Tiergartenstr 17, Heidelberg, 69121, Germany. Refereed. Microform: PQC. Reprint: PSC. *Indexed:* A01, A22, ABIn, AbAn, Agr, BRI, C45, E01, EngInd, ExcerpMed, FS&TA, IndVet, OceAb, S25. *Aud.:* Ac, Sa.

This journal covers a wide range of topics that qualify as applied microbiology and biotechnology including molecular biotechnology, genomics, proteomics, applied microbial physiology, bioprocess engineering, and environmental biotechnology. Most of the papers are original, peer-reviewed research articles; however, minireviews are an important component of this journal. Every recent issue contained at least one, and usually several, of these short five- to six-page review articles, that summarize and provide perspective on a research area or trend. A methods and protocols section publishes short articles that describe the development of a novel method and its potential impact on the field. As with many biotechnology journals, the focus is on the science rather than other issues, and so the journal would be of interest to scientists in the field.

837. *B M C Bioinformatics.* [ISSN: 1471-2105] 2000. irreg. Free. Ed(s): Dr. Melissa Norton. BioMed Central Ltd., 236 Gray's Inn Rd, London, WC1X 8HB, United Kingdom; info@biomedcentral.com; http://www.biomedcentral.com. Adv. Refereed. *Indexed:* A01, C45, IndVet. *Aud.:* Ac, Sa.

This is an open-access, peer-reviewed journal from BioMed Central (BMC), a publisher of many open-access journals that rely on author payment and institutional memberships for support. Bioinformatics combines biology with computer science to create a new field in which biological information is processed and analyzed using computers and computer algorithms. Instructions for authors state that this journal "publishes articles on the development, testing, or novel applications of computer and statistical methods for modeling and analysis of all kinds of biological data." Articles are published immediately upon acceptance, and there are no discrete issues. Volumes of the journal correspond to the year of publication. The online format allows authors to publish large data sets that readers can download and manipulate themselves. The journal publishes original peer-reviewed research articles and also methodology articles and articles that describe databases or software. BMC is one of the publishers creating gateways or web portals as described in this section's introduction. These gateways are built around topics such as "bioinformatics and genomics" and point readers to articles from several of BMC's journals. A supplement section reports proceedings of relevant workshops or conferences. Of interest to researchers in the bioinformatics field.

838. B M C Biotechnology. [ISSN: 1472-6750] 2000. irreg. Free. Ed(s): Dr. Melissa Norton. BioMed Central Ltd., 236 Gray's Inn Rd, London, WC1X 8HB, United Kingdom; info@biomedcentral.com; http://www.biomedcentral.com. Adv. Refereed. *Indexed:* A01, C45, EngInd, ExcerpMed, FS&TA, IndVet. *Aud.:* Ac, Sa.

This is another open-access journal from BioMed Central (BMC) where funding to publish comes from payment by the authors and institutional memberships. Like the other BMC journals, articles are published online upon acceptance, and volume numbers correspond to the year the article was published. *BMC Biotechnology* publishes original, peer-reviewed research articles in all areas of biotechnology from agricultural to pharmaceutical. Besides the journal's web site, BioMed Central has also created web gateways around topics such as stem cells, and these might point users to articles from *BMC Biotechnology* as well as other BMC journals. Since all are available for free online, there would be no access issues. Of interest to researchers in biotechnology.

Biofuels, Bioproducts, and Biorefining. See Energy section.

839. Bioinformatics. Incorporates (1993-2000): *International Conference on Intelligent Systems for Molecular Biology. Proceedings;* Formerly (until 1998): *Computer Applications in the Biosciences.* [ISSN: 1367-4803] 1985. fortn. EUR 2760. Ed(s): Alfonso Valencia, Alex Bateman. Oxford University Press, Great Clarendon St, Oxford, OX2 6DP, United Kingdom; enquiry@oup.co.uk; http://www.oxfordjournals.org/. Illus., adv. Sample. Refereed. Reprint: PSC. *Indexed:* A01, A22, Agr, C45, CompLI, E01, IndVet, OceAb. *Aud.:* Ac, Sa.

This is the leading and one of the oldest journals in the field of bioinformatics, and is an official publication of the International Society for Computational Biology. Bioinformatics is the collection, processing, and analysis of biological information using computers and computer algorithms. The subject matter can include genetic or genomic information, systems biology data, text mining, databases, and even bio-image informatics. Much of the information and data generated today in biotechnology is on a large scale, making manipulation by computers essential. While bioinformatics started out as a combination of biology and computer science, it has evolved into a scientific discipline in its own right. The journal publishes both original research and review articles about new developments in the field. Two sections within the journal, "Discovery Notes" and "Application Notes," publish shorter papers—respectively, one describes "biologically interesting discoveries made using computational techniques," and the other describes novel software, databases, or applications. Like other Oxford journals, this journal is also available in a mobile version that works for institutional as well as personal subscriptions.

Biomaterials. See Engineering and Technology/Biomedical Engineering section.

840. Biosensors and Bioelectronics. Formerly (until 1989): *Biosensors.* [ISSN: 0956-5663] 1985. 12x/yr. EUR 2726. Ed(s): Anthony P F Turner. Elsevier BV, Radarweg 29, PO Box 211, Amsterdam, 1000 AE, Netherlands; JournalsCustomerServiceEMEA@elsevier.com; http://www.elsevier.nl. Illus., adv. Refereed. *Indexed:* A01, A22, Agr, C&ISA, C45, CerAb, EngInd, ExcerpMed, IndVet. *Bk. rev.:* Occasional. *Aud.:* Ac, Sa.

This is a journal that covers an emerging interdisciplinary field. In general, bioelectronics integrates biological molecules with electronics to make functional devices. Some of those devices are biosensors, which are analytic or detection devices that couple biological or biologically-derived material with a transducer to transmit a digital electronic signal to indicate the presence of a specific substance. Biosensors and bioelectronics have been applied to problems in medicine, pharmaceuticals, the environment, food processing, or security. This journal publishes primarily original, peer-reviewed research articles as full papers or short communications. Often there is one review article per issue or even, occasionally, book reviews. Some issues have contained special topic sections or groups of papers from a conference. This journal would be of interest to research scientists.

841. Biotechnology Advances: research reviews. [ISSN: 0734-9750] 1983. 6x/yr. EUR 2298. Ed(s): M Moo-Young. Elsevier Inc., 360 Park Ave S, New York, NY 10010; usinfo-f@elsevier.com; http://www.elsevier.com. Adv. Sample. Refereed. Microform: PQC. *Indexed:* A01, A22, Agr, C&ISA, C45, CerAb, EngInd, IndVet. *Bk. rev.:* Occasional. *Aud.:* Ac, Sa.

This is a journal devoted to publishing reviews of important advances in all areas of biotechnology and would be of interest to students or researchers in industry, government, and academia. Each issue contains research review papers on such topics as tissue engineering, chemical engineering, food and agricultural technologies, bioremediation, environmental technologies, drug discovery, and genetic technologies. Special issues contain selected relevant conference presentations. Recent issues have focused on a theme such as biomedical innovation or biorefining.

842. Biotechnology and Bioengineering. Formerly (until 1962): *Journal of Biochemical and Microbiological Technology and Engineering.* [ISSN: 0006-3592] 1958. 18x/yr. GBP 5353. Ed(s): Douglas S Clark. John Wiley & Sons, Inc., 111 River St, MS 4-02, Hoboken, NJ 07030; info@wiley.com; http://www.wiley.com/WileyCDA/. Illus., index, adv. Refereed. Microform: PQC. Reprint: PSC. *Indexed:* A22, Agr, C&ISA, C45, CEA, CerAb, EngInd, ExcerpMed, FS&TA, IndVet, P02, S25. *Aud.:* Ac, Sa.

This journal covers every area of biotechnology: environmental, food, plant, pharmaceutical, medical, and industrial. Articles on topics such as tissue engineering, stem cells, biofuels, protein engineering, biosensors, bioinformatics, and bioremediation, all covered by many more narrowly focused journals mentioned in this section, are accepted, although the content of recent issues suggests that articles tend toward the bioprocess engineering, environmental biotechnology, and metabolic engineering side, rather than toward tissue or cell engineering. The first part of each issue is a "Spotlights" section highlighting the more noteworthy articles of that issue with a teaser paragraph. "Communications to the Editor" are shorter research papers found at the end of each issue. Issues may also contain perspectives or review articles. The journal covers only the scientific advancements in biotechnology and not the business, legal, or other sides of the field, and so is of interest primarily to scientists or engineers.

843. Briefings in Bioinformatics. [ISSN: 1467-5463] 2000. bi-m. EUR 772. Ed(s): Martin Bishop. Oxford University Press, Great Clarendon St, Oxford, OX2 6DP, United Kingdom; enquiry@oup.co.uk; http://www.oxfordjournals.org/. Adv. Sample. Refereed. Reprint: PSC. *Indexed:* A01, A22, B01, C45, E01, P02. *Bk. rev.:* Number and length vary. *Aud.:* Ac, Sa.

This is a review and case studies journal in the field of bioinformatics, in which biological information is processed and analyzed using computer algorithms. Most bioinformatics journals only contain original research articles of use to researchers in the bioinformatics field who know biology as well as computer science and who are developing new tools and programs. This journal claims to be unique in providing practical help and advice for the non-bioinformatics specialist who may be using or teaching the tools or databases but does not develop them. Articles can even be on such topics as bioinformatics education. There are occasional special issues on one topic, such as RNA analysis or plant genomics. The journal also contains some book and software/database reviews. Like other Oxford journals, this journal is also available in a mobile version that works for institutional as well as personal subscriptions.

844. *Current Opinion in Biotechnology.* [ISSN: 0958-1669] 1990. bi-m. EUR 2824. Ed(s): Jan van der Meer, Greg Stephanopoulos. Elsevier Ltd., Current Opinion Journals, The Blvd, Langford Ln, Kidlington, OX5 1GB, United Kingdom; JournalsCustomerServiceEMEA@elsevier.com; http://www.current-opinion.com. Illus., adv. Sample. Refereed. Vol. ends: No. 12. *Indexed:* A01, A22, AbAn, C45, E01, EngInd, ExcerpMed, IndVet, RRTA, S25. *Aud.:* Ac, Sa.

The *Current Opinion* series of journals is geared toward helping researchers keep up with the large amount of information published in their fields by providing authoritative, expert opinion on recent advances and annotations of select recently-published original papers. *Current Opinion in Biotechnology* covers all areas of biotechnology by dividing the subject into 11 topics, each of which is covered once a year. Each of the six issues per year reviews one or two of these topics, and an expert section editor is assigned to each: analytical biotechnology, plant biotechnology, food biotechnology, energy biotechnology, environmental biotechnology, systems biology, protein technologies and commercial enzymes, biochemical engineering, tissue and cell engineering, chemical biotechnology, and pharmaceutical biotechnology. The journal is geared toward scientists and focuses on scientific advances rather than on business or regulatory issues. It would also be excellent to use in the classroom to introduce advanced students to important topics.

845. *Drug Discovery Today.* Incorporates (in Dec.2004): *Drug Discovery Today. Targets;* Which was formerly (2002-Feb.2004): *Targets;* Incorporates (in Nov.2004): *Drug Discovery Today. Biosilico;* Which was formerly (2003-Mar.2004): *Biosilico.* [ISSN: 1359-6446] 1996. 24x/yr. EUR 4026. Ed(s): Steve L Carney. Elsevier Ltd., Trends Journals, 32 Jamestown Rd, London, NW1 7BY, United Kingdom; JournalsCustomerServiceEMEA@elsevier.com; http://www.elsevier.com. Sample. Refereed. Circ: 10790. *Indexed:* A01, A22, AbAn, C&ISA, CerAb, ExcerpMed. *Aud.:* Ac, Sa.

Similar to Elsevier's *Trends* series, this journal publishes reviews for scientists to help them maintain currency in their research area. The short front section contains editorials on current topics and perspectives pieces. The majority of the journal is the "Reviews" section, with both keynote and short reviews, focused on scientific discoveries and divided into sections such as "Gene to Screen," "Informatics," and "Postscreen." A final "Monitor" section highlights recent developments in medicinal chemistry. The associated *Drug Discovery Today* reviews collection contains four online-only themed review journals published quarterly. These are *Drug Discovery Today: Disease Models*; *Drug Discovery Today: Disease Mechanisms*; *Drug Discovery Today: Technologies*; and *Drug Discovery Today: Therapeutic Strategies.* Besides the scholarly journals, *Drug Discovery Today* is also available as a "digital magazine" at the web site http://drugdiscovery.com. The peer-reviewed digital magazine functions as a portal, and it features news and analysis, industry news, podcasts, educational webinars (in collaboration with experts from industry), and some highlighted research reviews from the *Drug Discovery Today* journals; it is also free to readers who work at organizations that meet qualifying criteria. The majority of review content from the *Drug Discovery Today* journals is not, however, free on this web site, and readers are pointed back to Elsevier's Science Direct platform for those. Geared toward both a research and industry audience.

846. *Gene Therapy.* [ISSN: 0969-7128] 1994. m. JPY 469400 EUR 2747 in Europe. Ed(s): Nick Lemoine, Joseph Glorioso. Nature Publishing Group, The MacMillan Bldg, 4 Crinan St, London, N1 9XW, United Kingdom; nature@nature.com; http://www.nature.com. Illus., adv. Sample. Refereed. *Indexed:* A01, A22, AbAn, C45, E01, ExcerpMed, IndVet. *Aud.:* Ac, Sa.

Gene Therapy is devoted to peer-reviewed papers on both the basic research and clinical applications of gene therapy, which involves the correction of diseases by replacing abnormal or faulty genes with normal ones. According to the journal's web site, an increasing number of gene therapy protocols are now entering the clinical trial stage. The bulk of the journal is research articles, but each issue might also contain an editorial and one or two reviews. Occasional special issues contain several review articles on one particular topic such as "gene therapy for chronic pain." An "Enabling Technology" section is for papers that describe new techniques. New articles are published weekly in the online version of this journal, and are later published in the archived print version. Of interest to scientific researchers and clinicians in this area.

847. *Genome Biology (Online).* Formerly (until 2001): *GenomeBiology.com (Online).* [ISSN: 1474-760X] 2000. bi-m. Ed(s): Clare Garvey. BioMed Central Ltd., Fl 6, 236 Gray's Inn Rd, London, WC1X 8HB, United Kingdom; info@biomedcentral.com; http://www.biomedcentral.com. Adv. Sample. Refereed. *Indexed:* ExcerpMed. *Aud.:* Ac, Sa.

BioMed Central (BMC) publishes this hybrid, online-only journal that incorporates open-access as well as subscription-based material. Each issue contains a section of commentary, reviews, and meeting reports. This part of the journal requires a subscription to access. All of the peer-reviewed original research articles are open access, however. These articles can be hypothesis-driven research articles or articles reporting methods or software research. The scope of the subject matter is genomic, proteomic, and computational research, as well as all areas of biology informed by these. The goal of the journal is to be a forum for publication of new research and for discussion and critical review of new developments in technologies and in the field. Publication of large datasets that are not necessarily accepted at other more traditional journals is encouraged. Because the journal is online-only, articles in *Genome Biology* are published as soon as they are available and are later compiled into a complete "issue" of the journal. Occasional supplemental issues on one particular topic are also published as open access.

Genome Research. See Biology/Genetics section.

848. *Genomics.* [ISSN: 0888-7543] 1987. m. EUR 1910. Ed(s): J Quackenbush. Academic Press, 3251 Riverport Ln, Maryland Heights, MO 63043; JournalCustomerService-usa@elsevier.com; http://www.elsevierdirect.com/brochures/academicpress/index.html. Adv. Refereed. *Indexed:* A01, A22, AbAn, Agr, C45, E01, ExcerpMed, IndVet. *Aud.:* Ac, Sa.

Focusing on the genome sciences and the technologies used to study genomes, this journal has both a basic science and an applied biotechnology bent. It is primarily a forum for the publication of original, peer-reviewed research in such areas as comparative or functional genomics, proteomics, bioinformatics, computational biology, and other genome technologies. Each issue usually also contains one or more articles that focus on methods and may also contain reviews. Of interest to scientific researchers.

849. *Human Gene Therapy.* [ISSN: 1043-0342] 1990. 18x/yr. USD 8237. Ed(s): James M Wilson. Mary Ann Liebert, Inc. Publishers, 140 Huguenot St, 3rd Fl, New Rochelle, NY 10801; info@liebertpub.com; http://www.liebertpub.com. Adv. Sample. Refereed. Vol. ends: Dec. Reprint: PSC. *Indexed:* A01, A22, E01, ExcerpMed. *Aud.:* Ac, Sa.

Like two other journals listed in this section, *Molecular Therapy* and *Gene Therapy,* this journal also publishes peer-reviewed scientific papers on all aspects of gene therapy, which involves the correction of diseases by replacing abnormal genes with normal ones. All stages of gene therapy research are covered, from laboratory investigations to clinical trials. It is the official journal of the European Society of Gene and Cell Therapy, as well as of several individual European countries' gene therapy societies. Besides the research articles, there are reviews, editorials, and commentaries. An interesting policy demonstrating the fast-moving nature of this field and demand from researchers for the latest information is the journal's "Instant Online" publishing of all manuscripts in unedited format within 72 hours of peer review and acceptance. Later copy editing and proofreading will yield a final archived version of the paper. In 2012, the journal expanded into two parts. The new "Human Gene Therapy Methods" is bimonthly and focuses on technological advances that promote the translation of research into therapeutic products. Of interest to scientific researchers or clinicians in this area.

850. *Journal of Biotechnology.* [ISSN: 0168-1656] 1984. 24x/yr. EUR 5275. Ed(s): A Puehler. Elsevier BV, Radarweg 29, PO Box 211, Amsterdam, 1000 AE, Netherlands; JournalsCustomerServiceEMEA@elsevier.com; http://www.elsevier.nl. Adv. Refereed. Microform: PQC. *Indexed:* A01, A22, Agr, C&ISA, C45, CerAb, EngInd, ExcerpMed, FS&TA, IndVet. *Aud.:* Ac, Sa.

This multidisciplinary journal is divided into sections covering all aspects of biotechnology: biochemical, biomedical, food, plant, agricultural, genomic, molecular biology, and bioprocess engineering. It provides for rapid publication of peer-reviewed research articles, both long and short. It particularly seeks to publish interdisciplinary articles that are not suitable for publication in a journal for a more specific discipline. The focus is on primary research articles rather than reviews or other types of articles. Of interest to researchers in many areas of biotechnology.

851. *Metabolic Engineering.* [ISSN: 1096-7176] 1998. 6x/yr. EUR 796. Ed(s): G N Stephanopoulos. Academic Press, 525 B St, Ste 1900, San Diego, CA 92101-4495; JournalCustomerService-usa@elsevier.com; http://www.elsevierdirect.com/brochures/academicpress/index.html. Adv. Refereed. *Indexed:* A01, A22, E01, EngInd, ExcerpMed, FS&TA. *Aud.:* Ac, Sa.

Metabolic engineering involves the alteration or manipulation of the metabolic pathways of organisms (often by genetic engineering) for commercial objectives, to produce chemicals or fuels for environmental, agricultural, or medical purposes. The research in this area is interdisciplinary, drawing on ideas and techniques from molecular biology, physiology, and biochemistry as well as engineering, bioinformatics, and computational biology. This journal is devoted to publishing only original peer-reviewed research and would be useful for research scientists.

852. *Molecular Therapy.* [ISSN: 1525-0016] 2000. m. EUR 1877 in Europe; USD 2181 in the Americas; JPY 321000 Japan. Ed(s): Dr. Malcolm K Brenner, Robert M Frederickson. Nature Publishing Group, The MacMillan Bldg, 4 Crinan St, London, N1 9XW, United Kingdom; nature@nature.com; http://www.nature.com. Adv. Sample. Refereed. *Indexed:* A01, A22, E01, ExcerpMed. *Aud.:* Ac, Sa.

The official publication of the American Society for Gene and Cell Therapy, this top journal has an international scope and publishes original, peer-reviewed papers on all aspects of gene, peptide, protein, oligonucleotide, and cell-based therapeutics research for human disease. These primary research articles can report basic or preclinical studies, translational research, or the results of clinical research. Besides these papers, each issue may also contain one or two review articles, commentaries, or a meeting report. In 2012, a brand-new, online-only, open-access companion journal, *Molecular Therapy: Nucleic Acids,* began to publish the same types of articles more specifically for a targeted audience of nucleic acids therapeutics researchers. Both journals would be of interest to scientists or clinicians working in this field.

853. *Nanomedicine.* [ISSN: 1743-5889] 2006. m. Future Medicine Ltd., Unitec House, 2 Albert Pl, London, N3 1QB, United Kingdom; info@futuremedicine.com; http://www.futuremedicine.com/. Adv. Sample. Refereed. *Indexed:* ExcerpMed. *Aud.:* Ac, Sa.

Covering medicine's "emerging scientific specialty born from nanotechnology, which has grown up in the fields of engineering, physics, chemistry, and biotechnology," this journal notes to authors that nanomedicine is still in its infancy, and it aims to be a tool to shape this exciting field. Nanomedicine offers new opportunities for novel approaches to the prevention and cure of diseases. The journal covers original research; pre-clinical testing; therapeutic applications; ethical, legal, and regulatory issues; and commercialization of nanomedical technology. Each issue might contain editorials, news, interviews, reviews, or research articles. Most of the editorials and news articles are freely available. Of interest to academic, industrial, and clinical researchers as well as those interested in legal and regulatory matters.

854. *Nature Biotechnology.* Formerly (until 1996): *Bio-Technology.* [ISSN: 1087-0156] 1983. m. EUR 3936 in Europe Academic institutions (Corporations, EUR 4912). Ed(s): Andrew Marshall. Nature Publishing Group, 75 Varick St, 9th Fl, New York, NY 10013; nature@natureny.com; http://www.nature.com. Illus., adv. Sample. Refereed. Microform: PQC. *Indexed:* A01, A22, Agr, BRI, C45, EngInd, ExcerpMed, FS&TA, IndVet. *Aud.:* Ga, Ac, Sa.

If a librarian wanted to buy only one journal in the field of biotechnology, this should be it, because it has something for everyone. This journal has one of the highest impact factors among biotechnology journals ranked by Thomson Scientific. The scope of the journal includes all of biotechnology from the agricultural and environmental to the biomedical. The latter part of the journal is devoted to peer-reviewed research papers, both short and long, on new developments in these areas. The beginning section of the journal is devoted to news from the business and research communities, and essays, comments, and articles covering the current political, ethical, legal, and societal issues surrounding biotechnology and new products. Regular columns include the "Bioentrepreneur" (with advice on building a business), profiles of people who have had an impact on some aspect of the field, a section with advice for those seeking patents with lists of recent patent applications, and a careers section. Another regular section covers the latest in computational biology. A "People" section at the end announces new appointments or retirements of CEOs and other important leaders at various biotechnology companies. The online version of the journal is designed as a web portal, containing the same sections as the printed version but organized differently, with highlighted articles and links to more resources. For instance, the "Bioentrepreneur" section of the portal links into the "Nature jobs" site with job listings and career advice from Nature Publishing's network of online resources. The web portal also advertises upcoming conferences and events and has a regularly updated blog called "Trade Secrets." The idea is that the site will act as a place for bench research scientists to interact with people on the commercial side of biotechnology. Some of the site's content is free, while content from the *Nature Biotechnology* journal is only available to subscribers. While the research articles and some other sections will be of most use to scientific academic and special libraries, the essays and news sections of both the printed journal and online web portal will be valuable to both business and public libraries.

855. *Nature Reviews. Drug Discovery.* [ISSN: 1474-1776] 2002. m. EUR 3936 in Europe academic institutions (Corporations, EUR 5654). Ed(s): Peter Kirkpatrick. Nature Publishing Group, The MacMillan Bldg, 4 Crinan St, London, N1 9XW, United Kingdom; NatureReviews@nature.com; http://www.nature.com. Adv. Sample. Refereed. *Indexed:* A01, A22, ExcerpMed. *Aud.:* Ga, Ac, Sa.

This journal is part of the *Nature Reviews* series of journals that are geared toward keeping researchers informed and up-to-date. There are four main sections. "Research Highlights" provides short updates on recently published research papers. The online version of the journal may contain more of these than the print version, because highlights are added continuously to the online journal. The larger "Reviews" section contains commissioned review articles by leading researchers in their field, and these have some added features. Specialized hyperlinked words in this section are explained in a glossary, and some of the references are annotated. There is usually one article published in each issue for the "Perspectives" section, which covers broader issues: opinions, implications of science on society, new developments, future directions, and business outlooks. At the beginning of each issue is a section for "News and Analysis," which contains current stories on the scientific or business aspects of drug discovery, and information on patents and the latest drugs. Interviews with key people might also be included. While not as much of a portal as *Nature Biotechnology,* there are links from the homepage of this journal to notice boards, conferences, and "Nature jobs." The journal is geared toward scientists in the field but also to non-scientists working in the pharmaceutical industry.

856. *Pharmacogenetics and Genomics.* Formerly (until 2005): *Pharmacogenetics.* [ISSN: 1744-6872] 1991. m. USD 2226 (print & online eds.). Ed(s): M J Ratain, M Schwab. Lippincott Williams & Wilkins, 530 Walnut St, Philadelphia, PA 19106; customerservice@lww.com; http://www.lww.com. Index, adv. Refereed. Circ: 137. *Indexed:* A01, A22, C45, E01, ExcerpMed, IndVet. *Aud.:* Ac, Sa.

This journal falls into the "drug discovery" group of biotechnology journals. Pharmacogenetics (or pharmacogenomics) is the study of how genetics affects people's and animals' responses to drugs. The ultimate goal is to use these genetic insights to improve drug delivery and therapy by tailoring drugs to individuals. This journal publishes primarily original research articles and short communications in this subject area, but also occasional mini-reviews. The journal is not very large—some recent issues contained less than seven articles. However, a comparatively high impact factor among journals on this subject indicates that at least some of these articles are being cited frequently. Only of interest to scientific researchers.

857. *Pharmacogenomics.* [ISSN: 1462-2416] 2000. m. Future Medicine Ltd., Unitec House, 2 Albert Pl, London, N3 1QB, United Kingdom; info@futuremedicine.com; http://www.futuremedicine.com/. Illus., adv. Sample. Refereed. *Indexed:* AbAn, ExcerpMed. *Aud.:* Ac, Sa.

The terms pharmacogenomics and pharmacogenetics are often used interchangeably to describe the study of genes that influence response to drugs and ways to use this knowledge to develop drugs tailored to individuals' genetic variations. This flagship journal of the publisher Future Medicine aims to comment on and analyze new developments in the field, publishing reports, review articles, company profiles, news, opinions, perspectives, editorials, and technology reports. Areas covered include emerging technologies for the use of genetic information for therapy or diagnosis, review of clinical data, and the impact of new initiatives. This journal is geared toward research scientists as well as non-scientists involved or interested in the pharmaceutical industry or clinical community. Authors are asked to keep this multidisciplinary audience in mind.

858. Plant Biotechnology Journal. [ISSN: 1467-7644] 2003. 9x/yr. Ed(s): Keith J Edwards. Wiley-Blackwell Publishing Ltd., 9600 Garsington Rd, Oxford, OX4 2DQ, United Kingdom; customerservices@blackwellpublishing.com; http://www.wiley.com/. Adv. Sample. Reprint: PSC. *Indexed:* A01, A22, Agr, C45, E01, IndVet. *Aud.:* Ac, Sa.

This journal is published in association with two societies, the Society for Experimental Biology and the Association of Applied Biologists. It publishes molecular plant sciences with a strong focus on application. Practical applications of plant studies can be found in such wide-ranging fields as agriculture, biodiversity, biomaterials, bioremediation, conservation, food sciences, forestry, pharmaceuticals, and medicine. A large number of the articles are devoted to genomics, functional genomics, and transgenic technologies. There are primary, peer-reviewed research articles, reviews, and special issues devoted to a single topic such as biofuels. Of interest to researchers in the field.

859. Protein Engineering Design and Selection (Online). Formerly (until 2004): *Protein Engineering (Online).* [ISSN: 1741-0134] 199?. bi-m. EUR 1386. Ed(s): Alan Fersht, Valerie Daggett. Oxford University Press, Great Clarendon St, Oxford, OX2 6DP, United Kingdom; enquiry@oup.co.uk; http://www.oxfordjournals.org. Refereed. *Aud.:* Ac, Sa.

Also called *PEDS,* this official journal of the Antibody Society "publishes research papers and review articles relevant to the engineering, design[,] and selection of proteins for use in biotechnology and therapy, and for understanding fundamental properties of activity, stability, folding, misfolding and disease." Original research articles appear to be the main focus. The journal claims to be a "community-based journal for protein scientists," promising that peer review will be done by other scientists working in areas very similar to that of the article being considered. No other non-traditional elements of this journal make it any more of a community than other scientific journals, and a blog that had been included on the web site years ago has since been abandoned. Of interest to researchers in the field.

Scientific American. See Science and Technology/General section.

860. Stem Cells and Development. Former titles (until 2004): *Journal of Hematotherapy & Stem Cell Research;* (until 1999): *Journal of Hematotherapy.* [ISSN: 1547-3287] 1992. 24x/yr. USD 2712. Ed(s): Graham C Parker. Mary Ann Liebert, Inc. Publishers, 140 Huguenot St, 3rd Fl, New Rochelle, NY 10801; info@liebertpub.com; http://www.liebertpub.com. Adv. Sample. Refereed. Reprint: PSC. *Indexed:* A01, A22, E01, ExcerpMed. *Aud.:* Ac, Sa.

This journal is primarily a forum for the publication of original, peer-reviewed research articles on human or animal stem cell research and its potential therapeutic applications. Besides the original research, which takes up most of each issue, there are occasionally other types of articles: comprehensive or concise reviews, letters to the editor, editorials, and even "Cutting Edge Communications" that warranted accelerated publication. Like other Mary Ann Liebert journals, "Instant Online" access is provided to peer-reviewed articles 72 hours after their acceptance for publication and before final copy editing. This journal would be of interest to research scientists in the field.

861. Stem Cells (Durham): the international journal of cell differentiation and proliferation. Formerly (until 1993): *International Journal of Cell Cloning.* [ISSN: 1066-5099] 1983. m. GBP 445. Ed(s): Martin J Murphy, Ann Murphy. AlphaMed Press, Inc., 318 Blackwell St, Ste 260, Durham, NC 27701; http://www.alphamedpress.org/. Adv. Refereed. Circ: 950. Reprint: PSC. *Indexed:* A22, ExcerpMed. *Aud.:* Ac, Sa.

Stem Cells is one of the leading and oldest journals in this specialty subject area and one of only three journals published by AlphaMed Press. It is co-published by Wiley-Blackwell and available on both platforms. The journal covers all aspects of stem cell research from basic laboratory investigations to the translation of findings to clinical care. Embryonic stem cells, adult tissue-specific stem cells, cancer stem cells, regenerative medicine, the stem cell niche, technology development, proteomics, and genomics of stem cells and translational and clinical research are the separate subsections of many issues. Most of the articles are original research reports, but there are occasional concise reviews of topics in any of these sections. A brand-new companion journal was launched in 2012 called "Stem Cells Translational Medicine," which publishes on clinical and translational topics in original research articles, commentary, and case studies. This journal also includes more protocols, policies, and standards for stem cell therapies. A "Stem Cells Portal" provides a separate way to access the original journal along with some other resources. News articles, headlines, featured resources, and articles that feature laboratories are included, and, presumably, the new companion journal will eventually be linked from the portal as well. Like some other portals discussed in this section, this was meant to be an interactive forum and a Facebook-like virtual meeting space; however, the functionality for that part of the site is not ideal, attracts spammers, and has yet to become successful. A good web portal requires more and different investment of writers and time than a traditional scientific journal.

862. Tissue Engineering. Parts A, B and C. Supersedes in part (in 2008): *Tissue Engineering.* [ISSN: 2152-4947] 1995. s-m. Part A & B - semi-monthly; Part C - monthly. USD 5885. Ed(s): Peter C Johnson, Antonios G Mikos. Mary Ann Liebert, Inc. Publishers, 140 Huguenot St, 3rd Fl, New Rochelle, NY 10801; info@liebertpub.com; http://www.liebertpub.com. Adv. Sample. Refereed. Reprint: PSC. *Aud.:* Ac, Sa.

This is the official journal of the Tissue Engineering and Regenerative Medicine International Society. The goal of this emerging field is eventually to be able to regenerate tissues or create new tissues and artificial organs using biological cells and biomaterials along with biotechnology techniques. Such current topics of research as nanobiotechnology, gene therapy, and stem cells are included. Much of this is still in the experimental rather than the clinical stage, but the field is growing by leaps and bounds. The journal is now in three parts. Part A is the original monthly journal, publishing peer-reviewed, hypothesis-driven research articles. Part B comes out six times a year and publishes reviews that give a broader and summarized view of the tissue engineering field, new developments, and new areas of research. Special issues cover one theme. Part C is monthly and can be subscribed to with the others or on its own. It publishes methodology-related research articles that address technical and scientific challenges in the development of tissue engineering products. As mentioned above for other Mary Ann Liebert journals, "Instant Online" access is provided to articles from all three parts of the journal within 72 hours of their acceptance for publication and before final copy editing. This demonstrates the demand for information and the fast-moving nature of this field. Research scientists in the field would be interested in all three parts of the journal.

863. Trends in Biotechnology. [ISSN: 0167-7799] 1983. m. EUR 2099. Ed(s): Paige Shaklee. Elsevier Ltd., Trends Journals, The Blvd, Langford Ln, Kidlington, Oxford, OX5 1GB, United Kingdom; JournalsCustomerServiceEMEA@elsevier.com; http://www.elsevier.com. Illus., adv. Sample. Refereed. Circ: 453. Vol. ends: No. 19. *Indexed:* A01, A22, Agr, C&ISA, C45, CerAb, EngInd, ExcerpMed, FS&TA, IndVet, RRTA. *Aud.:* Ac, Sa.

Part of the *Trends* journal series from Elsevier, this journal publishes commissioned, peer-reviewed, review articles by leading researchers. The reviews summarize and discuss recent scientific developments in all areas of biotechnology from agricultural and environmental to biomedical. Other types of articles include the "Opinions" articles that present a personal viewpoint on a research topic rather than a balanced review. "Science and Society" articles for a broader audience are included as options in the instructions for authors, but none of these have appeared recently. This journal is geared primarily to a scientific and academic research audience. Like several other biotechnology journals listed here, this journal is published on two separate platforms. The version on the ScienceDirect platform points users in a traditional way to volumes and issues. The second version is slightly more portal-like, although not really a complete portal as other publishers have developed. This site features "most-read" articles, "featured articles," podcasts, and job and conference announcements. It also points to articles in other journals by the same publisher.

■ BIRDS

See also Environment and Conservation; and Pets sections.

Kathryn Johns-Masten, Assistant Librarian, Penfield Library, SUNY Oswego, Oswego, NY 13126; kathryn.johnsmasten@oswego.edu

Introduction

The titles in this section will appeal to amateur birders, students of ornithology, and professional ornithologists. They encompass a wide range of geographic areas. Some focus on a specific area; others focus on specific types of birds—for example, waterbirds or predators. The titles appropriate for a general audience, or for those new to birding, provide color photographs and articles from ornithologists as well as fellow amateur birders. The professional academic journals contain in-depth articles that include scientific studies and field research.

Web sites provide birders with the ability to interact with each other, submit bird counts, listen to bird songs, and communicate with researchers on current projects. The majority of the electronic journals provide feature articles and multiple links to other sources.

"Birds have wings; they're free; they can fly where they want when they want, they have the kind of mobility people envy."

—Roger Tory Peterson

As the Internet evolves, more journals exhibit behaviors of birds—having both mobility and ability to fly to where they are needed. Therefore, these print and electronic publications were selected based on their appeal to a range of readers, from amateur to professional.

Basic Periodicals

Hs: *Bird Watcher's Digest, BirdWatching, Living Bird, Wildbird;* Ga: *Bird Watcher's Digest, Birding, BirdWatching, Living Bird;* Ac: *British Birds, Emu, Journal of Avian Biology, North American Birds, Wilson Journal of Ornithology.*

Basic Abstracts and Indexes

Biological Abstracts.

864. The Auk: a quarterly journal of ornithology. Supersedes (in 1884): *Nuttall Ornithological Club. Bulletin;* Which was formerly (until 1976): *Nuttall Ornithological Club. Quarterly Bulletin.* [ISSN: 0004-8038] 1884. q. USD 364 (print & online eds.). Ed(s): Mark Penrose, Michael Murphy. University of California Press, Journals Division, 2000 Ctr St, Ste 303, Berkeley, CA 94704; customerservice@ucpressjournals.com; http://www.ucpressjournals.com. Illus., index, adv. Refereed. Circ: 3398. Vol. ends: Oct (No. 4). Microform: IDC; PQC. *Indexed:* A01, A22, AnBeAb, BRI, C45, E01, IndVet, MLA-IB, OceAb, P02, PsycInfo, RRTA. *Bk. rev.:* 10, 500 words. *Aud.:* Ac, Sa.

The Auk has been published for more than 100 years and is a well-regarded journal that publishes original reports on the biology of birds. Research articles contain innovative empirical and theoretical findings. Topics include documentation, analysis, and interpretation of laboratory and field studies, and

theoretical or methodological developments. Commentary, letters, and book reviews provide additional information. Recommended for academic and special libraries that support ornithology, zoology, and ecology.

865. Bird Conservation International. [ISSN: 0959-2709] 1991. q. GBP 292. Ed(s): Phil Atkinson. Cambridge University Press, The Edinburgh Bldg, Shaftesbury Rd, Cambridge, CB2 8RU, United Kingdom; journals@cambridge.org; http://www.cambridge.org/uk. Adv. Sample. Refereed. Circ: 500. Reprint: PSC. *Indexed:* A22, C45, E01, IndVet, RRTA. *Aud.:* Ac, Sa.

The offical journal for BirdLife International with a goal to promote worldwide research and conservation action to ensure the protection of bird life and fragile environments. It publishes original peer-reviewed papers and reviews that deal with all aspects of the conservation of birds and their habitats. In addition, it uses birds to illustrate wider issues of biodiversity, conservation, and sustainable resource use. Recommended for academic and special libraries that support ornithology studies.

866. Bird Study: the science of pure and applied orinthology. Incorporates (in 1963): *Bird Migration;* Which was formerly (1934-1954): *British Trust for Ornithology. Bulletin.* [ISSN: 0006-3657] 1954. 4x/yr. GBP 221 (print & online eds.). Ed(s): Will Cresswell. Taylor & Francis, 4 Park Sq, Milton Park, Abingdon, OX14 4RN, United Kingdom; subscriptions@tandf.co.uk; http://www.tandfonline.com. Illus., index, adv. Refereed. Vol. ends: No. 3. Microform: PQC. Reprint: PSC. *Indexed:* A22, AnBeAb, C45, E01, IndVet, P02. *Bk. rev.:* 1, 50 words. *Aud.:* Ac, Sa.

This journal from the British Trust for Ornithology publishes high-quality original peer-reviewed research papers on all aspects of field ornithology. It especially covers patterns of distribution and abundance, movements, habitat preferences, developing field census methods, and ringing and other techniques for marking and tracking. This journal focuses on birds in the Western Palearctic, which includes Europe, North Africa, and the Middle East, although papers are accepted from any part of the world. Scientific reviews and critical book reviews are included. Recommended for the professional and for serious students of bird life.

Bird Talk. See Pets section.

867. Bird Watcher's Digest. [ISSN: 0164-3037] 1978. bi-m. USD 19.99; USD 4.99 newsstand/cover in US & Canada. Ed(s): Bill Thompson, III. Pardson, Inc., 149 Acme St, PO Box 110, Marietta, OH 45750; editor@birdwatchersdigest.com. Illus., adv. Vol. ends: Jul/Aug. Microform: PQC. *Bk. rev.:* 8, 50 words. *Aud.:* Hs, Ga.

Bird Watcher's Digest is a popular magazine that offers articles for the amateur birder written by ornithologists. Regular columns cover attracting birds, bird behavior, backyard birdwatching, and helpful hints for new birders. Other regular features include letters from readers, gardening tips, and wonderful color photographs. This magazine covers North American species and birding hotspots in North America and beyond. The field-guide size of this publication makes it convenient to carry outdoors. Recommended for general audiences.

868. Birding. [ISSN: 0161-1836] 1969. bi-m. Free to members. Ed(s): Ted Floyd. American Birding Association, 4945 N 30th St, Ste 200, Colorado Springs, CO 80919; members@aba.org; http://www.aba.org. Illus., index, adv. Refereed. Vol. ends: Dec (No. 6). *Bk. rev.:* 3, 200 words. *Aud.:* Ga, Ac.

This is the magazine of the American Birding Association, with a mission to educate the general public in the appreciation of birds and their relationship to the environment. It focuses on North American and foreign birdfinding, bird conservation, behavior, field identification techniques, and birder education. In addition, it includes reviews of books, media, and equipment. Extra features on the web provide additional information and reading. Recommended for scholars and ornithologists in the field.

869. *BirdWatching*. Formerly (until 2011): *Birder's World.* [ISSN: 2158-3838] 1987. bi-m. USD 36.95 combined subscription domestic (print & online eds.); USD 42.95 combined subscription Canada (print & online eds.); USD 44.95 combined subscription elsewhere (print & online eds.). Madavor Media, Llc., 85 Quincy Ave, Ste 2, Quincy, MA 02169; info@madavor.com; http://www.madavor.com. *Indexed:* A01, BRI. *Bk. rev.:* Number and length vary. *Aud.:* Hs, Ga.

BirdWatching (the new title was adopted recently) is geared toward enthusiasts new to birding as well as experienced birders, and offers readers superb color photography. Feature articles and regular columns cover identification tips, photography pointers, attracting birds, worldwide bird movement, and travel tips for birders. The web site contains a blog called "Field of View," photos of the week; a birding basics section; and surveys. It also provides links to learn about photographers, birding organizations, and resources. Highly recommended for the beginning birder.

870. *British Birds*. [ISSN: 0007-0335] 1907. m. GBP 99 (Individuals, GBP 53). Ed(s): Dr. Roger Riddington. B B 2000 Ltd., 4 Harlequin Gardens, St Leonards on Sea, TN37 7PF, United Kingdom; subscriptions@britishbirds.co.uk. Illus., index, adv. Sample. Refereed. Vol. ends: Dec. *Indexed:* A22, MLA-IB. *Bk. rev.:* 2, 200 words. *Aud.:* Ac.

British Birds is considered by many to be *"the journal of record in Britain,"* and publishes original research from the Western Palearctic, which includes Europe, North Africa, and the Middle East. Emphasis is given to areas of behavior, conservation, distribution, ecology, identification, movement, status, and taxonomy. Regular features include book reviews, news and comments, recent reports of rarities, and information on equipment and travel for birders. In addition, it publishes annual reports of the Rarities Committee and the Rare Breeding Birds Panel. Contributors include professionals and knowledgeable amateurs, and articles are written for all levels of birdwatcher.

871. *The Condor: an international journal of avian biology*. Formerly (until 1900): *Cooper Ornithological Club. Bulletin.* [ISSN: 0010-5422] 1899. q. USD 288 (print & online eds.). Ed(s): Philip Unitt, Michael Patten. University of California Press, Journals Division, 2000 Ctr St, Ste 303, Berkeley, CA 94704; customerservice@ucpressjournals.com; http://www.ucpressjournals.com. Illus., index, adv. Refereed. Circ: 1712. Vol. ends: Nov. Microform: PQC. *Indexed:* A01, A22, AnBeAb, BRI, C45, E01, IndVet, OceAb, P02, PsycInfo, RRTA. *Bk. rev.:* 1, 2,000 words. *Aud.:* Ac, Sa.

The Condor is an international journal that includes original research reports and review articles that focus on the biology of wild species of birds. Research reports contain substantial references, and many include detailed discussions of fieldwork and habitat. Other features include book reviews, news, and society announcements. Tables of contents and abstracts for issues from February 2001 to the present can be found on the Cooper Ornithological Society's web site. Recommended for institutions that support advanced ornithological research.

872. *Emu: austral ornithology*. [ISSN: 0158-4197] 1901. q. USD 558 combined subscription (print & online eds.); EUR 460 combined subscription (print & online eds.); GBP 320 combined subscription (print & online eds.). Ed(s): Kate Buchanan. C S I R O Publishing, 150 Oxford St, PO Box 1139, Collingwood, VIC 3066, Australia; publishing@csiro.au; http://www.publish.csiro.au/home.htm. Illus., index, adv. Sample. Refereed. Vol. ends: Dec. *Indexed:* A01, A22, Agr, AnBeAb, C45, E01, IndVet. *Bk. rev.:* 2, 1,000 words. *Aud.:* Ac, Sa.

Emu publishes original papers and reviews in all areas of ornithology, and is considered the premier journal for ornithological research in the Southern Hemisphere and adjacent tropics. While scholarly articles are the main feature, book reviews are also included. Topics range from effects of climate change on birds to DNA analysis. Students and researchers interested in the biology and management of birds will find it useful. The variety of species covered by this geographic area makes it a recommended title for research libraries that serve ornithologists.

873. *Ibis: the international journal of avian science*. [ISSN: 0019-1019] 1859. q. GBP 438. Ed(s): Paul F Donald. Wiley-Blackwell Publishing Ltd., The Atrium, Southern Gate, Chichester, PO19 8SQ, United Kingdom; customer@wiley.com; http://www.wiley.com/. Illus., index, adv. Sample. Refereed. Vol. ends: Oct. Reprint: PSC. *Indexed:* A22, Agr, AnBeAb, C45, E01, IndVet, MLA-IB, OceAb, P02, RRTA. *Bk. rev.:* 25, 300 words. *Aud.:* Ac, Sa.

The British Ornithologists' Union encourages active research and the publication of that research in its peer-reviewed journal. *Ibis* publishes original papers, reviews, and short communications on the cutting edge of ornithology, with an emphasis on conservation, ecology, ethology, taxonomy, and systematics of birds. Union conference proceedings are occasionally published as supplements to *Ibis.* Recommended for research and academic libraries that support ornithological research.

874. *Journal of Avian Biology*. Formerly (until 1994): *Ornis Scandinavica.* [ISSN: 0908-8857] 1970. bi-m. GBP 273. Ed(s): Thomas Alerstam, Jan-Ake Nilsson. Wiley-Blackwell Publishing, Inc., Commerce Pl, 350 Main St, Malden, MA 02148; info@wiley.com; http://onlinelibrary.wiley.com/. Adv. Refereed. Reprint: PSC. *Indexed:* A01, A22, Agr, AnBeAb, C45, E01, IndVet. *Aud.:* Ac, Sa.

The *Journal of Avian Biology* publishes empirical and theoretical research in all areas of ornithology, with an emphasis on ecology, behavior, and evolutionary biology. In addition to peer-reviewed research articles, the journal publishes short commentaries and communications, short point-of-view articles, and a forum for communication and comments. Topics include habitiat, conservation, distribution, migration, ecology, and behavior of birds. Recommended for academic and research libraries that support ornithological research.

875. *Journal of Field Ornithology*. Former titles (until 1980): *Bird-Banding;* (until 1930): *Northeastern Bird-Banding Association. Bulletin.* [ISSN: 0273-8570] 1930. q. GBP 241. Ed(s): Gary Ritchison. Wiley-Blackwell Publishing, Inc., 111 River St, Hoboken, NJ 07030; info@wiley.com; http://onlinelibrary.wiley.com/. Illus., index, adv. Sample. Refereed. Vol. ends: No. 4. Microform: PQC. Reprint: PSC. *Indexed:* A22, Agr, AnBeAb, C45, E01, IndVet. *Bk. rev.:* 4, 200 words. *Aud.:* Ac, Sa.

This journal of the Association of Field Ornithologists publishes original articles with a focus on the descriptive or experimental study of birds in their natural habitats. Bird banding, conservation, habitat, and fieldwork are emphasized. Technology used to perform or aid in the study of birds is discussed in detail, such as solar-powered transmitters and audio-video systems. Studies that involve participation by amateur ornithologists in research are encouraged. The association emphasizes conservation biology of birds. Recommended for academic and research collections.

876. *Journal of Ornithology*. Formerly (until 2004): *Journal fuer Ornithologie;* Which incorporated (1851-1858): *Naumannia.* [ISSN: 2193-7192] 1853. q. EUR 720 (print & online eds.). Ed(s): Franz Bairlein. Springer, Tiergartenstr 17, Heidelberg, 69121, Germany; orders-hd-individuals@springer.com; http://www.springer.com. Illus., adv. Refereed. Microform: IDC. Reprint: PSC. *Indexed:* A01, A22, Agr, C45, E01, IndVet, MLA-IB. *Aud.:* Ac, Sa.

The *Journal of Ornithology* has been published for over 150 years. It contains original papers, reviews, short notes, technical notes, and commentaries that cover all aspects of ornithology. The editorial board consists of subject editors from around the world and is international. Topics include behavior, ecology, environment, and conservation of birds. Recommended for institutions that support advanced ornithological research.

877. *The Journal of Raptor Research*. Former titles (until 1987): *Raptor Research;* (until 1972): *Raptor Research News.* [ISSN: 0892-1016] 1967. q. Free to members. Ed(s): Cheryl Dykstra. Raptor Research Foundation, Inc., O S N A, 5400 Bosque Blvd, Ste 680, Waco, TX 76710; business@osnabirds.org; http://raptorresearchfoundation.org/. Illus., index, adv. Sample. Refereed. Vol. ends: No. 4. *Indexed:* A22, AnBeAb, C45, IndVet, RRTA. *Bk. rev.:* 3, 800 words. *Aud.:* Ac, Sa.

The *Journal of Raptor Research* is an international scientific journal that publishes original peer-reviewed research reports and review articles focused on all aspects of predatory birds throughout the world. Features include book reviews, letters, short communications, and articles with extensive references.

Research includes raptor ecology, behavior, life history, and conservation. Raptor Research Foundation membership includes the newsletter *Wingspan*. Recommended for academic and research libraries.

878. *Living Bird.* Former titles (until 1991): *Living Bird Quarterly;* (until 1982): *Living Bird.* [ISSN: 1059-521X] 1962. q. Free to members. Ed(s): Tim Gallagher. Cornell University, Laboratory of Ornithology, 159 Sapsucker Woods Rd, Ithaca, NY 14850; cornellbirds@cornell.edu; http://www.birds.cornell.edu/. Illus., index, adv. *Indexed:* A22. *Aud.:* Hs, Ga, Ac.

Living Bird is published by the Cornell Laboratory of Ornithology and contains articles on all aspects of bird life, including biology, behavior, and environmental concerns. It reviews current research and activities related to ornithology, and includes birders' guides to various countries and travel adventures. The journal contains high-quality color photos, articles from experts in birding and ornithology, reviews of the latest books, binoculars, and equipment. The web site provides a multimedia gallery for some articles published in print. Recommended for amateur birders.

879. *The Loon.* Formerly (until 1964): *Flicker.* [ISSN: 0024-645X] 1929. q. Free to members. Minnesota Ornithologists' Union, James Ford Bell Museum of Natural History, University of Minnesota, Minneapolis, MN 55455; mou@moumn.org; http://moumn.org. Illus., index. Vol. ends: Winter. *Bk. rev.:* 1, 200 words. *Aud.:* Ga, Ac.

The Minnesota Ornithologists' Union (MOU) has a goal of promoting conservation and the natural-history study of birds in the Minnesota area. *The Loon* provides articles with extensive references that focus on all aspects of birding. Field studies, observation of birds, a seasonal report on bird migration, and book reviews are included. Although the journal concentrates on birds in the Minnesota area, it is one of the best regional bird journals available.

880. *North American Bird Bander.* Incorporates (1979-1981): *Inland Bird Banding;* Formed by the merger of (1938-1976): *E B B A News;* (1924-1976): *Western Bird Bander.* [ISSN: 0363-8979] 1976. q. Members, USD 25. Western Bird Banding Association, c/o C John Ralph, Redwood Sciences Lab, USFS, Arcata, CA 95521; cjralph@humboldt1.com; http://www.westernbirdbanding.org. Illus., index, adv. Sample. Vol. ends: Oct/Dec. Microform: PQC. *Bk. rev.:* 1, 250 words. *Aud.:* Ac, Sa.

This essential journal for the serious bird bander includes research from the Eastern, Inland, and Western Bird Banding Associations. Bird banding equipment, basics of banding, netting, and trapping are some of the topics covered. This journal also contains reports from banding stations and reports on original research by banders. Recent literature and books on banding, annual reports of the associations, regional news, and notes and comments are included. Recommended for professional ornithologists in the field.

881. *North American Birds.* Former titles (until 1999): *National Audubon Society Field Notes;* (until 1994): *American Birds;* (until 1971): *Audubon Field Notes.* [ISSN: 1525-3708] 1947. q. USD 60 (Members, USD 30; Non-members, USD 32). Ed(s): Ned Brinkley, Edward S Brinkley. American Birding Association, 4945 N 30th St, Ste 200, Colorado Springs, CO 80919; beview@aba.org; http://www.aba.org. Illus., index, adv. Vol. ends: Winter. Microform: PQC. *Indexed:* A22. *Aud.:* Ga, Ac, Sa.

North American Birds, called the "journal of record" for birders, publishes reports that cover all of the continent's bird life, including range extensions and contractions, migration patterns or seasonal occurrences of birds, and population dynamics. Regional reports contained in each issue provide articles that cover migration sightings and the effects of climate and weather patterns on bird movement specific to that region. Articles on outstanding bird records augment the regional reports. Color photos and information on tours are included. Recommended for academic libraries and special libraries that serve ornithologists.

Owl. See Children section.

882. *Pacific Seabirds.* Formerly (until 1994): *Pacific Seabird Group. Bulletin.* [ISSN: 1089-6317] 1974. s-a. Free to members. Ed(s): Vivian M Mendenhall. Pacific Seabird Group, c/o Lindsay Young, Treasurer, PO Box 61493, Honolulu, HI 96839-1493; info@pacificseabirdgroup.org; http://www.pacificseabirdgroup.org. Illus. Sample. Vol. ends: Fall (No. 2). *Bk. rev.:* 2,500 words. *Aud.:* Ac, Sa.

Pacific Seabirds is published by the Pacific Seabird Group to improve communication among Pacific seabird researchers. Topics relating to the conservation of seabirds in the Pacific Ocean and regional seabird research keep members and the general public informed. The journal covers the entire Pacific region (including Russia, Alaska, Canada, Southeast Asia, the west coast of the United States, and all Pacific Islands). It contains technical articles, reports, book reviews, artwork, and abstracts of papers presented at meetings. Recommended for researchers and academic libraries.

883. *Waterbirds: the international journal of waterbird biology.* Former titles (until 1999): *Colonial Waterbirds;* (until 1981): *Colonial Waterbird Group. Proceedings.* [ISSN: 1524-4695] 1977. 3x/yr. USD 50. Ed(s): Robert W Elner. Waterbird Society, 5400 Bosque Blvd, Ste 680, Waco, TX 76710; membership@osnabirds.org; http://www.waterbirds.org. Refereed. *Indexed:* A22, AnBeAb, C45, IndVet, OceAb, RRTA. *Bk. rev.:* Number and length vary. *Aud.:* Ac, Sa.

Waterbirds is an international scientific journal that publishes original research on all types of waterbird species living in marine, estuarine, and freshwater habitats internationally. It has been published by the Waterbird Society for over two decades, to promote and encourage communication about the world's waterbird population. Topics cover conservation, management, biology, and techniques used to study the world's waterbirds. Waterbirds include seabirds, wading birds, shorebirds, and waterfowl. Tables of contents for all issues since 1998 are available on the society's web site. Recommended for researchers and academic libraries.

884. *Western Birds: quarterly journal of Western Field Ornithologists.* Formerly (until 1973): *California Birds.* [ISSN: 0160-1121] 1973. q. Ed(s): Philip Unitt. Western Field Ornithologists, c/o Philip Unitt, San Diego Natural History Museum, PO Box 121390, San Diego, CA 92112; http://www.westernfieldornithologists.org. Illus., index, adv. Sample. Refereed. *Indexed:* A22. *Bk. rev.:* 1, 1,000 words. *Aud.:* Ga, Ac.

A quarterly journal that provides articles for both amateur and professional field ornithologists, while maintaining a high level of quality. This journal includes lengthy articles, reports, and book reviews. It covers topics on identification, conservation, behavior, population dynamics, migration status, geographic variation, effects of pollution, and census techniques. Reports and studies focus on birds from the Rocky Mountain and Pacific states and provinces, including Hawaii and Alaska, western Texas, northwestern Mexico, and the northeastern Pacific Ocean. Recommended for academic libraries and researchers interested in this geographic area.

885. *Wildbird.* [ISSN: 0892-5534] 1987. bi-m. USD 12.99 domestic; USD 18.99 foreign. BowTie, Inc., PO Box 6050, Mission Viejo, CA 92690; http://www.bowtieinc.com. Illus., index, adv. Vol. ends: Dec. *Indexed:* BRI. *Aud.:* Hs, Ga.

Wildbird continues a tradition of educating and entertaining readers. Focusing on North American birds and birding in the Western Hemisphere, it provides readers with information on backyard bird identification, and habitat conservation, and covers feeding and landscaping techniques to attract birds. A feature titled "Birding Hotspots" provides travel locations and tips for birders. Excellent color photographs are included. Highly recommended for a general audience.

886. *The Wilson Journal of Ornithology.* Former titles (until 2006): *The Wilson Bulletin;* (until 1894): *Wilson Ornithological Chapter of the Agassiz Association. Journal;* (until 1893): *Agassiz Association. Wilson Ornithological Chapter. Wilson Quarterly;* (until 1892): *Agassiz Association. Department of the Wilson Chapter. The Semi-annual;* (until 1981): *The Ornithologists' and Oologists' Semi-annual.* [ISSN: 1559-4491] 1889. q. Ed(s): Mary Bomberger Brown. Wilson Ornithological Society, c/o Dale Kennedy, Biology Department, Albion

College, Albion, MI 49224; DKennedy@albion.edu; http://www.wilsonsociety.org/. Illus., index. Refereed. Vol. ends: Dec. Microform: PQC. *Indexed:* A01, A22, AnBeAb, BRI, C45, E01, IndVet, MLA-IB, OceAb, P02. *Bk. rev.:* 3, lengthy. *Aud.:* Ac, Sa.

Since 1889, *The Wilson Journal of Ornithology* has provided scholarly research from around the world on all aspects of ornithology. It is a major journal in the field, containing articles with extensive references, footnotes, charts, maps, and shorter pieces focused on bird behavior. Articles are accessible to both professional and amateur ornithologists. Lengthy book reviews are found in the section titled "Ornithological Literature." Recommended for research libraries that serve ornithologists.

■ BLIND AND VISUALLY IMPAIRED

See also Disabilities section.

Camille McCutcheon, Librarian, Coordinator of Collection Management, University of South Carolina Upstate, 800 University Way, Spartanburg, SC 29303; FAX: 864-503-5601; CMcCutcheon@uscupstate.edu

Introduction

There are many print and electronic periodicals available to address the needs of blind and visually impaired individuals and their support networks. The intended audiences of these publications include individuals with low vision, parents of blind children, teachers and professionals who work with deaf-blind individuals, and blinded veterans of the U.S. Armed Forces. The subject matter of these periodicals varies widely, from poetry or prose submitted by the blind and visually impaired, to improvements in assistive technology, to ways to adjust to vision loss late in life, to tips on day-to-day living with blindness or a visual impairment. Other titles contain reprints and compilations of articles from mainstream newspapers and magazines.

Publishers of the resources featured in this section all have web sites and can be contacted via e-mail. In addition to the electronic journals, there are several other magazine titles that have current and back issues available online. Most of the publications included here are in the large-print format, which is 14-point type or higher. Other available formats for some of these titles include Braille, e-mail, digital text, digital Braille, press Braille, CD, USB flash drive, and podcast.

Basic Periodicals

FOR THE BLIND AND VISUALLY IMPAIRED. *Braille Book Review, Braille Monitor, Dialogue, Guideposts, The New York Times Large Print Weekly, Reader's Digest Large Print, Syndicated Columnists Weekly, Talking Book Topics.*

ABOUT THE BLIND AND VISUALLY IMPAIRED. *Journal of Visual Impairment and Blindness, Review.*

BASIC REFERENCE MATERIALS. *Library of Congress. National Library Service for the Blind and Physically Handicapped.*

ORGANIZATIONS.

American Council of the Blind, 2200 Wilson Boulevard, Suite 650, Arlington, VA 22201, acb.org, info@acb.org.

American Association of the Deaf-Blind, P.O. Box 2831, Kensington, MD 20891, www.aadb.org, aadb-info@aadb.org.

American Foundation for the Blind, 2 Penn Plaza, Suite 1102, New York, NY 10121, www.afb.org, afbinfo@afb.net.

American Printing House for the Blind, 1839 Frankfort Avenue, P.O. Box 6085, Louisville, KY 40206-0085, aph.org, info@aph.org.

Clovernook Center for the Blind and Visually Impaired, 7000 Hamilton Avenue, Cincinnati, OH 45231, www.clovernook.org.

Helen Keller National Center for Deaf-Blind Youths and Adults, 141 Middle Neck Road, Sands Point, NY 11050, http://www.hknc.org, hkncinfo@hknc.org.

Library of Congress, National Library Service for the Blind and Physically Handicapped, 1291 Taylor Street, N.W., Washington, DC 20011, www.loc.gov/nls, nls@loc.gov.

Lighthouse International, 111 E. 59th Street, New York, NY 10022-1202, lighthouse.org, info@lighthouse.org.

National Federation of the Blind, 200 East Wells Street at Jernigan Place, Baltimore, MD 21230, nfb.org.

Basic Abstracts and Indexes

Academic Search Premier

887. *A F B Directory of Services Database.* 1926. Free. American Foundation for the Blind, 2 Penn Plz, Ste 1102, New York, NY 10121; afbinfo@afb.net; http://www.afb.org. *Aud.:* Ga, Sa.

Provides information on organizations and agencies in the United States and Canada that offer services for people who are blind or visually impaired. Each organizational profile in this free online resource provides full contact information, including web site address and key personnel, as well as useful descriptions of services offered that help in identifying the appropriate agency. An excellent reference source. URL: www.afb.org

888. *AccessWorld (Online Edition): technology and people who are blind or visually impaired.* [ISSN: 1526-9574] 2000. m. Free. Ed(s): Lee Huffman. American Foundation for the Blind, 2 Penn Plz, Ste 1102, New York, NY 10121; afbinfo@afb.net; http://www.afb.org. Illus. *Aud.:* Ga, Sa.

AccessWorld has news and articles concerning technology for the blind and visually impaired. It also includes product reviews and information on access issues. The *AccessWorld* archives contain issues dating back to 2000 and are accessible via the American Foundation for the Blind web site. URL: www.afb.org

889. *The B V A Bulletin.* [ISSN: 0005-3430] 1946. q. Free. Ed(s): Stuart Nelson. Blinded Veterans Association, National Board of Directors, 477 H St, NW, Washington, DC 20001; bva@bva.org; http://www.bva.org. Illus. Sample. Vol. ends: Fall. *Aud.:* Sa.

Information in *The BVA Bulletin* is written by blinded veterans for blinded veterans. This publication contains news, legislation, feature articles, information from the President of the Blinded Veterans Association, recent and upcoming association activities, letters to the editor, and an "In Remembrance" section for blinded veterans who have recently died. The current issue, along with issues dating back to 2006, is accessible via the BVA web site. *The BVA Bulletin* is also available in 14-point type. URL: www.bva.org

890. *Braille Book Review.* [ISSN: 0006-873X] 1932. bi-m. Free to blind and physically handicapped. U.S. Library of Congress, National Library Service for the Blind and Physically Handicapped, 1291 Taylor St, NW, Washington, DC 20011; nls@loc.gov; http://www.loc.gov/nls. Illus., index. Sample. *Bk. rev.:* Number and length vary. *Aud.:* Ems, Hs, Ga, Sa.

Braille Book Review contains announcements of Braille books recently added to the Library of Congress collection along with news and developments in library services for blind individuals. The Braille edition includes one-line annotations from *Talking Book Topics* and a Braille order form. The current issue of *BBR*, along with back issues dating back to 1994, is accessible via the NLS web site. This publication is also available in the following formats: 14-point type, digital Braille, and press Braille. URL: www.loc.gov/nls

891. *The Braille Forum.* [ISSN: 0006-8772] 1962. 10x/yr. USD 25. Ed(s): Sharon Lovering. American Council of the Blind, 2200 Wilson Blvd, Ste 650, Arlington, VA 22201; info@acb.org; http://www.acb.org. Illus., adv. Sample. Vol. ends: Jun. *Aud.:* Sa.

The Braille Forum is a resource for blind and visually impaired individuals. It contains news, human interest stories, information about legislation, and announcements of new products and services. Information and updates about the American Council of the Blind (ACB) are also featured. The current issue, along with issues dating back to 2010, is accessible via the ACB web site. *The Braille Forum* is also available in the following formats: Braille, 16-point type, half-speed four-track cassette, IBM-compatible CD, podcast, and e-mail. URL: http://acb.org

892. *Braille Monitor: voice of the nation's blind.* [ISSN: 0006-8829] 1956. 11x/yr. Non-members, USD 25. Ed(s): Gary Wunder. National Federation of the Blind, 200 E Wells St, at Jernigan Pl, Baltimore, MD 21230; nfb@nfb.org; http://www.nfb.org. Illus., index, adv. Sample. Circ: 35000. Vol. ends: Dec. *Aud.:* Sa.

The leading publication of the National Federation of the Blind (NFB), the *Braille Monitor* is read by the blind, their families, and the professionals who serve them. The *Braille Monitor* contains recipes, human-interest stories, profiles of blind individuals, and highlights of NFB activities and programs. It also addresses concerns of the blind, such as civil rights, social issues, legislation, employment, and education, and provides information on technology and aids/appliances used by the blind. The current issue, along with issues dating back to 1957, is accessible via the NFB web site. Other available formats of the *Braille Monitor* include 14-point type, Braille, USB flash drive, an MP3 downloadable audio file, and e-mail. URL: http://nfb.org

893. *The Complete Directory of Large Print Books & Serials.* Formerly (until 1988): *Large Type Books in Print.* [ISSN: 0000-1120] 1970. a. USD 475 2013 ed. Grey House Publishing, 4919 Rte 22, PO Box 56, Amenia, NY 12501; books@greyhouse.com; http://www.greyhouse.com/. *Aud.:* Sa.

This resource is an excellent tool for determining the availability of large-print newspapers and periodicals. It lists all active large-print materials included in Bowker's *Books In Print* and Ulrich's databases. The directory contains two indexes for looking up newspaper and periodical titles. One index is arranged alphabetically by subject, the other alphabetically by title. URL: http://greyhouse.com

894. Connect! (Sands Point). 2010. 3x/yr. Free. Ed(s): Nishy Bhargavan, Nancy O'Donnell. Helen Keller National Center for Deaf - Blind Youths and Adults, 141 Middle Neck Rd, Sands Point, NY 11050; hkncinfo@hknc.org; http://www.hknc.org. *Aud.:* Ga, Sa.

CONNECT! is the electronic newsletter for the Helen Keller National Center for Deaf-Blind Youths and Adults (HKNC). Featured in the newsletter are activities at the HKNC and across the United States that would be of interest to deaf-blind individuals. The current issue of *CONNECT!*, along with issues dating back to 2009, is accessible via the HKNC web site. This publication is available in 24-point type and in Braille. URL: www.hknc.org

895. Deaf - Blind Perspectives. [ISSN: 1526-9841] 1993. s-a. Free. Ed(s): John Reiman, Peggy Malloy. Teaching Research Institute, 345 N Monmouth Ave, Monmouth, OR 97361; kenyond@wou.edu; http://www.tr.wou.edu/. Illus. Sample. *Bk. rev.:* Number and length vary. *Aud.:* Sa.

Deaf-Blind Perspectives contains announcements, articles, and essays on topics concerning the deaf-blind. According to the *Deaf-Blind Perspectives* web site, its "intended audience includes deaf-blind individuals, family members, teachers, and other service providers and professionals." The current issue, along with issues dating back to 1993, is accessible via the *Deaf-Blind Perspectives* web site. This publication is also available in Grade 2 Braille, 16-point type, standard print (12-point type), and e-mail. URL: http://nationaldb.org/dbp

896. Dialogue (Salem): a world of ideas for visually impaired people of all ages. Incorporates (1983-1995): *Lifeprints.* [ISSN: 1069-6857] 1961. q. USD 42. Ed(s): B T Kimbrough. Blindskills, Inc., PO Box 5181, Salem, OR 97304-0181; info@blindskills.com; http://www.blindskills.com. Adv. Sample. Vol. ends: Winter. *Bk. rev.:* Number and length vary. *Aud.:* Ga, Sa.

Dialogue contains informative articles written by people who are blind or visually impaired. Living with low vision, technology, sports and recreation, careers, education, and cooking are some of the topics covered. News and information on ways to obtain new products and services are also included. This publication is available in the following formats: 18-point type, four-track cassette, Braille, and e-mail. URL: http://blindskills.com

897. Future Reflections. [ISSN: 0883-3419] 1981. q. Free. Ed(s): Deborah Kent Stein. National Federation of the Blind, 200 E Wells St, at Jernigan Pl, Baltimore, MD 21230; nfb@nfb.org; http://www.nfb.org. Sample. *Indexed:* P01. *Aud.:* Sa.

Future Reflections is a resource for parents and educators of blind children. It contains profiles of blind children and their parents and educators, as well as information on the National Federation of the Blind (NFB). Also included are articles on issues concerning blind children, educational programs for blind students, and resources for parents and teachers. The current issue, along with issues dating back to 1981, is accessible via the NFB web site. *Future Reflections* is also available in the following formats: standard print (12-point type), USB flash drive, and e-mail. URL: http://nfb.org

898. Guideposts: true stories of hope and inspiration. [ISSN: 0017-5331] 1945. m. 11/yr. USD 16.97 domestic; USD 20.97 Canada; USD 31.97 elsewhere. Ed(s): Edward Grinnan. Guideposts, 39 Seminary Hill Rd, Carmel, NY 10512; http://www.guideposts.org. Illus., index, adv. Sample. Vol. ends: Mar. *Aud.:* Ga, Sa.

Guideposts, an inspirational, interfaith publication, presents first-person narratives that encourage readers to achieve their "maximum personal and spiritual potential." This publication is available on four-track cassette, in 15-point type, and in Braille. URL: www.guideposts.org

899. Library Resources for the Blind and Physically Handicapped: a directory with budget, staff and collections information and FY (year) statistics on readership and circulation. Formerly: *Directory of Library Resources for the Blind and Physically Handicapped.* [ISSN: 0364-1236] 1968. a. Free to blind and physically handicapped. U.S. Library of Congress, National Library Service for the Blind and Physically Handicapped, 1291 Taylor St, NW, Washington, DC 20011; nls@loc.gov; http://www.loc.gov/nls. Illus. Sample. *Aud.:* Sa.

This free directory contains budget, staff, and collections information and yearly statistics on readership and circulation. It is available in 14-point type and digital text. An excellent reference source. URL: www.loc.gov/nls

900. Musical Mainstream (Large Print Edition). Former titles (until Dec.1976): *New Braille Musician; Braille Musician.* [ISSN: 0364-7501] 1942. q. Free to blind and physically handicapped. U.S. Library of Congress, National Library Service for the Blind and Physically Handicapped, 1291 Taylor St, NW, Washington, DC 20011; nls@loc.gov; http://www.loc.gov/nls. Sample. *Bk. rev.:* Number and length vary. *Aud.:* Ga, Sa.

Musical Mainstream contains selected articles from national magazines about classical music, music criticism, and music teaching, and lists new National Library Service music acquisitions. This publication is available in 14-point type, audiocassette, digital Braille, and press Braille. URL: www.loc.gov/nls

901. New York Times Large Print Weekly. Formerly (until 2007): *New York Times Large Type Weekly.* 1967. w. Mon. USD 85.80 domestic; USD 288.60 foreign. Ed(s): Tom Brady. New York Times Company, 620 8th Ave, New York, NY 10018; letters@nytimes.com; http://www.nytimes.com. Illus., adv. Sample. Vol. ends: Feb. *Aud.:* Ga, Sa.

This publication contains selected articles that have appeared throughout the past week in *The New York Times.* Graphics and color photographs enhance stories on national and international news, science and health, business, the arts, and sports. An editorial and a crossword puzzle are also included. *The New York Times Large Print Weekly* is available in 16-point type. It is also available in Braille from the Clovernook Center for the Blind and Visually Impaired. URL: www.nytimes.com

902. Our Special: a braille magazine edited for and by blind women. [ISSN: 0030-6959] 1927. bi-m. USD 15. Ed(s): Dana Nichols. National Braille Press, 88 St Stephen St, Boston, MA 02115; orders@nbp.org; http://www.nbp.org. *Aud.:* Sa.

Our Special is a resource especially for blind women. It contains both original articles and ones reprinted from newspapers and women's magazines. Topics featured in *Our Special* include career issues, crafts, health, dating, cooking, travel, poetry, shopping, and fashion. *OS* is available in paper Braille and in electronic Braille. URL: www.nbp.org

903. Reader's Digest (Large Print for Easier Reading). Former titles (until 2001): *Reader's Digest (Large Print); Reader's Digest Large Type Edition.* 1964. m. USD 27.96 domestic; USD 53.91 Canada. Ed(s): Liz Vaccariello. Reader's Digest Association, Inc, Reader's Digest Rd, Pleasantville, NY 10570; http://www.rd.com. Adv. Circ: 500000 Paid. *Aud.:* Ga, Sa.

Reader's Digest Large Print contains in-depth feature articles and departments such as "Word Power," "@Work," "Off Base," and "Life's Funny." It is available in 16-point over 21.75 type. This periodical is also available from the American Printing House for the Blind (APH) on four-track cassette and in Braille. The advertising has been removed from the editions produced by the APH. URL: www.rd.com

904. Seeing It Our Way: a magazine of recipes, crafts, and much more! 1997. m. USD 30 (print or braille ed.). Ed(s): Casandra Leaman, Debra Marino. Horizons for the Blind, 125 Erick St, A103, Crystal Lake, IL 60014; mail@horizons-blind.org; http://www.horizons-blind.org. Circ: 50. *Aud.:* Ga, Sa.

Seeing It Our Way is a magazine published by Horizons for the Blind, an organization "dedicated to improving the quality of life for people who are blind or visually impaired by increasing accessibility to consumer products and services, education, recreation[,] and the cultural arts." Recipes, gardening, crafts, sports, technology, and poetry are some of the topics covered in *Seeing It Our Way*. This publication is available in 22-point type. URL: www.horizons-blind.org

905. Slate & Style. [ISSN: 1536-4321] 1982. q. USD 16. Ed(s): Bridgit Kuenning-Pollpeter. National Federation of the Blind, 200 E Wells St, at Jernigan Pl, Baltimore, MD 21230; nfb@nfb.org; http://www.nfb.org. *Bk. rev.:* Number and length vary. *Aud.:* Ga, Sa.

Slate & Style is a magazine published by the National Federation of the Blind Writers' Division. Although this publication features literary writing, it also contains information about other writing formats. Issues dating back to 2006 are accessible via the National Federation of the Blind Writers' Division web site. *Slate & Style* is available in the following formats: 14-point type, Braille, and e-mail. URL: www.nfb-writers-division.net

906. Syndicated Columnists Weekly. 1984. w. USD 24. Ed(s): Diane Croft. National Braille Press, 88 St Stephen St, Boston, MA 02115; orders@nbp.org; http://www.nbp.org. *Aud.:* Sa.

Syndicated Columnists Weekly contains the best editorials written by syndicated columnists that have appeared that week in major U.S. newspapers such as *The Wall Street Journal, The New York Times, The Washington Post,* and *The Boston Globe. SCW* is available in paper Braille and electronic Braille. URL: www.nbp.org

907. T X SenseAbilities: a quarterly publication about visual impairments and deafblindness for families and professionals. 2010. q. USD 10. Ed(s): David Wiley, Holly Cooper. Texas School for the Blind and Visually Impaired, 1100 W 45th St, Austin, TX 78756; htpp://www.tsbvi.edu. *Aud.:* Sa.

TX SenseAbilities is published by the Texas School for the Blind and Visually Impaired and by the Department of Assistive and Rehabilitative Services, Division for Blind Services. This newsletter contains articles, news, and announcements about visual impairments and deaf-blindness for families and professionals. The current issue, along with issues dating back to 2007, is accessible via the *TX SenseAbilities* web site. URL: www.tsbvi.edu/tx-senseabilities

908. Talking Book Topics. [ISSN: 0039-9183] 1935. bi-m. Free to blind and physically handicapped. U.S. Library of Congress, National Library Service for the Blind and Physically Handicapped, 1291 Taylor St, NW, Washington, DC 20011; nls@loc.gov; http://www.loc.gov/nls. Index. Sample. *Aud.:* Ems, Hs, Ga, Sa.

Talking Book Topics contains announcements of recorded books recently added to the Library of Congress collection, along with news and developments in library services for blind and physically handicapped individuals. One-line annotations from *TBT* are included in *Braille Book Review*. The current issue of *TBT*, along with issues dating back to 1997, is accessible via the NLS web site. This publication is also available in the following formats: audiocassette, 14-point type, and digital text. URL: www.loc.gov/nls

■ BOATS AND BOATING

See also Fishing; Hunting and Guns; and Sports sections.

Julia D. Ashmun, Managing Partner, Dirty Dog Software, P.O. Box 592, Danville, NH 03819; julia@dirtydogsoftware.com

Introduction

Magazines in this section will appeal to boaters in a variety of crafts, from paddle boats to yachts. There is something here for those who already own a boat, are thinking of owning a boat, charter boats, or enjoy crewing on boats. Titles here cover topics from boating safety, maintenance, skills, boat and equipment review, to the best vacation sites or rivers to paddle. Some titles cover general boating topics, while others focus on particular craft types (e.g., sailboats, powerboats, canoes, or yacht) or address particular aspects of boating (e.g., ocean navigation, cruising, or racing).

Many boating magazines are now available in abbreviated form on the web, but most titles listed here also have established, full, printed versions. Most of the abbreviated online sites have lacked feature materials in the past. *By-the-Sea* (www.by-the-sea.com) and *Practical Sailor* (www.practical-sailor.com) have made substantial improvements to quality and quantity of online articles and stories, and are among the best of this type of electronic publication.

As a side note, this year's section edits are being completed from the cockpit of my Mariner 39 sloop located in the light-blue waters of the Bahamas.

Basic Periodicals

Ems: *BoatSafe* and *BoatSafeKids;* Hs: *Boating World;* Ga: *Boating, Boating World, Boatworks, Canoe & Kayak, Cruising World, Practical Sailor, Sail, The Woodenboat;* Ac: *Boating World, Boatworks, Canoe & Kayak, Sail, The Woodenboat.*

Basic Abstracts and Indexes

Readers' Guide to Periodical Literature.

909. Blue Water Sailing: the worlds best cruising magazine. [ISSN: 1091-1979] 1996. m. USD 29.95 domestic; USD 44.95 Canada; USD 64.95 elsewhere. Ed(s): Valerie Adams Meffert. Blue Water Sailing, 747 Aquidneck Ave, Ste 201, Middletown, RI 02842. Adv. Circ: 52000. *Aud.:* Ga, Sa.

Focused on extended offshore sailing, this magazine is geared toward experienced blue water sailors. *Blue Water Sailing* includes practical tips for offshore seamanship; content on safety and design; gear and boat reviews; news; personal stories; and information on destinations. It has also added a regular column written by a veteran woman sailor, Suzanne Giesemann, who brings her perspective to the cruising experience. It also has special sections on aspects of offshore navigation, including articles on electronic navigation, electronic charts, raster versus vector charts, radar, GPS, etc. Departments include a "Captain's Log" (editorial), "Readers' Forum," "Blue Water Dispatches," "World Sailing Adventures," and "News and Notes"—stories of ideal regional destinations and best anchorages. Recommended for public libraries that serve offshore boaters. URL: www.bwsailing.com

910. *Boating.* Incorporates (in 1980): *Motorboat;* Which incorporated (in 1975): *Family Houseboating;* Formerly: *Popular Boating.* [ISSN: 0006-5374] 1956. m. USD 14 domestic; USD 24 foreign. Hachette Filipacchi Media U.S., Inc., 1633 Broadway, New York, NY 10019; flyedit@hfmus.com; http://www.hfmus.com. Illus., index, adv. Sample. Circ: 201536 Paid. Vol. ends: Dec. *Indexed:* A22, ASIP, BRI, C37, P02. *Aud.:* Ga.

The magazine with the highest circulation in the genre, *Boating* offers a wide range of information for power boaters. Most material is aimed at increasing boaters' knowledge, with regular features on seamanship, navigation, equipment, maintenance, and safety. A significant portion of the coverage is new-boat testing and evaluation. Other material includes articles on trips, recreational activities, and boating industry news. This is a highly polished, visually satisfying journal with extensive use of color and graphics, along with a substantial amount of advertising (generally integrated well with the text). The emphasis is on mid-sized to large boats, but there's also a broader perspective for power boaters, and it can be useful as part of a basic collection. URL: www.boatingmag.com

911. *Boating World.* Former titles (until 1991): *Boat Journal;* (until 1990): *Small Boat Journal.* [ISSN: 1059-5155] 1979. 8x/yr. USD 12 domestic; USD 15 Canada; USD 30 elsewhere. Ed(s): Alan Jones, Brain Quines. Duncan McIntosh Co. Inc., 17782 Cowan, Ste A, Irvine, CA 92614. Illus., index, adv. Sample. *Indexed:* BRI, IHTDI. *Aud.:* Hs, Ga.

The focus here is on power boats of 35 feet or less, a popular size for short trips, water-sports activities, and fishing. There's a very wide range of material on boats and equipment, activities on and off the water, and the general boating environment. Each issue contains a lengthy feature article on a special topic and an article focusing on a boat of the month. Articles offer practical advice for hands-on upkeep and maintenance, as well as consumer tips (such as buying a used boat or insuring boats). A colorful production, with good graphics and broad coverage. Because it focuses on boats of such a popular size, this publication merits strong consideration as part of a library's core collection. URL: www.boatingworldonline.com

912. *BoatSafeKids: boating courses, boating tips, boating safety, boating contests.* Formerly: *BoatSafe and BoatSafeKids.* 19??. m. Nautical Know How, Inc., 51 N 3rd St #240, Philadelphia, PA 19106; nkh@boatsafe.com; http://Boatsafe.com. *Aud.:* Ems, Hs, Ga.

This comprehensive web magazine, sponsored by International Marine Educators, Inc., is dedicated to promoting boating knowledge and safety. Its archive is full of articles on safety issues for boats and people, along with instructional material and narratives about navigation, equipment, boat maintenance, and boat handling. Other articles here deal with the same topics—but they're written specifically for children. The magazine has a state-by-state listing of boating regulations and online boating courses designed to satisfy most boating-education requirements. A very useful, free site for boaters, and one that will be helpful to public libraries for reference service. URL: www.boatsafe.com/kids

913. *Boatworks: how to rewire your boat.* Formerly: *Boatworks for the Hands-On Sailor.* 2004. q. USD 4.99 per issue elsewhere. Ed(s): Peter Nielsen. Source Interlink Companies, 6420 Wilshire Blvd, 10th Fl, Los Angeles, CA 90048; dheine@sourceinterlink.com; http://www.sourceinterlinkmedia.com. Adv. Circ: 75000. *Aud.:* Hs, Ga, Sa.

An outstanding publication, useful to boat owners and soon-to-be boat owners. There is excellent advice on what to look for in purchasing a boat and then how to go about maintaining it. Do-it-yourself articles are practical, informative, and—most importantly—accurate. They provide very hands-on information about maintenance and upgrading of sailboats, with lots of instructive illustrations including step-by-step guides to carrying out specific repairs and upgrades. This title will appeal to all types of boating enthusiasts; you don't need to have a yacht to get a lot out of it. Highly recommended for all public libraries with boating journal collections. URL: www.sailmagazine.com/boatworks/index.aspx

914. *By-the-Sea.* 1996. d. Free. By-the-Sea, PO Box 2804, Orleans, MA 02653. *Aud.:* Ga.

This web-based smorgasbord for boaters includes feature articles and stories, posts message boards, and lists boats for sale as well as boat builders and boat dealers. There's a huge amount of readily available, useful information. This is a title all those interested in boating will want to know about. URL: www.by-the-sea.com

915. *Canoe & Kayak: the #1 paddlesports resource.* Former titles (until 1993): *Canoe;* Which was Incorporated (in 1941): *American Canoeist.* [ISSN: 1077-3258] 1973. bi-m. USD 14.95 domestic; USD 27.95 Canada; USD 29.95 elsewhere. Ed(s): Frederick Reimers, Ross Prather. Source Interlink Companies, 950 Calle Amanecer, Ste C, San Clemente, CA 92673; dheine@sourceinterlink.com; http://www.sourceinterlinkmedia.com. Illus., adv. Sample. Circ: 47330 Paid. Vol. ends: Dec. *Indexed:* A22, SD. *Aud.:* Ga, Ac.

An excellent offering with information for canoe and kayak enthusiasts in all kinds of paddling environments. Primary emphasis is on descriptions of paddling trips, ranging from casual day outings to rigorous whitewater excursions. There is also considerable coverage of paddling techniques, skills, safety, and health. This is topped off by material on boat design and construction and new products and accessories. Articles often voice environmental concerns and are usually very thorough and well written. Tastefully done, the magazine is both informative and enjoyable to read. *Canoe & Kayak* will be appreciated by a wide audience. URL: www.canoekayak.com

916. *Cruising World.* [ISSN: 0098-3519] 1974. m. USD 28 domestic; USD 42 Canada; USD 64 elsewhere. Ed(s): Mark Pillsbury. Bonnier Corp., 55 Hammarlund Way, Middletown, RI 02842; http://www.bonniercorp.com. Illus., adv. Sample. Circ: 130000 Paid. Vol. ends: Dec. Microform: PQC. *Indexed:* A22, BRI, C37, P02, SD. *Bk. rev.:* 3, 50 words. *Aud.:* Ga.

This is a popular magazine dedicated to open-water sailing and enjoying the sailing life, while most of *Cruising World*'s content centers on descriptive narratives of cruising trips or on practical solutions and techniques for long-term cruising. Trip narratives convey a good sense of the open-water experience and provide interesting glimpses of the character, history, and culture of international areas visited. Practical material covers such topics as navigational techniques, fishing, and boat maintenance. Supporting material includes news items and reviews of new equipment and new boats. The writing is sound, the graphics are pleasing, and the overall quality of the magazine is good. This title is useful and informative, and with its emphasis on living on the water, it offers a different approach than most other boating magazines. URL: www.cruisingworld.com

917. *D I Y Boat Owner: the marine maintenance magazine.* [ISSN: 1201-5598] 1995. q. USD 21 domestic; USD 26 Canada. Ed(s): Jan Mundy. D I Y Boat Owner, PO Box 15282, Washington, DC 20003. Adv. Sample. *Aud.:* Ga, Sa.

A technical, how-to title for powerboat and sailboat owners aimed at increasing knowledge of boat maintenance, upgrade, and repair, *DIY* offers articles on engine maintenance, building projects, electrical problems, installing accessories, troubleshooting engines and electronics, rigging, hull and deck maintenance, and more. Also included are reviews and articles on equipment, tools, parts, and products. A solid title for any boating collection. URL: www.diy-boat.com

918. *Dockwalk.* Incorporates (2001-2005): *Captain's Log.* 1998. m. USD 75 domestic; USD 150 foreign. Ed(s): Lauren Beck, Steve Davis. Boat International Media, First Fl, 41-47 Hartfield Rd, London, SW19 3RQ, United Kingdom; info@boatinternational.co.uk; http://www.boatinternational.co.uk. Adv. *Aud.:* Ga, Sa.

This title has enabled captains and crew of super yachts to keep up to date on their industry as their jobs may take them around the world. It also incorporates industry stories in the "Captain's Log," as well as includes articles on social events, health, and activities for the crews. It is intended for captains and crew and is edited by writers with knowledge of crewing yachts. This is a good magazine for current crew, or those considering or researching this industry.

919. *Good Old Boat.* [ISSN: 1099-6354] 1998. bi-m. USD 39.95 in US & Canada; USD 49.95 elsewhere. Ed(s): Karen Larson. Partnership for Excellence, Inc., 7340 Niagara Ln N, Maple Grove, MN 55311; http://www.goodoldboat.com. Adv. Sample. *Bk. rev.:* Number and length vary. *Aud.:* Ga, Sa.

A good ol' magazine aimed at average, do-it-yourself sailors who are not sailing the latest and greatest new yachts but are instead "celebrating older-model sailboats." Like *The Woodenboat,* it has in-depth reviews about models of boats that include the history, design, biography of the designer(s), and articles about the owner(s) of that model, along with photos of the boat—inside and out—in an attractive, glossy format. Most material is focused on furthering a sailor's knowledge of boat maintenance, seamanship, and safety, and do-it-yourself improvement projects are routinely included. Issues include design lessons, book reviews, equipment reviews, and features about fellow sailors relating their experiences and favorite weekend or extended cruise spots. URL: www.goodoldboat.com

920. *Houseboat Magazine: the family magazine for American houseboaters.* 1971. m. USD 29.95 domestic; USD 44.95 Canada; USD 49.95 elsewhere. Ed(s): Brady L Kay. Harris Publishing, Inc. (Idaho Falls), 360 B St, Idaho Falls, ID 83402-3547; customerservice@harrispublishing.com; http://www.harrispublishing.com. Illus., adv. Circ: 25000. *Aud.:* Ga.

A publication focusing exclusively, and extensively, on houseboats, this title covers all facets of boat ownership and maintenance, interesting boating locales, and activities and lifestyles of houseboaters. One of the defining features of this magazine is its focus on a different destination in each issue, including some of the history, scenic qualities, and services found there. This is a thin but attractively packaged publication that fills a need for a unique group of boaters. Houseboats are seen most frequently on large lakes and rivers, especially in the Western and Midwestern regions, so libraries in those areas would be the most likely to consider this title. URL: www.houseboatmagazine.com

921. *Motor Boating.* Former titles (until 2000): *Motor Boating & Sailing;* (until 1970): *Motor Boating;* (until 1909): *Motor Boating Magazine.* [ISSN: 1531-2623] 1907. 10x/yr. USD 14 domestic; USD 24 Canada; USD 44 elsewhere. Ed(s): Peter A Janssen, Jeanne Craig. Bonnier Corp., 460 N Orlando Ave, Ste 200, Winter Park, FL 32789; http://www.bonniercorp.com. Illus., adv. Sample. Vol. ends: Jun/Dec. Microform: NBI; PQC. *Indexed:* A22, BRI, C37, MASUSE, P02. *Aud.:* Ga.

One of the oldest boating magazines currently published, this popular title is for powerboaters only. Its scope includes powerboats of all sizes. The emphasis is on reviews of new boats, with supporting material covering both the pleasure and the practical aspects of boating. A particularly useful feature is the "Boatkeeper" section, designed as a cut-out section for hands-on boaters and containing a number of practical ideas and applications for boat maintenance, upkeep, and problem solving. Like several other high-circulation boating magazines, this has abundant advertising plus classified and brokerage sections that take up close to half of each issue. This effectively obscures some of the informational content that has been relegated to the latter part of the magazine. Its web site has the table of contents for the current issue, but no material is available in full text; prior issues are not archived, but material from the "Boatkeeper" section is, and there is keyword search capability. URL: www.motorboating.com

922. *Ocean Navigator: marine navigation and ocean voyaging.* Formerly (until Dec. 1985): *Navigator.* [ISSN: 0886-0149] 1985. bi-m. USD 27.95 combined subscription domestic; USD 37.95 combined subscription Canada; USD 42.95 combined subscription elsewhere. Ed(s): Tim Queeney. Navigator Publishing LLC., 58 Fore St, Portland, ME 04101-4842; http://www.oceannavigator.com. Illus., adv. Sample. Circ: 44000 Paid and controlled. *Bk. rev.:* 2-4, 75-200 words. *Aud.:* Ga.

Ocean boating requires considerable navigational skills and knowledge, and this is the only magazine we know of whose major focus is on these. While primary content concerns the art, tools, and techniques of navigation and seamanship, there is also a good sampling of articles on other aspects of ocean voyaging, such as boat maintenance or inviting cruise destinations. Some articles give accounts of voyages in which navigational skills or equipment have been a significant or crucial factor in the trip's outcome. Most articles offer detailed, in-depth coverage and are interesting, informative, and sometimes instructional. Although most of the material applies to sailing craft, the navigational features can be valuable for all boaters. URL: www.oceannavigator.com

923. *PassageMaker: the trawler & ocean motorboat magazine.* [ISSN: 1095-7286] 1996. 8x/yr. USD 34.95 domestic; USD 48.95 Canada; USD 62.95 elsewhere. Ed(s): John Wooldridge, Christine Alhambra. PassageMaker Magazine, Inc., 105 Eastern Ave, Ste 103, Annapolis, MD 21403; http://www.passagemaker.com. Adv. *Aud.:* Ga, Sa.

Trawlers are an up-and-coming area of interest in boating, and this title is a good contribution to the literature. It includes recommended travel locations, human interest stories about cruisers and their boats, technical aspects of this type of boating (electronics, engine maintenance, anticipating and coping with weather, etc.). Each issue includes boat and equipment reviews, an editorial feature called "From the Pilothouse," a food section called "The Galley," and an update highlighting upcoming events of interest to trawler fans. This will be both a practical help and a cozy read for a growing segment of library readers: aging baby-boomers who don't relish the rigors of other kinds of boating are fast becoming trawler enthusiasts. URL: www.passagemaker.com

924. *Power and Motoryacht.* Formerly: *Guide to Marine Electronics.* [ISSN: 0886-4411] 1985. m. USD 11.97 domestic; USD 24.97 Canada; USD 26.97 elsewhere. Ed(s): Richard Thiel, Daine M Byrne. Source Interlink Companies, 261 Madison Ave, 6th Fl, New York, NY 10016; dheine@sourceinterlink.com; http://www.sourceinterlinkmedia.com. Illus., adv. Sample. Circ: 157000 Controlled. Vol. ends: Dec. *Indexed:* A22. *Aud.:* Ga, Sa.

This glossy magazine covers large powerboats in detail, with feature stories about new boats, boating techniques (a recent article is titled "Docking for Dummies"), powerboat electronics, "Gadgets and Gizmos" (special boating equipment), a boat testing resource, and an FYI page (a recent issue's page includes a note titled "Scams, Schemes, and Stolen Dreams," about the alarmingly increasing trend in boat thefts, as well as a quiz testing readers' knowledge about boat safety, a list of upcoming boat shows, and cautionary tips to keep boaters from getting into "deep water" while running the boat). Periodic special issues are largely devoted to single themes, such as a recent one dedicated to "everything engines," with articles ranging from how to buy horsepower to troubleshooting, reading rating sheets, how marine gears work, and "the future of fuel cells." Aimed at motorboat enthusiasts who may have more money than boating savvy and knowledge—and heartily recommended to libraries that serve them. URL: www.powerandmotoryacht.com

925. *Powerboat: the world's leading performance boating magazine.* Formerly (until 19??): *Power Boat.* [ISSN: 0032-6089] 1968. bi-m. USD 19.97 domestic; USD 25.97 Canada; USD 31.97 elsewhere. Ed(s): Jason Johnson, Gregg Mansfield. Nordskog Publishing, Inc., 2575 Vista Del Mar, Ventura, CA 93001; http://nordskogpublishing.com. Illus., adv. Sample. Vol. ends: Dec. *Aud.:* Ga.

This is an artfully done magazine targeted at high-performance powerboat enthusiasts, and its main focus is on evaluations of new boats, with an emphasis on performance features. Reviews are thorough and detailed, testing a boat's speed and handling characteristics, its construction and workmanship, and its interior design and overall impact. Many of these boats are also tested for their qualities as water-skiing boats. The magazine also features powerboat racing coverage, with commentary and results of racing events plus articles about significant figures in powerboat racing. Additional material includes information on products, accessories, and various watersports activities. The magazine has excellent photography and graphics, complemented by intelligent and informative writing. *Powerboat* is a very complete magazine for performance-minded boaters and would be a good complement to a basic collection.

926. *Practical Sailor: guide to sailing gear.* [ISSN: 0161-8059] 1974. m. USD 84 combined subscription in US & Canada (print & online eds.); USD 120 combined subscription elsewhere (print & online eds.). Ed(s): Darrell Nicholson. Belvoir Media Group, LLC, PO Box 5656, Norwalk, CT 06856; customer_service@belvoir.com; http://www.belvoir.com. Sample. *Indexed:* SD. *Aud.:* Ga, Sa.

Practical Sailor is the *Consumer Reports* of sailing. The focus is on reviewing equipment and supplies with a review of one sailboat (both new and old are covered in various issues). Most of the magazine is dedicated to reviewing equipment and supplies, such as the best bottom paint by region, and testing of hand-held radios, ladders, radar, autopilots, etc. The publication recently underwent a makeover, and now includes color photographs and appears in a glossier format. Sailboat reviews contain quotes from previous or existing customers about items they like or don't like; value/price graphs over the years starting with original cost; interior, exterior, hull, and manufacturing quality information; and how the boat handles under sail.

927. Sail. [ISSN: 0036-2700] 1970. m. USD 10 domestic; USD 23 Canada; USD 25 elsewhere. Ed(s): Peter Nielsen. Source Interlink Companies, 6420 Wilshire Blvd, 10th Fl, Los Angeles, CA 90048; dheine@sourceinterlink.com; http://www.sourceinterlinkmedia.com. Illus., adv. Sample. Circ: 170000 Paid. Vol. ends: Dec. *Indexed:* A22, BRI, P02. *Bk. rev.:* 1-2, 200 words. *Aud.:* Ga, Ac.

A very popular magazine that provides a balanced selection of material, with an emphasis on boating knowledge and skills as applied to equipment, maintenance, navigation, and seamanship. Articles address these issues in very practical terms. Another focus is on cruising and racing activities. These are usually narratives that describe interesting cruise destinations or situations that demonstrate sailing skills and experiences. The magazine's content applies to both small and large boats and to both novice and expert sailors. The consistent focus is on the enhancement of sailing skills. One of the boating periodicals with the highest circulation, this title contains a great deal of advertising that sometimes overwhelms the text. However, it is well done overall, and should be a core holding for most boating collections.

928. Sailing: the beauty of sail. Formerly: *Lake Michigan Sailing.* [ISSN: 0036-2719] 1966. m. USD 28 domestic; USD 39 Canada; USD 70 elsewhere. Ed(s): Bill Schanen. Port Publications, Inc., 125 E Main St, PO Box 249, Port Washington, WI 53074; ads@sailingmagazine.net. Illus., adv. Sample. Circ: 40000. Vol. ends: Aug. Microform: PQC. *Indexed:* A22, BRI. *Bk. rev.:* 2-4, 200-400 words. *Aud.:* Ga.

An oversized magazine combining lengthy feature articles with pictorial beauty. Its primary content is balanced between cruising locales and thorough reviews of boats and equipment. Additional material covers maintenance skills, sailing techniques, and racing news. What separates this magazine from others is its sense of artistry. Not only is it tastefully done, but the photography is often stunning. The large format allows full-page photos to convey the panorama of certain places or the sensation of skimming through the water. An interesting, enjoyable, and often instructive magazine that does a very good job of portraying the sailing experience.

929. Sailing World: the authority on performance sailing. Former titles (until 1986): *Yacht Racing and Cruising;* (until 1983): *Yacht Racing;* (until 1972): *One-Design and Offshore Yachtsman;* (until 1965): *One-Design Yachtsman.* [ISSN: 0889-4094] 1962. 9x/yr. USD 14.97 domestic; USD 23.97 Canada; USD 36.97 elsewhere. Ed(s): Dave Reed. Bonnier Corp., 55 Hammarlund Way, Middletown, RI 02842; http://www.bonniercorp.com. Illus., adv. Sample. Vol. ends: Dec/Jan. Microform: PQC. *Indexed:* BRI, C37, MASUSE. *Aud.:* Ga.

The definitive periodical for performance- and competition-oriented sailors. Its coverage includes narratives about competitive events and articles focusing on sailing techniques, boat technology, and racing tactics and strategies. The material is primarily oriented toward larger boats, but it is also applicable to smaller ones. Most articles are thorough and informative, with the intent of enhancing sailing skills and performance. The magazine also includes boat reviews and evaluations of high-performance equipment and gear. Racing news and results are included for many levels of competition. This is a visually appealing publication, with good photography, graphics, and layout design. The website largely links to racing news and events, but it does provide an index for all magazine issues since 1991 and an archive of selected published articles. Intended for serious sailors involved in competitions, this is an excellent choice for libraries near sailing centers.

930. Sea Kayaker: experience the world's waterways. [ISSN: 0829-3279] 1984. bi-m. USD 23.95 domestic; USD 25.95 Canada; USD 33.95 elsewhere. Sea Kayaker Inc., PO Box 17029, Seattle, WA 98127; sknewsletter@seakayakermag.com; http://www.seakayakermag.com. Illus., adv. Sample. Vol. ends: Dec. *Indexed:* SD. *Bk. rev.:* 1-2, 500 words. *Aud.:* Ga, Sa.

The only publication dedicated specifically to the sport of sea kayaking. It is interesting and informative, and its primary content is lengthy first-person narratives of paddling adventures and related aspects, such as conditioning and health, food, safety, and camping. Additional feature material is usually instructional, dealing with techniques such as navigation or paddling. Coverage is rounded out with reviews of new kayaks, equipment, and products. There are occasional articles on environmental issues or wildlife. Recommended for libraries located in coastal regions or near large, open bodies of water.

931. ShowBoats International. Formerly (until 198?): *Showboats.* [ISSN: 0749-2952] 1988. bi-m. USD 23.95 domestic; USD 38.95 Canada; USD 63.95 elsewhere. Ed(s): Jill Bobrow, Danielle C Wallin. CurtCo Robb Media LLC., 29160 Heathercliff Rd, Ste 200, Malibu, CA 90265; support@robbreport.com; http://www.curtco.com. Adv. Sample. Circ: 50000. *Indexed:* ABIn. *Aud.:* Ga, Sa.

A fantasyland for boating enthusiasts, this title reviews showboats—and we're not talking the kind that used to run on the Mississippi. Reviews include boat specs, interior and exterior photos, biographical material on the wealthy individual and corporate owners, and the manufacturers of these beauties. Advertising is glossy, extensive, and targeted at the well-heeled—think Maserati, AIG Private Client Group, and Hublot watches. These showboats are the highest of the high-end, high-concept vessels typically costing in the millions of dollars. Your readership will probably not be buying these boats, but true boating enthusiasts can always dream.

932. Trailer Boats: guiding avid boaters since 1971. [ISSN: 0300-6557] 1971. m. USD 16.97 domestic; USD 28.97 Canada; USD 41.97 domestic. Ed(s): Rebecca Stone, Ron Eldridge. Affinity Group Inc., 2575 Vista Del Mar, Ventura, CA 93001; info@affinitygroup.com; http://www.affinitygroup.com. Illus., adv. Sample. Circ: 102000 Paid. Vol. ends: Nov/Dec. Microform: PQC. *Indexed:* A22, BRI, P02. *Aud.:* Ga.

This magazine is dedicated to boats small enough to be towed on a trailer (generally powerboats less than 30 feet long). Content consists of thorough evaluations of new boats and engines and towing equipment and vehicles. It is the only boating resource that regularly features articles on towing vehicles and techniques and regulatory issues involved with towing. Additional material covers gear and accessories, seamanship, and boating activities. Much of the material has enough detail and technical description to make it very useful for boaters who do their own maintenance. The magazine is well written, has pleasing graphics, and is enjoyable to read. With its emphasis on those smaller, portable boats that are owned by a sizable segment of the boating community, this publication will appeal to a wide readership.

933. The Woodenboat: the magazine for wooden boat owners, builders and designers. [ISSN: 0095-067X] 1974. bi-m. USD 32. WoodenBoat Publications, Inc., 41 WoodenBoat Ln, PO Box 78, Brooklin, ME 04616; http://www.woodenboat.com. Illus., adv. Sample. Vol. ends: Nov/Dec. *Indexed:* A22, IHTDI. *Bk. rev.:* 2, 500-1,000 words. *Aud.:* Ga, Ac.

Modern boats are usually made of synthetic materials, but the tradition of building boats of wood still has a devoted following. This magazine is dedicated to preserving that tradition, and it is one of the finest and most informative of all boating periodicals. It covers the history, design, building, and preservation of wooden boats of any size or style. Feature articles range from highly detailed descriptions and plans for building or restoring a boat to historical pieces on a style of boat or a boat-building operation. Articles often include substantive biographical profiles of individuals prominent in some area of the wooden-boat industry. There is also material on wood technology and tools and techniques for working with wood. Detailed feature articles provide more depth than is usually found in boating periodicals. The color photography, illustrations, and design all lend a sense of artistry to the magazine. This stylish publication is a pleasure to read and should be in a core collection.

934. *Yachting: power and sail.* [ISSN: 0043-9940] 1907. m. USD 14 for 3 yrs. domestic; USD 26 Canada; USD 46 elsewhere. Ed(s): George Sass, Jr., Jason Wood. Bonnier Corp., 2 Park Ave, 9th Fl, New York, NY 10016; http://www.bonniercorp.com. Illus., adv. Sample. Vol. ends: Jun/Dec. Microform: PQC. *Indexed:* A22, BRI, C37, CBRI, MASUSE, P02, SD. *Aud.:* Ga.

This title's coverage emphasizes large, upscale yachts plus activities and lifestyles associated with those boats. It is intended for experienced, knowledgeable yachtsmen of both powerboats and sailboats and contains lengthy, well-written articles on a variety of boating topics. Evaluations of new boats are numerous, as are cruise narratives describing interesting, exotic, or out-of-the-way places to visit. There are a number of informational articles on boating know-how, especially relating to equipment. The magazine has high production values and a very good sense of style. There is an appreciable amount of advertising, with the latter half of each issue given over to ads for boat brokerages and chartering services. This is a sound, stylish, and useful magazine that represents the high end of boating very well.

■ BOOKS AND BOOK REVIEWS

See also Archives and Manuscripts; Bibliography; Library and Information Science; and Printing and Graphic Arts sections. Book reviews in subject areas are located within their specific subject areas (e.g., *Science Books and Films* in the Science and Technology section).

Pam Baker, Library Instruction Coordinator, California State University, Monterey Bay, 100 Campus Center, Seaside, CA 93955; pbaker@csumb.edu.

Jacqui Grallo, Reference and Instructional Technology Librarian, California State University, Monterey Bay, 100 Campus Center, Seaside, CA 93955; jgrallo@csumb.edu

Introduction

Even as writers, publishers, educators, employers, and the public debate the future of e-books versus print books, they all continue to acknowledge the importance of reading to our intellectual, social, and work lives. More than ever, librarians, educators, and parents need to encourage the love of books and reading in our future generations through print, traditional online access, or a burgeoning array of e-readers and other mobile devices.

Since lifelong readers are formed at every age, this section once again offers useful resources for finding and reviewing books for pre-readers through adults. Some publications listed in *MFL* have migrated online or added an online presence, and many of the publisher web sites continue the trend of offering enhanced features such as blogs, RSS feeds, YouTube videos, free e-newsletters, and searchable archives.

Most publisher web sites now include social networking tools such as Facebook, Twitter, LibraryThing, and Amazon Wishlist for sharing information and reader feedback. These can be powerful awareness tools at any age level: we never know which book could be the one that changed a life forever. As Oscar Wilde, the Irish playwright, novelist, and poet, once wrote, "It is what you read when you don't have to, that determines what you will be when you can't help it."

Basic Periodicals

Ems: *Book Links, Center for Children's Books. Bulletin, The Horn Book Magazine;* Hs: *Booklist, Kirkus Reviews;* Ga: *Booklist, Kirkus Reviews, New York Review of Books, New York Times Book Review, Publishers Weekly;* Ac: *Choice, New York Review of Books, New York Times Book Review, Publishers Weekly, T L S.*

Basic Abstracts and Indexes

Book Review Digest, Book Review Index, Children's Book Review Index, Library Literature.

935. *American Book Review.* [ISSN: 0149-9408] 1977. bi-m. USD 30 (Individuals, USD 24; USD 35 foreign). Ed(s): Jeffrey R Di Leo. University of Houston at Victoria, School of Arts & Sciences, 3007 N Ben Wilson, Victoria, TX 77901. Illus., adv. Sample. Circ: 5000. Vol. ends: Sep/Oct. *Indexed:* A01, A22, AmHI, ArtHuCI, BRI, CBRI, Chicano, E01, MLA-IB. *Bk. rev.:* 25-30, 500-2,500 words. *Aud.:* Ac, Sa.

Written and edited by writers for audiences interested in literature, *American Book Review* is dedicated to the review of fiction, poetry, and literary and cultural criticism from small, avant-garde, university, ethnic, and women's presses. Each bimonthly issue has a focus—examples include "Essential Asian American Literature" and "Fiction's Future"—though not all titles reviewed fall within it. Contributing editors include notable authors Rudolfo Anaya, Joyce Carol Oates, and Charles Simic, among others. A small amount of sample content is available on the *ABR* web site. Intended to "project the sense of engagement that writers themselves feel about what is being published," *ABR* is an important title for academic and large public library collections.

936. *Book Links: connecting books, libraries, and classrooms.* [ISSN: 1055-4742] 1991. q. American Library Association, 50 E Huron, Chicago, IL 60611; ala@ala.org; http://www.ala.org. Illus., index, adv. Vol. ends: Aug. *Indexed:* A01, A22, AmHI, BRI, C37, MASUSE. *Bk. rev.:* 50-75, 50-150 words. *Aud.:* Ems, Ga.

This quarterly supplement to *Booklist*, published by the ALA, is designed for teachers, librarians, reading specialists, and others with an interest in children's literacy development. *Book Links* reviews new and existing children's titles, always with an eye toward curriculum; each issue is focused on a particular curricular area. *Book Links* includes author and illustrator interviews and essays, as well as thematic bibliographies, organized by grade level, with related discussion questions and activities. It also features articles by educators on practical ways to connect young people with books. The web site offers a searchable index, some sample content, and a "Web Connections" section, which points to online resources that support content in each issue. Electronic full text of *Book Links* articles is included in the *Booklist Online* database. Appropriate for school and public libraries, as well as academic libraries with robust teacher education collections.

937. *Book Page.* 1988. m. Individuals, USD 30. Ed(s): Lynn Green. ProMotion, Inc., 2143 Belcourt Ave, Nashville, TN 37212; contact@bookpage.com. Illus., adv. Sample. Circ: 450000 Paid. *Indexed:* CBRI. *Aud.:* Ga.

A broad-based, inexpensive review of new books published every month, focusing on bestsellers and new books in a variety of categories. The magazine's goal is to "recommend the best books for readers of all types." It includes short review sections on mysteries, cooking, romance, audio books, and book club picks, as well as advice for readers on a variety of book-related topics. Longer review sections cover fiction, nonfiction, and children's books. Also included are feature articles on a variety of themes, author interviews and photos, and many colorful ads for new books. Bookpage.com posts all of the content from the current edition each month and features reviews, author interviews, and searchable indexes of reviews by genre and by author. Readers can follow *Bookpage* on Twitter, Facebook, and Bookcase, a blog by written by *Bookpage* editors. They may also sign up for free e-newsletters, access a special section that highlights children's books, or subscribe (have a login) to http://bookpage.com to watch author interviews on YouTube. Web exclusives on the web site include additional feature articles, reviews, and author interviews. An attractive, readable resource for public librarians and their readers. URL: http://bookpage.com

938. *Booklist.* Formerly (until 1969): *The Booklist and Subscription Books Bulletin;* Which was formed by the merger of (1930-1956): *Subscription Books Bulletin;* (1917-1956): *The Booklist;* Which was formerly (1905-1917): *A L A Booklist.* [ISSN: 0006-7385] 1969. bi-m. 22/yr. USD 147.50 domestic; USD 170 foreign; USD 9 per issue. Ed(s): Bill Ott. American Library Association, 50 E Huron, Chicago, IL 60611; customerservice@ala.org; http://www.ala.org. Illus., index, adv. Vol. ends: Sep. Microform: PQC. *Indexed:* A01, A07, A22, ABS&EES, AmHI, BRI, C37, CBRI, Chicano, GardL, I15, MASUSE, MLA-IB, P02. *Bk. rev.:* 200-250, 75-150 words. *Aud.:* Ems, Hs, Ga, Ac.

Published 22 times a year by the ALA, *Booklist* is the premier source of book and media reviews for librarians, educators, and the general reader. It features concise, engaging, recommended-only reviews of new and recent library materials in a variety of formats for youth and adults. Quality and anticipated demand are factors for inclusion, and special consideration is given to the needs of small and medium-sized libraries. Reviews contain critical evaluation of materials and point out limitations and weaknesses as appropriate. Explicit in *Booklist*'s selection policy is the philosophy that "any library collection must include both works of current interest and those of lasting value, regardless of their ideological point of view." Spotlight issues focus on popular genres, topics, and themes, such as graphic novels, biography, romance, and the like. Columns, interviews, special features, bibliographies, and full coverage of ALA awards and "best of" lists accompany the reviews. Each issue has a separate section of reference book reviews. The *Booklist* web site offers a few "Web Exclusives," as well as links to *Booklist* blogs and lists of award winners. The *Booklist Online* database, available separately by subscription, features searchable full text of over 130,000 reviews. An essential resource for school and public librarians, and an engaging and informative read for anyone interested in literacy, books, and reading.

939. *Bookmarks: for everyone who hasn't read everything.* [ISSN: 1546-0657] 2002. bi-m. USD 27.95 domestic; USD 37.95 Canada; USD 57.95 elsewhere. Ed(s): Jon Phillips. Bookmarks Publishing LLC, 1818 MLK Blvd, Ste 181, Chapel Hill, NC 27514; letters@bookmarksmagazine.com. Illus., adv. *Indexed:* B02, BRI. *Bk. rev.:* 55-65, 500 words. *Aud.:* Ga, Ac.

Since 2002, this bimonthly magazine has summarized and distilled hundreds of new published book reviews from more than 50 major publications for a comprehensive look at the latest fiction, nonfiction, and children's books. Every issue includes articles that cover classic and contemporary authors, "best-of" genre reading lists, reader recommendations, and book group profiles. Each book review contains author information, a plot summary, and a critical summary culled from select national and international reviews. In addition to the ratings given from the media reviews, each book review provides a one- to five-star summary rating from *Bookmarks* editors to aid book buyers with their selections. Bookmarksmagazine.com provides sections to browse reviews and read the latest reading guides, web reading lists, and favorite *Bookmarks* articles. The web site also contains access to a free book reviews newsletter and an archive of past issues that contains links to media reviews. A succinct and valuable resource for public and academic library selectors, as well as the general reader.

940. *BookWire: the book industry resource.* [ISSN: 0000-1759] 1999. irreg. approx. m. Free. R.R. Bowker LLC, 630 Central Ave, New Providence, NJ 07974; info@bowker.com; http://www.bowker.com. Adv. *Aud.:* Ga, Ac.

The newest version of *Bookwire, Bookwire Beta,* allows readers to search over 20 million book titles, including print, e-books, and audio books in the Bowker's Books in Print database. This web site provides category pages where readers can get information about bestsellers and new releases, or find titles that match their reading interests. A searchable Author Index links to author biographies, and a Reviews Index links to all titles available on Bookwire.com. When the reader clicks on a book title, she is provided with a "SEO Title Card" that contains author, title, publisher, and available formats information, as well as a short, simple description of the book. Each card also provides links to retailers where the reader can purchase the books online. Some titles contain reviews from other publications such as *Publisher's Weekly* or can be shared through e-mail or social networking sites such as Digg, AmazonWishlist, Facebook, LibraryThing, and more. A useful tool for libraries and readers to find and share book information in a variety of ways.

941. *Boston Review.* Formerly (until 1982): *New Boston Review.* [ISSN: 0734-2306] 1975. bi-m. USD 45 (Individuals, USD 25). Ed(s): Deborah Chasman, Joshua Cohen. Boston Critic, Inc., 35 Medford St, Ste 302, Somerville, MA 02143. Illus., index, adv. Sample. Circ: 170000 Paid and controlled. Vol. ends: Dec/Jan. Microform: LIB; PQC. *Indexed:* A22, AmHI, BRI, CBRI, MLA-IB. *Bk. rev.:* 20-25, 250-2,000 words. *Aud.:* Ga, Ac, Sa.

Recently relaunched in glossy, color magazine format, with its motto "Ideas Matter" emblazoned on the cover, *Boston Review* offers deep coverage of current affairs, and places book reviews alongside essays, fiction, and poetry. General readers and librarians alike will enjoy *Boston Review*'s high-level journalism and treatment of the literary arts. Like libraries, *Boston Review* is committed to promoting informed discourse and a variety of points of view. Much of the content of current and previous issues is available for free in full text, with reader comments, at the web site. Published six times a year and "putting important ideas to the test of reason," *Boston Review* is recommended for both academic and public libraries.

C M Magazine. See Canada section.

942. *Center for Children's Books. Bulletin.* Former titles (until 1958): *Children's Book Center. Bulletin;* (until 1950): *University of Chicago. Center for Instructional Materials. Service Bulletin;* (until 1947): *Children's Books Received by the Center for Instructional Materials.* [ISSN: 0008-9036] 1945. m. except Aug. USD 98. Ed(s): Deborah Stevenson. The Johns Hopkins University Press, 2715 N Charles St, Baltimore, MD 21218; http://www.press.jhu.edu. Illus., index, adv. Sample. Circ: 1876. Vol. ends: Jul/Aug. Microform: PQC. Reprint: PSC. *Indexed:* A22, BRI, CBRI, E01. *Bk. rev.:* 70, 50-100 words. *Aud.:* Ems, Hs, Ga, Ac.

Each year, the *Bulletin* reviews nearly 1,000 new books for children and young people of all ages. Each signed review gives concise summaries and critical evaluations on the book's content, reading level, strengths and weaknesses, and quality of format, as well as suggestions for curricular use. The *Bulletin* has developed explicit rating codes to aid library selector purchasing—a very useful tool in tight budget times. Regular features include an in-depth editorial on selected new titles and trends; reviews of new professional books; and an annual selection of the year's most distinguished books, the Blue Ribbon List. Author/title indexes are provided for each volume, as well as a unique "Subject and Use Index" to aid the reader in finding useful titles by subject, curricular use, and genre. The *Bulletin*'s web page includes links to the current "Big Picture" article, the *Bulletin* homepage archives, and an awards list. A thoughtful, essential source for school, public, or academic librarians who are responsible for selecting children's literature. URL: http://bccb.lis.illinois.edu/

943. *Choice: current reviews for academic libraries.* [ISSN: 0009-4978] 1963. m. USD 390 domestic; USD 510 foreign. Ed(s): Francine Graf, Irving E Rockwood. Association of College and Research Libraries, 50 E Huron St, Chicago, IL 60611; acrl@ala.org. Illus., index, adv. Refereed. Vol. ends: Jul/Aug. Microform: PQC. *Indexed:* BAS, BRI, CBRI, Chicano, MLA-IB, P02. *Bk. rev.:* 600, 100-250 words. *Aud.:* Ga, Ac.

Published monthly by the Association of College and Research Libraries, *Choice* magazine and its recently redesigned electronic counterpart, *Choice Reviews Online* (available separately by subscription), are arguably the most important collection development tools for academic librarians. *Choice* reviewers are not just subject experts; they are teaching faculty directly involved with undergraduate students and curricula. *Choice* publishes annually more than 7,000 concise reviews of academic titles, including books and electronic resources, and is often the first to comment on brand-new items. Reviews are organized by discipline. The "Summing Up" section of each review specifies the appropriate audience/academic level of each title, and offers a recommendation regarding purchase. *Choice* also features bibliographic essays, lists of significant forthcoming titles, and, each January, the prestigious and much-relied-on "Outstanding Academic Titles" list. Highly recommended for all libraries; essential for academic libraries that serve undergraduates.

944. *Criticas (Online): Spanish language authors and book reviews.* 2005. m. Free to qualified personnel. Media Source Incorporated, 160 Varick St, 11th Fl, New York, NY 10013; http://www.mediasourceinc.com. Adv. *Bk. rev.:* 100, 75-200 words. *Aud.:* Ga, Sa.

Library Journal and *School Library Journal* review the latest Spanish-language books for adults and children. Located under "Reviews" on the *LJ* web site, *Criticas: Spanish Language Authors and Book Reviews* provides English-language reviews of Spanish-language fiction, nonfiction, picture books, and titles in translation. The short, signed reviews give a brief summary and critique of each book. Adult titles are reviewed monthly, and children's titles every other month. Children's book reviews also appear in the following month's issue of *School Library Journal.* Although it no longer provides comprehensive coverage of the international Spanish-language publishing market, the current version is still a valuable resource for public and academic libraries that purchase Spanish-language books. URL: www.libraryjournal.com/csp/cms/sites/LJ/Reviews/Spanish/index.csp

945. *Horn Book Guide to Children's and Young Adult Books.* [ISSN: 1044-405X] 1989. s-a. USD 60 domestic; USD 77 Canada; USD 81 elsewhere. Ed(s): Roger Sutton. Horn Book, Inc., 56 Roland St, Ste 200, Boston, MA 02129; info@hbook.com; http://www.hbook.com. Illus., index, adv. Sample. Vol. ends: Jan/Jun. *Indexed:* BRI, CBRI. *Bk. rev.:* 2,000, 40-50 words. *Aud.:* Ems, Hs, Ga.

A comprehensive, companion publication to *Horn Book Magazine,* this indispensable magazine reviews over 2,000 titles—virtually every children's and young adult book published in the U.S. in a six-month period. Published each spring and fall, the *Horn Book Guide* publishes short critiques of fiction and nonfiction hardcover trade books published in the United States for young people. Signed reviews are concise—identifying strengths, weaknesses, and appropriate grade levels, as well as clearly rating the books on a scale from one to six (a triangular symbol marks titles with the highest ratings). Fiction titles are grouped by grade level, while nonfiction titles are arranged by Dewey Decimal subject area. Each issue includes notes on reviewers and useful indexes by author/illustrator, title, subject, series, etc. As a separate subscription, *Horn Book Online* is searchable by author, illustrator, title, subject, bibliographic data, and rating. A must for school libraries and public libraries that serve their school communities.

946. *The Horn Book Magazine: about books for children and young adults.* [ISSN: 0018-5078] 1924. bi-m. USD 72. Ed(s): Roger Sutton. Horn Book, Inc., 56 Roland St, Ste 200, Boston, MA 02129; info@hbook.com; http://www.hbook.com. Illus., index, adv. Sample. Vol. ends: Nov/Dec. Microform: NBI; PQC. *Indexed:* A01, A06, A22, ABS&EES, ASIP, BRI, C37, CBRI, Chicano, MLA-IB, P02. *Bk. rev.:* 70-120, 100-300 words. *Aud.:* Ems, Hs, Ga, Ac.

"Independent, opinionated, and stylish," *The Horn Book Magazine* is for anyone interested in literature—including fiction, nonfiction, poetry, and picture books—for children and young adults. Published bimonthly and engagingly written and illustrated, *The Horn Book Magazine* comprises commentary, articles, book reviews of selected new titles, and more. Reviews are gathered twice a year in the *Horn Book Guide* (see above), which is available in print and electronically. Most reviewers are teachers, professors, and/or librarians. The January/February issue features "Fanfare," a list chosen by the editors, of the past year's best children's and young adult books. The publication's web site offers selected pieces from the magazine, as well as links to the monthly newsletter, *Notes from the Horn Book,* and *Read Roger,* a blog by editor Roger Sutton. *The Horn Book Magazine* is recommended for school and public libraries, as well as academic libraries that serve teacher education students.

947. *The Journal of Electronic Publishing.* [ISSN: 1080-2711] 1995. 3x/yr. Free. Ed(s): Judith Turner. University of Michigan Library, Scholarly Publishing Office, 300 Hatcher N, 920 N University Ave, Ann Arbor, MI 48109; lib.spo@umich.edu; http://www.lib.umich.edu/spo/. Refereed. *Indexed:* ISTA. *Aud.:* Ac, Sa.

An open-access journal intended for academic audiences, students, and faculty. Since 1995, *JEP* has been committed to "providing a forum for research and discussion about contemporary publishing practices, and the impact of those practices upon users." Three times a year *JEP* publishes articles on its web site, hosted by the Scholarly Publishing Office of the University of Michigan Library. The editors describe the publication as "neither quite a magazine nor a journal," as it publishes both invited contributions from experts and practitioners and longer articles (some peer-reviewed) from scholars, publishers, and others who are writing about electronic publishing. This unique journal crosses both professional fields and academic disciplines to bring the reader an informed snapshot of current issues in scholarly electronic publishing. Recommended for academic libraries. URL: www.journalofelectronicpublishing.org/index.html

948. *Journal of Scholarly Publishing.* Formerly (until 1994): *Scholarly Publishing.* [ISSN: 1198-9742] 1969. q. USD 140. Ed(s): Tom Radko. University of Toronto Press, Journals Division, 5201 Dufferin St, Toronto, ON M3H 5T8, Canada; journals@utpress.utoronto.ca; http://www.utpjournals.com. Illus., index, adv. Sample. Refereed. Vol. ends: Jul. Microform: MML. *Indexed:* A01, A22, ArtHuCI, BAS, CBCARef, CLI, E01, FR, HEA, ISTA, MLA-IB. *Bk. rev.:* 1-4, 400-500 words. *Aud.:* Ac, Sa.

The *Journal of Scholarly Publishing,* from the University of Toronto Press, is the premier venue for contributions to the current publishing debate. Articles and essays address enduring problems as well as challenges brought about by recent technological advances and shifting funding considerations. *JSP* is international in scope, and takes both a philosophical and a pragmatic approach to issues in the world of academic publishing. *JSP* includes a small section of academic book reviews. Published quarterly, *JSP* will appeal to authors, editors, marketers, and publishers of scholarly books and journals, and is recommended for academic and research libraries.

949. *Kirkus Reviews.* Former titles (until 1991): *Jim Kobak's Kirkus Reviews;* (until 1985): *Kirkus Reviews;* (until 1969): *Kirkus Service;* (until 1967): *Virginia Kirkus' Service;* (until 1964): *Virginia Kirkus' Service. Bulletin;* (until 1955): *Virginia Kirkus' Bookshop Service. Bulletin.* [ISSN: 1948-7428] 1933. bi-w. USD 199 combined subscription domestic (print & online eds.); USD 229 combined subscription foreign (print & online eds.); USD 25 newsstand/cover. Ed(s): Elaine Szewczyk. Kirkus Media LLC, 6411 Burleson Rd, Austin, TX 78744; customers@kirkusreviews.com; http://www.kirkusreviews.com. Illus., index, adv. *Indexed:* A01, BRI, CBRI, MASUSE. *Aud.:* Ems, Hs, Ga, Ac.

Founded in 1933, *Kirkus Reviews* has been a respected source of book reviews for almost 80 years. Purchased in early 2010 from the Nielsen Company, it is now operated by Kirkus Media LLC, and continues to publish pre-publication reviews on the first and 15th of each month, in both digital and print formats. *Kirkus* publishes more than 500 book reviews each month, including fiction and nonfiction, and children's and young adult books. The reviews are written by specialists selected for their knowledge and expertise in their particular fields, and *Kirkus* editors assign a star to books of "remarkable merit." Separate, themed *Kirkus Supplements* are also offered multiple times each year. *Kirkus* began reviewing children's-book apps for the iPad at the end of 2010, and has recently made the decision to expand its coverage to book apps for adults. Archived reviews from the digital version of the magazine are available to online subscribers through the publisher's web site (see below). Free features include select full reviews under "Critic's Pick," "Browse Books" by genre, and "Browse Lists." An extremely useful collection development tool for public and academic libraries. URL: http://kirkusreviews.com

950. *Lambda Literary Review.* Former titles (until 2010): *Lambda Book Report;* (until 1991): *Lambda Rising Book Report.* 1987. q. Ed(s): William Johnson. Lambda Literary Foundation, PO Box 73910, Washington, DC 20056-3910; llf@lambdalit.org; http://www.lambdalit.org. Illus., adv. *Indexed:* A01, A22, AmHI, BRI, C37, C42, CBRI, GW, MASUSE, MLA-IB, P02. *Aud.:* Ga, Ac.

Prior to 2009, the *Lambda Book Report* was published in print by the Lambda Literary Foundation. Since the Foundation re-launched its web site in 2010, all book reviews are now on the web site under the section *Lambda Literary Review.* The Foundation "seeks to represent as wide a spectrum as possible of LGBTQ ideas and perspectives" by covering pertinent literature, poetry, interviews, and publishing-industry news. The signed, critical reviews are lengthy, covering fiction, nonfiction, young adult, poetry, and drama and more from the LGBTQ community. The publisher's web site (see below) functions as a portal for literary resources and events such as the Lambda Literary Awards, the Writers' Retreat for Emerging LGBT Voice, literary events, book groups, workshops for writers, and links to other publications, publishers, editors, and author web sites. A well-rounded and useful resource for book selectors interested in LGBTQ literature. URL: http://lambdaliterary.org

The Literary Review. See Literary Reviews section.

951. *London Review of Books.* [ISSN: 0260-9592] 1979. s-m. GBP 63.72 combined subscription domestic (print & online eds.); GBP 76.50 combined subscription in Europe (print & online eds.); USD 42 combined subscription United States (print & online eds.). Ed(s): Mary-Kay Wilmers. L R B Ltd., 28 Little Russell St, London, WC1A 2HN, United Kingdom; subs@lrb.co.uk. Illus., index, adv. Circ: 48269. Vol. ends: Dec. Microform: PQC. *Indexed:* A01, A22, AmHI, BEL&L, BRI, C37, CBRI, MLA-IB, RILM. *Bk. rev.:* 15-20, 1,500-2,500 words. *Aud.:* Ga, Ac.

LRB features lengthy, intelligent review essays by academics, writers, and journalists, and shorter reviews of art and film. Erudite and often witty, *LRB*'s essays place book reviews in context, offer thoughtful commentary, and function as literary and intellectual works in their own right. Readers will also enjoy the magazine's poetry and its spirited letters page. *LRB* is published twice each month, and boasts the largest circulation of any literary magazine in Europe, as well as a worldwide reach and an "unmatched international reputation." The web site has full text of some content from current and past issues; the electronic version of the current issue and the complete online archive are available to subscribers. Recommended for academic and larger public libraries.

MultiCultural Review. See Multicultural Studies section.

952. *New York Review of Books.* [ISSN: 0028-7504] 1963. 20x/yr. USD 69 domestic; USD 89 Canada; USD 109 elsewhere. Ed(s): Robert Silvers. N Y R E V, Inc., 435 Hudson St, 3rd Fl, New York, NY 10014; web@nybooks.com. Illus., adv. Circ: 135109. Vol. ends: Jan. Microform: PQC. *Indexed:* A&ATA, A01, A22, ABS&EES, AmHI, ArtHuCI, BRI, CBRI, MASUSE, MLA-IB, P02, RILM. *Bk. rev.:* 15-20, 2,000-3,500 words. *Aud.:* Ga, Ac, Sa.

Every two weeks *NYRB* publishes a new issue "based on the assumption that the discussion of important books [is] itself an indispensable literary activity." The *Review* includes essays and reviews of books and the arts, selected from a pantheon of American writers who have helped shape the political and cultural issues of the nation since the publication's inception in 1963. As a sampling, current issues contain offerings by the likes of Larry McMurtry, Diane Ravitch, E. L. Doctorow, and Nadine Gordimer. In addition to the reviews, interviews, and articles, the *Review* features original poetry and extensive advertising from publishers promoting newly published books. The web site (below) contains substantial content from back issues in its archive dating back to 1963, and hosts a blog written by *NYRB*'s contributing writers. An indispensable source for academic and larger public libraries. URL: http://nybooks.com

953. *New York Times Book Review.* Former titles (until 1923): *New York Times Book Review and Magazine;* (until 1920): *New York Times Review of Books;* (until 1911): *New York Times Saturday Review of Books and Art;* (until 1896): *New York Times Saturday Book Review Supplement.* [ISSN: 0028-7806] 1896. w. New York Times Company, 620 8th Ave, New York, NY 10018; letters@nytimes.com; http://www.nytimes.com. Illus., index, adv. Vol. ends: Dec. Microform: PQC. *Indexed:* A01, A22, ABS&EES, AmHI, ArtHuCI, BEL&L, BRI, CBRI, Chicano, GardL, MLA-IB, N01, NewsAb, P02. *Bk. rev.:* 45-50, 250-2,500 words. *Aud.:* Ga, Ac, Sa.

Highly influential, widely read, and intended for the educated reader, the *NYTBR* publishes detailed reviews of a very small percentage of the fiction and nonfiction books it receives from publishers and authors in the mail each week. The focus is on important and notable books, as well as identifying significant works from new authors. Books considered for review must be published in the United States and available via general-interest bookstores. Separate hardcover, paperback, and ebook bestseller lists are further divided into categories, including fiction, nonfiction, advice, children's, graphic, and more. *NYTBR* appears in the Sunday edition of *The New York Times,* and is also available separately by subscription. The online version, freely available via the *New York Times* web site, also includes excerpts, podcasts, and "Arts Beat Books," the *NYTBR* blog. An essential source for all libraries.

954. *Publishers Weekly: the international news magazine of book publishing.* Formerly (until 1873): *Publishers' and Stationers' Weekly Trade Circular;* Incorporates (in 1872): *American Literary Gazette and Publishers' Circular;* Which was formerly (until 1863): *American Publishers' Circular and Literary Gazette;* (until 1855): *Norton's Literary Gazette and Publishers' Circular.* [ISSN: 0000-0019] 1872. w. USD 249.99 domestic (Free to qualified personnel). Ed(s): Sonia Jaffe Robbins. PWxyz, LLC, 71 West 23 St. #1608, New York, NY 10010. Illus., index, adv. Sample. Vol. ends: Dec. Microform: CIS; PQC. *Indexed:* A01, A06, A22, ABIn, ABS&EES, B01, B02, B03, BAS, BRI, C37, C42, CBRI, Chicano, F01, GardL, MASUSE, MLA-IB, P02, RILM. *Bk. rev.:* 70, 50-150 words. *Aud.:* Ga, Ac, Sa.

One of the book industry's best-known newsmagazines, *PW* informs publishers, sellers, agents, and librarians on the creation, production, marketing, and sale of the books in all formats. Focusing mainly on the U.S., issues cover industry news and book industry statistics, and provide critical reviews of print, audio, and e-books as well as in-depth author interviews. Regular bestseller lists cover fiction and nonfiction hardbacks, mass market and trade paperbacks, and audio fiction and nonfiction. Weekly columns, calendars of book-related events, advertisements, and classifieds provide a wealth of current information, but the signed book reviews are the backbone of this weekly publication. Short and readable, these reviews critique each book and assign a star to notable titles. Subscribers get access to the weekly print edition of *PW,* and a digital edition via their iPad app and online. The web site (see below) offers free access to news stories from the print magazine as well as its blogs, newsletters, and the current week's bestsellers lists; however, most reviews, print features, articles, author interviews, listings, and columns are available exclusively to subscribers only. A core resource, especially for public libraries. URL: http://publishersweekly.com

955. *Rain Taxi: review of books.* [ISSN: 1535-9352] 1996. q. USD 15 domestic; USD 23 in Canada & Mexico; USD 30 elsewhere. Ed(s): Eric Lorberer. Rain Taxi, Inc., PO Box 3840, Minneapolis, MN 55403; orders@raintaxi.com. Illus., adv. Circ: 17000. *Aud.:* Hs, Ga, Ac.

Committed to promoting literature, art, and culture by reviewing innovative fiction, nonfiction, poetry, graphic novels, and more that "might otherwise get overlooked," *Rain Taxi* has been a winner of the Alternative Press Award for Best Arts & Literature Coverage, as well as received an Utne Independent Press Award. The print version is published quarterly and is available by paid subscription or for free at over 250 independent bookstores and other centers of literary life. The online version, also free, is published quarterly but offers completely different content from the print. Bonus features of the online edition include teaching tools, video author interviews, and a searchable archive. *Rain Taxi* is recommended for libraries with users interested in exploring beyond the literary mainstream.

956. *Reference and Research Book News.* Incorporates (1977-200?): *SciTech Book News;* (1989-1992): *University Press Book News.* [ISSN: 0887-3763] 1986. bi-m. USD 175. Ed(s): Shannon Hendrickson. Book News, Inc. (Portland), 5739 NE Sumner St, Portland, OR 97218; info@booknews.com; http://www.booknews.com. Illus. Vol. ends: Nov. *Indexed:* A01, BRI, C37, CBCARef, CBRI. *Bk. rev.:* 2,500, 25-75 words. *Aud.:* Ga, Ac.

Reference and Research Book News now incorporates *SciTech Book News* and, thus, covers new reference works as well as scholarly titles in the humanities, technology, engineering, medicine, agriculture, and physical, biological, and social sciences. Published bimonthly, this journal is designed for acquisitions librarians in academic, special, and public libraries, and its entries are organized by Library of Congress subject classification and include bibliographic data. Reviews are concise and descriptive, and are of books immediately available for purchase. Current issues are available for free online; the subscription-based *Book News Online* database holds over 280,000 reviews, with 18,000 more added each year. A useful, practical resource for collection development librarians.

957. *T L S: the Times literary supplement.* Formerly (until 1969): *Times Literary Supplement.* [ISSN: 0307-661X] 1902. w. Ed(s): James MacManus, Peter Stothard. Times Newspapers Ltd., 3 Thomas More Sq, London, E98 1XY, United Kingdom; custserv@timesonline.co.uk; http://www.timesonline.co.uk. Illus., index, adv. Vol. ends: Dec. Microform: RPI. *Indexed:* A01, A22, AmHI, ArtHuCI, BRI, CBRI, F01, MLA-IB, P02, RILM. *Bk. rev.:* Number and length vary. *Aud.:* Ga, Ac.

Published weekly for "lovers of literary culture," *TLS* "provides a unique record of developments in literature, politics, scholarship and the arts, and brings a unique seriousness to bear on the major intellectual debates of our time." U.K.-based *TLS* is global in scope and readership as it offers comprehensive coverage of recent and important publications as well as developments in the realms of theater, opera, exhibitions, and film. *TLS* is part of the *Sunday Times,* but is also available separately by subscription. The free web site features two blogs and full-text access to selected current content; subscribers may access the complete online current issue and archive. As *TLS* has set the standard for the authoritative literary review, it is an essential resource for libraries.

958. *The Women's Review of Books.* [ISSN: 0738-1433] 1983. bi-m. USD 95 (print & online eds.). Ed(s): Amy Hoffman. Old City Publishing, Inc., 628 N 2nd St, Philadelphia, PA 19123; info@oldcitypublishing.com; http://www.oldcitypublishing.com. Illus., index, adv. Sample. Circ: 15000 Paid. Vol. ends: Sep. Microform: PQC. *Indexed:* A01, A22, ABS&EES, AmHI, BRI, C37, C42, CBRI, FemPer, MASUSE, MLA-IB, P02, WSA. *Bk. rev.:* 15-20, 1,000-1,500 words. *Aud.:* Ac, Sa.

The *Women's Review of Books* admirably accomplishes its mission "to promote women's critical writing" by providing intelligent, accessible essays and signed, in-depth reviews of new books by and about women, on a bimonthly basis. The reviews cover an eclectic mix of new fiction, poetry, biographies of notable women, and a wide range of relevant nonfiction topics. Regular features showcase women's original photography, poetry, or artwork. *WRB's* web site (see below) contains full text of selected articles and images back to 2006; issues published three years ago and older are available through JSTOR as well. A rich, thought-provoking source of reviews, analyses, and commentary for academic and larger public libraries. URL: http://wcwonline.org/womensreview

■ BOTANY

See also Biology; and Ecology sections.

Kari Zhe-Heimerman, Librarian for the Sciences, Le Moyne College, 1419 Salt Springs Road, Syracuse, NY 13214

Introduction

Botany, also referred to as plant science, plant biology, or phytology, is the branch of biology focused on the study of plants. As a discipline, it examines a wide variety of organisms, including plants, algae, and fungi. It also encompasses many different levels of examination, from the molecular focus through to plant community interactions. Botany includes a large range of subdisciplines such as classification, structure, ecology, growth, physiology, genetics, metabolism, development, pathology, systematics, and evolution. Botany continues to grow and evolve as a discipline, with biochemistry, cellular and molecular biology, genetics, and ecological interactions gaining more significance within the field.

The aim of this section is to present a comprehensive collection of core botany titles that could support either general botany researchers, academic specialists, field scientists, industry specialists, or plant practitioners. The primary focus of this section is general botany journals that present current, original research, and review articles that cover a wide range of botanical topics. There are also a few specialty titles presented in areas of great botanical importance (such as systematics and ecology and pathology). These journals include international fora for plant research, as well as titles that focus on national developments in the field of botany. Most of the titles in this section are primarily suited for academic and special library collections, although a large or specialized public library may also have an interest in some of the key titles that are labeled accordingly.

Because of the wide range of topics and levels of study within botany, research in this area is often dependent on core botany titles as well as on general science, chemistry, agriculture, and ecology journals. Readers should note that this section limits itself to journals that have botany as their focus; however, the Biology, Ecology, and Chemistry sections of this edition of *MFL* will have further useful recommendations for those interested in comprehensive botany research.

Basic Periodicals

Ac: *American Journal of Botany, Annals of Botany, AoB Botany, International Journal of Plant Sciences.*

Basic Abstracts and Indexes

AGRICOLA, Biological Abstracts, Biological & Agricultural Index, BIOBASE, CAB Abstracts, Chemical Abstracts, Horticultural Science Abstracts, Science Citation Index.

959. *A O B Plants.* [ISSN: 2041-2851] 2009. m. Free. Ed(s): Mike Jackson. Oxford University Press, Great Clarendon St, Oxford, OX2 6DP, United Kingdom; enquiry@oup.co.uk; http://www.oxfordjournals.org. Refereed. *Aud.:* Ac, Sa.

AoB Plants is an international, peer-reviewed, open-access journal that publishes articles on a wide range of plant biology topics. This journal is written for both a specialized and interdisciplinary audience, and the range of topics covered indicates this commitment. Though topics need to be of current interest, they can range from the sub-cellular to the community level. This journal is published by Oxford Journals on behalf of the Annals of Botany company, and its mission is to provide an affordable, open-access route for the rapid publication of peer-reviewed manuscripts for the benefit of the international plant science community. The types of articles published include original research articles, point-of-view commentaries, technical articles, invited review articles, mini-reviews, and traditional review articles. Because of the general scope and wide intended audience, this publication will be of interest for public, academic, and special botany collections.

960. *American Journal of Botany.* Incorporates (19??-1982): *Botanical Society of America. Meeting. Abstracts;* Which was formerly (until 198?): *Botanical Society of America. Abstracts of Papers to be Presented at the Meetings;* (until 1977): *American Journal of Botany.* [ISSN: 0002-9122] 1914. m. USD 665 (print & online eds.). Ed(s): Judy Jernstedt, Amy McPherson. Botanical Society of America, Inc. (Columbus), Business Office, PO Box 299, St. Louis, MO 63166; bsa-manager@botany.org; http://www.botany.org. Illus., adv. Sample. Refereed. Microform: IDC; PMC. *Indexed:* A01, A22, AbAn, Agr, BRI, C45, OceAb, P02, RRTA, S25. *Bk. rev.:* Number and length vary. *Aud.:* Ac, Sa.

This internationally recognized journal publishes original, refereed research that addresses major questions of plant biology. Articles range from molecular to ecosystem level, and cover topics including structure, function, development, diversity, genetics, evolution, reproduction, and systematics. In addition to original research, the journal contains reviews, critiques, and analyses of controversial plant biology subjects. With its general focus on all plant groups and allied organisms, this journal is of interest to plant scientists in all areas of plant biology. Recommended for academic and special botany collection.

961. *Annals of Botany.* [ISSN: 0305-7364] 1887. m. EUR 1268. Ed(s): J S Heslop-Harrison, David Frost. Oxford University Press, Great Clarendon St, Oxford, OX2 6DP, United Kingdom; enquiry@oup.co.uk; http://www.oxfordjournals.org/. Illus., adv. Sample. Refereed. Microform: IDC; PMC. Reprint: PSC. *Indexed:* A01, A22, AbAn, Agr, C45, E01, FS&TA, OceAb, RRTA, S25. *Bk. rev.:* Number and length vary. *Aud.:* Ac, Sa.

This international journal publishes original and strikingly new research across the field of botany. Topics range from the molecular to ecosystem level, and include questions from all areas of botanical science, with particular emphasis on molecular, analytical, mathematical, and statistical techniques. Published monthly, the journal also produces at least one extra issue per year on a particular theme of interest in plant biology. The journal is managed by the Annals of Botany Company, a not-for-profit educational charity, and it is recognized for its rigorous review process. Articles include research papers, short communications, review articles (both invited and submitted), and book reviews. This journal is of interest to plant biology researchers across specialties and is recommended for academic and special botany collections.

962. *Annual Review of Plant Biology.* Former titles (until 2002): *Annual Review of Plant Physiology and Plant Molecular Biology;* (until 1988): *Annual Review of Plant Physiology.* [ISSN: 1543-5008] 1950. a. USD 269 (print or online ed.). Ed(s): Samuel Gubins, Sabeeha Merchant. Annual Reviews, PO Box 10139, Palo Alto, CA 94303; service@annualreviews.org; http://www.annualreviews.org. Refereed. Microform: PQC. Reprint: PSC. *Indexed:* A01, A22, Agr, C45, GardL. *Aud.:* Ac, Sa.

This highly cited journal presents reviews of the significant developments in plant biology each year. Since 1950, researchers have turned to *Annual Review of Plant Biology* for review articles covering a wide range of plant biology subdisciplines. These content areas include, but are not limited to, biochemistry, molecular biology, genetics and genomics, cell biology, plant ecology, methods, and model organisms. Plant biology is covered from the cellular to the community level, with a special focus on significant contributions to advancement in a particular year. This journal will be of great use to keep plant biology researchers aware of important advancements across the field. It should be a core component of an academic or special library collection that supports such researchers.

963. *B M C Plant Biology.* [ISSN: 1471-2229] 2000. m. Free. Ed(s): Dr. Melissa Norton. BioMed Central Ltd., 236 Gray's Inn Rd, London, WC1X 8HB, United Kingdom; info@biomedcentral.com; http://www.biomedcentral.com. Adv. Refereed. *Indexed:* A01, Agr, C45, FS&TA. *Aud.:* Ac, Sa.

This open-access, peer-reviewed journal publishes original articles on a wide variety of useful research contributions in the field of plant biology. Topics focus from the molecular to whole plant level, including all the levels between. Especially useful features of this online-only journal include large data sets, large numbers of illustrations and moving pictures, and data displayed in a form that can be manipulated by readers. This journal is freely available online, and offers comprehensive articles on topics of interest to general plant scientists and specialized botanists. It is recommended for all academic, special botany collections, and could prove a useful, free addition to a public library collection as well.

964. *The Botanical Review.* [ISSN: 0006-8101] 1935. q. EUR 176 (print & online eds.). Ed(s): Dennis W M Steven, Joy E Runyon. Springer New York LLC, 233 Spring St, New York, NY 10013; journals@springer-ny.com; http://www.springer.com. Illus., adv. Sample. Refereed. Vol. ends: Oct/Dec. Microform: IDC; PMC; PQC. Reprint: PSC. *Indexed:* A01, A22, Agr, BRI, C45, E01, P02, RRTA. *Aud.:* Ac, Sa.

This internationally recognized journal reviews current plant science research. Its detailed review articles cover a wide range of topics within the field of botany, including such topics as systematics, phytogeography, cladistics, evolution, physiology, ecology, morphology, paleobotany, and anatomy. The goal of the journal is to synthesize the current research done by various scientists on a particular topic within the field of plant biology in order to identify current gaps and research needs within that particular area. Articles are mainly by invitation (although submissions are accepted) and undergo rigorous review before publication. This journal will be of interest to any researcher in the field of plant biology, and is recommended for academic and special botany collections.

965. *Botany.* Former titles (until Jan.2008): *Canadian Journal of Botany;* (until 1950): *Canadian Journal of Research. Section C: Botanical Sciences;* Which superseded in part (in 1935): *Canadian Journal of Research.* [ISSN: 1916-2790] 1929. m. USD 1650. Ed(s): Christian R Lacroix. N R C Research Press, 1200 Montreal Rd, Bldg M-55, Ottawa, ON K1A 0R6, Canada; pubs@nrc-cnrc.gc.ca; http://pubs.nrc-cnrc.gc.ca. Illus., index, adv. Refereed. Circ: 1506. Vol. ends: Dec. Microform: MML; PMC; PQC. *Indexed:* A01, A22, ABS&EES, Agr, C37, C45, CBCARef, E01, EngInd, FS&TA, RRTA, S25. *Aud.:* Ac, Sa.

This well-respected international journal of botany has been a source of original research articles, review articles, and commentary in all areas of plant science since 1929. Topics covered include cell and molecular biology, ecology, mycology and plant-microbe interactions, phycology, physiology and biochemistry, structure and development, genetics, systematics, and phytogeography. The National Research Council of Canada, the journal's

publisher, ensures a rigorous peer-review process for each article. The journal is of interest to general and specialized plant science researchers, and is recommended for public, academic, or special botany collections.

966. *Brittonia.* Incorporates: *Taxonomic Index.* [ISSN: 0007-196X] 1931. q. EUR 160 (print & online eds.). Ed(s): Lawrence M Kelly, Joy E Runyon. Springer New York LLC, 233 Spring St, New York, NY 10013; service-ny@springer.com; http://www.springer.com. Illus., adv. Sample. Refereed. Circ: 700. Reprint: PSC. *Indexed:* A22, Agr, BRI, C45, E01. *Aud.:* Ac, Sa.

Brittonia is a widely indexed and important voice in systematic plant research. Since 1931, the staff of the New York Botanical Garden, along with other contributors, has used this journal to share original research focused on taxonomy, phylogeny, the diversity of plants, and the relationships of plants. Some articles are also available to readers freely via open-access options, depending on the author's choice. This journal will be of interest to researchers in the area of plant systematics, and is recommended for any academic or special library that supports such research.

967. *International Journal of Plant Sciences.* Former titles (until 1992): *Botanical Gazette;* (until 1876): *Botanical Bulletin.* [ISSN: 1058-5893] 1875. m. except Mar./Apr, Jul./Aug. and Nov./Dec. combined. USD 939 (print & online eds.). Ed(s): Patrick Herendeen, James Ellis. University of Chicago Press, 1427 E 60th St, Chicago, IL 60637; subscriptions@press.uchicago.edu; http://www.journals.uchicago.edu. Illus., index, adv. Sample. Refereed. Vol. ends: Nov. Microform: IDC. Reprint: PSC. *Indexed:* A01, A22, Agr, BRI, C45, FS&TA, GardL, P02, S25. *Bk. rev.:* Number and length vary. *Aud.:* Ac, Sa.

This journal, internationally recognized as a major forum for botany research, presents original, peer-reviewed research in all areas of the plant sciences. Intended to present new contributions in plant biology from around the world, the journal covers a wide variety of topics including biochemistry, cell biology, developmental biology, ecology, evolution, genetics, genomics, physiology, morphology and structure, systematics, plant–microbe interactions, and paleobotany. In addition, the journal publishes special issues on topics of current interest, including research presented at major botanical conferences. This journal is written for general and specialized plant biologists who are interested in current research in the field, and is recommended for any academic or special botany collection.

968. *Journal of Experimental Botany.* [ISSN: 0022-0957] 1950. m. plus special issue. EUR 2185. Ed(s): Christine Raines, Mary Traynor. Oxford University Press, Great Clarendon St, Oxford, OX2 6DP, United Kingdom; enquiry@oup.co.uk; http://www.oxfordjournals.org/. Illus., index, adv. Sample. Refereed. Circ: 560. Vol. ends: Dec. Microform: PQC. Reprint: PSC. *Indexed:* A01, A22, AbAn, Agr, C45, E01, EngInd, FS&TA, RRTA, S25. *Aud.:* Ac, Sa.

Published on behalf of the Society for Experimental Biology, this peer-reviewed journal is a forum for both primary research and review articles in the plant sciences. Topics cover a range of disciplines including plant physiology, biochemistry, molecular biology, and biophysics. The focus of these articles ranges from the molecular level to cellular through whole plant to community. Each issue also contains at least one "Perspective" article that reviews an area of current research controversy or interest. In addition to the monthly issues of the journal, at least one special issue is published each year that collects relevant articles from a current conference or meeting. There are open-access options available for authors in this journal, so some articles are freely available to the reader. This journal would be of interest to general or specialized researchers in plant biology, particularly those interested in the cutting-edge research in the field. Recommended for academic or special botany collections.

969. *Journal of Plant Interactions.* [ISSN: 1742-9145] 2005. q. GBP 310 (print & online eds.). Ed(s): Dr. Massimo Maffei. Taylor & Francis, 4 Park Sq, Milton Park, Abingdon, OX14 4RN, United Kingdom; subscriptions@tandf.co.uk; http://www.tandfonline.com. Adv. Sample. Refereed. Reprint: PSC. *Indexed:* A01, A22, C45, E01. *Aud.:* Ac, Sa.

This journal presents primary research and review articles focused on plant interactions with the surrounding environment. The following interactions are covered: plant–plant, plant–microorganism, plant–insect, plant–animal, plant–environment, and plant–soil. Also covered are biochemical, physiological, and molecular aspects. All submissions are subjected to a rigorous international peer-review process. The primary audiences for this journal include both plant biologists and ecologists. This journal is strongly recommended for academic and special botany collections, especially those collections where plant ecology is a focus.

970. Native Plants Journal. [ISSN: 1522-8339] 2000. 3x/yr. USD 145 (print & online eds.). Ed(s): R Kasten Dumroese. University of Wisconsin Press, Journal Division, 1930 Monroe St, 3rd Fl, Madison, WI 53711; journals@uwpress.wisc.edu; http://www.uwpress.org/. Illus., adv. Refereed. Circ: 1200. Reprint: PSC. *Indexed:* A01, A22, Agr, BRI, C45, E01, GardL, P02, RRTA. *Bk. rev.:* Number and length vary. *Aud.:* Ga, Ac, Sa.

This journal includes both peer-reviewed, primary research articles and general technical articles concerned with planting and growing North American native plants. It is published in full color, and topics cover a wide range, including conservation, restoration, reforestation, and landscaping with native plants. The journal aims to be a communication forum between academic researchers and field/nursery practitioners. As such, it focuses on practical scientific information about seed germination, planting techniques and tools, equipment, cultural techniques, seed collection, and fertilization. Also included are plant propagation protocols that give specific directions for growing particular native species. This journal is written for either researchers or practitioners interested in growing native plants, and it has wide appeal for any collection that supports users with that interest.

971. New Phytologist (Online). [ISSN: 1469-8137] 1998. 16x/yr. GBP 1839. Ed(s): Ian Woodward. Wiley-Blackwell Publishing Ltd., 9600 Garsington Rd, Oxford, OX4 2DQ, United Kingdom; customer@wiley.co.uk; http://www.wiley.com/. Refereed. *Bk. rev.:* Number and length vary. *Aud.:* Ac, Sa.

New Phytologist, published on behalf of the nonprofit New Phytologist Trust, is dedicated to the promotion of original and current plant science research. The journal presents peer-reviewed, original research on topics of current interest in plant science that fall into four major areas: physiology and development, environment, interaction, and evolution. These topics are covered at levels ranging from cellular to community. Other features of the journal include a forum section that hosts letters, commentary, and opinion pieces; short research reviews on topics of current interest; rapid reports; modeling/theory papers; and methods papers. Special issues of the journal are published to highlight key areas of current research. There are open-access options available to authors, so some of this journal's articles are freely available online. This journal is recommended for general plant scientists who need to keep up-to-date with current research developments and discussion. It would be key for any academic or special botany collection.

972. The Plant Cell. [ISSN: 1040-4651] 1989. m. Non-members, USD 500 (print & online eds.). Ed(s): Cathie Martin. American Society of Plant Biologists, 15501 Monona Dr, Rockville, MD 20855; info@aspb.org; http://www.aspb.org. Illus., index, adv. Sample. Refereed. Circ: 2300. *Indexed:* A01, A22, Agr, C45, EngInd, FS&TA, RRTA. *Aud.:* Ac, Sa.

The Plant Cell is a highly regarded source of cutting-edge original research that is of broad interest to all plant biologists, not just specialists. The journal places special emphasis on cellular biology, molecular biology, genetics, development, and evolution. Published monthly by the American Society for Plant Biologists, this journal prides itself on a rigorous but very expedient peer-review process that provides rapid turnaround on research articles. As part of the journals' mission to increase interactive discussion in the plant biology research community, the front section of the journal is devoted to commentaries, editorials, meeting reports, review articles, and summaries of featured research papers. There are some open-access articles available for this journal via the journal's web site. *The Plant Cell* is written for a general audience of plant biology researchers, and does not focus on articles written for or by specialists. Thus it is recommended for any public, academic, or special botany collection.

973. The Plant Journal. [ISSN: 0960-7412] 1991. s-m. GBP 2975. Ed(s): Christoph Benning. Wiley-Blackwell Publishing Ltd., 9600 Garsington Rd, Oxford, OX4 2DQ, United Kingdom; customerservices@blackwellpublishing.com; http://www.wiley.com/. Illus., adv. Sample. Refereed. Microform: PQC. Reprint: PSC. *Indexed:* A01, A22, Agr, C45, E01, EngInd, FS&TA, P02, RRTA. *Aud.:* Ac, Sa.

This journal, published in association with the Society for Experimental Biology, is one of the most highly cited by the general plant science community. *The Plant Journal* presents highly significant advances in international plant biology research. Topics covered range across the subdisciplines of modern plant biology, including molecular biology, cell biology, biochemistry, genetics, and protein function in plants. Original research articles, technical advance articles, and editorials are all included in the journal; special issues are published periodically on topics of current interest. There are open-access options available for some of the journal articles. This is a high-quality, rigorous, research publication written to keep any researcher with an interest in the wide range of plant biology fields up-to-date. This journal is suitable for academic or special botany collections.

974. Plant Physiology. [ISSN: 0032-0889] 1926. m. Members, USD 240; Non-members, USD 475 (print & online eds.); Students, USD 175). Ed(s): Donald R Ort, John Long. American Society of Plant Biologists, 15501 Monona Dr, Rockville, MD 20855; info@aspb.org; http://www.aspb.org. Illus., index, adv. Refereed. Circ: 2300. Microform: MIM; PMC; PQC. *Indexed:* A01, A22, AbAn, Agr, C45, EngInd, FS&TA. *Aud.:* Ac, Sa.

Plant Physiology is a highly regarded, international journal that presents basic research on how plants live, function, and interact with their biotic and abiotic environments. The topics covered include nutrition, metabolism, growth, development, reproduction, environmental physiology, stress physiology, biochemistry, genetics, and biophysics. These topics are covered from the molecular through ecosystem level, and all levels in between. Some articles are available for free via the journal's web site, and they are labeled accordingly. This journal is written for scientists interested in the physiology of plants, but presents a wide range of topics within that discipline. It is necessary for any academic or special botany collection that supports plant physiology researchers.

975. Taxon: international journal of plant taxonomy, phylogeny and evolution. [ISSN: 0040-0262] 1951. bi-m. Free to members. Ed(s): S Robert Gradstein. International Association for Plant Taxonomy, Institute of Botany, University of Vienna, Vienna, 1030, Austria; http://www.iapt-taxon.org. Illus., adv. Refereed. Circ: 2500. *Indexed:* A22, Agr, C45, GardL. *Bk. rev.:* Number and length vary. *Aud.:* Ac, Sa.

As the official journal of the International Association for Plant Taxonomy, this is an important source for current information regarding plant and fungal systematic botany. Topics covered include, but are not limited to, rubiaceae systematics, molecular phylogenetics, speciation and population genetics, morphology, taxonomy, methods and techniques, karyology, and nomenclature. In addition to original, peer-reviewed research articles and review articles, the journal also includes features such as proposals to conserve or reject names, proposals to amend the code, current reports on plant systematics from around the world, and book reviews. Written for an international research audience with a particular interest in taxonomy, phylogeny, systematics, and nomenclature, this journal will be of interest to academic and special botany collections that support such research interests.

976. Trends in Plant Science. [ISSN: 1360-1385] 1996. m. EUR 2264. Ed(s): Susanne C Brink. Elsevier Ltd., Trends Journals, The Blvd, Langford Ln, Kidlington, Oxford, OX5 1GB, United Kingdom; JournalsCustomerServiceEMEA@elsevier.com; http://www.elsevier.com. Illus., adv. Sample. Refereed. Circ: 465. Vol. ends: No. 6. *Indexed:* A01, A22, AbAn, Agr, C45, FS&TA, GardL. *Aud.:* Ac, Sa.

This highly cited journal presents review articles on a broad range of topics of current interest to both plant science researchers and technicians. Topics presented include (but are not limited to) growth, development, genetics, evolution, cell biology, biotechnology, physiology, metabolism, nutrition, pathology, systematics, and plant interactions with both abiotic and biotic environments. These topics are covered at levels ranging from molecular through cellular to ecosystem. Invited and refereed review articles as well as opinion articles focus on basic research topics or controversies that illuminate important developments on a particular specialty topic. Additionally, the "Update" section features research articles that highlight significant, recent research or technical advances. The journal is designed as a tool for academic and applied plant scientists across specialties to stay up-to-date with the latest plant biology research developments and discussions. It is appropriate for academic and special botany collections that serve either academic researchers or field technicians.

■ BUILDING AND CONSTRUCTION

See also Architecture; Home; and Interior Design and Decoration sections.

Nicholas Wharton, Head, Reference and Public Services, Mortensen Library, University of Hartford, 200 Bloomfield Ave., West Hartford, CT 06117

Introduction

As economic times remain unstable, libraries have a duty to offer the best information tools for local tradespeople to be able to improve, economize, and learn about the innovations, trends, and regulations that impact their livelihood. Construction, heavy or light, has a huge impact on the economic well-being of any geographic region. Offering access to that information to help contractors and designers promote business and prosper becomes the most difficult task for a librarian with limited budgets and space constraints.

This section focuses on trade magazines that have been chosen due to their impact or importance to the construction industry and, if added to collections, would fulfill the information needs of a library's community of builders. There are a vast number of trade journals available in print and online that do not make the list for the very same reasons that a librarian must choose what to add to its collection based on need, clientele, and space issues. The focus of this section is on the construction industry as it pertains to practical uses for large and small projects, refurbishing, new construction, and equipment (heavy and light), and it gets as specific as concrete construction or welding.

All of the magazines have common threads such as to propose ideas, expose best practices, and explain regulation changes. Many offer product information and reviews, opinion pieces, and success stories. All offer vivid photographs and diagrams of the ideas and products discussed. Article topics are current and relevant. The section is designed to help librarians make informed decisions on how to help patrons in the construction field continue to provide work, promote new ideas, and prosper in uncertain times.

The magazines all have an online presence, which may fill an immediate need for a library's patrons without the need to purchase an institutional subscription. All access to contents and other article information is available in each magazine for future procurement through interlibrary loan if not a subscriber. The scope of access to the online information varies depending on the rules of the publisher, as some online article access is fee-based, member-based, or free. All access to contents and other article information is available in each magazine for future procurement through interlibrary loan, if the inquirer is not a subscriber. The online presence commonly offers blogs, product information and reviews, archives of past issues, classifieds, job prospects, and usually advertisements.

These magazines of the building trade are important to all types of libraries. Most public libraries will need to carry some of the titles depending on the needs of its patrons. Academic libraries with engineering, architecture, and design programs will find these magazines and journals most important to building a well-rounded collection. The magazines highlighted in this section give a cross-section of the types of periodicals that are helpful and useful for the construction community. There are also other sections in *Magazines for Libraries* that contain crossover building and construction journals in the "Architecture," "Home," and "Interior Design and Decoration" sections.

Basic Periodicals

Sa: *Builder* (Washington), *Building Design & Construction, Constructor, Old-House Journal, Professional Builder.*

Basic Abstracts and Indexes

Applied Science and Technology Index, Engineering Index, T R I S Electronic Bibliographic Data Base.

977. A C I Materials Journal. Supersedes in part (until 1987): *American Concrete Institute. Journal.* [ISSN: 0889-325X] 1913. bi-m. USD 650 (Individuals, USD 161; Free to members). Ed(s): Rex C Donahey. American Concrete Institute, PO Box 9094, Farmington Hills, MI 48333; BKStore@concrete.org; http://www.concrete.org; Illus., index, adv. Sample. Refereed. *Indexed:* A22, C&ISA, CerAb, EngInd. *Aud.:* Ac, Sa.

The American Concrete Institute publishes the *Materials Journal* to inform professional masons and forms pourers, architects, and engineers on the latest trends in various aspects of concrete materials. The subjects include articles on best practices, proper mixes, types of reinforcements, and sealants and grouts to be used by professionals in the field. The *Materials Journal* is available full-text for a fee and archived back to 1905. Fees as of publication are $25 for members and $20 for non-members or via yearly subscription. Visit the ACI (www.concrete.org) web site for membership and subscription pricing. URL: www.concrete.org/PUBS/JOURNALS/MJHOME.ASP

978. A C I Structural Journal. Supersedes in part (until 1987): *American Concrete Institute. Journal.* [ISSN: 0889-3241] 1913. bi-m. USD 650 (Individuals, USD 161; Free to members). Ed(s): Rex C Donahey. American Concrete Institute, PO Box 9094, Farmington Hills, MI 48333; webmaster@aci-int.org; http://www.concrete.org. Illus., index, adv. Refereed. Microform: PQC. *Indexed:* A22, ApMecR, C&ISA, CerAb, EngInd, H24, P02. *Aud.:* Ac, Sa.

The American Concrete Institute publishes the *Structural Journal* to inform professional masons and forms pourers, architects, and engineers on the latest trends in various aspects of concrete reinforcement materials. Articles include information on types of reinforcements for concrete, structural integrity, and testing methodology for reinforced structural concrete used in industrial and home construction. The *Structural Journal* is available full-text for a fee and archived back to 1905. Fees as of publication are $25 for members and $20 for non-members or via yearly subscription. Visit the ACI (www.concrete.org) web site for membership and subscription pricing. URL: www.concrete.org/PUBS/JOURNALS/SJHOME.ASP

Air Conditioning, Heating & Refrigeration News. See Business and Finance/Trade and Industry section.

979. Builder (Washington): NAHB, the voice of America's housing industry. Incorporates (1978-1982): *Housing;* Which was formerly (until 1978): *House & Home;* (until 1952): *The Magazine of Building (House & Home Edition);* (until 19??): *Architectural Forum;* Supersedes in part (in 1981): *N A H B Builder;* Which was formerly (until 1980): *Builder;* Which superseded (in 1978): *N A H B Journal-Scope;* Which was formed by the merger of: *N A H B Journal; N A H B Washington Scope.* [ISSN: 0744-1193] 1942. m. Free to qualified personnel; USD 8 per issue. Ed(s): Denise Dersin. Hanley Wood, LLC, 1 Thomas Cir, NW, Ste 600, Washington, DC 20005; fanton@hanleywood.com; http://www.hanleywood.com. Illus., adv. Microform: PQC. *Indexed:* A22, ABIn, API, B02, BRI. *Aud.:* Ac, Sa.

Builder, published by the NAHB (National Association of Home Builders), serves designers, developers, architects, and contractors in innovations and best practices for new and restoration home construction. Product features, innovative designs, regulation information, cost analysis, and green construction are typical features and topics each month, and each April issue contains the "Buyer's Guide" issue. Print subscriptions are fee-based, and online access is free with online archive beginning in 2006. The web site offers a database of house plans, a link to online video instructions, and events and industry news information. URL: www.builderonline.com

980. Building Design & Construction: the magazine for the building team. Formerly (until 1958): *Building Construction.* [ISSN: 0007-3407] 1950. m. Free to qualified personnel. S G C Horizon LLC., 3030 W. Salt Creek Ln., Ste.201, Arlington Heights, IL 60005; tmancini@sgcmail.com; http://www.sgchorizon.com/. Illus., index, adv. Sample. Circ: 76006 Controlled. *Indexed:* A22, ABIn, ArchI, B01, B02, B03, BRI. *Aud.:* Ac, Sa.

The scope of *Building Design & Construction* reaches an audience for big-project construction, including developers, architects, and general contractors, with articles highlighting successful projects, new trends in design and engineering, legal issues, and going green. The *Building Design & Construction* web site offers a blog, job and education links, and extensive product information. The journal is available online and is archived back to 2010 with free access. URL: www.bdcnetwork.com

981. Buildings: the source for facilities decision-makers. Formerly (until 1947): *Buildings and Building Management;* Incorporates (1910-1958): *National Real Estate and Building Journal;* (199?-2002): *Building Interiors.* [ISSN: 0007-3725] 1906. m. USD 125 (Free to qualified personnel). Ed(s): Leah B Garris. Stamats Business Media, Inc., P O Box 1888, Cedar Rapids, IA 52406; http://www.stamats.com/. Illus., index, adv. Vol. ends: Dec. Microform: PQC. *Indexed:* A22, ABIn, B01, B02, BRI, C&ISA, CerAb. *Aud.:* Ac, Sa.

Buildings, with its web site (see below), informs developers, architects, general contractors, and building owners on trends in the building and construction industry, including restoration, retrofitting, and new construction. Articles range from informational to cost explanations to elevator efficiency. The magazine has been in continuous publication since 1906. The online magazine and web site offer extra points of entry to the building, restoration, and upkeep of buildings. A "Buyers Guide" and a "Resource Center" are offered on the web along with an RSS feed, a database of white papers, and several online newsletters. There is also a browsable menu for viewing articles from past issues back to December 2003, and a selection of featured facsimiles from archival issues even older. URL: www.buildings.com

982. Concrete Construction. Former titles (until 1999): *Aberdeen's Concrete Construction;* (until 1990): *Concrete Construction.* [ISSN: 1533-7316] 1956. m. USD 30 domestic; USD 39 in Canada & Mexico; USD 93 elsewhere. Ed(s): Tim Gregorski, Kate Hamilton. Hanley Wood, LLC, 8725 W Higgins Rd, Ste 600, Chicago, IL 60631; fanton@hanleywood.com; http://www.hanleywood.com. Illus., index, adv. Microform: PQC. *Indexed:* A22, B02, BRI, EngInd. *Aud.:* Ac, Sa.

Hanley-Wood publishes *Concrete Construction* to engage concrete pourers, contractors, architects, and engineers with new standards, trends, mixing formulas, and problems in the concrete construction industry. Each issue highlights a "Contractor to Watch," product news and reviews, and monthly feature articles. The online magazine has two "Web Exclusive" articles per issue. The web site has video guides to help with step-by-step instructions, and video models to aid practitioners in the field, as well as a blog and an "On the Job" section that goes in-depth into various aspects of concrete uses in construction. Current and past issues back to March 1950 are available free online. URL: www.concreteconstruction.net

983. Concrete International. Formerly: *Concrete International - Design and Construction.* [ISSN: 0162-4075] 1979. m. Free to members. Ed(s): Rex C Donahey, Keith A Tosolt. American Concrete Institute, PO Box 9094, Farmington Hills, MI 48333; webmaster@aci-int.org; http://www.concrete.org. Adv. Refereed. *Indexed:* A22, C&ISA, CerAb, P02. *Aud.:* Ac, Sa.

The American Concrete Institute publishes *Concrete International* to inform professionals in the industry about composites mixing, trends, and standards and best practices. Articles include topics such as highlighted finished structures, best practices, repair tutorials, and behaviors of different types of mortar and concrete with a "Products and Practices Spotlight" section. Also, the ACI web site has a free career center link for prospective job seekers and employers. *Concrete International* is available in print or online, with a searchable database of past issues dating back to 1979, and free access to its abstracts. URL: www.concreteinternational.com/pages/index.asp

984. Construction Equipment: ideas and insight for the equipment pro. Former titles: *Construction Equipment Magazine; Construction Equipment and Materials Magazine.* [ISSN: 0192-3978] 1949. 13x/yr. Free to qualified personnel. S G C Horizon LLC., 3030 W. Salt Creek Ln., Ste.201, Arlington Heights, IL 60005; tmancini@sgcmail.com; http://www.sgchorizon.com/. Illus., index, adv. Sample. Circ: 80000 Controlled. *Indexed:* A22, ABIn, B01, B02, B03, BRI. *Aud.:* Sa.

Construction Equipment caters to the contractors who will need to utilize heavy equipment to get the job done. Heavy equipment includes front-end loaders, dump trucks, hydraulic lifts, bulldozers, compressors, generators, portable heating systems, and the equipment attachments that may be needed. This area includes all the tools that a job site will require to clear, fill, heat, and electrify. Print and online subscriptions are free, and access to the online version, including archives back to July 2002, is available at no charge. The online articles have a simple search engine finding aid. The web site has advertisements and product information, equipment evaluations, and resources that include a blog, white papers, case studies, and videos. URL: www.constructionequipment.com

985. The Construction Specifier. [ISSN: 0010-6925] 1950. m. Free to qualified personnel. Construction Specifications Institute, 110 S Union St, Ste 100, Alexandria, VA 22314; csi@csinet.org; http://www.csinet.org. Illus., index. *Indexed:* A22, ArchI, C&ISA, CerAb, EngInd. *Aud.:* Sa.

The Construction Specifier covers the gamut of techniques used in new and remodeling construction and is geared to contractors, designers, and architects. Topics include innovations like "tilt-up" concrete techniques, code and standards changes, green building, and bidding advice. The print subscription is generally free; however, there is a fee for access to the articles in a pdf format. The online version of the journal utilizes a display program that mimics the page flipping of a paper journal, and the archive dates back to 2007. URL: www.constructionspecifier.com

986. Constructor: the construction management magazine. Supersedes in part (in 1922): *General Contractors Association. Bulletin;* Which was formerly (until 1921): *Associated General Contractors. Bulletin;* (until 1919): *General Contractors Association. Bulletin.* [ISSN: 0162-6191] 1919. bi-m. USD 95. Ed(s): Mark J Shaw. A G C, 2300 Wilson Blvd, Ste 400, Arlington, VA 22201; info@agc.org; http://www.agc.org. Illus., index, adv. *Indexed:* A22. *Aud.:* Sa.

Constructor serves general contractors of all construction types and is the major publication of the Associated General Contractors of America (AGC). The topics include product reviews, job management techniques, best practices, and estimating techniques. The web site offers access the current issues of the *Constructor* and the *Constructor Newsletter,* with access to archives of previous issues back to May/June 2012. Also, the site contains information about AGC, and offers access to the AGC of America News wire. URL: www.constructormagazine.com/

987. Contractor: the newsmagazine of mechanical contracting. [ISSN: 0897-7135] 1954. m. USD 99 domestic (Free to qualified personnel). Ed(s): Robert P Mader. Penton Media, Inc., 1300 E 9th St, Cleveland, OH 44114; information@penton.com; http://www.penton.com. Illus., adv. Circ: 50377 Controlled. *Indexed:* A22, ABIn, B01, B02, B03, BRI. *Aud.:* Sa.

Contractor caters to mechanical and general contractors and highlights issues in plumbing, heating systems, sustainable technologies, and green energies. Each issue has a featured article and several topical articles, plus a commentary section and a classified advertisement. The web site has information specific to the categories of plumbing, piping, hydronics, radiant, green, bath/kitchen, technology, tools, trucks, and management. It also has the capacity for mouse-scrolling subsets for easy access to the information, and an RSS feed. Subscriptions to the magazine are free to qualified personnel who are residents of the United States and Canada (and fees apply to others). There is free online access with archives back to January 2011. URL: http://contractormag.com

988. Custom Home. Incorporates (1987-1999): *Custom Builder;* Which was formerly (until 1987): *Progressive Builder;* (until 1986): *Solar Age;* Which incorporated (in 1985): *Progressive Builder;* (until 1976): *Solar News and Views.* [ISSN: 1055-3479] 1991. bi-m. USD 36 in US & Canada (Free to qualified personnel). Ed(s): Jennifer Lash. Hanley Wood, LLC, 1 Thomas Cir, NW, Ste 600, Washington, DC 20005; fanton@hanleywood.com; http://www.hanleywood.com. Illus., adv. *Indexed:* A22, BRI. *Aud.:* Sa.

Custom Home caters to home building for the unique building and living experiences. Custom home builders, architects, and land owners with varying interests in residential, individualized home-building will find the resources helpful in providing ideas for designing different-sized homes across the globe. Articles cover interior/exterior, landscaping, patios and hearths, vanishing pools, finishes, and fixtures. The web site has a scroll-over menu guide with information on "Houses," "Rooms," "Custom Touches," "Products," "Green," "CH Outdoors," "Business," "Builders," and "Architects." Print subscriptions are free to qualified builders and architects, and $36 for individuals. The online article access is free online and archived back to 2004. URL: www.customhomeonline.com

989. *E C & M.* Incorporates (in 2002): *Power Quality Assurance;* Formerly (until 199?): *Electrical Construction & Maintenance.* [ISSN: 1082-295X] 1901. m. USD 48 domestic (Free to qualified personnel). Ed(s): Michael Eby, Ellen Parson. Penton Media, Inc., 330 N Wabash Ave, Ste 2300, Chicago, IL 60611; information@penton.com; http://www.pentonmedia.com. Illus., adv. Circ: 104000 Controlled. *Indexed:* A22, ABIn, B01, B02, BRI, EngInd. *Aud.:* Ac, Sa.

E C & M (for "Electrical Construction and Maintenance") covers articles on industry news and trends, forecasts in markets, and industry reports with the electrical engineer and practitioner in mind for all types of building construction. The magazine also imparts opinions and reports on industry-standard releases. The web site has a scroll-over menu guide with information on "NEC" (standards), "Design," "Ops and Maintenance," "Contractor," "Safety," "Power Quality," "Training," "Basics," and "Products." Subscription is free in print or online, and there is an archive back to 2011. URL: http://ecmweb.com

The Family Handyman. See Do-It-Yourself section.

990. *H P A C Engineering.* Formerly (until 1999): *Heating, Piping and Air Conditioning;* Which incorporated (1915-1929): *American Society of Heating and Ventilating Engineers. Journal.* [ISSN: 1527-4055] 1929. m. USD 89 domestic (Free to qualified personnel). Ed(s): Scott Arnold. Penton Media, Inc., 1300 E 9th St, Cleveland, OH 44114; information@penton.com; http://www.penton.com. Illus., adv. Microform: PQC. *Indexed:* A01, A22, ABIn, ApMecR, B03, BRI, C&ISA, CerAb, EngInd. *Aud.:* Ac, Sa.

Mechanical systems engineers, designers, and architects will find great value in the resources and articles in the *HPAC Engineering* journal. Articles cover standards and best practices for heating, cooling, ventilation, and piping systems for mostly large projects and facilities maintenance. The web site contains the current issue, with a free archive back to 2012; newsletter access; and a searchable manufacturer's index called "Info-Dex." URL: www.hpac.com

991. *Journal of Light Construction (New England Edition).* Supersedes in part (in 1989): *The Journal of Light Construction;* Which was formerly (until 1988): *New England Builder.* [ISSN: 1050-2610] 1982. m. USD 39.95 domestic; USD 54.95 foreign. Hanley Wood, LLC, 186 Allen Brook Ln, Williston, VT 05495; fanton@hanleywood.com; http://www.hanleywood.com. Illus., index, adv. Sample. *Aud.:* Sa.

Journal of Light Construction provides information on remodeling and smaller jobs like decking, bathrooms, roofing, and additions. Contractors, builders, and remodelers will find "how to's," industry trends, types of tools and equipment to use, and different types of construction materials. The web site has special sections for help and a video feature and "JLCLive" (a residential construction show). The current issue is available free online, and you may purchase a USB containing the digital retrospective archive for $59.95 dating back to issue 1. URL: www.jlconline.com

992. *Masonry Construction.* Former titles: *Aberdeen's Magazine of Masonry Construction;* (until 1990): *Magazine of Masonry Construction.* 1988. 10x/yr. USD 30 domestic; USD 39 in Canada & Mexico; USD 93 elsewhere. Ed(s): Richard Yelton. Hanley Wood, LLC, 8725 W Higgins Rd, Ste 600, Chicago, IL 60631; fanton@hanleywood.com; http://www.hanleywood.com. Illus., index, adv. Circ: 30000 Paid. *Indexed:* A22, B02, BRI, C&ISA, CerAb, EngInd. *Aud.:* Sa.

Masons and bricklayers will find *Masonry Construction* of particular interest, with articles on all types of concrete, grout, and reinforcements, as well as industry trends and standards. Feature articles deal with "how to's" and displays of finished products. The web site contains free access to articles, a blog, "News" and products, an online "problem clinic," and article archives with a searchable interface back to 2006. URL: www.masonryconstruction.com

Old-House Journal. See Do-It-Yourself section.

993. *P M Engineer.* [ISSN: 1080-353X] 1994. m. USD 104 domestic (Free to qualified personnel). Ed(s): Bob Miodonski, Kelly Johnson. B N P Media, 2401 W Big Beaver Rd, Ste 700, Troy, MI 48084; portfolio@bnpmedia.com; http://www.bnpmedia.com. Adv. Sample. Circ: 26500. *Indexed:* B01, B02, BRI. *Aud.:* Ac, Sa.

Plumbing engineers, plumbing-system designers, and fire-system designers will find in *PM Engineer* information on trends, current practices, standard updates, and design features. The magazine highlights installation and guidelines for sprinkler systems, piping, drainage design, filtering systems, and old-fashioned plumbing. Each issue has an eye-catching "Cover Article," "Feature Article(s)," "New Products" reviews, and a listing of each columnist. Free access to access articles online occurs after signing up for a subscription, and there is access to archives back to 1998. The web site features blogs, "web exclusives," an e-newsletter, and multimedia demos and exposes on successful projects. URL: www.pmengineer.com

994. *Plumbing Engineer.* [ISSN: 0192-1711] 1973. m. USD 300 elsewhere (Free to qualified personnel). Ed(s): John Mesenbrink, James Schaible. T M B Publishing, 1838 Techny Ct, Northbrook, IL 60062; info@tmbpublishing.com; http://plumbingengineer.com/. Illus., adv. Circ: 25920 Controlled. *Indexed:* A22. *Aud.:* Ac, Sa.

Plumbing-system and fire-system designers and the traditional plumbing engineer will find *Plumbing Engineer* a valuable resource. It offers updates to code, trends in the field, product reviews, and green technologies. Article features include a "Designer's Guide," which has in-depth and anecdotal examples of problems faced in the field, and the "Code Classroom," with discussions of new developments of the plumbing codes. The web site has a scroll roll-over menu guide with information on "Current Issue," "Video and Webcasts," "Blogs," "More Resources" (including white pages and classifieds), "Archives (to 2007)," and "Advertisers." Online access to articles is free, and subscriptions come with various pricing. URL: www.plumbingengineer.com

995. *Professional Builder.* Former titles (until 1993): *Professional Builder and Remodeler;* (until 1990): *Professional Builder;* (until 1985): *Professional Builder and Apartment Business;* (until 1973): *Professional Builder;* (until 1968): *Practical Builder.* [ISSN: 1072-0561] 1936. m. plus "Construct", published 6 times per yr. Free to qualified personnel. S G C Horizon LLC., 3030 W. Salt Creek Ln., Ste.201, Arlington Heights, IL 60005; tmancini@sgcmail.com; http://www.sgchorizon.com/. Illus., adv. Sample. Circ: 120833. Microform: CIS. *Indexed:* A22, ABIn, B01, B02, BRI, C&ISA, CerAb. *Aud.:* Sa.

The Housing Zone Group of magazines publishes *Professional Builder* with architects and general contractors who work on new homes in mind. Features include articles on housing rules and codes, highlighted completed homes, and featured designers and architects. Each issue has several articles that review products for use in home construction. The www.housingzone.com web site offers a suite of home-building journals with online access as well as the features of blogs, videos, house plans, green technologies, and product highlights. The print subscriptions to all *Housing Zone*–related journals are free, and there is free online access to the archives dating back to June 1999. URL: www.housingzone.com/professionalbuilder/pubhome/

996. *Qualified Remodeler: best practices, products & design ideas.* Incorporates (1985-1991): *Kitchen and Bath Concepts.* [ISSN: 0098-9207] 1975. m. USD 81 domestic (Free to qualified personnel). Ed(s): Patrick O'Toole, Kenneth W Betz. Cygnus Business Media, Inc., PO Box 803, Fort Atkinson, WI 53538; http://www.cygnus.com. Illus., adv. Circ: 82510. *Indexed:* ABIn, B02, BRI. *Aud.:* Sa.

ForResidentialPros.com now publishes *Qualified Remodeler* along with several other trade magazines to help general contractors, carpenters, and restoration specialists with new regulations, green construction ideas, and best practices for remodeling. The web site has a web-exclusive article, blogs, and a "Media Center." Online issues go back to July 2012 and are fully accessible and searchable. Access to the ForResidentialPros.com web site is free, but by signing up for free, individuals get access to white papers, a newsletter, an e-magazine, "one click product information," and other "premium content." URL: www.forresidentialpros.com/magazine/qur/issue/2013/jun

997. Remodeling. Formerly (until 1985): *Remodeling World;* Incorporates (1983-1987): *Remodeling Contractor;* Which was formerly (until 1983): *Home Improvement Contractor;* (until 1976): *Home Improvements;* (until 1969): *Building Specialties and Home Improvements.* [ISSN: 0885-8039] 1982. m. USD 24.95 domestic (Free to qualified personnel). Hanley Wood, LLC, 1 Thomas Cir, NW, Ste 600, Washington, DC 20005; fanton@hanleywood.com; http://www.hanleywood.com. Illus., adv. Microform: PQC. *Indexed:* B02, BRI. *Aud.:* Sa.

Remodeling magazine is a Hanley-Wood publication for general contractors, carpenters, and restoration specialists to help guide them with innovations, techniques, and regulations for home renovations. Each issue has feature articles, product reviews, op-eds, and three sections designed for the practitioner: "Your Business," "Your Clients," and "Your Projects." The web site contains information on "Marketing," "Products," and "Training," and an entire section devoted to lead paint removal and issues. Other information includes a blog, information on management, an e-newsletter, and "Home Performance," which is more of a green construction section. The online journal is free to access, as are archives back to 2002. URL: www.remodeling.hw.net

This Old House. See Do-It-Yourself section.

998. Welding Journal. Former titles (until 1937): *American Welding Society Journal;* (until 1934): *American Welding Society. Journal;* (until 1922): *American Welding Society. Proceedings.* [ISSN: 0043-2296] 1922. m. Members, USD 6; Non-members, USD 90. Ed(s): Andy Cullison. American Welding Society, 550 N W LeJeune Rd, Miami, FL 33126; info@aws.org; http://www.aws.org. Illus., adv. Refereed. Microform: PMC; PQC. *Indexed:* A22, ApMecR, C&ISA, CerAb, EngInd. *Aud.:* Sa.

The American Welding Society (AWS) publishes the *Welding Journal,* which offers contractors and practitioners of metal fabrication and metal works the latest innovations and trends in welding and metal joining. Each issue contains new technology alerts, best practices, and regulation updates for the welder to improve technique and expand knowledge of the trade. To access articles online (with an archive of issues back to 2000), individuals must become a member of the AWS, with varying degrees of membership and costs offered. URL: www.aws.org/wj

■ BUSINESS AND FINANCE

General/Computer Systems and Forecasting/Ethics/International/Small Business/State and Regional/Trade and Industry/Banking/Insurance/Investment/Scholarly/Trade Journals

See also Accounting and Taxation; Advertising and Public Relations; Economics; Management, Administration, and Human Resources; and Real Estate sections.

Lisa Junghahn, Reference Librarian for Business & Corporate Law, Harvard Law School Library, 1545 Mass Ave., Cambridge, MA 02138; ljunghahn@law.harvard.edu

Introduction

This year, the Business and Finance section of *Magazines for Libraries* represents 10 percent fewer titles.

This culling reflects three publishing trends. The first is that many trade journals reproduce content for free and online. The second is that there are a greater amount of high-quality articles being made freely available online

through open-access initiatives. And finally, there has been a notable decline in some of the research and writing quality among publishers—likely owing to financial pressures and increased competition.

Traditional powerhouses, like *Barron's* and *The Economist,* continue to do well, with no major cancellations in the last year. What has changed, however, is the amount of companion information made available online. Thus, for any publication, even for the most esoteric academic journals, patrons will want to visit publication web sites for free additional content, like video interviews and colorful info-graphics.

Overall, business- and finance-related issues continue to grow in cultural relevance. Nearly five years after the 2008 economic crises, government and individual behavior suggests greater involvement in the markets and increased global interdependence. Thus, two new titles this year include *The Journal of Multinational Management* and *The Corporate Philanthropy Report.*

Basic Periodicals

GENERAL. Ga: *Barron's, Fast Company, Forbes, Fortune, Harvard Business Review, Industry Week, Wall Street Journal;* Ac: *Business History Review, Business Horizons, Journal of Business Research, Journal of Education for Business, Journal of Retailing.*

COMPUTER SYSTEMS AND FORECASTING. Ga: *CIO;* Ac: *International Journal of Forecasting.*

ETHICS. Ac: *Business and Society Review, Journal of Business Ethics.*

INTERNATIONAL. Ga: *The Economist, Financial Times, The Journal of Commerce;* Ac: *Journal of International Business Studies, Journal of World Business.*

SMALL BUSINESS. Ga: *Entrepreneur, Franchising World, Inc.;* Ac: *Entrepreneurship: Theory and Practice, Journal of Small Business Management.*

STATE AND REGIONAL. Will vary.

TRADE AND INDUSTRY. Will vary.

Basic Abstracts and Indexes

ABI/Inform, Business Abstracts, Business and Company Resource Center, Business and Industry, Business Source Complete.

General

999. American Journal of Business. Formerly (until 2007): *Mid-American Journal of Business;* Which was formed by the merger of (1971-1985): *Ball State Business Review;* (1929-1985): *Ball State Journal for Business Educators;* Which was formerly (until 1965): *Ball State Commerce Journal.* [ISSN: 1935-519X] 1985. q. EUR 189 combined subscription in Europe (print & online eds.); USD 259 combined subscription in the Americas (print & online eds.); AUD 289 combined subscription in Australasia (print & online eds.). Ed(s): Richard Reed, Susan F Storrud-Barnes. Emerald Group Publishing Ltd., Howard House, Wagon Ln, Bingley, BD16 1WA, United Kingdom; information@emeraldinsight.com; http://www.emeraldinsight.com. Illus., index. Refereed. Microform: PQC. *Indexed:* ABIn, B01, B02, B03, BRI. *Bk. rev.:* 1, length varies. *Aud.:* Ac.

This title is aimed at researchers, practicing managers, and instructors of general business administration in the United States. Articles running eight to ten pages in length are the norm. Issues include case studies, which are useful for gaining practical approaches to work.

1000. *Barron's: the Dow Jones business and financial weekly.* Former titles (until vol.74, no.13, 1994): *Barron's National Business and Financial Weekly;* (until 1942): *Barron's.* [ISSN: 1077-8039] 1921. w. USD 99; USD 149 combined subscription (print & online eds.). Ed(s): Robert Thomson, Richard Rescigno. Dow Jones & Company, 1 World Financial Ctr, 200 Liberty St, New York, NY 10281; http://www.dowjones.com. Illus., adv. Circ: 304689 Paid. Vol. ends: Dec. *Indexed:* A22, ABIn, ATI, B02, BRI, CBRI, NewsAb, P02. *Bk. rev.:* Number and length vary. *Aud.:* Ga.

This weekly newspaper format provides general business information that serves the needs of investors. Articles on current business, economic, and political trends are accompanied by reports on industries, individual companies, and people in the news. The "Market Week" center section covers securities analysis and performance statistics, including stock tables, economic indicators, commodities, money markets, and major indexes. This is a core business and investment title for public and academic libraries.

1001. *Bloomberg Markets.* Formerly (until 2000): *Bloomberg.* [ISSN: 1531-5061] 1992. 13x/yr. USD 29.95 domestic; USD 38.95 Canada; USD 54.95 elsewhere. Bloomberg Finance L.P., 499 Park Ave, New York, NY 10022; magazine@bloomberg.com; http://www.bloomberg.com. Adv. *Indexed:* ASIP. *Aud.:* Sa.

The subjects here are money, money-making, and how to build wealth. Regular features include financial predictions, international news, company profiles, Wall Street news, and op-ed pieces. Articles are global in scope, covering everything from the infrastructure of developed countries to the educational attainment and potential of populations in emerging markets. Pieces cover both macro-factors, like security in shipping lanes, and micro-factors, like management performance at specific companies. This serial is ideal for public libraries with a broad collection, and academic institutions with finance degree programs. URL: www.bloomberg.com/markets-magazine/

1002. *Business and Society Review: journal of the Center for Business Ethics at Bentley College.* Formerly (until 1974): *Business and Society Review/Innovation;* Which was formed by the merger of (1962-1973): *Innovation; Business and Society Review.* [ISSN: 0045-3609] 1972. q. GBP 267. Ed(s): Robert E Frederick. Wiley-Blackwell Publishing, Inc., 111 River St, Hoboken, NJ 07030; info@wiley.com; http://onlinelibrary.wiley.com/. Illus. Microform: PQC. Reprint: PSC. *Indexed:* A22, ABIn, B01, B02, BRI, C42, CLI, CompR, E01, L14, P02. *Aud.:* Ac.

This scholarly publication includes a dozen articles of 10–20 pages in length, which cover a wide range of ethical issues, corporate citizenship, and social responsibility. Some issues are thematic. Articles are of interest to business people, academics, and others involved in the contemporary debate about the proper role of business in society. Expect to find this title in academic collections that support business programs and in larger public libraries.

1003. *Business Communication Quarterly.* Former titles (until 1995): *Association for Business Communication. Bulletin;* (until 1985): *A B C A Bulletin (American Business Communication Association);* (until 1969): *A B W A Bulletin (American Business Writing Association).* [ISSN: 1080-5699] 1935. q. USD 466. Ed(s): Betty S Johnson, Melinda Knight. Sage Publications, Inc., 2455 Teller Rd, Thousand Oaks, CA 91320; info@sagepub.com; http://www.sagepub.com. Illus., index, adv. Sample. Refereed. Microform: PQC. Reprint: PSC. *Indexed:* A22, ABIn, B01, B02, BRI, E01, ERIC. *Bk. rev.:* 2-3, 750-1,000 words. *Aud.:* Ac.

This interdisciplinary journal is aimed primarily at an international readership involved directly in the teaching of business communication. As with its sister publication, *Journal of Business Communication,* submissions are invited from educators in a wide variety of fields, including management, rhetoric, organizational behavior, composition, speech, mass communication, psychology, linguistics, advertising, sociology, information technology, education, and history. Topics cover teaching methods in a variety of settings: technical institutes, community colleges, four-year colleges, universities, and corporate-training programs. Article formats include case studies of specific classroom techniques, reports on program development strategies, research on classroom teaching and assessment, and book reviews of textbooks and other titles of interest to faculty.

Business Economics. See Economics section.

1004. *Business Education Forum.* Incorporates in part (1963 -1982): *National Business Education Yearbook;* Formerly (until 1949): *U B E A Forum.* [ISSN: 0007-6678] 1947. q. Oct., Dec., Feb. & Apr. Free to members. National Business Education Association, 1914 Association Dr, Reston, VA 20191; nbea@nbea.org; http://www.nbea.org. Illus., index, adv. Vol. ends: Apr. Microform: PQC. *Indexed:* A22, ERIC. *Aud.:* Ac.

This is the official publication of the National Business Education Association. Articles range from 1,500 to 2,500 words and cover business education issues in high schools, technical schools, colleges, and universities. The "Curriculum Forum" section includes articles on accounting, basic business, communication, international business, marketing, methods, and technology. Special sections appear quarterly: research (October), student organizations (December), entrepreneurship (February), and administration and supervision (April). Association news, a professional leadership directory, and award announcements are also included.

1005. *Business History Review.* Formerly (until 1954): *Business Historical Society. Bulletin.* [ISSN: 0007-6805] 1926. q. GBP 144 (print & online eds.). Ed(s): Geoffrey G Jones, Walter A Friedman. Cambridge University Press, 32 Ave of the Americas, New York, NY 10013; information@cambridge.org; http://www.cambridge.org/us/. Illus., index, adv. Refereed. Circ: 2000. Vol. ends: No. 4. Microform: PQC. *Indexed:* A01, A22, ABIn, ABS&EES, B01, B02, BAS, BRI, CBRI, EconLit, IBSS, JEL, MLA-IB. *Bk. rev.:* 25-30, 750-1,000 words. *Aud.:* Ac.

Each issue is composed of three feature articles, of 40–50 pages in length, along with numerous book reviews. Subjects cover biographical profiles, corporate culture, and studies of specific industries, with emphasis on North American history. Photographs and illustrations appear on the cover and accompany some articles. The online archives offer article abstracts back to 1954, and pdf images of book reviews back to 2002. Of interest to all social scientists, historians, and fans of Americana. URL: www.hbs.edu/bhr

1006. *Business Horizons.* Supersedes in part (in 1958): *Indiana Business Review.* [ISSN: 0007-6813] 1957. 6x/yr. EUR 464. Ed(s): L F Miller, C M Dalton. Elsevier Inc., 360 Park Ave S, New York, NY 10010; usinfo-f@elsevier.com; http://www.elsevier.com. Illus., index, adv. Sample. Circ: 3000 Paid. Vol. ends: No. 6. Microform: PQC. Reprint: PSC. *Indexed:* A22, ABIn, ABS&EES, B01, B02, BAS, BLI, BRI, CBRI, P02. *Bk. rev.:* 0-3, 1,500 words. *Aud.:* Ga, Ac.

This bimonthly title is edited by the Kelley School of Business, Indiana University. Approximately ten scholarly articles, seven to ten pages in length, address a wide range of business disciplines, business ethics, and the impact of business on society. Editors strive to strike a balance between the practical and the academic; contributors are encouraged to avoid nontechnical language. Each issue contains a cumulative index for the current volume year. Of interest to all academic libraries.

1007. *Business Today (Princeton).* Formerly (until 1968): *Princeton Business Today.* [ISSN: 0007-7100] 1968. s-a. Free to qualified personnel. Ed(s): B J Sullivan. Foundation for Student Communication, Inc., 48 University Pl, Princeton, NJ 08544. Illus., adv. Circ: 200000. Microform: MIM; PQC. *Indexed:* A22. *Aud.:* Ga, Ac, Sa.

This student-run magazine serves as a forum for diverse topics and is designed to give undergraduates a broader understanding of business leadership, industry innovation, government policies, international perspectives, and career track advice. The content will appeal to a wider college audience, not just business majors. Ideal for browsing collections in academic libraries.

1008. *The Conference Board Review.* Formerly (until 2006): *Across the Board;* Which incorporated (in 1977): *Focus (New York, 1964);* Which superseded (in 1964): *National Industrial Conference Board. Preview;* Across the Board was formerly (until 1976): *Conference Board Record;* (until 1964): *Business Management Record.* [ISSN: 1946-5432] 1939. bi-m. Members, USD 39; Non-members, USD 59. Ed(s): Matthew

Budmen. Conference Board, Inc., 845 Third Ave, New York, NY 10022; atb@conference-board.org; http://www.conference-board.org. Illus., index, adv. Vol. ends: Dec. *Indexed:* A22, ABIn, ABS&EES, B01, B02, BAS, BLI, BRI. *Bk. rev.:* 1-2, 1,500 words. *Aud.:* Ga.

The Conference Board, whose membership is comprised of thousands of business leaders from around the world, has promoted a better understanding of the changing complexities of the business environment. Whereas this magazine offers best practices and analysis primarily to corporate executives, its content will also appeal to a more general audience. Articles are written in an accessible style, and address a wide range of subject matter. Only selected features and departments from the current and previous issues are available in full text at the web site. URL: www.tcbreview.com

Consumer Reports. See General Interest section.

1009. *Fast Company.* [ISSN: 1085-9241] 1995. 10x/yr. USD 9.97 domestic; USD 22 Canada; USD 46 elsewhere. Ed(s): Robert Safian. Fast Company, Inc., 7 World Trade Ctr, New York, NY 10007. Illus., adv. Circ: 725000 Paid. *Indexed:* A22, ABIn, B01, B02, BRI, C37, I15. *Aud.:* Ga.

Articles of varying lengths profile executives, managers, and business owners who drive innovation. Emphasis is placed on covering the new, novel, and trendy in the business world. The writing style is irreverent. Bold graphics and content that are pushed to the very edges of the page speak to a reader who is most likely comfortable with multitasking. Conclusions are frequently enumerated or distilled to bullet points; lists of companies or products are ranked, all for the purpose of providing information—fast. Online access to the current issue and archives is available at the web site, complemented by video and other web exclusives. URL: www.fastcomapany.com/

1010. *Forbes.* [ISSN: 0015-6914] 1917. bi-w. USD 29.99; USD 5.99 newsstand/cover. Forbes, Inc., 60 Fifth Ave, New York, NY 10011; readers@forbes.com; http://www.forbes.com. Illus., index. Vol. ends: Dec. Microform: PQC. *Indexed:* A01, A22, ABIn, ATI, AgeL, Agr, B01, B02, B03, BLI, BRI, C37, Chicano, F01, I15, MASUSE, P02. *Aud.:* Ga.

The focus of this title is on news and analysis that impact executives, managers, and investors. In addition to the cover story, a typical issue contains numerous short articles, each analyzing economic trends or profiling industries, corporations, and key individuals. Recurring sections include "Marketing," "Entrepreneurs," "Technology," "Money and Investing," and "Health." A subscription is complemented by occasional supplements: *Forbes Asia* and *Forbes Life,* containing lifestyle features. Current issue and archives content are available at the web site. A core title for both public and academic libraries. URL: www.forbes.com/forbes

1011. *Harvard Business Review.* [ISSN: 0017-8012] 1922. m. except Jul./Aug. USD 79 domestic; USD 99 Canada; USD 149 elsewhere. Ed(s): Adi Ignatius. Harvard Business School Publishing, 60 Harvard Way, Boston, MA 02163; corpcustserv@hbsp.harvard.edu; http://harvardbusiness.org/. Illus., index, adv. Vol. ends: Dec. Microform: PQC. *Indexed:* A22, ABIn, ABS&EES, ASIP, AbAn, B01, B02, BAS, BLI, BRI, CBRI, CompR, JEL, P02. *Bk. rev.:* Number and length vary. *Aud.:* Ga.

Each issue contains about a dozen articles, ten pages in length, along with a short case study. *HBR* provides readers with the current thinking of scholars and industry leaders on the topics of human resources management, manufacturing, strategic planning, globalization of markets, competitiveness, and related general business interests. Articles—although rarely containing footnotes—are highly regarded if not considered scholarly. This is a core business title for academic libraries and larger public libraries.

1012. *IndustryWeek: the management resource.* Incorporates (1985-1995): *Electronics;* Which was formerly (1984-1985): *Electronics Week;* (1930-1984): *Electronics.* [ISSN: 0039-0895] 1882. 22x/yr. USD 99 domestic (Free to qualified personnel). Ed(s): David Blanchard. Penton

Media, Inc., 1300 E 9th St, Cleveland, OH 44114; information@penton.com; http://www.penton.com. Illus., index, adv. Circ: 236248 Controlled. Vol. ends: Dec. Microform: PQC. *Indexed:* A01, A22, ABIn, B01, B02, B03, BRI, C&ISA, C42, CerAb, MASUSE, P02. *Aud.:* Ga.

This trade magazine profiles individuals and companies active in manufacturing industries. Approximately five feature articles in each issue cover a wide range of topics of interest to executives and managers, including innovation, competition, infrastructure, globalization, supply chains, distribution, labor relations, regulatory pressures, and best practices in management and marketing. Recurring departments address emerging technologies, leadership, e-business, continuous improvement, and economic policies. Features and departments from the current and previous issues are freely available online at the web site. Web-only content is highlighted alongside the magazine's table of contents. Of interest to all business collections. URL: www.industryweek.com

1013. *Journal of Business and Economic Statistics.* [ISSN: 0735-0015] 1983. q. GBP 149 (print & online eds.). American Statistical Association, 732 N Washington St, Alexandria, VA 22314; asainfo@amstat.org; http://www.amstat.org. Illus. Refereed. Vol. ends: Oct. Reprint: PSC. *Indexed:* A22, ABIn, B01, B02, CCMJ, EconLit, JEL, MSN, MathR. *Aud.:* Ac.

One of the official journals from the American Statistical Association, this scholarly title focuses on a broad range of topics in applied economics and business statistical problems. Using empirical methods, authors of these highly technical articles presume a reader's knowledge of mathematical theory. Topics covered include demand and cost analysis, forecasting, economic modeling, stochastic theory control, and impact of societal issues on wages and productivity. Recommended for academic libraries.

1014. *Journal of Business Research.* Formerly (until 1973): *Southern Journal of Business.* [ISSN: 0148-2963] 1966. 12x/yr. EUR 2639. Ed(s): Arch G Woodside, Michel Laroche. Elsevier Inc., 360 Park Ave S, New York, NY 10010; usinfo-f@elsevier.com; http://www.elsevier.com. Illus., index. Sample. Refereed. Circ: 1750 Paid. Vol. ends: Nov. Microform: PQC. *Indexed:* A22, ABIn, B01, BRI, IBSS, JEL, PsycInfo. *Aud.:* Sa.

Each issue presents a dozen articles 8–20 pages in length that cover theoretical and empirical advances in buyer behavior, finance, organizational theory and behavior, marketing, risk and insurance, and international business. Issues are frequently devoted to a theme, e.g., cross-cultural consumer studies, electronic marketing theory, Asian business research, etc. Emphasis is placed on linking theory with practical solutions. Intended for executives, researchers, and scholars alike.

Journal of Business Strategy. See Management and Administration section.

Journal of Consumer Research. See Advertising, Marketing, and Public Relations section.

1015. *Journal of Education for Business.* Former titles (until 1985): *The Journal of Business Education;* (until 1929): *The Business School Journal.* [ISSN: 0883-2323] 1928. bi-m. GBP 150 (print & online eds.). Ed(s): James L Morrison. Routledge, 325 Chestnut St, Ste 800, Philadelphia, PA 19106; customerservice@taylorandfrancis.com; http://www.tandfonline.com. Illus., adv. Refereed. Reprint: PSC. *Indexed:* A01, A22, ABIn, B01, B02, BRI, C42, CBRI, ERIC, P02, PsycInfo. *Bk. rev.:* Irregular; 500-750 words. *Aud.:* Ac.

This is a forum for authors reporting on innovative teaching methods and curricula or proposing new theories and analyses of controversial topics in accounting, communications, economics, finance, information systems, management, marketing, and other business disciplines, trends, and professional information. Each issue contains eight to ten features that aid educators in preparing business graduates who will need new competencies and leadership skills to thrive. This would be most interesting to higher-education administrators and faculty members.

1016. *Journal of Retailing.* [ISSN: 0022-4359] 1925. q. EUR 525. Ed(s): S Ganesan. Pergamon, The Blvd, Langford Ln, E Park, Kidlington, OX5 1GB, United Kingdom; JournalsCustomerServiceEMEA@elsevier.com; http://www.elsevier.com. Illus., adv. Sample. Refereed. Microform: PQC. Reprint: PSC. *Indexed:* A22, ABIn, B01, B02, BRI, C45, PsycInfo, RRTA. *Aud.:* Ac.

Each issue offers five or six articles, 20–25 pages in length. Retailing is defined as the act of selling products and/or services to consumers for their personal or family use. Thus, the scope of this journal is explicitly limited to consumer behavior, retail strategy, marketing channels, location analysis, the marketing mix, merchandise management, store and operations management, store atmospheric issues, and retail services. Other topics may be addressed so long as retailing is the focus of the submission. Examples include benchmarking retail productivity, supply chain management, marketing impact assessment, and public policy issues. There is liberal use of mathematical models for the benefit of other academicians; a general readership will appreciate the nontechnical executive summaries.

1017. *The Service Industries Journal.* Formerly (until 1983): *Service Industries Review.* [ISSN: 0264-2069] 1981. 16x/yr. GBP 1461 (print & online eds.). Routledge, 4 Park Sq, Milton Park, Abingdon, OX14 4RN, United Kingdom; subscriptions@tandf.co.uk; http://www.tandfonline.com. Adv. Sample. Refereed. Microform: PQC. Reprint: PSC. *Indexed:* A22, ABIn, B01, B02, B03, BRI, C45, E01, FS&TA, H&TI, RRTA. *Bk. rev.:* 5-6, 750-1,000 words. *Aud.:* Ac.

This title publishes research that contributes to the development of theory and resulting best practices in services, including management, human resources, logistics, and marketing. Service industries include retailing and distribution; financial services, including banking and insurance; hotels and tourism; leisure, recreation, and entertainment; professional and business services. Each issue contains approximately ten articles, 20–30 pages in length. The geographic emphasis is split between Europe and the United States. Of interest primarily to academic collections that support business-related degree programs.

Wall Street Journal. See Newspapers/General section.

Computer Systems and Forecasting

1018. *C I O: the magazine for information executives.* Incorporates (1995-1997): *WebMaster.* [ISSN: 0894-9301] 1987. 23x/yr. USD 95 in US & Canada (Free to qualified personnel). Ed(s): Brian Carlson, Elana Varon. C X O Media Inc., 492 Old Connecticut Path, PO Box 9208, Framingham, MA 01701; http://www.cxo.com/. Illus., adv. Circ: 140000. *Indexed:* A22, ABIn, B01, B02, B03, BRI, C&ISA, CerAb, CompLI, I15. *Aud.:* Ga.

This major trade title provides semi-monthly industry updates, news and events, tips, trends, and opinions by and for managing executives in the information technology and computer systems departments of medium-to-large organizations. Feature articles cover management skills, outsourcing, recruiting and other human resource management topics, emerging technologies, e-commerce, and IT strategies. Although aimed at the working professional, *CIO* is well suited for public libraries that serve the business community, and academic libraries that support advanced business degrees and computer science programs. Current and previous issues' content is available at the web site. URL: www.cio.com/magazine

Decision Sciences. See Management and Administration section.

1019. *Decision Support Systems.* [ISSN: 0167-9236] 1985. 8x/yr. EUR 1566. Ed(s): A B Whinston. Elsevier BV, North-Holland, Postbus 211, Amsterdam, 1000 AE, Netherlands; JournalsCustomerServiceEMEA@elsevier.com; http://www.elsevier.com. Illus., index, adv. Refereed. *Indexed:* A22, ABIn, B01, C&ISA, CerAb, CompLI, CompR, EngInd, ErgAb, PsycInfo. *Aud.:* Ac.

This is a highly technical and scholarly journal that covers the concept of using computers for supporting the managerial decision process. Articles discuss artificial intelligence, cognitive science, computer-supported cooperative work, database management, decision theory, economics, linguistics, management

science, mathematical modeling, operations management psychology, and user-interface management systems. The relatively high subscription price and theoretical focus limit holdings to academic libraries that offer programs in advanced business administration, MIS, or computer science.

eWEEK. See Computers and Information Technology/Popular Titles section.

1020. *Information & Management.* Incorporates (1981-1985): *Systems, Objectives, Solutions;* Former titles (until 1977): *Management Datamatics;* (until 1975): *Management Informatics;* (until 1972): *I A G Journal.* [ISSN: 0378-7206] 1968. 8x/yr. EUR 1127. Ed(s): E H Sibley. Elsevier BV, North-Holland, Postbus 211, Amsterdam, 1000 AE, Netherlands; JournalsCustomerServiceEMEA@elsevier.com; http://www.elsevier.com. Illus., index, adv. Refereed. Microform: PQC. *Indexed:* A22, ABIn, B01, CompLI, CompR, EngInd, FR, PsycInfo. *Bk. rev.:* Number and length vary. *Aud.:* Sa.

Aimed at managers, database administrators, and senior executives, this scholarly journal covers a wide range of developments in applied information systems, such as knowledge management, data mining, and CRM. Articles focus on trends in evaluation methodology and models; managerial policies, strategies, and activities of business, public administration, and international organizations; and guidelines on how to mount successful information technology initiatives through case studies. The technical nature of the writing will appeal primarily to researchers and practitioners active in the MIS field.

1021. *International Journal of Forecasting.* [ISSN: 0169-2070] 1985. 4x/yr. EUR 848. Ed(s): Rob J Hyndman. Elsevier BV, Radarweg 29, PO Box 211, Amsterdam, 1000 AE, Netherlands; JournalsCustomerServiceEMEA@elsevier.com; http://www.elsevier.com. Adv. Refereed. Microform: PQC. *Indexed:* A22, ABIn, B01, B02, BAS, BRI, EconLit, JEL, P61, RiskAb, SSA. *Bk. rev.:* Number and length vary. *Aud.:* Ac, Sa.

This official publication of the International Institute of Forecasters is the leading journal of forecasting for all aspects of business. It strives to bridge the gap between theory and practice for those policy and decision makers who utilize forecasting methods. Articles by international scholars are featured each quarter, along with notes, book and software reviews, and reviews of current research in forecasting. Although not published as often as the *Journal of Forecasting,* at half the cost, this title is an economical alternative. Recommended for academic libraries.

1022. *International Journal of Technology Management.* [ISSN: 0267-5730] 1986. 16x/yr. EUR 1382 (print or online eds.). Ed(s): Dr. M A Dorgham. Inderscience Publishers, PO Box 735, Olney, MK46 5WB, United Kingdom; editorial@inderscience.com; http://www.inderscience.com. Illus., index. Sample. Refereed. *Indexed:* A01, A22, ABIn, Agr, B01, B02, BRI, BrTechI, C&ISA, CerAb, CompLI, EngInd, IBSS, ISTA. *Bk. rev.:* Number and length vary. *Aud.:* Ac, Sa.

This refereed journal disseminates advances in the science and practice of technology management, with the goal of fostering communication between government officials, technology executives, and academic experts worldwide. Each issue contains research reports and case studies on technology transfers, supply chain management, sourcing, R&D systems, and information technology. Geared to academics, researchers, professionals, and policy makers, *IJTM* is best suited to academic libraries with advanced degree programs in the management and engineering sciences.

1023. *The Journal of Business Forecasting.* Formerly (until 2005): *Journal of Business Forecasting Methods and Systems.* [ISSN: 1930-126X] 1981. q. Free to members; Non-members, USD 95. Ed(s): Chaman L Jain. Graceway Publishing Co., PO Box 670159, Flushing, NY 11367. Illus., index, adv. Sample. Vol. ends: No. 4. Microform: PQC. *Indexed:* A22, ABIn, ATI, B01, B02, BRI, RiskAb. *Bk. rev.:* 1, 750 words. *Aud.:* Ac, Sa.

Executives and managers comprise the primary audience of this highly specialized publication. Clearly written and jargon-free articles provide practical information for decision makers on inventory control, supply chain management, production scheduling, budgeting, marketing strategies, and financial planning. Also featured are international and domestic economic outlooks and corporate earnings analysis by industry. Of most interest to academic business collections and corporate libraries.

1024. *Journal of Forecasting.* [ISSN: 0277-6693] 1982. 8x/yr. GBP 1027. Ed(s): Derek W Bunn. John Wiley & Sons Ltd., The Atrium, Southern Gate, Chichester, PO19 8SQ, United Kingdom; customer@wiley.com; http://www.wiley.com. Illus., adv. Sample. Refereed. Vol. ends: Nov. Reprint: PSC. *Indexed:* A22, ABIn, B01, B02, BRI, CCMJ, EconLit, EngInd, IBSS, JEL, MSN, MathR, P61, RiskAb, SSA. *Aud.:* Sa.

Edited by an international board of scholars, this title is multidisciplinary, welcoming submissions dealing with any aspect of forecasting: theoretical, practical, computational, and methodological. A broad interpretation of the topic is taken with approaches from various subject areas, such as statistics, economics, psychology, systems engineering, and social sciences, which are all encouraged. This journal presupposes a knowledge of mathematical theory; it is appropriate for academic and corporate libraries.

Long Range Planning. See Management and Administration section.

Ethics

1025. *Business & Professional Ethics Journal.* Incorporates (1992-2003): *Professional Ethics.* [ISSN: 0277-2027] 1981. q. USD 95. Ed(s): Robert Baum. Philosophy Documentation Center, PO Box 7147, Charlottesville, VA 22906. Illus., index, adv. Refereed. Reprint: PSC. *Indexed:* A22, B01, BRI, P02. *Bk. rev.:* Number and length vary. *Aud.:* Ac.

Published by the Center for Applied Philosophy and Ethics in the Professions, this journal is broadly interdisciplinary in aim. Lengthy articles explore "the similarities and differences between the ethical situations that arise in two or more professions," including marketing, health care, human resource management, global labor, socially responsible investing, and business ethics. Half of the issues are devoted to reprinting selected papers from professional ethics conferences around the globe. Because of the pervasive awareness of applied ethics in society, this journal will be useful in all academic libraries.

1026. *Business Ethics: a European review.* [ISSN: 0962-8770] 1992. q. GBP 946. Ed(s): Christopher Cowton. Wiley-Blackwell Publishing Ltd., The Atrium, Southern Gate, Chichester, PO19 8SQ, United Kingdom; customer@wiley.com; http://www.wiley.com/. Illus., adv. Sample. Refereed. Reprint: PSC. *Indexed:* A22, ABIn, B01, BRI, E01, IBSS, PsycInfo, RiskAb. *Bk. rev.:* Brief; number varies. *Aud.:* Ac.

This primarily European-focused journal provides a forum for dialogue through original theoretical research and refereed scholarly papers. The range of contributions reflects the variety and scope of ethical issues faced by businesses and organizations worldwide. Articles address ethical challenges and solutions, analyze business policies and practices, and explore the concept of good ethical thinking. Submissions that are responsive to changing concerns and emerging issues are encouraged. Interviews, brief book reviews, comments, and responses to previously published articles round out the content. Appropriate for academic institutions with a tradition of comparative studies.

1027. *Business Ethics Quarterly.* [ISSN: 1052-150X] 1991. q. USD 185 (Individuals, USD 25; Free to members). Ed(s): Gary R Weaver. Philosophy Documentation Center, PO Box 7147, Charlottesville, VA 22906; order@pdcnet.org; http://www.pdcnet.org. Sample. Refereed. Microform: PQC. Reprint: PSC. *Indexed:* A22, ABIn, ABS&EES, B01, B02, BRI, IBSS, P02, P61, SSA. *Bk. rev.:* 2-3, 1,000-2,000 words. *Aud.:* Ac.

This official journal of the Society for Business Ethics publishes peer-reviewed articles on a broad range of topics, including the internal ethics of business organizations; the role of business organizations in larger social, political, and cultural frameworks; and the ethical quality of market-based societies and market-based relationships. There are approximately four to six feature articles in each issue, accompanied by one or more review articles. Recognizing that

contributions to the better understanding of business ethics can come from any quarter, the journal encourages submissions from the humanities, social sciences, and professional fields. Of most interest to academic business collections.

1028. *Corporate Philanthropy Report.* Formerly (until 1986): *Corporate Philanthropy.* [ISSN: 0885-8365] m. GBP 2019. Ed(s): Nicholas King. John Wiley & Sons, Inc., One Montgomery St, Ste 1200, San Francisco, CA 94104-4594; info@wiley.com; http://www.wiley.com. Reprint: PSC. *Indexed:* B01. *Aud.:* Ac, Sa.

This monthly newsletter covers trends and best practices in corporate and foundation giving and provides grant-makers and nonprofits tools to measure the impact of charitable efforts. Each issue includes a "Spotlight" section, which is designed to give corporate grant-makers the latest news on what other companies are doing—or not doing—in the philanthropy sector, and also provide nonprofits insight into what corporations are funding and why.

1029. *Journal of Business Ethics.* Incorporates (1997-2004): *Teaching Business Ethics;* (1988-2004): *International Journal of Value-Based Management.* [ISSN: 0167-4544] 1982. 28x/yr. EUR 2773 (print & online eds.). Ed(s): Alex C Michalos. Springer Netherlands, Van Godewijckstraat 30, Dordrecht, 3311 GX, Netherlands; http://www.springer.com. Illus., adv. Refereed. Vol. ends: Dec. Microform: PQC. Reprint: PSC. *Indexed:* A22, ABIn, B01, BRI, E01, IBSS, P02, PsycInfo. *Aud.:* Ac.

This journal has aimed to improve the human condition by providing a public forum for discussion and debate about ethical issues related to business. The number of submissions and general interest in ethics have greatly expanded in recent years; two sister publications have been absorbed, and new section editors have been named to handle business law, codes of ethics, corporate governance, gender issues, philosophic foundations, small business, teaching business ethics, and value-based management. An important title for collections that support academic programs in business.

International

African Business. See Africa section.

1030. *Business Latin America: weekly report to managers of Latin American operations.* [ISSN: 0007-6880] 1966. w. Economist Intelligence Unit Ltd., 750 Third Ave, 5th Fl, New York, NY 10017; newyork@eiu.com; http://www.eiu.com. Illus. Sample. *Indexed:* A22, ABIn, B01. *Aud.:* Ac, Sa.

This newsletter format offers news briefs on political and economic developments in Mexico and other countries of Central America, South America, and the Caribbean. It provides important insights for companies that wish to operate in those countries/regions. The editorial board consists of executives from large multinational corporations. Each issue contains segments on various industry sectors; a "Country watchlist" that reports on negative economic indicators or regulatory developments by country; and "Databank," a topical statistical table, e.g., of statistics on tourist arrivals. This is a vital source of international business intelligence, although it is cost-prohibitive for all but the largest academic and corporate libraries. Similar titles exist from this publisher for other regions/countries: Africa, the Middle East, Asia, India, China, Europe, and Eastern Europe.

Business Strategy Review. See Management and Administration section.

1031. *Business Today.* [ISSN: 0974-3650] 1992. fortn. INR 650; INR 25 newsstand/cover. Living Media India Pvt. Ltd., F-14/15, Connaught Pl, New Delhi, 110 001, India. Adv. *Indexed:* ABIn, B01. *Aud.:* Ga.

India's leading fortnightly, which covers all aspects of Indian business, with an emphasis on information systems and technologies. Articles are written clearly for a general audience and are accompanied by colorful, detailed graphics. Each issue also includes news and trends, profiles of people, case studies, policy analysis, and discussions on career development. Of interest to larger public libraries and academic collections that support international business programs or South Asian Studies. The latest issue and archive content are available to view online. URL: www.business-today.com

Canadian Business. See Canada section.

1032. China Business Review. Formerly (until 1977): *U S China Business Review.* [ISSN: 0163-7169] 1974. bi-m. USD 89 combined subscription domestic (print & online eds.); USD 99 combined subscription foreign (print & online eds.). United States - China Business Council, 1818 N St, N W, Ste 200, Washington, DC 20036-2406; info@uschina.org; http://www.chinabusinessreview.com/. Illus., index, adv. Sample. Circ: 3500 Paid. Vol. ends: Nov/Dec (No. 6). Microform: PQC. *Indexed:* A22, ABIn, B01, B03, BAS, C42. *Aud.:* Ga, Sa.

This official magazine of the U.S.-China Business Council provides an in-depth picture of the China market, and unique insight into the business and investment environment in China, legal developments, impending legislation, and industrial-sector issues. Each issue contains a few articles that examine one particular topic. Topics include all sectors of the Chinese economy and all business issues, from human resources and management to operational issues and broader policy issues. Intellectual property-rights issues, looking after China's elderly, and the growing Chinese health-care industry are examples in recent issues. URL: www.chinabusinessreview.com/

The Economist. See Economics section.

Financial Times. See Newspapers/General section.

1033. Japan Spotlight: Economy, Culture & History. Formerly (until 2003): *Journal of Japanese Trade and Industry.* [ISSN: 1348-9216] 1982. bi-m. JPY 6000; JPY 1200 newsstand/cover. Japan Economic Foundation, 11th Fl, Jiji Press Bldg., 5-15-8 Ginza Chuo-Ku, Tokyo, 104-0061, Japan; info@jef.or.jp; http://www.jef.or.jp/. Illus., adv. Circ: 35000. *Indexed:* A22, B01, B02, B03, BAS, BRI. *Aud.:* Sa.

This journal covers not only economy, industry, and trade, but also international politics, history, culture, and other topics that fit the primary goal of the Japan Economic Foundation, i.e., to create a deeper understanding of Japan and the world. Writers include business executives, government officials, university professors, specialist researchers, and leading journalists. Current issue contents and searchable archives are available at the web site only to print subscribers. Recommended for academic collections that support programs in international business or Japanese Studies; a must for corporations doing business with Japan. URL: www.jef.or.jp/journal

1034. The Journal of Commerce. Incorporates (1923-2009): *Shipping Digest;* (1913-2009): *The Traffic World;* Formerly (until 2002): *J o C Week;* Which superseded in part (in 2000): *Journal of Commerce;* Which was formerly (until 1996): *Journal of Commerce and Commercial;* (until 1927): *Journal of Commerce.* [ISSN: 1542-3867] 1827. w. Free to members. Ed(s): Chris Brooks. Journal of Commerce, Inc., 2 Penn Plz E, Newark, NJ 07105; http://www.joc.com. Microform: PQC. *Indexed:* ABIn, B01, B02, BRI. *Aud.:* Ga.

This weekly provides authoritative editorial content for international business executives to help them plan their global supply chain and better manage their day-to-day international logistics and shipping needs. This information is delivered through news, analysis of the political landscape that surrounds the latest regulatory issues, case studies, and perspective pieces. Recommended for all international business and transportation collections. Page thumbnails from the digital edition can be viewed at the web site, but only selected full-screen content can be displayed to nonsubscribers. URL: www.joc.com

1035. Journal of International Business Studies. [ISSN: 0047-2506] 1970. 9x/yr. USD 498. Ed(s): John Cantwell. Palgrave Macmillan Ltd., Houndmills, Basingstoke, RG21 6XS, United Kingdom; orders@palgrave.com; http://www.palgrave.com. Adv. Refereed. Microform: PQC. Reprint: PSC. *Indexed:* A22, ABIn, ABS&EES, B01, B02, BAS, BRI, C&ISA, C37, CerAb, E01, EconLit, IBSS, JEL. *Bk. rev.:* Infrequent. *Aud.:* Ac.

Each issue contains a short editorial and eight empirical and hypothetical research articles, 15–20 pages in length, and research presented is cutting-edge and breaks new ground, rather than merely making an incremental contribution to international business research. Submissions should address real-world phenomena, problems, or puzzles and build on relevant prior research to highlight what is interesting and different. Contents can include occasional articles identified as "perspectives" that are deliberately controversial or challenging to mainstream views. Recommended for all academic business collections.

1036. Journal of Multinational Financial Management. [ISSN: 1042-444X] 1990. 5x/yr. EUR 497. Ed(s): S P Ferris. Elsevier BV, North-Holland, Postbus 211, Amsterdam, 1000 AE, Netherlands; JournalsCustomerServiceEMEA@elsevier.com; http://www.elsevier.com. Refereed. Microform: PQC. *Indexed:* A22, B01, EconLit, IBSS, JEL. *Aud.:* Ac, Sa.

Corporate executives buying and selling goods and services, and making financing and investment decisions across national boundaries, have developed policies and procedures for managing cash flows denominated in foreign currencies. These policies and procedures, and the related managerial actions of executives, change as new relevant information becomes available. This title offers original articles that deal with the management of the multinational enterprise. Some of the topics covered include: foreign exchange risk management; cost of capital; political risk assessment; international tax management; and international liability management.

1037. Journal of World Business. Formerly (until 1997): *Columbia Journal of World Business.* [ISSN: 1090-9516] 1965. q. EUR 568. Ed(s): J W Slocum, Jr., F Luthans. Pergamon, The Blvd, Langford Ln, E Park, Kidlington, OX5 1GB, United Kingdom; JournalsCustomerServiceEMEA@elsevier.com; http://www.elsevier.com. Illus., index, adv. Sample. Refereed. Vol. ends: No. 4. Microform: PQC. *Indexed:* A22, ABIn, ABS&EES, B01, B02, BLI, BRI, Chicano, EconLit, IBSS, JEL, PsycInfo. *Aud.:* Ac.

Each issue includes half-a-dozen articles written by leading academic researchers, top government officials, and prominent business leaders on issues related to financial markets, free trade, transition economies, emerging markets, privatization, joint ventures, mergers and acquisitions, human resource management, and marketing. Separate editorial review boards are designated for contributors in the United States, Europe, Latin America, and the Pacific Rim. Recommended for all academic collections that support international business studies.

1038. Latin Trade: your business source for Latin America. Formerly (until 1996): *U S - Latin Trade.* [ISSN: 1087-0857] 1993. bi-m. USD 109.95 domestic. Ed(s): Sabrina R Crow. Miami Media, 200 S Biscayne Blvd, Ste 1150, Miami, FL 33131. Illus., adv. Circ: 87000. *Indexed:* A01, A22, ABIn, B01, B02, B03, BRI, C42. *Bk. rev.:* Number and length vary. *Aud.:* Ac, Sa.

This pan-regional newsmagazine covers all aspects of corporate business in Central and South America. Feature articles tend to be few and short in length. Four departments fill out the remainder of each issue, providing timely information, statistics, and opinion pieces on people, companies, regulations, technology, import/export, travel destinations, and various trade and industry topics of the region. Special issues include the annual Bravo Awards, which recognize outstanding leadership in Latin America, and the annual ranking of Latin America's 100 largest publicly traded companies. The web site provides current economic indicators, along with a shallow archive of recently published articles. URL: www.latintrade.com

1039. Multinational Business Review. [ISSN: 1525-383X] 1993. q. EUR 189 combined subscription in Europe (print & online eds.); USD 259 combined subscription in the Americas (print & online eds.); GBP 149 combined subscription in the UK & elsewhere (print & online eds.). Ed(s): Hongxin Zhao, Alan M Rugman. Emerald Group Publishing Ltd., Howard House, Wagon Ln, Bingley, BD16 1WA, United Kingdom; information@emeraldinsight.com; http://www.emeraldinsight.com. Refereed. Microform: PQC. Reprint: PSC. *Indexed:* ABIn, B01. *Aud.:* Ac.

Publishes feature-length and shorter articles, as well as case studies that explore contemporary international issues in finance, accounting, management, marketing, and economics. By focusing on practical applications in operations management, investing, debt management, and importing and exporting, this journal provides a bridge between business theory and practice. Best suited for academic libraries that serve international business programs.

1040. *Project Finance (London).* Former titles (until 2011): *Project Finance and Infrastructure Finance;* (until 2007): *Project Finance;* Which was formed by the merger of (1992-1997): *Infrastructure Finance;* (1993-1997): *Project and Trade Finance;* Which was formerly (until 1993): *Trade Finance;* (until 1990): *Trade Finance and Banker International;* Which was formed by the merger of (1987-1989): *Trade Finance;* (1987-1989): *Banker International;* Which was formerly (until 1987): *Euromoney Bank Report.* [ISSN: 2049-7059] 1997. m. GBP 1650. Ed(s): Sean Keating, Tom Nelthorpe. Euromoney Institutional Investor Plc., Nestor House, Playhouse Yard, London, EC4V 5EX, United Kingdom; information@euromoneyplc.com; http://www.euromoneyplc.com/. Illus., adv. Microform: PQC. *Indexed:* A22, ABIn, B01, B02, B03, BLI. *Aud.:* Sa.

Self-proclaimed as "the global authority for the project finance industry," this trade title offers news and short features related to various infrastructure sectors: telecommunications, oil, gas, rail, roads, bridges, tunnels, water, ports, airports, stadia, property and tourism development, petrochemicals, mining, utilities, private and public partnerships (PPP), and private finance initiatives (PFI). Aimed at corporate insiders, this title might appeal to academic libraries that serve programs in international strategic planning and risk management. Online access to articles is limited to print subscribers. URL: www.projectfinancemagazine.com

1041. *Thunderbird International Business Review.* Formerly (until 1998): *International Executive;* Incorporates (1988-2001): *Global Focus;* Which was formerly (until 1999): *Global Outlook;* (until 1998): *Business and the Contemporary World.* [ISSN: 1096-4762] 1959. bi-m. GBP 477. Ed(s): Suzy Howell, Mary B Teagarden. John Wiley & Sons, Inc., 111 River St, MS 4-02, Hoboken, NJ 07030; info@wiley.com; http://www.wiley.com/WileyCDA/. Adv. Refereed. Microform: PQC. Reprint: PSC. *Indexed:* A22, ABIn, ABS&EES, B01. *Bk. rev.:* 0-8, 450-2,000 words. *Aud.:* Ac.

With the goal of exchanging ideas and research between scholars and practitioners worldwide, this refereed journal addresses the unique challenges of global human management, analysis of multinational corporations, small business development, marketing ethics, market entry, doing business in specific countries, and international trade policies. Of primary interest to libraries that support graduate degree programs in business or international relations.

Small Business

Black Enterprise. See African American section.

1042. *Entrepreneur (Irvine).* Former titles (until 1978): *International Entrepreneurs;* (until 1977): *Insider's Report.* [ISSN: 0163-3341] 1973. m. USD 15.97 domestic; USD 31.97 foreign; USD 4.99 newsstand/cover. Ed(s): Amy Cosper, Charlotte Jensen. Entrepreneur Media, Inc., 2445 McCabe Way, Ste 400, Irvine, CA 92614; subscribe@enterpreneurmag.com; http://www.entrepreneur.com. Illus., adv. Sample. Circ: 612108 Paid. *Indexed:* A22, B01, B02, BRI. *Aud.:* Ga.

A leading magazine that covers trends, issues, and problems associated with starting and running a business. Short features written in an engaging style include individual and company profiles; success stories; strategies for improvement; and rankings of top companies and individuals. News coverage includes national, global, women-oriented, industry-specific, and hot topics. Each issue contains tips on technology, money, management, and marketing; classified ads; and a products-and-services directory. The web site contains full-text features and columns from the current issue and archives, along with online exclusives. A core title for business collections in most public and academic libraries. URL: www.entrepreneur.com/magazine

1043. *Entrepreneurship & Regional Development.* [ISSN: 0898-5626] 1989. 10x/yr. GBP 747 (print & online eds.). Ed(s): Alistair R Anderson. Routledge, 4 Park Sq, Milton Park, Abingdon, OX14 4RN, United Kingdom; subscriptions@tandf.co.uk; http://www.tandfonline.com. Adv. Sample. Refereed. Reprint: PSC. *Indexed:* A22, ABIn, B01, E01, EconLit, IBSS, JEL. *Bk. rev.:* Infrequent. *Aud.:* Ac.

This title focuses on the diverse and complex characteristics of local and regional economies (primarily European) that lead to entrepreneurial vitality. It provides a multidisciplinary forum for researchers, students, and practitioners in the fields of entrepreneurship and small- to medium-sized enterprise (SME) development within the larger context of economic growth and development. Each issue contains four or five articles, each 15–25 pages in length. Of interest to academic collections that cater to small-business studies or economics.

1044. *Entrepreneurship: Theory and Practice.* Formerly (until 1988): *American Journal of Small Business.* [ISSN: 1042-2587] 1976. bi-m. GBP 428. Ed(s): D Bagby. Wiley-Blackwell Publishing, Inc., 111 River St, Hoboken, NJ 07030; info@wiley.com; http://onlinelibrary.wiley.com/. Illus., index, adv. Vol. ends: No. 4. Microform: PQC. Reprint: PSC. *Indexed:* A22, ABIn, ATI, B01, B02, E01, IBSS, RiskAb. *Aud.:* Ac.

Blending theoretical and applied methods, this official journal of the U.S. Association for Small Business and Entrepreneurship features refereed articles on a wide range of topics in the field of entrepreneurship studies, including creation of enterprises, management of small firms, and issues in family-owned businesses. Case studies, research notes, announcements, and guest editors' commentary occur sporadically throughout the year. Most appropriate for academic libraries.

1045. *Family Business Review.* [ISSN: 0894-4865] 1988. q. USD 451. Ed(s): Pramodita Sharma. Sage Publications, Inc., 2455 Teller Rd, Thousand Oaks, CA 91320; info@sagepub.com; http://www.sagepub.com. Illus., index, adv. Sample. Refereed. Vol. ends: No. 4. Reprint: PSC. *Indexed:* A22, ABIn, B01, BRI, C42, E01. *Bk. rev.:* Number and length vary. *Aud.:* Ac.

An international editorial board oversees this scholarly publication, which is dedicated to furthering knowledge and increasing interdisciplinary skills of educators, consultants, and researchers of family-owned businesses. Four features, comprised of method papers and case studies, are presented in each issue, along with invited commentaries, interviews, and book reviews. Occasional special issues are devoted to family-owned business practices in a particular region of the world. Recommended for academic libraries that support entrepreneurship programs.

1046. *Franchising World.* Former titles (until Dec.1990): *Franchising Opportunities;* (until Feb.1990): *Franchising Opportunities World;* (until 1989): *Franchising World; International Franchise Association. Quarterly Legal Bulletin; International Franchise Association. Legal Bulletin.* [ISSN: 1524-4814] 1960. m. Free to members; Non-members, USD 50. Ed(s): Terry Hill. International Franchise Association, 1501 K St, NW, Ste 350, Washington, DC 20005; ifa@franchise.org; http://www.franchise.org. Adv. Circ: 25600. Microform: PQC. *Indexed:* A22, ABIn, B01, B02, BRI. *Aud.:* Ga.

Official publication of the International Franchise Association. Each issue contains eight articles that offer practical advice for both franchisors and franchisees. Anybody interested in franchising as a small-business opportunity will want to consult this publication. Regular columns address management and operations, industry trends, case studies, legal and regulatory issues, minority ownership opportunities, international development, and association events and activities. Digital issues of the magazine from the past two years can be viewed at the web site by selecting "News" from the navigation bar. URL: www.franchise.org

1047. *Home Business Magazine: the home-based entrepreneur's magazine.* Formerly: *National Home Business.* [ISSN: 1092-4779] 1993. bi-m. USD 19 domestic; USD 39 Canada; USD 59 elsewhere. Ed(s): Stacy Ann Henderson, Sandy Larson. United Marketing & Research Company, Inc., 20664 Jutland Pl, Lakeville, MN 55044. Illus., adv. *Indexed:* B01. *Aud.:* Ga.

Featuring five or six articles on strategy, along with an individual success story, this magazine exudes practical advice. There is a strong online presence at the web site, a useful bookmark in libraries that do not subscribe to this bimonthly in print. Information is organized by channels: "Start Up," "Marketing/Sales," "Money Corner," "Management," "Home Office," "Telecommuting," and "Community." High-resolution digital images of recent issues permit online viewing page by page. Of most interest to public libraries. URL: www.homebusinessmag.com

1048. *Journal of Business Venturing: entrepreneurship, entrepreneurial finance, innovation and regional development.* [ISSN: 0883-9026] 1985. 6x/yr. EUR 1313. Ed(s): Dean A Shepherd, S Venkataraman. Elsevier Inc., 360 Park Ave S, New York, NY 10010; usinfo-f@elsevier.com; http://www.elsevier.com. Illus., index, adv. Sample. Refereed. Circ: 675 Paid and free. Microform: PQC. *Indexed:* A22, ABIn, B01. *Aud.:* Sa.

Leading scholars and practitioners contribute developed theoretical and empirical studies to fulfill the editor's stated aims of knowledge advancement in four key areas: entrepreneurship, new business development, industry evolution, and technology management. Approximately five refereed articles of 20–30 pages in length make up each issue. Occasionally included are invited papers by selected authors, with a topic of special concern. The last issue of each volume includes a cumulative index for the volume year. An important journal for academic libraries that support programs for advanced degrees in business.

1049. *Journal of Small Business Management.* [ISSN: 0047-2778] 1963. q. GBP 275. Ed(s): George T Solomon. Wiley-Blackwell Publishing, Inc., 111 River St, Hoboken, NJ 07030; info@wiley.com; http://onlinelibrary.wiley.com/. Illus., index, adv. Sample. Refereed. Vol. ends: Nov. Reprint: PSC. *Indexed:* A22, ABIn, B01, B02, BLI, BRI, C42, E01, IBSS, P02, PsycInfo, RiskAb. *Aud.:* Ac.

This official journal of the International Council for Small Business publishes research in entrepreneurship studies and fosters the exchange of ideas dealing with marketing, financing, accounting, management, education, technology, law, and cross-cultural ramifications. Each issue contains five or six rigorously researched articles aimed at the international academic community. Appropriate for academic institutions that offer advanced degrees in business administration.

1050. *Minority Business Entrepreneur.* [ISSN: 1048-0919] 1984. bi-m. USD 18. Ed(s): Emily Richwine. Minority Business Entrepreneur, 3528 Torrance Blvd, Ste 101, Torrance, CA 90503. Illus., index, adv. Vol. ends: No. 6. *Indexed:* ENW. *Bk. rev.:* Number and length vary. *Aud.:* Ga.

This title serves to inform, educate, and inspire business owners who are women or in an ethnic minority. Articles profile individual entrepreneurs, report on success stories, analyze failures, and provide best-practice examples designed to enhance small-business management. Typical articles describe corporate and government programs and the positive benefits of supplier diversity. Ideal for public libraries that serve small businesses; of interest to academic collections that support entrepreneurship programs.

1051. *Small Business Economics: an entrepreneurship journal.* [ISSN: 0921-898X] 1989. 8x/yr. EUR 1601 (print & online eds.). Ed(s): David B Audretsch, Zoltan J Acs. Springer New York LLC, 233 Spring St, New York, NY 10013; service-ny@springer.com; http://www.springer.com/. Illus., index, adv. Sample. Refereed. Microform: PQC. Reprint: PSC. *Indexed:* A22, ABIn, B01, BRI, E01, EconLit, IBSS, JEL. *Bk. rev.:* 0-1, 750-1,000 words. *Aud.:* Ac.

This title provides a forum for theoretical, empirical, and conceptual papers in entrepreneurship. The scope is interdisciplinary and cross-national research from a broad spectrum of disciplines and related fields, including economics, finance, management, psychology, regional studies, sociology, and strategy. Each issue features six to eight articles of research and analysis that address personal characteristics of entrepreneurs, new ventures and innovation, firms' life cycles, and the role played by institutions and public policies. Of most interest to academic libraries.

1052. *Technovation: the international journal of technological innovation, entrepreneurship and technology management.* [ISSN: 0166-4972] 1981. m. EUR 2148. Ed(s): Jonathan Linton. Pergamon, The Blvd, Langford Ln, E Park, Kidlington, OX5 1GB, United Kingdom; JournalsCustomerServiceEMEA@elsevier.com; http://www.elsevier.com. Illus., adv. Sample. Refereed. *Indexed:* A22, ABIn, B01, B02, BRI, C&ISA, CerAb, EngInd, IBSS, RiskAb. *Bk. rev.:* 1-3, 500-1,000 words. *Aud.:* Ac.

All facets of the process of technological innovation, from conceptualization through commercial utilization, are covered. Topics include technological trends and breakthroughs, availability of capital for new product development and introduction, displacement of existing products, management of entrepreneurial ventures, management of innovation in small and medium enterprises (SMEs), investment strategies related to new science- or technology-based innovations, the innovator as an individual and as a personality type, and technology transfer to developing nations. Case studies that illustrate how innovation occurs from business and technical standpoints are also included, together with reviews and analyses of governmental and industrial policy that inhibit or stimulate technological innovation. Recommended for academic collections that support small business studies.

State and Regional

Several states and major cities produce some form of business newsmagazine. The Alliance of Area Business Publications provides a directory of members' titles at its web site, www.bizpubs.org.

1053. *Los Angeles Business Journal.* [ISSN: 0194-2603] 1979. w. Mon. USD 99.95 combined subscription domestic (print & online eds.); USD 199 combined subscription foreign (print & online eds.). Ed(s): Laurence Darmiento, Charles Crumpley. California Business Journals, 5700 Wilshire Blvd, Los Angeles, CA 90036; https://www.pubservice.com/CJ.htm. Adv. Microform: PQC. *Indexed:* B02, BRI. *Aud.:* Ga.

This weekly newspaper covers local business activity in the second-largest metropolitan area in the United States. Regular columns feature articles on media and technology, small business, finance, investment, and real estate. Each issue has a special report that contains several brief articles on a specific industry or subject. Topical rankings of companies known as "The Lists," along with selected articles from the current newsstand issue, are now available online after free registration through the web site. Links are provided to regional editions that cover Orange County, San Diego, and the San Fernando Valley. URL: www.labusinessjournal.com

Trade and Industry

1054. *Air Conditioning, Heating & Refrigeration News: the HVACR contractor's weekly newsmagazine.* Incorporates: *Air Conditioning and Refrigeration Directory;* (in 2000): *Service & Contracting;* Which was formerly (until 1998): *Refrigeration Service and Contracting;* Which incorporated (in 1961): *Industrial Refrigeration;* Which was formerly (until 1953): *Ice and Refrigeration;* (in 1969): *Air Engineering;* Which superseded (in 1959): *Air Engineering Newsletter;* Formerly (until 1958): *Air Conditioning and Refrigeration News.* [ISSN: 0002-2276] 1926. w. USD 59 domestic; USD 117 Canada; USD 169 elsewhere. Ed(s): Mike Murphy, Kyle Gargaro. B N P Media, 2401 W Big Beaver Rd, Ste 700, Troy, MI 48084; portfolio@bnpmedia.com; http://www.bnpmedia.com. Illus., index, adv. Sample. Circ: 21693 Paid. Microform: CIS; PQC. *Indexed:* A22, ABIn, B01, B02, BRI. *Aud.:* Sa.

This tabloid-style magazine reports on heating, ventilating, and air conditioning (HVAC) industry news, with a half-dozen articles on training and education, contracting, manufacturing, and management. Regular departments include updates on energy matters, historical practices, views and opinions, industry newsmakers, and classified ads. Appropriate for public libraries that serve patrons in regions with active construction and renovation industries, as well as academic libraries that support programs in engineering, architecture, and related fields. The current issue and archives are available at the web site, which also offers breaking news, blogs, and video clips. URL: www.achrnews.com

Airline Business. See Transportation section.

Beverage Industry. See Food Industry section.

1055. *Beverage World: intelligence for the global drinks business.*
Incorporates (in 2002): *Beverage World International;* Former titles (until 1975): *Soft Drinks;* (until 1966): *National Bottler's Gazette.* [ISSN: 0098-2318] 1882. m. USD 89 domestic (Free to qualified personnel). Ed(s): Jeff Cioletti, Andrew Kaplan. Ideal Media LLC, PO Box 2054, Skokie, IL 60076; http://www.idealmediallc.com. Illus., index, adv. Circ: 34000. Vol. ends: Dec. Microform: PQC. *Indexed:* A22, ABIn, B01, B02, H&TI. *Aud.:* Sa.

This journal tracks all aspects of the global beverage industry: manufacturers, bottlers, distributors, and retailers of soft drinks, fruit juices, iced teas, coffees, wines, spirits, and bottled waters. Articles and interviews cover diverse topics, including industry statistics, market share, packaging, vending, quality control, consumer preferences, marketing efforts, and fleet management. Only the current digital edition is viewable at the web site; however, this web site does offer complementary special reports, new product profiles, and "Lists & Rankings." An ideal candidate for a large public library with a patron group involved in the beverage industry, and academic institutions with patrons looking for market and industry data. URL: www.beverageworld.com

Billboard. See Music/Popular section.

Boxoffice. See Films section.

Broadcasting & Cable. See Television, Video, and Radio section.

Builder. See Building and Construction section.

1056. *Chain Store Age: the news magazine for retail executives.* Former titles (until 1995): *Chain Store Age Executive with Shopping Center Age;* (until 1975): *Chain Store Age Executives Edition Including Shopping Center Age;* Which was formed by the merger of (1959-1964): *Chain Store Age (Executives Edition);* Which was formerly (until 1959): *Chain Store Age (Administration Edition);* (until 1928): *Chain Store Age;* (1962-1964): *Shopping Center Age.* [ISSN: 1087-0601] 1925. m. Free to qualified personnel. Ed(s): M Nannery, Katherine Field. Lebhar-Friedman, Inc., 425 Park Ave, New York, NY 10022; info@lf.com; http://www.lf.com. Illus., adv. Sample. Circ: 33499. Vol. ends: Dec. Microform: CIS. *Indexed:* A22, ABIn, B01, B02, B03, BRI, C42. *Aud.:* Sa.

This title, from the same publisher as *Retailing Today* (below in this section), serves the decision makers who manage chain stores and shopping centers. Nearly two dozen short articles in each issue discuss current news, events, and issues related to real estate, store planning, operations, electronic retailing, payment systems, related products, and technologies. Appropriate for larger public libraries and for academic libraries that support business programs. Free registration is required to access published article content and detailed industry data. URL: www.chainstoreage.com

1057. *Chemical Week.* Incorporates (in 2003): *Soap & Cosmetics. Blue book;* Former titles: *Chemical Industries Week;* (until 1951): *Chemical Industries;* (until 1933): *Chemical Markets.* [ISSN: 0009-272X] 1914. w. USD 149.97 domestic; USD 169.97 Canada; USD 449 elsewhere. Ed(s): Roberte Westervelt, Kate Phillips. Access Intelligence, LLC, 4 Choke Cherry Rd, 2nd Fl, Rockville, MD 20850; info@accessintel.com; http://www.accessintel.com. Illus., index, adv. Sample. Circ: 9533 Paid. Microform: PQC. *Indexed:* A&ATA, A01, A22, ABIn, Agr, B01, B02, B03, BRI, C&ISA, C42, CEA, CerAb, EngInd. *Aud.:* Sa.

Weekly news source for chemical manufacturers and related industries, including pharmaceuticals and plastics. A cover story, running two or three pages, accompanies brief business and finance news articles organized by region: United States/Americas, Europe/Mideast, and Asia/Pacific. Other sections cover construction projects, mergers and acquisitions, information technology, specialty chemical production, environmental issues, laws and

regulations, company and market profiles, management trends, and newsmakers in the industry. Online content of the magazine is restricted to current subscribers only at the web site. URL: www.chemweek.com

Constructor. See Building and Construction section.

ENR. See Engineering and Technology/Civil and Environmental Engineering section.

Farm Journal. See Agriculture section.

Fleet Owner. See Transportation section.

1058. *Footwear News.* [ISSN: 0162-914X] 1945. w. USD 72 domestic; USD 149 in Canada & Mexico; USD 295 elsewhere. Ed(s): Neil Weilheimer. Fairchild Publications, Inc., 750 3rd Ave, 3rd Fl, New York, NY 10017; customerservice@fairchildpub.com; http://www.fairchildpub.com. Illus., adv. Circ: 17189. *Indexed:* ABIn, B01, B02, B03, BRI, C42. *Aud.:* Sa.

The readership of this weekly includes designers, retailers, manufacturers, importers, wholesalers, suppliers, tanners, finishers, and members of related fields. It offers extensive coverage of trends in women's, men's, and children's footwear across the dress, casual, and athletic categories. A typical issue is more visual than textual in content; articles tend to be brief profiles of designer lines and manufacturers. The web site offers only a few features and current news items; it lacks the graphic punch of its print counterpart. Of most interest to libraries that collect in fashion design. URL: www.footwearnews.com

1059. *Global Cosmetic Industry.* Former titles (until 1999): *D C I;* (until 1997): *Drug and Cosmetic Industry;* (until 1932): *Drug Markets;* (until 1926): *Drug and Chemical Markets;* Drug and Cosmetic Industry incorporated (1957-1988): *Drug and Cosmetic Catalog;* Which was formerly (until 1957): *Drug and Cosmetic Review;* (until 1939): *Drug and Cosmetic Catalog.* [ISSN: 1523-9470] 1914. m. Free. Ed(s): Jeff Falk. Allured Publishing Corp., 336 Gundersen Dr, Ste A, Carol Stream, IL 60188; customerservice@allured.com; http://www.allured.com. Illus., index, adv. Circ: 15089. Vol. ends: Dec. Microform: PMC; PQC. *Indexed:* A22, ABIn, B01, B02, B03, BRI, C42. *Aud.:* Sa.

GCI, primarily intended for cosmetics and personal-care product professionals, is a showcase of research and development, market trends, and marketing efforts. Features are short and mix the practical (product application) with the technical (formulas and ingredient analysis). Of interest to academic collections that support marketing programs and to special libraries that support personal-care product manufacturers, marketers, and retailers. Also somewhat of interest to public libraries because of the practical information imparted to consumers, e.g., new product previews and general fashion forecasts. Current issue contents and archives are available at the web site. URL: www.gcimagazine.com

1060. *H F N.* Former titles (until 1995): *H F D - Home Furnishing Daily;* (until 19??): *H F D - Retailing Home Furnishings;* (until 1976): *Home Furnishings Daily;* (until 1929): *Women's Wear Daily. Saturday.* [ISSN: 1082-0310] 19??. w. Free to qualified personnel. Ed(s): Duke Ratliff, Warren Shoulberg. Macfadden Communications Group, LLC, 333 Seventh Ave, 11th Fl, New York, NY 10001; http://www.macfad.com. Illus., index, adv. Sample. Circ: 18111. *Indexed:* ABIn, B02, B03, BRI, C42. *Aud.:* Sa.

This is a key news source for suppliers, manufacturers, wholesalers, and retailers in and associated with the interior design industry. It covers the broad spectrum of what constitutes home furnishings. In addition to the obvious furniture, there are major appliances, housewares, tableware, bedding, floor coverings, lighting and decorative accessories, do-it-yourself decorating products, and giftware. Articles address new materials, products, and processes; news and newsmakers; market conditions; and industry trends. Online content at the web site is limited to article summaries from the current issue only. However, today's news briefs, job postings, and a trade-show calendar will nicely complement a paid print subscription. Of interest to larger business collections. URL: www.hfnmag.com

Logistics Management. See Transportation section.

1061. Packaging Digest. Incorporates (in 1985): *Packaging;* Which was formerly (until 1985): *Package Engineering Including Modern Packaging;* Which was formed by the merger of (1927-1979): *Modern Packaging;* (1956-1979): *Package Engineering;* Which incorporated (in 1974): *Package Engineering New Products;* Which was formerly (until 1973): *Package Engineering New Products News.* [ISSN: 0030-9117] 1963. m. Free to qualified personnel (print or online ed.). Canon Communications LLC, 1200 Jorie Blvd., Ste.230, Oak Brook, IL 60523; info@cancom.com; http://www.cancom.com. Illus., adv. Sample. Circ: 91681. Vol. ends: Dec. Microform: PQC. *Indexed:* A22, ABIn, B01, B02, B03, BRI, EngInd. *Aud.:* Sa.

Aimed at managers, marketers, and manufacturers in the packaging industry, this monthly tabloid presents the fusion of art, design, and functionality. Ten to 12 short articles feature company and product information; new materials, technologies, and manufacturing methods; environmental concerns; and retail display. Recurring departments report on industry news, pending legislation, regulatory pressures, and new product spotlights. Illustrations abound. Current and past issue articles, daily news updates, industry links, and a few web-based exclusives are available online at the web site. An important source for marketing and branding trends. URL: www.packagingdigest.com

1062. Progressive Grocer (New York, 2002). Formed by the merger of (1922-2002): *Progressive Grocer (New York, 1922);* (1979-2002): *Supermarket Business;* Which was formerly (1969-1979): *Supermarketing;* (1946-1969): *Food Topics.* 2002. m. USD 135 domestic (Free to qualified personnel). Ed(s): Meg Major. Stagnito Media, 570 lake Cook Rd, Ste 106, Deerfield, IL 60015; http://www.stagnitomedia.com. Illus., adv. Circ: 40082 Paid and controlled. *Indexed:* A22, ABIn, B01, B02, B03, BRI. *Aud.:* Ga, Sa.

Intended for the supermarket manager, this title covers such topics as personnel and labor issues, security, customer service, new products, store design, and market conditions in general. Retailers, both foreign and domestic, who utilize unique approaches to management are spotlighted in a "Store of the Month" feature. Articles are categorized as grocery, fresh food, or nonfoods business. Regular departments address consumer preferences, in-store promotions, technology, equipment, distribution, and issues unique to independent stores. Of interest to academic libraries that support marketing and management programs, and to public libraries because of the general appeal of food. Current issue contents, web exclusives, and daily news updates are available online at the web site. URL: www.progressivegrocer.com

1063. Recycling Today. Formed by the merger of (1990-1992): *Recycling Today (Scrap Market Edition);* (1990-1992): *Recycling Today (Municipal (Post-Consumer) Market Edition);* Both of which superseded in part (in May 1990): *Recycling Today;* Which was formerly (until 1963): *Secondary Raw Materials.* [ISSN: 1096-6323] 1992. m. Free to qualified personnel. Ed(s): Brian Taylor, DeAnne Toto. G I E Media Inc., 4020 Kinross Lakes Pky, Richfield, OH 44286; http://www.giemedia.com/pages/home/default.aspx. Illus., adv. Circ: 30000. *Indexed:* A22, B02, B03, BRI, C&ISA, CerAb, EngInd. *Aud.:* Sa.

This title addresses social, political, and environmental issues that impact, and are impacted by, recycling efforts from both a local and global perspective. Articles monitor trends in waste management technologies and processes, environmental regulations, and the volatility of recycled commodity prices. Each issue provides updates on the status of the nonmetallic, ferrous, nonferrous, paper, electronics, scrap, and construction/demolition debris sectors. Current issue contents and archives are available to subscribers at the web site; nonsubscribers may register there for free online access. URL: www.recyclingtoday.com/magazine

1064. Retail Merchandiser: strategies for growth. Formerly (until May 2000): *Discount Merchandiser.* [ISSN: 1530-8154] 1961. bi-m. Free to qualified personnel. Ed(s): Amanda Gaines. RedCoat Publishing, 900 Cummings Center, Ste 222-T, Beverly, MA 01915; http://www.redcoatpublishing.com/. Illus., adv. Circ: 20000. Vol. ends: Dec. *Indexed:* A22, ABIn, B01, B02, BRI. *Aud.:* Ac, Sa.

All aspects of merchandising are covered in this publication, including manufacturing, distribution, marketing, advertising, and sales. Articles discuss product lines, famous brands, private labels, store security, technology enhancements, staffing, and related issues. Industry news, newsmakers, and competition are spotlighted. The special convention issue contains 20 pages of editorial commentary on the current and future state of mass retailing. This is a useful publication for libraries that support professionals and some academics with a focus on retail and marketing.

1065. Retail Traffic. Formerly (until May 2003): *Shopping Center World;* Incorporates (1975-1991): *Shopping Center World Product and Service Directory.* [ISSN: 1544-4236] 1972. m. USD 109 domestic (Free to qualified personnel). Ed(s): David Bodamer. Penton Media, Inc., 249 W, 17th St, New York, NY 10011; information@penton.com; http://www.penton.com. Illus. Circ: 36553 Controlled. Microform: PQC. *Indexed:* A22, ABIn, B01, B02, B03, BRI. *Aud.:* Sa.

This trade title caters to commercial real estate executives, shopping center developers, owners and managers, retail chain store executives, construction personnel, marketing professionals, leasing agents, brokers, architects, and designers. Articles report on successful shopping center properties, projects proposed and underway, specific design elements and materials, financing, and retail store profiles. Regular departments include "Shows and Events," "Retail Design Trends," "Lease Language," "International News," and "Sales Figures of Major Retailers." Content is available online after free registration. URL: http://nreionline.com/

1066. Rock Products. Former titles (until 1994): *Rock Products Mining & Processing;* (until 1963): *Rock Products;* (until 1917): *Rock Products and Building Materials;* Rock Products incorporated (1896-1924): *Cement and Engineering News;* (1918-193?): *Concrete Products.* [ISSN: 0747-3605] 1897. m. USD 62 in US & Canada (Free to qualified personnel). Ed(s): Mark S Kuhar. Mining Media International, 8751 E Hampden Ave, Ste B-1, Denver, CO 80231; info@mining-media.com; http://www.mining-media.com. Illus., adv. Vol. ends: Dec. Microform: PQC. *Indexed:* A01, A22, ABIn, B02, EngInd, P02. *Aud.:* Ga, Ac, Sa.

Topics covered are associated with the quarried stone, sand, gypsum, lightweight aggregate, and earthmoving industries. Regular features include a handful of articles on manufacturing technologies, business practices, community relations, labor, regulatory, and safety issues. Additional trade-specific departments include industry news, environmental issues, a Washington letter, new products, and a calendar of events, in addition to an annual buyers' guide and dealer directory. Current and previous issues are available online at the web site. Apart from special libraries, this title is of interest to academic libraries that support civil engineering programs and public libraries in communities with quarry operations. URL: www.rockproducts.com

1067. Rubber World. Former titles (until 1954): *India Rubber World;* (until 1899): *India Rubber World and Electrical Trades Review.* [ISSN: 0035-9572] 1889. 16x/yr. USD 34 domestic; USD 39 Canada; USD 149 elsewhere. Ed(s): Jill Rohrer, Don R Smith. Lippincott & Peto, Inc., 1867 W Market St, Akron, OH 44313. Illus., adv. Vol. ends: Dec. Microform: PMC; PQC. *Indexed:* A22, B01, B02, BRI, C&ISA, EngInd. *Aud.:* Sa.

Feature articles provide up-to-date technical service information for rubber chemists and formulators, give R&D personnel current technical know-how, and inform plant engineering personnel about the latest equipment and production technology. Regular departments include "Business Briefs," "Patent News," "Market Focus," "Tech Service," "Process Machinery," "Supplies Showcase," "Meetings," and "Calendar of Events." The subscription includes additional quarterly issues devoted to special topics. Digital edition of the current issue is offered after free registration at the web site; articles from previous issues must be purchased. Libraries that support industrial marketing, chemistry, or engineering research and development should find this title useful in their collections. URL: www.rubberworld.com

Sea Technology. See Marine Science and Technology section.

Snack Food & Wholesale Bakery. See Food Industry section.

1068. *Special Events Magazine.* Formerly: *Special Events.* [ISSN: 1079-1264] 1982. m. USD 36 domestic (Free to qualified personnel). Ed(s): Lisa Hurley. Penton Media, Inc., 17383 Sunset Blvd, Ste A220, Pacific Palisades, CA 90272; information@penton.com; http://www.penton.com. Circ: 5763 Paid and controlled. *Indexed:* B01, B02, BRI. *Aud.:* Ga, Sa.

A resource for event professionals who design and produce social, corporate, and public events in hotels, resorts, banquet facilities, and other venues. Coverage of galas is extensive; photos are a feast for the eyes. Departments provide practical advice on event management and tout new products and innovative ideas. The publication has a cooperative alliance with the International Special Events Society. In each issue, five pages are reserved for news and promotion of the society's web site. Contents of the current and back issues are available online. URL: www.specialevents.com

1069. *Stores.* Former titles (until 1947): *National Retail Dry Goods Association. Bulletin;* (until 1925): *National Retail Dry Goods Association. Confidential Bulletin.* [ISSN: 0039-1867] 1912. m. USD 120 (print or online ed.) (Free to qualified personnel). Ed(s): Susan Reda. N R F Enterprises, Inc., 325 7th St, NW, Ste 1100, Washington, DC 20004. Illus., adv. Vol. ends: Dec. *Indexed:* A22, ABIn, B01, B03, BRI. *Aud.:* Sa.

This title features corporate and industry news for all kinds of retail chain stores and wholesale clubs, restaurants, drug stores, direct mail, and marketing firms engaged in specialty and general merchandising. The focus is on technology, management, and operations. Special issues include ranked lists of department stores in July and specialty chains in August, both including sales and earnings figures. Appropriate for larger public libraries and for academic libraries that support business programs. URL: www.stores.org

1070. *Textile World.* Incorporates (2001-2001): *Textile Industries;* Which was formerly (until 2001): *America's Textiles International;* (until 1986): *America's Textile;* Which was formed by the merger of (19??-1983): *America's Textiles. Knitter - Apparel;* (1971-1983): *America's Textiles. Reporter - Bulletin;* Which was formed by the merger of (1908-1971): *America's Textile Reporter;* (1933-1971): *Textile Bulletin;* Which was formerly (1911- 1933): *Southern Textile Bulletin;* Incorporated: *Fiber World;* (1973-1984): *Fiber Producer;* Which superseded: *Fiber Producer Buyer's Guide;* (1947-1984): *Textile Industries;* Former titles (until 1931): *Textile Advance News;* (until 1924): *Textiles;* (until 1923): *Posselt's Textile Journal;* (until 1921): *Textile World Journal;* Which was formed by the merger of (1903-1915): *Textile World Record;* (1894-1915): *Textile Manufacturers Journal.* [ISSN: 0040-5213] 1915. m. Free. Ed(s): Jim Borneman. Billian Publishing, Inc., 2100 Powers Ferry Rd, Ste 300, Atlanta, GA 30339; info@billian.com; http://www.billian.com. Illus., adv. Circ: 32340 Paid and controlled. Vol. ends: Dec. Microform: PMC; PQC. *Indexed:* A22, ABIn, B01, EngInd. *Aud.:* Sa.

Included in this title are reports on technologies such as yarn manufacturing; fabric forming; chemical treatment and finishing; industrial and specialty textiles; carpet manufacturing and marketing; manufacturing systems; and management issues on an international basis. Articles and advertisements introduce suppliers, new products, innovative techniques, and industry trends. Recurring departments provide industry news, statistics, legal developments, legislation, profiles of companies, interviews with executives, and occasional special reports. The current issue and archives are freely available online. URL: www.textileworld.com

1071. *W W D: the retailer's daily newspaper.* Incorporates (199?-2004): *Fairchild's Executive Technology;* (2000-2002): *W W D, The Magazine;* (2001-200?): *W W D Beautybiz;* Which was formerly (in 2001): *Beautybiz;* Former titles (until 1976): *Women's Wear Daily;* Which incorporated (1931-1940): *Retail Executive;* (until 1927): *Women's Wear.* [ISSN: 0149-5380] 1892. d. USD 99 domestic (print or online ed.); USD 312.70 Canada; USD 595 elsewhere). Ed(s): Edward Nardoza. Fairchild Publications, Inc., 750 3rd Ave, 3rd Fl, New York, NY 10017; customerservice@fairchildpub.com; http://www.fairchildpub.com. Illus., adv. Circ: 46728. Microform: PQC. *Indexed:* ABIn, B01, B02, B03, BRI, C42. *Aud.:* Ga.

This newspaper-format publication provides extensive coverage of the women's apparel and couture fashion industries. Each weekday issue of this "fashion bible" focuses on a rotating theme of accessories, ready-to-wear, sportswear, or beauty, along with commentary on the season's colors, styles, and fabrics. Designers are profiled and their runway shows are lavishly photographed. There is extensive reporting on the social scene that is intrinsic to the concept of "image." Manufacturing problems, marketing, distribution channels, and retail issues are discussed in brief. To view content from today's paper and previous issues at the web site requires a separate subscription. Of interest to libraries with a flair for fashion. URL: www.wwd.com

1072. *Wines and Vines.* Incorporates (198?-2008): *Wine East;* (1933-1950): *Wine Review;* Which incorporated: *Wine News;* Former titles (until 1935): *California Grape Grower;* (until 1933): *California Grower.* [ISSN: 0043-583X] 1919. m. USD 38 combined subscription domestic (print & online eds.); USD 48 combined subscription in Canada & Mexico (print & online eds.); USD 85 combined subscription elsewhere (print & online eds.). Ed(s): Jim Gordon. Hiaring Co., 65 Mitchell Blvd Ste A, San Rafael, CA 94903; info@winesandvines.com; http://www.winesandvines.com/. Illus., adv. Circ: 5142. *Indexed:* BRI. *Bk. rev.:* Number and length vary. *Aud.:* Sa.

Published since 1919, this trade title even managed to survive the lean years of Prohibition. Although aimed at wine producers, this monthly publication will be enjoyed by all wine aficionados. Each monthly issue includes topical industry news along with editorial columns on political, legal, and regulatory developments. Emphasis is on boutique wine production trends and techniques in North America, including profiles of notable winemakers and grape growers. The latest wine industry news headlines and print issue content are offered at the web site. URL: www.winesandvines.com

1073. *Wood & Wood Products: furniture, cabinets, woodworking and allied products management and operations.* Incorporates (in 1960): *The Wood-Worker;* (in 1960): *Veneers and Plywood;* Which was formerly (until 1934): *Veneers;* Formerly (until 1952): *Wood Combined with Wood Products;* Which was formed by the merger of (1946-1951): *Wood;* (190?-1951): *Wood Products.* [ISSN: 0043-7662] 1896. m. USD 55 in North America (Free to qualified personnel). Ed(s): Karen M Koenig, Michaelle Bradford. Vance Publishing Corp., PO Box 1400, Lincolnshire, IL 60069; info@vancepublishing.com; http://www.vancepublishing.com. Illus., adv. Circ: 48000. Microform: PQC. *Indexed:* A22, B01, B02. *Aud.:* Sa.

This publication is intended for management and operating personnel in the woodworking industry. Articles address machining trends and developments; management and marketing techniques; and automation, hardware, and design for the markets for residential furniture, business and institutional furniture, cabinet, millwork, and paneling. Archives, industry news, and other web exclusives are available at the web site. URL: www.woodworkingnetwork.com/wood-archives/wood-products-magazine

Banking

1074. *A B A Banking Journal.* Incorporates (2000-2010): *Community Banker (Washington, D.C. 2000);* Which was formerly (1995-1999): *America's Community Banker;* (1992-1995): *Savings & Community Banker;* Former titles (until 1979): *Banking;* (until 1934): *American Bankers Association Journal;* (until 1924): *American Bankers Association. Journal.* [ISSN: 0194-5947] 1908. m. USD 61 (print or online ed.) Free to qualified personnel; USD 31 per issue in US & Canada). Ed(s): William W Streeter, Steven Cocheo. Simmons-Boardman Publishing Corp., 345 Hudson St, New York, NY 10014. Illus., index, adv. Sample. Microform: PQC. *Indexed:* A22, ABIn, ATI, B01, B02, BLI, BRI, Chicano. *Bk. rev.:* Number and length vary. *Aud.:* Ac, Sa.

This legal industry magazine covers news, trends, and products in commercial and community banking. Columns report on community banking, compliance, mortgage lending, trusts, technology, new-product development, news and newsmakers, regulatory issues, and the general economy. A calendar of events is also included, and an annual issue ranks the top financial performers among the largest U.S. banks and thrifts. Recent feature articles examine keeping up on bank regulatory compliance, the national mortgage crisis, and risk management. URL: www.ababj.com/

1075. *American Banker: on focus and in depth.* Formerly (until 1887): *Thompson's Bank Note and Commercial Reporter;* Incorporates (in 2002): *Financial Services Marketing.* [ISSN: 0002-7561] 1836. d. USD 995 combined subscription (print & online eds.). Ed(s): Neil Weinberg. SourceMedia, Inc., One State St Plz, 27th Fl, New York, NY 10004; custserv@sourcemedia.com; http://www.sourcemedia.com. Illus., index, adv. *Indexed:* ATI, B01, B02, B03, BLI, BRI, C42, NewsAb. *Bk. rev.:* Number and length vary. *Aud.:* Ac, Sa.

This highly regarded daily financial paper reports on trade and industry news and newsmakers. It covers trends in community banking, mortgages, investment products, debt and credit, technology, ATMs, and finance. Bank ratings, marketing, court cases, regulations, and news about movers and shakers in the banking industry are also included. Because of the in-depth coverage of banking and the concise reports of related general business and industry news, this is a must for bankers and for academic as well as larger public libraries. URL: www.americanbanker.com/

1076. *The Banker.* [ISSN: 0005-5395] 1926. m. GBP 645 combined subscription (print & online eds.). Ed(s): Brian Caplen. The Financial Times Ltd., 1 Southwark Bridge, London, SE1 9HL, United Kingdom; help@ft.com; http://www.ft.com/. Illus., index, adv. Sample. Circ: 28974. Vol. ends: Dec. Microform: PQC. Reprint: SCH. *Indexed:* A22, ABIn, B01, B02, B03, BLI, BRI. *Bk. rev.:* Number and length vary. *Aud.:* Ac, Sa.

This international banking newsmagazine provides insights into the international retail and investment-banking climates. Each issue includes summary reports of economic and industry conditions in a dozen or more countries, along with brief reports that cover banking, capital markets, foreign exchange, derivatives, trade finance, risk analysis, technology, and interviews. Recent contents include discussions of covered bonds, the credit derivatives market, the strengthening of firms' compliance departments, and a host of other issues for each geographic region. Ranked lists of top banks and directories of foreign banks are often provided. This is a great choice for any academic or large public library whose patrons are interested in international finance, development, and banking news. URL: www.thebanker.com/

1077. *Banking and Finance Review.* [ISSN: 1947-7945] 2009. s-a. Ed(s): Joseph Farhat. Central Connecticut State University, Department of Finance, 1615 Stanley St, New Britain, CT 06050. Refereed. *Indexed:* B01, EconLit. *Aud.:* Ac, Sa.

This semi-annual, peer-reviewed journal publishes empirical and theoretical research in the fields of banking and finance. Topic areas include banking, capital markets, commodity markets, corporate finance, derivatives, financial institutions, insurance, international finance, investments, portfolio and security analysis, real estate, risk management, and other areas. The editorial board is made up of faculty from universities around the world. The web site offers free access to articles.

1078. *Credit Union Magazine: for credit union elected officials, managers and employees.* Formerly: *Credit Union Bridge.* [ISSN: 0011-1066] 1924. m. USD 64. Ed(s): Kathryn Kuehn. Credit Union National Association, Inc., PO Box 431, Madison, WI 53701; http://www.cuna.org. Illus., index, adv. Circ: 30900. Microform: PQC. *Indexed:* A22, ABIn, B01, BLI. *Aud.:* Ac, Sa.

This important trade magazine, produced by the Credit Union National Association, reports on news and newsmakers, new products and technologies, target markets, new services, and information related to credit unions in general. Recent topics include discussions of student loans, vehicle repossession, and measuring customer loyalty. This title is worthwhile for large public libraries and academic libraries that support finance programs or a campus credit union. The web site provides free articles from the current issue and archives.

1079. *Mortgage Banking: the magazine of real estate finance.* Formerly (until 1981): *Mortgage Banker;* Which superseded (in 1939): *M B A News Review.* [ISSN: 0730-0212] 1936. m. Members, USD 64; Non-members, USD 74. Ed(s): Janet Reilley Hewitt. Mortgage Bankers Association, 1331 L St, NW, Washington, DC 20005; info@mortgagebankers.org; http://www.mortgagebankers.org. Illus., index, adv. Sample. Vol. ends: Sep. Microform: CIS; PQC. *Indexed:* A22, ABIn, B01, B02, B03, BLI, BRI. *Aud.:* Ac, Sa.

This journal provides practical and timely articles about all aspects of real estate finance. Departments cover trends, technology, software, key people, the secondary mortgage market, statistics, sources of demographics and research, mortgage revenue bonds, and servicing. The companion web site highlights the current issue and provides a searchable archive. Libraries that support business programs that focus on real estate should consider this title. URL: www.newslibrary.com/sites/mbkb/

Insurance

1080. *Best's Review.* Formed by the merger of (1969-2000): *Best's Review. Life - Health Insurance Edition;* Which was formed by the merger of (1920-1969): *Best's Insurance News. Life - Health Edition;* Which was formerly (19??-1920): *Best's Life Insurance News;* (1964-1969): *Flitcraft Courant;* Which was formerly (until 1964): *Life Insurance Courant;* (until 19??): *Insurance Courant;* (1977-2000): *Best's Review. Property - Casualty Insurance Edition;* Which was formerly (until 1977): *Best's Review. Property - Liability Edition;* (until 1969): *Best's Insurance News. Fire and Casualty.* [ISSN: 1527-5914] 2000. m. USD 57; USD 15.50 per issue. A.M. Best Co., Ambest Rd, Oldwick, NJ 08858; http://www.ambest.com. Illus., index, adv. Vol. ends: Apr. *Indexed:* A22, ABIn, AgeL, B01, B02, B03, BRI, C42. *Aud.:* Ac, Sa.

This trade magazine provides wide coverage of the insurance industry under a single title. This integrated edition includes company and industry news, political and regulatory information, new-product announcements, newsmakers in the industry, and reports of court cases in each issue. This publication "best" represents the insurance industry as a whole, and therefore is a core title for large public and academic libraries.

1081. *Insurance: Mathematics and Economics.* [ISSN: 0167-6687] 1982. 6x/yr. EUR 1734. Ed(s): M J Goovaerts, H U Gerber. Elsevier BV, North-Holland, Postbus 211, Amsterdam, 1000 AE, Netherlands; JournalsCustomerServiceEMEA@elsevier.com; http://www.elsevier.com. Illus., index, adv. Sample. Refereed. Vol. ends: No. 4. Microform: PQC. *Indexed:* A22, ABIn, B01, CCMJ, EconLit, IBSS, JEL, MSN, MathR. *Aud.:* Ac, Sa.

Each issue contains five to eight papers of international interest, 10–15 pages in length, concerned with the theory of insurance mathematics or the inventive application of it, including empirical or experimental results. Articles evaluate mathematical and economic applications related to actuarial science and a variety of insurance-related concerns. Libraries that support programs in actuarial science, mathematics, and economics should evaluate this journal despite its hefty price.

1082. *Journal of Risk and Insurance.* Formerly (until 1964): *Journal of Insurance;* Which was formed by the merger of (1954-1957): *Review of Insurance Studies;* (1933-1957): *American Association of University Teachers of Insurance. Journal;* Which was formerly (until 1937): *American Association of University Teachers of Insurance. Proceedings of the Annual Meeting.* [ISSN: 0022-4367] 1957. q. GBP 303 (print or online ed.). Ed(s): Georges Dionne. Wiley-Blackwell Publishing, Inc., 111 River St, Hoboken, NJ 07030; info@wiley.com; http://onlinelibrary.wiley.com/. Illus., index. Sample. Refereed. Vol. ends: Dec. Microform: PQC. Reprint: PSC. *Indexed:* A22, ABIn, B01, B02, BRI, E01, EconLit, JEL, MCR, RiskAb. *Bk. rev.:* 1-3, 1,000+ words. *Aud.:* Ac.

This is the flagship journal of the American Risk and Insurance Association. Each issue contains roughly ten articles that present original theoretical and empirical research in insurance economics and risk management. The focus is on the organization of markets, managing pure risk, insurance finance, the economics of employee benefits, utility theory, insurance regulation, actuarial and statistical methodology, and economics of insurance institutions. Large public libraries and academic libraries that support business programs should consider this title.

1083. *Life Insurance Selling: field-tested solutions for today's strategic producer.* Incorporates: *Selling Insurance.* [ISSN: 0024-3140] 1926. m. Free to qualified personnel. Ed(s): Corey Dahl, Brian Anderson. Summit Business Media LLC, 475 Park Ave S, Sixth Fl, New York, NY 10016; jobs@summitbusinessmedia.com; http://www.summitbusinessmedia.com. Illus. Vol. ends: Dec. Microform: PQC. *Indexed:* ABIn, B02, BLI. *Aud.:* Sa.

This magazine for life and health insurance and financial-services producers provides practical and transferable sales ideas and information through both editorial content and advertising. Regular departments describe policies, books, sales aids, computer products, and educational programs designed for producers. This is one of the best introductions to life insurance sales as a career, and it provides important product information for producers.

1084. *National Underwriter. Life & Health.* Former titles (until 2004): *National Underwriter. Life and Health Financial Services;* (until 1986): *National Underwriter. Life and Health Insurance Edition;* (until 1970): *National Underwriter. Life Insurance Edition.* [ISSN: 1940-1345] 197?. bi-w. USD 249 (Free to qualified personnel). The National Underwriter Company, 5081 Olympic Blvd, Erlanger, KY 41018; customerservice@nuco.com; http://www.nationalunderwriter.com. Illus., adv. Vol. ends: Dec. Microform: PQC. *Indexed:* A22, ABIn, B01, B02, B03, BRI, C42. *Aud.:* Sa.

This is a core newspaper for the life, health, and financial-services segments of the insurance industry. A variety of topics are covered, including new product information; changes in the tax law; new federal and state legislation; company, agent, and brokerage activities; and trade association meetings. Special in-depth issues are offered throughout the year that focus on particularly hot topics or issues of importance. Public libraries with a balanced business collection and all academic libraries that support insurance programs should have this title. The companion web site offers current news and past issues. URL: www.nationalunderwriter.com/magazines

1085. *National Underwriter. P & C.* Former titles (until 2004): *National Underwriter. Property & Casualty - Risk & Benefits Management Edition;* (until 1989): *National Underwriter. Property and Casualty - Employee Benefits Edition;* (until 1986): *National Underwriter. Property and Casualty Insurance Edition;* (until 1970): *The National Underwriter;* (until 1917): *The Western Underwriter;* (until 1899): *Ohio Underwriter.* [ISSN: 1940-1353] 1896. w. USD 249 combined subscription (print & online eds.). The National Underwriter Company, 5081 Olympic Blvd, Erlanger, KY 41018; customerservice@nuco.com; http://www.nationalunderwriter.com. Illus. Vol. ends: Dec. Microform: PQC. *Indexed:* A22, ABIn, B01, B02, B03, BRI, C42. *Aud.:* Ac, Sa.

This is a core newspaper for the international property, casualty, and risk-management insurance industry. Regularly featured sections include industry trends, agent and broker activities, corporate risk management, employee benefits, product and marketing information, stock activity, international events, and reinsurance. In addition, special, in-depth issues throughout the year focus on hot topics or issues of importance. Public libraries with a balanced business collection and all academic libraries that support insurance programs should have this title. The companion web site offers current news and past issues.

Investment

1086. *Better Investing.* [ISSN: 0006-016X] 1951. m. Free to members; Non-members, USD 31. Ed(s): Adam Ritt. Betterinvesting, PO Box 220, Royal Oaks, MI 48068; corporate@betterinvesting.org; http://www.betterinvesting.org. Illus., index, adv. Sample. Microform: PQC. *Indexed:* A22, ABIn. *Bk. rev.:* Number and length vary. *Aud.:* Ga, Ac, Sa.

A popular choice for personal-investing collections in public libraries, this title presents news and information related to money management, investment clubs, and National Association of Investors Corporation (NAIC) events. Each issue includes an editorial, letters to the editor, "Ask Mr. NAIC," a growth-fund report, a technology report, and regional notices. The stocks and funds section includes an undervalued stock, a stock to study, a contrary opinion, a "five years ago stock to study," an undervalued stock, and an 18-month undervalued review. Public and academic libraries that serve individual investors or support investment courses should certainly consider this title. URL: www.betterinvesting.org/Public/StartLearning/BI+Mag/default.htm

1087. *C F A Digest.* [ISSN: 0046-9777] 1971. q. Members, USD 50; Non-members, USD 75. Ed(s): Maryann Dupes, Rodney N Sullivan. C F A Institute, 560 Ray C Hunt Dr, PO Box 3668, Charlottesville, VA 22903; info@cfainstitute.org; http://www.cfainstitute.org. Illus. Sample. *Indexed:* B01. *Aud.:* Ac, Sa.

The Association for Investment Management and Research, composed of the Institute of Chartered Financial Consultants and the Financial Analysts Federation, produces this digest. Each issue provides 600-word abstracts of 30 articles, drawn from a pool of more than 100 investment-related journals. Scholarly articles on alternative investments, corporate finance, corporate governance, debt investments, derivatives, equity investments, financial markets, investment theory, portfolio management, quantitative tools, and risk measurement and management are included. Publishers' names and addresses and article order forms are included. In each issue, the editor summarizes the general content and the uses of the research articles. This is a core title for academic libraries that support programs in investment and finance.

1088. *Euromoney (Print).* Incorporates (1989-2005): *Corporate Finance;* Which was formerly (1984-1989): *Euromoney Corporate Finance;* Incorporates (1991-2001): *Central European.* [ISSN: 0014-2433] 1969. m. GBP 475 combined subscription (print & online eds.); EUR 625 combined subscription (print & online eds.); USD 835 combined subscription (print & online eds.). Ed(s): Clive Horwood. Euromoney Institutional Investor Plc., Nestor House, Playhouse Yard, London, EC4V 5EX, United Kingdom; information@euromoneyplc.com; http://www.euromoneyplc.com/. Illus., index, adv. Sample. Vol. ends: Dec. Microform: PQC. *Indexed:* A22, ABIn, B01, B02, B03, BLI, BRI. *Bk. rev.:* Number and length vary. *Aud.:* Ac, Sa.

This title monitors the global financial marketplace, including financial institutions, securities, and commodities in established and emerging economies. It provides profiles of companies, industries, and the family trees and business interests of the people who control the wealth. Related aspects of international finance are covered. Each issue provides information from a dozen or more countries and regions. This is a core industry publication for anyone interested in international finance, and is appropriate for academic, special, and larger public libraries that support finance programs or professionals, especially with patrons seeking a comparative perspective. URL: www.euromoney.com/

1089. *Institutional Investor (America's Edition).* Incorporates (1972-1973): *Pensions;* (1970-1973): *Corporate Financing;* Which was formerly (until 1970): *Investment Banking and Corporate Financing.* [ISSN: 0020-3580] 1967. 10x/yr. GBP 367 combined subscription United Kingdom (print & online eds.); EUR 452 combined subscription in Europe (print & online eds.); USD 575 combined subscription elsewhere (print & online eds.). Ed(s): Thomas W Johnson, Michael Peltz. Institutional Investor, Inc., 225 Park Ave S, New York, NY 10003; http://www.institutionalinvestor.com. Illus., index, adv. Vol. ends: Dec. Microform: PQC. *Indexed:* A22, ABIn, ATI, B01, B02, B03, BLI, BRI, C42. *Bk. rev.:* 1-2, 1,000-1,500 words. *Aud.:* Ac, Sa.

This practitioner's magazine is known for its benchmark rankings and ratings of analysts, asset managers, banks, and country credit globally. These rankings are designed to assist financial professionals in making sound investment decisions. The journal provides detailed coverage of commercial and investment banking and many other areas of finance and investing. It also addresses policies, strategies, and the political activities in the social arenas that influence investment decisions. This publication is a must for academic and research libraries that support programs in business and finance.

1090. *Investor's Business Daily.* Formerly (until 1991): *Investor's Daily.* [ISSN: 1061-2890] 1984. d. (Mon.-Fri.). USD 319. Ed(s): Wesley Mann. Investor's Business Daily, Inc., 12655 Beatrice St, Los Angeles, CA 90066. Illus., adv. Circ: 264699. *Indexed:* ABIn, B01, B02, BLI, BRI. *Aud.:* Ga, Sa.

This daily newspaper provides timely information for individual and institutional investors. It reports on the economic, social, and political trends that drive markets and the individuals, companies, industries, and funds that make up the competitive landscape. Regular features include a weekly list of the 100 top-rated stocks, a list of stocks traded heavily by institutional investors, unbiased market analysis, profiles of innovative companies, and "Investor's Corner," lessons for successful investing. This newspaper is an excellent source for evaluating the global investment climate, and is a necessity for academic libraries that support business programs and for large public libraries.

1091. *Investors Chronicle.* Formerly (until 1975): *Investors Chronicle and Stock Exchange Gazette;* Which was formed by the merger of (1901-1967): *Stock Exchange Gazette;* (1914-1967): *The Money Market Review & Investors' Chronicle;* Which was formerly (until 1914): *The Money Market Review.* [ISSN: 0261-3115] 1967. w. GBP 145. Ed(s): John Hughman. The Financial Times Ltd., 1 Southwark Bridge, London, SE1 9HL, United Kingdom; help@ft.com; http://www.ft.com/. Illus., adv. Sample. Circ: 25731. Vol. ends: Dec. Microform: RPI; PQC. *Indexed:* ABIn, B02, BLI, BRI. *Bk. rev.:* Number and length vary. *Aud.:* Ac, Sa.

This weekly British financial newsmagazine has been providing private investors with market information since 1860. Articles are grouped by category under general business news, features, tips, markets, sectors, and companies. Stock tips, statistics, and a survey article appear in each issue. Special supplements are issued with a subscription that report on insurance, investing for children, and other topics of interest to investors. This title provides a more international perspective than most U.S.-produced magazines of its kind.

1092. *The Journal of Portfolio Management.* [ISSN: 0095-4918] 1974. q. USD 955 combined subscription domestic (print & online eds.); GBP 635 combined subscription United Kingdom (print & online eds.); EUR 765 combined subscription in Europe (print & online eds.). Ed(s): Frank J Fabozzi. Institutional Investor, Inc., 225 Park Ave S, 8th Fl, New York, NY 10003; info@iijournals.com; http://www.institutionalinvestor.com/. Illus., adv. Microform: PQC. *Indexed:* A22, ABIn, ATI, B01, B02, BLI, BRI, EconLit, JEL. *Bk. rev.:* Number and length vary. *Aud.:* Ac, Sa.

This journal for investment professionals is focused on all aspects of institutional investing. Substantive articles are written in a layperson's terms by both practitioners and academics. Articles are not longer than 20 pages each, and recent ones cover topics such as innovation and portfolio management, embedded tax liabilities and portfolio choice, and investing under inflation risk. Recommended for academic and large public libraries.

1093. *Kiplinger's Personal Finance: a guide to today's best bargains.* Former titles (until 2000): *Kiplinger's Personal Finance Magazine;* (until 1991): *Changing Times;* (until 1949): *Kiplinger Magazine.* [ISSN: 1528-9729] 1947. m. USD 12 (print or online ed.). Ed(s): Knight Kiplinger, Fred W Frailey. Kiplinger Washington Editors, Inc., 1729 H St, NW, Washington, DC 20006; magazine@kiplinger.com; http://www.kiplinger.com. Illus., index, adv. Sample. Circ: 850000 Paid. *Indexed:* A01, A22, ABIn, ATI, AgeL, B01, B02, BRI, C37, CBRI, MASUSE, P02. *Bk. rev.:* Number and length vary. *Aud.:* Ga, Ac, Sa.

Aimed at anyone who wants to take an active role in their own personal-finance decisions, this title offers practical strategies for investing, managing, and spending your money. Articles cover topics that range from paying for college to planning your retirement, and everything in-between. Regular departments monitor and report on mutual funds, money market funds, blue chips, and taxes. Personal-interest columns discuss travel, health, personal finances, and family finances. A handful of articles in each issue discuss general concerns related to investing. Special issues evaluate and chart mutual fund performance. The web site provides online access to selected content.

1094. *Morningstar FundInvestor.* Former titles (until 1999): *Morningstar Investor;* (until 1995): *Five Star Investor.* [ISSN: 1099-0402] 1992. m. USD 125 combined subscription (print & online eds.). Ed(s): Russel Kinnel. Morningstar, Inc., 22 W Washington St, Chicago, IL 60602; productinfo@morningstar.com; http://www.morningstar.com. *Indexed:* B01. *Aud.:* Ga, Ac, Sa.

The firm Morningstar produces both stock and mutual-fund investment newsletters and a user-friendly web site with helpful free content that includes fund data, calculators, and market news. The mutual fund title evaluated here comprises monthly issues that contain detailed coverage of the mutual fund industry, including 500 selected funds. This publication offers ratings, statistics, and interviews with top financial planners and fund industry leaders, as well as news, updates, and emerging trends in the industry. All public and academic libraries that provide investment information should have this title.

1095. *Pensions & Investments: the newspaper of corporate and institutional investing.* Former titles (until 1990): *Pensions and Investment Age;* (until 1981): *Pensions and Investments.* [ISSN: 1050-4974] 1973. bi-w. USD 259; USD 1129 combined subscription (print & online eds.). Ed(s): Joel Chernoff, Elizabeth Karier. Crain Communications, Inc., 711 Third Ave, New York, NY 10017; info@crain.com; http://www.crain.com. Illus., index, adv. Sample. Circ: 52039. Microform: CIS; PQC. *Indexed:* A22, ABIn, ATI, B01, B02, B03, BLI, BRI, C42. *Aud.:* Ga, Sa.

This weekly newsmagazine for money managers provides information, explanation, analysis, and updates on all aspects of pensions and institutional investments. Regular departments cover news, interviews, opinions, a "pensions and investments" index, and updates on newsmakers. The "Annual Databook" issue includes a ranking of top managers and funds, statistics on pension plans, mutual funds, savings plans, life insurance, and more. Recent feature articles address the state of municipal pension plans, the impact of same-sex marriage laws on pension planning, and overall retirement confidence.

1096. *Risk.* [ISSN: 0952-8776] 1987. m. GBP 767 domestic; EUR 1150 in Europe; USD 1395 elsewhere. Ed(s): Nick Sawyer. Incisive Financial Publishing Ltd., Haymarket House, 28-29 Haymarket, London, SW1Y 4RX, United Kingdom; customerservices@incisivemedia.com; http://www.incisivemedia.com/. Illus., adv. Sample. Vol. ends: Dec. *Indexed:* A22, ABIn, ATI, B01, BLI, RiskAb. *Bk. rev.:* Number and length vary. *Aud.:* Ac, Sa.

This journal provides mathematical detail in its discussions of all forms of risk, including currencies, interest rates, equities, commodities, and credit. Issues include a cover story, an organizational profile, an interview, news, and six to eight articles on fund management, options, and brokers. Topics include the credit market, equity derivatives, interest rate swaps, structured credit, and inflation. Public libraries with supporting demographics and academic libraries with programs in international business, economics, or finance should consider this title for its practitioner-oriented information.

1097. *The Street.com.* 1996. w. USD 229.95. Ed(s): Dave Kansas. TheStreet.com, 14 Wall St, New York, NY 10005; http://www.weissratings.com/. *Aud.:* Ga.

Since 1996, *The Street.com* has provided solid advice based on financial know-how rather than wild guesses about investments. The site offers insights and advice from well-known market watchers, first-rate analysis, and in-depth articles that will be of interest to anyone serious about Wall Street. *TheStreet.com* combines articles, tools, and video in an easily browsable format.

1098. *Worth.* Former titles (until 2006): *Robb Report Worth;* (until 2003): *Worth;* (until 1992): *Investment Vision;* Which incorporated (1985-1991): *Personal Investor.* [ISSN: 1931-9908] 1987. bi-m. USD 109 domestic; USD 149 Canada; USD 229 elsewhere. Ed(s): Richard Bradley. Sandow Media Corp., 360 Park Ave S, 17th Fl, New York, NY 10010; sandowinfo@sandowmedia.com; http://www.sandowmedia.com. Illus. *Bk. rev.:* Number and length vary. *Aud.:* Ga, Sa.

This personal investing magazine is aimed at high-net-worth individuals and their advisors. The magazine's features cover topics ranging from top wealth advisors, philanthropy, and tax havens, to profiles of CEOs and prominent business people. Even if you do not own a second home or a yacht, this publication provides savvy investment advice that could benefit all types of investors. Recommended for browsing collections in public libraries and larger academic libraries.

Scholarly

This section provides recommended purchases. To get more detailed evaluation and rankings of academic journals in the subject area, visit Harzing.com at www.harzing.com/jql.htm.

1099. *Applied Financial Economics.* [ISSN: 0960-3107] 1991. 24x/yr. GBP 3035 (print & online eds.). Ed(s): Mark P Taylor. Routledge, 4 Park Sq, Milton Park, Abingdon, OX14 4RN, United Kingdom; subscriptions@tandf.co.uk; http://www.tandfonline.com. Illus., index, adv. Sample. Refereed. Reprint: PSC. *Indexed:* A22, ABIn, B01, BAS, E01, EconLit, IBSS, JEL. *Aud.:* Ac, Sa.

This peer-reviewed journal serves as an international forum for applied research on financial markets (debt, equity, derivatives, foreign exchange) as well as corporate finance, market structure, and related areas. Each issue includes roughly a half-dozen articles, generally about ten pages in length, that focus on both developed markets and developing economies in Central and Eastern Europe. Topics also include econometric techniques as they relate to financial research, forecasting, and the intersection of real and financial economy. Recent articles look at the risk as measured in the financial industry, and pricing for particular instruments, such as options. This highly technical journal will be appreciated in academic and research libraries that support graduate programs or finance professionals.

1100. *Applied Mathematical Finance.* [ISSN: 1350-486X] 1994. bi-m. GBP 1320 (print & online eds.). Ed(s): Christoph Reisinger, Dr. Ben Hambly. Routledge, 4 Park Sq, Milton Park, Abingdon, OX14 4RN, United Kingdom; subscriptions@tandf.co.uk; http://www.tandfonline.com. Adv. Sample. Refereed. Reprint: PSC. *Indexed:* A22, ABIn, B01, BLI, CCMJ, E01, EconLit, JEL, MSN, MathR. *Aud.:* Ac, Sa.

Aimed at financial practitioners, academics, and applied mathematicians, this title includes 15- to 20-page articles by worldwide academics that are designed to encourage the "confident use" of applied mathematics and mathematical models for finance. Papers cover such topics as economic primitives (interest rates, asset prices, etc.), market behavior, market strategy (such as hedging), financial instruments, reviews of new developments in financial engineering, general mathematical finance, models and algorithms, new products, and reviews of practical tools. Recent articles explore modeling electricity prices with forward-looking capacity constraints, and trader behavior and its effect on asset price dynamics.

1101. *F M.* [ISSN: 0046-3892] 1972. q. GBP 251 (print & online eds.). Ed(s): Bill Christie. Wiley-Blackwell Publishing, Inc., 111 River St, Hoboken, NJ 07030; info@wiley.com; http://onlinelibrary.wiley.com/. Illus., index. Refereed. Vol. ends: Winter. Microform: PQC. Reprint: PSC. *Indexed:* A22, ABIn, ATI, B01, B02, BRI, E01, EconLit, IBSS, JEL. *Aud.:* Ac, Sa.

This is a core publication for financial management because of its high-quality, often groundbreaking research. Editors include the most widely published scholars in the field, and each volume addresses a variety of topics related to the practical applications and economic aspects of operating large public companies. Articles report on a range of topics, such as company ownership structures, takeover strategies and risks, and corporate finance solutions. Sources of data are provided, and some articles are presented as tutorials intended for classroom use. Strictly for academic and research libraries.

1102. *Financial Accountability & Management.* [ISSN: 0267-4424] 1985. q. GBP 504. Ed(s): Irvine Lapsley. Wiley-Blackwell Publishing Ltd., The Atrium, Southern Gate, Chichester, PO19 8SQ, United Kingdom; customer@wiley.com; http://www.wiley.com/. Adv. Sample. Refereed. Reprint: PSC. *Indexed:* A22, ABIn, ATI, B01, B02, BLI, E01, RiskAb. *Aud.:* Ac, Sa.

This interdisciplinary journal draws from the fields of economics, social and public administration, political science, management sciences, accounting, and finance. The focus is on financial accountability, accounting, and financial and resource management for governmental and nonprofit organizations. Articles discuss everything from optimal tax and audit structures to strategies for private–public financing, to public-sector adoption of corporate practices.

1103. *Financial Markets, Institutions and Instruments.* Former titles (until 1992): *Monograph Series in Finance and Economics;* (until 1977): *New York University, Center for the Study of Financial Institutions. Bulletin.* [ISSN: 0963-8008] 1928. 5x/yr. GBP 482. Ed(s): Mary Jaffier, Anthony Saunders. Wiley-Blackwell Publishing, Inc., 111 River St, Hoboken, NJ 07030; info@wiley.com; http://onlinelibrary.wiley.com/. Illus., adv. Sample. Refereed. Reprint: PSC. *Indexed:* A22, B01, BLI, E01, EconLit, IBSS, JEL, RiskAb. *Aud.:* Ac, Sa.

This journal attempts to bridge the gap between the academic and professional finance communities by covering topics that are relevant to both groups. Contributors include both financial practitioners and academics. Each issue has in-depth articles on a single topic, while the year-end issue features the year's most significant developments in corporate finance, money and banking, derivative securities, and fixed-income securities. A recent issue, for example, focuses on CEO bonus compensation and bank default risk. Recommended for academic and corporate libraries.

1104. *Government Finance Review.* Formed by the merger of (197?-1985): *Government Financial Management Resources in Review;* (1926-1985): *Governmental Finance;* Which was formerly (until 1971): *Municipal Finance.* [ISSN: 0883-7856] 1985. bi-m. USD 35. Ed(s): Anne Spray Kinney, Marcy Boggs. Government Finance Officers Association, 203 N LaSalle St, Ste 2700, Chicago, IL 60601; publications@gfoa.org; http://www.gfoa.org. Illus., index, adv. Circ: 16000 Paid. Microform: PQC. *Indexed:* A01, A22, ABIn, ATI, B01, B02, BLI, BRI. *Bk. rev.:* Number and length vary. *Aud.:* Ac, Sa.

The membership magazine of the Government Finance Officers Association of the United States and Canada reflects a broad spectrum of theory and practice in finance and financial management for state and local governments. Recent article topics include a 25-year retrospective of the GASB; the importance of cash-flow analysis in times of fiscal stress; and misunderstandings about accounting for capital assets. A core title for public-finance collections.

1105. *International Journal of Finance & Economics.* [ISSN: 1076-9307] 1996. q. GBP 520. Ed(s): Mark P Taylor, Michael P Dooley. John Wiley & Sons Ltd., The Atrium, Southern Gate, Chichester, PO19 8SQ, United Kingdom; customer@wiley.com; http://www.wiley.com. Illus., adv. Sample. Refereed. Vol. ends: Dec. Reprint: PSC. *Indexed:* ABIn, B01, BLI, C&ISA, CerAb, EconLit, JEL. *Bk. rev.:* 1, signed, 5,000 words. *Aud.:* Ac, Sa.

Each issue includes a small number of lengthy articles on topics related to some aspect of international finance. Each article has a 500-word nontechnical abstract. Occasionally, an article will be published that is academically rigorous but less technical. The content of this journal appears to be more empirical than theoretical; it is positioned as a step between practitioner and theoretical titles that focus on similar content. Recent article topics include the Euro as a reserve currency; announcement effects on exchange rates; and nonlinear interest rate dynamics and forecasting. Although pricey, this title is appropriate for international finance collections in larger libraries.

1106. *International Review of Economics & Finance.* [ISSN: 1059-0560] 1991. 4x/yr. EUR 556. Ed(s): C R Chen, H Beladi. Elsevier BV, North-Holland, Postbus 211, Amsterdam, 1000 AE, Netherlands; JournalsCustomerServiceEMEA@elsevier.com; http://www.elsevier.com. Illus., index. Refereed. Microform: PQC. Reprint: PSC. *Indexed:* A22, ABIn, B01, BAS, BLI, EconLit, JEL. *Bk. rev.:* Number and length vary. *Aud.:* Ac, Sa.

This journal presents a global perspective in empirical and theoretical papers on financial and market economics. Articles in recent issues explore country size and tax policy; privatizing by merger; and manager compensation related to cash flow. The half-dozen lengthy articles in each issue require a working knowledge of statistics to be fully appreciated. Libraries that support finance students and professionals will want to consider this title.

1107. *Journal of Accounting Auditing and Finance.* [ISSN: 0148-558X] 1977. q. USD 402. Sage Publications, Inc., 2455 Teller Rd, Thousand Oaks, CA 91320; info@sagepub.com; http://www.sagepub.com. Illus., adv. Refereed. Reprint: PSC. *Indexed:* A22, ABIn, ATI, B01, BLI, CLI, EconLit, JEL. *Aud.:* Ac.

This journal aims to publish high-quality original research in accounting and accounting issues that relate to finance, economics, and operations. Empirical, analytical, and experimental research is included. Recent topics include carbon business accounting, the role of auditor specialization, and a study of fiscal year-ends. Academic libraries that support accounting and finance programs should consider this title.

1108. *Journal of Applied Finance: theory, practice, education.* Formerly (until 2001): *Financial Practice and Education.* [ISSN: 1534-6668] 1991. s-a. Free to members. Ed(s): Betty J Simkins, Charles W Smithson. Financial Management Association International, University of South Florida, College of Business Administration, Ste 3331, Tampa, FL 33620; fma@coba.usf.edu; http://www.fma.org. Adv. Refereed. *Indexed:* ABIn, B01, BAS, BLI, EconLit, JEL. *Bk. rev.:* 2 to 3. *Aud.:* Ac, Sa.

This journal focuses on the theory, practice, and education of finance. Lengthy scholarly articles are geared to practitioners. Recent article topics include student-managed investment funds, the financial crisis and the U.S. auto industry, and sub-prime mortgages. Recommended for academic libraries that support finance programs.

1109. *Journal of Banking & Finance.* Incorporates (1985-1989): *Studies in Banking and Finance.* [ISSN: 0378-4266] 1977. 12x/yr. EUR 3660. Ed(s): I Mathur. Elsevier BV, North-Holland, Postbus 211, Amsterdam, 1000 AE, Netherlands; JournalsCustomerServiceEMEA@elsevier.com; http://www.elsevier.com. Illus., index, adv. Sample. Refereed. Vol. ends: Dec. Microform: PQC. *Indexed:* A22, ABIn, ATI, B01, BAS, BLI, BRI, EconLit, IBSS, JEL, RiskAb. *Bk. rev.:* Number and length vary. *Aud.:* Ac, Sa.

This journal aims to provide a platform for scholarly research that concerns financial institutions and the capital markets in which they function. Many of this journal's issues contain a special section of five or six themed articles, and an additional seven to ten regular papers on topics related to financial institutions, money, and capital markets. The editorial board includes top U.S. and international finance faculty, as well as some practitioners, mainly from the U.S. Federal Reserve system. Recent articles have discussed bank capital and financial constraints on private firms; ETF arbitrage; and corporate social responsibility in banking.

1110. *The Journal of Derivatives.* Incorporates (1992-1999): *The Journal of Financial Engineering.* [ISSN: 1074-1240] 1992. q. USD 695 combined subscription domestic (print & online eds.); GBP 470 combined subscription United Kingdom (print & online eds.); EUR 565 combined subscription in Europe (print & online eds.). Ed(s): Stephen Figlewski. Institutional Investor, Inc., 225 Park Ave S, 8th Fl, New York, NY 10003; info@iijournals.com; http://www.institutionalinvestor.com/. Illus., index, adv. *Indexed:* A22, ABIn, B01, B02, BLI, BRI, EconLit, JEL. *Aud.:* Ac, Sa.

Aimed at bridging the gap between academic theory and practice, this title is a leading analytical journal on derivatives. Readers need to be well versed in mathematics. Articles range from 10 to 20 pages in length, include charts and graphs, and offer analysis and evaluative commentary on all aspects of the use of derivatives: hedging, management of foreign exchange risk, maximization of transaction costs, measuring swap exposures on a balance sheet, comparison of price models, evaluation of new products, embedded options, arbitrage between cash and futures markets, and similar themes. An interesting recent article discusses how to apply academic derivatives theory and research to real-world problems. Suitable for libraries that support graduate finance programs or finance professionals.

1111. *Journal of Emerging Market Finance.* [ISSN: 0972-6527] 2002. 3x/yr. USD 357. Ed(s): Shubhashis Gangopadhyay, Bappaditya Mukhopadhyay. Sage Publications India Pvt. Ltd., B-1/I-1 Mohan Cooperative Industrial Estate Mathura Rd, PO Box 7, New Delhi, 110 044, India; info@sagepub.in; http://www.sagepub.in. Adv. Sample. Refereed. Reprint: PSC. *Indexed:* A22, E01, EconLit, IBSS, RiskAb. *Aud.:* Ac.

This journal aims to highlight the theory and practice of finance in emerging markets. Emphasis is on articles that are of practical significance, but the journal covers theoretical and conceptual topics as well. Recent articles examine such diverse topics as foreign institutional investor behavior in Turkey and fixed-income managed funds in Eastern Europe. Academic libraries that support global finance programs should consider this title.

1112. *The Journal of Finance.* [ISSN: 0022-1082] 1946. bi-m. Ed(s): Campbell R Harvey. Wiley-Blackwell Publishing, Inc., 111 River St, Hoboken, NJ 07030; info@wiley.com; http://onlinelibrary.wiley.com/. Illus., index. Sample. Refereed. Vol. ends: Dec. Microform: MIM; PQC. Reprint: PSC. *Indexed:* A22, ABIn, ATI, B01, B02, BLI, BRI, CBRI, E01, EconLit, IBSS, JEL, MathR, RiskAb. *Bk. rev.:* 3-4, 1,500-2,000 words. *Aud.:* Ac, Sa.

This is the official publication of the American Finance Association and is a core publication for business collections. It is one of the most widely cited academic journals in finance and economics. A single issue generally includes six to ten feature articles of 20–50 pages in length, plus six to ten shorter papers that report on original scholarly research, in addition to announcements, commentaries, and lectures. This journal highlights research from all major fields of financial research, and would be a welcome addition in large public and academic libraries.

1113. *Journal of Financial and Quantitative Analysis.* [ISSN: 0022-1090] 1966. bi-m. GBP 308. Ed(s): Stephen Brown, Hendrik Bessembinder. Cambridge University Press, The Edinburgh Bldg, Shaftesbury Rd, Cambridge, CB2 8RU, United Kingdom; information@cambridge.org; http://www.cambridge.org/uk. Illus., index, adv. Sample. Refereed. Vol. ends: Dec. Microform: PQC. Reprint: PSC. *Indexed:* A22, ABIn, ATI, B01, B02, BLI, EconLit, IBSS, JEL. *Aud.:* Ac, Sa.

In this academic journal, theoretical and empirical research on corporate finance, investments, financial markets, and related concepts are approached from a quantitative perspective. As articles tend to be data-heavy, knowledge of finance and statistics is needed to fully appreciate this journal. Academic libraries with extensive programs in finance or economics should consider this title.

1114. *Journal of Financial Economics.* [ISSN: 0304-405X] 1974. 12x/yr. EUR 3178. Ed(s): G William Schwert. Elsevier BV, North-Holland, Postbus 211, Amsterdam, 1000 AE, Netherlands; JournalsCustomerServiceEMEA@elsevier.com; http://www.elsevier.com. Illus., index, adv. Sample. Refereed. Vol. ends: No. 2. Microform: PQC. *Indexed:* A22, ABIn, ATI, B01, EconLit, IBSS, JEL. *Bk. rev.:* Number and length vary. *Aud.:* Ac, Sa.

The focus of this journal is on reports of analytical, empirical, or clinical research in capital markets, corporate finance, corporate governance, and economics of organizations and financial institutions. Feature articles are usually 15–50 pages long. Recent articles discuss corruption in bank lending, collateral pricing, and the effects of social norms on markets. Large academic libraries with graduate programs in finance and economics may be the only ones that will want to invest in this costly journal.

1115. *Journal of Financial Intermediation.* [ISSN: 1042-9573] 1990. q. EUR 813. Ed(s): G Pennacchi. Academic Press, 3251 Riverport Ln, Maryland Heights, MO 63043; JournalCustomerService-usa@elsevier.com; http://www.elsevierdirect.com/brochures/academicpress/index.html. Illus. Sample. Refereed. *Indexed:* A22, ABIn, B01, BLI, E01, EconLit, IBSS, JEL. *Aud.:* Ac, Sa.

The focus of this title is on the design of financial contracts and institutions. Research topics have included the theory of financial intermediation; informational bases for the design of financial contracts; the role of insurance firms in influencing allocations and the efficiency of market equilibrium; the economics of financial engineering; and interactions between real and financial decisions. Articles are 20–30 pages in length, and recent issues include articles on broad topics such as bank runs, pension funding, and credit derivatives. This journal would be appropriate for large public libraries that serve educated investors, and for many academic libraries.

1116. The Journal of Financial Research. [ISSN: 0270-2592] 1978. q. GBP 392. Ed(s): Gerald Gay, Jayant Kale. Wiley-Blackwell Publishing, Inc., 111 River St, Hoboken, NJ 07030; info@wiley.com; http://onlinelibrary.wiley.com/. Illus., index. Sample. Refereed. Microform: PQC. Reprint: PSC. *Indexed:* A22, ABIn, ATI, B01, B02, BRI, E01, EconLit, JEL, RiskAb. *Bk. rev.:* Number and length vary. *Aud.:* Ac, Sa.

This journal presents original research in investment and portfolio management, capital markets and institutions, and corporate finance, corporate governance, and capital investment. Each issue contains eight to ten articles that are 15–20 pages long. Recent articles examine the linkage between financial risk tolerance and risk aversion, mutual fund governance, and debt financing. Large academic libraries that support finance programs and public libraries that serve educated investors should consider this title.

1117. The Journal of Fixed Income. [ISSN: 1059-8596] 1991. q. USD 680 combined subscription domestic (print & online eds.); GBP 465 combined subscription United Kingdom (print & online eds.); EUR 555 combined subscription in Europe (print & online eds.). Ed(s): Stanley J Kon. Institutional Investor, Inc., 225 Park Ave S, 8th Fl, New York, NY 10003; info@iijournals.com; http://www.institutionalinvestor.com/. Illus., adv. *Indexed:* A22, ABIn, ATI, B01, B02, BLI. *Aud.:* Ac, Sa.

The associate editors are mostly academics from top universities and professionals from investment firms. Each issue contains six to ten articles, each about 20 pages long, that report original applied research on all aspects of fixed-income investing. Articles discuss market conditions and methods of analysis of a variety of fixed-income investments. Recent articles discuss return chasing in bond funds and inflation risk premiums. Libraries that support graduate finance programs or investment professionals should consider this title.

1118. The Journal of Futures Markets. [ISSN: 0270-7314] 1981. m. GBP 1596. Ed(s): Robert I Webb. John Wiley & Sons, Inc., 111 River St, MS 4-02, Hoboken, NJ 07030; info@wiley.com; http://www.wiley.com/WileyCDA/. Illus., index, adv. Sample. Refereed. Vol. ends: Dec. Reprint: PSC. *Indexed:* A22, ABIn, B01, B02, B03, BLI, BRI, EconLit, IBSS, JEL, P61, RiskAb, SSA. *Aud.:* Ac, Sa.

Each issue of this journal focuses on futures, options, and other derivatives. The articles range from the highly theoretical to the very practical. Recent topics discuss the effects of after-hours trading, employee stock options, and credit default swaps. Articles include charts and tables. Recommended for academic and research libraries that support finance programs.

1119. Journal of International Financial Management and Accounting. [ISSN: 0954-1314] 1989. 3x/yr. GBP 515. Ed(s): Richard Levich. Wiley-Blackwell Publishing Ltd., The Atrium, Southern Gate, Chichester, PO19 8SQ, United Kingdom; customer@wiley.com; http://www.wiley.com/. Illus., adv. Sample. Refereed. Reprint: PSC. *Indexed:* A22, ABIn, ATI, B01, E01, IBSS, RiskAb. *Bk. rev.:* 1-2, 1,500 words. *Aud.:* Ac, Sa.

Each issue contains three to five original research articles, each 20–30 pages long, on topics related to international aspects of financial management and reporting, banking and financial services, auditing, and taxation. Issues include an "Executive Perspective" (written by a practitioner), a case, comments concerning earlier papers, or a book review. Recent articles discuss choosing between IAS and U.S. GAAP accounting practices; the impact of the Euro on the European economy; and capital budgeting and political risk. Libraries that support finance programs and professionals may want to consider this specialized title.

1120. Journal of International Money and Finance: theoretical and empirical research in international economics and finance. [ISSN: 0261-5606] 1982. 8x/yr. EUR 1525. Ed(s): J Aizenman, P D McNelis. Pergamon, The Blvd, Langford Ln, E Park, Kidlington, OX5 1GB, United Kingdom; JournalsCustomerServiceEMEA@elsevier.com; http://www.elsevier.com. Illus., adv. Sample. Refereed. Microform: PQC. *Indexed:* A22, ABIn, B01, BLI, EconLit, IBSS, JEL, P02, RiskAb. *Bk. rev.:* Number and length vary. *Aud.:* Ac, Sa.

This publication presents research in all areas of international finance, monetary economics, and the increasing overlap between the two. Topics include foreign exchange, balance of payments, international markets, fiscal policy, foreign aid, and international economic institutions. Articles in recent issues discuss currency predictability; exchange-rate pass-through; and central bank swap line effectiveness. Each article is roughly 15–30 pages long. The scope of this journal makes it an appropriate choice for academic and research libraries.

1121. Public Finance Review. Formerly (until 1997): *Public Finance Quarterly.* [ISSN: 1091-1421] 1973. bi-m. USD 1136. Ed(s): James Alm. Sage Publications, Inc., 2455 Teller Rd, Thousand Oaks, CA 91320; info@sagepub.com; http://www.sagepub.com. Illus., adv. Refereed. Circ: 800 Paid. Microform: PQC. Reprint: PSC. *Indexed:* A22, ABIn, ATI, B01, B02, BRI, E01, EconLit, IBSS, JEL, P02, P61, RiskAb, SSA. *Bk. rev.:* Number and length vary. *Aud.:* Ac, Sa.

This scholarly journal explores the theory, policy, and institutions related to the allocation, distribution, and stabilization functions within the public sector of the economy. Each issue includes five lengthy articles in which authors present theoretical and empirical studies of the positive or normative aspects of (primarily) U.S. federal, state, and local government policies. Recent article topics include a history of tax collection, social security benefits, and public education. Academic libraries that support programs in public administration and finance should consider this title.

1122. Quantitative Finance. [ISSN: 1469-7688] 2001. m. GBP 2093 (print & online eds.). Ed(s): Michael Dempster. Routledge, 4 Park Sq, Milton Park, Abingdon, OX14 4RN, United Kingdom; subscriptions@tandf.co.uk; http://www.tandfonline.com. Adv. Sample. Refereed. Reprint: PSC. *Indexed:* A22, ABIn, B01, BLI, CCMJ, E01, EconLit, JEL, MSN, MathR. *Bk. rev.:* Number and length vary. *Aud.:* Ac, Sa.

This interdisciplinary journal presents original research that reflects the increasing use of quantitative methods in the field of finance. Just a few of the applications covered in this journal are experimental finance, price formation, trading systems, corporate valuation, risk management, and econometrics. This journal has a well-respected editorial board from universities and research institutions around the world, and this fact makes the journal a good pick to add depth to quantitative areas in finance collections of research libraries.

1123. The R M A Journal. Former titles (until Sep. 2000): *The Journal of Lending & Credit Risk Management;* (until 1996): *Journal of Commercial Lending;* (until 1992): *Journal of Commercial Bank Lending;* (until 1967): *Robert Morris Associates Bulletin.* [ISSN: 1531-0558] 1918. 10x/yr. Free to members; Non-members, USD 110. Ed(s): Kathleen M Beans. Risk Management Association, One Liberty Place, Ste 2300, 1650 Market St, Philadelphia, PA 19103-7398; customers@rmahq.org; http://www.rmahq.org/. Illus., index, adv. Circ: 3000 Paid. Vol. ends: Aug. *Indexed:* A22, ABIn, ATI, B01, B02, BLI, BRI. *Bk. rev.:* Number and length vary. *Aud.:* Ac, Sa.

The official journal of the Risk Management Association (RMA), this is a key source of information for commercial loan officers. It covers risk management issues in addition to commercial lending. Each issue contains 10–12 feature articles as well as regular departments on management strategies, commercial lending and risk management issues, accounting actions, and a cautionary case study. The RMA web site serves as a portal to all RMA products and services, including a searchable archive of journal articles. An essential title for libraries that support finance programs and banking professionals. URL: www.rmahq.org/tools-publications/the-rma-journal

1124. The Review of Financial Studies. [ISSN: 0893-9454] 1988. bi-m. GBP 318. Ed(s): Matthew Spiegel. Oxford University Press, Great Clarendon St, Oxford, OX2 6DP, United Kingdom; enquiry@oup.co.uk; http://www.oxfordjournals.org. Illus., adv. Sample. Refereed. Reprint: PSC. *Indexed:* A22, ABIn, B01, BLI, E01, EconLit, IBSS, JEL. *Bk. rev.:* 1, signed, 1,000-2,500 words. *Aud.:* Ac, Sa.

This scholarly journal interprets the scope of finance as to broadly allow for much interplay between finance and economics. Each issue presents a balance of new theoretical and empirical research in the form of 10–12 lengthy articles. Recent papers examine such topics as corporate leverage, corporate bond returns, and entangled financial systems. Academic libraries should consider this a core finance title.

1125. *Review of Quantitative Finance and Accounting.* [ISSN: 0924-865X] 1991. 8x/yr. EUR 1340 (print & online eds.). Ed(s): Cheng-Few Lee. Springer New York LLC, 233 Spring St, New York, NY 10013; service-ny@springer.com; http://www.springer.com/. Illus., adv. Sample. Refereed. Vol. ends: No. 4. Microform: PQC. Reprint: PSC. *Indexed:* A22, ABIn, ATI, B01, BLI, E01, EconLit, IBSS, JEL. *Aud.:* Ac, Sa.

The articles in this journal are original research that involves the interaction of finance with accounting and economic and quantitative methods. This interdisciplinary journal is international in scope and includes five or six lengthy articles per issue. A strong background in mathematics and economic statistics is required to understand these articles, so only specialists and research libraries should consider this journal for purchase.

Trade Journals

1126. *Business Credit.* Formerly: *Credit and Financial Management.* [ISSN: 0897-0181] 1898. 9x/yr. USD 54 domestic; USD 60 Canada; USD 65 elsewhere. Ed(s): Caroline Zimmerman. National Association of Credit Management, 8840 Columbia 100 Pky, Columbia, MD 21045; http://www.nacm.org. Illus., index, adv. Sample. Circ: 24000 Controlled. Vol. ends: Dec. Microform: PQC. *Indexed:* A22, ABIn, ATI, B01, B02, BLI, BRI. *Aud.:* Ac, Sa.

The target audience of this title is the corporate credit and financial professional, with additional emphasis on company finance in general. Each issue includes news on relevant issues, such as legislation, loss prevention, collections, and technology. Several feature articles present insights on such topics as mechanics liens and bonds, managing during the credit crunch, and credit insurance. Columns on international issues and on professionals at work, as well as member profiles, present a global yet personalized approach to industry issues. Articles in the international-affairs section give insight into the global-industry environment.

1127. *Financial Analysts Journal.* Formerly (until 1960): *The Analysts Journal.* [ISSN: 0015-198X] 1945. bi-m. USD 250 combined subscription domestic (print & online eds.). Ed(s): Richard M Ennis. C F A Institute, 560 Ray C Hunt Dr, PO Box 3668, Charlottesville, VA 22903; info@cfainstitute.org; http://www.cfainstitute.org. Illus., index, adv. Sample. Refereed. Circ: 100616 Paid. Vol. ends: Nov/Dec. Microform: PQC. *Indexed:* A22, ABIn, ATI, B01, B02, BRI, IBSS. *Bk. rev.:* 1-2, 500 words. *Aud.:* Ac, Sa.

Each issue of this title, which is aimed at academics and practitioners, contains nearly a dozen articles of varying length on financial and investment analysis. Primary emphasis is on valuation, portfolio management, market structure, market behavior, and professional conduct and ethics. Articles also involve accounting, economics, and securities law and regulations. Recent issues include articles on a simple theory of the financial crisis using Fischer Black, and measurement biases in hedge fund performance data. Association content, such as speeches, commentary, and association policy statements, is also included. The editorial board has representatives from highly respected universities and capital management firms. Suited for academic or public libraries that support finance programs or financial analysts.

1128. *Journal of Business Finance & Accounting.* [ISSN: 0306-686X] 1974. 10x/yr. GBP 1146. Ed(s): Peter F Pope, Martin Walker. Wiley-Blackwell Publishing Ltd., The Atrium, Southern Gate, Chichester, PO19 8SQ, United Kingdom; customer@wiley.com; http://www.wiley.com/. Illus., index, adv. Sample. Refereed. Vol. ends: Dec. Reprint: PSC. *Indexed:* A22, ABIn, ATI, B01, B02, E01, EconLit, IBSS, JEL, RiskAb. *Aud.:* Ac, Sa.

The scope of this journal covers both theoretical and empirical analysis of accounting and finance relating to financial reporting, asset pricing, financial markets and institutions, market microstructure, corporate finance, corporate governance, and the economics of internal organization and management control. Each issue delivers eight to ten research articles that are 15–20 pages in length. Even though this is a more expensive journal, the large number of articles and the variety of topics make it an impressive title.

1129. *Journal of Financial Planning.* Formerly (until 1988): *Institute of Certified Financial Planners. Journal.* [ISSN: 1040-3981] 1979. m. Free to members; Non-members, USD 119. Financial Planning Association, 4100 E Mississippi Ave Ste 400, Denver, CO 80246; http://www.fpanet.org. Illus., index, adv. Sample. Refereed. Vol. ends: No. 4. *Indexed:* A22, ABIn, ATI, AgeL, B01. *Aud.:* Ac, Sa.

This practitioner-focused title serves as a forum for the exchange of ideas and information related to the financial planning profession. Roughly a dozen short articles focus on professional issues, retirement, portfolio management, investment research, technology, noteworthy people, and strategies. Departments report on legal and legislative news, institutional resources, continuing education, letters to the editor, and contacts. The web site includes full-text articles from current and past issues, and features additional content that does not appear in the print edition. Academic and large public libraries that support programs, and professionals in insurance and finance, should consider this title.

1130. *Mergers & Acquisitions (New York, 1965): the dealmakers' journal.* Incorporates (1967-1967): *Mergers and Acquisitions Monthly.* [ISSN: 0026-0010] 1965. m. USD 1595. Ed(s): Ken MacFadyen. SourceMedia, Inc., One State St Plz, 27th Fl, New York, NY 10004; custserv@sourcemedia.com; http://www.sourcemedia.com. Illus., index, adv. Sample. Circ: 3000 Paid. *Indexed:* A22, ABIn, B01, B02, B03, C42, CLI, L14. *Aud.:* Ga, Sa.

Corporate mergers and acquisitions (M&A) are the specialized focus of this core trade magazine. Joint ventures are reported on, but are not regularly charted. Data are gathered from a number of sources, including Thomson's Merger and Corporate Transaction Database, and they are used to develop league tables that rank the leading financial advisers in the M&A industries, as well as sales volumes of target companies, industries most attractive to foreign investment, countries with the largest role in M&A in the United States, and the top transactions. Quarterly rosters give data on U.S. acquisitions by SIC code, foreign acquisitions in the United States, and U.S. acquisitions overseas. In addition, this title includes a feature cover story, guest articles from M&A professionals, current industry news, and the "industry's most comprehensive calendar of events."

1131. *Site Selection.* Former titles (until 1994): *Site Selection and Industrial Development;* (until 1984): *Site Selection Handbook;* (until 1977): *Industrial Development's Site Selection Handbook;* (until 1976): *Site Selection Handbook;* (until 1970): *Industrial Development's Site Selection Handbook;* Incorporated (in 1984): *Industrial Development;* Which was formerly (until 1967): *Industrial Development and Manufacturers Record;* Which was formed by the 1958 merger of: *Manufacturers Record;* (1954-1958): *Industrial Development.* [ISSN: 1080-7799] 1956. bi-m. USD 95 domestic (Free to qualified personnel). Ed(s): Mark Arend, Adam Bruns. Conway Data, Inc., 6625 The Corners Pky, Ste 200, Norcross, GA 30092; circulation@siteselection.com; http://www.conway.com. Illus., adv. Circ: 44000. Microform: PQC. *Indexed:* A22, ABIn, B01, B02, BRI. *Aud.:* Ac, Sa.

This title offers original research and analysis, interviews, and case studies for expansion-planning decision-makers: CEOs, corporate real estate executives, facility planners, human resource managers, and consultants. Industry overviews provide forecasts and address key topics such as new plant construction, utilities and other infrastructure concerns, political and business climates, and labor demographics. Detailed economic development reports on specific cities, states, regions, and foreign countries fill out each issue. Current and back issue content, along with exclusive web content, is offered at the web site. URL: www.siteselection.com

1132. *Venture Capital Journal: the only financial analyst of small business investment companies and venture capital companies.* Former titles: *Venture Capital; S B I C-Venture Capital; S B I C-Venture Capital Service.* [ISSN: 0883-2773] 1961. m. Ed(s): Lawrence Aragon. Thomson Financial Media, One State St Plaza, 27th Fl, New York, NY 10004; custserv@thomsonmedia.com; http://www.thomsonmedia.com. Adv. *Indexed:* A22, ABIn, B01, B02, BRI, C42. *Aud.:* Ac, Sa.

This is a core journal for libraries that cater to venture capitalists, entrepreneurs, or entrepreneurship programs. It offers news, analysis, and insight into the venture capital and private equity markets, with stories on recent deals, new sources of capital, and fund formations. There are profiles of leading venture capital firms and their portfolios, interviews with institutional investors, an event calendar, and up-to-date reports on the latest venture-backed IPOs. Recent issues have focused on angel investors, consumer goods, and health-care innovations.

1133. *Wall Street & Technology: for senior-level executives in technology and information management in securities and investment firms.* Formerly (until 1992): *Wall Street Computer Review;* Which Incorporated (in 1991): *Wall Street Computer Review. Buyer's Guide.* [ISSN: 1060-989X] 1983. m. USD 85 domestic (Free to qualified personnel). Ed(s): Gregory MacSweeney. TechWeb, Financial Technology Network, 11 W. 19th St., New York, NY 10011; http://www.techweb.com/. Illus., index, adv. Sample. Circ: 25000 Controlled. Vol. ends: Dec. *Indexed:* A22, ABIn, B01, B02, BLI, BRI, I15. *Aud.:* Ac, Sa.

This trade publication is one of an important group of niche titles that provide information on the technology of financial services (others include *Insurance & Technology* and *Bank Systems & Technology*). The technology and communications aspects of the financial-services industry are discussed in articles and departments that report on trading, regulation, and money management. Regular coverage includes risk management, trading and exchange, investment technology, inside operations, and a calendar. Recent articles discuss timely topics such as the credit crisis, data security, global markets, new software platforms, and IT outsourcing. The web site has current and past articles arranged by topic and type of article, plus a buyers' guide.

■ CANADA

Jessica Lange and Dawn McKinnon, McGill University Library, 3459 McTavish St., Montreal, PQ, Canada H3A 0C9; jessica.lange@mcgill.ca; dawn.mckinnon@mcgill.ca

Introduction

The Canada section consists of a selection of magazines that are published in Canada, containing articles about Canada, Canadians, and living in Canada. Titles include academic journals that showcase research about, or conducted in, Canada, as well as magazines for general audiences that cover all aspects of Canadian life, including politics, economics, arts and culture, geography, travel, and history. Split-run publications (foreign-published but with some Canadian content) are excluded. Many Canadian periodical publishers receive assistance from the federal government via the Canada Periodical Fund (CPF), as well as through provincial and municipal arts councils. For more magazines not included in this listing (or to learn more about the magazine industry in Canada), see the Professional Writers Association of Canada's directory of magazines (which lists over 2,000 titles published in Canada), Magazines Canada (www.magazinescanada.ca), or Masthead Online (www.mastheadonline.com).

Magazine trends noted in the previous editions of *MFL* continue, such as a decrease in the number of pages per issue and increased web content. Many magazines, particularly general-interest magazines, make a large amount of content available for free online. Many provide apps to view content, which can be downloaded to a mobile device, demonstrating a change in user habits: people want to read content in a variety of ways, not just on paper. Many sites also have online exclusives and publish this notice in their print journals; readers are encouraged to go online to view this extra content, which includes articles as well as contests, polls, and the ability to write comments and opinions

to create an online community for a shared interest or cause. Social networking tools such as the ability to post content to Twitter and Facebook are no longer added features, but rather, they are the norm on magazine sites now.

For academic journals, open access continues to play an important role, particularly for those journals published by universities or those that receive government funding. Free access to archival issues continues to be the norm. Despite the rise of freely available online content, there is continued presence of print readership in Canada, and the most popular magazines remain constant: *Canadian Living, Canadian Geographic,* and *Chatelaine* for English general-interest reading, and *L'Actualite* for news published in French, according to PMB.

Basic Periodicals

Hs, Ga, Ac: *Canadian Business, Canadian Geographic, Maclean's, The Walrus.*

Basic Abstracts and Indexes

Canadian Business & Current Affairs.

1134. *Above & Beyond.* [ISSN: 0843-7815] 1988. q. CAD 14; USD 17. Ed(s): Annelies Pool. Above & Beyond, P O Box 13142, Kanata, ON K2K 1X3, Canada. Adv. Circ: 1800 Paid. *Indexed:* BRI, C37. *Bk. rev.:* 1, 1 page, signed. *Aud.:* Hs, Ga.

Above & Beyond: Canada's arctic journal includes feature articles and information about living in Canada's Arctic, including arts, culture, education, business, government, the environment, and history particular to the North. Some articles are also on travel and wildlife. It includes many Inuit and Aboriginal authors, and a regular feature column from Mary Simon, Inuit Tapiriit Kanatmi's president. This magazine is provided in many northern flights, including all First Air flights. For nearly a quarter of a century, *Above & Beyond* has provided good general coverage of the Canadian Artic for a public library or general audience. The journal's web site provides some content of the current issues for free, or all content is available with a digital subscription. URL: www.arcticjournal.ca

1135. *Acadiensis: journal of the history of the Atlantic region.* [ISSN: 0044-5851] 1971. s-a. CAD 35 (Individuals, CAD 25). Ed(s): Stephen Dutcher, Bill Parenteau. University of New Brunswick, Department of History, Campus House, PO Box 4400, Fredericton, NB E3B 5A3, Canada; http://www.unbf.ca/arts/History. Illus., index, adv. Sample. Refereed. Vol. ends: Spring (No. 2). Microform: MML. *Indexed:* A22, ArtHuCI, BRI, C37, CBCARef, IBSS, MLA-IB. *Bk. rev.:* 2-4, 12-24 pages. *Aud.:* Ga, Ac.

Acadiensis is a scholarly journal devoted to the history of Atlantic Canada. The journal is bilingual and published twice a year, with research articles, book reviews and essays in history, geography, political science, folklore, literature, sociology, and economics of the Atlantic provinces (New Brunswick, Nova Scotia, Prince Edward Island, and Newfoundland and Labrador). Older issues (prior to 2004) contain bibliographies rather than book reviews. Free online access is available for the current issue and archives for the past five years. Select *Acadiensis* ebooks are available online for free as well. This journal is well suited for public libraries and academic libraries with programs in Canadian or Atlantic Studies, and history programs for the region. URL: http://journals.hil.unb.ca/index.php/Acadiensis/index

1136. *L'Actualite.* Incorporates (1971-1976): *Maclean;* Which was formerly (1961-1971): *Magazine Maclean;* Formerly (until 1960): *Ma Paroisse.* [ISSN: 0383-8714] 1976. 20x/yr. Ed(s): Carole Beaulieu. Rogers Publishing Ltd., 1200 McGill College Ave, Off 1700, Bureau 800, Montreal, PQ H3B 4G7, Canada; http://www.rogerspublishing.ca. Illus., adv. Circ: 175150. Microform: MML. *Indexed:* A22, BRI, C37, CBCARef, MLA-IB, PdeR. *Bk. rev.:* 1, 1-2 pages, signed. *Aud.:* Hs, Ga, Ac.

L'Actualite, the most popular French-language newsmagazine in Canada, is published 20 times a year and includes provincial, national, and global news; politics; business; and Quebec entertainment, as well as regular features on health, sports, travel, and food/wine. It also includes a Quebec cultural calendar for events in the province. Six times a year, an article on a Canadian region is included from Royal Canadian Geographical Society, with color photographs. January issues highlight Quebec personalities of the year and amateur photography contest winners. Some content is available free online, and online subscriptions are available for the full journal. The web site also contains additional information including contests, blogs, and readers' comments on articles. *L'Actualite* is suited for libraries who wish to offer publications in French, about French-Canadian and Quebec news and culture. URL: www.lactualite.com

1137. Alberta History. Formerly (until 1975): *Alberta Historical Review.* [ISSN: 0316-1552] 1953. q. Free to members. Ed(s): Hugh A Dempsey. Historical Society of Alberta, PO BOX 4035, Calgary, AB T2T 5M9, Canada; info@albertahistory.org; http://www.albertahistory.org/. Illus., index. Sample. Refereed. Vol. ends: No. 4. Microform: PQC. *Indexed:* A22, BRI, C37, CBCARef. *Bk. rev.:* 15-20, 1-2 pages. *Aud.:* Ga, Ac.

Alberta History includes primary source material and scholarly articles published by the Historical Society of Alberta (HSA). Issues are published quarterly and content is primarily about Alberta historical figures and events, and includes photographs and illustrations. The journal also includes book reviews on the subject and sometimes articles on current national issues. The journal's archives (1953–2004) are available for free online from the University of Alberta's Peel Prairie Province Collection (http://peel.library.ualberta.ca). This journal is recommended for large public libraries and to academic libraries with studies or collections specializing in Alberta or Canadian history.

1138. Arctic. [ISSN: 0004-0843] 1947. q. Free to members; Non-members, USD 25. Ed(s): Karen McCullough. Arctic Institute of North America, University of Calgary, 2500 University Dr N W, Calgary, AB T2N 1N4, Canada; arctic@ucalgary.ca; http://www.arctic.ucalgary.ca. Illus., index. Refereed. Vol. ends: Dec (No. 4). Microform: PQC. *Indexed:* A01, A22, ABS&EES, AbAn, BRI, C37, C45, CBCARef, IndVet, M&GPA, MLA-IB, OceAb, RRTA, S25. *Bk. rev.:* 7-10, 1-3 pages. *Aud.:* Ac.

Arctic is one of several publications from the Arctic Institute of North America (AINA), a global research center at the University of Calgary. This journal has been published for over 70 years, and includes peer-reviewed articles on research in polar and sub-polar regions (Nunavut, Alaska, Yukon, the Northwest Territories, and the Arctic Sea). Some articles are highly technical research and others are essays and commentary; both are on northern-related topics, including new books, people significant to the region, events and research in anthropology, astronomy, biology, ecology, education, engineering, fine arts, humanities, medicine, and paleoethnology. The journal is published quarterly and archives (from 1948 onward) are freely available through Open Journals Systems Archives (http://arctic.synergiesprairies.ca/arctic/index.php/arctic/index). A subscription is required for recent issues. *Arctic* is a member of the Canadian Association of Learned Journals. This journal is recommended for academic libraries with programs involving the North and specialized collections on this region.

1139. B C Studies: the British Columbian quarterly. [ISSN: 0005-2949] 1969. q. CAD 55 (Individuals, CAD 40; Students, CAD 25). Ed(s): Leanne Coughlin, Graeme Wynn. University of British Columbia, Buchanan E162, 1866 Main Mall, Vancouver, BC V6T 1Z1, Canada; write_us@bcstudies.com; http://www.interchange.ubc.ca/bcstudie. Illus., index, adv. Sample. Refereed. Circ: 600. Vol. ends: Summer. Microform: MML; PQC. Reprint: PSC. *Indexed:* A01, BRI, C37, CBCARef, IBSS. *Bk. rev.:* 4-20, 2-6 pages, signed. *Aud.:* Ga, Ac.

BC Studies covers British Columbia's current and past culture, economics, and politics. Published quarterly, this journal includes peer-reviewed articles, interviews, poetry, essays, book reviews, and bibliographies of books and journals relating to the province. Some issues are based on themes, such as aboriginal culture. The journal's web site provides table of contents listings for all issues, with many book reviews and content available for purchase. For its 40th anniversary, 40 of the journal's most influential articles were recorded and are available for free (www.bcstudies.com/audio.php). Although situated at the University of British Columbia, it's jointly managed by UBC, Simon Fraser University, and the University of Victoria, and it has been supported by the Canada Council, the Social Sciences and Research Council (SSHRC), and

Canadian Heritage funds. This journal is suitable for large public libraries and academic libraries that support programs on Canadian Studies or studies of British Columbia. URL: www.bcstudies.com/

1140. Border Crossings: a magazine of the arts. Formerly (until 1985): *Arts Manitoba.* [ISSN: 0831-2559] 1977. q. CAD 32 domestic (Students, CAD 24). Ed(s): Meeka Walsh. Arts Manitoba Publications Inc., 500-70 Arthur St, Winnipeg, MB R3B 1G7, Canada. Illus., index, adv. Vol. ends: No. 4. Microform: MML. *Indexed:* A07, A51, AmHI, BRI, C37, CBCARef. *Bk. rev.:* 1-3, 2 pages, signed. *Aud.:* Ga, Ac.

Border Crossings covers contemporary Canadian and international art and culture, including visual art, photography, writing, film, theater and performance, dance, music, architecture, and popular culture. This award-winning journal is in its 30th year of publication and has won 62 Gold and Silver medals at the National and Western Magazine Awards and four Maggie Awards (Manitoba Magazine Publishers' Association). It claims to publish only what is not published elsewhere, and content is covered in a variety of formats including articles, columns, reviews, profiles, interviews, drawings, essays, and poetry. It includes extensive color photographs and reproductions of artwork. Some current and archival content is available online for free. *Border Crossings* is published quarterly and is recommended to public libraries and academic libraries. URL: www.bordercrossingsmag.com

1141. British Columbia Magazine. Formerly (until 2002): *Beautiful British Columbia.* [ISSN: 1709-4623] 1959. q. CAD 19.95 domestic; CAD 28.95 foreign. Ed(s): Anita Willis. Tourism British Columbia, 1803 Douglas St, Victoria, BC V8T 5C3, Canada; cs@bcmag.ca. Illus., adv. Circ: 114156. *Indexed:* BRI, C37, CBCARef. *Aud.:* Hs, Ga.

British Columbia Magazine has been published for more than 50 years, and covers scenic geography and travel of British Columbia. Articles are liked as much for the high-quality color photographs as for the writing, which include articles on parks, wilderness, travel destinations, practical tips for outdoor life, and wildlife for the region. Many authors are from the province. The journal is published quarterly and select issues include the "Beautiful BC Traveller" supplement. The journal's web site includes some free full-text content (current and archival), a blog, photo gallery, contests, and more. This magazine has subscribers worldwide and would be of interest to high school and public libraries. URL: www.bcmag.ca

1142. C M Magazine: Canadian review of materials. Former titles (until 1995): *C M: Canadian Materials for Schools and Libraries;* (until 1980): *Canadian Materials.* [ISSN: 1201-9364] 1971. w. Free. Ed(s): Dave Jenkinson. Manitoba Library Association, 167 Houde Dr, Winnipeg, MB R3V 1C6, Canada; http://mla.mb.ca. Illus. *Indexed:* BRI, C37, CBCARef, CBRI. *Bk. rev.:* 30, 1 page, signed. *Aud.:* Ems, Ga, Ac.

CM Magazine is a free online journal that provides reviews for books and media (video and audio) by Canadian authors, illustrators, and publishers produced for children and adolescents. It is published in 22 issues, from September to June. In addition to author, title, and subject, the journal's content can also be searched by age/grade of the child. Previously published by the Canadian Library Association (CLA), it is now published by the Manitoba Library Association. This journal would be of interest to anyone who works with young children, including parents, teachers, and librarians who work in public libraries or academic libraries that support education programs. URL: www.umanitoba.ca/cm

1143. Canada. Statistics Canada. Canadian Social Trends. [ISSN: 0831-5698] 1986. s-a. CAD 39; CAD 24 per issue. Statistics Canada, 150 Tunney's Pasture Driveway, Ottawa, ON K1A 0T6, Canada; infostats@statcan.ca; http://www.statcan.gc.ca. Illus., index, adv. Vol. ends: No. 4. Microform: MML. *Indexed:* A01, C37, C45, CBCARef, P02, PdeR, RRTA. *Aud.:* Hs, Ga, Ac, Sa.

Canadian Social Trends contains the latest figures for major social indicators in Canada including social, economic, and demographic changes. This bilingual journal is published semi-annually by the Housing, Family, and Social Statistics Division of the Canadian government agency Statistics Canada. It consists primarily of statistics and charts, but also includes some articles on culture education, family, health, income, justice, labor, population, and trends. The

"Educator's Notebook" section gives resources and lesson plans for teachers. The publication is also available online. An important publication for all libraries. URL: http://dsp-psd.pwgsc.gc.ca/Collection-R/Statcan/11-008-XIE/11-008-XIE.html

1144. *Canada's History.* Formerly (until 2010): *The Beaver.* [ISSN: 1920-9894] 1920. bi-m. CAD 31.38 domestic; CAD 42.95 United States; CAD 50.95 elsewhere. Ed(s): Mark Reid. Canada's National History Society, University of Winnipeg, Bryce Hall, Main Fl, 515 Portage Ave, Winnipeg, MB R3B 2E9, Canada; memberservices@historysociety.ca; http://www.historysociety.ca. Illus., index, adv. Sample. Vol. ends: Dec/Jan (No. 6). Microform: MML. *Indexed:* A01, A22, BRI, C37, CBCARef, CBRI, MASUSE, P02. *Bk. rev.:* 3-6, 1-3 pages. *Aud.:* Hs, Ga, Ac.

Canada's History, formerly called *The Beaver,* is Canada's oldest history magazine. The journal was originally published by the Hudson's Bay Company but is now published bimonthly by the Canada's National History Society, a charitable organization devoted to popularizing Canadian history. The name change, in March 2010, was due to modern connotations of the word *beaver* that were causing problems with online access to the journal. Content includes feature articles on Canadian historical events, places and people as well as news, exhibit information, new publications and films. Many articles include high-quality photographs. Some current and archival content is available online, as well as podcasts, lesson plans, readers' comments, RSS feeds, and more. This journal is recommended to public libraries as well as school and academic libraries. URL: www.canadashistory.ca/Magazine.aspx

Canadian Art. See Art/General section.

1145. *Canadian Business.* Former titles (until 1977): *Canadian Business Magazine;* (until 1972): *Canadian Business;* (until 1933): *Commerce of the Nation;* Incorporates (1981-1982): *Energy.* [ISSN: 0008-3100] 1928. 18x/yr. CAD 21 domestic. Ed(s): Steve Maich, Conan Tobias. Rogers Publishing Ltd., One Mount Pleasant Rd., Toronto, ON M4Y 2Y5, Canada; http://www.rogerspublishing.ca. Illus., index, adv. Sample. Circ: 90652 Paid. Vol. ends: Dec (No. 12). Microform: MML. *Indexed:* A01, A22, ABIn, B01, B02, BRI, C37, CBCARef, F01, MASUSE, P02. *Bk. rev.:* 2-3, 1-3 pages. *Aud.:* Ga, Ac.

Canadian Business is Canada's leading business newsmagazine and includes articles on new business, market, investments, industry research, technology, economics, and human resources, as well as "Feature" articles on major players in business. Special issues include several rankings, such as "The Investor 500," a survey of Canada's 500 largest publicly traded companies; "The Tech 100," the top Canadian technology firms; the "MBA Guide," an annual review of Canadian MBA schools; and "Canada's 100 Wealthiest People." Published 18 times a year, the print edition covers online content, which also includes blogs, social media links, polls, videos, and podcasts. This journal is of interest to public libraries and academic libraries. URL: www.canadianbusiness.com

1146. *Canadian Dimension: for people who want to change the world.* [ISSN: 0008-3402] 1963. bi-m. CAD 39.99 (Individuals, CAD 29.99). Ed(s): Cy Gonick. Dimension Publishing Inc., 91 Albert St, Rm 2 B, Winnipeg, MB R3B 1G5, Canada. Illus., index, adv. Sample. Circ: 3200. Vol. ends: Nov/Dec (No. 6). Microform: MML; PQC. *Indexed:* A01, A22, BAS, BRI, C37, CBCARef, P02. *Bk. rev.:* 2-4, 1 page, signed. *Aud.:* Hs, Ga, Ac.

Canadian Dimensions is the oldest alternative and independently published magazine in Canada. It provides debate, opinion, personal stories, short reviews, cartoons, illustrations, photographs, and feature articles regarding "Left-wing political thought and discussion." Articles often challenge mainstream ideas and encourage debate to bring social change. Topics include the environment, the family, the division of labor in the home, food, community development, coalition building, and gender and racial inequalities. The journal's web site contains table of contents for the issues, a blog, and podcasts. *Canadian Dimensions* is published six times per year, including two double issues, and is suited for high school, public, and academic library collections. URL: http://canadiandimension.com

1147. *Canadian Ethnic Studies.* [ISSN: 0008-3496] 1969. 3x/yr. Ed(s): Jo Ann Cleaver, James S Frideres. Canadian Ethnic Studies Association, c/o Department of History, University of Calgary, 2500 University Dr, NW, Calgary, AB T2N 1N4, Canada. Illus., index, adv. Sample. Refereed. Vol. ends: No. 3. Microform: MML; PQC. Reprint: PSC. *Indexed:* A01, A22, A47, ABS&EES, AmHI, BRI, C37, CBCARef, E01, ENW, IBSS, IIBP, MASUSE, MLA-IB, P61, RILM, SSA. *Bk. rev.:* 15-20, 1-4 pages, signed. *Aud.:* Ga, Ac.

Canadian Ethnic Studies/Etudes ethniques au Canada is the official publication of the Canadian Ethnic Studies Association. This bilingual journal is published three times a year and includes refereed articles, conference reports, case studies, essays, opinions, memoirs, translations of primary sources, and film and book reviews relating to the study of ethnicity, immigration, history, and culture for ethnic groups in Canada. Some issues have a theme such as diversity and identity. Recommended for academic and large public libraries.

1148. *Canadian Gardening.* [ISSN: 0847-3463] 1990. 7x/yr. CAD 21.95 domestic; CAD 37.95 United States. Ed(s): Aldona Satterthwaite, Bonnie Summerfeldt. TC Media, 25 Sheppard Ave West, Ste 100, North York, Toronto, ON M2N 6S7, Canada; info@transcontinental.ca; http://www.medias-transcontinental.com. Adv. Circ: 135000 Paid. *Indexed:* CBCARef, GardL. *Bk. rev.:* 1-2, 1 page, signed. *Aud.:* Hs, Ga.

Canadian Gardening covers home gardening tips, plant information, techniques, descriptions, and photographs of all things related to flower and vegetable gardens in rural and urban locations. It also includes features on unique gardens, trends, and climate change. Regional gardening events and society meetings are also covered, along with a source (buying) guide. The journal's web site includes table of contents for issues back to 2007, and some available full-text content, as well as supplementary online material, such as articles, blogs, quizzes, a store, and sections including "What to do now" and "How to," offering tips. Published seven times a year (January, March through July, and October), this journal is suitable for libraries with patrons interested in beginner and advanced gardening, such as public libraries. URL: www.CanadianGardening.com

1149. *Canadian Geographic.* Formerly (until 1978): *Canadian Geographical Journal.* [ISSN: 0706-2168] 1930. bi-m. CAD 28.52 domestic; CAD 37.95 United States; CAD 59.95 elsewhere. Ed(s): Rick Boychuk. Canadian Geographical Enterprises, Ste 200, 1155 Lola St, Ottawa, ON K1K 4C1, Canada; editorial@canadiangeographic.ca. Illus., index, adv. Sample. Vol. ends: Nov/Dec (No. 6). *Indexed:* A01, A06, A22, ABS&EES, BAS, BRI, C37, CBCARef, CBRI, MASUSE, P02. *Bk. rev.:* 1-5, 1 page, signed. *Aud.:* Hs, Ga, Ac.

Canadian Geographic covers Canada's people, environment, resources, heritage, and geography (urban and physical). Since 1929, the Royal Canadian Geographical Society, a nonprofit educational organization, has been publishing this journal, which is issued bimonthly. Four times a year, it includes "Geographic Travel" supplements devoted to traveling to different places across the country. The magazine is renowned for its beautiful photographs, and every year it hosts photography contests in which the winners are published in the magazine. The journal's web site provides additional information on some feature articles, including interviews, photographs, videos, social networking tools, and indexes for subjects and contributors. Recommended for high school, public, and academic library collections. URL: www.canadiangeographic.ca

1150. *Canadian Historical Review.* Formerly (until 1920): *Review of Historical Publications Relating to Canada.* [ISSN: 0008-3755] 1896. q. USD 160. Ed(s): Jeffrey L McNairn, Suzanne Morton. University of Toronto Press, Journals Division, 5201 Dufferin St, Toronto, ON M3H 5T8, Canada; journals@utpress.utoronto.ca; http://www.utpjournals.com. Illus., index, adv. Sample. Refereed. Circ: 883. Vol. ends: Dec (No. 4). Microform: MML; PMC; PQC. *Indexed:* A01, A22, ABS&EES, AbAn, AmHI, ArtHuCI, BRI, C37, CBCARef, CBRI, E01, FR, IBSS, MLA-IB, P02, P61, RILM, SSA. *Bk. rev.:* 20-30, 1-3 pages, signed. *Aud.:* Ga, Ac.

Canadian Historical Review (*CHR*) has been published for over 115 years and is the primary scholarly journal on Canadian history. Articles are peer-reviewed and cover history on politics, environment, culture, religion, gender, and everyday events that impact Canadian institutions and society. Issues are published quarterly, and include book reviews written by historians and a bibliography of new books, media, and dissertations in the field. Abstracts are in both English and French; articles can be in either language. The journal's web site includes archives except for the current issue. *CHR* is recommended for academic libraries as well as large public libraries. URL: http://utpjournals.metapress.com/content/120322

1151. *Canadian House & Home.* Former titles (until 1984): *House and Home;* (until 1982): *House & Home Magazine;* (until 19??): *Moving House & Home.* [ISSN: 0826-7642] 1979. m. CAD 26.50 domestic; CAD 62.95 foreign; CAD 5.95 per issue. Ed(s): Kate Quetton, Suzanne Dimma. Canadian Home Publishers, 511 King St W, Ste 120, Toronto, ON M5V 2Z4, Canada; subscriptions@hhmedia.com. Adv. Sample. *Indexed:* BRI, C37, CBCARef. *Bk. rev.:* 5-10, 100 words. *Aud.:* Hs, Ga.

Canadian House & Home is dedicated to home decorating, fashion, and design. Issues include articles on home decor and renovation trends, practical information for organizing and updating spaces, gardening makeovers, recipes, and entertainment advice. A source (buying) guide is included. Articles are accompanied by full-color, full-page photographs of the re-designed spaces. This magazine is published by Lynda Reeves, a renowned Canadian designer. The web site provides additional photo galleries, videos, a blog, contests, polls, and other online tools. Back issues can be purchased, but content is not available for free. This magazine would be of interest to public libraries. URL: www.houseandhome.com

1152. *Canadian Issues.* Incorporates (1994-1999): *A C S Bulletin;* Which was formerly (until 1994): *A C S Newsletter;* (until 1982): *Association for Canadian Studies. Association Newsletter.* [ISSN: 0318-8442] 1975. q. Free to members; Non-members, USD 5. Association for Canadian Studies, 1822-A Sherbrooke W, Montreal, PQ H3H 1E4, Canada; general@acs-aec.ca; http://www.acs-aec.ca. Refereed. *Indexed:* BRI, C37, CBCARef, CEI, PdeR. *Bk. rev.:* 1-2, 1 page, signed. *Aud.:* Hs, Ga, Ac.

Canadian Issues/Themes Canadiens is a bilingual (French/English) journal on Canadian society, government, history, and economy. The journal contains mainly articles and opinion essays from academics, politicians, and lawyers. It is published quarterly by the Association for Canadian Studies, a nonprofit society dedicated to research, teaching, publishing, and the training of students in the field of Canadian Studies. Some issues are thematic, such as globalization. The journal's web site includes downloadable pdf versions back to 2010, and table of contents back to 2000. This journal is suited to high schools, public libraries, and academic libraries that require information on current and political events.

1153. *Canadian Living: smart solutions for everyday living.* [ISSN: 0382-4624] 1975. m. CAD 23.98 domestic; CAD 61.98 United States. TC Media, 25 Sheppard Ave West, Ste 100, North York, Toronto, ON M2N 6S7, Canada; info@transcontinental.ca; http://www.transcontinental-gtc.com/. Adv. Circ: 555118 Paid. *Indexed:* BRI, C37, CBCARef, GardL, P02. *Aud.:* Hs, Ga.

Canadian Living is Canada's most popular family magazine, with a subscription base of over half a million readers. While known for its "tested 'til perfect" recipes, articles are also devoted to health, fashion, beauty, relationships, parenting, and work–life balance. The magazine is published monthly and is favored by women, with sections devoted to different stages of life, including motherhood and life over 50. Although the web site content is not freely accessible by "back issue," much of the content from the print edition can viewed online. Additional content can also be viewed including videos, consumer reports, blogs, and social media tools. Recommended for public libraries. URL: www.canadianliving.com

1154. *Canadian Public Policy.* [ISSN: 0317-0861] 1975. q. USD 210. Ed(s): Herb Emery. University of Toronto Press, Journals Division, 5201 Dufferin St, Toronto, ON M3H 5T8, Canada; journals@utpress.utoronto.ca; http://www.utpjournals.com. Illus., index, adv. Sample. Refereed. Circ: 747. Vol. ends: Dec (No. 4). Microform: MML. *Indexed:* A01, A22, ABIn, B01, BRI, C37, CBCARef, E01, EconLit, JEL, P61, SSA. *Bk. rev.:* 15-25, 1-2 pages, signed. *Aud.:* Ga, Ac.

Canadian Public Policy is a bilingual (English/French) journal on economic and social policy and aims to "stimulate research and discussion of public policy problems in Canada." Articles are refereed, and content covers health care, taxes, education, and other policies of national concern. Issues also include reviews and editorials. The journal's web site includes searchable archives, providing free full-text access to previous issues (with a one-year delay on current issues). *CPP* is published quarterly and is recommended for academic and large public libraries with collections on Canadian Studies. URL: http://economics.ca/cpp/en

1155. *Canadian Wildlife.* Supersedes in part (in 2002): *International Wildlife;* Incorporates: *Wildlife Update;* Which was formerly: *Canadian Chronicle;* Which superseded: *Wildlife News.* [ISSN: 1201-673X] 1995. bi-m. CAD 24.95 domestic; CAD 45 United States; CAD 55 elsewhere. Canadian Wildlife Federation, 350 Michael Cowpland Dr, Kanata, ON K2M 2W1, Canada; info@cwf-fcf.org; http://www.cwf-fcf.org. Adv. *Indexed:* A01, BRI, C37, CBCARef, MASUSE. *Aud.:* Hs, Ga.

Canadian Wildlife contains articles on nature, animals, plants, and ecological issues, both in Canada and worldwide. Published bimonthly by the nonprofit Canadian Wildlife Federation (CWF), this magazine includes in-depth articles on scientists, climate change, wildlife management, and politics. Articles are accompanied by beautiful color photographs. The magazines web site contains some abridged content for issues in the past year, but full text is only available through subscriptions. Other educational resources can be found on the site, as it's a part of the larger CWF site. This magazine would be of interest to school and public libraries. URL: www.cwf-fcf.org/en/resources/magazines/canadian-wildlife

Canadian Woman Studies. See Gender Studies section.

Etudes Inuit Studies. See Native Americans section.

1156. *International Journal of Canadian Studies.* [ISSN: 1180-3991] 1990. s-a. CAD 70 domestic; USD 80 domestic; CAD 95 combined subscription domestic (print & online eds.). Ed(s): Claude Couture. University of Toronto Press, Journals Division, 5201 Dufferin St, Toronto, ON M3H 5T8, Canada; journals@utpress.utoronto.ca; http://www.utpjournals.com. Adv. Refereed. *Indexed:* BRI, C37, CBCARef, MLA-IB, P61, PdeR, RILM, SSA. *Aud.:* Ac, Ga.

The *International Journal of Canadian Studies* is a bilingual (English/French), multidisciplinary journal that covers the study of Canada. Issues are published semi-annually and include articles and essays on a variety of topics related to Canada. The journal is published by the International Council for Canadian Studies (www.iccs-ciec.ca) at the University of Alberta, which makes past issues available online (1990–2011) in pdf. This journal would be of interest to academic and large public libraries. URL: http://iec-csi.csj.ualberta.ca

1157. *Journal of Canadian Studies.* [ISSN: 0021-9495] 1966. 3x/yr. USD 140. Ed(s): Andrew Nurse, Christl Verduyn. University of Toronto Press, Journals Division, 5201 Dufferin St, Toronto, ON M3H 5T8, Canada; journals@utpress.utoronto.ca; http://www.utpjournals.com. Illus., index, adv. Refereed. Circ: 380. Vol. ends: No. 4. Microform: MML. *Indexed:* A01, A22, AmHI, ArtHuCI, BEL&L, BRI, C37, CBCARef, E01, FR, IBSS, MLA-IB, P02, RILM. *Bk. rev.:* 1-2, 8-15 pages, signed. *Aud.:* Ga, Ac.

The *Journal of Canadian Studies* is an academic, multidisciplinary periodical devoted to Canada and Canadian life (this includes, but is not limited to, Canadian culture, history, sociology, and political science). Published by the University of Toronto Press, this journal contains original research in both French and English, and attempts to fill in the gaps left by other academic Canadian journals by having a broad, interdisciplinary mandate. This journal is published three times a year, in the spring, fall, and winter. This journal is of interest to large public libraries and academic institutions with collections specializing in Canadian studies.

1158. *Labour: journal of Canadian labour studies - revue d'etudes ouvrieres Canadiennes.* [ISSN: 0700-3862] 1976. s-a. CAD 35. Ed(s): Bryan D Palmer. Canadian Committee on Labour History, Athabasca University, Peace Hills Trust Tower, Edmonton, AB T5J 3S8, Canada; cclh@athabascau.ca; http://www.cclh.ca. Illus., index, adv. Sample. Refereed. Vol. ends: No. 2. *Indexed:* A01, ABIn, ArtHuCI, B02, BRI, C37, CBCARef, IBSS. *Bk. rev.:* Number and length vary. *Aud.:* Ga, Ac.

Labour/Le Travail is a biannual academic journal published in the spring and fall of each year by the Canadian Committee on Labour History. Containing articles in both French and English, the journal contains articles, conference reports, review essays, and book reviews that focus on aspects of Canadian labor studies, including labor economics, industrial sociology, labor relations, and working-class history (with a particular focus on the history of Canadian workers). It also contains the minutes from the Annual Meeting of the Canadian Committee on Labour History. This journal is of interest to large public libraries and academic institutions with collections specializing in Canadian studies. Previous years' materials are available free online through the web site. URL: www.lltjournal.ca/index.php/llt/issue/archive

1159. *Literary Review of Canada: a review of Canadian books on culture, politics and society.* [ISSN: 1188-7494] 1991. 10x/yr. CAD 59 domestic; CAD 69 foreign. Literary Review of Canada Inc., 581 Markham St, Ste 3A, Toronto, ON M6G 2L7, Canada. Circ: 5000. *Indexed:* BRI, C37, CBCARef, MLA-IB. *Bk. rev.:* 12, 1-2 pages, signed. *Aud.:* Ac.

The *Literary Review of Canada* is a monthly magazine primarily devoted to providing detailed book reviews (fiction and nonfiction) of Canadian books. This magazine also contains poetry as well as essays on culture, politics, and books. Previous issues back to 2002 can be viewed online at the web site. This title is recommended for large public libraries and academic institutions. URL: http://reviewcanada.ca/magazine/archive/

1160. *Maclean's.* Former titles (until 1911): *Busy Man's Magazine;* (until 1905): *Business Magazine.* [ISSN: 0024-9262] 1905. w. CAD 49.95 domestic. Ed(s): Kenneth Whyte, Mark Stevenson. Rogers Publishing Ltd., One Mount Pleasant Rd., Toronto, ON M4Y 2Y5, Canada; RMS@rci.rogers.com; http://www.rogerspublishing.ca. Illus., index, adv. Sample. Circ: 355054. Microform: MML; NBI; PQC. *Indexed:* A01, A22, ABIn, B01, BRI, C37, CBCARef, CBRI, F01, MASUSE, P02. *Bk. rev.:* 1-2, 2-4 pages. *Aud.:* Hs, Ga, Ac.

Maclean's is a weekly, national newsmagazine that contains both editorial and opinion columns as well as investigative journalism pieces. Although *Maclean's* has a special focus on Canadian current affairs, it also contains articles on international news, business, health, arts and culture, politics, and social issues. Each issue also contains a short book review section. This magazine would be relevant to public libraries and academic institutions with an interest in Canadian current affairs. Many of articles are available online for free through the web site. URL: http://www2.macleans.ca/

1161. *Maisonneuve.* [ISSN: 1703-0056] 2002. q. CAD 24.99 domestic; CAD 36 United States; CAD 60 elsewhere. Ed(s): Derek Webster. Maisonneuve, 4413 Harvard Ave, Montreal, PQ H4A 2W9, Canada. Adv. *Indexed:* CBCARef. *Aud.:* Hs, Ga, Ac, Sa.

Maisonneuve is a quarterly magazine with a focus on arts, sciences, culture, and society. Commentary on the province of Quebec culture and society also figures prominently. The magazine contains essays, articles, photo essays, and comics, as well as fiction and poetry. The magazine has been called the "*New Yorker* for a new generation" and targets educated, urban readers. The magazine is very much a Quebec counterpart to the general-interest magazine *The Walrus*. This journal is of interest to large public libraries and academic institutions (notably those in Quebec).

1162. *Manitoba History.* Formerly (until 1980): *Manitoba Pageant.* [ISSN: 0226-5044] 1956. s-a. CAD 29.50 domestic (Free to members). Manitoba Historical Society, 61 Carlton St, Winnipeg, MB R3C 1N7, Canada; info@mhs.mb.ca; http://www.mhs.mb.ca/. Illus. Sample. Refereed. Circ: 1000. Vol. ends: Fall (No. 2). *Indexed:* A01, BRI, C37, CBCARef. *Bk. rev.:* 4-8, 1-3 pages. *Aud.:* Hs, Ga, Ac.

Manitoba History is a biannual academic journal published in the spring and winter by the Manitoba Historical Society. This journal contains feature-length articles as well as shorter general articles, essays, and book reviews (it also contains photographs and illustrations). The focus of the journal is on the political, social, economic, and cultural history of Manitoba and the Canadian West (British Columbia, Alberta, and Saskatchewan). This journal is of interest to large public libraries and academic institutions with collections specializing in Canadian history.

1163. *Newfoundland and Labrador Studies.* Formerly (until 2003): *Newfoundland Studies.* [ISSN: 1719-1726] 1985. s-a. CAD 30 (Individuals, CAD 20). Ed(s): Jeff Webb. Memorial University of Newfoundland, Department of English, Arts and Administration 3026, Elizabeth Ave, St. John's, NF A1C 5S7, Canada; irenew@plato.ucs.mun.can; http://www.ucs.mun.ca/~nflds/. Illus., index, adv. Sample. Refereed. Circ: 250. Vol. ends: Fall (No. 2). *Indexed:* BRI, C37, CBCARef, MLA-IB. *Bk. rev.:* 6-7, 2-5 pages, signed. *Aud.:* Ac.

Newfoundland and Labrador Studies is a biannual journal published in the spring and fall. The journal publishes essays in both French and English and on the topic of the society and culture of the province of Newfoundland and Labrador (both historical and present). The essays are intended for academic and general audiences with an interest in the province. The journal also contains book reviews as well as the presentation of one historical document (annotated and edited) per issue. This journal is of interest to large public libraries and academic institutions with collections that specialize in Canadian studies.

1164. *Ontario History.* Formerly (until 1947): *Ontario Historical Society. Papers and Records;* Incorporates (1944-1948): *Ontario Historical Society. Newsletter.* [ISSN: 0030-2953] 1899. s-a. CAD 42.80 (Individuals, CAD 32.10; Members, CAD 21.40). Ed(s): Thorold Tronrud. The Ontario Historical Society, 34 Parkview Ave, Willowdale, ON M2N 3Y2, Canada; ohs@ontariohistoricalsociety.ca; http://www.ontariohistoricalsociety.ca/. Illus., index, adv. Refereed. Vol. ends: Dec (No. 4). Reprint: PSC. *Indexed:* BRI, C37, CBCARef, MLA-IB. *Bk. rev.:* 5-12, 500-1,000 words. *Aud.:* Ga, Ac.

Ontario History is a biannual publication released in the spring and fall by the Ontario Historical Society. This academic, peer-reviewed journal focuses on the history and heritage of the province of Ontario. Each issue contains book reviews of books that focus on Canadian history (especially Ontario history). Each volume also contains an "Archival Sources" section that highlights one particular collection held in an Ontario archive. This journal is of interest to large public libraries and academic institutions with collections that specialize in Canadian history.

1165. *Outdoor Canada: the total outdoor experience.* [ISSN: 0315-0542] 1972. 8x/yr. CAD 17.95 domestic. Ed(s): Aaron Kylie, Patrick Walsh. TC Media, 25 Sheppard Ave West, Ste 100, North York, Toronto, ON M2N 6S7, Canada; info@transcontinental.ca; http://www.medias-transcontinental.com. Illus., adv. Sample. Circ: 93000 Paid. Microform: MML. *Indexed:* BRI, C37, CBCARef. *Aud.:* Ga.

Published six times a year, *Outdoor Canada* is leisure magazine devoted to hunting and fishing. This magazine contains articles, buyer's guides, and how-to articles, as well as travelogues. Articles are accompanied by photography. This magazine would be of interest to public libraries where hunting and fishing are significant activities in their community.

1166. *Policy Options.* [ISSN: 0226-5893] 1979. 10x/yr. CAD 47.60 domestic; CAD 67.60 United States; CAD 87.60 elsewhere. Ed(s): L Ian MacDonald. Institute for Research on Public Policy, 1470 Peel St, Ste 200, Montreal, PQ H3A 1T1, Canada; irrp@irrp.org; http://www.irpp.org. Illus., adv. Sample. Circ: 3000. Vol. ends: Dec (No. 10). *Indexed:* BRI, C37, CBCARef. *Bk. rev.:* 0-1, 500 words. *Aud.:* Ga, Ac.

Published ten times per year by the Institute for Research on Public Policy, *Policy Options* is a magazine devoted to politics and policy in Canada. Intended for "educated" readers, this magazine publishes articles in both French and English and contains accompanying photographs. This journal is of interest to large public libraries and academic institutions with collections that specialize in Canadian studies and political science.

1167. *Prairie Forum.* [ISSN: 0317-6282] 1976. s-a. CAD 28 (Individuals, CAD 23). Ed(s): Donna Grant. Canadian Plains Research Center, University of Regina, 3737 Wascana Pky, Regina, SK S4S 0A2, Canada; canadian.plains@uregina.ca; http://www.cprc.ca. Illus., index. Refereed. Vol. ends: Fall (No. 2). Microform: MML. *Indexed:* ABS&EES, BRI, C37, CBCARef, MLA-IB. *Bk. rev.:* 2-10, 2-4 pages. *Aud.:* Ga, Ac, Sa.

Prairie Forum is a biannual publication released in the spring and fall of each year. It is an interdisciplinary journal that focuses on Canada's prairie provinces (Alberta, Saskatchewan, and Manitoba). The journal is academic in nature and seeks to unite research on the Canadian prairies nature, environment, history, politics, and culture by not limiting its scope to one particular province. Past issues up to 2001 can be viewed online for free through ouRspace, hosted at the University of Regina: http://ourspace.uregina.ca/handle/10294/302. This journal is of interest to large public libraries and academic institutions with collections that specialize in Canadian studies.

1168. *Queen's Quarterly: a Canadian review.* [ISSN: 0033-6041] 1893. q. USD 40 (Individuals, USD 20; USD 6.50 per issue). Ed(s): Boris Castel. Queen's Quarterly, Queen's University, Kingston, ON K7L 3N6, Canada. Illus. Sample. Refereed. Vol. ends: No. 4. Microform: MML; PQC. *Indexed:* A22, ABS&EES, ArtHuCI, BAS, BEL&L, BRI, C37, CBCARef, CBRI, MLA-IB, P61, RILM, SSA. *Bk. rev.:* Number and length vary. *Aud.:* Ga, Ac.

Queen's Quarterly is a quarterly journal intended for educated readers (although the journal is more general-interest than academic in nature). The journal publishes articles, reviews, poetry, and fiction, as well as essays. The articles are interdisciplinary in nature and cover a range of topics including arts, culture, literature, politics, religion, science policy, and international relations. Although the content is Canadian-centric, many of the articles deal with issues, ideas, and people beyond Canada's borders. The journal contains accompanying photographs and illustrations. *Queen's Quarterly* is a cross between an intellectual general interest magazine and an academic journal, making it suitable for large public libraries and academic institutions.

1169. *Quill and Quire: Canada's magazine of book news and reviews.* Incorporates (in 1989): *Books for Young People.* [ISSN: 0033-6491] 1935. 10x/yr. CAD 79.50 domestic; CAD 125 foreign. Ed(s): Stuart Woods. St. Joseph Media, 111 Queen St E, Ste 320, Toronto, ON M5C 1S2, Canada; communications@stjoseph.com; http://www.quillandquire.com/. Illus., adv. Circ: 5400 Paid. Microform: MMP; MML. *Indexed:* BRI, C37, CBCARef, CBRI, MLA-IB. *Bk. rev.:* Number and length vary. *Aud.:* Hs, Ga, Ac.

The *Quill & Quire* is a magazine that focuses on all aspects of the Canadian book industry. The magazine is published ten times per year and contains articles, opinion pieces, and fiction and nonfiction book reviews (including book reviews for children and adolescents' books). The magazine also contains book bestseller lists, and is accompanied by photographs and illustrations. This magazine is recommended for public libraries and academic institutions as it would provide useful reviews, news, and information on Canada's book industry.

1170. *Report on Business Magazine.* Former titles (until 1985): *Report on Business; Report on Business 1000.* [ISSN: 0827-7680] 1984. 11x/yr. Ed(s): John Stackhouse, Derek DeCloet. Globe and Mail Publishing, 444 Front St W, Toronto, ON M5V 2S9, Canada; Newsroom@globeandmail.com; http://www.globeandmail.com. Illus., adv. Circ: 296544. *Indexed:* ABIn, BRI, C37. *Bk. rev.:* 1-3, 500 words, signed. *Aud.:* Hs, Ga, Ac.

Report on Business is a monthly publication by the Globe and Mail on business in Canada (including markets and trends in industry). The magazine contains essays, opinion pieces, and articles; and it contains many photographs and images. It is intended for a general audience with an interest in the Canadian business environment. Suitable for public libraries and academic institutions.

1171. *Revue d'Histoire de l'Amerique Francaise.* [ISSN: 0035-2357] 1947. q. Institut d'Histoire de l'Amerique Francaise, 261 Avenue Bloomfield, Montreal, PQ H2V 3R6, Canada; ihaf@ihaf.qc.ca; http://www.cam.org/~ihaf. Adv. Refereed. Microform: PQC. *Indexed:* ArtHuCI, BRI, C37, CBCARef, MLA-IB, PdeR. *Aud.:* Ac.

Founded by Quebecois historian Lionel Groulx in 1947, the *Revue d'Histoire de l'Amerique Francaise* is a scholary, peer-reviewed publication devoted to the history of Quebec, as well as francophones in North and South America. The journal is based out of the Institut d'Histoire de l'Amerique francaise (www.ihaf.qc.ca/IHAF) at the University of Montreal. Articles are written in French, and each issue contains a bibliography of the history of the French in America. Each issue also contains a section on archives, containing a description of the archive and its holdings. Although this publication and the Institute that maintains it appear to be active, this journal has not released any new issues since 2011. This journal is recommended for large public libraries and academic institutions with an interest in Canadian history, particularly in regions where there is a significant French population.

1172. *Saltscapes.* [ISSN: 1492-3351] 2000. bi-m. CAD 24.95. Ed(s): Heather White. Saltscapes Publishing Limited, 30 Damascus Rd, Ste 209, Bedford, NS B4A 0C1, Canada; subscriptions@saltscapes.com. Adv. *Aud.:* Hs, Ga.

Saltscapes is general-interest magazine focused on east-coast Canadian life and lifestyles. Published six times a year, *Saltscapes* contains articles on leisure, health, entertainment, food, history, and nature in Atlantic Canada, with a rural bias. This magazine is recommended for public libraries on Canada's east coast or in public libraries with an interest in Atlantic Canadian life and lifestyles.

1173. *Saskatchewan History.* [ISSN: 0036-4908] 1948. s-a. CAD 15 domestic; CAD 17.50 foreign. Saskatchewan Archives Board, Murray Building, University of Saskatchewan, Saskatoon, SK S7N 5A4, Canada; info.saskatoon@archives.gov.sk.ca; http://www.saskarchives.com/. Illus., index. Sample. Refereed. Vol. ends: No. 2. *Indexed:* BRI, C37, CBCARef, MLA-IB. *Bk. rev.:* 7-8, 1-2 pages. *Aud.:* Ga, Ac.

Saskatchewan History is a biannual publication released in the spring and winter. The articles are intended for a general and academic audience, and focus on some aspect of the history of the province of Saskatchewan. The magazine also includes book reviews, an editorial column, and news from the Saskatchewan Archives Board (SAB). Each article is accompanied by photographs. This journal is of interest to large public libraries and academic institutions with collections that specialize in Canadian history.

1174. *This Magazine.* Former titles (until 1998): *This Magazine - Education, Culture, Politics;* (until 1973): *This Magazine is About Schools.* [ISSN: 1491-2678] 1966. 6x/yr. USD 26.66 domestic; USD 40 foreign. Ed(s): Graham F Scott. Red Maple Foundation, 396-401 Richmond St W, Toronto, ON M5V 3A8, Canada. Illus., index, adv. Sample. Circ: 5000. Microform: MML; PQC. *Indexed:* A22, BRI, C37, CBCARef. *Bk. rev.:* 1-2 pages. *Aud.:* Hs, Ga, Ac.

This Magazine is a monthly general-interest magazine that focuses on social issues and activism in Canada while also featuring articles on arts, politics, and culture. It contains articles, essays, interviews, and reviews. Calling itself an "alternative journal," the magazine contains both investigative journalism and opinion pieces. *This Magazine* would be relevant to large public libraries and academic institutions with an interest in Canadian social issues.

1175. *Toronto Life.* Incorporates (1969-1982): *Toronto Calendar Magazine;* (1962-1966): *Ontario Homes and Living.* [ISSN: 0049-4194] 1966. m. CAD 24 domestic. Ed(s): Angie Gardos, Sarah Fulford. Toronto Life Publishing Co. Ltd., 111 Queen St East, Ste 320, Toronto, ON M5C 1S2, Canada; guides@torontolife.com; http://www.torontolife.com. Illus., index, adv. Sample. Microform: MML. *Indexed:* ASIP, BRI, C37, CBCARef. *Aud.:* Hs, Ga.

Toronto Life is a monthly magazine that contains articles on all aspects of living in Toronto and the Greater Toronto Area (GTA), including articles on municipal politics, entertainment, shopping, and real estate, as well as restaurant and store reviews. The magazine also caters to people seeking the city as a travel destination. Each issue contains a calendar of events for theater and nightlife. The magazine's web site provides some content from the print version as well as supplementary features. Suitable for public libraries, specifically those within the GTA. URL: www.torontolife.com/

University of Toronto Quarterly. See Literature section.

1176. *The Walrus.* [ISSN: 1708-4032] 2003. 10x/yr. CAD 29.75 domestic; CAD 37.75 United States; CAD 57.75 elsewhere. Ed(s): Jared Bland, John Macfarlane. Walrus, 19 Duncan St, Ste 101, Toronto, ON M5H 3H1, Canada. Adv. *Indexed:* CBCARef. *Bk. rev.:* Number and length vary. *Aud.:* Hs, Ga, Ac, Sa.

The Walrus is a monthly general-interest magazine. It contains a mix of essays and reviews, as well as fiction and poetry. The essays focus on all aspects of Canadian life: politics, culture, current affairs, technology, health, and business, etc. This magazine would be relevant for all public library and academic institutions with an interest in Canada and Canadian studies.

YES Mag. See Children section.

1177. *Zoomer Canada.* Former titles (until 2010): *Zoomer;* (until Oct. 2008): *C A R P;* (until 2008): *C A R P Fifty Plus;* (until 2001): *C A R P News Fifty Plus;* (until 1999): *C A R P News;* (until 1994): *C A R P;* (until 1992): *C A R P News;* (until 1986): *C A R P Newsletter.* [ISSN: 1928-0920] 1985. 9x/yr. CAD 19.95 domestic; CAD 79.95 foreign. Ed(s): Suzanne Boyd. Canadian Association of Retired Persons, 30 Jefferson Ave, Toronto, ON M6K 1Y4, Canada; support@carp.ca; http://www.carp.ca. Adv. *Indexed:* BRI, C37, CBCARef. *Aud.:* Ga, Ac, Sa.

Zoomer Canada is a magazine dedicated to the baby boomer demographic (person 50 years of age or older). This lifestyle magazine aims to help boomers "make the most out of life" and contains articles on health, food, fitness, money, culture, beauty, etc. Recommended for public libraries.

■ CARTOGRAPHY, GIS, AND IMAGERY

See also Environment and Conservation; Earth Sciences and Geology; and Geography sections.

Katherine H. Weimer, Curator, Map & GIS Library, Texas A&M University Libraries, College Station, TX 77843; k-weimer@library.tamu.edu

Introduction

Cartography, GIS (geographic information systems), and imagery are distinct yet interrelated fields. Cartography had its beginnings in early explorers and maintains its own distinct focus today, while evolving from print to digital forms. GIS, geographic information systems, are software and data that include a geographic reference and can be used in analysis and visualization. Imagery includes aerial photography, satellite imagery, and remote sensing and is applied in a variety of fields. Maps, imagery, and geo-locational devices are becoming a part of everyday life, and the study and science behind them is rapidly expanding. The web has also had a huge effect on the distribution of map and geographic information, with geocoded information finding its way into portals and mash-ups, all of which are an increasing portion of the scholarly discourse.

The collection, description, analysis, and applications of imagery and geographic data drive much of the journal literature. The fields of cartography, GIS, and imagery are interrelated in their desire to describe and analyze the earth and what is contained on it. The developments made in the area of cartography, GIS, and imagery support a range of disciplines, such as environmental studies, transportation, population, and health. The journals in this list are core to the subject matter; however, many also do include special theme issues that cover a wide variety of applications.

The titles support upper-level undergraduate through graduate and professional-level research. A study of GIScience journals was published in 2008—"GIScience Journals Ranking and evaluation: An International Delphi Study" by Caron et al.; it appeared in *Transactions in GIS,* volume 12, number 3. That paper is a thorough study on the topic, and is well worth reviewing when making selection decisions. For related titles, see the sections on Geography; Earth Sciences and Geology; and Environment and Conservation.

Basic Periodicals

Cartography and Geographic Information Science, Computers & Geosciences, GeoInformatica, IEEE Transactions on Geoscience and Remote Sensing, Imago Mundi, International Journal of Geographical Information Science, International Journal of Remote Sensing, Journal of Geographical Systems, Photogrammetric Engineering and Remote Sensing, Surveying and Land Information Science.

Basic Abstracts and Indexes

Geographical Abstracts, GEOBASE, GeoRef, Scopus.

1178. *A C S M Bulletin: promoting advancement in surveying and mapping.* Formerly (until 1981): *American Congress on Surveying and Mapping. Bulletin.* [ISSN: 0747-9417] 1950. bi-m. USD 100 domestic; USD 115 foreign; USD 126 combined subscription domestic (print & online eds.). Ed(s): Ilse Alipui. American Congress on Surveying and Mapping, 6 Montgomery Village Ave, Ste #403, Gaithersburg, MD 20879; infoacsm@acsm.net; http://www.acsm.net. Illus., adv. Circ: 8000. *Indexed:* A22. *Bk. rev.:* Number and length vary. *Aud.:* Ac, Sa.

This industry magazine covers current events in geospatial technologies and the related communities of geodesy, GIS, GPS, and other fields. It reflects the interest of four American Congress on Surveying and Mapping (ACSM) professional organizations: the American Association for Geodetic Surveying (AAGS), the Cartography and Geographic Information Society (CaGIS), the Geographic and Land Information Society (GLIS), and the National Society of Professional Surveyors (NSPS). This journal includes conference reports, book reviews, and association news. An online "Webmazine" is free. For academics and practitioners.

1179. *A R C News.* [ISSN: 1064-6108] 1987. q. Free. Ed(s): Thomas K Miller. Environmental Systems Research Institute, Inc., 380 New York St, Redlands, CA 92373; requests@esri.com. Adv. *Aud.:* Ac, Sa.

ARC News is a newsmagazine geared toward a range of GIS professionals, IT/ GIS support, researchers, and educators. It covers software updates, applications of GIS in industry and government, conferences, and trends in GIS teaching and learning. Its target audience is the Environmental Systems Research Institute (ESRI) user community, but others will find material of interest here. The electronic version offers articles that appear exclusively online, as well as web-only content and supplemental podcasts. URL: www.esri.com/news/arcnews/arcnews.html

1180. *Annals of G I S.* Formerly (until 2009): *Geographic Information Sciences.* [ISSN: 1947-5683] 1995. q. GBP 277 (print & online eds.). Ed(s): Hui Lin. Taylor & Francis, 4 Park Sq, Milton Park, Abingdon, OX14 4RN, United Kingdom; subscriptions@tandf.co.uk; http://www.tandfonline.com. Adv. Sample. Refereed. Reprint: PSC. *Indexed:* A01, S25. *Aud.:* Ac, Sa.

This is the official peer-reviewed journal of the International Association of Chinese Professionals in Geographic Information Sciences. Among the most cited articles are: "Geographic Information Systems and Science: Today and Tomorrow," "Map Mashups, Web 2.0 and the GIS Revolution," and "From GIS to Neogeography: Ontological Implications and Theories of Truth."

1181. *The Cartographic Journal: the world of mapping.* [ISSN: 0008-7041] 1964. q. GBP 420 (print & online eds.). Ed(s): Ken Field. Maney Publishing, Ste 1C, Joseph's Well, Hanover Walk, Leeds, LS3 1AB, United Kingdom; maney@maneypublishing.com; http:// maneypublishing.com/. Illus., index, adv. Sample. Refereed. Circ: 2000. Vol. ends: Dec. Reprint: PSC. *Indexed:* A01, A22, MLA-IB. *Bk. rev.:* Number and length vary. *Aud.:* Ac, Sa.

This long-standing peer-reviewed title is the official journal of the British Cartographic Society and is affiliated with the International Cartographic Association. The journal is international in scope and includes scholarly articles and professional papers on all aspects of cartography and mapping, such as symbology, projections, map use, and national mapping surveys, with articles also touching on spatial data analysis, geographical information systems, related remote-sensing technologies, and global-positioning systems. The journal also includes international cartographic news, book and software reviews, and a list of recent maps and atlases, and offers a fast-track publishing option. Geared toward scholarly readers.

1182. *Cartographic Perspectives.* Former titles (until 1989): *Cartographic Information;* (until 1987): *Map Gap.* [ISSN: 1048-9053] 1981. 3x/yr. Free to members. Ed(s): Patrick Kennelly. North American Cartographic Information Society, PO Box 399, Milwaukee, WI 53201; business@nacis.org; http://dev.nacis.org/. Refereed. *Indexed:* A01, MLA-IB. *Aud.:* Ga, Ac, Sa.

Cartographic Perspectives is the journal of the North American Cartographic Information Society, with members representing academia, cartographic publishers, and GIS and digital mapping communities, as well as educators, map curators, and librarians. The journal contains research and descriptive papers on all aspects of cartography, maps, and related topics in four sections: "Mapping: Methods & Tips"; "Cartographic Collections"; "Reviews"; and "Visual Fields." Appropriate for academic libraries that support a map collection or geography department, and for special libraries that support cartographic work.

1183. *Cartographica: the international journal for geographic information and geovisualization.* Incorporates (1964-1980): *Canadian Cartographer;* Which was formerly (until 1968): *Cartographer.* [ISSN: 0317-7173] 1964. q. USD 245. Ed(s): Nigel Waters. University of Toronto Press, Journals Division, 5201 Dufferin St, Toronto, ON M3H 5T8, Canada; journals@utpress.utoronto.ca; http://www.utpjournals.com. Illus., index. Sample. Refereed. Circ: 433. Vol. ends: No. 4. Microform: MML. *Indexed:* A01, A22, BRI, C37, CBCARef. *Bk. rev.:* Number and length vary. *Aud.:* Ac, Sa.

This quarterly, from the University of Toronto Press, publishes articles on cartographic thought, the history of cartography, and cartography and society, as well as material on geovisualization research. Regular issues include book reviews and listings of new cartographic publications that appear globally. Abstracts are in both English and French. A section, "Technical Notes and Ephemera," includes technical information, news items, and opinions. Recent theme issues include: "Internet Mapping" and "Indigenous Cartographies and Counter-Mapping." For a scholarly audience.

1184. *Cartography and Geographic Information Science.* Former titles (until Jan.1999): *Cartography and Geographic Information Systems;* (until 1990): *American Cartographer.* [ISSN: 1523-0406] 1974. 5x/yr. GBP 143 (print & online eds.). Ed(s): Ilse Genovese, Michael Leitner. Taylor & Francis, 4 Park Sq, Milton Park, Abingdon, OX14 4RN, United Kingdom; subscriptions@tandf.co.uk; http://www.tandfonline.com. Illus., adv. Refereed. Vol. ends: Oct. *Indexed:* A22, ABS&EES, BRI, EngInd. *Aud.:* Ac, Sa.

This is the official publication of the Cartography and Geographic Information Society (CaGIS), which is a member organization of the American Congress on Surveying and Mapping (ACSM). It "supports research, education, and practices that improve the understanding, creation, analysis, and use of maps and geographic information." *CaGIS* became one of the three official journals of the International Cartographic Association (ICA) in 2004, and has since expanded coverage globally, inviting international submissions to the journal, as well as international participation in the editorial and review processes. This journal "houses" the U.S. National Report to the ICA. Articles are broad-based, are not as technical as those in some other journals, and include cartographic representations, GIS, spatial analysis, web-based mapping, and other topics.

1185. *Computers & Geosciences: an international journal.* Incorporates (1985-1989): *C O G S Computer Contributions.* [ISSN: 0098-3004] 1975. 12x/yr. EUR 3093. Ed(s): M Piasek, J Caers. Pergamon, The Blvd, Langford Ln, E Park, Kidlington, OX5 1GB, United Kingdom; JournalsCustomerServiceEMEA@elsevier.com; http://www.elsevier.com. Illus., index, adv. Sample. Refereed. Vol. ends: Dec (No. 27). Microform: PQC. *Indexed:* A01, A22, C&ISA, C45, CerAb, CompLI, CompR, EngInd, M&GPA, RRTA, S25. *Bk. rev.:* Number and length vary. *Aud.:* Ac.

This highly rated scholarly journal contains research and application articles that describe new computation methods for the geosciences. It includes a range of methods such as those for geoscience information infrastructure, collection, representation, management, analysis, and visualization. It also contains articles on software development and on the scientific and social use of geoscience information. Recent special issues were on "Geospatial Cyberinfrastructure for Polar Research" and "Geocomputation of Mineral Exploration Targets."

1186. *Geo World.* Formerly (until 1998): *G I S World;* Which incorporated (1997-1997): *GeoDirectory. Vol. 1 Products and Services;* Which superseded in part (1989-1997): *G I S World Sourcebook;* Which was formerly (until 1995): *International G I S Sourcebook;* (until 1992): *G I S Sourcebook.* [ISSN: 1528-6274] 1988. m. Free to qualified personnel. Ed(s): Todd Danielson. M2Media360, 760 Market St, Ste 432, San Francisco, CA 94105. Illus., adv. Circ: 25050 Controlled. *Indexed:* A22, B02, BRI. *Aud.:* Sa.

Geo World offers news and updates on recent technological and application developments in geographic information systems. Articles also describe new and ongoing projects involving GIS, its management, and policy implications. Special columns focus on GIS case studies, business trends, news, software and web site reviews, schedules of events, and government geospatial data activities. Recent feature articles include "Going Google: A New Way to Visualize Transit Information" and "Introducing GPS III: The World Changing Technology is Ready to Improve." This magazine is important for any library—academic, public, or special—that supports work in any of the numerous applications of GIS. The online version contains some exclusive content. URL: http://geoplace.com

1187. *Geocarto International.* [ISSN: 1010-6049] 1986. 8x/yr. GBP 496 (print & online eds.). Ed(s): Bradley C Rundquist. Taylor & Francis, 4 Park Sq, Milton Park, Abingdon, OX14 4RN, United Kingdom; http://www.tandfonline.com. Illus., adv. Sample. Refereed. Reprint: PSC. *Indexed:* A01, A22, E01, M&GPA, S25. *Aud.:* Ac.

This journal is international in scope and features scholarly articles that focus on the research and application of remote sensing, GIS, geoscience, and cartography. Among its goals is to promote multidisciplinary research. It includes reviews, news, evaluation of equipment and software, and lists of events concerning remote sensing worldwide. Appropriate for academic libraries with collections that include remote sensing as well as GIS and environmental sciences.

1188. *Geodesy and Cartography.* Formerly (until 2011): *Geodezija ir Kartografija;* Supersedes in part (in 1994): *Vilniaus Technikos Universiteto. Geodezijos Katedros ir Geodezijos Instituto Darbai. Geodezijos Darbai;* Which was formerly (until 1993): *Vilniaus Technikos Universiteto. Mokslo Darbai. Geodezijos Darbai;* (until 1989): *Naucnye Trudy Vyssih Ucebnyh Zavedenij Litovskoj SSR. Trudy po Geodezii.* [ISSN: 2029-6991] 1963. q. GBP 190 (print & online eds.). Ed(s): Dr. Eimuntas Parseliunas, Dr. Arminas Stanionis. Taylor & Francis, 4 Park Sq, Milton Park, Abingdon, OX14 4RN, United Kingdom; subscriptions@tandf.co.uk; http://www.tandfonline.com. Reprint: PSC. *Indexed:* A01, C&ISA, CerAb, EngInd. *Aud.:* Ac, Sa.

This journal is co-published with Vilnius Gediminas Technical University. It includes original unpublished research articles on geodesy and cartography in the following languages: Lithuanian, English, German, French, and Russian. Among the most read papers in English are "Relief Modeling Methods for Topographic Plans in Urbanized Territories" and "Comparison Between Digital Photogrammetric Systems."

1189. *Geoinformatica: an international journal on advances of computer science for geographic information systems.* [ISSN: 1384-6175] 1997. q. EUR 974 (print & online eds.). Ed(s): Patrick Bergougnoux, Shashi Shekhar. Springer New York LLC, 233 Spring St, New York, NY 10013; service-ny@springer.com; http://www.springer.com/. Adv. Sample. Refereed. Reprint: PSC. *Indexed:* A01, A22, CompLI, E01, EngInd, S25. *Aud.:* Ac.

The aim of the journal is to "promote the most innovative results coming from the research in the field of computer science applied to geographic information systems." Among the topics addressed are spatial modeling and spatial databases, human–computer interfaces for GIS, digital cartography, space imagery in GIS, distribution and communication through GIS, and spatio-temporal reasoning. Computer advances are of wide and general-application domain.

1190. GIScience and Remote Sensing. Former titles (until 2004): *Mapping Sciences and Remote Sensing;* (until 1984): *Geodesy, Mapping and Photogrammetry;* (until 1973): *Geodesy and Aerophotography.* [ISSN: 1548-1603] 1962. bi-m. GBP 535 (print & online eds.). Ed(s): John R Jensen. Taylor & Francis, 4 Park Sq, Milton Park, Abingdon, OX14 4RN, United Kingdom; subscriptions@tandf.co.uk; http://www.tandfonline.com. Illus. Refereed. Reprint: PSC. *Indexed:* A22, C45, M&GPA, OceAb. *Aud.:* Ac, Sa.

This journal expanded to six issues per year and publishes original, peer-reviewed articles related to cartography, geographic information systems (GIS), remote sensing of the environment, geocomputation, spatial data mining and statistics, and geographic environmental modeling. The specialized content includes both basic and applied topics. Articles are written for scholarly audiences.

1191. I E E E Geoscience and Remote Sensing Letters. [ISSN: 1545-598X] 2004. q. USD 470; USD 565 combined subscription (print & online eds.). Ed(s): Paolo Gamba, Martin J Morahan. Institute of Electrical and Electronics Engineers, 445 Hoes Ln, Piscataway, NJ 08855; contactcenter@ieee.org; http://www.ieee.org. Adv. Refereed. *Indexed:* C&ISA, CerAb, EngInd, M&GPA, S25. *Aud.:* Ac.

This newer journal from the IEEE Geoscience and Remote Sensing Society includes an international editorial board and has shown tremendous growth in recent years. It has a high impact factor. *Letters* emphasizes "rapid turn around for shorter, high impact papers." Articles are published quickly online and follow that exposure with publication in the printed quarterly version, grouped by topic. Sections include "Research Review Letter"; and the papers in "Forward Look" address recent advances and new areas or research paths. The journal accommodates extended objects such as image animations and multimedia.

1192. I E E E Journal of Selected Topics in Applied Earth Observations and Remote Sensing. [ISSN: 1939-1404] 2008. q. USD 680; USD 815 combined subscription (print & online eds.). Ed(s): Ellsworth LeDrew. Institute of Electrical and Electronics Engineers, 445 Hoes Ln, Piscataway, NJ 08854; contactcenter@ieee.org; http://www.ieee.org. Adv. *Indexed:* M&GPA, S25. *Aud.:* Ac.

J-STARS is a new title, first published in 2008, and its focus is on remote sensing and Earth observations, and their use in understanding the Earth. This peer-reviewed journal is sponsored by the IEEE Geoscience and Remote Sensing Society (GRSS) and the IEEE Committee on Earth Observations. This journal strives to serve as a communication venue for the application themes that arise from the annual IEEE conferences and the collaboration of the two founding groups. *J-STARS* will publish the special issue topics formerly found in *Transactions.*

1193. I E E E Transactions on Geoscience and Remote Sensing. Formerly (until 1980): *I E E E Transactions on Geoscience Electronics.* [ISSN: 0196-2892] 1963. m. USD 1275; USD 1530 combined subscription (print & online eds.). Ed(s): Christopher S Ruf, Martin J Morahan. Institute of Electrical and Electronics Engineers, 445 Hoes Ln, Piscataway, NJ 08854; contactcenter@ieee.org; http://www.ieee.org. Illus., adv. Refereed. *Indexed:* A01, A22, ApMecR, B01, C&ISA, C45, CerAb, EngInd, M&GPA, MathR, OceAb, S25. *Aud.:* Ac, Sa.

The second-most-cited journal in remote sensing according to Journal Citation Report (2009), *IEEE Transactions on Geoscience and Remote Sensing* focuses on the techniques, theory, and concepts of sensing the Earth, oceans, atmosphere, and space. It also contains discussion of the processing, interpretation, and dissemination of the sensing data. *TGARS* has peer-reviewed technical and research papers, reviews, and correspondence articles. It is widely

indexed. Recent articles are "A First Assessment of Ice Bridge Snow and Ice Thickness Data Over Arctic Sea Ice" and "Potential of L-Band Radar for Retrieval of Canopy and Subcanopy Parameters of Boreal Forests." This journal is free to members of GRS or GRSS (Geoscience and Remote Sensing Society). Essential for libraries with remote sensing collections and geosciences collections.

1194. I S P R S Journal of Photogrammetry and Remote Sensing. Formerly (until 1989): *Photogrammetria.* [ISSN: 0924-2716] 1938. 6x/yr. EUR 788. Ed(s): George Vosselman. Elsevier BV, Radarweg 29, PO Box 211, Amsterdam, 1000 AE, Netherlands; JournalsCustomerServiceEMEA@elsevier.com; http://www.elsevier.nl. Illus., adv. Refereed. Microform: PQC. *Indexed:* A01, A22, C&ISA, CerAb, EngInd, PhotoAb, S25. *Bk. rev.:* Number and length vary. *Aud.:* Ac.

Referred to as *P&RS,* this is the official journal of the International Society for Photogrammetry and Remote Sensing (ISPRS). With a long publishing history and extensively indexed, this is among the highest-rated journals in the field. Papers published here that are winners of the society's Helava Award include "Automatic detection and Tracking of Pedestrians from a Moving Stereo Rig." Recent themed issues were on "Visualization and Exploration of Geospatial Data" and "Advancement in LIDAR Data Processing and Applications."

1195. Imago Mundi: the international journal for the history of cartography. [ISSN: 0308-5694] 1935. s-a. GBP 201 (print & online eds.). Ed(s): Dr. Catherine Delano-Smith. Routledge, 4 Park Sq, Milton Park, Abingdon, OX14 4RN, United Kingdom; subscriptions@tandf.co.uk; http://www.tandfonline.com. Illus., index, adv. Sample. Refereed. Reprint: PSC. *Indexed:* A01, A22, AmHI, ArtHuCI, E01, FR, MLA-IB. *Bk. rev.:* Number and length vary. *Aud.:* Ac, Sa.

Imago Mundi is the leading scholarly journal on early maps worldwide. Founded in 1935, it is interdisciplinary and has an international readership. It covers research and has occasional review articles about antique maps and historic cartography. Each issue includes book reviews, an indexed bibliography of current literature, and an extensive news-and-notices section on conferences, exhibits, map acquisitions, etc. The 2011 winner of the Imago Mundi Prize was "The Date of the Gough Map." The editorship is largely American and British, with an international editorial board. The full-text back issues through 2002 are available through JSTOR free of charge for current individual subscribers of the journal. *Imago Mundi* is important for academic libraries that support a geography department or map collection.

1196. International Journal of Applied Earth Observation and Geoinformation. Formerly (until 1999): *I T C Journal.* [ISSN: 1569-8432] 1973. 6x/yr. EUR 520. Ed(s): F van der Meer. Elsevier BV, Radarweg 29, PO Box 211, Amsterdam, 1000 AE, Netherlands; JournalsCustomerServiceEMEA@elsevier.com; http://www.elsevier.nl. Illus., adv. Refereed. *Indexed:* A01, A22, C&ISA, C45, CerAb, IndVet, M&GPA, PhotoAb, S25. *Bk. rev.:* Number and length vary. *Aud.:* Ac.

This publication had a long history as *ITC Journal,* and its aim is to present Earth observation data as acquired by remote sensing platforms, such as satellites or aircraft, which relate to the management of natural resources and environmental issues, such as industrial pollution, biodiversity, or natural hazards. With a very highly ranked impact factor, the journal encourages both discussion articles and review articles, especially those that emphasize economic and social issues related to developing countries. Recent special issues were "Retrieval of Key Eco-hyrological Parameters for Cold and Arid Regions" and "Geographic Object-based Image Analysis: GEOBIA."

1197. International Journal of Digital Earth: a new journal for a new vision. [ISSN: 1753-8947] 2008. bi-m. GBP 466 (print & online eds.). Ed(s): Guo Huadong. Taylor & Francis, 4 Park Sq, Milton Park, Abingdon, OX14 4RN, United Kingdom; subscriptions@tandf.co.uk; http://www.tandfonline.com. Adv. Sample. Refereed. Reprint: PSC. *Indexed:* A01, A22, C45, E01. *Bk. rev.:* Number and length vary. *Aud.:* Ac.

This peer-reviewed journal was founded by the International Society for Digital Earth in 2008, and has quickly gained a solid reputation. Its goal is to integrate and share information regarding digital Earth's science and technology. Specifically, it includes papers on digital Earth theory and framework, geoinformatics, visualization and simulation, data mining, and integration of remote-sensing GIS-GPS. Additionally, it includes topics on digital Earth in societal issues. Full research papers, shorter papers, reports, and book reviews are included. A number of papers are freely available as an "Editor's Choice" selection. Appropriate for libraries with geographic or information technology collections.

1198. International Journal of Geographical Information Science. Formerly (until 1997): *International Journal of Geographical Information Systems*. [ISSN: 1365-8816] 1987. m. GBP 2216 (print & online eds.). Ed(s): Brian Lees. Taylor & Francis, 4 Park Sq, Milton Park, Abingdon, OX14 4RN, United Kingdom; subscriptions@tandf.co.uk; http://www.tandfonline.com. Illus., index, adv. Sample. Refereed. Vol. ends: Dec. Reprint: PSC. *Indexed:* A01, A22, BrArAb, C45, CompLI, E01, ErgAb, NumL. *Aud.:* Ac.

IJGIS is highly ranked for impact in Journal Citation Reports. The focus of this journal is geographical information science (GISc) and geocomputation and is international in scope. It is of interest to those who research, design, analyze, and plan using GIS in natural resources and environmental studies, as well as those involved in the information and database management aspect of GIS. Free access is offered to members of the Association of American Geographers. Recent special issues were on "Data Intensive Geospatial Computing" and "Spatial Ecology." Appropriate for libraries with geography, GIS, or information science research collections.

1199. International Journal of Remote Sensing. Incorporates (1983-2001): *Remote Sensing Reviews*. [ISSN: 0143-1161] 1980. m. USD 11988 (print & online eds.); EUR 9592 (print & online eds.); GBP 6851 (print & online eds.). Ed(s): Giles Foody. Taylor & Francis, 4 Park Sq, Milton Park, Abingdon, OX14 4RN, United Kingdom; http://www.tandfonline.com. Illus., index, adv. Sample. Refereed. Vol. ends: Dec. Reprint: PSC. *Indexed:* A01, A22, C&ISA, C45, CerAb, E01, EngInd, M&GPA, OceAb, PhotoAb, RRTA, S25. *Aud.:* Ac.

This is the official journal of the Remote Sensing and Photogrammetry Society. It is a research journal, and its focus is on the science and technology of remote sensing and its applications. Topics include data collection, analysis, and interpretation; surveying from space; and use of remote sensing data. The top ten most-cited articles now are offered free online. The section "Remote Sensing Letters" split off to form its own journal of the same name [ISSN 2150-704X]. Editorship and authorship are international. Appropriate for remote-sensing professionals and academic libraries with collections that support environmental studies, geography, and related programs that study remote sensing.

1200. Journal of Geodesy. Formed by the merger of (1924-1995): *Bulletin Geodesique;* (1978-1995): *Manuscripta Geodaetica*. [ISSN: 0949-7714] 1995. m. EUR 1678 (print & online eds.). Ed(s): Roland A Klees. Springer, Tiergartenstr 17, Heidelberg, 69121, Germany. Adv. Refereed. Circ: 1200. Reprint: PSC. *Indexed:* A01, A22, E01, M&GPA, MathR, OceAb. *Aud.:* Ac, Sa.

The *Journal of Geodesy* is a peer-reviewed, international journal that covers scientific problems of geodesy and related sciences, such as positioning, reference frame, geodetic networks, and remote sensing. It is highly rated, has a long publishing history, and is widely indexed. Most downloaded articles are available for free and include "Zero-difference GPS Ambiguity Resolution at CNES-CLS IGS Analysis Center" and "Impact of Earth Radiation Pressure on GPS Position Estimates."

1201. Journal of Geographical Systems: geographical information, analysis, theory and decision. Formerly (until 1998): *Geographical Systems*. [ISSN: 1435-5930] 1999. q. EUR 413 (print & online eds.). Ed(s): Antonio Paez, Manfred M Fischer. Springer, Tiergartenstr 17, Heidelberg, 69121, Germany. Adv. Sample. Refereed. Reprint: PSC. *Indexed:* A01, A22, ABIn, B01, E01, EconLit, JEL. *Aud.:* Ac.

The journal covers geographical information and its analysis, and theory and decision systems. It has an international editorial board and gives special attention to regional issues. In addition, it encourages interdisciplinary research and seeks to foster interaction between theorists and GIS users and practitioners in regional science and related fields. *Journal of Geographical Systems* is widely indexed and ranks high on impact factors.

1202. Journal of Map & Geography Libraries: advances in geospatial information, collections, and archives. [ISSN: 1542-0353] 2004. 3x/yr. GBP 451 (print & online eds.). Ed(s): Katherine H Weimer, Paige G Andrew. Routledge, 325 Chestnut St, Ste 800, Philadelphia, PA 19106; customerservice@taylorandfrancis.com; http://www.tandfonline.com. Sample. Refereed. Reprint: PSC. *Indexed:* A01, A22, C&ISA, C45, CerAb, E01. *Aud.:* Ac.

Journal of Map & Geography Libraries covers a wide variety of map, cartography, and geospatial research and applications. It ranges from historic cartography and modern map publishing to emerging GIS and geospatial data topics. It is aimed primarily at the library and archives community, and its international board covers a wide span of cartographic and geospatial data–related specializations. Recent themed issues covered "Geographic Opportunities in Medicine" and "Crisis Mapping." Appropriate for libraries, archives, and universities with map or GIS collections and areas of specialization.

1203. Photogrammetric Engineering and Remote Sensing. Formerly (until 1975): *Photogrammetric Engineering*. [ISSN: 0099-1112] 1934. m. USD 440 domestic; USD 468 Canada; USD 450 elsewhere. Ed(s): Dr. Russell G Congalton. American Society for Photogrammetry and Remote Sensing, 5410 Grosvenor Ln, Ste 210, Bethesda, MD 20814-2160; asprs@asprs.org; http://www.asprs.org. Illus., index, adv. Refereed. Circ: 6300 Paid. Vol. ends: Dec. *Indexed:* A22, Agr, C&ISA, C45, CerAb, EngInd, M&GPA, PhotoAb, RRTA, S25. *Bk. rev.:* Number and length vary. *Aud.:* Ac, Sa.

PE&RS is the official journal of the American Society for Photogrammetry & Remote Sensing. Members receive the print version and have complete online access. Non-member access on the society's web page is limited to material older than 24 months and does not contain the complete peer-reviewed article. The journal covers new technologies and applications relating to photogrammetry, remote sensing, and spatial sciences. Included are book reviews, the columns "Grids" and "Datums," and "Headquarters and Industry" news.

1204. The Photogrammetric Record: an international journal of photogrammetry. [ISSN: 0031-868X] 1953. q. GBP 385. Ed(s): Stuart I Granshaw. Wiley-Blackwell Publishing Ltd., 9600 Garsington Rd, Oxford, OX4 2DQ, United Kingdom; customerservices@blackwellpublishing.com; http://www.wiley.com/. Illus., adv. Sample. Refereed. Reprint: PSC. *Indexed:* A01, A22, BrTechI, E01, EngInd, PhotoAb. *Aud.:* Ac, Sa.

The journal publishes review articles on current photogrammetric practices around the world. It is published on behalf of the Remote Sensing and Photogrammetry Society (RSPSoc) and includes an international board, with Europe heavily represented. The scope includes various applications of photogrammetry, including topographic mapping, spatial data acquisition, digital cartography, virtual reality, agriculture and forestry, and other subject-focused works.

1205. Remote Sensing Letters. [ISSN: 2150-704X] 2010. q. GBP 307 (print & online eds.). Ed(s): Arthur P Cracknell, Giles Foody. Taylor & Francis, 4 Park Sq, Milton Park, Abingdon, OX14 4RN, United Kingdom; subscriptions@tandf.co.uk; http://www.tandfonline.com. Illus. Refereed. *Indexed:* A01, C45. *Aud.:* Ac, Sa.

The journal is peer-reviewed with an international editorial board committed to the rapid publication of articles that advance the science and technology of remote sensing as well as its applications. It previously was printed as a section contained in the *International Journal of Remote Sensing* from 1983 to 2009, and expanded to eight issues per year in 2012. Articles cover sensor technology, image processing, and Earth-oriented applications.

Remote Sensing of Environment. See Environment and Conservation section.

1206. *Surveying and Land Information Science.* Former titles (until 2002): *Surveying and Land Information Systems;* (until 1990): *Surveying and Mapping;* (until 1944): *American Congress on Surveying and Mapping. Bulletin;* (until 1942): *National Congress on Surveying and Mapping. Bulletin;* (until 1941): *National Congress on Surveying and Mapping. Report on the ... Meeting.* [ISSN: 1538-1242] 1941. q. Free to members. Ed(s): Ilse Genovese, Steve Frank. American Congress on Surveying and Mapping, 6 Montgomery Village Ave, Ste #403, Gaithersburg, MD 20879; infoacsm@acsm.net; http://www.acsm.net. Illus., index, adv. Sample. Refereed. Vol. ends: Dec. Microform: PQC. *Indexed:* A22. *Bk. rev.:* Number and length vary. *Aud.:* Ac, Sa.

This journal is published by the National Society of Professional Surveyors, with the American Association for Geodetic Surveying and the Geographic and Land Information Society. Articles cover theoretical, technical, administrative, and policy developments in surveying, mapping, and land information systems (including geodesy and hydrography) through research articles, book reviews, current literature lists, and comments and discussion. Topics of current interest, such as global positioning systems (GPS) and total stations, are emphasized. There is a regular section on surveying and mapping education. Every four years, the journal publishes the *U.S. Report to the International Federation of Surveyors* (FIG). The *Proceedings of the Surveying Teachers Conference* is published biannually. Members of the supporting professional societies (NSPS, AAGS, or GLIS) receive the journal as part of their membership. *SaLIS* is important for any library—academic, public, or special—that supports research or teaching in any of the numerous applications of GIS and related technologies.

1207. *Transactions in G I S.* [ISSN: 1361-1682] 1996. bi-m. GBP 1094. Ed(s): Dr. John P Wilson. Wiley-Blackwell Publishing Ltd., 9600 Garsington Rd, Oxford, OX4 2DQ, United Kingdom; customer@wiley.co.uk; http://www.wiley.com/. Refereed. Reprint: PSC. *Indexed:* A01, A22, ABIn, B01, C45, E01, RRTA, S25. *Bk. rev.:* Number and length vary. *Aud.:* Ac.

Transactions in GIS is an international scholarly journal that contains original research articles, reviews, and brief notes on both applied and theoretical aspects of GIS development: collection, analysis, modeling, interpretation, and display of spatial data. Recently highlighted articles include "The Instructor Element in GIS Instruction at U.S. Colleges and Universities" and "Exploring the Boundaries of Web Map Services: The Example of the Online Injury Atlas for Ontario." The journal is very highly rated, extensively indexed, and geared toward academic and professional audiences.

U R I S A Journal. See Urban Studies section.

■ CHEMISTRY

General/Analytical/Inorganic/Organic/Physical

Amy Gullen, Life and Health Sciences Librarian, University of Dayton, 300 College Park Dr., Dayton, IL 45469; gullen@udayton.edu

Introduction

The United Nations Educational, Scientific and Cultural Organization (UNESCO) and the International Union of Pure and Applied Chemistry (IUPAC) partnered to declare 2011 the International Year of Chemistry, "a worldwide celebration of the achievements of chemistry and its contributions to the well-being of humankind," with a theme of "Chemistry—our life, our future." The objectives were to raise awareness and appreciation of chemistry's role in meeting world needs, and to interest youth in chemistry. Coinciding with the 100th anniversary of Madame Curie's Nobel Prize, the initiative also provides an opportunity to highlight the contributions of women to the discipline. Many journals have dedicated pages this year to related content.

In October 2004, the Chemical Sciences Roundtable of the Board on Chemical Sciences and Technology of the National Academy of Sciences sponsored a workshop, "Are Chemistry Journals Too Expensive and Inaccessible?" The published summary (Heindel et al., 2005, National Academies Press) describes the many challenges peculiar to chemistry, as well as those facing scholarly publishing in general. It is recommended reading as a primer on past, current, and proposed models of scholarly communication.

Among the challenges highlighted by Heindel et al. (2005) are the complex graphical information and the unique "language" of chemistry that requires both special authoring and special search and retrieval tools. Providing sufficient data to allow others to use published research is also challenging in traditional print formats. Such concerns were part of the rationale behind the now-defunct *Internet Journal of Chemistry. IJC*'s editor noted that the journal had intended to demonstrate the benefits of electronic over print publication—for example, with respect to graphical content not easily rendered in print. This SPARC leading-edge title ended its run in 2005, but innovation in online publishing in chemistry continues (SPARC is the Scholarly Publishing and Academic Resource Coalition).

Journal proliferation may also influence cost of and access to chemistry research. *Ulrich's Periodicals Directory* lists 81 active, English-language, refereed print journals with "chemistry" as part of the subject that began publication in 2000 or later, which is about 14 percent of the total such journals in *Ulrich's* that began publication within the last decade. Only 20 English-language, refereed print journals with "chemistry" as part of the subject are reported in *Ulrich's* as having ceased. Similarly, between 2005 and 2010, *Journal Citation Reports* added 74 titles to chemistry categories (analytical applied, inorganic/nuclear, medicinal, multidisciplinary, organic, physical, crystallography, and electrochemistry), which represent 13 percent growth in the number of chemistry titles tracked, with 37 percent growth in the total citable articles. The amount of information available for scientists to read and libraries to acquire is clearly growing.

Subdiscipline growth-trends are also interesting. Medicinal chemistry had the greatest percentage increase in titles (58 percent) and articles (68 percent) tracked since 2005. However, physical chemistry is the largest *JCR* category, both in number of titles and in articles tracked, and it also had the largest number of titles added (16) between 2005 and 2010. *JCR* also indicates physical chemistry had the greatest increase in impact, with 49 percent increase in aggregate impact factor, and 37 percent increase in median Impact Factor between 2005 and 2010. The *JCR* categories of electrochemistry and multidisciplinary chemistry also had remarkable increases (~45 percent) in aggregate Impact Factor between 2005 and 2010.

The chemistry journal literature has become more complex, as chemistry research thrives at interfaces with other disciplines. Identification of "chemistry" titles is a challenge. Active, refereed, English-language journals in *Ulrich's* with chemistry subject headings may also have subject headings involving engineering (61 of 550 titles, or 11 percent), physics (122 titles, or 22 percent), biology (42 titles, or 8 percent), or some form of medicine or pharmacy (37 titles, or 7 percent). Similarly, many titles reviewed in this section are found in *JCR* chemistry categories and other categories, including engineering, physics, biology, medicinal, nanoscience, and nanotechnology.

High-cost titles have faced targeted competition, and there are a growing number of open-access titles available, as well as open-access content within traditionally published titles. The American Chemical Society partnered with SPARC to develop *Organic Letters* (1999) and *Crystal Growth and Design* (2001) as alternatives to Elsevier's *Tetrahedron Letters* and *Journal of Crystal Growth*, respectively. *Organic Letters* now ranks well above *Tetrahedron Letters* by *JCR* impact factor. *Crystal Growth and Design* ranks second among crystallography titles by 2010 impact factor. Whether competition has kept prices down is difficult to assess, but the targets have continued publication. The outcome for libraries has been the need to purchase two titles, but the overall benefit to the discipline has been the publication of more research.

During review for the 16th edition of *MFL*, I reported that print issues for review were less readily available in libraries, as libraries trimmed costs by eliminating print subscriptions in favor of online packages. Some publishers are now finding the cost of producing print prohibitive. The American Chemical Society now prints most of their titles in a reduced two-pages-per-sheet format, a change implemented since the last edition of *MFL*. Subscribers were also offered incentives to replace print with online access. James Milne, editorial director of the Royal Society of Chemistry, indicated that RSC has "no plans to follow suit" (www.rsc.org/chemistryworld/News/2009/June/22060901.asp, retrieved July 2, 2009).

Much chemistry research is freely available online. Examples include *Aldrichimica Acta, Acta Crystallographica Section E: Structure Reports*

Online, the Beilstein Institute titles, and *Chemistry Central Journal.* Bentham publishes a number of open-access chemistry titles, which are excluded from this section in the wake of a 2009 incident involving another Bentham Open title accepting a "fake" paper, as reported on *The Scientist* news blog at www.the-scientist.com/blog/display/55756 (retrieved June 15, 2009).

Many publishers offer authors the option to pay to open-access articles. In August 2006, ACS introduced "AuthorChoice" to allow authors the option of paying to make their work openly available online. The Royal Society of Chemistry has Open Science; Wiley offers OnlineOpen. The result is access for researchers to at least a subset of chemistry content, whether or not their institutions subscribe. One result of the impact of the open-access movement and ongoing dialogue on scholarly publishing has been more options for authors, and more evident mechanisms for requesting permissions for authors and for readers. Some publishers (e.g., Elsevier, NRC) have partnered with the Copyright Clearance Center and have come to provide contextual "Rightslink" forms on their web sites.

Acquisition of packages can be more economical than title-by-title selection in many cases, in some ways rendering reviews of individual titles an anachronistic practice. Licensed online access for institutions is ubiquitous, and is offered in various combinations with and without print. Back files continue to fill in and are typically sold separately. Participation by many major publishers in digital archiving initiatives such as Portico, consortial print-archiving agreements, and the cost of maintaining subscriptions in two formats have, to some degree, quieted objections to cancelling print subscriptions.

Online value-added features make electronic journals attractive. Most titles reviewed here offer supplementary information online, including chemical image files, video content, and data sets. The widespread assignment of Digital Object Identifiers (DOIs) to research articles facilitates reference-linking both cited and citing articles. Forward linking may be through proprietary platforms; for example, Elsevier uses *Scopus* to link to citing articles. Nearly all journals reviewed here offer e-mail and RSS alerts of new content and other alerting functionality. Additional "Web 2.0" features, which allow readers to share articles via Facebook, Twitter, and other social networking venues can now be found on American Chemical Society and Wiley journal sites, but not on those of the Royal Society of Chemistry or Elsevier. The American Chemical Society now offers functionality for mobile devices via ACS Mobile, which is available for various smartphone and tablet platforms.

Other recent developments of interest in chemical information include the 2008 launch of the *SciFinder Web,* and the 2009 acquisition of ChemSpider from its originator Antony Williams by the Royal Society of Chemistry. *SciFinder* is the premier abstracting and indexing service for chemistry, and has long been offered only as a desktop client. The web version has added new functionality and customizable features for users, including an alerting service. From RSC's May 11, 2009, press release, "ChemSpider is a free online service providing a structure[-]centric community for chemists" and is "the richest single source of structure[-]based chemistry information." It was originally developed by Williams and a team of volunteers. The ChemSpider web site was relaunched under the RSC brand on its own web domain. This free federated search tool retrieves chemical formulas and structures, reference data and suppliers, patents, article citations, and content from Wikipedia. Web APIs, free to academic users, allow web developers to include ChemSpider searches in their own web services.

Reviewed in this section are 48 titles from 13 publishers, representing general chemistry and four subdisciplines. In annotations, if no mention of DOIs is made, the reviewer found no evidence of DOIs assigned. For more information on DOIs, see www.doi.org. *Journal Citation Reports* for 2007 (Thomson-ISI) was used to gather supporting evidence for inclusion and recommendation of journals; where impact factors and other *JCR* measures are mentioned outside of publisher quotes, they are from this source. OpenURL linking levels are reported from the targets-list compiled and posted by Ex Libris on its web site as found in April–June 2009; reporting these data does not constitute endorsement of Ex Libris or its link resolver. Most titles in this section are offered on platforms that are to some degree COUNTER-compliant for some usage reports, based on the list of vendors evaluated against Release 3 of the Code of Practice for Journals and Databases at www.projectcounter.org/compliantvendors.html, accessed May–July 2011. Compliant publishers/vendors in this section include ACS, RSC, Elsevier, Wiley, AIP, Thieme, Nature Publishing Group, and BioMed Central. For detailed information on usage statistics reporting, see www.projectcounter.org/compliantvendors.html.

Basic Periodicals

Ac: *Accounts of Chemical Research, Analytical Chemistry, Chemical Reviews, Inorganic Chemistry, Journal of Chemical Education, The Journal of Organic Chemistry, The Journal of Physical Chemistry Part A, American Chemical Society. Journal.*

Basic Abstracts and Indexes

Chemical Abstracts; Current Contents: Physical, Chemical, and Earth Sciences; Science Citation Index.

General

1208. *Accounts of Chemical Research.* [ISSN: 0001-4842] 1968. m. USD 775. Ed(s): Joan S Valentine. American Chemical Society, 1155 16th St N W, Washington, DC 20036; help@acs.org; http://pubs.acs.org. Illus., index, adv. Sample. Refereed. *Indexed:* A01, A22. *Aud.:* Ac, Sa.

Offers short, readable accounts of "basic research and applications in all areas of chemistry and biochemistry" that "describe current developments, clarify controversies, and link the latest advances with past and future research." One or more thematic special issues come out per year. In 2008, article abstracts were replaced with a conspectus that the publisher claims provides greater detail and improves retrieval in online searches; such items are longer than abstracts, and typically include an image. Ranked fourth among multidisciplinary chemistry journals by 2012 impact factor. Recommended for academic libraries that support chemistry programs and special libraries.

1209. *American Chemical Society. Journal.* Incorporates (1879-1913): *American Chemical Journal;* (1891-1893): *Journal of Analytical and Applied Chemistry;* Which was formerly (until 1891): *Journal of Analytical Chemistry.* [ISSN: 0002-7863] 1879. w. USD 4660. Ed(s): Peter J Stang, Sonja Krane. American Chemical Society, 1155 16th St N W, Washington, DC 20036; help@acs.org; http://pubs.acs.org. Illus., index, adv. Refereed. Microform: PMC. *Indexed:* A01, A22, ApMecR, BRI, EngInd, ExcerpMed, FS&TA, S25. *Bk. rev.:* Number and length vary. *Aud.:* Ac, Sa.

The flagship journal of the American Chemical Society is "devoted to the publication of research papers in all fields of chemistry" and publishes articles, communications, and book and software reviews. Most articles are accompanied by online supporting information, which includes text, image, and/or video files. Ranked 11th among multidisciplinary chemistry journals by 2012 impact factor. Strongly recommended for academic and research libraries that support chemistry programs.

1210. *Angewandte Chemie (International Edition).* Formerly (until 1998): *Angewandte Chemie: International Edition in English.* [ISSN: 1433-7851] 1961. 52x/yr. GBP 5648. Ed(s): Peter Goelitz. Wiley - V C H Verlag GmbH & Co. KGaA, Postfach 101161, Weinheim, 69451, Germany; info@wiley-vch.de; http://www.vchgroup.de. Illus., index, adv. Sample. Refereed. Circ: 3453 Paid and controlled. Vol. ends: Dec. Reprint: PSC. *Indexed:* A22, Agr, C45, EngInd, FS&TA. *Bk. rev.:* Typically 1 per issue, signed, 1-2 pages in length. *Aud.:* Ac, Sa.

The *International Edition* is the English translation of the German-language publication of the *Gesellschaft Deutscher Chemiker.* It offers review articles, highlights, communications, news, graphical abstracts, author profiles, and Nobel lectures in chemistry and related fields. Critically selected communications on current research results comprise the majority of content. Graphical abstracts, highlights, reviews, and minireviews are also published. Ranked seventh by 2012 impact factor among multidisciplinary chemistry journals. Recommended for academic and special libraries that support research in chemistry.

ChemComm. See *Chemical Communications.*

1211. *Chemical & Engineering News.* Former titles (until 1942): *American Chemical Society. News Edition;* (until 1940): *Industrial and Engineering Chemistry. News Edition.* [ISSN: 0009-2347] 1923. w. USD 273 (print & online eds.); Free to members. Ed(s): Rudy M Baum, Robin M Giroux. American Chemical Society, 1155 16th St N W, Washington, DC 20036; acspubs@acs.org; http://pubs.acs.org. Illus., index, adv. Refereed. Circ: 135156 Paid. *Indexed:* A&ATA, A01, A22, ABIn, Agr, B01, B02, B03, BRI, C&ISA, C42, CEA, CerAb, EngInd, FS&TA, P02, RILM. *Bk. rev.:* up to 1 per issue, 1-2 pages each, signed. *Aud.:* Ga, Ac, Sa.

A magazine of the American Chemical Society (ACS) that provides international coverage of "science and technology, business and industry, government and policy, education, and employment," with relevance to chemistry in concise, accessible articles. Content includes summarized research reports from chemistry and related disciplines and current events. "News of the Week" highlights news headlines with a chemistry focus, including references to published research. Regular sections address business, education, and government policy. Also included are award announcements and ACS news. Online version includes links to companies, agencies, individuals discussed, and cited research. Recommended for academic libraries that support science curricula, research libraries that support chemists, and larger public libraries.

1212. *Chemical Communications.* Former titles (until 1996): *Chemical Society. Chemical Communications. Journal;* (until 1972): *Chemical Communications;* Which superseded in part (in 1965): *Chemical Society. Proceedings;* Which superseded in part (in 1957): *Chemical Society. Journal;* Which was formerly (until 1924): *Chemical Society. Transactions. Journal;* Which superseded in part (in 1878): *Chemical Society. Journal;* Which was formerly (until 1862): *Chemical Society of London. Quarterly Journal;* (until 1849): *Chemical Society of London. Memoirs and Proceedings;* Which was formed by the merger of (1841-1843): *Chemical Society of London. Memoirs;* (1841-1843): *Chemical Society of London. Proceedings;* Chemical Society. Journal incorporated (1891-1914): *Chemical Society. Proceedings;* Which was formerly (1885-1891): *Chemical Society. Abstracts of the Proceedings.* [ISSN: 1359-7345] 1843. 100x/yr. GBP 3444 combined subscription (print & online eds.); USD 6428 combined subscription (print & online eds.). Ed(s): Robert D Eagling. R S C Publications, Thomas Graham House (290), Science Park, Milton Rd, Cambridge, CB4 0WF, United Kingdom; sales@rsc.org; http://www.rsc.org. Illus., adv. Refereed. Microform: PQC. *Indexed:* A01, A22, E01, ExcerpMed. *Aud.:* Ac, Sa.

"The largest publisher of high[-]quality communications within the general chemistry arena." The audience is "academic and industrial chemists in all areas of the chemical sciences." Feature review articles are also published. "Web themed issues on cutting[-]edge areas of chemical research" continue to be published throughout the year, as well as an annual "Emerging Investigator" issue. Now publishes 100 issues per year, which is much more frequent than other journals in this section. Recommended for libraries that support academic and industry chemists and related programs.

1213. *Chemical Reviews.* [ISSN: 0009-2665] 1924. m. USD 1430. Ed(s): Josef Michl. American Chemical Society, 1155 16th St N W, Washington, DC 20036; help@acs.org; http://pubs.acs.org. Illus., index, adv. Sample. Refereed. *Indexed:* A01, A22, ApMecR, EngInd, P02. *Aud.:* Ac, Sa.

Provides "comprehensive, authoritative, critical, and readable reviews of important recent research in organic, inorganic, physical, analytical, theoretical, and biological chemistry." Several thematic issues are published annually. This is a core title, ranked first among multidisciplinary chemistry titles by 2012 impact factor. Supporting information (primarily text) for some papers is available online at no charge. Recommended for academic libraries that serve chemistry departments and special libraries.

1214. *Chemical Society Reviews.* Formed by the merger of (1947-1972): *Chemical Society. Quarterly Reviews;* (1968-1972): *Royal Institute of Chemistry. Reviews;* Which was formerly (until 1968): *Royal Institute of Chemistry. Lecture Series;* (until 1961): *Royal Institute of Chemistry. Lectures, Monographs, and Reports.* [ISSN: 0306-0012] 1972. s-m. GBP 1296 combined subscription (print & online eds.); USD 2138 combined

subscription (print & online eds.). Ed(s): Robert D Eagling. R S C Publications, Thomas Graham House (290), Science Park, Milton Rd, Cambridge, CB4 0WF, United Kingdom; sales@rsc.org; http://www.rsc.org. Illus., adv. Refereed. *Indexed:* A01, A22, ApMecR, E01, FS&TA. *Aud.:* Ac, Sa.

"Publishes accessible, succinct[,] and reader-friendly articles on topics of current interest in the chemical sciences." This title includes both critical and tutorial reviews, the latter appropriate for advanced undergraduates or researchers new to the field, as well as experts. It publishes articles of social interest, broadening the potential reader base beyond research chemists. It also includes RSC Awards reviews. Guest-edited themed issues are published. It ranks second among multidisciplinary chemistry journals by 2012 impact factor. Recommended for academic and research libraries with chemistry collections.

1215. *Chemistry & Industry.* Incorporates (2001-2006): *In the Loop;* Which was formerly (until 2004): *S C I News;* Formerly (until 1932): *London. Society of Chemical Industry. Review Section. Journal;* Which superseded in part (in 1917): *London. Society of Chemical Industry. Journal;* Which was formerly (until 1882): *London. Society of Chemical Industry. Proceedings.* [ISSN: 0009-3068] 1881. m. Fortnightly until 2012. GBP 536. Ed(s): Neil Eisberg. Wiley-Blackwell Publishing Ltd., 9600 Garsington Rd, Oxford, OX4 2DQ, United Kingdom; customer@wiley.co.uk; http://www.wiley.com/. Illus., adv. Sample. Circ: 5500. Vol. ends: No. 24. *Indexed:* A22, B01, B02, BRI, BrTechI, C&ISA, CEA, CerAb, FS&TA. *Bk. rev.:* 1-5 per issue. Signed. *Aud.:* Ac, Sa.

"A news[-]breaking, topical and international chemistry-based magazine—bridging the gap between scientific innovation and industrial and consumer products." This is a useful current-awareness source for industrial chemists, tailored to industry needs and interests but accessible to a lay audience. Issues feature a number of regular sections including news, business, and commentary. "Highlights" summarize recent published research. Recommended for libraries that support academic and industry chemists.

1216. *Chemistry Central Journal.* [ISSN: 1752-153X] 2007. irreg. Free. BioMed Central Ltd., 236 Gray's Inn Rd, London, WC1X 8HB, United Kingdom; info@biomedcentral.com; http://www.biomedcentral.com. Adv. Refereed. *Indexed:* A01, A22, E01. *Aud.:* Ac, Sa.

This title is published independently on the BioMed Central platform, and it covers "research in all areas of chemistry." There are sections for organic, inorganic, physical, biological, analytical, environmental, materials and polymer, and food science chemistry. It offers authors rapid publication in an open-access medium. Authors pay processing charges for publication that are waived if author's institution is a BioMed Central member, or at the discretion of the publisher. It publishes full research articles, preliminary communications, methodology papers, commentary, and software reviews. Occasional supplements with meeting abstracts are published. Recommended for academic and special libraries that support research in chemistry.

1217. *Chemistry World.* Formerly (until 2004): *Chemistry in Britain;* Which was formed by the merger of (1957-1965): *Chemical Society. Proceedings;* Which superseded in part (in 1957): *Chemical Society. Journal;* (1950-1965): *Royal Institute of Chemistry. Journal;* Which was formerly (until 1950): *Royal Institute of Chemistry. Journal and Proceedings;* (until 1949): *Royal Institute of Chemistry of Great Britain and Ireland. Journal and Proceedings;* (until 1944): *Institute of Chemistry of Great Britain and Ireland. Journal and Proceedings;* (until 1920): *Institute of Chemistry of Great Britain and Ireland. Proceedings.* [ISSN: 1473-7604] 1965. m. GBP 845 combined subscription (print & online eds.); USD 1577 combined subscription (print & online eds.). R S C Publications, Thomas Graham House (290), Science Park, Milton Rd, Cambridge, CB4 0WF, United Kingdom; sales@rsc.org; http://www.rsc.org. Illus., adv. Refereed. *Indexed:* A&ATA, A22, BrTechI, FS&TA, RILM. *Bk. rev.:* 6 or more per month, signed. *Aud.:* Ga, Ac, Sa.

Covers research advances, international business news, and government policy as it affects the chemical science community and product applications. Includes job advertisements. Each issue contains several feature articles on timely or timeless topics related to chemistry, plus news items from current research and an opinion section. This title is an excellent source for current awareness in chemistry and the myriad related disciplines, and it is especially well suited for a broad academic audience that includes undergraduates and seasoned researchers. In January 2011, the Royal Society of Chemistry supplements *Highlights in Chemical Science, Highlights in Chemical Biology,* and *Highlights in Chemical Technology* moved to the *Chemistry World* news page, and are no longer published as separate supplements. Free supplementary content on the web site includes the *Chemistry World* blog. Recommended for academic libraries and research libraries that support chemists, as well as large public libraries.

1218. *Green Chemistry.* [ISSN: 1463-9262] 1999. m. GBP 1479 combined subscription (print & online eds.); USD 2762 combined subscription (print & online eds.). Ed(s): Sarah Ruthven. R S C Publications, Thomas Graham House (290), Science Park, Milton Rd, Cambridge, CB4 0WF, United Kingdom; sales@rsc.org; http://www.rsc.org. Adv. Refereed. *Indexed:* A01, A22, C45, E01. *Aud.:* Ac, Sa.

Publishes original research "that attempts to reduce the environmental impact of the chemical enterprise by developing a technology base that is inherently non-toxic to living things and the environment." Content is intended to be broadly accessible to chemists and technologists, including upper-level undergraduate students. Original research papers, communications, perspectives, and review articles are published; editorials and news (usually conference news) are also included. Institutional online access is available. Electronic supplementary information for articles is available free of charge and includes text and graphics. Recommended for academic libraries that support chemistry or environmental science curricula and research libraries that support chemists.

1219. *Journal of Chemical Education.* Incorporates (1896-1942): *New England Association of Chemistry Teachers. Report.* [ISSN: 0021-9584] 1924. m. Ed(s): Norbert J Pienta. American Chemical Society, 1155 16th St N W, Washington, DC 20036; help@acs.org; http://pubs.acs.org. Illus., index, adv. Sample. Refereed. Microform: PMC; PQC. *Indexed:* A&ATA, A01, A22, BRI, CBRI, ERIC, EngInd, MLA-IB, P02. *Bk. rev.:* One or more book/media reviews per issue. *Aud.:* Hs, Ac, Sa.

"The world's premier chemistry education academic journal." Monthly issues contain "a wide range of interesting articles and activities useful in both the classroom and laboratory." Topical coverage runs the gamut from classroom activities to scholarship of teaching and learning chemistry. True to its mission of supporting education, *JCE* has liberal use policies for print and online content. Highly recommended for academic libraries that support chemistry, chemistry education, or general science education curricula, as well as for high school and middle-school chemistry educators.

1220. *Journal of Physical and Chemical Reference Data.* [ISSN: 0047-2689] 1972. q. Ed(s): Donald R Burgess, Robert L Watters. American Institute of Physics, 1 Physics Ellipse, College Park, MD 20740; aipinfo@aip.org; http://www.aip.org. Illus., index, adv. Sample. Refereed. Vol. ends: Dec. *Indexed:* A22, ApMecR, P02. *Aud.:* Ac, Sa.

Published by the American Institute of Physics (AIP) for the National Institute of Standards and Technology (NIST), this journal has the aim "to provide critically evaluated physical and chemical property data, fully documented as to the original sources and the criteria used for evaluation, preferably with uncertainty analysis." It defines reference data as "the best available values for the relevant properties." Critical reviews of measurement techniques that evaluate available data accuracy may be included. This journal includes contributions that originate from the National Standard Reference Data System (NSRDS) as administered by NIST under the Standard Reference Data Act (Public Law 90-396). Recommended for academic and research libraries that support research in chemistry and related disciplines.

1221. *Macromolecules.* [ISSN: 0024-9297] 1968. bi-w. USD 3840. Ed(s): Timothy P Lodge. American Chemical Society, 1155 16th St N W, Washington, DC 20036; help@acs.org; http://pubs.acs.org. Illus., index, adv. Sample. Refereed. *Indexed:* A01, A22, C&ISA, EngInd, FS&TA. *Aud.:* Ac, Sa.

Publishes research on "fundamental aspects of macromolecular science including synthesis, polymerization mechanisms and kinetics, chemical modification, solution/melt/solid-state characteristics, and surface properties of organic, inorganic, and naturally occurring polymers." Comprehensive reports, brief communications, technical notes, and topical reviews (perspectives) are published. This title is ranked third by 2012 impact factor of 83 titles in *JCR*'s polymer science category. Supplementary information is available online at no charge, and includes text, data sets, and image files. Recommended for academic and research libraries that support polymer research.

1222. *Nano Today: an international rapid reviews journal.* [ISSN: 1748-0132] 2006. 6x/yr. EUR 1184. Ed(s): J Y Ying, Codelia Sealy. Elsevier Ltd, 32 Jamestown Rd, Camden, London, NW1 7BY, United Kingdom; corporate.sales@elsevier.com; http://www.elsevier.com. Adv. Sample. Refereed. *Indexed:* C&ISA, CerAb, EngInd, ExcerpMed. *Aud.:* Ac, Sa.

"Publishes original articles on all aspects of nanoscience and nanotechnology" in the form of review articles, rapid communications, and news and opinions. It has ranked second in nanoscience and nanotechnology, and fifth in multidisciplinary chemistry subject categories, based on impact factor in the 2012 *JCR*. Recommended for academic and research libraries that support nanotechnology.

1223. *Nature Chemistry.* [ISSN: 1755-4330] 2009. m. EUR 3936. Ed(s): Stuart Cantrill. Nature Publishing Group, The MacMillan Bldg, 4 Crinan St, London, N1 9XW, United Kingdom; nature@nature.com; http://www.nature.com. Illus., adv. Sample. Refereed. *Indexed:* A01. *Bk. rev.:* Approx. 1 per issue. *Aud.:* Ga, Ac, Sa.

A multidisciplinary chemistry journal that publishes primary research, reviews, news and research highlights from other journals, commentary, and "analysis of the broader chemical picture beyond the laboratory, including issues such as education, funding, policy, intellectual property, and the impact chemistry has on society." The publisher claims rapid production and independence from "academic societies and others with vested interests" as advantages for prospective authors. *Journal Citation Reports* data for 2012 ranks it third by impact among multidisciplinary chemistry titles. The publisher's web site hosts supplementary chemical information. Recommended for academic, research, and large public libraries.

1224. *Pure and Applied Chemistry.* Formerly: *International Congress of Pure and Applied Chemistry. Lectures.* [ISSN: 0033-4545] 1960. m. EUR 1630. Ed(s): Bernardo J Harold, John W Lorimer. Walter de Gruyter GmbH & Co. KG, Genthiner Str 13, Berlin, 10785, Germany; info@degruyter.com; http://www.degruyter.de. Illus., index. Sample. Refereed. Vol. ends: Dec. Microform: PQC. *Indexed:* A&ATA, A01, A22, C45, E01, FS&TA, IndVet. *Aud.:* Ac, Sa.

The official monthly journal of the International Union of Pure and Applied Chemistry (IUPAC) has "responsibility for publishing works arising from those international scientific events and projects that are sponsored and undertaken by the Union," and is the "designated medium for publication of recommendations, technical reports on standardization, recommended procedures, data compilations, and collaborative studies of IUPAC bodies." It also publishes proceedings of IUPAC-sponsored symposia and other events. Occasional special topic features with submission by invitation are published. All but the "current and most recently completed volumes" are freely available on the IUPAC web site. Authors may immediately "deposit copies of their own articles online" in the "IUPAC published pdf form." Technical reports and recommendations are open access upon publication. Recommended for academic and research libraries that support chemistry programs.

Analytical

1225. *American Society for Mass Spectrometry. Journal.* [ISSN: 1044-0305] 1990. 12x/yr. EUR 536 (print & online eds.). Ed(s): Michael L Gross. Springer New York LLC, 233 Spring St, New York, NY 10013; journals-ny@springer.com; http://www.springer.com. Illus., index, adv. Sample. Refereed. Circ: 5110 Paid. Vol. ends: Dec. *Indexed:* A01, A22, C&ISA, CerAb, EngInd, ExcerpMed, FS&TA. *Bk. rev.:* Occasionally 1 per issue, length varies, signed. *Aud.:* Ac, Sa.

Covers research on "fundamentals and applications" of mass spectrometry, in the disciplines of "chemistry, physics, geology, and environmental science as well as the biological, health, and life sciences." This title publishes research papers, communications, application notes, signed book reviews, accounts, and perspectives, the latter two typically invited by the editor. Annual society conference proceedings and a society directory are published in supplements. The society transferred the publisher to Springer in 2011. Content is free online after a 12-month embargo; some articles are published open access. Recommended for academic and research libraries that support chemistry programs.

1226. *The Analyst.* Incorporates (in 1996): *Analytical Communications;* Which was formerly (until 1996): *Analytical Proceedings;* (until 1980): *Chemical Society. Analytical Division. Proceedings;* (until 1975): *Society for Analytical Chemistry, Analytical Division, Chemical Society. Proceedings;* (until 1972): *Society for Analytical Chemistry. Proceedings.* [ISSN: 0003-2654] 1876. s-m. GBP 2160 combined subscription (print & online eds.); USD 4032 combined subscription (print & online eds.). Ed(s): May Copsey. R S C Publications, Thomas Graham House (290), Science Park, Milton Rd, Cambridge, CB4 0WF, United Kingdom; sales@rsc.org; http://www.rsc.org. Illus., adv. Sample. Refereed. Microform: PQC. *Indexed:* A&ATA, A01, A22, AbAn, C&ISA, C45, CerAb, E01, FS&TA, IndVet, S25. *Aud.:* Ac, Sa.

Offers "the latest developments in theory and application of analytical and bioanalytical techniques." Publishes urgent communications, full papers, and review articles on "interdisciplinary detection science." The emphasis is on rapid publication—typically 50 days from submission to publication for rapid communications, and 90 days from submission to publication for full articles. Communications may be subsequently featured in *Chemical Science* or *Chemical Technology*. Recommended for academic and research libraries that support chemistry programs.

1227. *Analytica Chimica Acta.* Incorporates: *Analytica Chimica Acta - Computer Technique and Optimization.* [ISSN: 0003-2670] 1947. 48x/yr. EUR 11373. Ed(s): R P Baldwin, L Buydens. Elsevier BV, Radarweg 29, PO Box 211, Amsterdam, 1000 AE, Netherlands; JournalsCustomerServiceEMEA@elsevier.com; http://www.elsevier.nl. Illus., index, adv. Sample. Refereed. Microform: PQC. *Indexed:* A01, A22, C&ISA, C45, CerAb, EngInd, ExcerpMed, FS&TA, IndVet, RRTA, S25. *Aud.:* Ac, Sa.

"Provides a forum for the rapid publication of original research, and critical reviews dealing with all aspects of fundamental and applied modern analytical science." The emphasis is on innovative methodologies, rather than application of existing methods to new systems. Reviews and invited articles are published. Special issues may feature proceedings from conferences or workshops. Recommended for libraries that support analytical chemistry research programs.

1228. *Analytical Chemistry.* Incorporates (1996-2000): *Analytical Chemistry News & Features;* Formerly (until 1948): *Industrial and Engineering Chemistry. Analytical Edition;* Which superseded in part (in 1929): *Industrial & Engineering Chemistry.* [ISSN: 0003-2700] 19??. s-m. USD 2025. Ed(s): Jonathan Sweedler. American Chemical Society, 1155 16th St N W, Washington, DC 20036; service@acs.org; http://pubs.acs.org. Illus., index, adv. Sample. Refereed. *Indexed:* A01, A22, BRI, C45, EngInd, FS&TA, IndVet, OceAb, P02, RRTA, S25. *Aud.:* Ac, Sa.

"Concerned with measuring important chemical things," this title publishes research on analytical theory or "any phase of analytical measurements and concepts thereof." Included in this journal are features, letters, news articles, and product reviews of interest to analytical chemists, in addition to accelerated and regular research articles and technical notes. Supporting information for some papers is available online. Recommended for academic libraries that support chemistry and related curricula.

Biosensors and Bioelectronics. See Biotechnology section.

1229. *Journal of Applied Crystallography.* [ISSN: 0021-8898] 1968. bi-m. GBP 539. Ed(s): A R Kaysser-Pyzalla. Wiley-Blackwell Publishing, Inc., Commerce Pl, 350 Main St, Malden, MA 02148; info@wiley.com; http://onlinelibrary.wiley.com/. Illus., adv. Sample. Refereed. Reprint: PSC. *Indexed:* A&ATA, A01, A22, C&ISA, CerAb, CompLI, E01. *Aud.:* Ac, Sa.

Publishes research in crystallographic methods and their "use in identifying structural and diffusion-controlled phase transformations, structure-property relationships, structural changes of defects, interfaces[,] and surfaces," as well as instrumentation and crystallographic apparatus development, theory and interpretation, and numerical analysis. Supplementary content accompanies articles, including three-dimensional images. Recommended for academic and research libraries that support chemistry programs.

1230. *Journal of Chromatography A.* Incorporates (1959-1971): *Chromatographic Reviews;* Supersedes (in 1958): *Chromatographic Methods.* [ISSN: 0021-9673] 1956. 52x/yr. EUR 16779. Ed(s): R W Giese, J G Dorsey. Elsevier BV, Radarweg 29, PO Box 211, Amsterdam, 1000 AE, Netherlands; JournalsCustomerServiceEMEA@elsevier.com; http://www.elsevier.nl. Illus., index, adv. Refereed. Microform: PQC. *Indexed:* A01, A22, Agr, C45, EngInd, ExcerpMed, FS&TA, IndVet, RRTA. *Aud.:* Ac, Sa.

Publishes "original research and critical reviews on all aspects of fundamental and applied separation science." Published here are primarily full-length research papers, but some short communications, discussions, technical notes, and invited review articles are also included. Articles are arranged by technique. Occasional symposium volumes are published. Its audience comprises analytical chemists, biochemists, clinical chemists, and others who are "concerned with the separation and identification of mixtures or compounds in mixtures."

Inorganic

1231. *Coordination Chemistry Reviews.* [ISSN: 0010-8545] 1966. 24x/yr. EUR 7156. Ed(s): Dr. A B P Lever. Elsevier BV, Radarweg 29, PO Box 211, Amsterdam, 1000 AE, Netherlands; JournalsCustomerServiceEMEA@elsevier.com; http://www.elsevier.nl. Illus., adv. Refereed. Vol. ends: No. 206 - No. 223. Microform: PQC. *Indexed:* A01, A22. *Aud.:* Ac, Sa.

This journal "[o]ffers rapid publication of review articles on topics of current interest and importance in coordination chemistry," which is interpreted broadly to include organometallic, theoretical, and bioinorganic chemistry. Themed special issues are published. Issues may also be dedicated to conference proceedings. This title ranks first by 2012 impact factor among the 43 titles in *JCR*'s inorganic and nuclear chemistry category. Issues are combined in pairs, so that only 12 pieces are published each year. The audience comprises inorganic and organometallic chemists. Recommended for academic and research libraries that support research in coordination chemistry.

1232. *Inorganic Chemistry: including bioinorganic chemistry.* [ISSN: 0020-1669] 1962. bi-w. USD 3835. Ed(s): Richard Eisenberg. American Chemical Society, 1155 16th St N W, Washington, DC 20036; help@acs.org; http://pubs.acs.org. Illus., index, adv. Refereed. *Indexed:* A01, A22, BRI. *Aud.:* Ac, Sa.

Publishes "experimental and theoretical reports on quantitative studies of structure and thermodynamics, kinetics, mechanisms of inorganic reactions, bioinorganic chemistry, and relevant aspects of organometallic chemistry, solid-state phenomena, and chemical bonding theory. Emphasis is placed on the synthesis, structure, thermodynamics, reactivity, spectroscopy, and bonding properties of significant new and known compounds." Brief communications, full articles, and invited award addresses are published. Each year, up to three thematic forum issues are published on a "multidisciplinary topic of growing interest." In the *JCR* category of inorganic and nuclear chemistry, *Inorganic Chemistry* ranked fifth by 2012 impact factor. Supplementary information for some papers, including text and images, is available online at no charge. A core title for academic and research libraries that support chemistry programs.

1233. *Inorganica Chimica Acta.* Incorporates: *Chimica Acta Reviews.* [ISSN: 0020-1693] 1967. 15x/yr. EUR 10397. Ed(s): R J Puddephat, U Belluco. Elsevier BV, Radarweg 29, PO Box 211, Amsterdam, 1000 AE, Netherlands; JournalsCustomerServiceEMEA@elsevier.com; http://www.elsevier.nl. Illus., index, adv. Sample. Refereed. Microform: PQC. *Indexed:* A01, A22. *Aud.:* Ac, Sa.

Publishes "research in all aspects of inorganic chemistry" in the form of full research articles, short research reports (notes), and regular reviews. Frequent "Protagonists in Chemistry" special issues provide profiles of researchers and collections of appropriately themed articles to honor them. Recommended for libraries that support research programs in inorganic chemistry.

1234. *Organometallics.* [ISSN: 0276-7333] 1982. bi-w. USD 3610. Ed(s): John A Gladysz. American Chemical Society, 1155 16th St N W, Washington, DC 20036; help@acs.org; http://pubs.acs.org. Illus., index, adv. Sample. Refereed. *Indexed:* A01, A22, EngInd. *Aud.:* Ac, Sa.

This journal records advances in organometallic, inorganic, organic, and materials chemistry. It covers "synthesis, structure, bonding, chemical reactivity and reaction mechanisms, and applications of organometallic and organometalloidal compounds." *Organometallics* publishes communications, mini-reviews, notes, and correspondence. It ranks within the top ten by 2012 impact factor in two *JCR* categories, organic chemistry (tenth of 55 titles) and inorganic and nuclear chemistry (sixth of 43 titles). Supporting information for some papers is available online at no charge, and includes text and images. Recommended for libraries that support research programs in organometallic, inorganic, organic, and materials chemistry.

Organic

1235. *Aldrichimica Acta.* Supersedes: *Kardinex Sheets.* [ISSN: 0002-5100] 1967. q. Free. Ed(s): Sharbil J Firsan. Aldrich, Sigma-Aldrich Corporation, 6000 N Teutonia Ave, Milwaukee, WI 53209; aldrich@sial.com; http://www.sigma-aldrich.com. Illus., adv. Sample. *Indexed:* A22. *Aud.:* Ac, Sa.

Publishes review articles on chemistry research written by chemists. Issues are typically thematic, "usually...involving organic, organometallic, bio-organic, or inorganic chemistry." The title began as a marketing tool for Aldrich, and it boasts the highest impact factor of organic chemistry titles for nine of the past ten years. Issues are available online at no charge. That and the fact that articles are all extensive reviews may account for the high impact of the title relative to other titles in its subcategory. Note that articles are not parsed on the online platform; each issue is offered as a single file. Recommended for academic and special libraries that support work in pure and applied chemistry.

1236. *Bioconjugate Chemistry.* [ISSN: 1043-1802] 1990. bi-m. USD 1230. Ed(s): Claude F Meares. American Chemical Society, 1155 16th St N W, Washington, DC 20036; help@acs.org; http://pubs.acs.org. Adv. Sample. Refereed. *Indexed:* A22, ExcerpMed, P02. *Aud.:* Ac, Sa.

Publishes articles, reviews, communications, technical notes, and comments on all aspects of the joining of different molecular functions by chemical or biological means. Recommended for libraries that support research or related programs in biochemistry and organic chemistry.

1237. *Biomacromolecules.* [ISSN: 1525-7797] 2000. m. USD 1850. Ed(s): Ann-Christine Albertsson. American Chemical Society, 1155 16th St N W, Washington, DC 20036; help@acs.org; http://pubs.acs.org. Adv. Refereed. *Indexed:* A01, A22, AbAn, EngInd, ExcerpMed. *Aud.:* Ac, Sa.

Publishes "interdisciplinary investigations exploring the interactions of macromolecules with biological systems and their environments[,] as well as biological approaches to the design of polymeric materials." Research articles comprise most of the content, but critical reviews, brief communications, and notes are also published. Ranked seventh among organic chemistry and fourth among polymer science titles by 2012 impact factor. Recommended for libraries that support polymer research or related programs in organic chemistry.

1238. *The Journal of Organic Chemistry.* [ISSN: 0022-3263] 1936. bi-w. USD 3150. Ed(s): C Dale Poulter. American Chemical Society, 1155 16th St N W, Washington, DC 20036; help@acs.org; http://pubs.acs.org. Illus., index, adv. Sample. Refereed. Vol. ends: Dec. *Indexed:* A01, A22, AbAn, BRI, EngInd, ExcerpMed, FS&TA. *Aud.:* Ac, Sa.

Publishes "novel, important findings of fundamental research in all branches of the theory and practice of organic and bioorganic chemistry," in full articles, notes, and perspectives. This title publishes "Brief Communications" of preliminary results that have warranted "immediate disclosure," and short reviews of current topics called "*JOC*Synopses," in addition to "Articles," "Notes," and "Perspectives." Supplementary information, including text and image files, is offered online. A core title for the subdiscipline, it is recommended for academic libraries that support graduate chemistry programs.

1239. *Natural Product Reports.* Formed by the merger of (1971-1984): *Biosynthesis;* (1970-1984): *The Alkalois;* (1969-1984): *Terpenoids and Steroids;* (1977-1984): *Aliphatic and Related Natural Product Chemistry;* Which superseded in part (in 1977): *Aliphatic Chemistry;* (in 1974): *Aliphatic, Alicyclic, and Saturated Heterocylic Chemistry. Part I. Aliphatic Chemistry.* [ISSN: 0265-0568] 1984. m. GBP 1138 combined subscription (print & online eds.); USD 2123 combined subscription (print & online eds.). Ed(s): Dr. Richard Kelly. R S C Publications, Thomas Graham House (290), Science Park, Milton Rd, Cambridge, CB4 0WF, United Kingdom; sales@rsc.org; http://www.rsc.org. Adv. Refereed. *Indexed:* A01, A22, Agr, E01, FS&TA. *Aud.:* Ac, Sa.

Primarily publishes reviews on "natural products research including isolation, structural and sterochemical determination, biosynthesis, biological activity and synthesis." This title includes review articles, shorter highlight articles, viewpoint articles, and hot-off-the-press articles. It has ranked first in organic chemistry and medical chemistry and 16th in biochemistry and molecular biology subject categories, based on impact factor in the 2012 *JCR*. Recommended for academic and research libraries that support organic chemistry research.

1240. *Organic Letters.* [ISSN: 1523-7060] 1999. bi-w. USD 4950. Ed(s): Amos B Smith, Carol Carr. American Chemical Society, 1155 16th St N W, Washington, DC 20036; help@acs.org; http://pubs.acs.org. Adv. Sample. Refereed. *Indexed:* A01, A22. *Aud.:* Ac, Sa.

Publishes brief reports of research on organic chemistry, organometallic and materials chemistry, physical and theoretical organic chemistry, natural products isolation and synthesis, new synthetic methodology, and bio-organic and medicinal chemistry. The emphasis is on rapid communication of research. Established in 1999 as a Scholarly Publishing and Academic Resource Coalition (SPARC) alternative to Elsevier's *Tetrahedron Letters,* it quickly eclipsed its target by at least one measure: by 2003, its impact factor was nearly twice that of *Tetrahedron Letters.* It has retained its lead over the competition, and ranks fifth by 2012 impact factor among 55 journals in *JCR*'s organic chemistry category (compared to 24th for *Tetrahedron Letters*). *Tetrahedron Letters* cost about $12,000 more than *Organic Letters.* However, major research institutions now likely subscribe to both titles. Supporting information, including text and image files, is available online at no charge. Recommended for academic and research libraries that support organic chemistry research.

1241. *Tetrahedron: the international journal for the rapid publication of full original research papers and critical reviews in organic chemistry.* [ISSN: 0040-4020] 1957. 52x/yr. EUR 15785. Pergamon, The Blvd, Langford Ln, E Park, Kidlington, OX5 1GB, United Kingdom; JournalsCustomerServiceEMEA@elsevier.com; http://www.elsevier.com. Illus., adv. Sample. Refereed. Microform: MIM; PQC. *Indexed:* A01, A22, C45, ExcerpMed, IndVet. *Aud.:* Ac, Sa.

Publishes experimental and theoretical research in "organic chemistry and its application to related disciplines, especially bio-organic chemistry." Its specific topical coverage includes organic synthesis, organic reactions, natural products chemistry, reaction mechanism, and spectroscopy. It publishes full research papers, commissioned critical reviews ("Tetrahedron Reports"), and "Tetrahedron Symposia-in-print." Other features include *Tetrahedron* Young

Investigator Award papers. It ranks 17th by 2012 impact factor among 55 journals in *JCR*'s organic chemistry category. It is widely accepted as a core title and is recommended for libraries that support substantial research programs in organic or bio-organic chemistry.

Physical

1242. *A C S Nano.* [ISSN: 1936-0851] 2007. m. USD 1625 domestic; USD 1769 foreign. Ed(s): Paul S Weiss, Heather Tierney. American Chemical Society, 1155 16th St N W, Washington, DC 20036; help@acs.org; http://pubs.acs.org. Adv. Sample. Refereed. *Aud.:* Ac, Sa.

This title "[p]ublishes comprehensive articles on synthesis, assembly, characterization, theory, and simulation of nanostructures (nanomaterials and assemblies, nanodevices, and self-assembled structures), nanobiotechnology, nanofabrication, methods and tools for nanoscience and nanotechnology, and self- and directed-assembly." Research articles, reviews, perspectives, and "conversations" with leading researchers in this emerging discipline are included. Most articles are accompanied by online supporting information, which includes text, image, and/or video files. Recommended for academic and research libraries.

Advanced Materials. See Engineering and Technology section.

1243. *Chemistry of Materials.* [ISSN: 0897-4756] 1989. bi-w. USD 2055. Ed(s): Leonard V Interrante. American Chemical Society, 1155 16th St N W, Washington, DC 20036; help@acs.org; http://pubs.acs.org. Illus., index, adv. Sample. Refereed. *Indexed:* A01, A22, C&ISA, EngInd. *Aud.:* Ac, Sa.

Publishes "fundamental research at the interface of chemistry, chemical engineering, and materials science," including "theoretical and experimental studies which focus on the preparation or understanding of materials with unusual or useful properties." Solid-state inorganic and organic chemistry, polymer materials, biomaterials, nanomaterials, coatings, thin films, and more are covered. Typical issues offer full articles and short communications. Occasional thematic issues are published. Supporting information for some papers is available online at no charge. Recommended for academic and research libraries that support materials-related research across a range of disciplines.

Journal of Catalysis. See Engineering and Technology/Chemical Engineering section.

1244. *Journal of Chemical Theory and Computation.* [ISSN: 1549-9618] 2005. bi-m. USD 1435. Ed(s): Donna Minton, Gustavo E Scuseria. American Chemical Society, 1155 16th St N W, Washington, DC 20036; help@acs.org; http://pubs.acs.org. Adv. Sample. *Indexed:* CCMJ, MSN, MathR. *Aud.:* Ac, Sa.

Initiated to provide a single forum for "articles, letters, and reviews reporting new theories based on physical laws, advances in computational methods, and important applications to problems in chemistry." This title reports on "new theories, methodology, and/or important applications in quantum electronic structure, molecular dynamics, and statistical mechanics." The intended audience is theoretical and computational chemists. This title ranks third by 2012 impact factor among titles in the "Physics, Atomic, Molecular & Chemical" category, but it is less competitive with other journals in *JCR*'s "Physical Chemistry" category. Supporting information is available for some papers online. Recommended for academic and research libraries that support theoretical chemistry research.

Journal of the American Society for Mass Spectrometry. See *American Society for Mass Spectrometry. Journal* under Chemistry/Analytical section.

1245. *Langmuir: the A C S journal of surfaces and colloids.* [ISSN: 0743-7463] 1985. bi-w. USD 5145. Ed(s): David G Whitten. American Chemical Society, 1155 16th St N W, Washington, DC 20036; help@acs.org; http://pubs.acs.org. Illus., index, adv. Sample. Refereed. *Indexed:* A01, A22, C&ISA, EngInd. *Aud.:* Ac, Sa.

Publishes research on surfactants and self-assembly, dispersions, emulsions, foams, adsorption, reactions, films, forces, biocolloids, biomolecular and biomimetic materials, nano- and meso-structured materials, polymers, gels, liquid crystals, interfacial charge transfer, charge transport, electrocatalysis, electrokinetic phenomena, bioelectrochemistry, sensors, fluidics, patterning, catalysis, and photonic crystals. This journal's issues offer brief letters and full articles, the latter arranged into topical categories: materials, colloids, electrochemistry, interfaces, biological interfaces, and devices and applications. Recommended for academic and research libraries that support research in physical chemistry.

1246. *Nano Letters.* [ISSN: 1530-6984] 2001. m. USD 1845. Ed(s): Charles M Lieber, A Paul Alivisatos. American Chemical Society, 1155 16th St N W, Washington, DC 20036; help@acs.org; http://pubs.acs.org. Adv. Sample. Refereed. *Indexed:* A01, A22, EngInd. *Aud.:* Ac, Sa.

"Reports on fundamental research in all branches of the theory and practice of nanoscience and nanotechnology." This title has ranked in the top eight titles in six different *JCR* subject categories based on impact factor, including multidisciplinary chemistry (eighth) and physical chemistry (fifth). Recommended for academic and research libraries that support research in physical chemistry.

Nature Materials. See Engineering and Technology/Materials Engineering section.

1247. *Physical Chemistry Chemical Physics.* Formed by the merger of (1991-1999): *Berichte der Bunsen-Gesellschaft;* Which was formerly (until 1991): *Berichte der Bunsengesellschaft fur Physikalische Chemie;* (until 1963): *Zeitschrift fuer Elektrochemie;* (1904-1952): *Zeitschrift fuer Elektrochemie und Angewandte Physikalische Chemie;* (1990-1999): *Chemical Society. Faraday Transactions. Journal;* Which was formed by the merger of (1972-1990): *Chemical Society. Faraday Transactions I. Journal;* (1972-1990): *Chemical Society. Faraday Transactions II. Journal;* Which incorporated (1972-1984): *Chemical Society. Faraday Symposia;* Which was formerly (until 1972): *Faraday Society. Symposia;* Both Faraday Transactions I. Journal and Faraday Transactions II. Journal superseded in part (in 1972): *Faraday Society. Transactions.* [ISSN: 1463-9076] 1999. 48x/yr. GBP 3562 combined subscription (print & online eds.); USD 6650 combined subscription (print & online eds.). R S C Publications, Thomas Graham House (290), Science Park, Milton Rd, Cambridge, CB4 0WF, United Kingdom; sales@rsc.org; http://www.rsc.org. Illus., adv. Refereed. *Indexed:* A22, C&ISA, CEA, E01. *Aud.:* Ac, Sa.

Publishes rapid communications, invited articles, and research papers on topics at the interface of physics and chemistry, including biophysical chemistry. This title's coverage includes "spectroscopy, dynamics, kinetics, statistical mechanics, thermodynamics, electrochemistry, catalysis, surface science, quantum mechanics, and theoretical developments." Frequent themed issues are published. The publisher claims this is "the fastest physical chemistry journal," with submission-to-publication time of less than 80 days. It is run by an ownership board with equal representation from 16 societies, mostly European and none North American. Recommended for academic and research libraries that support physical chemistry research.

■ CHILDREN

See also Classroom Magazines; Parenting; and Teenagers sections.

Lucy Duhon, Scholarly Communications Librarian, Carlson Library, The University of Toledo, Toledo, OH 43606; lucy.duhon@utoledo.edu

Introduction

According to the *United Nations World Population Prospects, 2010 Revision,* children (ages 0–14) currently make up one fifth (or 20.1 percent) of the United

States population. The other major English-speaking countries show slightly lower figures for this age group: Australia (19.0 percent), the U.K. (17.4 percent), and Canada (16.4 percent). While all areas of child population growth have slowed over the last decade, the U.S. child population in particular is projected to continue to remain stable or even trend downward slightly in the coming decade. The minority populations, however, continue to grow. Most strikingly, Hispanic children now make up 23 percent of the U.S. child population, as compared to non-Hispanic whites who make up 54 percent (in 1980 these figures were 9 percent and 74 percent, respectively). Other minority groups, such as Asians, are increasingly making up the new U.S. population of children as well. Meanwhile, the black population has also grown, but only moderately. While this last decade has seen only a small increase in the child population as compared to the mini baby-boom of the 1990s, children do continue to make up one-fifth of our people.

The large proportion of children in the population explains the mass market that exists in the children's magazine publishing industry, but recent factors such as demographic shifts, economic turbulence, and increasing online activity also explain its slight decline in recent years. Yet children continue to love to read, and increasingly they are contributing to the creativity of what is published; many magazines now employ children on their editorial boards.

The titles listed in this chapter include material appropriate for child readers (and pre-readers) up to about the age of 14. The vast bulk of titles listed are those published in English and in the United States. A few non-U.S. English titles have also been included as this listing is intended to reflect, roughly, the demographic profile of current subscribers to *MFL* as listed in WorldCat (where U.S., Canada, Australia, U.K., and other English-speaking countries predominantly subscribe). Librarians should recognize changes in demographics and changes in preferred reading, leisure, and learning habits when building their collections and services for children. They should pay attention to the need for increasingly varied cultural representations in children's magazine literature, so that changing populations are served accordingly. Having said this, most children's magazine publishers already seem to be doing a more than adequate job of integrating the concept of diversity into their product, and of representing minority cultures.

The past two years have again seen changes. A few more titles have gone under or are in a state of uncertainty. Many of those that remain report much smaller circulation figures. Listing changes since the last edition of *MFL* are based on the cessation, indefinite suspension, or uncertain status of the following: *Cousteau Kids; Crinkles; IndyKids; J J Express; Kahani; Know; Pack-o-Fun;* and *Yes.* Additions include the very popular *Beckett Game Strategyst* and *WW Kids* titles, and the award-winning *Magic Dragon.* The indexing service *Children's Magazine Guide* has also ceased publication as of August 2010, though it continues to provide access to existing content. Notably, while many publishers have raised their subscription prices substantially since the last edition of this reference book, a couple of the major publishing houses, such as Carus (which includes the Cobblestone and Cricket groups) and The Children's Better Health Institute, have actually managed to avoid subscriber increases and have even lowered some prices. A few magazines have decreased their publishing schedules or combined their issues, while others have increased their publishing frequencies.

Choosing titles for this chapter is always a challenge, due to their large number and similarity. Therefore, some lines have been drawn. As a general rule, the following categories of titles have been excluded from this listing: local, regional, or syndicated titles (of which there are hundreds, including different countries' versions of the same title); to some extent, "spin-off" titles ("little sisters" to main titles); unless they have very broad appeal, those more appropriately listed in a specific subject category (e.g., *Young Rider* [see Horses]); those with a political, proselytizing, or marketing agenda (note that this section only very selectively includes titles that feature TV characters); those better suited for older teens; teacher/classroom titles; those better meant for parents, other caretakers, or adult readers; and titles meant for all ages. Newsletter- and newspaper-type titles are also excluded unless they are significant publications. Magazines published by government entities are included only if they have a mass distribution, scope, or appeal. Except for a select few, web sites have also been excluded from this listing because of their sheer number. Only those with serially issued or continually updated content are listed here (or those that present themselves most like bona fide magazines, such as *Business News for Kids*).

Almost every magazine now includes supplementary online content above and beyond its print content anyway. Other titles excluded are those not generally picked up by public library systems and those whose publishers were deemed unresponsive or unreachable by the reviewer. As much as possible, this section is also an attempt to provide an equal balance of magazine offerings to interest both boys and girls.

As the magazine *Highlights* puts it, "children are the world's most important people." The future of a civilized society depends greatly on people who grow up informed, sensitive, and capable. Quality children's magazines will continue to be a great medium for reaching our youth and inspiring them also to reach out to their peers and eventually lead the next generation. Unfortunately, in this continuing era of tight budgets, librarians will have to be more selective than ever in providing these reading materials.

Luckily they have a wide range of titles from which to choose. Librarians will either have to commit to subscribing to more magazines than previously required to satisfy the needs of their young readers, or make difficult choices among similar, competing titles. This will likely enable the highest-quality and most innovative children's publications to thrive. It is hoped that the list below will provide a good reference point for beginning to make those choices.

Basic Periodicals

Adventure Box, AppleSeeds, Ask, Babybug, Big Backyard, Biography for Beginners, Boys' Life, Calliope, Chickadee, ChildArt, Chirp, Click, Cobblestone, Creative Kids, Cricket, Dig, Discovery Box, Discovery Girls, Faces, Highlights for Children, Highlights High Five, Kids Discover, Kiki, Ladybug, Magic Dragon, Muse, National Geographic Kids, National Geographic Little Kids, New Moon Girls, Odyssey, Owl, Ranger Rick, Skipping Stones, Spider, Sports Illustrated for Kids, Stone Soup, Story Box, Tessy and Tab Reading Club, The Magazine, Wild, Wild Animal Baby, Zoobies, Zoobooks, Zootles.

Basic Abstracts and Indexes

Children's Magazine Guide, MAS Ultra: School Edition, Middle Search, Primary Search, Readers' Guide to Periodical Literature, Vertical File Index.

1248. A Girl's World. 1996. m. Free. A Girl's World Productions, Inc., PO Box 153551, San Diego, CA 92195. *Bk. rev.:* Number and length vary. *Aud.:* Ems, Hs.

Written and edited by girls, this bright and extraordinarily creative and useful web site "where girls and teens rule the web!" encourages and empowers girls ages 7 to 17 from all over the world to become active contributors through a variety of opportunities. These include writing contests, articles, movie reviews, quizzes, opinion polls, essays, artwork, and crafts. Girls can even take online courses in babysitting or petsitting for a small additional fee. Meanwhile, regular columns such as "Advice Alley" and "Diaries" provide girls with much-appreciated social support and a way to feel connected. Advice topics cover everything from boy problems to family issues and all the tough stuff in between. In "Hot Stuff," they can read original interviews with celebrities and catch up on entertainment news. While the site is free, a $12 membership fee lets girls into the "Circle of Friends Pen Pal Club," which gives them the opportunity to connect with other girls around the world with similar experiences, problems, or challenges without making their contact information public. New to the site are sections "Whats Hot/What's Not!" and "New Voices," which showcase girls' poetry and short stories. In "Talkabout," girls are encouraged to share their views of current events, and in "Paws for Thought," they are invited to write essays about animals. Girls are also encouraged to submit their own movie and book reviews. Highly recommended for personal subscription use, but also a worthy resource for public libraries to promote.

1249. Adventure Box. [ISSN: 1366-9001] 1995. 10x/yr. GBP 40 domestic; GBP 74 foreign. Ed(s): Christine Auberger. Bayard Presse, 3-5 Rue Bayard, Paris, 75393 Cedex 08, France; redactions@bayard-presse.com; http://www.bayardpresse.com. Illus., adv. Sample. *Aud.:* 6-9 yrs.

Winner of a Parents' Choice award, this little magazine is "much more than a book!" At 72 pages, it is actually a substantial, softcover book designed "to get kids hooked on reading." Each issue is a high-quality, sewn softcover booklet, the bulk of which consists of an exciting 40-plus page story in several chapters. Story genres range from action to history to humor to macabre. Every page is beautifully illustrated, designed to keep newly independent readers engaged. In addition to the chapter story, regular departments include "Naturebox" (giving children a close-up on particular plants, for instance), and two mischievous yet gentle comic strips, one of which runs several pages long. These are meant to "stimulate children's literacy and reasoning in a fun way." The remainder of each issue is made up of literary and math puzzles and games. Also included are competitions and opportunities for reader input. The back cover quizzes children on the chapter story and the longer comic inside. Multicultural diversity seems to be adequately represented. There are several subscription options available, including one with accompanying CDs for an enhanced audio experience. The web site provides teachers with classroom guides and biographical information about the magazine's various authors and illustrators. Highly recommended for school and public libraries.

1250. *American Girl.* [ISSN: 1062-7812] 1992. bi-m. Ed(s): Barbara E Stretchberry. American Girl Publishing, 8400 Fairway Pl, Middleton, WI 53562; legalrequests@americangirl.com; http://www.americangirl.com. Illus. *Indexed:* ICM, MASUSE, P01. *Aud.:* 6-12 yrs.

As one of the largest-circulating titles dedicated exclusively to pre-teen girls, this highly engaging bimonthly is filled with activities. Boldly and simply illustrated, at 50 pages it "is packed with everything girls love!" This award-winning magazine strives to bolster self-esteem and encourage creativity by focusing on girls and their families and friendships, rather than on popular culture or silliness. Real girls are featured throughout, including on the cover. Activities include contests, quizzes, puzzles, and crafts, and reader participation is invited through letters, artwork, jokes, and real-life anecdotes. Both indoor and outdoor activities are encouraged as are trips to the library. Each issue also includes a fiction story of approximately 3,000 to 4,000 words, as well as nonfiction feature articles on real-life girls. Girls can speak their minds and offer advice in the "Help!" section. A variety of crafts and activities are offered in the "Girls Express" and "Here's How," departments where recent issues, for example, showed girls how to make a French braid or a movie. All instructions are tested by children and adults. Monthly contests solicit reader submissions, including short stories. Some issues include mini-mag facsimile cutouts for girls to use as props for their American Girl dolls. Also included are girl-centered polls and reviews. Highly recommended for both personal subscriptions and public libraries.

1251. *AppleSeeds.* [ISSN: 1099-7725] 1998. 9x/yr. USD 33.95. Cobblestone Publishing Company, 30 Grove St, Ste C, Peterborough, NH 03458; custsvc@cobblestone.mv.com; http://www.cobblestonepub.com. Illus., index. Sample. Vol. ends: May. *Indexed:* BRI, ICM, P01. *Bk. rev.:* 3-5, 20-40 words. *Aud.:* 6-9 yrs.

This glossy, richly illustrated, 34-page magazine combines history and social studies with the literary world. Aimed at the elementary-school level, it contains numerous articles of varying length. They feature factual, personal anecdotes from real diaries, accounts of life, and experiences from other times and lands, as well as historical fiction and folklore. The articles are written so as to bring young readers into the experience; in fact, "Applecorps" provides a way for readers to provide input into the magazine's content. A recent issue presented the American Civil War with stories, factual articles, and related content depicting life on both sides of the conflict. As with other Carus publications, whimsical cartoon characters are sprinkled throughout each issue, adding comments in thought bubbles. The magazine provides interesting sidebars, some focusing on special vocabulary words. One short book review is also included. Regular departments include "Your Turn," which brings readers into the discussion, and "Contest Corner." Illustrators contribute in a variety of styles, including cartoons. The back cover of each issue includes puzzles, quick tips, and facts relating to the theme inside. An annual subject index lists previous issues by theme, and all back issues are available online and fully searchable by registered subscribers. This magazine contains no advertisements. An advisory board made up of educational and subject specialists ensures the quality of this publication. Each issue also has an academic consulting editor. Highly recommended for both school and public libraries.

1252. *Aquila: the fun magazine for children who enjoy challenges.* [ISSN: 0965-4003] 1994. m. GBP 40 domestic; GBP 45 in Europe; GBP 55 elsewhere. Ed(s): Jackie Berry. New Leaf Publishing Ltd, Studio 2, 67A Willowfield Rd, Eastbourne, BN22 8AP, United Kingdom; office@aquila.co.uk. Illus., adv. Sample. *Aud.:* 8-13 yrs.

Dedicated to "encouraging children to reason and create, and to develop a caring nature," this larger-format, handsomely designed 24-page magazine contains articles on "science, arts and fun every month." Regular departments include "Science Scene" and "Things to Make." Recent issues, for instance, told readers about the science behind the chili pepper hotness rating scale, and provided instructions on building a compost bin. With plenty of white space and colorful, large, and simple illustrations and photographs, this magazine provides easy instructions for activities like growing a garden. Each issue includes two-page articles on sports, culture, history, and also one fiction story of approximately 1,000 to 1,500 words. The magazine also regularly features crafts, recipes, experiments, "brainfeeders," jokes, quizzes, and other activities that promote language learning and participation. "Over to You" features reader mail, and each issue has a competition and prizes. Uniquely, *Aquila* encourages the photocopying of its specially marked puzzle and leisure pages in order to "enable more than one reader" to complete the activities. Links are also provided to the magazine's web site for further information and activities. Pro-rated "taster" subscriptions are available, even to overseas subscribers. Recommended for public libraries.

1253. *Ask: arts and sciences for kids.* [ISSN: 1535-4105] 2002. 9x/yr. USD 33.95. Ed(s): Liz Huyck. ePals Publishing Company, 30 Grove St, Ste C, Peterborough, NH 03458; customerservice@caruspub.com. Illus., adv. Sample. *Indexed:* ICM, P01. *Aud.:* 6-9 yrs.

A high-gloss, joint venture between the Cricket Magazine Group and the Smithsonian Institution, this attractive, stunningly illustrated 34-page magazine aims to answer children's questions about the natural and manmade world around them. It focuses primarily on science, technology, and inventions. For instance, a recent issue was themed on robots. Departments include "Scoops" (a science and culture current events column), "Nestor's Dock" (an environmentally focused two-page comic strip), "Ask Jimmy and the Bug," and several pages' worth of contests, letters, and artwork. In "Contest and Letters," children's letters and contributed artwork span several pages. A web link takes subscribers to additional reader contributions online. Also included in the magazine are lengthy feature articles on science and history, accompanied by photos and animation graphics. The back cover consists of a comic. The themed issues also include hands-on activities related to featured articles. It contains no advertisements. Highly recommended for both school and public libraries.

1254. *Babybug.* [ISSN: 1077-1131] 1994. 9x/yr. USD 33.95. ePals Publishing Company, 30 Grove St, Ste C, Peterborough, NH 03458; customerservice@caruspub.com; http://www.cricketmag.com. Illus., adv. Sample. Vol. ends: Nov/Dec. *Aud.:* 0-3 yrs.

From the publishers of *Ladybug,* this small, sturdy, 24-page pocket-sized magazine with rounded page edges is "for babies who love to read and for adults who love to read to them." It contains nursery rhymes and simple two- to six-page stories, songs, and poems that are just right for infants and toddlers and their caretakers. Gently but brightly designed, frequently by award-winning illustrators, this magazine strives to "begin a lifelong love of books," and is indeed an excellent introduction to reading. Stories are several sentences long, and some continue from issue to issue. The back cover features several pictures that summarize the stories and concepts inside. As a beginner magazine, *Babybug* teaches children simple concepts about the world around them and fosters an appreciation for being read to, which is the foundation for reading and learning. Stories and poems also adequately reflect a multicultural perspective. The magazine's cover offers tips for adults, offering guidance on child development and reading through a special web site. Appropriate for public libraries.

1255. *Beckett Game Strategyst.* Former titles (until 2010): *Beckett Pokemon Unofficial Collector;* (until 2007): *Beckett Anime & Manga;* (until 2006): *Beckett Anime Unofficial Collector;* (until 2004): *Beckett Anime Collector;* (until 2003): *Beckett Pokemon & Anime Collector; Beckett Pokemon Collector.* [ISSN: 2157-2240] 1999. m. USD 19.95 domestic; USD 29.95 Canada; USD 5.99 per issue. Ed(s): Sean Kavanagh, Erin Lang Masercola. Beckett Media Llc, 4635 McEwen Rd, Dallas, TX 75244; subscriptions@beckett.com; http://www.beckett.com. *Aud.:* Ems, Ga.

Truly a "trade" magazine for young gamers, this full-color publication is chock-full of in-depth articles that cover a myriad of aspects of the online gaming world, and that offer tips and insight into specific games. The main part of the magazine consists of a variety of different lengths on topics ranging from how to get parents involved in their children's gaming activities, to subjects such as the comparison of two *Star Wars*–themed games. The reviews section offers numerous software, product, and app reviews, while "Game Guides" gives readers specific tips on succeeding and excelling in a wide variety of games. Advertising and product reviews are clearly marked. Each issue also has a price guide that consists of an extensive listing of gaming cards and their values. Hobby store directory information and classified advertisements are also listed. Each issue includes special "Giveaways"—software or upgrades readers can redeem by code. This magazine will be a welcome and very popular title in public library children's or teen's sections.

1256. *Biography for Beginners: sketches for early readers.* [ISSN: 1081-4973] 1995. s-a. USD 40. Ed(s): Laurie Harris. Favorable Impressions, PO Box 69018, Pleasant Ridge, MI 48069; danh@favimp.com; http://www.favimp.com. Illus., index. Sample. Vol. ends: May/Oct. *Aud.:* 6-9 yrs.

This award-winning, 112-page, library-bound reference work is written specifically for early elementary readers. Published in two small-format, library-bound issues per year, each contains eight biographical sketches. They cover a variety of high-profile people, including children's authors, actors, artists, musicians, sports stars, political figures, and scientists. Written "at grade level 3," using bold headings, age-appropriate vocabulary, and plenty of white space, this sturdy publication engages curious minds with interesting information about people they would like to know more about. Unfamiliar terms are defined for young readers, and pronunciation help is provided. The five- to seven-page sketches are substantial and generously illustrated, and include quotations. Information about the subject's early life and schooling is included within each sketch. Cumulative name, subject, and birthday indexes are included in each issue, while upcoming biographies are announced. Recent entries include a wide variety of personalities, from Louisa May Alcott to the Duke and Duchess of Cambridge, to Mitt Romney. There is even a space reserved in the 2012 schedule for an Olympic champion (to be announced at time of writing). Addresses and web sites are included for classroom writing projects. There are several biographical sub-series available too, from presidents of the United States to inventors, and more. Appropriate for school and public libraries.

1257. *Boys' Life: the magazine for all boys.* [ISSN: 0006-8608] 1911. m. USD 24 domestic; USD 45 foreign. Ed(s): J D Owen. Boy Scouts of America, 1325 W. Walnut Hill Ln, PO Box 152079, Irving, TX 75015; http://www.bsa.scouting.org. Illus., adv. Microform: NBI; PQC. *Indexed:* A22, BRI, C37, ICM, IHTDI, MASUSE, P01, P02. *Bk. rev.:* Number and length vary. *Aud.:* 8-18 yrs.

Published by the Boy Scouts of America, this magazine is filled with captivating informational articles of varying length on topics such as adventures, nature, technology, health, and good works. It also includes historical and faith-based stories and comics, as well as puzzles, mazes, games, and other activities for the various ranks of scouts. A recent issue covered the sport of fishing in depth, and included a chart of common species of freshwater fish. Other lengthy articles cover such topics as cyber safety, avoiding drugs, and getting a job. Also included are fiction stories of interest to boys. Most page spreads are filled with short bites of information for the busy boy. One regular feature is "True Stories of Scouts in Action," while brief comics in every issue include "Fitness First," which offers tips for staying healthy and "Merit Badge Minute," which helps boys advance toward badges in various areas of life. Other regular features include reader mail, and a "heads up" guide to sports, movies, and other happenings. Boys can complete a craft in the "Workshop" section. The magazine also features a classified ad section known as the "Tradin' Post." Limited commercial advertising at the end of each issue is aimed at scouts and their leaders. Most suitable for personal subscriptions and scouts, but true to its name, this magazine is of value to all boys.

1258. *Boys' Quest.* [ISSN: 1078-9006] 1995. bi-m. USD 32.95. Ed(s): Marilyn Edwards. Bluffton News Publishing & Printing Co., PO Box 227, Bluffton, OH 45817. Illus. Vol. ends: Apr/May. *Indexed:* C37, ICM, P01. *Aud.:* 5-14 yrs.

This small-format, glossy, 50-page magazine prides itself on no violence and no advertising. Among its goals is to "promote the development of the individual spirit, self-esteem, and self-confidence through example and experiences." It does this by helping boys identify and develop their interests and abilities, and by building confidence through literacy and reading comprehension "through exciting, lively articles[,] and projects." The magazine is designed to draw readers in by promoting fun, brainy activities revolving around a single theme. A recent issue, for instance, highlighted the topic of "fathers and sons." Articles are written to be read, not simply scanned. The illustrations, while not sophisticated, are bold and eye-catching. Some feature stories are presented in comic strip form. In addition to feature articles, regular departments include "Science," in which boys can conduct hands-on experiments, "Workshop," which gives them a project to complete, such as a humane mouse trap, and "Chef's Corner," where boys can try their baking or cookout skills. The "Puzzles" section includes word searches, logic puzzles, riddles, math teasers, hobby-related games, and more. This magazine offers plenty of fiction articles and poetry associated with the topic for that issue. *Boys' Quest* is one of the few publications dedicated exclusively to boys and is thus highly recommended for both personal subscriptions and public libraries.

1259. *Business News for Kids: today shapes tomorrow.* 2007. w. Free. Business News for Kids, http://www.businessnewsforkids.com. *Aud.:* 8-14 yrs.

Like a mini *Barron's* for children, *Business News for Kids* is a richly informative online weekly. The site's founder believes that "an early business education can keep kids' interest alive in money matters" and that "one day these kids will run businesses or work for one to make our economy stronger." Developed by an individual with editorial feedback from his sons, this child-friendly resource is as educational as it is enjoyable to browse. It employs the advice and input of business and economics professionals and scholars and draws from a variety of primary sources. A simple and colorful layout makes it easy to find such things as daily stock quotes, currency exchange rates, and major stock market index figures. Besides the major news stories of the day, the main sectors followed are: automotive, technology, environment, computer and electronics, and daily commodities. A running archive is maintained in which children can access recent historical market data and browse detailed articles on various topics written in a highly readable manner; topics range from understanding personal credit history to the basics of supply and demand. Cross-references from article to article are frequent and helpful. Children can learn so much from this site: from understanding the concept of the word *economy* to learning the concrete steps for creating their own business plan. A sidebar includes business fun facts. This "easy to understand business and economy news platform for kids of all ages" is free (no commercial use is permitted). It is highly recommended for promotion in libraries.

1260. *Calliope (Peru): exploring world history.* Formerly (until 1990): *Classical Calliope.* [ISSN: 1050-7086] 1981. 9x/yr. USD 33.95 domestic; USD 48.95 foreign. Ed(s): Rosalie F Baker, Charles Baker. Cobblestone Publishing Company, 30 Grove St, Ste C, Peterborough, NH 03458; custsvc@cobblestone.mv.com; http://www.cobblestonepub.com. Illus., index. Vol. ends: May. *Indexed:* A22, AmHI, BRI, ICM, MASUSE, P01. *Bk. rev.:* 5, 50-75 words. *Aud.:* 9-14 yrs.

This highly engaging, 50-page Parents' Choice Award–winning magazine allows elementary and middle school readers to explore world history amid stunning photographs and high-quality illustrations. Each issue covers, in depth, a particular topic or figure in history, with all the departments and features revolving around that topic. A recent themed issue on Greek mythology included an article comparing the *Iliad* and the *Odyssey,* a play involving the Cyclops, and several archaeological articles, as well as related suggested activities, quizzes, and puzzles. Regular departments include "Musings," "Map," "Fun with Words" (word origins and uses), and "Off the Shelf" (book reviews for further reading). Each issue also includes an informational "Ask CALLIOPE" page. Additional suggested resources are included in "On the Net," and "From Past to Present" makes the theme topic relevant to today. An annual subject index lists previous issues by theme, and all back issues are available online and fully searchable by registered subscribers. This magazine contains no advertisements. An advisory board made up of educational and subject specialists ensures the quality of this publication. Each issue also has an academic consulting editor. Highly recommended for both school and public libraries.

1261. *Chickadee.* [ISSN: 0707-4611] 1979. 10x/yr. CAD 34.95 in US & Canada; CAD 64.95 elsewhere. Ed(s): Mandy Ng. Bayard Canada, Owlkids, 10 Lower Spadina Ave, Ste 400, Toronto, ON M5V 2Z2, Canada; bayard@owl.on.ca; http://www.owlkids.com/. Illus., index, adv. Sample. Vol. ends: Dec. *Indexed:* BRI, C37, CBCARef, ICM, P01. *Bk. rev.:* Number and length vary. *Aud.:* 6-9 yrs.

A winner of several distinguished achievement awards, this bright and whimsical magazine helps early elementary school children learn about the world around them. It does this by bringing the world of nature, science, art, and culture to the beginning reader through factual and fiction articles, and more. Richly illustrated with cartoons, photographs, large typeface, and set off by plenty of white space, each issue presents a theme with humor and interesting facts. The emphasis is on fun. Regular departments include, "What Is It?," "Did You Know?," and "Animal of the Month." Children's tough science questions are addressed in the "Dr. Zed Science" page. Discovery pages consist of factual articles on science, geography, or culture. Each issue also includes a fiction story of approximately 500 to 1,000 words as well as a variety of puzzles, comics, crafts, and brief topic-related book reviews. Reader-submitted riddles and artwork make up "Chick and DEE's Clubhouse" section. There is some advertising. Recommended for school and public libraries, as well as personal subscriptions.

1262. *ChildArt.* [ISSN: 1096-9020] 1998. q. USD 30 domestic; USD 40 foreign. Ed(s): Carrie Foix, Ashfaq Ishaq. International Child Art Foundation, PO Box 58133, Washington, DC 20037; http://www.icaf.org/. Adv. Sample. *Indexed:* BRI, P01. *Aud.:* 8-12 yrs.

The mission of the International Child Art Foundation is "to prepare children for a creative and cooperative future," recognizing that art is the key to universal communication and understanding among cultures. *ChildArt* and its parent foundation encourage the nourishment of critical thinking skills and creativity in the pre-teen child, the age at which the child is most open to expansion and development. We live in the age of creativity, so this magazine "endeavors to create peace, utilizing the power of the arts to develop the innate creativity and intrinsic empathy of children." Realizing the importance of art and physical activity in addition to the hard disciplines, *ChildArt* "invites readers to explore different ways of being creative and to inspire artistry in everything they do." Issue themes are determined and planned by children, who then weave creativity and a sense of global understanding into each of them. Most content relates to specific peace and art activities around the globe, with articles about real-life accomplishments and groundbreaking events. More prominent now are contributions from famous world leaders and artists, such as Betty Ford or Eric Carle, for example. The magazine regularly features crafts and activities related to a particular theme. Cooperation and group activities are particularly encouraged. A complete full-color sample issue is available for download on the publisher's web site. Perhaps most appropriate in the classroom and school libraries, but sure to be of value in public libraries as well.

1263. *Chirp.* Formerly: *Tree House.* [ISSN: 1206-4580] 1992. 10x/yr. CAD 34.95 in US & Canada; CAD 64.95 foreign. Ed(s): Jackie Farquhar. Bayard Canada, Owlkids, 10 Lower Spadina Ave, Ste 400, Toronto, ON M5V 2Z2, Canada; bayard@owl.on.ca; http://www.owlkids.com/. Illus. Sample. *Bk. rev.:* Number and length vary. *Aud.:* 3-6 yrs.

A winner of several distinguished achievement awards and a Parents' Choice Honor Award, this publication from Bayard Canada offers "stories, crafts, comics, jokes and puzzles" for the youngest readers. It contains a variety of challenges and exciting activities for the various ability levels present in this very early age group. Each issue is loosely themed; one recent issue focused on nighttime, for example. The gentle but colorfully illustrated two-page comic, "Chirp and Friends," draws the very young child into reading. While "Let's Read" is a picturebook story made for readers to enjoy with their parents or caretakers, "Look and Learn" offers older readers new vocabulary on a particular topic related to the issue's theme. "Let's Move" gets children up and moving via a song and dance, while "Take a Trip" takes young readers to other cultures, even teaching them some foreign vocabulary. "Playhouse" features reader contributions and contest winners; and crafts, recipes, puzzles, and riddles round out each issue. This magazine promotes organic living and green values, and it encourages physical activity and movement. *Chirp* draws on Canada's leading parenting experts, and also employs an advisory committee of

25 parents from across North America. Some issues include very short book reviews. This magazine includes some tear-out and drawing pages. Nonetheless it is appropriate for public libraries, as well as personal subscriptions.

1264. *Click: opening windows for young minds.* [ISSN: 1094-4273] 1998. 9x/yr. USD 33.95 domestic; USD 48.95 foreign. ePals Publishing Company, 30 Grove St, Ste C, Peterborough, NH 03458; customerservice@caruspub.com; http://www.cricketmag.com. Illus., adv. Sample. Vol. ends: Dec. *Indexed:* ICM, P01. *Bk. rev.:* 12-16, length varies. *Aud.:* 3-6 yrs.

This glossy, 40-page magazine opens up the world of science, nature, history, and culture for the most elementary of learners. This is a joint publication of the Cricket Group and *Smithsonian Magazine,* and its themed issues are guided by comic-strip character "Click" the Mouse and his friends, as he leads children on different discovery adventures. Informational, fact-filled articles cover science, technology, and the surrounding world, aiming to satisfy a child's natural curiosity. For example, a recent issue presented readers with astronomy. Substantial theme-related stories satisfy the eager reader as well. This large-print magazine is generously illustrated with photographs and paintings alike. Articles vary in length and reading level, with fiction stories up to 1,000–1,200 words. The magazine also offers readers a "read together" feature that allows children to log in and listen as they read the longer pieces. End-of-issue take-out pages double as games for the reader. Special issues cover biographies. A helpful parent's companion section includes follow-up activities, plus additional related book titles. Appropriate for public libraries or individual subscriptions.

1265. *Cobblestone: discover American history.* [ISSN: 0199-5197] 1980. 9x/yr. USD 33.95 domestic; USD 48.95 foreign. Ed(s): Meg Chorlian. ePals Publishing Company, 30 Grove St, Ste C, Peterborough, NH 03458; customerservice@caruspub.com; http://www.cricketmag.com. Illus., index. Circ: 31000. Vol. ends: Dec. *Indexed:* A22, BRI, ICM, MASUSE, P01, P02. *Bk. rev.:* 10, length varies. *Aud.:* 9-14 yrs.

This richly illustrated, award-winning 50-page magazine for upper elementary and junior high school students focuses on American history. Issues are themed, exploring a single, highly-focused topic. Departments include the comic "Did You Know?," "The Past is Present," which brings history to life, and "Going Global," which compares cultures. "Digging Deeper" provides further reading, both in books and online; some reviews are provided by young readers. The "Fast Facts" and "Did You Know?" sidebars highlight additional snippets of information throughout the magazine. A recent issue focused on early explorers and presents numerous lengthy and factual articles and related topics, such as trade commodities. The magazine also offers theme-related craft ideas, puzzles, comics, brainteasers, and opportunity for reader feedback. An annual subject index points readers to the appropriately themed issues for the previous year, and all issues are available online and fully searchable by registered subscribers. Previous issues from the archive which are related to the topic are also listed for reference. This magazine contains no advertisements. An advisory board made up of educational and subject specialists ensures the quality of this publication. Each issue also has an academic consulting editor. Highly recommended for both school and public libraries.

1266. *Creative Kids: the national voice for kids.* Formerly (until 1986): *Chart Your Course.* [ISSN: 0892-9599] 1980. q. USD 19.95 domestic; USD 39.95 foreign. Ed(s): Lacy Compton. Prufrock Press Inc., PO Box 8813, Waco, TX 76714; info@prufrock.com; http://www.prufrock.com. Illus., adv. Vol. ends: Summer. *Indexed:* BRI, MASUSE. *Bk. rev.:* Number and length vary. *Aud.:* 8-14 yrs.

This remarkable 52-page magazine is created cover-to-cover by children; even its advisory board is composed entirely of children from around the world. Inside the pages of this small-format, understated publication are pages and pages of original fiction stories, essays (including photo essays), informational articles, poetry, artwork, puzzles, teasers, recipes, and other creative works submitted exclusively by child readers. Regular departments include "Write-On" (an opinion column) and "Under Review," which is a forum for children's book reviews (each issue features two to four substantial reviews of approximately 200–400 words). Children can find projects to undertake on their own in the "DIY" section, while "Science & Math Corner" features informational articles or essays they have written on hot topics in the sci-tech world. Each issue cover displays the art of children whose brief biographies appear inside, while additional reader artwork appears in the gallery on the inside covers. Opportunities for input on contest ideas are also provided. The summer issue is extra large. Like a "little magazine" for children, this publication, now in full color, is highly recommended for public libraries.

1267. Cricket: the realm of imagination. [ISSN: 0090-6034] 1973. 9x/yr. USD 33.95. ePals Publishing Company, 30 Grove St, Ste C, Peterborough, NH 03458; customerservice@caruspub.com; http://www.cricketmag.com. Illus., adv. Sample. Vol. ends: Jul/Aug. Indexed: A22, ICM, P01. Aud.: 9-14 yrs.

Winner of numerous awards, this beautifully illustrated, 50-page magazine for older elementary through junior high school readers specializes in literature, poetry, science fiction, folk tales, and fantasy, as well as historical and contemporary fiction. All content is that of internationally respected writers and artists. Substantial factual and scientific articles are presented as well. Most pieces run several pages in length and are as varied by topic as they are by illustrative style. Some fiction pieces run serially, spanning several issues. Regular features include "The Letterbox," which prints a large number of reader letters; "Favorite First Sentences," submitted by readers; "Cricket Country," a regular comic strip; and the closing "Old Cricket Says," which imparts wisdom on a topic. Readers vie for a spot in the "Cricket League," which presents story, photo, and poetry contest winners. The ever-present cartoon cricket character continues to reside in the margins, explaining unfamiliar terms to the reader. Each issue also offers plenty of joke and puzzle pastimes. A sample issue is available for viewing online. No library collection for children should be without this magazine.

1268. Dig. Formerly (until 2001): Archaeology's Dig. [ISSN: 1539-7130] 1999. 9x/yr. USD 33.95 domestic; USD 48.95 foreign. Ed(s): Rosalie Baker. ePals Publishing Company, 30 Grove St, Ste C, Peterborough, NH 03458; customerservice@caruspub.com; http://www.cricketmag.com. Illus. Sample. Vol. ends: Nov/Dec. Indexed: BRI, ICM, P01, P02. Bk. rev.: 3-5, 20-40 words. Aud.: 9-14 yrs.

Published in partnership with Archaeology Magazine, this glossy, richly illustrated 34-page publication introduces children to the world of history, culture, and anthropology. Lengthy feature articles are supported by stunning photographs and colorful illustrations, and are supplemented by related crafts and activities. A recent issue, for example, focused on board games throughout the millennia. Regular departments include "Ask Dr. Dig," which answers children's questions about archaeology, and "Stones and Bones," which are short pieces covering news, discoveries, facts, and myths on culture and history. Each month, the one-page "Art-i-facts" column highlights a "fantastic factoid about ancient sites, historical objects, and amazing discoveries." Brief book and web reviews are included in "Dig Facts." Also included are games, puzzles, and opportunities to submit artwork in "Dig Stuff." Additional activities, including a state-by-state guide to real archaeological events for readers to explore, are available on Dig's web site. This magazine contains no advertisements. An advisory board made up of educational and subject specialists ensures the quality of this publication. Each issue also has an academic consulting editor. Highly recommended for public libraries and personal subscriptions.

1269. Discovery Box. [ISSN: 1366-9028] 1995. 10x/yr. EUR 65 in Europe; EUR 72 elsewhere. Ed(s): Christine Auberger. Bayard Presse, 3-5 Rue Bayard, Paris, 75393 Cedex 08, France; redactions@bayard-presse.com; http://www.bayardpresse.com. Illus., adv. Sample. Aud.: 9-12 yrs.

Like its sister publications, this beautifully designed magazine is "more than a book!" It is a high-gloss, 56-page "journey through nature, science and history," designed to "stimulate children's curiosity and whet their appetite for learning." Each issue opens with a stunning "Photo Shoot" that takes readers onto a geographical or scientific adventure. Main features include well-researched articles on animals in their habitat, almanac-like articles on world regions (including culture and sport), and history and science articles, complete with experiments and their results. All are supplemented by lovely photographs and whimsical comics. "Fun Facts" offers snippets of history, science, and culture, and "Zoom In" takes readers on a close-up journey into a science, history, or nature topic, such as the human body. "Life Story" consists of a real-life article of a geographical or animal nature, while "Quick Look" is a two-page spread profiling a particular topic. A span of several DIY pages lets children try their

hand at crafts, recipes, experiments, and projects that help them discover nature, science, history, and the world around them up close. Several comic strips cover history and science while games, activities, and recipes round out the magazine. Most issues include also a magnificent full-color foldout poster as well as collectible pull-out cards. Multicultural diversity seems to be adequately represented. The back cover features a mini-quiz about the contents inside. Highly recommended for public libraries and great to help with school projects at home.

1270. Discovery Girls: a magazine created by girls, for girls. [ISSN: 1535-3230] 2000. bi-m. USD 22.95 domestic; USD 26 Canada; USD 32 elsewhere. Discovery Girls, 4300 Stevens Creek Blvd, Ste 190, San Jose, CA 95129. Illus., adv. Vol. ends: Oct. Indexed: ICM. Bk. rev.: Number and length vary. Aud.: 8-13 yrs.

Probably the largest-circulation title dedicated exclusively to pre-teen girls and a winner of several awards, this glossy bimonthly provides "a voice and a forum" for this delicate age group. Over half the content of this popular, 60-page magazine is actually generated by girls between the ages of 8 and 12, and all the girls depicted on its pages are readers. Recent issues have featured real readers by state, examining their trends, fashions, dreams, hobbies, and lingo. Most issues contain at least one article focusing on friendship, while quizzes let girls test their social savvy. Regular departments encouraging reader participation include "The Great Debate," which discusses topics such as bedtimes and summer homework. Other regular sections cover health and beauty and etiquette, while girls get to share their embarrassing moments. "The Worst Day" is place where girls can share their life-changing moments in essay form. Feature articles cover topics such as self-confidence and creativity. Each issue also includes a two-page fashion layout as well as a celebrity spread. This magazine also includes games, puzzles, and book and product reviews, stories, poems, and essays are solicited. Real girls have the opportunity to try for an appearance on the cover. A special, separately-priced seventh issue ("Survival Guide") is also published in June. Although somewhat more fashion- and pop-culture–oriented than similar girls' magazines, this is nonetheless a quality publication with substantial content. Includes advertising (which is clearly labeled as such). Recommended for public libraries.

1271. Faces: people, places, & cultures. Formerly: Faces Rocks. [ISSN: 0749-1387] 1984. 9x/yr. USD 33.95 domestic; USD 48.95 foreign. Ed(s): Marianne Carus, Elizabeth Crooker Carpentiere. ePals Publishing Company, 30 Grove St, Ste C, Peterborough, NH 03458; customerservice@caruspub.com; http://www.cricketmag.com. Illus., index. Circ: 12000 Paid. Indexed: A22, BRI, ICM, MASUSE, P01. Bk. rev.: 5, 35-50 words. Aud.: 9-14 yrs.

This award-winning 50-page publication introduces middle-grade readers to the beliefs, lifestyles, and cultures of people around the world. Glossy, colorful, thematic issues focus on a variety of cultures and countries. Each issue explores a theme in-depth, through informational articles, historical fiction, folk tales, photographs, maps, time lines, recipes, puzzles, crafts, and more. Regular departments include "High 5" (fascinating facts about the theme topic), "At a Glance," and a one-box comic called "Face Facts," a single-frame cartoon that offers a little-known fact or piece of triva related to the theme topic. "Ask Faces" allows readers to ask general questions about culture, geography, and science, while "Art Connection" suggests to readers a tie-in activity to the theme topic. Contests, reader polls, and guest book reviews of 100–200 words provide opportunities for reader participation. Additional content is available to subscribers online. This magazine contains no advertisements. An advisory board made up of educational and subject specialists ensures the quality of this publication. Each issue also has an academic consulting editor and is extensively indexed by various agencies. Highly recommended for both school and public libraries.

1272. Focus on the Family Clubhouse. [ISSN: 0895-1136] 1988. m. USD 19.99. Ed(s): Jesse Florea. Focus on the Family, 8605 Explorer Dr, Colorado Springs, CO 80920; http://www.family.org. Illus. Aud.: 8-14 yrs.

This engaging and fun, non-denominational Christian magazine for school-age children encourages them to follow their faith and to participate in activities with their families to foster closeness. It is written in a manner highly relevant to today's tween, containing exciting fiction stories, real-life accounts and biographies, and challenging puzzles and brainteasers. Regular departments include "Adventures in Odyssey," a series of science mystery stories with a Biblical tie-in, and "Adventures of Average Boy," consisting of short whimsical stories. This 32-page magazine also features advice pages such as "U Ask," as well as several reader-mail pages. Sprinkled throughout the engaging stories and inspirational articles is additional lighthearted content such as recipes, crafts, and reader-submitted jokes in "U Joke." The regular entertainment page, "High Voltage," answers children's pop-culture questions. Scripture is quoted frequently in relation to content. Advertising is minimal. Recommended for Christian faith-based school libraries and some public libraries as appropriate.

1273. Focus on the Family Clubhouse Jr. 1988. m. USD 19.99. Focus on the Family, 8605 Explorer Dr, Colorado Springs, CO 80920; http://www.family.org. Illus., adv. Circ: 90000 Paid. *Aud.*: 4-8 yrs.

A fun-filled, little-sister publication to *Clubhouse,* this 32-page magazine emphasizes character to very young children, within the context of family and based on Christian faith and values. It includes fiction stories of varying lengths, informational articles, games, crafts, contests and puzzles, and jokes and riddles, as well as a comic strip called "Poppy and Sam." A section called "You Said It" features reader mail and art. Stories teach children to get along well with others and to build strong and righteous relationships with their families, friends, and communities. Also included are some science, nature, and technology articles that incorporate faith. Issues are built loosely around a theme; for instance, a recent issue focused on fathers and their importance. A "WebExtras" page points to the magazine web site for additional activities. Some issues contain several pages of seatwork type activity also. Recommended for Christian faith-based school libraries and public libraries where appropriate.

1274. Fun for Kidz. [ISSN: 1536-898X] 2002. bi-m. USD 32.95. Ed(s): Marilyn Edwards. Bluffton News Publishing & Printing Co., 103 N Main St, Bluffton, OH 45817-0164. *Indexed:* BRI, C37, ICM, P01. *Aud.*: 5-14 yrs.

This small-format, glossy, 50-page magazine prides itself on no violence and no advertising. Its philosophy, in part, is to "encourage literacy and reading comprehension" and to instill traditional family values by providing "exciting, lively articles and projects." As a companion to its sister publications *Boys' Quest* and *Hopscotch for Girls, Fun for Kidz* encourages children to follow directions and solve problems by providing challenging puzzles and activities with real-life applications and meaning. Regular departments include "Science," in which children can conduct experiments or play games that help them learn facts. "Workshop" provides children with fun and tangible projects to complete. Of course, there are plenty of entertaining jokes and puzzles and comics too, as well as recipes. This magazine also includes plenty of fiction articles and poetry associated with the topic for that issue. A recent issue themed on horses offered fiction stories, tips on grooming, insights into horse psychology, instructions on how to draw a horse, and a sawhorse building project. All three publications from the Bluffton News Publishing and Printing Company are unique in their content and approach, and are therefore highly recommended for personal subscriptions, as well as for public libraries.

1275. Fun to Learn - Friends. Formerly (until 2010): *Fun to Learn - Playroom;* (until 2001): *Preschool Playroom.* [ISSN: 2155-5818] 2001. 8x/yr. USD 39.92 domestic. Ed(s): Sue Porritt. Redan Publishing, Inc., 908 Oak Tree Rd, Ste H, S Plainfield, NJ 07080; customerservice@redan.com; http://www.redan.com. Illus. *Aud.*: 2-6 yrs.

As a friend to many, this very bright and colorful magazine continues to feature familiar cartoon characters between its pages, from *Curious George, Scooby Doo,* and *Max & Ruby* to *Sesame Street* and others within its activity-filled pages. The Redan *Fun to Learn* suite of magazines pledges to "make learning fun," and aims to develop children's reading, math, cognitive, creative, and fine motor skills. Indeed, the magazine promotes early reading by featuring "read-together" stories and stories with pictures. It also includes lessons on how to draw and even promotes the fading art of penmanship. The primary colors are sure to capture anyone who picks up an issue. Each issue includes a 16-page, character-sponsored central workbook "designed to encourage practice in early learning skills." It contains alphabet, counting, coloring, and matching games and mazes, as well as parent–child activities. Readers may also send in artwork.

The proportionately high workbook nature of this publication may make it more suitable for preschools, homeschoolers, and individual subscribers, but it continues to remain hugely popular in public libraries.

Girls' Life. See Teenagers section.

1276. Highlights for Children: fun with a purpose. Incorporates (1953-1960): *Children's Activities;* Which was formerly (until 1953): *Children's Activities for Home and School.* [ISSN: 0018-165X] 1946. m. USD 34.44 domestic; USD 48.76 Canada. Ed(s): Christine French Cully. Highlights for Children, Inc., 1800 Watermark Dr, Columbus, OH 43216-0269; eds@highlights.com; http://www.highlights.com. Illus., index. Sample. Vol. ends: Dec. Microform: PQC. *Indexed:* A22, BRI, ICM, P01. *Aud.*: 6-12 yrs.

Nearing its seventh decade and the winner of numerous awards, including one from the National Conference of Christians and Jews, this 44-page classic continues to maintain high standards with excellent stories, articles, activities, and crafts. The magazine's mission is dedicated in part to "helping children grow in basic skills and knowledge, in creativeness, in ability to think and reason, in sensitivity to others, and in high ideals." The three main sections continue to be: "Fun to Read," "Fun to Do," and "Fun Things from You." Original pictures, poetry, and stories are solicited from readers in "Your Own Pages," while "Dear Highlights" gives readers an opportunity to express their concerns. The updated "Goofus and Gallant" now also includes readers' comments, while the longstanding "Hidden Pictures," "The Timbertoes," and "What's Wrong?" continue to charm especially the younger readers. "My Sci" gets children thinking about science concepts, and "Brain Play" gets kids thinking about everything under the sun. Some faith-based content is presented, especially during holidays. A special color-coded key in the table of contents guides parents and teachers to appropriate early, moderate, and advanced reading sections and indicates the "creative & critical thinking" and "social & emotional learning" rating of each section. A subscription to *Highlights for Children* grants access to http://HighlightsKids.com, where readers can access additional features. Highly recommended for personal subscriptions, but being "designed for use in the classroom," it is also indispensable for school and public libraries.

1277. Highlights High Five: celebrating early childhood. [ISSN: 1943-1465] 2007. m. USD 29.64 domestic. Ed(s): Christine French Cully. Highlights for Children, Inc., 1800 Watermark Dr, Columbus, OH 43216-0269; eds@highlights.com; http://www.highlights.com. Illus. Sample. *Aud.*: 2-6 yrs.

Only five years old, this high-quality offshoot of *Highlights* that "celebrates the early years of childhood" has already won several awards, including Parent's Choice and Preschool Periodical of the Year. Its mission in part is to encourage children's natural sense of wonder; promote their reasoning and self-expression, and their love of language; and help them grow in self-confidence. Its three main sections consist of "Reading," containing brief stories and poems; "Puzzles" (matching games, and silly pages to build observational skills); and "Activities," consisting of crafts, nutritional recipes, and other activities such as action rhymes to get children up and moving. The comic strip "The Adventures of Spot" resembles "The Timbertoes" in its simplicity and style. This magazine also contains a slightly simpler "My First Hidden Pictures" than what is found in its big sister magazine. It also regularly includes a read-aloud story in English and Spanish, which includes some vocabulary. Counting games, riddles, mazes, action rhymes, and silly pictures round out the magazine—which is sure to delight emerging readers and learners. Fold-out pages and crafts conclude each issue, and the back cover consists of an art gallery of pictures for children to find inside. Illustrations consist of a wide variety of styles and depict diversity adequately. This magazine is "designed for use in all the classrooms of early childhood, including daycare centers, preschools, schools, and the home." Highly recommended for personal subscriptions, but also indispensable for school and public libraries.

1278. Hopscotch (Bluffton): for girls. [ISSN: 1044-0488] 1989. bi-m. USD 32.95. Ed(s): Marilyn Edwards. Bluffton News Publishing & Printing Co., 103 N Main St, Bluffton, OH 45817-0164. Illus., adv. Sample. Vol. ends: Apr/May. *Indexed:* ICM, P01, P02. *Aud.*: 5-14 yrs.

This small-format, glossy, 50-page magazine prides itself on "no teen themes" and no advertising. Among its goals is to "identify and develop the...interests and individual abilities" of girls. It was created to "challenge young girls...to enjoy and make the utmost of those few and precious years of childhood." Girls with a wholesome grounding can more easily handle the pressures and difficulties that inevitably follow in adolescence. This magazine allows them to explore their own interests and abilities without the influence of the fast-paced world or peer pressure. It promotes old-fashioned values and skills such as handwriting a letter or conducting oneself with poise. Like its two companion publications from Bluffton, *Hopscotch* is meant "to be read, not scanned." Besides "Story Time," regular features include "Science," featuring hands-on experiments, "Potsy's Pen Pal Club," as well as reader mail in "Potsy's Post Office." "Craft" offers in-depth projects, such as building a Newton's Cradle. This magazine also includes plenty of fiction and nonfiction articles and poetry associated with the topic for that issue. Contained within its pages also are entertaining jokes and comics, personal quizzes, puzzles, brain-teasers, how-to's, and other activities, such as crafts and recipes with plenty of girl-appeal. Highly recommended for personal subscriptions, but also appropriate for public libraries.

1279. Humpty Dumpty Magazine. Formerly (until 1979): *Humpty Dumpty's Magazine for Little Children.* [ISSN: 0273-7590] 1952. bi-m. USD 19.98 domestic. Ed(s): Terry Webb Harshman. Children's Better Health Institute, 1100 Waterway Blvd, Indianapolis, IN 46202; editor@saturdayeveningpost.com; http://www.uskidsmags.com. Illus., index, adv. Vol. ends: Dec. Microform: PQC. *Indexed:* A22, BRI, ICM, P01. *Aud.:* 5-7 yrs.

The mission of this longstanding and award-winning newsprint magazine from *US Kids* is "to promote the healthy physical, educational, creative, social, and emotional growth of children in a format that is engaging, stimulating, and entertaining..." It employs an editorial advisory board that includes pediatricians and a certified dietician. Separated into three main sections called "I Can Read," "Things to See," and "I Can Do," each issue contains fiction, poetry, informational health articles, and easy science activities based on changing theme. Also included are coloring pages, spelling words, matching games, and puzzles, as well as crafts and recipes. The "Humpty Dumpty" character features in a teaching comic that runs throughout the issue. A very helpful regular feature is the "Ask Doctor Cory" column, which answers questions about very young readers' health concerns. In "Kids Helping Kids," readers can also now send in questions for other children's advice. This 36-page magazine includes a gallery of reader-submitted artwork and regular art contests. Because of the workbook nature of many of the activities in this magazine, it may be best suited for personal subscriptions, but it will continue to be popular in public libraries as well.

1280. Iguana: lee discubre disfruta. [ISSN: 1554-916X] 2005. m. USD 29.95 domestic; USD 29.95 Puerto Rico; USD 39.95 in Canada & Mexico. NicaGal LLC, PO Box 26432, Scottsdale, AZ 85255. Illus. *Aud.:* 7-12 yrs.

A winner of several awards, this 32-page, full-color, Spanish-language magazine, now published monthly, encourages children to "read, discover, and enjoy!" Its primary purpose is to preserve and promote a love of the Spanish language and pride in Latino culture. It "informs, instructs, and entertains" with original fiction stories and educational articles of varying length on science, mathematics, history, the natural world, arts, and culture. Everything is authored in Spanish; as a policy, the magazine does not publish translations. The inside front cover includes a short fact sheet on a topic, "Sabias Que?," while "Invenciones que Cambiaron el Mundo" spotlights life-changing inventions and discoveries. Another department greets children around the world, in "Ninos Alrededor del Mundo," while mythology is brought to life in a two-page regular comic, "Mitologia." Also included are one-page biographies of prominent individuals in the Hispanic and Latino world. And the animal kingdom is explored in "El Reino Animal." Children can try easy recipes in "La Cocina Chiquita," as well as try their hand at simple science experiments and crafts (or "manualidades"). The inside back cover provides "disfrutando" in the form of comics and a puzzle. Readers are encouraged to submit art and poetry. This important magazine is highly recommended for public libraries in areas with larger Hispanic populations.

1281. Indy Kids. [ISSN: 1943-1031] 2005. 5x/yr. Individuals, USD 10. Indymedia, PO Box 2281, New York, NY 10163; http://www.indymedia.org. *Bk. rev.:* 1-2. *Aud.:* Ems.

Now in its seventh year, this online bimonthly fills a niche in children's periodicals. Although politically unaffiliated, this "free paper for free kids" is activist in nature. Its aim is to "inform children on current news and world events" and to inspire in them a "passion for social justice and learning." Beautifully designed and sporting a clear and spare layout, this online publication is a pleasure to navigate with its highly interesting and sometimes provocative reading. Regular content is contributed by both children and adults, and it includes lengthy articles in sections labeled "Nation & World" and "Culture & Activism." Also included are science briefs, articles on food and nutrition, and a regular profile on an individual from another country, complete with a brief language lesson. Children are encouraged to provide feedback to posted news articles, and they frequently sound off in letters or in "Your Turn." Recent topics of discussion have included thoughts on the 9/11 anniversary and school segregation. Every issue includes a quick "Where in the World?" geography quiz that references locations mentioned in that issue's articles. Puzzles and games are tied directly to content; for example, a math story problem may revolve around the number of unemployed. This newspaper also includes lighter fare such as movie, documentary, and book reviews and recipes. The site is searchable, and a complete downloadable archive of past issues is freely available. One may opt to subscribe to the print edition for a nominal additional cost that covers mailing. This publication is funded by several progressive foundation grants and donors, but this information is clearly disclosed. The Association for Library Service to Children (ALSC, a division of The American Library Association) added *IndyKids!* to its "Great Websites for Kids" list in 2011. Recommended for public libraries.

1282. Jack and Jill. [ISSN: 0021-3829] 1938. bi-m. USD 19.98. Ed(s): Steven Slon. Children's Better Health Institute, 1100 Waterway Blvd, Indianapolis, IN 46202; editor@saturdayeveningpost.com; http://www.uskidsmags.com. Illus., adv. Microform: PQC. *Indexed:* A22, BRI, ICM, MASUSE, P01. *Bk. rev.:* Number and length vary. *Aud.:* 8-12 yrs.

One of the few remaining *US Kids* titles, this award-winning, 36-page magazine "promotes the healthy physical, educational, creative, social and emotional growth" of elementary-school-age readers. It employs an editorial advisory board that includes pediatricians and a certified dietician. This magazine recently revamped its look to emphasize a "green" attitude and "cool" content in an eye-catching layout that adequately represents multiculturalism and more up-to-date technology. Laid out in three main sections—"Stories & Articles," "Things to Do," and "Regular Features"—each issue contains well-illustrated informational, biographical, how-to, and fictional articles that combine fun with learning. Readers are provided with recipes, crafts, puzzles, games, and tips on exploring new skills, such as how to ride a mountain bike or conduct a science experiment. This magazine includes a jokes and riddles department with reader contributions, as well as a reader poetry page. It also allows for reader-submitted artwork and holds regular art contests. A product review page includes "good reads." Another regular feature includes the "Ask Dr. Cory" column, which answers questions on children's health concerns. In "Kids Helping Kids," readers can now also send in questions for other children's advice. Because of the workbook nature of some of the activities in this magazine, it may be best suited for personal subscriptions, but it will remain popular in public libraries as well.

1283. Junior Baseball. Formerly (until Jan.1999): *Junior League Baseball.* [ISSN: 1522-8460] 1996. bi-m. USD 17.70 domestic; USD 27.70 in Canada & Mexico; USD 47.70 elsewhere. Ed(s): Jim Beecher. JSAN Publishing LLC, 14 Woodway Ln, Wilton, CT 06897; publisher@juniorbaseball.com. Illus., adv. Vol. ends: Nov/Dec. *Bk. rev.:* 8-10, 20 words. *Aud.:* 5-17 yrs.

This 42-page trade-type magazine is directed at young players and their parents and coaches. Articles cover a range of topics from technique and safety to ethics, as well as real-life accounts of personalities and teams. A large portion of each issue consists of extensive, step-by-step tip pages on offense, defense, and pitching. Some columns are reserved for specific age groups: those labeled "Rookie Club" are meant for five- to eight-year-old readers, while "Triple A Squad" is aimed at older boys. This magazine also includes interviews with and biographies of famous players in "When I Was A Kid." In "Fun Food &

Fitness," boys are offered choices for healthy living and recipes. The regular "Collector's Corner" gives baseball enthusiasts advice on excelling in the quieter side of the sport. The "Coaches Clinics" department offers extensive tips on everything from specific play drills to earning players' respect, and the final column, "In the Stands," offers parenting and coaching advice from a sports psychologist. Product and book reviews are also included, while the "Game Room" provides puzzles for various age groups as well as a "Make The Call" story situation. A baseball equipment buyers' guide is published annually as part of one issue. Highly recommended for public libraries.

1284. *Kayak: Canada's history for kids.* [ISSN: 1712-3984] 2004. q. USD 29.98 domestic; USD 37.95 United States; USD 44.95 elsewhere. Ed(s): Nancy Payne. Canada's National History Society, University of Winnipeg, Bryce Hall, Main Fl, 515 Portage Ave, Winnipeg, MB R3B 2E9, Canada; http://www.historysociety.ca. Illus. Sample. *Indexed:* C37, P01. *Aud.:* 7-11 yrs.

This magazine is published by Canada's National History Society, and its mission is to introduce children to Canada's rich history, natural resources, and notable people through fresh writing and playful, animation-rich design. Each issue of this 36-page, pocket-size magazine centers on a particular theme, but it encompasses a variety of time periods, geographic locations, and cultural perspectives. For instance, a recent issue featured the *Titanic* disaster as its cover story, but included other sea disaster feature articles, fiction stories, and sidebars. Additionally, the regular departments "History Mystery" and "Backyard History" make history real to children, while "Then and Now" and "Here and There" show them that things were not always better in another time and place. The magazine celebrates diversity and gives children an appreciation of their own living conditions and the culture within their own backyards, as well as exposing them to that which may be different from their own. For instance, the magazine's title is subtitled with its Inuktitut translation. Word games, puzzles, jokes, fun facts, and contests are also included in every issue. Fact pages are clearly marked. Some issues vary slightly in size and format. Recommended for public libraries throughout North America.

1285. *Kids Discover.* [ISSN: 1054-2868] 1991. m. USD 26.95. Kids Discover, 149 5th Ave, 12th Fl, New York, NY 10010. Illus. *Indexed:* BRI, ICM, MASUSE, P01. *Aud.:* 6-12 yrs.

A winner of several major awards, this 20-page magazine is written for elementary and junior high school–age readers. It covers a wide variety of subject areas, including science, nature, technology, culture, and history. Like a mini-course, each issue is devoted in-depth to a single topic, and includes numerous short articles, diagrams, and activities concerning the theme. Color photographs and illustrations of a variety of styles are abundant and highly engaging. Also included are charts, timelines, and brief fact boxes. Each issue closes with do-it-yourself activities such as crafts and recipes, quizzes, puzzles, brainteasers, and games to reinforce learning. Also included is a list of further reading for both adults and children. Educational and subject consultants guide each issue. Although the publication is not very lengthy, it is densely printed and could use a small table of contents. Back issues may be purchased singly or in bulk. Recent issues have covered an array of topics as varied as Benjamin Franklin's life, ecology, and bees. Most useful for readers in the classroom, but also highly recommended for public libraries and homeschoolers.

1286. *KidSpirit Online: tackling life's big ideas together.* 2008. q. Free. Ed(s): Elizabeth Dabney Hochman. KidSpirit Magazine, 77 State St, Brooklyn, NY 11201; info@kidspiritmagazine.com. Illus., adv. *Bk. rev.:* Number and length vary. *Aud.:* 11-15 yrs.

Now moved to an online format with an annual print compilation, this lovely nonprofit e-journal and highly interactive web site explore deep-thinking children's big questions. They comprise a "free teen magazine and website for kids created by and for young people to tackle life's big ideas together." In it, they "share online writings, poetry, artwork, [and] volunteer opportunities[,] and examine their spiritual development in a non-affiliated and inclusive forum." *KidSpirit* helps teens examine the meaning of life, explore expressions of spirituality, and address worldly topics such as divorce and war. Guided by a children's editorial board and advised by professionals in children's spiritual development, this magazine focuses on a new theme with each issue, and asks (and allows readers to respond to) some universal big questions. Recent topics have included "competition and achievement," "rituals and traditions," "the

body in balance," and "finding your spirit in art." Children thus share their beliefs, values, traditions, questions, and advice with others around the world. In "The Big Question," a central theme is presented and expounded on, while the "Listen Up!" section allows child readers to weigh in briefly on the topic. Teens can also share their life-changing personal experiences in "Awesome Moments." Finally, a profiled expert is called on to provide "elder" advice on the themed topic in the closing department, "PerSpectives." Also included are reader-contributed poetry, book, and media reviews, as well as some lighthearted games and puzzles and a place to be goofy in "Goof Corner." Online membership is free and allows readers access also to a bulletin board and forums. This journal is connected with the progressive Christianity movement and seeks to celebrate religious diversity in an increasingly secular world. The separately available annual compilation (purchasable in the web site's online shop) is printed from well-managed forest resources and recycled materials. This perfect-bound print volume also includes "group guides" for assistance in the classroom or study groups.

1287. *Kiki.* [ISSN: 1941-6350] 2007. bi-m. USD 26. Ed(s): Jamie Bryant. B - Books, Ltd., 6977 5 Mile Road, Cincinnati, OH 45230; info@b-books.com info@kikimag.com info@kikimag.com info@kikimag.com. Illus., adv. Sample. *Bk. rev.:* 6-10, staff-written. *Aud.:* Ems.

With a move to a bimonthly schedule, this handsome, award-winning, designer magazine is slightly slimmer now than before. At 66 pages, it is high on style, but as the subtitles suggests, it is also big on substance. Its aim is to inspire and to elicit creativity and a drive for accomplishment in girls. With its square-backed perfect binding, it has the feel of an academic journal, and its bimonthly production means that each issue presents high-quality content. Its editorial mission in part is to "help each reader develop a sense of style that reflects her own personality." This is not to say that this magazine does not exude a certain undeniable fashion flair; it does, but it is combined with a respect for individuality and the "natural" girl. Girls depicted in the magazine are as real as they get and represent a diverse population. *Kiki* also pushes the message that "the world needs creators, inventors and doers." Thus it teaches girls not only how to take care of themselves and look their best, but also how to undertake things on their own. For instance, recent issues explained how to follow the stock market, and presented entrepreneurial success stories and profiles on brands and companies in "Biz Buzz." Other regular departments include "From the Studio," which presents articles on fashion (including a fix-it page for fashion near-disasters), and "World Beat," which explores other cultures. Articles in "Kiki Care" promote health and safety. Included also is a column of substantial, staff-written book reviews. Never short on business ideas or style savvy, this magazine is a must for ambitious tween and young teen girls who wish to "blend style and artistry with knowledge and creativity." Highly recommended for libraries.

1288. *Krash.* [ISSN: 1448-7985] 2005. m. AUD 44.95; AUD 5.95 newsstand/cover. Ed(s): Ash Krash. Nuclear Media and Publishing, Bondi Jct, PO Box 1382, Sydney, NSW 1355, Australia; info@nuclear.com.au; http://www.nuclear.com.au/. Adv. Circ: 65000. *Bk. rev.:* Number and length vary. *Aud.:* 8-14 yrs.

As there are so few publications just for boys, any magazine that can attract and keep their interest while informing them and getting them to read is to be commended. The highly entertaining *Krash* keeps them coming back for more! Known also as "the world's coolest boys' mag," this small-format, 84-page magazine is loaded with fun, facts, and activities of unique interest to boys. Included are articles on highly masculine pastimes such as wrestling and skateboarding, collecting, cars, action heroes, gaming, and science. Weird and wacky true stories from around the world can be found in its "Newz" section. The magazine also offers loads of competitions, gaming "cheats," and challenging puzzles and quizzes, as well as the necessary window on pop culture, with plenty of music and movie references. Comics and anime feature highly in the magazine. Of note is the opportunity for boys to share mortifying experiences in "Shame Shack," and to speak their minds in "Speak Up." Also included are boys' art contributions, jokes, and movie, game, and toy reviews. The magazine's web site is highly interactive. Note: This title may not be available to subscribers outside of Australia.

1289. *Ladybug: the magazine for young children.* [ISSN: 1051-4961] 1990. 9x/yr. USD 33.95 domestic; USD 48.95 foreign. ePals Publishing Company, 30 Grove St, Ste C, Peterborough, NH 03458; customerservice@caruspub.com; http://www.cricketmag.com. Illus., adv. Sample. Vol. ends: Aug. *Indexed:* ICM, P01. *Aud.:* 3-6 yrs.

Picking up where *Babybug* leaves off, this glossy 40-page magazine for very young children provides an introduction to the literary world. It consists mostly of highly engaging stories, songs, and poetry, accompanied by outstanding and varied illustrations by world-class artists. Probably one of the only children's magazines to do so, *Ladybug* includes in every issue a song with musical score; a link is provided also, for children to enjoy the song online. To accommodate various reading levels, articles range from very short stories with pictures filling in for words, to those several pages in length with challenging words. Some are fiction and some are factual. Many are cultural or folklore-oriented; for instance, a recent issue was themed on all things woolen. The culturally diverse "Max and Kate" takes newly independent readers on simple adventures. Meanwhile, the "Mop and Family" comic series helps children discover their world. Some lengthier stories are made for storytime with an adult. Special activity take-out pages at the end involve learning based on concepts within the issue. Children are encouraged to visit the magazine's web site for additional activities. Highly recommended for both public libraries and personal subscriptions.

1290. *The Magazine (Toronto): entertainment, life & stuff.* Former titles (until 2000): *Magazine not for Adults;* (until 1999): *Jr. Jays Magazine.* 1993. bi-m. CAD 36 domestic; CAD 40 United States; CAD 60 elsewhere. Knightscove Media Corpo., 643 Queen St East, Toronto, ON M4M 1G4, Canada. Illus. *Bk. rev.:* 4-10. *Aud.:* 8-13 yrs.

Now published less frequently but in a full-size format, this entertainment magazine for tweens is heavy on pop culture. Very densely and colorfully designed, it provides an abundance of reading material in small bites. It is good for busy lives or short attention spans, offering material of interest for both girls and boys. Although the emphasis is undeniably commercial, the magazine actually contains few advertisements. Each issue offers many departments and regular features. References to new movies, music, and pop culture characters and celebrities are frequent, and comics feature heavily. Book, DVD, music, gaming, and techno-gadget reviews span several pages every issue. The "ScreamGals" section offers weird, scary, or mysterious short news pieces, sure to please the tween set, while eye-catching, graphic "style" tip pages for both boys and girls are an added fun feature. But the magazine also contains short news pieces on nature, health, multiculturalism, and environmentalism. There are also plenty of opportunities for contests, puzzles, reader mail, and art, and the sharing of pet photos in the "Friends" pages. Two of the best features of this magazine are the departments "Eats" and "Earth," in the latter of which children can learn food facts and discover ways to help the environment. This magazine includes two additional annual activity issues. It may be best suited for personal subscriptions, but it will undoubtedly be highly popular in public libraries as well.

1291. *Magic Dragon: presenting young writers and artists.* 2005. q. USD 22; USD 5 per issue. Ed(s): Patricia Roesch. Association for Encouragement of Children's Creativity, PO Box 687, Webster, NY 14580; http://www.magicdragonmagazine.com/. Illus., adv. Vol. ends: Fall. *Aud.:* Ems, Ga.

Much in the style of *Skipping Stones,* but with a more "East Coast" attitude, this is a beautiful and very colorful literary and art magazine, printed on slightly heavier paper and spanning 34 pages. It is now in its eighth year, and its purpose is to "present writing and art created by children in the elementary school grades," with the objective "to encourage the development of creativity in children and to provide a medium to share their creative efforts...." The main editorial conviction is to teach children to be "unafraid to express their creative ideas," as partial preparation for life in the adult working world. The magazine consists of an abundance of large, full-color illustrations interspersed throughout with poetry of all types and styles, and stories and essays of varying lengths. Except for a small two-page spread that offers "Write It" tips and a specific art "How To," the entire content of the magazine consists of children's submissions. Each issue solicits new contributions from children, from stories to poems to artwork (including self-portraits and sculptures), jokes, riddles, and even games. The subject matter of the young contributors is unique and the

writing style fresh and sometimes edgy—surely a reflection of the loose rein encouraged by the publication. This magazine respects and portrays diversity as much as most magazines do, but—rather refreshingly—it allows these concepts to emerge more organically and subtly out of the children's contributions. Arguably, this publication's only drawback might be the overwhelming number of contributors from just a handful of states on the East Coast. Winner of a Parents' Choice Award, this title seems equally appropriate for boys and girls, and is highly recommended for public libraries, schools, and homes.

1292. *Muse (Chicago): the magazine of life, the universe and pie throwing.* [ISSN: 1090-0381] 1996. 9x/yr. USD 33.95. Ed(s): Alice Letvin. ePals Publishing Company, 30 Grove St, Ste C, Peterborough, NH 03458; customerservice@caruspub.com; http://www.cricketmag.com. Illus., adv. Vol. ends: Dec. *Indexed:* ICM. *Bk. rev.:* Number and length vary. *Aud.:* 10-15 yrs.

Another joint publication by the *Cricket Group* and the Smithsonian Institution, this glossy, 42-page "magazine of life, the universe, and pie throwing" engages elementary and middle-school–age readers with provocative topics and humor. Lengthy but highly interesting articles on science, history, and geography topics are supported by photographs, pictures, and diagrams, plus suggested further reading via web sites and book titles. Article subjects are varied but based on a loose theme within each issue. *Muse's* board of advisors includes a contributor from the journal *Science.* Regular departments include the comic strip "Kokopelli & Company," as well as "Bo's Page," which features several science, medicine, and technology news bites, one of which is always hilariously bogus! In "Q&A," readers may submit a challenging question to the *Science* editor, while "Muserology" is a two-page column written by and about a *Muse* reader each month. There is also an extensive reader mail section. Each issue has a new reader contest. The back cover consists of several brief book and product reviews. An advisory board made up of educational and subject specialists ensures the quality of this publication. Highly recommended for school and public libraries, as well as for personal subscriptions.

1293. *National Geographic Kids.* Formerly (until Oct.2002): *National Geographic World;* Which superseded (in 1975): *National Geographic School Bulletin;* Which was formerly (until 1961): *Geographic School Bulletins;* (until 1941): *Geographic News Bulletins.* [ISSN: 1542-3042] 1975. 10x/yr. USD 24.95 domestic; USD 29.95 foreign. Ed(s): Rachel Buchholz. National Geographic Society, PO Box 98199, Washington, DC 20090; ngsforum@nationalgeographic.com; http://www.nationalgeographic.com/. Illus., index, adv. Microform: PQC. *Indexed:* A22, BRI, C37, ICM, MASUSE, P01, P02. *Aud.:* 6-14 yrs.

The winner of numerous honors and awards, this high-interest, 36-page geography magazine from the National Geographic Society dares children to explore. It briefly covers topics in science, travel, wildlife, exploration, history, anthropology, careers, and biography, and includes just-for-fun articles. Departments include "Weird But True," "Sports Funnies," "Bet You Didn't Know," "Cool Inventions," and "What in the World?" One regular feature, "Guinness World Records," reports on recent records set by children, as well as strange animal and other facts. Each issue also includes tear-out collectors' cards. Also included is a regular two-page comic. Readers submit art in response to the magazine's request for a particular theme, and respond also to caption contests, while "My Shot" features winning children's photographs. There is some advertising. Recommended for public and school libraries, though perhaps this title is slightly better suited for personal subscriptions.

1294. *National Geographic Little Kids: the magazine for young explorers.* [ISSN: 1934-8363] 2007. 10x/yr. USD 24.95. Ed(s): Rachel Buchholz. National Geographic Society, 1145 17th St, NW, Washington, DC 20036; askngs@nationalgeographic.com; http://www.nationalgeographic.com/. *Indexed:* P01. *Aud.:* 3-6 yrs.

Winner of a Parents' Choice Gold Award, this small-format, 24-page magazine by the National Geographic Society is a very young child's introduction to the world of nature and culture, animal species, and geography. Just the right size for small hands, it "builds early learning skills" by engaging children with rhymes, brief stories, and factual articles about animals and people, accompanied by simple, colorful illustrations and stunning photographs. The feature article introduces children to a particular animal. Regular departments include "What Do You See?" and "What is Different?" Sorting, counting, naming and matching games, mazes, and simple science experiments all help to bring a small child's world to life as do logic, finding, and number pages. Included also are activity and craft pages and simple science experiments, as well as an alphabet and vocabulary lesson. Pages include links to online content. Highly recommended for personal subscriptions, but very popular in public libraries as well.

1295. *New Moon Girls.* Formerly (until 2008): *New Moon.* [ISSN: 1943-488X] 1993. bi-m. USD 44.95 combined subscription (print & online eds.). New Moon Publishing, PO Box 161287, Duluth, MN 55816. Illus., index, adv. Vol. ends: Jul/Aug. *Indexed:* BRI, C42, ICM, MASUSE. *Bk. rev.:* Number and length vary. *Aud.:* 8-14 yrs.

Now available online and in print, this magazine and safe social network is "where girls develop their full potential through self-discovery, creativity, and community." Advised by an all-girl editorial board, and employing mentors and interns, the magazine offers pre-teen and early adolescent girls a strong and positive experience and message. International and progressive in flavor and content, it features articles on customs, ceremonies, biographies, and women's work around the world. Feature articles cover topics such as the value of owning a pet, weather prediction, and the way of life in Wales (as part of the "global village"). Regular departments include "Check it Out" (a 400- to 500-word girl-submitted book review), "How Aggravating," where girls can voice concerns about injustices to the female gender, and "Howling at the Moon," where girls share inspirational anecdotes. "Voice Box" lets girls sound off about hot topics such as dating or allowance, and "Girl-Caught" lets girls share real-life product instances of either stereotyping or valuing females. Each issue also includes a roughly 1,000-word girl-written and illustrated fictional piece. Opportunities for reader participation include the submission of opinions, ideas, advice, book reviews, poetry, and fiction, as well as artwork and letters. "The Last Word" features interviews with inspirational female role models. Individual subscriptions cover 12-month online access and include six print issues. A complete sample issue is available online. Highly recommended for school and public libraries, as well as for personal subscriptions where girls can take advantage of *New Moon*'s web site for additional content and features.

1296. *Odyssey (Peru): adventures in science.* [ISSN: 0163-0946] 1979. 9x/yr. USD 33.95 domestic; USD 48.95 foreign. Ed(s): Marianne Carus, Elizabeth Lindstrom. ePals Publishing Company, 30 Grove St, Ste C, Peterborough, NH 03458; customerservice@caruspub.com; http://www.cricketmag.com. Illus., adv. Sample. *Indexed:* A22, BRI, ICM, P01. *Bk. rev.:* Number and length vary. *Aud.:* 9-14 yrs.

This award-winning, glossy, 50-page magazine engages upper elementary and middle-school students in all kinds of science. Each issue provides lengthy, factual articles that focus tightly on a particular theme. Included also are fiction stories of roughly 1,500 words, loosely based on the theme topic. The magazine incorporates scientific principles into everyday life, such as sports and social activities. Regular columns include "Brain Strain" (a science puzzler) and "Science Scoops" (several pages of short news items). In "Person to Discover," real scientists are profiled, while "Staying Healthy: It's a Science" presents a health topic loosely related to the issue's theme. Readers submit substantial book reviews in "Kids Picks," while "Ask Dr. Cyborg" allows them to submit advanced science questions to experts for discussion. The stunning color illustrations and photography throughout each issue add interest, while charts, sidebars, and inserts expand on unfamiliar terms. Reader participation is encouraged. This magazine contains no advertisements. An advisory board made up of educational and subject specialists ensures the quality of this publication. Each issue also features an academic consulting editor. Highly recommended for school and public libraries and personal subscriptions.

1297. *Owl: the discovery magazine for kids.* [ISSN: 0382-6627] 1976. 10x/yr. CAD 34.95 in US & Canada; CAD 64.95 elsewhere. Ed(s): Craig Battle. Bayard Canada, Owlkids, 10 Lower Spadina Ave, Ste 400, Toronto, ON M5V 2Z2, Canada; bayard@owl.on.ca; http://www.owlkids.com/. Illus., index. Sample. *Indexed:* BRI, C37, CBCARef, ICM, P01, P02. *Bk. rev.:* Number and length vary. *Aud.:* 9-13 yrs.

This brightly illustrated, award-winning discovery magazine is for pre- to young teens who have graduated from its companion magazine, *Chickadee*. At 40 pages, it is heavy on comics, jokes, and good-natured leg-pulling, and its weirdness factor and gross-out quotient is high—perfect fodder to keep the boys

reading. Otherwise, *Owl* contains entertaining and informative articles on science, nature, current events, and social studies. Each issue opens with a calendar of suggested activities, and draws readers in with a "Wow Shot" photograph featuring some aspect of science or nature. The two-page science spread "Weird Zone" highlights strange but true science stories and facts, while "Hot Topic" presents a controversial issue for discussion and debate (e.g., a recent discussion about "too much screen time"). Two regular comics appear, one of which is several pages long and has readers solving a mystery. Included are plenty of DIY projects and activities to interest both boy and girl readers, such as mixing your own toothpaste or making your own hand soap. Additionally, there are pen-pal opportunities, photography and art contests, an opinion page, and usually a removable poster. Book, game, and movie reviews in "What's Hot" include young reader submissions. In "Talk About it," readers participate in giving advice to one another. Issues contain minimal advertising. Highly recommended for school and public libraries and personal subscriptions.

Plays. See Theater section.

1298. *Ranger Rick.* Formerly (until 1983): *Ranger Rick's Nature Magazine.* [ISSN: 0738-6656] 1967. m. 10/yr. USD 19.95 domestic; USD 31.95 foreign. Ed(s): Mary Dalheim. National Wildlife Federation, 11100 Wildlife Ctr Dr, Reston, VA 20190; pubs@nwf.org; http://www.nwf.org. Illus., index, adv. Vol. ends: Dec. Microform: NBI; PQC. *Indexed:* A22, BRI, C37, CBCARef, ICM, MASUSE, P01, P02. *Aud.:* 7-14 yrs.

This high-interest, award-winning, 40-page nature magazine for elementary school readers is published by the National Wildlife Federation. It is filled with short stories and articles of varying length that are frequently supplemented by "fast fact" sidebars. Regular departments include "Ask Rick"; people, science, and nature making news in "The Buzz"; "Fakes and Foolers"; and "Be Out There," which encourages children to get out and explore nature on their own. "Ranger Rick's Adventures" is a four-page feature comic. Other regular features include reader mail, photo contests, recipes, informational articles, nature-related puzzles, games and riddles, and a couple of comic series. Feature articles may span several pages. Photographs are large and supporting illustrations are helpful. Some issues are loosely themed around a particular topic. The corresponding web site includes a number of departments and sample activities from the current month's print publication. This magazine is printed from well-managed forests and recycled products. Subscribers get an additional e-mailed newsletter called "The Buzz." Highly recommended for school and public libraries and for individual subscriptions.

1299. *Ranger Rick Jr.* Former titles (until 2012): *Big Backyard;* (until 2011): *Your Big Backyard.* [ISSN: 2169-2750] 1980. 10x/yr. USD 19.95. National Wildlife Federation, 11100 Wildlife Ctr Dr, Reston, VA 20190; pubs@nwf.org; http://www.nwf.org. Illus. *Indexed:* ICM. *Bk. rev.:* 1-2. *Aud.:* 3-6 yrs.

This award-winning 32-page magazine from the National Wildlife Federation contains informational articles written at levels appropriate for the very young reader. Interestingly, it boasts an editorial advisory board of over 25 children. Adventure stories for hesitant readers use inserted pictures, while "Ricky & Pals" consists of multi-page stories for more eager and capable readers. Accompanying photographs are very large and captivating. "Backyard Buddies" features reader-submitted photographs of their personal experiences with wildlife. The "Family Fun Guide" section includes recipes, songs, crafts, and other activities, and also reviews a "Book of the Month." Links to the web site feature crafts and recipes that relate to wildlife, while a "Green Hour" suggests old-fashioned ways to have fun. Also to be found within the pages are whimsical games and quizzes, cut-out activities including mini-booklets, and poetry. This magazine is an excellent introduction to wildlife and environmental topics. Note: This title is distributed also by the Canadian Wildlife Federation. It is printed in part using well-managed forests and recycled materials. Highly recommended for public libraries and personal subscriptions.

1300. *Skipping Stones: a multicultural literary magazine.* [ISSN: 0899-529X] 1988. 5x/yr. USD 35 (Individuals, USD 25). Ed(s): Arun Narayan Toke. Skipping Stones, Inc., 166 W 12th Ave, PO Box 3939, Eugene, OR 97403; info@skippingstones.org. Illus. Sample. *Indexed:* BRI, P01. *Bk. rev.:* 16, 30-50 words. *Aud.:* 8-14 yrs.

This award-winning, nonprofit, no-frills magazine "encourages cooperation, creativity and celebration of cultural and linguistic diversity." There is no other children's magazine quite like it. Its emphasis is on ethnic ties and nonviolence. Printed on recycled paper, it promotes a respect for self, others, and the environment. While most of the writing and artwork is contributed by children ages 8 to 15, it is unusual in that adults contribute as well. The magazine consists of 36 pages, and its regular departments include "Nature Poetry Page," "What's on Your Mind?," and "Skipping Stones Stew," which features reader poetry. Non-English writing is accompanied by a translation in order to promote language-learning. Also included are regular book reviews, essays, and exchanges of cultural traditions, such as recipes, games, and projects. "Bookshelf" is a column for parents and teachers, listing new multicultural books and videos for children as well as parent–teacher resources. This magazine also features pen-pal opportunities and letters to "Dear Hanna," seeking advice and guidance. As the magazine tends toward the progressive end of the political spectrum, it has an emphasis on both diversity and global equality. It employs a small board of student reviewers and recognizes budding young writers with its own youth honor award. Because of its unique content and high-quality submissions, it should be considered essential for school and public libraries.

1301. *Spider: the magazine for children.* [ISSN: 1070-2911] 1994. 9x/yr. USD 33.95. ePals Publishing Company, 30 Grove St, Ste C, Peterborough, NH 03458; customerservice@caruspub.com; http://www.cricketmag.com. Illus. Sample. Vol. ends: Dec. *Indexed:* ICM, P01. *Bk. rev.:* Number and length vary. *Aud.:* 6-9 yrs.

Another quality publication from the Cricket Group, this 40-page literary magazine is specially designed to engage newly independent readers. It features interesting informational articles and realistic, fantasy, and historical fiction by the very best children's authors. Like a mini *Cricket Magazine,* it also includes folk tales, historical fiction, multicultural stories, ethnic legends, poetry, crafts, and jokes and puzzles, as well as some factual articles. Issues are themed loosely around a certain topic. Gorgeous, colorful illustrations provided by world-class artists enhance the text, while insect characters inhabiting the margins add their own comments. In "Spider's Corner," children answer calls to submit artwork, poetry, and other creative expressions. "Ophelia's Last Word" offers children crafts, recipes, games, and activities that get them using their bodies. Special activity "takeout pages" at the end of each issue involve learning based on concepts within the issue. Highly recommended for both public libraries and personal subscriptions.

1302. *Sports Illustrated for Kids.* [ISSN: 1042-394X] 1989. m. 10/yr. USD 31.95 domestic. Ed(s): Bob Der. Sports Illustrated Group, 135 W 50th St, 4th Fl, New York, NY 10020. Illus., adv. *Indexed:* A22, BRI, C37, ICM, MASUSE, P01. *Aud.:* 8-14 yrs.

This commercial, 60-page publication is aimed at boys and girls interested in all kinds of sports. Chock-full of articles of varying lengths, it is colorful, with plenty of stunning, up-close action photographs from all angles. Articles include human-interest stories about professional athletes and other sports figures. A recent issue profiled basketball sensation Jeremy Lin. Regular departments (or "Favorites") include "Freeze Frame," which contains large full-color photographs that catch special sports moments in action; "SportsKids," which focuses on real-life boys and girls and their athletic achievements; and "Tips from the Pros," which offers advice on various sports plays. In "Go Figure," charts provide interesting statistics from all types of sports. The "End Zone" includes trivia quizzes, hypothetical game rule situations to "call," and wonderful reader-submitted artwork. A pull-out page of collector cards is also included in every issue. This magazine contains a large amount of advertising, but it is labeled as such. The accompanying online site contains content that changes at least daily and contains news, games, and interactive features. Highly recommended for school and public libraries, as well as personal subscriptions.

1303. *Stone Soup: the magazine by young writers and artists.* [ISSN: 0094-579X] 1973. bi-m. USD 37 domestic; USD 43 in Canada & Mexico; USD 49 elsewhere. Ed(s): William Rubel, Gerry Mandel. Children's Art Foundation, 245 Eighth Ave, Ste 256, New York, NY 10011; info@childrenartfoundation.org; http://www.childrenartfoundation.org. Illus., adv. Vol. ends: Summer. *Indexed:* BRI, ICM, P01. *Bk. rev.:* Number and length vary. *Aud.:* 8-13 yrs.

Called "*The New Yorker* of the 8 to 13 set," this smaller-format, 50-page magazine provides young writers and artists with a wonderful opportunity to submit their own creative work for publication. All of the stories, poetry, book reviews, and artwork found in it are the original work of the young contributors. Readers are encouraged to submit writing and artwork based on their own experiences and observations on issues they "feel most strongly about." This makes *Stone Soup* an amazing melting pot of real life, adventure, and imagination. This magazine publishes approximately eight original articles per issue, interspersed with several pages of original poetry and lengthy book reviews of about 500 words. Young contributors are encouraged to submit work that is "about imaginary situations or real ones." Profile photographs of the writers and artists appear alongside their creations. Contributors represent a diverse group, and the boy-to-girl ratio seems to be about one to four. "The Mailbox" allows readers to provide feedback on pieces they have read. The magazine's web site contains extensive content from past issues as well as some audio recordings. *Stone Soup* is also available in a Braille edition. Highly recommended for personal subscriptions and school libraries, especially.

1304. *Story Box: a read-aloud magazine to share with your child.* [ISSN: 1366-901X] 1995. 10x/yr. EUR 65 in Europe; EUR 72 elsewhere. Ed(s): Christine Auberger. Bayard Presse, 3-5 Rue Bayard, Paris, 75393 Cedex 08, France; redactions@bayard-presse.com; http://www.bayardpresse.com. Adv. Sample. *Aud.:* 3-6 yrs.

This glossy publication is designed as "a quality magazine to share and enjoy with children," and each issue centers on a picture book-length, read-aloud story. These highly engaging stories by top authors and illustrators range from historical folktales to imaginary adventures. Other departments include "Animal World," a beautifully illustrated multi-page spread that provides fascinating facts on a particular species, and "Wonder with WhizKid," in which a whimsical character explores children's burning questions with them about science and nature. Also included are plenty of age-appropriate "fun and games" to keep children busy, such as mazes, word and sequencing games, and dot-to-dot. "Time for a Rhyme" introduces little ones to "lively riddles and rhymes [to] encourage children to play with words and sounds." The futuristic comic hero "SamSam" takes children on far-out adventures to teach them growing-up lessons. Meanwhile "Polo" delights pre-readers with a wordless comic strip. As with the other *Box* magazines, the back cover features a mini-quiz related to the content inside. This magazine is an ideal and entertaining introduction to learning. Multicultural diversity seems to be adequately represented. There are several subscription options available, including one with accompanying CDs for an enhanced audio experience. As winner of the Parents' Choice Foundation's Gold Award, this magazine belongs in every public library.

1305. *Tessy and Tab Reading Club.* [ISSN: 1544-3485] 200?. s-m. USD 48. Ed(s): Kim Imas. Blue Lake Children's Publishing, Judy Johnston, PO Box 14669, Portland, OR 97293; http://www.bluelakepublishing.com. Illus., adv. *Aud.:* 2-6 yrs.

As the title indicates, the goal of this magazine is both to initiate pre-readers and to keep older children interested in reading the printed word. Very simply designed, with bold outlines and primary colors, this 16-page magazine is attractive and the reading is easy to enjoy. Each issue features a particular number and letter of the alphabet. Pictures are packed with detail to fascinate and hold the attention of very young children. A single story per issue encourages children to participate in learning about the world around them, doing hands-on activities such as baking and gardening. There is usually a featured letter, number, color, or activity in every issue. For example, a recent issue was themed on Halloween costumes and the color orange. Each issue closes with a short but fun comprehension quiz and finding game, and introduces useful new vocabulary based on that issue's letter. Young readers are encouraged to answer "story questions," to "find these things," and to "find these words." The back of every issue also lists three new vocabulary words of one, two, and three syllables. A very brief and pertinent "grown-up memo" appears on the back of every issue. The magazine is printed from well-managed forests and other controlled sources. Highly recommended for public libraries and personal subscriptions.

Time for Kids World Report. See Classroom Magazines/Social Studies and Current Events section.

1306. *Turtle Magazine for Preschool Kids: magazine for preschool kids.*
[ISSN: 0191-3654] 1979. bi-m. USD 19.98. Ed(s): Terry Webb
Harshman. Children's Better Health Institute, 1100 Waterway Blvd,
Indianapolis, IN 46202; editor@saturdayeveningpost.com; http://
www.uskidsmags.com. Illus., adv. Sample. Vol. ends: Dec. *Indexed*: P01.
Aud.: 3-5 yrs.

Written with a focus on health, safety, and physical fitness, this colorful
newsprint magazine is perfect for preschool children. Its mission in part is "to
promote the healthy physical, educational, creative, social, and emotional
growth of children in a format that is engaging, stimulating, and entertaining...."
Three main content sections make up the magazine. "Fun to Read" includes
articles and fiction stories of varying length and reading ability, including
stories with words and pictures. The "Fun to Do" section includes activities,
such as dot-to-dot, hidden pictures, mazes, matching games, spelling words,
simple science experiments, recipes, and coloring pages. "Family Craft Night"
gets children and their families involved in fun, hands-on projects, while "Fun
Food" presents creative ways to decorate food. "Fun to See" showcases things
like readers and their pets, and reader art. The *Turtle* character features in a
teaching comic that runs throughout the issue. And "Ask Doctor Cory" answers
health-related questions for parents, teachers, and children. This award-
winning, 36-page magazine employs an editorial advisory board that includes
pediatricians and a certified dietician. Due to its cut-out and workbook-style
activities, it may be best suited for personal subscriptions, although it remains
of enduring value to public libraries as well.

1307. *W W E Kids.* [ISSN: 1941-7047] 2008. 10x/yr. USD 19.95 domestic;
USD 25.95 Canada; USD 31.95 elsewhere. Ed(s): Matt Christensen.
World Wrestling Entertainment, Inc., 1241 E Main St, Stamford, CT
06902; http://www.com/. Illus. *Aud.*: Ems, Ga.

This slick, 34-page magazine is chiefly of interest to elementary school boys,
though apparently it has some regular girl readers. It features showtime
schedules in "The Main Event," gives highlight coverage in "Ringside Seats,"
and takes readers inside the "Locker Room" for in-depth interviews with their
heroes, who offer little more than entertaining insight into their success and
personalities (very little growing-up advice or "eat-your-veggies" type of
moralizing; it's strictly sports talk). The magazine also provides a plethora of
trivia, games, puzzles, projects, and ideas for physical activities related to
wrestling. It includes a regular space for the display of readers' artwork and
contest submissions. Finally, each issue profiles a famous wrestling star in
"Finishing Moves," including vitals, stats, strengths, and weaknesses. While
this magazine is primarily of entertainment value, it will probably have boys
flocking enthusiastically to the library for the latest issue and is therefore
recommended.

1308. *Wild: Canada's wildlife magazine for kids.* Formerly (until 1995):
Ranger Rick (Ottawa); Which superseded in part (in 1984): *Ranger Rick;*
Which was formerly (until 1982): *Ranger Rick's Nature Magazine.*
[ISSN: 1492-014X] 1967. 8x/yr. CAD 25 domestic; CAD 49 United
States; CAD 59 elsewhere. Canadian Wildlife Federation, 350 Michael
Cowpland Dr, Kanata, ON K2M 2W1, Canada; info@cwf-fcf.org;
http://www.cwf-fcf.org. Adv. *Indexed*: BRI, C37, MASUSE. *Aud.*: 5-13
yrs.

Published by the Canadian Wildlife Federation, this colorful, 36-page magazine
is generously illustrated with stunning photographs and other pictures to
captivate children's interest in the natural world around them. A two-page,
sparely designed table of contents points children directly to articles of interest
with thumbnail pictures. Articles are lengthy and fully illustrated. The center
page consists of a full-color wildlife poster. In "You Asked," readers may submit
questions for experts to respond to. They also have the opportunity to submit
letters and artwork. Another regular department includes "Moose & Weasel's
Pals at Risk," which profiles endangered and threatened species. The magazine
also includes jokes, games, puzzles, and quizzes appropriate for the various
reading levels. Answers are provided at the end of the issue. Highly
recommended for public libraries.

1309. *Wild Animal Baby.* [ISSN: 1526-047X] 1999. 10x/yr. USD 19.95
domestic; USD 31.95 foreign. Ed(s): Lori Collins. National Wildlife
Federation, 11100 Wildlife Ctr Dr, Reston, VA 20190; pubs@nwf.org;
http://www.nwf.org. Illus., adv. *Aud.*: 1-4 yrs.

Just right for infants and preschoolers, this small-format magazine brings the
world of wildlife to the earliest learners. Published by the National Wildlife
Federation, it includes brief informational articles on wild animals as well as
short, fictional read-aloud articles. Very simple matching, color, and counting
games are expertly incorporated into the pages, as are other concepts, such as
opposites and shapes. Interactive poems and games such as "I Spy" promote
parent–child interaction, and children are encouraged to use their bodies in
animal pretend play. Regular features include "Animal Shapes" and "What Do
You Say?," the latter of which teaches children animal sounds. In addition to
real-life animal picture stories, the short fiction stories in "Out And About" give
children the opportunity to have an encounter with nature. Each issue features
a letter of the alphabet on the back cover, represented by a wild animal. The end
of each issue challenges children to a hide-and-seek game, searching for
"Sammy Skunk" throughout the pages. A link to the publication's web site
encourages children to explore further. This very engaging and charming
publication is highly recommended for public libraries.

Young Rider. See Horses section.

1310. *Zoobies.* 2009. bi-m. USD 29.95 domestic; USD 35.95 Canada.
Ed(s): Beth Sycamore. Wildlife Education Ltd., 4110 Progress Blvd, Ste
2A, Peru, IL 61354; http://wildlife-ed.com. Illus., adv. *Aud.*: 0-2 yrs.

The newest member of the *Zoobooks* family, this sturdy little bimonthly
introduces infants to the animal world. Small but well-designed, it packs a lot
of information into its 24 pages, using simple but powerful words and pictures.
Learning sections cover various growth areas. The "Language and
Development" section teaches babies to use their words appropriately in a fun
animal context, such as learning the different movements a penguin can make.
The photographs are up-close and captivating. Numbers and colors, and
concepts such as similarities and opposites, use animals to teach within the
magazine's "Cognitive Development" pages. The "Social/Emotional
Development" pages engage babies with whimsical animal pictures and
gestures that echo human behavior. Also contained within this charming
magazine is a "rhyme time" section, as well as several "flip-pages" that open out
for a larger picture, game, or craft. The rear of each issue has advice for parents
on using the magazine optimally for playtime and also provides tips on being
"green." Highly recommended for public libraries.

1311. *Zoobooks.* [ISSN: 0737-9005] 1980. 10x/yr. USD 29.95. Wildlife
Education Ltd., 4110 Progress Blvd, Ste 2A, Peru, IL 61354; http://
wildlife-ed.com. Illus., adv. *Indexed*: ICM, P01. *Aud.*: 6-12 yrs.

Guided by scientific consultants, this award-winning, 18-page publication is
filled with interesting text and high definition illustrations that focus in-depth on
a new animal in every issue. Habitat and species variations are also discussed.
Stunningly illustrated with both full-color photographs and detailed drawings,
this magazine is appropriate for both very young readers and older ones ready
to absorb many new and exciting facts. Illustrations include musculoskeletal
diagrams of the animals presented to show their inner workings, as well as many
large and captivating photographs. Every issue contains a centerfold
photograph. Recent issues have covered animals such as pinnipeds and snakes.
"Kids Zooworks" invites reader contributions in art and creative writing. Each
issue also contains a four-page paper activity tear-out section filled with games,
puzzles, and crafts that further the learning on that month's topic. These pages
direct readers also to online activity pages at the "Secret Jungle" where
subscribers can access special online features, such as quizzes, games, and
many additional contributor poems and stories (the print issue provides a new
online password every month). Each issue announces the next month's animal.
Perfect for use in the classroom, in the home, and as a library resource for school
projects.

1312. *Zootles.* [ISSN: 1936-4342] 2006. bi-m. USD 29.95 domestic; USD
35.95 Canada. Ed(s): Edward Shadek. Wildlife Education Ltd., 4110
Progress Blvd, Ste 2A, Peru, IL 61354; http://wildlife-ed.com. Illus., adv.
Aud.: 2-6 yrs.

The little sister magazine to the wildly popular *Zoobooks, Zootles* is aimed at
pre-readers spending together-time with their parents, as well as beginning
readers. Each issue features a single letter of the alphabet and also a concept,
color, or number. Both themes are reinforced throughout every aspect of the
issue. The magazine includes fantastic nature photographs and clear, colorful

illustrations to accompany its brief science facts, and its prose, fiction, and poetry. The fiction stories are accompanied by high-quality picturebook illustrations and are just the right length for either the advanced early reader or the child being read to. The middle of each issue includes a separate "Resource Center" for parents, which provides to-do ideas to further build upon the educational articles contained within. Additionally, "Fun Pages" offer quizzes and puzzles. The end of each issue's "You Can Be A Scientist Too" gives children and parents tips on observing wildlife around them. The back cover features an animal comic that teaches children about the wonders of wildlife. Additional activity pages are available for subscribers online via password. For individual subscribers in particular, the downloadable "read-aloud" feature will very enjoyable. Highly recommended for public libraries, as well as individual subscriptions.

■ CIVIL LIBERTIES

General/Bioethics: Reproductive Rights, Right-to-Life, and Right-to-Die/ Freedom of Expression and Information/Freedom of Thought and Belief/ Groups and Minorities/Political-Economic Rights

See also Alternatives; News and Opinion; and Political Science sections.

Miriam Leigh, Medford, MA; miriam.leigh@gmail.com

Introduction

The journals reviewed in this section document the crucial role of civil liberties in democracy. Civil liberties—the rights to freedom of thought, expression, and action without interference from government—have been at the forefront of debate in the United States since the Founding Fathers wrote the Bill of Rights with the specific intent to safeguard individual liberties against the power of a strong central government.

Civil liberties have traditionally been concerned with freedom of expression and due process, but the specific focus has changed as public attitudes have shifted from one generation to the next. Civil liberties have expanded and, during times of national crisis such as war, have contracted. Judicial activism has had significant impact on civil liberties. The Warren Court (1953–1969) carved out the constitutional right of privacy that later became the basis of *Roe v. Wade*. The Burger Court shifted rightward and weakened civil liberties, notably in the area of criminal procedure protections.

Toward the end of the twentieth century, technology became the First Amendment battleground. Free speech on the Internet and the right to privacy relating to individuals' genetic profiles entered the debate. The terrorist attacks of September 11, 2001, and the USA PATRIOT Act, giving government unprecedented investigative powers, heightened civil liberties concerns. Government actions to prevent future terrorist attacks have made the defense of civil liberties more complex than at any time in our history.

In 1822, James Madison wrote, "A people who mean to be their own governors must arm themselves with the power which knowledge gives." Articles in journals in this section give historical review of civil liberties issues and also chronicle contemporary discussion by intellectuals and policymakers. Preservation of indigenous cultures, religion in the public sphere, the Arab Spring and similar popular uprisings, sex trafficking, autonomy for the elderly in institutional care, evangelizing in ethnic minority communities, changes to immigration policy, and the 2010 Affordable Care Act are issues that citizens, students, and scholars will want to fully explore in order to be more fully able to participate in American discourse and democracy. Journals in this section inform Americans about issues that touch on their daily lives and on the future of their country as well as issues faced by people all over the world.

Librarians should review titles in other sections of *Magazines for Libraries*, most notably the ones dedicated to individual groups (African Americans, Asian Americans, Disabilities, Latino Studies, Native Americans, and Women) to augment titles in this section.

Basic Periodicals

Hs: *Human Rights (Chicago), Liberty (Hagerstown), Newsletter on Intellectual Freedom, Reason;* Ga:*Cultural Survival Quarterly, Free Inquiry, Human Rights (Chicago), Index on Censorship, Liberty (Hagerstown), Newsletter on*

Intellectual Freedom, Northwestern Journal of International Human Rights, Reason, The International Journal of Human Rights; Ac: *American Journal of Bioethics, American Journal of Law & Medicine, Bioethics, Columbia Human Rights Law Review, Cultural Survival Quarterly, George Mason University civil rights law journal, Harvard Civil Rights—Civil Liberties Law Review, Human Rights (Chicago), Human Rights Law Review, Human Rights Quarterly, Index on Censorship, Issues in Law and Medicine, Journal of civil rights and economic development, Journal of human rights practice, Journal of Law and Religion, Journal of Law, Medicine, & Ethics, Law & Inequality, Newsletter on Intellectual Freedom, Northwestern Journal of International Human Rights, Reason, Seattle Journal for Social Justice, Stanford Journal of Civil Rights & Civil Liberties, The International Journal of Human Rights;* Sa: *American Journal of Bioethics, American Journal of Law & Medicine, Bioethics, Columbia Human Rights Law Review, Free Inquiry, Harvard Civil Rights—Civil Liberties Law Review, Human Rights Law Review, Human Rights Quarterly, Issues in Law and Medicine, Journal of civil rights and economic development, Journal of human rights practice, Journal of Law and Religion, Journal of Law, Medicine & Ethics, Law & Inequality, Northwestern Journal of International Human Rights, Seattle Journal for Social Justice, Stanford Journal of Civil Rights & Civil Liberties, The International Journal of Human Rights.*

Basic Abstracts and Indexes

Alternative Press Index.

General

1313. *Columbia Human Rights Law Review.* Formerly (until 1972): *Columbia Survey of Human Rights Law.* [ISSN: 0090-7944] 1967. 3x/yr. USD 65. Ed(s): Adam L Shpeen. Columbia University, School of Law, 435 W 116th St, New York, NY 10027; Admissions@law.columbia.edu; http://www.law.columbia.edu. Circ: 235. Microform: WSH; PMC. Reprint: WSH. *Indexed:* A22, ABS&EES, BRI, CLI, L14, MLA-IB. *Aud.:* Ac, Sa.

The student-run *Columbia Human Rights Law Review* is "one of the oldest and the most recognized human rights journals in the world." Published three times a year, it aims to analyze and discuss civil liberties in both a domestic and international context. The most recent issue is a single book-length article on the Texas execution of Carlos deLuna for a crime likely committed by another. Other recent topics have included laptop searches at international borders; sex trafficking of American Indian women and girls; and sexual orientation as a primary basis for asylum-seeking. Articles are dense and technical in nature, making them most appropriate in law libraries and libraries affiliated with law schools.

Criminal Justice Ethics. See Criminology and Law Enforcement section.

1314. *George Mason University. Civil Rights Law Journal.* [ISSN: 1049-4766] 1990. 3x/yr. USD 60 in US & Canada; USD 70 elsewhere. Ed(s): Megan Marinos, John Sandell. George Mason University, School of Law, 3401 N Fairfax Dr, Arlington, VA 22201; http:// www.law.gmu.edu. Circ: 149 Paid. Reprint: WSH. *Indexed:* A01, BRI, CLI, L14. *Aud.:* Ac, Sa.

The *George Mason University Civil Rights Law Journal* was founded in 1990, and "serves as a forum for thought-provoking scholarly articles written by leading academics." Recent articles have addressed such issues as the importance of Miranda rights even in terror cases; predictions on challenges to eminent domain; and victim impact statements in death penalty sentencing proceedings. Articles are of a complex legal nature, and thus would be most appropriate in a legal library or in the library at a law school. It is available both as a paid print subscription and for free at the web site. URL: http:// civilrightslawjournal.com/

1315. *Harvard Civil Rights - Civil Liberties Law Review.* [ISSN: 0017-8039] 1966. s-a. USD 31 domestic; USD 38 Canada; USD 40 elsewhere. Ed(s): Sharo Atmeh, Amanda Wittenstein. Harvard University, Law School, 1563 Massachusetts Ave, Cambridge, MA 02138; http:// www.law.harvard.edu/. Illus. Vol. ends: Summer. Microform: WSH; PMC; PQC. Reprint: WSH. *Indexed:* A01, A22, BRI, CLI, L14, P02, P61, SSA. *Aud.:* Ac, Sa.

This publication, the leading progressive law journal in the United States, focuses on civil rights and the American people's loss thereof. Written from a perspective of social justice, the *Harvard Civil Rights–Civil Liberties Law Review* offers dialogues on a variety of controversial topics. It was founded with the goal "to catalyze progressive thought and dialogue through publishing innovative legal scholarship and from various perspectives and in diverse fields of study." Recent issues explore the relationship between property ownership and identity as related to the current housing crisis; the effects of Wikileaks on investigative journalism; and a Constitutional approach to legal gender identity. In addition to its availability as a paid print subscription, the *CRCL* is available for free online at http://harvardcrcl.org/.

1316. *Human Rights (Chicago).* Incorporates (1969 -1978): *American Bar Association. Section of Individual Rights and Responsibilities. Newsletter; American Bar Association. Section of Individual Rights and Responsibilities. Edited Proceedings.* [ISSN: 0046-8185] 1970. q. USD 25 (Individuals, USD 18; Free to members). Ed(s): Angela Gwizdala, Deborah Flores. American Bar Association, 321 N Clark St, 20th Fl, Chicago, IL 60654; service@abanet.org; http://www.americanbar.org. Illus., index, adv. Microform: WSH. Reprint: WSH. *Indexed:* A01, A22, BRI, CLI, ENW, L14, P02. *Aud.:* Hs, Ga, Ac.

Human Rights, published quarterly by the American Bar Association–Section of Individual Rights and Responsibilities, focuses each issue on a single theme, offering in-depth coverage and a range of perspectives on each topic. Recent issues focus on such timely topics as changes in the education landscape in America; the world in the decade since the terrorist attacks of September 11, 2001; and the intersection of human sexuality and the law. Although this magazine is published primarily for section members, its formatting and accessible articles give it a broad appeal.

1317. *Human Rights Law Review.* Formerly (until 1994): *Student Human Rights Law Centre. Newsletter.* [ISSN: 1461-7781] 19??. q. EUR 338. Ed(s): David Harris. Oxford University Press, Great Clarendon St, Oxford, OX2 6DP, United Kingdom; enquiry@oup.co.uk; http://www.oxfordjournals.org/. Adv. Sample. Reprint: PSC; WSH. *Indexed:* A22, CJPI, E01, P61, SSA. *Bk. rev.:* 2, 1,500-2,200 words. *Aud.:* Ac, Sa.

Human Rights Law Review is published quarterly with the intent to "promote knowledge, awareness[,] and debate of human rights law and policy." It offers a range of articles, updates on recent cases, and book reviews on human rights issues around the world. This journal is written with an academic focus, but is also intended for a wider audience of anyone involved in human rights work. Recent issues have published articles on the effects that NGOs have on the Convention on the Rights of the Child; an anti-stereotyping approach suggested for the European Court of Human Rights; and a discussion of religion in the public sphere in modern European secular societies. Because of its broad appeal, this journal would be appropriate in any academic library.

1318. *Human Rights Quarterly.* Formerly (until 1981): *Universal Human Rights.* [ISSN: 0275-0392] 1979. q. USD 200. Ed(s): Bert B Lockwood, Jr., Anne Niehaus. The Johns Hopkins University Press, 2715 N Charles St, Baltimore, MD 21218; http://www.press.jhu.edu. Illus., index, adv. Sample. Refereed. Circ: 1010. Vol. ends: Nov. Microform: WSH; IDC; PQC. Reprint: PSC; WSH. *Indexed:* A01, A22, ABS&EES, BAS, BRI, CLI, E01, IBSS, L14, MLA-IB, P02, P61, RiskAb, SSA. *Bk. rev.:* 1-4, 1,100-3,000 words. *Aud.:* Ac, Sa.

Human Rights Quarterly, published by the Johns Hopkins University Press, offers award-winning articles in the field of human rights. It uses as its focus the Universal Declaration of Human Rights, publishing articles from experts in a variety of disciplines including the law and the humanities. It includes book reviews, essays, and analytical articles, intending to "provide decision makers with insight into complex human rights issues." Recent articles are on such topics as gay rights as seen through the lens of the persecution of homosexuals in Uganda; the challenges that are posed to human rights during states of emergency; and the rights of ethnic minorities in cases such as France's recent ban on the burka in public spaces. Although *Human Rights Quarterly* is intended primarily for policymakers, it is also edited to be of use to the "intelligent reader," making it extremely appropriate for any academic library.

Journal of Criminal Law & Criminology. See Law section.

1319. *Law & Inequality: a journal of theory and practice.* [ISSN: 0737-089X] 1981. s-a. USD 18 (Free to qualified personnel). Ed(s): Joseph Watson Steinberg, Jonathan Blackburn. University of Minnesota, Law School, 229 19th Ave S, Minneapolis, MN 55455; law@umn.edu; http://www.law.umn.edu. Illus., adv. Refereed. Vol. ends: Jun. Microform: WSH. Reprint: WSH. *Indexed:* A22, BRI, CJPI, CLI, L14. *Bk. rev.:* 1, 2,000 words. *Aud.:* Ac, Sa.

Law & Inequality, published twice a year under the umbrella of the University of Minnesota Law School, provides articles, essays, and letters "addressing issues of inequality in law and society." Recent topics include the policies of Big Ten schools regarding undocumented student applications; the condition of the Roma in Europe; and the effects of legally recognizing same-sex unions on health and well-being. Although most articles are written in the traditional legal format, they are also intended to appeal to a wider audience, both within and outside the legal community. Thus, *Law & Inequality* would be appropriate in both legal and academic libraries.

New Perspectives Quarterly. See News and Opinion section.

1320. *Northwestern Journal of International Human Rights.* [ISSN: 1549-828X] 2003. s-a. Free. Ed(s): Heather Scheiwe, Lee Hasselbacher. Northwestern University, School of Law, 375 E Chicago Ave, Chicago, IL 60611; admissions@law.northwestern.edu; http://www.law.northwestern.edu. Reprint: WSH. *Indexed:* A01, L14. *Aud.:* Ga, Ac, Sa.

The *Northwestern Journal of International Human Rights* is published twice a year, and is "dedicated to providing a dynamic forum for the discussion of human rights issues and international human rights law." The journal offers traditional legal articles as well as presentations from the Annual Transatlantic Dialogue conference between the Center for International Human Rights at Northwestern University School of Law and the Catholic University in Leuven, Belgium. Recent articles cover such topics as the ramifications of the Arab Spring on human rights; the progress of the labor movement in Iran; and the Mexican push for security to the detriment of human rights. It is available only in full text online, for free. URL: www.law.northwestern.edu/journals/jihr

Social Philosophy and Policy. See Philosophy section.

Social Theory and Practice. See Cultural Studies section.

1321. *Stanford Journal of Civil Rights & Civil Liberties.* [ISSN: 1553-7226] 2003. s-a. USD 36 domestic; USD 41 foreign; USD 21 per issue. Ed(s): Elena Maria Coyle, Louise Nutt. Stanford University, Stanford Law School, Stanford Law School, 559 Nathan Abbott Way, Stanford, CA 94305; communications@law.stanford.edu; http://www.law.stanford.edu/. *Aud.:* Ac, Sa.

The *Stanford Journal of Civil Rights & Civil Liberties,* published twice a year by the students of Stanford Law, has as its mission "to explore the changing landscape of the civil rights and civil liberties dialogue, the real[-]world implications of these changes on society, and the larger structural and systemic implications of these issues." The fall issue of each volume explores topics covered during the journal's annual symposium, while the spring issue contains a broader range of articles. The most recent issues explore whether or not same-sex marriage threatens religious liberty; an analysis of the history of civil rights activism and how it might be relevant today; and a faith-based penitentiary in Florida. Although its intended audience is the legal community, the articles are clear and the topics are highly relevant in today's world. This journal would be a good fit for both legal and academic libraries.

Bioethics: Reproductive Rights, Right-to-Life, and Right-to-Die

1322. *The American Journal of Bioethics.* [ISSN: 1526-5161] 2001. m. USD 1690 (print & online eds.). Ed(s): David Magnus. Routledge, 325 Chestnut St, Ste 800, Philadelphia, PA 19106; customerservice@taylorandfrancis.com; http://www.tandfonline.com. Illus. Refereed. Reprint: PSC. *Indexed:* A01, A22, E01, P61, SSA. *Bk. rev.:* Number and length vary. *Aud.:* Ac, Sa.

The *American Journal of Bioethics,* launched in 1999, has rapidly become one of the most widely read publications in the field. It offers three primary, or "target," articles and then several peer commentaries on each article, allowing for a varied and in-depth exploration of each topic. In addition, *AJOB* publishes book reviews and correspondence from readers. In 2007, this journal moved from being published six times per year to 12. Recent issues touch on such topics as premortem organ donation, the doctor–patient relationship, and the ethical implications of drug shortages. Readers will also enjoy the companion web site for thought-provoking news, editorials, and even a blog. The subscription price includes *AJOB Neuroscience* and *AJOB Primary Research* in a bundle. URL: www.bioethics.net

American Journal of Law & Medicine. See Law section.

1323. *Bioethics.* [ISSN: 0269-9702] 1987. 9x/yr. GBP 850. Ed(s): Udo Schueklenk, Ruth Chadwick. Wiley-Blackwell Publishing Ltd., The Atrium, Southern Gate, Chichester, PO19 8SQ, United Kingdom; customer@wiley.com; http://www.wiley.com/. Illus., adv. Sample. Refereed. Reprint: PSC. *Indexed:* A01, A22, ASSIA, BRI, E01, IBSS, P02, P61, PsycInfo, RiskAb, SSA. *Aud.:* Ac, Sa.

This journal, published under the aegis of the International Association of Bioethics, explores contemporary ethical concerns raised in the course of biomedical research. These debates reflect those in today's popular discourse. Topics include elective reduction of twin pregnancies, the effect of the economic downturn on academic bioethics, and cloning. Issues occasionally focus on a single theme, allowing authors to explore topics on a more in-depth level, such as last year's special issue on clinical ethics support services. Other recent topics include informed consent, an Islamic view on stem cell research, and autonomy for the elderly in institutional care. The articles are a mix of scientific studies and more accessible popular-style articles.

Hastings Center Report. See Public Health section.

1324. *Issues in Law and Medicine.* [ISSN: 8756-8160] 1985. 3x/yr. USD 99. Ed(s): James Bopp, Jr., Barry A. Bostrom. National Legal Center for the Medically Dependent and Disabled, Inc., Bopp, Coleson & Bostrom, 1 South Sixth St, Terre Haute, IN 47807-3510; bcb@bopplaw.com. Illus., adv. Refereed. Circ: 1000. Vol. ends: Spring. Microform: WSH. Reprint: WSH. *Indexed:* A01, A22, B01, BRI, CLI, L14, P02, SWR&A. *Bk. rev.:* 5, 200-1,000 words. *Aud.:* Ac, Sa.

Issues in Law and Medicine, a peer-reviewed journal aimed at attorneys, health-care workers, educators, and administrators, covers topics that explore the intersection of medical practice and the rights of both the patient and the care provider. Articles are typically highly technical, as the subject matter is legal in nature. Recent issues contain articles on the attempts by the FDA to reduce safety risks from opioid medications; the Presidentially-mandated Independent Medicare Advisory Committee; and the status of abortion rights if *Roe v. Wade* were overturned. This journal often offers debates on a controversial topic, publishing opposing viewpoints together.

1325. *The Journal of Law, Medicine & Ethics.* Formerly (until 1993): *Law, Medicine and Health Care;* Which was formed by the merger of (1973-1981): *Medicolegal News;* (1980-1981): *Nursing Law and Ethics.* [ISSN: 1073-1105] 1981. q. GBP 322. Ed(s): Kevin Outterson, Edward J Hutchinson. Wiley-Blackwell Publishing, Inc., 111 River St, Hoboken, NJ 07030; info@wiley.com; http://www.wiley.com/. Illus., adv. Sample. Refereed. Vol. ends: Winter. Microform: WSH; PQC. Reprint: PSC. *Indexed:* A01, A22, BRI, CLI, E01, H24, L14, P02, RiskAb. *Bk. rev.:* Number and length vary. *Aud.:* Ac, Sa.

Published quarterly by the American Society of Law, Medicine & Ethics, *The Journal of Law, Medicine & Ethics* aims to be "a leading peer-reviewed journal for research at the intersection of law, health policy, ethics, and medicine." Issues contain topical sections, publishing articles based on a single symposium. This allows the journal to explore a given subject in depth and from a variety of perspectives. Recent issues have discussed geriatric health care needs; disclosure of findings from medical research studies to participants; health-care reform; and end-of-life care. In addition to these symposium articles, each issue

also contains standalone articles, regular columns, a calendar of professional events, and the occasional book review. Articles are scholarly, and would be most appropriate in academic, legal, and medical libraries.

Freedom of Expression and Information

1326. *Index on Censorship: for free expression.* [ISSN: 0306-4220] 1972. q. USD 615. Ed(s): Jo Glanville. Sage Publications Ltd., 1 Oliver's Yard, 55 City Rd, London, EC1Y 1SP, United Kingdom; info@sagepub.co.uk; http://www.uk.sagepub.com. Illus., index, adv. Sample. Circ: 3000 Paid. Vol. ends: Nov/Dec. Reprint: PSC. *Indexed:* A01, A22, AmHI, ArtHuCI, BAS, BRI, E01, MASUSE, MLA-IB, P02, P61, RILM, SSA. *Aud.:* Ga, Ac.

In the last few years, we have seen an increase in protests, and with this, an increase in restrictions on speech and behavior. *Index on Censorship,* first conceived of in response to Soviet sham trials, reports on incidences of censorship from around the world, exploring controversial issues and bringing abuses to light. It seeks "to shed light on other challenges facing free expression, including religious extremism, the rise of nationalism, and Internet censorship." Recent topics include a manifesto by jailed dissident Aung San Suu Kyi; the Russian culture of secrecy; and the under-reporting of violence and murder in Mexico City. It offers creative works (poetry, fiction, plays), reports, editorials, and essays. Although it does explore these issues from an academic perspective, the writing is accessible and the information pertinent, making *Index on Censorship* suitable for a more general readership as well.

Journal of Information Ethics. See Library and Information Science section.

1327. *Newsletter on Intellectual Freedom (Online).* [ISSN: 1945-4546] bi-m. USD 50. American Library Association, 50 E Huron, Chicago, IL 60611; ala@ala.org; http://www.ala.org. *Bk. rev.:* 1-4, 500-700 words. *Aud.:* Hs, Ac, Ga.

Published by the American Library Association's Office of Intellectual Freedom, the *Newsletter on Intellectual Freedom* is the only journal that reports on challenges to materials from schools and libraries nationwide. It provides articles on pertinent topics such as the recent Arizona ethnic studies ban; censorship of youth materials in libraries; and the defeat of restrictive anti-piracy bills in the U.S. Senate. It also publishes regular features such as "Censorship Dateline," a state-by-state survey of challenges and bannings of library materials, and "From the Bench" and "Is It Legal?," which detail important changes in federal and state laws that affect librarians, teachers, students, authors, journalists, and artists. This periodical is available both in print format and in full text online. URL: www.members.ala.org/nif

Freedom of Thought and Belief

1328. *Free Inquiry.* [ISSN: 0272-0701] 1980. q. USD 31.50; USD 6.95 per issue. Ed(s): Paul Kurtz, Andrea Szalanski. Council for Secular Humanism, 3965 Rensch Rd, Amherst, NY 14228; info@secularhumanism.org; http://www.secularhumanism.org. Illus., index, adv. Vol. ends: Fall. Microform: PQC. *Indexed:* A01, A22, BRI, MLA-IB, P02. *Bk. rev.:* 3-5, 500-1,500 words. *Aud.:* Hs, Ga, Sa.

Free Inquiry is published as the mouthpiece of the Council for Secular Humanism. It takes as its focus the exploration of complex contemporary ethical issues through the lens of secular humanism. Its Statement of Purpose specifies that the journal's aim is "to promote and nurture the good life—life guided by reason and science, freed from the dogmas of god and state, inspired by compassion for fellow humans, and driven by the ideals of human freedom, happiness, and understanding." Recent articles cover such topics as the enhancement of human capabilities (including genetic or technological modifications); the concept of the United States as a Christian nation; and a secular humanist perspective on overpopulation. Sections in the magazine include letters to the editor, op-eds, feature articles, book reviews, poetry, and more. These timely articles reflect issues being discussed in the American popular press.

The Humanist. See Religion section.

Journal of Church and State. See Religion section.

1329. *Journal of Law and Religion.* [ISSN: 0748-0814] 1983. 3x/yr. GBP 98 (print & online eds.). Cambridge University Press, 32 Ave of the Americas, New York, NY 10013; information@cambridge.org; http://www.cambridge.org/us/. Illus., index, adv. Refereed. Microform: WSH; PMC. Reprint: WSH. *Indexed:* A01, A22, BRI, CLI, L14, P61, R&TA. *Bk. rev.:* 10-20, 2,000 words. *Aud.:* Ac, Sa.

Dedicated to exploring the intersection of law and religion, this journal offers an international perspective on relevant topics. In the Statement of Perspective, the editor identifies the six major focuses of the journal: historical, theoretical, ethical, global, professional, and spiritual. Published semi-annually, issues of the *Journal of Law and Religion* often focus on recent news, with topical articles, editorials, and legal papers from writers from a variety of religious and legal backgrounds. Recently, topics have explored the dual family law system (religious and civil) in Israel; the Jewish perspective on torture in warfare; and the current approach by the European Court of Human rights on freedom of religion and freedom of expression. Although this journal is largely intended for a legal audience, many of the articles can be enjoyed by the general public.

1330. *Liberty (Hagerstown): a magazine of religious freedom.* [ISSN: 0024-2055] 1906. bi-m. USD 7.95. Ed(s): Lincoln Steed. Review and Herald Publishing Association, 55 W Oak Ridge Dr, Hagerstown, MD 21740; info@rhpa.org; http://www.rhpa.org. Illus., adv. Circ: 200000. Vol. ends: Nov/Dec. Microform: PQC. *Indexed:* A22. *Aud.:* Hs, Ga.

Published six times per year by the Seventh Day Adventist Church, *Liberty* offers a variety of thought-provoking articles, essays, and editorials. Its "Declaration of Principles" states the journal's position that "[r]eligious liberty entails freedom of conscience: to worship or not to worship; to profess, practice, and promulgate religious beliefs, or to change them." This focus on the separation of church and state yields strong viewpoints on pressing contemporary topics. Recent issues of *Liberty* include articles on religious concerns about the Affordable Health Care Act of 2010; legal secularism; and civil disobedience in the Christian tradition. This magazine is highly readable, and is available both by print subscription and for free online. URL: www.libertymagazine.org

Groups and Minorities

The Advocate. See Gay, Lesbian, Bisexual, and Transgender section.

Children's Legal Rights Journal. See Sociology and Social Work/General section.

Columbia Journal of Gender and the Law. See Law section.

1331. *Cultural Survival Quarterly: world report on the rights of indigenous peoples and ethnic minorities.* Formerly (until 1981): *Cultural Survival Newsletter.* [ISSN: 0740-3291] 1976. q. USD 60 (Individuals, USD 19.95). Ed(s): Mark Cherrington. Cultural Survival, Inc., 215 Prospect St, Cambridge, MA 02139; culturalsurvival@cs.org; http://www.culturalsurvival.org/. Illus., index, adv. Vol. ends: Winter. Reprint: PSC. *Indexed:* A22, A47, ABS&EES, ENW, RILM. *Bk. rev.:* 1-3, 300-700 words. *Aud.:* Ga, Ac.

Cultural Survival Quarterly was founded as a society newsletter. Over the last 30-plus years, it has become an authoritative resource on important issues that affect indigenous and ethnic minority communities around the world. Recent topics covered include the use of media to preserve traditional cultures; indigenously-developed and managed ecotourism; and a language reclamation project on Cape Cod. This magazine publishes thought-provoking essays, book reviews, and photographs with the intent of expanding public understanding about indigenous rights and cultures, with writers from indigenous communities or working closely with indigenous groups. In addition to a paid print subscription, this journal is also available for free at http://www.culturalsurvival.org/publications/cultural-survival-quarterly.

National Black Law Journal. See Law section.

Political-Economic Rights

Clearinghouse Review. See Law section.

Employee Relations Law Journal. See Labor and Industrial Relations section.

1332. *The International Journal of Human Rights.* [ISSN: 1364-2987] 1997. 8x/yr. GBP 739 (print & online eds.). Ed(s): Frank Barnaby. Routledge, 4 Park Sq, Milton Park, Abingdon, OX14 4RN, United Kingdom; subscriptions@tandf.co.uk; http://www.tandfonline.com. Adv. Sample. Refereed. Circ: 9000. Reprint: PSC. *Indexed:* A01, A22, E01, IBSS, P61, RiskAb, SSA. *Aud.:* Ga, Ac, Sa.

Published eight times per year, the *International Journal of Human Rights* has an ambitiously broad scope. It covers a wide spectrum of topics, including "human rights and the law, race, religion, gender, children, class, refugees and immigration." Articles are academic but readable, designed to appeal to a range of readers such as academics, lawyers, politicians, NGO workers, activists, and the interested general public. The *Journal* primarily publishes original research, but also offers essays, comments, literature surveys, and more, with occasional special issues devoted to a single topic. Recent issues have covered such topics as human dignity in the Canadian Charter of Rights and Freedoms; the rights to reparations for victims of torture; and evangelization in indigenous communities in India.

1333. *Journal of Civil Rights and Economic Development.* Formerly (until 2010): *Saint John's Journal of Legal Commentary.* 1985. q. USD 22.95; USD 12.50 per issue. Ed(s): Daniel Perrone, Eileen Ward. St. John's Law Review Association, 8000 Utopia Pky, Jamaica, NY 11439; lawinfo@stjohns.edu; http://www.law.stjohns.edu/. Vol. ends: Summer. Reprint: WSH. *Indexed:* A22, BRI, CLI, L14, MLA-IB. *Aud.:* Ac, Sa.

Established in 2010 at St. John's Law School, the *Journal of civil rights and economic development* is committed to publishing on "issues of social, racial[,] and economic justice." Recent issues have covered such topics as past and present trends in prison sentencing; race considerations in child custody cases; and the use of health insurance exchanges to increase health equity under the Affordable Care Act of 2010. In addition to its availability in print form, this journal is available for free in full text at http://www.stjohns.edu/academics/graduate/law/journals_activities/jcred.

1334. *Journal of Human Rights Practice.* [ISSN: 1757-9619] 2009. 3x/yr. EUR 299. Ed(s): Brian Phillips, Paul Gready. Oxford University Press, Great Clarendon St, Oxford, OX2 6DP, United Kingdom; enquiry@oup.co.uk; http://www.oxfordjournals.org. Refereed. Circ: 2848 Paid. Reprint: PSC. *Aud.:* Ac, Sa.

Written primarily for human rights practitioners (NGO workers, anthropologists, etc.) and academics, the *Journal of Human Rights Practice* intends to "capture learning and communicate the lessons of practice across professional and geographical boundaries," in order to encourage and stimulate new approaches and ideas in the field. The *Journal* publishes interviews, research articles, review articles, book reviews, and more, allowing for a wide perspective. Recently covered topics include a human rights perspective on housing rights in Cameroon; the interactions between armed groups and human rights groups; and the current legal status of sex work and sex solicitation in Cambodia. The journal is academic but clearly written, and would be an appropriate fit in academic and legal libraries.

The Progressive. See News and Opinion section.

1335. *Reason: free minds and free markets.* [ISSN: 0048-6906] 1968. m. USD 14.97. Ed(s): Matt Welch. Reason Foundation, 5737 Mesmer Ave, Los Angeles, CA 90230; chris.mitchell@reason.org; http://reason.org/. Illus., index, adv. Vol. ends: Apr. Microform: PQC. *Indexed:* A01, A22, ABS&EES, BRI, CBRI, P02. *Bk. rev.:* 3-4, 1,500-2,500 words. *Aud.:* Hs, Ga, Ac.

Founded in 1968 as a student publication based at Boston University, *Reason* has since become an independent publication dedicated to "making a principled case for liberty and individual choice in all areas of human activity." It is published 11 times a year by the Reason Foundation, a nonprofit research organization dedicated to advancing libertarian principles, although the journal remains editorially independent. *Reason* is written for a general audience, with recent articles on such timely topics as the legal challenges to the Affordable Care Act; private industry solutions to traffic congestion; and an analysis of the income gap of recent years. The journal is available in full text online, although the most recent issue is available only at newsstands and by subscription.

The Review of Black Political Economy. See Labor and Industrial Relations section.

1336. *Seattle Journal for Social Justice.* [ISSN: 1544-1245] 2002. s-a. USD 40 (Individuals, USD 25). Ed(s): Sonja Carlson. Seattle University, School of Law, 901 12th Ave, PO Box 222000, Seattle, WA 98122; lawhelp@seattleu.edu; http://www.law.seattleu.edu. Refereed. Reprint: WSH. *Aud.:* Ac, Sa.

The *Seattle Journal for Social Justice* is published two times per year by the students of the Seattle University School of Law. It aims to cover a broad range of urgent problems of social justice through a variety of formats: research articles, creative writing, commentaries, essays, and even artwork. Recent articles have covered local compliance with the United States Immigration and Customs Enforcement's "Secure Communities" initiative; how best to engage legal students in disaster response; and approaches to combating human trafficking. The research articles are academic in style, but remain accessible to the non-legal reader, making this journal a good fit for both legal and academic libraries.

■ CLASSICAL STUDIES

See also Archaeology; Art; History; Linguistics; and Literature sections.

Tom Bruno, Associate Director for Resource Sharing and Reserves, Sterling Memorial Library, Yale University, New Haven, CT 06511

Introduction

While the field of Classical Studies enjoys a perennial appeal in higher education, interest in Ancient Greece and Rome among the general public and popular culture tends to be more cyclical in nature. Therefore, it is not surprising that journals published about the Classics fall into two general categories: those long-standing, peer-reviewed publications that serve as the chief vehicle of scholarly communication for faculty, graduate students, and independent researchers; and more popular (as well as more ephemeral) publications that are written with the educated layperson as its target audience.

Two smaller but nevertheless important categories include journals that are published primarily for educators in the Classics (especially teachers of high school Latin and Greek), as well as those publications that address topics from Ancient Greek and Roman culture—such as narrative fiction, poetry, drama, or dance—which are of interest to modern artists, contemporary scholars, and other performers who have been inspired by Classical artists and their themes.

The ongoing crisis in scholarly publishing has not been kind to many academic disciplines, and Classical Studies has proven to be no exception in this regard. In fact, several titles that were reviewed in this section two years ago have not produced any additional issues since that time, while others have attempted to move to an open-access format with varying levels of success. While the necessity of publication in peer-reviewed journals for the purposes of receiving tenure will ensure that the most respected of scholarly publications in Classical Studies will survive, it is difficult to predict how other titles will fare over the next few years.

Basic Periodicals

Hs: *Amphora, Classical Journal, Classical Outlook, Classical World, Greece and Rome.* Ac: *American Journal of Philology, American Philological Association. Transactions, Amphora, Classical Journal, Classical Outlook, Classical Philology, Classical World, Greece and Rome.*

Basic Abstracts and Indexes

L'Annee Philologique, Arts and Humanities Citation Index, Humanities Index, TOCS-IN.

1337. *American Journal of Philology.* [ISSN: 0002-9475] 1880. q. USD 185. Ed(s): David H J Larmour. The Johns Hopkins University Press, 2715 N Charles St, Baltimore, MD 21218; http://www.press.jhu.edu. Illus., index, adv. Sample. Refereed. Circ: 603. Vol. ends: Winter. Microform: IDC; PMC; PQC. Reprint: PSC. *Indexed:* A01, A22, AmHI, ArtHuCI, BRI, CBRI, E01, FR, IPB, MLA-IB, NumL, P02, RILM. *Bk. rev.:* 4-5, 2-5 pages. *Aud.:* Ac.

Founded in 1880 by American classical scholar Basil Lanneau Gildersleeve, the *American Journal of Philology* is a quarterly publication of the Johns Hopkins University Press. Each issue offers several scholarly articles that highlight the latest research in Greek and Roman literature, classical linguistics, and related topics in Greek and Roman history, society, religion, and philosophy; there are four or five book reviews as well. Recent articles have covered such topics as narrative and rhetoric in Homer's *Odyssey,* sexual ideology and creative authority in Heliodorus' *Aethiopica,* and chiasmus in the *Aeneid.* Few journals are as prestigious and influential to the field of Classical Studies as the *AJP,* making it an indispensable part of any academic library collection with a strong focus on Latin and Greek or the humanities.

1338. *American Philological Association. Transactions.* Supersedes in part (in 1974): *American Philological Association. Transactions and Proceedings;* Which was formerly (until 1897): *American Philological Association. Transactions.* [ISSN: 0360-5949] 1870. s-a. USD 125 (print or online ed.). Ed(s): Katharina Volk. The Johns Hopkins University Press, 2715 N Charles St, Baltimore, MD 21218; http://www.press.jhu.edu. Illus., adv. Sample. Refereed. Circ: 3040. Microform: PMC. *Indexed:* A01, A22, AmHI, ArtHuCI, E01, MLA-IB, P02, SSA. *Aud.:* Ac.

The official research publication of the American Philological Association, *Transactions* is the main clearinghouse of scholarship for the field of Classical Studies. This journal is now published two times a year, and each issue contains between six and ten articles on various topics in Greek and Latin literature, Classical philology, and ancient history. Each Autumn issue includes an address from the current APA President, as well. Recent articles have featured such topics as wind and time in Homeric epic, religious feasting in Apuleius' *Metamorphoses,* and music, order, and love in *Daphnis and Chloe.* Although it goes without saying that *Transactions* is an essential title for any library collection that supports studies of Ancient Greek and Latin, it is also an excellent snapshot of the current state of Classical Studies, and as such would be a welcome addition to any academic research library.

1339. *Ancient Narrative.* [ISSN: 1568-3532] 2001. 3x/yr. EUR 102 (Individuals, EUR 51). Ed(s): Dr. Maaike Zimmerman, Gareth Schmeling. Barkhuis Publishing, Zuurstukken 37, Eelde, 9761 KP, Netherlands; info@barkhuis.nl; http://www.barkhuis.nl. Refereed. *Aud.:* Ac.

A continuation of the *Petronian Society Newsletter* and the *Groningen Colloquia on the Novel, Ancient Narrative* is "an interdisciplinary peer-reviewed electronic journal publishing articles on Greek, Roman, and Jewish novels and narrative from the ancient and Byzantine periods." Although its focus primarily consists of Classical and religious scholarship, *Ancient Narrative* welcomes contributions from any scholars interested in the birth and development of narrative fiction. Authors are encouraged to revise their articles based on reader feedback; at the end of each year, the revised articles are made available in both electronic and print form. Recent issues have featured articles on topics such as storytelling in Apollodorus' *Against Neaira;* psychological conflicts and moral goodness in the Greek Novels; and the *Ephesiaca* as a Bildungsroman. Each issue also contains several reviews of recent monographs published in the field. *Ancient Narrative* has recently transitioned from a subscription-based publishing model to an open-access format—and while it is too early to tell whether this change will be successful, it is consistent with the editors' vision of facilitating scholarship as a fruitful dialog between authors and readers.

1340. *Arethusa.* [ISSN: 0004-0975] 1968. 3x/yr. USD 113. Ed(s): Madeleine S Kaufman, Martha Malamud. The Johns Hopkins University Press, 2715 N Charles St, Baltimore, MD 21218; http://www.press.jhu.edu. Illus., adv. Sample. Refereed. Circ: 315. Vol. ends: Fall. Microform: PQC. Reprint: PSC. *Indexed:* A22, AmHI, ArtHuCI, E01, MLA-IB, P02. *Aud.:* Ac.

Published three times a year by the Johns Hopkins University Press, *Arethusa* is an interdisciplinary journal that highlights literary and cultural studies of the ancient Graeco–Roman world. Each issue offers five to eight scholarly articles, with a focus on literary criticism. Recent issues have covered such topics as sacrifice and sorority in Sophocles' *Antigony,* a reading of Martial's epigrams through the lens of Pliny's *Natural History,* and the juxtaposition of Aztec and Roman empires in a recent exhibition at the Getty Villa in Malibu. *Arethusa* prides itself on embracing a mix of contemporary literary theory and more traditional modes of Classical scholarship—thus, it makes for a more accessible publication about Ancient Greek and Latin literature than those that emphasize philology and linguistics.

1341. *Arion: a journal of humanities and the classics.* [ISSN: 0095-5809] 1962. 3x/yr. USD 60 (print & online eds.). Ed(s): Nicholas Poburko, Herbert Golder. Boston University, 621 Commonwealth Ave, Boston, MA 02215; http://web.bu.edu/arion/. Illus., adv. Vol. ends: Fall. Reprint: PSC. *Indexed:* A22, AmHI, ArtHuCI, MLA-IB, RILM. *Bk. rev.:* 2-5, 5-20 pages. *Aud.:* Ac.

When Boston University launched its classics journal *Arion* in the Winter of 1990, editor Herbert Golder made the following editorial statement: "We are in a quest of freshness of vision, a distinction of thought (as opposed to professional group-think), rigor of imagination, and an energetic sense of the spaciousness of the classical tradition." More than 20 years later, *Arion* continues to push the envelope of Classical Studies, offering its erudite and eclectic mix of scholarly essays, reviews, and translations, as well as original fiction and poetry inspired by ancient authors and Classical themes. Recent issues have offered a breadth of topics, such as postmodernism and the Grand Narrative; the Greek invention of the human; and a comparison of the 2010 movie *Inception* and Book 6 of Virgil's *Aeneid.* Few academic publications in any discipline would make for scintillating reading to laypersons, but *Arion* is a notable exception to this rule, and would be an excellent addition to any large academic or public library's collection.

1342. *Bryn Mawr Classical Review (Online).* [ISSN: 1063-2948] 1990. irreg. Free. Ed(s): Camilla MacKay, James O'Donnell. Bryn Mawr College, 101 N Merion Ave, Bryn Mawr, PA 19010; info@brynmawr.edu; http://www.brynmawr.edu. Illus. Refereed. *Indexed:* AmHI. *Bk. rev.:* 1,500-2,000 words. *Aud.:* Ac.

Not a magazine or journal *per se,* the *Bryn Mawr Classical Review* is an open-access online collection of reviews of current scholarly work in the field of Classical Studies, including Ancient Greek and Roman archaeology. New book reviews are added irregularly and are written by experts in the respective field that each monograph addresses. The *BMCR* blog permits readers to comment on individual reviews, permitting some degree of interactivity between readers, reviewers, and occasionally the original authors of the books being reviewed as well. The *Bryn Mawr Classical Review* is one of the best resources available for keeping abreast of new books being published in the field, and thus could serve as a valuable tool for collection development as well.

1343. *Classical Antiquity.* Formerly (until 1982): *California Studies in Classical Antiquity.* [ISSN: 0278-6656] 1968. s-a. USD 239 (print & online eds.). Ed(s): Mark Griffith. University of California Press, Journals Division, 2000 Ctr St, Ste 303, Berkeley, CA 94704; customerservice@ucpressjournals.com; http://www.ucpressjournals.com. Illus., index, adv. Sample. Refereed. Circ: 581. Vol. ends: Oct. Microform: PQC. Reprint: PSC. *Indexed:* A01, A22, AmHI, ArtHuCI, E01, P02. *Aud.:* Ac.

A biannual publication of the University of California Press, *Classical Antiquity* is "a journal that combines the pleasures, politics, intellectualism, cultural production, sciences, and linguistics of European traditions, centuries past." Each issue features four or five articles about Classical Studies, with an emphasis on comparative literature and interdisciplinary studies. Recent topics have included doubles and masquerades in Cassius Dio's *Roman History,* the

structure of the Plutarchan book, and an investigation of historiographic evidence for the political management of Ancient Greek fisheries. In a field of publications that can often sag under the weight of their own scholarship, *Classical Antiquity* manages to strike a balance between respectable research and broader cultural relevance, making it a lively addition to most academic library collections.

1344. *The Classical Journal.* [ISSN: 0009-8353] 1905. q. USD 125 (print & online eds.). Ed(s): S Douglas Olson. Classical Association of the Middle West and South, Inc., c/o Anne H. Groton, St. Olaf College, Department of Classics, Northfield, MN 55057; newlands@stolaf.edu; http://www.camws.org. Illus., index, adv. Refereed. Vol. ends: May. *Indexed:* A06, A07, A22, AmHI, ArtHuCI, BRI, CBRI, IIMP, MLA-IB, NumL. *Bk. rev.:* 3-5, 1-5 pages. *Aud.:* Hs, Ac.

The Classical Association of the Middle West and South, the largest regional Classics association in the United States and Canada, has been publishing *The Classical Journal* for over 100 years. Each issue of this quarterly publication contains several articles that cover topics in Ancient Graeco–Roman literature, history, or culture (including book reviews), as well as articles that discuss teaching Greek and Latin in high schools and colleges. Recent issues have included articles about Athena and the Spartans at the conclusion of *Lysistrata,* ritual imagery in Plautus' *Epidicus,* and the motif of crane migration in Roman martial epic. While there are many Classical Studies publications that offer a healthy range of solid scholarship, *The Classical Journal*'s strong pedagogical focus makes it of special interest to library collections that support the education of future Greek and Latin teachers.

1345. *Classical Outlook.* Formerly (until 1936): *Latin notes.* [ISSN: 0009-8361] 1923. q. Free to members; USD 10 per issue. Ed(s): Mary C English. American Classical League, Miami University, Oxford, OH 45056; info@aclclassics.org; http://www.aclclassics.org. Illus., adv. Circ: 4250. Vol. ends: Summer. *Indexed:* A22, BRI, CBRI, MLA-IB. *Bk. rev.:* 6-8, 300-1,000 words. *Aud.:* Hs, Ac, Ga.

Classical Outlook, "the most widely circulated Classics journal in North America," is a quarterly publication of the American Classical League, which since 1919 has fostered the study of classical languages in the United States and Canada. This is primarily a journal for teachers, and each issue of *Classical Outlook* includes essays, scholarly articles, committee or research reports, classroom materials, and reviews of books or other media. Items are selected for publication by the editors for the dual purpose of offering information that can be used by active teachers of Latin and Greek and keeping ACL members up to date on recent scholarship in the field of Classical Studies. Thus, this journal is not only an essential tool for educators, but it can also provide an excellent overview to lay readers or other amateur enthusiasts for the Classics.

1346. *Classical Philology.* [ISSN: 0009-837X] 1906. q. USD 302 (print & online eds.). Ed(s): Elizabeth Asmis. University of Chicago Press, 1427 E 60th St, Chicago, IL 60637; subscriptions@press.uchicago.edu; http://www.journals.uchicago.edu. Illus., index, adv. Sample. Refereed. Vol. ends: Oct. Microform: IDC. Reprint: PSC. *Indexed:* A01, A22, AmHI, ArtHuCI, BRI, IPB, MLA-IB, NumL, P02. *Bk. rev.:* 4-6, 3-5 pages. *Aud.:* Ac.

A quarterly publication of the University of Chicago Press, *Classical Philology* is one of the most respected journals in the field of Classical Studies. From its statement of Editorial Policy, *CP* "is devoted to publishing the best scholarly thought on all aspects of Graeco-Roman antiquity, including literature, languages, anthropology, history, social life, philosophy, religion, art, material culture, and the history of classical studies." Each issue features four to six scholarly articles, a section on "Notes and Discussions," and several book reviews. Recent topics covered include leisure in Plato's *Laws,* Parmenides and the grammar of being, and astrology in Ancient Rome. *Classical Philology* is a first-rate academic journal with international repute, and is therefore a "must-have" for any library collection that supports the Classics.

1347. *The Classical Quarterly.* [ISSN: 0009-8388] 1906. s-a. GBP 162 (print & online eds.). Ed(s): Bruce Gibson, John Wilkins. Cambridge University Press, The Edinburgh Bldg, Shaftesbury Rd, Cambridge, CB2 8RU, United Kingdom; journals@cambridge.org; http://www.cambridge.org/uk. Illus., index, adv. Sample. Refereed. Microform: PQC. Reprint: PSC. *Indexed:* A01, A22, AmHI, ArtHuCI, BrArAb, E01, FR, IPB, MLA-IB, MSN, NumL, P02, RILM. *Aud.:* Ac.

One of the premier academic journals dedicated to classical scholarship, *The Classical Quarterly* is a biannual publication of the Classical Associate of Great Britain. Each issue of this journal features 20–30 articles, with a strong focus on philology. While there are no book reviews in *The Classical Quarterly*, these appear in *The Classical Review*, which is also published by the Classical Association. Recent issues have covered such topics as the Nile Cruise of Cleopatra VII; poetry and ritual in the Hymn to Dionysus in Sophocles' *Antigone*; and source citations in Thucydides. Although *Classical Quarterly* may not appeal to laypersons or amateur enthusiasts of the Classics, it is an indispensable resource for serious scholars and professional classicists.

1348. The Classical Review. [ISSN: 0009-840X] 1886. s-a. GBP 162 (print & online eds.). Ed(s): Neil Hopkinson, Roger Rees. Cambridge University Press, The Edinburgh Bldg, Shaftesbury Rd, Cambridge, CB2 8RU, United Kingdom; journals@cambridge.org; http://www.cambridge.org/uk. Illus., index, adv. Sample. Refereed. Microform: PMC; PQC. Reprint: PSC. *Indexed:* A01, A22, AmHI, ArtHuCI, BRI, CBRI, E01, IPB, MLA-IB, NumL. *Bk. rev.:* 150, 100-2,000 words. *Aud.:* Ac.

The Classical Review, also published by the Classical Association of Great Britain, is an annual collection of book reviews "covering the literatures and civilizations of ancient Greece and Rome." Each issue features about 150 reviews and 50 brief notes, providing an impressive swath of current scholarship in the Classics. Like the *Bryn Mawr Classical Review, Classical Review* is an important tool for any librarian seeking to build a strong collection in Classical Studies.

1349. Classical World. Formerly (until 1957): *The Classical Weekly;* Which superseded (in 1907): *The New York Latin Leaflet.* [ISSN: 0009-8418] 1907. q. USD 65. The Johns Hopkins University Press, 2715 N Charles St, Baltimore, MD 21218; http://www.press.jhu.edu. Illus., index, adv. Refereed. Vol. ends: Jun/Aug. Microform: MIM; PQC. Reprint: PSC. *Indexed:* A22, AmHI, ArtHuCI, BRI, CBRI, E01, IPB, MLA-IB, NumL. *Bk. rev.:* 15-20, 300-500 words. *Aud.:* Hs, Ac.

A quarterly publication of the Classical Association of the Atlantic States, *Classical World* covers the literature, history, and society of Ancient Greece and Rome, especially from a pedagogical perspective: "The ideal reader of Classical World is a scholarly teacher or a teaching scholar, and the ideal contributor has something to say to this reader." Every issue features original articles, research bibliographies, and reviews of scholarly monographs, textbooks, and other teaching materials; each issue also includes information about scholarships, fellowships, conferences, and other programming of interest both to teachers and students of the Classics. *Classical World* is a first-rate journal that would appeal to both high school and collegiate readers.

1350. Didaskalia. [ISSN: 1321-4853] 1994. irreg. Free. Ed(s): Amy R Cohen. Randolph College, 2500 Rivermont Ave, Lynchburg, VA 24503; helpdesk@randolphcollege.edu; http://www.randolphcollege.edu/. Illus. Refereed. *Bk. rev.:* 2-3, 1,000-2,000 words. *Aud.:* Ga, Ac.

Started in 1994 as a "notice board" for discussing productions of Ancient drama, *Didaskalia* is an online journal that features the study of all Greek and Roman performance, both ancient and modern. Each issue offers scholarly articles on the performance of Classical drama, dance, and music, as well as reviews of contemporary productions, previews of upcoming productions, and interviews with artists and scholars. *Didaskalia* also publishes opinion or essays reflecting personal views on aspects of ancient performance. Given the cultural importance of performance in the Classical world and the diachronic interplay between ancient Greek and Roman authors and modern artists, a publication such as *Didaskalia* is a wonderful resource for both scholars of ancient performance and contemporary performers.

1351. Greece and Rome. [ISSN: 0017-3835] 1931. s-a. GBP 118 (print & online eds.). Ed(s): Robert Shorrock, Vedia Izzet. Cambridge University Press, The Edinburgh Bldg, Shaftesbury Rd, Cambridge, CB2 8RU, United Kingdom; information@cambridge.org; http://www.cambridge.org/uk. Illus., adv. Sample. Refereed. Microform: PQC. Reprint: PSC. *Indexed:* A01, A22, AmHI, ArtHuCI, BRI, BrArAb, E01, IPB, MLA-IB, P02, RILM. *Bk. rev.:* 2-3, 500-1,000 words. *Aud.:* Hs, Ga, Ac.

Greece & Rome, another publication by the Classical Association of Great Britain, aims to deliver classical scholarship "to a wider audience." Each issue features several articles of general interest on various aspects of Greek and Roman literature, history, and culture. Reviews of recently published books are also included, as well as subject reviews that provide concise updates for different disciplines within the field of Classical Studies. Recent issues have covered a wide range of topics, such as playing ball in antiquity, commemoration and pilgrimage in the ancient world, and a discussion of whether posttraumatic stress disorder was prevalent among Roman soldiers. It is rare to find a journal that makes academic scholarship more accessible to the layperson without oversimplifying the subject matter, but *Greece & Rome* manages to challenge readers of all levels of expertise while at the same time engaging them.

1352. Mnemosyne: a journal of classical studies. [ISSN: 0026-7074] 1852. 6x/yr. EUR 757. Ed(s): G J Boter. Brill, PO Box 9000, Leiden, 2300 PA, Netherlands; cs@brill.nl; http://www.brill.nl. Illus., index. Refereed. Vol. ends: Nov. Microform: SWZ. Reprint: PSC. *Indexed:* A01, A22, AmHI, ArtHuCI, BRI, E01, FR, IPB, MLA-IB, P02, RILM. *Bk. rev.:* 10-12, 500-1,500 words. *Aud.:* Ac.

Published four times a year, *Mnemosyne* is one of the oldest journals in the field of Classical Studies. Each issue features four to six articles that focus primarily on ancient Greek and Latin philology, with extensive short notes and 10–12 book reviews. The subject matter is highly technical and requires subject expertise in Classical languages. Recent topics have included the spatial meaning of the Greek preposition *dia* with the accusative case in Homeric Greek; the interrogative use of the word *nam* in Early Latin; and a treatment of paradox and the marvelous in Augustan literature and culture. Although this journal will appeal only to a limited audience, *Mnemosyne* is the *ne plus ultra* of Classical philology, and thus is a required title for any college or university that offers advanced study in Greek or Latin.

1353. Phoenix (Toronto, 1946). [ISSN: 0031-8299] 1946. q. USD 140 (print & online eds.). Ed(s): Judith K Schutz, J Trevett. Classical Association of Canada, Trinity College, University of Toronto, Toronto, ON M5S 1H8, Canada; http://www.cac-scec.ca. Illus., index, adv. Refereed. *Indexed:* A22, ArtHuCI, CBCARef, FR, IPB, MLA-IB, NumL. *Bk. rev.:* 15-20, 500-1,000 words. *Aud.:* Ac.

Published by the University of Toronto Press for the Classical Association of Canada, *Phoenix* features "the literature, language, history, philosophy, religion, mythology, science, archaeology, art, architecture, and culture of the Greek and Roman worlds from earliest times to about AD 600." Each issue contains several articles and 15–20 book reviews written in English and French. Recent issues have covered topics including temporary propriety in Propertius; the significance of overlap in Strabo's *Geography*; and crossing the Rubicon and the outbreak of civil war in Cicero, Lucan, Plutarch, and Suetonius. With no recent publications from *Mouseion*, the Classical Association of Canada's other professional journal, *Phoenix* is now an essential resource for keeping abreast of scholarly research in the Classics in Canada, and as such is an excellent addition to any academic library collection.

■ CLASSROOM MAGAZINES

Art/Foreign Language/Language Arts/Life Skills/Mathematics/Science/Social Studies and Current Events/Teacher and Professional

See also Children; Education; and Teenagers sections.

Kacy Lundstrom, Instruction Coordinator, Utah State University, Logan, UT 84322-3000; kacy.lundstrom@usu.edu

Introduction

These magazines provide creative, hands-on ways for students in the K–12 classroom to enjoy learning. They also provide ways for teachers to support this learning, including providing teachers with tips and ideas for how they can facilitate learning by using these resources. These magazines give students introductory practice with discipline-specific vocabulary and research. They can also garner student interest in unique and visual ways, and can also help save teachers' time by providing ideas or specific instructions for lessons that are relevant and creative.

The magazines listed in this section target students and specify target ages relating to reading level. Some magazines are primarily or solely found in online formats, while nearly all have moved toward having a strong online presence. For easy identification of how these magazines would correspond with classroom content or student interests, sources are listed by subject.

Since the latest edition of *MFL*, one major change is the merger of the Weekly Reader company and Scholastic. Due to market pressures and decreasing school budgets, titles such as *Current Events, Current Science,* and *Weekly Reader* have been folded into related Scholastic publications. According to Scholastic's web site, this merger allows them to offer "a line of classroom magazines that combine the classic curriculum support of Weekly Reader with the educational expertise of Scholastic."

A number of these titles cater specifically to teachers, identifiable mainly by the integration of direct tips, lesson plans, and activities for how to use magazine content in the classroom. The titles can be found within the "Teacher and Professional" subsection. Suggestions for integration include ideas for (1) how to use unique art or current-event stories to stimulate critical thinking; (2) how to create collaborative learning opportunities for students; and (3) classroom discussion. Material is designed to help students meet learning objectives and to enrich classroom curriculum. To assist in giving specific instructions and guides for how to integrate magazine content into the classroom, many of these resources are accompanied by supplementary web sites, CDs, learning goals, and assessment ideas. Magazines such as *Scope* have new online interactive features, as well as classroom resources designed for use on a whiteboard or projector.

Most of the magazines in this section are published in the U.S., although similar magazines are also produced in other countries (e.g., Canada or Australia). One major foreign language publisher, Authentik Language Learning Resources Ltd., a campus company of Trinity College, Dublin, was also forced into liquidation due to market challenges.

The education pedagogy reflected in these magazines through its content and instruction ideas tends to mirror the goals of current pedagogy in today's educational research. Magazines that specifically focus on theory are listed in the "Education" section of this volume or in the corresponding subject discipline section, such as "Art," or "Marine Science and Technology."

The titles listed here are likely to be classroom subscriptions, while the titles that are more likely to be personal subscriptions are listed in the "Children" and "Teenagers" sections, although a number of those titles could also be applicable in a classroom setting. Subscriptions are available as classroom sets or at a discounted per-issue price.

Basic Periodicals

Select by subject and audience level.

Basic Abstracts and Indexes

Academic Search Premier, Children's Magazine Guide, Education Index, Education Research Complete, ERIC, InfoTrac, MAS Ultra-School Edition, Primary Search, Wilson OmniFile.

Art

Dramatics. See Theater section.

Instructor. See Education/General, K-12 section.

1354. Scholastic Art. Formerly (until 1992): *Art and Man;* Incorporates: *Artist Junior.* [ISSN: 1060-832X] 1970. 6x/yr. USD 8.95 for grade 7-12. Ed(s): Susanne McCabe. Scholastic Inc., 557 Broadway, 3rd Fl, New York, NY 10012; news@scholastic.com; http://www.scholastic.com. Illus., index. Sample. Circ: 245000. Vol. ends: Apr/May. *Indexed:* A22, ICM. *Aud.:* Ems, Hs.

This beautifully illustrated magazine introduces students to classical and contemporary art and artists from around the world. The "Artist of the Month" column features an interview with a student artist from among the winners of the Scholastic Art and Writing Award. Each issue features a "Masterpiece of the Month," with a poster of the featured artist's work in the teacher's edition and mini-posters in each student issue. "Art Spotlight" and "Critics Corner" are regular skills features. The new "Career Corner" page features an interview with an art professional, as well as a career profile with salary and education information and advice on what a student can do to prepare for a career in that particular field. The teacher's edition for grades 7–12 (free with orders of ten or more student subscriptions) includes discussion questions, an answer key for the skills sections, a lesson plan for the "Art Workshop," a reproducible question sheet for the featured theme, and a list of the National Content Standards for the Visual Arts to which each article correlates. An additional teacher's edition for working with students in grades 4–6 is also included. The web site includes an editorial calendar, with topics and artists for the year's upcoming issues, that teachers can use to plan future lessons. URL: http://teacher.scholastic.com

Stone Soup. See Children section.

Foreign Language

1355. Ciao Italia: il mensile per il tuo italiano. [ISSN: 0997-0290] 6x/yr. EUR 17.90. European Language Institute (E L I), Casella Postale 6, Recanati, 62019, Italy; editorial@elionline.com; http://www.elimagazines.com. Illus. *Aud.:* Ems, Hs.

One of many foreign-language magazines from this publisher, *Ciao Italia* is intended for students in their second year of Italian ("lower intermediate" level). Other magazines target various levels of language proficiency from elementary school through college. All include comic strips, puzzles, and games to teach vocabulary. Topical articles provide reading practice and enhance comprehension. Elementary-level magazines include colorful pictures, games, and classroom activities. Intermediate levels place greater emphasis on civilization and culture and contain articles about music, sports, movies, and the Internet. More advanced levels provide excerpts from contemporary literature, enhanced glossaries, and a wider variety of articles. Teachers' guides include reproducible activities as well as a list of the lessons, goals, and grammar to be covered in each of the year's issues. Audio CDs accompany classroom orders for most of the magazines. Other magazines from this publisher include: ITALIAN: *Azzurro,* for students of various ages beginning to learn Italian; *Ragazzi* (intermediate); *Tutti Insieme* (upper intermediate); and *Oggitalia,* for advanced students. GERMAN: *Fertig...los,* for students beginning to study German; *Kinder* (lower intermediate); *Freunde* (intermediate); and *Zusammen* (upper intermediate). SPANISH: *Vamos!,* for students beginning to study Spanish; *Chicos* (lower intermediate); *Muchachos* (intermediate); and *Todos Amigos* (upper intermediate). FRENCH: *Voila,* for beginning French in elementary school; *C'est Facile,* for the next level of beginning study; *Mome* (lower intermediate); *Jeunes* (intermediate); *Ensemble* (upper intermediate); and *Presse-Papiers,* for advanced students. LATIN: *Adulescens,* for students with a beginning knowledge of Latin; and *Iuvenis* (lower intermediate). RUSSIAN: *Davai,* for students studying Russian at an intermediate level. For students of English as a Second Language, ELI publishes *Ready for English,* for primary school; *Let's Start,* for secondary beginners; *A Tot for English* (lower intermediate to one year of English); *Kid* (intermediate to two years of English); *Teen* (upper intermediate to three years of English); and *Sure!,* for advanced students. The web site also includes teacher resources, such as reading texts, song lyrics, activities, and professional development materials. The "Play & Learn" section has games, comics, picture dictionaries, tests in the various languages, and e-mail postcards. URL: www.elimagazines.com

1356. Que Tal. Formerly: *Oye.* [ISSN: 0033-5940] 1966. bi-m. USD 7.99 per issue. Mary Glasgow Magazines, Westfield Rd, Southam, CV47 0RA, United Kingdom; orders@maryglasgowplus.com; http://maryglasgowplus.com. Illus. Sample. Microform: PQC. *Aud.:* Hs.

Distributed through Scholastic, this colorful Mary Glasgow (London) magazine is aimed at first-year students of Spanish. Teen-interest content—such as interviews, activities, puzzles, and games—helps build language proficiency and cultural awareness. "Teacher's Notes" (in English), free with class subscriptions, provides additional teaching ideas, background information to complement articles, reproducible worksheets, activities, and quizzes. For each title, two audio CDs (with tracks corresponding to each issue) include an engaging radio show format, games, contests, original songs for singing along, and an illustrated booklet with full audio transcripts. The price per student is $6.95 for six issues. Other Mary Glasgow magazines include: SPANISH: *Ahora,* for advanced beginners; and *El Sol,* for intermediate and advanced learners. FRENCH: *Allons-y!,* for beginners and near-beginners; *Bonjour,* for advanced beginners; *Ca Va?,* for intermediate; and *Chez Nous,* for advanced. GERMAN: *Das Rad,* for beginners and near-beginners; and *Schuss,* for intermediate. In addition, several Mary Glasgow titles are distributed only in Canada. *La Petite Press* is a French-language magazine for ages 7–11 with teacher's notes available in English or French. A series for English language learners includes *Click* (beginner level), *Crown* (pre-intermediate), *Team* and *Club* (intermediate), and *Current* (advanced).

Language Arts

Cricket. See Children section.

1357. Scholastic Action. [ISSN: 0163-3570] 1977. 14x/yr. USD 3.99 with 10 or more student subscr. Ed(s): Janice Behrans. Scholastic Inc., 557 Broadway, 3rd Fl, New York, NY 10012; news@scholastic.com; http://www.scholastic.com. Illus. Sample. Circ: 230000. *Indexed:* MASUSE, P01. *Aud.:* Hs.

Action is a reading and language arts magazine that covers teen topics for middle and high school students reading at a third- to fifth-grade level. Celebrity profiles, debate topics, and real-life skill activities provide engaging reading material for teens. A series of read-aloud plays based upon current movies, TV shows, and classic books is designed to be integrated into the curriculum and help students with decoding, fluency, and class participation. Every story is followed by a reading comprehension quiz. The "True Teen" nonfiction articles highlight teens who have overcome personal and social challenges. A teen advice column appears in every issue. Graphic organizers and other tools accompanying the articles help students to improve their reading comprehension and suggest strategies for reading, writing, and vocabulary building. The teacher's edition includes "Issue at a Glance," which ties articles to skills, activities, and related standards. It contains lesson plans and reproducible worksheets as well as a planning calendar. This magazine could also be useful for ESL students.

1358. Scholastic Let's Find Out. Formerly (until 1995): *My First Magazine.* [ISSN: 0024-1261] 19??. 32x/yr. USD 4.95. Scholastic Inc., 557 Broadway, 3rd Fl, New York, NY 10012; news@scholastic.com; http://www.scholastic.com. Illus. Sample. Circ: 615000. Vol. ends: May/Jun. *Aud.:* Ems.

Each month, *LFO* provides teaching ideas for the five critical areas of early reading: phonemic awareness, phonics, fluency, vocabulary, and comprehension in four themed issues. Pictures, stories, and activities help pre-K and kindergarten children discover the world around them. Regular sections include "Kids Can Do It," "Science," "People and Places," and "Early Reader." "My Rebus Reader" is a new mini-book format featured in each issue, which began in March 2009. There is also a section, "Look What I'm Learning at School" (which includes "Let's Find Out Goes Home"), that comprises activities to be done with parents or family, with instructions in both English and Spanish. Free classroom posters in full color are included in each issue. The teacher's guide, included with each subscription, contains cross-curricular activities, tips for teaching with the posters, NAEYC guidelines and connections to state and national standards, and links to additional resources.

1359. Scholastic Scope: the language arts magazine. Incorporates: *Read Magazine.* [ISSN: 0036-6412] 1964. bi-w. during school year. USD 8.99 for 9 issues. Ed(s): Diane Weber, Mary Harvey. Scholastic Inc., 557 Broadway, 3rd Fl, New York, NY 10012; news@scholastic.com; http://www.scholastic.com. Illus., adv. Sample. Circ: 424843. *Indexed:* A01, A22, ICM, P01. *Bk. rev.:* Number and length vary. *Aud.:* Ems.

Scholastic Scope, which absorbed Weekly Reader's *READ* when the two companies merged, provides literature and writing activities for sixth- to tenth-grade students, including read-aloud plays, writing workshops, vocabulary builders, and reading strategies. Each issue provides writing prompts, puzzles, a "Readers Theater" play, and regular features such as "You Be the Editor," which works on particular grammar elements such as pronouns or quotations, and the "Scope 100," challenging words taken from SAT/ACT lists. The "Having Your Say" writing program invites readers to submit their poetry, book reviews, music reviews, essays, and stories for publication in the magazine. Skill-building features and test-preparation lessons are tied to state and national standards. *Scholastic Scope* works on skills such as sequencing, listening, graph reading, and comprehension. The teacher's edition includes lesson plans with pre-reading activities and post-reading discussion questions, as well as reproducible pages. Now includes digital lessons on the web site. URL: www.scholastic.com/scopemagazine/index.html

1360. Storyworks. [ISSN: 1068-0292] 1993. 6x/yr. USD 3.99. Scholastic Inc., 557 Broadway, 3rd Fl, New York, NY 10012; http://www.scholastic.com. Illus. Sample. Vol. ends: Apr/May. *Indexed:* BRI, MASUSE, P01. *Bk. rev.:* 4-5, 125 words. *Aud.:* Ems.

A literature magazine for grades 3–6, *Storyworks* features fiction, nonfiction, poetry, plays, and illustrations by award-winning children's authors and artists. Activities that develop grammar, writing, vocabulary, and test-taking skills complement the readings. "Reviews by You" publishes students' reviews of books they've read. "Sentence Chef" and "Writing Rescue" provide writing skills exercises. "Word Nerd" introduces vocabulary, and "Grammar Cop" and "WordWorks" supply practice with grammatical concepts and parts of speech. "Micro Mystery" builds comprehension with reading for detail. Writing activities in the "Yesterday and Today" feature present side-by-side articles for students to compare and contrast an event or person from the past with the contemporary equivalent. Contests and author interviews offer students the opportunity to experience literature in more active and personal ways. In the teacher's guide, the feature "At a Glance" lists articles with corresponding themes and standards. The web site has additional lessons, quizzes, activities, and contests.

Life Skills

1361. Current Health Kids. Formerly (until 2010): *Current Health 1.* [ISSN: 2157-5916] 1974. 8x/yr. USD 39.95 per academic year. Weekly Reader Corporation, 3001 Cindel Dr, PO Box 8037, Delran, NJ 08075; customerservice@weeklyreader.com; http://www.weeklyreader.com. Illus. Sample. Circ: 300000 Paid. *Indexed:* A22, ICM, MASUSE, P01. *Aud.:* Ems, Hs.

This magazine is a wonderful resource for teachers looking for engaging material for health education. *Current Health 1* covers topics in personal health, fitness and exercise, diet and nutrition, diseases and disorders, and first aid and safety. Filled with full-color photographs, it focuses on health issues relevant to students and follows most state health curricula for grades 4–7. Articles focus on health factors such as body, mind, choices, and relationships. Features provide in-depth treatment of current topics such as the effects of sleep on health, walking for exercise, or how to maintain a healthy body image. Regular columns such as "Pulse," "Get Up and Go," and "Safety Zone" help students explore health-related issues and questions. The teacher's guide provides key objectives, links to National Health Education standards and relevant subject areas, and a planning calendar. The web site has reproducibles from the teacher's guides. *Current Health* is now also on Facebook, where teachers can share success stories and ideas for using the magazine. Meanwhile, *Current Health 2* [ISSN: 0163-156X] provides health information in a similar format for issues and health topics of interest to grades 7–12. There is an optional "Human Sexuality" supplement to complement *Current Health 2,* which explores sensitive issues such as relationships, peer pressure, and reproductive health from a teenager's perspective. It now offers free interactive digital editions of every issues. URL: www.weeklyreader.com/current-health-teens/

1362. Imagine (Baltimore): big ideas for bright minds. [ISSN: 1071-605X] 1993. 5x/yr. USD 50 (print or online ed.). Ed(s): Melissa Hartman. Johns Hopkins University, Center for Talented Youth, McAuley Hall, 5801 Smith Ave, Ste 400, Baltimore, MD 21209; ctyinfo@jhu.edu; http://cty.jhu.edu. Sample. *Indexed:* A22, E01. *Bk. rev.:* Number and length vary. *Aud.:* Hs.

Written for gifted students in grades 7–12, this exciting periodical is a five-time winner of the Parents Choice Gold Award. Each issue focuses on a general subject area, such as public health, politics and government, writing, philosophy, or "the art and science of games." Emphasis is given to activities that students can do *now* to pursue that interest, as well as career opportunities in that field. Each issue includes articles about summer programs and extracurricular activities across the country (written by student participants), student reviews of selective colleges, advice on planning for college, career profiles of accomplished professionals, puzzles, web resources, and book reviews written by students.

1363. *Scholastic Choices: personal development & living skills.*
Incorporates (in 1999): *Health Choices;* Supersedes (in 1985): *Co-Ed;* Incorporates (in 1991): *Forecast for the Home Economist;* Which superseded (in 1986): *Forecast for Home Economics;* (1963-1966): *Practical Forecast for Home Economics.* [ISSN: 0883-475X] 1956. 6x/yr. USD 4.75 for 10 copies or more. Ed(s): Maura Christopher. Scholastic Inc., 557 Broadway, 3rd Fl, New York, NY 10012; news@scholastic.com; http://www.scholastic.com. Illus., index, adv. Sample. Circ: 180000 Paid. Vol. ends: May. *Indexed:* A01, A22, BRI, ICM, MASUSE, P01. *Aud.:* Ems, Hs.

This life skills magazine for grades 7–12 features articles about health and nutrition, family life, decision making, careers, and personal development, using examples of interest to this age group. Weight and healthy lifestyles, sportsmanship and competition, teen pregnancy, and personal responsibility are some of the topics covered. Each article includes an activity that encourages students to apply what they've learned. Features include "Sticky Situation," in which students help other students as positive peer role models with issues such as substance abuse and personal relationships, and "Recipe 101," featuring recipes from an 18-year-old chef. The teacher's edition summarizes the articles, ties them to applicable standards, and provides discussion questions and additional activities for the featured stories. The tone is upbeat and not condescending; difficult issues are presented honestly. Because of the high interest of the subject matter, this magazine could be used as discussion material in a variety of subjects or settings—for example, language arts, health, or social studies.

Mathematics

1364. *Scholastic Dynamath.* Formerly (until 1982): *Scholastic Math Power.* [ISSN: 0732-7773] 1992. 8x/yr. USD 3.99 with 10 or more student subscr. Ed(s): Jack Silbert. Scholastic Inc., 557 Broadway, 3rd Fl, New York, NY 10012; news@scholastic.com; http://www.scholastic.com. Illus. Sample. Circ: 200000 Paid and free. Vol. ends: May. *Indexed:* P01. *Aud.:* Ems.

A workbook/magazine for grades 3–6, *Dynamath* reinforces basic math skills with colorful pictures, problems, and puzzles. Telling time, measurements, map reading, and problem solving are among the skills taught. Features include "Math on the Job," "Numbers in the News," and "Money Math" to help students with problem solving. The teacher's edition includes an answer key; lesson plans and extension activities; a "Problem of the Day" planning calendar to introduce math lessons with a warm-up exercise; and a table that correlates math features with national math standards (National Council for Teachers of Mathematics; NCTM).

1365. *Scholastic Math.* [ISSN: 0198-8379] 1980. 12x/yr. USD 3.99 price taken for grade 6-9. Ed(s): Jack Silbert. Scholastic Inc., 557 Broadway, 3rd Fl, New York, NY 10012; news@scholastic.com; http://www.scholastic.com. Illus. Sample. Circ: 200000 Paid. *Indexed:* ICM, MASUSE, P01. *Aud.:* Ems, Hs.

Scholastic Math for grades 6–9 is designed to prepare junior high students for pre-algebra. Math problems are illustrated in articles on current, real-world, age-appropriate topics. Features include "Fast Math" brainteasers, "Sports by the Numbers," "Math at Work," "Math in Literature," and "Math for Your Daily Life." Skills exercises, quizzes, and practice tests help prepare students for standardized tests. Movies, celebrities, sports, consumer math, and math-related

news make complex concepts accessible and entertaining. The teacher's edition contains teaching tips, extension activities, and a skills guide that correlates the articles to National Council for Teachers of Mathematics (NCTM) standards that are covered in each issue.

Science

1366. *National Geographic Explorer.* Formerly (until 2003): *National Geographic for Kids.* [ISSN: 1541-3357] 2001. 7x/yr. USD 3.95. Ed(s): Jacalyn Mahler, Dana Jensen. National Geographic Society, PO Box 98199, Washington, DC 20090; askngs@nationalgeographic.com; http://www.nationalgeographic.com/. Illus. Sample. *Indexed:* BRI, MASUSE. *Aud.:* Ems.

The National Geographic Society offers two editions of this colorful magazine, which helps students to develop nonfiction reading skills using science, social studies, and geography content. The *Pioneer Edition* is written at a second- to third-grade reading level and the *Pathfinder Edition* is written for fourth- to sixth-graders. Both editions look alike and feature the same topics, maps, graphs, and illustrations, but vary the text and concepts in terms of length and complexity. The editions can be used separately for a specific grade level or combined for differentiated instruction so that teachers can mix and match to address students' individual reading levels. The standards-based articles help teachers to meet NCLB goals. The "Teacher's Guide," included with each issue, contains suggested teaching strategies, "fast facts" about the featured subject matter, reproducible worksheets for checking comprehension, and extension activities for writing practice and making connections between disciplines. Supplementary content, such as games, e-cards, puzzles, and additional links can be found on the web site, as well as one article from each issue translated into Spanish (URL: www.nationalgeographic.com/ngexplorer). *National Geographic Young Explorer* [ISSN 1930-8116] is geared to a kindergarten–grade 1 reading level. This magazine develops literacy skills and introduces word patterns and rhymes through poetry while teaching standards-based science and social studies content. Designed for reluctant readers in grades 6–12, *National Geographic Extreme Explorer* [ISSN 1938-8004] uses engaging science and social studies–based stories and photographs to reinforce literacy skills. Specific reading strategies are highlighted at the beginning of each story.

1367. *Science News: magazine of the society for science and the public.* Former titles (until 1966): *Science News Letter; Science News Bulletin.* [ISSN: 0036-8423] 1922. 26x/yr. GBP 135 (print & online eds.). Ed(s): Tom Siegfried. Science Service, 1719 N St, NW, Washington, DC 20036; subnews@sciserv.org. Illus., index, adv. Circ: 133000 Paid. Vol. ends: Dec. Microform: PQC. *Indexed:* A01, A22, ABIn, Agr, BRI, C37, CBCARef, GardL, MASUSE, P02. *Bk. rev.:* 6-8, 125 words. *Aud.:* Hs, Ga.

Science News is packed with information about what's happening in the science community. Brief news articles that cover a broad spectrum of science can provide material for class discussion or student writing assignments. Sections include "Atom and Cosmos," "Body and Brain," "Matter and Energy," "Earth," "Numbers," "Humans," and "Science and Society." *Science News Online* provides an archive of past issues with free access to cover stories and additional access for subscribers. Also available on the web site are special features, such as blogs and book listings. RSS feeds are available for topic, department, blogs, and columns. The "Science News for Kids" section of the web site links to articles on topics of particular interest to younger readers. Although the magazine is not specifically aimed at K–12 students, it is very popular in middle and high schools, and is highly recommended. URL: www.sciencenews.org

1368. *Science World Current Science.* Incorporates: *Current Science;* Former titles: *Science World;* (until 1987): *Scholastic Science World;* (until 1974): *Science World (1965);* Which incorporated (1965-1968): *Senior Science (1965);* Which was formerly (1960-1965): *Science World. Edition 2;* Science World (1965) was formerly (until 1965): *Science World. Edition 1;* Both of which superseded in part (in 1960): *Senior*

Science. 1957. m. during school year. USD 9.25 per student. Scholastic Inc., 557 Broadway, 3rd Fl, New York, NY 10012; news@scholastic.com; http://www.scholastic.com. Illus., index, adv. Sample. Circ: 390298. Vol. ends: May. Microform: PQC. *Indexed:* A22, BRI, C37, ICM, MASUSE, P01, P02. *Aud.:* Ems, Hs.

Newly titled *Science World Current Science* due to its merger with Weekly Reader, this magazine shares articles and hands-on experiments for grades 6–10. Each issue features interesting articles on topics in the fields of physical, earth/space, life/health, and environmental sciences, as well as technology. Hands-on experiments with photos, diagrams, maps, graphs, and charts are regular features, as are puzzles, quizzes, and brain-teasers that help students understand scientific processes. Regular features include "I Want That Job," an interview with a career professional in the sciences, and "Gross Out," which looks at aspects of nature or scientific phenomena that may be outside our comfort zone or experience. The teacher's edition provides lesson plans and a table that connects content to appropriate National Science Education Standards. It also contains an answer key, reproducible skills pages, and additional quizzes to test vocabulary, reading comprehension, and understanding of graphs and maps.

1369. *SuperScience.* Formed by the merger of (1989-1997): *SuperScience Blue;* (1989-1997): *SuperScience Red.* 1997. 8x/yr. USD 6.95. Ed(s): Britt Norlander. Scholastic Inc., 557 Broadway, 3rd Fl, New York, NY 10012; http://www.scholastic.com. Illus., index. Sample. Vol. ends: Apr/May. *Indexed:* C37, ICM, MASUSE, P01. *Aud.:* Ems.

A cross-curricular science newsmagazine for grades 3–6, *SuperScience* is theme-based and includes many color photos that teach earth, life, and physical science concepts. Hands-on activities, experiments, and quizzes on the news stories actively engage students in the content. The teacher's guide provides background information, teaching strategies, discussion prompts, additional activities, reproducible worksheets, and answer keys. Regular features include "Science Mystery," where students read a fictional text, then use scientific method and data to solve the case; and the "You Asked" column, which answers a student-generated question in each issue. "Cool Science Jobs" features an interview with a scientist and gives information about preparation, skills, and salary for that career. Feature articles are tied to curriculum areas through process skills addressed in each activity (e.g., observe, compare, use numbers, hypothesize, etc.). *SuperScience* features help teachers meet local, state, and National Science Education standards.

Social Studies and Current Events

1370. *Biography Today (General Series): profiles of people of interest to young readers.* [ISSN: 1058-2347] 1992. 3x/yr. USD 64. Ed(s): Cherie D. Abbey. Omnigraphics, Inc., PO Box 31-1640, Detroit, MI 48231; info@omnigraphics.com; http://www.omnigraphics.com. Illus., index. Circ: 12000. Vol. ends: Sep (No. 3). *Indexed:* A01, F01, ICM, P01. *Aud.:* Ems.

This publication is written for the young reader, age nine and above, and each issue includes profiles of 10–12 current, high-interest individuals, many from the arts, sports, or politics. Each entry provides at least one picture of the person. Biographical information traces the person's life from childhood, including education, first jobs, marriage and/or family, memorable experiences, hobbies, and accomplishments (e.g., honors and awards). Each profile includes a short list of easily accessible print and online resources for further reading. A current address, as well as a web site URL, is provided where available. Librarians and teachers submit suggestions for subjects to be included. An advisory board composed of librarians, children's literature specialists, and reading instructors reviews each issue. A "Cumulative Names Index" in every issue contains the names of all individuals who have appeared in either the general series or a subject series. The web site includes the "Names Index" and three other cumulative indexes: "Cumulative General Index," "Places of Birth Index," and "Birthday Index." The edition of *Biography Today* reviewed here is the General Series, which is available as a three-issue subscription, hardcover annual cumulation, or subscription plus cumulation. Special subject series have been published in the following categories: artists, authors, business leaders, performing artists, scientists and inventors, sports figures, and world leaders, as well as a series in Spanish. These series expand and complement the general series but do not duplicate any of the entries. The subject series are available as

individual hardbound volumes, usually published annually. A one-year subscription for schools or libraries is $64. Hardbound annual cumulations can be purchased for $66. Individual volumes in the subject series are $39. *Biografias Hoy* ($39) presents biographical profiles written in Spanish. Profiles here follow the same style as in the *Biography Today General Series* and *Subject Series.* Highly recommended for elementary and middle school libraries, as well as children's collections in public libraries. URL: www.biographytoday.com

Cobblestone. See Children section.

1371. *Junior Scholastic.* Incorporates: *Current Events.* [ISSN: 0022-6688] 1937. bi-w. USD 3.99 for grade 6-8. Ed(s): Lee Baier, Susanne McCabe. Scholastic Inc., 557 Broadway, 3rd Fl, New York, NY 10012; news@scholastic.com; http://www.scholastic.com. Illus., index. Sample. Circ: 570000 Paid. *Indexed:* ICM, P01. *Aud.:* Ems.

Junior Scholastic merged with Weekly Reader's *Current Events.* It remains a colorful current events magazine for grades 6–8. *Junior Scholastic: Current Events* features U.S. and world news, American and world history, biographical profiles, and maps. Articles focus on people and topics in the news, and the many photos and illustrations help students understand complex issues. The U.S. news section covers a wide variety of topics from anthropology and the environment to sports and entertainment. The "Debate" feature presents a controversial question with pro and con viewpoints to initiate classroom discussion. "MapSearch" and "GeoSkills" provide examples of different types of maps and guidance in how to read them. Additional features include key vocabulary at the end of each article, and questions to encourage further analysis of the topics. The teacher's edition contains supplementary material for the stories in the issue with references to additional resources, skills masters, activities, quizzes, and answer keys. The *Junior Scholastic* page on the *Scholastic News* web site contains additional supporting material, such as test-prep and skills reproducibles and links to online resources. URL: www.scholastic.com/juniorscholastic

1372. *The New York Times Upfront (Student Edition): the news magazine for teens.* Formerly (until 1999): *Scholastic Update;* Which was formed by the merger of (1972-1983): *Scholastic Search;* (1920-1983): *Senior Scholastic;* Which incorporated: *American Observer; World Week.* [ISSN: 1525-1292] 1983. 14x/yr. USD 4.75 (Individuals, USD 15.95; Students, USD 4.70). Ed(s): Peter S Young. Scholastic Inc., 557 Broadway, 3rd Fl, New York, NY 10012; news@scholastic.com; http://www.scholastic.com. Illus., index, adv. Sample. Circ: 297029 Paid and free. Vol. ends: May. *Indexed:* A01, A22, BRI, MASUSE, P01, P02. *Aud.:* Hs.

Upfront is a newsmagazine for teens that features in-depth coverage of current events, entertainment, and trends. Informative articles about national and international events, special reports, and interviews encourage high school students to consider various points of view. Recent articles examine the presidential election, the impact of the economy on the U.S. auto industry, education of girls in Afghanistan, and twenty-first-century piracy. The teacher's edition includes lesson plans for the national, international, economy, and "times past" sections with teaching objectives, classroom strategies, writing prompts, and quizzes. "Cartoon Analysis" and "Photo Analysis" activities in the teacher's edition promote media literacy with thought-provoking questions. Each student issue includes political cartoons from around the country and a debate question with pro and con viewpoints. A subscription also includes two special series: "Coming of Age," which focuses on the challenges teens face in the world today, and "Immigration in America," about the current debate over who gets to be an American. The web site supplements the print newsletter and links to additional teacher resources. URL: http://teacher.scholastic.com/upfront

1373. *Scholastic News. Grade 5/6 Edition.* Formed by the merger of (1952-1998): *Scholastic News (Edition 6);* Which was formerly (until 1993): *Scholastic Newstime;* (until 1989): *Scholastic News (Newstime Edition);* (until 1982): *Scholastic Newstime;* (1941-1998): *Scholastic News (Citizen Edition);* Which was formerly (until 1982): *Scholastic News Citizen;* (until 1973): *Young Citizen.* [ISSN: 1554-2440] 1998. 24x/yr. Students, USD 1.99. Ed(s): Lucille Renwick. Scholastic Inc., 557 Broadway, 3rd Fl, New York, NY 10012; news@scholastic.com; http://www.scholastic.com. Illus., index. *Indexed:* ICM, P01. *Aud.:* Ems.

This colorful current-events weekly, published in several editions, targets various reading levels and interests. This magazine absorbed Weekly Reader when the company merged with Scholastic. *Scholastic News,* in first-grade and second-grade editions (32 issues per year), helps students learn phonics, vocabulary, fluency, and comprehension skills by introducing them to real-world events, seasons, and holidays. Grade 1 and 2 editions also include posters, take-home activity pages, graphic organizers for teachers, and three big issues on "pencil-friendly paper" each month for guided reading. Editions 3 and 4 (24 issues each per year) build on those skills and introduce science, history, and geography topics. Both include a "Test Prep Program" with online quizzes, reproducibles, and diagnostic tests to help focus on improving standardized testing skills. Grade 3 includes "Place in the News," a current events and geography feature, and "Find It," which comprises mini-lessons that provide an activity for each story. Grade 4 and the senior edition (for fifth- and sixth-grade students) focus on current events, civic awareness, and geography with features such as "News Zone" and "News Map." "Graph of the Week" incorporates charts and graphs that illustrate data on topics of interest to readers, such as popular sports activities or favorite format for books they read. Editions sometimes include two-sided posters, and all have teacher's guides with lesson plans, reproducible pages, and additional resources. All content can be extended with material from the *Scholastic News Online* web site (www.scholasticnews.com). Meanwhile, *Scholastic News English/Espanol* (Levels 1 and 2) has a flip format that lets students read in their native language and then flip the magazine over to read the same content in English. Every issue has "Exploring Your World" sidebars that connect topics to Latino cultures. The teacher's edition contains "Let's Learn English with Maya and Miguel," which comprises reproducible pages that are meant to reinforce spelling and vocabulary.

1374. *Time for Kids World Report.* Supersedes in part (in 1997): *Time for Kids.* 1995. 18x/yr. Students, USD 4.10. Time Inc., 1271 6th Ave., 22nd Fl., New York, NY 10020; information@timeinc.com; http://www.timeinc.com. Illus. Sample. Vol. ends: May. *Indexed:* ICM. *Bk. rev.:* Number and length vary. *Aud.:* Ems.

Time for Kids is a weekly newsmagazine that is published in three editions: *Big Picture* for grades K–1 (ages 4–7), *News Scoop* for grades 2–3 (ages 7–10), and *World Report* for grades 4–6 (ages 10–12). Each colorful issue is theme-based and contains articles, puzzles, and contests relating to the featured topic. Recent themes include "Green Schools," "Amazing Inventions," and "Animal Habitats." Issues also include spotlights on people with notable accomplishments, short book reports, and opinion columns. The web site contains highlights from the issues (including the cover story in both English and Spanish), quizzes, mini-lessons, a teacher's guide, and worksheets. *Time for Kids Around the World,* an eight-page magazine with a companion web site, integrates geography, reading, math, and science while introducing students to the people, languages, and culture of countries around the world. It is available to subscribers to the *World Report* and *News Scoop* editions for one dollar per student. URL: www.timeforkids.com

Teacher and Professional

Arts and Activities. See Education/Specific Subjects and Teaching Methods, The Arts section.

1375. *Internet at Schools: an educator's guide to technology and the web.* Former titles (until 2011): *MultiMedia & Internet at Schools;* (until 2003): *MultiMedia Schools.* [ISSN: 2156-843X] 1994. 5x/yr. USD 46.95 domestic; USD 61 in Canada & Mexico; USD 70 elsewhere. Ed(s): Kathie Felix, David Hoffman. Information Today, Inc., 143 Old Marlton Pike, Medford, NJ 08055; custserv@infotoday.com; http://www.infotoday.com. Illus., adv. Sample. Circ: 15000 Paid. *Indexed:* A01, A22, BRI, C37, I15. *Bk. rev.:* 4. *Aud.:* Ac, Sa.

A practical how-to magazine for librarians, teachers, and media specialists, *MultiMedia & Internet@Schools* reports on, reviews, and discusses a wide array of electronic media, including Internet resources and online services, library systems, curriculum software, and administrative systems and tools to improve learning. Articles and columns address issues associated with using electronic information resources in K–12 schools. Regular features include

"Cyberbee," informing on web resources for classroom use; "The Pipeline," which focuses on new technologies and new uses of current technologies; and various "Watch" columns, which highlight product and industry news. All are contributed by practicing educators who use new technologies in the classroom or media center. *MultiMedia & Internet@Schools* is addressed primarily to K–12 librarians and media specialists, but it also will be of interest to technology coordinators, principals, and other administrators. Register for a free account on the web site for links to current and archived content from the magazine, with free full text for some articles (the rest available on a pay-per-view basis) and all product reviews. Special discounts are available for first-time subscribers. You can also sign up to receive the *MMIS Xtra* newsletter via e-mail. URL: www.mmischools.com

1376. *Learning & Leading with Technology.* Former titles (until 1995): *The Computing Teacher; Oregon Computing Teacher.* [ISSN: 1082-5754] 19??. m. Members, USD 54; Non-members, USD 100. Ed(s): Kate Conley. International Society for Technology in Education, 1710 Rhode Island Ave NW, Ste 900, Washington, DC 20036; iste@iste.org; http://www.iste.org. Illus., index. Sample. Circ: 28809 Paid and controlled. Vol. ends: May. Microform: PQC. *Indexed:* A22, BRI, ERIC, I15. *Aud.:* Sa.

This membership publication that the International Society for Technology in Education (ISTE) calls its "flagship periodical" is for K–12 teachers and teacher educators with a broad range of experience in integrating technology into the classroom. Articles emphasize practical applications of technology. "Learning Connections" focuses on uses of technology for specific subjects (language arts, social studies, math, science, and physical education) and service learning. "Leading Connections" offers teacher-to-teacher advice on technology issues, professional development topics, and projects for the connected classroom. Each issue reviews new products and emerging technologies for teaching and learning. "Point/Counterpoint" provides opposing viewpoints on current education questions, and "Bloggers Beat" provides coverage of hot topics from bloggers and those who comment on their posts. The web site (www.iste.org) provides members with access to the full text of articles.

1377. *The Mailbox: the idea magazine for teachers.* [ISSN: 0199-6045] 1972. bi-m. USD 29.95 domestic; USD 40.95 foreign. The Education Center, Inc., PO Box 9753, Greensboro, NC 27429; customerservice@themailbox.com; http://www.theeducationcenter.com. Illus., index, adv. Sample. Vol. ends: Dec/Jan. *Aud.:* Sa.

A colorful and engaging resource for teachers, *The Mailbox* is published in five editions: "Preschool," "Kindergarten," "Grade 1," "Grades 2–3," and "Intermediate." The "Preschool" edition includes arts and crafts, story time, circle time, songs, and science, among other activities that promote counting and pre-reading skills. A fold-out centerfold activity is included in each issue. "Kindergarten and Grade 1," formerly a combined edition, is now two separate editions. The "Kindergarten" edition contains many reproducibles as well as a centerfold pullout, and focuses on basic skills in math, literacy and literature, science, and social studies. "Grade 1" builds on those skills, introducing two-digit addition, fractions, and themed writing ideas. The "Grade 2–3" edition takes the math, reading, science, and cross-curricular activities to the next level, with the introduction of more grammar and additional emphasis on comprehension. The "Intermediate" edition features activities in the broad subject areas as well as a "Seasonal" category, with writing prompts and skills practice relating to the holidays and events of the season. The "Teachers Resource" section in all of the editions includes resources for classroom displays, management tips and timesavers, and activities sent in by subscribers in "Our Readers Write." *Mailbox Companion Online* is a free online service for subscribers that complements the print issue and contains a homepage specifically for the subscriber's edition of the magazine, additional reproducibles, and other magazine extenders to complement the units in every issue. "The Mailbox Blog" is searchable by topic and keyword and provides information about news, publications, and areas of interest to teachers. Additionally, there is *Teacher's Helper: classroom skill builders* [ISSN 1078-6570]. 6/yr. USD 24.95. The Education Center, P.O. Box 9753, Greensboro, NC 27429-0753; www.themailbox.com. Illus. Vol. ends: Dec./Jan. *Aud:* Sa. Provides skill-based reproducible activity worksheets in four editions: "Kindergarten," "Grade 1," "Grades 2–3," and "Intermediate."

Mathematics Teacher. See Mathematics/General section.

1378. *Onestopenglish.* 200?. d. GBP 42; USD 68; EUR 53. Macmillan Education, Macmillan Oxford, Between Towns Rd, Oxford, OX4 3PP, United Kingdom; permissions@macmillan.com; http://www.macmillaneducation.com. Adv. *Aud.:* Sa.

Onestopenglish, a teacher's resource site published by Macmillan English Campus, part of the Macmillan Education Group, publishes materials developed for teachers of English as a first or second language. Currently there are over 420,000 users in over 100 countries. Materials are available in British and American English. There are three ways to access *Onestopenglish* resources: (1) You can browse the categories for free; all material is available for downloading for classroom use. (2) You can sign up as a registered user (also free) for access to expanded content, an interactive forum in which to share ideas with teachers around the world, and a monthly newsletter with up-to-date information about what's new on the site. Finally, (3) you can subscribe to the "Staff Room" for access to a database of over 6,500 resources searchable by age, level, and language focus. Resources include lesson plans, games, worksheets, and tips and suggestions for teachers of preschoolers through teenagers. Weekly news lessons from the *Guardian Weekly,* audio and podcasts, songs, games, music videos, and flashcards are also available, along with the series "Onestop Phonics." An individual subscription costs $62, and institutional subscriptions are based upon the number of teachers, starting at $288 for up to five teachers. A full-featured site for both English and ESL instruction, this is a very useful resource for teachers and students. URL: www.onestopenglish.com

1379. *Scholastic Early Childhood Today (Online).* [ISSN: 2168-2283] 1986. 8x/yr. Free. Scholastic Inc., 557 Broadway, 3rd Fl, New York, NY 10012; custserv@scholastic.com; http://www.scholastic.com. Adv. *Aud.:* Ac, Sa.

Early Childhood Today has transitioned from a print magazine to a solely online presence. The web site offers free access to a wealth of material from an archive that spans 22 years of serving early childhood professionals. *Early Childhood Today* features teaching tips and resources, online interactive learning activities, and management strategies. Articles focus on leadership issues as well as behavior and development. The "School-Home Connection" section includes articles about parent/teacher communication, as well as recommended send-home activities. The "Connect" section provides a discussion forum for teachers and tools for students to communicate as well. Professional resources include articles by experts in behavior and development in children from birth to age six, and reports from the field.

1380. *Scholastic.com.* Formerly: *Scholastic Network.* w. Scholastic Inc., 557 Broadway, 3rd Fl, New York, NY 10012; news@scholastic.com; http://www.scholastic.com. *Aud.:* Ems, Sa.

An excellent source of information and classroom resources with separate areas for each of its target audiences (kids, parents, teachers, administrators, and librarians), the *Scholastic.com* web site emphasizes participation and interaction. The teacher's section includes lesson plans, printables and mini-books, teaching tips, and activities for pre-K through 12th grade. Dropout prevention strategies, assessment in the differentiated classroom, and content area writing are some of topics covered under the "Teaching Strategies" section. The "Tools" section provides teaching templates for creating rubrics, flash cards, and graphic organizers. The site also includes a "Classroom Homepage Builder" and "TeacherShare," a free, worldwide learning network for K–8 classroom teachers to create, edit, collaborate on, and share classroom content. URL: www.scholastic.com/home/

School Arts. See Education/Specific Subjects and Teaching Methods, The Arts section.

1381. *Science and Children.* Formerly (until 1963): *Elementary School Science Bulletin.* [ISSN: 0036-8148] 1952. 9x/yr. Free to members. Ed(s): Valynda Mayes. National Science Teachers Association, 1840 Wilson Blvd, Arlington, VA 22201; pubinfo@nsta.org; http://www.nsta.org/. Illus., index, adv. Sample. Refereed. Circ: 21000. Vol. ends: May. *Indexed:* A22, BRI, ERIC, WSA. *Bk. rev.:* 6, 300 words. *Aud.:* Sa.

Science and Children is a peer-reviewed journal from the National Science Teachers Association (NSTA) for elementary science teachers, science teacher administrators, and teacher educators. It features articles that discuss pedagogy and educational issues relevant to science teaching. The table of contents indicates whether articles apply to particular grade ranges (K–2, 3–6, K–6, etc.). "In the News" highlights discoveries and current research of interest to the science community. Regular features include "Finds & Sites," a list of free or inexpensive materials, publications, and events; "Teaching Through Trade Books," activities inspired by children's literature; and "Every Day Science Calendar," a monthly calendar with "facts and challenges for the science explorer." "Science 101" experts answer teachers' questions about everyday science. "NSTA Recommends" reviews both student texts and professional literature for science teachers. These reviews and others are also available online. URL: www.nsta.org/recommends

1382. *Science Scope.* Formerly (until 19??): *Middle Jr. High Science Bulletin.* [ISSN: 0887-2376] 1978. 9x/yr. Free to members. Ed(s): Ken Roberts. National Science Teachers Association, 1840 Wilson Blvd, Arlington, VA 22201; pubinfo@nsta.org; http://www.nsta.org/. Illus., index, adv. Sample. Refereed. Circ: 18000. Vol. ends: May. *Indexed:* A22, BRI, ERIC. *Bk. rev.:* 3-4, 300 words. *Aud.:* Sa.

Produced by the National Science Teachers Association (NSTA), this is a professional journal for middle-level and junior high school science teachers. Peer-reviewed articles provide ready-to-use activities and teaching strategies for life science, physical science, and earth science. Regular features include "Science Sampler," descriptions and templates for classroom activities and field trips; "Tried and True," classic demonstrations and experiments; "Tech Trek," incorporating the latest technology in the classroom; "Scope on Safety," safety information for the classroom; and "Scope's Scoops," summaries of recent scientific news. "NSTA Recommends" highlights trade books. These reviews and others are available online. URL: www.nsta.org/recommends

The Science Teacher. See Astronomy section.

■ COMMUNICATION

See also Education; Journalism and Writing; Media and AV; and Television, Video, and Radio sections.

Laura A. Sullivan, Grants Coordinator, Northern Kentucky University, Steely Library, Highland Heights, KY 41099; FAX: 859-572-6181; sullivanl@nku.edu.

Nancy F. Campbell, Assistant to the Associate Provost for Library Services, Northern Kentucky University, Steely Library, Highland Heights, KY 41099; FAX: 859-572-6181; campbelln@nku.edu.

Michael J. Providenti, Web Development Librarian, Steely Library, Highland Heights, KY 41099; FAX: 859-572-6181; providenti@nku.edu

Introduction

This section features representative, critical publications in the discipline of communication. Titles chosen reflect scholarship and analysis in all fields of communication: mass, speech, interpersonal, organizational, rhetorical, and applied, among others. All titles of the National Communication Association are featured (it is the oldest and largest national organization to advance communication scholarship and education), including its online publications. In general, the list includes many well-known core periodicals within the discipline.

Six new titles have been added—*Advances in the History of Rhetoric*; *Communication Currents*; *Communication Methods & Measures*; *Communication Review*; *International Journal of Listening*; and *Journal of Communications Research*. These new titles will bring new dimension to the section. While it is recognized that there are numerous communication periodicals that focus on a specific type of communication, such as political, business, visual, health, etc., for purposes of consistency the current list concentrates on key, broad publications, although these titles publish articles on specialized communication areas. Emphasis is on academic titles, because that is where the concentration of communication journals lies. However, the necessary titles for larger public libraries are included here, as well.

Basic Periodicals

Ac: *Argumentation & Advocacy, Communication Education, Communication Monographs, Communication Quarterly, Communication Reports, Communication Research, Communication Research Reports, Critical Studies in Media Communication, Human Communication Research, Journal of Applied Communication Research, Journal of Communication, Quarterly Journal of Speech, Southern Communication Journal, Western Journal of Communication.*

Basic Abstracts and Indexes

Communication & Mass Media Complete, Communication Abstracts, ERIC, Humanities Index, PsycINFO, Social Sciences Index, Sociological Abstracts.

1383. *Advances in the History of Rhetoric.* [ISSN: 1536-2426] 1997. s-a. GBP 106 (print & online eds.). Ed(s): Ekaterina Haskins. Routledge, 325 Chestnut St, Ste 800, Philadelphia, PA 19106; customerservice@taylorandfrancis.com; http://www.tandfonline.com. Refereed. Circ: 160 Paid and controlled. *Indexed:* AmHI, MLA-IB. *Aud.:* Ac.

This journal, the annual research publication of the American Society for the History of Rhetoric, "welcomes contributions from scholars who take a historical approach to the study of rhetoric," including theory, discourse, criticism—across disciplines and across all historical periods. Recent subjects of articles have included feminist rhetoric, digital media, and Aristotle's theory of rhetoric. Recommended for academic libraries.

1384. *American Communication Journal.* [ISSN: 1532-5865] 1996. 3x/yr. Ed(s): Debbi Hatton. American Communication Association, c/o Dale Cyphert, College of Business Administration, Cedar Falls, IA 50614; acjournal@email.com; http://www.americancomm.org/. Refereed. *Bk. rev.:* Irregular. *Aud.:* Ac, Sa.

This title's goal is to be a primary online source for "interdisciplinary scholarship on communication." A new feature, called "Practitioners' Corner," seeks reports and research from authors who apply classroom theories and principles to the real world. A check of the journal's web site finds the following topics addressed in recent issues: media effects on body image, change and organizational discourse, news source credibility, and the image repair of Hillary Clinton.

1385. *Argumentation & Advocacy.* Formerly (until 1988): *American Forensic Association. Journal.* [ISSN: 1051-1431] 1964. q. Free to members. Ed(s): John Fritch, Catherine H Palczewski. American Forensic Association, PO Box 256, River Falls, WI 54022; amforensicassoc@aol.com; http://www.americanforensics.org. Illus. Sample. Refereed. Vol. ends: Spring. Microform: PQC. *Indexed:* A01, A22, AmHI, BRI, MLA-IB, P02. *Bk. rev.:* 2-5, lengthy. *Aud.:* Ac.

This "flagship" journal of the American Forensic Association advances the study of argumentation. Any research methodology is encouraged in the areas of argumentation theory (contemporary or historical), public and political argument, culture and argument, legal argument, interpersonal arguing, and forensics and pedagogy. Special issues occur occasionally (e.g., coming in 2013, "Political Campaign Debates in the 2012 Elections"), and book reviews are included. Article topics from recent issues include pharmaceutical advertising, climate change controversy, and conflict and stress. A title for academic collections.

1386. *Atlantic Journal of Communication.* Formerly (until 2004): *New Jersey Journal of Communication.* [ISSN: 1545-6870] 1993. 5x/yr. GBP 208 (print & online eds.). Ed(s): Gary P Radford. Routledge, 325 Chestnut St, Ste 800, Philadelphia, PA 19106; customerservice@taylorandfrancis.com; http://www.tandfonline.com. Illus., adv. Sample. Refereed. Reprint: PSC. *Indexed:* A01, A22, AmHI, E01. *Bk. rev.:* Number and length vary. *Aud.:* Ac, Sa.

The focus of this academic journal is on problems and issues in the field of communication studies, with particular concentration on theory, practice, and policy. Submissions are subject to a blind editorial review. Representative article topics from recent issues include hurtful teasing, religion and verbal aggression, communication and health concerns, and political humor and trust.

Broadcasting & Cable. See Television, Video, and Radio section.

Columbia Journalism Review. See Journalism and Writing/Journalism section.

1387. *Communication and Critical/Cultural Studies.* [ISSN: 1479-1420] 2004. q. GBP 236 (print & online eds.). Ed(s): James Hay. Routledge, 325 Chestnut St, Ste 800, Philadelphia, PA 19106; customerservice@taylorandfrancis.com; http://www.tandfonline.com. Sample. Reprint: PSC. *Indexed:* A22, ABIn, ArtHuCI, E01. *Bk. rev.:* 1 or more, lengthy. *Aud.:* Ac.

A journal of the National Communication Association, CCCS offers scholarship that focuses on communication and our democratic culture. Within that framework, topics may include class, race, ethnicity, gender, sexuality, the public sphere, the nation, globalization, and environment. The journal features "critical inquiry that cuts across academic boundaries to focus on social, political, and cultural practices from the standpoint of communication." Recent content includes "The Theatricality of Humanitarianism: A Critique of Celebrity Advocacy" and "Communication as Incarnation." CCCS publishes occasional reviews of major new books, as well. A relevant publication for today's world, this journal belongs in comprehensive communication collections.

1388. *Communication Currents: knowledge for comminicating well.* 2006. bi-m. Ed(s): Katherine Hawkins. National Communication Association, 1765 N St, NW, Washington, DC 20036; inbox@natcom.org; http://www.natcom.org. *Aud.:* Ac.

This online web magazine of the National Communication Association looks at current communication research that is published in scholarly journals of the NCA, and translates them into a "form understandable and usable for broad audiences, including communication experts working with lay audiences, instructors and students, the press, and other interested members of the public." In addition to the essays, there are two sections included—"Cross Current" provides short pieces (no more than 1,200 words), invited and solicited from NCA members, that assert a position on a contemporary communication issue. "Comments for Opening the Lines of Communication" are also short and are an opportunity for communication scholars to address "how communication issues are presented or positioned in the popular press and other media outlets." Submissions may be in response to a recent event, film, or book, for example, on a communication issue or may deal in general with a topical communication matter. An example of a recent research-based essay is "'I'm so fat!': The negative outcomes of Fat Talk"; and a "Cross Current" topic is "Forgetting Racial Injustice in Press Coverage of President Obama's Inauguration." Recommended title for its comprehensible presentation of timely communication research.

1389. *Communication Education.* Formerly (until 1976): *The Speech Teacher.* [ISSN: 0363-4523] 1952. q. GBP 279 (print & online eds.). Ed(s): Paul L Witt. Routledge, 325 Chestnut St, Ste 800, Philadelphia, PA 19106; customerservice@taylorandfrancis.com; http://www.tandfonline.com. Illus., index, adv. Sample. Refereed. Vol. ends: Oct. Microform: PQC. Reprint: PSC. *Indexed:* A01, A22, BRI, CBRI, E01, ERIC, MLA-IB, P02, PsycInfo. *Aud.:* Ac, Sa.

This journal covers original instructional communication scholarship in all methodologies. Areas of focus include technology in mediated instruction, classroom discourse, life-span development of communication competence, and diverse backgrounds of learners and teachers in instructional settings. The current editor intends to advance the areas of general instruction and, specifically, communication education by "encouraging systematic and programmatic research, theoretically grounded projects, rigorous literature reviews and meta-analyses, and interesting methodological and pedagogical papers." Research beyond the classroom, such as community service learning and instructional intervention activities, is also examined. Recent topics published include text message and cognitive learning, and the value of e-mail communication between students and teachers. This is a critical publication for communication faculty and researchers. Valuable for its focus, and a necessary resource for academic libraries.

1390. *Communication Methods and Measures.* [ISSN: 1931-2458] 2007. q. GBP 313 (print & online eds.). Ed(s): Andrew F Hayes. Routledge, 325 Chestnut St, Ste 800, Philadelphia, PA 19106; customerservice@taylorandfrancis.com; http://www.tandfonline.com. Adv. Sample. Refereed. Reprint: PSC. *Indexed:* A22, ABIn, E01. *Aud.:* Ac.

This title aims to bring attention to new developments in methodological tools and approaches. Editors encourage articles focused on "methods for improving research design and theory testing using quantitative and/or qualitative approaches." Subjects of recent publications include social network analysis, reliable data coding, the Monte Carlo method, student engagement studies, and communication in medicine. Recommended for upper-division studies in academic libraries.

1391. *Communication Monographs.* Formerly (until 1976): *Speech Monographs.* [ISSN: 0363-7751] 1934. q. GBP 227 (print & online eds.). Ed(s): Katherine Miller. Routledge, 325 Chestnut St, Ste 800, Philadelphia, PA 19106; customerservice@taylorandfrancis.com; http://www.tandfonline.com. Illus., index. Sample. Refereed. Vol. ends: Dec. Microform: PQC. Reprint: PSC. *Indexed:* A01, A22, BAS, E01, LT&LA, MLA-IB, P02, P61, PsycInfo, SSA. *Aud.:* Ac.

Communication Monographs publishes original research, theoretical papers, and original reviews on human communication processes. The journal seeks research that "bridge[s] boundaries that have traditionally separated scholars within the communication discipline," within rigorous review and high intellectual standards. Recent article topics include praise in parent–teacher interaction and communication research and new media. Recommended for academic libraries.

1392. *Communication Quarterly.* Formerly (until 1976): *Today's Speech.* [ISSN: 0146-3373] 1953. 5x/yr. USD 317 (print & online eds.). Ed(s): Benjamin R Bates. Routledge, 325 Chestnut St, Ste 800, Philadelphia, PA 19106; customerservice@taylorandfrancis.com; http://www.tandfonline.com. Illus., index, adv. Sample. Refereed. Vol. ends: Fall. Microform: PQC. Reprint: PSC. *Indexed:* A01, A22, AmHI, BRI, E01, F01, MLA-IB, P02, RILM. *Aud.:* Ac.

This journal publishes all types of refereed manuscripts (topical interest papers, research reports, state-of-the-art reviews, supported opinion, critical studies) that advance the understanding of human communication. A diverse, "eclectic" mix of topics is covered; recent articles focus on young children's perception of television news content, communication issues related to divorce, and negotiation in dating relationships. Six to eight articles are published in each issue. *Communication Quarterly* is a regional communication association publication and a core title for academic libraries.

1393. *Communication Reports.* [ISSN: 0893-4215] 1988. s-a. Ed(s): Dr. William F Sharkey. Routledge, 4 Park Sq, Milton Park, Abingdon, OX14 4RN, United Kingdom; subscriptions@tandf.co.uk; http://www.tandfonline.com. Illus., adv. Sample. Vol. ends: Summer. Reprint: PSC. *Indexed:* A01, A22, B01, E01, PsycInfo. *Aud.:* Ac.

This journal seeks short, original, data-based articles on broadly defined human communication topics. Theoretical or speculative reports are not accepted; rather, emphasis should be on research data analysis, and a submission should reflect this. Topics from recent issues include customer service structure, apprehension and college students, and swearing in the work environment. Recommended for academic collections.

1394. *Communication Research.* [ISSN: 0093-6502] 1974. bi-m. USD 1251. Ed(s): Michael E Roloff, Pamela Shoemaker. Sage Publications, Inc., 2455 Teller Rd, Thousand Oaks, CA 91320; info@sagepub.com; http://www.sagepub.com. Illus., index, adv. Sample. Refereed. Vol. ends: Dec. Reprint: PSC. *Indexed:* A01, A22, ABIn, AmHI, B01, B02, BRI, E01, F01, MLA-IB, P02, PsycInfo, RILM, SSA. *Aud.:* Ac.

The editorial goal of *Communication Research* is to publish articles that explore communication across societal systems, such as mass media, new technology, and intercultural, from a multidisciplinary perspective. A recent sampling of article topics includes minority influence in virtual groups, television use and self-esteem, and news coverage and voting decisions. Although a costly title, it should be required for academic collections.

1395. *Communication Research Reports.* [ISSN: 0882-4096] 1984. q. USD 278 (print & online eds.). Ed(s): Theodore A Avtgis. Routledge, 325 Chestnut St, Ste 800, Philadelphia, PA 19106; customerservice@taylorandfrancis.com; http://www.tandfonline.com. Illus., index, adv. Sample. Refereed. Microform: PQC. Reprint: PSC. *Indexed:* A22, E01. *Aud.:* Ac.

A publication of the Eastern Communication Association, *Communication Research Reports* publishes brief, empirical articles on human communication in a wide variety of areas, including intercultural, interpersonal, aging/life span, health, organizational, persuasive, mass, political, nonverbal, instructional, relational, or mediated. Articles emphasize reporting and interpretation of the results rather than theory. Recent topics include public-speaking fears, college students' use of social media, and teasing effects related to race and gender. For academic collections.

1396. *The Communication Review.* Formerly: *Communication (Langhorne).* [ISSN: 1071-4421] 1975. q. GBP 282 (print & online eds.). Ed(s): Bruce A Williams, Andrea L Press. Routledge, 325 Chestnut St, Ste 800, Philadelphia, PA 19106; customerservice@taylorandfrancis.com; http://www.tandfonline.com. Adv. Sample. Refereed. Reprint: PSC. *Indexed:* A01, A22, B01, E01, IBSS, MLA-IB. *Aud.:* Ac.

This title "seeks a synthesis of concerns traditional to the fields of communication and media studies." Scholarhip is sought in three divisions: communication and culture; communication as a social force; and communication and mind. The editors are particularly interested in "historical work, feminist work, and visual work." Recent submissions have included Twitter and social media, audience engagement, and women on reality television. Recommended for academic libraries.

1397. *Communication Studies.* Formerly (until 1989): *Central States Speech Journal.* [ISSN: 1051-0974] 1949. 5x/yr. GBP 233 (print & online eds.). Ed(s): Kim Powell. Routledge, 4 Park Sq, Milton Park, Abingdon, OX14 4RN, United Kingdom; subscriptions@tandf.co.uk; http://www.tandfonline.com. Illus., index, adv. Sample. Refereed. Vol. ends: Winter. Reprint: PSC. *Indexed:* A01, A22, E01, MLA-IB, P02, RILM. *Aud.:* Ac.

A publication of the Central States Communication Association, *Communication Studies* publishes high-quality original research on communication theory and research processes, with the expectation that the essays and studies advance human communication scholarship. There are no restrictions as to methodology or philosophy. Article topics vary (e.g., family communication, workplace bullying, and adult sibling relationships) and reflect communication studies in broad contexts. An important title for academic libraries.

1398. *Communication Teacher (Online).* Formerly (until 1999): *Speech Communication Teacher (Online).* [ISSN: 1740-4630] q. GBP 66. Ed(s): Cheri J Simonds. Routledge, 4 Park Sq, Milton Park, Abingdon, OX14 4RN, United Kingdom; subscriptions@tandf.co.uk; http://www.tandfonline.com. Adv. Sample. Refereed. *Aud.:* Ac.

Published by the National Communication Association, *Communication Teacher* is a quarterly publication dedicated to the identification, assessment, and promotion of quality teaching practices in the K–12, community college, and university communication classrooms. Additionally, the journal seeks original research that focuses on "communication education assessment on student learning, classroom practices, or program development." Recent article topics include teaching digital oratory, students and group projects, and social judgment theory. Each issue is available electronically to current subscribers in January, April, July, and October. Subscribers then receive a printed volume at the end of the year.

1399. *Communication Theory.* [ISSN: 1050-3293] 1991. q. GBP 694 (print & online eds.) Individuals, USD 70 (print & online eds.). Ed(s): Angharad N Valdivia. Wiley-Blackwell Publishing, Inc., 111 River St, Hoboken, NJ 07030; info@wiley.com; http://onlinelibrary.wiley.com/. Illus., adv. Sample. Refereed. Vol. ends: Nov. Reprint: PSC. *Indexed:* A22, BRI, E01, IBSS, MLA-IB, P02, P61, PsycInfo, SSA. *Aud.:* Ac, Sa.

This journal publishes "high quality, original research into the theoretical development of communication." Many disciplines are represented, including communication studies, psychology, cultural/gender studies, sociology, political science, philosophy, linguistics, and literature. Articles that examine technology, ethnicity and race, global and intercultural communication, gaming and intergroup studies are those works welcomed. Recent topics explored include multiracial naming, posture and affluence, and media effects theory. Recommended for larger research libraries.

1400. *Communication World.* Former titles (until 1982): *Journal of Communication Management;* (until 1981): *Journal of Organizational Communication;* (until 1974): *I A B C Journal.* [ISSN: 0744-7612] 1973. bi-m. Free to members; Non-members, USD 150. Ed(s): Natasha Nicholson, Sue Khodarahmi. International Association of Business Communicators, 601 Montgomery St, Ste 1900, San Francisco, CA 94111; http://www.iabc.com. Illus., adv. Vol. ends: Dec. *Indexed:* A01, A22, ABIn, B01, B02, BRI, F01. *Aud.:* Ga, Ac, Sa.

These official publications of the International Association of Business Communicators combine practical articles with global communication issues in the area of communication management. *CW* is published bimonthly, and its online version, *CW Online,* is updated regularly. Articles serve an international audience and include interviews with communication innovators and case studies on current topics. A wide variety of subjects is covered, including marketing communication, strategic planning, crisis communication, employee communication, public relations, career advice, and speechwriting/presentations. Both publications' goals are to "stay on the forefront of developments in the communication profession and report them in an informative, timely[,] and entertaining way to assist and inspire readers." Current article topics have included leaders' use of communication and cultural differences and internal communication. For large public libraries and academic business and communication collections.

1401. *Critical Studies in Media Communication.* Formerly (until 2000): *Critical Studies in Mass Communication.* [ISSN: 1529-5036] 1984. 5x/yr. GBP 255 (print & online eds.). Ed(s): Ronald L Jackson, Kent A Ono. Routledge, 325 Chestnut St, Ste 800, Philadelphia, PA 19106; customerservice@taylorandfrancis.com; http://www.tandfonline.com. Illus., index, adv. Sample. Refereed. Vol. ends: Dec. Reprint: PSC. *Indexed:* A01, A22, ABS&EES, AmHI, BRI, E01, F01, IBSS, MLA-IB, P02, P61, RILM, SSA. *Aud.:* Ac.

Critical Studies publishes original research and analytical and interpretive articles that reflect a concentration on mediated communication. Interest is in cross-disciplinary scholarship and "how media audiences, representations, institutions, technologies, and professional practices impact social justice and civic culture." Recent titles include "History of (Future) Progress: Hyper-Masculine Transhumanist Virtuality" and "Past Continuous: Newsworthiness and the Shaping of Collective Memory." A publication of the National Communication Association, this is a valuable source for academic libraries due to its expansive approach to mediated communication theory and research.

1402. *Discourse & Society: an international journal for the study of discourse and communication in their social, political and cultural contexts.* [ISSN: 0957-9265] 1990. bi-m. USD 1749. Ed(s): Teun A van Dijk. Sage Publications Ltd., 1 Oliver's Yard, 55 City Rd, London, EC1Y 1SP, United Kingdom; info@sagepub.co.uk; http://www.uk.sagepub.com. Adv. Sample. Refereed. Reprint: PSC. *Indexed:* A01, A22, BRI, E01, IBSS, MLA-IB, P02, P61, PsycInfo, SSA. *Bk. rev.:* Number and length vary. *Aud.:* Ac.

Discourse & Society is an international, multidisciplinary journal of discourse analysis. The journal studies "society through discourse and discourse through an analysis of its sociopolitical and cultural functions or implications." Social, political, or cultural problems of the day that require a multidisciplinary approach are featured. The journal requires accessibility as one criterion; that is,

articles should be accessible to readers of various levels of expertise and specialization, and to readers from varied disciplines and countries. Articles from a recent issue include "Bridging the gap: Interdisciplinary insights into the securitization of poverty" and "Journalists on the news: The structured panel discussion as a form of broadcast talk." Lengthy book reviews are included, and issues are occasionally devoted to special topics. An expensive title, but appropriate for research libraries.

1403. *Electronic Journal of Communication.* [ISSN: 1183-5656] 1990. q. Institutional members, USD 300; Individual members, USD 50. Ed(s): Teresa Harrison. Communication Institute for Online Scholarship, PO Box 57, Rotterdam Junction, NY 12150. Illus. Refereed. Circ: 2500000 Controlled. *Bk. rev.:* Occasional. *Aud.:* Ac, Sa.

Presented in English with French abstracts, this academic journal addresses all areas of communication studies including theory, research, practice, and policy. Each issue is devoted to a theme and has its own editor. Nonsubscribers may access the editor's introduction to the issue and view abstracts for each article. A subscription is required to access the articles and the search engine that indexes every word in the issue. Occasionally, an issue will include special features with book reviews.

Howard Journal of Communications. See African American section.

1404. *Human Communication Research.* [ISSN: 0360-3989] 1974. q. GBP 694 (print & online eds.) Individuals, USD 100 (print & online eds.). Ed(s): James E Katz. Wiley-Blackwell Publishing, Inc., 111 River St, Hoboken, NJ 07030; info@wiley.com; http://onlinelibrary.wiley.com/. Illus. Sample. Refereed. Vol. ends: Jun. Microform: PQC. Reprint: PSC. *Indexed:* A01, A22, B01, E01, ERIC, FR, MLA-IB, P02, P61, PsycInfo, SSA. *Aud.:* Ac, Sa.

This official journal of the International Communication Association offers a broad social science focus to the study of human communication. It is touted as one of the top ten journals in human communication, and articles emphasize human symbolic processes in the areas of interpersonal, nonverbal, organizational, intercultural, and mass communication; language and social interaction; new technologies; and health communication. Emphasis is on theory-driven research, human communication methodologies, and critical synthesis. The journal will appeal not only to communication studies scholars but also to those in psychology, sociology, linguistics, and anthropology. In fact, the editors welcome submissions from those within and outside the communication field. For large public and academic libraries.

1405. *International Journal of Communication.* [ISSN: 1932-8036] 2007. irreg. Free. Ed(s): Arlene Luck, Manuel Castells. University of Southern California, Annenberg Center for Communication, Annenberg Press, Kerckhoff Hall, 734 W Adams Blvd, Los Angeles, CA 90089; info@ijoc.org. Refereed. *Indexed:* BRI. *Bk. rev.:* Number and length vary. *Aud.:* Ac.

This international, online, academic, multimedia, peer-reviewed journal is broadly targeted at the many interdisciplinary aspects of communication rather than being narrowly focused on any particular subset of the discipline. Articles are presented in pdf format and are available without subscription. Users are encouraged to register with the site (so that the journal can collect usage statistics and users can be notified via e-mail of new issues), although there is no subscription fee. Along with the articles, book reviews are also published. Recommended for academic libraries.

1406. *International Journal of Listening.* Formerly (until 1995): *International Listening Association. Journal.* [ISSN: 1090-4018] 1987. 3x/yr. GBP 265 (print & online eds.). Ed(s): Margarete Imhof. Routledge, 325 Chestnut St, Ste 800, Philadelphia, PA 19106; customerservice@taylorandfrancis.com; http://www.tandfonline.com. Adv. Sample. Refereed. Reprint: PSC. *Indexed:* A01, A22, E01, ERIC. *Bk. rev.:* Number and length vary. *Aud.:* Ac.

The *International Journal of Listening,* an International Listening Association journal, publishes scholarship on listening in a wide range of contexts, including professional, interpersonal, public/political, media or mass communication, educational, intercultural, and international. Methodologies accepted are empirical, pedagogical, philosophical, and historical. The journal scope does not include listening as it pertains to speech and language pathology, hearing/auditory neurology, and strict cognitive psychology. Articles address listening as it relates to many disciplines (mass communication, intercultural communication, business communication, rhetorical studies, and so forth). A reader will find, on occasion, coverage on a "Special Topic," such as "Best Practices in the Teaching of Listening." Issues may include a "Book Review" section as well as a "Forum" section, where authors discuss current listening research from various viewpoints. Recommended for academic libraries.

1407. *Journal of Applied Communication Research.* Formerly (until 1981): *Journal of Applied Communications Research.* [ISSN: 0090-9882] 1973. q. GBP 263 (print & online eds.). Ed(s): Laura Stafford. Routledge, 325 Chestnut St, Ste 800, Philadelphia, PA 19106; customerservice@taylorandfrancis.com; http://www.tandfonline.com. Illus., adv. Sample. Refereed. Vol. ends: Nov. Microform: PQC. Reprint: PSC. *Indexed:* A01, A22, BRI, E01, ERIC, MLA-IB, P02, P61, PsycInfo, SSA. *Aud.:* Ac, Sa.

This journal publishes articles that bring communication theory and practice together. Articles report on actual communication situations or show results that can be applied to the solution of communication problems. Articles can be any of the following: original research applied to practical situations/problems; application articles that offer ways of improving or expanding upon a particular communication setting through specific research or theory; or commentaries on applied communication issues. Any methodological or theoretical approach is considered, although rigorous application is expected. Examples of articles include "How Audiences Seek Out Crisis Information: Exploring the Social-Mediated Crisis Communication Model" and "The crisis with no name: Defining the interplay of culture, ethnicity, and race on organizational issues and media outcomes." Valuable for its pertinent topics, and recommended for academic libraries.

1408. *Journal of Communication.* [ISSN: 0021-9916] 1951. q. USD 1072 print & online eds. Ed(s): Michael Pfau. Wiley-Blackwell Publishing, Inc., Commerce Pl, 350 Main St, Malden, MA 02148; info@wiley.com; http://onlinelibrary.wiley.com/. Illus., index, adv. Refereed. Circ: 6150 Paid. Microform: PQC. Reprint: PSC. *Indexed:* A01, A22, ABIn, ABS&EES, AmHI, B01, BAS, BRI, C45, CBRI, E01, F01, FR, IBSS, IIFP, MLA-IB, P02, P61, PsycInfo, RILM, SSA. *Bk. rev.:* 4 or more, length varies. *Aud.:* Ac.

Considered a flagship journal in the communication studies field, this publication is interdisciplinary and concentrates broadly on communication theory, research, practice, and policy. The journal is "especially interested in research whose significance crosses disciplinary and sub-field boundaries." Articles are written by scholars, professors from a variety of disciplines, and graduate and doctoral students. Recent articles include "Perceived Versus Actual Disagreement: Which Influences Deliberative Experiences?," "When Do People Misrepresent Themselves to Others? The Effects of Social Desirability, Ground Truth, and Accountability on Deceptive Self-Presentations," and "Internet Use and Democratic Demands: A Multinational, Multilevel Model of Internet Use and Citizen Attitudes About Democracy." There is an extensive book review section, with review essays and shorter book reviews. A necessary publication for large public libraries and academic libraries.

1409. *Journal of Communication Inquiry.* [ISSN: 0196-8599] 1974. q. USD 438. Ed(s): Meenakshi Gigi Durham, Hye Jin Lee. Sage Publications, Inc., 2455 Teller Rd, Thousand Oaks, CA 91320; info@sagepub.com; http://www.sagepub.com. Illus., adv. Sample. Refereed. Vol. ends: Oct. Reprint: PSC. *Indexed:* A01, A22, AmHI, B01, BRI, E01, MLA-IB, P02, P61, RILM, SSA. *Bk. rev.:* 1-3, lengthy. *Aud.:* Ac.

This journal approaches the study of communication and mass communication from cultural and historical perspectives. The interdisciplinary aspects of communication are emphasized, as articles reflect a variety of approaches, from philosophical to empirical to legal. International contributors regularly represent such diverse areas as mass communication, cultural studies, journalism, sociology, philosophy, and political science. The journal also publishes thematic special issues on any of the following critical topics:

deconstructing popular culture; technology and culture; feminist cultural studies; and race, media, and culture. Valuable for its commitment to providing a place for alternative viewpoints on communication and media studies. Includes critical essays and book reviews. For large research collections.

1410. *Journal of Communication Studies.* [ISSN: 1940-9338] 2008. irreg. USD 99.95 soft cover; USD 149 hard cover. Ed(s): Cary W Horvath. Marquette Books LLC, 3107 E 62nd Ave, Spokane, WA 99223; journals@marquettejournals.org; http://www.marquettebooks.com. Refereed. *Bk. rev.:* Number and length vary. *Aud.:* Ac.

This peer-reviewed scientific journal publishes theoretical and empirical papers, essays, and book reviews that advance an understanding of interpersonal, intercultural, or organizational communication processes and effects. Submissions may have a psychological, social, or cultural orientation. The journal is published in hard-copy form and in an open-access online version that is available at no charge to the public. Recent article titles include "A Burning Issue in Teaching: The Impact of Teacher Burnout and Nonverbal Immediacy on Student Motivation and Affective Learning" and "Message Design Logic, Goals, and Message Characteristics in Second-Request Messages." Recommended for academic libraries.

1411. *Journal of Communications Research.* [ISSN: 1935-3537] 2007. q. USD 195. Nova Science Publishers, Inc., 400 Oser Ave, Ste 1600, Hauppauge, NY 11788; nova.main@novapublishers.com; https://www.novapublishers.com. *Aud.:* Ac.

This journal provides research on language and social interaction, nonverbal communication, interpersonal communication, organizational communication and new technologies, mass communication, health communication, intercultural communication, and developmental issues in communication. Recently published articles include "Legal and Ethical Challenges of Corporate Social Networking" and "The Impact of E-Learning on End-Users Satisfaction." Recommended for academic libraries.

1412. *Journal of Computer-Mediated Communication.* [ISSN: 1083-6101] 1995. q. Free. Ed(s): Kevin B Wright. Wiley-Blackwell Publishing, Inc., 111 River St, Hoboken, NJ 07030; info@wiley.com; http://blackwellpublishing.com. Illus., index. Refereed. *Indexed:* A22, E01, PsycInfo. *Aud.:* Ac, Sa.

This journal provides a broad interdisciplinary forum for research and essays based on any of the social sciences on the topic of computerized communication. Each issue is devoted to a specific aspect of computer-mediated communication such as online journalism, electronic commerce, and Internet research. Examples of articles include "A Multimodal Framework for Analyzing Websites as Cultural Expressions" and "Newspapers and the Long-Term Implications of Hyperlinking." An integrated search engine is useful for the researcher searching for keywords or concepts across the full run of issues.

1413. *Journal of Intercultural Communication.* [ISSN: 1404-1634] 1999. q. Free. Ed(s): Jens Allwood, Miguel Benito. Immigrant Institutet, Katrinedalsgatan 43, Boraas, 50451, Sweden; info@immi.se; http://www.immi.se. Refereed. *Indexed:* IBSS. *Aud.:* Ac.

With a focus on the similarities and differences of global cultures and linguistic patterns, this journal promotes research that may have a positive impact on intercultural communication. Issues are published gradually to the web as articles are accepted for publication through a peer-review process. Examples of articles include "Negotiation Styles: Similarities and Differences between American and Japanese University Students" and "Confucian and Protestant Work Ethics Among Polish and Korean Employees and Small Business Owners." For those interested in submitting articles to the journal, statistics are presented to demonstrate the number of accepted and rejected articles broken down by nation of origin.

1414. *Journal of International and Intercultural Communication.* [ISSN: 1751-3057] 2008. q. GBP 168 (print & online eds.). Ed(s): Shiv Ganesh. Routledge, 325 Chestnut St, Ste 800, Philadelphia, PA 19106; customerservice@taylorandfrancis.com; http://www.tandfonline.com. Sample. Reprint: PSC. *Indexed:* A22, E01. *Aud.:* Ac.

Founded in 2008 by the National Communication Association, *JIIC* brings a strong "focus on international, intercultural, and indigenous communication issues" to the field. Scholarship is not limited to single cultures, as some nation-states may comprise multiple cultures. All types of communication are considered (i.e., interpersonal, mass) within the framework of a global perspective. The publication welcomes the following viewpoints: theoretical, experiential, historical, experimental, and analyses that are critical, discursive, and textual. Recommended for academic libraries.

1415. *Journal of Nonverbal Behavior.* Formerly (until 1979): *Environmental Psychology and Nonverbal Behavior.* [ISSN: 0191-5886] 1976. q. EUR 1071 (print & online eds.). Ed(s): Howard S Friedman. Springer New York LLC, 233 Spring St, New York, NY 10013; service-ny@springer.com; http://www.springer.com/. Illus., adv. Sample. Refereed. Vol. ends: Winter. Microform: PQC. Reprint: PSC. *Indexed:* A01, A22, E01, MLA-IB, P02, P61, PsycInfo, SWR&A. *Aud.:* Ac, Sa.

This specialized journal publishes research on the varying components of nonverbal communication—interpersonal, distance, gaze, facial expressiveness, kinesics, paralanguage, posture, gestures, and related behaviors. Research submitted can be empirical, theoretical, or methodological. The journal recognizes the interdisciplinary nature of nonverbal communication, and manuscripts are welcomed from a variety of research fields. Special issues are also published. An expensive but worthwhile title for comprehensive research collections.

1416. *Journal of Social and Personal Relationships.* [ISSN: 0265-4075] 1984. 8x/yr. USD 1933. Ed(s): Mario Mikulincer. Sage Publications Ltd., 1 Oliver's Yard, 55 City Rd, London, EC1Y 1SP, United Kingdom; info@sagepub.co.uk; http://www.uk.sagepub.com. Sample. Refereed. Reprint: PSC. *Indexed:* A01, A22, B01, E01, IBSS, P02, P61, PsycInfo, SSA. *Bk. rev.:* 0-3, length varies. *Aud.:* Ac.

This international journal publishes important scholarship on social and personal relationships. The nature of the field results in articles that are multidisciplinary in scope, drawing from social, clinical, and developmental psychology, sociology, and communication. Recent article titles include "Family Conflict from the Perspective of Adult Child Caregivers: The Influence of Gender" and "Relational Sacrifices in Romantic Relationships: Satisfaction and the Moderating Role of Attachment." Book reviews are often included, and issues are occasionally devoted to special topics. A necessary addition to fully round out a basic academic communication collection.

Journalism and Mass Communication Educator. See Journalism and Writing/Pedagogy section.

1417. *Mass Communication and Society.* Formerly (until 1998): *Mass Communications Review.* [ISSN: 1520-5436] 1973. bi-m. GBP 533 (print & online eds.). Ed(s): Stephen D Perry. Routledge, 325 Chestnut St, Ste 800, Philadelphia, PA 19106; customerservice@taylorandfrancis.com; http://www.tandfonline.com. Illus., adv. Sample. Refereed. Vol. ends: Summer/Fall. Reprint: PSC. *Indexed:* A01, A22, AmHI, BRI, E01, P61, PsycInfo, SSA. *Bk. rev.:* 1-2, lengthy. *Aud.:* Ac.

This is the official journal of the Mass Communication and Society Division of the Association for Education in Journalism and Mass Communication. Research and scholarship are published on mass communication theory from various perspectives, although the macrosocial and societal perspectives are encouraged. This is a cross-disciplinary publication drawing from sociology, law, philosophy, history, psychology, and anthropology. Articles sought must demonstrate how mass communication and its audiences interact. Special issues are occasionally published such as the recent one on "Olympics, Media, and Society." Book reviews on mass communication processes, media effects, and social impacts are also included. Worthwhile for academic collections.

Philosophy and Rhetoric. See Philosophy section.

1418. *Popular Communication: the international journal of media and culture.* [ISSN: 1540-5702] 2003. q. GBP 338 (print & online eds.). Ed(s): Jonathan Gray, Cornel Sandvoss. Routledge, 325 Chestnut St, Ste 800, Philadelphia, PA 19106; customerservice@taylorandfrancis.com; http://www.tandfonline.com. Adv. Sample. Refereed. Reprint: PSC. *Indexed:* A01, A22, E01, P61, SSA. *Bk. rev.:* 1-4, lengthy. *Aud.:* Ac, Sa.

Emphasis is, naturally, on popular communication and its texts, artifacts, audiences, events, and practices, including "the Internet, youth culture, representation, fandom, film, sports, spectacles, the digital revolution, sexuality, advertising/consumer culture, television, radio, music, magazines, and dance." The publication is relevant to many fields—mass communication, media studies, sociology, gender studies, etc. Diverse theoretical and methodological scholarly perspectives are encouraged. A reader will find a special issue once or twice a year, such as "Not Necessarily the News? Global Approaches to News Parody and Political Satire." Book reviews of both academic and nonacademic titles are included, as is an occasional review essay. A title to round out academic communication collections due to the continuing influence of popular culture in today's society.

1419. *Qualitative Research Reports in Communication.* [ISSN: 1745-9435] 2000. a. USD 52 per issue. Ed(s): Janie Harden Fritz. Routledge, 4 Park Sq, Milton Park, Abingdon, OX14 4RN, United Kingdom; subscriptions@tandf.co.uk; http://www.tandfonline.com. Adv. Sample. Refereed. Reprint: PSC. *Indexed:* A01, A22, E01. *Aud.:* Ac.

An Eastern Communication Association journal, *QRRC* publishes numerous qualitative and critical research essays that cover the spectrum of human communication topics (legal, interpersonal, rhetorical, intercultural, media, political, and organizational). The brief essays are 2,500 words or less. Recent articles are "Rapidly Recognizing Relationships: Observing Speed Dating in the South" and "Tall Poppies in the Workplace: Communication Strategies Used by Envious Others in Response to Successful Women." A solid title for academic collections.

1420. *Quarterly Journal of Speech.* Former titles (until 1928): *Quarterly Journal of Speech Education;* (until 1918): *Quarterly Journal of Public Speaking.* [ISSN: 0033-5630] 1915. q. GBP 187 (print & online eds.). Ed(s): Raymie E McKerrow. Routledge, 325 Chestnut St, Ste 800, Philadelphia, PA 19106; customerservice@taylorandfrancis.com; http://www.tandfonline.com. Illus., index, adv. Sample. Refereed. Vol. ends: Nov. Microform: PMC; PQC. Reprint: PSC. *Indexed:* A01, A22, ABS&EES, AmHI, BEL&L, BRI, CBRI, E01, ERIC, FR, LT&LA, MLA-IB, P02, P61, PsycInfo, RILM, SSA. *Bk. rev.:* 4 or more, lengthy. *Aud.:* Ac.

A respected and established journal in the field, *QJS* publishes articles "under rhetoric's broad purview." Our understanding of rhetoric has evolved beyond solely the traditional approach, and the journal embraces the fact that rhetoric "cuts across many different intellectual, disciplinary, and political vectors." Various forms of rhetoric are included, whether that be oral or written, direct or mediated, historical or contemporary. Of particular interest are essays that speak to the discourse of marginalized voices. Each issue may include a book review essay and additional critical book reviews. A necessary title for academic libraries.

1421. *The Review of Communication.* [ISSN: 1535-8593] 2001. q. GBP 195. Ed(s): Pat J Gehrke. Routledge, 325 Chestnut St, Ste 800, Philadelphia, PA 19106; customerservice@taylorandfrancis.com; http://www.tandfonline.com. Sample. Refereed. *Indexed:* A22, E01. *Bk. rev.:* Number and length vary. *Aud.:* Ac, Sa.

This refereed online-only publication from the National Communication Association provides "scholarship that advances the discipline of communication through the study of major themes that cross the disciplinary sub-fields." The journal touts uniqueness in its emphasis on broad trends, topics, and impasses in the examination of communication; and its studies may be historical, theoretical, philosophical, qualitative, quantitative, or syncretic. Also provides lengthy book review essays.

1422. *Rhetoric Society Quarterly.* Formerly (until 1976): *Rhetoric Society Newsletter.* [ISSN: 0277-3945] 1969. 5x/yr. GBP 199 (print & online eds.). Ed(s): Carolyn R Miller. Taylor & Francis Inc., 325 Chestnut St, Ste 800, Philadelphia, PA 19106; customerservice@taylorandfrancis.com; http://www.tandfonline.com. Illus., index, adv. Refereed. Vol. ends: Oct. Reprint: PSC. *Indexed:* A22, ArtHuCI, E01, MLA-IB, P02. *Bk. rev.:* 3 or more, length varies. *Aud.:* Ac.

A publication of the Rhetoric Society of America, *RSQ* presents cross-disciplinary scholarship on all aspects of rhetorical studies. Approaches to rhetoric include historical, theoretical, pedagogical, and practical criticism. Editorial expectations are that the scholarship submitted will advance and/or contribute to a multidisciplinary field. Special issues such as "Regional Rhetorics" occur occasionally as well. To serve its mission as a publication for the society, *RSQ* also publishes book reviews, announcements, and general information. A solid journal in its field, and recommended for academic collections.

1423. Southern Communication Journal. Former titles (until 1988): *Southern Speech Communication Journal;* (until 1971): *The Southern Speech Journal;* (until 1942): *Southern Speech Bulletin.* [ISSN: 1041-794X] 1935. 5x/yr. GBP 199 (print & online eds.). Ed(s): Mary Stuckey. Taylor & Francis Inc., 325 Chestnut St, Ste 800, Philadelphia, PA 19106; customerservice@taylorandfrancis.com; http://www.tandfonline.com. Illus., index, adv. Sample. Refereed. Vol. ends: Summer. Microform: PQC. Reprint: PSC. *Indexed:* A01, A22, BRI, E01, MLA-IB, P02, PsycInfo, RILM. *Bk. rev.:* Number and length vary. *Aud.:* Ac.

A well-established publication of a regional communication association, *SCJ* publishes original scholarly research on human communication. The journal is not limited to any topic, simply those topics of interest to scholars, researchers, teachers, and practitioners in the communication field. Any methodological and theoretical orientation is welcome, as long as the topic is established as important, the methodology is sound, and the theoretical viewpoint is appropriate. Recent articles illustrate the varied content, "Organization-Public Relationship: Satisfaction and Intention to Retain a Relationship with a Cell Phone Service Provider" and "First Lady International Diplomacy: Performing Gendered Roles on the World Stage." Book reviews are also included. A recommended title for academic libraries.

1424. Text and Performance Quarterly. Formerly (until 1989): *Literature and Performance.* [ISSN: 1046-2937] 1980. q. GBP 259 (print & online eds.). Routledge, 4 Park Sq, Milton Park, Abingdon, OX14 4RN, United Kingdom; subscriptions@tandf.co.uk; http://www.tandfonline.com. Illus., adv. Sample. Refereed. Vol. ends: Oct. Reprint: PSC. *Indexed:* A22, AmHI, ArtHuCI, E01, MLA-IB, P61, RILM. *Aud.:* Ac, Sa.

This journal publishes readable scholarship that examines and advances the study of performance as a "social, communicative practice; as a technology of representation and expression; and as a hermeneutic." Material is often presented in diverse styles, such as narratives, interviews, performance texts/scripts, and photographic essays. A variety of perspectives to performance are considered—historical, ethnographic, feminist, rhetorical, political, and aesthetic. The journal's sections may include "Original Articles," "Research Reports," "The Year in Books," and "The Performance Space," which analyzes performances from all types of venues. For comprehensive communication collections.

1425. Toastmaster. Formerly: *The Toastmasters International.* [ISSN: 0040-8263] 1933. m. Free to members. Ed(s): Suzanne Frey. Toastmasters International, PO Box 9052, Mission Viejo, CA 92690; letters@toastmasters.org; http://www.toastmasters.org/. Illus., index. Vol. ends: Dec. *Aud.:* Ga, Sa.

This is a monthly magazine for members of Toastmasters International, a nonprofit educational organization, although libraries may purchase a subscription. The publication provides helpful information and practical tips to those interested in acquiring and improving their communication and leadership skills. Articles have a how-to focus as they cover topics such as humor, speaking techniques, leadership, famous speakers, career development, presentation technology, and language usage. Since the majority of readers are experienced and knowledgeable public speakers, only well-researched and well-written articles are accepted for publication. The digital version allows viewers to read an article in a different language by clicking on the title of the article they wish to translate. Notices and articles about the activities of the organization are also included. Of benefit to business professionals and other people with these special interests, this is a title for public libraries.

1426. Vital Speeches of the Day. [ISSN: 0042-742X] 1934. m. USD 75 domestic; USD 95 foreign. Ed(s): Jennifer Dack Woolson, Thomas Dealy. McMurry, Inc., 1010 E Missouri Ave, Phoenix, AZ 85014; info@mcmurry.com; http://www.mcmurry.com. Adv. Sample. Circ: 9000 Paid and free. *Indexed:* A01, A22, ABIn, AgeL, B01, BAS, C37, MASUSE, P02. *Aud.:* Hs, Ga, Ac.

Vital Speeches prints the "best thought of the best minds on current national questions." Important speeches are presented by leaders in the fields of business, politics, education, government, and more. The speeches serve dual purposes—as models of excellent current oratory and as informative discussions on key issues. Current speeches are printed in full (unless otherwise stated), and editorial policy is committed to covering both sides of public questions. Examples of speeches are "We Will Remake America" by President Barack Obama and "It's Not Just About Us, It's About the Patients" by Nancy H. Nielsen, M.D., Ph.D., President of the American Medical Association. Not only is this title important for the general public, it is also an excellent resource for the student of public speaking. Recommended for public and academic libraries.

1427. Web Journal of Mass Communication Research. 1997. q. Free. Ed(s): Guido Stempel, Robert Stewart. Ohio University, E. W. Scripps School of Journalism, 32 Park Place, Athens, OH 45701; hodson@ohio.edu; http://scrippsjschool.org/. Refereed. *Aud.:* Ac, Sa.

The journal has narrowed its focus to "web-related communication themes" due to the influence the web has had in "shaping" mass communication. A new column that appears semi-regularly will highlight important web-related communication research published in other journals in the field. Each issue consists of a single article, such as "Uses of New Media Before 2011 By Egyptian Political Movements."

1428. Western Journal of Communication. Former titles (until 1992): *Western Journal of Speech Communication;* (until 1977): *Western Speech Communication;* (until 1975): *Western Speech.* [ISSN: 1057-0314] 1937. 5x/yr. Routledge, 4 Park Sq, Milton Park, Abingdon, OX14 4RN, United Kingdom; subscriptions@tandf.co.uk; http://www.tandfonline.com. Illus., index, adv. Sample. Refereed. Microform: PQC. Reprint: PSC. *Indexed:* A01, A22, BAS, E01, ERIC, MLA-IB, P02, PsycInfo. *Aud.:* Ac.

One of two scholarly journals of the Western States Communication Association, *WJC* publishes original scholarly articles in all areas of human communication, including rhetoric, communication theory, health, family, interpersonal, and small-group communication, language behavior, critical and cultural studies, oral interpretation, performance studies, freedom of speech, and applied communication. All methodological and theoretical perspectives are encouraged. Editorial policy encourages research that is accessible to both a scholarly audience and a learned public. A good title for academic libraries.

1429. Women's Studies in Communication. Formerly (until 1982): *O R W A C Bulletin.* [ISSN: 0749-1409] 1977. s-a. GBP 94 (print & online eds.). Ed(s): Valeria Fabj. Organization for Research on Women and Communication, c/o Bonnie Dow, Celeste Condit, Eds., Department of Speech Comm, CSU, Long Beach, CA 90840-2407; sdowney@sculb.edu; http://www.orwac.org/. Illus., adv. Refereed. Vol. ends: Fall. Reprint: PSC. *Indexed:* A01, A22, AmHI, BRI, C42, F01, FemPer, GW, MLA-IB, P02, RILM, WSA. *Bk. rev.:* Number and length vary. *Aud.:* Ac, Sa.

The editorial policy of *WSIC* states that it provides a "feminist forum for research, reviews, and commentary that advances our understanding of the relationships between communication and women, gender, sexuality and feminism." This journal seeks research where gender, power, class, race, ethnicity, nationality, and transnationalism "intersect." The publication is open to any methodology, perspective, scope, and context, as long as there is a connection between communication and gender/women/the feminine. Scholarship that empowers women and other marginalized groups is especially welcomed, and the editors encourage submissions from novice scholars. *WSIC* also includes a "Conversation and Commentary" section. As the official journal of the Organization for Research on Women and Communication, this is a worthwhile title for all-inclusive academic collections.

■ COMPUTERS AND INFORMATION TECHNOLOGY

Professional Journals/Popular Titles

See also Business; Electronics; Engineering and Technology; and Library and Information Science sections.

Nathan Mealey, Manager of Library Technologies, Portland State University Library, Portland, OR; mealey@pdx.edu

Introduction

The Computer and Information Technology section includes the core journals and magazines for academic and public library collections. Professional journals are oriented toward researchers and specialists in the field of computer science, and in most cases consist of highly technical, peer-reviewed content. Contrasted with these are the popular titles that are aimed at a wide array of technology consumers and decision makers. These titles focus on delivering practical, actionable information about the technology field and recent developments within it.

The last edition of *Magazines for Libraries* noted the significant changes that were occurring in the realm of information technology magazines, and in particular how publishers were responding to the increasing pressures created by digital technologies. This challenge has only intensified in the two years since then. Most significant has been the increasingly prominent role played by mobile devices and the distribution channel that they offer. With the rapid growth of mobile devices has come a host of applications that enable publishers to more easily reach consumers and to craft content specific to the medium. A number of the magazines included here have followed this path, creating digital editions that take advantage of the technologies built into mobile devices, often surpassing the capabilities of the print medium. In some cases, publishers have created their own mobile applications, enabling consumers to access both their magazine and associated content published through other channels, such as their blogs or books.

These changes have had their greatest effect on popular magazines, changing their publishing paradigm and thinning their overall number. In contrast, the number and range of scholarly technology journals has remained relatively constant. Open-access publishing has certainly impacted this field, and several of the journals listed below are published online and open-access, but no more so than in any other field. The biggest shift in scholarly technology journals is the changing scope of the subjects they address. New types of devices, social networking, cloud services, and ubiquitous computing are just a few examples of technologies that are fundamentally altering the nature of technology and computing, redefining what is being studied and how it is understood. Scholarly journals reflect this change through the changing scope of research that they publish and highlight. Looking back through the archives of these journals is an opportunity to observe the evolution of technology over the past several decades.

Basic Periodicals

Ga: *Information Week, Macworld, PC Magazine, PC World, Smart Computing;* Ac: *Association for Computing Machinery. Journal, The Computer Journal, Computerworld, Educause Review, Information Today.*

Basic Abstracts and Indexes

Computer and Control Abstracts, Computing Reviews, INSPEC, Internet & Personal Computing Abstracts.

C I O. See Business and Finance section.

Computers in Libraries, See Library and Information Science section.

Professional Journals

1430. *A C M Queue (Online).* [ISSN: 1542-7749] 2003. 11x/yr. Free. Association for Computing Machinery, Inc., 2 Penn Plz, Ste 701, New York, NY 10121; acmhelp@acm.org; http://www.acm.org. *Aud.:* Ac.

ACM Queue is a monthly magazine published by the Association for Computing Machinery that is aimed at practicing software engineers and is oriented toward addressing the "technical problems that loom ahead, helping readers to share and pursue innovative solutions [by taking] a critical look at current and emerging technologies, highlighting problems that are likely to arise, and posing questions that software engineers should be thinking about." Contributors include many significant researchers and practitioners from within the field, and topics cover a wide spectrum, including computing performance, development, visualization, networks, and power management. All articles are peer reviewed. This title is highly recommended for academic libraries, as the topics covered are of general and current interest within the field of computer science and the magazine's audience includes both students and researchers.

1431. *A C M Transactions.* q. Association for Computing Machinery, Inc., 2 Penn Plz, Ste 701, New York, NY 10121; acmhelp@acm.org; http://www.acm.org. *Aud.:* Ac.

ACM Transactions is the umbrella under which a collection of more than 30 discipline-specific journals are published by the Association for Computing Machinery. Each specific journal maintains a direct relationship to one of the ACM's many special-interest groups. For instance, the *ACM Transactions on Database Systems* is steered by the ACM Special Interest Group on Management and Organization of Data. Each of these quarterly journals focuses on original, previously unpublished research within the given discipline. Articles address new areas of research or new experiences with applications of existing research, and all articles are peer reviewed. Recommended for academic libraries.

1432. *A I Magazine.* [ISSN: 0738-4602] 1980. q. USD 280 (Individuals, USD 140; Students, USD 70). Ed(s): David B Leake. A A A I Press, 445 Burgess Dr, Ste 100, Menlo Park, CA 94025; info@aaai.org; http://www.aaai.org. Illus., index, adv. Refereed. Vol. ends: Dec. *Indexed:* A01, A22, ABIn, B01, B02, BRI, CompLI, CompR, EngInd, I15, P02. *Bk. rev.:* Number and length vary. *Aud.:* Ac.

This professional journal is the official publication of the Association for the Advancement of Artificial Intelligence. The organization itself has been active since 1979, and began publishing this journal in 1980. *AI Magazine* has maintained its quarterly release schedule ever since. The magazine features articles and book reviews, and the contents of each issue are typically centered on a specific subject. Recent examples include issues covering such topics as robotics, recommender systems, and predictive problem solving. Articles are all peer reviewed. Recommended for academic libraries.

1433. *Advances in Multimedia.* [ISSN: 1687-5680] 2007. USD 295. Ed(s): Ling Shao. Hindawi Publishing Corporation, 410 Park Ave, 15th Fl, PMB 287, New York, NY 10022; info@hindawi.com; http://www.hindawi.com. Refereed. *Indexed:* C&ISA, CerAb. *Aud.:* Ac, Sa.

Advances in Multimedia is an open-access, peer-reviewed journal that publishes both original research and review articles in all areas of multimedia. With the goal of providing comprehensive coverage of the field of multimedia research, this journal publishes articles on such topics as: data compression, multimedia storage and delivery, networking, communications, discovery algorithms and retrieval, and software design. The journal initiated publication in 2007, and produces the occasional special issue dedicated to a specific topic of interest as part of its regular publication schedule. All articles are available freely online, and print subscriptions are available as well. Recommended for academic libraries.

1434. *Advances in Software Engineering.* [ISSN: 1687-8655] 2008. USD 295. Hindawi Publishing Corporation, 410 Park Ave, 15th Fl, PMB 287, New York, NY 10022; orders@hindawi.com; http://www.hindawi.com. Refereed. *Aud.:* Ac, Sa.

Similar to *Advances in Multimedia,* this is an open-access, peer-reviewed journal that publishes both original research and review articles. The journal began publication in 2009, with the objective is to publish articles that provide wide coverage of all aspects of the field of software engineering. Recent articles have covered such topics as software development and testing, distributed software development, tools for software engineering, quality assurance in software engineering, and best practices in software development. Special issues dedicated to specific topics are occasionally published. All articles are available freely online, and print subscriptions are available as well. Recommended for academic libraries.

1435. *Association for Computing Machinery. Journal.* [ISSN: 0004-5411] 1954. bi-m. Free to members; Non-members, USD 270. Ed(s): Victor Vianu. Association for Computing Machinery, Inc., 2 Penn Plz, Ste 701, New York, NY 10121; acmhelp@acm.org; http://www.acm.org. Illus., index. Refereed. Microform: PQC. *Indexed:* A22, ABIn, B01, C&ISA, CCMJ, CerAb, CompLI, CompR, EngInd, MSN, MathR, P02. *Aud.:* Ac.

The *Journal of the Association for Computing Machinery* is a bimonthly publication of the Association for Computing Machinery that has been in continuous publication since 1954. The journal is a "best of" publication with the stated goal of including only "original research papers of lasting value in computer science." All articles are peer reviewed, and each article must meet the rigorous criteria of being "truly outstanding in its field and to be of interest to a wide audience." The articles included cover the entire spectrum of research in the field of computer science, broadly construed and changing over the course of time as computing technology evolves. As a result, this journal's contents are typically very timely and relevant. Recommended for academic libraries.

1436. *Communications of the A C M.* Formerly (until 1959): *Association for Computing Machinery. Communications.* [ISSN: 0001-0782] 1958. m. Free to members; Non-members, USD 224. Ed(s): Diane Crawford, Thomas E Lambert. Association for Computing Machinery, Inc., 2 Penn Plz, Ste 701, New York, NY 10121; acmhelp@acm.org; http://www.acm.org. Illus., index. Sample. Refereed. Vol. ends: No. 12. Microform: PQC. *Indexed:* A01, A22, ABIn, ABS&EES, ApMecR, B01, B02, BRI, C&ISA, CerAb, CompLI, CompR, EngInd, ErgAb, MLA-IB, MathR, P02. *Aud.:* Ac.

This monthly magazine published by the Association for Computing Machinery unites the full range of interests, ideas, and perspectives that are captured in both the ACM's numerous publications and diverse membership base. Similar to an organization such as Educause, the ACM's membership includes both information technology practitioners and academic researchers, and the breadth of topics and articles included in *Communications of the ACM* reflects this. The magazine has been in print continuously since 1958, and in recent years has adapted to take advantage of the web by developing distinct online and print versions that include both shared and unique content. Topics include news, opinion, research, practical applications, and coverage of leading and emerging trends in information technology. The more heavily research-oriented sections of the magazine ("review articles" and "contributed articles") are peer reviewed. Due to its wide range of content, the magazine is of relevant interest to both technology practitioners and researchers, and is recommended for both academic and public libraries.

1437. *Computer Graphics (Online).* Former titles (until 2006): *Computer Graphics (Print);* (until 1970): *S I G G R A P H Newsletter (Special Interest Group Graphics).* [ISSN: 1558-4569] 196?. q. USD 110. Association for Computing Machinery, Inc., 2 Penn Plz, Ste 701, New York, NY 10121; acmhelp@acm.org; http://www.acm.org. *Aud.:* Ac.

This scholarly journal is published quarterly by ACM SIGGRAPH, the Association for Computing Machinery's computer graphics special interest group, whose goal is to "promote the generation and dissemination of information on computer graphics and interactive techniques." The journal has been in publication since 1997, and is a leading voice on the broad range of topics and issues found under the umbrella of computer graphics. These include visual techniques as applied to art, movies, games, data manipulation and visualization, simulation, and more. Articles are contributed by members, and the journal's editorial board is made up of active members, although the contents are not formally peer-reviewed. Recommended for academic libraries.

1438. *Computer Graphics World.* Formerly (until 1980): *Computer Graphics (Eugene).* [ISSN: 0271-4159] 197?. m. USD 72 domestic; USD 98 in Canada & Mexico; USD 150 elsewhere. Ed(s): Karen Moltenbrey. C O P Communications, 620 W Elk Ave, Glendale, CA 91204; info@copprints.com; http://www.copprints.com. Illus., adv. Sample. Vol. ends: Dec. Microform: PQC. *Indexed:* A01, A22, B01, B02, B03, BRI, BrTechI, C37, EngInd, F01, I15, MASUSE, P02. *Aud.:* Ga, Ac.

This monthly magazine provides in-depth coverage of the world of computer graphics aimed at professionals in the field of computer graphics as applied to film, education, technology, art, music, and gaming. Each issue features a range of articles, from reviews to in-depth analyses, each devoted to exploring leading-edge graphics techniques including animation, visualization, and 3D modeling and their application in many different fields and industries. The accompanying web site features content that supplements specific articles from the print magazine, alongside additional content such as news, tutorials, and videos. The topics and tone of the magazine make it accessible to a wide audience, including practitioners, researchers, and consumers. Recommended for both public and academic libraries.

1439. *The Computer Journal.* [ISSN: 0010-4620] 1958. m. EUR 1556. Ed(s): Erol Gelenbe. Oxford University Press, Great Clarendon St, Oxford, OX2 6DP, United Kingdom; enquiry@oup.co.uk; http://www.oxfordjournals.org. Illus., index, adv. Sample. Refereed. Vol. ends: No. 8. Microform: PQC. Reprint: PSC. *Indexed:* A01, A22, ABIn, BRI, BrTechI, C&ISA, CerAb, CompLI, CompR, E01, EngInd, ErgAb, MLA-IB, MathR, P02. *Aud.:* Ac.

The Computer Journal is published by Oxford University Press on behalf of England's BCS—The Chartered Institute For IT. The journal is academically oriented. All articles are refereed, and journal's objective is to serve all branches of the computer science community by publishing high-quality papers concerning original research and new developments in the field of computer science. The journal publishes articles in three broad areas: (1) computer science, methods, and tools; (2) networks and computer systems; and (3) computational intelligence (this section was launched by the journal in 2010). There are also occasional topic-specific special issues. Recent special-issue topics included high-performance computing, network and system security, and digital forensics. This journal is highly regarded within the field, and is recommended for academic libraries.

1440. *Computer (New York).* Formerly (until 1970): *I E E E Computer Group News.* [ISSN: 0018-9162] 1966. m. USD 2095; USD 2620 combined subscription (print & online eds.). Ed(s): Carl K Chang, Judi Prow. Institute of Electrical and Electronics Engineers, 445 Hoes Ln, Piscataway, NJ 08854; contactcenter@ieee.org; http://www.ieee.org. Illus. Refereed. Vol. ends: Dec. *Indexed:* A01, A22, BRI, C&ISA, CerAb, CompLI, CompR, EngInd, ErgAb, P02. *Aud.:* Ac.

Computer magazine, published monthly by the IEEE Computer Society, brings together a compilation of articles that have been previously published in one of the Society's other peer-reviewed technical magazines. Articles published in *Computer* are edited to enhance readability, as the magazine is oriented toward a more general audience than their other topic-specific, technical magazines. The overall focus of the magazine is all aspects of computer science, including "research, trends, best practices, and changes in the profession." Recent issues have included articles discussing digital image content, delivery, and manipulation; parallel computing; green IT and sustainable computing; and recent trends in security technologies. Recommended for academic libraries.

1441. *Computers in Libraries: complete coverage of library information technology.* Formerly (until 1989): *Small Computers in Libraries;* Which incorporated (1986-1988): *Systems Librarian and Automation Review;* (1985-1987): *Bulletin Board Systems;* (1986-1987): *Public Computing.* [ISSN: 1041-7915] 1981. m. USD 99.95 (Individuals, USD 69.95). Ed(s): Kathy Dempsey. Information Today, Inc., 143 Old Marlton Pike, Medford, NJ 08055; custserv@infotoday.com; http://www.infotoday.com. Illus., index, adv. Circ: 6000. Vol. ends: Dec. *Indexed:* A01, A22, ABIn, B01, B02, B03, BRI, CLI, CompR, ERIC, FR, I15, ISTA, P02. *Aud.:* Ac.

Computers in Libraries is arguably the preeminent magazine dedicated to covering the intersection of technology and libraries. The magazine is published on a monthly basis by Information Today, who also host the annual Computers

In Libraries conference in Washington, D.C. The magazine's central focus is on the practical application of technologies for all types of libraries, including academic, public, school, and special libraries. Recently published articles address such topics as: digital library technologies, technology planning and strategies for libraries, cloud computing and libraries, mobile devices in libraries, and library uses for social media technologies. This journal is recommended for academic libraries, and is a highly recommended professional resource for library staff in all types of libraries.

1442. Educause Review. Former titles (until 2000): *Educom Review;* (until 1989): *Educom Bulletin;* (until 1984): *Educom.* [ISSN: 1527-6619] 1966. bi-m. USD 35 in North America; USD 60 elsewhere. Ed(s): D Teddy Diggs. Educause, 4772 Walnut St, Ste 206, Boulder, CO 80301; info@educause.com; http://www.educause.edu. Illus., index, adv. Sample. Refereed. Circ: 22000. Vol. ends: Dec. *Indexed:* A01, A22, ABIn, CompLI, ERIC, HEA, MLA-IB. *Aud.:* Ac.

Educause Review is published by Educause, a nonprofit organization that brings together IT leaders and professionals in academia. The magazine is published in both print and online formats on a bimonthly basis, six issues per year. The magazine's goal is to take a broad look at current development in the information technology industry and how they affect higher education and is aimed at a readership that includes administrators and managers in the technology field, as well as non-IT staff such as librarians, academic administrators and leaders, librarians, and faculty. Recent articles cover such topics as the impact of cloud computing on academic technology, knowledge management, copyright, and access to digital content, technological innovation, and assessing the impact of technology on student learning. Recommended for academic libraries.

1443. Human - Computer Interaction (Mahwah): a journal of theoretical, empirical, and methodological issues of user psychology and of system design. [ISSN: 0737-0024] 1985. q. GBP 597 (print & online eds.). Ed(s): Thomas P Moran. Taylor & Francis Inc., 325 Chestnut St, Ste 800, Philadelphia, PA 19106; customerservice@taylorandfrancis.com; http://www.tandfonline.com. Adv. Sample. Refereed. Reprint: PSC. *Indexed:* A01, A22, ABIn, B01, C&ISA, CerAb, CompLI, E01, EngInd, ErgAb, P61, PsycInfo, SSA. *Aud.:* Ac.

This interdisciplinary, scholarly journal brings together the work of researchers from the broad range of fields that contribute to the field of human–computer interaction, including interface development, cognitive science, system design, and user science. Topics covered include web-development and graphic design, users' cognitive perception of technology interfaces, software development, sense-making and technology, touch-based system design, and visual search methodologies. The magazine is published quarterly, and features occasional special issues that are dedicated to covering specific topics. Recent special issues include human–computer interaction and transnational issues, and assessing the impact of technology on our ability to understand and participate in the world around us. Recommended for academic libraries.

1444. Human Technology: an interdisciplinary journal on humans in I C T environments. [ISSN: 1795-6889] 2005. s-a. Free. Ed(s): Paivi Hakkinen. Jyvaskylan Yliopisto, Agora Center, University of Jyvaskyla, PO Box 35, Jyvaskyla, 40014, Finland. Refereed. *Indexed:* PsycInfo. *Aud.:* Ac.

Human Technology is an interdisciplinary and multidisciplinary journal established with the goal of "investigating the human role in existing and emerging technologies" through publishing original research exploring the human aspect of technology and crafting solutions to addressing its challenges. It began publication as a semi-annual, open-access journal in 2005, and remains so today. Articles include both original research and review articles, and cover a range of topics that illustrates the complexity of the field of human–computer interaction, including the social, psychological, educational, cultural, philosophical, cognitive scientific, and communication aspects of human-centered technology. All of the journal's contents are peer reviewed. Recommended for academic libraries.

1445. I E E E Transactions. m. I E E E Computer Society, 2001 L St NW, Ste 700, Washington, DC 20036; customer.service@ieee.org; http://www.computer.org. Refereed. *Aud.:* Ac.

Similar to the above entry for *ACM Transactions, IEEE Transactions* is the umbrella under which the IEEE Computer Society publishes many individual journals that cover separate aspects of the field of computer science. Each journal is oriented toward a specific aspect of computer science, including computer architecture, parallel and distributed computing, software engineering, computer graphics, learning technologies, mobile computing, multimedia, bioinformatics, and networking. Each of the titles publishes peer-reviewed original research. This collection of titles is recommended for academic libraries.

1446. Information Systems: databases: their creation, management and utilization. [ISSN: 0306-4379] 1975. 8x/yr. EUR 2138. Ed(s): Gottfried Vossen, Dr. Dennis Shasha. Pergamon, The Blvd, Langford Ln, E Park, Kidlington, OX5 1GB, United Kingdom; JournalsCustomerServiceEMEA@elsevier.com; http://www.elsevier.com. Illus., adv. Sample. Refereed. Vol. ends: No. 8. Microform: PQC. *Indexed:* A01, A22, C&ISA, CompLI, CompR, EngInd, RiskAb. *Aud.:* Ac.

Information Systems is a peer-reviewed journal that publishes research that explores the hardware and software that supports data-intensive computing applications. It is published eight times a year and includes a range of article types, including original research, reviews, and implementation papers. Articles cover the design and implementation of languages, data models, process models, algorithms, software and hardware for information systems, data mining, information retrieval, and cloud management of data. Of particular interest is the journal's strong focus on practice-based article topics: "All papers should motivate the problems they address with compelling examples from real or potential applications." The journal's online presence includes "virtual special issues" that compile previously published papers on a common theme. Recommended for academic libraries.

1447. Interactions (New York): experiences, people, technology. [ISSN: 1072-5520] 1994. bi-m. Free to members; Non-members, USD 210. Ed(s): Ron Wakkary, John Stanik. Association for Computing Machinery, Inc., 2 Penn Plz, Ste 701, New York, NY 10121; acmhelp@acm.org; http://www.acm.org. *Indexed:* A22, ABIn, C&ISA, CerAb, CompR, EngInd, ErgAb. *Aud.:* Ac.

Interactions is a bimonthly magazine published by the Association for Computing Machinery. Aimed at information technology professionals, its content articulates "the connections between experiences, people[,] and technology." The magazine is less formal than the ACM's scholarly research-oriented journals. Instead of focusing on the publishing of original or cutting-edge research, *Interactions* aims to publish articles, stories, and other less traditional content that illustrates the interconnections between technology and human experience. Recommended for academic libraries.

1448. Journal of Computer Science and Technology. [ISSN: 1000-9000] 1986. bi-m. EUR 1113 (print & online eds.). Ed(s): Guo-Jie Li, Zhi-Wei Xu. Springer New York LLC, 233 Spring St, New York, NY 10013; service-ny@springer.com; http://www.springer.com/. Illus., adv. Sample. Refereed. Circ: 6000. Reprint: PSC. *Indexed:* A22, ABIn, BRI, CCMJ, CompLI, E01, EngInd, MSN, MathR. *Aud.:* Ac.

The *Journal of Computer Science and Technology* is an academically-oriented, peer-reviewed, bimonthly magazine that publishes articles from "scientists and engineers in all aspects of computer science and technology." Papers are of original research, accompanied by occasional special issues devoted to conference proceedings, and cover a range of topics, including formal methods, algorithms and complexity, computer architecture, high-performance computing, software engineering, distributed computing systems, artificial intelligence, bioinformatics, data mining, database systems, information security, and computer graphics and visualization. Special issues dedicated to specific topics are published occasionally, and typically each non-issue is itself oriented around two or three general topics (e.g., distributed computing). The journal's web site includes access to tables of contents for all published issues, article abstracts, and full-text pdfs of each article. Recommended for academic libraries.

1449. *Journal of Database Management.* Formerly (until 1992): *Journal of Database Administration.* [ISSN: 1063-8016] 1990. q. USD 625 (Individuals, USD 220). Ed(s): Keng Siau. I G I Global, 701 E Chocolate Ave, Ste 200, Hershey, PA 17033; cust@igi-global.com; http://www.igi-global.com. Refereed. *Indexed:* A22, ABIn, B01, B02, BRI, C&ISA, CerAb, CompLI, E01, EngInd, I15. *Aud.:* Ac.

This peer-reviewed, professional journal is one of the leading sources of timely research in the field of database management. The journal publishes original research on database theory, systems design, and software engineering related to databases, and its mission is to "be instrumental in the improvement and development of theory and practice related to information technology and management of information resources." The journal publishes research articles, research notes, and research reviews on a broad range of topics, such as data warehousing and data mining, database models and query languages, bioinformatics, and systems analysis design. The journal is aimed at both researchers and database professionals, and so includes both theoretically-oriented research and concrete, actionable research. Recommended for academic libraries.

Journal of Digital Information. See Library and Information Science section.

1450. *Journal of Usability Studies.* [ISSN: 1931-3357] 2005. q. Free. Ed(s): Joe Dumas, Marilyn Tremaine. Usability Professionals' Association, 140 N Bloomingdale Rd, Bloomingdale, IL 60108; office@usabilityprofessionals.org; http://www.upassoc.org/. Refereed. *Indexed:* ErgAb. *Aud.:* Ac.

The *Journal of Usability Studies* is scholarly voice of the Usability Professionals Association, an organization that "supports people who research, design, and evaluate the user experience of products and services." This is an open-access, online journal that has been published quarterly since 2005. The journal's editorial goal is to "promote and enhance the practice, research, and education of user experience design and evaluation." Articles cover a broad range of topics within the realm of usability studies, including empirical studies, comparative analyses of methodologies, usability case studies, critical/discussion papers, opinion/editorials, and reports on research findings. All submissions are peer reviewed. Recommended for academic libraries.

1451. *Operating Systems Review.* Formerly (until 1970): *S I G O P S Bulletin.* [ISSN: 0163-5980] 1967. 3x/yr. USD 20. Ed(s): Jeanna Neefe Matthews. Association for Computing Machinery, Inc., 2 Penn Plz, Ste 701, New York, NY 10121; acmhelp@acm.org; http://www.acm.org. Illus., index, adv. *Indexed:* A22, C&ISA, CerAb, CompR, EngInd. *Aud.:* Ac.

Operating Systems Review is a publication of the Association for Computing Machinery's Special Interest Group on Operating Systems. Each issue is oriented around a specific theme, and articles are solicited by guest editors. Several types of articles are published, including polemics, works in progress, results of repeated research, historical accounts, novel approaches to operating system education, and tutorials. The journal's scope covers a range of subjects, including computer operating systems and architecture for multiprogramming, multiprocessing, and time sharing; resource management; evaluation and simulation; reliability, integrity, and security of data; communications among computing processors; and computer system modeling and analysis. Recent articles included such topics as cloud computing, distributed databases, peer-to-peer data sharing, and operating system virtualization. Recommended for academic libraries.

1452. *S I A M Journal on Computing.* [ISSN: 0097-5397] 1972. bi-m. USD 738 (print & online eds.). Ed(s): Madhu Sudan. Society for Industrial and Applied Mathematics, 3600 Market St, 6th Fl, Philadelphia, PA 19104; siam@siam.org; http://www.siam.org. Illus., adv. Sample. Refereed. Circ: 1487. Vol. ends: Dec. *Indexed:* A01, A22, ABIn, ApMecR, B01, C&ISA, CCMJ, CompLI, CompR, EngInd, MSN, MathR. *Aud.:* Ac.

This journal, published by the Society for Industrial and Applied Mathematics, provides coverage of "the most significant work going on in the mathematical and formal aspects of computer science and non-numerical computing." The

bimonthly journal was founded in 1972, and publishes articles that cover a very broad range of topics, including designing algorithms, data structures, computational complexity, computational algebra, robotics, artificial intelligence, mathematical aspects of programming languages, databases and information retrieval, cryptography, distributed computing, and parallel algorithms. Full tables of contents are available on the journal's web site, and access to full-text articles is available to subscribing institutions and individuals. Recommended for academic libraries.

1453. *Software: Practice and Experience.* [ISSN: 0038-0644] 1971. m. GBP 2699. Ed(s): R N Horspool, A J Wellings. John Wiley & Sons Ltd., The Atrium, Southern Gate, Chichester, PO19 8SQ, United Kingdom; customer@wiley.com; http://www.wiley.com. Illus., index, adv. Sample. Refereed. Vol. ends: No. 15. Reprint: PSC. *Indexed:* A22, BrTechI, C&ISA, CerAb, CompLI, CompR, EngInd. *Aud.:* Ac.

This peer-reviewed journal bills itself as a "vehicle for the dissemination and discussion of practical experience with new and established software for both systems and applications," oriented toward an audience of software engineers, systems programmers, and computer science educators. The journal is published monthly, and features articles that make a significant and original contribution "from which other persons engaged in software design and implementation might benefit." Published articles fall into one of several categories, including detailed accounts of software developments that may function as tutorials for others, brief reports on programming techniques applicable to a number of areas of software development, discussions of new techniques and tools aiding in software development, and methods and techniques coping with large-scale software development projects, alongside short communications of timely news items and brief reviews of a specific issue. Recent articles covered such topics as memory leak protection, validating program behavior, and new approaches to query search engines. Recommended for academic libraries.

Popular Titles

1454. *Baseline (New York): the fusion of business and technology.* [ISSN: 1541-3004] 2001. bi-m. USD 105 domestic (Free to qualified personnel). Ed(s): Lawrence M Walsh. Ziff Davis Enterprise Inc., 28 E 28th St, New York, NY 10016; http://www.ziffdavisenterprise.com/. Adv. Circ: 125100. *Indexed:* ABIn, B01, B02, BRI, C&ISA, CerAb, F01. *Aud.:* Ga.

Baseline is part of the Ziff-Davis collection of technology-related digital magazines. Focusing on the "fusion of business and technology," the magazine publishes articles aimed at decision makers, leaders, and technology managers in business and nonprofit environments. The scope of the magazine's content includes such topics as technology management, business-technology alignment, green IT, recent developments in business technology, and industry-specific analysis. A variety of articles are published, including informed opinion pieces, feature stories, case studies, and brief stories that focus on specific aspects of business technology. A full, freely available archive of past issues is available, and numerous white papers. This title is of interest to information technology professionals and decision-makers, and is recommended for public libraries.

1455. *Computerworld: newsweekly for information technology leaders.* [ISSN: 0010-4841] 1967. s-m. Mon. USD 129 in US & Canada (Free to qualified personnel). Ed(s): Scot Finnie, Mitch Betts. I D G Communications Inc., PO Box 9171, Framingham, MA 01701; teresina_cardamone@idg.com; http://www.idg.com/. Illus., adv. Vol. ends: Dec. Microform: PQC. *Indexed:* A01, A22, ABIn, B01, B02, BRI, C&ISA, C37, CerAb, I15, MASUSE, P02. *Aud.:* Ga.

Computerworld is a regular magazine aimed at working information professionals and business executives who are interested in staying abreast of current developments in technology and the intersection of business and technology. Each issue features articles that cover a range of topics, including case studies, recent product reviews, information security, and recent technology trends. The magazine is available via subscription, which is free to information professionals, and the *Computerworld* web site features a freely available archive of articles from past issues, and numerous additional articles that supplement the print version.

1456. eWEEK: the enterprise newsweekly. Incorporates (1994-2001): *Inter@ctive Week;* Formerly (until 2000): *P C Week.* [ISSN: 1530-6283] 1984. w. USD 195 domestic (Free to qualified personnel). Ziff Davis Enterprise Inc., 28 E 28th St, New York, NY 10016; http://www.ziffdavisenterprise.com/. Illus., adv. Circ: 400100 Paid and controlled. Microform: PQC. *Indexed:* A01, A22, B01, B02, BRI, C&ISA, C37, CerAb, I15, P02. *Aud.:* Ga.

This trade-oriented magazine is part of the Ziff-Davis Enterprise collection of publications. All aspects of the computer industry are covered, with a general orientation toward a readership composed of decision makers and technology leaders in business environments. Topics covered include IT infrastructure, virtualization, networking, enterprise applications, security, and other related subjects. The magazine is available via subscription, which is free to information professionals, and the *eWEEK* web site features numerous additional articles and news stories that supplement the print version. Recommended for high school and public libraries.

1457. Information Week (US Edition): business innovation powered by technology. Incorporates (in 2007): *Network Computing;* (2001-2007): *Optimize;* (1992-1995): *Open Systems Today;* Which was formerly (until 1992): *UNIX Today;* (until 1984): *Information Systems News.* [ISSN: 8750-6874] 1979. w. Free. Ed(s): Rob Preston. TechWeb, InformationWeek Business Technology Network, 600 Community Dr, Manhasset, NY 11030; http://www.techweb.com/home. Adv. Circ: 440000 Paid and controlled. *Indexed:* A01, A22, ABIn, B01, B02, B03, BRI, C&ISA, C42, CerAb, CompLI, I15. *Aud.:* Ga.

Information Week brings together the goals of business and technology to help organizations make sound strategic decisions. The magazine is oriented toward an audience that consists of decision-makers and technology specialists in both business and nonprofit organizations. The magazine covers the full scope of the technology landscape as it affects these organizations, providing current news items, analytical articles, case studies, and columns from regular contributors. Recent issues included articles covering such topics as information security, enterprise software, technology and business strategy, technology trends, and reviews of newly released mobile devices. The magazine is available via subscription, which is free to information professionals, and the *Information Week* web site features a freely available archive of numerous articles that supplement the print version. Recommended for both academic and public libraries.

1458. iPhone Life. 2008. bi-m. USD 15.97 combined subscription (print & online eds.). Ed(s): Alex Cequeae. Mango Life Media, 402 N B St, Ste 108, Fairfield, IA 52556. Illus., adv. *Aud.:* Ga.

This magazine covers the rapidly-changing world of iOS-related technology, specifically looking at the iPhone and iPad and the technology landscape they have created. It is published monthly in both a print and digital format. Each issue features a number of articles, including reviews of applications, games, and peripherals, tips and tricks, and case studies of iOS-device power-users. The magazine's companion web site does not repeat any of this content, and instead focuses on adding value by publishing timely news and reviews and aggregating iOS-related information from other sources. Recommended for public libraries.

1459. Linux Journal. [ISSN: 1938-3827] 1994. m. USD 29.50. Belltown Media, Inc., PO Box 980985, Houston, TX 77098; subs@linuxjournal.com. Adv. *Aud.:* Ga.

Linux Journal is the longest-running magazine devoted solely to coverage of the Linux operating system and the software and hardware related to it. It began publication in 1994 at the same time that the Linux operating system reached version 1.0, and has been in continuous publication ever since. In 2011, in response to changing usage patterns and demographics, the magazine switched to an all-digital format. Article topics include cloud computing, system administration, web development, security, virtualization, product reviews, and how-tos. The magazine also has a companion web site that offers a range of unique content, including unique articles, blogs, news, and videos, as well as articles that are drawn from the magazine itself. Recommended for public libraries.

1460. MacWorld. Incorporates (1985-1997): *MacUser.* [ISSN: 0741-8647] 1984. m. USD 19.97 in US & Canada; USD 44.97 elsewhere; USD 6.99 newsstand/cover. Ed(s): Dan Miller. Mac Publishing, L.L.C., 501 Second St, 5th Fl, San Francisco, CA 94107; customer_service@macworld.com; http://www.macworld.com. Illus. Vol. ends: Dec. Microform: NBI; PQC. *Indexed:* A01, A22, ABIn, B01, B02, B03, BRI, C37, I15, MASUSE, P02. *Aud.:* Hs, Ga.

Published monthly since 1984, *Macworld* is the leading magazine devoted to coverage of the Apple market, nearly doubling the circulation numbers of its nearest competitor. The magazine is a rich source for "news, reviews, help and how-to, videos, and podcasts for the Apple market, including the Mac, Mac software, Mac OS X, the iPod and iTunes, and the iPhone." It publishes a range of article types, including in-depth analyses, hardware and software reviews, surveys, and editorials and opinion pieces. The focus is on Apple hardware and related peripherals, software for Apple computers, and the computer industry as related to Apple and its products. An accompanying web site offers a wealth of information to supplement the print magazine. Recommended for public libraries.

1461. Online Searcher: information discovery, technology, strategies. Formed by the merger of (1977-2013): *Online;* (1993-2013): *Searcher.* [ISSN: 2324-9684] 2013. bi-m. USD 139 domestic; USD 154 in Canada & Mexico; USD 181 elsewhere. Ed(s): Marydee Ojala. Information Today, Inc., 143 Old Marlton Pike, Medford, NJ 08055; custserv@infotoday.com; http://www.infotoday.com. Illus., adv. Sample. Vol. ends: Dec. *Indexed:* A01, A22, ABIn, ABS&EES, B01, B02, B03, BRI, EngInd, FR, I15, ISTA, P02. *Aud.:* Ac, Sa.

Online is a bimonthly magazine oriented toward information professionals throughout the technology world. Each issue offers a range of articles including product reviews, case studies, evaluation, and "informed opinion about selecting, using, and evaluating information technology, with a focus on information delivery systems." Topics cover the broad sweep of information technology, including information delivery systems, informational databases and vendors, security, information technology research and current developments, information consumers and usage patterns, and search engine technology and vendors. Recent issues included articles on web analytics for business intelligence, mobile devices in libraries, the future of e-books, and the intersections of social media, searching, and privacy. The web site includes tables of contents, full text of selected articles, and additional content that supplements the magazine. Recommended for academic and public libraries.

1462. P C Magazine (Online). m. USD 19.99. Ziff Davis Media Inc., 28 E 28th St, New York, NY 10016; info@ziffdavis.com; http://www.ziffdavis.com. *Aud.:* Ga.

PC Magazine is part of the family of Ziff-Davis–published technology magazines that has gone 100 percent digital in recent years. The digital edition retains the same look and feel of the print edition, and is available in a range of formats for both mobile and desktop devices. The magazine covers all areas of technology, with emphasis on consumer technologies ranging from smart phones to network area storage devices. As with most consumer technology magazines, it includes a number of article types, such as reviews, tips and how-tos, editorials by prominent technology writers, and business-oriented case studies. Given the scope of the topics it covers, its long publishing history, and the prominence of its writers, this title is recommended for public libraries.

1463. P C World (Online). [ISSN: 1944-9143] . USD 19.97. I D G Communications Inc., 501 Second St, San Francisco, CA 94107. *Aud.:* Ga.

PC World is part of the same family of publications that includes *Macworld*. The magazine is oriented toward both business and home technology consumers, with a focus on offering industry news, product reviews, and technological solutions. Articles cover a broad range of topics and are not platform-specific, focusing on issues of relevance to users throughout the technology spectrum, with a particular emphasis on analysis and reviews of new technologies and products. Recent issues included articles that cover security and the Windows operating system; reviews of the best cell phones and smart-phones from each carrier; an evaluation of laptops as desktop replacements; and an analysis of new developments in wireless network technologies. An accompanying web site offers timely information to supplement the print magazine. Recommended for public libraries.

1464. *Smart Computing.* Formerly (until May 1997): *P C Novice.* [ISSN: 1093-4170] 1990. m. USD 29 domestic; USD 37 Canada; USD 69 elsewhere. Ed(s): Ronald D Kobler, Andrew Leibman. Sandhills Publishing Co., 120 W Harvest Dr, Lincoln, NE 68521; feedback@sandhills.com; http://www.sandhills.com. Illus., adv. Circ: 205837. Vol. ends: Dec. *Indexed:* A22, I15, P02. *Aud.:* Ga.

Smart Computing is a monthly magazine aimed at helping computer users improve their productivity with technology, and demystifying technology for the average user. Each issue includes sections devoted to answering readers' questions, tutorials on maximizing your computers' functionality, how-to articles on using various software applications, hardware and software reviews, and sections covering a further wide range of technology topics. Recent article topics include giving your Windows PC a tune-up to improve its performance; combating spyware; transitioning from a Windows PC to a Mac; and reviews of home-office printers and the latest crop of digital cameras. The accompanying web site provides a range of additional content to supplement the print edition. Recommended for high school and public libraries.

■ COOKING AND COOKERY

Caroline Mandler Lopez, Knowledge and Learning Services Librarian, Darien Library, 1441 Post Road, Darien, CT 06820; clopez@darienlibrary.org

Introduction

At the end of 2012, the National Restaurant Association surveyed over 1,800 chefs to predict what the "hottest" menu items would be in the coming year. This annual report serves to reveal emerging and existing trends in the culinary industry, giving us an inside look into this community, which ultimately influences the recipes and features that will be seen in periodicals and read in homes across America. The titles chosen for this year's Cooking and Cookery section represent an attempt to reflect these trends and encapsulate the best culinary periodicals for collections in libraries.

The main culinary themes for 2013 included environmental sustainability, children's nutrition, hyper-local or "farm to table" sourcing of ingredients, gluten-free alternatives, and a general emphasis on health and nutrition. Specific ingredients of interest were farm or estate-branded items, artisan and ethnic cheeses, non-wheat flour, and ancient grains like kamut and spelt.

These themes and ingredients are seen frequently throughout the periodicals reflected in this edition. Almost all include recipe indexes with specific nutritional breakdowns, or icons indicating whether they are health-conscious. Feature articles frequently focus on local farms and fresh, seasonal ingredients across the globe, especially in periodicals geared toward travel such as *Bon Appetit, Saveur,* and *La Cucina Italiana.* This edition also intentionally includes health- and nutrition-focused publications such as *Chop Chop Kids, Eating Well, Cooking Light,* and *Vegetarian Times.*

Each entry includes the publication's web site, which offers additional recipes, resources, and interactive features. All titles included in this edition are geared toward general library audiences, relevant to current culinary trends, and recommended for inclusion in library collections.

Basic Periodicals

Bon Appetit, Cook's Illustrated, Food & Wine.

Basic Abstracts and Indexes

Reader's Guide to Periodical Literature.

1465. *Bon Appetit: America's food and entertaining magazine.* [ISSN: 0006-6990] 1956. m. USD 15 domestic. Ed(s): Adam Rapoport. Conde Nast Publications, Inc., 4 Times Sq, 6th Fl, New York, NY 10036; http://www.condenast.com. Illus., index, adv. Sample. Circ: 1371495 Paid. Vol. ends: Dec. *Indexed:* A22, ASIP, BRI, C37, CBCARef, P02. *Aud.:* Ga, Ac, Sa.

One of the most recognizable and highly-regarded publications in the industry, *Bon Appetit* regularly incorporates travel and entertaining in addition to recipes and menu ideas from the "BA Kitchen." With a huge emphasis on notable restaurants and chefs from around the country, this title has many recipes that also come directly from the restaurants highlighted. Feature articles are always the standouts. The web site offers valuable content as well. Strongly recommended for public libraries. URL: www.bonappetit.com

1466. *ChopChop: the fun cooking magazine for families.* [ISSN: 2169-0987] 2010. q. USD 14.95. Ed(s): Catherine Newman. ChopChopKids, 32B Calvin Rd, Watertown, MA 02472. *Aud.:* Ems, Ga.

Relatively new to the culinary scene, *ChopChop* was first published in 2010, and won the 2013 James Beard Foundation Award for Publication of the Year. It is published by a nonprofit organization, ChopChopKids, whose mission is to inspire and teach kids to cook real food with their families and reduce childhood obesity. Available in both Spanish and English, it features fun, colorful recipes alongside valuable nutrition information. URL: www.chopchopmag.org/magazine

1467. *Cooking Light: the magazine of food and fitness.* Supersedes in part (in 1986): *Southern Living.* [ISSN: 0886-4446] 1966. m. USD 18 domestic; CAD 23 Canada; USD 4.99 newsstand/cover. Southern Progress Corp., 2100 Lakeshore Dr, Birmingham, AL 35209; http://www.southernprogress.com. Illus., index, adv. Sample. *Indexed:* A22. *Aud.:* Ga.

As the title suggests, *Cooking Light* places an emphasis on healthy recipes, nutrition tips, and fitness. The "Super Fast" section introduces 20-minute recipes, with a full collection available online. Recipes in the "Dinner Tonight" section include a helpful shopping list. Colorful features focus on variations of a specific dish or cooking strategy, such as "tacos" or "microwave cooking." An index at the back indicates whether recipes are kid-friendly, quick and easy, freezable, make-ahead, or vegetarian. Recommended for public libraries. URL: www.cookinglight.com

1468. *Cook's Illustrated.* Former titles (until 1992): *Cook's;* (until 1985): *The Cook's Magazine.* [ISSN: 1068-2821] 1980. bi-m. USD 24.95 domestic; USD 30.95 Canada; USD 36.95 elsewhere. Ed(s): Christopher Kimball. Boston Common Press, 17 Station St, Brookline, MA 02445; cooks@americastestkitchen.com. Illus., index. Sample. *Indexed:* H&TI. *Aud.:* Ga, Ac, Sa.

A trusted resource by home cooks, and most notably features in-depth, step-by-step instructions. The magazine is primarily in black-and-white, but clear images make recipes easy to follow, accompanied by written reflections from the editors and test cooks. There is also an emphasis on culinary equipment, offering ratings and comments that one might find in a standard consumer magazine such as *Consumer Reports.* Strongly recommended for public libraries. URL: www.cooksillustrated.com

1469. *La Cucina Italiana: good food for good living.* [ISSN: 1090-4484] 1996. bi-m. USD 38 in US & Canada; USD 42 elsewhere. Quadratum Publishing, 512 Seventh Ave, 41st Fl, New York, NY 10018; info@quadratumusa.com. Illus., index, adv. Circ: 140 Paid. Vol. ends: Nov/Dec. *Aud.:* Ga, Sa.

La Cucina Italiana is the go-to source for authentic, elegant, yet accessible Italian cooking. Readers can always count on beautiful features, which highlight specific ingredients and Italian locations. The magazine also includes cocktail and wine columns, with recommended Chiantis and other Italian wines, as well as cocktail recipes from notable Italian restaurants. The "Cooking School" is a valuable component as well, with in-depth, step-by-step instructions for making pasta or completing a recipe. URL: www.lacucinaitalianamagazine.com

1470. *Cuisine at Home.* Former titles (until 2001): *Cuisine;* (until 2000): *August Home's Cuisine.* [ISSN: 1537-8225] 1996. bi-m. USD 28 for 2 yrs. domestic; CAD 42 Canada; USD 32 elsewhere. Ed(s): Joy Taylor. August Home Publishing Co., PO Box 842, Des Moines, IA 50304; orders@augusthome.com; http://www.augusthome.com. Illus. Sample. Circ: 528 Paid. Vol. ends: Nov. *Aud.:* Ga, Ac, Sa.

Offers straightforward, accessible recipes with step-by-step instructions and pictures. There is a noticeable focus on seasonal recipes—for example, "Fast and Fresh Spring Menus" in a spring edition, and "Hot Soups for Cold Nights" during the winter months. One notable section is "Faster with Fewer," which incorporates minimal ingredients into simple recipes, but the magazine does also offer a range of more in-depth recipes for experienced or adventurous cooks. "Cuisine for Two" is another great addition, with recipes geared to just two people. URL: www.cuisineathome.com

1471. *Eating Well: where good taste meets good health.* [ISSN: 1046-1639] 1990. bi-m. USD 9.99. Eating Well, Inc., 6221 Shelburne Rd, Ste 100, Shelburne, VT 05482. Illus., index, adv. Vol. ends: Nov/Dec. *Aud.:* Ga, Sa.

Eating Well offers a wide range of health-inspiring articles and recipes, complemented by its exceptional photographs and layout. It features a recipe index with nutritional content and icons that indicate whether recipes are "Budget" (less than $3 per serving); ready in 45 minutes or less; "Gluten-Free"; "Heart Healthy"; "Healthy Weight"; and "High Fiber." Throughout the magazine there is a huge emphasis on fresh ingredients, as well as current reports on health issues. Strongly recommended for public libraries. URL: www.eatingwell.com

1472. *Every Day with Rachael Ray.* [ISSN: 1932-0590] 2005. m. 10 or 11 times x yr. USD 24 domestic; USD 29 foreign. Ed(s): Rachael Ray. Reader's Digest Association, Inc, Reader's Digest Rd, Pleasantville, NY 10570; letters@rd.com; http://www.rd.com. Adv. Circ: 650000 Controlled. *Aud.:* Ga.

Just as in her books and TV show, you'll find "Meals in Minutes," as well as other fast and budget-friendly ideas. A colorful recipe index at the beginning details whether recipes are "Fast," "Freezer-Friendly," "Gluten-Free," and "Vegetarian." In addition to recipes, the magazine also includes articles on kitchen renovations, DIY decor, party planning, and travel. There's even a something for pets. Recommended for public libraries. URL: www.rachaelraymag.com

1473. *Food & Wine.* Former titles (until 1983): *Monthly Magazine of Food and Wine;* (until 1981): *International Review of Food and Wine.* [ISSN: 0741-9015] 1978. m. USD 19.99 domestic; USD 31.99 Canada. Ed(s): Dana Cowin, Mary Ellen Ward. American Express Publishing Corp., 1120 Ave of the Americas, New York, NY 10036; ashields@amexpub.com; http://www.amexpub.com. Illus., index, adv. Sample. Circ: 958348 Paid. Vol. ends: Dec. *Indexed:* A22, ASIP. *Aud.:* Ga, Sa.

Food & Wine is a clear must-have for any library collection. It encompasses the entire culinary industry, including notable and up-and-coming chefs and restaurants, recipes, wines, and trends. There are also excerpts on kitchen designs and recommended tools and equipment. Recipes range from reinventions on "New Basics" to "Well-Being" and "Superfast." The "Wine" component of *Food & Wine* includes not only items of interest for wine-lovers, but also tasting tips on beer and cocktail recipes. Strongly recommended for public libraries. URL: www.foodandwine.com

1474. *Food Network Magazine.* [ISSN: 1944-723X] 2008. 10x/yr. USD 15. Ed(s): Maile Carpenter. Hearst Communications Inc., 1700 Broadway, 30th Fl, New York, NY 10019; http://www.hearst.com. *Aud.:* Ga.

With the ever-growing popularity of celebrity chefs comes the need for *Food Network Magazine*. It features behind-the-scenes articles on favorite cooking shows, as well as frequent interjections from recognizable Food Network chefs. Each issue also includes a calendar with seasonally-specific food activities as well as recipes under the headings of "Fun Cooking," "Weeknight Cooking," "Weekend Cooking," "Party Time," and "On the Road," which shows regional recipes. Recipes are organized in a convenient and colorful "Recipe Index." *Food Network Magazine* is high energy, with an emphasis on entertainment. Recommended for public libraries. URL: www.foodnetwork.com/food-network-magazine/package/index.html

1475. *Gastronomica: the journal of food and culture.* [ISSN: 1529-3262] 2001. q. USD 312 (print & online eds.). Ed(s): Darra Goldstein. University of California Press, Journals Division, 2000 Ctr St, Ste 303, Berkeley, CA 94704; customerservice@ucpressjournals.com; http://www.ucpressjournals.com. Illus., adv. Circ: 8784. *Indexed:* A01, A07, A22, AmHI, E01, FS&TA, H&TI, P02. *Aud.:* Ga, Ac, Sa.

Published by University of California Press, *Gastronomica* raises the bar for food writing. Lengthy articles accompanied by relevant photography and drawings are challenging, informative, and entertaining. A culinary *New Yorker* in a sense, this title features impressive contributors and engaging subjects, which set this award-winning journal apart time and time again. URL: www.gastronomica.org

1476. *Saveur.* [ISSN: 1075-7864] 1994. 9x/yr. USD 19.95 domestic; USD 29.95 Canada. Ed(s): James Oseland. Bonnier Corp., 15 E 32nd St, 12th Fl, New York, NY 10016; http://www.bonniercorp.com. Illus., index, adv. *Indexed:* BRI, H&TI. *Aud.:* Ga, Ac, Sa.

A widely regarded favorite of culinary experts, *Saveur* combines a love of food with writing and travel. The majority of the articles are written in essay form, and range from a half-page to several pages. They focus primarily on different travel locations and integrate relevant recipes. Sections include "Fare," "Cellar," "Classic," and "Pantry," among others. Recommended for public libraries with high interest in travel and culinary topics. URL: www.saveur.com

1477. *Taunton's Fine Cooking: for people who love to cook.* [ISSN: 1072-5121] 1994. bi-m. USD 29.95 in US & Canada; USD 36 elsewhere. Ed(s): Jennifer Armentrout. The Taunton Press, Inc., 63 South Main St, PO Box 5506, Newtown, CT 06470; publicrelations@taunton.com; http://www.taunton.com. Illus., index, adv. Circ: 240000 Paid. *Indexed:* ASIP, H&TI. *Bk. rev.:* Number and length vary. *Aud.:* Ga, Ac, Sa.

Comprised almost entirely of recipes, *Fine Cooking* puts a focus on cooking in a way that sets it apart from many other publications. "Make it Tonight" features several pages of recipes that are 30 minutes, start to finish. "Cook Fresh" introduces seasonal ingredients with tips on how to use them. Librarians and cookbook collectors will enjoy "The Reading List," which reviews new must-reads for food lovers. Also found in every issue are wine pairings and a recipe index with a complete nutritional breakdown. Recommended for public libraries. URL: www.finecooking.com

1478. *Vegetarian Times.* Incorporates (1975-1980): *Well-Being.* [ISSN: 0164-8497] 1974. 9x/yr. USD 14.95 domestic; USD 26.95 Canada; USD 38.95 elsewhere. Ed(s): Elizabeth Turner. Active Interest Media, 300 Continental Blvd, Ste 650, El Segundo, CA 90245; http://www.aimmedia.com/. Illus., adv. Microform: PQC. *Indexed:* A01, A22, Agr, BRI, C37, MASUSE, P02. *Aud.:* Ga, Sa.

Focused on green cooking as well as green living, *Vegetarian Times* will be enjoyed by vegetarians and omnivores alike. Colorful recipes and photographs showcase a range of cuisines, from Vietnamese to Indian, and more basic, family-friendly dinners as well. The "1 Food 5 Ways" section is a great feature, demonstrating how to make the most of certain ingredients. Recommended for public libraries. URL: www.vegetariantimes.com

■ CRAFT

General/Clay and Glass/Fiber/Jewelry - Metal/Knitting and Crochet/
Needlework/Quilting/Wood

*Alexandra Regan, Reference Librarian, Corvallis-Benton County Public
Library, Corvallis, OR 97330.*

*Mary Frances Angelini, Librarian of the Grossman Library, Division of
Continuing Education, Harvard University, 311 Sever Hall, Harvard
Yard, Cambridge, MA 02138; angelini@fas.harvard.edu.*

*Cheryl LaGuardia, Research Librarian, Widener Library, Harvard
University*

Introduction

Craft, which falls somewhere on the continuum between art and do-it-yourself,
is enjoying a resurgence with the rise of maker culture. Craft can be useful, as
in a quilt for a bed or a knitted scarf, but it shares with art a transformative
quality: skilled crafters can turn a ceramic bowl or a crocheted accessory into
an object of beauty.

Our modern understanding of craft may arise from the Arts and Crafts
Movement of the late nineteenth and early twentieth centuries, which was a
reaction against mass-produced domestic and decorative arts, and included
furniture and woodwork, stained glass, leatherwork, lacemaking, embroidery,
rug making and weaving, jewelry and metalwork, and enameling and ceramics.

There are many craft resources available online. They include sites by
individual crafters and stores selling items, as well as sites devoted to the
practice of a craft or a group of crafts (e.g., www.ravelry.com for knitters and
crocheters), museums, and exhibitions, to the still-extant guilds. All of these
resources are valuable, and while they do some of the same things as a
magazine, they fill quite a different niche from the traditional magazines listed
in this section, and are beyond the scope of this publication.

Most craft journals have online counterparts with many things freely
available, including videos, free or "bonus" projects, and even corrections
sections. They also may have publisher-sponsored blogs and community
listings for exhibitions and gatherings. They can be an excellent resource for
those wanting to reach out to others who craft.

Basic Periodicals

GENERAL. *American Craft, Craft.*

CLAY. *Ceramic Review.*

JEWELRY—METAL. *Beadwork.*

FIBER. *Piecework.*

WOOD. *Fine Woodworking, Woodsmith.*

Basic Abstracts and Indexes

*Art Index, ARTbibliographies Modern, Index to How to Do It Information, MAS
Ultra: School Edition.*

General

1479. *American Craft.* Former titles (until 1979): *Craft Horizons with Craft
World;* (until 1978): *Craft Horizons;* Incorporates: *Craft World.* [ISSN:
0194-8008] 1941. bi-m. USD 40 combined subscription domestic (print
& online eds.); USD 55 combined subscription foreign (print & online

eds.). Ed(s): Shannon Sharpe. American Craft Council, 72 Spring St,
New York, NY 10012; council@craftcouncil.org; http://
www.craftcouncil.org. Illus., adv. Microform: PQC. *Indexed:* A06, A07,
A22, A51, BAS, BRI, CBRI, MLA-IB, P02. *Bk. rev.:* 3-4, 500 words,
critical, signed. *Aud.:* Ac, Sa.

It would be difficult to overstate the depth and breadth of this journal. It covers
crafts from the contemporary to the historical, to the prehistoric in any medium,
and analyzes the current state of craft in America. While it concentrates on
American crafts and artisans, *American Craft* also looks at trends and artisans
from all over the world. This is one of the journals that treats craft, and all kinds
of crafts, as art. There are about five feature articles that focus on artists,
collectors, technique, the history of a genre or technique, or trends and
philosophies. The "Master Class" section looks at the work of practicing
artisans. The "Wide World of Craft" section explores the crafts of a
neighborhood or region. The "Exhibition" section reviews one or two exhibits
around the nation. The "Ideas" section looks at unusual directions or
innovations taken by artisans. Galleries and museums take out full-page ads to
list upcoming shows, whereas other magazines would have commercial ads;
and there are more gallery notices than there are articles. This is a beautiful,
glossy publication full of ideas, inspiration, and information for artists,
craftspeople, students, and the interested public. One caveat: If your collection
must choose between this magazine and something for a more specific crafting
group, such as knitters, it is recommended that the budget go for materials that
readers would find more immediately useful, however inspiring and entrancing
this magazine is.

Clay and Glass

1480. *Ceramic Review.* Formerly (until 1970): *C P A Newsheet.* [ISSN:
0144-1825] 19??. bi-m. Members, GBP 32; Non-members, GBP 36; GBP
7.50 per issue domestic. Ed(s): Bonnie Kemske. Ceramic Review
Publishing Ltd., 63 Great Russell St, London, WC1B 3BF, United
Kingdom. Illus., index, adv. *Indexed:* A06, A07, A22, A51, C&ISA,
CerAb. *Bk. rev.:* 5-6, critical. *Aud.:* Ac, Sa.

Ceramic Review is a beautiful, thought-provoking, and practical British journal
with global coverage. It includes technical and practical information about
methods, materials, and equipment for clay, glazes, and kilns. There are critical
articles on practicing potters, reviews of exhibitions, and tips and techniques.
There are also articles on historical influences and techniques and the craft as
it is practiced in other parts of the world. The ads (which are numerous but
confined to the front and back of the magazine), the classified section, and the
gallery listings are as critical to the magazine's functionality as are the articles
themselves—although they are not as useful for readers on the western shore of
the Atlantic. The web site has good general information and makes content
available for purchase. *Ceramic Review* belongs in most crafts collections, and
any ceramics collection.

1481. *Ceramics Monthly.* [ISSN: 0009-0328] 1953. 10x/yr. USD 34.95
domestic; USD 40 Canada; USD 60 elsewhere. Ed(s): Sherman Hall.
American Ceramic Society Inc., 600 N Cleveland Ave, Ste 210,
Westerville, OH 43082; customerservice@ceramics.org; http://
www.ceramics.org. Illus., index, adv. Microform: NBI; PQC. *Indexed:*
A&ATA, A01, A06, A07, A22, A51, ABS&EES, B02, BAS, BRI,
C&ISA, CBRI, CerAb, IHTDI, P02. *Bk. rev.:* . *Aud.:* Ga, Sa.

Ceramics Monthly is geared toward studio ceramics. Each issue features
developments in the ceramics field and "clay culture." It offers studio tips, tools,
and techniques; a "techno file" section; reviews of exhibitions; and a call-for-
entries section, which lists application deadlines for exhibitions from the
regional to the international. The numerous advertisements provide a great
resource for equipment and suppliers. The comprehensive web site includes free
content and the option to subscribe to a free daily newsletter. *Ceramics Monthly*
is a necessity in any ceramics collection, and an important part of any basic
crafts/decorative arts collection.

1482. *Glass on Metal: the enamelist's magazine.* [ISSN: 1083-6888] 1982.
5x/yr. USD 51.20 domestic; USD 52 in Canada & Mexico; USD 54
elsewhere. Ed(s): Tom Ellis. Enamelist Society, 650 Colfax Ave,
Bellevue, KY 41073; info@EnamelistSociety.org; http://
www.enamelistsociety.org. Illus., adv. Refereed. Vol. ends: Dec. *Indexed:*
A07, A51, B02, BRI. *Bk. rev.:* Occasional, descriptive and critical. *Aud.:*
Sa.

Enameling, while not as old an art or craft form as ceramics, was practiced by the ancient Egyptians as a decorative art. As with many old crafts, there is a guild or society that acts as organizing point for practitioners. *Glass on Metal* is a publication of one such group, the Enamelist Society. There are four to eight feature articles in each issue. Most articles are short, about two pages, and society news articles can run to three or four pages. The topics are varied, from works to gallery and museum reviews, to techniques and to news of the craft and artisans. The web site includes an introduction to enameling and some past articles. This is an unusual specialty journal that is well worth reviewing if your readers include jewelers, craftspeople, or metalworkers.

Fiber

1483. *Piecework.* [ISSN: 1067-2249] 1993. bi-m. USD 29.95; USD 6.99 newsstand/cover. Ed(s): Jeane Hutchins. Interweave Press, LLC., 201 E Fourth St, Loveland, CO 80537; customerservice@interweave.com; http://www.interweave.com/. Illus., adv. Circ: 26191 Paid. *Indexed:* A07, A47. *Bk. rev.:* 6-9, critical. *Aud.:* Ga, Sa.

The purpose of this magazine is to promote historical and ethnic handwork by providing articles on history, techniques, and individual items and people, and then offering a few projects based on the articles using techniques such as needlework, knitting, quilting, crocheting, beading, drawn thread, and other crafts. Entire issues may be devoted to a single theme. For example, the May/June 2013 issue is all about lace. The projects all have clear instructions and are well designed, although none are for the novice or timid crafters. This is not a magazine that will teach a technique in simple terms; if readers are at all shy about picking up new techniques, then some of the projects may be beyond them. The web site content is sparse. The magazine, however, is beautiful and inspiring and is devoted to the history and the current state of common and ethnic handicraft arts. It would be a wonderful addition to any craft collection.

1484. *Rug Hooking.* [ISSN: 1045-4373] 1989. 5x/yr. USD 34.95 (print or online ed.). Ed(s): Debra Smith. Stackpole Magazines, 5067 Ritter Rd, Mechanicsburg, PA 17055; stackpolemagazines@theoystergroup.ca; http://www.stackpolebooks.com/. Illus., index, adv. *Aud.:* Ga.

Rug Hooking is the magazine for the not-yet-lost craft of traditional rug hooking. This craft involves pulling or hooking strips of cloth through a fabric ground rather than the latch-hook projects most often sold in craft stores. There are "projects" with materials lists, but even the "Dear Beginning Rug Hooker" project assumes a basic level of familiarity with the techniques. They do not explain what is meant by a "hook" or how to put it through the cloth or attach the material. The designs are generally in the style called "primitive," although there are some exceptions. The articles focus on design, combining hooking with other techniques such as rug braiding and dyeing materials. This title is very interesting, and if there is a need for a new or unusual magazine in your craft collection, give *Rug Hooking* a try.

1485. *Sew News: the fashion how-to magazine.* [ISSN: 0273-8120] 1980. bi-m. USD 21.98 domestic; USD 27.98 Canada; USD 33.98 elsewhere. Ed(s): Ellen March. Creative Crafts Group, 741 Corporate Clr ,Ste A, Golden, CO 80401; http://www.creativecraftsgroup.com. Illus., adv. *Aud.:* Ga.

Sew News, which is available as both a print and digital subscription, specializes in presenting sewing ideas, inspirations, and techniques to both beginning and intermediate sewers. Features include garment construction, quick-to-make gifts, home decoration how-tos, and step-by-step instructions on current creative trends. The main drawback is the ads, which can be obtrusive. The web site is busy, but there are some attractive web-only extras such as patterns and projects.

1486. *Spin-Off: it's about making yarn by hand.* [ISSN: 0198-8239] 1977. q. USD 30; USD 7.99 newsstand/cover. Ed(s): Amy Clarke Moore. Interweave Press, LLC., 201 E Fourth St, Loveland, CO 80537; customerservice@interweave.com; http://www.interweave.com/. Illus., adv. Circ: 25535 Paid. *Indexed:* IHTDI. *Bk. rev.:* 5, 300-350 words, critical and descriptive. *Aud.:* Ga, Ac, Sa.

This magazine encompasses many aspects of fiber art. There are in-depth feature articles on various animal fibers (e.g., alpaca) and animals; rare breeds, their wool, and their historical/cultural importance; carding and spinning techniques; caring for items made from natural fibers; museums and their collections; and artist interviews. Each issue also contains four to eight projects. The extensive classified section lists everything from carding supplies to animals. There are ads throughout the magazine, and they are a distraction from the otherwise excellent content. At Interweave's web site, http://spinningdaily.com, there are free projects, a calendar of events, an index of past issues, and several blogs on spinning.

1487. *Threads: for people who love to sew.* [ISSN: 0882-7370] 1985. bi-m. USD 32.95 in US & Canada; USD 38.95 elsewhere; USD 6.99 per issue. The Taunton Press, Inc., 63 South Main St, PO Box 5506, Newtown, CT 06470; publicrelations@taunton.com; http://www.taunton.com. Illus., index, adv. Circ: 130000 Paid. Vol. ends: Dec. *Indexed:* ASIP, BRI, IHTDI. *Bk. rev.:* . *Aud.:* Ga, Sa.

Threads covers all aspects of sewing: clothing, non-clothing, measuring, software, tools and equipment, fabrics, decoration, machine embroidery, and so on. It bills itself as the source for the sewing community for beginners to experts, but beginners may find the emphasis on tailoring and structural details of sewing to be challenging. In addition to expert tips on using sewing machines and working with fabric, the magazine contains patterns, projects, and how-to advice on making dresses, pants, jackets, and more. There are regular columns such as "Notions" and "Tips." Advertising is found in the first and fourth quarter of the magazine, but not in the feature articles section. There is some free content such as videos on the web site, but many of the articles are available only to subscribers. A reliably excellent and important resource for sewers.

Jewelry - Metal

1488. *Art Jewelry.* [ISSN: 1547-2728] 2004. bi-m. USD 32.95 domestic; USD 40.95 Canada; USD 41.95 elsewhere. Ed(s): Hazel Wheaton. Kalmbach Publishing Co., 21027 Crossroads Circle, Waukesha, WI 53187; customerservice@kalmbach.com; http://www.kalmbach.com. Illus., adv. *Bk. rev.:* 2-3, 100-150, descriptive. *Aud.:* Ga, Sa.

This is a jewelry magazine for practitioners, and it encompasses the whole of jewelry making. Each issue includes four to seven projects articles, which are rated for difficulty and list required materials. In addition to metal, some projects incorporate clay and fiber. Regular columns include sections such as "Business Savvy" and "Metalsmithing 101," and best of all, there is the full-color photo "Gallery." The "Basics" section covers the introductory techniques that are used in the projects. As with *Lapidary Journal Jewelry Artist,* there are a lot of ads. The web site has some free content such as articles and videos, although much of it is only for users who register for a free account. Additional content is available only to magazine subscribers. Libraries should inquire if institutional access to the content is possible. This is a wonderful magazine to have in a jewelry or craft section.

1489. *Bead & Button: creative ideas and proffects for the art of beads and jewelry.* [ISSN: 1072-4931] 1994. bi-m. USD 28.95 domestic; USD 36.95 Canada; USD 42.95 elsewhere. Ed(s): Julia Gerlach. Kalmbach Publishing Co., 21027 Crossroads Circle, Waukesha, WI 53187; customerservice@kalmbach.com; http://www.kalmbach.com. Illus., adv. *Indexed:* IHTDI. *Aud.:* Ga.

Bead & Button is devoted to beading, and is focused mostly but not entirely on jewelry. All but one or two of the articles are projects; the others are artists' profiles or information on materials. The projects are very appealing, and the instructions are clear and well written. The regular columns include expert advice, a guide to techniques covered in the issue, and a technique guide with page numbers. The only drawback is that the layout is very crowded and overly busy, with ads scattered throughout the magazine. There is also a web site associated with the magazine; it requires free registration to access any meaningful content or features, and there are two levels of access: one for free and one with additional content for subscribers. It is worth contacting the publisher to see if your library can gain access to the web site on behalf of your readers. If your library is in need of a beading projects magazine, *Bead & Button* is an excellent choice.

1490. *Beadwork.* Incorporates (2003-2010): *Step by Step Beads;* Former titles (until Dec.2011): *Super Beadwork;* (until 1998): *Interweave Beadwork.* [ISSN: 1528-5634] 1996. bi-m. USD 29.95; USD 5.99 newsstand/cover. Ed(s): Melinda Barta. Interweave Press, LLC., 201 E Fourth St, Loveland, CO 80537; customerservice@interweave.com; http://www.interweave.com/. Illus., adv. Circ: 50988 Paid. *Aud.:* Ga.

This is a project magazine focused primarily on jewelry. There are eight to ten projects in each issue, two or three feature articles, and a variety of regular features such as readers' works and "The Challenge," in which two editors and two readers create a design out of the same set of materials. Each project has a materials and notions list, a list of techniques used, and clear directions that include diagrams. Projects are rated for difficulty. There is an online index available on the magazine's web site. There is some content, mostly projects, available online without registration—some of the projects are exclusive to the web site. The magazine's subtitle, "Inspired designs for the passionate beader," is a fitting description for this very good general-interest beading magazine, which is geared toward the beginner hobbyist rather than the professional.

1491. *Jewelry Stringing: making jewelry, bead by bead.* Formerly (until 2012): *Stringing.* [ISSN: 2165-3631] 2003. q. USD 31.95; USD 5.99 per issue. Ed(s): Danielle Fox. Interweave Press, LLC., 201 E Fourth St, Loveland, CO 80537; customerservice@interweave.com; http://www.interweave.com/. Adv. Circ: 40981 Paid. *Aud.:* Ga.

There are many beading magazines to choose from, but if you are looking for another one for the general reader, I recommend *Jewelry Stringing* for its clean, attractive design and dozens of projects. The projects are not rated for difficulty, but they are accessible to beginners. Projects are photographed beautifully, with instructions in the back of the magazine. There is also a regular "Sell & Tell" department, which offers tips for readers wanting to market and sell their jewelry. There are ads but they are unobtrusive.

1492. *Lapidary Journal Jewelry Artist.* Former titles (until 2007): *Jewelry Arts & Lapidary Journal;* (until Dec.2005): *Lapidary Journal.* [ISSN: 1936-5942] 1947. 9x/yr. USD 29.95; USD 6.99 newsstand/cover. Interweave Press, LLC., 201 E Fourth St, Loveland, CO 80537; customerservice@interweave.com; http://www.interweave.com/. Illus., adv. Circ: 25342 Paid. *Indexed:* A&ATA, A22, BRI, IHTDI, P02. *Aud.:* Ga.

This is a magazine for the jewelry-making practitioner. Lapidary is the art of cutting gems or stones, and this is the focus of the magazine. It covers all aspects of the craft, and some articles and projects are quite advanced. The majority of the articles are projects designed to teach technique, but there are also artist profiles and articles on the business side of jewelry making. The most advanced projects and articles are more difficult than any seen in *Art Jewelry*. There are ads throughout, and they somewhat detract from the presentation of the articles. Interweave Press has a "Jewelry Making Daily" web site that includes some online extras for the magazine. *Lapidary Journal Jewelry Artist* should be reviewed along with *Art Jewelry*, which is its primary competition. This would make an good addition to a collection if there is demand for another jewelry-making publication.

1493. *Step by Step Wire Jewelry.* [ISSN: 1555-9939] 2004. bi-m. USD 29.95; USD 5.99 newsstand/cover. Ed(s): Denise Peck. Interweave Press, LLC., 201 E Fourth St, Loveland, CO 80537; customerservice@interweave.com; http://www.interweave.com/. Illus., adv. Circ: 34216 Paid. *Aud.:* Ga.

Wire jewelry is a popular subject in public libraries, and if you already subscribe to *Art Jewelry* but want one that focuses exclusively on wire, I recommend this one. *Step by Step Wire Jewelry* teaches readers how to make attractive, inexpensive, and creative wire jewelry using tools, wire, stones, findings, beads, gems, jigs, pearls, and more. In addition to at least ten projects, issues contains some feature articles. In the issues reviewed for this edition, there was an article on tools and one on books for your jewelry library.

Knitting and Crochet

1494. *Cast On.* [ISSN: 1557-573X] 1984. 4x/yr. Free to members. Ed(s): Marrijane Jones, Jane Miller. Knitting Guild of America, 1100H, Brandywine Blvd, Zanesville, OH 43701; tkga@tkga.com; http://www.tkga.com. Illus., adv. *Indexed:* IHTDI. *Bk. rev.:* 2-4, descriptive. *Aud.:* Ga.

Cast On is the official publication of the Knitting Guild of America. It has recently refocused its content so that while there are still 9–12 patterns or designs in each issue, there are also at least six "teaching" articles. These cover everything from basics such as a picking up a dropped stitch to advanced knitwear design concepts. The "Stitch Anatomy" lesson and project are particularly well done and include a bibliography for further reading and learning. The "Guild" section, covering news, conventions, and individuals, has its own position near the back of the magazine, before the ads. *Cast On*'s refocus emphasizes that it is more than just a pattern magazine; it now better fills the teaching niche that other, more mainstream knitting magazines do not fill. The quality and variety of the projects, along with their very clear instructions, make *Cast On* an excellent choice for your collection, and, in fact, it is preferred over more mainstream "project" publications.

1495. *Crochet!* Formed by the merger of (199?-2002): *Annie's Crochet to Go;* Which was formerly (199?-199?): *Annie's Quick & Easy Crochet to Go;* (199?-199?): *Annie's Quick & Easy Pattern Club;* (1980-199?): *Annie's Pattern Club Newsletter;* (1999-2002): *Crochet Home & Holiday;* Which was formerly (1989-1999): *Crochet Home;* (1987-1989): *Crochet Fun.* [ISSN: 1539-011X] 2002. q. USD 23.95 domestic; USD 31.95 Canada. Ed(s): Carol Alexander. Annie's Publishing, 306 E Parr Rd, Berne, IN 46711; http://www.annies-publishing.com/. Adv. Circ: 68000. *Aud.:* Ga.

This is a very good, general-purpose crochet pattern magazine. And make no mistake: this is a pattern magazine, even though it is the official publication of the Crochet Guild of America, while there also appears to be no guild news. Most of the patterns are for clothing and accessories (purses, jewelry), although there are also patterns for home decor, including afghans and pillows. Every issue includes a "Beginner's Corner" project and a column designed to address crochet problems and questions from readers. The web site contains some free content, including tips and patterns. A good choice for your craft collection.

1496. *Inside Crochet.* [ISSN: 2040-1051] 2009. m. GBP 48 domestic; GBP 66 per issue in Europe; GBP 75 per issue elsewhere. Ed(s): Claire Montgomerie. Tailor Made Publishing Ltd., PO Box 6337, Bournemouth, BH1 9EH, United Kingdom; contact@tailormadepublishing.co.uk; http://www.tailormadepublishing.co.uk/. Illus., adv. *Aud.:* Ga, Sa.

This is a sophisticated crochet magazine with an attractive layout and appealing patterns, and each issue has articles and news. Regular columns include a beginner's guide to crochet. Although it is expensive for North American subscribers, it is one of the most inspiring crochet magazines out there.

1497. *Interweave Crochet.* [ISSN: 1937-0008] 2004. q. USD 26.95; USD 6.99 newsstand/cover. Ed(s): Marcy Smith. Interweave Press, LLC., 201 E Fourth St, Loveland, CO 80537; customerservice@interweave.com; http://www.interweave.com/. Adv. Circ: 45815 Paid. *Bk. rev.:* Approx. 6, descriptive, 60-150 words. *Aud.:* Ga.

Like many other Interweave Press publications, this one is a mixture of (predominantly) projects and four or so short feature articles. The feature articles may be on designers, techniques, history, or cultures. The projects are generally both stylish and timeless, and typically match the seasons: the spring 2013 issues features light, lacy designs. The winter 2012 issue includes mittens and hats, as well as projects inspired by Downton Abbey. Most patterns indicate a skill level, and all required materials are listed, including what yarn was used to crochet the model. The web site includes free videos and patterns. A good choice for your crochet section. Digital subscriptions are also available.

1498. *Interweave Knits.* [ISSN: 1088-3622] 1996. q. USD 26.95; USD 6.99 newsstand/cover. Ed(s): Lisa Shroyer. Interweave Press, LLC., 201 E Fourth St, Loveland, CO 80537; customerservice@interweave.com; http://www.interweave.com/. Illus., adv. Circ: 96237 Paid. *Bk. rev.:* 7, 100-150 words, descriptive. *Aud.:* Ga.

There is a tremendous amount of competition between knitting magazines as the craft gains popularity. *Interweave Knits* is recommended partly because there are many online extras and partly because the projects in this magazine are so appealing. There are three to five feature articles and 18 or more projects in each issue. The articles may be about fibers, artist profiles, or techniques, and there is a "News and Views" section; but the focus is clearly on the projects, which include sweaters, socks, dresses, scarves, purses, and household objects. Interestingly, projects are not rated for difficulty. The ads are numerous—if readers cannot find the product they are seeking, it will not be for lack of listings. The web site has a links to blogs, discussion forums, and free patterns. All in all, a fine addition to a knitting collection.

1499. Knit 'n Style: real fashion for real knitters. Formerly (until 1997): *Fashion Knitting.* [ISSN: 1096-5408] 1981. bi-m. USD 24.97 domestic; USD 36.97 Canada; USD 42.97 elsewhere. Ed(s): Penelope Taylor. All American Crafts, Inc., 7 Waterloo Rd, Stanhope, NJ 07874; dcohen@allamericancrafts.com; http://www.allamericancrafts.com. Illus., adv. Sample. Circ: 55000 Paid. *Aud.:* Ga.

This is a pattern magazine. There are five or so feature articles, but there are more than 25 patterns per issue. The feature articles may be about needles, yarn, yarn companies, designers, or knitting techniques. The patterns are tempting and attractive, and are rated for difficulty; and the instructions are well written. This magazine and *Interweave Knits* offer very similar projects, although *IK* has slightly more variety, so the two publications should be reviewed side by side. Choose the one that has patterns that your readers will enjoy the most, although this choice may be difficult. If there is room in the budget, choose both.

1500. Vogue Knitting International. Formerly (until 198?): *Vogue Knitting.* [ISSN: 0890-9237] 1982. q. USD 21.97 domestic; USD 25.97 Canada; USD 6.99 per issue domestic. Soho Publishing Company, 233 Spring St, 3rd Fl, New York, NY 10013; http://www.sohopub.com/. Illus., adv. *Aud.:* Ga.

This is a knitting magazine that is fairly evenly divided between patterns and feature articles. Non-pattern articles cover such topics as techniques, designer profiles, and yarns. As one would expect from a publication with the name *Vogue,* the magazine is an excellent resource for what is fashionable, both for clothing and home decor, and the projects are modeled in a photo spread with the instructions in the back of the magazine. The majority of the patterns are for clothing. The instructions are clear and easy to understand, are rated for difficulty, and have pictures of the yarns used in the project. The web site has an online learning section and links to other resources. *Vogue Knitting* is a fine choice for knitting patterns that are both trendy and timeless.

Needlework

1501. Cross-Stitch and Needlework. Former titles (until 2006): *Stitcher's World;* (until 1999): *The Stitchery Magazine.* [ISSN: 1932-2720] 1995. bi-m. USD 19.99 domestic; USD 21.99 Canada; USD 35.99 elsewhere. Baywood Publishing, 26 Austin Ave, PO Box 337, Amityville, NY 11701; info@baywood.com; http://www.baywood.com. *Aud.:* Ga.

The focus of this magazine is very much on cross-stitch at the expense of other types of needlework. There are still needlepoint, drawn thread, hardanger, and other types of needlework projects, but these projects are few in number, and they are easy and less interesting for it. The instructions are clear; and the charts are in color, come with complete materials lists, are rated for difficulty, and list the types of stitches used. There are also designer profiles and some wonderful columns about technique. There is some free online content at www.c-sn.com. This is still a solid magazine for a collection serving readers interested in needlework, and is a good supplement to *Just Cross Stitch.*

1502. Just Cross Stitch. [ISSN: 0883-0797] 1983. bi-m. USD 21. Ed(s): Christy Schmitz. Annie's Publishing, 306 E Parr Rd, Berne, IN 46711; http://www.annies-publishing.com/. Illus., adv. *Aud.:* Ga.

Just Cross Stitch is a project magazine, and a good one. In each of the two issues I reviewed, there were 13 projects and two needle-artist profiles. It is written for the intermediate to advanced-level hobbyist, and at least one project has a variety of stitches other than a plain cross stitch. As well, the designs are attractive; the instructions are clear; and all materials are listed.

1503. Lace. [ISSN: 0308-3039] 1976. q. Free to members. Ed(s): Susan Roberts. Lace Guild, The Hollies, 53 Audnam, Stourbridge, DY8 4AE, United Kingdom; hollies@laceguild.org; http://www.laceguild.demon.co.uk/. Illus. *Bk. rev.:* 3, 120-140 words, critical. *Aud.:* Ga.

This magazine is principally devoted to bobbin lace. While it is published in England by the Lace Guild, it is global in its scope, featuring works by lace makers from all the over the world. The content is varied; there are articles on lace makers, design issues, and collections, and there are also some projects that include pricking patterns. In addition, there are plentiful guild news and information about guild courses and workshops. Advertising is confined to the back so that it does not distract from the content. There is good online content with photographs and articles that include a recently revised and expanded "Craft of Lace" section. If there are lace makers in your community or you are looking for an interesting or unusual addition to your crafts collection, try reviewing this publication.

1504. Stitch. Formerly: *Stitch With the Embroiderers Guild.* [ISSN: 1467-6648] 1999. bi-m. GBP 25.50 domestic; GBP 30.60 in Europe; GBP 37.50 in the Americas. Ed(s): Kathy Troup. E G Enterprises Ltd., 1 Kings Rd, Walton on Thames, KT12 2RA, United Kingdom; administrator@embroiderersguild.com; http://www.embroiderersguild.com. Adv. *Bk. rev.:* 2-4. *Aud.:* Ga.

Stitch, a publication of the Embroiderers Guild of the U.K., is partly a project magazine (12 in the issue I reviewed), and partly a showcase of both contemporary and historical techniques. There are articles profiling craftspersons, as well as book and exhibition reviews. The goal of the magazine is to provide creative inspiration to the modern stitcher, and therefore most of the projects are fresh and contemporary in nature. The projects have easy-to-follow instructions for beginners and experienced stitchers, and each issue includes a stitch glossary and section with tips and techniques for completing the projects. *Stitch* doesn't entirely confine itself to embroidery; in the issue I reviewed, there were articles profiling other textile artists. If you are looking for another textile title for your collection, this is a good choice.

Quilting

1505. The Quilter Magazine: for yesterday, today, and tomorrow. Formerly (until 2000): *Traditional Quilter.* [ISSN: 1531-5630] 1989. 7x/yr. USD 24.97 domestic; USD 38.97 Canada; USD 45.97 elsewhere. Ed(s): Laurette Koserowski. All American Crafts, Inc., 7 Waterloo Rd, Stanhope, NJ 07874; dcohen@allamericancrafts.com; http://www.allamericancrafts.com. Illus., adv. Sample. Circ: 65000 Paid. *Bk. rev.:* 3, 100-125 words, descriptive. *Aud.:* Ga.

This is a pattern magazine. The majority of the patterns are for full-sized quilts, although there are some mini-quilts. There about 15 projects in every issue, with a good mix of traditional and modern styles. Some projects require special-order fabrics, and some have alternative suggestions at the end. All the projects were rated for skill level and had materials lists. In addition to the plethora of projects, there are a couple of articles on history or equipment, and offerings on tips and techniques; there is also a designer profile. The web site has free content that includes projects and articles. All in all, a very good choice for a quilting craft collection.

1506. Quilter's Newsletter Magazine: the magazine for quilt lovers. [ISSN: 0274-712X] 1969. bi-m. USD 17.97 domestic; USD 23.97 Canada; USD 29.97 elsewhere. Ed(s): Bill Gardner. C K Media LLC, 1450 Pony Express Rd, Bluffdale, UT 84065; info@ckmedia.com; http://www.ckmedia.com. Illus., adv. Circ: 180000. Vol. ends: Dec. *Indexed:* IHTDI. *Aud.:* Ga.

This magazine is for both the beginner and the experienced quilter. The first part of each issue comprises articles on such topics as techniques, exemplary quilts on various themes, quilters, museums and other quilt collections, and technical aspects of quilting such as needles, thimbles, and sewing machines. In the second half are projects rated for difficulty. The instructions are clear and easy to understand. The numerous ads seem to offer everything that a quilter could need or want. Articles are accompanied by color photographs. The web site has some online-only content, including free patterns as well as indexes to past articles and a listing of events and shows. There is additional free content such as ebooks available after creating an account. The magazine belongs in every quilting collection and in more general collections as well, given the popularity of this craft.

1507. *Quilting Arts.* [ISSN: 1538-4950] 2001. bi-m. USD 34.95. Ed(s): Patricia Bolton. Interweave Press, LLC., 201 E Fourth St, Loveland, CO 80537; customerservice@interweave.com; http://www.interweave.com/. Adv. *Aud.:* Ga, Sa.

This is a magazine for contemporary art quilters and covers the latest techniques in art and embellished quilting, wearable arts, mixed media, surface design, and other textile arts. Issues feature guest artists and teachers, and address a wide range of skills including surface embroidery, thread painting, stamping, and fabric painting. Edited by Patricia Bolton, host of *Quilting Arts TV* on PBS, each issue is filled with design inspiration from world-renowned artists, projects with step-by-step directions, gorgeous full-color photographs, and a department called "Minding Your Business" on the business side of quilting. If your library already has quilting pattern magazines and your patrons would appreciate the inspiration to be found in art quilting, then this is an excellent choice.

1508. *Quiltmaker: step-by-step patterns, tips & techniques.* [ISSN: 1047-1634] 1982. bi-m. USD 17.97 domestic; USD 23.97 Canada; USD 29.97 elsewhere. Ed(s): June Dudley, Brenda Bauermeister Groelz. C K Media LLC, 1450 Pony Express Rd, Bluffdale, UT 84065; info@ckmedia.com; http://www.ckmedia.com. Illus., index, adv. Sample. Circ: 175000. Vol. ends: Nov/Dec. *Indexed:* IHTDI. *Aud.:* Ga.

This is a project magazine. There are about 13 in each issue, with at least one quite challenging, and the rest either easy or intermediate. They range from variations on traditional patterns such as log cabin to modern watercolor designs, to quilted objects rather than quilts *per se*. All projects have materials lists and cutting guides. There is also a pullout section called "QM basic lessons," which guides beginners through the steps required to begin working on a project. There are ads throughout, but they are not overly intrusive. The web site has basic lessons, interviews, and some articles, but the online version is available only to subscribers. *Quiltmaker* is a very good choice for your quilting collection.

Wood

1509. *Fine Woodworking.* Incorporates (in 1998): *Home Furniture;* Which superseded (in 1997): *Taunton's Home Furniture;* (in 1996): *Fine Woodworking's Home Furniture;* Formerly (until 1993): *Fine Woodworking.* [ISSN: 0361-3453] 1975. bi-m. USD 34.95 in US & Canada; USD 41.95 elsewhere; USD 7.99 per issue. Ed(s): Mark Schofield, Asa Christiana. The Taunton Press, Inc., 63 South Main St, PO Box 5506, Newtown, CT 06470; publicrelations@taunton.com; http://www.taunton.com. Illus., index, adv. Sample. Circ: 292000 Paid. *Indexed:* A06, A07, A22, ASIP, IHTDI. *Bk. rev.:* 2-4, critical. *Aud.:* Ga, Sa.

Fine Woodworking is for the professional carpenter or cabinetmaker, those who would like to be, and those with an interest in this craft. It is also a great example of how to blend print and online content. The magazine uses projects as examples of techniques or as the basis of articles rather than as projects for the reader to do. Materials lists and measured drawings of projects are not provided in the print publication, but there are downloadable plans and multiple videos of projects on the web site. Other articles review tools and equipment and discuss their use, go into detail about particular techniques, look at designs of current or historic importance, and occasionally profile people or groups—past or present—of woodworkers who are important to the craft. There is an extensive Q & A section; and the "Methods of Work" and "Notes and Comment" sections are also substantial and have online chat-group counterparts. There are even two tables of contents, one each for print and online. Taunton Press has excellent production quality; thus, this magazine is a joy to read not only for content but also for presentation. This belongs in every craft collection.

1510. *Popular Woodworking Magazine.* Former titles (until 1985): *Popular Woodworker;* (until 1984): *Pacific Woodworker.* [ISSN: 0884-8823] 1981. 7x/yr. USD 24.95; USD 5.99 newsstand/cover. Ed(s): Megan Fitzpatrick. F + W Media Inc., 38 E 29th St, 3rd Fl, New York, NY 10016; contact_us@fwmedia.com; http://www.fwmedia.com/. Illus., adv. Circ: 132340 Paid. *Indexed:* IHTDI, MASUSE. *Aud.:* Ga.

Popular Woodworking has more articles than projects, although it has at least two projects in each issue. The articles are about techniques, such as ebonizing wood; tool reviews; or how a particular practitioner performs his or her craft. There are also regular columns on finishing and tricks of the trade. Compared with the projects in *Fine Woodworking,* those in this magazine are more approachable, and so the two magazines appeal to different segments of the woodworking readership. The online counterpart has videos to go with the print articles, and there is even a table of contents for the online site in the print magazine. This should be in every woodworking collection.

The Woodenboat. See Boats and Boating section.

1511. *Woodsmith.* [ISSN: 0164-4114] 1979. bi-m. USD 28 for 2 yrs. domestic; CAD 42 Canada; USD 32 elsewhere. Ed(s): Vince Ancona, Terry Strohman. August Home Publishing Co., 2200 Grand Ave, Des Moines, IA 50312; orders@augusthome.com; http://www.augusthome.com. Illus. Sample. Vol. ends: Dec. *Indexed:* IHTDI. *Aud.:* Ga.

This is an excellent resource for woodworking projects and well-written, detailed articles on techniques and tools of the trade. Each issue contains a weekend project, a designer series project, and an heirloom project with detailed instructions, cutting lists, and diagrams. The web site has online extras, listed by magazine issue, which include material and supplies lists and cutting diagrams and videos of some projects. In addition to having useful, well-designed projects, there is no advertising—a welcome change.

■ CRIMINOLOGY AND LAW ENFORCEMENT

See also Law; and Sociology and Social Work sections.

Susan Metcalf, Reference Librarian, Social Sciences Liaison, Western Carolina University, Cullowhee, NC 28723; metcalf@email.wcu.edu

Introduction

In the field of criminology, there are two basic types of magazines: scholarly journals, and trade and professional publications. Both types are reviewed in this section. Scholarly journals are sometimes published by commercial publishers in association with an academic society, and these relationships are noted in the reviews. These partnerships have flourished in the last decade or so, no doubt due to the presence of online versions of the journals and the technology needed to support that format. Sage Publications and Routledge are both examples of publishers that have successfully embraced this model.

Scholarly journals frequently favor empirical research over theoretical works and commentary, but there are several titles that provide both, and this is noted in the annotations. The intended audience for these journals comprises researchers and policy makers, and they are good choices for academic and special libraries. As one would expect, the trade magazine articles are the more practical, and would be of the most help to those who work in the field.

Most of the titles reviewed in this section are published in the United States, but international publications are included, and many of the U.S.-based journals publish content that is both international and interdisciplinary. Those two adjectives frequently appear in journal subtitles.

The present reviewers relied on five resources to determine which journals appear in this section, all of which proved very helpful and informative: (1) the previous edition of *Magazine for Libraries*; (2) *Ulrich's Directory of Periodicals*; (3) an article by Sorensen et al. entitled "An assessment of criminal justice and criminology journal prestige," published in the *Journal of Criminal Justice Education*; and (4) a report compiled by experts from the Australian & New Zealand Society of Criminology. The Australian Department of Education, Science, and Training tasked the society with ranking scholarly journals in their field. For this edition we added six new titles, discovered through the new tool Google Scholar Metrics, which lists the top journals by subject or discipline as calculated by its algorithms. Complete bibliographic information is provided below for the latter two publications.

In addition, the U.S. government's National Criminal Justice Reference Service is an excellent resource, and publishes numerous reports and statistical bulletins that are not reviewed here, primarily due to the vast number of them. Readers are referred to the service's web site at www.ncjrs.gov. Several of the most popular and important U.S. government publications are, however, reviewed, such as *Federal Probation*.

REFERENCES

Sorensen, J., Snell, C., and Rodriguez, J.J. (2006). "An assessment of criminal justice and criminology journal prestige." *Journal of Criminal Justice Education,* 17 (2), pp. 297–392.

Brown, M., and Daly, K. (2008, February 25). *Australian & New Zealand Society of Criminology Report on Criminology Bibliometrics Development.* Retrieved May 17, 2009, from www.anzsoc.org/publications/bibliometrics_report.pdf.

www.google.com/intl/en/scholar/metrics.html. Accessed June 6, 2013.

Basic Periodicals

Ga: *American Jails, Corrections Compendium, Corrections Today, F B I Law Enforcement Bulletin, Law and Order Magazine, Police Chief, Sheriff Magazine;* Ac: *The British Journal of Criminology, Crime & Delinquency, Criminal Justice & Behavior, Criminal Justice Ethics, Criminology, The Howard Journal of Criminal Justice, Journal of Offender Rehabilitation, Journal of Research in Crime and Delinquency, Justice Quarterly, Policing and Society, The Prison Journal.*

Basic Abstracts and Indexes

Criminal Justice Abstracts, Criminal Justice Periodicals Index, SocINDEX.

1512. *Aggression and Violent Behavior.* [ISSN: 1359-1789] 1996. bi-m. EUR 861. Ed(s): Vincent van Hasselt. Pergamon, The Blvd, Langford Ln, E Park, Kidlington, OX5 1GB, United Kingdom; JournalsCustomerServiceEMEA@elsevier.com; http://www.elsevier.com. Adv. Sample. Refereed. *Indexed:* A01, A22, ASSIA, CJPI, ExcerpMed, FR, H24, IBSS, P61, PsycInfo, RiskAb, SSA. *Aud.:* Ac, Sa.

Aggression and Violent Behavior is a bimonthly, peer-reviewed publication that has become one of the premier journals of the criminology field since its inception in 1996. The journal is a compilation of "substantive and integrative review articles, as well as summary reports of innovative ongoing clinical research programs on a wide range of topics relevant to the field of aggression and violent behavior." Reoccurring topics explored in this journal include homicide, family and workplace violence, sexual assault, and genetic and physiological associations with aggression. As a multidisciplinary periodical, *Aggression and Violent Behavior* holds significance for a variety of researchers and professionals, including those in criminal justice, psychology, sociology, social work, law, forensic studies, and many other fields. This publication is available in print, as well as online in its entirety via ScienceDirect.

1513. *American Jails.* [ISSN: 1056-0319] 1987. bi-m. Free to members. American Jail Association, 1135 Professional Ct, Hagerstown, MD 21740; http://www.aja.org. Illus., index, adv. Sample. Vol. ends: Nov/Dec. *Indexed:* A01, CJPI. *Bk. rev.:* 3-4; signed. *Aud.:* Ga, Ac, Sa.

American Jails is the official trade publication of the American Jail Association. It is published bimonthly, and the first issue was printed in 1987. The magazine's audience comprises association members and others employed by local correctional facilities. The content is thus directed at local, rather than state and federal, corrections; the latter constituents are covered by other journals that include *Corrections Compendium* and *Corrections Today*. Both are reviewed below. *American Jails'* content is typical of professional association publications. Included are industry and association news stories; a column that summarizes recent pertinent federal court cases; and policy advocacy and training opportunities. The majority of the articles address American concerns, but foreign coverage is occasionally provided. Each issue of the magazine has an editorial spotlight, and annual calendars of the subjects to be addressed are included on the association's web page at www.aja.org. Recent editorial spotlights feature "Being Careful Out There," which deals with physical and

mental illness in jails while maintaining personal health and wellness; "An Otherwise Mundane Day," on crisis management and preventing workplace complacency; and "Running an Intelligent Jail," on cutting costs without compromising security. There is also a column by the association's chaplain that discusses the spiritual care of inmates. Most issues contain in-depth articles that offer operational best-practice advice—for example, the March/April 2013 issue features an article on stress management. Research review articles and essays, sometimes authored by academics, appear in many issues, and they are written in clear language and fully referenced. This publication is a good choice for large public libraries, colleges and universities with criminal justice programs, and special libraries that serve the corrections industry.

1514. *Australian and New Zealand Journal of Criminology.* [ISSN: 0004-8658] 1968. 3x/yr. USD 550. Ed(s): Sharon Pickering. Sage Publications Ltd., 1 Oliver's Yard, 55 City Rd, London, EC1Y 1SP, United Kingdom; info@sagepub.co.uk; http://www.uk.sagepub.com. Illus., index, adv. Sample. Refereed. Vol. ends: No. 3. Reprint: PSC. *Indexed:* A01, A22, BRI, CBRI, CJPI, CLI, IBSS, L14, P61, PsycInfo, SSA. *Bk. rev.:* 3-5, 1,000 words; signed. *Aud.:* Ac, Sa.

Australian and New Zealand Journal of Criminology is the official journal of the Australian and New Zealand Society of Criminology (ANZSOC). It began as a quarterly publication in 1968, but since 1991, it has been published three times a year. The journal is "dedicated to advancing research and debate on a range of criminological problems and embraces diverse, methodological approaches, being home to a wide range of criminological and interdisciplinary work in the field of crime and criminal justice." As one would expect, most of the articles are authored by Australian or New Zealand faculty, and they cover issues pertaining to those countries, but articles by American, Canadian, and other international criminologists are sometimes included. Each issue contains six to eight peer-reviewed research articles, and frequently opens with an editorial introduction. There are special topic-focused issues that have guest editors who provide a summary introduction; the most recent example was an issue devoted to lethal violence. Book reviews are often included. Full-text access is available through Sage.

1515. *The British Journal of Criminology: an international review of crime and society.* Formerly (until 1960): *British Journal of Delinquency.* [ISSN: 0007-0955] 1950. bi-m. EUR 716. Ed(s): Pat Carlen. Oxford University Press, Great Clarendon St, Oxford, OX2 6DP, United Kingdom; enquiry@oup.co.uk; http://www.oxfordjournals.org/. Illus., adv. Sample. Refereed. Reprint: PSC; WSH. *Indexed:* A01, A22, BRI, CJPI, CLI, E01, IBSS, L14, P02, P61, PsycInfo, SSA. *Bk. rev.:* 8-10; signed. *Aud.:* Ac, Sa.

The British Journal of Criminology: An International Review of Crime and Society (BJC) is published by Oxford University Press under the auspices of the Centre for Crime and Justice Studies, an independent charity located at King's College, London. The journal was launched in 1950 as *The British Journal of Delinquency* and changed its title in 1960. It has evolved into one of the top academic criminology journals (for the rationale for this assessment, see the introduction to this section for information on selection/ranking criteria). The content has both an international and an interdisciplinary focus, and its advisory board is composed of academics from around the globe. The editorial policies do not prescribe that submissions be only original research, or empirically based, as is the case with many other peer-reviewed journals in this section, but that they "contribute new knowledge to an understanding of crime and society." Each issue contains from five to nine articles, and a number of scholarly book reviews. BJC is a valuable resource for academics and researchers in crime, whether they are from the fields of criminology, sociology, anthropology, psychology, law, economics, politics, or social work. It is also appropriate for professionals and policy makers.

1516. *Canadian Journal of Criminology and Criminal Justice.* Former titles (until 2003, vol.45): *Canadian Journal of Criminology;* (until 1978): *Canadian Journal of Criminology and Corrections;* (until 1971): *Canadian Journal of Corrections.* [ISSN: 1707-7753] 1958. q. USD 200. Ed(s): Peter J Carrington. University of Toronto Press, Journals Division, 5201 Dufferin St, Toronto, ON M3H 5T8, Canada;

journals@utpress.utoronto.ca; http://www.utpjournals.com. Illus., index. Sample. Refereed. Circ: 690. Vol. ends: Oct. Microform: PQC. *Indexed:* A01, A22, ASSIA, BRI, C37, CBCARef, CJPI, CLI, E01, IBSS, L14, P02, P61, PdeR, PsycInfo, SSA, SWR&A. *Bk. rev.:* 5-8, 500-1,000 words; signed. *Aud.:* Ac, Sa.

The *Canadian Journal of Criminology and Criminal Justice* is published quarterly by the University of Toronto Press for the Canadian Criminal Justice Association (CCJA). The articles are peer-reviewed and bilingual, available in French or English, with the abstract available in both languages. The journal's scope is broad—it seeks to be a "forum for inter-disciplinary discussion of all aspects of criminology," and the coverage is theoretical as well as empirical. Most of the articles relate directly to Canadian criminal justice concerns, but the research would be of interest to U.S. practitioners and criminal justice scholars and students. Each issue contains a listing of book reviews that are published in association with that issue and that are available free on the CCJA web site (www.ccja-acjp.ca/en/cjcr.html). This journal is available full-text from several vendors: Project Muse, EBSCOhost, and ProQuest.

1517. *Corrections Compendium.* [ISSN: 0738-8144] 1976. q. USD 72. Ed(s): Susan Clayton. American Correctional Association, 206 N Washington St, Ste 200, Alexandria, VA 22314; execoffice@aca.org; http://www.aca.org. Illus. Sample. Refereed. Vol. ends: Dec. *Indexed:* BRI, CJPI. *Bk. rev.:* Number and length vary. *Aud.:* Ga, Ac, Sa.

Corrections Compendium: The Peer-reviewed Journal of the American Correctional Association is published quarterly by the association (ACA). It publishes peer-reviewed research articles and commentary written by professionals in the field and by academic contributors. Each issue also contains an article that summarizes the results of a survey sent to ACA members concerning a current topic of interest, such as the status of correctional facilities' budgets. International profiles that look at corrections agencies around the world, book reviews, and a column devoted to professional news items are also provided. However, the association publishes the bulk of its professional news in another publication, *Corrections Today*, which is reviewed below. The ACA has served the corrections community since 1870 and has more than 20,000 active members. It also serves as an accrediting body and has an active professional certification program. *Corrections Compendium* is available in print from the association. ProQuest's Criminal Justice Periodicals database provides full-text access online from 2001 and indexing back to 1995. This journal is recommended for special and academic libraries that serve the criminal justice and correctional fields.

1518. *Corrections Today.* Former titles (until 1979): *American Journal of Correction;* (until 1954): *Prison World;* (until 1941): *Jail Association Journal.* [ISSN: 0190-2563] 1939. bi-m. Free to members. American Correctional Association, 206 N Washington St, Ste 200, Alexandria, VA 22314; jeffw@aca.org; http://www.aca.org. Illus., index, adv. Sample. Vol. ends: Dec. Microform: MIM; PQC. Reprint: PSC. *Indexed:* A01, A22, ABS&EES, BRI, CJPI, P02. *Bk. rev.:* 1, 300-500 words; signed. *Aud.:* Ga, Ac, Sa.

Corrections Today is a bimonthly trade magazine published by the American Correctional Association (ACA). Each issue contains several articles that cover the same subject. Recent topics include eco-friendly corrections, women in the corrections workforce, and professional development. These articles are written by professionals in the corrections industry and public agencies. Guest editorials, ACA news items, research notes, book reviews, and other columns are also provided. *Corrections Today* is a good resource for special libraries that serve the industry and academic libraries in institutions with a criminal justice department. It is available in print and online from the association. The online archive goes back to 2003. EBSCOhost and ProQuest's Criminal Justice Periodicals Index provides full-text access from 1994 to the present.

1519. *Crime & Delinquency.* Incorporates (1960-1972): *N C C D News;* Which was formerly (1955-1960): *N P P A News;* Former titles (until 1960): *National Probation and Parole Association Journal;* (until 1955): *National Probation and Parole Association. Yearbook;* (until 1947): *National Probation Association. Year Book;* (until 1929): *National Probation Association. Proceedings;* (until 1928): *National Probation Association. Annual Conference. Annual Report and Proceedings.* [ISSN: 0011-1287] 1915. 8x/yr. USD 1758. Ed(s): Paul E Tracy. Sage

Publications, Inc., 2455 Teller Rd, Thousand Oaks, CA 91320; info@sagepub.com; http://www.sagepub.com. Illus., index, adv. Sample. Refereed. Vol. ends: Oct. Microform: WSH; PMC. Reprint: PSC. *Indexed:* A01, A22, ABS&EES, BRI, CJPI, CLI, E01, ERIC, IBSS, L14, P02, P61, PsycInfo, RILM, RiskAb, SSA. *Aud.:* Ac, Sa.

Crime & Delinquency is one of the most highly respected journals in the study of criminology. The journal dates back to 1955, when it was published by the National Probation and Parole Association (NPPA). Sage began publishing the journal for the organization in 1984, and now works directly with the editor, who is not associated with the former NPPA (presently named the National Council on Crime and Delinquency.) The organization remains tied to the journal through the editorial board and sometimes compiles special issues. *Crime & Delinquency*'s articles are policy-oriented, and span the breadth of all criminal justice issues, including juvenile and adult offenders, victims, police and other law enforcement agencies, and crime prevention. They consist of qualitative or quantitative research, reviews of recent literature, debates of current issues, or discussions of future directions in the field. Contributors are primarily American academics from the disciplines of sociology, criminology, family therapy, social work, and other related subjects. However, some articles are written by international scholars, practitioners from public policy think tanks, or governmental agencies. The journal has an editorial policy requiring authors to present their conclusions, particularly statistical information, in a manner that is accessible to non-academic practitioners. Its audience is policy makers, academics, and criminal justice researchers in any setting. The quality of the articles and the clarity of the writing also make this an excellent resource for college students studying criminal justice, sociology, social work, counseling, or public administration. The journal is available in print and online from Sage. The online archive includes issues from 1955 to the present.

1520. *Crime, Law and Social Change: an interdisciplinary journal.* Formerly (until 1991): *Contemporary Crises;* Incorporates (1986-1992): *Corruption and Reform.* [ISSN: 0925-4994] 1977. 10x/yr. EUR 1512 (print & online eds.). Ed(s): Nikos Passas. Springer Netherlands, Van Godewijckstraat 30, Dordrecht, 3311 GX, Netherlands; http://www.springer.com. Illus., adv. Sample. Refereed. Microform: PQC. Reprint: PSC. *Indexed:* A22, ABIn, BAS, BRI, CJPI, E01, FR, IBSS, P61, RiskAb, SSA. *Bk. rev.:* Number and length vary. *Aud.:* Ac, Sa.

Crime, Law and Social Change is a well-regarded peer-reviewed journal. Its articles focus on the "political economy of organized crime" in all of its forms, including international, national, regional, or local. These articles are interdisciplinary essays and reviews, and they cover a broader range of topics than might first be expected. According to the publisher, primary topics include financial crime, political corruption, environmental crime, and the expropriation of resources from developing nations. The journal thoroughly covers the topic of human rights through reports on compensation and justice for survivors of mass murder and state-sponsored terrorism, essays on gender, racial, and ethnic equality, and a number of other related articles. Contributors are academics and practitioners from throughout the world. The number of articles per issue varies, from four to 12, and book reviews are included occasionally. Many issues have themes and are introduced by guest editors. For example, the May 2013 issue focuses on prosecutor and prosecution issues. Additional recent special issues cover "environmental crime," and "country or state development aid." *Crime, Law and Social Change* is available in print and online from Springer. EBSCOhost and ProQuest offer full-text access, with a one-year embargo. Springer's online archive begins with the first issues in 1977. Each volume has five numbered issues, although some issues are combined into one. This journal is recommended for academic libraries, due to the quality of its articles and its appeal to many other social science disciplines.

1521. *Criminal Justice & Behavior: an international journal.* Supersedes (in 1974): *Correctional Psychologist.* [ISSN: 0093-8548] 1973. m. USD 1073. Ed(s): Dr. Curt R Bartol. Sage Publications, Inc., 2455 Teller Rd, Thousand Oaks, CA 91320; info@sagepub.com; http://www.sagepub.com. Illus., index, adv. Sample. Refereed. Vol. ends: Dec. Microform: WSH; PMC; PQC. Reprint: PSC. *Indexed:* A22, ASSIA, BRI, CBRI, CJPI, CLI, E01, L14, P02, P61, PsycInfo, SSA. *Bk. rev.:* Number and length vary. *Aud.:* Ac, Sa.

Criminal Justice & Behavior: An International Journal is published monthly by Sage for the International Association for Correctional and Forensic Psychology. The journal "promotes scholarly evaluations of assessment, classification, prevention, intervention, and treatment programs to help the correctional professional develop successful programs based on sound and informative theoretical and research foundations." The journal began publishing monthly in 2007, and changed its editorial policy to include literature reviews, commentary, and other submissions, in addition to the empirical research that had been and remains its primary focus. It occasionally contains book reviews. Academics author the majority of articles for this journal, but behavioral scientists from medical institutions and public organizations contribute as well. Ranked as a first-tier journal (for rationale for this assessment, see section introduction for information on selection/ranking criteria), *CJB* is good choice for academic libraries and special libraries that serve criminal justice professionals. Available in print and online. The online archive goes back to volume one in 1974.

1522. Criminal Justice Ethics. [ISSN: 0731-129X] 1982. 3x/yr. GBP 149 (print & online eds.). Ed(s): Margaret Leland Smith, Jonathan Jacobs. Routledge, 325 Chestnut St, Ste 800, Philadelphia, PA 19106; customerservice@taylorandfrancis.com; http://www.tandfonline.com. Illus. Sample. Refereed. Vol. ends: Summer/Fall. Microform: PQC. Reprint: PSC. *Indexed:* A01, A22, BRI, CJPI, CLI, L14, P02. *Bk. rev.:* 1-2, review essays. *Aud.:* Ac, Sa.

Criminal Justice Ethics is published by Taylor & Francis in association with the Institute for Criminal Justice Ethics at John Jay College of Criminal Justice, the City University of New York. The articles are largely philosophical; in fact, many are authored by professors of philosophy or law. They stand in contrast to quantitative and empirical articles that populate many of the other scholarly journals in this section. The journal's editorial scope "includes topics relating to the police, the courts, corrections, and issues in legal philosophy." In 2010, the publication frequency changed from twice to three times a year. Recent issues cover topics such as private military and security companies as well as types of punishment and moral reform. This journal's coverage of ethical matters is excellent, and it is essential for law schools and highly recommended for other academic libraries. However, the content is more appropriate for faculty, graduate, and upper undergraduates than for freshmen.

1523. Criminal Justice Policy Review. [ISSN: 0887-4034] 1986. bi-m. USD 1301. Ed(s): David L Myers. Sage Publications, Inc., 2455 Teller Rd, Thousand Oaks, CA 91320; info@sagepub.com; http://www.sagepub.com. Adv. Refereed. Reprint: PSC. *Indexed:* A01, A22, CJPI, E01, P61, SSA. *Bk. rev.:* Number and length vary. *Aud.:* Ac, Sa.

Criminal Justice Policy Review (*CJPR*) was first published in 1986 by the Indiana University of Pennsylvania's criminology department. It is now published quarterly by Sage, but the current editor remains associated with that university. The editorial introduction to the first issue stated: "Because criminal justice policy is studied by scholars, debated by politicians, enacted into law by legislators, executed by scores of functionaries, and is the focus of diverse commentary from a broad range of interests[,] the CJPR wishes to be the medium through which all of these perspectives can be presented." The articles reflect this broad mission, and include essays, research (quantitative and qualitative), commentary, and interviews. Contributors are primarily academics; however, professionals are encouraged to submit, also. There are frequent special issues with guest editorials; recent ones covered the topics of drug policy research and the accountability movement in juvenile justice. This journal is highly recommended for academic and special libraries. It is available in print and online.

1524. Criminal Justice Review. [ISSN: 0734-0168] 1976. q. USD 353. Ed(s): Dean Dabney. Sage Publications, Inc., 2455 Teller Rd, Thousand Oaks, CA 91320; info@sagepub.com; http://www.sagepub.com. Adv. Sample. Refereed. Microform: PQC. Reprint: PSC; WSH. *Indexed:* A22, BRI, CJPI, CLI, E01, P61, RiskAb, SSA. *Bk. rev.:* 1-2 review essays, 15-20, 700-1,000 word, signed reviews. *Aud.:* Ac, Sa.

Criminal Justice Review is published by Sage in association with the Georgia State University College of Health and Human Sciences. It is a quarterly, peer-reviewed publication that is "dedicated to presenting a broad perspective on criminal justice issues within the domestic United States." The journal

publishes quantitative and qualitative research, research notes, and commentary, and encourages contributors who take an interdisciplinary approach. Each issue contains five to seven articles and a hefty book review section, frequently containing ten or more reviews. There are occasional special issues—the most recent presents research in honor of Gresham Sykes, a pioneer in the field of criminology. This journal would be a good choice for academic libraries with criminal justice departments, and may also be of interest to faculty and students in political science. It is available in print and online. The online archive goes back to the first issue in 1976.

1525. Criminal Justice Studies: a critical journal of crime, law and society. Formerly (until 2003): *The Justice Professional.* [ISSN: 1478-601X] 1986. q. GBP 293 (print & online eds.). Ed(s): Richard Tewksbury. Routledge, 325 Chestnut St, Ste 800, Philadelphia, PA 19106; customerservice@taylorandfrancis.com; http://www.tandfonline.com. Sample. Refereed. Reprint: PSC. *Indexed:* A22, B01, CJPI, E01, IBSS, P61, PsycInfo, RiskAb, SSA. *Aud.:* Ac, Sa.

Criminal Justice Studies: A Critical Journal of Crime, Law and Society is a quarterly journal that publishes articles that address "substantive" issues in criminal justice, public policy, administration, and public affairs. The articles may be quantitative or qualitative studies, research notes, literature reviews, or summary reports. Recent examples include "Knowledge and attitudes toward felon-voting rights" and several articles about workplace stress and job satisfaction among correctional staff. The journal is available online from Taylor and Francis, starting with volume 7, issue 2, when it was published under its original title *Justice Professional.* This journal would be useful to faculty and students in criminal justice and political science programs.

1526. Criminology: an interdisciplinary journal. Formerly (until 1970): *Criminologica.* [ISSN: 0011-1384] 1963. q. USD 263 (print & online eds.). Ed(s): Bianca Bersani, Denise Gottfredson. Wiley-Blackwell Publishing, Inc., 111 River St, Hoboken, NJ 07030; info@wiley.com; http://onlinelibrary.wiley.com/. Illus., index, adv. Sample. Refereed. Circ: 3569 Paid. Vol. ends: Nov. Microform: PQC. Reprint: PSC; WSH. *Indexed:* A01, A22, BRI, CJPI, CLI, E01, H24, IBSS, L14, P02, P61, PsycInfo, RiskAb, SSA, SWR&A. *Aud.:* Ac, Sa.

Criminology is a quarterly publication of the American Society of Criminology (ASC). It is consistently ranked as a first-tier criminology journal (see section introduction for information on selection/ranking criteria). The content is interdisciplinary, with articles from sociology, psychology, and other social sciences that "concern crime, deviant behavior, and related phenomena." Most of the articles are empirical studies, but theoretical discussions and literature reviews are also included. Most articles are authored by American academics and relate to U.S. crime and policies; however, this isn't always the case, as the society has international members and welcomes articles that cover international issues. An example is a recent article titled "Target choice during extreme events: A discrete spatial choice model of the 2011 London Riots." Other topics discussed in recent issues are the cycle of violence and child abuse, police culture and legitimacy, personality effect on criminal decision making, and juvenile delinquency issues. This journal is essential for academic libraries, and is useful for criminal justice, sociology, social work, and psychology programs. It is available online and in print from Wiley (formerly Blackwell). The online archive goes back to the first issue in 1963. The ASC also publishes *Criminology and Public Policy,* which is reviewed in this section.

1527. Criminology & Criminal Justice: an international journal. Formerly (until 2006): *Criminal Justice.* [ISSN: 1748-8958] 2001. 5x/yr. USD 939. Ed(s): Adam Crawford. Sage Publications Ltd., 1 Oliver's Yard, 55 City Rd, London, EC1Y 1SP, United Kingdom; info@sagepub.co.uk; http://www.uk.sagepub.com. Adv. Sample. Refereed. Reprint: PSC. *Indexed:* A01, A22, ASSIA, CJPI, CLI, E01, IBSS, P61, PsycInfo, SSA. *Bk. rev.:* 2-4. *Aud.:* Ac.

Criminology and Criminal Justice (*CCJ*) is the official journal of the British Society of Criminology. Launched in 2001 under the title *Criminal Justice, CCJ* is peer-reviewed and comes out five times per year. Although it is published under the auspices of a British society and the majority of authors are from U.K. universities, the journal also encourages submission of articles written by authors from other countries. Recent issues included contributions from the U.S., Canada, Denmark, and Norway. The articles can be theoretical or empirical, and discuss policy and practice from all areas of the study of criminal justice, including policing, prisons, drug use, crime prevention, and more. Most issues contain several book reviews. The journal is published by Sage, and is available online and in print. The online archives begin with volume 1. This journal is recommended for academic libraries with a criminal justice department.

1528. *Criminology and Public Policy.* [ISSN: 1538-6473] 2001. q. GBP 168 (print & online eds.). Ed(s): Shanna Van Slyke, Tom Blomberg. Wiley-Blackwell Publishing, Inc., 111 River St, Hoboken, NJ 07030; http://onlinelibrary.wiley.com/. Adv. Sample. Reprint: PSC; WSH. *Indexed:* A01, A22, CJPI, E01, FR, P02, P61, RiskAb, SSA. *Aud.:* Ac, Sa.

Criminology and Public Policy was first published in 2001 by the American Society of Criminology (ASC) as a forum to present policy-related research findings in a meaningful way to policy makers. The society also publishes *Criminology* (see above), which contains empirical research articles aimed at criminal justice researchers rather than at policy makers. Each issue of *Criminology and Public Policy* addresses several current policy issues, such as race, place and drug enforcement, fugitive safe-surrender programs, and employment-based reentry of prisoners into society. An editorial introduces each topic, followed by a research article, which is written in a slightly different format than is the case in most academic peer-reviewed journals due to its intended audience. Two or three related policy essays follow. Like its sister publication, this is a good choice for academic libraries and special libraries that serve those who study criminal justice policy issues. This journal would also be an excellent choice for undergraduates. The articles are scholarly but more accessible than those of other scholarly research journals. Available online and in print from Wiley (formerly Blackwell).

1529. *Critical Criminology: international journal.* Formerly (until 1996): *Journal of Human Justice.* [ISSN: 1205-8629] 1989. 4x/yr. EUR 517 (print & online eds.). Ed(s): Shahid Alvi. Springer Netherlands, Van Godewijckstraat 30, Dordrecht, 3311 GX, Netherlands; http://www.springer.com. Adv. Refereed. Reprint: PSC. *Indexed:* A22, BRI, C37, CBCARef, E01. *Bk. rev.:* 2, 1,500-2,500 words; signed. *Aud.:* Ac, Sa.

Critical Criminology is the official journal of two related professional bodies—the Division of Critical Criminology of the American Society of Criminology, and the Academy of Criminal Justice Sciences Section on Critical Criminology. The journal publishes articles that focus on "issues of social harm and social justice" that are written from alternative criminological perspectives, such as feminist, Marxist, and postmodernist. *Critical Criminology* is published quarterly, and each issue contains five to seven articles and scholarly, in-depth book and film reviews. There are occasional special issues with introductions by guest editors. The March 2012 issue was devoted to "restorative justice," with articles on the restoration of crime victims, victim-offender mediation, and school bullying and youth restoration issues. This journal provides interesting and provocative articles that would be of interest to faculty and students studying criminology, political science, and sociology, especially if they were interested in exploring alternative methodologies. It is favorably rated by the journal-ranking sources consulted for this review (see section introduction for information on selection/ranking criteria). This publication is available in print and electronically from Springer.

1530. *European Journal of Criminology.* [ISSN: 1477-3708] 2004. bi-m. USD 1152. Ed(s): Alex Sutherland, Julian Roberts. Sage Publications Ltd., 1 Oliver's Yard, 55 City Rd, London, EC1Y 1SP, United Kingdom; info@sagepub.co.uk; http://www.uk.sagepub.com. Adv. Sample. Refereed. Reprint: PSC. *Indexed:* A22, ASSIA, CJPI, E01, IBSS, P61, PsycInfo, RiskAb, SSA. *Aud.:* Ac, Sa.

European Journal of Criminology is offered by Sage in association with the European Society of Criminology. The society was formed in 2000 and the journal's first issue appeared in 2004 to address issues that were particularly relevant to that continent and its various member countries. The articles present scholarly research, including theoretical, quantitative, qualitative, or comparative studies. They contain evaluations of various criminological interventions, institutions, or political processes. Each issue has four to eight articles, and is sometimes thematic. The latest special-themed issue looked at urban security in Europe. The journal frequently includes a country survey that summarizes the featured country's criminal justice system, trends in crime and punishment, and major publications. This journal is recommended for academic libraries with programs concerned with European criminology, including political science, sociology, European studies, and criminal justice. Available in print and online.

1531. *F B I Law Enforcement Bulletin.* Formerly (until 1935): *Fugitives Wanted by Police.* [ISSN: 0014-5688] 1932. m. USD 53 domestic; USD 74.20 foreign. Ed(s): John E Ott. U.S. Federal Bureau of Investigation, 935 Pennsylvania Ave, NW, Washington, DC 20535; http://www.fbi.gov/. Illus., index. Sample. Vol. ends: Dec. Microform: MIM; PQC. *Indexed:* A01, A22, BRI, CJPI, P02. *Bk. rev.:* Occasional, 400-500 words. *Aud.:* Ga, Ac, Sa.

FBI Law Enforcement Bulletin is published monthly by the U.S. Federal Bureau of Investigation. The intended audience is clearly the U.S. law enforcement community. Each issue contains two to four articles and several recurring columns, which appear under the headings "Perspective," "Legal Digest," and "Leadership Spotlight," among others. Occasionally, issues will have a theme; and sometimes research results are reported. For example, the July 2012 issue includes several articles on psychopathy, written by university faculty as well as private consultants and business owners. The *Bulletin's* authors are usually professionals in the field or faculty at U.S. colleges and universities. Published since the 1930s, this publication is available online, but no longer in print as of December 2012. Online archives go back to 1999 and are available free at www.fbi.gov/publications/leb/leb.htm. This publication is a good choice for academic, public, and special libraries.

1532. *Federal Probation (Online): a journal of correctional philosophy and practice.* [ISSN: 1555-0303] 2004. 3x/yr. Free. Administrative Office of the United States Courts, Federal Corrections and Supervision Division, 1 Columbus Cir, NE, Washington, DC 20544; http://www.uscourts.gov. *Bk. rev.:* June and Dec. issues. *Aud.:* Ga, Ac, Sa.

Federal Probation is published three times a year by the Administrative Office of the United States Courts. It first appeared in 1937, and continued to be published in print until 2004. This publication is also freely available online, as are many U.S. federal documents. The contributors are scholars, practitioners, lawyers, and policy researchers. The articles are essays, policy analyses, and research studies. They are written using scholarly language, but are not laden with legal jargon beyond the comprehension of students. When appropriate, references are provided. Each September issue focuses on a special topic; the latest issue discusses topics related to "30th Anniversary of the Passage of the Pretrial Services Act of 1982." June and December issues contain a column that focuses on juvenile justice, and book reviews; and there is an annual index in December. This journal is an excellent resource for students, scholars, and practitioners, especially those that work with the courts.

1533. *Feminist Criminology.* [ISSN: 1557-0851] 2006. q. USD 691. Ed(s): Jana L Jasinski. Sage Publications, Inc., 2455 Teller Rd, Thousand Oaks, CA 91320; info@sagepub.com; http://www.sagepub.com. Adv. Sample. Refereed. Reprint: PSC. *Indexed:* A22, ASSIA, E01, FemPer, P61, PsycInfo, RiskAb, SSA. *Aud.:* Ac, Sa.

Feminist Criminology is a relatively new journal that presents criminological research from a feminist perspective. It is the official journal of the Division on Women and Crime of the American Society of Criminology, and was launched in 2006. The following excerpt from the introductory editorial of that inaugural issue explains the journal's scope and editorial intent: "The main aim of this journal will be to focus on research related to women, girls, and crime. Defined broadly, this includes research on women working in the criminal justice profession, women as offenders, women in the criminal justice system, women as victims, and theories and tests of theories related to women and crime. This journal will highlight scholarship that demonstrates the gendered nature of crime and the justice system. The main focus will be empirical research and theory, although we also welcome practice-oriented papers." *Feminist Criminology* was ranked in the top 50 journals (from a total of 152) by the Australian & New Zealand Society of Criminology in a journal-ranking survey report (see section introduction for information on selection/ranking criteria). This is impressive considering the journal's recent launch. However, recent issues have contained only three articles each. Earlier issues published four articles and had an editorial introduction. It is available in print and online from Sage at http://fcx.sagepub.com. Readers interested in this title should also consider *Women & Criminal Justice,* also reviewed in this section.

1534. *Homicide Studies: an interdisciplinary & international journal.* [ISSN: 1088-7679] 1997. q. USD 818. Ed(s): Wendy Regoeczi. Sage Publications, Inc., 2455 Teller Rd, Thousand Oaks, CA 91320; info@sagepub.com; http://www.sagepub.com. Illus., adv. Sample. Refereed. Reprint: PSC. *Indexed:* A01, A22, CJPI, E01, H24, PsycInfo, RiskAb. *Bk. rev.:* Occasional, signed, 800-1,000 words. *Aud.:* Ac, Sa.

Homicide Studies: An Interdisciplinary & International Journal is a quarterly publication of the Homicide Research Working Group, which was organized in 1991 at the American Society of Criminology meeting. The group saw its mission as interdisciplinary and international—much broader than just American criminology. Its goal, and the focus of the journal, is "to forge links between research, epidemiology, and practical programs to reduce levels of mortality from violence." The first issue of *Homicide Studies* appeared in 1997. Each issue contains four to seven articles; some include commentaries, responses to research articles, and book reviews. Examples of topics covered in recent articles are homicide recidivism, homicides associated with sexual violence, and prostitutes as victims of serial killers. Authors are academics, professionals, and policy experts from the fields of criminology, sociology, public health, anthropology, social work, and more. A good choice for academic and special libraries concerned with homicide crimes and policy. Available in print and online. URL: http://hsx.sagepub.com

1535. *The Howard Journal of Criminal Justice.* Former titles (until Feb.1984): *Howard Journal of Penology and Crime Prevention;* (until 1965): *Howard Journal.* [ISSN: 0265-5527] 1921. 5x/yr. GBP 519. Ed(s): Anita Dockley, Penny Green. Wiley-Blackwell Publishing Ltd., The Atrium, Southern Gate, Chichester, PO19 8SQ, United Kingdom; customer@wiley.com; http://www.wiley.com/. Illus., adv. Sample. Refereed. Vol. ends: Nov. Microform: PQC. Reprint: PSC. *Indexed:* A01, A22, AmHI, BRI, CJPI, CLI, E01, IBSS, L14, P61, PsycInfo, RiskAb, SSA. *Bk. rev.:* 5-8, 700-1,200 words. *Aud.:* Ac, Sa.

The Howard Journal of Criminal Justice is published by Wiley-Blackwell for the Howard League for Penal Reform, a U.K.-based charity founded in 1866. The journal is published five times a year, and each issue contains five or so in-depth articles relating to both theory and practice. These articles relate to "all aspects of the criminal justice process, penal policy, and crime prevention." As with other journals reviewed in this section, the editors seek to inform practitioners as well as academics, so the writing is clear and accessible. Contributors are U.K. academics for the most part, but the journal welcomes submissions written by practitioners, and occasionally U.S., Canadian, or other countries are represented. The articles are sometimes research-based, but commentary, essays, and reviews are included also. Each issue contains a summary of new policy developments titled "Penal Policy File"; a controversial short piece appropriately titled "Counterblast"; and numerous scholarly book reviews. It is available in print and online from Wiley. The online archive goes back to 1921. Although this journal is U.K.-based, the policies and issues discussed are applicable to U.S. criminal justice practitioners, faculty, and students.

1536. *International Criminal Justice Review.* [ISSN: 1057-5677] 1991. q. USD 353. Ed(s): Dean Dabney. Sage Publications, Inc., 2455 Teller Rd, Thousand Oaks, CA 91320; info@sagepub.com; http://www.sagepub.com. Adv. Sample. Refereed. Reprint: PSC; WSH. *Indexed:* A22, CJPI, E01, IBSS, P61, RiskAb, SSA. *Bk. rev.:* 15-20, 800-1,300 words; signed. *Aud.:* Ac, Sa.

The *International Criminal Justice Review* (*ICJR*) is a publication of Georgia State University's Department of Criminal Justice, which also publishes *Criminal Justice Review* (reviewed in this section). Sage is the publisher of both journals since 2005. The International Section of the Academy of Criminal Justice Sciences is now also professionally affiliated with *ICJR,* beginning with the June 2009 issue. This issue was a special one devoted to the subject of genocide, and some of the articles are based on papers delivered at the 2008 annual meeting of the academy, which was the impetus for its decision to join with Georgia State. The journal's articles focus on one particular country, or compare two or more countries. They may use quantitative or qualitative methodologies, and commentary is also welcome. The main criteria are that they present "system-wide trends and problems on crime and justice throughout the world." Each quarterly issue contains three to seven articles and 10–15 scholarly book reviews. Recent articles include using the British Crime Survey to measure ethnic differences in Welsh and British citizens' confidence in their criminal justice system; and Saudi Arabian use of counter-indoctrination to rehabilitate terrorists. The authors are academics from throughout the world; however, most are affiliated with U.S. universities. *ICJR* is available in print and online from Sage, back to the inaugural issue in 1991. URL: http://0-icj.sagepub.com

1537. *International Journal of Offender Therapy and Comparative Criminology.* Former titles (until 1972): *International Journal of Offender Therapy;* (until 1967): *Journal of Offender Therapy;* (until 1961): *Association for Psychiatric Treatment of Offenders. Journal.* [ISSN: 0306-624X] 1957. m. USD 1227. Ed(s): George Palermo. Sage Publications, Inc., 2455 Teller Rd, Thousand Oaks, CA 91320; info@sagepub.com; http://www.sagepub.com. Illus., index, adv. Sample. Refereed. Vol. ends: Winter. Microform: PQC. Reprint: PSC. *Indexed:* A01, A22, ABS&EES, ASSIA, AbAn, BRI, CJPI, CLI, E01, H24, L14, P02, P61, PsycInfo, RiskAb, SSA. *Bk. rev.:* Occasional, 300-1,000 words; signed. *Aud.:* Ac, Sa.

International Journal of Offender Therapy and Comparative Criminology publishes articles that focus on research and theory as they inform treatment practices for criminal offenders. The journal addresses three primary aspects of offender therapy—psychological, due to the preponderance of offenders with serious psychological disorders; genetic/biological, to help inform those treating offenders to recognize and deal with these factors; and environmental, which looks at the influences of offenders' life histories on their behavior. Examples of recent article topics include a study of a risk-assessment instrument and repeat offenders; the change of prisoners' social bonds during their incarceration and its effect on the success of their reentry to society; and a guest editorial that looks at how the role of psychologists in prison has evolved from a helper to a risk assessor. Contributors to this journal come from a variety of disciplines, and include psychologists, social workers, counselors, health scientists, legal studies scholars, sociologists, and medical professionals, as well as corrections and criminal justice researchers and policy makers. In keeping with the editorial intent to present articles from international scholars, research from other countries is included. Sage publishes this journal, which is available in print and online. The online archive is complete, beginning with volume 1 in 1966. URL: http://0-ijo.sagepub.com

1538. *Journal of Contemporary Criminal Justice.* [ISSN: 1043-9862] 1978. q. USD 663. Ed(s): Chris Eskridge. Sage Publications, Inc., 2455 Teller Rd, Thousand Oaks, CA 91320; info@sagepub.com; http://www.sagepub.com. Illus., adv. Sample. Refereed. Vol. ends: Nov. Reprint: PSC. *Indexed:* A01, A22, B01, CJPI, E01, IBSS, PsycInfo, RiskAb. *Aud.:* Ac, Sa.

Journal of Contemporary Criminal Justice is a quarterly journal that examines current criminal justice issues in-depth to inform academics, professionals, and policy makers. It is interdisciplinary, with contributors from most social science fields, including anthropology, criminology, economics, history, legal studies, political science, psychology, public administration and policy, sociology, and social work. Each issue tackles a single topic, and most have a guest editor who is an expert on that topic. For example, the May 2011 issue is subtitled "Forensic Science and Criminal Justice." The guest editor for this issue is a professor in the Criminal Justice Department at California State University, Long Beach. According to his web page at the university, he researches "the intersection of law with the social and forensic sciences, most frequently with an emphasis in forensic psychology and psychiatry." The guest editors for each issue write a detailed introductory essay that presents an overview of the topic at hand and the research that follows. Firearms and violent crime, sentencing reforms, and victimization are some topics of recent issues. Full text of all issues, dating back to 1978, are available from the journal's homepage. The journal's unique theme-based coverage makes this a good choice for academic and special libraries. URL: http://ccj.sagepub.com

1539. *Journal of Correctional Education.* Former titles (until 1974): *Correctional Education;* (until 1973): *Journal of Correctional Education.* [ISSN: 0740-2708] 1949. q. Free to members. Ed(s): John J Dowdell,

Russell L Craig. Ashland University, 401 College Ave, Ashland, OH 44805; http://www.ashland.edu/. Illus., index, adv. Sample. Refereed. Vol. ends: Dec. Microform: PQC. *Indexed:* A01, A22, CJPI, ERIC. *Aud.:* Ac, Sa.

The *Journal of Correctional Education* is published by Ashland University for the Correctional Education Association, whose members serve as educators for juveniles and adults in criminal justice settings. It is a quarterly publication, containing research articles, discussions, and guidelines on best practices, and reports that cover current issues and legislative updates. Examples of current articles are research on the therapeutic use of expressive writing for juvenile male inmates; and a discussion of the implementation of a technique called "response to intervention"—which is currently employed in public schools—in the juvenile justice setting. The articles are well written, and even the research articles are composed in language that is accessible to the layperson. The journal is available electronically; guests can browse the table of contents (with brief abstracts) for each issue going back to the first in 1951. It is also available full-text through ProQuest's Criminal Justice Periodicals database and EBSCOhost. In addition to correctional educators and other practitioners such as social workers, the journal would be helpful to those in academia studying criminal justice or related social-science disciplines. URL: www.ashland.edu/correctionaled/articles-search.php

1540. *Journal of Criminal Justice: an international journal.* [ISSN: 0047-2352] 1973. bi-m. EUR 1412. Ed(s): Matthew DeLisi. Pergamon, The Blvd, Langford Ln, E Park, Kidlington, OX5 1GB, United Kingdom; JournalsCustomerServiceEMEA@elsevier.com; http://www.elsevier.com. Illus., adv. Sample. Refereed. Microform: PQC. *Indexed:* A01, A22, ASSIA, BRI, CJPI, CLI, Chicano, L14, P02, P61, PsycInfo, SSA. *Aud.:* Ac, Sa.

Journal of Criminal Justice: An International Journal is published six times a year by Elsevier. Its scope is broad in that it covers all aspects and elements of criminology, but its editorial intent is to publish creative and innovative thought and research in the discipline. Each issue contains 10–15 articles, although some have more: July/August 2010 had over 50. There are special-themed issues; the most recent such issue presented research on addiction and the criminal justice system. Examples of topics addressed in recent articles include the analysis of public opinion research on attitudes toward intermediate sanctions (i.e., electric monitoring) and the differences between minority respondents; research on police behavior in encounters with juveniles versus encounters with adults; and female drug abusers and punishment in China. There was also a quantitative study of the effect of the moon on criminal activity. The majority of articles represent U.S.-based research, but many issues contains at least one article that analyzes international criminal justice concerns. The quality of the research and writing in this journal is excellent, and it belongs in academic libraries with criminal justice programs, and in special libraries interested in criminological research. More information is available at the web site. URL: www.sciencedirect.com/science/journal/00472352

1541. *Journal of Criminal Justice Education.* [ISSN: 1051-1253] 1990. q. GBP 423 (print & online eds.). Ed(s): George Higgins. Routledge, 4 Park Sq, Milton Park, Abingdon, OX14 4RN, United Kingdom; subscriptions@tandf.co.uk; http://www.tandfonline.com. Illus., index, adv. Sample. Refereed. Vol. ends: Fall. Reprint: PSC; WSH. *Indexed:* A01, A22, CJPI, E01. *Bk. rev.:* Number and length vary. *Aud.:* Ac, Sa.

The *Journal of Criminal Justice Education* (*JCJE*) is published by Routledge for the Academy of Criminal Justice Sciences, to serve as a "forum for the examination, discussion[,] and debate of a broad range of issues concerning post-secondary education in criminal justice, criminology, and related areas." Articles include reviews of various pedagogical approaches, such as concept mapping to teach criminological theory; or using classical literature to encourage students' independent thinking skills. There was also an analysis of different active-learning exercises, such as film analysis and jail tours. In addition to pedagogy, some articles address criminal justice departments' administrative concerns, such as a review of the characteristic of criminal justice scholars who are successful at obtaining research grants, and bibliometric and citation analysis of criminal justice journals. *JCJE* also contains book reviews and book review essays. In 2010, the journal became a quarterly publication; it had been published three times a year. More information is available at the web site. URL: www.tandf.co.uk/journals/titles/10511253.asp

Journal of Criminal Law & Criminology. See Law section.

1542. *Journal of Experimental Criminology.* [ISSN: 1573-3750] 2005. q. EUR 476 (print & online eds.). Springer New York LLC, 233 Spring St, New York, NY 10013; journals@springer-ny.com; http://www.springer.com. Refereed. Reprint: PSC. *Indexed:* A22, CJPI, E01, PsycInfo. *Aud.:* Ac.

Journal of Experimental Criminology was launched in 2005 to publish experimental and quasi-experimental research, systematic reviews, and other evidence-based methodologies in the disciplines of criminology and criminal justice. The journal is international in scope, with an editorial board from institutions that span the globe. However, the majority of article authors are individuals based in the United States. They include academics, practitioners from public-policy institutes, and individuals from think tanks. The articles include presentations of empirical research, articles that discuss research methodologies as they pertain to the discipline, and discussions of criminal justice problems and concerns. There are special issues; for example, December 2010 was devoted to experimental studies of violence against women.

1543. *The Journal of Forensic Psychiatry & Psychology.* Formerly (until 2003): *Journal of Forensic Psychiatry (Print).* [ISSN: 1478-9949] 1990. bi-m. GBP 735 (print & online eds.). Ed(s): Jenny Shaw. Routledge, 4 Park Sq, Milton Park, Abingdon, OX14 4RN, United Kingdom; subscriptions@tandf.co.uk; http://www.tandfonline.com. Adv. Sample. Refereed. Reprint: PSC. *Indexed:* A01, A22, ASSIA, CJPI, E01, ExcerpMed, FR, IBSS, PsycInfo. *Aud.:* Ac, Sa.

The *Journal of Forensic Psychiatry & Psychology* was first published in 1990 as the *Journal of Forensic Psychiatry*. As the journal became multidisciplinary, its aim has been to publish "papers relating to aspects of psychiatry and psychological knowledge (research, theory and practice) as applied to offenders and to legal issues arising within civil, criminal, correctional or legislative contexts." A variety of topics are explored in recent issues of this peer-reviewed publication, including anger management, weight management, and personality disorders of offenders. With an international scope, this publication is valuable to a number of legal, health, and academic institutions. This publication is available in print and online via Taylor & Francis Online, EBSCOhost, and other full-text databases.

1544. *Journal of International Criminal Justice.* [ISSN: 1478-1387] 2003. 5x/yr. EUR 658. Ed(s): Salvatore Zappala. Oxford University Press, Great Clarendon St, Oxford, OX2 6DP, United Kingdom; enquiry@oup.co.uk; http://www.oxfordjournals.org/. Adv. Sample. Reprint: PSC. *Indexed:* A22, BRI, CJPI, E01, L14. *Aud.:* Ac, Sa.

The *Journal of International Criminal Justice* was first published in 2003 by the Oxford University Press. The journal's mission is to address "the major problems of justice from the angle of law, jurisprudence, criminology, penal philosophy, and the history of international judicial institutions." New issues are published five times per year, and although this journal is not peer-reviewed, it provides a valuable forum for discussion of international law issues and trends. Special issues are published periodically. In 2012, a tenth-anniversary special issue entitled "Aggression: After Kampala" was released, as well as a tribute issue dedicated to Nino Cassese, a major contributor to the field of international criminal justice. *Journal of International Criminal Justice* is available in print and online via EBSCOhost, LexisNexis, Oxford University Press, and other full-text sources.

1545. *Journal of Interpersonal Violence: concerned with the study and treatment of victims and perpetrators of physical and sexual violence.* [ISSN: 0886-2605] 1986. 18x/yr. USD 1955. Ed(s): Jamie Hart, Jon R Conte. Sage Publications, Inc., 2455 Teller Rd, Thousand Oaks, CA 91320; info@sagepub.com; http://www.sagepub.com. Illus., index, adv. Sample. Refereed. Vol. ends: Dec. Reprint: PSC. *Indexed:* A01, A22, BRI, CJPI, E01, ERIC, P02, P61, PsycInfo, SSA, SWR&A. *Bk. rev.:* 1, 700-1,000 words; signed. *Aud.:* Ac, Sa.

Journal of Interpersonal Violence's subtitle states the journal is "concerned with the study and treatment of victims and perpetrators of physical and sexual violence," and this succinctly explains the unique editorial focus of this journal, on both the victims and offenders in interpersonal violence. Contributors are academics and practitioners from a variety of disciplines, including sociology, social work, public health and health administration, pediatrics, clinical psychology, and criminal justice. They are primarily associated with U.S. universities and policy centers; however, submissions from international researchers are frequently included. The articles "address the causes, effects, treatments, and prevention of all types of interpersonal violence." Recent examples of research that has appeared include an analysis of interviews with male social workers who counsel men who are batterers; a U.K. study of police interventions in domestic violence where children are involved; and a quantitative study of teachers and violence that they experience at school directed at them. In addition to research articles, the journal publishes regular features that include commentary, practice notes, discussions of methodology, and book reviews. The *Journal of Interpersonal Violence* is published monthly by Sage and available in print and online. The online archive goes back to the first issue in 1986, when it was a quarterly. The frequency increased to bimonthly in 1997, and then to monthly in 1999. This journal is useful for faculty, students, and practitioners, and is recommended for most academic libraries. URL: http://intl-jiv.sagepub.com

1546. *Journal of Offender Rehabilitation: a multidisciplinary journal of innovation in research, services, and programs in corrections and criminal justice.* Former titles (until 1990): *Journal of Offender Counseling, Services and Rehabilitation;* (until 1980): *Offender Rehabilitation.* [ISSN: 1050-9674] 1976. 8x/yr. GBP 1152 (print & online eds.). Ed(s): Creasie Finney Hairston. Routledge, 325 Chestnut St, Ste 800, Philadelphia, PA 19106; customerservice@taylorandfrancis.com; http://www.tandfonline.com. Illus., adv. Sample. Refereed. Circ: 328 Paid. Vol. ends: Spring/Summer. Microform: PQC. Reprint: PSC. *Indexed:* A01, A22, CJPI, E01, ERIC, P61, PsycInfo, SSA, SWR&A. *Aud.:* Ac, Sa.

Journal of Offender Rehabilitation is an interdisciplinary journal that publishes qualitative, quantitative, and theoretical articles covering research, services, and programs related to the treatment of offenders. Topics include "alternatives to incarceration; community reentry and reintegration; alcohol and substance abuse and mental health treatment interventions; service for correctional populations with special needs; recidivism prevention strategies," and more. Contributors come from the fields of criminal justice, psychology, psychosocial and community health, social work, and related fields, and include academics and practitioners. This journal is recommended for practitioners, and faculty and students, in the fields of social work, counseling, and therapy. It is published eight times a year by Routledge. Readers interested in this journal should also review the *International Journal of Offender Therapy* and *Comparative Criminology,* also reviewed in this section. URL: www.tandf.co.uk/journals/WJOR

1547. *Journal of Quantitative Criminology.* [ISSN: 0748-4518] 1984. q. EUR 1097 (print & online eds.). Ed(s): Julie Viollaz, James P Lynch. Springer New York LLC, 233 Spring St, New York, NY 10013; service-ny@springer.com; http://www.springer.com/. Illus., index, adv. Refereed. Vol. ends: Dec. Microform: PQC. Reprint: PSC. *Indexed:* A01, A22, ASSIA, CJPI, E01, P61, PsycInfo, SSA. *Aud.:* Ac, Sa.

The *Journal of Quantitative Criminology* (*JQC*) is a quarterly journal that presents studies that use quantitative research methodologies to investigate criminological concerns. Most articles are original research, but the journal also accepts critiques of quantitative methodologies and discussions of advances in the field of criminological research. The coverage is interdisciplinary, arising from the fields of sociology, statistics, political science, geography, economics, and engineering. Contributors are primarily U.S. academic criminologists; however, some are professors in related disciplines, or practitioners and researchers at public policy institutions. The first issue of *JQC* appeared in 1985, before the rise in popularity of quantitative research. Many of the scholarly journals reviewed in this section publish quantitative research, but this journal was the first to focus on it. It is ranked as first-tier journal (see section introduction for information on selection/ranking criteria), which speaks to quality of the articles. *JQC* is highly recommended to faculty, graduate students, and professionals interested in criminological research. The articles are a bit heavy for most undergraduates unless the students are statistically inclined. Available in print and online from Springer.

1548. *Journal of Research in Crime and Delinquency.* [ISSN: 0022-4278] 1964. q. USD 915. Ed(s): Julie Viollaz, Michael Maxfield. Sage Publications, Inc., 2455 Teller Rd, Thousand Oaks, CA 91320; info@sagepub.com; http://www.sagepub.com. Illus., index, adv. Sample. Refereed. Vol. ends: Nov. Microform: WSH; PMC. Reprint: PSC. *Indexed:* A01, A22, BRI, CJPI, CLI, E01, ERIC, IBSS, P02, P61, PsycInfo, RILM, SSA, SWR&A. *Aud.:* Ac, Sa.

Journal of Research in Crime and Delinquency is published quarterly by Sage in cooperation with the Rutgers School of Criminal Justice. From its inaugural issue in 1964 until volume 45 in 2008, the journal was sponsored by the National Council on Crime and Delinquency (NCCD). This U.S. nonprofit was founded in 1907 to promote research to support humane solutions to family, community, and justice problems. Rutgers faculty members have been the editors since the 1990s, and state that the scope and mission remains as it was under the NCCD watch. The journal publishes original research, research notes, and essays. It is ranked among the top criminal justice journals (see section introduction for information on selection/ranking criteria). Each issue contains three to five articles, and for the most part they present the results of original quantitative or qualitative research into delinquency. In February 2011, the journal resumed publishing special issues after a several-year hiatus. The theme for this latest issue was "Crime and Place." It presented criminal research using spatial analysis—for example, crimes committed on street corners. Examples of topics covered in other recent issues include gang membership; the theft of copper wire; the victimization of adolescents at school, based on an extensive dataset from Kentucky; a look at the development of delinquency in high-risk youth in the Netherlands using treatment data; and an essay on a new organizational theory applied to police organization. This journal would be helpful to anyone interested in current research on delinquency, including criminologists, social workers, and psychologists. Available online and in print from Sage. URL: http://0-jrc.sagepub.com

1549. *Justice Quarterly.* [ISSN: 0741-8825] 1984. bi-m. GBP 671 (print & online eds.). Ed(s): Clair Vaughn-Uding. Routledge, 4 Park Sq, Milton Park, Abingdon, OX14 4RN, United Kingdom; subscriptions@tandf.co.uk; http://www.tandfonline.com. Illus., adv. Sample. Refereed. Reprint: PSC; WSH. *Indexed:* A01, A22, CJPI, E01, P61, RiskAb, SSA. *Bk. rev.:* 2, 1,000-2,000 words, signed. *Aud.:* Ac, Sa.

Justice Quarterly is the official publication of the Academy of Criminal Justice Sciences, which also publishes the *Journal of Criminal Justice Education* (reviewed above). *Justice Quarterly* is highly regarded by criminal justice scholars and is ranked among the top criminal justice journals in surveys (see section introduction for information on selection/ranking criteria). The articles are multidisciplinary and employ a variety of quantitative, qualitative, and other empirical research methodologies. For example, in recent issues, a criminologist specializing in geospatial analysis looked at the geo-structure of terrorist cells; sociologists used longitudinal data to see if there is a relationship between dating and delinquency; and another article examined criminologists and their appearance as guest commentators on cable news shows. This journal belongs in all academic libraries, and is useful to all social science students and researchers. It is published by Routledge and available electronically and in print.

1550. *Law and Order Magazine: the magazine for police management.* [ISSN: 0023-9194] 1953. m. Free to qualified personnel. Ed(s): Yesenia Salcedo, Jennifer Gavigan. Hendon Publishing Company, 130 N Waukegan Rd, Ste 202, Deerfield, IL 60015; info@hendonpub.com; http://www.hendonpub.com. Illus., index, adv. Sample. Circ: 37000. Vol. ends: Dec. Microform: PQC. *Indexed:* A22, CJPI, P02. *Bk. rev.:* 0-5, 75-150 words. *Aud.:* Ga, Ac, Sa.

Law and Order is a monthly trade magazine for law enforcement professionals. The coverage is comprehensive and touches on all aspects of the profession, including equipment and products, training, techniques, office management, and best practices. Each issue has a thematic focus, and several articles touch on the same topic. For example, a recent focus was interoperability and data sharing. The articles covered the technology of interoperability, "rugged laptops," nationwide 4G networks, and new developments in land mobile radios. The magazine also contains a calendar of upcoming events, an editorial introduction, feature articles, product reviews, news, and other columns. The February issue includes an annual buyer's guide, with over 200 pages of manufacturer, product, and dealer listings. Many issues are available full-text through ProQuest's Criminal Justice Periodicals database, although (at time of writing) 2010 issues are not available. Some content is free online from the journal's web site. The publisher, Hendon, offers a searchable online archive of *Law and Order* and three other related magazines that it publishes. This magazine is useful for law enforcement professionals, especially those in management positions, and academic libraries that support programs that offer law enforcement courses and degrees. URL: www.hendonpub.com/ publications/lawandorder/

1551. *Law Officers' Bulletin.* [ISSN: 0145-6571] 1976. bi-w. Ed(s): Mary B Murphy. Pike & Fischer, Inc., 1010 Wayne Ave, Ste 1400, Silver Spring, MD 20910; customercare@pf.com; http://www.pf.com. Illus. Sample. Vol. ends: No. 26. *Indexed:* CJPI. *Aud.:* Ga, Ac, Sa.

The *Law Officers' Bulletin* is a monthly newsletter published by Thomson Reuters/West, one of the world's largest publishers of legal materials. It contains plain-language summaries of recent local, state, and federal court cases pertinent to police and other officers of the law. The issues covered relate to constitutional and statutory law, such as consent to search, or kidnapping and false imprisonment. Usually four cases are examined in-depth, and several more are given brief-synopsis write-ups. An interesting feature is "You be the Judge," where readers are invited to form an opinion on cases. The opinions of the actual judge are provided in the next issue. There are also special issues that focus on a recent hot topic. This bulletin is recommended for legal, state, municipal, and related special libraries, and academic libraries that serve institutions that offer legal and criminal justice programs. More information is available at http:// west.thomson.com/

1552. *Legal and Criminological Psychology.* [ISSN: 1355-3259] 1996. s-a. GBP 205 (print & online eds.). Ed(s): Paul Taylor. John Wiley & Sons Ltd., The Atrium, Southern Gate, Chichester, PO19 8SQ, United Kingdom; customer@wiley.com; http://www.wiley.com. Adv. Sample. Refereed. Reprint: PSC. *Indexed:* A01, A22, ASSIA, CJPI, E01, ExcerpMed, P61, PsycInfo, SSA. *Aud.:* Ac, Sa.

Legal and Criminological Psychology is one of 11 journals published by The British Psychological Society. The journal was first released in 1996, with two issues printed each year. According to the BPS, this publication's goal is to "advance professional and scientific knowledge defined broadly as the application of psychology to law and interdisciplinary enquiry [sic] in legal and psychological fields." Most of the articles featured in each journal issue contain original research, but book reviews, hot topic debates, and article commentary (with author response) are also included periodically. The range of topics discussed in this journal includes mental health and the law, management of offenders, witness and jury roles, crime detection and prevention, and aspects of deception. *Legal and Criminological Psychology* is available in print and online through EBSCOhost, Wiley-Blackwell, and other full-text providers.

1553. *National Institute of Justice Journal.* Superseded in part (in 1992): *National Institute of Justice Reports;* Which was formerly (until 1991): *N I J Reports;* (until 1983): *S N I: Selective Notification of Information.* [ISSN: 1067-7453] 1972. 3x/yr. Free. Ed(s): Philip Bulman. U.S. Department of Justice. National Institute of Justice, 810 Seventh St, NW, Washington, DC 20531; http://www.ojp.usdoj.gov/nij/. Illus. Sample. Circ: 80000. *Aud.:* Ga, Ac, Sa.

The National Institute of Justice is the research, development, and evaluation agency of the U.S. Department of Justice. It is charged with providing independent, evidence-based research and tools for crime control and on justice issues, especially on the state and local level. The *National Institute of Justice Journal* is published several times a year by the institute. Its intended audience is criminal justice professionals and policy makers, but college and advanced high school students researching current topics in criminal justice would find the journal useful as well. The articles are well written and clear. They present the results of recent research in language that the layperson can understand. The authors are U.S. government personnel, policy researchers, university professors, and other experts. Footnotes and citations are often included. Recent articles present the results of NIJ-funded research to investigate new technologies and determine if they can reduce injuries to both police and offenders when police officers have to use force; interview protocols for investigators of children involved in sexual abuse; research on the length of time

DNA can be collected in sexual assault cases; and more. The journal is available in print and online at www.nij.gov/nij/journals/267/welcome.htm. The online archive dates back to 1994. The institute's web site is www.nij.gov/

1554. *The Police Chief: professional voice of law enforcement.* Former titles (until 1953): *Police Chiefs News;* (until 1947): *Police Chiefs' Newsletter.* [ISSN: 0032-2571] 1934. m. Free to members; Non-members, USD 25. Ed(s): Charles E Higginbotham. International Association of Chiefs of Police, Inc., 515 N Washington St, Alexandria, VA 22314; information@theiacp.org; http://www.theiacp.org/. Illus., index, adv. Circ: 23382. Vol. ends: Dec. Microform: PQC. *Indexed:* A22, BRI, CJPI, P02. *Aud.:* Ga, Ac, Sa.

The Police Chief is the official publication of the International Association of Chiefs of Police, the world's oldest and largest police chief organization. The association has over 20,000 members in 89 countries. Contributors to the magazine are most often law enforcement professionals from local, state, and federal agencies, but some pieces are written by academics or professionals from related fields. The content is typical of trade and association magazines—association news; legislative updates and other legal news; new equipment, products, and technology reviews; training and professional development advice and best-practice examples; and employment opportunities. *The Police Chief* is published monthly, and is available in print and online. The online access is free and available back to September 2003, at the journal web site. This journal is recommended for all law enforcement special libraries and academic libraries that serve institutions offering a criminal justice degree. URL: http://policechiefmagazine.org

1555. *Police Quarterly.* [ISSN: 1098-6111] 1998. q. USD 691. Ed(s): Dr. John L Worrall. Sage Publications, Inc., 2455 Teller Rd, Thousand Oaks, CA 91320; info@sagepub.com; http://www.sagepub.com. Refereed. Reprint: PSC. *Indexed:* A01, A22, CJPI, E01, PsycInfo, RiskAb. *Bk. rev.:* 1-2, signed, 2-6 pages. *Aud.:* Ac, Sa.

Police Quarterly is published by Sage in association with the Police Executive Research Forum and the Police Section of the Academy of Criminal Justice Sciences. The former is a national membership organization of metropolitan, county, and state police executives. It was formed in 1977 to improve the profession through research and public policy debate. The latter is a section of a prominent international association of scholars and professionals, and is the publisher of two other journals reviewed in this section, *Justice Quarterly* and the *Journal of Criminal Justice Education*. The journal reviewed here, *Police Quarterly,* publishes research that is policy-oriented to inform both those in academia and practitioners. The articles are in the form of "theoretical contributions, empirical studies, essays, comparative analyses, critiques, innovative program descriptions, debates, and book reviews." An editorial introduction to a recent journal stressed the importance of articles to "test one or more empirical research questions" and have a clear relevance to policy. Thus the journal appears to be now favoring original research over essays and other non-empirical contributions. However, most articles appearing in the last few issues are already empirically based, so readers shouldn't see a major editorial shift. Examples of topics addressed recently include the limits to regional data sharing; the shared perceptions of gay and lesbian police officers; and the reasons behind policewomen's assertive or passive reactions to sexual harassment. Although this journal is perhaps too specialized for some academic libraries, it should be included in the collections of those that serve criminal justice students and faculty. It also should be considered by large public libraries and special libraries. URL: http://intl-pqx.sagepub.com

1556. *Policing and Society: an international journal of research & policy.* [ISSN: 1043-9463] 1990. 5x/yr. GBP 914 (print & online eds.). Ed(s): Martin Innes. Routledge, 4 Park Sq, Milton Park, Abingdon, OX14 4RN, United Kingdom; subscriptions@tandf.co.uk; http://www.tandfonline.com. Illus., adv. Sample. Refereed. Reprint: PSC. *Indexed:* A01, A22, ASSIA, CJPI, E01, IBSS, P61, PsycInfo, RiskAb, SSA. *Aud.:* Ac, Sa.

Policing and Society: An International Journal of Research & Policy is a quarterly journal that specializes in the study of policing institutions throughout the world. Coverage includes "social scientific investigations of police policy and activity; legal and political analyses of police powers and governance; and management[-]oriented research on aspects of police organization." There are occasional special issues; a recent one covered policing and peacekeeping. Each issue is truly international—for example, a recent one contained articles covering Ghana, the U.K., China, and the U.S. *Policing and Society* is published by Routledge, and more information is available at www.tandfonline.com/toc/gpas20/current

1557. ***Policing (Bingley): an international journal of police strategies and management.*** Formed by the merger of (1978-1996): *Police Studies;* (1981-1996): *American Journal of Police.* [ISSN: 1363-951X] 1978. q. EUR 3659 combined subscription in Europe (print & online eds.); USD 3829 combined subscription in the Americas (print & online eds.); GBP 2629 combined subscription in the UK & elsewhere (print & online eds.). Ed(s): Lorie A Fridell, Kim Lersch. Emerald Group Publishing Ltd., Howard House, Wagon Ln, Bingley, BD16 1WA, United Kingdom; emerald@emeraldinsight.com; http://www.emeraldinsight.com. Illus. Sample. Refereed. Microform: PQC. Reprint: PSC; WSH. *Indexed:* A01, A22, ABS&EES, ASSIA, CJPI, E01, H24, P61, RiskAb, SSA. *Bk. rev.:* 1, 900-1,500 words; signed. *Aud.:* Ac, Sa.

Policing: An International Journal of Police Strategies and Management looks at policing through an international lens. Each issue contains seven to ten refereed research articles, as well as a book review, reviews of important articles that appear in other journals, and a brief write-up of a police-related web site. The articles are interdisciplinary and cover all aspects of law enforcement, including training, policies, practice, technology, and more. A recent issue contained research on citizen support for community policing in China; a survey of the public's view of law enforcement in Turkey; and an analysis of a survey from the U.S. on police use of force and how it has changed over time. Although this is not a top-tier research journal, its articles are thorough and scholarly. It is good choice for academic libraries throughout the world that offer a criminal justice degree. The journal is available online from Emerald beginning with volume 20, 1997.

1558. ***Policing (Oxford): a journal of policy and practice.*** [ISSN: 1752-4512] 2007. 4x/yr. EUR 611. Ed(s): Peter Neyroud, P Waddington. Oxford University Press, Great Clarendon St, Oxford, OX2 6DP, United Kingdom; enquiry@oup.co.uk; http://www.oxfordjournals.org. Refereed. Reprint: PSC. *Indexed:* CJPI. *Bk. rev.:* 6; signed. *Aud.:* Ac, Sa.

Policing: A journal of policy and practice is a quarterly, peer-reviewed publication launched in 2007 by Oxford University Press. According to the journal's homepage, its audience is "senior police officers, researchers, policy makers[,] and academics." The primary editorial board is composed of U.K.-based academics, professionals, and policy analysts, although there is also an international editorial board with members from other European countries, the United States, Australia, and India. The journal's first issue was a special issue devoted to policing terrorism. Each subsequent issue has contained original research articles, usually around ten, and several scholarly book reviews. Many issues also have editorials and other opinion pieces, and some have case studies. Although this title is relatively new, this journal's prestigious publisher and the quality of its content should guarantee its success. Even with its U.K.-centered content, it is highly recommended for all academic libraries and special libraries that serve clientele interested in policing policy and theory.

1559. ***The Prison Journal: an international forum on incarceration and alternative sanctions.*** Supersedes (in 1921): *Journal of Prison Discipline and Philanthropy.* [ISSN: 0032-8855] 1845. q. USD 666. Ed(s): Rosemary L Gido. Sage Publications, Inc., 2455 Teller Rd, Thousand Oaks, CA 91320; info@sagepub.com; http://www.sagepub.com. Illus., index, adv. Sample. Refereed. Vol. ends: Dec. Microform: PQC. Reprint: PSC. *Indexed:* A01, A22, BRI, CJPI, E01, H24, P02, P61, PsycInfo, RiskAb, SSA. *Aud.:* Ac, Sa.

The Prison Journal: An International Forum on Incarceration and Alternative Sanctions was first published in 1921 by the Pennsylvania Prison Society, a social justice and prison reform organization founded in 1787. It remains the official publication of the society, and is now published by Sage. The journal's mission is to be a "central forum for studies, ideas, and discussions of adult and juvenile confinement, treatment interventions, and alternative sanctions." It is published quarterly, and each issue contains three to seven articles. Examples of recent papers include an essay condemning the practice of sentencing juveniles to life in prison without the possibility of parole; an evaluation of the use of radio frequency devices in prisons to prevent and investigate sexual assaults;

and an empirical evaluation of a psychometric instrument that measures group climate in prisons. There are topical special issues—a recent topic was children of incarcerated parents. The contributors are academics and practitioners from the United States and other countries, specializing in the fields of public administration and ethics, criminal justice studies, psychiatric nursing, and related disciplines. The articles are scholarly and written in clear language, making this journal a good choice for social science undergraduates. It is also appropriate for faculty and professionals who are interested in social justice issues as they apply to prisons. URL: http://intl-tpj.sagepub.com

1560. ***Probation Journal: the journal of community and criminal justice.*** Formerly (until 1974): *Probation.* [ISSN: 0264-5505] 1929. q. USD 814 (print & online eds.). Ed(s): Emma Cluley. Sage Publications Ltd., 1 Oliver's Yard, 55 City Rd, London, EC1Y 1SP, United Kingdom; info@sagepub.co.uk; http://www.uk.sagepub.com. Adv. Sample. Refereed. Reprint: PSC. *Indexed:* A22, CJPI, E01, RiskAb. *Bk. rev.:* 5-6, signed, 300-600 words. *Aud.:* Ga, Ac, Sa.

Probation Journal: The Journal of Community and Criminal Justice is a peer-reviewed journal published by Sage in association with Napo, a U.K.-based trade union and professional association for family court and probation staff. It was first published in 1929 (by an earlier incarnation of Napo) as a trade magazine. But it has evolved into a quarterly scholarly journal that addresses U.K. and international probation and related issues. Napo, although still involved in the publication of the journal, exercises no editorial control. Because this is a U.K. publication, most of the articles discuss issues directly related to that country, but the research and theory are applicable to an international audience; according to the journal's web site, it now has subscribers in 25 countries. The journal features articles that present the results of quantitative and qualitative research, discuss best practices, and present recent theoretical debates. Each issue also contains book reviews and a column, "In Court," that "reviews recent appeal judgements and other judicial developments that inform sentencing and early release." URL: http://0-prb.sagepub.com

1561. ***Psychology, Crime and Law.*** [ISSN: 1068-316X] 1994. 10x/yr. GBP 725 (print & online eds.). Ed(s): Dr. Theresa Gannon, Brian H Bornstein. Routledge, 4 Park Sq, Milton Park, Abingdon, OX14 4RN, United Kingdom; subscriptions@tandf.co.uk; http://www.tandfonline.com. Adv. Sample. Refereed. Reprint: PSC. *Indexed:* A01, A22, CJPI, E01, IBSS, PsycInfo. *Aud.:* Ac, Sa.

Psychology, Crime & Law is the official journal of the European Association of Psychology and Law (EAPL). Since its release in 1994, the journal's purpose has been "to promote the study and application of psychological approaches to crime, criminal and civil law, and the influence of law on behavior." Articles within this publication explore procedures and individuals of the law process from a psychological standpoint. For example, recent issues include studies of marital breakdown and its impact on criminal behavior and prisoner motivation practices. *Psychology, Crime & Law* is uniquely valuable to special libraries, such as law libraries, but is broad enough in scope that it is beneficial for academic institutions with criminal justice, law, or related programs of study. This publication is available in print as well as online through Taylor & Francis Online, EBSCOhost, and other full-text providers.

1562. ***Punishment & Society: the international journal of penology.*** [ISSN: 1462-4745] 1999. 5x/yr. USD 1073. Ed(s): Dirk van Zyl Smit, Alison Liebling. Sage Publications Ltd., 1 Oliver's Yard, 55 City Rd, London, EC1Y 1SP, United Kingdom; info@sagepub.co.uk; http://www.uk.sagepub.com. Adv. Sample. Refereed. Reprint: PSC. *Indexed:* A01, A22, CJPI, E01, IBSS, P61, RiskAb, SSA. *Bk. rev.:* 4-5, signed, lengthy. *Aud.:* Ac, Sa.

Punishment & Society: The International Journal of Penology is a highly regarded international and interdisciplinary journal that presents research on punishment, penal institutions, and penal control. A typical issue contains five or six articles and a number of scholarly book reviews and review symposiums. Recent articles include an update on a 20-year-old essay that compared the Dutch and British penal systems and found the former more humane; an editorial on mass incarceration; and a comparison of Chinese and American college students' view of the death penalty. This journal is recommended for all academic libraries that serve institutions with criminal justice departments, and related special libraries. It is available in print and online, going back to the first issue in 1999. URL: http://0-pun.sagepub.com

Sexual Abuse. See Psychology section.

1563. Sheriff Magazine. Formerly (until 1991): *National Sheriff;* Which superseded (in 1948): *Sheriffs' Newsletter.* [ISSN: 1070-8170] 19??. bi-m. Free to members; Non-members, USD 30. Ed(s): Susan Crow. National Sheriffs' Association, 1450 Duke St, Alexandria, VA 22314; publications@sheriffs.org; http://www.sheriffs.org/. Illus., adv. Sample. Vol. ends: Nov/Dec. *Indexed:* CJPI. *Aud.:* Ga, Ac, Sa.

Sheriff Magazine is the official publication of the National Sheriff Association (NSA). It is published for its members but also for other law enforcement and corrections officials. Coverage of NSA conferences and other association news is included, along with legislative updates, a calendar of industry events, and training opportunities. Each issue contains a brief biographical sketch entitled "Meet the Sheriff." The magazine's well-written, concise articles discuss successful law enforcement programs, best practices and procedures, and new research in law enforcement. For example, a recent issue contained an article written by an undersecretary from the U.S. Department of Homeland Security on efforts to get local law enforcement involved in national security; and a member of the Los Angeles sheriff department discussed the rights of newly arrested foreign nationals. Each year, usually in the January/February issue, a buyer's guide is included. *Sheriff Magazine* is available in print from the association at www.sheriffs.org/publications/SheriffMagazine.asp. ProQuest's Criminal Justice Periodicals database offers it full-text from volume 50, issue 4 (in 1998); it is indexed back to 1981. This magazine would be a good choice for academic libraries if their institutions offer criminal justice degrees, and for special libraries that serve those in law enforcement.

1564. Theoretical Criminology: an international journal. [ISSN: 1362-4806] 1997. q. USD 1054. Ed(s): Simon A Cole. Sage Publications Ltd., 1 Oliver's Yard, 55 City Rd, London, EC1Y 1SP, United Kingdom; info@sagepub.co.uk; http://www.uk.sagepub.com. Illus. Sample. Refereed. Vol. ends: Nov. Reprint: PSC. *Indexed:* A01, A22, CJPI, E01, IBSS, P02, P61, PsycInfo, RiskAb, SSA. *Bk. rev.:* 5, 1,400 words; signed. *Aud.:* Ac, Sa.

Theoretical Criminology, as the title suggests, looks at the theoretical aspects of criminology. Within that constraint, however, the coverage is interdisciplinary, international, and broad. For example, in a recent issue, a London-based professor of criminology and a colleague in social research looked at "the emergence of the security state as a successor to the liberal welfare state"; and a cultural criminologist looked at the culture of justice through the analysis of stand-up comedy and folk humor. Most issues contain three to six articles and a number of book reviews, usually seven or eight. There are special thematic issues; the latest was titled "Reinventing Penal Parsimony" and looked at what the editor termed an "era of penal excess." This journal is highly regarded by criminal justice scholars (see section introduction for information on selection/ranking criteria). It is recommended for academic libraries and practitioners interested in the subject. It is available in print and online, back to issue 1 in 1997 from Sage. URL: http://0-tcr.sagepub.com

1565. Trauma, Violence & Abuse (Online): a review journal. [ISSN: 1552-8324] 2000. q. USD 537. Ed(s): Jamie Hart, Jon R Conte. Sage Publications, Inc., 2455 Teller Rd, Thousand Oaks, CA 91320; info@sagepub.com; http://www.sagepub.com. Adv. Sample. Refereed. *Aud.:* Ac, Sa.

Trauma, Violence & Abuse (TVA) is a quarterly, peer-reviewed journal that is "devoted to organizing, synthesizing[,] and expanding knowledge on all forms of trauma, violence[,] and abuse." This journal is particularly useful for practitioners, as it is composed of review articles that summarize current practices and subjects of interest in the field. A number of topics are explored in this journal, including sexual abuse, domestic violence, child abuse, and post-traumatic stress disorder. The journal's interdisciplinary scope makes it useful to most academic institutions as well as to professionals in many fields, including criminology, psychiatry, psychology, social work, and law. Unfortunately, *Trauma, Violence & Abuse* ceased to be published in print in 2009, but the journal is still available online through Sage Publications.

1566. Trends and Issues in Crime and Criminal Justice. Incorporates in part (1990-1992): *Homicides in Australia.* [ISSN: 0817-8542] 1986. 20x/yr. Ed(s): Adam Graycar. Australian Institute of Criminology, GPO Box 2944, Canberra, ACT 2601, Australia; aicpress@aic.gov.au; http://www.aic.gov.au. *Indexed:* CJPI. *Aud.:* Ac, Sa.

Trends and Issues in Crime and Criminal Justice is a serial publication of the Australian Institute of Criminology, which is part of the Australian government. The institute publishes and makes freely available several serial publications and other reports, and its offered content and services are similar to that of the United States National Criminal Justice Research Service. The *Trends and Issues* homepage describes the publication as "concise, peer-reviewed papers on criminological topics for policy makers and practitioners." This journal first appeared in 1986, and the papers in the series are numbered, rather than dated per se. For the last few years, 18–20 studies have been published annually. They are data-rich, referenced, and scholarly, but as they are written for a non-academic audience, the language is straightforward and clear. Some recent titles are "Knife crime: Recent data on carriage and use" and "Crime families: Gender and the intergenerational transfer of criminal tendencies." These reports concern crime issues in Australia, but would be of interest to scholars and researchers elsewhere as well. URL: www.aic.gov.au/publications/current%20series/tandi.aspx

1567. Trends in Organized Crime. [ISSN: 1084-4791] 1995. q. EUR 416 (print & online eds.). Ed(s): Klaus Von Lampe. Springer New York LLC, 233 Spring St, New York, NY 10013; service-ny@springer.com; http://www.springer.com. Sample. Reprint: PSC. *Indexed:* A01, A22, ABS&EES, BRI, CJPI, E01, P61, SSA. *Bk. rev.:* 3; signed. *Aud.:* Ac, Sa.

Trends in Organized Crime is published by Springer in association with the International Association for the Study of Organized Crime (IASOC). The organization describes its members as "criminologists, researchers, working professionals, teachers, and students" from 23 countries, including the United States; Canada; major European, Middle Eastern, and Asian countries; South Africa; Australia; New Zealand; and more. The journal, which has been published since 1995, contains original research, essays and commentary, and analyses of current and historical organized-crime issues, along with pertinent reports from national governmental agencies. A recent special issue was devoted to human trafficking. Examples of other topics covered include organized crime in New Zealand; group involvement in the trade of illegal antiquities; and a presentation of a taxonomy of organized-crime groups. Book reviews and listings of related publications are included in each issue. In addition to the association's members, the journal is good resource for interested criminologists, policy makers, and academics.

Violence Against Women. See Gender Studies section.

1568. Women & Criminal Justice. [ISSN: 0897-4454] 1989. q. GBP 468 (print & online eds.). Ed(s): Frances P Bernat. Routledge, 325 Chestnut St, Ste 800, Philadelphia, PA 19106; customerservice@taylorandfrancis.com; http://www.tandfonline.com. Illus., adv. Sample. Refereed. Circ: 397 Paid. Vol. ends: No. 2. Microform: PQC. Reprint: PSC. *Indexed:* A22, BRI, C42, CJPI, E01, FemPer, GW, P61, SSA, WSA. *Bk. rev.:* 5-10, 500-1,500 words. *Aud.:* Ac, Sa.

Women & Criminal Justice is an international and interdisciplinary journal that covers all aspects of the intersection of women and criminal justice, be the women victims, professionals, or offenders. The articles present the results of qualitative and quantitative research, or are theoretical studies. Contributors are academics and professionals from the disciplines of women's studies, sociology, social work, criminal justice, law, and human rights. This title is published quarterly by Routledge, but with some irregularity. There are frequently double issues, and no issues were published in 2008. However, there were four issues in 2009, and the journal appears to have fully resumed publication. It is available from the publisher in print and online, and the full text is offered through EBSCOhost with a one-year embargo. This journal would be of interest to criminologists, sociologists, and those in gender studies. Readers should also consider *Feminist Criminology,* reviewed in this section.

■ CULTURAL STUDIES

See also History; Literature; and Political Science sections.

Vanette M. Schwartz, Social Sciences Librarian, 8900 Milner Library, Illinois State University, Normal, IL 6l790-8900; vmschwa@ilstu.edu

Introduction

The field of Cultural Studies is continually expanding into ever more diverse areas. Research, theories, and writing in Cultural Studies reflect the range of social sciences and humanities disciplines. Publications in Cultural Studies are inherently interdisciplinary and international, and include issues of race, class, and gender.

Many Cultural Studies journals blend philosophy, history, politics, and literature with social issues; others emphasize popular culture and future studies. Several publications focus on aesthetics, the arts, and criticism. Still others concentrate on a region of the world, on urban areas, or on specific populations such as children and young adults. Electronic Cultural Studies journals also offer varied formats, including an increasing number of photos, film clips, musical excerpts, and computer graphics. The open-access trend has broadened the spectrum of Cultural Studies literature by providing new avenues for scholars and students. The journal literature of Cultural Studies offers a unique combination of theoretical, philosophical, and critical writing for the academic community as well as for the general public.

Basic Periodicals

Hs: *The Futurist;* Ga: *The Futurist, Humanities, Journal of Popular Culture;* Ac: *American Quarterly, Critical Inquiry, Humanities, Journal of Popular Culture, Social Science Quarterly.*

Basic Abstracts and Indexes

America: History and Life, Humanities International Complete, MLA International Bibliography, PAIS International, SOCIndex, Sociological Abstracts.

1569. American Quarterly. [ISSN: 0003-0678] 1949. q. USD 170. Ed(s): Jih-Fei Cheng, Sarah Banet-Weiser. The Johns Hopkins University Press, 2715 N Charles St, Baltimore, MD 21218; http://www.press.jhu.edu. Illus., index, adv. Sample. Refereed. Circ: 4513. Vol. ends: Dec (No. 4). Microform: PQC. Reprint: PSC. *Indexed:* A01, A06, A22, AmHI, ArtHuCI, BAS, BEL&L, BRI, CBRI, Chicano, E01, F01, MLA-IB, P02, P61, RILM, SSA. *Bk. rev.:* 5-8, essay length. *Aud.:* Ac.

With a publication history spanning more than 60 years, this journal is unquestionably the premier publication in the field of American Studies. *American Quarterly* publishes lengthy research articles and review essays on American culture. Recent articles cover such topics as occupied Okinawa and U.S. colonialism; public narratives of voodoo in New Orleans; speculative freedom in colonial Liberia; academia and activism; and visual culture and the war on terror. In addition to book reviews, event reviews appear in most issues, covering art exhibitions and film festivals. Special issues are published each September, focusing on themes such as race, empire, and the crisis of the subprime; or sound clash—listening to American studies. This journal covers the activities of the American Studies Association, and serves as the major avenue of scholarship in the discipline.

1570. American Studies. Former titles (until 1971): *Midcontinent American Studies Journal;* (until 1962): *Central Mississippi Valley American Studies Association. Journal;* (until 1960): *Central Mississippi Valley American Studies Association. Bulletin;* Incorporates (1975-2004): *American Studies International;* Which was formerly (until 1975): *American Studies;* (until 1970): *American Studies News;* American Studies International Incorporated (1983-1996): *American Studies International Newsletter.* [ISSN: 0026-3079] 1957. q. USD 50 (Individuals, USD 35). Ed(s): David Katzman, Randal M Jelks. University of Kansas, American Studies Department, 213 Bailey Hall, Lawrence, KS 66045; amerst@ku.edu; http://americanstudies.ku.edu. Illus., index, adv. Refereed. Circ: 1200 Paid. Vol. ends: No. 3. Microform: PQC. *Indexed:* A01, A22, AmHI, BRI, E01, MLA-IB, P02, RILM. *Bk. rev.:* 10-45, 400-500 words, in some issues. *Aud.:* Ga, Ac.

The focus of *American Studies* is on broadly-based research on U.S. cultures and histories. Research articles on U.S. literature and the arts, politics, social issues, and popular culture are the foundation of this journal. Recent articles explore such topics as domestic novels of the 1920s, direct-action politics and U.S. punk collectives, technology and people with disabilities, and identity jokes. Some issues are devoted to a single theme, such as "Indigeneity at the Crossroads of American Studies." Review essays and book reviews appear in most issues. The Mid-America American Studies Association, the University of Kansas College of Liberal Arts and Sciences, and the Department of American Studies and the KU Libraries jointly sponsor *American Studies.* The aim of this journal is to be cross-disciplinary and to widen the field of American Studies discourse, including international and transnational coverage. Both specialists and nonspecialists will find engaging articles here.

1571. Atlantic Studies: literary, cultural and historical perspectives. [ISSN: 1478-8810] 2004. q. GBP 473 (print & online eds.). Routledge, 4 Park Sq, Milton Park, Abingdon, OX14 4RN, United Kingdom; subscriptions@tandf.co.uk; http://www.tandfonline.com. Adv. Sample. Refereed. Reprint: PSC. *Indexed:* A22, AmHI, E01, IBSS, MLA-IB. *Aud.:* Ac.

This international journal brings together scholarship on the cultures and societies of the overall Atlantic world, in particular the countries of Africa, the Americas, and Europe. It deals primarily with the areas of history and literature, along with cultural studies and critical theory, and includes both research studies and debate on current issues. *Atlantic Studies* is the official journal of the Society for Multi-Ethnic Studies: Europe and the Americas. Articles in recent issues cover topics such as oceanic studies, French Atlantic studies; memorializing the slave trade, the ruins of Havana; and the fall of the planter class. The diasporic, historical, and literary studies of ethnic groups in the Atlantic region form the basis for the writing in this journal. Recommended for academic libraries with an emphasis on this region.

Behaviour and Information Technology. See Psychology section.

1572. Body & Society. [ISSN: 1357-034X] 1995. q. USD 1051. Ed(s): Mike Featherstone, Tomoko Tamari. Sage Publications Ltd., 1 Oliver's Yard, 55 City Rd, London, EC1Y 1SP, United Kingdom; info@sagepub.co.uk; http://www.uk.sagepub.com. Adv. Sample. Refereed. Reprint: PSC. *Indexed:* A01, A22, E01, IBSS, P61, SSA. *Bk. rev.:* Occasional, 1-4 reviews, 500-1,000 words. *Aud.:* Ac.

This heavily theoretical publication covers disciplines from art and cultural history to health studies, sociology, and philosophy. Focusing on the social and cultural analysis of the human body, articles in this journal center on issues of feminism, technology, ecology, postmodernism, medicine, ethics, and consumerism. The Theory, Culture and Society Centre at Nottingham Trent University sponsors this journal, along with its joint publication, *Theory, Culture and Society.* Recent articles in *Body and Society* cover such topics as gender and healthy bodies, obesity, cosmetic surgery, medical tourism and the body, and affect studies. Special issues are also published on topics such as medicine, bodies and politics, and animation and automation. For scholars interested in a wide-ranging combination of theory, society, culture, and science.

1573. Cabinet. [ISSN: 1531-1430] 2000. q. USD 38 (Individuals, USD 32). Ed(s): Sina Najafi, Christopher Turner. Immaterial Incorporated, 181 Wyckoff St, Brooklyn, NY 11217. *Indexed:* A51, MLA-IB. *Aud.:* Ga, Ac.

The focus of *Cabinet* is the "margins of culture." An incredibly wide-ranging magazine, this publication covers primarily art and culture, but combines many other aspects in the mix. Both international and interdisciplinary, each issue contains regular columns and essays along with interviews, photography, works of art, and postcards. Issues begin with regular columns on "Colors," "Ingestion," and "Inventory," "Legend," and "Leftovers." The main section includes both articles and art projects ranging from crowd dynamics to cryptanalysis, and from political murals to social networking. A thematic section is featured in each issue on subjects such as trees, logistics, punishment and games. Contributors range from academics to freelance writers, artists, filmmakers, sound designers, and musicians. The magazine's web site contains a table of contents and information on contributors, along with additional readings, artwork, soundtracks, and musical works. This award-winning publication provides fascinating reading, along with engaging art and photography.

1574. Canadian Review of American Studies. Formerly (until 1970): *C A A S Bulletin*. [ISSN: 0007-7720] 1965. 3x/yr. USD 155. Ed(s): Priscilla L Walton. University of Toronto Press, Journals Division, 5201 Dufferin St, Toronto, ON M3H 5T8, Canada; journals@utpress.utoronto.ca; http://www.utpjournals.com. Illus., index, adv. Sample. Refereed. Circ: 289. Vol. ends: No. 3. *Indexed:* A01, A22, AmHI, ArtHuCI, CBCARef, E01, MLA-IB, P61, RILM, SSA. *Bk. rev.:* 2-3, 1,000-1,500 words. *Aud.:* Ac.

American culture from the perspective of our northern neighbors is the focus of this publication by the Canadian Association for American Studies, supported by Carleton University in Ottawa. This journal emphasizes cross-disciplinary studies of U.S. culture from both historical and contemporary perspectives. It also includes articles on the relationship between U.S. and Canadian cultures. Each issue includes research articles and review essays written primarily by Canadian academics, with some content by U.S. and international scholars. Many articles focus on literary works or films, while others explore social and cultural issues. Recent articles cover such topics as American antiwar poetry, tipping-point discourse, 9/11 and national states of emergency, and America's twenty-first-century economic agenda. Special issues are published occasionally on topics such as the politics of culture wars. Libraries with an emphasis on American Studies scholarship from varying viewpoints will want to include this journal in their collection.

1575. City, Culture and Society. [ISSN: 1877-9166] 2010. q. EUR 479. Ed(s): Masayuki Sasaki. Elsevier Ltd, The Boulevard, Langford Lane, Oxford, OX5 1GB, United Kingdom; journalscustomerserviceemea@elsevier.com; http://www.elsevier.com. *Indexed:* P61, SSA. *Aud.:* Ac.

With more than half the world's population currently living in cities, the study of urban areas has become increasingly important. The new publication *City, Culture and Society* focuses on "urban governance in the 21st century." The journal covers topics such as urban economics, sustainability, cultural technology, and social inclusion. International in scope, the journal has editorial board members from Europe, the Far East, Australia, the U.K., and the U.S. Each issue includes several original articles, with some issues covering a specific theme such as cultural heritage, urban sports facilities, poverty and homelessness, or the creative economy of cities. Other articles focus on a particular city such as Osaka, Japan, Haifa, Israel, or Melbourne, Australia. This journal will primarily interest academic libraries, but may also appeal to large public libraries.

1576. Communication, Culture & Critique. [ISSN: 1753-9129] 2008. q. GBP 694 Free to members. Ed(s): John Downing. Wiley-Blackwell Publishing Ltd., 9600 Garsington Rd, Oxford, OX4 2DQ, United Kingdom; customer@wiley.co.uk; http://www.wiley.com/. Reprint: PSC. *Indexed:* A22, E01. *Bk. rev.:* 1-2 in some issues; 2-3 pages in length. *Aud.:* Ac.

The International Communication Association developed this title as a complement to its four other journals. The editors aim to "provide an international forum for critical, interpretive, and qualitative research examining the role of communication and cultural criticism in today's world." Original research articles comprise the bulk of each issue, with review essays and commentary included occasionally. Article content varies from popular topics such as social networking and activist movements to more scholarly subjects, including conceptualizing journalistic criticism and the interview in audience research. Although many articles deal with the United States, some articles provide more international coverage of subjects, such as Finnish television culture or Brazilian music. This journal will be of interest to researchers and students in many areas of communication, as well as cultural studies in general.

1577. Comparative American Studies. [ISSN: 1477-5700] 2003. q. GBP 494 (print & online eds.). Ed(s): Nick Selby. Maney Publishing, Ste 1C, Joseph's Well, Hanover Walk, Leeds, LS3 1AB, United Kingdom; maney@maneypublishing.com; http://maneypublishing.com/. Adv. Refereed. Reprint: PSC. *Indexed:* A22, AmHI, E01, IBSS, MLA-IB, P61, SSA. *Bk. rev.:* 2-6 reviews, essay length. *Aud.:* Ac.

Scholarship on American Studies from outside the United States is the focus of *Comparative American Studies*. The journal aims to place the discourse on American culture in an international framework. With the contemporary focus on globalization and on the relationship between the United States and other nations, *Comparative American Studies* seeks to draw out the conflicts and common themes, especially in the areas of literature, film, popular culture, photography, and visual arts. Each issue contains six to eight articles on topics such as the presidency of Barack Obama, comparative border studies, and influence in American literature. Some articles cover comparative themes in the works of U.S., Canadian, and Latin American writers and artists. Since its beginning in 2003, this journal has filled a major gap in the literature of American Studies by providing a much-needed international viewpoint.

1578. Critical Discourse Studies: an interdisciplinary journal for the social sciences. [ISSN: 1740-5904] 2004. q. GBP 430 (print & online eds.). Ed(s): John E Richardson. Routledge, 4 Park Sq, Milton Park, Abingdon, OX14 4RN, United Kingdom; subscriptions@tandf.co.uk; http://www.tandfonline.com. Adv. Sample. Refereed. Reprint: PSC. *Indexed:* A22, AmHI, E01, IBSS, MLA-IB, P61, SSA. *Bk. rev.:* 2-3, 500-1,000 words. *Aud.:* Ac.

Reaching far beyond language and linguistic studies, this publication has something for every discipline in the social sciences, as well as literary and media studies and racial, ethnic, and gender studies. This journal aims to "publish critical research that advances our understanding of how discourse figures into social processes, social structures[,] and social change." Connecting academic research with discussion of practical and activist approaches is an additional goal of *Critical Discourse Studies*. Recent articles cover such topics as genealogy and discourse analysis in conversation, newspaper Op/Ed debates, the language of paramilitary groups, and neoliberalism as discourse. The final issue of the year concentrates on a specific topic such as critical analysis of musical discourse, or ethnography and critical discourse analysis. Each issue is primarily composed of original articles, with a few book reviews in many issues. This journal enhances the range of scholarship on critical discourse, a vital and expanding area of interdisciplinary study.

1579. Critical Inquiry. [ISSN: 0093-1896] 1974. q. USD 279 (print & online eds.). Ed(s): James W Williams, W J T Mitchell. University of Chicago Press, 1427 E 60th St, Chicago, IL 60637; subscriptions@press.uchicago.edu; http://www.journals.uchicago.edu. Illus., index. Sample. Refereed. Vol. ends: Summer. Microform: PMC; PQC. Reprint: PSC. *Indexed:* A01, A22, A51, ABS&EES, AmHI, ArtHuCI, BEL&L, BRI, MLA-IB, P02, P61, RILM, SSA. *Aud.:* Ac.

For nearly 40 years, *Critical Inquiry* has set the standard for publishing interdisciplinary criticism in the arts and humanities. Each issue includes several articles on topics from the arts, philosophy, literature, film, history, politics, and social issues. Some volumes include a special section or issue on a single topic such as the Occupy movement or photography as art. Recent issues include articles on such subjects as early video art, a colonial history of comparative literature, the genesis of iconology, and philology in literary and cultural studies. Most issues contain several original articles, along with critical responses to previous articles. A list of "Books of Critical Interest" is also in most issues. This journal provides a forum for both traditional and currently developing areas of criticism. In *Critical Inquiry,* authors engage in theoretical debate and spar in critical responses. A significant journal for most academic libraries.

1580. Critical Review (Philadelphia): a journal of politics and society. [ISSN: 0891-3811] 1987. q. GBP 293 (print & online eds.). Ed(s): Jeffrey Friedman. Routledge, 325 Chestnut St, Ste 800, Philadelphia, PA 19106; customerservice@taylorandfrancis.com; http://www.tandfonline.com. Illus., index. Sample. Refereed. Vol. ends: Fall. Microform: PQC. Reprint: PSC. *Indexed:* A22, ABIn, BRI, E01, EconLit, IBSS, JEL, P61, SSA. *Bk. rev.:* 1-3, review essays in some issues. *Aud.:* Ac.

This journal will interest academics in all areas of the social sciences, especially political scientists and economists. *Critical Review* focuses on political theory, while also including articles on political psychology, political economy, and public opinion. Contributors are primarily from U.S. academic circles, with a few authors from other countries. Articles are theoretical or historical but do not advocate or criticize proposed policies. Each issue concentrates on a particular theme, such as political dogmatism, capitalism and economics after the crisis, and deliberative democracy. Each issue contains several research articles or essays that are well written and extensively documented. Articles explore topics such as belief systems, media bias, and critical realism. One or more review essays are included in most issues. This journal presents lively writing and debate on major political, economic, and social ideas.

1581. Cross-Cultural Research: the journal of comparative social science. Former titles (until 1993): *Behavior Science Research;* (until 1974): *Behavior Science Notes.* [ISSN: 1069-3971] 1966. q. USD 728. Ed(s): Carol R Ember. Sage Publications, Inc., 2455 Teller Rd, Thousand Oaks, CA 91320; info@sagepub.com; http://www.sagepub.com. Illus., index, adv. Sample. Refereed. Vol. ends: Nov. Microform: PQC. Reprint: PSC. *Indexed:* A01, A22, A47, ABIn, ABS&EES, BAS, E01, FR, IBSS, MLA-IB, P02, P61, PsycInfo, RiskAb, SSA. *Aud.:* Ac.

Cross-Cultural Research aims to publish comparative studies in many areas of the social and behavioral sciences from anthropology, psychology, and sociology to political science, economics, human ecology, and evolutionary biology. The journal stresses the methodology of the research, and requires that articles include statistical measures linking dependent and independent variables. Recent articles have covered such topics as masculine gender role stress, romantic relationships, national culture, cross-national perspectives on suicide, marriage transactions, uncertainty in religious beliefs, and adaptation to societal differences in intelligence. Occasional special issues are published on such themes as evolutionary approaches to cross-cultural anthropology, workaholism, or behavioral control of school-age youth. The journal is sponsored by Human Relations Area Files, Inc., and is the official journal of the Society for Cross-Cultural Research. Scholars in many areas of the social sciences will find this publication valuable for its analysis and range of coverage.

1582. Cultural & Social History. [ISSN: 1478-0038] 2004. q. USD 444 (print & online eds.). Ed(s): John Arnold, David Nash. Bloomsbury Publishing plc, 50 Bedford Sq, London, WC1B 3DP, United Kingdom; contact@bloomsbury.com; http://www.bloomsbury.com. Illus., adv. Sample. Refereed. Reprint: PSC. *Indexed:* A22, ArtHuCI, BRI, E01, P61, SSA. *Bk. rev.:* 10-12, essay length. *Aud.:* Ac.

This journal is sponsored by the Social History Society and based in the United Kingdom. The purpose of this publication is to blend the historical study of culture and society beyond the traditional borders of these two areas of history. Although many articles focus on aspects of British or Irish history, the journal also has international coverage, including recent articles on Latin America, China, and India. Most contributors are from Britain, the United States, or Western Europe. Each issue includes research articles and other features such as a debate forum, review essays, and several individual book reviews. Articles cover such topics as gender and civility in early modern London, Chinese–Russian relations, teenagers in postwar Britain, army life in World War I, and consumer activism during the New Deal. By interweaving the cultural and social aspects of historical research, this journal is keeping pace with disciplinary trends. *Cultural & Social History* will be of interest to scholars and students in history and related areas such as literature, art, and cultural studies.

1583. Cultural Critique (Minneapolis, 1985): an international journal of cultural studies. [ISSN: 0882-4371] 1985. 3x/yr. USD 78 (Individuals, USD 30). Ed(s): John Mowitt, Simona Sawhney. University of Minnesota Press, Ste 290, 111 Third Ave S, Minneapolis, MN 55401; ump@umn.edu; http://www.upress.umn.edu. Illus., index, adv. Sample. Refereed. Vol. ends: Oct. *Indexed:* A22, ABS&EES, AmHI, ArtHuCI, BRI, E01, IBSS, MLA-IB, RILM. *Aud.:* Ac.

This journal focuses on analysis, interpretation, and debate of culture in the broadest sense. An international and interdisciplinary publication, *Cultural Critique* deals with aspects of culture from the political and economic to the ethical and artistic. Most contributors are scholars from U.S. institutions, although some international writers and researchers are included. Most issues are devoted to a single topic or a few main subjects. Some articles involve literary criticism, while others focus on sociological, anthropological, and philosophical issues. Both historical topics and contemporary social and aesthetic studies are included. Recent articles cover such subjects as financial crisis, human machines, and memories of historical trauma. *Cultural Critique* will appeal to scholars in literature, film, politics, media, art, and sociology.

1584. Cultural History. [ISSN: 2045-290X] 2012. s-a. GBP 63.50 (print & online eds.). Ed(s): Marjo Kaartinen, Kristine Steenbergh. Edinburgh University Press Ltd., 22 George Sq, Edinburgh, EH8 9LF, United Kingdom; journals@eup.ed.ac.uk; http://www.euppublishing.com. Refereed. *Bk. rev.:* Number and length vary. *Aud.:* Ac.

The International Society for Cultural History was established in 2008, with the organization's journal beginning in 2012. The aim of this publication is to serve as a forum for discussion and debate about the theory, methods, issues, and trends in this field of history. The journal is international in scope, although most authors and editorial board members are from Europe, Scandinavia, and the U.S. Each issue includes several research articles on topics such as Kipling and Buddhism; the needle trades in eighteenth-century European towns; women and cultural citizenship in nineteenth-century New Zealand; and attitudes toward collecting scientific artifacts in nineteenth-century England. Other articles on "cultural history—now" cover subjects including the entertainment age, and the difficulties and possibilities of cultural history. Each issue also includes several reviews, of different types; review essays discuss a group of books on a specific topic such as the history of emotions, while individual books are reviewed in both lengthy essays as well as in brief reviews. *Cultural History* provides a new venue of international writing for historians as well as for scholars in museums, galleries, and archives.

1585. Cultural Politics. [ISSN: 1743-2197] 2005. 3x/yr. USD 324. Duke University Press, 905 W Main St, Ste 18 B, PO Box 90660, Durham, NC 27701; subscriptions@dukeupress.edu; http://www.dukeupress.edu. Adv. Sample. Refereed. Reprint: PSC. *Indexed:* BRI, IBSS, MLA-IB, P61, SSA. *Bk. rev.:* 2 in some issues; 4-5 pages in length. *Aud.:* Ac.

In a contemporary world that links politics with virtually every aspect of society, this journal explores "what is cultural about politics and what is political about culture." Each issue consists of four to six articles on topics such as secrecy and transparency in U.S. politics, urban homelessness, assessing a revolution, and class struggle in film theory. Occasional special issues focus on an individual theme such as nuclear stories or the cultural politics of celebrity. The writing links philosophical and political discussions with literary works, performance media, and current online communication. The articles are engaging and provide a unique approach to the integration of culture with contemporary local, national, and transnational political issues. This journal will interest academics and students, especially in political science, but also in related areas of the social sciences, humanities, and fine arts.

1586. Cultural Sociology. [ISSN: 1749-9755] 2007. q. USD 725. Ed(s): David Inglis, Andrew Blaikie. Sage Publications Ltd., 1 Oliver's Yard, 55 City Rd, London, EC1Y 1SP, United Kingdom; info@sagepub.co.uk; http://www.uk.sagepub.com. Adv. Sample. Refereed. Reprint: PSC. *Indexed:* A22, E01, IBSS, MLA-IB, P61, SSA. *Bk. rev.:* 4-5, essay length. *Aud.:* Ac.

This journal merges the fields of sociology and cultural studies into a specialized publication. An official publication of the British Sociological Association, *Cultural Sociology* aims to "consolidate, develop[,] and promote the arena of sociological understandings of culture." The editors and contributors are primarily from universities in the United Kingdom, with some from the United States and Europe; however, the journal deals with sociology and culture internationally. Articles cover such topics as the sociology of perception, celebrity culture, popular music in the U.S. and Europe, and folk art and political power. Although scholarship in culture and sociology has been published in many other types of journals, this publication provides a gathering place for research and discourse in this expanding area. Scholars in sociology, cultural studies, gender studies, post-colonial studies, art history, history, and literary and film studies will find this journal of great interest.

1587. Cultural Studies. Formerly (until 1987): *Australian Journal of Cultural Studies.* [ISSN: 0950-2386] 1983. bi-m. GBP 639 (print & online eds.). Ed(s): Sindhu Zagoren, Lawrence Grossberg. Routledge, 4 Park Sq, Milton Park, Abingdon, OX14 4RN, United Kingdom; book.orders@tandf.co.uk; http://www.tandfonline.com. Illus., adv. Sample. Refereed. Vol. ends: Oct. *Indexed:* A01, A22, AmHI, ArtHuCI, BRI, C45, Chicano, E01, FR, IBSS, MLA-IB, P61, RILM, RRTA, SSA. *Bk. rev.:* 2-6; essay length. *Aud.:* Ac.

For over 25 years, *Cultural Studies* has consistently sought to be on the cutting edge of writing in this interdisciplinary area. Its aim is to "explore the relation between cultural practices, everyday life, material, economic, political, geographical and historical contexts." This journal emphasizes race, class, and gender, while addressing major questions of community, identity, agency, and change. Contributors are mainly from the United States, the United Kingdom, and Australia, with occasional articles by authors from other countries. Each issue contains several original articles, with book reviews included in some issues. Frequently, special issues concentrate on single themes such as transnationalism, the economic crisis, cultural studies in Ireland, and education and cultural studies. Articles have explored such topics as choosing to use drugs, celebrities and branding, developmentally disabled artists, and gender performance. *Cultural Studies* will be of interest to scholars and students seeking dynamic, international coverage of cultural issues.

1588. Cultural Studies - Critical Methodologies. [ISSN: 1532-7086] 2001. bi-m. USD 827. Ed(s): Norman K Denzin. Sage Publications, Inc., 2455 Teller Rd, Thousand Oaks, CA 91320; info@sagepub.com; http://www.sagepub.com. Adv. Sample. Refereed. Reprint: PSC. *Indexed:* A01, A22, AmHI, E01, IBSS, P61, SSA. *Aud.:* Ac.

While other titles concentrate on the wider range of cultural studies or the specific area of cultural critique, this journal combines both, with an emphasis on methodology. Such issues as "local and global, text and context, voice, writing for the other, and the presence of the author in the text" are the underlying focus of many contributions to this journal. Each issue is composed of several original articles on topics such as extremist group narratives; reflexivity; ethnographic choice; food as power; and music and performance studies. Analysis of popular culture, media, and new technologies is also integral to the writing in this publication. *Cultural Studies—Critical Methodologies* blends methodology with the full expanse of cultural studies and cultural critique to make a vital and engaging addition to the literature in this interdisciplinary field.

1589. Culture Unbound: journal of current cultural research. [ISSN: 2000-1525] 2009. irreg. Free. Linkoeping University Electronic Press, Linkoeping Universitet, Linkoeping, 58183, Sweden; ep@ep.liu.se; http://www.ep.liu.se. Refereed. *Bk. rev.:* Occasional. *Aud.:* Ac.

Based in Sweden, this journal combines scholarship from the academic units of the Advanced Cultural Studies Institute, the Swedish Cultural Policy Research Observatory, and the Department of Culture Studies at Linkoeping University. The aim of this publication is to offer "border-crossing cultural research, including cultural studies as well as other interdisciplinary and transnational currents." Each annual issue includes thematic sections, along with individual articles and occasional book reviews. Thematic sections range from signs of the city to literary public spheres, and from rural media spaces to fashion, market, and materiality. Other articles focus on topics such as digital media and the order of ethnography; foodscapes and children's bodies; and Ramadan in Istanbul. Contributors are primarily Swedish, European, and U.S. scholars. This open-access journal provides an international forum for cultural research and scholarship.

1590. Futures: the journal of policy, planning and futures studies. [ISSN: 0016-3287] 1968. 10x/yr. EUR 1447. Ed(s): T Fuller. Pergamon, The Blvd, Langford Ln, E Park, Kidlington, OX5 1GB, United Kingdom; JournalsCustomerServiceEMEA@elsevier.com; http://www.elsevier.com. Illus., adv. Sample. Refereed. Microform: PQC. *Indexed:* A22, ABIn, BRI, C45, ISTA, MLA-IB, P02, P61, RRTA, RiskAb, SSA. *Bk. rev.:* 2-4, 500-1,500 words. *Aud.:* Ac, Sa.

This journal covers future studies from a cultural, social, scientific, economic, political, and environmental perspective. *Futures* has an international advisory board, but authors are mainly from the United States and the United Kingdom, with some from other countries. The papers that begin each issue cover such subjects as portable fuel cells, the fine-art market, consumer education, and foresight and sustainability. Many volumes include special issues on such themes as community engagement, technology analysis, international business, global mindset change, and landscape visions. Shorter review articles, essays, and reports are included along with book reviews. *Futures* aims "to examine possible and alternative futures of all human endeavors." This journal will appeal to scholars in the sciences and social sciences and to members of the business and government communities.

1591. The Futurist: a journal of forecasts, trends, and ideas about the future. [ISSN: 0016-3317] 1967. bi-m. Free to members. Ed(s): Cynthia G Wagner, Edward S Cornish. World Future Society, 7910 Woodmont Ave, Ste 450, Bethesda, MD 20814; info@wfs.org; http://www.wfs.org/. Illus., index, adv. Sample. Vol. ends: Dec. Microform: PQC. *Indexed:* A01, A22, ABIn, AgeL, B01, B02, BRI, C37, CBRI, Chicano, EIP, MASUSE, P02, SWR&A. *Bk. rev.:* 1-3, 400-1,000 words. *Aud.:* Hs, Ga, Ac.

The World Future Society is perhaps the leading organization in future studies. For over 40 years, the society's popular publication, *The Futurist,* has been publishing articles and reports on many aspects of this interdisciplinary area. Each issue includes several engaging articles on such topics as technology's role in revolutions, solar power from the moon, imagineering, and personalized learning. Articles are written by noted researchers and writers in the field. The "World Trends and Forecasts" section offers brief reports in a variety of categories, including climate change, crime, health, and computing, as well as energy, cities, work, and governance. "Tomorrow in Brief" presents news items gleaned from government, university, and research institute web sites. The December issue includes an outlook section compiling forecasts for the coming year. This magazine will appeal to a range of readers from the general public to students at many levels.

Gender & Society. See Gender Studies section.

1592. History of the Human Sciences. [ISSN: 0952-6951] 1988. 5x/yr. USD 1559. Ed(s): James Good. Sage Publications Ltd., 1 Oliver's Yard, 55 City Rd, London, EC1Y 1SP, United Kingdom; info@sagepub.co.uk; http://www.uk.sagepub.com. Illus., index, adv. Sample. Refereed. Reprint: PSC. *Indexed:* A01, A22, AmHI, ArtHuCI, BRI, E01, IBSS, IPB, MLA-IB, P02, P61, PsycInfo, SSA. *Bk. rev.:* 1-2, essay length. *Aud.:* Ac.

Based on a broad definition of the human sciences, this publication offers a range of scholarly articles that link research from traditional social science disciplines including sociology, psychology, anthropology, and political science with the areas of philosophy, literary criticism, art history, linguistics, psychoanalysis, aesthetics, and law. Some issues focus on one theme, such as histories of science; the history of the science of consciousness; and neuroscience, power, and culture. Other issues cover a variety of topics, such as the therapeutic value of work; alienation theory; linguistics in the Cold War years; medicine and the history of sociology; and revisionism and meta-history. Reviews of individual books as well as review essays appear regularly. Most contributors are academics from British, European, and U.S. institutions. This journal will appeal to scholars and advanced students who are interested in the complex relationships between social science and humanities research.

1593. Humanities: the magazine of the national endowment for the humanities. [ISSN: 0018-7526] 1980. bi-m. USD 24 domestic; USD 33.60 foreign; USD 9 per issue domestic. U.S. National Endowment for the Humanities, 1100 Pennsylvania Ave, N W, Washington, DC 20506; info@neh.gov; http://www.neh.gov. Illus., index. Sample. Vol. ends: Nov/Dec. Microform: PQC. *Indexed:* A01, A07, A22, AmHI, C45, MASUSE, RILM. *Aud.:* Hs, Ga, Ac.

This publication reports on the activities and projects sponsored by the U.S. government's National Endowment for the Humanities (NEH). *Humanities* includes articles on history, literature, music, art, film, theater, and photography. Contributors are academics, freelance writers, and NEH staffers and administrators. Articles include such items as world's fairs during the Depression; a documentary on the freedom riders; the history of books and publishing; and the Popular Front and American culture. Specialized sections appear in many issues. "Statements" describes exhibits and programs sponsored by state humanities councils; and "In Focus" profiles various state leaders. "Curio" offers brief descriptions of NEH-funded publications and projects, while "Impertinent Questions" interviews authors and curators. This publication includes engaging, well-illustrated articles that will appeal to general readers, and offers information for scholars interested in obtaining NEH funding.

1594. *International Journal of Politics, Culture, and Society.* Formerly (until 1987): *State, Culture, and Society.* [ISSN: 0891-4486] 1984. q. EUR 1013 (print & online eds.). Ed(s): Elzbieta Matynia, Vera Zolberg. Springer New York LLC, 233 Spring St, New York, NY 10013; service-ny@springer.com; http://www.springer.com/. Illus., index, adv. Sample. Refereed. Vol. ends: Summer. Microform: PQC. Reprint: PSC. *Indexed:* A01, A22, BRI, E01, IBSS, P61, RiskAb, SSA, SWR&A. *Bk. rev.:* Essay length, in some issues. *Aud.:* Ac.

Scholarship derived from the "intersection of nations, states, civil societies, and global institutions and processes" forms the basis for this journal. Each issue includes essays and research articles on global and regional political issues, ethnic and religious groups, and social transformation and cultural changes as they impact societies in general. Recent articles cover issues such as the end of the nation-state; a French–American perspective on the arts and politics; and the future of democracy after 1989. Essay-length book reviews, or a review and commentary section, are included in some issues. The journal's editorial board is centered at the New School for Social Research, but contributors are drawn from many countries. Articles frequently cover political and social issues in the context of a particular nation or region. This publication will appeal to social scientists and scholars interested in societal change, especially as it relates to international political and cultural issues.

1595. *International Review of Social History.* Formerly (until 1956): *International Institute for Social History. Bulletin.* [ISSN: 0020-8590] 1937. 3x/yr. GBP 183. Ed(s): Aad Blok. Cambridge University Press, The Edinburgh Bldg, Shaftesbury Rd, Cambridge, CB2 8RU, United Kingdom; journals@cambridge.org; http://www.cambridge.org/uk. Adv. Refereed. Circ: 1200. Microform: PQC. Reprint: PSC. *Indexed:* A22, ABIn, ArtHuCI, BRI, E01, IBSS, MLA-IB, P02, P61, SSA. *Bk. rev.:* 8-12, 1,000 words, some essay length. *Aud.:* Ac.

For over 70 years, this journal has published much of the leading scholarship in social history. The International Institute for Social History, based in the Netherlands, sponsors the journal. Contributors are mainly from American and British institutions, with some from European countries. The research articles that begin each issue cover a range of countries, usually Britain, the United States, or European states, but also Africa, Israel, and Australia. Many articles explore issues of workers' groups and labor history, but other topics from transnational radicals to labor courts, and from worldwide migration and social class to refugees and rebel armies, are also included. Articles are in English, with occasional reviews in French or German. The extensive annotated bibliography of books on many aspects of social history is a vital section of this journal. Covering some 30 pages, the bibliography begins with a general section and is then subdivided by continent and country. The annual supplement is another strength of the journal; this special issue draws together articles on a major theme such as labor and work ethic in the fourteenth and fifteenth centuries, or current issues of globalization and environmental change and their impact on social history. The journal will appeal to historians and social scientists, especially scholars with an interest in labor history.

1596. *Jeunesse: Young People, Texts, Cultures.* Formerly (until 2009): *Canadian Children's Literature/Litterature Canadienne pour la Jeunesse.* [ISSN: 1920-2601] 1975. s-a. CAD 75. Ed(s): Larissa Wodtke. University of Winnipeg, Centre for Research in Young People's Texts and Culture, 515 Portage Ave, Winnipeg, MB R3B 2E9, Canada. Refereed. *Indexed:* A22, BRI, C37, CBCARef, CBRI, E01, MLA-IB. *Bk. rev.:* Review essays, 3-10 per issue. *Aud.:* Ac.

The aim of this journal is to provide scholarly articles on "cultural productions for, by, and about young people." Both interdisciplinary and international, *Jeunesse* publishes articles in English and French. This publication covers children's and young adult literature, art, and film, including material and digital culture focusing on the roles of "the child." Each issue has four or five articles on subjects ranging from themes in picture books, children's book series, and baby books to haunted doll houses and Disney's princess web site. One issue per year also includes a forum with divergent views on a common topic such as globalization, participation, and approaches to childhood studies. Each issue also includes lengthy review essays on one or more works, covering topics such as multiculturalism or the role of the outsider in Canadian young adult literature. *Jeunesse* offers a fresh perspective on international children's and young adult literature and culture. This journal will appeal most to scholars of children's literature, although some articles will also be of interest to librarians and elementary school teachers.

1597. *Journal for Early Modern Cultural Studies.* [ISSN: 1531-0485] 2001. s-a. USD 52 (Individuals, USD 35; Students, USD 20). University of Pennsylvania Press, 3905 Spruce St, Philadelphia, PA 19104; custserv@pobox.upenn.edu; http://www.upenn.edu/pennpress. Adv. Sample. Refereed. Circ: 450. Reprint: PSC. *Indexed:* A22, AmHI, BRI, E01, MLA-IB, P02. *Bk. rev.:* 2, 1,000-1,500 words. *Aud.:* Ac.

Although other publications in cultural-social studies also focus on history, this journal specializes in the era of the late fifteenth to the late nineteenth centuries. As the official publication of the Group for Early Modern Cultural Studies, this publication combines scholarship from many areas of the humanities, social sciences, and area studies with research on gender, colonialism and post-colonialism, and postmodernism. Editors and contributors are largely from U.S. and Canadian universities. Issues of the journal often emphasize an overall theme such as the rhetoric of plague; connections between Spanish and English literature and history; or climate and crisis. Recent articles focus on topics from illicit privacy and outdoor spaces to agricultural and medical manuals, and from cross-cultural marriage to historical fiction. This journal will be of interest to scholars in many disciplines whose research centers on the early modern time period.

1598. *Journal of Aesthetic Education.* [ISSN: 0021-8510] 1966. q. USD 142 (print & online eds.). Ed(s): Lisa Savage, Pradeep Dhillon. University of Illinois Press, 1325 S Oak St, Champaign, IL 61820; journals@uillinois.edu; http://www.press.uillinois.edu. Illus., index. Sample. Refereed. Vol. ends: Winter. Microform: MIM; PQC. *Indexed:* A07, A22, A51, AmHI, ArtHuCI, BAS, BEL&L, BRI, CBRI, E01, ERIC, MLA-IB, RILM. *Bk. rev.:* 3-5, 500-1,500 words. *Aud.:* Ac.

Journal of Aesthetic Education draws together the threads of philosophy, theory, and pedagogy as applied to the full range of the arts. The journal provides a forum to explore issues in aesthetic education, both in instructional settings and in society at large. Contributors cover issues of arts and humanities instruction, aesthetics and new communications media, and philosophy in aesthetics. Individual issues include articles on theory and philosophy, and analysis of specific works in literature, art, or music. Recent issues feature articles on such topics as aesthetic realism; art therapy; the influence of film music on audiences; art-house cinema and avant-garde film; and improvisational pedagogy. Special issues have covered themes from children's literature to pragmatism in aesthetics, to arts education curriculum projects. Some issues contain commentary sections with brief essays or responses to earlier articles. This journal will appeal to scholars and artists, as well as to teachers and administrators in arts education.

1599. *Journal of Aesthetics and Art Criticism.* [ISSN: 0021-8529] 1941. q. GBP 179. Ed(s): Susan Feagin. Wiley-Blackwell Publishing, Inc., 111 River St, Hoboken, NJ 07030; info@wiley.com; http://onlinelibrary.wiley.com/. Illus., index. Sample. Refereed. Vol. ends: Fall. Microform: MIM; PQC. Reprint: PSC. *Indexed:* A01, A06, A07, A22, A51, ABS&EES, AmHI, ArtHuCI, BAS, BRI, CBRI, E01, F01, FR, IIMP, IIPA, IPB, MLA-IB, P02, RILM. *Bk. rev.:* 7-15, 1,000-2,000 words. *Aud.:* Ac.

Although the title of this journal may indicate a quite specific publication, the *Journal of Aesthetics and Art Criticism* instead takes a very wide-ranging view. Both fine and decorative arts are covered, as well as film, photography, performance, and popular culture. Most issues include several research articles, occasional discussion segments, and book reviews. Articles cover theoretical and philosophical research on aesthetics, as well as critical analyses of specific works and artists, historical treatment of the arts, and social and political questions related to aesthetics. Some issues focus on one theme, such as the aesthetics of architecture, songs and singing, or variations on the narrative.

Individual articles cover such topics as suspense realism, word sculpture, street art, aesthetic deception, and digital art. As the journal of the American Society for Aesthetics, this publication will appeal to scholars in the philosophy of the arts, to critics of art, and more broadly to students of aesthetics.

Journal of American Ethnic History. See Multicultural Studies section.

1600. *Journal of American Studies.* Formerly (until 1967): *British Association for American Studies. Bulletin.* [ISSN: 0021-8758] 1956. q. GBP 291. Ed(s): Scott Lucas. Cambridge University Press, The Edinburgh Bldg, Shaftesbury Rd, Cambridge, CB2 8RU, United Kingdom; journals@cambridge.org; http://www.cambridge.org/uk. Illus., index, adv. Refereed. Circ: 2000. Vol. ends: Dec. Microform: PQC. Reprint: PSC. *Indexed:* A01, A22, AmHI, ArtHuCI, BRI, CBRI, E01, IBSS, IIBP, MLA-IB, P02, P61, RILM, SSA. *Bk. rev.:* 30-40, 250-750 words. *Aud.:* Ac.

American Studies from an international perspective is the focus of this publication. U.S. literary works, politics, history, and economics are covered, as are art, music, film, and popular culture. Most contributors are from British universities, although some articles are by U.S. and European authors. Many articles explore American literary classics or historical topics, but cross-disciplinary and comparative cultural studies are also included. Recent articles cover such topics as political blogs; jazz as an African American art form; compassionate conservatism; and changes in the American left. Each issue includes many book reviews; review essays also appear in some issues. The journal is sponsored by the British Association for American Studies. This journal will be of interest to scholars of American Studies in the U.S. and the U.K. as well as internationally.

1601. *Journal of British Studies.* Incorporates (1969-2005): *Albion.* [ISSN: 0021-9371] 1961. q. GBP 185. Ed(s): Elizabeth Elbourne, Brian Cowan. Cambridge University Press, 32 Ave of the Americas, New York, NY 10013; information@cambridge.org; http://www.cambridge.org/us/. Illus., index, adv. Sample. Refereed. Vol. ends: Oct. Microform: PQC. Reprint: PSC. *Indexed:* A01, A22, AmHI, ArtHuCI, BRI, BrArAb, IBSS, MLA-IB, P02, RILM. *Bk. rev.:* 3-5, essay length. *Aud.:* Ac.

Often described as "the premier journal devoted to the study of British history and culture," this publication includes a range of research articles, review essays, and book reviews. Although the editorial board is composed mainly of scholars from U.S. universities and colleges, contributors to the journal include authors from Canada, Australia, and Britain as well as other Western countries. Articles most often cover British history in combination with politics, economics, religion, and social issues. In addition, the journal includes articles on comparative history, gender and cultural studies, the arts, and health and disease. Geographically, most writing in this journal deals with England; however, some articles focus on Ireland and areas of the former British Empire. Recent articles cover such topics as civic pageantry, modernist architecture, women and conservative activism, and domestic service humor. Sponsored by the North American Conference on British Studies, this journal will be of significant interest internationally to students and scholars of the culture, society, and history of the United Kingdom.

1602. *Journal of Cultural Economy.* [ISSN: 1753-0350] 2008. 3x/yr. GBP 464 (print & online eds.). Ed(s): Tony Bennett, Michael Pryke. Routledge, 4 Park Sq, Milton Park, Abingdon, OX14 4RN, United Kingdom; subscriptions@tandf.co.uk; http://www.tandfonline.com. Adv. Sample. Refereed. Reprint: PSC. *Indexed:* A22, E01. *Bk. rev.:* Occasional essays. *Aud.:* Ac.

The Economic and Social Research Council's Centre for Research on Socio-Cultural Change is the sponsoring organization for this journal, which aims to be the "premiere [*sic*] forum for debating the relations between culture, economy[,] and the social in all their various manifestations." The editors are from the Open University in the U.K. and University of Western Sydney in Australia. Most issues include several scholarly articles, along with reviews and commentaries. Frequent special issues are published on topics such as "beyond liquidity"; transnational medical research; or performativity, economics, and politics. Individual articles cover topics ranging from ship disposal to

participation on the Internet, and from consumer testing of perfumes to cultural tourism. This publication will be of interest to scholars and students of economics and social sciences, as well as cultural aspects of these disciplines.

1603. *Journal of European Popular Culture.* [ISSN: 2040-6134] 2010. s-a. GBP 150 (Individuals, GBP 36). Ed(s): Owen Evans, Cristina Johnston. Intellect Ltd., The Mill, Parnall Rd, Fishponds, Bristol, BS16 3JG, United Kingdom; info@intellectbooks.com; http://www.intellectbooks.co.uk/. Adv. Sample. *Indexed:* AmHI. *Aud.:* Ac.

With the increase in popular culture worldwide has come not only a growing interest in writing on popular culture topics, but also a new publication. The *Journal of European Popular Culture* "investigates the creative cultures of Europe, present and past." This publication covers the full gamut of "European popular imagery" from literature, music, and art to film, media, and drama. Each issue contains five scholarly articles on topics such as reality television in Slovakia and film policy in Iceland, as well as articles on specific films and writers. Contributors are faculty members from British, Canadian, and European universities. As a complement to the long-running U.S. *Journal of Popular Culture,* this publication will appeal to academic audiences, as well as to readers interested in popular culture from the European perspective.

1604. *Journal of Popular Culture.* [ISSN: 0022-3840] 1967. bi-m. GBP 245. Ed(s): Gary C Hoppenstand. Wiley-Blackwell Publishing, Inc., 111 River St, Hoboken, NJ 07030; info@wiley.com; http://onlinelibrary.wiley.com/. Illus., index, adv. Sample. Refereed. Vol. ends: Spring. Microform: PQC. Reprint: PSC. *Indexed:* A01, A22, ABS&EES, AmHI, ArtHuCI, BAS, BEL&L, BRI, C45, CBRI, Chicano, E01, F01, FR, IBSS, IIMP, IIPA, MLA-IB, P02, P61, RILM, RRTA, SD, SSA. *Bk. rev.:* 15-20, 100-500 words. *Aud.:* Ga, Ac.

The articles in this journal explore popular culture and its effects on people and society as a whole. The journal brings to the forefront the aspects of "low culture" that fascinate and consume so much of contemporary U.S. and global society. Each issue contains several articles on a wide variety of topics ranging from comic books to Victorian novels, from television shows to popular movies, and from advertisements to rap music. In addition to its interdisciplinary coverage of U.S. culture, the *Journal of Popular Culture* also includes international coverage. Recent articles focus on pop nationalism in Korea; Tokyo street fashion; and American popular music in China. This journal is the official publication of the Popular Culture Association. Scholars studying popular literature, film, and television will be interested in this publication, as will students and general readers who are fans of pop culture.

1605. *Journal of the History of Ideas: an international quarterly devoted to intellectual history.* [ISSN: 0022-5037] 1940. q. USD 120 (print & online eds.) Individuals, USD 43 (print & online eds.); Students, USD 32). Ed(s): Robin Ladrach. University of Pennsylvania Press, 3905 Spruce St, Philadelphia, PA 19104; custserv@pobox.upenn.edu; http://www.pennpress.org. Illus., index, adv. Sample. Refereed. Vol. ends: Oct/Dec. Microform: PMC; PQC. *Indexed:* A01, A06, A07, A22, ABS&EES, AmHI, ArtHuCI, BAS, BRI, CBRI, CCMJ, E01, FR, IBSS, IPB, MLA-IB, MSN, MathR, P02, RILM. *Aud.:* Ga, Ac, Sa.

Intellectual history, very broadly defined, is the focus of this publication. The journal aims to cover a wide range of geographical areas, time periods, and methods, encompassing philosophy, literature, the social sciences, religion, and the arts. Each issue contains several scholarly articles that cover such topics as contemporary human rights, arts in the eighteenth century, and French philosophy. Most articles deal with philosophical writings, historiography, theology, scientific theories, or literary works. Contributors to the journal are academics, mostly historians, with some authors from the fields of philosophy, classics, and literature. This journal, sponsored by the Society for the History of Ideas, contains superior research and writing that will appeal to scholars in several areas of the humanities.

Journal of Thought. See Education/General, K-12 section.

1606. *Journal of Transnational American Studies.* [ISSN: 1940-0764] 2009. irreg. Free. University of California, Digital Library - eScholarship, http://www.escholarship.org. Refereed. *Indexed:* MLA-IB. *Aud.:* Ac.

Sponsored by the University of California at Santa Barbara's American Cultures and Global Contexts Center and Stanford University's Program in American Studies, the *Journal of Transnational American Studies* provides a forum for scholars in American Studies to "move beyond disciplinary and geographic boundaries." Each issue includes a "Forward" section, several original articles, and a closing "Reprise" section. The "Forward" section offers excerpts from new or upcoming publications that point to new developments in the field. The scholarly articles in each issue span a wide range of topics, from temperance discourse to African American studies in Europe, and from tabloid journalism in the war of 1898 to South Asian Americans after 9/11. The "Reprise" section provides reprinted online access to important works the field. This journal expands both the scope of American Studies and open access to new scholarship on transnationalism.

1607. *Journal of War and Culture Studies.* [ISSN: 1752-6272] 2008. q. USD 485 (print & online eds.). Ed(s): Debra Kelly, Nicola Cooper. Maney Publishing, Ste 1C, Joseph's Well, Hanover Walk, Leeds, LS3 1AB, United Kingdom; maney@maneypublishing.com; http://maneypublishing.com/. Adv. Sample. Reprint: PSC. *Indexed:* AmHI, MLA-IB. *Aud.:* Ac.

The culture of war, a unique focus in the area of Cultural Studies, is the subject of a new international and multidisciplinary journal. This publication "analyses the relationship between war and culture in the twentieth century and early decades of the twenty-first." The Group for War and Cultural Studies, based at the University of Westminster, publishes the journal. Each issue includes about ten scholarly articles on a wide range of topics related to armed conflict and the many people it involves. Many issues focus on a specific theme, such as the body at war; war and visual culture since 1900; the figure of the soldier; and the Spanish Civil War. Some articles deal with literary works on war, while others cover specific groups such as women nurses. Other studies focus on military officers, front-line soldiers, members of the resistance, and bonding among fighting men. Issues of the journal also include a "Noticeboard" that provides lists of recent books, museum exhibitions, forthcoming conferences, and web sites of centers for the study of war. Collections with an emphasis on military science and history will find this journal of interest.

1608. *Memory Studies.* [ISSN: 1750-6980] 2008. q. USD 666. Ed(s): Andrew Hoskins. Sage Publications Ltd., 1 Oliver's Yard, 55 City Rd, London, EC1Y 1SP, United Kingdom; info@sagepub.co.uk; http://www.uk.sagepub.com. Adv. Sample. Refereed. Reprint: PSC. *Indexed:* A22, ArtHuCI, E01. *Bk. rev.:* 4-6 (in most issues), 800-1,000 words. *Aud.:* Ac.

The question of how individuals, societies, and nations remember events and aspects of history has become a major area of scholarly research. The journal *Memory Studies* brings together a range of scholarship on remembering and forgetting. It is international in coverage, and its editors and editorial board are largely from the U.K., the U.S., and Australia, although scholars from Europe and Israel are also included. Each issue offers several scholarly articles on one or more topics or problems. Thematic issues appear often on subjects such as nostalgia and history, social memory, perpetrator memory, reconciliation and memory, and national collective memory. Some issues focus on a particular country such as Korea or Australia, or an event such as the 2005 London bombings or the oral history of 1968. Book reviews appear in each issue, along with occasional conference reviews and roundtable discussions. Although primarily for an academic audience, this journal will also appeal to non-specialists with an interest in how and why things are remembered.

1609. *The Midwest Quarterly: a journal of contemporary thought.* Supersedes (in 1959): *The Educational Leader.* [ISSN: 0026-3451] 1959. q. USD 15; USD 5 per issue. Ed(s): James B M Schick. Pittsburg State University, English Department, 406b Grubbs Hall, 1701 S Broadway, Pittsburg, KS 66762; http://www.pittstate.edu/department/english/. Index. Refereed. Vol. ends: Summer. Microform: PQC. *Indexed:* A01, A22, AmHI, ArtHuCI, BAS, BRI, MLA-IB, P02, RILM. *Bk. rev.:* 2-5, 500-750. *Aud.:* Ac.

For 50 years and counting, *Midwest Quarterly* has published both writings of literary analysis and a substantial amount of original poetry. Although many, but not all, articles in this publication are written by Midwesterners, the content of this journal has no geographical limitations. It focuses on "analytical and speculative treatment of its topics, rather than heavily documented research studies." Most articles analyze specific literary themes and works, although some cover philosophical, social, and historical topics. Recent articles explore the writings of authors from Mark Twain and William Faulkner to Toni Morrison and Kurt Vonnegut. Other articles cover such subjects as East German science and math textbooks; John the Baptist in contemporary fiction; and race and white college students in the Midwest. Poetry is a major emphasis of this journal, with each issue including several poems by well-known writers. This journal will appeal to poets as well as scholars in literature and the humanities in general.

1610. *Modern Intellectual History.* [ISSN: 1479-2443] 2004. 3x/yr. GBP 206. Ed(s): Anthony J La Vopa, Charles Capper. Cambridge University Press, The Edinburgh Bldg, Shaftesbury Rd, Cambridge, CB2 8RU, United Kingdom; journals@cambridge.org; http://www.cambridge.org/uk. Adv. Reprint: PSC. *Indexed:* A22, ArtHuCI, E01. *Bk. rev.:* 3-5 essays per issue, c. 5,000 words. *Aud.:* Ac.

The modern period of intellectual history, from 1650 to the present, is the focus of this journal. European and American history are the major areas of focus, but articles on transnational history of other regions are also included. The journal draws upon writings from a wide range of disciplines, including not only the social sciences and literature but also political thought, philosophy, religion, natural sciences, visual arts, communications, economic thought, anthropology, and music. Each issue contains several scholarly articles, along with review essays and an occasional forum containing articles and commentary on a specific theme. Recent articles cover the political thought of Habermas; location and evidence in modern historiography; European sculpture; American conservatism in the late nineteenth century; and ethics and beliefs of the Third Reich. This journal will be of interest to scholars in many disciplines, especially history, philosophy, and political science.

1611. *Modernism/Modernity.* [ISSN: 1071-6068] 1994. q. USD 165. Ed(s): Benjamin Madden, Jeffrey T Schnapp. The Johns Hopkins University Press, 2715 N Charles St, Baltimore, MD 21218; http://www.press.jhu.edu. Illus., index, adv. Sample. Refereed. Circ: 1136. Vol. ends: Sep. Reprint: PSC. *Indexed:* A01, A07, A22, A51, AmHI, ArtHuCI, BEL&L, BRI, E01, MLA-IB, P02, P61, RILM. *Bk. rev.:* 10-20, 500-1,500 words. *Aud.:* Ac.

This journal is an interdisciplinary forum for scholars of modernist studies to explore the theories, methods, philosophy, and history of the late nineteenth through the twentieth century. The coverage of *Modernism/Modernity* is international and cross-disciplinary, encompassing primarily the arts and history, along with other areas of the humanities. Many articles are devoted to literary works of modernist writers such as James Joyce, Zora Neale Hurston, E. M. Forster, Joseph Conrad, and William Faulkner. Other articles cover art, music, theater, philosophy, and politics. Recent articles focus on Brazilian theater and the avant-garde; modernism and obscenity; melodrama in film; and the United States and the cultural cold war. Some issues or sections center on a particular theme such as decadent aestheticism and modernism, fascism, or modernist authenticities. This publication is the journal of the Modernist Studies Association. It will appeal to academics and literary scholars studying this time period in general and its prominent writers and trends.

1612. *New Formations: a journal of culture/theory/politics.* [ISSN: 0950-2378] 1987. 3x/yr. GBP 225 (Individuals, GBP 40). Ed(s): Jeremy Gilbert. Lawrence & Wishart Ltd, 99a Wallis Rd, London, E9 5LN, United Kingdom; info@lwbooks.co.uk; http://www.lwbooks.co.uk. Illus., adv. Refereed. Vol. ends: Winter. *Indexed:* A01, A22, BRI, IBSS, MLA-IB, RILM. *Bk. rev.:* 2-3; 1,000-3,000 words, plus "Book Notes", 2-3, c. 500 words. *Aud.:* Ac.

As the subtitle suggests, this journal uses the basis of cultural studies and examines it through the critical lens of theory and politics. The purpose of this publication is to explore and critically investigate contemporary culture, its ideology, its politics, and its impact. Each issue includes several articles and essays, many of which focus on one specific theme, such as postmodernism, music and cultural theory, the left and twenty-first-century political projects, and ecocriticism and culture. Themes are explored from many points of view—from political and social to literary and philosophical. Articles range from modern applications of classical philosophy to popular culture essays.

New Formations provides a fresh perspective on historical and contemporary international culture and politics. This journal will be of interest to cultural studies scholars, especially in politics and philosophy.

1613. *Philosophy & Technology (Dordrecht, 1988).* Former titles (until 2011): *Knowledge, Technology and Policy;* (until 1998): *Knowledge and Policy;* (until 1991): *Knowledge in Society.* [ISSN: 2210-5433] 1988. q. EUR 356 (print & online eds.). Ed(s): Luciano Floridi. Springer Netherlands, Van Godewijckstraat 30, Dordrecht, 3311 GX, Netherlands; http://www.springer.com. Illus., index, adv. Refereed. Vol. ends: Winter. Reprint: PSC. *Indexed:* A01, A22, ABIn, BRI, CompLI, E01, P61, SSA. *Bk. rev.:* 2-6; 500-1,000 words. *Aud.:* Ac, Sa.

The impact of technology on individuals and the larger global society continues to grow exponentially. Formerly titled *Knowledge, Technology and Policy,* this journal has changed its title and focus completely. *Philosophy and Technology* covers "the conceptual nature and practical consequences of technologies," and "aims to publish the best research produced in all areas where philosophy and technology meet." Each issue includes several scholarly articles, with sections of an issue often centered on a specific theme such as the here and now, and the unpredictable effects of future technologies. Research article topics include theories of causality and the hidden side of the material world. Authors are primarily from universities in the U.S., U.K., and European countries, with a few from China, Japan, and India. This journal will be of interest to those teaching and researching ethical and philosophical issues of current and developing technologies.

1614. *Public Culture: an interdisciplinary journal of transnational cultural studies.* [ISSN: 0899-2363] 1988. 3x/yr. USD 262. Ed(s): Claudio Lomnitz, Plaegian Alexander. Duke University Press, 905 W Main St, Ste 18 B, PO Box 90660, Durham, NC 27701; subscriptions@dukeupress.edu; http://www.dukeupress.edu. Illus., index, adv. Sample. Refereed. Vol. ends: Spring. Reprint: PSC. *Indexed:* A01, A22, A47, ABS&EES, AmHI, ArtHuCI, E01, IBSS, MLA-IB, P02, P61, RILM, SSA. *Aud.:* Ac.

This journal focuses on cultural studies from a global perspective. *Public Culture* includes research articles and essays on cultural, social, and political issues including contemporary media, urban issues, consumerism, and advertising. Articles cover such topics as the privatization of risk or sexual politics in the public sphere. Photos, drawings, and paintings often accompany articles. Each issue begins with editorials in a section called "Doxa at Large." Individual articles and themed sections cover such issues as financial prediction; a subaltern middle class; cartography of China; Qatar's national graphic identity; and South Africa in the age of AIDS. Photo-essays included in most issues focus on topics such as racial issues in France; indigenous housing; and urban planning in Shanghai. Sponsored by New York University's Institute for Public Knowledge, this publication will appeal to readers with an interest in globalization and the internationalization of cultural studies.

1615. *Renaissance Quarterly.* Incorporates (1954-1974): *Studies in the Renaissance;* Formerly (until 1967): *Renaissance News.* [ISSN: 0034-4338] 1954. q. USD 202 (print & online eds.). Ed(s): Erika Suffern. University of Chicago Press, 1427 E 60th St, Chicago, IL 60637; subscriptions@press.uchicago.edu; http://www.journals.uchicago.edu. Illus., index, adv. Sample. Refereed. Vol. ends: Winter. Microform: PQC. Reprint: PSC. *Indexed:* A01, A06, A07, A22, AmHI, ArtHuCI, BEL&L, BRI, CBRI, E01, MLA-IB, P02, RILM. *Bk. rev.:* 40-50, 400-500 words. *Aud.:* Ac.

As the leading journal in Renaissance studies, this publication offers research studies, review essays, and a large section of book reviews. Literary works and themes are the focus of many articles, in addition to specialized studies in the arts, religion, or social aspects of the Renaissance. Recent articles cover such topics as the history of early modern science; witchcraft in early modern Venice; landscape painting in the seventeenth century; and women in sixteenth-century Italy. Review essays and reviews of individual works make up nearly half of each issue. English-language works predominate, but some titles in French and Italian are included. As the official publication of the Renaissance Society of America, reports of society meetings are also included. This journal will interest scholars and students of the Renaissance both for its scholarly articles and extensive reviews of current books.

1616. *Representations.* [ISSN: 0734-6018] 1983. q. USD 310 (print & online eds.). Ed(s): David Henkin, Ian Duncan. University of California Press, Journals Division, 2000 Ctr St, Ste 303, Berkeley, CA 94704; customerservice@ucpressjournals.com; http://www.ucpressjournals.com. Illus., adv. Refereed. Circ: 965. Microform: PQC. Reprint: PSC. *Indexed:* A01, A07, A22, A51, AmHI, ArtHuCI, BEL&L, E01, MLA-IB, P61, RILM, SSA. *Aud.:* Ac.

For over 25 years, *Representations* has provided a multidisciplinary forum for scholars of literature, culture, and history. Most issues include several articles on a variety of topics, with occasional issues focusing on one particular theme. Many articles analyze aspects of a particular literary or philosophical writing, while other essays examine historical, political, or social issues. Recent articles explore topics ranging from the Spanish Civil War to Berlin's urban spaces, and from miracles in the Middle Ages to the death and fossils. The essays are written in a very engaging style and present original perspectives on literary, historical, or social subjects. Occasional special issues focus on such themes as "New World Slavery and the Matter of the Visual," "Forms of Asia," and a forum on fear beyond the disciplines. Most contributors are scholars in English or other areas of the humanities. This journal will appeal to a wide range of academics, especially in literature and the humanities.

1617. *The Sixties: a journal of history, politics and culture.* [ISSN: 1754-1328] 2008. s-a. GBP 182 (print & online eds.). Ed(s): Jeremy Varon, John McMillian. Routledge, 325 Chestnut St, Ste 800, Philadelphia, PA 19106; customerservice@taylorandfrancis.com; http://www.tandfonline.com. Sample. Reprint: PSC. *Bk. rev.:* 8-10 per issue; 2-3 pages in length. *Aud.:* Ga, Ac.

The decade of the 1960s, along with the years just before and after, has come to symbolize a period of major social, political, and cultural change. This journal looks at the history and politics of the time, but also at "the ways the 1960s continue to be constructed in contemporary popular culture." Each issue begins with original research articles on topics such as women in the civil rights movement, cultural feminism, the Poor People's Campaign, and Chicano history. Although most articles focus on the United States, the journal has also included articles on the the Iranian student movement; China's Red Guards; and the Red Cross in the Vietnam war. Special forums are occasionally offered on topics such as the 1960s and the 2008 presidential election. Reviews of books, movies, and art exhibitions are also included. Some issues conclude with interviews or conversations with major political figures or activists from this decade. The journal will appeal to a wide range of scholars and students interested in the 1960s, especially in the disciplines of history, sociology, media, and politics.

Social Epistemology. See Philosophy section.

1618. *Social Identities: journal for the study of race, nation and culture.* [ISSN: 1350-4630] 1995. bi-m. GBP 780 (print & online eds.). Ed(s): Toby Miller, Pal Ahluwalia. Routledge, 4 Park Sq, Milton Park, Abingdon, OX14 4RN, United Kingdom; subscriptions@tandf.co.uk; http://www.tandfonline.com. Illus., index, adv. Sample. Refereed. Vol. ends: Dec. Reprint: PSC. *Indexed:* A01, A22, E01, IBSS, MLA-IB, P61, PsycInfo, SSA. *Bk. rev.:* 1-3, essay length. *Aud.:* Ac.

Current international conflicts and hostilities underscore the critical role of race and ethnicity in contemporary societies. *Social Identities* provides a forum to address global racial, ethnic, and national issues in the context of social and cultural studies. Postmodernism and postcolonialism underscore much of the writing in this journal, as do the theories of how racial, national, and cultural identities are developed, changed, and affected by political and economic power. Each issue begins with several research articles on topics ranging from Muslim Palestinian women to Mexican identity in the U.S, and from media images of South Africa to the National Museum of the American Indian. Special issues are published occasionally on such themes as post-colonial Europe; Foucault 25 years after his death; carnivals and the carnivalesque; and migrants from eastern Europe to the U.K. after 2004. Contributors are mainly from U.S. and U.K. universities, with some writers from Latin America, the Middle East, and Africa. This journal will be of interest to scholars and students in many disciplines, especially politics, history, and sociology, but also humanities and the arts.

1619. *Social Justice Research.* [ISSN: 0885-7466] 1986. q. EUR 923 (print & online eds.). Ed(s): Curtis D Hardin. Springer New York LLC, 233 Spring St, New York, NY 10013; service-ny@springer.com; http://www.springer.com/. Illus., index, adv. Refereed. Vol. ends: Dec. Microform: PQC. Reprint: PSC. *Indexed:* A01, A22, BAS, BRI, CJPI, E01, IBSS, P61, PsycInfo, SSA. *Bk. rev.:* 2-3, essay length. *Aud.:* Ac.

The theory and practice of social justice has become an expanding area of contemporary social science research and scholarship. This journal aims to explore "the origins, structures[,] and consequences of justice in human affairs." This publication takes a cross-disciplinary view of justice, covering social science and policy studies nationally and internationally. Each issue includes articles on the application of justice to such areas as human rights, conflict of interest, immigration policies, and public views of restorative justice. Recent articles cover topics such as citizens fighting back; fairness in transport pricing policies; theories of implicit race bias; and the justice sensitivity inventory. The articles are well written and thoroughly documented. Contributors are mainly from U.S., Canadian, and European universities. As the official journal of the International Society for Justice Research, this publication will be of interest to scholars in the social sciences, particularly in political science, criminal justice, sociology, and law.

1620. *Social Science History.* [ISSN: 0145-5532] 1976. q. USD 192. Ed(s): Terri C Fain, Douglas L Anderton. Duke University Press, 905 W Main St, Ste 18 B, PO Box 90660, Durham, NC 27701; subscriptions@dukeupress.edu; http://www.dukeupress.edu. Illus., index, adv. Sample. Refereed. Vol. ends: Winter. Reprint: PSC. *Indexed:* A01, A22, ABS&EES, ArtHuCI, BAS, E01, IBSS, P61, SSA. *Aud.:* Ac.

Social aspects of history have become a major focus of contemporary scholarship within the discipline. This publication focuses on interdisciplinary studies that combine history with the fields of sociology, economics, political science, anthropology, and geography. Articles include "a blend of empirical research and theoretical work," as well as comparative and methodological studies. Research covers the family, demography, economic issues, social classes, the labor force, crime, and poverty. Each issue includes articles on such subjects as revolutionary waves, school desegregation, ethnohistory as a discipline, and the gender gap in voter registration and turnout. Frequently, an entire issue or a section thereof is devoted to a single theme, such as economics for history; taking stock and moving ahead in history and the social sciences; and railways and political economy in Britain, France, and the U.S. Many articles focus on U.S. historical research, but British and European history are also covered. As the official journal of the Social Science History Association, this journal will have broad appeal not only to historians, but also to scholars in related social science fields.

1621. *Social Science Information.* Formerly (until 1962): *International Social Science Council. Information.* [ISSN: 0539-0184] 1954. q. USD 1030. Ed(s): Anna Rocha Perazzo. Sage Publications Ltd., 1 Oliver's Yard, 55 City Rd, London, EC1Y 1SP, United Kingdom; info@sagepub.co.uk; http://www.uk.sagepub.com. Illus., index, adv. Sample. Refereed. Vol. ends: Dec. Reprint: PSC. *Indexed:* A22, A47, ASSIA, BAS, C45, E01, FR, IBSS, MLA-IB, P02, P61, RRTA, SSA. *Aud.:* Ac.

With an international focus, this journal publishes research on theory and method in the social sciences, often emphasizing comparative and cross-cultural research. Articles on such subjects as evolution and error theory, Bourdieuan sociology, privacy in digital society, and ethnographic fieldwork in Brazil indicate the range of issues covered by *Social Science Information.* Occasionally, special issues or symposia are published on such topics as a generalized science of humanity, digitization and transfer, and rules of collective decision. Special sections on the areas of rationality and society, biology and social life, studies of science, theory and methods, and trends and developments appear in various issues. The text of articles may be in English or French. This journal is affiliated with the Maison des Sciences de l'Homme in Paris, and will appeal to researchers across a broad spectrum of the social sciences.

1622. *The Social Science Journal.* Formerly (until 1976): *The Rocky Mountain Social Science Journal.* [ISSN: 0362-3319] 1963. q. EUR 538. Ed(s): S A Carson. Pergamon, The Blvd, Langford Ln, E Park, Kidlington, OX5 1GB, United Kingdom;

JournalsCustomerServiceEMEA@elsevier.com; http://www.elsevier.com. Illus., adv. Sample. Refereed. Reprint: PSC. *Indexed:* A01, A22, ABS&EES, AbAn, B01, BRI, Chicano, IBSS, P02, P61, PsycInfo, RiskAb, SSA, SWR&A. *Aud.:* Ac.

Although this publication began as a regional journal, over the past 48 years of its history *The Social Science Journal* has expanded into a national and international forum. This journal publishes research articles, statistical analyses, and case studies. Articles on society, history, economics, politics, and gender are included, along with coverage of social theories, research methods, and curricular issues. Representative articles have covered such subjects as group structure in voluntary organizations; the presidential vote in the Mexico–U.S. border region; child care among couples with young children; property crime and economic conditions; and 15 years of the Chiapas conflict. Research notes on works-in-progress are also included, covering topics such as capitalism and the global financial crisis, media coverage of school shootings, measuring religion in Japan, and home prices and the 2008 presidential election. As the official publication of the Western Social Science Association, this journal will be of interest to scholars and students in all geographical areas and in many fields of the social sciences and beyond.

1623. *Social Science Quarterly.* Former titles (until 1968): *Southwestern Social Science Quarterly;* (until 1931): *Southwestern Political and Social Science Quarterly.* [ISSN: 0038-4941] 1920. 5x/yr. GBP 313. Ed(s): Nita Lineberry, Robert Lineberry. Wiley-Blackwell Publishing, Inc., 111 River St, Hoboken, NJ 07030; info@wiley.com; http://onlinelibrary.wiley.com/. Illus., index, adv. Sample. Refereed. Vol. ends: Dec. Microform: PQC. Reprint: PSC. *Indexed:* A01, A22, ABIn, ABS&EES, B01, BAS, BRI, CBRI, Chicano, E01, EconLit, FR, H24, IBSS, JEL, MLA-IB, P02, P61, PsycInfo, RiskAb, SSA. *Bk. rev.:* 10-15, 500 words. *Aud.:* Ga, Ac.

For about 90 years, *Social Science Quarterly* has published top-quality research in a wide range of the social sciences. The journal is international in scope and covers social and public policy issues, including both theoretical approaches and quantitative research. General-interest articles explore such topics as the state welfare policies and abortion; immigration and crime rates; social demography of Internet dating; and the impact of gaming on Indian Nations. Often, articles are grouped around a specific theme such as politics, race and ethnicity, human behavior, or comparative perspectives. In 2004, the journal began to publish an additional supplementary issue at the end of the year that focused on themes such as inequality and poverty, health policy, women and politics, and environmental culture and attitudes. This journal offers superior coverage of contemporary social questions from a research standpoint. *Social Science Quarterly* is the official publication of the Southwestern Social Science Association. This journal will interest scholars and students, as well as policy researchers.

1624. *Social Science Research.* [ISSN: 0049-089X] 1972. bi-m. EUR 1208. Ed(s): W Kane, James D Wright. Academic Press, 3251 Riverport Ln, Maryland Heights, MO 63043; JournalCustomerService-usa@elsevier.com; http://www.elsevierdirect.com/brochures/academicpress/index.html. Illus., index, adv. Sample. Refereed. Vol. ends: Dec. *Indexed:* A01, A22, BAS, Chicano, E01, IBSS, P02, P61, PsycInfo, SSA. *Aud.:* Ac.

Although qualitative studies have expanded in the social sciences, much of the current research in these fields remains heavily quantitatively-based. This journal covers quantitative research studies as well as methodologies in all areas of the social sciences. Empirical research is the focus of this publication, especially research that emphasizes cross-disciplinary issues or methods. Each issue offers lengthy articles grouped into varying thematic areas, including the enduring significance of race, cross-national studies, survey methods, environmental sociology, social inequalities, migration and immigration, gender studies, family and youth, and political sociology. Contributors are drawn from both U.S. colleges and universities, as well as from universities abroad and from private research groups. *Social Science Research* will appeal to scholars and upper-level students in the disciplines of sociology, economics, politics, criminal justice, and demography.

1625. *Social Text.* [ISSN: 0164-2472] 1979. q. USD 270. Ed(s): Livia Tenzer, Anna McCarthy. Duke University Press, 905 W Main St, Ste 18 B, PO Box 90660, Durham, NC 27701; subscriptions@dukeupress.edu; http://www.dukeupress.edu. Illus., adv. Sample. Vol. ends: Winter. Reprint: PSC. *Indexed:* A01, A22, ABS&EES, AmHI, E01, FR, MLA-IB, P61, RILM, SSA. *Aud.:* Ac.

Social Text offers a cutting-edge perspective on current political, social, and cultural trends and issues. Addressing cultural theory with an emphasis on "questions of gender, sexuality, race and the environment" is the journal's focus. Contributors are largely U.S. scholars, critics, artists, and writers, although works of international writers are also included. Articles deal with such topics as identification cards in Palestine/Israel; U.S. immigration policy and deportation; Muslim women in American popular literature; and internally displaced peoples. Special issues on a single theme are common, and have covered such subjects as inter-species, dislocations across the Americas, the politics of recorded sound, and media and the political forms of religion. *Social Text* places current social issues in the larger context of national and international cultural transformation. This journal will appeal to scholars and students interested in the latest cultural theory applied to the critical areas of race, sex, and class.

1626. *Social Theory and Practice: an international and interdisciplinary journal of social philosophy.* [ISSN: 0037-802X] 1970. q. USD 55 (Individuals, USD 28; Students, USD 20). Ed(s): Margaret Dancy. Florida State University, Department of Philosophy, 151 Dodd Hall, Tallahassee, FL 32306; journals@mailer.fsu.edu; http://whttp://www.fsu.edu/~philo/. Illus., index, adv. Sample. Refereed. Microform: PQC. *Indexed:* A01, A22, ABS&EES, BRI, FR, IBSS, IPB, MLA-IB, P02, P61, SSA. *Aud.:* Ac.

Social Theory and Practice has been published by the Department of Philosophy at Florida State University for about 40 years. This journal seeks to address "theoretical and applied questions in social, political, legal, economic, educational and moral philosophy." The articles examine theories of historical figures in philosophy including Kant, Mill, Hegel, and Locke, as well as more contemporary theorists such as Fischer, Rawls, Habermas, and Foucault. Other writings address questions on social identity, human rights, terrorism and retribution, relating morals and politics, parental responsibilities, and disabilities. Occasional special issues have appeared on topics such as self-deception, as well as theory and circumstances in social justice. Most contributors are from American and Canadian universities. The writing is scholarly and encompasses a broad range of the humanities and social sciences, as well as public policy issues. This journal will be of interest to scholars and students of philosophy, but also to academics in many other disciplines.

1627. *South Asian History and Culture.* [ISSN: 1947-2498] 2010. q. GBP 338 (print & online eds.). Routledge, 4 Park Sq, Milton Park, Abingdon, OX14 4RN, United Kingdom; subscriptions@tandf.co.uk; http://www.tandfonline.com. Adv. Sample. Refereed. *Indexed:* AmHI, BAS. *Bk. rev.:* 1-3 review essays, 8-10 book reviews in some issues. *Aud.:* Ac.

This multidisciplinary journal focuses on the countries of India, Pakistan, Bangladesh, Sri Lanka, Nepal, and other parts of South Asia. It blends the traditional disciplines of history, economics, and politics with more contemporary areas of gender studies, minority rights, and sexuality studies. The publication also includes research on film, media, photography, sports, medicine, and the environment as related to this region of the world. Authors and editors are primarily from India, Australia, the U.K., and the U.S. Each issue contains research articles and book reviews, with some issues featuring commentary, interviews, and photo essays. Special themed issues are published frequently on subjects ranging from health, religion, minorities, and transnationalisms to Gujarat beyond Gandhi, and gender and masculinities and television. Other articles focus on topics such as Muslim resistance, the Cold War in the region, and Hindu temples. This publication is aimed at historians and scholars in other social sciences and humanities disciplines.

1628. *Southern Quarterly: a journal of the arts in the south.* [ISSN: 0038-4496] 1962. q. USD 35 (Individuals, USD 25). Ed(s): Ann Branton, Douglas Chambers. University of Southern Mississippi, 118 College Dr, Box 5078, Hattiesburg, MS 39406; gcadmissions@usm.edu; http://www.usm.edu. Illus., index. Refereed. Vol. ends: Summer. Microform: PQC. *Indexed:* A01, A22, ABIn, AmHI, BEL&L, BRI, F01, JEL, MLA-IB, P02, RILM. *Bk. rev.:* 4-10, 400-1,000 words. *Aud.:* Ga, Ac.

The arts and culture of the Southern United States is the focus of this journal, including the areas of the fine arts, film, photography, and popular culture, as well as folklore, history, anthropology, and material culture. Each issue presents articles on Southern writers and artists, including interviews, critical analyses of particular works, or themes from Southern literature, music, visual arts, or cultural studies. Frequently, special issues or features on one theme or author are published. Recent special issues have focused on humor in the South; the writing of Robert Morgan; and the centenary of Eudora Welty. *Southern Quarterly* also contains review essays and bibliographies, along with photographic essays, book reviews, and occasional film and exhibition reviews. "A Bibliography of the Visual Arts and Architecture" appears in the fall issue of each volume. *Southern Quarterly* is a fascinating and thoroughly enjoyable publication for readers in the South and across the country.

1629. *Systems Research and Behavioral Science.* Formed by the merger of (1984-1997): *Systems Research;* (1956-1997): *Behavioral Science.* [ISSN: 1092-7026] 1997. bi-m. GBP 485. Ed(s): M C Jackson. John Wiley & Sons Ltd., The Atrium, Southern Gate, Chichester, PO19 8SQ, United Kingdom; customer@wiley.com; http://www.wiley.com. Illus., adv. Sample. Refereed. Vol. ends: No. 4. Microform: PQC. Reprint: PSC. *Indexed:* A22, ABIn, B01, B02, BAS, BRI, C&ISA, CerAb, IBSS, PsycInfo. *Bk. rev.:* 5-6, 700-1,000 words, in some issues. *Aud.:* Ac.

This is the official journal of the International Federation for Systems Research. Its purpose is to publish theoretical and empirical articles on "new theories, experimental research, and applications relating to all levels of living and non-living systems." The journal has a very broad, interdisciplinary scope, covering systems in society, organizations, and business and management, as well as systems related to social cognition, modeling, values, and the quality of life. Each issue includes research articles on such topics as facilitating conservation planning, organizational cooperation for cultural heritage, and relational benefits in an e-business environment. Some issues include shorter news items or research notes, along with book reviews. Special issues appear occasionally on such subjects as metaphors in knowledge management, livable sustainable systems, and systems methodology and social development. The well-written and documented articles range from highly technical studies to theoretical approaches. This journal will be of interest to scholars as well as researchers in business, government, and technology.

1630. *Thesis Eleven: critical theory and historical sociology.* [ISSN: 0725-5136] 1980. bi-m. USD 1099. Sage Publications Ltd., 1 Oliver's Yard, 55 City Rd, London, EC1Y 1SP, United Kingdom; info@sagepub.co.uk; http://www.uk.sagepub.com. Illus., index, adv. Sample. Refereed. Vol. ends: Nov. Microform: PQC. Reprint: PSC. *Indexed:* A01, A22, E01, IBSS, IPB, P02, P61, SSA. *Bk. rev.:* 4-6, 1,000-3,000 words. *Aud.:* Ac.

For over 30 years, *Thesis Eleven* has published some of the leading work in the field of social theory. The journal is international and interdisciplinary, with a focus on "cultivating diverse critical theories of modernity." Incorporating both social sciences and liberal arts disciplines, from sociology and politics to philosophy, cultural studies, and literature, this publication includes European social theory as well as theory from other areas of the world. The editors are from Australian universities, while contributors to the journal are primarily from Europe, Canada, Australia, and the United States. Several research articles make up each issue, along with review essays and book reviews. Shorter essays or commentaries on earlier articles are also included. Recent articles have focused on topics such as sustainable development and environmental politics; the sociology of art; open-source knowledge and university rankings; colonial liberalism and Western Marxism; and academic entrepreneurship and the creative economy. This journal will appeal to academics, especially in the fields of sociology, politics, and philosophy.

1631. *World Future Review: a journal of strategic foresight.* Formed by the merger of (1985-2009): *Futures Research Quarterly;* Which was formerly (until 1985): *World Future Society. Bulletin;* (1979-2009): *Future Survey;* Which was formerly (until 1979): *Public Policy Book Forecast.* [ISSN: 1946-7567] 1967. bi-m. USD 362. Ed(s): Timothy C Mack. Sage Publications, Inc., 2455 Teller Rd, Thousand Oaks, CA 91320; info@sagepub.com; http://www.sagepub.com. Illus., adv. Refereed. *Indexed:* A01, A22. *Bk. rev.:* 1 - 2, essay length. *Aud.:* Ga, Ac.

A publication from the World Future Society, this journal "provides a forum for all who are professionally involved with the theory, methodology, practice[,] and use of futures research." Scholarly articles form the basis for the journal, which also seeks to "promote public understanding and education in the methods and applications of futures research." The editors and authors are primarily from the United States, with some from Great Britain and Western Europe. Recent articles have covered such topics as the future of climate change; competitive intelligence; twenty-first-century economics; the ecology of the mind; and future systems engineering. The "Abstracts" section highlights new books, articles, blog postings, and other reports on futurist issues. These shorter descriptions, some 10–20 per issue, are grouped into subject areas such as business, environment, food, politics, methods, and social change. This journal will appeal to the academic community and to non-specialists interested in developments in futurist studies.

■ DANCE

Mary Augusta Thomas, Deputy Director, Smithsonian Institution Libraries, Washington, DC 20560-0154

Introduction

Journals in dance keep pace with the trends that have emerged in the past two years, continuing to meet the needs of students, researchers, dance professionals and dance audiences. Now, most dance journals offer both print and web versions with additional content, making them accessible to a wide and diverse group of readers.

Social media has energized the dance community. National Dance Week 2012 featured a flashmob competition that included companies from Korea and the U.K. as well as those across America. Dance U 101 (www.danceu101.com) is for those heading off to dance programs in colleges and universities. At Dance 212 (www.dance212.com), daily online episodes follow real dancers in New York City as they study, live, and strive to make it as professionals.

There are independent web sites such as www.goethe.de/tanzconnexions; this one provides choreographers, dancers, and dance enthusiasts with a wealth of information on contemporary dance in the Asia-Pacific region and the European-influenced German dance scene. Based on a joint project of Goethe-Institutes in Australia, Indonesia, Malaysia, New Zealand, the Philippines, Singapore, Thailand, and Vietnam, tanzconnexions seeks to shed light on local artists, working methods, and infrastructure in the fields of dance and choreography in Southeast Asia, Australia, and New Zealand.

For the public, dance competitions remain among the most popular programs on television. England has a long tradition of competitive dance, while in the United States, competitive dance for school-age children is growing in popularity. In June, *Bun Heads* joined the new season lineup on commercial television. As more international dance companies perform across the country, Zumba and other dance workouts are debuting on the list of the top 20 predicted fitness trends for 2012. For adults, classes in African dance, Afro-Caribbean dance, and Latin dance and salsa are all available nationwide.

At colleges and universities, supporters of varied traditions in dance are working together to keep the entire art form strong. Dance research must include the work of international scholars whose publications appear in most of the recommended journals. Other national resources include www.danceusa.org for Dance/USA, a national service organization for professional dance.

Basic Periodicals

Ems: *Dance Magazine;* Hs: *Dance Magazine, Dance Spirit, Pointe;* Ga: *Dance Magazine, Dance Spirit, Dance Teacher, Dance Today!, Pointe;* Ac: *Ballet Review, Dance Chronicle, Dance Research Journal, Dance Theatre Journal, Dancing Times, Pointe;* Sa: *American Journal of Dance Therapy, Dance Research Journal, Dance Teacher, DanceView.*

Basic Abstracts and Indexes

American Bibliography of Slavic and Eastern European Studies (ABSEES), Arts and Humanities Citation Index, Current Contents, Humanities Index, International Index to the Performing Arts, Music Index.

1632. *American Journal of Dance Therapy.* Supersedes (in 1977): *American Dance Therapy Association. Monograph.* [ISSN: 0146-3721] 1968. s-a. EUR 501 (print & online eds.). Ed(s): Susan Loman, Christina Devereux. Springer New York LLC, 233 Spring St, New York, NY 10013; service-ny@springer.com; http://www.springer.com/. Illus., index, adv. Sample. Refereed. Reprint: PSC. *Indexed:* A22, BRI, E01, IIPA, P02, PsycInfo, RILM. *Bk. rev.:* 4-5, 500 words. *Aud.:* Ac, Sa.

Behavior, movement, and physical and mental health are closely linked. Essays and original research in this journal reflect the important role of dance/movement therapy in therapeutic practice. Articles present original, scholarly research on the psychology of movement and dance, which is intertwined with other areas of dance research. The relationship between movement and psychological health is a continuing subject for research that seeks to evaluate and promote use of dance in therapy with physical and mental illness, societal problems, and domestic violence. Recent issues include conference proceedings from national and international meetings of clinicians, researchers, educators, and well-established students. Journal contributors come from all groups. This is a good source for administrators, psychiatrists, psychologists, social workers, and creative-arts therapists in the disciplines of music, art, and drama.

1633. *American SquareDance.* Former titles (until 1972): *New Square Dance;* (until 1968): *Square Dance;* (until 1966): *American Squares.* [ISSN: 0091-3383] 1945. m. USD 27.50 domestic; USD 69.50 Canada; USD 92.50 elsewhere. Ed(s): Bill Boyd. American Squaredance, 34 E Main St, Apopka, FL 32703. Illus., adv. Microform: PQC. *Indexed:* A22. *Bk. rev.:* Occasional, short. *Aud.:* Hs, Ga.

For 67 years, this small-format magazine has covered square dance worldwide. Regular features report on contra dance and round dance, as well as square dance. A recent editorial noted that square dance organizations need to stay current with the times, and respond to their members. Contributors cover conventions, clubs, and dance news. The "Caller Lab" presents tips on steps and patterns. Each issue also includes notes on travel, events, and a calendar of dances.

1634. *Ballet Review.* [ISSN: 0522-0653] 1965. q. USD 25 domestic; USD 33 foreign. Ed(s): Marvin Hoshino. Dance Research Foundation, Inc., 37 W 12th St 7J, New York, NY 10011; info@balletreview.com; http://www.balletreview.com. Illus., adv. *Indexed:* A22, ABS&EES, AmHI, ArtHuCI, BRI, IIPA, MLA-IB, RILM. *Bk. rev.:* Number and length vary. *Aud.:* Ac, Sa.

Founded by Arlene Croce, renowned dance critic for *The New Yorker,* this periodical remains central to academic and specialized collections. Modern dance and avant-garde companies, in addition to ballet companies, are featured in "big city" reviews written by both critics and practitioners. The clear, readable, well-researched text, often with unusual historic or contemporary black-and-white photographs and drawings, and the contributions of leading dance historians and critics like George Dorris, combine to lend credibility to this journal as a major resource for dance criticism. Each issue contains six or seven articles on dance history, trends in dance criticism, and biographical features on important dancers, dance music on disc, costumes, and company performances.

1635. *Contact Quarterly: a vehicle for moving ideas.* Formerly (until 1976): *Contact Newsletter.* [ISSN: 0198-9634] 1975. q. Free to members. Ed(s): Melinda Buckwalter, Nancy Stark Smith. Contact Collaborations, Inc., PO Box 603, Northampton, MA 01061; info@contactquarterly.com; http://www.contactquarterly.com. Illus., index, adv. Sample. *Indexed:* IIPA. *Bk. rev.:* Number and length vary. *Aud.:* Ac, Sa.

Started 37 years ago as a print journal to discuss the then relatively unknown field of dance improvisation, *Contact Quarterly* is the "longest living, independent, artist-made, not-for-profit, reader-supported magazine devoted to the dancer's voice." A print annual, a chapbook, and an annual dance directory combine with the online journal to present the latest techniques and performances in contemporary movement arts. This may be the only dance performance magazine to deal with a broad range of social issues, providing studies on the philosophical and psychological dimensions of movement for all people, including those with mental or physical disabilities. Fiction and poetry are included, along with pieces on health and alternative healing, to emphasize the all-encompassing nature of movement. The editors cover worldwide events, festivals, and schools, documenting what teachers of movement improvisation are doing internationally. URL: www.contactquarterly.com

1636. Dance Chronicle: studies in dance & the related arts. Formerly (until 1977): *Dance Perspectives.* [ISSN: 0147-2526] 1959. 3x/yr. GBP 787 (print & online eds.). Ed(s): Joellen A Meglin, Lynn Matluck Brooks. Taylor & Francis Inc., 325 Chestnut St, Ste 800, Philadelphia, PA 19106; customerservice@taylorandfrancis.com; http://www.tandfonline.com. Illus., index, adv. Sample. Circ: 450. Vol. ends: Winter. Microform: RPI. Reprint: PSC. *Indexed:* A01, A22, ABS&EES, AmHI, ArtHuCI, BRI, E01, IIPA, MLA-IB, P02, RILM. *Bk. rev.:* 3-5 signed, 500-1,000 words. *Aud.:* Ac, Sa.

With topics ranging in time from classical antiquity to Broadway, and recent numbers featuring Zen koan and Kafka, this is the oldest journal devoted exclusively to scholarship in dance. The peer-reviewed research found here is essential for serious students of dance history, choreography, performance, and criticism. The contents address all periods and styles of dance and the interplay between dance and music. Detailed research on costuming and staging is presented. The style is highly polished and readable, with extensive references to sources for further study. Dance experts, established dance historians, and scholars review books in lengthy and carefully supported articles. Recent exhibitions on dance history are reviewed here as well. Contents of several other scholarly dance journals are listed, along with books received. Although this is the most expensive dance journal, it must be included in any comprehensive dance collection.

1637. Dance Europe: the international dance magazine. 1995. 11x/yr. GBP 68. Ed(s): Emma Manning. Dance Europe, PO Box 12661, London, E5 9TZ, United Kingdom. Adv. *Bk. rev.:* 1 signed, 500-1,000 words. *Aud.:* Hs, Ga, Ac, Sa.

Dance Europe, founded in 1995, published 11 times a year in London in Spanish and English, considers its audience "anyone who loves to dance." The editorial policy is to provide "unbiased platforms for dance throughout Europe and beyond," and many of the contributors are professional dancers or ex-dancers. Handsomely designed and illustrated, it covers ballet and modern dance from many of the smaller companies across Europe. It includes reviews from Asia with a Japanese summary page and a South African report. Well-written interviews with dancers and choreographers provides access to European trends for U.S. students. There are previews of the dance season and interviews with well-known and lesser-known dancers, lists of auditions, and a performance diary. *Dance Europe* may be the broadest source for worldwide professional performance that is currently available. The online version includes numerous links to auditions and jobs, training, and news about dancers and companies. URL: www.danceeurope.net

1638. Dance Magazine. Former titles (until 1948): *Dance;* (until 1945): *Dance Magazine;* (until 1943): *Dance;* (until 1942): *The American Dancer;* Incorporates (in 2006): *Dance Annual Directory;* Which was formerly (until 2004): *Stern's Directory;* (until 2000): *Stern's Performing Arts Directory;* (until 1989): *Performing Arts Directory;* (until 1986): *Dance Magazine Annual;* (until 1974): *Dance Magazine;* (until 1970): *Dance Magazine Annual.* [ISSN: 0011-6009] 1927. m. USD 34.95 domestic; USD 46.95 Canada; USD 66.95 foreign. Ed(s): Wendy Perron. DanceMedia, LLC., 333 7th Ave, New York, NY 10001; http://dancemedia.com. Illus., index, adv. Sample. Vol. ends: Dec. Microform: PQC. *Indexed:* A01, A06, A22, ABS&EES, AmHI, ArtHuCI, BRI, C37, CBRI, F01, IIPA, MASUSE, P02, RILM. *Bk. rev.:* 250-2,500 words. *Aud.:* Ems, Hs, Ga, Ac.

Dance Magazine remains the one journal that any collection must include to provide information on current dance in performance and dance education in the United States. It offers in-depth coverage of all regions and companies, and its sections on people, events, an annual audition calendar, and even gossip make this journal a basic tool. As the oldest continuously published dance periodical (more than 80 years) in the country, it attracts leading dance writers from all over the world and is the first magazine consulted by professionals and dance aficionados. Because of its panoramic coverage of ballet, modern, and theatrical styles throughout the country, it is required reading for the professional dancer and teacher. Each issue provides "Dancefinder" listings of jobs and schools

nationwide. Online, editors offer vast additional content, including blogs, a dance search engine, a career and learning resource guide, and up-to-the-minute reviews. URL: www.dancemagazine.com

1639. Dance Research Journal. Formerly (until 1975): *C O R D News.* [ISSN: 0149-7677] 1969. s-a. GBP 114. Ed(s): Mark Franko. Cambridge University Press, 32 Ave of the Americas, New York, NY 10013; information@cambridge.org; http://www.cambridge.org/us/. Illus., adv. Sample. Refereed. Reprint: PSC. *Indexed:* A01, A22, ABS&EES, AmHI, ArtHuCI, BRI, CBRI, E01, IIPA, MLA-IB, P02, RILM, SD. *Bk. rev.:* Lengthy. *Aud.:* Ac, Sa.

Dance Research Journal, published by the Congress on Research in Dance for its members, is a semi-annual, academic, peer-reviewed journal, providing a source for serious study of the work of international dance scholars. Handsome graphic design combines with articles by well-regarded dance historians at major institutions to present current research that employs quantitative and qualitative analysis of international dance and related fields. With its focus on scholarship in dance, this journal includes dance studied through ethnography, linguistics, and semiotics. Papers are well documented and usually accompanied by bibliographies. One of the strongest attributes is the book review section, which contains many in-depth reviews that are signed and often accompanied by additional references, making this journal a major source for bibliographic information. A regular feature lists papers of major conferences and descriptions of research collections and archives. Research ranges from migration of peoples to teaching styles in contact/improvisation.

1640. Dance Spirit: inspiring a new generation of dancers. [ISSN: 1094-0588] 1997. 10x/yr. USD 16.95 domestic; USD 35 Canada; USD 45 elsewhere. Ed(s): Kate Lydon. DanceMedia, LLC., 333 7th Ave, New York, NY 10001; http://dancemedia.com. Adv. Sample. Circ: 93066 Paid and controlled. *Indexed:* A01, IIPA, MASUSE. *Aud.:* Hs, Ga, Ac, Sa.

The editors of *Dance Spirit* want their audience to be anyone who loves to dance. This includes dancers in training; dance teachers; and beginning professional dancers from the Broadway stage to the ballet, to graduate dance programs. Keeping the journal's aim at a younger audience, editors employ a lively style, with short features illustrated with intense graphics and color photography. This journal meets the needs of those in high school on dance teams or those learning tap dance, swing dance, ballroom dancing, and hip hop. *Dance Spirit* covers the entire field of dance practice, teaching, and competition. Each issue includes news on dance competitions, business and agents, and dance events. The publisher also produces *Dance Magazine, Dance Teacher,* and *Pointe.*

1641. Dance Teacher: the magazine for dance professionals. Formerly (until 1999): *Dance Teacher Now.* [ISSN: 1524-4474] 1979. m. USD 24.95 domestic; USD 38 Canada; USD 48 elsewhere. Ed(s): Karen Hildebrand. DanceMedia, LLC., 333 7th Ave, New York, NY 10001; http://dancemedia.com. Illus., index, adv. *Indexed:* ABS&EES, IIPA. *Bk. rev.:* 3, 250 words. *Aud.:* Ga, Ac.

Dance Teacher is the only national magazine addressed to dance teachers of all disciplines. Features cover tap, ballroom, Irish dance, aerobics, ballet, hip hop, and modern performance. Recent issues have added articles on dance history to enhance teaching and ground the profession. Profiles of dance teaching institutions, a higher-education guide, classified advertising for training courses, and good articles on dance music make this a fine resource for all dance teachers. Online, the magazine includes dance videos, blogs, and a tip of the day. DanceMedia LLC is responsible for a string of dance-related publications that range from ballet to cheerleading. Since this journal includes the business of teaching dance, it reviews proper flooring and provides information on creating the dream studio, selling studios, producing publicity, and financing. The content is useful for teachers with students from grade school through college. URL: www.dance-teacher.com

1642. Dance Theatre Journal. Formerly (until 1983): *Labanews.* [ISSN: 0264-9160] 1981. q. GBP 25 (Individuals, GBP 15; GBP 4 per issue domestic). Ed(s): Martin Hargreaves. Laban, Creekside, London, SE8 3DZ, United Kingdom; info@laban.org; http://www.laban.org. Illus., index, adv. Vol. ends: Dec. *Indexed:* A22, ArtHuCI, IIPA, RILM. *Bk. rev.:* Number and length vary. *Aud.:* Ga, Ac, Sa.

Dance Theatre is a sophisticated journal that aims both to cover dance and to foster critical debate among a community of dance intellectuals. It focuses on current thinking about live art; and covers contemporary dance and dance theater in Europe, with recent examples from Dublin to Kupio, Finland. The articles concentrate on the intersections of dance, drama, music, and visual art. Interviews with performance artists and in-depth articles encompass the entire setting of dance performances, detailing not only choreography but cutting-edge design for costumes, sets, lighting, and music. In a 2012 issue, two invited guest editors focused on dance films as performance. Ballet, modern dance, and contemporary hybrids are described in a lively fashion for performers, dance writers, and a general audience. Well-written text and visually stimulating photographs support the lengthy signed reviews and interviews.

1643. *Dance Today!* Formerly (until 2001): *Ballroom Dancing Times.* [ISSN: 1475-2336] 1956. m. GBP 19.25 domestic. Ed(s): Nicola Rayner. Dancing Times Ltd., 45-47 Clerkenwell Green, London, EC1R 0EB, United Kingdom; dt@dancing-times.co.uk; http:// www.dancing-times.co.uk. Illus., adv. Vol. ends: Sep. *Indexed:* IIPA. *Aud.:* Ga, Sa.

The editors of *Dance Today!* claim the magazine to be *the* publication for people who love to dance and watch dancing. For ballroom/social dancers in England, this remains the main source for news on national competition. Features include any kind of partner dance: flamenco, sequence, musical theater, and salsa, as well as ballroom dance. Since there is a current craze for dance competition and televised competitions, the most useful sections for dancers and judges are the well-illustrated and well-described scripts and sequences performed by competition winners. Tips on how to improve ballroom dancing may benefit any amateur or professional. As a spinoff of *Dancing Times,* this magazine is part of a tradition going back to 1894 and in general publication since 1910.

1644. *DanceView: a quarterly review of dance.* Formerly (until 1992): *Washington Danceview.* [ISSN: 1077-0577] 1979. q. Individuals, USD 30. Ed(s): Alexandra Tomalonis. DanceView, PO Box 34435, Washington, DC 20043. Illus. Vol. ends: Winter. *Indexed:* ABS&EES, IIPA. *Bk. rev.:* Number and length vary. *Aud.:* Ac, Sa.

DanceView covers companies and dance events worldwide. It includes thoughtful, in-depth interviews with dancers, often conducted by other dancers and dance writers, and reviews of exhibitions and other forms of research on dance and dance history. Its contributors, George Jackson, Robert Greskovic, and others, are professional dance critics who provide analysis of the major companies in the United States, England, and occasionally Russia. There is research value in the interviews. For example, a recent issue contains an analysis of Merrill Ashley's approach to coaching dancers in Balanchine's actual movements for a piece, a good source in the future. Features include regular reports from New York, London, and the Bay Area. Each issue provides overviews of the season, video reviews, and complete book reviews that are a satisfying read. This would be a good addition to serious dance collections that serve dance devotees. Its online counterpart, subtitled *Writers on Dance,* posts short reviews and features blogs by important dance critics in New York, the San Francisco Bay area, and Washington, D.C. URL: www.danceviewtimes.com

1645. *Dancing Times.* Incorporates (1930-1934): *The Amateur Dancer;* (19??-19??): *Dancing & the Ballroom;* (1964-19??): *The Ballet Annual and Year Book;* Which was formerly (1947-1964): *The Ballet Annual.* [ISSN: 0011-605X] 1910. m. GBP 32.45 domestic. Ed(s): Jonathan Gray. Dancing Times Ltd., 45-47 Clerkenwell Green, London, EC1R 0EB, United Kingdom. Illus., adv. *Indexed:* A22, ArtHuCI, IIPA, MLA-IB, RILM. *Bk. rev.:* 4-5. *Aud.:* Hs, Ga, Ac.

Britain remains a major center for dance performance, with a strong audience for contemporary dance, which is fully reflected in *Dancing Times,* the oldest continuing periodical on dance in existence. In its second century, *Dancing Times* continues to inform readers interested in theatrical/classical dance, especially British companies and the season. Because dance students from the United States often study abroad, the coverage of British dance schools is especially valuable. Regular sections are devoted to dance on video and television. "Into Dance!" is a regular section for children that makes dance themes more approachable by profiling young dancers and recent ballets. The editors provide an online format, access to full-text articles, additional content, and an RSS feed. URL: www.dancing-times.co.uk

1646. *Folk Music Journal.* Formerly (until 1965): *English Folk Dance and Song Society. Journal;* Which was formed by the merger of (1927-1932): *English Folk Dance Society. Journal;* Which was formerly (1914-1927): *English Folk Dance Society. Journal;* (1899-1932): *Folk-Song Society. Journal.* [ISSN: 0531-9684] 1932. a. Free to members; Non-members, GBP 7.50. Ed(s): David Atkinson. English Folk Dance and Song Society, Cecil Sharp House, 2 Regents Park Rd, London, NW1 7AY, United Kingdom; info@efdss.org; http://www.efdss.org/. Illus., index, adv. Refereed. Microform: PQC. Reprint: PSC. *Indexed:* A01, A22, AmHI, ArtHuCI, BRI, IIMP, IIPA, MLA-IB, P02, RILM. *Bk. rev.:* Number varies, 500 words, signed; shorter notices section. *Aud.:* Ac, Sa.

In 1911, Cecil Sharp formed the English Dance and Song Society, which serves to "collect, research and preserve our heritage of folk dances, songs, and music." The journal's consistently well-written style makes it of interest to historians, to the audience for folk music and dancing, and to the many people who are active in folk music and dance as a hobby. The emphasis on considering dance and music together reflects the interdisciplinary approach in most current dance scholarship and incorporates social and cultural history. Scholarly reviews of new books and sound recordings are, in effect, research essays. Subscribers become members of the society and also receive the quarterly *English Dance and Song,* which contains shorter informational articles, events calendars, and news items. According to its editors, the *Folk Music Journal* is "set to enjoy a further century at the forefront of cultural studies. The *Journal* is also embracing the World Wide Web without relinquishing its role as a printed journal of record." The journal's web site now carries multimedia items in support of articles in the print issues, access to the Vaughn Williams library, and other resources.

Journal of Physical Education, Recreation and Dance. See Sports section.

1647. *Pointe: ballet at its best.* Formerly (until 2000): *Points.* [ISSN: 1529-6741] 2000. bi-m. USD 16.95 domestic; USD 25 Canada; USD 35 elsewhere. Ed(s): Hanna Rubin. DanceMedia, LLC., 333 7th Ave, New York, NY 10001; http://dancemedia.com. Illus., adv. *Indexed:* ABS&EES, IIPA, MASUSE, P02. *Aud.:* Hs, Ga, Ac, Sa.

The stated purpose for *Pointe,* published six times a year, is to empower ballet dancers to achieve career goals, technical prowess, and artistic self-confidence. The focus is on individual dancers as opposed to companies, with articles that discuss the business of ballet. Subjects range from contracts to technique, as well as the most recent developments in health care and the prevention of injuries, each handled by a practitioner/expert in the field. Since the focus is on working dancers and students, this journal's style is crisp and clear, with very good photographs and illustrations. *Pointe* will also inform the ballet fan who wants to understand more about the dancer's craft and preparations for performance. The web site contains the content of the print publication, and as do others from DanceMedia, it includes blogs, additional services, and professional information for subscribers. URL: www.pointemagazine.com

■ DEATH AND DYING

See also Medicine section.

Patricia Newland, Catalog/Technical Services Librarian, Francis Harvey Green Library, West Chester University of Pennsylvania, West Chester, PA 19383; Hospice volunteer; pnewland@wcupa.edu

Introduction

Although death, dying, and bereavement touch all library users, most periodicals devoted to these topics are aimed at academic or professional audiences, and almost every title reviewed here is relevant to one or both of these audiences. These journals will be read by faculty and students in a wide range of disciplines and by practitioners caring for the dying: physicians, nurses, clergy, therapists, social workers, and hospice staff. Highly interdisciplinary journals such as *Death Studies* and *Omega,* publish research from the fields of psychology, sociology, education, religion, anthropology, and others. They are essential for academic and research libraries with programs in these fields. Publications such as *Journal of Hospice & Palliative Nursing* and *Journal of Palliative Medicine* are chiefly aimed at practitioners and students in the health professions. These journals publish research on pain management and care of the dying and are essential for libraries that support medical schools and nursing programs, as well as for hospital libraries. Studies on bereavement and psychological issues involving the dying and their caretakers are covered in both types of publications; students and faculty in counseling and social work, as well as professionals in either field, will benefit from academic and special libraries that collect both.

Recent changes in publishers have resulted in online access to almost all these titles. In addition, there are now several peer-reviewed, open-access online journals aimed at practitioners and students in the health professions. The journals reviewed here are published in the United States, Canada, Great Britain, Australia, and New Zealand. Contributions are in English. These contributions, however, cover issues involved in death, dying, and bereavement throughout the world, and they are written by an international group of researchers. In addition, a cross-cultural perspective on death, dying, and bereavement is prominent not only in interdisciplinary journals such as *Death Studies* but also in journals aimed at those working in medical fields. The diverse nature of the population in the countries in which they are published is reflected in these journals' contents.

Basic Periodicals

Ac, Sa: *American Journal of Hospice and Palliative Medicine; Death Studies; European Journal of Palliative Care; Journal of Hospice and Palliative Nursing; Journal of Palliative Care; Journal of Palliative Medicine; Mortality; Omega: Journal of Death and Dying; Palliative & Supportive Care; Palliative Medicine; Suicide and Life-Threatening Behavior.*

Basic Abstracts and Indexes

AgeLine, CINAHL, Family Index, MEDLINE, PsycINFO, Scopus, Social Work Abstracts.

1648. The American Journal of Hospice and Palliative Medicine. Former titles (until 2004): *The American Journal of Hospice and Palliative Care;* Which incorporated (2002-2003): *Journal of Terminal Oncology;* (until 1990): *The American Journal of Hospice Care.* 1983. 8x/yr. USD 925. Ed(s): Robert E Enck. Sage Publications, Inc., 2455 Teller Rd, Thousand Oaks, CA 91320; info@sagepub.com; http://www.sagepub.com/. Illus., index. Sample. Refereed. Reprint: PSC. *Indexed:* A22, AgeL, E01, PsycInfo, SWR&A. *Bk. rev.:* Number and length vary. *Aud.:* Ga, Ac, Sa.

Published by Sage, this peer-reviewed journal, available in print and online, offers original research, case reports, news briefs, book reviews, discussion of ethical issues, and life stories of patients and hospice workers. Hospice in an international context is a regular topic of research. The contents are generally aimed at practitioners and students in the health care and counseling professions. Recent articles include "Improving Cultural Competency among Hospice and Palliative Care Volunteers: Recommendations for Social Policy," "Level of Consciousness in Dying Patients. The Role of Palliative Sedation: A Longitudinal Prospective Study," and "Palliative Care and Support for Persons with HIV/AIDS in 7 African Countries: Implementation Experience and Future Priorities." Tables of contents and abstracts from volume 1 (1984), as well as a sample issue, are available on the journal's web site. URL: http://ajh.sagepub.com

1649. B M C Palliative Care. [ISSN: 1472-684X] 2002. irreg. Free. BioMed Central Ltd., 236 Gray's Inn Rd, London, WC1X 8HB, United Kingdom; info@biomedcentral.com; http://www.biomedcentral.com. Illus., adv. Refereed. *Indexed:* A01, ExcerpMed. *Aud.:* Ac, Sa.

This online open-access journal primarily publishes peer-reviewed original research studies and study protocols in the areas of palliative medicine, medical ethics, and hospice care. Professionals in the health care and counseling fields, as well as students and faculty in programs preparing practitioners in those fields, would be interested in this journal. Recently published articles include "Developing and Testing a Strategy to Enhance a Palliative Approach and Care Continuity for People Who Have Dementia: Study Overview and Protocol," "Outcomes 'Out of Africa': The Selection and Implementation of Outcome

Measures for Palliative Care in Africa," and "Cancer Carepartners: Improving Patients' Symptom Management by Engaging Informal Caregivers." The full text of all articles, in html and pdf formats, is available from the journal's web site. Links are provided for related articles from this and other journals; frequently accessed articles are identified. Articles can be searched in a variety of ways; free registration is required to save searches or for e-mail alerts. The journal is widely indexed in databases in the field. URL: www.biomedcentral.com/bmcpalliatcare

1650. Bereavement Care: an international journal for those who help bereaved people. [ISSN: 0268-2621] 1982. 3x/yr. GBP 154 (print & online eds.). Ed(s): Kate Mitchell. Routledge, 4 Park Sq, Milton Park, Abingdon, OX14 4RN, United Kingdom; subscriptions@tandf.co.uk; http://www.tandfonline.com. Illus. Sample. Refereed. Reprint: PSC. *Indexed:* A01, A22, E01. *Bk. rev.:* Number and length vary. *Aud.:* Ac, Sa.

Published by Routledge in association with Cruse Bereavement Care, this peer-reviewed journal, available in print and online, contains original research, case studies, and book, article, and media reviews that would be of interest to those involved in hospice care, counseling, pastoral care, or social work. Recent articles include "Using the Biographical Grid Method to Explore Parental Grief Following the Death of a Child," "Workplace Support for Traumatically Bereaved People," and "Waves: A Psycho-Educational Programme for Adults Bereaved by Suicide." A sample issue and tables of contents and abstracts beginning with volume 1 (1982) can be found on the journal's web site. URL: www.tandf.co.uk/journals/titles/02682621.asp

1651. Compassion and Choices Magazine. Former titles (until 2005): *End-of-Life Choices;* (until 2002): *Timelines;* (until 1994): *Hemlock Quarterly.* [ISSN: 1949-8829] 1980. q. Free to members. Compassion & Choices, PO Box 101810, Denver, CO 80250; info@compassionandchoices.org; http://www.compassionandchoices.org. Illus., adv. *Bk. rev.:* Number and length vary. *Aud.:* Ga.

Compassion and Choices Magazine, a publication of the organization of the same name, fosters the work of the organization and is aimed at a general adult audience as well as lawmakers and health-care workers. A recent issue describes the work of Dr. Peter Goodwin, who was influential in the passing of Oregon's Death with Dignity Act. The print edition is a benefit of membership in the organization; the current issue is available online from a link on the organization's web site. URL: https://www.compassionandchoices.org/

1652. Death Studies: counseling - research - education - care - ethics. Formerly (until 1985): *Death Education.* [ISSN: 0748-1187] 1977. 10x/yr. GBP 626 (print & online eds.). Ed(s): Robert A Neimeyer. Routledge, 325 Chestnut St, Ste 800, Philadelphia, PA 19106; customerservice@taylorandfrancis.com; http://www.tandfonline.com. Illus., index. Sample. Refereed. Vol. ends: Dec. Microform: PQC. Reprint: PSC. *Indexed:* A01, A22, AbAn, BRI, E01, ERIC, MLA-IB, P02, P61, PsycInfo, SSA, SWR&A. *Bk. rev.:* Number and length vary. *Aud.:* Ac, Sa.

Death Studies is available in print and online; the print journal is now published twice a year, with five numbers in each. This peer-reviewed interdisciplinary journal would interest researchers and students in disciplines as varied as medicine, philosophy, anthropology, religion, psychology, sociology, and education. It contains original research, news from the field, best practices, and in-depth book reviews. Original research examines beliefs about and reactions to death and bereavement in the context of age, gender, and ethnicity. Cross-cultural similarities and differences are the subject of investigation in every issue. Recent studies include "Helpful Aspects of Bereavement Support for Adults Following an Expected Death: Volunteers' and Bereaved People's Perspectives," "Suicide Bulletin Board Systems Comparison between Japan and Germany," and "Visiting the Site of Death: Experiences of the Bereaved after the 2004 Southeast Asian Tsunami." *Death Studies* publishes occasional thematic issues or special sections such as the recent "Death Acceptance." A sample copy and tables of contents and abstracts from volume one (1977) to the present are available on the journal's web site. URL: www.tandf.co.uk/journals/titles/07481187.html

1653. *European Journal of Palliative Care.* [ISSN: 1352-2779] 1994. bi-m. GBP 425 (print & online eds.). Ed(s): Julia Riley. Hayward Medical Communications Ltd., 8-10 Dryden St, Covent Garden, London, WC2E 9NA, United Kingdom; edit@hayward.co.uk; http://www.hayward.co.uk. Illus., adv. *Bk. rev.:* Number and length vary. *Aud.:* Ac, Sa.

This publication, available in print and online, is an official journal of the European Association for Palliative Care. The association's empirical research focus is primarily the domain of the journal *Palliative Medicine,* which the association also sponsors. *European Journal of Palliative Care* serves as a vehicle for communication about the work of the organization and related events within the European palliative care community. The journal publishes review articles in English on current research in palliative care, book reviews, and news updates. These multidisciplinary articles are not limited in geographic scope, and there is a notable concern for palliative care in developing countries. An interesting feature is the case study masterclass. Each issue describes a clinical case and asks the reader to respond to questions posed about the case; in the next issue, specialists in the field provide answers to these questions, based on the actual conduct of the case. An example is Case 59, "Managing Renal Failure at Home near the End of Life." These case studies could be useful for both practitioners and students in the field of palliative medicine. Recent articles include "Preventing Iatrogenic Pain in Oncology Patients: Considerations and Solutions," "The Path to Developing Unified Palliative Care Services in India," and "Schooling of Children with a Life-Limiting or Life-Threatening Illness." Tables of contents and brief summaries are available beginning with volume 1 (1994) on the journal's web site; the full text of articles can be searched as well. There are several subscription options, including one for short-term access. URL: www.haywardpublishing.co.uk/ejpc_.aspx

1654. *Grief Matters: the Australian journal of grief and bereavement.* [ISSN: 1440-6888] 1998. 3x/yr. Free to members. Ed(s): Christopher Hall. Australian Centre for Grief and Bereavement, McCulloch House, Monash Medical Centre, Clayton, VIC 3168 , Australia; info@grief.org.au; http://www.grief.org.au/. Illus., adv. Vol. ends: Summer. *Bk. rev.:* Number and length vary. *Aud.:* Ac, Sa.

This journal is a publication of the Australian Centre for Grief and Bereavement, which provides grief and bereavement-related education in Australia. Articles from an international group of researchers focus on psychological, social, and ethical issues involved in grief and bereavement. *Grief Matters* contains research articles, book reviews, and abstracts of relevant articles in other journals. Each issue has a theme, such as the recent "Grief in Schools" and "Grief of First Nation Peoples." Recent articles include "Grief and the American Indian," "Grieving Styles: Gender and Grief," and "A Voyage in the Grief Labyrinth: The Impact of Grief on University Students' Academic Progress and Overall Wellbeing." The journal would interest practitioners and students in the fields of mental health, social work, and pastoral work. Tables of contents for volume 1 (1998) to the present are available on the journal's web site. URL: www.grief.org.au/resources/grief_matters

1655. *Illness, Crisis, and Loss.* [ISSN: 1054-1373] 1991. q. USD 754 (print & online eds.) Individuals, USD 118 (print & online eds.). Ed(s): Jason L Powell. Baywood Publishing Co., Inc., 26 Austin Ave, PO Box 337, Amityville, NY 11701; info@baywood.com; http://www.baywood.com. Illus., adv. Sample. Refereed. *Indexed:* A01, A22, ASSIA, E01, P61, PsycInfo, SSA. *Bk. rev.:* Number and length vary. *Aud.:* Ac, Sa.

This peer-reviewed journal, sponsored by the Center for Death Education and Bioethics, is published in print and online by Baywood Publishing, publisher of *Omega: Journal of Death and Dying.* The scope of *Illness, Crisis, and Loss* extends beyond issues related to death and dying, but many of its articles focus on psychological, social, and ethical issues involved in death, dying, and bereavement. Regular features include "Commentaries" and "Voices," personal reflections on experience with illness and the dying. This interdisciplinary journal would interest practitioners and students in the fields of counseling, social work, medicine, and ethics. Recent articles reflect the coverage of death and bereavement: "Understanding Grief Following Pregnancy Loss: A Retrospective Analysis Regarding Women's Coping Responses," "Life Will Never Be the Same Again: Examining Grief in Survivors Bereaved by Young Suicide," and "Diversity in Death: Body Disposition and Memorialization." Some issues are organized thematically, such as the recent one on the Chinese experience of loss and bereavement. Tables of contents and article abstracts

beginning with volume 7 (1999) are available from a link on the journal's web site. A sample issue can be downloaded or a print issue requested after free registration. URL: www.baywood.com/journals/previewjournals.asp?id=1054-1373

1656. *The Internet Journal of Pain, Symptom Control and Palliative Care.* [ISSN: 1528-8277] 2000. s-a. Free. Ed(s): Peter Lierz. Internet Scientific Publications, Llc., 23 Rippling Creek Dr, Sugar Land, TX 77479; wenker@ispub.com ; http://www.ispub.com/. Refereed. *Indexed:* A01. *Aud.:* Ac, Sa.

An early open-access online-only publication in the field, this peer-reviewed journal publishes original research, literature reviews, and case reports on pain control and palliative medicine for the dying. It would interest all those studying or working in the area of pain management and palliative care. The journal is indexed, and the full text of articles is fully or partially available in the databases of major vendors; it is also accessible through the Directory of Open Access Journals. Recent articles include "The Prevalence of Pain in Patients Attending Melanoma Outpatient Clinics," "Are We Making Progress? One Medical School's Assessment of an Evolving Integrated Palliative Medicine Curriculum," and "Establishing Palliative Care for American Indians as a Public Health Agenda." URL: www.la-press.com/palliative-care-research-and-treatment-journal-j86

1657. *Journal of Hospice and Palliative Nursing.* [ISSN: 1522-2179] 1999. bi-m. USD 265 (print & online eds.). Ed(s): Dr. Betty Rolling Ferrell. Lippincott Williams & Wilkins, 530 Walnut St, Philadelphia, PA 19106; customerservice@lww.com; http://www.lww.com. Adv. Refereed. Circ: 9057. *Aud.:* Ac, Sa.

This peer-reviewed publication, available in print and online, is the official journal of the Hospice and Palliative Nurses Association (HPNA). Previously published bimonthly, the journal is expanding to eight issues a year. It features original research in care of the dying, case studies, literature reviews, and HPNA news and position papers. Two new sections have been added: "Research and Practice: Partners in Care Series" and "Symptom Management Series." Each issue has at least one continuing education (CE) test based on an article in the issue: for example, the article "Symptom Management of Spiritual Suffering in Pediatric Palliative Care." Nurses completing the test send it and the registration fee to the publisher, an accredited provider of continuing education for nurses, and receive CE hours after passing the test. Recent research articles include "Palliative Care in the Neonatal Intensive Care Setting: Our Past and Our Future," "Choice Intention Regarding Hospice Care Based on the Theory of Reasoned Action," and "The Experiences and Care Preferences of People with Diabetes at the End of Life: A Qualitative Study." Tables of contents and abstracts from volume 1 (1999) to the present are available on the journal's web site, as is full text searching of the journal's contents. Some issues offer free access to an individual article. URL: www.jhpn.com

1658. *Journal of Loss & Trauma: international perspectives on stress and coping.* Incorporates (1994-2006): *Stress, Trauma and Crisis;* Which was formerly (until 2004): *Crisis Intervention and Time-Limited Treatment;* Formerly (until 2001): *Journal of Personal & Interpersonal Loss.* [ISSN: 1532-5024] 1996. 5x/yr. GBP 460 (print & online eds.). Ed(s): John H Harvey. Routledge, 325 Chestnut St, Ste 800, Philadelphia, PA 19106; customerservice@taylorandfrancis.com; http://www.tandfonline.com. Adv. Sample. Refereed. Reprint: PSC. *Indexed:* A01, A22, ASSIA, E01, ERIC, PsycInfo. *Bk. rev.:* Number and length vary. *Aud.:* Ac, Sa.

Previously titled *Journal of Personal & Interpersonal Loss,* the *Journal of Loss & Trauma* incorporated *Stress, Trauma, and Crisis* in 2007. This peer-reviewed journal is published five times a year online and twice a year in print. Similar to *Illness, Crisis, and Loss,* its scope is wider than issues involved in death, dying, and bereavement. It does, however, publish many articles on these issues, including the recent "Continuing Bonds and Psychosocial Adjustment in Pet Loss," "Responses to Loss and Health Functioning Among Homicidally Bereaved African Americans," and "Beliefs in Reincarnation and the Power of Fate and Their Association with Emotional Outcomes among Bereaved Parents of Fallen Soldiers." The journal's interdisciplinary content would interest practitioners, faculty, and students in the fields of counseling, social work, and health. A sample issue and tables of contents and abstracts beginning with volume 1 (1996) are available on the journal's web site. URL: www.tandf.co.uk/journals/titles/15325024.asp

1659. *Journal of Pain & Palliative Care Pharmacotherapy.* Formerly (until 2002): *Journal of Pharmaceutical Care in Pain & Symptom Control;* Incorporates (1985-2002): *The Hospice Journal.* [ISSN: 1536-0288] 1993. q. GBP 509 (print & online eds.). Ed(s): Arthur G Lipman. Informa Healthcare, 52 Vanderbilt Ave, New York, NY 10017; healthcare.enquiries@informa.com; http://www.informahealthcare.com. Illus., adv. Sample. Refereed. Circ: 529 Paid. Reprint: PSC. *Indexed:* A01, A22, E01, ExcerpMed, PsycInfo. *Bk. rev.:* Number and length vary. *Aud.:* Ac, Sa.

This peer-reviewed journal on the management of pain in both chronic and acute illness, as well as in the dying, is published by Informa Healthcare and is available in print and online. Aimed chiefly at practitioners in medical fields, it includes original research, review articles, news updates, and reviews of books, web sites, and other media. Special reports cover legal issues and standards involved in pain management. Among the features are sections such as "Narratives in Pain and Palliative Care," "Evidence-Based Pain Management and Palliative Care," and "Patient Education and Self-Advocacy: Questions and Responses on Pain Management." Recent articles include "Levodropropizine in the Management of Cough Associated with Cancer or Nonmalignant Chronic Disease—A Systematic Review," "Computational Opioid Prescribing: A Novel Application of Clinical Pharmacokinetics," and "Profit-Driven Drug Testing." Tables of contents and summaries beginning with volume 1 (1993) are available on the journal's web site. URL: http://informahealthcare.com/ppc

1660. *Journal of Palliative Care.* [ISSN: 0825-8597] 1985. q. CAD 130 (Individuals, CAD 90). Ed(s): Dr. David J Roy, Alison Ramsey. Centre for Bioethics - Clinical Research Institute of Montreal, 4565 chemin Queen Mary, Montreal, PQ H3W 1W5, Canada; http://www.criugm.qc.ca. Illus. Sample. Refereed. Vol. ends: Winter. Microform: MML. *Indexed:* A22, BRI, C37, CBCARef, PsycInfo, RILM. *Bk. rev.:* Number and length vary. *Aud.:* Ac, Sa.

Published by the Centre de recherche of the Institut universitaire de geriatrie de Montreal, this peer-reviewed journal contains original research, reviews of current issues in the field, case reports, and features such as "Global Exchange" and "Reflections from the Bedside." Offering an international perspective on hospice care and palliative medicine, this journal would be of interest to health professionals involved with the dying, as well as to practitioners and students in social work and counseling. There are occasional thematic issues, such as "Palliative Care for Persons Living and Dying with Dementia." Recent articles include "End-of-Life Care for the Dying Child: What Matters Most to Parents," "Can Addressing Death Anxiety Reduce Health Care Workers' Burnout and Improve Patient Care?," and "Palliative Cancer Patients' Experience of Physical Activity." All articles are in English; abstracts are in both English and French. Tables of contents are available from 2009 (volume 25) to the present on the journal's web site. URL: www.criugm.qc.ca/journalofpalliativecare/

1661. *Journal of Palliative Medicine.* [ISSN: 1096-6218] 1998. m. USD 1368. Ed(s): Charles F von Gunten, Lisa Pelzek-Braun. Mary Ann Liebert, Inc. Publishers, 140 Huguenot St, 3rd Fl, New Rochelle, NY 10801; info@liebertpub.com; http://www.liebertpub.com. Illus., adv. Sample. Refereed. Vol. ends: Dec. Reprint: PSC. *Indexed:* A01, A22, AbAn, E01, ExcerpMed, PsycInfo. *Bk. rev.:* Number and length vary. *Aud.:* Ac, Sa.

Published monthly in print and online, this peer-reviewed publication is an official journal of the Hospice and Palliative Nurses Association. It is also the official journal of the Center to Advance Palliative Care and ANZSPM, i.e., the Australian & New Zealand Society of Palliative Medicine. It covers palliative care for the dying and ethical and legal issues involved in end-of-life care. It would interest professionals in the health-care and counseling fields, as well as students and faculty in programs preparing health, counseling, and social work practitioners. Each issue includes original research, reviews of current practice and research, case studies, book and media reviews, and columns recounting personal experiences of practitioners working with the dying. "Fast Facts and Concepts" columns such as "Borderline Personality Disorder in Palliative Care"

offer background information on a wide range of topics. Recent research articles include "Physical Function in Hospice Patients and Physiotherapy Interventions: A Profile of Hospice Physiotherapy," "Mapping Children's Palliative Care around the World: An Online Survey of Children's Palliative Care Services and Professionals' Educational Needs," and "Addressing Parental Bereavement Support Needs at the End of Life for Infants with Complex Chronic Conditions." Sample issues, occasional free articles within other issues, and tables of contents going back to volume 1 (1998) are available on the journal's web site. URL: www.liebertpub.com/jpm

1662. *Journal of Social Work in End-of-Life & Palliative Care.* Formerly (until 2005): *Loss, Grief & Care.* [ISSN: 1552-4256] 1986. q. GBP 395 (print & online eds.). Ed(s): Ellen L Csikai. Routledge, 325 Chestnut St, Ste 800, Philadelphia, PA 19106; customerservice@taylorandfrancis.com; http://www.tandfonline.com. Illus., adv. Sample. Refereed. Vol. ends: Winter. Microform: PQC. Reprint: PSC. *Indexed:* A01, A22, ASSIA, E01, PsycInfo, SSA, SWR&A. *Bk. rev.:* Number and length vary. *Aud.:* Ac, Sa.

Published in print and online, this peer-reviewed journal, affiliated with the Social Work in Hospice and Palliative Care Network, offers original research, invited papers, and reviews of the literature on the role of social workers in assisting individuals with terminal or chronic illnesses and their families. A regular column, "Reflections," offers personal perspectives, in the form of poetry, essays, or case studies, on social workers' experiences in palliative care. While social work practitioners and faculty and students in social work programs are the primary audience for this publication, many articles would also interest health professionals in other disciplines. Thematic issues such as "Partners in Palliative Care: Enhancing Ethics in Care at the End of Life" are published occasionally. Recent articles include "Identifiable Grief Responses in Persons with Alzheimer's Disease," "Caring for People with Intellectual Disabilities and Life-Limiting Illness: Merging Person-Centered Planning and Patient-Centered, Family-Focused Care," and "Interdisciplinary Perceptions of the Social Work Role in Hospice: Building upon the Classic Kulys and Davis Study." A sample issue and tables of contents and abstracts beginning with volume 1 (2005), as well as nine volumes beginning with volume 1 (1987) under the journal's former name, *Loss, Grief & Care,* are available on the journal's web site. URL: www.tandf.co.uk/journals/WSWE

1663. *Mortality: promoting the interdisciplinary study of death and dying.* [ISSN: 1357-6275] 1996. q. GBP 517 (print & online eds.). Ed(s): Carol Komaromy, Arnar Arnason. Routledge, 4 Park Sq, Milton Park, Abingdon, OX14 4RN, United Kingdom; subscriptions@tandf.co.uk; http://www.tandfonline.com. Illus., adv. Sample. Refereed. Reprint: PSC. *Indexed:* A01, A22, AmHI, E01, P61, PsycInfo, SSA. *Bk. rev.:* Number and length vary. *Aud.:* Ac, Sa.

Available in print and online, this interdisciplinary, peer-reviewed publication is the official journal of the Association for the Study of Death and Society. It would be of interest to those in counseling, social work, and the health professions, as well as faculty and students in disciplines such as psychology, sociology, anthropology, religion, and literature. Original research covers customs related to mourning, end-of-life care, treatment of the dead, and other topics to do with death and dying. Occasional thematic issues, such as "Music and Death," treat their topics in depth. Recent articles include "Creative Songwriting in Therapy at the End of Life and in Bereavement," "Joining a Right-to-Die Society: Motivation, Beliefs and Experiences," and "Speaking of the Dead." A sample issue and tables of contents and abstracts beginning with volume 1 (1996) are available on the journal's web site. The full text of the articles in these volumes can be searched from the web site. An interesting feature of the journal's web site is the "virtual themed issue," which, with an editorial by an expert in the field, gathers together articles from *Mortality* that address specific themes; examples include "Death and the Media" and "Gender and Death." URL: www.tandf.co.uk/journals/titles/13576275.asp

1664. *Omega: Journal of Death and Dying.* [ISSN: 0030-2228] 1970. 8x/yr. USD 599 (print & online eds.) Individuals, USD 166 (print & online eds.). Ed(s): Kenneth J Doka. Baywood Publishing Co., Inc., 26 Austin Ave, PO Box 337, Amityville, NY 11701; info@baywood.com; http://www.baywood.com. Illus., index. Sample. Refereed. Vol. ends: No. 4. *Indexed:* A01, A22, ASSIA, AgeL, BRI, MLA-IB, P02, P61, PsycInfo, RILM, SSA. *Bk. rev.:* Number and length vary. *Aud.:* Ac, Sa.

An early journal in the field, *Omega* is published in print and online. It is an official journal of the Association for Death Education and Counseling. Its peer-reviewed content is interdisciplinary and would interest not only therapists, social workers, and health professionals, but also students and faculty in such disciplines as anthropology, psychology, sociology, and religion. Original research examines cross-cultural perspectives on dying, grief, and customs related to death and mourning. Recent articles include "Does the Internet Change How We Mourn and Die?," "Healing Components of a Bereavement Camp: Children and Adolescents Give Voice to Their Experiences," "Islamic Death Rituals in a Small Town Context in the Netherlands: Explorations of a Common Praxis for Professionals," and "Conversations, Coping, & Connectedness: A Qualitative Study of Women Who Have Experienced Involuntary Pregnancy Loss." Tables of contents beginning with volume 1 (1970) are available on the journal's web site; citations and abstracts for these volumes are searchable by keyword. A sample issue is available online; a print copy can be requested. URL: http://baywood.com/journals/previewjournals.asp?id=0030-2228

1665. *Palliative & Supportive Care.* [ISSN: 1478-9515] 2003. q. Ed(s): William Breitbart. Cambridge University Press, The Edinburgh Bldg, Shaftesbury Rd, Cambridge, CB2 8RU, United Kingdom; journals@cambridge.org; http://www.cambridge.org/uk. Adv. Refereed. Reprint: PSC. *Indexed:* A22, E01. *Aud.:* Ac, Sa.

Available in print and online, this peer-reviewed journal is published by Cambridge University Press. The journal focuses on psychological, social, spiritual, and ethical issues involved in bereavement and in the care of the dying and their families/caretakers. Its interdisciplinary content would interest therapists, social workers, educators, and health professionals. It contains original research, review articles, case reports, and personal experiences in the form of essays, poetry, or fiction. Some issues have special thematic sections, such as the section "Vulnerability and Palliative Care." Recent articles include "'Our Best Hope Is a Cure.' Hope in the Context of Advance Care Planning," "Assessment of Self-Efficacy for Caregiving: The Critical Role of Self-Care in Caregiver Stress and Burden," and "Heightened Vulnerabilities and Better Care for All: Disability and End-of-Life Care." A sample issue and tables of contents and abstracts from volume 1 (2003) to the present are available on the journal's web site. URL: http://journals.cambridge.org/action/displayJournal?jid=PAX

1666. *Palliative Care: Research and Treatment.* [ISSN: 1178-2242] 2008. irreg. Free. Ed(s): Parag Bharadwaj. Libertas Academica Ltd., PO Box 302-624, Auckland, 1330, New Zealand; editorial@la-press.com; http://www.la-press.com. Refereed. *Indexed:* A01. *Bk. rev.:* Number and length vary. *Aud.:* Ac, Sa.

This open-access, peer-reviewed, online journal publishes original research, practitioner perspectives, case reports, and reviews of books and media on the practice and scientific/policy aspects of palliative medicine. It would interest all those studying or working in the area of palliative care. The journal is indexed and the full text of articles is available in the databases of major vendors; it is also accessible through the Directory of Open Access Journals. Recent articles include "Cancer Pain and Its Management: A Survey on Interns' Knowledge, Attitudes and Barriers," "Subjective Definitions of Problems and Symptoms in Palliative Care," and "Thai Medical Students' Self Assessment of Palliative Care Competencies." URL: www.la-press.com/palliative-care-research-and-treatment-journal-j86

1667. *Palliative Medicine: a multiprofessional journal.* [ISSN: 0269-2163] 1987. 10x/yr. USD 2353. Ed(s): Catherine Walshe. Sage Publications Ltd., 1 Oliver's Yard, 55 City Rd, London, EC1Y 1SP, United Kingdom; info@sagepub.co.uk; http://www.uk.sagepub.com. Illus., index, adv. Sample. Refereed. Vol. ends: Dec. Reprint: PSC. *Indexed:* A01, A22, ASSIA, E01, ExcerpMed, PsycInfo. *Bk. rev.:* Number and length vary. *Aud.:* Ac, Sa.

This publication, available in print and online, is the peer-reviewed research journal of the European Association for Palliative Care, which also sponsors the *European Journal of Palliative Care*. The journal's coverage of palliative care is international in scope. *Palliative Medicine* contains research articles, case studies, and book reviews of interest to those working in all areas of palliative care. Recent articles include "Illicit Drug Use as a Challenge to the Delivery of End-of-Life Care Services to Homeless Persons: Perceptions of Health and

Social Services Professionals," "Experiences of Dying, Death and Bereavement in Motor Neurone Disease: A Qualitative Study," and "Factors Associated with Perceived Barriers to Pediatric Palliative Care: A Survey of Pediatricians in Florida and California." A sample issue and tables of contents and abstracts beginning with volume 1 (1987) are available on the journal's web site. URL: http://pmj.sagepub.com

1668. *Suicide and Life-Threatening Behavior.* Former titles (until 1976): *Suicide;* (until 1975): *Life Threatening Behavior.* [ISSN: 0363-0234] 1970. bi-m. GBP 517. Ed(s): Thomas E Joiner. John Wiley & Sons, Inc., 111 River St, MS 4-02, Hoboken, NJ 07030; info@wiley.com; http://www.wiley.com/WileyCDA/. Illus., index, adv. Sample. Refereed. Microform: PQC. Reprint: PSC. *Indexed:* A01, A22, BRI, Chicano, E01, ERIC, FR, P02, P61, PsycInfo, RILM, SSA. *Bk. rev.:* Number and length vary. *Aud.:* Ac, Sa.

The official journal of the American Association of Suicidology, *Suicide and Life-Threatening Behavior* is now published by Wiley. A peer-reviewed publication, it is available in print and online. The journal is interdisciplinary, drawing from the fields of sociology, psychology, statistics, biology, religion, and public health. Practitioners and students in the fields of mental health, social work, and pastoral work would find this journal of interest, as would physicians, nurses, and others in the field of medicine. It contains original research and case studies that examine suicide, attempted suicide, and other life-threatening acts and their effects on the social networks in which a suicidal person is involved. Suicide is considered in a variety of contexts, including age, gender, ethnicity, and nationality. Recent articles include "'Let Me Count the Ways': Fostering Reasons for Living Among Low-Income, Suicidal, African American Women," "Suicide in the Army National Guard: An Empirical Inquiry," "High School Bullying as a Risk for Later Depression and Suicidality," and "Mental Disorders and Communication of Intent to Die in Indigenous Suicide Cases, Queensland, Australia." A sample issue and tables of contents and abstracts beginning with volume 1 (1971) are available on the journal's web site. URL: http://eu.wiley.com/WileyCDA/WileyTitle/productCd-SLTB.html

■ DISABILITIES

See also Education; and Medicine and Health sections.

Beth McDonough, Research and Instruction Librarian/Education Liaison, Hunter Library, Western Carolina University, Cullowhee, NC 29723; bmcdono@email.wcu.edu

Introduction

Several magazines in this section focus more on ability than disability, providing positive support and helpful informaton for people with disabilities and their caregivers and families. Others are academic journals that strive to support research and evidence-based clinical practice. Whether they target a general or academic audience, these publications demonstrate a careful cultural sensitivity toward people with a range of disabilities, even while dealing with associated issues in a forthright manner. The increasing quality and quantity of publications in this area are indicative of the growing awareness and acceptance of disabled people that have occurred in the wake of the landmark passage of the Americans with Disabilities Act in 1990.

Basic Periodicals

Adapted Physical Education Quarterly; American Annals of the Deaf; American Journal on Intellectual and Developmental Disabilities; Review of Disability Studies; Sports 'n Spokes.

Basic Abstracts and Indexes

Academic Search Premier, CINAHL, Education Abstracts, ERIC, Linguistics and Language Behavior Abstracts, PsycINFO, SocIndex, SPORTDiscus.

1669. Ability. Formerly (until 200?): *Ability Journal.* [ISSN: 1062-5321] 1992. bi-m. USD 29.70 in US & Canada; USD 6.95 per issue. Ed(s): Chet Cooper, Pamela Johnson. C.R. Cooper Publishing, 8941 Atlanta Ave, Huntington Beach, CA 92646. Illus., adv. *Aud.:* Hs, Ga, Sa.

Upbeat and empowering, *Ability*'s bimonthly issues include articles ranging from celebrity interviews and consumer health to the latest in assisted living and political coverage. It nicely fulfills its mission "to provide new insights into our individual levels of ability." Colorful layouts that incorporate photographs and graphic design elements add flair, with cover stories that feature prominent celebrities, politicians, business leaders, athletes, or similar role models with stories to tell about facing and surmounting challenges related to disabling health conditions. Contributors come from a wide range of backgrounds and often write in the first person. Regular editorial features include interviews, humor, and a crossword puzzle. This is a good choice for libraries that collect popular magazines. Available in print and online by individual subscription. The online version is an exact reproduction of the print.

AccessWorld (Online Edition). See Blind and Visually Impaired section.

1670. Adapted Physical Activity Quarterly. [ISSN: 0736-5829] 1984. q. USD 502 (print & online eds.). Ed(s): Marcel Bouffard. Human Kinetics, Inc., 1607 N Market St, Champaign, IL 61820; info@hkusa.com; http://www.humankinetics.com. Illus., index, adv. Sample. Refereed. Vol. ends: Oct. Reprint: PSC. *Indexed:* A01, A22, C45, ERIC, PsycInfo, RILM, SD. *Bk. rev.:* Number and length vary. *Aud.:* Ac, Sa.

This research journal offers readers "the latest scholarly inquiry related to physical activity for individuals with disabilities." Each issue features primary research articles, an essay-length book or media review, a digest of research published in other journals, and a calendar of upcoming events of interest to health and physical education professionals. This is the official journal of the International Federation of Adapted Physical Activity. The journal is multidisciplinary in scope, inviting research from the fields of corrective therapy, gerontology, health care, occupational therapy, pediatrics, physical education, dance, sport medicine, physical therapy, recreation, and rehabilitation. "The focus of the adaptation may be upon equipment, activity, facilities, methodology and/or setting." An annual index is published in print each October, and the journal is searchable on the publisher's web site. The web site also provides access to tables of contents and abstracts. The journal is widely indexed. Available in print and digital formats. Recommended for academic libraries.

1671. ADDitude: living well with attention deficit. [ISSN: 1529-1014] 2000. 4x/yr. USD 24.99; USD 6.95 newsstand/cover domestic; USD 7.95 newsstand/cover Canada. Ed(s): Wayne Kalyn. New Hope Media, LLC, 39 W 37th St, 15th Fl, New York, NY 10018; http://www.newhopemedia.com. Adv. Circ: 50000. *Bk. rev.:* 2-3 per issue. *Aud.:* Hs, Ga, Sa.

This readable quarterly magazine is of interest to children and adults with ADD and their families. Subscriptions include a resource guide published each September. Colorful layouts deliver three or four cover stories; more than a dozen regular columns, such as self-help, legal issues, and relationship advice; and many additional articles presented in four sections, parenting, treatment, adults, and school. Many articles are written in the first person by people with ADD, family members, and authors of current books. Articles are interspersed with punchy lists such as the recent "Five office stress busters" or "Four ways to master math facts." Each issue features letters from readers and a reader poll. There is an annual guide to schools and camps. The web site offers free access to web-exclusive content. The magazine is not indexed in any known databases. Recommended for public libraries.

1672. American Annals of the Deaf. Formerly (until 1886): *American Annals of the Deaf and Dumb.* [ISSN: 0002-726X] 1847. q. USD 133 (print & online eds.). Ed(s): Peter V Paul. Gallaudet University Press, College Hall, 4th Floor, 800 Florida Avenue, NE, Washington, DC 20002; gupress@gallaudet.edu; http://gupress.gallaudet.edu. Illus., index, adv. Sample. Refereed. Vol. ends: Dec. Microform: PQC. *Indexed:* A01, A22, AbAn, BRI, E01, ERIC, MLA-IB, P02, PsycInfo. *Aud.:* Ac, Sa.

This is a professional journal that targets teachers, administrators, and researchers in the field of deaf education. It is the official publication of the Council of American Instructors of the Deaf and the Conference of Educational Administrators of Schools and Programs for the Deaf. The scope of the journal extends beyond education to include such topics as communication methods and strategies; language development; mainstreaming and residential schools; parent–child relationships; and teacher training and teaching skills. Each regular issue opens with an editorial. In addition to *Annals*' four issues each year (spring, summer, fall, and winter), subscriptions include an annual reference issue with a directory of deaf education schools; information on programs in the United States and Canada; and demographic data about the schools and students who are deaf or hard of hearing. The publisher web site includes indexes by subject, author, and individual issue, and an annual print index is published in the winter issue. This is an essential resource for libraries that serve populations who are deaf or that support professional preparation for those entering the deaf education field.

1673. American Journal on Intellectual and Developmental Disabilities. Former titles (until 2008): *American Journal on Mental Retardation (Print);* (until 1987): *American Journal of Mental Deficiency;* (until 1939): *American Association on Mental Deficiency. Proceedings and Addresses of the Annual Session.* [ISSN: 1944-7515] 1876. bi-m. USD 287 print & online eds. for schools & public libraries. Ed(s): Leonard Abbeduto. American Association on Intellectual and Developmental Disabilities, 501 3rd St, NW, Ste 200, Washington, DC 20001; orders@allenpress.com; http://www.allenpress.com. Illus., adv. Refereed. Circ: 8000. Vol. ends: Nov. Microform: PQC. *Indexed:* A22, BRI, CBRI, Chicano, ERIC, FR, MLA-IB, PsycInfo, SWR&A. *Aud.:* Ac, Sa.

This peer-reviewed journal is dedicated to multidisciplinary scholarly research into the causes, treatments, and preventions of intellectual disabilities. Articles include empirical research on characteristics of people with intellectual and developmental disabilities, systematic reviews of relevant research literature, and evaluative research on new treatments. It is published bimonthly by the American Association on Intellectual and Developmental Disabilities. The journal is widely indexed, including the Education Resources Information Center (ERIC), which is a free database on the Internet. Recommended for academic libraries that serve researchers and professionals in the mental health field.

1674. Autism Spectrum Quarterly. Former titles (until 2004): *Jenison Autism Journal;* (until 2002): *The Morning News.* [ISSN: 1551-448X] 2004. q. USD 29.95 in US & Canada; USD 32 United Kingdom; KWD 15 in the Middle East. Ed(s): Diane Twachtman-Cullen, Kim R Newgass. Starfish Specialty Press, PO Box 799, Higganum, CT 06441. Adv. *Bk. rev.:* Number and length vary. *Aud.:* Ga, Sa.

Self-described as a "magajournal" on the publisher's web site, *Autism Spectrum Quarterly* seeks to "bridge the gap between research and general autism communities," with a focus on making the latest research understandable to laymen. It offers a blend of research, interviews, parenting articles, book and product reviews, and scientific news. Authors include researchers, professionals, parents of exceptional children, and individuals with Autism Spectrum Disorder. The magazine is published four times yearly, in February, May, August, and November. The publisher's web site includes an online search feature; however, the magazine is not indexed in any known library databases. The lack of indexing and peer review makes this title most suitable for public libraries.

Behavior Modification. See Psychology section.

The Braille Forum. See Blind and Visually Impaired section.

1675. Education and Training in Autism and Developmental Disabilities. Former titles (until 2010): *Education and Training in Developmental Disabilities;* (until 2003): *Education and Training in Mental Retardation and Developmental Disabilities;* (until 1994): *Education and Training in Mental Retardation;* (until 1987): *Education and Training of the Mentally Retarded.* [ISSN: 2154-1647] 1966. q. USD 195 Free to members. Ed(s):

Stanley H Zucker. Council for Exceptional Children, Division on Developmental Disabilities, 1110 N Glebe Rd., Ste 300, Arlington, VA 22201; http://www.dddcec.org/. Illus., index, adv. Sample. Refereed. Circ: 6000 Paid. Vol. ends: Dec. Microform: PQC. *Indexed:* A22, ERIC, PsycInfo, SWR&A. *Aud.:* Ac, Sa.

This is the official journal of the Division on Autism and Developmental Disabilities, Council for Exceptional Children. It is published four times a year in March, June, September, and December. The December issue includes an annual author and title index. Each issue features a dozen or so scholarly research articles concerning identification, assessment, educational programming, characteristics, training of instructional personnel, habilitation, prevention, community understanding, and legislation. Content includes qualitative and quantitative empirical research and critical reviews of the literature. Formerly published as *Education and Training in Developmental Disabilities,* the new title demonstrates increased focus on Autism Spectrum Disorder. It is published in print and online formats. This title is widely indexed in library databases including ERIC and PsychInfo, which makes it an excellent choice for academic libraries. The publisher has developed a comprehensive, topical article index on its web site.

Exceptional Parent. See Family section.

1676. *Hearing Health: the voice on hearing issues.* Formerly (until 1992): *Voice.* 1984. q. Free. Voice International Publications, Inc., 641 Lexington Ave, Fl 15, New York, NY 10022. Illus., adv. *Aud.:* Sa.

Hearing Health is a quarterly consumer magazine with articles that focus primarily on news about the latest hearing loss research and products and services available to people who are deaf or hard of hearing. Each issue includes special features, such as the summer camp issue, along with several regular columns, such as "Meet the Researcher," which profiles scientists researching hearing loss. Topics include managing hearing loss, assistive technology, personal interest and success stories, and disability rights and education. The web site provides access to the full content of each issue. Subscriptions are free with registration and include both print and online access. Although published by a nonprofit, charitable organization dedicated to deafness research, *Hearing Health* is an odd cross between a consumer and a trade magazine. It is an optional purchase for libraries that serve a significant population of individuals with hearing problems.

1677. *Intellectual and Developmental Disabilities: journal of policy, practice, and perspectives.* Formerly (until 2007): *Mental Retardation.* [ISSN: 1934-9491] 1963. bi-m. USD 273 (print & online eds.) for schools & public libraries. Ed(s): Stephanie Dean, Steven Taylor. American Association on Intellectual and Developmental Disabilities, 501 3rd St, NW, Ste 200, Washington, DC 20001; anam@aaidd.org; http://www.aamr.org. Illus., index, adv. Sample. Refereed. Circ: 6000. Vol. ends: Dec. *Indexed:* A01, A22, FR, MLA-IB, PsycInfo. *Aud.:* Ac, Sa.

This peer-reviewed publication is described by the publisher as a "journal of policy, practices, and perspectives for professionals, clinicians, and other support staff interested in intellectual disabilities and related developmental disabilities." Each bimonthly issue has articles in the categories of policy, practice, and perspective. It also includes abstracts of the articles in French. Periodically, the meeting minutes of the Board of Directors of the American Association on Intellectual and Developmental Disabilities, publisher of the journal, are provided. It is widely indexed, including the Educational Resources Information Center (ERIC) database, which is freely available on the Internet. Recommended for academic libraries.

Journal of Developmental Education. See Education/Higher Education section.

Journal of Learning Disabilities. See Education/Educational Psychology and Measurement, Special Education, Counseling section.

Learning Disability Quarterly. See Education/Educational Psychology and Measurement, Special Education, Counseling section.

1678. *P N.* Formerly (until 1992): *Paraplegia News;* Which incorporated: *Journal of Paraplegia.* 1946. m. USD 26 domestic; USD 38 foreign. P V A Publications, 2111 E Highland Ave, Ste 180, Phoenix, AZ 85016; info@pnnews.com; http://www.pvamagazines.com. Illus., index, adv. Vol. ends: Dec. *Indexed:* BRI, P02, SD. *Aud.:* Ga, Ac, Sa.

This consumer magazine targets individual with spinal cord injuries, family members, and caregivers. Each monthly issue features news, research, and information about new products, disability legislation, veteran's affairs, accessible travel, assistive technology, housing, employment, and health care. Published by the Paralyzed Veterans of America, the magazine is international in scope and is dedicated to "better wheelchair living." The web site features tables of contents and article abstracts for each issue and is searchable. The content is varied, interesting, and of great potential use to wheelchair users and their caregivers. An attractive option for public libraries.

1679. *Palaestra: forum of sport, physical education and recreation for those with disabilities.* [ISSN: 8756-5811] 1984. q. USD 31.95 (Individuals, USD 21.95). Ed(s): David P Beaver, William Bruce Lorton. Challenge Publications, Ltd., Circulation Department, PO Box 269, Bushnell, IL 61422; challpub@macomb.com. Illus., index, adv. Microform: PQC. *Indexed:* A01, A22, BRI, P02, SD. *Bk. rev.:* 5-7, 150-200 words. *Aud.:* Ac, Sa.

The magazine's title is Ancient Greek for "sport school" or "gymnasium." Each issue includes four or five feature articles with an emphasis on teaching adapted physical education and a dozen regular departments, such as legislative updates, travel, editorials, sports nutrition, and book and video reviews. Articles are of interest to individuals with disabilities, their caregivers, and professionals in the field. It is published four times each year in cooperation with the Adapted Physical Activity Council of the American Alliance for Health, Physical Education, Recreation, and Dance, the U.S. Paralympics Division of the U.S. Olympic Committee, and the Education Committee of the North American Riding for the Handicapped Association. The table of contents and article abstracts from the most current issue are available on the publisher's web site; but there is no archive, and the web site is not searchable. Recommended for libraries that cater to in-service or pre-service physical education teachers, and for large public libraries.

Remedial and Special Education. See Education/Educational Psychology and Measurement, Special Education, Counseling section.

1680. *The Review of Disability Studies.* [ISSN: 1553-3697] 2003. q. USD 100 (Individuals, USD 50; Students, USD 25). Ed(s): Robert A. Stodden, Megan A Conway. University of Hawaii at Manoa, Center on Disability Studies, 1776 University Ave, UA 4-6, Honolulu, HI 96822; http://www.cds.hawaii.edu. Adv. Refereed. *Bk. rev.:* Number and length vary. *Aud.:* Ac, Sa.

This peer-reviewed, quarterly academic journal is surprisingly readable and interesting. Articles are international and interdisciplinary in scope, with recent topics such as a qualitative study of Maasai with disabilities in Tanzania and an analysis of the protrayal of individuals with disabilities in American literature. Reviews of books, music, and film are included, as well as a new section that features selected abstracts of disability-related dissertations. The journal also sometimes includes poetry, artwork, short stories, and photography. The full text of the journal is freely available on the publisher's web site; however, the search engine on the site is a mediocre tool for locating individual articles. Indexing is limited to SocIndex and TOC Premier, and the journal does not appear to publish a print index. Recommended for academic libraries.

1681. *Sports 'n Spokes: the magazine for wheelchair sports and recreation.* [ISSN: 0161-6706] 1975. bi-m. USD 21 domestic; USD 27 foreign. Ed(s): Richard Hoover. P V A Publications, 2111 E Highland Ave, Ste 180, Phoenix, AZ 85016; info@pnnews.com; http://www.pvamagazines.com. Illus., index, adv. Sample. *Indexed:* SD. *Aud.:* Hs, Ga, Sa.

Packed with stories of disability-defying athletic feats, this magazine is an interesting read. Each bimonthly issue includes a wide range of sports from the traditional basketball, golf, and tennis to the less-well-known fencing, fishing, and rugby. Colorful photographs add to the action. Coverage is inclusive of women, men, and youth, and extends to international events. Four or five feature articles anchor the magazine, with regular departments such as letters to the editor and a calendar of events. Personality profiles and assistive technology are also included. Recent issues showcase the Paralympics, and a review of the latest trends and technology in wheelchair design. Expanded content and limited full text are freely available on the publisher's web site, along with an article search feature. Highly recommended for public libraries, and an interesting supplemental purchase for recreational reading in academic and special libraries, depending on their missions.

1682. *Topics in Language Disorders.* [ISSN: 0271-8294] 1980. q. USD 364 (print & online eds.). Ed(s): Katherine G Butler, Nickola Wolf-Nelson. Lippincott Williams & Wilkins, Two Commerce Sq, 2001 Market St, Philadelphia, PA 19103; customerservice@lww.com; http://www.lww.com. Illus., adv. Sample. Refereed. Vol. ends: Aug. *Indexed:* A01, A22, BRI, ERIC, MLA-IB, PsycInfo. *Aud.:* Ac, Sa.

This double-blind, peer-reviewed, scholarly journal targets researchers and clinicians in the field of language development and disorders. Articles for each thematic issue are invited by the editors. The journal strives to "provide relevant information to support theoretically sound, culturally sensitive, research-based clinical practices." Recent themes include end-of-life considerations in clinical practice with adults and treatment approaches for children with Autism Spectrum Disorders. The publisher's web site offers a free e-mail table-of-contents alert and access to a keyword search of journal content. It is widely indexed. In collaboration with the Continuing Education Board of the American Speech-Language-Hearing Association, the publisher offers continuing education credit to subscribers and non-subscribers on passing a short test based on the topical issue and the payment of a small fee. Recommended for academic libraries that support advanced studies in language development.

■ DO-IT-YOURSELF

See also Building and Construction; Craft; Home; and Interior Design and Decoration sections.

Carrie M. Macfarlane, Head of Research and Instruction, Middlebury College, Middlebury, VT 05753; cmacfarl@middlebury.edu

Introduction

Do-it-yourself projects are as popular as ever. Penny-pinching homeowners, brand-averse millennials, and off-the-grid environmentalists are equally motivated to avoid buying in to modern consumer culture. The magazines in this chapter provide guidance to all. Browse through and you'll find intriguing and easy-to-follow advice on tasks ranging from repainting wooden shutters to building a motorized go-cart to planting storm-resistant trees.

Doing it yourself can be a good outlet for artistic talents, too. These magazines support the creative urge by showing readers how to choose paint colors, make a woodblock print, or redecorate a room. They all share a common goal: to provide inspiration to those who want to be able to rely on themselves to get a job done.

You'll notice that some publications are geared toward a specific audience. Is your library in an urban or a rural setting? Do you count new homeowners among your users? Are you in the vicinity of a historic district? Consider these factors when you choose your subscriptions, and do-it-yourselfers will thank you as they head home to tackle their projects. Magazines are putting lots of content on their web sites, Facebook and Pinterest pages these days, so it should be easy to select even without waiting for a sample issue.

For professionals and dedicated hobbyists, consult other sections in this volume, such as Building and Construction, and Craft. For patrons interested in homemaking, entertaining in the home, and interior design, useful titles can be found in sections such as Home, and Interior Design and Decoration.

Basic Periodicals

Ga: *BackHome, The Family Handyman, ReadyMade, This Old House.*

Basic Abstracts and Indexes

Index to How to Do It Information, Readers' Guide to Periodical Literature.

1683. *BackHome: your hands-on guide to sustainable living.* [ISSN: 1051-323X] 1990. bi-m. USD 21.97 domestic; USD 31.97 Canada; USD 41.97 elsewhere. WordsWorth Communications Inc., 315 East Seventh St, Cincinnati, OH 45202; http://www.wordsworthweb.com. Illus. *Aud.:* Ga.

BackHome will appeal to the environmentally conscious do-it-yourselfer. It's built from the ground up, with articles submitted by everyday readers who want to help like-minded folks gain more control over their personal health and their impact on the world. Each issue is packed with new ideas. Small tasks, such as maintaining a chemical-free lawn, are described in casual stories, while larger jobs such as building a chicken coop provide enough advice to get most people started. The table of contents and a link to the *BackHome* radio program are available on the magazine's web site. Recommended for public libraries that serve small-town and rural communities.

1684. *Better Homes and Gardens Do-It-Yourself: ideas for your home and garden.* 1968. q. USD 19.97 for 2 yrs. domestic; USD 23.97 Canada. Ed(s): Linda Hallam. Meredith Corporation, 1716 Locust St, Des Moines, IA 50309; patrick.taylor@meredith.com; http://www.meredith.com. Adv. Circ: 450000 Paid. *Aud.:* Ga.

This glossy quarterly features advice for home-decorating, remodeling, and gardening hobbyists. Projects are both approachable and affordable, with detailed instructions and photos. One recent issue showed readers how to sew a trendy pouf ottoman stuffed with fabric scraps. A great way to dispose of discarded towels! This magazine is recommended for public libraries that have a large *Better Homes and Gardens* readership. The do-it-yourself section of the web site has a blog with feeds from relevant publications, tips, and projects.

1685. *Extreme How-To: the enthusiast's guide to home improvement.* [ISSN: 1540-5346] 2002. 9x/yr. USD 18.97 combined subscription in US & Canada (print & online eds.); USD 4.99 newsstand/cover in US & Canada). Ed(s): Matt Weber. Latitude3 Media, 1111 Edenton St, Birmingham, AL 35242; http://www.latitude3.com. Adv. *Aud.:* Ga.

Homeowners with some carpentry and repair skills will find this magazine full of useful information regarding home and auto maintenance. Recent issues have included tips on building a deck, reviews of the best flooring tools, and advice on how to plan a bathroom remodel. All instructions assume prior fix-it experience. If your library is frequented by builders, carpenters, and serious do-it-yourselfers, this magazine might be a good fit. The web site has how-to videos and guides, Q&A, and the full text of back issues.

1686. *The Family Handyman: tons of projects, tips and tools.* Incorporates (in 1951): *Home Garden's Natural Gardening Magazine;* Which was formerly (until 1972): *Home Garden;* (until 1967): *The Flower Grower.* [ISSN: 0014-7230] 1951. 10x/yr. USD 10 domestic; USD 15.98 in Canada & Mexico; USD 29 elsewhere. Ed(s): Ken Collier, Spike Carlsen. Home Service Publications, Inc., 2915 Commers Dr, Ste 700, Eagan, MN 55121-2398; editors@thefamilyhandyman.com; http://www.familyhandyman.com. Illus., index, adv. Circ: 1000000 Paid. Vol. ends: Dec. *Indexed:* A22, BRI, IHTDI, P02. *Aud.:* Ga.

Dedicated do-it-yourselfers can advance from novice to intermediate to expert, all in this one publication. Issues are packed with illustrated step-by-step instructions for projects and repairs for the home and garden, helpful tips, and reviews of new products. Instructions include a complexity ranking (simple to advanced), estimated cost, and time required. Highly recommended for all public libraries. The magazine's web site offers a significant amount of content, including a categorized collection of full-text how-to articles, DIY forums, and a blog.

1687. *Handy.* Former titles (until 2000): *Handyman How-To;* (until 2000): *American How-To.* [ISSN: 1531-569X] 1993. bi-m. Free to members. Ed(s): Larry Okrend. North American Media Group, Inc., 12301 Whitewater Dr, Minnetonka, MN 55343; mail@handymanclub.com; http://www.northamericanmediagroup.com/. Adv. Sample. Circ: 1001544. *Aud.:* Ga.

Meticulously labeled and captioned photos, illustrated cutting lists, and up-to-the-minute product reviews signal the earnest nature of this do-it-yourself magazine of the Handyman Club of America. Carpentry projects teach the basics so that readers can build a replica or design their own. Recent issues have featured a contemporary-style extension table, a practical planter box, and wire-feed welding tips. If your library acquires a membership, this magazine will be delivered through the mail just as with any other subscription. Libraries that serve serious do-it-yourselfers may want to check it out. Current and past issues can be searched on the web site.

1688. *Make: technology on your time.* [ISSN: 1556-2336] 2005. q. USD 34.95 combined subscription domestic (print & online eds.); USD 39.95 combined subscription Canada (print & online eds.); USD 49.95 combined subscription elsewhere (print & online eds.). Ed(s): Mark Frauenfelder, Shawn Connally. O'Reilly Media, Inc., 1005 Gravenstein Hwy N, Sebastopol, CA 95472; http://www.oreilly.com/. Illus., adv. *Aud.:* Ga.

Judging from the proliferation of online how-to videos, at-home hackers are an ambitious bunch. This magazine is meant for them. Each issue is filled with challenging DIY projects like converting a Roomba into a spy bot, building a better Nerf gun, and developing new applications for the Microsoft Kinect. Contributors place a consistent emphasis on bringing up the next generation of "makers" with projects that will appeal to kids, too. Online at http://makezine.com, readers will find extras such as featured articles, a blog, an online store, and a discussion forum. Recommended for academic and public libraries that specialize in engineering and technology, and all libraries trying to reach an alternative group of do-it-yourselfers.

Mother Earth News. See Environment and Conservation section.

1689. *Old-House Journal.* [ISSN: 0094-0178] 1973. bi-m. USD 16.95 domestic; USD 31.97 Canada; USD 51.97 elsewhere. Restore Media LLC, 1054 31st St, NW, Ste 430, Washington, DC 20007; info@restoremedia.com; http://www.restoremedia.com/. Illus., adv. *Indexed:* A&ATA, A22, API, BRI, GardL, IHTDI. *Aud.:* Ga.

Designers, homeowners, and wannabes all will enjoy paging through the content-rich issues of *Old House Journal*. An article about restoring a privately-owned Frank Lloyd Wright home is a perfect illustration of the beauty of this well-rounded magazine: it is as appealing to real do-it-yourselfers as it is to armchair enthusiasts. Step-by-step instructions, product reviews, and advice make it easy to highly recommend this title for libraries in communities with old and historic homes. The web site offers an enormous amount of content, including the full text of selected feature articles, a product directory, a photographic dictionary of house styles, and user forums.

1690. *This Old House.* Incorporates (in 2001): *Today's Homeowner Solutions;* Which was formerly (until 2001): *Today's Homeowner;* (until 1996): *Home Mechanix;* (until 1984): *Mechanix Illustrated;* Which incorporated: *Electronics Illustrated.* [ISSN: 1086-2633] 1995. 10x/yr. USD 16 domestic; CAD 26 Canada. Ed(s): Donna Sapolin. Time Inc., 1271 Ave of the Americas, New York, NY 10020; information@timeinc.com; http://www.timeinc.com. Illus., adv. Circ: 672754 Paid. *Indexed:* C37, MASUSE, P02. *Aud.:* Ga.

This Old House offers a full complement of advice for owners of old homes. With full-scale carpentry projects, practical decorating tips, and Q & A–style tricks of the trade, the magazine lives up to the reputation of the long-running television show from which it originated. Recent issues have featured tips on adding color to a room, instructions for installing a garden path, and examples of successful kitchen renovations. Most projects are appropriate for weekend do-it-yourselfers, but instructions are careful to advise calling in a professional when a job becomes too big. If your patrons are interested in house and yard maintenance and interior design, then this publication should be in your collection. The web site offers categorized projects, product reviews, and a discussion board.

■ EARTH SCIENCES AND GEOLOGY

See also Agriculture; Engineering and Technology; Geography; and Pale-ontology sections.

Edward F. Lener, Associate Director for Collection Management and College Librarian for the Sciences, University Libraries, Virginia Tech, P.O. Box 90001, Blacksburg, VA 24062; lener@vt.edu.

Flora G. Shrode, Government Documents & Science Subject Librarian, Merrill-Cazier Library, Utah State University, Logan, UT 84322; flora.shrode@usu.edu

Introduction

Due to heavy media coverage of natural disasters such as floods, earthquakes, and landslides, geologic hazards such as these are often the first thing that comes to mind when one mentions the earth sciences. In fact, this is only one part of the picture. The earth sciences touch on many aspects of daily life, from the water we drink to the energy and mineral resources that power our industries and transportation. Research ranges from field reconnaissance, using such traditional tools as rock hammer, compass, and hand lens, to advanced computer-modeling techniques and laboratory equipment designed to simulate conditions deep within the earth. The earth sciences are also highly interdisciplinary, drawing on work in biology, chemistry, geography, physics, and mathematics.

As a general rule, publications in the earth sciences tend to have a long life span of usefulness. The importance of older literature is reflected by the fact that indexing coverage in the American Geosciences Institute's GeoRef database extends well over 200 years for North America. Of course, while much of the older research and descriptive material are still valid, new theories and analytical techniques are more refined and often allow for a better understanding of the processes involved. Also, the increasing use of color illustrations and computer-generated graphics in earth science journals can help readers to grasp complex visual information more easily.

The number of publications for general audiences continues to be limited, but there are many excellent academic and specialist journals in the field. When selecting materials in the earth sciences, it is also necessary to consider the issues of geographic coverage and time frame. Work done at sites from around the world and examining different periods of geologic history are essential to developing a well-rounded collection. Obtaining a good mix of both theoretical and applied research is also important.

Most earth science journals now offer full text of articles online. The GeoScience World collection, launched in 2005, features a growing title list, including those of many professional societies in the field. Back-file coverage also continues to improve. The full list may be viewed at the GeoScience World web site (www.geoscienceworld.org).

The American Geosciences Institute maintains a list of "priority journals." These are serial titles recommended by the GeoRef Users Group Steering Committee to receive the highest priority for database indexing as new issues come out. These are indicated in the annotations where applicable. While this is a good indication of the importance of these titles, one should always be cautious about relying too heavily on any single selection criterion. For the full list of priority journals, go to the American Geosciences Institute's web site (www.agiweb.org/georef/about/journals.html).

Basic Periodicals

Hs, Ga: *EARTH; Geology Today, Rocks and Minerals;* Ac, Sa: *Geological Society. Journal, Geological Society of America. Bulletin, Geology, Geophysics, The Journal of Geology.*

Basic Abstracts and Indexes

GeoRef.

1691. *A A P G Bulletin.* Former titles (until 1974): *The American Association of Petroleum Geologists Bulletin;* (until 1967): *American Association of Petroleum Geologists. Bulletin;* (until 1918): *Southwestern Association of Petroleum Geologists. Bulletin.* [ISSN: 0149-1423] 1917.

m. Free to members. Ed(s): Andrea Sharrer. American Association of Petroleum Geologists, PO Box 979, Tulsa, OK 74101; info@aapg.org; http://www.aapg.org. Illus., index. Refereed. Microform: PMC; PQC. *Indexed:* A22, ABS&EES, C&ISA, EngInd, OceAb. *Bk. rev.:* 0-4, 300-700 words, signed. *Aud.:* Ac, Sa.

This serves as the official journal of the American Association of Petroleum Geologists (AAPG) and is targeted toward the association's members, as well as other professionals in the field. The high-quality research and technical articles address such topics as reservoir characterization, well logging, depositional environments, and basin modeling. The AAPG Datapages Archive offers full-text content from 1917 forward for subscribers or by pay-per-view. Citations are available on GeoScience World from 1921 forward, with full text for 2000 to the present. Readers may register for free RSS feeds or e-mail alerts. Suitable for academic and specialized collections. A GeoRef priority journal.

1692. *American Journal of Science: an international earth science journal.* Former titles (until 1880): *American Journal of Science and Arts;* (until 1820): *American Journal of Science.* [ISSN: 0002-9599] 1818. 10x/yr. USD 195 (print & online eds.) Individuals, USD 75 (print & online eds.); Students, USD 35 (print & online eds.). Ed(s): Danny M Rye, Page C Chamberlain. American Journal of Science, 217 Kline Geology Laboratory, Yale University, PO Box 208109, New Haven, CT 06520. Illus., index. Sample. Refereed. Vol. ends: Dec (No. 10). Microform: PMC; PQC. *Indexed:* A01, A22, BRI, OceAb, P02. *Aud.:* Ac, Sa.

The oldest continuously published journal in the United States devoted to geology and related sciences. It publishes articles from around the world, presenting results of major research from all earth sciences. Readers are primarily earth scientists in academia and government institutions. There are occasional special issues, with some past topics including functional morphology and evolution, Proterozoic evolution and environments, frontiers in petrology, and studies in metamorphism. These designated special volumes and special issues are made available free of charge in digital form. The journal's web site provides free table of contents and abstracts, along with full text for subscribers, from 1896 to the present. Readers may register for free e-mail alerts. Appropriate for academic and research collections. A GeoRef priority journal.

1693. *The American Mineralogist (Print): an international journal of earth and planetary materials.* Former titles (until 1916): *The Mineral Collector;* (until 1894): *Minerals;* (until 1893): *Mineralogists' Monthly;* (until 1890): *Exchanger's Monthly.* [ISSN: 0003-004X] 188?. 8x/yr. USD 875 (print & online eds.). Ed(s): Rachel A Russell, Jennifer A Thomson. Mineralogical Society of America, 3635 Concorde Pkwy Ste 500, Chantilly, VA 20151; business@minsocam.org; http://www.minsocam.org. Illus., index, adv. Sample. Refereed. Vol. ends: Nov/Dec (No. 11 - No. 12). Reprint: PSC. *Indexed:* A01, A22, BRI, OceAb, P02, PhotoAb. *Bk. rev.:* 0-3, 500-1,200 words, signed. *Aud.:* Ac, Sa.

A key title in the field of mineralogy, this journal is an official publication of the Mineralogical Society of America. Research articles cover many topics, including crystal structure, crystal chemistry, and mineral occurrences and deposits. Work in closely related areas such as crystallography, petrology, and geochemistry is also included. In addition, most issues include a section that features newly named minerals, with a brief description and citation to the literature for each of them. Tables of contents for journal issues published from 1916 to the present are available on the Mineralogical Society web site. Full text of articles published from 1916 to 1999 is freely accessible online; the latest years are accessible only to subscribers and society members. The GeoScience World web site also provides full text to subscribers from 1998 forward, and readers may register for free RSS feeds or e-mail alerts. A GeoRef priority journal.

1694. *Annales Geophysicae: atmospheres, hydrospheres and space sciences.* Formed by the merger of (1983-1988): *Annales de Geophysicae. Serie A: Upper Atmosphere and Space Sciences;* (1983-1988): *Annales Geophysicae. Serie B: Terrestrial and Planetary Physics;* Both of which superseded in part (in 1985): *Annales Geophysicae;* Which was formed by the merger of (1944-1983): *Annales de Geophysique;* (1948-1983): *Annali di Geofisica.* [ISSN: 0992-7689]

1983. m. EUR 2050; EUR 154 newsstand/cover. Ed(s): Wlodek Kofman. Copernicus GmbH, Bahnhofsallee 1e, Goettingen, 37081, Germany; info@copernicus.org; http://www.copernicus.org. Illus., index, adv. Sample. Refereed. Circ: 600. Vol. ends: Dec (No. 12). *Indexed:* A01, A22, M&GPA, S25. *Aud.:* Ac, Sa.

This open-access journal of the European Geosciences Union (EGU) presents research articles and short communications on a broad range of topics in geophysics. Areas of major emphasis include atmospheric physics and dynamics, the magnetosphere and ionosphere of the earth, solar and heliospheric physics, and the oceans and their physical interactions with the land and air. Special issues may feature conference papers or an in-depth report on selected geophysical studies. This monthly also makes extensive use of color illustrations where appropriate. Online access is available for articles published from late 1996 forward. Readers may sign up for free RSS feeds and topical e-mail alerts.

1695. *Applied Geochemistry.* [ISSN: 0883-2927] 1986. m. EUR 1646. Ed(s): Ron Fuge. Pergamon, The Blvd, Langford Ln, E Park, Kidlington, OX5 1GB, United Kingdom; JournalsCustomerServiceEMEA@elsevier.com; http://www.elsevier.com. Illus., adv. Sample. Refereed. Microform: PQC. *Indexed:* A01, A22, C45, EngInd, RRTA, S25. *Bk. rev.:* 0-2, 400-2,000 words. *Aud.:* Ac, Sa.

This international journal emphasizes research in geochemistry and cosmochemistry that has practical applications to such areas as environmental monitoring and preservation, waste disposal, and exploration for resources. Reports of original research, rapid communications, and some reviews are published in the fields of inorganic, organic, and isotope geochemistry. This title is the official publication of the International Association of GeoChemistry, and some issues include reports of association activities. This journal is appropriate for academic or corporate research collections. The web site provides free access to tables of contents and abstracts for issues published from 1986 to the present, with full-text articles available to subscribers through ScienceDirect. Readers may register for a free account to receive alerts for specific searches or when new issues become available. A GeoRef priority journal.

1696. *Basin Research.* [ISSN: 0950-091X] 1988. bi-m. GBP 944. Ed(s): Peter van der Beek, Brian Horton. Wiley-Blackwell Publishing Ltd., The Atrium, Southern Gate, Chichester, PO19 8SQ, United Kingdom; customer@wiley.com; http://www.wiley.com/. Illus., index, adv. Sample. Refereed. Vol. ends: No. 4. Microform: PQC. Reprint: PSC. *Indexed:* A01, A22, C45, E01, S25. *Bk. rev.:* 0-4, 500-1,500 words, signed. *Aud.:* Ac, Sa.

This journal is a joint publication of the European Association of Geoscientists and Engineers and the International Association of Sedimentologists. It features interdisciplinary work on sedimentary basins that addresses such important issues as sediment transport, fluid migration, and stratigraphic modeling. Special thematic issues are also published from time to time. Free tables of contents and abstracts can be found on the web site beginning with 1988, with the full text of articles available for subscribers. Recommended for comprehensive collections, but libraries on a tight budget may first want to consider its more general counterpart, *Sedimentology,* also published by Wiley-Blackwell, for the International Association of Sedimentologists. Readers may register for a free account to receive RSS feeds or e-mail alerts about new journal content.

1697. *Biogeosciences.* [ISSN: 1726-4170] 2003. m. EUR 1160; EUR 106 newsstand/cover. Copernicus GmbH, Bahnhofsallee 1e, Goettingen, 37081, Germany; info@copernicus.org; http://www.copernicus.org. Refereed. *Indexed:* C45, IndVet, M&GPA, S25. *Aud.:* Ac, Sa.

This open-access journal launched in 2004 is dedicated to the publication of research articles, short communications, and review papers on all aspects of the interactions of biological, chemical, and physical processes with the geosphere, hydrosphere, and atmosphere. Some topics include biogeochemistry, global elemental cycles, gas exchange, interactions between microorganisms and rocks, biomineralization, and responses to global change. The web site also allows for interactive discussion of recent article postings, and readers may register for a free account to receive RSS feed or e-mail alerts about new journal content.

1698. *Boreas: an international journal of quaternary research.* [ISSN: 0300-9483] 1972. q. GBP 245. Ed(s): Jan A Piotrowski, Karen Luise Knudsen. Wiley-Blackwell Publishing, Inc., Commerce Pl, 350 Main St, Malden, MA 02148; info@wiley.com; http://onlinelibrary.wiley.com/. Illus., index, adv. Sample. Refereed. Vol. ends: Dec (No. 4). Microform: PQC. Reprint: PSC. *Indexed:* A01, A22, AbAn, BrArAb, C45, E01, M&GPA, NumL. *Bk. rev.:* 0-3, 500-1,200 words, signed. *Aud.:* Ac, Sa.

Sponsored by a partnership of geologists in several Nordic countries, this journal deals exclusively with research on the Quaternary period. This extends from about two million years ago to the present, and many of the topics covered, such as climatic variations and sea-level changes, are of particular relevance today. Other papers examine the stratigraphy, glacial dynamics and landforms, and the flora and fauna of the period. Full-text web access beginning with 1972 is available from Wiley-Blackwell to subscribers, with some content also offered on EBSCOhost. Readers may register to receive free alerts via e-mail or RSS feeds. A GeoRef priority journal.

1699. *Bulletin of Volcanology.* Formerly (until 1984): *Bulletin Volcanologique.* [ISSN: 0258-8900] 1924. 8x/yr. EUR 1936 (print & online eds.). Ed(s): T H Druitt, J Stix. Springer, Tiergartenstr 17, Heidelberg, 69121, Germany. Illus., index, adv. Sample. Refereed. Vol. ends: Jul (No. 8). Reprint: PSC. *Indexed:* A01, A22, BRI, E01. *Aud.:* Ac, Sa.

The official journal of the International Association of Volcanology and Chemistry of the Earth's Interior. As suggested by its title, the emphasis is on volcanoes, including their characteristics, behavior, and associated hazards. Coverage is international in scope and includes related material on magmatic systems and igneous petrology. Through early 2011, issues also contain a summary of recent volcanic activity based on data from the Smithsonian Institution's Global Volcanism Network. The web site offers free tables of contents and abstracts as well as full-text access from 1937 forward for subscribers. Readers may register for a free account to receive table of content alerts via e-mail, or sign up for an RSS feed. A GeoRef priority journal.

1700. *Canadian Journal of Earth Sciences.* [ISSN: 0008-4077] 1963. m. CAD 1630. Ed(s): Dr. Ali Polat. N R C Research Press, 1200 Montreal Rd, Bldg M-55, Ottawa, ON K1A 0R6, Canada; pubs@nrc-cnrc.gc.ca; http://pubs.nrc-cnrc.gc.ca. Illus., index, adv. Refereed. Circ: 1572. Vol. ends: Dec (No. 12). Microform: MML; PMC; PQC. *Indexed:* A01, A22, C&ISA, C37, CBCARef, CerAb, E01, EngInd, FR, M&GPA, S25. *Aud.:* Ac, Sa.

This journal is published monthly by the National Research Council of Canada. The majority of its articles are in English, and those in French include English abstracts. Articles are more technical than those found in *Geoscience Canada.* As one might expect, for site-specific topics the focus is heavily on Canadian geology, but many of the underlying principles are transferable to other regions. The web site offers free tables of contents and abstracts from 1964 on, with full-text access for subscribers. Readers may sign up for RSS feeds or e-mail alerts to learn when new content is published. A GeoRef priority journal.

1701. *Canadian Mineralogist.* Formerly (until 1957): *Contributions to Canadian Mineralogy.* [ISSN: 0008-4476] 1921. bi-m. CAD 525 (print & online eds.); Free to members. Ed(s): Vicki Loschiavo. Mineralogical Association of Canada, 490 Rue de la Couronne, Quebec, PQ G1K 9A9, Canada; office@mineralogicalassociation.ca; http://www.mineralogicalassociation.ca. Illus. Sample. Refereed. Vol. ends: Dec. *Indexed:* A22, C&ISA, CerAb, EngInd. *Bk. rev.:* 0-2, 300-1,000 words. *Aud.:* Ac, Sa.

Publishes research papers on crystallography, geochemistry, mineralogy, mineral deposits, and petrology. This title averages one thematic issue each year, usually reporting on symposia sponsored by the Mineralogical Association of Canada. Articles are primarily in English, while some include French summaries. Abstracts for papers from 1957 to present are available on the GeoScience World web site, with full text for subscribers. Readers may register for free RSS feeds or e-mail alerts. A GeoRef priority journal.

1702. *Canadian Petroleum Geology. Bulletin.* Former titles (until 1963): *Alberta Society of Petroleum Geologists. Journal;* (until 1955): *A S P G News Bulletin.* [ISSN: 0007-4802] 1953. q. Free to members;

Non-members, CAD 150. Ed(s): Denis Lavoie, Denise Then. Canadian Society of Petroleum Geologists, 600, 640 8th Ave S W, Calgary, AB T2P 1G7, Canada; http://www.cspg.org. Illus., index, adv. Refereed. Vol. ends: Dec (No. 4). *Indexed:* A22, EngInd. *Bk. rev.:* 0-4, 500-1,200 words, signed. *Aud.:* Ac, Sa.

This is the official publication of the Canadian Society of Petroleum Geologists, and many of its issues devote some space to society business, such as awards and a report of activities. More importantly, the journal also features high-quality research articles on various aspects of petroleum geology in a wide range of geologic environments. Articles are well illustrated and feature color where appropriate. Regional coverage emphasizes Canada and Alaska, but the title is still a valuable addition to larger academic or special libraries. Abstracts and tables of contents are available for free from 1965 to the present, and online access is available through GeoScience World from 2000 to the present. Readers may register for free e-mail alerts when new journal content is published. The AAPG Databases Archive offers full-text coverage from 1953 forward for subscribers or by pay-per-view. A GeoRef priority journal.

1703. *Chemical Geology.* Incorporates (in 1993): *Chemical Geology. Isotope Geoscience Section;* Which was formerly (1983-1985): *Isotope Geoscience.* [ISSN: 0009-2541] 1966. 44x/yr. EUR 5399. Ed(s): Bernard Bourdon, Jeremy Fein. Elsevier BV, Radarweg 29, PO Box 211, Amsterdam, 1000 AE, Netherlands; JournalsCustomerServiceEMEA@elsevier.com; http://www.elsevier.nl. Illus., index, adv. Sample. Refereed. Vol. ends: No. 4. Microform: PQC. *Indexed:* A01, A22, C&ISA, CerAb, OceAb, S25. *Aud.:* Ac, Sa.

This title serves as an official publication of the European Association for Geochemistry. It has an international scope and aims to provide broad coverage of the growing field of organic and inorganic geochemistry, including reports about Earth and other planets. Papers address topics such as low-temperature geochemistry, organic/petroleum geochemistry, analytical techniques, isotope studies, environmental geochemistry, and experimental petrology and geochemistry. The web site provides free access to tables of contents and abstracts from the journal's inception in 1966, and full-text access from is available through ScienceDirect. Readers may register for a free account to receive table of content alerts via e-mail, or sign up for an RSS feed. A GeoRef priority journal.

1704. *Clay Minerals.* Formerly (until 1965): *Clay Minerals Bulletin.* [ISSN: 0009-8558] 1947. q. GBP 411 (print & online eds.); Free to members. Mineralogical Society, 12 Baylis Mews, Amyand Park Rd, Twickenham, TW1 3HQ, United Kingdom; info@minersoc.org; http://www.minersoc.org. Illus., index, adv. Refereed. Circ: 500. Vol. ends: Dec (No. 4). *Indexed:* A01, A22, C&ISA, CerAb, E01, EngInd. *Bk. rev.:* 0-2, 600-1,000 words, signed. *Aud.:* Ac, Sa.

Published by the Mineralogical Society of Great Britain, this journal represents the combined efforts of several clay research groups based primarily in Europe. Papers are occasionally written in French, German, or Spanish but are predominantly in English. Many articles focus on research concerning hydrothermal interactions related to clay weathering and diagenesis. Analytical techniques and their use in the determination of structure and physical properties of clay minerals are also emphasized. The society's web site offers a free full-text archive for the years from 1950 to 1999, and issues from 1998 forward are available to subscribers via Ingenta. Abstracts from mid-1975 onward, and full text from mid-1996 forward, are available online to subscribers of GeoScience World. Readers may register to receive free e-mail alerts or RSS feeds about new journal content. A GeoRef priority journal.

1705. *Clays and Clay Minerals.* Former titles (until 1965): *Clays and Clay Minerals;* (until 1953): *National Conference on Clays and Clay Technology. Proceedings.* [ISSN: 0009-8604] 1952. bi-m. Free to members. Ed(s): Joseph W Stucki, Kevin Murphy. The Clay Minerals Society, PO Box 460130, Aurora, CO 80046; cms@clays.org; http://www.clays.org. Illus., index. Refereed. Vol. ends: Dec (No. 6). Reprint: PSC. *Indexed:* A22, C&ISA, C45, CerAb, EngInd, S25. *Aud.:* Ac, Sa.

This journal serves as the official publication of the Clay Minerals Society and was originally issued as an annual proceedings volume. Clays are important because of their unusual chemical and physical properties, and this journal focuses on all aspects of clay science. The web site of the society offers an archive with free access to articles from 1952 to 2001. Coverage is offered on Ingenta to subscribers from 2002 forward. GeoScience World offers free tables of contents and abstracts beginning with 1975, and subscribers may view full text from 2000 onward. Readers may register for a free account and receive RSS feeds or e-mail alerts when new journal content is published. Coverage is similar to that of *Clay Minerals,* but with a greater emphasis on interdisciplinary applications. Together, the two journals provide very thorough coverage of the field. A GeoRef priority journal.

1706. *The Compass (Norman).* Former titles (until 1984): *The Compass of Sigma Gamma Epsilon;* (until 1921): *Sigma Gamma Epsilon Compass.* [ISSN: 0894-802X] 1920. q. Free to members. Society of Sigma Gamma Epsilon, c/o James C Walters, Sigma Gamma Epsilon, Department of Earth Science, Cedar Falls, IA 50614; walters@uni.edu; http://www.uni.edu/earth/SGE/info.html. Illus., index. Sample. Refereed. *Aud.:* Ac.

Sigma Gamma Epsilon is an honorary scientific society devoted to the earth sciences. Published since 1920, this quarterly presents society- and chapter-related news and historical information. This small journal also features research articles on a wide range of topics, with many of them written by students presenting their findings. Research papers are refereed and indexed in the major sources. Long only offered in print form, this title became available online in 2012.

Computers & Geosciences. See Cartography, GIS, and Imagery section.

1707. *Contributions to Mineralogy and Petrology.* Former titles (until 1965): *Beitraege zur Mineralogie und Petrographie;* (until 1957): *Heidelberger Beitraege zur Mineralogie und Petrographie.* [ISSN: 0010-7999] 1947. m. EUR 4865 (print & online eds.). Ed(s): J Hoefs, T L Grove. Springer, Tiergartenstr 17, Heidelberg, 69121, Germany. Illus., index, adv. Refereed. Vol. ends: No. 6. Microform: PQC. Reprint: PSC. *Indexed:* A01, A22, E01, P02. *Aud.:* Ac, Sa.

This journal provides in-depth technical coverage on the petrology and genesis of all major rock types. Heavy emphasis is placed on geochemistry, and many of the articles consist of theoretical and experimental work such as determining mineral phase relations and chemical equilibria. Related areas such as isotope geology and element partitioning are also featured. The publisher's web site offers free tables of contents and abstracts from 1947 on, with full-text access for subscribers. Readers may register for free table-of-contents alerts via e-mail or RSS feed. Some content is also available via EBSCOhost. A GeoRef priority journal.

1708. *Cretaceous Research.* [ISSN: 0195-6671] 1980. bi-m. EUR 1708. Ed(s): C J Wood, P J Harries. Academic Press, 32 Jamestown Rd, Camden, London, NW1 7BY, United Kingdom; corporate.sales@elsevier.com; http://www.elsevier.com/. Illus., index, adv. Sample. Vol. ends: Dec (No. 6). Reprint: PSC. *Indexed:* A22, E01. *Bk. rev.:* 0-2, 700-1,000 words, signed. *Aud.:* Ac, Sa.

Like *Quaternary Research,* this journal is interdisciplinary and focuses on a single major geological time period. The Cretaceous Period ended about 65 million years ago, a time best known for the extinction of the dinosaurs. Several of the articles focus on this "K/T boundary," but this is by no means the only subject covered. Stratigraphy and paleontology, in particular, receive considerable attention. Special topical issues on significant sites or geologic events during the Cretaceous Period are also featured. The web site provides free access to tables of contents and abstracts beginning with 1980 issues. Full-text articles from 1980 to the present are available to subscribers through ScienceDirect. Recent articles often include a graphical abstract. Readers may register to receive free e-mail alerts or RSS feeds when new issues are published.

1709. *E O S.* Formerly (until 1969): *American Geophysical Union. Transactions.* [ISSN: 0096-3941] 1919. w. GBP 609. John Wiley & Sons, Inc., 111 River St, MS 4-02, Hoboken, NJ 07030; info@wiley.com; http://www.wiley.com. Illus., index, adv. Sample. Vol. ends: No. 52. *Indexed:* A&ATA, A22, C&ISA, CerAb, M&GPA. *Bk. rev.:* 0-2, 100-400 words. *Aud.:* Ac, Sa.

This tabloid-format weekly publishes on items of current interest in geophysics research. Along with the feature articles, there are announcements from the American Geophysical Union, news, book reviews, a calendar of events, and information on grants, fellowships, and employment opportunities. A hardcover volume published annually contains the articles, news, and editorials from the weekly issues. The web site provides full-text access from 1969 forward for subscribers. Readers may register for free table-of-contents alerts via e-mail or RSS feed. Recommended for academic and corporate libraries. A GeoRef priority journal.

1710. *Earth: the science behind the headlines.* Former titles (until 2008): *Geotimes;* (until 1956): *Geological News Letter.* [ISSN: 1943-345X] 1956. m. USD 36 domestic; USD 50.50 newsstand/cover per issue Canada; USD 81 newsstand/cover per issue elsewhere. Ed(s): Christopher M Keane. American Geological Institute, 4220 King St, Alexandria, VA 22302; agi@agiweb.org; http://www.agiweb.org. Illus., index, adv. Sample. Circ: 15000. Vol. ends: Dec (No. 12). Microform: PQC. *Indexed:* A01, A22, BRI, C&ISA, CerAb, M&GPA, OceAb, P02. *Bk. rev.:* 1-3, 500-1,000 words. *Aud.:* Ga, Ac, Sa.

This monthly magazine provides reports on geoscience research and education, recent geological phenomena, political developments, technological advances, and other news. Articles are aimed at both geologists and the general public. Books, maps, audiovisual material, and software are reviewed. Issues also include classified ads, and these along with many news items are freely accessible at the journal's web site. Readers may access full content online from 2008 forward through a subscription to the digital edition. Strongly recommended for academic and corporate collections, as well as for larger public libraries. A GeoRef priority journal. URL: www.earthmagazine.org/

1711. *Earth and Planetary Science Letters.* [ISSN: 0012-821X] 1966. 48x/yr. EUR 5370. Ed(s): T Elliott, G M Henderson. Elsevier BV, Radarweg 29, PO Box 211, Amsterdam, 1000 AE, Netherlands; JournalsCustomerServiceEMEA@elsevier.com; http://www.elsevier.nl. Illus., index. Sample. Refereed. Vol. ends: No. 4. Microform: PQC. *Indexed:* A01, A22, BrArAb, C&ISA, CerAb, EngInd, M&GPA, OceAb, S25. *Aud.:* Ac, Sa.

Publishes research in physical, chemical, and mechanical properties of the Earth's crust and mantle, atmosphere, and hydrosphere, as well as papers on lunar studies, plate tectonics, ocean floor spreading, and continental drift. The journal focuses on shorter communications with rapid turnaround. The publisher's web site offers free access to tables of contents and article abstracts from 1966 to the present. Data sets and other supplementary content are provided online. Full-text articles from 1966 forward are available to subscribers via ScienceDirect. Readers may register for free e-mail alerts or an RSS feed when new journal content is available. A GeoRef priority journal.

1712. *Earth Surface Processes and Landforms.* Formerly (until 1981): *Earth Surface Processes.* [ISSN: 0197-9337] 1976. 15x/yr. GBP 2459. Ed(s): S N Lane. John Wiley & Sons Ltd, The Atrium, Southern Gate, Chichester, PO19 8SQ, United Kingdom; customer@wiley.com; http://www.wiley.com. Illus., index, adv. Sample. Refereed. Vol. ends: No. 13. Microform: PQC. Reprint: PSC. *Indexed:* A22, C&ISA, C45, CerAb, EngInd, FR, RRTA, S25. *Bk. rev.:* 0-2, 200-600 words, signed. *Aud.:* Ac, Sa.

This wide-ranging journal publishes on all aspects of earth surface science and geomorphology. This encompasses the complex process of landform evolution by the processes of weathering, erosion, transport, and deposition. Landslides and other natural hazards are also considered. Much of the work is highly interdisciplinary in nature and shows in what way different chemical, mechanical, and hydrologic factors have interacted to shape the landscape both in the past and in the present. Free tables of contents and abstracts from 1976 forward are provided at the web site, with full-text access for subscribers. Readers may register for free e-mail alerts or RSS feeds. A GeoRef priority journal.

1713. *Economic Geology and the Bulletin of the Society of Economic Geologists.* Formerly (until 1930): *Economic Geology;* Which superseded in part (in 1906): *American Geologist.* [ISSN: 0361-0128] 1905. 8x/yr. Free to members. Ed(s): Mabel J Peterson, Lawrence D Meinert. Society of Economic Geologists, Inc., 7811 Shaffer Pky, Littleton, CO 80127; seg@segweb.org; http://www.segweb.org. Illus., index. Sample. Refereed. Vol. ends: Dec (No. 8). Microform: PMC; PQC. *Indexed:* A22, EngInd, S25. *Bk. rev.:* 0-4, 600-1,000 words. *Aud.:* Ac, Sa.

Articles feature research on theoretical and experimental aspects of economic geology; these are balanced with papers on field research. This bulletin also contains selected tables of contents from journals in related fields and a calendar of relevant events. GeoScience World provides free tables of contents and abstracts from 1905 forward, and with full-text articles for all years available for subscribers. Readers may register for free e-mail alerts or RSS feeds when new journal content is published. A GeoRef priority journal.

1714. *Elements (Quebec): an international magazine of mineralogy, geochemistry, and petrology.* Formed by the merger of (1985-2005): *The Lattice;* (1961-2005): *M A C Newsletter; C M S News.* [ISSN: 1811-5209] 2005. bi-m. USD 150 Free to members. Ed(s): Pierrette Tremblay. Mineralogical Association of Canada, 490 Rue de la Couronne, Quebec, PQ G1K 9A9, Canada; office@mineralogicalassociation.ca; http://www.mineralogicalassociation.ca. Adv. Sample. Refereed. *Indexed:* A22, C&ISA, C45, CerAb. *Aud.:* Ac, Sa.

Elements is a joint effort among over a dozen professional societies in the mineralogical sciences. Issues are thematic in nature—for example, urban geochemistry, mine wastes, impact craters, water resources, and specific rock or mineral types. This title includes news of society events, short courses, awards, and conference reports. Full text from 2005 forward is available online through the GeoScience World platform. Readers may register for free e-mail alerts or RSS feeds. A GeoRef priority journal.

1715. *Engineering Geology.* Incorporates (1983-1991): *Mining Science and Technology.* [ISSN: 0013-7952] 1965. 28x/yr. EUR 2595. Ed(s): R Shiemon, G B Crosta. Elsevier BV, Radarweg 29, PO Box 211, Amsterdam, 1000 AE, Netherlands; JournalsCustomerServiceEMEA@elsevier.com; http://www.elsevier.nl. Illus., index, adv. Sample. Refereed. Vol. ends: No. 4. Microform: PQC. *Indexed:* A01, A22, ApMecR, C&ISA, CerAb, EngInd, OceAb, S25. *Bk. rev.:* 0-2, 500-1,000 words. *Aud.:* Ac, Sa.

This international journal publishes studies relevant to engineering geology and related topics, such as environmental concerns and geological hazards. These include research papers, case histories, and reviews. The web site provides free access to tables of contents and abstracts beginning with 1965 issues. Full-text articles are available to libraries that subscribe via ScienceDirect. Readers may register for an account and receive alerts for search results or new issues of the journal. A GeoRef priority journal.

1716. *Environmental and Engineering Geoscience.* Former titles (until 1995): *Association of Engineering Geologists. Bulletin;* (until 1968): *Engineering Geology.* [ISSN: 1078-7275] 1963. q. Members, USD 60 (print & online eds.); Non-members, USD 225). Ed(s): Ira D Sasowsky, Abdul Shakoor. Geological Society of America, PO Box 9140, Boulder, CO 80301; editing@geosociety.org; http://www.geosociety.org. Illus., index, adv. Sample. Refereed. Vol. ends: Dec (No. 4). *Indexed:* A22, C&ISA, CerAb, OceAb, S25. *Bk. rev.:* 0-9, 800-3,000 words. *Aud.:* Ac, Sa.

This quarterly publishes research articles and technical papers and notes in areas of interest to hydrologists, environmental scientists, and engineering geologists. Topics include site selection, feasibility studies, design or construction of civil engineering projects, waste management, and ground water. Appropriate for corporate and academic collections. Free tables of contents and abstracts are available on the GeoScience World web site from 1995 to the present, with full-text coverage from 2000 onward for subscribers. Readers may sign up for free e-mail alerts or RSS feeds when new issues are published. A GeoRef priority journal.

1717. *Environmental Earth Sciences.* Former titles (until 2010): *Environmental Geology;* (until 1993): *Environmental Geology and Water Sciences;* (until 1984): *Environmental Geology.* [ISSN: 1866-6280] 1975. 24x/yr. EUR 3652 (print & online eds.). Ed(s): James W Lamoreaux. Springer, Tiergartenstr 17, Heidelberg, 69121, Germany. Illus., index, adv. Sample. Refereed. Microform: PQC. Reprint: PSC. *Indexed:* A22, Agr, BRI, C45, E01, EngInd, OceAb, S25. *Bk. rev.:* 2-7, 300-1,800 words, signed. *Aud.:* Ac, Sa.

The application of geological principles and data to environmental issues has become an increasingly important area of emphasis. This international journal includes both research articles and applied technical reports on specific cases and solutions. Much of the work is multidisciplinary in nature and covers such areas as soil and water contamination, radioactive waste disposal, remediation techniques, and the effects of mining and industrial activities. Special topical issues often focus in greater detail on one of these specific subject areas; some examples are carbon dioxide storage, karst hydrology, and integrated water-resource management. The web site offers tables of contents and abstracts from 1975 to the present, with full-text access available for subscribers or individual purchase. E-mail alerts and RSS feeds are available to track new additions. A GeoRef priority journal, listed under its earlier title of *Environmental Geology.*

1718. *Environmental Geosciences.* Former titles (until 1995): *A A P G Division. Environmental Geosciences Journal.* [ISSN: 1075-9565] 1994. q. USD 292 (print & online eds.); Free to members. Ed(s): Kristin M Carter. American Association of Petroleum Geologists, PO Box 979, Tulsa, OK 74101; info@aapg.org; http://www.aapg.org. Adv. Refereed. *Indexed:* A01, A22, E01, S25. *Aud.:* Ac, Sa.

This quarterly is published by AAPG's Division of Environmental Geosciences. Research articles focus on a range of environmental issues such as carbon capture, groundwater monitoring, pollution remediation, and site characterization. Full-text coverage is available on the AAPG Datapages web site from 2001 forward, with online access to society members and subscribers. GeoScience World offers full text from 1997 onward, along with e-mail alerts and RSS feeds for new content. A GeoRef priority journal.

1719. *Episodes: journal of international geoscience.* Supersedes: *International Union of Geological Sciences. Geological Newsletter.* [ISSN: 0705-3797] 1978. q. Ed(s): Hongren Zhang. Geological Society of India, No 63, 12th Cross, Basappa Layout, Gavipuram, Bangalore, 560019, India; gsocind@gmail.com ; http://www.geosocindia.org. Illus., index, adv. Sample. Refereed. Vol. ends: Dec (No. 4). *Indexed:* A22, C45, M&GPA. *Bk. rev.:* 0-4, 500-1,500 words. *Aud.:* Ga, Ac, Sa.

Articles generally have more international orientation than those in *EARTH,* and cover developments of regional and global importance in earth science research programs and techniques, organizations, and science policy. The International Union of Geological Sciences (IUGS) is a large nongovernmental scientific organization that facilitates international and interdisciplinary cooperation in the earth sciences, promoting and supporting study of geological problems of worldwide significance. Many issues include brief reports from international conferences and meetings. The full text of articles is accessible from 1978 forward via the IUGS web site (http://iugs.org/).

1720. *European Journal of Mineralogy: an international journal of mineralogy, geochemistry and related sciences.* Formed by the merger of (1950-1988): *Fortschritte der Mineralogie;* (1968-1988): *Rendiconti della Societa Italiana di Mineralogia e Petrologia;* (1878-1988): *Bulletin de Mineralogia;* Which was formerly (until 1978): *Societe Francaise de Mineralogie et de Cristallographie. Bulletin;* (until 1949): *Societe Francaise de Mineralogie. Bulletin;* (until 1886): *Societe Mineralogique de France. Bulletin.* [ISSN: 0935-1221] 1988. 6x/yr. EUR 389 combined subscription (print & online eds.). Ed(s): Christian Chopin. E. Schweizerbart'sche Verlagsbuchhandlung, Johannesstr 3A, Stuttgart, 70176, Germany; order@schweizerbart.de; http://www.schweizerbart.de. Illus., index, adv. Sample. Refereed. Vol. ends: Nov/Dec (No. 6). *Indexed:* A22, C&ISA, CerAb. *Aud.:* Ac, Sa.

The result of a cooperative publication effort among several European mineralogical societies, this journal replaced these groups' individual journals when it began publication in 1989. Papers are international in scope, with an emphasis on European localities. They cover a wide range of topics in mineralogy, petrology, and crystallography. Free tables of contents from 1989 forward are available, along with full text for subscribers on GeoScience World. Readers may register for free e-mail alerts or RSS feeds. A GeoRef priority journal.

1721. *G3: Geochemistry, Geophysics, Geosystems: an electronic journal of the earth sciences.* [ISSN: 1525-2027] 1999. m. GBP 814. Wiley-Blackwell Publishing, Inc., 111 River St, Hoboken, NJ 07030; info@wiley.com; http://onlinelibrary.wiley.com/. *Indexed:* C45, IndVet, S25. *Aud.:* Ac, Sa.

Sponsored by the American Geophysical Union and the Geochemical Society, this electronic-only journal publishes original research, reviews, and technical briefs in geophysics and geochemistry. The focus is on interdisciplinary work that pertains to understanding the earth as a system, and contributions span a wide range of topics. Many submissions include material such as large data sets, sound clips, or movies that could not be included in a print journal. Some articles are organized into "themes," much as in special issues of more traditional journals. Full-text articles from late 1999 to the present are available for subscribers, along with free access to tables of contents and abstracts on the journal's web site. Readers may register for free e-mail alerts or RSS feeds. A GeoRef priority journal.

1722. Geo-Marine Letters: an international journal of marine geology. [ISSN: 0276-0460] 1980. bi-m. EUR 1246 (print & online eds.). Ed(s): Burg W Flemming. Springer, Tiergartenstr 17, Heidelberg, 69121, Germany. Illus., index, adv. Sample. Refereed. Vol. ends: No. 4. Microform: PQC. Reprint: PSC. *Indexed:* A01, A22, BRI, E01, EngInd, OceAb, P02, S25. *Bk. rev.:* 0-3, 700-1,200 words, signed. *Aud.:* Ac, Sa.

Newer analytical techniques and advanced equipment have opened up the vast areas of the earth under the oceans to intensive study. *Geo-Marine Letters* publishes studies and reviews "dealing with processes, products, and techniques in marine geology, geophysics, and geochemistry." Some topics of coverage include depositional environments, sedimentary processes, stratigraphy, continent–ocean margins, deep-sea sedimentation, and post-depositional movement. Other areas of emphasis include marine geochemistry and geophysics. The web site offers free tables of contents and abstracts from 1981 to the present, with full-text access available for subscribers or individual purchase. Readers may register for an account to receive free e-mail alerts or RSS feeds when new issues are published.

1723. Geobiology (Online). [ISSN: 1472-4669] 2003. bi-m. GBP 470. Ed(s): Kurt Konhauser. Wiley-Blackwell Publishing Ltd., The Atrium, Southern Gate, Chichester, PO19 8SQ, United Kingdom; customer@wiley.com; http://www.wiley.com/. Adv. Sample. Refereed. *Aud.:* Ac, Sa.

This interdisciplinary journal focuses on the complex interaction of life and the geology of Earth over time. Topics include the origin of life, evolutionary ecology, and the sedimentary rock record. Occasional special issues cover such topics as anaerobic photosynthetic ecosystems and microbes in paleoenvironments. Tables of contents and abstracts are available free on the web from 2003 forward, with full-text access for subscribers. A GeoRef priority journal.

1724. Geochemical Transactions. [ISSN: 1467-4866] 2000. irreg. Free. Ed(s): Ken B Anderson, Martin Schoonen. BioMed Central Ltd., 236 Gray's Inn Rd, London, WC1X 8HB, United Kingdom; info@biomedcentral.com; http://www.biomedcentral.com. Adv. Refereed. *Indexed:* A01, A22, E01, M&GPA, S25. *Aud.:* Ac, Sa.

The official journal of the Geochemistry Division of the American Chemical Society, this open-access electronic publication is freely available online and compares favorably with other titles in the field. *Geochemical Transactions* publishes peer-reviewed articles on topics in chemistry related to terrestrial and extraterrestrial systems such as organic geochemistry, inorganic geochemistry, marine and aquatic chemistry, chemical oceanography, biogeochemistry, applied geochemistry, astrobiology, and environmental geochemistry. Free RSS feeds and e-mail alerts are available. An important electronic journal for academic libraries that support earth science research and teaching.

1725. Geochemistry: Exploration, Environment, Analysis. [ISSN: 1467-7873] 2001. q. GBP 327.55 combined subscription domestic (print & online eds.); GBP 315 combined subscription foreign (print & online eds.); USD 630 combined subscription foreign (print & online eds.). Ed(s): Gwendy Hall. Geological Society Publishing House, Unit 7, Brassmill Enterprise Ctr, Brassmill Ln, Bath, BA1 3JN, United Kingdom. Illus. Refereed. *Indexed:* C45, S25. *Aud.:* Ac, Sa.

This quarterly is produced by the Geological Society of London and the Association of Applied Geochemists. It covers the application of geochemistry to the exploration and study of mineral resources. Some topics include geochemical exploration, sampling and analytical techniques, and dispersion processes in and around mineralized deposits. Full text for subscribers is available on GeoScience World, along with free abstracts going back to volume 1. Readers may register to receive free alerts via e-mail when new journal content is published. The journal is also available online as part of the Lyell Collection from the Geological Society of London. Recommended for academic and special libraries. A GeoRef priority journal.

1726. Geochemistry International. Formerly (until 1963): *Geochemistry.* [ISSN: 0016-7029] 1956. m. EUR 5378 (print & online eds.). Ed(s): Erik Galimov. M A I K Nauka - Interperiodica, Profsoyuznaya ul 90, Moscow, 117997, Russian Federation; compmg@maik.ru; http://www.maik.ru. Illus., index, adv. Refereed. Circ: 675. Vol. ends: Dec (No. 12). Microform: PQC. Reprint: PSC. *Indexed:* A22, E01, EngInd, OceAb, S25. *Aud.:* Ac, Sa.

The American Geophysical Union and the American Geosciences Institute together with the Russian Academy of Sciences sponsor publication of this journal. Articles are translated from the Russian journal *Geokhimiya.* Concentrating on the geology of the Eurasian continent, research papers in the journal address theoretical and applied topics such as cosmochemistry; geochemistry of magmatic, metamorphic, hydrothermal, and sedimentary processes; organic geochemistry; and chemistry of the environment. Occasional reports appear from symposia and international meetings. Full text is available to subscribers through SpringerLink, beginning with 2006. Readers may register for free e-mail alerts or RSS feeds. Appropriate for comprehensive collections.

1727. Geochimica et Cosmochimica Acta. [ISSN: 0016-7037] 1950. s-m. EUR 3646. Ed(s): M Norman. Pergamon, The Blvd, Langford Ln, E Park, Kidlington, OX5 1GB, United Kingdom; JournalsCustomerServiceEMEA@elsevier.com; http://www.elsevier.com. Illus., adv. Sample. Refereed. Microform: PQC. *Indexed:* A01, A22, C&ISA, C45, CerAb, IndVet, M&GPA, OceAb, S25. *Aud.:* Ac, Sa.

Publishes research papers in the areas of terrestrial geochemistry, meteoritics, and planetary geochemistry. Topics include chemical processes in Earth's atmosphere, hydrosphere, biosphere, and lithosphere; organic and isotope geochemistry; and lunar science. The web site provides free access to tables of contents and abstracts beginning with 1950 issues, with full-text articles available to subscribers on ScienceDirect. Readers may register for free alerts via e-mail or RSS feeds. Appropriate for academic and corporate research collections. A GeoRef priority journal.

1728. Geofluids (Online). [ISSN: 1468-8123] 2001. q. GBP 517. Ed(s): Craig Manning, Richard Worden. Wiley-Blackwell Publishing Ltd., The Atrium, Southern Gate, Chichester, PO19 8SQ, United Kingdom; customer@wiley.com; http://www.wiley.com/. Adv. Sample. Refereed. *Aud.:* Ac, Sa.

Geofluids emphasizes the chemical, mineralogical, and physical aspects of subsurface fluids in the Earth's crust. Some areas of focus include composition and origin of fluids, groundwater flow regimes, rock fracturing and structural controls on fluid migration, and the geochemistry of dissolution, transport, and precipitation. Free tables of contents and abstracts can be found on the web site, along with full text for subscribers from the first volume forward. Readers may sign up for free e-mail alerts or RSS feeds to keep up with new journal content.

1729. Geological Journal. Formerly (until 1964): *Liverpool and Manchester Geological Journal;* Which was formed by the merger of (1926-1950): *Manchester Geological Association. Journal;* (1874-1950): *Liverpool Geological Society. Proceedings;* Which was formerly (until 1874): *Liverpool Geological Society. Abstract. Proceedings.* [ISSN: 0072-1050] 1951. bi-m. GBP 1029. Ed(s): I D Somerville. John Wiley & Sons Ltd., The Atrium, Southern Gate, Chichester, PO19 8SQ, United Kingdom; customer@wiley.com; http://www.wiley.com. Illus., index, adv. Sample. Refereed. Reprint: PSC. *Indexed:* A22, S25. *Bk. rev.:* 0-7, 500-2,000 words. *Aud.:* Ac, Sa.

This journal provides broad coverage of geology with an emphasis on interdisciplinary work and regional case studies. The United Kingdom and other areas of Europe receive the most attention, although studies from around the world are included. This title is a good complement to others of a general nature, such as *Geology* or *Geological Magazine,* and is appropriate for comprehensive collections. Free tables of contents and abstracts from 1951 to the present are provided on the web site, along with full-text access for subscribers. Readers may register for free e-mail alerts or RSS feeds announcing new journal content.

1730. Geological Magazine. Formerly (until 1864): *Geologist.* [ISSN: 0016-7568] 1842. bi-m. GBP 705. Ed(s): M B Allen, Graham E Budd. Cambridge University Press, The Edinburgh Bldg, Shaftesbury Rd, Cambridge, CB2 8RU, United Kingdom; journals@cambridge.org; http://www.cambridge.org/uk. Illus., index, adv. Sample. Refereed. Circ: 1700. Vol. ends: Nov (No. 6). Microform: BHP. Reprint: PSC. *Indexed:* A01, A22, BRI, C45, E01, MASUSE, P02. *Bk. rev.:* 5-12, 100-500 words. *Aud.:* Ac, Sa.

A strong general journal in the field, this title publishes research and review articles in all areas of earth sciences, and emphasizes interdisciplinary papers of interest to geologists from several specialties. Each issue also features several signed book reviews. GeoScience World offers free tables of contents and abstracts from 1940 forward, and subscribers may view full text of articles from 2000 to present. Readers may sign up for free e-mail alerts or RSS feeds announcing new journal content. Cambridge University Press offers a digitized archive extending back to 1864. A GeoRef priority journal.

1731. Geological Society. Journal. Incorporates (1952-1971): *Geological Society of London. Proceedings;* Which superseded in part (in 1971): *Geological Society of London. Quarterly Journal;* Which was formerly (until 1845): *Geological Society of London. Proceedings.* [ISSN: 0016-7649] 1826. bi-m. GBP 1280.83 combined subscription domestic (print & online eds.); GBP 1212 combined subscription foreign (print & online eds.); USD 2424 combined subscription foreign (print & online eds.). Ed(s): Quentin Crowley. Geological Society Publishing House, Unit 7, Brassmill Enterprise Ctr, Brassmill Ln, Bath, BA1 3JN, United Kingdom. Illus., adv. Refereed. Vol. ends: Nov (No. 6). *Indexed:* A01, A22, BrArAb, M&GPA, P02. *Aud.:* Ac, Sa.

This is the flagship journal of the Geological Society of London, one of the oldest geological societies in the world. It is international in scope, with papers covering the full range of the earth sciences. These include both full-length research articles and shorter, rapid-publication "specials." The editors also often publish thematic sets of papers as all or part of an issue. Top-quality throughout and heavily cited, this journal is highly recommended for academic and special library collections. Free tables of contents and abstracts are available on GeoScience World, along with full text for subscribers from 1971 forward. Readers may sign up for free e-mail alerts or RSS feeds. Archival coverage back to 1845 is available as part of the Lyell collection. A GeoRef priority journal.

1732. Geological Society of America Bulletin. Formerly (until 1961): *Geological Society of America. Bulletin.* [ISSN: 0016-7606] 1890. bi-m. Members, USD 85 (print & online eds.); Non-members, USD 825 (print & online eds.). Ed(s): Jill Rothenberg. Geological Society of America, PO Box 9140, Boulder, CO 80301; editing@geosociety.org; http://www.geosociety.org. Illus., adv. Sample. Refereed. Vol. ends: Dec (No. 12). Microform: PMC; PQC. *Indexed:* A01, A22, C&ISA, C45, CerAb, EngInd, M&GPA, OceAb, P02, S25. *Aud.:* Ac, Sa.

This journal is the more research-oriented periodical published by the Geological Society of America (GSA) and contains longer articles than does *Geology.* Although coverage of international projects is included, work in North America is emphasized. Large-format inserts (usually maps) appear in some issues. The GSA web site provides tables of contents and article abstracts beginning in 1918, with full-text access from 1945 forward for subscribers or individual purchase. Also included is a free data repository of supplementary files for selected articles. Similar coverage is also available on GeoScience World, with full-text articles from 1945 forward and abstracts back to 1918. Readers may sign up for free e-mail alerts or RSS feeds about new articles. Strongly recommended for academic and corporate collections. A GeoRef priority journal.

1733. Geology (Boulder). [ISSN: 0091-7613] 1973. m. Members, USD 85 (print & online eds.); Non-members, USD 825 (print & online eds.). Ed(s): Lyne Yohe. Geological Society of America, PO Box 9140,

Boulder, CO 80301; editing@geosociety.org; http://www.geosociety.org. Illus., adv. Sample. Refereed. Vol. ends: Dec (No. 12). Microform: PQC. *Indexed:* A01, A22, BRI, EngInd, M&GPA, OceAb, P02, S25. *Aud.:* Ac, Sa.

This title publishes short, thought-provoking articles on a wide range of geological topics of interest to a broad audience. *Geology* is oriented more toward new investigations and recent discoveries in the field than is *Geological Society of America Bulletin.* A "Research Focus" feature highlights additional information on research issues related to selected articles. Abstracts are accessible on the GSA web site from 1973 to the present, with full-text access for subscribers or for purchase. Full text is also available on GeoScience World from 1973 forward. Readers may sign up for e-mail alerts or RSS feeds to stay up-to-date with new journal content. Strongly recommended for academic and corporate collections. A GeoRef priority journal.

1734. Geology Today. [ISSN: 0266-6979] 1985. bi-m. GBP 575. Ed(s): Peter Doyle. Wiley-Blackwell Publishing Ltd., The Atrium, Southern Gate, Chichester, PO19 8SQ, United Kingdom; customer@wiley.com; http://www.wiley.com/. Illus., index, adv. Sample. Refereed. Microform: PQC. Reprint: PSC. *Indexed:* A01, A22, BRI, C37, E01, MASUSE, P02, S25. *Bk. rev.:* 0-10, 200-500 words. *Aud.:* Ga, Ac.

Published on behalf of the Geologists' Association and the Geological Society of London, this journal is similar in many respects to *EARTH.* News and current awareness briefings are provided and supplemented by short feature articles. The latter often gravitate toward popular topics, but are generally well written and illustrated. Free tables of contents with abstracts can be found on the web site beginning with 1985. Full-text access is available from Wiley-Blackwell for subscribers, and articles are also available for individual purchase. Readers may sign up for free e-mail alerts or RSS feeds to keep up with new content. Some content is also available on EBSCOhost.

1735. Geomorphology. [ISSN: 0169-555X] 1987. 44x/yr. EUR 3033. Ed(s): R A Marston, A Plater. Elsevier BV, Radarweg 29, PO Box 211, Amsterdam, 1000 AE, Netherlands; JournalsCustomerServiceEMEA@elsevier.com; http://www.elsevier.nl. Illus., adv. Sample. Refereed. Microform: PQC. *Indexed:* A01, A22, C&ISA, C45, CerAb, FR, OceAb, RRTA, S25. *Bk. rev.:* 0-3, 500-1,000 words. *Aud.:* Ac, Sa.

Publishes research papers, review articles, and book reviews on landform studies of all types and scales, including extraterrestrial settings. Special issues present papers on such topics as sediment sources, erosion by water, and effects of climate change and land use on geomorphic processes. The web site provides free access to tables of contents and abstracts from 1987 onward, and full-text access is available to subscribers through ScienceDirect. Readers may register to receive free e-mail alerts or RSS feeds to track new articles. Appropriate for academic collections. A GeoRef priority journal.

1736. Geophysical Journal International. Formerly (until 1989): *Geophysical Journal;* Which was formed by the merger of (1986-1987): *Annales Geophysicae. Series B: Terrestrial and Planetary Physics;* (1958-1987): *Royal Astronomical Society Geophysical Journal;* Which was formerly (until 1958): *Royal Astronomical Society. Monthly Notices. Geophysical Supplement;* (1986-1987): *Annales Geophysicae. Series A: Upper Atmosphere and Space Sciences.* [ISSN: 0956-540X] 1958. m. EUR 2071. Ed(s): J Trampert. Oxford University Press, Great Clarendon St, Oxford, OX2 6DP, United Kingdom; jnl.orders@oup.co.uk; http://www.oxfordjournals.org. Illus., adv. Sample. Refereed. Microform: PQC. Reprint: PSC. *Indexed:* A01, A22, C&ISA, CerAb, E01, M&GPA, MSN. *Bk. rev.:* 0-2, 700-1,500 words, signed. *Aud.:* Ac, Sa.

Formed by a merger of three journals, this title continues the numbering of the *Geophysical Journal of the Royal Astronomical Society.* It endeavors to "promote the understanding of the earth's internal structure, physical properties, processes[,] and evolution." Subject areas covered include seismology, crustal structure, geomagnetism, and rock rheology. Tables of contents and abstracts can be found on the web site from 1958 forward, with full-text access available for subscribers. Readers may register for free e-mail alerts about new journal content. A GeoRef priority journal.

1737. Geophysical Prospecting. [ISSN: 0016-8025] 1953. bi-m. GBP 908. Ed(s): Tijmen Jan Moser. Wiley-Blackwell Publishing Ltd., The Atrium, Southern Gate, Chichester, PO19 8SQ, United Kingdom; customer@wiley.com; http://www.wiley.com/. Illus., adv. Sample. Refereed. Microform: PQC. Reprint: PSC. *Indexed:* A01, A22, C&ISA, C45, E01, EngInd. *Aud.:* Ac, Sa.

Published on behalf of the European Association for Geoscientists and Engineers, *Geophysical Prospecting* covers research on geophysics as applied to exploration. Many articles report on work in the oil and mineral industries and have a practical emphasis. However, the journal is also appropriate for academic researchers in geophysics. Free tables of contents and abstracts from 1953 to the present are available at the web site, along with full-text access for subscribers. Readers may sign up for free e-mail alerts or RSS feeds to track new journal content. Some content is also available on EBSCOhost.

1738. Geophysical Research Letters. [ISSN: 0094-8276] 1974. s-m. USD 4368. Ed(s): Eric Calais. Wiley-Blackwell Publishing, Inc., 111 River St, Hoboken, NJ 07030; info@wiley.com; http://onlinelibrary.wiley.com/. Illus., index. Sample. Refereed. Vol. ends: Dec. *Indexed:* A22, C&ISA, C45, CerAb, EngInd, M&GPA, OceAb, RRTA, S25. *Aud.:* Ac, Sa.

This journal is aimed at scientists in diverse disciplines related to geophysics, and issues contain topics such as atmospheric science, oceans, and climate; solid earth and planets; and hydrology and climate. Manuscripts are of limited length in order to expedite review and publication. Special sections address hot topics of broad interest to the geophysics research community. Full-text articles from 1974 to the present are available for subscribers from Wiley-Blackwell. The web site offers free access to tables of contents and abstracts back to 1974 and allows readers to register for free e-mail alerts and RSS feeds for new journal content. A GeoRef priority journal.

1739. Geophysics. Formerly (until 1936): *Society of Petroleum Geophysicists. Journal.* [ISSN: 0016-8033] 1931. bi-m. USD 580 (print & online eds.) Corporations, USD 995). Ed(s): Vladimir Grechka. Society of Exploration Geophysicists, PO Box 702740, Tulsa, OK 74170; meetings@seg.org; http://www.seg.org. Illus., index, adv. Refereed. Vol. ends: Nov/Dec (No. 6). Microform: PQC. *Indexed:* A22, ApMecR, C&ISA, EngInd, M&GPA, S25. *Aud.:* Ac, Sa.

Published by the Society of Exploration Geophysicists, this is one of the leading journals in the field. Many of the articles focus on seismic data acquisition, processing, and interpretation. Other areas such as mechanical properties of rock, borehole geophysics, and remote sensing are also covered. Extensive use is made of color figures and illustrations. Access to tables of contents and article abstracts from 1936 to the present are free on the SEG Digital Library, with full-text articles for all years available to subscribers. GeoScience World also features abstracts from 1936 forward, but full-text access begins with 2000. Readers may sign up for free e-mail alerts or RSS feeds. Highly recommended. A GeoRef priority journal.

1740. Geoscience Canada. Formerly (until 1974): *Geological Association of Canada. Proceedings.* [ISSN: 0315-0941] 1948. q. Individuals, CAD 50; Members, CAD 40; Non-members, CAD 185. Ed(s): Reginald A Wilson. Geological Association of Canada, c/o Dept. of Earth Sciences, Memorial Univ. of Newfoundland, St. John's, NF A1B 3X5, Canada; gac@mun.ca; http://www.gac.ca. Illus., adv. Sample. Refereed. Vol. ends: Dec (No. 4). Microform: PQC. *Indexed:* A01, A22, BRI, C37, C45, EngInd, M&GPA. *Bk. rev.:* 1-7, 400-1,200 words, signed. *Aud.:* Ac, Sa.

This engaging quarterly is the main journal of the Geological Association of Canada (GAC) and is geared toward the nonspecialist. Many of the papers deal with historical and policy issues related to the geology of Canada. Others address topics of broader interest, such as sedimentation processes, glacial geology, geothermal energy, and plate tectonics. For many years, this journal has published an excellent series on mineral deposit models; other series feature such topics as environmental marine geoscience, igneous rock associations, and even geology and wine. Full text of articles is available to GAC members and subscribers from 1974 to present. Free online summaries, often in both English and French, are available.

1741. Geosphere. [ISSN: 1553-040X] 2005. bi-m. Non-members, USD 150. Ed(s): Bridgette Moore. Geological Society of America, PO Box 9140, Boulder, CO 80301; editing@geosociety.org; http://www.geosociety.org. *Indexed:* A01, M&GPA, OceAb, S25. *Aud.:* Ac, Sa.

Casting a broad net, *Geosphere* publishes research articles in all fields of earth and geosciences, especially papers that take advantage of the online format to include multimedia files, color illustrations, and links to supplementary data. Themes in recent special issues include modeling of geologic systems, magma intrusions, and marine geology. All article abstracts and are freely available online, with full text for subscribers on the web site. Full-text access from 2005 forward is also available to subscribers on GeoScience World. Readers may set up an e-mail alert or RSS feed to receive notification when new issues are published. Some content is available on EBSCOhost. A GeoRef priority journal.

Geothermics. See Energy section.

1742. Ground Water. [ISSN: 0017-467X] 1963. bi-m. GBP 386. Ed(s): Mary P Anderson. Wiley-Blackwell Publishing, Inc., 111 River St, Hoboken, NJ 07030; info@wiley.com; http://onlinelibrary.wiley.com/. Illus., index. Sample. Refereed. Vol. ends: Nov/Dec (No. 6). Microform: PQC. Reprint: PSC. *Indexed:* A01, A22, AbAn, Agr, BRI, C&ISA, C45, CerAb, E01, EngInd, M&GPA, P02, S25. *Bk. rev.:* 0-5, 300-800 words, signed. *Aud.:* Ac, Sa.

This is an official journal of the Association of Ground Water Scientists and Engineers, a division of the National Ground Water Association. Emphasis is on ground water hydrology in aquifers and other geologic environments. Physical and chemical interactions and solution transport are also given considerable attention. Monitoring and remediation techniques, however, are largely dealt with in its sister publication, *Ground Water Monitoring and Remediation*. Full text of all volumes is available online to subscribers, while tables of contents and abstracts are freely online. Readers may sign up to receive alerts via RSS feed when new articles are published. A GeoRef priority journal.

1743. Hydrogeology Journal. Formerly: *Applied Hydrogeology*. [ISSN: 1431-2174] 1992. bi-m. EUR 1127 (print & online eds.). Ed(s): Clifford Voss. Springer, Tiergartenstr 17, Heidelberg, 69121, Germany. Illus., index, adv. Sample. Refereed. Vol. ends: No. 6. Reprint: PSC. *Indexed:* A01, A22, Agr, BRI, C&ISA, CerAb, E01, S25. *Bk. rev.:* 0-2, 300-800 words, signed. *Aud.:* Ac, Sa.

This journal addresses an important area of interest in the earth sciences. *Hydrogeology Journal* is the official journal of the International Association of Hydrogeologists, and publishes theoretical and research-oriented papers, as well as applied reports. The first issue of each year is often a thematic one. Recent topics include insights from environmental tracers in groundwater systems, saltwater and freshwater interactions in coastal aquifers, and hydrogeoecology and groundwater-dependent ecosystems. The web site offers full-text access for all volumes for subscribers, free tables of contents and abstracts, and an option to sign up for alerts when new articles are published.

1744. Hydrological Processes (Online). [ISSN: 1099-1085] 1986. s-m. GBP 2985. Ed(s): Malcolm G Anderson. John Wiley & Sons Ltd., The Atrium, Southern Gate, Chichester, PO19 8SQ, United Kingdom; customer@wiley.com; http://www.wiley.com. Adv. Sample. Refereed. *Bk. rev.:* 0-1, 500-1,000 words. *Aud.:* Ac, Sa.

This international journal publishes original scientific and technical papers in hydrology. Articles present research on physical, biogeochemical, mathematical, and methodological aspects of hydrological processes, as well as reports on instrumentation and techniques. Occasional special issues focus on a theme; recent examples include flood risk and uncertainty, tracer applications in sediment research, and "Catchments in the future North: interdisciplinary science for sustainable management in the twenty-first century." The journal includes a rapid-communications section called "HPToday" that provides invited commentaries, letters to the editor, refereed scientific briefings, and more. As of 2011, this journal has been published only online, and subscribers may view volumes from 1986 online, or articles are available on a pay-per-view basis. Readers may sign up to receive alerts when new articles are published. A GeoRef priority journal.

1745. *Hydrological Sciences Journal.* Former titles (until 1982): *Hydrological Sciences Bulletin;* (until 1972): *International Association of Scientific Hydrology. Bulletin;* (until 1958): *Bulletin de l'Association Internationale d'hydrologie Scientifique;* (until 1957): *Bulletin d'information de l'Association Internationale d'hydrologie Scientifique.* [ISSN: 0262-6667] 1956. 8x/school-academic yr. GBP 568 (print & online eds.). Ed(s): Zbigniew W Kundzewicz, Demetris Koutsoyiannis. Taylor & Francis, 4 Park Sq, Milton Park, Abingdon, OX14 4RN, United Kingdom; subscriptions@tandf.co.uk; http://www.tandfonline.com. Illus., index, adv. Sample. Refereed. Vol. ends: Dec (No. 6). Reprint: PSC. *Indexed:* A01, A22, C&ISA, C45, EngInd, M&GPA, S25. *Bk. rev.:* Number and length vary. *Aud.:* Ac, Sa.

This official journal of the International Association of Hydrological Sciences publishes scientific papers primarily written in English, as well as some in French. The range of topics covered is quite broad and includes modeling of hydrologic systems, use of water resources, runoff and erosion, and groundwater pollution and chemistry. The journal also features announcements, book reviews, and a handy "diary" of forthcoming hydrology-related events. The web site offers free tables of contents and abstracts, along with author and keyword indexes. Full text for recent volumes is available to subscribers, with open access for older issues.

1746. *Hydrology and Earth System Sciences.* [ISSN: 1027-5606] 1997. m. EUR 1160; EUR 106 newsstand/cover. Ed(s): Murugesu Sivapalan, Hubert H G Savenijeh. Copernicus GmbH, Bahnhofsallee 1e, Goettingen, 37081, Germany; info@copernicus.org; http://www.copernicus.org. Refereed. *Indexed:* Agr, C45, M&GPA, RRTA, S25. *Aud.:* Ac, Sa.

This interdisciplinary journal takes a broad approach and publishes research in all areas of hydrology, with an emphasis on interactions with physical, chemical, and biological processes. Topics covered include the hydrological cycle, transport of dissolved and particulate matter, water budgets and fluxes, climate and atmospheric interactions, and the effects of human activity. Papers are reviewed and discussed in the open-access journal *Hydrology and Earth System Sciences Discussions* (HESSD); once accepted, the papers appear in *HESS*. Articles in special issues address themes such as remote sensing in hydrological sciences, river systems and watersheds, and advances in flood forecasting. This open-access journal makes full text freely available online to all. A GeoRef priority journal.

Icarus. See Astronomy section.

1747. *International Geology Review.* [ISSN: 0020-6814] 1958. m. GBP 1405 (print & online eds.). Ed(s): W Gary Ernst. Taylor & Francis Inc., 325 Chestnut St, Ste 800, Philadelphia, PA 19106; customerservice@taylorandfrancis.com; http://www.tandfonline.com. Illus., index, adv. Refereed. Vol. ends: Dec (No. 12). Reprint: PSC. *Indexed:* A01, A22, E01. *Aud.:* Ac, Sa.

This monthly publication features in-depth review articles and original research. Specific areas of emphasis include petrology, tectonics, and mineral and energy resources. Coverage is global in scope, but the editors particularly encourage submission of papers about parts of the world such as Africa, Asia, and South America, making this an especially useful resource for those geographic areas. Readers may set up alerts via e-mail or RSS feed to learn when new content is published. Tables of contents and article abstracts are freely available online for all volumes. Full text is available online to subscribers. A GeoRef priority journal.

1748. *International Journal of Coal Geology.* [ISSN: 0166-5162] 1981. 16x/yr. EUR 2831. Ed(s): C O Karacan, S Dai. Elsevier BV, Radarweg 29, PO Box 211, Amsterdam, 1000 AE, Netherlands; JournalsCustomerServiceEMEA@elsevier.com; http://www.elsevier.nl. Illus., adv. Sample. Refereed. Vol. ends: No. 4. Microform: PQC. *Indexed:* A01, A22, C&ISA, EngInd. *Bk. rev.:* 0-2, 500-1,000 words. *Aud.:* Ac, Sa.

Publishes both basic and applied research articles on the geology and petrology of coal from around the world. Some areas of special focus are the geology of coal measures, coal genesis and modern coal-forming environments, and coalbed gases. Proceedings of symposia appear in some issues. The web site

provides free access to tables of contents and abstracts for all volumes. Full-text articles are also available online through ScienceDirect. Readers may set up alerts via RSS feed or using their ScienceDirect user account to learn when new articles are published. Appropriate for comprehensive research collections. A GeoRef priority journal.

1749. *International Journal of Earth Sciences.* Formerly (until 1998): *Geologische Rundschau.* [ISSN: 1437-3254] 1910. bi-m. EUR 1375 (print & online eds.). Ed(s): Wolf-Christian Dullo. Springer, Tiergartenstr 17, Heidelberg, 69121, Germany. Illus., index, adv. Sample. Refereed. Vol. ends: Dec (No. 4). Microform: BHP. Reprint: IRC; PSC. *Indexed:* A01, A22, Agr, E01, S25. *Aud.:* Ac, Sa.

This journal publishes "process-oriented original and review papers on the history of the earth." Some areas of particular focus include tectonics, volcanology, sedimentology, mineral deposits, and surface processes. Coverage is international in scope but with emphasis on Europe. Examples of thematic-issue topics include rocks, fabrics, and magnetic anisotropy; from embryonic tectonics and geosynclines to modern concepts of rifting, spreading, and alpine orogenesis; and long-term rift evolution. A special supplementary volume issued in 2002 featured milestone papers from the early history of the journal, with English translations. The web site offers tables of contents and abstracts for all volumes and full-text access for subscribers. Readers may set up alerts to receive tables of contents when new issues are published. Listed as a GeoRef priority journal under its earlier title, *Geologische Rundschau.*

1750. *Journal of Applied Geophysics.* Formerly (until 1992): *Geoexploration.* [ISSN: 0926-9851] 1963. 12x/yr. EUR 1591. Ed(s): M Chouteau, A Pugin. Elsevier BV, Radarweg 29, PO Box 211, Amsterdam, 1000 AE, Netherlands; JournalsCustomerServiceEMEA@elsevier.com; http://www.elsevier.nl. Illus., adv. Refereed. Microform: PQC. *Indexed:* A01, A22, EngInd, M&GPA, OceAb, S25. *Aud.:* Ac, Sa.

Originally published with mining geophysicists as its target audience, this journal now emphasizes environmental, geotechnical, engineering, and hydrological aspects of geophysics and petrophysics, including soil and rock mechanical properties. Special issues focus on current topics and conference reports. Article abstracts include research highlights, a list of three to four bullet points that present the essence of the article. The web site provides free access to tables of contents and abstracts for all volumes. Full-text articles are available to subscribers through ScienceDirect, and new publication alerts are available via RSS feed or from a ScienceDirect user account.

1751. *Journal of Geochemical Exploration.* [ISSN: 0375-6742] 1972. 12x/yr. EUR 1955. Ed(s): J Hoogewerff, B De Vivo. Elsevier BV, Radarweg 29, PO Box 211, Amsterdam, 1000 AE, Netherlands; JournalsCustomerServiceEMEA@elsevier.com; http://www.elsevier.nl. Illus., index. Sample. Refereed. Vol. ends: No. 3. Microform: PQC. *Indexed:* A01, A22, EngInd. *Bk. rev.:* 0-2, 800-2,000 words. *Aud.:* Ac, Sa.

This journal emphasizes the application of geochemistry to the exploration and study of mineral resources and related fields, including geochemistry of the environment. Papers present international research on geochemical exploration, sampling and analytical techniques, geoinformatics, and geochemical distributions and mapping. Free access to tables of contents and article abstracts for all volumes is available on the web site. Full-text articles are available online through ScienceDirect. Readers may set up alerts via RSS feed or using their ScienceDirect user account to learn when new articles are published. Appropriate for comprehensive and research collections. A GeoRef priority journal.

1752. *Journal of Geodynamics.* [ISSN: 0264-3707] 1984. 10x/yr. EUR 2113. Ed(s): R Stephenson. Pergamon, The Blvd, Langford Ln, E Park, Kidlington, OX5 1GB, United Kingdom; JournalsCustomerServiceEMEA@elsevier.com; http://www.elsevier.com. Adv. Sample. Refereed. Microform: PQC. *Indexed:* A01, A22, M&GPA. *Aud.:* Ac, Sa.

This journal provides an international forum for research in the solid earth sciences with an emphasis on large-scale processes. Papers address a wide range of topics, such as physical properties of rocks and changes with pressure and temperature, mantle convection and heat flow, plate tectonics and kinematics, and magma generation, transport, and emplacement. Occasional issues report on symposia or feature a special topic. Recent examples are the medical geology perspective on the risk associated with volcanism and brownfields, molecular aspects of humic substances and biological functionality in soil ecosystems, and phytoremediation of polluted soils. Tables of contents and abstracts are available free on the web site for all volumes. Full text is available for subscribers through ScienceDirect, and readers may set up alerts via RSS feed, or using their ScienceDirect user account to learn when new articles are published.

1753. The Journal of Geology. [ISSN: 0022-1376] 1893. bi-m. USD 273 (print & online eds.). Ed(s): Barbara J Sivertsen, David Rowley. University of Chicago Press, 1427 E 60th St, Chicago, IL 60637; subscriptions@press.uchicago.edu; http://www.journals.uchicago.edu. Illus., index, adv. Sample. Refereed. Vol. ends: Nov. Microform: PMC; PQC. Reprint: PSC. *Indexed:* A01, A22, BRI, OceAb, P02, S25. *Bk. rev.:* 0-4, 300-750 words. *Aud.:* Ac, Sa.

This prestigious journal, published since 1893, is a core title for academic and special libraries. Articles address a broad range of topics in the discipline of geology, and are chosen in part for their wide applicability or use of innovative approaches and methods. Both the full-length articles and the shorter geological notes reflect high editorial standards, adding to the archival value of this outstanding publication. Tables of contents and abstracts are available free on the web site, and full text is accessible to subscribers (via the JSTOR platform). Readers may sign up to receive alerts via e-mail or RSS feed when new issues are published. A GeoRef priority journal.

1754. Journal of Geophysical Research. Former titles (until 1949): *Terrestrial Magnetism and Atmospheric Electricity;* (until 1899): *Terrestrial Magnetism.* [ISSN: 0148-0227] 1896. m. Wiley-Blackwell Publishing, Inc., 111 River St, Hoboken, NJ 07030; info@wiley.com; http://onlinelibrary.wiley.com/. Refereed. *Indexed:* A22, C&ISA, CerAb, M&GPA, OceAb, S25. *Aud.:* Ac, Sa.

This comprehensive, interdisciplinary journal presents research on the physics and chemistry of the earth, its environment, and the solar system. *JGR* is published in seven sections that may be purchased as a package or separately (sections feature atmospheres, biogeosciences, earth surface, oceans, planets, solid earth, and space physics). Individual issues often contain special sections with multiple papers devoted to one topic. Tables of contents and abstracts are freely available, while subscribers may view full-text articles. Readers may sign up to receive publication alerts via e-mail or RSS feed. Parts *B: Solid Earth, C: Oceans,* and *E: Planets* are GeoRef priority journals.

1755. Journal of Geophysics and Engineering. [ISSN: 1742-2132] 2004. bi-m. GBP 1004 (print & online eds.). Ed(s): Shouli Qu, Yanghua Wang. Institute of Physics Publishing Ltd., Temple Circus, Temple Way, Bristol, BS1 6HG, United Kingdom; custserv@iop.org; http://ioppublishing.org. Sample. Refereed. *Indexed:* C45, M&GPA, S25. *Aud.:* Ac, Sa.

This quarterly publishes research articles in all areas of geophysics, with an emphasis on applied science and engineering. It covers topics like geodynamics, seismology, mineral exploration, and reservoir geophysics. Engineering papers focus on the study of the subsurface in such areas as petroleum engineering, rock mechanics, remote sensing, instrumentation, and sensor design. Subscribers may view full text of all articles, while abstracts and reference lists are freely available. Readers may get alerts about newly published articles via RSS feed or by setting up an account on the IOPScience site.

1756. Journal of Geoscience Education. Formerly (until 1996): *Journal of Geological Education.* [ISSN: 1089-9995] 1951. 5x/yr. USD 135 (Individuals, USD 55; Free to members). Ed(s): Julie Libarkin. National Association of Geoscience Teachers, c/o Carleton College B-SERC, One North College St, Northfield, MN 55057; lgoozen@carleton.edu; http://www.nagt.org. Illus., index, adv. Refereed. Vol. ends: Nov (No. 5). Microform: PQC. *Indexed:* A01, A22. *Bk. rev.:* 5-10, 200-800 words. *Aud.:* Ac, Sa.

Earth science teachers are the target audience for this journal, which reports on techniques, resources, and innovations useful for pedagogy and assessment. Recent special issues have included preparing future geoscience teachers, global geoscience education, and teaching geoscience in the context of culture and place. The National Association of Geoscience Teachers web site makes author and subject indexes available back to 1980, along with the full text of volumes since 2001 and a growing number of articles digitized back to 1979. Readers can sign up for e-mail alerts or RSS feeds to learn about newly published articles. A GeoRef priority journal.

1757. Journal of Glaciology. Formerly (until 1947): *Association for the Study of Snow and Ice. Papers and Discussions.* [ISSN: 0022-1430] 19??. bi-m. Free to members; Non-members, GBP 346 (print & online eds.). Ed(s): T H Jacka. International Glaciological Society, Scott Polar Research Institute, Lensfield Rd, Cambridge, CB2 1ER, United Kingdom; igsoc@igsoc.org; http://www.igsoc.org/. Illus., index. Refereed. *Indexed:* A22, M&GPA, S25. *Bk. rev.:* 0-1, 600-1,200 words. *Aud.:* Ac, Sa.

This journal of the International Glaciological Society publishes findings and theories on all aspects of snow and ice, with particular emphasis on studies of glaciers and their formation, movement, and changes over time. Many issues also include one or more papers covering "Instruments and Methods," which describe new techniques and equipment for glacial investigation. Free table-of-contents information is available on the society web site for volumes since 1999 and for a few as far back as 1949. Subscribers may view the full text of articles in digitized volumes, and nonsubscribers may purchase articles (alerts announcing new papers are available via RSS feed). Appropriate for comprehensive academic and specialized collections.

1758. Journal of Hydrology. [ISSN: 0022-1694] 1963. 64x/yr. EUR 7544. Ed(s): P Baveye, K P Georgakakos. Elsevier BV, Radarweg 29, PO Box 211, Amsterdam, 1000 AE, Netherlands; JournalsCustomerServiceEMEA@elsevier.com; http://www.elsevier.nl. Illus., index, adv. Sample. Refereed. Vol. ends: No. 4. Microform: PQC. *Indexed:* A01, A22, Agr, ApMecR, C&ISA, C45, CerAb, EngInd, M&GPA, OceAb, RRTA, S25. *Aud.:* Ac, Sa.

Publishes research papers and reviews on topics related to all areas of the hydrological sciences, such as physical, chemical, biogeochemical, and systems aspects of surface and groundwater hydrology. Special issues focus on such topics as the transfer of pollutants, historical data in flood-risk analysis, and catchment research. Tables of contents and abstracts are available on the web site for all volumes, and full-text articles are available through ScienceDirect (readers may set up alerts via RSS feed or using their ScienceDirect account). Appropriate for comprehensive academic and research collections. A GeoRef priority journal.

1759. Journal of Metamorphic Geology. [ISSN: 0263-4929] 1983. 9x/yr. GBP 1610. Wiley-Blackwell Publishing Ltd., The Atrium, Southern Gate, Chichester, PO19 8SQ, United Kingdom; customer@wiley.com; http://www.wiley.com/. Illus., adv. Sample. Refereed. Vol. ends: Nov (No. 6). Reprint: PSC. *Indexed:* A01, A22, E01, P02. *Aud.:* Ac, Sa.

This title publishes papers on a full range of metamorphic topics. Research is presented on properties of metamorphic minerals, theoretical and experimental studies of metamorphic reactions, structural deformation and geochemical changes associated with metamorphism, and regional analysis of metamorphic terrains. The web site provides free tables of contents and abstracts for all volumes; full-text access to articles is available for subscribers. Alerts are available via RSS feed or through an account on the publisher's site. A GeoRef priority journal.

Journal of Paleontology. See Paleontology section.

1760. Journal of Petroleum Geology. [ISSN: 0141-6421] 1978. q. GBP 424 (print & online eds.). Ed(s): Christopher Tiratsoo. Wiley-Blackwell Publishing Ltd., The Atrium, Southern Gate, Chichester, PO19 8SQ, United Kingdom; customer@wiley.com; http://www.wiley.com/. Illus., index, adv. Sample. Refereed. Vol. ends: Oct (No. 4). Reprint: PSC. *Indexed:* A01, A22, E01, EngInd, OceAb. *Bk. rev.:* 0-3, 500-1,200 words, signed. *Aud.:* Ac, Sa.

This quarterly presents research on the geology of oil and gas, with emphasis on regions outside of North America. Topics include petroleum exploration and development, basin evolution and modeling, and reservoir evaluation. Each issue includes a calendar of international events. Free tables of contents and abstracts are available on the web site for all volumes, and full text is available to subscribers. Readers may sign up to receive journal issue tables of contents via e-mail. A GeoRef priority journal.

1761. *Journal of Petrology.* [ISSN: 0022-3530] 1960. m. EUR 1686. Ed(s): Marjorie Wilson. Oxford University Press, Great Clarendon St, Oxford, OX2 6DP, United Kingdom; enquiry@oup.co.uk; http://www.oxfordjournals.org/. Illus., index, adv. Sample. Refereed. Circ: 380. Vol. ends: Dec (No. 12). Microform: PQC. Reprint: PSC. *Indexed:* A01, A22, BAS, E01, OceAb. *Bk. rev.:* 0-2, 600-1,000 words, signed. *Aud.:* Ac, Sa.

This journal features research in igneous and metamorphic petrology and is recommended for academic and special libraries. Subjects covered include magmatic processes, petrogenesis, trace element and isotope geochemistry, and experimental studies and theoretical modeling. Occasional issues feature special themes or publish selected papers from conferences. Tables of contents with abstracts are available for all volumes on the web site, and full-text articles are available to current subscribers. Readers may sign up to receive alerts via e-mail or RSS feed. A GeoRef priority journal.

1762. *Journal of Quaternary Science.* [ISSN: 0267-8179] 1986. 8x/yr. GBP 1244. Ed(s): A J Long. John Wiley & Sons Ltd., The Atrium, Southern Gate, Chichester, PO19 8SQ, United Kingdom; customer@wiley.com; http://www.wiley.com. Illus., index, adv. Sample. Refereed. Vol. ends: No. 8. Microform: PQC. Reprint: PSC. *Indexed:* A22, C&ISA, C45, CerAb, M&GPA, S25. *Bk. rev.:* 2-10, 300-1,000 words, signed. *Aud.:* Ac, Sa.

Published for the Quaternary Research Association, this journal focuses on the earth's history during the last two million years. This time period is the same as that covered by the journal *Boreas,* and there are many similarities between the two journals. Papers span a wide range of topics, and many are interdisciplinary in nature. In particular, there is an emphasis on the stratigraphy, glaciation, and paleoclimatology of the period. Occasional special issues often focus on a particular region or environment. Full-length research papers, short contributions intended for rapid communication, and invited reviews are all included. Free tables of contents and abstracts for all volumes are provided on the web site, along with access to full-text articles for subscribers. Readers may sign up to receive alerts when new articles are published. A GeoRef priority journal.

1763. *Journal of Sedimentary Research.* Formed by the merger of (1994-1996): *Journal of Sedimentary Research. Section A: Sedimentary Petrology and Processes;* (1994-1996): *Journal of Sedimentary Research. Section B: Stratigraphy and Global Studies;* Both of which superseded in part (in 1994): *Journal of Sedimentary Petrology.* [ISSN: 1527-1404] 1996. bi-m. Free to members; Non-members, USD 625 (print, online & CD-ROM eds.). Ed(s): Melissa B Lester, Gene Rankey. Society for Sedimentary Geology (S E P M), 4111 S Darlington, Ste 100, Tulsa, OK 74135; foundation@sepm.org; http://www.sepm.org. Illus., adv. Refereed. *Indexed:* A22, C45, M&GPA, OceAb, S25. *Bk. rev.:* 0-3, 200-600 words. *Aud.:* Ac, Sa.

This monthly journal of the Society for Sedimentary Geology publishes papers on topics from all branches of sedimentary geology, including the process of transport and deposition, inherent characteristics of sediments themselves, and their impacts on other aspects of the geologic record. These range from detailed papers that concentrate on very specific, often small-scale topics to big-picture reports about research on larger spatial and temporal scales. Tables of contents, abstracts, and full-text searching are available on the web site for all volumes; subscribers have access to full-text articles via GeoScience World. A GeoRef priority journal.

1764. *Journal of Seismology.* [ISSN: 1383-4649] 1997. q. EUR 574 (print & online eds.). Ed(s): T Dahm. Springer Netherlands, Van Godewijckstraat 30, Dordrecht, 3311 GX, Netherlands; http://www.springer.com. Adv. Refereed. Microform: PQC. Reprint: PSC. *Indexed:* A01, A22, BRI, C&ISA, CerAb, E01, H24, RiskAb, S25. *Aud.:* Ac, Sa.

This international journal specializes in the study of earthquakes and their occurrence. Areas of particular focus include seismicity, fault systems, earthquake prediction, seismic hazards, and earthquake engineering. Many papers are regional or historical studies. However, broader theoretical work is also included, along with short communications on new analytical techniques and instrumentation. The web site provides free table of contents and abstracts for all volumes, and subscribers may view full text of articles. Readers may sign up for alerts via RSS feed.

1765. *Journal of Structural Geology.* [ISSN: 0191-8141] 1979. m. EUR 2268. Ed(s): C W Passchier. Pergamon, The Blvd, Langford Ln, E Park, Kidlington, OX5 1GB, United Kingdom; JournalsCustomerServiceEMEA@elsevier.com; http://www.elsevier.com. Illus., adv. Sample. Refereed. Microform: PQC. *Indexed:* A01, A22, ApMecR, C&ISA, CerAb, EngInd, S25. *Bk. rev.:* 0-2, 500-1,000 words. *Aud.:* Ac, Sa.

This international journal publishes research and review articles on structural geology, tectonics, and the associated rock deformation processes. Some specific topics include faults, folds, fractures, strain analysis, rock mechanics, rheology, and theoretical and experimental modeling. Regional structural accounts are published when they are of broad interest. Tables of contents and article abstracts are accessible free on the web site for all volumes, and full-text articles are available through ScienceDirect. Readers may set up alerts via RSS feed or using their ScienceDirect user account to learn when new articles are published. A GeoRef priority journal.

1766. *Journal of Volcanology and Geothermal Research.* [ISSN: 0377-0273] 1976. 40x/yr. EUR 4051. Ed(s): M T Mangan, J W Neuberg. Elsevier BV, Radarweg 29, PO Box 211, Amsterdam, 1000 AE, Netherlands; JournalsCustomerServiceEMEA@elsevier.com; http://www.elsevier.nl. Illus., index, adv. Sample. Refereed. Vol. ends: No. 4. Microform: PQC. *Indexed:* A01, A22, EngInd, S25. *Aud.:* Ac, Sa.

Publishes research on geochemical, petrological, geophysical, tectonic, and environmental aspects of volcanic and geothermal activity. Special issues often address particular processes, locales, or topics such as volcanic gases, magma genesis, and risk assessment. Tables of contents and abstracts are available free on the web site for all volumes, and full-text articles are accessible through ScienceDirect. Readers may set up alerts via RSS feed or using their ScienceDirect user account to learn when new articles are published. A GeoRef priority journal.

Lethaia. See Paleontology section.

1767. *Lithos.* [ISSN: 0024-4937] 1968. 28x/yr. EUR 2202. Ed(s): I Buick, A C Kerr. Elsevier BV, Radarweg 29, PO Box 211, Amsterdam, 1000 AE, Netherlands; JournalsCustomerServiceEMEA@elsevier.com; http://www.elsevier.nl. Illus., index, adv. Sample. Refereed. Vol. ends: No. 4. Microform: PQC. *Indexed:* A01, A22. *Bk. rev.:* 1-3, 800-1,000 words. *Aud.:* Ac, Sa.

Publishes research papers, reviews, discussions, and book reviews in the fields of mineralogy, geochemistry, and petrology. Occasional special issues feature proceedings of meetings or focus on specific topics such as large igneous provinces (LIPs) and supercontinents; peralkaline rocks and carbonatites, with special reference to the East African riftgeology of ophiolites; and reports from the seventh Hutton Symposium on granites and related rocks. Free access to tables of contents and article abstracts for all volumes is available on the web site. Full-text articles are accessible through ScienceDirect. Readers may set up alerts via RSS feed, or use their ScienceDirect user account to learn when new articles are published. A GeoRef priority journal.

1768. *Lithosphere.* [ISSN: 1941-8264] 2009. bi-m. Members, USD 60; Non-members, USD 450 (print & online eds.). Ed(s): Matt Hudson, Jon D Pelletier. Geological Society of America, 3300 Penrose Pl, PO Box 9140, Boulder, CO 80301; pubs@geosociety.org; http://www.geosociety.org. Refereed. *Aud.:* Ac, Sa.

Launched in 2009, this journal in the solid earth sciences focuses on tectonic processes in the crust and upper mantle, and publishes papers about feedback relationships among geomorphic, lithospheric, and upper-mantle processes. It includes a mix of short articles, longer research papers, and invited reviews. Abstracts from all issues are freely available online, and subscribers may view full text. Alerts to new content are available via e-mail or RSS feed. This journal is part of the GeoScience World collection and has been identified as a GeoRef priority journal.

1769. Marine and Petroleum Geology. Former titles (until 1984): *Underwater Information Bulletin;* (until 1974): *Underwater Journal Information Bulletin.* [ISSN: 0264-8172] 1971. 10x/yr. EUR 2864. Ed(s): O Catouneanu. Elsevier Ltd, 32 Jamestown Rd, Camden, London, NW1 7BY, United Kingdom; corporate.sales@elsevier.com; http://www.elsevier.com. Illus., index, adv. Sample. Refereed. Microform: PQC. *Indexed:* A01, A22, C&ISA, CerAb, EngInd, OceAb. *Aud.:* Ac, Sa.

Comprising a multidisciplinary forum for those concerned with marine and petroleum geology, this journal presents papers that focus on research in areas of basin analysis, geophysical interpretation, estimation of reserves, sedimentology, stratigraphy, continental margins, and well logging. Seismic sections and full-color illustrations enhance journal text. Thematic issues are occasionally published on selected basins or depositional environments. Tables of contents and abstracts for all volumes are available free at the web site, and full-text articles are accessible through ScienceDirect. Publication alerts are available via RSS feed or with a ScienceDirect user account.

Marine Geology. See Marine Science and Technology section.

1770. Mathematical Geosciences. Former titles (until 2008): *Mathematical Geology;* (until 1986): *International Association for Mathematical Geology. Journal.* [ISSN: 1874-8961] 1969. 8x/yr. EUR 1600 (print & online eds.). Ed(s): Roussos Dimitrakopoulos. Springer, Tiergartenstr 17, Heidelberg, 69121, Germany; subscriptions@springer.com; http://www.springer.com. Illus., adv. Refereed. Vol. ends: Nov (No. 8). Microform: PQC. Reprint: PSC. *Indexed:* A01, A22, ApMecR, BRI, C&ISA, CCMJ, CerAb, E01, MSN, MathR, S25. *Bk. rev.:* 0-5, 400-700 words, signed. *Aud.:* Ac, Sa.

Techniques and methods to analyze large amounts of numerical data efficiently are crucial to research in the earth sciences. As suggested by the title, papers in *Mathematical Geosciences,* the official journal of the International Association for Mathematical Geology, are primarily concerned with the application of quantitative methods in the earth sciences. Some specific areas of concentration include modeling and simulation, fluid mechanics, filtering techniques, fractals, and spatial analysis. Tables of contents and article abstracts for all volumes are on the web site, with full-text access available for subscribers and the option to sign up for alerts via RSS feed. Listed as a GeoRef priority journal under its earlier title, *Mathematical Geology.*

Meteoritics and Planetary Science. See Astronomy section.

1771. Mineralium Deposita: international journal of geology, mineralogy, and geochemistry of mineral deposits. [ISSN: 0026-4598] 1966. 8x/yr. EUR 2090 (print & online eds.). Ed(s): Patrick Williams, Bernd Lehmann. Springer, Tiergartenstr 17, Heidelberg, 69121, Germany. Illus., index, adv. Sample. Refereed. Vol. ends: No. 8. Microform: PQC. Reprint: PSC. *Indexed:* A01, A22, BRI, E01. *Bk. rev.:* 0-5, 400-700 words, signed. *Aud.:* Ac, Sa.

This is the official journal of the Society for Geology Applied to Mineral Deposits. It focuses on economic geology, including field studies, mineralogy, experimental and applied geochemistry, and ore deposit exploration. Many of the illustrations are in color, especially those of mineral thin sections. Coverage is international in scope and includes such often under-represented areas as Africa, Asia, Australia, and South America. Occasional thematic issues cover selected ore deposits or other relevant topics. The web site offers free tables of contents and abstracts for all volumes and full-text access articles for subscribers. Readers may sign up for alerts via RSS feed. A GeoRef priority journal.

1772. Mineralogical Magazine. Formerly (until 1969): *Mineralogical Magazine and Journal of the Mineralogical Society.* [ISSN: 0026-461X] 1876. bi-m. GBP 430 (print & online eds.). Ed(s): M D Welch. Mineralogical Society, 12 Baylis Mews, Amyand Park Rd, Twickenham, TW1 3HQ, United Kingdom; http://www.minersoc.org. Illus., index, adv. Sample. Refereed. Circ: 2000. Vol. ends: Dec (No. 6). Microform: BHP. *Indexed:* A01, A22, E01, EngInd. *Bk. rev.:* 3-8, 500-900 words. *Aud.:* Ac, Sa.

Published by the Mineralogical Society, this well-respected journal has been in print for 137 years. Topics covered span not only the field of mineralogy but also related areas such as geochemistry and petrology. Both full-length original research papers and shorter letters for rapid communication are included. Along with *American Mineralogist,* this title is highly recommended for larger academic library collections. A free archive featuring abstracts and full text of articles from 1876 to 1999 is available on the web site of the Mineralogical Society. Tables of contents and abstracts from 1998 to the present are available through Ingenta; subscribers may view full-text articles from multiple sources, including GeoScience World. Publication alerts are available via RSS feed. A GeoRef priority journal.

1773. The Mineralogical Record. [ISSN: 0026-4628] 1970. bi-m. USD 190 (Individuals, USD 62). Ed(s): Wendell E Wilson. Mineralogical Record, Inc., 7413 N Mowry Pl, Tucson, AZ 85741. Illus., index, adv. Sample. Refereed. Vol. ends: Nov/Dec (No. 6). Microform: PQC. *Indexed:* A01, A22, BRI, P02. *Bk. rev.:* 0-4, 100-800 words. *Aud.:* Ga, Ac, Sa.

Publishes both nontechnical and technical articles for mineral collectors, curators, and researchers. Each issue has numerous high-quality color photographs, and many of the advertisements use arresting images. Reports from mineral shows around the world appear in a column called "What's New in Minerals," and articles include topics such as minerals of a particular region, equipment used by mineralogists, and historically significant mines. Occasional supplements highlight mineral collections. The International Mineralogical Association publishes abstracts of new mineral descriptions in *The Mineralogical Record.* The web site provides searchable tables of contents back to the first issue, published in 1970. Recommended for larger public and academic libraries.

1774. Natural Hazards and Earth System Sciences. [ISSN: 1561-8633] bi-m. EUR 630; EUR 116 newsstand/cover. Ed(s): Fausto Guzzetti. Copernicus GmbH, Bahnhofsallee 1e, Goettingen, 37081, Germany; info@copernicus.org; http://www.copernicus.org. Refereed. *Indexed:* C45, M&GPA, RiskAb, S25. *Aud.:* Ac, Sa.

The interactive, open-access journal from the European Geosciences Union publishes interdisciplinary research concerning the detection, monitoring, risk assessment, and impact of natural hazards. Topics include flooding, landslides, tsunamis, earthquakes, avalanches, and volcanic eruptions. Full text is available to all on the web site for this open-access, peer-reviewed journal.

1775. Nature Geoscience. [ISSN: 1752-0894] 2008. m. EUR 3936 in Europe; USD 4958 in the Americas; GBP 2544 in the UK & elsewhere. Ed(s): Heike Langenberg. Nature Publishing Group, The MacMillan Bldg, 4 Crinan St, London, N1 9XW, United Kingdom; nature@nature.com; http://www.nature.com. Adv. Sample. Refereed. *Indexed:* C45, M&GPA, OceAb, S25. *Bk. rev.:* 0-3, 600-900 words, signed. *Aud.:* Ac, Sa.

This monthly, launched in 2008, carries on the tradition of quality of its namesake. Coverage spans all major areas of the earth sciences, with an emphasis on interdisciplinary work. Articles include primary research, reviews, research highlights, news, and commentary. Tables of contents and abstracts are freely accessible on the web site, and full-text articles are available to subscribers or for individual purchase. Publication alerts are available by registering for a free account with *Nature* or via RSS feed. A GeoRef priority journal.

1776. Netherlands Journal of Geosciences. Former titles: *Geologie en Mijnbouw;* (until 1931): *Mijnwezen;* (until 1928): *Mijnwezen en Metallurgie;* (until 1925): *Mijnwezen;* Incorporates (1946-1999): *Nederlands Instituut voor Toegepaste Geowetenschappen T N O.*

Mededelingen; Which was formerly (until 1997): *Rijks Geologische Dienst. Mededelingen;* (until 1977): *Rijks Geologische Dienst. Mededelingen. Nieuwe Serie;* (until 1968): *Geologische Stichting. Mededelingen. Nieuwe Serie.* 1921. q. EUR 298 (Individuals, EUR 80). Ed(s): W Z Hoek. Netherlands Journal of Geosciences Foundation, PO Box 80015, Utrecht, 3508 TA, Netherlands. Illus., index, adv. Refereed. Vol. ends: No. 4. Microform: SWZ; PQC. *Indexed:* A22, E01, OceAb, S25. *Aud.:* Ac, Sa.

This is the official journal of the Royal Geological and Mining Society of the Netherlands, and it represents a merger of two titles, *Geologie en Mijnbouw* and *Mededelingen Nederlands Instituut voor Geowetenschappen–TNO.* It began publication in March 2000. Articles feature research on geology and mining, with an emphasis on the Netherlands, the North Sea, and neighboring areas. A special strength is in geological aspects of coastal and deltaic lowlands, both ancient and modern. Tables of contents, abstracts, supplementary material, and full-text articles are available on the web site for registered subscribers.

1777. *Organic Geochemistry.* [ISSN: 0146-6380] 1977. m. EUR 4187. Ed(s): L R Snowden, J R Maxwell. Pergamon, The Blvd, Langford Ln, E Park, Kidlington, OX5 1GB, United Kingdom; JournalsCustomerServiceEMEA@elsevier.com; http://www.elsevier.com. Illus., adv. Sample. Refereed. Microform: PQC. *Indexed:* A01, A22, C&ISA, C45, EngInd, IndVet, S25. *Bk. rev.:* 0-2, 300-1,000 words. *Aud.:* Ac, Sa.

The official journal of the European Association of Organic Geochemists, this monthly publishes papers on all aspects of organic geochemistry, including biogeochemistry, environmental geochemistry, and geochemical cycling. Types of articles include original research papers, comprehensive reviews, technical communications and notes, and meeting announcements. The web site provides free tables of contents and article abstracts for all volumes. Full-text articles are available through ScienceDirect, and publication alerts are available via a user account or RSS feed. A GeoRef priority journal.

Palaeontology. See Paleontology section.

1778. *Petroleum Geoscience.* [ISSN: 1354-0793] 1994. q. GBP 301.72 combined subscription domestic (print & online eds.); GBP 257 combined subscription foreign (print & online eds.); USD 514 combined subscription foreign (print & online eds.). Ed(s): Phil Christie. Geological Society Publishing House, Unit 7, Brassmill Enterprise Ctr, Brassmill Ln, Bath, BA1 3JN, United Kingdom. Illus., adv. Refereed. Circ: 5000. Vol. ends: Nov (No. 4). *Indexed:* A22, C&ISA, CerAb. *Bk. rev.:* 0-6, 250-600 words, signed. *Aud.:* Ac, Sa.

This quarterly is published by the Geological Society of London and the Petroleum Division of the European Association of Geoscientists and Engineers. It covers a full range of geoscience aspects involved in the "exploration, exploitation, appraisal, and development of hydrocarbon resources." Coverage is international in scope and includes both theoretical and applied articles. Color is used to good effect for many illustrations. Tables of contents and abstracts are freely available online. Full-text articles are available to subscribers, and publication alerts are available via e-mail or RSS feed. A GeoRef priority journal.

1779. *Physics and Chemistry of Minerals.* [ISSN: 0342-1791] 1977. 10x/yr. EUR 3063 (print & online eds.). Ed(s): C McCammon, P C Burnley. Springer, Tiergartenstr 17, Heidelberg, 69121, Germany. Illus., index, adv. Sample. Refereed. Vol. ends: No. 10. Microform: PQC. Reprint: PSC. *Indexed:* A01, A22, E01, EngInd. *Aud.:* Ac, Sa.

This technical journal focuses on the chemistry and physics of minerals and related solids. Some areas of emphasis include atomic structure, mineral surfaces, spectroscopy, chemical reactions and bonding, and analysis of physical properties. Recommended for larger academic or special libraries. The web site offers free access to tables of contents and article abstracts for all volumes; full-text access to articles is available to subscribers. Readers may sign up for publication alerts via RSS feed. A GeoRef priority journal.

1780. *Physics of the Earth and Planetary Interiors.* [ISSN: 0031-9201] 1967. 24x/yr. EUR 3628. Ed(s): D Rubie, K Zhang. Elsevier BV, Radarweg 29, PO Box 211, Amsterdam, 1000 AE, Netherlands; JournalsCustomerServiceEMEA@elsevier.com; http://www.elsevier.nl. Illus., index. Sample. Refereed. Vol. ends: No. 124 - No. 129. Microform: PQC. *Indexed:* A01, A22, EngInd, M&GPA. *Bk. rev.:* 0-1, 300-800 words. *Aud.:* Ac, Sa.

This journal is devoted to studies of the planetary physical and chemical processes, and the papers it contains present observational and experimental studies, along with theoretical interpretation. Occasional special issues present papers from symposia or thematic reports on special topics. Some recent examples include deep slab and mantle dynamics; planetary magnetism, dynamo, and dynamics; and proceedings of the Study of the Earth's Deep Interior (SEDI) symposium. The web site offers free access to tables of contents and abstracts for all volumes, and full-text articles are available through ScienceDirect, which offers publication alerts through a user account or RSS feed. A GeoRef priority journal.

1781. *Precambrian Research.* [ISSN: 0301-9268] 1974. 32x/yr. EUR 3752. Ed(s): P A Cawood, R R Parrish. Elsevier BV, Radarweg 29, PO Box 211, Amsterdam, 1000 AE, Netherlands; JournalsCustomerServiceEMEA@elsevier.com; http://www.elsevier.nl. Illus., index, adv. Sample. Refereed. Vol. ends: No. 4. Microform: PQC. *Indexed:* A01, A22. *Bk. rev.:* 0-2, 200-600 words. *Aud.:* Ac, Sa.

The Precambrian era is believed to have lasted for some four billion years, representing the bulk of Earth's history on the geological time scale. This journal emphasizes interdisciplinary studies and publishes research on all aspects of the early history and development of Earth and its planetary neighbors. Topics include the origin of life, evolution of the oceans and atmosphere, the early fossil record, paleobiology, geochronology, and Precambrian mineral deposits. Free tables of contents and abstracts are available on the web site for all volumes, and full-text articles are available through ScienceDirect, which offers publication alerts via RSS feed or a user account. A GeoRef priority journal.

1782. *Pure and Applied Geophysics.* Formerly: *Geofisica.* [ISSN: 0033-4553] 1939. m. EUR 3274 (print & online eds.). Ed(s): Renata Dmowska, Brian J Mitchell. Birkhaeuser Verlag AG, Viaduktstr 42, Postfach 133, Basel, 4051, Switzerland; info@birkhauser.ch; http://www.birkhauser.ch/journals. Illus. Refereed. Vol. ends: No. 4. Reprint: PSC. *Indexed:* A01, A22, ApMecR, BAS, BRI, E01, M&GPA, S25. *Bk. rev.:* 0-12, 400-1,200 words, signed. *Aud.:* Ac, Sa.

Often referred to as *PAGEOPH,* this journal features full-length papers on all aspects of geophysics, including solid earth, atmospheric, and ocean sciences. Special issues, sometimes representing multiple numbers within a volume, feature themes like tsunami science, mesoscale processes, earthquake physics, properties of fractured rock, and induced seismicity. The web site offers free tables of contents and abstracts from 1939 forward and access to full-text articles for subscribers. Readers may sign up for alerts via RSS feed. Strongly recommended for academic and special libraries. A GeoRef priority journal.

1783. *Quarterly Journal of Engineering Geology and Hydrogeology.* Formerly (until 2000): *Quarterly Journal of Engineering Geology.* [ISSN: 1470-9236] 1967. q. GBP 909.96 combined subscription domestic (print & online eds.); GBP 579 combined subscription foreign (print & online eds.); USD 1157 combined subscription foreign (print & online eds.). Geological Society Publishing House, Unit 7, Brassmill Enterprise Ctr, Brassmill Ln, Bath, BA1 3JN, United Kingdom. Illus., adv. Refereed. Circ: 4000. Vol. ends: Nov (No. 4). *Indexed:* A22, C&ISA, CerAb, EngInd, S25. *Bk. rev.:* 0-7, 300-800 words, signed. *Aud.:* Ac, Sa.

Upholding the high standards of publications from the Geological Society of London, this title focuses specifically on geology as applied to civil engineering, mining, and water resources. This makes it of value to both engineers and earth scientists. Coverage is international in scope. In addition to original research, it includes review articles, technical notes, and lectures. Tables of contents and abstracts are freely available on the web for all volumes, and subscribers may view full-text articles from multiple vendors including GeoScience World. A GeoRef priority journal.

1784. *Quaternary International.* [ISSN: 1040-6182] 1989. 36x/yr. EUR 1412. Ed(s): N R Catto. Pergamon, The Blvd, Langford Ln, E Park, Kidlington, OX5 1GB, United Kingdom; JournalsCustomerServiceEMEA@elsevier.com; http://www.elsevier.com. Illus., adv. Sample. Refereed. Microform: PQC. *Indexed:* A01, A22, M&GPA. *Aud.:* Ac, Sa.

Publishes international, interdisciplinary research on global climate and the succession of glacial and interglacial ages during the Quaternary period, approximately the last two million years of the earth's history. This title reports on studies of environmental changes and interactions, with appropriate connections to both present processes and future climatological implications. Most issues are thematic, often presenting collected papers from symposia and workshops sponsored by the International Union for Quaternary Research. Free access to tables of contents and abstracts is available on the web site for all volumes, and full-text articles are accessible through ScienceDirect. Publication alerts are available via RSS feed or with a ScienceDirect user account.

1785. *Quaternary Research.* [ISSN: 0033-5894] 1970. bi-m. EUR 1397. Ed(s): K Stewart-Perry, D B Booth. Academic Press, 3251 Riverport Ln, Maryland Heights, MO 63043; JournalCustomerService-usa@elsevier.com; http://www.elsevierdirect/brochures/academicpress/index.html. Illus., index, adv. Sample. Refereed. Vol. ends: Nov (No. 3). *Indexed:* A01, A22, AbAn, Agr, BrArAb, C&ISA, C45, CerAb, E01, FR, IndVet, M&GPA, OceAb, RRTA, S25. *Bk. rev.:* 0-2, 500-1,000 words. *Aud.:* Ac, Sa.

Papers in this journal present interdisciplinary studies in the earth and biological sciences that span the Quaternary period. Articles explore a diverse range of topics related to the recent past, including botany, climatology, ecology, geochemistry and geophysics, geochronology, geomorphology, and glaciology. Free tables of contents and abstracts for articles for all volumes are available on the web site. Full-text articles are accessible through ScienceDirect, and publication alerts are available via RSS feed or with a ScienceDirect user account. Recommended for college and university libraries. A GeoRef priority journal.

1786. *Rocks and Minerals: mineralogy, geology, lapidary.* [ISSN: 0035-7529] 1926. bi-m. GBP 129 (print & online eds.). Ed(s): Marie E Huizing. Taylor & Francis Inc., 325 Chestnut St, Ste 800, Philadelphia, PA 19106; customerservice@taylorandfrancis.com; http://www.tandfonline.com. Illus., index, adv. Refereed. Vol. ends: No. 6. Reprint: PSC. *Indexed:* A01, A22, BRI, CBRI, E01, MASUSE. *Bk. rev.:* 0-7, 100-800 words, signed. *Aud.:* Hs, Ga, Ac, Sa.

The official publication of Eastern Federation of Mineralogical and Lapidary Societies, this magazine features spectacular full-color photographs, accessible articles, and a modest price, making it a strong candidate for libraries of all sizes. The emphasis is on minerals more than on rocks, and the specimens featured are generally of "museum quality." There is also a considerable amount of other material to interest collectors, such as mineral localities, sample preparation, and historical background. In addition, museum notes, announcements, and a calendar of upcoming events are included. Available online from multiple vendors, with varying years of coverage.

1787. *Sedimentary Geology.* [ISSN: 0037-0738] 1967. 40x/yr. EUR 4167. Ed(s): M R Bennett, G J Weltje. Elsevier BV, Radarweg 29, PO Box 211, Amsterdam, 1000 AE, Netherlands; JournalsCustomerServiceEMEA@elsevier.com; http://www.elsevier.nl. Illus., index, adv. Sample. Refereed. Vol. ends: No. 4. Microform: PQC. *Indexed:* A01, A22, C&ISA, CerAb, OceAb, S25. *Bk. rev.:* 0-4, 300-3,000 words. *Aud.:* Ac, Sa.

Publishes research papers on all aspects of sediments and sedimentary rocks, provided they are of broad interest or applicability. Examples of topics addressed include analytical techniques such as numerical modeling; regional studies of sedimentary systems and basin; and sediment transport and deposition. There are occasional special issues, with recent ones having focused on aspects of carbonates, sediment dynamics, and tsunami deposits, among

other subjects. Tables of contents and abstracts are available at the web site for all volumes. Full-text articles are available through ScienceDirect, and publication alerts are available via RSS feed or from a ScienceDirect user account. A GeoRef priority journal.

1788. *Sedimentology.* [ISSN: 0037-0746] 1962. 7x/yr. GBP 1141. Ed(s): Peter K Swart, S Rice. Wiley-Blackwell Publishing Ltd., The Atrium, Southern Gate, Chichester, PO19 8SQ, United Kingdom; customer@wiley.com; http://www.wiley.com/. Illus., index, adv. Sample. Refereed. Vol. ends: Dec (No. 6). Microform: PQC. Reprint: PSC. *Indexed:* A01, A22, Agr, C45, E01, OceAb, S25. *Aud.:* Ac, Sa.

This publication is the official journal of the International Association of Sedimentologists. Full-length papers deal with every aspect of sediments and sedimentary rocks. These are well illustrated and of consistently high quality. This journal is recommended for academic and special library collections. Free tables of contents and abstracts from volume one forward are accessible on the web site. Full-text articles are available for subscribers, and readers may sign up to receive alerts when new articles are published. A GeoRef priority journal.

1789. *Seismological Society of America. Bulletin.* [ISSN: 0037-1106] 1911. bi-m. USD 565 (print & online eds.). Ed(s): Carol Mark, Andrew Michael. Seismological Society of America, 201 Plaza Professional Bldg, El Cerrito, CA 94530-4003; info@seismosoc.org; http://www.seismosoc.org. Illus., index. Sample. Refereed. Circ: 2500 Paid. Vol. ends: Dec (No. 6). *Indexed:* A22, ApMecR, CCMJ, E01, EngInd, MSN, MathR. *Aud.:* Ac, Sa.

Publishes research papers, reviews, short notes, comments, and replies in the areas of seismology, earthquake geology, and earthquake engineering. Specific topics include investigation of earthquakes, theoretical and observational studies of seismic waves, seismometry, earthquake hazard and risk estimation, and seismotectonics. The web site provides free tables of contents and some abstracts from 1911 to the present, while full text is available to subscribers and society members via GeoScience World. A GeoRef priority journal.

1790. *Stratigraphy.* [ISSN: 1547-139X] 2004. q. USD 780 (print & online eds.) Members, USD 450 (print & online eds.). Ed(s): John A Van Couvering. Micropaleontology Press, 256 Fifth Ave, New York, NY 10001; http://micropress.org/. Refereed. *Aud.:* Ac, Sa.

This is the journal of record for the North American Commission on Stratigraphic Nomenclature. It publishes research articles on all aspects of stratigraphy, including chronostratigraphy, biostratigraphy, cyclostratigraphy, sequence stratigraphy, tectonostratigraphy, chemostratigraphy, lithostratigraphy, and others. Tables of contents and abstracts of recent issues are freely accessible online, while subscribers may view full text.

1791. *Tectonics.* [ISSN: 0278-7407] 1982. bi-m. Ed(s): Kip V Hodges, Onno Oncken. Wiley-Blackwell Publishing, Inc., 111 River St, Hoboken, NJ 07030; info@wiley.com; http://onlinelibrary.wiley.com/. Illus., index. Sample. Refereed. Vol. ends: Dec (No. 6). *Indexed:* A22, P02. *Aud.:* Ac, Sa.

Cosponsored by the American Geophysical Union (AGU) and the European Geosciences Union, this journal publishes reports of original analytical, synthetic, and integrative studies on the structure and evolution of the terrestrial lithosphere. Emphasis is on continental tectonics, including such topics as thrusting and faulting, mountain building, volcanism, and rifting. Full-text articles from 1982 (vol. 1) to the present are available for subscribers. Readers may sign up to receive publication alerts via e-mail or RSS feed. A GeoRef priority journal.

1792. *Tectonophysics.* [ISSN: 0040-1951] 1964. 68x/yr. EUR 6571. Ed(s): M Liu, H Thybo. Elsevier BV, Radarweg 29, PO Box 211, Amsterdam, 1000 AE, Netherlands; JournalsCustomerServiceEMEA@elsevier.com; http://www.elsevier.nl. Illus., adv. Sample. Refereed. Vol. ends: No. 327 - No. 343. Microform: PQC. *Indexed:* A01, A22, C&ISA, CerAb, M&GPA, OceAb, S25. *Bk. rev.:* 0-3, 400-1,500 words. *Aud.:* Ac, Sa.

Publishes research papers on the geology and physics of the earth's crust and interior, addressing topics such as regional and plate tectonics, seismology, crustal movements, rock mechanics, and structural features. Journal issues often include large-scale geological maps, seismic sections, and other diagrams. The web site provides free access to tables of contents and abstracts from volume one forward. Full-text articles are also available through ScienceDirect, and readers may set up alerts via RSS feed or using their ScienceDirect user account. A GeoRef priority journal.

1793. Terra Nova: the European journal of geosciences. Supersedes in part (in 1989): *Terra Cognita.* [ISSN: 0954-4879] 1981. bi-m. GBP 790. Wiley-Blackwell Publishing Ltd., The Atrium, Southern Gate, Chichester, PO19 8SQ, United Kingdom; customer@wiley.com; http://www.wiley.com/. Illus., index, adv. Sample. Refereed. Vol. ends: No. 6. Microform: PQC. Reprint: PSC. *Indexed:* A01, A22, E01, P02. *Aud.:* Ac, Sa.

Terra Nova is the result of a collaboration among 19 national geoscience societies throughout Europe. It primarily features short, original research papers that cover the solid earth and planetary sciences, including interfaces with the hydrosphere and atmosphere. Free tables of contents and abstracts are available on the web site from volume one forward, with full-text articles accessible to subscribers. Readers may sign up to receive alerts when new articles are published.

1794. Water Resources Research. [ISSN: 0043-1397] 1965. m. Ed(s): Praveen Kumar. Wiley-Blackwell Publishing, Inc., 111 River St, Hoboken, NJ 07030; info@wiley.com; http://onlinelibrary.wiley.com/. Illus., index. Sample. Refereed. Vol. ends: No. 12. *Indexed:* A22, ABIn, Agr, ApMecR, C45, EconLit, EngInd, JEL, M&GPA, OceAb, RRTA, S25. *Aud.:* Ac, Sa.

Articles present interdisciplinary research on water-related studies that spans the social and natural sciences. Areas of focus include the physical, chemical, and biological sciences in hydrology, as well as economics, policy analysis, and law. Issues include original research articles along with technical notes, commentaries, and replies. Full-text articles from all volumes are available for subscribers on the American Geophysical Union web site, with tables of contents and abstracts freely accessible. Readers may sign up for alerts to new publications via e-mail or RSS feed. A GeoRef priority journal.

■ ECOLOGY

See also Biology; Botany; Physiology; and Zoology sections.

Kristen LaBonte, Life Sciences Librarian, Davidson Library, University of California Santa Barbara, Santa Barbara, CA 93106-9010

Introduction

Ecology is an interdisciplinary biological science that studies species, systems, and/or ecosystems and the relationships between them and other systems, such as the physical environment. Studies vary from the micro to the macro and can range from examining an aspect of a gene to the functioning of a biome. Ecologists often conduct field and laboratory research on behavior, evolution, physiology, and genetics, and the science is applied in the fields of natural resources management, conservation biology, resource economics, public health, and conservation policy.

Journals can be broad and comprehensive in scope but can be narrowly focused on an application or field of study, such as *Restoration Ecology* or *Molecular Ecology.* Most have rigorous standards for peer review, with strict deadlines to ensure timely dissemination of research that may be featured as a pre-print on the publication's web site prior to being formally published. Some articles within paid, subscription-based journals are open access, and many journal web sites offer RSS feeds.

Basic Periodicals

Ac: *Ecology, Journal of Animal Ecology, Journal of Ecology, Trends in Ecology and Evolution.*

Basic Abstracts and Indexes

Academic Search Premier, AGRICOLA, Aquatic Sciences and Fisheries Abstracts, Biological Abstracts, BIOSIS, Current Contents/Life Sciences, Expanded Academic ASAP, Science Citation Index, Web of Science, Zoological Record.

1795. Acta Oecologica. Formed by the merger of (1980-1990): *Oecologia Applicata;* (1980-1990): *Oecologia Generalis;* (1966-1990): *Acta Oecologica. Oecologia Plantarum;* Which was formerly (until 1980): *Oecologia Plantarum.* [ISSN: 1146-609X] 1981. 6x/yr. EUR 659. Ed(s): R. Arditi. Elsevier Masson, 62 Rue Camille Desmoulins, Issy les Moulineaux, Cedex 92442, France; infos@elsevier-masson.fr; http://www.elsevier-masson.fr. Refereed. Circ: 1000. Microform: MIM; PQC. *Indexed:* A01, A22, C&ISA, C45, CerAb, IndVet, OceAb, RRTA, S25. *Aud.:* Ac, Sa.

Acta Oecologica publishes studies in all areas of ecology, including evolutionary, conservation, ecosystem, population, and community ecology. Empirical or theoretical papers are sought for publication, but combinations are desired. Review papers are also published. There is a forum section for short papers on current issues in ecology, feedback on previously published papers, and comments on new books (although book reviews are not published). The journal is available in print and online. URL: www.sciencedirect.com/science/journal/1146609X

African Journal of Ecology. See Africa section.

1796. American Midland Naturalist. Formerly (until Apr.1909): *The Midland Naturalist.* [ISSN: 0003-0031] 1909. q. USD 95 (Individuals, USD 55; Students, USD 35). Ed(s): William E Evans. University of Notre Dame, Department of Biological Sciences, Rm 285 GLSC, PO Box 369, Notre Dame, IN 46556; biology.biosadm.1@nd.edu; http://www.nd.edu. Illus., index. Refereed. Microform: IDC; PQC. *Indexed:* A01, A22, Agr, AnBeAb, BRI, C45, E01, GardL, IndVet, P02, RRTA, S25. *Aud.:* Ac, Sa.

American Midland Naturalist publishes original field and experimental biology articles as well as "review articles of a critical nature on topics of current interest in biology." It covers all areas of natural history and publishes many articles on biodiversity. The scope is ecology, evolution, and the natural environment. Published since 1909 by the University of Notre Dame, this academic journal no longer is limited in geographic scope to the middle of America. Rather, it covers the North American continent and has occasional articles from other continents. Two volumes containing two issues each are published per year. The issues are composed of many full-length articles and a few short "Notes and Discussions." All subject areas related to plant and animal ecology are covered in this diverse journal. The journal is available in print and online through BioOne (since 1998) and JSTOR (1909–2008). URL: www.bioone.org/loi/amid

1797. The American Naturalist. [ISSN: 0003-0147] 1867. m. USD 707 (print & online eds.). Ed(s): Judith L Bronstein. University of Chicago Press, 1427 E 60th St, Chicago, IL 60637; subscriptions@press.uchicago.edu; http://www.journals.uchicago.edu. Illus., index. Sample. Refereed. Microform: IDC; PMC; PQC. Reprint: PSC. *Indexed:* A01, A22, AbAn, Agr, AnBeAb, BRI, C45, GardL, IndVet, MLA-IB, MathR, OceAb, P02. *Aud.:* Ac, Sa.

Advancing the knowledge of organic evolution and examining broad biological principles comprise the focus of *The American Naturalist.* Articles relating to "community and ecosystem dynamics, evolution of sex and mating systems, organismal adaptation, and genetic aspects of evolution" are published. The journal emphasizes articles in "sophisticated methodologies and innovative theoretical syntheses." The journal has recently revived the section called "Natural History Miscellany," which includes notes pertaining to the natural history of a species that also have "relevance to important or conceptual issues or understanding of the dimensions of biological diversity." The enhanced electronic edition offers a citation manager, RSS, pdfs, direct Medline and CrossRef linking, table and figure galleries, free text to recent electronic articles, and ASCII versions of tables. Published for the American Society of

Naturalists, this journal is appropriate for academic libraries and professionals. The journal is available in print and online with some open-access articles. URL: www.journals.uchicago.edu/loi/an

1798. *Animal Conservation: the rapid publication journal for quantitative studies in conservation.* [ISSN: 1367-9430] 1998. bi-m. GBP 374. Ed(s): Trenton WJ Garner, Iain Gordon. Wiley-Blackwell Publishing Ltd., 9600 Garsington Rd, Oxford, OX4 2DQ, United Kingdom; customerservices@blackwellpublishing.com; http://www.wiley.com/. Adv. Sample. Refereed. Reprint: PSC. *Indexed:* A01, A22, Agr, C45, E01, IndVet, RRTA. *Aud.:* Ac, Sa.

Conservation of animal species and their habitats is the focus of this peer-reviewed journal, published by the Zoological Society of London. Quantitative studies on species, populations, and communities that are either theoretical or empirical are published, with less emphasis on specific species and more on "new ideas and findings that have general implications for the scientific basis of conservation." The journal covers topics on population biology, epidemiology, evolutionary ecology, population genetics, biodiversity, biogeography, palaeobiology, conservation economics, sociology, and anthropology. Editorials, feature papers, commentaries, responses, and original articles are available in print and online. URL: www.wiley.com/bw/journal.asp?ref=1367-9430

1799. *Annual Review of Ecology, Evolution and Systematics.* Formerly (until 2003): *Annual Review of Ecology and Systematics.* [ISSN: 1543-592X] 1970. a. USD 246 (print or online ed.). Ed(s): Samuel Gubins, Douglas J Futuyma. Annual Reviews, PO Box 10139, Palo Alto, CA 94303; service@annualreviews.org; http://www.annualreviews.org. Refereed. Microform: PQC. Reprint: PSC. *Indexed:* A01, A22, Agr, C45, M&GPA, S25. *Aud.:* Ac, Sa.

Annual Review of Ecology, Evolution, and Systematics is a core academic journal that provides review articles in one volume each year. The reviews summarize the primary literature on a subject and create conclusions as well as highlight conflicts of previous research. It is a critical starting point in conducting research for ecologists, and is also a great resource for undergraduate assignments. The reviews are written by distinguished authors and editors in the field and are highly cited. The journal is available in print and online. URL: http://arjournals.annualreviews.org/loi/ecolsys

1800. *Applied Soil Ecology.* [ISSN: 0929-1393] 1994. 9x/yr. EUR 1794. Ed(s): C A M van Gestel, H Insam. Elsevier BV, Radarweg 29, PO Box 211, Amsterdam, 1000 AE, Netherlands; JournalsCustomerServiceEMEA@elsevier.com; http://www.elsevier.nl. Index. Refereed. Microform: PQC. *Indexed:* A01, A22, Agr, C45, IndVet, RRTA, S25. *Aud.:* Ac, Sa.

Applied Soil Ecology features articles on the function of soil organisms and their association with soil processes, soil structure, soil fertility, nutrient cycling, and agricultural productivity, along with the "impact of human activities and xenobiotics on soil ecosystems and bio(techno)logical control of soil-inhabiting pests, diseases, and weeds." Original research and review articles are published in the journal, and the web site offers journal news, conferences, most downloaded articles, most cited articles, special issues, and recent articles. This peer-reviewed journal is recommended for academic and special libraries. Available online and in print. URL: www.elsevier.com/locate/apsoil

1801. *Aquatic Toxicology.* [ISSN: 0166-445X] 1981. 20x/yr. EUR 3262. Ed(s): R S Tjeerdema, M J Nikinmaa. Elsevier BV, Radarweg 29, PO Box 211, Amsterdam, 1000 AE, Netherlands; JournalsCustomerServiceEMEA@elsevier.com; http://www.elsevier.nl. Illus., adv. Refereed. *Indexed:* A01, A22, AbAn, Agr, C45, ExcerpMed, FS&TA, IndVet, OceAb, S25. *Aud.:* Ac, Sa.

Increasing the knowledge and understanding of the impact of toxicants on aquatic organisms and ecosystems is the aim of *Aquatic Toxicology.* This journal publishes field and laboratory studies that relate to the "mechanisms of toxicity and the responses to toxic agents in aquatic environments at the community, species, tissue, cellular, subcellular, and molecular levels, including aspects of uptake, metabolism[,] and excretion of toxicants." The journal has special issues pertaining to specific topics or proceedings related to symposia; and each

regular issue is made up exclusively of research articles. It is recommended for academic and special libraries, and is available online and in print. URL: www.journals.elsevier.com/aquatic-toxicology/

1802. *Basic and Applied Ecology.* [ISSN: 1439-1791] 2000. 8x/yr. EUR 683. Ed(s): Teja Tscharntke. Urban und Fischer Verlag, Loebdergraben 14a, Jena, 07743, Germany; info@urbanfischer.de; http://www.urbanundfischer.de. Adv. Refereed. Circ: 1850 Paid and controlled. *Indexed:* A22, Agr, AnBeAb, C&ISA, C45, CerAb, E01, IndVet, RRTA. *Aud.:* Ac, Sa.

This is the official journal of the Ecological Society of Germany, Austria, and Switzerland, but ecologists from around the world are invited to publish articles on broad ecological topics from all geographical areas. Original contributions and minireviews are included in the journal, which "provides a forum in which significant advances and ideas can be rapidly communicated to a wide audience." The web site features recent articles, the top ten cited articles, and special issues. This journal is recommended for special and academic libraries, and is available online and in print. URL: www.elsevier.com/locate/baae

Behavioral Ecology. See Zoology section.

Behavioral Ecology and Sociobiology. See Zoology section.

1803. *Biological Conservation.* [ISSN: 0006-3207] 1969. 12x/yr. EUR 3847. Ed(s): R B Primack. Elsevier BV, Radarweg 29, PO Box 211, Amsterdam, 1000 AE, Netherlands; JournalsCustomerServiceEMEA@elsevier.com; http://www.elsevier.nl. Illus., adv. Sample. Refereed. Microform: PQC. *Indexed:* A01, A22, Agr, C&ISA, C45, CerAb, GardL, IndVet, OceAb, RRTA. *Bk. rev.:* Number and length vary. *Aud.:* Ac, Sa.

Shifting conservation science into conservation practice is a goal of the journal *Biological Conservation,* which is interdisciplinary and international in scope. Articles published span "a diverse range of fields that contribute to the biological, sociological, and economic dimensions of conservation and natural resource management." Areas of focus are broad and encompass various aspects of biological conservation to aid in policy making and decision processes. For example, topics covered may include ecological restoration, resource economics, impacts on biodiversity from global change, invasive organism spread, or ecological reserve design. Journal issues have sections for letters to the editor, reviews, regular papers, short communications, and book reviews, or may have a special section on a given topic. The journal is appropriate for institutions with natural resource managers, environmental policy makers, environmental scientists, and ecologists. Available in print and online. URL: www.elsevier.com/locate/biocon

1804. *Biotropica.* Formerly (until 1969): *Association for Tropical Biology. Bulletin.* [ISSN: 0006-3606] 1969. bi-m. GBP 291. Ed(s): Jaboury Ghazoul. Wiley-Blackwell Publishing, Inc., 111 River St, Hoboken, NJ 07030; info@wiley.com; http://www.wiley.com/. Adv. Sample. Refereed. Microform: PQC. Reprint: PSC. *Indexed:* A22, Agr, AnBeAb, C45, E01, IndVet, M&GPA, RRTA, S25. *Bk. rev.:* Number and length vary. *Aud.:* Ac, Sa.

Biotropica, the official journal of the Association for Tropical Biology and Conservation, publishes original research on the behavior, population biology, and evolution of tropical organisms and the conservation, ecology, and management of tropical ecosystems. Academic papers are divided into sections for tropical biology and tropical conservation, alongside reviews of current topics, commentaries that initiate debate and discussions, book reviews, and short communication insights. The journal is available online and in print, and is suggested for academic and public libraries that serve researchers interested in tropical biology and conservation. URL: www3.interscience.wiley.com/journal/118501466/home

1805. *Conservation Biology.* [ISSN: 0888-8892] 1986. bi-m. GBP 719 (print or online ed.). Ed(s): Ellen Main, Gary K Meffe. Wiley-Blackwell Publishing, Inc., 111 River St, Hoboken, NJ 07030; info@wiley.com; http://onlinelibrary.wiley.com/. Illus., index, adv. Sample. Refereed. Reprint: PSC. *Indexed:* A01, A22, Agr, AnBeAb, BRI, C45, E01, GardL, IndVet, OceAb, P02, RRTA, S25. *Aud.:* Ac, Sa.

The Society for Conservation Biology publishes this journal, which is focused on the science and practice of examining and preserving Earth's biological diversity. Articles define key issues of conservation relating to ecosystems or species in any geographic region, with emphasis given to those that have a scope beyond that particular ecosystem or species. The journal publishes papers in nine sections: contributed papers, research notes, reviews, essays, conservation practice and policy, comments, diversity, letters, and invited book reviews. *Conservation Biology* is an important title for institutions that serve professional physical geographers, environmental scientists, and ecologists. The journal is available online and in print. URL: www.wiley.com/bw/journal.asp?ref=0888-8892

Diversity and Distributions: a journal of conservation biogeography. See Geography section.

1806. *Ecography: pattern and diversity in ecology.* Formerly (until 1992): *Holarctic Ecology.* [ISSN: 0906-7590] 1978. bi-m. Ed(s): Carsten Rahbek. Wiley-Blackwell Publishing, Inc., Commerce Pl, 350 Main St, Malden, MA 02148; info@wiley.com; http://onlinelibrary.wiley.com/. Illus., adv. Refereed. Reprint: PSC. *Indexed:* A01, A22, Agr, C45, E01, IndVet, RRTA, S25. *Aud.:* Ac, Sa.

Contemporary ecological spatial and temporal patterns are the primary focus of this academic journal. Issued by the Nordic Ecological Society OIKOS, *Ecography* publishes "studies of population and community ecology, macroecology, biogeography, and ecological conservation." Among those are four types of articles: original research papers; forum papers (short papers or commentaries); review and syntheses papers (emphasizing current topics); and software notes. The journal is recommended for academic and special libraries and is available in print and online. URL: www.wiley.com/bw/journal.asp?ref=0906-7590&site=1

1807. *Ecological Applications.* [ISSN: 1051-0761] 1991. 8x/yr. USD 360 with less than 2500 FTE (print & online eds.). Ed(s): David Schimel. Ecological Society of America, 1990 M St, NW, Ste 700, Washington, DC 20036; esahq@esa.org; http://www.esa.org. Illus., adv. Microform: PQC. *Indexed:* A22, Agr, AnBeAb, C45, FS&TA, GardL, IndVet, M&GPA, RRTA, S25. *Aud.:* Ac, Sa.

Ecological Applications, a journal of the Ecological Society of America, stands apart from most other ecology journals in that its articles "explicitly discuss the applications or implications of the work in regard to policy, management, or the analysis and solution to major environmental problems." The journal contains articles that describe original and significant research and communications of short length for urgent application and scientific debate. There are also invited features, forums, and letters to the editor. The journal is a core title for university and special libraries with scholars and practitioners in the ecological and environmental science fields. It is available online and in print. URL: http://esapubs.org

1808. *Ecological Complexity.* [ISSN: 1476-945X] 2004. 4x/yr. EUR 702. Ed(s): Sergei Petrovskii. Elsevier BV, Radarweg 29, PO Box 211, Amsterdam, 1000 AE, Netherlands; JournalsCustomerServiceEMEA@elsevier.com; http://www.elsevier.nl. Refereed. *Indexed:* C45. *Aud.:* Ac, Sa.

Ecological Complexity is an interdisciplinary, peer-reviewed journal that focuses on "all aspects of biocomplexity in the environment, theoretical ecology, and special issues on topics of current interest." Quantitative research that integrates social and natural processes that are applied at broad spatial-temporal scales are published in this relatively new journal. Ecologists with interest in integrated and quantitative research will find this journal of particular interest, along with those whose research intersects natural and socioeconomic systems. It is also appropriate for "mathematical and theoretical ecologists, biophysicists, computational biologists (in ecological informatics), landscape ecologists, conservation biologists, complex systems scientists, and resource managers." The journal is available in print and online. URL: www.elsevier.com/locate/issn/1476945X

1809. *Ecological Indicators.* [ISSN: 1470-160X] 2001. 6x/yr. EUR 727. Ed(s): F M Mueller. Elsevier BV, Radarweg 29, PO Box 211, Amsterdam, 1000 AE, Netherlands; JournalsCustomerServiceEMEA@elsevier.com; http://www.elsevier.nl. *Indexed:* A01, C&ISA, C45, CerAb, EngInd. *Aud.:* Ac, Sa.

Sound management practices can be informed by the assessment and monitoring of environmental and ecological indicators and indices. *Ecological Indicators* "provides a forum for the discussion of the applied scientific development and review of traditional indicator approaches as well as for theoretical, modelling[,] and quantitative applications such as index development." The journal publishes original research papers, review articles, short notes and case studies, viewpoint articles, letters to the editor, and book reviews; and it features special themed issues. It is available online and in print, and is recommended for academic and special libraries. URL: www.journals.elsevier.com/ecological-indicators/

1810. *Ecological Modelling.* [ISSN: 0304-3800] 1975. 24x/yr. EUR 5157. Ed(s): B D Fath. Elsevier BV, Radarweg 29, PO Box 211, Amsterdam, 1000 AE, Netherlands; JournalsCustomerServiceEMEA@elsevier.com; http://www.elsevier.nl. Illus., index, adv. Refereed. Microform: PQC. *Indexed:* A01, A22, C&ISA, C45, CerAb, EngInd, FS&TA, IndVet, OceAb, RRTA, S25. *Bk. rev.:* Number and length vary. *Aud.:* Ac, Sa.

Ecological processes and sustainable resource management are described through the use of systems analysis and mathematical models in *Ecological Modelling.* The journal publishes works with a strong emphasis on "process-based models embedded in theory with explicit causative agents," rather than on models that only have correlative or statistical descriptions. Basic ecosystem functions are described using "mathematical and conceptual modelling, systems analysis, thermodynamics, computer simulations, and ecological theory." Research articles, review articles, short communications, letters to the editor, and book reviews are published, and the activities of the International Society of Ecological Modelling are supported by the journal. The journal is available online and in print, and is recommended for special libraries and academic institutions that have research spanning between ecology and mathematical modeling. URL: www.elsevier.com/locate/ecolmodel

1811. *Ecological Monographs.* [ISSN: 0012-9615] 1931. q. USD 191 with less than 2500 FTE (print & online eds.). Ed(s): Aaron M Ellison. Ecological Society of America, 1990 M St, NW, Ste 700, Washington, DC 20036; esahq@esa.org; http://www.esa.org. Illus., adv. Refereed. Microform: IDC; PMC; PQC. *Indexed:* A01, A22, AbAn, Agr, AnBeAb, C45, GardL, M&GPA, OceAb, P02, S25. *Aud.:* Ac, Sa.

Published by the Ecological Society of America, *Ecological Monographs* features "complex, multi-faceted studies that demand greater length than those published in *Ecology* or *Ecological Applications.*" The article length is generally more than 16 printed pages, and the content typically includes many factors that describe complicated ecological processes and phenomena. The journal's mission states that papers published "will provide integrative and complete documentation of major empirical and theoretical advances in the field and will establish benchmarks from which future research will build." It is available online and in print. URL: http://esapubs.org

1812. *Ecology.* Formerly (until 1920): *Plant World;* Which incorporated (1893-1900): *The Asa Gray Bulletin.* [ISSN: 0012-9658] 1897. m. USD 935 (print & online eds.); Free to members. Ed(s): Donald R Strong. Ecological Society of America, 127 W State St, Ste 301, Ithaca, NY 14850; esa_journals@cornell.edu; http://www.esa.org. Illus., index, adv. Refereed. Vol. ends: Dec. Microform: IDC; PMC; PQC. *Indexed:* A01, A22, AbAn, Agr, AnBeAb, BRI, C45, CBRI, FS&TA, GardL, IndVet, M&GPA, OceAb, P02, S25. *Bk. rev.:* Number and length vary. *Aud.:* Ac, Sa.

Ecology focuses on the publishing of concise articles that contain "research and synthesis that lead to generalizations potentially applicable to other species, populations, communities, or ecosystems." Research and synthesis papers from all areas of ecology are published "with particular emphasis on papers that develop new concepts in ecology that test ecological theory or lead to an increased appreciation for the diversity of ecological phenomena." The publication provides reports, concept and synthesis articles, full-length articles, notes, comments, data papers, book reviews, and books and monographs received. The journal is a core title for academic and special libraries that support ecologists. It is available online and in print. URL: http://esapubs.org

Ecology and Society. See Environment and Conservation section.

1813. *Ecology Letters.* [ISSN: 1461-023X] 1998. m. GBP 1497. Ed(s): Marcel Holyoak. Wiley-Blackwell Publishing Ltd., The Atrium, Southern Gate, Chichester, PO19 8SQ, United Kingdom; customer@wiley.com; http://www.wiley.com/. Adv. Sample. Refereed. Reprint: PSC. *Indexed:* A01, A22, Agr, C45, E01, IndVet, P02, RRTA. *Aud.:* Ac, Sa.

Current worldwide ecological research is rapidly published in *Ecology Letters.* The concise, primary literature published in this scholarly journal relates to new developments in ecology or is general-interest in scope. Research that tests clearly stated hypotheses has priority in being granted publication. There are three sections: "Letters: exciting findings in fast-moving areas"; "Ideas and Perspectives: novel essays for a general audience"; and "Reviews: syntheses of important subjects which merit urgent coverage." This is an important journal for academic libraries that serve an ecology department. Available in print and online. URL: www.wiley.com/bw/journal.asp?ref=1461-023x

Ecology of Freshwater Fish. See Fish, Fisheries & Aquaculture section.

1814. *Ecosystems.* [ISSN: 1432-9840] 1998. 8x/yr. EUR 835 (print & online eds.). Ed(s): Stephen R Carpenter, Monica G Turner. Springer New York LLC, 233 Spring St, New York, NY 10013; journals@springer-ny.com; http://www.springer.com/. Illus., adv. Sample. Refereed. Reprint: PSC. *Indexed:* A01, A22, AbAn, Agr, C45, E01, RRTA, S25. *Aud.:* Ac, Sa.

Ecosystem science, which incorporates "fundamental ecology, environmental ecology[,] and environmental problem solving" is published in this academic journal. Spatial and temporal scales of all sizes are examined in large experiments, theoretical research, modeling, comparative research, and long-term investigations. Natural and social processes are integrated in research that can be terrestrial or aquatic. The journal mainly features research articles, but also publishes editorials, special features on complex topics, and invited mini-reviews of emerging topics. It is available in print and online. URL: www.springer.com/life+sciences/ecology/journal/10021

Evolution: international journal of organic evolution. See Biology/General section.

1815. *Evolutionary Ecology.* [ISSN: 0269-7653] 1987. bi-m. EUR 949 (print & online eds.). Ed(s): John A Endler. Springer Netherlands, Van Godewijckstraat 30, Dordrecht, 3311 GX, Netherlands; http://www.springer.com. Adv. Refereed. Reprint: PSC. *Indexed:* A22, AbAn, Agr, AnBeAb, C45, E01, FS&TA, IndVet, OceAb. *Aud.:* Ac, Sa.

The focus of *Evolutionary Ecology* is on the ecological influences on evolutionary processes, as well as the evolutionary influences on ecological processes. Behavioral and population ecology are explored in respect to evolutionary aspects, and the journal publishes empirical and theoretical articles on all systems and organisms. Research articles, ideas and perspectives, review articles, and comments on recent articles are published in this academic journal, which is recommended for academic and special libraries. The journal is available in print and online. URL: http://springerlink.metapress.com/openurl.asp?genre=journal&issn=0269-7653

Forest Ecology and Management. See Forestry section.

1816. *Freshwater Biology (Print).* [ISSN: 0046-5070] 1971. m. GBP 3603. Ed(s): Dr. Alan G. Hildrew, Dr. Colin R. Townsend. Wiley-Blackwell Publishing Ltd., The Atrium, Southern Gate, Chichester, PO19 8SQ, United Kingdom; customer@wiley.com; http://www.wiley.com/. Illus., index, adv. Sample. Refereed. Microform: PQC. Reprint: PSC. *Indexed:* A01, A22, Agr, C45, E01, IndVet, RRTA, S25. *Bk. rev.:* 0-3, 500-2,000 words. *Aud.:* Ac, Sa.

Freshwater Biology publishes standard research papers related to all ecological aspects of surficial inland waters. Studies can be focused at any level in the ecological hierarchy that relate to "micro-organisms, algae, macrophytes, invertebrates, [and] fish and other vertebrates, as well as those concerning whole ecosystems and related physical and chemical aspects of the environment." Review articles and discussion (editorial) papers are printed and special issues dedicated to a topic or theme are also occasionally published. Applied science papers related to the management and conservation of inland waters are also published. This journal is appropriate for academic and special libraries that support ecologists, limnologists, biologists, and environmental scientists. It is available online and in print. URL: www.wiley.com/bw/journal.asp?ref=0046-5070

1817. *Functional Ecology.* [ISSN: 0269-8463] 1987. bi-m. GBP 876. Ed(s): Charles W Fox, Ken Thompson. Wiley-Blackwell Publishing Ltd., 9600 Garsington Rd, Oxford, OX4 2DQ, United Kingdom; customerservices@blackwellpublishing.com; http://www.wiley.com/. Adv. Sample. Refereed. Microform: PQC. Reprint: PSC. *Indexed:* A01, A22, Agr, AnBeAb, C45, E01, IndVet, OceAb, S25. *Aud.:* Ac, Sa.

This journal has articles focused on the relationship between the development of organisms and their function in the environment. Standard papers, forum articles, and reviews with an emphasis on life history, anatomical, and physiological characteristics in relationship to an ecosystem or community are published. Current issues are divided into sections that may have *Functional Ecology* spotlight, perspectives, plant morphology, behavioral ecology, evolutionary biology, plant physiological ecology, animal physiological ecology, evolutionary ecology, animal morphology and coloration, plant growth and development, and community ecology. This peer-reviewed journal is recommended for academic and special libraries and is available in print and online. URL: www.functionalecology.org/

1818. *Global Change Biology.* [ISSN: 1354-1013] 1995. m. GBP 2926 (print or online ed.). Ed(s): Steve Long. Wiley-Blackwell Publishing Ltd., The Atrium, Southern Gate, Chichester, PO19 8SQ, United Kingdom; customer@wiley.com; http://www.wiley.com/. Adv. Sample. Refereed. Reprint: PSC. *Indexed:* A01, A22, Agr, C45, E01, FS&TA, IndVet, M&GPA, P02, RRTA, S25. *Aud.:* Ac, Sa.

Biological systems interfacing with the physical environment are the central focus of this academic journal. The scope is from the micro to the macro, and it covers topics that include atmospheric pollution, ocean warming, land-use change, climate change, carbon sequestration, and global food security. Primary research articles "which integrate across levels of organization to provide a mechanistic understanding" are the main feature, but the journal also publishes technical papers, mini-reviews, and opinion articles. The journal is available online and in print. URL: www.wiley.com/bw/journal.asp?ref=1354-1013

1819. *Global Ecology and Biogeography: a journal of macroecology.* Formerly (until 1999): *Global Ecology and Biogeography Letters.* [ISSN: 1466-822X] 1991. m. GBP 4603 (print & online eds.). Ed(s): David J Currie. Wiley-Blackwell Publishing Ltd., 9600 Garsington Rd, Oxford, OX4 2DQ, United Kingdom; customerservices@blackwellpublishing.com; http://www.wiley.com/. Illus., adv. Sample. Refereed. Reprint: PSC. *Indexed:* A01, A22, Agr, AnBeAb, C45, E01, IndVet, S25. *Aud.:* Ac, Sa.

Global Ecology and Biogeography: a journal of macroecology is an academic journal that "focuses on the emerging field of macroecology: the study of broad, consistent patterns in the ecological characteristics of organisms and ecosystems." Articles published within this journal are wide in scope and focus on global or regional issues that pertain to biodiversity, ecology, and biogeography. This peer-reviewed publication is appropriate for institutions with faculty that study global change, biodiversity, geography, ecology, biogeography, and environmental science. It is available in print and online. URL: www.blackwellpublishing.com/geb

Human Ecology. See Environment and Conservation section.

1820. *Hydrobiologia: the international journal of aquatic sciences.* Incorporates (in 2003): *Journal of Aquatic Ecosystem Stress and Recovery;* Which was formerly (1991-1997): *Journal of Aquatic Ecosystem Health;* Incorporated (1992-2000): *International Journal of Salt Lake Research.* [ISSN: 0018-8158] 1948. 21x/yr. EUR 12301 (print & online eds.). Ed(s): Koen Martens. Springer Netherlands, Van Godewijckstraat 30, Dordrecht, 3311 GX, Netherlands; http://www.springer.com. Adv. Refereed. Microform: PQC. Reprint: PSC. *Indexed:* A01, A22, Agr, AnBeAb, C45, E01, EngInd, FS&TA, IndVet, OceAb, RRTA, S25. *Bk. rev.:* Number and length vary. *Aud.:* Ac, Sa.

Limnology, oceanography, systematic, and aquatic ecology topics are covered at the levels of molecular, organism, community, and ecosystem. In addition to hypothesis-driven and theoretical research, reviews and opinions are published in this peer-reviewed journal, which is aimed at a "broad hydrobiological audience." The journal had special issues and guest editors and publishes over 15 volumes each year. Regular volumes are divided into sections for review papers and primary research papers, and the most downloaded articles are offered for free. This peer-reviewed journal is recommended for academic and special libraries and is available in print and online.

1821. *Journal of Animal Ecology.* [ISSN: 0021-8790] 1932. bi-m. GBP 837. Wiley-Blackwell Publishing Ltd., The Atrium, Southern Gate, Chichester, PO19 8SQ, United Kingdom; customer@wiley.com; http://www.wiley.com/. Illus., index, adv. Sample. Refereed. Vol. ends: Nov. Microform: PQC. Reprint: PSC. *Indexed:* A01, A22, AbAn, Agr, AnBeAb, C45, E01, FS&TA, IndVet, MathR, RRTA, S25. *Bk. rev.:* 0-8, 300-1,200 words. *Aud.:* Ac, Sa.

The British Ecological Society offers original research related to all aspects of animal ecology in this journal. The topics of evolutionary ecology, behavioral ecology, population ecology, molecular ecology, community ecology, and physiological ecology are covered to support long-term ecological research. In addition, "field, laboratory, and theoretical studies based upon terrestrial freshwater or marine systems" are included. Each article has a numbered point-by-point overview instead of a standard abstract, which allows browsing to be more efficient. The journal is appropriate for academic programs that focus on animal ecology and for professionals. It is available in print and online. URL: www.journalofanimalecology.org

1822. *Journal of Ecology.* [ISSN: 0022-0477] 1913. bi-m. GBP 880. Ed(s): Andrea J. Baier. Wiley-Blackwell Publishing Ltd., 9600 Garsington Rd, Oxford, OX4 2DQ, United Kingdom; customerservices@blackwellpublishing.com; http://www.wiley.com/. Illus., index. Sample. Refereed. Circ: 1800. Vol. ends: Dec. Microform: PQC. Reprint: PSC. *Indexed:* A01, A22, Agr, AnBeAb, BRI, BrArAb, C45, E01, GardL, OceAb, P02, RRTA, S25. *Aud.:* Ac, Sa.

The British Ecological Society offers original research related to the ecology of plants in the *Journal of Ecology.* Experimental papers using any kind of ecological approach are published, along with those focusing on theoretical approaches or papers with historical or descriptive accounts. The journal has a broad scope and an international audience. Each article has a numbered, point-by-point overview instead of an abstract, which makes browsing more efficient. Papers from all geographical regions are published, along with essay reviews and forum (opinion) articles. The journal is appropriate for academic programs related to plant ecology and for professionals. It is available online and in print. URL: www.journalofecology.org

1823. *Landscape Ecology.* [ISSN: 0921-2973] 1987. 10x/yr. EUR 1331 (print & online eds.). Ed(s): Jianguo Wu. Springer Netherlands, Van Godewijckstraat 30, Dordrecht, 3311 GX, Netherlands; http://www.springer.com. Adv. Refereed. Reprint: PSC. *Indexed:* A22, Agr, BRI, C45, E01, GardL, IndVet, RRTA. *Aud.:* Ga, Ac, Sa.

The development and maintenance of sustainable landscapes, informed by the understanding of the relationships between ecological processes and spatial patterns is the primary focus of *Landscape Ecology.* Transdisciplinary and interdisciplinary studies are published that aggregate "expertise from biological, geophysical, and social sciences to explore the formation, dynamics[,] and consequences of spatial heterogeneity in natural and human-dominated landscapes." The peer-reviewed journal informs researchers and practitioners in the fields of landscape design and planning, biodiversity conservation, broad-scale ecology, and ecosystem management. It is available in print and online. URL: www.springer.com/life+sciences/ecology/journal/10980

Marine Ecology - Progress Series. See Marine Science and Technology/Marine Biology section.

1824. *Molecular Ecology.* [ISSN: 0962-1083] 1992. s-m. GBP 4368. Ed(s): Loren Rieseberg. Wiley-Blackwell Publishing Ltd., 9600 Garsington Rd, Oxford, OX4 2DQ, United Kingdom; customerservices@blackwellpublishing.com; http://www.wiley.com/. Illus., adv. Sample. Refereed. Microform: PQC. Reprint: PSC. *Indexed:* A01, A22, AbAn, Agr, C45, E01, IndVet, P02, RRTA. *Aud.:* Ac, Sa.

Important questions in ecology, behavior, evolution, and conservation are addressed in *Molecular Ecology.* Papers published must employ molecular genetic techniques to address the research issue. Each journal has a concentration on primary research articles, but also may have invited reviews, opinion articles (perspectives), and commentaries. The journal's featured research topics include population and conservation genetics, molecular adaptation, speciation and hybridization, phylogeography, kinship parentage and behavior, ecological interactions, ecological genomics, and genetically modified organisms and their release. Institutions that serve molecular ecologists should include this journal in their collection. The journal is available online and in print. URL: www.wiley.com/bw/journal.asp?ref=0962-1083

1825. *Oecologia.* Formerly: *Zeitschrift fuer Morphologie und Oekologie der Tiere.* [ISSN: 0029-8549] 1924. 16x/yr. EUR 6175 (print & online eds.). Ed(s): Roland Brandl, Craig W Osenberg. Springer, Tiergartenstr 17, Heidelberg, 69121, Germany. Illus., adv. Sample. Refereed. Microform: PQC. Reprint: PSC. *Indexed:* A01, A22, AbAn, Agr, AnBeAb, C45, E01, IndVet, OceAb, S25. *Aud.:* Ac, Sa.

Oecologia publishes "innovative ecological research of general interest" related to plant and animal ecology aimed at an international audience. Issues are divided into the sections of "Concepts," "Reviews and Syntheses," "Views and Comments," "Original Papers," "Special Topics," and "Methods." Categories of published manuscripts include physiological ecology, behavioral ecology, population ecology, plant–animal interactions, community ecology, ecosystem ecology, global change ecology, and conservation ecology. It is appropriate for scholars and professionals and is available online and in print. URL: www.springer.com/life+sciences/ecology/journal/442

1826. *Oikos (Malden): a journal of ecology.* [ISSN: 0030-1299] 1948. m. GBP 985. Ed(s): Dries Bonte. Wiley-Blackwell Publishing, Inc., Commerce Pl, 350 Main St, Malden, MA 02148; info@wiley.com; http://onlinelibrary.wiley.com/. Illus., adv. Sample. Refereed. Reprint: PSC. *Indexed:* A01, A22, Agr, AnBeAb, C45, E01, IndVet, OceAb, P02, S25. *Aud.:* Ac, Sa.

The Nordic Ecologic Society publishes *Oikos: a journal of ecology.* Theoretical and empirical work related to all aspects of ecology from all regions of the world can be accepted for publication. *Oikos* publishes articles that emphasize "theoretical and empirical work aimed at generalization and synthesis across taxa, systems[,] and ecological disciplines." The journal has a "forum" section for syntheses and reviews, a "horizons" section for essays, and a "brevia" section for comments on published articles. Articles are available online ahead of print in the "EarlyView" feature. The forum section is "an arena for challenging current thinking on ecological issues by revising established concepts and received knowledge through critical experiments or new theory so that new ground can be broken." Horizons papers are original and novel and explore developing ideas and concepts that point research in a new direction. The brevia papers "broaden and widen the scope of published contributions or debate controversial findings." *Oikos* is appropriate for academic institutions with an ecology program or for professionals. It is available online and in print. URL: www.blackwellpublishing.com/oik

1827. *Restoration Ecology.* [ISSN: 1061-2971] 1993. bi-m. GBP 575. Ed(s): Richard Hobbs, Susan A Yates. Wiley-Blackwell Publishing, Inc., 111 River St, Hoboken, NJ 07030; info@wiley.com; http://onlinelibrary.wiley.com/. Adv. Sample. Refereed. Microform: PQC. *Indexed:* A01, A22, Agr, C45, E01, GardL, IndVet, RRTA, S25. *Aud.:* Ac, Sa.

The Society for Ecological Restoration International publishes the journal *Restoration Ecology*. Topics in interdisciplinary science are covered in the journal, which "addresses global concerns" yet also highlights specific issues within ecological communities. Articles based in marine, freshwater, and terrestrial ecology are integrated with social science "in the fight to not only halt ecological damage, but also to ultimately reverse it." Restoration practitioners and academic researchers will find valuable information that can be applied on a variety of spatial and temporal scales. The journal is available online and in print. URL: www.wiley.com/bw/journal.asp?ref=1061-2971

1828. *Trends in Ecology & Evolution.* [ISSN: 0169-5347] 1986. m. EUR 2351. Ed(s): Paul Craze. Elsevier Ltd., Trends Journals, The Blvd, Langford Ln, Kidlington, Oxford, OX5 1GB, United Kingdom; JournalsCustomerServiceEMEA@elsevier.com; http://www.elsevier.com. Illus., adv. Sample. Refereed. Circ: 955. Vol. ends: No. 16. *Indexed:* A01, A22, AnBeAb, C45, FS&TA, IndVet, RRTA. *Bk. rev.:* Number and length vary. *Aud.:* Ac, Sa.

Trends in Ecology & Evolution is a highly regarded journal that focuses on current developments in ecology and evolutionary science. It spans topics in microbiology to global evolution and features pure and applied science articles. The journal "is the major forum for coverage of all the important issues concerning organisms and their environments." Features include updates, a forum, letters, responses to letters, book reviews, and opinion. This is a core journal for university and college libraries that have ecology, evolution, microbiology, biology, and environmental studies departments. It can be found in print and online. URL: www.elsevier.com/locate/tree

1829. *The Wildlife Professional.* [ISSN: 1933-2866] 2007. q. Free to members. Ed(s): Lisa Moore. Alliance Communications Group, 810 E 10th St, PO Box 368, Lawrence, KS 66044; info@allenpress.com; http://allenpress.com/. Adv. Circ: 8300 Paid. *Aud.:* Ga, Ac, Sa.

Published as a free membership benefit to The Wildlife Society, this magazine is aimed to keep the professional wildlife manager informed of "critical advances in wildlife science, conservation, management, and policy." Each issue has a theme highlighted by a cover story, along with an in-focus topic area, rotating features, and departments with items like policy watch, field notes, and photos from readers. This magazine is recommended for college and academic libraries with wildlife programs and for special libraries, such as career centers. It is available in print and online, dating back to the origin of the magazine in 2007. URL: www.wildlife.org/publications/twp

■ ECONOMICS

Gwyneth Crowley, Librarian for Economics, Sociology, Anthropology and Women's, Gender and Sexuality Studies, Social Science Libraries and Information Service, Yale University

Introduction

.

Basic Periodicals

Ga: *The American Prospect, Challenge, The Economist, The Journal of Economic History, Journal of Economic Literature, O E C D Observer, World Bank Research Observer;* Ac: *Brookings Papers on Economic Activity, Economic History Review, The Economic Journal, Economica, Journal of Economic Literature, Journal of Economic Theory, Journal of Political Economy, O E C D Observer, Quarterly Journal of Economics, RAND Journal of Economics, The World Bank Economic Review.*

Basic Abstracts and Indexes

ABI/Inform, Business Abstracts, EconLit, International Bibliography of the Social Sciences, PAIS International, Social Science Citation Index, World Agricultural Economics and Rural Sociology.

1830. *The American Economic Review.* Formed by the 1911 merger of: *American Economic Association Quarterly; Economic Bulletin.* [ISSN: 0002-8282] 1911. 5x/yr. USD 420. Ed(s): Jane Voros, Robert A Moffitt. American Economic Association, 2014 Broadway, Ste 305, Nashville, TN 37203; aeainfo@vanderbilt.edu; http://www.vanderbilt.edu/AEA/. Illus., index, adv. Refereed. Circ: 27000. Vol. ends: Dec. Microform: MIM; PMC; PQC. *Indexed:* A22, ABIn, ABS&EES, Agr, B01, B02, BAS, BLI, BRI, CBRI, Chicano, EconLit, F01, IBSS, JEL, P02. *Aud.:* Ac, Sa.

The premier journal of the American Economic Association, American Economic review, is a must for any college, university or special library. In 2011, the American Economic Association announced that it ended it double blind peer review and will now only be single blind reviewed. Since this spends up the publishing time, forthcoming articles can be viewed online as soon as they are available. With the field of economic becoming increasingly interdisciplinary, the following titles title from a recent issue illustrate this point: Preferences and Incentives of Appointed and Elected Public Officials: Evidence from State Trial Court Judges" and "A Theory of Strategic Voting in Runoff Elections" Traditional fare is , of course, included. Titles include: Why Don't the Poor Save More? Evidence from Health Savings Experiments" and "The Dynamic Effects of Personal and Corporate Income Tax Changes in the United States".

American Statistical Association. Journal. See Statistics section.

1831. *Brookings Papers on Economic Activity.* [ISSN: 0007-2303] 1970. s-a. USD 90 (Individuals, USD 55; USD 35 per issue). Ed(s): Justin Wolfers, David H Romer. Brookings Institution Press, 1775 Massachusetts Ave, NW, Washington, DC 20036; communications@brookings.edu; http://www.brookings.edu. Illus., index. Refereed. Microform: PQC. *Indexed:* A22, ABIn, ABS&EES, B01, B02, BRI, E01, EconLit, JEL, P02. *Aud.:* Ga, Ac, Sa.

The Brookings Institution has been described as liberal-centrsit or independent organization. It has been ranked as one of the most influential think tanks in the world and has been cited by the right and left wing. The esteemed journal is a forum for "nonpartisan research, education, and publication in economics, government, foreign policy, and the social sciences generally." It also works to help develop "sound public policies and to promote public understanding of issues of national importance." The journal is composed exclusively of invited contributions and "articles, reports, and highlights of the discussions from conferences of the Brookings Panel on Economic Activity." Highly recommended for universities and colleges.

1832. *Business Economics: designed to serve the needs of people who use economics in their work.* [ISSN: 0007-666X] 1965. q. USD 288. Ed(s): Robert Thomas Crow. Palgrave Macmillan Ltd., Houndmills, Basingstoke, RG21 6XS, United Kingdom; orders@palgrave.com; http://www.palgrave.com. Illus., adv. Sample. Refereed. Vol. ends: Oct. Microform: PQC. Reprint: PSC. *Indexed:* A22, ABIn, Agr, B01, B02, BLI, BRI, E01, EconLit, JEL, P02. *Bk. rev.:* 1-4, 1,000-1,500 words. *Aud.:* Ga, Ac.

Published by the National Association for Business Economists, this refereed journal provides articles, analyses, summaries, best practices on business issues. Each issue has features on statistics, industries and markets, economics at work and book reviews. Signed book reviews are included. All of it is very accessible to the non-economist. Papers are mostly invited. Academic and large public libraries should consider this journal for their collections.

1833. *Challenge (Armonk): the magazine of economic affairs.* Former titles (until 1954): *Challenge Magazine;* (until 1952): *Popular Economics.* [ISSN: 0577-5132] 1950. bi-m. USD 420 (print & online eds.). Ed(s): Jeffrey Madrick. M.E. Sharpe, Inc., 80 Business Park Dr, Armonk, NY 10504; custserv@mesharpe.com; http://www.mesharpe.com. Illus., index, adv. Sample. Refereed. Vol. ends: Nov/Dec. Microform: PQC. Reprint: PSC. *Indexed:* A22, ABIn, B01, B02, BAS, BRI, E01, EconLit, IBSS, JEL, P02. *Bk. rev.:* 1, 2-4 pages. *Aud.:* Hs, Ga, Ac.

Challenge presents a "wide range of views on national and international economic affairs in the belief that an informed dialogue can result in more rational and effective public policy." Many agree this is the "insightful and eclectic" journal to keep you informed on the latest economic policy and issues. Written in a clear, nontechnical manner, the articles are by prestigious economists and well-respected scholars, and the editorial board includes four Nobel laureates. In-depth book reviews are also included. Highly recommended for high school, public, academic, and government libraries.

1834. *Economic Development and Cultural Change.* [ISSN: 0013-0079] 1952. q. USD 393 (print & online eds.). Ed(s): John Strauss, Agnes L Brawn. University of Chicago Press, 1427 E 60th St, Chicago, IL 60637; subscriptions@press.uchicago.edu; http://www.journals.uchicago.edu. Illus., index, adv. Sample. Refereed. Vol. ends: Jul. Microform: PMC; PQC. Reprint: PSC. *Indexed:* A22, ABIn, ABS&EES, ASSIA, AbAn, Agr, B01, B02, BRI, C45, EconLit, IBSS, JEL, P02, P61, RRTA, SSA. *Bk. rev.:* 8-9, lengthy. *Aud.:* Ga, Ac, Sa.

From the University of Chicago Press comes this "multidisciplinary journal of development economics that disperses scientific evidence about policy issues related to economic development." Articles are on developing nations in regard to the social and economic forces that affect culture. Book reviews are included. Scholars and researchers in economics, sociology, political science, and geography know this journal is very important.

Economic Geography. See Geography section.

1835. *The Economic History Review: a journal of economic and social history.* [ISSN: 0013-0117] 1927. q. GBP 256. Ed(s): Stephen Broadberry, Phillipp Schofield. Wiley-Blackwell Publishing Ltd., The Atrium, Southern Gate, Chichester, PO19 8SQ, United Kingdom; customer@wiley.com; http://www.wiley.com/. Illus., index, adv. Sample. Refereed. Vol. ends: Nov. Microform: IDC; PQC. Reprint: PSC. *Indexed:* A22, ABIn, AmHI, ArtHuCI, B01, B02, BRI, BrArAb, E01, EconLit, IBSS, JEL, NumL, P02. *Bk. rev.:* 28-40, 600-1,200 words. *Aud.:* Ga, Ac, Sa.

A typical issue of *Economic History Review* contains a long essay in the "Surveys and Speculations" section that "discusses a particular problem in economic and social history in an adventurous way," five to six articles, and "Notes and Comments," as well as a plethora of signed book reviews. This journal has increased in recent years in size and scope, including social history in its coverage, so it is even more useful to researchers. This well-written, easy-to-understand journal is recommended to historians, students, and researchers alike.

1836. *The Economic Journal.* [ISSN: 0013-0133] 1891. 8x/yr. GBP 436 (print or online ed.). Wiley-Blackwell Publishing Ltd., The Atrium, Southern Gate, Chichester, PO19 8SQ, United Kingdom; customer@wiley.com; http://www.wiley.com/. Illus., index, adv. Sample. Refereed. Vol. ends: Nov. Microform: PMC; PQC. Reprint: PSC. *Indexed:* A22, ABIn, Agr, B01, B02, BAS, BRI, C45, CBRI, E01, EconLit, IBSS, JEL, P02, RRTA, RiskAb. *Bk. rev.:* 25, lengthy. *Aud.:* Ac, Sa.

This classic and frequently cited periodical continues to be a preeminent source on economic issues, both theoretical and empirical. Each issue typically contains 9–11 papers. A discussion forum, datasets, and book notes can be found on its web site. Selected papers from the annual conference of the Royal Economic Society (the journal's sponsor) and the Association of University Teachers of Economics comprise an annual issue. A recent issue has these sexier-sounding articles: "Sustaining Cooperation in Trust Games," "Equilibrium in the Jungle," and "A Theory of Clearance Sales." Highly recommended for academic, government, business, and financial libraries.

1837. *The Economic Record.* [ISSN: 0013-0249] 1925. q. GBP 232 (print or online ed.). Ed(s): Jeffrey Sheen. Wiley-Blackwell Publishing Asia, 155 Cremorne St, Richmond, VIC 3121, Australia; melbourne@wiley.com; http://www.wiley.com/. Illus., index, adv. Sample. Refereed. Vol. ends: Dec. Reprint: PSC. *Indexed:* A22, ABIn, B01, B02, BAS, BRI, E01, EconLit, IBSS, JEL, P02. *Bk. rev.:* 3-7, lengthy; signed. *Aud.:* Ac, Sa.

Published by the Economic Society of Australia (and also covering New Zealand), this is a general economics journal that provides a forum for research on the Australian economy. The articles have a very long citation half-life. This journal publishes theoretical, applied, and policy papers in all fields of economics. Six articles are typical, and book reviews are included. Recommended for economists and university libraries with international interests.

1838. *Economica.* [ISSN: 0013-0427] 1921. q. GBP 281. Wiley-Blackwell Publishing Ltd., The Atrium, Southern Gate, Chichester, PO19 8SQ, United Kingdom; customer@wiley.com; http://www.wiley.com/. Illus., index, adv. Sample. Refereed. Vol. ends: Nov. Reprint: PSC. *Indexed:* A22, ABIn, B01, B02, BAS, BRI, E01, EIP, EconLit, IBSS, JEL, P02, P61, RiskAb, SSA. *Bk. rev.:* 5-11, 275-1,800 words. *Aud.:* Ac, Sa.

A top economics journal, this is published on behalf of the London School of Economics and Political Science. This highly cited journal is international in scope and covers "all branches of economics." Some recent topics are risk aversion, educational investments, school quality, and consumption risk-sharing. In addition to the articles, the journal contains numerous book reviews and an annual author/title index. Recommended for academic libraries, professional economists, and researchers.

1839. *The Economist.* [ISSN: 0013-0613] 1843. w. 51/yr. USD 160; USD 2.74 combined subscription per issue (print & online eds.); USD 2.19 per issue. Ed(s): Daniel Franklin. The Economist Newspaper Ltd., 25 St James's St, London, SW1A 1HG, United Kingdom; intelligentlife@economist.com; http://www.economist.com. Illus., index, adv. Sample. Vol. ends: Dec. Microform: PQC. *Indexed:* A01, A06, A22, ABIn, AmHI, B01, B02, B03, BAS, BLI, BRI, BrTechI, C37, C45, CBCARef, CBRI, Chicano, F01, IndVet, MASUSE, P02, RRTA. *Bk. rev.:* 3-4, 450-500 words. *Aud.:* Ems, Hs, Ga, Ac, Sa.

One of the most read journals in the world, this magazine was founded more than 150 years ago to support free trade and is read in more than 180 countries. It is well respected and authoritative for information on "world politics, global business, finance and economics, science and technology, and the arts." It includes 16 news categories, including summaries on politics and business, short articles on world leaders, science, technology, finance and economics, surveys of countries and regions, and obituaries, etc. Well known in the back of each issue are handy economic, financial, and market indicators. A must-have for all libraries.

1840. *The Economists' Voice.* [ISSN: 1553-3832] 2004. a. EUR 246. Walter de Gruyter GmbH & Co. KG, Genthiner Str 13, Berlin, 10785, Germany; info@degruyter.com; http://www.degruyter.de. Sample. *Indexed:* A22, C&ISA, CerAb, E01, EconLit, JEL. *Aud.:* Ga, Ac, Sa.

The Economists' Voice was created in 2004 to provide a nonpartisan forum for leading economists on important issues. Articles are 600–2,000 words in length, and are accessible to the general reader. The journal publishes several columnists with varying political viewpoints and a "Features" section written by a professional economist. The journal is peer reviewed. Dialogue is encouraged, and letters to the editor are welcome. Economists, policy makers and analysts, and students of economics will be interested in this online journal. It is heartily recommended for academic and public libraries. URL: www.bepress.com/ev

Energy Economics. See Energy section.

The Energy Journal. See Energy section.

Gender and Development. See Gender Studies section.

Harvard Business Review. See Business and Finance/General section.

1841. *History of Political Economy.* [ISSN: 0018-2702] 1969. q. USD 586. Ed(s): Paul Dudenhefer, Kevin D Hoover. Duke University Press, 905 W Main St, Ste 18 B, PO Box 90660, Durham, NC 27701; subscriptions@dukeupress.edu; http://www.dukeupress.edu. Illus., index, adv. Sample. Refereed. Vol. ends: Winter. Microform: MIM; PQC. Reprint: PSC. *Indexed:* A22, ABIn, B01, B02, BAS, BRI, CCMJ, E01, EconLit, FR, IBSS, JEL, MSN, P02, P61, SSA. *Bk. rev.:* 3-7, 1-3 pages. *Aud.:* Ga, Ac, Sa.

This is the leading journal in its field, and its scholarly articles focus on topics such as the development of economic thought, the historical background behind major figures, and the interpretation of economic theories. Early political economists such as Marshall, Adam Smith, Keynes, Malthus, Ricardo, and Marx are heavily featured. Each issue usually has six or seven articles and signed book reviews. Recommended for academic libraries.

1842. *I M F Economic Review.* Former titles (until 2010): *I M F Staff Papers;* (until 1999): *International Monetary Fund. Staff Papers.* [ISSN: 2041-4161] 1950. q. USD 248. Ed(s): Pierre Olivier Gourinchas. Palgrave Macmillan Ltd., Houndmills, Basingstoke, RG21 6XS, United Kingdom; orders@palgrave.com; http://www.palgrave.com. Illus., adv. Sample. Refereed. Microform: CIS; PQC. Reprint: PSC. *Indexed:* A01, A22, ABIn, B01, B02, BAS, BLI, BRI, E01, EIP, EconLit, JEL, P02. *Aud.:* Ga, Ac, Sa.

This official research journal for the International Monetary Fund is written for a "general audience including policymakers and academics." The authors are IMF staff, primarily professional economists, and invited guests. The "Special Data" section has had an increasing presence. An example is "Core Inflation: Measurement and Statistical Issues in Choosing Among Alternative Measures," by Mick Silver. The focus on policy is illustrated by these two recent titles: "Labor Policies to Raise Employment" and "Foreign Aid Policy and Sources of Poverty: A Quantitative Framework." Starting in June 2007, this journal was to be published online with Palgrave-Macmillan. A great bargain for large public, special, and academic libraries.

Journal of Banking & Finance. See Business and Finance/Scholarly section.

Journal of Business and Economic Statistics. See Business and Finance/General section.

Journal of Business Ethics. See Business and Finance/Ethics section.

1843. *Journal of Comparative Economics.* [ISSN: 0147-5967] 1977. q. EUR 1061. Ed(s): G Roland, D M Berkowitz. Academic Press, 3251 Riverport Ln, Maryland Heights, MO 63043; JournalCustomerService-usa@elsevier.com; http://www.elsevierdirect.com/brochures/academicpress/index.html. Illus., index, adv. Sample. Refereed. Vol. ends: Dec. *Indexed:* A22, ABIn, ABS&EES, B01, BAS, BRI, E01, EconLit, IBSS, JEL, P02. *Bk. rev.:* 2-23, 500-2,000 words. *Aud.:* Ac, Sa.

This major journal is published for the Association for Comparative Economic Studies. While it is "devoted to the analysis and study of contemporary, historical, and hypothetical economic systems, primarily socialist and transition economies," it has a new orientation on the "comparison of economic effects of the various institutions of capitalism on law, politics, culture," and this will broaden its perspective. Each issue has at least eight articles, five or six lengthy signed book reviews, and an author index for each volume. Recommended for universities and large institutions with international programs.

Journal of Consumer Research. See Advertising, Marketing, and Public Relations section.

1844. *Journal of Economic Growth.* [ISSN: 1381-4338] 1996. q. Ed(s): Oded Galor. Springer New York LLC, 233 Spring St, New York, NY 10013; service-ny@springer.com; http://www.springer.com/. Adv. Refereed. Reprint: PSC. *Indexed:* A22, ABIn, Agr, B01, BAS, E01, EconLit, IBSS, JEL, RiskAb. *Aud.:* Ac, Sa.

The scope is simple: economic growth and dynamic macroeconomics. Empirical and theoretical, this journal deals with international economics, growth models, urban economics, migration, and development. It ranks very high in the widely recognized RepEc (Research Papers in Economics) and the *Journal Citation Reports.* There are prominent researchers on the editorial board, including (among others) Alberto Alesina, Philippe Aghion, Robert Barro, Paul Romer, Jagdish Bhagwati, and Paul Krugman. Highly recommended for academic and special libraries.

1845. *The Journal of Economic History.* Incorporates (1941-1950): *Tasks of Economic History.* [ISSN: 0022-0507] 1941. q. GBP 192. Ed(s): Paul W Rhode, Jean-Laurent Rosenthal. Cambridge University Press, The Edinburgh Bldg, Shaftesbury Rd, Cambridge, CB2 8RU, United Kingdom; journals@cambridge.org; http://www.cambridge.org/uk. Illus., index. Refereed. Circ: 3300. Vol. ends: Dec. Microform: MIM; PQC. Reprint: PSC. *Indexed:* A01, A06, A22, ABIn, ABS&EES, Agr, ArtHuCI, B01, B02, BAS, BRI, CBRI, Chicano, E01, EconLit, IBSS, JEL, MLA-IB, P02, RiskAb. *Bk. rev.:* 39-63, 600-1,800 words. *Aud.:* Ac, Sa.

This journal is the official publication of the Economic History Association in Great Britain. Of interest to economists and economic, social, and demographic historians, the journal has a broad coverage in terms of methodology and geography, including such topics as "money and banking, trade manufacturing, technology, transportation, industrial organization, labor, agriculture, servitude, demography, education, economic growth, and the role of government and regulation." This excellent journal will appeal to the student and the general public. Recommended for colleges, universities, and public libraries.

1846. *Journal of Economic Literature.* Formerly (until 1968): *Journal of Economic Abstracts.* [ISSN: 0022-0515] 1963. q. Free to members; Non-members, USD 455. Ed(s): Mary Kay Akerman, Roger Gordon. American Economic Association, 2014 Broadway, Ste 305, Nashville, TN 37203; http://www.vanderbilt.edu/AEA/. Illus., index, adv. Circ: 17267 Paid. Vol. ends: Dec. Microform: PQC. *Indexed:* A22, ABIn, ABS&EES, B01, B02, BRI, C45, CBRI, EconLit, IBSS, JEL, P02. *Bk. rev.:* 40, lengthy. *Aud.:* Ac, Sa.

The *Journal of Economic Literature* is received by all members of the American Economic Association (AEA) and libraries everywhere. It contains four to six research articles written by outstanding economists, numerous book reviews, and new book listings by JEL classification. *e-JEL,* the electronic edition, has the current issue hyperlinks. The December issue lists dissertations and recipients of doctoral degrees in economics conferred in U.S. and Canadian universities during the previous academic year. Highly recommended for colleges, universities, and larger public and special libraries.

1847. *Journal of Economic Theory.* [ISSN: 0022-0531] 1969. bi-m. EUR 4634. Ed(s): Christian Hellwig, Karl Shell. Academic Press, 3251 Riverport Ln, Maryland Heights, MO 63043; JournalCustomerService-usa@elsevier.com; http://www.elsevierdirect.com/brochures/academicpress/index.html. Adv. Sample. Refereed. *Indexed:* A22, ABIn, B01, CCMJ, E01, EconLit, IBSS, JEL, MSN, MathR, P02, RiskAb. *Aud.:* Ac, Sa.

This well-established, heavily-cited, core scholarly journal publishes "research on economic theory and emphasizes the theoretical analysis of economic models, including the related mathematical techniques." There are usually four to six articles followed by notes, comments, letters to the editor, announcements, a list of papers to appear in forthcoming issues, and an author index. An excellent journal for libraries that support theoretical economics. Still a must!

1848. *Journal of Economics.* Formerly (until 1986): *Zeitschrift fuer Nationaloekonomie.* [ISSN: 0931-8658] 1930. 9x/yr. EUR 1822 (print & online eds.). Ed(s): G Corneo, Dieter Boes. Springer Wien, Sachsenplatz 4-6, Vienna, 1201, Austria; journals@springer.at; http://www.springer.at. Illus., index, adv. Sample. Refereed. Circ: 1000 Paid. Microform: PQC. Reprint: PSC. *Indexed:* A22, ABIn, Agr, B01, BRI, E01, EconLit, IBSS, JEL, MathR, P02, RiskAb. *Bk. rev.:* 6-8, lengthy. *Aud.:* Ac.

Focusing on mathematical economic theory, this excellent journal has technical articles that cover mainly microeconomics and some macroeconomics. The level of difficulty is from medium to hard, in its own estimation. The typical issue has five extensive articles and six to eight lengthy book reviews. Additional supplemental issues are devoted to current issues. Authors are academic and international. For well-versed economists and readers in large academic libraries.

1849. *Journal of Environmental Economics and Management.* [ISSN: 0095-0696] 1975. 6x/yr. EUR 1898. Ed(s): C F Mason. Academic Press, 3251 Riverport Ln, Maryland Heights, MO 63043; JournalCustomerService-usa@elsevier.com; http://www.elsevierdirect.com/brochures/academicpress/index.html. Illus., adv. Refereed. *Indexed:* A01, A22, ABIn, Agr, B01, B02, C&ISA, C45, CerAb, E01, EconLit, EngInd, IBSS, JEL, P02, RRTA, S25. *Aud.:* Ac, Sa.

This is the official journal of the Association of Environmental and Resource Economists. Devoted to the worldwide coverage of theoretical and empirical research, it "concentrates on the management and/or social control of the economy in its relationship with the management and use of natural resources and the natural environment." The majority of authors are academic economists, and it includes interdisciplinary papers from fields of interest. Recommended for university and large public libraries.

The Journal of Finance. See Business and Finance/Scholarly section.

Journal of Financial and Quantitative Analysis. See Business and Finance/Scholarly section.

Journal of Financial Economics. See Business and Finance/Scholarly section.

1850. *Journal of Human Development and Capabilities.* Formerly (until 2009): *Journal of Human Development.* [ISSN: 1945-2829] 2000. q. GBP 397 (print & online eds.). Ed(s): Siddiq Osmani. Routledge, 4 Park Sq, Milton Park, Abingdon, OX14 4RN, United Kingdom; subscriptions@tandf.co.uk; http://www.tandfonline.com. Adv. Sample. Refereed. Reprint: PSC. *Indexed:* A01, A22, E01, EconLit, IBSS, JEL, P61, SSA. *Aud.:* Ac, Sa.

This refereed journal was started in 2000, and its contents reflect human development as a new school of thought in economics, and thus it is a must-purchase for academic libraries. Its scope encompasses the challenges of dealing with development and poverty eradication, including human well-being, markets, growth, social justice, and human rights. Amartya Sen is on the editorial advisory board; he won the 1998 Nobel Prize in Economics for his "contributions to welfare economics." Affiliated with the United Nations Development Programme, this journal will be gaining circulation and respect.

1851. *Journal of Institutional and Theoretical Economics.* Formerly (until 1986): *Zeitschrift fuer die Gesamte Staatswissenschaft.* [ISSN: 0932-4569] 1844. q. EUR 364 (Individuals, EUR 179). Ed(s): Yvan Lengwiler. Mohr Siebeck GmbH & Co. KG, Wilhelmstr 18, Tuebingen, 72074, Germany; info@mohr.de; http://www.mohr.de. Illus., index, adv. Refereed. Circ: 1070 Paid and controlled. Reprint: SCH. *Indexed:* A22, ABIn, B02, BAS, BRI, EconLit, IBSS, JEL. *Bk. rev.:* 10-14, 600-2,200 words. *Aud.:* Ga, Ac, Sa.

As institutional economics has grown in importance, this leading journal, with its diversity of opinions, has covered the "economics of property rights and of institutional evolution, transaction cost economics, contract theory, economic history and interdisciplinary studies." Articles and book reviews may be in English or German, but most are in English; papers have a summary in both languages. Notable are the papers from the Symposium on New Institutional Economics, presented in a single issue annually. Recommended for large public and university libraries.

Journal of Labor Economics. See Labor and Industrial Relations section.

Journal of Law and Economics. See Law section.

1852. *Journal of Money, Credit & Banking.* [ISSN: 0022-2879] 1969. 8x/yr. GBP 388 (print & online eds.). Wiley-Blackwell Publishing, Inc., 111 River St, Hoboken, NJ 07030; info@wiley.com; http://onlinelibrary.wiley.com/. Illus., index. Sample. Refereed. Vol. ends: Feb/Nov. Microform: PQC. Reprint: PSC. *Indexed:* A22, ABIn, ATI, B01, B02, BLI, BRI, E01, EconLit, IBSS, JEL, P02, RiskAb. *Bk. rev.:* 1-5, 2-4 pages. *Aud.:* Ac, Sa.

A classic, this widely read and cited journal presents "major findings in the study of monetary and fiscal policy, credit markets, money and banking, portfolio management, and related subjects." Ben Bernanke, Chairman of the Federal Reserve Board, is on the advisory board. A newer section called "Shorter Papers, Discussions, and Letters" is for quickly publishing concise new results, models, and methods. Online is a data archive for papers' empirical findings. Both JSTOR and Project Muse have archives. Recommended for policy makers, professional and academic economists, and bankers.

1853. *Journal of Political Economy.* [ISSN: 0022-3808] 1892. bi-m. USD 506 (print & online eds.). Ed(s): Philip Reny, Connie Fritsche. University of Chicago Press, 1427 E 60th St, Chicago, IL 60637; subscriptions@press.uchicago.edu; http://www.journals.uchicago.edu. Illus., index, adv. Sample. Refereed. Vol. ends: Dec. Microform: MIM; PMC; PQC. Reprint: PSC. *Indexed:* A22, ABIn, B01, B02, BAS, BLI, BRI, C45, CBRI, ERIC, EconLit, IBSS, JEL, MLA-IB, P02, P61, RRTA, SSA. *Bk. rev.:* 1-2, 2-4 pages. *Aud.:* Ac, Sa.

One of the most prestigious economic journals, the *Journal of Political Economy* publishes "analytical, interpretive, and empirical studies" in such traditional areas as monetary theory, fiscal policy, labor economics, planning and development, micro- and macroeconomics theory, international trade and finance, industrial organization, the history of economic thought, and social economics. Authors are from international academic institutions and government agencies such as the Federal Reserve Board. Each issue includes five or six articles, occasionally followed by review articles, comments, and book reviews. It would be wise for academic and larger public libraries to subscribe to this publication.

Journal of Risk and Insurance. See Business and Finance/Insurance section.

Journal of Transport Economics and Policy. See Transportation section.

1854. *Kyklos: international review for social sciences.* [ISSN: 0023-5962] 1947. q. GBP 476. Ed(s): Rene L Frey. Wiley-Blackwell Publishing Ltd., The Atrium, Southern Gate, Chichester, PO19 8SQ, United Kingdom; customer@wiley.com; http://www.wiley.com/. Illus., index, adv. Sample. Refereed. Vol. ends: Nov. Microform: PQC. Reprint: PSC. *Indexed:* A01, A22, ABIn, B01, B02, BAS, BRI, E01, EconLit, IBSS, JEL, P02. *Bk. rev.:* 15-20, 550-1,600 words. *Aud.:* Ga, Ac, Sa.

This journal is widely recognized around the world, and published by an international nonprofit organization whose main purpose is "to analyze socio-economic problems of our time and to bridge the gap between scholarship and economic policy makers by means of public conferences and publications." Authors are mostly international, and a new "Forum of Ideas" calls for short essays that show new and unconventional ideas, even if they are not fully worked out or formalized in a neat model. Each issue has about seven articles. Researchers, economists, sociologists, policy makers, and students appreciate this journal; it is also for larger public libraries.

1855. *Land Economics.* Formerly (until 1948): *The Journal of Land and Public Utility Economics.* [ISSN: 0023-7639] 1925. q. USD 290 (print & online eds.). Ed(s): Meg Hannah, Daniel W Bromley. University of Wisconsin Press, Journal Division, 1930 Monroe St, 3rd Fl, Madison, WI 53711; journals@uwpress.wisc.edu; http://www.uwpress.org. Illus., index, adv. Refereed. Vol. ends: Nov. Microform: PQC. Reprint: PSC. *Indexed:* A22, ABIn, Agr, B01, B02, BAS, BRI, C45, EconLit, IBSS, JEL, P02, RRTA, RiskAb, S25. *Bk. rev.:* 1-2, 1-6 pages. *Aud.:* Ac, Sa.

Land Economics is "dedicated to the study of land use, natural resources, public utilities, housing, and urban land issues." It is one of oldest American economic journals and was started by Richard Ely, the founder of the American Economic Association. Topics here include "transportation, energy, urban and rural land use, housing, environmental quality, public utilities, and natural resources." Highly recommended for scholars and economists in government, business, finance, and universities.

Meridians. See Gender Studies section.

1856. *National Institute Economic Review.* [ISSN: 0027-9501] 1959. q. USD 745. Ed(s): Martin Weale. Sage Publications Ltd., 1 Oliver's Yard, 55 City Rd, London, EC1Y 1SP, United Kingdom; info@sagepub.co.uk; http://www.uk.sagepub.com. Illus., index, adv. Sample. Refereed. Reprint: PSC. *Indexed:* A22, ABIn, B01, B02, BRI, E01, EconLit, IBSS, JEL, P61, RiskAb, SSA. *Aud.:* Ga, Ac, Sa.

This periodical was established in 1959 and is from one of Britain's oldest established independent economic research institutes. It covers quantitative research that illustrates a "deeper understanding of the interaction of economic and social forces that affect peoples' lives so that they may be improved." The institute receives no funding from private or public sources. There are six basic sections: "Economic Overview," "Commentary," "The UK Economy," "The World Economy," "Research Articles," and "Main Economic Events." The last is a statistical appendix that gives series information on the GDP, output volumes, prices, unemployment, imports and exports, monthly economic indicators, and financial indicators. Strongly recommended for libraries with large economics collections or those that support international studies.

National Tax Journal. See Accounting and Taxation/Taxation section.

1857. *O E C D Observer.* [ISSN: 0029-7054] 1962. q. EUR 77 combined subscription (print & online eds.); GBP 60 combined subscription (print & online eds.); USD 102 combined subscription (print & online eds.). Organisation for Economic Cooperation and Development (O E C D), 2 Rue Andre Pascal, Paris, 75775 Cedex 16, France; sales@oecd.org; http://www.oecd.org. Illus., index, adv. Circ: 25000. Vol. ends: Dec/Jan. *Indexed:* A22, ABIn, B01, B02, BRI, EIP, P02, P61, PdeR, SSA. *Bk. rev.:* 1-2. *Aud.:* Hs, Ga, Ac.

The Organisation for Economic Co-operation and Development (OECD), an international organization composed of 30 member-countries, "is a unique forum permitting governments of the industralised democracies to study and formulate the best policies possible in all economic and social spheres." In contributing to this goal, it "collects and analyses a unique body of data that allows comparison of statistics across countries and provides macro-micro economic research and policy advice in fields that mirror policy-making ministries in governments." All of this research is made available through a large publishing mechanism, and this publication is part of that mechanism. Other excellent publications include *OECD Foreign Trade Statistics, OECD Main Economic Indicators, OECD Economic Studies,* and *OECD Economic Outlook.* The *OECD Observer* is written for a popular audience. It has a wealth of information on the member countries, and it also covers transitional economies, dynamic nonmember economies, and the developing world. It has a wide scope, encompassing "economic growth, labour markets, education, social policy, demography, industry, services, energy, finance trade, fiscal policy, public-sector management, environment, science and technology, investment and multinational enterprises, transport, agriculture and fisheries, taxation, competition and consumer policy, research and development, urban affairs, telecommunications, tourism, and rural development." Every issue has an editorial, articles on a theme, and additional titles. A very useful feature is the two to six pages of current statistics on the GDP, the consumer price index, and the leading indicators. Highly recommended for high school, academic, and public libraries.

Post-Communist Economies. See Slavic Studies section.

Post-Soviet Affairs. See Slavic Studies section.

1858. *The Quarterly Journal of Economics.* [ISSN: 0033-5533] 1886. q. EUR 465. Ed(s): Robert J. Barro, Lawrence F. Katz. Oxford University Press, 2001 Evans Rd, Cary, NC 27513; jnlorders@oup-usa.org; http://www.oxfordjournals.org. Illus., index, adv. Refereed. Circ: 3000 Paid. Vol. ends: Nov. Microform: PQC. Reprint: PSC. *Indexed:* A22, ABIn, B01, B02, BAS, C45, E01, EconLit, IBSS, JEL, MathR, P02, RRTA, RiskAb, SWR&A. *Aud.:* Ac, Sa.

Founded in 1886, this is "the oldest journal of economics in the English language"; it is also the second-highest-cited of all economic journals. The traditional focus on microtheory has been "expanded to include both empirical and theoretical macroeconomics." Statistical methods and models are often used. A typical issue has 11 lengthy articles, which are sometimes controversial and always interesting. The authors are leading American economists, often affiliated with Harvard. This prestigious journal is essential for libraries that serve professionals, academic economists, and students of economics.

1859. *RAND Journal of Economics.* Former titles (until 1984): *Bell Journal of Economics;* (until 1975): *Bell Journal of Economics and Management Science.* [ISSN: 0741-6261] 1970. q. GBP 216 (print & online eds.). Ed(s): James R Hosek. Wiley-Blackwell Publishing, Inc., 111 River St, Hoboken, NJ 07030; info@wiley.com; http://www.wiley.com/. Illus., index, adv. Sample. Refereed. Vol. ends: Winter. Microform: PQC. Reprint: PSC. *Indexed:* A22, ABIn, B01, B02, BRI, C45, CompR, E01, EconLit, IBSS, JEL, MathR, RRTA. *Aud.:* Ac, Sa.

Published by the RAND Corporation, this journal supports and encourages research "in the behavior of regulated industries, the economic analysis of organizations, and applied microeconomics." Empirical and theoretical papers in law and economics are accepted. Authors are usually connected to American universities. Each issue typically contains about 13 articles; there could be symposium papers as well. Highly recommended for large academic, government, business, and public libraries.

The Review of Black Political Economy. See Labor and Industrial Relations section.

Review of Financial Studies. See Business and Finance/Scholarly section.

1860. *Review of World Economics.* Formerly (until 2003): *Weltwirtschaftliches Archiv.* [ISSN: 1610-2878] 1914. q. Ed(s): Harmen Lehment, Horst Siebert. Springer, Tiergartenstr 17, Heidelberg, 69121, Germany. Illus., index, adv. Refereed. Circ: 1800. Vol. ends: No. 4. Reprint: PSC. *Indexed:* A22, ABIn, B01, BAS, BRI, E01, EconLit, IBSS, JEL, RiskAb. *Bk. rev.:* 10-16, 700-2,100 words. *Aud.:* Ac, Sa.

Internationally renowned and affiliated with the esteemed Kiel Institute of World Economics, *Review of World Economics* focuses on the empirical. Topics include "trade and trade policies, international factor movements and international business, international finance, currency systems and exchange rates, monetary and fiscal policies in open economies, economic development, technological change and growth." Well-known scholars contribute. Each issue has six or seven articles, shorter papers, comments, reports, book reviews, and announcements of new books. An excellent choice for international economists and graduate students.

Theory and Decision. See Philosophy section.

Transitions Online. See Slavic Studies section.

1861. *The World Bank Economic Review.* [ISSN: 0258-6770] 1986. 3x/yr. EUR 272. Ed(s): Jaime de Melo. Oxford University Press, 2001 Evans Rd, Cary, NC 27513; http://www.oxfordjournals.org. Illus. Sample. Refereed. Microform: PQC. Reprint: PSC. *Indexed:* A22, ABIn, B01, BAS, C45, E01, EconLit, IBSS, JEL, P61, RiskAb. *Aud.:* Ac, Sa.

A very widely read scholarly publication, *The World Bank Economic Review* is a professional journal for the dissemination of World Bank–sponsored research on policy analysis and choice. The international readers are "economists and social scientists in government, business, international universities, and development research institutions." Policy is emphasized over theoretical or methodological issues. Readers need to be familiar with economic theory and analysis but not necessarily proficient in mathematics. Six to nine articles are written by World Bank staff and economists. There are occasionally special issues by non–World Bank specialists. Highly recommended for academic libraries and larger public libraries.

1862. *The World Bank Research Observer.* [ISSN: 0257-3032] 1986. s-a. EUR 202. Ed(s): Emmanuel Jimenez. Oxford University Press, Great Clarendon St, Oxford, OX2 6DP, United Kingdom; enquiry@oup.co.uk; http://www.oxfordjournals.org/. Illus., adv. Sample. Refereed. Microform: CIS; PQC. Reprint: PSC. *Indexed:* A22, ABIn, ABS&EES, B01, E01, EconLit, IBSS, JEL. *Aud.:* Ga, Ac, Sa.

Written for the nonspecialist, and published by the World Bank, this journal is intended for anyone who has an interest in development issues. Articles are written by well-established economists, and key issues in development economics research and policy are examined. Surveys of the latest literature and World Bank research are included. The editorial board is drawn from the international community of economists. Each issue has six to eight articles. Highly recommended for public and academic libraries.

■ EDUCATION

General, K-12/Comparative Education and International/Educational Psychology and Measurement, Special Education, Counseling/Higher Education/Homeschooling/Specific Subjects and Teaching Methods

See also Classroom Magazines; and Parenting sections.

Deborah S. Garson, Head of Research and Instruction Services, Monroe C. Gutman Library, Graduate School of Education, Harvard University, Cambridge, MA 02138.

Mark Shelton, Head of Collection Development, Monroe C. Gutman Library, Graduate School of Education, Harvard University, Cambridge, MA 02138

Introduction

As a field, education is both interdisciplinary and inclusive of teaching and learning for pre-K to older learners. Within the social sciences, education relates particularly to the fields of psychology and sociology, as the selection of titles below indicates. By virtue of the teaching and learning components of education, however, the connections to other fields are evident, and readers may wish to examine subject-specific sections of this publication. As a discipline, the field of education is grounded in the traditional research frameworks of philosophy, theory, and methodology that form the basis for applications in many types of educational settings.

The education journals represent a broad range of publications, from the academic and scholarly to those intended for practical applications in the classroom and other learning environments. Contents of journals reflect current educational trends and issues, as well as historical analyses of educational theory and practice. Current topics focus on educational reform, e-learning principles and practices, teacher and student assessment, global trends in education, international education, educational counseling, and educational technology.

Publishers are responding to current journal research needs and authors' publishing opportunities as well as their own for-profit requirements by developing electronic collections comparable to the print versions, with all the technological enhancements available to them. A wide variety of options is available for any user of journal collections, ranging from subscription-based models to freely available titles or collections. With the development of the open-access journals, there have been some innovative publishers' responses as well as institutional responses. These initiatives are reflective of the current movement to provide to a global audience open-access journals in education as well as in all disciplines.

Basic Periodicals

Ems (teachers): *The Elementary School Journal, Middle School Journal, The Reading Teacher, School Arts, Teaching K-8*; Hs (teachers): *The American*

Biology Teacher, American Secondary Education, English Journal, The High School Journal, History Teacher; Ga: *Change, The Education Digest, Phi Delta Kappan*; Ac: *Academe, American Journal of Education, The Chronicle of Higher Education, College English, Harvard Educational Review, Teachers College Record.*

Basic Abstracts and Indexes

Education Index, Resources in Education.

General, K-12

1863. *American Educational Research Journal.* [ISSN: 0002-8312] 1964. bi-m. USD 922. Ed(s): Lois Weis. Sage Publications, Inc., 2455 Teller Rd, Thousand Oaks, CA 91320; info@sagepub.com; http://www.sagepub.com. Illus., adv. Sample. Refereed. Vol. ends: Winter. Microform: PQC. Reprint: PSC. *Indexed:* A22, ABIn, Chicano, E01, ERIC, FR, HEA, PsycInfo, RILM. *Aud.:* Ac.

Within each issue, articles are published in two sections under separate editorships and editorial boards: "Social and Institutional Analysis" and "Teaching, Learning, and Human Development." This journal addresses an audience of researchers, practitioners, and policymakers from many disciplines, and its articles are lengthy and substantive, generally 20–30 or more pages long, representing the publication's stated focus on original empirical and theoretical studies and analyses in education. In the first section, the research centers on major political, cultural, social, economic, and organizational issues in education. This section is followed by articles that examine various aspects of teaching, learning, and human development in different types of educational settings. Eight or nine articles per issue provide in-depth research findings and analyses with extensive notes, tables, figures, and references. This is an essential resource for advanced undergraduates, graduate students, and academicians. URL: www.aera.net/Publications/Journals/iAmericanEducationalResearchJournali/tabid/12607/Default.aspx

1864. *American Educator.* [ISSN: 0148-432X] 1977. q. USD 10; USD 2.50 per issue. Ed(s): Lisa Hansel. American Federation of Teachers, 555 New Jersey Ave, NW, Washington, DC 20001; online@aft.org; http://www.aft.org. Illus., adv. Circ: 900000. Vol. ends: Fall. *Indexed:* A22, ABS&EES, BRI, ERIC, MLA-IB. *Bk. rev.:* 1, 2,500 words. *Aud.:* Ga, Ac.

Aimed at an audience of teachers and other school and higher-education professionals, this American Federation of Teachers publication contains a variety of articles on topics for a wide range of reader interests. There are opinion pieces on parenting and on student attitudes; practical and informational articles for applications in school settings; and discussions on the national or international school scene, covering such topics as pedagogy versus content, Finland's approach to teacher preparation, state standards, and schools with low test scores. Issues often have biographical essays and tributes to important historical figures, educators, and authors that are helpful for professional development and classroom use. Recommended for public, academic, and school libraries. URL: www.aft.org/pubs-reports/american_educator/index.htm

1865. *American Journal of Education.* Former titles (until 1979): *School Review;* (until 1893): *School and College.* [ISSN: 0195-6744] 1893. q. USD 184 (print & online eds.). Ed(s): Emily Crawford, Melanie Fedri. University of Chicago Press, 1427 E 60th St, Chicago, IL 60637; subscriptions@press.uchicago.edu; http://www.journals.uchicago.edu. Illus., index. Sample. Refereed. Vol. ends: Aug. Microform: PMC; PQC. Reprint: PSC. *Indexed:* A01, A22, BRI, CBRI, Chicano, ERIC, MLA-IB, P02, P61, PsycInfo, SSA. *Bk. rev.:* 3-5, 500 words. *Aud.:* Ga, Ac.

This journal publishes scholarly articles on educational topics meant to encourage discussion and debate among scholars and practitioners. Articles range from the methodological, philosophical, and theoretical to matters of administration and policy in the schools. Historical and current perspectives for all school settings are represented. Particularly emphasized are research reports, theoretical statements, philosophical arguments, critical syntheses, and integration of educational inquiry, policy, and practice. Articles have focused on teachability culture; in-state resident tuition policies; immigrants and American schools; youth–adult partnerships in schools; privatized school management;

and the relationship between high school graduation and the various state policies of assessment and accountability. The book reviews are lengthy, and most issues also have a review essay. This is a basic title for graduate students, faculty, and practitioners. URL: www.journals.uchicago.edu/AJE/home.html

1866. *American School Board Journal.* Incorporates (1979-1996): *Executive Educator;* (in 1928): *Modern Public Buildings.* [ISSN: 0003-0953] 1891. m. USD 47 combined subscription domestic (print & online eds.); USD 53 combined subscription Canada (print & online eds.); USD 72 combined subscription elsewhere (print & online eds.). Ed(s): Glenn Cook, Kathleen Vail. National School Boards Association, 1680 Duke St, Alexandria, VA 22314; info@nsba.org; http://www.nsba.org. Illus., index, adv. Sample. Circ: 41197 Paid. Vol. ends: Dec. Microform: PQC. *Indexed:* A01, A22, RILM. *Bk. rev.:* 1, 300-1,200 words. *Aud.:* Ga, Sa.

This journal of the American School Boards Association publishes articles on current issues in the field and topics in the news. Authored by faculty and practitioners, articles are directed at an audience of school board members and school administrators. Some topics have been student achievement; board members and time management; mentoring new administrators; and issues of homework. Regular departments include letters from readers, research findings on particular topics, school law rulings on specific cases, a new section of education news and trends, and book reviews. Special supplements for subscribers of *ASBJ* are the Magna Awards, a yearly recognition of programs for major school district initiatives nationwide, and the annual supplement, *Education Vital Signs,* which focuses on school data. Recommended for school, public, and academic libraries with an education program. URL: www.asbj.com

1867. *American Secondary Education.* [ISSN: 0003-1003] 1970. 3x/yr. USD 30 domestic; USD 40 foreign. Ed(s): James A Rycik. American Secondary Education, Ashland University, Dwight Schar College of Education Rm 231, Ashland, OH 44805; http://www.ashland.edu. Adv. Sample. Refereed. Microform: PQC. *Indexed:* A01, A22, ERIC. *Bk. rev.:* Number and length vary. *Aud.:* Ac.

This journal examines current secondary school issues for teachers, administrators, and all those involved in public and private secondary education. Written by practitioners and researchers in the field, articles focus on theories, research, and practice, with discussions on such topics as academic literacy for ESL students; experiences of Latina/o students; the impact of online discussion; ethics issues in U.S. history textbooks; special education teachers at the secondary level; implementing critical-thinking instruction; a qualitative study of magnet schools; and teaching through assessment and feedback. Most issues have a column for an opinion or commentary, and suggestions on techniques for handling student harassment in a high school setting. Book reviews are included. It is a mix of scholarly and practical articles. Recommended for school and academic libraries with an education program. URL: www1.ashland.edu/coe/about-college/american-secondary-education-journal

1868. *Childhood Education.* Incorporates (1981-1991): *A C E I Exchange.* [ISSN: 0009-4056] 1924. bi-m. GBP 107 (print & online eds.). Ed(s): Anne Watson Bauer. Routledge, 325 Chestnut St, Ste 800, Philadelphia, PA 19106; customerservice@taylorandfrancis.com; http://www.tandfonline.com. Illus., adv. Refereed. Microform: PMC; PQC. Reprint: PSC. *Indexed:* A01, A22, BRI, CBRI, ERIC, P02. *Bk. rev.:* 40-50, 75-400 words; signed. *Aud.:* Ga, Ac, Sa.

The Association for Childhood Education International's refereed journal is focused on the development and education of children from birth through early adolescence (age 13). It is geared toward an audience of teachers, teacher educators, parents, child care workers, administrators, librarians, and others with an interest in the field. The editors encourage articles on practices in the classroom and in other settings, international programs and practices, and reviews of research, and are written by authors from many countries, and a variety of different organization and institutions. Articles have covered a wide range of useful topics, including encouraging empathy, developing social skills through music, intentional mathematics teaching, and cyberbullying. Columns address issues in education, the needs of parents, and teaching strategies. This journal includes reviews of books for children, reviews and lists of professional books, special publications and reports, and discussions on technology in the classroom. Highly recommended for school, public, and academic libraries. URL: http://www.acei.org/childhood-education

1869. *The Clearing House: a journal of educational strategies, issues, and ideas.* Former titles (until 1936): *Junior-Senior High School Clearing House;* (until 1929): *The Junior High Clearing House;* (until 1928): *The Junior High School Clearing House;* (until 1923): *The Junior High Clearing House.* [ISSN: 0009-8655] 1920. bi-m. GBP 124 (print & online eds.). Routledge, 325 Chestnut St, Ste 800, Philadelphia, PA 19106; customerservice@taylorandfrancis.com; http://www.tandfonline.com. Illus., index, adv. Refereed. Reprint: PSC. *Indexed:* A01, A22, BRI, E01, ENW, ERIC, MLA-IB, P02. *Aud.:* Ac.

This peer-reviewed and well-indexed journal is geared to the interests of middle-level, junior, and high school teachers and administrators. The articles are based on research and school practices. Theoretical articles also appear. There is an emphasis on instructional techniques and leadership, school law, curriculum, gifted and talented and disability programs, education trends, and testing and measurement. Some issues have a special section with articles that focus on a special theme. Occasionally, there are articles that present opinions on current issues of concern and debate. Articles are authored by academicians, administrators, and consultants in the field. Recommended for school libraries and academic libraries with education programs. URL: www.tandfonline.com/loi/vtch20

1870. *Curriculum Review.* Former titles (until 1976): *C A S Review;* (until 1975): *C S Review.* [ISSN: 0147-2453] 1960. m. USD 169. PaperClip Communications, 125 Paterson Ave, Little Falls, NJ 07424; info@paper-clip.com; http://www.paper-clip.com. Illus., adv. Sample. Vol. ends: Sep/May. Microform: PQC. *Indexed:* A01, A22, BRI, CBRI, ERIC, MLA-IB. *Bk. rev.:* 15-25, 150-500 words. *Aud.:* Ga, Ac.

This is a practical report issued monthly during the school year. It aims to assist K–12 teachers and administrators with ideas for the classroom, stimulus fund guidelines, raising funds, tips on resources, information about successful schools and projects, and news in the area of federal education budget information. There are columns that present readers' ideas and experiences; technology updates; useful techniques that point out what's working in schools and classrooms; some highlights of education news; interviews with educators; and reviews of school web sites. A section on resources for the classroom provides an abstract of useful books for students. This is a useful publication for school libraries and libraries that serve programs in undergraduate or graduate education. URL: www.curriculumreview.com/

1871. *Early Childhood Education Journal.* Formerly (until 1995): *Day Care and Early Education.* [ISSN: 1082-3301] 1973. 6x/yr. EUR 863 (print & online eds.). Ed(s): Mary Renck Jalongo. Springer Netherlands, Van Godewijckstraat 30, Dordrecht, 3311 GX, Netherlands; http://www.springer.com. Illus., adv. Sample. Refereed. Vol. ends: Summer. Microform: PQC. Reprint: PSC. *Indexed:* A01, A22, BRI, CBRI, Chicano, E01, ERIC, P02, PsycInfo, SWR&A. *Bk. rev.:* 1-5, 50-500 words; signed. *Aud.:* Ac, Sa.

Intended for early childhood practitioners such as classroom teachers and child-care providers, this peer-reviewed publication focuses on the education and care of young children from birth through age eight. The journal publishes articles that address the issues, trends, policies, and practices of the field. Contributors have covered topics of curriculum; immigrant children; neuroscience and play; literacy education and policy; school to home literacy connections; child-care programs; administration; staff development; and child development. Highly recommended for academic libraries that serve education programs and for libraries that serve early childhood professional institutions or organizations.

1872. *Education.* [ISSN: 0013-1172] 1880. q. Ed(s): Phillip Feldman. Project Innovation, Inc., Spring Hill Sta, PO Box 8508, Mobile, AL 36689; http://www.projectinnovation.biz. Index, adv. Refereed. Microform: PMC; PQC. *Indexed:* A01, A22, BRI, Chicano, ERIC, MLA-IB, P02, P61, SSA. *Aud.:* Ac.

This journal presents a wide range of studies and theoretical papers on all areas of teaching and learning in the school and university settings. Teacher preparation is a primary area of focus for the journal as well as innovation in the school. Brief and lengthy articles cover such topics as teaching/learning patterns of educators, character education, bullying, instructional technology, parental involvement, university support for teacher professional development, strategic leadership, and class participation. Articles are included with content that address research with an international focus. Recommended for school and academic libraries. URL: www.projectinnovation.com/Education.html

1873. Education and Urban Society: an independent quarterly journal of social research. [ISSN: 0013-1245] 1968. bi-m. USD 1110. Ed(s): Charles J Russo. Corwin Press, Inc., 2455 Teller Rd, Thousand Oaks, CA 91320; info@sagepub.com; http://www.corwinpress.com. Illus., index, adv. Sample. Refereed. Vol. ends: Aug. Microform: PQC. Reprint: PSC. *Indexed:* A01, A22, ASSIA, Chicano, E01, ERIC, FR, IBSS, P02, P61, PsycInfo, RiskAb, SSA, SWR&A. *Aud.:* Ac, Sa.

This peer-reviewed journal provides a multidisciplinary forum for research articles focused on the role of education in society. The intended audience includes school board members, sociologists, educational administrators, urban anthropologists, political scientists, and other professionals in fields aligned with education. The emphasis is on current issues in the field and new ideas regarding educational practices. The relationship between society and the educator is emphasized. Topics have included such subjects as school choice, alternative certification pathways, constituent values and school policy, serving culturally and linguistically diverse students, and resources in financially distressed schools. This is an important resource for academic libraries. URL: http://eus.sagepub.com

1874. The Education Digest: essential readings condensed for quick review. [ISSN: 0013-127X] 1935. 9x/yr. USD 32 domestic; USD 42 foreign. Ed(s): Pam Moore. Prakken Publications, Inc., 832 Phoenix Dr, Ann Arbor, MI 48107. Illus., index, adv. Sample. Microform: PQC. *Indexed:* A01, A22, BRI, C37, ERIC, P02, RILM. *Bk. rev.:* 2-3, of varying length. *Aud.:* Ga, Ac.

This publication provides a condensation of current articles on the themes chosen for the individual-issue *ED* issues. It thus allows educators, students, and other interested readers an opportunity to quickly update their knowledge of particular education topics such as teacher shortages, education reform, and diversity. In addition, there are regular columns with free-ranging discussions on technology, policy, capsules of education news in Washington and elsewhere, and books/media reviews. This is a handy, pocket-sized resource that is useful for school and public libraries. URL: www.eddigest.com

1875. Education Finance and Policy. [ISSN: 1557-3060] 2005. q. USD 364 (print & online eds.). Ed(s): Dan Goldhaber, Thomas A Downes. M I T Press, 55 Hayward St, Cambridge, MA 02142; journals-cs@mit.edu; http://mitpress.mit.edu. Adv. *Indexed:* A22, E01, ERIC, EconLit. *Aud.:* Ac.

This publication is the official journal of the American Education Finance Association. It includes scholarly articles that will inform and impact research and policy in the area of education finance. Articles present theoretical, statistical, and qualitative research from many different viewpoints. Authors have addressed the issues in school choice policy; teacher layoffs; value-added modeling; national board certification and teachers' career paths; salaries of public school teachers; the field of school finance; inflation's effect on wages and school finance equity; training and labor markets; and teacher retirement decisions and pension incentives. Policy briefs have focused on current education issues such as funding special education, year-round schooling, college financial aid, and educational accountability systems. Recommended for academic and research institutions. URL: www.mitpressjournals.org/efp

1876. Education Policy Analysis Archives. [ISSN: 1068-2341] 1993. a. Free. Ed(s): Gustavo E Fischman. Arizona State University, Mary Lou Fulton Teachers College, PO Box 37100, Phoenix, AZ 85069; education@asu.edu; http://education.asu.edu. Refereed. *Indexed:* ERIC, HEA. *Aud.:* Ac.

A peer-reviewed journal that publishes articles on educational policy at all educational levels worldwide. Articles are in Spanish, Portuguese, or English. The journal will be of interest to researchers, practitioners, policymakers, and development analysts. Article abstracts appear at the beginning of each article. Issues cover topics of social pedagogy; teacher preparation; in-school feeding programs; computer skills and digital media usage by students; and social policies and educational inclusion. Highly recommended for academic libraries. URL: http://epaa.asu.edu/ojs/

1877. Education Week: American education's newspaper of record. [ISSN: 0277-4232] 1981. 37x/yr. USD 74.94 combined subscription domestic (print & online eds.); USD 135.94 combined subscription Canada (print & online eds.); USD 208.84 combined subscription elsewhere (print & online eds.). Ed(s): Karen Diegmueller, Caroline Hendrie. Editorial Projects in Education Inc., 6935 Arlington Rd, Ste 100, Bethesda, MD 20814-5233; http://www.edweek.org. Illus., index, adv. Sample. Vol. ends: Aug. *Indexed:* A01, A22, BRI, ERIC, P02. *Aud.:* Ga, Ac.

This weekly provides full coverage of state and national education news in a newspaper format. There are articles on current topics and issues in the field, information about recent education reports, profiles and interviews, and weekly commentaries. It contains letters to the editor; events listings; advertisements, including for books and curriculum products and services; and job postings. From time to time, there is an in-depth report that appears as a series. *EW* also provides several special issues, such as the yearly review of education in the 50 states, *Quality Counts*. This is essential weekly reading for graduate education students, educators, and administrators in the field. Highly recommended for school, public, and academic libraries. URL: www.edweek.org

1878. Educational Administration Quarterly: the journal of leadership for effective & equitable organizations. [ISSN: 0013-161X] 1964. 5x/yr. USD 897. Ed(s): Linda E Skrla. Corwin Press, Inc., 2455 Teller Rd, Thousand Oaks, CA 91320; info@sagepub.com; http://www.corwinpress.com. Illus., index, adv. Sample. Refereed. Vol. ends: Nov. Microform: PQC. Reprint: PSC. *Indexed:* A01, A22, E01, ERIC, FR, P02, PsycInfo. *Bk. rev.:* 0-3, essay length. *Aud.:* Ac, Sa.

The *EAQ* seeks scholarly articles that include empirical investigations, conceptual and theoretical perspectives, policy and legal analyses, reviews of research and practice, and analyses of methodology related to broad concepts of leadership and policy issues of educational organizations. The editors are especially interested in papers on educational leadership; governance and reform in colleges of education; teaching of educational administration; and the professional preparation of educational administrators. Faculty, principals, and teachers, national and international, have contributed research articles on topics such as: designing for learning social justice; rethinking instructional leadership; teaching sexual orientation; and urban school reform. The articles are lengthy, generally 20–30 pages, with extensive references, and with tables and figures. Some issues have a book review or review essay. This journal is published in cooperation with the University Council for Educational Administration and the University of Kentucky. Highly recommended for academic and school libraries. URL: http://eaq.sagepub.com

1879. Educational Assessment, Evaluation and Accountability. Formerly (until 2008): *Journal of Personnel Evaluation in Education.* [ISSN: 2150-1939] 1987. q. EUR 464 (print & online eds.). Ed(s): Lejf Moos, John MacBeath. Springer Netherlands, Van Godewijckstraat 30, Dordrecht, 3311 GX, Netherlands; http://www.springer.com. Illus., index, adv. Sample. Refereed. Vol. ends: Dec. Microform: PQC. Reprint: PSC. *Indexed:* A22, E01, ERIC, HEA. *Aud.:* Ac, Sa.

Offers discussion and analyses of current issues, programs, and research on evaluation, assessment, and accountability in education settings, both national and international. This journal encourages studies that focus on the theory, research, values, and practice of evaluation and assessment pertaining to K–12 teachers, students, administrators, support personnel, and faculty in colleges and universities. Articles have looked at high-stakes testing; standards-based performance appraisal systems; analysis of letters of reference; web sites that let students rate faculty; and selection of teacher education programs. Occasional special-themed issues are published. Occasional editorial notes are included. Recommended for academic libraries. URL: www.springer.com/education+&+language/journal/11092

1880. *Educational Evaluation & Policy Analysis.* [ISSN: 0162-3737] 1979. q. USD 377. Ed(s): Dominic Brewer, Susanna Loeb. Sage Publications, Inc., 2455 Teller Rd, Thousand Oaks, CA 91320; info@sagepub.com; http://www.sagepub.com. Illus., adv. Sample. Refereed. Vol. ends: Winter. Microform: PQC. Reprint: PSC. *Indexed:* A22, E01, ERIC, PsycInfo. *Bk. rev.:* 1-2, 500-1,200 words. *Aud.:* Ac.

This journal of the American Educational Research Association publishes theoretical and practical articles for the interest and benefit of researchers who are involved in educational evaluation, decision making, or policy analysis. In brief, the editorial instructions for submission indicate that contributions should include economic, demographic, financial, and political analyses of education policies; syntheses of policy studies, evaluation theories, and methodologies; results of important evaluation efforts; and overviews of evaluation studies. Authored by faculty, graduate students, and professionals in the field, well-referenced articles have covered such topics as the effects of NCLB on school resources and practices; incentive pay programs; effects of summer instruction; and the effects of professional development intervention on teaching practices. An important resource for academic libraries. URL: www.aera.net/Publications/Journals/iEducationalEvaluationandPolicyAnaysisi/tabid/12608/Default.aspx

1881. *The Educational Forum.* Supersedes (in 1936): *The Kadelpian Review;* Which was formerly (until 1927): *The Kadelpian Quarterly Review;* (until 1926): *Kappa Delta Pi Record.* [ISSN: 0013-1725] 1921. q. GBP 108 (print & online eds.). Ed(s): Carrie Gaffney. Routledge, 4 Park Sq, Milton Park, Abingdon, OX14 4RN, United Kingdom; subscriptions@tandf.co.uk; http://www.tandfonline.com. Illus., index, adv. Sample. Refereed. Microform: MIM; PQC. Reprint: PSC. *Indexed:* A22, BRI, CBRI, E01, ERIC, MLA-IB. *Bk. rev.:* 1-3, 700-1,600 words. *Aud.:* Ga, Ac.

This journal of the Kappa Delta Pi, International Honor Society in Education, has as its mission to provide thought-provoking scholarly essays and research on issues of importance for educational improvement. It serves as a forum for discussion by providing differing viewpoints and seeks to stimulate dialogue. The audience is education scholars, university faculty and graduate students in education, educational leaders, K–12 practitioners, and the general educational community. There are themed issues, such as "Politics of Policy in Teacher Education," with an introductory overview of the theme. Issues are generally organized into sections: editorial, research reports, essays, and book reviews. This is a valuable resource for undergraduate and graduate education libraries and K–12 schools. URL: www.kdp.org/publications/theeducationalforum/index.php

1882. *Educational Horizons.* Formerly (until 1953): *Pi Lambda Theta Journal.* [ISSN: 0013-175X] 1921. q. Free to members; Non-members, USD 29. Pi Lambda Theta, Inc., PO Box 7888, Bloomington, IN 47407; plt@pdkintl.org; http://www.pilambda.org/. Illus., index, adv. Sample. Refereed. Vol. ends: Summer. Microform: PQC. *Indexed:* A22, ERIC. *Aud.:* Ga, Ac.

This magazine aims to serve as a forum for the professional development of beginning teachers, education graduate students, and prospective teachers. The content will address education practices in support of excellent teaching. Issues generally have a primary article of focus. These articles address such topics as collaborating with parents of students with disabilities; tackling climate change in the science classroom; and networking tips to advance career goals. The magazine includes news about Pi Lambda Theta, and regular features present commentaries on topics such as classroom management, sharing teaching knowledge, the job hunt, and legal talk. There are also short commentaries by teachers explaining why they teach. This is a good mix of readable articles and columns for academic, public, and school libraries. URL: http://pilambda.org/benefits/publications/educational-horizons/

1883. *Educational Leadership.* Formed by the merger of (1928-1943): *Educational Method;* Which was formerly (1921-1928): *Journal of Educational Method;* (1935-1943): *Curriculum Journal;* Which was formerly (1930-1935): *News Bulletin.* [ISSN: 0013-1784] 1943. 8x/yr. USD 39 (Free to members). Ed(s): Marge Scherer. Association for Supervision and Curriculum Development, 1703 N Beauregard St, Alexandria, VA 22311; member@ascd.org; http://www.ascd.org. Illus., adv. Circ: 160000. Vol. ends: May. Microform: PQC. *Indexed:* A01, A22, BRI, C37, CBRI, Chicano, ERIC, MASUSE, MLA-IB, P02. *Bk. rev.:* 5, 300 words. *Aud.:* Ga, Ac, Sa.

EL's focus is on educators with leadership roles in elementary, middle, secondary, and higher education and all those with an interest in curriculum, instruction, supervision, leadership, and new trends and practices. Authored by teachers, administrators, higher education faculty, and other professionals in the field, articles and essays (generally three to six pages) are organized under such themes as the principalship; faces of poverty; technology-rich learning; the common core; and teacher evaluation. Departments include a section on perspectives written by the editor, a research feature that provides an article/commentary, book reviews, letters to the editor, a principal's column, and descriptions of useful web sites. Each issue contains a wide selection of illustrated and referenced articles, and advertisements of interest to teachers and administrators. This is an important resource for academic, public, and school libraries. URL: www.ascd.org/publications/educational-leadership.aspx

1884. *Educational Researcher.* [ISSN: 0013-189X] 1972. 9x/yr. USD 493. Ed(s): Steven R Yussen. Sage Publications, Inc., 2455 Teller Rd, Thousand Oaks, CA 91320; info@sagepub.com; http://www.sagepub.com. Illus., index, adv. Sample. Refereed. Vol. ends: Dec. Microform: PQC. Reprint: PSC. *Indexed:* A22, E01, ERIC, HEA, MLA-IB, PsycInfo. *Bk. rev.:* 1-3, 1,000 words. *Aud.:* Ac.

This American Educational Research Association (AERA) journal publishes scholarly articles of significance to educational researchers from many disciplines. The features section contains articles that may report, analyze, or synthesize research inquiries or explore developments of importance to the field of research in education. The journal consists of featured research articles, research reviews or essays, and briefs. Commentaries are found in the public forum section or the letters section. Responses to articles within an issue may appear, offering a dialogue that highlights divergent approaches and interpretations. Book reviews are included in most issues, as well as some reviews of multimedia, web sites, etc. This title provides AERA news, with annual meeting highlights, council minutes, and meeting events. Contains advertisements for job openings. An important journal for graduate education students, faculty, and researchers in the field. URL: www.aera.net/Publications/Journals/iEducationalResearcheri/tabid/12609/Default.aspx

1885. *Educational Studies.* [ISSN: 0013-1946] 1970. bi-m. GBP 352 (print & online eds.). Ed(s): Rebecca A Martusewicz, Pamela K Smith. Routledge, 325 Chestnut St, Ste 800, Philadelphia, PA 19106; customerservice@taylorandfrancis.com; http://www.tandfonline.com. Illus., index. Sample. Refereed. Microform: PQC. Reprint: PSC. *Indexed:* A01, A22, ABS&EES, BRI, CBRI, E01, ERIC, MLA-IB, P61, PsycInfo, SSA. *Bk. rev.:* 2-3 per issue, 2,000 words. *Aud.:* Ac.

Educational Studies has expanded its traditional book review format to include academic articles that focus on the interdisciplinary field of educational foundations as well as media reviews, essay reviews, and poetry that address pedagogical issues in the social foundations classroom. Articles may focus on teaching within this field, analyze research methodologies, or report on significant findings. Articles have discussed qualitative research in education; images of people in textbooks; community building in social justice work; and the socialist revolution. The time-exposure section provides a glimpse of a historically interesting image, illustration, or publication. There are also special theme issues. A valuable journal for undergraduate and graduate education students and faculty. URL: www.educationalstudies.org/publications.html

1886. *Educational Theory: a medium of expression.* [ISSN: 0013-2004] 1951. q. GBP 186. Ed(s): Nicholas C Burbules. Wiley-Blackwell Publishing, Inc., 111 River St, Hoboken, NJ 07030; info@wiley.com; http://onlinelibrary.wiley.com/. Illus., index, adv. Refereed. Circ: 1455 Paid. Vol. ends: Fall. Microform: PQC. Reprint: PSC. *Indexed:* A01, A22, BRI, CBRI, E01, ERIC, IPB, MLA-IB. *Bk. rev.:* 1-2, essay length. *Aud.:* Ac.

Founded by the John Dewey Society and the Philosophy of Education Society, this journal fosters ongoing development of educational theory and discussion of theoretical problems in the education profession. *ET* seeks scholarly articles and studies on the educational foundations of education and related disciplines that contribute to the advancement of educational theory. Issues may present articles on a single theme, or there may be a collection of articles on a variety of topics. Special symposium issues have guest editors who focus on the special topic. Recommended for academic libraries. URL: http://onlinelibrary.wiley.com/journal/10.1111/(ISSN)1741-5446

1887. *The Elementary School Journal.* Former titles (until 1914): *The Elementary School Teacher;* (until 1902): *The Elementary School Teacher and Course of Study;* (until 1901): *The Course of Study.* [ISSN: 0013-5984] 1900. q. USD 226 (print & online eds.). Ed(s): Russell Gersten, Greg Scherban. University of Chicago Press, 1427 E 60th St, Chicago, IL 60637; subscriptions@press.uchicago.edu; http://www.journals.uchicago.edu. Illus., index, adv. Sample. Refereed. Microform: PMC; PQC. Reprint: PSC. *Indexed:* A01, A22, Chicano, ERIC, MLA-IB, P02, PsycInfo. *Aud.:* Ac.

The *ESJ* seeks original studies that provide data about school and classroom processes in elementary or middle schools, as well as articles that focus on educational theory and research and the implications for teaching. Articles that relate research in child development, cognitive psychology, and sociology to school learning and teaching are also included. This publication is directed toward an audience of researchers, teacher educators, and practitioners. Articles with references, data, and tables have covered a wide range of topics, such as common mathematics standards in the United States; enhancing the intensity of vocabulary instruction; and teachers' use of scientifically based instruction. A major title for academic and school libraries. URL: www.press.uchicago.edu/ucp/journals/journal/esj.html

Gender and Education. See Gender Studies section.

1888. *Harvard Educational Review.* Formerly (until 1937): *The Harvard Teachers Record.* [ISSN: 0017-8055] 1931. q. USD 217 (Individuals, USD 59). Harvard University, Graduate School of Education, 8 Story St, 1st Fl, Cambridge, MA 02138; http://www.gse.harvard.edu. Illus., index. Refereed. Vol. ends: Nov. Microform: PQC. *Indexed:* A01, A22, BAS, BRI, CBRI, Chicano, ERIC, FR, MLA-IB, P02, P61, PsycInfo, SSA, SWR&A. *Bk. rev.:* Number and length vary. *Aud.:* Ac.

HER, a journal of opinion and research, seeks articles on teaching and practice in the United States and international educational settings. Articles and other contributions are authored by teachers, practitioners, policymakers, scholars, and researchers in education and related fields. Authors have focused on such topics as the Obama Administration and education; urban schools; No Child Left Behind; educating immigrant children; women of color in STEM; teacher unions and state testing scores; and methods for ethnographic research. Contains book reviews of recent publications. *HER* is published by an editorial board of doctoral students at the Harvard Graduate School of Education. Highly recommended for academic libraries. URL: www.hepg.org/main/her/Index.html

1889. *The High School Journal.* Formerly (until 1918): *The North Carolina High School. Bulletin.* [ISSN: 0018-1498] 1910. bi-m. USD 66. Ed(s): Scott Morrison. University of North Carolina Press, 116 S Boundary St, Chapel Hill, NC 27514; uncpress@unc.edu; http://www.uncpress.unc.edu. Illus., index, adv. Sample. Refereed. Circ: 900. Vol. ends: Apr/May. Microform: PQC. *Indexed:* A01, A22, BRI, E01, ERIC, PsycInfo. *Bk. rev.:* 1, 500 words. *Aud.:* Ac.

Managed by the students and faculty at the School of Education at the University of North Carolina at Chapel Hill, this journal seeks reflective articles that examine the field of secondary education and report on research, informed opinions, and, occasionally, successful practices. Special issues have focused on particular topics, such as high schools in the twenty-first century and the use of narratives for teaching. Other issues contain a collection of topics of interest for teacher educators and other professionals and individuals interested in adolescent growth and development and secondary schools. Authors have researched implementing schoolwide positive behavior support; creating a college culture in urban high schools; perspectives about academic reading; student learning, engagement, and movitation in the high school biology lab. Recommended for school and academic libraries that serve education programs. URL: http://uncpress.unc.edu/

1890. *History of Education Quarterly.* Formerly (until 1961): *History of Education Journal.* [ISSN: 0018-2680] 1949. q. GBP 114 (print & online eds.). Ed(s): James D Anderson. Wiley-Blackwell Publishing, Inc., Commerce Pl, 350 Main St, Malden, MA 02148; info@wiley.com; http://onlinelibrary.wiley.com/. Illus., index, adv. Sample. Refereed. Vol. ends: Winter. Reprint: PSC. *Indexed:* A01, A22, BAS, E01, ERIC, MLA-IB, P02. *Bk. rev.:* 5-10, 500 words. *Aud.:* Ac.

This publication of the international and scholarly History of Education Society covers topics that span the history of education, both formal and nonformal, including the history of childhood, youth, and the family. The articles are universal in scope and greatly vary in content and time period. There are two or three lengthy articles per issue, in addition to a historiographical essay. Research topics have included oral histories of education; narrative history and theory; charity education in the eighteenth century; race and gender in higher education, 1940–55; social history of the school principal; American women's higher education from 1945 to 1965; Asian Americans in the history of education; a study of Amherst College from 1850 to 1880; national identity in mid-Victorian Wales; and religious schooling in America. Offers an average of ten book reviews per issue. This is a major journal for education historians. Recommended for academic libraries. URL: http://ojs.ed.uiuc.edu/index.php/heq

1891. *Independent School.* Former titles (until 1976): *Independent School Bulletin;* (until 1941): *Secondary Education Board. Bulletin.* [ISSN: 0145-9635] 1935. q. Members, USD 32; Non-members, USD 54. Ed(s): Michael Brosnan. National Association of Independent Schools, 1620 L St, NW, Ste 1100, Washington, DC 20036; info@nais.org; http://www.nais.org. Adv. Microform: PQC. *Indexed:* A01, A22, ERIC, MLA-IB. *Bk. rev.:* 2. *Aud.:* Ac, Sa.

IS is published to provide an open forum for the exchange of general information about elementary and secondary education and to focus particularly on independent schools. Each issue has a theme, and recent themes include safe school; leading from the middle; experiential learning; and elementary education in complex times. Issues feature news and research articles that report on such topics as humane education; developing a professional culture in school; what we teach; school culture and climate; athletics and education; the public purpose of private schools; and sexuality education. Contains interviews, profiles, opinion pieces, and a narrative section about books. Each issue includes an insert of *The Reporter,* the independent school newsletter of the National Association of Independent Schools. Recommended for academic, public, and school libraries. URL: www.nais.org/Articles/Pages/Independent-School-Magazine.aspx

1892. *Instructor (New York).* Formed by the merger of (1996-1999): *Instructor: Primary Edition;* (1996-1999): *Instructor: Intermediate Edition;* Both of which superseded in part (1981-1996): *Instructor;* Which was formerly (until 1989): *Instructor and Teacher;* (until 1989): *Instructor;* (until 1986): *Instructor and Teacher;* Which was formed by the merger of (1931-1981): *Instructor;* (1972-1981): *Teacher;* Which was formerly: *Grade Teacher.* [ISSN: 1532-0200] 1981. bi-m. 8/yr. USD 8. Ed(s): Mark Bregman. Scholastic Inc., 557 Broadway, 3rd Fl, New York, NY 10012; custserv@scholastic.com; http://www.scholastic.com. Illus., index, adv. Sample. Circ: 525000. *Indexed:* A01, A22, B02, BRI, C37, CBRI, ERIC, P02. *Bk. rev.:* 10, 50-100 words. *Aud.:* Ga.

This resource for elementary and middle school teachers includes helpful articles with information for professional development, as well as tips, strategies, lesson plans, and activities for use in the classrooms. A section on ready-to-use material includes a poster, reproducible activities, theme units, and a variety of aids for classroom projects. Issues have featured math software, heroes of history, summer reading lists, end-of-the-year activities, and a teacher's technology guide with information about software, hardware, and multimedia reference tools. They have also featured articles and strategies for teaching science. Issues are packed with advertisements for all types of products for classroom use. Recommended for school libraries and academic libraries that serve education programs. URL: http://teacher.scholastic.com/products/instructor

1893. *Journal of Classroom Interaction.* Formerly (until 1976): *Classroom Interaction Newsletter.* [ISSN: 0749-4025] 1965. s-a. USD 49.50 (Individuals, USD 40). Ed(s): Dr. H Jerome Freiberg. Journal of

Classroom Interaction, c/o H Jerome Freiberg, College of Education, University of Houston, Houston, TX 77204. Illus., index. Sample. Refereed. Vol. ends: Winter. Microform: PQC. *Indexed:* A22, ERIC, P02, PsycInfo. *Aud.:* Ac.

This semi-annual journal publishes articles on empirical research and theory that deal with observation techniques, student and teacher behavior, and other issues connected with classroom interaction. Geared for an audience of faculty, practitioners, and graduate education students, this journal has presented a range of investigations and studies authored by national and international researchers and teacher educators. Each issue contains three articles. Topics have included addressing the social and academic behavior of students with emotional and disability issues; embracing cooperative learning practices; and the validity and reliability of tests. Themed issues have focused on mathematics in elementary and secondary-school classrooms and democratic classroom practices. Recommended for academic and school libraries. URL: www.jciuh.org/

1894. *Journal of Education.* Formerly (until 1881): *New England Journal of Education;* Which was formed by the merger of (1848-1875): *The Massachusetts Teacher;* (1855-1875): *The R I Schoolmaster;* (18??-1875): *College Courant;* (1871-1875): *The Connecticut School Journal;* Which was formerly (1838-1853): *Connecticut Common School Journal.* [ISSN: 0022-0574] 1875. 3x/yr. USD 45 (Individuals, USD 35; USD 15 per issue domestic). Ed(s): Lynne Larson, Roselmina Indrisano. Boston University, School of Education, Two Silber Way, Boston, MA 02215; bused@bu.edu; http://www.bu.edu/sed. Illus. Refereed. Vol. ends: Fall. Microform: PQC. *Indexed:* A01, A22, BRI, CBRI, ERIC, MLA-IB, P02. *Bk. rev.:* 1, essay length. *Aud.:* Ac.

The journal was established in 1875, and follows a historic tradition of addressing policies and practices in the field. It has a focus on research, scholarship, reflection, and analysis for an audience of scholars and practitioners. Its editorial board seeks to publish a wide range of topics; and each issue addresses an important theme or topic. Recent issues have highlighted collaborative learning, graphic novels, fostering social and cultural capital in urban youth, and math coaching in rural schools. The journal invites readership suggestions for potential subjects relevant to the field of education. URL: www.bu.edu/journalofeducation/

1895. *The Journal of Educational Research.* [ISSN: 0022-0671] 1920. bi-m. GBP 192 (print & online eds.). Routledge, 325 Chestnut St, Ste 800, Philadelphia, PA 19106; customerservice@taylorandfrancis.com; http://www.tandfonline.com. Illus., index, adv. Refereed. Microform: PMC. Reprint: PSC. *Indexed:* A01, A22, ABIn, BAS, BRI, Chicano, E01, ERIC, FR, HEA, MLA-IB, PsycInfo. *Bk. rev.:* 2 per issue, 1,000-1,200 words. *Aud.:* Ac.

JER publishes research articles that are expressly relevant to educational practice in elementary and secondary schools. Targeting teachers, counselors, supervisors, administrators, curriculum planners, and educational researchers, the journal looks at cutting-edge theories and practices. Articles by national and international faculty have provided studies on seeking peer support; the academic benefits of Advanced Placement programs; the impact of fonts on education; and supporting instructional improvement in low-performing schools. This title contains five or six well-illustrated and referenced articles per issue. A valuable resource for academic and school libraries. URL: www.tandfonline.com/toc/vjer20/current

1896. *Journal of Thought.* [ISSN: 0022-5231] 1966. q. USD 100 (Individuals, USD 50). Ed(s): Douglas J Simpson. Caddo Gap Press, 3145 Geary Blvd, PMB 275, San Francisco, CA 94118; info@caddogap.com; http://www.caddogap.com. Illus., index. Refereed. Vol. ends: Winter. Microform: PQC. *Indexed:* A22, BRI, P02. *Bk. rev.:* 1 per issue, essay format. *Aud.:* Ac.

This journal reflectively and philosophically examines worldwide educational issues and problems from the perspectives of many different disciplines. It welcomes the work of scholars that represent a variety of methodologies, approaches, cultures, and nationalities. Essays that offer analyses and critiques of arguments or that report on significant research of interest to the field are encouraged. The articles are written by and directed at an audience of faculty in higher education institutions and practitioners. Issues may explore a variety of

topics or offer a common thematic thread, such as the achievement gap. Each issue contains an essay introduction by the editor. Recommended for academic libraries. URL: www.journalofthought.com/

1897. *Kappa Delta Pi Record.* Supersedes in part (in 1964): *The Educational Forum;* Which superseded (in 1936): *Kadelpian Review;* Which was formerly (until 1927): *The Kadelpian Quarterly Review;* (until 1926): *Kappa Delta Pi Record.* [ISSN: 0022-8958] q. GBP 65 (print & online eds.). Ed(s): Kathie-Jo Arnoff. Routledge, 711 3rd Ave, 8th Fl., New York, NY 10017; customerservice@taylorandfrancis.com; http://www.tandfonline.com. Illus. Refereed. Circ: 25000. Reprint: PSC. *Indexed:* A22, ERIC, P02. *Bk. rev.:* Number and length vary. *Aud.:* Ac.

This publication of the Kappa Delta Pi International Honor Society in Education offers articles on current issues, classroom practices, and general educational concerns about teaching and learning. The research articles will be of interest to national and international educator professionals who work at all levels and fields related to education. Articles are authored by faculty, teachers, administrators, parents, and others involved in the schools. Themed issues have featured articles on middle and high school topics such as flexible schedules and specific teacher preparation programs. Non-themed issues have offered articles on pre-service teaching; education reform efforts; tips for publishing research findings; and the classroom environment. Includes information about Kappa Delta Pi, letters to the editor, opinion pieces, a section on programs in practice, curriculum, and book reviews. Recommended for school and academic libraries. URL: www.kdp.org/publications/kdprecord/index.php

1898. *Middle School Journal.* Formerly: *Midwest Middle School Journal.* [ISSN: 0094-0771] 1970. 5x/yr. Free to members. Ed(s): David Virtue. National Middle School Association, 4151 Executive Pky, Ste 300, Westerville, OH 43081; info@nmsa.org; http://www.nmsa.org. Illus., index, adv. Sample. Refereed. Vol. ends: May. *Indexed:* A22, ERIC. *Bk. rev.:* 1-4, 500-1,800 words. *Aud.:* Ga, Ac.

The articles in this official journal of the National Middle School Association are focused on middle-level education and the educational and developmental needs of youngsters aged 10–15. Written by teacher educators and professionals in the field and directed at an audience of practitioners, articles report on successful programs or discuss effective practices and research applications, and there are reflective essays. Issues may be thematic or of general interest to the readership. Coverage of topics has included the common core in the middle grades, middle-level teacher education and professional development, purposeful learning opportunities for students, and enhancing literacies. Discussions have centered on advisory sessions for urban young adolescents; interdisciplinary team training for middle grades teachers; aggressive students; national board certification; and equity in mathematics classrooms. Departments include an editorial and a section on "What Research Says." Recommended for school libraries and academic libraries that serve education programs. URL: www.amle.org/Publications/MiddleSchoolJournal/tabid/435/Default.aspx

1899. *Mind, Brain, and Education.* [ISSN: 1751-2271] 2007. q. GBP 231 (print & online eds.). Ed(s): Kurt W. Fischer, David B Daniel. Wiley-Blackwell Publishing, Inc., 111 River St, Hoboken, NJ 07030; info@wiley.com; http://onlinelibrary.wiley.com/. Adv. Sample. Refereed. Reprint: PSC. *Indexed:* A22, E01, ERIC, PsycInfo. *Aud.:* Ac.

The International Mind, Brain, and Education Society created this interdisciplinary, peer-reviewed journal that combines education, biology, and cognitive science to introduce the new field of mind, brain, and education. Research and practice in the area of mind, brain, and education are meant to contribute to the synergy between scientific research and educators' practical knowledge. The journal includes a section on the teaching brain that presents articles on how the brain affects the teaching process. This journal targets an audience comprising educators, school personnel, teacher educators, educational policy professionals, and researchers in general, who wish to explore careful, high-quality research and practice-based evaluation relevant to education. Highly recommended for academic and research institutions. URL: http://onlinelibrary.wiley.com/journal/10.1111/(ISSN)1751-228X

1900. *Momentum (Washington).* Supersedes in part (in 1970): *N C E A Bulletin.* [ISSN: 0026-914X] 19??. q. USD 20 domestic; USD 25 in Canada & Mexico; USD 30 elsewhere. National Catholic Educational Association, 1005 N Glebe Rd, Ste 525, Arlington, VA 22201; nceaadmin@ncea.org; http://www.ncea.org. Illus., adv. Microform: PQC. *Indexed:* A22, C26, Chicano, P02. *Bk. rev.:* 3-6, 400-600 words. *Aud.:* Sa.

Geared to Catholic educators and parents, this journal offers news and articles pertinent to current issues in education, with a particular focus on Catholic schools. Each issue includes feature articles written by Catholic educators. A special section presents articles on such topics as leadership and professional development, sports and spirituality, promoting civil discourse, social justice, the learning process, Catholic identity, the vocation of Catholic education, and Catholic education and public policy. Written by teachers, administrators, clergy, and professionals in the field, the articles provide practical news and information about school programs and practices for K–12 schools. Recommended for parochial school libraries and academic libraries that serve education programs. URL: www.ncea.org/publications/momentum

1901. *Multicultural Perspectives.* [ISSN: 1521-0960] 1999. q. GBP 282 (print & online eds.). Ed(s): Penelope L Lisi. Routledge, 325 Chestnut St, Ste 800, Philadelphia, PA 19106; customerservice@taylorandfrancis.com; http://www.tandfonline.com. Illus., adv. Sample. Reprint: PSC. *Indexed:* A01, A22, E01, ERIC. *Bk. rev.:* Number and length vary. *Aud.:* Ac.

This official journal of the National Association for Multicultural Education is geared to an audience of K–12 educators, social scientists, social service personnel, and teacher educators, and all those involved in multicultural education. Articles are written primarily by college and university faculty, and have focused on American Indian females and their stereotypes; teaching for social justice; culturally relevant pedagogy; ideologies of religion and diversity; and rethinking safe schools. Includes reviews of books and other media. Each issue includes feature articles, reviews, program descriptions, and other pieces by and for multicultural educators and activists around the world. Highly recommended for school and academic libraries. URL: http://nameorg.org/publications/

1902. *N A S S P Bulletin.* Formerly (until 1972): *National Association of Secondary School Principals. Bulletin.* [ISSN: 0192-6365] 1916. q. USD 356. Ed(s): Pamela Salazar. Sage Publications, Inc., 2455 Teller Rd, Thousand Oaks, CA 91320; info@sagepub.com; http://www.sagepub.com. Illus. Refereed. Vol. ends: Dec. Microform: PQC. Reprint: PSC. *Indexed:* A01, A22, BRI, CBRI, E01, ERIC, P02, RILM. *Aud.:* Ac.

This publication of the National Association of Secondary School Principals supports the decision-making and practices of middle-level and high school principals. Its articles address current issues and emphasize effective administration and leadership. Issues contain research and scholarly articles authored by faculty and professionals in the field. These articles are of enduring interest to educators as they help promote student learning and achievement, provide insight for strategic planning and decision-making in schools, and provide contemporary perspectives on educational reform and policies. Articles have explored such issues as evaluation and supervision of co-teaching; the relationship between student engagement and cognitive rigor; leadership via an oriented compass model; development and implementation of a teacher performance incentive initiative; and secondary school administrators' attitudes toward confidentiality in school counseling. Highly recommended for school and academic libraries that serve education programs. URL: http://bul.sagepub.com/

1903. *N A S S P Leadership for Student Activities.* Former titles (until 1988): *Student Activities;* (until 1983): *Student Advocate.* [ISSN: 1040-5399] 1974. m. Free to members. National Association of Secondary School Principals, 1904 Association Dr, Reston, VA 20191; publications2@principals.org; http://www.principals.org. *Indexed:* A22, P02. *Aud.:* Ac.

This publication of the National Association of Secondary School Principals Department of Student Activities is geared for student activities advisers and student leaders. Articles that are written by teachers, student council advisers, guidance counselors, and educational consultants offer practical information about successful programs for developing student leadership. Articles have discussed programs for the student council; a specific high school leadership conference; local area organizations that teach leadership; how to identify and develop leaders; and student profiles. Issues include leader resources, middle-level activities, projects, national news, scholarships and awards, information about school honor societies, and an exchange of information about activities. Recommended for school libraries. URL: www.njhs.us/Leadership-for-Student-Activities-Magazine

1904. *NewsLeader.* Former titles (until 1999): *N A S S P Newsleader;* (until 1981): *N A S S P Newsletter.* 1971. m. Sep.-May. Free to members. Ed(s): Sarah Mckibben. National Association of Secondary School Principals, 1904 Association Dr, Reston, VA 20191; publications2@principals.org; http://www.principals.org. Illus., index. Vol. ends: May. *Aud.:* Ac.

In a newspaper format, this publication provides articles on current issues, news, and events for an audience of school leaders in middle-level and high school education. It also includes coverage of the National Association of Secondary School Principals (NASSP) conferences, awards, organizational events, speeches, and elections, and available professional opportunities, as well as and NASSP activities to influence federal education policy. This is an important resource for secondary school principals, as is the NASSP web site, which provides timely complementary information.

1905. *Peabody Journal of Education.* Formerly (until 1970?): *Peabody Journal of Education.* [ISSN: 0161-956X] 1923. 5x/yr. GBP 465 (print & online eds.). Ed(s): Robert Crowson. Routledge, 325 Chestnut St, Ste 800, Philadelphia, PA 19106; customerservice@taylorandfrancis.com; http://www.tandfonline.com. Illus., adv. Sample. Refereed. Vol. ends: Summer. Reprint: PSC. *Indexed:* A01, A22, BAS, Chicano, E01, ERIC, MLA-IB, P61, PsycInfo, SSA. *Aud.:* Ga, Ac.

PJE seeks to enhance the understanding and practice among institutions and individuals concerned with human learning and development. Articles are focused primarily on educational research, practice, and policy. The journal is one of America's oldest educational publications. Issues focus on themes with contributed articles by practitioners, academicians, policymakers, and researchers and scholars in the social sciences. The intended audience is similarly broad and diverse. Topics explored include contesting equity in the twenty-first century; state-level education policy; centralization of American education policy; and school leadership and change in East Asia. Lengthy and well-referenced articles offer in-depth examination of the selected themes. An important journal for academic libraries. URL: http://peabody.vanderbilt.edu/faculty/pje/

1906. *Phi Delta Kappan.* Formerly (until 1916): *National News Letter of Phi Delta Kappa;* Which Superseded (in 1915): *Phi Delta Kappa Inter-Chapter News Letter.* [ISSN: 0031-7217] 1915. 8x/yr. USD 75 (Individuals, USD 68; Students, USD 34). Ed(s): Joan Richardson, David M. Ruetschlin. Phi Delta Kappa International, 408 N Union St, Bloomington, IN 47405; customerservice@pdkintl.org; http://www.pdkintl.org. Illus., index, adv. Vol. ends: Sep/Jun. Microform: CIS; PQC. *Indexed:* A01, A22, ABS&EES, BRI, C37, CBRI, Chicano, ERIC, MLA-IB, P02. *Aud.:* Ga, Ac.

PDK publishes articles on education research and leadership, with an emphasis on classroom practice, policy, research, professional issues, and innovations in education. Authored by faculty, practitioners, independent researchers, and consultants in the field, articles report on research or provide commentary on topics of concern and interest for educators at all levels. Articles have focused on reform before NCLB; leading by learning; principals as solo performers; the effective and reflective principal; and the common core. A section titled "Backtalk" provides an opportunity for readers to submit comments on *PDK* articles. There are regular columnists who contribute to the magazine. News from Phi Delta Kappa is also included. This is an important resource for educators. URL: www.kappanmagazine.org/

1907. *Principal (Alexandria).* Formerly (until Sep.1980): *National Elementary Principal.* [ISSN: 0271-6062] 1921. 5x/yr. Free to members. Ed(s): Vanessa St Gerard. National Association of Elementary School Principals, 1615 Duke St, Alexandria, VA 22314; naesp@naesp.org; http://www.naesp.org. Illus., index, adv. Circ: 28000. Vol. ends: May. Microform: PQC. *Indexed:* A22, Chicano, ERIC. *Bk. rev.:* 2 per issues; 350 words. *Aud.:* Ac.

This journal is published to serve elementary and middle school principals and educators. Articles are written by teachers, principals, administrators, and other professionals to address current issues and to present ideas and information for practical applications in the schools. Regular columns include feature articles and commentaries for practitioners, parents and schools, ten to teen, the reflective principal, and school law issues. Books of interest to principals are reviewed. Articles have discussed crossing language barriers; transitioning from teacher to principal; assessing progress toward college and career readiness; and time management. Issues may also have a theme, such as teacher and staff development; the achievement gap; mathematics instruction; and the Common Core. Recommended for school and academic libraries that serve education programs. URL: www.naesp.org/publications-0

1908. Principal Leadership. Formed by the merger of (2000-2009): *Principal Leadership (High School Edition);* Which was formerly (until 2000): *The High School Magazine;* (2000-2009): *Principal leadership (Middle Level Edition);* Which was formerly (until 2000): *Schools in the Middle;* The High School Magazine and Schools in the Middle superseded in part (1964-1999): *Curriculum Report.* [ISSN: 2156-2113] 2000. m. Free to members. National Association of Secondary School Principals, 1904 Association Dr, Reston, VA 20191; publications2@principals.org; http://www.principals.org. *Indexed:* BRI, CBRI. *Aud.:* Ac.

This title replaces two former NASSP publications, *Schools in the Middle* and *The High School Magazine.* The stated focus is supporting school leaders' real needs, offering them practical, hands-on strategies for improving their schools in a constantly evolving educational environment. Issues have provided articles, authored by practitioners and professionals in the field, that address breakthrough schools; equity and access; teacher evaluations; and knowledge sharing. Regular columns include a discussion of a legal problem; a focus on digital issues; support for instructional leaders; a student services column; and a bit of humor. Nonetheless, this is a title recommended for school and academic libraries that serve education programs. URL: www.nassp.org/knowledge-center/publications/principal-leadership

1909. Radical Teacher: a socialist and feminist journal on the theory and practice of teaching. [ISSN: 0191-4847] 1975. 3x/yr. USD 83 (print & online eds.). University of Illinois Press, 1325 S Oak St, Champaign, IL 61820; journals@uillinois.edu; http://www.press.uillinois.edu. Illus., adv. Refereed. Vol. ends: Winter. *Indexed:* A01, A22, BRI, C42, E01, MLA-IB. *Bk. rev.:* 1-2, 1,000-2,000 words. *Aud.:* Ac, Sa.

This journal presents articles written by and for educational workers at all education levels in a variety of institutional settings. Since 1975, the journal has provided a forum for the exploration and discussion of critical teaching practice, the political economy of education, and institutional struggles. Some issues have emphasized particular themes such as teaching with technology; teaching in carceral institutions; and studying and teaching in the corporate university. Several regular columns are reviews of books for professional reading, current education news, and teaching notes. Recommended for school and academic libraries that serve education programs. URL: www.radicalteacher.org

1910. Review of Educational Research. [ISSN: 0034-6543] 1931. q. USD 461. Ed(s): Gaea Leinhardt. Sage Publications, Inc., 2455 Teller Rd, Thousand Oaks, CA 91320; info@sagepub.com; http://www.sagepub.com. Illus., index, adv. Refereed. Vol. ends: Winter. Microform: PMC; PQC. Reprint: PSC. *Indexed:* A01, A22, Chicano, E01, ERIC, FR, HEA, LT&LA, MLA-IB, P02, PsycInfo. *Aud.:* Ac.

RER publishes critical reviews and interpretations of educational research literature on substantive and methodological issues. The reviews of research relevant to education may be from any discipline. Authored by faculty, doctoral students, and professionals in the field, well-referenced articles have reviewed employees' involvement in work-related learning; reading interventions for students with reading disabilities; assessment feedback in higher education; and the effects of school racial composition on K–12 mathematics outcomes. Four to five articles per issue offer thought-provoking reviews and analyses for the American Educational Research Association (AERA) members and readers of this AERA publication. Highly recommended for academic libraries. URL: www.aera.net/Publications/Journals/iReviewofEducationalResearchi/tabid/12611/Default.aspx

1911. Roeper Review: a journal on gifted education. [ISSN: 0278-3193] 1978. q. GBP 98 (print & online eds.). Ed(s): Dr. Don Ambrose. Routledge, 325 Chestnut St, Ste 800, Philadelphia, PA 19106; customerservice@taylorandfrancis.com; http://www.tandfonline.com. Illus., index, adv. Sample. Refereed. Vol. ends: Jun. Reprint: PSC. *Indexed:* A01, A22, BRI, Chicano, E01, ERIC, PsycInfo, RILM. *Bk. rev.:* 2 to 3 per issue; 200-800 words. *Aud.:* Ga, Ac, Sa.

As the mission and contents indicate, this journal publishes articles that reflect on research, observation, experience, theory, and practice with regard to the growth, emotions, and education of gifted and talented learners. The internationally focused articles seek to put more attention on giftedness, talent development, and creativity. Faculty authors and professionals have written articles that address issues such as theories and philosophical analyses pertinent to giftedness, talent, and creativity; gender issues; curriculum studies; instructional strategies; educational psychology; elementary/early childhood/secondary education of the gifted; emotional, motivation, and affective dimensions of gifted individuals; differentiating instruction; teacher education; tests, measurement, and evaluation; and program development. Some themed issues are published. Issues generally include a section that presents one or more in-depth research articles and/or a brief research article. An interview with a noted person in the field is also included. Book reviews and a column on hot topics also appears. This is an informative and important journal in gifted education. Recommended for academic libraries that serve education programs. URL: www.roeper.org/page.aspx?pid=1222

1912. School Administrator: the monthly magazine for school system leaders. Incorporates: *D C Dateline.* [ISSN: 0036-6439] 1943. m. 11/yr. Members, USD 9; Non-members, USD 10. Ed(s): Liz Griffin, Jay P Goldman. American Association of School Administrators, 801 N Quincy St, Ste 700, Arlington, VA 22208; info@aasa.org; http://www.aasa.org. Adv. *Indexed:* A22, BRI, ERIC, P02. *Bk. rev.:* Number and length vary. *Aud.:* Ac.

This monthly magazine for school leaders from the American Association of School Administrators (AASA) is focused on topics and news related to school district administration, and is directed primarily at an audience of school superintendents. Authored by superintendents, faculty, and other professionals, articles provide practical information and discussions on important topics and often support a particular theme. Issues have offered articles on second-chance dropouts; grit, character, and other noncognitive skills; college and workforce readiness; and career and technical education. Sections of the magazine provide commentary from the frontlines, and news and information from AASA. Issues contain an insert, the AASA *Bulletin: A Supplement to the School Administrator,* which includes organization news, conference news, calls for proposals, and job postings. An important resource for school and academic libraries that serve education programs. URL: www.aasa.org/SchoolAdministrator.aspx

1913. Teachers College Record: a professional journal of ideas, research and informed opinion. Former titles (until 1970): *Columbia University. Teachers College. The Record;* (until 1967): *Teachers College Record;* Which incorporated (1910-1914): *The Household Arts Review;* Which was formerly (1908-1910): *The Domestic Art Review.* [ISSN: 0161-4681] 1900. m. USD 730 (Individuals, USD 85 (print & online eds.); Free to members). Ed(s): Gary Natriello, Jeff Frank. EBSCO Publishing, 10 Estes St, PO Box 682, Ipswich, MA 01938; information@ebscohost.com; http://www.ebscohost.com. Illus., index, adv. Sample. Refereed. Microform: MIM; PQC. *Indexed:* A01, A22, BRI, CBRI, Chicano, E01, ERIC, HEA, MLA-IB, P02, PsycInfo. *Bk. rev.:* 6-8, 750 words. *Aud.:* Ac.

TCR is a scholarly journal of research, analysis, and commentary on a broad range of issues and topics in the field of education. Articles have focused on policy; the politics of testing; the market model of education reform; the cognitive complexity of English language instructing; and the effects of inequality and poverty on teachers and schooling. *TCR* also publishes themed issues, such as an issue focused on the critical discourse and pedagogy of techno-knowledge. One issue is entirely devoted to book reviews, organized topically under administration, assessment and evaluation, curriculum, diversity, early childhood education, higher education, learning, research methods, social context, teacher education, teaching, and technology. Highly recommended for academic libraries. URL: www.tcrecord.org/

1914. *Theory into Practice.* Supersedes (in 1962): *Educational Research Bulletin.* [ISSN: 0040-5841] 1922. q. GBP 141 (print & online eds.). Ed(s): Eric M Anderson. Routledge, 325 Chestnut St, Ste 800, Philadelphia, PA 19106; customerservice@taylorandfrancis.com; http://www.tandfonline.com. Illus., index, adv. Sample. Refereed. Microform: PQC. Reprint: PSC. *Indexed:* A01, A22, B01, BRI, E01, ERIC, MLA-IB. *Aud.:* Ac.

Focusing on the important issues in education, each issue of *TIP* is theme-based and offers a comprehensive overview of the particular education topic, with articles representing a range of viewpoints on the subject. A guest editor with that specific subject expertise develops the theme. Articles authored by faculty and other professionals in the field are directed at an audience of teachers, education researchers, students, professors, and administrators. Editors provide an introduction to the topic for each issue. Some of the recent themes the journal has dealt with includes effective professional development of teachers of culturally diverse students; education in and through music; the future of critical literacies; and qualitative research in the twenty-first century. A section at the end of each issue provides additional resources for use in the classroom. These resources are based on the articles in the same issue. Recommended for academic libraries that serve education programs. URL: www.tandfonline.com/loi/htip20

1915. *Today's Catholic Teacher.* [ISSN: 0040-8441] 1967. bi-m. USD 15.95 domestic (Free to qualified personnel). Ed(s): Mary Noschang, Betsy Shepard. Peter Li Education Group, 2621 Dryden Rd, Ste 300, Dayton, OH 45439; service@peterli.com; http://www.peterli.com. Illus., adv. Sample. Vol. ends: Apr. *Indexed:* A22, P02. *Aud.:* Ac.

Addressing K–12 Catholic school teachers, this journal provides articles on special topics such as digital textbooks; bullying; math instruction; Common Core assessment; social networks; and cloud computing. Each article looks at the issues from a Catholic perspective and meant to help the practitioner succeed in the classroom. It also contains practical articles that are related to classroom activities. It includes news, ideas for class projects, resources, and other helpful aids for academic and religious lesson plans, and a column on technology in the classroom. It contains extensive advertising information on products and services for classroom use. Recommended for Catholic school libraries. URL: www.catholicteacher.com/

1916. *Urban Education.* [ISSN: 0042-0859] 1966. bi-m. USD 1169. Corwin Press, Inc., 2455 Teller Rd, Thousand Oaks, CA 91320; info@sagepub.com; http://www.corwinpress.com. Illus., adv. Sample. Refereed. Vol. ends: Jan. Microform: PQC. Reprint: PSC. *Indexed:* A01, A22, BRI, Chicano, E01, ERIC, FR, P02, P61, PsycInfo, RiskAb, SSA, SWR&A. *Bk. rev.:* 2, 10 pages. *Aud.:* Ac.

This journal provides articles that examine issues of concern for inner-city schools. Issues are presented from a gender-balanced and racially diverse perspective. Subjects include: student motivation and teacher practice; restructuring in large urban schools; school-to-work programs; and mental health needs of urban students. Topics explored have been about developing urban teachers of color; initiating RTI in urban schools; diversity and the school choice process; and an analysis of urban charter schools. Includes book reviews and an editorial. Recommended for academic libraries. URL: http://uex.sagepub.com

1917. *Voices from the Middle.* [ISSN: 1074-4762] 1994. q. USD 75. Ed(s): Doug Fisher, Diane Lapp. National Council of Teachers of English, 1111 W Kenyon Rd, Urbana, IL 61801; customerservice@ncte.org; http://www.ncte.org. Sample. Refereed. Circ: 9000 Paid. *Indexed:* BRI, ERIC. *Bk. rev.:* Number and length vary. *Aud.:* Ac.

Recognizing that middle school teachers are challenged with "a unique set of circumstances and issues," this journal is dedicated to supporting the middle school language arts teacher. Each issue provides a forum for the sharing of ideas, practices, reflections, solutions, and theories from classroom teachers and others involved with reading, writing, speaking, and listening in the visual and language arts at the middle school level. Thematic issues consider middle school topics such as tolerance, grouping in middle school, background knowledge and vocabulary, and new literacies. Each issue has a featured

theoretical article, with additional articles focused on classroom practices for sixth through eighth grades. Specifically, this is for middle schools with a professional library, as well as education libraries. URL: www.ncte.org/journals/vm

1918. *Y C - Young Children.* Former titles (until 2002): *Young Children;* (until 1964): *Journal of Nursery Education;* (until 1956): *National Association for Nursery Education. Bulletin;* (until 1950): *N A N E Bulletin;* (until 1948): *National Association for Nursery Education. Bulletin.* [ISSN: 1538-6619] 1945. bi-m. Free to members. National Association for the Education of Young Children, PO Box 97156, Washington, DC 20090; naeyc@naeyc.org; http://www.naeyc.org. Illus., index, adv. Refereed. Vol. ends: Sep. Microform: PQC. *Indexed:* A22, Agr, ERIC, MLA-IB, P02. *Bk. rev.:* 1-8, 400-800 words. *Aud.:* Ac.

This journal of the National Association for the Education of Young Children (NAEYC) addresses an audience of teachers and directors of programs involved with children from birth through age eight within child care, preschool, Head Start, and primary grade settings. It is also directed at teacher educators, local and state decision-makers, and researchers in child development. Practical articles provide ideas for teaching children and administering programs, and scholarly articles refer to current research and theory as a basis for practical recommendations. Articles also describe program changes that have occurred as an outcome of experts' experience and research about how young children learn. Essays discuss important issues and ideas concerning the education, care, and development of young children. Issues include NAEYC organization information, and brief book reviews of professional publications, as well as children's books. Recommended for school, public, and academic libraries. URL: www.naeyc.org/yc/

Comparative Education and International

1919. *Adults Learning.* Former titles (until 1989): *Adult Education;* (until 1934): *Journal of Adult Education.* [ISSN: 0955-2308] 19??. q. GBP 67 (Individuals, GBP 41). The National Institute of Adult Continuing Education (NAICE), Chetwynd House, 21 De Montfort St, Leicester, LE1 7GE, United Kingdom; enquiries@niace.org.uk; http://www.niace.org.uk. Illus., index, adv. Sample. Vol. ends: Jun. *Indexed:* A01, A22, ERIC, MLA-IB. *Bk. rev.:* 6-7, 500 words. *Aud.:* Ac, Sa.

This official publication of the National Institute of Adult Continuing Education (NIACE) in England and Wales provides national news of conferences and events, notes or reviews, commentaries, and brief articles on current issues in the field. The magazine targets adult education practitioners and policymakers. Articles by adult education consultants, university professors, and NIACE personnel have discussed older adult career reviews; adult learning for the world; the decline in part-time higher education; volunteerism; and lifelong learning. Recommended for academic and public libraries. URL: www.niace.org.uk/publications

1920. *Australian Journal of Education.* [ISSN: 0004-9441] 1957. 3x/yr. USD 651. Ed(s): Glenn Rowley. Sage Publications Ltd., 1 Oliver's Yard, 55 City Rd, London, EC1Y 1SP, United Kingdom; info@sagepub.co.uk; http://www.uk.sagepub.com. Illus., index, adv. Sample. Refereed. Vol. ends: Nov. Reprint: PSC. *Indexed:* A01, A22, BRI, ERIC, FR, HEA, MLA-IB. *Aud.:* Ac.

AJE publishes papers on the theory and practice of education that utilize various methodologies and conceptual frameworks. Embracing all fields of education and training, it aims to inform educational researchers as well as educators, administrators, and policymakers about issues of contemporary concern in education. Its main focus is on Australian education. The authors represent an international corps of scholars from a broad range of disciplines, such as philosophy, psychology, political science, economics, history, anthropology, medicine, and sociology. Articles have discussed Indian higher education students in Australia; bullying, victimization, and adolescents; boarding in Australian schools; national test performance; and vocational education and training. Recommended for academic libraries. URL: www.acer.edu.au/press/aje

1921. *British Educational Research Journal.* Supersedes in part (in 1978): *Research Intelligence.* [ISSN: 0141-1926] 1978. bi-m. GBP 1311 (print & online eds.). Wiley-Blackwell Publishing Ltd., The Atrium, Southern Gate, Chichester, PO19 8SQ, United Kingdom; customer@wiley.com; http://www.wiley.com/. Illus., index, adv. Sample. Refereed. Reprint: PSC. *Indexed:* A01, A22, E01, ERIC, FR, IBSS, LT&LA, P02, P61, PsycInfo, SSA. *Bk. rev.:* Number and length vary. *Aud.:* Ac, Sa.

This major publication of the British Educational Research Association is interdisciplinary in its approach and includes reports of case studies, experiments and surveys, discussions of conceptual and methodological issues and of underlying assumptions in educational research, accounts of research in progress, and book reviews. Scholarly articles are primarily focused on British educational research, although the journal's scope is international. Articles have examined how educational interventions can address religious intolerances; inclusive education policy; the effects of tuition fees on student mobility; the prevalence of streaming in U.K. primary schools; and sources of differential participation rates in school science. Recommended for academic libraries. URL: www.bera.ac.uk/berj.html

1922. *British Journal of Educational Studies.* [ISSN: 0007-1005] 1952. q. GBP 497 (print & online eds.). Ed(s): James Arthur. Routledge, 4 Park Sq, Milton Park, Abingdon, OX14 4RN, United Kingdom; subscriptions@tandf.co.uk; http://www.tandfonline.com. Illus., index, adv. Sample. Refereed. Circ: 1300. Vol. ends: Nov. Microform: PQC. Reprint: PSC. *Indexed:* A01, A22, BAS, E01, ERIC, IBSS, MLA-IB, P02. *Bk. rev.:* 16 per issue, 500-1,000 words. *Aud.:* Ac.

BJES publishes scholarly, research-based articles on education that draw particularly upon historical, philosophical, and sociological analysis and sources. An international education journal from the U.K., it addresses the wide range of perspectives in the areas of educational philosophy, history, psychology, sociology, management, administration, and comparative studies. They are also written for an audience of nonspecialists in the field, in keeping with the journal's interest in clearly expressed and nontechnical contributions to scholarship. Articles have discussed participation in higher education; technology-mediated collaborative learning environments for culturally and linguistically diverse children; privatizing of school-based education in England; and educational effects on individual life chances. Recommended for academic libraries. URL: www.soc-for-ed-studies.org.uk/journal/

1923. *British Journal of Sociology of Education.* [ISSN: 0142-5692] 1980. bi-m. GBP 1536 (print & online eds.). Routledge, 4 Park Sq, Milton Park, Abingdon, OX14 4RN, United Kingdom; subscriptions@tandf.co.uk; http://www.tandfonline.com. Illus., index, adv. Sample. Refereed. Reprint: PSC. *Indexed:* A01, A22, ASSIA, E01, ERIC, FR, IBSS, P02, P61, PsycInfo, RILM, SSA. *Bk. rev.:* Number and length vary. *Aud.:* Ac, Sa.

This journal publishes high-quality original, theoretically informed analyses of the relationship between education and society. From an international perspective, the journal addresses the major global debates on the social impact of educational policy and practice. International academic authors have contributed articles on lesbian and gay teachers' experiences in Irish schools; conceptualizing curriculum differentiation in higher education; languages, cultural capital, and school choice; and practicing leadership in newly multi-ethnic schools. Each issue generally contains a review essay, an extended review, and a review symposium on a major book or a collection of books. Recommended for academic libraries. URL: www.tandfonline.com/loi/cbse20

1924. *Canadian Journal of Education.* Formerly (until 1976): *Canadian Society for the Study of Education. Bulletin.* [ISSN: 0380-2361] 1974. q. Free to members. Ed(s): Julia Ellis. Canadian Society for the Study of Education, 260 Dalhousie St, Ste 204, Ottawa, ON K1N 7E4, Canada; csse-scee@csse.ca; http://www.csse.ca. Illus., index. Refereed. Vol. ends: Fall. Microform: MML. *Indexed:* A22, BRI, C37, CEI, ERIC, P02, PsycInfo. *Bk. rev.:* 3-7, 600-1,500 words. *Aud.:* Ac.

CJE publishes bilingual articles that are broadly but not exclusively related to Canadian education. Included are short research notes, discussions on topics, and book reviews. Articles are published either in English or French, with the abstracts in both languages. The journal publishes issues on early, lifelong, and Francophone education, and from rural, aboriginal, cultural, pre-service, and

inclusive perspectives. Topics covered have been teacher perspectives on inclusive classrooms in rural Canada; high school students with intellectual disabilities; service learning and student engagement; electronic storybooks; academic entitlements in the context of learning styles; and internationally educated teachers in Manitoba schools. This is an important and well-indexed Canadian education journal. Recommended for academic libraries. URL: http://ojs.vre.upei.ca/index.php/cje-rce/index

1925. *Child Education Plus.* Formerly (until 2007): *Child Education;* Incorporates (2007-200?): *Junior Education Plus;* Which was formerly (until 2007): *Junior Education;* (until 1977): *Teachers World;* (2008-200?): *Literacy Time Plus Ages 5-7;* Which was formerly (until 2007): *Literacy Time. Ages 5 to 7;* (2002-2007): *Literacy Time. Years 1 to 2;* (2008-200?): *Literacy Time Plus Ages 7-9;* Which was formerly (until 2007): *Literacy Time. Ages 7 to 9;* (1998-2007): *Literacy Time. Years 3 to 4;* (2008-200?): *Literacy Time Plus Ages 9-11;* Which was formerly (until 2007): *Literacy Time. Ages 9 to 11;* (1999-2007): *Literacy Time. Years 5 to 6.* [ISSN: 1755-8891] 1924. m. GBP 19.98 combined subscription domestic (print & online eds.); GBP 25.98 combined subscription in Wester Europe; (print & online eds.); GBP 28.98 combined subscription worldwide (print & online eds.). Scholastic Ltd., FREEPOST (SCE 2665), Windrush Park, Range Road, Witney, OX29 0YZ, United Kingdom; enquiries@scholastic.co.uk; http://www.scholastic.co.uk. Illus., index, adv. Vol. ends: Dec. Microform: PQC. *Indexed:* A22. *Bk. rev.:* 15-20, 50-200 words. *Aud.:* Ac.

This publication provides lesson plans, colorful posters, and reproducible activities geared for classroom use in primary schools in the United Kingdom. Articles offer tips on teaching strategies and ideas to enhance the curriculum. Throughout, there is useful current information about U.K. education news, publications, and resources. Each monthly issue is organized with activities under literacy, arts workshop, project, and numeracy. Book reviews include professional reading and children's books. Recommended for school and public libraries. URL: http://education.scholastic.co.uk/child_education

1926. *Chinese Education and Society.* Formerly (until Jan.1993): *Chinese Education.* [ISSN: 1061-1932] 1968. bi-m. USD 1539 (print & online eds.). Ed(s): Gerard A Postiglione, Stanley Rosen. M.E. Sharpe, Inc., 80 Business Park Dr, Armonk, NY 10504; custserv@mesharpe.com; http://www.mesharpe.com. Illus., index, adv. Sample. Refereed. Vol. ends: Nov/Dec. Microform: PQC. Reprint: PSC. *Indexed:* A01, A22, BAS, E01, ERIC, FR. *Aud.:* Ac, Sa.

This journal provides unabridged English translations of important articles on education in China from Chinese sources including scholarly journals, newspapers, and collections of articles in book form. It provides the Chinese thinking on policy and practice, reform and development, pedagogical theory and methods, higher education, and schools and families, as well as the education for diverse social groups across different demographics and minorities. Articles have covered such topics as rethinking the national education reform blueprint; the massification of higher education in Taiwan; basic education curriculum reform and teachers challenges in China; and a study of 30 years of entrance exam reform in Shanghai. Recommended for academic libraries. URL: www.mesharpe.com/mall/results1.asp?acr=ced

1927. *Comparative Education: an international journal of comparative studies.* [ISSN: 0305-0068] 1964. q. GBP 1143 (print & online eds.). Ed(s): Fred Friedberg. Routledge, 4 Park Sq, Milton Park, Abingdon, OX14 4RN, United Kingdom; subscriptions@tandf.co.uk; http://www.tandfonline.com. Illus., index, adv. Sample. Refereed. Vol. ends: Oct. Reprint: PSC. *Indexed:* A01, A22, BAS, E01, ERIC, FR, IBSS, P02, P61, SSA. *Bk. rev.:* Number and length vary. *Aud.:* Ac, Sa.

This international journal provides current information and analyses of significant world problems and trends in the field of education, with particular emphasis on comparative analysis of educational issues in national, international, and global contexts. It also has an interest in the associated disciplines of government, management, sociology, technology, and communications, with a view to the impact of these areas on educational policy decisions. The instructions to contributors have a long list of suggested themes, including educational reform, post-compulsory education, curricular content, education for the disadvantaged, higher education, ideological and religious interventions, and teacher preparation. Article topics have addressed such topics as the role of basic education in post-conflict recovery; school tracking and educational inequality in Switzerland; and changing grassroots communities and lifelong learning in Japan. Special issues have examined the dialogue of the East and the West, as well as education outcomes and poverty. Includes book reviews. Recommended for academic libraries. URL: www.tandfonline.com/toc/cced20/current

1928. *Comparative Education Review.* [ISSN: 0010-4086] 1957. q. USD 312 (print & online eds.). Ed(s): David Post. University of Chicago Press, 1427 E 60th St, Chicago, IL 60637; subscriptions@press.uchicago.edu; http://www.journals.uchicago.edu. Illus., index, adv. Sample. Refereed. Vol. ends: Nov. Microform: PQC. Reprint: PSC. *Indexed:* A01, A22, ABS&EES, BAS, BRI, C45, ERIC, FR, P02, P61, SSA. *Bk. rev.:* 9-11, 800-2,000 words. *Aud.:* Ac.

The official journal of the Comparative and International Education Society, this publication seeks to advance knowledge of education policies and practices throughout the world and the teaching of comparative education studies. Articles authored by international faculty and researchers have discussed the social, economic, and political forces that shape education throughout the world. Issues contain one or more essay reviews and a number of book reviews. Special issues have addressed fair access to higher education and the local and the global in reforming teaching and teacher education. An annual supplemental bibliography on comparative and international education is included. Recommended for academic libraries. URL: www.press.uchicago.edu/ucp/journals/journal/cer.html

1929. *Current Issues in Comparative Education.* [ISSN: 1523-1615] 1998. s-a. Free. Ed(s): Matthew Hayden. Columbia University, Teachers College, 525 W 120th St, New York, NY 10027; webcomments@tc.columbia.edu; http://www.tc.columbia.edu/. *Indexed:* ERIC. *Bk. rev.:* Number and length vary. *Aud.:* Ac.

An international open-access journal dedicated to publishing scholarly debate and discussion on educational policies and comparative studies. With academic and practical experience–based contributions, the journal has a wide and diverse audience. Each themed issue has a minimum of five articles with an online commentary. Issue topics have included education in small states; education and economic crises; early childhood care and education; and cosmopolitanism and comparative education. The articles are written by professors, researchers, students, advocates, policymakers, and practitioners from around the world. Recommended for academic libraries. URL: www.tc.columbia.edu/cice/

1930. *Curriculum Inquiry.* Formerly (until 1976): *Curriculum Theory Network.* [ISSN: 0362-6784] 1971. q. GBP 391. Ed(s): Dennis Thiessen, Elizabeth Campbell. Wiley-Blackwell Publishing, Inc., 111 River St, Hoboken, NJ 07030; info@wiley.com; http://onlinelibrary.wiley.com/. Illus., index, adv. Sample. Refereed. Circ: 760 Paid. Vol. ends: Winter. Reprint: PSC. *Indexed:* A01, A22, CEI, E01, ERIC, P02. *Bk. rev.:* 1-2, essay length. *Aud.:* Ac.

This journal, sponsored by the Ontario Institute for Studies in Education of the University of Toronto, focuses on the study of educational research, development, evaluation, and theory. Within each issue, international authors from a variety of disciplines offer articles on a wide range of issues and topics such as curriculum development, educational policy, and teacher education. Articles have addressed such topics as neuroscience and education; exploring how teachers' emotions interact with intercultural texts; reading the Bible as a pedagogical text; developing an integrated arts curriculum in Hong Kong; and teaching as a performative act. Equally important in this journal are critical book reviews, for which there are extensive instructions for in-depth essays. Editorial introductions are substantive. Recommended for academic libraries. URL: http://onlinelibrary.wiley.com/journal/10.1111/(ISSN)1467-873X

1931. *Discourse (Abingdon): studies in the cultural politics of education.* [ISSN: 0159-6306] 1980. 5x/yr. GBP 643 (print & online eds.). Ed(s): Victoria Carrington, Martin Mills. Routledge, 4 Park Sq, Milton Park, Abingdon, OX14 4RN, United Kingdom; subscriptions@tandf.co.uk; http://www.tandfonline.com. Illus., adv. Sample. Refereed. Reprint: PSC. *Indexed:* A01, A22, AmHI, E01, ERIC, MLA-IB, P61, SSA. *Bk. rev.:* Number and length vary. *Aud.:* Ac, Sa.

With its emphasis on international critical inquiry and dialogue on the cultural politics of education, this journal offers scholarly articles from around the world on a range of current topics of interest and concern that further the debate around the social, cultural, and political dynamics of education. Articles have discussed boys' peer dynamics and neighborhood risk; adventure learning and indigenous cultural competence; and new health imperatives and their impact on education. Several themed issues are produced each year, with opinion pieces related to the topic being covered. Includes review essays and book reviews. Recommended for academic libraries. URL: www.tandfonline.com/toc/cdis20/current

1932. *Economics of Education Review.* [ISSN: 0272-7757] 1981. bi-m. EUR 1157. Ed(s): Elchanan Cohn. Pergamon, The Blvd, Langford Ln, E Park, Kidlington, OX5 1GB, United Kingdom; JournalsCustomerServiceEMEA@elsevier.com; http://www.elsevier.com. Illus., adv. Sample. Refereed. Microform: PQC. *Indexed:* A01, A22, B01, BAS, ERIC, EconLit, HEA, JEL. *Aud.:* Ac.

EER provides a forum in which to share ideas and research findings in the economics of education and to create an interaction between economists and scholars interested in decisions surrounding the economics of education. It also seeks to encourage theoretical, empirical, and policy research that points out the role of economic analysis for an improved understanding of educational problems and issues. The articles are authored by international faculty, and are documented with references, tables, and other data, and they cover a wide range of topics. Articles have focused on the effectiveness of extended day programs; college decisions and financial aid; long-run impacts of early childhood education; the willingness to pay to reduce school bullying; state teacher union strength and student achievement; and responses of private and public schools to voucher funding. Recommended for academic libraries. Publisher URL: www.journals.elsevier.com/economics-of-education-review/

1933. *Educational Research.* [ISSN: 0013-1881] 1958. q. GBP 406 (print & online eds.). Ed(s): Felicity Fletcher-Campbell, Frances Brill. Routledge, 4 Park Sq, Milton Park, Abingdon, OX14 4RN, United Kingdom; subscriptions@tandf.co.uk; http://www.tandfonline.com. Illus., index, adv. Sample. Refereed. Vol. ends: Nov. Microform: SWZ. Reprint: PSC. *Indexed:* A01, A22, E01, ERIC, FR, IBSS, LT&LA, MLA-IB, PsycInfo. *Bk. rev.:* 1, 1,000-1,200 words. *Aud.:* Ac.

This journal is published by the National Foundation for Education Research in England and Wales (NFER), a major British research institution. It seeks articles on contemporary issues in education that convey research findings in language that is understandable to both scholars and its non-expert readership. With its objective of comprehensively describing for readers the problems and the research outcomes of a wide range of concerns in all areas of education, this forum for NFER is meant to assist professionals in making practical decisions and to aid those people concerned with mediating research findings to policymakers and practitioners. Faculty authors and researchers have written articles on routes toward Portuguese higher education; enhancing student engagement in student experience surveys; the role of education in economic growth; and the school choice market in China. Some special issues organized around a theme are also published. This publication also includes reviews of research, discussion pieces, short research reports, and book reviews. Recommended for academic libraries. URL: www.tandf.co.uk/journals/titles/00131881.asp

1934. *European Education.* Formerly (until 1991): *Western European Education.* [ISSN: 1056-4934] 1969. q. USD 1102 (print & online eds.). Ed(s): Iveta Silova, Noah W Sobe. M.E. Sharpe, Inc., 80 Business Park Dr, Armonk, NY 10504; custserv@mesharpe.com; http://www.mesharpe.com. Illus., adv. Sample. Refereed. Vol. ends: Dec. Reprint: PSC. *Indexed:* A01, A22, E01, ERIC, MLA-IB. *Bk. rev.:* Number and length vary. *Aud.:* Ac.

This publication contains selected articles from major journals drawn from the member states of the Council of Europe and is published in association with the Comparative Education Society in Europe (CESE). Articles focus on both education within member states and on the impact of European education globally. It includes research reports and documents (some abridged) from various research centers and school systems. Its education scope is broad with articles that are theoretical and empirical studies, interdisciplinary perspectives, and critical examinations of the impact of political, economic, and social forces on education. Themed issues have addressed educational metamorphoses in post-Soviet Ukraine; historical perspectives on European education outside Europe; continuing struggle over the meanings of the Shoah in Europe; and the new educational assessment regimes in Eurasia. Article topics have addressed educational sector changes in Europe, state ideology in kindergarten curriculum, and the outcome of a compulsory educational policy change on educational attainment. Recommended for academic libraries. URL: www.mesharpe.com/mall/results1.asp?ACR=eue

1935. European Journal of Education: research, development and policy. Formerly (until 1979): *Paedagogica Europaea.* [ISSN: 0141-8211] 1965. q. GBP 1297. Ed(s): Jean-Pierre Jallade, Jean Gordon. Wiley-Blackwell Publishing Ltd., The Atrium, Southern Gate, Chichester, PO19 8SQ, United Kingdom; customer@wiley.com; http://www.wiley.com/. Illus., index, adv. Sample. Refereed. Reprint: PSC. *Indexed:* A01, A22, ASSIA, E01, ERIC, FR, HEA, P02. *Aud.:* Ac.

The European Institute for Education and Social Policy, a nonprofit organization with expertise in the analysis of education and training policies in Europe and in the partner countries of the European Union, produces this journal. The aim is to offer a European perspective on policymaking. The journal focuses on European research and policy analysis that are of interest to policymakers and international organizations in Europe. The journal seeks to contribute to the policy debate at the national and Europeean level by providing comparative up-to-date data; examine, compare, and assess education policies, trends, and reforms across Europe; and disseminate policy debates and research results. Each issue has a theme; *EJE* is a thematic journal with five to eight articles that address the selected theme. A second section of each issue includes articles on other themes. Recommended for academic libraries. URL: http://onlinelibrary.wiley.com/journal/10.1111/(ISSN)1465-3435

1936. Higher Education: the international journal of higher education and educational planning. [ISSN: 0018-1560] 1971. 12x/yr. EUR 1313 (print & online eds.). Ed(s): Grant Harman. Springer Netherlands, Van Godewijckstraat 30, Dordrecht, 3311 GX, Netherlands; http://www.springer.com. Illus., index, adv. Sample. Refereed. Vol. ends: No. 4. Microform: PQC. Reprint: PSC. *Indexed:* A01, A22, ABIn, BRI, E01, ERIC, HEA, IBSS, LT&LA, MLA-IB, P02, P61, SSA. *Bk. rev.:* Number and length vary. *Aud.:* Ac.

This publication provides a forum for the exchange of information, experiences, and research results worldwide among professionals in the field of higher education studies. Developments in higher education institutions at all levels, both public and private, and across the world are reported. International authors reflect on higher education problems and issues; offer comparative reviews and analyses of country policies and education systems; and consider how these contributions may impact future planning. They address problems of teachers, students, administrators, and policymakers. Articles have discussed the determinants of international student mobility; barriers to and facilitators of female deans' career advancement in Vietnam; the Bologna process; religious affiliation and university satisfaction; and the discourse around global university rankings. Includes book reviews. Recommended for academic libraries. Publisher URL: http://link.springer.com/journal/10734

1937. International Journal of Leadership in Education: theory & practice. [ISSN: 1360-3124] 1998. q. GBP 472 (print & online eds.). Ed(s): Duncan Waite. Routledge, 4 Park Sq, Milton Park, Abingdon, OX14 4RN, United Kingdom; subscriptions@tandf.co.uk; http://www.tandfonline.com. Adv. Sample. Refereed. Reprint: PSC. *Indexed:* A01, A22, B01, E01, ERIC. *Aud.:* Ac.

This international journal provides a forum for theoretical and practical discussions of educational leadership. It considers conceptual, methodological, and practical issues in a variety of settings. Its stated goal is to publish cutting-edge research on instructional supervision, curriculum and teaching development, and educational administration. It presents alternative theoretical perspectives, methodologies, and leadership experiences. Its broad definition of leadership includes teachers as leaders, shared governance, site-based decision-making, and community–school collaborations. Issue sections include peer-reviewed, theoretically-based research papers; practical shorter articles from

academicians and practitioner-researchers; and commentary. Special theme-based issues are published. Recommended for academic libraries. URL: www.tandfonline.com/toc/tedl20/current

1938. International Review of Education. [ISSN: 0020-8566] 1955. bi-m. EUR 515 (print & online eds.). Ed(s): Virman Man. Springer Netherlands, Van Godewijckstraat 30, Dordrecht, 3311 GX, Netherlands; http://www.springer.com. Illus., index, adv. Sample. Refereed. Vol. ends: Dec (No. 6). Microform: PQC. Reprint: PSC. *Indexed:* A01, A22, BAS, BRI, E01, ERIC, FR, IBSS, LT&LA, P61, SSA. *Bk. rev.:* 4-6 per issue, of varying lengths. *Aud.:* Ac.

Edited by the UNESCO Institute for Lifelong Learning, Hamburg, this publication is directed at institutes of education, teacher-training institutions and ministries, nongovernment organizations, and individuals throughout the world. It provides an international forum for scholarly articles on the comparative theory and practice of formal and informal education as it relates to lifelong learning and education. Several journal issues have focused on work and learning research; literacy in the information age; and education and human rights. Article contributors have discussed public university entry in Ghana; language of instruction in Tanzania; turning around low-performing private universities in China; private supplementary tutoring and its implications for policymakers in Asia; and globalization, transnational policies, and adult education. A few articles within an issue may be non-English, but with an English abstract. Includes book reviews. Recommended for academic libraries. Publisher URL: http://link.springer.com/journal/11159

1939. J E T: Journal of Educational Thought. Formerly: *Journal of Educational Thought.* [ISSN: 0022-0701] 1967. 3x/yr. CAD 125. Ed(s): Ian Winchester. University of Calgary, Faculty of Education, 2500 University Dr NW, Calgary, AB T2N 1N4, Canada; http://www.educ.ucalgary.ca. Illus., adv. Sample. Refereed. Microform: MML; PQC. Reprint: PSC. *Indexed:* A22, CEI, MLA-IB, P02. *Bk. rev.:* 6-8, both short reviews and essay reviews. *Aud.:* Ac.

This international qualitative journal presents speculative, critical, and historical research concerning the theory and practice of education. Subject areas explored by mainly Canadian and American faculty vary widely and include administration, comparative education, curriculum, evaluation, instructional methodology, intercultural education, philosophy, psychology, and sociology. All articles have French and English abstracts, with occasional articles entirely in French. Each issue contains an editorial, articles, and book reviews. Recommended for academic libraries. URL: http://educ.ucalgary.ca/node/14

1940. Journal of Philosophy of Education. Former titles (until 1978): *Philosophy of Education Society of Great Britain. Proceedings;* (until 1971): *Philosophy of Education Society of Great Britain. Annual Conference. Proceedings.* [ISSN: 0309-8249] 1966. q. GBP 705. Wiley-Blackwell Publishing Ltd., The Atrium, Southern Gate, Chichester, PO19 8SQ, United Kingdom; customer@wiley.com; http://www.wiley.com/. Illus., index, adv. Sample. Refereed. Vol. ends: No. 2. Reprint: PSC. *Indexed:* A01, A22, E01, ERIC, FR, P02. *Bk. rev.:* 1-2 per issue, 1,000-2,000 words. *Aud.:* Ac.

This journal is published for the Philosophy of Education Society of Great Britain. Authors discuss basic philosophical issues related to education, or they may provide critical examinations of current educational practices or policies from a philosophical perspective. The journal promotes rigorous thinking on education, and the philosophical and ideological forces that shape the field. The authors are international, as is the editorial board. Articles have focused on such topics as the aesthetic and moral character of Oakeshott's educational writings; the epistemology of narrative research in education; children, praise, and the reactive attitudes; and philosophy in primary schools. Special issues devoted to a particular theme have presented articles on the lure of psychology; education and the growth knowledge; and policy. Generally includes a book review or review article. Recommended for academic libraries. URL: http://onlinelibrary.wiley.com/journal/10.1111/(ISSN)1467-9752

1941. Prospects: quarterly review of comparative education. Formerly: *Prospects in Education.* [ISSN: 0033-1538] 1969. q. EUR 134 (print & online eds.). Ed(s): Clementina Acedo. Springer Netherlands, Van Godewijckstraat 30, Dordrecht, 3311 GX, Netherlands; http://www.springer.com. Illus. Reprint: PSC. *Indexed:* A22, E01, ERIC. *Aud.:* Ac.

This publication of the UNESCO International Bureau of Education provides articles on education throughout the world by scholars, practitioners, policymakers, and administrators. In addition to theoretical and research-based analysis of comparative education, the journal focuses on policy implementation and bridging the gap between the policymakers and the theorists and researchers. Themed issues have focused on comparing learner performance in Southern Africa; education, fragility, and conflict; and internationalization of teacher education. Each issue begins with at least one opening article that offers an opinion on a controversial topic. Some issues have a section that discusses education trends based on particular case studies—for example, the international baccalaureate; education data in conflict-affected countries; and internationalization of in-service teacher training in Quebec. This journal is currently available in a number of foreign language editions: Arabic, Chinese, French, Russian, and Spanish. Recommended for academic libraries. URL: www.ibe.unesco.org/en/services/online-materials/publications/prospects.html

1942. Times Educational Supplement. [ISSN: 0040-7887] 1910. w. GBP 49 domestic; GBP 210 in Europe; GBP 255 elsewhere. T S L Education Ltd., 26 Red Lion Sq, London, WC1R 4HQ, United Kingdom; info@tsleducation.com; http://www.tsleducation.co.uk. Illus., index, adv. Microform: RPI. *Indexed:* A01, BRI, CBRI, LT&LA, P02, RILM. *Aud.:* Ac, Sa.

TES is the British version of the American publication, *Education Week*. It is the United Kingdom's major weekly publication for news concerning "primary, secondary, and further education." It includes background analyses of a wide range of current issues in education, local and national news, and a section on job openings for predominantly K–12 and also higher-education positions. A section called "TES Professional" provides many different teaching tips and strategies for educators. "TES Life," found at the end of each issue, provides a window into a day of the teaching life of a professional somewhere in the world. This title provides frequent special supplements to the news edition, such as separate job advertising supplements that include international openings. Highly recommended for academic libraries. URL: www.tes.co.uk

1943. Times Higher Education. Formerly (until 2008): *Times Higher Education Supplement.* 1971. w. GBP 49 domestic; GBP 98 in Europe; GBP 120 elsewhere. T S L Education Ltd., 26 Red Lion Sq, London, WC1R 4HQ, United Kingdom; info@tsleducation.co.uk; http://www.tsleducation.co.uk. Illus., index, adv. Microform: RPI. *Indexed:* A01, A22, AmHI, BRI, LT&LA, MLA-IB. *Bk. rev.:* Number varies per issue; 300-1,200 words. *Aud.:* Ac.

This title is the British version of the American publication *Chronicle of Higher Education.* THES states it is "designed specifically for professional people working in higher education and research." Articles cover a range of higher-education topics, including leadership, governmental policy, international news and views, scientific theory, and copyright. There are two or three feature articles, which includes the covers story. The news section covers the latest week's news with several special news columns such as "Campus Roundup." A culture section covers the arts and includes book reviews. There is an opinions section that includes letters from readers. As with the *Chronicle of Higher Education,* THES includes job advertisements with some international vacancies. This British weekly is a standard for any academic library, higher education institute, or organization. URL: www.thes.co.uk

Educational Psychology and Measurement, Special Education, Counseling

1944. Applied Measurement in Education. [ISSN: 0895-7347] 1988. q. GBP 481 (print & online eds.). Ed(s): Kurt Geisinger. Routledge, 325 Chestnut St, Ste 800, Philadelphia, PA 19106; customerservice@taylorandfrancis.com; http://www.tandfonline.com. Illus., adv. Sample. Refereed. Vol. ends: No. 4. Reprint: PSC. *Indexed:* A01, A22, E01, ERIC, PsycInfo. *Aud.:* Ac.

This research journal's prime mission is to improve communication between theory and practice. Articles will address original research studies, innovative strategies for solving educational measurement problems, and integrative reviews of current approaches to contemporary measurement issues. The

intended audience of researchers and practitioners will find articles on applied research, educational measurement problems and considered solutions, and research reviews of current issues in testing. Research studies with accompanying tables, figures, graphs, and other supporting material address topics such as experimental test of student verbal reports and teacher evaluations, construct comparability in multilanguage assessments, and use of student learning as formative assessment. A recent special issue's theme title was "Teachers' and Administrators' Use of Evidence of Student Learning to Take Action." Contributors are from academic and testing institutions such as the American Council of Testing and the Education Testing System. Strongly recommended for libraries that serve teachers and related education professionals. URL: https://www.erlbaum.com/shop/tek9.asp?pg=products&specific=0895-7347

1945. Counselor Education and Supervision. [ISSN: 0011-0035] 1961. q. GBP 141. Wiley-Blackwell Publishing, Inc., 111 River St, Hoboken, NJ 07030; info@wiley.com; http://www.wiley.com/. Illus., index, adv. Refereed. Circ: 3200. Vol. ends: Jun. Microform: PQC. Reprint: PSC. *Indexed:* A01, A22, BRI, C42, ERIC, PsycInfo. *Bk. rev.:* Number and length vary. *Aud.:* Ac, Sa.

This official publication of the Association for Counselor Education and Supervision (ACES) is designed for professionals engaged in the teaching and supervising of counselors. The journal's scope encompasses a broad range of workplaces, from schools to agencies, to private institutions. Each issue contains about six articles written by authors predominantly from academe. Articles range from pedagogical methods to practical teaching methods, such as counselor educators' gatekeeping responsibilities and student rights; counselor attitudes toward evidence-based practices; guidelines for operating counselor education and supervision training clinics; an investigation of African American counselor education students' challenging experiences; and using screenwriting techniques for realistic role plays. The journal has two regularly featured sections: one on counselor preparation, and the other on counselor supervision. The inclusion of ACES executive council minutes supports the professional orientation of the journal. A focused journal for a specific audience. URL: www.unco.edu/ces

1946. Educational Measurement: Issues and Practice. Supersedes: *National Council on Measurement in Education. Measurement News;* Formerly: *N C M E Newsletter.* [ISSN: 0731-1745] 1982. q. Ed(s): Steve Ferrara. Wiley-Blackwell Publishing, Inc., 111 River St, Hoboken, NJ 07030; info@wiley.com; http://onlinelibrary.wiley.com/. Illus. Refereed. Vol. ends: Winter. Reprint: PSC. *Indexed:* A01, A22, E01, ERIC, P02, PsycInfo. *Bk. rev.:* 1, 5,000 words. *Aud.:* Ac.

A journal of the National Council on Measurement in Education (NCME) that is designed to both highlight and inform its professional audience on issues and practices in the field of educational measurement. Each issue contains three articles that range in length from five to ten pages. Journal articles cover such topics as educational assessment knowledge and skills for teachers; the impact of an argument-based approach to validity; testing rubrics for elementary school students' writing; standard-setting methods as measurement processes; models of cognition used in educational measurement; security of web-based assessments; practice analysis for credentialing examinations; the meaning of student achievement in relation to the TIMSS international survey data; evaluation criteria for teacher certification tests; large-scale testing in other countries; and issues in large-scale writing assessments. As a membership publication, the journal also reports on NCME member activities, the annual conference, and organizational news. This journal supports practitioners in the field of testing. URL: www.ncme.org/pubs/emip.ace

1947. Educational Psychology Review. [ISSN: 1040-726X] 1989. q. EUR 876 (print & online eds.). Ed(s): Daniel H Robinson. Springer New York LLC, 233 Spring St, New York, NY 10013; service-ny@springer.com; http://www.springer.com/. Illus., adv. Sample. Refereed. Vol. ends: Dec. Microform: PQC. Reprint: PSC. *Indexed:* A01, A22, BRI, E01, ERIC, PsycInfo. *Aud.:* Ac, Sa.

An international peer-reviewed publication that supports the field of general educational psychology. Averaging four to six substantial and well-referenced articles per issue, this journal covers the history, the profession, and the issues of the educational psychology field. A special issue recently covered advancing cognitive-load theory through interdisciplinary research. The peer-reviewed journal has addressed such issues as impact of APA and AERA guidelines on effect size reporting; motivational experiences model of stereotype threat; a review of research on school bullying; visualization strategies for reading comprehension; and causal modeling analyses in educational psychology. Article authors are predominantly from institutions of higher education. Academic libraries that serve education and psychology faculty and graduate students will want this title. Publisher URL: www.springerlink.com

1948. *J E M.* Former titles (until 1978): *Journal of Educational Measurement;* (until 1964): *National Council on Measurement in Education. Yearbook.* [ISSN: 0274-838X] 19??. q. USD 428 (print & online eds.). Ed(s): James E Carlson. Wiley-Blackwell Publishing, Inc., 111 River St, Hoboken, NJ 07030; info@wiley.com; http://onlinelibrary.wiley.com/. Illus., index. Sample. Refereed. Vol. ends: Winter. Microform: PQC. Reprint: PSC. *Indexed:* A01, A22, ASSIA, Chicano, E01, ERIC, HEA, P61, PsycInfo, SSA. *Bk. rev.:* 2, 600-1,200 words. *Aud.:* Ac.

Published by the National Council on Measurement in Education, this journal intends to "promote greater understanding and improved use of measurement techniques." The journal's content format is based on research studies and reports on educational measurement such as item clusters and computerized adaptive testing; scaling performance assessments; assessing the dimensionality of NAEP reading data; trace lines for testlets; toward a psychometrics for testlets; and high school socioeconomic status's effect on SAT scores and grade-point average. There is a review section for books, software, and published tests and measurements. In addition, the journal asks for and publishes comments on previously published articles and reviews. The authors come from a broad range of testing and measurement backgrounds, such as the National Board of Medical Examiners, Microsoft Corporation, Research Triangle Institute, and CTB/McGraw-Hill. A scholarly research journal for those in the field of educational testing and measurement. URL: www.ncme.org/pubs/jem.ace

1949. *Journal of Educational and Behavioral Statistics.* Formerly (until 1994): *Journal of Educational Statistics.* [ISSN: 1076-9986] 1976. bi-m. USD 554. Ed(s): Sandip Sinharay, Matthew Johnson. Sage Publications, Inc., 2455 Teller Rd, Thousand Oaks, CA 91320; info@sagepub.com; http://www.sagepub.com. Illus., index, adv. Sample. Refereed. Microform: PQC. Reprint: PSC. *Indexed:* A22, E01, ERIC, PsycInfo. *Aud.:* Ac.

This journal is sponsored by the American Educational Research Association and the American Statistical Association. Intended for the statistician working in the field of educational or behavioral research, the journal publishes papers on methods of analysis, as well as reviews of current methods and practices. *JEBS*'s articles inform readers about the use of statistical methods: the "why, when, and how" of statistical methodology. Four to five articles are included per issue, along with the occasional column titled "Teachers Corner," which presents brief essays on the teaching of educational and behavioral statistics. Articles have addressed issues such as estimation of school effects; scaling procedures in NAEP; a case study in Path analysis; overview of the National Assessment of Educational Progress; parametric alternatives to the analysis of variance; designing cluster randomized crossover trials; using a multilevel latent Markov Rasch model for assessing school performance; and an interview with Karl Gustav Joreskog. A focused journal important to those in academe, whether researcher or practitioner. URL: www.apa.org/journals/edu

1950. *Journal of Educational Psychology.* [ISSN: 0022-0663] 1910. q. USD 574 (Individuals, USD 179). Ed(s): Arthur C Graesser. American Psychological Association, 750 First St, NE, Washington, DC 20002; journals@apa.org; http://www.apa.org. Illus., adv. Sample. Refereed. Circ: 2500. Vol. ends: Feb. Microform: PMC; PQC. Reprint: PSC. *Indexed:* A01, A22, Chicano, ERIC, FR, HEA, LT&LA, MLA-IB, P02, P61, PsycInfo, SSA. *Aud.:* Ac.

The journal's stated purpose is to publish current research as well as theoretical and review articles in the field of educational psychology. Each issue has 15–20 well-referenced research articles supported by tables, figures, and appendixes. Most articles have multiple authors. Article coverage includes learning, cognition, instruction, motivation, social issues, emotion, and special populations at all education levels. The journal has published articles on such

topics as what makes a good student; guided retrieval practice of educational materials; influences of text and reader characteristics on learning in science texts; effects of speaker variability on learning for EFL learners; learning vocabulary from television; learning with animation and illusions of understanding; and a study that identified and described middle school students' goals. Published by the American Psychological Association, this is an academic research journal for students, researchers, and practitioners in the field of educational psychology.

1951. *The Journal of Experimental Education.* [ISSN: 0022-0973] 1932. q. GBP 159 (print & online eds.). Ed(s): Rayne Sperling. Routledge, 325 Chestnut St, Ste 800, Philadelphia, PA 19106; customerservice@taylorandfrancis.com; http://www.tandfonline.com. Illus., index, adv. Refereed. Microform: PMC. Reprint: PSC. *Indexed:* A01, A22, Chicano, E01, ERIC, FR, HEA, MASUSE, MLA-IB, PsycInfo. *Aud.:* Ac.

This journal publishes basic and applied-research studies that use quantitative or qualitative methodologies in the behavioral, cognitive, and social sciences. Intended for researchers and practitioners, the journal is dedicated to promoting educational research in areas such as teaching, learning, and schooling in the United States and abroad. Contributed articles are divided into three sections: learning, instruction, and cognition; motivation and social processes; and measurement, statistics, and research design. Articles have covered such topics as being labeled "nerd"; constructing motivation through choice, interest, and interestingness; note-taking with computers; do films affect learning?; exploration feedback versus correct-answer feedback; a writing intervention to combat stereotype threat; academic-integrity responsibility and the frequency of cheating; exploring teachers' beliefs about teaching knowledge; motivation and self-regulation as predictors of achievement; cooperative college examinations; the effects of test anxiety on college students; and video case construction with pre-service teacher education programs. A journal intended for and useful to the professional researcher in the field of education and related social sciences. URL: www.heldref.org/jexpe.php

1952. *Journal of Learning Disabilities.* [ISSN: 0022-2194] 1967. bi-m. USD 282. Ed(s): H Lee Swanson. Sage Publications, Inc., 2455 Teller Rd, Thousand Oaks, CA 91320; info@sagepub.com; http://www.sagepub.com. Illus., adv. Sample. Refereed. Vol. ends: Dec. Microform: PQC. Reprint: PSC. *Indexed:* A01, A22, ASSIA, BRI, Chicano, E01, ERIC, FR, HEA, MLA-IB, PsycInfo, SSA. *Aud.:* Ac, Sa.

Dedicated to the field of learning disabilities, the journal publishes articles on practice, research, and theory. Articles are organized into categories such as feature articles, instructional/intervention, research, definitional issues, assessment, and special issues. Each issue averages about six to eight well-referenced articles. In covering the multidisciplinary field of learning disabilities, articles have presented topics such as private speech use in arithmetical calculation; a number sense program to develop kindergarten students' number proficiency; the mediating role of technology; learning disability assessment across ethnic groups; impaired visual attention in children with dyslexia; inattentive behavior in young children; gifted students with learning disability diagnoses; identifying interventions to address reading difficulties of children with learning disabilities; and examining an apprenticeship relationship in a collaborative writing context. A recent special issue covers I.Q. discrepancy and the LD diagnosis. Includes a classified advertising section with professional position postings. A professional calendar lists seminars and conferences on learning disabilities. An academic journal that covers the field. URL: www.ingentaconnect.com/content/proedcw/jld

1953. *Learning Disability Quarterly.* [ISSN: 0731-9487] 1978. q. USD 187. Ed(s): Diane Pedrotty Bryant, Brian R Bryant. Sage Publications, Inc., 2455 Teller Rd, Thousand Oaks, CA 91320; info@sagepub.com; http://www.sagepub.com. Illus. Refereed. Vol. ends: Fall. Reprint: PSC. *Indexed:* A01, A22, Chicano, ERIC, MLA-IB, PsycInfo. *Aud.:* Ac, Sa.

Published by The Council for Learning Disabilities, an international organization, this journal focuses on educational practices and theories as applied to disabilities. Articles represent a broad range of formats, including assessment or remediation reports; literature reviews; theory and issue papers; original or applied research; and professional education program models. With usually six articles an issue, the journal contents cover professional development, current issues in the field, the development of effective teaching methods, teaching in inclusive classrooms, and increasing student achievement. Journal topics have included: identification of learning-disabled students; a new definition of learning disabilities; problems of identification of learning disabilities; and writing and writing instruction for students with learning disabilities. Figures, tables, and appendixes support the research methodology used by authors. An important journal of value to both the academician and practitioner.

1954. *Professional School Counseling.* Formed by the merger of (1965-1997): *Elementary School Guidance and Counseling;* (1953-1997): *School Counselor;* Which superseded (1953-1954): *Elementary Counselor.* [ISSN: 1096-2409] 1997. bi-m. Free to members; Non-members, USD 115. American School Counselor Association, 1101 King St, Ste 625, Alexandria, VA 22314; asca@schoolcounselor.org; http://www.schoolcounselor.org. Illus., index. Sample. Refereed. Vol. ends: May. *Indexed:* A01, A22, BRI, Chicano, ERIC, PsycInfo, SWR&A. *Bk. rev.:* Number and length vary. *Aud.:* Ga, Ac.

The journal is dedicated to presenting the most current theory, research, practice, techniques, materials, and ideas for school counselors. Articles are research-based, but the journal also publishes theoretical and philosophical pieces, as well as literature reviews. Each issue has eight or more articles. Article topics have included comprehensive school-counseling programs; evaluation of ASCA national model school counseling programs in Utah; supporting student spirituality; interpersonal and predictors of peer victimization; school counselors and child abuse reporting; reducing rumor spreading in a junior high school; school counselor consultation; narrative theory; the counseling of at-risk adolescent girls; and the importance of promoting a professional identity. A regular feature, "Perspectives from the Field," gives a brief overview of current issues or practices of concern to school counselors. Books and other resources are reviewed. This is a very relevant title for school counselors or other professionals concerned with the well-being of all elementary and high school students. URL: www.schoolcounselor.org/content.asp?contentid=235

1955. *Psychology in the Schools.* [ISSN: 0033-3085] 1964. 8x/yr. GBP 448. Ed(s): David E McIntosh. John Wiley & Sons, Inc., 111 River St, MS 4-02, Hoboken, NJ 07030; info@wiley.com; http://www.wiley.com/WileyCDA/. Illus., index, adv. Sample. Refereed. Vol. ends: Oct. Microform: PQC. Reprint: PSC. *Indexed:* A01, A22, ABS&EES, ASSIA, Chicano, ERIC, FR, PsycInfo. *Bk. rev.:* 1-5, 600-2,000 words. *Aud.:* Ac.

This peer-reviewed journal is intended for the school practitioner and others working in educational institutions, including psychologists, counselors, and administrators. Articles are organized into categories of evaluation and assessment, educational practices and problems, strategies for behavioral change, and general issues. Categories are indicative of article content, such as evaluation and assessment, that focuses on testing practices and issues. Recent articles cover provision of counseling services among school psychologists; intervention and prevention of harassment of LGBTQ youth; preparing school psychologists for crisis intervention; assessing giftedness with the WISC-III and SB-IV; teacher behavior toward failing students; a review of diversity research literature in school psychology from 2000 to 2003; predicting reading levels for low-SES English-speaking children; the validity of office discipline referrals; a review of research and recommendations with type 1 diabetes mellitus; looking at early screening profile validity; and the learning and study strategies of college students with ADHD. Two special issues are published annually that cover current topics such as resilience in the schools and cognitive behavioral therapy in the schools. Occasional test and book reviews. An important journal for school and academic libraries. URL: www3.interscience.wiley.com/cgi-bin/jhome/32084

1956. *Remedial and Special Education.* Formed by the merger of (1981-1984): *Topics in Learning and Learning Disabilities;* (1980-1984): *Exceptional Education Quarterly;* (1978-1983): *Journal for Special Educators;* Which was formed by the 1978 merger of: *Special Children; Journal for Special Educators of the Mentally Retarded;* Which was formerly: *Digest of the Mentally Retarded;* Incorporates: *Retarded Adult.* [ISSN: 0741-9325] 1984. bi-m. USD 260. Ed(s): Michael Wehmeyer.

Sage Publications, Inc., 2455 Teller Rd, Thousand Oaks, CA 91320; info@sagepub.com; http://www.sagepub.com. Illus., index. Sample. Refereed. Microform: PQC. Reprint: PSC. *Indexed:* A01, A22, ASSIA, BRI, E01, ERIC, PsycInfo. *Bk. rev.:* Number and length vary. *Aud.:* Ac, Sa.

A journal dedicated to the issues and practices of remedial and special education. Each issue averages five to six articles, which may be literature reviews, position papers, or research reports. Topics cover a broad range of issues concerning the population of underachieving and exceptional individuals. Recent article topics include school predictors of violent criminality in adulthood; teaching students with disabilities basic finance skills; a support model for new teachers of students with disabilities; social skills interventions for young children with disabilities; inclusive schooling and community-referenced learning; mediated activities and science literacy; charter school enrollment of students with disabilities; and the legal and practical issues of high school graduation for students with disabilities. A special series considers peer-mediated instruction and intervention. Contributing authors are predominantly academics, including graduate students. Book reviews and a professional calendar are regular features. A journal of importance for the special education teacher and regular classroom teacher, as well as those teaching in the field.

1957. *Studies in Educational Evaluation.* [ISSN: 0191-491X] 1975. q. EUR 913. Ed(s): P van Petegem. Pergamon, The Blvd, Langford Ln, E Park, Kidlington, OX5 1GB, United Kingdom; JournalsCustomerServiceEMEA@elsevier.com; http://www.elsevier.com. Illus., adv. Sample. Refereed. Microform: PQC. *Indexed:* A01, A22, ASSIA, ERIC, HEA, RILM. *Bk. rev.:* Number and length vary. *Aud.:* Ac.

An internationally authored journal that publishes original reports on evaluation studies for practitioners, students, and researchers. Focused on presenting both empirical and theoretical studies, the journal seeks articles that report on international educational systems, evaluation practices, and current evaluation issues of educational programs, institutions, and personnel and student assessment. Additionally, the journal covers topics both general to the field and specific to a country or countries. Topics presented have included assessing conceptual knowledge; uses of the Student-in-the-Arts questionnaire; effectiveness of a dual-language science test for bilingual learners; changing students' assessment preferences; teacher licensing examinations; attitudes toward school self-evaluation; anti-bullying programs; evaluation of professional development programs for science and mathematics teachers; school composition and achievement in primary education; evaluation of an alternative teacher-licensing assessment program; program evaluation using video; and Brazil's basic education evaluation system. A special issue covered "Assessment for Learning" with nine commissioned papers. The issue covered wide-ranging perspectives on the subject, including an article on "Afl" origins, reviews, and definitions, as well as two empirical studies abut the facilitation or challenges with implementing "Afl." Book reviews and brief abstracts of evaluation studies are included in each issue. This is a focused journal with international coverage that is recommended for libraries that serve testing and education organizations or institutions.

Higher Education

1958. *A A U W Outlook.* Former titles (until 1989): *Graduate Woman;* (until 1978): *A A U W Journal;* (until 1962): *American Association of University Women. Journal;* (until 1921): *Association of Collegiate Alumnae. Journal;* (until 1911): *Association of Collegiate Alumnae. Publications.* [ISSN: 1044-5706] 1884. q. Free to members. American Association of University Women, 1111 16th St, NW, Washington, DC 20036; connect@aauw.org; http://www.aauw.org. Illus., adv. Vol. ends: Nov/Dec. *Bk. rev.:* 1-2, 200-500 words. *Aud.:* Ga, Ac, Sa.

Published by the American Association of University Women for its members, this magazine informs and promotes the organization's mission of "equity for all women and girls, lifelong education, and positive societal changes." Regular features include an equity watch and "President's Message." Illustrated throughout with photos, the magazine has classified ads that include job opportunities. Featured brief articles have considered AAUW in the postwar era; prospects for women's issues in the New Congress; women and street harassment; 30 years of Title IX; AAUW members' reflections on voting experiences over eight decades; and the Violence Against Women Act. Member surveys, the President's Message, and an issue devoted to the AAUW's annual conference exemplify the outreach focus of the magazine to its members. An important magazine for academic libraries and for libraries that serve women's organizations. URL: www.aauw.org/resource/aauw-outlook/

1959. Academe. Incorporates (1967-1979): *Academe;* Former titles (until 1979): *A A U P Bulletin;* (until 1956): *American Association of University Professors. Bulletin;* (until 1943): *American Association of University Professors. Bulletin.* [ISSN: 0190-2946] 1915. bi-m. Free to members; Non-members, USD 80. Ed(s): Michael Ferguson. American Association of University Professors, 1133 Nineteenth St, NW, Ste 200, Washington, DC 20036; aaup@aaup.org; http://www.aaup.org. Illus., index, adv. Vol. ends: Nov/Dec. Microform: PMC; PQC. *Indexed:* A01, A22, ERIC, HEA, MLA-IB, P02, P61, SSA. *Bk. rev.:* 3-4, 800-1,500 words. *Aud.:* Ac.

The journal of the American Association of University Professors (AAUP) is dedicated to presenting faculty views on issues concerning higher education. Each issue has a theme such as globalization and the university, ethics and higher education, professors and intellectual property, and assessment and accountability of faculty and institutions. Five or six featured articles cover such important topics as human costs of layoffs, women's progress in academic leadership and athletics, copyrighted materials and the web, diversity and affirmative action, part-time and non–tenure-track faculty, and faculty retirement policy. Regular departments report on government policy and legislation pertaining to higher education, current legal issues facing academe, book reports, and censured higher education administrations. The association provides brief reports on its committees, its council, and annual meetings. The invaluable annual report on the "economic status of the profession" keeps the higher education professional informed as to faculty economic well-being. New and noteworthy items of interest are highlighted in a regular column titled "Nota Bene." Some content is available online only. A required journal for all academic libraries and special libraries. URL: www.aaup.org/reports-and-publications/academe

1960. Change: the magazine of higher learning. Formerly (until 1970): *Change in Higher Education.* [ISSN: 0009-1383] 1969. bi-m. GBP 155 (print & online eds.). Ed(s): Margaret A Miller. Routledge, 325 Chestnut St, Ste 800, Philadelphia, PA 19106; customerservice@taylorandfrancis.com; http://www.tandfonline.com. Illus., index, adv. Circ: 12868 Paid. Reprint: PSC. *Indexed:* A01, A22, BRI, C42, CBRI, Chicano, E01, ERIC, HEA, MLA-IB, P02. *Aud.:* Ac.

A magazine for the practitioner, *Change* presents views and opinions on current higher education issues. This journal is intended for all practitioners in higher education institutions, organizations, and government offices, and its focus is on discussion and analysis of educational programs and practices. Articles cover all aspects of higher education, including technology, teaching and learning, curriculum, students, educational philosophy, economics and finance, higher education management and administration, public policy, and the social role of higher education. Each issue contains about six articles, ranging from a brief point of view to a featured article. Article topics have included increasing enrollments and the economy; grouping faculty according to academic interests; executive searches and the use of consultants; the demographics of higher education; pay equity for faculty; academic audits; evaluating state higher education performance; and changing admissions policies. Regular departments feature an editorial and a column of items of current interest to those in the field. A title important to all those in the field of higher education from administrators to department heads to faculty. URL: www.changemag.org

1961. The Chronicle of Higher Education. [ISSN: 0009-5982] 1966. w. 49/yr. USD 82.50 domestic; USD 175 Canada; USD 295 elsewhere. Ed(s): Philip Semas, David Wheeler. Chronicle of Higher Education, Inc., 1255 23rd St, NW, Ste 700, 7th Fl, Washington, DC 20037; help@chronicle.com. Illus., index, adv. Sample. Vol. ends: Aug. Microform: CIS; PQC. *Indexed:* A&ATA, A01, A22, ABS&EES, Agr, BRI, C37, C42, CBRI, Chicano, ERIC, F01, MLA-IB, P02, RILM. *Aud.:* Ga, Ac.

Published weekly, *The Chronicle of Higher Education* is academe's resource for news and information. Although the journal is intended for higher education faculty and administrators, the contents are relevant for others interested in the field of higher education, such as researchers, students, federal and state legislators, government policymakers, and taxpayers. This weekly is organized into sections: current developments and issues in higher education; regular features on faculty, research, money and management, government and politics, international, students, and athletics; the chronicle review, with letters to the editor and opinion articles; listings of coming events; and the section on career networking, with hundreds of job listings. Additionally, twice a year "Events in Academe" indexes meetings, events, and deadlines for fellowships, grants, papers, and prizes. An annual almanac issue covers facts and statistics about U.S. higher education at both the national and state level. *CHE* is available online with additional sections like blogs, career-building tools, and a searchable archive with content back to the 1970s. The online version is updated every weekday. A required standard for all academic libraries, as well as higher education institutions and organizations. URL: http://chronicle.com

1962. College and University. Former titles (until 1947): *American Association of Collegiate Registrars. Journal;* (until 1937): *American Association of Collegiate Registrars. Bulletin;* (until 1925): *American Association of Collegiate Registrars. National Meeting. Proceedings;* (until 1914): *American Association of Collegiate Registrars. Annual Meeting.* [ISSN: 0010-0889] 1910. q. USD 100 Free to members; (Non-members, USD 80). Ed(s): Louise Lonabocker, Heather Zimar. American Association of Collegiate Registrars and Admissions Officers, One Dupont Circle, N W, Ste 520, Washington, DC 20036-1135; pubs@aacrao.org; http://www.aacrao.com. Illus., index, adv. Vol. ends: Summer. Microform: PQC. *Indexed:* A22, BRI, CBRI, ERIC, HEA, MLA-IB. *Bk. rev.:* Number and length vary. *Aud.:* Ac.

This journal of the American Association of Collegiate Registrars and Admissions Officers publishes scholarly and educational policy articles. The journal's focus is emerging and current issues, innovative practices and techniques, and administrative information technology in the profession. Each issue contains three or four featured articles. Regular features are letters to the editor, guest commentary, and book reviews. Articles have included a two-part series on helicopter parents; enrollment management; meritocracy; enterprise administration systems; student–institution fit; and the relationship between athletics and application yield. Articles reflect the professional experience of the contributing academic authors. This journal is required for libraries that serve those working or studying in the field of higher education admissions and registration. URL: www.aacrao.org/publications/college_and_university_journal.aspx

1963. College Teaching. Formerly (until 1985): *Improving College and University Teaching.* [ISSN: 8756-7555] 1953. q. GBP 132 (print & online eds.). Ed(s): Scott P Simkins, Barbara J Millis. Routledge, 325 Chestnut St, Ste 800, Philadelphia, PA 19106; customerservice@taylorandfrancis.com; http://www.tandfonline.com. Illus., adv. Refereed. Reprint: PSC. *Indexed:* A01, A22, BRI, E01, ERIC, HEA, MLA-IB. *Aud.:* Ac.

Improving student learning is the core focus of this journal, with an emphasis on providing new and practical strategies to faculty and instructors in all disciplines. Interdisciplinary full-length articles report research on instructional methods, assessment, evaluation, educational technology, course design, and classroom management. One to two short, 500-word quick-fix articles in each issue provide solutions to common instructional problems. The occasional commentary gives authors a chance to reflect on teaching. Recent articles have addressed topics such as creating a dynamic syllabus; increasing interest in research by undergraduate students; using the classroom to model real world work experiences; and note-restructuring. With a broad range of topics, this journal covers the higher education classroom. An important and informative tool for higher education instructors. URL: www.tandfonline.com/toc/vcol20/current

1964. Community College Journal. Former titles (until 1992): *Community, Technical, and Junior College Journal;* (until 1985): *Community and Junior College Journal;* (until 1972): *Junior College Journal.* [ISSN: 1067-1803] 1930. bi-m. Free to members; Non-members, USD 34. Ed(s):

Cheryl Gamble. American Association of Community Colleges, One Dupont Cir, NW, Ste 410, Washington, DC 20036; http://www.aacc.nche.edu. Illus., index, adv. Sample. Circ: 10000. Vol. ends: Jun/Jul. Microform: PQC. *Indexed:* A22, ERIC, HEA, MLA-IB. *Bk. rev.:* 4-7, 100-300 words. *Aud.:* Ac.

As the advocate for community colleges, the American Association of Community Colleges publishes this journal to support the advancement of community colleges as institutions of higher learning. The journal contents include feature articles, opinion pieces, news items, and issues in the field of higher education. Each issue is dedicated to a theme with five or six brief articles. Recent themes include re-imagining the community college; whole-system thinking; skills matching; training the nation's technical workforce; and igniting innovation. The intended audience of presidents, board members, administrators, faculty, and staff at two-year institutions is presented with practical content. Articles focus on trends and issues in the field such as training future faculty, leadership, campus security, community colleges and changing technology needs, and the public image of community colleges. For all community college libraries and graduate education program libraries that support those working in or preparing to work in the field. URL: www.aacc.nche.edu/Publications/CCJ/Pages/default.aspx

1965. *Community College Review.* [ISSN: 0091-5521] 1973. q. USD 327. Ed(s): Jim Palmer. Sage Publications, Inc., 2455 Teller Rd, Thousand Oaks, CA 91320; info@sagepub.com; http://www.sagepub.com. Illus., adv. Sample. Refereed. Vol. ends: Spring. Microform: PQC. Reprint: PSC. *Indexed:* A01, A22, BRI, E01, ERIC, HEA, MLA-IB. *Bk. rev.:* Number and length vary. *Aud.:* Ac.

With an international appeal, this referred journal publishes scholarly research focused on community colleges, both in the United States and internationally. With an emphasis on issues of policy, administration, and education, the journal includes blind peer-reviewed qualitative and quantitative research studies, essays, literature reviews, and book reviews. Integrating theory and practice, articles are meant to further the study and understanding of community college students, administrators, and faculty, and the educational environment of community college. Recent articles have focused on skills and trajectories of developmental learners; using the community college's web site as a virtual advisor; and the impact of student success courses. An important title for libraries that serve the higher education community, the journal supports the work of administrators, faculty, graduate students, researchers, and policymakers with an interest in community colleges. URL: http://crw.sagepub.com

1966. *Innovative Higher Education.* Formerly (until 1983): *Alternative Higher Education.* [ISSN: 0742-5627] 1976. 5x/yr. EUR 967 (print & online eds.). Ed(s): Libby V Morris. Springer Netherlands, Van Godewijckstraat 30, Dordrecht, 3311 GX, Netherlands; http://www.springer.com. Illus., index, adv. Sample. Refereed. Vol. ends: Summer. Microform: PQC. Reprint: PSC. *Indexed:* A01, A22, E01, ERIC, HEA, MLA-IB. *Aud.:* Ga, Ac.

A refereed academic journal dedicated to emerging and current trends in higher education. Its focus is on providing practitioners and scholars with current strategies, programs, and innovations to enhance the field of higher education. The publication focuses on articles that: consider current innovative trends and practices with application beyond the context of higher education; discuss the effect of innovations on teaching and students; present scholarship and research methods broadly defined; and cover practice and theory appropriate for both faculty and administrators. Recent issues feature topics relevant to the field, such as new technology-based teaching platforms; impediments to degree completion; athletics and academics; and program assessment. This scholarly journal is highly recommended for libraries at higher education institutions or organizations. URL: www.springer.com/education+%26+language/higher+education/journal/10755

1967. *Journal of College Student Development.* Formerly (until 1988): *Journal of College Student Personnel;* Which superseded (in 1959): *Personnel-o-Gram.* [ISSN: 0897-5264] 19??. bi-m. USD 165. Ed(s): John M Braxton. The Johns Hopkins University Press, 2715 N Charles St,

Baltimore, MD 21218; http://www.press.jhu.edu. Illus., adv. Sample. Refereed. Circ: 501. Vol. ends: Nov. Microform: PQC. Reprint: PSC. *Indexed:* A22, Chicano, E01, ERIC, HEA, MLA-IB, PsycInfo, RILM, SWR&A. *Bk. rev.:* 0-4, 700-1,000 words. *Aud.:* Ac, Sa.

This publication of the American College Personnel Association is focused on student development, professional development, administrative issues, and innovative programs to enhance student services at institutions in the United States and internationally. Authors contribute quantitative or qualitative research articles, research reviews, and essays on theoretical, organizational, and professional topics. Shorter research studies present tools and methods that administrators may find useful in providing services. Each issue generally contains about seven articles with a wide range of college student topics of interest, such as the student aggression and victimization; emotion skills; personal and sociocultural stressors on international students; and student outcomes predictors. Includes book reviews and international research. A professional journal recommended for academic libraries. URL: www.jcsdonline.org

1968. *Journal of Computers in Mathematics and Science Teaching.* [ISSN: 0731-9258] 1981. q. USD 185 (Members, USD 55; USD 25 student members). Ed(s): Chris Marks, Gary Marks. Association for the Advancement of Computing in Education, PO Box 1545, Chesapeake, VA 23327; info@aace.org. Illus. Refereed. *Indexed:* A22, CompLI, CompR, ERIC, I15, P02, PsycInfo. *Aud.:* Ac, Sa.

An academic journal that provides a venue for information on using information technology in teaching mathematics and science. It is published by the Association for the Advancement of Computing in Education, and its aim is to promote the teaching and learning of computing technologies. With an international authorship, the journal is directed to faculty, researchers, classroom teachers, and administrators. Article format includes research papers, case studies, courseware experiences, review papers, evaluations, and opinions. Issues have four to six well-referenced articles on such topics as: teaching finite mathematics; use of screencasting to transform pedagogy; integrating multimedia into the third-grade math curriculum; and high school physics education. A subject-specific journal of value to both practitioner and researcher at all education levels. URL: www.aace.org/pubs/jcmst/default.htm

1969. *Journal of Developmental Education.* Formerly (until 1984): *Journal of Developmental and Remedial Education.* [ISSN: 0894-3907] 1978. 3x/yr. USD 40 (Individuals, USD 34). Appalachian State University, National Center for Developmental Education, Appalachian State University, ASU Box 32098, Boone, NC 28608; hoffmankm@appstate.edu; http://www.ncde.appstate.edu/index.htm. Illus., index, adv. Refereed. Vol. ends: Jan. *Indexed:* A01, A22, ERIC, HEA, MLA-IB. *Aud.:* Ac, Sa.

The National Center for Developmental Education's publication is dedicated to the education of the academically at-risk college community. The intended readers are educators involved with academically at-risk college students, including faculty, administrators, and others at postsecondary institutions. Basic skills education is the primary content focus. There is an emphasis on articles that relate educational theory to the practice of teaching, evaluative studies, and the dissemination of research and news in the field. In addition to about four articles per issue, there are regularly featured columns that focus on developing critical thinking, computer uses, latest news and developments, and innovative classroom methods. An important title for all academic libraries. URL: http://ncde.appstate.edu/publications/journal-developmental-education-jde

1970. *Journal of Higher Education.* [ISSN: 0022-1546] 1930. bi-m. USD 270. Ed(s): Scott L Thomas. Ohio State University Press, 180 Pressey Hall, 1070 Carmack Rd, Columbus, OH 43210-1002; info@osupress.org; http://www.ohiostatepress.org. Illus., adv. Refereed. Circ: 4200 Paid. Microform: PMC; PQC. *Indexed:* A01, A22, BRI, CBRI, Chicano, E01, ERIC, HEA, MLA-IB, P02, SWR&A. *Bk. rev.:* 2-4, 700-1,500 words. *Aud.:* Ac.

A membership journal for several higher-education associations, this is the standard title in the field of higher education. It publishes research or technical papers, professional practice papers, literature reviews, and policy papers of interest to faculty, administrators, and program managers. Article content focuses on topics of interest and importance to the higher education community.

A small number of substantial articles cover the current trends and issues in the field such as university rankings; state higher-education governance structures; spending on higher education; and access and equity. Occasional special issues examine topics in depth, such as research and methodology, the faculty in the new millennium, or higher education's social role in the community at large. Each issue contains several lengthy book reviews and a review essay. A highly recommended journal for all libraries that serve higher education institutions and organizations. URL: https://ohiostatepress.org/index.htm?journals/jhe/jhemain.htm

1971. *Journal of Student Affairs Research and Practice.* Former titles (until 2010): *N A S P A Journal;* (until 1970): *N A S P A.* [ISSN: 1949-6591] 1963. q. EUR 149. Walter de Gruyter GmbH & Co. KG, Genthiner Str 13, Berlin, 10785, Germany; info@degruyter.com; http://www.degruyter.de. Refereed. Circ: 6500. *Indexed:* A22, HEA. *Bk. rev.:* 4 per issue. *Aud.:* Ac, Sa.

This journal is the voice of NASPA, an association of student affairs administrators. This journal focuses on relevant and practical information in support of student affairs administrators at all levels. Critical and current articles explore national social, political, and financial issues and challenges that connect student affairs to the broader world. Innovations on research and scholarship articles connect research and theory to student affairs practice. Recent topics include the impact of first year seminars; male peer educators; and sorority/fraternity issues. The "International Feature" articles provide research on international issues that affect higher education and student affairs. Each section include three or four articles, and may include literature reviews and essays. Reviews focus on all forms of media. Appropriate for all academic libraries. URL: www.degruyter.com/view/j/jsarp

1972. *Liberal Education.* Former titles (until 1958): *Association of American Colleges. Bulletin;* Which incorporated (19??-1951): *College and Church;* (until 1940): *Association of American Colleges. Bulletin;* (until 1931): *Association of American Colleges. Bulletin.* [ISSN: 0024-1822] 1915. q. Individuals, USD 50; Members, USD 10; Non-members, USD 14. Association of American Colleges and Universities, 1818 R St NW, Washington, DC 20009; pub_desk@aacu.org; http://www.aacu.org. Illus., index. Vol. ends: Nov/Dec. Microform: PQC. *Indexed:* A01, A22, BRI, ERIC, HEA, MLA-IB. *Aud.:* Ac.

A journal of the Association of American Colleges and Universities, dedicated to improving undergraduate education. This journal is a voice of the association and a resource for the higher education community, and its contents highlight liberal education theory and its practical application. Articles seek to improve undergraduate education by focusing on institutional change, leadership, teaching and learning, and faculty innovation. Three sections include a featured topic with three or four supporting articles, a perspective section with how-to pieces, and an opinion article. Featured topics have been about what employers want from college graduates; student learning; and liberal education for sustainability. For all libraries that serve the undergraduate education community and graduate schools of education. URL: www.aacu.org/liberaleducation/index.cfm

1973. *Research in Higher Education.* [ISSN: 0361-0365] 1973. 8x/yr. EUR 1350 (print & online eds.). Ed(s): John Smol. Springer Netherlands, Van Godewijckstraat 30, Dordrecht, 3311 GX, Netherlands; http://www.springer.com. Illus., adv. Refereed. Vol. ends: No. 4. Microform: PQC. Reprint: PSC. *Indexed:* A01, A22, E01, ERIC, HEA, P02, PsycInfo. *Aud.:* Ac.

The journal of the Association for Institutional Research is dedicated to improving the functioning of higher education institutions. Articles are written for an audience of higher education personnel, including institutional planners and researchers, administrators, and student personnel specialists who wish to have a better understanding of higher education institutions for the purpose of improved decision-making, effectiveness, and efficiency. Professional papers focus on quantitative studies of higher education procedures. Areas of focus include administration and faculty, curriculum and instruction, student characteristics, alumni, and recruitment and admissions. Each issue contains about five lengthy, well-referenced articles that address subjects such as alumni role identity; the department head's decision autonomy; impact of dual

enrollment on academic performance; and faculty member engagement in undergraduate research. A standard journal for all academic libraries and higher education institutions and organizations. URL: http://link.springer.com/journal/11162

1974. *The Review of Higher Education.* Formerly (until 1978): *Higher Education Review.* [ISSN: 0162-5748] 1977. q. USD 180. Ed(s): Alia Salis Nicole Reyes, Amaury Nora. The Johns Hopkins University Press, 2715 N Charles St, Baltimore, MD 21218; http://www.press.jhu.edu. Illus., adv. Sample. Refereed. Circ: 2034. Microform: PQC. Reprint: PSC. *Indexed:* A01, A22, E01, ERIC, HEA, MLA-IB, P02, PsycInfo. *Bk. rev.:* 12-18 per issue, essay length. *Aud.:* Ac.

The Association for the Study of Higher Education publishes this scholarly journal to report on the issues and trends that affect the field of higher education. The *RHE* contains peer-reviewed articles, essays, studies, and research findings. Issues are analyzed, examined, investigated, and described in articles that focus on topics important to the study of higher education. Recent issues have included articles on faculty–doctoral student relationships; a new college president's transitional processes; work–life balance and culture; and college student engagement. The review essay looks at recently published titles on a topic such as a historical perspective on higher education planning. Available in an online edition. Numerous book reviews are included. An important journal to inform all those working or interested in the field of higher education. URL: www.press.jhu.edu/journals/review_of_higher_education

Homeschooling

1975. *Eclectic Homeschool Online.* 1996. irreg. Eclectic Homeschool Association, PO Box 5304, Fallon, NV 89407-5304. *Aud.:* Ga.

Published from a Christian perspective, this magazine promotes creative homeschooling through unique resources, teaching methods, and online tips. In addition to articles and news on homeschooling, an extensive listing of reviews of resources is provided. A recent issue contains articles on summer reading programs; planning for the next school year; crafts for July; and a homeschool cookbook. Recommended for public libraries and the homeschooling community. URL: http://eclectichomeschool.org/

1976. *Home Education Magazine.* [ISSN: 0888-4633] 1984. bi-m. USD 26; USD 6.50 per issue. Ed(s): Helen E Hegener. Home Education Magazine, PO Box 1083, Tonasket, WA 98855. Illus., adv. Sample. Vol. ends: Dec. *Aud.:* Ga.

This journal is one of the oldest homeschooling magazines, providing focused and extensive coverage of homeschooling. Each issue presents feature articles, columns by various contributors, political commentary, and issues affecting homeschooling; and it acts as a resource to homeschooling families, supporters, educators, researchers, and policymakers. Columns and articles have covered such topics as sustaining homeschooling for the long haul; homeschooling and divorce; tax credits for homeschoolers; science fair participation; and helping children to learn to ask good questons. It also contains interviews, resources, and reviews. The web site offers subscription information, current issue content, a blog, and an archive of selected articles and columns. The September-October 2013 issue promises a shift with new and young writers, fresh ideas, and more support for homeschooling. Highly recommended for public libraries and the homeschooling community. URL: http://homeedmag.com/

1977. *Home Educator's Family Times.* 1993. bi-m. USD 15. Ed(s): Jane R Boswell. Home Educator's Family Times, Inc., PO Box 6442, Brunswick, ME 04011; famtimes@blazenetme.net; http://www.homeeducator.com/. Adv. *Aud.:* Ga.

A homeschool publication that focuses on new or veteran homeschool families. Its content covers research on education and homeschool issues, homeschool strategies, how-to articles, special education needs, and recommended curriculum resources. The article archives currently date back to 1995 with selected issues. Current issue articles cover such topics as predicting homeschool success; adventure of raising boys; college and homeschooling; evaluating learning progress; and homeschooling and family unity. The site offers news items related to homeschooling, previous issues' articles; and an online support group. Recommended for public libraries and the homeschooling community. URL: www.homeeducator.com/

1978. *Homeschooling Today: a journal of home discipleship.* [ISSN: 1073-2217] 1992. bi-m. Ed(s): Kara Murphy. Family Reformation, LLC., PO Box 244, Abingdon, VA 24212; http://www.familyreformation.org. Sample. *Aud.:* Ga.

Established in 1992, this magazine founded by homeschooling parents is focused on the mechanics, mission, and metrics of homeschooling, and integrates Christian concepts into the content. A recent issue concentrates on the Ark and the flood, and uses the topic as a basis for exploring literature and storms. Other issues have covered homeschooling for single parents; life after homeschooling; homeschooling special-needs children; the church as a support group; and the Jamestown legacy as a unit study. Sections include a blog, literature, parenting, resources, reviews, and special needs. Recommended for public libraries and the homeschooling community. URL: www.homeschooltoday.com/

1979. *Practical Homeschooling.* [ISSN: 1075-4741] 1993. bi-m. USD 29 USD 17.95 domestic. Home Life, Inc., PO Box 1190, Fenton, MO 63026. Adv. *Indexed:* BRI, C37. *Aud.:* Ga.

This magazine provides practical how-to information for the homeschooling community. The three to four feature articles in each issue have focused on topics such as Common Core standards for curriculum; homeschool methods; college admissions and homeschooling transcripts; summer camps; and top resources and reading materials. Columns cover such topics as reading readiness; the importance of cursive handwriting; astronomy lessons; increasing a student's vocabulary; and getting kids interested in classical music. Offers detailed product reviews, news shorts, and special features such as how other families homeschool. URL: www.home-school.com/

Specific Subjects and Teaching Methods

ADULT EDUCATION

1980. *Adult Education Quarterly: a journal of research and theory.* Formerly (until 1983): *Adult Education;* Which was formed by the merger of (1942-1950): *Adult Education Journal;* (1936-1950): *Adult Education Bulletin;* Both of which superseded in part (in 1941): *Journal of Adult Education;* Which was formerly (until 1929): *American Association for Adult Education. Journal.* [ISSN: 0741-7136] 1950. q. USD 417. Sage Publications, Inc., 2455 Teller Rd, Thousand Oaks, CA 91320; info@sagepub.com; http://www.sagepub.com. Illus., index, adv. Sample. Refereed. Vol. ends: Summer. Microform: PQC. Reprint: PSC. *Indexed:* A01, A22, BRI, CBRI, E01, ERIC, MLA-IB, PsycInfo. *Bk. rev.:* 3, 1,000 words. *Aud.:* Ac, Sa.

A quarterly refereed journal dedicated to promoting the practice and understanding of adult and continuing education. Geared to practitioners at all levels of adult and continuing education, policymakers, scholars, and students, the journal aims to be inclusive regarding adult and continuing education topics and issues. Interdisciplinary and internationally focused articles, as well as critical problem-oriented research reports of value to practitioners, are of particular interest. In addition to qualitative and quantitative research reports, the journal publishes theoretical and philosophical analyses, critical literature reviews, position statement essays, book reviews, and editorials. Recent research includes studies on learning and refugees; theoretical frameworks for lifelong learning with an indigenous people; what is genre; cultural values and politics in planning adult educational programs in Korea; and a review of research on leadership development and social capital. Book reviews consider publications that are indirectly related, such as cultural studies, work and the economy, distance learning, and international development. A standard title for academic libraries, as well as adult education organizations. URL: http://aeq.sagepub.com

Educational Media International. See Media and AV section.

1981. *Journal of Adolescent & Adult Literacy.* Former titles (until 1995): *Journal of Reading;* (until 1964): *Journal of Developmental Reading.* [ISSN: 1081-3004] 1957. 8x/yr. GBP 95 (print & online eds.). Ed(s): Emily Neil Skinner, Margaret Carmody Hagood. John Wiley & Sons, Inc., 111 River St, MS 4-02, Hoboken, NJ 07030; info@wiley.com; http://onlinelibrary.wiley.com/. Illus., index, adv. Refereed. Circ: 14425. Vol. ends: May. Microform: PQC. Reprint: PSC. *Indexed:* A01, A22, ABS&EES, BEL&L, BRI, CBRI, Chicano, ERIC, MLA-IB, P02, P61, RILM, SSA. *Bk. rev.:* 2, 800 words. *Aud.:* Ac.

A peer-reviewed journal dedicated to providing a forum for educators working in the field of literacy and language arts for older learners. This title is published by the International Reading Association, and its focus is on innovative methods of teaching and researching literacy, and the issues and concerns of literacy professionals. Original articles present practical, theoretical, or research topics such as critical literacy and ethics of student media productions; reading choice in a high school; disciplinary literacy; designing assessments; and the reading behavior of junior secondary students during school holidays. Each issue includes practical instructional ideas; student and teacher resource reviews; information on how to apply technology and media in the classroom; and reflections on current reading research, issues, and trends. Each issue contains lengthy reviews of books for adolescents, professional materials, and classroom materials. Recommended for school and academic libraries. URL: www.reading.org/publications/journals/jaal

1982. *Journal of Research and Practice for Adult Literacy, Secondary, and Basic Education.* Former titles (until 2012): *Adult Basic Education and Literacy Journal;* (until 2007): *Adult Basic Education;* (until 1991): *Adult Literacy and Basic Education.* [ISSN: 2169-0480] 1977. 3x/yr. USD 109 (Members, USD 35; Non-members, USD 65). Ed(s): Jim Berger. Commission on Adult Basic Education, PO Box 620, Syracuse, NY 13206; info@coabe.org; http://www.coabe.org/. Illus. Refereed. Microform: PQC. *Indexed:* A01, A22, BRI, ERIC. *Bk. rev.:* 1, 1,000 words; signed. *Aud.:* Ac, Sa.

A peer-reviewed scholarly journal dedicated to improving educators' efforts with adult literacy. The journal's audience consists of adult educators working in volunteer-based, community-based, and institution-based literacy programs. Written for the practitioner, this journal publishes critical essays, research reviews, and theoretical or philosophical articles. With an emphasis on practical relevance and thought-provoking research articles, contents have considered dropping out of vocational education in Kuwait; literacy-content knowledge expertise among adult education providers; literacy skills acquisition and use; domestic abuse and adult education; modeling professional development for adult literacy providers; skills for successful literacy performance; cognitive approaches to adult literacy; testing adult literacy; and a resource review of learning and violence web site. A highly recommended title for libraries that serve adult literacy educators. URL: www.coabe.org/html/abeljournal.html

Learning & Leading with Technology. See Classroom Magazines/Teacher and Professional section.

1983. *New Horizons in Adult Education & Human Resource Development.* Formerly (until 2006): *New Horizons in Adult Education.* [ISSN: 1939-4225] 1987. q. Free. Ed(s): Douglas H Smith, Tonette S Rocco. Wiley-Blackwell Publishing, Inc., 111 River St, Hoboken, NJ 07030; info@wiley.com; http://www.wiley.com/. Refereed. *Indexed:* ERIC. *Bk. rev.:* Number and length vary. *Aud.:* Ac.

With an emphasis on adult education, human resource development, and related topics, this journal seeks to publish research and practical reports that explore organizational, group, and individual learning at all levels and locations. Rural, urban, and international environments in which the relevant learning occurs are fully acceptable contexts for research published in this journal. This title includes sections filled with research manuscripts; essays that give perspectives on people, practice, research, and teaching; point/counterpoint essays; book reviews; and practical news and notes. All of this comes together to support the work of faculty, students, researchers, and practitioners. Recently published articles have covered: information consumption and literacy; trends in the opportunity costs of U.S. higher education; and barriers to higher education. Occasional special-topics issues are also published on relevant subjects such as "Conflicts, Collaborations, and LGBTQ Cultural Work in Adult Education and

Human Resource Development." With its international coverage, this resource is a standard for all those working or interested in the fields of adult education and human resource development as separate fields or as intersecting fields. URL: http://education.fiu.edu/newhorizons/index.html

THE ARTS

1984. Art Education. Incorporates (1970-1980): *Art Teacher.* [ISSN: 0004-3125] 1948. bi-m. Free to members. Ed(s): Flavia Bastos. National Art Education Association, 1916 Association Dr, Reston, VA 20191; info@arteducators.org; http://www.naea-reston.org. Illus., index, adv. Refereed. Vol. ends: Nov. Microform: PQC. *Indexed:* A07, A22, A51, BRI, ERIC. *Aud.:* Hs, Ac.

This bimonthly journal of the National Art Education Association supports the association's goal of promoting art education. Articles on current issues and exemplary practices in visual arts education serve the professional needs and interests of art educators at all educational levels. Theme-focused issues have addressed topics such as re-imagining art education; creativity and imagination; and the impact of place on art education and those involved in it. In addition to the four or five themed articles, each issue has instructional resources, including shop window displays, four full-color art reproductions, and a lesson plan. Position advertisements are a regular item. Highly recommended for school and academic libraries. URL: www.naea-reston.org

1985. Arts and Activities: the nation's leading arts education magazine. Formerly (until 1955): *Junior Arts and Activities.* [ISSN: 0004-3931] 1932. 10x/yr. USD 40 domestic; USD 90 foreign. Publishers Development Corp., 12345 World Trade Dr., San Diego, CA 92128. Illus., index, adv. Sample. Circ: 22000. Microform: PQC. *Indexed:* A01, A07, A22, BRI, C37, ERIC, P02. *Bk. rev.:* 2-6, 50-100 words. *Aud.:* Ems, Hs, Ga, Ac.

A magazine dedicated to providing an exchange of professional experiences, opinions, and new ideas for art educators. Contributors share strategies for art instruction, approaches to art history, techniques for engaging students in evaluating art, and programs and lessons to expand students' appreciation of art. Articles have covered a broad range of topics such as learning styles in the classroom, children as art teachers, artist trading cards, art appreciation, ceramics, computer art, drawing and painting, mixed media, papier-mache, collage, and three-dimensional design. Each issue has a major theme with multiple articles addressing the theme. Recent themes include protecting the planet through art; summery ideas and summer art; creative three-dimensional ideas; a smart project for color media; and constructing in clay. A regular feature is a pullout clip-and-save art print. For the practitioner, the magazine publishes an annual buyers' guide and a listing of summer art programs. Recommended for school libraries and academic libraries with art education programs. URL: http://artsandactivities.com/

1986. Arts Education Policy Review. Former titles (until 1992): *Design for Arts in Education;* (until 1977): *Design;* (until 1930): *Design-Keramic Studio;* (until 1924): *Keramic Studio.* [ISSN: 1063-2913] 1899. q. GBP 166 (print & online eds.). Ed(s): Colleen Conway. Routledge, 325 Chestnut St, Ste 800, Philadelphia, PA 19106; customerservice@taylorandfrancis.com; http://www.tandfonline.com. Illus., index, adv. Refereed. Microform: PQC. Reprint: PSC. *Indexed:* A01, A06, A07, A22, BRI, ERIC, IIPA, MLA-IB, P02, RILM. *Bk. rev.:* 1, essay length. *Aud.:* Ac.

This journal provides a forum for the discussion of arts education policy issues in grades pre-K–12, nationally and internationally. With a focus on presenting current and controversial ideas and issues, articles focus on the application of policy analysis to arts education topics. Contributors present a broad range of perspectives and ideas on arts education. Articles have covered topics such as evolution of public arts education; cognition and student learning through the arts; high-stakes testing and art education; merit pay and the music teacher; the importance of dance education; factors that influence retention, turnover, and attrition of K–12 music teachers; and teaching and fostering creativity. One special topic issue focused on the professional development of experienced music teachers. Readership includes teachers, university faculty, education

students, graduate students, policymakers, and others interested in arts in education. Recommended for all school and academic libraries. URL: www.tandf.co.uk/journals/titles/10632913.asp

1987. School Arts: the art education magazine for teachers. Formerly (until 1935): *School Arts Magazine.* [ISSN: 0036-6463] 1901. 9x/yr. USD 24.95. Ed(s): Nancy Walkup. Davis Publications, Inc. (Worcester), 50 Portland St, Printers Bldg, Worcester, MA 01608; contactus@davis-art.com; http://www.davis-art.com. Illus., index, adv. Sample. Vol. ends: May/Jun. Microform: NBI; PQC. *Indexed:* A01, A06, A07, A22, B02, BRI, CBRI, ERIC, MLA-IB, P02. *Aud.:* Ems, Hs, Ga, Ac.

A magazine dedicated to inspiring art and classroom teachers at the elementary and secondary level. Issues, often with a theme, address topics such as: elementary and high school studio lessons; environment and nature; interdisciplinary connections; and managing the art classroom. Short, focused articles present curriculum ideas and plans; art technique applications; exemplary art programs; instruction and assessment methods; teaching art to special populations; and professional development. With the practitioner as audience, the magazine contains classroom instructional materials organized by educational level, and extensive advertisements for art materials. Each issue includes different showcases of materials and resources, including showcases on clay, web sites, and technology. Highly recommended for all school libraries. URL: www.davisart.com/portal/schoolarts/sadefault.aspx

1988. Studies in Art Education: a journal of issues and research. [ISSN: 0039-3541] 1959. q. Members, USD 26; Non-members, USD 33. National Art Education Association, 1916 Association Dr, Reston, VA 20191; info@arteducators.org; http://www.naea-reston.org. Illus., index, adv. Refereed. Vol. ends: Summer. Microform: PQC. *Indexed:* A07, A22, A51, ERIC. *Bk. rev.:* 1-3, 500-1,000 words. *Aud.:* Ac.

Published by the National Art Education Association, this scholarly refereed journal supports the association's goal to promote art education through professional development and to disseminate knowledge and information about the field. The journal reports on historical, philosophical, or empirical research in the field of art education, as well as applicable research in related disciplines. An interdisciplinary approach to art education is a focus of the journal's content. Issues cover a wide variety of topics, and reflect the trends and issues of art education research. Articles have examined learning and teaching art through social media; urban arts practice; mass media through video art education; disability studies and art education; inherent creativity in early childhood; an examination of the re-conceptualization of art education; and multicultural art education. Highly recommended for all academic libraries. URL: www.arteducators.org/research/studies

1989. Visual Arts Research: educational, historical, philosophical and psychological perspectives. Former titles (until 1982): *Review of Research in Visual Arts Education;* (until 1975): *Review of Research in Visual and Environmental Education.* [ISSN: 0736-0770] 1973. s-a. USD 70 (print & online eds.). Ed(s): Elizabeth M Delacruz. University of Illinois Press, 1325 S Oak St, Champaign, IL 61820; journals@uillinois.edu; http://www.press.uillinois.edu. Illus., adv. Refereed. *Indexed:* A07, A22, E01, PsycInfo. *Aud.:* Ac.

A journal dedicated to research on teaching and learning in the visual arts. Article contents cover critical and cultural studies, curriculum research and development, art education history, research, and theory, aesthetics, and phenomenology. A regular column reports on published dissertations that are relevant to the field of visual arts instruction. Academic contributors, predominantly from the United States, present papers concerned with current issues and ideas such as artistic development in context; children's drawings in Egypt; a billboard poetry project; the novice art teacher; changing adolescent attitudes in the art classroom; and generation and gender aesthetic responses to popular illustrations. One issue each year is dedicated to a special topic. A recent special issue focused on visual arts research, while another dealt with mentoring doctoral research. A focused journal for a specific audience of faculty, students, and researchers. URL: www.press.uillinois.edu/journals/var.html

BIOLOGY

1990. *The American Biology Teacher.* [ISSN: 0002-7685] 1938. 9x/yr. USD 225 (print & online eds.). Ed(s): Cheryl S Merrill, William Leonard. University of California Press, Journals Division, 2000 Ctr St, Ste 303, Berkeley, CA 94704; customerservice@ucpressjournals.com; http://www.ucpressjournals.com. Illus., index, adv. Refereed. Vol. ends: Nov/Dec. Microform: PQC. *Indexed:* A01, A22, ABS&EES, Agr, BRI, E01, ERIC, GardL, P02, RILM. *Bk. rev.:* 4-8, 300-800 words. *Aud.:* Ems, Hs, Ac.

This is the official journal of the National Association of Biology Teachers, and it is aimed at teachers of high school and undergraduate biology students. Most authors are biology educators (mainly at the college level, though some are high school teachers) or professional biologists. The journal publishes two or three feature articles monthly. These may include reviews of biology research or topics of current interest, discussion of social and ethical issues in biology education, results of studies on teaching techniques, or approaches for use in the classroom. The "Inquiry & Investigations" section includes four to six articles that focus on specific projects for the laboratory or field. Curricular and laboratory-based activities are presented in the "How-To-Do-It" section. Upcoming focused issues will address population biology, physiology, and microbiology. Most issues have reviews of audiovisual materials or computer resources in "Classroom Media Reviews." "Biology Today" presents essays by the section editor on interesting topics of current interest. Announcements and society news are also featured. Given the concern about science education in this country, this title should be of interest to anyone teaching undergraduate introductory biology courses, junior and senior high teachers, and even parents homeschooling older children. URL: www.nabt.org/websites/institution/index.php?p=26

COMMUNICATION ARTS

1991. *College Composition and Communication.* [ISSN: 0010-096X] 1950. q. USD 75. Ed(s): Kathleen B Yancey. National Council of Teachers of English, 1111 W Kenyon Rd, Urbana, IL 61801; customerservice@ncte.org; http://www.ncte.org. Illus., index, adv. Sample. Refereed. Circ: 8000. Vol. ends: Dec. Microform: PQC. *Indexed:* A22, AmHI, ArtHuCI, BRI, CBRI, ERIC, MLA-IB. *Bk. rev.:* 1, essay length. *Aud.:* Ac.

This academic journal, published by the Conference on College Composition and Communication, addresses the issues and concerns of college composition instructors. Articles provide a forum for critical work on the study and teaching of college-level composition and reading. Article content covers all aspects of the profession, including teaching practices, the historical or institutional background of an educational practice, and current issues and trends in related disciplines. Although focused on those responsible for the teaching of composition at the college level, this journal will be of interest to administrators of composition programs, community college instructors, researchers, technical writers, graduate assistants, and others involved with college writing instruction. Each issue contains featured articles, review essays, book reviews, and contributor responses to published research theory or practice. Contributors have considered local assessment; feminist historiography and digital humanities; adult students and process knowledge transfer; graduate-level writing instruction; negotiating cultural identities through language; research centers as change agents; resisting age bias in digital literacy research; and enacting and transforming local language policies. Some content has free access. A highly recommended title for academic libraries. URL: www.ncte.org/cccc/about

1992. *College English.* Supersedes (in 1939): *English Journal (College Edition);* Which superseded in part (in 1928): *English Journal.* [ISSN: 0010-0994] 1912. bi-m. USD 75. Ed(s): Kelly Ritter. National Council of Teachers of English, 1111 W Kenyon Rd, Urbana, IL 61801; customerservice@ncte.org; http://www.ncte.org. Illus., index. Sample. Refereed. Vol. ends: Dec. Microform: PMC; PQC. *Indexed:* A01, A22, AmHI, ArtHuCI, BEL&L, BRI, ERIC, LT&LA, MLA-IB, P02. *Bk. rev.:* 1-3, essay length. *Aud.:* Ac.

This refereed professional journal of the College Section of the National Council of Teachers of English (NCTE) provides a forum for scholars on teaching English. Topics covered include, but are not limited to, literature, linguistics, literacy, critical theory, reading theory, rhetoric, composition, pedagogy, and professional issues. Each issue has three or four articles as well as occasional opinion pieces, book reviews, reader comments and author responses, and NCTE news and announcements. Authors have published literary articles on topics such as "speaking white"; language differences in student writing; world literature pedagogy; poverty in literature; and autism and rhetoric. Other issues have covered special topics such as contingent faculty, and Chinese rhetoric. A standard for all academic libraries. URL: www.ncte.org/journals/ce

1993. *English Education.* Formerly (until 1969): *Conference on English Education. Selected Addresses Delivered.* [ISSN: 0007-8204] 1963. q. USD 75. Ed(s): Lisa Scherff, Leslie S Rush. National Council of Teachers of English, 1111 W Kenyon Rd, Urbana, IL 61801; customerservice@ncte.org; http://www.ncte.org. Illus., index, adv. Sample. Refereed. Circ: 2700. Vol. ends: Dec. Microform: PQC. *Indexed:* A22, ERIC, MLA-IB. *Aud.:* Ac.

Dedicated to the education of teachers of English, reading, and language arts, the Conference on English Education focuses its journal on pre-service training and in-service development. Issues relevant to the profession are considered, such as pre-service and in-service education, professional development, student teacher evaluation, English curriculum, and trends in teacher education programs nationwide. Each issue has three or four articles that cover such topics as building multiliterate and multilingual writing practices; connecting across classrooms, communities, and disciplines; the challenges of beginning teachers' teaching writing and grammar; using theater to engage cultural identity; the role of history in English education; positioning students as readers and writers; and English education program assessment. Readership is aimed at a broad range of teacher education personnel, including college and university instructors of teachers; in-service educators; teacher consultants; curriculum coordinators; and classroom teachers supervising student teachers. A highly recommended journal for libraries that serve education programs. URL: www.ncte.org/journals/ee

1994. *English Journal.* [ISSN: 0013-8274] 1912. bi-m. USD 75 domestic; USD 85 Canada; USD 90 elsewhere. Ed(s): Julie A Gorlewski, David A Gorlewski. National Council of Teachers of English, 1111 W Kenyon Rd, Urbana, IL 61801; customerservice@ncte.org; http://www.ncte.org. Illus., index, adv. Sample. Refereed. Circ: 18000. Vol. ends: Dec. Microform: PMC; PQC. *Indexed:* A01, A22, BRI, CBRI, Chicano, ERIC, LT&LA, MLA-IB, P02. *Bk. rev.:* 5-9, 500-700 words. *Aud.:* Ac.

A publication of the National Council of Teachers of English (NCTE), this journal serves an audience of middle school, junior high school, and senior high school teachers, as well as supervisors and teacher educators. This refereed publication covers current practices and theory in teaching composition, reading skills, oral language, literature, and varied media use. Featured articles may focus on a particular issue or topic, while regular columns review books and classroom material. Current and/or upcoming issues cover: the capacity and audacity of English; examining assessment; teaching English in a democratic society; literacy and literature; and development of professional educators. The journal also provides a forum for the exchange of teaching suggestions and ideas; and informs as to NCTE news and activities. There are 15 or more articles per issue, and the featured topic is well covered with respect to both practical applications and theoretical perspectives. Article topics have included robo-grading and writing instruction; haiku in the classroom; digital literacy; videogames in the classroom; and how to awaken creativity in students. A recommended journal for school and academic libraries. URL: www.ncte.org/journals/ej

1995. *Kairos: a journal of rhetoric, technology and pedagogy.* [ISSN: 1521-2300] 1996. s-a. Free. Ed(s): Cheryl Ball. Kairos. Refereed.
Indexed: ERIC, MLA-IB. *Aud.:* Ac, Sa.

As a leading journal in the field of English studies, this peer-reviewed, open-access journal has a large international readership and seeks to explore the intersection of pedagogy, technology, and rhetoric. The scholarly works published utilize rhetoric, digital technology and media, and these works are authored specifically for the World Wide Web. The journal's contributions cover empirical research reports, narratives on teaching with technology, theoretical essays, commentary, and print, software, and media reviews. Many issues have a themed focus, and include regular columns for news and announcements. Themes have addressed rhetoric, technology, and the military; the tenth anniversary issue; disability and technology; writing in globalization; and issues of new media. Features have considered critical issues in digital scholarship; manifestos as scholarship; and rhetoric, technology, and the military. A highly recommended resource for the secondary education and higher education community. URL: www.technorhetoric.net/about.html

1996. *Language Arts.* Former titles (until 1975): *Elementary English;* (until 1947): *Elementary English Review.* [ISSN: 0360-9170] 1924. bi-m. USD 75. Ed(s): Peggy Albers, Amy S Flint. National Council of Teachers of English, The Ohio State University, School of Teaching and Learning, 333 Arps Hall, 1945 N. High St., Columbus, OH 43210; customerservice@ncte.org; http://www.ncte.org. Illus., index, adv. Sample. Refereed. Circ: 10000. Vol. ends: Dec. Microform: PQC. *Indexed:* A01, A22, BRI, CBRI, Chicano, ERIC, LT&LA, MLA-IB, P02. *Bk. rev.:* 30-35 children's books and 5-7 professional books. *Aud.:* Ac.

A title published by the National Council of Teachers of English for elementary teachers and teacher educators of language arts. Original articles focus on all aspects of language arts learning and teaching from preschool through middle school–age levels. Issues are theme-focused, with the exception of a single non-themed issue per volume. Recent themes consider inquiries and insights; language arts in a 2.0 world; stories of achievement; locating standards in language arts education; and the rights of readers. Each issue gives classroom strategies, methods, research reports, and opinions. Recommended for school and academic libraries that serve an education program. URL: www.ncte.org/journals/la

1997. *Learning, Media & Technology (Online).* Incorporates (2001-2005): *Education, Communications & Information (Online);* Formerly (until 2005): *Journal of Educational Media (Online).* [ISSN: 1743-9892] q. GBP 849. Ed(s): Neil Selwyn, Rebecca Eynon. Routledge, 4 Park Sq, Milton Park, Abingdon, OX14 4RN, United Kingdom; subscriptions@tandf.co.uk; http://www.tandfonline.com. Refereed. *Bk. rev.:* Number and length vary. *Aud.:* Ac.

Educational theory and practices have always relied on the varied media and technology that are available. This online journal explores the interaction of learning, pedagogy, and educational practice with all of the different kinds of media and technology and the relevant debates associated with these interactions. In addition to empirical studies, the journal also publishes literature reviews and policy critiques. The four to five critically analytic studies published in each issue have examined such topics as texting as a venue for personalized youth support; challenges of participatory media for youths at-risk; Twitter usage in the large lecture hall; making Dutch students media-conscious; using game-based learning to support struggling readers; and a review of why university lecturers enhance their teaching with technology. Annually, one issue of the journal is devoted to a special topic. Some recent topics include city youth and the pedagogy of participatory media; the future of learning design, and learning and researching in the digital world. Book reviews and a viewpoints section are also included. Highly recommended for academic and research institutions. URL: www.tandfonline.com/loi/cjem20

1998. *Literacy Research and Instruction.* Former titles (until 2008): *Reading Research and Instruction;* (until 1985): *Reading World;* (until 1971): *The Journal of the Reading Specialist;* (until 1962): *College Reading Association. Newsletter.* [ISSN: 1938-8071] 1961. q. GBP 109 (print & online eds.). Ed(s): Parker Fawson, Brad Wilcox. Taylor & Francis Inc., 325 Chestnut St, Ste 800, Philadelphia, PA 19106; customerservice@taylorandfrancis.com; http://www.tandfonline.com. Illus., index, adv. Sample. Refereed. Reprint: PSC. *Indexed:* A22, ERIC, P02, PsycInfo. *Bk. rev.:* Number and length vary. *Aud.:* Ac.

A refereed journal of the College Reading Association, which publishes articles on reading research and related literacy fields. There is an emphasis on practice and research of interest literacy and reading educators. Articles include discussions of current issues, research reports, instructional practices, book

reviews, and news from the field. Each issue has four or five lengthy articles on such topics as reading motivation; improving young children's writing; text-based questioning; content validity for a literacy coach performance-evaluation instrument; comprehension after oral and silent reading; a literature review focused on the practice of writing the dissertation; pre-service tutors and first-grade instruction; and the influence of literacy-based science instruction on adolescents' interest and participation in science. Highly recommended for school and academic libraries that serve education programs. URL: www.tandfonline.com/loi/ulri20

1999. *Reading Improvement: a journal for the improvement of reading teaching.* Formerly (until 164): *Reading in High School.* [ISSN: 0034-0510] 1963. q. USD 50 (Individuals, USD 40). Ed(s): Phillip Feldman. Project Innovation, Inc., Spring Hill Sta, PO Box 8508, Mobile, AL 36689; http://www.projectinnovation.biz. Illus., index, adv. Sample. Refereed. Vol. ends: Winter. Microform: PQC. *Indexed:* A01, A22, Chicano, ERIC, MLA-IB. *Bk. rev.:* 0-3, 200-300 words. *Aud.:* Ac.

A journal dedicated to improving the pedagogy and practice of the teaching of reading. Covering all levels of instruction, the journal publishes investigative reports and theoretical papers. Each issue contains five to seven articles that cover a broad range of topics, such as vocabulary instruction modification to support low-socioeconomic students; using semantic mapping to facilitate reading instruction; childrens' language and literacy development through shared reading; supporting reading goals through visual arts; and data-based instruction in reading. Recommended for school and academic libraries. URL: www.projectinnovation.biz/ri.html

2000. *Reading Research Quarterly.* [ISSN: 0034-0553] 1965. q. GBP 98 (print & online eds.). Ed(s): Ian Wilkinson, David Bloome. International Reading Association, 800 Barksdale Rd, PO Box 8139, Newark, DE 19714; customerservice@reading.org; http://www.reading.org. Illus., index, adv. Refereed. Circ: 12280. Vol. ends: Fall. Microform: PQC. Reprint: PSC. *Indexed:* A01, A22, BRI, ERIC, FR, LT&LA, MLA-IB, PsycInfo. *Bk. rev.:* 1, varies in length. *Aud.:* Ac.

Published by the International Reading Association, *RRQ* is a peer-reviewed scholarly journal dedicated to presenting and examining the issues of literacy for all learners. Articles include qualitative and quantitative research, integrative reviews, and conceptual pieces that promote and contribute to the understanding of literacy and literacy research. Each issue reflects a broad range of academic literacy research, with topics and issues such as promoting early literacy; response-based framework for helping middle-school struggling readers; classroom observations of teachers' literacy instruction; young children's literacy practices in a virtual world; comprehension and learning from refutation and expository texts; promises and problems of teaching with popular culture; and text complexity and oral reading prosody in young readers. Letters to the editor and commentaries contribute to the journal's dialogue on literacy research. Available online. Highly recommended for academic and school libraries. URL: www.reading.org/General/Publications/Journals/RRQ.aspx

2001. *The Reading Teacher.* Formerly (until 1951): *International Council for the Improvement of Reading Instruction. Bulletin.* [ISSN: 0034-0561] 1948. 8x/yr. GBP 95 (print & online eds.). Ed(s): Maria Mallette, Diane Barone. International Reading Association, 800 Barksdale Rd, PO Box 8139, Newark, DE 19714; customerservice@reading.org; http://www.reading.org. Illus., index, adv. Refereed. Circ: 46000. Vol. ends: May. Microform: PQC. Reprint: PSC. *Indexed:* A01, A22, AmHI, BRI, C37, CBRI, Chicano, ERIC, MLA-IB, P02, RILM. *Bk. rev.:* Number and length vary. *Aud.:* Ga, Ac.

A peer-reviewed journal by the International Reading Association, *RT* considers practices, research, and trends in literacy education and related disciplines. This journal is published for educators and other professionals involved with literacy education for children to the age of 12. Individual issues have three or four featured articles, teaching tips, digital literacies in the classroom, toolbox, by educators for educators, and children's book review columns, as well as the occasional annotated bibliography of books and children's literary work. The journal's goal to promote and affect literacy education is realized with article topics such as teaching with interactive picture e-books; building a community of readers; meeting the reading challenges of science textbooks in the primary grades; extending readers' theater; supporting informational writing in the elementary grades; and exploring the culture of reading among primary school teachers in Botswana. An important journal for school and academic libraries. URL: www.reading.org/General/Publications/Journals/RT.aspx

2002. *Research in the Teaching of English.* [ISSN: 0034-527X] 1967. q. USD 75. Ed(s): Mary Juzwik, Ellen Cushman. National Council of Teachers of English, 1111 W Kenyon Rd, Urbana, IL 61801; customerservice@ncte.org; http://www.ncte.org. Illus., adv. Sample. Refereed. Circ: 4200. Vol. ends: Dec. Microform: PQC. *Indexed:* A22, ERIC, LT&LA, MLA-IB. *Aud.:* Ac.

RTE's definition of research in the teaching of English is broad and inclusive. The journal is dedicated to publishing multiple approaches to conducting research such as teacher-based research, historical articles, narratives, and current methodology. Additionally, the journal seeks articles that consider literacy issues regardless of language, within schools or other settings, and in other disciplines, and explore the relationship between learning and language teaching. General themes are supported with scholarly, well-referenced articles. A recent issue addressed writing research outside the U.S. Articles for the themed issue included: integrated literacies in a Kenyan girls' secondary school journalism club; Indonesian street children's writing; and thought processes of multilingual writers. A semi-annual selected bibliography of recent research in the teaching of English further supports *RTE*'s mission. Recommended for academic libraries. URL: www.ncte.org/journals/rte

2003. *T E S L - E J.* [ISSN: 1072-4303] 1994. q. Free. Ed(s): Maggie Sokolik. T E S L - E J, University of California, Berkeley, Technical Communication Program, College of Engineering, Berkeley, CA 94720. Illus., index. Refereed. *Indexed:* BRI, CBRI, ERIC, MLA-IB. *Bk. rev.:* Reviews of media, books, and teacher resources; number and length vary. *Aud.:* Ac.

A refereed academic journal focused on the research and practice of English as a second or foreign language. *TESL-EJ* covers a broad range of issues from research to classroom practices for all education levels. Wide-ranging topics that are covered include language assessment, second-language acquisition, applied socio- and psycholinguistics, and EFL and ESL pedagogy. Issues present original articles, book or media reviews, and a forum for discussion. Featured articles range from nine to 25 pages in length. Authors have written on such issues as current status of ELT in Mexico's higher education institutions; the supervisory process of EFL teachers (a case study); expressive vocabulary development of immigrant preschoolers; classrooms as complex adaptive systems; improving speaking fluency for international teaching assistants; repair strategies usage of primary elementary ESL students; and "problematizing" the hybrid classroom for ESL/EFL students. A standard journal for the field of ESL. URL: http://tesl-ej.org/

ENVIRONMENTAL EDUCATION

2004. *The Journal of Environmental Education.* Formerly (until 1971): *Environmental Education.* [ISSN: 0095-8964] 1969. q. GBP 164 (print & online eds.). Routledge, 325 Chestnut St, Ste 800, Philadelphia, PA 19106; customerservice@taylorandfrancis.com; http://www.tandfonline.com. Illus., index. Refereed. Reprint: PSC. *Indexed:* A01, A22, BRI, E01, ERIC, P02, PsycInfo, S25. *Bk. rev.:* 1-2, 500 words. *Aud.:* Ac, Sa.

With a focus on environmental education, this journal publishes original articles that promote and inform on instruction, theory, methods, and practice from primary grades through college. Peer-reviewed research articles include project reports, programs, review articles, critical essays, analyses, and qualitative or quantitative studies. The emphasis is on how to instruct on environmental issues and how to evaluate existing programs. There are four to six articles per issue, and topics have included: influencing citizen scientists intent with climate change; wildfire education program identification of behavior change; a model of early childhood environmental education; environmental literacy in teacher training; teaching through modeling; building environmental literacy; developing effective environmental education; considering culture as a determinant of environmental attitudes; and examining a meta-analysis of classroom interventions and improved environmental behavior. Regular

columns include a review of resources and a summary of a current innovative research study. Readership consists of teachers and others involved with environmental education programs for schools, parks, camps, recreation centers, and businesses. A recommended title for schools and programs that serve environmental education. URL: www.tandfonline.com/toc/vjee20/current

MORAL EDUCATION

2005. *Journal of Moral Education.* Formerly (until 1971): *Moral Education.* [ISSN: 0305-7240] 1969. q. GBP 259 (print & online eds.). Ed(s): Darcia Narvaez. Routledge, 4 Park Sq, Milton Park, Abingdon, OX14 4RN, United Kingdom; subscriptions@tandf.co.uk; http://www.tandfonline.com. Illus., index, adv. Sample. Refereed. Vol. ends: Dec. Reprint: PSC. *Indexed:* A01, A22, ASSIA, E01, ERIC, FR, HEA, IBSS, P02, P61, PsycInfo, R&TA, SSA. *Bk. rev.:* 5-10, 600-1,500 words. *Aud.:* Ac.

A journal focused on all aspects of moral education and development. A multidisciplinary approach and inclusive age range contribute to the journal's broad content scope. Authors provide philosophical analyses, empirical research reports, evaluations of educational practice, and overviews of international moral education theories and practices. Five or six articles per issue cover moral education research such as engagement with moral beauty; teaching care ethics; promotion of moral ideas in schools; moral and political identity; peace education; and children's development of moral and social knowledge. Curriculum materials and book reviews, as well as special thematic issues, further the academic value of the journal. A standard journal for all academic libraries. URL: www.tandfonline.com/toc/cjme20/current

SOCIAL STUDIES (INCLUDING HISTORY AND ECONOMICS)

2006. *The History Teacher.* [ISSN: 0018-2745] 1967. q. USD 63 (Individuals, USD 32; Students, USD 22). Ed(s): Richard H Wilde, Jane A Dabel. Society for History Education, California State University, 1250 Bellflower Blvd, PO Box 1578, Long Beach, CA 90840; lazarowi@csulb.edu. Illus., index, adv. Sample. Refereed. Vol. ends: Aug. *Indexed:* A01, A22, ABS&EES, BAS, Chicano, ERIC, MLA-IB. *Bk. rev.:* 10-15, 600-1,200 words. *Aud.:* Ac.

A membership journal of the Society for History Education, this title is dedicated to the teaching of history in the primary, secondary, and higher education classroom. The journal focuses on professional analyses of current and innovative teaching techniques. Each issue includes a featured article and one or two additional articles. Some recent featured articles have dealt with teaching medieval European society with chess; the Magna Carta in American history; using technologies and media to engage and elicit changes in thinking; and the importance of local history in the rural setting. A recent issue's special feature offered 2012 National History Day prize essays. Multiple shorter items fill the sections on the craft of teaching and the state of the profession. An extensive review section covers textbooks, readers, films, computer programs, and other material. Recommended for academic libraries. URL: www.thehistoryteacher.org/

2007. *The Journal of Economic Education.* [ISSN: 0022-0485] 1969. q. GBP 158 (print & online eds.). Ed(s): William B Walstad. Routledge, 325 Chestnut St, Ste 800, Philadelphia, PA 19106; customerservice@taylorandfrancis.com; http://www.tandfonline.com. Illus., index, adv. Refereed. Reprint: PSC. *Indexed:* A22, ABIn, B01, B02, BRI, E01, ERIC, EconLit, JEL. *Aud.:* Ac.

This journal offers original articles on innovations in, and evaluations of, teaching techniques, materials, and programs in economics. This journal is designed for instructors of beginning through graduate-level economics courses, and issues feature sections on research, economic instruction, economic content, and features and information. Contributed articles include theoretical and empirical studies, substantive issues, new ideas, innovations in pedagogy, interactive exemplary material, and reports on the status and events that influence academic economists. Recent article topics explore principles of economics textbook in the financial crisis; econometrics as a capstone economics course; test of economic literacy; teaching bank runs with classroom experiments; microeconomics and psychology; teaching and assessment methods in undergraduate economics; student performance in undergraduate economics; and trends in undergraduate economics degrees. Innovative teaching materials that utilize interactive technologies are presented in the "Online" section of the electronic version of the journal. Recommended for academic libraries. URL: www.tandfonline.com/loi/vece20

2008. *Social Education.* [ISSN: 0037-7724] 1937. 7x/yr. Free to members. Ed(s): Michael Simpson. National Council for the Social Studies, 8555 16th St, Ste 500, Silver Spring, MD 20910; publications@ncss.org; http://www.ncss.org. Illus., index, adv. Sample. Vol. ends: Nov/Dec. Microform: PQC. *Indexed:* A01, A22, ABS&EES, BAS, BRI, CBRI, ERIC, MLA-IB, P02, RILM. *Bk. rev.:* 1-6, 200-800 words. *Aud.:* Ac.

This is a journal published by the National Council for the Social Studies (NCSS) to support the council's mission "to provide leadership, service, and support" for social studies instructors. Its content is focused on classroom practices at all levels: elementary, middle, high school, and university. Featured articles have presented using historical fiction in the elementary classroom; water education in the Netherlands; teaching with visualization tools; teaching economics in the current economy; using primary sources to teach world history; connections for classroom teaching; a consideration of the practice and theory of instructional technology; and a ten-year study of citizenship education in five countries. One recent feature article was written by the U.S. Secretary of Education explaining why social studies is essential to a well-rounded education. A 2013 issue included the NCSS position statement on revitalizing civic learning in the schools. Significant journal content is given to classroom curriculum materials. The magazine regularly includes book reviews, lesson plans, pull-outs, and notable Internet resources. Highly recommended for school and academic libraries that serve education programs. URL: www.socialstudies.org/socialeducation

2009. *The Social Studies: a periodical for teachers and administrators.* Former titles (until 1953): *Social Studies for Teachers and Administrators;* (until 1951): *The Social Studies;* (until 1934): *Historical Outlook;* (until 1918): *History Teacher's Magazine.* [ISSN: 0037-7996] 1909. bi-m. GBP 135 (print & online eds.). Ed(s): Ronald A Banaszak. Routledge, 325 Chestnut St, Ste 800, Philadelphia, PA 19106; customerservice@taylorandfrancis.com; http://www.tandfonline.com. Illus., index. Refereed. Microform: PQC. Reprint: PSC. *Indexed:* A01, A22, BRI, CBRI, E01, ENW, ERIC, P02, P61, RILM, SSA. *Bk. rev.:* 0-1, 400 words. *Aud.:* Ac.

This peer-reviewed journal publishes articles concerned with the subjects of social studies, social sciences, history, and interdisciplinary studies for grades K–12 and above. The journal seeks articles that give new perspectives, practical applications, and insights on issues concerning social studies curricula, learning, and instruction. Articles dealing with current issues or historical ideas significant to the social sciences are also published. With five to seven articles per issue, *TSS* covers a broad range of topics from research-based to classroom practice. Articles have focused on media literacy and cultural studies in social studies curricula; citizenship as seen through the lens of the "Hunger Games"; maps as primary sources in the classroom; learning history with museums; promoting critical thinking and inquiry using maps; Wernher von Braun and "the Space Race"; teaching about Navajo citizenship and sovereignty; and retooling the social studies classroom for the current generation. A special issue dealt with the challenges of teaching 9/11. Recommended for school and academic libraries. URL: http://www.tandfonline.com/toc/vtss20/current#.UeBFUKxsuSo

TEACHER EDUCATION

2010. *Action in Teacher Education.* [ISSN: 0162-6620] 1978. bi-m. GBP 169 (print & online eds.). Routledge, 325 Chestnut St, Ste 800, Philadelphia, PA 19106; customerservice@taylorandfrancis.com; http://www.tandfonline.com. Illus., index, adv. Sample. Refereed. Vol. ends: Winter. Microform: PQC. Reprint: PSC. *Indexed:* A22, ERIC. *Aud.:* Ac.

This is a refereed journal published by the Association of Teacher Educators, an organization dedicated to the improvement of teacher education for both school and higher education instructors. Intended to serve as a forum for issues, ideas, and trends concerning the improvement of teacher education, this journal is for

the practitioner. Articles are focused on the theory, practice, and research of teacher education. With practitioners as audience, the content is on the applications and implications of research and practice. Issues are both thematic and non-thematic, with 6–12 articles per issue. Themed issues have featured teacher education programs; media literacy education; partnerships; alternative routes to certification; indigenous perspectives on teacher education; reflective practices; preparation and professional development of teachers and the impact on student learning; and three different perspectives on teaching and teacher education. Non-themed issues have covered a broad range of issues, from professional development schools to student teachers as reflective thinkers to teachers as mentors. For all school and academic libraries. URL: http://education.ou.edu/action

2011. *Journal of Education for Teaching: international research and pedagogy.* Formerly (until 1981): *British Journal of Teacher Education.* [ISSN: 0260-7476] 1975. q. GBP 1028 (print & online eds.). Routledge, 4 Park Sq, Milton Park, Abingdon, OX14 4RN, United Kingdom; subscriptions@tandf.co.uk; http://www.tandfonline.com. Adv. Sample. Refereed. Reprint: PSC. *Indexed:* A01, A22, E01, ERIC, HEA, LT&LA, MLA-IB, P02. *Aud.:* Ac.

JET publishes original articles on the subject of teacher education. The journal's definition of teacher education is inclusive of initial training, in-service education, and professional staff development. Primarily British, but with an international orientation, the journal seeks to promote academic discussion of issues, trends, research, opinion, and practice on teacher education. Contributors have assessed such issues as transforming teacher education; learning to teach in a context of education reform; learners' expectations of their first year in college; promoting teacher reflection; teaching controversial issues and teacher education in England and South Africa; and the importance of collegiality and reciprocal learning in the professional development of beginning teachers. Each issue also contains a research-in-practice article. Annually, one issue is devoted to a special topic. Recent special topics have dealt with the work of teacher education regarding policy, practice, and institutional conditions; academic work and identities in teacher education; and international perspectives on research in initial teacher education. Recommended for all academic libraries. URL: www.tandfonline.com/loi/cjet20

2012. *Journal of Teacher Education: the journal of policy, practice, and research in teacher education.* [ISSN: 0022-4871] 1950. 5x/yr. USD 590. Corwin Press, Inc., 2455 Teller Rd, Thousand Oaks, CA 91320; info@sagepub.com; http://www.corwinpress.com. Illus., adv. Sample. Refereed. Vol. ends: Nov/Dec. Microform: PQC. Reprint: PSC. *Indexed:* A01, A22, BRI, CBRI, Chicano, E01, ERIC, FR, MLA-IB, P02. *Bk. rev.:* 0-1, essay length up to 3,800 words. *Aud.:* Ac.

A professional journal of the American Association of Colleges for Teacher Education, *JTE* considers teacher education as a field of study. As noted in the journal's subtitle, the focus is on policy, practice, and research in teacher education. The journal focuses on helping future teachers deal with the issues, challenges, and demands of the future instructional environment. Recent articles have addressed such topics as using rehearsals to support beginning teachers, teacher learning in a context of educational change; knowledge expectations in mathematics teacher preparation programs in South Korea and the United States; understanding teachers' desires to teach in the urban environment; and developing a framework for professional ethics courses in teacher education. Themed issues have considered teacher learning and standards-based instruction; multicultural education; and teacher education and society with scholarly papers integrating research, practice, and theory on the topic. Occasionally, essay-length book reviews are included. Highly recommended for all libraries that serve teacher education programs. URL: http://jte.sagepub.com/

2013. *Teacher Education Quarterly.* Formerly (until 1983): *California Journal of Teacher Education.* [ISSN: 0737-5328] 1972. q. USD 150 (Individuals, USD 75; Free to members). Ed(s): Thomas G Nelson. Caddo Gap Press, 3145 Geary Blvd, PMB 275, San Francisco, CA 94118; caddogap@aol.com; http://www.caddogap.com. Illus., adv. Sample. Refereed. Vol. ends: Fall. Microform: PQC. *Indexed:* A22, ERIC, MLA-IB. *Aud.:* Ac.

A refereed research journal that focuses on current educational research and practice, as well as educational policy and reform issues. It is published by the California Council on Teacher Education, an organization dedicated to supporting and promoting teacher educators. *TEQ* supports the council's mission with relevant, interesting, and challenging articles related to the field of teacher education and teacher professional development. Contributors from university researchers to teacher education practitioners cover issues such as collaborative professional development's impact on teacher practice; technological innovations in teaching and learning; shaping new models of teacher education; moving teacher education to urban schools; progressive teacher education; and research on teacher development. Each issue has a special theme with articles that showcase innovative and practical research and solutions useful to the scholar and the practitioner. A recent themed issue examined entering, preparing for, and leaving the teaching profession. Recommended for all libraries that serve teacher education programs. URL: www.teqjournal.org/

2014. *Teaching and Teacher Education: an international journal of research and studies.* [ISSN: 0742-051X] 1985. 8x/yr. EUR 1597. Ed(s): M L Hamilton, J Clandinin. Pergamon, The Blvd, Langford Ln, E Park, Kidlington, OX5 1GB, United Kingdom; JournalsCustomerServiceEMEA@elsevier.com; http://www.elsevier.com. Illus., adv. Sample. Refereed. Microform: PQC. *Indexed:* A01, A22, ASSIA, ERIC, PsycInfo. *Aud.:* Ac.

This international journal covers all aspects and levels of teaching, teachers, and teacher education. With its broad coverage, the journal is of value to all concerned with teaching, including researchers in teacher education, educational and cognitive psychologists, and policymakers and planners. The journal is committed to promoting teaching and teacher education through the publication of theory, research, and practice, and is of interest to all involved or connected with teaching. Academic authors support the journal's commitment, with scholarly articles that range from classroom practice to professional development, to pre-service teachers. Each issue contains 10–15 articles focused on topics such as beliefs about teaching; language teachers; teacher professional development over ten years; building caring relationships between a teacher and students; student teachers' skills in the implementation of collaborative learning; a teacher's working-environment fit as a framework for burnout; and how pre-service teachers observe teaching on video. Special issues, virtual and print, have considered equity and social justice; teacher education for inclusive education; and teaching learning and development in the U.K. Recommended for all libraries that serve teacher education programs. URL: www.sciencedirect.com/science/journal/0742051X

2015. *Teaching Education.* [ISSN: 1047-6210] 1987. q. GBP 398 (print & online eds.). Ed(s): Diane Mayer, Carmen Luke. Routledge, 4 Park Sq, Milton Park, Abingdon, OX14 4RN, United Kingdom; subscriptions@tandf.co.uk; http://www.tandfonline.com. Illus., index, adv. Sample. Refereed. Reprint: PSC. *Indexed:* A22, E01, ERIC. *Bk. rev.:* 2, 800 words to essay length. *Aud.:* Ac.

Dedicated to providing a forum for innovative practice and research in teacher education, this journal focuses on challenge and change in teacher education. Contributors address social, cultural, practical, and theoretical issues of teacher education from school to university, and on the transformation of teacher education. The journal's contents include critical and theory-based research; scholarly reflections on current teacher education issues; innovative approaches to undergraduate and graduate teaching; new practices in the K–12 classroom; and reviews of scholarly works. Research and scholarship topics have addressed a case study of a career in education that began with "Teach for America"; pre-service teachers preparation for parent engagement; Latino parents and teachers; a content analysis of lesbian, gay, bisexual, and transgender topics in multicultural education textbooks; and investigating Finnish teacher educators. A recent special issue focused on family, school, community engagement, and partnerships. Innovative approaches to curriculum have included a study of critical liberal education in a socially diverse university setting. Recommended for all academic libraries. URL: www.tandf.co.uk/journals/cTED

TECHNOLOGY

2016. *Educational Technology: the magazine for managers of change in education.* Former titles (until 1966): *Teaching Aids News;* (until 1961): *Teaching Aids Newsletter.* [ISSN: 0013-1962] 1961. bi-m. USD 199

domestic; USD 229 foreign. Ed(s): Laurence Lipsitz. Educational Technology Publications, 700 Palisade Ave, PO Box 1564, Englewood Cliffs, NJ 07632; edtecpubs@aol.com. Illus., adv. Sample. Vol. ends: Nov/Dec. *Indexed:* A22, CompLI, ERIC, I15. *Bk. rev.:* 0-3, 300-500 words. *Aud.:* Ac.

This magazine publishes articles that report on research and practical applications in the field of educational technology. It is focused on a readership of school administrators, trainers, designers, and others involved with educational technology. With nine or ten articles per issue, various aspects of educational technology are covered, such as: instructional design cases; beyond digital natives; risks of open scholarship; McLuhan's legacy; ICT in schools—what rationale?; educational technology during economic downturns; connecting improved learning outcomes and scholarly communications; and knowledge management for teachers. Recent new features include a column of interviews with visionary leaders who have done innovative work with educational technology; a conference reports section of pertinent papers of interest to the field; and biographical studies of historical figures in educational technology. There are also occasional columns by leaders from interdisciplinary fields related to educational technology, and special issues on developing trends in the field. A special issue focused on highly mobile computing. Recommended for all academic and school libraries. URL: www.asianvu.com/bookstoread/etp/

2017. *Educational Technology Research & Development.* Formed by the merger of (1978-1989): *Journal of Instructional Development;* (1978-1989): *Educational Communications and Technology Journal;* Which was formerly (unil 1978): *A V Communication Review;* (until 1964): *Audio Visual Communication Review.* [ISSN: 1042-1629] 1989. bi-m. EUR 322 (print & online eds.). Ed(s): J Michael Spector, Michael J Hannafin. Springer New York LLC, 233 Spring St, New York, NY 10013; service-ny@springer.com; http://www.springer.com/. Illus., index, adv. Refereed. Vol. ends: No. 4. Microform: PQC. Reprint: PSC. *Indexed:* A01, A22, BRI, E01, ERIC, FR, PsycInfo. *Bk. rev.:* 0-2, essay length. *Aud.:* Ac.

A publication of the Association for Educational Communications and Technology, the journal serves to promote educational technology and its application to the learning process, and focuses entirely on research and development in educational technology. Each issue has five or six articles that cover research, both practical aspects and applied theory, and development topics, including planning, implementation, evaluation, and management. Recent topics include team-based complex problem–solving; emotions and information problem-solving; content of educational technology curricula; understanding international graduate student isolation in traditional and online environments; and a study of learning and motivation in a new media-enriched environment for middle school science. A regular department features issues and trends in the field of educational technology in other countries. Each issue also includes book reviews, international reviews, and research abstracts. Recommended for all academic and school libraries. URL: www.aect.org/intranet/publications/index.asp

2018. *From Now On: the educational technology journal.* 1990. m. Free. Ed(s): Jamie McKenzie. F N O Press, 917 12th St, Network 609, Bellingham, WA 98225; mckenzie@fromnowon.org. *Bk. rev.:* Infrequently. *Aud.:* Ems, Hs, Ga.

A journal committed to the use of technologies for information literacy and for student learning and reasoning. Articles are written for a broad audience of parents, educators, administrators, and others involved with educational technology. Issues containing one to three articles have covered the topics of assessment, curriculum, grants, research, staff development, technology planning, virtual museums, and web site development. Short, concise articles have focused on laptop writing and thinking; learning to trust amateurs; digital pedagogy; combating mental brownout in the classroom; and the importance of libraries and librarians. A recent open issue examined plagiarism and how to combat it. Recommended for school and academic libraries. URL: http://fno.org/may2013/cov.html

2019. *Journal of Educational Computing Research.* [ISSN: 0735-6331] 1985. 8x/yr. USD 630 (print & online eds.) Individuals, USD 245 (print & online eds.). Ed(s): Robert H Seidman. Baywood Publishing Co., Inc., 26 Austin Ave, PO Box 337, Amityville, NY 11701; info@baywood.com; http://www.baywood.com. Illus., index. Sample. Refereed. *Indexed:* A22, CompLI, ERIC, MLA-IB, PsycInfo. *Aud.:* Ac.

This refereed journal publishes original articles on various aspects of educational computing: the outcome effects of educational computing applications; development and design of new hardware and software; interpretation and implications of research; and theory and history. Informative interdisciplinary articles are intended for a readership of practitioners, researchers, scientists, and educators from classroom teachers to faculty. Each issue's well-referenced articles advance knowledge and practice in the field of educational computing with empirical research, analyses, design and development studies, and critical reviews. Authors have presented recent research on digital writing and diversity; laptop use and scores on standardized tests; self-regulated learning and externally generated feedback with hypermedia; gender differences in the use of laptops in higher education; maximizing online supported learning; and how time-compressed narration in multimedia instruction impacts recall. A special issue has focused on recommender systems and group awareness tools. This journal is appropriate for libraries that support education programs. URL: www.baywood.com/journals/previewjournals.asp?id=0735-6331

2020. *Journal of Interactive Media in Education.* [ISSN: 1365-893X] 1996. irreg. Free. Open University, Knowledge Media Institute, Walton Hall, Milton Keynes, MK7 6AA, United Kingdom. Illus. Refereed. *Indexed:* ERIC, PsycInfo. *Bk. rev.:* Occasional, 1,600 words; signed. *Aud.:* Ac.

A journal focused on the role and contribution of interactive media to the field of learning. With an interest in the integration of technology and education, the journal publishes articles that develop theory, critique existing work, or analyze various aspects of educational technology. Articles have presented research on technology-enhanced learning in the sciences; and explored curation as a core competency. Other coverage has been of a pilot study using Second Life as practice for pre-service teachers; a look at emotional responses to technology; and a research investigation of the temporal nature of learning. Articles can have an interactive component, such as examples of interactive media or access to qualitative data. Special issues focus on open educational resources; researching computing and learning; and comparing educational modeling languages. Book reviews include responses by authors or other readers. Recommended for academic libraries. URL: http://www-jime.open.ac.uk/

2021. *Meridian (Raleigh): a middle school computer technologies journal.* [ISSN: 1097-9778] 1998. s-a. Free. Ed(s): Beckey Reed. North Carolina State University, 203 Peele Hall, Campus Box 7103, Raleigh, NC 27695; undergrad_admissions@ncsu.edu; http://www.ncsu.edu. *Aud.:* Ems, Sa.

A journal focused on the research and practice of computer technology in all elementary and secondary levels. Articles feature research, practical application, commentary, and book excerpts for the middle school practitioner, administrators, and others involved with middle school students. Two issues a year consider topics and issues such as technology usage in the middle school; teachers' perspectives and attitudes of the one-laptop-per-teacher initiative; and the influence of gender on computer simulation outcomes. The journal also includes an article with an international perspective that is written by international authors. An important journal for teachers from kindergarten through high school, and appropriate for libraries that support education and educational technology programs. URL: www.ncsu.edu/meridian/index.html

2022. *Tech Directions: linking education to careers.* Former titles (until 1992): *School Shop - Tech Directions;* (until 1990): *New School Shop - Tech Directions;* (until 1989): *School Shop;* (until 1948): *School Shop for Industrial Arts and Vocational Education Teachers.* [ISSN: 1062-9351] 1941. 10x/yr. USD 30 domestic (Free to qualified personnel). Ed(s): Susanne Peckham. Prakken Publications, Inc., 832 Phoenix Dr, Ann Arbor, MI 48107; vanessa@techdirections.com. Illus., index, adv. Sample. Vol. ends: May. Microform: PQC. *Indexed:* A01, A22, ABIn, B01, ERIC, P02. *Bk. rev.:* 6, 150 words. *Aud.:* Ga, Ac.

A publication focused on the fields of technology, industrial, and vocational education. Contributors cover teaching techniques, school-to-work transition, industrial arts, and current issues in the field. The magazine is intended for technology, vocational-technical, and applied science educators at all educational levels, and its articles and columns are curriculum-oriented. Articles in this magazine focus on teaching techniques, classroom projects, laboratory/classroom administrative procedures, and issues facing the applied educational technology field. Topics have included building homes for the homeless; materials and tools management; heat-loss experiments; a kayak design challenge; fuel-cell–powered go-karts; digital photography; laser projects; and the job-cost estimation process. An annual buying guide is also provided. Readers will also find cartoons, funny anecdotes, puzzles, and brain teasers that educators can use. Recommended for academic and school libraries with vocational education programs. URL: www.techdirections.com

2023. *Techniques.* Former titles (until 1999): *American Vocational Association.Techniques;* (until 1996): *Vocational Education Journal;* (until 1985): *VocEd;* (until 1978): *American Vocational Journal;* (until 1945): *A V A Journal and News Bulletin;* (until 1935): *American Vocational Association. News Bulletin.* [ISSN: 1527-1803] 1926. 8x/yr. Free to members; Non-members, USD 48. Association for Career and Technical Education, 1410 King St, Alexandria, VA 22314; acte@acteonline.org; http://www.acteonline.org. Adv. *Indexed:* A01, A22, BRI, ERIC, P02. *Bk. rev.:* 1, 500 words. *Aud.:* Ga, Ac, Sa.

Published by the Association for Career and Technical Education (ACTE), this magazine covers issues of career and technical education. Content is aimed at ACTE members with current news about legislation, profiles of educators, featured articles about programs and issues, and association news and events. Recent issues have examined student leadership; current teaching practices; promising practices; at-risk students; credentialing; college and career readiness; apprenticeships; adult education and retraining; alternative energy; guidance and career development; emerging careers; online education and distance learning; the role of service learning; and teacher recruitment and retention. Recommended for all libraries that serve career and technical education programs. URL: www.acteonline.org/techniques.aspx

2024. *Technology and Engineering Teacher.* Former titles (until 2010): *The Technology Teacher;* (until 1983): *Man, Society, Technology;* (until 1970): *Journal of Industrial Arts Education;* (until 1964): *The Industrial Arts Teacher.* [ISSN: 2158-0502] 1939. 8x/yr. Free to members. Ed(s): Kathleen B de la Paz, Kathie F Cluff. International Technology and Engineering Educators Association, 1914 Association Dr, Ste 201, Reston, VA 20191; iteea@iteea.org; http://www.iteea.org/. Illus., index, adv. Sample. Refereed. Vol. ends: May/Jun. Microform: PQC. *Indexed:* A01, A22, BRI, ERIC. *Bk. rev.:* 1, 100 words. *Aud.:* Ac.

This is the journal of the International Technology Education Association, and its goal is to be a resource tool for technology education practitioners. The audience ranges from elementary school to high school classroom teachers, as well as teacher educators. Article content is focused on the sharing of classroom ideas and applications. With the practitioner as audience, article content has covered engineering at the elementary level; STEM education methodology; recruitment of women and girls to the STEM classroom; learning from engineering failures; exploring hydrogen fuel-cell technology; designing technology activities that teach mathematics; gender-friendly technology education; and creating a creative classroom. A section on classroom challenges showcases interesting projects such as radio-controlled cars, creating an electric vehicle, creating a greenhouse, and developing a watershed. As a membership journal, it also includes association events and news. Recommended for all school and academic libraries. URL: www.iteea.org/Publications/ttt.htm

■ ELECTRONICS

Paula M. Storm, Assistant Professor; Science Technology Librarian, Bruce T. Halle Library, Eastern Michigan University, Ypsilanti, MI 48197; FAX: 734-487-8861; pstorm@emich.edu

Introduction

Trade magazines and journals in the field of electronics range in perspective from technical and scientific to business and consumer. Readers from a variety of backgrounds and educational levels use these publications as a way to keep current in this rapidly changing environment. Those in business need to know how to incorporate electronic equipment into their workflow, how to monitor the electronics industry, and how to improve, assemble, or package their electronic products.

Readers with technical and scientific backgrounds will want to keep current on trends and research, and also to use these journals to communicate their own research findings. Consumers will find the trade magazines invaluable in obtaining information on construction and repair, and explanations, reviews, and ratings of new products. Public librarians who collect in the area of electronics will want to include the trade magazines, and those in an academic environment will supplement those titles with scholarly journals, especially those published by IEEE.

Basic Periodicals

Electronic News; IEEE Transactions on Consumer Electronics; IEEE Transactions on Electron Devices; IEEE Transactions on Industrial Electronics; IEEE Transactions on Power Electronics; Institute of Electrical and Electronics Engineers. Proceedings; International Journal of Electronics; Solid-State Electronics.

Basic Abstracts and Indexes

ABI/Inform, Applied Science and Technology Abstracts, Business and Company ASAP, Business Source Premier, Compendex, Computer Database, Electronics and Communications Abstracts, IEEE Computer Society Digital Library, INSPEC, Physics Abstracts, ScienceDirect, Scopus, Web of Science.

2025. *AudioXpress: the audio technology authority.* Formed by the merger of (1989-2001): *Glass Audio;* (1980-2001): *Speaker Builder;* (1996-2001): *Audio Electronics;* Which was formerly (1970-1996): *Audio Amateur.* [ISSN: 1548-6028] 2001. m. USD 37 domestic; USD 49 per issue Canada; USD 72 per issue elsewhere. Ed(s): Edward T Dell, Jr. Audio Amateur Corporation, 305 Union St, PO Box 876, Peterborough, NH 03458; custserv@audioxpress.com. Illus., adv. Sample. *Indexed:* IHTDI. *Bk. rev.:* Number and length vary. *Aud.:* Hs, Ga.

For the do-it-yourself audiophile, *AudioXpress* covers subjects that range from amplifiers to vacuum tube technology. Articles feature new projects as well as tips to help upgrade current equipment. Includes reviews of equipment and columns with advice from experts in audio technology.

2026. *Digital Signal Processing.* [ISSN: 1051-2004] 1991. bi-m. EUR 901. Ed(s): F J Harris, M Rangaswamy. Academic Press, 3251 Riverport Ln, Maryland Heights, MO 63043; JournalCustomerService-usa@elsevier.com; http://www.elsevierdirect.com/brochures/academicpress/index.html. Illus., adv. Sample. Refereed. *Indexed:* A01, A22, CompLI, E01, EngInd. *Bk. rev.:* Number and length vary. *Aud.:* Ac, Sa.

Digital Signal Processing consists of peer-reviewed research articles and reviews that cover new technologies in the field. This journal is for electronic engineers, scientists, and business managers engaged in digital signal processing. The diverse subjects covered include digital signal processing applications in biomedicine, astronomy, telecommunications, geology, and biology. This journal is available online via Swets, EBSCOhost, Elsevier, and other vendors.

2027. *E E Times: the industry newspaper for engineers and technical management.* [ISSN: 0192-1541] 1972. w. USD 280 domestic (Free to qualified personnel). Ed(s): Junko Yoshida. United Business Media Llc, TechInsights, Inc., 600 Harrison St, 6th Fl, San Francisco, CA 94107; pmiller@techinsights.com; http://www.techinsights.com. Adv. Circ: 140000. *Indexed:* A01, A22, ABIn, B01, B03, BRI, C&ISA, C42, CerAb, EngInd. *Bk. rev.:* Number and length vary. *Aud.:* Ga, Ac, Sa.

This trade publication is focused on the key trends and news in the electronics industry. Written for engineers and technical managers, it is a weekly tabloid that contains statistics, charts, and tables on the electronics industry sector. A free online subscription is available. Also available via Gale, Lexis/Nexis, ProQuest, and other vendors. URL: www.eetimes.com

2028. *Electronic Design.* Incorporates (1941-2007): *E E Product News.* [ISSN: 0013-4872] 1952. bi-w. USD 120 domestic (Free to qualified personnel). Ed(s): Joe Desposito. Penton Media, Inc., 1300 E 9th St, Cleveland, OH 44114; information@penton.com; http://www.penton.com. Illus., index, adv. Sample. Circ: 145000 Controlled. Vol. ends: No. 28. Microform: PQC. *Indexed:* A01, A22, ABIn, B01, B02, B03, BRI, C&ISA, CerAb, EngInd, I15. *Bk. rev.:* Number and length vary. *Aud.:* Ac, Sa.

Electronic Design features short, practical articles on various subjects of interest to design engineers such as electronic design automation, test and measurement, and communications. Two longer features include "Design Solutions," written by contributors who provide more in-depth advice and problem solutions, and "Technology Report," which addresses current topics in the world of electronic design. Full text is available online via Gale, ProQuest, and other vendors. It is free to qualified subscribers. URL: www.electronicdesign.com

Electronic House. See Home section.

2029. *Electronics.* [ISSN: 2079-9292] 2012. q. Free. Ed(s): Dr. Mostafa Bassiouni. M D P I AG, Postfach, Basel, 4005, Switzerland; http://www.mdpi.com. Refereed. *Bk. rev.:* Number and length vary. *Aud.:* Ac.

This open-access, peer-reviewed, English-language journal is published in Switzerland by Molecular Diversity Preservation International (MDPI). It covers all aspects of electronics. It is available online from MDPI.

2030. *Electronics and Communications in Japan.* Formed by the merger of (1985-2008): *Electronic and Communications in Japan. Part 1: Communications;* (1985-2008): *Electronic and Communications in Japan. Part 2: Electronics;* (1989-2008): *Electronic and Communications in Japan. Part 3: Fundamental Electronic Science;* All of which superseded in part (1963-1985): *Electronic and Communications in Japan.* [ISSN: 1942-9533] 2008. m. GBP 10665. Ed(s): Hironori Hirata. Wiley-Blackwell Publishing, Inc., 111 River St, Hoboken, NJ 07030; info@wiley.com; http://www.wiley.com/. Adv. Sample. Reprint: PSC. *Indexed:* A01, B01, C&ISA, CerAb. *Aud.:* Ac, Sa.

This scholarly journal publishes original research in the area of electronics. The articles are translated from the Japanese, from papers originally published in the *Transactions of the Institute of Electronics, Information and Communication Engineers of Japan.* Available online via EBSCOhost, Wiley-Blackwell, and Swets.

2031. *Electronics Letters.* [ISSN: 0013-5194] 1965. bi-w. GBP 1756. Ed(s): Ian H White, Christofer Toumazou. The Institution of Engineering and Technology, Michael Faraday House, Six Hills Way, Stevenage, SG1 2AY, United Kingdom; journals@theiet.org; http://www.theiet.org/. Illus., index, adv. Sample. Refereed. Vol. ends: No. 25. *Indexed:* A01, A22, B01, C&ISA, EngInd. *Aud.:* Ac, Sa.

Electronics Letters contains short research papers that address the most current international developments in electronics. This journal is published by the Institution of Engineering and Technology, an association formed by the joining together of the IEE (Institution of Electrical Engineers) and the IIE (Institution of Incorporated Engineers). Each issue contains about 30 refereed papers that cover both the science and technology of electronics. Full text is available online from a variety of vendors.

2032. *Elektor.* Former titles (until 2007): *Elektor Electronics;* (until 1984): *Elektor.* [ISSN: 1757-0875] 1974. 11x/yr. Free to members. Elektor Electronics (Publishing), Regus Brentford, 1000 Great West Rd, Brentford, TW8 9HH, United Kingdom; sales@elektor-electronics.co.uk; http://www.elektor.com. Illus., adv. Circ: 17500. *Indexed:* A22. *Bk. rev.:* Number and length vary. *Aud.:* Ga, Ac, Sa.

Elektor is a magazine for both consumers and professional engineers. The articles focus on current projects in the electronics industry and newsworthy new products in electronics technology.

2033. *Embedded Systems Design: creative solutions for senior systems designers and their teams.* Formerly (until 2005): *Embedded Systems Programming.* [ISSN: 1558-2493] 1988. m. USD 55 domestic (Free to qualified personnel). Ed(s): Rich Nass. United Business Media Llc, TechInsights, Inc., 600 Harrison St, 6th Fl, San Francisco, CA 94107; pmiller@techinsights.com; http://www.techinsights.com. Adv. Circ: 45000. *Indexed:* A01, A22, B01, B02, BRI, CompLI, I15. *Bk. rev.:* Number and length vary. *Aud.:* Ac, Sa.

Embedded Systems Design is a magazine for electronic systems designers who are responsible for selecting, integrating, and building hardware and software components and systems for their companies. Each issue contains short articles that highlight featured products, and longer feature articles that address specific problems encountered by system designers. Available full-text online via ProQuest, Dow Jones Factiva, and Gale.

2034. *Engineering & Technology.* Incorporates (2007-2008): *I E T Manufacturing;* Which was formerly (until 2007): *Manufacturing Engineer;* (1921-1989): *Production Engineer;* (2004-2008): *Information Professional;* (2003-2008): *Power Engineer;* Which was formerly (1987-2002): *Power Engineering Journal;* (2007-2008): *I E T Electronics;* Which was formerly (Jun.2003-Jul.2007): *Electronics Systems & Software;* (200?-2008): *Engineering Management;* Which was formerly (1991-200?): *Engineering Management Journal;* (2007-2008): *Control & Automation;* Which was formerly (1990-2007): *Computing & Control Engineering;* Which incorporated (1983-1992): *Computer-Aided Engineering Journal;* (2003-2008): *Communications Engineer;* Which was formerly (until 2003): *Electronics & Communication Engineer;* (until 1998): *Institution of Electronic and Radio Engineers. Journal;* (until 1985): *Radio and Electonic Engineer;* (1939-1963): *British Institute of Radio Engineers. Journal;* Which incorporated: *Insitution of Electronic and Radio Engineers. Proceedings;* Engineering & Technology was formed by the merger of (1988-2006): *I E E Review;* Which incorporated (in 2003): *I E E News;* Which incorporated: *Interlink;* I E E Review was formerly (until 1987): *Electronics and Power;* (1949-1954): *Institution of Electrical Engineers. Journal;* Which incorporated (1949-1954): *Institution of Electrical Engineers. Proceedings. Part 1: General;* (1941-1948): *Institution of Electrical Engineers. Journal. Part 1: General;* (1941-1948): *Institution of Electrical Engineers. Journal. Part 2: Power Engineering;* (1941-1948): *Institution of Electrical Engineers. Journal. Part 3: Radio and Communication Engineering;* Part 1, 2 & 3 superseded in part (in 1940): *Institution of Electrical Engineers. Journal;* Which was formerly (until 1888): *Society of Telegraph Engineers and Electricians. Journal; Students Quarterly;* (1998-2006): *Engineering Technology;* Which was formed by the merger of (1973-1998): *Electrotechnology;* Which was formerly (1966-1972): *Electrical & Electronics Technician Engineers;* (1988-1998): *Mechanical Incorporated Engineer;* Which was formed by the merger of (1981-1988): *Mechanical Engineering Technology;* (1973-1988): *General Engineer;* Which was formerly (until 1972): *Institution of General Technician Engineers. Journal;* (until 1971): *Junior Institution of Engineers. Journal and Record of Transactions;* (1990-1998): *Electronic and Electrical Engineering;* Which was formerly (until 1990): *Electrical and Electronics Incoporated Engineer;* (until 1983): *Incorporated Engineer; I E E I E Bulletin;* (until 1962): *I E E T E Bulletin.* [ISSN: 1750-9637] 2006. 18x/yr. USD 1370. Ed(s): Dickon Ross, Dominic Lenton. The Institution of Engineering and Technology, Michael Faraday House, Six Hills Way, Stevenage, SG1 2AY, United Kingdom; journals@theiet.org; http://www.theiet.org/. Adv. *Indexed:* A01, A22, B01, C&ISA, EngInd. *Bk. rev.:* Number and length vary. *Aud.:* Ga, Ac, Sa.

Published by the Institution of Engineering and Technology, this monthly publication targets professional engineers. In addition to regular features such as news, research and development, events, and editorials, articles by high-profile contributors are included on a variety of subjects ranging from from technology to management. This title is available in print and via IEEE, the IET Digital Library, EBSCOhost, and other vendors.

2035. *Everyday Practical Electronics.* Incorporates (1971-1998): *E T I - Electronics Today International;* Which was formerly (until 1989): *Electronics Today International;* (until 1972): *Electronics Today;* Formerly (until 1995): *Everyday with Practical Electronics;* Which

incorporates: *Electronics Monthly;* Which was formed by the merger of (1971-1992): *Everyday Electronics;* (1964-1992): *Practical Electronics.* [ISSN: 1367-398X] 1992. m. GBP 37.90 domestic; GBP 44 foreign. Ed(s): Michael Kenward. Wimborne Publishing Ltd., Sequoia House, 398a Ringwood Rd, Ferndown, BH22 9AU, United Kingdom; enquiries@wimborne.co.uk. Illus., adv. Circ: 20544 Paid. *Bk. rev.:* Number and length vary. *Aud.:* Ga.

Everyday Practical Electronics (EPE) Online is a magazine from the United Kingdom for electronics and computer enthusiasts. Each issue contains numerous building projects in electronics, for every level of expertise.

Home Theater. See Television, Video, and Radio/Home Entertainment section.

2036. *I E E E Electron Device Letters.* Formerly (until Feb.1980): *Electron Device Letters.* [ISSN: 0741-3106] 1980. m. USD 1400; USD 1680 combined subscription (print & online eds.). Ed(s): Yuan Taur, Martin J Morahan. Institute of Electrical and Electronics Engineers, 445 Hoes Ln, Piscataway, NJ 08854; contactcenter@ieee.org; http://www.ieee.org. Illus., index, adv. Sample. Refereed. *Indexed:* A22, C&ISA, CerAb, EngInd. *Bk. rev.:* Number and length vary. *Aud.:* Ac, Sa.

This journal is published by the IEEE Electron Device Society. It publishes original research and significant contributions relating to the theory, design, and performance of electron and ion devices, solid-state devices, integrated electronic devices, and optoelectronic devices and energy sources. In 2010, *IEEE Electron Device Letters* was ranked 15th in impact factor in journals that cover electrical and electronics engineering, according to the annual *Journal Citation Report.* Available online from IEEE.

2037. *I E E E Journal of Quantum Electronics.* [ISSN: 0018-9197] 1965. m. USD 2315; USD 2780 combined subscription (print & online eds.). Ed(s): Robert J Lang, Mona Mittra. Institute of Electrical and Electronics Engineers, 445 Hoes Ln, Piscataway, NJ 08854; contactcenter@ieee.org; http://www.ieee.org. Illus., index, adv. *Indexed:* A01, A22, B01, BRI, C&ISA, CerAb, EngInd. *Bk. rev.:* Number and length vary. *Aud.:* Ac, Sa.

Each issue highlights specific subjects, and the articles are grouped accordingly. Published by the IEEE Lasers and Electro-Optics Society, this journal covers technology in which quantum electronic devices are used. Available online via IEEE.

2038. *I E E E Journal on Emerging and Selected Topics in Circuits and Systems.* [ISSN: 2156-3357] 2011. q. USD 955; USD 1145 combined subscription (print & online eds.). Ed(s): Massoud Pedram. Institute of Electrical and Electronics Engineers, 3 Park Ave, 17th Fl, New York, NY 10016; corporate-communications@ieee.org; http://www.ieee.org. Adv. *Aud.:* Ac.

This new journal, published by IEEE, has an emphasis on developing new areas in circuits and system technology. There are special issues on specific topics including the theory, analysis, design, tools, and implementation of circuits and systems.

2039. *I E E E Journal on Selected Topics in Signal Processing.* [ISSN: 1932-4553] 2007. bi-m. USD 1380; USD 1656 combined subscription (print & online eds.). Ed(s): Vikram Krishnamurthy, Martin J Morahan. Institute of Electrical and Electronics Engineers, 445 Hoes Ln, Piscataway, NJ 08854; contactcenter@ieee.org; http://www.ieee.org. Adv. *Bk. rev.:* Number and length vary. *Aud.:* Ac, Sa.

This publication from the IEEE contains solicited papers on special topics on all aspects of signal processing. Useful for academics and practitioners in electronics and electrical engineering.

I E E E Signal Processing Magazine. See Engineering and Technology section.

2040. *I E E E Transactions on Circuits and Systems. Part 1: Regular Papers.* Formed by the merger of (1992-2004): *I E E E Transactions on Circuits and Systems Part 1: Fundamental Theory and Applications;* (1992-2004): *I E E E Transactions on Circuits and Systems Part 2:*

Analog and Digital Signal Processing; Both of which superseded in part (in 1992): *I E E E Transactions on Circuits and Systems;* Which was formerly (until 1974): *I E E E Transactions on Circuit Theory;* (until 1963): *I R E Transactions on Circuit Theory;* (until 1955): *I R E Professional Group on Circuit Theory. Transactions.* [ISSN: 1549-8328] 1952. m. USD 1195; USD 1435 combined subscription (print & online eds.). Ed(s): Wouter A Serdijn, Mona Mittra. Institute of Electrical and Electronics Engineers, 445 Hoes Ln, Piscataway, NJ 08854; contactcenter@ieee.org; http://www.ieee.org. Illus., index, adv. Sample. Refereed. Vol. ends: No. 12. *Indexed:* A01, A22, B01, C&ISA, CCMJ, CerAb, CompLI, EngInd, MSN, MathR. *Bk. rev.:* Number and length vary. *Aud.:* Ac, Sa.

Published by the IEEE Circuits and Systems Society, *IEEE Transactions on Circuits and Systems* contains peer-reviewed papers on the theory and applications of circuits and systems, both analog and digital. Articles contain numerous charts and tables, as well as short biographies of the authors. Available online via IEEE.

2041. *I E E E Transactions on Circuits and Systems. Part 2: Express Briefs.* Formerly (until 2004): *I E E E Transactions on Circuits and Systems Part 2: Analog and Digital Signal Processing;* Which superseded in part (in 1992): *I E E E Transactions on Circuits and Systems;* Which was formerly (until 1973): *I E E E Transactions on Circuit Theory;* (until 1962): *I R E Transactions on Circuit Theory;* (until 1954): *I R E Professional Group on Circuit Theory. Transactions.* [ISSN: 1549-7747] 1952. m. USD 1140; USD 1365 combined subscription (print & online eds.). Ed(s): Yong Lian. Institute of Electrical and Electronics Engineers, 445 Hoes Ln, Piscataway, NJ 08854; contactcenter@ieee.org; http://www.ieee.org. Illus., index, adv. Sample. Refereed. Vol. ends: No. 12. *Indexed:* A01, A22, B01, C&ISA, CerAb, CompLI, EngInd. *Aud.:* Ac, Sa.

The intent of *IEEE Transactions on Circuits and Systems. Part 2: Express Briefs* is rapid dissemination of original innovations and ideas on the subject of digital and analog circuits and systems. If an article is accepted, it is scheduled to be published four months from the date of receipt. Authors may send more in-depth articles to the sister publication *IEEE Transactions on Circuits and Systems. Part 1: Regular Papers,* (above in this section). Available online via IEEE.

I E E E Transactions on Components, Packaging and Manufacturing Technology. See Engineering and Technology section.

2042. *I E E E Transactions on Computer - Aided Design of Integrated Circuits and Systems.* [ISSN: 0278-0070] 1982. m. USD 1330; USD 1595 combined subscription (print & online eds.). Ed(s): Sachin Sapatnekar, Martin J Morahan. Institute of Electrical and Electronics Engineers, 445 Hoes Ln, Piscataway, NJ 08854; contactcenter@ieee.org; http://www.ieee.org. Adv. Refereed. *Indexed:* A01, A22, B01, C&ISA, CerAb, CompLI, EngInd. *Aud.:* Ac, Sa.

Published by the IEEE Circuits and Systems Society, this journal contains articles on analog, digital, optical, or microwave integrated circuits that emphasize the practical applications and the resulting products of original research. All such research papers are published in this journal, whereas briefer papers that report recent important results are published in the *IEEE Transactions on Circuits Systems. Part 2: Express Briefs.*

2043. *I E E E Transactions on Consumer Electronics.* Former titles (until 1975): *I E E E Transactions on Broadcast and Television Receivers;* (until 1963): *I R E Transactions on Broadcast and Television Receivers;* (until 1955): *I R E Professional Group on Broadcast and Television Receivers. Transactions.* [ISSN: 0098-3063] 1953. q. USD 380; USD 455 combined subscription (print & online eds.). Ed(s): Wayne C Luplow. Institute of Electrical and Electronics Engineers, 445 Hoes Ln, Piscataway, NJ 08854; contactcenter@ieee.org; http://www.ieee.org. Illus., index, adv. Sample. Refereed. Vol. ends: Nov. *Indexed:* A01, A22, B01, C&ISA, CerAb, CompLI, EngInd, MathR. *Bk. rev.:* Number and length vary. *Aud.:* Ac, Sa.

This IEEE publication emphasizes new technology in consumer electronics. Consumer electronics includes products and components used for leisure, education, or entertainment. Many of the papers in this journal have been presented at the International Conference on Consumer Electronics. It is available online via IEEE.

2044. *I E E E Transactions on Electromagnetic Compatibility.* Former titles (until 1964): *I E E E Transactions on Radio Frequency Interference;* (until 1963): *I R E Transactions on Radio Frequency Interference.* [ISSN: 0018-9375] 1963. q. USD 525; USD 630 combined subscription (print & online eds.). Ed(s): Heyno Garbe, Martin J Morahan. Institute of Electrical and Electronics Engineers, 445 Hoes Ln, Piscataway, NJ 08854; contactcenter@ieee.org; http://www.ieee.org. Illus., index, adv. Sample. Refereed. Vol. ends: Nov. *Indexed:* A01, A22, B01, C&ISA, CerAb, EngInd, MathR. *Bk. rev.:* Number and length vary. *Aud.:* Ac, Sa.

Topics covered in this journal include measurement techniques and standards, spectrum conservation and utilization, and equipment and systems related to electromagnetic compatibility. This IEEE publication includes correspondence, brief articles, and longer papers. Available in full text online via IEEE and EBSCOhost.

2045. *I E E E Transactions on Electron Devices.* Former titles (until 1963): *I R E Transactions on Electron Devices;* (until 1955): *I R E Professional Group on Electron Devices. Transactions.* [ISSN: 0018-9383] 1952. m. USD 2235; USD 2680 combined subscription (print & online eds.). Ed(s): Douglas P Verret, Martin J Morahan. Institute of Electrical and Electronics Engineers, 445 Hoes Ln, Piscataway, NJ 08854; contactcenter@ieee.org; http://www.ieee.org. Illus., index, adv. Sample. Refereed. Vol. ends: No. 12. *Indexed:* A01, A22, B01, C&ISA, CerAb, CompLI, EngInd, MathR. *Bk. rev.:* Number and length vary. *Aud.:* Ac, Sa.

The IEEE Electron Device Society publishes this monthly journal, which covers the theory, design, performance, and reliability of electron devices. Two types of papers are selected for inclusion: peer-reviewed, in-depth regular papers; and briefs covering preliminary results or reporting of recently completed projects. There is also a section for letters to the editor. According to the JCR 2010 report, this journal is #9 in the Electrical and Electronic Journal category for Eigenfactor Score. Full text is available online through the IEEE and from EBSCOhost.

2046. *I E E E Transactions on Industrial Electronics.* Former titles (until 1982): *I E E E Transactions on Industrial Electronics and Control Instrumentation;* (until 1964): *I E E E Transactions on Industrial Electronics;* (until 1963): *I R E Transactions on Industrial Electronics;* (until 1955): *I R E Professional Group on Industrial Electronics. Transactions.* [ISSN: 0278-0046] 1953. m. USD 1375; USD 1650 combined subscription (print & online eds.). Ed(s): Mo-Yuen Chow, Jeffrey F Cichocki. Institute of Electrical and Electronics Engineers, 445 Hoes Ln, Piscataway, NJ 08854; contactcenter@ieee.org; http://www.ieee.org. Illus., index, adv. Sample. Refereed. Vol. ends: Nov. *Indexed:* A01, A22, ApMecR, B01, C&ISA, CerAb, EngInd, MathR. *Bk. rev.:* Number and length vary. *Aud.:* Ac, Sa.

Each issue of *IEEE Transactions on Industrial Electronics* features a special section of reviewed papers covering a specific topic on the application of electronics to industrial and manufacturing systems and processes. Each section is preceded by a guest editorial that explains the special topic that is to be covered. Following the special section papers are papers on various topics, letters, and comments. As in all *IEEE Transactions* journals, short biographies and photos of authors are included. The 2010 JCR lists this journal #9 in Impact Factor in the electrical and electronics journal category. Online availability is via IEEE and from EBSCOhost.

2047. *I E E E Transactions on Power Electronics.* [ISSN: 0885-8993] 1986. bi-m. USD 1239; USD 1486 combined subscription (print & online eds.). Ed(s): Frede Blaabjerg. Institute of Electrical and Electronics Engineers, 445 Hoes Ln, Piscataway, NJ 08854; contactcenter@ieee.org; http://www.ieee.org. Illus., index, adv. Sample. Vol. ends: Oct. *Indexed:* A01, A22, B01, C&ISA, CerAb, EngInd, P02. *Bk. rev.:* Number and length vary. *Aud.:* Ac, Sa.

Published by the Power Electronics Society of the IEEE, *IEEE Transactions on Power Electronics* has the highest impact factor of any journal in power electronics, according to its editor-in-chief, Frede Blaabjerg. This publication contains both long research papers and shorter letters that introduce new developments and ideas. JCR 2010 ranks this journal #10 in Impact Factor for electrical and electronic journals. Online availability is via IEEE and from EBSCOhost.

2048. *I E T Power Electronics.* [ISSN: 1755-4535] 2008. 9x/yr. GBP 551. Ed(s): Brian Mellitt. The Institution of Engineering and Technology, Michael Faraday House, Six Hills Way, Stevenage, SG1 2AY, United Kingdom; journals@theiet.org; http://www.theiet.org/. Adv. Refereed. *Aud.:* Ac, Sa.

This journal contains articles on the current research and development in power electronics, circuits, devices, techniques, and the performance management of power systems. It received its first Impact Factor of 1.018 for 2011.

2049. *Institute of Electrical and Electronics Engineers. Proceedings.* Former titles (until 1963): *Institute of Radio Engineers. Proceedings;* (until 1939): *Institute of Radio Engineers. Proceedings;* (until 1913): *Wireless Institute. Proceedings of the Meeting Held.* [ISSN: 0018-9219] 1913. m. USD 1075; USD 1290 combined subscription (print & online eds.). Ed(s): Robert J Trew, James Calder. Institute of Electrical and Electronics Engineers, 445 Hoes Ln, Piscataway, NJ 08854; contactcenter@ieee.org; http://www.ieee.org. Illus., index, adv. Vol. ends: Dec. *Indexed:* A22, C&ISA, CerAb, EngInd, ErgAb, M&GPA, MLA-IB, MathR. *Aud.:* Ga, Ac, Sa.

Published since 1913 and renowned as the most highly cited general-interest journal in electrical engineering and computer science, the *Proceedings of the IEEE* contains in-depth tutorial and review articles in the areas of electrical engineering and technology. Its alternate title is *Proceedings of the I E E E.* Included are survey articles that review an existing technology. Each issue focuses on a special topic, preceded by an editorial that reviews the included papers. Articles are written for the IEEE member or the general reader who has some background in electrical engineering. Available online via IEEE and from EBSCOhost.

2050. *International Journal of Computer Technology and Electronics Engineering.* [ISSN: 2249-6343] 2011. irreg. Free. National Institute of Science Communication and Information Resources, Dr. K.S. Krishnan Marg, New Delhi, 110 012, India; http://www.niscair.res.in/. Refereed. *Aud.:* Ac.

This is a new, open-access academic journal published in India that contains original research papers.

2051. *International Journal of Electrical and Electronics Engineering Research.* [ISSN: 2250-155X] 2011. q. INR 5000 domestic; USD 300 foreign. Ed(s): Jayasudha Manivannan. Transstellar Journal Publications and Research Consultancy Private Ltd., Transstellar Enclave, 12, Periya Kannara St, Mayiladuthurai, 609 001, India; ceo@tjprc.org; http://www.tjprc.org. Illus., adv. Refereed. Circ: 20 Paid. *Bk. rev.:* Number and length vary. *Aud.:* Ac.

This is an English-language journal published in India that covers research in electronics and electrical engineering.

2052. *International Journal of Electronics.* Supersedes in part (in 1965): *Journal of Electronics and Control;* Which was formerly (until 1957): *Journal of Electronics.* [ISSN: 0020-7217] 1955. m. GBP 2757 (print & online eds.). Ed(s): Ian Hunter, Dr. Alaa Abunjaileh. Taylor & Francis, 4 Park Sq, Milton Park, Abingdon, OX14 4RN, United Kingdom; http://www.tandfonline.com. Illus., index, adv. Sample. Refereed. Reprint: PSC. *Indexed:* A01, A22, ApMecR, B01, C&ISA, CerAb, E01, EngInd, MathR. *Bk. rev.:* Number and length vary. *Aud.:* Ac, Sa.

International Journal of Electronics originates in the United Kingdom and publishes articles in these topic areas of electronics: solid state, power, analogue, RF and microwave, and digital. Each issue contains fewer than ten full-length papers that report a theoretical or experimental perspective on one of the above topics. Full text is available online via various vendors including EBSCOhost and Swets.

2053. *International Journal of Industrial Electronics and Drives.* [ISSN: 1757-3874] 2009. q. EUR 494 (print or online eds.). Ed(s): Ehab H E Bayoumi. Inderscience Publishers, PO Box 735, Olney, MK46 5WB, United Kingdom; editorial@inderscience.com; http://www.inderscience.com. Sample. Refereed. *Aud.:* Ac, Sa.

This journal contains research work in the area of industrial electronics, power converters, and drives. It is available online via EBSCOhost and Ingenta.

2054. *Journal of Active and Passive Electronic Devices.* [ISSN: 1555-0281] 2005. q. EUR 635 (print & online eds.) Individuals, EUR 148). Ed(s): Robert Castellano. Old City Publishing, Inc., 628 N 2nd St, Philadelphia, PA 19123; info@oldcitypublishing.com; http://www.oldcitypublishing.com. Adv. Sample. Refereed. *Bk. rev.:* Number and length vary. *Aud.:* Ac, Sa.

International in scope, this is a relatively new academic journal that fills the subject gap of active and passive electronic devices. This peer-reviewed journal includes review articles, short communications, long articles, and book reviews on the subject of electronic components. Full text is available online via EBSCOhost and Old City Publishing Co.

2055. *Journal of Electrical and Electronics Engineering.* Formed by the merger of (2005-2007): *Universitatea din Oradea. Analele. Fascicula Electrotehnica. Sectiunea Inginerie Electrica;* (1999-2007): *Universitatea din Oradea. Analele. Fascicula Electrotehnica, Sectiunea Electronica;* Both of which superseded in part (1993-1999): *Analele Universitatii din Oradea. Fascicula Electrotehnica;* Which superseded in part (1991-1992): *Analele Universitatii din Oradea. Fascicula Electrotehnica si Energetica;* Which superseded in part (1976-1990): *Lucrari Stiintifice - Institutul de Invatamant Superior Oradea. Seria A, Stiinte Tehnice, Matematica, Fizica, Chimie, Geografie;* Which was formed by the merger of (1971-1973): *Lucrari Stiintifice - Institutul Pedagogic Oradea. Geografie;* (1971-1973): *Lucrari Stiintifice - Institutul Pedagogic Oradea. Matematica, Fizica, Chimie;* Both of which superseded in part (1969-1970): *Lucrari Stiintifice - Institutul Pedagogic Oradea. Seria A;* Which superseded in part (1967-1968): *Lucrari Stiintifice - Institutul Pedagogic Oradea.* [ISSN: 1844-6035] 2008. a. Free to qualified personnel. Ed(s): Teodor Leuca. Editura Universitatii din Oradea, Str Universitatii 1, Geotermal Bldg., 2nd Fl., Oradea, 410087, Romania; editura@uoradea.ro; http://webhost.uoradea.ro/editura/. Illus., index. Sample. *Indexed:* A01, C45. *Aud.:* Ac, Sa.

This peer-reviewed journal contains original papers in the fields of electronics and electrical engineering. Published in Romania, it has an international scope. This is an open-access journal.

2056. *Journal of Electrical and Electronics Engineering.* [ISSN: 2250-2424] 2011. q. INR 7000 (Individuals, INR 5000). Ed(s): Manivannan Sethuraman, Jayasudha Manivannan. Transstellar Journal Publications and Research Consultancy Private Ltd., Transstellar Enclave, 12, Periya Kannara St, Mayiladuthurai, 609 001, India; ceo@tjprc.org; http://www.tjprc.org. Illus., adv. Refereed. Circ: 20 Paid. *Bk. rev.:* Number and length vary. *Aud.:* Ac.

This new English-language journal is published in India and contains research and review articles on all aspects of electrical engineering.

2057. *Journal of Electronic and Electrical Engineering.* [ISSN: 0976-8106] 2010. s-a. USD 425. Ed(s): Dr. Deeraj Joshi. Bioinfo Publications, B-23/7, Kendriya Vihar, Sector-11, Kharghar, Navi Mumbai, 410 210, India; editor@bioinfo.in; http://www.bioinfo.in. Refereed. *Aud.:* Ac.

Published in India, this English-language journal contains both research and review articles on all aspects of electronics. It is available through EBSCO.

2058. *Journal of Electronic Materials.* [ISSN: 0361-5235] 1972. m. EUR 768 (print & online eds.). Ed(s): Suzanne E Mohney. Springer New York LLC, 233 Spring St, New York, NY 10013; journals@springer-ny.com; http://www.springer.com. Illus., index, adv. Sample. Refereed. Vol. ends: No. 12. Microform: PQC. Reprint: PSC. *Indexed:* A22, C&ISA, CerAb, E01, EngInd, P02. *Bk. rev.:* Number and length vary. *Aud.:* Ac, Sa.

This journal is published by the The Minerals, Metals and Materials Society (TMS) and the Institute of Electrical and Electronics Engineers (IEEE). Written for practicing materials engineers and scientists, the *Journal of Electronic Materials* contains peer-reviewed technical papers about new developments in the science and technology of the materials used in electronics, as well as review papers, letters, and selected papers from conferences and meetings of TMS. Several special issues are published during the year containing articles that focus on the same aspect of electronic materials. Available in full text from ProQuest, EBSCOhost, Springer-Verlag, and other vendors.

2059. *Journal of Electronics Cooling and Thermal Control.* [ISSN: 2162-6162] 2011. q. USD 156. Ed(s): Dayong Gao, Shu-shen Lu. Scientific Research Publishing, Inc., PO Box 54821, Irvine, CA 92619; service@scirp.org; http://www.scirp.org. Refereed. *Aud.:* Ac.

This journal contains original research, technical notes, and reviews about electronic cooling and thermal system control technology in the computer and electronics industries.

2060. *Journal of Low Power Electronics.* [ISSN: 1546-1998] 2005. s-a. Ed(s): Patrick Girard. American Scientific Publishers, 26650 The Old Rd, Ste 208, Valencia, CA 91381-0751; order@aspbs.com; http://www.aspbs.com. Refereed. *Bk. rev.:* Number and length vary. *Aud.:* Ac, Sa.

Journal of Low Power Electronics is a peer-reviewed journal with a focus on recent research in the area of low-power electronics, including optoelectronic and electromagnetic devices, wireless communications, VLSI systems, computer systems, signal processing, and more. Full text is available from Ingenta and EBSCOhost.

2061. *Journal of Low Power Electronics and Applications.* [ISSN: 2079-9268] 2010. q. Free. Ed(s): Alexander Fish. M D P I AG, Postfach, Basel, 4005, Switzerland; http://www.mdpi.com. Refereed. *Aud.:* Ac.

This open-access, English-language journal contains papers related to low-power electronics. Published in Switzerland, it is available from Molecular Diversity Preservation International, and through the Directory of Open Access Journals.

2062. *Journal of Nanoelectronics and Optoelectronics.* [ISSN: 1555-130X] 2006. q. Ed(s): Alexander A Balandin. American Scientific Publishers, 26650 The Old Rd, Ste 208, Valencia, CA 91381-0751; order@aspbs.com; http://www.aspbs.com. Refereed. *Bk. rev.:* Number and length vary. *Aud.:* Ac, Sa.

This peer-reviewed journal, first published in 2006, contains research and review articles on nanoscale and optoelectronic devices and materials. Published by American Scientific Publishers, it is international and interdisciplinary in scope. Special issues highlighting a single subject are published regularly. Indexed in Web of Science, Compendex, SCOPUS, and Current Contents. Full text is available online via Ingenta and EBSCO.

2063. *Journal of Quantum Electronics and Spintronics.* [ISSN: 1949-4882] 2010. q. USD 295. Ed(s): M I Miah. Nova Science Publishers, Inc., 400 Oser Ave, Ste 1600, Hauppauge, NY 11788; nova.main@novapublishers.com; https://www.novapublishers.com. Refereed. *Aud.:* Ac.

This peer-reviewed, international journal publishes original theoretical and experimental research, as well as reviews related to quantum electronic and spin properties. Subject matter also includes quantum electronic and spintronic devices and applications.

2064. *Journal of Technology & Science.* [ISSN: 1944-1894] 2008. w. USD 2295 in US & Canada; USD 2495 elsewhere; USD 2525 combined subscription in US & Canada (print & online eds.). NewsRx, 2727 Paces Ferry Rd SE, Ste 2-440, Atlanta, GA 30339; pressrelease@newsrx.com; http://www.newsrx.com. Adv. Sample. *Aud.:* Ga, Sa.

This publication disseminates the latest news and research in the electronics industry, including news on nanotechnology and robotics.

2065. *Microelectronics Journal.* Formerly (until 1978): *Microelectronics;* Incorporates (1983-1991): *Journal of Semi-Custom I Cs;* (1983-1991): *Semi-Custom I C Yearbook.* [ISSN: 0959-8324] 1967. 12x/yr. EUR 2479. Ed(s): Bernard Courtois. Elsevier Ltd, 32 Jamestown Rd, Camden, London, NW1 7BY, United Kingdom; corporate.sales@elsevier.com; http://www.elsevier.com. Illus., index, adv. Sample. Refereed. *Indexed:* A01, A22, C&ISA, EngInd. *Bk. rev.:* Number and length vary. *Aud.:* Ac, Sa.

International in scope, *Microelectronics Journal* covers research on and applications of microelectronics circuits, systems, physics, and devices. Review articles are included, as are papers that present an unusual or new system design or device. Papers are peer reviewed and contain an abstract and keywords. Available in print only.

2066. *Microelectronics Reliability.* Formerly (until 1964): *Electronics Reliability & Microminiaturization.* [ISSN: 0026-2714] 1962. m. EUR 4362. Ed(s): N D Stojadnovic. Pergamon, The Blvd, Langford Ln, E Park, Kidlington, OX5 1GB, United Kingdom; JournalsCustomerServiceEMEA@elsevier.com; http://www.elsevier.com. Illus., adv. Sample. Refereed. Microform: PQC. *Indexed:* A01, A22, C&ISA, EngInd. *Bk. rev.:* Number and length vary. *Aud.:* Ac, Sa.

Microelectronics Reliability is composed of research articles discussing the most current research results and related information on microelectronic device reliability. Topics covered include physics and analysis; evaluation and prediction; design, packaging, and testing; modeling and simulation; and methodologies and assurance. The majority of the remaining articles are primarily case studies. Special issues are sporadically published that report on significant conferences or timely topics in the area of microelectronics. Book reviews are also included in many of the issues. Electronic availability is provided from a number of vendors.

2067. *Nuts & Volts: exploring everything for electronics.* Formerly (1999): *Nuts & Volts Magazine.* [ISSN: 1528-9885] 1980. m. USD 26.95 combined subscription domestic (print & online eds.); USD 33.95 combined subscription Canada (print & online eds.); USD 44.95 combined subscription elsewhere (print & online eds.). Ed(s): Bryan Bergeron. T & L Publications, 430 Princeland Ct, Corona, CA 92879; display@NutsVolts.com. Illus., adv. Sample. *Indexed:* IHTDI. *Bk. rev.:* Number and length vary. *Aud.:* Hs, Ga.

Written for the electronics hobbyist, design engineer, and electronics technician, *Nuts & Volts* contains information on equipment and do-it-yourself projects in robotics, lasers, circuit design, computer control, automation, and data acquisition. There are also columns that feature new technology, products, and electronics news. Available in print and online. URL: www.nutsvolts.com

2068. *Progress in Quantum Electronics: an international review journal.* [ISSN: 0079-6727] 1969. bi-m. EUR 1517. Ed(s): J G Eden. Pergamon, The Blvd, Langford Ln, E Park, Kidlington, OX5 1GB, United Kingdom; JournalsCustomerServiceEMEA@elsevier.com; http://www.elsevier.com. Adv. Sample. Refereed. Microform: PQC. *Indexed:* A01, A22, C&ISA, EngInd. *Bk. rev.:* Number and length vary. *Aud.:* Ac, Sa.

Progress in Quantum Electronics is an international journal that contains review articles on current topics in quantum electronics and its applications. The papers are either theoretical or experimental in focus and emphasize various aspects of physics, technology, and engineering related to quantum electronics. Potential readers would include materials scientists, solid state scientists, optical scientists, and electrical and electronic engineers. It is available online from numerous vendors.

2069. *Radioelectronics and Communications Systems.* [ISSN: 0735-2727] 1977. m. EUR 3029 (print & online eds.). Ed(s): Yaroslav K Trokhimenko. Allerton Press, Inc., 18 W 27th St, New York, NY 10001; journals@allertonpress.com; http://www.allertonpress.com. Illus. Sample. Refereed. *Indexed:* A22, E01, EngInd. *Bk. rev.:* Number and length vary. *Aud.:* Ac, Sa.

Radioengineering and electronics are the focus of this scholarly journal, published by Allerton Press. Articles include those that report new research in microwave technology, solid-state electronics, radioengineering systems, integral circuit technology, quantum electronics, radiolocation and radionavigation systems, and biomedical electronics. Importantly, many of the articles report research on subjects that not too long ago would have been classified information.

2070. *Semiconductor Science and Technology.* [ISSN: 0268-1242] 1986. m. GBP 2054 (print & online eds.). Ed(s): K Nielsch. Institute of Physics Publishing Ltd., Dirac House, Temple Back, Bristol, BS1 6BE, United Kingdom; custserv@iop.org; http://iopublishing.org. Illus. Sample. Refereed. Vol. ends: No. 12. *Indexed:* A01, A22, C&ISA, CompLI, EngInd. *Bk. rev.:* Number and length vary. *Aud.:* Ac, Sa.

Published by the Institute of Physics, *Semiconductor Science and Technology* is an international journal that covers semiconductor research and its applications. Research papers, review articles, and rapid communications are all peer reviewed and are written for the scientist or engineer. Occasionally, an issue will cover a specific topic; two such special issues were "Carbon Nanotubes" and "Optical Orientation." Full text is available online from a number of vendors.

2071. *Solid-State Electronics: an international journal.* [ISSN: 0038-1101] 1960. m. EUR 4110. Pergamon, The Blvd, Langford Ln, E Park, Kidlington, OX5 1GB, United Kingdom; JournalsCustomerServiceEMEA@elsevier.com; http://www.elsevier.com. Illus., adv. Sample. Refereed. Microform: MIM; PQC. *Indexed:* A01, A22, C&ISA, EngInd. *Bk. rev.:* Number and length vary. *Aud.:* Ac, Sa.

This international journal consists of collections of original research papers that cover the theory, design, physics, modeling, measurement, preparation, evaluation, and applications of solid-state electronics, crystal growth, semiconductors, and circuit engineering. The letters, review papers, and research papers emphasize the new and innovative and the connection of theory and practice. Full text is available online from Elsevier, EBSCO, and other vendors.

2072. *Solid State Technology.* Incorporates (2001-2011): *Small Times;* (1992-2008): *Advanced Packaging;* Which was formerly (1984-1992): *Hybrid Circuit Technology;* Former titles (until 1968): *Semiconductor Products and Solid State Technology;* (until 1962): *Semiconductor Products.* [ISSN: 0038-111X] 1958. 9x/yr. USD 258 domestic (Free to qualified personnel). Ed(s): Peter Singer. PennWell Corporation, 1421 S Sheridan Rd, Tulsa, OK 74112; Headquarters@PennWell.com; http://www.pennwell.com. Illus., index, adv. Sample. Circ: 41136. Vol. ends: No. 12. *Indexed:* A01, A22, ABIn, B01, B02, B03, C&ISA, CerAb, EngInd, P02, RiskAb. *Bk. rev.:* Number and length vary. *Aud.:* Ac, Sa.

Solid State Technology is a trade magazine for managers and engineers in the semiconductor manufacturing industry. Each issue covers the news and technology of such topics as nanotechnology, MEMS, flat panel displays, atomic layer deposition, wafers, and waste handling, as well as the materials, software, products, and processes used in the manufacturing of semiconductors. Occasional special issues cover the state of the industry in specific geographic regions, or report on important conferences and trade shows. Available online from a variety of vendors.

■ ENERGY

Sharon L. Siegler, Engineering Librarian, Lehigh University Library & Technology Services, Fairchild/Martindale Library, 8A Packer Ave., Bethlehem, PA 18015; FAX: 610-758-6524; sls7@lehigh.edu

Introduction

Recent years have seen a resurgence in new "energy" journal titles. A quick search in *Ulrichsweb* shows that, in the last three years, more new energy journals and magazines (approximately 71 titles) have appeared than in the ten years that immediately followed the 1973 "energy crisis" (approximately 62). Most of the post-1973 titles featured oil and nuclear power sources, although there were a few that covered solar, wind, and even sustainable energy. The big thrust then was in legal, economic, and policy issues. The current crop is concerned with renewable, sustainable, and environmentally friendly fuel sources and the systems that make these and the "traditional" fuels viable in today's world.

Unfortunately, the trend to lower subscription prices (or, at least, lower price increases) has gone, replaced by a return to double-digit percentage increases. A few Open Access titles have appeared, but most have too few issues (or articles, since these tend to be online publications) to adequately review. Another trend is the movement to "online only" with 16 of the 71 new titles in that category. In this vein, although most of the long-time "trade magazines" still produce a print copy, the print issues are notably skimpy, and the bulk of these magazines are obviously becoming "online only" themselves. This may be a boon to public, small academic, and small industry libraries, since online access often provides better access for users and lower processing costs for libraries.

This section cannot possibly cover all of the types of energy, its applications, nor its aspects (engineering, policy, economics, etc.); the goal here is to review the major publications in the major areas, with some attention to new developments. Most of the titles reviewed are research journals; a few of the multitudinous trade magazines are included as examples.

Basic Periodicals

Ga: *Home Power, Power Engineering, World Oil;* Ac: *Energy, Energy & Environmental Science, Energy & Fuels, The Energy Journal, Journal of Energy Engineering.*

Basic Abstracts and Indexes

Applied Science and Technology Abstracts, Engineering Index, Web of Science.

2073. *Advanced Energy Materials.* [ISSN: 1614-6832] 2011. 6x/yr. EUR 1625. Ed(s): Martin Ottmar, Eliza-Beth Lerch. Wiley - V C H Verlag GmbH & Co. KGaA, Postfach 101161, Weinheim, 69451, Germany; info@wiley-vch.de; http://www.wiley-vch.de. Refereed. *Aud.:* Ac.

Begun as a section of *Advanced Materials, Advanced Energy Materials* became a journal in its own right in 2011. The focus of the journal is "materials used in all forms of energy harvesting, conversion[,] and storage," but the applications are largely for renewable energy sources or, more generally, non–carbon based. The point is to find the correct materials to use for specific types of energy generation, such as which organics work best in organophotovoltaic systems, or what materials can handle the problems of generating and storing hydrogen (embrittlement, pressurization, temperature). Beyond the choosing of materials is the implementation, such as how the layering of catalytic material affects electrode performance. Issues are comprised of reviews, communications, and full articles. The reviews are lengthy, the communications are relatively short (four or six pages on average), and the articles range from 5 to 15 pages. Some articles include "supplementary material" that may be as simple as a graphic or as complex as datasets. The delay from submission to online publication is short (about three months), but add another three months for the "official" journal issue. The title is too new to have an Impact Factor, but the editor projects that it will be around 8 in 2013 (2012 release), which would make it high-ranking in the field. More to the point, it fills a niche in the energy field, and will be useful in cross-disciplinary collections as well.

2074. *Applied Energy.* [ISSN: 0306-2619] 1975. m. EUR 3925. Ed(s): J Yan. Pergamon, The Blvd, Langford Ln, E Park, Kidlington, OX5 1GB, United Kingdom; JournalsCustomerServiceEMEA@elsevier.com; http://www.elsevier.com. Illus., adv. Sample. Refereed. Microform: PQC. *Indexed:* A01, A22, ApMecR, C&ISA, EngInd. *Aud.:* Ac.

Applied Energy discusses energy conversion, conservation, and management from the engineering point of view. Research here is not to develop new energy sources, but to better utilize the ones presently in use. Issues average 40–50 articles, with occasional reviews and short communications. Articles in recent issues discuss the impact of carbon tax on energy and economic growth in

China; flywheel-based energy storage devices for wind power; and long-term forecasting of hourly electricity consumption. Authors are almost exclusively academics or from government-sponsored research institutions. With some exceptions, the lag time between receipt and online publication has lengthened from a short two months to about six, still respectably current. One of the top ten energy titles in Impact Factor, it is also one of the top ten in price, and it should be considered only for an extensive academic library collection.

2075. *Applied Thermal Engineering: design, processes, equipment, economics.* Former titles (until 1996): *Heat Recovery Systems and C H P;* (until 1987): *Journal of Heat Recovery Systems.* [ISSN: 1359-4311] 1981. s-m. EUR 3123. Ed(s): D A Reay. Pergamon, The Blvd, Langford Ln, E Park, Kidlington, OX5 1GB, United Kingdom; JournalsCustomerServiceEMEA@elsevier.com; http://www.elsevier.com. Adv. Sample. Refereed. Microform: PQC. *Indexed:* A22, ApMecR, B01, C&ISA, CEA, CerAb, EngInd. *Aud.:* Ac, Sa.

This journal covers thermal energy applications in depth, from the theoretical ("mathematical modeling of steady-state operation of a loop heat pipe") to the extremely practical ("fast response heat[-]pump water heater using [a] thermostat made from shape memory alloy"). In general, work involves energy production and large-scale use (such as manufacturing or building heating plants). Although the journal is academic in thrust, often co-authors will work for commercial concerns; the editor himself maintains a private practice as well as an academic appointment. Articles average less than ten pages but can be lengthy. The lag time between submission and electronic publication is often within two to four months of receipt, but print readers can expect to wait another three or four months. Occasionally, an issue is devoted to the proceedings of a conference, but the bulk of the papers are current, independent research. Oddly, beginning in 2012, there are multiple volumes (of one or two issues each) instead of one volume with 18 issues. The total number of articles and pages is about the same. Those libraries with strong interests in energy and mechanical engineering would find this a welcome title, but compare it to *Applied Energy* (also in this section).

2076. *Biofuels, Bioproducts and Biorefining.* [ISSN: 1932-104X] 2007. bi-m. GBP 627. Ed(s): Bruce E Dale. John Wiley & Sons Ltd., The Atrium, Southern Gate, Chichester, PO19 8SQ, United Kingdom; customer@wiley.co.uk; http://www.wiley.com. Adv. Sample. Refereed. Reprint: PSC. *Indexed:* C&ISA, C45, CerAb. *Aud.:* Ac, Sa.

Since its initial publication in 2007, this journal has rapidly become an important title in energy and is currently ranked tenth in the ISI energy category. It is a mix of engineering and business, which may be the important factor in its appeal. With many colorful illustrations and a magazine layout, *Biofpr,* as it calls itself, is in the style of many professional society magazines, rather than a scholarly journal. The scope is larger than biomass as fuel, and includes using biomass for carbon reduction and integrating biomass fuel into power systems. Most of each issue is composed of articles, but there are several regular sections: business highlights, technology news, patents, modeling and analysis (formerly "market trends"), interviews, and the occasional commentary. The articles are categorized as features, perspectives, and reviews. The economic/political articles slightly outnumber the technical material, but both topic areas have complex titles, such as "Cost estimate for biosynfuel production via biosyncrude gasification" and "Comparative analysis of efficiency, environmental impact, and process economics for mature biomass refining scenarios." The modeling and analysis section often highlights a particular fuel type; the patent section will not only list and discuss new patents of interest, but also illustrate trends in number of patents in various countries. Libraries that subscribe to *Biomass & Bioenergy* (also reviewed in this section) will find this title a useful addition. Libraries that have little in the bioenergy area might find that this fills the gap. As this is one of the few titles that have actually dropped in price, it is worth a second look.

2077. *Biomass & Bioenergy.* [ISSN: 0961-9534] 1991. m. EUR 2402. Ed(s): R P Overend, C P Mitchell. Pergamon, The Blvd, Langford Ln, E Park, Kidlington, OX5 1GB, United Kingdom; JournalsCustomerServiceEMEA@elsevier.com; http://www.elsevier.com. Adv. Sample. Refereed. Microform: PQC. *Indexed:* A01, A22, Agr, C45, EngInd, RRTA. *Aud.:* Ac.

As the title indicates, the coverage of this journal is very mixed. Some articles will appeal mostly to agribusiness endeavors, discussing harvesting methods, agricultural waste, pesticide runoff, and the like. Others will appeal to the energy engineer, with BTU figures and combustion problems associated with biofuels. Still others will appeal to economists and managers, with long-range forecasting of biofuel production and usage. It is also environmentally friendly in several senses of the term, as seen in "Kudzu: A new source of carbohydrate for bioethanol production," which may turn a landscape pest into an asset. Authors are from academia and government-sponsored research laboratories, with a wide range of backgrounds: engineering, agriculture, economics, and more. The publication lag remains high (approximately two years), even with early posting on the web site. Institutions with strong agriculture as well as energy collections will find this a core title. Some geographic areas will have a strong interest in this type of energy source, while others will find this a niche topic. Libraries looking for broader coverage should consider *Biofuels, Bioproducts and Biorefining,* also reviewed in this section.

2078. *Energies.* [ISSN: 1996-1073] 2008. m. Free. Ed(s): Dr. Enrico Sciubba, Mr. Tony Xu. M D P I AG, Postfach, Basel, 4005, Switzerland; http://www.mdpi.com. Refereed. *Indexed:* A01, C45. *Aud.:* Ac.

A successful Open Access title, *Energies* has as broad a scope as its title suggests. Largely a technical research journal, it also covers policy and management. As well as the primary sources (fossil and renewable), articles discuss the theory of energy (thermodynamics), exploration, delivery, and conversion systems (from boilers to power plants). Environmental issues are raised, but usually in the contexts of policy or management. The title has a good Impact Factor (1.865 in 2011, the latest available), which puts it in the middle of the "Energy and Fuels" category; and it is cited by a wide range of energy-related research journals, and many libraries subscribe. One troublesome issue is the very short delay between article submission and publication, which is often less than two months. Authors, of course, find this a plus, but it is difficult to see how peer review by more than one reviewer can be accomplished in such a short time. The online interface has several good features, such as article-download statistics, versioning, and links to more works by the same authors, but it lacks links to cited references. As an Open Access title, the "subscription price" fits all budgets, but libraries should judge it on how it fits their collection goals.

2079. *Energy.* [ISSN: 0360-5442] 1976. 15x/yr. EUR 3384. Ed(s): Henrik Lund. Elsevier Ltd, 32 Jamestown Rd, Camden, London, NW1 7BY, United Kingdom; corporate.sales@elsevier.com; http://www.elsevier.com. Illus., index, adv. Sample. Refereed. Vol. ends: Dec. Microform: PQC. *Indexed:* A01, A22, BAS, BrTechI, C&ISA, C45, CerAb, EngInd, RRTA. *Aud.:* Ac.

One of the first scholarly journals in the energy field, this title covers the full spectrum: all types of energy sources, all aspects of energy production, and economic/political/social factors. *Energy* emphasizes development, assessment, and management of energy programs. Most papers involving technical matter average fewer than eight pages; those concerned with economic issues tend to be twice as long. Technical issues often have an economic or societal aspect; economic issues often have a technical flavor. Periodically, an issue will be devoted to a theme (such as "World Energy Systems") or a symposium (such as "Sustainable Development of Energy, Water and Environment"). Bibliographies, maps, and statistics abound; graphs and tables are often in color. On average, articles are published within six months of receipt, although some take much longer. RSS feeds, open-URL linking, social bookmarking, citations, related articles, and downloading to citation managers are added features. A primary journal, but expensive for all except large academic or industry libraries.

2080. *Energy and Buildings.* [ISSN: 0378-7788] 1978. 12x/yr. EUR 2444. Ed(s): B B Todorovic. Elsevier S.A., PO Box 564, Lausanne, 1001, Switzerland. Illus., index, adv. Sample. Refereed. Vol. ends: No. 6. Microform: PQC. *Indexed:* A01, A22, API, C&ISA, EngInd, ErgAb. *Aud.:* Ac, Sa.

The emphasis here is on the "buildings," with the "energy" portion largely devoted to energy conservation, architectural design for passive energy use/ savings, use of solar energy, manipulation of lighting, insulation materials, and cost/benefit analyses for energy consumption. "Sustainability" has been added to the mix, and the journal is also a likely source for distributed energy material, so often used in multi-occupant facilities. The buildings can be anything from high-rise complexes to grass huts, and from classrooms in the tropics to crawlspaces in Finland. Although scholarly in treatment, this journal is practical in outlook; articles have discussed energy consumption in old school buildings, low-cost insulation, pressure air-flow models for ventilation, and heat transfer in insulated concrete walls. Occasionally a theme issue is published, such as "Cool roofs, cool pavements, cool cities, and cool world" (only the first three categories were addressed). Authorship is international. Articles tend to be short (six to ten pages). Not for all collections, this title is best for libraries with interest in civil engineering or architecture, as well as energy.

2081. *Energy & Environment.* [ISSN: 0958-305X] 1990. 8x/yr. GBP 518; GBP 560 combined subscription (print & online eds.). Ed(s): Sonja Boehmer-Christiansen. Multi-Science Publishing Co. Ltd., 5 Wates Way, Brentwood, CM15 9TB, United Kingdom; info@multi-science.co.uk; http://www.multi-science.co.uk. Illus. Sample. Refereed. *Indexed:* A22, C&ISA, CerAb, EngInd, M&GPA. *Aud.:* Ac.

This is a difficult journal. It is described by its editor as an interdisciplinary journal aimed at scientists, engineers, and social scientists, discussing energy's impact on the environment. More to the point, the editor sees it as a forum for all parties to discuss the issues, and actively encourages and publishes their debates. To that end, "Viewpoints and technical communications" is a regular issue feature. Most of the articles are sociopolitical or socioeconomic; the technology issues are raised but, perforce, this is done at a relatively superficial level. The articles themselves are scholarly treatments, and extensively documented, but the authors vary in level of expertise. Very few institutions subscribe to this title, but it deserves a wider audience; regardless of the merits of the debates published here, the fact that the debates occur should help drive out bad science, bad politics, bad economics, and bad blood. Recommended with reservations to libraries with strong programs in economics and politics, as well as energy.

2082. *Energy & Environmental Science.* [ISSN: 1754-5692] 2008. m. GBP 1325 combined subscription (print & online eds.); USD 2524 combined subscription (print & online eds.). R S C Publications, Thomas Graham House (290), Science Park, Milton Rd, Cambridge, CB4 0WF, United Kingdom; sales@rsc.org; http://www.rsc.org. Adv. Refereed. *Indexed:* A22, C45, E01, OceAb, S25. *Aud.:* Ac.

The title of this journal should actually be *Energy, Environmental Science, and Chemistry* because the coverage is all from the chemist's perspective. Only in its fifth year, it is now ranked number two in the ISI's "Energy and Fuels" category. Treatment ranges from a review article on organic tandem solar cells to "Photocatalytic water splitting by RuO2-loaded metal oxides and nitrides with d0- and d10-related electronic configurations," which requires an advanced chemistry degree even to understand the title. The online version is excellent, with full-color images in the abstracts (with the option to invoke or turn off, saving online bandwidth), pdf or html versions, internal links, and links to full text of the references. The newest feature is a tabbed display for articles, table of contents, special issues, and "most read" options, making navigation simpler and providing more content on a single screen. The entire journal can be searched by field or full text; chemical structure searching is also available through a still-in-development system. Social bookmarking, RSS feeds, export to bibliographic managers, and finding cites to particular articles are supported. The title is included in some Royal Society of Chemistry packages, but the regular price limits this to collections with strong chemistry and energy programs.

2083. *Energy & Fuels.* [ISSN: 0887-0624] 1987. bi-m. USD 1615. Ed(s): Michael T Klein. American Chemical Society, 1155 16th St N W, Washington, DC 20036; help@acs.org; http://pubs.acs.org. Illus., index, adv. Sample. Refereed. *Indexed:* A22, C&ISA, EngInd. *Bk. rev.:* 1, 1,000 words. *Aud.:* Ac, Sa.

One of the many American Chemical Society (ACS) journals, this is a scholarly publication interested in both the discovery of non-nuclear fuels and their development as power sources. Each issue's content is arranged by category. "Biofuels and Biomass," "Catalysis & Kinetics," "Combustion," "Environmental and Carbon Dioxide Issues," "Fossil Fuels," and "Renewable Energy" predominate, but "Efficiency and Sustainability," "Hydrogen,"

"Process Engineering," and others appear often. Individual issues often contain selected papers from symposia, reviews, and "communications" (brief notes on techniques). Authorship is from academia and includes chemists and geologists as well as engineers. Publication is often within two months of manuscript subscription but can be longer. The site has tabbed views, RSS feeds, social bookmarking, DOI links, html and three types of pdf views, citation alerts, related articles, other articles by the same authors, and the option to download references to the major bibliographic managers. This is a core, quality title.

2084. *Energy Conversion and Management.* Former titles (until 1980): *Energy Conversion;* (until 1968): *Advanced Energy Conversion.* [ISSN: 0196-8904] 1961. 12x/yr. EUR 5303. Ed(s): J Denton, S Sahin. Elsevier Ltd, 32 Jamestown Rd, Camden, London, NW1 7BY, United Kingdom; corporate.sales@elsevier.com; http://www.elsevier.com. Illus., index, adv. Sample. Refereed. Vol. ends: No. 18. Microform: PQC. *Indexed:* A01, A22, ApMecR, C45, CEA, EngInd, RRTA. *Aud.:* Ac, Sa.

Another of the many energy-related scholarly publications in the Elsevier stable, this journal is concerned with technical development of all types of fuels and energy resources, ranging from hydrocarbons though biomass, solar, wind, and other renewable sources. The topics are defined broadly, so that titles representing published papers include both "Piezoelectric energy harvesting" and "Conversion of waste rubber to the mixture of hydrocarbons in the reactor with molten metal." While its sister publication, *Energy: the international journal,* discusses large-scale management issues, *Energy Conversion* presents detailed technical papers on the ultimate production of many of the same resources. Authorship is international. The lag between article submission and acceptance is now quite short (three to six months on average), although some articles spend more time in the review process. Article length has shortened considerably, with most averaging under ten pages, instead of the 20-plus of previous years. Although one of the most expensive titles in the field, this publication has a relatively high subscription base, probably because of the emphasis on application and its wide coverage of energy sources.

2085. *Energy Economics.* Incorporates (1996-2001): *Journal of Energy Finance and Development.* [ISSN: 0140-9883] 1979. 6x/yr. EUR 1427. Ed(s): R S J Tol, B W Ang. Elsevier BV, North-Holland, Postbus 211, Amsterdam, 1000 AE, Netherlands; JournalsCustomerServiceEMEA@elsevier.com; http://www.elsevier.com. Illus., index, adv. Sample. Refereed. Vol. ends: No. 6. Microform: PQC. *Indexed:* A22, ABIn, B01, EconLit, EngInd, IBSS, JEL, P61, SSA. *Aud.:* Ac.

True to its name, this scholarly journal discusses the economic and tax issues of energy, generally on the macro scale. Recent issues feature "Do petrol prices rise faster than they fall when the market shows significant disequilibria?" (what we all suspect), "The carbon rent economics of climate policy," and "The liquidity of oil stocks." Definitely international in scope, the lengthy articles have covered Indian coal, oil-price sticker shock in Europe, price rigidity in the New Zealand petroleum industry, and the Colombian electricity market. Although other types of fuel sources appear occasionally, most issues deal with oil, coal, and the electricity markets. The average time from submission to online publication of an article is still one year, but the print issue now appears about four months later instead of after yet another year's delay. This is a journal for larger collections with an active local interest in economics; other libraries should consider *The Energy Journal* (also reviewed in this section).

2086. *Energy Engineering.* Former titles (until 1980): *Building Systems Design;* (until 1969): *Air Conditioning, Heating and Ventilating;* (until 1955): *Heating and Ventilating;* (until 1929): *The Heating and Ventilating Magazine.* [ISSN: 0199-8595] 1904. bi-m. GBP 276 (print & online eds.). Taylor & Francis Inc., 325 Chestnut St, Ste 800, Philadelphia, PA 19106; customerservice@taylorandfrancis.com; http://www.tandfonline.com. Illus., index. Sample. Refereed. Vol. ends: No. 6. Microform: PMC; PQC. Reprint: PSC. *Indexed:* A22, C&ISA, CerAb, E01, EngInd. *Aud.:* Ac, Sa.

This is the energy magazine for the plant engineer, high-rise building supervisor, and town engineer. Articles range from tips on energy auditing to financing renewable energy projects. Most articles are written by practitioners or consultants, but some are by academics. Some have lengthy reference lists and others are obviously "expert-advice" columns. Over the years, coverage has broadened from HVAC fine-tuning and lighting system adjustments to include alternative fuels, fuel cells, cogeneration, energy control systems, and "green systems." Two other journals from the same publisher (which are not reviewed in this section) are *Strategic Planning for Energy and the Environment* and *Cogeneration and Competitive Power Journal*; the former is addressed to managers, and the latter discusses the technical aspects of "cogeneration" (using the byproduct of one power source to produce yet another form of energy). The publisher provides web access to all of its journals with a browsable, searchable interface; "guest users" may access tables-of-contents and abstracts. Users who register can obtain an alerting service and pay-per-view of individual articles. This is a good choice for a large public library and/or undergraduates in an engineering curriculum.

2087. *The Energy Journal.* [ISSN: 0195-6574] 1980. q. Free to members; Non-members, USD 475. Ed(s): Adonis Yatchew, Lester Hunt. International Association for Energy Economics, 28790 Chagrin Blvd, Ste 350, Cleveland, OH 44122; iaee@iaee.org; http://www.iaee.org. Illus., index, adv. Sample. Refereed. Vol. ends: No. 4. Microform: PQC. *Indexed:* A01, A22, ABIn, B01, B02, BRI, CBRI, EconLit, EngInd, JEL, RiskAb. *Bk. rev.:* 4, 1,000 words. *Aud.:* Ac.

The journal of the International Association for Energy Economics, this is a scholarly publication that covers the economic and social/political aspects of energy. Generally, this means electric power, oil, and natural gas, but there is some attention to renewable sources. Currently, there is much attention paid to climate and carbon emission issues, electricity demand/distribution economics, and energy consumption patterns. Articles are lengthy, often more than 20 pages, with extensive bibliographies, and they use charts and graphs as illustrations. Authors are from the international academic and government-policy community. Announcements of association conferences and book reviews complete the issues. There are occasional special issues (often available for free online). The web site includes tables of contents and subject category indexes for the entire run of the journal, plus the option for subscribers to download issues rather than receive them by mail. This title is available in full text from several sources, and the subscription price has not increased in three years; a good choice for libraries with strong energy and economics programs.

2088. *Energy Law Journal.* [ISSN: 0270-9163] 1980. s-a. Free to members; Non-members, USD 35. Ed(s): Robert S Fleishman, Harvey L Reiter. University of Tulsa, College of Law, 3120 E 4th Pl, Tulsa, OK 74104; news@utulsa.edu; http://www.utulsa.edu/law. Adv. Microform: WSH. Reprint: WSH. *Indexed:* A22, ABIn, B01, BRI, CLI, L14. *Bk. rev.:* 2, 1,000 words. *Aud.:* Ac, Sa.

As much about economics and environment as about law, the *Energy Law Journal* is a scholarly work devoted to lengthy analyses of energy issues and how they affect the law or how the law affects them. Issues are not only reviewed but debated as well. Papers are written by attorneys, judges, and experts from government agencies. Most of the discussions involve U.S. law, but there are occasional works specific to other countries or international in scope. Emphasis is on electricity supply with some attention to oil, natural gas, the environment, and alternative energy forms, such as hydrogen. Book reviews, committee reports on energy and administrative law, and what passes for short notes in the legal world (such as "Exxon shrugged: how a 200 year old statute torments the Titans," in 15 pages) round out the issues. The complete run of issues may be browsed or searched via keyword. A special feature is a list of "cited cases," instances where articles from the *Journal* are cited in opinions, cases, and other legal documents. Pdfs are freely available for all issues. Widely owned by law libraries and with a very modest price, it deserves consideration by libraries with strong energy collections and public-policy collections.

2089. *Energy Policy.* [ISSN: 0301-4215] 1973. 12x/yr. EUR 3023. Ed(s): N France. Elsevier Ltd, 32 Jamestown Rd, Camden, London, NW1 7BY, United Kingdom; corporate.sales@elsevier.com; http://www.elsevier.com. Illus., index, adv. Sample. Refereed. Vol. ends: No. 15. Microform: PQC. *Indexed:* A22, ABIn, ABS&EES, B01, B02, BRI, C45, EconLit, EngInd, IBSS, P02. *Aud.:* Ac.

This journal should be compared with *Energy Economics,* also from Elsevier. First, the emphasis is on renewable energy forms (such as wind, solar, biomass), as opposed to the primarily oil and electric power interests of its sister title. Second, the theme is policy decisions by government and by industry as opposed to financial considerations. Renewable energy, carbon emissions, and energy efficiency are current topics. Both publications have international authorship and interest, but *Energy Policy* often discusses specific countries and regions while *Energy Economics* is often global in focus. Publication lag is very short, often only two to three months. While most of the articles are research reports, many issues also contain a "Viewpoints" section with one or two persuasive analyses. Recommended for libraries with international relations and public policy collections in conjunction with energy research.

2090. *Energy Sources. Part A. Recovery, Utilization, and Environmental Effects.* Supersedes in part (in 2006): *Energy Sources;* Which incorporated (1974-1991): *Energy Systems and Policy.* [ISSN: 1556-7036] 1973. 20x/yr. GBP 3397 (print & online eds.). Ed(s): James G Speight. Taylor & Francis Inc., 325 Chestnut St, Ste 800, Philadelphia, PA 19106; customerservice@taylorandfrancis.com; http://www.tandfonline.com. Illus., index, adv. Sample. Refereed. Reprint: PSC. *Indexed:* A01, A22, BAS, C&ISA, C45, CerAb, E01, EngInd, M&GPA. *Aud.:* Ac.

Energy Sources split into two sections in January 2006. *Part A,* still the major section with 20 issues per year, retained the technical papers; *Part B* (also reviewed in this section) covers economics, policy, and planning. Librarians are usually not pleased when a title splits because, aside from the cataloging headaches and user confusion, there is also an automatic price increase. In this case, it is still possible to subscribe to each part separately, so that libraries that emphasize the technical aspects of energy are not required to accept the policy addition (and vice versa). There is also a combined subscription option. The journal's theme is fuel sources: carbon-based (petroleum, natural gas, oil tars and shales, organic waste), nuclear, wind, solar, and geothermal. The aspects are extraction and conversion to energy, and what is reported is "completed" research as opposed to theory or in-process updates. Recent articles concerned green energy from biogas in a sewage treatment plant; flue gas analysis from coal combustion; and geothermal energy in Saudi Arabia. Issue topics tend to clump, with a string of issues devoted to carbon-based fuels, then a single issue that covers mostly other forms. Dates are now provided for the publishing process from submission to online publication; the delay is over two years and often three, despite the publisher's stated aim for rapid publication. With a middle-of-the-pack Impact Factor and an average annual price increase in the double digits, this title should only be considered for the comprehensive collection.

2091. *Energy Sources. Part B. Economics, Planning, and Policy.* Supersedes in part (in 2006): *Energy Sources;* Which incorporated (1974-1991): *Energy Systems and Policy.* [ISSN: 1556-7249] 1973. q. GBP 264 (print & online eds.). Ed(s): James G Speight. Taylor & Francis Inc., 325 Chestnut St, Ste 800, Philadelphia, PA 19106; customerservice@taylorandfrancis.com; http://www.tandfonline.com. Sample. Refereed. Reprint: PSC. *Indexed:* A01, A22, C&ISA, C45, CerAb, E01, EngInd. *Aud.:* Ac.

Energy Sources split in 2006 into *Parts A* and *B. Part A* is the "parent" title and is also reviewed in this section (and *Part B* is really a new journal, since the volume numbering begins with one. Unlike many title splits, it is possible to subscribe to each title separately or to get both at a reduced price. *Part A* contains the highly technical papers; *Part B* contains the analysis papers. This does not mean that they are light reading; recent titles include "Diversification of crude oil import sources as determinant factors in the pricing of petroleum products" and "Optimal long-term electricity price forecasting." Many of the articles published so far are reviews in nature. Like its sister publication, *Part B* now has long delays between article submission and publication, a mid-rank Impact Factor, and double-digit price increases (although *Part B* is modestly priced).

2092. *Energy Systems.* [ISSN: 1868-3967] 2010. 4x/yr. EUR 309 (print & online eds.). Ed(s): Panos Pardalos. Springer, Tiergartenstr 17, Heidelberg, 69121, Germany; subscriptions@springer.com; http://www.springer.com. Refereed. Reprint: PSC. *Indexed:* ABIn. *Aud.:* Ac.

Although articles may mention specific energy sources or production process, this is primarily a "mathematical modeling" journal devoted to the systems of distributing and using energy. Many articles include "grid" or "wind" in their titles, implying the chief energy form is electricity. The treatment is highly mathematical and the authors are just as likely to be economists as engineers. Indeed, combinations of academic researchers and production supervisors are also common. Lag time between submission and publication averages six months, but it can be as much as one year. Issues are skimpy, with only four to six articles, but they are relatively lengthy at about 20 pages each. This title will be a good fit in both industry and academic libraries with interests in electric power production.

2093. Fuel: the science and technology of fuel and energy. Formerly (until 1948): *Fuel in Science and Practice.* [ISSN: 0016-2361] 1922. 12x/yr. EUR 4304. Ed(s): John W Patrick, E Suuberg. Elsevier Ltd, The Boulevard, Langford Lane, Oxford, OX5 1GB, United Kingdom; journalscustomerserviceemea@elsevier.com; http://www.elsevier.com. Illus., index, adv. Sample. Refereed. Vol. ends: No. 15. Microform: PQC. *Indexed:* A01, A22, ApMecR, BrTechI, C&ISA, CerAb, EngInd. *Bk. rev.:* Number and length vary. *Aud.:* Ac.

One of the oldest professional journals devoted to energy sources, *Fuel* publishes highly technical articles on coal (and coal tar), petroleum (oil, oil shale, oil sands, and derivatives), natural gas, and more than a trace of biomass. Most of the articles concern the production of electrical energy, but there is some attention to transportation (gasoline, diesel fuel, and the like). Authorship is international and largely academic, with some coauthors from commercial enterprises. The articles are under ten pages, well referenced, and illustrated with charts, tables, and line drawings, some in color to enhance readability. Most of each issue is devoted to "full papers," but the occasional review article, brief communication, or book review pops up. The extra issues in this "monthly" are proceedings of conferences. This is a relatively expensive title but is useful in a number of engineering disciplines and has a proven track record. Libraries that subscribe to this title should also consider its sister publication, *Fuel Processing Technology,* also reviewed in this section.

2094. Fuel Cells (Online). [ISSN: 1615-6854] bi-m. GBP 696. Ed(s): Ulrich Stimming. Wiley - V C H Verlag GmbH & Co. KGaA, Postfach 101161, Weinheim, 69451, Germany; info@wiley-vch.de; http://www.wiley-vch.de. Refereed. *Aud.:* Ac.

A highly technical journal in a highly technical field, *Fuel Cells* is also highly ranked in the ISI Impact Factor for the energy and fuels category. The average issue is composed of original research, but special issues on a theme, such as new ceramic materials, often include one or two review articles and editorial comment on the topic. Original articles are short, averaging five or six pages; review articles are much lengthier at 10–15 pages. Illustrations are gray-scale. The journal's scope covers everything about fuel cells from "their molecular level to their applications," but most articles appear to address very specific issues on the laboratory scale. Beginning in 2011, the journal dropped its print version and became online only. Relatively inexpensive for a scholarly journal in a specialized field, this one still requires a strong local interest.

2095. Fuel Processing Technology. [ISSN: 0378-3820] 1978. 12x/yr. EUR 3193. Ed(s): A Boehman. Elsevier BV, Radarweg 29, PO Box 211, Amsterdam, 1000 AE, Netherlands; JournalsCustomerServiceEMEA@elsevier.com; http://www.elsevier.nl. Illus., index. Sample. Refereed. Microform: PQC. *Indexed:* A01, A22, C&ISA, CerAb, EngInd. *Aud.:* Ac.

Fuel Processing Technology should be compared to its sister publication, *Fuel* (also reviewed in this section). The two titles cover the same types of fuels: hydrocarbons (coal, oil, shale) and biomass. The first title emphasizes "processing" (the conversion of the raw materials to higher forms of fuels) and the second title also includes papers similar in scope. However, *Fuel Processing Technology* uses a less theoretical approach. The articles make for dense reading, with such titles as "Towards a comprehensive thermodynamic database for ash-forming elements in biomass and waste." However, there are occasional review articles and special issues, such as "Impacts of fuel quality on power production and environment." Article authorship, length, illustration, and referencing are also similar; the lag between paper submission and online averages less than six months. Consider the pair of these titles for those libraries with strong programs in petroleum technology, as well as energy.

2096. Geothermics: international journal of geothermal research and its applications. [ISSN: 0375-6505] 1972. q. EUR 1614. Ed(s): A Ghassemi. Pergamon, The Blvd, Langford Ln, E Park, Kidlington, OX5 1GB, United Kingdom; JournalsCustomerServiceEMEA@elsevier.com; http://www.elsevier.com. Illus., adv. Sample. Refereed. Microform: PQC. *Indexed:* A01, A22, C&ISA, C45, CerAb, EngInd, S25. *Aud.:* Ac.

Geothermal energy sources are more widespread than is commonly thought. Iceland comes to mind, and perhaps New Zealand, but many countries have geothermal hot spots. Yellowstone is the obvious one in the United States, but Alaska is also a geothermal locale. Obviously of specialized research interest, this topic also intrigues consumers because of the novelty and the idea of "free energy." In recent years, private homes have begun using ground loop heat exchangers instead of heat pumps; this is basically the same idea but with a more stable environment and fewer moving parts. Most of the articles in *Geothermics* are practical in nature: applied research. Topics include using ground-coupled condensers in air conditioning systems, problems associated with boreholes, surveys of geothermal sites, and similar items. Articles average about ten pages, with color illustrations where appropriate. This is a good title for a strong mechanical engineering collection, as well as for energy.

2097. Home Energy. Formerly (until 1988): *Energy Auditor and Retrofitter.* [ISSN: 0896-9442] 1984. bi-m. USD 75 (print or online ed.); USD 85 combined subscription (print & online eds.). Ed(s): Iain Walker, Jim Gunshinan. Energy Auditor and Retrofitter, Inc., 2124 Kittredge St, #95, Berkeley, CA 94704. Illus., adv. Sample. Circ: 5000. Vol. ends: Nov/Dec. *Indexed:* BRI. *Aud.:* Ga, Sa.

Home Energy is published by a nonprofit organization, which states that its mission is "to provide objective and practical information for residential energy conservation." Originally intended for the professional home remodeler, since 1997 it has addressed the homeowner as well, partly with consumer guide information and partly with self-help tips. The thrust is efficient use of energy, not necessarily the source of energy, so that home insulation, lighting, water usage, and the like are considered. Each issue has a few articles that are factual in nature, cite publications or refer to web links, and include many photographs and line illustrations. The rest of the issue is "Trends," covering product information, an events calendar, industry news, and briefs. The web site is not just a reproduction of the printed product, but includes a do-it-yourself tips section, a blog, and a training directory. Only subscribers have access to the current content, although the 1993–99 archive (searchable) has many free articles. There is an extensive list of short, colorfully illustrated information articles for both the consumer and the contractor, plus links to sites of interest. With its wide geographic range, even in states where the winter sun can be hard to find, this is good title for any public library.

2098. Home Power. [ISSN: 1050-2416] 1987. bi-m. USD 24.95 domestic; USD 34.95 foreign; USD 8.95 per issue. Ed(s): Claire Anderson. Home Power, Inc., PO Box 520, Ashland, OR 97520. Illus., adv. *Aud.:* Ga, Sa.

Home Power has revamped itself several times over its 25-year history. The current version is better organized and more "professional" than the early years (although the early years had many offbeat and fun articles). The magazine promulgates "homemade" electric power using renewable energy resources (solar, wind, water). Two new sections cover energy-efficient vehicles and "home efficiency." Many articles are success stories from the readership. *Home Power* solicits articles but does not offer payment, but the author keeps some publication rights. The web site includes the full digital versions of all issues (free with a three-year subscription), some useful files/data from earlier issues, links to related sites, and job and "experts" lists. The archives are searchable by keyword, and many of the articles are available for free. An excellent choice for public libraries and two-year colleges with technical programs.

2099. I E E E Power & Energy Magazine. Formed by the merger of (1988-2003): *I E E E Computer Applications in Power;* (1981-2003): *I E E E Power Engineering Review.* [ISSN: 1540-7977] 2003. bi-m. USD 460; USD 550 combined subscription (print & online eds.). Ed(s): Melvin I Olken. Institute of Electrical and Electronics Engineers, 445 Hoes Ln, Piscataway, NJ 08854; contactcenter@ieee.org; http://www.ieee.org. *Indexed:* A22, C&ISA, CerAb, EngInd. *Bk. rev.:* 1, 1,000 words. *Aud.:* Ac, Sa.

This title is another of the highly relevant, highly useful *IEEE Magazines* series (as distinct from the often dense *IEEE Transactions*). It is designed for the "electric power professional." Each issue is based on a theme chosen by the editor, then illustrated with three or four articles. This journal is executed in the usual colorful, glossy style of the *IEEE Magazines,* and its articles are eight to ten pages in length but with minimal references (often simply URLs). The treatment is suitable for undergraduates and professionals outside the electric power field. The remainder of the issues includes letters, columns (the "Leader's Corner," the "Guest Editorial"), society and industry news, book reviews, new products, and an events calendar. The IEEEXplore site identifies the content type of each title on the contents page, an exceedingly welcome addition when the titles themselves are ambiguous. Well worth considering for many libraries, especially for those where the equivalent *IEEE Transactions* are either too expensive or too weighty.

2100. *I E E E Transactions on Energy Conversion.* Supersedes in part (in 1986): *I E E E Transactions on Power Apparatus and Systems;* Which was formed by the merger of (1952-1963): *Power Apparatus and Systems;* (1952-1963): *American Institute of Electrical Engineers. Transactions. Part 3. Power Apparatus and Systems;* Which superseded in part (in 1952): *American Institute of Electrical Engineers. Transactions.* [ISSN: 0885-8969] 1986. q. USD 990; USD 1190 combined subscription (print & online eds.). Ed(s): Scott D Sudhoff, Martin J Morahan. Institute of Electrical and Electronics Engineers, 445 Hoes Ln, Piscataway, NJ 08854; contactcenter@ieee.org; http:// www.ieee.org. Adv. Refereed. *Indexed:* A01, A22, B01, C&ISA, CerAb, EngInd, M&GPA. *Aud.:* Ac.

The thrust of this journal is efficient conversion of energy-producing mechanisms (usually motors in small or large scale) to electrical energy. Therefore, it contains a significant number of articles that cover wind, solar, and renewable energy production problems. As usual with *IEEE Transactions* publications, the papers are written for and by academics, but there are highly practical problems under discussion, such as "Full load efficiency estimation of refurbished induction machines from no-load testing." Large engineering collections will be pleasantly surprised to discover they have a good, economical source of material on niche energy topics. Commercial entities in solar or wind power will find this an inexpensive source of research material. It is also a good title for those electric-car enthusiasts found in engineering schools. This title should be considered in conjunction with the new *IEEE Transactions on Smart Grid* (also reviewed in this section) and the *IEEE Transactions on Power Delivery* (not reviewed in this section), as all three deal with generation and delivery of electricity.

2101. *I E E E Transactions on Smart Grid.* [ISSN: 1949-3053] 2010. q. USD 570; USD 685 combined subscription (print & online eds.). Ed(s): Mohammad Shahidehpour. Institute of Electrical and Electronics Engineers, 445 Hoes Ln, Piscataway, NJ 08854; contactcenter@ieee.org; http://www.ieee.org. Adv. *Aud.:* Ac, Sa.

A relatively new addition to the IEEE stable of energy titles, *Smart Grid* (begun in 2010) sounds like a journal for a small set of specialists. Certainly it could not be of interest to anyone outside of electrical engineering. In fact, though, the aim of the journal is to be cross-disciplinary, and it is cited by *Applied Energy, Energy Policy, Renewable Energy,* and even *Neural Computing Applications.* The reason for these cites is that *Smart Grid* models the power loads and distributions across the entire system, and those models can be used in other applications such as siting plug-ins for hybrid vehicles. As does *Energy Systems* (also reviewed in this section), this journal seeks the best ways to use the energy we now produce. In contrast with *Energy Systems,* economists are unlikely to submit articles to this highly technical publication, although, with an article title such as "Autonomous demand-side management based on game-theoretic energy consumption scheduling," they could. Libraries with strong energy and electrical/power engineering will be best served by this title; others may prefer *Energy Systems* for its wider scope.

2102. *I E E E Transactions on Sustainable Energy.* [ISSN: 1949-3029] 2010. 4x/yr. USD 755; USD 905 combined subscription (print & online eds.). Ed(s): Dr. Bikash C Pal. Institute of Electrical and Electronics Engineers, 445 Hoes Ln, Piscataway, NJ 08854; contactcenter@ieee.org; http://www.ieee.org. Adv. Refereed. *Aud.:* Ac.

Another new addition to the IEEE energy titles, *Sustainable Energy* concentrates on articles that demonstrate how to implement wind, photovoltaic, wave, and renewable energy forms and add them to the energy grid. The current emphasis is on wind, with many articles covering the integration of wind power with the more conventional systems. The treatment may be modeling, such as in "Game theoretic approaches for hybrid power system planning," or practical, such as a "Microcontroller-based power management system." The articles

themselves are highly mathematical, with the most exciting illustration often is just a bar graph. This will be a useful title for engineering collections, but libraries that seek broader coverage of renewable energy sources will prefer *Renewable Energy* or *Renewable and Sustainable Energy Reviews* (both reviewed in this section).

2103. *I E T Renewable Power Generation.* [ISSN: 1752-1416] 2007. bi-m. GBP 370. Ed(s): David Infield. The Institution of Engineering and Technology, Michael Faraday House, Six Hills Way, Stevenage, SG1 2AY, United Kingdom; journals@theiet.org; http://www.theiet.org/. Adv. Refereed. *Aud.:* Ac.

IET Renewable Power Generation, no longer a fledgling, has an Impact Factor that ranks it a respectable middle-of-the-pack title in energy and fuels. Specifically, this research journal discusses the practical generation of power from several renewable energy sources, from both the technical and the managerial sides of the system. The scope of the journal also includes solar, marine current, geothermal, biomass, wind, wave, photovoltaic, and fuel-cell power sources. Unlike many new titles that have overview articles with broad outlines, *IET Renewable Power Generation* got down to business from the start. This bodes well for future issues. Now a bimonthly, this journal has a reasonable price (but compare it to the IEEE publications also reviewed in this section), and its coverage of the energy outliers will be of value to institutions with active research in these fields.

2104. *Institution of Mechanical Engineers. Proceedings. Part A: Journal of Power and Energy.* Formerly (until 1990): *Institution of Mechanical Engineers. Proceedings. Part A: Journal of Power Engineering;* Which superseded in part (in 1988): *Institution of Mechanical Engineers. Proceedings. Part A: Power and Process Engineering;* Which superseded in part (in 1983): *Institution of Mechanical Engineers. Proceedings;* Which incorporated (1948-1970): *Institution of Mechanical Engineers. Automobile Division. Proceedings;* Which was formerly (until 1948): *Institution of Automobile Engineers, London. Proceedings;* (until 1906): *Incorporated Institution of Automobile Engineers. Proceedings.* [ISSN: 0957-6509] 1983. 8x/yr. USD 2968. Sage Publications Ltd., 1 Oliver's Yard, 55 City Rd, London, EC1Y 1SP, United Kingdom; info@sagepub.co.uk; http://www.uk.sagepub.com. Illus., index. Sample. Refereed. Vol. ends: No. 6. Microform: PMC; PQC. Reprint: PSC. *Indexed:* A01, A22, ApMecR, BrTechI, C&ISA, CerAb, E01, EngInd, MathR, OceAb. *Bk. rev.:* 3, 500 words. *Aud.:* Ac, Sa.

Normally, the journal of a professional society outside the United States would not be included in this section, especially when there are relevant titles available from U.S. equivalents (*IEEE Transactions on Energy Conversion* and *Journal of Solar Energy Engineering,* also reviewed in this section). However, this publication is well worth consideration for a broadly based energy collection. First, it covers a lot of territory: electric power, wind power, ocean wave energy, power production from coal, nuclear energy, gas, fuel cells, and solar energy. Its focus is the conversion of energy forms into electricity; much of the content concerns the design and upkeep of mechanical systems that do the actual conversion. Second, although the publisher is a British society, the journal has an international authorship made up of a combination of academic and industry researchers. Third, it has a relatively rapid turnaround time (often less than three months) from submission to publication. Fourth, the articles are readable (it is indexed in *Applied Science and Technology Abstracts*), well referenced, and well illustrated. A rarity in these times, there are even extensive book reviews. Its major shortcoming is that it is relatively expensive for a college library. Most university collections will already have it, as part of the complete IME *Proceedings,* and therefore at a cheaper rate. Now published by Sage for the Institution of Mechanical Engineers it enjoys all of the features of the Sage web site.

2105. *International Journal of Energy Research.* [ISSN: 0363-907X] 1977. 15x/yr. GBP 3679. Ed(s): I Dincer. John Wiley & Sons Ltd., The Atrium, Southern Gate, Chichester, PO19 8SQ, United Kingdom; customer@wiley.com; http://www.wiley.com. Adv. Sample. Refereed. Microform: PQC. Reprint: PSC. *Indexed:* A01, A22, ApMecR, BrTechI, C&ISA, CerAb, EngInd, OceAb. *Aud.:* Ac.

This is an exceedingly eclectic title. The "aims and scope" for this journal are to discuss energy issues with all types of researchers: engineers, scientists, developers, planners, and policy makers. However, the content is quite technical; an engineering degree will be quite helpful. Article subjects range from cost-efficient control strategies for a confectionery plant (management) to phase-change drywall systems (practical), to performance studies of combustion of gas cycle and rankine cycle engines (thermodynamics); these were all in one issue. Exergy (energy available for use), carbon emission, and sustainability are the current focus topics. Articles range from short to 20 or more pages. Not only are the authors international, but it is not unusual to find an article co-authored by a team from three or more institutions. Issues are composed of research articles, technical notes, and the occasional review. As it is, the price makes this a hard title to justify; once again, it has the dubious distinction of being the most expensive journal reviewed in this section, if not in the entire energy field, without the saving distinction of the high Impact Factor of other titles. For the comprehensive academic collection.

2106. *International Journal of Green Energy.* [ISSN: 1543-5075] 2004. q. GBP 1336 (print & online eds.). Ed(s): Xianguo Li. Taylor & Francis Inc., 325 Chestnut St, Ste 800, Philadelphia, PA 19106; customerservice@taylorandfrancis.com; http://www.tandfonline.com. Adv. Sample. Refereed. Reprint: PSC. *Indexed:* A22, C&ISA, C45, CerAb, E01, EngInd. *Aud.:* Ac.

This journal publishes research on "the forms and utilizations of energy that have no, minimal, or reduced impact on environment and society." To that end, a large percentage of the articles deal with wind, solar, biomass, and other alternative/renewable sources. Financial considerations play a part, illustrated by the wonderful merger of economics and technology in the article title "Carbon credits required to make manure biogas plants economic." That title is also indicative of the niche subjects that might make or break the journal. These are not mainstream research thrusts, but the journal has an Impact Factor that is higher than those for a number of coal, oil, and nuclear energy titles. Libraries with interests in sustainable development as well as energy should consider this one.

2107. *International Journal of Hydrogen Energy.* [ISSN: 0360-3199] 1976. 24x/yr. EUR 3886. Ed(s): E A Veziroglu. Elsevier Ltd, 32 Jamestown Rd, Camden, London, NW1 7BY, United Kingdom; corporate.sales@elsevier.com; http://www.elsevier.com. Illus., adv. Sample. Refereed. Microform: PMC; PQC. *Indexed:* A01, A22, C&ISA, EngInd. *Aud.:* Ac.

This may be the only journal (there are a few magazines) devoted to hydrogen as an energy source, and, as such, it covers both the technical aspects and the social aspects (economics, environment, and international impact). Each issues averages 40 papers, categorized as dealing with economy, electrolysis, solar, chemical/thermochemical, biology, storage, several types of fuel cells, and many others. There is also a goodly number of articles on hydrogen-powered vehicles. Recent articles include "Manganese oxide based thermochemical hydrogen production cycle" and "Review on solid oxide fuel cell models." Several issues each year include conference papers or are organized around a theme such as "Emerging Materials Technology: Materials in Clean Power System." This is a niche area in energy research, but a very active one, and this title has a high Impact Factor. A good title for a strong energy collection.

2108. *International Journal of Photoenergy.* [ISSN: 1110-662X] 1999. a. USD 695. Hindawi Publishing Corporation, 410 Park Ave, 15th Fl, PMB 287, New York, NY 10022; hindawi@hindawi.com; http:// www.hindawi.com. Refereed. *Indexed:* A01, C&ISA, C45, CerAb. *Aud.:* Ac.

This is a journal with an extremely narrow focus, but one that has caught the attention of many in the photovoltaic and/or solar energy field in its short publishing life. Aimed at the chemistry/chemical engineering researcher, articles cover fine details in photoreactivity, degradation, and, conversely, energizing of materials due to "photoenergy." This is precisely why some researchers in solar energy, fuel cells, and the like read and cite this journal. Resolving materials problems in these fields is critical to success, and much of this is uncharted territory. The web site has some nice features, such as RSS feeds, links to references through the publisher and through Google Scholar, and even a "how to cite" format. There are no volumes or issues; articles are

published online as soon as they pass review, which is generally within two months. It is possible to search all articles (and determine which were published in a given year) when a specific reference is needed. This is an Open Access publication (a print version is available via subscription), but the treatment is so specialized that only libraries with strong solar/photovoltaic collections will find it useful.

2109. *Journal of Energy Engineering.* Former titles (until 1983): *American Society of Civil Engineers. Energy Division. Journal;* (until 1979): *American Society of Civil Engineers. Power Division. Journal;* Which superseded in part (in 1956): *American Society of Civil Engineers. Proceedings.* [ISSN: 0733-9402] 1873. q. USD 388. Ed(s): Hilary I Inyang. American Society of Civil Engineers, 1801 Alexander Bell Dr, Reston, VA 20191; http://www.asce.org. Illus., adv. Refereed. Microform: PQC. *Indexed:* A01, A22, BRI, C&ISA, CerAb, EngInd, M&GPA. *Aud.:* Ac, Sa.

This journal is part of the American Society of Civil Engineers collection of engineering journals and has been focused on energy since 1983. The primary interest is "planning, development, management, and finances of energy-related programs"; this translates to construction of power plants, energy efficiency of buildings, selecting/implementing the optimal power source for a project, and regulatory/environmental issues. Articles usually address the part, rather than the whole, such as "Virtual wind speed sensor for wind turbines," where the sensor is the object of inquiry. Because of the AIP decision to reduce the Scitation system to AIP publications, this journal is now served from the ASCE Library, whose underlying software was designed by Atypon (which also works with many other sci/tech publishers). One of the features of the new design is tabs; there is a tab for "most cited" and another for "most viewed," and none of the titles on the one list is in the other. This is probably true for many journals, but it's a good reminder that citation counts are just one of many decision criteria. Compare this title to *Energy and Buildings* for coverage and relevancy to local collections.

2110. *Journal of Power Sources.* [ISSN: 0378-7753] 1976. 24x/yr. EUR 6338. Ed(s): Z Ogumi, C K Dyer. Elsevier S.A., PO Box 564, Lausanne, 1001, Switzerland. Refereed. Microform: PQC. *Indexed:* A01, A22, C&ISA, CerAb, EngInd. *Aud.:* Ac.

Think photovoltaics: the power sources here are fuel cells and batteries for portable power supplies, electric vehicles, satellites, and the like. This journal discusses the conversion of energy from solar, wind, and other sources into storage devices such as fuel cells. Much of the work involves materials properties, electrochemical reactions, and the application of photovoltaics to practical devices. Issues are lengthy, often running to 500 pages, and the publication lag is quite short, sometimes under two months between submission and online publication. The contents are arranged in subject sections, then divided by topic (fuel cells, batteries, review, etc.). This is convenient for the reader, but the pagination is then out of order—with, say, the article on pages 1–4 in the section on fuel cells, after the article on pages 63–73 in the reviews section. Conference proceedings as such have not appeared in the last two years; these are all original articles. This is a high Impact Factor journal, but quite expensive (although not on a cost-per-page basis); libraries with strong engineering collections as well as renewable-energy interests should consider it. However, it should be compared with *Progress in Photovoltaics* (also reviewed in this section).

2111. *Journal of Renewable and Sustainable Energy.* [ISSN: 1941-7012] 2009. bi-m. Ed(s): John A Turner, P Craig Taylor. American Institute of Physics, 1 Physics Ellipse, College Park, MD 20740; aipinfo@aip.org; http://www.aip.org. Adv. Sample. Refereed. *Indexed:* A01, S25. *Aud.:* Ac, Sa.

A number of new energy-related journals and magazines have appeared recently that feature "sustainable" in their titles. Some of them have only been in existence for less than a year, so it is difficult to evaluate them for library collections. The *Journal of Renewable and Sustainable Energy* appears to be the best of the lot in terms of quality and variety of content, range of topics, and its own sustainability. As part of the American Institute of Physics (AIP) journals collection, it is likely to continue long after "sustainable" ceases to be the fashion. Other titles of interest, though, include the *IEEE Transactions on Sustainable Energy* and *Renewable and Sustainable Energy Review* (both reviewed in this section). The new AIP journal contains peer-reviewed articles, which average 15–20 pages, on topics such as solar space heating in a passive house; blended biodiesel fuel; economical inverters for grid-tied generators; and treatment of wastewater by solar power to alleviate water scarcity. Authors are largely from academia; the lag from submission to publication is usually less than six months. The online version of the journal includes a blog, podcasts, a newsletter, interviews, and energy-related news clips, thus separating the research material from the topical. This will be a welcome addition to academic libraries with interests in renewable energy forms, sustainable development, and systems engineering.

2112. *Journal of Solar Energy Engineering.* [ISSN: 0199-6231] 1980. q. Feb., May., Aug., & Nov. USD 388 combined subscription domestic (print & online eds.); USD 425 combined subscription foreign (print & online eds.); USD 116 per issue. Ed(s): Gilles Flamant. A S M E International, Two Park Ave, New York, NY 10016; CustomerCare@asme.org; http://www.asme.org. Illus., index. Sample. Refereed. Vol. ends: Nov. Microform: PQC. *Indexed:* A01, A22, ApMecR, BRI, C&ISA, CEA, CerAb, EngInd. *Aud.:* Ac, Sa.

This is an engineering research journal, with short articles (around six pages) on applied research into solar energy production, materials used in solar energy, and applications of solar energy to other engineering problems. Most readers are familiar with the use of solar power to dry fruits and heat water, but many will be surprised to learn that it can also be used in aluminum smelting and fullerene synthesis. The journal should really be titled "Solar and Wind Energy"; every issue has an article or two on wind power. Recent articles range from "Simulation of thunderstorm downbursts and associated wind turbine loads" to "Parametric study of a flat plate wick[–]assisted heat pipe solar collector." This is a good value for the research dollar, and it will be useful at industrial as well as academic sites.

2113. *Nuclear Engineering International.* Formerly (until 1968): *Nuclear Engineering;* Which incorporated (1956-1968): *Nuclear Power.* [ISSN: 0029-5507] 1956. m. GBP 299 domestic; EUR 510 in Europe; USD 557 elsewhere. Ed(s): Will Dalrymple. Wilmington Media & Entertainment, Progressive House, 2 Maidstone Rd, Foots Cray, Sidcup, DA14 5HZ, United Kingdom; investorinfo@wilmington.co.uk; http://www.wilmington.co.uk/. Illus., index, adv. Refereed. Microform: PQC. *Indexed:* A22, ABIn, ApMecR, B02, B03, BRI, BrTechI, C&ISA, CerAb, EngInd, H24, RiskAb. *Aud.:* Ac, Sa.

There are many research journals devoted to nuclear energy, but few devoted to the nuclear industry. A number of "power plant" titles include nuclear (as well as coal, oil, etc.) as fuel sources. *Nuclear Engineering International* is perhaps the earliest magazine in the field; certainly it is among the longest running. Although produced by a British trade press, it is, perforce, international in coverage and orientation. The web site includes the standard features: news, buyers guide, upcoming events, trade shows, and links. It also features videos, including freely available videos of the Fukushima Daiichi plant post-tsunami. For years, the magazine has published "wallcharts" of nuclear plants; many of these, covering all types of reactors, are available for sale as pdfs or prints, providing useful illustrations for nuclear engineering courses. Thanks go, however, to the University of New Mexico's Digital Collections for making low-resolution, color versions available for free (see http://econtent.unm.edu/cdm/search/collection/nuceng). Feature articles are short (two or three pages) with a mix of technical updates, economic trends, and safety issues: in short, anything that affects a nuclear power plant. The subscription price is about three times that of the average specialty trade magazine, precluding most public and academic library purchases, but the web site has many free features and it is indexed in the standard abstract services.

2114. *Nuclear Technology.* Former titles (until 1971): *Nuclear Applications and Technology;* (until 1969): *Nuclear Applications.* [ISSN: 0029-5450] 1965. m. USD 1870 (print & online eds.). Ed(s): Nicholas Tsoulfanidis. American Nuclear Society, Inc., 555 N Kensington Ave, La Grange Park, IL 60526; members@ans.org; http://www.ans.org. Illus., index. Refereed. Vol. ends: No. 3. *Indexed:* A&ATA, A22, C&ISA, CerAb, EngInd, H24. *Bk. rev.:* Occasional. *Aud.:* Ac, Sa.

One of several publications from the American Nuclear Society (ANS), *Nuclear Technology* publishes papers on applications of research to the nuclear field, as opposed to theoretical work; the scope includes medical use as well as a power source. Each issue is subdivided into sections, such as nuclear reactor safety, fission reactors, radioactive waste management, and others as appropriate. The layout is crisp and has such features as keyword descriptors at the head of each paper, which help the reader target relevant papers. The authorship is international, often from industry, and the publication lag averages about one year. Brief author biographies are included after the bibliographies. Papers average 10–15 pages; there are per-page charges to defray the society's expenses. Occasionally, technical notes (one- or two-page items) and papers from conferences are included. Book reviews are encouraged but rarely appear. Libraries with active physics researchers will probably have all of the ANS publications; others may prefer the specialized titles.

2115. *Oil & Gas Journal.* Formerly (until 1910): *Oil Investors' Journal.* [ISSN: 0030-1388] 1902. w. Free to qualified personnel; USD 109 combined subscription domestic (print & online eds.). Ed(s): Bob Tippee. PennWell Corporation, 1455 West Loop South, Houston, TX 77027; patrickM@pennwell.com; http://www.pennwell.com. Illus., index, adv. Circ: 101695 Paid. Vol. ends: No. 52. *Indexed:* A22, ABIn, B02, B03, BRI, C&ISA, CEA, EngInd, H24, OceAb, P02, RiskAb. *Aud.:* Ga, Ac, Sa.

Decade after decade, this has been a reliable source for topical industry news, special features, and lots of data. Articles comprise a large portion of the contents, either short reviews (one to three pages) by staff writers or somewhat longer, referenced papers by industry specialists. Each issue follows the section format of focus articles, general interest news, exploration and development, drilling and production, and processing and transportation, with columns on equipment and statistics. There are a number of annually repeating issues, such as forecast and review or worldwide refining. The best section for librarians is the multi-page statistics analysis at the end of each paper issue. American Petroleum Institute data and prices (crude and refined, U.S. and world regions) are reported weekly, but other analyses pop up from time to time, such as country-by-country current/previous-year production comparison figures. For many years it was included in the *Web of Science* (formerly *Science Citation Index*) because its content was primary for the industry. The web site no longer offers free samples; all material requires a user login. There are several subscription packages: basic print includes access to 12 months of earlier material; an upgraded print version is twice the cost but includes full access to the archives; and the digital version is cheaper but uses a cumbersome ID/password system. The print version is found in aggregator databases, but the online version is superior, with daily updates.

2116. *Power Engineering.* Former titles (until 1950): *Power Generation;* (until 1947): *Power Plant Engineering;* Which was formed by the merger of (1896-1917): *Practical Engineer; Power Plant.* [ISSN: 0032-5961] 1896. m. USD 95 domestic (Free to qualified personnel). Ed(s): David Wagman. PennWell Corporation, PO Box 3271, Northbrook, IL 60065; Headquarters@PennWell.com; http://www.pennwell.com. Illus., index, adv. Circ: 64000. Vol. ends: Dec. *Indexed:* A01, A22, ABIn, ApMecR, B01, B02, BRI, C&ISA, CerAb, EngInd. *Aud.:* Ga, Ac, Sa.

One of those trade magazines that have been around forever, partly because it knows how to change with the times, *Power Engineering* is concerned with the electric power–producing industry with a concentration on solid fuels, and with a section featuring "renewables." Although it does not ignore the "big picture," its focus is on running the power plant. In addition to short articles, it is chock-full of ads, industry briefs, and regular columns on the environment, business, and field notes (which plant is doing what about which). The articles are often by staff writers, but can also be tips from experts in the industry. Although they usually do not include references, the articles are well illustrated with color photographs, charts, tables, and line drawings. The buyers' guide is continuously updated and freely available on the web. Other features include the "Project of the Year," the big industry conference, Power-Gen, webcasts, podcasts, and white papers. Access to the archives search and articles is free, but features such as the "white papers" require a subscription. The web site is actually a combination of three PennWell titles: *Power Engineering, Power Engineering International,* and *Cogeneration & On-Site Power Production,* which sometimes makes it difficult to determine what is the actual source of the information. Aside from the scope, the major difference between this magazine and *Power* (also reviewed in this section) is the latter's special reports.

2117. *Power (Houston).* Incorporates (1977-2007): *International Power Generation;* (1976-2007): *Middle East Electricity;* (1981-2007): *European Power News;* Which was formerly (1976-1981): *Power Generation Industrial.* [ISSN: 0032-5929] 1882. m. Free. Ed(s): Robert Peltier, Gail Reitenbach. The TradeFair Group, Inc., 11000 Richmond, Ste 500, Houston, TX 77042; info@tradefairgroup.com; http://www.tradefairgroup.com/. Illus., index, adv. Vol. ends: No. 9. Microform: PQC. *Indexed:* A01, A22, ABIn, ApMecR, B01, B02, B03, BRI, C&ISA, CerAb, EngInd. *Aud.:* Ga, Ac, Sa.

After more than a century of publication, McGraw-Hill sold *Power* to the TradeFair Group (Houston, Texas) in 2006. In some areas, there have been some big changes, but much of the familiar format remains. The big changes are in the web layout; there are tabbed topic areas (coal, gas, smart grid, etc.) where the stories are listed in reverse chronological order. Alternatively, there are still dated issues that have the feature articles and various departments (global monitor, operations and management, new products, and more). Every other issue seems to have a "special report" on something, and there are annual features, such as the "Plant of the Year Award" and the "Top Plants" survey. The concentration is on "traditional" power plants, which run on fossil fuels or nuclear power, but renewable energy sources are also included. Although technical, the articles are written with management in mind, which makes them approachable for the undergraduate or lay reader. They are also often illustrated with statistics difficult to find elsewhere. Few articles have references; the author's credentials and e-mail contact are the "cited sources." There are columns on fuels, labor, the environment, and the latest technologies and management practices. Obviously a rival to *Power Engineering* (also in this section), *Power* seems to have the edge on in-depth special issues, but these are not available at the web site except to registered subscribers.

2118. *Progress in Energy and Combustion Science: an international review journal.* [ISSN: 0360-1285] 1975. bi-m. EUR 2335. Ed(s): Norman A Chigier. Pergamon, The Blvd, Langford Ln, E Park, Kidlington, OX5 1GB, United Kingdom; JournalsCustomerServiceEMEA@elsevier.com; http://www.elsevier.com. Illus., index, adv. Sample. Refereed. Microform: PQC. *Indexed:* A01, A22, ApMecR, C&ISA, C45, CEA, EngInd. *Aud.:* Ac.

This is a review journal that publishes papers on efficient combustion of fuels (fossil and biomass), with the aim of conserving resources and protecting the environment. Although much of the "conserving" is for power-plant energy production, a fair percentage of coverage is devoted to jets and internal combustion engines. Articles are not for the fainthearted; the editors solicit papers from experts in the field, and they do a thorough job. Many articles are lengthy, and it is not unusual for an issue to have only three or four papers, each of 40 pages or more. This journal is heavily illustrated with tables and charts, and many of these include color for emphasis and easy reading, a virtue of electronic publishing. Thus, this title is consumed by the academic market, but some papers are deliberately designed for the practicing engineer or manager. This is an expensive publication, but with a very high Impact Factor (number one in energy and fuels for the last six years), and well worth considering for the complete research collection.

2119. *Progress in Photovoltaics: research and applications.* [ISSN: 1062-7995] 1993. 8x/yr. GBP 1228. Ed(s): Martin A Green, Tim M Bruton. John Wiley & Sons Ltd., The Atrium, Southern Gate, Chichester, PO19 8SQ, United Kingdom; customer@wiley.com; http://www.wiley.com. Adv. Sample. Refereed. Microform: PQC. Reprint: PSC. *Indexed:* C&ISA, CerAb, EngInd. *Aud.:* Ac.

For "photovoltaics" in the title, the reader should substitute the term "solar cells." Issues are arranged by "accelerated," research, applications, and "broader perspective" articles. "Accelerated" is reserved for papers that show significant improvements in technique or reliability, innovations, and/or new theories. There is a deliberate mix of academics, practitioners, and policy makers on the review board to provide the same mix in the journal. Issues are divided into research, broad perspectives, and applications. Although the editors state that part of the intended readership is policy makers, generally the articles

are highly technical and narrowly focused. About once a year there will be a theme issue on such topics as "Cu-Chalcogenide Solar Cells." The photovoltaics literature survey section, culled from other research journals in the field, is very current and appears in each issue. This is a good title for universities with strong interests in energy and electrical engineering.

2120. *Public Utilities Fortnightly: energy, money, power.* Incorporates (2000-2003): *Fortnightly's Energy Customer Management;* Former titles (until 1994): *Public Utilities Reports. Fortnightly;* (until 1993): *Public Utilities Fortnightly;* (until 1929): *Public Utilities Reports Fortnightly.* [ISSN: 1078-5892] 1928. m. USD 169 domestic; USD 199 foreign. Ed(s): Michael T Burr, Lori A Burkhart. Public Utilities Reports, Inc., 8229 Boone Blvd, Ste 400, Vienna, VA 22182; pur_info@pur.com; http://www.pur.com. Adv. Circ: 6500 Paid. Microform: PQC. *Indexed:* A22, ABIn, B02, B03, BRI, CLI, L14. *Aud.:* Ga, Sa.

This classic title hasn't been "fortnightly" since 2003; it is now a monthly, at least for the print version. Gone are the flimsy newsprint pages (pink, if memory serves), replaced by glossy paper, full-color layouts, and eye-catching advertisements. Issues have three or four articles and several columns. The articles average four pages, often with nicely formatted data, and, unless they are opinion pieces, they include numerous references. This is a magazine for the investor, addressing new plant technology, regulatory issues, international economics, and supply/distribution problems for electricity, natural gas, nuclear power, and other large-scale energy suppliers. The brevity of the articles, coupled with the overview approach, makes this a useful source for undergraduates as well. The web site has tables of contents for issues back to 1995; the entire set is searchable, but full text is restricted to subscribers.

2121. *Renewable & Sustainable Energy Reviews.* [ISSN: 1364-0321] 1997. m. EUR 1871. Ed(s): Dr. Lawrence L Kazmerski. Pergamon, The Blvd, Langford Ln, E Park, Kidlington, OX5 1GB, United Kingdom; JournalsCustomerServiceEMEA@elsevier.com; http://www.elsevier.com. Adv. Sample. Refereed. *Indexed:* A01, EngInd. *Aud.:* Ac.

This publication is a mix of engineering, economics, and policy journal, which, as the title suggests, features review articles. However, the length of the reviews varies considerably: some are over 30 pages, and others are as short as seven. The average is now around ten pages; two years ago it was 30. Publication is speedy, often only two months between submission and online publication. Authors are either faculty at universities or researchers for government-supported organizations. The energy sources covered are biomass, geothermics, hydrogen, hydroelectric, ocean/tide, solar, and wind. Illustrations are often tables and graphs, which serve as an excellent data source. Libraries should compare this title with its sister publication *Renewable Energy* as well as with *Renewable Energy World* and *Journal of Renewable and Sustainable Energy* (all reviewed in this section) to determine which title(s) may be most useful for their collections.

2122. *Renewable Energy: an international journal.* Formerly (until 1991): *Solar and Wind Technology.* [ISSN: 0960-1481] 1984. m. EUR 3103. Ed(s): A A M Sayigh, L Sayigh. Pergamon, The Blvd, Langford Ln, E Park, Kidlington, OX5 1GB, United Kingdom; JournalsCustomerServiceEMEA@elsevier.com; http://www.elsevier.com. Illus., adv. Sample. Refereed. Microform: PQC. *Indexed:* A01, A22, C&ISA, C45, EngInd, RRTA, S25. *Bk. rev.:* 1, 1,000 words. *Aud.:* Ac.

At the other end of the spectrum from such magazines as *Home Power* and *Windpower Monthly* (also reviewed in this section), in both type of content and price, *Renewable Energy* is a scholarly publication. Originally emphasizing solar and wind energy (and still heavily cited in the major solar energy titles), it now includes ocean wave and geothermal material. The intended audience includes manufacturers as well as academics and policy groups. A small percentage of the articles is nontechnical, covering social, political, and economic aspects of renewable energy development; but most articles are technical in nature, and the focus is on implementation rather than theory. The authorship is international, with a high rate of Third World contributors, reflecting the sites that emphasize development and use of low-cost (economically and environmentally) power sources.

2123. Renewable Energy World. Incorporates (1996-1998): *Sustainable Energy Industry Journal.* [ISSN: 1462-6381] 1996. bi-m. USD 133 in Europe (Free to qualified personnel). Ed(s): David Appleyar. PennWell Corporation, 1421 S Sheridan Rd, Tulsa, OK 74112; Headquarters@PennWell.com; http://www.pennwell.com. Illus., adv. Sample. Circ: 15000 Controlled. *Aud.:* Ac, Sa.

A colorful trade publication with a well-designed web presence, this magazine covers all of the "renewable" energy sources, but emphasizes solar and wind. The coverage is international, both in terms of articles and of suppliers: it's easy to find wind power companies in, say, Colombia. This journal is designed for the practitioner rather than the scholar, and issues are crammed with current news, include ten or so articles, and contain the usual conference/trade show announcements, letters, editorials, and the like. The web site includes links to suppliers, related material, archives of selected articles from back numbers, and a few videos. The articles themselves often have the kinds of tables, charts, and engineering data that are hard to acquire elsewhere. Articles (and the archives) are free to all, but some features require a subscription. Of interest to those in the related industries, it is free to industry professionals.

2124. Resource and Energy Economics. Formerly (until 1993): *Resources and Energy.* [ISSN: 0928-7655] 1978. 4x/yr. EUR 924. Ed(s): S Smulders, J F Shogren. Elsevier BV, North-Holland, Postbus 211, Amsterdam, 1000 AE, Netherlands; JournalsCustomerServiceEMEA@elsevier.com; http://www.elsevier.com. Illus., index, adv. Sample. Refereed. Microform: PQC. *Indexed:* A22, ABIn, B01, C45, EconLit, EngInd, JEL, M&GPA. *Aud.:* Ac.

This journal should be compared with its sister publication *Energy Economics* (also reviewed in this section). *Resources and Energy Economics* emphasizes use of resources, of which energy is just one. The papers are scholarly and lengthy (often more than 20 pages). Recent topics include renewable energy subsidies and the effect of biofuel policies on the feedstock market. Publication delay has increased again, now averaging over one year. Libraries whose interest is primarily in energy will prefer *Energy Economics,* while those with strong economics and/or business collections should consider both journals.

2125. Solar Energy. Formerly (until Jan.1958): *The Journal of Solar Energy, Science and Engineering.* [ISSN: 0038-092X] 1957. 12x/yr. EUR 3506. Ed(s): D Yogi Goswami. Elsevier Ltd, The Boulevard, Langford Lane, Oxford, OX5 1GB, United Kingdom; http://www.elsevier.com. Illus., index, adv. Sample. Refereed. Vol. ends: No. 6. Microform: MIM; PQC. *Indexed:* A01, A22, API, Agr, ApMecR, BRI, C&ISA, EngInd, M&GPA, P02. *Bk. rev.:* 1, 500 words. *Aud.:* Ac.

Solar Energy was once the premier journal in solar research, encompassing biomass and wind energy, as well as the engineering and physical aspects of solar energy. In early 2009, the editors revised the journal's scope to limit the publication of articles on solar radiation and solar resource assessment to novel and universally applicable techniques, resulting in articles' reflecting advances in modeling techniques that render inadequate the "data analysis" approach of earlier years. This title is strictly a scholarly publication, and most of its authors are academics from all of the engineering disciplines, with a few applied physicists included for good measure. Illustrations are limited to charts, tables, and line drawings, although an occasional candid photograph of field work appears; many of these are enhanced with adept use of color. Every few months, there is a topical issue (such as "Organic photovoltaics and dye[-]sensitized solar cells") and the occasional "brief note," a brief methodology description. Publication lag time can be over a year, but most of the lag seems to be in the review process; once accepted, an article is promptly published. Institutions with emphasis on materials and electronics might prefer its sister publication, *Solar Energy Materials & Solar Cells* (also reviewed in this section).

2126. Solar Energy Materials & Solar Cells. Formerly (until 1992): *Solar Energy Materials;* Incorporates (1979-1991): *Solar Cells.* [ISSN: 0927-0248] 1979. 12x/yr. EUR 3506. Ed(s): C M Lampert. Elsevier BV, North-Holland, Postbus 211, Amsterdam, 1000 AE, Netherlands; JournalsCustomerServiceEMEA@elsevier.com; http://www.elsevier.com. Illus., index. Sample. Refereed. Vol. ends: No. 4. Microform: PQC. *Indexed:* A01, A22, C&ISA, CerAb, EngInd. *Bk. rev.:* 1, 500 words, signed. *Aud.:* Ac.

Aptly named, this journal publishes highly technical papers on the materials used in solar energy production and products. Aside from solar cells, it includes light control (smart windows), optical and photochemical properties of materials, and photothermal devices (used in energy storage). Unlike *Progress in Photovoltaics* (also reviewed in this section), this is an applications-centered publication. Recent articles discuss the problem of damp-heat in the breakdown of solar cells; materials for high temperature energy storage; and carbon nanotubes for three-dimensional photovoltaic cells. Publication can be swift (within two months of submission) or as long as a year's lag. This is one of the top ten most-cited journals in energy, but it is best for scholarly collections that encompass materials chemistry as well as energy.

2127. Solar Today: leading the renewable energy revolution. Formerly: *A S E S News.* [ISSN: 1042-0630] 1987. 9x/yr. Free to members. Ed(s): Corey Dahl, Regina Johnson. American Solar Energy Society, Inc., 4760 Walnut St, Ste 106, Boulder, CO 80301; ases@ases.org; http://www.ases.org. Illus., index, adv. Circ: 18424 Paid. Vol. ends: Nov/Dec. *Indexed:* A22. *Aud.:* Ga, Sa.

This is the members' magazine for the American Solar Energy Society, the "local" for the international, which publishes *Solar Energy.* The latter is for researchers; *Solar Today* is for everybody. As is true of many magazines in the solar field, wind power is included as an also-ran. Many of the articles describe success stories on a small scale, such as "Passive Solar House." Others take the larger view, covering potential world markets for wind energy or green power. Although the topics may be technical, the treatment usually is not. The letters section is extensive, there are lots of ads (for both the contractor and the homeowner), and society news and conference programs complete the issue. The web site includes links to conferences and events, educational and informational sites, government agencies, utilities, businesses (by specialty), and society business and information on the annual National Solar Tour (formerly the National Tour of Solar Buildings). There is also a "digital version" of the print magazine with the same content but a glossy display. To top it off, video interviews are now featured. This is an inexpensive title suitable for public libraries, but academic institutions will be better served by *Solar Energy* or *Solar Energy Materials & Solar Cells.*

2128. Wind Energy. [ISSN: 1095-4244] 1998. 8x/m. GBP 537. Ed(s): Scott Schreck, Rebecca Barthelmie. John Wiley & Sons Ltd., The Atrium, Southern Gate, Chichester, PO19 8SQ, United Kingdom; customer@wiley.com; http://www.wiley.com. Adv. Sample. Refereed. Reprint: PSC. *Indexed:* EngInd. *Aud.:* Ac.

For many years, there were only two scholarly journals covering wind sources of energy, the *Journal of Wind Engineering & Industrial Aerodynamics* and *Wind Engineering* (also reviewed in this section). *Wind Energy* was launched in 1998, evidently in direct competition with *Wind Engineering.* They both cover the technical aspects of generating power from wind sources; they both have an international scope, include papers authored largely by academic institutions and government-funded agencies, have lengthy articles and references, and include the occasional historical or economic review. The chief differences between the two journals are price (*Wind Energy* costs twice as much as *Wind Engineering*) and inclusion in ISI's *Web of Science* (*Wind Engineering* is not). However, *Wind Energy* cites *Wind Engineering* and vice versa. Libraries with large collections may want both, but the less expensive title seems the best bet.

2129. Wind Engineering. [ISSN: 0309-524X] 1977. bi-m. GBP 405; GBP 424 combined subscription (print & online eds.). Ed(s): Jon McGowan. Multi-Science Publishing Co. Ltd., 5 Wates Way, Brentwood, CM15 9TB, United Kingdom; info@multi-science.co.uk; http://www.multi-science.co.uk. Sample. Refereed. *Indexed:* A22, ApMecR, C&ISA, CerAb, EngInd. *Aud.:* Ac.

Wind Engineering claims to be the oldest English-language journal devoted entirely to the technical issues of wind power, which is largely true, although the *Journal of Wind Engineering & Industrial Aerodynamics* has been in existence longer, beginning as the *Journal of Industrial Aerodynamics.* Topics covered are wind turbines, turbine blade design, and economic and historical aspects of wind energy, and there is a good deal of emphasis on wind farms and offshore wind energy production. It is very similar in coverage and quality to *Wind*

Energy (also reviewed in this section), and libraries with restricted budgets or tangential interest in wind power will want to carefully compare the two, especially as *Wind Engineering* offers a discount for libraries whose faculty publish in the journal.

2130. *Windpower Monthly.* [ISSN: 0109-7318] 1985. m. USD 250; USD 436 inc. on-line ed.; USD 550 inc. subc. to Windstats Newsletter. Ed(s): Ben Walker. Haymarket Publishing Ltd., 174 Hammersmith Rd, London, W6 7JP, United Kingdom; info@haymarket.com; http://www.haymarket.com. Illus., adv. Sample. Circ: 5000. Vol. ends: No. 12. *Aud.:* Ac, Sa.

Begun in Denmark, distributed from the United States, and with a web site originating in the United Kingdom, *Windpower Monthly* is truly an international publication. The audience is wind energy businesses, investors, and power plant component manufacturers. Although each issue will have a small number of articles (one of which is the "Focus Article"), the bulk of the magazine is devoted to wind energy news reports, arranged by regions/countries of the world. Some of the news is technical ("Blades Built by Robots"), but most of it is economic or policy news. The "Windicator," a quarterly supplement, is a chart of wind power capacity worldwide, identifying industrial, political, technical, and economic trends. A new feature is "Windpower TV," which comprises video reports and interviews. The magazine also publishes the *Windstats* newsletter, available at an extra cost. One of the few magazines for the wind energy "trade," it is useful only for large collections.

2131. *World Oil.* Former titles (until 1947): *The Oil Weekly;* (until 1918): *Gulf Coast Oil News.* [ISSN: 0043-8790] 1916. m. USD 149 domestic. Ed(s): Michael David. Gulf Publishing Co., PO Box 2608, Houston, TX 77252; publications@gulfpub.com; http://www.gulfpub.com. Illus., adv. Circ: 35393. Microform: PQC. *Indexed:* A22, ABIn, B01, B02, B03, BRI, C&ISA, EngInd. *Aud.:* Ac, Sa.

One of the many petroleum-related trade magazines (see the *Oil & Gas Journal* in this section), this one covers oil around the world. Each issue follows the pattern of focus articles, feature articles, columns (such as "What's New in Production" and "International Politics"), news, and departments. Focus and feature articles are short (two or three pages), but they are well illustrated in color. The web site includes supplements (such as "Deepwater Technology") and case studies, plus extensive statistics (both production and price), reference tables, forecasts, and analyses, most requiring registration and some requiring a paid subscription. The data alone are worth the price of subscription. An excellent, inexpensive addition to a good energy collection.

■ ENGINEERING AND TECHNOLOGY

General/Biomedical Engineering/Chemical Engineering/Civil and Environmental Engineering/Computer, Control, and Systems Engineering/Electrical Engineering/Industrial and Manufacturing Engineering/Materials Engineering/Mechanical Engineering/Nuclear Engineering

See also Aeronautics and Space Science; Atmospheric Sciences; Biology; Chemistry; Computers and Information Technology; Earth Sciences; Mathematics; Physics; Robotics; and Science and Technology sections.

Theresa Calcagno, IT & Engineering Librarian, George Mason University, Fairfax, VA 22030

Introduction

The subdisciplines of engineering do not exist in a vacuum. As the pace of scientific discovery and technological innovation have increased in the past century, engineering has become increasingly interdisciplinary and dependent on other scientific and engineering fields. In the past century, the number of engineering subdisciplines has increased, and some disciplines that were in their infancy in the early twentieth century, e.g., electrical engineering, have matured, grown, and diversified beyond their original scope. Some subdisciplines, such as biomedical, nuclear, and environmental engineering, did not even exist in 1900. They have grown rapidly in the last 50 years as the needs of an increasingly connected global society demanded solutions to medical problems, to the need for more electric power–generation capacity, or to the prevention or remediation of major (and not-so-major) environmental disasters.

The engineering research literature does not exist in a vacuum either. As engineering has grown and evolved, so has the engineering literature. The scopes of engineering journal offerings in 2013 reflect the increasing interdependence on other disciplines. This is very evident in journals related to computing and numerical methods. Biomedical engineering journals combine mechanical or electrical engineering with biology, chemistry, physics, and materials research. Environmental engineering journals may publish research that is steeped in water resources, chemistry, and biology. Thus, it is imperative that researchers are aware of scholarly resources in research fields other than their own disciplines. The following list includes cross-references to help selectors identify publications that are not "engineering" but are important to engineers nevertheless.

Changes in the publishing world, i.e., mergers and acquisitions, have resulted in fewer publishers of engineering research papers. The major providers of research information to engineers include professional engineering societies, e.g., IEEE, ACM, ASCE, and ICE, and commercial publishers like Elsevier and Springer. Small professional societies are also a source of research information and may publish their own journals, or outsource them to a commercial publisher.

Another change in scholarly publishing in recent years is the evolution of "open access" publishing. Its increasing importance is reflected in the number of journals that are technically "hybrid" journals because they offer authors either open access or traditional publication (both including peer review) for publishing their research. The fact that high-impact journals from major publishers, including society publishers, are offering the open-access option underscores the importance of the open-access movement.

The journals in the following list reflect the changing face of engineering and engineering literature. For the vast majority, the online version was reviewed. Electronic journals are easier for a user to search, making a researcher's work more easily found. In addition, they allow both publishers and authors to include additional content that cannot be provided in print. This includes user access to special groupings of papers (e.g., most cited, related, or open-access), topical podcasts, embedded video, datasets or other supplemental materials, article metrics, linking of references, etc.

"Altmetrics," metrics tracking a researcher's impact by tracking online mentions of his/her research, is becoming more important, and is now included in several of the journals on the list. Altmetrics capture the impact of research *outside* the research community by tracking blogs, bookmarks, Twitter feeds, links to a researcher's information, etc. This is a relatively new metric, but it will become more important and accurate as the tracking services evolve in the near future.

This year's list also includes trade publications, e.g., *ENR* and *Advanced Materials and Processes,* and membership publications, e.g., *ASEE Prism* and *Nuclear News.* These magazines, while not peer-reviewed research publications, are a very important source of industry news, statistics, and applications of research. They frequently contain overview articles that discuss new research or developments in the field. In addition, they usually have eye-catching editorial layouts, color photographs, and engaging graphics.

What does the future hold for engineering research and its literature? Both will become more and more interdisciplinary, blurring the lines between engineering and hard science, as well as between different engineering subdisciplines. Research will be presented online and value will be added by the inclusion of additional research- and subject-related content, interactive media, and additional metrics to track its impact.

Basic Periodicals

BIOMEDICAL ENGINEERING. Ac, Sa: *Biotechnology and Bioengineering.*

CHEMICAL ENGINEERING. Ga, Ac, Sa: *A I Ch E Journal.*

CIVIL ENGINEERING. Ac, Sa: *Civil Engineering* (Reston), *E N R.*

COMPUTER, CONTROL, AND SYSTEMS ENGINEERING. Ac, Sa: *Association for Computing Machinery. Journal.*

ELECTRICAL ENGINEERING. Ac, Sa: *IEEE Journals, Proceedings, and Transactions.*

MANUFACTURING ENGINEERING. Ac, Sa: *Journal of Manufacturing Systems.*

MATERIALS ENGINEERING. Ac, Sa: *Journal of Materials Research, Metallurgical and Materials Transactions A.*

MECHANICAL ENGINEERING. Ac, Sa: *Mechanical Engineering.*

NUCLEAR ENGINEERING. Ga, Ac, Sa: *Nuclear Engineering International.*

Basic Abstracts and Indexes

Applied Science and Technology Index, Computer & Control Abstracts, Engineering Index (Compendex), INSPEC, Metals Abstracts.

General

2132. *A S E E Prism.* Formed by the merger of (1974-1991): *Engineering Education News;* (1924-1991): *Engineering Education;* Which was formerly (until 1969): *Journal of Engineering Education.* [ISSN: 1056-8077] 1991. 9x/yr. Free to members. Ed(s): Mark Matthews. American Society for Engineering Education, 1818 N St, NW, Ste 600, Washington, DC 20036; http://www.asee.org. Illus., index, adv. Circ: 12000. Microform: CIS; PQC. *Indexed:* A22, ApMecR, C&ISA, CerAb. *Bk. rev.:* Number and length vary. *Aud.:* Ga, Ac, Sa.

An engaging and informative magazine, *ASEE Prism* (ASEE URL: www.prism-magazine.org/default.cfm) is free to members of the American Society for Engineering Education (ASEE). *Prism* has regular features and original articles that highlight and discuss trends in engineering and engineering education. Articles are well written and illustrated. The journal is published in print and online; online issues are open-access with a one-month lag. It includes display advertising for products and services as well as a classified section highlighting jobs for engineering faculty. Readers include college and university administrators and engineering faculty, professional engineers, and K–12 educators.

2133. *The Bridge (Washington).* [ISSN: 0737-6278] 1969. q. Free. Ed(s): Ronald M Latanision, Carol Arenberg. National Academy of Engineering, 500 5th St NW, Washington, DC 20001; http://www.nae.edu. Circ: 6500. *Indexed:* C&ISA, CerAb, S25. *Aud.:* Ga, Ac, Sa.

The Bridge is an online-only, open-access publication published quarterly by the National Academy of Engineering (NAE) (www.nae.edu/19582/bridge.aspx). The journal's intent is to stimulate discussion among NAE members, policymakers, educators, and others. To do this, the journal publishes opinions and analyses of engineering research, education, and practice; policy related to science and engineering; and engineering's role in society. Individual issues are devoted to one subject, e.g., STEM education, urban sustainability, or frontiers of engineering. This publication will appeal to engineering faculty, policy makers, and educators, as well as anyone interested in the role of engineering and technology in society. Print copies may be obtained directly from the NAE.

2134. *Computer Methods in Applied Mechanics and Engineering.* [ISSN: 0045-7825] 1970. 52x/yr. EUR 8601. Ed(s): Thomas J R Hughes, Manolis Papadrakakis. Elsevier BV, Radarweg 29, PO Box 211, Amsterdam, 1000 AE, Netherlands; JournalsCustomerServiceEMEA@elsevier.com; http://www.elsevier.com. Illus., index, adv. Refereed. Vol. ends: No. 190. Microform: PQC. *Indexed:* A01, A22, ApMecR, C&ISA, CCMJ, CerAb, CompLI, CompR, EngInd, MSN, MathR. *Aud.:* Ac, Sa.

Computer Methods in Applied Mechanics and Engineering (Elsevier URL: www.journals.elsevier.com/computer-methods-in-applied-mechanics-and-engineering/) publishes original papers relating to the use of advanced mathematical techniques and modeling for research in mechanics and engineering. The journal covers computational methods of any type that simulate complex physical problems. Specific areas of interest include: mechanics (solid and structural, fluid, biomechanics, geomechanics and quantum), heat transfer, acoustics, electromagnetics, and more. The online version (reviewed herein; ISSN 0045-7825) features recent articles, most-downloaded, most-cited, highlighted, and open-access articles. Special-topical issues are also available. Individual articles feature CrossMark tracking, which identifies the most current version for each paper, social media–sharing options, and eReader formats. This journal will appeal to researchers in science and engineering who use computational methods to model physical systems and problems.

Engineering & Technology. See Electronics section.

2135. *International Journal for Numerical Methods in Engineering.* Formerly (until 1969): *Numerical Methods in Engineering.* [ISSN: 0029-5981] 19??. 52x/yr. GBP 7192. Ed(s): Ted Belytschko, Rene de Borst. John Wiley & Sons Ltd., The Atrium, Southern Gate, Chichester, PO19 8SQ, United Kingdom; customer@wiley.com; http://www.wiley.com. Illus., index, adv. Sample. Refereed. Microform: PQC. Reprint: PSC. *Indexed:* A22, ApMecR, C&ISA, CCMJ, CerAb, CompLI, EngInd, MSN, MathR. *Bk. rev.:* Number and length vary. *Aud.:* Ac, Sa.

The *International Journal for Numerical Methods in Engineering* (Wiley Online Library, URL: http://onlinelibrary.wiley.com/journal/10.1002/(ISSN)1097-0207) publishes original papers that discuss important developments in numerical methods used to solve engineering problems. Papers focus on engineering problems in solids, multi-physics, multi-scale, and multi-disciplinary problems. The online version (reviewed herein; ISSN 1097-0207) features links to early-view, most-read, and most-cited articles. Authors can choose to publish their papers open access. Individual articles include linked references, citation tracking, and social media–sharing options. Readers of this journal will include engineers and scientists studying computational and numerical methods to solve problems in engineering and applied mathematicians.

2136. *International Journal of Engineering Science (Online).* [ISSN: 1879-2197] 1963. m. Ed(s): K R Rajagopal, M Kachanov. Elsevier Inc., 1600 John F Kennedy Blvd, Philadelphia, PA 19103; usinfo-f@elsevier.com; http://www.elsevier.com. Illus. *Aud.:* Ac, Sa.

The core interest of the *International Journal of Engineering Science* (Elsevier URL: www.journals.elsevier.com/international-journal-of-engineering-science/) is the modeling of materials and their responses, but it publishes articles from many areas of engineering and is especially interested in publishing research that is multidisciplinary in nature. The journal also publishes review articles and special issues devoted to a specific engineering sub-field. The online version (reviewed herein; ISSN 1879-2197) features recent, most-downloaded, most-cited, and open-access articles. Individual articles include citing and related articles, linked references, and "CrossMark" tracking, which identifies the most current version of an article. Articles are also available in eReader format and social media–sharing is included. This journal will appeal to engineering researchers in many subfields, but especially those researching and modeling materials.

Issues in Science and Technology See Science and Technology/History and Philosophy of Science section.

2137. *Journal of Engineering Education.* [ISSN: 1069-4730] 1993. q. Individuals, USD 25. Ed(s): Jack R. Lohmann. Wiley-Blackwell Publishing, Inc., 111 River St, Hoboken, NJ 07030; info@wiley.com; http://www.wiley.com/. Adv. Refereed. *Indexed:* A01, A22, EngInd, P02. *Aud.:* Ac, Sa.

The *Journal of Engineering Education* (*JEE*) publishes and disseminates original papers related to engineering education. Areas of interest include: epistemologies, learning mechanisms, learning systems, diversity and inclusiveness, and assessment. This title is published quarterly in print and online, and recent issues included papers on assessment of capstone courses; analysis of a multidisciplinary capstone design class; engineering education reform; and a study of how well engineering graduate students learn in research groups. In 2013, the online version (reviewed herein; ISSN 2168-9830) moved to the Wiley Online Library platform (http://onlinelibrary.wiley.com/journal/10.1002/(ISSN)2168-9830). Online features include access to current and past issues, and recently published articles. Individual articles feature linked references, citation tracking, and social media–sharing options. *JEE* is international in scope and will appeal to anyone interested in engineering education and the recruitment of students to engineering through educational activities in the K–12 levels.

2138. *Journal of Engineering Mathematics.* [ISSN: 0022-0833] 1966. m. EUR 1752 (print & online eds.). Ed(s): H K Kuiken. Springer Netherlands, Van Godewijckstraat 30, Dordrecht, 3311 GX, Netherlands; http://www.springer.com. Illus., index, adv. Refereed. Microform: PQC. Reprint: PSC. *Indexed:* A22, ApMecR, C&ISA, CCMJ, CerAb, E01, EngInd, MSN, MathR. *Bk. rev.:* Number and length vary. *Aud.:* Ac, Sa.

The *Journal of Engineering Mathematics* online (Springer URL: www.springer.com/physics/classical+continuum+physics/journal/10665) promotes the use of mathematics to solve physical problems, especially in applied and engineering science. The research papers published employ a variety of mathematical techniques (including ordinary and partial differential equations, integral equations, asymptotics, numerical analysis, and more) to solve problems in continuum mechanics, fluid mechanics, solid mechanics, heat and mass transfer, rheology, shock waves, biomedical and geophysical engineering, and more. The online version (reviewed herein; ISSN 1573-2703) features access to current and past issues and online-first and open-access articles. Social media–sharing options are provided. This journal will appeal especially to physical scientists and engineers who are using advanced mathematical methods to solve physical problems.

2139. *Journal of Testing and Evaluation.* Formerly (until 1973): *Journal of Materials;* Which incorporated (in 1966): *Gillett Memorial Lecture;* Journal of Materials superseded in part (in 1961): *American Society for Testing and Materials. Proceedings;* Which was formerly (until 1961): *American Society for Testing Materials. Proceedings;* (until 1945): *American Society for Testing Materials. Proceedings of the Annual Meeting;* (until 1902): *International Association for Testing Materials. American Section. Bulletin.* [ISSN: 0090-3973] 1966. bi-m. USD 490 (print & online eds.) Individuals, USD 305 (print & online eds.). Ed(s): Dr. M R Mitchell. A S T M International, 100 Barr Harbor Dr, PO Box C700, W Conshohocken, PA 19428; service@astm.org; http://www.astm.org. Illus., index, adv. Refereed. Vol. ends: Nov. Microform: PMC; PQC. *Indexed:* A22, ApMecR, C&ISA, CerAb, E01, EngInd, RILM. *Aud.:* Ac, Sa.

The *Journal of Testing and Evaluation* (*JOTE*) is an ASTM International publication (URL: www.astm.org/DIGITAL_LIBRARY/JOURNALS/TESTEVAL/), and it provides a multidisciplinary forum for the publication of research on performance, characterization, and evaluation of materials. Papers include discussions of new methods and data (and their evaluation), and reports of users' experiences with test methods. In addition to research papers, *JOTE* publishes review articles, technical notes, research briefs, and commentary. Major topic areas include fatigue and fracture, and mechanical and fire testing. The online version (reviewed herein; ISSN 1945-7553) of this journal is the official publication for citation purposes. Available through the ASTM Standards and Digital Library, it features first-look articles and access to current and past issues. Individual articles are cross-referenced with applicable ASTM standards. The information in this journal will appeal to scientists and engineers interested in testing and evaluation of materials.

2140. *Leadership and Management in Engineering.* [ISSN: 1532-6748] 2001. q. USD 290. Ed(s): William M Hayden. American Society of Civil Engineers, 1801 Alexander Bell Dr, Reston, VA 20191; http://www.asce.org. Adv. Refereed. *Indexed:* A22, B01, C&ISA, CerAb, EngInd. *Aud.:* Ga, Ac, Sa.

Leadership and Management in Engineering is published quarterly by the American Society of Civil Engineers' Committee on Professional Practice, and it examines issues and trends in leadership and management and their application to engineering. The journal provides articles of interest to practicing professionals in many engineering fields and industry sectors. Topics include leadership, teamwork, team building, communications, decision making, motivational techniques, and more. The journal also has recurring columns on: "Leadership on the Entry Level," "Ethical Issues in Civil Engineering," "Engineering Legends," "Education in Practice," and "Engineering Your Future." Engineers in any field and general readers who are interested in learning more about leadership and management in engineering will be interested in this journal. (This review is of the online version [ISSN 1943-5630].) URL: http://ascelibrary.org/journal/lmeeaz

Measurement Science and Technology. See Physics section.

National Academy of Sciences. Proceedings. See Biology/General section.

R & D Magazine. See Science and Technology/General section.

Science and Engineering Ethics. See Science and Technology/History and Philosophy of Science section.

Biomedical Engineering

American Chemical Society. Journal. See Chemistry/General section.

2141. *Annals of Biomedical Engineering.* Incorporates (1976-1978): *Journal of Bioengineering.* [ISSN: 0090-6964] 1972. m. EUR 1353 (print & online eds.). Ed(s): Kyriacos A Athanasiou, Holly Ober. Springer New York LLC, 233 Spring St, New York, NY 10013; journals@springer-ny.com; http://www.springer.com/. Illus., index, adv. Refereed. Microform: PQC. Reprint: PSC. *Indexed:* A22, Agr, ApMecR, BRI, C&ISA, CerAb, E01, EngInd. *Bk. rev.:* Number and length vary. *Aud.:* Ac, Sa.

Annals of Biomedical Engineering (Springer URL: http://link.springer.com/journal/10439), the official journal of the Biomedical Engineering Society (BMES), publishes original research and review articles related to bioengineering and biomedical engineering. Special issues devoted to specific topics are also published. Recent articles discussed biomaterials, medical imaging, tissue engineering, biomechanics, drug delivery, bioelectricity, nanomedicine and modeling (computational, statistical, multi-linear, predictive), and more. The online version (reviewed herein; ISSN 1573-9686) provides access to "Latest Articles" and "Online First Articles." Authors can opt to publish articles as open access through Springer's "Open Choice" option. Articles in this journal will appeal to researchers in all areas of biomedical engineering.

Biochemistry. See Biology/Biochemistry and Biophysics section.

2142. *Biomaterials.* Incorporates (1986-1995): *Clinical Materials;* Which incorporated (in 1991): *Critical Reviews in Biocompatibility.* [ISSN: 0142-9612] 1980. 36x/yr. EUR 6776. Ed(s): D F Williams. Elsevier BV, Radarweg 29, PO Box 211, Amsterdam, 1000 AE, Netherlands; JournalsCustomerServiceEMEA@elsevier.com; http://www.elsevier.nl. Illus., adv. Refereed. Microform: PQC. *Indexed:* A01, A22, BrTechI, C&ISA, C45, CerAb, EngInd, ExcerpMed, IndVet. *Bk. rev.:* Number and length vary. *Aud.:* Ac, Sa.

Biomaterials, a core journal on the topic (Elsevier URL: www.journals.elsevier.com/biomaterials/), is an important international journal that covers research related to biomaterials and their applications. It publishes peer-reviewed original research papers, reviews and opinion papers discussing biomaterials, their applications in clinical medicine, and issues surrounding their use. Papers in each issue are divided into categories linking biomaterials to medical device performance, regenerative medicine, cancer, diagnostics, drug delivery, and more. The online version (reviewed herein; ISSN 1878-5905) includes articles in press, most-downloaded, most-cited, and open-access articles and "CrossMark" version tracking. Individual articles include linked references, citing and related articles, and eReader versions. Social media–sharing is also available. This journal is recommended reading for bioengineering and biomedical researchers who are interested in materials for use in a clinical setting.

2143. *Biomedical Microdevices.* [ISSN: 1387-2176] 1998. bi-m. EUR 725 (print & online eds.). Ed(s): Mauro Ferrari. Springer New York LLC, 233 Spring St, New York, NY 10013; service-ny@springer.com; http://www.springer.com/. Adv. Sample. Reprint: PSC. *Indexed:* A22, Agr, E01, EngInd, ExcerpMed. *Aud.:* Ac, Sa.

Biomedical Microdevices (Springer URL: www.springer.com/engineering/biomedical+engineering/journal/10544) is unique because it is the first publication to focus on the medical applications of micro and nanotechnology. It publishes scholarly articles that cover everything from the initial design through modeling and clinical validation of micro-fabricated systems. Research areas covered include Micro-Electro-Mechanical Systems (MEMS), micro-fabrication, and nanotechnology. Particular areas of interest include neural stimulation, bioseparation, biosensors, tissue engineering, drug delivery systems, and more. The online version (reviewed herein; ISSN 1572-8781) features access to "Online First" articles and "Latest Articles." Authors can publish open-access articles using the "Open Choice" option. Biomedical scientists and engineers who are researching and developing micro- and nanotechnology applications for use in medicine will want to read this journal.

Biophysical Journal. See Biology/Biochemistry and Biophysics section.

Biotechnology and Bioengineering. See Biotechnology section.

2144. *I E E E Pulse.* Former titles (until 2010): *I E E E Engineering in Medicine and Biology Magazine;* (until Jun. 1982): *Engineering in Medicine and Biology;* (until 1982): *I E E E - E M B S Newsletter.* [ISSN: 2154-2287] 1962. bi-m. USD 650; USD 780 combined subscription (print & online eds.). Ed(s): Michael R Neuman. Institute of Electrical and Electronics Engineers, 445 Hoes Ln, Piscataway, NJ 08854; contactcenter@ieee.org; http://www.ieee.org. Illus., adv. *Indexed:* A22, C&ISA, CerAb, EngInd, H24. *Bk. rev.:* Number and length vary. *Aud.:* Ga, Ac, Sa.

Published by the IEEE Engineering in Medicine and Biology Society, *IEEE Pulse* (IEEE Xplore URL: http://ieeexplore.ieee.org/xpl/RecentIssue.jsp?punumber=5454060) helps readers stay up-to-date on biomedical engineering topics. The magazine publishes general-interest pieces such as news items, book reviews, patent descriptions, and correspondence, as well as technical articles on topics including technologies and methods in biomedical engineering, clinical engineering, new products, and more. Articles may include color photographs and illustrations. *Pulse* is available both in print and online (reviewed herein; ISSN 2154-2317), and limited display and classified advertising are included in the print version. The current issue can be downloaded from the EMBS web site (www.embs.org/publications/ieee-pulse). This magazine will appeal to biomedical engineers and researchers as well as students in the field.

2145. *I E E E Transactions on Biomedical Engineering.* Former titles (until 1964): *I E E E Transactions on Bio-Medical Electronics;* (until 1963): *I R E Transactions on Bio-Medical Electronics;* (until 1961): *I R E Transactions on Medical Electronics;* (until 1955): *I R E Professional Group on Medical Electronics. Transactions.* [ISSN: 0018-9294] 1953. m. USD 1965; USD 2360 combined subscription (print & online eds.). Ed(s): Bruce C Wheeler, Jeffrey E Cichocki. Institute of Electrical and Electronics Engineers, 445 Hoes Ln, Piscataway, NJ 08854; contactcenter@ieee.org; http://www.ieee.org. Illus., adv. Refereed. *Indexed:* A01, A22, ApMecR, B01, C&ISA, CerAb, EngInd, ErgAb, ExcerpMed, MathR. *Aud.:* Ac, Sa.

IEEE Transactions on Biomedical Engineering (IEEE Xplore URL: http://ieeexplore.ieee.org/xpl/RecentIssue.jsp?punumber=10) is a leading journal in the field, and is published by the IEEE Engineering in Medicine and Biology Society. It publishes peer-reviewed research and practical papers that discuss many aspects of biomedical engineering. Topics of interest include biomedical signal processing, imaging and image processing, neural engineering, tissue engineering, biomedical modeling and computing, micro- and nanotechnology, robotics, emerging biomedical engineering topics, and more. The online version of the journal (reviewed herein; ISSN 1558-2531) provides access to latest, popular, and early-access articles. Individual articles include linked references, similar papers, citing articles information, and article metrics. Special topical issues and sections are sometimes featured. Readers of this journal will include biomedical research scientists and engineers as well as practitioners in the field.

International Journal of Medical Robotics and Computer Assisted Surgery. See Robotics section.

The International Journal of Robotics Research. See Robotics section.

JAMA: The Journal of the American Medical Association. See Medicine section.

2146. *Journal of Biomaterials Applications.* [ISSN: 0885-3282] 1986. 8x/yr. USD 2386. Ed(s): Jonathan Knowles. Sage Publications Ltd., 1 Oliver's Yard, 55 City Rd, London, EC1Y 1SP, United Kingdom; info@sagepub.co.uk; http://www.uk.sagepub.com. Sample. Refereed. Reprint: PSC. *Indexed:* A01, A22, C&ISA, CerAb, E01, EngInd. *Aud.:* Ac, Sa.

The *Journal of Biomaterials Applications* (Sage URL: http://jba.sagepub.com) focuses on new and emerging technologies in biomaterials for surgical and medical devices and products. It publishes peer-reviewed papers that discuss all aspects of biomaterials research: development and manufacture of new technologies and their clinical applications, as well as materials properties and performance evaluation and application; and more. The online version (reviewed herein; ISSN 1530-8022) features forthcoming articles, a collection of review articles, and a collection of high-impact articles from previous years. Open-access publishing is available to authors; each issue includes an index by author. This journal will appeal to biomaterials and medical researchers who are interested in new and emerging biomaterials and their use in medical instruments and their clinical applications.

2147. *Journal of Biomechanics.* [ISSN: 0021-9290] 1968. 16x/yr. EUR 5063. Ed(s): Dr. Farshid Guilak. Pergamon, The Blvd, Langford Ln, E Park, Kidlington, OX5 1GB, United Kingdom; JournalsCustomerServiceEMEA@elsevier.com; http://www.elsevier.com. Illus., adv. Sample. Refereed. Microform: PQC. *Indexed:* A01, A22, AbAn, ApMecR, C&ISA, C45, EngInd, ErgAb, ExcerpMed, H24, IndVet, RILM, SD. *Bk. rev.:* Number and length vary. *Aud.:* Ac, Sa.

The *Journal of Biomechanics* (Elsevier URL: www.journals.elsevier.com/journal-of-biomechanics) publishes peer-reviewed, original research that focuses on the use of mechanics in the investigation of biological problems. A wide variety of research topics will be considered, including the biomechanics of cells, systems, injury, and sports, functional tissue engineering, and more. The journal publishes original articles, surveys, book reviews, invited perspective articles, and letters. Available in print and online, the online version (reviewed herein; ISSN 0021-9290) highlights recent, most-cited, most-downloaded, and open-access articles, and special thematic issues. Individual articles include color illustrations and photographs, linked references, citing and related articles, and eReader format downloads. Because of its interdisciplinary nature, this journal will appeal to researchers in several fields, including biomedical engineering, mechanical engineering, medicine, and physics.

2148. *Journal of Biomedical Materials Research. Part A.* Supersedes in part (in 2003): *Journal of Biomedical Materials Research;* Which incorporated (1990-1995): *Journal of Applied Biomaterials.* [ISSN: 1549-3296] 1967. 10x/yr. GBP 5546. Ed(s): James M Anderson. John Wiley & Sons, Inc., 111 River St, MS 4-02, Hoboken, NJ 07030; info@wiley.com; http://www.wiley.com/WileyCDA/. Illus., adv. Refereed. Reprint: PSC. *Indexed:* ApMecR, C&ISA, CerAb, ExcerpMed. *Aud.:* Ac, Sa.

The *Journal of Biomedical Materials Research[,] Part A* (Wiley http://onlinelibrary.wiley.com/journal/10.1002/(ISSN)1552-4965) publishes peer-reviewed, original research articles, review articles, and technical notes on the performance and evaluation of biomaterials, their behavior in living systems, and the response of blood and tissue to them. The journal, which is international in scope, is the official journal of the Society for Biomaterials (U.S.), the Japanese Society for Biomaterials, the Australasian Society for Biomaterials, and the Korean Society for Biomaterials. Topics include the science and technology of materials (alloys, polymers, and ceramics) and reprocessed tissues in surgery, dentistry, artificial organs, and medical devices. Articles on interdisciplinary topics, e.g., tissue engineering, are also encouraged. The online version (reviewed herein; ISSN 1552-4965) includes access to early-view, accepted, and open-access articles. Individual articles include linked references, citing articles, and social media–sharing options. A related journal, *Journal of Biomedical Materials Research[,] Part B,* publishes research on applied biomaterials.

The Journal of Cell Biology. See Biology/Cell and Molecular Biology section.

2149. *Medical & Biological Engineering & Computing.* Incorporates (in 1998): *Cellular Engineering;* Which was formerly (until 1995): *Journal of Cellular Engineering;* Former titles (until 1977): *Medical and Biological Engineering;* (until 1966): *Medical Electronics and Biological Engineering;* Which was formed by the merger of: *Biological Engineering; Medical Electronics.* [ISSN: 0140-0118] 1962. bi-m. EUR 1528 (print & online eds.). Ed(s): Jos A Spaan. Springer, Tiergartenstr 17, Heidelberg, 69121, Germany; subscriptions@springer.com; http://www.springer.com. Illus., adv. Refereed. Circ: 1300. Microform: PQC. Reprint: PSC. *Indexed:* A01, A22, ABIn, Agr, ApMecR, B01, C&ISA, CompLI, E01, EngInd, ErgAb. *Aud.:* Ac, Sa.

Medical & Biological Engineering & Computing (Springer URL: http://link.springer.com/journal/11517) is an official publication of the International Federation of Medical and Biological Engineering. This publication covers all topics related to biomedical and clinical engineering. Articles discuss experimental and theoretical developments in the field, and report on emerging technologies and advances in computing techniques related to biomedical science and technology. Review articles and technical notes are also included. The online version (reviewed herein; ISSN 1741-0444) features a "Rapid Communications" category and a "Controversies" section that provides a forum to readers to exchange views on selected issues.

2150. *Physics in Medicine and Biology.* [ISSN: 0031-9155] 1956. s-m. GBP 2183 (print & online eds.). Ed(s): S R Cherry. Institute of Physics Publishing Ltd., Dirac House, Temple Back, Bristol, BS1 6BE, United Kingdom; custserv@iop.org; http://ioppublishing.org. Illus. Sample. Refereed. Reprint: IRC. *Indexed:* A01, A22, AbAn, C45, EngInd, IndVet. *Aud.:* Ac, Sa.

Physics in Medicine and Biology (IOPScience URL: http://iopscience.iop.org/0031-9155) is a peer-reviewed journal that publishes original research on the application of physics to medicine, physiology, and biology. Specific topics covered by the journal include biomedical imaging, image reconstruction, image analysis, radiotheraphy physics, other applications of radiation medicine, and more. Content includes research papers, review papers (invited), technical notes, and comments and replies. Available both in print and online, the online version (reviewed herein; ISSN 1361-6560) is a "hybrid open access" journal.

Other online features include "Most Read" and "Most Cited" articles. This journal will appeal to biomedical scientists and engineers working in radiobiology, radiotherapy, radiation dosimetry, and radiation protection, biomedical imaging and optics, and more.

Tissue Engineering. Part A. See Biotechnology section.

Chemical Engineering

2151. *A I Ch E Journal.* [ISSN: 0001-1541] 1955. m. GBP 1436. Ed(s): Stanley I Sandler. John Wiley & Sons, Inc., 111 River St, MS 4-02, Hoboken, NJ 07030; uscs-wis@wiley.com; http://www.wiley.com/WileyCDA/. Illus., index, adv. Refereed. Circ: 3000 Paid. Vol. ends: Dec. Reprint: PSC. *Indexed:* A22, Agr, ApMecR, C&ISA, CEA, CerAb, EngInd, MathR, S25. *Bk. rev.:* Number and length vary. *Aud.:* Ac, Sa.

The *AIChE Journal,* published by the American Institute of Chemical Engineers (Wiley URL: http://onlinelibrary.wiley.com/journal/10.1002/(ISSN)1547-5905), is a leading peer-reviewed research journal that publishes research and review papers, R&D notes, and book reviews in chemical engineering and related fields (biotechnology, electrochemical engineering, and environmental engineering). Research papers and R&D notes are arranged by topical areas that include: biomolecular engineering, bioengineering, biochemical, biofuels and food; Inorganic Materials; Particle Technology and Fluidization; Process Systems; Reaction Engineering; Soft Materials; Thermodynamics and Molecular-Scale Phenomena; and Transport Phenomena and Fluid Mechanics. The online version (reviewed herein; ISSN 1547-5905) provides quick access to early-view, accepted, most-accessed, and most-cited articles. Individual articles feature linked references, citing articles, and social media sharing options. The target audience for this journal is researchers and practitioners in academia and industry in chemical, electrochemical, and environmental engineering.

2152. *Biochemical Engineering Journal.* [ISSN: 1369-703X] 1998. 15x/yr. EUR 2006. Ed(s): Colin Webb, M Taya. Elsevier BV, Radarweg 29, PO Box 211, Amsterdam, 1000 AE, Netherlands; JournalsCustomerServiceEMEA@elsevier.com; http://www.elsevier.nl. Refereed. *Indexed:* A01, A22, C45, EngInd, ExcerpMed, FS&TA, IndVet. *Aud.:* Ac, Sa.

The *Biochemical Engineering Journal* (Elsevier URL: www.journals.elsevier.com/biochemical-engineering-journal/) is a peer-reviewed journal that publishes original research papers, review articles, and short communications on the chemical engineering aspects of biological processes. Research areas covered in recent issues include microbial fuel cells, modeling of reversible bioconversions, fermentation, ethanol production, phosphorous removal in an aquaculture system, and more. The online version (reviewed herein; ISSN 1369-703x) features access to most-downloaded, most-cited, open-access, and recent articles. Special issues are also available. Individual articles include citing and related articles, linked references, eReader formats, and social media sharing. Readers of this journal will include researchers in chemical engineering, bioengineering, biology, and chemistry interested in engineering biological processes.

Chemical & Engineering News. See Chemistry/General section.

2153. *Chemical Engineering and Technology.* Formerly (until 1987): *German Chemical Engineering.* [ISSN: 0930-7516] 1978. m. GBP 2712. Ed(s): Barbara Boeck. Wiley - V C H Verlag GmbH & Co. KGaA, Postfach 101161, Weinheim, 69451, Germany; info@wiley-vch.de; http://www.wiley-vch.de. Adv. Sample. Refereed. Circ: 1000 Paid and controlled. Reprint: PSC. *Indexed:* A22, C&ISA, CEA, CerAb, EngInd. *Aud.:* Ac, Sa.

Chemical Engineering & Technology (Wiley URL: http://onlinelibrary.wiley.com/journal/10.1002/(ISSN)1521-4125) publishes experimental and theoretical information that covers all areas of chemical and process engineering, biotechnology, and process equipment design. This peer-reviewed journal, which is associated with the German publication *Chemie Ingenieur Technik,* publishes original research, review articles, and short communications. Recent articles discussed materials science, fluid dynamics, numerical modeling and simulation, mass transfer, biofuels, catalysts and catalytic reactions, and more. Special topical issues are issued periodically. The online version (review herein; ISSN 1521-4125) provides access to early-view, most-accessed, and most-cited articles. Individual articles include linked references, citing articles, and social media options. This journal is recommended reading for chemical and process engineers, industrial chemists, biotechnologists, and designers of process plant equipment.

2154. Chemical Engineering Communications. [ISSN: 0098-6445] 1973. m. GBP 5079 (print & online eds.). Ed(s): William N Gill. Taylor & Francis Inc., 325 Chestnut St, Ste 800, Philadelphia, PA 19106; customerservice@taylorandfrancis.com; http://www.tandfonline.com. Adv. Sample. Refereed. Reprint: PSC. *Indexed:* A01, A22, C&ISA, CEA, CerAb, E01, EngInd, S25. *Aud.:* Ac, Sa.

Chemical Engineering Communications (Taylor & Francis URL: www.tandfonline.com/action/aboutThisJournal?journalCode=gcec20) is a peer-reviewed journal that publishes original articles that discuss basic and applied research results in chemical engineering. The journal seeks articles that discuss progress in all areas of chemical engineering as well as semiconductor processing, materials engineering, bioengineering, and more. Other types of articles published include review papers, short communications, and commentaries and discussion of previously published research. In recent issues, articles discussed the Fischer-Tropsch process, kinetic modeling, acetylene hydrogenation for ethylene production, laminar mixed convection, synthesis gas production, and more. The online version (reviewed herein; ISSN 1563-5201) features easy access to latest, most-read, most-cited articles, and linked references. Authors can publish their articles open access; thematic special issues are also published. Readers of this journal will include researchers in chemical engineering, bioengineering, and industrial chemistry.

2155. Chemical Engineering Journal. Former titles (until 1996): *Chemical Engineering Journal and Biochemical Engineering Journal;* (until 1983): *Chemical Engineering Journal.* [ISSN: 1385-8947] 1970. 30x/yr. EUR 3932. Ed(s): J Santamaria, M Deshusses. Elsevier BV, Radarweg 29, PO Box 211, Amsterdam, 1000 AE, Netherlands; JournalsCustomerServiceEMEA@elsevier.com; http://www.elsevier.nl. Illus., adv. Refereed. Microform: PQC. *Indexed:* A01, A22, C45, CEA, EngInd, FS&TA, MathR, RRTA. *Aud.:* Ac, Sa.

The international journal *Chemical Engineering Journal* (Elsevier URL: www.journals.elsevier.com/chemical-engineering-journal/) seeks contributions that discuss original and novel research or new developments in chemical engineering. This is a well-regarded, peer-reviewed publication, and its contents highlight three areas of chemical engineering: chemical-reaction engineering (reaction kinetics, multiphase reactors, types of reactors, etc.), environmental chemical engineering (pollution control, bioenergy, clean process technology, etc.), and materials synthesis and processing. The journal publishes original research articles, review articles, and short communications. The online version (reviewed herein; ISSN 1385-8947) features access to recent articles, open-access, most-downloaded, and most-cited articles. Special, thematic issues are also available. Individual articles feature color illustrations, citing and related articles, eReader formats and social media–sharing options. Readers of this journal will include chemical engineering researchers interested in new research advances in the areas covered by the journal.

2156. Chemical Engineering Science. [ISSN: 0009-2509] 1951. 18x/yr. EUR 7546. Ed(s): A P J Middelberg. Pergamon, The Blvd, Langford Ln, E Park, Kidlington, OX5 1GB, United Kingdom; JournalsCustomerServiceEMEA@elsevier.com; http://www.elsevier.com. Illus., adv. Sample. Refereed. Microform: PQC. *Indexed:* A01, A22, ApMecR, BrTechI, C&ISA, CEA, CerAb, EngInd. *Bk. rev.:* Number and length vary. *Aud.:* Ac, Sa.

Chemical Engineering Science (Elsevier URL: www.journals.elsevier.com/chemical-engineering-science/) is a peer-reviewed journal that publishes original papers discussing fundamental research in chemical engineering and critical reviews of cutting-edge developments in the field. The journal covers biotechnology, chemicals, nanotechnology, specialty chemicals, and more. Major research areas covered include biomolecular and biological engineering; biochemical and bioprocess engineering; energy, water, environment, and sustainability; materials engineering; particle technology; process systems

engineering; reaction engineering and catalysis; and separations science and technology. The online version (reviewed herein; ISSN 0009-2509) features access to special issues and most-downloaded, most-cited, and recent articles. Individual articles include citing and related articles, linked references, eReader formats, and social media–sharing options. The broad coverage of this journal will make it very appealing to industrial and academic researchers working in the areas of chemical and process engineering.

Chemical Week. See Business and Finance/Trade and Industry section.

Fuel. See Energy section.

2157. Industrial & Engineering Chemistry Research. Formed by the merger of (1962-1987): *Industrial and Engineering Chemistry Process Design and Development;* (1962-1987): *Industrial and Engineering Chemistry Fundamentals;* (1978-1987): *Industrial and Engineering Chemistry Product Research and Development;* Which was formerly (until 1978): *Product R & D;* (until 1969): *I & E C Product Research and Development.* [ISSN: 0888-5885] 1987. w. USD 2995. Ed(s): Donald R Paul, David J Smith. American Chemical Society, 1155 16th St N W, Washington, DC 20036; help@acs.org; http://pubs.acs.org. Illus., adv. Refereed. *Indexed:* A01, A22, C&ISA, CEA, EngInd, FS&TA, S25. *Aud.:* Ac, Sa.

The American Chemical Society journal, *Industrial & Engineering Chemistry Research* (ACS URL: http://pubs.acs.org/page/iecred/about.html), is an important source of research information in the fields of applied chemistry and chemical engineering. This title is published weekly, and the online version of the journal (reviewed herein; ISSN 1520-5045) features access to just-accepted manuscripts and "Articles ASAP," articles published online ahead of print, most-read articles, and special-topical and festschrift issues. Some articles are open access. Papers published in the journal discuss fundamental research (reaction kinetics, catalysis, thermodynamics, and more), process design, product research and development, and new areas of science and technology related to chemical engineering. The types of papers in the journal include original research, research notes, reviews, and more. The audience for this journal is chemists and chemical engineers in industry and academia.

2158. Journal of Catalysis. [ISSN: 0021-9517] 1962. 16x/yr. EUR 7944. Ed(s): E Iglesia. Academic Press, 3251 Riverport Ln, Maryland Heights, MO 63043; JournalCustomerService-usa@elsevier.com; http://www.elsevierdirect.com/brochures/academicpress/index.html. Illus., adv. Sample. Refereed. *Indexed:* A01, A22, CEA, E01, EngInd. *Bk. rev.:* Number and length vary. *Aud.:* Ac, Sa.

The *Journal of Catalysis* (Elsevier URL: www.journals.elsevier.com/journal-of-catalysis) is the foremost publication of research in catalysis and is highly ranked in annual journal rankings. It publishes original research, priority communications, and research notes that cover the fields of homogeneous and heterogeneous catalysis. Recent issues have included articles that discuss reaction kinetics, selective catalytic reduction, cooperative catalysts, methanol synthesis using copper catalysts, preparation of hierarchical zeolites, and more. The web site of the online version (reviewed herein; ISSN 0021-9517) provides access to most-downloaded, most-cited, and recent articles, as well as special, topical issues and job advertisements. Some contributions are published as open-access articles. Individual articles include citing and related articles and events, linked references, eReader formats, and social media–sharing options. Chemists and chemical engineers in industry and academia are the target audience for this journal.

2159. Journal of Chemical & Engineering Data. Formerly (until 1959): *Chemical & Engineering Data Series.* [ISSN: 0021-9568] 1956. m. USD 1340. Ed(s): Joan F Brennecke. American Chemical Society, 1155 16th St N W, Washington, DC 20036; help@acs.org; http://pubs.acs.org. Illus., index, adv. Sample. Refereed. *Indexed:* A01, A22, CEA, EngInd. *Bk. rev.:* Number and length vary. *Aud.:* Ac, Sa.

The *Journal of Chemical & Engineering Data* (http://pubs.acs.org/page/jceaax/about.html) is published monthly by the American Chemical Society. The journal's scope covers research on the properties (physical, thermodynamic, and transport) of well-defined materials and complex mixtures, and publishes articles with experimental data and the evaluation and validation of property values. Thermophysical properties of materials, molecular simulation, and molecular mechanics calculations are also accepted. The content types include articles, short articles, correlations, and reviews. Book reviews are also published. This title is available in print and online, and the online version (reviewed herein; ISSN 1520-5134) features color illustrations, "Articles ASAP," and some open-access articles. Researchers can set up an ACS ChemWorx account (free) to save their research, and social media–sharing options are available.

The Journal of Chemical Physics. See Physics section.

Journal of Physical and Chemical Reference Data. See Chemistry/ General section.

Langmuir. See Chemistry/Physical section.

Macromolecules. See Chemistry/General section.

Physical Review Letters. See Physics section.

Physics of Fluids. See Physics section.

Civil and Environmental Engineering

The ASCE Library provides electronic access to all 33 journals that are published by the American Society of Civil Engineers. This core group of journals represents the backbone for any academic library that supports a civil engineering department. From the *Journal of Engineering Mechanics,* which was first published in 1875, to the *Journal of Nanomechanics and Micromechanics,* which was introduced in 2011, the ASCE Library will often prove to be the first stopping place for both the practicing engineer and the academic researcher.

2160. *American Water Works Association. Journal.* Former titles (until 1948): *American Water Works Association. Proceedings of the Annual Convention;* (until 1902): *American Water Works Association. Report. Proceedings. Annual Meeting.* [ISSN: 0003-150X] 1881. m. Free to members. Ed(s): Laura High, Marcia Lacey. American Water Works Association, 6666 W Quincy Ave, Denver, CO 80235; custsvc@awwa.org; http://www.awwa.org. Illus., adv. Refereed. Vol. ends: Dec. Microform: PMC; PQC. *Indexed:* A22, ABIn, EngInd, FS&TA, S25. *Aud.:* Ga, Ac, Sa.

The *Journal of the American Water Works Association* is the premier journal of the American Water Works Association (AWWA). Published monthly, the journal publishes articles on new technologies and research (peer-reviewed) in the water industry, information on new regulations and contemporary practices, industry news, best practices, management, and more. Article types include research articles, interviews, case studies, forecasts, and more. This title is available in print and online (reviewed herein; ISSN 2164-4535), and online access is free to members of the AWWA. Features of the online version include online-first and most-read articles and social media–sharing options. The broad scope of coverage of this journal will appeal to researchers, managers, and operators in the field of water treatment and wastewater management. URL: www.awwa.org/publications/journal-awwa.aspx

2161. *Cold Regions Science and Technology.* [ISSN: 0165-232X] 1979. 15x/yr. EUR 1808. Ed(s): G W Timco. Elsevier BV, Radarweg 29, PO Box 211, Amsterdam, 1000 AE, Netherlands; JournalsCustomerServiceEMEA@elsevier.com; http://www.elsevier.nl. Refereed. Microform: PQC. *Indexed:* A01, A22, ApMecR, C&ISA, CerAb, EngInd, M&GPA, S25. *Aud.:* Ac, Sa.

Cold Regions Science and Technology (Elsevier URL: www.elsevier.com/ locate/coldregions) publishes original research and review articles related to the scientific and technical problems found in cold environments. Areas emphasized include applied science (physics, chemistry, mechanics of ice, ice-water, snow, and more) and related topics in earth science, materials science,

engineering, and more. Topical special issues are also published. Available in print and online, the online version (reviewed herein; ISSN 0165-232X) includes CrossMark version tracking and most-downloaded, most-cited, recent, and open-access articles. Individual articles feature linked references, citing and related articles, eReader formats, and social media–sharing options. This journal provides a venue for interdisciplinary exchange of ideas so it will appeal to a wide range of researchers, in both science and engineering (civil, mechanical, etc.).

2162. *Computer-Aided Civil and Infrastructure Engineering.* Formerly (until 1998): *Microcomputers in Civil Engineering.* [ISSN: 1093-9687] 1986. 10x/yr. GBP 1024. Ed(s): Hojjat Adeli. Wiley-Blackwell Publishing, Inc., 111 River St, Hoboken, NJ 07030; info@wiley.com; http://www.wiley.com/. Illus., adv. Sample. Refereed. Reprint: PSC. *Indexed:* A01, A22, C&ISA, CerAb, E01, EngInd, H24. *Aud.:* Ac, Sa.

Computer-Aided Civil and Infrastructure Engineering (Wiley URL: http:// onlinelibrary.wiley.com/journal/10.1111/(ISSN)1467-8667) is a top peer-reviewed civil engineering journal that bridges the disciplines of civil and infrastructure engineering and computer science and IT. It publishes papers that discuss original research, state-of-the-art reviews, novel industrial applications, and computers in education. Topics include the use of artificial intelligence, modeling, neural network computing, robotics, and more in construction, environmental, transportation infrastructure engineering, and more. Special topical issues are also published. The online version (reviewed herein; ISSN 1467-8667) features access to early-view and open-access papers, and current and previous issues. Individual articles include linked references and citing articles. A keyword tag cloud facilitates browsing papers, and social media–sharing is enabled. Readers of this journal will include civil engineers who are active in construction and infrastructure engineering, and interested in the application of computational methods in these areas.

2163. *Computers & Structures: solids, structures, fluids, multiphysics.* [ISSN: 0045-7949] 1971. 16x/yr. EUR 7603. Ed(s): B H V Topping, K J Bathe. Pergamon, The Blvd, Langford Ln, E Park, Kidlington, OX5 1GB, United Kingdom; JournalsCustomerServiceEMEA@elsevier.com; http://www.elsevier.com. Illus., adv. Sample. Refereed. Microform: PQC. *Indexed:* A01, A22, ApMecR, C&ISA, CCMJ, CerAb, CompLI, CompR, EngInd, MSN, MathR. *Aud.:* Ac, Sa.

Computers & Structures (Elsevier URL: www.journals.elsevier.com/ computers-and-structures) aims to have an impact on the advancement and use of simulations in mechanics. To do so, it publishes original research that discusses the development and use of computational methods to solve problems in engineering and the sciences. Areas of particular interest are mechanics, solids, fluids, and multiphysics. The journal seeks papers that discuss novel techniques or provide insight into important computational methods. Review papers are also accepted. Available in print and online, the online version (reviewed herein; ISSN 1879-2243) provides access to most-cited, most-downloaded, recent, and open-access articles, special issues, and related conferences. This journal will appeal to researchers in engineering and applied science who are studying the mechanics of solids and fluids.

2164. *E N R: the construction weekly.* Formerly (until 1987): *Engineering News-Record;* Which incorporated (1898-1918): *Contractor;* (in 1928): *Sanitary Engineer;* Engineering News-Record was formed by the merger of (1902-1917): *Engineering News;* Which was formerly (until 1902): *Engineering News and American Railway Journal;* (until 1888): *Engineering News and American Contract Journal;* (until 1882): *Engineering News;* (until 1875): *Engineer, Architect and Surveyor;* (until 1874): *Engineer and Surveyor;* (1910-1917): *Engineering Record;* Which was formerly (until 1910): *Engineering Record, Building Record and Sanitary Engineer;* (until 1897): *Engineering Record, Building Record & the Sanitary Engineer;* (until 1890): *Engineering & Building Record and the Sanitary Engineer;* (until 1887): *Sanitary Engineer and Construction Record;* (until 1886): *Sanitary Engineer;* (until 1880): *Plumber & Sanitary Engineer.* [ISSN: 0891-9526] 1917. w. 46/yr. USD 82 combined subscription domestic (print & online eds.); USD 89 combined subscription Canada (print & online eds.); USD 195 combined subscription elsewhere (print & online eds.). Ed(s): Janice L Tuchman,

John J Kosowatz. McGraw-Hill Construction Dodge, 2 Penn Plaza, 25th Fl, New York, NY 10121; http://www.fwdodge.com. Illus., adv. Circ: 71255 Paid. Microform: PQC. *Indexed:* A01, A22, ABIn, B01, B02, BRI, C&ISA, CerAb, EngInd. *Bk. rev.:* Number and length vary. *Aud.:* Ga, Ac, Sa.

ENR or *Engineering News Record* (McGraw-Hill URL: http://enr.construction.com/) is a "go to" trade magazine for engineers in the construction industry. *ENR* publishes construction news in areas including power and industrial, equipment, business management, environment, and more. In addition, the magazine publishes annual lists of the top contractors, design firms, construction management firms, environmental firms, and more. Regular departments include "Washington Observer," "Construction Week," "People," "Equipment Tracks," and "Trends and Construction Economics," which is a good source of materials costs, and includes construction cost and building costs indices. Available in print and online, this magazine will appeal to civil engineers, construction engineers, project managers and more. (This review is of the online version.)

2165. Earthquake Engineering & Structural Dynamics. [ISSN: 0098-8847] 1972. 15x/yr. GBP 3262. Ed(s): Anil K Chopra, Masayoshi Nakashima. John Wiley & Sons Ltd., The Atrium, Southern Gate, Chichester, PO19 8SQ, United Kingdom; customer@wiley.com; http://www.wiley.com. Illus., index, adv. Sample. Refereed. Microform: PQC. Reprint: PSC. *Indexed:* A22, ApMecR, C&ISA, CerAb, EngInd, H24, S25. *Bk. rev.:* Number and length vary. *Aud.:* Ac, Sa.

Earthquake Engineering & Structural Dynamics (Wiley URL: http://onlinelibrary.wiley.com/journal/10.1002/(ISSN)1096-9845) is the journal of the International Association for Earthquake Engineering, and it publishes original papers that focus on either research or design, and on subjects related to all aspects of earthquake engineering. The journal covers seismology, the characteristics of ground motion, wave propagation, tsunamis, behavior of structures, structural dynamics, seismic code requirements, and more. This title is available both in print and online, and the online version (reviewed herein; ISSN 1096-9845) provides easy access to "Early View," "Most Accessed," and "Most Cited" papers. Individual articles feature linked references, citation tracking, and social media–sharing options. Authors can publish their papers open-access using the "OnlineOpen" option. This journal is recommended reading for architects, engineers, researchers, and engineering faculty working in civil and mechanical engineering.

Engineering Geology. See Earth Sciences and Geology section.

2166. Environmental Science & Technology. Incorporates (1991-1993): *Environmental Buyers' Guide.* [ISSN: 0013-936X] 1967. s-m. USD 2220. Ed(s): Matt Hotze, Jerald Schnoor. American Chemical Society, 1155 16th St N W, Washington, DC 20036; help@acs.org; http://pubs.acs.org. Illus., index, adv. Sample. Refereed. *Indexed:* A01, A22, ABIn, ABS&EES, Agr, B01, BRI, C45, EngInd, ExcerpMed, FS&TA, H24, IndVet, M&GPA, OceAb, P02, RRTA, RiskAb, S25. *Bk. rev.:* Number and length vary. *Aud.:* Ac, Sa.

Environmental Science & Technology (ACS URL: http://pubs.acs.org/toc/esthag/47/9) is a peer-reviewed journal from the American Chemical Society, and it publishes original research, review, and news articles related to a variety of environmental disciplines. Research offerings include original research papers, critical reviews, policy analyses, and more. News and feature articles provide information and commentary on issues, trends, and advances in environmental science. This title is available in print and online, and the online version (reviewed herein; ISSN 1520-5851) features access to "Most Read Articles," "Articles ASAP," just-accepted manuscripts, and some open-access articles. Researchers can set up an ACS ChemWorx account (free) to save their research, and social media sharing options are available. This journal will appeal to environmental engineers and scientists, environmental researchers, policy makers, and others.

IEEE Transactions on Intelligent Transportation Systems. See Transportation section.

2167. Journal of Hydraulic Engineering (Reston). Formerly (until 1983): *American Society of Civil Engineers. Hydraulics Division. Journal;* Which superseded in part (in 1956): *American Society of Civil Engineers. Proceedings.* [ISSN: 0733-9429] 1873. m. USD 1472. Ed(s): Terry W Sturm. American Society of Civil Engineers, 1801 Alexander Bell Dr, Reston, VA 20191; http://www.asce.org. Illus., adv. Refereed. Microform: PQC. *Indexed:* A01, A22, ApMecR, BRI, C&ISA, C45, CerAb, EngInd, M&GPA, OceAb, RRTA, S25. *Aud.:* Ac, Sa.

The *Journal of Hydraulic Engineering* (ASCE URL: http://ascelibrary.org/journal/jhend8) is published by the American Society of Civil Engineers. This peer-reviewed journal publishes original, technical papers that discuss hydraulic engineering problems and their solutions, technical notes that describe a problem, and discussions of previously published papers. Case studies are also accepted. Specific topics of interest include free-surface and contained fluid flow, multiphase flow, and heat and gas transfer. This title is available in print and online (reviewed herein; ISSN 1943-7900), and the online version allows researchers to create a free account to save research, create and share lists of articles, and set up targeted search alerts of newly published research. This journal will appeal to hydraulic engineers, both researchers and practitioners alike.

Journal of Hydrology. See Earth Sciences and Geology section.

2168. Journal of Soils and Sediments: protection, risk assessment and remediation. [ISSN: 1439-0108] 2001. bi-m. EUR 420 (print & online eds.). Ed(s): Zhihong Xu, Ulrich Foerstner. Springer, Tiergartenstr 17, Heidelberg, 69121, Germany; orders-hd-individuals@springer.com; http://www.springer.com. Adv. Refereed. Circ: 2000 Paid and controlled. Reprint: PSC. *Indexed:* A22, Agr, BRI, C45, E01, OceAb, RRTA, S25. *Aud.:* Ac, Sa.

The *Journal of Soils and Sediments* (Springer URL: www.springer.com/environment/soil+science/journal/11368) publishes peer-reviewed research on contaminated, intact or disturbed, soils and sediments. Research topics of particular interest include the effects caused by disturbance and contamination of soils and sediments; strategies and technologies for prediction, prevention, and protection; treatment, remediation, and reuse; international regulation and legislation; and more. Special, topical issues are also published. This title is available both in print and online, and the online version (reviewed herein; ISSN 1614-7480) features access to open-access articles and "Online First Articles." Individual articles include linked references, related content, and supplementary material. This journal is multidisciplinary in scope. Readers will include scientists in the physical, biological, and environmental sciences; environmental engineering, waste, and remediation specialists; lawyers; and others working in academia, research, industry, government, and more.

2169. Sustainability: Science, Practice, & Policy. [ISSN: 1548-7733] 2005. s-a. Free. ProQuest, 789 E Eisenhower Pky, PO Box 1346, Ann Arbor, MI 48106; info@proquest.com; http://www.proquest.com. Refereed. *Indexed:* ABIn, C45, P61, SSA. *Bk. rev.:* Number and length vary. *Aud.:* Ac, Sa.

Sustainability: Science, Practice, & Policy (SSPP) is an online, open-access, peer-reviewed journal (Proquest URL: http://sspp.proquest.com/). It is published twice a year, and its aim is to disseminate research about new sustainability practices and to provide a venue for the cross-disciplinary discussion of scientific research, practice, and policy related to sustainability. Contributions published by the journal include research papers, policy debates, book reviews, and community essays. Recent issues have included papers on teaching sustainability, measuring sustainable development, carbon offset programs, social sustainability, and more. The journal's web site includes access to all issues of SSPP, the SSPP blog, and access to sustainability data and resources. This journal will appeal to readers in any discipline, but especially readers in the sciences, social sciences, engineering, and public policy who are interested in advancing sustainability.

2170. Water Research. Supersedes in part (in 1967): *Air and Water Pollution;* Which was formerly (until 1963): *International Journal of Air and Water Pollution;* (until 1961): *International Journal of Air Pollution.* [ISSN: 0043-1354] 1958. 20x/yr. EUR 6452. Ed(s): Mogens Henze, Mark van Loosdrecht. I W A Publishing, Alliance House, 12 Caxton St,

London, SW1H 0QS, United Kingdom; publications@iwap.co.uk; http://www.iwapublishing.com. Illus., index, adv. Sample. Refereed. Vol. ends: Dec (No. 35). Microform: MIM; PQC. *Indexed:* A01, A22, AbAn, Agr, C&ISA, C45, CerAb, EngInd, ExcerpMed, FS&TA, IndVet, OceAb, RRTA, S25. *Bk. rev.:* Number and length vary. *Aud.:* Ac, Sa.

Water Research (Elsevier URL: www.journals.elsevier.com/water-research), the journal of the International Water Association (IWA), is a leading international journal related to water quality. It publishes peer-reviewed research papers that discuss water and wastewater treatment processes, environmental restoration, modeling techniques, public health, water quality standards, and water quality analysis, using various methodologies. This title is available in print and online, and the online version (reviewed herein; ISSN 0043-1354) highlights access to special issues; related conferences; most-downloaded, most-cited, open-access, and recent articles; and videos. Individual articles include linked references, citing, and related articles. The target audience for this journal comprises researchers and practitioners in physical, biological, and environmental science and engineering who are interested in water quality, pollution management, water quality standards, and analytical techniques.

Computer, Control, and Systems Engineering

2171. *A C M Journal of Experimental Algorithmics.* [ISSN: 1084-6654] 1996. m. Free to members; Non-members, USD 199. Ed(s): Giuseppe F Italiano. Association for Computing Machinery, Inc., 2 Penn Plz, Ste 701, New York, NY 10121; acmhelp@acm.org; http://www.acm.org. Illus. Refereed. *Indexed:* C&ISA, CCMJ, CerAb, CompLI, MSN, MathR. *Aud.:* Ac, Sa.

The *ACM Journal of Experimental Algorithmics* is a peer-reviewed, online-only journal published by the Association for Computing Machinery (ACM). This journal publishes high-quality papers on experimental research on discrete algorithms and data structures. Topics of interest include: combinatorial optimization, computational biology and geometry, graph manipulation, network, design, routing and scheduling, and more. Recent papers have reported research on route planning and alternative routes, pattern matching, selection algorithms for graphics processing, and more. Selected papers from relevant ACM conferences may also be included. A unique feature on the journal's web site is free access to the JEA Research Code Repository, which archives code, data, and test files that accompanied published algorithmic papers. Alternative ways to access the journal are available through the HTTP, ftp, and ftpmail protocols. URL: www.jea.acm.org/

2172. *A C M Transactions on Computer - Human Interaction.* [ISSN: 1073-0516] 1994. q. Free to members; Non-members, USD 180. Ed(s): Shumin Zhai. Association for Computing Machinery, Inc., 2 Penn Plz, Ste 701, New York, NY 10121; acmhelp@acm.org; http://www.acm.org. Refereed. *Indexed:* A22, ABIn, C&ISA, CerAb, CompLI, CompR, EngInd, ErgAb, PsycInfo. *Aud.:* Ac, Sa.

ACM Transactions on Computer-Human Interaction is a multidisciplinary journal devoted to interactive system design and development. Published quarterly, the journal publishes high-quality contributions related to the creation of effective human–computer interfaces for many purposes. Topics of interest include the human aspects of interaction with computers, software and hardware architectures, iterative techniques and evaluation, processes of user interface design, and individual users and groups of users. The online version (reviewed herein; ISSN 1557-7325) is available through the ACM Digital Library (URL: http://dl.acm.org/citation.cfm?id=J756&picked=prox) and provides access to current and previous issues, special topical issues, linked references, citation tracking, article metrics, and social media sharing options. This journal is recommended for researchers studying human–computer interaction in information systems, artificial intelligence, software engineering, and other disciplines. ACM URL: http://tochi.acm.org/

2173. *Artificial Intelligence.* [ISSN: 0004-3702] 1970. 18x/yr. EUR 2887. Ed(s): A G Cohn. Elsevier BV, Radarweg 29, PO Box 211, Amsterdam, 1000 AE, Netherlands; JournalsCustomerServiceEMEA@elsevier.com; http://www.elsevier.com. Illus., adv. Refereed. Microform: PQC. *Indexed:* A01, A22, C&ISA, CCMJ, CerAb, CompLI, CompR, EngInd, MSN, MathR. *Aud.:* Ac, Sa.

Artificial Intelligence (Elsevier URL: www.journals.elsevier.com/artificial-intelligence/) is the foremost research publication in the world devoted to artificial intelligence (AI). This peer-reviewed journal publishes papers that contain current research results, discussions of systems or architectures integrating multiple technologies, and applications of AI. Specific topics of interest include: artificial intelligence and philosophy, cognitive aspects of artificial intelligence, heuristic search, computer vision, machine learning, and others. Annually, the journal publishes a volume of survey articles and hosts a report of results from AI competitions. Special, topical issues are also published. The online version (reviewed herein; ISSN 1872-7921) features access to most-downloaded, most-cited, recent, and open-access articles. This journal will appeal to a variety of readers including applied and theoretical researchers in artificial intelligence specialists, computer scientists, cognitive scientists, psychologists, and more.

Association for Computing Machinery. Journal. See Computers and Information Technology/Professional Journals section.

2174. *Automatica (Online).* [ISSN: 1873-2836] m. Ed(s): T Basar. Pergamon, The Blvd, Langford Ln, E Park, Kidlington, OX5 1GB, United Kingdom; JournalsCustomerServiceEMEA@elsevier.com; http://www.elsevier.com. *Bk. rev.:* Number and length vary. *Aud.:* Ac, Sa.

Automatica (Elsevier URL: www.journals.elsevier.com/automatica/), a publication of the International Federation of Automatic Control (IFAC), is a well-regarded, peer-reviewed research journal in the area of control systems. It publishes original theoretical or experimental research that reports on R&D in control systems. Research topics cover a broad spectrum, and include: theory and design of control systems and components, distributed control, adaptive control, system reliability, fault detection, fuzzy and expert systems, computers for control systems in industrial processes such as aircraft, traffic, power systems, agriculture, and more. Papers include review, research and tutorial papers, brief papers, technical communiques, and book and software reviews. Special, topical issues are also published. The online version (reviewed herein; ISSN 1873-2836) includes access to most-downloaded, most-cited, open-access, and recent articles, and special issues. Individual articles include citing and related articles, linked references, and CrossMark version tracking. Social media sharing and eReader formats also available. This publication is recommended for researchers and practitioners in control engineering in any industry sector.

2175. *Control Engineering: covering control, instrumentation, and automation systems worldwide.* [ISSN: 0010-8049] 1954. m. Free to qualified personnel. C F E Media, 1111 W. 22nd St., Ste.250, Oak Brook, IL 60523; http://www.cfemedia.com/. Illus., adv. Sample. Circ: 157289. *Indexed:* A01, A22, ABIn, B01, B02, B03, BRI, C&ISA, C42, CEA, CerAb, EngInd. *Bk. rev.:* Number and length vary. *Aud.:* Ga, Ac, Sa.

Control Engineering (CFE Media URL: www.controleng.com/) is an important trade magazine that covers news, new products, information systems, software and hardware, standards, and other topics of interest to control engineers. Non-English editions are also available on the web site. The digital edition (reviewed herein; ISSN 2163-4076) offers free access to the full text of magazine articles and provides social media–sharing options. Articles may contain color illustrations and figures, embedded videos, and references to web sites for related industry organizations and additional information. Recent issues have included articles on industry news and events, safety and risk management, PLC software, energy management, industrial wireless components, robots, asset management, and more. Case studies, regular editorials, and columns are also included. Industry-related display advertising is accepted. This engaging publication is recommended reading for control engineers in any manufacturing industry using control instrumentation and automatic systems.

2176. *I E E E Transactions on Fuzzy Systems.* [ISSN: 1063-6706] 1993. bi-m. USD 1750; USD 2050 combined subscription (print & online eds.). Ed(s): Chin-Teng Lin. Institute of Electrical and Electronics Engineers, 445 Hoes Ln, Piscataway, NJ 08854; contactcenter@ieee.org; http://www.ieee.org. Adv. Refereed. *Indexed:* A22, C&ISA, CerAb, CompLI, EngInd, M&GPA. *Aud.:* Ac, Sa.

IEEE Transactions on Fuzzy Systems (IEEE URL: http://ieeexplore.ieee.org/servlet/opac?punumber=91) is published bimonthly by the IEEE Computational Intelligence Society. This peer-reviewed journal covers the theoretical foundations, design, and applications of fuzzy systems in fields including aerospace, power generation, signal processing and analysis, transportation, and more. Recent papers discussed computational modeling, stochastic systems, fault tolerant control, fuzzy neural models, fuzzy cognitive maps, and more. The online version (reviewed herein; ISSN 1063-6706) highlights latest-published, popular, and early-access papers. Linked references, citation tracking, and article metrics are also provided for individual papers. This journal will appeal to systems engineers and researchers interested in the development and application of fuzzy systems in a variety of fields.

2177. I S A Transactions. [ISSN: 0019-0578] 1961. 4x/yr. EUR 496. Ed(s): R R Rhinehart. Elsevier Inc., 360 Park Ave S, New York, NY 10010; usinfo-f@elsevier.com; http://www.elsevier.com. Illus., index, adv. Sample. Refereed. Microform: PQC. *Indexed:* A22, EngInd, H24, RiskAb. *Aud.:* Ac, Sa.

ISA Transactions (Elsevier URL: www.journals.elsevier.com/isa-transactions/), a journal of the International Society of Automation (ISA), is a peer-reviewed publication that focuses on the state-of-the-art and advances in automation and measurement. It publishes papers on automation and measurement research, practice and applications, tutorials and reviews, technical notes, and more; special topical issues are also published. Topics covered include measurement, signal processing, filtering, data compression and rectification, and automation system reliability, quality, maintenance management, and more. Papers discussing equipment and techniques that support measurement and automation are also published. The online version (reviewed herein) features access to special issues and most-cited and recent articles. Individual articles provide access to citing, related articles, and reference works. This journal will appeal to researchers and practitioners in academia and industry who are interested in automation and measurement.

2178. The Journal of Artificial Intelligence Research. [ISSN: 1076-9757] 1993. 2x/yr. USD 90 vol.40. Ed(s): Adnan Darwiche, Dr. Steven Minton. A A A I Press, 445 Burgess Dr, Ste 100, Menlo Park, CA 94025; info@aaai.org; http://www.aaai.org. Illus., adv. Refereed. *Indexed:* CCMJ, EngInd, MSN, MathR. *Aud.:* Ac, Sa.

The Journal of Artificial Intelligence Research (*JAIR*) is a peer-reviewed, open-access journal published by the Association for the Advancement of Artificial Intelligence (AAAI). *JAIR* publishes research articles, survey articles, and technical notes related to all areas of artificial intelligence. All articles published by the journal are freely available on the *JAIR* web site (http://www.jair.org/) or can be purchased in print from the AAAI Press. Online versions are published as soon as the final copy is received from the author. The web site also features recently published research and survey articles. *JAIR* issues three volumes per year and authors are encouraged to include data appendices for posting online with their final papers. Recent volumes included papers on Bayesian network structure learning, modeling numeric resource flows, multi-agent systems, intersection management in urban road networks, and more. This journal will appeal to researchers who are investigating the use of artificial intelligence to solve problems in many different fields.

2179. Journal of Graph Algorithms and Applications. [ISSN: 1526-1719] 1997. a. Free. Ed(s): Roberto Tamassia, Ioannis G Tollis. Brown University, Department of Computer Science, 115 Waterman St, 4th Fl, PO Box 1910, Providence, RI 02912; dept@cs.brown.edu; http://www.cs.brown.edu. Illus. Refereed. *Indexed:* CCMJ, MSN, MathR. *Aud.:* Ac, Sa.

The *Journal of Graph Algorithms and Applications* is a refereed, gold open-access publication that strives to publish high-quality research related to the design and analysis of graph algorithms, and experiences with and applications of graph and network algorithms (http://jgaa.info/index.jsp; ISSN 1526-1719). Regular and concise research papers, as well as survey papers, are published online with no authors' fees. The journal's web site features free access to current and past volumes of the journal (varying number of issues), recently published papers, lists of editors and journal advisors, news, and more. Authors are encouraged to add appendices (including animations, corrections, examples,

implementations, and more) to their articles after online pbulication. Areas of application for the research published include social networks, bioinformatics, software engineering, VLSI Circuits, economic networks, databases, computer systems, and more.

Robotics and Autonomous Systems. See Robotics section.

2180. Systems Engineering: the journal of the International Council on Systems Engineering. [ISSN: 1098-1241] 1998. q. GBP 623. Ed(s): Andrew P Sage. John Wiley & Sons, Inc., 111 River St, MS 4-02, Hoboken, NJ 07030; info@wiley.com; http://www.wiley.com/WileyCDA/. Adv. Refereed. Reprint: PSC. *Indexed:* A01, C&ISA, CerAb, EngInd. *Aud.:* Ac, Sa.

Systems Engineering is published quarterly by the International Council on System Engineering (INCOSE) and is available online through Wiley (URL: http://onlinelibrary.wiley.com/journal/10.1002/(ISSN)1520-6858). This peer-reviewed journal is an important source of multidisciplinary information related to systems engineering, and product and process management and services. Recent issues included research articles or case studies on system dynamics, strategic requirements engineering, simulation of human–robot teams, complex adaptive systems, system-of-systems acquisition, requirements management, and more. The online version (reviewed herein; ISSN 1520-6858) features early-view articles, citation tracking, and linked references. This publication is recommended for systems engineers, systems programmers, and computer system developers.

Electrical Engineering

The Institute of Electrical and Electronics Engineers (IEEE) publications are core to any engineering collection, and are among the most highly cited journals in engineering. This society produces technical periodicals, conference papers, standards, reports, tutorials, and other specialized publications. The flagship journal, *Proceedings of the IEEE* [0018-9219], is a monthly that presents papers that have broad significance and long-range interest in all areas of electrical, electronics, and computer engineering. The *Index to IEEE Publications* is an annual publication that indexes by author and subject all the publications of the society. All of the content mentioned here can be found in the full-text, subscription-based electronic product called IEEE Xplore. Check for current products at http://shop.ieee.org/store.

2181. I E E E Network: the magazine of global internetworking. [ISSN: 0890-8044] 1987. bi-m. USD 580; USD 695 combined subscription (print & online eds.). Ed(s): Ioanis Nikolaidis. Institute of Electrical and Electronics Engineers, 445 Hoes Ln, Piscataway, NJ 08854; contactcenter@ieee.org; http://www.ieee.org. Illus., adv. Vol. ends: No. 6. *Indexed:* A01, A22, B01, BRI, C&ISA, CerAb, CompLI, EngInd, P02. *Bk. rev.:* Number and length vary. *Aud.:* Ga, Ac, Sa.

IEEE Network (IEEE URL: http://ieeexplore.ieee.org/servlet/opac?punumber= 65) is a scholarly journal devoted to disseminating information and discussion of new ideas on networks (protocols, architecture, control, implementation), protocol development and validation, and more. This title is published six times a year by the IEEE Communications Society, and the online version (reviewed herein; ISSN 1558-156X) provides access to current and past issues, latest-published, and popular articles. Special issues are published, and recent topics include video over mobile networks, computer network visualization, and wire and wireless network virtualization. Brief book and multimedia reviews, and guest editorials, are also published. This journal is recommended for computer and electrical engineers and IT professionals in academia and industry.

2182. I E E E Transactions on Antennas and Propagation. Former titles (until 1963): *I R E Transactions on Antennas and Propagation;* (until 1955): *I R E Professional Group on Antennas. Transactions.* [ISSN: 0018-926X] 1952. m. USD 1665; USD 2000 combined subscription (print & online eds.). Ed(s): Michael A Jensen. Institute of Electrical and Electronics Engineers, 445 Hoes Ln, Piscataway, NJ 08854; contactcenter@ieee.org; http://www.ieee.org. Illus., adv. Refereed. *Indexed:* A01, A22, B01, BRI, C&ISA, CCMJ, CerAb, CompLI, EngInd, M&GPA, MSN, MathR. *Aud.:* Ac, Sa.

IEEE Transactions on Antennas and Propagation (IEEE URL: http://ieeexplore.ieee.org/servlet/opac?punumber=8) is a leading international journal, and publishes peer-reviewed papers that report on experimental and theoretical research on antennas and electromagnetic wave propagation. Shorter communications are also accepted. Specific topics of interest include design and development of antennas, wave scattering and diffraction, remote sensing, applied optics, space-based communication, and more. The online version (reviewed herein; ISSN 1558-2221) includes access to current and past issues; early-access, latest-published, and popular articles; article metrics; citation tracking; and linked references. Special issues are also published. The intended audience for this journal is academic and industry researchers in electrical engineering and telecommunications.

2183. *I E E E Transactions on Pattern Analysis and Machine Intelligence.* [ISSN: 0162-8828] 1979. m. Ed(s): Ramin Zabih. Institute of Electrical and Electronics Engineers, 445 Hoes Ln, Piscataway, NJ 08854; contactcenter@ieee.org; http://www.ieee.org. Adv. *Indexed:* A01, A22, B01, C&ISA, CerAb, CompLI, CompR, EngInd. *Aud.:* Ac, Sa.

IEEE Transactions on Pattern Analysis and Machine Intelligence (IEEE URL http://ieeexplore.ieee.org/servlet/opac?punumber=34) is published monthly by the IEEE Computer Society, and is a peer-reviewed research journal that covers important research in computer vision and pattern analysis. This highly-cited journal publishes both short and long research papers on topics that include computer vision, image understanding, pattern analysis and recognition, machine learning, medical image analysis, face and gesture recognition, search techniques, and more. The online edition (reviewed herein; ISSN 1939-3539) provides access to most-popular, latest, and early-access articles; and to article downloads and citation tracking. Special, topical issues are also published. Non-subscribers can search the journal (www.computer.org/portal/web/tpami), read abstracts of papers, and purchase papers if necessary. This journal will appeal to researchers working in the area of artificial intelligence.

2184. *I E E E Transactions on Power Systems.* Supersedes in part (in 1986): *I E E E Transactions on Power Apparatus and Systems;* Which was formed by the merger of (1952-1963): *American Institute of Electrical Engineers. Transactions on Power Apparatus and Systems. Part 3;* Which superseded in part (1952): *American Institute of Electrical Engineers. Transactions;* (1952-1963): *Power Apparatus and Systems.* [ISSN: 0885-8950] 1986. q. USD 1260; USD 1515 combined subscription (print & online eds.). Ed(s): Antonio J Conejo. Institute of Electrical and Electronics Engineers, 445 Hoes Ln, Piscataway, NJ 08854; contactcenter@ieee.org; http://www.ieee.org. Adv. *Indexed:* A01, A22, B01, C&ISA, CerAb, EngInd, M&GPA. *Aud.:* Ac, Sa.

IEEE Transactions on Power Systems (IEEE URL: http://ieeexplore.ieee.org/servlet/opac?punumber=59) is a scholarly journal that covers many facets of the electric power-generation industry, including requirements, planning, analysis, operation, transmission, and more. This title is published six times per year by the IEEE Power & Energy Society, and the online version (reviewed herein; ISSN 1558-0679) features access to current and past issues; early-access, latest-published, and popular articles; article metrics; citation tracking; and linked references. Recent articles discussed simulation modeling for long-term capacity investment, merger analysis in wholesale power markets, photovoltaic systems, power system stability, power generation planning, adaptation modeling, and more. Readers of this publication will include electrical engineers, planners, and economists working in the electric generation sector.

2185. *I E E E Wireless Communications Magazine.* Formerly (until 2002): *I E E E Personal Communications.* [ISSN: 1536-1284] 1994. bi-m. USD 670; USD 825 combined subscription (print & online eds.). Ed(s): Hsiao-Hwa Chen. Institute of Electrical and Electronics Engineers, 445 Hoes Ln, Piscataway, NJ 08854; contactcenter@ieee.org; http://www.ieee.org. Adv. *Indexed:* A22, C&ISA, CerAb, EngInd. *Bk. rev.:* Number and length vary. *Aud.:* Ga, Ac, Sa.

IEEE Wireless Communications Magazine (IEEE URL: www.comsoc.org/wirelessmag) is published by the IEEE Communications Society, and is not to be confused with the research journal *IEEE Transactions on Wireless Communications* [ISSN 1536-1276]. *Wireless Communications Magazine* [ISSN 1536-1284] covers all technical and policy areas related to wireless communications including mobile phones, protocols, messaging, personalized

traffic filtering, and more. Recent articles have discussed cognitive cellular networks, multi-cellular cooperation, remote health monitoring, personal satellite communication, and more. Policy issues discussed may include spectrum allocation, industry structure, and evolution of technology. Published bimonthly, the journal includes contributed articles, book reviews, research literature scans, and special topical issues. The online version (reviewed herein; ISSN 1558-0687) provides access to latest-published and popular articles, and current and past issues of the magazine. This magazine is recommended for researchers, practitioners, and policy makers working on wireless communication applications and issues.

Institute of Electrical and Electronics Engineers. Proceedings. See Electronics section.

2186. *International Journal of Wireless Information Networks.* Formerly (until 1994): *International Journal of Wireless Communication.* [ISSN: 1068-9605] 1994. q. EUR 683 (print & online eds.). Ed(s): Kaveh Pahlavan. Springer New York LLC, 233 Spring St, New York, NY 10013; service-ny@springer.com; http://www.springer.com/. Adv. Sample. Refereed. Reprint: PSC. *Indexed:* A01, A22, CompLI, E01, EngInd. *Aud.:* Ac, Sa.

The *International Journal of Wireless Information Networks* (Springer URL: www.springer.com/engineering/electronics/journal/10776) is a peer-reviewed research journal that focuses on wireless information networks. It publishes submissions on various types of information networks, including sensor, mobile ad-hoc, and wireless LANs; performance prediction modeling; security and privacy concerns; and more. Recent papers have discussed wireless technologies in health care, localization technologies, intrusion detection, modeling techniques, and more. Paper types published include invited openings, overview reports, technical (research) papers, and letters. Special topical issues are also published. The online version (reviewed herein; ISSN 1572-8129) features access to latest, online-first, and open-access articles; links to related content; supplementary material (if available); and linked references. Social media–sharing options are available. This journal will be read by telecommunications and network researchers at universities and research laboratories, engineers working in the field, and members of the technical community.

2187. *Neural Networks.* [ISSN: 0893-6080] 1988. 10x/yr. EUR 2262. Ed(s): Deliang Wang, Kenji Doya. Pergamon, The Blvd, Langford Ln, E Park, Kidlington, OX5 1GB, United Kingdom. Illus. Sample. Refereed. Microform: PQC. *Indexed:* A01, A22, C&ISA, CompLI, CompR, EngInd, ExcerpMed, PsycInfo, RILM. *Bk. rev.:* Number and length vary. *Aud.:* Ac, Sa.

Neural Networks (Elsevier URL: www.journals.elsevier.com/neural-networks/) is the official journal of the International Neural Network Society, European Neural Network Society, and the Japanese Neural Network Society. This peer-reviewed journal publishes original research papers, covering the complete scope of neural networks, that are assigned to specific sections: "Cognitive Science," "Neuroscience," "Learning Systems," "Mathematical and Computational Analysis," and "Engineering and Applications." The online version (reviewed herein; ISSN 1879-2782) highlights special issues; recent, most-downloaded, and most-cited articles; and related conferences. Authors can publish their articles open-access. Individual articles provide access to citing and related articles, related reference works; downloading in eReader format may be available. The broad scope of this international journal will attract neural network researchers from many fields including psychology, neurobiology, engineering, mathematics, and more.

2188. *Optical Engineering.* Former titles (until 1972): *S P I E Journal;* (until 1962): *S P I E Newsletter.* [ISSN: 0091-3286] m. USD 1175 (print & online eds.). Ed(s): Dr. Ron C Driggers. S P I E - International Society for Optical Engineering, 1000 20th St, Bellingham, WA 98225; spie@spie.org; http://spie.org. Illus., index, adv. Refereed. Circ: 9000 Controlled. *Indexed:* A01, A22, C&ISA, CerAb, EngInd, PhotoAb. *Bk. rev.:* Number and length vary. *Aud.:* Ac, Sa.

Optical Engineering (SPIE URL: http://spie.org/x867.xml) is a publication of the International Society for Optics and Photonics (SPIE). Published monthly, this journal focuses on optical science and engineering and practical applications. Specific topics generally fall into one of the following areas: "Imaging Components, Systems and Processing"; "Instrumentation, Techniques and Measurement"; "Optical Design and Engineering"; "Lasers, Fiber Optics, and Communications"; and "Materials, Photonic Devices and Sensors." Papers that discuss emerging technologies and applications are also of interest. The journal publishes research papers, letters, tutorials, and reviews. The online edition (reviewed herein; ISSN 1560-2303) highlights top downloaded and featured articles. Individual articles feature access to related journal and proceedings articles and related book chapters. Authors can opt to publish their research open-access. Readers of this journal will be from many different fields, including electrical and biomedical engineering, telecommunications, physics, astronomy, and more.

Progress in Quantum Electronics. See Electronics section.

2189. *S I A M Journal on Imaging Sciences.* [ISSN: 1936-4954] 2008. q. USD 353. Ed(s): Jean-Michel Morel. Society for Industrial and Applied Mathematics, 3600 Market St, 6th Fl, Philadelphia, PA 19104; siam@siam.org; http://www.siam.org. Sample. Refereed. *Indexed:* MSN. *Aud.:* Ac, Sa.

The *SIAM Journal on Imaging Sciences* (SIAM URL: www.siam.org/journals/siims.php) is a peer-reviewed, online-only research journal that covers all areas of imaging science. The journal seeks innovative papers on both applications and the fundamentals of the field related to image formation, image processing, image analysis, image interpretation, computer graphics and visualization, and more. It includes access to current and past issues, issues in progress, recently published and most-read articles, and CrossRef linking of references. Readers can create a free account that they can use to save research and citations, and track citations. Readers of this journal will include engineers and scientists in a variety of fields who are researching the applications of imaging science.

Semiconductor Science and Technology. See Electronics section.

Industrial and Manufacturing Engineering

2190. *Computers & Industrial Engineering.* [ISSN: 0360-8352] 1977. m. EUR 3672. Ed(s): Mohamed Dessouky. Pergamon, The Blvd, Langford Ln, E Park, Kidlington, OX5 1GB, United Kingdom; JournalsCustomerServiceEMEA@elsevier.com; http://www.elsevier.com. Illus., adv. Sample. Refereed. Microform: PQC. *Indexed:* A22, ABIn, B01, B02, B03, C&ISA, CerAb, CompLI, CompR, EngInd, ErgAb. *Bk. rev.:* Number and length vary. *Aud.:* Ac, Sa.

Computers & Industrial Engineering (Pergamon URL: www.journals.elsevier.com/computers-and-industrial-engineering/) provides an international forum for the exchange of ideas among industrial engineers. The journal publishes peer-reviewed research about the development and application of new computerized methodologies for solving industrial engineering problems. Topics discussed in recently published papers include material handling systems, data-driven modeling, team formation, robotic cellular manufacturing systems, integrated production systems, product line optimization, and more. The online version (reviewed herein; ISSN 1879-0550) features access to most-downloaded, most-cited, recent, and open-access articles, calls for papers, and access to special issues. Social media–sharing options are available. Article features include access to citing and related articles, linked references, and downloadable eReader format versions. Academic researchers, faculty, and practitioners of industrial engineering in many sectors will find many useful papers in this journal.

2191. *I E E E Transactions on Components, Packaging and Manufacturing Technology.* Formed by the merger of (1999-2011): *I E E E Transactions on Advanced Packaging;* Which was formerly (until 1999): *I E E E Transactions on Components, Packaging and Manufacturing Technology, Part B: Advanced Packaging;* Which superseded in part (in 1994): *I E E E Transactions on Components, Hybrids and Manufacturing Technology;* Which was formed by the merger of (1972-1978): *I E E E Transactions on Manufacturing Technology;* (1971-1978): *I E E E Transactions on Parts, Hybrids, and Packaging;* Which was formerly (until 1971): *I E E E Transactions on*

Parts, Materials and Packaging; Which was formed by the merger of (1963-1965): *I E E E Transactions on Product Engineering and Production;* Which was formerly (until 1963): *I R E Transactions on Product Engineering and Production;* (until 1961): *I R E Transactions on Production Techniques;* (1963-1965): *I E E E Transactions on Component Parts;* Which was formerly (until 1963): *I R E Transactions on Component Parts;* (until 1955): *I R E Professional Group on Component Parts. Transactions;* (1999-2011): *I E E E Transactions on Components and Packaging Technologies;* (1999-2011): *I E E E Transactions on Electronics Packaging Manufacturing.* [ISSN: 2156-3950] 2011. bi-m. USD 1365; USD 1640 combined subscription (print & online eds.). Institute of Electrical and Electronics Engineers, 445 Hoes Ln, Piscataway, NJ 08854; contactcenter@ieee.org; http://www.ieee.org. Adv. Refereed. *Indexed:* A01, A22, B01, C&ISA, CerAb, EngInd. *Aud.:* Ac, Sa.

Published monthly by the IEEE Components, Packaging and Manufacturing Technology Society, *IEEE Transactions on Components, Packaging and Manufacturing Technology* (IEEE URL: http://ieeexplore.ieee.org/servlet/opac?punumber=5503870) publishes papers that report developments related to the design, modeling, and analysis of electronic, photonic, and MEMS packaging, as well as developments in passive components, thermal management, device reliability, electronics parts manufacture, and more. Application areas covered include aerospace, communication, networking and broadcast, computer hardware/software, photonics and electro-optics, robotics and control systems, and more. The online version (reviewed herein; ISSN 2156-3950) provides readers with access to recent, most-popular, and early-access articles. Individual papers include linked references, citation tracking, article metrics, and links to related content (in IEEE Xplore).

Industry Week. See Business and Finance/General section.

2192. *International Journal of Machine Tools and Manufacture: design, research & application.* Formerly (until 1987): *International Journal of Machine Tool Design and Research;* Which superseded: *Advances in Machine Tool Design and Research.* [ISSN: 0890-6955] 1961. 12x/yr. EUR 3703. Ed(s): T A Dean. Elsevier Inc., 360 Park Ave S, New York, NY 10010; JournalCustomerService-usa@elsevier.com; http://www.elsevier.com. Illus., adv. Sample. Refereed. Circ: 1000 Paid and controlled. Microform: PQC. *Indexed:* A01, A22, ApMecR, BrTechI, C&ISA, CerAb, EngInd. *Aud.:* Ac, Sa.

The *International Journal of Machine Tools and Manufacture* (www.journals.elsevier.com/international-journal-of-machine-tools-and-manufacture/) publishes peer-reviewed research that discusses significant advances to the current state-of-the-art in manufacturing engineering. Topics covered by the journal include the essential mechanics of processes, e.g., material removal and deformation, performance of machine tools, tool design and reliability, micromanufacture, and more. Research on other areas of process science or manufacturing will be considered. Features of the online version (reviewed herein; ISSN 1879-2170) include access to recent, most-popular, most-cited, and open-access articles, and special issues. Individual articles include citing and related article information, social media–sharing, and eReader formats for download. Because this journal covers both the research and its applications, it will appeal to both researchers and practitioners in industrial and manufacturing engineering.

2193. *Journal of Manufacturing Processes.* [ISSN: 1526-6125] 1999. q. EUR 443. Ed(s): S G Kapoor. Elsevier Ltd, 32 Jamestown Rd, Camden, London, NW1 7BY, United Kingdom; corporate.sales@elsevier.com; http://www.elsevier.com. Adv. Refereed. *Indexed:* ABIn. *Aud.:* Ac, Sa.

The *Journal of Manufacturing Processes* (Elsevier URL: www.journals.elsevier.com/journal-of-manufacturing-processes/) is a quarterly publication of the Society of Manufacturing Engineers (SME), and it publishes original research and reviews that focus on the current and future state of research that advance the state-of-the-art in manufacturing processes. Recently, nano- and micro-scale manufacturing have become more important, and this is reflected in the scope of the journal. Topics of particular interest include fabrication at the meso, micro, and nano scales; advanced manufacturing processes; rapid prototyping; process modeling and simulation; tribology; and more. The online version (reviewed herein; ISSN 2212-4616) highlights special, topical issues on emerging technology, and most-cited and recent articles. Individual articles include color illustrations, information about citing and related articles, eReader format downloads, social media–sharing, and linked references.

2194. *Journal of Manufacturing Systems.* [ISSN: 0278-6125] 1982. q. EUR 827. Ed(s): S J Hu. Elsevier Ltd, 32 Jamestown Rd, Camden, London, NW1 7BY, United Kingdom; corporate.sales@elsevier.com; http://www.elsevier.com. Illus., index, adv. Sample. Refereed. *Indexed:* A22, ABIn, ApMecR, B01, EngInd. *Aud.:* Ac, Sa.

Published quarterly by the Society of Manufacturing Engineers (SME), the *Journal of Manuacturing Systems* (Elsevier URL: www.journals.elsevier.com/journal-of-manufacturing-systems/) seeks to publish original research on state-of-of-the art basic and applied research of manufacturing at the systems level. In addition, papers discussing the design of novel manufacturing systems, or those addressing global challenges in manufacturing systems, are also sought. Specific topics covered by this peer-reviewed journal include manufacturing strategy, sustainable manufacturing, quality management, control and information systems, micro- and nano-manufacturing systems, and more. Features of the online version (reviewed herein; ISSN 1878-6642) include access to special issues, most-downloaded, most-cited, and recent articles. Individual articles include color illustrations, citing and related articles, linked references, eReader format downloads, and social media–sharing.

2195. *Journal of Quality Technology: a quarterly journal of methods, applications and related topics.* Supersedes in part (in 1968): *Industrial Quality Control.* [ISSN: 0022-4065] 1944. q. Members, USD 30; Non-members, USD 45. Ed(s): Enrique Del Castillo. American Society for Quality, 600 North Plankinton Ave, P O Box 3005, Milwaukee, WI 53203; help@asq.org; http://www.asq.org. Illus., index, adv. Refereed. Circ: 22000. Reprint: PSC. *Indexed:* A22, ABIn, B01, C&ISA, CerAb, EngInd, FS&TA. *Bk. rev.:* Number and length vary. *Aud.:* Ga, Ac, Sa.

The *Journal of Quality Technology* (ASQ URL: http://asq.org/pub/jqt/) is a peer-reviewed publication from the American Society for Quality (ASQ). This journal publishes research articles, case studies, book reviews, and letters to the editor that focus on the application of statistical methods to quality control, reliability, and related topics. Recent articles have discussed the use of finite element models in micromachining; application of analytical methods including Bayesian, Markov, and conjoint analyses; Monte Carlo simulation; product design; statistical process control; and more. The online version reviewed herein (available through ProQuest) provides access to linked references, related articles, and options for tagging articles. Researchers can create a free account to save their results or create tags. This journal will appeal to researchers and engineers who are interested in the use of statistical methods and mathematical models to advance quality control in manufacturing and industry.

2196. *Manufacturing Engineering.* Former titles (until 1975): *Manufacturing Engineering and Management;* (until 1970): *Tool and Manufacturing Engineer;* (until 1960): *Tool Engineer;* (until 1935): *American Society of Tool Engineers. Journal.* [ISSN: 0361-0853] 1932. m. Free to members; Non-members, USD 12. Ed(s): James D Destefani, Brian J Hogan. Society of Manufacturing Engineers, One SME Dr, PO Box 930, Dearborn, MI 48121; service@sme.org; http://www.sme.org. Illus., adv. Circ: 102500 Controlled. Microform: PQC. *Indexed:* A22, ABIn, ApMecR, B01, C&ISA, CerAb, EngInd. *Bk. rev.:* Number and length vary. *Aud.:* Ga, Ac, Sa.

Manufacturing Engineering is a monthly trade journal published by the Society of Manufacturing Engineers (SME). Free subscriptions to the print and digital editions are available at the magazine's web site (SME URL: www.sme.org/manufacturingengineering/). Recent articles discussed issues and trends in manufacturing; advances in manufacturing processes and technologies; additive manufacturing; productivity and efficiency enhancement; workforce development; micromanufacturing; manufacturing statistics and forecasts; automation; and more. Regular departments include "Newsdesk," "Tech Front," and "Product Previews." In addition, "Shop Solutions" provides case histories. The SME web site version of the magazine contains additional content (special

reports, videos, and more). With its practical focus, this magazine will be most useful to manufacturing engineers and managers who are active in any manufacturing sector. (Note: This magazine is also available through ProQuest.)

2197. *Packaging Technology and Science.* [ISSN: 0894-3214] 1988. 8x/yr. GBP 1341. Ed(s): David Shires, Diana Twede. John Wiley & Sons Ltd., The Atrium, Southern Gate, Chichester, PO19 8SQ, United Kingdom; customer@wiley.com; http://www.wiley.com. Adv. Sample. Refereed. Microform: PQC. Reprint: PSC. *Indexed:* A22, C&ISA, C45, CerAb, EngInd, FS&TA, H24. *Aud.:* Ac, Sa.

Packaging Technology and Science (Wiley URL: http://onlinelibrary.wiley.com/journal/10.1002/(ISSN)1099-1522) publishes peer-reviewed research and review articles on developments in packaging and packaging research. Areas of interest include research related to the packaging of food, medical products, machinery and machine tools, and chemicals and hazardous substances, as well as packaging materials, packaging machinery, new manufacturing processes, and more. The online version (reviewed herein; ISSN 1099-1522) provides access to early-view, most-accessed, most-cited, and open-access articles. Individual articles have linked references, citation tracking, and social media–sharing options. The journal, affiliated with the International Association of Packaging Research Institutes (IAPRI), also publishes selected papers from the IAPRI annual conferences. Due to its broad scope, this journal will appeal to researchers and practitioners in many different areas, including packaging engineers, food scientists, polymer and material scientists, toxicologists, environmental scientists, regulatory officials, and more.

2198. *Plant Engineering: the problem-solving resource for plant engineers.* [ISSN: 0032-082X] 1947. m. Free to qualified personnel. C F E Media, 1111 W. 22nd St., Ste.250, Oak Brook, IL 60523; http://www.cfemedia.com/. Illus., adv. Sample. Circ: 90063. *Indexed:* A01, A22, ABIn, B01, B02, BRI, C&ISA, CEA, CerAb, H24. *Bk. rev.:* Number and length vary. *Aud.:* Ga, Ac, Sa.

The trade magazine *Plant Engineering* (CFE Media URL: www.plantengineering.com/) is available to readers via a free print or online subscription. The web site version (reviewed herein; ISSN 1558-2957) provides full-text access to current and past issues of the magazine. Recent articles discussed counterfeit electrical parts, process safety, additive manufacturing, OSHA inspections, filter cleaning technologies, lean manufacturing, energy management, and more. Regular departments include "InFocus," "InPractice," "Electrical Solutions," and "Automation Solutions." Other features of the magazine's web site include access to industry news, blogs, related content links, a media library, and a case-study database for sharing solutions to plant problems. Social media–sharing options are provided. This publication will appeal to industrial plant managers and engineers in many different manufacturing sectors. (Note: This magazine is also available through aggregators including ProQuest, EBSCO, and DowJones.)

2199. *Quality Progress.* Supersedes in part (in 1968): *Industrial Quality Control.* [ISSN: 0033-524X] 1944. m. Members, USD 55; Non-members, USD 80. American Society for Quality, 600 North Plankinton Ave, P O Box 3005, Milwaukee, WI 53203; help@asq.org; http://www.asq.org. Illus., index, adv. Circ: 80374. Reprint: PSC. *Indexed:* A01, A22, ABIn, B01, B02, BRI, C&ISA. *Bk. rev.:* Number and length vary. *Aud.:* Ga, Ac, Sa.

Quality Progress (ASQ URL: www.asq.org/qualityprogress/index.html) is the membership magazine of the American Society for Quality (ASQ) and is available to subscribers on the ASQ web site as well through aggregators including ProQuest and EBSCO. This monthly publication includes feature articles, regular columns, and departments ("Standards Outlook," "Statistics Roundtable," "Expert Answers," "Keeping Current," "QP Toolbox," and more) and book reviews. Recent articles covered evaluation of manufacturing processes, continuous improvement process, statistical methods for process control, risk management, new product development, and more. The publication's web site includes additional material (some of which is open access) including career information, case studies, quality glossary, history of quality, and more. This magazine will appeal to many different readers, including engineers, technologists, and practitioners in many fields interested in quality assessment and improvement.

Materials Engineering

2200. Acta Materialia. Incorporates (1992-1999): *Nanostructured Materials;* Former titles (until 1996): *Acta Metallurgica et Materialia;* (until 1990): *Acta Metallurgica.* [ISSN: 1359-6454] 1953. 20x/yr. EUR 4291. Pergamon, The Blvd, Langford Ln, E Park, Kidlington, OX5 1GB, United Kingdom; JournalsCustomerServiceEMEA@elsevier.com; http://www.elsevier.com. Illus., adv. Sample. Refereed. Microform: PQC. *Indexed:* A01, A22, ApMecR, C&ISA, CerAb, EngInd, RILM. *Bk. rev.:* Number and length vary. *Aud.:* Ac, Sa.

Acta Materialia (Elsevier URL: www.journals.elsevier.com/acta-materialia/) publishes original, peer-reviewed research papers and overviews that explore the relationship between the processing and the structure and properties of inorganic materials at all scales. Papers covering the mechanical or functional behavior of inorganic solids are accepted, and particular emphasis is placed on discussions of material properties that are based on experimentation, simulation, and modeling. Research relating material properties to the mechanisms of processing or their structure and chemistry is also accepted. The online version (reviewed herein; ISSN 1843-2453) includes access to most-cited, most-downloaded, and recent articles, special issues, podcasts, and materials news. Individual articles are technical in nature and feature color illustrations, citing and related articles, eReader formats for download, and social media sharing. This journal will appeal to academic and industrial researchers working on the characterization of materials.

2201. Advanced Materials. [ISSN: 0935-9648] 1989. s-m. GBP 6135. Ed(s): Peter Gregory, Lisa Wylie. Wiley - V C H Verlag GmbH & Co. KGaA, Postfach 101161, Weinheim, 69451, Germany; info@wiley-vch.de; http://www.wiley-vch.de. Adv. Sample. Refereed. Reprint: PSC. *Indexed:* A22, C&ISA, CerAb, EngInd. *Aud.:* Ac, Sa.

The high-impact journal *Advanced Materials* publishes peer-reviewed research that encompasses all areas of materials science. This international journal is multidisciplinary and accepts discussions of novel research and important advances in materials science as well as communications, research reports, progress reports, and more for publication. Recent articles discussed transparent thin-film transistors, silver nanoparticles, materials for nanobiotechnology, polymer solar cells, new anode materials, and more. Features of the online version (reviewed herein; ISSN 1521-4095) include early-view, most-accessed, and open-access articles. "Virtual Issues" provide topical access to articles in important areas. Individual articles include unique cover art, color illustrations, linked references, tracking of citations and altmetrics, and supplemental information (if any). This important journal is recommneded for materials researchers in academia and industry who are researching materials applications across many disciplines.

2202. Advanced Materials & Processes. Incorporates (1986-1989): *Guide to Engineered Materials;* (in 1989): *Metal Progress;* Which superseded in part (in 1933): *The American Society for Steel Treating. Transactions;* Which was formed by the merger of (1918-1920): *American Steel Treaters Society. Journal;* (1917-1920): *Steel Treating Research Society. Proceedings.* [ISSN: 0882-7958] 1983. m. Free to members. A S M International, 9639 Kinsman Rd, Materials Park, OH 44073; CustomerService@asminternational.org; http://asmcommunity.asminternational.org. Illus. Vol. ends: Jun/Dec. *Indexed:* A01, A22, BRI, C&ISA, CerAb, EngInd. *Aud.:* Ac, Sa.

Advanced Materials and Processes (*AMP*) (ASM URL: www.asminternational.org/portal/site/www/membership/benefits/amp/) is a trade magazine published by ASM International. The magazine is free in print to ASM members and available free online (reviewed herein; ISSN 2161-9425) for all interested readers (it is also available through sources including EBSCO). It publishes technical and news articles related to materials processing and new developments related to materials and manufacturing processes. Recent articles discussed developments in nondestructive testing, microscale fatigue testing,

thermal spray coatings, high-performance supercapacitors, automotive materials and applications, and more. Regular departments include "Industry News," "Products & Literature," "Of Material Interest" (highlighting new or interesting materials), and more. This magazine is engaging and informative. Articles are well written and not overly technical. Materials engineers and scientists and nontechnical personnel working in academia and industry will benefit from reading this magazine.

Applied Physics Letters. See Physics section.

Chemistry of Materials. See Chemistry/Physical section.

Journal of Applied Physics. See Physics section.

2203. Journal of Composite Materials. [ISSN: 0021-9983] 1967. 28x/yr. USD 8097. Ed(s): H Thomas Hahn. Sage Publications Ltd., 1 Oliver's Yard, 55 City Rd, London, EC1Y 1SP, United Kingdom; info@sagepub.co.uk; http://www.uk.sagepub.com. Illus., index. Sample. Refereed. Microform: PQC. Reprint: PSC. *Indexed:* A01, A22, ApMecR, C&ISA, CerAb, E01, EngInd. *Aud.:* Ac, Sa.

The *Journal of Composite Materials* (Sage URL: http://jcm.sagepub.com/) is a leading international journal on advanced composite materials, and it publishes peer-reviewed, original research papers that discuss advances in materials, processing, analysis testing, and more. Specific areas covered by the journal include bonding, ceramic-matrix composites, coatings, design of materials and components, environmental effects, modeling, non-destructive evaluation, nanotechnology, and more. The online version (reviewed herein; ISSN 1530-793X) features online-first articles, review papers, podcasts, and more on its web site. New content alerts via e-mail or RSS feed are available after creating a free account. Individual articles provide access to similar articles in the journal, linked references, and social media–sharing options. This journal is an important journal for materials researchers and engineers working in universities, research organizations, and industry.

Journal of Electronic Materials. See Electronics section.

2204. Journal of Materials Research. [ISSN: 0884-2914] 1986. m. GBP 1127 (print & online eds.). Ed(s): Gary L Messing. Cambridge University Press, 32 Ave of the Americas, New York, NY 10013; information@cambridge.org; http://www.cambridge.org/us/. Illus., index, adv. Refereed. Vol. ends: Dec. *Indexed:* A22, ABIn, ApMecR, C&ISA, CerAb, EngInd. *Aud.:* Ac, Sa.

The *Journal of Materials Research* (Cambridge URL: http://journals.cambridge.org/action/displayJournal?jid=JMR), a Materials Research Society journal, publishes peer-reviewed, original research and invited papers, rapid communications, and review papers that discuss advances and developments in the scientific understanding of materials. It seeks contributions related to the synthesis and processing of materials, material microstructure and properties, and other interdisciplinary materials-research topics. Special, topical issues are also published. Recent papers discussed ductility of nanocrystalline metals, microstructural and optical properties of materials, techniques for synthesizing materials, and more. The online version (reviewed herein; ISSN 2044-5326) highlights most-cited, first-view, and most-downloaded articles. Individual articles include color illustrations, links to related articles, supplemental materials (if any), linked references, and more. Materials researchers in academia and research centers, especially those working on micro- and nanostructure materials, will be very interested in this publication.

2205. Journal of Materials Science. Incorporates (1993-2004): *Interface Science;* (1982-2003): *Journal of Materials Science Letters.* [ISSN: 0022-2461] 1966. s-m. EUR 11084 (print & online eds.). Ed(s): C Barry Carter. Springer New York LLC, 233 Spring St, New York, NY 10013; service-ny@springer.com; http://www.springer.com/. Illus., index, adv. Refereed. Vol. ends: Dec. Reprint: PSC. *Indexed:* A&ATA, A01, A22, ApMecR, BRI, C&ISA, CerAb, E01, EngInd, RILM. *Aud.:* Ac, Sa.

Springer's *Journal of Materials Science* (www.springer.com/materials/journal/10853) is a peer-reviewed publication that publishes original research papers, short communications, and reviews that discuss research on the structure, properties, and uses of materials and their relationships. This international journal is interdisciplinary, and topics cover crystallography, characterization and evaluation of materials, and mechanics of materials, as well as a variety of materials including metals, ceramics, glasses, composites, and more. Special topical issues are also published. The online version (reviewed herein; URL 1573-4803) provides access to current and previous issues, to online-first, popular, and open-access articles. Individual articles include color illustrations, linked references, related content, supplementary materials (if any), and social media–sharing options. The multidisciplinary nature of this journal will appeal to materials researchers and professionals in many different disciplines in academic, research, and industrial settings.

2206. *M R S Bulletin.* Incorporates: *J M R Abstracts.* [ISSN: 0883-7694] 1976. m. GBP 350 (print & online eds.). Ed(s): Judith A Meiksin, Elizabeth L Fleischer. Cambridge University Press, 32 Ave of the Americas, New York, NY 10013; information@cambridge.org; http://www.cambridge.org/us/. Illus., adv. Refereed. *Indexed:* A22, C&ISA, CerAb, EngInd, RILM. *Aud.:* Ac, Sa.

Published by the Materials Research Society, the *MRS Bulletin* (Cambridge URL: http://journals.cambridge.org/action/displayIssue?jid=MRS&tab=currentissue) is an important journal in this field, and it publishes peer-reviewed original research on advanced materials. Free to MRS members, the journal features topical issues containing research papers, overview articles, news, and more focusing on the state-of-the-art in materials research. Recent issue topics include metal hydrides for energy applications; paper-based technology; Ziegler-Natta catalysis; materials for neural interfaces; and more. Highlights of the online version (reviewed herein; ISSN 1938-1425) include access to the journal archive, and to most-downloaded and most-cited papers and the technical themes for future issues. Individual articles include access to related articles, linked references, e-book download or cloud storage options, content alerts, and social media sharing. Readers of this high-impact journal will include engineers and materials scientists in a variety of disciplines.

2207. *Materials Today.* [ISSN: 1369-7021] 1998. 12x/yr. EUR 557. Ed(s): C Sealy. Elsevier BV, Radarweg 29, PO Box 211, Amsterdam, 1000 AE, Netherlands; JournalsCustomerServiceEMEA@elsevier.com; http://www.elsevier.nl. *Indexed:* A01, C&ISA, CerAb, EngInd. *Bk. rev.:* Number and length vary. *Aud.:* Ac, Sa.

Materials Today (Elsevier URL: www.materialstoday.com/) is both an open-access review magazine and a portal to additional materials science information on the Internet. Digital editions of the magazine are freely available on the web site, along with links to emerging materials science developments in webinars, white papers, podcasts, newscasts, blogs, and more. The magazine publishes research and review papers, and news on the latest developments in materials science as well as book reviews, comments, and editorials. Topics covered include the use of a wide variety of materials in fields including biomaterials, electronic materials, nanotechnology, ceramics, polymers, composites, and more. The digital edition (reviewed herein; ISSN 1873-4103) is interesting to read, with full-color illustrations and photographs. Researchers and students in materials science in many different fields will benefit from the content published in the magazine and on the web site.

2208. *Nature Materials.* [ISSN: 1476-1122] 2001. m. EUR 3936 in Europe; USD 4958 in the Americas; GBP 2544 in the UK & elsewhere. Ed(s): Vincent Dusastre. Nature Publishing Group, The MacMillan Bldg, 4 Crinan St, London, N1 9XW, United Kingdom; nature@nature.com; http://www.nature.com. Adv. Sample. Refereed. *Indexed:* A01, A22, C&ISA, CerAb, EngInd. *Aud.:* Ac, Sa.

In 2012, *Nature Materials* (Nature Publishing URL: www.nature.com/nmat/index.html) was ranked the number 1 journal in materials science. This highly-cited journal provides a forum for the exchange of original, peer-reviewed materials science research across disciplines. Research covers all aspects of materials science, and specific topics include engineering and structural materials; organic materials; biomedical and biomolecular materials; optoelectronic materials; semiconducting materials; thin films; and many more. The design, synthesis, and processing of materials are also covered. The online version (reviewed herein; ISSN 1476-4660) highlights access to current and past issues, access to advanced publication papers, content-alerting services, job postings, lists of events, and more. Individual papers include links to related

content, linked references, and altmetrics tracking. Because of its broad scope and focus on cutting-edge research, this important journal will appeal to engineers and scientists in many areas of academia and industry.

2209. *Progress in Materials Science.* Formerly (until 1961): *Progress in Metal Physics.* [ISSN: 0079-6425] 1949. 8x/yr. EUR 2496. Ed(s): B Cantor, Tetsuo Mohri. Pergamon, The Blvd, Langford Ln, E Park, Kidlington, OX5 1GB, United Kingdom; JournalsCustomerServiceEMEA@elsevier.com; http://www.elsevier.com. Sample. Refereed. Microform: PQC. *Indexed:* A01, A22, ApMecR, C&ISA, CerAb, EngInd. *Aud.:* Ac, Sa.

The high-impact, review journal *Progress in Materials Science* (Pergamon URL: www.journals.elsevier.com/progress-in-materials-science/) publishes lengthy review papers by experts that discuss recent advances in materials science and their engineering applications. Review topics include the relationship of microstructure to material properties; modeling of processes; experimental modeling that enhances the understanding of the effects of microstructure mechanisms on macroscopic properties; and more. Recent reviews discussed biocompatible implant surfaces, smart materials, mechanically alloyed nanocomposites, inorganic semiconductor nanowires, and more. The online version of the journal (reviewed herein: ISSN 1873-2208) includes access to recent, most-cited, and most-downloaded articles, and special issues. Individual articles include information on citing and related articles, linked references, and eReader format downloads. This review journal is important to researchers and engineers in materials science, because it provides an overview of new research and its applications in a concise format.

Solid-State Electronics. See Electronics section.

Mechanical Engineering

2210. *Acta Mechanica.* Formerly (until 1965): *Oesterreichisches Ingenieur-Archiv.* [ISSN: 0001-5970] 1946. 28x/yr. EUR 6775 (print & online eds.). Ed(s): F Ziegler, N Aksel. Springer Wien, Sachsenplatz 4-6, Vienna, 1201, Austria; journals@springer.at; http://www.springer.at. Illus., adv. Sample. Refereed. Circ: 600 Paid. Microform: PQC. Reprint: PSC. *Indexed:* A01, A22, ApMecR, BRI, C&ISA, CerAb, E01, EngInd, MathR, P02. *Aud.:* Ac, Sa.

The focus of *Acta Mechanica* (Springer URL: http://link.springer.com/journal/707) is theoretical and applied mechanics. A leading journal in mechanical engineering, it publishes peer-reviewed original research, occasional invited review papers, and brief communications. Topics of interest include classical mechanics and recently developed and emerging areas of mechanics, including non-Newtonian fluid dynamics, micromechanics, nanomechanics, smart materials, and more. Articles on applied mathematics dealing with mechanics and papers that discuss related fields, e.g., thermodynamics, will also be considered. The online version (reviewed herein; ISSN 1619-6937) features access to the journal archive, and latest articles. Individual articles provide access to related content, linked references, supplementary materials (if any), and social media–sharing options. Because of its mathematical and technical nature, the audience for this journal will be researchers in physics, mechanical engineering, and mechanics in academia, industry, and other research centers.

2211. *Engineering Fracture Mechanics: an international journal.* [ISSN: 0013-7944] 1968. 18x/yr. EUR 5895. Ed(s): K-H Schwalbe, A R Ingraffea. Pergamon, The Blvd, Langford Ln, E Park, Kidlington, OX5 1GB, United Kingdom; JournalsCustomerServiceEMEA@elsevier.com; http://www.elsevier.com. Illus., adv. Sample. Refereed. Microform: PQC. *Indexed:* A01, A22, ApMecR, C&ISA, CerAb, EngInd, S25. *Bk. rev.:* Number and length vary. *Aud.:* Ac, Sa.

The journal *Engineering Fracture Mechanics* (Pergamon URL: www.journals.elsevier.com/engineering-fracture-mechanics/) is an international, peer-reviewed research journal that focuses on fracture mechanics. It publishes papers that discuss fracture behavior in both conventional and emerging engineering material systems. Recent papers have addressed cohesive zone modeling, thermo-mechanical fatigue, stress singularity, crack propagation, scaled boundary finite element method, and more. The online version (reviewed herein; ISSN 1873-7315) provides access to highlighted, most-downloaded, most-cited, open-access, and recent articles, content alerts, and RSS feeds. Special issues are published, and a blog and events listing are also available. Individual articles include linked references, links to citing and related papers, ebook download options, and social media–sharing. Because this journal has a broad focus, it will appeal to engineers, scientists, and practitioners in academia, industry, and government studying fracture mechanics in a variety of materials.

2212. *Experimental Mechanics.* [ISSN: 0014-4851] 1961. bi-m. EUR 953 (print & online eds.). Ed(s): Horacio D Espinosa. Springer New York LLC, 233 Spring St, New York, NY 10013; service-ny@springer.com; http://www.springer.com/. Illus., adv. Refereed. Circ: 3000 Paid and controlled. Microform: PQC. Reprint: PSC. *Indexed:* A01, A22, ApMecR, C&ISA, CerAb, E01, EngInd. *Aud.:* Ac, Sa.

Experimental Mechanics (Springer URL: www.springer.com/materials/ mechanics/journal/11340) publishes peer-reviewed research in all areas of mechanics related to the design and implementation of experiments to characterize materials, structures, and systems. Areas of interest include optical/ electron microscopy, reliability and failure analysis, micro/ nanoelectromechanical systems, health monitoring of structures and systems, mechanics of materials, bio and nanotechnologies, and many others. As the official publication of the Society for Experimental Mechanics, it publishes review articles, brief technical notes, open-access papers, and articles about emerging technologies that are significant to society. The online version (reviewed herein; ISSN 1741-2765) provides access to online first articles, current and past issues, and special issues. Individual papers include color illustrations, linked references, related content, supplementary material (if any), and social media–sharing options. This journal's focus on experimentation and its interdisciplinary nature will make it very attractive to mechanics researchers in physics, engineering, and other scientific fields who work in academia or industry.

2213. *I E E E Journal of Microelectromechanical Systems.* [ISSN: 1057-7157] 1992. bi-m. USD 945; USD 1135 combined subscription (print & online eds.). Ed(s): Richard S Mullerr, Jeffrey F Cichocki. Institute of Electrical and Electronics Engineers, 445 Hoes Ln, Piscataway, NJ 08854; contactcenter@ieee.org; http://www.ieee.org. Adv. *Indexed:* A01, A22, ApMecR, C&ISA, CerAb, CompLI, EngInd. *Aud.:* Ac, Sa.

The *IEEE Journal of Microelectromechanical Systems* (IEEE URL: http:// ieeexplore.ieee.org/servlet/opac?punumber=84) publishes original research that discussing advances in the methods, technologies, and applications of microelectromechanical systems (MEMS). This title is published by several IEEE societies (Electron Devices; Industrial Robotics; Robotics and Automation), and research topics it covers include micromechanics, microdynamical systems, microsensing, materials for microsystems, and more. The journal also covers applications of MEMS in a variety of fields including biomedical engineering, communications, micropower devices, and more. The online version (reviewed herein; ISSN 1941-0158) provides access to popular, latest-published, and early-access articles, journal content alerts, and RSS feeds. Individual articles contain linked references, citing and similar articles, article metrics, and social media–sharing options. This journal has a unique focus that will appeal to MEMS researchers and engineers in academia, research centers, and industry.

IEEE - ASME Transactions on Mechatronics. See Robotics section.

2214. *International Journal of Heat and Mass Transfer.* [ISSN: 0017-9310] 1960. s-m. EUR 7921. Ed(s): W Minkowycz. Pergamon, The Blvd, Langford Ln, E Park, Kidlington, OX5 1GB, United Kingdom; JournalsCustomerServiceEMEA@elsevier.com; http://www.elsevier.com. Illus., adv. Sample. Refereed. Microform: MIM; PQC. *Indexed:* A01, A22, ApMecR, C&ISA, CEA, CerAb, EngInd. *Bk. rev.:* Number and length vary. *Aud.:* Ac, Sa.

The *International Journal of Heat and Mass Transfer* (Pergamon URL: www.journals.elsevier.com/international-journal-of-heat-and-mass-transfer/) provides a global forum for researchers and engineers to exchange ideas in heat and mass transfer. This important scholarly journal publishes original research papers, reviews, short communications, news, and more. Recent articles

addressed heat-transfer enhancement, simulation of turbulent-free convection, ways to reduce and enhance the evaporation ability of different nanoparticles, improving high-temperature heat-capture in gasification plants, and more. The online version (reviewed herein; ISSN 1879-2189) features access to open-access, most-cited, most-downloaded, and recent articles and journal-content alerts. Individual articles feature citing and related articles, linked references, color illustrations, eReader formats, and social media–sharing. This journal will appeal to researchers and practitioners in academia and industry working on problems of heat and mass transfer.

2215. *International Journal of Plasticity.* [ISSN: 0749-6419] 1985. 12x/yr. EUR 3297. Ed(s): Akhtar S Khan. Pergamon, The Blvd, Langford Ln, E Park, Kidlington, OX5 1GB, United Kingdom; http://www.elsevier.com. Illus., adv. Sample. Refereed. Microform: PQC. *Indexed:* A01, A22, ApMecR, C&ISA, CerAb, EngInd. *Aud.:* Ac, Sa.

The highly regarded *International Journal of Plasticity* (Pergamon URL: www.journals.elsevier.com/international-journal-of-plasticity/) publishes peer-reviewed, original research papers that cover all aspects of plastic deformation (damage and fracture behavior and mechanics, thermodynamics, macro/ microscopic phenomena, and more) in isotropic and anisotropic materials. Experimental, numerical, or theoretical papers that detail the plastic behavior of solids are encouraged. The online version (reviewed herein; ISSN 1879-2154) highlights open-access, most-recent, most-cited, and most-downloaded article and access to special, topical issues. Individual articles contain linked references, citing and related articles links, ebook format downloads, and social media–sharing. Readers of this journal will include scientists and engineers in academia and industry interested in plastic deformation of materials.

2216. *Journal of Fluid Mechanics.* [ISSN: 0022-1120] 1956. s-m. GBP 3163. Ed(s): M G Worster. Cambridge University Press, The Edinburgh Bldg, Shaftesbury Rd, Cambridge, CB2 8RU, United Kingdom; journals@cambridge.org; http://www.cambridge.org/uk. Illus., index, adv. Refereed. Circ: 2100. Microform: PMC; PQC. Reprint: PSC. *Indexed:* A22, ApMecR, C&ISA, CCMJ, CEA, CerAb, E01, EngInd, M&GPA, MSN, MathR, S25. *Bk. rev.:* 3, length varies. *Aud.:* Ga, Ac, Sa.

The international publication *Journal of Fluid Mechanics* (Cambridge URL: http://journals.cambridge.org/action/displayJournal?jid=FLM) is a peer-reviewed journal that publishes theoretical, computational, or experimental research in all areas of fluid mechanics. Papers in each issue focus on either the fundamentals of fluid mechanics or the application of fluid mechanics to other disciplines, e.g., aerospace, biology, chemical and mechanical engineering, hydraulics, and more. The online version (reviewed herein; ISSN 1465-7645) features access to the current and past issues, open-access articles, "Focus on Fluids" review articles, and "JFM Rapids"—which are short, high-impact research papers that are published with a short turnaround time. Individual articles include links to related content, linked references, social media–sharing, article metrics, and altmetrics. The broad scope of the research published in this journal, and its applicability in many different fields, makes appeal to scientists, engineers, and practitioners in many different disciplines in academia and industry.

2217. *Journal of Mechanical Design.* Formerly (until 1990): *Journal of Mechanisms, Transmissions and Automation in Design;* Which superseded in part (in 1983): *Journal of Mechanical Design.* [ISSN: 1050-0472] 1978. m. USD 739 combined subscription domestic (print & online eds.); USD 805 combined subscription foreign (print & online eds.); USD 74 per issue. Ed(s): Shapour Azarm. A S M E International, Two Park Ave, New York, NY 10016; CustomerCare@asme.org; http://www.asme.org. Sample. Refereed. *Indexed:* A01, A22, ApMecR, BRI, C&ISA, CerAb, EngInd. *Bk. rev.:* Number and length vary. *Aud.:* Ac, Sa.

The *Journal of Mechanical Design*, published by ASME International (ASME URL: http://mechanicaldesign.asmedigitalcollection.asme.org/journal.aspx), is scholarly research journal focused on all aspects of mechanical system design with special emphasis on design synthesis. Design topics covered by the journal include automation, design innovation, and design of: systems for energy, power and fluid handling; direct contact systems; and robotic systems. Contents include in-depth, original research articles, technical briefs, design innovation papers, book reviews and editorials. The online version (reviewed herein; ISSN

1528-9001) provides access to current and past issues, newest articles, popular content, accepted manuscripts, topic collections and content alerting services. Individual articles include public access articles, related content, linked references, and social media sharing options. This journal will appeal to academic researchers and industrial engineers and designers across many disciplines.

Journal of Power Sources. See Energy section.

2218. *Mechanical Engineering.* Incorporates (1982-1988): *Computers in Mechanical Engineering;* Former titles (until 1919): *American Society of Mechanical Engineers. Journal;* (until 1908): *American Society of Mechanical Engineers. Proceedings.* [ISSN: 0025-6501] 1880. m. USD 144; USD 40 per issue. Ed(s): John G Falcioni. A S M E International, Two Park Ave, New York, NY 10016; CustomerCare@asme.org; http://www.asme.org. Illus., index, adv. Microform: PMC; PQC. *Indexed:* A01, A06, A22, ABIn, ApMecR, B01, BRI, C&ISA, CCMJ, CerAb, EngInd, M&GPA, P02, RILM, S25. *Bk. rev.:* Number and length vary. *Aud.:* Ga, Ac, Sa.

Mechanial Engineering, the flagship magazine of ASME, is an engaging publication with informative articles on a wide variety of topics related to mechanical engineering. Recent issues contained articles on waste-to-energy plants for solid waste disposal, driverless cars, solar wires, a field unit for testing for HIV, public perceptions of engineers, career-related articles, interviews, ASME division news, legislative news, and more. Articles are technical, but are clearly written and contain photographs and graphics that support the text. Readers will include individuals interested in innovations in engineering as well as engineers and researchers. ASME members can access this publication online, and it is also available in ProQuest or EBSCO databases.

Progress in Energy and Combustion Science. See Energy section.

2219. *Wear.* [ISSN: 0043-1648] 1958. 24x/yr. EUR 9129. Ed(s): I M Hutchings. Elsevier BV, Radarweg 29, PO Box 211, Amsterdam, 1000 AE, Netherlands; JournalsCustomerServiceEMEA@elsevier.com; http://www.elsevier.nl. Illus., adv. Refereed. Vol. ends: No. 249 - No. 251. Microform: PQC. *Indexed:* A01, A22, ApMecR, C&ISA, CerAb, EngInd. *Aud.:* Ac, Sa.

The international, peer-reviewed journal *Wear* (Elsevier URL: www.journals.elsevier.com/wear/) publishes original research on wear, friction, lubrication, contact phenomena, and surface characterization. Topics of interest include design and materials selection to control wear and friction; tribology of natural biological and artificial implanted materials; lubricants, surface physics, and chemistry related to wear and friction; and more. Contributions published by the journal comprise full-length original research papers, short communications, and reviews. The online version (reviewed herein; ISSN 1873-2577) highlights special issues; recent, most-cited, most-downloaded, and open-access articles; related conference information; and news. Individual articles include links to citing and related articles, linked references, eReader format downloads, and social media–sharing options. This journal will appeal to researchers in academia and industry who are studying wear and friction in many different systems.

Nuclear Engineering

Arms Control Today. See Peace and Conflict Studies section.

2220. *I E E E Transactions on Nuclear Science.* Former titles (until 1963): *I R E Transactions on Nuclear Science;* (until 1955): *I R E Professional Group on Nuclear Science. Transactions.* [ISSN: 0018-9499] 1954. bi-m. USD 2070; USD 2485 combined subscription (print & online eds.). Ed(s): Paul V Dressendorfer. Institute of Electrical and Electronics Engineers, 445 Hoes Ln, Piscataway, NJ 08854; contactcenter@ieee.org; http://www.ieee.org. Illus., adv. *Indexed:* A01, A22, B01, BRI, C&ISA, CerAb, EngInd, MathR. *Aud.:* Ac, Sa.

IEEE Transactions on Nuclear Science (IEEE URL: http://ieeexplore.ieee.org/ servlet/opac?punumber=23) is sponsored by the IEEE Nuclear and Plasma Sciences Society. Articles published by this scholarly journal cover the theory and applications of nuclear science and engineering. Topics of interest include instruments for detecting and measuring radiation, particle accelerators and their control systems, applications of nuclear medicine, and more. Features of the online version (reviewed herein; ISSN 1558-1578) include latest-published, popular, and early-access articles, and special issues of symposia and conference papers. Linked references, citing articles, article metrics, and social media–sharing options are available for individual articles. In the past, this journal has been a high-impact journal. The audience for this journal comprises academic and industry researchers, engineers, and practitioners in fields including nuclear medicine, nuclear power, physics, and more.

2221. *International Journal of Pressure Vessels and Piping: design, manufacture and operation of pressurised components; structural Integrity; plant life management.* Incorporates (1980-1991): *Res Mechanica.* [ISSN: 0308-0161] 1973. m. EUR 4967. Ed(s): Robert A Ainsworth. Elsevier Ltd, 32 Jamestown Rd, Camden, London, NW1 7BY, United Kingdom; corporate.sales@elsevier.com; http://www.elsevier.com. Illus., adv. Sample. Refereed. Microform: PQC. *Indexed:* A01, A22, ApMecR, C&ISA, CEA, CerAb, EngInd, H24, RiskAb. *Aud.:* Sa.

The *International Journal of Pressure Vessels and Piping* (Elsevier URL: www.journals.elsevier.com/international-journal-of-pressure-vessels-and-piping) is a peer-reviewed research journal that covers the latest research on the engineering of pressure vessels of all sizes. It publishes original, applied research and review articles on pressure vessel engineering, design methods, construction of pressure vessels, inspection, management and maintenance, and more. The online version (reviewed herein; ISSN 1879-3541) features most-cited, most-downloaded, open-access, and recent articles, news, related conference information, and job information. Individual articles include color illustrations, linked references, citing and related articles, eReader formats, and social media–sharing. Readers of this journal will include engineers and practitioners in any industry that uses pressure vessels, as well as pressure vessel manufacturers and researchers in academia.

2222. *Journal of Nuclear Materials.* [ISSN: 0022-3115] 1959. 36x/yr. EUR 9406. Ed(s): L K Mansur, C Lemaignan. Elsevier BV, North-Holland, Postbus 211, Amsterdam, 1000 AE, Netherlands; JournalsCustomerServiceEMEA@elsevier.com. Illus., adv. Refereed. Microform: PQC. *Indexed:* A01, A22, C&ISA, CerAb, EngInd, H24. *Aud.:* Ac, Sa.

Materials used in nuclear applications is the focus of the *Journal of Nuclear Materials* (Elsevier URL: www.journals.elsevier.com/journal-of-nuclear-materials/). It publishes original, peer-reviewed research and critical review papers on materials research related to nuclear reactors and particle accelerators. Specific topics covered include fission and fusion reactor materials, materials aspects of the fuel cycle, nuclear waste materials performance, and more. Papers that discuss the theoretical, experimental, computational, or applied aspects of nuclear materials are also accepted. The online version (reviewed herein; 1873-4820) highlights recent, most-cited, most-downloaded, and open-access articles, special issues, related conference information, and news. Podcasts and webinars are also offered. Individual articles have color illustrations, citing and related articles, linked references, eReader formats, and social media–sharing. This journal will appeal to engineers and scientists conducting materials research or working in academic and other research centers devoted to nuclear energy and its applications.

2223. *Journal of Nuclear Science and Technology.* [ISSN: 0022-3131] 1964. bi-m. GBP 358 (print & online eds.). Ed(s): Toyohiko Yano. Taylor & Francis Asia Pacific (Singapore), 240 MacPherson Rd. #08-01, Pines Industrial Bldg., Singapore, 348574, Singapore; info@tandf.com.sg; http://www.taylorandfrancis.com.sg/. Illus., index, adv. Refereed. Circ: 1350. Reprint: PSC. *Indexed:* A22, C&ISA, CerAb, EngInd. *Aud.:* Ac, Sa.

Published by the Atomic Energy Society of Japan, this journal features academic articles in nuclear energy that are focused on the following areas: designing, manufacturing, testing, operating or analyzing facilities, equipment, devices, etc., with an eye to practical value. URL: www.aesj.or.jp/publication/jnst.html

2224. Kerntechnik: independent journal for nuclear engineering, energy systems, radiation and radiological protection. Formerly (until 1987): *Atomkernergie - Kerntechnik;* Which was formed by the merger of (1956-1979): *Atomkernenergie;* (1968-1979): *Kerntechnik;* Which incorporated (1955-1970): *Atompraxis;* Kerntechnik was formerly (1960-1968): *Kerntechnik, Isotopentechnik und -Chemie;* (1960-1960): *Kerntechnik und Isotopentechnik;* (1959-1960): *Kerntechnik.* [ISSN: 0932-3902] 1979. bi-m. EUR 1098 combined subscription (print & online eds.); EUR 285 newsstand/cover. Ed(s): Annemarie Schmitt-Hannig. Carl Hanser Verlag GmbH & Co. KG, Kolbergerstr 22, Munich, 81679, Germany; info@hanser.de; http://www.hanser.de. Illus., adv. Circ: 1000. *Indexed:* A22, C&ISA, EngInd, FS&TA. *Aud.:* Sa.

The focus here is research and development in nuclear engineering, energy systems, radiation, and radiological protection. Topics include the design, operation, safety, and economics of nuclear-power stations, research reactors, and simulators and their components, as well as the complete fuel cycle. Radiation means the application of ionizing radiation in industry, medicine, and research. Topics in radiological protection cover the biological effects of ionizing radiation; the system of protection for occupational, medical, and public exposures; the assessment of doses; operational protection and safety programs; management of radioactive wastes; and decommissioning and regulatory requirements. The articles are published almost exclusively in English. URL: www.nuclear-engineering-journal.com/web/index.asp?navid= 20090820941372&task=010

2225. Nuclear Engineering and Design: an international journal devoted to the thermal, mechanical, materials, and structural aspects of nuclear fission energy. Formerly (until 1966): *Nuclear Structural Engineering.* [ISSN: 0029-5493] 1965. 12x/yr. EUR 7591. Ed(s): Y A Hassan, D Bestion. Elsevier BV, Radarweg 29, PO Box 211, Amsterdam, 1000 AE, Netherlands; JournalsCustomerServiceEMEA@elsevier.com; http:// www.elsevier.nl. Adv. Refereed. Vol. ends: No. 203 - No. 210. Microform: PQC. *Indexed:* A01, A22, ApMecR, C&ISA, CerAb, EngInd, H24, RiskAb. *Aud.:* Sa.

Nuclear Engineering and Design (Elsevier URL: www.journals.elsevier.com/ nuclear-engineering-and-design) is a peer-reviewed journal that publishes original research on all aspects of nuclear fission energy. Contributions covering engineering, design, construction, and safety of fission reactors throughout the reactor life cycle are sought. Some of the topics covered include engineering mechanics, materials engineering, structural plant design, engineering of reactor components, safety analysis and risk assessment, reactor control systems, nuclear waste disposal, and others. The online version (reviewed herein; ISSN 1872-759X) features recent, most-cited, open-access, and most-downloaded articles; information on related conferences; and access to special, topical issues (sometimes including conference papers). Individual articles include citing and related articles, linked references, CSV-downloadable tables, eReader formats for download; and social media–sharing. This journal is recommended reading for nuclear engineers and research scientists interested in new designs, developments, and applications of nuclear fission.

Nuclear Engineering International. See Energy section.

2226. Nuclear Instruments & Methods in Physics Research. Section A: Accelerators, Spectrometers, Detectors, and Associated Equipment. Supersedes in part (in 1984): *Nuclear Instruments and Methods in Physics Research;* Which was formerly (until 1981): *Nuclear Instruments and Methods;* (until 1958): *Nuclear Instruments.* [ISSN: 0168-9002] 1957. 42x/yr. EUR 10889. Ed(s): W Barletta. Elsevier BV, North-Holland, Postbus 211, Amsterdam, 1000 AE, Netherlands; JournalsCustomerServiceEMEA@elsevier.com. Illus., index, adv. Refereed. Vol. ends: No. 456 - No. 474. Microform: PQC. *Indexed:* A&ATA, A01, A22, C&ISA, EngInd. *Aud.:* Ac, Sa.

The design, manufacture, and performance of instruments is the focus of *Nuclear Instruments & Methods in Physics[,] Section A* (Elsevier URL: www.journals.elsevier.com/nuclear-instruments-and-methods-in-physics-research-section-a-accelerators-spectrometers-detectors-and-associated-equipment/). This peer-reviewed journal publishes papers on scientific instruments, including particle accelerators, ion sources, and more, as well as instruments to detect and analyze radiation from high-energy processes and

nuclear decay and instruments for use with experiments at nuclear reactors. Special issues are also published. The online version (reviewed herein; ISSN 1872-9576) features recent, most-downloaded, and most-cited papers; special issues; upcoming conferences; and news. Individual papers include citing and related articles, linked references, and eReader formats. This specialized journal will appeal to scientists and engineers working in the area of high-energy or nuclear physics, nuclear power, and nuclear research facilities, as well as researchers interested in applying these types of instruments in other areas of research.

2227. Nuclear Instruments & Methods in Physics Research. Section B: Beam Interactions with Materials and Atoms. Supersedes in part (in 1984): *Nuclear Instruments and Methods in Physics Research;* Which was formerly (until 1981): *Nuclear Instruments and Methods;* (until 1958): *Nuclear Instruments.* [ISSN: 0168-583X] 1957. 24x/yr. EUR 11549. Ed(s): M B H Breese, C Trautmann. Elsevier BV, Radarweg 29, PO Box 211, Amsterdam, 1000 AE, Netherlands; JournalsCustomerServiceEMEA@elsevier.com; http://www.elsevier.com. Illus., index, adv. Refereed. Vol. ends: No. 173 - No. 185. Microform: PQC. *Indexed:* A01, A22, C&ISA, CerAb, EngInd, RILM. *Bk. rev.:* Number and length vary. *Aud.:* Ac, Sa.

Nuclear Instruments & Methods in Physics[,] Section B (Elsevier URL: www.journals.elsevier.com/nuclear-instruments-and-methods-in-physics-research-section-b-beam-interactions-with-materials-and-atoms/) focuses on the ways in which materials interact at all levels with energetic beams. Topics of interest in this peer-reviewed journal include the modification of materials by energetic beams (atomic/molecular ions, neutrons, positrons, and more), atomic collisions in solids, physics and chemistry of beam interactions, collision cascades, analysis of materials using energetic radiation, and more. The online version (reviewed herein; ISSN 1872-9584) highlights recent, most-cited, and most-downloaded papers; special issues; and upcoming, related conferences. Individual papers include color illustrations, citing and related articles, linked references, and eReader formats.

2228. Nuclear News. Incorporates (198?-1995): *American Nuclear Society News.* [ISSN: 0029-5574] 1959. m. USD 550 (print & online eds.). Ed(s): Betsy Tompkins. American Nuclear Society, Inc., 555 N Kensington Ave, La Grange Park, IL 60526; members@ans.org; http://www.ans.org. Illus., adv. Circ: 10958 Paid. *Indexed:* A22, C&ISA, CerAb, EngInd. *Bk. rev.:* Number and length vary. *Aud.:* Ga, Ac, Sa.

Nuclear News is the membership magazine for the American Nuclear Society (www.ans.org). This publication focuses on the global nuclear industry, publishing overview and feature articles, news, special reports, and more. Topics covered include plant operations and maintenance, security, waste management, non-power uses of nuclear science, and more. Special-topical issues are published, and an annual special issue is the *Nuclear News Buyers Guide.* The magazine also includes news, calls for papers, events calendar, information on new products, and more. Regular sections include power, security, waste management, isotopes and radiation, fuel, and more. This informative magazine is recommended for nuclear engineers in industry; nuclear researchers in academia who track industry developments; and non-technical readers who work in areas associated with the nuclear industry. This magazine is also available to members and subscribing institutions online.

2229. Nuclear Science and Engineering: research and development related to peaceful utilization of nuclear energy. [ISSN: 0029-5639] 1956. 9x/yr. USD 1525 (print & online eds.). Ed(s): Dan G Cacuci. American Nuclear Society, Inc., 555 N Kensington Ave, La Grange Park, IL 60526; members@ans.org; http://www.ans.org. Illus. Refereed. *Indexed:* A22, ApMecR, C&ISA, CerAb, EngInd, H24. *Bk. rev.:* Number and length vary. *Aud.:* Ac, Sa.

Published by the American Nuclear Society (ANS), *Nuclear Science and Engineering* (ANS URL: www.ans.org.mutex.gmu.edu/pubs/journals/nse/) is a peer-reviewed publication that focuses on current nuclear energy research. It publishes technical papers, critical reviews, notes, and computer code abstracts that cover all aspects of peaceful applications of nuclear energy and radiation. Recent articles discussed instrumentation for fast breeder reactors; a computer model of primary coolant water chemistry in a supercritical water reactor; fault detection in nuclear systems; Monte Carlo code for the study of radiation damage by neutrons; and more. The content of the journal tends to be very mathematical, and it includes papers discussing the application various modeling methods to research issues in nuclear science. The online version (reviewed herein; ISSN 1943-748X) provides free abstracts for the journal's full run, full-text access for subscribers, and paper purchase options for non-subscribers. Because of its highly technical nature, the main audience for this journal is nuclear scientists and engineers conducting research in nuclear science.

Nuclear Technology. See Energy section.

■ ENVIRONMENT AND CONSERVATION

See also Biology; Fishing; Hiking, Climbing, and Outdoor Recreation; Hunting and Guns; and Sports sections.

Diane T. Sands, Assistant Librarian, Leonard Library, San Francisco State University, San Francisco, CA 94132; dsands@sfsu.edu

Introduction

The backbone of this section lies firmly in scholarly research journals. Ecosystem change has broad implications for health and sustainability at local, regional, and global scales. Environment- and conservation-focused periodicals are helping readers make sense of the abundant information available. Environmental news journals have value-added, online components to supplement traditional subscriptions.

Environment and conservation comprise an interdisciplinary topic that cannot be covered in one section of *MFL*, thus readers should look to the sections "Zoology," "Science and Technology," "Travel and Tourism," and "Urban Studies," among others, for further suggestions.

Basic Periodicals

Conservation; Ecology and Society; Environmental Hazards; Environment and Energy Daily; Environment: Science and Policy for Sustainable Development; Green Teacher; Restoration Ecology.

Basic Abstracts and Indexes

Academic Search Premier, AGRICOLA, BIOSIS, Ecology Abstracts, Environment Index, Environmental Sciences and Pollution Management, Forestry Abstracts, GEOBASE, LexisNexis, Pollution Abstracts, ProQuest Research Library, Risk Abstracts Online, Water Resources Abstracts, Web of Science.

2230. *Ambio: a journal of the human environment.* [ISSN: 0044-7447] 1972. 8x/yr. EUR 364 (print & online eds.). Ed(s): Elisabeth Kessler. Springer Netherlands, Van Godewijckstraat 30, Dordrecht, 3311 GX, Netherlands; http://www.springer.com. Illus., index, adv. Refereed. Circ: 4000. Vol. ends: Dec. Reprint: PSC. *Indexed:* A01, A22, ABIn, AbAn, BRI, C45, CBRI, CJPI, E01, FS&TA, H24, IndVet, M&GPA, OceAb, RRTA, RiskAb, S25. *Aud.:* Ac, Sa.

"Significant developments in environmental research, policy[,] and related activities" are the core areas for this peer-reviewed journal. Sponsored by the Royal Swedish Academy of Sciences, this internationally focused publication contains topics that range from ecology, environmental economics, and geological sciences to hydrology, water resources, and earth sciences.

American Forests. See Forestry section.

2231. *American Water Resources Association. Journal.* Formerly (until 1997): *Water Resources Bulletin;* Which incorporated: *American Water Resources Association. Water Resources Newsletter.* [ISSN: 1093-474X] 1965. bi-m. GBP 352 (print & online eds.). Ed(s): Kenneth Lanfear.

Wiley-Blackwell Publishing, Inc., 111 River St, Hoboken, NJ 07030; info@wiley.com; http://onlinelibrary.wiley.com/. Illus. Sample. Microform: PQC. Reprint: PSC. *Indexed:* A01, A22, Agr, BAS, C45, E01, EngInd, M&GPA, MLA-IB, OceAb, RRTA, S25. *Bk. rev.:* Number and length vary. *Aud.:* Ac, Sa.

The *Journal of the American Water Resources Association* (*JAWRA*) "is dedicated to publishing original papers [that are] characterized by their broad approach to water resources issues." Each issue of this highly respected, scholarly journal consists of a group of feature articles that are related to a designated topic. Additional articles relate to water chemistry, economic and policy issues, hydrology, or pollution and conservation.

BackHome. See Do-It-Yourself section.

2232. *Biodiversity and Conservation.* [ISSN: 0960-3115] 1991. 14x/yr. EUR 3307 (print & online eds.). Ed(s): David L Hawksworth. Springer Netherlands, Van Godewijckstraat 30, Dordrecht, 3311 GX, Netherlands; http://www.springer.com. Illus., adv. Refereed. Reprint: PSC. *Indexed:* A22, Agr, BRI, C45, E01, GardL, IndVet, RRTA, S25. *Aud.:* Ac, Sa.

This peer-reviewed, academic journal is international in scope and explores "all aspects of biological diversity; [including] its description, analysis[,] and conservation." Technical articles use extensive analysis of data and statistics to examine the human impact on biodiversity. It incorporates political, economic, and social perspectives. Includes editorials and research notes.

2233. *ClimateWire.* 2008. d. Ed(s): John Fialka. Environment and Energy Publishing, LLC, 122 C St, N W, Ste 722, Washington, DC 20001; pubs@eenews.net; http://www.eenews.net. Adv. Sample. *Aud.:* Hs, Ga, Ac, Sa.

This is an online news daily that covers state, local, and international programs, policies, and funding issues related to climate change. It includes scientific findings and ecological and economic impacts of climate change. "[It b]rings readers unmatched coverage of the debate over climate policy and its effects on business, the environment, and society."

Climatic Change. See Atmospheric Sciences section.

Conservation Biology. See Ecology section.

2234. *Conservation (Malden): best minds, best writing.* Former titles (until 2007): *Conservation in Practice;* (until 2002): *Conservation Biology in Practice.* [ISSN: 1936-2145] 2000. q. GBP 44 (print & online eds.). Ed(s): Kathy Kohm. Wiley-Blackwell Publishing, Inc., 111 River St, Hoboken, NJ 07030; info@wiley.com; http://onlinelibrary.wiley.com/. Index. Sample. *Indexed:* A22, C45, E01, GardL, IndVet, S25. *Bk. rev.:* Number and length vary. *Aud.:* Hs, Ga, Ac, Sa.

Published by the Society for Conservation Biology, *Conservation* presents articles on current topics such as effects of the economy on conservation, the carbon footprint, and local food. Photographs, illustrations, and brief news items are featured alongside lengthier articles, and all contribute to a publication that is engaging enough to be a general-interest magazine.

2235. *E: the environmental magazine.* [ISSN: 1046-8021] 1990. bi-m. USD 24.95. Ed(s): Doug Moss, Brita Belli. Earth Action Network, 28 Knight St, Norwalk, CT 06851. Illus., adv. Sample. Vol. ends: Nov/Dec. *Indexed:* A01, A22, ABS&EES, ASIP, BRI, C37, CBRI, MASUSE, P02. *Aud.:* Hs, Ga, Ac, Sa.

E: the environmental magazine is a general-interest magazine with an international scope that would be a welcome addition to public libraries. It includes articles that address larger environmental issues and a section with shorter items that provide tips for a more sustainable lifestyle.

2236. *EcoHealth: conservation medicine: human health: ecosystem sustainability.* Formed by the merger of (2000-2004): *Global Change and Human Health;* (1995-2004): *Ecosystem Health.* [ISSN: 1612-9202] 2004. q. Ed(s): Bruce A Wilcox. Springer New York LLC, 233 Spring St, New York, NY 10013; journals@springer-ny.com; http://www.springer.com/. Refereed. Reprint: PSC. *Indexed:* A22, BRI, C45, E01, H24, IndVet, RRTA, RiskAb. *Bk. rev.:* Number and length vary. *Aud.:* Ac, Sa.

This is "[a]n international, peer-reviewed journal focused on the integration of knowledge at the interface between ecological and [human] health sciences." Articles explore the effects of research and practices as they apply ecosystem principles to addressing health and sustainability challenges, and its coverage ranges from public health practice and human and veterinary medicine, to rural and urban development and planning. *EcoHealth* hopes to reach researchers, policy makers, and educators.

2237. *The Ecologist (Online).* 2006. m. GBP 20. Ed(s): Mark Anslow. Ecosystems Ltd., 102 D Lana House Studios, 116-118 Commercial St, London, E1 6NF, United Kingdom. Adv. *Aud.:* Hs, Ga, Ac.

A magazine for activists interested in environmental issues in the broadest sense. It tackles everything from war to eating local foods. There are lively articles that don't hesitate to show their bias. *The Ecologist* is available exclusively in electronic format. Print production ceased after the July 2009 issue.

Ecology. See Ecology section.

2238. *Ecology and Society: a journal of integrative science for resilience and sustainability.* Formerly: *Conservation Ecology.* [ISSN: 1708-3087] 1997. s-a. Free. Ed(s): Lance Gunderson, Carl Folke. Resilience Alliance Publications, PO Box 40037, Waterloo, ON N2J 4V1, Canada; questions@consecol.org; http://www.consecol.org. Illus. Refereed. *Indexed:* A01, C45, CBCARef, IndVet, RRTA, S25. *Bk. rev.:* Number and length vary. *Aud.:* Ac, Sa.

Articles in this open-access, electronic, peer-reviewed journal take a healthy interdisciplinary approach. They are published as accepted in an "Issue in Progress" capacity—which is an advantage unique to electronic publications. They are also written for a wide audience that includes "an array of disciplines from the natural sciences, social sciences, and the humanities [that are] concerned with the relationship between society and the life-supporting ecosystems." It includes occasional special features and groups of articles on the same theme.

Ecosystems. See Ecology section.

2239. *Electronic Green Journal: professional journal on international environmental information.* Formerly (until 1994): *Green Library Journal.* [ISSN: 1076-7975] 1992. s-a. Free. University of California, Los Angeles, Library, Powell Library Building, Los Angeles, CA 90095-1450. Illus. Sample. Refereed. *Indexed:* A01, BRI, C45, CBRI. *Bk. rev.:* Number and length vary. *Aud.:* Ga, Ac, Sa.

Providing open access to scholarly, international environmental information since 1994, this publication includes book reviews, opinion pieces, articles, and semi-regular columns. It is "[a] professional peer-reviewed publication devoted to disseminating information concerning environmental protection, conservation, management of natural resources, and ecologically-balanced regional development."

2240. *Environment: science and policy for sustainable development.* Former titles (until 1969): *Scientist and Citizen;* (until 1964): *Nuclear Information.* [ISSN: 0013-9157] 1958. bi-m. GBP 141. Ed(s): Margaret Benner. Taylor & Francis Inc., 325 Chestnut St, Ste 800, Philadelphia, PA 19106; customerservice@taylorandfrancis.com; http://www.tandfonline.com. Illus., adv. Refereed. Reprint: PSC. *Indexed:* A01, A22, ABIn, Agr, BRI, C37, C45, CBRI, E01, IBSS, M&GPA, MASUSE, P02, RRTA. *Bk. rev.:* Number and length vary. *Aud.:* Hs, Ga, Ac, Sa.

Environment explores both ecological and social aspects of environmental issues. Scientific research is presented, accompanied by photographs, illustrations, and understandable explanations that are accessible to those who want to stay current on questions of environmental policy. This is a general-interest publication that provides peer-reviewed articles, editorials, essays, and suggestions for interesting web sites, books, and articles.

2241. *Environment and Development Economics.* [ISSN: 1355-770X] 1996. bi-m. GBP 298. Ed(s): Anastasios Xepapadeas. Cambridge University Press, The Edinburgh Bldg, Shaftesbury Rd, Cambridge, CB2 8RU, United Kingdom; journals@cambridge.org; http://www.cup.cam.ac.uk/. Illus., adv. Refereed. Circ: 1950 Controlled. Reprint: PSC. *Indexed:* A22, ABIn, B01, BAS, E01, EconLit, JEL. *Aud.:* Ac, Sa.

Each issue of *Environment and Development Economics* provides a mix of scientific and policy papers, with a heavy emphasis on economic theory and modeling. This academic journal focuses on "the environmental problems associated with economic development," particularly of developing countries.

2242. *Environment and Energy Daily (Online): the best way to track congress.* [ISSN: 1540-790X] 1999. d. Ed(s): Kevin Braun, Dan Berman. Environment and Energy Publishing, LLC, 122 C St, N W, Ste 722, Washington, DC 20001; pubs@eenews.net; http://www.eenews.net. Adv. *Aud.:* Ga, Ac, Sa.

This online news source provides the latest on environmental and energy legislation and federal agency appropriations in daily online updates. It provides a breakdown of where lawmakers stand on the issues, notice of floor votes, a calendar of committee schedules, and comprehensive analysis of major bills.

2243. *Environment, Development and Sustainability: a multidisciplinary approach to the theory and practice of sustainable development.* [ISSN: 1387-585X] 1999. bi-m. EUR 477 (print & online eds.). Ed(s): Bhaskar Nath, David Pimentel. Springer Netherlands, Van Godewijckstraat 30, Dordrecht, 3311 GX, Netherlands; http://www.springer.com. Refereed. Reprint: PSC. *Indexed:* A22, ABIn, Agr, BRI, C45, E01, IBSS, RRTA, S25. *Aud.:* Ac, Sa.

Environmental and social impacts of development are considered in this international, multidisciplinary journal. Articles cover myriad angles of the environmental impacts related to socioeconomic development, particularly in developing and developed areas. Topics include the current state of marine fisheries, community organizing and community-led initiatives, and rainwater harvesting in environmentally degraded areas.

2244. *Environment Matters (Online).* [ISSN: 1564-5878] 1996. a. The World Bank, 1818 H St NW, Washington, DC 20433; books@worldbank.org; http://www.worldbank.org. *Aud.:* Ga, Ac.

This annual review from the World Bank includes overviews of work in the WB's six regions, feature articles with a different theme each year, and viewpoints from within the organization.

2245. *Environmental Conservation: an international journal of environmental science.* [ISSN: 0376-8929] 1974. q. GBP 485. Ed(s): Nicholas V C Polunin. Cambridge University Press, The Edinburgh Bldg, Shaftesbury Rd, Cambridge, CB2 8RU, United Kingdom; journals@cambridge.org; http://www.cambridge.org/uk. Illus., adv. Sample. Refereed. Circ: 1800. Vol. ends: Winter. Microform: PQC. Reprint: PSC. *Indexed:* A22, BAS, C&ISA, C45, E01, EngInd, IndVet, M&GPA, OceAb, P02, RRTA, S25. *Bk. rev.:* Number and length vary. *Aud.:* Ac, Sa.

A peer-reviewed, academic journal, *Environmental Conservation* has an international scope. It includes brief "Comments," lengthier "Papers," and book reviews. Articles span a broad range of topics, from individual species to fisheries management, deforestation rates, and global trends.

2246. *Environmental Ethics: an interdisciplinary journal dedicated to the philosophical aspects of environmental problems.* [ISSN: 0163-4275] 1979. q. USD 36 per vol. Ed(s): Eugene C Hargrove. Environmental Philosophy, Inc., 1155 Union Cir, 310980, University of North Texas, Denton, TX 76203; cep@unt.edu; http://www.cep.unt.edu. Illus., index, adv. Sample. Refereed. Vol. ends: Winter. Microform: PQC. *Indexed:* A01, A22, Agr, AmHI, BRI, IPB, MLA-IB, P02, R&TA, S25. *Bk. rev.:* Number and length vary. *Aud.:* Ac.

Environmental Ethics is a peer-reviewed academic journal that examines environmental issues through a philosophical lens, while still making them accessible to all levels of readers. Issues consist of feature articles, discussion papers, and book reviews.

2247. *Environmental Hazards: human and policy dimensions.* Formerly (unitl 2006): *Global Environmental Change Part B: Environmental Hazards;* Which superseded in part (in 1999): *Global Environmental Change.* [ISSN: 1747-7891] 1990. q. GBP 335 (print & online eds.). Ed(s): Edmund Penning-Rowsell. Earthscan Ltd., Dunstan House, 14a St Cross St, London, EC1N 8XA, United Kingdom; earthinfo@earthscan.co.uk; http://www.earthscan.co.uk/. Adv. Sample. Refereed. Reprint: PSC. *Indexed:* A01, C45, H24, IBSS, M&GPA, OceAb, S25. *Aud.:* Ac, Sa.

Written for academics and those with an interest in regulations and governance, *Environmental Hazards* also considers sociological responses to disasters and associated potential policy implications. This international, peer-reviewed publication "addresses the full range of hazardous events from extreme geological, hydrological, atmospheric[,] and biological events such as earthquakes, floods, storms[,] and epidemics to technological failures and malfunctions such as industrial explosions, fires[,] and toxic material releases."

2248. *Environmental Justice.* [ISSN: 1939-4071] 2008. bi-m. USD 683. Ed(s): Sylvia Hood Washington. Mary Ann Liebert, Inc. Publishers, 140 Huguenot St, 3rd Fl, New Rochelle, NY 10801; info@liebertpub.com; http://www.liebertpub.com. Adv. Sample. Refereed. Reprint: PSC. *Indexed:* C45, H24. *Aud.:* Hs, Ac, Sa.

This journal is appropriate for community planners and organizers, academic libraries, and public health professionals. *Environmental Justice* "provides a channel for research, debate, and discussion of the equitable treatment and involvement of all people, especially minority and low-income populations, with respect to the development, implementation, and enforcement of environmental laws, regulations, and policies." It is international in scope, and its topics include siting for nuclear power plants, cleanup of toxic environments in low-income areas, disparities in grocery stores between racially dissimilar communities, and community health issues and their underlying environmental causes.

2249. *Environmental Science & Policy.* [ISSN: 1462-9011] 1998. 8x/yr. EUR 1090. Ed(s): Dr. J C Briden. Elsevier Inc., 360 Park Ave S, New York, NY 10010; usinfo-f@elsevier.com; http://www.elsevier.com. Illus., adv. Sample. Refereed. *Indexed:* C&ISA, C45, CerAb, ExcerpMed, IBSS, RRTA. *Bk. rev.:* Number and length vary. *Aud.:* Ac, Sa.

Environmental Science and Policy is written for those "who are instrumental in the solution of environmental problems," including non-governmental and governmental organizations, and business and academic research labs. It also considers the interplay between environmental, social, and economic issues. Topics include current research and theories on social learning; public participation; methods for carbon sequestration; and the pros and cons of biofuels.

Ethics, Policy & Environment. See Geography section.

Global Biogeochemical Cycles. See Marine Science and Technology/Ocean Science section.

Global Change Biology. See Ecology section.

Global Ecology and Biogeography: a journal of macroecology. See Ecology section.

Green Places. See Landscape Architecture section.

2250. *Green Teacher: education for planet earth.* [ISSN: 1192-1285] 1991. q. USD 32 in US & Canada; AUD 45 Australia; NZD 55.25 New Zealand. Ed(s): Gail Littlejohn, Tim Grant. Green Teacher, 95 Robert St, Toronto, ON M5S 2K5, Canada. Illus., adv. Sample. *Indexed:* BRI, C37, CEI, P02. *Bk. rev.:* Number and length vary. *Aud.:* Hs, Ga, Ac.

Green Teacher is a magazine primarily for elementary through high school educators. Articles about global and local environmental issues are geared toward all educators, making it easy to merge lessons into existing school subjects or in students' time outside of school, including at camps, day care, or at home. Activities are designed to empower and engage students to become part of the solution. Recommended for school and public libraries.

2251. *Greenwire.* Former titles: *Environment and Energy Newsline; Environment and Energy Update.* [ISSN: 1540-787X] 1997. d. Ed(s): Kevin Braun, Cyril T Zaneski. Environment and Energy Publishing, LLC, 122 C St, N W, Ste 722, Washington, DC 20001; pubs@eenews.net; http://www.eenews.net. *Aud.:* Hs, Ga, Ac, Sa.

Greenwire is a daily online news source for the latest in "environmental and energy action." Language is neutral and coverage of issues is balanced. Recommended for academic libraries and special libraries with an environmental focus. The web site is broken into sections ("Top Stories," "Politics," "Business," "Finance and Technology," "States," "International"), and each headline is tagged with the major issue (forests, water, coal, climate, energy policy) that should enable readers to find articles of interest at a glance.

2252. *High Country News: for people who care about the West.* [ISSN: 0191-5657] 1970. bi-w. USD 29.95 combined subscription (print & online eds.). Ed(s): Jonathan Thompson. High Country Foundation, 119 Grand Ave, PO Box 1090, Paonia, CO 81428. Illus., index, adv. Circ: 22637 Paid. Vol. ends: Dec. *Indexed:* M&GPA, S25. *Bk. rev.:* Number and length vary. *Aud.:* Hs, Ga, Ac, Sa.

High Country News is an award-winning, "nonprofit media organization that covers the important issues and stories that define the American West. Its mission is to inform and inspire people—through in-depth journalism—to act on behalf of the West's diverse natural and human communities." A good choice for public libraries, particularly in the western United States.

2253. *Human Ecology (New York): an interdisciplinary journal.* [ISSN: 0300-7839] 1972. bi-m. EUR 1510 (print & online eds.). Ed(s): Ludomir Lozny, Daniel G Bates. Springer New York LLC, 233 Spring St, New York, NY 10013; service-ny@springer.com; http://www.springer.com/. Illus., index, adv. Refereed. Reprint: PSC. *Indexed:* A01, A22, A47, Agr, BAS, BRI, C45, E01, P02, P61, RRTA, SSA. *Bk. rev.:* Number and length vary. *Aud.:* Ac, Sa.

This peer-reviewed journal focuses on the "interaction between people and their environment." Articles examine the problems of adaptation in urban environments, and scrutinize the effects of population density on environmental quality, social organization, and health. International in focus, this journal is recommended for academic libraries.

Journal of Environmental Economics and Management. See Economics section.

The Journal of Environmental Education. See Education/Specific Subjects and Teaching Methods: Environmental Education section.

2254. *Journal of Environmental Health.* Former titles (until 1963): *Sanitarian's Journal of Environmental Health;* (until 1962): *Sanitarian.* [ISSN: 0022-0892] 1938. 10x/yr. USD 135 domestic (Free to members). Ed(s): Nelson Fabian. National Environmental Health Association, 720 S Colorado Blvd, Ste 1000-N, Denver, CO 80246; staff@neha.org; http://www.neha.org. Illus., adv. Refereed. Microform: PQC. *Indexed:* A01, A22, AbAn, BRI, C&ISA, C45, CerAb, FS&TA, H24, IndVet, P02, RRTA, S25. *Aud.:* Ac, Sa.

From the National Environmental Health Association comes this peer-reviewed journal, with articles concerning the public health field. Published ten times per year, this publication "keeps readers up-to-date on current issues," and offers research in such fields as air quality, food safety and protection, occupational safety and health, and water quality. Recommended for both academic and public libraries.

The Journal of Wildlife Management. See Zoology/General section.

2255. Land Letter: the newsletter for natural resource professionals.
[ISSN: 0890-7625] 1982. fortn. Ed(s): Kevin Braun, Daniel Cusick. Environment and Energy Publishing, LLC, 122 C St, N W, Ste 722, Washington, DC 20001; pubs@eenews.net; http://www.eenews.net. Adv. *Aud.:* Hs, Ga, Ac, Sa.

Land Letter is a weekly news source that provides objective coverage of U.S. environmental issues. It is recommended for special and academic libraries whose users work on natural resources policy or research. "Considered a 'must-read' by people who track and influence energy, environmental[,] and climate policy."

2256. Linkages Update. Former titles: *Linkages; Earth Negotiations Bulletin; Earth Summit Bulletin.* 1992. bi-w. Free. Ed(s): Lynn Wagner, Pamela Chasek. International Institute for Sustainable Development (I I S D), 161 Portage Ave E, 6th Fl, Winnipeg, MB R3B 0Y4, Canada; http://www.iisd.ca. *Aud.:* Hs, Ga, Ac, Sa.

Linkages "is a bi-weekly e-newsletter that delivers the latest information on international environment and sustainable development issues." Published by the International Institute for Sustainable Development, this online publication makes the most of the Listserv format. Libraries with constituents that need to keep abreast of environmental and sustainability issues will find this publication useful.

2257. Local Environment: the international journal of justice and sustainability. [ISSN: 1354-9839] 1996. 10x/yr. GBP 904 (print & online eds.). Ed(s): Julian Agyeman. Routledge, 4 Park Sq, Milton Park, Abingdon, OX14 4RN, United Kingdom; subscriptions@tandf.co.uk; http://www.tandfonline.com. Adv. Sample. Refereed. Reprint: PSC. *Indexed:* A01, A22, C45, E01, IBSS, IndVet, RRTA. *Aud.:* Ac, Sa.

Local Environment: the international journal of justice and sustainability is a refereed journal that "is a forum for the examination, evaluation[,] and discussion of the environmental, social[,] and economic policies and strategies which will be needed in the move towards 'Just Sustainability' at local, national[,] and global levels." Recommended for academic libraries with an urban planning focus, and for libraries that support local policymakers and community advocates.

2258. Mother Earth News: the original guide to living wisely. [ISSN: 0027-1535] 1970. bi-m. USD 14.95 domestic; USD 27.95 Canada; USD 31.95 elsewhere. Ed(s): Cheryl Long, John Rockhold. Ogden Publications, Inc., 1503 SW 42nd St, Topeka, KS 66609; http://www.ogdenpubs.com. Illus., index, adv. Sample. Circ: 410344 Paid. *Indexed:* A01, A22, B02, B03, BRI, C37, C42, GardL, IHTDI, MASUSE, P02. *Aud.:* Hs, Ga.

Public libraries are the best location for this general interest magazine, which is aimed at do-it-yourself environmentalists. It contains classified and other advertising. Online content enhances the magazine with blogs, daily content, and an interactive garden planner.

2259. Natural Hazards Review. [ISSN: 1527-6988] 2000. q. USD 388. Ed(s): Kathleen Tierney, Vilas Mujumdar. American Society of Civil Engineers, 1801 Alexander Bell Dr, Reston, VA 20191; http://www.asce.org. Adv. Refereed. *Indexed:* A22, C&ISA, C45, CerAb, EngInd, H24, RiskAb. *Bk. rev.:* Number and length vary. *Aud.:* Ac, Sa.

International in scope, this journal is recommended for academic libraries. It is published by the American Society of Civil Engineers and the Hazards Center at the University of Colorado at Boulder. *Natural Hazards Review* is "dedicated to bringing together the physical, social, and behavioral sciences; engineering; and the regulatory and policy environments to provide a forum for cutting edge, holistic, and cross-disciplinary approaches to natural hazards loss and cost reduction."

2260. The Natural Resources Journal. [ISSN: 0028-0739] 1961. q. USD 40 domestic; USD 45 foreign; USD 15 per issue. Ed(s): Reed Benson. University of New Mexico, School of Law, MSC11 6070, 1 University of New Mexico, Albuquerque, NM 87131; http://lawschool.unm.edu. Illus., index, adv. Refereed. Vol. ends: Fall. Microform: WSH; PMC. Reprint: WSH. *Indexed:* A01, A22, ABS&EES, Agr, BAS, BRI, CBRI, CLI, EconLit, IBSS, JEL, L14, P02, P61, S25, SSA. *Bk. rev.:* Number and length vary. *Aud.:* Ac, Sa.

Published by the University of New Mexico School of Law, *Natural Resources Journal* "is an international, interdisciplinary forum devoted to the study of natural and environmental resources." Policy-oriented, this peer-reviewed academic journal provides analysis of both policy issues and legal cases.

Ranger Rick. See Children section.

2261. Remote Sensing of Environment: an interdisciplinary journal.
[ISSN: 0034-4257] 1969. 12x/yr. EUR 3895. Ed(s): Marvin E Bauer. Elsevier Inc., 360 Park Ave S, New York, NY 10010; usinfo-f@elsevier.com; http://www.elsevier.com. Illus., index, adv. Sample. Refereed. Vol. ends: Mar/Dec. *Indexed:* A01, A22, Agr, C&ISA, C45, CerAb, CompR, EngInd, M&GPA, OceAb, PhotoAb, RRTA, S25. *Bk. rev.:* Number and length vary. *Aud.:* Ac, Sa.

Remote sensing involves collecting environmental data without coming into physical contact with the environment, including through satellite imaging, aerial photography, and radar. This interdisciplinary journal "serves the remote sensing community with the publication of results on theory, science, applications[,] and technology of remote sensing of Earth resources and environment." It includes peer-reviewed articles, and is recommended for academic libraries.

Restoration Ecology. See Ecology section.

■ EUROPE

General/Newspapers

See also Latin America and Spain; and Slavic Studies sections.

Sarah Roberts, Library Assistant, Physics Research Library, Harvard College Library, Harvard University, Cambridge, MA 02138.

Cheryl LaGuardia, Research Librarian, Widener Library, Harvard University

Introduction

The Europe section covers a range of journals, magazines, and newspapers that focus on Western Europe, with an emphasis on artistic, literary, cultural, and historical themes and topics. Numerous journals contain a comparative structure, and most provide scholarly articles about regional cultural influences, accomplishments, and styles dating from the Middle Ages to the present day. Dutch, French, German, Italian, and Scandinavian regions are especially highlighted in this section. Also included are two international, Western Europe–based newspapers, and several magazines published by Western European cultural societies, both of which offer news, information, and cultural review sections for a more generally-based audience.

The interdisciplinary scope of this section necessitates selectivity, and the journals, magazines, and newspapers listed have been included based on librarian recommendations and their selection for inclusion in earlier editions of *Magazines for Libraries.*

Basic Periodicals

Central European History, The Germanic Review, Journal of European Studies, Scandinavian Review, Yale French Studies.

Basic Abstracts and Indexes

Annual Bibliography of English Language Literature (ABELL), Arts and Humanities Citation Index, BHA: Bibliography of the History of Art, British Humanities Index, Current Contents, FRANCIS, Humanities Index, IBZ, MLA International Bibliography, PAIS International, RILM Abstracts of Music Literature, Zeitungs-Index.

General

2262. Central European History. Formerly (until 1968): *Journal of Central European Affairs.* [ISSN: 0008-9389] 1941. q. GBP 149 (print & online eds.). Ed(s): Kenneth Ledford, Catherine Epstein. Cambridge University Press, The Edinburgh Bldg, Shaftesbury Rd, Cambridge, CB2 8RU, United Kingdom; journals@cambridge.org; http://www.cambridge.org/uk. Illus., index, adv. Refereed. Reprint: PSC. *Indexed:* A01, A22, ABS&EES, AmHI, ArtHuCI, BRI, CBRI, E01, IBSS, MASUSE, MLA-IB, RILM. *Bk. rev.:* 20, length varies. *Aud.:* Ac.

This journal is published for the Central European History Society and provides articles, book reviews, and essays from international scholars on a wide range of topics, examining the history of Austria, Germany, and German-speaking regions of Central Europe. This scholarly and refereed journal covers cultural, diplomatic, economic, intellectual, military, political, and social issues and topics within and related to Central Europe from the medieval period to the present day, and it is recommended for academic research libraries. This journal is also available electronically, and the publisher's web site can be accessed at http://journals.cambridge.org.ezp-prod1.hul.harvard.edu/action/displayJournal?jid=CCC, where articles can be submitted, browsed by latest issue, back issues, most-downloaded, or most-cited filters. They can also be downloaded or purchased depending on readers' membership or institutional affiliation status. The web site also offers special tools, sales information, a search widget, and related links, and allows readers to sign up for content alerts.

2263. Contemporary French Civilization. [ISSN: 0147-9156] 1976. 3x/yr. GBP 88 (print & online eds.). Ed(s): Denis M Provencher, Jean-Philippe Mathy. Liverpool University Press, 4 Cambridge St, Liverpool, L69 7ZU, United Kingdom; lup@liv.ac.uk; http://www.liverpooluniversitypress.co.uk/. Illus., adv. Refereed. *Indexed:* A22, AmHI, FR, MLA-IB, RILM. *Bk. rev.:* Number and length vary. *Aud.:* Ac.

Contemporary French Civilization publishes articles, book reviews, essays, and information in both French and English on topics related to French culture, civilization, and language, and to the Francophone world in general. This refereed journal strives to reach a diverse audience by providing broad, interdisciplinary content inclusive of all French and Francophone cultures worldwide. Interviews, research articles, annotated bibliographies, and book reviews are highlights. This journal is recommended for any academic library that supports French Studies, and is also available as an e-journal. The publisher's web site can be accessed at www.liverpooluniversitypress.co.uk/index.php?option=com_content&view=article&id=47%3Acontemporary-french-civilization&catid=8&Itemid=21. Here, readers can browse content by subject areas, submit articles, acquire subscription information, and download or purchase articles depending on membership status.

Deutschland. See *Magazin-Deutschland.de* in International Magazines section.

2264. Dutch Crossing: a journal of low countries studies. [ISSN: 0309-6564] 1977. 3x/yr. GBP 191 (print & online eds.). Ed(s): Carol Fehringer, Ulrich Tiedau. Maney Publishing, Ste 1C, Joseph's Well, Hanover Walk, Leeds, LS3 1AB, United Kingdom; maney@maneypublishing.com; http://maneypublishing.com/. Illus., index. Sample. Refereed. Reprint: PSC. *Indexed:* A22, ArtHuCI, LT&LA, MLA-IB, P61, SSA. *Bk. rev.:* 12, length varies. *Aud.:* Ac.

This scholarly, peer-reviewed, multidisciplinary journal is the official publication of the Association for Low Countries Studies. It covers the Dutch language, Dutch literature, history and art of the Low Counties, politics, Dutch as a foreign language, and social and cultural issues of the Netherlands and Flanders. It strives to encourage scholarship among young and established researchers in order to "enhance the profile of Low Countries Studies and of Dutch and Flemish culture in the English-speaking world." Areas of topical coverage include Belgium, the Netherlands, and parts of the Americas, Southeast Asia, and Southern Africa, where Dutch has historically had an impact. Entries include book reviews, conference papers, research reports, and Dutch literary works translated into English. All articles are written in English. *Dutch Crossing* is also available as an ejournal, and is recommended for academic libraries that support research in European Studies and the Low Countries. The publisher's web site can be accessed at http://maneypublishing.com/index.php/journals/dtc/

The Economist. See Economics section.

2265. Edinburgh Review. Formerly (until 1985): *New Edinburgh Review.* [ISSN: 0267-6672] 1969. 3x/yr. GBP 35 (Individuals, GBP 20; GBP 7.99 per issue). Edinburgh Review, 22A Buccleuch Pl, Edinburgh, EH8 9LN, United Kingdom. Illus., adv. Refereed. Microform: PMC; PQC. *Indexed:* AmHI, BEL&L, MLA-IB. *Bk. rev.:* Number and length vary. *Aud.:* Ga, Ac.

Considered the leading journal of ideas from Scotland, and Edinburgh's oldest literary journal, the *Edinburgh Review* was founded in 1802 and became one of the nineteenth century's most influential British magazines. Publication ceased in 1929 but resumed in 1969, with the journal's title *New Edinburgh Review,* only to return to its earlier title, *Edinburgh Review,* in 1985. Throughout the course of this history, the review has published the works of such influential literary figures as Carlyle, Gladstone, Macaulay, and Scott. Balancing its Scottish focus with international coverage of intellectual debate, *Edinburgh Review* contains short fiction, poetry, and reviews, and is considered to have contributed greatly to the development of modern standards of literary criticism and the development of the modern periodical. Online access to this periodical can be found at the web site, where readers can browse extracts, subscribe, read featured articles, learn about upcoming events, and submit articles and reviews. Recommended for general and academic audiences. URL: http://edinburgh-review.com

Elsevier. See International Magazines section.

L'Espresso. See International Magazines section.

2266. L'Esprit Createur. [ISSN: 0014-0767] 1961. q. USD 95. Ed(s): Maria Minich Brewer, Daniel Brewer. The Johns Hopkins University Press, 2715 N Charles St, Baltimore, MD 21218; http://www.press.jhu.edu. Illus., index, adv. Sample. Refereed. Circ: 343. Microform: PQC. Reprint: PSC. *Indexed:* A22, AmHI, ArtHuCI, BRI, CBRI, E01, FR, MLA-IB. *Bk. rev.:* Number and length vary. *Aud.:* Ac.

L'Esprit Createur is a peer-reviewed scholarly journal that contains book reviews and critical essays focusing on Francophone literature, criticism, and culture. This American publication, with articles in both English and French, explores "all periods of French literature and thought," and "has been analyzing and documenting contemporary French and Francophone Studies for half a century." With a host of eminent past and present contributors who represent a variety of critical approaches and methodologies, *L'Esprit Createur* examines such topics as culture, film, and literature, and ranks among the premier literary and critical publications of its kind. Also available as an ejournal, this journal is highly recommended for all academic research libraries. Access, subscription, and submission information is available on the publisher's web site, at http://www.press.jhu.edu.ezp-prod1.hul.harvard.edu/journals/lesprit_createur/

2267. European History Quarterly. Formerly (until 1984): *European Studies Review.* [ISSN: 0265-6914] 1971. q. USD 875. Ed(s): Laurence Cole, Lucy Riall. Sage Publications Ltd., 1 Oliver's Yard, 55 City Rd, London, EC1Y 1SP, United Kingdom; info@sagepub.co.uk; http://www.uk.sagepub.com. Illus., index, adv. Sample. Refereed. Reprint: PSC. *Indexed:* A01, A22, ABS&EES, AmHI, ArtHuCI, BRI, E01, IBSS, NumL, P02, P61, SSA. *Bk. rev.:* 8-10, length varies. *Aud.:* Ac.

European History Quarterly is a peer-reviewed, quarterly journal with an "international reputation as an essential resource on European history." This journal contains articles on a variety of topics associated with European history and social and political thought from the late Middle Ages to the present day, with submissions written by prominent scholars from Europe and North America. Topics have included "Cold War Europe, Hero Cults, and the Politics of the Past: Comparative European Perspectives," and "Europe and Latin America in the 1820s," for example. Issues typically contain about six scholarly contributions and an extensive book review section, with occasional feature review articles and historiographical essays. This journal is recommended for all academic libraries, and is also available as an ejournal. Podcasts, an index of special issues, as RSS feed, and submission and subscription access can be found on the publisher's web site at http://ehq.sagepub.com.ezp-prod1.hul.harvard.edu/

2268. *Eurozine: the netmagazine.* [ISSN: 1684-4637] 1998. irreg. Ed(s): Carl Henrik Fredriksson. eurozine, Rembrandtstr 31/10, Vienna, 1020, Austria. *Aud.:* Ga, Ac.

Eurozine is both a network of European cultural journals and a netmagazine, published with the support of the European Union. *Eurozine* is designed to serve as an "independent cultural platform" to promote European journals, foster communication, and provide a critical space for transnational debate. This platform aims to spread and promote aesthetic, cultural, political, and philosophical thought between European languages, in order to "stimulate a common cultural discourse among an international readership." Linking "up more than 80 partner journals and just as many associated magazines and institutions from nearly all European countries," *Eurozine* provides access to almost 100 periodicals, including *Kritika & Kontext, Mittelweg36, Ord & Bild, Revista Critica, Samtiden, Transit,* and *Wespennest.* The site is well organized, with all articles, including some from archival issues, searchable by keyword and able to be read in html or pdf format. There are biographies of contributors and an impressive list of European cultural journals, with links to their web sites, in addition to headlines from the news, editorials, focal points, and a social media presence. This netmagazine and portal is recommended for general or academic audiences wishing to stay abreast of the current cultural debate in Europe. URL: www.eurozine.com

L'Express. See International Magazines section.

2269. *Forum Italicum: a journal of Italian studies.* [ISSN: 0014-5858] 1967. s-a. USD 211. Ed(s): Mario B Mignone. Sage Publications, Inc., 2455 Teller Rd, Thousand Oaks, CA 91320; info@sagepub.com; http://www.sagepub.com. Illus. Sample. Refereed. Reprint: PSC. *Indexed:* A22, ArtHuCI, BRI, MLA-IB. *Bk. rev.:* 15-20, length varies. *Aud.:* Ac.

Forum Italicum, published in the United States, is a journal of peer-reviewed, scholarly articles encompassing Italian Studies topics such as Italian culture, language, and literature. Issues typically contain five or six scholarly articles, in addition to notes, reviews, poetry, prose, and literary translations. Established in 1967 by M. Ricciardelli, this journal was created with the intention of serving as a meeting-place for scholars to debate and discuss Italian Studies topics. Students and young scholars are encouraged to contribute. The publisher's web site provides information about the distinguished editorial board and subscriptions, and offers a comprehensive, searchable bibliography of past and current issues, including pdf files of book reviews. This journal is also available as an ejournal and is highly recommended for academic libraries that support Italian and European Studies. URL: www.sagepub.com.ezp-prod1.hul.harvard.edu/journals/Journal202152

2270. *France.* [ISSN: 0958-8213] 1990. m. GBP 23.99 domestic; GBP 38.70 in Europe; GBP 40.70 elsewhere. Ed(s): Carolyn Boyd. Archant Life Ltd., Archant House, 3 Oriel Rd, Cheltenham, GL50 1BB, United Kingdom; http://www.archantlife.co.uk. Illus., adv. *Aud.:* Ga.

France magazine is marketed to readers as "the next best thing to being there!," and is filled with glossy photos, articles about weekend getaways, a food and wine section, holiday destination ideas, and articles about France's culture and history. Additional topics include "insider tips" for travelers, a monthly language section for improving one's French, and film reviews and interviews. The magazine's web site provides article summaries and tables of contents dating back to 1990, and also includes a number of useful links to information

about traveling to France, French real estate, French food, and special offers and contests. Published for British Francophiles, the web site and magazine are nevertheless helpful for Americans who may wish to steep themselves in French (tourist) culture. Recommended for a general audience. URL: www.completefrance.com/magazines/france-magazine

2271. *French Historical Studies.* [ISSN: 0016-1071] 1958. q. USD 232. Ed(s): Patricia M. E. Lorcin. Duke University Press, 905 W Main St, Ste 18 B, PO Box 90660, Durham, NC 27701; subscriptions@dukeupress.edu; http://www.dukeupress.edu. Illus., index, adv. Sample. Refereed. Reprint: PSC. *Indexed:* A01, A22, AmHI, ArtHuCI, BRI, E01, MLA-IB, P02, RILM. *Bk. rev.:* Essays. *Aud.:* Ac.

French Historical Studies, the official journal of the Society for French Historical Studies, is "the leading journal on the history of France" and publishes monographic articles, commentaries, and research notes that cover French history from the Middles Ages to the present day. This journal offers a diverse format consisting of review essays, bilingual abstracts of journal articles, special issues, forums, bibliographies of dissertations and recent French history publications, and conference, prize, and fellowship announcements. It would be of interest primarily to French historians and scholars, and is recommended for academic libraries. Occasional special issues are supervised by guest editors, and the journal is also available in electronic format. The publisher's web site provides society news and links to special/back issues, and submission and access information. URL: www.dukeupress.edu/Catalog/ViewProduct.php?viewby=journal&productid=45611

2272. *French History.* [ISSN: 0269-1191] 1987. q. EUR 365. Ed(s): Julian Wright, Penny Roberts. Oxford University Press, Great Clarendon St, Oxford, OX2 6DP, United Kingdom; enquiry@oup.co.uk; http://www.oxfordjournals.org/. Illus., adv. Sample. Refereed. Reprint: PSC. *Indexed:* A22, ArtHuCI, E01, P61, SSA. *Bk. rev.:* 20, length varies. *Aud.:* Ac.

French History is a peer-reviewed journal published on behalf of the U.K. Society for the Study of French History, and it provides a "broad perspective on contemporary debates from an international range of scholars, and covers the entire range of French history from the early Middle Ages to the twentieth century." The editorial board is composed of international scholars who support the journal's goal of creating an international research forum for anyone interested in French history. Issues contain research articles that cover a range of French history-related topics across the arts and social sciences, and "a book reviews section that is an essential reference for any serious student of French history." The web site at Oxford University Press provides tables of contents and full text (for subscribers only) from the first volume (1987) to the present, a reader services section, and submission and subscription information. Recommended for academic libraries, this title is also available as an ejournal. URL: http://fh.oxfordjournals.org.ezp-prod1.hul.harvard.edu/

2273. *French Review.* [ISSN: 0016-111X] 1927. bi-m. Free to members; Non-members, USD 55. Ed(s): Christopher P Pinet, Wynne Wong. American Association of Teachers of French, Mailcode 4510, Southern Illinois University, Carbondale, IL 62901; aatf@frenchteachers.org; http://www.frenchteachers.org. Adv. Refereed. Circ: 10300. Microform: PMC; PQC. *Indexed:* A22, AmHI, ArtHuCI, BRI, CBRI, FR, LT&LA, MLA-IB, RILM. *Aud.:* Ac.

The *French Review* is the official journal of the American Association of Teachers of French (AATF). According to the journal's web site, the *French Review* has "the largest circulation of any scholarly journal of French and Francophone studies in the world." Each issue contains articles and reviews on French and Francophone literature, society and culture, linguistics, cinema, technology, and pedagogy. There are occasional special issues covering topics such as Martinique and Guadeloupe, Quebec, and France-Algeria; and one annual issue is devoted to annual reviews. The web site is informational but contains tables of contents for issues dating back to 1999, society announcements, and a guide for authors. Recommended for academic libraries. URL: http://frenchreview.frenchteachers.org/

2274. *German Life and Letters.* [ISSN: 0016-8777] 1936. q. GBP 423. Wiley-Blackwell Publishing Ltd., The Atrium, Southern Gate, Chichester, PO19 8SQ, United Kingdom; customer@wiley.com; http://www.wiley.com/. Illus., index, adv. Sample. Refereed. Reprint: PSC. *Indexed:* A01, A22, AmHI, ArtHuCI, E01, MLA-IB, RILM. *Aud.:* Ac.

German Life and Letters has long been considered a leading journal in German Studies, offering a variety of English- and German-language "articles dealing with literary and non-literary concerns in the German-speaking world." Literature, politics, social history, language, and the visual arts are frequent article topics, with contributors covering "German thought and culture from the Middle Ages to the present." Thematic issues are published irregularly but have covered a wide variety of topics, ranging from German cinema to "Exilliteratur." The publisher's journal web site provides a free online cumulative index of issues dating from 1936 to 2006, with abstracts and full text available from 1997 to the latest edition, but reserved for institutions with current subscriptions. This journal is recommended for academic libraries that support research in German Studies, and is also available as an ejournal. URL: http://onlinelibrary.wiley.com.ezp-prod1.hul.harvard.edu/journal/10.1111/%28ISSN%291468-0483/homepage/ProductInformation.html

2275. *The German Quarterly.* [ISSN: 0016-8831] 1928. q. GBP 125 (print & online eds.). Ed(s): Dr. James L Rolleston. Wiley-Blackwell Publishing, Inc., 111 River St, Hoboken, NJ 07030; info@wiley.com; http://onlinelibrary.wiley.com/. Index. Sample. Refereed. Microform: PMC; PQC. Reprint: PSC. *Indexed:* A01, A07, A22, ABS&EES, AmHI, ArtHuCI, BRI, CBRI, E01, LT&LA, MLA-IB, RILM. *Bk. rev.:* 35, length varies. *Aud.:* Ac.

The German Quarterly is a refereed journal published on behalf of the American Association of Teachers of German (AATG), whose aim is to serve "as a forum for all sorts of scholarly debates—topical, ideological, methodological, [and] theoretical, of both the established and the experimental variety, as well as debates on recent developments in the profession." Along with scholarly articles on German culture, history, language, and literature throughout history, the journal provides special reports and extensive book reviews of academic publications, and encourages essays "employing new theoretical or methodological approaches, essays on recent developments in the field, and essays on subjects that have recently been underrepresented." The publisher's journal web site provides an index to issues dating back to 2005 and links to the AATG-sponsored web site for the journal. The *German Quarterly* should be included in any academic library that supports German Studies, and is also available as an ejournal. URLs: www.germanquarterly.aatg.org; or http://onlinelibrary.wiley.com.ezp-prod1.hul.harvard.edu/journal/10.1111/%28ISSN%291756-1183/homepage/ProductInformation.html

2276. *German Studies Review.* [ISSN: 0149-7952] 1978. 3x/yr. USD 65 (print or online ed.). Ed(s): Sabine Hake. The Johns Hopkins University Press, 2715 N Charles St, Baltimore, MD 21218; http://www.press.jhu.edu. Illus., adv. Sample. Refereed. Circ: 1800. *Indexed:* A01, A22, ABS&EES, AmHI, ArtHuCI, BRI, IBSS, MLA-IB, RILM. *Bk. rev.:* 60. *Aud.:* Ac.

German Studies Review is the scholarly journal of the "German Studies Association (GSA), the world's largest academic association devoted to the interdisciplinary and multidisciplinary study of the German-speaking countries." This is a refereed journal that covers interdisciplinary scholarship in Austrian, German, and Swiss history, cultural studies, literature, political science, and economics; and issues generally contain about six articles and a large section of reviews of academic book publications. This journal is also available electronically, and the publisher's journal web site includes tables of contents and abstracts for current issues, along with pricing, submission, subscription, and indexing/abstracting information. Recommended for academic libraries that support research in German Studies. URL: www.press.jhu.edu.ezp-prod1.hul.harvard.edu/journals/german_studies_review/

2277. *The Germanic Review: literature, culture, theory.* [ISSN: 0016-8890] 1925. q. GBP 170 (print & online eds.). Ed(s): Andreas Gailus, Johannes von Moltke. Taylor & Francis Inc., 325 Chestnut St, Ste 800, Philadelphia, PA 19106; customerservice@taylorandfrancis.com; http://www.tandfonline.com. Illus., index, adv. Sample. Refereed. Vol. ends: Winter. Microform: PQC. Reprint: PSC. *Indexed:* A01, A22, ABS&EES, AmHI, ArtHuCI, BRI, E01, MLA-IB, P02, RILM. *Bk. rev.:* 3-9, length varies. *Aud.:* Ac.

The Germanic Review is a refereed scholarly journal that features contributors from leading research institutes in the U.S., Canada, U.K., France, Australia, and Germany. Articles cover such topics as German culture, literature, identity, historical memory, and literary theory, as well as reviews of recent German Studies publications. Most articles are written in English, but all-German articles are occasionally published. This journal is also available as an ejournal, and the publisher's journal web site includes tables of contents and preview pages for issues dating back to 1974, a search feature that can filter by most-read and most-cited articles, and submission and subscription information. Published since 1925, *The Germanic Review* is an important title for libraries that support German Studies, and is recommended for academic libraries. URL: www.tandfonline.com.ezp-prod1.hul.harvard.edu/loi/vger20

L'Hebdo. See International Magazines section.

Iceland Review. See International Magazines section.

2278. *Irish University Review: a journal of Irish studies.* Formerly (until 1970): *University Review.* [ISSN: 0021-1427] 1954. s-a. GBP 50 (print & online eds.). Ed(s): Dr. John Brannigan. Edinburgh University Press Ltd., 22 George Sq, Edinburgh, EH8 9LF, United Kingdom; journals@eup.ed.ac.uk; http://www.euppublishing.com. Illus., adv. Refereed. Circ: 1200. *Indexed:* A22, ArtHuCI, BRI, MLA-IB, RILM. *Bk. rev.:* 10, length varies. *Aud.:* Ac.

The *Irish University Review: a journal of Irish studies* was established in 1970 as a journal of Irish literary criticism. With an emphasis on contemporary Irish literature, this refereed, scholarly, literary journal "is affiliated to [sic] the International Association for the Study of Irish Literatures (IASIL), whose members receive the journal as a benefit of association membership." Contributions consist of literary essays, poetry, short fiction, interviews with authors, poets, and playwrights, and a large section of book reviews. The semi-annual issues are regularly devoted to Irish authors or themes, "particularly submissions which expand the range of authors and texts to receive critical treatment." Meanwhile, the book reviews enable readers to stay abreast of current Irish literary trends. This journal is recommended for academic libraries. It is also available as an ejournal, and the publisher's journal web site provides tables of contents for recent issues, and submission and subscription information. URL: www.euppublishing.com.ezp-prod1.hul.harvard.edu/journal/iur

2279. *Italica.* Formerly (until 1926): *American Association of Teachers of Italian. Bulletin.* [ISSN: 0021-3020] 1924. q. Free to members. Ed(s): Andrea Ciccarelli. American Association of Teachers of Italian (A A T I), c/o Andrea Ciccarelli, Editor, Dept. of French and Italian, Indiana University, Blomington, IN 47405-6601, IN 47405-6601; aati@utoronto.ca; http://www.aati-online.org/. Adv. Refereed. Microform: PQC. *Indexed:* A22, BRI, LT&LA, MLA-IB, RILM. *Bk. rev.:* Number and length vary. *Aud.:* Ac.

Italica publishes interdisciplinary and comparative studies-based scholarly articles on topics including Italian cinema, culture, linguistics, and literature, and is the official journal of the American Association of Teachers of Italian (AATI). Issues also include "a section devoted to translations of Italian major works/ authors, cultural debates, and interviews." Authors are generally from North America, as contributing preference is given to AATI members. The web site of the AATI provides a variety of information related to the teaching of Italian, and its section on *Italica* is mostly informational, with the tables of contents of some volumes available. Archival issues may be accessed through JSTOR. This journal is also available as an ejournal, and is recommended for academic libraries. URL: www.aati-online.org/

2280. *Journal of European Studies (Chalfont Saint Giles).* [ISSN: 0047-2441] 1971. q. USD 941. Ed(s): John Flower. Sage Publications Ltd., 1 Oliver's Yard, 55 City Rd, London, EC1Y 1SP, United Kingdom; info@sagepub.co.uk; http://www.uk.sagepub.com. Illus., index. Sample. Refereed. Microform: PQC. Reprint: PSC. *Indexed:* A01, A22, ABIn, AmHI, ArtHuCI, BRI, E01, FR, MLA-IB, P02. *Bk. rev.:* 30, length varies. *Aud.:* Ac.

The *Journal of European Studies* is a peer-reviewed, interdisciplinary journal that covers the literature and cultural history of Europe since the Renaissance. Published quarterly since 1971, *JES* is led by an international editorial board, guaranteeing the quality of articles and review essays. *JES* publishes most articles in English, with occasional contributions in French or German, and provides review essays and notices that offer "a wide and informed coverage of many books that are published on European cultural themes." The web site at Sage Publications provides access to tables of contents for issues from 1971 to the latest issue, with full-text access provided to users with subscription access, in addition to an index of special issues, a note from the editor and subscription and submission information. This journal is also available as an ejournal, and is recommended for all research libraries. URL: http://jes.sagepub.com.ezp-prod1.hul.harvard.edu

Knack. See International Magazines section.

The Literary Review. See Literary Reviews section.

2281. New German Critique. [ISSN: 0094-033X] 1973. 3x/yr. USD 203. Ed(s): Andreas Huyssen, David Bathrick. Duke University Press, 905 W Main St, Ste 18 B, PO Box 90660, Durham, NC 27701; subscriptions@dukeupress.edu; http://www.dukeupress.edu. Illus., index, adv. Sample. Microform: PQC. Reprint: PSC. *Indexed:* A01, A22, ABS&EES, AmHI, ArtHuCI, MLA-IB. *Aud.:* Ac.

The *New German Critique* is an interdisciplinary journal that covers twentieth and twenty-first century German studies subjects, "including literature, film, and media; literary theory and cultural studies; Holocaust studies; art and architecture; political and social theory; and philosophy." Issues are theme-oriented and include up to eight lengthy scholarly articles. This journal is available electronically, and the publisher's web site is mostly informational, providing tables of contents for back issues as well as special issues, an RSS feed, and subscription and submission information. This journal is highly recommended for all academic libraries, in particular those that support collections in contemporary criticism, philosophy, German Studies, and comparative literature. URL: http://ngc.dukejournals.org.ezp-prod1.hul.harvard.edu/

New Statesman. See News and Opinion section.

2282. Nineteenth Century French Studies. [ISSN: 0146-7891] 1972. s-a. 2 double issues. USD 99. Ed(s): Marshall C Olds. University of Nebraska Press, 1111 Lincoln Mall, Lincoln, NE 68588; pressmail@unl.edu; http://www.nebraskapress.unl.edu. Illus., index, adv. Refereed. Circ: 450. Microform: PQC. *Indexed:* A01, A07, A22, AmHI, ArtHuCI, BRI, E01, FR, MLA-IB, RILM. *Bk. rev.:* 10, length varies. *Aud.:* Ac.

Nineteenth Century French Studies is an independent, peer-reviewed, scholarly journal that covers all aspects of nineteenth-century French literature and criticism. This journal examines new trends, reviews (in both French and English), and promising research findings in a variety of disciplines, and strives to acquaint readers with "professional developments in nineteenth-century French studies." This title is also available electronically, and the publisher's web site provides information about submissions, guidelines, and subscriptions, as well as free access to an archive of abstracts of all articles published since the journal's inception, in addition to a news and a reviews section. The journal is available in full text online through Project Muse and other large serials aggregators. A premier resource for nineteenth-century French literary scholarship, this journal is highly recommended for academic libraries that support research in French literature. URL: www.unl.edu/ncfs

Norseman. See *Norwegians Worldwide* in International Magazines section.

Le Point. See International Magazines section.

2283. Il Politico: rivista italiana di scienze politiche. Formerly (until 1941): *Annali di Scienze Politiche.* [ISSN: 0032-325X] 1928. 3x/yr. Rubbettino Editore, Viale Rosario Rubbettino 10, Soveria Mannelli, 88049, Italy; segreteria@rubettino.it; http://www.rubbettino.it. Illus., index, adv. Sample. *Indexed:* A22, BAS, IBSS, JEL, P61. *Aud.:* Ac.

Published in Italian and English as a continuation of *Annali di Scienze Politiche* (*Annals of Political Sciences*), *Il Politico* is generally recognized as one of the more important periodicals in the field of Italian studies, with an emphasis on theory. *Il Politico* is renowned for the quality of its articles, written by internationally renowned authors, and for its wealth of research notes and reviews. The essays include brief summaries in English. Its web site is in Italian and is purely informational. This journal is recommended for academic and research libraries that support Italian studies. URL: www.giuffre.it/

Profil. See International Magazines section.

2284. Revue des Deux Mondes: litterature, histoire, arts et sciences. Former titles (until 1982): *Nouvelle Revue des Deux Mondes;* (until 1972): *Revue des Deux Mondes.* [ISSN: 0750-9278] 1829. m. Individuals, EUR 75.50; Students, EUR 53.50. Ed(s): Michel Crepu. Societe de la Revue des Deux Mondes, 97 rue de Lille, Paris, 75007, France. Illus., index, adv. Circ: 15000. *Indexed:* A22, BAS, IBSS, MLA-IB, RILM. *Bk. rev.:* 2, length varies. *Aud.:* Ga, Ac.

The *Revue des Deux Mondes* was first published in 1829 with the objective of welcoming "ideas related to France and the world emanating from other European countries." Truly multidisciplinary, it covers a variety of world issues such as the promotion of literary and artistic creations, important political debates, travel tales, social progress, economics, and science. Providing commentary and analysis on world events, the journal has accumulated over the years an impressive list of contributors, including Balzac, Baudelaire, Hugo, Fenimore Cooper, Heine, and Tocqueville. The web site is in French, though some parts are able to be translated into English, and is largely informational with an accessible archives, news, boutique, and theme sections. Older archival issues of the *Revue* are available in digital format from the Bibliotheque Nationale's digital library portal, Gallica. The *Revue des Deux Mondes* is one of few publications worldwide that may rightly claim to be a cultural institution. An essential title for large public libraries and research libraries. URL: www.revuedesdeuxmondes.fr/home/english.php

2285. Rivista di Letterature Moderne e Comparate. Formerly (until 1954): *Rivista di Letterature Moderne.* [ISSN: 0391-2108] 1946. q. EUR 69 domestic. Ed(s): A Pizzorusso. Pacini Editore SpA, Via A Gherardesca 1, Ospedaletto, 56121, Italy; pacini.editore@pacinieditore.it; http://www.pacinimedicina.it. Illus., adv. Sample. *Indexed:* A22, ArtHuCI, FR, MLA-IB. *Bk. rev.:* 13, length varies. *Aud.:* Ac.

Established by Carlo Pellegrini and Vittorio Santoli in 1946, *Rivista di Letterature Moderne e Comparate* is an academic journal whose scope covers the entire spectrum of Western literature since the Renaissance. Comparative in theme and covering the research of comparatists in both Europe and North America, articles are written in Italian, French, German, and English. Each issue contains about six scholarly articles and numerous book reviews that cover cultural topics in comparative literature, with a focus on European works, traditions, and perspectives. The December issue contains an index for the entire previous year. The publisher's journal web site is in Italian and is informational. Recommended for academic libraries that support programs in comparative literature. URL: www.pacinieditore.it/?p=1295

2286. Scandinavian Journal of History. Incorporates (1955-1980): *Excerpta Historica Nordica.* [ISSN: 0346-8755] 1976. 5x/yr. GBP 293 (print & online eds.). Ed(s): Guomundur Halfdanarson. Routledge, 4 Park Sq, Milton Park, Abingdon, OX14 4RN, United Kingdom; subscriptions@tandf.co.uk; http://www.tandfonline.com. Illus., adv. Sample. Reprint: PSC. *Indexed:* A01, A22, AmHI, ArtHuCI, E01, FR, IBSS. *Bk. rev.:* Number and length vary. *Aud.:* Ac.

The *Scandinavian Journal of History* is published for the Historical Associations of Denmark, Finland, Iceland, Norway, and Sweden, and the Scandinavian subcommittees of the International Committee of Historical Sciences. The journal "presents articles on Scandinavian history and review essays surveying themes in recent Scandinavian historical research," and although most authors are Scandinavian, all articles and reviews are published in English. Articles comparing Scandinavian phenomena, culture, and processes to those in other parts of Europe and the world are of particular interest. This journal also contains a books-reviewed section at the back of each issue, and polemical communications and review essays are encouraged for submission. Available as an ejournal as well as print, this journal is recommended for academic libraries that support Scandinavian Studies. The publisher's journal web site provides abstracts and tables of contents for browsing, as well as journal history, readership, and submission and subscription information; also there are news and offers. URL: www.tandfonline.com/action/aboutThisJournal?show=aimsScope&journalCode=shis20#.Uc3kuYIrrvY

2287. *Scandinavian Review.* Formerly (until 1975): *The American-Scandinavian Review.* [ISSN: 0098-857X] 1913. 3x/yr. Free to members; Non-members, USD 15. American-Scandinavian Foundation, 58 Park Ave, 38th St, New York, NY 10016; info@amscan.org; http://www.amscan.org/. Illus., index, adv. Sample. Microform: PQC. *Indexed:* A01, A06, A22, ENW, MLA-IB, P02, RILM. *Bk. rev.:* 2-5, 450 words. *Aud.:* Hs, Ga, Ac.

Scandinavian Review is published by the American-Scandinavian Foundation (ASF), whose mission is to promote an "international understanding through educational and cultural exchange between the United States and Denmark, Finland, Iceland, Norway, and Sweden." The magazine is issued to members of ASF, but is also available by subscription and in ejournal format. The magazine covers all aspects of contemporary life in Scandinavia, with an "emphasis on areas in which Scandinavian achievement is renowned: art and design, industrial development, commercial, political, economic and social innovation." The primary goal of this magazine is to provide information, news, and insights about Scandinavia that are rarely read about or seen in American media; and regular features include articles on particular themes or persons, cultural and historical informational articles, and reviews of Nordic books. Submissions are authored by leading journalists and writers from Scandinavia and North America and from other European countries, and subscription information and samples of articles can be found on the ASF web site. Because this magazine offers information rarely found in American media about Nordic countries and Scandinavian culture, it would be an excellent addition to any collection that supports European Studies. URL: www.amscan.org

The Spectator. See News and Opinion section.

Der Spiegel. See International Magazines section.

Suomen Kuvalehti. See International Magazines section.

2288. *Yale French Studies.* [ISSN: 0044-0078] 1948. s-a. Ed(s): Lawrence R Schehr, Michael A Johnson. Yale University Press, PO Box 209040, New Haven, CT 06520; customer.care@triliteral.org; http://yalepress.yale.edu/home.asp. Illus., adv. Sample. Microform: PQC. Reprint: PSC. *Indexed:* A01, A22, ABS&EES, AmHI, ArtHuCI, FR, MLA-IB, P02, RILM. *Aud.:* Ac.

Yale French Studies is one of the premier journals on French literature, thought, and civilization in the English language, and is "the oldest English-language journal in the United States devoted to French and Francophone literature and culture." Each volume is distinct and focuses on a single theme or author, and is conceived and written by a guest editor(s). Although essays are mostly contributed by North American scholars, articles by the most well-known contemporary French authors and critics have also been included. This journal, which is also available as an ejournal, provides a multidisciplinary approach to literature that includes French-speaking cultures outside of France, and has covered such topics as "Crime Fiction; Surrealism; Contemporary Writing for the Stage; and Memory in Postwar French and Francophone Culture." The full text is accessible through JSTOR with a two-year wall, and the publisher's journal web site is mainly informational. This journal is indispensable for any academic library that supports the study of French culture. URLs: http://french.yale.edu/yale-french-studies; http://yalepress.yale.edu/yupbooks/book.asp?isbn=9780300118230

Newspapers

Newspapers are popular among Europeans. It has been reported that an average of 31 million newspapers are sold in Germany each day, and 80 percent of the German population over the age of 14 reads at least one newspaper daily. Like Germany, the rest of Western Europe has an appetite for reading newspapers. To stay competitive, newspaper publishers have created user-friendly and continuously updated web versions of their products, while adding more color and innovative designs to their print editions. Although this subsection is brief, it presents newspapers that either have high international readership or are cited as the nation's newspaper of record.

See also the Newspapers section, and check the index for specific titles not included here.

The Guardian. See Newspapers/General section.

2289. *International Herald Tribune: the global edition of the New York Times.* [ISSN: 0294-8052] 1887. 6x/w. EUR 485 combined subscription (print & online eds.). Ed(s): Michael Getler. International Herald Tribune, 6 bis, rue des Graviers, Neuilly-sur-Seine, Cedex 92521, France; http://www.iht.com. Illus. Circ: 234722 Paid. Microform: PQC. *Indexed:* B02, B03, BRI, RILM. *Aud.:* Ga, Ac.

Published for American expatriates since 1887, the *International Herald Tribune* is the product of a unique collaboration between *The New York Times* and a number of premier international newspapers, among them *El Pais, Le Figaro,* and the *Moscow Times.* This newspaper was initially only available in select locations (e.g., Paris in the 1920s), but is now printed in 38 locations and sold in more than 160 countries. In the fall of 2013, it will be renamed the *International New York Times.* The well-organized web site presents the news with different emphases depending on selected regions of interest, and provides free access to selected full-text articles, blog entries, editorials, puzzles, weather forecasts, and classifieds. The world's most international paper, the *International Herald Tribune* presents a unique summary of world news. Recommended for general reader audiences. URL: http://global.nytimes.com/

2290. *The Irish Times (Special Edition).* Incorporates (19??-2003): *The Irish Times (City Edition);* Supersedes in part (in 19??): *The Irish Times.* [ISSN: 1393-3515] 1859. d. EUR 2 newsstand/cover; GBP 1.25 newsstand/cover in Northern Ireland. Irish Times Ltd., 24-28 Tara St, PO Box 74, Dublin, 2, Ireland; enquiries@irishtimes.com. Illus., adv. Microform: PQC. *Aud.:* Ga, Ac.

Published since 1859, *The Irish Times* established itself as Ireland's premier independent newspaper in 1974 when it was transferred from private ownership to ownership by the charitable Irish Times Trust, which was created to keep the newspaper free "from any form of personal or party, political, commercial, religious or other sectional control." With correspondents all over the world, the paper covers national and international news, economics, media, politics, technology, sports, the arts, and any other issue of general interest. The fully developed web site provides access to selected articles in full text, blogs, editorials, videos, and galleries. This newspaper is recommended for research and large public libraries or those catering to a large Irish community. URL: www.irishtimes.com

TLS: the Times literary supplement. See Books and Book Reviews section.

■ FAMILY

See also Lesbian, Gay, Bisexual, and Transgender; Marriage and Divorce; Parenting; Psychology; and Sociology and Social Work sections.

Erin K. McCaffrey, Electronic Services Librarian, Regis University, 3333 Regis Blvd., D-20, Denver, CO 80221; emccaffr@regis.edu

Introduction

The literature related to family studies presents a broad representation of what constitutes "family." A variety of intimate and partner relationship structures represent the modern family, some of which are very different from traditional representations of the family. Definitions of gender roles within the family have changed. The current family literature addresses multigenerational families, family therapy, parent–child relationships, gender issues, family caregivers, the family in a global context, family violence, substance abuse, and cross-cultural examinations of the family. Family therapy training and supervision continue to receive greater attention, as do therapy and treatment.

According to the report *America's Children: Key National Indicators of Well-Being, 2011* on ChildStats.gov, the number of children living with two married parents has gradually decreased, while the number of children living with only their mother has increased slightly between 1980 and 2010. Of children not living with either parent, over half of those children lived with a grandparent. Marriage rates have declined as the average age of first marriage has increased. Data issued in April 2012 in the U.S. Census Bureau 2010 Census Briefs *Households and Families: 2010* indicates that the average American family household size has stayed the same over the last decade. For the first time, husband–wife families increased yet fell below 50 percent of all households in the United States; opposite-sex unmarried-partner and same-sex partner households both increased. Multigenerational households have increased, as well as families with a female householder. Single-parent child-bearing and -rearing are common.

Here, periodicals that address the broad definition of the contemporary family, as well as family studies and family therapy, are the focus. Family studies periodicals tend to fall into either the popular or the scholarly category. The popular magazines in this area concentrate on practical self-help for families. Many of the periodicals in this category offer table-of-contents information and selected full text on their web sites. Periodicals in the scholarly category are devoting greater coverage to outside influences on the family. There has been an increase in content addressing economic factors and their impact on families. Of the scholarly journals represented here, content ranges from theory and research to practice and application.

Periodicals related to family and marriage are included in other sections of this volume, such as Marriage and Divorce, Parenting, Psychology, Sociology and Social Work, and Gay, Lesbian, Bisexual, and Transgender.

Basic Periodicals

Ga: *FamilyFun, Parenting, Parents;* Ac: *Family Process, Family Relations, Journal of Comparative Family Studies, Journal of Family Issues, Journal of Family Psychology, Journal of Marriage and Family;* Sa: *Families in Society, Journal of Marital and Family Therapy.*

Basic Abstracts and Indexes

Family & Society Studies Worldwide, Family Studies Abstracts, PsycINFO, Social Sciences Citation Index, Social Sciences Index, Social Work Abstracts, Sociological Abstracts.

2291. American Journal of Family Therapy. Former titles (until 1979): *International Journal of Family Counseling;* (until 1977): *Journal of Family Counseling.* [ISSN: 0192-6187] 1973. 5x/yr. GBP 256 (print & online eds.). Ed(s): S Richard Sauber. Routledge, 325 Chestnut St, Ste 800, Philadelphia, PA 19106; customerservice@taylorandfrancis.com; http://www.tandfonline.com. Illus., index, adv. Sample. Refereed. Vol. ends: Winter. Microform: PQC. Reprint: PSC. *Indexed:* A01, A22, BRI, E01, P02, P61, PsycInfo, SSA, SWR&A. *Bk. rev.:* 0-4, 600-1,200 words. *Aud.:* Ac, Sa.

The *American Journal of Family Therapy* publishes five issues per year and intends to be "the incisive, authoritative, independent voice" in family therapy. The journal is interdisciplinary in scope and its readership includes marriage and family therapists, counselors, clinical social workers, psychiatrists, psychologists, allied health and mental health practitioners, physicians, nurses, and clergy practitioners. Regular sections include "Family Law Issues in Family Therapy Practice," "Family Behavioral Medicine and Health," "Family Measurement Techniques," and "Continuing Education and Training," as well as book and media reviews. Recent topics represent the changing field of family therapy and encompass medical family therapy in cancer care; the ethics of family therapy; couples and money; children's daytime behavior problems in relation to bedtime routine and practices; and the effects of parental military deployment on child well-being. There is also coverage of substance abuse, child custody, and domestic violence. This journal is highly recommended for academic libraries that seek more than one scholarly family therapy journal.

2292. Child & Family Behavior Therapy. Formerly (until 1982): *Child Behavior Therapy.* [ISSN: 0731-7107] 1978. q. GBP 817 (print & online eds.). Ed(s): Cyril M Franks, Charles Diament. Routledge, 325 Chestnut St, Ste 800, Philadelphia, PA 19106; customerservice@taylorandfrancis.com; http://www.tandfonline.com. Illus., adv. Sample. Refereed. Circ: 387 Paid. Vol. ends: No. 4. Microform: PQC. Reprint: PSC. *Indexed:* A01, A22, E01, ERIC, FR, P02, P61, PsycInfo, SSA, SWR&A. *Bk. rev.:* 1-4, 600-2,200 words. *Aud.:* Ac, Sa.

Child & Family Behavior Therapy is intended for family therapists, counselors, child psychologists, teachers, social workers, researchers, and others interested in utilizing behavior therapy techniques when working with difficult children and adolescents. This peer-reviewed journal is published quarterly, and each issue contains three to four articles, as well as brief reports. Researchers will find the considerable book reviews helpful. Articles are lengthy and scientific, yet practical in approach, and include original research, clinical applications, and case studies. Recent articles include "Maternal ADHD: Parent-Child Interactions and Relations with Child Disruptive Behavior," "Parents May Hold the Keys to Success in Immersion Treatment of Adolescent Obesity," "Sport-Based Group Therapy Program for Boys with ADHD or with Other Behavioral Disorders," "Evaluation of Foster Parent Training Programs: A Critical Review," and "Parent-Child Interactions in Anxious Families." Recommended for academic libraries.

Child & Family Social Work. See Sociology and Social Work/Social Work and Social Welfare section.

2293. Contemporary Family Therapy: an international journal. Formerly (until 1986): *International Journal of Family Therapy.* [ISSN: 0892-2764] 1979. q. EUR 1059 (print & online eds.). Ed(s): Dorothy S Becvar. Springer New York LLC, 233 Spring St, New York, NY 10013; service-ny@springer.com; http://www.springer.com/. Adv. Refereed. Reprint: PSC. *Indexed:* A01, A22, ABS&EES, ASSIA, BRI, E01, FR, P61, PsycInfo, SSA, SWR&A. *Aud.:* Ac.

Contemporary Family Therapy offers current developments in family therapy practice, theory, and research. The interactions among family systems, society, and individuals are examined, with investigation of fundamental factors such as family value systems, ethnicity, race, religious background, and social class. Recent topics include treating depression in men; incorporating universal design to increase accessibility of instruction in couple and family therapy; military marriages; family therapy and medical issues; spirituality in couple and family therapy; stepfamily education; factors influencing therapy dropout; and home-based family therapy models. This journal is published quarterly and international in scope, and the editorial board includes broad geographic representation and international advisory editors. Recommended for academic libraries that support family therapy and sociology programs.

2294. Exceptional Parent: the magazine for families and professionals caring for people with special needs. [ISSN: 0046-9157] 1971. m. USD 19.95. Ed(s): Rick Rader. Exceptional Parent, 700 Broadway Ste 76, Westwood, NJ 07675-1674. Illus., index, adv. Sample. Vol. ends: Dec. Microform: PQC. *Indexed:* A22, BRI, ERIC, P02. *Bk. rev.:* Number and length vary. *Aud.:* Ga, Sa.

Exceptional Parent originally focused on children with disabilities; the magazine later expanded its scope to include adults with disabilities. Focusing on making life easier for those with disabilities, it serves individuals with disabilities as well as their families and caregivers, in addition to physicians, educators, and therapists. Informative articles cover topics such as pet therapy, new assistive technologies, strategies for couples, accessibility, home improvement, military families, bullying, mobility, music therapy, health-care policy issues, newborn screening programs, living with a disability, autism, and estate and tax planning. There are also book reviews. *Exceptional Parent* publishes an annual resource guide; and additional news and resources are available on its web site. Recommended for large public libraries.

Families in Society. See Sociology and Social Work/Social Work and Social Welfare section.

2295. *Family & Consumer Sciences Research Journal.* Formerly (until 1995): *Home Economics Research Journal;* Which incorporates (1962-1991): *Titles of Dissertations and Theses Completed in Home Economics.* [ISSN: 1077-727X] 1972. q. GBP 420. Ed(s): Dr. Sharon A DeVaney. John Wiley & Sons, Inc., 111 River St, MS 4-02, Hoboken, NJ 07030; info@wiley.com; http://www.wiley.com/WileyCDA/. Illus., index, adv. Sample. Refereed. Circ: 800 Paid. Vol. ends: Jun. Microform: PQC. Reprint: PSC. *Indexed:* A&ATA, A22, Agr, BRI, E01, P02, P61, PsycInfo, SSA. *Aud.:* Ac.

An official publication of the American Association of Family and Consumer Sciences, *Family & Consumer Sciences Research Journal* presents theory, research, and philosophy of family and consumer sciences. Published quarterly, the journal provides scholarly peer-reviewed articles, as well as specialized research and occasional themed issues. Research areas include family economics and management, child and family studies, education, human development, and teacher education. Recent articles include "Newlyweds' Unexpected Adjustment to Marriage," "Rituals in Unmarried Couple Relationships: An Exploratory Study," "Which Low- and Moderate-Income Families Purchase Life Insurance?," and "Neighborhood, Parenting, and Individual Qualities Related to Adolescent Self-Efficacy in Immigrant Families." There is also a special issue on the influence of technology on individuals and families. The journal also publishes virtual issues, highlighting a selection of articles on a particular topic from prior issues. Content is aimed at professionals, scholars, researchers, and students of family and consumer sciences. Recommended for academic libraries.

The Family Handyman. See Do-It-Yourself section.

2296. *The Family Journal: counseling and therapy for couples and families.* [ISSN: 1066-4807] 1993. q. USD 871. Ed(s): Stephen Southern. Sage Publications, Inc., 2455 Teller Rd, Thousand Oaks, CA 91320; info@sagepub.com; http://www.sagepub.com. Adv. Sample. Refereed. Reprint: PSC. *Indexed:* A01, A22, ASSIA, E01, ERIC, P61, PsycInfo, RiskAb, SSA, SWR&A. *Bk. rev.:* Number and length vary. *Aud.:* Ac, Sa.

The Family Journal: Counseling and Therapy for Couples and Families presents an assortment of practice, research, and theory in each issue, and this blend of coverage, from a family systems perspective, serves practitioners, educators, and researchers involved with couple and family counseling and therapy. This is the official journal of the International Association of Marriage and Family Counselors. In addition to articles, regular sections include counselor training, techniques to share, case consultation, ethics, literature reviews, and book reviews, as well as the new student contribution section. Some recent features are "Adult Children of Divorce and Relationship Education: Implications for Counselors and Counselor Educators," "Parenting Styles and Children's Emotional Intelligence: What Do We Know?," "Preparing School Counseling Students to Aid Families: Integrating a Family Systems Perspective," "Vietnamese American Immigrant Parents: A Pilot Parenting Intervention," and "African American Grandchildren Raised in Grandparent-Headed Families: An Exploratory Study." Interviews with leaders in family therapy are also published here. Recommended for academic libraries.

2297. *Family Process.* [ISSN: 0014-7370] 1962. q. GBP 373 (print & online eds.). Ed(s): Evan Imber-Black. Wiley-Blackwell Publishing, Inc., 111 River St, Hoboken, NJ 07030; info@wiley.com; http://onlinelibrary.wiley.com/. Illus., index, adv. Sample. Refereed. Circ: 2061 Paid. Vol. ends: Dec. Reprint: PSC. *Indexed:* A01, A22, AbAn, E01, FR, P61, PsycInfo, RiskAb, SSA, SWR&A. *Aud.:* Ac, Sa.

Family Process began publication when the field of family therapy was in its infancy. This journal is a major resource for over 50 years, and in it, mental health and social service professionals will find research and clinical ideas on a wide range of psychological and behavioral problems. The journal publishes original articles, including on training in couple and family therapy; family interaction; clinical research; and theoretical contributions in the broad area of family therapy. Recent special sections include the origins of *Family Process,* "Ethical challenges for researchers and practitioners—realizing social justice" and "Integrative Problem Centered Metaframeworks." Recent topics include

parenting; collaborative family-oriented services; theory, practice, and research from a new generation; couples and families; qualitative and quantitative research in family relationships; parenting in Mexican-American families; and complexities and challenges in family configurations. A virtual issue celebrating the 50th anniversary of the journal was published in 2011, compiling editors' picks from the past 50 years. Highly recommended for academic libraries that support family therapy, social work, psychiatry, and psychology programs.

2298. *Family Relations: interdisciplinary journal of applied family studies.* Former titles (until 1980): *Family Coordinator;* (until 1968): *Family Life Coordinator;* (until 1959): *The Coordinator.* [ISSN: 0197-6664] 1952. 5x/yr. Individuals, USD 136 (print & online eds.); Students, USD 58 (print & online eds.). Ed(s): Ronald Sabatelli. Wiley-Blackwell Publishing, Inc., 111 River St, Hoboken, NJ 07030; info@wiley.com; http://onlinelibrary.wiley.com/. Illus., index. Refereed. Microform: PQC. Reprint: PSC. *Indexed:* A01, A22, AgeL, Agr, BRI, CBRI, Chicano, E01, ERIC, IBSS, P02, PsycInfo, RiskAb, SSA, SWR&A. *Bk. rev.:* 7-18, 500-800 words. *Aud.:* Ac, Sa.

Family Relations is an applied scholarly journal, focusing on diverse families and family issues. One of three journals published by the National Council on Family Relations (NCFR), it publishes empirical studies, conceptual analysis, and literature reviews that emphasize "family research with implications for intervention, education, and public policy." Articles are interdisciplinary in scope and focus on a wide range of family issues, including cross-cultural issues, intergenerational family relations, parent offspring relations, and aging. Recent topics include diverse experiences in parenting; distress in couple relationships; men and fatherhood; parenting and child development; lesbian and gay families; relationship quality in couples; family and work balance; educating couples and families; and families at risk. There is also a special issue on relationship dissolution within a contemporary context. Readers are scholars and practitioners, including researchers, marriage and family therapists, educators, and family practitioners. NCFR members can access full-text articles through the NCFR web site. *Family Relations* is an excellent resource that is routinely cited; it is highly recommended for academic libraries with programs that address psychology, family studies and family research, or social work.

2299. *Family Science: global perspectives on research, policy and practice.* [ISSN: 1942-4620] 2010. q. GBP 313 (print & online eds.). Ed(s): Judith Semon Dubas. Taylor & Francis, 4 Park Sq, Milton Park, Abingdon, OX14 4RN, United Kingdom; subscriptions@tandf.co.uk; http://www.tandfonline.com. *Indexed:* IBSS. *Aud.:* Ac.

Family Science is the official journal of the European Society on Family Relations, and its first issue was published in 2010. The journal's vision is "to become the leading international outlet for reporting research on the family." The target audience includes practitioners, family scientists, and policy specialists. Articles are interdisciplinary in scope, coming from research in psychology, sociology, anthropology, and economics. Some recent articles are "Coparenting cooperation and child adjustment in low-income mother-grandmother and mother-father families," "Parental attachment and romantic relationships in emerging adults: The role of emotional regulation processes," "Daily hassles, sacrifices, and relationship quality for pregnant cohabitors," "Divorce in Europe and the United States: Commonalities and differences across nations," and "Bereavement in family context: Coping with the loss of a loved one." A thematic issue on fathers was published in 2011. Recommended for academic libraries.

Family Therapy Networker. See *Psychotherapy Networker.*

FamilyFun. See Parenting section.

2300. *Journal of Child and Family Studies.* [ISSN: 1062-1024] 1992. bi-m. EUR 837 (print & online eds.). Ed(s): Nirbhay N Singh. Springer New York LLC, 233 Spring St, New York, NY 10013; service-ny@springer.com; http://www.springer.com/. Adv. Refereed. Reprint: PSC. *Indexed:* A01, A22, ASSIA, BRI, C45, E01, ERIC, IBSS, P02, P61, PsycInfo, RiskAb, SSA, SWR&A. *Bk. rev.:* Number and length vary. *Aud.:* Ac, Sa.

The *Journal of Child and Family Studies* addresses all aspects of emotional disorders pertaining to children and adolescents, including diagnosis, rehabilitation, treatment, prevention, and their effects on families. Recent articles include "Support Networks of Single Puerto Rican Mothers of Children with Disabilities," "Strengths of Aboriginal Foster Parents," "Family Concerns and Involvement During Kindergarten Transition," "Maternal Depressive Symptoms When Caring for a Child with Mental Health Problems," and "Measuring Attitudes Toward Acceptable and Unacceptable Parenting Practices." There are also special issues on wraparound services. This journal is international in scope, and health-care practitioners and clinicians will find the basic and applied research, policy issues, and program evaluation useful. Recommended for academic libraries, particularly those that support programs related to child and adolescent mental health.

2301. *Journal of Comparative Family Studies.* [ISSN: 0047-2328] 1970. bi-m. USD 525 (Individuals, USD 275). Ed(s): George Kurian, James White. University of Calgary, Department of Sociology, 2500 University Dr N W, Calgary, AB T2N 1N4, Canada; http://soci.ucalgary.ca/. Illus., index, adv. Refereed. Vol. ends: No. 4. Microform: MIM; MML; PQC. *Indexed:* A01, A22, BAS, BRI, C37, CBCARef, Chicano, IBSS, P02, P61, PsycInfo, RILM, SSA. *Bk. rev.:* 0-10, 400-1,300. *Aud.:* Ac.

Aimed at family counselors, social psychologists, anthropologists, and sociologists, the *Journal of Comparative Family Studies* "provides a unique cross-cultural perspective on the study of the family." The editorial board and authors are international in representation and abstracts are provided in English, French, and Spanish. The journal publishes articles, book reviews, and research notes. Recent articles include "Emerging Adulthood in Israeli Families: Individual-Social Tasks and Emotional-Relational Challenges," "Memories of Home: Family in the Diaspora," "Gender Role Disruption and Marital Satisfaction among Wives of Chinese International Students in the United States," and "Chinese Similes and Metaphors for Family," and "Work-Family Conflict in the Nordic Countries: A Comparative Analysis." The journal also publishes special issues on selected themes, such as global research on parenting, family diversity and gender, and the Indian family. Highly recommended for academic libraries that serve social psychology, sociology, multicultural studies, or anthropology programs.

Journal of Divorce & Remarriage. See Marriage and Divorce section.

2302. *Journal of Family and Economic Issues.* Former titles (until 1991): *Lifestyles;* (until 1984): *Alternative Lifestyles.* [ISSN: 1058-0476] 1978. q. EUR 944 (print & online eds.). Ed(s): Jing Xiao. Springer New York LLC, 233 Spring St, New York, NY 10013; service-ny@springer.com; http://www.springer.com/. Illus., adv. Refereed. Vol. ends: Winter. Reprint: PSC. *Indexed:* A22, ABIn, Agr, BRI, CJPI, E01, EconLit, FR, IBSS, JEL, P61, PsycInfo, RiskAb, SSA, SWR&A. *Bk. rev.:* Number and length vary. *Aud.:* Ac, Sa.

The *Journal of Family and Economic Issues* presents interdisciplinary research, integrative theoretical articles, and critical reviews that address the family and its economic environment. Book reviews are included. The journal is international in scope, and articles investigate family economic issues in developing and transition economies. The journal publishes special, thematic issues on topics such as health, economics, and the family; family finance; and family and economic issues in East Asia. Many articles explore family management and the relationship between work and family life. Recent topics include couples' financial management practices; financial capability in children; intra-family gift transfers in rural Mulawi; family structure and conflict among single and partnered parents; food security and insecurity in families; the influence of government assistance on marital quality and income; and contemporary fathers and their engagement in childcare. Recommended for academic libraries.

2303. *Journal of Family Communication.* [ISSN: 1526-7431] 2001. q. GBP 329 (print & online eds.). Ed(s): Loreen N Olson. Routledge, 325 Chestnut St, Ste 800, Philadelphia, PA 19106; customerservice@taylorandfrancis.com; http://www.tandfonline.com. Adv. Sample. Refereed. Reprint: PSC. *Indexed:* A01, A22, E01, PsycInfo, SSA. *Aud.:* Ac.

The *Journal of Family Communication* examines all aspects of communication in the family. These aspects include "the intersection between families, communication, and social systems, such as mass media, education, health care, and law [and] policy." The journal presents articles related to family communication pedagogy and applied family communication, empirical reports, and theoretical and review essays. The journal's readership includes family therapists, counselors, communication researchers, social psychologists, and sociologists. Special issues are occasionally published; recent issues include "Family Communication and Culture." Current articles address topics concerned with the division of domestic labor; paternity leave and changing masculinities; communication around financial issues in families; relational satisfaction and in-laws; and adult sibling relationships. Recommended for academic libraries.

2304. *Journal of Family History: studies in family, kinship and demography.* Supersedes (in 1976): *The Family in Historical Perspective.* [ISSN: 0363-1990] 1972. q. USD 865. Ed(s): Roderick Phillips. Sage Publications, Inc., 2455 Teller Rd, Thousand Oaks, CA 91320; info@sagepub.com; http://www.sagepub.com. Illus., index, adv. Sample. Refereed. Vol. ends: Oct. Reprint: PSC. *Indexed:* A01, A22, ABS&EES, AmHI, BRI, E01, IBSS, P02, P61, PsycInfo, SSA, SWR&A. *Bk. rev.:* 4-8, 800-1,200 words. *Aud.:* Ac.

Interdisciplinary in scope and published in association with the National Council on Family Relations, this journal publishes contributions that represent the international perspective of historically based research on family, kinship, and population. Review essays, debates, book reviews, research notes, and thematic symposia are regular features. Scholarly research articles present viewpoints in relation to culture, gender, race, class, and sexuality. Recent articles include "Marrying in the City in Times of Rapid Urbanization," "Social Mobility and Reproduction Among Nineteenth-Century Colorado Silver Prospectors," "Daily Chicken: The Cultural Transmissions of Bourgeois Family Values in Adaptations of Literary Classics for Children, 1850-1950," and "Surnames and Gender in Japan: Women's Challenges in Seeking Own Identity." A thematic issue, "From Past Patterns of Divorces to Present: New Light on the Divorce Transition," was published in 2011. Recommended for academic libraries.

2305. *Journal of Family Issues.* [ISSN: 0192-513X] 1980. m. USD 1720. Ed(s): Constance Shehan. Sage Publications, Inc., 2455 Teller Rd, Thousand Oaks, CA 91320; info@sagepub.com; http://www.sagepub.com. Illus., index, adv. Sample. Refereed. Vol. ends: Nov. Microform: WSH; PMC. Reprint: PSC. *Indexed:* A01, A22, Agr, Chicano, E01, ERIC, HEA, P02, P61, PsycInfo, RiskAb, SSA, SWR&A. *Aud.:* Ac, Sa.

Published monthly, the *Journal of Family Issues* publishes current research, analyses, and theory from an interdisciplinary perspective, exploring the institutional and social forces that influence marriage and families today. Articles and advocacy pieces represent any topic related to modern family issues and marriage. Recent articles address transracial versus intercountry adoption; boys' household work in single-mother households; work–family balance; parent and adult child relationships; race and gender differences in dating rituals; clergy spouses; limiting children's television viewing time; and intergenerational attitudes toward marriage. Recent special issues include "Experiences, Stress, and Resilience in the Face of Disasters: Children, Teachers, Older Adults and Families" and "Irish Voices: Families in a Globalizing Economy." This scholarly journal is highly recommended for academic libraries.

2306. *Journal of Family Psychology.* [ISSN: 0893-3200] 1987. bi-m. USD 508 (Individuals, USD 167). Ed(s): Nadine J Kaslow. American Psychological Association, 750 First St, NE, Washington, DC 20002; journals@apa.org; http://www.apa.org. Illus., index, adv. Sample. Refereed. Circ: 2300. Vol. ends: Feb. Reprint: PSC. *Indexed:* A01, A22, ASSIA, FR, P02, P61, PsycInfo, SSA, SWR&A. *Aud.:* Ac, Sa.

The *Journal of Family Psychology* provides original scholarly articles devoted to the study of the family system "from multiple perspectives and to the application of psychological methods to advance knowledge related to family research, patterns and processes, and assessment and intervention." Published by the American Psychological Association, it is regarded as an important journal in family research. The journal addresses such topics as stigma within the context of same-sex relationships; facing HIV as a family; parent–child relationship quality in difficult economic times; family attachment and military deployment; divorce; infidelity; father–daughter relationships; and families' experiences of multisystemic therapy processes. Recent special sections include "U.S. Military Operations: Effects on Military Members' Partners and Children" and "Advances in Mixed Methods in Family Psychology: Integrative and Applied Solutions for Family Science." Meanwhile, a special section on "Genetics and Epigenetics in a Family Context" is forthcoming. Occasionally, the journal publishes literature reviews, case studies, or theoretical articles, but the focus of the journal is empirical research that addresses behavioral, biological, cognitive, emotional, and social variables. Widely indexed, this journal is highly recommended for academic libraries.

2307. *Journal of Family Psychotherapy: the official journal of the International Family Therapy Association.* Formerly (until 1988): *Journal of Psychotherapy and the Family.* [ISSN: 0897-5353] 1985. q. GBP 614 (print & online eds.). Ed(s): Terry S Trepper. Routledge, 325 Chestnut St, Ste 800, Philadelphia, PA 19106; customerservice@taylorandfrancis.com; http://www.tandfonline.com. Adv. Sample. Refereed. Circ: 272 Paid. Microform: PQC. Reprint: PSC. *Indexed:* A01, A22, E01, ExcerpMed, FR, P61, PsycInfo, SSA, SWR&A. *Bk. rev.:* Number and length vary. *Aud.:* Ac, Sa.

The *Journal of Family Psychotherapy* is the official journal of the International Family Therapy Association. The journal fills a niche in the marriage and family therapy literature, focusing on a case study orientation. Case studies, strategies currently in clinical practice, applied research, and program reports are written by clinicians for practicing clinicians. The journal is divided into sections that include "Family Therapy and Mental Health," "Family Therapy Around the World," "Intervention Interchange," and "Media Reviews." Thematic issues are published in each volume year, providing in-depth coverage of a current topic such as "Systemic Interventions in Substance-Abuse Treatment." Recent articles address mindfulness practice and emotionally focused couple therapy; narrative therapy within the field of family therapy; cyberspace betrayal; and clinical implications for work with interfaith couples. Recommended for academic libraries that support marriage and family therapy programs.

2308. *Journal of Family Theory & Review.* [ISSN: 1756-2570] 2009. q. Ed(s): Robert Milardo. John Wiley & Sons, Inc., 111 River St, MS 4-02, Hoboken, NJ 07030; info@wiley.com; http://www.wiley.com/WileyCDA/. Reprint: PSC. *Indexed:* A22, E01. *Bk. rev.:* Number and length vary. *Aud.:* Ac.

A newer addition to the field of family studies literature, the *Journal of Family Theory and Review* is one of three publications of the National Council on Family Relations. Multidisciplinary and international in scope, the journal "publishes original contributions in all areas of family theory, including new advances in theory development, reviews of existing theory, and analyses of the interface of theory and method." Families are defined broadly and inclusively; recent articles include "Attachment, Identity, and Intimacy: Parallels Between Bowlby's and Erikson's Paradigms," "Theoretical Perspectives on Sibling Relationships," "Doing Family, Doing Gender, Doing Religion: Structured Ambivalence and the Religion-Family Connection," "Mothers' Part-Time Employment: Child, Parent, and Family Outcomes," and "Imprisoned Fathers and Their Family Relationships: A 40-Year Review from a Multi-Theory View." Book reviews, as well as integrative and theory-based reviews of content areas, are included. Recommended for academic libraries.

2309. *Journal of Family Therapy.* [ISSN: 0163-4445] 1979. q. GBP 334. Ed(s): Mark Rivett. Wiley-Blackwell Publishing Ltd., The Atrium, Southern Gate, Chichester, PO19 8SQ, United Kingdom; customer@wiley.com; http://www.wiley.com/. Illus., index, adv. Sample. Refereed. Vol. ends: Nov. Reprint: PSC. *Indexed:* A01, A22, ASSIA, E01, FR, P61, PsycInfo, RiskAb, SSA. *Bk. rev.:* 1-4, 500-1,200 words. *Aud.:* Ac, Sa.

Published on behalf of the Association for Family Therapy and Systemic Practice in the U.K., the *Journal of Family Therapy* seeks to advance "the understanding and treatment of human relationships constituted in systems such as couples, families, professional networks, and wider groups." International contributions to each issue include research papers, training articles, and book reviews, and represent all schools of thought within family therapy. The journal

also publishes an annual article that reviews current themes in couples and family therapy literature. Recent papers include "Family and social networks after bereavement: experiences of support, change and isolation," "Bringing forth spirituality dialogues in family therapy education," "Review and reflections on 40 years of family therapy development in Taiwan," and "Engaging reluctant adolescents in family therapy: an exploratory study of in-session processes of change." A special issue devoted to qualitative research was published in 2011. Recommended for academic libraries that call for original research in family therapy.

2310. *Journal of Family Violence.* [ISSN: 0885-7482] 1986. 8x/yr. EUR 1141 (print & online eds.). Ed(s): Vincent B Van Hasselt, Michel Hersen. Springer New York LLC, 233 Spring St, New York, NY 10013; service-ny@springer.com; http://www.springer.com/. Illus., index, adv. Refereed. Vol. ends: Dec. Microform: PQC. Reprint: PSC. *Indexed:* A01, A22, ASSIA, BRI, CJPI, Chicano, E01, FR, H24, IBSS, P02, P61, PsycInfo, RiskAb, SSA. *Bk. rev.:* 0-4, 300-1,000 words. *Aud.:* Ac, Sa.

Interdisciplinary in scope, this journal addresses "clinical and investigative efforts concerning all forms of family violence and its precursors, including spouse-battering, child abuse, sexual abuse of children, incest, abuse of the elderly, marital rape, domestic homicide, the alcoholic marriage, and general family conflict." Case studies, papers, review articles, and theoretical discussions are included. Its clinical and research reports draw from clinical and counseling psychology, criminology, marital counseling, psychiatry, public health, law, social work, and sociology. Just a few topics recently addressed are abusive dating relationships in a college setting; characteristics of couple violence in China; a historical review of interventions for intimate partner violence; violence during pregnancy; sexual minority stressors and same-sex intimate partner violence; and violent family environments. Recommended for academic libraries, especially those that support criminology, counseling, or social work programs.

Journal of Feminist Family Therapy. See Psychology section.

2311. *Journal of G L B T Family Studies.* [ISSN: 1550-428X] 2005. 5x/yr. GBP 612 (print & online eds.). Ed(s): M Paz Galupo. Routledge, 325 Chestnut St, Ste 800, Philadelphia, PA 19106; customerservice@taylorandfrancis.com; http://www.tandfonline.com. Refereed. Reprint: PSC. *Indexed:* A01, A22, E01, GW, IBSS, P61, PsycInfo, SSA. *Aud.:* Ac, Sa.

The *Journal of GLBT Family Studies* is a more recent addition to the family studies literature. Content is interdisciplinary in scope and is directed to practitioners, researchers, and academics in family therapy, social work, human services, psychology, and counseling. The journal addresses "the vital issues facing gay, lesbian, bisexual, and transgender individuals and their families." Topics examine family structure, family policy, extended family relationships, sexual identity, gender roles, alternative family structures, couple and relationship issues, and high-risk issues such as sexual abuse. Recent articles include "Same-Sex Couples in Poland: Challenges of Family Life," "Family Therapy with GLBT Youths: Kite in Flight Revisited," and "Growing Up in a Lesbian Family: The Life Experiences of the Adult Daughters and Sons of Lesbian Mothers." Special issues are published occasionally, such as "GLBTQ Issues in Foster Care and Adoption: Contemporary Research, Policy, and Practice" and "Mixed-Orientation Marriages: Challenges of Individual Spouses and GLB-Straight Couples in Diverse Contexts." Recommended for academic libraries.

2312. *Journal of Marital and Family Therapy.* Formerly (until 1979): *Journal of Marriage and Family Counseling.* [ISSN: 0194-472X] 1975. q. GBP 258 (print & online eds.). Ed(s): Ronald Chenail. Wiley-Blackwell Publishing, Inc., 111 River St, Hoboken, NJ 07030; info@wiley.com; http://onlinelibrary.wiley.com/. Illus., index, adv. Refereed. Vol. ends: Oct. Microform: PQC. Reprint: PSC. *Indexed:* A01, A22, ASSIA, BRI, E01, ERIC, P02, PsycInfo, SSA, SWR&A. *Bk. rev.:* 3-10, 300-1,000 words, signed. *Aud.:* Ac, Sa.

As the leading family therapy journal, this widely circulated journal "publishes articles on research, theory, clinical practice, and training in marital and family therapy." Published quarterly by the American Association for Marriage and Family Therapy, the practical articles, focused on clinical topics, are directed to marriage and family therapists. Recent articles include "Compassion Fatigue in Marriage and Family Therapy: Implications for Therapists and Clients," "Understanding the Experience of Black Clients in Marriage and Family Therapy," "Natural Disasters: An Assessment of Family Resiliency Following Hurricane Katrina," "Does Family Matter to HIV-Positive Men Who Have Sex With Men?," and "Couple and Family Interventions in Health Problems." A current issue contained a special section on emotionally focused therapy. Topics related to clinical techniques and marriage and family therapy practice are often included. An essential title for academic libraries that support programs in marriage and family therapy.

2313. *Journal of Marriage and Family.* Former titles (until 1964): *Marriage and Family Living;* (until 1941): *Living.* [ISSN: 0022-2445] 1939. 5x/yr. USD 1043 (print & online eds.). Ed(s): David H Demo. Wiley-Blackwell Publishing, Inc., 111 River St, Hoboken, NJ 07030; info@wiley.com; http://onlinelibrary.wiley.com/. Illus., index, adv. Refereed. Circ: 4365 Paid. Microform: PQC. Reprint: PSC. *Indexed:* A01, A22, ABS&EES, AgeL, Agr, BRI, C45, CBRI, Chicano, E01, ERIC, FR, IBSS, MLA-IB, P02, P61, PsycInfo, RiskAb, SSA, SWR&A. *Bk. rev.:* 7-21, 600-1,000 words. *Aud.:* Ac, Sa.

According to *Essential Science Indicators,* the *Journal of Marriage and Family* is in the top ten of the Most-Cited Journals in Social Sciences, 1997-2007. A leading resource in family studies, it is one of three publications of the National Council on Family Relations. Contributors come from a diverse array of social science fields, including psychology, anthropology, sociology, history, and economics. It presents original research, theory, critical discussion, research interpretation, and reviews related to marriage and the family. Here, marriage and family encompass other forms of close relationships. All family-related topics are represented, including marital satisfaction among new mothers; low-income families; middle- and later-life families; children's health and well-being; family support; families with young children; family structure and family stability; transnational families; intimate unions over the life course; intergenerational relationships; and cohabitation and marriage. A virtual issue was published in 2011, highlighting the journal's 20 most highly cited articles published between 2001 and 2010. Widely indexed and frequently cited, this journal is highly recommended for all academic libraries.

Parents. See Parenting section.

2314. *Psychotherapy Networker: the magazine for today's helping professional.* Formerly (until Mar.2001): *Family Therapy Networker;* (until 1982): *Family Therapy Network Newsletter;* (until 197?): *Family Therapy Practice Network Newsletter; Family Shtick.* [ISSN: 1535-573X] 197?. bi-m. USD 18 domestic; USD 24 foreign. Ed(s): Brett Topping, Richard Simon. Family Therapy Network, Inc., 5135 MacArthur Blvd NW, Washington, DC 20016; http://www.psychotherapynetworker.org/. Illus., adv. Circ: 55000. Vol. ends: Nov. *Indexed:* A22, MLA-IB, SWR&A. *Bk. rev.:* Number and length vary. *Aud.:* Ac, Sa.

Family therapy is a significant subject included in *Psychotherapy Networker.* It is a trade publication aimed at therapists, and its mission is to inspire therapists and to connect therapists with their colleagues. It provides practical information for therapists with its feature articles, case studies, clinical methods, and career information, as well as regular columns that address family matters, the business of therapy, consultation, and networking. The articles, while written for therapists, are also likely to appeal to general readers interested in psychology; and many articles are accessible through the publication's web site. Recent cover stories examine the mindfulness movement, couples therapy, dilemmas of twenty-first–century childrearing, and emotion in the consulting room. Reviews of self-help and therapy books are included, as well as current popular film reviews written from a therapist's perspective. The magazine recently celebrated 30 years of publication. Because of its broad appeal, *Psychotherapy Networker* is recommended for academic and special libraries.

Sexual and Relationship Therapy. See Sexuality section.

Studies in Family Planning. See Family Planning section.

■ FAMILY PLANNING

See also Family and Marriage; Health and Fitness; Population Studies; and Pregnancy sections.

Serin Anderson, Collection Development & Administrative Services Librarian, University of Washington–Tacoma, Tacoma, WA 98402; serin@uw.edu

Introduction

Family planning, maternal health, and reproductive health are often terms used almost interchangeably for topics dealing with global women's health care. Improving maternal health, as one of the eight Millennium Development Goals, is a top priority for countries worldwide. Yet, in a 2009 World Health Organization report, *Women and health: today's evidence, tomorrow's agenda,* family planning issues are still among the top ten causes of death for women and girls around the world. These include neonatal infections, prematurity/low birthweight, and HIV/AIDS.

This compilation of journals and magazines pulls together a primarily academic list of titles that focus on both North American and international reproductive health issues. These titles will be of particular interest for libraries that serve patrons interested in global health and population studies.

Basic Periodicals

Conceive, Studies in Family Planning.

Basic Abstracts and Indexes

Academic OneFile; Academic Search Premier; CINAHL; Family Index; PubMed.

2315. *Birth: issues in perinatal care.* Formerly (until 1982): *Birth and the Family Journal.* [ISSN: 0730-7659] 1973. q. GBP 428. Ed(s): Diony Young. Wiley-Blackwell Publishing, Inc., 111 River St, Hoboken, NJ 07030; info@wiley.com; http://onlinelibrary.wiley.com/. Illus., index, adv. Sample. Refereed. Vol. ends: Dec. Microform: PQC. Reprint: PSC. *Indexed:* A01, A22, ASSIA, C45, E01, PsycInfo, RiskAb. *Bk. rev.:* 2-3. *Aud.:* Ac, Sa.

A top-ranked journal for nursing, pediatrics, and obstetrics/gynecology, *Birth: Issues in Perinatal Care* is a multidisciplinary, refereed journal that includes original research, editorials, and media/book reviews. The journal's focus is on child-bearing women, and it covers a broad range of topics from women and infant health to the effects of information on family planning decisions. Free online access to this journal is available in developing countries through the World Health Organization's HINARI initiative. Highly recommended for academic and research libraries that provide support for nursing and medical colleges and programs.

2316. *Conceive Magazine (Florida).* [ISSN: 1550-8900] 2004. q. USD 11.20 domestic; USD 24 Canada; USD 32 elsewhere. Ed(s): Emily Kruckemyer. Bonnier Corp., 460 N Orlando Ave, Ste 200, Winter Park, FL 32789; http://www.bonniercorp.com. Adv. *Aud.:* Ga.

An easy-to-browse, popular magazine, *Conceive* will appeal to a wide variety of individuals and couples planning for parenthood. This title focuses on topics related to conception, fertility, and adoption, while a companion web site, www.conceiveonline.com, provides additional support, including blogs, reviews, and forums. Many parenting magazines include some information about pre-conception health and issues, but this title provides focused articles and advertising (such as the annual list, "50 Best Fertility and Adoption Friendly Companies") for the many people trying to conceive. Now owned by the Bonnier Corporation, this quarterly title rounds out a parenting "trilogy" that includes *Parenting, BabyTalk,* and *Working Mother.* Recommended for public libraries.

2317. *The European Journal of Contraception and Reproductive Health Care.* [ISSN: 1362-5187] 1996. bi-m. GBP 721 (print & online eds.). Ed(s): Dr. Jean-Jacques Amy. Informa Healthcare, Guardian House, 119 Farringdon Rd, London, EC1R 3DA, United Kingdom; healthcare@informa.com; http://informahealthcare.com/. Adv. Refereed. Reprint: PSC. *Indexed:* A01, A22, AbAn, E01, ExcerpMed, P02, PsycInfo. *Aud.:* Ac, Sa.

Although most of the articles for this peer-reviewed journal deal with topics and research specific to European Union citizens, it also includes research from Africa, the Middle East, and more. *The European Journal of Contraception & Reproductive Health Care* primarily includes research articles, at least one editorial, and occasional case reports or review articles. Recommended for academic libraries.

Fertility Today See Pregnancy section.

2318. *International Perspectives on Sexual and Reproductive Health.* Former titles (until 2009): *International Family Planning Perspectives;* (until 1979): *International Family Planning Perspectives and Digest;* (until 1978): *International Family Planning Digest.* [ISSN: 1944-0391] 1975. q. USD 50 (Individuals, USD 40). Ed(s): Patricia Donovan, Frances A Althaus. Alan Guttmacher Institute, 125 Maiden Ln, 7th Fl, New York, NY 10038; info@guttmacher.org; http://www.guttmacher.org. Illus., adv. Refereed. Microform: PQC. *Indexed:* A01, A22, ASSIA, BAS, C42, C45, EIP, FR, IBSS, P61, SSA. *Aud.:* Ac, Sa.

This is a quarterly journal focused on peer-reviewed research throughout the developing world, including Africa, Latin America, Asia, and the Caribbean. *International Perspectives on Sexual and Reproductive Health* features articles on contraception, fertility, and family planning policies and programs, as well as reproductive and maternal/child health. It also includes special reports and opinion articles that tackle significant population and health issues around the world. It is co-published by the Guttmacher Institute, a World Health Organization Collaborating Centre, and Wiley-Blackwell. Highly recommended for academic and research libraries, particularly those with any programs related to population studies and global public health. All research articles include summaries in Spanish and French.

2319. *Journal of Family Planning and Reproductive Health Care.* Former titles (until 2001): *British Journal of Family Planning;* (until 1977): *Journal of Family Planning Doctors.* [ISSN: 1471-1893] 1974. q. USD 355 (Individuals, USD 223 (print & online eds.). Ed(s): Anne Szarewski. B M J Group, BMA House, Tavistock Sq, London, WC1H 9JR, United Kingdom; support@bmjgroup.com; http://group.bmj.com. Illus., adv. Sample. Refereed. *Indexed:* AbAn, C45, ExcerpMed, IndVet, RRTA. *Bk. rev.:* 2-5, length varies. *Aud.:* Ac.

From the Royal College of Obstetricians and Gynaecologists in Great Britain, the *Journal of Family Planning and Reproductive Health Care* offers an interesting mix of research, news, and opinion on reproductive health and family planning. Issues include regular research articles, columns such as the "View from Primary Care," and the "History of Contraception," in addition to editorials and reviews on everything from fiction books to nonfiction books, journal articles, and blogs. Articles often cover topics with broad interest such as "Approaches to family planning in Muslim Communities." Recommended for academic libraries.

2320. *Perspectives on Sexual and Reproductive Health.* Formerly (until 2002): *Family Planning Perspectives.* [ISSN: 1538-6341] 1969. q. GBP 180 (print & online eds.). Ed(s): Patricia Donovan, Dore Hollander. Wiley-Blackwell Publishing, Inc., 111 River St, Hoboken, NJ 07030; info@wiley.com; http://onlinelibrary.wiley.com/. Illus., index. Sample. Refereed. Vol. ends: Nov/Dec. Microform: CIS; PQC. Reprint: PSC. *Indexed:* A01, A22, ASSIA, Agr, BRI, C42, C45, Chicano, E01, H24, P02, P61, PsycInfo, RiskAb, SSA, SWR&A. *Bk. rev.:* Number and length vary. *Aud.:* Ac, Sa.

This title, formerly known as *Family Planning Perspectives,* should be part of any academic or research collection that supports public health, nursing/ medicine, family studies, or social work/counseling programs. It is a peer-reviewed journal, which includes both quantitative and qualitative research in areas such as fertility, adolescent pregnancy, abortion, sexual behavior, sexually transmitted disease, family planning, and reproductive health. Each issue also features an awareness column called "FYI," which includes news briefs with at least one associated citation for further reading. Co-published by the Guttmacher Institute, a World Health Organization Collaborating Centre, and Wiley-Blackwell.

2321. *Studies in Family Planning.* Incorporates: *Current Publications in Family Planning.* [ISSN: 0039-3665] 1963. q. GBP 164 (print & online eds.). Ed(s): Gary Bologh. Wiley-Blackwell Publishing, Inc., 111 River St, Hoboken, NJ 07030; info@wiley.com; http://onlinelibrary.wiley.com/. Illus., index. Sample. Refereed. Vol. ends: Dec. Microform: PQC. Reprint: PSC. *Indexed:* A01, A22, ABS&EES, ASSIA, AbAn, BAS, BRI, C42, C45, Chicano, E01, EIP, EconLit, H24, IBSS, JEL, P02, P61, PsycInfo, RiskAb, SSA. *Bk. rev.:* 3-4. *Aud.:* Ac, Sa.

A peer-reviewed quarterly with an international focus on developing countries, *Studies in Family Planning* publishes original research and reports, commentary, and book reviews. It also routinely includes snapshots of survey data on at least two countries from the Demographic and Health Surveys. These 200+ surveys are issued in more than 75 countries and focus on population, health, HIV, and nutrition. Highly recommended for academic and research libraries, particularly those with programs related to population studies and global public health.

■ FASHION AND LIFESTYLE

Vang Vang, Instruction and Outreach Services Librarian, Henry Madden Library, 5200 N. Barton Ave., M/S 34, California State University– Fresno, Fresno, CA 93740-8014; vangv@csufresno.edu.

Leta Hendricks, Human Ecology Librarian, The Ohio State University Libraries, Columbus, OH 43210.

Cheryl LaGuardia, Research Librarian, Widener Library, Harvard University

Introduction

The modern *Fashion and Life Style* magazine began in 1909 with the purchase of *Vogue* magazine by Conde Montrose Nast. Publisher Nast used the idea of class or lifestyle to develop a readership with common interests: fashion, beauty, health, home, and leisure. Nast also used business means to advertise products that would appeal to the readership. Nast's successful marketing formula of advertising and cultivating readership still influences the contents of popular magazines today.

In 1916, Nast launched a British edition of *Vogue,* followed by the publication of *Paris Vogue* in 1921. The globalization of fashion magazines occurred in the postmodern era with technological developments in printing and shipping.

The contemporary *Fashion and Lifestyle* magazine began in 2005 with the Meredith Corporation's launch of its Integrated Marketing division. Integrated offers outside clients app development, video production, web design, and social media capabilities. Likewise, major publishing houses are evolving into diversified publishing and marketing companies.

In 2011, Conde Nast launched Conde Nast Ideactive. The company has redefined itself beyond its core business of ad-page sales with a new marketing services division. Conde Nast Digital Creations has had internal success with developing communication, e-commerce, and studio technology for its publications. The commercially successful Style.com, a branded "mega" site, grouped *Brides, Glamour, Lucky, Teen Vogue, Vogue,* and *W Magazine,* all of them featuring fashion, beauty, and shopping. Style.com connects with the readers, sells subscriptions, and encourages renewals.

The sites and networks are not mere extensions of the magazines but a virtual dynamic resource. The same creative use of digital media by exploiting its marketing capabilities that Conde Nast already offers its advertisers, the company will offer to outside clients.

The global love of the Internet brought about the transition from analog print news and entertainment to digital communications and new technology. The great publishing houses of Conde Nast, Hearst, Marshall, and Hachette all now have internal digital technology divisions developed to combat sagging subscription rates, increase development of social media sites and web sites, and make other digital enhancements for immediate and virtual access. As with most methods of communication, digital is the fashionable way to go.

Basic Periodicals

Complex, Cosmopolitan, Elle, Essence, Family Circle, Glamour, G Q, Good Housekeeping, Jade, Latina, Marie Claire, Maxim, Redbook, Seventeen, Vogue.

Basic Abstracts and Indexes

Berg Fashion Library, Design and Applied Arts Index, MasterFILE Premier, Readers' Guide to Periodical Literature.

2322. Allure. [ISSN: 1054-7711] 1991. m. USD 12 domestic; USD 35 Canada; USD 40 elsewhere. Ed(s): Linda Wells. Conde Nast Publications, Inc., 4 Times Sq, 6th Fl, New York, NY 10036; http://www.condenast.com. Illus., adv. Sample. Circ: 1091147 Paid. Vol. ends: Feb. Microform: PQC. *Indexed:* BRI. *Aud.:* Ga.

Allure, "The Beauty Expert," provides readers with a thorough guide to beauty advice on hair and skin care, cosmetics and beauty products, and appearance trends. Issues include sections on Body News, Mood News, Editors' Favorite product finds, Fashion Bulletins, Fashion Cravings, celebrity photo shoots, and more features on hair, makeup, and styles. There's also an annual "Free Stuff" issue. *Allure* is well connected with its web site, social networks, and a free iPad app. URL: www.allure.com/

2323. Cosmopolitan. Supersedes in part (in 1952): *Hearst's International Combined with Cosmopolitan;* Which was formed by the merger of (1921-1925): *Hearst's International;* Which was formerly (until 1921): *Hearst's;* (until 1914): *Hearst's Magazine;* (until 1912): *Hearst's Magazine, the World To-day;* (until 1912): *World To-day;* (1886-1925): *The Cosmopolitan.* [ISSN: 0010-9541] 1886. m. USD 15; USD 3.99 newsstand/cover. Hearst Magazines, 300 W 57th St, 12th Fl, New York, NY 10019; HearstMagazines@hearst.com; http://www.hearstcorp.com/magazines/. Illus., adv. Vol. ends: Dec. Microform: PQC. *Indexed:* A22, BRI, C37, MASUSE, P02. *Bk. rev.:* 4-6; brief, 500 words. *Aud.:* Ga, Ac.

Cosmopolitan, Cosmo, carries on the sexual revolution of feminist editor Helen Gurley Brown, whose tenure was 1965–97. Candid columns, articles, and surveys discuss modern sexual relationships. The magazine remains the young career woman's lifestyle guide on fashion and beauty; health and fitness; popular culture and entertainment; and relationships and romance. *Cosmopolitan* is published in 32 languages and 63 editions, and is distributed globally. The fully integrated web site and social media networks provide advice for the socially active *Cosmo* girl. Sister publications include *Allure, Elle, Glamour,* and *Lucky* magazines. *Cosmopolitan's* United States, Spanish, and French editions are highly recommended for academic and public libraries. URL: www.cosmopolitan.com/

2324. Country Woman. Former titles (until 1987): *Farm Woman;* (until 1986): *Farm Woman News;* (until 1985): *Farm Wife News.* [ISSN: 0892-8525] 1971. bi-m. USD 14.98 domestic; USD 19.98 Canada; USD 25.98 elsewhere. Ed(s): Lori Lau Grzybowski, Ann Kaiser. Reiman Media Group, Inc., 5400 S 60th St, Greendale, WI 53129; rpsubscustomercare@custhelp.com; http://www.reimanpub.com. Illus., adv. Sample. Circ: 2300000 Paid. Vol. ends: Dec. *Aud.:* Hs, Ga.

Country Woman celebrates the North American rural lifestyle. Many of the articles are written by country women. Topics include country cooking and entertaining; fiction and poetry; gardening and decorating; crafts and hobbies; rural businesses and volunteering; and reader remembrances and profiles. The companion web site provides contest entry forms, antique advice, and recipe submissions. Recommended for high school and public libraries. URL: www.countrywomanmagazine.com/

2325. Details. [ISSN: 0740-4921] 1982. 11x/yr. USD 7.97 domestic; USD 30 Canada; USD 42.95 elsewhere. Ed(s): Daniel Peres. Fairchild Publications, Inc., 750 3rd Ave, 3rd Fl, New York, NY 10017; customerservice@fairchildpub.com; http://www.fairchildpub.com. Illus., adv. Sample. Circ: 458536 Paid. Vol. ends: No. 12. *Indexed:* BRI, MLA-IB. *Aud.:* Ga, Ac.

Details is a lifestyle magazine marketed to the young urban career man. The magazine's columns and features cover arts and film; celebrities and style; clothing and grooming; entertaining and finance; health and fitness; innovations and gadgets; popular culture and trends; and sex and relationships. The companion web site and blog continue the discussions on celebrity, culture, current events, fatherhood, masculinity, and style. Recommended for public libraries. URL: www.details.com/

2326. Elle (New York). [ISSN: 0888-0808] 1985. m. USD 10; USD 4.25 newsstand/cover. Hearst Magazines, 300 W 57th St, 12th Fl, New York, NY 10019; HearstMagazines@hearst.com; http://www.hearst.com. Illus., adv. Vol. ends: Aug. *Indexed:* A22, ASIP, BRI, C37. *Bk. rev.:* 8-12, brief. *Aud.:* Hs, Ga.

The *Elle* Global Network is marketed to the affluent and career-driven woman. *Elle (American Edition)* began publication in 1985, 40 years after the first French edition. Magazine topics include beauty and health-product ratings; celebrity and popular culture features; horoscope and trend analyses; and designer and fashion runway reviews. *Elle's* ability to connect with women's whole lives and the well-balanced editorial approach of personal style and personal power is the key to the publication's success. The companion web site and social media networks, digital editions, and iPad app provides access to topical guides and updates. Recommended for public libraries. URL: www.cosmopolitan.com/

2327. Essence (New York): the magazine for today's black woman. [ISSN: 0014-0880] 1970. m. USD 47.88 domestic; USD 34.96 Canada; USD 13.99 newsstand/cover. Ed(s): Angela Burt-Murray. Essence Communications Inc., 1500 Broadway, 6th Fl., New York, NY 10036-4015; info@essence.com; http://www.essence.com. Illus., adv. Circ: 950000 Paid. Vol. ends: Dec. Microform: PQC. *Indexed:* A01, A22, BRI, C37, CBRI, ENW, MASUSE, MLA-IB, P02. *Bk. rev.:* 4-5, 75 words; 6, 15 words; unsigned. *Aud.:* Hs, Ac, Sa.

Essence, The Magazine for Today's Black Woman, has a new mission and tone under Constance C.R. White, the new editor-in-chief. Celebrity lives, beauty tips, and fashion news now comprise the magazine's major feature articles and columns. African American culture, politics, spirituality, and social issues occasionally appear as news items and articles. *Essence* reflects marketing trends of other fashion and lifestyle magazines by focusing on personalities, careers, clothing, consumption, finance, healthy living, and family. The companion web site ("*Essence:* fierce, fun and fabulous") is a networked portal to social media and digital apps. Recommended for academic, high school, and public libraries. URL: www.essence.com/

2328. Flare (Toronto): Canada's fashion magazine. Formerly (until 1979): *Miss Chatelaine.* [ISSN: 0708-4927] 1979. m. CAD 14.95 domestic. Ed(s): Lisa Tant. Rogers Publishing Ltd., One Mount Pleasant Rd, 8th Fl, Toronto, ON M4Y 2Y5, Canada; http://www.rogerspublishing.ca. Illus., adv. Circ: 151646 Paid. Vol. ends: Dec. Microform: MML. *Indexed:* BRI, C37, CBCARef. *Aud.:* Hs, Ac, Ga.

Flare, "Canada's Fashion Authority," is a fashion and lifestyle magazine, marketed to young Canadian women. The magazine celebrates Canadian athletes, authors, designers, models, musicians, thespians, and other notables. Every issue cover features Canadian and international celebrities, including Amanda Seyfried, Coco Rocha, Channel Iman, Nelly Furtado, Sasha Pivovarova, and Lady Gaga. *Flare* covers trends in beauty, careers, entertainment, fashion, fitness, and Canadian popular culture. The web site, social media, and digital edition provide access to blogs, bridal tips, contests, newsletters, shopping guides, and videos. Recommended for high school and public libraries.

2329. Glamour (New York). Incorporates (1935-2001): *Mademoiselle;* (in 1959): *Charm;* Formerly (until 1941): *Glamour of Hollywood.* [ISSN: 0017-0747] 1939. m. USD 12 domestic; USD 36 Canada; USD 45 foreign. Ed(s): Cynthia Leive, Jill Herzig. Conde Nast Publications, Inc., 4 Times Sq, 6th Fl, New York, NY 10036; magpr@condenast.com; http://www.glamour.com. Illus., adv. Sample. Circ: 2354973 Paid. Vol. ends: Dec. Microform: PQC. *Indexed:* A22, BRI, C37, P02. *Bk. rev.:* 5, 75 words, unsigned. *Aud.:* Hs, Ga, Ac.

Glamour magazine provides real-world personal care and style guides for today's American woman. The magazine publishes information on trends in beauty, dating, diet, fashion, health, money, and shopping. The companion web site, digital edition, and iPad app furnish sections on fashion and beauty; youth and weddings; do's and don'ts; blogs and videos; health and fitness; and sex, love, and life. Recommended for public libraries. URL: www.glamour.com/

2330. *Harper's Bazaar.* [ISSN: 0017-7873] 1867. 10x/yr. USD 10; USD 3.99 newsstand/cover. Ed(s): Glenda Bailey. Hearst Magazines, 300 W 57th St, 12th Fl, New York, NY 10019; HearstMagazines@hearst.com; http://www.hearstcorp.com/magazines/. Illus., adv. Vol. ends: Dec. Microform: NBI; PMC; PQC. *Indexed:* A22, BRI, C37, MASUSE, MLA-IB, P02. *Bk. rev.:* Number and length vary. *Aud.:* Hs, Ga, Ac.

Harper's Bazaar, America's first fashion magazine, targets the affluent American woman. The magazine's rich visual past includes the photography by Richard Avedon, Peter Lindbergh, Man Ray, and Solve Sundsbo, as well as illustrations by Erte and Andy Warhol. *Harper's Bazaar*'s motto, "Where Fashion Gets Personal," reflects the sophisticated taste of readers in their purchasing the best from the best, from casual to couture. Each issue features articles and photographic spreads of provocative stylists and renowned designers. The convergent web site, social media networks, digital edition, and iPad app provides readers with up-to-date information on the world of beauty and fashion. Recommended for public libraries. URL: www.harpersbazaar.com/

2331. *InStyle.* [ISSN: 1076-0830] 1994. m. USD 23.88 domestic; CAD 34 Canada. Ed(s): John Huey, Maria Baugh. Time Inc., 1271 Ave of the Americas, New York, NY 10020; information@timeinc.com; http://www.timeinc.com. Illus., adv. Circ: 1660193 Paid. *Indexed:* BRI, C37, MASUSE. *Aud.:* Ga.

InStyle, a newsstand beauty magazine, targets active women who want immediate information to tips and step-by-step guides to cosmetic products; skin care techniques; make-up applications; hair styling; shopping deals; and wardrobe assembly. The magazine features celebrity interviews; style-setter photo shoots; and tours of homes of the rich and famous. The companion web site, social media, and iPad app provide quick access to celebrity spottings, fashion news, and shopping deals. URL: www.instyle.com

2332. *Jade Magazine: a fresh perspective for Asian women.* 1999. bi-m. JADE Magazine Inc., Village Station, PO Box 915, New York, NY 10014; info@jademagazine.com. *Bk. rev.:* Number and length vary. *Aud.:* Sa.

Started by two ambitious Asian-American women, *Jade* is an e-zine designed to create a place to address young English-speaking Asian women's issues and interests, highlight their contributions, and confront the stereotypes surrounding them. *Jade* has grown in readership, receiving over 10,000 unique visitors every month. Many features are common to women's fashion and beauty magazines: career, fitness, family, legal issues, personal finance, relationships, beauty, fashion, and health, but all are addressed from a unique Asian perspective. In addition to the more usual women's magazine features, *Jade* also provides daily updates of world news relevant to its readership, events of interest in Asia, Canada, and the United States, and "Open Mike," where readers can share their views. The current online issue is available at no charge; however, articles from past issues are for sale. URL: www.jademagazine.com/

2333. *Latina (New York).* [ISSN: 1099-890X] 1996. 10x/yr. USD 9.97 domestic; USD 29.97 foreign. Latina Media Ventures, LLC, 625 Madison Ave, 3rd Fl, New York, NY 10022. Illus., adv. *Bk. rev.:* Number and length vary. *Aud.:* Hs, Ga, Ac, Sa.

Latina is the first bilingual lifestyle publication for bi-cultural Hispanic women in the United States. The magazine identifies trends in fashion and beauty; health and fitness; food and recipes; and media and politics. *Latina* celebrates modern Hispanic women by featuring articles rooted in Latin traditions and U.S. history. *Latina* places on its covers celebrities, cultural heroines, star

athletes, business moguls, style icons, civil rights leaders, and academic achievers. The successful web site, social media sites, and accompanying iPad app are marketed for acculturated users by offering interactive forums and tools in the lifestyle sections, and by spotlighting U.S. Latino culture and history in web articles. Recommended for public libraries. URL: www.latina.com/

2334. *Lucky: the magazine about shopping and style.* [ISSN: 1531-4294] 2000. m. USD 3.99 newsstand/cover. Ed(s): Brandon Holley. Conde Nast Publications, Inc., 4 Times Sq, 6th Fl, New York, NY 10036; talktous@luckymag.com; http://www.condenast.com. Adv. Sample. *Indexed:* BRI. *Aud.:* Ga.

Lucky, "The Magazine About Shopping & Style," was inspired by popular Japanese shopping magazines. The magazine targets readers who love to shop for apparel, cosmetics, and home-decorating bargains. *Lucky* showcases celebrity beauty and fashion style; shopping basics and boutique guides; and real-life advice for what and how to wear. The companion web sites include the magazine's web site; *Lucky* Magazine on Facebook; the *Lucky* blogs, newsletter, and tutorials; and the *Lucky* iPad shopping app. Recently, *Lucky* partnered with ThisNext (www.thisnext.com/) to form an integrated shopping and social media site. This co-branded site enables women to shop together offline and online. URL: www.luckymag.com/

2335. *Marie Claire.* [ISSN: 1081-8626] 1994. m. USD 10; USD 3.50 newsstand/cover. Hearst Magazines, 300 W 57th St, 12th Fl, New York, NY 10019; HearstMagazines@hearst.com; http://www.hearst.com. Illus., adv. *Indexed:* BRI. *Bk. rev.:* 2-3, 25 words. *Aud.:* Hs, Ga.

Marie Claire magazine offers advice to the modern woman on celebrity and stylist interviews; fashion and pop culture trends; hair and skin care; health and fitness; sex and romance; and careers and wardrobe. There are also occasional features on women's social and political issues. The web site is a portal to "Games & Giveaways," "Sex & Relationships," "Horoscopes," "Fashion, Hair & Beauty," "Virtual Hairstyle and Makeup Makeover," "Health & Fitness," and the "Sex and the Single Guy Blog." It also leads to the digital magazine edition; social media networks; and the iPad app. Recommended for public libraries.

2336. *Maxim (Print).* [ISSN: 1092-9789] 1997. m. USD 17.97 for 3 yrs. domestic; USD 47.97 Canada; USD 5.99 newsstand/cover. Dennis Digital, Inc, 1040 Ave of the Americas, 12th Fl, New York, NY 10018. Illus., adv. Sample. Circ: 2535884 Paid. Vol. ends: Dec. *Bk. rev.:* 5, 200 words, signed. *Aud.:* Ga.

Maxim has found its way onto some library periodical racks, although it's usually found on magazine newsstands. It is a slick, good-looking magazine that will attract male readers. The provocative cover does the trick, but there's as much meat as cheesecake within. Health, holidays, sports, technology, investing, fashion, and sex are all grist for the *Maxim* mill. All types of media are reviewed. A fascination with the slightly offbeat is also apparent. Inquisitive librarians and readers may check out the title through its full-text web site, at www.maxim.com/amg/.

2337. *Men's Journal.* [ISSN: 1063-4657] 1992. m. USD 11.88. Wenner Media, Inc., 1290 Ave of Americas, New York, NY 10104. Illus., adv. Circ: 700000 Paid. *Indexed:* BRI. *Bk. rev.:* 4, 200 words, signed. *Aud.:* Hs, Ga.

A publication for the active male, *Men's Journal* consists of about equal parts sports, action, and travel reading, with a hint of savoring the good life. Known for its outstanding photography and exceptional writing, it is aimed at the active man who wants to get the most out of life. An article about American heroes may stand side-by-side with one about climbing Mt. Everest, along with columns on the latest innovations in digital and other equipment, sports, fashion trends, health, grooming, sex, cars, books, and music. URL: www.mensjournal.com/

2338. *More (New York).* [ISSN: 1094-7868] 1997. 10x/yr. USD 20 for 2 yrs. domestic; USD 30 for 2 yrs. Canada. Ed(s): Lesley Jane Seymour. Meredith Corporation, 1716 Locust St, Des Moines, IA 50309; patrick.taylor@meredith.com; http://www.meredith.com. Illus., adv. Circ: 1200000. *Indexed:* AgeL. *Bk. rev.:* Number and length vary. *Aud.:* Ga, Sa.

More is geared to a target audience of women who are 40-plus. Articles focus on the positive aspects of that time of life, such as health, fashion for all sizes and shapes, travel, relationships, and beauty tips. The "Notebook" section highlights trends, films, books, travel, and the arts, suggesting that the content is geared to women with more leisure time and a fair amount of disposable income on their hands. Interior decorating is also a focus, with work and career de-emphasized. Health-related news and information is a particular strength, through both the "Vital & Vibrant" section and lengthy articles that focus on such issues as breast cancer and osteoporosis. Relationship stories focus on love and sex in middle age, and parenting adult children. The web site highlights events and promotions, the current issue, and a reader panel. URL: www.more.com/

O: The Oprah Magazine. See General Interest section.

2339. Redbook. Incorporates (1928-1983): *American Home.* [ISSN: 0034-2106] 1903. m. USD 8; USD 3.99 newsstand/cover. Ed(s): Jill Herzig. Hearst Magazines, 300 W 57th St, 12th Fl, New York, NY 10019; HearstMagazines@hearst.com; http://www.hearst.com. Illus., index, adv. Circ: 2227957 Paid. Microform: NBI; PQC. *Indexed:* A22, BRI, C37, MASUSE, P02. *Aud.:* Ac, Ga.

Redbook targets readers who have married and outgrown *Cosmo* but do not yet place themselves among the readership of more traditional titles such as *Ladies' Home Journal* and *Good Housekeeping.* The magazine offers great tips on fashion, clothing, gifts, sex, makeup, and shopping. Most of the articles are not just about how you look, but also about how to take care of yourself emotionally and physically. The web site is similar in content but focuses a bit more on sex and marriage. Reader polls, chat, and advice columns complete the site. URL: www.redbookmag.com/

2340. Vogue. Incorporated (from Mar. 1936 to Feb. 1983): *Vanity Fair;* Which was formerly (until 1914): *Dress & Vanity Fair.* [ISSN: 0042-8000] 1892. m. USD 15 domestic; USD 50 Canada; USD 70 elsewhere. Ed(s): Anna Wintour. Conde Nast Publications, Inc., 4 Times Sq, 6th Fl, New York, NY 10036; http://www.condenast.com. Illus., index, adv. Sample. Circ: 1224131·Paid. Vol. ends: Dec. *Indexed:* A06, A22, BRI, C37, MLA-IB, P02. *Bk. rev.:* 3-4, 100-200 words. *Aud.:* Ga, Ac.

Vogue started as a society paper in 1892 and since then has become an elite women's lifestyle and fashion magazine. Its layout is beautiful and glossy, as with most expensive fashion magazines, and its advertising content is extremely prolific. In fact, *Vogue* is one of the most advertised-in magazines in the world. Every conceivable tie-in to the fashion industry is included: clothing, footwear, accessories, jewelry, makeup, cosmetics, and medications to make one look and feel younger. The magazine is sectioned into four parts that include articles on haute couture, designers, makeup, and hair trends. It also covers current events such as museum openings and book and film reviews. A core fashion title for public libraries. URL: www.vogue.com/

■ FICTION: GENERAL/MYSTERY AND DETECTIVE

General/Mystery and Detective

Rebecca H. Wingfield, Bibliographic Specialist for North America, Widener Library, Harvard University, Cambridge, MA 02138; rwingfie@fas.harvard.edu

Introduction

The magazines included in this section publish a wide range of original fiction by established and emerging writers. Content varies from literary and experimental fiction to genre fiction, including romance and mystery fiction. While fiction is heavily emphasized in these publications, many also publish poetry, essays, and other nonfiction. Many of these publications also feature book reviews, author interviews, and other features of interest to fans and writers of fiction. Small independent publishers or university presses or departments generally publish these magazines. Despite being print-based, many of these publications make effective use of the online environment for promoting creative fiction, providing companion web sites that offer additional multimedia content.

Basic Periodicals

GENERAL. Ga, Ac: *Fiction, Fiction International, Narrative, Zoetrope.*

MYSTERY AND DETECTIVE. Ga, Ac: *Mystery Scene, The Strand Magazine.*

Basic Abstracts and Indexes

MLA International Bibliography, Mystery Short Fiction.

General

These magazines represent a diverse range of approaches to publishing high-quality fiction, poetry, and prose. Some magazines feature relatively accessible fiction and poetry with broad appeal, while others lean toward more radical literary experimentations that push at the boundaries of literature and art, and/or explore the role of the digital environment in storytelling. All of these magazines have relatively small circulation and cater to an avid readership. Also included in this section are magazines that specialize in romance fiction and often feature extensive reviews of romance fiction.

2341. Affaire de Coeur: the magazine that brings you honest reviews. [ISSN: 0739-3881] 1979. m. USD 36 domestic; USD 65 Canada; USD 6 per issue. Ed(s): Louise B Snead. Snead, Inc., 3976 Oak Hill Rd, Oakland, CA 94605; sseven1@att.net. Adv. *Bk. rev.:* Number and length vary. *Aud.:* Ga.

Affaire de Coeur magazine has been serving female readers of all genres of romance fiction for over 30 years. Each issue contains features on the romance genre, writing and publication advice, author interviews, and plenty of book reviews for avid readers of romance fiction. The book reviews are arranged by genre and include reviews of contemporary, historical, young adult, and paranormal romance, as well as erotica. There's something here for every romance reader! The web site features subscription information, author interviews, a blog, and more. URL: http://adcmagazine.com/

2342. Fiction. [ISSN: 0046-3736] 1972. s-a. USD 24; USD 12 per issue. Ed(s): Mark Jay Mirsky, Steve Rosenstein. Fiction Inc., c/o City College of NY, Department of English, New York, NY 10031. Illus., index. Microform: PQC. *Indexed:* A22, AmHI. *Aud.:* Ga, Ac.

Published out of the City University of New York, *Fiction* features an impressive array of stories by notable and up-and-coming writers. Eschewing any particular school of fiction, the magazine nonetheless aims "to bring the experimental to a broader audience." Each issue features a range of high-quality stories, including new short fiction, previously published stories, works in translation, and book excerpts. Recent past contributors have included Harold Brodkey, Henry Roth, Julio Cortazar, William Powers, and John Barth. Fiction is an excellent addition for large public libraries and academic libraries. The web site contains submission guidelines, subscription information, an archive of stories previously published in *Fiction,* and news and commentary from the editors. URL: www.fictioninc.com/

2343. Fiction International. [ISSN: 0092-1912] 1973. a. USD 16 per issue. Ed(s): Harold Jaffe. San Diego State University Press, 5500 Campanile Dr, San Diego, CA 92182; http://sdsupress.sdsu.edu/. Illus. Microform: PQC. *Indexed:* A22, AmHI, BRI, CBRI, MLA-IB. *Aud.:* Ga, Ac.

Fiction International features a unique blend of "fiction, non-fiction, indeterminate prose, and visuals" that emphasizes "formal innovation and progressive politics." Each issue contains original fiction, nonfiction, and creative visual art by established and emerging writers and artists. Past issues of *Fiction International* have featured the work of well-known formal innovators, including Kathy Acker and Robert Coover. Issues often revolve around specific themes, past examples of which have included "Walls," "About seeing," and

"The Artist in Wartime." This annual publication is recommended for academic and large public libraries with an interest in collecting contemporary experimental fiction. The web site contains subscription information, submission guidelines, and links to *FI*'s media presence elsewhere on the web, including a blog, a Twitter feed, and a Goodreads profile. URL: http://fictioninternational.sdsu.edu/index.html

Glimmer Train. See Little Magazines section.

Jacket 2. See Literary Reviews section.

2344. *The Long Story.* [ISSN: 0741-4242] 1982. a. USD 13 for 2 yrs. Ed(s): R Peter Burnham. Long Story, 18 Eaton St, Lawrence, MA 01843. Sample. *Indexed:* AmHI. *Aud.:* Ga, Ac.

The Long Story bills itself as "the only literary magazine in America devoted strictly to long stories," of 8,000–20,000 words. This annual features eight to ten pieces of long fiction and a smattering of poems on varying themes, with a preference for humanistic stories of "common folks" and "a perspective on current society." The web site lists the table of contents of the current issue, gives subscription and submission information, and provides a cumulative index. Recommended for libraries that support creative writing programs and larger public libraries with strong fiction collections. URL: www.longstorylitmag.com/longstorylitmag/LongStory.html

2345. *Narrative Magazine.* 2003. irreg. Free. Ed(s): Tom Jenks, Carol Edgarian. Narrative Magazine. *Aud.:* Ga, Ac.

Since its founding as a nonprofit organization in 2003, *Narrative* has dedicated itself to "to advancing literary arts in the digital age by supporting the finest writing talent and encouraging readership across generations, in schools, and around the globe." In addition to publishing fiction, poetry, and nonfiction, *Narrative* sponsors fiction and poetry contests. Although it's primarily an online magazine, *Narrative* publishes a print annual in the winter. The online magazine features an impressive library of free stories by emerging and well-known writers. As a way of exploring the impact of new technologies on conventional forms, the print and online versions also publish "iPoems" and "iStories" of no more than 150 words, a length that should fit within a couple of screens on a smart phone. Recent issues have published new fiction from literary luminaries, such as Russell Banks, Joyce Carol Oates, Sherman Alexie, and C.D. Wright. A "Narrative Backstage" section on the web site may also be accessed for a small donation and features audio and video files of author readings, unpublished works-in-progress, and discussions on writing. URL: www.narrativemagazine.com/

2346. *Painted Bride Quarterly.* [ISSN: 0362-7969] 1973. a. USD 15. Drexel University, Department of English and Philosophy, 3141 Chestnut St, Philadelphia, PA 19104. Adv. Circ: 1000 Paid. *Indexed:* AmHI. *Aud.:* Ga.

Published out of Drexel University, *Painted Bride Quarterly* is one of the country's longest-running literary magazines. *PBQ* is an independent, community-based, nonprofit magazine that publishes a wide range of genres. Issues often feature a theme, past examples of which include issues on "Style," "Displacement," and "Food." *PBQ* is published quarterly online and annually in print. Each issue includes fiction, poetry, and prose from emerging and established authors. The web site features online issues, submission information, news, and information on writing contests. URL: http://pbq.drexel.edu/

2347. *Ploughshares.* [ISSN: 0048-4474] 1971. 3x/yr. USD 39. Ed(s): Ladette Randolph. Emerson College, 120 Boylston St, Boston, MA 02116; http://www.emerson.edu. Illus., adv. Sample. Vol. ends: Dec. Microform: PQC. *Indexed:* A01, A22, ABS&EES, AmHI, ArtHuCI, BRI, MLA-IB, P02. *Aud.:* Ga, Ac.

Long recognized as a springboard for talented new writers, *Ploughshares* continues to publish new fiction, poetry, and prose by established and up-and-coming writers. Each issue is often guest-edited by a "prominent writer, who explores personal visions, aesthetics, and literary circles." The guest editor may solicit up to half of the stories and poems, while the other half are chosen from unsolicited submissions. This unique editorial policy aims to provide a means

"for challenging provincial or fashionable tastes, and, in particular, for showcasing unknown and under promoted writers." Guest editors of recent issues have included Alice Hoffman, Colm Toibin, and Patricia Hampl. Every issue of *Ploughshares* features fiction, poetry, nonfiction, essays, and book recommendations. *Ploughshares* is published three times a year: the spring and winter issues contain a combination of poetry and prose, while the fall issue features prose. Highly recommended for academic and public libraries. The web site contains information on subscriptions, submissions, a blog, and multimedia section, consisting of video of talks by guest editors. URL: www.pshares.org/

2348. *Romantic Times Book Reviews: the magazine for fiction lovers.* Former titles (until 2006): *Romantic Times Book Club;* (until May 2002): *Romantic Times Magazine; Romantic Times;* Which incorporated (1986-1991): *Rave Reviews.* [ISSN: 1933-0634] 1981. m. USD 29.95 domestic; USD 65 foreign. Ed(s): Faygie Levy. Romantic Times Publishing Group, 55 Bergen St, Brooklyn, NY 11201. Illus., adv. Circ: 135000. *Bk. rev.:* 120-170, 50-250 words. *Aud.:* Ga.

For more than 30 years, *Romantic Times Book Reviews* magazine has kept romance readers, writers, publishers, and booksellers informed about romance fiction in all its forms. Each glossy issue features articles, authors, writing advice, book news, and, of course, book reviews of romance in all its guises. The comprehensive book reviews section is organized around romance subgenres, including contemporary romance, erotic romance, and historical romance, along with mainstream fiction, mystery and suspense, science fiction and fantasy, young adult, and more. This magazine is a great resource for public libraries with a romance-reading public. The extensive web site features additional information on authors and books, a community forum for readers, and a section of resources for aspiring writers. URL: www.rtbookreviews.com/

2349. *The Storyteller.* [ISSN: 1523-6021] 1996. q. Ed(s): Regina Williams. Storyteller Magazine, 2441 Washington Rd, Maynard, AR 72444. *Aud.:* Sa.

Billing itself a "Magazine for all writers," *Storyteller Magazine* is unique in the care it makes to nurture new literary talent. Each issue of *Storyteller Magazine* contains well-crafted short stories in a wide range of genres, poetry, essays, and other nonfiction. Tony Hillerman, Jodi Thomas, and David Marion Wilkinson have published in this family-oriented magazine. The web site provides subscription information and submission guidelines and tips for writers. URL: www.thestorytellermagazine.com

2350. *Thema.* [ISSN: 1041-4851] 1988. 3x/yr. USD 20 domestic; USD 30 foreign. Ed(s): Virginia Howard. Thema Literary Society, 4312 Napoli Dr, Metairie, LA 70002. *Indexed:* AmHI. *Aud.:* Ga.

This delightfully quirky magazine is "designed to stimulate creative thinking." *Thema* takes up a different theme in each issue with the aim of providing a forum for established and emerging artists, serving as a source of material for creative writing teachers, and entertaining readers with its uniquely eclectic collection of pieces. Each issue features poetry, short fiction, art, photography, and other creative pieces inspired by a unique theme. Past theme-based issues have been devoted to themes such as "Who keeps it tidy?," "White Wine Chilling," and "The Perfect Cup of Coffee." The web site includes subscription and submission information. URL: http://themaliterarysociety.com/

2351. *Zoetrope: all-story.* [ISSN: 1091-2495] 1997. q. USD 24 in North America; USD 40 elsewhere; USD 8 per issue. A Z X Publications, 916 Kearny St, San Francisco, CA 94133. Illus., adv. *Aud.:* Ga, Ac.

Founded by Adrienne Brodeur and Francis Ford Coppola, *Zoetrope* is an art and literary magazine that aims to "explore the intersection of story and art, fiction and film." This beautifully designed magazine features a fascinating amalgam of art and fiction from well-known and emerging writers. In addition, the editors invite contemporary artists to be guest designers, making the visual look of the magazine as intriguing as its fictional content. Each issue features a short story that was adapted into a screenplay, such as Daphne du Maurier's short story "The Birds," which was later adapted into the Hitchcock film of the same name. This magazine is recommended for academic libraries that support creative writing, film production, and/or art programs. The web site features subscription information, submission guidelines, and table of contents information on the current issue and back issues. URL: www.all-story.com/index.cgi

Mystery and Detective

Magazines included in this section are devoted to some aspect of mystery and detective fiction, covering a wide range of subgenres, including suspense fiction, thrillers, whodunits, and hard-boiled crime fiction. Many of these periodicals publish original short mystery and detective fiction, as well as criticism, author interviews, book reviews, and other information of interest to readers and writers in the mystery genre. Although some publications feature criticism and may be of interest to academic audiences, these publications are generally directed at a general audience.

2352. *Alfred Hitchcock's Mystery Magazine.* [ISSN: 0002-5224] 1956. 10x/yr. USD 32.97 domestic; USD 42.97 foreign. Penny Publications LLP, 6 Prowitt St, Norwalk, CT 06855; customerservice@pennypublications.com; http://www.pennypublications.com. Illus., adv. Vol. ends: Dec. *Indexed:* AmHI, MSF. *Bk. rev.:* 300-500 words. *Aud.:* Ga.

This classic, digest-sized magazine features short mystery stories of every kind from whodunits to suspense to hardboiled crime fiction. Founded in 1956, *AHMM* continues to publish mystery fiction by up-and-coming and award-winning authors. Stories vary in length from "short-shorts to novellas." While the emphasis is on new, original stories, issues occasionally feature "mystery classics" from bygone eras. Each issue includes short stories, book reviews, puzzles, and story contests. The web site has submission guidelines, links to a podcast series of author readings and interviews, information on the current issue, and an excerpt from one of the stories in the current issue. A must-have subscription for public libraries and other libraries with a mystery-reading public. URL: www.themysteryplace.com/ahmm/

2353. *Baker Street Journal: an irregular quarterly of sherlockiana.* [ISSN: 0005-4070] 1946. q. USD 38.50 domestic; USD 49 foreign. Ed(s): Steven Rothman. The Sheridan Press, PO Box 583, Zionsville, IN 46077; circulation@thesheridanpress.com; http://www.thesheridanpress.com. Illus., index, adv. Microform: PQC. *Indexed:* A22, AmHI, BEL&L, MLA-IB. *Bk. rev.:* 1-10, 30-90 words. *Aud.:* Ga.

The *Baker Street Journal* is the official publication of the major Sherlock Holmes fan association in the United States. Describing itself as an "irregular quarterly of Sherlockiana," the *BSJ* features both scholarly articles and lighter fare devoted to the character and world of Sherlock Holmes in the original stories and in popular culture more broadly, including film and television. In addition to articles, each issue features reports on Holmes-related events and book news and reviews. The web site features subscription information, submission guidelines, a table of contents for the most recent issue, select articles from the most recent issue, and links to a calendar of Holmes-related events. URL: www.bakerstreetjournal.com/home.html

2354. *Clues: a journal of detection.* [ISSN: 0742-4248] 1980. q. USD 120 (print & online eds.) Individuals, USD 40 (print & online eds.). Ed(s): Margaret Kinsman, Elizabeth Foxwell. McFarland & Company, Inc., PO Box 611, Jefferson, NC 28640; info@mcfarlandpub.com; http://www.mcfarlandpub.com. Illus. Refereed. *Indexed:* A22, ABS&EES, AmHI, MLA-IB, P02. *Bk. rev.:* 0-60, 40-300 words. *Aud.:* Ac.

Clues is a peer-reviewed journal that features scholarly articles on all aspects of the mystery and detective fiction genre in print, television, and film. Each issue contains literary criticism, essays, and book reviews. Special issues focus on particular themes related to mystery fiction, past and present. Recent special issues have focused on paranormal fiction, Alfred Hitchcock, and adaptation; future special issues will tackle the topics of Tana French and Irish crime fiction and "the global crime scene." The "only American scholarly journal on mystery fiction," *Clues* is a must-read for academics and students interested in the mystery genre. The web site provides submission, publication, and subscription information. URL: www.mcfarlandbooks.com/customers/journals/clues-a-journal-of-detection/

2355. *Crimespree Magazine.* [ISSN: 1551-5826] 2004. bi-m. USD 32 domestic; USD 42 Canada and UK; USD 50 elsewhere. Ed(s): Ruth Jordan, Jon Jordan. Crimespree Magazine, 536 S 5th St, Ste 1 A, Milwaukee, WI 53204; info@crimespreemag.com; http://www.crimespreemag.com. *Bk. rev.:* Number and length vary. *Aud.:* Ga.

Produced by "mystery fans from all over the map," *Crimespree Magazine* features interviews and other creative features, great short crime fiction, book and media reviews, news on mystery fiction and film, and even crime-fiction–related recipes. Additional news, features, and giveaways appear on the companion web site. URL: http://crimespreemag.com/

2356. *Ellery Queen's Mystery Magazine: the world's leading mystery magazine.* Former titles (until 1988): *Ellery Queen;* (until 1981): *Ellery Queen's Mystery Magazine.* [ISSN: 1054-8122] 1941. 10x/yr. USD 32.97 domestic; USD 42.97 foreign. Penny Publications LLP, 6 Prowitt St, Norwalk, CT 06855; customerservice@pennypublications.com; http://www.pennypublications.com. Illus., adv. *Indexed:* AmHI, MSF. *Bk. rev.:* 8-12, 30-70 words. *Aud.:* Ga, Ac.

From its beginnings in 1941, *Ellery Queen Mystery Magazine* has offered readers short mystery fiction with a literary bent, often featuring the work for leading mystery and crime writers. Each issue is chock-full of short fiction and also features book reviews, occasional poetry, and a "department of first stories" section that features the first published work by talented new writers. *EQMM* is recommended for public libraries and academic libraries that support creative writing programs. The web site features reviews, subscription information, submission guidelines, and *EQMM* podcasts featuring readings and dramatizations of stories that appear in the magazine. URL: www.themysteryplace.com/eqmm/

2357. *Mystery Scene.* [ISSN: 1087-674X] 1985. 6x/yr. USD 32 domestic; USD 42 Canada; USD 65 elsewhere. Ed(s): Brian Skulpin, Kate Stine. Mystery Scene Magazine, 331 W. 57th St, Ste 148, New York, NY 10019-3101; info@mysteryscenemag.com. Illus., adv. Circ: 8000. *Indexed:* MLA-IB. *Bk. rev.:* 10-15, 45-80 words. *Aud.:* Ga, Sa.

With coverage that spans past mystery masters and contemporary writers, *Mystery Scene* bills itself as "the oldest, largest, and most authoritative guide to the crime fiction genre." This lively magazine is aimed at a broad audience consisting of readers and authors of mysteries, booksellers, and publishers. Each issue contains publishing news, in-depth features, interviews, articles by well-known authors, and reviews of books, films, television shows, audio books, juvenile mystery fiction, short stories, and reference works. The web site has details on subscribing, contributing, and advertising, as well as the table of contents of the latest issue. URL: www.mysteryscenemag.com/

2358. *Over My Dead Body!* [ISSN: 1067-2540] 1993. q. USD 12. Ed(s): Cherie Jung. Over My Dead Body!, PO Box 1778, Auburn, WA 98071-1778. Illus., adv. Circ: 1000. *Bk. rev.:* Number and length vary. *Aud.:* Ga.

Currently publishing online only, *Over My Dead Body* features short mystery fiction "from cozy to hardboiled and everything in between." In addition to stories, the web site features interviews with writers, author profiles and interviews, and book and movie reviews. URL: www.overmydeadbody.com/

2359. *Sherlock Holmes Journal.* [ISSN: 0037-3621] 1952. s-a. Free. Ed(s): Roger Johnson. Sherlock Holmes Society of London, c/o Roger Johnson, Mole End, 41 Sandford Rd, Chelmsford, CM2 6DE, United Kingdom; rojerjohnson@yahoo.co.uk; http://www.sherlock-holmes.org.uk/. Illus. *Bk. rev.:* 5-10, 80-700 words. *Aud.:* Ga.

The *Sherlock Holmes Journal* is the official publication of the Sherlock Holmes Society of London, a literary and social society devoted to Sherlock Holmes and his world. The journal features well-researched critical and historical articles and Holmes-related news, as well as reviews of books, plays, television shows, and films on Holmes-related topics. The journal also documents the transactions, meetings, dinners, and excursions and activities of the Sherlock Holmes Society, giving it a more sociable feel. The society's web site includes subscription information, the current issue's table of contents, a calendar of events, and the latest Sherlock Holmes Society newsletter. URL: www.sherlock-holmes.org.uk/journal.php

2360. *The Strand Magazine (Birmingham).* [ISSN: 1523-8709] 1891. q. USD 19.95 domestic; USD 47 foreign. Ed(s): Andrew F Gulli. Strand Magazine (Birmingham), PO Box 1418, Birmingham, MI 48012. Adv. *Indexed:* MSF. *Aud.:* Ga.

The venerable *Strand Magazine* traces its origins back to George Newnes' late Victorian magazine, perhaps best known as the popularizer of Sherlock Holmes. Styling itself as "a magazine for mystery and short story lovers," the new, revitalized *Strand Magazine* publishes works on and about some of the best-known contemporary crime and mystery writers. Each issue of this glossy magazine includes fiction, in-depth author interviews, and other articles of interest to mystery fans. Recent issues included works by Elmore Leonard, Laura Lippman, and Alexander McCall Smith. The reviews section in each issue covers the latest crime and mystery releases, including books, audiobooks, and films. URL: www.strandmag.com

2361. Thrilling Detective. 1998. q. Ed(s): Kevin Burton Smith. Thrilling Detective, 3053 Rancho Vista Blvd, Ste 116, Palmdale, CA 93551; http://thrillingdetective.com. *Bk. rev.:* Number and length vary. *Aud.:* Ga.

Although *Thrilling Detective* no longer publishes fiction, it still serves as an excellent resource for fans of private eye fiction. Each online issue features essays, reviews of books, films, and television shows in the detective genre. The web site has some excellent additional resources, including short essays on notable "private eyes and other tough guys" that have graced the genre and short essays on important films, television shows, and radio programs featuring private eyes. URL: http://thrillingdetective.com/index.html

■ FICTION: SCIENCE FICTION, FANTASY, AND HORROR

Laura A. Saloiye, Lead Readers' Services Librarian, Masland Library, University: Cairn University; lsaloiye@cairn.edu

Introduction

No longer a set of genres that inspires academic derision, science fiction, fantasy, and horror have now moved into mainstream media. It is now almost impossible for the modern viewer or reader to ignore the expanding radius of this genre's influence. Television is full to overflowing with television shows that delve into this rich and full world; *Game of Thrones, Doctor Who, Merlin, The Walking Dead,* and more have brought this world into our homes. What makes this genre so relevant is its ability to explore questions that cannot be answered through contemporary fiction.

The publications in this genre continue to grow in density and number, and the same can be said for its growing fan base, both academically and in trade publications. The fiction, art, poetry, and books included in this section offer a vast array of material characterized by the supernatural, frightening, and magical.

Through scholarly studies, speculative fiction, and entertainment publications, we get to explore strange new worlds, contemplate what it means to be human, and at times see our fears come to life. The broader audience can now read and review these materials in print, electronic, or webzine form.

Basic Periodicals

Analog Science Fiction & Fact (print edition), *Fantasy & Science Fiction, Science Fiction Studies.*

Basic Abstracts and Indexes

Arts & Humanities Citation Index, Book Review Index, MLA International Bibliography, PIO: Periodicals Index Online.

2362. Albedo One. Formerly (until 1991): *F T L.* [ISSN: 0791-8534] 1993. q. EUR 25 domestic; EUR 32 foreign. Ed(s): John Kenny. Albedo One, c/o David Murphy, 2 Post Rd., Lusk, Ireland; bobn@yellowbrickroad.ie; http://www.albedo1.com/. Circ: 180. *Aud.:* Ga, Sa.

An Irish import, *Albedo One* features a number of Irish authors as well as authors and stories from around the world. This title features an interesting array of sub-genres within the science fiction and fantasy genre. *Albedo One* features a wonderfully impressive list of award winners as contributors and authors in its

40+ issue history. This title would be appropriate for science fiction collections or with collections with Irish Literature. While not as explicit as some, this title would not be recommended for collections catering to children.

2363. Analog Science Fiction & Fact. Former titles (until 1991): *Analog Science Fiction Science Fact;* (until 1965): *Analog Science Fact - Science Fiction;* (until 1961): *Astounding Science Fiction;* (until 19??): *Astounding Science Fact & Fiction;* (until 1960): *Astounding Science-Fiction;* (until 1938): *Astounding Stories;* (until 19??): *Astounding Stories of Super-Science;* (until 1932): *Astounding Stories;* (until 1931): *Astounding Stories of Super-Science.* [ISSN: 1059-2113] 1930. 12x/yr. USD 34.97 domestic (print or online ed.); USD 44.97 foreign (print or online ed.); USD 4.49 per issue. Ed(s): Trevor Quachri, Stanley Schmidt. Dell Magazines, 475 Park Ave S, 11 Fl, New York, NY 10016; delleditorial@pennypublications.com; http://www.pennydellpuzzles.com. Illus., index, adv. Sample. Circ: 50000 Paid. Vol. ends: Dec. Microform: PQC. *Indexed:* A22, ASIP, BRI, CBRI, P02. *Aud.:* Hs, Ga, Ac.

When thinking about the titles in the SF genre, there are a couple that should come to mind; one of the first should be *Analog,* now the longest continuously published SF title from America. It has had a few title changes, but it has maintained its integrity as a publication of worth since its inception in 1930. *Analog* has a rare and wondrous ability to draw the reader in while maintaining excellent writing standards, blending fact and fiction seamlessly. This title has an obscene number of award nominations, and is recommended for all science fiction collections. Additional content can be found online. URL: www.analogsf.com/

2364. Andromeda Spaceways Inflight Magazine. [ISSN: 1446-781X] 2002. q. AUD 48 domestic; AUD 68 foreign; AUD 12.95 newsstand/cover per issue. Andromeda Spaceways Publishing Co-Op, PO Box 7311, Kaleen, ACT 2617, Australia. Adv. *Bk. rev.:* 5-10, 100-500 words. *Aud.:* Hs, Ga.

Andromeda Spaceways is an award-winning magazine from Australia. In it, the reader will find imaginative stories, poetry, scholarly essays, and reviews that are rooted in Australia's classic storytelling history. This title should appeal to a wide variety of readers; however, due to the language and some adult themes, it would not be appropriate for a young audience. An electronic version of the magazine is now available by subscription. There are additional benefits to the web site as well, including podcasts, letters, and forums that allow fans of the magazine to interact at a more intensive level. URL: www.andromedaspaceways.com

2365. Apex Magazine. [ISSN: 2157-1406] 2009. m. USD 19.95; USD 2.99 newsstand/cover per issue. Ed(s): Lynne M Thomas, Jason Sizemore. Apex Publications, PO Box 24323, Lexington, KY 40524; http://www.apexbookcompany.com. Illus. *Aud.:* Ga.

Apex Magazine would best be described as speculative, poignant, eerie, and a tiny bit melancholy. Short stories, interviews, poetry, and the occasional essay fill the pages of this title. General audiences consisting of older high school through adult would be the target audience. Published monthly, this magazine is available electronically through a number of online retailers.

2366. Bards and Sages Quarterly. [ISSN: 1944-4699] 2009. q. Ed(s): Julie A Dawson. Bards and Sages Publishing.201 Leed Ave, Bellmawr, NJ 08031; admin@bardsandsages.com; http://www.bardsandsages.com/. Adv. *Aud.:* Ga, Sa.

On the surface, this periodical seems like lighter fare; however, it doesn't take long for the reader to realize that it is anything but light—instead, terms like dark, eerie, and horrific might be better adjectives. These tales are told with great flair and just enough details to make them terrifying. Not recommended for young readers, this title may be appropriate for academic collections with horror or storytelling collections. Available electronically or in print.

2367. Black Gate: adventures in fantasy literature. [ISSN: 1531-7854] 2001. q. USD 29.95 domestic; CAD 56 Canada; USD 88 elsewhere. Ed(s): John O'Neill. New Epoch Press, 815 Oak St, St Charles, IL 60174; john@blackgate.com ; http://www.blackgate.com. Illus. *Bk. rev.:* Number and length vary. *Aud.:* Hs, Ga, Ac.

Explore old and new worlds within the pages of this generous title. Short fiction and book reviews comprise the bulk of this magazine, with an amusing comic strip at the end. Its pages are filled with well-written, fantastical stories of mythology, horror, and far-off worlds from reputable authors. Primarily made up of epic fantasy fiction, it nevertheless has an excellent variety of fiction, with a short biography for each author. *Black Gate* would be most appropriate for general audiences; however, it wouldn't be out of place in a fantasy literature collection.

2368. Black Static. Formerly (until 2007): *The Third Alternative.* [ISSN: 1753-0709] 1994. bi-m. GBP 24 domestic; GBP 27 in Europe; GBP 30 elsewhere. Ed(s): Andy Cox. T T A Press, 5 Martins Ln, Witcham, Ely, CB6 2LB, United Kingdom; info@ttapress.demon.co.uk; http://ttapress.com. Illus., adv. *Bk. rev.:* 15-25, 500-1,000 words. *Aud.:* Ga, Ac.

Dark, mysterious, and eerie, *Black Static* is a scintillating import from the United Kingdom. This title features a mix of excellent fiction, and film and book reviews. The reviews present unbiased opinions of recent releases in film and fiction, helping the discriminating viewer choose between the masses of new titles published each year. This title is recommended for any horror collection in both academic and public libraries.

2369. Cemetery Dance. [ISSN: 1047-7675] 1988. bi-m. USD 27; USD 5 newsstand/cover per issue. Cemetery Dance Publications, 132 B Industry Ln, Unit 7, Forest Hill, MD 21050. Illus., adv. Vol. ends: Winter. *Bk. rev.:* 20-40, 200-5,000 words. *Aud.:* Ga.

This long-standing, award-winning publication, now celebrating 25 years, includes essays, short stories, and artwork, as well as news and reviews. With a long history in horror, this title has a good combination of established and up-and-coming writers. Readers of horror will appreciate the six to eight original stories published in each issue and the in-depth interviews with the authors, while fans of the broader genre of science fiction will have an interest in this journal's news articles, interviews, and reviews of movies, software, and recent books. Not for the faint of heart, this title is best in general collections, but an academic collection with a horror section should have this on its shelves.

2370. Clarkesworld Magazine. [ISSN: 1937-7843] 2006. m. Free. Wyrm Publishing, PO Box 172, Stirling, NJ 07980. *Aud.:* Hs, Ga, Ac.

Clarkesworld is published monthly as a webzine, or you can download the ebook form through Amazon (.mobi) or Weightless books (.epub or .mobi). Each month the reader can expect at least two original short stories, a number of nonfiction pieces, original art, editorials, and podcasts. The quality of writing is stellar, with a some articles incorporating videos or podcasts to enhance the discussion. *Clarkesworld* is a must for anyone who is interested in reading reviews about the broader science fiction, fantasy, and horror world. One of the joys of webzine publishing is the ability to promote forums, and this title is no exception. Having received several awards and nominations, this is a publication not to be missed. URL: http://clarkesworldmagazine.com/

2371. ConNotations (Phoenix): the bi-monthly science fiction, fantasy, horror. [ISSN: 1082-7765] 1990. bi-m. USD 25. Ed(s): Patti Hultstrand. Central Arizona Speculative Fiction Society, Central Arizona Speculative Fiction Society, PO Box 62613, Phoenix, AZ 85082; info@casfs.org; http://www.casfs.org. Adv. Circ: 4000. *Bk. rev.:* Number and length vary. *Aud.:* Ga.

Published by the Central Arizona Speculative Fiction Association, this short news magazine is now available via the web and in print. Filled with news of upcoming and past conventions, with plenty of reviews covering books, comics, movies, and television media, this title will keep the reader current in the genre. While *ConNotations*' focus is speculative SF, it does cover the broader range of this genre as well. If you live in or near to Arizona and have a SF, fantasy, and horror collection, then this is a title that would benefit your community.

2372. Daily Science Fiction. 2010. d. Free. Ed(s): Jonathan Laden. Daily Science Fiction, info@dailysciencefiction.com; http://dailysciencefiction.com/. *Aud.:* Hs, Ga.

If you are looking for great science fiction and fantasy at a very reasonable price—free, then this is a publication worth signing up for the long term. Or if you would rather have a nice sit-down with your Kindle, then you can purchase monthly digests through Amazon for a very reasonable price. The stories within the daily e-mail or monthly digest feature Hugo Award–winning authors and a number of different genres: science fiction, fantasy, speculative, alternative history, slip-stream, and everything in-between. If your library has a page for science fiction and fantasy, then this would be an excellent web site to include among the links of recommended sources.

2373. Dead Reckonings. [ISSN: 1935-6110] 2007. s-a. USD 15. Ed(s): Jack Madison Haringa, S T Joshi. Hippocampus Press, PO Box 641, New York, NY 10156; http://www.hippocampuspress.com/. *Bk. rev.:* Number and length vary. *Aud.:* Hs, Ga, Ac.

Nominated for the International Horror Guild Award, this journal features reviews of titles that feature the best offerings from the horror genre. These well-written, unbiased reviews spare little from the readers, clearly portraying the negative and positive aspects of each title. With content cleverly written and insightful, this title allows discerning readers a chance to review the best literature of the field before purchasing. *Dead Reckonings* is a necessity for any collection that holds significant works in the horror field.

2374. Doctor Who Magazine. Former titles (until 1985): *The Official Doctor Who Magazine;* (until 1984): *Doctor Who Monthly;* (until 1982): *Doctor Who;* (until 1980): *Doctor Who Weekly.* [ISSN: 0957-9818] 1979. 13x/yr. GBP 43.89 domestic; GBP 61.65 in Europe; GBP 83.02 elsewhere. Panini UK Ltd., Brockbourne House, 77 Mount Ephraim, Tunbridge Wells, TN48BS, United Kingdom; customercare@panini.co.uk; http://www.paninicomics.co.uk. Adv. Circ: 34674. *Aud.:* Ems, Hs, Ga.

This magazine is inspired by the long-running television show from the United Kingdom whose recent return has sparked a new phenomenon in the United States. After 40 years on TV and over 400 issues, this magazine reviews and explores everything related to the "Doctor Who" world. It includes cast and producer interviews and progress reports on all past and present doctors and their companions. It is designed to keep fans up-to-date with upcoming television episodes, books, audio materials, and spin-offs in the ever-expanding "Doctor Who" world. This title would be most appropriate in a general setting, and would be of interest to a wide range of ages.

2375. The Edgar Allan Poe Review. Former titles (until 2000): *P S A Newsletter (Poe Studies Association);* (until 1978): *Poe Studies Association. Newsletter.* [ISSN: 2150-0428] 1973. s-a. USD 125 (print or online ed.). Poe Studies Association, c/o Barbara Cantalupo, Penn State Lehigh Valley, Center Valley, PA 18034; bac7@psu.edu; http://www2.lv.psu.edu/psa. Illus. Refereed. *Indexed:* AmHI, MLA-IB. *Bk. rev.:* Number and length vary. *Aud.:* Hs, Ga, Ac.

One of the scholarly titles dedicated to Edgar Allan Poe, this title comes from Penn State Lehigh Valley. Filled with scholarly essays and creative responses, these articles cover all aspects of Poe's life and work. The essays are well written and researched, and the reviews are lengthy. Serious Poe scholars will find this journal invaluable for their research, and those new to Poe will learn a great deal about one of the founders of fantasy/horror fiction. A section on the Poe Studies Association news is included in each edition.

2376. Electric Velocipede. [ISSN: 1949-2030] 2001. s-a. USD 25 domestic for 4 issues; USD 30 Canada for 4 issues; USD 35 elsewhere for 4 issues. Ed(s): John Klima. Night Shade Books, 1661 Tennessee St, #3H, San Francisco, CA 94107; info@nightshadebooks.com; http://www.nightshadebooks.com/. Adv. *Aud.:* Ga.

Electric Velocipede is an eclectic blend of mythology, fantasy, and speculative fiction. As a 2009 Hugo Award–winner, it contains well-written short stories, poetry, and nonfiction pieces. The fiction featured in this publication is speculative in nature, and runs through the gamut of human emotions. 2011 marked the last print issue; all future issues can be found online. URL: www.electricvelocipede.com

2377. Extrapolation. [ISSN: 0014-5483] 1959. 3x/yr. GBP 48 (print & online eds.); Free to members. Liverpool University Press, 4 Cambridge St, Liverpool, L69 7ZU, United Kingdom; lup@liv.ac.uk; http:// www.liverpooluniversitypress.co.uk/. Index, adv. Sample. Refereed. Vol. ends: Dec. Microform: PQC. *Indexed:* A01, A22, ABS&EES, AmHI, ArtHuCI, BEL&L, BRI, CBRI, MLA-IB, P02. *Bk. rev.:* 3-5, 300-1,500 words. *Aud.:* Ga, Ac.

This is an international, peer-reviewed journal that publishes articles and book reviews on science fiction and speculative fiction. With a 50-year history, *Extrapolation* was one of the first peer-reviewed journals containing well-written pieces that cover a wide variety of topics within the genre. Its reviews include print, film, television, comics, and videogames. It would be appropriate for any higher education library with an interest in the genres of speculative fiction or science fiction. *Extrapolation* would also be relevant for a public library's science fiction collection.

2378. Fangoria. [ISSN: 0164-2111] 1978. 10x/yr. USD 54.47 domestic; USD 63.97 foreign. Ed(s): Michael Gingold, Anthony Timpone. Starlog Communications, 250 W 49th St, 3rd Fl Ste 304, New York, NY 10019. Illus. Circ: 214500 Paid. *Bk. rev.:* Number and length vary. *Aud.:* Ga.

A horrific horror magazine for the masses. Fans of the genre will appreciate the gory indulgence of its glossy pages and full-color illustrations. Reviewing movies, plays, film, and occasionally classic horror history, *Fangoria* will appeal to those interested in new movies and in books representing the mainstream media more than the alternative experiments of the genre. Some adult content is included, so it would not be recommended for young audiences.

2379. Fantasy & Science Fiction. Formerly (until 1987): *The Magazine of Fantasy and Science Fiction;* Incorporates: *Venture Science Fiction.* [ISSN: 1095-8258] 1949. bi-m. USD 34.97 domestic; USD 46.97 foreign. Spilogale, Inc., P O Box 3447, Hoboken, NJ 07030. Illus., adv. Sample. Microform: PQC. *Indexed:* A01, AmHI, BRI, C37, CBRI, F01, MASUSE, MLA-IB, P02. *Bk. rev.:* 5-10, 200-1,000 words. *Aud.:* Hs, Ga, Ac.

Any true aficionado of the genre has heard of *Fantasy & Science Fiction.* This publication features a variety of writers from the most prestigious names in the business to up-and-coming authors. Celebrating 60 years in print, this title is known for publishing the very best in fantasy short stories. It also provides current book and film reviews. *Fantasy and Science Fiction* belongs in all collections with an interest in the genre, and would be suitable for both academic and general audiences. Readers can also pursue their passion online through the publication's web site to find additional articles and ideas. URL: www.sfsite.com/fsf

2380. Femspec. [ISSN: 1523-4002] 1999. s-a. USD 95 (Individuals, USD 40). Ed(s): Batya Weinbaum. Femspec, 1610 Rydalmount Rd, Cleveland Heights, OH 44118. Adv. Refereed. Circ: 300. *Indexed:* AmHI, BRI, FemPer, GW, MLA-IB. *Bk. rev.:* 2, essay length, signed. *Aud.:* Ga, Ac.

FemSpec provides a critical look at the scholarly and fictional works relating to feminist studies, science fiction, and fantasy. It would be appropriate for feminist, women's, or gender studies collections, as it contains many historical pieces and references to feminist mythology and ethnology. This interdisciplinary journal includes short fiction, poetry, and a generous book review section.

2381. Focus (London, 1979). [ISSN: 0144-560X] 1979. 3x/yr. Free to members. Ed(s): Martin McGrath. British Science Fiction Association Ltd., 61 Ivycroft Rd, Warton, Tamworth, B79 0JJ, United Kingdom; bsfamembership@yahoo.co.uk; http://www.bsfa.co.uk. *Aud.:* Ga, Ac.

This is the membership magazine of the British Science Fiction Association Ltd. Its focus is on improving writing for the genre. The articles all involve information about the art and craft of storytelling. Its broad content discusses everything from horror to sex, from crafting strange new worlds to patterns of speech. If you are interested in professional opinion on science fiction writing, this would be a good title to check out. Would be appropriate for collections with writing departments, science fiction, or horror collections.

2382. Foundation: the international review of science fiction. [ISSN: 0306-4964] 1972. 3x/yr. Free to members. Ed(s): Graham Sleight. Science Fiction Foundation, University of Reading, Department of History, Faculty of Letters and Social Science, Reading, RG1 5PT, United Kingdom; http://www.sf-foundation.org/. Illus., index. Refereed. Vol. ends: Dec. *Indexed:* MLA-IB. *Bk. rev.:* 10-15, 500-2,500 words. *Aud.:* Ga, Ac.

This international, peer-reviewed journal is published three times a year in the United Kingdom. The writing is impressive, containing detailed, relevant articles, essays, and reviews. Filled with established authors in the field, this is a critical publication for any science fiction collection. Published by the Science Fiction Foundation, this scholarly title is an excellent resource for academic or research collections.

2383. Greatest Uncommon Denominator Magazine. [ISSN: 1932-8222] 2007. s-a. USD 12. Ed(s): Julia Bernd. Greatest Uncommon Denominator Magazine, PO Box 1537, Laconia, NH 03247; editor@gudmagazine.com. Illus. *Aud.:* Ga, Ac.

This journal of poetry, fiction, and art is a wonderful source for science fiction and fantasy writing. It is well written and demonstrates a love of the written word. *GUD* offers a splendid collection of the fantastical. It is eclectic, yet still has a sophistication that sets it apart from many other titles. The poetry is varied and takes you across many genres. The art offerings present a brilliant new world to explore and add an ambience that completes the package. It is recommended for all libraries with a science fiction and fantasy collection, but it would be equally in place in language and arts collections. This title was on a brief sabbatical, but was supposed to restart with the Spring 2012 volume.

2384. Horrorhound. [ISSN: 1557-556X] 2005. bi-m. USD 34. Ed(s): Nathan Hanneman. HorrorHound Ltd., PO Box 710, Milford, OH 45150. Adv. *Bk. rev.:* Number and length vary. *Aud.:* Ga.

HorrorHound contains in-depth articles about horror movies, books, and interviews with the men and women who have influenced the horror field and its special effects. Also included are toy reviews, collector spotlights, comics, DVD reviews, convention updates and news, reviews of upcoming games, and apps from the *HorrorHound* company. The magazine's web site includes additional information and forums for its readers. Due to the startling images found here, it is not recommended for young readers.

2385. Interzone: science fiction and fantasy. Incorporates (in 1994): *Nexus;* (1991-1993): *Million.* [ISSN: 0264-3596] 1982. bi-m. GBP 24 domestic; EUR 27 in Europe; USD 30 elsewhere. Ed(s): Andy Cox. T T A Press, 5 Martins Ln, Witcham, Ely, CB6 2LB, United Kingdom; info@ttapress.demon.co.uk; http://ttapress.com. Illus., adv. Sample. *Bk. rev.:* 7-10, 100-500 words. *Aud.:* Ga, Ac.

Interzone is a glossy British magazine that explores the ramifications of space/time and fantasy, and is currently celebrating its 30th year in publication. In full color, this title features well-written pieces of fiction and art that perfectly mesh to create a stunning creative piece. Additional features are found online, including current book and film reviews. Recommended for all fans of the genre and for all science fiction and fantasy collections.

2386. Journal of the Fantastic in the Arts. Former titles (until 1988): *Fantasy Review;* (until 1984): *Fantasy.* [ISSN: 0897-0521] 1984. 3x/yr. Free to members; Non-members, USD 35. Ed(s): Brian Attebery. International Association for the Fantastic in the Arts, c/o Brian Attebery, Idaho State University, Pocatello, ID 83209; iafareg@gmail.com; http://www.iafa.org. Illus., index, adv. Sample. Refereed. Reprint: PSC. *Indexed:* A07, AmHI, BRI, MLA-IB. *Bk. rev.:* 5-10, 1,000-1,500 words. *Aud.:* Ga., Ac.

The *Journal of the Fantastic in the Arts* is an interdisciplinary, scholarly title. It contains beautifully written essays and reviews that examine the arts (drama, film, dance, architecture, and popular media). It explores everything from Lovecraft to Tolkien, zombies to J.K. Rowling; this title has something for both a general audience and serious scholars. *JFA* is recommended for all scholarly collections that recognize and promote the genres of science fiction and fantasy. The quality of its articles and the relevancy of its material make this journal accessible to all readers.

2387. *Lady Churchill's Rosebud Wristlet.* [ISSN: 1544-7782] 1996. s-a. USD 20 for 2 yrs. domestic; USD 20 for 2 yrs. foreign. Small Beer Press, 150 Pleasant St., #306, Easthampton, MA 01027; info@lcrw.net; http://www.lcrw.net/. Adv. *Indexed:* AmHI. *Bk. rev.:* Number and length vary. *Aud.:* Ga, Ac.

This small press title has a fanciful name to go with its eclectic contents. Each issue contains short comics, short fiction, and poetry, as well as a humorous advice column. The stories share a certain dark poignancy, ranging from the suspenseful to the humorous, and never forgetting the fantastical. *LCRW* would be appropriate for any academic collection that has an interest in writing and creative expression.

2388. *Locus (Oakland): the magazine of the science fiction and fantasy field.* [ISSN: 0047-4959] 1968. m. USD 72. Ed(s): Liza Groen Trombi. Locus Publications, 34 Ridgewood Ln, Oakland, CA 94611. Illus., index, adv. Sample. Vol. ends: Dec. *Indexed:* BRI, CBRI, MLA-IB. *Bk. rev.:* 15-30, 200-1,000 words. *Aud.:* Hs, Ga, Ac.

Containing trade news, articles, reviews, and annual reading lists, *Locus* is a vital resource for authors, publishers, and enthusiasts of science fiction and fantasy. This magazine features exhaustive lists of forthcoming books and science fiction magazines from North America and Europe. Also included are interviews with established genre authors, reports of conventions and awards, and listings of past and upcoming events. The web version of this publication allows free access to samples from the current issue in addition to its own news and reviews. URL: www.locusmag.com

2389. *Lovecraft Annual.* [ISSN: 1935-6102] 2007. a. USD 15. Ed(s): S T Joshi. Hippocampus Press, PO Box 641, New York, NY 10156; http://www.hippocampuspress.com/. *Indexed:* MLA-IB. *Bk. rev.:* Number and length vary. *Aud.:* Hs, Ga, Ac.

As the name implies, this annual publication explores all matters concerning the great horror writer Howard Phillips Lovecraft. If you rejoice in all things "Lovecraftian," or wish to discover the roots of horror fiction, this journal would be one to add depth to your collection. Also featured are a number of book reviews about or related to H.P. Lovecraft. Recommended for collections that emphasize science fiction, fantasy, and horror fiction studies.

2390. *Mythlore.* Incorporates (1964-1972): *Tolkien Journal.* [ISSN: 0146-9339] 1969. s-a. Members, USD 35; Non-members, USD 43. Ed(s): Janet Brennan Croft. Mythopoeic Society, PO Box 71, Napoleon, MI 49261; http://www.mythsoc.org. Index, adv. Sample. Refereed. Circ: 660. *Indexed:* A22, AmHI, BEL&L, BRI, MLA-IB. *Bk. rev.:* 3-10, 100-300 words. *Aud.:* Hs, Ga, Ac.

Mythlore is an absolutely lovely scholarly title. It discusses mythic and fantasy elements in literature with an emphasis on Tolkien, Williams, and Lewis. This title provides invaluable research for contemporary scholarship. Featuring critical articles, poetry, and art, it is suitable for anyone exploring fantasy and mythology. Readers from high school to college will appreciate the historical mythology found in its pages.

2391. *New York Review of Science Fiction.* [ISSN: 1052-9438] 1988. m. USD 40 domestic; USD 44 Canada; USD 47 in Europe. Ed(s): David G Hartwell. Dragon Press, PO Box 78, Pleasantville, NY 10570; dgh@tor.com; http://www.nyrsf.com. Illus., adv. Circ: 1000 Paid. *Indexed:* MLA-IB. *Bk. rev.:* 8-15, 1,000-3,500 words. *Aud.:* Ga, Ac.

This frequent Hugo Award nominee is one of the best-written monthly reviews in the science fiction, fantasy, and horror genres. Published 12 times a year, it contains well-written essays and reviews that provide the reader with insightful opinions about themes and upcoming titles within the field. *NYRSF* is recommended for all science fiction or fantasy collections in both public and academic libraries.

2392. *On Spec: the Canadian magazine of the fantastic.* [ISSN: 0843-476X] 1989. q. CAD 24 domestic; USD 25 United States; USD 35 elsewhere. Ed(s): Diane Walton. Copper Pig Writers' Society, P O Box 4727, Edmonton, AB T6E 5G6, Canada; http://www.icomm.ca/onspec/. Illus., index, adv. Circ: 600 Paid. *Aud.:* Ga, Ac.

Created as a venue for English-speaking Canadian science fiction writers to explore their genre, *On Spec* has a wonderful editorial team to help new writers develop their craft. It supports fantastical literature from a Canadian point of view. For over 20 years, *On Spec* has been helping readers suspend their disbelief through fantastical and speculative fiction. This title contains award-winning science fiction, fantasy, horror, and poetry. Now available electronically as well as in print. Appropriate for a variety of audiences.

2393. *Poe Studies (Online).* Formerly (until 2008): *Poe Studies - Dark Romanticism (Online).* [ISSN: 1754-6095] a. GBP 91. Ed(s): Scott Peeples, Jana L Argersinger. Wiley-Blackwell Publishing, Inc., Commerce Pl, 350 Main St, Malden, MA 02148; info@wiley.com; http://onlinelibrary.wiley.com/. Sample. Refereed. Circ: 500 Paid. *Bk. rev.:* Number and length vary. *Aud.:* Hs, Ga, Ac.

Published annually, this biographical title provides a dialogue on all things related to Edgar Allan Poe. *Poe Studies* is broader in its approach than the *EAP Review*, covering his social life and influences in addition to his creative works. Throughout the journal, readers will find engaging discussion about the theoretical and philosophical issues in Poe's works and his contributions to modern literature. If you have a nineteenth-century literature collection, or interest in Early American literature, or if you just want to learn more about Mr. Poe, this title belongs in your collection.

2394. *Polluto.* 2008. s-a. GBP 14.99 domestic; GBP 16.99 United States; GBP 18.99 elsewhere. Ed(s): Adam Lowe, Victoria Hooper. Dog Horn Publishing, 45 Monk Ings, Birstall Batley, WF17 9HU, United Kingdom; editor@polluto.com; http://www.polluto.com/. *Aud.:* Sa.

This title portrays the dark, twisted, and anti-societal view of the world filled with sex, props, and mind-bending twists. Unafraid to travel the road less trod, *Polluto* knows no boundaries; queers, prostitution, sex slavery, obese dominatrixes—no topic is sacred. If you enjoy tiptoeing on the edges of social taboos, this title has you covered. For that reason, *Polluto* would not be advised for collections that cater to young readers, as the contents are rather explicit. If you have a collection that addresses GLBT or Queer Studies, or sexually deviant practices, this title may fit in better there.

2395. *Rue Morgue.* [ISSN: 1481-1103] 1997. 11x/yr. USD 74.95 per academic year in US & Canada; USD 103.95 per academic year elsewhere. Ed(s): Dave Alexander. Marrs Media, Inc., 2926 Dundas St W, Toronto, ON M6P 1Y8, Canada; jessa@rue-morgue.com. Adv. *Aud.:* Hs, Ga.

Rue Morgue features music, movies, interviews, and television reviews, as well as specialty features including weird statistics and morbid facts. In full color throughout, this title will most likely appeal to anyone with an interest in horror and the macabre. *Rue Morgue* travels throughout Canada and the United States to provide the best coverage of the horror field. Fans of the title will be pleased with the extras provided on the web site. Forums, band coverages, and interviews are some of the extras that you will find online. URL: http://rue-morgue.com

2396. *Sci Fi.* Formerly (until 1999): *Sci-Fi Entertainment.* [ISSN: 1527-5779] 1994. bi-m. USD 14.95 domestic; USD 19.95 elsewhere. N B C Universal, 100 Universal City Plaza, Universal City, CA 91608; nbcuniversalviewerfeedback@nbcuni.com; http://www.nbcuni.com. Illus., adv. Sample. Circ: 75000. *Bk. rev.:* 5-10, 800-1,000 words. *Aud.:* Hs, Ga.

This engaging title features sci-fi television and movie news as well as in-depth cast interviews. *Sci Fi*'s focus is on the news and upcoming offerings from network shows and upcoming motion pictures. The articles offer a variety of interviews and reviews that should appeal to a broad audience, informing readers of possible plot twists and providing insider's information. The wide coverage gives viewers up-to-the-minute coverage of video's brightest stars.

2397. *Science Fiction Studies.* [ISSN: 0091-7729] 1973. 3x/yr. USD 65 (print & online eds.). S F - T H, Inc., c/o Arthur B. Evans, Department of Modern Languages, Greencastle, IN 46135; aevans@depauw.edu. Illus., index, adv. Sample. Refereed. Vol. ends: Dec. *Indexed:* A01, A22, ABS&EES, AmHI, ArtHuCI, BRI, C37, CBCARef, CBRI, F01, MLA-IB, P02. *Bk. rev.:* 10-20, 500-3,000 words. *Aud.:* Ac.

A long-standing scholarly journal, *Science Fiction Studies* publishes articles and book reviews. From sexuality to blogging, from anthropology to feminist studies, this journal has broad coverage of science fiction studies. Thoroughly reviewed and edited, this journal would be appropriate for any collection with an emphasis in this area. Tables of contents and article abstracts for current and past issues since 1973 are available on the publication's companion web site, with a three-year blackout. URL: www.depauw.edu/sfs

2398. SciFiNow. [ISSN: 1753-3147] 2007. 13x/yr. GBP 45.80 domestic; GBP 75 in US & Canada; GBP 65 elsewhere. Ed(s): Aaron Asadi. Imagine Publishing Ltd., Richmond House, 33 Richmond Hill, Bournemouth, BH2 6EZ, United Kingdom; http://www.imagine-publishing.co.uk. Adv. *Bk. rev.:* Number and length vary. *Aud.:* Hs, Ga.

SciFiNow is a brilliant import, written by fans for fans of the science fiction, horror, cult television, and fantasy genres. It is a large magazine that celebrates the explosion and growth of sci-fi TV and film. It was voted best magazine of 2010 in Great Britain, and its topics include everything from Stephen King to Buck Rogers, from *Tron* to *True Blood.* Cast and director interviews provide insider information about current and past television and film productions. Fans of the genre will love its size, glossy pictures, and up-to-date reviews. This magazine is well worth your attention.

2399. Shimmer Magazine. [ISSN: 1933-8864] 2005. q. USD 22. Ed(s): Beth Wodzinski, Anne Zanoni. Shimmer Magazine, PO Box 58591, Salt Lake City, UT 84158-0591; info@shimmerzine.com; http://www.shimmerzine.com. *Aud.:* Ga.

Shimmer Magazine is wonderfully crafted, blending elements of modern fiction and the speculative with ease. The beautiful, and often melancholy short fiction in this publication is dark, as is the artwork. It is available in print or electronic format. Several stories have been reprinted in *Best American Fantasy* and Rich Horton's *Year's Best Fantasy and Science Fiction.* This title is well worth a look, but may not be appropriate for younger audiences.

2400. Space and Time. [ISSN: 0271-2512] 1966. q. USD 20 combined subscription in US & Canada (print & online eds.). Ed(s): Hildy Silverman. Space and Time, 1308 Centennial Ave, Ste 101, Piscataway, NJ 08854. Illus., adv. Sample. Circ: 1500 Paid. *Bk. rev.:* Number and length vary. *Aud.:* Hs, Ga.

Space and Time is a quarterly journal that provides fiction, poetry, book reviews, and the occasional interview. Over 40 years in print, this magazine contains stories that are dark, magical, and speculative. Fans of the magazine should go to the title's companion web site for further reading. *Space and Time* would be appropriate for any collection with similar titles. This title is appropriate for any collection, as the stories are relatively free of expletives and sexuality. URL: www.spaceandtimemagazine.com

2401. Star Trek. [ISSN: 1357-3888] 1995. 8x/yr. GBP 29.99. Titan Magazines, Titan House, 144 Southwark St, London, SE1 0UP, United Kingdom; titanmagazines@servicehelpline.co.uk; http://www.titanmagazines.co.uk/. Adv. *Aud.:* Ga.

The official guide to Gene Roddenberry's space saga, *Star Trek* is an unparalleled source for information about the cast and characters from the series and movies. There is so much in this title, and it provides everything a Trekkie needs to be up-to-date. This title is a must for any fan. Its retrospective look at various actors throughout the years is fantastic, reminding viewers of guest appearances they may have forgotten about since the original viewing. The "Federation" news is important for anyone wanting to see what may be coming out in the future.

2402. Strange Horizons. 2000. w. Free. Ed(s): Susan Marie Groppi, Gerry Allen. Strange Horizons. *Bk. rev.:* 15-20. *Aud.:* Ga, Ac.

Strange Horizons is a weekly online title, publishing articles, art, reviews, and poetry that are speculative in nature. It focuses on investigating the underlying meaning or message within science fiction and fantasy works. Extremely well-written for a free online publication, the content is relevant and timely. *Strange Horizons* has made a name for itself with numerous reprints in other printed collections of stories and articles. It is fully archived, allowing new readers to explore past and present articles. URL: www.strangehorizons.com

2403. Sybil's Garage. [ISSN: 1557-9735] 2004. irreg. USD 12. Ed(s): Matthew Kressel. Senses Five Press, 76 India St, Apt A8, Brooklyn, NY 11222; info@sensesfive.com; http://www.sensesfive.com. *Aud.:* Ga.

Sybil's Garage is unique in that it recommends a song for each story, allowing the reader to discover the tone of the story before reading. In each issue, there is fiction and poetry that is speculative in nature, with the majority of pieces categorized under the slipstream genre. The themes and language may make this title somewhat risky for a high school audience, though it would probably be enjoyed. The storytelling is tight and descriptive. It would be appropriate for any speculative fiction collection. Due to its one-man press operation, the frequency of this title is in question. This may prove to be too problematic for academic collections, but for individuals who have to buy their copies one at a time, it is still something to consider.

2404. Tangent Online: the genre's premiere review magazine for short sf & fantasy. Formerly (until 1997): *Tangent (Print).* 1993. bi-m. Ed(s): David A Truesdale. Tangent, 4601 Wallace, #4, Kansas, MO 64129. Adv. *Bk. rev.:* 60-75, 500-2,000 words. *Aud.:* Hs, Ga, Ac.

For the critical reader, *Tangent Online* is an invaluable web site that reviews most of the short fiction, magazines, and journals in the field. With an impressive history in reviewing the best of science fiction and fantasy, this title has garnered four Hugo awards and multiple nominations for its reviews and interviews. If you would like to know more about the publications and authors in the field, this is one of the first places to look. Readers can access the site without a subscription. URL: www.tangentonline.com

2405. Vector. Incorporates (1980-1992): *Paperback Inferno;* Which was formerly (until 1980): *Paperback Parlour.* [ISSN: 0505-0448] 1958. bi-m. Free to members. Ed(s): Niall Harrison. British Science Fiction Association Ltd., 61 Ivycroft Rd, Warton, Tamworth, B79 0JJ, United Kingdom; bsfamembership@yahoo.co.uk; http://www.bsfa.co.uk. Illus., adv. Sample. Circ: 1000. Vol. ends: Dec. *Bk. rev.:* 15-25, 200-1,000 words. *Aud.:* Hs, Ga, Ac.

Vector is a journal published by the British Science Fiction Association (BSFA). Its scholarly and critical tone offers the reader a wide variety of topics by the genre's best authors. If you want to be current on articles, books, and their authors, this is one of the titles you'll want in your collection. As it is from the British SFA, it does have a focus on British SF authors. This title is recommended for any SF collection, and especially for British collections. To find out more about what is going on currently, interested readers should check out the journal's blog, Torque Control, found at the web site. URL: http://vectoreditors.wordpress.com/

2406. Weird Tales. Former titles (until 1998): *Worlds of Fantasy and Horror;* (until 1994): *Weird Tales.* 1923. bi-m. USD 24 domestic; USD 48 foreign. Ed(s): John G. Betancourt, Stephan H Segall. Wildside Press, 9710 Traville Gateway Dr #234, Rockville, MD 20850; weirdtales@comcast.net ; http://www.wildsidepress.com/. Illus., adv. Circ: 8000 Paid. *Bk. rev.:* Number and length vary. *Aud.:* Hs, Ga.

Weird Tales is a magazine that will appeal to a wide variety of readers. With everything from H.P. Lovecraft to George R.R. Martin, this brilliantly strange title has more than enough material to satisfy hardcore science fiction and fantasy fans. It has an impressive history; the first edition started in 1923, and it won an impressive number of Hugo nominations. It is a unique and appealing magazine. Short stories, interviews, reviews, music, and comics round out its pages. For those interested in more information or selections from the print edition, *Weird Tales* has a web site. URL: www.weirdtalesmagazine.com

■ FILMS

Caroline M. Kent, Director of Research Support and Instruction, Charles E. Shain Library, Connecticut College, New London, CT 06320

Introduction

It is fascinating that a wholly visual medium such as film can generate such a huge body of print publications (digital or not)! Of course, since it is a visual medium, the publications themselves are indeed beautiful, and this may help keep them alive longer than in a discipline that is predominantly text-based. But approaching this body of publications is daunting, to say the least.

Film magazines can be approached logically by dividing them into those publications that address a more academic market or formal film studies programs, and those that address the needs of the film buff. True fan magazines have not been included here, although there are some magazines that address the fans of a particular film genre such as American film classics. There are clear, strong relationships to other disciplines, such as screenwriting (creative writing), animation (art), film music, etc., and many of those journals have been included here. There are also a multitude of business-related publications and technical journals; a few of these have also been included. Any library developing its film journal collection should look carefully at the research and curricula of the programs it serves when determining which few of the many titles should be purchased.

If the number of print journals is daunting, the number of digital publications is almost overwhelming. A visual medium like film logically gives birth to materials in other visual media, such as the web. Not surprisingly, however, this turns out to be very valuable; because of the huge popularity of film, even libraries that serve serious film studies programs could, in the past, barely dip into the ocean of international publications on film. The rapid increase in film-interest portals and e-journals around the world can help fill this gap.

In many ways, the liberal use of the Internet greatly increases our access to important sources in film, sources that were previously unavailable. There are electronic publications on Cuban film and portals in Urdu and Tamil and Russian—the vast majority of countries have a movie industry, and this is reflected on the web. Some of these publications are true electronic journals; many are gateways. As a footnote, it is noteworthy that there seems to be rapid transition of much of the industry news and business information to web sites that promise direct and daily delivery of financial and legal information. This is something to watch....

Gateways or research portals are obviously not the purview of this publication; but we cannot ignore the growing importance of portals such as the Internet Movie Database (www.imdb.com). Making them harder and harder to deal with, portals are also becoming hybrid, including a wide variety of web-publishing formats. There are film sites on the web that contain materials that are truly serial in nature, that are portals to other sources, and that are blogs. Cartoon Brew (www.cartoonbrew.com) is a site in blog format, in which the editors keep the content focused on issues, books, and news of interest to the art end of animation. Print publication ain't what it used to be, and neither is electronic publishing. It is shifting as you read this. This is not news to libraries, but we have yet to comfortably accommodate all these new formats—and we must.

Basic Periodicals

Hs: *Animation Magazine, Film Comment, Film Quarterly;* Ga: *Cineaste, Classic Images, Film Comment, Film Quarterly, Sight and Sound;* Ac: *Cineaste, Cinema Journal, Film Comment, Film Quarterly, Journal of Film and Video, Sight and Sound.*

Basic Abstracts and Indexes

Film & Television Literature Index, International Index to Film Periodicals.

2407. *Alphaville: journal of film and screen media.* [ISSN: 2009-4078] 2011. Free. Ed(s): Laura Rascaroli. University College Cork, Film Studies at UCC, O'Rahilly Bldg G28, Cork, Ireland; http://www.ucc.ie. Refereed. *Aud.:* Ac.

This new, fully online, and open-access journal seeks to be "a dynamic international forum open to the discussion of all aspects of film history, theory and criticism through multiple research methodologies and perspectives. *Alphaville* aims to cultivate inspiring, cutting-edge research, and particularly welcomes work produced by early career researchers in Film and Screen Media." This is a beautifully designed online publication, and its presentation is, well, cool! The articles are far-reaching and international in nature. Some recent article titles are "Who's Got the 'Reel' Power? The Problem of Female

Antagonisms in Blaxploitation Cinema" and "Egyptian Film Censorship: Safeguarding Society, Upholding Taboos." Best audience for this fascinating publication will be serious film studies programs. URL: www.alphavillejournal.com

2408. *American Cinematographer: the international journal of motion imaging.* [ISSN: 0002-7928] 1920. m. USD 29.95. A S C Holding Corporation, PO Box 2230, Hollywood, CA 90078; office@theasc.com; http://www.ascmag.com/. Illus., index, adv. Vol. ends: Dec. Microform: PQC. *Indexed:* A06, A07, A22, ABS&EES, F01, IIFP, IIPA, RILM. *Bk. rev.:* 5-6, 150 words. *Aud.:* Sa.

This monthly publication of the American Society of Cinematographers not only provides current industry information, but also provides lots of interviews with cinematographers of current releases and a behind-the-scenes look at the technical details used to achieve a particular shot. Working cameramen can get reviews of new equipment on the market, and film buffs and burgeoning cinematographers can get detailed information about their new favorite films. Book and DVD reviews, classified ads, and an ad index are in each issue. Titles of recent articles include "Boldly Captured, Dan Mindel shoos anamorphic and large formats on *Star Trek Into Darkness*" and "Living Large, Simon Duggan brings stereoscopic perspectives to *The Great Gatsby*." This journal is for collections that address the needs of film studies programs and filmmakers.

2409. *Animation Magazine: the news, business, technology & art of animation.* Formerly (until 1987): *Animation News.* [ISSN: 1041-617X] 19??. m. USD 55 domestic; USD 70 in Canada & Mexico; USD 85 elsewhere. Ed(s): Ramin Zahed, Mercedes Milligan. Terry Thoren Publications, D B A Animation Magazine, 30941 W. Agoura Rd., Ste 102, Westlake Village, CA 91361; sales@animationmagazine.net. Illus., adv. *Indexed:* A07, F01. *Bk. rev.:* 1-2, 300-500 words. *Aud.:* Ga, Sa.

Although this claims to be a fan magazine, the level of technical detail and technical ads indicate that it as much an industry magazine. Not too surprisingly for a magazine about a visual art form, it is a gorgeous and fun publication, with wonderful glossy illustrations that have wide appeal. It contains articles on animation's use in feature films, games, and television. There are copious ads, film reviews, and regular articles on industry business and conferences. There is also an annual section on animation academic programs. Titles of recent feature articles include "Gollum, You Never Looked Better" to "Everything You Wanted to Know about Kickstarter." Any academic library with a strong, varied art program should consider purchasing this title, as well as any special or academic library that services a film production population.

2410. *Black Camera: an international film journal.* [ISSN: 1536-3155] 1985. s-a. USD 119 (print & online eds.). Ed(s): Michael T Martin. Indiana University Press, 601 N Morton St, Bloomington, IN 47404; iupress@indiana.edu; http://iupress.indiana.edu. Illus. Circ: 1000. Reprint: PSC. *Indexed:* A22, E01, F01, IIBP, IIFP, IIPA, MLA-IB. *Bk. rev.:* 3-4, 500-1,000 words. *Aud.:* Ac.

The original *Black Camera* was a newsletter, predominantly focused on American Black film. This new series has turned the title into a glossy, substantive, peer-reviewed academic journal. It covers all Black film, from African film to sites of the African diaspora. It is an excellent journal, filling a niche that had been empty after the death of its first iteration. The included articles are rich and diverse. Some titles of recent articles include "Black Glamour and the Hip-Hop Renaissance: Idlewild's Debt to *Tuning into Precious*: The Black Women's Empowerment Adaptation and the Interruptions of the Absurd." There are excellent book reviews, which are, like the rest of the journal, directed at an academic audience. For any academic library that addresses a film or African American or African Studies departments.

2411. *Boxoffice Pro: the business of movies.* Formerly (until 2011): *Boxoffice;* Which incorporated (1920-1977): *Boxoffice (Eastern Edition);* (19??-1977): *Boxoffice (Southeast Edition);* (19??-1977): *Boxoffice (Southwest Edition);* (1932-1977): *Boxoffice (National Executive Edition);* (19??-1977): *Boxoffice (New England Edition).* [ISSN: 2325-1492] 1920. m. USD 59.95 domestic; USD 74.95 in Canada & Mexico; USD 135 elsewhere. Ed(s): Ken Bacon. Boxoffice Media, LLC., 230 Park Ave., Ste. 1000, New York, NY 10169. Illus., adv. Vol. ends: Dec. *Indexed:* ABIn, BRI, F01, IIPA. *Aud.:* Sa.

For more than 90 years, *Boxoffice* has been required reading for every serious player in the industry, from theater owners to studio executives. There is coverage of industry news (national and international), box office grosses, production data on new Hollywood releases, and financial information on the major studios. Also included are numerous reviews of new Hollywood feature films; interviews with filmmakers, screenwriters, executives, actors, producers, and directors; and up-to-date festival information. Although it covers all areas of the film industry, it is definitely skewed toward, as its current subtitle says, the business of movies. It lists current and upcoming studio release charts by month. There are short reviews with "exploitips," a guide to new products, and news on concessions. The magazine is also now promising certain types of timely information (such as financials) directly via e-mail. Highly recommended for libraries that need complete coverage of the Hollywood film industry.

2412. Bright Lights (Online): film journal. Formerly (until 1995): *Bright Lights (Print)*. 1974. q. Free. Ed(s): Gary Morris. Bright Lights, PO Box 420987, San Francisco, CA 94142-0987; brightlightswriters@gmail.com. Illus., adv. *Indexed:* F01, IIFP. *Bk. rev.:* Number and length vary. *Aud.:* Ga, Ac.

"A popular-academic hybrid of movie analysis, history and commentary, looking at classical and commercial, independent, exploitation, and international film from a wide range of vantage points from the aesthetic to the political. A prime area of focus is on the connection between capitalist society and the images that reflect, support, or subvert it—movies as propaganda." I admit, I love this site more every time a look at it. It gets broader, edgier, and more interesting! Included on this site are some highly unusual genres, such as "tranny cinema." It has feature articles, film reviews, book reviews, filmmaker interviews, and film festival coverage. Unlike some online film journals, this publication has also caught onto the power of its web-based format, and includes not only stills, but clips from films. Titles of recent articles include "The Horrible Gatsby, the Bland Gatsby, and the Surprisingly Good Gatsby," "August and Everything After A Half-Century of Surfing in Cinema," and "Depth Takes a Holiday, Good Bad Movies." Any library with serious filmgoing patrons should consider linking to this edgy, interesting journal.

2413. Camera Obscura: feminism, culture, and media studies. [ISSN: 0270-5346] 1976. 3x/yr. USD 176. Ed(s): Ryan Bowles. Duke University Press, 905 W Main St, Ste 18 B, PO Box 90660, Durham, NC 27701; subscriptions@dukeupress.edu; http://www.dukeupress.edu. Illus., adv. Sample. Refereed. Vol. ends: Sep. Reprint: PSC. *Indexed:* A01, A07, A22, A51, AmHI, ArtHuCI, BAS, C42, E01, F01, FemPer, GW, IIFP, IIPA, MLA-IB, RILM. *Bk. rev.:* Number and length vary. *Aud.:* Ac.

This title "seeks to provide a forum for dialogue and debate on media, culture, and politics. Specifically, the journal encourages contributions in the following areas: analyses of the conjunctions among gender, race, class, sexuality, and nation, as these are articulated in film, television, popular culture, and media criticism and theory; new histories of film, television, popular culture, and media criticism and theory, as well as contemporary interventions in these fields; [and] politically engaged approaches to visual culture, media production, and contemporary constructions of feminism—inside the academy and in popular culture." Articles are well documented and accompanied by detailed notes. Titles of some recent articles include "Deanna Durbin and the Mismatched Voice," "Queer/Palestinian Cinema: A Critical Conversation on Palestinian Queer and Women's Filmmaking," and "Diasporic Erotic: Love, Loss, and the Cop." A recommended addition to academic film collections.

2414. Canadian Journal of Film Studies. [ISSN: 0847-5911] 1990. s-a. CAD 45 (Individuals, CAD 35). Film Studies Association of Canada, Department of Art History and Communication Studies, McGill University, Arts Building W225, Montreal, PQ H3A 2T6, Canada; http://www.film.queensu.ca/FSAC/CJFS.html. Illus. Refereed. *Indexed:* A07, ArtHuCI, CBCARef, F01, IIFP, IIPA, MLA-IB. *Bk. rev.:* Number and length vary. *Aud.:* Ac.

The stated aim of this publication is "to promote scholarship on Canadian film and television while . . . publishing articles, book reviews[,] and archival materials relevant to all aspects of film and television." There are good book reviews and lengthy essays in English (or occasionally in French) that cover Canadian as well as global cinema. Some recent article titles include "Camera-

Witness: Women's Documentary Responses to the Polytechnique Murders" and "The Thing About Obomsawin's Indianness: Indigenous Reality and the Documentary Burden of Education at the National Film Board of Canada." For serious academic film collections.

2415. Cineaction! [ISSN: 0826-9866] 1985. 3x/yr. USD 40 (Individuals, USD 21). Cineaction!, 40 Alexander St, Ste 705, Toronto, ON M4Y 1B5, Canada. Illus., index. Sample. *Indexed:* BRI, C37, CBCARef, F01, IIFP, IIPA, MLA-IB. *Bk. rev.:* Number and length vary. *Aud.:* Ac.

This title examines film from various viewpoints. Each issue focuses on a central theme, and forthcoming themes are announced, encouraging the submission of articles. In addition to scholarly articles on film theory, there are interviews with filmmakers, film reviews, book reviews, and reports from international film festivals. Some recent article titles include "Dostoevsky's Journey to Iran," "Seeing[-]Eye Gods CCTV and Surveillance in Tati's and Kubrick's 1960s Space Odysseys," and "Man(n) of the West(ern)." For library collections that address the needs of serious students of film and filmmakers.

2416. Cineaste: America's leading magazine on the art and politics of the cinema. [ISSN: 0009-7004] 1967. q. USD 36 (Individuals, USD 20). Ed(s): Gary Crowdus, Rahul Hamid. Cineaste Publishers, Inc., 243 Fifth Ave, Ste 706, New York, NY 10016. Illus., index, adv. Vol. ends: Fall. Microform: PQC. *Indexed:* A01, A07, A22, ABS&EES, ArtHuCI, BRI, C37, Chicano, F01, IIFP, IIPA, MASUSE, MLA-IB, P02. *Bk. rev.:* Number and length vary. *Aud.:* Ga, Ac.

This publication bills itself as "America's leading magazine on the art and politics of the cinema." It provides interviews with actors and filmmakers, as well as film, home video, and book reviews. Recent article titles include "Me and *Mr. Mom*: A Second Look at a Stay-at-Home Stereotype" and "*The Act of Killing*: An Interview with Joshua Oppenheimer." For serious film studies collections.

2417. Cinefex. [ISSN: 0198-1056] 1980. q. USD 36 combined subscription domestic (print & online eds.); USD 48 combined subscription in Canada & Mexico (print & online eds.); USD 52 combined subscription elsewhere (print & online eds.). Cinefex, PO Box 20027, Riverside, CA 92516. Illus., adv. Vol. ends: Dec. *Indexed:* F01, IIFP, IIPA. *Aud.:* Sa.

"*Cinefex* is a quarterly magazine devoted to motion picture special effects. Since 1980 it has been a bible to professionals and enthusiasts, covering the field like no other publication. Profusely illustrated in color, with as many as 180 pages per issue, *Cinefex* offers a captivating look at the technologies and techniques behind many of our most popular and enduring movies." For the professional, there is a profusion of ads for services and products related to special visual effects. And not too surprisingly, this journal has an astounding web site! Titles of recent articles include "*Iron Man*: Rough Around the Edges" and "*White House Down*: To the Rescue." For any library that serves the needs of a film studies program.

2418. Cinema Journal. Formerly (until 1967): *Society of Cinematologists. Journal.* [ISSN: 0009-7101] 1961. q. USD 183. Ed(s): Will Brooker. University of Texas Press, Journals Division, PO Box 7819, Austin, TX 78713; journals@uts.cc.utexas.edu; http://www.utexas.edu/utpress/journals/journals.html. Illus., index, adv. Refereed. Vol. ends: Aug. *Indexed:* A01, A06, A07, A22, ABS&EES, ArtHuCI, B02, BRI, E01, F01, IIFP, IIPA, MLA-IB, RILM. *Bk. rev.:* Number and length vary. *Aud.:* Ac.

This title "presents recent scholarship by Society for Cinema and Media Studies members. The journal publishes essays on a wide variety of subjects from diverse methodological perspectives. A Professional Notes section informs . . . readers about upcoming events, research applications, and the latest published research." For all film collections that address the needs of film studies programs.

2419. Cinema Scope: expanding the frame on international cinema. [ISSN: 1488-7002] 1999. q. USD 40 CAD 21.40 domestic. Ed(s): Andrew Tracy, Mark Peranson. Cinema Scope Publishing, 465 Lytton Blvd, Toronto, ON M5N 1S5, Canada. Illus., adv. *Indexed:* F01, IIFP, MLA-IB. *Bk. rev.:* Number and length vary. *Aud.:* Ac, Sa.

"An independently published quarterly jam-packed with interviews, features, and essays on film and video, *CS* is geared to cinephiles looking for an intelligent forum on world cinema. With unparalleled depth and breadth, *CS* is a real alternative in today's Canadian film scene." Includes DVD reviews, book reviews, and film festival reviews. Titles of recent articles include "Soft in the Head: The Films of Nathan Silver," "Love Letters from a Spanish Monomaniac: The Labyrinthine Legacy of Jess Franco," and "Pretending That Life Has No Meaning: Paul Schrader's *The Canyons*." For any film journal collection that addresses the needs of serious film aficionados and students.

2420. *Cinematiq: the quarterly resource magazine with a distinct perspective on black cinema.* [ISSN: 2162-0814] 2011. q. USD 8.95 per issue. Brown Ross, Ed. & Pub., Long Island University, Long Island, NY 11120. Adv. *Aud.:* Ga, Ac.

This interesting journal has a slightly different slant from its erudite counterpart, *Black Camera*. While intelligently written, and beautifully produced, it does not seek to hit quite so directly at the academic market. It also isn't simply about Black cinema; it is also intended to look at the portrayal of Blacks in other cinemas. One recent article title is "Ava Duvernay, Changing the game with AFFRM!" In addition to feature articles, it includes movie reviews and movie previews, and even has clips from new films on its web site. The publication frequency makes the journal's longevity seem slightly...fragile. Given the interesting nature of its content, we can only hope it succeeds. For academic programs that support film studies and/or African-American Studies.

2421. *Classic Images.* Former titles (until 1979): *Classic Film - Video Images;* (until 1978): *Classic Film Collector;* (until 1966): *Eight MM Collector.* [ISSN: 0275-8423] 1962. m. USD 52 domestic; USD 78 in Canada & Mexico; USD 108 elsewhere. Ed(s): Bob King. Muscatine Journal, 301 E Third St, Muscatine, IA 52761; http://www.muscatinejournal.com. Illus., index, adv. Vol. ends: Dec. Microform: PQC. *Indexed:* A22, F01, IIFP, IIPA, MLA-IB. *Bk. rev.:* Number and length vary. *Aud.:* Ga.

As "[t]he film fan's bible," this is the publication for people who love older, classic films. Each tabloid-format issue is approximately 80 pages in length. It has biographical articles on film stars, illustrated with black-and-white production and publicity stills. There are regular monthly features: video and DVD reviews, book reviews, articles on music in film, obituaries, and "this month in movie history." For film buffs and collectors, it has an advertisers' index for film festivals, conventions, video companies, publishers, and memorabilia merchants. Recent articles include "Toronto Film Society: One of the Oldest and Best," and "Lottie Briscoe, Octavia Handworth, Ormi Hawley, Helen Marten: Lubin's Lovely Ladies." Its tabloid format makes it dubious for an archiving library, but if a public library serves a large population of film buffs, this would be a good choice. Besides, one can always choose the digital format!

2422. *Documentary (Los Angeles).* Formerly (until 2006): *International Documentary.* [ISSN: 1559-1034] 1986. q. Free to members; Non-members, USD 45. Ed(s): Thomas White. International Documentary Association, 1201 W 5th St, Ste M320, Los Angeles, CA 90017; http://www.documentary.org/. Illus., adv. Sample. Vol. ends: Nov. *Indexed:* F01, IIFP. *Aud.:* Ac, Sa.

This publication of the International Documentary Foundation intends to "promote nonfiction film and video and to support the efforts of documentary makers around the world." It provides membership news and reports on festivals. Feature articles on aspects of the documentary filmmaking process are published with the doc filmmaker in mind. Ads for pre- and post-production services, festivals, and classes in documentary filmmaking are included. Columns formerly included in each issue, but now available on the web site, are North American broadcast and cable premieres, events and screenings, calls for entries, funding, and jobs and opportunities. Examples of some recent articles include "*The Art of Killing*: How Much Truth Comes from the Lie that Tells the Truth?" and "Unsung Heroes: *Twenty Feet from Stardom* Hails the Singers behind the Hits." Libraries that address either film studies or television journalism should consider this title.

2423. *Editors Guild Magazine.* 19??. bi-m. USD 45 domestic; USD 65 foreign. Ed(s): Tomm Carroll. Steven Jay Cohen, IATSE Local 700 MPEG, 7715 Sunset Blvd, Ste 200, Hollywood, CA 90046. Adv. *Aud.:* Sa.

This is the official magazine of the Editors Guild. It covers industry events that impact guild members. There are interviews with editors, assessments of new equipment and technologies, and a section on technical tips. Regular features in each issue include an index of advertisers, announcements and obituaries, and new signatories. Recent articles include "The Great Sequelization of Hollywood Film Part 1: Serial Thrillers" and "The Iron Men of Post-Production." For serious industry and academic film studies collections.

2424. *Film Comment.* Formerly (until 1962): *Vision.* [ISSN: 0015-119X] 19??. bi-m. Ed(s): Laura Kern, Gavin Smith. Film Society of Lincoln Center, 70 Lincoln Center Plz, New York, NY 10023; filminfo@filmlinc.com; http://www.filmlinc.com. Illus., index, adv. Circ: 40000. Vol. ends: Nov/Dec. Microform: NBI; PQC. *Indexed:* A01, A06, A07, A22, ABIn, ABS&EES, AmHI, ArtHuCI, BRI, C37, CBRI, F01, IIFP, IIPA, MASUSE, MLA-IB, P02, RILM. *Bk. rev.:* Number and length vary. *Aud.:* Hs, Ga, Ac.

This publication by the Film Society of Lincoln Center gives excellent coverage of filmmaking in the United States and abroad (although if you don't live in New York City, this publication will make you want to move there!). It contains feature articles, reviews, screenings, etc. Some examples of recent articles: "Intolerance: On Westerns in general and John Ford's in particular, the non-malleable nature of the&#8200

ast, and why Quentin Tarantino shouldn't teach film history," and "Cahiers du CineMAD: *MAD* magazine's movie parodies perfected the art of the hand-drawn film review for juveniles of all ages." For academic collections and public libraries that address the needs of serious film buffs.

2425. *Film Criticism.* [ISSN: 0163-5069] 1976. 3x/yr. USD 30 (Individuals, USD 25; USD 40 foreign). Ed(s): Lloyd Michaels. Allegheny College, 520 N Main St, Meadville, PA 16335; campus@alleg.edu; http://www.allegheny.edu. Illus., adv. Sample. Refereed. Vol. ends: Spring. *Indexed:* A01, A07, A22, ABS&EES, AmHI, ArtHuCI, BRI, CBRI, F01, IIFP, IIPA, MLA-IB, RILM. *Bk. rev.:* Number and length vary. *Aud.:* Ac.

As it celebrates its 36th year of publication, this journal also celebrates its status as the third-oldest film magazine in the country. This refereed journal publishes articles that examine and re-examine films from a variety of critical, political, and aesthetic viewpoints. Unusual aspects of films and symbolism are discussed in great detail. Occasionally, the body of work of a specific filmmaker is analyzed. Recent titles include "Kiarostami's *Shirin* and the Aesthetics of Ethical Intimacy," "*The Girl with the Dragon Tattoo* (2009/2011), and the New 'European Cinema,'" and "*A Film Unfinished*: Yael Hersonki's Re-Representation of Archival Footage from the Warsaw Ghetto." There are book reviews in most issues. For academic libraries that serve film studies programs.

2426. *Film History: an international journal.* [ISSN: 0892-2160] 1987. q. USD 279.50 (print & online eds.). Ed(s): Richard Koszarski. Indiana University Press, 601 N Morton St, Bloomington, IN 47404; journals@indiana.edu; http://iupress.indiana.edu. Illus., index, adv. Sample. Refereed. Circ: 800. Vol. ends: Dec. Reprint: PSC. *Indexed:* A01, A07, A22, BRI, E01, F01, IIFP, IIMP, IIPA, MLA-IB. *Bk. rev.:* Number and length vary. *Aud.:* Ac.

"The subject of *Film History* is the historical development of the motion picture, and the social, technological[,] and economic context in which this has occurred. Its areas of interest range from the technical and entrepreneurial innovations of early and pre-cinema experiments, through all aspects of the production, distribution, exhibition[,] and reception of commercial and non-commercial motion pictures. In addition to original research in these areas, the journal will survey the paper and film holdings of archives and libraries worldwide, publish selected examples of primary documentation (such as early film scenarios)[,] and report on current publications, exhibitions, conferences[,] and research in progress. Most future issues will be devoted to comprehensive studies of single themes." Titles of recent articles include "The Pleasures and Perils of Big Data in Digitized Newspapers," "Senses of Success and the Rise of the Blockbuster," and "Invisible by Design: Reclaiming Art Nouveau for the Cinema." For academic libraries with film studies collections.

2427. Film Journal International. Former titles (until 1996): *Film Journal;* (until 1979): *Independent Film Journal.* [ISSN: 1526-9884] 1934. m. USD 65 domestic; USD 120 foreign. Ed(s): Kevin Lally, Robert Sunshine. Nielsen Business Publications, 770 Broadway, New York, NY 10003; bmcomm@nielsen.com; http://www.nielsenbusinessmedia.com. Illus., index, adv. Circ: 9200. Vol. ends: Dec. *Indexed:* A07, B02, BRI, C37, F01, IIPA, MLA-IB. *Aud.:* Sa.

The intended audience for this publication is exhibitors: news, articles, and advertisements all relate to aspects of exhibition and concessions. The articles on specific film titles are written for a broader audience, but the main intent is to report on box-office potential. Each issue includes film reviews, film company news, new posts, new products, a buying and booking guide, trade talk, and an index of advertisers. For special libraries and film studies programs that address the business and promotional aspects of filmmaking.

2428. Film Quarterly. Former titles (until 1958): *The Quarterly of Film, Radio and Television;* (until 1951): *The Hollywood Quarterly.* [ISSN: 0015-1386] 1945. q. USD 250 (print & online eds.). Ed(s): Rob White. University of California Press, Journals Division, 2000 Ctr St, Ste 303, Berkeley, CA 94704; customerservice@ucpressjournals.com; http://www.ucpressjournals.com. Illus., index, adv. Sample. Refereed. Circ: 3591. Vol. ends: Oct. Microform: PQC. Reprint: PSC. *Indexed:* A01, A06, A07, A22, ABS&EES, AmHI, ArtHuCI, BRI, CBRI, E01, F01, IIFP, IIPA, MLA-IB, P02, RILM. *Bk. rev.:* Number and length vary. *Aud.:* Ga, Ac.

"International in coverage and reputation, *Film Quarterly* offers lively and penetrating articles covering the entire field of film studies. Articles include interviews with innovative film- and videomakers, writers, editors[,] and cinematographers; readable discussion of issues in contemporary film theory; definitive, thoughtful reviews of international, avant garde, national cinemas, and documentaries; and important approaches to film history." Now also available online. Recent titles include "*The Hunger Games* and other Precarious Dystopias," "*Melancholia* and the Comedy of Abandon," and "*Boardwalk Empire*: America Through a Bifocal Lens." For academic libraries that serve film studies programs.

2429. Film Score Monthly: your soundtrack source since 1990. [ISSN: 1077-4289] 1990. bi-m. USD 36.95 domestic; USD 42.95 in Canada & Mexico; USD 50 elsewhere. Ed(s): Tim Curran. Film Score Monthly, 6311 Romaine St, Ste 7109, Hollywood, CA 90038; lukas@filmscoremonthly.com; http://www.filmscoremonthly.com. Illus. Sample. *Indexed:* F01, IIMP, IIPA, RILM. *Aud.:* Sa.

Film Score Monthly provides information for those interested in what is happening in the film music industry: current news, record-label updates on releases, upcoming assignments (who's scoring what for whom), and CD reviews. There are feature articles on composers and behind-the-scenes looks at film music production. Some recent titles include: "The Horrors of High School Film Music" and "What about Bob...Bornstein? Paramount's Film Music Librarian." For libraries that serve serious film studies programs or communities.

2430. Filmmaker: the magazine of independent film. Formed by the 1992 merger of: *Off-Hollywood Report; Montage.* [ISSN: 1063-8954] 1992. q. USD 18. Ed(s): Jason Guerrasio, Scott Macaulay. Filmmaker, 68 Jay St, Ste 425, Brooklyn, NY 11201. Illus., adv. Sample. Circ: 42000. *Indexed:* A07, F01, IIPA. *Bk. rev.:* Number and length vary. *Aud.:* Sa.

This title is directed toward those interested in independent, smaller-budgeted films and filmmaking. Lesser-known films currently being released are profiled in each issue, along with independent filmmaker interviews and current film festival news. There are advertisements for film products, pre- and postproduction services, and film festivals, plus a handy advertisers' index. Some recent articles are: "Secrets of the Glam Squad" and "Meeting Ingmar Bergman." This is a nice addition to any collection that supports a film program.

2431. Films of the Golden Age. [ISSN: 1083-5369] 1995. q. USD 19.80 domestic; USD 30 in Canada & Mexico; USD 38 elsewhere. Ed(s): Bob King. Muscatine Journal, 301 E Third St, Muscatine, IA 52761; http://www.muscatinejournal.com. Illus., adv. Vol. ends: Winter. *Indexed:* F01, IIFP. *Aud.:* Ga.

How many of us start our interest in film with an addiction to old films? No matter how academic our original interest becomes, publications such as *Films of the Golden Age* have continuing appeal. This publication covers what it defines as the "golden age," that is, films produced in the studio era, from the 1930s through the 1950s. There are biographical articles on both stars and directors. Each issue is chock-full of illustrations, many of them unusual. Public libraries and academic libraries with general film collections should consider purchasing this. One caveat: its large, newspaper format will make processing and storage painful. But then...digital access is simple!

2432. Gorilla Film Magazine. [ISSN: 2049-8616] 2011. q. Gorilla Film Magazine Ltd., Flat 4, 40 Hackney Rd, London, E2 7PA, United Kingdom; ad@gorillafilmmagazine.com. Adv. *Aud.:* Ga, Ac.

In explaining the origin of this journal, the editors say, "In the 1880s, the motion picture camera allowed individual images to be stored on a single reel, leading to the invention of the motion picture projector. Cinema proved popular, and people began to have opinions about it. Not long after, the written word was invented, and was used as a medium for manic-depressives and alcoholics to express their opinions on film. One such people [sic] was called Jonathan Gorilla, who, it is said, looked up at a bird in a tree one day and was inspired to create a magazine totally devoted to short, or low[-]budget films..." And from that, this journal's humor, aesthetic, and sense of fun can clearly be seen. The web site encourages people to submit their films, their writing, their reviews. Will this publication last? I certainly hope so; for an industry that takes itself as seriously as film, this is a delightful and sometimes serious contribution. Articles include "The Launch of *Act of Terror*: An Interview with Fat Rat Films" and "Five Great Horror Films by Non-Horror Film Makers." For libraries that support film studies programs, or populations interested in alternative and street-smart publications.

2433. Griffithiana. [ISSN: 0393-3857] 1978. s-a. EUR 80 (Individuals, EUR 40). Ed(s): Peter Lehman, Davide Turconi. Cineteca del Friuli, Via G. Bini, Palazzo Gurisatti, Gemona, 33013, Italy; griffithiana@cinetecadelfriuli.org; http://cinetecadelfriuli.org. Illus., adv. Refereed. Circ: 2500. *Indexed:* AmHI, F01, IIFP, IIPA, MLA-IB. *Bk. rev.:* Number and length vary. *Aud.:* Ac.

"An international journal of film history, *Griffithiana* is devoted to the study of animation and silent cinema. It features articles by prominent international film scholars, historians, archivists, and journalists, as well as comprehensive filmographies and reviews of international cinema books. Many issues showcase newly rediscovered and restored films presented at the Pordenone Film Festival." The articles are published in both Italian and English.

2434. indieWIRE: filmmakers, biz, fans. 1995. d. Ed(s): Eugene Hernandez, Brian Brooks. indieWIRE LLC, 73 Spring St, Ste 403, New York, NY 10012. Adv. *Aud.:* Ga, Ac, Sa.

This is an excellent example of the hybrid nature of electronic publishing. Is it a magazine? a newspaper? a mere newsletter? a portal? It contains blogging, but is not a blog per se. *indieWIRE* offers special coverage of the major independent film festivals in such places as Los Angeles and Tribeca. It has routine coverage of special areas, such as world cinema and queer cinema. It includes film business news and information on releases and people. Its articles may be brief, but they are substantive, and all materials are archived. Well, whatever it is, it makes anyone interested in film jump up and down. It is, in fact, probably the most up-to-date place for industry information on independent films. This is an invaluable link for any library that supports a film studies or production program.

2435. Journal of Film and Video. Former titles (until 1984): *University Film and Video Association. Journal;* (until 1982): *University Film Association. Journal;* (until 1968): *University Film Producers Association. Journal.* [ISSN: 0742-4671] 1949. q. USD 95 (print & online eds.). Ed(s): Stephen Tropiano. University of Illinois Press, 1325 S Oak St, Champaign, IL 61820; journals@uillinois.edu; http://www.press.uillinois.edu. Illus., index, adv. Refereed. Microform: PQC. *Indexed:* A01, A07, A22, ABS&EES, ArtHuCI, BRI, E01, F01, IIFP, IIPA, MLA-IB, P02. *Aud.:* Ac.

This refereed journal "focuses on scholarship in the fields of film and video production, history, theory, criticism, and aesthetics." It is the official publication of the University Film and Video Association. In its call for papers, it requests "articles about film and related media, problems of education in these fields[,] and the function of film and video in society." Some recent titles include "Writing *The Simpsons*: A Case Study of Comic Theory" and "Screenwriting Representation: Teaching Approaches to Writing Queer Characters." For academic audiences.

2436. Journal of Popular Film and Television. Formerly (until 1978): *The Journal of Popular Film.* [ISSN: 0195-6051] 1972. q. GBP 133 (print & online eds.). Ed(s): Michael T Marsden, Gary R Edgerton. Routledge, 325 Chestnut St, Ste 800, Philadelphia, PA 19106; customerservice@taylorandfrancis.com; http://www.tandfonline.com. Illus., index, adv. Refereed. Reprint: PSC. *Indexed:* A01, A06, A07, A22, ABS&EES, AmHI, ArtHuCI, BRI, C42, CBRI, E01, F01, IIFP, IIPA, MLA-IB, P02, RILM. *Bk. rev.:* Number and length vary. *Aud.:* Ga, Ac.

This title "is dedicated to popular film and television in the broadest sense. Concentration is upon commercial cinema and television: stars, directors, producers, studios, networks, genres, series, the audience, etc." Articles are accompanied by acknowledgements, with notes and works cited. Recent article titles include "*Bad Teacher* is Bad for Teachers," "What Popular Films Teach Us About Values: Locked Inside with the Rage Virus," and "Challenging *Waiting for Superman* Through Detournement." Book reviews are also included. For serious film and communications libraries.

2437. Journal of Religion and Film. [ISSN: 1092-1311] 1997. s-a. Free. Ed(s): Kathryn Schwartz, Michele Desmarais. University of Nebraska at Omaha, Department of Philosophy and Religion, 60th & Dodge Streets, Omaha, NE 68182; unonews@unomaha.edu; http://www.unomaha.edu/wwwphrel/. Adv. Refereed. *Indexed:* BRI, F01, MLA-IB. *Aud.:* Ga, Ac.

The *Journal of Religion and Film* "examines the description, critique, and embodiment of religion in film." The editors "invite articles and discussion on a variety of film types, commercial and academic, foreign and documentary, classic and contemporary." Peer-reviewed articles and analyses of films that stress spiritual aspects are presented. Some recent articles include "Echoes of a Storyteller," "Shinto and Buddhist Metaphors in Departures," and "Satanic but not Satan: Signs of the Devilish in Contemporary Cinema." For academic collections.

2438. Jump Cut: a review of contemporary media. 1974. a. Free. Ed(s): John Hess, Julia Lesage. Jump Cut Associates, PO Box 865, Berkeley, CA 94701. Illus. Refereed. Microform: PQC. *Indexed:* IIPA. *Bk. rev.:* 4-5, 500-1,000 words. *Aud.:* Ga, Ac, Sa.

This journal has a definite editorial viewpoint: as its byline says, its editors have been "looking at media in its social and political context. Pioneers since 1974, analyzing media in relation to class, race, and gender." And that certainly describes its content. Its articles often take a radical, thought-provoking perspective on media in general and on film in particular. Recent articles include "Migrant Workers, Women, and China's Modernization on Screen," "The Chilean Student Movement of 2011: Camila Vallejo and the media," and "Postmodern geekdom as simulated ethnicity." Ever interesting, ever edgy, this should be considered by libraries with large film studies collections.

2439. Moviemaker: the art and business of making movies. Formerly (until 200?): *Movie Maker Magazine.* 1993. bi-m. USD 18 domestic; USD 28 Canada; USD 44 elsewhere. Ed(s): Timothy E Rhys, Jennifer M Wood. Moviemaker Pub., 174 Fifth Ave, Ste 300, New York, NY 10010. Illus., adv. *Indexed:* IIPA. *Aud.:* Ac, Sa.

This title features articles on producers, actors, and directors. It also covers independent film industry issues, such as copyright, technical instruction, festivals, shorts, and documentaries. There are ads for film equipment and services, with an advertisers index. Recent articles include "How to Earn a Living Making Documentaries" and "Sean Baker Addresses the Porn Industry in *Starlet*." This is a good title for collections that support a film studies program.

2440. Quarterly Review of Film and Video. Formerly (until 1989): *Quarterly Review of Film Studies.* [ISSN: 1050-9208] 1976. 5x/yr. GBP 948 (print & online eds.). Ed(s): Wheeler Winston Dixon, Gwendolyn Audrey Foster. Routledge, 325 Chestnut St, Ste 800, Philadelphia, PA 19106; customerservice@taylorandfrancis.com; http://www.tandfonline.com. Illus., index, adv. Sample. Refereed. Reprint: PSC. *Indexed:* A01, A07, A22, ABS&EES, AmHI, BRI, CBRI, E01, F01, IIFP, MLA-IB, P02. *Bk. rev.:* Number and length vary. *Aud.:* Ac.

This refereed journal is international and interdisciplinary in scope. It publishes "critical, historical, and theoretical essays, book reviews, and interviews in the area of moving[-]image studies[,] including film, video, and digital image studies." Titles of recent feature articles include "I love you, Brom Bones: Beta Male Comedies and American Culture," and "Seeing Life in Disney's Mutual Affection Images." For academic libraries.

2441. Script (Calabasas): where film begins. [ISSN: 1092-2016] 1995. bi-m. USD 24.95 domestic; USD 32.95 in Canada & Mexico; USD 44.95 elsewhere. Ed(s): Shelly Mellott, Andrew Schneider. Final Draft, Inc., 26707 W Agoura Rd, Ste 205, Calabasas, CA 91302; http://www.finaldraft.com/. Illus., adv. *Indexed:* F01. *Aud.:* Sa.

The explanation given for the title is "the (i) in *Scr(i)pt* is used to honor the screenwriter . . . [and] our message to you is that we recognize you as the genesis of film—the inspiration." This publication is for those who are beyond asking for examples of the standard script format. Interviews and articles are included of/by writers of currently released films as well, which makes it a source of practical information for both established and burgeoning screenwriters. Unlike many journals with a digital counterpart, this publication is still careening around for its best home (it now offers its FaceBook site as a point of entry). But despite that, it continues to offer interesting content. For film studies and writing center collections.

2442. Senses of Cinema. [ISSN: 1443-4059] 1999. q. Free. Senses of Cinema Inc., AFI Research Collection, School of Media and Communication, RMIT University, GPO Box 2476V, Melbourne, VIC 3001, Australia; editor@sensesofcinema.com. Adv. Refereed. *Indexed:* F01, MLA-IB. *Bk. rev.:* Number and length vary. *Aud.:* Ac, Sa.

Senses of Cinema is "an online film journal devoted to the serious and eclectic discussion of cinema." It receives financial assistance from the Australian Film Commission, and it has a slight (increasingly slight) down-under, Aussie bias (the "Festivals" section is divided into "international festivals" and "Australian festivals"). The journal is building up a "Great Directors" database, with a critical essay on each director along with a filmography, bibliography, and web resources. It includes book and DVD reviews. Some titles of recent feature articles include "Sirk, Hollywood and Genre," and "Bodies in Filmic Space: The *Mise en Scene* of 'Courtship Readiness' in *The Big Sleep*." An excellent choice for film studies collections. URL: www.sensesofcinema.com

2443. Sight and Sound: the international film magazine. Incorporates (1934-1991): *Monthly Film Bulletin;* (1948-1949): *Monthly Film Strip Review.* [ISSN: 0037-4806] 1932. m. GBP 45 combined subscription domestic (print & online eds.); GBP 68 combined subscription foreign (print & online eds.); GBP 4.50 newsstand/cover. British Film Institute, 21 Stephen St, London, W1T 1LN, United Kingdom; publishing@bfi.org.uk; http://www.bfi.org.uk. Illus., adv. Vol. ends: Dec. Microform: MIM; PQC; WMP. *Indexed:* A01, A06, A07, A22, AmHI, ArtHuCI, BRI, CBRI, F01, IIFP, IIPA, MLA-IB, P02. *Bk. rev.:* Number and length vary. *Aud.:* Ga, Ac.

The journal is published under the auspices of the eminent British Film Institute. It is particularly good in the area of film reviews and credits; it consistently gives the most complete credit listings of any film periodical. Coverage includes major film festivals and filmmakers, American and foreign. It also publishes detailed articles and interviews with directors who are not usually found in popular movie magazines. Some recent article titles include "Man on fire: Tony Scott," and "Second Youth: The Golden Age of Nikkatsu Studios." For all academic film studies programs, and for public libraries with serious filmgoing populations.

2444. *The Velvet Light Trap.* [ISSN: 0149-1830] 1971. s-a. USD 120. University of Texas Press, Journals Division, PO Box 7819, Austin, TX 78713; journals@uts.cc.utexas.edu; http://www.utexas.edu/utpress/journals/journals.html. Illus., index. Refereed. Vol. ends: Sep. Microform: PQC. *Indexed:* A01, A22, AmHI, B02, BRI, E01, F01, IIFP, IIPA, MLA-IB, P02, P61, SSA. *Bk. rev.:* Number and length vary. *Aud.:* Ac.

This journal just gets better and better! It is "devoted to investigating historical questions that illuminate the understanding of film and other media." Issues often have a single theme, e.g., "Censorship and Regulation," or "Comedy." Articles and interviews are of a scholarly nature and include notes. The content is edited by graduate students in film studies from Austin and Madison. Some recent articles have been "The Lost Studio of Atlantis: Norman Bel Geddes's Failed Revolution in Television Form," "Dissecting *Bambi*: Multiplanar Photography, the Cel Technique, and the Flowering of Full Animation," and "*Kung Fu Panda*: Animated Animal Bodies as Layered Sites of (Trans)National Identities." Book reviews are provided in each issue. Recommended for academic collections.

2445. *Written By.* Former titles (until 1997): *Writers Guild of America, West. Journal;* (until 1988): *W G A West Newsletter.* [ISSN: 1092-468X] 1965. bi-m. USD 40 domestic; USD 45 in Canada & Mexico; USD 50 elsewhere. Ed(s): Richard Stayton, Christina McBride. Writers Guild of America, West, 7000 W Third St, Los Angeles, CA 90048; http://www.wga.org/. Illus. *Indexed:* F01, IIPA. *Aud.:* Sa.

The official publication of the Writers Guild of America West, this title "actively seeks material from Guild members and other writers." It covers current events and creative issues that affect screen and television writers, and offers biographical articles on writers and analyses of current films. Some recent titles of articles include "You Can't Make This Stuff Up, Chris Terrio's Career is Exfiltrated," and "Solving *Pi*[:] David Magee Adapts the Impossible." A good title for libraries that support a screenwriting program.

■ FIRE PROTECTION

Lian Ruan, Director/Head Librarian, Illinois Fire Service Institute Library, University of Illinois at Urbana–Champaign, 11 Gerty Drive, Champaign, IL 61820; lruan@illinois.edu.

Diane Richardson, Reference and Training Librarian, Illinois Fire Service Institute Library, University of Illinois at Urbana–Champaign, 11 Gerty Drive, Champaign, IL 61820; dlrichar@illinois.edu.

David Ehrenhart, Archivist and Metadata Librarian, Illinois Fire Service Institute Library, University of Illinois at Urbana–Champaign, 11 Gerty Drive, Champaign, IL 61820; ehrenha1@illinois.edu

Introduction

Firefighters and emergency responders respond to emergencies and save lives. Their responsibilities cover a wide range of emergencies like firefighting, emergency medical care, aircraft crashes, earthquakes, floods, hurricanes, tornadoes, hazardous materials incidents, civil disturbances, rescue operations, explosions, terrorism, and other emergency responses.

This section includes fire protection journals with a national or international perspective. The titles selected here primarily focus on firefighters, emergency responders, and fire service administrators. Articles cover key topics in the fire service, such as firefighter training, firefighting operations, fire safety, hazardous materials, fire management, leadership, incidents, and news, etc. Most magazines use an informative format including featured articles, columns, and news. This section also includes a peer-reviewed and internationally recognized scholarly journal for fire science and fire safety engineering researchers and academic programs.

Basic Periodicals

Ac: *Fire Chief, Fire Engineering, Fire Protection Engineering, Fire Technology, N F P A Journal;* Sa: *Fire Engineering, Fire Protection Engineering, FireRescue Magazine, Fire Technology, Firehouse, Industrial Fire World, N F P A Journal.*

Basic Abstracts and Indexes

Chemical Abstracts, Engineering Index.

2446. *Fire Engineering: the journal of fire suppression and protection.* Formerly (until 1926): *Fire Protection;* Incorporates (1903-1926): *Fire and Water Engineering.* [ISSN: 0015-2587] 1877. m. USD 29 domestic; USD 42 Canada; USD 64 elsewhere. Ed(s): Bobby Halton. PennWell Corporation, 21-00 Rte 208 S, Fair Lawn, NJ 07410; Headquarters@PennWell.com; http://www.pennwell.com. Illus., index, adv. Sample. Circ: 57351 Paid. *Indexed:* A01, A22, ABIn, B03, C&ISA, CerAb, EngInd. *Aud.:* Ac, Sa.

With a history that dates back over 130 years, *Fire Engineering* is a monthly periodical that provides fire and emergency service professionals worldwide with training, education, and management information written by experts in the fire service. Feature articles focus on "lessons learned" from a wide variety of situations that a fire or emergency services professional might encounter, including vehicle extrication, structural collapse rescue, or hazardous materials operations. In addition to the feature articles, regular sections are devoted to emergency medical services, volunteer firefighters, and new technologies. Each issue also includes a "Web Watch" section, in which fire service resources from the Internet are highlighted. The online version of the magazine provides frequently updated content, including daily news, calendars of industry events, and articles from the current print issue. *Fire Engineering* is highly recommended for fire service personnel and fire departments, as well as public, academic, and special libraries that serve fire protection and prevention professionals.

2447. *Fire Protection Engineering.* [ISSN: 1524-900X] 1998. q. GBP 346 (print & online eds.) Individuals, GBP 339; Free to members). Ed(s): Ronald L Alpert. Society of Fire Protection Engineers, 7315 Wisconsin Ave, Ste 620E, Bethesda, MD 20814; sfpehqtrs@sfpe.org; http://www.sfpe.org. Illus., adv. Vol. ends: Fall. *Indexed:* B02, BRI. *Bk. rev.:* 200-300 words. *Aud.:* Ac, Sa.

The quarterly publication *Fire Protection Engineering* serves as the "Official Magazine of the Society of Fire Protection Engineers." Feature articles are scholarly in nature and closely examine specific issues in the field while maintaining an accessible format and writing style that is understandable to those without a background in fire protection engineering. Articles examine issues relating to the design of fire protection systems, current codes and standards relevant to the field, and emerging technologies. In addition to the articles, recurring sections include opinion articles, current publications in the field, industry news, and an ad index to products advertised in the issue. The online version of the magazine provides access to all articles from the print version as well as case studies, information on webinars for professional development, and access to a free "FPE Emerging Trends" monthly newsletter distributed in the off-months of the print magazine. *Fire Protection Engineering* is recommended for special and academic libraries that support fire prevention and protection training programs.

2448. *Fire Technology.* [ISSN: 0015-2684] 1965. q. EUR 541 (print & online eds.). Ed(s): John M Watts, Jr. Springer New York LLC, 233 Spring St, New York, NY 10013; service-ny@springer.com; http://www.springer.com/. Illus., index, adv. Sample. Refereed. Vol. ends: Oct (No. 4). Microform: PQC. Reprint: PSC. *Indexed:* A01, A22, ABIn, Agr, BRI, E01, EngInd, H24, P02, RiskAb. *Bk. rev.:* 1, 250-500 words. *Aud.:* Ac, Sa.

Published quarterly, *Fire Technology* is a peer-reviewed journal with both an interdisciplinary and international scope that focuses on fire safety science and engineering. It is published in conjunction with the National Fire Protection Association. Issues of *Fire Technology* are composed of original papers, both theoretical and empirical, that address subjects such as materials testing, fire modeling, human behavior in fires, municipal and wildland fire protection, fire risk analysis, fire detection, and loss statistics. Each year a special issue addresses facets of a single topic. Past special issues have been devoted to pedestrian and evacuation dynamics, the World Trade Center, smoke control in buildings and tunnels, and fire suppression. The "Online First Articles" section of the digital edition of the magazine features articles that have not been assigned to a print issue. *Fire Technology* is highly recommended for academic libraries that support fire safety and engineering disciplines, and for special libraries that support fire prevention and protection training programs.

2449. *Firehouse (Fort Atkinson).* [ISSN: 0145-4064] 1976. m. USD 24.95 domestic (Free to qualified personnel). Ed(s): Harvey Eisner, Elizabeth Friszell-Neroulas. Cygnus Business Media, Inc., 1233 Janesville Ave, PO Box 803, Fort Atkinson, WI 53538; http://www.cygnus.com. Illus., adv. Circ: 76139. Vol. ends: Dec. *Indexed:* ABIn, B02, BRI. *Aud.:* Sa.

Firehouse provides fire and emergency service professionals with information on current news stories and events relevant to their profession. Monthly issues contain features that detail significant fires and emergencies, training tips, developments in fire service higher education, and interviews with fire chiefs about tough issues facing the profession. Regular columns discuss politics, emergency medical service issues, close calls encountered by firefighters, and professional development topics for fire officers. The online version contains up-to-date news articles and line-of-duty deaths, blogs, podcasts, webcasts, and weekly training drills that can be utilized by fire departments. *Firehouse* is highly recommended for fire service personnel and fire departments, as well as public, academic, and special libraries that serve fire protection and prevention professionals.

2450. *FireRescue Magazine.* Incorporates (1997-2008): *Wildland Firefighter;* Formed by the merger of (1984-1997): *Firefighter's News;* (1989-1997): *Rescue;* Which was formerly (until 1989): *Rescue Magazine.* [ISSN: 1094-0529] 1997. m. USD 48. Ed(s): Tim Sendelbach. Elsevier Public Safety, 525 B St, Ste 1800, San Diego, CA 92101. Adv. *Aud.:* Sa.

FireRescue Magazine, with the subtitle "Read It Today. Use It Tomorrow," is dedicated to the purpose of helping firefighters excel in every facet of emergency response. To that end, it interprets the latest emergency response technology, research, and information into skills and solutions firefighters and fire officers can use on the job. A unique feature of this magazine is color photographs of emergency response situations captioned with solution tips. Also, each editorial is a training lesson, and even the "About the cover" paragraph contains a tactical tip. Columns and feature articles are written by fire service veterans and address such practical topics as fireground strategy and tactics, extrication, hazardous materials, training, personnel issues, and technology. Other monthly sections include a wildland/urban interface feature, a letter/response column, a tools/news/techniques section, classified ads, and sections that review new products and report deliveries of new equipment to specific fire departments. The print edition connects to the online edition by providing URLs for additional *FireRescue* articles by featured authors. The online edition provides tags with each article summary, facilitating searches for recent related articles. This excellent magazine, a media partner of the International Association of Fire Chiefs, is highly recommended for special and large public libraries, academic libraries that support fire protection and prevention training programs, and fire and emergency medical services professionals.

2451. *Industrial Fire World.* [ISSN: 0749-890X] 1985. bi-m. USD 29.95 (Free to qualified personnel). Ed(s): Anton Riecher. Industrial Fire World, PO Box 9161, College Station, TX 77842. Adv. Sample. *Aud.:* Sa.

Industrial Fire World, published quarterly, provides personnel in the industrial fire protection field with the latest information on techniques and technology related to all aspects of industrial emergency response. Regular columns are devoted to emergency medical response, hazardous materials, risk assessment, and training. Each issue also provides a log of international industrial incidents, including injury and fatality reports. Feature articles by leaders in the field address the most up-to-date technological innovations in industrial fire fighting, changes in governmental regulations that affect firefighters, and training practices and opportunities. Issues contain in-depth coverage of a recent or historical industrial emergency incident, including photographs and "lessons learned." An industrial service directory is also published regularly. Full text of some current articles are made available at the Fireworld.com web site. *Industrial Fire World* is highly recommended for special libraries supporting industrial emergency response teams and training programs.

2452. *N F P A Journal.* Formed by the merger of (1984-1991): *Fire Command;* Which was formerly (until 1984): *Fire Service Today;* (until 1981): *Fire Command;* (until 1970): *Firemen;* (until 1946): *Volunteer Firemen;* (1965-1991): *Fire Journal;* Which was formerly (until 1965): *Quarterly of the National Fire Protection Association.* [ISSN: 1054-8793] 1991. bi-m. Free to members. Ed(s): Scott Sutherland. National Fire Protection Association, 1 Batterymarch Park, Quincy, MA 02269; custserv@nfpa.org; http://www.nfpa.org. Illus., index, adv. Sample. Circ: 82871 Controlled. Vol. ends: Nov/Dec. Microform: PQC. *Indexed:* A22, P02. *Aud.:* Ac, Sa.

NFPA Journal is the bimonthly membership magazine of the National Fire Protection Agency (NFPA), a nonprofit organization that produces codes and standards accepted as professional standards related to fire, building, and electrical safety. Regular columns and feature articles address safety-related public education programs, alarm systems, structural firefighting operations, sprinkler systems, fire code compliance, and issues related to NFPA 70E, the *Electrical Safety in the Workplace* standard. Overviews of recent reports issued by the Fire Analysis and Research Division of NFPA, short summaries of recent significant or fatal fires, and reviews of noteworthy historical disasters are also published in each issue. Statistical reports of United States fire loss, large-loss fires, multiple death fires, and firefighter injuries and fatalities are published annually. A buyer's guide, which includes a guide to NFPA standards, is also published annually. The journal is available both online and as a digital edition at NFPA.org. *NFPA Journal* is highly recommended for academic and special libraries that support fire prevention and protection training programs, and for fire service leaders and public administrators.

■ FISH, FISHERIES, AND AQUACULTURE

Wenli Gao, Instructional Services Librarian, Morrisville State College, P.O. Box 902, Eaton Street, Morrisville, NY 13408; gaow@morrisville.edu

Introduction

Publications in this section cover marine and freshwater fish, exploitable shellfish, and their respective fisheries. Topics include, but are not limited to, biology, ecology, genetics, health, psychology, population genetics, economics, management, and culture. Some publications cover a variety of topics, while some focus on certain aspects of aquaculture, such as nutrition, disease, environment, physiology, and biochemistry.

Most titles in this section focus on fish and fisheries in North America, but some have an international and global perspective. Some publications in this section focus on Japan and Asia, too. So this section really covers a broad range of aquaculture topics. Those publications will be useful for scholars all around the world.

Publications in this section are not only written for scholars. Although some publications focus on research, there are some that serve as an overview of the aquaculture industry and will be of interest to those working in the business and management side of the industry. They will be useful also for people who are interested in opening or maintaining the business and making profits.

The types of publications in this section are also versatile. There are trade magazines with advertisements and scholarly journals with mostly original research. Review articles, technical papers, and short communications are also included in some publications. The language in most of the publications is not for the general publication, although the editors of some of them encourage less jargon.

Overall, the Fish, Fisheries, and Aquaculture section contains publications that will be useful for scholars around the world, and people working in the industry or interested in working in the industry.

Basic Periodicals

Ac, Sa: *American Fisheries Society. Transactions, Aquaculture Research, Fish and Fisheries, Fishery Bulletin, Journal of Applied Aquaculture, Marine Fisheries Review, North American Journal of Fisheries Management, Reviews in Fisheries Science.*

Basic Abstracts and Indexes

ASFA Aquaculture Abstracts, Biological Abstracts.

2453. American Fisheries Society. Transactions. Former titles (until 1900): *American Fisheries Society. Proceedings;* (until 1899): *American Fisheries Society. Minutes;* (until 1897): *American Fisheries Society. Transactions;* (until 1895): *American Fish-Cultural Association. Transactions;* (until 1878): *American Fish Culturists' Association. Transactions;* (until 1876): *American Fish Culturists' Association. Proceedings.* [ISSN: 0002-8487] 1872. bi-m. Individuals, USD 43. Ed(s): Dennis R DeVries, Richard J Beamish. American Fisheries Society, 5410 Grosvenor Ln, Ste 110, Bethesda, MD 20814; alerner@fisheries.org; http://www.fisheries.org. Illus., index, adv. Refereed. Vol. ends: No. 6. Reprint: PSC. *Indexed:* A22, AnBeAb, C45, IndVet, OceAb, RRTA, S25. *Bk. rev.:* Number and length vary. *Aud.:* Ac, Sa.

Published bimonthly by the American Fisheries Society, this journal publishes papers on all aspects of fisheries science, including, but not limited to, biology, ecology, genetics, health, psychology, population genetics, economics, and culture. It covers marine and freshwater fish, exploitable shellfish, and their respective fisheries. Each issue includes refereed original research papers, making it an important journal for those studying aquaculture.

2454. Aquacultural Engineering. [ISSN: 0144-8609] 1982. 6x/yr. EUR 1337. Ed(s): Dr. J van Rijn, J Colt. Elsevier BV, Radarweg 29, PO Box 211, Amsterdam, 1000 AE, Netherlands; JournalsCustomerServiceEMEA@elsevier.com; http://www.elsevier.nl. Illus., index, adv. Refereed. Vol. ends: No. 6. Microform: PQC. *Indexed:* A01, A22, Agr, C&ISA, C45, CerAb, EngInd, IndVet, OceAb, RRTA, S25. *Aud.:* Ac, Sa.

Published bimonthly, *Aquacultural Engineering* is the official journal of the Aquacultural Engineering Society. This journal publishes original research papers, review articles, and short communications related to the design and development of aquacultural systems for both freshwater and marine facilities. The journal aims to apply the knowledge gained from basic research that potentially can be translated into commercial operations. Topics covered include construction experiences and techniques, engineering and design of aquacultural facilities, and materials selection and their uses. This publication would be useful for those studying marine life and those interested in the design and construction of fisheries.

2455. Aquaculture. Incorporates (1990-1996): *Annual Review of Fish Diseases.* [ISSN: 0044-8486] 1972. 48x/yr. EUR 5747. Ed(s): E M Donaldson, G Hulata. Elsevier BV, Radarweg 29, PO Box 211, Amsterdam, 1000 AE, Netherlands; JournalsCustomerServiceEMEA@elsevier.com; http://www.elsevier.nl. Illus., index, adv. Refereed. Microform: PQC. *Indexed:* A01, A22, Agr, C45, FS&TA, IndVet, OceAb, P02, RRTA, S25. *Bk. rev.:* Number and length vary. *Aud.:* Ac, Sa.

Published semi-monthly, *Aquaculture* is an international journal for freshwater and marine researchers interested in the exploration, improvement, and management of all aquatic food resources. Types of articles include original research papers, review articles, technical papers, and short communications. This journal covers all aspects of aquaculture, including diseases, genetics, nutrition, physiology and endocrinology, production science, and sustainability and society. It carries articles that are international in scope. The journal is aimed at aquaculturalists and scientists who desire a better understanding of the issues facing those in the field.

2456. Aquaculture Economics & Management. [ISSN: 1365-7305] 1997. q. GBP 361 (print & online eds.). Taylor & Francis, 4 Park Sq, Milton Park, Abingdon, OX14 4RN, United Kingdom; http://www.tandfonline.com. Adv. Sample. Refereed. Reprint: PSC. *Indexed:* A01, A22, Agr, B01, C45, E01, EconLit, JEL, OceAb, S25. *Aud.:* Ac, Sa.

Aquaculture Economics & Management is the official journal of the International Association of Aquaculture Economics and Management. Published quarterly, this journal includes peer-reviewed papers that address the economic issues related to aquaculture in both the public and private sectors. Topics covered include farm management, consumer behavior, pricing, and government policy. Unlike other titles in this section, this journal does not cover the biological or ecological aspects of aquaculture. It would be useful for those studying business, economics, or public policy as these fields relate to the field of aquaculture.

2457. Aquaculture Environment Interactions: international and multidisciplinary journal. [ISSN: 1869-215X] 2010. 6x/yr. EUR 199 combined subscription (print & online eds.). Ed(s): Marianne Holmer, Tim Dempster. Inter-Research, Nordbuente 23, Oldendorf, 21385, Germany; ir@int-res.com; http://www.int-res.com. Refereed. *Indexed:* C45. *Aud.:* Ac, Sa.

Aquaculture Environment Interactions is a multidisciplinary international forum for primary research studies on environmental sustainability of aquaculture. It focuses on inter-actions between aquaculture and the environment from local to ecosystem scales, at all levels of organization and investigation. It is useful for researchers in environmental science, and researchers interested in the environmental aspect of aquaculture.

2458. Aquaculture Nutrition. [ISSN: 1353-5773] 1995. bi-m. GBP 716. Ed(s): Dr. Rune Waagbo, Genevieve Corraze. Wiley-Blackwell Publishing Ltd., The Atrium, Southern Gate, Chichester, PO19 8SQ, United Kingdom; customer@wiley.com; http://www.wiley.com/. Illus., index, adv. Sample. Refereed. Vol. ends: No. 4. Reprint: PSC. *Indexed:* A01, A22, Agr, C45, E01, IndVet, OceAb. *Aud.:* Ac, Sa.

Published bimonthly, this international journal provides a global perspective on the nutrition of all cultivated aquatic animals. Topics range from extensive aquaculture to laboratory studies of nutritional biochemistry and physiology. The articles included in the journal are technical and the focus of the journal is narrow, so it would be of most value to those researchers who are studying nutritional aspects of aquaculture.

2459. Aquaculture Research. Former titles (until 1995): *Aquaculture and Fisheries Management;* (until 1985): *Fisheries Management.* [ISSN: 1355-557X] 1970. m. GBP 2372. Ed(s): Dr. Ronald W Hardy, Dr. Shi-Yen Shiau. Wiley-Blackwell Publishing Ltd., The Atrium, Southern Gate, Chichester, PO19 8SQ, United Kingdom; customer@wiley.com; http://www.wiley.com/. Illus., index, adv. Sample. Refereed. Vol. ends: No. 12. Microform: PQC. Reprint: PSC. *Indexed:* A01, A22, Agr, C45, E01, IndVet, OceAb, RRTA. *Bk. rev.:* Number and length vary. *Aud.:* Ac, Sa.

Aquaculture Research publishes hypothesis-driven papers on applied or scientific research that is relevant to freshwater aquaculture, brackish-water aquaculture, and marine aquaculture. With an international scope, this journal covers both faunistic and floristic aquatic organisms and includes review articles, reports on original research, short communications, technical papers, and book reviews. The journal invites young scientists to submit short communications based on their own research. As a journal with a global perspective and wide range of coverage, it is recommended for people seeking a broad understanding of aquaculture.

Aquatic Conservation (Online). See Marine Science and Technology section.

2460. Canadian Journal of Fisheries and Aquatic Sciences. Former titles (until 1980): *Fisheries Research Board of Canada. Journal;* (until 1937): *Biological Board of Canada. Journal;* (until 1934): *Contributions to Canadian Biology and Fisheries; Contributions to Canadian Biology.* [ISSN: 0706-652X] 1901. m. CAD 1740. Ed(s): Rolf D Vinebrooke, Yong Chen. N R C Research Press, 1200 Montreal Rd, Bldg M-55, Ottawa, ON K1A 0R6, Canada; pubs@nrc-cnrc.gc.ca; http://pubs.nrc-cnrc.gc.ca. Illus., index, adv. Refereed. Circ: 3000. Vol. ends: No. 12. Microform: PQC. *Indexed:* A01, A22, AnBeAb, C37, C45, CBCARef, E01, FS&TA, IndVet, OceAb, RRTA, S25. *Aud.:* Ac, Sa.

Published since 1901, *Canadian Journal of Fisheries and Aquatic Sciences* is considered a core publication for those studying the multidisciplinary field of aquatic sciences. This journal is published monthly, and each issue includes articles, rapid communications, and perspectives. Subjects covered include current research on cells, organisms, populations, ecosystems, or processes that affect aquatic systems. Supplements are sometimes devoted to conference proceedings or to single topics. Though the material covered is academic in nature, this journal is a must-have for those studying aquaculture.

2461. *Diseases of Aquatic Organisms*. [ISSN: 0177-5103] 1985. 15x/yr. EUR 995 combined subscription (print & online eds.). Ed(s): Sven Klimpel, Alex Hyatt. Inter-Research, Nordbuente 23, Oldendorf, 21385, Germany; ir@int-res.com; http://www.int-res.com. Refereed. *Indexed:* A22, AbAn, C45, IndVet, OceAb, RRTA. *Aud.:* Ac, Sa.

Diseases of Aquatic Organisms is a leading journal in its field. It is international and interdisciplinary, including information about animals, plants, and microorganisms in marine, limnetic, and brackish habitats. It covers diseases that affect all facets of life—at the cell, tissue, organ, individual, population, and ecosystem level. It is an indispensable source of information for all who are concerned with health of humans, animals, plants and microorganisms, environmental protection, resource management, ecosystem health, conservation of organisms and habitats, and aquafood production. Those who will find this journal useful include physicians, veterinarians, environmental biologists, fishery biologists and ecologists, aquaculturalists, pathologists, parasitologists, microbiologists, botanists, and zoologists.

2462. *Ecology of Freshwater Fish*. [ISSN: 0906-6691] 1992. q. GBP 549. Ed(s): Asbjoern Voellestad, Javier Lobon-Cervia. Wiley-Blackwell Publishing, Inc., Commerce Pl, 350 Main St, Malden, MA 02148; info@wiley.com; http://onlinelibrary.wiley.com/. Illus., adv. Refereed. Reprint: PSC. *Indexed:* A01, A22, Agr, AnBeAb, C45, E01, IndVet, RRTA, S25. *Bk. rev.:* Number and length vary. *Aud.:* Ac, Sa.

Published quarterly, *Ecology of Freshwater Fish* publishes original articles on all aspects of fish ecology and fishery sciences in lakes, rivers, and estuaries. This journal publishes reports of studies, research papers, theoretical papers and studies, articles, letters, reviews, and proceedings of papers. Subjects include issues related to ecologically-oriented studies of behavior, genetics, and physiology and the conservation, development, and management of recreational and commercial fisheries. As many journals related to aquaculture deal primarily with oceanic fish life, this journal serves as a useful addition to the collections of researchers looking for information beyond the ecology of oceanic fish life.

2463. *Environmental Biology of Fishes*. [ISSN: 0378-1909] 1976. m. EUR 2983 (print & online eds.). Ed(s): David L G Noakes. Springer Netherlands, Van Godewijckstraat 30, Dordrecht, 3311 GX, Netherlands; http://www.springer.com. Adv. Refereed. Microform: PQC. Reprint: PSC. *Indexed:* A22, Agr, AnBeAb, BRI, C45, E01, IndVet, OceAb, RRTA, S25. *Bk. rev.:* Number and length vary. *Aud.:* Ac, Sa.

This monthly journal publishes original studies on the ecology, life history, epigenetics, behavior, physiology, morphology, and evolution of marine and freshwater fishes. It includes editorials, papers, brief communications, essays, and critical book reviews. This journal would be most useful for serious researchers studying aquaculture.

2464. *Fish and Fisheries*. [ISSN: 1467-2960] 2000. q. GBP 604. Ed(s): Paul J B Hart, Tony J Pitcher. Wiley-Blackwell Publishing Ltd., The Atrium, Southern Gate, Chichester, PO19 8SQ, United Kingdom; customer@wiley.com; http://www.wiley.com/. Adv. Sample. Refereed. Reprint: PSC. *Indexed:* A01, A22, Agr, C45, E01, IndVet, OceAb, RRTA. *Aud.:* Ac, Sa.

Taking an interdisciplinary approach to the subject of fish and fisheries, *Fish and Fisheries* provides critical synthesis of major physiological, molecular, ecological, and evolutionary issues relating to the interdisciplinary study of fish. It publishes discussion papers, review papers, commentaries, and letters that cover a wide range of research. Published quarterly, this journal aims to appeal to a wide range of people involved in all aspects of the study and conservation of fish, with coverage that is both interdisciplinary and global. *Fish and Fisheries* is a must-have for all of those interested in the biology, conservation, and exploitation of fish.

2465. *Fish Physiology & Biochemistry*. [ISSN: 0920-1742] 1986. 4x/yr. EUR 768 (print & online eds.). Ed(s): Patrick Kestemont. Springer Netherlands, Van Godewijckstraat 30, Dordrecht, 3311 GX, Netherlands; http://www.springer.com. Illus., index. Refereed. Vol. ends: No. 4. Reprint: PSC. *Indexed:* A22, Agr, C45, E01, IndVet, OceAb, RRTA, S25. *Aud.:* Ac, Sa.

Fish Physiology & Biochemistry publishes original research papers in all aspects of the physiology and biochemistry of fishes. Contents covered include experimental work in biochemistry and structure of organisms, organs, tissues, and cells, nutritional, osmotic, ionic, respiratory and excretory homeostasis, and more. It contains papers, brief communications, reviews, editorials, and announcements, and has an international audience. Additionally, this journal includes both invited and unsolicited reviews. With its international focus and its in-depth study of fish, this publication is a must-have title for researchers interested in physiology and biochemistry aspects of fish.

2466. *Fisheries*. Supersedes (in 1976): *American Fisheries Society. Newsletter.* [ISSN: 0363-2415] 1948. m. GBP 106. Ed(s): Beth Beard. American Fisheries Society, 5410 Grosvenor Ln, Ste 110, Bethesda, MD 20814; alerner@fisheries.org; http://www.fisheries.org. Illus., index, adv. Refereed. Circ: 9800 Paid. Vol. ends: No. 12. Reprint: PSC. *Indexed:* A01, A22, BRI, C45, IndVet, OceAb, RRTA. *Bk. rev.:* Number varies. *Aud.:* Ac, Sa.

Fisheries is the official trade magazine of the American Fisheries Society. It features peer-reviewed technical articles on all aspects of aquatic resource–related subjects. It focuses more on professional issues, new ideas and approaches, education, economics, administration, and law. Issues also contain AFS news, current events, book reviews, editorials, letters, job notices, chapter activities, and a calendar of events. It has more advertisements than other publications in this section. *Fisheries* offers an overview of the fisheries industry, but it is not focused on aquaculture research.

2467. *Fisheries Management and Ecology*. [ISSN: 0969-997X] 1994. bi-m. GBP 794. Ed(s): Hal Schramm, I Cowx. Wiley-Blackwell Publishing Ltd., The Atrium, Southern Gate, Chichester, PO19 8SQ, United Kingdom; customer@wiley.com; http://www.wiley.com/. Illus., index, adv. Sample. Refereed. Vol. ends: No. 4. Reprint: PSC. *Indexed:* A01, A22, Agr, C45, E01, IndVet, OceAb, RRTA, S25. *Bk. rev.:* Number and length vary. *Aud.:* Ac, Sa.

With an international perspective, *Fisheries Management and Ecology* presents papers that cover all aspects of the management, ecology, and conservation of inland, estuarine, and coastal fisheries. Published bimonthly, this journal publishes full research papers as well as management and ecological notes. It is best suited for people interested in fish conservation or those working with, or interested in working with, the management side of fisheries.

2468. *Fisheries Research*. [ISSN: 0165-7836] 1982. 18x/yr. EUR 2986. Ed(s): A D McIntyre. Elsevier BV, Radarweg 29, PO Box 211, Amsterdam, 1000 AE, Netherlands; JournalsCustomerServiceEMEA@elsevier.com; http://www.elsevier.nl. Illus., index, adv. Refereed. *Indexed:* A01, A22, C45, IndVet, OceAb, RRTA, S25. *Bk. rev.:* Number and length vary. *Aud.:* Ac, Sa.

Fisheries Research takes a multidisciplinary approach to the study of fish. It publishes papers in the areas of fisheries science, fishing technology, fisheries management, and relevant socioeconomics. It includes theoretical and practical papers as well as reviews and viewpoint articles. This publication is an important resource for fisheries scientists, biological oceanographers, gear technologists, economists, managers, administrators, policy makers, and legislators.

2469. *Fisheries Science*. [ISSN: 0919-9268] 1994. bi-m. EUR 777 (print & online eds.). Ed(s): Takafumi Arimoto. Springer Japan KK, No 2 Funato Bldg, 1-11-11 Kudan-kita, Tokyo, 102-0073, Japan; orders@springer.jp; http://www.springer.jp. Sample. Refereed. Circ: 5400. Reprint: PSC. *Indexed:* A01, A22, ABIn, Agr, C45, E01, FS&TA, IndVet, P02. *Aud.:* Ac, Sa.

Fisheries Science, a bimonthly journal, is the official publication of the Japanese Society of Fisheries Science. With a focus on Asia, and an emphasis on Japan, this journal covers the entire field of fisheries science. It includes original articles, short papers, and review articles on subjects like fisheries, biology, aquaculture, environment, chemistry and biochemistry, and food science and technology. It includes on average more than 180 articles per volume. Though it has a narrow geographical focus, the breadth of topics covered makes this journal an important publication in the field of aquaculture.

2470. *Fishery Bulletin.* Former titles (until 1971): *Fishery Bulletin of the Fish and Wildlife Service;* (until 1941): *Bureau of Fisheries. Bulletin;* (until 1904): *United States Fish Commission. Bulletin.* [ISSN: 0090-0656] 1881. q. USD 36 domestic; USD 50.40 foreign; USD 21 per issue domestic. Ed(s): Sharyn Matriotti. U.S. National Marine Fisheries Service, Scientific Publications Office, 7600 Sand Point Way, N E, Bin C15700, Seattle, WA 98115; http://spo.nwr.noaa.gov/. Illus. Refereed. Vol. ends: No. 4. Microform: PQC; NTI. *Indexed:* A01, A22, C45, FS&TA, IndVet, OceAb, RRTA, S25. *Aud.:* Ac, Sa.

Published quarterly by the National Oceanic and Atmospheric Administration (NOAA), *Fishery Bulletin* has existed since 1881. It is an official publication of the U.S. Government, under various titles, and is the U.S. counterpart to other highly regarded governmental fisheries-science publications. Though it includes articles and notes about other countries, this journal has a decidedly American point of view. The journal features both articles that reflect original research and interpretative articles for all interdisciplinary fields that bear on marine fisheries and marine mammal science. This is the most general of the fisheries-related journals published by NOAA, and it would be good for those interested in fisheries science in the United States.

2471. *Journal of Applied Aquaculture.* [ISSN: 1045-4438] 1992. q. GBP 494 (print & online eds.). Ed(s): Paul B Brown. Taylor & Francis Inc., 325 Chestnut St, Ste 800, Philadelphia, PA 19106; customerservice@taylorandfrancis.com; http://www.tandfonline.com. Illus., adv. Sample. Refereed. Circ: 181 Paid. Vol. ends: No. 4. Reprint: PSC. *Indexed:* A01, A22, Agr, C45, E01, FS&TA, IndVet, OceAb, RRTA. *Aud.:* Ac, Sa.

Published quarterly, this journal is a platform for the sharing of practical information needed by researchers to meet the needs of investors, farm managers, extension agents, and policy makers working to adapt aquaculture theory to achieve economic and food-security objectives in the real world. This journal contains both original research papers and process papers, and it occasionally publishes issues focused on a single subject. Examples of topics included in this journal are practical diet formulation and food conversion efficiencies, feed manufacturing, techniques to minimize stress, and techniques for the management of genetic quality in broodstock. This publication is more accessible to farmers and non-specialists (in addition to professional aquaculture researchers), because technical jargon is kept to a minimum, and tables and figures that facilitate comprehension are encouraged.

2472. *Journal of Applied Ichthyology (Print).* Incorporates: *Archive of Fishery and Marine Research.* [ISSN: 0175-8659] 1984. bi-m. GBP 734. Ed(s): D Schnack, Dr. H Rosenthal. Wiley-Blackwell Verlag GmbH, Kurfuerstendamm 57, Berlin, 10707, Germany; verlag@blackwell.de; http://www.blackwell.de. Index. Refereed. Circ: 340. Reprint: PSC. *Indexed:* A01, A22, Agr, C45, E01, FS&TA, IndVet, OceAb, RRTA. *Bk. rev.:* Number and length vary. *Aud.:* Ac, Sa.

Journal of Applied Ichthyology publishes papers that are oriented toward practical application rather than pure research. Topics covered include development and management of fisheries resources, ecotoxicology, genetics, and fisheries in developing countries. Emphasis is placed on the application of scientific research findings, while special consideration is given to ichthyological problems occurring in developing countries. Article formats include original articles, review articles, short communications, technical reports, and book reviews. With its international coverage and focus on the practical applications of aquaculture research, this journal would be good for people working in fisheries or those interested in learning about the practical side of aquaculture and fisheries.

2473. *Journal of Aquariculture and Aquatic Sciences.* Formerly (until 1982): *Journal of Aquariculture.* [ISSN: 0733-2076] 1980. irreg. USD 140 (Individuals, USD 70). Ed(s): John Farrell Kuhns. The Written Word, 7601 E Forest Lake Dr, N W, Parkville, MO 64152; JFK@compuserve.com. Illus., index, adv. Refereed. *Indexed:* S25. *Bk. rev.:* Number and length vary. *Aud.:* Ac, Sa.

Journal of Aquariculture and Aquatic Sciences publishes scientific papers, short communications, correspondence, and aids that are of interest to those studying both aquaculture and aquariculture. Topics covered in this journal will be of interest to those involved in all aspects of the field, including research scientists, aquarium curators, and breeders and farmers of fish. Although the journal is still active, irregular publication makes it hard to follow.

2474. *Journal of Aquatic Animal Health.* [ISSN: 0899-7659] 1989. q. GBP 265 (print & online eds.). Ed(s): Jeffrey C Wolf, Vicki S Blazer. American Fisheries Society, 5410 Grosvenor Ln, Ste 110, Bethesda, MD 20814; alerner@fisheries.org; http://www.fisheries.org. Illus., adv. Refereed. Reprint: PSC. *Indexed:* A22, C45, IndVet, OceAb. *Aud.:* Ac, Sa.

Journal of Aquatic Animal Health is a publication of the American Fisheries Society. It carries research papers on the causes, effects, treatments, and prevention of diseases of marine and freshwater organisms, particularly fish and shellfish. Published quarterly, it also examines the environmental and pathogenic aspects of fish and shellfish health. An important resource for those studying ichthyology.

2475. *Journal of Fish and Wildlife Management.* [ISSN: 1944-687X] 2010. s-a. Free. Ed(s): Dr. John Wenburg. U.S. Department of the Interior, Fish and Wildlife Service, Dept of the Interior, 1849 C St N W, Washington, DC 20240; fisheries@fws.gov; http://www.fws.gov. *Aud.:* Ac, Sa.

Journal of Fish and Wildlife Management is a freely accessible journal that covers the practical application and integration of science to conservation and management of native North American fish, wildlife, plants, and their habitats. Article types include articles, notes, surveys, and issues and perspectives. This journal would be of interest to those working in the practical aspect of fish and wildlife.

2476. *Journal of Fish Biology.* [ISSN: 0022-1112] 1969. 14x/yr. GBP 2519. Ed(s): J F Craig. Wiley-Blackwell Publishing Ltd., The Atrium, Southern Gate, Chichester, PO19 8SQ, United Kingdom; customer@wiley.com; http://www.wiley.com/. Illus., index, adv. Sample. Refereed. Reprint: PSC. *Indexed:* A01, A22, AnBeAb, C45, E01, FS&TA, IndVet, OceAb, RRTA. *Bk. rev.:* Number and length vary. *Aud.:* Ac, Sa.

Journal of Fish Biology, the official journal of the Fisheries Society of the British Isles, seeks to cover all aspects of fish biology research. This journal includes review articles and book reviews, and seeks papers of interest to those studying fish around the world. Topics covered include behavior, ecology, genetics, physiology, population studies, and toxicology. With its international scope and breadth of coverage, this journal is recommended for those engaged in research in nearly every area of aquaculture.

2477. *Journal of Fish Diseases.* [ISSN: 0140-7775] 1978. m. GBP 1507. Ed(s): R Wootten, R J Roberts. Wiley-Blackwell Publishing Ltd., The Atrium, Southern Gate, Chichester, PO19 8SQ, United Kingdom; customer@wiley.com; http://www.wiley.com/. Illus., index, adv. Sample. Refereed. Vol. ends: No. 9. Microform: PQC. Reprint: PSC. *Indexed:* A01, A22, Agr, C45, E01, IndVet, OceAb. *Bk. rev.:* Number and length vary. *Aud.:* Ac, Sa.

Journal of Fish Diseases is the premier journal dedicated to the diseases of fish and shellfish. This journal is international in its coverage of disease in wild and cultured fish and shellfish. Published monthly, *Journal of Fish Diseases* includes review articles, short communications, scientific papers, and book reviews. Areas of interest regularly covered by the journal include host–pathogen relationships, studies of fish pathogens, pathophysiology, diagnostic methods, therapy, epidemiology, and descriptions of new diseases. This title would be useful to environmental researchers or fish pathologists.

2478. *Journal of Fisheries and Aquaculture.* [ISSN: 0976-9927] 2010. s-a. USD 425. Ed(s): Dr. Yeong Yik Sung. Bioinfo Publications, B-23/7, Kendriya Vihar, Sector-11, Kharghar, Navi Mumbai, 410 210, India; editor@bioinfo.in; http://www.bioinfo.in. Refereed. *Indexed:* A01, C45. *Aud.:* Ac, Sa.

The Journal of Fisheries and Aquaculture publishes all the latest and outstanding research articles, reviews, and letters in all areas of fisheries and aquaculture. Each issue contains a series of timely, in-depth articles by leaders in the field, covering a wide range of the integration of multidimensional challenges of research, including integration issues regarding fisheries and aquaculture. Because of its wide coverage, researchers may find it useful, as well as people interested in fisheries and aquaculture.

2479. *The Journal of Shellfish Research.* Formerly (until 1981): *National Shellfisheries Association. Proceedings;* Which superseded (in 1954): *National Shellfisheries Association. Papers Delivered at the Convention;* Which was formerly (until 1953): *National Shellfisheries Association. Addresses Delivered at the Convention;* (until 1947): *National Association of Fisheries Comissioners. Minutes of the ... Annual Convention.* [ISSN: 0730-8000] 1981. 3x/yr. USD 293 Free to members. Ed(s): Sandra E Shumway. National Shellfisheries Association, Inc., PO Box 465, Hanover, PA 17331; pubsvc@tsp.sheridan.com; http://www.shellfish.org/. Illus., index. Refereed. *Indexed:* A22, C45, IndVet, OceAb, RRTA. *Aud.:* Ac, Sa.

As the name implies, *The Journal of Shellfish Research* focuses solely on research related to shellfish. It is the official publication of the National Shellfisheries Association. Areas of research covered in this journal include aquaculture, biology, ecology, and management. Published three times per year, with an occasional special issue, this journal often includes abstracts of technical papers presented at conferences related to shellfish research. The journal targets individuals interested in basic research, commercial production, and resource management.

2480. *Marine Fisheries Review.* Former titles (until 1972): *Commercial Fisheries Review;* (until 1946): *Fishery Market News.* [ISSN: 0090-1830] 1939. q. USD 21 domestic; USD 29.40 foreign; USD 12 per issue domestic. U.S. National Marine Fisheries Service, Scientific Publications Office, 7600 Sand Point Way, N E, Bin C15700, Seattle, WA 98115; http://spo.nwr.noaa.gov/. Illus., index. Refereed. Vol. ends: No. 4. Microform: CIS; NTI. *Indexed:* A01, A22, AmStI, B01, B02, BRI, FS&TA, OceAb, S25. *Aud.:* Ac, Sa.

An official publication of the U.S. government since 1939, *Marine Fisheries Review* focuses on applied aspects of marine fisheries. It publishes review articles, research reports, significant progress reports, technical notes, and news articles on fisheries science, engineering and economics, commercial and recreational fisheries, marine mammal studies, aquaculture, and U.S. and foreign fisheries developments. Emphasis, however, is on in-depth review articles and practical or applied aspects of marine fisheries, rather than pure research. This journal's focus on practical application means that it might not be useful for biologists or researchers. It would, however, be a good resource for those looking to get into the fisheries business for fun or profit.

2481. *North American Journal of Aquaculture.* Formerly (until 1999): *Progressive Fish-Culturist;* Which incorporated (1935-1937): *Fish Culture.* [ISSN: 1522-2055] 1934. q. GBP 265 (print & online eds.). Ed(s): Christopher C Kohler, Bruce A Barton. American Fisheries Society, 5410 Grosvenor Ln, Ste 110, Bethesda, MD 20814; alerner@fisheries.org; http://www.fisheries.org. Illus., index, adv. Refereed. Vol. ends: No. 4. Microform: PQC. Reprint: PSC. *Indexed:* A22, C45, IndVet, OceAb, RRTA, S25. *Bk. rev.:* Number and length vary. *Aud.:* Ac, Sa.

The North American Journal of Aquaculture is a quarterly journal that publishes research in all areas of fish culture. This international journal carries papers on all areas of fish and other aquatic organisms. It covers a wide range of topics, including nutrition and feeding, broodstock selection and spawning, drugs and chemicals, and health and water quality. This journal is an excellent resource for researchers interested in aquaculture in North America and the global aquaculture community.

2482. *North American Journal of Fisheries Management.* [ISSN: 0275-5947] 1981. bi-m. Individuals, USD 43. Ed(s): Carolyn A Griswold, Stephen C Riley. American Fisheries Society, 5410 Grosvenor Ln, Ste 110, Bethesda, MD 20814; alerner@fisheries.org; http://www.fisheries.org. Illus., index, adv. Refereed. Vol. ends: No. 4. Reprint: PSC. *Indexed:* A22, AnBeAb, C45, OceAb, S25. *Aud.:* Ac, Sa.

North American Journal of Fisheries Management is published bimonthly to promote communication between managers of both marine and freshwater fisheries. An official journal of American Fisheries Society, this title covers the maintenance, enhancement, and allocation of fisheries resources. The journal documents successes and failures of fisheries programs and explores ways in which fisheries can be managed to best protect fish and fisheries resources. It helps convey practical management experience to others. With a focus on fishery best practices, it will appeal to those running fisheries.

2483. *Reviews in Aquaculture (Online).* [ISSN: 1753-5131] 2009. q. GBP 386. Ed(s): Albert Tacon, Sena De Silva. John Wiley & Sons, Inc., 111 River St, MS 4-02, Hoboken, NJ 07030; http://www.wiley.com. Refereed. *Aud.:* Ac, Sa.

Published quarterly, *Reviews in Aquaculture* contains peer-reviewed articles that relate to all aspects of aquaculture. Subjects covered include market trends, genetics and aquaculture, aquaculture practices, biology and culture of species, health management, and policy development. Though it is limited in the types of material it publishes, this journal attempts to be comprehensive in its coverage of the field of aquaculture. *Reviews in Aquaculture* would be most useful to scientists and aquaculturalists interested in keeping current on the latest research developments in the field.

2484. *Reviews in Fish Biology and Fisheries.* [ISSN: 0960-3166] q. EUR 1011 (print & online eds.). Ed(s): Jennifer L Nielsen. Springer Netherlands, Van Godewijckstraat 30, Dordrecht, 3311 GX, Netherlands; http://www.springer.com. Adv. Refereed. Reprint: PSC. *Indexed:* A01, A22, ABIn, Agr, AnBeAb, BRI, C45, E01, IndVet, OceAb, RRTA. *Bk. rev.:* Number and length vary. *Aud.:* Ac, Sa.

Of all the academic journals in this section, this may be the most accessible. Published quarterly, *Reviews in Fish Biology and Fisheries* is an international journal that publishes review articles on varied aspects of fish and fisheries biology. It also includes book reviews, correspondence, and accounts of relevant papers delivered at conferences. Topics include evolutionary biology, taxonomy, stock identification, genetics, functional morphology, fisheries development, and exploitation and conservation. This journal's audience is those in the field of aquaculture and those with an interest in biology but not necessarily aquaculture. This journal would be useful to a wide range of people, from the general population to the seasoned academic researcher.

2485. *Reviews in Fisheries Science.* [ISSN: 1064-1262] 1993. q. GBP 817 (print & online eds.). Ed(s): Sandra E Shumway. Taylor & Francis Inc., 325 Chestnut St, Ste 800, Philadelphia, PA 19106; customerservice@taylorandfrancis.com; http://www.tandfonline.com. Illus., index. Sample. Refereed. Vol. ends: No. 4. Reprint: PSC. *Indexed:* A01, A22, C&ISA, C45, CerAb, E01, IndVet, OceAb, P02, RRTA. *Bk. rev.:* Number and length vary. *Aud.:* Ac, Sa.

Published quarterly, *Reviews in Fisheries Science* covers nearly every aspect of aquaculture. It provides an important forum for the publication of up-to-date reviews that cover the broad range of subject areas in fisheries science. These areas include management, aquaculture, taxonomy, behavior, stock identification, genetics, nutrition, and physiology. This publication includes reviews, historical articles, and original research. Because of its broad scope and its commitment to covering the current issues of interest to those studying aquaculture, this publication is essential for serious researchers in the field, as well as those interested in learning more about aquaculture.

Tropical Fish Hobbyist. See Pets section.

2486. *World Aquaculture Society. Journal.* Former titles (until 1986): *World Mariculture Society. Journal;* (until 1981): *World Mariculture Society. Proceedings;* (until 1974): *World Mariculture Society. Proceedings of the Annual Meeting;* (until 19??): *World Mariculture*

Society. *Proceedings of the Annual Workshop.* [ISSN: 0893-8849] 1986. bi-m. GBP 278. Ed(s): Carl Webster. Wiley-Blackwell Publishing, Inc., 111 River St, Hoboken, NJ 07030; info@wiley.com; http://onlinelibrary.wiley.com/. Illus., adv. Sample. Refereed. Vol. ends: No. 4. Reprint: PSC. *Indexed:* A22, Agr, C45, E01, IndVet, OceAb, RRTA. *Aud.:* Ac, Sa.

This is the official journal of the World Aquaculture Society, an international organization with over 2,500 members in over 80 countries. The journal contains review and research articles, communications, and research notes all focused on the culture of aquatic plants and animals. Topic covers nutrition, disease, genetics and breeding, physiology, environmental quality, culture systems engineering, husbandry practices, and economics and marketing, as well as a number of other topics related to the culture of aquatic organisms. Though the articles in this journal are aimed at academics, the broad range of topics covered and the global coverage make it accessible to those wishing to get a big-picture understanding of the field of aquaculture.

■ FISHING

Michael R. Blake, *Digital Resources Librarian and Assistant Librarian of the John G. Wolbach Library of the Harvard-Smithsonian Center for Astrophysics, 60 Garden Street, Cambridge, MA 02138*

Introduction

There are many different types of fishing, and consequently a rather large number of fishing magazines available to the curious of mind, the general reader, the sports enthusiast, and the dedicated fisher. Whether it is bait fishing with a homemade cane pole and bobber, spin fishing with a Mepps or Rapala lure, gigging in the shallows for flounder, traveling to the next state over to noodle for flatheads or to exotic places to fly fish with flies, or heading out to the deep blue sea with 50-pound wire leaders to fish for sailfish and marlin, there is a title available to prepare you for the time of your life.

Fishing magazines can usually be categorized into three types; general, geographic, or focused on a single type of species or type of fishing. General titles include *Field & Stream, Outdoor Life, Gray's Sporting Journal,* and *Sport Fishing.* Geographic titles include over 20 state fish-and-game titles by Intermedia Outdoors, such as *New England Game & Fish* or *Oklahoma Fish and Game* and *Eastern Fly Fishing.* Titles that focus on a single type of species or type of fishing include *Musky Hunter* and *Fly Tyer,* just to name a few. Many fishing groups and organizations have their own publications; the Federation of Fly Fishers has *Flyfisher,* and the American Museum of Fly Fishing has *The American Fly Fisher.*

Since the last edition of *Magazines for Libraries,* many fishing titles have ceased publication. The printed magazine market is shrinking. Some titles are surviving by consolidating with other titles, while others are migrating to an online venue.

Many well-regarded titles have a companion web presence. The online editions take full advantage of the electronic environment and add music, video, photographs, and links to additional content not available in print, such as tutorials with step-by-step procedures to tie the latest hatch fly on a given river.

There are new fishing "magazines" available only electronically. One title, *Catch Magazine,* located at www.catchmagazine.net, is worth mentioning. With the subtitle *Official Journal of Fly Fishing Photography & Film,* it presents beautiful images, both still and in motion.

The titles listed in this section are recommended for public libraries or for personal subscription.

Basic Periodicals

Ems: *Field & Stream, Outdoor Life;* Hs, Ga, Ac: *American Fly Fisher, Fly Fisherman, Gray's Sporting Journal.*

Basic Abstracts and Indexes

MasterFILE Premier.

2487. American Angler. Former titles (until 1991): *American Angler and Fly Tyer;* (until 1988): *Fly Tyer.* [ISSN: 1055-6737] 1978. bi-m. USD 19.95 combined subscription domestic (print & online eds); USD 29.95 combined subscription Canada (print & online eds); USD 39.95 combined subscription elsewhere (print & online eds). Ed(s): Russ Lumpkin, Phil Monahan. Morris Multimedia, Inc., PO Box 34, Boulder, CO 80329; http://www.morris.com. Circ: 41164 Paid. *Bk. rev.:* 5-8; 150-200 words. *Aud.:* Hs, Sa.

Anyone wishing to become a fly fisher, or those expert in the field, will find *American Angler* the first publication encountered. Dedicated to fly fishers and fly tyers of all levels, the magazine focuses on trout and salmon. There are occasionally articles on warm water and saltwater species. Regular contributors are fly fishing authorities. Columns and departments cover every aspect of fly fishing, conservation updates, and new gear. Where and how to fish are features in every issue. Articles are well written, enjoyable, and accompanied by fine photo illustrations. An online equivalent contains extra content and online forums expanding the coverage of the print. A must-have for all libraries that serve a fly fishing population.

2488. American Fly Fisher. 1974. q. Free. Ed(s): Kate Achor. The American Museum of Fly Fishing, 4104 Main St, Manchester, VT 05254; amff@amff.com; http://www.amff.com/. *Bk. rev.:* Number and length vary. *Aud.:* Hs, Ga, Ac, Sa.

American Fly Fisher is a research-level magazine published by the American Museum of Fly Fishing in Manchester, Vermont. Each issue contains three or four in-depth articles, and may contain "Notes from the Library," obituaries, book reviews, and "Museum News." This magazine presents the history of fly fishing, rod building, fly tying, club histories, and fisher biographies. The in-depth articles are well written, are usually illustrated with period images, and frequently provide a long list of end notes. Recommended for libraries that support history and fly fishers.

2489. Bassmaster Magazine. [ISSN: 0199-3291] 1968. 11x/yr. USD 25. E S P N Publishing, Inc., PO Box 10000, Lake Buena Vista, FL 32830. Illus., adv. Circ: 600000 Paid. *Aud.:* Hs, Ga.

Bassmaster focuses on all aspects of bass fishing. The boats, the rods, the tackle, and the tournaments are given in-depth coverage. Regular departments present tackle tips, fishing strategies, advice from fishing professionals, moon charts, best spots to fish, and cartoons. This magazine covers the infectious enthusiasm bass fishers have for their sport. Recommended for any library.

2490. Eastern Fly Fishing. 2005. bi-m. USD 29.95 domestic; USD 36.95 Canada; USD 44.95 elsewhere. Ed(s): Steve Probasco, John Shewey. Northwest Fly Fishing, LLC., PO Box 12275, Salem, OR 97309; http://www.matchthehatch.com/. Adv. Circ: 30457 Paid. *Aud.:* Hs, Ga, Ac, Sa.

Eastern Fly Fishing provides very detailed articles on fishing locations. Although the title says "Eastern," the coverage of geographic areas is much more expansive. Each issue contains four to eight features, instructions for tying several flies, and a photographic essay. Recently the editors added a section titled "Urban Angler." Each feature article details a location with a map, launching sites, a popular fly for the location, instructions to complete the fly on your own, and a story about the place. The "Urban Angler" articles start from a city, using it as a hub, then branching out to explore all the local and not-too-distant waters available to the fisher. Sidebars provide restaurant reviews, pubs, local attractions, and points of interest. The magazine provides detailed information to help create a great fishing experience. The title has now added more flies and fly tying instructions. Recommended for any "Eastern" library.

Field & Stream. See Hunting and Guns section.

2491. Fish & Fly: for the adventure angler. [ISSN: 1535-6353] 4x/yr. USD 16.95 domestic; USD 24.95 Canada; USD 36.95 elsewhere. Ed(s): Thomas R Pero. Turnstile Publishing Company, 1500 Park Center Dr, Orlando, FL 32835. Adv. Sample. *Aud.:* Hs, Ga.

Heavily illustrated feature articles cover four main topics from all over the world: trout, steelhead, salmon, and saltwater. The in-depth articles focus on places to catch fish, fishing essays, interviews, fly tying, recipes for flies, and stories. Departments include "Feature Fly," "Home Waters," letters, and angling literature. Frequently included are short pieces on angling history. Recommended for libraries with fly fishing enthusiasts.

2492. Fly Fusion: North America's fly-fishing authority. [ISSN: 1916-1034] 2004. q. CAD 24.95 domestic; USD 23.85 United States; USD 35.85 elsewhere. Ed(s): Derek Bird. Fly Fusion Ltd., 100, 2250 - 162 Ave SW, PO Box 24030, Calgary, AB T2Y 0J9, Canada. Adv. Circ: 72000 Paid. *Aud.:* Ac, Ga, Sa.

Dedicated to fly fishers and fly tyers of all levels, *FlyFusion* provides well written articles accompanied by fine photography. Where and how to fish are features in each issue, along with "Profiles" of well-known fly fishing enthusiasts. This Canadian publication provides a unique look from across the border.

2493. Fly Rod & Reel. Formerly (until 1989): *Rod and Reel.* [ISSN: 1045-0149] 1979. q. USD 23.95 domestic; USD 33.95 foreign; USD 6.99 per issue. Down East Enterprise, Inc., PO Box 679, Camden, ME 04843. Illus., adv. Sample. Vol. ends: Dec. *Bk. rev.:* 3-4; 200-400 words. *Aud.:* Hs, Ga.

Fly Rod & Reel is a stable, high-quality magazine that primarily covers the Americas. Each issue offers four to eight feature articles. All subjects related to fly fishing are covered. Issues rotate features among fishing techniques, useful gear, and flies. Regular departments include "Salt Water," letters, casting techniques, conservation news, new gear, fly tying, and essays. Each issue contains well-written book reviews. Although the dominant subject is fly fishing, this title contains advice suitable for any angler.

2494. The Flyfish Journal. [ISSN: 1947-4539] 2009. q. USD 39.99 domestic; USD 50.99 per issue Canada; USD 89.99 per issue elsewhere. Ed(s): Ben Romans. Funny Feelings, LLC, PO Box 2806, Bellingham, WA 98227; http://www.funnyfeelingsllc.com. Illus., adv. *Aud.:* Hs, Ga.

An addition to any fly fisher's collection, indeed any fisher's collection, this title is for anyone trying to learn the sport, from those looking for the next exotic place to land that unusual fish, to the armchair angler interested in a fictional respite. *The Flyfish Journal* is beautiful! Have it on your shelves for the avid fly fisher or for the general public. Articles cover all species of fish from the traditional trout and salmon, to the exotic Peacock Bass or Manchurian Trout. Each issue begins with five to seven gorgeous photographs, and continues throughout with high-quality images and text that feeds the reader's obsession. Well worth the yearly subscription.

2495. Musky Hunter. Formerly (until 19??): *Musky Hunter Magazine.* [ISSN: 1079-3402] 1989. bi-m. USD 21.95 domestic; USD 24.95 foreign; USD 7 per issue. Ed(s): Jim Saric. Esox Promotions, Inc, 7978 Hwy 70 E, PO Box 340, St Germain, WI 54558. Adv. *Aud.:* Hs, Sa.

Devoted to the musky-fishing enthusiast, this specialized title focuses on fishing for the elusive muskellunge. Containing eight to ten feature articles and multiple departments, each issue entices the fisher with fishing methods, new gear, tournament catches, and larger-than-life pictures. "Lure Doctor" and "Joe Bucher's Moon Secrets" are two sections that provide fishing information for just this species. Since this fish is found in northern areas of the United States or in Canada, this area is the title's primary market. Recommended for libraries near the northern waters and down the Mississippi and Ohio River valleys, wherever the muskellunge are found.

Outdoor Life. See Hiking, Climbing, and Outdoor Recreation section.

Tropical Fish Hobbyist. See Pets section.

2496. Trout. [ISSN: 0041-3364] 1959. q. Free to members. Ed(s): Steven R Kinsella. Trout Unlimited, 1300 N 17th St, Ste 500, Arlington, VA 22209; trout@tu.org; http://www.tu.org/. Illus., adv. Circ: 125000 Paid. *Aud.:* Hs, Ga, Ac, Sa.

Trout provides in-depth articles that cover every aspect of trout, salmon, and coldwater fisheries. Articles on the restoration of habitats, removal of dams, and the workings of Trout Unlimited are included in six to eight feature articles.

Profiles of great fishers, well-known fishing writers, and artists are provided in features, as well as department essays such as "The Art of Angling" and "Native Fish." Recommended for any coldwater fishing enthusiast.

■ FOLKLORE

Jean Piper Burton, Technical Services Librarian, FH Green Library, West Chester University of Pennsylvania, West Chester, PA 19383

Introduction

Folklore can be defined as cultural materials that are part of a group of people and are passed by oral communication, customary example, and imitation. Folk traditions can be a part of many generations, or of recent developments in pop culture. Because everyone is part of some folk culture group, there is interest in the subject on the part of both layperson and scholar.

To accommodate both the general reader and the researcher, there are a wide variety of publications with differing scopes. Some of the titles are concerned with a specific geographic area, some take a historical perspective, and some are research oriented. The titles reviewed here try to represent this variety. In recent years there has been an ever-increasing volume of folklore resources on the web. Most societies and many individual folklorists have their own web page. Some of the journals can be found in e-format but require a paid subscription. Articles from some of the titles are available as full text through electronic indexing services.

The journals described below as electronic journals are samples of e-journals in the area of folklore. They were selected as samples because they are published by known institutions, provide content through free access, and indicate continuing activity. An excellent portal that will connect to both free and fee-based journals, as well as related web sites, is Open Folklore (www.openfolklore.org).

Basic Periodicals

Hs: *The Foxfire Magazine;* Ga: *Journal of American Culture, Storytelling Magazine;* Ac: *Ethnologies, Folklore, Journal of American Folklore, Journal of Folklore Research.*

Basic Abstracts and Indexes

America: History and Life, Historical Abstracts, Humanities Index, MLA International Bibliography.

2497. Asian Ethnology. Former titles (until 200?): *Asian Folklore Studies;* (until 1963): *Folklore Studies.* [ISSN: 1882-6865] 1942. s-a. JPY 6000 (Individuals, JPY 3000). Nanzan University, Anthropological Institute, 18 Yamazato-cho, Showa-ku, Nagoya, 466-8673, Japan; nuai@ic.nanzan-u.ac.jp; http://www.nanzan-u.ac.jp/JINRUIKEN/index.html. Illus., adv. Refereed. Circ: 350. Vol. ends: No. 2. Microform: IDC. *Indexed:* A01, A22, A47, AmHI, ArtHuCI, BAS, BRI, ENW, FR, IBSS, MLA-IB, P02, RILM. *Bk. rev.:* 30, 1,000 words. *Aud.:* Ac.

This journal publishes scholarly research on the folklore of Asian nations, including literary works and the oral tradition; it also discusses folkloric aspects of belief, cultural customs, and art. The journal includes scholarly articles, research materials, communications, and lengthy book reviews. Some of the articles are purely descriptive accounts or retellings of folk tales; others are more analytic, based on research, including surveys and textual analysis or comparative study. Recent topics are ritual practice and environmental changes, Korean cinema as viewed by different social classes, and pop ghazal music. Some issues are thematic. Abstracts are included. Back issues are accessible online from the journal's web site. Recommended for academic libraries with an interest in Asian literature or arts, folklore, or children's literature.

2498. Children's Folklore Review. Formerly (until 1988): *The Children's Folklore Newsletter.* 1979. a. Free to members. Ed(s): Elizabeth Tucker. Binghamton University, Department of English, PO Box 6000, Binghamton, NY 13902; info@binghamton.edu; http://www2.binghamton.edu/english. *Indexed:* MLA-IB. *Bk. rev.:* Number and length vary. *Aud.:* Ga, Ac.

Published by the Children's Folklore Section of the American Folklore Society, this title covers "all aspects of children's traditions: oral, customary, and material." Articles may also deal with the use of folklore in children's literature, education, and pop culture. Issues contain articles and book reviews. It appears that there is only one issue per year, as indicated on the journal's web site; however, the publisher is trying to post past issues on the web. There is also an e-newsletter available on the web site that contains news of the Society and its members, plus a lengthy editorial. The most recent topic was children's games and hiking narratives. This is a good title for those doing research in children and folklore, especially since titles that deal strictly with children's lore are not plentiful. It is also a good source for those working in critical review of children's literature as a genre.

2499. Craft + Design Enquiry. [ISSN: 1837-445X] a. Free. Ed(s): Jenny Deves. Craft Australia Research Centre, Ste.7, Level 1, The National Press Club, 16 National Circuit, Barton, ACT 2600, Australia. Refereed. *Indexed:* A07. *Bk. rev.:* Number and length vary. *Aud.:* Ac.

Published by the Craft Research Center of Australia, this is an open-access journal. The scope includes articles on all areas of craft and design practices. From its publishing history, this journal appears to be a recent online creation. It is published annually, and contributions are peer-reviewed. Issues are thematic and have included migratory practices, cross-cultural exchange, and sustainability. It is a worthwhile title for those interested in design as well as folklore.

2500. Cultural Analysis: an interdisciplinary forum on folklore and popular culture. [ISSN: 1537-7873] 2000. irreg. Free. Cultural Analysis, University of California at Berkeley, 232 Kroeber Hall, Berkeley, CA 94720. Refereed. *Indexed:* BRI, RILM. *Aud.:* Ac.

This is an "interdisciplinary, peer-reviewed journal dedicated to investigating expressive and everyday culture." The electronic journal includes research articles, notes, reviews, and responses. It is designed to be cross-disciplinary and international in scope, with approximately one volume per year. Available free on the web, the journal is produced in both html and pdf formats, but publication of new issues can be erratic. Some feature articles are followed by critics' responses. Articles cover topics from many world cultures. Each article is abstracted. Reviews average 1,500 to 2,000 words. Some issues are thematic. One of the strengths of this publication is its diversity of authorship, with contributors from around the world. This journal seems to have developed a solid foundation for web access. Recommended for academic libraries with cultural studies programs. URL: http://socrates.berkeley.edu/~caforum

2501. Ethnologies. Formerly (until 1998): *Canadian Folklore.* [ISSN: 1481-5974] 1979. s-a. Free to members. Ed(s): Laurier Turgeon. Folklore Studies Association of Canada, 12 Tessier Pl, St. John's, NF A1C 1X1, Canada; cfc@celat.ulaval.ca; http://www.celat.ulaval.ca/acef/learn.htm. Illus., adv. Refereed. Vol. ends: No. 2. *Indexed:* AmHI, BRI, C37, CBCARef, IBSS, MLA-IB, RILM. *Bk. rev.:* Number and length vary. *Aud.:* Ac.

This journal is published by the Folklore Studies Association of Canada, and each issue is devoted to a specific topic. Themes are wide ranging, from the historic and traditional to current trends in the field. The most recent issue dealt with tourism. In the copies reviewed, the number of articles in French and in English varied, but abstracts for each article were in both languages. The current issue is listed on the web page, and introduction and abstracts for each article are available for viewing. However, accessing the full journal requires a subscription, and the journal is now issued biannually. Current issues listed on the web are dated 2010. Links to past issues were dead links. This title is for academic libraries that support folk studies programs and for large public libraries with strong folk and culture collections, particularly with an interest in Canadian folklore.

2502. Folklore. Formed by the merger of (1888-1890): *Archaeological Review;* (1883-1890): *The Folk-Lore Journal;* Which was formerly (1878-1883): *The Folk-Lore Record.* [ISSN: 0015-587X] 1890. 3x/yr. GBP 372 (print & online eds.). Ed(s): Patricia Lysaght. Routledge, 4 Park Sq, Milton Park, Abingdon, OX14 4RN, United Kingdom; subscriptions@tandf.co.uk; http://www.tandfonline.com. Illus., adv. Sample. Refereed. Microform: PMC. Reprint: PSC. *Indexed:* A01, A22, A47, AbAn, AmHI, ArtHuCI, BEL&L, BRI, BrArAb, E01, FR, IBSS, MLA-IB, NumL, P02, P61, RILM, SSA. *Bk. rev.:* 20, 500-700 words. *Aud.:* Ac.

A British publication, this scholarly journal considers itself a forum for European folk studies and culture, but also includes some articles on American folklore. Topics in recent issues include: popular Scottish songs; childrens' role in house blessings; spirits and stone; and outlaw legends and modern American lore. In addition to articles, some issues include papers from meetings of the Folklore Society. Bibliographies, articles on recipients of awards in the field, and book reviews may also be included. For libraries that provide research materials in the area of folk studies.

2503. Folklore. [ISSN: 1406-0949] 1996. q. Free. Ed(s): Andres Kuperjanov, Mare Koiva. Eesti Kirjandusmuuseum, Vanemuise St 42-235, Tartu, 51003, Estonia; kirmus@kirmus.ee; http://www.kirmus.ee/. Illus. Refereed. *Indexed:* AbAn, MLA-IB. *Bk. rev.:* Number and length vary. *Aud.:* Ga, Ac.

This journal is the publication of the Folklore Department of the Institute of the Estonian Language and is not to be confused with the British Folklore Society's journal of the same name. Articles cover a wide variety of topics, and some issues are thematic. Some issues include book reviews and news. There is a special emphasis on Estonia and neighboring regions. The real appeal is the free electronic version of this publication. Articles are done as pdf files, to provide illustrations as well as text. There is online access to both current and back issues. An editorial note welcomes contributors from all countries and contributions on all aspects of folklore. Submission guidelines include a listing of software requirements. This is a worthy journal and one of the better ones with full online access. It has a strong record of continuing publication. Recommended for academic and general adult readers. URL: www.folklore.ee/folklore

2504. Folklore Forum (Online). Formerly (until 2004): *Folklore Forum (Print).* 1968. s-a. Free. Ed(s): Tabatha Lingerfelt, Monica Foote. Folklore & Ethnomusicology Publications, Inc., 504 N Fess Ave, Bloomington, IN 47408; folkpub@indiana.edu; https://www.indiana.edu/~folkpub/. Illus., adv. Refereed. Vol. ends: No. 2. *Indexed:* ABS&EES, AmHI, BAS, MLA-IB, RILM. *Bk. rev.:* 5-7, 500-600 words. *Aud.:* Ac.

As defined on the web site, "Folklore Forum is a space for the free exchange of ideas on the cutting edge of folklore, folklife[,] and ethnomusicology, [and] a space where up-and-coming scholars can interrogate existing paradigms and cultivate a rich intellectual landscape with a multi-disciplinary perspective." This journal has morphed to a more web-friendly form. Abstract of articles and reviews are posted on the main page, with links to full views. Each entry is tagged, and there is ability to post comments. Back issues of the print journal are available under the archives link. Some issues are thematic, and recent issues contain more book reviews than articles. Considering that this is a free forum for current topics in folklore research and book reviews, it is a good addition for libraries with interest in folklore. URL: http://folkloreforum.net/

The Foxfire Magazine. See Teenagers section.

2505. Journal of American Culture. Former titles (until 2003): *Journal of American and Comparative Culture;* (until 2000): *Journal of American Culture.* [ISSN: 1542-7331] 1978. q. GBP 197. Ed(s): Kathy Merlock Jackson. Wiley-Blackwell Publishing, Inc., 111 River St, Hoboken, NJ 07030; info@wiley.com; http://onlinelibrary.wiley.com/. Illus., adv. Sample. Refereed. Vol. ends: No. 4. Microform: PQC. Reprint: PSC. *Indexed:* A01, A22, ABS&EES, AmHI, BRI, CBRI, E01, F01, IIMP, IIPA, MLA-IB, P02, P61, RILM, SSA. *Bk. rev.:* 20-30, 300-500 words. *Aud.:* Ga, Ac.

As the official journal of the American Cultural Association, this publication intends to "promote and facilitate American culture in its broadest sense." There is a mix of historic and present-day material. Articles cover traditional folklore themes and pop culture. Topics in recent issues have included tattoos, the lore of Johnny Appleseed, and vampire lovers in popular novels. Some issues are thematic. Most issues include a few essays and short book reviews. With its wide variety of topics and accessible writing style, this title will be of interest to the general reader and the student of folklore or popular culture.

2506. *Journal of American Folklore.* [ISSN: 0021-8715] 1888. q. USD 175 (print & online eds.). Ed(s): Giovanna P Del Negro, Harris M Berger. University of Illinois Press, 1325 S Oak St, Champaign, IL 61820; journals@uillinois.edu; http://www.press.uillinois.edu. Illus., index, adv. Refereed. Vol. ends: No. 4. Microform: MIM; PMC; PQC. *Indexed:* A01, A07, A22, A47, ABS&EES, AmHI, ArtHuCI, BEL&L, BRI, CBRI, Chicano, E01, FR, IIMP, IIPA, MLA-IB, P02, P61, RILM, SSA. *Bk. rev.:* 10, 500-700 words. *Aud.:* Ga, Ac.

As the official publication of the American Folklore Society, this journal puts an emphasis on the United States. However, the scope of this journal is worldwide and varied. Articles past and present include such topics as legends of Hurricane Katrina, bridal lamentations in China, and scrapbooking. Occasional issues are devoted to a single theme. Reviews are lengthy and cover both books and media; there is also a section titled creative writing that features original works. One of journal's goals is to "push the boundaries, explore the borders, and expand the parameters of folklore." Academic libraries should select this title for their basic collection, and large public libraries will also want to consider it.

2507. *Journal of Cultural Geography.* [ISSN: 0887-3631] 1980. 3x/yr. GBP 137 (print & online eds.). Ed(s): Alyson L Greiner. Routledge, 325 Chestnut St, Ste 800, Philadelphia, PA 19106; customerservice@taylorandfrancis.com; http://www.tandfonline.com. Illus., adv. Sample. Refereed. Vol. ends: No. 2. Reprint: PSC. *Indexed:* A01, A22, BAS, BRI, C45, E01, FR, IBSS, MLA-IB, RILM. *Bk. rev.:* 12, 400-500 words. *Aud.:* Ac.

This journal's articles discuss the influences of culture on the physical world. Topics vary widely, from the historic to current pop culture. Recent topics have included Inuit economics, Maroi geographical self, local travelers, and theme parks. Some issues are thematic. Most contributors are professors or graduate students. In addition to articles, there are book reviews and occasional annotated bibliographies. This title should appeal to a wide variety of readers. A good pick for academic libraries and larger public libraries.

2508. *Journal of Folklore Research: an international journal of folklore and ethnomusicology.* Former titles (until 1983): *Folklore Institute. Journal;* (until 1964): *Midwest Folklore;* (until 1951): *Hoosier Folklore;* (until 1946): *Hoosier Folklore Bulletin.* [ISSN: 0737-7037] 1942. 3x/yr. USD 90.75 (print & online eds.). Ed(s): Moira Smith. Indiana University Press, 601 N Morton St, Bloomington, IN 47404; journals@indiana.edu; http://iupress.indiana.edu. Illus., index, adv. Refereed. Circ: 450. Vol. ends: No. 3. Microform: PQC. Reprint: PSC. *Indexed:* A01, A22, A47, AmHI, ArtHuCI, BEL&L, BRI, E01, FR, IBSS, IIMP, IIPA, MLA-IB, P61, RILM, SSA. *Bk. rev.:* Number and length vary. *Aud.:* Ac.

"Devoted to the study of the world's traditional creative and expressive forms, the *Journal of Folklore Research* provides an international forum for current theory and research among scholars of folklore and related fields." International in scope, the journal covers a wide variety of topics, including the cash wedding gift and the role of sign language for deaf children's identity. Abstracts of articles are available on the institution's web site, but full-text articles are only available on fee-based databases. Reviews of books, media, museum exhibits, and web sources are available by e-mail subscription and on the web site. Although this title is important for libraries that serve academic folklore research and folklore programs, it does have a noticeable lag time in publication. The newest or "current" issue was from 2010.

2509. *Louisiana Folklore Miscellany.* [ISSN: 0090-9769] 1958. a. Free to members. Ed(s): Carolyn Ware. Louisiana Folklore Society, c/o Dept of English, Louisiana State University, Baton Rouge, LA 70803; http://www.louisianafolklife.org/lafolkloresociety.html. *Indexed:* MLA-IB. *Aud.:* Ga, Ac.

Published under the auspices of the Louisiana Folklore Society, this is described on the Society's web site as a publication of "articles, notes, and commentaries on all aspects of Louisiana folklore and folklife." What makes this journal a standout among Southern folklore journals is its wide variety of Southern cultural topics. It is an excellent source for articles on Cajun and Creole social life and customs. Issues have included such topics as the Mardi Gras mask market; African-Americans and baseball; and the Vietnamese community and Hurricane Katrina. The Society's web site offers full text of some articles. This is a great publication for general readers and folklore researchers interested in the traditions of the South. Highly recommended as a Southern folklore title.

2510. *Marvels & Tales: a journal of fairy-tale studies.* Formerly (until 1996): *Merveilles et Contes.* [ISSN: 1521-4281] 1987. s-a. USD 126 (print & online eds.). Ed(s): Donald P Haase. Wayne State University Press, The Leonard N Simons Bldg, 4809 Woodward Ave, Detroit, MI 48201; http://wsupress.wayne.edu/. Illus. Refereed. *Indexed:* A01, A22, AmHI, BRI, E01, IBSS, MLA-IB. *Bk. rev.:* Number and length vary. *Aud.:* Ac.

According to its editorial statement, this journal is "committed to promoting advances in fairy-tale studies." Covering a wide variety of cultural groups and disciplines, this journal contains up to five lengthy articles, plus translations of tales and numerous reviews that cover both print and media. Article topics have included fearless children and monsters, ghosts, animal–human hybrids, and the queen and Rumpelstiltskin. Some issues are organized by themes—fairy tales and translations. A scholarly journal for academic folklore programs or strong children's literature programs.

2511. *New Directions in Folklore.* Formerly (until 1997): *Impromptu Journal.* [ISSN: 2161-9964] 19??. s-a. Free. Ed(s): Trevor J Blank. New Directions in Folklore, c/o Trevor J. Blank, Ed., Pennsylvania State University, W356 Olmsted Building, Middletown, PA 19711; newdirectionsinfolklore@gmail.com. Refereed. *Bk. rev.:* Number and length vary. *Aud.:* Ac.

This title has returned after a hiatus of over five years and is in partnership with the American Folklore Society, Indiana University Libraries, and IUScholarWorks. It is published biannually, and its editors are hoping that, with growth, it will become a quarterly publication. Articles are peer reviewed and cover various topics, often looking at contemporary culture. Each issue contains articles and reviews. Recent issue themes have included humor, quilt making, and web 2.0. For libraries that support folklore or pop cultural programs.

2512. *North Carolina Folklore Journal.* Formerly (until 1973): *North Carolina Folklore.* [ISSN: 0090-5844] 1948. s-a. Free to members. Ed(s): Dr. Carmine Prioli. North Carolina Folklore Society, P O Box 62271, Durham, NC 27715; info@ncfolkloresociety.org; http://www.ncfolkloresociety.org/. Illus. Refereed. Vol. ends: No. 2. *Indexed:* A22, FR, IIMP, IIPA, MLA-IB, RILM. *Bk. rev.:* 1-2, 300 words. *Aud.:* Ga, Ac.

This title is published by the North Carolina Folklore Society, and its scope includes "studies of state folklife, collections of verbal and musical lore, analyses of the use of folklore in literature, and articles whose innovative approach or exemplary methodology is pertinent to local folklife study." Topics include the historical, the traditional, and the contemporary. Issues can be thematic, delving into all aspects of a subject from geographic and occupational influences to community and domestic life. There are reviews for books and media, and also for exhibits. Although not lengthy, the articles are well written. This journal is a good choice for those interested not only in North Carolina folk culture but also in the folklore of southern Appalachia and the Southeastern coast. Its easy reading style makes it a title for both general and academic library audiences. It is a bit slow in publication.

2513. *Now & Then (Johnson City): the Appalachian magazine.* [ISSN: 0896-2693] 1984. 2x/yr. USD 25 (Individuals, USD 15). Ed(s): Randy Sanders, Fred Sauceman. East Tennessee State University, Center for Appalachian Studies and Services, PO Box 70556, Johnson City, TN 37614-0556. Circ: 1500. *Indexed:* MLA-IB, RILM. *Bk. rev.:* 5, 500 words. *Aud.:* Ga.

Sponsored by the Center for Appalachian Studies and Services, this journal is probably the best source on folk culture relating to Appalachia. It is a nice mix of articles, essays, poetry, interviews, and photographs that cover views of past and present folk life. Recent thematic issues have covered serving and public service. Reviews are limited, but additional titles are listed under "Books in Brief" and "Music in Brief." Current events of the region are listed in an accompanying newsletter. An excellent title, recommended for libraries of the region and for others that support interest in its folk culture.

2514. Oral Tradition (Online). [ISSN: 1542-4308] 1986. irreg. Free. Ed(s): Vicki Polansky. Slavica Publishers, Inc., Indiana University, 2611 E 10th St, Bloomington, IN 47408; slavica@indiana.edu; http://www.slavica.com/. *Indexed:* AmHI. *Aud.:* Ac.

This journal describes its purpose as a "comparative and interdisciplinary focus for studies of oral literature and related fields by publishing research and scholarship on the creation, transmission, and interpretation of all forms of oral tradition expression." Articles are worldwide in scope, with subjects ranging from ancient epics and religious texts to modern drama and e-texts. Some issues are thematic. The issues are available in full text on the journal's web site, with links to the Center for Studies in Oral Tradition. This scholarly title is for academic libraries that support folk literature programs.

2515. Storytelling Magazine. Incorporates: *Inside Story;* Which was formerly: *Yarnspinner;* Formerly (until 1989): *National Storytelling Journal.* [ISSN: 1048-1354] 1984. 5x/yr. Free to members. National Storytelling Network, PO Box 795, Jonesborough, TN 37659. Illus., index, adv. *Aud.:* Hs, Ga.

Issues are a mix of articles, stories, news, and advertisements. Usually the stories section has a central theme. Reviews and suggested readings are from print, media, and Internet sources. The news section deals with all aspects of the National Storytelling Network, listing conferences, awards, and calls for stories. There are a fair number of advertisements in the magazine, but all are pertinent to storytellers. A good source for storytellers and teachers, as well as librarians.

2516. Tennessee Folklore Society Bulletin. Formerly (until 1937): *Tennessee Folklore Society. Bulletin.* [ISSN: 0040-3253] 1935. s-a. Free to members. Ed(s): Brent Cantrell. Tennessee Folklore Society, c/o Jubilee Community Arts, 1538 Laurel Ave, Knoxville, TN 37916; info@tennesseefolklore.org; http://www.tennesseefolklore.org. Illus., index. Refereed. Vol. ends: No. 2. *Indexed:* IIMP, IIPA, MLA-IB, RILM. *Bk. rev.:* 2-3, 600 words. *Aud.:* Ga, Ac.

Most of the articles in this journal pertain to folk culture in Tennessee and neighboring states. However, there are occasional pieces on folklore outside the United States, and some issues are thematic. In addition to articles, there are reviews of books and media and a section that lists coming events. Issues also usually contain a section listing publications available from the Tennessee Folklore Society. Although publication lags, this journal is a good source for Tennessee libraries and others in the surrounding geographic region.

2517. Voices (Schenectady). Formed by the merger of (1980-1999): *New York Folklore Newsletter;* (1975-1999): *New York Folklore;* Which was formerly (until 1974): *New York Folklore Quarterly.* [ISSN: 1551-7268] 2000. s-a. Free to members. Ed(s): Eileen Condon. New York Folklore Society, PO Box 764, Schenectady, NY 12301; nyfs@nyfolklore.org; http://www.nyfolklore.org. Refereed. *Indexed:* IIPA, MLA-IB, P02. *Aud.:* Ga, Ac.

Published by the New York Folklore Society, *Voices* covers New York State and surrounding regions. Most issues include feature articles, columns, interviews, poetry, art, reviews, and all things related to folklore. The scope of the publication includes a wide variety of topics from bagels to a family history quilt. The editors view the journal as publishing "peer-reviewed, research-based articles, written in an accessible style, on topics related to traditional art and life, including ethnic culture." Issues are accessible online through the Society's web page. For libraries that are interested in Northeastern folklore, this is a good title.

2518. Western Folklore. Formerly (until 1947): *California Folklore Quarterly.* [ISSN: 0043-373X] 1942. q. Free to members. Ed(s): Robert Glenn Howard. Western States Folklore Society, c/o Elliott Oring, PO Box 3557, Long Beach, CA 90803; http://www.westernfolklore.org. Adv. *Indexed:* A01, A22, ABS&EES, AmHI, ArtHuCI, BEL&L, BRI, CBRI, Chicano, FR, IIMP, IIPA, MLA-IB, P02, RILM. *Bk. rev.:* Number and length vary. *Aud.:* Ga, Ac.

This title's geographic scope includes California and neighboring regions. Most issues are composed of articles and reviews. Some may have a thematic approach. Topics cover all aspects of folklore, taking a wide interpretation of the subject. Reviews are numerous and vary in length from several paragraphs to several pages. The table of contents for each issue is available on the Society's web site. Although publication lags, this journal is a good addition for both academics and the sophisticated general reader.

■ FOOD AND NUTRITION

Diane T. Sands, Assistant Librarian, Leonard Library, San Francisco State University, San Francisco, CA 94132; dsands@sfsu.edu

Introduction

The bulk of the titles in this section are aimed at academic libraries, especially those that support research in the health sciences. Publications in this section may include articles on health policy; food supply safety; healthy eating behaviors; food allergies; obesity; new treatments; medications and their effects; technical discussions of cutting-edge research in nutrition; and lighter articles that describe more general issues in the nutrition and health fields. While some titles are appropriate for well-versed general audiences, libraries that support researchers in nutrition or health professionals will best benefit from these titles and their range of content.

Basic Periodicals

Ga: *Nutrition Today, Vegetarian Journal;* Ac: *American Dietetic Association. Journal, American Journal of Clinical Nutrition, Annals of Nutrition and Metabolism, The British Journal of Nutrition, The Journal of Nutrition, Nutrition Reviews.*

Basic Abstracts and Indexes

Biological Abstracts, CAB Abstracts, Current Contents/Life Sciences, MEDLINE, Nutrition Abstracts and Reviews.

2519. Academy of Nutrition and Dietetics. Journal. Former titles (until 2012): *American Dietetic Association. Journal;* (until 1925): *American Dietetic Association. Bulletin.* [ISSN: 2212-2672] 19??. 12x/yr. USD 623. Ed(s): Dr. Linda Snetselaar. Elsevier Inc., 360 Park Ave S, New York, NY 10010; JournalCustomerService-usa@elsevier.com; http://www.elsevier.com. Illus., index, adv. Sample. Refereed. *Indexed:* A01, A22, Agr, BRI, C45, Chicano, FS&TA, H&TI, H24, IndVet, P02, RRTA, SD, SWR&A. *Bk. rev.:* Number and length vary. *Aud.:* Ac, Sa.

The American Dietetic Association (ADA) is the world's largest organization of food and nutrition professionals. Access to the full text of this official association journal is available to ADA members and professional subscribers at the journal's web site; tables of contents and abstracts are free to all. Aimed at professional nutritionists and dietitians, the refereed reports include original research on diet therapy, community nutrition, and education and training; reports of association activities and conferences; columns that focus on professional advice; and articles approved for continuing-education credits (codes are provided). Appropriate for collections that support professional or research populations in the health sciences.

2520. *American College of Nutrition. Journal.* [ISSN: 0731-5724] 1982. bi-m. GBP 235 (print & online eds.). Ed(s): John J Cunningham, Dr. Richard R Caldwell. American College of Nutrition, 300 S Duncan Ave, Ste 225, Clearwater, FL 33755; office@amcollnutr.org; http://www.am-coll-nutr.org/jacn/jacn.htm. Illus., adv. Refereed. *Indexed:* A22, Agr, C45, ExcerpMed, FS&TA, RRTA, SD. *Bk. rev.:* Number and length vary. *Aud.:* Ac, Sa.

This official journal of the American College of Nutrition focuses on original and innovative research in nutrition, with useful application for researchers, physicians, and other health professionals. Tables of contents and article abstracts can be found at no charge online, along with full-text articles available to subscribers. Professionals and investigators focused on current nutrition research will find scholarly articles that describe clinical and laboratory reports, as well as critical reviews on pertinent nutrition topics that highlight key teaching points.

2521. *The American Journal of Clinical Nutrition.* Formerly (until 1954): *Journal of Clinical Nutrition;* Incorporates (1950-1958): *National Vitamin Foundation, Nutrition Symposium Series.* [ISSN: 0002-9165] 1952. m. USD 585 (print & online eds.). Ed(s): Dennis M Bier, Darren T Early. American Society for Nutrition, 9650 Rockville Pike, Bethesda, MD 20814; info@nutrition.org; http://www.nutrition.org. Illus., index, adv. Refereed. Circ: 3350. Microform: PMC; PQC. *Indexed:* A22, ABS&EES, AbAn, Agr, BRI, C45, Chicano, ExcerpMed, FS&TA, IndVet, P02, RRTA. *Bk. rev.:* 1-4, 500-1,000 words. *Aud.:* Ac, Sa.

The American Society for Clinical Nutrition has as its primary focus the publication of basic and clinical studies relevant to human nutrition. Articles are often grouped into subject areas such as obesity and eating disorders, aging, or cardiovascular disease risk. Supplements to *AJCN* are published on occasion, and these contain proceedings from internationally recognized conferences on clinical nutrition. The web site provides access to tables of contents and abstracts. Subscribers have full access to editorials, book reviews, and full-text articles, as well as access to articles in press (published weekly). This journal is appropriate for health science collections that support professional or research populations.

2522. *Annals of Nutrition and Metabolism: European journal of nutrition, metabolic diseases and dietetics.* Formed by the merger of (1947-1981): *Annales de la Nutrition et de l'Alimentation;* (1970-1981): *Nutrition and Metabolism;* Which was formerly (1959-1969): *Nutritio et Dieta.* [ISSN: 0250-6807] 1981. 8x/yr. CHF 3636. Ed(s): Ibrahim Elmadfa. S. Karger AG, Allschwilerstr 10, Basel, 4055, Switzerland; karger@karger.ch; http://www.karger.ch. Illus., index, adv. Sample. Refereed. Circ: 1200. *Indexed:* A01, A22, AbAn, Agr, C45, E01, ExcerpMed, FS&TA, RRTA. *Aud.:* Ac, Sa.

Basic and clinical reports that offer new information relating to human nutrition and metabolic diseases (including molecular genetics) are the focus of this peer-reviewed publication. Papers present original findings that deal with problems such as the consequences of specific diets and dietary supplements, and nutritional factors in the etiology of metabolic and gastrointestinal disorders. All articles are published electronically ahead of print copies, with full text available online to subscribers. The web site also includes free access to tables of contents, abstracts, and full text of selected "must-read" articles. Health science collections that support research populations will benefit from access to this journal.

2523. *The British Journal of Nutrition: an international journal of nutritional science.* [ISSN: 0007-1145] 1947. 24x/yr. GBP 1432 (print & online eds.). Ed(s): Philip C Calder. Cambridge University Press, The Edinburgh Bldg, Shaftesbury Rd, Cambridge, CB2 8RU, United Kingdom; journals@cambridge.org; http://www.cambridge.org/uk. Illus., index, adv. Refereed. Circ: 2230. Microform: SWZ; PMC; PQC. Reprint: PSC. *Indexed:* A22, AbAn, Agr, C45, E01, ExcerpMed, FS&TA, IndVet, P02, RRTA. *Bk. rev.:* 1-2, 500 words, signed. *Aud.:* Ac, Sa.

This international, peer-reviewed journal focuses on human and clinical nutrition research, animal nutrition, and basic science as applied to nutrition. It addresses the multidisciplinary nature of nutritional science, and includes material from all of the specialties involved in nutrition research, including

molecular and cell biology and the emerging area of nutritional genomics. Tables of contents and abstracts are freely available on the web site. This journal is appropriate for health science collections that support professional or research populations.

2524. *European Journal of Clinical Nutrition.* Formerly (until 1988): *Human Nutrition. Clinical Nutrition;* Which superseded in part (in 1982): *Journal of Human Nutrition;* Which was formerly (until 1976): *Nutrition;* (until 1951): *Nutrition, Dietetics, Catering.* [ISSN: 0954-3007] 1947. m. EUR 1299 in Europe; USD 1635 in the Americas; JPY 222400 Japan. Ed(s): Manfred J Muller. Nature Publishing Group, The MacMillan Bldg, 4 Crinan St, London, N1 9XW, United Kingdom; nature@nature.com; http://www.nature.com. Illus., adv. Sample. Refereed. *Indexed:* A01, A22, AbAn, Agr, BRI, C45, E01, ExcerpMed, FS&TA, P02, RRTA, RiskAb. *Bk. rev.:* 1-3, length varies, signed. *Aud.:* Ac, Sa.

This journal is appropriate for health science collections that support professional or research populations. *EJCN* is an international, peer-reviewed journal that publishes articles about human and clinical nutrition. The scope of the journal includes original articles, short communications, and case reports based on clinical, metabolic, and epidemiological studies that describe methodologies, mechanisms, relationships, and benefits of nutritional interventions for disease and health promotion. The web site provides one free issue, selected free articles and reviews, and weekly online advance publications that are available to subscribers.

2525. *The Journal of Nutrition.* [ISSN: 0022-3166] 1928. m. USD 810 (print & online eds.). Ed(s): Dr. A Catherine Ross. American Society for Nutrition, 9650 Rockville Pike, Bethesda, MD 20814; info@nutrition.org; http://www.nutrition.org. Illus., index, adv. Refereed. Circ: 1850. Vol. ends: Dec. Microform: PMC; PQC. *Indexed:* A01, A22, AbAn, Agr, BRI, C45, ExcerpMed, FS&TA, IndVet, P02, RRTA. *Bk. rev.:* Number and length vary. *Aud.:* Ac, Sa.

Original research in nutrition is the focus of this scholarly journal, with articles geared toward research professionals. It is the first scientific journal created solely for the publication of nutrition research, and its contents range from peer-reviewed research reports on all aspects of experimental nutrition, critical reviews, and commentaries, to symposia and workshop proceedings. The web site contains access to articles in press (updated weekly) and full text for subscribers; tables of contents and abstracts are available to all.

2526. *Journal of Nutrition Education and Behavior.* Formerly (until 2002): *Journal of Nutrition Education.* [ISSN: 1499-4046] 1969. 6x/yr. USD 477. Ed(s): Karen Chapman-Novakofski. Elsevier Inc., 360 Park Ave S, New York, NY 10010; usinfo-f@elsevier.com; http://www.elsevier.com. Illus., index, adv. Sample. Refereed. *Indexed:* A01, A22, Agr, BRI, C37, C45, CBCARef, ERIC, FS&TA, H&TI, MLA-IB, P02, PsycInfo, RRTA, SD. *Aud.:* Ac, Sa.

This official journal of the Society for Nutrition Education (SNE) is a refereed scientific periodical aimed at all professionals with an interest in nutrition education and dietary/physical activity behaviors. Articles document and disseminate original research on emerging issues and practices that are relevant to nutrition education and behavior worldwide. Access is available via the web site to full-text articles from 2006 to the present for subscribers and SNE members; access to abstracts is complimentary, as are certain open-access articles.

2527. *The Journal of Nutritional Biochemistry.* Supersedes (in 1990): *Nutrition Reports International.* [ISSN: 0955-2863] 1970. 12x/yr. USD 2442. Ed(s): Dr. Bernhard Hennig. Elsevier Inc., 360 Park Ave S, New York, NY 10010; usinfo-f@elsevier.com; http://www.elsevier.com. Illus., index, adv. Sample. Refereed. Circ: 1000 Paid. Vol. ends: Dec. Microform: PQC. *Indexed:* A01, A22, Agr, C45, ExcerpMed, FS&TA, H24, IndVet, RRTA. *Aud.:* Ac, Sa.

Devoted to advancements in nutritional science, *The Journal of Nutritional Biochemistry* presents experimental nutrition research as it relates to biochemistry, neurochemistry, molecular biology, toxicology, physiology, and pharmacology. Health science collections that support professionals and researchers will find this to be a good selection. It periodically publishes on emerging issues, conference summaries, experimental methods, symposium reports, metabolic pathways, and short communications.

2528. Nutrition: an international journal of applied and basic nutritional science. Formerly (until 1987): *Nutrition International.* [ISSN: 0899-9007] 1985. 12x/yr. USD 1204. Ed(s): Dr. Michael M Meguid, D Spadaro. Elsevier Inc., 360 Park Ave S, New York, NY 10010; usinfo-f@elsevier.com; http://www.elsevier.com. Adv. Sample. Refereed. Circ: 650 Paid. Vol. ends: No. 17. *Indexed:* A01, A22, AbAn, Agr, C45, ExcerpMed, FS&TA, RRTA. *Aud.:* Ac, Sa.

Articles in this scholarly journal focus on advances in nutrition research and science; new and advancing technologies in clinical nutrition practice; encouraging the application of the techniques of outcomes research; and meta-analyses of problems in patient-related nutrition. Many issues are available online. Tables of contents and indexes can be accessed without a subscription. This journal is appropriate for health science collections that support professional or research populations.

2529. Nutrition Research: an international publication for nutrition to advance food and life science research. Incorporates (1975-1993): *Progress in Food and Nutrition Science;* Which was formerly: *International Encyclopedia of Food and Nutrition.* [ISSN: 0271-5317] 1981. 12x/yr. USD 2473. Ed(s): Bruce A Watkins. Elsevier Inc., 360 Park Ave S, New York, NY 10010; usinfo-f@elsevier.com; http://www.elsevier.com. Illus., adv. Sample. Refereed. Circ: 580 Paid. Vol. ends: Dec (No. 21). *Indexed:* A01, A22, Agr, C45, ExcerpMed, FS&TA, H24, RRTA, RiskAb. *Aud.:* Ac, Sa.

This is a scholarly journal for global communication of nutrition and life sciences research on food and health, with articles on the study of nutrients during growth; reproduction; athletic performance; and aging and disease. Academic or health science libraries that support nutrition research will find this title valuable. The journal's principal focus is on publishing research that advances the understanding of nutrients in food for improving the human condition. Abstracts, tables of contents, and one sample issue are available to all online; subscribers can access full text.

2530. Nutrition Reviews. [ISSN: 0029-6643] 1942. m. GBP 313 (print & online eds.). Ed(s): Naomi Fukagawa, Allison Worden. International Life Sciences Institute, One Thomas Cir, NW 9th Fl, Washington, DC 20005; ilsi@ilsi.org; http://www.ilsi.org. Illus., index. Sample. Refereed. Microform: PQC. Reprint: PSC. *Indexed:* A01, A22, AbAn, Agr, BRI, C45, E01, ExcerpMed, FS&TA, H&TI, P02, RRTA, SD. *Aud.:* Ac, Sa.

While this monthly scholarly journal is appropriate for libraries that support research in the health sciences, the writing is accessible to knowledgeable consumers as well. It offers in-depth coverage of nutrition topics, including experimental and clinical nutrition research, food science, food and nutrition legislation, and policy as developed by national and international bodies. Supplements contain proceedings from the World Congress of Public Health Nutrition. Abstracts, tables of contents, and free sample articles are available online to all.

2531. Nutrition Today. [ISSN: 0029-666X] 1966. bi-m. USD 325 (print & online eds.). Ed(s): Johanna T Dwyer, Randi Konikoff Beranbaum. Lippincott Williams & Wilkins, 530 Walnut St, Philadelphia, PA 19106; customerservice@lww.com; http://www.lww.com. Illus., index, adv. Refereed. Circ: 1732. *Indexed:* A01, A22, Agr, BRI, C45, FS&TA, P02, RRTA. *Aud.:* Ga, Ac, Sa.

This title is appropriate for all health science collections and is accessible to an educated general audience. Informative articles cover topics such as the role of bioactive food ingredients in chronic diseases, sports nutrition, the food business, communicating nutrition, the politics of food, food in culture, and articles approved for continuing-education credits (codes are provided). The web site has links to all CE-credit articles published in *Nutrition Today* under one tab.

2532. World Review of Nutrition and Dietetics. [ISSN: 0084-2230] 1964. irreg. Ed(s): B Koletzko. S. Karger AG, Allschwilerstr 10, Basel, 4055, Switzerland; karger@karger.ch; http://www.karger.ch. Refereed. *Indexed:* A22, Agr, FS&TA. *Aud.:* Ac, Sa.

This series, filled with comprehensive reviews of topics related to nutrition, is a good addition to academic or health science collections. Tables of contents and indexes are available online without a subscription, along with many free article excerpts. Volumes in this series consist of exceptionally thorough reviews on single specific topics, which are selected as either fundamental to improved understanding of human and animal nutrition, or relevant to problems of social and preventive medicine.

■ FOOD INDUSTRY

Margaret E. (Bess) Robinson, Associate Professor, University of Memphis Libraries, University of Memphis, Memphis, TN 38152; merobnsn@memphis.edu.

Cheryl LaGuardia, Research Librarian, Widener Library, Harvard University

Introduction

Even as the obesity rate continues to grow—for adults and children—current trends suggest that today's consumers are thinking more contemplatively about food: where it comes from, the circumstances under which it was raised, what is in it, and whether it fits their understanding of "healthy." Interest in organic food and the local food movement is reflected in the increasing numbers (and benefits) of farmers' markets and community-sustained agriculture programs. Palates continue to evolve thanks to international influences and the exciting new flavors being developed. Regulations, production, processing, sustainability, ingredients, labeling, safety, transportation, marketing, and portion control are among the topics in the food industry that researchers, practitioners, and educators are addressing through innovative technologies and new products.

The food industry is vast, and is covered in just about every conceivable type of periodical—from academic/scholarly publications to newspapers, and from trade/business-to-business and newsletter/bulletins to those targeting consumers. Publishers' web sites often offer non-subscribers free access to an astonishing amount of information. Please see the "Beer, Wine, and Spirits," "Cooking and Cookery," "Food and Nutrition," and "Hospitality/Restaurant" sections of *Magazines for Libraries* for additional food- and beverage-related entries.

This section describes a selection of trade journals, newsletters, and peer-reviewed publications particularly relevant to industry insiders, researchers, educators, and students; some may be of interest to the general reader. It also provides an idea of what is available at the respective publishers' web sites.

The publications present news (such as company profiles, technology, and legislation); industry analysis; trends (for instance, in production, sustainability, marketing, and retail); and research (e.g., food safety and product development) to those involved with—and interested in—all facets of the food industry.

Basic Periodicals

Ac: *Critical Reviews in Food Science and Nutrition, Food Engineering, Food Protection Trends, Food Technology;* Sa: *Dairy Foods, Food Engineering, Food Technology, Journal of Food Protection, The National Provisioner, Prepared Foods.*

Basic Abstracts and Indexes

ABI/INFORM Global, Business Source Premier, CINAHL, Current Contents, Food Science & Technology Abstracts, General Business File ASAP, General OneFile, General Reference Center Gold.

2533. Beverage Industry. Former titles (until 1972): *Soft Drink Industry;* (until 1966): *Bottling Industry;* Incorporates (in 199?): *Beverage Industry Annual Manual;* Which was formerly (until 1973): *Soft Drink Industry Annual Manual.* [ISSN: 0148-6187] 1946. m. Free to qualified personnel. Ed(s): Jessica Jacobsen. B N P Media, 2401 W Big Beaver Rd, Ste 700, Troy, MI 48084; http://www.bnpmedia.com. Illus., index, adv. Microform: PQC. *Indexed:* A22, ABIn, B01, B02, B03, BRI, H&TI. *Aud.:* Ac, Sa.

Beverage Industry is a big, colorful cornucopia of the latest news on the research and development, production, packaging, marketing, distribution, and retail behind just about every conceivable potable liquid imaginable in North America. This monthly trade magazine spotlights companies (and their manufacturing plants) and includes articles on consumer and industry trends, new technology and products, ingredient innovations, and operations. The regular "Up Close With..." column features top companies and their executives; "Plant Focus" showcases specific plants; and there's a classified ad section and an index to the considerable advertisements throughout. Visitors to the publisher's web site may access the digitized version of most issues back to May 2009. They may also see titles and selected content from archived issues back to November 2007, and search for stories by keyword. URL: www.bevindustry.com/

2534. Candy Industry: the global resource, from manufacturing to retailing. Former titles (until 1982): *Candy and Snack Industry; Candy and Baked Snack Industry; Candy.* [ISSN: 0745-1032] 1874. m. Free to qualified personnel (print or online ed.). Ed(s): Bernard Pacyniak. B N P Media, 155 N Pfingsten Rd, Ste 205, Deerfield, IL 60015; http://www.bnpmedia.com. Illus., index, adv. Sample. Circ: 104 Paid. Vol. ends: Dec. Microform: PQC. *Indexed:* A22, ABIn, B01, B02, B03, BRI, FS&TA. *Aud.:* Ac, Sa.

The trade publication *Candy Industry* provides news and analysis on all aspects of the global confectionery industry. Colorful, easy-to-read issues deliver the latest developments in manufacturing, new products, industry trends and related technologies, research and development, and processing and packaging, and include a pullout section, *Retail Confectioner,* aimed at retailers. Readers are also informed of international conferences and trade shows. Each monthly publication includes an ad index and classified ad section, and "wraps" with "Candy Wrapper," an interview with a leader in the confection field. The publisher's web site includes an archive of digitized issues back to March 2008, selected content of most issues back to November 2007, and the ability to search available content by keyword. URL: http://candyindustry.com

2535. Cereal Foods World. Formerly: *Cereal Science Today.* [ISSN: 0146-6283] 1956. bi-m. Nov.-Dec. combined. Free to members; Non-members, USD 420. Ed(s): Jody Grider. A A C C International, 3340 Pilot Knob Rd, St. Paul, MN 55121; aacc@scisoc.org; http://www.aaccnet.org. Illus., index, adv. Refereed. Vol. ends: Dec. Microform: PQC. *Indexed:* A22, ABIn, Agr, C45, FS&TA. *Aud.:* Ac, Sa.

Published bimonthly by AACC (the American Association of Cereal Chemists) International, *Cereal Foods World* focuses on current research and advances in grain-based food science. Articles written by and for food industry professionals worldwide report on related technology, product innovations, developments in food production, and industry trends. Association news, updates on people and companies of interest to readers, and an advertisers index round out the publication. Contains technical language and figures. The table of contents, abstracts, and selected content from the current issue and past issues back to 2006; selected digitized content of a sample issue; and keyword-searchable abstracts back to 2006 are available at the publisher's web site (http://aaccnet.org). Print and online subscriptions are available. Access to digitized issues back to January-February 2006 is restricted to AACC International members with an online subscription.

2536. Critical Reviews in Food Science and Nutrition. Former titles: *C R C Critical Reviews in Food Science and Nutrition; C R C Critical Reviews in Food Technology.* [ISSN: 1040-8398] 1970. 10x/yr. GBP 2118 (print & online eds.). Ed(s): Fergus M Clydesdale. Taylor & Francis Inc.,

325 Chestnut St, Ste 800, Philadelphia, PA 19106; customerservice@taylorandfrancis.com; http://www.tandfonline.com. Illus., index. Refereed. Vol. ends: Dec. Reprint: PSC. *Indexed:* A01, A22, Agr, C&ISA, C45, CerAb, E01, FS&TA, RRTA, SD. *Aud.:* Ac, Sa.

With an impressive five-year Impact Factor of 6.261 (2012 Journal Citation Reports), *Critical Reviews in Food Science and Nutrition* is written by and for food scientists, nutritionists, and health professionals. The print version is published quarterly; the online, monthly—except for October. Articles address topics as varied as new technologies, and the relationship of diet and disease, health, and behavior. There is also coverage of antioxidants; food safety; new ingredients and food products; government regulation and policy; food processing; and microbiological concerns. Academic/scholarly in nature, this scientific journal uses technical language and has supporting figures and tables throughout. The publisher's web site (http://tandfonline.com) offers free access to articles from a sample copy, the five most-cited articles from 2009 to 2011, and the tables of contents and abstracts of articles for issues back to the inaugural issue in 1970.

2537. Dairy Foods: innovative ideas for dairy processors. Incorporates (in 2007): *Dairy Field;* Which was formerly (until 1991): *Dairy Field Today;* (until 1990): *Dairy Field;* (until 1979): *Dairy & Ice Cream Field;* (1965-1967): *Ice Cream Field & Ice Cream Trade Journal;* Which was formed by the merger of (1922-1965): *Ice Cream Field;* (1905-1965): *Ice Cream Trade Journal;* Dairy & Ice Cream Field incorporated (1917-1968): *Ice Cream Review;* (1911-1968): *Milk Dealer;* Which incorporated (in 1967): *Manufactured Milk Products Journal;* Which was formerly (until 1962): *The Milk Products Journal;* (until 1953): *The Butter, Cheese and Milk Products Journal;* (1932-1950): *National Butter & Cheese Journal;* Which was formed by the merger of (1930-1932): *National Cheese Journal;* (1930-1932): *Concentrated Milk Industries;* (1930-1932): *National Butter Journal;* All three of which superseded in part: *Butter and Cheese Journal;* Which incorporated (1927-1928): *World's Butter Review;* Butter and Cheese Journal was formerly (1910-1928): *Butter Cheese and Egg Journal;* Dairy Foods was formerly (until 1986): *Dairy Record;* Which incorporated (1890-1950): *Creamery Journal;* (in 1981): *American Dairy Review;* Which was formerly (until 1965): *American Milk Review;* (until 1960): *American Milk Review and Milk Plant Monthly;* Which was formed by the merger of (1930-1958): *Milk Plant Monthly;* Which was formerly (until 1930): *Creamery and Milk Plant Monthly;* (1939-1958): *American Milk Review (Year);* Which superseded in part (in 1939): *American Produce Review;* Which was formerly (until 1937): *American Creamery & Poultry Produce Review;* (1897-1930): *New York Produce Review and American Creamery.* [ISSN: 0888-0050] 1958. m. Free to qualified personnel. Ed(s): Jim Carper. B N P Media, 155 N Pfingsten Rd, Ste 205, Deerfield, IL 60015; http://www.bnpmedia.com. Illus., index, adv. Circ: 22507. Vol. ends: Dec. Microform: PQC. *Indexed:* A22, ABIn, B01, B02, B03, BRI, C45, FS&TA. *Aud.:* Ac, Sa.

The monthly trade publication *Dairy Foods* presents information on all facets of processing, distributing, and marketing milk and the milk-related products that fuel the dairy industry. Cover stories often profile a processor and describe that company's plant equipment and technology. Easily-understood and well-illustrated articles provide news and analysis of industry-related trends and technologies, and information on such topics as marketing, packaging, regulations, food safety, health, flavors, ingredients, sustainability, and transportation and logistics—often through interviews with people working in those areas. Issues include sections for new products, supplier news, and classified ads, and an index to the extensive advertisements; usually there are show previews. Links to most digitized issues back to August 2008, major content of issues back to January 2003, and keyword searching for articles are available from the web site. URL: http://dairyfoods.com

2538. Emerging Food R & D Report. [ISSN: 1050-2688] 1990. m. USD 365 domestic; USD 385 foreign. Food Technology Intelligence, Inc., 215 Godwin Ave, PO Box 322, Midland Park, NJ 07432; ftiinfo@ftipub.com; http://www.ftipub.com. Sample. *Indexed:* B01, B02. *Aud.:* Ac, Sa.

An information-packed, eight-page monthly newsletter, *Emerging Food R&D Report* comprises innovative food-related developments and technologies being discovered by food researchers in government, academic, and corporate labs worldwide. Examples of new products and processes in recent issues include "Plant-derived antimicrobial compounds effective in killing *E. coli* on apples," "Reduce hardness of water to better remove bacteria from chicken skin," "Modified atmosphere packaging, cryogenic conditions retain freshness of oyster meat," "Quantitative PCR helps dairy processors improve yogurt quality," "Trout skin waste leads to gelatin-based edible film," and "Higher levels of healthy compound found in new broccoli variety." For potential collaborators, each of an issue's 10–12 developments includes the names and contact information of the researchers whose findings are highlighted. A sample issue is available online (www.ftipub.com/food/emergingfood); subscribers may choose to receive issues in print or electronically.

2539. *Food Engineering: the magazine for operations and manufacturing management.* Former titles (until 1998): *Chilton's Food Engineering;* (until 1977): *Food Engineering;* (until 1951): *Food Industries.* [ISSN: 1522-2292] 1928. m. Free to qualified personnel (print or online ed.). Ed(s): Joyce Fassl. B N P Media, 2401 W Big Beaver Rd, Ste 700, Troy, MI 48084; http://www.bnpmedia.com. Illus., index, adv. Vol. ends: Dec. Microform: CIS; PQC. *Indexed:* A22, ABIn, B01, B02, B03, BRI, FS&TA, H&TI. *Aud.:* Ac, Sa.

Published since 1928, *Food Engineering* continues to inform readers of trends and updates in engineering R&D, technology, new products, regulations, and manufacturing and plant operations, and how they affect food processing, packaging, and safety; sustainability; and other issues related to the food and beverage manufacturing industry in North America. This monthly trade journal profiles a variety of production, processing, and packaging facilities. It includes industry news, a calendar of national and international events, a classified section, and a comprehensive ad index. The language is reasonably technical; the publication is well-illustrated with color photographs and clear graphics. Cover-to-cover access to current issues—and most issues back to July 2008—is available on the publication's web site, as are selected cover stories, articles, and departments from most (non-digitized) issues back to January 1999, and the option to search for articles by keyword. URL: http://foodengineeringmag.com

2540. *Food Protection Trends: science and news from the International Association for Food Protection.* Former titles (until 2003): *Dairy, Food and Environmental Sanitation;* (until 1989): *Dairy and Food Sanitation; Food and Fieldmen.* [ISSN: 1541-9576] 1980. bi-m. USD 286 domestic; USD 301 in Canada & Mexico; USD 316 elsewhere. Ed(s): Lisa K. Hovey. International Association for Food Protection, 6200 Aurora Ave, Ste 200W, Des Moines, IA 50322-2864. Illus., adv. Microform: PQC. *Indexed:* A22, ABIn, Agr, C45, FS&TA, H24, IndVet, RRTA, RiskAb. *Bk. rev.:* Number and length vary. *Aud.:* Ac, Sa.

Food Protection Trends is published primarily for the members of the International Association for Food Protection (IAFP) and covers topics of interest to food industry employees or regulators, food science educators, and researchers. As of January 2013, each bimonthly issue includes four peer-reviewed articles on applied research and applications of current technology. There are also special-interest pieces of a more general or practical nature having to do with food safety or protection; industry and association news; new products; and an interview with an IAFP member. There are also updates on government regulations and sanitary design, and a calendar of upcoming events worldwide. The association's web site (http://foodprotection.org) provides links to a digitized sample issue and to a keyword- or author-searchable archive of summaries, and complete reference information of articles back to 2006.

2541. *Food Technology: advancing food & health through sound science.* [ISSN: 0015-6639] 1947. m. USD 190 domestic; USD 199.50 foreign. Ed(s): Bob Swientek, Mary Ellen Kuhn. Institute of Food Technologists, 525 W Van Buren, Ste 1000, Chicago, IL 60607; http://www.ift.org. Illus., index, adv. Circ: 28400 Paid. Vol. ends: Dec. Microform: PQC. *Indexed:* A01, A22, Agr, BRI, C45, EngInd, FS&TA, H&TI, H24, IndVet, P02. *Aud.:* Ac, Sa.

Published by the Institute of Food Technologists (IFT), the monthly magazine *Food Technology* provides coverage on the areas of developing, improving, processing, applying, packaging, and regulating ingredients. In addition, in-depth feature articles and columns such as "Food, Medicine & Health," "Nutraceuticals," "Food Safety & Quality," and "Consumer Trends" give readers current scientific research and development in food and how it is used,

and news and analysis of emerging trends and how they affect the food industry. Issues include eye-catching photos and effective graphics, a classified section, news about upcoming events, and an advertisers index. Members of the IFT and subscribers may view the full content online; others may access the pdf version of the current issue only. Tables of contents of archived issues back to July 1999—and the opportunity to do article searches—are on the IFT web site. URL: http://ift.org/food-technology.aspx

2542. *Journal of Food Protection.* Former titles (until 1977): *Journal of Milk and Food Technology;* (until 1947): *Journal of Milk Technology.* [ISSN: 0362-028X] 1937. m. USD 424 domestic; USD 444 in Canada & Mexico; USD 474 elsewhere. Ed(s): Lisa K. Hovey. International Association for Food Protection, 6200 Aurora Ave, Ste 200W, Des Moines, IA 50322-2864; info@foodprotection.org; http://www.foodprotection.org. Illus., index, adv. Refereed. Microform: PMC; PQC. *Indexed:* A01, A22, ABIn, AbAn, Agr, C45, FS&TA, H&TI, H24, IndVet, RRTA, RiskAb. *Aud.:* Ac, Sa.

Journal of Food Protection, the monthly publication of the International Association for Food Protection (IAFP) since 1937, comprises food microbiology-related research and review articles written by and for food science and safety professionals from all over the world who are interested in protecting the safety and quality of food. Refereed contributions examine topics such as causes and control of foodborn illness, food hazards and contamination, food spoilage, microbiological food quality, and food industry wastes. Academic/scholarly in nature, this scientific journal uses technical language and supporting figures and tables. It is available in print and/or online. The publisher's web site provides basic citation information for the top ten articles (based on number of downloads) from recent years, and information about the journal's Impact Factor according to Journal Citation Report data. URL: http://foodprotection.org/publications/journal-of-food-protection

2543. *Kashrus Magazine.* Former titles (until 1990): *Kashrus;* (until 1985): *Kashrus Newsletter.* [ISSN: 1074-3502] 1980. 5x/yr. USD 25 domestic; USD 30 Canada; USD 39 elsewhere. Ed(s): Rabbi Yosef Wikler. Kashrus Institute, PO Box 204, Brooklyn, NY 11204; info@kashrusmagazine.com. Illus., adv. Sample. *Indexed:* IJP. *Aud.:* Ga.

Readers interested in kosher foods—for religious or personal reasons (such as allergies or dietary restrictions)—will find in each issue of *KASHRUS Magazine* up-to-date, authoritative information on more than 100 products researched in collaboration with a kosher organization. Consumer alerts communicate concerns such as mislabeled products, unauthorized use of kosher symbols, pareve/dairy clarifications, and liquor and pharmaceutical updates. A product index allows readers to quickly locate information in a given issue. Stories and articles ("5 Current Kosher Trends On Campus"; "3 U.S. Lawsuits Bring Kosher to Inmates"; "Poor But Not Forgotten With Help From Kosher Food Pantries") focus on a variety of kosher-related matters. Subscribers receive annually a *Kosher Supervision Guide,* a *Kosher Travel Guide,* and a *Passover Shopping Guide.* Selected features from previous issues and additional information appear on the publication's web site. URL: http://kashrusmagazine.com

2544. *The National Provisioner: the authority on the business of meat and poultry processing.* [ISSN: 0027-996X] 1891. m. Free to qualified personnel (print or online ed.). Ed(s): Andy Hanacek. B N P Media, 155 N Pfingsten Rd, Ste 205, Deerfield, IL 60015; http://www.bnpmedia.com. Illus. Sample. *Indexed:* A22, ABIn, B01, B02, B03, C42. *Aud.:* Ac, Sa.

The National Provisioner covers all aspects of the meat, poultry, pork, and seafood processing industry. This self-described technical editorial magazine features articles on regulations and legislation; food safety; meat science; new products; and processing- and packaging-related technologies. The "Tech Showcase" introduces equipment, supplies, and industry news. The monthly publication includes interviews with principals from a variety of types of processing facilities, previews of industry events such as conventions and trade shows, classified ads, and an extensive advertisers index. Some issues include special reports ("State of the Industry") or supplements ("The 2013 Food Safety Report"). The publisher's web site offers access to digitized issues back to February 2010; selected content from the current and random issues back to April 2008; and the opportunity to find articles using keywords. URL: http://provisioneronline.com

2545. *Natural Foods Merchandiser: new ideas, trends, products for the natural and organic foods industry.* Incorporates (in 2001): *New Product Review; Nutrition Science News.* [ISSN: 0164-338X] 1979. 12x/yr. Free. Ed(s): Christine Kapperman. New Hope Natural Media, 1401 Pearl St, Boulder, CO 80302; customerservice@newhope.com; http://www.newhope.com. Illus. Circ: 500 Paid. *Indexed:* ABIn, B01, B02, B03, C42. *Aud.:* Ac, Sa.

To those interested in natural and organic products, *Natural Foods Merchandiser* (*NFM*) delivers information related to the growth of this sector of the food industry in general and of the retail end in particular. The monthly trade magazine reports on a variety of innovations and ideas through statements from and interviews with retailers and industry experts, articles based on consumer trends and scientific research, and columns such as "Secret Shopper" and "Checkout: A Retail Case Study." Recent topics included applications of new technology, flavors, diet and health, genetically modified food labeling, social media, "showrooming," challenges for independent retailers, and employee management strategies. Natural products industry and show news, an extensive new product showcase, and an advertiser's index complete each issue. The publication's annual market overview comes out in June. Subscription information is available at the publisher's web site. URL: http://newhope360.com/natural-foods-merchandiser

2546. *Prepared Foods: product development trends and technologies for formulators and marketers.* Incorporates (in 1986): *Food Plant Equipment;* Former titles (until 1984): *Processed Prepared Foods;* Which Incorporated (in 1981): *Food Development;* Which was formerly (until 19??): *Food Product Development;* (until 1977): *Canner Packer.* [ISSN: 0747-2536] 1895. m. Free to qualified personnel (print or online ed.). Ed(s): Bob Garrison, Julia M Gallo-Torres. B N P Media, 155 N Pfingsten Rd, Ste 205, Deerfield, IL 60015; http://www.bnpmedia.com. Illus., index, adv. Sample. Vol. ends: Dec. Microform: PQC. *Indexed:* A22, B01, B02, B03, FS&TA, H&TI. *Aud.:* Ac, Sa.

Focusing on the development and introduction of new food and beverage products worldwide, *Prepared Foods* features an approachable writing style, enticing color photographs, and clear graphics. Typically, the table of contents includes one or more articles under the categories of "New Product Trends," "Culinary Creations," "Ingredient Challenges," "R&D Applications," and "Nutrasolutions (A Section on Solutions for the Development and Marketing of Nutritional Products)." Articles report on consumer and market trends, news, regulations, seminars and conferences, and solutions to various business challenges. An index facilitates locating advertisers. While those interested must qualify to create an account to see the digital version of the magazine back to July 2008, anyone may see selected content (such as cover stories, features, columns, R&D applications, products, and departments) in non-digitized versions back to January 2001, and search for articles by keyword. URL: http://preparedfoods.com

2547. *Refrigerated and Frozen Foods: business and technology solutions for cold chain professionals.* Formerly (until 19??): *Dairy and Frozen Foods.* [ISSN: 1061-6152] 1990. 7x/yr. Free to qualified personnel (print or online ed.). Ed(s): Marina Mayer. B N P Media, 155 N Pfingsten Rd, Ste 205, Deerfield, IL 60015; portfolio@bnpmedia.com; http://www.bnpmedia.com. Adv. Sample. *Indexed:* ABIn, B02, B03, C45. *Aud.:* Ac, Sa.

Cold food safety; cold supply chain and logistics; and cold technology are just the tip of the iceberg for *Refrigerated & Frozen Foods,* whose focus is "value-added convenience chilled and frozen foods." Seven times a year, this trade publication reports additionally on packaging equipment and materials, new retail products, and cold energy management; features interviews with professionals from various category sectors; and provides show previews and advertisements related to temperature-sensitive food. Cover stories range from the "State of the Industry" and the "Top 150 Food Processors" to reports on best practices, recalls, food plants, and key processors. *Refrigerated & Frozen Foods* is available in print and online; the publisher's web site provides access to digitized issues back to May 2009, selected content of older issues back to January 2008, and a keyword search option to locate articles. URL: http://refrigeratedfrozenfood.com

2548. *Snack Food & Wholesale Bakery: production, technology & product development solutions for a changing industry.* Former titles (until Jul.1997): *Snack & Bakery Foods;* (until Jan.1997): *Snack Food;* (until 1967): *Biscuit and Cracker Baker;* (until 1950): *The Cracker Baker.* [ISSN: 1096-4835] 1912. m. Free to qualified personnel (print or online ed.). Ed(s): Lauren R Hartman. B N P Media, 2401 W Big Beaver Rd, Ste 700, Troy, MI 48084; http://www.bnpmedia.com. Illus., index, adv. Sample. Circ: 14854. Vol. ends: Dec. *Indexed:* ABIn, B02, B03, BRI. *Aud.:* Ac, Sa.

Easy to read and well-illustrated, the trade publication *Snack Food & Wholesale Bakery* reports on matters related to the large-volume commercial and wholesale snack and baked goods industries. Most monthly issues highlight a company (and profile its plant); regular features cover market trends, ingredient technology, and processing technology. Health and wellness, food safety, new products, packaging, and details of upcoming shows are consistent topics. The June and July issues ("State of the Bakery Industry" and "State of the Snack Industry" reports, respectively) discuss trends in various sectors of these ever-expanding markets. The October issue is the annual "Buyer's Guide." There's an ad index. Digitized copies of most issues back to September 2008, selected content of issues back to January 2008, and the means to search for articles online are available at the publisher's web site. URL: http://snackandbakery.com

■ FORENSICS

Jim Hodgson, Collection Management, Widener Library, Harvard University, Cambridge, MA 02138; hodgson@fas.harvard.edu

Introduction

Forensics, or forensic science, is the study and application of scientific method to any subject of public discourse or legal proceeding. One aspect of this is crime scene investigation (CSI). The scope of publications covered here includes CSI and law enforcement, medical forensics and forensic psychology, and digital forensics. The purpose is to provide information for the most general journals, with an emphasis on criminology. Journals that have a strictly medical or engineering focus are not included.

Basic Periodicals

The Australian Journal of Forensic Sciences; The British Journal of Forensic Practice; Digital Investigation; Forensic Magazine; Forensic Science International; Forensic Science Review; International Journal of Legal Medicine (Legal Medicine); Journal of Forensic and Legal Medicine; Journal of Forensic Sciences; Medicine, Science and the Law; Science and Justice.

Basic Abstracts and Indexes

Biology Digest; BIOSIS Previews; Criminal Justice Abstracts; Criminal Justice Periodical Index; MEDLINE; Science Citation Index.

2549. *Forensic Magazine.* [ISSN: 1553-6262] 2004. bi-m. USD 120 in US & Canada (Free to qualified personnel). Ed(s): Chris Janson. Vicon Publishing, Inc., 4 Limbo Ln, Amherst, NH 03031; http://www.viconpublishing.com. Adv. *Aud.:* Hs, Ga, Sa.

This journal publishes narratives about criminal investigations around the world. Some cases are examined in detail, along with short articles that cover new developments, opinions, and recaps. Almost all of the subjects are related to popular interests—for example, DNA databases, war crimes, and terrorism. The articles are well-written—although sometimes dramatized—case reports by professionals, which are suitable for people working in law enforcement and for readers interested in CSI stories. A print version is available, and there is free online access at www.forensicmag.com with advertising alongside. Public library reference desks will find the site approachable for topical CSI questions and interests.

2550. *Forensic Science International: an international journal dedicated to the applications of genetics in the administration of justice.* Former titles (until vol.13, no.1, 1979): *Forensic Science; Journal of Forensic Medicine.* [ISSN: 0379-0738] 1972. 30x/yr. EUR 4038. Ed(s): P Saukko. Elsevier Ireland Ltd, Elsevier House, Brookvale Plaza, E. Park, Shannon, Ireland. Illus. Refereed. Microform: PQC. *Indexed:* A01, A22, AbAn, BRI, C45, CJPI, CLI, ExcerpMed, IndVet, L14. *Bk. rev.:* 0-3, signed. *Aud.:* Ac, Sa.

Published in Ireland, this title was among the earliest journals devoted to forensic science, and it was also one of the first available online, through Gale. Coverage includes original research papers, literature review articles, and case reports on the legal aspects of general forensics disciplines. It also features (per the mission statement) "investigations of value to public health in its broadest sense, and the important marginal area where science and medicine interact with the law." The online presence includes the upcoming issue as well as recently-accepted articles in press. A recent sample article is titled, "The forensic relevance of hypothermia in living persons—Literature and retrospective study." Medical forensics coverage in this journal is so comprehensive that it can be esoteric, and a full understanding of most articles requires a strong medical or science background on the part of the reader. Many of the subjects are not suitable to topical or popular interest in criminology. There are occasional book reviews.

2551. *International Journal of Legal Medicine (Online).* [ISSN: 1437-1596] 1998. bi-m. Springer, Haber Str 7, Heidelberg, 69126, Germany; orders-hd-individuals@springer.com; http://www.springer.com. *Aud.:* Ac, Sa.

"Legal medicine" originated in the nineteenth-century German revolution in record-keeping, science, and publishing. Most of the articles relate to medical forensics and lab techniques, but some are specific to criminology, and all are relevant to criminal forensics. The online site includes articles not yet assigned to an issue. A strong medical or science background is helpful, but the wide variety of topics recommends this journal for inclusion in a core list of forensics publications.

2552. *Journal of Forensic Sciences.* Formerly (until 1956): *The American Academy of Forensic Sciences. Proceedings.* [ISSN: 0022-1198] 1956. bi-m. GBP 387 (print & online eds.). Ed(s): Michael A Peat. Wiley-Blackwell Publishing, Inc., 111 River St, Hoboken, NJ 07030; info@wiley.com; http://onlinelibrary.wiley.com/. Illus., index, adv. Refereed. Microform: PQC. Reprint: PSC. *Indexed:* A&ATA, A01, A22, AbAn, BRI, C&ISA, C45, CJPI, CLI, CerAb, E01, H24, IndVet, L14, PsycInfo, RILM, RRTA, RiskAb. *Bk. rev.:* 0-5, signed. *Aud.:* Ac, Sa.

This journal was one of several that began in the 1950s devoted to forensic science, and it presents papers, case reports, and technical notes in anthropology, criminalistics, "general," odontology, pathology and biology, psychiatry, engineering, questioned document, digital and multimedia sciences, and toxicology. It also includes case reports, as well as correspondence and letters to the editor. Most articles require a strong medical or professional criminology background, and most are esoteric rather than popular in subject matter, but some are relevant to overall development of the field, e.g., this recent sample title: "Expert Interpretation of Bitemark Injuries—A Contemporary Qualitative Study."

2553. *Medicine, Science and the Law.* [ISSN: 0025-8024] 1960. q. USD 276 (print & online eds.). Sage Publications Ltd., 1 Oliver's Yard, 55 City Rd, London, EC1Y 1SP, United Kingdom; info@sagepub.co.uk; http://www.uk.sagepub.com. Adv. Sample. Refereed. *Indexed:* A22, BRI, CLI, L14. *Bk. rev.:* 0-2. *Aud.:* Ac, Sa.

This small-format journal presents a wide variety of readable articles intended to "advance the knowledge of forensic science and medicine." Interactions between society and medicine are discussed, and case studies analyze causes of death in the aggregate and for individuals. There is coverage of medical devices and techniques, reviews of current forensic practices, and literature reviews of specific topics. A regular feature, "Law and Science," abstracts specific cases, and there are occasional book reviews.

2554. *Science and Justice.* Formerly (until 1995): *Forensic Science Society. Journal.* [ISSN: 1355-0306] 1960. q. EUR 328. Ed(s): L Barron. Elsevier Ltd, 32 Jamestown Rd, Camden, London, NW1 7BY, United Kingdom; corporate.sales@elsevier.com; http://www.elsevier.com. Illus., index, adv. Sample. Refereed. *Indexed:* A22, BRI, CJPI, CLI, ExcerpMed, L14. *Bk. rev.:* 0-4, signed. *Aud.:* Sa.

Forensic Science Society. Journal began in 1960, and was among the earliest U.S. publications dedicated to CSI. In 1995, it changed its name to *Science and Justice* and switched to a larger, glossy format. This journal is international in scope. Topics covered include CSI practice, theory, and analysis. Well-written articles are presented with a strong emphasis on science as applied to criminology, including literature reviews of specific topics, and upcoming U.K. events. Articles are written from a scientific perspective but are intended for a general audience, so readers are not required to have a strong science background. Authors may pay a fee to opt to make their articles openly accessible via the ScienceDirect platform.

■ FORESTRY

Bonnie E. Avery, Forestry and Natural Resources Librarian, Oregon State University Libraries, Room 121, The Valley Library, Corvallis, OR 97331-4501; bonnie.avery@oregonstate.edu

Introduction

A broad definition of forestry would include the study of trees, forests, and the habitat they provide, as well as their use by people. Modern, "science-based" forestry began in the nineteenth century, when Europeans looked for specialists who could address questions on wood supply and extraction both at home and in their colonies. The threat of forest loss and wood scarcity created concern for increased forest growth as well as management techniques that would improve yield.

By 1891, the United States had established publicly-owned forest reserves. In 1900, the Society of American Foresters was established, as was the first School of Forestry in North America at Yale University. The U.S. Forest Service was formed three years later. This combination of professional, scholarly, and governmental resources continues to provide the core of U.S. forestry research today.

Since the mid-1940s, the scope of forestry has grown in response to economics, demography, politics, and social change, as well as developments in related fields of study. While German was the primary language of forestry in the nineteenth century, since World War II most research has been reported in English. Knowledge of international research and practices has grown in importance since the 1980s, particularly as broader trade in forest products influenced the health of forests. In addressing global forest concerns, international and local researchers have begun to "discover" reservoirs of indigenous knowledge concerning native forests and their use. Today the Internet exposes researchers to a wealth of information in other languages as well. Locating these publications can be difficult, and language can be a barrier for those who only read English.

Modern forestry education has a tradition of integrating concepts from a variety of disciplines and creating new specialties. These include forest genetics, forest ecology, forest recreation, forest economics, forest engineering, urban forestry, plantation forestry, forest pathology, and wood science. Often, the questions addressed in forestry are interdisciplinary or require a deep understanding of complementary disciplines. As a result, a forestry collection is most useful when it is in close proximity to a sound collection in the natural, environmental, and agricultural sciences. Likewise, users of a wood science or forest engineering collection will rely on access to other collections in the physical sciences and civil, mechanical, and chemical engineering.

Finally, to address the interaction of humans and the forest as a multipurpose natural resource, whether looking at income generation, recreational use, traditional knowledge and practices, conservation strategies, or sustainable practices, a forest researcher will need access to collections in the social sciences.

Given these assumptions about access to other collections, we can define a distinct serial literature for forestry. First, it is anchored in the history of forestry and is composed largely of government document series and international and nongovernmental organization report series. In comparison to these, trade, professional, and specialized scholarly journals constitute a highly regarded yet small portion of the serial information sources in forestry.

The list of periodicals included here does not include government publications, although these are an important source of technical as well as scientific information. Governmental agencies such as the regional research and experiment stations of the U.S. Forest Service provide vital information on all aspects of forestry in series titles such as the regional *General Technical Reports*. These are numerous and now are published electronically and made available by the Forest Service on their *TreeSearch* web site. Electronic versions of many Canadian government forestry report series are also available free via the web. In addition, Canadian libraries that focus on forestry benefit from their access to the National Research Council of Canada's many serial publications.

Although important sources of information, the statistical series and serials available from nongovernmental, nonprofit international organizations, as well as from research institutions, have not been included in this listing. Several statistical series and *The State of the World's Forests* are available as searchable datasets and in full text on the Food and Agriculture Organization (FAO) Forestry Sector web site.

There are numerous serial report publications now available via the Internet from other nongovernmental, nonprofit agencies. These are particularly important for coverage of international forestry. The FAO Forestry Sector web site will help identify and serve as a portal to many of these resources, as will the "Forestry AgNIC" web site.

This selection of scholarly, academic, and trade journals for forestry is representative and by no means exhaustive. In 2001, faculty members in the College of Forestry at Oregon State University were asked to list their most used or "top ten" journals. This confirmed the multidisciplinary underpinnings of forestry. It also provided the core set of scholarly titles for this list to which I have added a few titles in subsequent years. In general when selecting scholarly titles, I look for those with high-impact factor rankings or journals with a long citation half-life as provided by the *Journal Citation Reports* from Thomson ISI. When deciding between comparable titles, I consider the journal subscription price, and give preference to professional society publications over journals from commercial publishers. For the 21st edition of *MFL*, I referred to an article by an Australian forest researcher for a new perspective (Vanclay, J. [2008] Ranking forestry journals using the h-index. *Journal of Infometrics*, 2[4], 326-334).

No forestry collection is complete, and many academic libraries have established open-access repositories as a means of archiving and making available their local institutional scholarship for the greater good. When signing a copyright transfer agreement with the journal publisher, authors need to retain their right to deposit a version of their article with their home institution. I have included information on these "author rights" taken from publisher web sites and from the *SHERPARoMEO* web site. These policies can change as publishers merge or take over an imprints for other reasons. I encourage checking publisher and *SHERPARoMEO* web sites for updates.

When updating this section, I look for titles that reflect changing concerns and new regions of interest. The *Directory of Open Access Journals* (*DOAJ*), which serves as an inexpensive entre to many international society publications and research journals. As with any journal claiming to be "scholarly," attention must be paid to the editorial and peer-review process employed. Added in this edition are *Forest Systems* and *International Journal of Forestry Research*, both peer-reviewed, open-access publications.

Removed with this edition are the *American Christmas Tree Journal* and the *Forest Land Owner Magazine*. While important to their individual audiences, these two publications offer little to non-member subscribers in the way of an added-value web site and are not available electronically. Also removed after a good deal of deliberation is *Environmental History*, an excellent publication, sponsored in part by the Forest History Society (FHS); the forest history content of this journal seems to be in decline. However, I would encourage all public libraries to provide access to the *Forest History Today Magazine*, an excellent annual publication available on the FHS web site. Finally, to correct a selection error from the previous edition, *Mathematical and Computational Forestry and Natural Resource Science* has been removed because it has proven to be too narrowly focused, based on a review of new articles added since 2010.

Forestry is an exciting and ever-changing field of study. For anyone new to managing a forestry collection, I recommend *Literature of Forestry and Agroforestry*, published by Cornell University Press in 1996. It provides a useful history of the field, and identifies both monographs and serials that have defined "science-based forestry" during the last century. It serves as a good foundation for considering new areas of research and how best to provide a wide array of "evidence-based" forestry information in the future.

Basic Periodicals

Hs: *American Forests, Journal of Forestry, Unasylva.* Ga: *American Forests, Canadian Forest Industries, Eastern Native Tree Society Bulletin, Journal of Forestry, National Woodlands, Unasylva.* Ac, Sa: *Agricultural and Forest Meteorology, Agroforestry Systems, Arboriculture and Urban Forestry, Arborist News, BC Journal of Ecosystems and Management, Canadian Journal of Forest Research, Fire Ecology, Forest Ecology and Management, Forest Policy and Economics, Forest Products Journal, Forest Science, Forest Systems, Forestry Chronicle, iForest, International Forestry Review, International Journal of Forestry Research, IAWA Journal, International Journal of Forest Engineering, International Journal of Wildland Fire, Journal of Forestry, Journal of Sustainable Forestry, New Forests, Northern Journal of Applied Forestry, Revista Arvore, Silva Fennica, Small-Scale Forestry, Southern Journal of Applied Forestry, Tree Physiology, Trees, Western Journal of Applied Forestry Wood and Fiber Science, Wood Material Science and Engineering.*

Basic Abstracts and Indexes

Academic Search Premier, AGRICOLA, Biological and Agricultural Index, CAB Abstracts, Forest Science Database, Google Scholar, Treesearch.

2555. Agricultural and Forest Meteorology. Formerly (until 1984): *Agricultural Meteorology.* [ISSN: 0168-1923] 1964. 16x/yr. EUR 3851. Ed(s): X Lee. Elsevier BV, Radarweg 29, PO Box 211, Amsterdam, 1000 AE, Netherlands; JournalsCustomerServiceEMEA@elsevier.com; http://www.elsevier.nl. Illus., index, adv. Sample. Refereed. Microform: PQC. *Indexed:* A01, A22, Agr, C&ISA, C45, CerAb, FR, M&GPA, RRTA, S25. *Bk. rev.:* 1-3, 500-800 words. *Aud.:* Ac, Sa.

This international journal covers meteorology as it is used in the agricultural, forest, and soil sciences. Articles emphasize research relevant to the practical problems of forestry, agriculture, and natural ecosystems. Topics include the effect of weather on forests, soils, crops, water use, and forest fires; the effect of vegetation on climate and weather; and canopy micrometeorology. This journal is heavily used by specialists working in these areas and as a result has high impact metrics in the ISI Web of Knowledge. Beginning with 2010, 12 volumes appear annually, each comprising a single issue. While this is an expensive journal, a number of thematic, special issues are available for purchase as monographs. Options for online access are available through Elsevier's SciVerse platform. Authors may archive their accepted manuscript (post–peer review) on their personal or institutional server, but must acknowledge the published source, must link to the journal homepage, and may not use the publisher's pdf version.

2556. Agroforestry Systems. Incorporates (1972-1999): *Agroforestry Forum;* Which was formerly (until 1992): *Agroforestry in the U K.* [ISSN: 0167-4366] 1982. 9x/yr. EUR 1627 (print & online eds.). Ed(s): Shibu Jose. Springer Netherlands, Van Godewijckstraat 30, Dordrecht, 3311 GX, Netherlands; http://www.springer.com. Adv. Refereed. Microform: PQC. Reprint: PSC. *Indexed:* A22, Agr, BRI, C45, E01, GardL, RRTA, S25. *Bk. rev.:* Occasional, 500-1,500 words. *Aud.:* Ac, Sa.

Sponsored in part by the World Agroforestry Center (formerly the International Center for Research in Agroforestry or ICRAF), this is an international, refereed journal. It has grown in reputation during its 20 years of publication, and is currently highly cited in the research literature. Three volumes are published annually, each consisting of three issues. Included in each issue are seven to ten reports of original research, critical reviews, and short communications, with periodic book reviews and announcements. Topics include basic and applied research on indigenous species and multipurpose trees, and techniques for integrating systems of trees, crops, and livestock. For inclusion, research results and information presented must have application beyond the specific location studied. This journal would complement collections that support agriculture and environmental studies as well as forestry, particularly those with an international development focus. Online access is available via SpringerLink.

FORESTRY

Authors may archive their accepted manuscript (post–peer review) on their personal or institutional server, but must acknowledge the published source, must link to the journal homepage, and may not use the publisher's pdf version.

2557. American Forests: protecting and restoring forests for life.
Incorporates (1990-1995): *Urban Forests;* Which was formerly (until 1990): *Urban Forest Forum;* (until 1988): *National Urban Forest Forum;* (until 1986): *National Urban and Community Forestry Forum;* Formerly (until 1931): *American Forests and Forest Life;* (until 1924): *American Forestry;* (until 1910): *Conservation;* (until 1908): *Forestry & Irrigation;* Which was formed by the merger of (1900-1901): *National Irrigation;* Which was formerly (until 1897): *The National Advocate;* (1895-1902): *The Forester;* Which was formerly (until 1985): *New Jersey Forester.* [ISSN: 0002-8541] 1895. q. Free to members. American Forests, 734 15th St NW Ste 800, Washington, DC 20005; info@amfor.org; http://www.americanforests.org. Illus., index, adv. Vol. ends: Winter. Microform: PQC. *Indexed:* A01, A06, A22, ABIn, Agr, B01, B02, BRI, C37, CBRI, EngInd, GardL, MASUSE, P02. *Aud.:* Hs, Ga, Ac.

This quarterly magazine is the membership organ for one of the oldest conservation organizations in the United States, American Forests. It is also made available free via the publisher web site. Feature articles are intended for a general audience and address tree planting, tree species profiles, and current policy controversies, as well as the practical aspects of current research and how-to articles. Typical of this magazine's well-illustrated and easily read features are recent articles on the role of urban forests in urban planning and on wildfire recovery efforts in the Southwest. The organization sponsors the work of the "Global ReLeaf Center," "Forest Policy Center," and "Urban Forest Center," and maintains the "National Register of Big Trees." Editorial emphasis is placed on coverage of forests and trees located "on land where people live, work, and relax." Further explanation of sponsored programs and memberships are available on the organization's web site, as is an archive of many of the magazine's articles. Authors retain copyrights to their writings in this publication.

2558. Arboriculture & Urban Forestry. Formerly (until 2006): *Journal of Arboriculture;* Which was formed by the merger of (1935-1975): *Arborist's News;* (1929-1975): *International Shade Tree Conference. Proceedings of the Annual Meeting.* [ISSN: 1935-5297] 1975. bi-m. Free to members. International Society of Arboriculture, PO Box 3129, Champaign, IL 61826; isa@isa-arbor.com; http://www.isa-arbor.com. Illus., index. Sample. Refereed. Vol. ends: Nov. *Indexed:* A01, A22, Agr, C45, GardL, RRTA. *Aud.:* Ac, Sa.

This bimonthly journal (formerly, *Journal of Arboriculture*) is published by the International Society of Arboriculture (ISA). Each issue includes four to six research papers intended for the practitioner, and although scientific in nature, they are accessible to the interested layperson. Articles regularly cover such topics as green space, sustainable urban forestry, control of invasive species, landscaping, etc., and would be of interest to urban policymakers as well as urban foresters and park administrators. Of interest to homeowners and gardeners are topics such as street tree inventories, the effect of vegetation on energy use, and topping of trees. Included in each issue is "Arboriculture Abstracts," which summarizes relevant articles in related journals. Authors transfer their copyrights to ISA, and no statement is available on author rights to self-archive. With a two-year lag, articles are available in an open-access back file from 1975 forward.

2559. Arborist News. [ISSN: 1542-2399] 1992. bi-m. Free to members. Ed(s): Aaron Bynum. International Society of Arboriculture, PO Box 3129, Champaign, IL 61826; isa@isa-arbor.com; http://www.isa-arbor.com. Adv. Circ: 20627. *Indexed:* C45, GardL. *Aud.:* Ga, Ac.

This bimonthly publication covers news of interest to the tree-care professional and is the membership publication of the International Society of Arboriculture. Regular features include the "Tree Industry Calendar"; professional profiles; summaries of articles published in the journal *Arboriculture & Urban Forestry*; the "Climbers Corner"; and "European News." Continuing-education articles feature general tree care, current tree-health problems, and business aspects of arboriculture. Selected articles are available in full text on the society's web site, as is membership information needed for subscribing. Articles are timely and

readable and would be useful for the general homeowner as well as for the professional arborist. This publication is suitable for a general collection or public library. With a one-year lag, an open-access back file beginning with 2000 for this publication is available online from the ISA web site.

2560. B C Journal of Ecosystems and Management. [ISSN: 1488-4666] 2001. 3x/yr. Ed(s): Julie Schooling. FORREX Forest Research Extension Society, 235 1st Ave, Ste 702, Kamloops, BC V2C 3J4, Canada; http://www.forrex.org. *Indexed:* C45, RRTA. *Aud.:* Ac, Sa.

This peer-reviewed journal is published by FORREX Forest Research Extension Partnership three times a year. Its mission is to inform readers about innovative approaches to sustainable ecosystem management, and it provides a forum for commentary on current issues and challenges. A modest subscription fee is required for the print edition, while the online version is free to all. This journal is aimed at decision makers in the policy, management, and operations areas, as well as practitioners, professionals, researchers, and natural resource users. Each journal contains research results, indigenous knowledge, management applications, socioeconomic analyses, and scholarly opinions. While the emphasis is on applications to British Columbia, articles from the Pacific Northwest states are considered for publication, and certainly articles on species common to the wider region are included. Issues include eight to ten articles categorized as one of the following: editorial comments/perspectives, research reports, discussion papers, popular summaries, and extension notes. This is an open-access journal that uses creative commons attribution licensing. This should allow authors to archive the published version of their articles, with attribution to the original published version.

2561. Canadian Biomass. Supersedes in part (in 201?): *Canadian Forest Industries;* Which incorporated (1992-2010): *Canadian Wood Products;* and was formed by the merger of (1940-1964): *Timber of Canada;* (1921-1964): *Canada Lumberman;* Which was formerly (until 1921): *Canada Lumberman and Woodworker;* (1880-1905): *Canada Lumberman.* [ISSN: 2290-3097] 1964. bi-m. CAD 48 domestic (Free to qualified personnel). J C F T Forest Communications, 105 Donly Dr S, PO Box 530, Simcoe, ON N3Y 4N5, Canada. Illus., adv. Vol. ends: Dec. Microform: MML; PQC. *Indexed:* A22. *Aud.:* Ac, Sa.

This Canadian trade journal serves as the journal of record for the Canadian Woodlands Forum of the Forest Products Association of Canada (formerly the Canadian Pulp and Paper Association). It focuses on the full range of activities associated with logging technology and harvesting systems. Articles are of current interest, and editorial features are common and may give this publication broad appeal among those interested in industry practices suitable for North America. Topics or features such as environmentally sound road building, wood certification, current forest harvesting practices, and tests of new logging equipment are included regularly, and would be of interest to students in forestry or environmental policy. Regular features also include reviews of new products and literature. The current issue can be viewed online, and a sampling of articles from 2007 forward is available on the journal's web site, as is subscription information for this bimonthly publication.

2562. Canadian Journal of Forest Research. [ISSN: 0045-5067] 1970. m. CAD 1740. Ed(s): Pierre Bernier, Dr. Daniel Kneeshaw. N R C Research Press, 1200 Montreal Rd, Bldg M-55, Ottawa, ON K1A 0R6, Canada; pubs@nrc-cnrc.gc.ca; http://pubs.nrc-cnrc.gc.ca. Illus., index, adv. Sample. Refereed. Circ: 862. Vol. ends: Dec. Microform: MML; PQC. *Indexed:* A01, A22, Agr, C37, C45, CBCARef, E01, EngInd, P02, RRTA, S25. *Aud.:* Ac, Sa.

Consistently in the top ten forestry journal rankings as issued by Institute for Scientific Information, this refereed journal should be a core title for any research collection in this area. It is international in scope, and its articles are in English with French summaries, and report on primary research that addresses an array of questions; they are also accompanied by extensive bibliographies. Each issue is composed of 15–20 articles, often authored by researchers at universities, government forestry agencies, or other research institutions. Subscription information and tables of contents are available on the web site of the National Research Council of Canada (NRC). After a 12-month period, articles in this journal are included in EBSCO's Academic Search packages. Access to the full back file is available for purchase via a package with other NRC publications. The plan is to make the file open-access once digitization costs are covered. A site license for online-only access is available. As of 2009, copyright in all articles among the NRC Research Press journals remains with the authors who may archive their accepted manuscripts, but not use the publisher's version.

2563. Eastern Native Tree Society. Bulletin. [ISSN: 1933-799X] 2006. q. Free to members. Ed(s): Dr. Don Bragg. Eastern Native Tree Society, c/o Don C Bragg, Eic, USDA Forest Service-SRS, Monticello, AR 71656; http://www.nativetreesociety.org/. *Aud.*: Ga, Ac.

This friendly journal is available free from the Eastern Native Tree Society web site. The society is a "cyberspace interest group devoted to the documentation and celebration of trees and forests of eastern North America." It also serves as an archive of information on specific trees and stands of trees, and serves as an arbiter of "big tree disputes." The society's broad geographic scope has led to the formation of a subgroup, the "Western Native Tree Society." The *Bulletin* typically includes announcements, one to three feature articles, prose or poetry, a field report, one to three pieces on "notable trees and forests," and an editorial. Recent feature articles cover the ancient Cypress of the Carolina coastal plains and the documenting of rare forests remnants. Articles are illustrated with fine photography. This publication serves as a good representative of citizen scientist groups that both public and academic libraries might include to promote local knowledge and interests.

2564. Fire Ecology. [ISSN: 1933-9747] 2005. s-a. Ed(s): Jan van Wagtendonk, Michael Medler. Association for Fire Ecology, PO Box 4388, Davis, CA 95617; afe@fireecology.net; http://www.fireecology.net. Refereed. *Indexed*: Agr. *Bk. rev.*: Occasional. *Aud.*: Ac, Sa.

Published twice annually by the Association of Fire Ecology, this is an open-access, peer-reviewed journal. Its coverage includes research, education, management, and policies related to fire as a fundamental ecological process. Some issues are thematic; these have included issues on fire history in California, fire in the Southwest, and remote sensing applications for investigations of fire attributes. Contributions include original research papers, short communications, opinion and response pieces, and discussions of practices and applications in fire ecology. The geographic scope is largely North America.

2565. Forest Ecology and Management. [ISSN: 0378-1127] 1977. 24x/yr. EUR 5446. Ed(s): P M Attiwill. Elsevier BV, Radarweg 29, PO Box 211, Amsterdam, 1000 AE, Netherlands; JournalsCustomerServiceEMEA@elsevier.com; http://www.elsevier.nl. Illus., index, adv. Sample. Refereed. Microform: PQC. *Indexed*: A22, Agr, C&ISA, C45, CerAb, EngInd, RRTA, S25. *Aud.*: Ac, Sa.

This refereed journal is perhaps most representative of the multidisciplinary nature of forestry. As of 2012, there are 24 volumes published each year, and issues numbering is no longer used. Each volume consists of 30 or more articles. The journal reports on the "application of biological, ecological[,] and social knowledge to the management of man-made and natural forests." Volumes are often thematic, and typical articles report on research related to tree growth, nutrient cycling, landscape ecology, the forest as habitat, the effect of logging practices, and numerous other subjects. Online access is available through Elsevier's SciVerse platform. The heavy use of this journal by scholars and researchers makes it a core title for research-based forestry collections despite its high cost. Authors may archive their accepted manuscript (post–peer review) on their personal or institutional server, but must acknowledge the published source, must link to the journal homepage, and may not use the publisher's pdf version.

2566. Forest Policy and Economics. [ISSN: 1389-9341] 2000. 8x/yr. EUR 610. Ed(s): M Krott. Elsevier BV, Radarweg 29, PO Box 211, Amsterdam, 1000 AE, Netherlands; JournalsCustomerServiceEMEA@elsevier.com; http://www.elsevier.nl. Refereed. *Indexed*: A22, Agr, B01, C45, EngInd, RRTA. *Aud.*: Ac, Sa.

This refereed journal is issued in collaboration with the European Forest Institute (EFI) and fills a niche in the forestry literature by addressing policy issues in an international context. It covers economics and planning as they apply to the forests and forest industries sector, and it seeks to "enhance communications amongst researchers, legislators, decision-makers, and other

professionals concerned with formulating and implementing policies for the sector." As of 2012, only volume numbering is used. Each volume consists of ten or more articles, as well as occasional conference announcements and EFI news. Special thematic issues have covered such topics as forest and nature-based recreation and tourism; integrating forest products with ecosystem services; and emerging economic mechanisms for global forest governance. As a moderately priced, scholarly forestry title, it will be an important addition to research collections, but may also be useful for large public library collections where forestry is an important part of the economy. Online access is available through Elsevier's SciVerse platform. Authors may archive their accepted manuscript (post–peer review) on their personal or institutional server, but must acknowledge the published source, must link to the journal homepage, and may not use the publisher's pdf version.

2567. Forest Products Journal. Former titles (until 1955): *Forest Products Research Society. Journal*; (until 1951): *Forest Products Research Society. Proceedings of the National Annual Meeting.* [ISSN: 0015-7473] 1947. m. Free to members; Non-members, USD 155. Forest Products Society, 2801 Marshall Ct, Madison, WI 53705; erin@forestprod.org; http://www.forestprod.org. Illus., index, adv. Sample. Refereed. Vol. ends: Nov/Dec. Microform: PMC; PQC. *Indexed*: A&ATA, A22, ABIn, Agr, B01, B02, BRI, C45, EngInd, RRTA. *Bk. rev.*: 0-1, 1,000-2,000 words. *Aud.*: Ac, Sa.

Sponsored by the Forest Products Society, this refereed journal is well respected for its technical coverage of research in wood science and technology. The journal is issued ten times a year. Each includes 10–12 technical articles on an array of topics that include management, processes, solid wood products, composites and manufactured wood products, and fundamental disciplines. To put these articles in perspective, a short statement on the relevance of each article is given under the heading "Practicalities and Possibilities." In addition to association news and classified ads, regular feature columns report on international research literature, new publications and computer applications, patents, codes, standards, and regulatory changes. The featured article from each of the most recent three issues is available in full text on the society's web site. Earlier articles are available to society members only through a user ID and password. This lack of IP recognition access may be a problem for libraries that wish to provide online access to their users. Alternative online access is available via the aggregator databases in EBSCO. Although this journal is a technical publication, many of its articles would be useful to engineers, economists, and those wishing to keep abreast of the forest products industry. There is no information available on the journal web site concerning author rights regarding archiving.

2568. Forest Science: a bimonthly journal of research and technical progress. [ISSN: 0015-749X] 1955. bi-m. USD 375 (Individuals, USD 130; Members, USD 99 (print & online eds.). Ed(s): Matthew Walls, Edwin J Green. Society of American Foresters, 5400 Grosvenor Ln, Bethesda, MD 20814; safnet@safnet.org; http://www.safnet.org/. Illus., index, adv. Sample. Refereed. Vol. ends: Dec. Microform: PQC. *Indexed*: A22, Agr, C45, EngInd, P02, RRTA, S25. *Bk. rev.*: 2-3, 1,000 words. *Aud.*: Ac, Sa.

This bimonthly refereed journal is one of five journals sponsored by the Society of American Foresters. Each issue includes 15–25 articles that report on scientific results from both theoretical and applied research related to silviculture, soils, biometry, disease, recreation, photosynthesis, tree physiology, and all aspects of management and harvesting. This journal is international in scope, and its articles are both highly cited and consistently cited over a long period of time. It enjoys wide respect within the forestry scientific community and is heavily used by researchers, practitioners, and students alike, who consider it a core title for their work. The general format is open to a wider audience, and articles are readable, making the journal accessible to the general reader as well. The journal is available online via *Ingenta* with a full electronic back set. Subscription information is available from the society's web site, as is a good deal of other information about the society. Authors may archive their accepted manuscript (post–peer review) on their personal or institutional server, but must acknowledge the published source, must link to the journal homepage, and may not use the publisher's pdf version.

2569. Forest Systems. Former titles (until 2009): *Investigacion Agraria. Sistemas y Recursos Forestales;* (until 1985): *Instituto Nacional de Investigaciones Agrarias. Anales. Serie Forestal;* (until 1980): *Instituto*

Nacional de Investigaciones Agrarias. Anales. Serie Recursos Naturales; Which superseded in part (1952-1970): *Instituto Nacional de Investigaciones Agronomicas. Anales.* [ISSN: 2171-5068] 1974. 3x/yr. Free. Ed(s): Ricardo Alia. Ministerio de Educacion y Ciencia, Instituto Nacional de Investigacion y Tecnologia Agraria y Alimentaria (I N I A), Carretera de la Coruna km. 7.5, Madrid, 28040, Spain. Refereed. *Indexed:* C45, RRTA. *Aud.:* Ac, Sa.

This quarterly, peer-reviewed journal aims to integrate multidisciplinary research with forest management. Preference is given to papers that bring together two or more approaches or disciplines. All aspects of forestry are covered, including genetics, ecology, silviculture, management and policy, and wood and non-wood forest products. Articles are in either Spanish and English, with abstracts in both languages. A quick sampling of articles reveals that most are in English. Occasional special thematic issues include a recent one on trends in modeling to address forest management and environmental challenges in Europe. This journal has been added in 2012 to the Forestry section because it represents the open-access model that many research institutions are using to provide additional peer-reviewed venues for publishing whose content is accessible to anyone. It does not appear that the editors of this open-access journal have elected to use creative commons licensing, nor is it clear what author rights are retained after publication with respect to archiving outside the journal site.

2570. *The Forestry Chronicle.* Incorporates (19??-1967): *Canadian Institute of Forestry. Annual Report.* [ISSN: 0015-7546] 1925. bi-m. USD 230 (print or online ed.). Ed(s): Ron Ayling. Canadian Institute of Forestry, c/o The Canadian Ecology Centre, 6905 Hwy, 17 West, PO Box 430, Mattawa, ON P0H 1V0, Canada; cif@cif-ifc.org; http://www.cif-ifc.org. Illus., index, adv. Sample. Refereed. Vol. ends: Nov/Dec. *Indexed:* A22, Agr, C45, EngInd, RRTA. *Bk. rev.:* 1-10, 500-1,500 words. *Aud.:* Ac, Sa.

Published by the Canadian Institute of Forestry, this refereed journal includes both peer-reviewed articles and membership news. Bimonthly issues include 10-15 articles in English and, less frequently, in French with English summaries. In recent issues, the ratio of "Professional Papers" to "Scientific and Technical Papers" is two to one. Papers focus on applied and scientific research and occasionally include conference presentations. Announcements of recent publications, forestry education programs, and professional and institute news are regularly included. Online access to this publication is available with a subscription and includes an archive back to 2002. The intended audience for this journal is the professional forester; however, given its modest price, it is an accessible publication for collections that serve undergraduates and the general public. Authors may deposit their accepted manuscript (post–peer review) on their personal or institutional server six months after publication, but must acknowledge the published source, must link to the journal homepage, and not use the publisher's pdf version.

2571. *I A W A Journal.* Former titles (until 1993): *I A W A Bulletin; I A W A Publications.* [ISSN: 0928-1541] 1931. q. EUR 240. Ed(s): E A Wheeler, P Baas. Brill, PO Box 9000, Leiden, 2300 PA, Netherlands; cs@brill.nl; http://www.brill.nl. Refereed. *Indexed:* A22, C45, RRTA. *Bk. rev.:* 2-3, 500-1,000 words. *Aud.:* Ac, Sa.

Published by the International Association of Wood Anatomists, this refereed journal covers topics in wood anatomy such as the micro-structure of wood, bark, and related plant products, including bamboo, rattan, and palms basic to the study of forest products. It is published quarterly, and each issue is comprised of eight to ten well-documented, illustrated articles on the anatomy and properties of a variety of species, as well as association news, announcements of conferences and workshops, and two or three book reviews. An open-access back file of issues is available with a two-year lag from the publisher's web site. For specialized and research collections, this highly cited journal is an important and inexpensive addition.

2572. *iForest: biogeosciences and forestry.* [ISSN: 1971-7458] 2007. q. Free. Societa Italiana di Selvicoltura ed Ecologia Forestale (S I S E F), Dipartimento di Produzione Vegetale, Via dell'Ateneo Lucano 10, Potenza, 85100, Italy; http://www.sisef.it. Refereed. *Indexed:* A01. *Aud.:* Ac, Sa.

This peer-reviewed journal is one of a growing number of open-access titles in forestry whose articles are easily found via Google Scholar. It is sponsored by the Italian Society of Silviculture and Forestry Ecology, which also publishes an Italian counterpart, *Forest@.* The scope of this new title is broad and includes forest ecology, biodiversity and genetics, ecophysiology, silviculture, forest inventory and planning, forest protection and monitoring, forest harvesting, landscape ecology, forest history, and wood technology. Of particular interest is research on sustainable management of forest ecosystems. Although the journal is published in Italy, articles are in English, and include reports of original research; reviews; short communications or brief reporting of research findings; progress reports by individual authors on specific topics; and commentaries on recently published research results. Each issue of this journal contains 10–15 articles that cover a diverse range of topics and geography. Although it is a research journal, many articles are accessible to the interested novice. In addition to Google Scholar, it is indexed by CABI and provides an RSS feed option. While this is an open-access title, it is not clear what rights the author retains regarding archiving of the publisher version of the article.

2573. *The International Forestry Review.* Former titles (until 1999): *Commonwealth Forestry Review;* (until 1962): *Empire Forestry Review;* (until 1946): *Empire Forestry Journal;* (until 1923): *Empire Forestry.* [ISSN: 1465-5489] 1921. q. Free to members. Ed(s): Alan Pottinger. Commonwealth Forestry Association, The Crib, Dinchope, Craven Arms, SY7 9JJ, United Kingdom; cfa@cfa-international.org; http://www.cfa-international.org. Illus., adv. Refereed. *Indexed:* A22, C45, RRTA. *Bk. rev.:* 5-7, 300-500 words. *Aud.:* Ga, Ac, Sa.

Formerly the *Commonwealth Forestry Review,* this refereed journal is published quarterly by the Commonwealth Forestry Association (CFA). Each issue features 6–12 papers that report on a wide range of research conducted, for the most part, in Asia and Africa. Also regularly featured are short opinion pieces under the heading "Comment," five to seven book reviews, and translations of article summaries in French and Spanish. Occasional issues focus on themes such as "Community Forestry." One of the goals of CFA is to foster public interest in forestry. For that reason, this modestly priced and well-indexed journal is a good introduction to forestry concerns from an international as well as a scientific point of view. Online access is available a subscription to BioOne. Author rights are restricted to archiving the authors' accepted manuscripts if prior permission is sought from the publisher.

2574. *International Journal of Forest Engineering.* Formerly (until 2000): *Journal of Forest Engineering.* [ISSN: 1494-2119] 1989. s-a. GBP 210 (print & online eds.). Ed(s): Marvin R Pyles. University of New Brunswick, Faculty of Forestry and Environmental Management, 28 Dineen Dr, PO Box 4400, Fredericton, NB E3B 53, Canada; forem@unb.ca; http://www.unbf.ca/forestry/. Illus. Refereed. Vol. ends: Jul. *Indexed:* Agr, C45. *Aud.:* Ac, Sa.

Although articles on forest engineering appear in other forestry journals, this journal is unique in being devoted to the research aspects of this field. The composition of its editorial board is representative of its international scope. Each issue contains, on average, eight technical papers, along with occasional technical notes and reviews. Among topics covered are forest operations including harvesting, stand management, machine design, road design and construction, and wood engineering and processing. The column "Tell us about your organization" may prove useful for librarians who wish to better acquaint themselves with this field. Free full-text access is available for the first ten volumes from the journal's web site. Online access to subsequent volumes is made available via a subscription managed by the Forest Products Society, and this capacity can now accommodate IP recognition. Modestly priced, this is an important addition to library collections that support practitioners and researchers in forest operations. Authors do not retain the right to archive any version of their articles.

2575. *International Journal of Forestry Research.* [ISSN: 1687-9368] 2008. USD 195. Hindawi Publishing Corporation, 410 Park Ave, 15th Fl, PMB 287, New York, NY 10022; info@hindawi.com; http://www.hindawi.com. Refereed. *Indexed:* C45, S25. *Aud.:* Ac, Sa.

This is a peer-reviewed, open-access journal that publishes original research articles as well as review articles in all areas of forestry research. This is a relatively new title among many from this open-access publisher, and it is unclear how it will measure up in the long term. However, this is a journal that students and faculty are considering when looking for a reasonably priced open-access venue. When the home institution becomes a member of Hindawi, the author fees are waived. Recent calls for papers in special issues include "Eucalyptus Beyond Its Native Range" and "REDD+ Mechanism in Developing Countries." The journal uses a Creative Commons Attribution license, assuring authors the right to archive the published version of their articles when properly cited.

2576. *International Journal of Wildland Fire.* [ISSN: 1049-8001] 1991. 8x/yr. USD 1540 combined subscription (print & online eds.); EUR 1290 combined subscription (print & online eds.); GBP 890 combined subscription (print & online eds.). Ed(s): Stefan Doerr, Susan G Conard. C S I R O Publishing, 150 Oxford St, PO Box 1139, Collingwood, VIC 3066, Australia; publishing@csiro.au; http://www.publish.csiro.au/home.htm. Index, adv. Sample. Refereed. *Indexed:* A22, Agr, C45, E01, H24, M&GPA, RRTA, RiskAb. *Aud.:* Ac, Sa.

This peer-reviewed journal is published commercially by the Commonwealth Scientific and International Research Organisation Australia (CSIRO). It is presented under the auspices of the International Association of Wildland Fire and has an editorial board representative of North America, Australia, and Europe. Among the areas covered on a regular basis are fire ecology, fire behavior, and fire management systems, as well as modeling of fire in relation to history, climate, landscape, and ecosystems. The journal is well indexed. The increased and sustained interest in fire management in relation to forested lands makes this publication a desirable addition to both specialized forestry collections and academic collections. Relative to other journals in this field, it is modestly priced. A subscription to the print version includes online access. Online-only access is available at a reduced annual fee, and multi-site licenses are available. Authors may archive their accepted manuscript (post–peer review) on their personal or institutional server, but must acknowledge the published source, must link to the journal homepage, and may not use the publisher's pdf version.

2577. *Journal of Forestry.* Formed by the merger of (1902-1916): *Forestry Quarterly;* (1905-1916): *Society of American Foresters. Proceedings.* [ISSN: 0022-1201] 1902. 8x/yr. USD 204 (print & online eds.) Individuals, USD 85; Free to members). Ed(s): Matthew Walls, W Keith Moser. Society of American Foresters, 5400 Grosvenor Ln, Bethesda, MD 20814; safnet@safnet.org; http://www.safnet.org/. Illus., index, adv. Sample. Refereed. Vol. ends: Dec. *Indexed:* A22, Agr, C45, EngInd, GardL, P02, RRTA, S25. *Bk. rev.:* 5-10, 100 words; 0-1, lengthy. *Aud.:* Hs, Ga, Ac.

This is the membership journal of the Society of American Foresters. Issues are often thematic, with an annual "Professional Resource Guide" included. Past themes include ethics, GIS, fire, and sustainable development. Feature articles undergo peer review but are written for a broad audience. Regular features include member "Commentary"; "Discussion"; and "Departments," which include "Forest Health," "Research in Review," and "Forestry Reports," useful for librarians wishing to keep up with the literature of forestry. A newer feature is the "Journal for Forestry Quiz," which allows member readers to gain continuing forestry education credit hours. Both the writing and range of topics covered make this an important addition to public and college libraries, as well as collections that serve the professional forester and researcher. This journal could also be a useful addition to a secondary school library. The journal is available online via *Ingenta* with a full electronic back set. Subscription information is available from the society's web site, as is a good deal of other information about the society. Authors may archive their accepted manuscript (post–peer review) on their personal or institutional server, but must acknowledge the published source, must link to the journal homepage, and may not use the publisher's pdf version.

2578. *Journal of Sustainable Forestry.* [ISSN: 1054-9811] 1993. 8x/yr. GBP 810 (print & online eds.). Ed(s): Graeme P Berlyn. Taylor & Francis Inc., 325 Chestnut St, Ste 800, Philadelphia, PA 19106; customerservice@taylorandfrancis.com; http://www.tandfonline.com. Illus., index, adv. Sample. Refereed. Microform: PQC. Reprint: PSC. *Indexed:* A01, A22, AbAn, Agr, C45, E01, EngInd, GardL, RRTA, S25. *Bk. rev.:* Occasional, brief. *Aud.:* Ac, Sa.

This international journal is refereed and focuses on research that promotes the sustainability of forests for their products (both wood and non-wood), as well as research that contributes to sustainable agroforestry. It fills a niche in the commercial journal market. Two or more of the four issues that make up each volume may be combined to serve as the record of a conference that covers an unusual topic, such as recent issues on "Conflict and Cooperation: Tools for Governing Tropical Forests"; "Biofuels and Avoided Deforestation—New Dynamics to the Tropical Forests"; and "Conservation and the Agricultural Frontier: Integrating Forests and Agriculture in the Tropics." These multi-issue titles are often made available as monographs as well. It can be argued that this journal can be forgone because more of this material is now available on the web; however, the fact that this journal is well indexed in the bibliographic databases used by students makes it particularly important for academic collections. This imprint is now owned by Taylor & Francis. Authors may deposit their accepted manuscript (post–peer review) on their personal or institutional server 12 months after publication, but must acknowledge the published source, must link to the journal homepage, and may not use the publisher's pdf version.

2579. *National Woodlands.* Formerly (until 1979): *National Woodlands Magazine.* [ISSN: 0279-9812] 1978. q. Members, USD 45; Non-members, USD 35. Ed(s): Eric A Johnson. National Woodland Owners Association, 374 Maple Ave E Ste 310, Vienna, VA 22180; info@woodlandowners.org; http://www.woodlandowners.org. Illus., adv. Circ: 2500. Vol. ends: Oct. *Aud.:* Ga.

This quarterly magazine serves the membership of the National Woodland Owners Association. This association monitors government activities related to its membership, and works with nonprofit groups and professional societies to communicate the concerns and interests of nonindustrial, private woodlot owners. Each issue includes three to five feature articles on such topics as income tax and carbon credits, forest ownership patterns, and restoration projects, as well as regular political news columns and insert reports from both the United States and Canada. Regular departments include "Non-industrial Forestry Commentary," "Conservation News Digest," "National Historic Lookout Register," and updates to the "National Directory of Consulting Foresters." The magazine has a broad geographic focus within the United States and Canada. An inexpensive addition to a general collection, it serves to represent the point of view of the nonindustrial forest landowner. Membership and subscription information is available from the association's web site, as is the full text of articles from 1999 through 2010.

2580. *New Forests: journal of biology, biotechnology, and management of afforestation and reforestation.* [ISSN: 0169-4286] 1986. bi-m. EUR 1008 (print & online eds.). Ed(s): Stephen W Hallgren. Springer Netherlands, Van Godewijckstraat 30, Dordrecht, 3311 GX, Netherlands; http://www.springer.com. Illus., index, adv. Sample. Refereed. Microform: PQC. Reprint: PSC. *Indexed:* A22, Agr, C45, E01, EngInd. *Aud.:* Ac, Sa.

This refereed journal is international in scope and is intended for an audience of scientists and practitioners. Six issues in two volumes appear annually. Each contains eight to ten papers that report on the findings of original research. "New forests" refers to the reproduction of trees and forests by reforestation or afforestation, whether for the purposes of resource protection, timber production, or agroforestry. Topics included are silviculture, plant physiology, genetics, biotechnology, propagation methods and nursery practices, ecology, economics, and forest protection. This journal enjoys a good reputation among researchers and should be considered a core title for a research collection. Archival full-text access to issues is available via SpringerLink for an additional fee through the publisher's web site. Authors may archive their accepted manuscript (post–peer review) on their personal or institutional server, but must acknowledge the published source, must link to the journal homepage, and may not use the publisher's pdf version.

2581. *Northern Journal of Applied Forestry.* [ISSN: 0742-6348] 1984. q. USD 170 (Individuals, USD 75). Ed(s): Matthew Walls, Kim C Steiner. Society of American Foresters, 5400 Grosvenor Ln, Bethesda, MD 20814; safnet@safnet.org; http://www.safnet.org. Illus., index, adv. Sample. Vol. ends: Dec. *Indexed:* Agr, C45, EngInd, RRTA. *Aud.:* Ac, Sa.

This is one of three regional applied research journals from the Society of American Foresters. It is targeted toward the professional forester or forest landowner in the Canadian and American Northeast and Midwest and the boreal forests of these areas. Emphasis is on management practices and techniques. Quarterly issues contain six to ten peer-reviewed articles on such topics as pest and disease control, wildlife management, and harvesting practices, all focusing on practical research to help the practitioner better manage forests of the region. All three regional journals are modest in price and are important for a research and teaching collection. In areas where forests are an important part of the local economy, a general collection would be strengthened with the addition of the geographically appropriate title. The journal is available online via *Ingenta* with a full electronic back set. Subscription information is available from the society's web site, as is a good deal of other information about the society. Authors may archive their accepted manuscript (post–peer review) on their personal or institutional server, but must acknowledge the published source, must link to the journal homepage, and may not use the publisher's pdf version.

2582. *Revista Arvore.* [ISSN: 0100-6762] 1977. bi-m. Universidade Federal de Vicosa, Campus Universitario, Vicosa, 36570-000, Brazil; reitoria@mail.ufv.br; http://www.ufv.br. *Indexed:* C45, RRTA. *Aud.:* Ac, Sa.

This well-indexed technical and scientific journal is published bimonthly by the Sociedade de Investigacoes Florestais (SIF) in Brazil. It contains original papers on all aspects of forestry and forest products. Among other things, this journal offers a local perspective on issues related to the fate of tropical forests, particularly in the Brazilian Amazon. The text of most articles is in Portuguese; however, informative abstracts are available in English. This journal is typical of the growing number of institutionally based and discipline-specific publications from other countries that are being made available via the Directory of Open Access Journals. The journal uses Creative Commons Attribution licensing, so authors retain the right to archive the published version of their articles.

2583. *Silva Fennica.* [ISSN: 0037-5330] 1926. q. EUR 230 (Individuals, EUR 100). Ed(s): Eeva Korpilahti. Suomen Metsatieteellinen Seura, PO Box 18, Helsinki, 01301, Finland; sms@helsinki.fi; http://www.metla.fi/org/sms/. Illus. Refereed. Circ: 1150. *Indexed:* C45, EngInd, RRTA. *Bk. rev.:* Occasional. *Aud.:* Ac, Sa.

This is a classic, international, peer-reviewed forestry journal is now fully open access. It is published quarterly, with an occasional fifth issue, by the Finnish Forest Research Institute and the Finnish Society of Forest Science. All aspects of forestry are covered, with a special interest in the boreal forests. Special issues have focused on wood quality, uneven-aged forest management, disturbance dynamics, climate change, and biodiversity. A typical issue includes 10–12 articles published in English. Issues back to 1994 are available from the publication web site, with a link to earlier issues back to 1929, in the University of Helsinki's institutional repository, "HELDA."

2584. *Small-Scale Forestry.* Formerly (until 2007): *Small-Scale Forest Economics, Management and Policy.* [ISSN: 1873-7617] 2002. q. EUR 413 (print & online eds.). Ed(s): J. Bliss, H. Karppinen. Springer Netherlands, Van Godewijckstraat 30, Dordrecht, 3311 GX, Netherlands; http://www.springer.com. Refereed. Reprint: PSC. *Indexed:* A22, BRI, C&ISA, C45, CerAb, E01, RRTA. *Bk. rev.:* 2-3, substantive. *Aud.:* Ga, Ac, Sa.

This peer-reviewed journal began in 2002 as an effort to address the need to disseminate research findings on management of small-scale private-forest woodlots within the International Union of Forest Research Organizations (IUFRO). Issues include eight to ten articles on topics related to social and economic aspects of private woodlot management and two to three substantive book reviews. With international coverage and a very modest subscription cost, this journal has the potential to be a welcome addition to academic collections. It should also be of use to general collections where management of private woodlots plays a role in the local economy. It is now hosted by SpringerLink, on whose web site the table of contents and abstracts of recent issues can be viewed. Authors may archive their accepted manuscript (post–peer review) on their personal or institutional server, but must acknowledge the published source, must link to the journal homepage, and may not use the publisher's pdf version.

2585. *Southern Journal of Applied Forestry.* [ISSN: 0148-4419] 1977. q. USD 170 (Individuals, USD 75). Ed(s): Matthew Walls, Ian A Munn. Society of American Foresters, 5400 Grosvenor Ln, Bethesda, MD 20814; safnet@safnet.org; http://www.safnet.org. Illus., index, adv. Sample. Refereed. Vol. ends: Nov. *Indexed:* A22, Agr, C45, EngInd, RRTA, S25. *Aud.:* Ac, Sa.

This is one of three regional, applied-research journals from the Society of American Foresters. It is targeted toward the professional forester and forest landowner in a geographic region ranging from Oklahoma and East Texas east to Virginia and Kentucky. Emphasis is on management practices and techniques in this region, where plantation forests are more common. Quarterly issues contain six to ten peer-reviewed articles on such topics as pest and disease control, wildlife management, and harvesting practices, all focusing on practical research to help the practitioner better manage forests of the region. All three regional journals are modest in price and are important for a research and teaching collection. In areas in which forests are an important part of the local economy, a general collection would be strengthened with the addition of the geographically appropriate title. This journal is available online via *Ingenta* with a full electronic back set. Subscription information is available from the society's web site, as is a good deal of other information about the society. Authors may archive their accepted manuscript (post–peer review) on their personal or institutional server, but must acknowledge the published source, must link to the journal homepage, and may not use the publisher's pdf version.

2586. *Tree Physiology: an international botanical journal.* [ISSN: 0829-318X] 1986. m. EUR 2571. Ed(s): Ram Oren, Sari Palmroth. Oxford University Press, Great Clarendon St, Oxford, OX2 6DP, United Kingdom; enquiry@oup.co.uk; http://www.oxfordjournals.org/. Illus., index, adv. Sample. Refereed. Reprint: PSC. *Indexed:* A01, A22, Agr, C45, GardL. *Bk. rev.:* 0-3, 300-500 words. *Aud.:* Ac, Sa.

This refereed journal is international in scope and distribution. It is a medium for disseminating theoretical and experimental research results as well as occasional review articles. Each issue consists of eight to ten papers that deal with an array of topics related to tree physiology, including genetics, reproduction, nutrition, and environmental adaptation, as well as those relevant to environmental management, biotechnology, and the economic use of trees. This is an important journal for forest science and botany collections. Online access to the full text of this journal is available. The publisher's web site also provides a cumulative index for downloading. This journal is now an Oxford University Press imprint. Authors may archive their accepted manuscript (post–peer review) on their personal or institutional server, but must acknowledge the published source, must link to the journal homepage, and may not use the publisher's pdf version.

2587. *Trees: structure and function.* [ISSN: 0931-1890] 1987. bi-m. EUR 2683 (print & online eds.). Ed(s): Ulrich E Luettge, Robert D Guy. Springer, Tiergartenstr 17, Heidelberg, 69121, Germany. Illus., index, adv. Sample. Refereed. Vol. ends: Sep. Reprint: PSC. *Indexed:* A22, Agr, C45, E01, EngInd. *Aud.:* Ac, Sa.

This international, refereed journal is narrowly focused but highly regarded among physiologists in the scholarly community of forestry, horticulture, and botany. Each of its six annual issues includes eight to ten articles on original research in the physiology, biochemistry, functional anatomy, structure, and ecology of trees and woody plants. Review articles are included selectively, as are papers on pathology and technological problems that add to a basic understanding of the structure and function of trees. An online edition of the journal, along with a table-of-contents alerting service, is available on the publisher's web site, Springerlink. Authors may archive their accepted manuscript (post–peer review) on their personal or institutional server, but must acknowledge the published source, must link to the journal homepage, and may not use the publisher's pdf version.

2588. *Unasylva: international journal of forestry and forest products.* [ISSN: 0041-6436] 1947. q. USD 26. Food and Agriculture Organization of the United Nations (F A O), Viale delle Terme di Caracalla, Rome, 00153, Italy; publications-sales@fao.org; http://www.fao.org. Illus., index. Sample. Vol. ends: Dec. Microform: CIS. *Indexed:* A22, BAS, C45, M&GPA, RRTA, S25. *Bk. rev.:* 2-5, 300 words. *Aud.:* Hs, Ga, Ac.

Available in French, Spanish, and English, this international journal is published by the Food and Agriculture Organization (FAO) of the United Nations to promote better understanding of issues in international forestry. Articles are well illustrated and readable, and will have broad appeal to an audience that includes students, policymakers, and professional foresters. Each quarterly issue consists of 8–12 articles that usually address a theme such as perceptions of forests, sustainable forest management, illegal logging, forest-dependent peoples, etc. Regular departments include new books; reports on FAO forestry activities; and news in the "world of forestry." This would be a good addition to general, high school, and college libraries as well as research collections. The full text of articles in each issue of the journal since 1947 is available on the FAO web site. Though this is an open-access journal, it is not clear whether the Creative Commons licensing is used, and therefore author rights to archive the published version of their articles are unclear.

2589. *Western Journal of Applied Forestry.* [ISSN: 0885-6095] 1986. q. USD 170 (Individuals, USD 75). Ed(s): Matthew Walls, Keith A Blatner. Society of American Foresters, 5400 Grosvenor Ln, Bethesda, MD 20814; safnet@safnet.org; http://www.safnet.org. Illus., adv. Sample. Refereed. Vol. ends: Oct. *Indexed:* A01, Agr, C45, EngInd, RRTA. *Aud.:* Ac, Sa.

This is one of three regional, applied-research journals from the Society of American Foresters. It is targeted toward the professional forester and landowner in western North America. Emphasis is on management practices and techniques. Quarterly issues contain six to ten peer-reviewed articles on such topics as pest and disease control, wildlife management, and harvesting practices, all focusing on practical research to help the practitioner better manage forests of the region. All three regional journals are modest in price and are important for a research and teaching collection. In areas where forests are an important part of the local economy, a general collection would be strengthened with the addition of the geographically appropriate title. The journal is available online via *Ingenta* with a full electronic back set. Subscription information is available from the society's web site, as is a good deal of other information about the society. Authors may archive their accepted manuscript (post–peer review) on their personal or institutional server, but must acknowledge the published source, must link to the journal homepage, and may not use the publisher's pdf version.

2590. *Wood and Fiber Science.* Formed by the merger of (1969-1983): *Wood and Fiber;* (1968-1983): *Wood Science.* [ISSN: 0735-6161] 1983. q. Free to members; Non-members, USD 250. Ed(s): Frank C Beall. Society of Wood Science and Technology, PO Box 6155, Monona, WI 53716; vicki@swst.org; http://www.swst.org. Illus., index, adv. Sample. Refereed. Vol. ends: Oct. Microform: PQC. *Indexed:* A22, C45, EngInd. *Bk. rev.:* 1-3, 400-600 words. *Aud.:* Ac, Sa.

This refereed journal is the product of the Society of Wood Science and Technology (SWST). Typical of the range of subjects covered by the 12–15 articles in each issue are processing testing; modeling applied to oriented strandboard; wood adhesives; moisture movement; use of engineered wood products in Japan; and properties of wood–plastic composites, plus one or two book reviews. This journal is modestly priced and highly regarded by wood scientists and wood technologists. Particularly with the increase in international research coverage, it is also useful for those interested in following new developments in these areas for product marketing. This journal is recommended for comprehensive research collections and for collections that need an economical representative title in this area. For subscribers, the full run of this journal (1969 to date) is available electronically. Authors do not retain the right to archive any version of their articles published in this journal.

2591. *Wood Material Science and Engineering.* [ISSN: 1748-0272] 2006. q. GBP 197 (print & online eds.). Ed(s): Dr. Dick Sandberg. Taylor & Francis, 4 Park Sq, Milton Park, Abingdon, OX14 4RN, United Kingdom; subscriptions@tandf.co.uk; http://www.tandfonline.com. Adv. Sample. Refereed. Reprint: PSC. *Indexed:* A22, C45, E01. *Aud.:* Ac, Sa.

This modestly priced journal addresses the science and engineering associated with wood as sustainable building materials. It is devoted to the application of wood for construction purposes and as products; the development of engineered wood products; and eco-efficient design and production. Issues generally include an editorial of broader interest, and four to six articles that report either original research or a review of current research. Most recently, issues have been combined. This is a Taylor and Francis imprint. Authors may deposit their accepted manuscript (post–peer review) on their personal or institutional server 12 months after publication, but must acknowledge the published source, must link to the journal home page, and may not use the publisher's pdf version.

■ GAMES AND GAMING

See also Computers and Information Technology; and Sports sections.

Davis S. Carter, Engineering Librarian & Video Game Archivist, University of Michigan Library, 2281 Bonisteel Blvd., Ann Arbor, MI, USA, 48109-2094; superman@umich.edu

Introduction

Game playing is a fundamental human activity. Evidence of board games have been found in archeological sites that date as far back as 3500 BCE. Modern games take on many forms, from board and card games to modern electronic and video games; as would be expected, magazines covering the area of games and gaming reflect this diversity.

In the video game space, the past few years have shown a shift away from printed publications as many players and consumers now turn to online sources for information. Magazines devoted to a particular gaming platform are rapidly become extinct; both *Nintendo Power* and *Playstation: The Official Magazine* ceased publication in late 2012, leaving *Official Xbox Magazine* as the sole remaining official magazine devoted to a single gaming platform. Several general purpose video game magazines such as *Game Informer Magazine* still remain and have branched out beyond platforms and handhelds to also include areas such as mobile and online gaming.

The past several years have aslo shown a dramatic rise in the interest of games as a subject of serious study in the academy. Academic publications such as *Journal of Gaming & Virtual Worlds*, *Games and Culture: A Journal of Interactive Media*, and *Simulation & Gaming* offer papers on research, criticism and commentary on aspects of game design, game theory, and relation of games to society.

Traditional games such as chess and bridge continue to enjoy devoted followings, and publications such as *Chess Life* and *Bridge Bulletin* cater to those games' serious devotees.

Basic Periodicals

Ga: *The Bridge World, Chess Life, Game Informer Magazine, PC Gamer.*

Basic Abstracts and Indexes

Academic Search Premier, MasterFILE Premier.

2592. *A C F Bulletin.* [ISSN: 1045-8034] 1952. bi-m. USD 25 domestic; USD 35 Canada; USD 40 elsewhere. Ed(s): Charles C Walker. American Checker Federation, PO Box 365, Petal, MS 39465. Illus. Circ: 1000. *Aud.:* Ems, Hs, Ga, Ac.

The *ACF Bulletin* is the bimonthly newsletter of the American Checker Federation (ACF) and is available through membership in the ACF. Notifications of upcoming and events and tournaments, obituaries, player standings, a marketplace, and game transcripts make this publication a one-stop shop for the serious checker player. Sample issues and archived game analysis, strategy, and transcripts are available on the Federation's web site at http://usacheckers.com.

2593. *Battlefleet: the journal of the Naval Wargames Society.* 1966. q. Free to members. Ed(s): Christopher White. Naval Wargames Society, c/o Peter Colbeck, Down House, 76, Church Rd, Bristol, BS36 1BY, United Kingdom; http://www.navalwargamessociety.org. *Aud.:* Hs, Ga.

Battlefleet: The Journal of the Naval Wargames Society is published quarterly and contains naval wargaming scenarios, reviews, and notices of interest to wargame consumers and members of the Society. This publication would be of interest to public libraries with active wargamers, particularly in the United Kingdom.

2594. The Bridge Bulletin. Former titles: *American Contract Bridge League. Bulletin;* (until 1993): *Contract Bridge Bulletin.* [ISSN: 1089-6376] 1935. m. Free to members. Ed(s): Brent Manley. American Contract Bridge League, 2990 Airways Blvd, Memphis, TN 38116; service@acbl.org; http://www.acbl.org. Illus., adv. Sample. Circ: 150000 Paid. *Bk. rev.:* 3, 50 words. *Aud.:* Ga.

Published by the American Contract Bridge League, *The Bridge Bulletin* contains regular columns, feature articles, player profiles, tournament listings, and game-play scenarios and advice for contract and duplicated bridge. Definitely worth considering, especially for public libraries in North America.

2595. Bridge Magazine. Incorporates (1980-200?): *International Popular Bridge Monthly;* Which was formerly (until 1980): *Popular Bridge Monthly;* Former titles (until 1993): *Bridge (Sutton Coldfield);* (until 1989): *Bridge International;* (until 1984): *Bridge Magazine;* (until 1930): *Auction Bridge Magazine;* Bridge Magazine incorporated: *British Bridge World.* [ISSN: 1351-4261] 1926. m. GBP 44.95 domestic; GBP 54.95 in Europe; GBP 60 in US & Canada. Ed(s): Mark Horton. Chess & Bridge Ltd., 369 Euston Rd, London, NW1 3AR, United Kingdom; info@chess.co.uk; http://www.chess.co.uk. Illus., adv. *Bk. rev.:* Number and length vary. *Aud.:* Ga, Ac, Sa.

Bridge Magazine is well laid out and easy to read. Featuring strategy and game analysis, player profiles, and tournament listings, this magazine is aimed at intermediate and advanced-level players. Recommended for public libraries that serve established bridge clubs or players. The journal's web site is worth a look, and features a variety of bridge-related items for sale. URL: www.bridgeshop.com

2596. The Bridge World: the magazine no bridge player should be without. [ISSN: 0006-9876] 1929. m. USD 99. Ed(s): Jeff Rubens. Bridge World Magazine Inc., PO Box 299, Scarsdale, NY 10583; mail@bridgeworld.com; http://www.bridgeworld.com. Illus., adv. Circ: 7800. *Bk. rev.:* Number and length vary. *Aud.:* Ga.

Tournament reports, book reviews, articles on strategy and defense, and player standings combine to make *The Bridge World* an excellent resource. Practice exercises, humor, and feature articles round out the content to make this publication the must-have bridge magazine. The web site has subscription information, a glossary, and an excellent introduction to the game. URL: www.bridgeworld.com

2597. Card Player. [ISSN: 1089-2044] 1988. bi-w. USD 39.95; USD 4.95 per issue. Shulman, Barry and Jeff, 6940 O'Bannon Dr, Las Vegas, NV 89117. Illus., adv. Circ: 5000 Paid. *Aud.:* Ga.

Though a little ad-heavy, *Card Player* is a worthwhile purchase. This biweekly glossy will appeal to both amateur and serious card players. It contains European and North American poker news, industry happenings, player profiles and interviews, poker strategy and analysis, and tournament information. Rich online content supplements the print magazine. URL: www.cardplayer.com

2598. Chess Life. Formerly (until 1980): *Chess Life and Review.* [ISSN: 0197-260X] 1969. m. Free to members. Ed(s): Daniel Lucas. United States Chess Federation, PO Box 3967, Crossville, TN 38557; feedback@uschess.org; http://main.uschess.org/. Illus., index, adv. Vol. ends: Dec. Microform: PQC. *Indexed:* A22, MLA-IB. *Bk. rev.:* 2-3, 250 words. *Aud.:* Hs, Ga, Ac.

The most polished and professional-looking of the chess magazines reviewed here, *Chess Life* bills itself as the world's most widely read chess magazine. Published by the United States Chess Federation, this magazine is a worthy purchase with its feature articles, game analysis, player profiles, and tournament listings. *Chess Life for Kids,* launched in 2006, is also worth considering. URL: www.uschess.org

2599. Chess Life for Kids. [ISSN: 1932-5894] 2006. bi-m. Free to members. Ed(s): Glenn Peterson. United States Chess Federation, PO Box 3967, Crossville, TN 38557; feedback@uschess.org; http://main.uschess.org/. *Aud.:* Ems, Hs.

Published by the United States Chess Federation (the publishers of *Chess Life*), *Chess Life for Kids* is a colorful, fun magazine aimed at children 12 and under. Featuring many of the same elements included in *Chess Life,* the kids' version has tournament listings, game analysis, feature articles, and player profiles. A worthy addition to public library collections.

2600. The Citizens' Companion: the voice of civilian reenacting. [ISSN: 1075-9344] 1993. bi-m. USD 30 domestic; USD 48 foreign. Ed(s): Connie Payne. Camp Chase Publishing Co., Inc., The Civil War Courier, PO Box 625, Morristown, TN 37814; campchase@aol.com; http://www.campchase.com. Adv. Sample. *Aud.:* Hs, Ga.

This companion publication to *Camp Chase Gazette* focuses on civilian reenactors of the Civil War instead of on their military counterparts. Interesting historical articles on topics such as fashion and food will likely intrigue those interested in this period of history. Some articles and news items are posted on the web site. URL: www.citizenscompanion.com

2601. Game Informer Magazine. [ISSN: 1067-6392] 1991. m. USD 14.99 combined subscription (print or online ed.). Ed(s): Andrew McNamara. Game Informer Magazine, 724 N First St, 4th Fl, Minneapolis, MN 55401-2885; customerservice@gameinformer.com; http://www.gameinformer.com. Adv. Circ: 200000 Paid. *Aud.:* Hs, Ga.

Billing itself as "The World's #1 Video Game Magazine," *Game Informer Magazine* is a solid choice for most public library collections. This heavily illustrated magazine focuses primarily on issues related to console gaming and announcements of upcoming systems and games. It contains the expected content in terms of previews, reviews, and articles on how the games are made, but it also provides feature articles on topics such as gender in gaming and on the history of popular gaming franchises, such as The Sims. It also includes interviews with industry leaders. Beyond console gaming, interesting forays are also made into PC gaming, Internet games, and mobile gaming such as Bejeweled Blitz and Farmville, that are attracting casual gamers in droves.

2602. Games and Culture: a journal of interactive media. [ISSN: 1555-4120] 2006. bi-m. USD 713. Ed(s): Douglas Thomas. Sage Publications, Inc., 2455 Teller Rd, Thousand Oaks, CA 91320; info@sagepub.com; http://www.sagepub.com. Adv. Sample. Refereed. Reprint: PSC. *Indexed:* A22, ArtHuCI, E01, P61, PsycInfo, SSA. *Aud.:* Ac, Sa.

The academic journal *Games and Culture* takes a more theoretical approach to gaming than the other periodicals reviewed here. This quality publication cuts across disciplines to examine issues such as race, gender, and community in the gaming context. Too academic for most public libraries, but a worthy purchase for college or university library collections.

2603. Journal of Gaming & Virtual Worlds. [ISSN: 1757-191X] 2009. 3x/yr. GBP 235 (Individuals, GBP 36). Ed(s): Eben Muse, Astrid Ensslin. Intellect Ltd., The Mill, Parnall Rd, Fishponds, Bristol, BS16 3JG, United Kingdom; info@intellectbooks.com; http://www.intellectbooks.co.uk/. Adv. Sample. Refereed. *Bk. rev.:* Number and length vary. *Aud.:* Ac.

A worthy addition to the scholarly literature on games and gaming, the peer-reviewed *Journal of Gaming & Virtual Worlds* contains substantial book and game reviews, conference reports, interviews, and interesting articles on a wide range of topics such as sex and gender in virtual worlds, narrative modes, the use of different video game genres, and in-game suicide. Recommended for college and university libraries, because many articles transcend the world of gaming and virtual worlds and would appeal to scholars in many other disciplines.

2604. Miniature Wargames. [ISSN: 0266-3228] 1983. m. Pireme Publishing Ltd., 1 Carrara House, Cemetery Rd, Nottingham, NG9 8AP, United Kingdom. Illus., index, adv. *Bk. rev.:* Number and length vary. *Aud.:* Hs, Ga.

A respected publication that covers miniature wargaming in the United Kingdom, *Miniature Wargames* is packed with colorful illustrations and modeling advice for collectors of military miniatures. The articles cover all historical periods, and naval modeling is also covered in detail. This magazine has something for everyone who might be interested in miniatures. The journal's web site has links to editorials, reviews, and information on vendors of miniatures. URL: www.wargames.co.uk

2605. *New in Chess Magazine.* Supersedes in part (in 1984): *Schaakbulletin (Amsterdam).* [ISSN: 0168-8782] 1968. 8x/yr. EUR 76.50 in the European Union; GBP 64.50 United Kingdom; USD 98 in North America. Interchess B.V., PO Box 1093, Alkmaar, 1810 KB, Netherlands; nic@newinchess.com; http://www.newinchess.com/. Illus., adv. Sample. Vol. ends: Jan. *Bk. rev.:* 3, 100 words. *Aud.:* Hs, Ga, Ac.

More European in focus than the other chess magazines reviewed here, *New in Chess* is well balanced with extensive game reviews and analysis, well-written feature articles, columns by the big names in chess, and chess news and trends. The magazine's web site has valuable content, including a large database of free online chess games and an extensive online store. URL: www.newinchess.com

2606. *Official Xbox Magazine.* [ISSN: 1534-7850] 2001. m. USD 24.95 combined subscription domestic; USD 29.95 combined subscription Canada. Ed(s): Francesca Reyes. Future U S, Inc., 4000 Shoreline Ct, Ste 400, South San Francisco, CA 94080; http://www.futureus.com. Adv. Sample. Circ: 407927 Paid. *Aud.:* Hs, Ga.

As the official organ of the Xbox community, this monthly magazine offers news, previews, and reviews of games for the popular Xbox gaming system. While directed at the loyal Xbox gamer, this image-heavy magazine contains plenty of content of interest to more casual players as well. New releases are promoted heavily, but the magazine also includes feature articles about big new releases, events, and gaming culture (with an Xbox slant, naturally). There are also letters from gamers with informative responses, along with numerous reader polls and elements to get input from the Xbox community. Games, downloadable content, and Xbox-related product reviews are an excellent feature. While often effusive, reviews can be critical; they list the pros and cons of games as well as a numerical review. Downloadable content is rated, alternatively, "buy," "fanboy only," or "deny." This magazine includes ads but, for the most part, these mesh seamlessly with the content.

2607. *P C Gamer.* Former titles (until May 1994): *Game Player's P C Entertainment;* (until 1991): *Game Player's P C Strategy Guide; Game Player's M S - D O S Strategy Guide; Game Player's Guide to M S - D O S Computer Games.* [ISSN: 1080-4471] 1988. m. USD 19.95 domestic; USD 29.95 Canada; USD 39.95 elsewhere. Future U S, Inc., 4000 Shoreline Ct, Ste 400, South San Francisco, CA 94080; http://www.futureus.com. Adv. Circ: 200000 Paid. *Aud.:* Hs, Ga, Ac.

Focusing on games for the personal computer, *PC Gamer* contains game previews, sneak peaks, ratings, and feature articles. Game hints and cheats are also included, but you will find much more of that type of content at the magazine's web site. Recommended for public libraries. URL: www.gamesradar.com

2608. *Simulation & Gaming: an international journal of theory, design and research.* Formerly (until 1990): *Simulation and Games.* [ISSN: 1046-8781] 1970. bi-m. Ed(s): David Crookall. Sage Publications, Inc., 2455 Teller Rd, Thousand Oaks, CA 91320; info@sagepub.com; http://www.sagepub.com. Illus., index, adv. Sample. Refereed. Vol. ends: Dec. Microform: PQC. Reprint: PSC. *Indexed:* A01, A22, ABIn, ABS&EES, B01, BRI, CompLI, CompR, E01, ERIC, IBSS, P02, P61, PsycInfo, RiskAb. *Aud.:* Ac.

An official journal of the Association for Business Simulation and Experiential Learning, *Simulation & Gaming* serves as a multidisciplinary journal exploring simulation and gaming methodologies used in education, training, consultation and research. Topics such as virtual reality, educational games, video games and industrial simulators are considered. Issues include theoretical and applied articles, conceptual papers, empirical studies, game reviews, news and notes.

■ GARDENING

See also Agriculture; and Home sections.

Rex J. Krajewski, Head of Library Information Services, Simmons College, 300 The Fenway, Boston, MA 02115; krajewsk@simmons.edu

Introduction

The National Gardening Association reports that participation in gardening in the United States is growing, up 3 percent in 2011 over the previous year. Even more dramatic was the 17 percent increase in food gardening from 2008 to 2009, which was after a 10 percent growth from 2007 to 2008! Experts expect this growth trend to continue into the foreseeable future, as folks continue to grapple with environmental concerns, the depressed economy, and changing values.

More new gardeners means the need for more information. In recent years, print and online gardening magazines have responded to the need for more information on the topic—and potential readership growth. Some magazines have retooled their content, others have reformatted, but most have begun presenting gardening information for a more diverse spectrum of readers: young and old, urban and rural, newbie and experienced. Most recently, publications are responding to the desire more folks have to grow their own food with more coverage of not only vegetable and herb gardening, but also topics like home fruit and nut production, small livestock-keeping, and the integration of edibles into ornamental gardens.

Gardeners are a curious and information-loving bunch, and gardening magazines have long reflected the breadth and depth of knowledge available. Literature about gardening tends to encompass the topic's interdisciplinary nature. Gardeners seek to know more about the science of gardening from fields such as agriculture, horticulture, and biochemistry. Ideas about design and aesthetics come from the worlds of art, architecture, history, and landscaping. Political aspects are covered with respect to issues such as water use and environmental sustainability; and there is coverage of seed and plant copyright and GMO (genetically modified organisms). For example, many of the magazines included here have recently featured stories about the threat of colony collapse disorder on honey bees and municipal regulations on backyard chickens.

Magazines about gardening may focus on a single aspect or may integrate multiple aspects. Specific topics of magazines might be defined by species, as in *The Rose*; by region, as in *Northern Gardener*; by environment, as in *Rock Gardener*; or by purpose, as in *Garden Design*. Even multidisciplinary, or generalist, titles tend to espouse a perspective. So, for example, *Organic Gardening* deals with many different kinds of gardening, including ornamentals, vegetables, and water gardening, but it does so on the assumption that all will be done using organic techniques and principles.

When choosing magazines on gardening, readers are likely to be attracted to the angle and focus. Libraries should be aware of the interests of gardeners in their user population and choose accordingly. In addition to titles that cater to local interests, libraries should have generalist gardening titles from a number of different perspectives to satisfy diverse needs and interests. Provided here is just such a list of core generalist titles.

Please note that region-specific titles, those that deal with the growing needs and conditions of a particular area, have been left off this list. Consider such titles based on the region where your library patrons live. It should be noted, though, that increasingly, general gardening magazines are treating relevant topics from a number of different regional perpectives, rendering regionally specific titles less unique.

There are very few strictly electronic journals in the realm of gardening magazines, though it should be noted that most print garden magazines have some kind of online presence. These might take the form of selected articles and content available to everyone for free, or all articles and content available to subscribers for free.

Another variation would be extra content available online to subscribers, such as guides, reader communities or blogs, free offers, and reference material. As well, garden magazines are increasingly active in social networks such as Twitter and Facebook, so readers can find additional information and more regular updates via social media. It is worthwhile for libraries to investigate what garden magazines of interest offer information online, and consider linking to these online resources via library catalogs, subject guides, or other resource-finding vehicles for patrons.

One surprising thing is that there have not been many new serial magazines published on the topic of gardening. Instead, publishers have produced irregular "special publications," such as *The Edible Gardener* from the publishers of *The English Garden*; *Dream Garden Rooms* from Meredith Publishers; or *Garden Doctor* from Better Homes and Gardens. Libraries are unlikely to collect titles such as these, as they are not readily available from subscription services or book jobbers.

Basic Periodicals

Ga: *The American Gardener, BBC Gardeners' World Magazine, Fine Gardening, Garden Gate, Gardening How-To, Horticulture, HortIdeas, National Gardening, Organic Gardening.*

Basic Abstracts and Indexes

Garden, Landscape & Horticulture Index.

2609. The American Gardener. Former titles (until 1996): *American Horticulturist;* (until 1972): *American Horticultural Magazine;* (until 1960): *National Horticultural Magazine.* [ISSN: 1087-9978] 1922. bi-m. Members, USD 10; USD 8 per issue. Ed(s): Mary Yee, David J Ellis. American Horticultural Society, 7931 E Boulevard Dr, Alexandria, VA 22308; http://www.ahs.org. Illus., index, adv. Circ: 20000 Paid. Vol. ends: Nov/Dec. Microform: PQC. *Indexed:* A01, A22, BRI, GardL, MASUSE, P02. *Bk. rev.:* 3, 500 words. *Aud.:* Ga, Ac.

The American Gardener is the official publication of the American Horticultural Society. It includes regular features on such topics as design, regional issues, conservation, and habitat gardening. Reviews, regional calendars, and vibrant photography round out this mainstay among gardening magazines. A unique perspective offered by *The American Gardener* is the attention paid to gardening for children and families. The magazine is designed for serious gardeners, so topics are treated in great detail, and articles provide sound information.

2610. B B C Gardeners' World. [ISSN: 0961-7477] 1991. m. GBP 3.70 newsstand/cover. Immediate Media Co. Ltd., Media Ctr, 201 Wood Ln, London, W12 7TQ, United Kingdom; enquiries@immediatemedia.co.uk; http://www.immediatemedia.co.uk. Illus., index, adv. Sample. Circ: 265238 Paid. Vol. ends: Feb. *Indexed:* GardL. *Aud.:* Ga.

BBC Gardeners' World Magazine is part of a multimedia gardening experience from the British media outlet BBC. Because the magazine is so closely aligned with television, the Internet, and radio, it features celebrity contributors like "Ground Force" alum Alan Titchmarsh. This magazine is aimed at a broad market, and articles cover a wide range of gardening topics. Regular features include the "Fresh Ideas" section, which offers "creative projects, garden design tips, new plants and great shopping ideas for a brighter and better garden"; "What to Do Now," which offers a planting and project schedule for Britain's gardening season; and "Problem Solving," a forum for readers to submit questions and receive expert advice.

2611. Birds & Blooms: beauty in your own backyard. [ISSN: 1084-5305] 1995. bi-m. USD 14.98 domestic; CAD 19.98 Canada; USD 25.98 elsewhere. Ed(s): Heather Lamb. Reiman Media Group, Inc., 5400 S 60th St, Greendale, WI 53129; rpsubscustomercare@custhelp.com; http://www.reimanpub.com. Illus., adv. Circ: 1400000 Paid. *Indexed:* GardL. *Aud.:* Ga.

Through the lens of creating landscapes that are hospitable to animals—especially birds—this magazine will satisfy many of today's ornamental gardeners, as well as wildlife enthusiasts and eco-conscious homeowners. *Birds & Blooms* is similar to other gardening magazines, though its emphasis on native plants, pesticide- and petrochemical-free additives, and non-destructive maintenance techniques is not a new editorial priority for this

publication. Setting this magazine apart from other gardening magazines is the bird and wildlife information and features. With useful information, creative ideas, and amazing pictures, *Birds & Blooms* is an important part of any gardening magazine collection.

Canadian Gardening. See Canada section.

2612. Country Gardens. Formerly (until 2003): *Country Home Country Gardens.* [ISSN: 1068-431X] 1992. 4x/yr. USD 19.97 for 2 yrs. domestic; USD 29.97 Canada. Meredith Corporation, 1716 Locust St, Des Moines, IA 50309; patrick.taylor@meredith.com; http://www.meredith.com. Illus., adv. Circ: 325000 Paid. *Indexed:* GardL. *Bk. rev.:* 500 words. *Aud.:* Hs, Ga, Ac.

Country Gardens is a product of the well-known mainstream publisher of *Better Homes and Gardens.* With an emphasis on successful personal experiences, this magazine would inspire and motivate even novice gardeners. Tips and projects are basic enough to be tackled by anyone. A more advanced gardener might go to another source for more cutting-edge or sophisticated information, but everyone would enjoy the lush photography and illustrations. Another universally appealing feature is that advertisements are limited to a separate section in the back of the magazine.

2613. The English Garden. [ISSN: 1361-2840] 1997. m. GBP 28.99 domestic; GBP 3.75 per issue; AUD 9.50 per issue. Ed(s): Tamsin Westhorpe. Archant Specialist Ltd., Archant House, Oriel Rd, Cheltenham, GL50 1BB, United Kingdom; miller.hogg@archant.co.uk; http://www.archant.co.uk/business_specialist.aspx. *Indexed:* GardL. *Aud.:* Hs, Ga, Ac.

As its subtitle says, *The English Garden* is "for everyone who loves beautiful gardens." Filled with the requisite tips and ideas, this magazine excels in offering information on enjoying gardens, such as ideas on gardens to visit and descriptions of storied estates. Indeed, regardless of whether or not the style of garden you enjoy is "English," this publication will inspire you with its beautiful, breathtaking images.

2614. Garden Design: the fine art of residential landscape architecture. [ISSN: 0733-4923] 1982. 7x/yr. USD 11.97 domestic; USD 19.97 Canada; USD 32.97 elsewhere. Bonnier Corp., 460 N Orlando Ave, Ste 200, Orlando, FL 32789; http://www.bonniercorp.com. Illus., adv. Vol. ends: Nov/Dec. *Indexed:* A07, A22, BRI, GardL. *Bk. rev.:* 3-5, 300 words. *Aud.:* Ga.

From its title, it should be clear that the focus of *Garden Design* is design and landscaping in gardens. In fact, if one were to choose a single magazine to represent this perspective on gardening, this would be it. Inspiration is provided by photographs and reports of upscale gardens, but practical advice, ideas, and strategies are given for gardeners of all levels and tastes. The product reviews are for cutting-edge and trendy garden design tools and accessories, and advertisements follow suit. This well-written publication is a must-read for anyone interested in garden design or in just looking at pictures and descriptions of beautiful gardens.

2615. Garden Gate. [ISSN: 1083-8295] 1995. bi-m. USD 20 domestic; CAD 32 Canada; CAD 30 elsewhere. Ed(s): Kristin Beane-Sullivan, Steven Nordmeyer. August Home Publishing Co., PO Box 842, Des Moines, IA 50304; orders@augusthome.com; http://www.augusthome.com. Illus. Sample. *Indexed:* GardL, IHTDI. *Aud.:* Hs, Ga, Ac.

The unique feature of this general gardening magazine is that it does not include advertisements. Therefore, it appears smaller than other comparable magazines, but, in fact, it contains just as much information in each issue. Articles tend to be practical in nature, including a lot of how-to narratives supported by color photographs and sketches. Although *Garden Gate* may not provide as sophisticated or cutting-edge content as some other magazines of its type, it is a good, basic gardening periodical.

2616. *Gardening How-To.* [ISSN: 1087-0083] 1996. bi-m. Free to members. Ed(s): Gail Johnson, Amy Sitze. North American Media Group, Inc., 12301 Whitewater Dr, Minnetonka, MN 55343; namghq@namginc.com; http://www.northamericanmediagroup.com/. Adv. Sample. Circ: 674702. *Indexed:* GardL. *Bk. rev.:* Number and length vary. *Aud.:* Ga.

Gardening How-To is the official magazine of the National Gardening Club, which is a paid membership association of home gardening enthusiasts. In many ways, it is not unlike other general consumer magazines, but it has more reader-contributed content, including book and product reviews. The how-to and science of horticulture information are more basic than in some other gardening magazines, but where this publication really shines is in its inclusion of "good ideas," i.e., helpful tips and strategies for more effective and efficient gardening. Much of this advice comes from other club members, so content is being generated by the audience.

2617. *Gardens Illustrated.* [ISSN: 0968-8927] 1993. m. GBP 35.88; GBP 3.99 newsstand/cover. Immediate Media Co. Ltd., Tower House, Fairfax St, Bristol, BS1 3BN, United Kingdom; enquiries@immediatemedia.co.uk; http://www.immediatemedia.co.uk. Adv. Circ: 33783 Paid. *Indexed:* GardL. *Aud.:* Hs, Ga, Ac, Sa.

As its name implies, *Gardens Illustrated*'s specialty is its visual depiction of gardens and gardening. While the photography in the magazine is exceptional, the narrative is every bit as worthwhile as the pictures. Gardens from all over the world provide a backdrop for inspiration and information. Regular features include plant profiles, news, product reviews, and recipes.

2618. *Green Prints: the weeder's digest.* [ISSN: 1064-0118] 1990. q. USD 19.97. Ed(s): Pat Stone. Green Prints, PO Box 1355, Fairview, NC 28730. Illus., adv. Sample. Vol. ends: Winter. *Indexed:* GardL. *Aud.:* Ems, Hs, Ga, Ac.

Green Prints: The Weeder's Digest is a title that fulfills a unique role among gardening magazines. Rather than being a how-to publication or one that inspires primarily with stunning imagery, this magazine offers a collection of personal narratives on the topic of gardening. Essays, stories, quotations, relevant ads, and black-and-white illustrations all serve to provide the perfect companion to readers who can't get enough of all things having to do with gardening.

2619. *The Heirloom Gardener Magazine.* [ISSN: 1548-1085] 2003. q. USD 12. Ed(s): Emilee Gettle. RareSeeds Publishing, 2278 Baker Creek Rd, Mansfield, MO 65704; seeds@rareseeds.com; http://rareseeds.com/. *Indexed:* GardL. *Aud.:* Hs, Ga, Ac.

Since 2003, *The Heirloom Gardener* has been a magazine dedicated to home heirloom gardeners. Interest in heirloom gardening is steadily growing as people become more aware of issues like native heritage and garden history. Also, as concern grows about genetically modified plants, heirloom species have garnered more attention. This magazine's appeal continues to grow. Covering topics listed above, as well as related concerns like organic gardening and preservation, *The Heirloom Gardener* would be a nice addition to a generalist gardening magazine collection, because it views the topic through a somewhat alternative lens. The magazine includes charming illustrations reminiscent of old-time seed catalogs. An interesting note: The magazine does not accept advertising from the tobacco, chemical, or automobile industries, or those it sees as counter to its view on responsible citizenship and sustainability.

2620. *Horticulture: the art and science of smart gardening.* [ISSN: 0018-5329] 1904. bi-m. USD 29.95; USD 5.99 newsstand/cover. Ed(s): Meghan Shinn. F + W Media Inc., 10151 Carver Rd, Ste 200, Blue Ash, OH 45242; contact_us@fwmedia.com; http://www.fwmedia.com/. Illus., adv. Circ: 87010 Paid. *Indexed:* A01, A22, ASIP, BRI, C37, CBRI, GardL, IHTDI, MASUSE, P02. *Bk. rev.:* 3, 500 words. *Aud.:* Ga, Ac.

Horticulture is one of the oldest titles in this list, and it could serve as a representative archetype of gardening magazines. While it is beautifully illustrated with inspiring color photographs, the strength of this title is as an information source. Reading this magazine makes one feel like a smarter, better-informed gardener with a scientific understanding, artistic knowledge, and technical savvy. Regular features include "Pest Watch," "Plant Index and Pronunciation Guide," and product reviews. *Horticulture* has has long defined standards for gardening magazines, and is leading the way in addressing regional needs with content that is specific to major growing regions in the United States.

2621. *HortIdeas.* [ISSN: 0742-8219] 1984. bi-m. USD 25 domestic; USD 32 in Canada & Mexico; USD 42 elsewhere. Ed(s): Patricia Williams, Gregory Williams. HortIdeas Publishing, 750 Black Lick Rd, Gravel Switch, KY 40328; gwill@mis.net; http://www.users.mis.net/~gwill. Index. Sample. Vol. ends: Dec. *Indexed:* GardL. *Bk. rev.:* 3, 500 words. *Aud.:* Ga.

A unique title, *HortIdeas* could almost be understood as an abstracting service for the average grower. Editors "gather the information from hundreds of popular and technical sources, worldwide, and rewrite it so that you can understand it and use it." The idea behind this publication is that there is a lot of good information out there about gardening and horticulture that the average gardener or small-scale grower would never have time to read. So, the staff at *HortIdeas* scans popular and technical publications about gardening, horticulture, agriculture, forestry, ecology, and more to find the very best and most useful information. And that is what this magazine provides: distilled, easy-to-read, and up-to-date on the latest research and ideas, and the most important information. There are no color photographs, basic how-to articles, experiential narratives, or advertisements.

2622. *Hortus: a gardening journal.* [ISSN: 0950-1657] 1987. q. GBP 38; GBP 9.50 per issue. The Bryansground Press, Bryan's Ground, Stapleton, Presteigne, LD8 2LP, United Kingdom. Illus., index, adv. Sample. Vol. ends: Winter. *Indexed:* GardL. *Bk. rev.:* Varying number; 1,000 words. *Aud.:* Ga, Ac.

Hortus is a publication that is inspired by and indulges in the artistic side of gardening. Itself a beautiful specimen, the journal is in black-and-white on ochre-colored paper. While topics such as historical and notable gardens, plant introductions, gardeners of note, and ideas worth sharing are included, much of the content comes from the place where gardens intersect with art. For example, books about how to garden are reviewed, but so is fiction that features gardens. *Hortus* is for those who believe gardening is a high art, but also for those who only occasionally enjoy losing themselves in the beauty of gardens.

2623. *Organic Gardening.* Former titles (until 2003): *O G;* (until 2001): *Organic Gardening;* (until 1988): *Rodale's Organic Gardening;* (until 1985): *Organic Gardening;* (until 1978): *Organic Gardening and Farming;* Which was formed by the merger of (1949-1954): *Organic Farmer;* (1943-1954): *Organic Gardening;* Which was formerly (until 1943): *Organic Farming and Gardening.* 1954. bi-m. USD 23.94 for 2 yrs. domestic; CAD 29.94 for 2 yrs. Canada; USD 84 for 2 yrs. elsewhere. Ed(s): Ethne Clarke. Rodale, Inc., 33 E Minor St, Emmaus, PA 18098; info@rodale.com; http://www.rodaleinc.com. Illus., index, adv. Vol. ends: Dec. Microform: NBI; PQC. *Indexed:* A01, A22, Agr, BRI, C37, GardL, IHTDI, MASUSE, P02. *Aud.:* Ga.

While its focus is on organic gardening techniques, all gardeners will find something to like in this magazine. *Organic Gardening* recently reworked its image to keep up with its growing readership. Color sketches and gorgeous photographs serve the very practical purpose of illustrating the narrative. The articles are thorough and informative, and often provide reference to a source for more information on a topic. *Organic Gardening* harkens back to its roots as a vehicle for communication and education provided by J.I. Rodale, the early advocate of organic agriculture and sustainability; and it also covers political and social topics that impact these areas. If you are an organic gardener, *Organic Gardening* is a must; it treats gardening naturally and organically from every angle. If you are a gardener of any sort, it is a great read that offers new ideas and inspiration.

2624. *Soiled & Seeded: cultivating a garden culture.* [ISSN: 1925-0452] 2010. q. Ed(s): Barbara Ozimec. Soiled And Seeded Natural Heritage Explorations, 2084 Pen St, Oakville, ON L6H 3L3, Canada; donate@soiledandseeded.com. Adv. *Aud.:* Ga.

Soiled & Seeded is a unique title among the selections in this section. It is the most overtly political magazine, aimed mainly at urban gardeners. Its stated purpose—in a manifesto—shows its intent: "to expand the conventional approach to gardens and the practice of gardening." Published in Canada, *Soiled & Seeded* is international in scope, highlighting horticultural projects and topics from all over the world. This publication focuses less on how-to and science, and more on can-do and community. Stories discuss people reclaiming front lawns for food production, individuals starting community gardens, and villages celebrating native crops. Again, in the words of the manifesto, *Soiled & Seeded* is "cultivating a garden culture not based on decorative, hi-gloss scenarios, but rather one that restores our connection to the natural world and redefines our relationship to plants."

2625. Studies in the History of Gardens & Designed Landscapes: an international quarterly. Formerly (until 1998): *The Journal of Garden History.* [ISSN: 1460-1176] 1981. q. GBP 722 (print & online eds.). Ed(s): John Dixon Hunt. Routledge, 4 Park Sq, Milton Park, Abingdon, OX14 4RN, United Kingdom; subscriptions@tandf.co.uk; http://www.tandfonline.com. Illus., index, adv. Sample. Refereed. Vol. ends: Winter. Reprint: PSC. *Indexed:* A&ATA, A01, A07, A22, API, ArtHuCI, BrArAb, GardL, MLA-IB, NumL. *Bk. rev.:* Number and length vary. *Aud.:* Ac.

Studies in the History of Gardens & Designed Landscapes is a scholarly journal on garden history. Readers of this publication are almost exclusively scholars in garden history or related topics such as art, architecture, design, or other histories. The journal's "main emphasis is on documentation of individual gardens in all parts of the world," although it includes other topics such as design, horticulture, technique, and conservation. Also, it is well known for its book reviews. Photography and other illustration are included.

2626. Taunton's Fine Gardening. Formerly (until 19??): *Fine Gardening.* 1988. bi-m. USD 29.95 in US & Canada; USD 36 elsewhere; USD 6.99 per issue. Ed(s): Michelle Gervais. The Taunton Press, Inc., 63 South Main St, PO Box 5506, Newtown, CT 06470; publicrelations@taunton.com; http://www.taunton.com. Illus., index, adv. Circ: 202163 Paid. *Indexed:* ASIP, BRI, CBRI, GardL, IHTDI. *Bk. rev.:* 4, 250 words. *Aud.:* Ga.

Don't be fooled by the descriptive adjective in the title of *Fine Gardening*. As far as this publication is concerned, *all* gardening is "fine." Most articles are practical—for example, providing information about plants, step-by-step directions on projects, and techniques for effective gardening. While there are a lot of ads in this magazine, they are appropriate to the content. The publication is sleek in appearance—the color photographs and illustrations are stunning, design ideas are hip, and product features are trendy. However, the content is well written and the information sound, so this general gardening magazine lives up to its own hype.

■ GAY, LESBIAN, BISEXUAL, AND TRANSGENDER

Hilary Kline, Manager of Reformatting Support Services, Preservation and Imaging Department, Harvard College Library, Widener Library, Harvard University, Cambridge, MA 02138; kline@fas.harvard.edu

Introduction

It is my goal in this section to select titles that appeal to a broad general audience, rather than to niche readers. The titles that you won't find here are many of the very narrowly focused scholarly publications like *Journal of LGBT Issues in Counseling, Journal of LGBT Youth,* and *Law & Sexuality.* All of these have a defined place in the literature, but I felt they were too narrow for this section.

Also, not included in this section are titles dealing with travel, such as *Out Traveler* and *Passport.* There is a lot of information available for free on their web sites and many others, thus it felt it was redundant to give them full reviews.

As I was reviewing the section, I was beginning to feel that it was too heavily weighted toward the lesbians, so I was glad to be able to include a new title, *Instinct,* in this edition; this title is aimed at the gay male audience.

Lastly, there were two titles that I discovered rather late and will look into more fully for the next edition of *MFL.* They are *Original Plumbing* and *Frock.* Both target the transgender community; since that is one area that seems rather poorly represented, I wanted to give these two titles a mention. Also, a really good informative web site is *TransHealth,* www.trans-health.com, which covers a variety of topics specific to the trans community.

Basic Periodicals

Hs: *The Advocate, Out;* Ga: *The Advocate, Curve, The Gay & Lesbian Review Worldwide, Out;* Ac: *The Advocate, Curve, The Gay & Lesbian Review Worldwide, Journal of Homosexuality.*

Basic Abstracts and Indexes

Academic Search Premier, Alternative Press Index, Expanded Academic ASAP, GenderWatch, LGBT Life, MasterFILE Premier.

2627. The Advocate (Los Angeles, 1967). Formerly (until 1970): *Los Angeles Advocate.* [ISSN: 0001-8996] 1967. m. USD 19.95 domestic; USD 34.95 foreign. Regent Entertainment Media Inc., 10990 Wilshire Blvd, Penthouse 1800, Los Angeles, CA 90024; info@regententertainment.com; http://www.regententertainment.com. Illus., adv. *Indexed:* A01, A22, BRI, C42, CBRI, F01, GW, MASUSE, MLA-IB, P02. *Bk. rev.:* 1-5, 50-100 words. *Aud.:* Hs, Ga, Ac.

If your library owns only one GLBT title, this should be it. *The Advocate* is the most important and widely read newsmagazine that focuses on GLBT issues in the United States. A recent issue includes the article "The Kids Are Not All Right" and "Philadelphia v. The Boy Scouts." You can get a good idea of the magazine's depth and breadth at its web site; topic sections include "Politics," "Op-Ed," "A&E," "Women Crime," "Health," "Art," and "Travel," but the print copy should be in every library that serves adults in the United States. It is important to note that the print edition of *The Advocate* is no longer available separately; it must be purchased with the print edition of *Out.* URL: www.advocate.com

2628. Curve. Formerly (until 1996): *Deneuve.* [ISSN: 1087-867X] 1991. 10x/yr. USD 24.95 domestic; USD 36.95 Canada; USD 59.95 elsewhere. Ed(s): Dane Anderson-Minshall. Outspoken Enterprises, Inc., 1550 Bryant St, Ste 510, San Francisco, CA 94103. Illus., adv. *Indexed:* BRI, C42, MLA-IB. *Bk. rev.:* 4-6, 100-400 words. *Aud.:* Hs, Ga, Ac.

Curve is the thinking lesbian's *People.* Yes, it's slick and glossy, but it brings together in one place all the photos, interviews, ads, and inside information about the celebs you want to read about, as well as public figures you might not otherwise hear about. Check out the web site to get the flavor; topic sections include "Interviews," "Travel," "Advice," "Family," and "Events," but the print publication is still more complete. Recommended for public library collections. URL: www.curvemag.com

2629. The Gay & Lesbian Review Worldwide: a bimonthly journal of history, culture, and politics. Formerly (until 2000): *Harvard Gay & Lesbian Review.* [ISSN: 1532-1118] 1994. bi-m. USD 22 domestic; USD 32 in Canada & Mexico; USD 42 elsewhere. Ed(s): Richard Schneider, Jr. Gay & Lesbian Review Worldwide, PO Box 180300, Boston, MA 02118. Illus., adv. *Indexed:* A01, A22, AmHI, BRI, C42, F01, GW, MLA-IB, RILM. *Bk. rev.:* 10-15, 500-1,000 words. *Aud.:* Ga, Ac.

The mission of the *Review* "is to provide a forum for enlightened discussion of issues and ideas of importance to lesbians and gay men; to advance gay and lesbian culture by providing a quality vehicle for its best writers and thinkers; and to educate a broader public on gay and lesbian topics." Regular sections include "Features," "Reviews," "Poems & Departments," and "BTW." Each issue is organized on a theme, with essays and book reviews supporting that theme. A recent issue was themed "Americana," and included the articles "Riot at the Black Cat," "Lesbian Subcultures before Stonewall," and "Of Beefcake and Beauty Queens." The web site archives the table of contents of the recent printed copies and includes some full-text articles. The easiest way to describe the *Review* is to say it is *The New Yorker* for gays.

2630. *Instinct.* [ISSN: 1096-0058] 1997. m. USD 9.95. Ed(s): Mike Wood. Instinct Publishing, 303 N Glenoaks Blvd, Ste L120, Burbank, CA 91502; http://instinctmagazine.com/. Adv. Sample. *Aud.:* Ga.

This is a monthly publication aimed at gay men that includes the sections "Up Front," "Mix," "Goods," "Interaction," "Soapbox," "Inside Features," "Instinct Travel," and "Fashion." Two recent articles are "AIDS/LifeCycle: Inspiring Us All...One Mile At A Time" and "Flame On," which tells of the burgeoning gays and lesbians in comic books. This title is very similar in appearance and content to *Out*.

2631. *Journal of Homosexuality.* [ISSN: 0091-8369] 1974. m. GBP 1866 (print & online eds.). Ed(s): John Elia. Routledge, 325 Chestnut St, Ste 800, Philadelphia, PA 19106; customerservice@taylorandfrancis.com; http://www.tandfonline.com. Illus., adv. Sample. Refereed. Circ: 811 Paid. Microform: PQC. Reprint: PSC. *Indexed:* A01, A22, ASSIA, AbAn, AmHI, BRI, C42, CBRI, E01, GW, H24, HEA, IBSS, MLA-IB, P02, P61, PsycInfo, RILM, RiskAb, SSA, SWR&A, WSA. *Bk. rev.:* 4, 2,000-5,000 words. *Aud.:* Ac, Sa.

This peer-reviewed scholarly publication aims to "publish thought-provoking scholarship by researchers, community activists, and scholars who employ a range of research methodologies and who offer a variety of perspectives to continue shaping knowledge production in the arenas of lesbian, gay, bisexual, transgender (LGBT) studies and queer studies." This journal is generally divided into three major sections: the largest section contains scholarly articles, sometimes encompassing a theme; the second section consists of book reviews; and the third section is an annotated bibliography of references. Two recent articles are "Unmet Mental Health and Substance Abuse Treatment Needs of Sexual Minority Elders" and "Deconstructing the Silences: Gay Social Memory." The audience of this journal is definitely the academic and/or special library sectors.

2632. *Lesbian Connection.* [ISSN: 1081-3217] 1974. bi-m. Free. Elsie Publishing Institute, PO Box 811, E Lansing, MI 48826; elsiepub@aol.com. Illus., adv. Sample. *Bk. rev.:* 2-4, 200-300 words. *Aud.:* Ga.

This is a bimonthly free publication; however, a suggested donation of $42 per year is always welcome. *Lesbian Connection* is a grassroots lesbian network and readers' forum. Each issue is made up of the letters, responses, articles, reviews, etc., from subscribers. It also includes information and ads for lesbian festivals, events, and businesses; information on lesbian land and retirement communities; and the popular comic strips "Dykes To Watch Out For" by Alison Bechdel and "Bitter Girl" by Joan Hilty. According to the web site, a recent issue includes the articles "Lesbian Weddings—Part I" and "Coming Out at Work." *LC* has been publishing since 1974 with the simple goal of connecting the lesbian community worldwide. URL: www.lconline.org

2633. *Lesbian News.* [ISSN: 0739-1803] 1975. m. USD 45 domestic; USD 65 Canada; USD 95 elsewhere. Ed(s): Ella Matthes, Zoe Edgerton. L N Publishing Inc., PO Box 55, Torrance, CA 90507; theln@sbcglobal.net. Illus., adv. *Indexed:* A01, MASUSE. *Bk. rev.:* 8-10, 300-500 words. *Aud.:* Ga.

LN is another national publication, although with a decidedly L.A. bent, that has been around since the mid-70s. The current web site tends to look more like a social networking site, but I was able to download a pdf of the current issue of the magazine. I did not find any subscription information or other information about the publication (goals, target audience, etc.). The issue that I viewed had three main sections, "Features," "Inside LN," and "Lifestyles," as well as a cover story. Topics that are included are books, music, poetry, and self-help, to name a few. URL: www.lesbiannews.com

2634. *Out.* [ISSN: 1062-7928] 1992. m. USD 9.97 domestic; USD 24.97 foreign. Regent Entertainment Media Inc., 10990 Wilshire Blvd, Penthouse 1800, Los Angeles, CA 90024; info@regententertainment.com; http://www.regententertainment.com. Illus., adv. Microform: PQC. *Indexed:* GW, MLA-IB. *Bk. rev.:* 6-9, 50-400 words. *Aud.:* Hs, Ga, Ac.

Out is published by the same company that publishes *The Advocate,* so you will definitely see the similarities in the two web sites. *Out* is more focused on a young gay male audience, while *The Advocate* is more bipartisan. The sections included in the magazine are "Features," "Fashion," "Foreground," "Symposium," "Surveillance," and "Departments." Music, theater, and the arts, as well as fashion, are showcased. Two recent articles are "Two Men Talking," featuring Edmund White and John Irving, and "The 25 SONGS of Summer."

2635. *Whosoever: an online magazine for gay, lesbian, bisexual and transgendered christians.* 1996. bi-m. Free. Ed(s): Candace Chellew-Hodge. Whosoever. *Aud.:* Hs, Ga, Ac.

Whosoever started as a print magazine, surviving in that format for just under a year. Now as a free online magazine, it is reaching many more GLBT Christians. The vision of Whosoever Ministries, Inc., is "to provide a safe and sacred space for gay, lesbian, bisexual[,] and transgender Christians to reclaim, rekindle[,] and grow their relationship with God." Regular sections of the bimonthly publication include "Cover Stories," "Features," "From the Pulpit," and "Holy Humor." Two recent articles are "Will These Supremes Care About 'Equal Justice for All?'" and "Christianity Affirms Same-Sex Love." Find it at http://whosoever.org/

■ GENDER STUDIES

See also Gay, Lesbian, Bisexual, and Transgender; and Sexuality sections.

Lilith R. Kunkel, Library Director, Salem Campus Library, Kent State University Salem Regional Campus, 2491 State Route 45 S., Salem, OH 44460; FAX: 330-337-4144; lkunkel@kent.edu.

Cheryl LaGuardia, Research Librarian, Widener Library, Harvard University

Introduction

Gender studies is a field of study that grew out of women's studies programs established in the 1970s, and has developed as an increasingly sophisticated area of academic inquiry that focuses on issues of sex and gender and their intersection with race, class, religion, culture, art, politics, and nationality across time and place. From its inception, it has been interdisciplinary and activist in outlook. It encompasses the study of masculinities and men's studies and queer studies as well as women's studies. It can be literary, humanistic, or scientific in its approach.

Gender studies programs vary greatly in their blending of theoretical, empirical, and applied studies. They also vary in their sexual politics and in their attention to diversity. They are shaped by third-wave feminism (though not all scholarship is necessarily feminist) and by changing debates about gender in both the discipline and the larger cultural context. Postcolonial and postmodern discourse has brought increased attention to gender in transcultural and global contexts.

In choosing gender studies periodicals, selectors need to consider not only the complicated nature of the field, but also current trends in publishing. Most notable are the continued growth of web-based publishing, the increased availability of online full-text, and the growing number of open-access scholarly journals. Online tables of contents, RSS feeds, and email alert services make the content of both print and electronic periodicals more accessible while blogs and other web based features enhance content and promote discussion. The content of some e-journals may be difficult to access through article databases and major search engines, however. Specialized databases such as *Contemporary Women's Issues, Gender Abstracts,* and *Women's Studies International* may provide better access, but at a price beyond the reach of smaller libraries.

The titles listed here have been selected to represent the variety and scope of gender studies. This section includes few publications that deal with sexuality; these are covered in the "Gay, Lesbian, Bisexual, and Transgender" section and the "Sexuality" section. It also does not include online publications such as *The Feminist Majority Foundation* that are excellent sources for current news and information but are not truly periodical in nature. Well-established health publications are now included in the "Health and Fitness" "Medicine" sections. Journals focusing on law and genedr such as the *Harvard Journal of Law and Gender* are included in the "Law" section.

Basic Periodicals

MEN'S STUDIES. Ga: *Harvard Men's Health Watch*; Sa: *The Aging Male, International Journal of Men's Health, The Journal of Men's Health, Journal of Men's Studies, Men and Masculinities, Psychology of Men and Masculinity.*

FEMINIST AND WOMEN'S STUDIES. Hs: *Ms., Feminist Formations*; Ga: *Frontiers, Herizons, Ms.*; Ac: *Critical Matrix, Feminist Studies, Frontiers, Gender and Education, Gender and History, Gender Issues, Genders, Hypatia, Journal of Women's History, Ms., Feminist Formations, Signs, Violence Against Women, Women & Health, Women in Sport and Physical Activity Journal, Women's Studies Quarterly.*

SPECIAL INTEREST. Ac: *Media Report to Women.*

Basic Abstracts and Indexes

Ac: *Contemporary Women's Issues, Feminist Periodicals, GenderWatch, Studies on Women and Gender Abstracts, Violence & Abuse Abstracts, Women Studies Abstracts, Women's Studies International.*

2636. *Affilia: journal of women and social work.* [ISSN: 0886-1099] 1986. q. USD 739. Ed(s): Fariyal Ross-Sheriff, Christine Flynn Saulnier. Sage Publications, Inc., 2455 Teller Rd, Thousand Oaks, CA 91320; info@sagepub.com; http://www.sagepub.com. Illus., adv. Sample. Refereed. Vol. ends: Nov. Reprint: PSC. *Indexed:* A01, A22, BRI, CJPI, E01, FemPer, P02, PsycInfo, SSA, SWR&A, WSA. *Bk. rev.:* 7-14, 350-900 words; signed. *Aud.:* Ac, Sa.

This scholarly journal addresses the concerns of social work and its clients from a feminist perspective. It aims to provide the knowledge and tools needed to improve the delivery of social services through research reports, empirical articles, opinion pieces, and book reviews. Issues also include news updates and literary works. Full text is available through Sage Journals Online to institutions with print subscriptions. The publisher also offers a table-of-contents alert service and advance online publication of forthcoming articles.

The Aging Male. See Geriatrics and Gerontological Studies section.

2637. *Asian Journal of Women's Studies.* [ISSN: 1225-9276] 1995. q. USD 145 (Individuals, USD 60). Ed(s): Philwha Chang, Jieun Roh. Ewha Womans University, Asian Center for Women's Studies, #11-1, Daehyun-dong, Seodaemun-gu, Seoul, 120-750, Korea, Republic of; acwsewha@ewha.ac.kr; http://home.ewha.ac.kr/~acws/eng/. Adv. Sample. Refereed. Circ: 700 Paid and controlled. *Indexed:* FemPer, GW, MLA-IB. *Bk. rev.:* 2, 800-1,000 words; signed. *Aud.:* Ac.

This interdisciplinary journal from the Asian Center for Women's Studies provides a feminist perspective on women's issues in Asia and throughout the world. It aims to communicate scholarly ideas and "to develop women's studies in Asia and expand the horizon of Western-centered women's studies." It includes scholarly articles, country reports, notes on teaching and research, and book reviews. A new "Special Corner: Voices from Asian Feminist Activism" section presents narratives by activists and young scholars on their individual and collective experiences.

2638. *Atlantis: a women's studies journal - revue d'etudes sur les femmes.* [ISSN: 0702-7818] 1975. s-a. Ed(s): Katherine Side, Annalee Lepp. Mount Saint Vincent University, Institute for the Study of Women, Halifax, NS B3M 2J6, Canada; http://www.msvu.ca/en/home/community/communityservices/instituteforthestudyofwomen.aspx. Illus., index. Refereed. Vol. ends: Spring/Summer. Microform: MML. *Indexed:* A22, AmHI, BRI, C37, CBCARef, FemPer, MLA-IB, WSA. *Bk. rev.:* 8, length varies; signed. *Aud.:* Ac.

Atlantis is an established Canadian journal that provides scholarly, critical, and creative writing in English and French about women and women's studies. Publication alternates between general, open, and special issues. One recent open issue featured articles on women's paid employment in a range of contemporary and historical contexts. Its perspective is international and interdisciplinary. Contributors are academics, artists, and feminists. The content of current and archived issues can be accessed through Open Journal Systems.

2639. *Australian Feminist Studies.* [ISSN: 0816-4649] 1985. q. GBP 629 (print & online eds.). Ed(s): Mary Spongberg. Routledge, Level 2, 11 Queens Rd, Melbourne, VIC 3004, Australia; enquiries@tandf.com.au; http://www.routledge.com. Adv. Sample. Refereed. Reprint: PSC. *Indexed:* A01, A22, AmHI, E01, F01, FemPer, IBSS, P61, SSA. *Bk. rev.:* 6-8, 500 words, essay length; signed. *Aud.:* Ac.

This international, peer-reviewed journal focuses on feminist scholarship, teaching, and practice. Its contents include research articles, reviews, critiques, and correspondence, as well as news, conference reports, and discussions of feminist pedagogy. Some articles fall within familiar disciplinary boundaries, while others are interdisciplinary. Others offer interesting insights into women's studies and feminist issues in Australia. A recent special issue featured papers on masculinity presented at a 2010 conference on "Transforming Gender" held in Adelaide. A free contents-alerting service is available from the publisher.

The Beltane Papers: a journal of women's mysteries. See Spirituality and Well-Being section.

2640. *Canadian Woman Studies.* Formerly (until 1981): *Canadian Women's Studies.* [ISSN: 0713-3235] 1978. q. Ed(s): Luciana Ricciutelli. Inanna Publications and Education Inc., 210 Founders College, York University, 4700 Keele St, North York, ON M3J 1P3, Canada; http://www.yorku.ca/inanna/about.html. Illus., adv. Refereed. Vol. ends: Winter (No. 4). Microform: MML. *Indexed:* ABS&EES, AmHI, BRI, C37, C42, CBCARef, FemPer, GW, MLA-IB, WSA. *Bk. rev.:* 7, 600-1,100; signed. *Aud.:* Ac, Sa.

This bilingual, feminist quarterly "was founded with the goal of making current writing and research on a wide variety of feminist topics accessible to the largest possible community of women." Issues are theme-based and include scholarly and experiential articles, art, creative writing, and book reviews. Coverage is international. The editors encourage submissions that deal with the diverse lives of "women of color, Aboriginal women, immigrant women, working class women, women with disabilities, lesbians, and other marginalized women."

Columbia Journal of Gender and the Law. See Law section.

2641. *Culture, Society and Masculinities.* [ISSN: 1941-5583] 2009. s-a. Individuals, USD 50. Ed(s): Diederik F Janssen. Men's Studies Press, PO Box 32, Harriman, TN 37748; publisher@mensstudies.com; http://www.mensstudies.com. Refereed. *Indexed:* GW, P61, SSA. *Aud.:* Ac, Sa. ;ITCS&M ;ROis a peer-reviewed academic journal published semi-annually in print and digital formats by the Men's Studies Press. It aims to place gender and masculinities studies in broader historical, political, sociological, and/or theoretical frameworks. Studies are social, cultural, and/or international. They offer ?comparative views and works that rethink, elaborate, or critique existing ideas and concepts of locality, globalization and regionalization?? Articles present research in cultural psychology, cross-cultural and trans-cultural studies, postcolonial studies, international conflict studies, and gender policy studies. This publication complements the more limited focus of the *Journal of Men's Studies.* A new issue alerting service is available from the publisher's web site. URL: http://www.mensstudies.com/content/121105/

2642. *Differences: a journal of feminist cultural studies.* [ISSN: 1040-7391] 1989. 3x/yr. USD 186. Ed(s): Denise Davis, Elizabeth Weed. Duke University Press, 905 W Main St, Ste 18 B, PO Box 90660, Durham, NC 27701; subscriptions@dukeupress.edu; http://www.dukeupress.edu. Illus., adv. Sample. Refereed. Vol. ends: Fall. Reprint: PSC. *Indexed:* A01, A22, AmHI, ArtHuCI, BRI, C42, E01, FemPer, GW, IBSS, MLA-IB, P02, P61, SSA, WSA. *Aud.:* Ac.

This scholarly journal focuses on how concepts and categories of "difference" are produced and operate within culture and over time. The main, but not exclusive, focus is women and gender. Articles are interdisciplinary and often theoretical. Special issues have included "Psychoanalysis and the Question of Social Change" and "God and Country." Some issues include "Critical Exchanges" between scholars on key issues. Published by Duke University Press, with full text available online to institutions with print subscriptions.

2643. *European Journal of Women's Studies.* [ISSN: 1350-5068] 1994. q. USD 998. Ed(s): Hazel Johnstone, Gail Lewis. Sage Publications Ltd., 1 Oliver's Yard, 55 City Rd, London, EC1Y 1SP, United Kingdom; info@sagepub.co.uk; http://www.uk.sagepub.com. Illus., adv. Sample. Refereed. Vol. ends: Nov. Reprint: PSC. *Indexed:* A01, A22, ABS&EES, AmHI, E01, FemPer, GW, IBSS, MLA-IB, P02, P61, PsycInfo, SSA, WSA. *Bk. rev.:* 2-10, length varies; signed. *Aud.:* Ac.

This interdisciplinary, academic journal publishes theoretical and thematic articles as well as open letters, book reviews, and conference reports that deal with women and feminism in the European context. Some issues focus on specific issues such as gender and transnationalism, race and ethnicity, and religion and politics. Articles are published in English, but Dutch, French, German, Italian, and Spanish articles are also refereed and may be published in translation. Full text is available through Sage Journals Online.

Feminism & Psychology. See Psychology section.

2644. *Feminist Collections: a quarterly of women's studies resources.* [ISSN: 0742-7441] 1980. q. USD 65 (Individuals, USD 35). Ed(s): JoAnne Lehman, Phyllis Holman Weisbard. University of Wisconsin at Madison, Women's Studies Librarian, Memorial Library, Rm.430, 728 State St., Madison, WI 53706; wiswsl@library.wisc.edu; http://womenst.library.wisc.edu/. Illus., adv. Vol. ends: Summer. *Indexed:* A01, A22, BRI, C42, GW, HEA, MLA-IB, WSA. *Bk. rev.:* Number varies, essay length; signed. *Aud.:* Ac, Sa.

Feminist Collections is a key resource for research and teaching in women's studies. It provides reviews of books, periodicals, audiovisuals, and online resources. Regular features include "New Reference Works in Women's Studies." "E-Sources on Women and Gender" provides notices of new web sites, blogs, and other digital or online resources, while "Periodical Notes" provides information about new publications, special issues, and ceased publications. A print subscription includes *Feminist Periodicals*, an online current-contents listing service, and *New Books on Women & Feminism*. Available in full text from volume 16, number 1 (Fall 1994) in the databases *Contemporary Women's Issues* and *GenderWatch*.

2645. *Feminist Economics.* [ISSN: 1354-5701] 1995. q. GBP 402 (print & online eds.). Ed(s): Diana Strassmann, Gunseli Berik. Routledge, 4 Park Sq, Milton Park, Abingdon, OX14 4RN, United Kingdom; subscriptions@tandf.co.uk; http://www.tandfonline.com. Illus., adv. Sample. Refereed. Vol. ends: No. 3. Reprint: PSC. *Indexed:* A01, A22, ABIn, AmHI, B01, BAS, C42, E01, EconLit, FemPer, IBSS, JEL, P61, SSA. *Bk. rev.:* Number and length vary. *Aud.:* Ac.

This journal offers feminist insights into the relationship between gender and power in the economy and in the discipline of economics. Its goals are "not just to develop illuminating theories but to improve the conditions of living for all children, women, and men," and to provide "an open forum for dialogue and debate about feminist economic perspectives." Coverage is cross-cultural and global. A recent issue, for example, includes a critical evaluation of the U.N.'s gender inequality index and research articles on the effect of gender on mortgage choice in the United States, gender and poverty risk in Europe, reciprocity in caring work in Australian residential aged care facilities. An upcoming special issue will focus on sex work and human trafficking. Book reviews are also included. Recommended for academic and research libraries.

2646. *Feminist Formations.* Formerly (until 2010): *National Women's Studies Association. Journal.* [ISSN: 2151-7363] 1988. 3x/yr. USD 165. Ed(s): Erin Durban-Albrecht, Sandra K Soto. The Johns Hopkins University Press, 2715 N Charles St, Baltimore, MD 21218; http://www.press.jhu.edu. Illus., adv. Sample. Refereed. Circ: 1286. Reprint: PSC. *Indexed:* A01, A22, AmHI, BRI, C42, CBRI, Chicano, E01, FemPer, GW, MLA-IB, P02, RILM, WSA. *Bk. rev.:* 9-12, brief and essay length; signed. *Aud.:* Ac.

The journal of the National Women's Studies Association, formerly *NWSA Journal,* publishes interdisciplinary, multicultural scholarship in women's studies. It seeks to connect feminist scholarship and theory with activism and teaching. In addition to research articles, its contents include articles about the theory and teaching of women's studies and reviews of books, teaching materials, and films. One recent special issue focuses on gendered experiences of schooling in a variety of local contexts across the globe. Covers now feature "politically charged feminist artwork." Tables of contents updates are available via e-mail and RSS feed through Project Muse.

Feminist Media Studies. See Television, Video, and Radio section.

2647. *Feminist Review.* [ISSN: 0141-7789] 1979. 3x/yr. USD 671. Palgrave Macmillan Ltd., Houndmills, Basingstoke, RG21 6XS, United Kingdom; orders@palgrave.com; http://www.palgrave.com. Illus., adv. Sample. Refereed. Reprint: PSC. *Indexed:* A01, A22, AmHI, BRI, C42, E01, FR, FemPer, GW, IBSS, MLA-IB, P02, P61, RILM, SSA. *Bk. rev.:* 4-17, length varies; signed; online only. *Aud.:* Ga, Ac.

This is a key feminist journal, published in Great Britain, that seeks "to unite research and theory with political practice, and contribute to the development of both." It publishes academic articles, feminist analysis, dialogues, review essays, interviews, creative writing, and book reviews on issues related to gender, sexuality, race, and class. Its perspective is international and interdisciplinary. Recent special issues have focused on water and conflict. Contents pages and a contents-alerting service are available from the publisher's web site. Book reviews are now published only in the online edition, and are available for free along with articles selected from the journal archives by the *Feminist Review Collective.*

2648. *Feminist Studies.* [ISSN: 0046-3663] 1972. 3x/yr. USD 263 (Individuals, USD 40 (print & online eds.); Students, USD 20 (print & online eds.). Ed(s): Karla Mantilla. Feminist Studies, Inc., 0103 Taliaferro Hall, University of Maryland, College Park, MD 20742. Illus., index, adv. Refereed. Vol. ends: Fall (No. 3). Microform: PQC. Reprint: PSC. *Indexed:* A01, A07, A22, ABS&EES, ASSIA, AmHI, BAS, BRI, C42, Chicano, FemPer, GW, IBSS, MASUSE, MLA-IB, P02, P61, RILM, SSA, WSA. *Bk. rev.:* 0-1, essay length; signed. *Aud.:* Ac.

Feminist Studies seeks to promote discussion among feminist scholars, activists, and writers, to develop an interdisciplinary body of knowledge and theory, and to change women's condition. It is both scholarly and political in its coverage. Contents include scholarly research from all disciplines, essays, interviews, commentaries, creative writing, full-color art works, and book reviews. Published by an editorial collective in association with the University of Maryland's Women's Studies Program, this is a core resource for women's studies programs. Contents pages are available from the publisher's web site. Full text is available through *GenderWatch* from 1990 to date.

2649. *Feminist Teacher: a journal of the practices, theories, and scholarship of feminist teaching.* [ISSN: 0882-4843] 1984. 3x/yr. USD 129 (print & online eds.). Ed(s): Monica Barron. University of Illinois Press, 1325 S Oak St, Champaign, IL 61820; journals@uillinois.edu; http://www.press.uillinois.edu. Adv. Refereed. *Indexed:* A01, A22, BRI, C42, E01, ERIC, FemPer, GW, MLA-IB, P02, P61, SSA, WSA. *Bk. rev.:* Number and length vary. *Aud.:* Hs, Ga, Ac.

This journal from the University of Illinois Press addresses the theory and practice of feminist teaching and considers "issues such as multiculturalism, interdisciplinarity, and distance learning in a feminist context." It is directed toward teachers and administrators at all levels and includes articles, book reviews, review essays, course descriptions, syllabi, and bibliographies. The "Teaching Resources" section offers information about online, audiovisual, and other resources, while the "Teaching Notes" section provides information about teaching strategies and current classroom issues.

2650. *Feminist Theology.* [ISSN: 0966-7350] 1992. 3x/yr. USD 547. Sage Publications Ltd., 1 Oliver's Yard, 55 City Rd, London, EC1Y 1SP, United Kingdom; info@sagepub.co.uk; http://www.uk.sagepub.com. Adv. Sample. Refereed. Reprint: PSC. *Indexed:* A01, A22, E01, R&TA. *Bk. rev.:* 6-8, length varies; signed. *Aud.:* Ac, Sa.

Feminist Theology provides an interdisciplinary and feminist perspective on theology, biblical studies, and the sociology of religion. It is a refereed, academic journal that aims to be accessible to a wide range of readers. Contents include articles and conference papers on various aspects of theology and practice. While its main focus is on Christianity, coverage includes Judaism, Islam, and Buddhism as well. There is a free contents-alerting service. Full text is available through Sage Journals Online.

2651. *Feminist Theory: an international interdisciplinary journal.* [ISSN: 1464-7001] 2000. 3x/yr. USD 693. Sage Publications Ltd., 1 Oliver's Yard, 55 City Rd, London, EC1Y 1SP, United Kingdom; info@sagepub.co.uk; http://www.uk.sagepub.com. Illus., index, adv. Sample. Refereed. Vol. ends: Dec. Reprint: PSC. *Indexed:* A22, E01, FemPer, IBSS, P61, PsycInfo, SSA. *Bk. rev.:* Number and length vary; signed. *Aud.:* Ac.

This international journal focuses on the critical examination and discussion of diverse feminist theoretical and political positions across the humanities and social sciences. Written by feminists from around the world, its contents include articles, shorter "think pieces" on topical issues, interchanges between theorists, and book reviews. Free contents-alerting service. Full text is available through Sage Journals Online.

2652. *Frontiers (Lincoln): a journal of women studies.* [ISSN: 0160-9009] 1975. 3x/yr. USD 182 (print & online eds.). Ed(s): Judy Tzu-Chun Wu, Guisela Latorre. University of Nebraska Press, 1111 Lincoln Mall, Lincoln, NE 68588; pressmail@unl.edu; http://www.nebraskapress.unl.edu. Illus., index. Refereed. Circ: 350. Microform: PQC. *Indexed:* A01, A22, ABS&EES, AmHI, BAS, BRI, Chicano, E01, FR, FemPer, GW, MLA-IB, P02, P61, RILM, SSA, WSA. *Aud.:* Ac.

This multicultural, cross-disciplinary journal is a mix of scholarly work, personal essays, and creative works that examine "the critical intersections among... gender, race, sexuality, and transnationalism." This well known journal has published a number of landmark articles throughout its history and has now expanded its geographic and comparative focus. Full text is available through *GenderWatch* and Project Muse, as well as through various EBSCO and ProQuest products.

2653. *Gender and Development.* Formerly (until 1995): *Focus on Gender.* [ISSN: 1355-2074] 1993. 3x/yr. GBP 273 (print & online eds.). Ed(s): Caroline Sweetman. Routledge, 4 Park Sq, Milton Park, Abingdon, OX14 4RN, United Kingdom; subscriptions@tandf.co.uk; http://www.tandfonline.com. Adv. Sample. Reprint: PSC. *Indexed:* A01, A22, AbAn, C45, E01, FemPer, IBSS, P61, RiskAb, SSA. *Bk. rev.:* brief, 750 words. *Aud.:* Ac, Sa.

This Oxfam journal is concerned with the relationship between gender and economic development. Issues are thematic and include articles, case studies, conference reports, interviews, resources, and book reviews. Articles are directed toward development practitioners, policy makers, and academics. A "Resources" section provides an annotated listing of relevant publications. A "Views, Events, and Debates" section features interviews, organizational profiles, reports of events, and responses from readers. Contents pages are available free of charge on the publisher's web site. Full text is available to subscribers through the publisher's web site.

2654. *Gender and Education.* [ISSN: 0954-0253] 1989. 7x/yr. GBP 1559 (print & online eds.). Routledge, 4 Park Sq, Milton Park, Abingdon, OX14 4RN, United Kingdom; subscriptions@tandf.co.uk; http://www.tandfonline.com. Illus., adv. Sample. Refereed. Vol. ends: Dec (No. 4). Reprint: PSC. *Indexed:* A01, A22, ASSIA, C42, E01, ERIC, FemPer, IBSS, LT&LA, P02, P61, RiskAb, SSA. *Bk. rev.:* 9-15, 500-1,000 words; signed. *Aud.:* Ac.

Gender and Education is an international journal that publishes multidisciplinary educational research with gender as a main category of analysis. It is committed to promoting feminist scholarship and practice in gender and education. Education is broadly defined as encompassing formal and informal education at all levels and within all contexts throughout the world. Tables of contents and an e-mail contents-alerting service are available on the publisher's web site. Full text is available online, to institutions with print subscriptions, through the publisher's web site.

2655. *Gender and History.* [ISSN: 0953-5233] 1989. 3x/yr. GBP 482. Wiley-Blackwell Publishing Ltd., The Atrium, Southern Gate, Chichester, PO19 8SQ, United Kingdom; customer@wiley.com; http://www.wiley.com/. Illus., adv. Sample. Refereed. Vol. ends: Nov. Reprint: PSC. *Indexed:* A01, A22, AmHI, E01, FemPer, IBSS, MLA-IB, P61, SSA, WSA. *Bk. rev.:* Number varies, essay length; signed. *Aud.:* Ac.

This peer-reviewed journal offers "research and writing on the history of femininity and masculinity and of gender relations." It has a broad chronological and geographical scope and reflects a variety of perspectives. It covers both specific episodes in gender history and broader methodological questions. Special issues focus on themes such as "Gender and the City before Modernity" and "Historicising Gender and Sexuality." It provides review essays and extensive book reviews. Articles are rigorous and readable. Some are in translation. Tables of contents of past issues and a sample issue are available on the publisher's web site.

2656. *Gender & Society.* [ISSN: 0891-2432] 1987. bi-m. USD 908. Ed(s): Joya Misra. Sage Publications, Inc., 2455 Teller Rd, Thousand Oaks, CA 91320; info@sagepub.com; http://www.sagepub.com. Illus. Sample. Refereed. Vol. ends: Dec. Reprint: PSC. *Indexed:* A22, ABS&EES, BRI, Chicano, E01, FemPer, IBSS, P02, P61, PsycInfo, RiskAb, SSA, WSA. *Bk. rev.:* Number varies, essay length; signed. *Aud.:* Ac.

This official publication of Sociologists for Women in Society publishes articles that "analyze gender and gendered processes in interactions, organizations, societies, and global and transnational spaces." This peer-reviewed journal publishes qualitative, quantitative, and comparative-historical research articles. It also includes book reviews and occasionally features a "book review symposium" featuring critical evaluations of the same or thematically related works. Articles are available electronically via Sage Journals Online. Some articles are available in advance of print publication through Sage's OnlineFirst service. The journal's website offers podcasts of authors discussing their work and a blog. *ISI Journal Citation Reports* ranks this journal among the top women's studies journals.

2657. *Gender Issues.* Formerly (until 1998): *Feminist Issues.* [ISSN: 1098-092X] 1980. q. EUR 375 (print & online eds.). Ed(s): R J Simon. Springer New York LLC, 233 Spring St, New York, NY 10013; service-ny@springer.com; http://www.springer.com. Illus. Refereed. Vol. ends: Fall. Microform: PQC. Reprint: PSC. *Indexed:* A01, A22, ABIn, ABS&EES, BRI, C37, E01, FemPer, GW, MASUSE, MLA-IB, P02, P61, SSA, WSA. *Bk. rev.:* 2, essay length; signed. *Aud.:* Ac.

Gender Issues "publishes basic and applied research on the relationships between men and women; on similarities and differences in socialization, personality, and behavior." Its coverage is interdisciplinary and international. Contributors come from the social sciences. One recent issue includes misogyny, living apart together relationships, and gender socialization in wilderness recreation advertising while another includes articles on gender disparities in the pricing of personal care products, self-induces abortion in the 21st century U.S., and the meaning of being a childless woman in Australian society. The journal also includes book reviews. Full text is available to individuals and members of subscribing institutions through the publisher's web site. Some articles are available ahead of print publication through the publisher's Online First service.

Gender, Place and Culture. See Geography section.

2658. *Gender, Technology & Development.* [ISSN: 0971-8524] 1997. 3x/yr. USD 382. Ed(s): N Veena. Sage Publications India Pvt. Ltd., B-1/I-1 Mohan Cooperative Industrial Estate Mathura Rd, PO Box 7, New Delhi, 110 044, India; info@sagepub.in; http://www.sagepub.in. Illus., index, adv. Sample. Refereed. Vol. ends: Nov. Reprint: PSC. *Indexed:* A22, E01, FemPer, IBSS, P61, RiskAb, SSA. *Bk. rev.:* 4, length varies; signed. *Aud.:* Ac.

This international, refereed journal focuses on gender relations and technological development in non-Western societies and cultures, particularly Asia. Its intended audience is academics and people working in development and natural resource management. In addition to scholarly articles, it includes book reviews, research notes, and conference reports. A "News and Events" section provides information on current issues. One special issue each year focuses on a theme, such as "Gender and Space" and "Women in National Politics in Asia. Tables of contents of recent issues are available on the publisher's web site.

2659. Gender, Work and Organization. [ISSN: 0968-6673] 1994. bi-m. GBP 757. Ed(s): Deborah Kerfoot, David Knights. Wiley-Blackwell Publishing Ltd., The Atrium, Southern Gate, Chichester, PO19 8SQ, United Kingdom; customer@wiley.com; http://www.wiley.com/. Illus., adv. Sample. Refereed. Vol. ends: No. 4. Reprint: PSC. *Indexed:* A01, A22, ABIn, B01, E01, ErgAb, FemPer, IBSS, P61, PsycInfo, RiskAb, SSA. *Bk. rev.:* Number and length vary; signed. *Aud.:* Ac.

This interdisciplinary journal publishes social science research and theoretical articles relating to gender and work. It is concerned with "gender relations at work, the organization of gender[,] and the gendering of organizations." Recent special issues have looked at "Researching Gender, Inclusion and Diversity in Contemporary Professions and Professional Organizations" and "Gender and Change." The journal also includes review articles and book reviews. Its focus is international and it includes coverage of new technologies. Content pages and free e-mail table of contents alerts are available on the publisher's web site.

2660. Genders (Online). [ISSN: 1936-3249] s-a. Free. Ed(s): Ann Kibbey, Carol Siegel. University of Colorado, Campus Box 226, Boulder, CO 80309. Refereed. *Indexed:* AmHI, FemPer. *Bk. rev.:* Number varies, essay length; signed. *Aud.:* Ga, Ac.

This e-journal from the University of Colorado publishes "essays about gender and sexualities in relation to artistic, semiotic, political, literary, social, ethnic, racial, economic, rhetorical or legal concerns." Contents include essays on how sexuality is used to support or protect various cultural institutions; historical and cross-cultural analyses of contemporary gender issues; interviews; and discussions of particular works of art, literature, or film. URL: www.genders.org

Harvard Men's Health Watch. See Health and Fitness section.

2661. Hawwa: journal of women of the Middle East and the Islamic world. [ISSN: 1569-2078] 2003. 3x/yr. EUR 300. Ed(s): Amira Sonbol. Brill, PO Box 9000, Leiden, 2300 PA, Netherlands; cs@brill.nl; http://www.brill.nl. Refereed. Reprint: PSC. *Indexed:* A22, E01, FemPer, MLA-IB, RiskAb. *Bk. rev.:* Number and length vary. *Aud.:* Ac.

This peer-reviewed journal publishes articles on women and gender issues in the Middle East and the Islamic world. It includes theoretical and methodological, as well as topical, articles and book reviews. Its main focus is on the contemporary era, but about one third of the submissions deal with the pre-modern era. One recent special issue looks at the intersection of justice and gender. Table of contents alerts are available through e-mail and RSS feed. Full text is available online through the publisher's web site and Ingenta Select.

2662. Hecate: an interdisciplinary journal of women's liberation. [ISSN: 0311-4198] 1975. s-a. AUD 154 (Individuals, AUD 35). Ed(s): Carole Ferrier. Hecate Press, PO Box 6099, St Lucia, QLD 4067, Australia. Refereed. *Indexed:* A01, A22, AmHI, BEL&L, BRI, FemPer, GW, MLA-IB, P02, WSA. *Aud.:* Ga, Ac.

This international journal—from Hecate Press and the University of Queensland's Research Centre for Women, Gender, Culture and Social Change—offers a feminist and generally radical perspective on women's experiences in Australia and in the Pacific region. It focuses on history, culture, sexuality, and politics. Contents include essays, interviews, and short stories, poems, and other creative works. The journal also publishes the annual *Hecate's Australian Women's Book Review*. Full text is available through *Academic Search Complete* and *Women's Studies International*.

2663. Herizons: women's news & feminist views. Formerly (until 1981): *Manitoba Women's Newspaper*. [ISSN: 0711-7485] 1980. q. CAD 25.94 domestic; CAD 33.94 foreign. Ed(s): Penni Mitchell. Herizons, PO Box 128, Winnipeg, MB R3C 2G1, Canada. Illus., adv. Circ: 4200. *Indexed:* A01, BRI, C37, C42, CBCARef, FemPer, GW, MASUSE. *Bk. rev.:* 4, 550 words; signed. *Aud.:* Ga, Ac.

This popular Canadian feminist magazine covers the Canadian women?s movement and topics of interest to feminists worldwide. Recent issues include articles by feminist writers and activists on veganism for children, the crunch in eldercare, crimes against women in India, and older woman-younger man relationships. Diffferent sections cover news, opinion, art, music, literature, health, and sexuality. Selected articles from the current and previous issues are posted on the magazine's web site. Full text is available through *Academic Search Complete* and *Women's Studies International*.

2664. Hypatia: a journal of feminist philosophy. Supersedes in part (in 1986): *Women's Studies International Forum;* Which was formerly (until 1982): *Women's Studies International Quarterly*. [ISSN: 0887-5367] 1978. q. GBP 155. Ed(s): Alison Wylie, Lori Gruen. Wiley-Blackwell Publishing, Inc., Commerce Pl, 350 Main St, Malden, MA 02148; info@wiley.com; http://onlinelibrary.wiley.com/. Illus. Sample. Refereed. Vol. ends: Fall. Reprint: PSC. *Indexed:* A01, A07, A22, ABS&EES, AmHI, ArtHuCI, BRI, C42, E01, FemPer, GW, MLA-IB, P02, P61, SSA, WSA. *Bk. rev.:* 3-5, 1,000-1,500 words; signed. *Aud.:* Ac.

This peer-reviewed journal publishes scholarly research in feminist philosophy and provides a perspective not available in many women's studies journals. It draws on traditions and methods within the discipline but is also interdisciplinary in outlook. It seeks to promote feminist discourse in philosophy and to represent the work of women philosophers, while it also serves "as a resource for the wider women's studies community, for philosophers generally, and for all those interested in philosophical issues raised by feminism." A recent special issue on the "Crossing Borders" presents scholarship on issues raised by globalization. considers the implications of bodily differences or vulnerability. The journal also includes book reviews and "Musings" on controversial issues. Table of contents alerts are available through e-mail and RSS feed from the publisher's web site. Online access to current content is only available through Wiley InterScience. Some open-access articles are available online without a paid subscription.

2665. International Feminist Journal of Politics. [ISSN: 1461-6742] 1999. q. GBP 507 (print & online eds.). Ed(s): Shannon Stettner, Teresia Teaiwa. Routledge, 4 Park Sq, Milton Park, Abingdon, OX14 4RN, United Kingdom; subscriptions@tandf.co.uk; http://www.tandfonline.com. Adv. Sample. Refereed. Reprint: PSC. *Indexed:* A01, A22, E01, FemPer, IBSS, P61, SSA. *Aud.:* Ac.

This peer-reviewed journal publishes "research at the intersection of politics, international relations, and women's studies." Articles by feminist scholars from across the world investigate issues of women, gender, and sexuality in the context of international relations, globalization, development, politics, and culture. Articles may be disciplinary or interdisciplinary in focus. The journal's "Conversations" section seeks to promote dialogue and debate. The publication also includes first-person narratives, interviews, letters, photographs, conference reports, and media reviews. The book review section contains review articles as well as reviews of individual works. One recent special issue looks at " Rethinking Masculinity and Practices of Violence in Conflict Settings." Another provides a critical examination of U.N. Security Council Resolution 1325 on women, peace, and security Now included in *Social Sciences Citation Index*, this is a good choice for larger gender studies collections.

2666. International Journal of Gender, Science and Technology. [ISSN: 2040-0748] 2009. 3x/yr. Free. Ed(s): Clem Herman. Open University, Walton Hall, Milton Keynes, MK7 6AA, United Kingdom; http://www.open.ac.uk. *Indexed:* FemPer. *Aud.:* Ga, Ac, Sa.

This online, open-access journal from the United Kingdom's Open University Press focuses on gender issues in science and technology and on "the intersections of policy, practice and research." Science and technology are broadly defined to also include engineering, construction, and the built environment. Coverage is international in scope. Contents include research and theoretical papers, case studies, "perspectives" essays, book reviews, and podcasts. Recent issues have addressed topics such as perceptions of workplace climate in the blogs of women scientists, the portrayal of women scientists in contemporary crime fiction, a gender perspective on authors and editors in mathematics journals, and engaging girls in STEM careers. This publication is of particular interest for science educators and others concerned with developing gender equality and diversity in the sciences. URL: http://genderandset.open.ac.uk/index.php/genderandset/

International Journal of Men's Health. See Health and Fitness section.

2667. *Intersections: gender and sexuality in Asia and the Pacific.* [ISSN: 1440-9151] 1998. q. Free. Ed(s): Carolyn Brewer. Australian National University, Research School of Pacific and Asian Studies, Gender Relations Centre, 2nd Fl, HC Coombs Bldg., Canberra, ACT 0200, Australia; http://rspas.anu.edu.au/grc/index.php. Illus., index, adv. Refereed. *Indexed:* AmHI, IBSS, MLA-IB, P61, SSA. *Bk. rev.:* 2-7, essay length; signed. *Aud.:* Ac.

This refereed electronic journal, now based at Australian National University, provides a forum for research and teaching about the multiple historical and cultural gender patterns of Asia. Issues are theme-based and include research articles, commentary, discussion papers, interviews, poetry, and book and film reviews. Papers include photos, maps, or artistic reproductions as well as video or sound. One recent issue on "Post-Colonial and Contemporary Sexual Contact Zones in East Asia and the Pacific" presents case studies that examine how notions of gender and sexuality interact in cross-cultural encounters. Another looks at "Islam and Gender Relations in Indonesia." Author and geographic indexes, as well as filmographies and a selected bibliography, are available on the journal's web site.

Journal of Feminist Studies in Religion. See Religion section.

2668. *Journal of Gender Studies.* [ISSN: 0958-9236] 1991. q. GBP 566 (print & online eds.). Ed(s): Blu Tirohl, John Mercer. Routledge, 4 Park Sq, Milton Park, Abingdon, OX14 4RN, United Kingdom; subscriptions@tandf.co.uk; http://www.tandfonline.com. Illus., index, adv. Sample. Refereed. Vol. ends: Nov. Reprint: PSC. *Indexed:* A01, A22, AmHI, BRI, C42, E01, FemPer, IBSS, MLA-IB, P02, P61, PsycInfo, RiskAb, SSA, SWR&A. *Bk. rev.:* 8-33, 300-1,500 words; signed. *Aud.:* Ac.

This peer-reviewed, interdisciplinary, feminist journal uses gender as a framework for analysis in the natural and social sciences, the arts, and popular culture. Research articles come from around the world. They provide a variety of perspectives on social and cultural definitions of gender and gender relations. Book reviews, and a "Forum" featuring interviews, debates, or responses to articles, are also included. An article-alert service is available via e-mail and RSS feed from the publisher's web site. Tables of contents are also available online.

2669. *Journal of International Women's Studies.* 1999. s-a. Ed(s): Frances Ward-Johnson, Diana Fox. Bridgewater State College, Boyden Hall, 131 Summer St, Bridgewater, MA 02325; http://www.bridgew.edu. Refereed. *Indexed:* C42. *Bk. rev.:* 0-2, essay length; signed. *Aud.:* Ac.

This online, open-access journal provides an opportunity for scholars, activists, and students to bridge "the conventional divides of scholarship and activism: 'western' and 'third world' feminisms," by exploring "the relationship between feminist theory and various forms of organizing." Contents grow out of conferences and activist meetings and include research articles, essays, and film and book reviews. One special issue each year features new writings in feminist and women's studies from the Feminist and Women's Studies Association's essay competition. URL: www.bridgew.edu/SoAS/jiws

2670. *Journal of Men, Masculinities and Spirituality.* [ISSN: 1177-2484] 2007. s-a. Free. Journal of Men, Masculinities and Spirituality, http://www.jmmsweb.org/?q=user/2. Refereed. *Indexed:* A01, BRI. *Bk. rev.:* 3-5, 800-1500 words. *Aud.:* Ac, Sa.

JMMS is an open-access, online, scholarly, peer-reviewed, interdisciplinary journal that addresses the study of men and masculinities in the context of religion and spirituality. Its approach is broadly inclusive. Papers address the full spectrum of masculinities and sexualities, and look at Eastern, indigenous, and new religious movements and other spiritualities as well as monotheistic religions. They examine both historical and contemporary phenomena and offer speculative essays about future spiritualities. This journal is more specialized than mainstream men's studies journals such as *Men and Masculinities* or the *Journal of Men's Studies.* It is appropriate for libraries supporting specialized study and research in gender and religion. Content is also aggregated through Ebsco and Gale-Cengage. URL: http://www.jmmsweb.org/

2671. *Journal of Men's Studies: a scholarly journal about men and masculinities.* [ISSN: 1060-8265] 1992. 3x/yr. USD 220. Ed(s): Dr. James A Doyle. Men's Studies Press, PO Box 32, Harriman, TN 37748; publisher@mensstudies.com; http://www.mensstudies.com. Illus., adv. Sample. Refereed. Circ: 390 Paid. Vol. ends: May. *Indexed:* A01, A22, AmHI, BRI, C42, GW, MLA-IB, P61, PsycInfo, SD, SSA. *Bk. rev.:* 4, 800 words. *Aud.:* Ac, Sa.

This journal publishes peer-reviewed scholarly research in men?s studies. Its approach is interdisciplinary and cross-cultural. Each issue includes 5-7 research articles that offer political, social, cultural, and/or historical perspectives on men and masculinities. Articles examine the intersections of class, culture, race, and sexual orientation in defining men's experiences. A recent special issue provides an overview of 20 years of men and masculinities scholarship. Substantial book reviews are also included. This is a leading academic journal in the field and belongs in academic and research libraries. Available in print and online.

2672. *Journal of Women, Politics & Policy: a quarterly journal of research & policy studies.* Formerly (until 2005): *Women & Politics.* [ISSN: 1554-477X] 1980. q. GBP 506 (print & online eds.). Ed(s): Heidi Hartmann. Routledge, 325 Chestnut St, Ste 800, Philadelphia, PA 19106; customerservice@taylorandfrancis.com; http://www.tandfonline.com. Illus., adv. Sample. Refereed. Circ: 566 Paid. Vol. ends: No. 4. Microform: PQC. *Indexed:* A01, A22, ABS&EES, BRI, C42, Chicano, E01, FemPer, GW, IBSS, P02, P61, SSA, SWR&A, WSA. *Bk. rev.:* 5-14, 600 words; essay length; signed. *Aud.:* Ac, Sa.

This peer-reviewed journal (formerly *Women & Politics*) is "devoted to the advancement of knowledge about women's political participation and about the development of public policies that affect women and their families." Its approach is multidisciplinary and international. It takes special interest in "the intersection of gender, race/ethnicity, class, and other dimensions of women's experiences." Contents include research and theoretical articles by social scientists and public policy experts, as well as book reviews. Widely covered by indexing/abstracting services. Tables of contents and a contents-alert service are available on the publisher's web site.

2673. *Journal of Women's History.* [ISSN: 1042-7961] 1989. q. USD 140. Ed(s): Mary Berkery, Jean H Quataert. The Johns Hopkins University Press, 2715 N Charles St, Baltimore, MD 21218; http://www.press.jhu.edu. Illus., adv. Sample. Refereed. Circ: 572. Vol. ends: Winter. Microform: PQC. Reprint: PSC. *Indexed:* A01, A22, ABS&EES, AmHI, ArtHuCI, BRI, C42, E01, FemPer, GW, IBSS, MLA-IB, P02, P61, RILM, SSA, WSA. *Bk. rev.:* 2-4, essay length; 23-120 brief abstracts. *Aud.:* Ac.

This journal features theoretical and research articles about women and gender throughout world history. It is committed to ??expanding the boundaries of women?s and gender history to insure geographic diversity and comparative perspectives.? It publishes research articles and essays on methodological and theoretical topics as well as commentary, review essays, and book reviews. One recent special issue looks at " Women?s Autobiography in South Asia and the Middle East.? The journal has added online virtual forums and discussions to supplement and extend the print edition. Table of contents alerts are available via e-mail or RSS feed from the publisher's web site. Full text is available online from 1999 on. An important journal for historical collections.

Media Report to Women. See Television, Video, and Radio section.

2674. *Men and Masculinities (Online).* [ISSN: 1552-6828] 1998. 5x/yr. USD 664. Ed(s): Michael S Kimmel. Sage Publications, Inc., 2455 Teller Rd, Thousand Oaks, CA 91320; info@sagepub.com; http://www.sagepub.com. Adv. Refereed. *Bk. rev.:* 6, 1,500 words; signed. *Aud.:* Ac, Sa.

Men and Masculinities is an important, peer-reviewed publication that ?presents empirical and theoretical articles that use both interdisciplinary and multidisciplinary approaches, employ diverse methods, and are grounded in current theoretical perspectives within gender studies. Contents include articles, essays, research notes, and book reviews. A recent special issue looks at men, masculinity, and responsibility. Now published only online, it offers early access to forthcoming articles and an e-mail alert system. This title provides the comprehensive coverage of men's studies essential for academic and research library collections.

2675. *Menstuff: the national men's resource.* Former titles (until 1996): *Menstuff (Print);* (until 1993): *National Men's Resource Calendar;* (until 1992): *Men's Resource Hotline Calendar;* (until 1988): *Men's Resource Hotline.* 1985. m. Free. National Men's Resource Center, PO Box 800, San Anselmo, CA 94979-0800; menstuff@menstuff.org; http://www.menstuff.org. Illus. *Bk. rev.:* Up to 20, 100 words. *Aud.:* Ga, Sa.

Menstuff is the online publication of the National Men's Resource Center, an organization providing information about men and men's issues to a diverse men's community. It is concerned with positive change in male roles and relationships and supports men's rights and mutually empowering relationships among all people. *Menstuff* is a useful (but not particularly scholarly) resource for information on more than 300 men's issues and provides more than 2000 links to men's organizations throughout the world. It includes current news and articles as well as weekly and monthly opinion columns. Some content is updated daily. It also provides a directory of contact information for people wishing to take action.

2676. *Meridians: feminism, race, transnationalism.* [ISSN: 1536-6936] 2000. s-a. USD 133 (print & online eds.). Ed(s): Elizabeth Hanssen, Paula J Giddings. Indiana University Press, 601 N Morton St, Bloomington, IN 47404; journals@indiana.edu; http://iupress.indiana.edu. Adv. Sample. Refereed. Circ: 300. Reprint: PSC. *Indexed:* A01, A22, AmHI, BRI, E01, FemPer, GW, IIBP, MLA-IB, P02, P61, SSA. *Aud.:* Ga, Ac.

This interdisciplinary journal publishes scholarship and creative work by and about women of color in U.S. and international contexts. It also examines the interplay of feminism, race, and transnationalism. Contents include articles, essays, discussions of topical issues, interviews, reports, creative works, and media reviews. Edited at Smith College and published by Indiana University Press. Tables of contents and some abstracts are available on the publisher's web site. Full text is available through Project Muse.

Michigan Journal of Gender and Law. See Law section.

Ms. See News and Opinion section.

2677. *Nashim: a journal of Jewish women's studies and gender issues.* [ISSN: 0793-8934] 1998. s-a. USD 86.50 (print & online eds.). Ed(s): Deborah Greniman. Indiana University Press, 601 N Morton St, Bloomington, IN 47404; iupress@indiana.edu; http://iupress.indiana.edu. Adv. Refereed. Circ: 1000. Reprint: PSC. *Indexed:* A01, A22, AmHI, BRI, E01, FemPer, GW, IJP, MLA-IB, P61, SSA. *Bk. rev.:* Number and length vary. *Aud.:* Ac.

This journal "provides an international, interdisciplinary academic forum in Jewish women's and gender studies." Each issue is based on a theme such as "Feminist Receptions of Biblical Women" or "Sex, Violence, Motherhood, and Modesty: Controlling the Jewish Woman and Her Body." Contents include articles, review essays, and book and literary pieces relating to women/feminism/gender and Judaism. Academic articles predominate. *Nashim* is published by the Hadassah-Brandeis Institute; the Schechter Institute of Jewish Studies, Jerusalem; and Indiana University Press.

2678. *New Male Studies.* [ISSN: 1839-7816] 2012. 3x/yr. Free. Ed(s): Miles Groth. Australian Institute of Male Health and Studies, PO Box 512, St Peters, SA 5069, Australia; http://aimhs.com.au. Refereed. *Aud.:* Ac, Sa.

New Male Studies is a new, open-access, peer-reviewed online journal from the Australian Institute of Male Health and Studies (University of New South Wales). It publishes research, essays, opinion pieces, interviews, podcasts, and book reviews in the areas of male health and men?s studies. Its approach is multidisciplinary and global. A recent issue included articles on male victims of domestic violence, the health status and behaviors of Australian farming men, male teachers? perspectives on best practices for teaching boys in single-sex Canadian classrooms, and representations of marriage, family, masculinity and fatherhood in popular culture. Contributors are scholars and writers in the areas of anthropology, biology, economics, education, history, law, literature, medicine, psychology and sociology. Not yet indexed by the leading academic article databases, this resource provides an interesting, global perspective on men, masculinity, and gender.

2679. *Nora: Nordic journal of women's studies.* [ISSN: 0803-8740] 1993. q. GBP 154 (print & online eds.). Ed(s): Pauline Stoltz, Kirsten Hvenegard-Lassen. Taylor & Francis Scandinavia, PO Box 3255, Stockholm, 10365, Sweden; victoria.babbit@se.tandf.no; http://www.tandf.co.uk/journals/scandinavia/index.asp. Illus., adv. Sample. Refereed. Reprint: PSC. *Indexed:* A01, A22, ASSIA, E01, FemPer, GW, IBSS, MLA-IB, P61, SSA. *Bk. rev.:* 6, 700 words to essay length; signed. *Aud.:* Ac.

This journal focuses on gender and women's studies in Nordic countries, both historically and in the present. But it also "acknowledges the need to speak across borders, challenging academic, linguistic[,] and national limits and boundaries." Its approach is interdisciplinary and international. Content includes research articles, review essays, and short communications. Review essays and book reviews provide access to works published in Nordic languages as well as in English. An article-alert service and tables of contents are available on the publisher's web site.

2680. *Outskirts (Online): feminisms along the edge.* Formerly (until Nov.1996): *Outskirts (Print).* [ISSN: 1445-0445] 1996. s-a. Free. Ed(s): Alison Bartlett. University of Western Australia, Centre for Women's Studies, 35 Stirling Hwy, Crawley, W.A. 6009, Australia; general.enquiries@uwa.edu.au; http://www.chloe.uwa.edu.au/. Sample. Refereed. *Indexed:* GW. *Bk. rev.:* Number and length vary. *Aud.:* Ac.

This is a refereed, feminist, cultural-studies e-journal issued from the English Department of the University of Western Australia. Its focus is on a broad range of issues in "feminisms along the edge." Contents include research articles, commentaries, conference reports, and reviews of performances and books. This publication is also a useful resource for information on teaching women's studies in Australia. Full text is available online from 1996 forward. URL: www.chloe.uwa.edu.au/outskirts

2681. *Politics & Gender.* [ISSN: 1743-923X] 2005. q. GBP 184. Ed(s): Aili Mari Tripp, Kathleen Dolan. Cambridge University Press, The Edinburgh Bldg, Shaftesbury Rd, Cambridge, CB2 8RU, United Kingdom; journals@cambridge.org; http://www.cambridge.org/uk. Adv. Reprint: PSC. *Indexed:* A22, E01, FemPer, GW, IBSS, P61, RiskAb, SSA. *Bk. rev.:* Number and length vary. *Aud.:* Ac.

Published by Cambridge University Press for the Women and Politics Research section of the American Political Science Association, this journal "aims to represent the full range of questions, issues, and approaches on gender and women across the major subfields of political science[,] including comparative politics, international relations, political theory, and U.S. politics." Most issues include book reviews. This important journal for academic and research libraries addresses key gender issues in politics and political science.

2682. *Psychology of Men & Masculinity.* [ISSN: 1524-9220] 2000. q. USD 410 (Individuals, USD 110). Ed(s): Ronald F Levant. American Psychological Association, 750 First St, NE, Washington, DC 20002; journals@apa.org; http://www.apa.org. Adv. Sample. Circ: 700. Vol. ends: Dec. Reprint: PSC. *Indexed:* ASSIA, PsycInfo, SSA. *Aud.:* Ac, Sa.

This American Psychological Association?s Society journal publishes research, theory, and clinical scholarship relating to men's psychology across the lifespan, race, ethnicity, and time. Articles address issues relating to male gender role socialization, identity, development, mental health, behavior, interpersonal relationships, sexuality and sexual orientation. Rigorously peer-reviewed, this journal is important for libraries supporting research and study in psychology and/or gender studies.

2683. Religion and Gender. [ISSN: 1878-5417] 2011. s-a. Free. Ed(s): Anne-Marie Korte, Burkhard Scherer. IWFT Vrouwennetwerk Theologie, Universiteit Utrecht, Faculteit Godgeleerdheid, Heidelberglaan 2, kamer 1206, Utrecht, 3584 CS, Netherlands; iwft@uu.nl; http://www.iwft.nl. Refereed. *Aud.:* Ac, Sa.

Religion and Gender 'rois a refereed, open-access journal initially funded by a grant from the Netherlands Organisation for Scientific Research (NWO). The journal is committed to the study of religion and gender from an interdisciplinary perspective. It looks at multiple manifestations of religion in varied contexts throughout the world with particular attention to contemporary or emerging issues. Its outlook is postmodern, postcolonial, and post-secular. Each issue is focuses on a specific theme. Recent themes have included gender religion, and migration and religion and masculinities. Contents include high quality research articles in the humanities and social sciences, invited keynote articles by outstanding scholars, and critical book reviews. The rigorous peer-review process and high editorial standards make this an important journal for academic libraries supporting research in gender and religion. URL: http://www.religionandgender.org/index.php/rg

2684. Resources for Feminist Research. Formerly (until 1979): *Canadian Newsletter of Research on Women.* [ISSN: 0707-8412] 1972. s-a. CAD 80 (Individuals, CAD 38). Ed(s): Philinda Masters. University of Toronto, Ontario Institute for Studies in Education, 252 Bloor St W, Toronto, ON M5S 1V6, Canada. Illus., index, adv. Refereed. Vol. ends: Winter. Microform: MML. *Indexed:* A22, AmHI, BRI, C37, C42, CBCARef, FemPer, GW, MLA-IB, P61, SSA, WSA. *Bk. rev.:* 5-20, length varies; signed. *Aud.:* Ac.

This bilingual (English/French) journal from the Ontario Institute for Studies in Education/University of Toronto addresses a range of issues relating to gender, sexuality, ethnicity, nationality, and class. It publishes two double issues a year. Contents include feminist research articles, reports of work in progress, bibliographies, and book reviews. A useful resource for understanding women's studies and feminist issues in the Canadian and international contexts. Full text is available through *GenderWatch.*

Sex Roles. See Sociology and Social Work section.

2685. Signs: journal of women in culture and society. [ISSN: 0097-9740] 1975. q. USD 381 (print & online eds.). Ed(s): Miranda Outman-Kramer, Mary Hawkesworth. University of Chicago Press, 1427 E 60th St, Chicago, IL 60637; subscriptions@press.uchicago.edu; http://www.journals.uchicago.edu. Illus., index, adv. Sample. Refereed. Vol. ends: Summer. Microform: PMC; PQC. Reprint: PSC. *Indexed:* A01, A22, ABS&EES, AmHI, BAS, BRI, CBRI, Chicano, F01, FR, FemPer, IBSS, MLA-IB, P02, P61, PsycInfo, RILM, SSA, WSA. *Bk. rev.:* 2-12, 1,200-2,000 words; signed. *Aud.:* Ac.

This leading journal from the University of Chicago Press publishes path-breaking interdisciplinary articles on gender, sexuality, race, class, ethnicity, and nationality. It publishes articles that express different, often contradictory, viewpoints. Contents include research articles, review essays, research reports, book reviews, letters/comments, editorials, primary documents, and notes. Some issues include "Comparative Perspectives Symposia" or other sets of articles on themes such as "Romani Feminism" or "Women in Contemporary Russia." A recent special issue on "Intersectionality: Theorizing Power, Empowering Theory" provides a critical assessment of this theoretical approach to understanding social identities and systems ofoppression. The journal's online blog offers announcements, links to open-access content,and other resources that supplement and extend the print edition. Table of contents alerts are available via e-mail or RSS feed.

2686. Social Politics: international studies in gender, state, and society. [ISSN: 1072-4745] 1994. q. EUR 245. Ed(s): Kyle Schafer, Ann Shola Orloff. Oxford University Press, Great Clarendon St, Oxford, OX2 6DP, United Kingdom; enquiry@oup.co.uk; http://www.oxfordjournals.org/. Illus., index, adv. Sample. Refereed. Vol. ends: No. 3. Microform: PQC. Reprint: PSC. *Indexed:* A22, E01, FemPer, GW, IBSS, P02, P61, SSA. *Bk. rev.:* Essay length, signed. *Aud.:* Ac, Sa.

This journal applies a feminist and gender perspective to the analysis of social policy, the state, and society. It is interdisciplinary and multicultural in scope. It is concerned with emerging issues such as globalization, transnationality, migrations, and the restructuring of capitalisms and states. Contents include research articles as well as articles on policy perspectives. Recent special issues have looked at "New Times, New Spaces: Gendered Transformations of Governance, Economy, and Citizenship" and "Limits to Progress and Change: Reflections on Latin American Social Policy." The publisher's web site provides advance access to some articles, tables of contents, article abstracts, and an e-mail or RSS feed contents-alerting service.

2687. Spectrum: a journal on Black men. [ISSN: 2162-3244] 2012. s-a. USD 98.50 (print & online eds.). Ed(s): Molly Reinhoudt, Judson L Jeffries. Indiana University Press, 601 N Morton St, Bloomington, IN 47404; journals@indiana.edu; http://iupress.indiana.edu. *Aud.:* Ac,Sa.

Spectrum is a new, multidisciplinary research journal from Indiana University Press. It focuses on the broad range of issues shaping black men?s experiences, including gender, masculinities, race, and ethnicity. Contents include empirical research, theoretical analysis, literary criticism, essays, review essays, and book reviews. It is a traditional, peer-reviewed scholarly journal available with an online presence that includes article summaries and supplementary audio and/or visuals. It is of particular interest for the perspective on black masculinities it brings to academic libraries supporting African American and gender studies programs. URL: http://www.jstor.org/action/showPublication?journalCode=spectrum

2688. Studies in Gender and Sexuality. [ISSN: 1524-0657] 2000. q. GBP 211 (print & online eds.). Ed(s): Muriel Dimen. Routledge, 325 Chestnut St, Ste 800, Philadelphia, PA 19106; customerservice@taylorandfrancis.com; http://www.tandfonline.com. Adv. Sample. Refereed. Reprint: PSC. *Indexed:* A01, A22, E01, FemPer, GW, MLA-IB, P61, PsycInfo, SSA. *Aud.:* Ac.

This journal looks at gender and sexuality from the perspectives of feminism, psychoanalytic theory, developmental research, and cultural studies. It is directed toward promoting interdisciplinary dialogue among clinicians, developmental researchers, and academics. Contents represent a variety of theoretical, clinical, and methodological approaches, including psychoanalytic theory. Some issues offer roundtable discussions and sets of papers on topics such as maternal desire or aging and desire. Contents pages and e-mail or RSS feed tables-of-contents notifications are available on the publisher's web site. Full text is available from 2000 on.

2689. Transitions (Minneapolis). [ISSN: 0886-862X] 1981. bi-m. Free to members; Non-members, USD 30. Ed(s): Kevin Young. National Coalition of Free Men, PO Box 582023, Minneapolis, MN 55458; ncfm@ncfm.org; http://www.ncfm.org. Illus. Sample. *Indexed:* GW. *Bk. rev.:* 1, 500 words; signed. *Aud.:* Ga, Sa.

This publication is the official newsletter of the National Coalition for Men (formerly the National Coalition of Free Men), a non-profit men's rights organization concerned with raising awareness of discrimination against men in divorce, child custody, and public policy; defending men's rights, and challenging what it perceives to be the feminist agenda. *Transitions* began publication in 1981. It offers an interesting alternative view to feminist and/or activist women?s publications. Back issues are available online in pdf format at the journal's web site.

2690. Violence Against Women: an international and interdisciplinary journal. [ISSN: 1077-8012] 1995. m. USD 1300. Ed(s): Claire M Renzetti. Sage Publications, Inc., 2455 Teller Rd, Thousand Oaks, CA 91320; info@sagepub.com; http://www.sagepub.com. Illus., adv. Sample. Refereed. Vol. ends: Dec. Reprint: PSC. *Indexed:* A01, A22, BRI, CJPI, E01, FemPer, H24, IBSS, P02, P61, PsycInfo, RiskAb, SSA. *Bk. rev.:* 2, essay length; signed. *Aud.:* Ga, Ac, Sa.

This journal publishes empirical research and cross-cultural and historical analyses of violence against women and girls. It is concerned with both well-known and lesser-known forms of violence and seeks to promote dialogue among people of diverse backgrounds working in various fields and disciplines. Contents include research articles, review essays, and clinical, legal, and research notes, as well as book reviews. A recent special issue looks at gender-based violence in the Middle East and North Africa. The journal's web site offers forthcoming articles that are published online ahead of print, and podcasts that feature discussions between selected authors and the journal editor. It also offers a contents-alerting service. Full-text articles are available to members of institutions with print subscriptions.

2691. *Wagadu: a journal of transnational women's and gender studies.* [ISSN: 2150-2226] 2004. q. Free. Ed(s): Mechthild Nagel, Tiantian Zheng. State University of New York at Cortland, P. O. Box 2000, Cortland, NY 13045; http://www.cortland.edu/. Refereed. *Bk. rev.:* Number and length vary. *Aud.:* Ac.

This free, open-acess, peer-reviewed journal provides a postcolonial and transnational perspective on race and gender issues. It is intended as "a medium of exchange and information for scholars and activists." Contents include articles written around a single theme, such as "Sexual Violence and Armed Conflict: Gender, Society, and the State," "Gender Equity in Higher Education," and "Demystifying Sex Work and Sex Workers." Book reviews are also included. Articles are predominantly in English, with abstracts in English, Spanish, and French. Readers can register to receive notification of a new issue of the journal by e-mail. URL: http://appweb.cortland.edu/ojs/index.php/Wagadu/index

2692. *Women: a cultural review.* [ISSN: 0957-4042] 1990. 4x/yr. GBP 414 (print & online eds.). Routledge, 4 Park Sq, Milton Park, Abingdon, OX14 4RN, United Kingdom; subscriptions@tandf.co.uk; http://www.tandfonline.com. Adv. Sample. Reprint: PSC. *Indexed:* A01, A22, AmHI, BRI, C42, E01, FemPer, GW, IBSS, MLA-IB, P61. *Bk. rev.:* Number and length vary. *Aud.:* Ac.

The focus of this British journal is on "the role and representation of gender and sexuality in the arts and culture, with a particular focus on the contemporary world." It looks at "the theory and politics of sexual difference in literature, the media, history, education, law, philosophy, psychoanalysis[,] and the performing and visual arts." Contents include research articles, essays, review essays, and interviews. Two special issues a year are thematic. The journal also includes book reviews and a listing of new titles in the study of gender and culture. Occasionally it publishes special issues such as "Reading Jean Rhys" and "Moving Feminism: How to 'Trans? the National?" The publisher's web site provides tables of contents and an article-alert service.

2693. *Women & Environments International Magazine.* Former titles (until 2001): *W E International;* (until 1998): *Women and Environments;* (until 1980): *Women and Environments International Newsletter.* [ISSN: 1499-1993] 1976. s-a. CAD 35. Ed(s): Karla Orantes. Institute for Women's Studies and Gender Studies, Faculty of Environmental Studies, York University, HNES Bldg, Rm 234, Toronto, ON M3J 1P3, Canada. Illus. Microform: CML. *Indexed:* A01, A22, BRI, C37, CBCARef, FemPer, GW, MASUSE, P02, WSA. *Bk. rev.:* 1-4, 175-400 words. *Aud.:* Ga, Ac.

This Canadian magazine brings together academic research and theory and community activism involving "women's multiple relationships with their environments." Its perspective is feminist, environmental, and anti-racist. Issues focus around themes such as "Asbestos Production" and "Gender and Foo Seurity." Contents include feature stories, research articles, essays, interviews, news updates, book and movie reviews, art, and poetry. Each issue includes listings of selected print resources and organizations and web sites relevant to the theme. Th journal's web site prvides a listig of importantarticles frm pst isss but is not up-to-date. Full text is available through *Academic Search* and *GenderWatch.*

Women and Music. See Music section.

Women & Therapy. See Psychology section.

2694. *Women, Gender, and Families of Color.* [ISSN: 2326-0939] 2013. s-a. USD 90 (print & online eds.). Ed(s): Jennifer Hamer. University of Illinois Press, 1325 S Oak St, Champaign, IL 61820; journals@uillinois.edu; http://www.press.uillinois.edu. Adv. Refereed. *Aud.:* Ga, Ac.

This online interdisciplinary peer-reviewed journal broadens the scope of its well respected predecessor, *Black Women, Gender, and Families,* to include Black, Latina, Indigenous, and Asian American women, gender, and families in its analytical focus. It "[p]ublishes theoretical and empirical research from history, the social and behavioural sciences, and humanities?[as well as] comparative and transnational research, and analyses of domestic social, political, economic, and cultural policies and practices within the United States." The inaugural issue included four articles by new and established scholars on health issues affecting Latino and African American women and families. *WGFC* is important for its explorations of the intersections of race, gender and class. Recommended for academic libraries supporting black or women's or gender studies programs and for larger public libraries.

Women in Sport and Physical Activity Journal. See Sports section.

2695. *Women's History Review.* [ISSN: 0961-2025] 1992. 6x/yr. GBP 539 (print & online eds.). Ed(s): June Purvis. Routledge, 4 Park Sq, Milton Park, Abingdon, OX14 4RN, United Kingdom; subscriptions@tandf.co.uk; http://www.tandfonline.com. Illus., index, adv. Sample. Refereed. Vol. ends: Dec. Reprint: PSC. *Indexed:* A01, A22, AmHI, ArtHuCI, BRI, E01, FemPer, MLA-IB, P61, SSA. *Bk. rev.:* 5-8, length varies; signed. *Aud.:* Ac.

This British journal provides an interdisciplinary, feminist perspective on women and gender relations in history. Coverage is international and emphasizes the nineteenth, twentieth, and twenty-first centuries. The journal includes research articles, viewpoint essays, review essays, and book reviews. Tables of contents and abstracts are available on the publisher's web site. Content alerts are available through e-mail or RSS feed.

2696. *Women's Studies: an interdisciplinary journal.* [ISSN: 0049-7878] 1972. 8x/yr. GBP 909 (print & online eds.). Ed(s): Wendy Martin. Taylor & Francis Inc., 325 Chestnut St, Ste 800, Philadelphia, PA 19106; customerservice@taylorandfrancis.com; http://www.tandfonline.com. Illus., adv. Sample. Refereed. Microform: MIM. Reprint: PSC. *Indexed:* A01, A22, ABS&EES, AbAn, AmHI, ArtHuCI, BRI, E01, F01, FemPer, GW, IBSS, MLA-IB, RILM, WSA. *Bk. rev.:* Number and length vary. *Aud.:* Ac.

This journal publishes research articles, critical essays, and book reviews that focus largely on women in literature and the arts. It is also interdisciplinary in outlook and includes articles on historical topics and current issues in feminist scholarship. Contents also include poetry, short stories, and film and book reviews. Occasional issues focus on special topics such as "Men and Masculinities in Women's Studies," "What is the Woman Artist Today?" and "Gender and Religion: Towards Diversity." Tables of contents and a contents-alerting service are available on the publisher's web site.

2697. *Women's Studies International Forum.* Formerly (until 1982): *Women's Studies International Quarterly;* Incorporates (1982-1986): *Feminist Forum;* Which was formerly (until 1982): *Women's Studies International Quarterly Forum.* [ISSN: 0277-5395] 1978. bi-m. EUR 929. Ed(s): Kalwant Bhopal. Pergamon, The Blvd, Langford Ln, E Park, Kidlington, OX5 1GB, United Kingdom; JournalsCustomerServiceEMEA@elsevier.com; http://www.elsevier.com. Illus., adv. Sample. Refereed. Microform: PQC. *Indexed:* A01, A22, ABS&EES, AmHI, BAS, BRI, FemPer, IBSS, MLA-IB, P02, P61, PsycInfo, SSA, WSA. *Bk. rev.:* 6-10, length varies; signed. *Aud.:* Ac.

This expensive journal offers truly global coverage of women's studies and feminist research. It publishes research and theoretical articles, review essays, and book reviews. One or more theme-based issues a year address special topics such as "Reintegrating gender in European studies" and "Gender, culture and work in global cities: Researching 'transnational' women." The publisher's web site offers tables of contents, abstracts, and a contents-alerting service.

2698. Women's Studies Quarterly. Formerly (until 1981): *Women's Studies Newsletter*. [ISSN: 0732-1562] 1972. s-a. USD 75. Feminist Press, CUNY, 365 5th Ave, Ste 5406, New York, NY 10016; http://www.feministpress.org. Illus., adv. Sample. Refereed. Vol. ends: Fall/Winter (No. 3 - No. 4). Reprint: PSC. *Indexed:* A01, A22, ABS&EES, BRI, Chicano, E01, F01, FemPer, GW, MLA-IB, P02, P61, SSA, WSA. *Bk. rev.:* 0-5, 1,000-1,800 words; signed. *Aud.:* Ga, Ac.

This journal from Feminist Press provides an international and cross-cultural perspective on women, gender, and sexuality. Its contents include research articles from multiple disciplines and articles about teaching. Theme-based issues provide diverse viewpoints and in-depth coverage of contemporary feminist topics. The journal also includes fiction, poetry, and representations of the visual arts, as well as conference reports, news alerts, and book reviews. Summary information about current issues is available on the publisher's web site. Full text is available through *Project MUSE, JStor,* and *GenderWatch.*

2699. X Y: Men, Masculinities and Gender Politics. 1990. irreg. X Y: Men, Masculinities and Gender Politcs, PO Box 473, Blackwood, SA 5051, Australia. *Bk. rev.:* 1, 200 words; signed. *Aud.:* Ac, Sa.

Originally a print journal published between 1990 and 1998 in Canberra, Australia, *XY: Men, Sex, Politics,* continues now as a non-profit web site containing new articles on issues from fathering and men?s health to the relationships between masculinity, class, race and sexuality, to domestic violence. It also includes 60 of the best articles from the print journal. *XY* functions as a forum for debate and discussion and as a clearinghouse for reports, articles, and other information. It also hosts several blogs on men, masculinities, and gender issues. Content reflects a variety of feminist positions and is of interest to readers and contributors around the world. The style is accessible to lay readers.

■ GENEALOGY

International and Ethnic-Interest Journals/National and Regional Journals

See also Canada; Europe; and History sections.

Scott Andrew "Drew" Bartley, www.yourgenealogist.com.

Erika Nosike, Countway Library, Harvard Medical School.

Cheryl LaGuardia, Research Librarian, Widener Library, Harvard University

Introduction

Genealogy continues to be a very popular hobby; it ranks as one of the most popular types of searches on the Internet, and as the second-most popular hobby in America at the time of this writing. So every public library needs at least a basic genealogical research collection, which should include access for library patrons to one of the major genealogical databases (Ancestry.com, FamilySearch, U.S.GenWeb, RootsWeb, World Vital Records, etc.), as well as access to some of the latest articles written on the subject.

Coverage by genealogical periodicals runs the gamut of topics across geographical locations, ethnicities, and time periods. It includes scholarly journals, commercial publications, how-to manuals, society newsletters, and a mixture of all of these. This section aims at presenting a basic, core list of publications, some of which should be offered to users of practically every public library, and many special and academic libraries.

The best meta-site for all things genealogical continues to be Cyndi's List, at www.CyndisList.com.

As used herein, the term *scholarly* is used to designate journals that properly footnote each genealogically significant event to a primary source, so that readers may go directly to that source.

Basic Abstracts and Indexes

MasterFILE Premier (EBSCOhost); MLA International Bibliography; Periodicals Index Online (ProQuest).

International and Ethnic-Interest Journals

2700. Afro-American Historical and Genealogical Society. Journal. [ISSN: 0272-1937] 1980. s-a. Ed(s): Sylvia Polk-Burriss. Afro-American Historical and Genealogical Society, PO Box 73067, Washington, DC 20056. Illus., index, adv. Vol. ends: Summer/Fall. *Indexed:* IIBP. *Bk. rev.:* 10/yr. *Aud.:* Sa, Ac.

This scholarly journal is "committed to documenting and preserving the African and African American experience by publishing historical and genealogical subject matter of interest to the African American family researcher, and facilitating the dissemination of historical and genealogical resources that will assist the African American family researcher" (from the web site at www.aahgs.org/journal.htm). Content discusses detailed methodologies for African American ancestry research, and includes depository materials, reports of archives, and family genealogies. Primary source transcriptions, along with their data analysis, are also included. Annual indexes for 1990–2008 and a cumulative index for 1980–90 are available online. Recommended for all public libraries.

2701. American-Canadian Genealogist. q. Institutional members, USD 50; Individual members, USD 35. American-Canadian Genealogical Society, PO Box 6478, Manchester, NH 03108-6478; editor@acgs.org. *Bk. rev.:* Number and length vary. *Aud.:* Ga.

The *American-Canadian Genealogist* is the official quarterly journal of the American-Canadian Genealogical Society and is sent to all society members. Regular sections include letters to the editor, messages from the President and the Editor, book reviews, material "From Other Publications," "Queries," "New Members," "Etoile d'Acadie," and a "Readers' Forum." Material focuses on Acadian, French-Canadian, and Franco-American family history and genealogy, and the editorial board encourages all members to submit articles for publication.

2702. The Augustan Omnibus. Former titles (until 20??): *The Augustan; Augustan Society Omnibus;* Which was formed by the merger of (1974-1986): *Irish-American Genealogist;* (1977-1986): *Plymouth Colony Genealogist;* (1977-1986): *Italian Genealogist;* (1977-1986): *Eastern & Central European Genealogist;* (1977-1986): *French Genealogist;* (1977-1986): *Spanish American Genealogist;* (1977-1986): *Be-Ne-Lux Genealogist;* (1982-198?): *Journal of Ancient & Medieval Studies;* (19??-1986): *Scottish-American Genealogist;* (1975-198?): *The Augustan;* Which superseded in part (1973-1974): *Augustan;* Which was formed by the 1972 merger of: *Forebears;* (196?-197?): *Coat-Arm;* (1970-1972): *Colonial Genealogist;* Which was formerly (1967-1969): *Beetle Gazette;* (19??-198?): *Chivalry;* (1976-198?): *Heraldry;* (1981-198?): *Royalty and Monarchy;* (1982-198?): *Genealogical Library Journal;* (1975-198?): *Colonial Genealogist;* (19??-198?): *English Genealogist;* Which was formerly (1975-19??): *English Genealogist Helper;* (1976-198?): *Germanic Genealogist;* Which was formerly (until 197?): *Germanic Genealogist Helper.* 1972. s-a. Non-members, USD 30. Augustan Society, Inc., PO Box 771267, Orlando, FL 32877-1267; hq@augustansociety.org; http://www.augustansociety.org. Illus., index, adv. Sample. Vol. ends: No. 4. *Bk. rev.:* 10/yr. *Aud.:* Sa.

The Augustan Omnibus is the official journal of the Augustan Society, "a group of scholars who focus in the fields of genealogy, heraldry, chivalry, royalty & nobility, and history with an emphasis on the period before 1600." The journal has gone by a number of names since its inception in the 1960s, and at various times in its history, the Augustan Society has published many different titles, including *The Augustan,* the *Augustan Society Information Bulletin,* the *Augustan Society Omnibus, Chivalry, Forebears, Genealogical Library Journal, Heraldry, Journal of Ancient & Medieval Studies, Journal of Ancient Egyptian Studies, Journal of Heraldic Studies, Journal of Royal & Noble Genealogy, The Royalist, Be-Ne-Lux Genealogist, The Colonial Genealogist, "Cuestiones," Eastern & Central European Genealogist, French Genealogist, English Genealogist, Germanic Genealogist, Irish-American Genealogist, Italian Genealogist, Nordmaendene, Plymouth Colony Genealogist, Scottish-American Genealogist,* and *Spanish-American Genealogist.* All of those titles are now combined in *The Augustan Omnibus,* and plans are "to continue this merged publication, as it encourages cross-disciplinary studies and may inspire readers to explore topics unfamiliar to them."

2703. *Avotaynu: the international review of Jewish genealogy.* [ISSN: 0882-6501] 1985. q. USD 38 in North America; USD 46 elsewhere. Avotaynu Inc., 155 N Washington Ave, Bergenfield, NJ 07621; info@avotaynu.com; http://www.avotaynu.com. Illus., adv. Vol. ends: Winter. *Indexed:* IJP. *Bk. rev.:* 15/yr. *Aud.:* Ga, Ac.

A scholarly journal devoted to Jewish genealogy, *Avotaynu* publishes 300+ articles annually to aid researchers. Methodology suggestions, queries (also known as "Ask the Experts"), and Internet help are common features. Contributing editors from 15 countries around the world regularly gather the information that appears here, and the editors maintain strong ties to officials at institutions that contain genealogical data throughout the world, including the YIVO Institute, American Jewish Archives, American Jewish Historical Society, U.S. National Archives, U.S. Library of Congress, U.S. Holocaust Memorial Museum, Leo Baeck Institute, U.S. Holocaust Museum, Yad Vashem, and Central Archives for the History of the Jewish People. An index to the first 24 volumes is available for major articles (see www.avotaynu.com/indexsum.htm).

National and Regional Journals

2704. *The American Genealogist.* Formerly (until 1932): *New Haven Genealogical Magazine.* [ISSN: 0002-8592] 1922. q. USD 40. Ed(s): Joseph C Anderson, III. American Genealogist, PO Box 398, Demorest, GA 30535-0398. Illus., index. Refereed. Circ: 1920 Paid and free. Vol. ends: Oct. Microform: PQC. *Indexed:* A22, BRI, CBRI. *Bk. rev.:* 40/yr. *Aud.:* Ga, Ac.

This scholarly journal focuses on colonial American families and genealogical methodology. Included are some medieval and royal articles and European origins. There is a query section, but ancestor tables are no longer published. The yearly and published indexes are only available for the first 60 volumes (presently out of print).

2705. *Association of Professional Genealogists Quarterly.* Former titles (until 1991): *A P G Quarterly; A P G Newsletter;* Supersedes (1975-1979, vol.5, no.3): *Professional Genealogists' News Bulletin.* [ISSN: 1056-6732] 1979. q. USD 65 domestic. Ed(s): Matthew Wright. Association of Professional Genealogists, PO Box 350998, Westminster, CO 80035-0998. Illus., adv. Circ: 1400. Vol. ends: Dec. *Bk. rev.:* 25/yr. *Aud.:* Sa.

A journal aimed at the professional genealogist, this title covers the spectrum of topics for running a genealogy business, from how-to articles to marketing strategies. Recent articles include "Simple, Smart Strategies for Bringing in Business," "Online and Print Marketing Opportunities," "Don't Sell Your Research Services Short," "Personal Branding for Professionals," "My Professional Journey: What Are You Going to Do Now?," and "Is a Blog Genealogical Writing?" The journal web site is at www.apgen.org/publications/index.html#Quarterly; and the parent site for the association (at www.apgen.org/index.html) includes an index for finding a professional genealogist by name, location, research specialty, and geographic specialty. For professional genealogists and those seeking to become same.

2706. *Eastman's Online Genealogy Newsletter.* [ISSN: 1544-4090] 1996. w. Free. Ed(s): Richard Eastman. MyFamily.com Inc., 360 West 4800 N, Provo, UT 84604; http://www.myfamilyinc.com/. *Bk. rev.:* Number and length vary. *Aud.:* Ga.

This e-newsletter discusses everything genealogical from new books in the field to electronic products, interesting news items, and upcoming events. Much of the content is free and searchable on the site. Included in the subscription price are the "plus" editions, which have more detailed articles and advice. The subscription price allows those sections to be searched online. Recommended for all public libraries and to individuals.

2707. *Family Chronicle: the magazine for families researching their roots.* [ISSN: 1209-4617] 199?. bi-m. USD 25 in US & Canada; USD 45 elsewhere; USD 4.17 per issue. Ed(s): Edward Zapletal. Moorshead Magazines Ltd., PO Box 194, Niagara Falls, NY 14304; http://www.moorshead.com. Adv. Sample. *Indexed:* BRI, C37, CBCARef. *Aud.:* Ga.

This popular magazine is perfect for general public library collections; it's aimed at the genealogy beginner but includes enough substance to interest the expert researcher as well. Content is best revealed by a glance at the latest issue's table of contents: "Reflections on a Life" (a study of letters, diaries, and memorabilia left in an attic long ago); "Doubtful Notes, Debtors, and Deadbeats" (a look at how promissory notes can supplement your research); "Anne McGill's Long Journey" (how the chance discovery of a family Bible led to solving the mystery of a grandmother's immigration from Ireland in the 1920s); "The Canadian Immigration Museum at Pier 21" (a look at the historic immigration processing facility and family history research center located in Halifax, Nova Scotia); "Sailing in their Wake" (the author recommends "living the history" of your ancestors through sailing, railroads, planes, and more); "Militia and Volunteers in the Early Indian Wars" (how to find genealogical records left by the Indian Wars east of the Mississippi); "The Value of Art in Research" (which shows how researching your ancestors' pastimes can reveal a great deal about how they lived); "Engaging Children with Genealogy and Family History" (in which the author gives examples of how young children can get involved in family history research—at home or in the community); "Some Thoughts on Family History Writing" (a genealogist reflects on the importance of documenting your family history for the sake of future generations); and "The Golden Age of Cemeteries" (in which the author suggests these are the best of times for cemetery research). There's something for just about every genealogical researcher here—even an online index at https://www.familychronicle.com/fullindex.htm.

2708. *The Genealogist.* [ISSN: 0197-1468] 1980. s-a. USD 25 domestic; USD 43 foreign. Ed(s): Gale Ion Harris, Charles M Hansen. American Society of Genealogists, PO Box 519, Williamstown, WA 01267; ASG.Sec@gmail.com; http://www.fasg.org/. Index. Sample. Refereed. Vol. ends: Fall. *Aud.:* Ac, Sa.

A highly respected scholarly journal that deals with European origins, royal and medieval ancestry, difficult genealogical problems, complete descendant genealogies, and related studies that are considered too lengthy by other scholarly journals in the field. Founded in 1980 as a private enterprise with an irregular publishing schedule, it became the official journal of the American Society of Genealogists (ASG) in 1997 (volume 11). Under the aegis of ASG, it has consistently maintained its semi-annual publication as well as its longstanding quality. This is a journal for all academic libraries and public libraries with a major focus in genealogy.

2709. *New England Historical and Genealogical Register.* Former titles (until 1874): *New England Historical & Genealogical Register and Antiquarian Journal;* (until 1853): *New England Historical & Genealogical Register;* (until 1847): *New Hampshire Repository.* [ISSN: 0028-4785] 1845. q. Free to members. Ed(s): Henry Hoff. New England Historic Genealogical Society, 99 Newbury St, Boston, MA 02116; membership@nehgs.org; http://www.newenglandancestors.org. Illus., index, adv. Vol. ends: Oct. Microform: PQC. *Indexed:* MLA-IB. *Bk. rev.:* 50/yr. *Aud.:* Ga, Ac.

The doyenne of scholarly genealogical journals, this remains the model against which other journals are compared. The *Register*'s primary focus is colonial New England families, their European origins, and some medieval and royal ancestry for New Englanders. New England primary source material is also abstracted and published. Book reviews are detailed and scholarly. There is a yearly index and cumulative indexes for volumes 1–50 and 51–148. The CD-ROM of the first 148 volumes is full-text and searchable. Microfilms have been created in blocks of five years per reel. Recommended for both academic and public libraries. All issues from volume 1 (1847) to present are available online. URL: www.americanancestors.org

2710. *Southern Genealogist's Exchange Society Quarterly.* Formerly (until 2004): *The Southern Genealogist's Exchange Quarterly.* [ISSN: 1933-1010] 1957. q. Free to members. Southern Genealogist's Exchange Society, Inc., PO Box 2801, Jacksonville, FL 32203; sges@juno.com; http://www.sgesjax.com/. Illus., index. Vol. ends: Dec. *Bk. rev.:* 150/yr. *Aud.:* Ga.

Although this is a regional journal covering 12 southern states (Virginia, West Virginia, North Carolina, South Carolina, Georgia, Florida, Kentucky, Tennessee, Alabama, Mississippi, Arkansas, and Louisiana), there's material available here that will be of interest to genealogists outside the region. Included in this journal from the Southern Genealogist's Exchange Society (SGES) are census records, cemetery listings, queries, Revolutionary War and other war records, letters, Bible and church records, marriage records, mortality schedules, area research tips, professional listings predating the nineteenth century, and orphanage listings, etc. Queries are published, and the web site of the SGES (www.sgesjax.org/) includes a superb research directory with direct links to archives (such as Ancestry.com and Family Search), cemetery research sites, genealogy blogs (the SGES has one of their own at www.sgesjax.org/category/blog/), further research resources, and links to local genealogical societies. Recommended for public libraries everywhere.

■ GENERAL INTEREST

See also Alternatives; Canada; Europe; and News and Opinion sections.

Amber Paranick, Library of Congress, Washington, DC; ampa@loc.gov.

Donna Scanlon, Library of Congress, Washington, DC; dscanlon@loc.gov

Introduction

"General Interest" implies that the topics will appeal to a broad audience. What is collected here are magazines that cover a wide array of topics that will likely appeal to a large audience. Many of these titles have become staples in American publishing and are some of the oldest continually published magazines available.

These magazines cover topics such as news, health, beauty, politics, culture, celebrities, arts, and travel, and there is something here for every type of reader. We know that in the current economic environment, decisions on what to keep have become more difficult, and it is our hope that this collection will make those decisions easier.

Within the pages of these publications is information that will keep us abreast of current events in the world, provide information so that we may form opinions, or bring order to our thoughts, lives, and homes. Some titles are starting points of research for students from grade school to college.

Basic Periodicals

Hs: *Newsweek, Smithsonian;* Ga: *The Atlantic, National Geographic, The New Yorker, Newsweek, Reader's Digest, TV Guide, Vanity Fair;* Ac: *The Atlantic, Harper's, The New Yorker, The Wilson Quarterly.*

Basic Abstracts and Indexes

MAS Ultra: School Edition, ProQuest Research Library, Readers' Guide to Periodical Literature.

2711. The Atlantic Monthly (Boston, 1993). Former titles (until 1993): *The Atlantic (Boston, 1981);* (until 1981): *The Atlantic Monthly (1971);* (until 1971): *The Atlantic (Boston, 1932);* (until 1932): *The Atlantic Monthly (1857);* Which incorporated (1866-1878): *The Galaxy;* (in 1910): *Putnam's Magazine;* (until 1909): *Putnam's & the Reader;* (until 1908): *Putnam's Monthly;* (until 1907): *Putnam's Monthly & the Critic;* (until 1906): *The Critic;* Which incorporated (in 1905): *Literary World;* The Critic was formerly (in 1884): *Critic & Good Literature;* Which was formed by the merger of (1881-1884): *Critic; Good Literature.* [ISSN: 1072-7825] 1857. 10x/yr. USD 24.50; USD 5.95 newsstand/cover. Ed(s): James Bennet. Atlantic Monthly Co., 600 New Hampshire Ave, N W, Washington, DC 20037. Illus., index, adv. Circ: 459600 Paid. Vol. ends: Jun/Dec. *Indexed:* A01, A06, A22, ABIn, ABS&EES, AmHI, BAS, BRI, C37, CBCARef, CBRI, F01, MASUSE, MLA-IB, P02, RILM. *Bk. rev.:* 3-5, 1,000 words. *Aud.:* Hs, Ga, Ac.

The Atlantic Monthly has been published for over 150 years and is a regarded as an American periodical that has truly set the standard for outstanding writing throughout its long publishing history. The magazine contains book reviews, literary critiques, and articles on myriad national and international topics, such as technology, arts, food, travels, religion, politics, and science. You can access even more content through its robust web site and blog, "The Atlantic Wire," which offers the "authoritative guide to the news and ideas that matter most right now." Now with the "Atlantic eReader," you can take a digital version (containing most articles and images found in the print edition of the print magazine) auto-delivered wirelessly to your reading device. Older issues from November 1995 to the present are available on the magazine's web site for free, along with notable articles from 1857 to 1995. Its premium archive (1857–present) is available via a third party for a small fee, and a selection of pre-1923 articles can be freely accessed via HathiTrust (http://catalog.hathitrust.org/Record/000597656). A digital edition has just been released for tablet readers. *The Atlantic* is truly a staple for all libraries. URL: www.theatlantic.com

2712. AudioFile: the magazine for people who love audiobooks. [ISSN: 1063-0244] 1992. bi-m. USD 19.95 combined subscription domestic (print & online eds.); USD 34.95 combined subscription Canada (print & online eds.); USD 54.95 combined subscription elsewhere (print & online eds.). Ed(s): Jennifer M Dowell, Robin F Whitten. AudioFile, 37 Silver St, PO Box 109, Portland, ME 04112. Illus., adv. Sample. *Indexed:* BRI. *Bk. rev.:* 150 per issue. *Aud.:* Hs, Ga, Ac.

The use of audiobooks in today's society has grown tremendously and is evident in every generation. *AudioFile,* a decade-old magazine that caters to those who love audiobooks, provides reviews of audio presentations, awards, interviews of authors and narrators, lists of new releases, and resources for product information. It is important to note that *AudioFile* does not critique the written material. There are various subscription packages available, such as a basic subscription for libraries on a tight budget. Along with a subscription, you gain access to the full web site, archive, and reference guides. *AudioFile* is highly recommended for all libraries that serve audiobooks, but especially for those libraries that have programs that serve audiobooks to the blind and physically handicapped populations. URL: http://audiofilemagazine.com

2713. Consumer Reports. Incorporates (in 1947): *Bread & Butter;* Formerly (until 1942): *Consumers Union Reports.* [ISSN: 0010-7174] 1936. m. except s-m. Dec. USD 29 domestic; CAD 39 Canada; USD 36 elsewhere. Ed(s): Greg Daugherty, Robert Tiernan. Consumers Union of the United States, Inc., 101 Truman Ave, Yonkers, NY 10703; http://www.consumersunion.org. Illus., index. Sample. Circ: 4100000 Paid. Vol. ends: Dec. Microform: NBI. *Indexed:* A01, A22, ABIn, AgeL, Agr, B01, B02, BLI, BRI, C37, CBCARef, F01, MASUSE, P02. *Aud.:* Hs, Ga, Ac.

Consumer Reports is the go-to publication for reviews on numerous products from home appliances to health products to electronics to vehicles. The monthly magazine has been making us more informed shoppers since 1936, and its mission is "to work for a fair, just, and safe marketplace for all consumers and to empower consumers to protect themselves." Feature columns articles include the popular "Up Front," "Special Reports," "Ask the Experts," and "Lab Tests." The magazine's "Auto" issue, published every April, is immensely popular. After you read the reviews and articles, the last page offers a humorous side of the marketplace with advertisement goofs, glitches, and gotchas submitted by readers. You can choose between a print or online subscription. A print subscription contains 13 issues (including the April "Auto" issue and *Annual Buying Guide 2013*) for USD 29.00. *CR*'s free web site offers helpful information; however, only subscribers have full access to exclusive online features that are not available to the general public. URL: www.consumerreports.org

2714. Contexts: understanding people in their social worlds. [ISSN: 1536-5042] 2002. q. USD 269. Ed(s): Arlene Stein, Jodi O'Brien. Sage Publications, Inc., 2455 Teller Rd, Thousand Oaks, CA 91320; info@sagepub.com; http://www.sagepub.com. Adv. Sample. Reprint: PSC. *Indexed:* A22, ABS&EES, ASIP, E01, ENW, P61, SSA. *Bk. rev.:* 2-3 per issue. *Aud.:* Ga, Ac.

Contexts is published by the American Sociological Association and is edited by Jodi O'Brien of Seattle University and Arlene Stein of Rutgers, The State University of New Jersey. But don't let this fact fool you into believing that this magazine is geared solely to an academic audience. Essentially, this is a quarterly magazine that makes cutting-edge sociological ideas and research accessible to general readers. The magazine serves as the "public face of sociology." Feature articles tend to focus on serious topics that affect modern life, such as climate change, gender issues, and reproduction around the world. The journal also incorporates lighthearted, but thought-provoking, pieces into its cultural reviews, such as making better helmets, reality TV stars, and slow food. In addition to the articles, there are book reviews, news within the field, and photo essays, all of which make *Contexts* a well-rounded magazine that will interest all types of readers. It is a perfect addition to a public library's magazine collection. Take *Contexts* with you on the go by subscribing to the title's podcast. URL: www.contexts.org

2715. Daedalus. Formerly (until 1955): *American Academy of Arts and Sciences. Proceedings.* [ISSN: 0011-5266] 1955. q. USD 136 (print & online eds.). Ed(s): Phyllis S Bendell. M I T Press, 55 Hayward St, Cambridge, MA 02142; journals-cs@mit.edu; http://mitpress.mit.edu. Illus., adv. Refereed. Microform: PQC. *Indexed:* A01, A22, ABS&EES, AmHI, ArtHuCI, BAS, BRI, BrArAb, CBRI, Chicano, E01, FR, IBSS, MLA-IB, P02, SWR&A. *Aud.:* Ac.

Daedalus was founded by the American Academy of the Arts and Sciences in 1955. The quarterly journal "draws on the enormous intellectual capacity of the American Academy, whose Members are among the nation's most prominent thinkers in the arts, sciences, and the humanities, as well as the full range of professions and public life." Each of its issues addresses a theme such as judicial independence, the global nuclear future, mass incarceration, the economy, the military, and race in today's society, with authoritative essays. Some of the more recent issues are titled "Science in the 21st Century," "Protecting the Internet as a Public Commons," and "American Democracy and the Common Good." It's clear from its nondescript cover that this magazine's main focus is on content, and the journal now includes poetry, fiction, interviews, and comments. This journal is geared toward the academic library, but it will also suit the public library's introspective reader and lifelong learner. URL: www.mitpressjournals.org/loi/daed

2716. Esquire. Former titles (until 1979): *Esquire Fortnightly;* (until 1978): *Esquire.* [ISSN: 0194-9535] 1933. 11x/yr. USD 8; USD 4.99 newsstand/cover. Hearst Magazines, 300 W 57th St, 12th Fl, New York, NY 10019; HearstMagazines@hearst.com; http://www.hearstcorp.com/magazines/. Illus., adv. Vol. ends: Dec. Microform: PQC. *Indexed:* A01, A22, BEL&L, BRI, C37, CBRI, F01, MASUSE, MLA-IB, P02, RILM. *Aud.:* Ga, Ac.

Esquire is a refined lifestyle magazine written primarily for the male audience. It delves into an array of topics that would interest the modern and well-informed man, such as art, current events, entertainment, food, fashion, health, politics, sports, and dating. The e-magazine, made specifically for e-book devices, allows readers to watch exclusive videos and photos, listen to recommended music, read book reviews, and swipe in 360 degrees around the best new cars, the best new clothes, and so much more. Its web site boosts a selection of the magazine's feature articles and videos, along with "Politics," "Style," and "Food" blogs. Recommended for all libraries. URL: www.esquire.com

2717. Fortune. Incorporates: *Fortune C N E T. Technology Review;* Which was formerly (until 2001): *Fortune. Technology Guide;* (until 2000): *Fortune. Technology Buyer's Guide.* [ISSN: 0015-8259] 1930. 20x/yr. CAD 26.34 Canada; USD 19.99 combined subscription domestic (print & online eds.). Time Inc., 1271 Ave of the Americas, New York, NY 10020; information@timeinc.com; http://www.timeinc.com. Illus., adv. *Indexed:* A01, A06, A22, ABIn, ABS&EES, ATI, AgeL, Agr, B01, B02, BLI, BRI, C37, CBRI, Chicano, I15, MASUSE, MLA-IB, P02. *Aud.:* Ga.

Not strictly for the business-minded professional or student, *Fortune* magazine's content includes interviews of executives and offers personal finance information and covers social-interest pieces such as social media in health care, environmental issues, and hydraulic fracturing. The highly-anticipated annual April issue includes the Fortune 500 ranking. Its digital-component features (available from the web and the tablet version) include information on conferences and leadership opportunities, and lists the top businessperson(s) of the year, the top 100 places to work, and the world's most admired companies.

2718. G Q (New York): gentlemen's quarterly for men. Formerly (until 1983): *Gentlemen's Quarterly.* [ISSN: 0016-6979] 1957. m. USD 15 domestic. Ed(s): Jim Nelson. Conde Nast Publications, Inc., 4 Times Sq, 6th Fl, New York, NY 10036; http://www.condenast.com. Illus., adv. Sample. Circ: 915173 Paid. Vol. ends: Winter. Microform: PQC. *Indexed:* A22, ASIP, BRI, IIFP, P02, RILM. *Aud.:* Hs, Ga, Ac.

GQ's advice to its readers is to "Look Sharp, Live Smart." Also known as *Gentleman's Quarterly*, it continues to live up to the standards that it set forth in 1957 when it first began. This title primarily caters to an urban male audience. Readers can connect with the magazine via various social media channels and download the latest issue through devices that handle e-magazines. Not only does it offer readers advice on fashion and dating, it provides articles on the best restaurants and entertainment, news and politics, and material for the casual browser. Highlights on the web site include the increasingly popular daily "StreetStyle" column, and most-read feature articles on topics such as interviews with "Top Chef" contestants and athletes; top female models of the century; and video excerpts from the magazine's recently published "Comedy Issue." Recommended for academic and public libraries alike.

2719. Grit: rural American know-how. Supersedes in part (in 1907): *Pennsylvania Grit;* Which was formerly (until 1887): *Sunday Grit;* (until 1884): *Grit Daily Sun and Banner.* [ISSN: 0017-4289] 1882. bi-m. USD 14.95. Ed(s): K C Compton. Ogden Publications, Inc., 1503 SW 42nd St, Topeka, KS 66609; http://www.ogdenpubs.com. Illus., adv. Sample. *Indexed:* BRI. *Bk. rev.:* Number and length vary. *Aud.:* Ems, Hs, Ga.

Initially started as a newspaper in 1882, *Grit: American Life and Customs* has been publishing content that focuses on rural communities, featuring inspirational thoughts, readers' true stories, book reviews, crafts, recipes, outdoor life, and much more. This magazine is now produced in color, and its feature articles include recipes using local food, do-it-yourself projects, and gardening and farming hints. The magazine's web site contains practical advice on the household and offers video webinars on a variety of topics such as tool and equipment reviews. User-generated content available on *Grit*'s blogs contain practical advice for the experienced and novice farmer alike. Recommended for rural and public libraries. URL: www.grit.com

2720. Harper's. Former titles (until 1976): *Harper's Magazine;* (until 1913): *Harper's Monthly Magazine;* (until 1900): *Harper's New Monthly Magazine;* Which incorporated (1850-1852): *International Magazine of Literature, Art, and Science;* Which was formerly (until Dec.1850): *International Miscellany of Literature, Art, and Science;* (until Oct.1850): *International Weekly Miscellany of Literature, Art, and Science.* [ISSN: 0017-789X] 1850. m. Ed(s): Ellen Rosenbush. Harpers Magazine, 666 Broadway, 11th Fl, New York, NY 10012; http://www.harpers.org. Illus., adv. Vol. ends: Jun/Dec. Microform: NBI; PMC; PQC. *Indexed:* A01, A06, A22, ABS&EES, BEL&L, BRI, C37, CBCARef, CBRI, F01, MASUSE, MLA-IB, P02, RILM. *Bk. rev.:* 3-5. *Aud.:* Hs, Ga, Ac.

Harper's is the second-oldest continuously published monthly magazine in the U.S., and is the oldest general-interest monthly in America, featuring works on art, literature, and culture. It's been published since 1950 and continues to offer voices from up-and-coming writers, as well as distinguished authors. Feature articles are thought-provoking and entertaining, such as "Glaciers for Sale: A Global Warming Get-Rich-Quick Scheme." The magazine offers works of fiction by notable authors, photo essays, book reviews, crossword puzzles, and the infamous "Harper's Index"—a monthly list of ironic factoids. Along with a subscription comes access to the *Harper's* archive. Readers can opt for digital-only subscription. Readers may subscribe to the print edition of *Harper's* and receive access to the magazine's digital archive, or opt for a digital subscription only (without access to the magazine's 163 years of content). Historical articles (those published in pre-1923 issues) may be accessed through the HathiTrust web site: http://catalog.hathitrust.org/Record/000505748

2721. Mental Floss. [ISSN: 1543-4702] 2001. bi-m. USD 24.97. Ed(s): Neely Harris. Mental Floss L L C, PO Box 528, Novelty, OH 44072. Illus., adv. *Aud.:* Hs, Ga, Ac.

Mental Floss, a magazine for knowledge junkies, was started by Duke University students who yearned for a fun, educational magazine. Not only is this magazine fun to browse, it also delivers readable articles about intellectual ideas and theories in a way that anyone can understand. With features for the

"Right and Left Brain," readers learn about the arts and sciences. The "Scatterbrain" feature gives ten straight pages of raw trivia, while the "Learn to Spin the Globe" section provides insight into religion, history, and world culture. This magazine inspires us to learn more about the world we live in. The *Mental Floss* web site provides articles that answer the major quandaries we've always pondered, but never took the time to research. Highlights include amazing facts, big questions, knowledge feed, lists, and quizzes. Highly recommended for all libraries. URL: www.mentalfloss.com

2722. *Money (New York).* [ISSN: 0149-4953] 1972. m. plus special issue. USD 47.88. Time Inc., 1271 Ave of the Americas, New York, NY 10020; information@timeinc.com; http://www.timeinc.com. Illus., adv. *Indexed:* A01, A22, ABIn, ATI, AgeL, B01, B02, BLI, BRI, C37, CBRI, MASUSE, P02. *Aud.:* Ga, Ac.

One of the best magazines around for personal finance, *Money* offers us a wide range of investment and money management advice, with a mix of articles, regular columns, and interviews. The use of plain English to explain the terminology used by financial planners makes the complex issues of finance and investment easier to understand. This magazine covers all aspects of money management from retirement planning to how and where to invest, and it includes how to find the "best deals on everything" (as highlighted in a recent issue). All this adds to the popularity of this magazine. With a focus on the casual investor, this is an excellent resource for managing personal finances and is essential for public libraries. Content from the magazine can also be found on the CNN/*Money* web site, which is a service of CNN, *Money,* and *Fortune* magazine. URL: http://money.cnn.com

2723. *Mother Jones.* [ISSN: 0362-8841] 1976. bi-m. USD 12 domestic; USD 22 Canada; USD 24 elsewhere. Ed(s): Clara Jeffery, Monika Bauerlein. Foundation for National Progress, 222 Sutter St, Ste 600, San Francisco, CA 94108. Illus., adv. Circ: 240000. Vol. ends: Dec. Microform: NBI; PQC. *Indexed:* A01, A22, ASIP, BRI, C37, C42, CBRI, Chicano, MASUSE, MLA-IB, P02, RILM, WSA. *Aud.:* Hs, Ga, Ac.

The aim of *Mother Jones* is simply stated—"Smart, Fearless Journalism"—as it covers politics, current affairs, environmental issues, health, media, and culture. An organization with both a print and online presence, *Mother Jones* delves into major topics with abandon. The progressive publication, featuring stories not found anywhere else, is a frequent winner of awards from the American Society of Magazine Editors. Its publishing frequency is bimonthly, but its web site offers original reporting 24/7. We think it's a good addition for any library, as it will undoubtedly fill the need for an alternative open-minded perspective on the world in which we live. URL: www.motherjones.com

2724. *National Geographic.* Formerly (until 1959): *The National Geographic Magazine.* [ISSN: 0027-9358] 1888. m. USD 15 domestic; CAD 20 Canada. Ed(s): Chris Johns. National Geographic Society, 1145 17th St, NW, Washington, DC 20036; http://www.nationalgeographic.com/. Illus., index, adv. Circ: 9500000 Paid. Vol. ends: Jun/Dec. *Indexed:* A&ATA, A01, A06, A22, A47, ABS&EES, AbAn, BEL&L, BRI, C37, F01, GardL, ICM, MASUSE, MLA-IB, P02. *Aud.:* Ems, Hs, Ga, Ac, Sa.

National Geographic is a magazine that provides us with a closer look at our world. Its motto reads: "inspiring people to care about our planet since 1888." Contributors have fulfilled this promise to us by providing articles on culture, animals, the environment, science, and space. You'll continually browse this title for the award-winning photographs and maps published within that truly bring the subjects to life. *National Geographic* is meant for all age groups and the magazine's web site, blogs, and social media channels provide up-to-the-minute coverage of daily news stories, videos, user-submitted photographs, and sections on adventure, travel, and the environment. A digital subscription is also available. *National Geographic* is quite possibly one of the most well-known magazines, and is a definite must for all libraries. URL: www.nationalgeographic.com

2725. *The New Yorker.* [ISSN: 0028-792X] 1925. 47x/yr. USD 59.99 domestic (print or online ed.); USD 90 Canada; USD 120 elsewhere). Ed(s): David Remnick. Conde Nast Publications, Inc., 4 Times Sq, 6th Fl, New York, NY 10036; http://www.condenast.com. Illus., adv. Sample. Circ: 1004040 Paid. Vol. ends: Dec. Microform: PQC. *Indexed:* A01, A06, A22, ABS&EES, AgeL, BEL&L, BRI, C37, CBRI, Chicano, F01, GardL, IIMP, IIPA, MASUSE, MLA-IB, P02, RILM. *Bk. rev.:* 5-7, 200-3,000 words. *Aud.:* Hs, Ga, Ac.

The New Yorker has been a premier publication since it began in 1925. Going beyond the events, reviews, and cultural life of New York City, this magazine has built up an audience beyond New York. Well known for its illustrated and topical covers, *The New Yorker* continues to provide some of the best cartoons, essays, fiction, and poetry, as well as articles from best-selling authors. Readers of this magazine are sure to find something of interest in each issue. *The New Yorker* also has an online site, with podcasts, videos, puzzles, and a complete archive of articles that are accessible to subscribers and that are also available for purchase. A must for all libraries. Now available for smartphones, tablets (iPad, Kindle Fire, Nook), and an audio edition of selected pieces from audible.com. URL: www.newyorker.com

Newsweek (Online). See News and Opinion section.

2726. *O: The Oprah Magazine.* [ISSN: 1531-3247] 2000. m. USD 15; USD 4.50 newsstand/cover. Hearst Magazines, 300 W 57th St, 12th Fl, New York, NY 10019; HearstMagazines@hearst.com; http://www.hearst.com. Illus., adv. *Indexed:* BRI, C37. *Bk. rev.:* 3-5. *Aud.:* Ga.

This magazine from Oprah Winfrey touches on the topics of everyday life that appeal to women. Every issue of *O: The Oprah Magazine* has a section on entertainment, advice, style, health, books, connections, and a final thought from Oprah called "What I Know For Sure." In each issue, readers will find timely articles and updates on upcoming trends and products; a book section that includes book reviews on hot new releases, as well as lists of forthcoming titles; and celebrity picks. The web site ties the magazine into the rest of Oprah's media empire and includes online contests, inspirations, and videos. There's also a link to Oprah's book club that includes Oprah's picks, and books from the TV show and from the magazine. A great addition for public libraries. URL: www.oprah.com/magazine

2727. *Pacific Standard.* Formerly (until 2012): *Miller-McCune.* [ISSN: 2165-5197] 2008. bi-m. USD 14.95 domestic; USD 26.95 foreign; USD 5.99 per issue. Ed(s): Maria Streshinsky. Miller-McCune Center for Research, Media and Public Policy, PO Box 698, Santa Barbara, CA 93102; info@miller-mccune.org; http://www.miller-mccune.org/. Illus., adv. Sample. *Indexed:* BRI. *Aud.:* Hs, Ga, Ac.

Started in 2008, *Pacific Standard* is somewhat of a newcomer to the world of magazines in print. Feature articles mostly fall into the political realm, yet this title features articles on education, health, economy, culture, and science. The magazine sets out to explore academic and research-based solutions to current social issues, in areas including politics, social problems, science, and economics.

2728. *People (New York).* Formerly (until 2002): *People Weekly.* [ISSN: 0093-7673] 1974. 54x/yr. USD 62 combined subscription (print & online eds.). Time Inc., 1271 Ave of the Americas, New York, NY 10020; information@timeinc.com; http://www.timeinc.com. Illus., adv. *Indexed:* A01, A22, BRI, C37, CBCARef, CBRI, MASUSE, P02. *Aud.:* Ga.

Published weekly since 1974, *People* magazine offers readers of all ages a glimpse into the lives of celebrities and other notable persons. Popular culture stories are published alongside human interest stories. This highly illustrated magazine also publishes weekly movie, music, and television reviews. Its web site contains celebrity news, photographs, pets, and babies. Special editions include "Style Watch" and "Most Beautiful People." Recommended for all libraries.

2729. *Popular Mechanics.* Former titles (until 1959): *Popular Mechanics Magazine;* Which incorporated (in 1923): *Illustrated World;* (in 1931): *Science and Invention;* (until 1913): *Popular Mechanics.* [ISSN: 0032-4558] 1902. 11x/yr. USD 12; USD 4.50 newsstand/cover. Hearst Magazines, 300 W 57th St, 12th Fl, New York, NY 10019; HearstMagazines@hearst.com; http://www.hearst.com. Illus., index, adv. Vol. ends: Dec. Microform: NBI; PQC. *Indexed:* A&ATA, A01, A06, A22, BRI, C37, CBCARef, IHTDI, MASUSE, P02. *Aud.:* Hs, Ga.

An excellent source for the "do it yourself" person in all of us, *Popular Mechanics* features sections on automotive, home improvement, outdoors, science, technology, and "DIY Central." This magazine is geared to those looking to embark on "do it yourself" projects, so the articles are not cluttered with technical language, and they include photos and diagrams as guides for the reader. *Popular Mechanics*' regular features include sections on "Home How-To," "Automotive," "Technology," "Science," and "Adventure," along with feature articles that touch on recent events and related technology. Since 1902, this magazine has been providing articles in science and technology. The web site features most of the articles from the current issue, as well as user communities, blogs, and videos. An iPad edition is also available. Essential for all public libraries. URL: www.popularmechanics.com

Prologue. See Archives and Manuscripts section.

2730. *Reader's Digest (U.S. Edition).* [ISSN: 0034-0375] 1922. 10x/yr. USD 12. Reader's Digest Association, Inc, Reader's Digest Rd, Pleasantville, NY 10570; letters@rd.com. Illus., index. Sample. Vol. ends: Dec. Microform: PQC. *Indexed:* A06, A22, BRI, C37, MASUSE, MLA-IB, P02. *Aud.:* Ems, Hs, Ga.

Reader's Digest has been a favorite of American households since 1922. With regular offerings of amazing and inspirational stories, interviews, and puzzles and quizzes that keep our minds alert, as well as tips on maintaining our health, *Reader's Digest* has become a staple in our homes. This publication provides book excerpts to whet our appetite for highly anticipated new releases. Available in large-print, iPad, and Kindle Fire editions. The web site has a similar feel to the magazine, but provides different material with cooking tips, recipes, photos, and games. *Reader's Digest* is essential for all public libraries. URL: www.rd.com

2731. *Saturday Evening Post.* Formerly (until 1839): *Atkinson's Evening Post and Philadelphia Saturday News;* Which was formed by the merger of (1836-1838): *Philadelphia Saturday News and Literary Gazette;* (1833-1839): *Atkinson's Saturday Evening Post;* Which was formerly (until 1833): *Atkinson's Saturday Evening Post and Bulletin;* Which was formed by the merger of (1827-1832): *Saturday Bulletin;* (1831-1832): *Atkinson's Saturday Evening Post;* Which was formerly (until 1831): *Saturday Evening Post;* Incorporates (1976-19??): *Country Gentleman;* Which superseded in part (1955-1956): *Farm Journal and Country Gentleman;* Which was formed by the merger of (1898-1955): *Country Gentleman;* Which was formerly (until 1898): *Cultivator & Country Gentleman;* Which was formed by the merger of (1834-1865): *Cultivator;* Which incorporated (1842-1844): *Central New-York Farmer;* (1831-1839): *Genesee Farmer;* (1853-1865): *Country Gentleman;* (1945-1955): *Farm Journal;* Which was formerly (until 1945): *Farm Journal and Farmer's Wife;* Which was formed by the merger of (1877-1939): *Farm Journal;* (1935-1939): *Farmer's Wife Magazine;* Which was formerly (until 1935): *Farmer's Wife.* [ISSN: 0048-9239] 1821. bi-m. USD 14.98. Benjamin Franklin Literary and Medical Society, Inc., 1100 Waterway Blvd, Indianapolis, IN 46202. Illus., adv. Vol. ends: Dec. *Indexed:* A01, A06, A22, BRI, C37, CBRI, F01, MASUSE, MLA-IB, P02. *Aud.:* Ems, Hs, Ga.

Beginning with Benjamin Franklin's *Pennsylvania Gazette* in 1721, *The Saturday Evening Post* has been taking us through the events and cultural changes that have shaped America. We all recall the famous and endearing covers that were painted by Norman Rockwell or illustrated by J.C. Leyendecker, N.C. Wyeth, Charles Livingston Bull, or John E. Sheridan. *The Saturday Evening Post* has featured short stories and commentary by the likes of F. Scott Fitzgerald, Sinclair Lewis, and Ring Lardner, to name just a few. Early issues tackled political controversy, morality, and various commercial interests. Today the magazine provides readers with articles on art, entertainment, health, family, people, places, trends, and opinions. With an appeal to older Americans for the nostalgia, the magazine also appeals to a younger generation with the fun, games, and cartoons. The web site provides online versions of past articles on a variety of topics. Recommended for public libraries. URL: www.saturdayeveningpost.com

2732. *Smithsonian.* [ISSN: 0037-7333] 1970. m. USD 12 domestic; USD 25 Canada; USD 38 elsewhere. Ed(s): Terence Monmaney, Alison C McLean. Smithsonian Magazine, Capital Gallery, Ste 6001, MRC 513, PO Box 37012, Washington, DC 20013; MagazinePermissions@si.edu. Illus., index, adv. Microform: PQC. *Indexed:* A01, A22, A51, ABS&EES, AbAn, AmHI, ArtHuCI, BEL&L, BRI, C37, CBCARef, CBRI, Chicano, F01, GardL, MASUSE, MLA-IB, P02, RILM. *Aud.:* Hs, Ga, Ac.

Putting the reader in touch with "fascinating and intriguing" aspects of history, science, nature, and art, the *Smithsonian Magazine* is always a popular choice. Providing us with opportunities, through the stunning photography and articles, to travel from our favorite chair, we can explore the latest archaeological dig or travel to places we have only dreamed of visiting. Since 1970, we have enjoyed the thoughtful journalism that is as diverse as the Institute. The web site provides additional content, photos and videos of the day, games to keep our minds entertained, and the archive of past issues. This is a wonderful addition for all libraries. An iPad edition is now available. URL: www.smithsonianmag.com

2733. *T V Guide.* [ISSN: 0039-8543] 1953. w. USD 16.50. Gemstar - TV Guide International, 1211 Ave of the Americas, New York, NY 10036. Illus., index, adv. *Indexed:* A22, ASIP, BRI, P02. *Aud.:* Ga.

Since 1953, households have been depending on *TV Guide* to keep us informed on what's on television each night. While still providing our nightly television listings, this weekly magazine also provides us with exclusive interviews with the stars of our favorite programs, and keeps us up-to-date with the latest news on our favorite programs and behind-the-scenes looks. *TV Guide* not only feeds our television viewing desires, but it also feeds our mind with the weekly crossword puzzle. The web site provides us the information in the weekly guide, and so much more—interviews, a guide for viewing full episodes online, and photos of our favorite stars, complete with red-carpet coverage. With 56 issues a year, this continues to be a must for public libraries. URL: www.tvguide.com

2734. *Town & Country (New York).* Former titles (until 1901): *Home Journal;* (until 1846): *Morris's National Press;* Incorporates (1901-1992): *Connoisseur.* [ISSN: 0040-9952] 1846. 11x/yr. USD 10 domestic; USD 34 foreign; USD 4.50 newsstand/cover. Hearst Magazines, 300 W 57th St, 12th Fl, New York, NY 10019; HearstMagazines@hearst.com; http://www.hearst.com. Illus., adv. Vol. ends: Dec. *Indexed:* A06, A07, A22, ASIP, BAS, BRI, C37, MASUSE, MLA-IB, P02, RILM. *Bk. rev.:* Number and length vary. *Aud.:* Ga.

Since 1846, *Town & Country* has been "America's premier lifestyle magazine for the affluent." Known as the "authority on the meaning of modern society, and why it matters," it showcases this seductive world of exceptional people and exclusive places, as well as fashion, travel, design, beauty, health, the arts, and antiques. Over the years *Town & Country* has highlighted the achievements of some of the country's most famous people. Sections include "Style," "Society," "Leisure," and "The Scene," which covers parties, events, and weddings; these are just a few of the spectacular items gracing its pages. Available in both print and online.

2735. *Travel & Leisure.* Former titles (until 1971): *Travel and Camera;* (until 1969): *U.S. Camera & Travel;* (until 1964): *U.S. Camera;* Which incorporated (in 19??): *Travel & Camera;* (until 1941): *U.S. Camera Magazine.* [ISSN: 0041-2007] 1971. m. USD 19.99. Ed(s): Nancy Novogrod, Laura Teusink. American Express Publishing Corp., 1120 Ave of the Americas, New York, NY 10036; ashields@amexpub.com; http://www.travelandleisure.com. Illus., index, adv. Sample. Circ: 975505 Paid. Vol. ends: Dec. Microform: PQC. *Indexed:* A22, ASIP, BRI, H&TI, P02. *Aud.:* Ga.

Travel magazines have reached an all-time popularity level. Though the content of *Travel & Leisure* is unique, distinguishing it from other popular travel magazines while still being accessible, it is a solid choice for public libraries and academic libraries alike.

2736. *Utne Reader: understanding the next evolution.* Former titles (until 2006): *Utne;* (until Nov. 2002): *Utne Reader.* 1984. bi-m. USD 29.95 domestic; USD 50 Canada; USD 55 elsewhere. Ed(s): David Schimke, Keith Goetzman. Ogden Publications, Inc., 1624 Harmon Place, Ste 330, Minneapolis, MN 55403; http://www.ogdenpubs.com. Illus., adv. Circ: 100000 Paid. *Indexed:* A01, A22, ABS&EES, BRI, CBRI, IIMP, IIPA, MASUSE, MLA-IB, P02. *Bk. rev.:* Number and length vary. *Aud.:* Hs, Ga, Ac.

For more than 25 years, the *Utne Reader* (now with Utne.com) has been a "[digest] of independent ideas and alternative culture. Not right, not left, but forward thinking." *Utne* is most interested in creating a conversation about everything from the environment to the economy, from politics to pop culture. It gleans through approximately 1,500 magazines, newsletters, journals, weeklies, zines, and more to locate the most essential stories, interviews, and cultural criticism to present to readers in one handy place. The magazine groups material in sections such as emerging ideas (feature articles), mindful living (helpful tips), gleanings (article reprints), and mixed media (reviews of music, books, film, and more). The *Utne Reader* offers writings from sources that do not reach a wide audience and is a nice supplement to mainstream newsmagazines. The web site provides access to some of the articles from the print issue, as well as blogs for "Mind & Body," "Science & Technology," and "Arts & Culture." URL: www.utne.com

2737. *Vanity Fair.* Formerly (until 1914): *Dress & Vanity Fair.* [ISSN: 0733-8899] 1913. m. USD 18 combined subscription (print & online eds.). Ed(s): Graydon Carter. Conde Nast Publications, Inc., 4 Times Sq, 6th Fl, New York, NY 10036; magpr@condenast.com; http://www.condenast.com. Illus., adv. Sample. Vol. ends: Dec. *Indexed:* A22, ASIP, BRI, C37, F01, P02, RILM. *Aud.:* Ga.

What may appear to many as a fashion and celebrity magazine, *Vanity Fair* is so much more. It covers the latest in politics, highlights new businesses, surveys international affairs, and looks back through history at noteworthy events, all in thought-provoking and informative ways throughout its pages. This magazine also allows its readers to keep up on what's new in literature, film, television, style, and, of course, all manner of culture. Covering topics from the ivory trade and its impact to new arrivals on the Hollywood scene, this is one publication that has managed to hold its own with more serious magazines and still keep its readers current on cultural issues. Available in print and online, it's a favorite addition to most public libraries. The web site offers exclusive content including "The VF Daily Column," "Most Popular" articles, and an "In the News" feature that links *VF* stories to current events. URL: www.vanityfair.com

2738. *The Village Voice.* [ISSN: 0042-6180] 1955. w. Ed(s): Tony Ortega. Village Voice Media, Inc., 80 Maiden Lane, Ste 2105, New York, NY 10038. Illus., adv. Vol. ends: Dec. Microform: PQC. *Indexed:* A22, ASIP, BRI, CBRI, Chicano, F01, IIMP, IIPA, P02, RILM. *Aud.:* Ga, Ac.

The Village Voice was founded in 1955 by Dan Wolf, Ed Fancher, and Norman Mailer as showcasing "free-form, high-spirited[,] and passionate journalism into the public discourse." This recipient of three Pulitzer prizes, the National Press Foundation Award, and the George Polk Award continues to hold onto its "no-holds-barred reporting and criticism." The *Voice* has earned a reputation for its groundbreaking investigations of New York City politics; and it is the authoritative source on all that New York has to offer as the premier expert on New York's cultural scene, with its coverage of local and national politics, and its opinionated arts, culture, music, dance, film, and theater reviews; its daily web dispatches; and its comprehensive entertainment listings. The web site, www.villagevoice.com, "has twice been recognized as one of the nation's premier online sites for journalistic quality and local content. The site is a past winner of both the National Press Foundation's Online Journalism Award and the Editor and Publisher Eppy Award for Best Overall US Weekly Newspaper Online." Available in print, online, and microform. Highly recommended for public libraries. URL: www.villagevoice.com

2739. *The Wilson Quarterly (Online): surveying the world of ideas.* [ISSN: 2328-529X] 1978. q. USD 15.99. Ed(s): Steven Lagerfeld. Woodrow Wilson International Center for Scholars, Woodrow Wilson Plaza, 1300 Pennsylvania Ave, NW, Washington, DC 20004-3027; http://www.wilsoncenter.org/. Illus. *Bk. rev.:* 5-7 per quarterly issue. *Aud.:* Ga, Ac.

The Wilson Quarterly is known for providing "a nonpartisan and non-ideological window on the world of ideas." Within its pages, you will find the writings and thinking of scholars, specialists, and others in an effort to assist the public in dealing with the overload of information found today, as well as a way to help it follow developments within "significant realms of knowledge." The subjects covered by this magazine include politics and policy, culture, religion, science, and others that impact our everyday lives. *Wilson Quarterly* went 100 percent online in 2012 and is also available in Kindle, Nook, iPad, and Android editons. URL: www.wilsonquarterly.com/

■ GEOGRAPHY

See also Cartography, GIS, and Imagery; Globalization; Population Studies; and Travel and Tourism sections.

Fred Burchsted, Research Librarian, Services for Academic Programs, Widener Library, Harvard University, Cambridge, MA 02138; burchst@fas.harvard.edu

Introduction

The mission of geography is to understand the world from a spatial perspective. This spatial view brings together highly diverse people—students of glacial landforms with literary scholars. Economics, politics, women's studies, literature, cultural heritage preservation, and many other subjects can be viewed geographically. Although geography is classed as a social science, many geographers, such as geomorphologists and biogeographers, study the natural world. Spatial aspects of the human–environment relations, together with regional studies, are firmly within the realm of geography.

As the problems facing the world—whether environmental, economic, or geopolitical—have become more global, the discipline of geography increasingly has taken an engaged turn. Thus, intersections of climate change, economics, and geopolitics take a central position in geographical research and teaching.

I have attempted in this section to include periodicals from the full range of geographic specialties. Technical aspects of geography, cartography, GIS, etc., are treated in a separate section of this volume ("Cartography, GIS, and Imagery").

Geo-Guide (Gottingen State and University Library; see http://geo-leo.de/e-zeitschriften/geographie/) offers a list of electronic journals in geography and cartography.

Since 1938, the American Geographical Society Library at the University of Wisconsin–Milwaukee listed publications received—including books, periodical articles, pamphlets, maps and atlases, and government documents—in *Current Geographical Publications*. The print version ceased with the December 2003 issue. It currently exists as a list of links to tables-of-contents of current issues of geographical journals. It was cumulated (1985–2005) in the Online Geographical Bibliography (GEOBIB); both are available on the American Geographical Society Library web site (http://www4.uwm.edu/libraries/AGSL/index.cfm).

Basic Periodicals

Hs: *Geographical, National Geographic;* Ga: *Explorers Journal, Geographical, National Geographic;* Ac: *Association of American Geographers. Annals, Geographical Review, Institute of British Geographers. Transactions, The Professional Geographer.*

Basic Abstracts and Indexes

Geographical Abstracts.

2740. *Acme: an international e-journal for critical geographies.* [ISSN: 1492-9732] 2002. s-a. Free. University of British Columbia - Okanagan, 3333 University Way, Kelowna, BC V1V 1V7, Canada. Adv. Refereed. *Indexed:* A01, IBSS. *Aud.:* Ac.

A journal of radical approaches to spatial relationships involved in inequality and social justice. Coverage is aimed at fostering social and political change. Articles approach geography from anarchist, anti-racist, environmentalist, feminist, Marxist, postcolonial, queer, and other perspectives. The articles are largely in English, but may be in French, Italian, German, or Spanish. Frequent special issues are on particular themes. The editorial board is international with a Canadian emphasis. Of interest to any library that supports a geography department with a political or social orientation.

2741. *Antipode: a radical journal of geography.* [ISSN: 0066-4812] 1969. 5x/yr. GBP 650. Ed(s): Andrew Kent, Wendy Lamer. Wiley-Blackwell Publishing Ltd., The Atrium, Southern Gate, Chichester, PO19 8SQ, United Kingdom; customer@wiley.com; http://www.wiley.com/. Illus., index, adv. Sample. Refereed. Vol. ends: Oct. Reprint: PSC. *Indexed:* A01, A22, E01, FR, IBSS, M&GPA, P61, SSA. *Bk. rev.:* 3-6, 1,200-2,400 words, signed. *Aud.:* Ac.

Antipode publishes articles from a variety of radical ideological positions, offering dissenting perspectives on environmentalism, feminism, postcolonialism, postmodernism, race, urbanism, war, and other topics. Most issues include focused groups of papers. This journal is devoted to fostering social and political change through activist scholarship and free discussion. Editors and authors are American and British, with an international editorial board. *Antipode Online,* the journal's new web site, offers several features, including some free content, interviews and book reviews, and links to left-wing journals and organizations. This journal is important for academic libraries that support geography and political science departments. URL: www.antipode-online.net

2742. *Applied Geography: putting the world's human and physical resource problems in a geographical perspective.* [ISSN: 0143-6228] 1981. 10x/yr. EUR 941. Ed(s): Jay D Gatrell. Pergamon, The Blvd, Langford Ln, E Park, Kidlington, OX5 1GB, United Kingdom; JournalsCustomerServiceEMEA@elsevier.com; http://www.elsevier.com. Illus., adv. Sample. Refereed. Microform: PQC. *Indexed:* A01, A22, C45, RRTA, S25. *Aud.:* Ac, Sa.

Applied Geography focuses geographical thought and methods on human problems that have a spatial component, by fostering an understanding of the underlying systems, whether human or physical. Coverage includes resource management, environmental problems, agriculture, and urban and regional planning. The target audience is planners and policymakers, as well as academics. The editorship is British, with a British/American/international editorial board. Authorship is international with a British emphasis. Important for libraries that support academic geography departments or agencies concerned with policy and planning.

2743. *Arab World Geographer.* [ISSN: 1480-6800] 1998. q. CAD 180 (Individuals, CAD 69; Students, CAD 52). Ed(s): Ghazi-Walid Falah, Virginie Mamadouh. A W G PUBLISHING, 1215 Stonesthrow Way, Wadsworth, OH 44281. Refereed. *Indexed:* C45, IBSS. *Aud.:* Ac, Sa.

Arab World Geographer publishes articles on geographical research, both theoretical and applied, on all aspects, cultural and physical, of the human environment in the Arab countries. There is an emphasis on application of research to policy and on the publication of work by Arab geographers. The editorship is American, with an international editorial board. Authorship is international. Important for academic libraries that support geography departments or Middle Eastern Area Studies programs.

2744. *Area.* [ISSN: 0004-0894] 1969. q. GBP 225. Ed(s): Madeleine Hatfield, Kevin Ward. Wiley-Blackwell Publishing Ltd., The Atrium, Southern Gate, Chichester, PO19 8SQ, United Kingdom; customer@wiley.com; http://www.wiley.com/. Illus., adv. Sample. Refereed. Vol. ends: Dec. Reprint: PSC. *Indexed:* A01, A22, BAS, BrArAb, C45, E01, FR, IBSS, IndVet, NumL, RRTA, SD. *Bk. rev.:* 6-20, 1,000-2,000 words, signed. *Aud.:* Ac.

Published on behalf of the Royal Geographical Society, *Area* is a scholarly journal that features short research and discussion articles on topics of current professional interest and expressions of opinion by geographers on public questions—largely human geography, but some physical. Groups of several articles that focus on special subjects are often published. The "Observation" section features short reviews and opinion pieces on subjects of current debate. This journal aims at a free discussion of geographical ideas, results, and methodology. Authorship and editorship are British. Important for libraries that support a geography department.

2745. *Association of American Geographers. Annals.* [ISSN: 0004-5608] 1911. bi-m. USD 2042 (print & online eds.). Ed(s): Robin Maier. Routledge, 325 Chestnut St, Ste 800, Philadelphia, PA 19106; customerservice@taylorandfrancis.com; http://www.tandfonline.com.

Illus., index, adv. Sample. Refereed. Vol. ends: Dec. Microform: PQC. Reprint: PSC. *Indexed:* A01, A22, ABS&EES, Agr, BAS, BRI, C45, CBRI, E01, FR, IBSS, IndVet, M&GPA, MLA-IB, P02, RRTA, S25. *Bk. rev.:* 10-20, 750-2,000 words, signed. *Aud.:* Ac.

The *Annals* is often considered the leading American research journal in geography. Covering all areas of geography worldwide, it offers research articles, commentaries on published articles, book review forums, and occasional review articles and map supplements. Emphasis is on integrative and cross-disciplinary papers. The editorship/authorship is largely American, with some international editors and contributors. Important for all academic and for large public libraries.

2746. *Australian Geographer.* [ISSN: 0004-9182] 1928. q. GBP 445 (print & online eds.). Routledge, Level 2, 11 Queens Rd, Melbourne, VIC 3004, Australia; http://www.routledge.com. Illus., index, adv. Sample. Refereed. Circ: 1200. Vol. ends: Nov. Reprint: PSC. *Indexed:* A01, A22, AbAn, BAS, C45, E01, FR, IBSS, MLA-IB, RRTA, S25. *Aud.:* Ac.

Published under the auspices of the Geographical Society of New South Wales, *Australian Geographer* offers research articles on human and physical geography, focusing on environmental studies. There is a strong Australian concentration, but with articles on the broader Asia-Pacific and Antarctic regions. Occasional special issues on focused topics are published. Editorship/authorship is largely Australian. Important for academic libraries that support geography departments, and environmental or area studies programs with Australasian interests.

Cartographic Perspectives. See Cartography, GIS, and Imagery section.

Cartography and Geographic Information Science. See Cartography, GIS, and Imagery section.

2747. *Cultural Geographies: a journal of cultural geographies.* Formerly (until 2002): *Ecumene.* [ISSN: 1474-4740] 1994. q. USD 943. Ed(s): Tim J Cresswell, Dydia DeLyser. Sage Publications Ltd., 1 Oliver's Yard, 55 City Rd, London, EC1Y 1SP, United Kingdom; info@sagepub.co.uk; http://www.uk.sagepub.com. Illus., index, adv. Sample. Refereed. Vol. ends: Oct. Reprint: PSC. *Indexed:* A01, A22, AmHI, C45, E01, IBSS, MLA-IB, P02, P61, RRTA, SSA. *Bk. rev.:* 4-8, 700-1,300 words, signed. *Aud.:* Ac.

Drawing on contributors from a wide range of disciplines, *Cultural Geographies* explores thought on the perception, representation, and interpretation of the earth and on "the cultural appropriation of nature, landscape, and environment." Interest in these themes comes from a variety of artistic, humanistic, environmental, and geographical communities. The section "Cultural Geographies in Practice" offers critical reflections from practitioners and academics on how civic, policy, and artistic practices relate to cultural geography. The editorship is American and British with international editorial/advisory boards. The authorship is international, with the United States, Canada, and the United Kingdom most heavily represented. Important for libraries that support geography departments, and for environmental and cultural studies programs.

2748. *CyberGEO: revue euroeenne de geographie/European journal of geography.* [ISSN: 1278-3366] 1996. irreg. Free. Ed(s): Christine Kosmopoulos. CyberGeo, 13 rue du Four, Paris, 75006, France. *Indexed:* FR. *Bk. rev.:* 10-20/year, 200-800 words, signed. *Aud.:* Ac.

This is a free online journal that publishes articles on the whole range of geography. It offers authors quick publication and immediate reader feedback. The results of reader feedback may be incorporated into or added to articles. There is an associated discussion mailing list. The web site has an English version. Articles have English summaries and are in French, English, and other languages. The editorial board is European, largely French. Of interest to any library that supports a geography department, especially with theoretical or European interests.

2749. *Diversity and Distributions: a journal of conservation biogeography.* Formerly (until 1998): *Biodiversity Letters.* [ISSN: 1366-9516] 1993. bi-m. USD 8497 combined subscription domestic (print & online eds.); GBP 4603 combined subscription United Kingdom (print & online eds.); EUR 5846 combined subscription in Europe (print & online eds.). Ed(s): David M Richardson. Wiley-Blackwell Publishing Ltd., 9600 Garsington Rd, Oxford, OX4 2DQ, United Kingdom; customerservices@blackwellpublishing.com; http://www.wiley.com/. Illus., adv. Sample. Refereed. Reprint: PSC. *Indexed:* A01, A22, Agr, C45, E01, IndVet, P02, RRTA. *Aud.:* Ac, Sa.

Although more closely tied to ecology, the spatial distribution of plants and animals has longstanding connections with geographical thought. *Diversity and Distributions'* particular mission is the application of biogeographical theories and methods to conservation problems. Editors are American and British; the editorial board is international. Sister journals are the *Journal of Biogeography*, which publishes articles in all areas of the field, and *Global Ecology and Biogeography* (see Ecology section), which focuses on macroecology.

Earth Interactions. See Atmospheric Sciences section.

Earth Surface Processes and Landforms. See Earth Sciences and Geology section.

2750. *Economic Geography.* [ISSN: 0013-0095] 1925. q. GBP 164. Ed(s): Joanne Miller. Wiley-Blackwell Publishing, Inc., 111 River St, Hoboken, NJ 07030; info@wiley.com; http://onlinelibrary.wiley.com/. Illus., index, adv. Sample. Refereed. Vol. ends: Oct. Microform: PMC; PQC. Reprint: PSC. *Indexed:* A01, A22, ABIn, ABS&EES, B01, B02, BAS, BRI, C45, CBRI, E01, EconLit, FR, IBSS, JEL, P02, P61, RRTA, SSA. *Bk. rev.:* 5-10, 800-1,800 words, signed. *Aud.:* Ac.

Economic Geography publishes theoretical articles and empirical papers that make a contribution to theory. Topics include geopolitics, international finance, land use, agriculture, and urban and regional development, with an emphasis on recent approaches that involve gender, environmental issues, and industrial change. The editors wish to make *EG* a focus for debate on the current diversity of theories in economic geography. The editorship and authorship are largely American/British/Commonwealth. Important for libraries that support academic geography and economics departments or urban and regional planning programs.

2751. *Ethics, Policy & Environment: a journal of philosophy and geography.* Formerly (until Jan. 2011): *Ethics, Place and Environment*; Incorporates (1997-2005): *Philosophy amd Geography.* [ISSN: 2155-0085] 1998. 3x/yr. GBP 358 (print & online eds.). Ed(s): Nick Barker. Routledge, 4 Park Sq, Milton Park, Abingdon, OX14 4RN, United Kingdom; subscriptions@tandf.co.uk; http://www.tandfonline.com. Illus., index. Sample. Refereed. Vol. ends: Oct. Reprint: PSC. *Indexed:* A01, A22, E01, GardL, IBSS, P61, SSA. *Bk. rev.:* 4-8, 600-2,000 words, signed. *Aud.:* Ac.

This scholarly journal of geographical and environmental ethics is concerned with human behavior in social/cultural and physical/biological environments. Emphases are on ethical problems of geographical and environmental research, ethical implications of environmental legislation, and business ethics from a geographical/environmental perspective. Both research and review articles are published, together with sets of short communications on special topics, including debates, conference reports, commentaries on published papers, opinions, and book reviews. This publication absorbed the journal *Philosophy & Geography* in 2005. The editorial board and authors are largely American/British/Commonwealth, with some broader international representation. Important for academic libraries that support geography or philosophy departments, and for any library that supports an environmental studies program.

2752. *European Journal of Geography.* [ISSN: 1792-1341] 2010. 3x/yr. Ed(s): Kostis C. Koutsopoulos. European Association of Geographers (EUROGEO), http://www.eurogeography.eu. Refereed. *Aud.:* Ac, Sa.

The *European Journal of Geography*, produced by the European Association of Geographers, is a peer-reviewed, open-access journal that publishes theoretical and empirical articles that foster research, teaching, and application of geographical work with a European dimension. It aims at a unified approach to European geographical studies. Edited in Greece, with a Europe-wide editorial board.

2753. *Explorers Journal.* [ISSN: 0014-5025] 1921. q. Free to members; Non-members, USD 29.95. Ed(s): Angela M H Schuster. Explorers Club, 46 E 70th St, New York, NY 10021; president@explorers.org; http://www.explorers.org/. Illus., index, adv. Refereed. Vol. ends: Dec. Microform: PQC. *Indexed:* A22. *Bk. rev.:* 5-7, 100-400 words, signed. *Aud.:* Hs, Ga, Ac.

The Explorers Club, a learned society devoted to the advancement of exploration, promotes all areas of field research by publishing in its journal scholarly articles of high literary and aesthetic quality that communicate the excitement of exploration and field research. The articles are accessible to nonspecialist readers, and feature high-quality color illustrations. Also included are brief notes on new discoveries and news of exploration and explorers. Useful for academic and public libraries and for libraries of institutions that undertake overseas field research.

2754. *Gender, Place and Culture: a journal of feminist geography.* [ISSN: 0966-369X] 1994. 8x/yr. GBP 1159 (print & online eds.). Ed(s): Robyn Longhurst. Routledge, 4 Park Sq, Milton Park, Abingdon, OX14 4RN, United Kingdom; subscriptions@tandf.co.uk; http://www.tandfonline.com. Illus., index, adv. Sample. Refereed. Vol. ends: Dec. Reprint: PSC. *Indexed:* A01, A22, AmHI, C42, C45, E01, FemPer, IBSS, MASUSE, P02, P61, RILM, SSA. *Bk. rev.:* 5-12, 900-1,500 words, signed. *Aud.:* Ac.

Gender, Place and Culture provides a forum for research and debate concerning the connections of geography and gender issues. Topics include the spatial aspects of gender relations; oppression structures; gender construction and politics; and relations between gender and ethnicity, age, class, and other social categories. Articles are theoretical or empirical, but with implications for theory. The journal emphasizes the relevance of its subject area for feminism and women's studies. The "Viewpoint" feature offers commentaries on published papers, debates, and other short items. Editorship and authorship are largely American, British, and Commonwealth. Important for academic libraries that support geography departments or programs in women's or cultural studies.

Geo World. See Cartography, GIS, and Imagery section.

2755. *Geoforum.* [ISSN: 0016-7185] 1970. bi-m. EUR 1510. Ed(s): Gavin Bridge. Pergamon, The Blvd, Langford Ln, E Park, Kidlington, OX5 1GB, United Kingdom; JournalsCustomerServiceEMEA@elsevier.com; http://www.elsevier.com. Illus., adv. Sample. Refereed. Microform: PQC. *Indexed:* A22, BAS, C45, FR, IBSS, IndVet, P61, RILM, RRTA, SSA. *Aud.:* Ac, Sa.

Geoforum addresses the management of the physical and social human environment by focusing on the spatial organization of economic, environmental, political, and social systems on scales from the global to the local. It emphasizes international, interdisciplinary, and integrative approaches and applications to policy. Issues generally focus on special subjects. Appropriate for libraries that support programs in urban/regional planning and environmental programs, as well as in academic geography.

2756. *Geographical.* [ISSN: 0016-741X] 1935. m. GBP 54 domestic; GBP 69 in Europe; GBP 78 elsewhere. Ed(s): Geordie Torr. Geographical Magazine Limited, Rm 320, Q W, Great W Rd, London, TW8 0GP, United Kingdom. Illus., adv. Vol. ends: Dec. Microform: WMP. *Indexed:* A01, A22, AmHI, BAS, BRI, C37, H&TI, MASUSE, P02. *Bk. rev.:* 3-5, 150-300 words, signed. *Aud.:* Ga.

The official magazine of the Royal Geographical Society (RGS), *Geographical* publishes colorfully illustrated, popular but scholarly articles on field research in geography, anthropology, environmental studies, and natural history, and on subjects of geographical interest worldwide. Regular features include brief articles on climate change, photography, items from the RGS collection, interesting destinations, etc. The "I'm a Geographer" section offers interviews. The magazine carries news of the activities of the society. The editorship and authorship are largely from the United Kingdom. Important for academic and public libraries, and for libraries that support overseas field research.

2757. Geographical Analysis: an international journal of theoretical geography. [ISSN: 0016-7363] 1969. q. GBP 208. Ed(s): Daniel Griffith. Wiley-Blackwell Publishing, Inc., 111 River St, Hoboken, NJ 07030; info@wiley.com; http://onlinelibrary.wiley.com/. Illus., index. Sample. Refereed. Vol. ends: Jan/Oct. Microform: PQC. Reprint: PSC. *Indexed:* A01, A22, Agr, BAS, BRI, E01, FR. *Bk. rev.:* Occasional, 700-1,200 words, signed. *Aud.:* Ac.

Geographical Analysis publishes methodological articles and new applications of mathematical and statistical methods in geography, including spatial data analysis and spatial econometrics. The editorship is largely American and British; authorship is international. Appropriate for college and university libraries with programs in quantitative social science research and in geography.

2758. The Geographical Journal. Former titles (until 1893): *Royal Geographical Society and Monthly Record of Geography. Proceedings;* (until 1879): *Royal Geographical Society of London. Proceedings;* Royal Geographical Society of London. Proceedings incorporated (1832-1880): *Royal Geographical Society of London. Journal;* Royal Geographical Society of London. Proceedings incorporated (1874-1878): *Geographical Magazine;* Which was formerly (until 1874): *Ocean Highways;* (1870-1872): *Our Ocean Highways.* [ISSN: 0016-7398] 1857. q. GBP 203. Ed(s): Madeleine Hatfield, Klaus Dodds. Wiley-Blackwell Publishing Ltd., The Atrium, Southern Gate, Chichester, PO19 8SQ, United Kingdom; customer@wiley.com; http://www.wiley.com/. Illus., index, adv. Sample. Refereed. Vol. ends: Nov. Microform: PQC. Reprint: PSC. *Indexed:* A01, A06, A22, A47, AmHI, BAS, BRI, BrArAb, C45, CBRI, E01, FR, IBSS, M&GPA, NumL, P02, RRTA, S25. *Bk. rev.:* 1-8, 400-600 words, signed. *Aud.:* Ga, Ac.

This journal of the Royal Geographical Society publishes articles on all aspects of geography, with an emphasis on environment and development. Book reviews, society news, meeting reports, and a substantial section on news of the profession are included. There are frequent topic-focused special issues. Editorship is British; authors are increasingly international. Important for any library that supports geography or area studies departments.

2759. Geographical Review. Former titles (until 1916): *American Geographical Society. Bulletin;* (until 1901): *American Geographical Society of New York. Journal;* (until 1872): *American Geographical and Statistical Society. Journal.* [ISSN: 0016-7428] 1859. q. GBP 184. Ed(s): Craig E Colten. John Wiley & Sons, Inc., 111 River St, MS 4-02, Hoboken, NJ 07030; info@wiley.com; http://www.wiley.com/WileyCDA/. Illus., index, adv. Refereed. Circ: 3000. Vol. ends: Oct. Microform: PMC; PQC. Reprint: PSC. *Indexed:* A01, A06, A22, ABS&EES, AbAn, BAS, BRI, BrArAb, C45, CBRI, Chicano, E01, FR, IBSS, MASUSE, MLA-IB, P02. *Bk. rev.:* 14-16, 600-2,000 words, signed. *Aud.:* Ga, Ac.

A publication of the American Geographical Society, *Geographical Review* publishes research articles and numerous book reviews. Regular features include "Geographical Record," which comprises short, sharply focused review articles; and "Geographical Field Note," which comprises short, local case studies. This journal is designed to present the results of geographical research to the interested nonprofessional as well as to academics. Authorship is largely American and Canadian. Important for most academic and large public libraries.

2760. Geography. Formerly (until 1927): *Geographical Teacher.* [ISSN: 0016-7487] 1901. 3x/yr. Free to members; Non-members, GBP 84. Geographical Association, 160 Solly St, Sheffield, S1 4BF, United Kingdom; info@geography.org.uk; http://www.geography.org.uk. Illus., index, adv. Refereed. Vol. ends: Oct. *Indexed:* A01, A22, AmHI, BAS, BRI, BrArAb, EIP, FR, NumL, P02, S25. *Bk. rev.:* 10-15, 250-500 words, signed. *Aud.:* Ac.

This is the major journal of the Geographical Association, the society devoted to the teaching of geography in Britain at the college and secondary levels. Articles present research results with classroom applications, report on ongoing changes in the Earth's human and physical geography, and discuss environmental, policy, and quality issues in geographical education. "This Changing World" features short articles on contemporary issues. A new emphasis began in 2008 on fostering communication among geographical subdisciplines. Relatively new features include "Challenging Assumptions," which is devoted to debunking popular myths, and "Spotlight," which was planned to offer in-depth reviews of educational resources. The editorship and authorship are British. Useful in any library that supports a geography department or teacher education program.

2761. Geography and Natural Resources. [ISSN: 1875-3728] 2007. q. EUR 633 (print & online eds.). Ed(s): V M Plyusnin. M A I K Nauka - Interperiodica, Profsoyuznaya ul 90, Moscow, 117997, Russian Federation; compmg@maik.ru; http://www.maik.ru. Refereed. Reprint: PSC. *Indexed:* M&GPA, S25. *Aud.:* Ga, Ac.

Geography and Natural Resources emphasizes regional nature management and environmental protection; geographical forecasting; and modeling, mapping, and monitoring approaches. Coverage relates largely to Russia and Central Asia. The editorial board is largely from Russia, Ukraine, and Belarus. English translation is from the Russian version.

2762. GeoJournal: an international journal on human geography and environmental sciences. [ISSN: 0343-2521] 1977. bi-m. EUR 1855 (print & online eds.). Ed(s): Daniel Z Sui. Springer Netherlands, Van Godewijckstraat 30, Dordrecht, 3311 GX, Netherlands; http://www.springer.com. Illus., index, adv. Refereed. Vol. ends: No. 4. Microform: PQC. Reprint: PSC. *Indexed:* A22, ABIn, BAS, BRI, C45, E01, EngInd, FR, H&TI, IBSS, M&GPA, OceAb, RRTA, S25. *Bk. rev.:* 0-8, 800-1,000 words, signed. *Aud.:* Ac, Sa.

GeoJournal applies the methods and results of human geography and allied fields to problems of social/environmental change and technological development. Applications to forecasting and planning are emphasized. There are frequent special issues with guest editors and occasional review articles. The editors and authors are international. Important for libraries that support geographical/environmental research or management/planning with a spatial emphasis.

Imago Mundi. See Cartography, GIS, and Imagery section.

2763. Institute of British Geographers. Transactions. Former titles (until 1965): *Institute of British Geographers. Transactions and Papers;* (until 1946): *Institute of British Geographers. Transactions.* [ISSN: 0020-2754] 1935. q. GBP 431. Ed(s): Madeleine Hatfield, Alison Blunt. Wiley-Blackwell Publishing Ltd., The Atrium, Southern Gate, Chichester, PO19 8SQ, United Kingdom; customer@wiley.com; http://www.wiley.com/. Illus., index, adv. Sample. Refereed. Vol. ends: No. 4. Reprint: PSC. *Indexed:* A01, A22, BAS, BrArAb, C45, E01, FR, IBSS, NumL. *Bk. rev.:* 4-6, 900-1,200 words, signed. *Aud.:* Ac.

The major journal of the leading British research-oriented geographical society, now joined with the Royal Geographical Society, and one of the leading geographical journals. Editorials discuss current trends in geographical research. Although general in scope, this title publishes more human than physical geography. Important for any library that supports a geography department.

2764. International Journal of Health Geographics. [ISSN: 1476-072X] 2002. irreg. Free. Ed(s): Maged N Kamel Boulos. BioMed Central Ltd., 236 Gray's Inn Rd, London, WC1X 8HB, United Kingdom; info@biomedcentral.com; http://www.biomedcentral.com. Adv. Refereed. *Indexed:* A01, AbAn, C45, H24, IndVet, RRTA, RiskAb. *Aud.:* Ac, Sa.

The *International Journal of Health Geographics* is an open-access, peer-reviewed online journal on all aspects of geospatial information systems and science applications with an emphasis on interdisciplinary topics. Editorship is British, with an international editorial board.

2765. *Island Studies Journal.* [ISSN: 1715-2593] 2006. 2x/yr. Free. Ed(s): Godfrey Baldacchino. University of Prince Edward Island, Institute of Island Studies, 550 University Ave, Charlottetown, PE C1A 4P3, Canada; iis@upei.ca; http://www.upei.ca/~iis/about.htm. Sample. Refereed. *Indexed:* A01, P61, SSA. *Aud.:* Ac, Sa.

Emanating from the University of Prince Edward Island, *Island Studies Journal* is devoted to the interdisciplinary and comparative study of all social/cultural/economic aspects of islands. This journal emphasizes islands as parts of broader patterns, thus focusing on island–island and island–mainland linkages. It includes a strong interest in sustainability and developing sets of best practices. The editorial board is international, with Commonwealth/U.S. emphasis. The web site offers a blog on island-related news. Of interest to any library that supports a geography department or a program in island or coastal studies.

2766. *Journal of Geography.* Formed by the merger of (1897-1902): *The Journal of School Geography;* (1900-1902): *American Bureau of Geography. Bulletin.* [ISSN: 0022-1341] 1902. bi-m. USD 224 (print & online eds.). Ed(s): Catherine M Lockwood. Taylor & Francis Inc., 325 Chestnut St, Ste 800, Philadelphia, PA 19106; customerservice@taylorandfrancis.com; http://www.tandfonline.com. Illus., index, adv. Sample. Refereed. Vol. ends: Dec. Microform: PQC. Reprint: PSC. *Indexed:* A22, BAS, E01, ERIC, MLA-IB, RILM. *Bk. rev.:* 2-5, 500-600 words, signed. *Aud.:* Ac.

As the official journal of the National Council for Geographic Education, the *Journal of Geography* is concerned with geographical teaching at all levels. It offers articles on teaching methods and strategies, as well as educational policy, and contains teaching resources and news of the profession. The "Teacher's Notebook" section offers K–12 teaching strategies. Occasional special-theme sections are published. The editorship and authorship are largely American. Useful in any library that supports a geography department or teacher education program.

2767. *Journal of Historical Geography.* [ISSN: 0305-7488] 1975. q. EUR 712. Ed(s): Graeme Wynn, Felix Driver. Elsevier Ltd, 32 Jamestown Rd, Camden, London, NW1 7BY, United Kingdom; corporate.sales@elsevier.com; http://www.elsevier.com. Illus., index, adv. Sample. Refereed. Vol. ends: Oct. Reprint: PSC. *Indexed:* A01, A22, AbAn, BAS, BRI, BrArAb, CBRI, Chicano, E01, FR, NumL, P02. *Bk. rev.:* 15-30, 500-750 words, signed. *Aud.:* Ac.

Journal of Historical Geography publishes research papers, methodological contributions, commentaries on published papers, news of the specialty, and occasional review articles. Subjects treated include reconstruction of past human environments, instances of environmental change, geographical aspects of imagination and culture in the past, and historical methodology. Applications to historic preservation are discussed. The editorship and authorship are American, British, and Commonwealth. Important for academic libraries that support geography or history departments.

2768. *Journal of Latin American Geography.* Former titles (until 2002): *Conference of Latin Americanist Geographers. Yearbook;* (until 1984): *Conference of Latin Americanist Geographers. Proceedings;* (until 197?): *Conference of Latin Americanist Geographers. Publication Series.* [ISSN: 1545-2476] 1971. 3x/yr. USD 120. Ed(s): David J Robinson. University of Texas Press, Journals Division, PO Box 7819, Austin, TX 78713; journals@uts.cc.utexas.edu; http://www.utexas.edu/utpress/journals/journals.html. Illus., adv. *Indexed:* A01, A22, BRI, E01. *Bk. rev.:* 5-6, 1,000 words, signed. *Aud.:* Ac.

This journal publishes articles on all aspects of Latin American, but largely human, geography, with an emphasis on interdisciplinary approaches. The "Forum" section offers a variety of short articles, including preliminary reports of field or archival work, descriptions of field courses, and seminar or conference reports. There are occasional film reviews, as well as a regular section on web site reviews that was added in 2010. The awards section profiles recipients of several awards from the Conference of Latin Americanist Geographers.

Journal of Transport Geography. See Transportation section.

National Geographic. See General Interest section.

2769. *Physical Geography.* [ISSN: 0272-3646] 1980. bi-m. GBP 410 (print & online eds.). Ed(s): Carol Harden. Taylor & Francis, 4 Park Sq, Milton Park, Abingdon, OX14 4RN, United Kingdom; subscriptions@tandf.co.uk; http://www.tandfonline.com. Illus., index. Refereed. Vol. ends: Dec. Reprint: PSC. *Indexed:* A22, FR, M&GPA, S25. *Aud.:* Ac.

Physical Geography offers research papers on geomorphology, climatology, soil science, biogeography, and related subjects. Coverage is worldwide. Review articles, as well as methodological and discussion papers, are also published. The editors and editorial board are American/Canadian. Important for academic libraries that support geography, geology, or environmental studies departments.

2770. *Polar Geography.* Former titles (until 1995): *Polar Geography and Geology;* (until 1980): *Polar Geography.* [ISSN: 1088-937X] 1977. q. GBP 273 (print & online eds.). Ed(s): Mark Carper. Taylor & Francis Inc., 325 Chestnut St, Ste 800, Philadelphia, PA 19106; customerservice@taylorandfrancis.com; http://www.tandfonline.com. Illus. Sample. Reprint: PSC. *Indexed:* A22, FR, M&GPA, OceAb. *Bk. rev.:* Occasional, 400-600 words, signed. *Aud.:* Ac, Sa.

Polar Geography publishes scholarly research on physical and human geography of the polar regions, with some emphasis on the Russian Arctic. Particular attention is paid to contextualizing results of international research projects and to interactions of the polar regions with the global climate system. Long papers and substantial review articles are welcomed. Some translations of Russian articles and sources are published. The editorship is American, with an international editorial board; authorship is international.

2771. *Political Geography: an interdisciplinary journal for all students of political studies with an interest in the geographical and spatial aspects of politics.* Formerly (until 1992): *Political Geography Quarterly.* [ISSN: 0962-6298] 1982. bi-m. EUR 1589. Ed(s): John O'Loughlin. Pergamon, The Blvd, Langford Ln, E Park, Kidlington, OX5 1GB, United Kingdom; JournalsCustomerServiceEMEA@elsevier.com; http://www.elsevier.com. Illus., adv. Sample. Refereed. Microform: PQC. *Indexed:* A01, A22, BRI, FR, IBSS, P61, SSA. *Bk. rev.:* 3-6, 800-1,400 words, signed. *Aud.:* Ac.

This title includes traditional, quantitative, political, economic, poststructuralist, and other approaches. Contributions from nongeographers on spatial aspects of politics are encouraged. Debates on topics of wide interest are published, as are special issues. The "Book Forum" offers multiple reviews of a major new book. The editorship and authorship are largely British and American. Important for academic libraries that support geography, political science, or international relations departments.

2772. *Population, Space and Place (Online).* Formerly (until 2004): *International Journal of Population Geography (Online).* [ISSN: 1544-8452] 2004. bi-m. GBP 683. John Wiley & Sons Ltd., 9600 Garsington Rd, Oxford, OX4 2DQ, United Kingdom; customer@wiley.co.uk; http://www.wiley.com. Refereed. *Bk. rev.:* 3-4, 800-1,500 words, signed. *Aud.:* Ac.

Population, Space and Place publishes research and review articles, book reviews, and articles on current debates. Topics covered include migration, the geography of fertility/mortality, population modeling and forecasting, environmental issues, spatial aspects of labor, housing, minority groups, and historical demography. The planning and policy implications of population research are emphasized. Articles originating in allied disciplines are published. The editorship is largely British, with an international advisory board; the authorship is international. Important for any library that supports research in geography or population studies, or in social science generally.

2773. *The Professional Geographer.* [ISSN: 0033-0124] 1949. q. USD 2042 (print & online eds.). Ed(s): Robin Maier, Barney Warf. Routledge, 325 Chestnut St, Ste 800, Philadelphia, PA 19106; customerservice@taylorandfrancis.com; http://www.tandfonline.com. Illus., index. Sample. Refereed. Vol. ends: Nov. Microform: PQC. Reprint: PSC. *Indexed:* A01, A22, ABS&EES, AbAn, BAS, BRI, E01, FR, IBSS, M&GPA, P02. *Bk. rev.:* 4-7, 700-1,200 words, signed. *Aud.:* Ac.

A publication of the Association of American Geographers, *The Professional Geographer* publishes short research papers and essays on all aspects of geography. New approaches and alternative perspectives are emphasized. "Focus" is a section for collections of short articles on special topics. The "Commentary" section discusses issues of current interest. Important for all academic and for large public libraries.

2774. Progress in Human Geography. Supersedes in part (in 1977): *Progress in Geography.* [ISSN: 0309-1325] 1969. bi-m. USD 1176. Ed(s): Roger Lee. Sage Publications Ltd., 1 Oliver's Yard, 55 City Rd, London, EC1Y 1SP, United Kingdom; info@sagepub.co.uk; http://www.uk.sagepub.com. Illus., index. Sample. Refereed. Vol. ends: No. 4. Reprint: PSC. *Indexed:* A01, A22, ABIn, BAS, BrArAb, C45, E01, FR, IBSS, P02, P61, RRTA, S25, SSA. *Bk. rev.:* 9-21, 700-1,600 words, signed. *Aud.:* Ac.

This journal publishes review articles on trends and developments in human geography and related work in other disciplines. The articles cover the full international literature and discuss possible applications. Editorship and authorship are largely British, Commonwealth, and American, with an international advisory board. This journal is important for academic libraries that support social science research and geography departments, as well as for large public libraries. Sage also issues a similar title, *Progress in Physical Geography* [ISSN: 0309-1333], which is important for libraries that serve geography and geology departments and environmental studies programs.

2775. Singapore Journal of Tropical Geography. Former titles (until 1980): *Journal of Tropical Geography; (until 1958): Malayan Journal of Tropical Geography.* [ISSN: 0129-7619] 1953. 3x/yr. GBP 221. Ed(s): Tim Bunnell, David Higgitt. Wiley-Blackwell Publishing Asia, 155 Cremorne St, Richmond, VIC 3121, Australia; melbourne@wiley.com; http://www.wiley.com/. Illus., adv. Sample. Refereed. Reprint: PSC. *Indexed:* A01, A22, BAS, C45, E01, EIP, FR, IBSS, IndVet, MLA-IB, P61, RRTA, SSA. *Bk. rev.:* 4-6, 400-600 words, signed. *Aud.:* Ac.

Edited at the Department of Geography of the University of Singapore, this journal treats, largely, human geography and spatial aspects of development from an interdisciplinary perspective. Papers from scholars outside of geography are welcome. Authorship is international. Important for academic libraries that support geography departments or area studies programs with interests in the Old World tropics.

Surveying and Land Information Science. See Cartography, GIS, and Imagery section.

2776. Terrae Incognitae: the journal for the history of discoveries. [ISSN: 0082-2884] 1969. s-a. GBP 176 (print & online eds.). Ed(s): Marguerite Ragnow. Maney Publishing, Ste 1C, Joseph's Well, Hanover Walk, Leeds, LS3 1AB, United Kingdom; maney@maneypublishing.com; http://maneypublishing.com/. Illus., index. Refereed. Circ: 600. Reprint: PSC. *Indexed:* A22. *Bk. rev.:* 15-20, 300-1,000 words, signed. *Aud.:* Ac.

This scholarly journal covers the worldwide history of discovery and exploration. It publishes research articles, book reviews, and a bibliography of current literature. Its web site hosts a subject index for vols. 1–28 (1969–96). The editorship is American, Canadian, and British; authorship is international. Important for academic libraries that support geography and history departments.

2777. Tijdschrift voor Economische en Sociale Geografie. [ISSN: 0040-747X] 1910. 5x/yr. GBP 307. Ed(s): Frank van Oort, Bouke van Gorp. Wiley-Blackwell Publishing Ltd., The Atrium, Southern Gate, Chichester, PO19 8SQ, United Kingdom; customer@wiley.com; http://www.wiley.com/. Illus., index, adv. Sample. Refereed. Vol. ends: No. 5. Reprint: PSC. *Indexed:* A01, A22, C45, E01, FR, FS&TA, IBSS, MLA-IB, P61, RILM, RRTA, RiskAb, SSA. *Bk. rev.:* 2-5, 1,000-1,500 words, signed. *Aud.:* Ac.

Published under the auspices of the Royal Dutch Geographical Society, *TESG* offers scholarly articles and subject-focused issues on human geography, emphasizing new approaches that emanate from both Continental and Anglo-American traditions. Special sections discuss Dutch and European geographical

trends. Each issue carries maps that illustrate Netherlands human geography. The editorship is largely Dutch; authorship is international. Important for academic libraries that support geography departments or area studies programs with interests in Western Europe.

■ GERIATRICS AND GERONTOLOGICAL STUDIES

Patricia L. Markley, Associate Librarian at Siena College, Loudonville, NY 12211-1462; markley@siena.edu

Introduction

Geriatrics is the branch of medicine that relates to the health of older people and medical changes or disorders that may result through the aging process. Gerontology is the study of aging and older people. As fields of study, geriatrics and gerontology are growing—in no small part because of the rapidly growing elderly population. Geriatrics and gerontology are almost by definition interdisciplinary in nature, so it is not surprising that many specialized journals dealing with aging have arisen and that many different, subject-specific databases index these journals.

Although *Abstracts in Social Gerontology* and *AgeLine* are the major indexes specifically for geriatrics and gerontology, most other major indexes will touch on aging. Depending on the focus of research, the major indexes in psychology, sociology, social work, medicine, education, women's studies, and others will be useful. The journals listed in this section constitute only a sample of the many quality publications available in geriatrics and gerontology. They have been chosen to represent the various areas of specialization within the field. Most journals listed here are valuable primarily to students, educators, scholars, and practitioners in geriatrics and gerontology, but several are of interest to the general public.

Basic Periodicals

A A R P: the magazine, Ageing International, Generations, The Gerontologist, International Journal of Aging & Human Development, Journal of the American Geriatrics Society, Journals of Gerontology: Series A and B.

Basic Abstracts and Indexes

Abstracts in Social Gerontology, AgeLine.

2778. A A R P the Magazine. Formed by the merger of (2001-2003): *My Generation;* (2002-2003): *A A R P Modern Maturity;* Which was formerly (until Mar.2002): *Modern Maturity;* Which incorporated (in 1960): *We;* (1955-1960): *Journal of Lifetime Living;* Which was formerly (1935-1955): *Journal of Living;* (1977-1986): *Dynamic Years;* Which was formerly (1965-1977): *Dynamic Maturity.* [ISSN: 1541-9894] 2003. bi-m. Free to members. American Association of Retired Persons (A A R P), 601 E St, NW, Washington, DC 20049; ageline@aarp.org; http://www.aarp.org. Adv. Sample. *Indexed:* AgeL, BRI, P02. *Aud.:* Ga.

This lifestyle magazine is included with membership in the American Association of Retired Persons (AARP). It covers a wide range of topics from the areas of health, entertainment, personal finance, government and law, and consumer affairs, among others. Regular short columns and sections include "What's New," "The Mail," "AARP & You," "Health," "Family & Friends," "Just for Fun," "Money," "Between Us," and "Big 5-Oh." Each issue has several longer feature articles as well, with at least one profiling a famous person over 50. Some recent feature articles are "Life's a Kick When You're Diane Keaton," "Age-Proof Your Brain," "Sharon Stone," and "Best Movies for Grownups." Recommended for public libraries.

2779. Activities, Adaptation & Aging: the journal of activities management. [ISSN: 0192-4788] 1980. q. GBP 708 (print & online eds.). Ed(s): Linnea Couture. Routledge, 325 Chestnut St, Ste 800, Philadelphia, PA 19106; customerservice@taylorandfrancis.com; http://www.tandfonline.com. Illus. Sample. Refereed. Microform: PQC. Reprint: PSC. *Indexed:* A01, A22, ASSIA, AgeL, C45, E01, MCR, P61, PsycInfo, RILM, RRTA, SD, SSA, SWR&A. *Bk. rev.:* 5-7, 1-4 pages, signed. *Aud.:* Ac, Sa.

An international journal "for activity directors and all health care professionals concerned with the enhancement of the lives of the aged." Its content includes formal and informal research on a wide variety of topics related to the therapeutic value of activities for the older adult: "such important topics as evidence-based practice, evaluation, assessment of psychosocial history, culture and its influence on meaningful activity, activities and caregivers, volunteerism, and successful aging" in institutional and community settings. Included are research findings, case studies, and program evaluations, plus book and media reviews, announcements, and news. This journal presents information and methodologies from the disciplines of physical therapy, art and music therapy, and recreational and occupational therapy; social work; nursing; psychiatry; and medicine. Recent articles are "Contribution of Relaxation on the Subjective Well-Being of Older Adults," "Sudoku and Working Memory Performance for Older Adults," "Interdisciplinary Methods of Treatment of Depression in Older Adults: A Primer for Practitioners," "Deconditioning and Fibromyalgia: A Pilot Study," and "Physical Activity of Older People: An Investigation of a Retirement Center in Olomouc, Czech Republic." Appropriate for relevant special libraries and academic libraries that support gerontological programs.

2780. Age and Ageing. [ISSN: 0002-0729] 1972. bi-m. EUR 501. Ed(s): Roger Francis. Oxford University Press, Great Clarendon St, Oxford, OX2 6DP, United Kingdom; enquiry@oup.co.uk; http://www.oxfordjournals.org/. Illus., adv. Sample. Refereed. Reprint: PSC. Indexed: A01, A22, ASSIA, AgeL, BRI, C45, E01, ErgAb, ExcerpMed, H24, P02, P61, RRTA, RiskAb, SSA. Bk. rev.: 2-3, 100-400 words, signed. Aud.: Ac, Sa.

Associated with the British Geriatrics Society, this international, peer-reviewed journal "includes research on [aging] and clinical, epidemiological[,] and psychological aspects of later life." It is written for clinicians and other health professionals. Original research articles and commissioned reviews are presented in the following sections: "Research Papers" and "Short Reports" (previously "Research Letters") to report original findings; "Reviews" and "Systematic Reviews"; and "Case Reports" and "Clinical Reminders." There are also "Conference Reports," "Editorials," "Commentaries," "Website and Book Reviews," and "Letters to the Editor." Examples of a few recent articles: "Measures of Everyday Competence in Older Adults with Cognitive Impairment: A Systematic Review," "Detection of Falls Using Accelerometers and Mobile Phone Technology" (a research paper), "Longitudinal Changes in Serum Lipids in Older People: The Turku Elderly Study 1991-2006" (a research letter), "Recurrent Strokes Caused by a Malpositioned Pacemaker Lead" (a case report), and "Sexuality in Older Age: Essential Considerations for Healthcare Professionals" (a review). Appropriate for medical libraries and any other library that maintains a geriatric medicine collection.

2781. Ageing and Society. [ISSN: 0144-686X] 1981. 8x/yr. GBP 376. Ed(s): Christina R Victor. Cambridge University Press, The Edinburgh Bldg, Shaftesbury Rd, Cambridge, CB2 8RU, United Kingdom; information@cambridge.org; http://www.cambridge.org/uk. Illus., index, adv. Sample. Refereed. Microform: PQC. Reprint: PSC. Indexed: A01, A22, AgeL, BRI, C45, E01, IBSS, P02, P61, PsycInfo, RRTA, SSA. Bk. rev.: 4-6, 1-4 pages, signed. Aud.: Ac.

Ranked 15th by Thomson Reuters for January–February 2011, for top journals in the field of gerontology. Associated with the Centre for Policy on Aging and the British Society of Gerontology, this international, peer-reviewed journal has an interdisciplinary focus, and thus it "has readers from many academic social science disciplines, and from clinical medicine and the humanities." Emphasis is placed on "the understanding of human ageing and the circumstances of older people in their social and cultural contexts." The journal publishes original research articles, book reviews, review articles, and guest editorials, as well as special issues. Examples of two recent special issues are "Wellbeing, Independence and Mobility" and "Rethinking Theoretical and Methodological Issues in Intergenerational Family Relations Research." A few examples of recent articles are "Understanding Ageing in Sub-Saharan Africa: Exploring the Contribution of Religious and Secular Social Involvement to Life Satisfaction" (original research), "The Challenges of Conducting Focus-group Research among Asian Older Adults" (review article), and "Elder Abuse in Long-term Care Residences and the Risk Indicators" (original research). Appropriate for academic libraries that support programs in sociology, global studies, or gerontology.

2782. Ageing International: information bulletin of the International Federation on Ageing. [ISSN: 0163-5158] 1973. q. EUR 345 (print & online eds.). Ed(s): S Levkoff. Springer New York LLC, 233 Spring St, New York, NY 10013; service-ny@springer.com; http://www.springer.com/. Illus., index, adv. Sample. Vol. ends: Winter. Reprint: PSC. Indexed: A01, A22, ABIn, AgeL, BRI, E01, ErgAb, P61, SSA. Aud.: Ga, Ac, Sa.

This peer-reviewed journal is devoted to improving the lives of older people regionally and globally. It specifically aims to reduce "the implementation gap between good science and effective service, between evidence-based protocol and culturally suitable programs, and between unique innovative solutions and generalizable policies." The range of subject areas is wide: housing, finances, health care, employment and retirement, technology, long-term care, death and dying, culture and aging, and elder abuse and neglect, among other topics. There are occasional special, thematic issues, the most recent being "Public Health, Healthcare Policy, Financing & Economics." The journal publishes long and short articles that report on original research, program reviews, review articles, interviews, and commentaries. Some recent articles are "University Students' Views and Practices of Ageism," "Quality Measures for the U.S. Hospice System," and "Ageing in Africa: Past Experiences and Strategic Directions." Appropriate for large public libraries, special libraries that focus on public and health policy, and academic libraries that support gerontology and public-health programs.

2783. Ageing Research Reviews. [ISSN: 1568-1637] 2001. 4x/yr. EUR 904. Ed(s): M P Mattson. Elsevier Ireland Ltd, Elsevier House, Brookvale Plaza, E. Park, Shannon, Ireland. Indexed: A01, A22, AbAn, ExcerpMed. Aud.: Ac, Sa.

Given the top impact ranking by Thomson Reuters for January–February 2011, in the field of gerontology, this journal is written for scientists and scholars interested in the biology of aging. The journal seeks to provide "critical reviews and viewpoints on emerging findings on mechanisms of ageing and age-related disease." Articles focus on the cellular and molecular mechanism of the aging process and age-related diseases or application of research in these areas in medicine. There are special issues, the most recent being "Exercise and Ageing." The number of articles per issues varies, but is usually about 12. A few recent articles are: "The Aging Musculoskeletal System and Obesity-related Considerations with Exercise," "AMP-activated Protein Kinase (AMPK) Controls the Aging Process via an Integrated Signaling Network," "Birds and Longevity: Does Flight Driven Aerobicity Provide an Oxidative Sink?," and "Cell Delivery in Cardiac Regenerative Therapy." Appropriate for medical and academic libraries.

2784. The Aging Male. [ISSN: 1368-5538] 1998. q. GBP 399 (print & online eds.). Ed(s): Bruno Lunenfeld. Informa Healthcare, Guardian House, 119 Farringdon Rd, London, EC1R 3DA, United Kingdom; healthcare@informa.com; http://informahealthcare.com/. Illus., adv. Sample. Refereed. Reprint: PSC. Indexed: A01, A22, AgeL, E01, ExcerpMed, P02, SD. Aud.: Ac, Sa.

Sponsored by the International Society for the Study of the Aging Male, this multidisciplinary, peer-reviewed journal covers a broad range of topics related to older men's health, but tends heavily toward biomedical topics. Regular features include editorials, original research articles, review articles, and "other appropriate educational materials," as well as conference paper and poster session abstracts. Titles of a few recent articles: "Sopranos But Not Tenors Live Longer," "Significant Association between Serum Dihydrotestosterone Level and Prostate Volume Among Taiwanese Men Aged 40-79 Years," "Mild Thyroid Hormone Excess is Associated with a Decreased Physical Function in Elderly Men," and "Telomere Length and Type 2 Diabetes in Men: A Premature Aging Syndrome." Appropriate for research and medical libraries, as well as practicing health-care professionals.

2785. American Geriatrics Society. Journal. Supersedes (in 1952): American Therapeutic Society. Transactions. [ISSN: 0002-8614] 1953. m. GBP 745. Ed(s): Flory Ferns-James, Dr. Thomas T Yoshikawa. Wiley-Blackwell Publishing, Inc., 111 River St, Hoboken, NJ 07030; info@wiley.com; http://www.wiley.com/. Illus., index, adv. Sample. Refereed. Vol. ends: Dec. Microform: PQC. Reprint: PSC. Indexed: A01, A22, AgeL, BRI, C45, E01, ExcerpMed, H24, P02, PsycInfo, RRTA, RiskAb, SWR&A. Aud.: Ac, Sa.

Ranked second by Thomson Reuters for January–February 2011, in the field of gerontology. This international, peer-reviewed journal from the American Geriatrics Society is intended primarily for medical practitioners. Its primary goal is "to publish articles that are relevant in the broadest terms to the clinical care of older persons." It addresses a wide range of issues related to biomedical, psychological, and social aspects of aging, in addition to diseases and disorders commonly encountered. The majority of articles included are reports on original clinical investigations ("Clinical Investigations," "Brief Reports," and "Brief Methodological Reports"). But also, every issue contains other types of articles, such as reviews, editorials, letters to the editor, and descriptive reports on service, programs, and models of geriatric care. Beginning in 2012, three new sections were to appear: "Clinical Management of the Geriatric Patient" (evidence-based papers), "Updates on Aging" (short reviews), and "Controversies in Geriatrics and Gerontology" (opposing viewpoints). Supplements appear occasionally, usually devoted to papers from conferences or "from projects or initiatives with older adults." Some recent articles: "Effect of Patient Perceptions on Dementia Screening in Primary Care," "Nocturnal Hypokinesia and Sleep Quality in Parkinson's Disease," "Quality of Care Provided in a Special Needs Plan Using a Nurse Care Manager Model," and "Fever of Unknown Origin in an Elderly Adult with Lipid Overload Syndrome." This is a core journal for geriatrics and gerontology and, therefore, appropriate for medical libraries and academic libraries that support pre-med, gerontology, sociology, or psychology programs.

2786. *American Journal of Geriatric Psychiatry.* [ISSN: 1064-7481] 1993. m. USD 1468. Ed(s): Dilip V. Jeste. Elsevier Inc., 360 Park Ave S, New York, NY 10010; usinfo-f@elsevier.com; http://www.elsevier.com. Illus., index, adv. Sample. Refereed. Microform: PQC. *Indexed:* A22, AbAn, AgeL, ExcerpMed, PsycInfo. *Bk. rev.:* Number and length vary. *Aud.:* Ac, Sa.

Ranked fifth by Thomson Reuters for January–February 2011, in the field of gerontology. From the American Association for Geriatric Psychiatry, this peer-reviewed journal covers topics such as "the diagnosis and classification of the psychiatric disorders of later life, epidemiological and biological correlates of mental health of older adults, psychopharmacology, and other somatic treatments." Each issue has about ten articles, primarily "Regular Research Articles" and "Brief Reports" (reporting on the results of original research studies), "Clinical Review Articles" ("evidence-based, state-of-the-art overviews"), and "Special Articles" ("usually overview articles that synthesize existing knowledge on a topic"). Examples of recent articles are "Psychological Impact of the Tsunami on Elderly Survivors" (a "Regular Research Article"), "The Riddle of Psychiatric Disorders in Parkinson Disease: From Phenomenology to Treatment" (an "Editorial"), "Demographic, Clinical, and Functional Factors Associated with Antidepressant Use in the Home Healthcare Elderly" (a "Brief Report"), and "Pharmacologic Treatment of Apathy in Dementia" (a "Special Article"). Appropriate for academic and medical libraries.

2787. *Canadian Journal on Aging.* [ISSN: 0714-9808] 1982. q. GBP 128. Ed(s): Margaret J Penning. Cambridge University Press, The Edinburgh Bldg, Shaftesbury Rd, Cambridge, CB2 8RU, United Kingdom; journals@cambridge.org; http://journals.cambridge.org. Illus., adv. Sample. Refereed. Vol. ends: Winter. *Indexed:* A22, ABIn, AgeL, BRI, C37, CBCARef, E01, ERIC, IBSS, P61, PsycInfo, RiskAb, SSA, SWR&A. *Bk. rev.:* Number and length vary. *Aud.:* Ac, Sa.

Ranked 20th by Thomson Reuters for January–February 2011, in the field of gerontology. This international, peer-reviewed journal is associated with the Canadian Association on Gerontology. It presents articles on "aging concerned with biology, educational gerontology, health sciences, psychology, social sciences, and social policy and practice." The journal is multidisciplinary in approach, so authors are encouraged to highlight in their articles the value of the work for professionals in other fields. Emphasis is on Canadian research, but non-Canadian authors are included, too. Regular features include "Editorials," "Articles," "Research Notes" (long and short reports on original research or theoretical papers), "Policy and Practice Notes" (clinical and policy-related articles), and "Book Reviews." Most papers are in English, with one or two each issue in French. Some recent articles are "Unequal Social Engagement for Older Adults: Constraints on Choice," "Rural Long-term Care Work, Gender, and

Restructuring," "Social Commitment Robots and Dementia," and "Income Replacement in Retirement: Longitudinal Evidence from Income Tax Records." Appropriate for academic libraries for which an emphasis on Canada would be of interest.

2788. *Clinical Gerontologist: the journal of aging and mental health.* Former titles: *Journal of Aged Care;* (until 1981): *Aged Care and Services Review.* [ISSN: 0731-7115] 1977. 5x/yr. GBP 921 (print & online eds.). Ed(s): Larry W Thompsom, Dolores E Gallagher-Thompson. Routledge, 325 Chestnut St, Ste 800, Philadelphia, PA 19106; customerservice@taylorandfrancis.com; http://www.tandfonline.com. Illus., index, adv. Sample. Refereed. Vol. ends: Summer. Microform: PQC. Reprint: PSC. *Indexed:* A01, A22, ASSIA, AbAn, AgeL, E01, FR, MCR, P61, PsycInfo, SSA, SWR&A. *Bk. rev.:* Number and length vary. *Aud.:* Ac, Sa.

This peer-reviewed journal is associated with psychologists in long-term care and written for "psychologists, physicians, nurses, social workers, and counselors (family, pastoral, and vocational) who address the issues commonly found in later life." The journal's focus is on providing practitioners with current information that is applicable in daily assessment and management of mental disorders in the elderly. It consists of articles that report on original empirically-based research, literature reviews, and case studies on a broad range of topics related to the mental health of older people. Typical topics are diversity and aging, spirituality, depression, education and the aged, changing roles and older people, and caregiving. Additional regular features are "Clinical Comments" (brief clinical reports from practitioners), "New and Emerging Professionals" (articles by students, postdoctoral fellows, or new faculty), and reviews of books, media, or software. Titles of recent articles are "Marital Satisfaction and Personality Traits in Long-Term Marriages: An Exploratory Study" (a regular article), "Behavioral Activation with Bereaved Older Adults: Unique Clinical Considerations" (a "Clinical Comment"), "Late-Onset Schizophrenia: A Review for Clinicians" (a review article), and "A Preliminary Comparison of Three Cognitive Screening Instruments in Long Term Care: The MMSE, SLUMS, and MoCA" (a "New and Emerging Professionals" article). Appropriate for medical and academic libraries.

2789. *Educational Gerontology: an international journal.* [ISSN: 0360-1277] 1976. m. GBP 629 (print & online eds.). Ed(s): Nieli Langer. Routledge, 325 Chestnut St, Ste 800, Philadelphia, PA 19106; customerservice@taylorandfrancis.com; http://www.tandfonline.com. Sample. Refereed. Microform: PQC. Reprint: PSC. *Indexed:* A01, A22, AgeL, E01, ERIC, MLA-IB, PsycInfo. *Bk. rev.:* 0-1, 1-2 pages, signed. *Aud.:* Ac, Sa.

Written for "gerontologists, adult educators, behavioral and social scientists, and geriatricians," this international, peer-reviewed journal covers topics in "gerontology, adult education, and the social and behavioral sciences." Specifically, it focuses not on the education of professionals who will work with older people, but on education and the learning process of older people, broadly understood. It publishes reports on current original research, review articles, and reviews of books and other media. Occasional special issues appear, such as "Sustainable Senior Living" and "Mentoring in Clinical Geropsychology." Several recent articles are "Age Stereotypes about Emotional Resilience at Work," "Correlates of Geriatric Loneliness in Philippine Nursing Homes: A Multiple Regression Model," "Students Connecting with the Elderly: Validation as a Tool," and "Virtual Models of Long-term Care." Appropriate for academic libraries that support education or gerontology programs.

The Elder Law Journal. See Law section.

2790. *Generations (San Francisco).* [ISSN: 0738-7806] 1976. q. USD 110. American Society on Aging, 71 Stevenson St, Ste 1450, San Francisco, CA 94105; info@asaging.org; http://www.asaging.org. Illus., adv. Sample. Refereed. Microform: PQC. Reprint: PSC. *Indexed:* A01, A22, AgeL, BRI, CBRI, MLA-IB, P02, P61, SSA, SWR&A. *Aud.:* Ga, Ac.

This journal from the American Society on Aging is written for "practitioners and researchers in the field of aging" and is devoted to "in-depth research, practical applications, and valuable insights" in subject areas related to aging and public health. Each issue has a prominent scholar as guest editor and focuses on a particular theme, for example: "Medications and Aging" and

"Ritual in Later Life: Its Role, Significance, and Power." Most articles are literature reviews, overviews of a particular topic, or argumentative papers, not reports on original research. Some recent articles are "How Does Cash and Counseling Affect the Growth of Participant-directed Services?," "Reflections of a Disability Activist," "New Symptoms in Older Adults: Disease or Drug?," and "Charting Late-Life Affective Disorders." Recommended for academic libraries and public or special libraries that serve professionals, policy makers, or members of the public concerned with aging and public health.

2791. *The Gerontologist: a journal of the Gerontological Society of America.* [ISSN: 0016-9013] 1961. bi-m. EUR 369. Ed(s): Rachel Pruchno. Oxford University Press, 2001 Evans Rd, Cary, NC 27513; jnlorders@oup-usa.org; http://www.us.oup.com. Illus., index, adv. Sample. Refereed. Microform: PQC. Reprint: PSC. *Indexed:* A01, A22, AgeL, BRI, Chicano, ERIC, MLA-IB, P02, P61, PsycInfo, SSA, SWR&A. *Bk. rev.:* 2, 2-6 pages, signed. *Aud.:* Ac, Sa.

Ranked sixth by Thomson Reuters for January–February 2011, in the field of gerontology. From the Gerontological Society of America, this peer-reviewed journal presents a "multidisciplinary perspective on human aging through the publication of research and analysis in gerontology, including social policy, program development[,] and service delivery." There are articles from a wide range of disciplines, such as social sciences, biomedical fields, the humanities, economics, education, and the law. Each issue contains 10–14 articles of several types: "Research Articles" and "Brief Reports" (on original research), "The Forum" (review or viewpoint articles on a hot topic), "Practice Concepts" (on innovative practices or programs), "Policy Studies," "Letters to the Editor," "Book Reviews," and "Guest Editorials." It does occasionally have special thematic issues or supplements; for example, "The Science of Recruitment and Retention Among Ethnically Diverse Older Adults." Examples of recent articles are "Aging Well and the Environment: Toward an Integrative Model and Research Agenda," "Adapting Stanford's Chronic Disease Self-Management Program to Hawaii's Multicultural Population," and "Primary Care Clinician Expectations Regarding Aging." A core journal for any library that covers geriatrics or gerontology.

2792. *Gerontology: international journal of experimental, clinical, behavioral, regenerative and technical gerontology.* Formed by the 1976 merger of: *Gerontologia; Gerontologia Clinica.* [ISSN: 0304-324X] 1957. bi-m. CHF 1829.50. Ed(s): George Wick. S. Karger AG, Allschwilerstr 10, Basel, 4055, Switzerland; karger@karger.ch; http://www.karger.ch. Index, adv. Refereed. Circ: 900. *Indexed:* A01, A22, AbAn, C45, E01, ExcerpMed, H24, IndVet, PsycInfo, RRTA, RiskAb. *Bk. rev.:* 0-1, 1 page. *Aud.:* Ac, Sa.

Ranked ninth by Thomson Reuters for January–February 2011, in the field of gerontology. From the International Association of Gerontology and Geriatrics, this peer-reviewed journal draws "topical contributions from diverse medical, biological, behavioural and technological disciplines" regarding aging in humans and animals. The main body of the journal is divided into several sections: usually "Clinical Section," "Experimental Section," "Behavioural Science Section," and "Regenerative and Technological Section." Within those sections are original papers, short review papers, commentary, opposing viewpoints papers, and "Short Communication" (brief reports on research). Most articles are reports on original studies, secondary data analyses, or literature reviews. Other regular features are editorials, letters to the editor, book reviews, "Images in Gerontology," and "Announcements." Titles of recent articles are "Effects of a Salsa Dance Training on Balance and Strength Performance in Older Adults: A Mini-Review," "Prostate-specific Antigen Screening for Prostate Cancer in Older Men in the United States of America" (debate), "Inducible Nitric Oxide Synthase-Activated Mitochondrial Apoptotic Pathway in Hypoxic and Aged Rat Hearts" (original paper), and "The Grandmother Effect" (viewpoint). Suitable for research and medical libraries.

2793. *Gerontology & Geriatrics Education: the official journal of the Association for Gerontology in Higher Education.* [ISSN: 0270-1960] 1980. q. GBP 673 (print & online eds.). Ed(s): Judith L Howe, Kelly Niles-Yokum. Routledge, 325 Chestnut St, Ste 800, Philadelphia, PA 19106; customerservice@taylorandfrancis.com; http://www.tandfonline.com. Illus., index. Sample. Refereed. Reprint: PSC. *Indexed:* A01, A22, AbAn, AgeL, E01, ERIC, MLA-IB, P61, PsycInfo, SSA. *Aud.:* Ac, Sa.

This peer-reviewed journal is from the Association for Gerontology in Higher Education, the educational unit of the Gerontological Society of America. Specifically, it is concerned with the education of gerontologists and other professionals who will work with older people. Its intended audience consists of students, educators, practicing professionals in direct-care and administration, and policy-makers. Included are review articles, articles reporting on original research, and reports on programs, through which it fosters "the exchange of information related to research, curriculum development, course and program evaluation, classroom and practice innovation, and other topics with educational implications for gerontology and geriatrics." The journal occasionally releases a special issue, such as "Accreditation in Gerontology: Opportunities & Challenges." Some recent articles are "Quality Assurance in Gerontological and Geriatric Training Programs: The European Case," "The Great Plains IDEA Gerontology Program: An Online, Interinstitutional Graduate Degree," "Health Care Workforce Development in Rural America: When Geriatric Expertise is 100 Miles Away," and "A Community-based Approach for Integrating Geriatrics and Gerontology into Undergraduate Medical Education." Valuable for research and academic libraries that support academic programs in education, social work, or gerontology.

2794. *International Journal of Ageing and Later Life.* [ISSN: 1652-8670] 2006. s-a. Free. Ed(s): Lars Anderson. Linkoeping University Electronic Press, Linkoeping Universitet, Linkoeping, 58183, Sweden; ep@ep.liu.se; http://www.ep.liu.se. Refereed. *Indexed:* P61, SSA. *Bk. rev.:* Number and length vary. *Aud.:* Ac, Sa.

Ranked 18th by Thomson Reuters for January–February 2011, in the field of gerontology. This open-access electronic journal is published with the support of the Swedish Council for Working Life and Social Research. Articles go through a double-blind review process before publication. The journal is intended for an international audience and is focused on "social and cultural aspects of ageing and later life development." It publishes primarily lengthy articles that "aim at advancing the theoretical and conceptual debate on research," but also prints empirically or methodologically based articles, editorials, and book reviews. There are usually three or four articles and one to three book reviews per issue. A few recent article titles are: "The Critical Use of Narrative and Literature in Gerontology," "How Do Unfamiliar Environments Convey Meaning to Older People? Urban Dimensions of Placelessness and Attachment," "A Critical Assessment of Generational Accounting and its Contribution to the Generational Equity Debate," and "Ethno-cultural Diversity in Home Care Work in Canada: Issues Confronted, Strategies Employed." Suitable for for relevant special libraries and academic libraries.

2795. *The International Journal of Aging & Human Development: a journal of psychosocial gerontology.* Formerly (until 1973): *Aging and Human Development.* [ISSN: 0091-4150] 1970. 8x/yr. USD 599 (print & online eds.) Individuals, USD 166 (print & online eds.). Ed(s): Bert Hayslip, Jr. Baywood Publishing Co., Inc., 26 Austin Ave, PO Box 337, Amityville, NY 11701; info@baywood.com; http://www.baywood.com. Illus., index. Sample. Refereed. *Indexed:* A01, A22, AbAn, AgeL, BAS, BRI, Chicano, ERIC, FR, MLA-IB, P02, P61, PsycInfo, RILM, SSA, SWR&A. *Aud.:* Ac, Sa.

This peer-reviewed journal emphasizes "psychological and social studies of aging and the aged"; however, its scope is quite broad. The journal also publishes "research that introduces observations from other fields that illuminate the 'human' side of gerontology, or utilizes gerontological observations to illuminate in other fields." Each issue contains four to six articles, mostly original research, but occasionally secondary analysis or review articles. Examples of recent articles are "Caregivers' Retirement Congruency: A Case for Caregiver Support," "Validation of Self-Image of Aging Scale for Chinese Elders," "The Association between Routinization and Cognitive Resources in Later Life," and "Aging Well Socially Through Engagement with Life: Adapting Rowe and Kahn's Model of Successful Aging to Chinese Cultural Context." This journal is a core journal for academic libraries that support programs in gerontology, psychology, social work, or sociology.

Johns Hopkins Medical Letter Health after 50. See Health and Fitness section.

2796. *Journal of Aging and Health: an interdisciplinary research forum.* [ISSN: 0898-2643] 1989. 8x/yr. USD 871. Ed(s): Kyriakos S Markides. Sage Publications, Inc., 2455 Teller Rd, Thousand Oaks, CA 91320; info@sagepub.com; http://www.sagepub.com. Illus., index, adv. Refereed. Reprint: PSC. *Indexed:* A01, A22, AbAn, AgeL, C45, E01, H24, P02, P61, PsycInfo, RRTA, SSA. *Aud.:* Ac, Sa.

Ranked 12th by Thomson Reuters for January–February 2011, in the field of gerontology. This international, peer-reviewed journal covers a wide range of topics related to health and aging—for example, diet and nutrition, long-term care, mental health, disease prevention, and health-care services. These topics are examined from the perspective of various disciplines: psychology, medicine, sociology, demography, and social work, to name just a few. Most of the eight or nine articles per issue report on original research (based on newly conducted research or secondary data analysis), but occasional review or methodological articles appear, as well. Recent articles include "Trajectories of Social Engagement and Mortality in Late Life," "The Influence of Community and Built Environment on Physical Activity," and "Body Mass Index and Long-Term Mortality in an Elderly Mediterranean Population." This journal provides broad coverage of gerontology and is appropriate for all academic libraries.

2797. *Journal of Aging and Physical Activity.* [ISSN: 1063-8652] 1993. q. USD 502 (print & online eds.). Ed(s): Julia S Glahn, Jennifer L Etnier. Human Kinetics, Inc., 1607 N Market St, Champaign, IL 61820; info@hkusa.com; http://www.humankinetics.com. Illus., adv. Sample. Refereed. Vol. ends: Oct. Reprint: PSC. *Indexed:* A22, AbAn, AgeL, ErgAb, PsycInfo, SD. *Aud.:* Ac, Sa.

Ranked 14th by Thomson Reuters for January–February 2011, in the field of gerontology. From the International Society for Aging and Physical Activity, this peer-reviewed journal focuses on the relationship between physical activity and the well-being of older people. The focus of the journal is on "articles that can contribute to an understanding of (a) the impact of physical activity on physiological, psychological, and social aspects of older adults and (b) the effect of advancing age or the aging process on physical activity among older adults." The journal has a multidisciplinary approach, presenting "articles from the biological, behavioral, and social sciences, as well as from fields such as medicine, clinical psychology, physical and recreational therapy, health, physical education, and recreation." The vast majority of articles are reports on original research, but rarely a scholarly review, case study, or letter to the editor appears. There are five to eight articles per issue. Recent articles include "What Sustains Long-Term Adherence to Structured Physical Activity After a Cardiac Event?," "Comparison of the IPAQ-Short Form and Accelerometry Predictions of Physical Activity in Older Adults," "Does Yoga Engender Fitness in Older Adults? A Critical Review," and "A Case Study on the Perception of Aging and Participation in Physical Activities of Older Chinese Immigrants in Australia." Appropriate for research libraries, medical libraries, and academic libraries that support programs in physical therapy or physical education.

2798. *Journal of Aging & Social Policy: a journal devoted to aging & social policy.* [ISSN: 0895-9420] 1989. q. GBP 615 (print & online eds.). Ed(s): Robert P Geary, Francis G Caro. Routledge, 325 Chestnut St, Ste 800, Philadelphia, PA 19106; customerservice@taylorandfrancis.com; http://www.tandfonline.com. Illus. Sample. Refereed. Microform: PQC. Reprint: PSC. *Indexed:* A01, A22, AbAn, AgeL, BRI, E01, H24, P02, P61, RiskAb, SSA, SWR&A. *Bk. rev.:* 0-1, 4-6 pages, signed. *Aud.:* Ac, Sa.

This international, peer-reviewed journal is intended for "educators, practitioners, researchers, and administrators who work with the elderly." The articles it presents analyze the development and implementation of programs for older people and factors that affect the process. Each issue's five to eight articles cover social policy around the world at all levels of government. It is interdisciplinary in nature and covers a wide variety of policy issues that affect older people, such as housing, retirement, health care, and transportation. It examines the policymaking process by "examining the interplay of political and economic forces, legal and regulatory constraints, the pressure of special interests, and the influence of constituencies." One issue every year is devoted to a single theme. Some recent thematic issues are "Critical Essays on Health Care Reform: The Affordable Care Act, Long-Term Care, and Elders" and "The Aging Workforce: Challenges for Societies, Employers, and Older Workers." Examples of recent articles are "Transitions from Home Care to Nursing Home:

Unmet Needs in a Home- and Community-Based Program for Older Adults," "Environmental and Policy Change to Support Healthy Aging," and "Toward Health Reform for Seniors in Bermuda: Historical Constraints on Political Possibilities." A core journal for libraries with collections in gerontology, public policy, social work, or sociology.

2799. *Journal of Aging Studies.* [ISSN: 0890-4065] 1987. q. EUR 556. Ed(s): J Gubrium. Pergamon, The Blvd, Langford Ln, E Park, Kidlington, OX5 1GB, United Kingdom; JournalsCustomerServiceEMEA@elsevier.com; http://www.elsevier.com. Adv. Sample. Refereed. Microform: PQC. Reprint: PSC. *Indexed:* A01, A22, AgeL, MLA-IB, P02, P61, PsycInfo, RiskAb, SSA. *Bk. rev.:* Number and length vary. *Aud.:* Ga, Ac, Sa.

Ranked 17th by Thomson Reuters for January–February 2011, in the field of gerontology. This multidisciplinary, peer-reviewed journal covers the subject of aging broadly. "Articles need not deal with the field of aging as a whole, but with any defensibly relevant topic pertinent to the aging experience and related to the broad concerns and subject matter of the social and behavioral sciences and the humanities." Emphasis is on innovation and critique "regardless of theoretical or methodological orientation or academic discipline." The types and number (10–15) of articles vary, but they include empirical, theoretical, and critical analyses, as well as book reviews. There are occasional special sections, such as "Innovative Approaches to International Comparisons." Some recent articles are "Space, time, and self: Rethinking Aging in the Contexts of Immigration and Transnationalism," "The Silent Impact of Ageist Communication in Long Term Care Facilities: Elders' Perspectives on Quality of Life and Coping Strategies," and "Elder Self Neglect: A Geriatric Syndrome or a Life Course Story?" This journal provides broad coverage of aging and is a core title for all libraries that collect in gerontology, sociology, or psychology.

2800. *Journal of Applied Gerontology.* [ISSN: 0733-4648] 1982. 8x/yr. USD 1299. Ed(s): Joseph E Gaugler, Bethany Gerdin. Sage Publications, Inc., 2455 Teller Rd, Thousand Oaks, CA 91320; info@sagepub.com; http://www.sagepub.com. Illus., index, adv. Refereed. Vol. ends: Dec. Reprint: PSC. *Indexed:* A22, AgeL, BRI, E01, ExcerpMed, H24, P02, P61, PsycInfo, RiskAb, SSA. *Aud.:* Ac, Sa.

This international, peer-reviewed journal is produced by the Southern Gerontological Society and "features articles that focus on research applications intended to improve the health and quality of life of older persons or to enhance our understanding of age-related issues that will eventually lead to such outcomes." Information presented is intended to have "clear and immediate applicability to the health, care, and quality of life of older persons." All disciplines of gerontological research, policy, and practice are treated, such as caregiving, physical activity, housing, mental health, ethnicity, and retirement. The concept of applicability is interpreted broadly to include useful information on practice, methodology, theory, and policy. Each issues consists of four to eight articles, almost all reports on original research. The journal does print "Brief Reports" and the occasional editorial. Recent articles include "How Gender and Religion Influence Alcohol Use in Elderly Korean Immigrants," "Larimer County Alliance for Grandfamilies: A Collaborative Approach to Meeting a Community Need," and "Nursing Home Deficiency Citations for Abuse." Suitable for academic and medical libraries.

2801. *Journal of Cross-Cultural Gerontology.* [ISSN: 0169-3816] 1986. q. EUR 643 (print & online eds.). Ed(s): Margaret A Perkinson. Springer New York LLC, 233 Spring St, New York, NY 10013; service-ny@springer.com; http://www.springer.com/. Illus., index, adv. Sample. Refereed. Microform: PQC. Reprint: PSC. *Indexed:* A01, A22, AgeL, BRI, E01, IBSS, P61, PsycInfo, RiskAb, SSA. *Aud.:* Ac, Sa.

This international, peer-reviewed journal provides a venue for analysis of the process and problems of aging from a global, interdisciplinary perspective. Emphasis is placed on research findings, theoretical issues, and applications dealing with non-Western populations, subcultures, and ethnic minorities in Western societies, and comparative analysis. Contributions come from a wide variety of disciplines, such as history, anthropology, sociology, political science, psychology, demography, and health. Each issue of the journal is composed of five or six lengthy research articles, but it may also contain brief reports or editorials. Some recent articles are "Suicidal and Depressive Symptoms in Filipino Home Care Workers in Israel," "Bodies, Technologies, and Aging in

Japan: Thinking about Old People and their Silver Products," and "Health Perception and Health Behaviors of Elderly Tibetans Living in India and Switzerland." This is a core title for research and academic libraries with collections in geriatrics and gerontology, and it is also appropriate for libraries that support sociology or global studies curricula.

2802. *Journal of Elder Abuse & Neglect.* [ISSN: 0894-6566] 1988. 5x/yr. GBP 766 (print & online eds.). Ed(s): Karen Stein. Routledge, 325 Chestnut St, Ste 800, Philadelphia, PA 19106; customerservice@taylorandfrancis.com; http://www.tandfonline.com. Illus., adv. Sample. Refereed. Microform: PQC. Reprint: PSC. *Indexed:* A01, A22, AgeL, BRI, C45, CJPI, E01, H24, IndVet, P02, P61, PsycInfo, RiskAb, SSA, SWR&A. *Bk. rev.:* Number and length vary. *Aud.:* Ac, Sa.

A peer-reviewed journal that is devoted to research on the causes, effects, treatment, and prevention of elder abuse from an international and interdisciplinary perspective. It is written for an audience of "professionals in social work, nursing, medicine, law, gerontology, adult protective services, criminal justice, sociology, psychology, domestic violence, counseling, ethics, public policy, aging network, research, practitioner, educator, student, and policymakers." The articles published are primarily reports on original research or literature reviews, but may also analyze specific conceptual models and programs related to clinical practice, international issues, public policy, or education and training. Issues may contain book reviews. Specific topics vary widely. Articles may address tools and programs for evaluating, treating, or preventing abuse of older people. Some issues are devoted to a special topic, for example, "Elder Abuse in Canada: Reports from a National Roundtable Discussion." Examples of recent articles are "Aggression Exhibited by Older Dementia Clients Toward Staff in Japanese Long-Term Care," "Financial Exploitation of Older Persons in Adult Care Settings: Comparisons to Physical Abuse and the Justice System's Response," "Essential Data Elements for Reporters of Elder Abuse," and "Conceptual Model and Map of Psychological Abuse of Older Adults." Appropriate for academic, medical, and law libraries.

2803. *Journal of Geriatric Psychiatry and Neurology.* Formerly (until 1988): *Topics in Geriatrics.* [ISSN: 0891-9887] 1982. q. USD 659. Ed(s): Alan M Mellow. Sage Publications, Inc., 2455 Teller Rd, Thousand Oaks, CA 91320; info@sagepub.com; http://www.sagepub.com/. Illus., adv. Sample. Refereed. Reprint: PSC. *Indexed:* A01, A22, C37, CBCARef, E01, ExcerpMed, PsycInfo. *Aud.:* Ac, Sa.

This peer-reviewed journal is written for clinicians who care for the elderly and researchers in neurology and/or psychiatry. The journal addresses "all aspects of the psychiatric and neuralgic care of aging patients, including age-related biologic, neuralgic, and psychiatric illness; psychosocial problems; forensic issues; and family care." Examples of specific topics covered are Alzheimer's disease and other forms of dementia, depression, addiction, sleep disorders, bereavement, evaluative methods, drug therapies, genetics, neuroimaging, caregivers, economics of neuropsychiatric care, and ethics. A typical issue contains seven to nine reports of original research, clinical reviews, case reports, and/or editorials. The approach to topics covered is broad and practical: emphasis is on presenting information from a wide range of the allied sciences that will be useful to the clinician in daily practice. There is the occasional special issue, such as "Late-Life Bipolar Disorder: Advances in Treatment, Conceptualization, and Research Methodology." Some recent articles are "Are Vascular Risk Factors Associated with Post-Stroke Depressive Symptoms?," "The IQCODE versus a Single-Item Informant Measure to Discriminate Between Cognitively Intact Individuals and Individuals with Dementia or Cognitive Impairment," and "Acute Bipolar I Affective Episode Presentation across Life Span." Appropriate for medical and academic libraries.

2804. *Journal of Gerontological Nursing: for nursing care of older adults.* [ISSN: 0098-9134] 1975. m. USD 325. Ed(s): Donna M Fink. Slack, Inc., 6900 Grove Rd, Thorofare, NJ 08086; customerservice@slackinc.com; http://www.slackinc.com. Illus., index. Sample. Refereed. Vol. ends: Dec. Microform: PQC. *Indexed:* A22, AgeL, BRI. *Aud.:* Ac, Sa.

This journal is written for gerontological nurses, but is also of interest to researchers and educators in gerontological nursing. Although a peer-reviewed journal, it has a magazine format with many color graphics and sidebars. The focus is "on the practice, research, theory, and/or teaching of gerontological nursing across the continuum of care." The journal is intended to be a complete guide to all aspects of the field, with emphasis on currency and practical value. All articles are required to discuss clinical implications of the information being presented. The journal is divided into sections, including "geropharmacology, clinical concepts, diagnosis: dementia, legal issues, public policy, research briefs, and technology innovations, as well as a Continuing Nursing Education quiz." Some recent articles are "Custodial Grandparents Raising Grandchildren: Lack of Legal Relationship is a Barrier for Services," "Worker Injuries and Safety Equipment in Ohio Nursing Homes," "Long-Term Care Nurse Role Models in Clinical Nursing Education: The ECLEPs Experience," and "Identifying Geriatric Malnutrition in Nursing Practice: The Mini Nutritional Assessment (MNA): An Evidence-Based Screening Tool." Appropriate for medical libraries and academic libraries that support nursing programs.

2805. *Journal of Gerontological Social Work.* [ISSN: 0163-4372] 1978. 8x/yr. GBP 1287 (print & online eds.). Ed(s): Amanda Barusch, Carmen Morano. Routledge, 325 Chestnut St, Ste 800, Philadelphia, PA 19106; customerservice@taylorandfrancis.com; http://www.tandfonline.com. Illus., adv. Sample. Refereed. Circ: 640 Paid. Microform: PQC. Reprint: PSC. *Indexed:* A01, A22, AgeL, BRI, E01, H24, P02, P61, PsycInfo, RiskAb, SSA, SWR&A. *Bk. rev.:* 1, 2-3 pages, signed. *Aud.:* Ac, Sa.

From the Association for Gerontology Education in Social Work, this peer-reviewed journal seeks to present "consistent, quality articles devoted to social work practice, theory, administration, and consultation in the field of aging." Its audience consists of social work practitioners, supervisors, administrators, and consultants along the entire range of service settings. Any topic related to social work with older people may be covered, such as mental health services, public welfare coordination of services for the elderly, crisis intervention, substance abuse, diversity, law, public policy, and social work education. Each issue contains five to seven articles: most are reports on original research, but a few are theoretical, review articles, editorials, and book reviews. There are occasional special thematic issues—for example, "Aging with Disability." Examples of recent articles are "Nursing Home Social Services Directors and Elder Abuse Staff Training," "The Third-Age African American Seniors: Benefits of Participating in Senior Multipurpose Facilities," "Voluntary and Involuntary Driving Cessation in Later Life," and "A Conceptual Framework for Differential Use of Mediation and Family Therapy Interventions with Older Adults and their Families." Appropriate for any library with a collection emphasis on gerontology or social work.

2806. *Journal of Nutrition in Gerontology and Geriatrics.* Formerly (until Jan. 2011): *Journal of Nutrition for the Elderly.* [ISSN: 2155-1197] 1980. q. GBP 752 (print & online eds.). Ed(s): Connie Bales. Routledge, 325 Chestnut St, Ste 800, Philadelphia, PA 19106; customerservice@taylorandfrancis.com; http://www.tandfonline.com. Illus. Sample. Refereed. Vol. ends: Summer. Microform: PQC. Reprint: PSC. *Indexed:* A01, A22, AgeL, Agr, C45, E01, FS&TA, MCR, PsycInfo, SWR&A. *Aud.:* Ga, Ac, Sa.

This peer-reviewed journal presents information and analysis related to nutrition and older people in clinical or community settings. Articles included are long and brief reports on original research, review articles, editorials, and notes on newly available findings. Nutrition is covered broadly, with articles in areas such as "preventive nutrition, nutritional interventions for chronic disease, aging effects on nutritional requirements, nutritional status and dietary intake behaviors, nutritional frailty and functional status, usefulness of supplements, programmatic interventions, transitions in care and long term care, and community nutrition issues." Rarely, the journal publishes a special issue, most recently: "Food Security in Older Adults." Some recent articles are "Nutritional Screening Tools as Predictors of Mortality, Functional Decline, and Move to Higher Level Care in Older People: A Systematic Review," "Ensuring Vitamin D Supplementation in Nursing Home Patients: A Quality Improvement Project," "Evaluating Nutrition Risk Factors and Other Determinants of Use of an Urban Congregate Meal Program by Older African Americans," and "Nutritional Status of Older Persons Presenting in a Primary Care Clinic in Nigeria." Appropriate for medical libraries and academic libraries that support curricula in gerontology or nutrition.

2807. *Journal of Religion, Spirituality & Aging: the interdisiplinary journal of practice, theory & applied research.* Former titles (until 2004): *Journal of Religious Gerontology;* (until vol.7, 1990): *Journal of*

Religion and Aging. [ISSN: 1552-8030] 1985. q. GBP 454 (print & online eds.). Ed(s): James W Ellor. Routledge, 325 Chestnut St, Ste 800, Philadelphia, PA 19106; customerservice@taylorandfrancis.com; http://www.tandfonline.com. Illus. Sample. Refereed. Vol. ends: Fall. Reprint: PSC. *Indexed:* A01, A22, ASSIA, AgeL, E01, P61, PsycInfo, R&TA, SSA. *Bk. rev.:* 0-5, 1-3 pages, signed. *Aud.:* Ga, Ac, Sa.

This interdisciplinary, interfaith, peer-reviewed journal is intended for both religious and secular professionals who work with the elderly and their families, but also for scholars within academic disciplines related to religious studies. In four to six articles per issue, the journal aims to provide discussion of current practices, theory, and information regarding spirituality, religion, and aging through research, clinical, theoretical, and methodological articles, case studies, editorials, and the occasional special double issue. Typical topics addressed are religious activities in retirement communities, preaching to the elderly, worship with mentally and physically disabled older people, grief, death, long-term care, and support systems for families. Recent special issues are: "Ageing and Spirituality: Resistance, Resilience, and Change" and "Training Clergy to Surf the Age Wave." Some recent articles are "Ageing and Identity Dilemmas for Men," "Praying for Health by Older Adults in the United States: Differences by Ethnicity, Gender, and Income," "Reading Luke for Community Formation Against Ageism," and "Challenges Faced by Staff in Faith-Based Agencies When Dedicated Volunteers Age in Place." This journal is appropriate for theological seminary libraries, academic libraries that support religious studies or social work curricula, and public libraries that serve a large aging population.

2808. *Journal of Women and Aging: the multidiciplinary quarterly of psychosocial practice, theory & research.* [ISSN: 0895-2841] 1989. q. GBP 514 (print & online eds.). Ed(s): J Dianne Garner. Routledge, 325 Chestnut St, Ste 800, Philadelphia, PA 19106; customerservice@taylorandfrancis.com; http://www.tandfonline.com. Illus., adv. Sample. Refereed. Microform: PQC. Reprint: PSC. *Indexed:* A01, A22, AbAn, AgeL, BRI, C42, E01, FemPer, GW, H24, P02, P61, PsycInfo, RiskAb, SSA, SWR&A, WSA. *Bk. rev.:* 1-2, 1-3 pages, signed. *Aud.:* Ga, Ac.

Ranked 19th by Thomson Reuters for January–February 2011, in the field of gerontology. The stated goal of this peer-reviewed journal is to provide "practitioners, educators, researchers, and administrators with a comprehensive guide to the unique challenges facing women in their later years." This journal is multidisciplinary, publishing articles from gerontology, medicine, psychology, sociology, and social work. Articles selected for publication may be research, clinical, or review articles. Sample topics are osteoporosis, domestic violence, hysterectomy and menopause, breast cancer, and terminal illness. Every issue has an editorial, about five articles, and one or two book reviews. Examples of recent articles are "Health and Cultural Determinants of Voluntary HIV Testing and Counseling Among Middle-Aged and Older Latina Women," "Menopause Symptoms' Predictors: The Influence of Lifestyle, Health- and Menopause-Related, and Sociodemographic Characteristics," "An Ecological Synthesis of Research on Older Women's Experiences of Intimate Partner Violence," and "Gender Differences in the Relationship of Social Activity and Quality of Life in Community-Dwelling Taiwanese Elders." Useful for students, educators, researchers, practitioners, and administrators, this journal is appropriate for academic libraries, especially those that desire strong collections in gerontology, women's studies, social work, or sociology.

2809. *Journals of Gerontology. Series A: Biological Sciences & Medical Sciences.* Supersedes in part (in 1995): *Journal of Gerontology.* [ISSN: 1079-5006] 1946. m. EUR 986. Ed(s): Stephen B Kritchevsky, Rafael de Cato. Oxford University Press, 2001 Evans Rd, Cary, NC 27513; jnlorders@oup-usa.org; http://www.us.oup.com. Illus., index, adv. Sample. Refereed. Vol. ends: Dec. Microform: PQC. Reprint: PSC. *Indexed:* A01, A22, AgeL, C45, CBRI, ErgAb, IndVet, P02, PsycInfo, RRTA, SWR&A. *Aud.:* Ac, Sa.

Ranked fourth by Thomson Reuters for January–February 2011, in the field of gerontology. This peer-reviewed journal is designed for "gerontological researchers, educators, and practitioners in biological, medical, behavioral, and social sciences and the humanities." It is divided into two parts (with separate paging): "Biological Sciences," which is devoted to the biological aspects of aging; and "Medical Sciences," which covers medical aspects of aging. Its mission is "to promote the scientific study of aging, to encourage exchanges

among researchers and practitioners from various disciplines related to gerontology, and to foster the use of gerontological research in forming public policy." "Biological Sciences" covers biochemistry, biodemography, cellular and molecular biology, comparative and evolutionary biology, endocrinology, exercise science, genetics, immunology, morphology, neuroscience, nutrition, pathology, pharmacology, and physiology. "Medical Sciences" covers basic medical sciences, clinical epidemiology, clinical research, and health-services research from professions such as medicine, dentistry, allied health sciences, and nursing. The journal contains full and brief reports on original research, but also theoretical or review articles, editorials, letters to the editor, and invited special articles. Some recent articles are "A Procedure for Creating a Frailty Index Based on Deficit Accumulation in Aging Mice," "A Significant Relationship between Plasma Vitamin C Concentration and Physical Performance among Japanese Elderly Women," "Age-Associated Alteration in Innate Immune Response in Captive Baboons," and "Risk of Continued Institutionalization After Hospitalization in Older Adults." A core journal for geriatrics and gerontology.

2810. *Journals of Gerontology. Series B: Psychological Sciences & Social Sciences.* Supersedes in part (in 1995): *Journal of Gerontology.* [ISSN: 1079-5014] 1946. bi-m. EUR 442. Ed(s): Merril Silverstein, Bob G Knight. Oxford University Press, 2001 Evans Rd, Cary, NC 27513; jnlorders@oup.usa.org; http://www.us.oup.com. Illus., index. Sample. Refereed. Vol. ends: Nov. Microform: PQC. Reprint: PSC. *Indexed:* A01, A22, ASSIA, AgeL, C45, CBRI, ErgAb, FR, P02, P61, PsycInfo, RRTA, SSA, SWR&A. *Aud.:* Ac, Sa.

Ranked eighth by Thomson Reuters for January–February 2011, in the field of gerontology. This international, peer-reviewed journal is published by the Gerontological Society of America and is the companion journal to *Journals of Gerontology. Series A: Biological Sciences and Medical Sciences.* It also is divided into two parts, each with separate pagination: "Psychological Sciences" and "Social Sciences." "Psychological Sciences" covers applied, clinical, counseling, developmental, experimental, and social psychology related to aging and the elderly. Articles are expected to demonstrate the theoretical or methodological implications of the research results reported. They may also relate psychological aspects of aging to other disciplines. Four types of articles are included: lengthy articles on original research, brief reports on original research, invited reviews and position papers, and articles on theory or methodology. The second section, "Social Sciences," covers topics related to aging in various social science disciplines, such as anthropology, demography, economics, epidemiology, geography, political science, public health, social history, social work, and sociology. The types of articles published in this journal are: lengthy articles or brief reports on original research, review articles, articles on theory or methodology, commentary or letters to the editor, and editorials. Examples of recent articles are "Human Behavior Change Following Chronic Illness in Middle and Later Life," "The Impact of Transportation Support on Driving Cessation Among Community-Dwelling Older Adults," "Examining Positive and Negative Perceptions of Older Workers: A Meta-Analysis," and "Does Race Influence Conflict Between Nursing Home Staff and Family Members of Residents?" A core title for geriatrics and gerontology.

2811. *Kiplinger's Retirement Report: your guide to a richer retirement.* [ISSN: 1075-6671] 1994. m. USD 39.95 combined subscription (print or online ed.). Ed(s): Rachel L Sheedy, Susan B Garland. Kiplinger Washington Editors, Inc., 1729 H St, NW, Washington, DC 20006; http://www.kiplinger.com. Sample. *Indexed:* ATI, AgeL, B01, B02, BRI. *Aud.:* Ga.

This consumer-oriented newsletter is written for the general public and, therefore, consists of short informational articles with graphics. The newsletter addresses a variety of financial topics as they would interest the older adult: investments, taxes, retirement benefits, and health. Each issue has about ten articles and is divided into sections, such as "Investing," "Benefits," "Taxes," "Estate Planning," "Retirement Living," "Managing Your Finances," and "Your Health." Other regular features are "Information to Act On" and "Your Questions Answered." Some recent feature articles are "A New Chapter of Pension Plan Woes," "Five Tech Stocks With Solid Records," "Need Medicare Help? Check These Sites," "Insurance for Those Who Live Too Long," and "Will Your Life Insurer Pay Promised Benefits?" Recommended for public libraries or a library that serves a large older population.

2812. *Long-Term Living.* Former titles (until 2008): *Nursing Homes;* (until 1991): *Nursing Homes and Senior Citizen Care;* (until 1986): *Nursing Homes.* [ISSN: 1940-9958] 1950. m. Free to qualified personnel. Ed(s): Patricia Sheehan. Vendome Group, LLC, 6 E 32nd St, 8th Fl, New York, NY 10016; info@vendomegrp.com; http://www.vendomegrp.com/. Illus., adv. Microform: PQC. *Indexed:* A01, A22, ABIn, AgeL, B01, B02, BRI, P02. *Aud.:* Sa.

This monthly trade journal is designated specifically for the continuing care professional: "owners, executives, administrators, and directors." The journal seeks to publish articles from long-term managers and supervisors on a wide range of topics related to long-term care—for example, Medicare, new products, law, finance, staffing and training, and innovations in service. It presents five to eight feature articles per issue, plus several brief, timely informational articles, and opinion pieces, organized under regular headings, such as "Field Studies," "Community," "Tech Notes," "Exemplars in LTC," and "Care Management." Some recent articles are "Memory Care Drives LTC Development," "Running a Senior Care Internship Program," "Controlling Infection Through Design," and "The Essential Components of Preparedness and Compliance." Appropriate for libraries that serve long-term care professionals and others concerned with the well-being of people in long-term care facilities.

2813. *Physical & Occupational Therapy in Geriatrics: current trends in geriatric rehabilitation.* [ISSN: 0270-3181] 1980. q. GBP 588 (print & online eds.). Ed(s): Ellen Dunleavey Taira. Informa Healthcare, 52 Vanderbilt Ave, New York, NY 10017; healthcare.enquiries@informa.com; http://www.informahealthcare.com. Illus., adv. Sample. Refereed. Microform: PQC. Reprint: PSC. *Indexed:* A01, A22, ASSIA, AgeL, E01, MCR, MLA-IB, PsycInfo, RILM, RiskAb, SD, SSA, SWR&A. *Aud.:* Ac, Sa.

This peer-reviewed journal is written for and by allied health professionals. It is intended to provide opportunities to share "information, clinical experience, research, and therapeutic practice." Its scope is broad: "the entire range of problems experienced by the elderly; and the current skills needed for working with older clients." Each issue contains five to eight articles: reports on original research, clinical practice, or review articles. Some recent articles are "The Use of Music to Improve Exercise Participation in People with Dementia: A Pilot Study," "Promoting Fall Self-Efficacy and Fall Risk Awareness in Older Adults," "Testing the Feasibility of Using Odors in Reminiscence Therapy in Japan," and "A Passive Monitoring System in Assisted Living Facilities: 12-Month Comparative Study." This journal is valuable for medical libraries and academic libraries with collections in physical therapy, occupational therapy, geriatrics and gerontology, or social work.

2814. *Psychology and Aging.* [ISSN: 0882-7974] 1986. q. USD 546. Ed(s): Ulrich Myer, Paul Duberstein. American Psychological Association, 750 First St, NE, Washington, DC 20002; journals@apa.org; http://www.apa.org. Illus., index, adv. Sample. Refereed. Microform: PQC. Reprint: PSC. *Indexed:* A01, A22, ASSIA, AgeL, ErgAb, ExcerpMed, FR, P02, PsycInfo, SWR&A. *Aud.:* Ac, Sa.

Ranked third by Thomson Reuters for January–February 2011, in the field of gerontology. This international, peer-reviewed journal from the American Psychological Association is devoted to the physiological and behavioral aspects of adult development and aging. It includes lengthy articles and brief reports on original research, theoretical analyses, clinical case studies, and editorials. Articles may be written on applied, biobehavioral, clinical, educational, experimental, methodological, and psychosocial research. Some recent articles are "Let Me Guess How Old You Are: Effects of Age, Gender, and Facial Expression on Perceptions of Age," "The Relationship between Identity, Intimacy, and Midlife Well-being: Findings from the Rochester Adult Longitudinal Study," "Altering Mindset can Enhance Motor Learning in Older Adults," and "Genetic and Environmental Influences on Odor Identification Ability in the Very Old." A core title for libraries with collections in geriatrics and gerontology, psychology, or sociology.

2815. *Research on Aging: an international bimonthly journal.* [ISSN: 0164-0275] 1979. bi-m. USD 1042. Ed(s): Debra Parker Oliver. Sage Publications, Inc., 2455 Teller Rd, Thousand Oaks, CA 91320; info@sagepub.com; http://www.sagepub.com. Illus., index, adv. Sample. Refereed. Reprint: PSC. *Indexed:* A01, A22, AbAn, AgeL, E01, IBSS, P02, P61, PsycInfo, RiskAb, SSA, SWR&A. *Aud.:* Ac, Sa.

Ranked 11th by Thomson Reuters for January–February 2011, in the field of gerontology. A peer-reviewed journal for scholars, researchers, and practitioners. It is interdisciplinary in approach, with articles from sociology, history, psychology, anthropology, economics, social work, political science, criminal justice, geriatrics, and public health. Research and review articles cover topics in all these fields as they relate to aging and the elderly, such as age discrimination, Alzheimer's disease, caretaking, and the aging workforce. The journal publishes full and brief reports on original research, systematic literature reviews, meta-analyses, and editorials. Each issue has five to eight articles. Among recent articles are "Comparison of Inflammatory, Metabolic, and Anthropometric Parameters in Elderly Women With and Without Insulin Resistance," "Residential Context, Social Relationships, and Subjective Well-Being in Assisted Living," and "Older Adults' Spiritual Needs in Health Care Settings: A Qualitative Meta-Synthesis." A core journal in gerontology for academic libraries.

2816. *Social Security Bulletin.* Incorporates (in 1988): *Monthly Benefit Statistics;* Which incorporated (1974-19??): *Supplemental Security Income for the Aged, Blind, and Disabled. Monthly Statistics.* [ISSN: 0037-7910] 1937. q. USD 56 domestic; USD 78.40 foreign; USD 13 per issue domestic. Ed(s): Karyn M Tucker. U.S. Social Security Administration, Office of Research, Evaluation and Statistics, 500 E St, S W, 8th Fl, Washington, DC 20254; http://www.ssa.gov/policy/about/ORES.html. Illus., index. Sample. Vol. ends: Dec. Microform: CIS; MIM; PMC; PQC. Reprint: WSH. *Indexed:* A01, A22, ABIn, AgeL, AmStI, B01, B02, BRI, CLI, EconLit, JEL, L14, MCR, P02, P61, SSA, SWR&A. *Aud.:* Ga, Ac, Sa.

This governmental quarterly is available in paper and open-access online formats. It is written "to promote the discussion of research questions and policy issues related to Social Security and the economic well-being of the aged." Its intended audience is broad: government and business people; students, educators, and scholars; and the general public. Most articles are written by researchers and analysts connected with the Social Security Administration, but the "Perspectives" section prints articles from outside the agency. The journal contains articles that describe and analyze the changing aging population and the economic, demographic, social, and medical factors that affect their economic security. Other items assess Social Security programs, as well as other programs and tools that may be of value to aging Americans before and after retirement. All papers are required to be written in accessible, nontechnical language and must have a clearly stated connection to public policy. Sample titles: "Raising Household Saving: Does Financial Education Work?," "The Retirement Prospects of Divorced Women," "Caregiver Credits in France, Germany, and Sweden: Lessons for the United States," and "The Growth in Social Security Benefits Among the Retirement-Age Population from Increases in the Cap on Covered Earnings." Recommended for all libraries.

2817. *Topics in Geriatric Rehabilitation.* [ISSN: 0882-7524] 1985. q. USD 424 (print & online eds.). Ed(s): Carole B Lewis. Lippincott Williams & Wilkins, Two Commerce Sq, 2001 Market St, Philadelphia, PA 19103; customerservice@lww.com; http://www.lww.com. Illus., adv. Sample. Refereed. *Indexed:* A22, AgeL, ExcerpMed. *Aud.:* Ac, Sa.

Specifically intended for "the health care professional practicing in the area of geriatric rehabilitation," this peer-reviewed journal may be of interest to other health professionals who work with older people. The journal's general scope is very broad, although most issues focus on a particular subject. Each issue contains six to ten research articles that report the results of "clinical, basic, and applied research," and review articles. Emphasis in each article is placed on the practical value of the information presented, so that the reader can use that information in the daily treatment of elderly clients. The themes of two recent issues are "Cancer Rehabilitation" and "Alzheimer Disease Cognitive-Communication Interventions." Recent articles include "Self-report Measures of Mobility," "RHEA, a Nonpharmacological Cognitive Training Intervention in Patients With Mild Cognitive Impairment: A Pilot Study," "Upper Quadrant Impairments Associated With Cancer Treatment," and "Measuring Walking Speed: Clinical Feasibility and Reliability." Appropriate for medical libraries, research libraries, and academic libraries that support geriatric, gerontology, social work, or physical therapy curricula.

Travel 50 & Beyond. See Travel and Tourism section.

■ GLOBALIZATION

Judi Tidwell, Reference/Instruction Librarian, Broward College, Davie, FL; jtidwell@broward.edu

Introduction

When the culture, customs, education, politics, media, economics, health, environmental disasters, revolutions, wars, triumphs, and achievements of one country affect another, we call it *globalization*. Simply put, this encompasses how we have looked at the world since the Internet put us in constant and immediate contact with strangers from across the planet. Anyone with a device and access point can share their hopes, viewpoints, rants, pranks, cats, and dance moves with the world.

In truth, globalization has been a phenomenon since the first trade routes opened between distant towns. And yet, only recently has it become such a prevalent part of society that academics have begun to study it in earnest. Nearly all of the magazines and journals contained in this volume will have some element in their publication that touches on the reality of globalization. From advertising to zoology, the people writing, reading, editing, and publishing are looking at the bigger picture.

However, the magazines and journals that follow this introduction are specific in their global focus. Here you will find journals about the health issues that affect the planet (*Global Journal of Health*), or global business practices (*Competition and Change*). There are journals that look at the study of globalization as a discipline (*Journal of International and Global Studies*), and those that hope to help shape ethical arguments concerning political involvements (*Ethics and Global Politics*).

Every one of the selections contained herein has an electronic version; many are solely online, while some are even open access. From general interest to highly rigorous academic research, there is something here for everyone because, after all, this is the section for Globalization.

Basic Periodicals

Ga: *Global Dialogue* (Online), *Global-e*. Ac, Sa: *Global Media and Communication*, *Global Networks* (Oxford), *Globality Studies Journal*, *Globalizations*.

Basic Abstracts and Indexes

ABI/Inform, CSA Sociological Abstracts, EBSCOhost, Elsevier BV, IngentaConnect, ProQuest 5000, SocINDEX.

2818. *Competition & Change: the journal of global business and political economy.* [ISSN: 1024-5294] 1996. q. GBP 387 (print & online eds.). Ed(s): Jane Hardy. Maney Publishing, Ste 1C, Joseph's Well, Hanover Walk, Leeds, LS3 1AB, United Kingdom; maney@maneypublishing.com; http://maneypublishing.com/. Adv. Refereed. Reprint: PSC. *Indexed:* A22, ABIn, B01, E01, EconLit, JEL. *Aud.:* Ac, Sa.

This peer-reviewed journal is one of the first to have embraced globalization as an area for specific study. Although the editorial board is mostly made up of business and economics professors, the articles "use a variety of social science perspectives to develop understanding of broad business issues around globalization and financialization [*sic*] and their impact on economic organization and performance, social conditions, labour[,] and policy frameworks." Published in the United Kingdom since 1996, with an online edition since 2002 [ISSN 1477-2221], this roughly-quarterly journal has included themed issues, reviews, and position pieces, as well as short items of relevant news. Solidly academic and pertinent to international students, faculty, and researchers who are concerned with the impact globalization has on commerce and trade, *Competition and Change* is an excellent choice.

2819. *Ethics & Global Politics.* [ISSN: 1654-4951] 2008. q. Free. Ed(s): Eva Erman. Co-Action Publishing, Ripvaegen 7, Jaerfaella, 17564, Sweden; info@co-action.net; http://www.co-action.net. Refereed. *Indexed:* P61, SSA. *Bk. rev.:* Number and length vary. *Aud.:* Ac, Sa.

Combining philosophy with political theory, *Ethics & Global Politics* publishes original research with the aim to contribute to the study of the role of morality within the current global environment. The content categories vary, including critical debates, invited editorials, research articles, essays, notes, and book reviews; also, there is one special thematic issue per year. Everything, with the exception of the book reviews and editorials, is subjected to a double-blind peer-review process. The online edition [ISSN 1654-6369] is free, archived and open-access, providing the reader with a variety of formats including pdf, html, xml, and the recent addition of ePub for mobile devices. Supported by a grant from the Swedish government, *Ethics & Global Politics* "does not favour any theoretical perspective or political problem[,] but emphasizes the importance of closing the gap between moral and democratic theory, on the one hand, and contemporary empirical problems on the global arena, on the other." This makes this title an excellent source of balanced research for academics studying, and specialized audiences for, international politics.

2820. *Global Dialogue (Online).* Formerly (until 2009): *Global Dialogue (Print).* [ISSN: 1986-2601] s-a. USD 96 (Individuals, USD 30). Ed(s): Paul Theodoulou. Centre for World Dialogue, 39 Riga Fereou St, Ag Omologitae, P.O. Box 23992, Nicosia, CY-1687, Cyprus; info@worlddialogue.org. *Indexed:* ABIn, IBSS, MLA-IB, P61, SSA. *Bk. rev.:* Number and length vary. *Aud.:* Hs, Ga, Ac.

Previously a quarterly magazine, *Global Dialogue* went fully online, semi-annual and free, with the Winter/Spring edition in 2010. Completely archived and presented exclusively in html format, the articles, editorials, and book reviews are available without subscription. Each issue of *Global Diaglogue* aims at creating an open discussion on one particular global problem, or on the impact globalization is having on the economy, politics, society, and culture of a specific country. The goal is to "...examine conflicts and issues wherever they arise...to illuminate the forces at work internationally that are shaping today's world." Openly accessible and easily navigated, *Global Dialogue* is a good resource for intelligent readers looking for an international take on current global conflicts.

2821. *Global-e: a global studies journal.* [ISSN: 1932-8060] 2007. m. Free. University of Illinois at Urbana-Champaign, Center for Global Studies, 302 International Studies Bldg, 910 S Fifth St, Champaign, IL 61820; global-studies@illinois.edu; http://cgs.illinois.edu/. *Indexed:* A01. *Aud.:* Ga, Ac.

Global-e is a different kind of online journal. It began as a collaborative publication between the global studies programs at the University of Illinois, the University of North Carolina, and the Universities of Wisconsin at Madison and Milwaukee. The articles are called featured postings because the entire publication is shaped more like a blog than a traditional journal. This blog format allows readers to comment and interact with the information published, and facilitates corrections or the addition of notes to even the archived posts. The frequency of these blog entries went from monthly to "every few weeks in early 2009[,] with the aim of providing a forum for timely commentary regarding global events, processes, and issues." Then they took a hiatus in 2012 as the funding for this Title VI project ran out. However, the archived entries remained accessible, and in May 2013, *Global-e* returned, "with a new look, new leadership, and new publishing objectives that put the user experience front and center." Now run by a consortium of 26 university global/transnational studies departments that span five continents, this free open-forum blog continues to encourage discussion and debate about global events, processes, and issues. The new team of editors plan to roll out some new features including "sections devoted to classroom resources, job postings, and items of professional interest, such as conferences and publishing news. Finally, we will be complementing our web materials with a social media presence on Twitter and Facebook." Despite the informal format and the focus on social media, the entries in *Global-e* are informed and researched, and focus on "public issues, theoretical debates, methodological challenges, and curricular concerns." Written by professors of communication, anthropology, political science, sociology, global studies, English, law, geography, media, and cultural studies (and also by several Ph.D. candidates), the entries cover a broad range of interdisciplinary perspectives on globalization. The unique blog format may take some getting used to, but both general audiences and academics will benefit from the academic and accessible content.

2822. Global Journal of Health Science. [ISSN: 1916-9736] 2009. s-a. Ed(s): Trisha Dunning. Canadian Center of Science and Education, 4915 Bathurst St, Unit 209-309, Toronto, ON M2R 1X9, Canada; info@ccsenet.org; http://www.ccsenet.org. Sample. Refereed. Circ: 200 Paid. *Indexed:* C37, P02. *Aud.:* Ac, Sa.

One interesting factor about *Global Journal of Health Science* is its inclusion of equality as a pertinent area of health research. Most health journals publish empirical research, experiments, and administration and staffing issues, which this title does include, but it also focuses on the sociological impact that health services and professionals have on the world. The aim is to "[e]ncourage and publish research and studies in the fields of public health, community health, environmental health, behavioral health, health policy, health service, health education, health economics, medical ethics, health protection, and equity in health." The online version [ISSN 1916-9744] is archived and offers the peer-reviewed articles for free in pdf. Searchable by issue, author, and title, the online version also allows readers to create free profiles for setting up alerts and receiving e-mails of the table of contents of current publications. *Global Journal of Health Science* is an excellent choice for academics and professionals looking for articles that cover hard science within a sociological global environment.

2823. Global Media and Communication. [ISSN: 1742-7665] 2005. 3x/yr. USD 720. Sage Publications Ltd., 1 Oliver's Yard, 55 City Rd, London, EC1Y 1SP, United Kingdom; info@sagepub.co.uk; http://www.uk.sagepub.com. Adv. Sample. Refereed. Reprint: PSC. *Indexed:* A22, E01, F01, IBSS. *Bk. rev.:* Number and length vary. *Aud.:* Ac, Sa.

Global Media and Communication is an international peer-reviewed journal that supplies a "forum for articulating critical debates and developments in the continuously changing global media and communication environment." The articles cover a wide range of topics, including (but not limited to) public policy changes, international relations, and resistance to a transnational free market. The online edition [ISSN 1742-7673] is accessible only through subscription, but for those subscribed, it has the ability to create e-mail alerts and RSS feeds, and there is a feature that tracks the "Most Read" and the "Most Cited," which is a help for serious researchers. *Global Media and Communication* contains articles; book, film, and television reviews; and opinion essays. It is an excellent resource for academics, researchers, and students interested in the international debates on communication and global policies.

2824. Global Networks (Oxford): a journal of transnational affairs. [ISSN: 1470-2266] 2001. q. GBP 397. Ed(s): Dr. Alisdair Rogers. Wiley-Blackwell Publishing, Inc., Commerce Pl, 350 Main St, Malden, MA 02148; info@wiley.com; http://onlinelibrary.wiley.com/. Adv. Sample. Refereed. Reprint: PSC. *Indexed:* A01, A22, E01, EconLit, EngInd, IBSS, JEL, P61, RiskAb, SSA. *Bk. rev.:* Number and length vary. *Aud.:* Ac, Sa.

Global Networks is a highly academic, peer-reviewed research journal that covers "global networks, transnational affairs[,] and practices, and their relation to wider theories of globalization." Contributors come from a wide cross-section of scholarship, including anthropology, geography, international political economy, business studies, and sociology. The online format for *Global Networks* [ISSN 1471-0374] allows for so many special features of customization that the subscription fee almost seems reasonable. You can create a profile to get e-mail alerts, RSS feeds, and APA citation, and track where the article you are reading has been cited (frequently with links to the subsequent articles). It also provides author information, direct linking to the Copyright Clearance Center, and a journal search feature that exceeds the most comprehensive indices. *Global Networks* is a quarterly published journal that will appeal to professionals and rigorous academics who are interested in transnationalism and the social impact of globalization.

Global Social Policy. See Sociology and Social Work/General section.

2825. Globality Studies Journal: global history, society, civilization. [ISSN: 1557-0266] 2005. irreg. Free. Ed(s): Wolf Schafer. State University of New York at Stony Brook, Center for Global History, Department of History, S-329 Ward Melville Social and Behavioral Sciences, Stony Brook, NY 11794; listserv@lists.sunysb.edu; http://www.stonybrook.edu/globalhistory. *Bk. rev.:* Number and length vary. *Aud.:* Ac, Sa.

Globality Studies Journal is a free online journal presented in html and pdf formats and includes a section for book reviews, editorials, a blog, feature articles, author search, and an index to help search through it all. Published by the Center for Global and Local History at Stony Brook University in New York, the journal is "committed to interdisciplinary analyses of global history and society, global civilization[,] and local cultures." Although the entire page looks similar to a blog, the journal is closed to comments, and publishes original research articles outside of its board of editors. There is, however, a separate blog attached to the *Globality Studies Journal* page called *EuroPoint*, in which the editor, Wolf Schafer, presents information to counteract his belief that current reporting "about the European Union (EU) in the United States is crisis-driven and one-sided." He is committed to presenting an in-depth European Union perspective on trends, regional policy debates, cultural events, and economic issues and policies that affect the entire EU. Both the journal and its blog cover theoretical trans-global topics that will be useful for researchers and academics of interdisciplinary studies.

2826. Globalization and Health. [ISSN: 1744-8603] 2004. irreg. Free. Ed(s): Emma Pitchforth, Greg Martin. BioMed Central Ltd., 236 Gray's Inn Rd, London, WC1X 8HB, United Kingdom; info@biomedcentral.com; http://www.biomedcentral.com. Adv. Refereed. *Indexed:* A01, C45, ExcerpMed, H24. *Bk. rev.:* Number and length vary. *Aud.:* Ac, Sa.

This specialized journal focuses on the effect that globalization has had on health issues. Open-access and peer-reviewed, *Globalization and Health* is an international forum "for high[-]quality original research, knowledge sharing[,] and debate on the topic of globalization and its effects on health, both positive and negative." Proposing to present a balanced view on global health issues, the journal includes research, book reviews, editorials, and debate and commentary articles. The articles are available in html, pdf, ePub, and PubMed for free. There is also a designation for "highly accessed" articles, which tracks the most viewed in the past month to give readers insight into what is currently trending. The intended audience comprises professionals and academic researchers in the fields of political science, international health, and public safety.

2827. Globalizations. [ISSN: 1474-7731] 2004. bi-m. GBP 548 (print & online eds.). Ed(s): Barry Gills. Routledge, 4 Park Sq, Milton Park, Abingdon, OX14 4RN, United Kingdom; subscriptions@tandf.co.uk; http://www.tandfonline.com. Adv. Sample. Refereed. Reprint: PSC. *Indexed:* A01, A22, E01, IBSS, P61, SSA. *Bk. rev.:* Number and length vary. *Aud.:* Ac, Sa.

Globalizations is a general-purpose subscription-based journal that attempts to broaden the meaning of globalization beyond economics. The online version [ISSN 1474-774X] is archived and provides the ability to track views and citations of each article. Readers can also see the most read and most cited articles, which will help in tracking information trends. *Globalizations* frequently produces special issues that focus on one particular aspect of globalization, or on a specific current global crisis. The journal "encourages the exploration and discussion of multiple interpretations and multiple processes that may constitute many possible globalizations, [and] many possible alternatives." Open to contribution from all disciplines, this peer-reviewed journal presents multiple interpretations of similar topics and concepts for academics and general readers, to deepen their understanding of globalization.

2828. Journal of Global Ethics. [ISSN: 1744-9626] 2005. 3x/yr. GBP 299 (print & online eds.). Ed(s): Sirkku Hellsten, Christien van den Anker. Routledge, 4 Park Sq, Milton Park, Abingdon, OX14 4RN, United Kingdom; subscriptions@tandf.co.uk; http://www.tandfonline.com. Adv. Sample. Refereed. Reprint: PSC. *Indexed:* A22, E01, IBSS, P61, SSA. *Aud.:* Ac, Sa.

The *Journal of Global Ethics* is a subscription-based periodical from Routledge under the publishing group Taylor & Francis. Free sample copies are available from the online version [ISSN 1744-9634], and you can browse the table of contents, reading the abstracts of all archived and current articles before being prompted to purchase the pdf. With a subscription, you will have access to editorials and articles, including the special issues. There is also a link to "related articles," which searches through other Taylor & Francis journals looking for similar subjects or authors. The online edition also tracks the citation count and views per article, so that researchers can track information trends.

And the references are resplendent with active links. As for the content, the *Journal of Global Ethics* "draws chiefly on the disciplines of philosophy, political science, sociology, theology, economics[,] and law and covers diverse topics such as human rights, international development, biomedical, economic[,] and environmental issues," which will be valuable to any students or scholars of international studies.

2829. *Journal of International & Global Studies.* [ISSN: 2158-0669] 2009. s-a. Free. Ed(s): Raymond Scupin. Lindenwood University, 209 S Kingshighway, St Charles, MO 63303; http://www.lindenwood.edu. *Indexed:* A01. *Bk. rev.:* Number and length vary. *Aud.:* Ga, Ac, Sa.

The *Journal of International and Global Studies,* created by Lindenwood University, provides an open-access, peer-reviewed online forum for a multidisciplinary look at the impact and implications of globalization on the different regions of the world. "One of our goals is to help undermine the fragmentation of specialization within the international academy by emphasizing broad interdisciplinary approaches to the comprehension of globalization in all of its many different forms and implications for different regions of the world." The semi-annual issues contain academic essays intended for general and professional audiences, and a plethora of book reviews that far exceeds the amount in most publications. This extensive book review section would make this title a valuable collection development tool for academic and public libraries with an interest in expanding the breadth and scope of their globalization title selections.

2830. *New Global Studies.* [ISSN: 1940-0004] 2007. 3x/yr. EUR 185. Walter de Gruyter GmbH & Co. KG, Genthiner Str 13, Berlin, 10785, Germany; info@degruyter.com; http://www.degruyter.de. Refereed. *Indexed:* P61, SSA. *Bk. rev.:* Number and length vary. *Aud.:* Ac, Sa.

Combining anthropology and history, *New Global Studies* takes a unique multidisciplinary approach to globalization, focusing on the social patterns that have developed over time and locality. This historical perspective brings something new to the study of globalization, and casts "increasing light on the common history of humankind." The online version [ISSN 1940-0004] allows readers to access the abstracts and select articles without subscription, and the journal adjusts content categories to accommodate submissions including peer-reviewed articles, commentaries, editor forum, book reviews, documentation, reportage, and review essays for researchers and academics.

■ GOVERNMENT PERIODICALS—FEDERAL

Rosemary L. Meszaros, Professor and Coordinator, Government Information and Law, Western Kentucky University, Bowling Green, KY 42101; 270-745-6441; rosemary.meszaros@wku.edu

Introduction

The U.S. Government Printing Office, known by its acronym, GPO, maintains the Federal Depository Library Program, consisting of 1,250 libraries across the country. In 2011, GPO celebrated 150 years of service in its book, *Keeping America Informed: The U.S. Government Printing Office: 150 Years of Service to the Nation.*

The might of the Internet has spurred talk of the demise of GPO, but it seems that GPO has used this powerful medium in furtherance of government information access. At first, the untamed aspect of the Internet made it difficult to harness. But GPO has made significant progress in keeping the Federal Depository Library Program a vital means for giving citizens access to government information.

One very disturbing trend has been the austere budget outlook for GPO and agencies such as the Bureau of the Census. We have witnessed the demise of *Statistical Abstract of the United States,* a vital source of data for businesses, government, and researchers. This is a tremendous loss for the country.

GPO is archiving online resources under a Persistent Uniform Resource Locator (PURL). See www.fdlp.gov/collections/building-collections/614-purls for an explanation. This move counterbalances the apprehension experienced by some in the depository community concerning the stability of online access.

GPO continues to publish and disseminate federal government reports, studies, testimony, hearings, analyses, and surveys—in short, the very words uttered and written by our federal public servants. The many federal agencies in the executive branch, the Congress and its agencies, and the Supreme Court all offer something for every interest. Law, military, politics, education, environment, business, economics, agriculture, weather, science, demographics, large print, audio and Braille bibliographies, consumer information, and statistics—all are represented in the array of magazines and journals that GPO publishes; or distributes, whether in paper form, in microform, or on the Internet; or sells.

GPO maintains a gateway web site, *FDLP (Federal Depository Library) Desktop, www.fdlp.gov/.*

The Essential Titles for Public Use in Paper Format is a list that GPO has compiled that recognizes the necessity for some titles to remain available in print. Several depository libraries have assisted with the electronic transition.

Two gateways seek to facilitate access to web-based information: *USA.gov* from the General Services Administration, www.usa.gov; and the Library of Congress's web site, http://loc.gov. Finally, the Federal Citizen Information Center in Pueblo, Colorado, www.pueblo.gsa.gov, continues to provide quick and easy access to its consumer publications.

GPO marches on with digital dissemination despite draconian budget cuts.

Basic Periodicals

Ga: *U.S. Congress. Congressional Record; U.S. Office of the Federal Register. Compilation of Presidential Documents;* Ac: *MMWR: Morbidity and Mortality Weekly Report.*

Basic Abstracts and Indexes

LexisNexis, PAIS International.

Agricultural Research. See Agriculture section.

2831. *Alcohol Research: current reviews.* Former titles (until 2012): *Alcohol Research & Health;* (until 1999): *Alcohol Health & Research World.* [ISSN: 2168-3492] 1973. 3x/yr. USD 33 domestic; USD 46.20 foreign; USD 13.75 per issue domestic. U.S. National Institute on Alcohol Abuse and Alcoholism, 5635 Fishers Ln, MSC 9304, Bethesda, MD 20892; NIAAAPressOffice@mail.nih.gov; http://www.niaaa.nih.gov. Illus., index. Refereed. Vol. ends: No. 4. *Indexed:* A01, A22, Agr, AmStI, C42, CJPI, Chicano, MASUSE, P02, PsycInfo, SWR&A. *Aud.:* Ac, Sa.

Each issue is devoted to a particular topic in alcohol research, e.g., children of alcoholics, chronobiology, circadian rhythms and alcohol use, and alcohol and comorbid mental health disorders. This quarterly, peer-reviewed scientific journal is available in full text from 1994 to date on the web site of the National Institute on Alcohol Abuse and Alcoholism. URL: www.niaaa.nih.gov/ Publications/AlcoholResearch

Amber Waves. See Agriculture section.

The Astronomical Almanac. See Astronomy section.

2832. *Cityscape (Washington, D.C.): a journal of policy development and research.* [ISSN: 1936-007X] 1994. 3x/yr. Free. U.S. Department of Housing and Urban Development, Office of Policy Development and Research, PO Box 23268, Washington, DC 20026; helpdesk@huduser.org; http://www.huduser.org/portal/. *Indexed:* ABIn, JEL. *Aud.:* Ga, Ac, Sa.

Cityscape: A Journal of Policy Development and Research strives to share HUD-funded and other research on housing and urban policy issues with scholars, government officials, and others who are involved in setting policy and determining the direction of future research. This refereed journal focuses on innovative ideas, policies, and programs that show promise in revitalizing cities and regions, renewing their infrastructure, and creating economic opportunities. A typical issue consists of articles that examine various aspects of a theme of particular interest to its audience, such as home equity conversion mortgage or reverse mortgage, personal bankruptcy exemption laws, mortgage availability, housing discrimination, assisted housing, etc. It has been online since its first issue in August 1994. URL: www.huduser.org/portal/periodicals/cityscape.html

2833. *Common Ground (Washington, DC): preserving our nation's heritage.* Former titles (until 1996): *Federal Archeology;* (until 1994): *Federal Archeology Report.* [ISSN: 1087-9889] 1988. q. Free. U.S. Department of the Interior, National Park Service, National Center for Cultural Resources, 1849 C Street NW 2286, Washington, DC 20240; http://www.nps.gov/. *Indexed:* A07. *Aud.:* Ga, Ac, Sa.

This award-winning magazine from the National Parks Service archaeology program has had two name changes: from *Common Ground: Archeology and Ethnography in the Public Interest* and, prior to that, *Federal Archaeology.* Expanding its scope beyond archaeology and ethnography, *Common Ground* now offers an in-depth look at the nationwide effort to preserve our heritage in all its forms. Stories focus not only on preservation, but on the people making it happen—on public and tribal lands and in cities, towns, and neighborhoods across the nation. Readers will find a wealth of useful information—from the nuts and bolts of approaches that work, to where to get grants, to the latest research findings. It is written in a jargon-free, to-the-point style. Quality artwork and photography provide an intimate portrait of America's heritage. Full text online; archived online since 2003. URL: http://commonground.cr.nps.gov/Index.cfm

2834. *Congressional Record: proceedings and debates of the Congress.* Former titles (until 1873): *Congressional Globe;* (until 1833): *Register of Debates in Congress;* (until 1824): *United States. Congress. Debates and Proceedings;* (until 1789): *United States. Continental Congress. Journal.* [ISSN: 0363-7239] 1774. d. USD 503 domestic; USD 704.20 foreign. U.S. Government Printing Office, 732 N Capitol St, NW, Washington, DC 20401; http://www.gpo.gov. Illus., index. *Aud.:* Ac, Sa.

The *Congressional Record* is the most widely recognized published account of the debates, proceedings, and activities of the United States Congress. Currently averaging more than 200 pages a day, it is a substantially verbatim account of the proceedings of Congress. It is published daily when either or both houses of Congress are in session. It may be thought of as the world's largest daily newspaper, because it contains an account of everything that is said and done on the floors of the House and Senate, extensive additional reprinting of inserted materials, and, since 1947, a resume of congressional activity (the *Daily Digest*). Available and searchable online through *FDsys* from 1994 to current at www.gpo.gov/fdsys/search/home.action; and through the Library of Congress's THOMAS database from 1989 to present at http://thomas.loc.gov.

2835. *Daily Compilation of Presidential Documents.* Formerly (until 2009): *Weekly Compilation of Presidential Documents (Online).* [ISSN: 1946-6986] 1965. w. USD 133 domestic; USD 186.20 foreign. National Archives and Records Administration, U.S. Office of the Federal Register, 8601 Adelphi Rd, College Park, MD 20740; http://www.federalregister.gov. Illus., index. Circ: 7000. Vol. ends: No. 52. *Indexed:* A01, A22, Chicano, MASUSE, P02. *Aud.:* Ga, Ac, Sa.

As of January 29, 2009, the *Weekly Compilation of Presidential Documents* was replaced by the *Daily Compilation of Presidential Documents.* Now it is more often referred to as *Compilation of Presidential Documents.* This is the authoritative source for all presidential communications, including proclamations, executive orders, speeches, press conferences, communications to Congress and Federal agencies, statements regarding bill signings and vetoes, appointments, nominations, reorganization plans, resignations, retirements, acts approved by the president, nominations submitted to the Senate, White House announcements, and press releases. It is only in electronic form from the U.S. Government Printing Office's GPOAccess: www.gpoaccess.gov/presdocs/index.html. GPOAccess will also maintain the *Weekly Compilation of Presidential Documents* from 1993 to January 26, 2009, at www.gpo.gov/fdsys/search/home.action.

2836. *Emerging Infectious Diseases (Print).* [ISSN: 1080-6040] 1995. m. Free. Ed(s): D Peter Drotman. U.S. Department of Health and Human Services, Centers for Disease Control and Prevention, 1600 Clifton Rd, Atlanta, GA 30333; http://www.cdc.gov. Illus. Refereed. Vol. ends: No. 4. *Indexed:* A01, A22, ABS&EES, BRI, C45, ExcerpMed, FS&TA, IndVet, RRTA, RiskAb. *Bk. rev.:* Number and length vary. *Aud.:* Ga, Sa.

This is a monthly peer-reviewed journal that tracks and analyzes disease trends. It has a very high citation rate and ranking in its field. In addition to dispatches on the latest epidemiology of infectious diseases, the issues contain research articles, columns, letters, commentary, and book reviews. Available in full text beginning with its inaugural issue in 1995 from the Centers for Disease Control and Prevention web site. URL: www.cdc.gov/ncidod/eid/index.htm

2837. *Engineer (Fort Leonard Wood): the professional bulletin of Army engineers.* [ISSN: 0046-1989] 1971. q. USD 24. Ed(s): Shirley Bridges, Rick Brunk. U.S. Army Maneuver Support Center, Development Support Department, MANSCEN Directorate of Training, 464 Manscen Loop, Ste 2661, Fort Leonard Wood, MO 65473; leon.engineer@conus.army.mil; http://www.wood.army.mil. *Indexed:* A01, A22, ABIn, BRI, C&ISA, CerAb, P02. *Bk. rev.:* Number and length vary. *Aud.:* Sa.

Engineer is a professional-development bulletin designed to provide a forum for exchanging information and ideas within the Army engineer community. Articles are by and about officers, enlisted soldiers, warrant officers, Department of the Army civilian employees, and others. Writers discuss training, current operations and exercises, doctrine, equipment, history, personal viewpoints, or other areas of general interest to engineers. Articles may share good ideas and lessons learned or explore better ways of doing things. In addition to regular columns from the Commandant of the U.S. Army Engineer School and from the Command Sergeant Major, and a book review column, there is also a column entitled "Dedication," which lists those in the Army Corps of Engineers who have been lost in the global war on terrorism. Full-text electronic coverage as of 2003. URL: www.wood.army.mil/Eengrmag/default.html

2838. *English Teaching Forum.* Former titles (until 2000): *U.S. Department of State. Bureau of International Information Programs. Forum;* (until 1982): *United States. International Communication Agency. Forum;* (until 197?): *United States Information Agency. Forum;* (until 1978): *English Teaching Forum.* [ISSN: 1559-663X] 1963. q. USD 21 domestic; USD 29.40 foreign. U.S. Department of State, Bureau of Education and Cultural Affairs, 2201 C St NW, Washington, DC 20520. Illus. Circ: 100000. *Indexed:* A22, ERIC, LT&LA, MLA-IB. *Bk. rev.:* 4. *Aud.:* Ga, Ac, Sa.

A quarterly journal published by the U.S. Department of State for teachers of English as a foreign or second language. Over 60,000 copies of the magazine are distributed in 100 countries. Most of the authors published in the journal are classroom teachers and regular readers of the journal. Submissions from English-language teachers around the world are welcomed. Book reviews are a half-page in length. Articles from issues of the *Forum* dating back to 1993 are available online through *GPO Access* or directly at the U.S. Department of State web site. URL: http://exchanges.state.gov/englishteaching/forum-journal.html

Environmental Health Perspectives. See Public Health section.

F B I Law Enforcement Bulletin. See Criminology and Law Enforcement section.

Federal Probation. See Criminology and Law Enforcement section.

2839. *Federal Reserve Bulletin.* [ISSN: 0014-9209] 1915. q. USD 25 domestic; USD 35 foreign. U.S. Federal Reserve System, Board of Governors, 20th St and Constitution Ave, NW, Washington, DC 20551; regs.comments@federalreserve.gov; http://www.federalreserve.gov. Circ: 26000. Microform: CIS; MIM; PMC; PQC. Reprint: WSH. *Indexed:* A01, A22, ABIn, AmStI, B01, B02, BLI, CLI, EconLit, JEL, P02. *Aud.:* Ac, Sa.

Staff members of the Board of Governors of the Federal Reserve prepare the articles for this publication. In general, they report and analyze economic developments, discuss bank regulatory issues, and present new data. Available in full text online since 1996 on the Federal Reserve Board web site. The quarterly *paper* version of the *Bulletin* is no longer published. However, the board produces an annual compilation in print for sale. URL: www.federalreserve.gov/pubs/general.htm

Fishery Bulletin. See Fish, Fisheries, and Aquaculture section.

2840. *Heritage News.* [ISSN: 1555-2748] 2003. m. Free. U.S. Department of the Interior, National Park Service, National Center for Cultural Resources, 1849 C Street NW 2286, Washington, DC 20240; http://www.nps.gov/. *Aud.:* Ga, Ac, Sa.

Heritage News is a monthly e-newsletter published by the National Park Service to deliver timely information on topics that include grant opportunities, new laws or policies, events, and activities of interest to the national heritage community. It updates its sister publications *Common Ground: Preserving Our Nation's Heritage* and *CRM: The Journal of Heritage Stewardship.* Also includes information on significant legislation. Online since August 2003. URL: http://heritagenews.cr.nps.gov/index/Index.cfm

Humanities: the magazine of the national endowment for the humanities. See Cultural Studies section.

2841. *M M W R.* Formerly (until 1976): *U.S. National Communicable Disease Center. Morbidity and Mortality.* [ISSN: 0149-2195] 1951. w. USD 373 domestic; USD 522.20 foreign. Ed(s): Frederic E Shaw, Teresa F Rutledge. U.S. Department of Health and Human Services, Centers for Disease Control and Prevention, 1600 Clifton Rd, Atlanta, GA 30333; http://www.cdc.gov. Illus., index. Microform: CIS; PQC. *Indexed:* A01, A22, AmStI, C42, C45, FS&TA, IndVet, P02, RRTA. *Aud.:* Ac, Sa.

Contains data on specific diseases as reported by state and territorial health departments, and reports on infectious and chronic diseases, environmental hazards, natural or human-generated disasters, occupational diseases and injuries, and intentional and unintentional injuries. Also included are reports on topics of international interest and notices of events of interest to the public health community. No longer distributed in paper to federal depository libraries. However, a print subscription may be purchased. Available online from 1982 on the Centers for Disease Control's own web site. URL: www.cdc.gov/mmwr/

Marine Fisheries Review. See Fish, Fisheries, and Aquaculture section.

Mariners Weather Log. See Marine Science and Technology section.

Military History. See Military section.

Military Review. See Military section.

2842. *National Institute of Standards and Technology. Journal of Research (Online).* [ISSN: 2165-7254] 1904. bi-m. Free. Ed(s): Robert A Dragoset, Sabrina Springer. U.S. Department of Commerce, National Institute of Standards and Technology, 100 Bureau Dr, Stop 2500, Gaithersburg, MD 20899; inquiries@nist.gov; http://www.nist.gov. *Aud.:* Ac, Sa.

This journal reports on National Institute of Standards and Technology (NIST) research and development in metrology and related fields of physical science, engineering, applied mathematics, statistics, biotechnology, and information technology. Papers cover a broad range of subjects, with the major emphasis on measurement methodology and the basic technology that underlies standardization. Also included, on occasion, are articles on topics closely related to the institute's technical and scientific program. NIST was formerly the National Bureau of Standards. Full text of all articles since 1948 is available on the NIST web site. URL: http://nist.gov/publication-portal.cfm

Occupational Outlook Quarterly. See Occupations and Careers section.

2843. *On Safety.* Former titles (until 2009): *The Safety Review;* (until 200?): *Consumer Product Safety Review;* (until 1996): *N E I S S Data Highlights; N E I S S News.* 1976. q. Free. U.S. Consumer Product Safety Commission, Washington, DC 20207. Circ: 1300 Paid. *Indexed:* AmStI. *Aud.:* Ga, Sa.

With its new title, *OnSafety,* this quarterly journal has become a blog that offers an in-depth look at the latest hazards associated with 15,000 types of consumer products under the agency's jurisdiction, both home and recreational products, as well as the most significant current product recalls. Available from its first issue in summer 1996 to its current issue. URL: www.cpsc.gov/onsafety/cpsr.html

Parameters. See Military section.

2844. *Peace Watch.* Formerly (until 1994): *United States Institute of Peace. Journal.* [ISSN: 1080-9864] 1988. 3x/yr. Ed(s): Elizabeth Harper. U.S. Institute of Peace, 1200 17th St NW, Ste 200, Washington, DC 20036-3011; http://www.usip.org. Illus. Circ: 15000. Vol. ends: Oct (No. 6). *Indexed:* ABS&EES. *Aud.:* Ga, Ac, Sa.

The U.S. Institute of Peace is an independent, nonpartisan federal institution created by Congress to promote the prevention, management, and peaceful resolution of international conflicts. Articles are written by the institute's staff and focus on news of conflicts worldwide, as well as report on symposia held under the sponsorship of the institute. Full text since December 2007 is available online at its web site. URL: www.usip.org/publications/

Prologue. See Archives and Manuscripts section.

Public Health Reports. See Public Health section.

Public Roads. See Transportation section.

Science & Technology Review. See Science and Technology section.

2845. *State Magazine.* Former titles (until 1996): *State;* (until 1980): *U.S. Department of State. Newsletter.* [ISSN: 1099-4165] 1961. m. except Aug.-Sep. combined issue. USD 48 domestic; USD 67.20 foreign. Ed(s): Rob Wiley. U.S. Department of State, 2201 C St NW, Washington, DC 20520. Illus. Microform: MIM; PQC. *Indexed:* A22, ABS&EES. *Aud.:* Ga, Sa.

State Magazine is published to facilitate communication between management and employees of the State Department at home and abroad, and to acquaint employees with developments that may affect operations or personnel. The magazine is also available to persons interested in working for the Department of State and to the general public. While the magazine serves the members of the State Department, it contains interesting articles about people and places all over the world. Online since 2000. URL: www.state.gov/m/dghr/statemag

2846. *Treasury Bulletin.* Incorporates (in 1945): *Annual Report on the Financial Condition and results of the Operations of the Highway Trust Fund.* [ISSN: 0041-2155] 1939. q. USD 26 domestic; USD 36.40 foreign. U.S. Department of the Treasury, Financial Management Service, 3700 East West Highway, Rm 515C, Hyattsville, MD 20782; http://www.fms.treas.gov. Circ: 1900. Microform: CIS; PMC. *Indexed:* ABIn, AmStI, B01, BLI. *Aud.:* Ga, Sa.

This is a quarterly synopsis of U.S. Department of the Treasury activities, covering financing operations, budget receipts and expenditures, debt operations, cash income and outgo, IRS collections, capital movements, yields of long-term bonds, ownership of federal securities, and other Treasury activities. There are lots of charts and graphs. Regular features include "Profile of the Economy," "Market Yields," "International Statistics," "Capital Movements," "Foreign Currency Positions," and "Federal Debt." Online since March 1996. URL: www.fms.treas.gov/bulletin/index.html

U.S. Bureau of Labor Statistics. Monthly Labor Review Online. See Labor and Industrial Relations section.

■ GOVERNMENT PERIODICALS—STATE AND LOCAL

General/State and Municipal Associations

See also Political Science; and Urban Studies sections.

Rosemary L. Meszaros, Professor and Coordinator, Government Information and Law, Western Kentucky University, Bowling Green, KY 42101; FAX: 270-745-6175; rosemary.meszaros@wku.edu

Introduction

Documents librarians who specialize in state and local governments are detectives at heart. Since only six states (California, Florida, Michigan, South Carolina, Texas, and Virginia) maintain a depository program similar to that of the federal government, the librarians sleuthing through the Internet will discover a hidden trove of periodical treasures. In fact, many states use the Internet as their publishing medium of choice. The cost savings especially are an attractive alternative to print for tight budgets. The fears about retention of archives are appearing in many of the titles in these government periodical sections.

The periodicals in this section cover a variety of local and state issues. They are necessarily narrowly focused and offer a home-grown coverage that national periodicals do not. Budgeting, the environment, infrastructure, technology, telecommunications, and health care are common topics. Besides these communal concerns, some of the periodicals feature articles on how the policies of the federal government may impact local issues, such as unemployment as affected by stimulus packages. Many also profile state and local government officials.

While some of the periodicals in this section may be of interest primarily to state and local officials, most are of interest to residents of the areas. A companion section in this volume is Urban Studies.

Basic Periodicals

Ga: *Nation's Cities Weekly;* Ac: *Governing, State and Local Government Review, State Legislatures.*

Basic Abstracts and Indexes

LexisNexis, PAIS International, Urban Studies Abstracts, Worldwide Political Science Abstracts.

General

American City & County. See Urban Studies section.

2847. Capitol Ideas. Former titles (until 2010): *State News;* (until 2004): *State Government News;* Which incorporated (in 1978): *Legislative Session Sheet; States and Nation;* Which was formerly (until 1962): *Washington Bulletin;* (until 1961): *Washington Legislative Bulletin;* (199?-2001): *State Trends;* Which was formerly (until 199?): *State Trends Bulletin.* [ISSN: 2152-8489] 1958. bi-m. USD 42; USD 7 per issue. Ed(s): Mary Branham. Council of State Governments, 2760 Research Park Dr, PO Box 11910, Lexington, KY 40578; info@csg.org; http://www.csg.org/. Illus., adv. Vol. ends: Nov/Dec. Microform: WSH. *Indexed:* A01, A22, BRI. *Aud.:* Ga, Sa.

For more than 50 years, *Capitol Ideas* magazine, formerly titled *State News,* has been a source of nonpartisan information. It offers updates and in-depth analyses of state programs, policies, and trends in the executive, legislative, and judicial branches. It covers areas such as budget shortfalls, health and human services, environment and natural resources, agriculture and rural policy, public safety and justice, education, energy, transportation, telecommunications, digital government, fiscal policy, economic development, state leadership, state management and administration, federalism and intergovernmental relations, interstate relations, election coverage, emergency management, and more. Online since 2000. URL: www.csg.org/pubs/statenews.aspx

2848. CommonWealth: politics, ideas and civic life in Massachusetts. 1996. q. USD 50. Ed(s): Bruce Mohl. The Massachusetts Institute for a New Common Wealth, 18 Tremont St, Ste 1120, Boston, MA 02108; info@massinc.org; http://www.massinc.org. *Bk. rev.:* Number and length vary. *Aud.:* Ga, Ac, Sa.

The mission of MassINC, publisher of *CommonWealth,* is to develop a public agenda for Massachusetts that promotes the growth and vitality of the middle class. MassINC has four primary initiatives: economic prosperity, lifelong learning, safe neighborhoods, and civic renewal. The publication includes articles, interviews, news, and book reviews. *CommonWealth* calls itself the Bay State's leading political magazine. A *Boston Globe* journalist has called it "snazzy and fair-minded." Web access has been available since summer 1996. Subscribers to the print version are asked for a USD 50 donation to become a friend of MassINC. Online access is free, but registration is required. URL: www.massinc.org

2849. Connection (Phoenix). 2003. m. Free. Ed(s): Mary Vinzant. League of Arizona Cities and Towns, 1820 West Washington St, Phoenix, AZ 85007; league@azleague.org; http://www.azleague.org. *Aud.:* Ga, Ac, Sa.

The League of Arizona Cities and Towns, a voluntary membership organization of the incorporated municipalities in Arizona, through its publication it;Connection aims to provide vital services and tools to all its members, focusing principally on representing the interests of cities and towns before the legislature, and secondarily providing technical and legal assistance, coordinating shared services, and producing high-quality conference and educational events. All issues are online. URL: www.azleague.org/newsletr/connect/

2850. County News (Washington). Formerly (until 1973): *N A C O News and Views.* [ISSN: 0744-9798] 1970. s-m. Ed(s): Beverly Schlotterbeck. National Association of Counties, 25 Massachusetts Ave, NW, Washington, DC 20001; http://www.naco.org. Illus. Vol. ends: Dec. *Aud.:* Sa.

Published by the National Association of Counties (NACo), this journal evaluates issues and policies of interest to county officials nationwide. Sections include "Financial Services News," "HR (Human Resources) Doctor," "Job Market," "News from the Nation's Counties," "Notices," "NACo on the Move," "Profiles in Service" (profiles of county officials), "Research News," "Web Watch," and "Classifieds." Full text is available online since January 2005 at NACo's web site. URL: www.naco.org/CountyNewsTemplate.cfm?Section=County_News

2851. Empire State Report: the magazine of politics and policy for New York State. Former titles (until 1989): *Changing Faces;* (until 1985): *Empire State Report Weekly;* (until 1983): *Empire State Report;* (until 1979): *Empire;* (until 1978): *Empire State Report.* [ISSN: 0747-0711] 1974. 10x/yr. USD 19.95 domestic; USD 75 foreign. Empire State Report Inc, PO Box 9001, Mt Vernon, NY 10552-9001. Circ: 15600 Paid and controlled. *Indexed:* A22. *Bk. rev.:* Number and length vary. *Aud.:* Ga, Ac, Sa.

This magazine of politics, policy, and the business of government in New York State reaches the state's senior municipal and town executives and financial decision makers (mayors, town supervisors, village managers, comptrollers, etc.). Readers also include statewide elected officials, state agency and authority heads, state government managers and senior staff, local and town government officials, public school and college/university administrators, private association executives, and business leaders across the state. *Empire State Report* dissects legislative issues from all angles and presents ideas in an objective fashion to incite balanced and beneficial change. Not available online.

2852. I C M A Public Management Magazine. Former titles (until 2007): *Public Management;* Which incorporated (in 1970): *International City Management Association. Annual Conference. Proceedings;* (until 1926): *City Manager Magazine;* (until 1923): *City Manager Bulletin.* 1919. m. 11/yr. Free to members; Non-members, USD 46. Ed(s): Beth Payne.

International City/County Management Association, 777 N Capitol St NE, Ste 500, Washington, DC 20002; info@icma.org; http://icma.org/en/icma/home. Illus., adv. Circ: 9500. Vol. ends: Dec. Microform: MIM; PQC. *Indexed:* A22, ABIn, B01, BRI, P02, P61, SSA. *Aud.:* Ga, Sa.

The International City/County Management Association (ICMA) is the publisher of *PM*. ICMA is the professional and educational organization for chief appointed managers, administrators, and assistants in cities, towns, counties, and regional entities throughout the world. Feature articles are written from the local government manager's point of view. The intent of the articles is to allow other local government managers to adapt solutions to fit their own situations. Regular sections include letters to the editor, profiles of individual officials and corporate entities, an ethics column, and FYI news briefs. Articles online are passworded, but are available to ICMA members and subscribers to *Public Management*. Online since 2003. URL: www.icma.org/pm/info/about.cfm

2853. *Illinois Issues.* [ISSN: 0738-9663] 1975. m. 10/yr. USD 35.95 domestic; USD 94.95 foreign. Ed(s): Dana Heupel. University of Illinois at Springfield, PO Box 19243, Springfield, IL 62794-9243; http://www.uis.edu. Illus., adv. Circ: 6500. Vol. ends: Dec. *Bk. rev.:* 1, 1,000 words. *Aud.:* Ga, Ac.

This magazine's mission is to provide fresh, provocative analysis of public policy in Illinois. With a special focus on Illinois government and politics, it pays close attention to current trends and legislative issues, and examines the state's quality of life. It also engages its readers in dialogue, enhancing the quality of public discourse in Illinois. A not-for-profit monthly magazine published by the University of Illinois at Springfield, *Illinois Issues* also sponsors and promotes other appropriate public-affairs educational activities. Available in full text online since March 2002. The web site also features a blog. URL: http://illinoisissues.uis.edu/index.html

2854. *M A Co News.* 1971. USD 25. Montana Association of Counties, 2715 Skyway Dr, Ste A, Helena, MT 59602; maco@mtcounties.org; http://www.mtcounties.org. *Aud.:* Ga, Ac, Sa.

Online since August 2001, this journal offers news of all Montana counties. In each issue, there is a highlighted article of newsworthy interest. The issues feature interviews with officials, reportage of important trends, and attention to conferences held in the state. Not confining itself exclusively to local news, the journal also covers issues of national importance. Available online. URL: www.mtcounties.org/news

2855. *Maine Policy Review.* [ISSN: 1064-2587] 1991. 3x/yr. 0 Donation. Ed(s): Ann Acheson. Margaret Chase Smith Center for Public Policy, University of Maine, 5784 York Complex, Bldg 4, Orono, ME 04469-5784; mcsc@umit.maine.edu; http://www.umaine.edu/mcsc/mpr.htm. *Aud.:* Ga, Ac, Sa.

A joint publication of the Margaret Chase Smith Center for Public Policy at the University of Maine. The majority of articles in *Maine Policy Review* are written by Maine citizens, many of whom are readers of the journal. It publishes independent analyses of public policy issues relevant to Maine by providing accurate information and thoughtful commentary. Issues range from snowmobiling to housing. Most issues since 1991 are on the web site. URL: www.umaine.edu/mcsc/MPR/archives/Archive.htm

2856. *Nation's Cities Weekly.* Formed by the merger of (1978-1978): *City Weekly;* (1963-1978): *Nation's Cities.* [ISSN: 0164-5935] 1978. w. Free to members; Non-members, USD 96. Ed(s): Cindy Hogan. National League of Cities, 1301 Pennsylvania Ave, NW, Ste 550, Washington, DC 20004; http://www.nlc.org. Illus., adv. Circ: 30000 Paid and free. Vol. ends: Dec. Microform: PQC. *Indexed:* A01, A22, B02, BRI, P02. *Aud.:* Ga, Sa.

This tabloid provides up-to-the-minute news on how national developments will affect cities, in-depth reports and case studies on how local governments are finding innovative solutions to today's municipal problems, and special editorial features by urban affairs experts. It includes regular reporting on developments in Congress and the Executive branch, the courts, and state government. To supplement this extensive coverage, *Nation's Cities Weekly* provides special reports throughout the year on key topics of interest to local

government leaders on finance, the environment, housing, technology, economic development, and telecommunications, as well as extensive coverage of the National League of Cities' two annual conventions. Regular monthly columns feature news about technologies, products, and services of interest to local governments and a roundup of news about how cities are solving today's problems and improving services to citizens. Online since 2009 on the National League of Cities web site. URL: www.nlc.org/articles/current_issue.aspx

2857. *North Carolina Insight.* 1978. s-a. USD 40. Ed(s): Mebane Rash. North Carolina Center for Public Policy Research, Inc., 5 W Hargett St, Ste 701, Raleigh, NC 27602; http://www.nando.net/insider/nccppr. Adv. Circ: 1000 Paid. *Aud.:* Ga, Ac, Sa.

The mission of the North Carolina Center for Public Policy Research is to create a more well-informed public and more effective, accountable, and responsive government by examining public policy issues that face North Carolina and enrich the dialogue among three constituencies: the public, the media, and policy makers. Based on its research and published studies, the center sometimes makes recommendations on public policy issues. *North Carolina Insight* features pro-and-con debates on issues such as education, the lottery, infrastructure, funding for the arts, voter turnout, and elections. Now available online with archives back to volume 1 in 1978.

2858. *Pennsylvania Township News.* [ISSN: 0162-5160] 1948. m. USD 36. Ed(s): Ginni Linn. Pennsylvania State Association of Township Supervisors, 4855 Woodland Dr, Enola, PA 17025; psatsweb@psats.org; http://www.psats.org. Illus., adv. Circ: 10000 Paid and free. Vol. ends: Dec. *Aud.:* Sa.

Regular features of *Pennsylvania Township News* include "Legislative Update," "Environmental Digest," "Newsworthy Items," "One Source Municipal Training" (a listing and description of courses offered to township officials), and a "Questions & Answers" column. Articles deal with common interests to the over 1,450 Pennsylvania member townships: stormwater drainage, animal control, recycling, etc. There are also interviews with top-ranking township officials. Table of contents is online. Articles are available online to subscribers only.

2859. *Privatization Watch.* Formerly (until 1988): *Fiscal Watchdog.* 1976. m. Ed(s): Leonard Gilroy. Reason Foundation, 5737 Mesmer Ave, Los Angeles, CA 90230; chris.mitchell@reason.org; http://reason.org/. Adv. *Aud.:* Ga, Ac.

Each issue concerns a specific topic: health care, bailouts, recession, education, environment, corrections, public safety, and other subjects of interest. This journal is published by the Public Policy Institute of the Reason Foundation, a libertarian public policy think tank promoting choice, competition, and a dynamic market economy as the foundation for human dignity and progress. Coverage of public-private partnerships is worldwide. Articles are full-text online since 2004, at www.reason.org/pw.shtml. There is also a blog where comments can be posted.

2860. *State and Local Government Review: a journal of research and viewpoints on state and local government issues.* Formerly (until 1976): *Georgia Government Review.* [ISSN: 0160-323X] 1968. q. USD 248. Ed(s): Michael Scicchitano. Sage Publications, Inc., 2455 Teller Rd, Thousand Oaks, CA 91320; info@sagepub.com; http://www.sagepub.com. Illus., index. Refereed. Vol. ends: Fall. Reprint: PSC. *Indexed:* A22, E01, P61, SSA. *Bk. rev.:* 1, 1,000 words. *Aud.:* Ac, Sa.

State and Local Government Review is jointly sponsored by the Carl Vinson Institute of Government of the University of Georgia and the Section on Intergovernmental Administration and Management (SIAM) of the American Society for Public Administration (ASPA). SIAM is the section of ASPA that is dedicated to state and local as well as intergovernmental teaching and research. Membership in SIAM includes a subscription to *State and Local Government Review*. Issues include feature stories and the "Practitioner's Corner," which offers practical advice for government officials on issues such as local government, social equity, sustainability, federalism, telecommunications, utility deregulation, etc. This is one of the few scholarly journals in this field. Contents and abstracts of articles are available for the most recent issue. Full text is available for previous issues from 1993 forward through the Carl Vinson Institute of Government. Online for subscribers since 1993. Abstracts only, 1993–96; abstracts and full text, 1997 to the present. URL: www.cviog.uga.edu/publications/slgr/issues.php

2861. *State Legislatures.* [ISSN: 0147-6041] 1975. m. 10/yr. USD 49 domestic; USD 55 Canada. Ed(s): Edward Smith. National Conference of State Legislatures, 7700 E First Pl, Denver, CO 80230; http://www.ncsl.org/. Illus., adv. Circ: 18200. Vol. ends: Dec. *Indexed:* A01, A22, BRI, MASUSE, P02. *Aud.:* Ga, Ac.

The trends, issues, solutions, personalities, innovations, and challenges of managing a state—they will all be found in *State Legislatures* magazine, published by the National Conference of State Legislatures. This national magazine of state government and policy provides lively, insightful articles that encompass vital information on public policies. From agriculture to cloning to transportation, it covers a wide variety of topics. Only excerpts are available online for nonsubscribers; full access is for subscribers. URL: www.ncsl.org/magazine

2862. *State Net Capitol Journal: news & views from the 50 states.* [ISSN: 1521-8457] 1998. w. Free to qualified personnel. Ed(s): Rich Ehisen. State Net, 2101 K St, Sacramento, CA 95816; info@statenet.com; http://www.statenet.com. *Aud.:* Ga, Ac, Sa.

State Net produces *State Net Capitol Journal,* which provides a comprehensive look at the issues and politics that drive state governments all over the country. The 50-state edition covers major trends in the spotlight, from Augusta to Honolulu, and features original reporting from its team of editors, from governors' agendas to legislative hot topics. It also provides an entertaining and informative array of notes and quotes, selecting information from numerous publications around the country. Subscriptions are free to qualified readers, that is, government affairs professionals. URL: www.statenet.com/capitoljournal

2863. *Virginia Review.* Formerly (until 1981): *Virginia Municipal Review.* [ISSN: 0732-9156] 1924. bi-m. USD 18. Ed(s): James M Smith. JS Publications, Inc., 7307 Belmont Stakes Dr, Midlothian, VA 23112. Illus., adv. Circ: 5000 Paid and controlled. Vol. ends: Nov/Dec. *Aud.:* Sa.

This journal has a new publisher and is revamping its web site. It has gone totally digital. A professional journal for officials at all levels of government in the Commonwealth of Virginia, *Virginia Review* prints articles that describe specific problems faced by localities and how the problems were solved, as well as employee relations, planning for growth, and economic development, among other topics. Each issue focuses on a specific theme. The journal does not include political articles or those that have the sole purpose of selling a product or concept. Online since March/April 2004. URL: www.vareview.com/index2.asp

State and Municipal Associations

State and municipal associations are the providers of common ground for local officials to exchange ideas and information in a discussion forum on issues of mutual interest. Shaping the content of the periodicals are the common issues of budget shortfalls, legislation, growth, lotteries, crime, traffic, energy, the environment, telecommunications, and leadership. Many of the periodicals contain helpful features such as a calendar of events and a legal advice column. The usual tone is positive, even with consideration of dire issues. The periodicals take a matter-of-fact perspective on confronting and solving problems. The principal audience for these periodicals comprises practitioners and observers of local government.

2864. *Actionlines Magazine.* 19??. 2x/yr. USD 50. Indiana Association of Cities and Towns, 200 S Meridian, Ste 340, Indianapolis, IN 46225; http://www.citiesandtowns.org. Adv. Circ: 4500. *Aud.:* Ga, Ac, Sa.

Actionlines is the official magazine of the Indiana Association of Cities and Towns. It includes relevant, timely articles about issues that affect Indiana cities and towns and municipal government. It accepts proposals and articles from association members, municipal members, affiliate groups, state agencies, and others. Not available online.

2865. *Alabama Municipal Journal.* Formerly (until 1953): *Alabama Local Government Journal.* [ISSN: 0002-4309] 1935. m. USD 24; USD 2 per issue. Ed(s): Carrie Banks. Alabama League of Municipalities, PO Box 1270, Montgomery, AL 36102; perryr@alalm.org; http://www.alalm.org. Illus. Circ: 4500 Paid and controlled. Vol. ends: Jun. *Aud.:* Sa.

This periodical is from the Alabama League of Municipalities. Its articles highlight the practical issues faced by local governments in Alabama and spotlight common problems, solutions, trends, and legal information. It offers reprints of speeches and articles from other publications from time to time. Unrestricted Internet access since the September 2002 issue. URL: www.alalm.org

2866. *Cities and Villages.* Formerly (until 1970): *Ohio Cities and Villages.* [ISSN: 0009-7535] 1953. bi-m. Free to members. Ed(s): Cynthia L Grant. Ohio Municipal League, 175 S Third St, Ste 510, Columbus, OH 43215; cgrant@omlohio.org; http://www.omlohio.org/. Illus., index, adv. *Aud.:* Ga, Ac, Sa.

The official publication of the Ohio Municipal League, *Cities and Villages* is read by officials who are directly involved in every aspect of municipal management and service. The magazine keeps the leadership of Ohio's cities and villages informed on current developments and the latest techniques for solving municipal problems. Not available online.

2867. *City & Town.* Formerly: *Arkansas Municipalities.* [ISSN: 0193-8371] 1947. m. USD 20; USD 1.67 newsstand/cover per issue. Ed(s): Andrew Morgan. Arkansas Municipal League, PO Box 38, North Little Rock, AR 72115-0038; jkw@arml.org; http://www.arml.org. Illus., index, adv. Circ: 6800 Paid and free. Vol. ends: Dec. *Aud.:* Sa.

Designed to provide a forum for municipal officials to exchange ideas and compare notes on accomplishments and problems in Arkansas, *City & Town* is sent to elected officials; city administrators and managers; police chiefs, fire chiefs, and other department heads; and state officials, local newspapers, chambers of commerce, and other offices and persons who are interested in municipal affairs. Employment opportunities and classified ads are spotlighted in the "Municipal Mart" section. Selected articles for 2005 and pdf full text from 2006 appear online. URL: www.arml.org/publications_city_town.html

2868. *City Scan (Bismarck).* Formerly (until 1996): *North Dakota League of Cities Bulletin.* [ISSN: 1094-5784] 1969. 10x/yr. Free to qualified personnel. Ed(s): Connie Sprynczynatyk. North Dakota League of Cities, 410 E. Front Ave., Bismarck, ND 58504; http://www.ndlc.org/. Illus., adv. Circ: 2850. *Aud.:* Sa.

Written specifically for city and park district officials and designed to promote best municipal practices, this magazine regularly features information about technology, cost-saving ideas, innovative programs, leadership issues, and products and services that help city leaders increase the efficiency and effectiveness of municipal operations. Selected articles are online only. URL: www.ndlc.org/index.asp

2869. *Cityscape (Des Moines).* Formerly (until 1995): *Iowa Municipalities.* [ISSN: 1088-5951] 1960. m. Free to members. Ed(s): Betsy Knoblock. Iowa League of Cities, 317 Sixth Ave, Ste 800, Des Moines, IA 50309-4111. Illus., adv. Circ: 5500 Paid. Vol. ends: Jun. *Indexed:* AmStI, JEL. *Aud.:* Sa.

Cityscape is part of the membership benefits of the Iowa League of Cities. The publication contains articles about city government issues in Iowa, and serves as a communication tool for local government officials. Some of the articles featured in *Cityscape* are available online in a Q&A section on the league's web site. Full text is available online only to members.

2870. *Colorado Municipalities.* [ISSN: 0010-1664] 1925. bi-m. USD 150; USD 25 per issue. Ed(s): Traci Stoffel. Colorado Municipal League, 1144 Sherman St, Denver, CO 80203; cml@cml.org; http://www.cml.org. Illus., adv. *Bk. rev.:* Number and length vary. *Aud.:* Ga, Ac, Sa.

This is the flagship magazine of the Colorado Municipal League. Its target audience is Colorado municipal government officials. Each issue runs to about 30 pages, and is packed with in-depth coverage of the topics and issues important to those officials. Available online only to members.

2871. *Connecticut Town & City.* 19??. bi-m. Free to members; Non-members, USD 18. Connecticut Conference of Municipalities, 900 Chapel St, 9th Fl, New Haven, CT 06510; ccm@ccm-ct.org; http://www.ccm-ct.org. Adv. Circ: 7700. *Aud.:* Sa.

This journal reports on major intergovernmental issues, new ideas in municipal management, and cost-saving measures by towns. Regular features include "Regional and Intermunicipal Cooperation," "Innovative Ideas For Managing Local Governments," "Civic Amenities" (which includes beautification projects, noise and litter abatement, and other ideas to make communities better places), "Volunteers," "Municipal Ethics Quiz," "What's New," and "Public-Private Cooperation." This is the only periodical devoted exclusively to issues that concern Connecticut's municipal market. Available online to members only.

2872. *Creating Quality Cities.* Formerly (until 199?): *City Report.* 19??. 9x/yr. Free to members. Ed(s): Ken Harward. Association of Idaho Cities, 3100 S Vista Ave, Ste 310, Boise, ID 83705; http://www.idahocities.org. Adv. *Aud.:* Ga, Ac, Sa.

This newsletter is of interest to government officials and citizens alike. Content includes news; job openings in city government from around Idaho; a calendar of events listing conferences, workshops, and institutes; profiles of city officials; grant opportunities; and a Q&A section on legislative issues. Online issues begin with February 2007. Issues from March 2004 are no longer available online. Go to the web site www.idahocities.org and click AIC Publications.

2873. *Georgia's Cities.* Former titles: *Urban Georgia; Georgia Municipal Journal.* 1951. m. 10/yr. Ed(s): Amy Henderson. Georgia Municipal Association, 201 Pryor St, S W, Atlanta, GA 30303-3606; info@gmanet.com; http://www.gmanet.com. Adv. Circ: 7300 Free. *Aud.:* Ga, Ac, Sa.

Georgia's Cities is sometimes referred to as *Georgia's Cities Newspaper* and resembles a newspaper in layout. The articles follow the newspaper format; there are several columns including a Q&A, district roundup, and city desk. Online since February 2008. Older issues (2006–07) are no longer available online. URL: www.gmanet.com/georgia_cities_newspaper

2874. *Illinois Municipal Review: the magazine of the municipalities.* [ISSN: 0019-2139] 1922. m. Qualified personnel, USD 5. Ed(s): Larry Frang. Illinois Municipal League, PO Box 5180, Springfield, IL 62705-5180; gkoch@iml.org; http://www.iml.org. Illus., adv. Circ: 13500 Controlled. Vol. ends: Dec. *Aud.:* Sa.

A legal Q&A, municipal calendar, exchange column, editorials, and a variety of articles of interest to local Illinois government officials make up this long-running magazine. Available online back to 1997. Current issues are at www.iml.org/spps/sitepage.cfm?catID=19. URL: www.lib.niu.edu/ipo/imlistyrs.html

2875. *Kansas Government Journal.* [ISSN: 0022-8613] 1914. m. USD 30. Ed(s): Kimberly Winn. League of Kansas Municipalities, 300 S W Eighth St, Topeka, KS 66603-3912; kgulley@lkm.org; http://www.lkm.org. Illus., index, adv. Circ: 6200 Paid. Vol. ends: Dec. *Aud.:* Sa.

This periodical keeps Kansas officials up-to-date on federal and statewide legislation, as well as on economic developments and budgetary procedures that impact municipalities. It also focuses on new ways of solving problems and assisting citizens. A subject index appears in the December issue. Available online since 1914. URL: www.lkm.org/publications/

2876. *Kentucky City Magazine.* Former titles (until 2009): *City Magazine;* (until 199?): *Kentucky City;* (until 1968): *Kentucky City Bulletin.* 1929. bi-m. Ed(s): Terri Johnson. Kentucky League of Cities, 101 E Vine St, Ste 600, Lexington, KY 40507-3700; city@klc.org; http://www.klc.org. Illus., adv. Circ: 27100 Controlled. *Aud.:* Sa.

Award-winning *City Magazine* has transitioned to *Kentucky City Magazine* in 2009. In 2011 it was retooled and redesigned. Published by the Kentucky League of Cities, it is Kentucky's only magazine dedicated specifically to city and municipal issues. It covers critical topics; profiles people; and reports on events and innovative initiatives and practices in Kentucky's cities. For example, it reviews significant bills; runs articles on funeral protests; covers (in respective stories) the 2010 Census, copyright infringement, and public showing of movies; profiles Kentucky cities; and includes a colorful calendar of events. Online since 2004. URL: www.klc.org

2877. *Local Focus.* m. Free to members; Non-members, USD 44. Ed(s): Kevin Toon. League of Oregon Cities, 1201 Court St, NE, Ste 200, Salem, OR 97301; loc@orcities.org; http://www.orcities.org. *Aud.:* Ga, Ac, Sa.

This journal presents regular updates on state and federal matters. It also includes League of Oregon Cities news; city happenings and best practices; feature articles; a calendar of events; reference to helpful publications; summaries of legal cases; and a list of job openings. Issues since January 2005 are available online. URL: www.orcities.org/Publications/Newsletters/tabid/873/Default.aspx

2878. *Louisiana Municipal Review.* [ISSN: 0164-3622] 1938. m. USD 12; USD 1.50 per issue. Ed(s): Tom Ed McHugh. Louisiana Municipal Association, PO Box 4327, Baton Rouge, LA 70821; lamunicipalassociation@compuserve.com; http://www.lamunis.org. Adv. Circ: 3300 Paid and controlled. *Aud.:* Ga, Ac, Sa.

The official publication of the Louisiana Municipal Association, a statewide league of villages, towns, and cities in Louisiana, *Louisiana Municipal Review* serves as a medium of exchange of ideas and information on municipal affairs for the public officials of Louisiana. It includes news articles, features, obituaries, and a column written by the state's governor. Online for one calendar year. URL: http://lma.org/LMR/lmr.htm

2879. *Minnesota Cities.* Formerly (until 1976): *Minnesota Municipalities.* [ISSN: 0148-8546] 1916. 10x/yr. USD 43. Ed(s): Claudia Hoffacker. League of Minnesota Cities, 145 University Ave W, St Paul, MN 55103; webmaster@lmnc.org; http://www.lmnc.org. Illus., adv. Circ: 7300 Controlled. *Aud.:* Ga, Ac, Sa.

The League of Minnesota Cities' monthly magazine includes articles on a wide range of city-related topics. Each issue is based on a theme—for example, human resources, technology, and winter.

2880. *Mississippi Municipalities.* [ISSN: 0026-6337] 1955. q. Mississippi Municipal League, 600 E Amite St, Ste 104, Jackson, MS 39201-1906. Illus., adv. *Aud.:* Ga, Ac, Sa.

Mississippi Municipalities contains feature articles as well as an auditor's column and a column on tax collections. The second issue is the annual conference issue. Some archived issues are online. URL: www.mmlonline.com

2881. *Missouri Municipal Review.* [ISSN: 0026-6647] 1936. bi-m. USD 25 (Free to qualified personnel). Ed(s): Katie Bradley. Missouri Municipal League, 1727 Southridge Dr, Jefferson City, MO 65109; info@mocities.com; http://www.mocities.com. Illus., index, adv. Circ: 6400. *Aud.:* Ga, Ac, Sa.

Designed to meet the needs and interests of municipal officials in Missouri, this publication features articles on all phases of municipal government and serves as a medium through which member officials can exchange ideas on current issues. Selected articles are available online. Three special issues are published each year: "Parks and Recreation" (May), "Public Works" (June), and "Pre-Conference" (August). Feature articles only are online. URL: www.mocities.com/default.asp?SectionID=53

2882. *Municipal Advocate.* Formerly (until 1988): *Municipal Forum.* [ISSN: 1046-2422] 1980. q. Members, USD 49; Non-members, USD 99. Ed(s): John Ouellette. Massachusetts Municipal Association, 60 Temple Place, Boston, MA 02111. Adv. Circ: 4525. *Aud.:* Ga, Ac, Sa.

This publication presents in-depth articles about important and timely municipal issues, such as budgeting, technology, management, infrastructure maintenance, education, and legal issues. An emphasis is placed on innovative solutions and problem-solving strategies. Selected feature articles from the latest two years are available online.

2883. *Municipal Bulletin.* 1941. bi-m. Ed(s): Jennifer Purcell. New York Conference of Mayors and Municipal Officials, 119 Washington Ave, Albany, NY 12210; info@nycom.org; http://www.nycom.org/. Circ: 7000. *Aud.:* Ga, Ac, Sa.

Municipal Bulletin is a resource for expanded coverage of NYCOM activities and events. It reports on legislative and other developments at the state and federal levels, and presents in-depth analysis of special issues, affiliate news, and the latest information on the municipal legal front. Available online only to members.

2884. *Municipal Maryland.* Formerly: *Maryland Municipal News.* [ISSN: 0196-9986] 1948. 9x/yr. USD 40. Ed(s): Karen Bohlen. Maryland Municipal League, Inc., 1212 West St, Annapolis, MD 21401. Adv. Circ: 2000. *Aud.:* Ga, Ac, Sa.

Municipal Maryland features articles on a variety of city/town topics, such as downtown revitalization, public works, financial management, conducting effective council meetings, consensus building, legal and personnel issues, recreation, and public safety. Regular columns include "Small Town News," "Innovations," and "City Beat" (news about large municipalities). The November issue features articles that summarize the general sessions and most of the workshops from the Maryland Municipal League's annual summer convention. Registration information for the annual convention is published in the March issue; registration information for the league's legislative conference is published in the July/August issue. Selected articles are available online since 2003. URL: www.mdmunicipal.org/publications/magazine.cfm

2885. *Municipal Research News: resources for Washington cities and towns.* 1991. q. Free to qualified personnel. Ed(s): Connie Elliot. Municipal Research Service Center, 2601 4th Ave, Ste 800, Seattle, WA 98121-1280; mrsc@mrsc.org. *Aud.:* Ga, Ac, Sa.

This is a product of the Municipal and Research Services Center, a private, nonprofit organization based in Seattle. Its mission is to promote excellence in Washington local government through professional consultation, research, and information services. All of the information and research services are available free of charge to elected officials and staff of Washington city and county governments, as well as to officials and staff of Special Purpose Districts that are members of WAPHD, WASWD, or the Enduris Insurance Pool. Online since March 1991. URL: www.mrsc.org/publications/mrscNewsletter.aspx

2886. *The Municipality.* Formerly (until 1916): *Wisconsin Municipality.* [ISSN: 0027-3597] 1900. m. USD 18; USD 1.75 per issue. Ed(s): Jean Staral. League of Wisconsin Municipalities, 122 W Washington Ave, Ste 300, Madison, WI 53703; http://www.lwm-info.org. Illus., index, adv. Circ: 9600 Paid and controlled. Vol. ends: Dec. *Aud.:* Sa.

From mosquito control to complex legal matters, this periodical showcases issues of interest to local government officials in Wisconsin. News about local officials, web links of interest, and a calendar are also included. Full text of the current edition can be found on the web under "Resources" at www.wileague.govoffice2.com.

2887. *Nebraska Municipal Review.* [ISSN: 0028-1905] 1930. m. USD 50; USD 5 per issue. Ed(s): Lynn Marienau. League of Nebraska Municipalities, 1335 L St, Lincoln, NE 68508; info@lonm.org; http://www.lonm.org. Illus., adv. Circ: 3300. *Bk. rev.:* Number and length vary. *Aud.:* Ga, Ac, Sa.

This official publication of the League of Nebraska Municipalities features articles on laws and issues that affect local government, government officials, leadership, and training. Not available online.

2888. *New Hampshire Town & City.* [ISSN: 0545-171X] 19??. 10x/yr. Members, USD 22; Non-members, USD 30; USD 3 per issue. Ed(s): Eleanor M Baron. New Hampshire Municipal Association, 25 Triangle Park Dr, PO Box 617, Concord, NH 03301; info@nhlgc.org; http://www.nhlgc.org. Adv. Circ: 3500. *Aud.:* Ga, Ac, Sa.

Provides local officials and others with 40–60 pages of timely information on legal issues, legislative issues, upcoming programs, and services of the local government center. Selected articles from past issues are available online through topical links, such as "Finance and Taxation," "Land Use," "Liability," and "Governance." URL: www.nhlgc.org/LGCWebSite/InfoForOfficials/townandcityarticles.htm

2889. *New Jersey Municipalities.* [ISSN: 0028-5846] 1917. m. Oct.-Jun. Members, USD 16; Non-members, USD 20. Ed(s): William G Dressel, Jr. New Jersey State League of Municipalities, 222 W State St, Trenton, NJ 08608. Illus., index, adv. Circ: 8200. Vol. ends: Dec. *Aud.:* Sa.

Typical lead articles are on such topics as public–private partnerships, energy, and urban sprawl. Columns include "Legal Q&A," "Legislative Update," "Labor Relations," "Washington Watch," job notices, and a calendar. Selected articles since January 2007 are available online. URL: www.njslom.org/maghome.html

2890. *New Mexico Municipal League. Municipal Reporter.* [ISSN: 0028-6257] 1959. m. Free. Ed(s): Roger Makin, William F Fulginiti. New Mexico Municipal League, PO Box 846, Santa Fe, NM 87504; http://nmml.org. *Aud.:* Ga, Ac, Sa.

The New Mexico Municipal League has produced this monthly newsletter for many years. There is a link to municipal job openings, and a regular column, "HR Insights," tackles personnel policy and problems in a Q&A format. Online publication begins with the June 2010 issue. URL: http://nmml.org/publications/

2891. *Oklahoma Cities & Towns Newsletter.* 1970. m. Members, USD 15; Non-members, USD 30. Ed(s): Carolyn Stager, Jimi Layman. Oklahoma Municipal League, 201 NE 23d, Oklahoma City, OK 73105; http://www.oml.org. *Aud.:* Sa.

This contains news, announcements of institutes and workshops for town and city officials, a section on grants and loans, and a spotlight on Oklahoma Municipal League members. Online since 2004.

2892. *Quality Cities.* Formerly: *Florida Municipal Record.* [ISSN: 0892-4171] 1928. 6x/yr. Members, USD 10; Non-members, USD 20. Ed(s): Beth Mulrennan. Florida League of Cities, Inc., 301 S Bronough St, Ste 300, Tallahassee, FL 32301. Illus., adv. Circ: 4700 Paid. Vol. ends: May. *Aud.:* Ga, Sa.

Quality Cities serves as a medium for exchange of ideas and information for Florida's municipal officials. Reporting addresses legislation that affects cities, current municipal issues, and innovative local-government ideas. The two summer issues cover the post-legislative session report and the Florida League of Cities conference. Not available online.

2893. *Review (Ann Arbor).* Formerly (until 2008): *Michigan Municipal Review.* [ISSN: 1941-532X] 1928. 10x/yr. Free to members. Michigan Municipal League, 1675 Green Rd, Ann Arbor, MI 48106; http://www.minl.org/. Illus., index, adv. Circ: 11300 Controlled. Vol. ends: Dec. Microform: PQC. *Indexed:* A22. *Aud.:* Sa.

This periodical aims to provide a forum to Michigan officials for the exchange of ideas and information. Municipal officials, consultants, legislators, and staff members of the Michigan Municipal League contribute to the publication. Want ads, a marketplace column, a municipal calendar, and legal spotlights round out the issues. Online since 2007. www.mml.org/resources/publications/mmr/index.html

2894. *South Dakota Municipalities.* [ISSN: 0300-6182] 1934. m. Free to members; Non-members, USD 30. Ed(s): Yvonne A Taylor, Carrie A Harer. South Dakota Municipal League, 214 E Capitol Ave, Pierre, SD 57501; http://www.sdmunicipalleague.org/. Adv. Circ: 3000. *Aud.:* Ga, Ac, Sa.

The magazine contains articles on legislation, court decisions, attorney general opinions, and issues that affect municipal operations on a daily basis. Every issue has a column by the Director and the President of the League, as well as a Washington report and risk-sharing news. Available online since 2008. URL: www.sdmunicipalleague.org/

2895. *Tennessee Town and City.* [ISSN: 0040-3415] 1950. s-m. Members, USD 6. Ed(s): Carole Graves. Tennessee Municipal League, 226 Capitol Blvd, Ste 710, Nashville, TN 37219-1894; gstahl@tml1.org; http://www.tml1.org. Illus., index, adv. Circ: 6250 Controlled. *Aud.:* Ga, Ac, Sa.

Tennessee Town and City looks like a newspaper. It has numerous photographs of the subjects of its news items. There is a classified ad section. In addition to distribution by subscription, free copies of *Tennessee Town and City* can be picked up in various newspaper stands in Nashville in the Legislative Plaza and the State Capitol. Online since July 2006. URL: www.tml1.org/issues.php?ID=9

2896. *Texas Town & City.* Former titles (until 1994): *T M L Texas Town & City;* (until 1984): *Texas Town & City;* (until 1959): *Texas Municipalities.* [ISSN: 1084-5356] 1914. 11x/yr. Members, USD 15; Non-members, USD 30. Ed(s): Karla Vining. Texas Municipal League, 1821 Rutherford Ln, Ste 400, Austin, TX 78754. Illus., adv. Circ: 11015. *Aud.:* Ga, Ac, Sa.

The official publication of the Texas Municipal League, this sets its sights on alerting member cities to important governmental or private sector actions or proposed actions that may affect city operations. The magazine has several feature articles, a legal Q&A, and a "Small Cities Corner." A sample issue is online, but no other issues are available online. URL: www.tml.org/pub_ttc.html

2897. *The Touchstone.* Former titles (until 1991): *Legislative Bulletin;* (until 1984): *Alaska Municipal League. Newsletter.* 19??. q. Free to members. Ed(s): Jeremy Woodrow. Alaska Municipal League, 217 Second St, Ste 200, Juneau, AK 99801; info@akml.org; http://www.akml.org. *Aud.:* Ga, Ac, Sa.

Legislative matters, job openings, a business card section, and news of the Alaska Municipal League's conference dominate this official newsletter. When the Alaska State Legislature is in session, *The Touchstone* is supplemented by the electronic weekly *AML Legislative Bulletin.* These publications are sent free to member municipalities, associates, and affiliates. Available online since January 2006. URL: www.akml.org/touchstone.html

2898. *U S Mayor.* Former titles (until 1989): *Mayor;* (until 1971): *United States Municipal News.* [ISSN: 1049-2119] 1934. s-m. USD 35. Ed(s): Tom Cochran, Ed Somers. United States Conference of Mayors, 1620 Eye St, NW, Washington, DC 20006; info@usmayors.org; http://usmayors.org/. Illus., adv. Circ: 9000. *Aud.:* Sa.

Although its present title includes the word *newspaper,* this publication takes the form of a newsletter or newsmagazine. Sections include "Front Page," "Executive Director's Column," other articles, and a calendar of events. Online since August 1996. URL: www.usmayors.org/uscm/us_mayor_newspaper

2899. *V L C T News.* 2000. m. Free to members; Non-members, USD 60. Ed(s): Allyson Barrieau. Vermont League of Cities & Towns, 89 Main St, Ste 4, Montpelier, VT 05602-2948; info@vlct.org; http://www.vlct.org. *Aud.:* Sa.

Legal and regulatory info, staff news, job vacancies, and classifieds. Online since January 2000. URL: www.vlct.org/aboutvlct/vlctnews/

2900. *Virginia Town & City.* [ISSN: 0042-6784] 1966. m. Free to members. Virginia Municipal League, PO Box 12164, Richmond, VA 23241; e-mail@vml.org; http://www.vml.org/. Illus. *Bk. rev.:* Number and length vary. *Aud.:* Ga, Ac, Sa.

Each issue has about three or four major articles on topics such as the environment, the bailout, the digital divide, terrorism, budgets, urban planning, and records management. Available on the web since 2010. URL: www.vml.org/VTC/VTCindex.html

2901. *W A M News.* Former titles (until 1979): *W A M News Bulletin;* (until 1961): *News Bulletin.* 19??. m. Free to members. Ed(s): Ginger Newman. Wyoming Association of Municipalities, 315 W 27th St, Cheyenne, WY 82001. Circ: 2000. *Aud.:* Ga, Ac, Sa.

WAM News is the official newsletter of the Wyoming Association of Municipalities and serves as an exchange of ideas and information for officials of municipalities. It has a broad audience of local and state elected officials, along with state agencies, businesses, and associations involved in local government. In addition to news, there is a calendar of events, a professional directory, and municipal ads, including job vacancies. The last three issues are online. URL: www.wyomuni.org

2902. *Western City.* Former titles (until 1976): *Western City Magazine;* (until 1960): *Western City;* (until 1930): *Hydraulic Engineering;* (until 1927): *Modern Irrigation.* [ISSN: 0279-5337] 1924. m. USD 39 domestic (Students, USD 26.50). Ed(s): Jude Hudson, Eva Spiegel. League of California Cities, 1400 K St, 4th Floor, Sacramento, CA 95814; http://www.cacities.org. Illus., index, adv. Circ: 9466. Vol. ends: Dec. *Aud.:* Sa.

Both practical ideas and bigger-picture policy issues and trends are the twin foci of coverage of *Western City.* The magazine's stated mission is to support and serve elected and appointed city officials (and those interested in local government), and to examine the policy, process, and fiscal issues that affect local government. It does the latter from a number of angles, including individual city success stories, legal analyses, and statewide perspectives. Online since September 2006. URL: www.westerncity.com/

■ HEALTH AND FITNESS

Journals and Magazines/Newsletters

Krista Schmidt, Research and Instruction Librarian/STEM Liaison, Hunter Library, Western Carolina University, Cullowhee, NC 28723; kschmidt@email.wcu.edu

Introduction

Health, fitness, and wellness continue to be popular and critically important to many individuals and communities. Luckily, a wealth of magazines and journals exists to meet the needs of these health- and fitness-conscious patrons. Librarians who select periodicals for inclusion in their collections can choose from a variety of popular and scholarly resources: from slick popular lifestyle magazines to double-blind peer-reviewed journals, to newsletters that bridge the divide between practicing professionals and the public.

The Health and Fitness section of *Magazines for Libraries* features the top publications currently published on health and fitness topics. While these resources address many similar subjects, each periodical has unique features that make it appropriate and useful for different venues and audiences. Resource selectors should also remember that while the titles included here represent some of the best-known and most-respected publications, they are a sampling of the many health and fitness periodicals available to today's audiences.

Basic Periodicals

Consumer Reports on Health, Fitness, The Harvard Health Letter, Health, Prevention, Self, Shape.

Basic Abstracts and Indexes

CINAHL, Health Source: Consumer Edition, MEDLINE.

Journals and Magazines

This section includes both scholarly and popular periodicals. Content and aim vary widely, from academic journals that publish double-blind, peer-reviewed articles to glossies that may appear to be more advertisements than content. This content-balanced list provides suggestions that will help almost every type of library meet patron needs and interests.

2903. *Childhood Obesity.* Former titles (until 2010): *Obesity and Weight Management;* (until 2009): *Obesity Management.* [ISSN: 2153-2168] 2005. bi-m. USD 492. Ed(s): David L Katz, Vicki Cohn. Mary Ann Liebert, Inc. Publishers, 140 Huguenot St, 3rd Fl, New Rochelle, NY 10801; info@liebertpub.com; http://www.liebertpub.com. Adv. Sample. Refereed. Reprint: PSC. *Indexed:* A22, BRI, C45, E01. *Bk. rev.:* Number and length vary. *Aud.:* Ac, Sa.

Childhood Obesity—a scholarly journal—focuses on obesity in children and teenagers and combines original research articles with case reports, research reports, reviews, interviews, editorials, etc. The wide range of topics addressed by *Childhood Obesity* are from a U.S.-centric viewpoint, though international perspectives can be found, particularly in the "Global Childhood Obesity Update" section. This journal is aimed at health-care professionals; however, much of the content will be of interest to the general public and is written in a style that is not beyond the layperson's understanding. Recommended for medical/health-sciences libraries, academic libraries, and larger public libraries.

2904. *Fitness: mind - body - spirit for women.* Formerly (until 1992): *Family Circle's Fitness Now.* [ISSN: 1060-9237] 1983. 11x/yr. USD 16.97 for 2 yrs. domestic; USD 29.97 Canada. Ed(s): Denise Brodey, Betty Wong. Meredith Corporation, 125 Park Ave, 25th Fl, New York, NY 10017; patrick.taylor@meredith.com; http://www.meredith.com. Illus., adv. Sample. Circ: 1574067 Paid. *Indexed:* BRI. *Aud.:* Hs, Ga.

Fitness is a well-known, popular magazine that focuses on a fitness-based lifestyle for women under 40. *Fitness's* slick appearance—replete with high-energy, enthusiastic headlines—enhances solid content that includes not only fitness topics such as workout routines and gear reviews, but also healthy diet advice (recipes abound) and women's overall physical and mental health. Like other fitness-based magazines, beauty and fashion articles are nestled among the fitness-focused content, giving *Fitness* broader appeal to its target demographic. Recommended for public libraries.

2905. *Health.* Formed by the merger of (1990-1992): *In Health;* (1981-1991): *Health;* Which was formerly (until 1981): *Family Health;* Which incorporated (1950-1976): *Today's Health;* Which was formerly (until 1950): *Hygeia.* [ISSN: 1059-938X] 1992. 10x/yr. USD 12; USD 1 per issue. Ed(s): Theresa Tamkins. Time Inc., 1271 Ave of the Americas, New York, NY 10020; information@timeinc.com; http://www.timeinc.com. Illus., adv. *Indexed:* A01, A22, BRI, C37, CBCARef, MASUSE, MLA-IB, P02, SD. *Aud.:* Ga, Ac.

Health is one of the best-known publications in the health- and fitness-consumer magazine genre. Within its sleek pages, a variety of lifestyle subjects are addressed—including fitness, nutrition, and beauty—and all are written on with a bright and friendly tone. *Health* teems with exercise tips, healthy recipes, and product reviews/suggestions, and there are often celebrity interviews that focus on the celebrity's routine to maintain health and well-being. Though *Health*'s target demographic is the over-30 woman, its content will appeal to women of all ages. Recommended for public libraries, medical/health-sciences libraries, and academic libraries that need a solid consumer-oriented health magazine.

2906. *International Journal of Men's Health.* [ISSN: 1532-6306] 2002. 3x/yr. USD 220. Ed(s): Miles Groth. Men's Studies Press, PO Box 32, Harriman, TN 37748; publisher@mensstudies.com; http://www.mensstudies.com. Index, adv. Sample. Refereed. *Indexed:* A01, ASSIA, BRI, C45, ExcerpMed, GW, PsycInfo, RRTA. *Bk. rev.:* Number and length vary. *Aud.:* Ac, Sa.

International Journal of Men's Health is a scholarly journal with a focus on men's health and related topics. It is published only three times a year, and in it, readers will find research articles and brief reports that focus on the physical and mental health of men from around the globe and from a variety of socioeconomic backgrounds. The research articles undergo a double-blind peer-review process and will be useful for researchers, practitioners, and other health-care professionals. Book reviews of scholarly monographs are included on an irregular basis. Recommended for medical/health-sciences libraries and academic libraries.

2907. *International Journal of Women's Health.* [ISSN: 1179-1411] 2009. irreg. Free. Ed(s): Elie D Al-Chaer. Dove Medical Press Ltd., Beechfield House, Winterton Way, Macclesfield, SK11 0JL, United Kingdom; http://www.dovepress.com. Refereed. *Indexed:* ExcerpMed. *Aud.:* Ac, Sa.

International Journal of Women's Health is an open-access, peer-reviewed journal focusing on health-care topics of concern to women. Though the content is primarily related to the physical health of women, mental and emotional health issues are also addressed. Readers will find a mix of original research articles, case reports, reviews, short reports, and letters. As the title indicates, coverage is international in scope, and health issues addressed affect all socioeconomic strata. Recommended for medical/health-sciences libraries and larger academic libraries.

2908. *Journal of Physical Activity & Health.* [ISSN: 1543-3080] 2004. 8x/yr. USD 912 (print & online eds.). Ed(s): Loretta DiPietro, Harold W Kohl, III. Human Kinetics, Inc., 1607 N Market St, Champaign, IL 61820; orders@hkusa.com; http://www.humankinetics.com. Adv. Refereed. Circ: 458 Paid. *Indexed:* PsycInfo, SD. *Aud.:* Ac, Sa.

Journal of Physical Activity & Health (*JPAH*) is a double-blind peer-reviewed journal that contains research and review articles, technical notes, and public health practice reports all related to adult and child physical activity. International in coverage, *JPAH* also produces supplements and special issues one to two times a year, in which all articles focus on a single theme, such as self-reporting gaps in active and sedentary behavior. Recommended for medical/health-sciences libraries and academic libraries.

2909. *Men's Health: tons of useful stuff.* Formerly (until 1987): *Prevention Magazine's Guide to Men's Health.* [ISSN: 1054-4836] 1986. 10x/yr. USD 24.94 domestic; CAD 39.50 Canada; USD 49.07 elsewhere. Ed(s): David Zinczenko, Peter Moore. Rodale, Inc., 733 Third Ave, 15th Fl, New York, NY 10022; customer_service@rodale.com; http://www.rodaleinc.com. Illus., adv. Circ: 1804949 Paid. Vol. ends: Dec (No. 10). *Indexed:* A01, A22, BRI, C37, GW, MASUSE, P02. *Aud.:* Hs, Ga.

Men's Health is a glossy magazine directed at young to middle-aged men interested in reading uncomplicated information related to a variety of fitness and health topics. The content is lifestyle-oriented and includes nutrition/recipe articles, gym workouts and routines, men's mental and physical health topics, sex and relationship advice, and even some fashion articles. *Men's Health* content is supplemented with short topic-specific quizzes, advice columns, and celebrity interviews. The amount of actual useful information and advice found in *Men's Health* is belied by the sleek, ad-heavy appearance. *Men's Health* has a robust web site that is organized very similarly to the magazine. Recommended for public libraries.

2910. *Prevention.* [ISSN: 0032-8006] 1950. m. USD 21.97 domestic; USD 32 Canada; USD 42.97 elsewhere. Ed(s): Diane J Salvatore. Rodale, Inc., 33 E Minor St, Emmaus, PA 18098; info@rodale.com; http://www.rodaleinc.com. Illus., index, adv. Sample. Vol. ends: Dec. Microform: PQC. *Indexed:* A01, A22, AgeL, BRI, C37, MASUSE, P02. *Aud.:* Hs, Ga.

With more than six decades of publication, *Prevention* remains a cornerstone periodical in the healthy-lifestyle magazine arena. It continues to provide information and advice that is both useful and straightforward, and like many consumer-oriented health and fitness magazines today, *Prevention* focuses on overall lifestyle aspects. This means readers can find articles on topics ranging from beauty to healthy diets to exercise, mental/emotional health, and sexual health/well-being. Much of the content is contained within brief articles, though there are usually several longer and more in-depth pieces in each issue. Recommended for public libraries.

2911. *Self.* Incorporates (in 2000): *Women's Sports & Fitness;* Which was formed by the merger of (1997-1998): *Conde Nast Sports for Women;* (1984-1998): *Women's Sports and Fitness;* Which was formerly (1979-1984): *Women's Sports.* [ISSN: 0149-0699] 1979. m. USD 8 domestic; USD 30 Canada; USD 35 elsewhere. Ed(s): Lucy Danziger. Conde Nast Publications, Inc., 4 Times Sq, 6th Fl, New York, NY 10036; http://www.condenast.com. Illus., adv. Sample. Circ: 1495033 Paid. Vol. ends: Dec. Microform: PQC. *Indexed:* A22, BRI, C37, P02. *Aud.:* Hs, Ga.

Though *Self* is among the best-known and popular magazines in the health and fitness world, the magazine has been re-vamped in spring 2013 to broaden its appeal to younger women and update its feel. Though some of the update is for aesthetic purposes, *Self* is aiming to shift its focus to more lifestyle-oriented content—think more fashion and beauty features (*New York Times,* February 10, 2013), though fitness and healthy eating are still fundamental to the magazine's content. The magazine's style remains quite casual and chatty, and qualified experts are still consulted for much of the advice provided. Recommended for public libraries.

2912. *Shape.* [ISSN: 0744-5121] 1981. m. USD 14.97 domestic; USD 29.97 Canada; USD 41.97 foreign. Ed(s): Katherine M Tomlinson, Elizabeth Tuner. A M I - Weider Publications, 21100 Erwin St, Woodland Hills, CA 91367; http://www.americanmediainc.com. Illus., adv. Sample. Circ: 1650000 Paid. Vol. ends: Aug. *Indexed:* A22, BRI, C37, P02, SD. *Aud.:* Hs, Ga.

Shape is a women's fitness magazine that is requisite for any periodical collection that serves the general public. The majority of *Shape*'s articles are focused on fitness and its many aspects (exercise, healthy eating, etc.), but the fashion, beauty, and healthy living pieces interspersed among the fitness articles make for a balanced reading experience. The fitness tips, information, and routines are all presented in an easy-to-read-and-follow format, and generally have accompanying illustrative materials, usually photographs. For those interested in the nutrition aspect of fitness, *Shape* includes plenty of recipes along with detailed nutritional information. Recommended for public libraries or academic libraries with a popular periodicals collection.

2913. *Women's Adventure.* Formerly: *Dandelion.* [ISSN: 1945-1946] 2003. bi-m. USD 17.95 domestic; USD 27.90 Canada; USD 39.90 elsewhere. Ed(s): Christian nardi. Big Earth Publishing, 1722 14th St, Ste 180, Boulder, CO 80302; info@womensadventuremagazine.com; http://www.bigearthpublishing.com. Adv. Circ: 78000 Paid and controlled. *Aud.:* Ga.

Women's Adventure (*WA*) is a great resource for physically active women of any age. *WA*'s content spans the interests of its target audience by including gear reviews and tips, profiling new or trending physical activities (e.g., ice canoe racing, highlining), safety and health advice, and articles that profile both sportswomen and environmental stewards. *WA*'s web presence is also to be recommended. Not only does it contain additional information that readers will appreciate, but the full text of issues is available for browsing online after a short embargo. Recommended for public libraries.

2914. *Women's Health.* [ISSN: 0884-7355] 2005. 10x/yr. USD 11.99 domestic; CAD 23.97 Canada. Ed(s): Michele Promaulayko. Rodale, Inc., 733 Third Ave, 15th Fl, New York, NY 10022; customer_service@rodale.com; http://www.rodaleinc.com. Adv. Sample. Circ: 1350000 Paid. *Indexed:* BRI. *Aud.:* Ga.

Women's Health (*WH*) is a popular magazine that targets women 35 and under who are interested in both health and fitness themes, as well as those who are interested in lifestyle topics such as beauty, fashion, and relationships. *WH* does a good job of intermingling content, and like many similar magazines, it still bases advice and suggestions for workouts, diet, and other health topics on professional/expert opinion. Longtime readers will notice that in April 2013, *WH* added several new features—including additional self-help content—in an effort to continue to increase its appeal to a wider audience. Recommended for public libraries.

Women's Health Issues. See Public Health section.

Newsletters

One unique aspect of the health and fitness publishing world is the variety and number of newsletters published. These are generally published by a respected medical/health-sciences institution or organization and, with very few exceptions, are completely advertisement-free. Health and fitness newsletters also are rife with expertise; staffing and editorial boards are populated heavily with M.D.s, Ph.D.s, and other professional/specialty degrees. By definition, newsletters are short, so expect most to fall in the 10- to 15-page range. Though newsletters may present more collection management difficulties, they are often gems that should be in many collections.

Child Health Alert, merged with *Pediatrics for Parents.* See Parenting section.

2915. *Consumer Reports on Health.* Formerly (until 1991): *Consumer Reports Health Letter.* [ISSN: 1058-0832] 1989. m. USD 24 combined subscription (print & online eds.). Ed(s): Melissa Virrill, Ronni Sandroff. Consumers Union of the United States, Inc., 101 Truman Ave, Yonkers, NY 10703; http://www.consumersunion.org. Illus., index. Sample. Circ: 360000. Vol. ends: Dec. *Indexed:* A01, A22, ABIn, B01, C37, MASUSE, P02. *Aud.:* Ga.

This newsletter provides adults with expert health advice and information. *Consumer Reports on Health* (*CRH*) consists of brief articles intended to provide adult consumers with informed evaluations and recommendations. Topics range from nutrition and fitness to aging and environmental health issues. *CRH*'s expert writers also address and debunking health myths/ misperceptions that abound in today's society. Readers who appreciate an "ask the expert" question-and-answer section will like "On Your Mind," where reader questions are answered. Recommended for public libraries, medical/ health-sciences libraries, and academic libraries that serve programs in the health sciences.

2916. *Environmental Nutrition: the newsletter of food, nutrition and health.* Formerly (until 1986): *Environmental Nutrition Newsletter.* [ISSN: 0893-4452] 1977. m. USD 39 domestic; USD 49 Canada; USD 59 elsewhere. Ed(s): Sharon Palmer. Belvoir Media Group, LLC, PO Box 5656, Norwalk, CT 06856; customer_service@belvoir.com; http://www.belvoir.com. Illus., index. Sample. *Indexed:* A01, A22, Agr, BRI, P02. *Aud.:* Ga, Ac, Sa.

Environmental Nutrition (*EN*) provides reviews, recommendations, and advice on all matters related to adult nutrition. *EN* contains a mix of brief articles and news updates. There is also a Q&A section in which readers' questions are answered. This sensible newsletter, written by experts, can help consumers make informed and healthy choices about their overall nutrition. The browseability of *EN* is enhanced through an end-of-year index of topics. Recommended primarily for public libraries, though *EN* may be useful for medical/health-sciences libraries or academic libraries that support nutrition programs.

2917. *The Harvard Health Letter.* Formerly (until 1990): *Harvard Medical School Health Letter.* [ISSN: 1052-1577] 1975. m. USD 29 combined subscription (print & online eds.). Ed(s): Anthony L Komaroff, Peter Wehrein. Harvard Health Publications Group, 10 Shattuck St, Ste 612, Boston, MA 02115; hhp@hms.harvard.edu; http://www.health.harvard.edu. Illus., index. Sample. Vol. ends: Oct. *Indexed:* A01, A22, Agr, BRI, C37, MASUSE, P02. *Bk. rev.:* Number and length vary. *Aud.:* Ga, Ac, Sa.

Harvard Medical School's *Harvard Health Letter* reports the latest news and information on the physical aspects of adult health and wellness. Written and edited by medical experts, *Harvard Health Letter* informs and advises readers on a host of topics, including new research findings, treatments for a variety of physical ailments, and medical myth-busting. Each issue contains a Q&A section in which an individual question is answered by a medical specialist. Recommended for public libraries, academic libraries, and medical/health-sciences libraries.

2918. *Harvard Men's Health Watch.* [ISSN: 1089-1102] 1996. m. USD 28 combined subscription (print & online eds.). Ed(s): Anthony L Komaroff, Dr. Harvey B Simon. Harvard Health Publications Group, 10 Shattuck St, Ste 612, Boston, MA 02115; hhp@hms.harvard.edu; http://www.health.harvard.edu. *Indexed:* A01. *Aud.:* Ga, Sa.

Harvard Men's Health Watch is an excellent men's consumer-health–oriented newsletter produced by Harvard Medical School. *HMHW* reports on a very broad spectrum of men's physical health issues, and readers will find the latest reports on medical news and research to be eminently readable and useful. There is an "ask the doctor" segment that is always popular with health consumers. Like most of the other Harvard Medical School newsletters targeted to a specific audience, *Harvard Men's Health Watch* has a wider appeal than just its target demographic of older adult males. Recommended for public libraries, academic libraries, and medical/health-sciences libraries.

2919. *Harvard Women's Health Watch.* [ISSN: 1070-910X] 1993. m. USD 28 combined subscription (print & online eds.). Ed(s): Dr. Celeste Robb-Nicholson, Anthony L Komaroff. Harvard Health Publications Group, 10 Shattuck St, Ste 612, Boston, MA 02115; hhp@hms.harvard.edu; http://www.health.harvard.edu. *Indexed:* A01, BRI, MASUSE. *Aud.:* Ga, Ac, Sa.

Harvard Women's Health Watch reports on topics that relate to the physical and mental health of adult women. Readers will find general-interest items alongside articles that detail recent research advances, findings, and/or treatments that present an impact on a specific area of women's health care. *Harvard Women's Health Watch* also includes a question-and-answer section with responses from an expert, generally an M.D. Recommended for public, academic, and medical/health-sciences libraries.

2920. *Johns Hopkins Medical Letter Health after 50.* [ISSN: 1042-1882] 1989. m. USD 15 domestic; CAD 24 Canada; CAD 39 elsewhere. Rebus Inc., 632 Broadway, 11th Fl, New York, NY 10012; health_after_50@enews.com. Illus. Sample. Vol. ends: Feb. *Indexed:* A22. *Aud.:* Ga, Ac.

Health after 50 disseminates expert opinion-based health information and advice to the growing over-50 population. Like other newsletters associated with respected medical institutions, *Health after 50* serves as a reliable source for health information consumers through its educational articles and health news reviews. Topics range widely though the focus remains mainly on age-related health issues for both men and women. The *de rigueur* reader/expert question-and-answer section can also be found in each issue. Recommended for public libraries, medical/health-sciences libraries, or academic libraries that support gerontology programs.

2921. *Tufts University Health & Nutrition Letter: the friedman school of nutrition science and policy.* Formerly (until 1997): *Tufts University Diet & Nutrition Letter (Print).* [ISSN: 1526-0143] 1983. m. USD 24 domestic. Ed(s): David A Fryxell, Irwin H Rosenberg. Tufts University, PO Box 5656, Norwalk, CT 06856; Tuftsbooks@customfulfillment.com. Illus. Sample. Microform: PQC. *Indexed:* A01, Agr, BRI, MASUSE, P02, SD. *Aud.:* Ga, Ac, Sa.

Tufts University Health & Nutrition Letter provides articles, reports, and advice ranging across the spectrum of nutrition-based health issues. Redesigned and updated in December 2012, this authoritative newsletter is more polished-looking and has slightly shifted its focus to emphasize more heavily the link between nutrition and physical/mental health. It produces an occasional supplement that takes an in-depth look at a single health issue or concern. Recommended for medical libraries, public libraries, and academic libraries that support health-science programs.

2922. *University of California, Berkeley. Wellness Letter: the newsletter of nutrition, fitness, and stress management.* [ISSN: 0748-9234] 1984. m. USD 24. Health Letter Associates, Prince St Sta, PO Box 412, New York, NY 10012. Illus. Sample. Vol. ends: Sep. *Indexed:* A01, P02. *Aud.:* Hs, Ga.

Articles and news items in the *UC Wellness Letter* (*UCWL*) address a wide range of adult-oriented health topics, including diet and nutrition, fitness, and physical health. The expert contributors to *UCWL* evaluate and report recent research using a layperson-friendly approach. Its authors also tackle common health myths, dispense advice, and answer readers' questions. Health-conscious folks from all walks of life will find the expert reporting to be useful and matter-of-fact. Recommended for public libraries.

■ HEALTH CARE ADMINISTRATION

See also Health Professions; and Nursing sections.

Emily Bell, Research Librarian, Services for Academic Programs, Harvard College Library; emilybell@fas.harvard.edu

Introduction

This professional field is occupied by a broad range of practitioners, and executive and financial officers. Medical students are a strong secondary audience. Journals in this field address health-care industry concerns from a variety of perspectives and in multiple ways. Some are strictly scholarly in nature, while others have a more trade-publication feel and rely more on graphics and small bursts of information to inform their busy multitasking audience. All aim to inform; most claim to spark thoughtful debate and aid in decision making.

Most titles here will be of service to academic libraries that support medical, dental, public health, health administration, bioscience, or health-care administration programs. Several are almost required to properly support the work of researchers associated with these programs.

Many of the included titles are provided to practitioners or association members at no cost or as part of membership. These might be most relevant to hospital libraries, as they are leaders in highlighting upcoming trends and practices.

A few of these publications are suited to a public library setting in which patrons may simply want an overview of the current state of finance and business practices in medical administration. Weeklies are good sources of emerging trends and current information.

All the titles included here are peer reviewed. Some have leanings toward health-care policy and keep an eye on government involvement, but most focus solidly within the realm of business and finance, quality and safety, management models, and implementation of new technologies, especially legally required ones like Electronic Health Records. Most editorial boards consist mainly of academics, with a few members of U.S. government agencies and a sprinkling of executives from corporate health care.

Most items require subscription-based access. Others have limited free access to their online archives, or distribute print copies among licensed practices. All have web sites that describe in more depth the publication and subscription options. Increasing numbers of these sites include supplementary material and social media access, further developing readers' involvement with their brand.

Basic Periodicals

Ac: *Health Care Management Review, Modern Healthcare;* Sa: *The Joint Commission Journal on Quality and Patient Safety, Journal of Healthcare Management, The Journal of Nursing Administration.*

Basic Abstracts and Indexes

CINAHL, MEDLINE.

2923. *Dental Economics.* Former titles (until 1967): *Oral Hygiene / Dental Economics;* (until 196?): *Oral Hygiene;* Which superseded (in 196?): *Dental Headlight.* [ISSN: 0011-8583] 1911. m. USD 132 domestic (Free to qualified personnel). Ed(s): Kevin Henry, Joseph A Blaes. PennWell Corporation, 1421 S Sheridan Rd, Tulsa, OK 74112; Headquarters@PennWell.com; http://www.pennwell.com. Illus., index, adv. Sample. Circ: 104166. *Indexed:* A22, ABIn, ATI. *Aud.:* Ac, Sa.

The web site and print edition are ad-heavy, which isn't surprising in a publication that's free to clinicians. This journal has a focus on the business aspects of dental practice, with writing aimed at clinicians who are not necessarily business-savvy. Its strength is in helping private practitioners stay current with business and management in their field, from staffing to services, and from electronic records management to social media. Each issue includes descriptions of sponsored medical products, which at times make the publication itself read like paid endorsements. The publication and a supplement, *Dental Office,* are complimentary to dental offices, with current and archived issues back to 1995 also freely available on the web site. Older issues are available through paid vendors. New features include a "digital mag format" available in full text only to subscribers. URL: www.dentalecomonics.com

2924. Frontiers of Health Services Management. [ISSN: 0748-8157] 1984. q. USD 110 domestic; USD 120 foreign; USD 32 per issue. Ed(s): Margaret F Schulte. Health Administration Press, 1 North Franklin St, Ste 1700, Chicago, IL 60606; ache@ache.org; http://www.ache.org/hap.cfm. Illus. Sample. Vol. ends: Summer. Microform: PQC. *Indexed:* A22, ABIn, B01. *Aud.:* Ac, Sa.

Scholarly in tone, this publication is suited to both an academic and an administrative planning audience. It presents each issue as a "bookazine": as substantial as a book, as condensed as a magazine. Each of the quarterly issues focuses on a current health-care topic and consists of a feature article and three first-person commentaries, followed by a response from the feature's author. Articles and commentaries cite references. Differing viewpoints are permitted. Recent issues have addressed chronic disease management and coordination among medical systems; medical apology; and electronic mergers and acquisitions. URL: www.ache.org/pubs/frontiers.cfm

2925. H F M Magazine. Former titles: *Healthcare Financial Management;* (until 1982): *Hospital Financial Management;* (until 1968): *Hospital Accounting.* 1946. m. USD 150 USD 280 foreign. Ed(s): Eric Reese. Healthcare Financial Management Association, 3 Westbrook Corporate Ctr, Ste 700, Westchester, IL 60154; http://www.hfma.org. Illus., index. Sample. Vol. ends: Dec. Microform: PQC. *Indexed:* A22, ABIn, ATI, AgeL, B01, B02, B03, BRI. *Bk. rev.:* Number and length vary. *Aud.:* Ac, Sa.

The official journal of the Healthcare Financial Management Association, this magazine is published monthly with an extra "Buyer's Resource Guide" issue each year. *HFM's* focus is finance, with an eye toward politics and government and practice management. Recent issues included a feature on the *Titanic;* one physician's musings on the relationship between leadership and basketball; speculation on the future of local hospitals as the center of the care-delivery system; and an article entitled "Avoiding the Performance Improvement Trap." With articles written by experts in the field, the magazine proposes to address the issues of working physicians. The tone is businesslike but friendly. URL: www.hfma.org/hfm

2926. Health Care Management Review. [ISSN: 0361-6274] 1976. q. USD 393 (print & online eds.). Ed(s): L Michele Issel. Lippincott Williams & Wilkins, 530 Walnut St, Philadelphia, PA 19106; customerservice@lww.com; http://www.lww.com. Illus., adv. Sample. Refereed. Circ: 691. Vol. ends: Fall. Microform: PQC. *Indexed:* A22, ABIn, B02, BRI, MCR. *Bk. rev.:* Number and length vary. *Aud.:* Ac, Sa.

Health Care Management Review calls itself "state of the art" in the field that is referred to in a recent article as "health care management science." Most articles consist of completed research relevant to health-care administration, leadership, management, and business practices. Each presents an abstract, including background, methodology, findings, and implications, as well as a bibliography. Aimed at both practitioners and researchers, the journal presents the application of current theory in controlled settings. *HCMR* publishes the "Best Theory to Practice" paper, chosen annually by the Health Care Administration Division of the Academy of Management. Recent issues included "Empowering leadership, perceived organizational support, trust, and job burnout for nurses: A study in an Italian general hospital" and "Innovative culture in long-term care settings: The influence of organizational characteristics." In 2012, the journal was expected to start publishing ahead-of-print articles. URL: http://journals.lww.com/hcmrjournal

2927. The Health Care Manager. Former titles (until 1999): *The Health Care Supervisor;* (until 1982): *The Health Care Supervisors Journal.* [ISSN: 1525-5794] 1982. q. USD 436 (print & online eds.). Ed(s): Charles R McConnell. Lippincott Williams & Wilkins, 530 Walnut St, Philadelphia, PA 19106; customerservice@lww.com; http://www.lww.com. Illus., adv. Refereed. Vol. ends: Jun. *Indexed:* A22, ABIn, B01, B02, BRI, PsycInfo. *Bk. rev.:* Number and length vary. *Aud.:* Ac, Sa.

The Health Care Manager recommends itself to those who are responsible for a staff and budget, primarily middle and lower-level managers, in any functional area of a health-care setting. It focuses on current health-care industry concerns such as electronic records management and quality in long-term care facilities, but also on basic management issues like revenue cycles; personnel recruitment, retention, staffing, and scheduling; planning techniques; delegation of authority; and program implementation. Each article contains an abstract, but not all articles have references, depending on how scholarly the focus. Article length and difficulty level are generally limited, with the busy manager's needs in mind. URL: http://journals.lww.com/healthcaremanagerjournal

2928. Hospitals & Health Networks. Incorporates (1999-2003): *Health Forum Journal;* Which was formerly (until 1999): *Healthcare Forum Journal;* (until 1987): *Healthcare Forum;* (until 1985): *Hospital Forum;* Formerly (until 1993): *Hospitals.* [ISSN: 1068-8838] 1936. m. USD 102 domestic (Free to qualified personnel). Ed(s): Bill Santamour. Health Forum, Inc., 155 N Wacker Dr, Ste 400, Chicago, IL 60606; hfcustsvc@healthforum.com; http://www.healthforum.com. Illus., index. Sample. Vol. ends: Dec. Microform: PQC. *Indexed:* A01, A22, ABIn, AgeL, B01, B02, B03, BRI, C42, MCR, P02. *Bk. rev.:* Number and length vary. *Aud.:* Ga, Ac, Sa.

Also known as *H&HN, Hospitals and Health Networks* is busy but pleasant. It has the feel of a slick magazine (despite its cover's satin/matte finish) and is ad-and-graphics-heavy on the inside. There are fold-out glossy ads in the center of each issue, plus fold-out content. Information is short and clipped, or managed in bursts with color graphics and illustrations for the MTV mind. The main content is solid. A recent main story has been about the importance and effective management of physician documentation for successful conversation to the new medical coding system. Another piece has been on the use of mobile wireless technology in the hospital setting. Monthly features include the end piece, "DataDig," with small bites of statistics and accompanying graphics. Billed as "the flagship" publication of the American Hospital Association. URL: www.hhnmag.com/hhnmag_app/index.jsp

2929. Inquiry (Rochester): the journal of health care organization, provision and financing. [ISSN: 0046-9580] 1963. q. USD 203 (print & online eds.). Ed(s): Kevin P Kane, Ronny Frishman. Excellus Health Plan, Inc., PO Box 527, Glenview, IL 60025; https://www.excellusbcbs.com. Illus., index, adv. Sample. Refereed. Vol. ends: Winter. Microform: PQC. *Indexed:* A22, ABIn, AgeL, B01, B02, BRI, EconLit, JEL, MCR. *Bk. rev.:* Number and length vary. *Aud.:* Ac, Sa.

Focusing on the health-care industry at large, this publication calls each winter for research papers on topical industry concerns, then publishes thematically linked articles in each issue of the next volume. Issues open with "The View From Here," a documented editorial from editor Alan C. Monheit. Introductions provide an overview of each article in the issue, tying them together with the overarching theme. Articles are well researched and documented, and have multiple authors. The publication concerns itself with public policy issues, scholarly communication, and original research in the areas of health-care organization, provision, and financing. Because of the broad scope of the writing, the journal is appropriate for any audience within the field of health care. Issues end with book reviews. URL: www.inquiryjournalonline.org/

2930. Journal of Health Care Finance. Formerly (until 1994): *Topics in Health Care Financing.* [ISSN: 1078-6767] 1974. q. USD 399; USD 150 per issue. Ed(s): James J Unland. Aspen Publishers, Inc., 76 Ninth Ave, 7th Fl, New York, NY 10011; ASPEN-CustomerService@wolterskluwer.com; https://www.aspenpublishers.com. Illus. Sample. Vol. ends: Summer. Microform: PQC. *Indexed:* A22, ABIn, AgeL, B01, B02, BRI, ExcerpMed, MCR. *Aud.:* Ac, Sa.

Composed of well-researched and -documented scholarly articles, this journal aims to position itself at the forefront of practical matters in U.S. and international health-care business and finance. Articles contain introductions, author-provided keywords, and documentation. Recent topics have included inner-city hospital closures; microeconomics and health in Pakistan; a comparison of U.S. and Canadian health-care systems; and health-care marketplace reform. URL: www.aspenpublishers.com/Product.asp?catalog_name=Aspen&product_id=SS10786767

2931. *Journal of Healthcare Management.* Former titles (until 1998): *Hospital and Health Services Administration;* (until 1976): *Hospital Administration.* [ISSN: 1096-9012] 1956. bi-m. USD 125 domestic; USD 135 foreign; USD 35 per issue. Ed(s): Stephen O'Connor. Health Administration Press, 1 North Franklin St, Ste 1700, Chicago, IL 60606; ache@ache.org; http://www.ache.org/hap.cfm. Illus. Sample. Refereed. Microform: PQC. *Indexed:* A01, A22, ABIn, B01, B02, BRI, ExcerpMed, MCR, P02. *Bk. rev.:* Number and length vary. *Aud.:* Ac, Sa.

The American College of Healthcare Executives has established a formula for each issue of this scholarly publication. Each issue features an editorial, an interview with a health-care executive or academic, and relevant papers on business and finance in health care, accompanied by evidence-based empirical data and proposal of strategic solutions. Each article is accompanied by a "Practitioner Application," a piece written by a health-care practitioner, which puts the article in practical perspective for the reader from a colleague's point of view. Issues also include theoretical pieces like the recent "Innovation or stagnation? Crossing the creativity gap in healthcare." Recent interviewees include a University of Minnesota School of Public Health professor; the Commanding General of the U.S. Army Medical Department Center and School; and the President and CEO of Group Health Cooperative, who is also a Fellow of the American College of Healthcare Executives. This publication is suitable for practitioners at all levels who are concerned with health-care finance and/or administration, and for students learning about the field. URL: www.ache.org/PUBS/jhmsub.cfm

2932. *M G M A Connexion.* Former titles (until 2001): *Medical Group Management Journal;* (until 1987): *Medical Group Management;* (until 1960): *National Association of Clinic Managers. Bulletin.* [ISSN: 1537-0240] 1953. 10x/yr. Free to members. Medical Group Management Association, 104 Inverness Terr E, Englewood, CO 80112; support@mgma.com; http://www.mgma.com. Illus., index, adv. Sample. Vol. ends: Nov/Dec. Microform: PQC. *Indexed:* A22, MCR. *Aud.:* Ac, Sa.

In *MGMA Connexion,* several issues per year highlight one featured topic, which is covered by an in-depth article and accompanying departmental pieces. The current year's editorial calendar is made available with featured topics, so that writers can work with them in mind. Recent topics have included business operations, risk management, informational management, and organizational governance. These issues also include the standard columns and departments included in the regular magazine. Though heavy on advertising, this publication is rich in information of use to the health-care manager or administrator. It covers timely concerns such as ICD-10 and questions about financial loss, as well as practical advice on new technology, such as the application mobile devices in the health-care setting. URL: www.mgma.com/mc/default.aspx?id=9100

2933. *Medical Economics.* [ISSN: 0025-7206] 1923. s-m. Free to qualified personnel. Ed(s): Erich Burnett. Advanstar Communications, Inc., 6200 Canoga Ave, 2nd Fl, Woodland Hills, CA 91367; info@advanstar.com; http://www.advanstar.com. Illus., adv. Vol. ends: Dec. Microform: RPI; PQC. *Indexed:* A22, ABIn, B01, B02, BRI, MCR. *Aud.:* Ac, Sa.

Heavy on advertising, color, and images—as many virtually free publications are—this publication is nevertheless a useful guide to the current state of its major topic. It is of use to anyone who wants to stay abreast of issues in health-care finance and economics. Information is presented in consumer-magazine format rather than in a scholarly manner, and issues are composed of bite-sized articles scattered among a few features. Recent issues have addressed doctors with addictions; the use of QR codes in medical practice; workflow problems; a physician's experience in Haiti; and retirement planning. In the last year, the journal has concerned itself with EHR implementation, including checklists, descriptions of personal experiences, and examples of successful implementation and other pieces designed to ease the way for the health-care practitioner to make the major and sometimes controversially mandatory adjustment to electronic health records. URL: www.memag.com/memag

2934. *Modern Healthcare: the newsmagazine for administrators and managers in hospitals, and other healthcare institutions.* Formed by the merger of (1967-1976): *Modern Healthcare (Long-Term Care);* Which superseded (in 1974): *Modern Nursing Home;* Which was formerly (until 1967): *Modern Nursing Home Administrator;* (until 1966): *Nursing Home Administrator;* (until 1950): *Nursing Home Magazine;* (1913-1976): *Modern Healthcare (Short-Term Care);* Which superseded (in 1974): *Modern Hospital.* [ISSN: 0160-7480] 1976. w. USD 164 domestic; USD 255 Canada; USD 218 elsewhere. Ed(s): Neil McLaughlin, David Burda. Crain Communications, Inc., 150 N Michigan Ave, Chicago, IL 60601; info@crain.com; http://www.crain.com. Illus., index. Sample. Vol. ends: Dec. *Indexed:* A01, A22, ABIn, API, AgeL, B01, B02, B03, BRI, C42. *Aud.:* Ga, Ac, Sa.

A weekly trade magazine with a cover like a newsmagazine, *Modern Healthcare* is intentionally breezy, to recommend itself to busy executives. It nevertheless addresses the spectrum of health-care industry trends and concerns. It particularly includes regular regional reports from the Northeast, Midwest, South, and West. It also features regular columns and departments, including technology, policy, financial, and legal news. There are three special issues a year, and occasional additional supplements. The publication is a good resource for anyone who wants to inform him or herself on the current names, issues, and happenings in health-care administration and finance. URL: www.modernhealthcare.com

2935. *Nursing Administration Quarterly.* [ISSN: 0363-9568] 1976. q. USD 456 (print & online eds.). Ed(s): Barbara J Brown. Lippincott Williams & Wilkins, 530 Walnut St, Philadelphia, PA 19106; customerservice@lww.com; http://www.lww.com. Illus. Refereed. Vol. ends: Summer. Microform: PQC. *Indexed:* A22, BRI. *Bk. rev.:* Number and length vary. *Aud.:* Ac, Sa.

Particularly focused on selected advancements in nursing, which foster opportunities for the advancement of the nursing industry and leadership roles for nurses in the medical community, this publication is a major forum for nursing scholars, executives, and educators in which to publish their research. Issues are thematic and offer viewpoints from editor Barbara Brown, as well as from guest editors with particular perspectives on the topic, followed by well researched and documented scholarly articles. Regular book reviews provide added value, and the advertisements are nonintrusive. Highly recommended for its nursing focus. URL: www.naqjournal.com

2936. *Nursing Economics: the journal for health care leaders.* [ISSN: 0746-1739] 1983. bi-m. USD 100. Ed(s): Kenneth J Thomas, Donna M Nickitas. Jannetti Publications, Inc., E Holly Ave, PO Box 56, Pitman, NJ 08071; http://www.ajj.com/jpi. Illus., index, adv. Sample. Refereed. Vol. ends: Nov. *Indexed:* A01, A22, ABIn, BRI. *Aud.:* Ac, Sa.

Spelled with a dollar sign in place of the final S, *Nursing Economics* directs its efforts toward information and analyses of current and emerging best practices in the nursing aspect of the health-care industry. Regular features include a "continuing nursing education series," which contains articles and exercises qualifying for CME credits, and columns such as "Nursing Informatics" and "Human Resource Solutions," which addresses HR problems from a manager's perspective and invites readers' input. This journal should be of significant practical and strategic value to anyone involved in advanced nursing or the administration of nurses. While *Nursing Administration Quarterly* creates a scholarly forum, *Nursing Economics* concerns itself more with daily experience. URL: www.nursingeconomics.net

■ HEALTH PROFESSIONS

See also Health Care Administration; Medicine; Nursing; and Public Health sections.

Eleanor P. Randall, Science Reference Librarian, ret., Baron-Forness Library, Edinboro University of Pennsylvania, Edinboro, PA 16444; eprandall@edinboro.edu

Introduction

The growth of health-profession specialties is reflected in many sections of *Magazines for Libraries;* some of the issues are universal to the health professions. Titles included in this section reflect the economic, educational, political, and social conditions that uniformly impact a cross-section of health professions.

Most magazines now have an Internet presence, with some online only. Functionality of the site renders some titles valuable in providing continuing growth in the profession through blogs, RSS feeds, and sharing capabilities. The online-only journals selected for this edition of *MFL* have enhanced communication by and between health professionals, while most maintain peer-reviewed standards in publishing.

Journals published by both recognized professional organizations and trade publications continue to expand research and understanding within the discipline and by those contemplating a health-care career.

Basic Abstracts and Indexes

CINAHL, MEDLINE.

2937. *American Dental Association. Journal.* Formery (until 1939): *The Journal of the American Dental Association and the Dental Cosmos;* Which was formed by the merger of (1859-1937): *The Dental Cosmos;* Which superseded (in 1859): *Dental News Letter;* (1922-1937): *American Dental Association. Journal;* Which was formerly (until 1922): *National Dental Association. Journal;* (until 1915): *National Dental Association. Official Bulletin.* [ISSN: 0002-8177] 1913. m. USD 169 (Individuals, USD 134; USD 17 per issue domestic). Ed(s): Dr. Michael Glick. American Dental Association, 211 E Chicago Ave, Lower Level, Chicago, IL 60611; adapub@ada.org; http://www.ada.org. Illus., index, adv. Refereed. Circ: 148622 Paid. Vol. ends: Dec. Microform: PQC. *Indexed:* A01, A22, BRI, MCR, MLA-IB, P02. *Aud.:* Ac, Sa.

The monthly *JADA* is considered the nation's foremost dental journal. A subscription is included with membership in the ADA (American Dental Association; www.ada.org). Peer-reviewed research articles on current practices in general dentistry are included, as are clinical reports and dental research in specialty areas such as cosmetic and aesthetic dentistry. Also offered in each issue is a continuing education program with related articles. Recurring topics include the role of dentistry as it relates to the overall general health of patients, and the legal implications of practice management. Sections include "Views," "Letters to the Editor," and "News." Illustrations are in color, and a dental calendar of events is provided.

American Journal of Nursing. See Nursing section.

International Nursing Review. See Nursing section.

2938. *The Internet Journal of Allied Health Sciences and Practice: a journal dedicated to allied health professional practice and education.* [ISSN: 1540-580X] 2003. q. Free. Ed(s): Dr. Richard E Davis, Guy M Nehrenz. Nova Southeastern University, 3200 S University Dr, Fort Lauderdale, FL 33328; ron@nsu.nova.edu; http://www.nova.edu. Refereed. *Bk. rev.:* Number and length vary. *Aud.:* Ac, Sa.

IJAHSP/The Internet Journal of Allied Health Sciences and Practice is a scholarly online forum for the advancement of allied health professionals. Articles focus on the science and practice of allied health and may involve global issues, as well as conceptual and research articles. Peer-reviewed articles are archived with a search option (SiteLevel.com) and Open Access on the Internet. No advertising is accepted. This journal is funded and supported as a public and professional service to the medical Internet community by Nova Southeastern University and a volunteer editorial board, a review board, and the College of Allied Health and Nursing. URL: http://ijahsp.nova.edu

2939. *Journal of Midwifery & Women's Health.* Former titles (2000): *Journal of Nurse - Midwifery;* (until 1973): *American College of Nurse - Midwives. Bulletin;* (until 1969): *American College of Nurse - Midwifery. Bulletin.* [ISSN: 1526-9523] 1955. 6x/yr. GBP 342. Ed(s): Frances E Linkis. Wiley-Blackwell Publishing, Inc., 111 River St, Hoboken, NJ 07030; info@wiley.com; http://onlinelibrary.wiley.com/. Illus., index. Sample. Refereed. Vol. ends: Nov/Dec. Microform: PQC. Reprint: PSC. *Indexed:* A22, ASSIA, AbAn, ExcerpMed, PsycInfo. *Bk. rev.:* Number and length vary; online. *Aud.:* Ac, Sa.

The *Journal of Midwifery & Women's Health* presents research and current knowledge across a broad range of topics. The May/June issue comprises special single-topic "Continuing Education" issues and is accessible online. The "Journal Reviews" section examines articles that are published in other journals and are reviewed by volunteer editors for their pertinent content and research validity. *JMWH* is the official journal of the American College of Nurse Midwives.

2940. *Minority Nurse: the career and education resource for minority nursing professionals, students and faculty.* Former titles (until 1999): *M N;* (until 1998): *Minority Nurse.* 1993. q. Individuals, USD 19.95; Free to qualified personnel. Ed(s): Pam Chwedyk. Career Recruitment Media, Inc., 211 W Wacker Dr, Ste 900, Chicago, IL 60606; info@careermedia.com; http://www.careermedia.com. Adv. *Aud.:* Ga, Ac, Sa.

Minority Nurse publishes regular columns such as the "Academic Forum," "2nd Opinion," and "Self-Exam." Topics include diversity concerns in nursing schools, the health of minority nurses, special reports, and feature articles on nursing careers, scholarship, and employment opportunities. Medical centers, the nation's largest hospitals, and 1,800 nursing programs receive complimentary copies. Personal, paid subscriptions are available. Recommended readership includes academic counselors, administrators, nursing students, and health professionals, regardless of minority status. The *Minority Nurse* homepage describes the magazine's purpose as providing information needed by all minority nurses on diversity in the profession—"from the classroom to the bedside." The browse feature online enables searching of articles published since 2005. URL: www.minoritynurse.com/about/magazine.html

2941. *Nursing Forum: an independent voice for nursing.* [ISSN: 0029-6473] 1961. q. GBP 168. Ed(s): Patricia S Yoder-Wise. Wiley-Blackwell Publishing, Inc., 111 River St, Hoboken, NJ 07030; info@wiley.com; http://www.wiley.com/. Illus., adv. Sample. Refereed. Microform: PQC. Reprint: PSC. *Indexed:* A01, A22, ASSIA, AbAn, E01. *Aud.:* Ac, Sa.

Nursing Forum provides essential reading on contemporary nursing issues for nursing students, educators, nurse recruiters, staff development nurses, and nurse practitioners and others who are interested in the profession of nursing. Editors are internationally known and contribute a global perspective to many critical issues that face the nursing profession. The new feature "Creative Controversy" establishes a topic forum for continuing discussion and feedback from readers. Feature articles include clinical and research-based studies. Suitable for all nurses, particularly advanced-practice nurses (APNs) and nurse educators.

2942. *Nursing Outlook.* Supersedes (in 1953): *Public Health Nursing;* Which was formerly (until 1931): *Public Health Nurse;* (until 1918): *Public Health Nurse Quarterly;* (until 1913): *Visiting Nurse Quarterly of Cleveland.* [ISSN: 0029-6554] 1909. bi-m. USD 285. Ed(s): Marion E Broome. Mosby, Inc., 1600 John F. Kennedy Blvd, Ste 1800, Philadelphia, PA 19103; http://www.us.elsevierhealth.com. Illus., index, adv. Sample. Refereed. Vol. ends: Nov/Dec. Microform: PQC. *Indexed:* A22, ASSIA, Chicano, E01, MCR, SWR&A. *Aud.:* Ac.

Nursing Outlook is of primary interest to practicing nurses, nurse educators, and administrators worldwide. "President's Message," "From the Editor," and the "Commentary" and "News" columns support the mission of the American Academy of Nurses to serve the public and the nursing profession by advancing health policy and practice through the generation, synthesis, and dissemination of nursing knowledge. An online advanced-search feature is the option of searching Medline and *Nursing Outlook* simultaneously. Complimentary abstracts, full-text editorials, and online special features are provided at this site. URL: www.nursingoutlook.org

2943. *Online Journal of Issues in Nursing.* [ISSN: 1091-3734] 1996. 3x/yr. Free. Ed(s): Harrcet Coeling. American Nurses Association, 8515 Georgia Ave, Ste 400, Silver Spring, MD 20910; http://www.nursingworld.org. Refereed. *Indexed:* A01, AbAn. *Aud.:* Sa.

OJIN publishes a selection of invited, peer-reviewed papers on topics that affect nursing research, education, and practice. The Internet format enables readers to submit letters to the editor, articles submitted on a volunteer basis by authors to represent various viewpoints, and other commentaries. These latter submissions are posted daily after being peer reviewed. This interactive format enables a more thorough discussion of the ramifications of the topic that was presented earlier, to which the later submissions respond.

2944. ***P T in Motion.*** Formerly (until 2009): *P T - Magazine of Physical Therapy.* [ISSN: 1949-3711] 1993. m. Free to members. Ed(s): Donald N Tepper. American Physical Therapy Association, 1111 N Fairfax St, Alexandria, VA 22314; aps@apta.org; http://www.apta.org. Adv. Circ: 70340 Paid. *Indexed:* A01, A22, BRI, P02, SD. *Bk. rev.:* Number and length vary. *Aud.:* Ac, Sa.

PT in Motion is a forum for professional issues that the physical therapist faces. This journal provides legislative, health-care, human interest, and association news. Topics include the patient–therapist relationship and issues relating to the changing health-care environment. Some of the magazine's regular features are "Ethics in Action," "Compliance Matters," and "Viewpoints." June 2012 saw the launch of *PT in Motion Extra,* designed to complement the magazine with sharing functionality, index view, posting of comments, and an audio version of the magazine.

2945. ***Policy, Politics & Nursing Practice.*** [ISSN: 1527-1544] 2000. q. USD 590. Ed(s): David M Keepnews. Sage Publications, Inc., 2455 Teller Rd, Thousand Oaks, CA 91320; info@sagepub.com; http://www.sagepub.com. Adv. Refereed. Reprint: PSC. *Indexed:* A01, A22, ASSIA, E01, PsycInfo. *Bk. rev.:* Number and length vary. *Aud.:* Ac, Sa.

Policy, Politics & Nursing Practice explores health policy issues through an analysis of legislative and regulatory processes as they impact nursing practice and the health-care delivery system. The journal includes discussion and debates of international health policy issues, diversity, and the equality of health care. Included are interviews, commentaries, case studies, research papers, and evidence-based studies of health policy. The interdisciplinary nature of this journal is reflected in the scope of health and related professions of authors who publish in this journal. *Policy, Politics, & Nursing Practice* offers OnlineFirst, by which forthcoming articles are published online before they are scheduled to appear in print.

2946. ***Rehabilitation Nursing.*** Formerly (until 1981): *A R N Journal.* [ISSN: 0278-4807] 1975. bi-m. GBP 161. Ed(s): Dr. Elaine Tilka Miller. John Wiley & Sons, Inc., 111 River St, MS 4-02, Hoboken, NJ 07030; info@wiley.com; http://onlinelibrary.wiley.com/. Illus., adv. Refereed. Microform: PQC. *Indexed:* A22. *Aud.:* Ac.

The mission of the Association of Rehabilitation Nurses is to support the growth of the specialty. Articles range from administration and research to education and clinical topics; nursing perspectives, resource reviews, and product information; and continuing education opportunities in every issue. *Rehabilitation Nursing* aims to increase awareness of new trends in products and services for individuals with disabilities or chronic illness. Related specialties such as wound-care nursing, caregiver educators, and palliative care professionals would benefit from pertinent materials in this title.

■ HIKING, CLIMBING, AND OUTDOOR RECREATION

See also Boats and Boating; Fishing; Hunting and Guns and Sports sections.

Jennifer Sundheim, Assistant Director, University of Washington Tacoma Library, 1900 Commerce Street, Tacoma, WA 98402; sundheim@uw.edu

Introduction

The magazines reviewed here are commercial English-language titles published in North America with a focus on hiking, climbing, and general outdoor recreation. The magazines are readily available to libraries through stand-alone subscriptions (publications requiring society or club memberships prior to obtaining a subscription are not included); and all titles have a broad geographic scope (smaller regional or local-interest publications were eliminated). Both recreational and competitive/professional-content–level publications are included. Whenever possible, the stated mission and scope of the magazine are quoted so as to make the target audience of the publication clear.

Outdoor recreation, in terms of publications below, is defined as camping or general adventure magazines that will include much information on camping and trekking. For publications dedicated to specific outdoor recreation activities such as kayaking or skiing, see the Boats and Boating or Sports sections respectively.

Basic Periodicals

Hs: *Outside (Santa Fe);* Ga: *Backpacker, Climbing, Outside (Santa Fe), Rock & Ice.*

Basic Abstracts and Indexes

MasterFILE Premier, ProQuest Research Library.

2947. ***Alpine Athena: a women's climbing magazine.*** 2011. q. Free. Ed(s): Genevieve S Hathaway. Alpine Athena, LLC., submissions@alpineathena.com; http://www.alpineathena.com/. Illus. *Bk. rev.:* 500-1,000 words in length. *Aud.:* Sa.

Alpine Athena "is a core-focused woman's alpinism magazine dedicated to the woman climber, alpinist and mountaineer." The newest publication to emerge in the climbing literature with a start in 2011, this online-only title is striving "to be the leading voice for the woman climber." Every issue has feature articles and gear reviews. Book reviews, interviews, letters to the editor, how-to's, and event reports vary in coverage by issue. The online interface is sleek, clean, and well organized. The magazine can be "subscribed to" or followed on FaceBook, Twitter, RSS, and e-mail newsletter. The price is right for libraries, with the magazine being freely available so long as patrons do not mind reading online.

2948. ***Alpinist Magazine.*** [ISSN: 1540-725X] 2002. q. USD 49.95; USD 17.95 per issue. Ed(s): Michael Kennedy, Katie Ives. Alpinist LLC, 60 Main St, Ste 201, Jeffersonville, VT 05464. Adv. *Aud.:* Sa.

The *Alpinist* significantly describes itself as "an archival-quality, quarterly publication dedicated to world alpinism and adventure climbing. The pages of *Alpinist* capture the art of ascent in its most powerful manifestations, presenting an articulation of climbing and its lifestyle that matches the intensity of the pursuit itself." It is true; the publication is as much an art-level design and photography publication worthy of archiving as it is a climbing magazine. Each issue contains feature articles, gear reviews, climbing technique write-ups, and interviews. Most online back-issue content is limited to subscribers. An additional "premier monthly electronic newletter" entitled *High Camp* is also available to subscribers to supplement the print. The publication is rarely available in retail establishments, so the only way individuals can get access to the publication would be through a subscription or library holding, and this publication is best suited to libraries with extensive outdoor recreation collections.

2949. ***Backpacker: the outdoor at your doorsteps.*** Incorporates (1977 -198?): *Backpacker Footnotes;* (19??-1979): *Wilderness Camping.* [ISSN: 0277-867X] 1973. 9x/yr. USD 15.95 domestic; USD 23.95 Canada; USD 36.95 elsewhere. Ed(s): Jonathan Dorn, Anthony Cerretani. Active Interest Media, 2520 55th St, Ste 210, Boulder, CO 80301; http://www.aimmedia.com/. Illus., adv. Sample. Circ: 500000 Paid. Vol. ends: Nov/Dec. Microform: PQC. *Indexed:* A22, BRI, C37, MASUSE, P02, SD. *Aud.:* Hs, Ga, Sa.

The stated mission of *Backpacker* is "We inspire and enable people to enjoy the outdoors by providing the most trusted and engaging information about backcountry adventure in North America." Published since 1973, the magazine is well known in the hiking world and is a staple of outdoor sporting–goods retailers, and it is for sale in most airports and can even be found in many grocery stores. Typical issues contain sections on hiking destinations and on skills for backcountry camping; gear reviews; and profiles of people involved in backcountry activities. Special themed issues are also produced. April is the month of the annual "Gear Guide." The web site provides access to the current issue, including featured articles, as well as the content of some past issues, a directory of hikes from across North America, blogs, and videos. Through the Google Magazines project, full-text back issues of the period 1973–2009 are freely available.

2950. *Climbing.* [ISSN: 0045-7159] 1970. 9x/yr. USD 14.95 domestic; USD 29.95 Canada; USD 34.95 elsewhere. Ed(s): Dougald MacDonald. Active Interest Media, 300 Continental Blvd, Ste 650, El Segundo, CA 90245; http://www.aimmedia.com/. Illus., adv. Sample. Circ: 38263 Paid. Vol. ends: Dec/Jan. *Indexed:* P02. *Bk. rev.:* 2-3, 200 words. *Aud.:* Ga, Sa.

Climbing stays true to its title, focusing on the activity of climbing in all forms—alpine, bouldering, sport, and traditional climbing. The one dalliance is photography, but any information on photography serves only to enable better climbing pictures. Typical issues contain features on climbing locales, technical climbing tips, equipment write-ups, climber profiles, and brief reviews of climbing books and videos. The "Gear Guide" releases in April and a "Photo Annual" issue comes out in the summer. Access to online issues requires an electronic subscription. Freely available on the web site are climbing news, indexing of past issues, blogs, photography, and a database of climbs.

Field & Stream. See Hunting and Guns section.

2951. *Gripped: the climbing magazine.* [ISSN: 1488-0814] 1999. bi-m. USD 25.95. Gripped Publishing Inc., 344 Bloor St, Unit 510, Toronto, ON M5S 3A7, Canada; info@gripped.com; http://gripped.com. Adv. *Bk. rev.:* 2-4, 200-300 words. *Aud.:* Ga, Sa.

Gripped sports the subtitle "The climbing magazine," but sometimes you will find it referred to as "Canada's climbing magazine." Published out of Toronto, *Gripped* features climbing news, gear reviews, articles on climbing destinations, and issues and reviews on books and media. The web site provides access to the current issue, climbing news, a calendar of events, and the ability to order back print issues.

National Geographic Traveler. See Travel and Tourism section.

2952. *Outdoor Life: the source for hunting and fishing adventure.* Incorporates: *Fisherman;* (in 1927): *Outdoor Recreation;* Which was formerly (until 1924): *Outer's Recreation;* (until 1919): *Outer's Book-Recreation;* Incorporates (in 1907): *Pacific Sportsman;* Which was formerly (until 1904): *Pacific Coast Sportman.* [ISSN: 0030-7076] 1898. m. USD 39.90 domestic; USD 26 Canada; USD 45 elsewhere. Ed(s): Todd W Smith. Bonnier Corp., 2 Park Ave, 9th Fl, New York, NY 10016; http://www.bonniercorp.com. Illus., adv. Sample. Circ: 750000 Paid. Vol. ends: Dec. Microform: NBI; PQC. *Indexed:* A01, A22, BRI, C37, MASUSE, P02. *Aud.:* Hs, Ga, Sa.

The subtitle of *Outdoor Life* is "The source of hunting and fishing adventure." To that end, each issue has dedicated sections for hunting, fishing, shooting, and gear news. An additional section called "Snap Shots" often details readers' real-life experiences while hunting and fishing. Featured articles cover things such as tactics for giant buck hunting and big-game safaris. A gear issue comes out in late summer. The web site provides access to some of the magazine content and the standard blog and video fare, as well as offers a message board and an additional Q & A.

2953. *Outside (Santa Fe).* Formerly (until 1980): *Mariah - Outside;* Which was formed by the merger of (1976-1979): *Mariah;* (1977-1979): *Outside (San Francisco).* [ISSN: 0278-1433] 1979. m. USD 19.95 domestic; CAD 35 Canada; USD 1.66 per issue domestic. Ed(s): Lawrence J Burke, Michael Roberts. Mariah Media Inc., 400 Market St, Santa Fe, NM 87501; letters@outsidemag.com. Illus., adv. Circ: 687916. Microform: PQC. *Indexed:* A01, A22, ASIP, P02, SD. *Aud.:* Hs, Ga, Ac.

With quality writing and wide coverage on all things athletic, *Outside* has become a standard title in most public libraries. The magazine describes itself as "America's leading active-lifestyle and adventure-travel magazine." It says it is "dedicated to covering the people, activities, gear, art, and politics of the world outside." While its featured topics can be far-ranging, the journalistic

coverage is more in-depth than that of most magazines. *Outside* publishes writers such as John Krakauer and Sebastian Junger, and the subjects of articles have often shown up later as full-length books and/or feature films. Special "Buyer's Guide" issues with gear reviews are produced annually. The web site features access to ten years of the magazine's archive, as well as additional article features, blogs, videos, photos, and podcasts.

2954. *Rock & Ice: the climber's magazine.* [ISSN: 0885-5722] 1984. 8x/yr. USD 29.95 combined subscription domestic (print & online eds.). Ed(s): Alison Osius. Big Stone Publishing, 417 Main St, Unit N, Carbondale, CO 81623; http://www.bigstonepub.com. Illus., adv. Vol. ends: Nov/Dec. *Bk. rev.:* 3-6, 300-500 words. *Aud.:* Ac, Sa.

Rock & Ice claims to be "the only climber-owned and operated climbing magazine." The Western Publishers Association voted it the "Best Consumer Outdoor Recreation" magazine in 2005. Each issue has climbing news, photography, gear and book reviews, an accident analysis report, featured climbs, and advice on sports injuries and climbing techniques. It is perhaps because of the standard analysis and review columns, that a search of WorldCat shows this publication to be a preferred title for academic libraries if they are going to subscribe to a climbing magazine. For special issues, once a year in June the magazine puts out *Ascent*—a collection of longer articles on people and events in "the climbing life." The web site provides access to the current issue and archives that range several years back. There are also directories for guides, gear, and gyms.

2955. *Trail Runner: one dirty magazine.* [ISSN: 1526-3134] 1999. bi-m. USD 19.95 combined subscription (print & online eds.). Ed(s): Elinor Fish, Michael Benge. Big Stone Publishing, 417 Main St, Unit N, Carbondale, CO 81623; http://www.bigstonepub.com. Circ: 2900 Paid. *Aud.:* Ac, Sa.

Like the magazine *Rock & Ice*, *Trail Runner* is a Big Stone Publishing production. And just as *Rock & Ice* establishes its authority with the claim "Built by Climbers," *Trail Runner* states that it is "written by trail runners for trail runners." It also claims to be "the only magazine dedicated to the off-road running community." There is another trail running magazine from the United Kingdom that has been in print for some time called *Trail Running*; however, for North America this is the publication (the magazine *Runner's World* does a special single issue per year on off-road trail running). Standard content for *Trail Runner* includes information on trail running skills, nutrition, and injury rehabilitation; runner interviews; gear reviews; and information on trail travel destinations. Special themed issues are produced each year. Between December and January, the big "Race" issue is put out, listing more than 1,000 trail races slated for the coming year. June is when the annual "Gear Guide" appears. The web site provides free access to scanned images of back issues, a calendar of race events, a forum board, and sign-up for a bimonthly e-mail newsletter.

2956. *Wend: beyond adventure.* [ISSN: 1933-3056] 2006. 5x/yr. USD 21 domestic. Ed(s): Stiv Wilson. Wend Magazine, 2001 NW 19th Av, Ste 103B, Portland, OR 97209; publisher@wendmag.com; http://www.wendmag.com. *Bk. rev.:* 6, 200 words. *Aud.:* Hs, Ga.

Wend describes itself as "a forum for real people, writing real stories about real adventures and real environmental issues. ... Our mission is to educate and inspire..." Each issue features outdoor adventure by foot, wheel, or paddle, colorfully photographed in some exotic locale; an article on food within a particular culture; reviews of outdoor gear made in a sustainable manner; six book reviews; and several pages of "fashion spreads" for outdoor clothing. The web site features access to the current issue, a blog, and limited gear information. *Wend* would be a good title for academic libraries that support students and faculty who are traveling abroad and thinking about cultural and sustainability issues.

Women's Adventure. See Health and Fitness section.

2957. *Woodall's Camping Life Magazine: America's family camping magazine.* Incorporates (in 2008): *Woodall's Tenting Directory;* Which was formerly (until 2008): *Woodall's Plan It - Pack It - Go;* (until 1993): *Woodall's Tent Camping Guide;* (until 1990): *Woodall's Tenting Directory.*

2008. 8x/yr. USD 14.97 domestic; USD 22.97 Canada; USD 30.97 elsewhere. Ed(s): Sylvia Alarid, Stuart Bourdon. Woodall Publications Corp., 20700 Belshaw Ave, Carson, CA 90746; info@woodallpub.com; http://www.woodalls.com. Adv. *Aud.:* Ga.

Woodall's Camping Life states, "Our magazine is focused on serving the needs of the family-style camper and others who explore the nation's parks, rivers, and forests." In short, this is the magazine for the recreational vehicle (RV) and drive-in camping crowd. Issues feature articles on campground locations throughout the United States; brief wildlife profiles; stories on campside cookery; and "gear" reviews on everything from hiking boots and kayaks to RVs and trailer hitches. The web site offers some access to the magazine content, as well as databases on campgrounds, tow ratings, recipes, gear reviews, and a camping checklist.

■ HISTORY

American History/World History/Interdisciplinary Interests/General History

Loraine Wies, Periodicals/Acquisitions Library, Schaffer Library, Union College, Schenectady, NY 12308.

Ellen Fladger, Head of Special Collections, Schaffer Library, Union College, Schenectady, NY 12308.

Elizabeth Z. Bennett, Librarian for History and History of Science, Princeton University Library, Princeton NJ 08544

Introduction

In a field of such broad interest to varied audiences, it is difficult to single out a handful of magazines and journals. History, for both a general and an academic audience, is served by hundreds of periodicals. Some are focused on very specific times (*Eighteenth Century Life*), places (*French History*), or themes (*Journal of the History of Sexuality*). This section presents magazines and journals that cover the field broadly, from an international perspective, or focus on a theme such as economic, social, or gender history.

American libraries will want a deeper selection of journals on American history, including journals that cover specific periods like the Civil War. It is noteworthy that there are now also many journals that cover the diversity of the American experience. And any library with an adult audience should also consider subscribing to periodicals that cover local and regional history. A list of these follows, arranged by state. There are also some excellent regional periodicals, listed at the end.

Alabama Review, Alaska History, Journal of the Southwest [Arizona], *Arkansas Historical Quarterly, California History, Colorado Heritage, Connecticut History, Delaware History, Florida Historical Quarterly, Georgia Historical Quarterly, Idaho Yesterdays, Illinois Heritage, Journal of Illinois History, Illinois State Historical Society Journal, Indiana Magazine of History, Annals of Iowa: a quarterly journal of history, Kansas History: a journal of the central plains, Kentucky Ancestors, Louisiana History, Maine History, Maryland History Magazine, Historical Journal of Massachusetts/Massachusetts Historical Review, Michigan Historical Review, Minnesota History, Journal of Mississippi History, Missouri Historical Review, Montana: the magazine of western history, Nebraska History, Nevada Historical Society Quarterly, New Jersey History (Rutgers), New Mexico Historical Review, New York History: quarterly journal of the New York State Historical Association, North Carolina Historical Review, North Dakota History, Ohio History, Chronicles of Oklahoma, Oregon Historical Quarterly, Pennsylvania History: a journal of Mid-Atlantic States, Rhode Island History, South Carolina Historical Magazine, South Dakota History, Tennessee Historical Quarterly, Southwestern Historical Quarterly* [Texas], *Utah Historical Quarterly, Vermont History, Virginia Magazine of History and Biography, West Virginia History, Wisconsin Magazine of History, Annals of Wyoming.*

REGIONAL:

Journal of Southern History, Journal of the West: an illustrated quarterly of Western American history and culture, New England Quarterly, Pacific Historical Review, True West, Western Historical Quarterly.

Basic Periodicals

Ems: *American History* (Leesburg); Hs: *American History, History Today;* Ga: *American History* (Leesburg), *History News, History Today;* Ac: *American Historical Review, English Historical Review, Hispanic American Historical Review, The Historian (East Lansing),* History, History Today, Journal of American History, Journal of Contemporary History, Journal of Modern History, Journal of Urban History, William and Mary Quarterly.

Basic Abstracts and Indexes

America: History and Life, Arts and Humanities Citation Index, Historical Abstracts, ProQuest Research Library.

American History

2958. *American Heritage.* [ISSN: 0002-8738] 1947. q. USD 17.95. Ed(s): Edwin S Grosvenor. American Heritage, 416 Hungerford Dr, Ste 216, Rockville, MD 20850. Illus., index, adv. *Indexed:* A01, A06, A22, ABS&EES, AmHI, ArtHuCI, BEL&L, BRI, C37, CBRI, F01, MASUSE, MLA-IB, P02, RILM. *Bk. rev.:* 2-10. *Aud.:* Ems, Hs, Ga, Ac.

Now more than 60 years old, *American Heritage* is the most widely distributed magazine for general readers interested in American history, heavily illustrated and with "accessible and engaging writing by the nation's leading historians." Besides the feature articles, there are news items and reviews. Currently, *AH* also has an ongoing feature commemorating the 150th anniversary of the Civil War. Suitable for all libraries.

2959. *American History (Leesburg).* Formerly (until 1995): *American History Illustrated.* [ISSN: 1076-8866] 1966. bi-m. USD 21.95. Ed(s): Roger Vance. Weider History Group, 19300 Promenade Dr, Leesburg, VA 20176-6500; comments@weiderhistorygroup.com; www.historynet.com. Illus., index, adv. Circ: 70000. *Indexed:* A01, A22, AmHI, ArtHuCI, BRI, C37, IIFP, MASUSE, P02, RILM. *Bk. rev.:* 2-29, 200-300 words. *Aud.:* Ems, Hs, Ga.

Written for a general audience, *American History* covers a wide range of topics in brief, well-written, and attractively illustrated articles. Each issue has six or so feature articles, plus shorter pieces on news about American history, historic firsts, artifacts, and important encounters. This title also includes short book and media reviews and information on historic sites. Very readable, and balanced in its approach to potentially controversial topics and current political issues. Recommended for public and school libraries.

2960. *Civil War History.* [ISSN: 0009-8078] 1955. q. USD 75. Ed(s): Mary D Young, Lesley J Gordon. Kent State University Press, 1118 Library, PO Box 5190, Kent, OH 44242; http://upress.kent.edu. Illus., index. Refereed. Microform: MIM; PQC. *Indexed:* A01, A22, AmHI, ArtHuCI, BEL&L, BRI, E01, IIBP, MLA-IB, P02. *Bk. rev.:* 7-13, 1-2 pages. *Aud.:* Ga, Ac.

The American Civil War is still of very wide interest to all audiences. *Civil War History* covers "not only the War Between the States but the events leading up to it and the results flowing from it." Each issue includes two to four articles, on topics like "Black Northerners' Debates over Enlistment in the American Civil War" or "The Nature of Preservation: The Rise of Authenticity at Gettysburg." It has in-depth book reviews, mostly of academic books, but also some of books for a general audience. Recommended for college libraries.

2961. *Civil War Times: a magazine for persons interested in the American Civil War, its people, and its era.* Formerly (until 2002): *Civil War Times Illustrated;* Which incorporates (1958-1962): *Tradition;* (until 1962): *Civil War Times.* [ISSN: 1546-9980] 1959. bi-m. USD 21.95. Ed(s): Chris Lewis. Weider History Group, 19300 Promenade Dr, Leesburg, VA 20176-6500; comments@weiderhistorygroup.com; www.historynet.com. Illus., index, adv. Circ: 64500. *Indexed:* A01, A22, BRI, MASUSE. *Bk. rev.:* 2-3, length varies. *Aud.:* Hs, Ga.

Civil War publications have a large and loyal readership, and *Civil War Times* is one of the most popular. The extensive use of illustrations supplements coverage of such topics as the use of photography, artillery, and music, although numerous advertisements sometimes make it difficult to follow a story from one part of the magazine to another. Regular features such as "Gallery," "Travel," and "My War," as well as book reviews, enhance the magazine's appeal. Intended primarily for the general reader and Civil War enthusiast, this publication would also be helpful to high school and junior college students beginning research on a Civil War topic.

2962. Diplomatic History: the journal of the Society for Historians of American Foreign Relations. [ISSN: 0145-2096] 1977. 5x/yr. EUR 397. Ed(s): Robert D Schulzinger, Thomas W Zeiler. Oxford University Press, Great Clarendon St, Oxford, OX2 6DP, United Kingdom; enquiry@oup.co.uk; http://www.oxfordjournals.org. Illus., adv. Sample. Refereed. Circ: 2267 Paid. Vol. ends: Oct. Reprint: PSC. *Indexed:* A01, A22, ABS&EES, AmHI, ArtHuCI, BAS, BRI, E01, IBSS, P02, P61, SSA. *Bk. rev.:* 4-5, 3-8 pages. *Aud.:* Ac, Sa.

Diplomatic History is published by the Society for Historians of American Foreign Relations. It covers U.S. international history, diplomacy, security, and foreign relations, broadly defined. In addition to well-researched articles, there are forums on special topics like "Gender and Sexuality in American Foreign Relations." Some issues include commentary on specific articles or broad themes, often with a response from the author. Each issue also includes book reviews. Written for an academic audience, but much of the material is relevant for anyone interested in current U.S. foreign policy.

Ethnohistory. See Multicultural Studies section.

Journal of African American History. See African American section.

2963. The Journal of American History. Formerly (until 1964): *The Mississippi Valley Historical Review (Print).* [ISSN: 0021-8723] 1914. q. EUR 230. Ed(s): Edward T Linenthal. Oxford University Press, 1215 E Atwater Ave, Bloomington, IN 47401; custserv.us@oup.com; http://www.oup.com/us. Illus., index, adv. Refereed. Circ: 9000. Vol. ends: Dec. Microform: PMC; PQC. Reprint: PSC. *Indexed:* A01, A22, ABS&EES, AmHI, ArtHuCI, BAS, BRI, CBRI, Chicano, MLA-IB, P02, RILM. *Bk. rev.:* 100, 1-5 pages. *Aud.:* Ac, Sa.

JAH is published by the Organization of American Historians and is the leading journal in American history, in contrast to the *American Historical Review,* which covers world history. Because the OAH includes not only academic historians, but also teachers, public historians, and curators of historic sites and archives, *JAH* includes not only academic articles that cover American history very broadly, but also essays on pedagogy and the practice of public history. Articles are supplemented by an extensive section of book, museum exhibit, and web site reviews. Essential for any academic library, and especially valuable for colleges preparing future history teachers.

2964. Journal of the Gilded Age and Progressive Era. [ISSN: 1537-7814] 2002. q. GBP 85 (print & online eds.). Ed(s): Alan Lessoff. Cambridge University Press, 32 Ave of the Americas, New York, NY 10013; http://www.cambridge.org/us/. Refereed. Reprint: PSC. *Indexed:* RILM. *Bk. rev.:* Number and length vary. *Aud.:* Ac.

This journal covers "all aspects of U.S. history for the time period from 1865 through 1920." This is a period that tends to fall between journals, so it is welcome to have something that covers this era. Most issues include three or four articles, plus a few in-depth book reviews. There is a companion web site with digital material that relates to the articles, which is especially useful for teaching. Suitable for academic libraries.

2965. Magazine of History. [ISSN: 0882-228X] 1985. q. EUR 39. Ed(s): Carl R Weinberg. Oxford University Press, 2001 Evans Rd, Cary, NC 27513; http://www.oxfordjournals.org. Illus., adv. Refereed. Circ: 6000. Microform: PQC. Reprint: PSC. *Indexed:* A01, A22, BRI. *Bk. rev.:* 2-4, 1/2-1 page. *Aud.:* Hs, Ga, Ac.

Published by the Organization of American Historians, this is a sister publication to the more academic *Journal of American History.* Its purpose is to enhance the teaching of U.S. history in the classroom by providing "practical

teaching strategies." Each issue focuses on a theme in U.S. history; recent themes include "The 1950s," "History Wars," and "The Civil War at 150: Turning Points." Especially recommended for colleges with teacher preparation programs.

2966. Reviews in American History. [ISSN: 0048-7511] 1973. q. USD 165. Ed(s): Denise Thompson-Slaughter, Thomas P Slaughter. The Johns Hopkins University Press, 2715 N Charles St, Baltimore, MD 21218; http://www.press.jhu.edu. Illus., index, adv. Sample. Circ: 1662. Vol. ends: Dec. Microform: PQC. Reprint: PSC. *Indexed:* A01, A22, ABS&EES, AmHI, ArtHuCI, BRI, CBRI, E01, P02. *Bk. rev.:* 30-40, lengthy. *Aud.:* Ac, Sa.

RAH specializes in longer high-quality critical book reviews, usually about 20 per issue; plus, it offers essay reviews of several books, e.g., "American Military History: A Look at the Field." The reviews generally place the book(s) in historiographic context, making them useful not only for staying current, but also as starting points for further research. The books reviewed reflect the perspectives of a wide range of subfields in American history. This makes *RAH* a useful supplement to online book review sites such as H-NET. Written for an academic audience; also useful as a collection development resource.

2967. William and Mary Quarterly: a magazine of early American history and culture. Former titles (until 1944): *William and Mary College Quarterly Historical Magazine;* (until 1894): *William and Mary College Quarterly Historical Papers.* [ISSN: 0043-5597] 1892. q. USD 95 (print & online eds.). Ed(s): Erin Michaela Bendiner, Christopher Grasso. Omohundro Institute of Early American History & Culture, PO Box 8781, Williamsburg, VA 23187; ieahc1@wm.edu; http://oieahc.wm.edu/. Illus., index, adv. Refereed. Circ: 3479. Vol. ends: Oct. Microform: PQC. Reprint: PSC. *Indexed:* A01, A06, A22, AmHI, ArtHuCI, BRI, CBRI, MLA-IB, P02, R&TA, RILM. *Bk. rev.:* 13-20, 1,000 words. *Aud.:* Ac, Sa.

WMQ is the oldest and most prestigious journal for scholarship on North America from the colonial period through about 1820. Although it is essentially a journal for historians, it also publishes work from other disciplines, such as material culture, political science, and literature. The quality of the writing and editing is high. There are occasional forums with groups of articles; one recent example is "Colonial historians and American Indians." The journal also publishes articles on sources and source interpretation, and some articles have online supplements. Each issue also includes book reviews and review essays. Highly recommended for any academic library.

World History

2968. British Heritage. Incorporates (1979): *British History Illustrated.* [ISSN: 0195-2633] 1974. bi-m. USD 21.95. Ed(s): Dana Huntley. Weider History Group, 19300 Promenade Dr, Leesburg, VA 20176-6500; comments@weiderhistorygroup.com; www.historynet.com. Illus., index, adv. Circ: 40000. *Indexed:* A01, A22, BRI, C37, MASUSE. *Bk. rev.:* 3-4, 300-400 words. *Aud.:* Hs, Ga.

Published by the Weider History Group, which also publishes several other history magazines for a general audience (*Civil War Times, Military History,* and *American History*), *British Heritage* is an unusual combination of history for a general audience and travel planning advice. Most articles feature historic sites or places, together with information on travel, hotels, and nearby attractions. Anglophile readers and armchair travelers will enjoy the short, well-illustrated articles.

2969. The English Historical Review. [ISSN: 0013-8266] 1886. q. EUR 439. Ed(s): Martin Conway, Catherine Holmes. Oxford University Press, Great Clarendon St, Oxford, OX2 6DP, United Kingdom; enquiry@oup.co.uk; http://www.oxfordjournals.org/. Illus., index, adv. Sample. Refereed. Vol. ends: Nov. Microform: IDC; PMC; PQC. Reprint: PSC. *Indexed:* A01, A22, AmHI, ArtHuCI, BAS, BRI, BrArAb, CBRI, E01, MLA-IB, NumL, P02, P61, SSA. *Bk. rev.:* Number and length vary. *Aud.:* Ac, Sa.

The venerable *EHR* began publication in 1886, making it one of the oldest continuously published history journals. Articles tend to focus on British history, but the journal also cover European history, world history, and the

Americas (including U.S. foreign policy, but excluding books on the internal politics of the U.S.). *EHR* covers history from the early medieval period onward. There are essay reviews, e.g., "The Decline of Violence in the West," in-depth book reviews, and shorter notices of newly published books. Plus, there is an annual summary of international periodical literature published in the previous 12 months. Authoritative, respected, and essential for libraries at colleges and universities that teach British and European history.

2970. *Hispanic American Historical Review.* [ISSN: 0018-2168] 1918. q. USD 474. Ed(s): Sara Lickey. Duke University Press, 905 W Main St, Ste 18 B, PO Box 90660, Durham, NC 27701; subscriptions@dukeupress.edu; http://www.dukeupress.edu. Illus., index, adv. Sample. Refereed. Microform: MIM; PMC; PQC. Reprint: PSC. *Indexed:* A01, A22, AmHI, ArtHuCI, BRI, CBRI, E01, IBSS, MLA-IB, NumL, P02. *Bk. rev.:* Number and length vary. *Aud.:* Ac.

HAHR is the premier journal in the field of Latin American history from the colonial period onwards, and covers "every facet of scholarship on Latin American history and culture." There are substantive articles and an extensive section of book reviews, including reviews of books in Spanish. Recommended for academic libraries.

2971. *Historical Journal.* Formerly (until 1958): *Cambridge Historical Journal.* [ISSN: 0018-246X] 1923. q. GBP 348. Ed(s): Julian Hoppit. Cambridge University Press, The Edinburgh Bldg, Shaftesbury Rd, Cambridge, CB2 8RU, United Kingdom; journals@cambridge.org; http://www.cambridge.org/uk. Illus., index, adv. Circ: 1300. Vol. ends: Dec. Microform: PQC. Reprint: PSC. *Indexed:* A01, A22, AmHI, ArtHuCI, BAS, BEL&L, BRI, BrArAb, E01, IBSS, MLA-IB, NumL, P02, P61, SSA. *Bk. rev.:* 5-28, lengthy. *Aud.:* Ac.

This journal's articles cover world history since 1500 broadly, including political, cultural, and economic perspectives. European history dominates, but there are also articles on topics concerning Africa, Asia, and South America. Many articles reflect an interdisciplinary approach. Rather than publishing book reviews, *THJ* prefers substantive historiographical reviews and essay reviews that cover a number of books on related topics, e.g., "The Protestant minority in Southern Ireland" or "Mercantile networks in the early modern world." Academic audience.

2972. *History: the journal of the Historical Association.* [ISSN: 0018-2648] 1912. q. USD 331 (print & online eds.). Ed(s): Joseph Smith. Wiley-Blackwell Publishing Ltd., 9600 Garsington Rd, Oxford, OX4 2DQ, United Kingdom; customer@wiley.co.uk; http://www.wiley.com/. Illus., adv. Sample. Refereed. Vol. ends: Oct. Microform: MIM; IDC; PQC. Reprint: PSC. *Indexed:* A01, A22, AmHI, ArtHuCI, BAS, BRI, BrArAb, E01, IBSS, MLA-IB, NumL, P02. *Bk. rev.:* 36-95, lengthy; number varies. *Aud.:* Ac, Sa.

The mission of the Historical Association, a British society, is to "support the study, teaching[,] and enjoyment of history at all levels." The HA publishes several journals, and *History* is its journal for an academic and scholarly audience. Unsurprisingly, British history accounts for the bulk of the articles, but the journal reflects a wide range of approaches and contributions from social, political, cultural, economic, and ecclesiastical historians. Under a new editorial team since 2011, *History* has introduced review articles and special issues—a recent issue focused on the Balkans—and essays on records and archives. However, although book reviews were once a feature of this journal, there are no book reviews in the two most recent issues.

2973. *History Today.* [ISSN: 0018-2753] 1951. m. GBP 49; GBP 74 combined subscription (print & online eds.). Ed(s): Paul Lay. History Today Ltd., 25 Bedford Ave, London, WC1B 3AT, United Kingdom. Illus., index, adv. Sample. Vol. ends: Dec. Microform: NBI. *Indexed:* A01, A06, A22, AmHI, ArtHuCI, BAS, BEL&L, BRI, BrArAb, C37, CBRI, MASUSE, MLA-IB, NumL, P02, RILM. *Bk. rev.:* 3-7. *Aud.:* Ga, Ac.

This beautifully illustrated popular magazine, published in Britain, is written for a general audience but is also valuable for academic researchers. Each issue includes several substantive articles, which generally cover a wide range of times, places, and topics. Recent issues include articles on "Why Englishmen

fought in the American Civil War," "Hitler's turncoat tutor," and "Asia and the old world order." There is an emphasis on British history, but world history is also covered. Many of the articles are written by academic historians, and generally include recommended further reading, making this a good resource for undergraduates and high school students. There are also essays, news, reviews (of books, media, and exhibitions), and letters to the editor. The style is exceptionally readable. Recommended for all libraries.

2974. *History Workshop Journal.* Formerly (until 1995): *History Workshop.* [ISSN: 1363-3554] 1976. s-a. EUR 208. Oxford University Press, Great Clarendon St, Oxford, OX2 6DP, United Kingdom; enquiry@oup.co.uk; http://www.oxfordjournals.org/. Illus., adv. Sample. Refereed. Reprint: PSC. *Indexed:* A22, ArtHuCI, E01, GW, MLA-IB, P61, RILM, SSA. *Bk. rev.:* 10-20, length varies. *Aud.:* Ga, Ac, Sa.

HWJ is the flagship journal of the "history workshop" movement, and champions the perspective of "history from below," i.e., history from the perspective of ordinary people rather than elites. Articles address a wide range of topics in European history. Beyond the usual academic articles, *HWJ* also publishes essays on research and the writing of history; articles regarding history in social and political context ("History on the Line"); and conference reports, as well as roughly half a dozen book reviews per issue. Recent issues are complemented by *History Workshop Online*, which publishes "conversations and disputations amongst historians, curators, activists, and others who aim to put past and present into critical dialogue." *HWJ* is academically rigorous, but written for a wider audience, and would be appropriate for most academic libraries.

2975. *The International History Review.* [ISSN: 0707-5332] 1979. q. GBP 264 (print & online eds.). Ed(s): Andrew Williams, Lucian Ashworth. Routledge, 4 Park Sq, Milton Park, Abingdon, OX14 4RN, United Kingdom; subscriptions@tandf.co.uk; http://www.tandfonline.com. Illus., adv. Refereed. Reprint: PSC. *Indexed:* A01, A22, ABS&EES, AmHI, ArtHuCI, BAS, BRI, C37, CBCARef, IBSS, MLA-IB. *Bk. rev.:* 70-80, length varies. *Aud.:* Ac.

The editors of the *IHR* seek to create a bridge between historical research and the study of international relations. The journal publishes articles on political and diplomatic history, especially on "the history of current conflicts and conflicts of current interest," such as a recent article titled "To the Shores of Tripoli: America, Qaddafi, and Libyan Revolution 1969–89." The journal also covers the intellectual history of international thought and international relations theory, as well as the history of international organizations. Most issues contain in-depth book reviews or review essays. Much of the content is about the twentieth century, but there are occasional articles on earlier periods. For an academic audience.

The Journal of African History. See Africa section.

2976. *Journal of Contemporary History.* [ISSN: 0022-0094] 1966. q. USD 1002. Ed(s): Stanley Payne, Richard J Evans. Sage Publications Ltd., 1 Oliver's Yard, 55 City Rd, London, EC1Y 1SP, United Kingdom; info@sagepub.co.uk; http://www.uk.sagepub.com. Illus. Sample. Refereed. Microform: PQC. Reprint: PSC. *Indexed:* A01, A22, ABS&EES, AmHI, ArtHuCI, BAS, BRI, E01, IBSS, MLA-IB, P02, P61, SSA. *Bk. rev.:* 6-12. *Aud.:* Ga, Ac.

JCH covers twentieth-century world history after World War I. While most articles are on European political and cultural history, there is an occasional article on America or other parts of the world. In addition to articles, there are also book reviews and review articles. This journal is for an academic audience, but is well-written and intelligible to the non-specialist. Recent articles include "Gender, Citizenship and Civil Defence in Britain 1937-1941" and "Journalists and the Stirring of Australian Public Diplomacy: The Colombo Plan Towards the 1960s."

2977. *Journal of Early Modern History: contacts, comparisons, contrasts.* [ISSN: 1385-3783] 1997. 6x/yr. EUR 366. Ed(s): Simon Ditchfield. Brill, PO Box 9000, Leiden, 2300 PA, Netherlands; cs@brill.nl; http://www.brill.nl. Refereed. Reprint: PSC. *Indexed:* A01, A22, ArtHuCI, E01. *Bk. rev.:* 5-10; vary in length. *Aud.:* Ac.

Established in 1996, *JEMH* covers world history from 1300 to 1800, and it is a key journal for this relatively recently-established academic field. In general there are three or four articles in each issue, and in some issues, book reviews supplement the scholarly articles. Some articles are comparative; many address contacts between cultures; and others address specific topics in particular times and places, e.g., "Porcelain and the Material Culture of the Mongol-Yuan Court" or "Professional Lobbying in Eighteenth-century Brussels." Special issues cover broader topics like "Piracy in Asian Waters" or "Speech and Oral Culture." This fairly specialized journal is suitable for an academic audience with an interest in this period.

2978. *Journal of Global History.* [ISSN: 1740-0228] 2005. 3x/yr. GBP 198 (print & online eds.). Ed(s): William Gervase Clarence-Smith, Peer Vries. Cambridge University Press, The Edinburgh Bldg, Shaftesbury Rd, Cambridge, CB2 8RU, United Kingdom; journals@cambridge.org; http://www.cambridge.org/uk. Adv. Reprint: PSC. *Indexed:* A22, ArtHuCI, E01, IBSS. *Bk. rev.:* Number and length vary. *Aud.:* Ac.

This journal covers world history, particularly from the point of view of interactions between peoples, countries, and cultures. The editors are broadly interested in "global change over time, together with the diverse histories of globalization." Recent articles examine the global history of the diamond trade; the histories of international organizations (from the League of Nations to the Oddfellows and the Rotary club); and the British colonial press in Africa. Each issue includes about eight articles, and some in-depth book reviews. Written for an academic audience.

Journal of Latin American Studies. See Latin America and Spain section.

2979. *Journal of Medieval History.* [ISSN: 0304-4181] 1975. 4x/yr. GBP 557 (print & online eds.). Ed(s): C M Woolgar. Elsevier BV, Radarweg 29, PO Box 211, Amsterdam, 1000 AE, Netherlands; JournalsCustomerServiceEMEA@elsevier.com; http://www.elsevier.nl. Illus., index. Refereed. Microform: PQC. Reprint: PSC. *Indexed:* A01, A22, AmHI, ArtHuCI, BrArAb, FR, MLA-IB, NumL. *Aud.:* Ac, Sa.

The European Middle Ages is well represented in popular culture and mythology (like video games), and this is a key journal for the academic study of medieval history. Each issue contains roughly a half-dozen articles on topics that cover the entire span from the fall of Rome to the Renaissance. Topics include political and military history, religion, and social and intellectual history. No book reviews. Academic audience.

2980. *The Journal of Modern History.* [ISSN: 0022-2801] 1929. q. USD 339 (print & online eds.). Ed(s): Mary van Steenbergh, John W Boyer. University of Chicago Press, 1427 E 60th St, Chicago, IL 60637; subscriptions@press.uchicago.edu; http://www.journals.uchicago.edu. Illus., index, adv. Sample. Refereed. Vol. ends: Dec. Microform: PMC; PQC. Reprint: PSC. *Indexed:* A01, A22, ABS&EES, AmHI, ArtHuCI, BAS, BEL&L, BRI, CBRI, IBSS, MLA-IB, P02, P61, RILM, SSA. *Bk. rev.:* 40-50, 1-2 pages. *Aud.:* Ac, Sa.

Covers the the history of Europe since the Renaissance, from the varied perspectives of intellectual, cultural, and political history. Some articles concern the history of specific countries or events, and others look at broader topics such as "Europe in the 1950s: The Anxieties of Beginning Again." Other recent articles range from "The Balkan Revolutionary Age" to "The French Hygiene Offensive of the 1950s." In addition to several articles, close to half of each issue is signed book reviews. Recommended for an academic audience.

2981. *Journal of World History: official journal of the World History Association.* [ISSN: 1045-6007] 1990. q. USD 120. Ed(s): Jerry H Bentley. University of Hawaii Press, 2840 Kolowalu St, Honolulu, HI 96822; uhpjourn@hawaii.edu; http://www.uhpress.hawaii.edu. Illus., adv. Sample. Refereed. Circ: 1282. *Indexed:* A01, A22, AmHI, ArtHuCI, BRI, E01, IBSS, MLA-IB, P61, SSA. *Bk. rev.:* 10, 1-4 pages. *Aud.:* Ac, Sa.

Published by the World History Association, this journal covers an exceptionally wide range of geography and time—one recent issue ranges from 1415 to 1978. Many articles are comparative or transnational in focus, discussing a topic across many countries or cultures. Each issue also includes

book reviews, both short and long. A good choice for any academic library that serves teaching and research on world history, and an excellent resource for understanding the range of topics addressed by world historians.

2982. *Past & Present: a journal of historical studies.* [ISSN: 0031-2746] 1952. q. EUR 313. Ed(s): Steve Smith, Lyndal Roper. Oxford University Press, Great Clarendon St, Oxford, OX2 6DP, United Kingdom; enquiry@oup.co.uk; http://www.oxfordjournals.org/. Illus., index, adv. Sample. Refereed. Reprint: PSC. *Indexed:* A01, A22, AmHI, ArtHuCI, BAS, BEL&L, BRI, BrArAb, E01, FR, IBSS, MLA-IB, NumL, P02, P61, SSA. *Bk. rev.:* Occasional review essay. *Aud.:* Ac, Sa.

Past & Present was founded in 1952 by a group of Marxist historians, to focus on social and economic history, in a period when most academic journals primarily addressed political history. It covers historical, social, and cultural change in the widest possible range of times and places. Articles like "Christian Civilization and the Confucian Church: The Origin of Secularist Politics in Modern China" or "Recycling in Britain after the Fall of Rome's Metal Economy" indicate the breadth of topics. The journal has been unusually open to publishing work that might generate controversy, including "constructive debates on controversial topics." There are no book reviews, but the journal features an occasional review essay. Unusually readable.

Interdisciplinary Interests

2983. *Comparative Studies in Society and History: an international quarterly.* [ISSN: 0010-4175] 1958. q. GBP 174 (print & online eds.). Ed(s): David Akin, Andrew Shryock. Cambridge University Press, The Edinburgh Bldg, Shaftesbury Rd, Cambridge, CB2 8RU, United Kingdom; journals@cambridge.org; http://www.cambridge.org/uk. Illus., index, adv. Refereed. Vol. ends: Nov. Microform: PQC. Reprint: PSC. *Indexed:* A01, A22, A47, ABIn, ABS&EES, AmHI, ArtHuCI, BAS, BRI, C45, E01, FR, IBSS, MLA-IB, P02, P61, RILM, RRTA, SSA. *Bk. rev.:* 0-5, 1 page. *Aud.:* Ac, Sa.

International in scope, *CSSH* is a forum for "interpretation concerning problems of recurrent patterning and change in human societies through time and the contemporary world." Articles are paired in themes like "being Chinese abroad" or "modes of insurrection." Most articles incorporate a theoretical or social science perspective, drawing on fields like anthropology, history, political science, and sociology. The result is a stimulating mix of approaches, making this journal appropriate for academic history collections and also for libraries that focus on the social sciences. Each issue also includes a few in-depth book reviews.

2984. *Environmental History.* Formed by the merger of (1990-1996): *Environmental History Review;* Which was formerly (until 1990): *Environmental Review;* Which incorporated (1974-198?): *Environmental History Newsletter;* (1990-1996): *Forest and Conservation History;* Which was formerly (until 1990): *Journal of Forest History;* (until 1974): *Forest History.* [ISSN: 1084-5453] 1996. q. EUR 213. Ed(s): Nancy Langston. Oxford University Press, 2001 Evans Rd, Cary, NC 27513; http://www.oxfordjournals.org. Illus., index, adv. Sample. Refereed. Vol. ends: Oct. Microform: PQC. Reprint: PSC. *Indexed:* A22, Agr, ArtHuCI, C45, GardL, MLA-IB, P02, RRTA. *Bk. rev.:* Number and length vary. *Aud.:* Ac.

Published jointly by the Forest History Society and the American Society for Environmental History, this is the premier journal in this relatively new field. The focus is on "international articles that portray human interactions with the natural world over time." Recent issues have included articles on organic farming in Nazi Germany and on the "right to fish" movement. Some issues include a "Gallery" section with essays on an image. Each issue also includes an extensive section of book reviews, and some issues also include a very valuable listing of "new scholarship"—regarding books, articles, dissertations, and archival sources.

Gender and History. See Gender Studies section.

2985. *History and Theory: studies in the philosophy of history.* [ISSN: 0018-2656] 1960. q. GBP 239. Ed(s): Brian C Fay. Wiley-Blackwell Publishing, Inc., 111 River St, Hoboken, NJ 07030; info@wiley.com; http://onlinelibrary.wiley.com/. Index, adv. Sample. Refereed. Vol. ends: Dec. Microform: PQC. Reprint: PSC. *Indexed:* A01, A06, A22, ABS&EES, AmHI, ArtHuCI, BAS, BRI, CBRI, E01, FR, IBSS, IPB, MASUSE, MLA-IB, P02, P61, RILM, SSA. *Bk. rev.:* Number varies; essay length. *Aud.:* Ac, Sa.

This journal features articles on theory and philosophy of history, historiography, methodology, time and culture, and related topics. In-depth, article-length review essays go beyond the usual scope of a book review; some issues include a "book forum," which has multiple articles about the same book. Brief book reviews are also included, along with abstracts of articles that originally appeared in Chinese journals. There is an annual theme issue, on a topic like "Tradition and history." This title is for specialists, not the general reader, but the articles are of very high quality.

Isis. See Science and Techology section.

Journal of Interdisciplinary History. See Interdisciplinary Studies section.

2986. *Journal of Social History.* [ISSN: 0022-4529] 1967. q. EUR 123. Ed(s): Peter Stearns. Oxford University Press, 2001 Evans Rd, Cary, NC 27513; custserv.us@oup.com; http://www.oxfordjournals.org. Illus., adv. Refereed. Circ: 1000. Vol. ends: Summer. Microform: MIM; PQC. Reprint: PSC. *Indexed:* A01, A22, ABS&EES, AmHI, ArtHuCI, BAS, BRI, CBRI, E01, IBSS, P02, P61, RILM, SSA. *Bk. rev.:* 25-30, lengthy. *Aud.:* Ac, Sa.

JSH covers social history worldwide, including issues of gender, class, and race, but also topics like migration, recreation, and government social policy. The emphasis is on the eighteenth, nineteenth, and twentieth centuries, but occasionally articles on the early modern period are published. In most issues, articles are grouped by topic, e.g., "Urban issues" or "Gender and labor." Each issue also contains in-depth book reviews. This title features occasional special issues, e.g., "The Politics of Suicide," plus there is an annual essay competition for graduate students. For an interdisciplinary academic audience, this is an influential journal in this subfield.

2987. *Journal of the History of Sexuality.* [ISSN: 1043-4070] 1990. q. USD 288. Ed(s): Mathew Kuefler. University of Texas Press, Journals Division, PO Box 7819, Austin, TX 78713; journals@uts.cc.utexas.edu; http://www.utexas.edu/utpress/journals/journals.html. Illus., adv. Refereed. Vol. ends: Nov. *Indexed:* A01, A22, ABS&EES, AmHI, ArtHuCI, BRI, E01, FR, GW, IBSS, MLA-IB. *Bk. rev.:* 11-16, 2-3 pages. *Aud.:* Ac, Sa.

This journal seeks to illuminate sexuality "in all its expressions, recognizing differences of class, culture, gender, race, and sexual preference" within a scope transcending "temporal and geographic boundaries." Articles include studies on "The Physician and the Fallen Woman: Medicalizing Prostitution in the Polish Lands" and "Cross-Dressing in a Russian Orthodox Monastery: The Case of Mariia Zakharova." The entire content reflects first-rate scholarship. Occasionally, there is a critical commentary or debate relevant to a previous article. The book reviews, book lists, and review essays provide a comprehensive bibliographic source.

2988. *Journal of Urban History.* [ISSN: 0096-1442] 1974. bi-m. USD 1197. Ed(s): David R Goldfield. Sage Publications, Inc., 2455 Teller Rd, Thousand Oaks, CA 91320; info@sagepub.com; http://www.sagepub.com. Illus., index, adv. Refereed. Vol. ends: Sep. Reprint: PSC. *Indexed:* A01, A22, ABS&EES, AmHI, ArtHuCI, BAS, BRI, CBRI, E01, IBSS, IIBP, P02, P61, RILM, SSA, SWR&A. *Bk. rev.:* 3-4, essay length. *Aud.:* Ac.

This journal is focused on "the history of cities and urban societies throughout the world." The emphasis is primarily on modern history, post-1800, but coverage is international. There are book reviews and excellent longer review essays on "new interpretations and developments in urban history." Occasional theme issues or sections of issues appear, e.g., "Suburban Diversity in Postwar America" or "Cities and Nationalisms." In a largely urbanized America, this journal is appropriate for most academic libraries.

Journal of Women's History. See Gender Studies section.

2989. *Radical History Review.* Former titles (until 1975): *M A R H O Newsletter*; (until 1974): *Mid-Atlantic Radical Historians' Organization. Newsletter*; *Mid-Atlantic Radical Historians' Newsletter.* [ISSN: 0163-6545] 1973. 3x/yr. USD 196. Ed(s): Atiba Pertilla. Duke University Press, 905 W Main St, Ste 18 B, PO Box 90660, Durham, NC 27701; dukepress@duke.edu; http://www.dukeupress.edu. Illus., adv. Sample. Refereed. Reprint: PSC. *Indexed:* A01, A22, ABS&EES, AmHI, ArtHuCI, BAS, BRI, E01, IBSS, MLA-IB, P02, P61, RILM, SSA. *Bk. rev.:* Number and length vary. *Aud.:* Ac.

This journal is managed by an "editorial collective" and is intentionally provocative. Articles address issues of gender, race, sexuality, imperialism, and class, in both Western and non-Western history. Each issue has a theme, like "Walker, Voyeurs, and the Politics of Urban Space" or "Haitian Lives/Global Perspectives." The journal is divided into subsections such as "Interventions" or "Reflections," and a section called "Curated Spaces" often addresses art as a form of doing history. There are also interviews, book and media reviews, and essays on teaching. The style is sometimes heavy on jargon, but the unusual perspective, links to current events, and the diversity of topics makes this title stimulating reading. Appropriate for academic libraries.

General History

2990. *American Historical Review.* [ISSN: 0002-8762] 1895. 5x/yr. EUR 288. Ed(s): Rob Schneider. Oxford University Press, 2001 Evans Rd, Cary, NC 27513; jnlorders@oup-usa.org; http://www.oxfordjournals.org. Illus., index, adv. Sample. Refereed. Vol. ends: Dec. Microform: PQC. Reprint: PSC. *Indexed:* A01, A06, A22, ABS&EES, AbAn, AmHI, ArtHuCI, BAS, BRI, BrArAb, CBRI, Chicano, EconLit, F01, IBSS, JEL, MASUSE, MLA-IB, NumL, P02, RILM. *Bk. rev.:* 250-275, 450 words. *Aud.:* Ac, Sa.

AHR is the official publication of the American Historical Association. It is the most prestigious academic history journal in the U.S., and covers every field of historical study worldwide. Occasional features bring together a group of articles on related topics with commentary, most recently, "Transnational Lives in the Twentieth Century." There is also an annual "conversation" on a topic like the historical study of emotions, presenting the views of several historians together. About half of each issue is an exceptional section of book reviews, arranged by subfield, which is very valuable for anyone trying to keep current in this field. Essential for any academic library.

Economic History Review. See Economics section.

2991. *The Historian (East Lansing): a journal of history.* [ISSN: 0018-2370] 1938. q. GBP 166. Ed(s): Kees Boterbloem. Wiley-Blackwell Publishing, Inc., 111 River St, Hoboken, NJ 07030; info@wiley.com; http://onlinelibrary.wiley.com/. Illus., adv. Sample. Refereed. Vol. ends: Aug. Microform: PQC. Reprint: PSC. *Indexed:* A01, A22, ABS&EES, AmHI, ArtHuCI, BAS, BRI, BrArAb, CBRI, E01, MASUSE, MLA-IB, NumL, P02, RILM. *Bk. rev.:* 40-60, 400-500 words. *Aud.:* Ga, Ac.

Published by Phi Alpha Theta, an American honor society for undergraduate and graduate students and professors of history, *The Historian* has four substantive articles in each issue, on a very wide range of topics. The choice of topics is a good match for undergraduate interests, and this journal is recommended for a college audience. Approximately half the articles are about American history. There is also an especially extensive section of book reviews, arranged geographically. The reviews are briefer than in some academic journals, but provide a good survey of current publishing in the field.

2992. *Historical Research.* Formerly (until 1987): *University of London. Institute of Historical Research. Bulletin.* [ISSN: 0950-3471] 1923. q. GBP 228. Ed(s): Miles Taylor. Wiley-Blackwell Publishing Ltd., The Atrium, Southern Gate, Chichester, PO19 8SQ, United Kingdom; customer@wiley.com; http://www.wiley.com/. Illus., adv. Sample. Refereed. Vol. ends: Nov. Microform: IDC. Reprint: PSC. *Indexed:* A01, A22, AmHI, ArtHuCI, BrArAb, E01, MLA-IB, NumL, P02. *Aud.:* Ac, Sa.

Historical Research has been published by the prestigious British Institute for Historical Research since 1923. It covers a broad time span, from medieval to twentieth-century history. Articles reflect a variety of approaches, including of social, political, urban, intellectual, and cultural history. While most articles are on British history, there are some on Europe and other areas of the world, like "The women pro-Boers: gender, peace and the critique of empire in the South African war." The online version also offers "virtual special issues" of articles on a particular topic or theme that have previously published in the journal. No book reviews.

The History Teacher. See Education section.

2993. *History (Washington): reviews of new books.* [ISSN: 0361-2759] 1972. q. GBP 185 (print & online eds.). Ed(s): Miriam Aronin. Routledge, 325 Chestnut St, Ste 800, Philadelphia, PA 19106; customerservice@taylorandfrancis.com; http://www.tandfonline.com. Illus., index, adv. Refereed. Reprint: PSC. *Indexed:* A01, A22, ABS&EES, BRI, CBRI, Chicano, E01, MASUSE. *Bk. rev.:* Number varies; 450 words. *Aud.:* Hs, Ga, Ac.

This journal is entirely devoted to book reviews, about 30 per issue, and it is a key resource for current awareness and collection development in the field of history. It covers world history in all periods. Most issues also feature essay reviews of several related books, on a theme like the Holocaust or environmental history.

The Public Historian. See Archives and Manuscripts section.

■ HOME

See also Do-It-Yourself; and Interior Design and Decoration sections.

Sarah Fagan, Library Assistant, Physics Research Library, Harvard University, Cambridge, MA 02138.

Darla A. White, Records Manager and Archivist, Center for the History of Medicine, Countway Library, Harvard Medical School, Boston, MA 02155

Introduction

Magazines within this section focus on the home and the diverse range of topics associated with home life. These topics include, but are not limited to, architecture, arts and crafts, collecting, domestic life, entertaining, food, gardening, health and wellness, interior decorating and design, and renovation. Several of these magazines contain articles that cover numerous home-centric topics within their pages, such as *Family Circle* and *Good Housekeeping*, which appeal to broad reader audiences, while others primarily focus on more specific topics, styles, or aspects of the home and home life, such as *Cottages and Bungalows* and *Electronic House: Fast Track to the Connected Lifestyle*. *Home Cultures* offers a scholarly perspective and is a peer-reviewed journal, international in scope, that explores connections between such disciplines as architecture, gender and cultural studies, social history, art history, and geography, all within an overall home cultures framework. All magazines listed in this section, with the exception of the *Home Cultures* journal, have companion web sites that offer a variety of additional home-oriented articles, photos, videos, blogs, and how-to or DIY guides. *Home Cultures* does provide article abstracts and table of contents information online, but an electronic subscription is required to obtain electronic full-text articles. This journal and each magazine provides a dynamic array of information for a wide variety of home-life interests and homemaking abilities, and as people continue to take care of and have pride in their homes and gardens and domestic lives, there will continue to be a market for resources that provide information on everything from growing plants to undertaking budget-friendly home renovations, and from cooking healthy meals to choosing paint schemes, among many other topics. The goal in compiling this list has been to provide a variety of resources that cover as many home-themed topics as possible. Since the last edition of *Magazines for Libraries* was published, *Country Almanac: Country Almanac Magazine* has ceased publication and has thus been removed from this list. In addition, two magazines were added since the previous edition, including *Cottages and Bungalows*, a useful and creative magazine that provides information about small-space living areas and vintage-themed home design, and *Martha Stewart Living*, a thorough resource filled with instructional and inspirational articles regarding all aspects of home life.

Basic Periodicals

Ga: *Better Homes and Gardens, House Beautiful, Martha Stewart Living, Real Simple.*

Basic Abstracts and Indexes

Readers' Guide to Periodical Literature.

2994. *Backwoods Home Magazine: practical ideas for self reliant living.* [ISSN: 1050-9712] 1989. bi-m. USD 24.95. Ed(s): Ilene Duffy, Dave Duffy. David J. Duffy, Ed. & Pub., PO Box 712, Gold Beach, OR 97444. Illus., adv. Vol. ends: Dec. *Indexed:* BRI. *Bk. rev.:* 1, 200 words. *Aud.:* Ga.

Written "for people who have a desire to pursue personal independence, self-sufficiency, and their dreams," *Backwoods Home Magazine* is particularly geared toward back-to-the-land and do-it-yourself enthusiasts. With a range of topics including home-building projects, emergence preparedness, farm and garden projects, and economics for those living outside traditional market structures, as well as regular columns on practical firearms and food canning and storage advice, *Backwoods Home* is geared toward a libertarian audience and those focused on rural living. Examples of recent articles include "Making Maple Syrup," "Zombie Apocalypse," and "Homestead burnout—what it is and how to avoid it." Though most articles lack an overtly political focus, the editor's "My View" column highlights current issues in domestic politics while reinforcing *Backwoods Home*'s themes of self-reliance and personal freedom. With a Kindle subscription newly available and an online radio show at www.preparednessradionetwork.com, *Backwoods Home Magazine* is most likely appropriate for public libraries whose patrons are interested in these topics.

2995. *Better Homes and Gardens.* Formerly (until 1924): *Fruit, Garden and Home.* [ISSN: 0006-0151] 1922. m. USD 5.99 domestic. Ed(s): Gayle Goodson Butler, Kitty Morgan. Meredith Corporation, 1716 Locust St, Des Moines, IA 50309; patrick.taylor@meredith.com; http://www.meredith.com. Illus., adv. Vol. ends: No. 12. *Indexed:* A22, BRI, C37, GardL, IHTDI, P02. *Aud.:* Hs, Ga, Ac.

Better Homes and Gardens is a well-known family-oriented magazine catering to indoor and outdoor living tips and inspiration. Featuring do-it-yourself articles on redecorating, health and beauty, cleaning, and home organization, *Better Home and Gardens* provides accessible information on a variety of subjects. Themed issues feature seasonally appropriate planting ideas, decorating tips, and meal planning. The regular cooking articles highlight vegetarian friendly recipes for special occasions and every day, with calorie counts and nutrition information included. A companion web site (see below) includes video instructions for projects featured in the print edition, dozens of cooking, decorating, holiday, and craft ideas for kids and adults as well as contests, connections to social media, and coupons and savings on purchases made through the web site. *Better Homes and Gardens* is a popular magazine and would be appropriate for public libraries. URL: www.BHG.com

2996. *Cottages & Bungalows.* [ISSN: 1941-4056] 2007. 10x/yr. USD 24.95. Ed(s): Jicki Torres. Beckett Media Llc, 2400 E Katella Ave, Ste 300, Anaheim, CA 92806; customerservice@beckett.com; http://www.beckett.com. Illus., adv. *Aud.:* Ga.

Spotlighting small living areas, *Cottages and Bungalows* is an innovative resource that provides creative ideas and information about vintage materials and vintage-inspired design themes that can be used to create dynamic small-space living areas that encompass both style and functionality. This magazine is filled with glossy photo spreads, along with real-life, small-space living and redesign testimonials, remodeling guides, do-it-yourself tutorials, and crafting ideas. It is a valuable resource for readers who want to make a small living area's design more dynamic and useful. Articles offer information about finding new uses for and refurbishing vintage furniture and fabrics, small-home and room makeovers, vintage-inspired paint-color schemes, simple weekend projects, seasonal design ideas, arts and crafts, and caring for classic small homes and antique furniture, all with a focus on vintage-inspired simplicity and workmanship. There is an overall theme of doing more with less, specifically regarding one's budget and living space size. There are also excellent product reviews and special features about cottage and bungalow communities, historically sensitive new homes, and cottage and bungalow destinations. In addition to the print magazine, there is a newly relaunched companion web site (see below), which offers useful information on such topics as interior decorating, renovating old and/or small living spaces, DIY guides, crafts, and entertaining, all accompanied by photos and how-to videos and reflecting the print magazine's simplistic, DIY approach to making one's small living space useful, functional, and stylish. This magazine would appeal to arts and crafts enthusiasts, small-space dwellers and homeowners, art students, and anyone interested in retro, vintage designs and homes, and is appropriate for any public library. URL: http://cottagesandbungalowsmag.com

2997. Country Living (New York). Formerly (until 198?): *Good Housekeeping's Country Living.* [ISSN: 0732-2569] 1978. 10x/yr. USD 12; USD 4.50 newsstand/cover. Hearst Magazines, 300 W 57th St, 12th Fl, New York, NY 10019; HearstMagazines@hearst.com; http://www.hearst.com. Illus., adv. Circ: 1651937 Paid. Vol. ends: Dec. *Indexed:* BRI, C37, GardL, MASUSE, P02. *Aud.:* Ga.

With a focus on simple Americana and down-home style, *Country Living* is a lifestyle magazine that features home decorating, collectibles, travel and real estate, and simple healthy recipes. Budget and style conscious, *Country Living* highlights decorating, shopping, and collecting items made in America, from antique stores and flea markets. Glossy photographs illustrate articles on indoor/outdoor remodeling projects, simple DIY, and home makeovers for under $100. A recent feature article, "Growing the Ultimate Kitchen Garden," included interviews with the professional chefs that contributed to the project, as well as plans, planting guides, and recipes featuring the vegetables planted. The recipes are health-conscious and vegetarian-friendly, and include calorie counts and nutrition information. The robust companion web site (see below) includes dozens of home-decorating, DIY, food, and entertaining ideas, and outdoor-living ideas. How-to videos are also included on the web site, supplemental to projects featured in the magazine. *Country Living* also hosts annual Country Living Fairs throughout the United States, which are promoted through the magazine and web site, and are a center for vendors, live music, book signings, demonstrations, and food in the country living theme. This magazine is appropriate for most public library audiences. URL: www.countryliving.com

2998. Dwell. [ISSN: 1530-5309] 2000. 10x/yr. USD 19.95 domestic; USD 39.95 Canada; USD 59.95 elsewhere. Dwell LLC, 40 Gold St, San Francisco, CA 94133; feedback@dwell.com; http://www.dwell.com. Illus., adv. Circ: 300000 Paid. *Indexed:* ASIP. *Aud.:* Ga.

Dwell, a modern interior-design magazine, features stylish home remodels from around the globe. A sleek and minimalist design aesthetic guides home goods and furniture reviews, with a detailed pro and con review of products in the "Dwell Reports" section. Articles feature "after" photographs of home renovation projects that are typically undertaken by architect or designer owners. Inspirational in design, most "Dwellings" highlight distinctive use of space, materials, or location, with an emphasis on sustainability and customization. Prefabricated homes are a common feature of magazine, with an annual issue devoted to innovative design with ready-made home models. Reports from international design shows and events are featured, including interviews with up-and-coming designers and reviews of show collections or newly released products. *Dwell*'s web site features free access to back issues with complete articles and robust slideshows, online interviews, and ideas for modern design well beyond the features of the print edition. *Dwell* is appropriate for public libraries and academic libraries with a design or architecture focus. URL: www.dwell.com

2999. Early American Life: traditions, period style, antiques, architecture, history. Former titles (until 2001): *Early American Homes;* (until 1996): *Early American Life.* [ISSN: 1534-2042] 1970. bi-m. plus special issue. USD 23 domestic; USD 33 Canada; USD 4.99 per issue. Ed(s):

Jeanmarie Andrews. Firelands Media Group LLC, PO Box 221228, Shaker Heights, OH 44122; http://www.firelandsmedia.com. Illus., adv. Circ: 100000. *Indexed:* A01, A22, ASIP, AmHI, BRI, IHTDI, MASUSE, MLA-IB, P02, RILM. *Aud.:* Ga.

Colonial life, memorabilia, and restored homes feature prominently in *Early American Life*. Appealing to hobbyists and historians, the magazine includes glossy photographs in multi-page features on period antiques, artwork, restoration projects, and Colonial era history and folklore. Articles are written in an accessible and easy-to-read format, and recent issues cover such topics as New England's first snuff mill; a historical overview of the War of 1812; period home renovation projects in Connecticut, Tennessee, and Pennsylvania; and early American animal portraiture. A companion web site highlights subscription information, and offers a few free articles and resources from the recent issue; there are also interactive tools to leave comments, send a letter to the editor, and an online version of "Reader's Exchange," a discontinued feature from the print magazine. *Early American Life* is appropriate for public and some academic libraries. URL: www.ealonline.com

3000. Electronic House: fast track to the connected lifestyle. [ISSN: 0886-6643] 1986. 8x/yr. USD 12.95 domestic; USD 12.95 Canada. Ed(s): Steve Castle, Lisa Montgomery. E H Publishing, Inc., 111 Speen St, Ste 200, PO Box 989, Framingham, MA 01701; info@ehpub.com; http://www.ehpub.com. Illus., adv. Sample. Circ: 75000. *Indexed:* IHTDI. *Aud.:* Ga, Sa.

Focused on technology, *Electronic House* provides information on home networking, home computing, home entertainment, and home electronics. These are broad topics, and feature articles might highlight topics as varied as automated home furnishings, "smart glass," reviews of specific equipment, or how to install modern equipment in historical homes. Many high-end electronic systems are reviewed, and though there are articles aimed at the "budget conscious" as well, the majority of electronic homes/rooms profiles are luxury environments belonging to sports or entertainment professionals. The web site features blogs, editorials, slide shows, product reviews, and lots of helpful articles on topics like energy management, audio, lighting, and other gadgets necessary to support a cutting-edge, efficient, and exciting electronic home environment. Appropriate for public libraries. URL: www.electronichouse.com

Elle Decor. See Interior Design and Decoration section.

3001. Family Circle. Former titles (until 1962): *Everywoman's Family Circle;* (until 1958): *The Family Circle;* Which incorporated: *Everywoman's.* [ISSN: 0014-7206] 1932. 15x/yr. USD 19.98. Ed(s): Linda Fears. Meredith Corporation, 1716 Locust St, Des Moines, IA 50309; patrick.taylor@meredith.com; http://www.meredith.com. Illus., adv. Circ: 4000000. Vol. ends: Dec. *Indexed:* A22, ASIP, BRI, IHTDI, P02. *Aud.:* Ga.

Accompanied by a robust suite of online features, *Family Circle* magazine and its web site provide tips and tools for busy families. Featuring concise articles on home, health, and family fun, this glossy magazine prominently features advertising for various personal and home products. *Family Circle* also carries its magazine articles on its dynamic companion web site, which features anytime tips on food, holidays, home, teens, health, family, style, and a "Momster" blog highlighting advice to/from moms, with a helpful comments-from-readers component. Particularly notable is the "Food" section, which includes a variety of healthy seasonal dishes prepared with a minimum of processed ingredients. *Family Circle* is appropriate for public libraries. URL: www.familycircle.com

3002. Good Housekeeping. Former titles (until 1919): *Good Housekeeping Magazine;* (until 1909): *Good Housekeeping.* [ISSN: 0017-209X] 1885. m. USD 7.97; USD 3.49 newsstand/cover. Hearst Magazines, 300 W 57th St, 12th Fl, New York, NY 10019; HearstMagazines@hearst.com; http://www.hearstcorp.com/magazines/. Illus., adv. Circ: 4668818 Paid. Vol. ends: Jun/Dec. Microform: NBI; PQC. *Indexed:* A01, A22, BRI, C37, IHTDI, MASUSE, MLA-IB, P02. *Aud.:* Hs, Ga, Ac.

With a 125+ year history, *Good Housekeeping* promotes advice, tips, and recommendations for the everyday to moms and families. The Good Housekeeping Institute and the Good Housekeeping Seal provide quality assurance and product evaluations on most household items, which are prominently featured throughout the glossy pages. Features include health and beauty advice, seasonal home and garden projects, celebrity interviews, renovation projects, and self-improvement ideas. A regular "good food" section includes entertaining advice, microwave cooking ideas, and budget-friendly everyday recipes. Most recipes are vegetarian friendly and include calorie and nutrition information. The print magazine is supported by an extensive online presence at its web site, where readers may learn more about the products featured and reviewed in the magazine; and helpful web tools include a "stain buster," "diet matchmaker," and "air conditioner BTU calculator." Appropriate for public libraries. URL: www.goodhousekeeping.com

3003. Home Cultures: the journal of architecture, design and domestic space. [ISSN: 1740-6315] 2004. 3x/yr. USD 406 (print & online eds.). Ed(s): Victor Buchli, Setha Low. Bloomsbury Publishing plc, 50 Bedford Sq, London, WC1B 3DP, United Kingdom; contact@bloomsbury.com; http://www.bloomsbury.com. Adv. Sample. Refereed. Reprint: PSC. *Indexed:* A01, A07, A47, A51, ArtHuCI, BRI, IBSS, P61, SSA. *Bk. rev.:* Number and length vary. *Aud.:* Ac.

Home Cultures is an interdisciplinary peer-reviewed scholarly journal that examines the connections between "home" as a physical space and human culture across time. International in scope, the journal brings together disciplines such as history, architecture, anthropology, religious studies, gender and cultural studies, social history, literary studies, art history, and geography, to highlight the concept of "home" as both a "highly fluid and contested site of human existence that reflects and reifies identities and values." Recent articles have included such titles as "The House as a Place of Work in Early Modern Rural England," "Gender, Space, and Place: The Experience of Service in the Early Modern English Household c. 1580-1720," and "Curtains and the Soft Architecture of the American Post War Domestic Environment." An introductory essay, written by the editors, contextualizes the articles in each issue. Through its parent publisher, Berg Publishers, article abstracts and sample issues can be purchased online. Academic libraries that support a diverse social science curriculum would be the most appropriate audience for *Home Cultures*.

3004. House Beautiful. Incorporates (in 1902): *Domestic Science Monthly;* (in Jan.1908): *Indoors and Out;* (in 1910): *Modern Homes;* (in Mar.1912): *American Suburbs;* (in Jan.1934): *Home and Field.* [ISSN: 0018-6422] 1896. 10x/yr. USD 15; USD 4.99 newsstand/cover. Hearst Magazines, 300 W 57th St, 12th Fl, New York, NY 10019; HearstMagazines@hearst.com; http://www.hearstcorp.com/magazines/. Illus., adv. Circ: 844258 Paid. Vol. ends: No. 12. Microform: NBI; PQC. *Indexed:* A06, A22, BRI, C37, GardL, MASUSE, P02. *Aud.:* Ga.

House Beautiful focuses on luxury and high-end domestic style with a focus on entertaining, design, and home goods. Interviews with decorators and stylists walk readers though glamorous interior design projects, reviewing in great detail the decoration and furniture in the photographs. "Tablescapes," wallpaper samples, and seasonal color palettes emphasize the design aesthetic of the magazine and serve as connections to the entertaining and cooking features in each magazine. In one issue, gourmet recipes for turkey, canapes, and cocktails give a do-it-yourself feel to high-end entertaining. A popular recurring series in the magazine has been the "Makeover" section, where a complete small house is restyled room by room, indoors and outdoors, with a new space featured each month. A regular "Kitchen of the Month" highlights great design and style in the heart of the home. The *House Beautiful* web site is an extensive collection of step-by-step instructions for home decorating and small renovation projects, as well as photo galleries of kitchen, decorated home spaces, gift guides, and organizing tips. Appropriate for public libraries. URL: www.housebeautiful.com

3005. Ladies' Home Journal. Formerly (until 1889): *Ladies Home Journal and Practical Housekeeper.* [ISSN: 0023-7124] 1883. m. USD 16.97; USD 2.49 newsstand/cover. Ed(s): Diane Salvatore, Jennifer Mirsky. Meredith Corporation, 1716 Locust St, Des Moines, IA 50309; patrick.taylor@meredith.com; http://www.meredith.com. Illus., adv. Circ: 4169444 Paid. Vol. ends: Dec. *Indexed:* A22, BRI, C37, MASUSE, MLA-IB, P02. *Bk. rev.:* Number and length vary. *Aud.:* Hs, Ga, Ac.

Marketed toward the working woman whose many hats include mother, daughter, girlfriend, and wife, the newly redesigned *Ladies' Home Journal* maintains a focus on women's lives and interests. Book reviews, nutrition and health features, and real-life stories are highlighted in a magazine that includes both self-improvement/lifestyle topics and home decorating as recurring themes. For example, articles recently published include "Take Control of Your Money, Health & Happiness" and "Sexy Spring Shoes (That Won't Wreck Your Feet)." Celebrity profiles include stories of charitable endeavors, personal transformations, and life lessons. Practical fashion, beauty, and marriage advice are also featured. The web site maintains dozens of freely available stories running on similar themes, but also includes hairstyle tutorials, gift and charity ideas, and a personal story section called *Divine Caroline*, where readers may submit short stories and essays to be considered for inclusion in the print publication. Appropriate for a public library audience. URL: www.LHJ.com

3006. Martha Stewart Living. [ISSN: 1057-5251] 1990. m. USD 24 domestic; CAD 38 Canada; CAD 4.99 newsstand/cover. Ed(s): Pilar Guzman. Martha Stewart Living Omnimedia LLC, 601 W 26th St, 10th Fl, New York, NY 10001; help@mstewart.customersvc.com; http://www.marthastewart.com. Illus., adv. Sample. Circ: 1861604 Paid. Vol. ends: No. 12. *Indexed:* BRI, GardL. *Bk. rev.:* Number and length vary. *Aud.:* Ga.

Martha Stewart Living is a detailed and thorough magazine overflowing with articles on every topic involved with maintaining a stylish, appealing, and organized household. Martha Stewart is synonymous with high-quality, reliable, authoritative advice and instruction on a wide variety of home-centric topics, and *Martha Stewart Living* combines this homemaking knowledge and advice into a valuable resource that covers such topics as gardening, home decorating, cooking, arts and crafts, entertaining, collecting, renovating, health and wellness, and interior design, all with a focus on quality, encouragement, instruction, and a do-it-yourself-better attitude. There are also additional features on weddings, pets, and seasonal recipes and entertaining. The articles are in-depth, with accompanying glossy photo spreads, and many ideas and tips function as do-it-yourself guides. Examples of article topics include garden planting and maintenance tips, party themes and decoration ideas, architectural design, living space organization, interior and exterior paint color schemes, etiquette, and seasonal craft projects. A companion web site (see below) offers an array of how-to instructional guides, photos, videos, design ideas, landscape guides, entertaining ideas, a "New Today" column that features the newest ideas and themes, blogs and blog recommendations, prize give-aways, a digital magazine and mobile apps page, book reviews, and links to Martha Stewart television programming and additional Martha Stewart subject-specific magazines. This magazine could be of interest to a wide demographic, from new homeowners to expert hostesses, and would be appropriate for any public library. URL: www.marthastewart.com

3007. Real Simple. [ISSN: 1528-1701] 2000. m. USD 28.95 domestic; CAD 34.95 Canada. Ed(s): Sarah Humphreys, Kristin van Ogtrop. Time Inc., 1271 Ave of the Americas, New York, NY 10020; information@timeinc.com; http://www.timeinc.com. Illus., adv. Sample. Circ: 1950000 Paid. *Indexed:* BRI, C37, P02. *Aud.:* Ga.

Real Simple's motto, "Life Made Easier," is pervasive throughout the magazine's feature articles on time-saving tips, work–life balance, daily routines, and home, decorative, beauty, and fashion "trends worth trying." Cost-conscious product reviews and recommendations, as well as before-and-after room makeovers, maintain the magazine's focus on domestic space and improvement. Inspirational stories, quotes, and a regular "Life Lessons" essay contest provide balance and reflective themes for those harried readers who are likely drawn to the magazine's articles on "Food Storage 101," "How to be More Optimistic," and "The Organized Home Office." The companion web site includes how-to videos, slideshows of organizational tips, entertaining ideas, and examples of home and self-improvement projects. Readers are encouraged to respond online with product reviews, ideas for decorating, etiquette and life issue advice. *Real Simple* is recommended for public libraries. URL: www.realsimple.com

This Old House. See Do-It-Yourself section.

3008. *Traditional Home.* Formerly (until 1985): *Traditional Home Ideas.* [ISSN: 0883-4660] 1978. 8x/yr. USD 12. Ed(s): Ann Omvig Maine, Michael Diver. Meredith Corporation, 1716 Locust St, Des Moines, IA 50309; patrick.taylor@meredith.com; http://www.meredith.com. Illus., adv. Sample. Circ: 950000. Vol. ends: No. 6. *Aud.:* Ga.

Traditional Home focuses on luxury-home goods and interior design, and includes features on society events, profiles of inspirational entrepreneurs and philanthropists, and grand homes elegantly and lavishly decorated. Information on collectables (e.g., cigarette cases), classic updates on design trends, meal-pairing guides, and eco-friendly tips for pets and children help to elevate this magazine from simply color palette and showroom reviews to one that celebrates a traditional luxury lifestyle. Celebrity profiles are featured, though not prominently. A companion web site features colorful slide shows of photographs and feature articles from the print edition. Additionally, "Design Centers" for both "color" and "kitchen" themes are featured, providing ideas and tips on specific themes like "colorful kitchens," "backsplashes," and "storage ideas." *Traditional Home* would most likely be appropriate for public libraries whose patrons are interested in interior decorating and design and luxury lifestyles. URL: www.traditionalhome.com

3009. *Victorian Homes.* [ISSN: 0744-415X] 1982. bi-m. USD 19.95 domestic; USD 34.95 Canada; USD 44.95 elsewhere. Ed(s): Meryl Schoenbaum, Rebecca Ittner. Beckett Media Llc, 2400 E Katella Ave, Ste 300, Anaheim, CA 92806; customerservice@beckett.com; http://www.beckett.com. Illus., adv. Circ: 100000 Paid. Vol. ends: No. 6. *Indexed:* GardL. *Bk. rev.:* Number and length vary. *Aud.:* Ga, Sa.

This year *Victorian Homes* celebrates its 30th anniversary of highlighting information, ideas, and style from the late nineteenth and early twentieth centuries. The magazines for owners and fans of houses and furnishings from the Victorian period, *Victorian Homes* includes articles on restoration, decoration, style, history, and renovation. There is also a recurring do-it-yourself theme to most articles, with tips on collecting, building/crafting decorations, and how to create your own Victorian themed party, holiday furnishings, or gifts. Recent articles included "Decorating with Victoriana" and "Victorian Splendor in New Orleans." Restoration articles feature a variety of topics like window or porch spindle repair; and occasional articles highlight meticulous restoration projects, and possibly include appropriately themes recipe from the homeowner's region or family. This niche publication is most likely suitable for public libraries whose patrons are interested in this topic. The web site features subscription information and letters from the editor. URL: www.victorianhomesmag.com

3010. *Woman's Day.* [ISSN: 0043-7336] 1937. 15x/yr. USD 7.99; USD 2.99 newsstand/cover. Ed(s): Elizabeth Mayhew. Hearst Magazines, 300 W 57th St, 12th Fl, New York, NY 10019; HearstMagazines@hearst.com; http://www.hearst.com. Illus., adv. Vol. ends: Dec. *Indexed:* A01, A22, ASIP, BRI, C37, IHTDI, MASUSE, P02. *Aud.:* Ga.

With over 75 years in the domestic magazine industry, *Woman's Day*'s motto is to "Live Well Everyday." To this end, this popular magazine provides lifestyle, health, food, and beauty advice to a middle-class audience. Including celebrity lifestyle interviews, a book-of-the-month feature, room makeovers, and fun party tips along with product evaluations and frugal everyday meal recipes, *Woman's Day* is a staple among supermarket glossy magazines. Feature articles frequently highlight real-life stories of weight loss, relationships, and family. A robust web site at supports the print edition with a blog, coupons, and giveaways, as well as games, in addition to articles and slide shows based on the print edition. Digital subscriptions are available. *Woman's Day* is most suitable for a public library audience. URL: www.womansday.com

■ HORSES

Linda Collins, Head of Reader Services, Widener Library, Harvard University, Cambridge, MA 02138

Introduction

The American Horse Council reports that there are 9.2 million horses in the United States. Diverse equine interests represent an economically significant $39 billion industry that provides 460,000 full-time equivalent jobs.

Man has enjoyed a long and vibrant history with the horse. The horse has attained a stature unparalleled by other animals. He has provided transportation, been a partner in battle, helped with agriculture, and been a source of food. He participates in sports, entertainment, and recreation, and has been and will always be a companion animal.

The country is a melting pot of equine activity, with one in every 63 people involved in the industry in some way, including everything from horse racing, show jumping, and trail riding to breeding, Western reining, and dressage. Across the country, 4-H and Pony Clubs continue to introduce children to riding, showing, and the basics of horse care and management. From general-interest to breed-specific titles, there are journals to support all types of equine activities and interests.

Basic Periodicals

Ga: *Equus, Horse & Rider, Horse Illustrated, Practical Horseman, Western Horseman.*

Basic Abstracts and Indexes

Reader's Guide to Periodical Literature.

3011. *American Farriers Journal.* [ISSN: 0274-6565] 1974. 8x/yr. USD 47.95 in North America; USD 79.95 elsewhere. Ed(s): Pat Tearney, Frank Lessiter. Lessiter Publications, 225 Regency Ct, Ste 200, Brookfield, WI 53045; info@lesspub.com; http://www.lesspub.com/. Adv. *Aud.:* Sa.

This trade publication features articles of interest not only to farriers but to equine practitioners and all those who manage horses. Article topics include current therapies, the latest in shoeing techniques, the anatomy and physiology of the horse, and information about national trade shows and conferences. Where there are horses, there are farriers. This publication is a valuable resource for all those involved in the care of horses from the hoof on up.

3012. *The American Quarter Horse Journal.* Former titles (until Jun.2001): *Quarter Horse Journal;* (until 1953): *Quarter Horse and the Quarter Horse Journal;* Which was formed by the merger of (1948-1949): *Quarter Horse Journal;* (1946-1949): *Quarter Horse.* [ISSN: 1538-3490] 1948. m. USD 25 domestic; USD 50 Canada; USD 80 elsewhere. American Quarter Horse Association, PO Box 200, Amarillo, TX 79168. Illus., index, adv. Sample. Circ: 67000. Vol. ends: Sep. Microform: PQC. *Bk. rev.:* 3, 250 words. *Aud.:* Sa.

This comprehensive journal is the official publication of the American Quarter Horse Association. Covering all disciplines, it speaks to the versatility of this popular horse. With more registered quarter horses than any other breed, this journal has a strong following. This is a large publication that is conveniently divided into color-coded sections based on interest or discipline. Because the quarter horse plays an important and influential role in many cross-breeding programs, the stallion issue is of interest to horsemen across the country.

3013. *The American Saddlebred.* [ISSN: 0746-6153] 1983. 5x/yr. Non-members, USD 50. American Saddlebred Horse Association (A S H A), 4093 Iron Works Pike, Lexington, KY 40511; saddlebred@asha.net; http://www.asha.net. Illus., adv. Sample. Circ: 7200. Vol. ends: Dec. *Bk. rev.:* 2, 150 words. *Aud.:* Sa.

As the official journal of the American Saddlebred Horse Association, this publication does not stray far from its primary focus—the breeding, training, showing, and promotion of these flashy, charismatic horses. The journal serves as the primary communication tool of the association and serves as a platform for interesting discussions and continued education. The articles are well written and include a broad range of topics including everything from legal responsibilities to understanding the direction of the breed, past and present. Exceptional color photographs enhance the cover. Included are a calendar of events, classified ads, and association notes and updates. This publication is a must for all American Saddlebred enthusiasts and libraries in regions where this style of horsemanship is particularly prevalent.

3014. *Appaloosa Journal.* Formerly: *Appaloosa News.* [ISSN: 0892-385X] 1946. m. USD 39.95 domestic. Ed(s): Diane Rice. Appaloosa Horse Club, 2720 W Pullman Rd, Moscow, ID 83843-0903; journal@appaloosa.com; http://www.appaloosa.com. Adv. Sample. Circ: 21340 Paid and free. Vol. ends: Dec. Microform: PQC. *Indexed:* A22. *Aud.:* Sa.

Appaloosa Journal is the official publication of the national breed association and registry for Appaloosa horses. The association has a stated mission to advance and improve the breeding and performance of the Appaloosa horse. To this end, the journal includes information on Appaloosa breeding, listing leading sires and incentive programs. An extensive show calendar includes class lists for each event and current national standings. Feature articles on training help to improve the performance of the horse. Each issue has information on all the disciplines of this versatile breed, including Appaloosa stakes racing and news from the regional associations.

3015. *Arabian Horse World: the magazine for owners, breeders and admirers of fine horses.* [ISSN: 0003-7494] 1960. m. USD 40 domestic; USD 72 Canada; USD 88 elsewhere. Ed(s): Mary Jane Parkinson. Source Interlink Companies, 1316 Tamson Dr, Ste 101, Cambria, CA 93428; dheine@sourceinterlink.com; http://www.sourceinterlinkmedia.com. Illus., index, adv. Sample. Circ: 7117. Vol. ends: Dec. *Indexed:* BRI. *Aud.:* Sa.

Arabians are one of the oldest purest breeds and have been admired for centuries for their classic beauty, strength, and stamina. *Arabian Horse World* is a publication as exquisite as the breed it represents. Artistic color photographs enhance every issue. Profiles of top breeders, leading sires, and prominent Arabian farms are featured. The versatility of the Arab is apparent, with articles on racing and endurance riding. This comprehensive journal often has over 300 pages and is of particular interest to those involved in the breeding of these lovely horses.

3016. *The Blood-Horse.* Formerly (until 1928): *Thoroughbred.* [ISSN: 0006-4998] 1916. w. USD 99 domestic; USD 164 Canada; USD 269 elsewhere. The Blood-Horse, Inc., 3101 Beaumont Ctr Cir, Lexington, KY 40513; customerservice@bloodhorse.com; http://www.bloodhorse.com. Illus., index, adv. Sample. Vol. ends: Dec. Microform: PQC. *Indexed:* A22. *Aud.:* Sa.

The Blood-Horse is the primary publication of the international thoroughbred industry. Published for over 90 years, this weekly journal dedicates itself to the improvement of thoroughbred breeding and racing. This is the bible of the sport of horse racing. It is of interest to racing professionals, those involved in breeding programs, handicappers, and fans. Race results, statistics, information on top lineage, sales, and biographies fill each issue. It is a must for all communities with ties to the thoroughbred industry. The electronic version includes news, racing results, and sales and breeding information, and has links to stud farms. There is a 12-month archive for subscribers. URL: www.bloodhorse.com

3017. *Carriage Journal.* [ISSN: 0008-6916] 1963. 5x/yr. Membership, USD 65. Ed(s): Jill Ryder. Carriage Association of America, Inc., 177 Pointers Auburn Rd, Salem, NJ 08079. Illus., index, adv. Sample. Circ: 3200. Vol. ends: Spring. *Bk. rev.:* 3-4, 500 words. *Aud.:* Sa.

Published by the Carriage Association of America five times a year, this journal has a very international feel with reports from England, South Africa, Germany, Argentina, and many other countries. It is apparent that carriage horse enthusiasts will travel great distances in pursuit of their sport. Articles are extremely well researched and authoritative, and cover a vast array of topics in great detail. Black-and-white photographs accompany most articles. An updated calendar lists events, trips, shows, and sales. Classified ads include everything from harnesses to horses to carriages. Because of its commitment to carriages from Roman times to the present, this publication may be of interest to historians as well as to driving enthusiasts.

3018. *The Chronicle of the Horse.* Former titles (until 1961): *The Chronicle;* (until 1939): *Horse.* [ISSN: 0009-5990] 1937. w. USD 59 combined subscription domestic (print & online eds.); USD 79 combined subscription foreign (print & online eds.). Ed(s): Tricia Booker. Chronicle of the Horse, Inc., PO Box 46, Middleburg, VA 20118; subscriptions@chronofhorse.com. Illus., index, adv. Sample. Circ: 1480 Paid. Vol. ends: Dec. Microform: PQC. *Indexed:* A22. *Bk. rev.:* Occasionally, 3-4, 300 words. *Aud.:* Ga, Sa.

This weekly publication is to the show-horse crowd what *The Blood-Horse* is to thoroughbred racing enthusiasts, a primary source for events, results, and the participants. Focusing on show jumping, dressage, eventing, driving, and hunter jumpers, this is a first-rate professional publication. The extensive classified ads offer horses, ponies, real estate, jobs, vans, and trailers. Each issue is packed with interesting feature articles on the personalities involved in the sport. The online version provides access to the same reliable source of current news and results for the entire sport-horse community. URL: www.chronofhorse.com

3019. *Cutting Horse Chatter.* Former titles (until Apr. 1993): *Cutting Horse;* (until 1992): *Cuttin' Hoss Chatter.* [ISSN: 1081-0951] 1948. m. National Cutting Horse Association, 260 Bailey Ave, Fort Worth, TX 76107; http://www.nchacutting.com. Illus. Sample. Vol. ends: Dec. *Aud.:* Sa.

Cutting Horse Chatter is the official publication of the governing body of the sport of cutting, a competition that comes from the Western tradition of cattle handling. Published for over 60 years, much of the business of the National Cutting Horse Association is carried on in the journal. Half of the almost 400 pages are devoted to show results, standings, upcoming events, and issues related to association management. Feature articles include training issues, personality profiles, and cattle management. Interest in the sport of cutting continues to increase across the country and is not limited to the traditional Western states.

3020. *The Draft Horse Journal.* [ISSN: 0012-5865] 1964. q. USD 35 domestic; USD 43 Canada; USD 45 elsewhere. Ed(s): Lynn Telleen. Draft Horse Journal, PO Box 670, Waverly, IA 50677. Illus., index, adv. Sample. Vol. ends: Winter. *Bk. rev.:* 1, 200 words. *Aud.:* Sa.

This quarterly publication represents the heavyweight division: Belgians, Percherons, Clydesdales, Shires, and other draft breeds. Focusing on breeding and sales, it also covers the draft horse shows and the county fair circuit of horse pulls. Feature articles discuss the nuances of the eight-horse hitch, harness and tack, and the past use of these big horses in logging, agriculture, and transportation. *The Draft Horse Journal* is a unique and important resource that boasts subscribers from all over the world. It is also available to subscribers online.

3021. *Dressage Today.* [ISSN: 1079-1167] 1994. m. USD 19.95 domestic; USD 32.95 Canada; USD 34.95 elsewhere. Ed(s): Patricia Lasko. Source Interlink Companies, 6420 Wilshire Blvd, 10th Fl, Los Angeles, CA 90048; dheine@sourceinterlink.com; http://www.sourceinterlinkmedia.com. Illus., adv. Sample. Circ: 47610 Paid. *Indexed:* BRI, SD. *Bk. rev.:* 1-2, 300 words. *Aud.:* Ga, Sa.

Dressage brings the training and riding of the horse to an art form. At the most advanced levels, it is the pinnacle of harmony between horse and rider, but the basic levels of dressage training can serve as the foundation for all other styles of riding. *Dressage Today* features articles related to the sport of dressage, but also includes a wealth of training information that easily relates to all other disciplines. Interviews with leaders in the sport, information on national and international competitions, and articles on the selection and care of the dressage horse are just some of the contents. As the nationwide interest in dressage grows, this journal enjoys increasing popularity.

Equine Veterinary Journal. See Veterinary Science.

3022. *Equus.* [ISSN: 0149-0672] 1977. m. USD 19.95 domestic; USD 32.95 Canada; USD 34.95 elsewhere. Ed(s): Laurie Prinz. Source Interlink Companies, 656 Quince Orchard Rd, Ste 600, Gaithersburg, MD 20878; dheine@sourceinterlink.com; http://www.sourceinterlinkmedia.com. Illus., index, adv. Sample. Circ: 144394 Paid. *Indexed:* A22, BRI, SD. *Aud.:* Ga.

If you were to select only one general horse publication, this is the classic. A repeat winner of the American Horse Publications Awards, *Equus* provides horsemen with sound advice on horse health and management. Feature articles by leaders in the industry are consistently well written and researched. "The Medical Front" is a monthly column describing the latest therapies, drugs, and procedures in laymen's terms. "Case Reports" are particularly good horse/human-interest stories. *Equus* has licensed veterinarians on its editorial board to ensure the accuracy of the medical reports. This publication has wide appeal to a broad range of horse enthusiasts and is well indexed.

3023. Hoof Beats. [ISSN: 0018-4683] 1933. m. Non-members, USD 35. Ed(s): Nicole Kraft, T J Burkett. United States Trotting Association, 750 Michigan Ave, Columbus, OH 43215; editorial@ustrotting.com; http://www.ustrotting.com. Illus., index, adv. Sample. Vol. ends: Feb. *Bk. rev.:* 1, 300 words. *Aud.:* Sa.

Hoof Beats is as important to the standardbred racing industry as *The Blood-Horse* is to thoroughbred racing. The official publication of the United States Trotting Association, this monthly publication carries features about leading drivers and winning trotters and pacers. Also included are regular articles on the business of the sport, including legislative changes that affect parimutuel wagering and taxes. Information on top stallions, successful breeding lines, and statistics round out the offerings. This is an important publication for any area with ties to the harness racing community.

3024. Hoofcare & Lameness: the journal of equine foot science. Former titles (until 1992): *Hoofcare and Lameness Quarterly Report;* (until 1991): *F Y I.* [ISSN: 1076-4704] 1985. q. USD 59 domestic; USD 69 in Canada & Mexico; USD 79 elsewhere. Ed(s): Fran Jurga. Hoofcare Publishing, 19 Harbor Loop, PO Box 6600, Gloucester, MA 01930; webinquiry@hoofcare.com. Illus. *Bk. rev.:* 3-4, 250 words. *Aud.:* Ac, Sa.

This journal of equine foot science is a focused quarterly publication for the professional farrier, veterinarian, or anyone involved with the care of the performance horse. "No hoof, no horse" is the popular saying that this publication addresses. Their international board of consulting editors is not shy about challenging conventional practice and hoof care theory. This scholarly journal's 15-year index is a virtual who's who and what's what in the history of horseshoeing and lameness. If you are interested in examining the horse from the ground up, this is an excellent place to begin. *Hoofcare & Lameness* also has a web presence with access to news and events, book and video reviews, and past articles. URL: www.hoofcare.com

3025. The Horse: your guide to equine health care. Formerly (until 1995): *Modern Horse Breeding.* [ISSN: 1081-9711] 1984. m. USD 24 domestic; USD 37.80 Canada; USD 65 elsewhere. Ed(s): Chad Mendell, Kimberly S Brown. The Blood-Horse, Inc., PO Box 919003, Lexington, KY 40591. *Aud.:* Ga, Ac, Sa.

Published by The Blood-Horse, Inc., this independent journal relies on the expertise of the American Association of Equine Practitioners to bring the latest research directly to the barn. Focusing on health, it has regular features on sports medicine, nutrition, and equine behavior. It includes reports from recent symposiums, association meetings, and current research. This is an important publication of interest to equine practitioners and horse owners who are concerned about the health and welfare of their animals.

3026. Horse & Rider. Incorporates (1981-1991): *Performance Horseman.* [ISSN: 0018-5159] 1968. m. USD 15.95 domestic; USD 28.95 Canada; USD 30.95 elsewhere. Ed(s): Darrell Dodds. Source Interlink Companies, 2000 S Stemmons Freeway, Ste 101, Lake Dallas, TX 75065; dheine@sourceinterlink.com; http://www.sourceinterlinkmedia.com. Illus., index, adv. Circ: 161596 Paid. Vol. ends: Dec. *Indexed:* A22, BRI, C37, MASUSE, P01, P02, SD. *Bk. rev.:* 1, 50 words. *Aud.:* Ga.

Horse & Rider is a self-proclaimed magazine for the Western rider, but its broad scope makes it so much more. Articles include training tips from professionals across the disciplines, the latest information on horse care, and regular features on horse professionals from chiropractors to authors. This is a high-quality publication with wonderful photographs enhancing the feature articles. It is well written and researched. A comprehensive index published annually in the January issue is an extremely useful tool and makes this a publication a valuable resource well worth collecting.

3027. Horse Illustrated. [ISSN: 0145-9791] 1976. m. USD 10 domestic; USD 28 foreign. Ed(s): Liz Moyer, Elizabeth Moyer. BowTie, Inc., 2401 Beverly Blvd, PO Box 57900, Los Angeles, CA 90057; adtraffic@bowtieinc.com; http://www.bowtieinc.com. Illus., index, adv. Sample. Circ: 197772 Paid and controlled. Vol. ends: Dec. *Bk. rev.:* 2, 150 words. *Aud.:* Ga.

This general-interest horse magazine does an exceptional job of providing articles of interest for all disciplines. Whether the focus is Western pole bending or top-level dressage, the articles always find the common ground and are accompanied by rich color photographs. Regular columns include the latest industry news and guest editorials on controversial topics. This is a great all-around publication that will be of interest to all horse owners and enthusiasts from novices to experienced horsemen.

3028. Horse Journal: the product, care and service guide for people who love horses. Formerly (until 199?): *Michael Plumb's Horse Journal.* [ISSN: 1097-6949] 1994. m. USD 24 combined subscription domestic (print & online eds.); USD 33 combined subscription Canada (print & online eds.); USD 38 combined subscription elsewhere (print & online eds.). Ed(s): Cynthia Foley. Belvoir Media Group, LLC, PO Box 5656, Norwalk, CT 06856; customer_service@belvoir.com. Illus., index. Sample. Vol. ends: Dec. *Indexed:* BRI. *Aud.:* Ga.

This publication describes itself as the product, care, and service guide for people who love horses. It is the *Consumer Reports* of the equine crowd, accepting no commercial advertising. The product recommendations are unbiased and firmly based on field trials and experience. In an authoritative, no-nonsense style, articles inform readers on nutrition, health care, training, and the latest technological advances. Every issue is packed with valuable practical advice. Individual subscribers have access to *Horse Journal* online.

3029. The Morgan Horse. Formerly (until 1951): *Morgan Horse Magazine.* [ISSN: 0027-1098] 1941. m. USD 31.50 domestic; USD 53.50 in Canada & Mexico; USD 61.50 elsewhere. American Morgan Horse Association, 122 Bostwick Rd, Shelburne, VT 05482; info@morganhorse.com; http://www.morganhorse.com. Illus., index, adv. Sample. Circ: 15000. Vol. ends: Jan. *Bk. rev.:* 2, 100 words. *Aud.:* Sa.

As the official journal of the Morgan Horse Breed Association, this publication has all the information one needs for the breeding, showing, or just plain enjoyment of this versatile horse. Articles include information about the Morgan in harness, as a park horse, and in the hunter/jumper division as well as English and Western pleasure; and dressage. Included are extensive show results and regional reports. Leading personalities past and present are profiled, as well as prominent Morgan horse farms. The popularity of this breed has spread from its origins in Vermont and enjoys a strong following across the country.

3030. N R H A Reiner. [ISSN: 0199-6762] 1980. bi-m. Non-members, USD 35. Ed(s): Kathy Swan. National Reining Horse Association, 3000 NW Tenth St, Oklahoma, OK 73107-5302; dwall@nrha.com; http://www.nrha.com. Illus., adv. Sample. Circ: 6000. *Aud.:* Sa.

The National Reining Horse Association (NRHA) is the governing body of the sport of reining. The mission of the association is to enforce the standards of competition and educate the public on the proper performance of a reining horse. *NRHA Reiner,* the association's official publication, presents association news and regional reports that include highlights of the major reining events across the country. Proper training is emphasized, as well as communication between horse and rider. The sport of reining is growing, with enthusiasts nationwide in over 350 sanctioned events.

3031. Paint Horse Journal. [ISSN: 0164-5706] 1962. m. USD 75. Ed(s): Jennifer Nice. American Paint Horse Association, PO Box 961023, Ft. Worth, TX 76161-0023; ddodds@apha.com; http://www.apha.com. Illus., index, adv. Sample. Circ: 32000 Paid. Vol. ends: Dec. *Bk. rev.:* 1-3, 200 words. *Aud.:* Sa.

The official publication of the American Paint Horse Association, this is the magazine for owners and breeders who appreciate a little splash of color in their barn. The popularity of the paint horse has skyrocketed in recent years, making it the second-largest registered breed in the country, just behind the American

Quarter Horse. The breeding of paints is a study in genetics, and this journal is an important resource that includes all recent research in this area. Covering all aspects of breeding, training, showing, and racing, this journal is a must for paint horse enthusiasts.

3032. Polo Players' Edition. 19??. m. USD 45 domestic; USD 61.42 Canada; USD 78 elsewhere. Ed(s): Gwen Rizzo. Rizzo Management Corp., 9011 Lake Worth Rd, Ste B, Lake Worth, FL 33467. Adv. *Aud.:* Ga.

This is a magazine by polo players for polo players. Articles include advice on training for players and their horses, reports on events, and features on celebrity players. More important are tournament results, the calendar of upcoming matches, and news from the polo scene. The polo community's commitment to philanthropy is evidenced by the number of articles reporting on fundraising and other charitable events. Published within *Polo Players' Edition* is the *USPA Bulletin,* the official publication of the U.S. Polo Association. *Polo Players Edition* is also available online.

3033. Practical Horseman. Incorporates (in 1972): *Pennsylvania Horse.* [ISSN: 0090-8762] 1973. m. USD 19.95 domestic; USD 32.95 Canada; USD 34.95 elsewhere. Ed(s): Sandra Oliynyk. Source Interlink Companies, 656 Quince Orchard Rd, Ste 600, Gaithersburg, MD 20878; dheine@sourceinterlink.com; http://www.sourceinterlinkmedia.com. Illus., adv. Sample. Circ: 65195 Paid. *Indexed:* BRI, SD. *Aud.:* Ga.

Practical Horseman bills itself as the "number one resource for English riders," and there is no better in its class. The articles on training of both horse and rider are comprehensive and accompanied by exceptional color photographs. The monthly jumping clinic is a great exercise in developing a keen eye for evaluating the athleticism of both horse and rider. The journal is packed full of sage advice for beginners and seasoned professionals alike. It also serves as a platform for discussion on topics that affect the industry. This publication is valuable for those involved in any aspects of English riding, from the trail to the show ring.

3034. Saddle & Bridle: the oldest name in show horse magazine. [ISSN: 0036-2271] 1927. m. USD 79. Ed(s): Mary Bernhardt. Saddle and Bridle, Inc., 375 Jackson Ave., St. Louis, MO 63130-4243. Illus., adv. Circ: 5200 Paid. *Bk. rev.:* Number and length vary. *Aud.:* Sa.

Saddle and Bridle is the oldest publication devoted to showing gaited horses. For more than 80 years, owners of saddlebreds, hackneys, roadsters, and other gaited breeds have relied on it as a major resource for show results, sales, and breeding information. This publication features the champions of the sport and the people behind these elegant animals. Articles explain and examine show rules, provide information on breeding, training, and horse care, and feature those involved in the sport. Regional editors from all parts of the country closely follow the show circuit. This is a tried-and-true journal for those involved in showing all types of gaited horses.

3035. Strides. Formerly (until 2011): *N A R H A Strides.* [ISSN: 2167-5058] 1995. q. Free to members; Non-members, USD 34. Professional Association of Therapeutic Horsemanship International, PO Box 33150, Denver, CO 80233; pathintl@pathintl.org; http://www.pathintl.org. Illus., adv. *Aud.:* Sa.

Formerly known as the North American Riding for the Handicapped Association, this association is now called the Professional Association of Therapeutic Horsemanship International (PATH Intl.). *Strides,* the association journal, concerns itself with industry standards, program accreditation, and certification of instructors. Articles include a wide range of topics, such as the correct training of horses for use in these types of programs, insurance policy limitations and general liability, crisis management, and a definition of terms used in therapeutic applications. It also features very heartwarming success stories of young riders who gain increased confidence and physical ability as a direct result of their participation in a therapeutic riding program. This publication would be of interest to administrators of handicapped riding facilities, mental health professionals, instructors, barn managers, volunteers, fundraisers, sponsors, and the participants and their parents.

3036. The Trail Rider. Former titles (until 198?): *Trail Rider;* (until 1986): *The New England Trail Rider.* [ISSN: 0892-3922] 19??. 8x/yr. USD 15.95 domestic. Ed(s): Rene Riley. Horse Media Group, 908 Main St, Ste 300, Louisville, CO 80027; http://www.horsemediagroup.com. Adv. *Indexed:* BRI. *Aud.:* Sa.

This publication is as rough and ready as the horsemen it's written for. Billed as America's premier trail riders' information source, it concerns itself with endurance, competitive and recreational trail riding, and the horses bred and sold for this purpose. The protection of the land and trails they ride on is also a major focus, as well as popular destinations for trail-riding adventures and vacations.

3037. Western Horseman. [ISSN: 0043-3837] 1936. m. USD 24; USD 2 per issue. Ed(s): Fran D Smith, A J Mangum. Western Horseman, Inc., PO Box 7980, Colorado Springs, CO 80933. Illus., index. Sample. Vol. ends: Dec. Microform: PQC. *Indexed:* A22, P02. *Bk. rev.:* 3-4, 300 words. *Aud.:* Ga.

This granddaddy of the industry bills itself as "the world's leading horse magazine since 1936" and has the readership to prove it. A tremendously popular general-interest horse magazine with a decidedly Western slant, this publication features a wide array of articles that cover training, health care, equipment, events, ranching, and personality profiles. There is something here for everyone, including a column for the young horsemen. A "Political Watch" informs readers of legislative changes affecting horse owners. There's also a column on Western art. Each issue includes product reviews, a cartoon of the month, a calendar of events, show results, and classified ads. *Western Horseman* online includes a search engine for equestrian events across the country, current point standings, and a link to numerous breed registries. URL: www.westernhorseman.com

3038. Young Rider: the magazine for horse and pony lovers. [ISSN: 1098-2442] 1994. bi-m. USD 12.99 domestic; USD 21.99 foreign; USD 3.99 per issue. Ed(s): Lesley Ward. BowTie, Inc., 2401 Beverly Blvd, PO Box 57900, Los Angeles, CA 90057; adtraffic@bowtieinc.com; http://www.bowtieinc.com. Illus., adv. Circ: 82699 Paid. *Bk. rev.:* 1, 100 words. *Aud.:* Ems.

Young Rider is arguably the best equine publication for young people. Directed toward readers aged eight to 14 years old, the articles are informative, interesting, and intelligent. The magazine is valuable for English riders, Western riders, those who show, those who compete in gymkhanas, children who ride at public stables, and those who just plain like horses. The articles are colorfully presented and accompanied by many photographs. There is an ever-present emphasis on safety and responsible behavior. Each edition includes large removable color posters. The magazine is not heavy with advertisements and those included are always age-appropriate. Overall, this is a wonderful publication for young people who are interested in horses.

■ HOSPITALITY/RESTAURANT

Amy J. Watson, Information Specialist, PPG Industries Inc., GBDC Library, 400 Guys Run Road, Cheswick, PA 15024; amywatson@ppg.com

Introduction

According to the May 2011 *DataMonitor Industry Market Research* report on "Global Hotels, Restaurants & Leisure," this field grew by 3.7 percent in 2010 to reach a value of $2.284 billion. The leading revenue source for the industry in 2010 was the restaurant market, which accounted for 68.7 percent of the sector's value, up from 68.2 in 2009. A little more than a third of the industry value comes from the Americas, and this is reflected well by the titles reviewed in this section, many of which have an international focus on the industry.

As was the case during preparation of the previous edition of this section, this industry continues to struggle with the global economic downturn, which has impacted the titles available in the field. Several historically key titles either have migrated to online-only versions, or have ceased publication entirely.

It is optimistically forecast that the performance of this sector will accelerate, with a predicted 23 percent increase by 2015 (over 2010 statistics). It is a hope that as the economy changes in coming years, new publications will come forth to replace those that have folded, potentially more with international focuses.

The magazines and journals in this section cover both the hotel and restaurant industries with a variety of focuses and depths. There are several refereed journals that offer research and analysis from a high-quality, in-depth perspective. Additionally, the diverse assortment of trade publications keeps those in the industry abreast of cutting-edge information and breaking news. A wide array of information needs are covered, with titles that address such topics as management, human resources, hospitality trends, design and decor, and security issues. The majority of titles listed have accompanying web sites that offer useful additional information and interactive tools.

Basic Periodicals

Ac: *The Cornell Hospitality Quarterly, International Journal of Hospitality & Tourism Administration;* Sa: *Restaurant Hospitality, Restaurant Startup and Growth, Restaurant Business.*

Basic Abstracts and Indexes

Hospitality and Tourism Index; Leisure, Recreation and Tourism Abstracts.

3039. Catering Magazine: the magazine for catering professionals. [ISSN: 1098-089X] bi-m. USD 65 domestic; USD 125 elsewhere. Ed(s): Sara Perez Webber. G P Publishing, 60 E Rio Salado Parkway, Ste 900, Tempe, AZ 85281. Illus., adv. Circ: 20000 Paid and free. *Indexed:* H&TI. *Aud.:* Sa.

This title continues to be a must-have trade journal for catering and special events professionals. Issues balance informative content that is useful to businesses with impressive photography and coverage of cutting-edge trends. Most issues are themed and provide examples of stellar catered special events. At first glance, heavy advertising is present, but even this is lush and interesting. Well recommended.

3040. Chef: the magazine for foodservice professional. Former titles (until 1994): *Chef Institutional;* (until 1971): *Chef Magazine.* [ISSN: 1087-061X] 1956. 8x/yr. USD 32 domestic. Ed(s): Brent Frei. Talcott Communications Corporation, 233 N Michigan Ave, Ste 1780, Chicago, IL 60601; talcottpub@talcott.com; http://www.talcott.com. Illus., adv. *Indexed:* H&TI. *Aud.:* Sa.

This title packs an informative punch in a slim volume, especially when complemented by exclusive online content. Issues cover regional highlights as well as culinary trends with complimentary recipes. Feature articles cover new technologies in depth as well as well written profiles of culinary pros in a variety of positions. Remains highly recommended as a trade journal for libraries that serve those in the culinary fields.

3041. Cornell Hospitality Quarterly: hospitality leadership through learning. Formerly (until 2008): *The Cornell Hotel & Restaurant Administration Quarterly.* [ISSN: 1938-9655] 1960. q. USD 571. Ed(s): J Bruce Tracey. Sage Publications, Inc., 2455 Teller Rd, Thousand Oaks, CA 91320; info@sagepub.com; http://www.sagepub.com. Illus., index, adv. Sample. Refereed. Vol. ends: Nov/Dec (No. 42). Reprint: PSC. *Indexed:* A22, ABIn, ABS&EES, B01, B02, BAS, BRI, C45, E01, FS&TA, H&TI, PsycInfo, RRTA. *Aud.:* Ac, Sa.

Perhaps the most key scholarly journal in the hospitality field, this title remains a potentially singular subscription for special libraries. Issues cover a variety of themed refereed topics across the broad hospitality field—gaming, food service, hotels —as well as specialty areas such as marketing and HR.

3042. Foodservice and Hospitality: Canada's hospitality business magazine. Former titles (until 1972): *Foodservice Hospitality Canada;* (until 1971): *C R A Magazine.* [ISSN: 0007-8972] 1968. m. USD 55 per issue domestic; USD 80 per issue United States; USD 100 per issue elsewhere. Ed(s): Rosanna Caira. Kostuch Media Ltd., 101-23 Lesmill Rd, Don Mills, ON M3B 3P6, Canada; http://www.kostuchmedia.com. Illus. *Indexed:* ABIn, C37, H&TI. *Aud.:* Sa.

This monthly Canadian trade journal is recommended to school libraries with an international focus on hospitality education. Of the trade titles reviewed in this section, it has the strongest content for the business practitioner, as well as solid editorial and news coverage. Other standout features include venue and professional profiles as well as solid trend coverage.

3043. Hospitality Design. Former titles (until 1992): *Restaurant - Hotel Design International;* (until 1988): *Restaurant and Hotel Design;* (until 1982): *Restaurant Design.* [ISSN: 1062-9254] 1979. 9x/yr. Ed(s): Michael Adams. Nielsen Business Publications, 770 Broadway, New York, NY 10003; bmcomm@nielsen.com; http://www.nielsenbusinessmedia.com. Illus., adv. Microform: PQC. *Indexed:* A07, A22, ABIn, B01, B02, BRI, H&TI. *Aud.:* Sa.

Of the titles reviewed in this section, this is the most lushly photographed and a treat for the eyes. It is advertising-heavy, but the ads flow seamlessly through the content, portraying luxury and cutting-edge hospitality design accommodation. Design inspiration is geared toward the high-end consumer, but will inspire all. Recommended for libraries that support either hospitality or design programs.

3044. Hospitality Style. [ISSN: 1945-6301] 2008. q. USD 48 domestic; USD 70 Canada; USD 92 elsewhere. Ed(s): Mary Scoviak. S T Media Group International, Inc., 11262 Cornell Park Dr, Cincinnati, OH 45242; http://www.stmediagroup.com. *Aud.:* Sa.

While similar in scope to other design titles reviewed in this section, this title provides a crisper, more streamlined layout and focus. Eye-catching photography and design features balance nicely with more editorial content than is seen in other design titles. Recommended for both design- and hospitality-focused libraries.

3045. International Journal of Contemporary Hospitality Management. Formerly (until 1990): *Journal of Contemporary Hospitality Management.* [ISSN: 0959-6119] 1989. 7x/yr. EUR 10939 combined subscription in Europe (print & online eds.); USD 13439 combined subscription in the Americas (print & online eds.); GBP 7369 combined subscription in the UK & elsewhere (print & online eds.). Ed(s): Dr. Fevzi Okumus. Emerald Group Publishing Ltd., Howard House, Wagon Ln, Bingley, BD16 1WA, United Kingdom; emerald@emeraldinsight.com; http://www.emeraldinsight.com. Index. Sample. Refereed. Reprint: PSC. *Indexed:* A22, ABIn, B01, C45, E01, ErgAb, H&TI, IndVet, PsycInfo, RRTA. *Aud.:* Ac, Sa.

This is an international scholarly journal that aims to communicate the latest developments on management of hospitality operations worldwide. Subject areas include operations, marketing, and finance. Target market ranges from hospitality managers to educators and researchers. For academic libraries that support hospitality research.

3046. International Journal of Hospitality and Tourism Administration. Supersedes (in 2000): *Journal of International Hospitality, Leisure and Tourism Management.* [ISSN: 1525-6480] 1997. q. GBP 363 (print & online eds.). Ed(s): Clayton W Barrows. Routledge, 325 Chestnut St, Ste 800, Philadelphia, PA 19106; customerservice@taylorandfrancis.com; http://www.tandfonline.com. Adv. Refereed. Circ: 173 Paid. Microform: PQC. Reprint: PSC. *Indexed:* A01, A22, B01, C45, E01, FR, H&TI, RRTA. *Aud.:* Ac, Sa.

This peer-reviewed and scholarly title represents a broad, general, yet international focus on a wide variety of hospitality management issues. Articles are in-depth scientific explorations into their fields of research, and are well cited, often with supplementary charts or graphs. Recommended for academic and special libraries that support research in the hospitality fields.

3047. International Journal of Hospitality Management. [ISSN: 0278-4319] 1982. q. EUR 1061. Ed(s): Abraham Pizam. Pergamon, The Blvd, Langford Ln, E Park, Kidlington, OX5 1GB, United Kingdom; JournalsCustomerServiceEMEA@elsevier.com; http://www.elsevier.com. Adv. Sample. Refereed. Microform: PQC. *Indexed:* A22, C45, H&TI, PsycInfo, RRTA. *Aud.:* Ac, Sa.

This scholarly research journal discusses trends in a variety of areas relative to the hospitality industry. Analysis and research are well written and reflect current management issues internationally. This journal is unique in application, while it is a research journal first, and it feels approachable to those in general management in the field. Recommended to libraries that support hospitality programs.

3048. Journal of Hospitality and Tourism Technology. [ISSN: 1757-9880] 2010. 3x/yr. EUR 419 combined subscription in Europe (print & online eds.); USD 579 combined subscription in the Americas (print & online eds.); GBP 369 combined subscription in the UK & elsewhere (print & online eds.). Ed(s): Dr. Cihan Cobanoglu. Emerald Group Publishing Ltd., Howard House, Wagon Ln, Bingley, BD16 1WA, United Kingdom; emerald@emeraldinsight.com; http://www.emeraldinsight.com. Reprint: PSC. *Indexed:* ABIn. *Aud.:* Ac, Sa.

This relatively new scholarly journal reaches a niche in the hospitality field while addressing the increasing presence of technology in every aspect of our lives. Article topics are broad in scope, but well written and researched. Topics range from e-business to virtual technology, to social media, to end-user technology. While it may appear to be of a limited subject-area interest, as technology continues to invade our lives, the relevance of this title will only increase.

3049. Journal of Hospitality Marketing and Management. Formerly (until 2008): *Journal of Hospitality & Leisure Marketing.* [ISSN: 1936-8623] 1992. 8x/yr. GBP 727 (print & online eds.). Ed(s): Dogan Gursoy. Routledge, 325 Chestnut St, Ste 800, Philadelphia, PA 19106; customerservice@taylorandfrancis.com; http://www.tandfonline.com. Illus., index. Sample. Refereed. Vol. ends: Winter. Microform: PQC. Reprint: PSC. *Indexed:* A01, A22, ABIn, B01, C45, E01, H&TI, RRTA. *Bk. rev.:* Number and length vary. *Aud.:* Ac, Sa.

The strength of this scholarly journal may be the special issues and the niche research represented in those issues. While it is not immediately obvious by title, the international scope of this research should also be noted. Content focuses on the relationship between marketing and hospitality, and does so in well-researched scientific publications. Recommended for both marketing and hospitality library collections.

3050. Lodging Hospitality: ideas for hotel developers & operators. Former titles: *Hospitality Lodging; Hospitality-Food and Lodging; Hospitality-Restaurant and Lodging; American Motel Magazine.* [ISSN: 0148-0766] 1949. 15x/yr. USD 80 domestic (Free to qualified personnel). Ed(s): Ed Watkins. Penton Media, Inc., 9800 Metcalf Ave, Overland Park, KS 66212-2216; information@penton.com; http://www.penton.com. Illus., index, adv. Sample. Circ: 50976 Controlled. Vol. ends: Dec. Microform: CIS; PQC. *Indexed:* A22, ABIn, B01, B02, B03, BRI, C42, H&TI. *Aud.:* Sa.

This trade journal is geared toward hotel developers and operators who wish to keep an eye on the trends and innovations in the field. Well balanced between editorial content and advertising, the regular departments (technology, back of house) remain standouts. The online version is a good complement to the print edition.

3051. Restaurant Business: street smarts for the entrepreneur. Formerly (until 1974): *Fast Food.* [ISSN: 0097-8043] 1902. m. USD 99 domestic (Free to qualified personnel). Ed(s): Sam Smith. C S P Business Media, LLC, 90 Broad St, New York, NY 10004; cspinquire@cspnet.com; http://www.monkeydish.com/. Illus., adv. Circ: 77000 Controlled. Microform: CIS; PQC. *Indexed:* A22, ABIn, Agr, B01, B02, BRI, C42, Chicano, FS&TA, H&TI. *Aud.:* Sa.

As trade journals go, this is an excellent resource for the restaurant industry. Very high-quality business articles address current issues and trends to an impressive degree. While this title is new to this section with this edition, we strongly recommend it to libraries that support hospitality programs. Regular columns are reliable in content, but the standout here is the thumb-on-the-pulse content.

3052. Restaurant Hospitality. Former titles (until 1976): *Hospitality, Restaurant;* (until 1967): *American Restaurant Hospitality;* (until 1962): *American Restaurant Magazine;* (until 1928): *American Restaurant.* [ISSN: 0147-9989] 1919. m. USD 80 domestic; USD 100 Canada; USD 150 elsewhere. Ed(s): Michael Sanson. Penton Media, Inc., 9800 Metcalf Ave, Overland Park, KS 66212-2216; information@penton.com; http://www.penton.com. Illus., adv. Circ: 119300 Controlled. Vol. ends: Dec. Microform: PQC. *Indexed:* A22, ABIn, B01, B02, B03, BRI, FS&TA, H&TI. *Bk. rev.:* Number and length vary. *Aud.:* Sa.

This trade journal sets itself apart from others reviewed in this section through the ease and readability of the articles. Also unique to this title is the inclusion of a wide range of recipes, often up to a quarter of the issue. Content includes regular columns on current affairs, rising stars, and equipment selection. Recommended as a key resource, especially in light of the complementing online version.

3053. Restaurant Startup & Growth. [ISSN: 1552-9746] 2004. m. USD 39.95 domestic. Ed(s): Barry K Shuster. Specialized Publications Company, 5215 Crooked Rd, Parkville, MO 64152. Adv. *Aud.:* Sa.

While this is technically a trade journal, where this title excels is in how detailed and research-oriented the articles are. More approachable than some of the scholarly, peer-reviewed titles reviewed here, this is a technically focused journal with the aim of helping restaurant owners find success. Strongly recommended.

3054. Tourism Analysis. [ISSN: 1083-5423] 1996. bi-m. USD 675 (print & online eds.). Ed(s): Geoffrey I. Crouch, Muzaffer Uysal. Cognizant Communication Corporation, 18 Peeksill Hollow Rd, PO Box 37, Putnam Valley, NY 10579; inquiries@cognizantcommunication.com; http://www.cognizantcommunication.com. Refereed. *Indexed:* C45, H&TI, RRTA. *Bk. rev.:* Number and length vary. *Aud.:* Ac, Sa.

This journal is a high-level scholarly resource that aims to be a research forum for the fields of leisure, recreation, tourism, and hospitality, with an international scope. Content leans toward research for researchers more than for everyday practitioners. Recommended for academic institutions with in-depth hospitality collections.

3055. Tourism, Culture & Communication. [ISSN: 1098-304X] 1998. 3x/yr. USD 390 (print & online eds.). Ed(s): Anne-Marie Hede, Brian King. Cognizant Communication Corporation, 18 Peeksill Hollow Rd, PO Box 37, Putnam Valley, NY 10579; inquiries@cognizantcommunication.com; http://www.cognizantcommunication.com. *Indexed:* C45, H&TI, RRTA. *Bk. rev.:* Number and length vary. *Aud.:* Ac, Sa.

This is a scholarly research journal that places no restriction on content or range beyond relation to tourism and hospitality. Topics lean into far-reaching niches that find no home elsewhere, therefore this journal is good for very in-depth research and researchers. Occasional theme issues blend regular subject areas nicely. Recommended for academic libraries with in-depth hospitality collections.

3056. Tourism in Marine Environments. [ISSN: 1544-273X] 2004. q. USD 495 (print & online eds.). Ed(s): Michael Luck. Cognizant Communication Corporation, 18 Peeksill Hollow Rd, PO Box 37, Putnam Valley, NY 10579; inquiries@cognizantcommunication.com; http://www.cognizantcommunication.com. Refereed. *Indexed:* C45, RRTA. *Aud.:* Ac, Sa.

Truly a niche journal, this title aims to cover a variety of hospitality issues as specific to marine settings. Beyond that restriction, its content is broad—ranging across tourism, environmental issues, marketing, economics, and more. An example of a special issue would be the "Scuba Diving Tourism" volume. For academic libraries that have an incredibly in-depth collection to support hospitality issues.

■ HUMAN RESOURCES

Nancy McGuire, Instructional Services Librarian, Mack Library at Bob Jones University, Greenville, SC 29614; ncmcguir@bju.edu

Introduction

Human resources magazines reach out to the many HR professionals across the work world emphasizing areas that affect the workforce, such as recruiting, hiring models, compensation and incentives, training, employee development, wellness programs, and legal issues to attract, motivate, and retain employees. Choosing the publications that attract and encourage the patrons of our library community interested in business and employee information is vital.

Basic Periodicals

H R Magazine, People & Strategy, Public Personnel Management, Training, Workspan.

Basic Abstracts and Indexes

Book Review Index, EBSCO AgeLine, EBSCO Business Source Complete, EBSCO Education Research Complete, Gale Educator's Reference Complete, ProQuest eLibrary.

3057. H R Magazine. Formerly (until 1990): *Personnel Administrator;* Which superseded (in 1956): *Journal for Personnel Administration.* [ISSN: 1047-3149] 1956. m. USD 70 domestic; USD 90 Canada; USD 125 elsewhere. Ed(s): Desda Moss, Nancy M Davis. Society for Human Resource Management, 1800 Duke St, Alexandria, VA 22314-3499; shrm@shrm.org; http://www.shrm.org. Illus., index, adv. Circ: 239832 Paid. Vol. ends: Dec. *Indexed:* A22, ABIn, AgeL, B01, B02, BRI, CBRI. *Bk. rev.:* 1, 600 words. *Aud.:* Ac, Sa.

H R Magazine is the flagship magazine for the Society for Human Resource Management (SHRM), with 250,000 members. The periodical has well-written articles in a glossy, monthly magazine format. Short, timely articles inform the HR community of pertinent changes in their profession and provide information for interested employees. All employees and business students interested in the human resource field may appreciate information contained in this periodical. A typical issue has nearly 24 articles and 40 HR-related advertisements. Recent articles include "Maximum Health Benefits, Global Pay, Telecommuting," emphasizing changes and possible solutions in the upcoming year. "Benefits Strategies Grow and HR Leads the Way" stresses the partnership of company and HR for the good of the employees. "Be a Strategic Performance Consultant" encourages the use of strategy and empowerment of the workforce for the good of the organization. "Disclosing HR Metrics: How Much Information is Too Much?" discusses whether or not to make internal information available to the public. Members of the Society for Human Resource Management have access to more information online. The SHRM member is encouraged to access the online version for more information. URL: www.shrm.org/HRmagazine

3058. People & Strategy. Formerly (until 2008): *Human Resource Planning.* [ISSN: 1946-4606] 1978. q. Free to members; Non-members, USD 150. Ed(s): Anna Tavis. Human Resource Planning Society, 401 N Michigan Ave, Ste 2200, Chicago, IL 60611; info@hrps.org; http://www.hrps.org. Illus., index, adv. Vol. ends: No. 4. *Indexed:* A22, ABIn, B01, B02, BRI. *Bk. rev.:* 4, 1,000 words. *Aud.:* Ac, Sa.

People & Strategy is published quarterly by the nonprofit Human Resource Planning Society. Experts in the field of human resources and academics write articles and publish research studies for this magazine. Communication and growth articles gear themselves to the employees' health and development. Recent articles include "A Tribute to Stephen R. Covey," written by his son; "Managing by Values: The Leadership Spirituality Connection," "Being Purposeful in Turbulent Environments," "Building Strength and Resilience," "Capturing Success, Not Taking the Blame," and "Priming the Talent Pipeline." There seems to be minimal advertising. Viewing the pdf version shows that the layout is readable and pleasing to the eye. This journal would be useful in business academic libraries and corporate libraries. URL: www.hrps.org/?page=PeopleStrategy

3059. Public Personnel Management. Formerly (until 1973): *Personnel Administration and Public Personnel Review;* Which was formed by the merger of (1940-1972): *Public Personnel Review;* (1938-1972): *Personnel Administration.* [ISSN: 0091-0260] 1972. q. USD 259. Ed(s): Edward P French. Sage Publications, Inc., 2455 Teller Rd, Thousand Oaks, CA 91320; info@sagepub.com; http://www.sagepub.com. Illus., index. Refereed. Vol. ends: Winter. Microform: MIM; PQC. *Indexed:* A22, ABIn, B01, B02, BRI, CBRI, PsycInfo. *Aud.:* Ac, Sa.

Research studies and articles comprise the content of this journal, which concentrates on HR issues. Recent articles include "Compressed Workweeks—Strategies for Successful Implementation," an article pertaining to the U.S.; "Antecedents of the Voluntary Performance of Employees: Clarifying the Roles of Employee Satisfaction and Trust"—research from Taiwan; "Leisure Ethic, Money Ethic, and Occupational Commitment Among Recreation and Park Professionals: Does Gender Make a Difference?," an article pertaining to the U.S.; "An Issue of Public Affairs Management: The Effect of Time Slack and Need for Cognition on Prediction of Task Completion"—research from China; "The Impact of Organizational Values on Organizational Citizenship Behaviors"—research from China; and "The Impact of the Service Staff's Recruitment and Service Characteristics in Public Mental Acceptance: Evidence from the Host Recruitment and TV Program Features," research from China. The last issue of 2012 has 11 articles contained in 127 pages. Each article has an extensive bibliography. No advertising is in the journal. All articles were viewed using an online database.

3060. Training: the source for professional development. Formerly (until 1974): *Training in Business and Industry.* [ISSN: 0095-5892] 1964. m. USD 79 combined subscription domestic (print & online eds.); USD 89 combined subscription Canada (print & online eds.); USD 159 combined subscription elsewhere (print & online eds.). Lakewood Media Group, 27020 Noble Rd, PO Box 247, Excelsior, MN 55331; http://www.mach1businessmedia.com. Illus., index, adv. Circ: 40585. Vol. ends: Dec. *Indexed:* A22, ABIn, Agr, B01, B02, BRI, ERIC. *Bk. rev.:* 1-3, 750 words. *Aud.:* Sa.

The online version is colorful and easy to navigate. Design is professional and pleasing to the eye. The issue reviewed highlighted the top 125 companies, with 71 companies advertising in the online version of 132 pdf pages. The top five companies featured include "Verizon's #1 Calling," "Jiffy Lube's Training Drive," "Coldwell Banker's Sold on Training," "Farmer's Comprehensive Training Policy," and "CHG Healthcare's RX for Success." A recent issue showed a table of contents of 29 articles that can be linked to from the web site. This title includes articles such as "Face Time Still Rules," "Get More Done In and Out of the Office," "Drilling Down into the Skills Gap," "Last Word: Embrace Social Media Carefully," and "Soapbox: Quality vs. Quantity." The glossy, nicely designed magazine can be purchased by libraries for patrons who appreciate reading a paper magazine. The magazine has articles for anyone in the world of work, but especially for those who train others to work. The web site is full of information pertaining to training. URL: www.trainingmag.com/

3061. Workspan. [ISSN: 1529-9465] m. USD 100 domestic; USD 125 foreign. Ed(s): Michele Kowalski. WorldatWork, 14040 N Northsight Blvd, Scottsdale, AZ 85260; customerrelations@worldatwork.org ; http://www.worldatwork.org/. Illus., index, adv. *Indexed:* ABIn, ATI. *Aud.:* Ac, Sa.

Workspan, published monthly, has timely, well-written articles from a professional perspective for a readership of 30,000 members and others interested in the human resources field. The emphasis on effective communication is vitally important to attract, motivate, and retain members of the workforce. The focus of the World at Work organization, which publishes *Workspan,* is "compensation, benefits, work-life effectiveness, and total rewards; strategies to attract, motivate and retain an engaged and productive workforce." Recent articles include "Boost Engagement with Next Generation Workplace Wellness," "Salesforce Retention," "How to Custom Fit Your New Pay Structure," "The Case for Understanding Extrinsic and Intrinsic Motivation," and "Four Ways to Get Employees to Stick Around." A compilation of articles published by World at Work Press, *Attraction and Retention,* is an excellent idea. Even if you are not in business nor specifically belong to a Human Resources department, the articles are excellent for those of us in HR and still privileged to work. Advertisements are informative and apropos to the field of human resources, with many of them advertising their own organization. The World at Work web site has many online resources for members of the organization and articles available to the public. URL: www.worldatwork.org/workspan

■ HUMOR

Donna Burton, Associate Professor, Schaffer Library, Union College, Schenectady, NY 12308; burtond@union.edu.

Christine K. Oka, Library Instruction Coordinator, 270 Snell Library, Northeastern University, Boston, MA 02115; c.oka@neu.edu

Introduction

In this age of political correctness, the line between funny and offensive has gotten harder to navigate than ever, and the balancing act for libraries may be a slightly tricky one in this genre.

These publications present humor in its various forms (parody, satire, anecdotes, poetry, etc.), or delve into those technical or scholarly resources that take humor seriously and study, analyze, and interpret it rather than generate it.

Readers may note that *The Onion* has been removed from the section for this edition. Since much of the material in the print is replicated and/or expanded online, and since the print ain't cheap (over $200 as of this writing), a print subscription probably shouldn't be considered vital unless there is patron demand in public and academic libraries. We do, however, continue to recommend the web site, at www.theonion.com.

Basic Periodicals

Hs: *Mad*; Ga: *Mad*; Ac: *The Annals of Improbable Research*.

Basic Abstracts and Indexes

Reader's Guide to Periodical Literature.

3062. *The Annals of Improbable Research: resarch that makes people LAUGH and then THINK.* [ISSN: 1079-5146] 1995. bi-m. USD 37 domestic; USD 46 in Canada & Mexico; USD 59 elsewhere. Ed(s): Marc Abrahams. Annals of Improbable Research, PO Box 380853, Cambridge, MA 02238; info@improbable.com; http://www.improbable.com. Illus. Sample. Refereed. *Aud.:* Hs, Ac, Sa.

This journal requires detailed perusal—the wit and humor abound. For example, the letters to the editor, or rather "Exhalations from our Readers," is titled "AIR Vents" (acronymic pun intended), and at the end of the magazine reside the enigmatic "Unclassified Ads," with the caveat for one to "Proceed at your own risk." Colorful, glossy front and back covers relate to the special themes treated in each issue, and the back sports a generally unanswerable "What is this picture?" challenge (with answers, fortunately, in the front). The rest of the publication, running 30 pages, is solely in black-and-white text—likewise the illustrations, diagrams, or photographs; and there is no outside advertising. Serious research is lampooned, and "many of the other articles are genuine, too, but [the editors] don't know which ones." Don't miss the web site, which has a monthly newsletter (*mini-AIR*), a weekly newspaper column, a blog, the "Improbable Research TV" series, and issue "airchives" from volume one (1995), with sample articles viewable in each issue up to 2004. This title is excellent for college and large public libraries, and even high school libraries (since the editors encourage copying, sharing, and discussing favorite articles with classes, as advocated in the *AIR* Teachers' Guide). URL: http://improbable.com/magazine/

3063. *The Believer.* [ISSN: 1543-6101] 2003. 9x/yr. USD 45 domestic; USD 75 foreign. Ed(s): Heidi Julavits, Ed Park. McSweeney's, 849 Valencia St, San Francisco, CA 94110; custservice@mcsweeneys.net; http://www.mcsweeneys.net. Illus. *Indexed:* MLA-IB. *Bk. rev.:* Number and length vary. *Aud.:* Ac, Sa.

"*The Believer* is a monthly magazine where length is no object." This note from the web site succinctly summarizes this title. It includes articles, poems, book reviews, interviews, and columns, with illustrations, photographs, or other art sprinkled throughout; and the two- and three-column text format is elegantly simple, clean, and free of advertising. The tables of contents from the inaugural March 2003 issue to the present are available on the web, with excerpts from almost everything and full text for some things. Contributors cover a broad spectrum of novelists, poets, musicians, actors, and freelancers, and can be searched by issue or name. The editors state that they focus on writers and books they like and give people and books the benefit of the doubt. Its appeal will be for those with literary or artistic interests, in large public or academic libraries. URL: www.believermag.com

3064. *Humor Times.* Formerly (until 200?): *Comic Press News.* [ISSN: 1937-299X] 1991. m. USD 18.95 domestic; USD 33.95 Canada; USD 50.95 elsewhere. Ed(s): James Israel. Comic Press News, PO Box 162429, Sacramento, CA 95816; info@humortimes.com; http://www.humortimes.com. Illus., adv. *Aud.:* Ga, Ac.

According to the *HT* "About Us" page, "The country's finest editorial cartoonists take a look at what's happening on the world stage, while adding their own commentary via the irreverent art of cartooning." This title should be considered for high schools (a few lesson plans are offered using editorial cartoons, and special subscription rates are available, depending on location), public libraries, and academic institutions; it is of national interest, and certainly for anyone looking for excellent political and social satire on current events. URL: www.humortimes.com

3065. *Journal of Irreproducible Results: the science humor magazine.* [ISSN: 0022-2038] 1955. irreg. USD 39. Ed(s): Norman Sperling. Journal of Irreproducible Results, 413 Poinsettia Ave, San Mateo, CA 94403-2803. Illus., index, adv. Circ: 2000. Vol. ends: No. 6. *Indexed:* A22. *Aud.:* Ac, Sa.

Although 70 percent of *JIR* readers have doctorates, you don't have to be a rocket scientist to enjoy this magazine. However, since it is subtitled "The Science Humor Magazine," a ready sense of humor and an interest or background in the sciences certainly wouldn't hurt. Colorful covers, black-and-white illustrations (drawings, photos, diagrams, and charts), and the wide-ranging variations in font types inside make for interesting viewing, uncomplicated by little, if any, advertising. Articles in every issue present fresh ideas from worldwide contributors, and these range from such subjects as "The decline and fall of the species *Pasta pasta*" to "How to narrow your search, or Oh crap, how can I read 5,000 articles by tomorrow." There is also "A taxonomic scale of cluedness in humans" and "Therapuetic benefits of beer for recovery from traumatic injury." *JIR*'s editor, Norman Sperling, states that readers will "get more new ideas, perspectives, and viewpoints per issue from *JIR* than from any other scientific publication." *JIR* can spur new insights into real science." Occasional poems and song parodies are included, as are crossword puzzles and cartoons. Back issues are available for purchase but are not archived online (except for some "Favorites") or indexed on the web site or commercially. *JIR* is both interesting and fun and should be in the collections of college, university, hospital, and research libraries and considered by high school and public libraries as well. URL: www.jir.com

3066. *Light: a quarterly of light verse.* [ISSN: 1064-8186] 1992. q. USD 24. Ed(s): Lisa Markwart. The Foundation for Light Verse, PO Box 7500, Chicago, IL 60680-7500; http://www.lightquarterly.org. Illus., adv. *Indexed:* AmHI, BRI. *Bk. rev.:* Number and length vary. *Aud.:* Ga.

According to the *Light* web site, this is the "...only publication in America to print funny, topical, and above all readable poems. They're metrical (usually) and enjoyable (always)." The publication's goal is to discard "...what is obscure and dreary, and restore lightness, understandability, and pleasure to the reading of poems." Even non–poetry lovers can enjoy these light and amusing poems; there is everything from parodies to puns to limericks to haiku and sonnets. Each quarterly issue contains poems that are all by the "Featured Poet" for that quarter. The subsequent pages contain groups of poems categorized under playful titles such as "Lit Crit Snits," "Amorous Dings and Pings," "Premature Decrepitude," and "Pure Naughtiness." The journal concludes with "Reviews and Reflections," a section of book reviews and related ruminations, followed by very abbreviated letter and news sections. Advertising is absent, and the web site exists mostly to take care of subscription and submission business, but it does provide issue excerpts back to 1997, and a discussion forum. This title would be a good selection for an academic library or a large public library. Occasional poems may not be appropriate for all ages. URL: http://lightquarterly.org

3067. *Mad.* [ISSN: 0024-9319] 1952. q. USD 14.99 domestic; USD 20.99 foreign. Ed(s): John Ficarra. E.C. Publications, Inc., 1700 Broadway, New York, NY 10019. Illus. Circ: 500000 Paid. *Aud.:* Hs, Ga.

This enduring favorite of the boomer and subsequent generations' adolescents and young adults, and written by "the usual gang of idiots," is now much more contemporary-looking, with graphics delivered in glossy color throughout the magazine, but with an occasional black-and-white nostalgia trip thrown in. Perennial favorites such as the clever fold-in back cover, "Spy vs. Spy," and the "marginals," the tiny cartoon sketches that have one perusing literally every inch of this magazine, continue to amuse. With fun poked at virtually anything from current movies, TV shows, and other pop culture icons, to dating to politics and the surefire parent/child relationships, very little is sacred in the world of *MAD,* enabling it to stay fresh and funny and contemporary. Although this may not look quite like your dad's (or granddad's) *MAD,* some things never change. One thing that has changed, however, is that *MAD* is now quarterly rather than monthly. There is an online presence, but it's not very heavily populated with "*MAD*ness." Sure to be popular in school and public libraries; the main problem may be keeping it around until the next quarter's issue.

3068. *Studies in American Humor: the journal of the American Humor Studies Association.* Incorporates (1974-1984): *American Humor.* [ISSN: 0095-280X] 1974. s-a. Membership, USD 20. Ed(s): Ed Piacentino. American Humor Studies Association, c/o Joseph Alvarez, Sec-Treas, 900 Havel Ct, Charlotte, NC 28211-4253; joe_alvarez@cpcc.cc.nc.us; http://www.slu.edu/academic/ahsa/journalhome.htm. Illus., index, adv. Refereed. *Indexed:* AmHI, BRI, MLA-IB. *Bk. rev.:* 2-4, 400-600 words. *Aud.:* Ac.

This journal was founded over 35 years ago by the American Humor Studies Association. Its "New Series" "...publishes essays, review essays, and book reviews on all aspects of American humor." The journal is peer reviewed and is indexed in several literature indexes such as Humanities Index and MLA, with no advertising and occasionally black-and-white cartoons, drawings, or photographs. Representative articles include "Humor in *Uncle Tom's Cabin*," " 'Through the Rube Goldberg Crazy Straw': ethnic mobility and narcissistic fantasy in *Sarah Silverman: Jesus is magic,*" "Wits and Wags in Southern Literature," and " 'Don't Laugh! Act as if it was all right!' and other comical interruptions in *Little Women.*" The tables of contents from the "New Series" for the dates 1994 to 2010 are on the web site. The subscription rate is very reasonable, and includes membership in the association. Recommended for research, academic, and possibly for larger public libraries.

■ HUNTING AND GUNS

Christine K. Oka, Library Instruction Coordinator, 270 Snell Library, Northeastern University, Boston, MA 02115; c.oka@neu.edu

Introduction

Stop at any large bookstore or newsstand and prepare to be inundated with periodicals that specialize in a wide range of hunting, such as for elk, whitetail, wild turkey, and waterfowl, and an even larger selection of titles related to guns: handguns, blackpowder guns, revolvers, muzzle-loaders, and automatic rifles, to name a few.

How does one decide what a library should have when the economic environment and budgets require libraries to reduce hours, services, collections, or all three? For this edition, most of the magazines listed were included because they provided overviews or appealed to a wide range of readers. Accessible articles on firearms, technical data and field testing, gun legislation, land management, conservation, adventure hunting, concealed carry, and safety were considered a priority. Many of these titles have associated web sites and offer selected online access to feature articles; see individual entries for the relevant URLs.

Basic Periodicals

Hs, Ga, Ac: *American Hunter, American Rifleman, Field & Stream, Guns & Ammo.*

Basic Abstracts and Indexes

Readers' Guide to Periodical Literature.

3069. *American Hunter.* [ISSN: 0092-1068] 1973. m. Members, USD 9.95. National Rifle Association of America, 11250 Waples Mill Rd, Fairfax, VA 22030; membership@nrahq.org; http://home.nra.org. Illus. Sample. Vol. ends: Dec. *Indexed:* A22, P02. *Bk. rev.:* 1-4, 500 words. *Aud.:* Hs, Ga, Ac.

According to the National Rifle Association (NRA), *American Hunter,* the official journal of the NRA, is about "tactics, adventure, great places to hunt, the latest hunting gear, and a special emphasis on the guns hunters love; all delivered by experts in the field." This magazine is loaded with information for hunters of all types of prey, especially pheasant, turkey, deer, and elk, as well as other big game. It also well serves gun collectors. Departments and columns in each issue include the "NRA President's Column"; "Gear"; "Armed Citizen"; and "Political Report," which has news and survey information about Second Amendment rights. Articles reflect the content diversity, such as practical feature articles on "Tactics & Technique," "Destination & Adventure," and "Guns & Shooting"; and personal stories, such as "My First Pair of Deer"—a young girl writing about her experience taking down her first doe and buck ("He was a 5 x 6. I was so excited"). Recommended for any hunter and any library that serves users with an interest in hunting and guns. Access to some of the feature articles is available online at www.americanhunter.org, where there are also videos, blogs, hunting news, gear reviews, and links to Twitter, Facebook, and Flickr.

3070. *American Rifleman.* Former titles (until 1923): *Arms and the Man;* (until 1906): *Shooting and Fishing;* (until 1888): *Rifle.* [ISSN: 0003-083X] 1885. m. Free to members; Non-members, USD 15. N R A Publications, 11250 Waples Mill Rd, Fairfax, VA 22030; publications@nrahq.org; http://www.nrapublications.org. Illus. Sample. Vol. ends: Dec. Microform: PQC. *Indexed:* A22, BRI, P02. *Bk. rev.:* 3-7, 150-250 words. *Aud.:* Hs, Ga, Ac.

American Rifleman is one of two magazines published by the National Rifle Association, and safety is one of its key issues. Articles cover a range of topics, such as handguns, shotguns, rifles, military weapons, law enforcement, gun collecting, and product reviews. There are more than 12 regular departments and columns, as well as feature articles. There are "blogs" by *American Rifleman* Editor in Chief Mark Keefe, handgun reporting by Field Editor Wiley Clapp, and work by blogger Paul Rackely, writing "The RackAttack," which provides tips and tactics for training and self-defense. The publication capitalizes on mobile technology, with mobile platforms for Apple, Droid, or Blackberry. Recommended for any gun enthusiast and for public libraries. Access to some feature articles (videos, blogs, and a newsletter) is available online. URL: www.americanrifleman.org/

3071. *Field & Stream.* Formed by the 2003 merger of: *Field & Stream. Northeast Edition; Field & Stream. Far West Edition; Field & Stream. West Edition; Field & Stream. South Edition; Field & Stream. Midwest Edition;* All of which superseded in part (in 1984): *Field & Stream;* Which incorporated: *Living Outdoors;* Which was formerly: *Western Field and Stream;* Which incorporated: *Field and Stream.* [ISSN: 1554-8066] 2003. m. USD 12 domestic; USD 26 Canada; USD 45 elsewhere. Ed(s): Mike Toth, Jean McKenna. Bonnier Corp., 2 Park Ave, 9th Fl, New York, NY 10016; http://www.bonniercorp.com. Adv. *Indexed:* A01, BRI, MASUSE, P02. *Bk. rev.:* 4-6, 200-300 words. *Aud.:* Ems, Hs, Ga.

More than a monthly magazine for hunting and fishing enthusiasts. Each issue of *Field & Stream* "celebrates the outdoor experience with great stories, compelling photography, and sound advice, and it honors the traditions hunters and fishermen have passed down for generations." If a library had to limit its hunting and fishing holdings to one periodical—this is it. Each issue contains departments with well written and accessible information from different perspectives: "People," in which readers share their opinions, photos, and stories; and "Experts," who write on subjects such as survival, conservation, rifles, shotguns, and fishing. The "Close Calls" column contains personal experiences recalled by ordinary hunters and fishermen. The experiences are inclusive; a recent issue contained pictures of beaming women hunters with their elk prizes. A favorite section is the "Skills" department, which is packed with "tips, tricks[,] and advice you need this month" on projects, tactics, skills, and gear. More than survival, a recent issue included a recipe for "wild boar stew with salsa verde." Highly recommended for high school and public libraries for its broad and practical coverage. The web site has links for purchasing content for iPad, Kindle, and Nook devices. URL: www.fieldandstream.com/

3072. Guns & Ammo. Incorporates (1995-1996): *Performance Shooter.* [ISSN: 0017-5684] 1958. m. Ed(s): Jim Bequette. Intermedia Outdoors, Inc., 512 7th Ave, 11th Fl, New York, NY 10018; customerservice@imoutdoors.com; http://www.imoutdoorsmedia.com. Illus., index, adv. Vol. ends: Dec. Microform: PQC. *Indexed:* A22, BRI. *Aud.:* Hs, Ga, Ac.

Guns & Ammo covers the practical applications of firearms and emphasizes their safe and proper use. Coverage is accessible to all levels of shooter experience (hunting, collectible guns, firearm education, and competitive shooting), with articles examining the specifications and technical design of a wide variety of firearms (from handguns to automatic rifles); ammunition and reloading; and securing firearms. Readers can see the broad scope of this magazine in the departments in each issue, such as "Handgunning"; "G&A Reloads," a review of bullets; "Modern Sporting Rifles," in this case, automatic rifles; and "Rounds Downrange," along with a surprising articles. One such article found in a recent issue is "France: Epicenter of fashion, cuisine and—you'd better believe it—small arms development." Selected feature articles are available online at the web site, which also offers links to reviews, shooting, and online videos produced by *Guns & Ammo.* Recommended for libraries that serve hunting and gun enthusiasts. URL: www.gunsandammo.com/

Outdoor Life. See Hiking, Climbing, and Outdoor Recreation section.

3073. Rifle: sporting firearms journal. Formerly: *Rifle Magazine.* [ISSN: 0162-3583] 1968. bi-m. USD 19.97. Ed(s): Dave Scovill. Wolfe Publishing Co., 2180 Gulfstream, Ste A, Prescott, AZ 86301; wolfepub@riflemag.com. Illus., adv. Sample. Vol. ends: Dec. *Aud.:* Hs, Ga.

Published bimonthly, *Rifle* covers everything of interest to hunting and rifle enthusiasts with substantial reviews of rifles, cartridges, shooting gear (such as scopes), and collectible rifles. Articles could cover step-by-step directions for light gunsmithing; the history of the Weatherby Mark V rifle; and "Little Bighorn Battle Rifles and Carbines: What Archaeological Finds Have Revealed." All articles are well written by the knowledgeable staff and contributors, and they are highlighted with color photographs that show the details of shooting gear and cartridges, and display the craftsmanship of the rifles. While articles are not online, a sampling from the latest issue may be found at the web site. Recommended for large public libraries. URL: www.riflemagazine.com

3074. Shooting Sportsman. [ISSN: 1050-5717] 1987. bi-m. USD 33 domestic; USD 53 per issue Canada. Ed(s): Ralph Stuart. Down East Enterprise, Outdoor Group Publications, PO Box 1357, Camden, ME 04843. Illus., adv. Sample. *Bk. rev.:* 700-1,000 words. *Aud.:* Sa.

International in scope, *Shooting Sportsman* is a glossy, full-color magazine dedicated to bird hunting and shotguns. Departments in each issue include "From the Editor"; "Letters"; coverage of specialized topics related to "Game and Gun Gazette"; and "Hunting Dogs." Articles cover a range of wingshooting from clays to quail, partridge, pheasant, and duck. Also thoroughly covered is the craftsmanship of shotguns made around the world. Articles are accessible to connoisseurs as well as to the interested general reader. A recent issue included "The Legacy of Westley Richards: Celebrating 200 years of gunmaking innovation," about a company in Birmingham, England; and "Harboring Birds," a story about shooting at Nova Scotia's Fox Harb'r Resort. There was also a beautifully photographed section about "Dreams of Africa." Access to selected articles from the magazine web site at www.shootingsportsman.com/ is available after you register for an account. There is a free, online companion magazine, *Sporting Shot,* at www.shootingsportsman.com/sporting-shot, covering the same type of topics as the print, but with dynamic and interactive features, including slide shows and videos. *Shooting Sportsman* is recommended for large public libraries.

3075. Sports Afield: the premier hunting adventure magazine. Former titles (until 1940): *Sports Afield with Rod and Gun; Sports Afield.* [ISSN: 0038-8149] 1887. bi-m. USD 24.97 domestic; USD 49.97 foreign. Ed(s): Diana Rupp. Sports Afield, Inc., 15621 Chemical Ln, Bldg B, Huntington Beach, CA 92649; letters@sportsafield.com. Illus., adv. Sample. *Indexed:* A01, A22, BRI, P02. *Bk. rev.:* 500-800 words. *Aud.:* Hs, Ga.

Founded in 1887, *Sports Afield* published its first issue in January 1888 with the intent "to help propagate the true spirit of gentle sportsmanship, to encourage indulgence in outdoor recreations[,] and to assist in the dissemination of knowledge regarding natural history, photography, firearms, and kindred subjects." The magazine has evolved over time, looking at conservation issues before they became politically correct. Famous writers who have worked for *Sports Afield* include Zane Grey and mystery writer Earle Stanley Gardner, who became known for his articles on the rights of gun owners and hunters. Today, *Sports Afield* is a high-end, glossy magazine, providing the armchair adventurer and the serious big-game hunter with stories on popular hunting destinations, the latest gadgets and gear. Departments include the "Conservation Corner," "Rifles," "Shotguns," "New Gear Review," and "The Traveling Hunter." Recent features covered Africa: "Central African Adventure," "Leopards of the Moyowosi," and "Enough Gun: Kilimanjaro's new doctari rifle is the ultimate tool for African hunting." All articles are accompanied by color and breathtaking photography. The magazine web page has teasers to encourage visitors to subscribe to the magazine for complete content. Recommended for large public libraries. URL: www.sportsafield.com

3076. Women & Guns Magazine. [ISSN: 1045-7704] 1989. bi-m. USD 18 domestic; USD 38 foreign. Ed(s): Peggy Tartaro. Second Amendment Foundation, 12500 NE 10th Pl, Bellevue, WA 98005; AdminForWeb@saf.org; http://www.saf.org. Illus., adv. Sample. Vol. ends: No. 6. *Bk. rev.:* 1, 300 words. *Aud.:* Sa.

Women & Guns is published bimonthly by the Second Amendment Foundation (www.saf.org), a nonprofit, tax-exempt organization "dedicated to promoting a better understanding about our Constitutional heritage to privately own and possess firearms." Touted as "the world's first firearms publication for women," the magazine focuses on firearms for that specific audience. Most issues include pieces on gear and gadgets and on training; book reviews; and personal stories about women in the gun and firearms safety industry. It also includes "Legally Speaking," a column that discusses firearms and Second Amendment issues; in a recent issue, it examined the question, "Should or when should kids be introduced to toy guns?" In addition to the use of guns in recreation and sports, the magazine includes defensive strategies, emphasizing the importance of training and mental preparation; practical issues related to concealed carry; historical firearms; first aid; and handgun and rifle reviews. Selected articles from past and present issues are accessible online. URL: www.womenshooters.com/

■ INFORMATICS

Khue Duong, Science Librarian, California State University, Long Beach, 1250 Bellflower Blvd., Long Beach, CA 90840

Introduction

Combining computer science, information science, mathematics, and statistics with study of the ethical and social aspects of complex information systems, the interdisciplinary field of informatics focuses on the design, application, use, and impact of information technology. By gathering, manipulating, storing, retrieving, and classifying information, informatics practitioners develop human-centered uses for information technology to solve specific problems as diverse as DNA analysis, medical records storage and retrieval, smartphone applications, or disaster preparedness and response.

Informatics has a widespread presence not only in health care, public health, and biomedical sciences but also in chemistry, astronomy, and even the social sciences and journalism. As the field evolves, special concentrations arise, notably in specializations such as user experience research, data mining, information retrieval and management, social computing, and human computer interaction.

Basic Periodicals

Bioinformatics; Computers, Informatics, Nursing (CIN); Journal of Chemical Information and Modeling; Journal of the American Medical Informatics Association (JAMIA); Neuroinformatics.

Basic Abstracts and Indexes

BIOBASE, BIOSIS, CINAHL, Current Contents/Clinical Medicine, Current Contents/Engineering Computing & Technology, EMBASE, Information Science and Technology Abstracts, INSPEC, LISTA, MEDLINE, PsycINFO, PubMed, Science Citation Index, Scopus.

3077. American Medical Informatics Association. Journal: a scholarly journal of informatics in health and biomedicine. [ISSN: 1067-5027] 1994. bi-m. USD 662 (print & online eds.) Individuals, USD 332 (print & online eds.). Ed(s): Lucila Ohno-Machado. B M J Group, BMA House, Tavistock Sq, London, WC1H 9JR, United Kingdom; support@bmjgroup.com; http://group.bmj.com. Illus., adv. Sample. Refereed. *Indexed:* A22, CompLI, ErgAb, ExcerpMed, ISTA. *Bk. rev.:* Number and length vary. *Aud.:* Ac, Sa.

A top-ranked journal in biomedical and health informatics, *JAMIA* is the official journal of the American Medical Informatics Association (AMIA). Emphasizing informatics research and systems that help to advance biomedical science and to promote health, the journal includes articles in the areas of clinical care, clinical research, translational science, implementation science, imaging, education, consumer health, public health, and policy. *JAMIA* articles describe innovative informatics research and systems that help to advance biomedical science and to promote health. Case reports, perspectives, and reviews also help readers stay connected with the most important informatics developments in implementation, policy, and education. Topics covered by some of the most downloaded papers include the role of medical bioinformatics in the advancement of clinical and translational medicine; usability of personal health record (PHR) systems; and secure protocol in protecting personal information and minimizing errors in medical records. All content published in *JAMIA* is deposited with PubMed Central with a 12-month embargo. Authors may pay an unlocked fee to make the article free immediately after publication on the *JAMIA* web site and PubMed Central. This title is highly recommended for both hospital libraries and health-focused academic libraries. AMIA membership includes both a print and online subscription to *JAMIA*.

3078. B M C Medical Informatics and Decision Making. [ISSN: 1472-6947] 2001. irreg. Free. Ed(s): Dr. Melissa Norton. BioMed Central Ltd., 236 Gray's Inn Rd, London, WC1X 8HB, United Kingdom; info@biomedcentral.com; http://www.biomedcentral.com. Illus., index, adv. Refereed. *Indexed:* A01. *Bk. rev.:* Number and length vary. *Aud.:* Ac, Sa.

BMC Medical Informatics and Decision Making is an open-access, peer-reviewed journal that considers articles in relation to the design, development, implementation, use, and evaluation of health information technologies and decision-making within the health-care setting. The publication cycle of this electronic-only journal is fast, since manuscript submission and peer review are done electronically. Large data sets, illustrations, and moving pictures can be included and read directly by other software packages, so as to allow readers to manipulate the data for themselves. Frequently discussed topics include mobile health apps, computerized clinical documentation systems, management of electronic health records, and application of a PICO framework in evidence-based medicine.

Bioinformatics. See Biotechnology section.

3079. Computers, Informatics, Nursing. Formerly (until 2002): *Computers in Nursing;* Incorporates (1998-2002): *C I N Plus.* [ISSN: 1538-2931] 1983. bi-m. USD 449 (print & online eds.). Ed(s): Dr. Leslie H Nicoll. Lippincott Williams & Wilkins, 530 Walnut St, Philadelphia, PA 19106; customerservice@lww.com; http://www.lww.com. Illus., index, adv. Circ: 1898. Microform: PQC. *Indexed:* A22. *Aud.:* Ac, Sa.

Originally designed as a forum for communication among nurses who use computers, *CIN: Computers, Informatics, Nursing* has become a high-quality, peer-reviewed journal that focuses on computer technology in contemporary nursing practice, education, research, and administration. The year 2011 marks the journal's transition to a more active online presence. Whereas new original content is published online each month, *CIN* continues to publish bimonthly print collections of articles grouped by relevant themes. Accepted manuscripts are fast-tracked for online publication ahead of print. In addition, the supplementary section, "CIN Plus," provides quick-access and "how to" pieces on practical issues in, and applications of, nursing-informatics computing tools. Recent topics of discussion include building patient relationships using smartphone applications; the role of informatics in nursing education; and enhancing oncology care and survivorship through informatics. The journal is an endorsed member benefit of AMIA, HIMSS, and all other member organizations of the Alliance for Nursing Informatics (ANI). Members of the ANI are eligible to receive the journal at a reduced subscription rate.

3080. International Journal of Medical Informatics. Formerly (until 1997): *International Journal of Bio-Medical Computing.* [ISSN: 1386-5056] 1971. 12x/yr. EUR 3201. Ed(s): J Talmon, C Safran. Elsevier Ireland Ltd, Elsevier House, Brookvale Plaza, E. Park, Shannon, Ireland. Illus., adv. Refereed. *Indexed:* A01, A22, AbAn, C45, CompLI, CompR, EngInd, ExcerpMed, IndVet, MathR. *Aud.:* Ac, Sa.

The official journal of the European Federation of Medical Informatics (EFMI), the *International Journal of Medical Informatics* publishes original results and interpretative reviews, focusing on the evaluation of information systems in health-care settings. Specific coverage of this peer-reviewed journal includes electronic medical-record systems, hospital information systems, computer-aided medical-decision support systems, and educational computer-based programs in medicine, as well as the clinical, ethical, and socioeconomic aspects of information technology (IT) applications in health care. The journal periodically publishes special issues that concentrate on themes such as mining clinical and biomedical text and data; security in health-information systems; or human-factors engineering for health-care applications. Potential audience groups include researchers in medicine and those in health policy and administration, and medical educators.

3081. Journal of Biomedical Informatics. Formerly (until 2001): *Computers and Biomedical Research.* [ISSN: 1532-0464] 1969. bi-m. EUR 1227. Ed(s): Dr. E H Shortliffe. Academic Press, 3251 Riverport Ln, Maryland Heights, MO 63043; JournalCustomerService-usa@elsevier.com; http://www.elsevierdirect.com/brochures/academicpress/index.html. Illus., index, adv. Sample. Refereed. *Indexed:* A22, ApMecR, C&ISA, C45, CerAb, CompR, E01, EngInd, ExcerpMed. *Bk. rev.:* Irregular. *Aud.:* Ac, Sa.

Since its name change in 2001, the *Journal of Biomedical Informatics* shifted its focus toward underlying methods across biomedical domains rather than system descriptions or summary evaluations. Whereas the peer-reviewed articles are motivated by applications in the biomedical sciences (for example, clinical medicine, health care, population health, imaging, and translational bioinformatics), the journal emphasizes reports of new methodologies and techniques with general applicability and those that form the basis for the evolving science of biomedical informatics. The journal periodically produces special-theme issues that highlight topics such as community-driven curation of ontologies and knowledge bases; biomedical complexity and error; and biomedical natural-language processing. The potential audience includes researchers in medicine, bioinformatics, computer science, and professionals in health policy, administration, and management.

3082. Journal of Chemical Information and Modeling. Former titles (until 2005): *Journal of Chemical Information and Computer Sciences;* (until 1975): *Journal of Chemical Documentation.* [ISSN: 1549-9596] 1961. bi-m. USD 915. Ed(s): William L Jorgensen. American Chemical Society, 1155 16th St N W, Washington, DC 20036; help@acs.org; http://pubs.acs.org. Adv. Sample. Refereed. *Indexed:* A22, Agr, C&ISA, CEA, CompLI, EngInd, MSN, P02. *Bk. rev.:* Irregular. *Aud.:* Ac, Sa.

Published by American Chemical Society Publications, the *Journal of Chemical Information and Modeling* produces peer-reviewed papers that focus on the methodology and applications of chemical informatics and molecular modeling. Specific topics include the representation and searching of chemical databases, molecular modeling, computer-aided molecular design of new materials, catalysts, or ligands, and development of new computational methods or efficient algorithms for chemical software. The coverage also extends to analyses of biological activity and other issues related to drug discovery. The online interface lists the most-read and most-cited articles as well as "Just Accepted" manuscripts. The "ACS Author Choice" option allows authors to pay a one-time fee to make their papers freely accessible online. Highly ranked in the "Computer Science, Information Systems" category by *Journal Citation Report,* the journal helps computational chemists, computer scientists, and information specialists stay current with recent developments in this multidisciplinary field.

3083. *Journal of Cheminformatics.* [ISSN: 1758-2946] 2009. irreg. Free. Ed(s): David J Wild, Christoph Steinbeck. Chemistry Central, Fl 6 236 Gray's Inn Rd, London, WC1X 8HL, United Kingdom; info@chemistrycentral.com; http://www.chemistrycentral.com/. Refereed. *Indexed:* A01. *Bk. rev.:* Irregular. *Aud.:* Ac, Sa.

Established in early 2009, the *Journal of Cheminformatics* is an open-access, peer-reviewed, online journal that addresses all aspects of cheminformatics and molecular modeling, including chemical information systems, software, and databases; computer-aided molecular design; chemical structure representations; and data-mining techniques. Chemistry Central Ltd., in association with BioMed Central, creates this journal as a forum for scientists to publish their research rapidly in an open-access medium. Published material may include electronic supplementary material such as data sets, spectra, or graphical chemical structures. The journal offers different types of articles including primary research; coverage of a database or software feature; and methodology articles that describe a new experimental method, test, or procedure. The potential audience includes academic and industrial groups involved in computational chemistry and cheminformatics.

3084. *NeuroInformatics.* [ISSN: 1539-2791] 2002. q. EUR 529 (print & online eds.). Ed(s): Giorgio Ascoli. Humana Press, Inc., 999 Riverview Dr, Ste 208, Totowa, NJ 07512; humana@humanapr.com; http://humanapress.com/journals.pasp. Illus. Sample. Refereed. Reprint: PSC. *Indexed:* A22, E01, PsycInfo. *Aud.:* Ac, Sa.

Neuroinformatics publishes articles and reviews with an emphasis on data structure and software tools related to analysis, modeling, integration, and sharing in all areas of neuroscience research. Coverage includes, per the journal's self-description, "theory and methodology, including discussions on ontologies, modeling approaches, database design, and meta-analyses; descriptions of developed databases and software tools, and of the methods for their distribution; relevant experimental results, such as reports accompanied by the release of massive data sets; computational simulations of models integrating and organizing complex data; and neuroengineering approaches, including hardware, robotics, and information theory studies." The journal also publishes independent "tests and evaluations" of available neuroscience databases and software tools. With the "Open Choice" option, authors can pay an open-access fee to make their articles freely available. The journal also provides "Online First" articles, which are made available before print publication. Frequent topics of discussion include clinical neuroinformatics, computer algorithms to facilitate neuron reconstruction, and Digital Reconstruction of Axonal and Dentritic Morphology (DIADEM). Recommended for both hospital libraries and health-focused academic libraries.

■ INTERDISCIPLINARY STUDIES

Courtney L. Young, Head Librarian, Greater Allegheny Campus Library, The Pennsylvania State University, McKeesport, PA 15132; cly11@psu.edu

Introduction

Interdisciplinary studies reflects the growth in scholarship that applies multiple approaches, as well as the scholastic conversations taking place across disciplines. This section is a complement to sections that focus on and incorporate diverse fields of study.

While racial and gender diversity are often equated with interdisciplinary studies, broader disciplines within the sciences, social sciences, and humanities are also bridging the gaps. The publications included in this section focus on cross-disciplinary education and the facilitation of conversations among educators in a variety of fields.

The emphasis of the journals included here is on science, approaches to education, and the understanding that one approach is really a strategy among many approaches. A large number of journals include "interdisciplinary" as a subtitle but are better suited for other sections. A challenge in editing this section was the large number of journals with a sporadic publishing history or journals that had simply ceased publishing.

Consider these publications when building and maintaining a collection to support interdisciplinary studies. In addition to the journals recommended, explore the many sections that more directly focus on specific disciplines and types of diversity. Your suggestions for expanding this list are encouraged.

Basic Periodicals

Ac: *Issues in Integrative Studies.*

Basic Abstracts and Indexes

Academic Search Premiere, Project MUSE, ProQuest Research Library.

American Quarterly. See Cultural Studies section.

American Studies. See Cultural Studies section.

Clio. See History/Interdisciplinary Interests section.

Critical Inquiry. See Cultural Studies section.

Discourse. See Education/Comparative Education and International section.

Environmental Ethics. See Environment and Conservation section.

Film & History. See Films section.

Inquiry: An Interdisciplinary Journal of Philosophy. See Philosophy section.

3085. *Interdisciplinary Environmental Review.* [ISSN: 1521-0227] 1999. 4x/yr. EUR 494 (print or online eds.). Ed(s): Demetri Kantarelis. Inderscience Publishers, PO Box 735, Olney, MK46 5WB, United Kingdom; editorial@inderscience.com; http://www.inderscience.com. Refereed. *Indexed:* S25. *Bk. rev.:* Number and length vary; signed. *Aud.:* Ac.

Published by the Interdisciplinary Environmental Association, *IER* publishes "research and survey papers" in all disciplines that concern the "natural environment." Each annual issue features seven or eight articles. Scholarship on ethics, religion, gender, and globalization as they relate to the environment represent a handful of the diverse topics covered. Submission information encourages authors to write their manuscripts in a manner that will "facilitate communication between disciplines." This journal is relevant to a variety of researchers.

3086. *Interdisciplinary Literary Studies: a journal of criticism and theory.* [ISSN: 1524-8429] 1999. s-a. USD 191 (print & online eds.). Ed(s): Kenneth Womack. Pennsylvania State University Press, 820 N University Dr, University Support Bldg 1, Ste C, University Park, PA 16802; info@psupress.org; http://www.psupress.org. Adv. Reprint: PSC. *Indexed:* MLA-IB. *Bk. rev.:* Number and length vary; signed. *Aud.:* Ac.

This journal publishes research that explores "the interconnections between literary studies and other disciplines, ideologies, and cultural methods of critique." Scholarship focuses on discussions of the "pedagogical possibilities of interdisciplinary literary studies." Also includes book reviews and interviews with important scholars in the field.

3087. *Interdisciplinary Science Reviews.* [ISSN: 0308-0188] 1976. q. GBP 625 (print & online eds.). Ed(s): Willard McCarty. Maney Publishing, Ste 1C, Joseph's Well, Hanover Walk, Leeds, LS3 1AB, United Kingdom; maney@maneypublishing.com; http://maneypublishing.com/. Adv. Refereed. Reprint: PSC. *Indexed:* A01, A22, C&ISA, CerAb, RILM. *Bk. rev.:* Number and length vary; signed. *Aud.:* Ac.

Founded in 1976, *ISR* aims to "foster inclusive pluralistic appreciation and understanding of scientific activity." Submissions by scholars with diverse research interests in the physical and biological sciences, social sciences, and humanities advance that goal. Faculty and researchers from around the world contribute frequently. Special issues are often published, with themes including "Science and Poetry" and "Neuroscience: the humanities and arts." Most issues are heavily illustrated. Book reviews and letters to the editor round out each issue. A fascinating and essential journal for interdisciplinary collections.

3088. *Interdisciplinary Studies in Literature and Environment.* [ISSN: 1076-0962] 1993. s-a. EUR 124. Ed(s): Kyhl Lyndgaard, Scott Slovic. Oxford University Press, 198 Madison Ave, New York, NY 10016; http://www.us.oup.com. Adv. Refereed. Reprint: PSC. *Indexed:* AmHI, ArtHuCI, MLA-IB. *Bk. rev.:* Number and length vary; signed. *Aud.:* Ac.

Another journal with a focus on the increasing research and scholarship on the environment, *ISLE* "seeks to bridge the gap between scholars, artists, students, and the public." Published since 1993 by the Association for the Study of Literature and Environment, *ISLE* bridges the gap with scholarship on advertising, poetry, religion, the environment, and representations of nature in literature. Also includes book reviews and an annotated list of recently published books in the field.

3089. *Issues in Integrative Studies: an interdisciplinary journal.* [ISSN: 1081-4760] 1982. a. Free to members. Ed(s): Stuart Henry. Association for Integrative Studies, Miami University, 501 E High St, Oxford, OH 45056; aisorg@muohio.edu; http://www.units.muohio.edu/aisorg. Refereed. *Indexed:* HEA. *Bk. rev.:* Number and length vary; signed. *Aud.:* Ac.

While other journals take an interdisciplinary approach to the study of disciplines, research in *Issues in Integrative Studies* explores what, exactly, the field of interdisciplinary studies is all about. Each publication examines the challenges of exploring this area of study, including "interdisciplinary theory and methodology; the nature, means, and problems of integrative research, especially on the human experience; and special pedagogical approaches for enhancing interdisciplinary/integrative comprehension, perspectives, knowledge, and utilization." This is an impressive, key journal for institutions with interdisciplinary studies programs. It is equally applicable to institutions with education programs.

3090. *Journal of Interdisciplinary History.* [ISSN: 0022-1953] 1969. q. USD 340 (print & online eds.). Ed(s): Ed Freedman, Robert I Rotberg. M I T Press, 55 Hayward St, Cambridge, MA 02142; journals-cs@mit.edu; http://mitpress.mit.edu. Illus., adv. Refereed. Microform: PQC. Reprint: SCH. *Indexed:* A01, A22, ABS&EES, AmHI, ArtHuCI, BAS, BRI, BrArAb, CBRI, E01, FR, IBSS, MLA-IB, NumL, P02, P61, RILM, SSA. *Bk. rev.:* 30-45, 2-3 pages, signed. *Aud.:* Ac, Sa.

Incorporating "contemporary insights on the past," articles in this journal employ a diverse approach to analysis and methodology in historical scholarship. Sample titles of articles, clearly influenced by an interdisciplinary approach to research, include "Reconceptualizing the Republic: Diversity and Education in France, 1945–2008"; "Nutritional Success on the Great Plains: Nineteenth-Century Equestrian Nomads"; and "Antebellum Farm-Settlement Patterns: A Three-Level Approach to Assessing the Effects of Soils." Book

reviews, research notes, and review essays continue to be a strength of the journal. While it remains an important journal in the discipline of history, the *Journal of Interdisciplinary History* is a solid contributor to the field of interdisciplinary studies.

Journal of the History of Ideas. See Cultural Studies section.

Literature and History. See History/Interdisciplinary Interests section.

Philosophy and Literature. See Philosophy section.

3091. *Race, Gender & Class: an interdisciplinary journal.* Formerly (until 1995): *Race, Sex and Class.* [ISSN: 1082-8354] 1993. q. USD 60 (Individuals, USD 40; USD 24 per issue). Ed(s): Christiane Charlemaine, Jean Ait Belkhir. The University at New Orleans, Sociology Department, Milneburg Hall Room 170, 2000 Lakeshore Dr, New Orleans, LA 70148; jbelkhir@suno.edu; http://rgc.uno.edu/. Circ: 1200. *Indexed:* ENW, FemPer, GW, HEA, IIBP, MLA-IB, P61, SSA, SWR&A. *Bk. rev.:* Number and length vary; signed. *Aud.:* Ac.

This interdisciplinary, multicultural journal publishes articles and review essays focused on issues of race, gender, and class in society, including climate change, the environment, health, and psychology. *Race, Gender & Class* aims to publish materials that "have practical implications, direct or indirect, for education" and "that are accessible to undergraduates in introductory and general education classes." Annual proceedings of the Race, Gender & Class Conference are also published here. Unusual for its focus on race and class. Limited coverage in indexes.

Social Theory and Practice. See Cultural Studies section.

■ INTERIOR DESIGN AND DECORATION

See also Home section.

Holly Stec Dankert, Readers' Services Librarian, John M. Flaxman Library, School of the Art Institute of Chicago, 37 S. Wabash, Chicago, IL 60603; FAX: 312-899-1851; hdankert@saic.edu

Introduction

Shelter magazines are targeted toward two audiences—professional designers and consumers. This section focuses on trade magazines for professionals but includes consumer-oriented magazines that play an important role in providing product information and trends to practitioners, while bringing design principles to everyone. Both types of magazines are central to interior design.

Trade publications serve to inform decorators, designers, and architects of current practices, trends, and new products and services in both commercial and residential interiors. Most of these trade titles include reader-service information, professional development opportunities, new technology advancements in furnishings and materials, calendars of professional events, and reviews of new publications in interior design. In addition, these publications provide many full-color illustrations of interiors and the materials used for their creation. The field's professional literature is best suited to academic libraries that offer degrees in interior design or decorating and public and special libraries that support their local design community.

Consumer-oriented titles target the affluent buyer as well as the professional decorator or designer, and generally devote a great deal more copy space to photography of the featured interiors and to advertisements that highlight furnishings, appliances, wall coverings, textiles, flooring, and interior architecture. Many from this second group focus on the homes of celebrities and renowned designers or collections of art, antiques, and custom furnishings, and they are almost exclusively devoted to residential interiors.

The hallmark of all titles in this section is the extensive use of lush, full-color illustrations. The web sites of the trade titles continue to provide more relevant content to their constituents than do the consumer titles, which provide subscriber services and some content that augments the print issues. Magazines in this section will appeal to all library users, but are aimed at working designers and a clientele in search of professional design services.

Basic Periodicals

Ga: *Architectural Digest;* Ac: *Architectural Digest, Contract, Interior Design, Interiors & Sources, Journal of Interior Design.*

Basic Abstracts and Indexes

Art Abstracts, Art Index, Avery Index to Architectural Periodicals, Design and Applied Arts Index.

Abitare. See Architecture section.

3092. *American Style: art - craft - travel - interior design.* [ISSN: 1078-8425] 1994. bi-m. USD 19.99 domestic; USD 29.99 Canada; USD 35.99 elsewhere. Ed(s): Hope Daniels. Rosen Group, 3000 Chestnut Ave, Ste 304, Baltimore, MD 21211; http://www.americanstyle.com. Illus., adv. Sample. Vol. ends: Summer. *Aud.:* Ga, Sa.

Highlighting contemporary craft, craft collectors, and the artists who create studio craft art, *American Style* provides designers, decorators, and collectors with beautifully photographed residential interiors. Each issue features the homes of collectors, artists, and gallery owners, giving prominence to the objects they collect or create. Both online and print issues provide lists of galleries, fairs, tours, walks, and events by region. Blending art and interior design, *American Style* is recommended for all public and academic libraries that serve collectors or the design community. URL: www.americanstyle.com

3093. *Architectural Digest.* [ISSN: 0003-8520] 1920. m. USD 20 domestic. Ed(s): Margaret Russell. Conde Nast Publications, Inc., 4 Times Sq, 6th Fl, New York, NY 10036; http://www.condenast.com. Illus., adv. Vol. ends: Dec. Microform: PQC. *Indexed:* A&ATA, A01, A06, A07, A22, ABS&EES, AmHI, ArtHuCI, BRI, C37, F01, GardL, IIFP, MASUSE, MLA-IB, P02, RILM. *Aud.:* Ga, Ac.

Under the guiding hand of new editor Margaret Russell (former editor of *Elle Decor*), *Architectural Digest* (*AD*) has been streamlined, yet continues the traditions of this flagship magazine of interior design, as Russell states: "*AD* is still a dream book: it's about the dream of living well." Featured are lavish interiors of homes owned by the rich and famous. *AD* is international in scope, and each issue features residences exquisitely furnished with expensive antiques, objets d'art, and premium designer furniture. Occasional issues are devoted to a theme; not to be missed is the summer issue devoted to American country houses and the January "AD100" issue listing the top architects and designers. *Architectural Digest* is aimed at the rich and cosmopolitan, with its glossy advertising of luxury products; its showcase for antiques, designer, and collector items; and its sophisticated international locations. Many readers, regardless of income, will find it appealing. A standard design magazine recommended for all libraries. URL: www.architecturaldigest.com

3094. *Atomic Ranch: midcentury marvels.* [ISSN: 1547-3902] 2004. q. USD 19.95 domestic; USD 27.95 Canada; USD 37.95 elsewhere. Ed(s): Michelle Gringeri-Brown. Atomic Ranch, 3125 SE Rex St, Portland, OR 97202. Adv. *Aud.:* Ga, Ac, Sa.

Modern, postwar, ranch homes, and their furnishings are the focus of *Atomic Ranch.* This journal often highlights renovations and makeovers for enthusiasts of mid-century housing with photographic spreads in glorious color. Recent issues include an atomic age subdivision in Missouri on the historical register; Isamu Noguchi furnishings; and contemporary masters creating new mid-century–style products. Fun departments let readers keep up with cool stuff, "ranch dressing" (all your vintage furniture questions answered), and more modern wisdom. Chock-full of advertising for new products and appliances plus sources for vintage furnishings, *Atomic Ranch* is a great source for mid-twentieth-century interiors. Appropriate for all libraries.

3095. *Contract: inspiring commercial design solutions.* Former titles (until 2000): *Contract Design;* (until 1990): *Contract.* [ISSN: 1530-6224] 1960. m. USD 94 domestic; USD 99 Canada; USD 184 elsewhere. Ed(s): Jennifer Thiele Busch, Danine Alati. Nielsen Business Publications, 770 Broadway, New York, NY 10003; ContactCommunications@nielsen.com; http://www.nielsenbusinessmedia.com. Illus., adv. Sample. Circ: 30000. Vol. ends: Dec. *Indexed:* A07, ABIn, B01, B02, BRI. *Bk. rev.:* Number and length vary. *Aud.:* Ac, Sa.

Focusing on commercial interiors, *Contract* is an important magazine for industry information aimed at the design professional. Carefully lit, full-color interior photos illustrate trends in corporate, retail, hospitality, health care, entertainment, government, educational, and institutional design. *Contract* also covers new-product information on floor and wall coverings, textiles, lighting, and furniture. Professional designers will value the wide variety of briefs on current practices, resources, materials, trends, and industry news. An annual source guide/brand report comes out in December of each year. Most useful is the web site, which offers current design projects, industry updates, a vendor database, conferences, trade shows, and professional associations. The web site offers everything needed to stay current in nonresidential design, plus the table of contents and some articles from the current issue at no charge. Aimed at the architecture and design community, this core title is a must-have for all libraries that serve architects, design professionals, and students. URL: www.contractmagazine.com

Dwell. See Home section.

3096. *Elle Decor.* [ISSN: 1046-1957] 1989. 10x/yr. USD 10; USD 5.99 newsstand/cover. Hearst Magazines, 300 W 57th St, 12th Fl, New York, NY 10019; HearstMagazines@hearst.com; http://www.hearst.com. Illus., adv. Sample. Vol. ends: Nov. *Indexed:* A22, ASIP, C37. *Aud.:* Ga.

Elle Decor captures a young and chic spirit that functions like a fashion magazine for your home. Posh interiors, modern renovations, urban townhomes, and country retreats that are highlighted by colorful photography are the focus of this journal's articles, which feature artists and designers and their young, affluent clients. *Elle Decor* includes a panoply of artful objects, kitchen gadgets, bed-and-bath linens, furniture, and fixtures for the style-conscious individual. Each issue includes trend-setting designs that are inspirational and attainable. Resource contacts and reader services make this title valuable for both professionals and do-it-yourself decorators. The web site includes an archive of content from the ceased *Metropolitan Home,* as well as decorating and remodeling tips, and shopping and entertaining advice. Suitable for public libraries and all libraries that serve design professionals.

3097. *Frame.* [ISSN: 1388-4239] 1997. bi-m. EUR 99 (Students, EUR 79). Frame Publishers, Laan der Hesperiden 68, Amsterdam, 1076 DX, Netherlands; http://www.frameweb.com. Illus., adv. Circ: 36000. *Bk. rev.:* 5-7, 300 words. *Aud.:* Sa.

A glossy European magazine bursting with full-color photos, *Frame: The Great Indoors* focuses on sleek, ultra-contemporary designed objects and interiors from around the world. *Frame* succeeds in looking very different from other professional interiors magazines, and is enhanced with artful advertising for a wide range of international furniture, lighting, and designed objects. Regular features include an in-depth portrait of new interior designers and architects, a handful of articles on new commercial interiors and furnishings, and a multitude of briefs on new industrial designs from mobile homes to bars and museums. The web site gives much of the print content at no cost, but with very few illustrations. Recommended for design collections. URL: www.framemag.com

3098. *Interior Design.* Former titles (until 1950): *Interior Design and Decoration;* (until 1937): *The Decorators Digest.* [ISSN: 0020-5508] 1932. 15x/yr. USD 59.95 domestic; USD 87 Canada; USD 187 elsewhere. Ed(s): Helene Oberman. Sandow Media Corp., 360 Park Ave S, 17th Fl, New York, NY 10010; sandowinfo@sandowmedia.com; http://www.sandowmedia.com. Illus. Circ: 73370. *Indexed:* A01, A06, A07, A22, ABIn, ArchI, B02, BRI, C37, P02. *Bk. rev.:* 4-5, 150 words. *Aud.:* Ac, Sa.

Interior Design is renowned for its extensive coverage of commercial and residential interior design projects. The print edition offers broadly themed issues—the positivity issue, offices, fashion—with lengthy feature articles on notable projects or design firms with beautifully shot interiors. Regular departments include "Headliners," contacts, books, and the latest innovations in furnishings from international manufacturers. A subscription includes fall and spring "Market Tabloids" and the annual "Interior Design Buyers Guide." The web site serves the professional interior design community with new products, projects, industry giants, events, and archives of the print edition. Filled with color illustrations and industry advertising, it is recommended for all libraries and a must-have for those that support the interior design community. URL: www.interiordesign.net

3099. Interiors and Sources. Former titles (until 2004): *I S Magazine;* (until 2002): *Interiors & Sources.* [ISSN: 1943-8648] 1990. bi-m. USD 45 domestic (Free to qualified personnel; Students, USD 25). Ed(s): Jamie Nicpon, Robert Nieminen. Stamats Business Media, PO Box 1888, Cedar Rapids, IA 52406; salesmf@meetingsmedia.com; http://www.stamatscommunications.com/. Illus., index, adv. Sample. Circ: 27800 Controlled. Vol. ends: Nov/Dec. *Indexed:* A07. *Aud.:* Ac, Sa.

IS is geared toward the professional designer and architect, providing "excellence in commercial design." Each issue features a designer or project, and photo essays on relevant topics for design problems, such as aging or obesity in health care or sustainability in any design. Regular departments include "EnvironDesign Notebook," association forums, product sources, and industry news, delivering relevant and timely information to design professionals. The journal's web site is full of helpful content, from case studies (free for registered users) and webinars, to sustainable design resources and archives. Recommended for academic libraries with a design focus and public libraries that serve the local interior design/architecture community. URL: www.interiorsandsources.com

3100. Journal of Interior Design. Formerly (until 1993): *Journal of Interior Design Education and Research.* [ISSN: 1071-7641] 1976. 3x/yr. GBP 291 (print & online eds.). Ed(s): Margaret Portillo. Wiley-Blackwell Publishing, Inc., 111 River St, Hoboken, NJ 07030; info@wiley.com; http://onlinelibrary.wiley.com/. Illus., index, adv. Sample. Refereed. Reprint: PSC. *Indexed:* A07, A22, A51, E01, ErgAb. *Bk. rev.:* 4-5, 500 words. *Aud.:* Ac.

Journal of Interior Design is the only scholarly title for the interior design profession. Published by the Interior Design Educators Council, it focuses on education, practice, research, and theory, providing scholars and teachers with a forum for "scientific applications of design principles," historical research, and design processes in theory and practice. Each issue contains three to five articles that explore a wide variety of topics in interiors, from case studies to historic reviews. The council's web site provides annual conference, membership, graduate program, and other information pertinent to design educators. Recommended for all academic collections that serve design programs. URL: www.idec.org

3101. The World of Interiors. Formerly (until 1982): *Interiors.* [ISSN: 0264-083X] 1981. m. GBP 4.40 per issue. Ed(s): Rupert Thomas, Camilla Belton. Conde Nast Publications Ltd., Vogue House, Hanover Sq, London, W1S 1JU, United Kingdom; newbusiness@condenast.co.uk; http://www.condenast.co.uk. Illus., adv. Vol. ends: Dec. *Indexed:* A07, A22, RILM. *Bk. rev.:* 5-6, 500 words. *Aud.:* Ga, Sa.

This lush British monthly offers international coverage of residential interior design. Regular departments with catchy titles provide design trends, auction and fair dates, merchandise, and suppliers for the U.K. market. Articles often feature renowned personalities and showcase royal abodes, historic homes, modern penthouses, and gardens from the whimsical to the formal that are located throughout the world, predominantly in Britain. Fine art and antiques collections are also featured. Aimed at designers in the United Kingdom and their clients, this journal is best suited to large libraries that serve the design community.

■ INTERNATIONAL MAGAZINES

Elizabeth McKeigue, Co-Interim University Librarian for Public Services, Santa Clara University, Santa Clara, CA 95051; emckeigue@scu.edu.

Joanne Clymer, Library Help Services Supervisor, Santa Clara University, Santa Clara, CA 95051; jclymer@scu.edu

Introduction

This section recommends a list of popular general-interest magazines representing multiple nations and languages. The primary criteria for selection is the appeal these titles would have in American libraries, either for studying another language, for learning about another culture, or for foreign-born nationals wanting to stay in touch with news and culture from home.

The languages represented here include those frequently taught in American secondary schools and in universities, including English, Spanish, French, German, and Italian.

Titles included in this section have been chosen because of the high percentage of foreign-born nationals in the United States who speak, in addition to the languages already named, Chinese, Russian, Arabic, Portuguese, Serbo-Croatian, and Russian. I recommend reviewing other sections in *Magazines for Libraries* that focus on a particular geographic area or a specific country (e.g., Canada, Asia, Europe) for references to general-interest periodicals for those areas. For example, most general-interest magazines in Spanish can be found in the Latin America section or in the General Interest: Non-English Language section. Another criterion for selection for the titles in this section is that they are indexed in major American-produced indexes like Factiva, LexisNexis, and Academic Search Premier.

In addition, these magazines have been recommended because they offer robust content on their web sites, often for free, that make generous use of multimedia and utilize the latest widgets for sharing links and getting newsfeeds.

Recommendations from experts and natives of foreign countries are welcome, so these may please feel free to contact us.

Basic Periodicals

Ga: *The Economist* (United Kingdom), *Elsevier* (Netherlands), *L'Espresso* (Italy), *L'Express* (France), *Hello!* (United Kingdom), *Impacto* (Mexico), *Ogonek* (Russia), *Paris Match* (France), *Proceso* (Mexico), *The Spectator* (United Kingdom), *Der Spiegel* (Germany), *Stern* (Germany).

Basic Abstracts and Indexes

Factiva, IBZ, LexisNexis.

3102. Ahlan! (Arabic Edition). [ISSN: 1728-3051] w. Ed(s): Katie Heskett. I T P Consumer Publishing, PO Box 500024, Dubai, United Arab Emirates; info@itp.com; http://www.itp.com. *Aud.:* Ga.

In Arabic, from the United Arab Emirates. Alternate edition [ISSN: 1727-5431] is also available in English. *Ahlan!* is as similar in scope as it is in title to Britain's *Hello!* magazine (*ahlan* means *hello* in Arabic). Offering fashion, royalty, and celebrity news, *Ahlan!* is available online only, by subscription. Recommended for libraries that support an Arabic-speaking population or Arabic-language programs.

3103. Bunte. Incorporates: *Bunte Oesterreich;* Formerly: *Bunte Illustrierte.* [ISSN: 0172-2050] 1948. w. EUR 166.40; EUR 3.20 newsstand/cover. Ed(s): Patricia Riekel. Bunte Entertainment Verlag GmbH, Arabellastr 23, Munich, 81925, Germany; birgit.peters@burda.com; http://www.burda.com. Illus., adv. Sample. Circ: 656038 Paid. *Aud.:* Ga.

In German, from Germany. *Bunte* is the German equivalent of *People* magazine. It gives you entertainment news, style advice, and paparazzi photos of royalty, all with a European focus. It's great for students of German who are looking for some "fun" reading. Although the major focus is on European celebrities and royalty, there are also sections on sports, business, technology, travel, and health. Online, you'll find some of the same features of the print magazine and lots of photos of internationally famous people with their children. The travel advice section online is particularly good. Recommended for libraries that support elementary German-language programs or that cater to a German-speaking population. URL: www.bunte.de

3104. *Caras.* [ISSN: 0104-396X] 1993. w. BRL 400. Editora Abril, S.A., Avenida das Nacoes Unidas 7221, Pinheiros, Sao Paulo, 05425-902, Brazil; abrilsac@abril.com.br; http://www.abril.com.br. Illus., adv. *Bk. rev.:* Number and length vary. *Aud.:* Ga.

In Portuguese, from Brazil. If *Bunte* is Germany's *People* magazine, then *Caras* is the Brazilian *Bunte*! This magazine provides news and general-interest stories. Contents include feature articles and interviews with and photographs of celebrities. While each issue is just as likely as any American "celebrity" magazine to include reports on the pregnancies of Hollywood actresses, the focus of *Caras* is almost entirely on the stars of the booming entertainment culture and industry of Latin America. There are even some stories about ordinary people as newsmakers. Rich with advertising, photos, book reviews, film and some theater reviews, and music reviews, *Caras* is pretty to look at and great for popular culture news from Brazil. The web site provides a wealth of free content, including videos and news feeds. Recommended for public libraries that serve Brazilian Portuguese-speaking communities and for academic libraries that support Portuguese-language programs. URL: http://caras.uol.com.br

Contenido. See Latin America and Spain section.

3105. *Dani.* [ISSN: 1512-5130] 1992. w. Ed(s): Vildana Selimbegovic. Civitas d.o.o., Skenderija 31A, Sarajevo, 71000, Bosnia & Herzegovina. Illus., adv. *Bk. rev.:* Number and length vary. *Aud.:* Ga.

In Serbo-Croatian, from Bosnia and Herzegovina. *Nezavisni* is a weekly magazine that has been in print since 1992. It is also known by the English translation of its title, *Independent Magazine Dani*. Articles include such content as news (from Bosnia and Herzegovina and beyond); coverage of social issues; interviews; and book, film, music, video, DVD, and television reviews. Recommended for public libraries that serve an immigrant Balkan population and for academic libraries that support Slavic Studies programs.

The Economist. See Economics section.

3106. *Elsevier.* Incorporates (in 1998): *Elseviers Weekblad;* Formerly (until 1987): *Elseviers Magazine*. [ISSN: 0922-3444] 1944. w. EUR 219.95; EUR 4.95 newsstand/cover per issue. Reed Business bv, Postbus 152, Amsterdam, 1000 AD, Netherlands; info@reedbusiness.nl; http://www.reedbusiness.nl. Illus., adv. Circ: 129519. *Indexed:* A22. *Aud.:* Ga.

In Dutch, from the Netherlands. A primary newsmagazine in the Netherlands, *Elsevier* is the publication that lent its name to the well-known publishing company. Articles present research and commentary on a variety of social, political, and cultural topics. This glossy magazine is easily browsable and is probably most reminiscent of *Time* or *Newsweek*. Many issues focus on business and the European economy. Another popular topic is American politics, particularly the relationship between the United States and the European Union. *Elsevier* is an excellent resource for Dutch-reading students of Europe and politics. Recommended for research and large academic libraries.

3107. *L'Espresso: settimanale di politica, cultura, economia.* [ISSN: 0423-4243] 1955. w. EUR 59 domestic. Gruppo Editoriale l' Espresso SpA, Via Cristoforo Colombo 149, Rome, 00147, Italy; espresso@espressoedit.it; http://www.espressoedit.it. Illus., adv. Sample. Microform: PQC. *Indexed:* A22. *Aud.:* Ga.

In Italian, from Italy. This newsmagazine provides articles on a variety of general-interest topics, such as art, culture, business, health, society, sports, and world news (from an Italian point of view). There is a regular feature on the activities of the Vatican. Although heavy on advertising, this magazine nonetheless provides nice photographic essays, detailed articles, and reviews. The well-designed web site has full text of current issues that are freely available (in both Italian and English) and includes a section of blogs on various

topics (in Italian only). The web site also has video and audio files freely available. Strongly recommended for libraries that serve Italian-speaking patrons or students of Italian. URL: www.espressonline.it

3108. *L'Express.* [ISSN: 0014-5270] 1953. w. Ed(s): Denis Jeambar. Groupe Express-Roularta, 29 Rue de Chateaudun, Paris, 75308, France; http://www.groupe-exp.com. Illus., adv. Sample. Microform: PQC. *Indexed:* BRI, PdeR. *Aud.:* Ga.

In French, from France. In print since 1953, this news and current affairs magazine offers investigative articles and point-of-view pieces on a variety of political and social debates, both in France and the wider world. Specific sections include world news, French issues, society, science and health, media (television and film), and photographic essays. Like its Italian counterpart *L'Espresso*, *L'Express* has a very good web site, and complete articles from the current edition are available for free. Both the print and the online versions include advertising, and articles are frequently punctuated with photos, graphs, charts, and illustrations. Highly recommended for large public and most academic libraries. URL: www.lexpress.fr

3109. *Focus (Munich): das moderne Nachrichtenmagazin.* [ISSN: 0943-7576] 1993. w. EUR 182; EUR 3.70 newsstand/cover. Ed(s): Uli Baur. Focus Magazin Verlag GmbH, Arabellastr 23, Munich, 81925, Germany; medialine@focus.de; http://www.focus.de. Illus., adv. Sample. Circ: 576268 Paid. *Indexed:* A22. *Aud.:* Ga, Ac.

In German, from Germany. This newsmagazine includes in-depth reporting on world news (from a German perspective), business, technology, health, culture, and sports. *Focus* also has an annual ranking of the top German universities. Each issue includes many photographs, statistics, charts, and graphs. The letters to the editor give a good idea of current topics of political debate in Germany. The online version includes full text of the current issue for free. The online version also features a blog and video downloads of recent news stories from "Focus Online TV." Recommended primarily for academic and research libraries. Public libraries may want to consider this magazine if they support a user population of German speakers. URL: www.focus.de

3110. *L'Hebdo: magazine suisse d'information.* [ISSN: 1013-0691] 1981. w. CHF 225; CHF 5.90 newsstand/cover. Ed(s): Alain Jeannet. Ringier Romandie, Pont Bessieres 3, Case postale 3733, Lausanne, 1002, Switzerland; ringier.romandie@ringier.ch; http://www.ringier.ch. Illus., adv. Sample. Circ: 44979 Paid and controlled. *Aud.:* Ga.

In French, from Switzerland. *L'Hebdo* covers news, culture, technology, and business from a Swiss perspective. There is a German-language version of this publication called *Die Woche* that has essentially the same content. *L'Hebdo* includes lots of advertising, photos, and illustrations, both in print and on the web. Only the current issue is available in full online. Articles focus primarily on societal and political issues. Features include science and technology, the world, society, culture, business, media (film and TV), and travel. The web site features a blog written by the journalists at *L'Hebdo*. Recommended for large public and academic libraries. URL: www.hebdo.ch

3111. *Iceland Review: the magazine of Iceland.* Former titles (until 1985): *Atlantica and Iceland Review;* (until 1967): *Iceland Review*. [ISSN: 1670-004X] 1963. q. USD 40. Ed(s): Pall Stefansson. Heimur hf., Borgartuni 23, Reykjavik, 105, Iceland; heimur@heimur.is; http://www.heimur.is. Illus., adv. Sample. Circ: 20000. *Indexed:* RILM. *Bk. rev.:* Number and length vary. *Aud.:* Ga.

In English and some Icelandic, from Iceland. Articles in *Iceland Review* focus on Icelandic nature, culture, art, literature, and daily life. The online version includes daily news stories. Each issue includes advertising, interviews, classifieds, book reviews, and still, after all these years, at least one mention of Bjork. The primary focus of the magazine is promoting tourism in Iceland. Articles highlight the activities in Iceland that make it a unique travel experience, such as hiking, bathing in outdoor hot springs, or surfing. Recommended for libraries that support Scandinavian Studies or libraries that serve a significant population of Scandinavian Americans. URL: www.icelandreview.com

3112. *Knack.* [ISSN: 0772-3210] 1971. w. EUR 183. Roularta Media Group, Meiboomlaan 33, Roeselare, 8800, Belgium; info@roularta.be; http://www.roularta.be. Illus., adv. *Aud.:* Ga, Ac.

In Dutch, from Belgium. This glossy popular magazine covers news, politics, business, literature, films, celebrity news, and sports in Belgium. Each issue of *Knack* includes lists of the top-selling books, films, music, and films in Belgium. Those lists and the full text of most articles from the current issue are also found on the web. Sections include news this week, film, music, TV and radio, books, letters, lifestyle, business and finance, and sport. Recommended for large public libraries and for large academic libraries that support European Studies programs. URL: www.knack.be

Maclean's. See Canada section.

3113. *Magazin-Deutschland.de (English Edition).* Former titles (until 2009): *Deutschland (English Edition); (until 1993): Scala; (until 1973): Scala International.* 1961. bi-m. Ed(s): Peter Hintereder. Frankfurter Societaet, Frankenallee 71-81, Frankfurt Am Main, 60327, Germany; verlag@fsd.de; http://www.fsd.de. Illus., adv. *Indexed:* A22. *Bk. rev.:* Number and length vary. *Aud.:* Ga.

In English, from Germany. This primarily English-language magazine is great way for non–German-speaking Germany lovers to learn about today's Germany. It is published six times a year by Societats-Verlag, Frankfurt am Main, in cooperation with the Federal Foreign Office, Berlin. Articles focus on political, economic, scientific, and cultural events in Germany, and are written by German journalists. The magazine also includes advertising, photos, interesting photographic essays, and book and film reviews. The content-rich online version is available in a variety of languages, including French, Arabic, Spanish, and Portuguese. Highly recommended for large public and all academic libraries. URL: www.deutschland.de/en

3114. *Al- Majalla.* Formerly (until 200?): *Al- Majalla (Print).* 1980. w. Saudi Research & Publishing Co., P O Box 478, Riyadh, 11411, Saudi Arabia; editorial@majalla.com; http://www.srpc.com/main. Illus., adv. Circ: 92860 Paid. *Aud.:* Ga.

In Arabic, from Saudi Arabia. This weekly magazine is available online with all content accessible for free. It covers news, business, culture, and social issues of the Arab world. It is recommended for libraries with an Arabic-speaking population and for libraries that support Arabic language programs. URL: www.majalla.com/ar

3115. *The Monthly: Australian politics, society and culture.* [ISSN: 1832-3421] 2005. m. AUD 69.95 domestic; AUD 109.95 foreign. Ed(s): John van Tiggelen. The Monthly Pty Ltd, 37-39 Langridge St, Collingwood, VIC 3066, Australia; enquiries@themonthly.com.au. Adv. Circ: 21766. *Bk. rev.:* Number and length vary. *Aud.:* Ga.

In English, from Australia. This news and culture magazine is like a mash-up of *Vanity Fair, The New Yorker,* and *The Atlantic* for Australians. With well-researched and informative articles, *The Monthly* opens a window onto Australian culture, politics, and society that will appeal to native Australians and Australiophiles alike. Regular features include news commentary, book and media reviews (including film and theater), interviews, and essays from regular columnists. Recommended for large public or academic libraries.

3116. *Norwegians Worldwide.* Formerly (until 2012): *Norseman;* Incorporates (1907-1984): *Nordmanns-forbundet.* [ISSN: 1893-0042] 1943. 4x/yr. NOK 450 (Students, NOK 350). Ed(s): Anne C Wangberg. Nordmanns-Forbundet, Raadhusgatan 23 B, Oslo, 0158, Norway; norseman@norseman.no; http://www.norseman.no. Illus., adv. *Indexed:* MLA-IB. *Bk. rev.:* Number and length vary. *Aud.:* Ga.

In English and some Norwegian, from Norway. Written more for Norwegian Americans than for Norwegians, *Norwegians Worldwide* includes feature articles, interviews, photos, advertising, illustrations, and book reviews. The focus is primarily on cultural and historical issues. It is published by Nordmanns Forbundet under the patronage of His Majesty the King of Norway. Included are letters to the editor, articles on business (particularly shipping), Norway's relationship to the United States and Norwegian Americans, the history of

Norway and Scandinavia, travel, and sports. Recommended for libraries that support a population of Scandinavian Americans, or academic libraries that support Scandinavian Studies programs.

3117. *Novoe Vremya: ezhenedel'nyi zhurnal.* [ISSN: 0137-0723] 1943. w. Ed(s): Evginiya Al'bats. Izdatel'stvo Novoe Vremya, Tverskoi bul'var, dom 14, stroenie 1, Moscow, 125009, Russian Federation. Illus., adv. Microform: BHP; EVP; MIM; PQC. *Indexed:* RILM. *Bk. rev.:* Number and length vary. *Aud.:* Ga.

In Russian, from Russia. This magazine includes feature articles on a variety of topics of interest to Russian emigres and to students of the Russian language. It is packed with glossy photos and advertising, as well as charts, illustrations, and book, film, and music reviews. Recommended for public libraries that serve a Russian-speaking population and for academic libraries that support Slavic Studies programs.

3118. *Oggi.* [ISSN: 0030-0705] 1945. w. Ed(s): Pino Belleri. R C S Periodici, Via San Marco 21, Milan, 20121, Italy; info@periodici.rcs.it; http://www.rcsmediagroup.it/siti/periodici.php. Illus., adv. *Indexed:* MLA-IB. *Aud.:* Ga.

In Italian, from Italy. This current-affairs journal features articles by some of Italy's top journalists. Published since 1945, *Oggi* is the traditional weekly magazine of the Italian family. As such, it features investigative reports and interviews of interest to most Italians.

3119. *Ogonek.* [ISSN: 0131-0097] 1899. w. Ed(s): Vladimir Pekin. Izdatel'stvo Ogonek, Bumazhnyi pr 14, Moscow, 101456, Russian Federation. Illus., adv. Vol. ends: Dec. *Indexed:* CDSP, MLA-IB. *Aud.:* Ga, Ac.

In Russian, from Russia. Published since 1899, this weekly magazine features articles on current news events and interviews with people in the news. Highly recommended for libraries that serve a Russian-speaking population and for most academic libraries.

3120. *Paris Match.* Former titles (until 1976): *Nouveau Paris Match; (until 1972): Paris Match.* [ISSN: 0397-1635] 1949. w. EUR 96. Ed(s): Didier Rapaud. Hachette Filipacchi Associes S.A., 149/151 Rue Anatole France, Levallois-Perret, 925340, France; segolene.delloye@lagardere-active.com; http://www.lagardere.com. Illus., adv. *Indexed:* MLA-IB, PdeR. *Aud.:* Ga.

In French, from France. *Paris Match* is one of the most widely read magazines in France. With its combination of news, current affairs, celebrity interviews, and great photography, this magazine is also a favorite of Francophones (and Francophiles) all over the world. There is a stylish web site where one can find a number of articles from the current and past issues in full text without a subscription. It is also one of the few commercial web sites with a bare minimum of annoying pop-up advertisements. Highly recommended for public and academic libraries everywhere. URL: www.parismatch.com

3121. *Le Point.* [ISSN: 0242-6005] 1972. w. EUR 98 domestic; EUR 139 in Belgium & Luxembourg; EUR 149 in Europe. Ed(s): Jean Schmitt. Le Point, 74 av. du Maine, Paris, 75014, France; cyber@lepoint.tm.fr; http://www.lepoint.fr. Illus. Microform: PQC. *Indexed:* A22, PdeR. *Aud.:* Ga, Ac.

In French, from France. The primary competitor of *L'Express* for the distinction of being France's top newsmagazine, *Le Point* has been covering news and current-interest stories since 1972. Main features include editorials, letters, world news, news from France, society, business, economics, and media/technology. Most issues also include essays on travel, food, wine, cinema, literature, and art. The table of contents can be found online, but one must subscribe to the magazine to receive electronic access to the full text of the current issue. *Le Point* is an important resource for the study of current events and issues in France. Highly recommended for large public libraries and most academic libraries. URL: www.lepoint.fr

Proceso. See Latin America and Spain section.

3122. *Profil: das unabhaengige Nachrichtenmagazin Oesterreichs.* [ISSN: 1022-2111] 1970. w. EUR 129.90; EUR 3.50 newsstand/cover. Verlagsgruppe News Gesellschaft mbH, Taborstr 1-3, Vienna, 1020, Austria; schuh-haunold.angela@news.at; http://www.verlagsgruppenews.at. Illus., adv. Sample. Circ: 92984 Paid. *Aud.:* Ga.

In German, from Austria. This popular newsmagazine features Austrian current-affairs issues, world news, sport, people, money, weather, technology, women's issues, food and wine, travel, home and garden, and classifieds. The print version includes ample advertising, photos (especially of celebrities), and illustrations. There is also a separate section devoted to TV and film reviews. Recommended as a good, light news and entertainment magazine, especially in public or school libraries that support the study of the German language. Also available online. URL: www.profil.at

The Spectator. See News and Opinion section.

3123. *Der Spiegel.* [ISSN: 0038-7452] 1947. w. EUR 208 domestic; EUR 262.20 per issue in Europe; EUR 340.60 per issue elsewhere. Ed(s): Wolfgang Buechner. Spiegel-Verlag Rudolf Augstein GmbH und Co. KG, Brandstwiete 19, Hamburg, 20457, Germany. Illus., adv. Sample. *Indexed:* A22, BAS. *Aud.:* Ga, Ac.

In German, from Germany. Packed with over 200 pages of text, this magazine is one of the most popular in Germany. With text entirely in German, each issue includes many articles (both short pieces and longer features) on politics (both German and worldwide), business, current affairs, culture, technology, and sport. Think of this journal as *Time* magazine in German. *Der Spiegel* is known for its superior investigative reporting, especially in the area of German and European politics. The online version is updated daily and includes the full text of the current weekly print issue. If you can purchase just one magazine in German, this should be it. Strongly recommended for academic, research, and public libraries. URL: www.spiegel.de

3124. *Stern.* [ISSN: 0039-1239] 1948. w. EUR 174.20; EUR 3.70 newsstand/cover. Ed(s): Dominik Wichmann. Gruner + Jahr AG & Co, Am Baumwall 11, Hamburg, 20459, Germany; info@gujmedia.de; http://www.guj.de. Illus., adv. Sample. Circ: 816961 Paid. Microform: ALP; PQC. *Aud.:* Ga, Ac.

In German, from Germany. *Stern* is a current-affairs magazine that provides articles on news and culture but seems to focus primarily on lifestyle issues, particularly stories about ordinary Germans faced with extraordinary circumstances. Articles report from both both scientific and humanistic points of view. A unique feature of *Stern* is its bestseller list that ranks the week's 20 most popular books, films, DVDs, and music CDs in Germany. The electronic version includes the full text of the current issue and an archive of articles that have appeared in the past six months. As one of the most intellectually accessible magazines in Germany, *Stern* is highly recommended for academic and public libraries. URL: www.stern.de

3125. *Suomen Kuvalehti.* [ISSN: 0039-5552] 1916. w. EUR 49. Ed(s): Tapani Ruokanen. Otavamedia Ltd., Maistraatinportti 1, Helsinki, 00015, Finland; asiakaspalvelu@otavamedia.fi ; http://www.otavamedia.fi. Illus., adv. Circ: 101380. *Bk. rev.:* Number and length vary. *Aud.:* Ga, Ac.

In Finnish, from Finland. This newsmagazine is the most popular and well-respected in Finland. It is reminiscent of other newsmagazines known for their strong current-affairs reporting such as *Der Spiegel, Time, L'Express,* etc. Most articles focus on politics, economics, and culture, in Finland and abroad. Each issue includes ample advertising, and articles are illustrated with charts, graphs, statistics, and photos. Issues generally include book reviews. The online version provides the full text of articles in all issues since early 2003. Recommended for large public libraries and academic libraries that support Slavic, Scandinavian, or European Studies. URL: www.suomenkuvalehti.fi

■ JOURNALISM AND WRITING

Journalism/Writing/Pedagogy

Caroline M. Kent, Director of Research Support and Instruction, Shain Library, Connecticut College, New London, CT 06320; ckent@conncoll.edu

Introduction

Writing is changing. Writing is changing because *reading* is changing. We are all seeing it in our students, our children, and our patrons, but as of yet, we don't know, absolutely, what is happening. We do know *why* it is happening: The materials in online environments are altering how we read, and therefore how we write.

We know people are not writing as well as they once did. Sometimes it seems as if we are returning to a very old, post-medieval way of thinking about written language. That is, grammar and spelling are falling into a place in which creativity, change, and personalization all seem to be equally valued with, or more valued than, standardization. And exacerbating this is that copy editing is dying as a profession. Authors are expected to do much more of this themselves, and the result is that we have all found mistakes in major newspapers, and in books from good publishers.

The good news is that thanks to the web, reading and writing (of a sort) is increasingly pervasive in everyone's lives. In the last edition, I wrote "The web is in chaos." I would now say: The web *IS* chaos. It is an inconceivably huge melange of fascinating user-produced content.

Many of the publications listed in this section concentrate on conventional journalism and writing as we have known them, although you'll find that many of the articles in them explore new global and cooperative venues for self-expression (blogging) and community creation of documents (wikis). The writing journals listed here are directed more to individual practitioners, while the journalism titles tend more toward the academic. I look forward, with eager anticipation, to what the next two years will bring, and what I will report for you then!

Basic Periodicals

JOURNALISM. Ga: *American Journalism Review, Columbia Journalism Review, Editor and Publisher;* Ac: *Columbia Journalism Review, Editor and Publisher, Newspaper Research Journal.*

WRITING. Hs: *Writer's Digest;* Ga: *Poets & Writers Magazine, Writer's Digest;* Ac: *Poets & Writers Magazine.*

PEDAGOGY. Hs: *Communication, Journalism Education Today;* Ac: *Assessing Writing, Journalism and Mass Communication Educator.*

Basic Abstracts and Indexes

Communication Abstracts, Humanities Index, MLA International Bibliography, Readers' Guide to Periodical Literature.

3126. *Journal of Mass Communication and Journalism.* [ISSN: 2165-7912] 2011. m. Free. Ed(s): Clarence W Thomas. Omics Publishing Group, 5716 Corsa Ave, Ste 110, Westlake, Los Angeles, CA 91362; info@omicsonline.org; http://www.omicsonline.org. *Aud.:* Ac.

This new journal seeks to become "a broad-based journal [that] was founded on two key tenets: To publish the most exciting researches with respect to the subjects of [m]ass communication & [j]ournalism. Secondly, to provide a rapid turn-around time possible for reviewing and publishing, and to disseminate the articles freely for research, teaching[,] and reference purposes." In keeping with these aims, it is, in fact, an open-access journal, only available on the web and freely available. It seeks to contribute an international scope to the issues. Some recent articles are "The Rumors of Television's Demise Have Been Greatly Exaggerated: What the Data Say about the Future of Television Content in a

Child's Digital World" and "Photojournalism in Pakistan: Ethics and Responsibilities Analysis of Urdu Newspapers Front Pages." The OMICS web site provides metrics, Google Translator, varying available formats, links to Twitter, and Facebook. Is this what all journals may eventually look like? We might say...PLEASE. Recommended for academic libraries with collections for journalism and communications programs.

Journalism

3127. American Journalism. [ISSN: 0882-1127] 1982. q. GBP 252 (print & online eds.). Ed(s): Jim Martin. Taylor & Francis Inc., 325 Chestnut St, Ste 800, Philadelphia, PA 19106; customerservice@taylorandfrancis.com; http://www.tandfonline.com. Adv. Refereed. *Indexed:* A22, AmHI. *Bk. rev.:* 8-10, 500-1,000 words. *Aud.:* Ac.

This small scholarly journal always seems to be packed with fascinating articles—fascinating not just to media historians, but also to anyone interested in cultural history. Some recent article titles include "The Woman Citizen: A Study of How News Narratives Adapt to a Changing Social Environment," "Reporters and 'Willing Propagandists': AEF Correspondents Define Their Roles," and "A Light Out of This World: Awe, Anxiety, and Routinization in Early Nuclear Test Coverage, 1951-1953." The writing is livelier than that found in many scholarly journals (perhaps because of the journalistic orientation of many of the authors), but this in no way detracts from the serious nature of the publication. Given that its articles cross disciplinary lines, and given that the journal is well indexed, it should be purchased by any academic library with serious history programs and media-history collections.

3128. American Journalism Review (Online). . American Journalism Review, 1117 Journalism Bldg, University of Maryland, College Park, MD 20742; editor@ajr.umd.edu; http://www.ajr.org. *Bk. rev.:* 1-2, 700-1,000 words. *Aud.:* Hs, Ga, Ac.

This glossy little journal provides interesting articles that are newsy and accessible to most readers. It essentially consists of reporters reporting on reporting, and in this age of blogging and social media, that in itself can be very interesting. Some recent articles include "Journalism in the Crucible" and "The Bloomberg Juggernaut." There are regular columns such as "Free Press," "Online Frontier," "First Amendment Watch," and "Books." It is important to note that a substantial number of the opinion and editorial pieces are available online at *AJR*'s web site. This is a good choice for high school libraries, college and university libraries, and public libraries that serve the needs of active news journalists.

3129. Columbia Journalism Review. Incorporates: *More Magazine; Public Interest Alert; Media and Consumer.* [ISSN: 0010-194X] 1961. bi-m. USD 19.95 domestic; USD 27.95 foreign. Ed(s): Mike Hoyt, Brent Cunningham. Columbia University, Graduate School of Journalism, 2950 Broadway, 116th St, New York, NY 10027; http://www.journalism.columbia.edu. Illus., index, adv. Vol. ends: No. 6. Microform: PQC. *Indexed:* A01, A22, ABIn, ABS&EES, AmHI, B01, BRI, CBRI, CLI, F01, P02. *Bk. rev.:* 4-6, 100-300 words; 1-2, 1,000-2,000 words. *Aud.:* Hs, Ga, Ac.

This wonderfully accessible, well-edited journal also has an excellent web site where many of its articles are archived in full text. Coverage ranges from journalistic practice to articles of both national and international newsworthiness. It is also one of the publications that is taking on the issues of digital versus print reporting very effectively. Some recent article titles include "The Newspaper That Almost Seized the Future: *The San Jose Mercury News,* Silicon Valley's own daily, was poised to ride the digital whirlwind. What happened?" and "Pirate Radio, Mayan Style: Indigenous stations want to come in from the cold." The book review section is a particularly rich one. Each issue not only contains four to six short (100- to 300-word) book reports, but also one or two extensive, in-depth reviews. Despite its high academic pedigree, this magazine would be a very good choice not only for college and university libraries but also for high school libraries (at an excellent price!). Public libraries that serve populations with high interest in current events should also consider it.

3130. Editor & Publisher. Incorporates (1894-1927): *Fourth Estate;* (1892-1924): *Newspaperdom;* (1884-1907): *Journalist.* [ISSN: 0013-094X] 1901. m. Formerly (until 2004): w. USD 65 combined subscription domestic (print & online eds.); USD 85 combined subscription foreign (print & online eds.). Ed(s): Shawn Moynihan, Mark Fitzgerald. Editor & Publisher Co., Inc., 17782 Cowan, Ste A, Irvine, CA 92614; circulation@editorandpublisher.com; http://www.editorandpublisher.com. Illus., index, adv. Sample. Circ: 14700 Paid and controlled. Vol. ends: Dec. *Indexed:* A01, A22, ABIn, B01, B02, BRI, Chicano, P02. *Aud.:* Ac, Sa.

This glossy magazine lays claim to being "America's oldest journal covering the newspaper industry." Articles are newsy, sometimes rather light, and directed at industry leaders. In keeping with its format as news for executives, there are many short columns and departments. University libraries that address the needs of future journalists and editors should consider purchasing this magazine. It would also be appropriate for special industry libraries.

3131. Extra! [ISSN: 0895-2310] 1987. m. USD 19 domestic; USD 31 foreign. Ed(s): Julie Hollar, Jim Naureckas. Fairness & Accuracy In Reporting (F.A.I.R.), 112 W, 27th St, 10th Fl, New York, NY 10001; fair@fair.org; http://www.fair.org. Adv. *Aud.:* Ga, Ac.

FAIR (Fairness and Accuracy In Reporting) is an anti-censorship watch group, working to create balance in media reporting. Its main publication, *Extra!,* is edgy and fascinating and includes articles about current events and discussions of accuracy in news reporting. Some recent articles are "New Media—but Familiar Lack of Diversity[:] Women, people of color still marginalized online," "Gender Focus: Being Transgender in American Media," and "INetwork TV's Attention Deficit After Gadhafi." Like most news reporting, this publication is not scholarly in nature, but it should be added to any library collection that serves the needs of journalists or journalism students.

3132. Grassroots Editor: journal for newspeople. Formerly: *Grassroots.* [ISSN: 0017-3541] 1960. q. Free to members. International Society of Weekly Newspaper Editors, c/o Chad Stebbins, Institute of International Studies, Missouri Southern State College, Joplin, MO 64801; http://www.mssu.edu/iswne/. Illus., index, adv. Sample. Vol. ends: Winter. Microform: PQC. *Indexed:* A22. *Aud.:* Ac, Sa.

There's always been a special place in this country for the editors of small, local newspapers. Perhaps that place is mythological, but the idea of it remains an important American icon. This thoughtful publication is directed at the editorial and writing staffs of weekly community newspapers in the United States. Recent article titles include "Believers, nonbelievers and fence straddlers: Community newspapers and the Web in 2012" and "A radical thought: Ask folks to pay for the news they're reading." Public libraries in cities with community newspapers should consider purchasing this inexpensive publication. In addition, academic libraries that support serious journalism programs should buy it.

Index on Censorship. See Civil Liberties/Freedom of Expression and Information section.

3133. International Journal of Press / Politics. Formerly (until 2008): *The Harvard International Journal of Press / Politics.* [ISSN: 1940-1612] 1996. q. USD 548. Ed(s): Silvio Waisbord. Sage Publications, Inc., 2455 Teller Rd, Thousand Oaks, CA 91320; info@sagepub.com; http://www.sagepub.com. Illus., adv. Sample. Refereed. Vol. ends: Fall. Reprint: PSC. *Indexed:* A01, A22, B01, E01, P61, SSA. *Bk. rev.:* 4-6, 100-250 words, signed. *Aud.:* Ac.

This journal strives to address the academic needs of journalists, politicians, and political scientists. It is heavily academic, with well-written, well-referenced, refereed articles. In addition to the feature articles, issues often lead off with a substantive interview with a well-known practitioner. Recent articles include "Double Vision: Election News Coverage on Mainstream and Indigenous Television in New Zealand" and "Between Usefulness and Legitimacy: Media Coverage of Governmental Intervention during the Financial Crisis and Selected Effects." Academic libraries in colleges or universities with strong political science, communication, or journalism programs will want this title.

3134. *Journal of Mass Media Ethics: exploring questions of media morality.* [ISSN: 0890-0523] 1985. q. GBP 464 (print & online eds.). Ed(s): Lee Wilkins. Routledge, 325 Chestnut St, Ste 800, Philadelphia, PA 19106; customerservice@taylorandfrancis.com; http://www.tandfonline.com. Illus., adv. Sample. Refereed. Microform: PQC. Reprint: PSC. *Indexed:* A01, A22, AmHI, B01, BRI, E01, F01, P02, P61, SSA. *Bk. rev.:* Number and length vary. *Aud.:* Ac.

As we watch the growing confusion between reporting and media experts with government sources, we learn quickly that ethical behavior and moral positioning is critical for our journalists. This academic journal does not take positions, but rather includes articles that articulate conflicts and present and define ethical issues. Some recent articles include "The Ethics of Lobbying: Testing an Ethical Framework for Advocacy in Public Relations" and "Ethics Management in Public Relations: Practitioner Conceptualizations of Ethical Leadership, Knowledge, Training and Compliance." It includes a varying number of substantive book reviews, and case studies. Appropriate for academic libraries that serve communications and journalism departments.

3135. *Journalism & Mass Communication Quarterly.* Former titles (until 1995): *Journalism Quarterly;* (until 1928): *The Journalism Bulletin;* (until 1924): *American Association of Teachers of Journalism. Monthly News letter.* [ISSN: 1077-6990] 1915. q. USD 311. Ed(s): Dan Riffe. Sage Publications, Inc., 2455 Teller Rd, Thousand Oaks, CA 91320; info@sagepub.com; http://www.sagepub.com. Illus., adv. Refereed. Vol. ends: Winter. Microform: PQC. Reprint: PSC. *Indexed:* A01, A22, ABIn, ABS&EES, AmHI, B01, BAS, BRI, CBRI, F01, IBSS, MLA-IB, P02, P61, RILM. *Bk. rev.:* 12-25, 700-1,200 words. *Aud.:* Ac.

This scholarly publication "strives to be the flagship journal of the Association for Education in Journalism and Mass Communication." Its articles develop theory, introduce new ideas, and work to challenge the boundaries of the existing bodies of research. Its issues often contain themes, such as "Advertising Effects," "Copyright Law," and "Research Methodology." Some recent titles of articles include "You Really, Truly, Have to be There: Video Journalism as a Social and Material Construction" and "Framing Immigration: Geo-ethnic Context in California Newspapers." This is an interesting journal, filled with thoughtful, well-researched articles. Any library that serves academic programs in communications and journalism should subscribe to it.

3136. *Journalism Studies.* [ISSN: 1461-670X] 2000. bi-m. GBP 990 (print & online eds.). Ed(s): Bob Franklin, Bob Franklin. Routledge, 4 Park Sq, Milton Park, Abingdon, OX14 4RN, United Kingdom; subscriptions@tandf.co.uk; http://www.tandfonline.com. Adv. Sample. Refereed. Reprint: PSC. *Indexed:* A01, A22, E01, IBSS. *Bk. rev.:* 8-12, 800-1,200 words. *Aud.:* Ac.

This British journal, published in association with the European Journalism Training Association, is geared to serious journalists and journalism historians. Some recent articles include "Rethinking Journalistic Authority: Walter Cronkite and ritual in television news," "The New, Old Journalism: Narrative writing in contemporary newspapers," and "Truth and Objectivity in Journalism: Anatomy of an endless misunderstanding." It contains regular columns such as "Debate," "Reviews," and "Feature Review." Yes, this *is* a relatively expensive journal—expensive enough that some academic libraries will decide not to purchase it. But for university libraries that serve strong journalism programs, it is invaluable. Full text is available online.

3137. *News Media and the Law.* Supersedes (in 1977): *Press Censorship Newsletter.* [ISSN: 0149-0737] 1973. q. USD 30; USD 7.50 per issue. Ed(s): Kathleen Cullinan, Jane Kirtley. Reporters Committee for Freedom of the Press, 1101 Wilson Blvd, Ste 1100, Arlington, VA 22209; rcfp@rcfp.org; http://www.rcfp.org. Illus., index. Sample. Vol. ends: Fall. Microform: PQC. *Indexed:* A01, A22, CLI, L14, P02. *Aud.:* Sa.

This title's mission is to assist news reporters in understanding their legal rights and professional obligations. It covers particular stories in the news where the media is in court, and contains many articles that are educational in nature. Recent articles include "Stolen Valor: Are lies protected under the First Amendment?" and "Copyright police: Why Righthaven fell apart." This journal is important to libraries that address the education of journalists, and to those that address the needs of professional journalists.

3138. *Newspaper Research Journal.* [ISSN: 0739-5329] 1979. q. USD 70 (Individuals, USD 60). Ed(s): Dr. Sandy Utt, Dr. Elinor Kelley Grusin. University of Memphis, Department of Journalism, 300 Meeman Journalism Bldg, Memphis, TN 38152; https://umdrive.memphis.edu/g-journalism. Illus. Refereed. Vol. ends: Fall. Microform: PQC. *Indexed:* A01, A22, BRI, P02. *Bk. rev.:* 3-5, 500-750 words. *Aud.:* Ac.

This scholarly journal addresses the needs of both the journalism student and the serious media practitioner. Its articles are well written, interesting, and often practical. Sometimes an entire issue will be dedicated to a particular topic. In others, there is a wide selection of articles, such as "Photojournalists Enjoy Web Work, Additional Autonomy," "TV News Framing Supports Societal Poverty Solutions," and "Newspaper Editorial Stands on Broadcast Indecency Regulation: Profits Over Principles?" Libraries that support serious journalism programs should consider this journal.

3139. *Nieman Reports.* [ISSN: 0028-9817] 1947. q. USD 25 domestic; USD 35 foreign. Ed(s): Melissa Ludtke. Nieman Foundation, Harvard University, 1 Francis Ave, Cambridge, MA 02138; http://www.nieman.harvard.edu. Illus., index. Vol. ends: Dec. *Indexed:* A01, A22, ABIn, B01, BEL&L, BRI, P02. *Bk. rev.:* 3-6, 700-1,500 words, signed. *Aud.:* Ga, Ac.

This title publishes articles intended to be thought-provoking discussions for practitioners on current events and issues surrounding the profession of journalism. The breadth of its articles, however, should give it a much wider audience. Some recent titles include "To Kill a Story[:] After Chauncey Bailey was murdered, journalists banded together to finish his investigation," "How a tightly paywalled, social-media-ignoring, anti-copy-paste, gossipy news site became a dominant force in Nova Scotia," and "Aggregation is deep in journalism's DNA." It contains excellent book reviews and alumni reports for Harvard's Nieman fellows. This journal should be purchased by academic libraries that serve journalism programs, as well as ones with active public service programs. Public libraries that serve well-read audiences should also consider it.

3140. *Poynter: a group weblog by the sharpest minds in online media/ journalism/publishing.* Formerly (until 2012): *E-Media Tidbits.* d. Free. The Poynter Institute, 801 Third St South, St. Petersburg, FL 33701; http://www.poynter.org. *Aud.:* Ac, Sa.

The Poynter Institute, located in St. Petersburg, Florida, has played an increasingly important role in newspaper development in the United States. *Poynter* began its electronic life as a newsletter. It has now morphed into a blog entitled *E-Media Tidbits* and is an interesting example of how legitimate "self-publishing" can be. Both past issues and current entries are archived and available on the web site. It is also the penultimate example of a media web site that has gradually taken us from a traditional format all the way to a constantly updated site with excellent content. Discussions include current events, opinions on web and journalism issues, and interesting observations on the technology used by writers and journalists. Take a look. You will be fascinated! This site should be considered by any special or academic collection that supports a journalism program.

3141. *Quill (Greencastle): a magazine for the professional journalist.* [ISSN: 0033-6475] 1912. bi-m. USD 72. Ed(s): Scott Leadingham. Society of Professional Journalists, 3909 N Meridian St, Indianapolis, IN 46208; spj@spj.org; http://www.spj.org/. Illus., index, adv. Sample. Vol. ends: Dec. Microform: PQC. *Indexed:* A01, A22, ABIn, AmHI, B01, BRI, P02. *Aud.:* Sa.

Quill is the official publication of the Society of Professional Journalists, and as such it contains articles and commentary of wide interest. Its annual education issue will be of particular interest to academics, but many of the research articles would be accessible to any reader. Academic and special libraries that serve practicing journalists and journalism educators should purchase this title.

Writing

Creative Screenwriting. See Films section.

3142. *The Internet Writing Journal.* [ISSN: 1095-3973] 1997. m. Free. Writers Write, Inc., 100 Highland Park Village, Ste 200, Dallas, TX 75205; http://www.writerswrite.com/journal. Illus., adv. *Bk. rev.:* Number varies, 150-200 words. *Aud.:* Ga.

The Internet Writing Journal is billed as "The Online Monthly Magazine for Writers and Book Lovers since 1997." Like many online publications, it is a mix of frequently updated content and static information. The most interesting parts are the frequent interviews with well-known authors and the now-ubiquitous blog, "The IWJ Blog: Commentary on books, entertainment and writing." It also includes good book reviews and a number of secondary blogs and columns. There are copious advertisements, some of which appear to be featured sections or at least services recommended by the journal. There are also many classifieds and job listings, as well as information on events and awards. Back issues are archived. This a good site that has cleaned up its presentation and organization in the last two years. Highly recommended for public libraries that serve writing communities.

3143. *Mslexia: for women who write.* [ISSN: 1473-9399] 1999. q. GBP 27.50 domestic; GBP 34 in Europe; GBP 40 elsewhere. Mslexia Publications Ltd., PO Box 656, Newcastle upon Tyne, NE99 1PZ, United Kingdom; postbag@mslexia.co.uk. Illus., adv. Circ: 9000. *Bk. rev.:* Number and length vary. *Aud.:* Hs, Ga, Ac, Sa.

The term *Mslexia* was coined to express the condition of "women being unable to get into print easily." This interesting journal not only seeks to address this issue, but also to give women a forum so that they can get into print. It includes feature articles, relevant book reviews, new writing, and editorial opinion. It has an obvious British bias, but that should not preclude American libraries from buying it. It talks technology, writing technique, and the art of writing. Its content is thoughtful, sometimes edgy, and always interesting. Some recent articles include "The curse of the disappearing floor: Scarlett Thomas' worst mistakes" and "How to be a Great Reviewer." For academic libraries with good writing programs, and for large public libraries that serve the interests of a writing community.

3144. *Poets & Writers Magazine.* Formerly (until 1987): *Coda: Poets and Writers Newsletter.* [ISSN: 0891-6136] 1972. bi-m. USD 14.95 domestic; USD 24.95 Canada; USD 30.95 elsewhere. Ed(s): Suzanne Pettypiece, Mary Gannon. Poets & Writers, Inc., 90 Broad St, Ste 2100, New York, NY 10004; http://www.pw.org. Illus., adv. Circ: 71000. Microform: PQC. *Indexed:* A01, A22, AmHI, BRI, MLA-IB, P02. *Aud.:* Ga, Ac.

The content of this important publication is specifically directed to the interests of poets and writers of serious fiction; each issue contains interviews with important authors, some venerable, some new. There are articles directed at the creative writing process, although this is not a how-to journal for the uninitiated. Some recent articles have been "A Day in the Life of a Literary Agency: Behind the Scenes at Folio Literary Management," "Me, You, and Charles Yu: A Profile of Charles Yu," and "First Fiction 2012." Regular departments include "News and Trends," "The Literary Life," and "The Practical Writer." There is an extensive and invaluable "Resources" section that includes grants and awards, conferences and residencies, and classifieds. All academic libraries should subscribe to this journal, and public libraries that serve populations of writers should also have it.

Scr(i)pt: Where Film Begins. See Films section.

3145. *Technical Communication Quarterly.* Formerly (until 1992): *Technical Writing Teacher.* [ISSN: 1057-2252] 1973. q. GBP 245 (print & online eds.). Ed(s): Amy Koerber. Routledge, 325 Chestnut St, Ste 800, Philadelphia, PA 19106; customerservice@taylorandfrancis.com; http://www.tandfonline.com. Illus., adv. Sample. Refereed. Vol. ends: Fall. Microform: PQC. Reprint: PSC. *Indexed:* A01, A22, ABIn, B01, E01, MLA-IB, P02, PsycInfo. *Bk. rev.:* 1-2, 1,000 words. *Aud.:* Ac, Sa.

This title publishes refereed articles on teaching and research methodologies, historical research, ethics, practical methodologies, digital applications, etc.—all as they relate to technical communication practices. Recent titles include "From the Workplace to Academia: Nontraditional Students and the Relevance of Workplace Experience in Technical Writing Pedagogy" and

"Moving From Artifact to Action: A Grounded Investigation of Visual Displays of Evidence during Medical Deliberations." Any academic library that supports a technical writing program should have this journal.

3146. *The Writer.* [ISSN: 0043-9517] 1887. m. USD 32.95 domestic; USD 42.95 Canada; USD 44.95 elsewhere. Madavor Media, Llc., 85 Quincy Ave, Ste 2, Quincy, MA 02169; http://www.madavor.com. Illus., index, adv. Vol. ends: Dec. *Indexed:* A01, A22, AmHI, BRI, C37, MASUSE, MLA-IB, P02. *Bk. rev.:* Number and length vary. *Aud.:* Hs, Ga, Ac.

Although not as substantive as *Writer's Digest* or *Poets and Writers*, this publication is well designed and has great appeal. It contains columns of general interest, such as "Dear Writer" and "How I Write." The articles are much more in the how-to vein than those in the more serious literary writing magazines, articles such as "Third-person limited offers flexibility." There are also book reviews and classified ads of interest to writers. The magazine's primary market is probably beginning writers, and it is therefore best placed in high school, public, and college libraries.

3147. *The Writer's Chronicle.* Former titles (until 1998): *A W P Chronicle;* (until 1989): *A W P Newsletter.* [ISSN: 1529-5443] 197?. bi-m. Free to members; Non-members, USD 20. Ed(s): David W Fenza, Supriya Bhatnagar. Association of Writers & Writing Programs, Mail Stop 1E3, George Mason University, Fairfax, VA 22030; awp@awpwriter.org; http://www.awpwriter.org. Illus., adv. Sample. Circ: 32000. *Indexed:* AmHI. *Aud.:* Ga, Ac.

The Writer's Chronicle is aimed at a broad audience, with its "information designed to enlighten, inform, and entertain writers, editors, students, and teachers of writing." It contains many interviews and feature articles that have wide appeal, as well as actual fiction and poetry. Some recent articles include "What Writers Need to Know About Electronic Publishing," ".Anything! How the Next Dotcom Boom Might Cost Writers More Than Just Their Money," and "Shirley Jackson & Her Demon Lover." Academic libraries and any public library that supports a population of creative writers should consider this journal.

3148. *Writer's Digest.* Formerly (until 1921): *Successful Writing.* [ISSN: 0043-9525] 1920. 8x/yr. USD 29.96; USD 5.99 newsstand/cover. Ed(s): Jessica Strawser. F + W Media Inc., 38 E 29th St, 3rd Fl, New York, NY 10016; contact_us@fwmedia.com; http://www.fwmedia.com/. Illus., adv. Circ: 66932 Paid. Microform: MIM; PQC. *Indexed:* A22, ASIP, BRI, IHTDI, P02. *Aud.:* Hs, Ga, Ac.

If a library can purchase only one writing journal, *Writer's Digest* should be it. It contains a huge amount of information on all types of nontechnical writing, interviews, and feature articles on issues of interest to writers such as book doctoring and copyright. There is market information, classifieds, and advertisements galore. Its glossy format is newsy and would be interesting even to the non-writer. An example of a recent feature article is "Writer for Hire, Your Guide to Opportunities that Pay Off Big." All public libraries and academic libraries that serve writing programs should have this title.

3149. *Writing That Works: the business communications report.* Formed by the merger of: *Desktop Publishing Users' Report; Communications Concepts;* Which was formerly: *Quick Report; Writing Concepts;* Which incorporated (1990-1995): *Hospital Editors' Idea Exchange;* (in Mar. 1995): *Editors' Forum; Communications Manager;* Which was formerly (until 1990): *Communications Concepts.* 19??. bi-m. USD 119. Ed(s): John De Lellis. Communications Concepts, Inc., 7481 Huntsman Blvd, Ste 720, Springfield, VA 22153; cci.dayton@pobox.com; http://www.communication-concepts.com. *Aud.:* Ga.

Everything that many writers hate about writing for business is clearly outlined as requirements for publication in this journal: quick, easy to read, short sentences, bulleted points. As an author of serious fiction, my teeth gnash as I read this publication. However, there are a large number of people in this country who are responsible for clear communications in a business setting. *Writing That Works* is a small but very useful publication that would fulfill many needs for corporate writers. It specifically outlines (neatly bulleted, of course) the types of articles it publishes: techniques, style issues (editing, grammar, usage), publication management, PR and marketing strategy, and online publishing. For public libraries that serve large business communities.

Written By. See Films section.

Pedagogy

3150. *Across the Disciplines.* Formed by the merger of (2000-2004): *Academic Writing;* (1994-2004): *Language and Learning Across the Disciplines.* [ISSN: 1554-8244] 2004. irreg. Free to qualified personnel. Ed(s): Michael Pemberton, Sharon Quiroz. W A C Clearinghouse, c/o Michael Pemberton, Department of Writing and Linguistics, PO Box 8026, Statesboro, GA 30460; Mike.Palmquist@ColoState.edu; http://wac.colostate.edu/. Refereed. *Indexed:* MLA-IB. *Bk. rev.:* Occasional, 1,000-1,500 words. *Aud.:* Ac.

"*Across the Disciplines,* a refereed journal devoted to language, learning, and academic writing, publishes articles relevant to writing and writing pedagogy in all their intellectual, political, social, and technological complexity." Despite that mouthful of words, this is an excellent web-based publication that is actually now an amalgam of two former e-journals, *Academic Writing* and *Language and Learning Across the Disciplines.* Archives for the current and the previous journals are all available online. The interesting content includes discussions of both academic writing and pedagogy. It is predominantly a pedagogical publication, but since most academics teach writing in the context of courses, it should have broad appeal. Some titles from recent issues include "The (In)Visible World of Teaching Assistants in the Disciplines: Preparing TAs to Teach Writing" and "Connected, Disconnected, or Uncertain: Student Attitudes about Future Writing Contexts and Perceptions of Transfer from First Year Writing to the Disciplines." For those of us who live with the complexities of traditional academic language, and who watch our students and faculty struggle to write between conflicting traditions on interdisciplinary topics, this journal fills a significant gap. Any academic library of merit should consider linking to this title.

3151. *Assessing Writing.* [ISSN: 1075-2935] 1994. q. EUR 372. Ed(s): L Hamp-Lyons. Pergamon, The Blvd, Langford Ln, E Park, Kidlington, OX5 1GB, United Kingdom; JournalsCustomerServiceEMEA@elsevier.com; http://www.elsevier.com. Adv. Sample. Refereed. Reprint: PSC. *Indexed:* A01, A22, ERIC, MLA-IB. *Bk. rev.:* 1-3, 1,000-2,000 words. *Aud.:* Ac.

This substantive refereed journal strives to publish articles on writing and the teaching of writing from an international perspective. That makes it a somewhat more theoretical journal than a "how-to" publication, but does not detract from its quality. Recent article titles include "Placing data in the hands of discipline-specific decision makers: Campus-wide writing program assessment," "Rater effects: Ego engagement in rater decision-making," and "Challenges in assessing the development of writing ability: Theories, constructs and methods." Given the journal's cost, many academic libraries will choose not to purchase it. But for those with strong writing programs, this is a title worth considering.

3152. *Communication: Journalism Education Today.* Former titles (until 1998): *C: J E T;* (until 1977): *Communication: Journalism Education Today;* Which incorporated (19??-1968): *J E A Digest.* [ISSN: 1536-9129] 1967. q. Free to members. Ed(s): Bradley Wilson. Journalism Education Association, Inc., 103 Kedzie Hall, Kansas State University, Manhattan, KS 66506; jea@spub.ksu.edu; http://www.jea.org. Illus., adv. *Indexed:* A22. *Aud.:* Hs, Ac.

Communication: Journalism Education Today is published by the Journalism Education Association, whose members range from high school- through university-level journalism practitioners; but this journal's focus is on the younger student. It includes some research articles, but also many pieces on curriculum development, lesson planning, and tips for teachers and young practitioners. Some recent articles include "Teaching with Facebook" and

"Working in social media." Recommended without reservation for high school libraries; college-level libraries should evaluate it from a sample issue. Some academic libraries with strong teacher-training programs should also consider its purchase.

3153. *Computers and Composition: an international journal.* [ISSN: 8755-4615] 1983. 4x/yr. EUR 466. Ed(s): Kristine L Blair. Elsevier Ltd, 32 Jamestown Rd, Camden, London, NW1 7BY, United Kingdom; corporate.sales@elsevier.com; http://www.elsevier.com. Adv. Sample. Refereed. Vol. ends: No. 18. Reprint: PSC. *Indexed:* A01, A22, CompLI, MLA-IB. *Bk. rev.:* 1-4, 2,500-3,000 words. *Aud.:* Ac.

This journal "is devoted to exploring the use of computers in writing classes, writing programs, and writing research." It looks at these issues from pedagogical, psychological, and social points of view. Articles may discuss legal or ethical issues or interface design. In keeping with the journal's charge, the editors also maintain an excellent web site that includes not only a complete archive but also supplementary materials and discussions, including blogs on various issues. Some recent articles include "Networking, Storytelling and Knowledge Production in First-Year Writing," "The posthuman grant application," and "Film School for Slideware: Film, Comics, and Slideshows as Sequential Art." Any academic library that serves a school of education or writing programs should purchase this title.

3154. *Journalism & Mass Communication Educator.* Formerly (until 1995): *The Journalism Educator.* [ISSN: 1077-6958] 1958. q. USD 214. Ed(s): Dane S Claussen. Sage Publications, Inc., 2455 Teller Rd, Thousand Oaks, CA 91320; info@sagepub.com; http://www.sagepub.com. Illus., index. Refereed. Vol. ends: Winter. Microform: CIS; PQC. Reprint: PSC. *Indexed:* A01, A22, BRI, ERIC, P02, P61, SSA. *Bk. rev.:* 10-12, 250-500 words. *Aud.:* Ac.

This title focuses on issues of interest to the faculty of communications and journalism programs. Each issue includes research articles and some focused book reviews, often following a theme. Some recent articles include "Poynter's News Delivers What You Expect, Your Own Institution Perhaps Not" and "The Personality of Plagiarism." Recommended for academic libraries that serve communications and journalism programs.

■ LABOR AND INDUSTRIAL RELATIONS

See also Business; Disabilities; Economics; and Occupations and Careers sections.

Terence K. Huwe, Director of Library and Information Resources, Institute for Research on Labor and Employment, University of California–Berkeley, 2521 Channing Way, #5555, Berkeley, CA 94720-5555; thuwe@library.berkeley.edu

Introduction

Labor and industrial relations is an area of study that looks at the past, present, and future of work and working life. It has its roots in the nineteenth century, when the Industrial Revolution triggered the emergence of Marxism and socialism, and the concept of unbridled capitalism rewrote the social contract of the times. As labor-management struggles over wages and conditions of work intensified, "labor market institutions" were created. These include unions, government agencies that regulate work, and employer coalitions (such as the Pacific Maritime Association) that do battle with organized labor. These institutions have become part of society, and remain vibrant during the twenty-first century.

Since World War II, the field has been evolving rapidly, just as the nature of work has been constantly changing. Labor and industrial relations research is now concerned not only with labor-management issues, but with every aspect of employment. The field attracts a large roster of sociologists, economists, business professors, city planners, demographers, anthropologists, engineers (studying occupational safety), public health professors, and historians. All of these specialists find common interest in studying how work shapes history and our everyday lives.

One of the enduring legacies of this field is its identification of the concept of the "employment relationship." Just as relationships with family and friends govern private life, the employment relationship encompasses the social (and legal) contracts that bind people and their employers together. Understanding the employment relationship and how to manage it has become a central and constant challenge for modern business. The employment relationship has continued to be a powerful paradigm, and it remains applicable both to the traditional and the "digital" work styles that we now take for granted.

The most important trends in industrial relations are often front-page news. "Globalization" is regarded as an employment issue, with job security, job growth, and protectionism driving international debate. "Offshoring" of employees remains a constant, and U.S. manufacturers have migrated much of their factory capacity to Mexico and other lower-wage nations. It is not uncommon for various nations such as China, Mexico, and Brazil to compete as sites for major new facilities. This poses a double-edged sword for organized labor. On one hand, many unions are against offshoring, NAFTA, and unbridled free trade. Yet on the other hand, American trade unionists are reaching out to workers abroad, looking for mutual gains. During 2011, an interesting new trend appeared: repatriation of jobs that were sent overseas. American manufacturing has grown in recent times, and employers are now seeing benefits in building the domestic workforce, with an emphasis on skilled labor at a high level of expertise.

The overall percentage of unionized workers in the United States has been steadily dropping for years, and labor has been trying new and daring moves to turn the trend around. These include organizing new immigrants and considering "associate membership" for non-union workers.

Collaboration between labor groups and broader social movements is a growing phenomenon, with the "green" movement leading the way. Indeed, labor unions were early collaborators with environmentalists, in part because the link between occupational health and pollution is so evident. Unions have also been exploring ways to partner with the nonprofit organizations that reach out to new immigrants.

This concerted effort to build broad coalitions is a calculated response to a long, difficult period for unions, which has been marked by ideological battles between pro- and anti-union thinkers. "Free market" proponents have long argued that the economy should be unfettered and allowed to evolve without organized labor's input. During 2010 and 2011, the states of Wisconsin, Ohio, and Indiana saw conservative initiatives that were aimed at reducing the power of collective bargaining by public employees. This move triggered a recall election for the governor of Wisconsin, and also triggered new research about the impact of employee costs on state budgets. The ensuing debate has been rich and vocal, and continues at the time of this writing.

The new ferment has contributed to a resurgence in the relevance of "center" and "center-left" political thinkers who study labor issues. Industrial relations researchers tend to favor various types of labor-management cooperation, because study in the field requires comprehensive assessments of all stakeholders, including workers, managers, shareholders, and even capital markets. Some experts argue that a healthy labor movement is in fact a crucial social institution, and that unions have a rightful role that promotes social stability.

As a result of the dynamic conditions facing the employment sector, researchers are best served by a three-pronged approach in their discovery process. The most effective searches encompass (1) journals; (2) union publications, social advocacy publications, and the general press; and (3) open-web publications from a wide variety of nongovernmental organizations. The latter includes groups like Common Cause, the Economic Policy Institute, LabourStart, and the Brookings Institution, to name a few.

The core resources of labor and industrial relations have been stable even as new entrants appear at a steady pace, mostly in a multidisciplinary context. Cornell's *Industrial and Labor Relations Review* and Berkeley's *Industrial Relations: A Journal of Economy and Society* continue as the most prestigious journals of peer-reviewed literature. Scholarship found in these publications is often dense, yet most issues include in-depth analyses of workforce events and trends, such as minimum and "living" wages. *New Labor Forum* (founded in 1997) and *Working USA* take a more populist approach. They focus on real-world issues in plain English, challenging the reader to look at everyday working life with new eyes. The *Daily Labor Report,* published by Bloomberg BNA, is a key practitioner's tool for labor lawyers and human resources professionals. It offers extensive information on all aspects of work, in daily

print issues and also online. The labor movement has embraced the Internet, and many substantive, content-rich web sites have proliferated accordingly.

Labor and employment issues are deeply affected by the law. Cases are litigated in court, and also before "administrative law judges," who review the regulations of a large number of agencies such as the Equal Employment Opportunity Commission, the National Labor Relations Board, etc. Consequently, there are many high-quality legal publications that are aimed both at academics and attorneys. These include *Labor Law Journal, Labor Notes, Employee Benefits Journal,* and the *Daily Labor Report.* Most of these titles are available online, although "moving walls" will apply in some cases for resources like JSTOR and other vendors with licensing strictures. Many larger aggregators of digital resources, themselves a rapidly evolving breed, offer comprehensive access to the literature of labor and industrial relations.

Finally, since the turn of the century, web-based government information has become much more accessible and easy to use. The U.S. Bureau of Labor Statistics (www.bls.gov) pays close attention to its web site, constantly improving its search functionality. In recent years, the BLS site has become much more effective in pinpointing hard-to-find statistics (such as the monthly employment turnover rate). In recent years, many information-rich government web sites have added analytical tools that enable research to extract and manipulate statistics directly, which is an interesting trend and is well worth watching over time. Unionstats.com (www.unionstats.com) has vastly eased the challenge of building tabular data about the workforce. It is also worth noting that many libraries provide finding tools such as web "pathfinders." These are very useful subject guides to the literature of industrial relations, and often they lead to the best sources of quality information on the open web.

Basic Periodicals

Hs: *Bulletin of Labour Statistics;* Ga: *America at Work, LaborNet, Labor's Heritage, U.S. Bureau of Labor Statistics. Monthly Labor Review;* Ac: *Bulletin of Labour Statistics, Industrial and Labor Relations Review, Labor History, LaborNet, World of Work;* Sa: *Benefits Quarterly, Employee Relations Law Journal, Japan Labour Bulletin.*

Basic Abstracts and Indexes

ABI/INFORM, America: History and Life, Business Periodicals Index, Econlit, Expanded Academic ASAP, PAIS International, Social Sciences Index, Sociological Abstracts.

3155. A F L - C I O Now. 2006. w. Free. A F L - C I O, 815 16th St, N W, Washington, DC 20006; http://www.aflcio.org. *Aud.:* Ga, Ac, Sa.

AFL-CIO Now has morphed from a free weekly e-newsletter into a much more interactive blog. The blog continues to highlight various initiatives and political objectives of the AFL-CIO, along with other union movement news. Articles are archived by subject, with headings including "Corporate Watch," "Learn About Unions," and "Legislation & Politics." Political reporting about congressional initiatives and campaigns has been increased, which makes this blog a good starting point to learn about current events in the world of labor. The content is primarily about the AFL-CIO and does not cover other organizations.

Academy of Management Journal. See Management, Administration, and Human Resources/General section.

3156. Benefits Quarterly. [ISSN: 8756-1263] 1985. q. Free to members; Non-members, USD 125. Ed(s): Jack L VanDerhei. International Society of Certified Employee Benefit Specialists, Inc., 18700 W Bluemound Rd, PO Box 209, Brookfield, WI 53008; iscebs@iscebs.org; http://www.iscebs.org. Illus., index, adv. Sample. Circ: 13000. Vol. ends: Dec. *Indexed:* A01, A22, ABIn, AgeL, B01, B02, BRI. *Bk. rev.:* 6-8, 200-500 words. *Aud.:* Sa.

This journal aims to provide a full-service news resource for all practitioners and students studying benefits and compensation. Articles offer a range of in-depth analyses of employee benefits issues. The text features pithy "pull quotes" and is formatted effectively for quick scanning. Articles explore breaking trends and new developments, frequently including case studies or strategic suggestions for practitioners. The editors also analyze legislative developments and court rulings that affect compensation issues. "Legal Update" and "Employee Benefits Bookshelf" features help readers stay current on legal news and new publications.

3157. *Berkeley Journal of Employment and Labor Law: a continuation of industrial relations law journal.* Formerly (until 1993): *Industrial Relations Law Journal.* [ISSN: 1067-7666] 1976. s-a. USD 47 USD 25 per issue. Ed(s): Brandon Rees, Ed Takashima. University of California, Berkeley, School of Law, Boalt Hall Rm 5, Berkeley, CA 94720-7200; journalpublications@law.berkeley.edu; http://www.law.berkeley.edu. Illus., index. Sample. Refereed. Circ: 650 Paid. Vol. ends: Dec. Microform: WSH; PQC. Reprint: WSH. *Indexed:* A22, ABIn, B01, B02, BRI, CLI, L14. *Bk. rev.:* Number and length vary. *Aud.:* Ac, Sa.

This law review has built a reputation for pragmatic writing that is aimed at attorneys who may not be employment law specialists, but need quality information on the law. The editors also publish articles with the educated citizen-researcher in mind. Articles cover all aspects of labor law, including "discrimination, traditional labor law, the public sector, international and comparative labor law, benefits, and workforce participation." The editors make an effort to address issues in a balanced fashion, with both management and labor perspectives taken into consideration. The journal provides a useful analysis of recent legal developments. Some issues deal with a single topic, such as the impact of NAFTA. The editors also survey labor and employment literature and provide abstracts of important articles in other journals.

3158. *British Journal of Industrial Relations: an international journal of employment relation.* [ISSN: 0007-1080] 1963. q. GBP 454. Ed(s): John Godard, Thomas Gaston. Wiley-Blackwell Publishing Ltd., The Atrium, Southern Gate, Chichester, PO19 8SQ, United Kingdom; customer@wiley.com; http://www.wiley.com/. Illus., index, adv. Sample. Refereed. Vol. ends: Dec. Reprint: PSC. *Indexed:* A22, ABIn, B01, B02, BAS, BRI, E01, EconLit, ErgAb, FR, IBSS, JEL, P61, SSA. *Aud.:* Ac, Sa.

This journal addresses a broad spectrum of trends in the field of industrial relations, and has changed with the times to reflect the evolving nature of the field. Its articles balance empirical studies and theoretical issues, underscoring the fact that the field is composed of many academic disciplines, chiefly economics, business, and sociology. The editors argue that traditional styles of collective bargaining now compete with "new forms of management, new methods of pay determination, and changes in government policies." Each issue has four or five substantive articles and several shorter features. Most authors provide extensive tables and charts to support their arguments. This journal is aimed at academics who have an awareness of the deeper issues in industrial relations, and therefore it may not be easily accessible to the casual reader.

3159. *Bulletin of Labour Statistics: supplementing the annual data presented in the Year Book of Labour Statistics.* [ISSN: 0007-4950] 1965. 4x/yr. CHF 105; USD 84. I L O, 4 Route des Morillons, Geneva, 1211, Switzerland; ilo@ilo.org; http://www.ilo.org. Illus., index. Vol. ends: No. 4. *Aud.:* Ac, Sa.

A tripartite agency of the United Nations, the International Labour Organization (ILO) is led by a board composed of management, labor, and government. The ILO is an important source of information about global labor trends, and this bulletin is one of its most important publications. It provides country-level data on employment, unemployment, hours of work, wages, and the consumer price index. It is also one of the few publications that offers meaningful international comparisons of various national workforce issues. Coverage of Eastern Europe and the former Soviet republics has increased its value as a ready-reference tool for statistics seekers. Each issue features a couple of in-depth articles about statistical data issues, as most nations collect data by various means. The ILO publishes articles in English, French, and Spanish.

3160. *Daily Labor Report.* Former titles: *Daily Economic Reports on Current Trends Affecting Management and Labor; Washington Daily Reporter: Labor Section; Washington Daily Reporter System: Daily Labor Report.* [ISSN: 0418-2693] 1941. d. USD 11476. Ed(s): Victoria Roberts. Bloomberg B N A, 1801 S Bell St, Arlington, VA 22202; bnaplus@bna.com; http://www.bna.com. Sample. *Bk. rev.:* Short listings of new publications. *Aud.:* Ac, Sa.

The *Daily Labor Report* is published by Bloomberg BNA. When Bloomberg acquired the Bureau of National Affairs, Inc., it became one of the leading players in labor law publishing. The publication appears every working day of the year, and is designed to provide labor lawyers, unionists, and government officials with all the information they need about the world of work. It is broken into several separately paginated sections (e.g., A1, B1, C1, etc.) that cover distinct areas of news. These include headlines, legal developments, regulatory developments, new reports and publications of interest, and the full text of important legal opinions. The editorial direction of this journal has been very active and customer-focused, and as a result, this is a "must have" for labor lawyers. Moreover, it covers the entire United States, with detailed information at the state and local level. The *DLR* often publishes groundbreaking new studies that are issued by government agencies and think tanks. When it does so, it always includes URLs, telephone numbers, and even names of individuals to contact. Subscriptions include print-only and print-plus-digital, and rates are high, as one expects in the legal market. It is worth noting that the *DLR* web version is updated throughout the day, offering real-time news. This publication is essential for lawyers and practitioners, but would also make a very useful addition to a central reference collection that is heavily used by patrons with legal and employment questions.

3161. *Dispute Resolution Journal.* Formerly (until 1993): *Arbitration Journal.* [ISSN: 1074-8105] 1937. q. USD 150 domestic; USD 164 Canada; USD 183 elsewhere. Ed(s): Susan Zuckerman. American Arbitration Association, 1633 Broadway, 10th Fl, New York, NY 10019; websitemail@adr.org; http://www.adr.org/. Illus., index, adv. Vol. ends: Dec. Microform: PQC. *Indexed:* A22, ABIn, B01, B02, BRI, CLI, L14, SD. *Aud.:* Ga, Ac, Sa.

Alternative dispute resolution (ADR) has emerged as a viable legal strategy to apply, instead of starting out with, litigation. The workplace generates a hefty percentage of all lawsuits, and therefore ADR is often cast as a better alternative to litigation. *Dispute Resolution Journal* is published by the American Arbitration Association, and highlights new developments in the field as well as creative strategies for keeping litigants out of court. Articles explore negotiation, mediation, final offer arbitration, and any other alternative to impasse. The journal also explores industrial trends, including developments in construction, technology, commerce, and health care. Since federal law allows for public employees to utilize alternative dispute resolution, public-sector issues figure highly in the article mix. Not all contributors are attorneys; expert authors hail from international relations, business, finance, construction, insurance, and technology. The articles are incisive and include good footnotes that facilitate further research. This title would be an important addition for law libraries, business libraries, and general social science collections.

3162. *Economic and Industrial Democracy: an international journal.* [ISSN: 0143-831X] 1980. q. USD 1160. Ed(s): Jan Ottosson, Lars Magnusson. Sage Publications Ltd., 1 Oliver's Yard, 55 City Rd, London, EC1Y 1SP, United Kingdom; info@sagepub.co.uk; http://www.uk.sagepub.com. Adv. Sample. Refereed. Reprint: PSC. *Indexed:* A22, ABIn, B01, BAS, E01, EconLit, IBSS, JEL, P61, RiskAb, SSA. *Bk. rev.:* Number and length vary. *Aud.:* Ga, Ac.

This journal has an international scope but also includes substantive articles about U.S. conditions. The prefatory material for each paper includes an abstract and a set of keywords, facilitating a handy, item-level guide. Each issue includes at least one book review. Recent issues have focused on large-scale topics, such as job insecurity in Europe, with many perspectives on the topic. Recent articles include "High Commitment Management Strategies Re-examined: The Case for Indian Call Centres," "Non-Union Employee Representation, Union Avoidance and the Managerial Agenda," and "Soft Skill and Employability: Evidence from UK Retail."

3163. *Employee Benefit Plan Review.* Incorporates (1999-2003): *Compensation & Benefits Report;* (1984-2002): *Compensation & Benefits Management.* [ISSN: 0013-6808] 1946. m. USD 359; USD 45 per issue. Ed(s): Steven A Meyerowitz. Aspen Publishers, Inc., 76 Ninth Ave, 7th Fl, New York, NY 10011; ASPEN-CustomerService@wolterskluwer.com; https://www.aspenpublishers.com. Illus., index. Vol. ends: Jun. Microform: PQC. *Indexed:* A22, ABIn, AgeL, B01, B02, BRI. *Aud.:* Ga, Ac, Sa.

This publication is top-ranked in its area of specialization, and is written both for specialists and generalists. Academics can find useful real-world case studies here, and human resources practitioners can rely upon it to stay current with employee benefits developments. In addition to a strong focus on current practice, the editors include a healthy balance of articles that address new and emerging trends that may not yet have hit the workplace. Issues are organized by topic, and include sections on laws, regulations, and new practices. Legal news is aimed at the non-lawyer, but does not oversimplify the nature of the legal issues to a fault. Most contributors are human resources professionals, with some academics contributing "think" pieces now and then. This title is very useful for labor, business, and law libraries, but it would also be useful for central reference collections, particularly when county law libraries are not located nearby.

3164. *Employee Relations Law Journal.* Incorporates (2000-2002): *Employee Rights Quarterly.* [ISSN: 0098-8898] 1975. q. USD 499. Ed(s): Steven A Meyerowitz. Aspen Publishers, Inc., 76 Ninth Ave, 7th Fl, New York, NY 10011; ASPEN-CustomerService@wolterskluwer.com; https://www.aspenpublishers.com. Illus., index. Vol. ends: Spring. Microform: WSH; PMC; PQC. *Indexed:* A22, ABIn, B01, B02, BLI, BRI, CLI, L14, SD. *Aud.:* Ac, Sa.

This journal targets human resources managers, in-house counsel, and employment law specialists, and offers a comprehensive means for them to keep up with the rapid pace of change in workplace issues. Authors strike an analytical and practical note without sinking too far into technical discourse. Well-known professionals contribute signed, short "Literature Review" essays. The journal covers a wide range of "hot" labor issues, including personnel management techniques, legal compliance, and court cases. Recent articles address such topics as family medical leave, sexual harassment, age discrimination, and alternative dispute resolution. This is the sort of publication that could be consulted for quick reading and "brushing up," although it also offers some real substance for those moments when time allows a more thoughtful perusal. This journal is a top choice for selectors who must make difficult decisions with limited funds.

3165. *European Journal of Industrial Relations.* [ISSN: 0959-6801] 1995. q. USD 1165. Ed(s): Richard Hyman. Sage Publications Ltd., 1 Oliver's Yard, 55 City Rd, London, EC1Y 1SP, United Kingdom; info@sagepub.co.uk; http://www.uk.sagepub.com. Adv. Sample. Refereed. Reprint: PSC. *Indexed:* A22, B01, E01, EconLit, IBSS, JEL, P02, P61, RiskAb, SSA. *Bk. rev.:* Occasional. *Aud.:* Ac.

This journal publishes substantive articles on contemporary issues that affect European labor. Recent articles touch on nearly every aspect of working life in the European Union, which is grappling with the challenges of expansion, monetary policy, and the impact of free movement of workers among member states. Recent articles include "Social Risk Protection in Collective Agreements: Evidence from the Netherlands" and "Cross-Border Cooperation Under Asymmetry: The Case of an Interregional Trade Union Council."

3166. *Government Employee Relations Report.* [ISSN: 0017-260X] 1963. w. USD 1944. Ed(s): James F Fitzpatrick. Bloomberg B N A, 1801 S Bell St, Arlington, VA 22202; bnaplus@bna.com; http://www.bna.com. Sample. *Indexed:* A22. *Bk. rev.:* Number and length vary. *Aud.:* Ac, Sa.

Government Employee Relations Report, another publication of Bloomberg BNS, offers one-stop news as well as qualitative and quantitative information for government unions and management. It is separately paginated (A1, B1, C1, etc.) by topics, which include legal news, federal news, collective bargaining, feature reports, and more. The editors cover all levels of government, so this publication is a great source for finding out what's happening at the state and local levels in faraway districts. Reporting is balanced between labor and management perspectives. Government information collections, public policy libraries, and law libraries would all benefit from this publication.

3167. *I C F T U Online.* 200?. d. International Confederation of Free Trade Unions (I C F T U), 5 Boulevard du Roi Albert II, Brussels, 1210, Belgium; http://www.icftu.org. *Aud.:* Ga, Sa.

The International Confederation of Free Trade Unions (ICFTU) represents 157 million trade union members in 148 countries and territories. This online resource replaces their previous published version. The resource provides information on actions and activism on numerous fronts, such as condemnation of labor rights abuses in Mexico, child labor abuse in Kyrgyzstan, and fighting for worker rights in Indonesia. Broader international news that affects workers shows up as well, such as developments in AIDS prevention. Content can be sorted by date, country, subject, or type.

3168. *Indian Journal of Industrial Relations: a review of economic & social development.* [ISSN: 0019-5286] 1964. q. INR 1800. Ed(s): N K Nair. Publishing India Group, Plot No-56, 1st Fl, Deepali Enclave, Near Deepali Chowk, New Dehi, 110 034, India. Refereed. Circ: 865 Paid. *Indexed:* B01, B02, BAS, BRI, IBSS, P61, SSA. *Bk. rev.:* Number and length vary. *Aud.:* Ac, Sa.

A preeminent publishing vehicle for South Asian academics who study the workplace, this journal encapsulates the latest industrial relations research in the world's most populous democracy. It includes full-length articles that focus on issues such as best practices, collective bargaining, and management strategies; and such more specific topics as new high-technology employment in India. It also provides case studies and book reviews. The scholarship is solid and provides a closer look at the conditions of work in the developing world.

3169. *Industrial and Labor Relations Review.* [ISSN: 0019-7939] 1947. q. USD 250 (print & online eds.) Individuals, USD 70 (print & online eds.); Free to members). Ed(s): Brian Keeling, Tove H Hammer. Cornell University, New York State School of Industrial and Labor Relations, 158 Ives Hall, Ithaca, NY 14853; ilrconferencecenter@cornell.edu; http://www.ilr.cornell.edu. Illus., index. Refereed. Vol. ends: Jul. Microform: WSH; PQC. Reprint: WSH. *Indexed:* A22, ABIn, ABS&EES, B01, B02, BAS, BRI, C42, CBRI, CLI, Chicano, EconLit, IBSS, JEL, L14, P02, P61, SSA, WSA. *Bk. rev.:* Number and length vary. *Aud.:* Ac, Sa.

This multidisciplinary journal is one of the preeminent scholarly publications in the field of industrial relations. Its empirical studies reflect all aspects of industrial relations, and researchers can rely upon it to guide them to the most important issues of the day. Articles are quantitative, dense, and statistical, which means that a literature search could begin here and move outward to other journal titles. The content is international in scope. Articles reflect "all aspects of the employment relationship, including collective bargaining, labor law, labor markets, social security and protective labor legislation, management and personnel, human resources, worker participation, workplace health and safety, organizational behavior, comparative industrial relations, and labor history." As is the case with all of the most scholarly publications in this field, readers will require a commanding knowledge of statistics and economic theory to follow many of the offerings. The book review section offers in-depth, subject-based literature reviews that track the latest publications in the field. This scholarly journal is required for serious academic collections.

3170. *Industrial Relations: a journal of economy and society.* Formerly (until 1961): *Civilian Defense.* [ISSN: 0019-8676] 1942. q. GBP 305. Ed(s): Trond Petersen, Steven Raphael. Wiley-Blackwell Publishing, Inc., 111 River St, Hoboken, NJ 07030; info@wiley.com; http://onlinelibrary.wiley.com/. Illus., index, adv. Sample. Refereed. Vol. ends: Fall. Microform: PQC. Reprint: PSC. *Indexed:* A22, ABIn, B01, B02, BRI, CLI, Chicano, E01, EconLit, ErgAb, H24, IBSS, JEL, L14, P02, P61, PsycInfo, SSA, SWR&A. *Bk. rev.:* Brief notes. *Aud.:* Ac.

The substantive and wide-ranging articles in this journal deal with all aspects of employee–employer relationships. The publication leans heavily in the direction of economic analysis, and thus requires a deeper knowledge of economic principles in many cases. Many authors address the challenge of how to bring theory into practice, or explore how real-world events may be explained utilizing theory. Each issue has a column on Internet resources and a survey of recent publications. The scope of the articles is international, although most deal with American scenarios. In addition to economics, authors hail from sociology, business administration, psychology, and history. Although the authors are clearly involved in a conversation with each other and not with the average reader, the overall editorial strategy for this publication has balanced "plain English" with complex theory. Therefore, readers can expect to find a substantial amount of accessible scholarship here. This journal competes with

Cornell's *Industrial and Labor Relations Review* for the top slot as "most frequently cited" journal in the field of industrial relations. It recently celebrated 50 years of publishing with a new cover as well as some new editorial strategies. These include sponsoring conferences and selecting topics on which to focus in depth in single issues. This is a valuable journal in the field and should be part of academic collections and large public library collections.

3171. Industrial Worker. [ISSN: 0019-8870] 1909. 10x/yr. USD 24 (Individuals, USD 18). Ed(s): Peter Moore. Industrial Workers of the World, PO Box 13476, Philadelphia, PA 19101-3476; ghq@iww.org; http://iww.org. Illus. Circ: 4300 Paid. Vol. ends: Dec. Microform: BHP; PQC. *Indexed:* ABIn. *Aud.:* Ga, Ac.

This tabloid-style newspaper, now enjoying a new life as a vibrant web site, is the public voice of the Industrial Workers of the World (IWW). It is unabashedly partisan in its editorial direction. Precisely for this reason, it is closely read by both labor activists and academics. As one of the most radical labor newspapers in print and online, it brings an important ideological perspective to any collection, whatever the politics of the region. World labor news is covered in depth, as is news from local unions in the United States. Authors are very much concerned with organizing strategies, the "strike tool," and other longtime labor strategies. Rank-and-file union members are frequent contributors, and the editor is an elected official with a two-year term.

3172. International Labor and Working-Class History. Formerly (until 1976): *European Labor and Working Class History. Newsletter.* [ISSN: 0147-5479] 1972. s-a. GBP 98. Ed(s): Peter Winn. Cambridge University Press, The Edinburgh Bldg, Shaftesbury Rd, Cambridge, CB2 8RU, United Kingdom; journals@cambridge.org; http://www.cambridge.org/uk. Illus., index, adv. Refereed. Circ: 900. Reprint: PSC. *Indexed:* A22, ABIn, ABS&EES, AmHI, ArtHuCI, BAS, Chicano, E01, P61, SSA. *Bk. rev.:* Number varies; essay length. *Aud.:* Ac.

This journal's essays are dense and scholarly, and generally carry the ideological perspective that "doing history" requires a rethinking of how we look at history itself. The editors argue that it is crucial to "change the character of historical conversation by expanding its scope, enlarging its scope and changing its terms." They attempt to do so by exploring a common subject from a variety of viewpoints, presenting the reader with an array of data from which to draw conclusions. Topics include globalization's impact on workers' rights, social class privilege, unions, and working-class politics. Substantive articles are matched with short reports of work in progress, short features, and critical commentary on material presented in earlier issues. Book reviews are also prominently included. Special-theme issues take one topic and provide deep analysis. The journal is globally focused, but also pays close attention to work and family issues, work performed at home or in sweatshops by women or underage workers, and the impact of cultural values on employment.

3173. International Labour Review. [ISSN: 0020-7780] 1921. q. GBP 220 (print & online eds.). Ed(s): Mark Lansky. Wiley-Blackwell Publishing Ltd., The Atrium, Southern Gate, Chichester, PO19 8SQ, United Kingdom; customer@wiley.com; http://www.wiley.com/. Illus., index, adv. Sample. Refereed. Vol. ends: Nov/Dec. Microform: CIS; PMC; PQC. Reprint: PSC; WSH. *Indexed:* A22, ABIn, ASSIA, B01, B02, BAS, BRI, C45, CBRI, E01, EIP, EconLit, ErgAb, GW, IBSS, JEL, MCR, P02, P61, SSA. *Bk. rev.:* Number and length vary. *Aud.:* Ac, Sa.

The International Labour Organization (ILO) is an important publisher that addresses international issues in industrial relations and the trade union movement. The ILO's *Review* focuses heavily on developing countries that do not receive much attention from U.S.- and European-based journals. Contributors include academics, labor leaders, government officials, nongovernmental organization (NGO) leaders, and technical experts. The ILO tracks many controversial issues such as the worldwide incidence of child labor. This publication is often the best place to start a search on issues that span national boundaries. The editors publish a literature review, which is unusual in that it provides a means to find international literature. Tables of contents and article abstracts are online from 1996 to the present, and subscribers to the print edition have full online access as well.

3174. Japan Labour Bulletin. [ISSN: 0021-4469] 1962. m. JPY 4320 domestic. Ed(s): H. Sakashita. Japan Institute of Labour, Shinjuku Monolith, P.O. Box 7040, Tokyo, 163-0926, Japan; http://www.jil.go.jp. Illus., index. Circ: 3100. Vol. ends: Dec. *Aud.:* Ac, Sa.

Published by the Japan Institute of Labour, a division of the Japanese Ministry of Labour, this concise English-language newsletter covers all aspects of working life in Japan. Its features are short and well written, and report on major topics such as labor economy, labor policy, working conditions, and trends in industrial relations. Many issues take one topic and provide an in-depth analysis of it. Recent special topics include labor law and social policy, social security, and human resource developments. This journal stands alone as the "must have" title for Japanese workplace issues, and you will find it on the shelf in every labor library.

3175. Journal of Collective Negotiations. Formerly (until 2006): *Journal of Collective Negotiations in the Public Sector.* [ISSN: 2167-7816] 1972. q. USD 430 (print & online eds.) Individuals, USD 117 (print & online eds.). Ed(s): David A Dilts, Loretta Schorr. Baywood Publishing Co., Inc., 26 Austin Ave, PO Box 337, Amityville, NY 11701; info@baywood.com; http://www.baywood.com. Illus., index. Sample. Refereed. Vol. ends: Dec. *Indexed:* A22, ABIn, B01, B02, BRI, CLI, L14, P61, SSA. *Aud.:* Ac, Sa.

Public-sector unions are the fastest growing segment of the labor movement, and the interplay between unionized workers and shrinking government budgets means that this area is the frequent subject of analysis. Since 2010, public sector unions have seen substantial "pushback" from right-wing advocacy groups, even is former "bastion" states such as Wisconsin and Ohio. This recent activity reaffirms the importance of public sector trade unionism, whatever the political beliefs of the reader. This journal covers the challenges of contract negotiations, impasse resolution, strikes and lockouts, grievance issues, and contract administration. It is noteworthy that the overall editorial policy calls for the analysis of public-sector work issues in the greater context of society. Contributors include negotiators, public office holders, and academics. The tone of this journal is active and collaborative, and it seeks to provide a forum for the free exchange of ideas. Articles tend to be pragmatic, seeking solutions to complex problems that affect both public policy and employee morale. This is the "one-stop" source for information on public-sector labor issues, and therefore is a necessary addition to any labor or law library. Subscribers have online access to full text of the entire contents of the journal.

3176. The Journal of Human Resources. [ISSN: 0022-166X] 1965. q. USD 275 (print & online eds.). Ed(s): Jan Levine Thal, William N Evans. University of Wisconsin Press, Journal Division, 1930 Monroe St, 3rd Fl, Madison, WI 53711; journals@uwpress.wisc.edu; http://www.uwpress.org/. Illus., index, adv. Refereed. Circ: 2000. Microform: MIM; PQC. Reprint: PSC. *Indexed:* A22, ABIn, AgeL, B01, B02, C42, Chicano, ERIC, EconLit, IBSS, JEL, MCR, P02, SWR&A. *Aud.:* Ac.

This is an academic journal with a strong emphasis on data and statistical analysis. It presents excellent original research on subjects such as disparities in incomes among various ethnic groups, and the relationship between child labor and family economic status. The editors strive to maintain a high degree of rigor and critical analysis; in some cases, tabular data can run several pages in length. Library subscription to this journal includes access to the electronic edition, which is available from the University of Wisconsin Press–Highwire Press. A full run of the journal (founded in 1966) is available via JSTOR.

3177. Journal of Labor Economics. [ISSN: 0734-306X] 1983. q. USD 412 (print & online eds.). Ed(s): Paul Oyer, Maggie Newman. University of Chicago Press, 1427 E 60th St, Chicago, IL 60637; subscriptions@press.uchicago.edu; http://www.journals.uchicago.edu. Illus., index, adv. Sample. Refereed. Vol. ends: Oct. Microform: PQC. Reprint: PSC. *Indexed:* A22, ABIn, B01, B02, EconLit, IBSS, JEL, P02. *Bk. rev.:* Number and length vary. *Aud.:* Ac, Sa.

This journal's editors recognize that the interplay between the economy, broad social trends, and private behavior is complex and requires multidisciplinary study. Articles can be either highly theoretical or applied, as authors explore labor market institutions (such as unions, management, and government) from a variety of perspectives. Topics cover a wide range of labor economics issues, varying from changes in the supply and demand of labor services, to the distribution of income, to the impact of public-policy decisions. Not a layperson's sourcebook, this journal requires a working knowledge of economic theory. The quality of the scholarship and the diversity of the material covered make this an excellent addition to academic collections.

3178. *Journal of Labor Research.* [ISSN: 0195-3613] 1980. q. EUR 358 (print & online eds.). Ed(s): Robert J Newman. Springer New York LLC, 233 Spring St, New York, NY 10013; journals@springer-ny.com; http://www.springer.com. Illus., index, adv. Refereed. Reprint: PSC. *Indexed:* A22, ABIn, B01, B02, BRI, E01, EconLit, IBSS, JEL, P02, P61, SD, SSA. *Aud.:* Ac, Sa.

This top-ranked journal takes the challenge of exploring the "employment relationship" very seriously, and offers hard-hitting articles by academics and practitioners. Authors rely heavily on economic theory and statistical analysis, and the lay reader may find this a challenge. Nonetheless, this journal is widely cited and is a necessary addition to the labor library. Most issues feature a symposium that brings together several articles that present a variety of viewpoints on a trend or policy issue. Recent topics include hospital workers, a new look at labor history of the American South, union wage effects in the public sector, and family leave.

3179. *Journal of Workplace Rights.* Formerly (until 2008): *Journal of Individual Employment Rights.* [ISSN: 1938-4998] 1992. q. USD 373 (print & online eds.) Individuals, USD 117 (print & online eds.). Ed(s): Joel P Rudin. Baywood Publishing Co., Inc., 26 Austin Ave, PO Box 337, Amityville, NY 11701; info@baywood.com; http://www.baywood.com. Sample. Refereed. *Indexed:* A01, B01, BRI, CLI, L14, P61, SSA. *Aud.:* Ac.

The *Journal of Workplace Rights* is the new title of the former *Journal of Individual Employee Rights.* It is dedicated to the idea that human rights should be upheld in the workplace, which requires input from both management and the workforce itself. Its definition of human rights is based on the Universal Declaration of Human Rights as passed by the United Nations in 1948. Topics of interest to the editors run through the full range of industrial relations issues, including job security, discrimination, living wages, collective bargaining, privacy, workplace democracy, and intellectual property rights. The editors also give special attention to doctoral students and non-tenured faculty members as authors, because they possess fewer rights and privileges than tenured professors do. Recent articles include "Accommodating Difference? British Unions and Polish Migrant Workers," "The Mexican Glass Ceiling and the Construction of Equal Opportunities: Narratives of Women Managers," and "Labor Arbitrations and Coworker Sexual Harassment: Looking at the Assessment of Mitigating Factors through a Feminist Lens."

3180. *Labor (Durham): studies in working-class history of the Americas.* [ISSN: 1547-6715] 2004. q. USD 374. Ed(s): Leon Fink. Duke University Press, 905 W Main St, Ste 18 B, PO Box 90660, Durham, NC 27701; subscriptions@dukeupress.edu; http://www.dukeupress.edu. Adv. Sample. Refereed. Reprint: PSC. *Indexed:* MLA-IB, P61, SSA. *Aud.:* Ga, Ac, Sa.

This relatively new journal provides a fresh venue for labor historians to publish articles about labor history in the Americas, although the emphasis is on the United States. The editors intend to cover not only industrial labor history, but also agricultural work, slavery, unpaid and domestic labor, the informal work sector, and the professions. Issues usually match one or more colorful historical articles, as well as a hard-hitting piece about current affairs. Examples of recent articles include "Ducking for Cover: Chicago's Irish Nationalists in the Haymarket Era," "A 'Labor History' of Mass Incarceration," and "Labor History and Abolitionism."

3181. *Labor History.* Incorporates (1967-1968): *Labor Historians Newsletter;* Formerly (1960): *The Labor Historian's Bulletin.* [ISSN: 0023-656X] 1953. 5x/yr. GBP 336 (print & online eds.). Ed(s): Craig Phelan. Routledge, 4 Park Sq, Milton Park, Abingdon, OX14 4RN, United Kingdom; subscriptions@tandf.co.uk; http://www.tandfonline.com. Illus., adv. Sample. Refereed. Reprint: PSC. *Indexed:* A22, ABIn, ABS&EES, AmHI, ArtHuCI, B01, B02, BRI, Chicano, E01, EconLit, IBSS, JEL, P02, P61, RILM, SSA. *Aud.:* Ac, Sa.

This journal publishes original research about the history of work and how it is represented in literature. It also explores the historical record of labor systems, the social production of labor, occupational culture, and folklore. Authors focus primarily on American labor, but the growing interest in transnational movements is showing up as an additional focus for the editors. This journal is the most important venue for scholars who are interested in presenting new ideas about labor history. The journal's reputation is built on its solid scholarly research and writing, yet it avoids limiting itself to a narrow focus. As the standard journal for this area of study, it is a natural fit in large public libraries and academic collections.

3182. *Labor Law Journal: to promote sound thinking on labor law problems.* Incorporates (1999-2001): *Journal of Alternative Dispute Resolution in Employment.* [ISSN: 0023-6586] 1949. q. USD 329; USD 50 per issue. Ed(s): Matthew A Pavich. C C H Inc., 2700 Lake Cook Rd, Riverwoods, IL 60015; cust_serv@cch.com; http://www.cchgroup.com/. Illus., index. Vol. ends: Dec. Microform: PQC. *Indexed:* A22, ABIn, B01, B02, BRI, CLI, L14. *Aud.:* Ac, Sa.

This quarterly journal reviews the complex relationship of law, labor, management, and the economy. Its editorial goal is to provide pragmatic thinking about employment law issues. The editors strive for a neutral stance, publishing articles that are useful to lawyers and lay practitioners alike. The content is written by labor experts from management, unions, government, the bar, and the academy. It covers domestic, foreign, and international labor issues. One special feature is "Who's What in Labor," publicizing current appointments to positions of interest within government, unions, and management. The journal also highlights important decisions, regulations, and news developments in the areas of labor–management relations, equal employment opportunity, job safety and health, and employment and training.

3183. *Labor Notes.* [ISSN: 0275-4452] 1979. m. USD 35 (Individuals, USD 24). Ed(s): Mischa Gaus. Labor Education & Research Project, 7435 Michigan Ave, Detroit, MI 48210. Illus. *Indexed:* A22, ABIn. *Aud.:* Ga, Ac, Sa.

Labor Notes is one of the hardest-hitting titles in labor news coverage, directed by the slogan "Putting the Movement Back in the Labor Movement." It carries news and opinion about rank-and-file struggles that are written by participants and observers, and has a 31-year history. Contributors freely explore the contradictions and nuances of the different forces involved in labor issues. The publication prides itself on its independence, and is equally critical of failings within unions and management. There is a steady supply of controversial op-ed pieces, guest editorials, and a lively letters section. In addition to the magazine, there is an active blog that offers extensive commentary and additional articles.

3184. *Labor Studies Journal.* [ISSN: 0160-449X] 1976. q. USD 414. Ed(s): Robert Bruno, Michelle Kaminski. Sage Publications, Inc., 2455 Teller Rd, Thousand Oaks, CA 91320; info@sagepub.com; http://www.sagepub.com. Illus. Refereed. Vol. ends: Winter. Microform: PQC. Reprint: PSC. *Indexed:* A22, ABIn, ABS&EES, B01, B02, BRI, E01, IBSS, P61, RILM, SSA. *Bk. rev.:* 7-12, 400-2,700 words. *Aud.:* Ac, Sa.

This publication successfully acts as a bridge between academic researchers and labor practitioners. Hosted by West Virginia University, it is also the official journal of the United Association for Labor Education (UALE). Papers presented at the annual UALE conference are published in *LSJ*. It is a multidisciplinary journal that publishes material based on research about work, workers, labor organizations, labor studies, and worker education in the United States and internationally. The content covers diverse research methods, both qualitative and quantitative. The articles are directed at a general audience, including union, university, and community-based labor educators, and labor activists and scholars from across the social sciences and humanities.

3185. *LaborNet.* d. LaborNet, http://www.labornet.org. *Aud.:* Ga, Ac, Sa.

LaborNet describes itself as a "global online communication for a democratic, independent labor movement." This site offers a lively source of news, opinions, and resources. The format lists top-level stories with just a headline that links to primary sources. Some of the material is from mainstream publications, but links also emphasize independent media sources. Most importantly, the

LaborNet editorial staff writes much of the content themselves. A top-level menu offers breaking news by U.S. developments and global news, which is useful for researchers who have international topics to explore.

3186. *Labour Education.* [ISSN: 0378-5467] 1964. q. CHF 55; USD 44. I L O, 4 Route des Morillons, Geneva, 1211, Switzerland; ilo@ilo.org; http://www.ilo.org. Illus. Circ: 2500. Vol. ends: No. 4. *Indexed:* A22. *Bk. rev.:* Occasional. *Aud.:* Ac, Sa.

Labour Education is published by the Bureau for Workers' Activities (ACTRAV). This outfit is a branch of the International Labour Office, which is the executive secretariat of the International Labour Organization. A quarterly review, *Labour Education* is published in three languages (English, Spanish, and French). It is devoted to news and analysis of global efforts to improve workers' lives. The content is useful to both union and nonunion workers, covering a broad range of topics. These include training and education programs, current events, trade union rights, social justice organizing, and legislation. The publication also includes reviews of relevant resources, such as books, articles, and videos.

3187. *LabourStart.* 1998. d. Free. Ed(s): Eric Lee. Eric Lee, Ed. & Pub.. Adv. *Aud.:* Ga, Ac, Sa.

This electronic resource is billed as the site "where trade unionists start their day on the [N]et." The "e-zine" aggregates and disseminates labor news in 17 languages. The site provides a long chronological list of "This Week's Top Stories" listed by country. There is also a "Book of the Day" feature, a "Photo of the Week," and a wide array of discussion forums and FAQs. On balance, it gives the reader a thorough overview of the global issues that are of primary concern to labor activists.

3188. *Monthly Labor Review Online.* [ISSN: 1937-4658] m. Free. U.S. Department of Labor, Bureau of Labor Statistics, 441 G St, NW, Washington, DC 20212. *Bk. rev.:* Occasional. *Aud.:* Ga.

Monthly Labor Review Online continues a long tradition of excellence in digital form. This journal is the top scholarly/professional journal of the Bureau of Labor Statistics (BLS), and it attracts prestigious authors. Full-text versions are available in pdf format, both at the article and full-issue levels. Articles include links to related Bureau of Labor Statistics programs and data, and author e-mail links are embedded. "The Editor's Desk," a useful review of new BLS data and research, is updated each business day. The content is informative and neutral, covering current labor statistics, book reviews, publications received, and a section called "Labor Month in Review." Content searching is facilitated by an index of articles published in print since 1988, as well as an archive of past issues.

3189. *NATLEX.* 1984. 1 Base Vol(s) irreg. I L O, 4 Route des Morillons, Geneva, 1211, Switzerland; ilo@ilo.org; http://www.ilo.org. *Aud.:* Ac, Sa.

NATLEX is the database of national labor, Social Security, and related human rights legislation maintained by the International Labour Organization's (ILO) International Labour Standards Department. This resource operates primarily like a database portal for foreign and international labor law, and therein lies its strength. The records in *NATLEX* are extensive: over 80,000 records covering over 196 countries and territories. It also provides abstracts of legislation and relevant citation information. Each record appears in only one of the three official ILO languages (English/French/Spanish). The data are indexed by keywords and by subject classifications, and viewers may browse for labor legislation by country or by subject. Where possible, the full text of the law or a relevant electronic source is linked to the record.

3190. *New Labor Forum: a journal of ideas, analysis and debate.* [ISSN: 1095-7960] 1997. 3x/yr. USD 359. Ed(s): Steve Fraser, Paula Finn. Sage Publications, Inc., 2455 Teller Rd, Thousand Oaks, CA 91320; info@sagepub.com; http://www.sagepub.com/. Illus., adv. Refereed. *Indexed:* A01, A22, B01, E01, P61, SSA. *Bk. rev.:* Number and length vary. *Aud.:* Ga, Ac.

Bold and provocative, this journal is of the sort that gets locked up for safekeeping and placed on two-hour reserve. Otherwise it manages to "disappear," which is a testament to its popularity. Subtitled "A Journal of Ideas, Analysis, and Debate," this publication invites controversy and does not eschew strong rhetoric. Articles from union organizers mingle with those of tenured faculty. Topics such as labor union revitalization and new labor-community coalition building are examples of the controversial issues that the editors take on. Fresh ideas abound, such as approaching high-tech globalized distribution as a union organizing opportunity, or exploring the future of the "strike weapon" as a strategic tool.

3191. *New Technology, Work & Employment.* [ISSN: 0268-1072] 1986. 3x/yr. GBP 359. Ed(s): Philip Taylor, Debra Howcroft. Wiley-Blackwell Publishing Ltd., The Atrium, Southern Gate, Chichester, PO19 8SQ, United Kingdom; customer@wiley.com; http://www.wiley.com/. Adv. Sample. Refereed. Reprint: PSC. *Indexed:* A22, ABIn, ASSIA, B01, CompLI, E01, ErgAb, IBSS, P61, RiskAb, SSA. *Aud.:* Ga.

Technology has brought sweeping changes to the way most people work, and this internationally edited, interdisciplinary journal assesses the impact of technology in the workplace. Articles balance solid academic work with readable text. Topics includes automation of retail distribution, telecommuting in small and medium-sized firms, management style and worker autonomy, and teamwork in factory assembly lines.

Occupational Outlook Quarterly. See Occupations and Careers section.

3192. *Our Times Magazine.* [ISSN: 0822-6377] 1981. bi-m. CAD 40 (Individuals, CAD 25; CAD 6 per issue). Ed(s): Lorraine Endicott. Our Times Labour Publishing Inc., #407 - 15 Gervais Dr, Toronto, ON M3C 1Y8, Canada; office@ourtimes.ca. Adv. Microform: MML. *Indexed:* BRI, C37, CBCARef. *Bk. rev.:* Number and length vary. *Aud.:* Ga.

Two-way trade in goods and services between the United States and Canada has surpassed $441 billion, making it the largest trading relationship in the world. Despite that, relatively few labor researchers in the United States invest time and effort in studying Canadian employment issues. *Our Times,* subtitled "Canada's Independent Labour Magazine," addresses issues that affect Canadian working people and the organizations that serve them. Articles cover a broad array of topics, including labor history, gender and racial struggles within the labor movement, NAFTA, and occupational safety and health. This publication offers readers an excellent starting point for learning all about labor and industrial relations in Canada.

3193. *Relations Industrielles.* Formerly (until 1950): *Bulletin des Relations Industrielles.* [ISSN: 0034-379X] 1945. q. CAD 135.54 (Individuals, CAD 67.72; CAD 39.51 per issue domestic). Ed(s): Claudine Leclerc, Paul-Andre Lapointe. Universite Laval, Department of Industrial Relations, Pavillon DeSeve, bureau 3129, 1025, av des Sciences-Humaines, Quebec, PQ G1V 0A6, Canada; info@riir.ulaval.ca; http://www.rlt.ulaval.ca/. Illus., index. Refereed. *Indexed:* A22, ABIn, B01, B02, BRI, C37, CLI, IBSS, P61, PdeR, SSA. *Bk. rev.:* Number and length vary. *Aud.:* Ac, Sa.

This scholarly journal is published by the industrial relations department of Canada's Universite Laval in Quebec. *Relations Industrielles* is an interdisciplinary publication that carries articles on all aspects of the world of work. Articles appear in either French or English, accompanied by a full summary in the other language and a shorter summary in Spanish. Each issue (numbering over 200 pages) includes reviews of significant books in the field and a bibliography of recent articles published throughout the world. Although predominantly covering Canadian issues, it also ventures into foreign and international topics as well. Recent articles include "Work and Citizenship in Mexico in the Era of Globalization," "Sexual Orientation Provisions in Canadian Collective Agreements," and "Recruitment Strategies and Union Exclusion in Two Australian Call Centres."

3194. *The Review of Black Political Economy.* [ISSN: 0034-6446] 1970. q. EUR 326 (print & online eds.). Ed(s): Cecilia Conrad. Springer New York LLC, 233 Spring St, New York, NY 10013; service-ny@springer.com; http://www.springer.com/. Illus. Refereed. Microform: PQC. Reprint: PSC. *Indexed:* A22, ABIn, B01, B02, BRI, Chicano, E01, EconLit, IBSS, IIBP, JEL, P02, P61, SSA. *Bk. rev.:* Occasional. *Aud.:* Ac.

The Review of Black Political Economy examines issues related to the economic status of African American and Third World peoples. It identifies and analyzes policies designed to reduce racial economic inequality. The journal also appraises public and private policies designed to advance economic opportunities. The articles and occasional book reviews cover such ground as inequalities in small business loans, analysis of preferential procurement programs, the impact of structural adjustment in the Caribbean, and the participation of women and people of color in union apprenticeship training programs.

3195. *Social Policy: organizing for social and economic justice.* [ISSN: 0037-7783] 1970. q. USD 185 (Individuals, USD 45). Labor Neighbor Research and Training Center, PO Box 3924, New Orleans, LA 70177. Illus., adv. Vol. ends: Winter. Microform: PQC. *Indexed:* A01, A22, ASSIA, BRI, Chicano, IBSS, MCR, MLA-IB, P02, P61, SSA, SWR&A. *Bk. rev.:* Number and length vary. *Aud.:* Ga.

This is an unabashedly partisan magazine, presenting news and analysis on various social change movements. Since labor is a key component of social justice work, each issue carries at least one article on worker organizing. One of the publication's strengths is a broad and balanced view of the role played by conventional unions. Recently covered topics have included organizing across language barriers; innovative organizing strategies applied in the city of Los Angeles; and immigrants as a target population for labor organizing.

3196. *Union Democracy Review.* Formerly (until 1972): *Union Democracy in Action.* [ISSN: 1077-5080] 1961. bi-m. Free to members; Non-members, USD 30. Ed(s): Herman Benson. Association for Union Democracy, Inc., 104 Montgomery St., Brooklyn, NY 11225; info@uniondemocracy.org; http://www.uniondemocracy.com. Sample. *Aud.:* Ga, Ac, Sa.

The Association for Union Democracy (AUD) is a nonprofit organization dedicated to advancing the principles and practices of democratic trade unionism in the North American labor movement. It is a nonpartisan organization and does not support or endorse candidates for union office or particular policies within unions. Rather, AUD supports actions that strengthen the democratic process, promote membership participation, support free speech, and encourage fair elections so that union members can shape and steer the direction of their union. *UDR* is AUD's published voice, and serves as a vital clearinghouse for this movement.

3197. *Work, Employment & Society.* [ISSN: 0950-0170] 1987. bi-m. USD 748. Ed(s): Mark Stuart, Irena Grugulis. Sage Publications Ltd., 1 Oliver's Yard, 55 City Rd, London, EC1Y 1SP, United Kingdom; info@sagepub.co.uk; http://www.uk.sagepub.com. Sample. Refereed. Microform: PQC. Reprint: PSC. *Indexed:* A22, ABIn, ASSIA, E01, ErgAb, H24, IBSS, P61, PsycInfo, SSA. *Bk. rev.:* Number and length vary. *Aud.:* Ac.

This British entry is heavily dominated by the sociological study of work, and this is a value point for labor researchers. It addresses work in the broadest possible sense, and it includes a wide array of articles that explore global and transnational employment trends. This is the sort of journal that citizen-researchers and students may consult to get the big picture, and that academics consult to stay current with their international colleagues. Recent articles explore management trends with significant impact on workers, such as "total quality management," the impact of technology on work, and disabilities in the workplace. For full-service research collections, this journal is a valuable addition.

3198. *Workforce Management.* Former titles (until 2003): *Workforce;* (until 1997): *Personnel Journal;* (until 1927): *Journal of Personnel Research.* [ISSN: 1547-5565] 1922. m. USD 79 domestic (Free to qualified personnel). Ed(s): John Hollon. Crain Communications, Inc., 1155 Gratiot Ave, Detroit, MI 48207; info@crain.com; http://www.crain.com. Illus., index, adv. Vol. ends: Dec. *Indexed:* A01, A22, ABIn, Agr, B01, B02, B03, BLI, BRI, C42, CBRI, P02. *Aud.:* Ga.

Workforce Management provides practical information about the impact of current events on human relations. The format is akin to commercial magazine publishing, with rich graphics, pull-text boxes, and a vibrant letters section. One section covers the trends, problem-solving strategies, and resources necessary for action; another covers legal briefings; and a third distills economic data into a usable form for human resources professionals. Topics covered include employer-provided child care, personnel practices at "big box" retailers, and the impact of changed overtime pay regulations.

3199. *Workindex.* 1997. d. Free. Ed(s): Kristen B Frasch, David Shadovitz. Human Resources Executive, Ste 500, 747 Dresher Rd, PO Box 980, Horsham, PA 19044; jdd10@cornell.edu ; http://www.hreonline.com/ HRE/index.jsp. Illus., adv. *Bk. rev.:* Number varies, brief. *Aud.:* Ac, Sa.

Workindex describes itself as a "dynamic list of 5,000 web sites for human resources professionals." It is produced by *Human Resource Executive* magazine. This site is a useful portal for news and resources oriented to the human resources community. Multiple, redundant navigation tools help viewers find what they are looking for, and when all else fails, there's a category or keyword search box. The Martin P. Catherwood Library at Cornell's School of Industrial and Labor Relations handles the site indexing, which contributes significantly to the information architecture and ease in retrieving documents.

3200. *Working U S A: the journal of labor and society.* [ISSN: 1089-7011] 1997. q. GBP 238. Ed(s): Immanuel Ness. Wiley-Blackwell Publishing, Inc., 111 River St, Hoboken, NJ 07030; info@wiley.com; http:// onlinelibrary.wiley.com/. Sample. Refereed. Reprint: PSC. *Indexed:* A22, ABIn, B01, B02, BRI, E01, EconLit, JEL, RiskAb. *Bk. rev.:* Number and length vary. *Aud.:* Ac, Sa.

In operation for over 14 years, this publication has made waves as a publishing venue for a large number of progressive academics and policymakers. It bills itself as an instrument for studying the workplace with the needs and concerns of "working people" in mind, and this is reflected in the topics it covers. In many cases, authors express partisan viewpoints, in contrast to the more arid language typically employed by many scholarly journals. Recent article topics include organizing temporary workers, labor education's challenges, and home-care worker issues. Authors are careful to write in plain English, yet offer solid scholarship that is footnoted and enhanced with tables and charts. This journal has earned a place as a core title both for industrial relations collections and for general business collections.

3201. *World of Work: the magazine of the ILO.* Formerly (until 1992): *I L O Information.* [ISSN: 1020-0010] 1965. 3x/yr. Free. Ed(s): Hans von Rohland. I L O, 4 Route des Morillons, Geneva, 1211, Switzerland; ilo@ilo.org; http://www.ilo.org. Illus. Vol. ends: Dec. *Indexed:* A22, ABIn, B01, BRI, CBRI, P61, SSA. *Bk. rev.:* Number and length vary. *Aud.:* Ga.

Although this magazine is published by the International Labour Organization (ILO), its editorial masthead is careful to note that it is not the ILO's official voice. It does, however, explore a wide range of topics addressed by the ILO. Each issue includes an extensive cover story ("Decent Work for Africa's Development," "World Day Against Child Labor"), numerous general articles, and brief book reviews.

■ LANDSCAPE ARCHITECTURE

Patrick Tomlin, Art and Architecture Library, Virginia Tech, 100 Cowgill Hall, Blacksburg, VA 24062-9001; tomlinl@vt.edu

Introduction

The literature of landscape architecture is rapidly growing and highly interdisciplinary, reflective of the diversity of the profession from which it originates. Although it encompasses elements of architecture and design, is informed by environmental studies and the social sciences, and embraces the challenges presented by new technologies as well as a long-standing commitment to the preservation of the past, landscape architecture has been fundamentally shaped by how humans see themselves in relation to the natural world.

Landscape architecture journals cover this wide terrain, and range in scope and subject matter from historical case studies and detailed analyses of contemporary projects to the politics of sustainability and the impact of global warming on the practice of landscape architects. The following journals offer a representative sampling of the periodical literature in this field.

While smaller in number than journals published in architecture or the visual arts, landscape architecture periodicals vary greatly in content and design. Nevertheless, like journals in those disciplines, many landscape architecture publications are as much visual as textual in nature: readers will find that almost all are heavily illustrated with images, drawings, plans, and photographs, as the one fundamentally contributes to the meaning of the other. The majority of landscape architecture journals featured below, moreover, display a discernible international flavor, which reflects the European origins of their publication and the profession's own increasingly global visibility and scale of operation. Accordingly, these journals often publish summaries or entire texts of articles in multiple languages for an international readership.

Professional and scholarly societies publish, or are directly affiliated with, nearly half of the landscape journals reviewed in this section. These include publications with sustained analysis of the history of landscape architecture, such as the monograph *Dumbarton Oaks Papers* from the Colloquium on the History of Landscape Architecture, as well as periodicals that focus on contemporary design and research issues like *Landskab* and the *Journal of Landscape Architecture*. Nevertheless, given the relatively small number of journals in the field, there is little useful distinction between "scholarly" and "non-scholarly" journals. Even those "glossy" titles that are characterized by their sophisticated production levels and high-quality design, and that frequently focus on new and relatively unknown projects rather than architectural history, are usually edited and written by educators and researchers who are also practitioners, firm leaders, and theorists. The audience for these publications will consist primarily of landscape architecture students and faculty, as well as practicing landscape architects. Those working in contiguous fields such as land conservation, urban planning, and environmental science will likely find such publications of interest as well.

Currently, print remains the dominant format for landscape architecture journals, though this appears to be quickly changing, as publishers offer more and more content, including access to older volumes, on the web. The list below will be most useful to libraries that serve academic programs in landscape architecture, architecture, urban design, and environmental studies. Those suitable for a public library with a strong architecture collection or landscape architecture component have been indicated as such.

Basic Periodicals

Ac: *Landscape Architecture, Landscape Journal;* Sa: *Landscape and Urban Planning, Landscape Research, Topos.*

Basic Abstracts and Indexes

Avery Index to Architectural Periodicals; Garden, Landscape and Horticulture Index; Geographical Abstracts; ICONDA.

3202. *Anthos: vierteljahres-Zeitschrift fuer Freiraumgestaltung, Gruen und Landschaftsplanung.* [ISSN: 0003-5424] 1962. q. CHF 89 (Students, CHF 49). Ed(s): Stephanie Perrochet. Bund Schweizer Landschaftsarchitekten und Landschaftsarchitektinnen, Rue du Doubs 32, La Chaux-de-Fonds, 2300, Switzerland; bsla@bsla.ch; http://www.bsla.ch. Illus., adv. Circ: 5000. Vol. ends: Dec. *Indexed:* A22, API, GardL. *Bk. rev.:* 10. *Aud.:* Ac, Sa.

This official publication of the L'Union Suisse des Service des Parc et Promenades provides coverage of current developments in landscape architecture around the globe. The content of each volume of *Anthos* centers on a specific theme or particular aspect of the profession; a recent issue, for example, focuses on environmental design in the Alps. Content also includes articles on individual landscape projects, a book review section, and information about notable competitions, awards, and individual architects. Written in German and French, with portions published in English, *Anthos* represents the Federation Suisse des Architectes Paysagiste (FSAP) and the

German Bund Schweizer Landschaftsarchitekten und Landschaftsarchitektinnen (BSLA). Its international perspective makes this publication a valuable contribution to an academic architecture library collection.

3203. *Colloquium on the History of Landscape Architecture. Papers.* 1972. irreg. Dumbarton Oaks, Research Library and Collection, 1703 32nd St, NW, Washington, DC 20007; DoaksBooks@doaks.org; http://www.doaks.org/publications.html. Refereed. *Aud.:* Ac, Sa.

This monograph serial gathers papers originally presented at the annual colloquium on landscape architecture organized by Harvard's Dumbarton Oaks in Washington, D.C. Begun in 1971, the series has achieved a reputation for its notable contributors, erudite scholarship, and high-quality production. Essays in each volume address an overarching theme, each usually focusing on one aspect of the history of landscape architecture, but the *Papers* as a whole has addressed a striking variety of topics over the past four decades: archaeological evidence from Pompeii, Islamic garden traditions, and individual landscape architects such as Beatrix Jones Farrand. Essays are accompanied by bibliographic matter, illustrations, and information about the contributor. Volumes are relatively small in size, rarely amounting to more than 150 pages, but the series is an essential component of any library collection that supports a program in landscape architecture. Any landscape architecture or garden history research library should own the complete set.

3204. *Garten und Landschaft: Zeitschrift fuer Landschaftsarchitektur.* [ISSN: 0016-4720] 1890. m. Individuals, EUR 132; Students, EUR 87; EUR 13 newsstand/cover. Ed(s): Robert Schaefer. Callwey Verlag, Streitfeldstr 35, Munich, 81673, Germany; a.hagenkord@callwey.de; http://www.callwey.de. Illus., index, adv. Circ: 5106 Paid and controlled. Vol. ends: Dec. *Indexed:* A22, GardL. *Bk. rev.:* 4. *Aud.:* Ac, Sa.

This German-language journal is published by the Deutsche Gesellschaft fuer Gartenkunst und Landschaftskulture (German Society for Garden Design and Landscape Architecture). *Garten und Landschaft* provides information about working landscape architects (principally European) and articles focusing on contemporary landscape design in Germany. A portion of the articles included in the journal discuss aspects of a specific theme such as sustainability, or concentrate on projects within an individual city. Additional features include local news items, book reviews, notices of symposia and job openings, exhibitions, and other special events. Most content is written by landscape architects or recognized scholars in the field. Each issue is substantially illustrated with color and black-and-white reproductions. Some English-language summaries are present. An archive of older issues is available in electronic format for subscribers on the journal's German-language web site. *Garten un Landschaft* is a well-designed and relevant periodical for any library collection with a strong landscape architecture component. URL: www.garten-landschaft.de

3205. *Green Places: dedicated to improving public space.* Former titles (until Nov.2003): *Landscape Design;* (until 1971): *Institute of Landscape Architects. Journal;* (until 1946): *Institute of Landscape Architects. War-Time Journal;* (until 1941): *Landscape and Garden.* [ISSN: 1742-3716] 1934. 10x/yr. GBP 65 domestic (Students, GBP 53 in UK). Landscape Design Trust, PO Box 651, Redhill, RH1 9AJ, United Kingdom; info@landscape.co.uk; http://www.landscape.co.uk. Illus., index, adv. Sample. Vol. ends: Jun. *Indexed:* A07, A22, API, BRI, GardL. *Bk. rev.:* 2-6. *Aud.:* Ga, Ac.

Formerly published by the Landscape Design Trust, *Green Places* is now the product of GreenSpace Forum, a British charity organization whose mission is "to improve parks and green spaces by raising awareness, involving communities[,] and creating skilled professionals." This journal is published ten times a year, and each issue highlights current public landscape projects across the United Kingdom and, on occasion, other European locations. Despite its glossy appearance and numerous photographs, *Green Places* devotes substantial scholarly attention to environmental issues of interest to many landscape architecture researchers, including "green" park design, the ecological impact of tourism, and sustainable urban planning. Other features and columns include book reviews, notices of regional events, and debates between practicing landscape architects or environmental experts on topical concerns. An important publication for academic architecture libraries, *Green Places* would also make a unique contribution to a public library with an emphasis on art and architecture or urban studies materials.

3206. *Journal of Landscape Architecture.* [ISSN: 1862-6033] 2006. s-a. GBP 202 (print & online eds.). Ed(s): Robert Schaefer. Callwey Verlag, Streitfeldstr 35, Munich, 81673, Germany; a.hagenkord@callwey.de; http://www.callwey.de. Adv. Refereed. Reprint: PSC. *Bk. rev.:* 6. *Aud.:* Ac, Sa.

Published by the European Council of Architecture Schools, *JoLA* often presents an interdisciplinary range of topics, including cultural landscapes, land conservation, and urban design. Each issue is typically composed of four or five articles, two thematic columns, book reviews, and announcements for conferences and international special events in landscape architecture. Special columns include "Thinking Eye," a visual presentation of a landscape architect's research project, "Under the Sky," an empirical analysis of a constructed landscape, and "JoLA Lab," a lecture or textual criticism by a noted scholar or practitioner. Articles are written primarily by landscape architecture scholars. Extremely well designed and with plenty of full-color illustrations, drawings, and maps, *JoLA* has quickly assumed a place alongside other highly regard publications in the field, making it an important addition to research library collections that support landscape architecture programs. Its consistent quality of production, international scope, and high level of scholarship suggest that it will become an important publication in landscape architecture studies.

3207. *Landscape.* [ISSN: 1742-2914] 2004. q. Free to members; Non-members, GBP 25. Landscape Institute, 33 Great Portland St, London, W1W 8QG, United Kingdom; paull@landscapeinstitute.org; http://www.landscapeinstitute.org. Adv. *Aud.:* Ac, Sa.

This quarterly journal, published by the Landscape Institute, focuses principally on events and projects in U.K. landscape architecture. Compact and attractively designed, *Landscape* typically features five or six regular components, including an events diary; "In Design," an examination of new projects; an obituary column; "Elements," a list of leading suppliers of a featured project; and "My Favorite Landscape," a brief ruminative column in which an architect or designer is selected to highlight a site or design of personal importance. The remainder of the magazine consists of four to five articles on various U.K. firms or thematic topics, ranging from the rejuvenation of historic town squares to waterfront design. This title would be desirable for any research collection with an international focus in landscape architecture.

3208. *Landscape and Urban Planning.* Incorporates (in 1988): *Reclamation and Revegetation Research;* (in 1986): *Urban Ecology;* Formerly (until 1986): *Landscape Planning.* [ISSN: 0169-2046] 1974. 20x/yr. EUR 2439. Ed(s): J R Rodiek. Elsevier BV, Radarweg 29, PO Box 211, Amsterdam, 1000 AE, Netherlands; JournalsCustomerServiceEMEA@elsevier.com; http://www.elsevier.nl. Illus., index, adv. Refereed. *Indexed:* A22, C&ISA, C45, CerAb, EngInd, GardL, IndVet, RRTA, S25. *Bk. rev.:* 2-4. *Aud.:* Ac, Sa.

Landscape and Urban Planning focuses attention on "the interrelated nature of problems posed by nature and human use of land." Interdisciplinary and international in approach, the publication has traditionally presented a diverse array of issues over the years, ranging from landscape ecology in Sweden to landscape planning in Asia and urban design in rural New England. Thematic issues are published on occasion; individual articles frequently include black-and-white maps, charts, and diagrams with infrequent color illustrations. Intended primarily for a specialized academic landscape architecture audience, *Landscape and Urban Planning* would also be of benefit for any research collection that supports urban and environmental studies, geography, or planning. Electronic full-text versions of articles are available with a subscription.

3209. *Landscape Architecture.* [ISSN: 0023-8031] 1910. m. USD 75 (Individuals, USD 59; USD 9 per issue). Ed(s): Lisa Speckhardt, J William Thompson. American Society of Landscape Architects, 636 Eye St, NW, Washington, DC 20001; info@asla.org; http://www.asla.org. Illus., index, adv. Sample. Vol. ends: Dec. *Indexed:* A06, A07, A22, API, ArchI, ArtHuCI, EIP, GardL. *Bk. rev.:* 4. *Aud.:* Ac, Sa.

Landscape Architecture is the flagship journal of the American Society of Landscape Architects (ASLA). Although its coverage does occasionally extend to international topics and projects, the journal focuses principally on one activity in the United States. Article topics range from individual landscape architecture projects to theoretical issues concerning urban design and planning; many issues concentrate on land conservation and environmental sustainability. Although most articles are fairly brief—few exceed ten pages—the journal is heavily illustrated throughout with color photographs, maps, plans, and drawings. Typical of many society-based publications in the field, book reviews, product analyses, and columns on professional practice round out each volume. One issue per year is devoted to the winners of the ASLA awards in various categories of design, practice, and communication. Aimed at the professional landscape architect, *Landscape Architecture* is an essential publication for an academic library with a research-level collection in the subject.

3210. *Landscape Architecture Australia.* Formerly (until 2006): *Landscape Australia.* [ISSN: 1833-4814] 1971. q. AUD 53 in Australia & New Zealand; AUD 88 elsewhere; AUD 16 per month in Australia & New Zealand. Ed(s): Cameron Bruhn. Architecture Media Pty Ltd., Level 6, 163 Eastern Rd, South Melbourne, VIC 3205, Australia; publisher@archmedia.com.au; http://www.archmedia.com.au. Illus., index, adv. Sample. *Indexed:* API, GardL. *Bk. rev.:* 2. *Aud.:* Ac.

The official journal of the Australian Institute of Landscape Architects (AILA), *Landscape Architecture Australia* addresses current issues within the profession and provides information on the contemporary projects and designs in Australian landscape architecture. It includes multiple illustrated feature articles on practitioners, firms, environmental policies, and more. Regularly appearing sections include book reviews, product reviews, news items, special events, and an annual summary of the AILA National and State Project Awards. Although its scope is necessarily limited to its geographic purview, this journal is recommended for any research library with specialized interests in landscape architecture or a particular focus on Australian culture.

3211. *Landscape Journal: design, planning, and management of the land.* [ISSN: 0277-2426] 1982. s-a. USD 225 (print & online eds.). Ed(s): David G Pitt, Lance M Neckar. University of Wisconsin Press, Journal Division, 1930 Monroe St, 3rd Fl, Madison, WI 53711; journals@uwpress.wisc.edu; http://www.uwpress.org/. Illus., index, adv. Refereed. Circ: 2000. Microform: PQC. Reprint: PSC. *Indexed:* A07, A22, API, Agr, B01, E01, GardL, S25. *Bk. rev.:* 8. *Aud.:* Ac.

Landscape Journal is published by the Council of Educators in Landscape Architecture (CELA), an international body composed of scholars and practitioners active in landscape architecture education and research. As its subtitle suggests, the publication's scope encompasses all areas of practice related to landscape architecture. Articles on the theory and practice of design, planning, and management of the environment around the world are staples. *Landscape Journal* is edited by faculty in the University of Minnesota's Department of Landscape Architecture, and published by the University of Wisconsin Press. Each issue consists of four to six articles and a series of brief reviews of books, conferences, and new technology. Articles contain abstracts and black-and-white illustrations, photographs, tabular data, and drawings. The journal's contributors comprise scholars, educators, or practitioners in the field. Unlike many landscape architecture periodicals, *Landscape Journal* frequently includes articles on historical research topics, making it an appropriate selection for an academic architecture library.

3212. *Landscape Research.* Formerly (until 1976): *Landscape Research News.* [ISSN: 0142-6397] 1968. bi-m. GBP 764 (print & online eds.). Ed(s): Maggie Roe. Routledge, 4 Park Sq, Milton Park, Abingdon, OX14 4RN, United Kingdom; subscriptions@tandf.co.uk; http://www.tandfonline.com. Illus., adv. Sample. Refereed. Reprint: PSC. *Indexed:* A22, API, B01, BrArAb, C45, E01, GardL, NumL, RRTA, S25. *Bk. rev.:* 4, 600-800 words. *Aud.:* Ac, Sa.

Published by Routledge, *Landscape Research* combines "original research papers with reflective critiques of landscape practice." International and multidisciplinary, the journal covers a wide variety of scholarly topics related to landscape architecture, including environmental design, ecology and environmental conservation, land survey, behavioral and cultural studies, and archaeology and history. Volumes are occasionally devoted to a single theme, and typically contain four to seven individual research articles or case studies contributed by scholars in the field. A book reviews section, consisting of four or five brief reviews, closes out each issue. *Landscape Research* is available in print and electronic formats, and is ideally suited for an academic library collection with students and faculty active in landscape research.

3213. *Landscapes.* Former titles (until 1999): *Landscape Architectural Review;* (until 1980): *Ontario Association of Landscape Architects Review.* [ISSN: 1492-9600] 1975. q. CAD 25; USD 25. Ed(s): Judy Lord. Naylor (Canada), Inc., 100 Sutherland Ave, Winnipeg, MB R2W 3C7, Canada. Illus., index, adv. Circ: 1400. Vol. ends: Dec. *Indexed:* A01, CBCARef, GardL. *Bk. rev.:* Number and length vary. *Aud.:* Ac, Sa.
This quarterly, the journal of the Canadian Society of Landscape Architects (CSLA), focuses primarily on contemporary landscape architecture in Canada. Volumes contain discussion and review of thematic topics. Recent issues include forums on "Montreal's Evolving Urban Vision" and "The Residential Landscape" from a Canadian viewpoint. The subjects of the scholarly articles range from landscape design and planning to the environmental sciences and aspects of professional practice, with some attention devoted to landscape and architectural history. Written primarily by academics and practitioners, the journal's content includes case studies, editorials, book reviews, and a list of recent and forthcoming events such as conferences and competitions. Each year, one issue is devoted to winners of the annual CSLA awards. When coupled with the U.S. journal *Landscape Architecture, Landscapes* offers readers an extensive view into contemporary North American landscape architecture (with the exception of Mexican examples, of course), making it a solid resource for an academic audience but also appropriate for general readers and researchers. Text is in French and English; some articles are written in French with summaries in English. All English-language articles are accompanied by French summaries.

3214. *Landskab: tidsskrift for planlaegning af have og landskab, review for garden and landscape planning.* Formerly (until 1968): *Havekunst.* [ISSN: 0023-8066] 1920. 8x/yr. DKK 930 domestic; DKK 990 in Europe; DKK 934 elsewhere. Ed(s): Annemarie Lund. Arkitektens Forlag, Pasteursvej 14,4, Copenhagen V, 1799, Denmark; arkfo@arkfo.dk; http://www.arkfo.dk. Illus., index, adv. Sample. Vol. ends: Dec. *Indexed:* API. *Bk. rev.:* 2-4. *Aud.:* Ac, Sa.
Published by the Association of Danish Landscape Architects, *Landskab* provides readers extensive coverage of current international projects in landscape architecture and urban design. Although texts are written in Danish, most articles are accompanied by summaries in English. Color photographs, drawings, plans, and details appear extensively throughout. Book reviews are included, but do not appear in every issue. *Landskab* is an appealing publication for any researcher or specialist interested in international, but particularly Danish and Scandinavian, landscape architecture.

Studies in the History of Gardens & Designed Landscapes. See Gardening section.

3215. *Topos: European landscape magazine.* [ISSN: 0942-752X] 1992. q. EUR 120 domestic (Students, EUR 86.20). Ed(s): Robert Schaefer. Callwey Verlag, Streitfeldstr 35, Munich, 81673, Germany; a.hagenkord@callwey.de; http://www.callwey.de. Illus., index, adv. Circ: 4839 Paid. *Indexed:* A22, API. *Bk. rev.:* Number and length vary. *Aud.:* Ac, Sa.
A well-designed and amply illustrated publication, *Topos* covers contemporary international landscape architecture and urban design. While other journals claim to report on international developments in the field yet rarely go beyond Europe and North America, *Topos* engages a truly striking assortment of geographical regions, from Argentina to Dubai, and from China to Zambia. Individual issues center on an individual theme (recent examples include "Culturescapes," "Crisis Landscapes," and "Making Space"), with several brief articles that explore different aspects of it. Additional features include a news column, competition and awards notices, and book reviews. Multiple individual projects or firms are also discussed in brief (two- or three-page) articles. The publication's uniquely international focus, exceptional book reviews, and

overall high quality of production make it an essential purchase for any landscape architecture collection, whether general or academic in nature. Although the journal was previously published in German and English, texts now appear solely in English.

■ LATIN AMERICA AND SPAIN

Michael Scott, Bibliographer for Latin American Studies and Iberian Languages, Lauinger Library, Georgetown University, 37th & O Streets NW, Washington, DC 20057.

Cheryl LaGuardia, Research Librarian, Widener Library, Harvard University

Introduction

The abstracts in this section discuss popular periodicals published in and about Latin America and Spain. As with everywhere else in the world, Latin American and Iberian magazines and journals are facing a rapidly changing and ever-more specialized market. In recent years, many Latin American countries' telecommunications have improved greatly, and therefore more and more publications in these countries have moved to focus on their online presence; and yet print still reigns there in the end, especially with popular general-audience titles. However, Spain's publishing houses have greatly suffered in recent years because of the country's financial problems, and many periodicals there are moving completely online simply to save money on paper.

For general-audience titles chosen here, the presentation is often quite similar to those found in American English-language publications. Glossy home decorating magazines, neon-bright teen magazines, and somber yet highly readable newsmagazines are the norm in Latin American and Iberia, just as here. The magazines' web sites often act as a supplement to the print version, but some of the print titles, such as *Veja* and *America economia,* offer a considerable amount of material for free online, and will likely be entirely virtual within the next few years. Also, just as with American publications, many of these magazines are using social networking sites to link to online versions of their articles. Nonetheless, even with improved telecommunications systems in Latin America mentioned above, many people do not have home access to a computer, so the print version will continue to be the primary source of revenue for the near future.

Academic journals are continuing in much the same vein. Print continues for now, but because of ever-increasing access to full-text articles via online databases (as well as current economic realities), many of these journals will likely move more and more online within the next few years. Following the trend in academia itself, these journals are becoming increasingly interdisciplinary in focus as well. Film studies, queer studies, and migration studies, in addition to the more usual literary and linguistic analyses, are all common topics in the journals listed below.

Latin American and Iberia are, of course, large regions, and therefore this list is far from exhaustive, and acts merely as a guide. If you wish to look at a broader scope of more journals, consider looking at the "Media" section of the Latin American Network Information Center (LANIC), based at the University of Texas at Austin (http://lanic.utexas.edu/subject/media/). Just as in the U.S., you might check Latin American and Iberian university press sites if you need more specialized or regionally-focused academic journals.

You can readily subscribe to all of these magazines and journals via their web sites or via book vendors based in the U.S., Latin America, and Iberia. Spanish, of course, has now become the second lingua franca of the United States. And given Brazil's rapid economic and political rise over the past few years, Portuguese is quickly sharing center stage with Spanish, hence the addition of the Brazilian magazine *Veja.* Other magazines, such as *Cristina,* that were discussed in previous editions of *MFL* have ceased publication, and still others have become more tabloid-like and have been left out of this year's edition.

Basic Periodicals

Ga: *America economia, Americas* (English edition), *Hola, TV y novelas, Tu, Vanidades;* Ac: *Hispanic Review, Historia mexicana, Journal of Latin American Studies, Latin American Literary Review, Latin American Research Review.*

Basic Abstracts and Indexes

Hispanic American Periodicals Index (HAPI).

3216. Alto Nivel. [ISSN: 1665-7977] m. Ed(s): Ulises Navarro. Iasa Communications, Rosaleda #34, Colonia Lomas Altas, 11950, Mexico; bbracamonte@iasanet.com.mx; http://www.iasanet.com.mx/. Adv. *Aud.:* Ga, Ac.

Alto Nivel deals primarily with Mexican and Latin American business news. Topics within its scope include government business policy, entrepreneurship, the economy within Mexico and abroad, women in business, banking, technology trends, career advice, and biographical profiles of successful businesspeople. Recommended for public libraries that serve large Latino/Chicano populations, as well as academic libraries that support international business programs with a particular focus on Latin America. (MS)

3217. America Economia. 1986. s-m. USD 260 United States. AmericaEconomia, Av Apoquindado 4499, Piso 10, Santiago, Chile; http://www.americaeconomia.com. *Aud.:* Ga, Ac.

America Economia is a renowned business and economics magazine, similar in scope and content to *The Economist.* Besides in-depth economic reporting and analysis, the magazine also covers business education in Latin America, politics, and economic and educational rankings; and includes opinion columns and blogs. Recommended for public libraries that serve populations interested in Latin American business, and academic libraries that serve Latin American–focused international business programs. (MS)

3218. The Americas. [ISSN: 0003-1615] 1944. q. Ed(s): Don Stevens, Eric Zolov. Academy of American Franciscan History, 1712 Euclid Ave, Berkeley, CA 94709; acadafh@aol.com; http://www.aafh.org. Illus., index, adv. Refereed. Circ: 1000. *Indexed:* A01, A22, ABS&EES, AmHI, ArtHuCI, BRI, CBRI, E01, MLA-IB, P02, RILM. *Bk. rev.:* 15, 500-700 words. *Aud.:* Ac.

Different from *Americas,* published by the Organization of the American States, *The Americas* is a well-respected journal of Latin American History, published by the Academy of American Franciscan History and edited at Drexel University. Each issue usually contains several book reviews and in-depth academic articles, often relating to the indigenous peoples of the region. Other common topics include the history of the Catholic Church, Latin Americans of African descent, and intellectual history. One recent addition is interviews with a Latin American historians. Highly recommended for academic libraries that serve Latin American Studies programs, especially those with a strong indigenous focus. (MS)

3219. Americas (English Edition). Former titles (until 1949): *Pan American Union. Bulletin;* (until 1910): *International Bureau of the American Republics. Bulletin;* (until 1908): *International Bureau of the American Republics, International Union of American Republics. Monthly Bulletin;* (until 1902): *Bureau of the American Republics. Monthly Bulletin;* (until 1893): *Bureau of the American Republics. Special Bulletin.* [ISSN: 0379-0940] 18??. bi-m. USD 25 domestic; USD 31 foreign. Organization of American States, 1889 F St, NW, Washington, DC 20006; svillagran@oas.org; http://www.oas.org. Illus. Sample. Microform: PQC. *Indexed:* A01, A06, A22, AmHI, BAS, BRI, C37, MASUSE, MLA-IB, P02. *Bk. rev.:* 2-3, 600-1,200 words. *Aud.:* Hs, Ga, Ac.

This magazine, published by the Organization of American States, has good coverage of current events and cultural and political topics throughout all of Latin America. Many articles discuss the work being done by the OAS and partner organizations, and others simply highlight an interesting cultural event or information about lesser-known but still fascinating places in the region. In some ways, the journal acts as publicity for the organization itself, but it is still recommended for a variety of general readers, especially high schools with strong Spanish-language programs and/or many Latino/Chicano students, and also for general reading in both public and academic libraries. A Spanish-language edition is also available by subscription. (MS)

Ancient Mesoamerica. See Archaeology section.

3220. Automovil Panamericano. 1995. m. MXN 480. Editorial Motorpress Televisa, Av Vasco de Quiroga 2000, Edif E, Mexico, Col Santa Fe, Mexico City, 01210, Mexico; automovil.panamericano@editorial.televisa.com.mx. Circ: 52700 Paid. *Aud.:* Ga.

Although naturally focused on the Mexican auto industry, *Automovil panamericano* also reviews new cars manufactured around the world. Other topics include Mexican government policy on highways and car travel; car racing; and, on occasion, even general transit issues and automobile insurance. Highly recommended for public libraries that serve large Spanish-speaking populations. (MS)

3221. Caras. Formerly (until 1992): *Tal Cual.* [ISSN: 0328-4301] 1980. w. Editorial Perfil S.A., Chacabuco 271, Buenos Aires, 1069, Argentina; perfilcom@perfil.com.ar; http://www.perfil.com.ar. Adv. Circ: 150000 Paid and controlled. *Aud.:* Ga.

Caras is an Argentine general-interest magazine, somewhat like the American publication *People.* Celebrities and other famous people take center stage in this magazine, with stories about the various dramatic (and perhaps less-than-dramatic) events in their lives, all accompanied by many color photos. The publication is naturally but not entirely focused on Argentina; successful Latinos and Spaniards from around the world are regularly featured. Articles are in clear and direct Spanish, and may actually be a great teaching tool in undergraduate classrooms. Recommended mostly, however, for public libraries that serve Spanish-speaking populations. (MS)

3222. Caribbean Quarterly. [ISSN: 0008-6495] 1949. q. University of the West Indies, PO Box 130, Kingston, 7, Jamaica; http://www.uwi.edu. Index, adv. Microform: PQC. Reprint: PSC. *Indexed:* AmHI, BRI, IIBP, IIPA, MLA-IB, RILM. *Bk. rev.:* Number and length vary. *Aud.:* Ga, Ac.

According to the journal itself, *Caribbean Quarterly* "publishes scholarly articles, personal and critical essays, public lectures, poetry, short fiction[,] and book reviews." This journal is published by the University of West Indies, and its focus is primarily (but far from exclusively) on the English-speaking Caribbean. A recent issue, for example, included articles mostly about Jamaica and Barbados, yet there were two articles about the Dominican Republic and the Caribbean coast of Colombia. Highly recommended for academic libraries, and also for public libraries that serve Caribbean or Caribbean-heritage patrons. (MS)

3223. Casa y Estilo Internacional. [ISSN: 1521-8287] 1994. bi-m. USD 29.94. Ed(s): Jose Alfonso Nino, Ugo Campello. Linda International Publishing, 12182 SW 128th St, Miami, FL 33186; info@estilonet.com. Adv. *Aud.:* Ga.

This Miami-based publication bills itself as the "number one Spanish-language magazine dedicated to interior design and lifestyles." Similar in presentation and scope to *Architectural Digest* or *House & Garden,* this bimonthly publication is filled with photographs of beautiful homes and articles about them, some belonging to celebrities. Other topics covered include food and cooking, travel, shopping tips, and practical decorating advice. Recommended for public libraries that serve Spanish-speaking populations. (MS)

3224. Chasqui: revista de literatura latinoamericana. [ISSN: 0145-8973] 1972. s-a. USD 35 (Individuals, USD 25). Ed(s): David W Foster. Chasqui, c/o Darrell B. Lockhart, Foreign Languages & Literatures, MS 0100, Reno, NV 89557-0100; lockhart@unr.edu. Illus., adv. Refereed. *Indexed:* A01, A22, AmHI, ArtHuCI, BRI, MLA-IB, RILM. *Bk. rev.:* 25-30, 500-3,000 words. *Aud.:* Ac.

Chasqui is devoted entirely to Latin American literature of all periods and regions, and articles may be in English, Spanish, or Portuguese. The articles tend to be more theory-focused, and often deal with queer and/or gender studies themes. The journal has an excellent selection of book reviews from both Latin American and U.S. publishers, as well review essays written in the style of *The New York Review of Books* and similar publications. Highly recommended for academic libraries with strong Latin American literature programs. (MS)

3225. *Colonial Latin American Review.* [ISSN: 1060-9164] 1992. 3x/yr. GBP 468 (print & online eds.). Ed(s): Kris Lane. Routledge, 4 Park Sq, Milton Park, Abingdon, OX14 4RN, United Kingdom; subscriptions@tandf.co.uk; http://www.tandfonline.com. Illus., index, adv. Sample. Refereed. Reprint: PSC. *Indexed:* A01, A22, A47, AbAn, AmHI, ArtHuCI, E01, MLA-IB, P61, SSA. *Bk. rev.:* Number and length vary. *Aud.:* Ac.

This interdisciplinary academic journal deals primary in the historical and political milieu of colonial Latin America, yet within this context, literature and the arts are treated as well. Each issue also contains at least several book reviews, and articles are written in English, Spanish, or Portuguese. *CLAR* would provide excellent support for Latin American Studies programs/ departments, as well as history, literature, and art history departments that have a strong focus on Latin America. (MS)

3226. *Contenido.* [ISSN: 0010-7581] 1963. m. Editorial Contenido S.A., Darwin 101, Nueva Cobertura, Mexico City, 11590, Mexico; ecsa@data.net.mx; http://www.contenido.com.mx. Illus., adv. *Aud.:* Ga, Ac.

This newsmagazine naturally focuses on Mexico, but other topics such as international relations (especially with the United States), health, and science are also covered. It is similar to the American magazines *Time* and *Newsweek,* although as it is a monthly publication, its articles tend to be more in-depth and analytical. Highly recommended for public libraries that serve Spanish-speaking patrons, and also for academic libraries that serve academic programs that have a particularly strong focus on Mexico. (MS)

3227. *Cuadernos Hispanoamericanos.* [ISSN: 0011-250X] 1948. m. Agencia Espanola de Cooperacion Internacional (A E C I), Avenida Reyes Catolicos 4, Madrid, 28040, Spain; http://www.aecid.es/es/. Illus. Reprint: PSC. *Indexed:* A22, ArtHuCI, MLA-IB, RILM. *Bk. rev.:* Number and length vary. *Aud.:* Ga, Ac.

Different from many academic publications, *Cuadernos hispanoamericanos* contains original essays, poetry, and fiction, as well as more traditional articles that deal with literary analysis and history, all by leading Latin American writers and academics. For those seeking the region's latest philosophical and literary trends, the journal is hard to surpass. Interviews and themed issues are also common. Highly recommended for academic libraries with strong programs in Latin American studies and literature, and because of the large amount of original content, perhaps also for large public libraries that serve large Hispanic populations. (MS)

3228. *Feminaria.* 1988. irreg. Ed(s): Lea Fletcher. Feminaria Editora, C.C. 402, Buenos Aires, 1000, Argentina; feminaria@fibertel.com.ar; http://www.latbook.com.ar. Refereed. *Bk. rev.:* Number and length vary. *Aud.:* Ga, Ac.

This is one of the longest-running feminist journals produced in Latin America. It focuses particularly on feminist literature, but current events, broader social issues, interviews with writers and activists, and translations from non-Spanish-speaking academics are also included. Geographically, it focuses on Argentina, of course, but nearly all issues discuss feminism from a worldwide perspective. It is mostly academic in tone and scope, and therefore it is an excellent addition to academic libraries that serve Latin American literature and women's studies programs, and but it is also recommended for public libraries that serve an activist Latina community. (MS)

3229. *Frontera Norte.* [ISSN: 0187-7372] 1989. s-a. USD 55 (Individuals, MXN 500). Ed(s): Gerardo Ordonez Barba. El Colegio de la Frontra Norte, A.C., Carretera Escenica Tijuana-Ensenada, km. 18.5, San Antonio del Mar, Tijuana, 22560, Mexico; http://www.colef.mx/. Illus. Refereed. Circ: 500. *Indexed:* A01, Chicano, P61, SSA. *Bk. rev.:* Number and length vary. *Aud.:* Ac.

This academic journal mostly focuses on U.S./Mexico border issues, although Mexico's relations with other countries are also discussed on occasion. Given recent events in the region, articles currently focus on security and political issues, but there are also others that discuss the economics, culture, and other

less immediately pressing issues as well. Vital for academic collections that serve departments that teach and research these same issues (Latin American Studies, security studies, etc.), and also for programs that focus on Border Studies in general. (MS)

3230. *Gestos: revista de teoria y practica del teatro hispanico.* [ISSN: 1040-483X] 1986. s-a. USD 50. Ed(s): Juan Villegas. University of California, Irvine, Department of Spanish and Portuguese, Irvine, CA 92697; http://www.humanities.uci.edu. Illus. Refereed. *Indexed:* A22, IIPA, MLA-IB. *Bk. rev.:* 8-10, 500-1,000 words. *Aud.:* Ac.

Gestos is a well-respected academic journal that deals with Hispanic theater. Articles cover all literary time periods and geographic areas, and are split evenly between being written in English and Spanish. Besides the articles themselves, each issue contains summaries and reviews of recent publications, as well as a list of new titles that the journal has received, which may aid in collection development. Highly recommend for academic libraries. (MS)

3231. *Hispanic Journal (Indiana).* [ISSN: 0271-0986] 1979. s-a. Ed(s): Liliana Jurewiez. Indiana University of Pennsylvania, Department of Foreign Languages, Sutton Hall, Indiana, PA 15705; http://www.iup.edu/ spanish/publications/default.aspx. Refereed. *Indexed:* A22, AmHI, MLA-IB, RILM. *Bk. rev.:* Number per issue varies; 550-1,750 words. *Aud.:* Ac.

Hispanic Journal covers literary and linguistics topics from both Iberia and Latin America, with a slight emphasis on nineteenth through twenty-first century literature. A helpful feature is a bibliography of books and journals that the journal has received recently, which may aid in collection development decisions. Highly recommended for academic libraries. (MS)

Hispanic Journal of Behavioral Sciences. See Psychology section.

3232. *Hispanic Review: a quarterly journal devoted to research in the Hispanic languages and literatures.* [ISSN: 0018-2176] 1933. q. USD 93 (print & online eds.) Individuals, USD 55 (print & online eds); Students, USD 30). Ed(s): Linda Grabner. University of Pennsylvania Press, 3905 Spruce St, Philadelphia, PA 19104; custserv@pobox.upenn.edu; http://www.pennpress.org. Illus., adv. Sample. Refereed. Vol. ends: Fall. *Indexed:* A01, A06, A07, A22, AmHI, ArtHuCI, BRI, E01, FR, MASUSE, MLA-IB, P02, RILM. *Bk. rev.:* Number and length vary. *Aud.:* Ac.

This is one of the premier academic journals on Hispanic literature and culture. Articles cover all time periods and regions (although balanced about evenly between Spain and Spanish-speaking America), and are either in Spanish or English. Some articles are more general in nature, such as on a literary theory topic or intellectual history. At least a few book reviews are included in each issue. Highly recommended for academic libraries. (MS)

3233. *Hispanofila: ensayos de literatura.* [ISSN: 0018-2206] 1957. 3x/yr. USD 50. Ed(s): Anne Abell, Fred M Clark. University of North Carolina at Chapel Hill, Department of Romance Languages and Literature, CB 3170, 238 Day Hall, Chapel Hill, NC 27599; romlpub@unc.edu; http://roml.unc.edu/. Illus., index, adv. Refereed. Vol. ends: May. Microform: PQC. *Indexed:* A01, A22, AmHI, ArtHuCI, BRI, MLA-IB. *Bk. rev.:* Number and length vary. *Aud.:* Ac.

This journal publishes academic articles, summaries, and reviews of new titles in the field of Hispanic literatures. Articles are in Spanish or English, and cover all time periods and literary genres. Recommened for academic libraries. (MS)

3234. *Historia Mexicana.* [ISSN: 0185-0172] 1951. 4x/yr. Ed(s): Beatriz Moran Gortari. Colegio de Mexico, A.C., Departamento de Publicaciones, Camino al Ajusco 20, Col. Pedregal Santa Teresa, Mexico City, 10740, Mexico; http://www.colmex.mx. Illus., index, adv. Refereed. Vol. ends: Jun. *Indexed:* A22, A47, AmHI, ArtHuCI, BAS, Chicano, IBSS, P61, SSA. *Bk. rev.:* 2-8, 500-2,000 words. *Aud.:* Ac.

This Spanish-language journal is published by the Colegio de Mexico, and is one of the "go-to" publications on Mexican history. Occasionally there are themed issues, but usually each number deals with a wide variety of historical topics. Critical essays, book reviews and summaries, bibliographies of received publications, and abstracts of the main articles in both English and Spanish are also often included. Highly recommended for academic libraries, especially those that serve institutions with a strong focus on Mexican history and culture. (MS)

3235. *Hola.* [ISSN: 0214-3895] 1944. w. USD 140. Empresa Editora Hola, S.A., C. Velazquez, 98 3o., Madrid, 28006, Spain. Illus., adv. Sample. *Aud.:* Ga.

The main focus of *Hola* is celebrity gossip and lifestyles, but each issue also contains information about both men's and women's fashion, food, interior decorating, and even current events and politics. It is somewhat like a combination of the American magazines *People* and *Time,* with more emphasis on the celebrity side of things. Recommended for public libraries with Spanish-speaking patrons. (MS)

3236. *Journal of Latin American Cultural Studies.* Formerly (until 1995): *Travesia.* [ISSN: 1356-9325] 1992. 4x/yr. GBP 706 (print & online eds.). Ed(s): Fernando Sdrigotti. Routledge, 4 Park Sq, Milton Park, Abingdon, OX14 4RN, United Kingdom; subscriptions@tandf.co.uk; http://www.tandfonline.com. Illus., adv. Sample. Refereed. Reprint: PSC. *Indexed:* A01, A22, AmHI, ArtHuCI, E01, MLA-IB, P61, SSA. *Bk. rev.:* Varies by issue. *Aud.:* Ac.

Articles in this academic journal often take a multidisciplinary approach; film, popular culture, racial politics, and new ways of looking at canonical works are just a few topics in recent issues. Some issues also contain reprints of earlier articles for rereading, and others contains book reviews or review essays as well. Highly recommended for universities and colleges with Latin American Studies programs, especially those with particular strengths in film, literature, and historical studies.

3237. *Journal of Latin American Studies.* [ISSN: 0022-216X] 1969. q. GBP 292. Ed(s): Gareth A Jones, Rory Miller. Cambridge University Press, The Edinburgh Bldg, Shaftesbury Rd, Cambridge, CB2 8RU, United Kingdom; journals@cambridge.org; http://www.cambridge.org/uk. Illus. Refereed. Vol. ends: Nov. Microform: PQC. Reprint: PSC. *Indexed:* A01, A22, A47, ABIn, AmHI, ArtHuCI, BRI, C45, Chicano, E01, IBSS, MLA-IB, P02, P61, RRTA, RiskAb, SSA. *Bk. rev.:* 22-28, 350-2,000 words. *Aud.:* Ga, Ac.

The articles in *JLAS* chiefly focus on the social sciences, history, international relations, politics, indigenous peoples, and specific topics such as colonization/decolonization and land reform. One valuable aspect of the journal is the many book reviews that cover a wide variety of recent publications. Highly recommended for academic libraries that serve Latin American Studies programs (especially programs focused on the topics listed above) and, because of its breadth, possibly for public libraries that serve Latino/Chicano populations. (MS)

3238. *Latin American Business Review.* [ISSN: 1097-8526] 1998. q. GBP 355 (print & online eds.). Ed(s): Lucilia Silva, Denise Dimon. Routledge, 325 Chestnut St, Ste 800, Philadelphia, PA 19106; customerservice@taylorandfrancis.com; http://www.tandfonline.com. Adv. Sample. Refereed. Reprint: PSC. *Indexed:* A01, A22, ABIn, B01, E01, IBSS, RiskAb. *Aud.:* Ga, Ac.

This journal contains academic articles on Latin American business culture, trends, and practices. Articles are in English, and cover all parts of Latin America, including non–Spanish-speaking countries. Highly recommended for libraries that serve international business programs in Latin America, and recommended specialized public library collections. (MS)

3239. *Latin American Indian Literatures Journal: a review of American Indian texts and studies.* Supersedes (in 1985): *Latin American Indian Literatures.* [ISSN: 0888-5613] 1977. s-a. USD 51 (Individuals, USD 30). Ed(s): Mary H Preuss. Pennsylvania State University at McKeesport, 4000 University Dr, McKeesport, PA 15132-7698; mhp1@psu.edu. Illus., adv. Refereed. Circ: 300 Paid. *Indexed:* A22, A47, AmHI, ArtHuCI, MLA-IB, RILM. *Bk. rev.:* 3-5, 500-1,500 words. *Aud.:* Ac.

This academic journal is about the literature, mythology, and oral tradition of Latin American indigenous peoples. Articles are generally in English, but French, Spanish, and Portuguese appear from time to time as well. It is truly multidisciplinary, with articles by anthropologists, historians, literary scholars, and political scientists. Book reviews also appear in each issue. Highly recommended for libraries that serve Latin American Studies programs and/or Spanish departments with an especially strong focus on indigenous literature, culture, and history. (MS)

3240. *Latin American Literary Review.* [ISSN: 0047-4134] 1972. s-a. USD 51. Ed(s): Yvette E Miller. Latin American Literary Review Press, PO Box 17660, Pittsburgh, PA 15235; http://www.lalrp.org. Illus., index. Refereed. Microform: PQC. *Indexed:* A01, A22, AmHI, BRI, Chicano, MLA-IB, P02. *Bk. rev.:* 4-6, 90-100 words. *Aud.:* Ac.

As one can infer from the title, this prestigious journal chiefly is about Latin American literature, especially from the nineteenth century until the present day. Articles are in English, Spanish, or Portuguese, and excellent book reviews are often included as well. Highly recommended for academic libraries. (MS)

3241. *Latin American Perspectives: a journal on capitalism and socialism.* [ISSN: 0094-582X] 1974. bi-m. USD 732. Ed(s): Ronald H Chilcote. Sage Publications, Inc., 2455 Teller Rd, Thousand Oaks, CA 91320; info@sagepub.com; http://www.sagepub.com. Illus. Refereed. Microform: PQC. Reprint: PSC. *Indexed:* A22, ABIn, BRI, Chicano, E01, IBSS, MLA-IB, P02, P61, RILM, RiskAb, SSA. *Bk. rev.:* Number and length vary. *Aud.:* Ga, Ac.

Each issue of *Latin American Perspectives* focuses on a single theme, and articles often deal with topics on the Latin American diaspora, including the United States and other countries. The overall tone is academic, but given its multidisciplinary approach, general readers may enjoy reading about popular culture via hip-hop music, contemporary and experimental film, and other less traditional forms of expression. Articles are in English, but abstracts are in both English and the language of the country considered in the article (Portuguese for Brazil, etc.). Highly recommended for academic libraries that serve highly multidisciplinary programs in Latin American Studies, and for large public libraries. (MS)

3242. *Latin American Research Review.* [ISSN: 0023-8791] 1965. 3x/yr. Free to members. Ed(s): Philip Oxhorn. Latin American Studies Association, 416 Bellefield Hall, University of Pittsburgh, Pittsburgh, PA 15260; lasa@pitt.edu; http://lasa.international.pitt.edu/. Illus., index, adv. Sample. Refereed. *Indexed:* A01, A22, ABIn, ABS&EES, AmHI, B01, BRI, Chicano, E01, FR, IBSS, IIBP, MLA-IB, P02, P61, RILM, SSA. *Aud.:* Ga, Ac.

This journal, the official publication of the Latin American Studies Association, deals with a broad range of topics in each issue. Indigenous studies, literary criticism, historical analysis, and sociological quality-of-life studies all have appeared in recent issues. Each issue also includes review essays, in which scholars write about topics using recent publications as the base of discussion. Highly recommended for academic libraries that serve Latin American Studies departments or programs, and also for public libraries that serve large Latino/Chicano populations. (MS)

Latina (New York). See Fashion and Lifestyle section.

3243. *Letras Femeninas.* [ISSN: 0277-4356] 1975. s-a. Free. Arizona State University, School of International Letters & Cultures, 851 South Cady Mall, PO Box 870202, Tempe, AZ 85287; acereda@asu.edu; http://silc.asu.edu/. Illus. *Indexed:* MLA-IB. *Bk. rev.:* Number and length vary. *Aud.:* Ac.

Articles in *Letras femeninas* looks at the gamut of Hispanic literature from a feminist perspective. Each issue covers virtually all regions and time periods, all dealing with women and their relation to literary culture. Many issues contain summaries and reviews of newly published monographs, as well. Not as activist-oriented as *Feminaria,* nonetheless *Letras femeninas* strongly asserts the place of feminism in the academy. Highly recommended for academic libraries that serve Latin American literature and/or women's studies programs.

3244. Letras Libres. [ISSN: 1606-5913] 1999. m. MXN 500 domestic; USD 80 in US & Canada; USD 110 elsewhere. Ed(s): Enrique Krauze. Editorial Vuelta, SA de CV, Presidente Carranza 210, Coyoacan, Mexico, D.F., 04000, Mexico. Circ: 30000. *Aud.:* Ga, Ac.

Letras libres is a multicolor, glossy publication that is probably most similar to the American publication *The New Yorker.* Its focus is primarily literary, including many summaries and reviews of new titles, but politics, the fine arts, media, and opinion pieces figure prominently as well. Geographically, the publication mostly covers Mexico, but most issues deal with other Latin America and even famous non–Spanish-language writers and events. Articles are almost always by the foremost current Latin American writers and intellectuals. Highly recommended for public libraries that serve a Spanish-speaking population, and also for academic libraries that serve institutions with strong Latin American and comparative literature programs.

3245. Luso - Brazilian Review. [ISSN: 0024-7413] 1963. s-a. USD 193 (print & online eds.). Ed(s): Severino J Albuquerque, Ellen W Sapega. University of Wisconsin Press, Journal Division, 1930 Monroe St, 3rd Fl, Madison, WI 53711; journals@uwpress.wisc.edu; http://www.uwpress.org/. Illus. Refereed. Circ: 2000. Microform: PQC. Reprint: PSC. *Indexed:* A01, A22, AmHI, ArtHuCI, E01, MLA-IB, P61, RILM, SSA. *Bk. rev.:* 5, 700 words. *Aud.:* Ga, Ac.

Luso-Brazilian Review publishes articles (in both English and Portuguese) on Portuguese, Brazilian, and Luso-African literatures, linguistics, and cultures. It is the oldest publication of its kind in the United States. The focus is primarily on literary studies, but issues often contain articles on Lusophone history, politics, or other social sciences. While it is an academic journal, and therefore best suited to academic libraries that serve Latin American and Lusophone studies, the journal may be popular in public libraries that serve large Luso/Brazilian-American populations. (MS)

3246. Mexican Studies. [ISSN: 0742-9797] 1985. s-a. USD 202 (print & online eds.). Ed(s): Jaime E Rodriguez. University of California Press, Journals Division, 2000 Ctr St, Ste 303, Berkeley, CA 94704; customerservice@ucpressjournals.com; http://www.ucpressjournals.com. Illus., index, adv. Refereed. Reprint: PSC. *Indexed:* A01, A22, A47, AmHI, ArtHuCI, BRI, Chicano, E01, ENW, MLA-IB, P02, P61, RILM, SSA. *Bk. rev.:* Number and length vary. *Aud.:* Ga, Ac.

This journal covers the history, economics, politics, and culture of Mexico, with a bit more of an emphasis on the social sciences. Articles are in English or Spanish and cover all regions and historical time periods. Some issues contain book reviews or a bibliography of books received. Highly recommended for academic libraries that serve academic programs with a strong emphasis on Mexico, and possibly recommended for large public libraries that serve Mexican or Mexican-American populations. (MS)

3247. Mexico Desconocido. [ISSN: 0187-1560] 1976. m. MXN 240 domestic; USD 60 United States; USD 70 in Europe. Ed(s): Beatriz Quintanar Hinojosa. Editorial Mexico Desconocido S.A.de C.V., Monte Pelvoux 110, Planta Jardin, Lomas de Chapultepec, Mexico City, 11000, Mexico. Illus., index, adv. Circ: 64000. *Aud.:* Ga.

A lavishly illustrated and carefully designed journal, *Mexico Desconocido* celebrates the lesser-known beauties of Mexico, covering the art, music, culture, and customs of Mexican regions and cultures that generally get little attention from tourists. The color photo essays are stunning and the articles are written in an informative yet engaging style. The magazine is justly celebrated for its efforts, having received a number of national awards from the Mexican government for its efforts to promote and preserve traditional Mexican arts and folklore. Excerpts from the print magazine are available from the magazine's web site in English and Spanish; however, the reader may be tempted to skip the text and go straight to the beautiful photos. Recommended for public libraries, although students of Mexican culture and history may also appreciate this journal, making it appropriate for academic libraries as well. (OO)

3248. N A C L A Report on the Americas. Former titles (until 1993): *Report on the Americas;* (until 1991): *N A C L A Report on the Americas;* (until 1977): *N A C L A's Latin America and Empire Report;* (until 1971): *N A C L A Newsletter.* [ISSN: 1071-4839] 1967. q. USD 60

(Individuals, USD 36). Ed(s): Pablo Morales. North American Congress on Latin America, Inc., 38 Greene St, 4th Fl, New York, NY 10013; nacla@nacla.org; http://www.nacla.org. Illus., adv. Refereed. Vol. ends: Jul/Jun. Microform: PQC. *Indexed:* A01, A22, BRI, P02, RILM. *Bk. rev.:* Number and length vary. *Aud.:* Ga, Ac.

This is chiefly a political science, history, and current affairs journal published by the North American Congress on Latin America. Each issue centers on a specific topic, mostly from a social sciences and historical perspective, and articles are often less academic in tone than those of other journals with the same sort of coverage. Issues surrounding racial minorities and women are also often given particular attention, many times with an activist point of view. U.S. and Latin American relations are also a common topic. Recommended for academic libraries that serve Latin American studies programs or departments, and also for public libraries that serve politically active Chicano/Latino populations and their allies. (MS)

3249. Problemas del Desarrollo: revista latinoamericana de economia. [ISSN: 0301-7036] 1969. q. Universidad Nacional Autonoma de Mexico, Instituto de Investigaciones Economicas, Torre II de Humanidades 5o Piso, Ciudad Universitaria, Mexico City, 04510, Mexico; revprode@servidor.unam.mx; http://probdes.iiec.unam.mx. Illus., index, adv. Refereed. *Indexed:* A01, A22, B01, EconLit, IBSS, JEL. *Bk. rev.:* 1-10, 800-1,500 words. *Aud.:* Ac.

As one can guess from its title, this Spanish-language academic journal contains articles about economic development issues, particularly in Latin America. General economics issues are also often discussed, such as the growing relationship between Latin America and China, and the effects of economic uncertainty in the region. Vital for libraries that serve Latin American Studies programs that specialize in political economy and economic developement, as well as economics departments with a particularly strong focus on Latin America. (MS)

3250. Proceso: semanario de informacion y analisis. [ISSN: 0185-1632] 1976. w. MXN 660; USD 150 United States; USD 350 in Europe. Ed(s): Rafael Rodriguez Castaneda. Comunicacion e Informacion S.A. de C.V. (CISA), Fresas 13, Col Del Valle, Mexico City, 03100, Mexico; buzon@proceso.com.mx; http://www.proceso.com.mx/. Illus., adv. Sample. *Bk. rev.:* 1, lengthy. *Aud.:* Ga, Ac.

This newsmagazine naturally chiefly focuses on Mexican politics and culture, but international issues and events are treated in depth. Similar to *Time* or *Newsweek, Proceso* is aimed toward a general readership, and articles are highly analytical and in-depth. Highly recommended for public libraries that serve Latino and Chicano populations, and also for academic libraries that serve departments and programs that have a strong focus on Mexico. (MS)

3251. Review (New York, 1968): literature and arts of the Americas. Formerly (until 1987): *Review - Center for Inter-American Relations.* [ISSN: 0890-5762] 1968. s-a. GBP 161 (print & online eds.). Ed(s): Daniel Shapiro. Routledge, 325 Chestnut St, Ste 800, Philadelphia, PA 19106; orders@taylorandfrancis.com; http://www.tandfonline.com. Illus., adv. Sample. Refereed. Microform: PQC. *Indexed:* A22, AmHI, ArtHuCI, E01, MLA-IB, RILM. *Bk. rev.:* 9-12, 900-1,200 words. *Aud.:* Ga, Ac, Sa.

This a leading English-language journal on contemporary arts and literature in the Americas. Each issue focuses on a particular topic, place, and/or time period, and articles tend to be written in a kind of "public scholar" tone. Each issue also contains numerous reviews of recently published monographs. Highly recommended for both public, academic, and arts libraries. (MS)

3252. Revista Canadiense de Estudios Hispanicos. [ISSN: 0384-8167] 1970. 3x/yr. CAD 60. Ed(s): Richard Young. Revista Canadiense de Estudios Hispanicos, Dept of Language, Literatures & Cultures, McGill University, Montreal, PQ H3A 3RI, Canada. Illus., index, adv. Refereed. Vol. ends: Spring. *Indexed:* A22, MLA-IB, RILM. *Bk. rev.:* 10-15, 500-1,500 words. *Aud.:* Ac.

This prestigious academic journal covers a broad variety of topics (literature, linguistics, cultural studies, etc.) within the field of Hispanic Studies. Issues often focus on a specific event or topic, and are generally in Spanish, although English and other languages appear from time to time as well. All time periods and places are also represented, often even within a single issue. On occasion, there are articles particularly about Canada's relations with the Hispanic world. Highly recommended for academic libraries, especially those that serve doctoral programs in Hispanic studies. (MS)

3253. Revista de Critica Literaria Latinoamericana. [ISSN: 0252-8843] 1975. s-a. USD 65 (Individuals, USD 35). Ed(s): Jose Antonio Mazzotti. Latinoamericana Editores, Department of Spanish and Portuguese, 5319 Dwinelle Hall, Berkeley, CA 94720-2590. Refereed. *Indexed:* A01, A22, AmHI, ArtHuCI, MLA-IB, RILM. *Bk. rev.:* Number and length vary. *Aud.:* Ac.

This highly respected, long-standing scholarly journal switched hands in 2010, moving from Dartmouth to Tufts University's Romance Languages Department and acquiring a beautifully organized and designed new web page. Issues are available online for free from 1998 on; however, the print edition is still a valuable resource. Each issue includes an excellent book review section, and may also include editorials by prominent scholars and interviews with literary figures. Combining literary and cultural criticism with keen sociohistorical analysis, *RCLL* is an indispensable resource for academic libraries that support Latin American Studies and literature programs, but would not be out of place in a public library with a research-oriented clientele. (OO)

3254. Revista de Indias. [ISSN: 0034-8341] 1940. 3x/yr. Ed(s): Consuelo Naranjo Orovio. Consejo Superior de Investigaciones Cientificas (C S I C), Departamento de Publicaciones, Vitruvio 8, Madrid, 28006, Spain; publ@csic.es; http://www.publicaciones.csic.es. Illus., index. *Indexed:* A22, A47, ArtHuCI, BAS, MLA-IB, RILM. *Bk. rev.:* Number and length vary. *Aud.:* Ac.

Published continuously since 1940, *Revista de Indias* publishes articles about the political and cultural history of Latin America, and these often, but not exclusively, focus on colonial- and Independence-era topics. Articles are in Spanish, English, or Portuguese. Many articles also deal with political and cultural relations between Iberia and Latin America. Recommended for academic libraries that have history departments with strong programs in Latin American history, and for multidisciplinary programs in Hispanic studies, especially those that specialize in Transatlantic topics. (MS)

3255. Revista de Occidente. [ISSN: 0034-8635] 1923. m. USD 200 foreign. Ed(s): Jose Varela Ortega. Fundacion Jose Ortega y Gasset, Fortuny 53, Madrid, 28010, Spain; comunicacion@fog.es; http://www.ortegaygasset.edu/. Illus., index, adv. *Indexed:* A22, ArtHuCI, MLA-IB, RILM. *Bk. rev.:* 1-3, 500-1,250 words. *Aud.:* Ga, Ac.

Founded in 1923 by the eminent Spanish philosopher Jose Ortega y Gasset, *Revista de Occidente* contains articles on a variety of cultural topics. Spanish and Latin American literature is discussed, of course, but other features make appearances, too—articles on non–Spanish language literature and film, author interviews, and general philosophical and cultural essays. It is fairly similar in style and content to *The Paris Review* and comparable publications, although it is perhaps slightly more outright-scholarly. Issues often contain original literary works as well. Highly recommended for academic libraries that serve Hispanic literature, linguistics, and comparative literature programs, and also for public libraries that serve Spanish-speaking populations. (MS)

3256. Revista Iberoamericana (Print). [ISSN: 0034-9631] 1938. q. USD 195 combined subscription (print & online eds.). International Institute of Ibero-American Literature, 1312 Cathedral of Learning, University of Pittsburgh, Pittsburgh, PA 15260; http://www.pitt.edu/~hispan/iili/. Illus. Refereed. Microform: PQC. Reprint: PSC. *Indexed:* A22, ArtHuCI, MLA-IB, RILM. *Bk. rev.:* 15-20, 500-3,500 words. *Aud.:* Ac.

While many issues of *Revista iberoamericana* cover a range of topics, some issues consider a particular theme or writer in Latin American literature. Articles are chiefly in Spanish, but may appear in Portuguese or English, and often focus on twentieth-century or contemporary literature. The many book reviews and summaries that appear in each issue are also of great use to scholars and librarians alike. The journal's intensely academic tone is especially suited to libraries that serve graduate programs and faculties that research and write on Hispanic-American literature, especially that of past century or so. Highly recommended. (MS)

3257. T V y Novelas. [ISSN: 0188-0683] 1982. bi-w. Editorial Televisa, Vasco de Quiroga 2000, Edificio E, Mexico City, 01210, Mexico; info@editorialtelevisa.com; http://www.esmas.com/editorialtelevisa/. Adv. Circ: 145000 Paid. *Aud.:* Ga.

Falling somewhere in between the American magazines *People* and *Entertainment Weekly*, *TV y Novelas* (the "Novelas" refers to *telenovelas*) mostly contains celebrity gossip from both the Latin American and Anglo-American regions, as well as TV and film news, and articles and photography on the latest fashion trends. Recommended for public libraries that serve Spanish-speaking populations, and possibly for academic libraries that serve programs with a particular focus on Latin American media culture. (MS)

3258. Tu. Former titles: *Tu Internacional; Tu.* 1980. m. Editorial Televisa, Vasco de Quiroga 2000, Edificio E, Mexico City, 01210, Mexico; info@editorialtelevisa.com; http://www.esmas.com/editorialtelevisa/. Illus., adv. Circ: 190000. *Aud.:* Ga.

This teen magazine focuses on both Latino/Chicano and Anglo teen celebrities, as well as providing style tips and advice for its young readers. It is very similar in content and presentation to the American magazine *Tiger Beat,* with very bright graphics, many photographs, and short articles. Recommended for public libraries that serve Spanish-speaking patrons. (MS)

3259. Vanidades. 1961. bi-w. Editorial Televisa, Vasco de Quiroga 2000, Edificio E, Mexico City, 01210, Mexico; info@editorialtelevisa.com; http://www.esmas.com/editorialtelevisa/. Illus., adv. Sample. Circ: 891000 Paid. *Aud.:* Ga.

Vanidades covers a broad range of women's issues, and has been in print for more than 50 years. Each issue contains a great amount of information on beauty, fashion, work, and home life and cooking. Each issue is adapted according to the local nationality; there are American, Mexican, Dominican, and other editions. Highly recommended for public libraries that serve Spanish-speaking populations. (MS)

3260. Veja. Formerly: *Veja e Leia.* [ISSN: 0100-7122] 1968. w. BRL 51.30 combined subscription (print & online eds.). Editora Abril, S.A., Avenida das Nacoes Unidas 7221, Pinheiros, Sao Paulo, 05425-902, Brazil; abrilsac@abril.com.br; http://www.abril.com.br. Illus., adv. Microform: PQC. *Indexed:* B03. *Aud.:* Ga, Ac.

Veja is basically the Brazilian equivalent of the American magazines *Time* and *Newsweek*. Each issue focuses on both Brazilian and international politics, and also includes articles on education, history, popular culture, the arts, and opinion pieces as well. Highly recommended for public libraries that serve Brazilian or Brazilian-American patrons, and also academic libraries that serve Latin American Studies programs that have a particular focus on Brazil. (MS)

3261. Wadabagei: a journal of the Caribbean and its diasporas. [ISSN: 1091-5753] 1998. 3x/yr. USD 80 (Individuals, USD 30). Ed(s): J.A George Irish, Holger Henke. Lexington Books, 4501 Forbes Blvd, Ste 200, Lanham, MD 20706; lexingtonbooks@rowman.com; http://www.lexingtonbooks.com/. Adv. Refereed. *Indexed:* AmHI, ENW, IBSS, IIBP, MLA-IB, P61, SSA. *Bk. rev.:* Number and length vary. *Aud.:* Ga, Ac.

Wadabagei is an academic journal dedicated to the study of the people of the Caribbean and their diaspora. All languages and nationalities are represented, and articles cover popular, literary, historical, and political culture all in nearly equal amounts. Each issue contains at least one book review as well. Recommended for academic libraries that serve Latin American programs with a Caribbean focus, and also for other multidisciplinary programs such as migration studies. Also recommended for public libraries that serve large Caribbean populations. (MS)

■ LATINO STUDIES

Lisa Gardinier, Latin American & Iberian Studies Librarian, University of Iowa, 100 Main Library, Iowa City, IA 52240; lisa-gardinier@uiowa.edu

Introduction

Like other fields of ethnic and area studies, Latino studies is an inherently interdisciplinary field. Thus, research concerning Latinos is scattered through the mainstream scholarly literature, as well as the specific titles listed here. Some titles, such as *Aztlan* or the *Bilingual Research Journal,* have been around for decades, but many titles are much newer, having appeared within the past 15 years, and they have quickly established strong reputations and academic respect, while allowing for, arguably, a more authentic voice and discussion among peer scholars. As one reviews the list, it is apparent that education and law are well represented, as they reflect major concerns of the Latino population in the United States.

As noted in previous editions of *Magazines for Libraries,* electronic publishing has created an instability that has not yet settled, and the field of Latino studies is no exception, in both popular and scholarly publishing. Very recently, as I was reviewing titles for inclusion, *Hispanic Business,* long a basic title in the field, published its last print issue and will be exclusively online. *Latin Beat,* long a core title on the Latin music scene, has been exclusively electronic since 2009. Electronic publishing is a complex environment with formats that are ever-changing: is it a blog, a web site, an electronic magazine, or a journal? While researching titles included in long-ago editions of *MFL,* I stumbled across *Pocho.com,* the Internet reincarnation of a seminal Chicano zine from the early 1990s. To impose some order, I limited the electronic-only publications that I included in this list to scholarly journals, though that criterion is likely a very inadequate rule.

Latino communities maintain a vibrant set of local news media. I strongly advise public and academic librarians alike to search out their local Latino news outlets, in both English and Spanish, both in the interest of serving Latino patrons and in order to preserve and document the local community through a distinctive perspective. Research for this section found local news publications, both print and online, across the United States, in large urban areas as well as in small population centers.

Basic Periodicals

Aztlan, Journal of Latinos and Education, Latino Studies, People en Espanol, Poder Hispanic.

Basic Abstracts and Indexes

Alternative Press Index, America: History and Life, Chicano Database, Ethnic Newswatch, Hispanic American Periodicals Index (HAPI).

3262. *The Association of Mexican-American Educators Journal.* s-a. Ed(s): Antonio Camacho, Oscar Jimenez-Castellanos. A M A E Inc., 634 S Spring St, Ste 908, Los Angeles, CA 90014; ExecutiveDirector@amae.org; http://amaejournal.asu.edu/. Refereed. *Bk. rev.:* 1. *Aud.:* Ac, Sa.

The *AMAE Journal* is an open-access, refereed journal published by the Association of Mexican-American Educators and hosted by the Mary Lou Fulton Teachers College at Arizona State University. It is intended to be a forum in which to address research and issues of importance to Mexican-American and Latino children and their families, to inform academia as well as other stakeholders involved in education. Recent articles have addressed undocumented students; professional development of science teachers in immigrant communities; and school finance. Issues also regularly include a book review, a short essay, and/or poetry. URL: http://amaejournal.asu.edu/

3263. *Aztlan: a journal of Chicano studies.* [ISSN: 0005-2604] 1970. s-a. USD 195 (print & online eds.). Ed(s): Chon A Noriega. University of California, Los Angeles, Chicano Studies Research Center Press, 193 Haines Hall, Los Angeles, CA 90095; aztlan@csrc.ucla.edu; http:/ www.chicano.ucla.edu. Illus., adv. Refereed. Circ: 700 Paid. Microform: LIB. *Indexed:* A01, A22, AmHI, BRI, CBRI, Chicano, ERIC, MLA-IB, P02, P61, RILM, SSA. *Bk. rev.:* 1-7, 350-1,000 words. *Aud.:* Ac.

Published since 1970, *Aztlan* is a well-respected journal of refereed scholarly articles from the humanities, social sciences, and arts with a focus on Chicano studies. Each issue includes an "Editor's Commentary," "Essays," "Dossier" (a collection of articles on a similar theme), an "Artist's Communique" by the artist of the cover illustration, and book reviews. Articles examine the intersection of Chicano studies with anthropology, Latino studies, and literature,

among other disciplines. Recent topics include Chicana women in politics; immigration; ethnic studies in public schools; Chicano community art initiatives; and Chicano literature. Highly recommended for academic libraries, as it is a core title in its field.

3264. *Berkeley La Raza Law Journal.* Formerly (until 2001): *La Raza Law Journal.* [ISSN: 1544-9882] 1987. s-a. USD 53. Ed(s): David Abella, Steve Valenzuela. University of California, Berkeley, School of Law, West Basement - Rm 20, Berkeley, CA 94720; journalpublications@law.berkeley.edu; http://www.law.berkeley.edu. Refereed. Circ: 250 Paid. Reprint: WSH. *Indexed:* A01, BRI, CLI, Chicano, L14. *Aud.:* Ac, Sa.

As one of the few law reviews in the United States focused on Latino issues, the *Berkeley La Raza Law Journal* declares its mission "to provide an open forum for the analysis of legal issues affecting the Latina/o community; to publish articles written by Latina/o students, scholars, and practitioners; to serve as a legal research resource." It is also of note that the *BLRLJ* has a special interest in encouraging future law students through an undergraduate fellowship. Recent articles include "Erasing Race, Dismissing Class: San Antonio Independent School District v. Rodriguez" and "Improving Legal Aid to Rural Communities in California." Back issues are available on the journal web site. Recommended for academic libraries that support Latino studies collections. URL: www.boalt.org/LRLJ

3265. *Bilingual Research Journal.* Former titles (until 1992): *N A B E Journal;* (until 1979): *N A B E.* [ISSN: 1523-5882] 1975. 3x/yr. GBP 147 (print & online eds.). Ed(s): Maria E Franquiz, Alba Ortiz. Routledge, 325 Chestnut St, Ste 800, Philadelphia, PA 19106; customerservice@taylorandfrancis.com; http://www.tandfonline.com. Illus., adv. Refereed. Reprint: PSC. *Indexed:* A01, A22, BRI, Chicano, ERIC, LT&LA, MLA-IB, P02. *Bk. rev.:* 1-2, 800-2200 words. *Aud.:* Ac.

The scope of the *Bilingual Research Journal* goes beyond Latino studies to all language-minority children and youth, but a significant number of the articles concern the education of Latino students. Topics include language politics, pedagogical approaches, and multilingualism. Recent articles include, "Vamos a jugar counters! Learning mathematics through funds of knowledge, play, and the third space" and "The role of bilingual education teachers in preventing inappropriate referrals of ELLs to special education: Implications for response to intervention." *BRJ* is peer-reviewed and publishes three issues per year. Highly recommended for academic libraries.

Chicana/o Latina/o Law Review. See Law section.

3266. *Harvard Journal of Hispanic Policy.* Former titles (until 1993): *Journal of Hispanic Policy;* (until 1987): *Journal of Hispanic Politics.* [ISSN: 1074-1917] 1985. a. USD 40 (Individuals, USD 20). Ed(s): Joe Carreon, Octavio Gonzalez. Harvard University, John F. Kennedy School of Government, 79 John F Kennedy St, PO Box 142, Cambridge, MA 02138; cpl@ksg.harvard.edu; http://www.hks.harvard.edu/. Adv. Refereed. *Indexed:* A01, BRI, Chicano, ENW, ERIC, P02. *Bk. rev.:* 1-2. *Aud.:* Ac, Sa.

HJHP is a student-edited annual publication at the Harvard Kennedy School that strives to be a nonpartisan review of politics and policy that affect U.S. Latinos. It publishes a vibrant mix of commentary, interviews, and research articles written by young researchers and graduate students alongside established academics, politicians, and professionals. Recent articles include "Social Security: Strengthening a Vital Safety Net for Latinos," "The Interplay between Prejudice against Latinos and Policy: A Social Psychological Perspective," and "Preserving Latino Heritage: An Interview with Ken Salazar." Back issues are available on the journal web site. Recommended for academic libraries and large public libraries. URL: www.hks.harvard.edu/kssgorg/hjhp/

3267. *Harvard Latino Law Review.* [ISSN: 1542-460X] 1993. a. Individuals, USD 30; USD 35 per issue elsewhere. Ed(s): Alissa Del Riego, Adrianna C Rodriguez. Harvard Law School, 1563 Massachusetts Ave, Cambridge, MA 02138; http://www.law.harvard.edu. *Indexed:* A01, BRI, L14, P61. *Aud.:* Ac, Sa.

The *Harvard Latino Law Review* is a student-edited law journal that focuses on legal issues of Latinos in the United States. In addition to scholarly articles, *HLLR* publishes conference papers and panel transcripts and occasional interviews. Recent articles have discussed immigration law; accommodations for non–English-speakers; and LatCrit theory. Recommended for academic libraries that support Latino Studies collections.

Hispanic Journal of Behavioral Sciences. See Psychology section.

3268. *Hispanic Network Magazine: a Latino lifesyle, business and employment magazine.* [ISSN: 1550-6444] 199?. q. USD 16; USD 4.50 per issue. Ed(s): Christine Stossel. DiversityComm, Inc., 18 Technology Dr., Ste 170, Irvine, CA 92618; info@hnmagazine.com; http://diversitycomm.net/. Adv. *Aud.:* Hs, Ga.

Hispanic Network is a human resources magazine published by DiversityComm, Inc., which also publishes similar titles focused on the black, veteran, and female workforce. While prominent sponsorships on its web site and advertisements adjacent to articles leave the connection between content and advertising less than transparent, this journal is still of significant value for its short, concise articles about Hispanic impact on and experience in various industries. *HN* also includes a regular section of summaries and photos from recent conferences of Hispanic-oriented professional and advocacy organization, such as the National Council of La Raza and the Society of Mexican Engineers & Scientists. The web site also hosts job listings. Back issues are available on the magazine's web site. Despite the murky policy on advertising and content, *Hispanic Network* would be a valuable addition to public and school libraries that serve a Hispanic population. URL: http://hnmagazine.com/

3269. *Hispanic Outlook in Higher Education.* [ISSN: 1054-2337] 1990. bi-w. except Jun. Jul. & Aug. USD 19.95. Hispanic Outlook in Higher Education Publishing Company, Inc., 80 Rte 4 E, Ste 203, Paramus, NJ 07652. Illus., adv. Sample. Refereed. *Indexed:* Chicano, ENW. *Bk. rev.:* Number and length vary. *Aud.:* Sa.

Published since 1990, the *Hispanic Outlook in Higher Education* is a biweekly publication that provides news and analysis on higher education as it impacts Hispanic students, staff, and faculty. Articles are short (one to four pages long) and cover topics specific to Hispanic higher education as well as general higher education trends of interest. There are 11 themed issues each year, including on health professions, graduate education, and women in higher education. It also produces an annual ranking of universities by number of degrees conferred to Hispanic students at bachelor's, master's, and doctoral levels. Recommended for academic libraries that serve education programs and/or Hispanic populations.

3270. *Journal of Hispanic Higher Education.* [ISSN: 1538-1927] 2002. q. USD 525. Ed(s): Esther Elena Lopez-Mulnix, Michael William Mulnix. Sage Publications, Inc., 2455 Teller Rd, Thousand Oaks, CA 91320; info@sagepub.com; http://www.sagepub.com. Adv. Sample. Refereed. Reprint: PSC. *Indexed:* A01, A22, Chicano, E01, ERIC, MLA-IB, PsycInfo. *Aud.:* Ac.

The *Journal of Hispanic Higher Education* publishes research concerning the entire spectrum of higher education as it relates to Hispanic students and faculty, particularly at Hispanic-serving institutions. It is especially interested in research with a multicultural and interdisciplinary approach. Recent articles have explored service learning, academic achievement, educational leadership training, and student motivation. While articles are in English, abstracts are in both English and Spanish. Recommended for academic libraries.

3271. *The Journal of Latino-Latin American Studies.* Formerly (until 2003): *Latino Studies Journal.* [ISSN: 1549-9502] 1990. q. USD 70 (Individuals, USD 60; Students, USD 50). Ed(s): Maria M Arbelaez. The Journal of Latino-Latin American Studies, 287-L Arts and Sciences Hall, University of Nebraska at Omaha, Omaha, NE 68182-0271. Adv. Refereed. *Indexed:* A01, BRI, Chicano. *Bk. rev.:* Varies. *Aud.:* Ac.

JOLLAS is largely focused on Latinos in the United States, with occasional articles on Latin America, centered on transnational political, economic, and social issues. Recent articles have discussed immigrant labor in the meatpacking industry; Afro-Hondurans in New Orleans; Latino immigrant identity, and religion and marriage among urban Latinos. Recommended for academic libraries.

3272. *Journal of Latinos and Education.* [ISSN: 1534-8431] 2002. q. GBP 332 (print & online eds.). Ed(s): Enrique G Murillo, Jr. Routledge, 325 Chestnut St, Ste 800, Philadelphia, PA 19106; customerservice@taylorandfrancis.com; http://www.tandfonline.com. Adv. Sample. Refereed. Reprint: PSC. *Indexed:* A01, A22, E01, ERIC, MLA-IB, PsycInfo. *Bk. rev.:* Varies. *Aud.:* Ac.

The *Journal of Latinos and Education* is a quarterly refereed journal focused on creating an interdisciplinary forum for researchers, policymakers, and other stakeholders interested in the education of Latinos, from preschool students to university faculty. The journal solicits articles on policy, practice, and original research, as well as creative works within the overall scope. A recent issue was dedicated to the role and identity of Hispanic-serving institutions in higher education. Other articles have examined de facto segregated schools and research motivation of Latino faculty in STEM disciplines. *JLE* encourages creativity in reoccurring sections such as "Alternative Formats," in which an author recently traced her educational trajectory from Chicago's Little Village to doctoral studies; and "Voces," which recently featured the *testimonio* of working-class Latina scholars. Highly recommended for academic libraries.

Latina (New York). See Fashion and Lifestyle section.

3273. *Latino Leaders: the national magazine of the successful Hispanic American.* [ISSN: 1529-3998] 1999. bi-m. Ed(s): Wendy Pedrero. Ferraez Publications of America, Corp., Invierno 16, Merced Gomez, 01600, Mexico. Circ: 100000. *Indexed:* BRI. *Aud.:* Ga.

As the title implies, *Latino Leaders* is interested in today's Latino leadership and the cultivation of future Latino leaders. Recent issues have profiled Latino leaders in academia, business, politics, and technology, as well as the primary challenges and opportunities for creating a new generation of leadership. Though much of the subject material comes from the business world, the focus is on the human side of business. *Latino Leaders* is a full-color glossy magazine, published six times per year, and also available in a digital edition. Recommended for public libraries.

3274. *Latino Policy & Issues Brief.* [ISSN: 1543-2238] 2002. irreg. USD 10 per issue. Ed(s): Chon A Noriega. University of California, Los Angeles, Chicano Studies Research Center Press, 193 Haines Hall, Los Angeles, CA 90095; press@chicano.ucla.edu; http:/www.chicano.ucla.edu. *Aud.:* Ac.

Latino Policy & Issues Briefs are concise four-page single article research summaries. Recent titles include "Not Quite a Breakthrough: The Oscars and Actors of Color, 2002-2012" and "Undergraduate Student Response to Arizona's Anti-ethnic Studies Bill: Implications for Mental Health." All briefs are available for download online. Recommended for academic libraries. URL: www.chicano.ucla.edu/press/briefs/current.asp

3275. *Latino Studies.* [ISSN: 1476-3435] 2003. q. USD 858. Ed(s): Karen Benita Reyes, Lourdes Torres. Palgrave Macmillan Ltd., Houndmills, Basingstoke, RG21 6XS, United Kingdom; orders@palgrave.com; http://www.palgrave.com. Illus., adv. Sample. Refereed. Reprint: PSC. *Indexed:* A22, ABIn, E01, ENW, IBSS, MLA-IB, P02, P61, SSA. *Bk. rev.:* 4-9, 750-1,500 words. *Aud.:* Ac.

In just ten years of publication, *Latino Studies* has established itself as a prominent peer-reviewed journal in its interdisciplinary field. Its stated focus is "the lived experience and struggles of Latinas and Latinos for equity, representation, and social justice" in the tradition of activist scholarship. Besides traditional scholarly articles, it also features regular reports from the field, essays on pedagogy and curriculum, and reflections on historical groundbreaking scholarship and events in the context of contemporary Latino scholarship. Also of note, *Latino Studies* publishes the most book reviews of any scholarly journal in the field. Highly recommended for academic libraries.

3276. People en Espanol. [ISSN: 1096-5750] 1997. 11x/yr. USD 14.96 domestic; CAD 36.89 Canada. Ed(s): Armando Lucas Correa. Time Inc., 1271 Ave of the Americas, New York, NY 10020; information@timeinc.com; http://www.timeinc.com. Adv. Circ: 500000. *Aud.:* Ga.

Like its weekly English-language sister magazine *People*, this title is focused on celebrity news, human interest stories, fashion, and reviews of beauty supplies and other consumer products, all in Spanish, of course. The celebrities in the pages of *People en Espanol* are familiar to the Latino media, both foreign and U.S. Latinos. *People en Espanol* also runs an annual "Most Beautiful People" issue. Complete issues are by subscription only but a significant number of articles are available on the magazine's web site. Highly recommended for public libraries. URL: www.peopleenespanol.com/

3277. Poder Hispanic. Formed by the merger of (1988-2010): *Hispanic;* (2000-2010): *Poder.* [ISSN: 2156-5139] 2011. 6x/yr. USD 12.95 domestic. Ed(s): Jose Fernando Lopez, David Adams. ET Publishing International, 6355 NW 36th St, Miami, FL 33166. Illus., adv. *Indexed:* A01, A22, BRI, Chicano, ENW, MASUSE, P02. *Bk. rev.:* 6-8, 50-100 words. *Aud.:* Ga.

Poder Hispanic is the product of the merger of *Hispanic* with the ceased title *Poder* in 2010. Continuing in *Hispanic*'s path as an English-language magazine focused at the upwardly-mobile Latino professional, *Poder Hispanic* carries articles on politics, entertainment, business, and culture. Regular sections include "Intelligence Gathering," highlighting national and international news in short articles and infographics; "Hispanic Enterprise," featuring business trends and profiles of Latino professionals and organizations; and "Time Well Spent," comprising reviews and news of books, media, and travel. Recent feature articles cover public schools, the financial side of *telenovelas,* and a ranking of 100 influential Hispanic figures. While complete issues are available by subscription only, many articles are available on the magazine's web site. Highly recommended for public and academic libraries that serve Latino patrons. URL: www.poder360.com

3278. Texas Hispanic Journal of Law and Policy. Formerly (until 1998): *Hispanic Law Journal.* [ISSN: 1547-4887] 1994. a. USD 30 per issue domestic; USD 40 per issue foreign. Ed(s): Jasmine Wightman. University of Texas at Austin, School of Law Publications, 727 E Dean Keeton St, Austin, TX 78705; Publications@law.utexas.edu; http://www.utexas.edu/law/publications/. Adv. Circ: 250. Reprint: WSH. *Indexed:* A01. *Aud.:* Ac, Sa.

This title focuses on the analysis of legal issues and public policy relevant to the Hispanic community and strives to be a neutral forum for such topics. Articles in recent issues have addressed the legal status of Puerto Rico, undocumented migrants, racial profiling, and the legal implications of ESL classrooms. Recommended for academic libraries that support Latino Studies collections.

3279. Urban Latino Magazine. Formerly (until 1998): *Urban.* [ISSN: 1531-6602] 1994. bi-m. USD 16; USD 24.99 combined subscription (print & CD-ROM eds.). Urban Latino Magazine, 10 Jay St Ste 206, Brooklyn, NY 11201. Illus., adv. *Bk. rev.:* Number and length vary. *Aud.:* Hs.

Urban Latino focuses largely on Latino entertainment and culture in the New York metropolitan area, but it includes articles on national Latino figures, general interest stories, and product and fashion reviews. Recent issues have included interviews with Carmelo Anthony, Taboo of the Black-Eyed Peas, and John Leguizamo; a history of the recently reopened Copacabana nightclub; and a profile of a halfway house with successful re-entry programs. Regular sections include "Mixer," featuring a liquor and cocktail recipes; fashion and grooming tips and products; and "Urban Sofrito Reviews," which includes reviews of books, music, movies, video games, and technology. Despite its regional focus, *Urban Latino* has national appeal and would find readers in public libraries that serve Latino communities.

■ LAW

Late Donald J. Dunn, Dean & Professor of Law, University of La Verne College of Law, 320 East D Street, Ontario, CA 91764.

Kim Dulin, Associate Director For Collection Development And Digital Initiatives, Harvard Law School Library and Co-Director Of The Harvard Library Innovation Laboratory, Harvard Law School Library, Areeda 526, 1545 Massachusetts Avenue, Cambridge, MA 02138.

Caitlin Elwood, Library Assistant, Harvard College Library, Lamont Library, Cambridge, MA 02138.

Michelle Pearse, Research Librarian for Open Access Initiatives and Scholarly Communication, Harvard Law School Library, 1545 Massachusetts Avenue, Cambridge, MA 02138

Introduction

The number of law journals currently being published is overwhelming. In assessing what journals might be appropriate for a library, one must have an understanding of the various types of legal periodicals available and the needs of the audience. An academic library might be more interested in scholarly legal periodicals, while a corporate library would probably be more interested in practice-oriented publications. This section represents a selection of the longer-standing, popular, or unique law journals and is not meant to be comprehensive.

The typical law school law review is the most prevalent and pervasive type of law journal in legal literature in this country. It is unique in that it is usually edited by law students, but with law professors and legal scholars writing feature articles. (Some of the top-tier law reviews are experimenting with faculty peer review, and a new project called Peer Reviewed Scholarship Marketplace [www.legalpeerreview.org/] attempts to facilitate review of author submissions by subject matter experts.) Most law schools have one general-interest law review (e.g., *Columbia Law Review*), but many have also developed journals with a more specific subject focus (e.g., *Columbia Journal of Race and Law*).

An increasing number of law reviews are also using the Internet to supplement their print publications. Often referred to as "online companions," these web resources often provide opportunities for commentary on material already published in the journal or on completely new topics. There are also interesting collaborative online projects such as the Legal Workshop (www.lawschool.cornell.edu/research/cornell-law-review/the-legal-workshop.cfm), which aggregates "op-ed versions of articles published by participating law reviews," and which are "written for a generalist audience, combining the best elements of print and online publication."

One can also find quality legal scholarship in peer-reviewed or refereed journals, most often published by professional organizations or learned societies, university presses, or commercial publishers.

There are various sources that "rank" legal journals. When looking at them, one must keep in mind the methodology used. One useful source is Washington and Lee Law School's web site "Law Journals: Submissions and Ranking" (http://lawlib.wlu.edu/LJ), which includes its own ranking of journals by various criteria, as well as submission information and tables of contents for individual titles with links to full-text sources. Some law reviews are also included in the Social Science Citation Index by Web of Science (Thomson Journal Citation Reports). Google Scholar's new journal ranking service includes law journals.

As in other disciplines, the open-access movement is continuing to take great hold in the field of law, but the degree to which journals are "open" varies. Many law reviews are making their contents freely available on the web. Individually, legal scholars (and their institutions) often disseminate their articles at various stages of publication through the Legal Scholarship Network (of the Social Science Research Network) and other repositories.

Some libraries might have patrons who need information that is more relevant to legal practice. Bar associations publish journals that often contain news and current events related to the practice of law. There are also commercial publications, usually focused on a specific area of practice and geared toward practicing lawyers. Finally, legal newspapers and other news sources can offer insight into relevant legal events and development in the legal profession or industry.

The primary focus of this section is English-language, U.S. journals; however, with the globalization of the law school curriculum and legal practice in general, foreign law journals and international law journals continue to proliferate and make a significant impact on the literature. (A good index for foreign legal periodicals is *Index to Foreign Legal Periodicals*. There are also legal indexes for specific jurisdictions, such as *Legal Journals Index through WestlawUK* for the United Kingdom and *Index to Canadian Legal Periodical Literature*.)

There are various electronic collections for law periodicals. HeinOnline offers a fairly extensive law journal library collection in pdf that usually goes back to the first volume for most titles, although there is sometimes a "wall" for current content. JSTOR has a law collection, which is fairly selective but might be growing. EBSCO also offers a full-text option with its *Index to Legal Periodicals and Books* database. LexisNexis Academic has a legal research module with a broad range of law reviews/journals and legal news sources. Many aggregator databases often have a decent selection of law journal titles among their sources. Finally, Google Scholar (http://scholar.google.com) is covering a significant number of legal journals, and the ABA's Legal Technology Resource Center has created a useful Google Custom Search of law reviews on the web: www.americanbar.org/groups/departments_offices/legal_technology_resources/resources/free_journal_search.html. Law school subscriptions to Lexis and Westlaw include full-text journal files, but the contents often only go back to approximately the 1990s or so.

Those interested in following the practices within law journal publishing might want to follow Brian Leiter, PrawfsBlawg, and the Faculty Lounge.

Basic Periodicals

Ga: *A B A Journal, The National Law Journal, The Practical Lawyer, Trial;* Ac: *A B A Journal, Business Lawyer, Columbia Law Review, Harvard Law Review, Law and Contemporary Problems, The National Law Journal, University of Chicago Law Review, Yale Law Journal.*

Basic Abstracts and Indexes

Current Law Index; Index to Foreign Legal Periodicals; Index to Legal Periodicals and Books; Index to Legal Periodicals and Books Retrospective; LegalTrac.

3280. *A B A Journal.* Formerly (until 1984): *American Bar Association. Journal;* Which incorporated (1908-1915): *American Bar Association. Comparative Law Bureau. Annual Bulletin.* [ISSN: 0747-0088] 1915. m. USD 120 (Individuals, USD 75; USD 7 per issue). Ed(s): Allen Pusey, Edward A Adams. American Bar Association, 321 N Clark St, Chicago, IL 60654; service@abanet.org; http://www.americanbar.org. Illus., index, adv. Sample. Refereed. Vol. ends: Dec. Microform: WSH; PQC. Reprint: WSH. *Indexed:* A01, A22, ABIn, ABS&EES, ATI, B01, B02, BAS, BRI, CBRI, CJPI, CLI, Chicano, L14, MLA-IB, P02. *Bk. rev.:* 2-4, 2,000 words. *Aud.:* Ga, Ac, Sa.

Distributed to members of the American Bar Association (ABA), this magazine is designed to be of interest to all segments of the legal profession. It usually contains several timely feature articles, along with sections that address various aspects of law and legal practice, such as the following: "President's Message," where the ABA president expounds on major legal issues; "Supreme Court Report," which discusses pending and recently decided cases in the U.S. Supreme Court; and "Ethics," which highlights professional responsibility development and ethical issues in the legal profession. The journal also has a useful web site including news features, a "blawg" (legal blogs), a directory, and social networking features.

3281. *Administrative Law Review (Chicago).* Formerly (until 1960): *Administrative Law Bulletin.* [ISSN: 0001-8368] 1949. q. Members, USD 10; Non-members, USD 40. Ed(s): Kevin Gauntt Barker, Farhan Ali. American Bar Association, Administrative Law and Regulatory Practice Section, 740 15th St, NW, 8th Fl, Ste 885, Washington, DC 20005; Anne.Kiefer@americanbar.org; http://www.abanet.org/adminlaw. Illus., index. Refereed. Vol. ends: Fall. Microform: WSH. Reprint: WSH. *Indexed:* A22, B01, BRI, CLI, L14, P02. *Bk. rev.:* Occasional, length varies. *Aud.:* Ac, Sa.

Administrative law is concerned with government authorities other than courts and legislative bodies. Administrative agencies—national, state, and local—promulgate rules and regulations and issue decisions that govern our daily lives. Consequently, the power wielded by these agencies is often immense. This journal is published jointly by the Section of Administrative Law and Regulatory Practice of the American Bar Association and its student staff members at the Washington College of Law of American University. It discusses all aspects of administrative law, including such topics as consumer protection regulation; administrative rule-making; immigration law; banking and currency regulation; and energy and environmental, insurance, and postal regulations.

3282. *American Criminal Law Review.* Former titles (until 1971): *American Criminal Law Quarterly;* (until 1963): *Criminal Law Quarterly.* [ISSN: 0164-0364] 1962. q. USD 30 domestic; USD 40 foreign; USD 10 per issue. Ed(s): Adam L Small, Ryan H Lehrer. Georgetown University Law Center, 600 New Jersey Ave, NW, Washington, DC 20001; http://www.law.georgetown.edu. Illus., index. Refereed. Vol. ends: No. 4. Microform: WSH; PQC. Reprint: WSH. *Indexed:* A01, A22, ABS&EES, B02, BRI, CJPI, CLI, L14, P02. *Bk. rev.:* Occasional, lengthy. *Aud.:* Ac, Sa.

Criminal law is an area that changes frequently, depending upon the political climate and the current membership of the U.S. Supreme Court. This journal, edited by students from the Georgetown University Law Center, includes articles, notes, project reports, and symposia that focus on some of the more complicated issues in the criminal law area. A regular feature is an annual survey of white-collar crime. It has launched an online companion.

3283. *American Journal of Comparative Law.* [ISSN: 0002-919X] 1952. q. USD 67 domestic (Free to members). Ed(s): Mathias W Reimann. American Society of Comparative Law, University of California, 394 Boalt Hall, Berkeley, CA 94720; http://www.comparativelaw.org. Illus., index. Refereed. Vol. ends: Fall. Microform: PQC. Reprint: WSH. *Indexed:* A22, ABS&EES, B02, BAS, BRI, CLI, IBSS, L14, P61, SSA. *Bk. rev.:* 6-10, 1,200-5,000 words. *Aud.:* Ac, Sa.

Comparative law, as the topic suggests, compares the laws of one or more nations with those of another, or discusses one jurisdiction's law in order for the reader to understand how it might differ from that of the United States or some other country. This widely respected publication features articles by major scholars and comments by law student writers. It has a useful survey on "Choice of Law in American Courts."

3284. *American Journal of International Law.* [ISSN: 0002-9300] 1907. q. USD 237 (print & online eds.). American Society of International Law, 2223 Massachusetts Ave, NW, Washington, DC 20008; services@asil.org; http://www.asil.org. Illus., index, adv. Refereed. Vol. ends: Oct. Microform: WSH; IDC; PQC. Reprint: WSH. *Indexed:* A01, A22, ABS&EES, B02, BAS, BRI, CLI, IBSS, L14, MLA-IB, P02, S25. *Bk. rev.:* 15-20. *Aud.:* Ac, Sa.

This highly respected English-language journal, which features a prestigious board of editors, focuses on all aspects of private and public international law. An annual volume averages over 1,000 pages and contains discussions on international organizations, foreign-relations law, and international conventions and protocols. In addition to the major articles and numerous book reviews, the "Current Developments" section addresses major news events, and recent cases are discussed in "International Decisions." "Contemporary Practice of the United States Relating to International Law," which analyzes international issues by subject, is arranged according to the *Annual Digest of United States Practice in International Law,* published by the U.S. Department of State.

3285. *American Journal of Jurisprudence: an international forum for legal philosophy.* Former titles (until 1969): *Natural Law Forum;* (until 1956): *Natural Law Institute. Proceedings.* [ISSN: 0065-8995] 1947. a. EUR 115. Ed(s): Gloria A Krull, John Finnis. University of Notre Dame, Law School, PO Box 780, Notre Dame, IN 46556; ndlaw@nd.edu; http://law.nd.edu/. Illus., index. Refereed. Microform: WSH; PMC; PQC. Reprint: WSH. *Indexed:* A01, A22, BRI, CLI, L14, MLA-IB, P61, SSA. *Bk. rev.:* 3-5, 2,000-7,000 words. *Aud.:* Ac, Sa.

Jurisprudence is the philosophy or formal science of law and can be an important topic for those studying law-related disciplines. This annual publication by the Natural Law Institute of the Notre Dame Law School is devoted exclusively to legal philosophy. Also published by the school are the *Notre Dame Law Review, The Journal of Legislation, Notre Dame Journal of Law, Ethics & Public Policy,* and *Journal of College and University Law.*

3286. *American Journal of Law & Medicine.* [ISSN: 0098-8588] 1975. q. USD 250 (Individuals, USD 140; Free to members). Ed(s): Alexander J Burakoff, Sara Hanson. American Society of Law, Medicine & Ethics, 765 Commonwealth Ave, Ste 1634, Boston, MA 02215; info@aslme.org; http://www.aslme.org. Illus., index, adv. Refereed. Vol. ends: Winter. Microform: WSH; PMC. Reprint: WSH. *Indexed:* A01, A22, BRI, CLI, L14, MCR, P02. *Bk. rev.:* Occasional. *Aud.:* Ac, Sa.

Published by the American Society of Law, Medicine, and Ethics (ASLME) and affiliated with Boston University School of Law, this publication attempts to foster communication among those in the law and medical fields. This was one of the first interdisciplinary journals to focus on issues that affect the legal and health-care professions, and it continues to be one of the most respected. The journal includes articles from both professionals and students, and emphasizes current issues in health law and policy. Its "Recent Developments in Health Law" section includes discussions of recent health law cases. ASLME also publishes *The Journal of Law, Medicine and Ethics.*

3287. *The American Lawyer: the United States leading legal monthly.* [ISSN: 0162-3397] 1979. m. 10/yr. Ed(s): Aric Press, Maryann Saltser. A L M, 120 Broadway, 5th Fl, New York, NY 10271; customerservices@incisivemedia.com; http://www.incisivemedia.com/. Illus., index, adv. Vol. ends: Dec. *Indexed:* A01, A22, ASIP, B01, BRI, CLI, L14. *Bk. rev.:* Usually 1. *Aud.:* Ga, Ac, Sa.

In the past, this newspaper-turned-magazine has been viewed as tabloid news for the legal profession. While it is still fairly sensational with its brazen or "cute" headlines and article and department titles, it does have a better reputation for its investigative reporting. The publisher also provides many supplements and surveys that appeal to those researching the legal industry or job market, such as salary surveys and lists of top law firms. (There is also a fairly expensive online product called ALMResearch Online, which provides reports and data about the legal profession and marketplace.) The publisher's web site has a related blog (Am Law Daily) that is useful for legal news. LexisNexis recently became the exclusive third-party online distributor of the broad collection of current and archived versions of ALM's legal news publications. URL: www.americanlawyer.com/amlaw_daily.jsp

Berkeley Journal of Employment and Labor Law. See Labor and Industrial Relations section.

3288. *Berkeley Technology Law Journal.* Formerly (until 1996): *High Technology Law Journal.* [ISSN: 1086-3818] 1986. 3x/yr. USD 85 USD 27 per issue. Ed(s): Taras M. Czebiniak, Michelle Ma. University of California, Berkeley, School of Law, Journal Publications, 2850 Telegraph Ave, Ste 561, #7220, Berkeley, CA 94705-7220; journalpublications@law.berkeley.edu; http://www.law.berkeley.edu. Illus., index. Refereed. Circ: 450. Vol. ends: Fall. Microform: WSH; PQC. Reprint: WSH. *Indexed:* A01, A22, ABIn, B01, BRI, CLI, IBSS, L14. *Bk. rev.:* Occasional, 2,500 words. *Aud.:* Ac, Sa.

Established in 1986 by students at the University of California (Berkeley) School of Law, this journal is devoted to covering issues related to the intersection of law and technology. It is one of the most respected of the law and technology journals, and is a good source for those wanting to keep abreast of the hot topics in this area. One issue a year, the *Annual Review of Law and Technology,* focuses exclusively on the most recent developments in the field, published in collaboration with the Berkeley Center for Law and Technology.

3289. *Boston University Law Review.* [ISSN: 0006-8047] 1921. 5x/yr. USD 40 domestic; USD 50 foreign. Ed(s): Jill Hamers, Bret A Finkelstein. Boston University, School of Law, 765 Commonwealth Ave, Boston, MA 02215; http://www.bu.edu/law/. Illus., index, adv. Refereed. Vol. ends: Dec. Microform: WSH. Reprint: WSH. *Indexed:* A01, A22, B02, BRI, CLI, L14. *Bk. rev.:* Occasional, lengthy. *Aud.:* Ac, Sa.

Among the older law reviews in the country, this student-edited journal is traditional in coverage and format. It features consistently high-quality articles on a wide spectrum of topics by noted authorities, notes by student members of the *Review,* and occasional book reviews. Boston University School of Law also publishes the *American Journal of Law & Medicine* jointly with the American Society of Law and Medicine (see above in this section), *Annual Review of Banking and Financial Law, Boston University International Law Journal, Journal of Science and Technology Law,* and *Public Interest Law Journal.*

3290. *The Business Lawyer.* [ISSN: 0007-6899] 1946. q. Free to members; Non-members, USD 65. Ed(s): Dixie L Johnson. American Bar Association, Section of Business Law, 321 North Clark St, Chicago, IL 60654; businesslaw@americanbar.org; http://www.americanbar.org/ groups/business_law.html. Illus., adv. Microform: MIM; WSH. Reprint: WSH. *Indexed:* A22, ABIn, B01, B02, BLI, BRI, CLI, L14, P61, SSA. *Aud.:* Ac, Sa.

This is a highly regarded and valued journal for business law issues, which can comprise a variety of topics such as commercial law, securities, partnership, finance law, etc. Focusing on developing trends and case law analysis, the journal often contains special reports, surveys, changes to model acts, and task-force/committee reports.

3291. *California Law Review.* [ISSN: 0008-1221] 1912. bi-m. USD 50 (Individuals, USD 45; USD 11 per issue). Ed(s): Jose L. Lopez, Joey L Hipolito. University of California, Berkeley, School of Law, 40 Boalt Hall, Berkeley, CA 94720; http://www.law.berkeley.edu. Illus., index. Refereed. Circ: 1650 Paid. Vol. ends: Dec. Microform: WSH; PQC. Reprint: WSH. *Indexed:* A01, A22, ABIn, B01, B02, BRI, CJPI, CLI, Chicano, L14, P02. *Bk. rev.:* Occasional, length varies. *Aud.:* Ac, Sa.

Consistently ranked among the top ten law reviews, this University of California (Berkeley) publication was the first student-edited law review published west of the Mississippi, and from its inception it included both male and female editors. Each volume includes six issues, and articles cover a wide range of topics from business law to tribal sovereignty. This school also publishes *Berkeley Journal of Gender Law and Justice, Ecology Law Quarterly,* and *Berkeley Technology Law Journal* (for the latter two, see above and below in this section), as well as *Berkeley Journal of African-American Law & Policy, Asian American Law Journal, Berkeley Business Law Journal, Berkeley Journal of Employment and Labor Law, Berkeley Journal of International Law, Berkeley Journal of Criminal Law, Berkeley Journal of Middle Eastern Islamic Law,* and *Berkeley La Raza Law Journal.*

3292. *The Cambridge Law Journal.* [ISSN: 0008-1973] 1921. 3x/yr. GBP 100. Ed(s): David J Ibbetson. Cambridge University Press, The Edinburgh Bldg, Shaftesbury Rd, Cambridge, CB2 8RU, United Kingdom; journals@cambridge.org; http://www.cambridge.org/uk. Illus., index, adv. Circ: 1600. Vol. ends: Nov. Microform: PQC. Reprint: PSC; WSH. *Indexed:* A01, A22, BRI, CJPI, CLI, E01, IBSS, L14, P61, RiskAb, SSA, SWR&A. *Bk. rev.:* 30, 1,200-1,500 words. *Aud.:* Ac, Sa.

Considered by many legal scholars to be the best British legal periodical, this publication reverses the format used by its American counterparts—that is, the student case notes and comments precede the longer scholarly articles. The book reviews, both cogent and forceful, serve as excellent aids in collection development for materials from the United Kingdom.

3293. *Chicano/a - Latino/a Law Review.* Former titles (until 2006): *Chicano Latino Law Review;* (until 1991): *Chicano Law Review.* 1972. a. USD 25 per issue domestic; USD 30 per issue foreign. University of California, School of Law, 385 Charles E. Young Dr, 1242 Law Bldg, Los Angeles, CA 90095; http://www.law.ucla.edu/home/. Illus., index, adv. Microform: LIB. Reprint: WSH. *Indexed:* A01, A22, BRI, CLI, Chicano, L14. *Bk. rev.:* Occasional, essay length. *Aud.:* Ac, Sa.

This publication of Chicano–Latino law students at UCLA School of Law, like *Berkeley La Raza Law Journal,* is a law-related publication specifically established to address issues concerning the Mexican American community and the broader-based Latino community. As a forum for an underrepresented minority in the legal community, this publication is important because of its particular perspective. It identifies and analyzes legal issues that affect the

Latino community and focuses on how these legal issues have an impact on the political and cultural interaction of the United States and Latin America. Other journals related to legal issues affecting Hispanic Americans include *Harvard Latino Law Review* and *Texas Hispanic Journal of Law and Policy*.

Children's Legal Rights Journal. See Sociology and Social Work/ General section.

3294. *Clearinghouse Review: journal of poverty law and policy.* [ISSN: 0009-868X] 1967. bi-m. Individuals, USD 400 (print & online eds.). National Clearinghouse for Legal Services, Inc., 50 E Washington, Ste 500, Chicago, IL 60602; http://www.povertylaw.org. Illus., index. Vol. ends: Apr. Microform: PQC. *Indexed:* A22, AgeL, BRI, CLI, L14, MCR, SWR&A. *Aud.:* Ga, Ac, Sa.

This journal serves the dual purpose of being the professional journal for attorneys who represent low-income clients in the Legal Services Corporation (LSC) grantee offices across the country, as well as providing authoritative articles on poverty law for the rest of the legal community. Published by the Sargent Shriver National Center on Poverty Law, this publication includes feature articles on a variety of issues including disability benefits, consumer protection, elder law, civil rights, public housing, and federal and state income assistance programs. This organization also hosts a useful web site, Poverty Law Library. URL: www.povertylaw.org/poverty-law-library

3295. *Clinical Law Review.* [ISSN: 1079-1159] 1994. s-a. USD 24 domestic; USD 26 foreign; USD 14 per issue domestic. New York University School of Law, 40 Washington Sq S, New York, NY 10012; law.moreinfo@nyu.edu; http://www.law.nyu.edu. Refereed. Reprint: WSH. *Indexed:* A01, BRI, CLI, L14. *Aud.:* Ac, Sa.

"Practical skills," "hands-on," "lawyering," and "real world" are words that help describe clinical legal education. This peer-edited journal, jointly sponsored by NYU School of Law, the Clinical Legal Education Association, and the Association of American Law Schools, fills a need by discussing the special forms of academic pedagogy required for successful clinical education experiences.

3296. *Columbia Journal of Gender and the Law.* [ISSN: 1062-6220] 1991. 3x/yr. USD 65. Ed(s): Rosalie Fazio, Liane Tai Rice. Columbia University, School of Law, 435 W 116th St, New York, NY 10027; Admissions@law.columbia.edu; http://www.law.columbia.edu. Illus. Reprint: WSH. *Indexed:* CLI, FemPer, GW, L14. *Bk. rev.:* Number varies, essay length, signed. *Aud.:* Ac, Sa.

This law review takes an interdisciplinary approach to the interplay between gender and the law. Articles reflect a broad definition of feminism and feminist jurisprudence and address issues that affect all races, ethnicities, classes, sexual orientations, and cultures. Contributors are judges, law professors, law students, and scholars from other disciplines.

3297. *Columbia Journal of Law & the Arts.* Former titles (until 2001): *Columbia - V L A Journal of Law & the Arts;* (until 1985): *Art and the Law.* [ISSN: 1544-4848] 1974. q. USD 45 domestic; USD 53 foreign; USD 12 per issue domestic. Ed(s): Lauren Gallo, Anthony Cheng. Columbia University, School of Law, 435 W 116th St, New York, NY 10027; Admissions@law.columbia.edu; http://www.law.columbia.edu. Illus., index, adv. Vol. ends: Summer. Microform: WSH. Reprint: WSH. *Indexed:* A22, BRI, CLI, F01, L14. *Aud.:* Ac, Sa.

As the subtitle of this publication indicates, coverage is sufficiently broad to include a multitude of issues relating to the arts and entertainment industry. The articles in each issue present enlightening, out-of-the-mainstream legal scholarship devoted to the interests of artists and attorneys whose specialty is serving artists. It has a "Law and the Arts" blog covering current developments. URL: www.lawandarts.org/ There are several other journals of the same genre that would be worthy of consideration, including *Hastings Communications and Entertainment Law Journal, UCLA Entertainment Law Review,* DePaul's *Journal of Art and Entertainment Law, Harvard Journal of Sports and Entertainment Law,* and *Vanderbilt Journal of Entertainment and Technology Law.*

3298. *Columbia Law Review.* [ISSN: 0010-1958] 1901. 8x/yr. USD 54 domestic (Free to members). Ed(s): Z Julius Chen, Kara Maguire. Columbia Law School, 435 W 116th St, New York, NY 10027; Admissions@law.columbia.edu; http://www.law.columbia.edu/. Illus., index. Refereed. Vol. ends: Dec. Microform: WSH. Reprint: WSH. *Indexed:* A01, A22, ABIn, ABS&EES, B01, B02, BRI, CBRI, CLI, IBSS, L14, MLA-IB, P02, P61, RiskAb, SSA. *Bk. rev.:* Occasional, essay length. *Aud.:* Ac, Sa.

A prestigious law review from an equally prestigious law school with a long and distinguished history, this publication follows the traditional model of lead articles by professionals, comments and notes by students, and occasional scholarly book review essays. Recent issues address such diverse topics as perceptual segregation, judicial elections, and local property law. The journal also has an online publication called *Sidebar* (www.clrsidebar.org). Columbia University School of Law publishes many other student journals: *American Review of International Arbitration, Columbia Business Law Review, Columbia Human Rights Law Review, Columbia Journal of Environmental Law, Columbia Journal of Law & the Arts* (for the latter, see above in this section), *Columbia Journal of Law and Social Problems, Columbia Journal of Transnational Law, Columbia Journal of Gender and Law, Columbia Journal of Asian Law, Columbia Journal of East European Law, Columbia Science and Technology Law Review, National Black Law Journal,* and *Columbia Journal of European Law.*

3299. *Conflict Resolution Quarterly.* Formerly (until 2001): *Mediation Quarterly.* [ISSN: 1536-5581] 1983. q. GBP 229. Ed(s): Susan Summers Raines. John Wiley & Sons, Inc., 111 River St, MS 4-02, Hoboken, NJ 07030; info@wiley.com; http://www.wiley.com/WileyCDA/. Adv. Refereed. Microform: PQC. Reprint: PSC. *Indexed:* A01, A22, ABIn, ABS&EES, B01, E01, IBSS, L14, P61, PsycInfo, SSA. *Aud.:* Ac, Sa.

A publication of the Association for Conflict Resolution (ACR), this journal is well respected among those practicing in alternative dispute resolution and negotiation. The ACR is a nonprofit membership organization dedicated to enhancing the practice and public understanding of conflict resolution.

3300. *Cornell Law Review.* Formerly (until 1967): *Cornell Law Quarterly.* [ISSN: 0010-8847] 1915. bi-m. USD 45; USD 15 per issue. Ed(s): Christine I Lee, Eduardo F Bruera. Cornell University, Cornell Law School, 127 Myron Taylor Hall, Ithaca, NY 14853; lawlib@cornell.edu; http://www.law.cornell.edu/. Index, adv. Refereed. Vol. ends: No. 6. Microform: WSH. Reprint: WSH. *Indexed:* A22, B02, BLI, BRI, CJPI, CLI, L14. *Aud.:* Ac, Sa.

Another traditional, student-edited law review that features lengthy, heavily researched articles by preeminent scholars and shorter pieces by student authors, this journal "strives to publish novel scholarship that will have an immediate and lasting impact on the legal community." Recent articles include "Pain as Fact and Heuristic: How Pain Neuroimaging Illuminates Moral Dimensions of Law" and "Children's Rights & a Capabilities Approach: The Question of Special Priority." Cornell Law School also publishes *Cornell International Law Journal* and *Cornell Journal of Law and Public Policy.* Cornell is also responsible for the *Journal of Empirical Legal Studies* (see below in this section).

3301. *Duke Law Journal.* Formerly (until 1957): *Duke Bar Journal.* [ISSN: 0012-7086] 1951. 8x/yr. USD 50 domestic; USD 56 foreign. Ed(s): Jeffrey M Chemerinsky, Sarah Ribstein. Duke University, School of Law, Science Dr & Towerview Rd, PO Box 90371, Durham, NC 27708; publications@law.duke.edu; http://www.law.duke.edu/. Illus., index, adv. Refereed. Vol. ends: Dec. Microform: WSH; PMC. Reprint: WSH. *Indexed:* A01, A22, B02, BRI, CLI, L14. *Bk. rev.:* Occasional, lengthy. *Aud.:* Ac, Sa.

A student-edited review that usually appears fairly high up in most law journal rankings, *Duke Law Journal* has a well-known "Annual Administrative Law Issue" that discusses and evaluates recent developments in administrative law. The Duke University School of Law has been providing free online access to all of its student-edited journals since 1996. Other law reviews published by the school include the influential *Law and Contemporary Problems* (see below in this section), *Duke Journal of Comparative & International Law, Duke Journal of Constitutional Law and Public Policy, Duke Environmental Law & Policy*

Forum, Duke Journal of Gender Law & Policy, Duke Law & Technology Review, and the *Alaska Law Review* (because Alaska has no law school, its bar association selected the Duke University School of Law).

3302. *Ecology Law Quarterly.* [ISSN: 0046-1121] 1971. q. USD 60 USD 16 per issue. Ed(s): Sara Clark, Christine Malumphy. University of California, Berkeley, School of Law, 313 Boalt Hall, Berkeley, CA 94720-7200; journalpublications@law.berkeley.edu; http://www.law.berkeley.edu. Illus., index. Refereed. Circ: 1150 Paid. Vol. ends: No. 4. Microform: WSH; PMC. Reprint: WSH. *Indexed:* A01, A22, B02, BRI, CLI, L14, OceAb, S25. *Bk. rev.:* Occasional, 500-1,000 words. *Aud.:* Ac, Sa.

When the environment became a major concern following Earth Day in 1970, the law students at Boalt Hall were among the first to address law-related ecological issues via a law review. They are to be commended for their long-standing commitment to these matters. Throughout its history, this journal has featured consistently high-quality pieces by scholars and students that cover such diverse topics as biodiversity, global warming, and wastewater discharge. Consistent with the theme of preserving the environment and its natural beauty and resources, the cover of each issue is enhanced by an Ansel Adams photograph. Its online-only *Ecology Law Currents* "features short-form commentary and analysis on timely environmental law and policy issues."

3303. *The Elder Law Journal.* [ISSN: 1070-1478] 1993. s-a. USD 25 domestic; USD 35 foreign. Ed(s): Jeffrey Kimball Paulsen, Robert R Kiepura. University of Illinois at Urbana-Champaign, College of Law, 504 E Pennsylvania Ave, Champaign, IL 61820; djhnsn1@law.illinois.edu; http://www.law.uiuc.edu. Refereed. Reprint: WSH. *Indexed:* AgeL, BRI, CLI, L14. *Aud.:* Ac, Sa.

Legal issues facing the elderly will likely become more prominent in legal academia and practice as the baby boomers get older. This law review is the "oldest scholarly publication in the country dedicated to addressing elder law issues." Topics related to elder law that could be found in this journal include estate/financial issues, Medicare and Medicaid, nursing home issues, and health law. Other publications of the University of Illinois School of Law include the *University of Illinois Law Review,* the *University of Illinois Journal of Law, Technology & Policy,* and the *Comparative Labor Law & Policy Journal.*

3304. *Emory Law Journal.* Formerly (until 1974): *Journal of Public Law.* [ISSN: 0094-4076] 1952. bi-m. USD 40 domestic; USD 45 foreign. Ed(s): Michael L Eber, Jennifer Kwon. Emory University, School of Law, 1301 Clifton Rd, Atlanta, GA 30322; publications@law.emory.edu; http://www.law.emory.edu. Illus., index. Sample. Vol. ends: No. 4. Microform: WSH; PMC; PQC. Reprint: WSH. *Indexed:* A01, A22, B02, BRI, CLI, L14. *Bk. rev.:* Occasional, lengthy. *Aud.:* Ac, Sa.

The School of Law of Emory University has a national reputation with a national and international focus. Its long-standing primary journal, traditional in nature, reflects the school's scholarly bent. Articles and student notes and occasional review essays address any legal topic. Also published by the school are *Emory International Law Review* and *Emory Bankruptcy Developments Journal.*

Employee Relations Law Journal. See Labor and Industrial Relations section.

3305. *Environmental Law (Portland).* [ISSN: 0046-2276] 1970. q. USD 40 domestic; USD 48 foreign; USD 10 per issue domestic. Ed(s): Adrienne L. Thompson. Lewis & Clark College, Northwestern School of Law, 10015 SW Terwilliger Blvd, Portland, OR 97219; http://law.lclark.edu/. Illus., index. Vol. ends: Oct. Microform: WSH; PQC. Reprint: WSH. *Indexed:* A22, BRI, C&ISA, CLI, CerAb, IBSS, L14, OceAb, S25. *Bk. rev.:* Occasional, lengthy. *Aud.:* Ac, Sa.

Environmental law is one of the most rapidly developing and frequently changing areas of the law. The Lewis and Clark Law School has built environmental law as its specialty. Its program is consistently rated at or near the top. The school's journal is consistent with the school's focus, and it is the oldest legal journal devoted exclusively to issues of environmental concern such as ecosystems, endangered species, and the Clean Water Act. While each issue is

hefty, often exceeding 300 pages, it is printed on unbleached, 100 percent recycled, 50 percent post-consumer paper with soy ink. It has an online companion that has selected articles and essays from the print journal, an archive of its Ninth Circuit case review and online conversation. The school also publishes the *Lewis and Clark Law Review* and *Animal Law Review.*

3306. *Family Law Quarterly.* Former titles (until 1967): *American Bar Association. Section of Family Law. Proceedings of the Section;* (until 1964): *American Bar Association. Section of Family Law. Summary of Proceedings.* [ISSN: 0014-729X] 1959. q. Free to members; Non-members, USD 79.95. Ed(s): Linda D Elrod, Deborah Eisel. American Bar Association, 321 N Clark St, 20th Fl, Chicago, IL 60654; service@abanet.org; http://www.americanbar.org. Illus., index, adv. Refereed. Circ: 11000 Controlled. Vol. ends: Winter. Microform: WSH; PMC; PQC. Reprint: WSH. *Indexed:* A01, A22, ABIn, BRI, CJPI, CLI, L14. *Bk. rev.:* Occasional, 500-1,500 words. *Aud.:* Ac, Sa.

The American Bar Association's (ABA) Section of Family Law has as its purpose "to promote the objectives of the American Bar Association by improving the administration of justice in the field of family law by study, conferences, and publication of reports and articles with respect to both legislation and administration." This publication, under the editorship of students at Washburn University School of Law, is one of the principal means toward that end. Issues discuss such topics as divorce, parentage, international custody and support, property rights, artificial reproductive technology, domestic torts, and adoption. The annotated "Summary of the Year in Family Law" is found in the Winter issue. *The Family Advocate,* also published by this ABA section, is a more basic magazine that offers practical advice for attorneys practicing family law.

3307. *Fordham Law Review.* [ISSN: 0015-704X] 1914. 6x/yr. Ed(s): Amanda L Houle, Frank D'Angelo. Fordham University, School of Law, 140 W 62nd St, New York, NY 10023; http://law.fordham.edu/. Refereed. Microform: WSH; PQC. Reprint: WSH. *Indexed:* A22, ABS&EES, B02, BLI, BRI, CLI, L14, P61, SSA. *Aud.:* Ac, Sa.

Well respected and frequently cited, the *Fordham Law Review* follows a different format than most traditional law reviews. Although feature articles and notes are included, some issues lead with an essay written by a noted scholar, followed by a discussion section with responses to the scholar. Fordham also publishes *Fordham Environmental Law Journal, Fordham Intellectual Property, Media & Entertainment Law Review, Fordham International Law Journal, Fordham Journal of Corporate and Financial Law, The Common Good,* and *Fordham Urban Law Journal.*

3308. *G P Solo.* Formerly (until 2000): *General Practice, Solo, and Small Firm Lawyer: The Complete Lawyer;* Which was formed by the merger of (1984-1998): *Compleat Lawyer;* Which was formed by the merger of (1966-1984): *Docket Call;* (1964-1984): *Law Notes for the General Practitioner;* (1997-1998): *Best of A B A Sections. General Practice, Solo & Small Firm Section;* (1997-1998): *Technology and Practice Guide.* [ISSN: 1528-638X] 1998. 8x/yr. USD 135 domestic; USD 145 foreign. Ed(s): Jennifer J Rose, Robert M Salkin. A B A Publishing, 750 N Lake Shore Dr, Chicago, IL 60611; service@abanet.org; http://www.americanbar.org. Illus., index, adv. *Indexed:* A01, A22, ABIn, BRI, CLI, L14. *Aud.:* Ga, Ac, Sa.

Although law is becoming more and more specialized, there are still a substantial number of attorneys engaged in general practice. This magazine caters to the needs of the general practitioner by providing timely, concise articles on all aspects of substantive law, news of the American Bar Association (ABA) section and committee activities, and updates relating to legislation, ethics, taxes, and solo practice. This publication is a good companion to the ABA's *Law Practice* (see below in this section).

3309. *George Washington Law Review.* Formerly (until 1932): *Constitutional Review.* [ISSN: 0016-8076] 1932. 6x/yr. USD 40 domestic; USD 44 foreign. Ed(s): Mark Taticchi, Andrew J Welz. The George Washington University Law School, 2008 G St, N W, 2nd Fl, Washington, DC 20052. Illus., index, adv. Refereed. Vol. ends: Aug. Microform: WSH; PMC. Reprint: WSH. *Indexed:* A22, B02, BAS, BRI, CLI, L14. *Bk. rev.:* Occasional, lengthy. *Aud.:* Ac, Sa.

This law review tends to contain three or four articles, often with an emphasis on federal law. The school also publishes the *George Washington International Law Review, International Law in Domestic Courts* (with Oxford University Press), *American Intellectual Property Law Association Quarterly Journal* (with the American Intellectual Property Law Association), *Federal Circuit Bar Journal* (official journal for the Federal Circuit Bar Association and the United States Court of Appeals for the Federal Circuit (CAFC)), *Journal of Energy and Environmental Law* (with the Environmental Law Institute), and the *Public Contact Law Journal* (with the ABA).

3310. *Georgetown Journal of Legal Ethics.* [ISSN: 1041-5548] 1987. q. USD 40; USD 12.50 per issue. Ed(s): Matthew U Scherer, Joshua Bachrach. Georgetown University Law Center, 600 New Jersey Ave, NW, Washington, DC 20001; http://www.law.georgetown.edu. Illus., index. Refereed. Vol. ends: Spring. Microform: WSH. Reprint: WSH. *Indexed:* A01, A22, ABIn, B01, BRI, CLI, L14. *Bk. rev.:* Occasional, lengthy. *Aud.:* Ac, Sa.

Ours is a litigious society, and the bad acts of a few reflect adversely on many in the professional realm. Every law school in the country is required to offer a course in professional responsibility, sometimes called legal ethics. Professional responsibility is a separate requirement on the multistate bar examination. This student-edited journal endeavors to heighten awareness of ethical issues within the legal community by providing scholarly articles, student notes and comments, and other information of interest to members of the bar. Recent topics covered in the journal include privatizing public interest law and the ethics of willful ignorance.

3311. *Georgetown Law Journal.* [ISSN: 0016-8092] 1912. bi-m. USD 45 domestic; USD 60 foreign. Ed(s): Matthew Berns, Elana Newberger. Georgetown University Law Center, 600 New Jersey Ave, NW, Washington, DC 20001; http://www.law.georgetown.edu. Illus., index. Refereed. Microform: WSH. Reprint: WSH. *Indexed:* A01, A22, B01, B02, BLI, BRI, CLI, L14, MLA-IB, RiskAb. *Aud.:* Ac, Sa.

This journal, the oldest from the District of Columbia law schools, is among several published by Georgetown University and has an outstanding reputation for producing traditional legal scholarship. Articles by noted authorities and student research pieces are lengthy, well documented, and influential. Its "Annual Review of Criminal Procedure" is monumental in scope and depth. This journal is among the more frequently cited—by courts and other legal journals—in the country. The school also publishes *American Criminal Law Review* (see above), *Georgetown Journal of International Law* (which subsumed the *Journal of Law and Policy in International Business*), *Georgetown Journal of Legal Ethics,* and *The Tax Lawyer* (for some of these four, see above and below in this section), as well as *Georgetown Immigration Law Journal, Georgetown International Environmental Law Review, Georgetown Journal of Gender and the Law, Georgetown Journal of Law and Modern Critical Race Perspectives, Georgetown Journal on Poverty Law & Policy,* and *Georgetown Journal of Law and Public Policy.* It recently launched an online companion called Res Ipsa Loquitur (http://georgetownlawjournal.org/ipsa-loquitur/), which features blog posts, article responses, and debates.

3312. *The Green Bag: an entertaining journal of law.* [ISSN: 1095-5216] 1889. q. USD 40 domestic; USD 60 foreign. Ed(s): Ross E Davies, David M Gossett. The Green Bag, Inc., 6600 Barnaby St, NW, Washington, DC 20015. *Indexed:* BRI, L14. *Bk. rev.:* 2-4. *Aud.:* Ga, Ac, Sa.

Green bags were once a required accessory for lawyers and law students. The bags, used to carry legal papers and casebooks, were considered the lawyer's "repository of knowledge." From 1889 to 1914, a journal known as *The Green Bag* was published and widely read by members of the bar. It contained short articles penned by scholars, practitioners, and judges discussing legal issues of interest at the time. Many of the articles were light, and some issues even included verse. *The Green Bag* was resurrected in 1997 with the hope of filling the gap in legal publishing between the scholarly law journals and the more practitioner-oriented legal magazines. Its creators describe it as a place for scholars to toss out creative thoughts or make an argument with fewer than 50 footnotes. Contributors to the new version of *The Green Bag* range from famous legal scholars to judges to general practitioners. Articles are varied; some

discuss serious legal issues of the day and some are light. More recently, the publishers of the *Green Bag* recently launched *The Journal of Law: A Periodical Laboratory of Legal Scholarship*—"[a] bundle of small, unconventional law journals, all published together in one volume." URL: http://journaloflaw.us/

Harvard Civil Rights—Civil Liberties Law Review. See Civil Liberties/ General section.

3313. *Harvard International Law Journal.* Former titles (until 1967): *The Harvard International Law Club. Journal;* (until 1962): *The Harvard International Law Club. Bulletin;* (until 1961): *Harvard International Law Club. Bulletin.* [ISSN: 0017-8063] 1959. s-a. USD 40 domestic; USD 50 foreign. Ed(s): Michael Gibaldi, Yonina Alexander. Harvard University, Law School, 1541 Massachusetts Ave, Cambridge, MA 02138; http://www.law.harvard.edu/. Refereed. Microform: WSH; PQC. Reprint: WSH. *Indexed:* A22, ABS&EES, B02, BAS, BRI, CLI, L14, P61, SSA. *Aud.:* Ac, Sa.

Harvard International Law Journal is the oldest and often considered to be the most-cited student-edited journal of international and comparative law. The journal has a robust web site with op-eds, responses to articles, and live blogs. As it indicates, *ILJ* "publishes articles on international, comparative, and foreign law, the role of international law in U.S. courts, and the international ramifications of U.S. domestic law."

3314. *Harvard Journal of Law & Gender.* Formerly (until 2005): *Harvard Women's Law Journal.* [ISSN: 1558-4356] 1977. s-a. USD 32 domestic; USD 44 foreign; USD 15 per issue domestic. Ed(s): Daniella Genet, Stefani Johnson. Harvard University, Law School, 1563 Massachusetts Ave, Cambridge, MA 02138; http://www.law.harvard.edu/. Microform: WSH; PMC. Reprint: WSH. *Indexed:* A01, A22, BRI, CLI, FemPer, L14, P61, SSA. *Bk. rev.:* Number and length vary. *Aud.:* Ac, Sa.

This law journal addresses a broad range of gender-related topics. Contents include academic articles that analyze feminist legal issues and essays based on personal experience. Issues also include case comments, notes on controversial or current topics, and book reviews.

3315. *Harvard Journal of Law and Public Policy.* [ISSN: 0193-4872] 1978. 3x/yr. USD 45 domestic; USD 50 foreign. Ed(s): Christopher M Thomas, Peter Schmidt. Harvard Society for Law and Public Policy, Inc., Harvard Law School, 1541 Massachusetts Ave, Cambridge, MA 02138; http://www.law.harvard.edu. Illus., index. Refereed. Vol. ends: No. 3. Microform: WSH; PMC. Reprint: WSH. *Indexed:* A01, A22, B01, B02, BRI, CLI, L14, P02, P61, SSA. *Bk. rev.:* Occasional. *Aud.:* Ac, Sa.

This journal is published by the Harvard Society for Law and Public Policy, a conservative and libertarian student group. Articles included reflect the journal's conservative philosophy. Many issues are symposia issues, such as a recent one that focused on essays on judicial independence. The contributors over the years have included conservative politicians and Supreme Court justices. This is a good source for viewpoints that are alternatives to those often found in student-edited law reviews. Harvard Law's *Unbound* and *Harvard Law and Policy Review* provide progressive and more left-leaning perspectives/ voices.

3316. *Harvard Journal on Legislation.* Formerly (until 1964): *Selected Drafts.* [ISSN: 0017-808X] 1958. s-a. USD 32 domestic; USD 44 foreign; USD 15 per issue domestic. Ed(s): Olivia Jennings. Harvard University, Law School, 1563 Massachusetts Ave, Cambridge, MA 02138; http://www.law.harvard.edu/. Illus., index. Refereed. Vol. ends: Summer. Microform: WSH; PQC. Reprint: WSH. *Indexed:* A01, A22, B02, BRI, CLI, L14, P61, SSA. *Bk. rev.:* Occasional. *Aud.:* Ac, Sa.

This is one of the oldest of Harvard Law School's several student-edited law reviews. According to the journal's publication policy, it specializes in the analysis of legislation and the legislative process by focusing on legislative reform and on organizational and procedural factors that affect the efficacy of legislative decision-making. The journal publishes articles that examine a public-policy problem of nationwide significance and propose legislation to resolve it. It also publishes a biannual "Congress Issue," which includes policy essays written by members of Congress. A section devoted to recent developments provides analysis of recent statutory interpretations and discussions of recent statutory enactments.

3317. Harvard Law Review. [ISSN: 0017-811X] 1887. 8x/yr. USD 200 (Individuals, USD 55). Harvard Law Review Association, Gannett House, 1511 Massachusetts Ave, Cambridge, MA 02138. Illus., index. Refereed. Vol. ends: Jun. Microform: WSH; PQC. Reprint: WSH. *Indexed:* A01, A22, ABIn, ABS&EES, B01, B02, BLI, BRI, CBRI, CLI, IBSS, L14, MLA-IB, P02, P61. *Bk. rev.:* Occasional, essay length. *Aud.:* Ac, Sa.

Harvard Law School's primary law journal is steeped in tradition. It continues to be the law school–produced law review that is most widely subscribed to. Previous members/editors/Presidents of this journal have gone on to great things, including being President of the United States (e.g., Barack Obama). Articles are chosen from an enormous pool of submissions. A highly regarded and useful regular feature is its annual evaluation of U.S. Supreme Court decisions of the term recently completed, accompanied by charts and statistical analyses. The journal also recently developed an online companion called "The Forum," which publishes timely responses to recent articles or ideas that do not lend themselves to the traditional law review format. Other journals edited by students at the school are *Harvard Journal on Legislation* and *Harvard Journal of Law and Public Policy* (for both, see above in this section); *Harvard Journal on Racial and Ethnic Justice* and *Harvard Civil Rights–Civil Liberties Law Review* (for the latter, see Civil Liberties section); *Harvard Environmental Law Review; Harvard Human Rights Journal; Harvard International Law Journal; Harvard Journal of Law and Gender; Harvard Journal of Law and Public Policy* (for previous three, see above in this section); *Harvard Journal of Law and Technology; Harvard Latino Law Review; Harvard Law and Policy Review; Harvard National Security Journal* (see below); *Harvard Business Law Review; Harvard Negotiation Law Review; Journal of Sports and Entertainment Law*; and *Unbound.*

3318. Harvard National Security Journal. [ISSN: 2153-1358] 2010. irreg. Ed(s): Brian Clampitt, Kait Michaud. Harvard Law School, 1563 Massachusetts Ave, Cambridge, MA 02138; hllr@law.harvard.edu; http://www.law.harvard.edu. *Aud.:* Ac.

As its web site notes, the *Harvard National Security Journal* (*NSJ*) "is a student-edited online journal dedicated to improving scholarship and discourse in the field of national security." The journal is affiliated with the Harvard Law School–Brookings Project on Law and Security (www.law.harvard.edu/programs/about/project-on-law-and-security/) and has a sister blog publication called Lawfare (www.lawfareblog.com/), founded by professors Benjamin Wittes, Jack Goldsmith, and Robert Chesney.

3319. Howard Law Journal. [ISSN: 0018-6813] 1955. 3x/yr. USD 34 domestic; USD 44 foreign; USD 12 per issue. Ed(s): Valerie L Collins, Jennifer D Thomas. Howard University, School of Law, 2900 Van Ness St, NW, Washington, DC 20008; http://www.law.howard.edu/. Illus., index. Vol. ends: No. 3. Microform: WSH; PMC. Reprint: WSH. *Indexed:* A22, BRI, CLI, IIBP, L14, RiskAb. *Bk. rev.:* 1-2, lengthy. *Aud.:* Ac, Sa.

Howard University is the second-oldest law school in our nation's capital, and its student body is predominantly African American. The editors of its *Journal* describe it as dedicated to promoting the civil and human rights of all people, in particular those groups who have been the target of subordination and discrimination, which is identical to the school's mission. Howard Law School also publishes the *Human Rights and Globalization Law Review.*

Human Rights. See Civil Liberties/General section.

3320. International Journal of Law in Context. [ISSN: 1744-5523] 2005. q. GBP 267. Ed(s): Michael Freeman, David Nelken. Cambridge University Press, The Edinburgh Bldg, Shaftesbury Rd, Cambridge, CB2 8RU, United Kingdom; journals@cambridge.org; http://www.cambridge.org/uk. Adv. Reprint: PSC. *Indexed:* A01, A22, ABIn, E01, RiskAb. *Aud.:* Ac, Sa.

This journal focuses on interdisciplinary legal studies with articles on the intersection of law and other disciplines such as science, literature, humanities, philosophy, sociology, psychology, ethics, history, and geography. It is a companion to Cambridge University Press's *Law in Context* book series. An example of a recent article is "Calculating claims: Jewish and Muslim women navigating religion, economics[,] and law in Canada."

3321. Iowa Law Review. Former titles (until 1925): *Iowa Law Bulletin;* (until 1915): *State University of Iowa. Law Bulletin.* [ISSN: 0021-0552] 1891. 5x/yr. USD 46 domestic; USD 54 foreign; USD 10 per issue domestic. Ed(s): Matthew J Donnelly, Jessica R Reese. University of Iowa, College of Law, 190 Boyd Law Bldg, Iowa City, IA 52242; http://www.law.uiowa.edu/. Illus., index. Refereed. Vol. ends: No. 5. Microform: WSH; PMC. Reprint: WSH. *Indexed:* A01, A22, B02, BRI, CLI, L14. *Bk. rev.:* Occasional, essay length. *Aud.:* Ac, Sa.

It may surprise some to learn that the University of Iowa College of Law, founded in 1865, is the oldest law school west of the Mississippi. The standards used to select the students for the *Review* are among the most rigorous in the country. Due to the College of Law's academic excellence and its longevity, its primary journal has a well-deserved reputation for publishing outstanding legal scholarship. Iowa law students also edit the *Journal of Corporation Law, Journal of Gender, Race & Justice,* and *Transnational Law & Contemporary Problems.*

Issues in Law and Medicine. See Civil Liberties/Bioethics: Reproductive Rights, Right-to-Life, and Right-to-Die section.

Journal of Air Law and Commerce. See Transportation section.

3322. Journal of Civil Law Studies. [ISSN: 1944-3749] 2008. s-a. Free. Ed(s): Olivier Moreteau, Agustin Parise. Louisiana State University, Paul M. Hebert Law Center, 1 E Campus Dr, Baton Rouge, LA 70803; info@law.lsu.edu; http://www.law.lsu.edu. *Indexed:* BRI, L14. *Bk. rev.:* Number and length vary. *Aud.:* Ac, Sa.

As comparative and foreign law becomes more prevalent in the U.S. law school curriculum, there is greater demand for articles that deal with different legal systems. This journal comes out of a U.S. law school and invites "articles dealing with civil law topics, [and the] relationship of civil law and common law in mixed, civil[-]law or common[-]law jurisdictions...especially where [they offer] a comparative perspective or overview." Articles may be written in English, French, or Spanish.

Journal of Criminal Justice. See Criminology and Law Enforcement section.

3323. Journal of Criminal Law & Criminology. Supersedes in part (in 1973): *Journal of Criminal Law, Criminology and Police Science;* Which was formerly (until 1951): *Journal of Criminal Law & Criminology;* Which incorporated (1930-1932): *American Journal of Police Science;* (until 1931): *American Institute of Criminal Law and Criminology. Journal.* [ISSN: 0091-4169] 1910. q. USD 50 domestic; USD 60 foreign. Ed(s): Adair Crosley, Polina Liberman. Northwestern University, School of Law, 375 E Chicago Ave, Chicago, IL 60611; law-web@law.northwestern.edu; http://www.law.northwestern.edu. Illus., index. Refereed. Microform: WSH; PQC. Reprint: WSH. *Indexed:* A01, A22, BRI, CJPI, CLI, IBSS, L14, P02, P61, SSA. *Bk. rev.:* 0-4, lengthy. *Aud.:* Ac, Sa.

This journal dates back over 90 years and is among the first of the subject-specialty law school reviews. Both its long history and the quality of its content make it a leader in the field and among the most frequently cited legal journals. Edited by students of Northwestern University School of Law, the journal is divided into "Criminal Law" and "Criminology" sections, written by law professionals and social scientists respectively, with a separate section of student-written "Comments." One issue per year contains a highly respected, heavily analytical review of U.S. Supreme Court decisions pertaining to criminal law and criminal procedure.

3324. *Journal of Dispute Resolution.* Formerly (until 1988): *Missouri Journal of Dispute Resolution.* [ISSN: 1052-2859] 1984. s-a. USD 35. Ed(s): Christina Semmer, Brittany Barrientos. University of Missouri at Columbia, School of Law, 203 Hulston Hall, Columbia, MO 65211; mulawhelpdesk@missouri.edu; http://www.law.missouri.edu/. Illus., index, adv. Vol. ends: No. 2. Microform: WSH. Reprint: WSH. *Indexed:* A22, BRI, CLI, L14. *Bk. rev.:* Number and length vary. *Aud.:* Ac, Sa.

Alternative Dispute Resolution (ADR), which involves ways in which parties can avoid litigation (such as negotiation, mediation, and arbitration), has been a significant topic for a number of years. This student-edited journal is published by the University of Missouri–Columbia School of Law in conjunction with the Center for the Study of Dispute Resolution. Since this journal's inception in 1984, there have been other journals focusing on this topic, such as the *Harvard Negotiation Law Review* and the *Ohio State Journal on Dispute Resolution.*

3325. *Journal of Empirical Legal Studies.* [ISSN: 1740-1453] 2004. q. GBP 380. Ed(s): Dawn M Chutkow. Wiley-Blackwell Publishing, Inc., 111 River St, Hoboken, NJ 07030; info@wiley.com; http://onlinelibrary.wiley.com/. Adv. Sample. Refereed. Reprint: PSC. *Indexed:* A22, E01, L14, RiskAb. *Aud.:* Ac, Sa.

Published on behalf of the Society for Empirical Legal Studies and Cornell Law School, this is a peer-edited, refereed, interdisciplinary journal that focuses on empirical studies of the legal system that would interest scholars in a diverse range of law and law-related fields. With the rise in empirical studies and data analysis in both graduate and undergraduate programs, this would be a good law-related journal for academic libraries.

3326. *Journal of Health & Life Sciences Law (Online).* 200?. q. USD 149. Ed(s): Robert W Miller, Kara Kinney Cartwright. American Health Lawyers Association, 1620 Eye St NW, 6th Fl, Washington, DC 20006; MbrDept@healthlawyers.org; http://www.healthlawyers.org. *Aud.:* Ac, Sa.

Legal issues related to health comprise an area of law that has exploded over the years. Accordingly, we have seen a fair number of journals dedicated to issues related to health-care law. Published by American Health Lawyers Association through LexisNexis, this one is the oldest, and it is fairly expensive. It had been published in collaboration with Saint Louis University School of Law, but the school's Center for Health Law Studies and a student editorial board now publish *Saint Louis University Journal of Health Law & Policy.* Other publications related to this topic include *Berkeley Journal of Health Care Law,* Catholic University's *Journal of Contemporary Health Law and Policy,* Duke's *Journal of Health Politics, Policy and Law,* DePaul's *Journal of Health Care Law,* Case Western's *Health Matrix,* University of Maryland's *Journal of Health Care Law and Policy,* and Cleveland State's *Journal of Law and Health.*

3327. *Journal of Labor and Employment Law.* Formerly (until 2009): *Labor Lawyer;* Which incorporated (in 1985): *American Bar Association. Section of Labor and Employment Law. Committee Reports;* Which was formerly (until 1979): *American Bar Association. Section of Labor Relations Law. Committee Reports;* (until 1970): *American Bar Association. Section of Labor Relations Law. Program of the Annual Meeting, Committee Reports;* (until 1966): *American Bar Association. Section of Labor Relations Law. Proceedings; Officers, Committees, Roster.* [ISSN: 2156-4809] 19??. 3x/yr. Free to members; Non-members, USD 45. Ed(s): Seth Thompson. American Bar Association, Labor and Employment Law Section, 321 N Clark St, Chicago, IL 60610; laborempllaw@abanet.org; http://www.abanet.org/labor. Illus., index. Vol. ends: Fall. Microform: WSH. Reprint: WSH. *Indexed:* A22, ABIn, B01, BRI, CLI, L14, P02. *Bk. rev.:* Occasional, lengthy. *Aud.:* Ac, Sa.

Another of the many American Bar Association section publications and edited at the University of Minnesota Law School, this journal is devoted to labor and employment law and is intended to provide practitioners, judges, administrators, and the interested public with balanced discussions of topical interest within the parameters of the journal's scope. Each issue contains six to eight articles that cover diverse topics, such as sexual harassment, labor unions, and employment law. Most articles are written by those practicing in the field and are practitioner oriented.

3328. *The Journal of Law and Economics.* [ISSN: 0022-2186] 1958. q. USD 145 (print & online eds.). Ed(s): Maureen Callahan, Anup Malani. University of Chicago Press, 1427 E 60th St, Chicago, IL 60637; subscriptions@press.uchicago.edu; http://www.journals.uchicago.edu. Illus., index, adv. Sample. Refereed. Vol. ends: Oct. Microform: WSH; PQC. Reprint: PSC; WSH. *Indexed:* A22, ABIn, B01, B02, BAS, BLI, C45, CLI, EconLit, IBSS, JEL, L14, P02, RRTA, RiskAb. *Aud.:* Ac, Sa.

Since the University of Chicago Law School is known for its strong law and economics perspective, it is not surprising that this long-standing journal is well respected and widely referenced. It is not for casual reading because articles are rife with statistical analysis and formulas. Its broad range of topics include economic analysis of regulation and the behavior of regulated firms, the political economy of legislation and legislative processes, law and finance, corporate finance and governance, and industrial organization.

Journal of Law and Policy in International Business. See *Georgetown Journal of Law.*

Journal of Law and Religion. See Civil Liberties/Freedom of Thought and Belief section.

3329. *Journal of Legal Analysis.* [ISSN: 2161-7201] 2009. s-a. Ed(s): J Mark Ramseyer. Oxford University Press, 198 Madison Ave, New York, NY 10016; orders.us@oup.com; http://www.us.oup.com. Refereed. Reprint: PSC. *Aud.:* Ac, Sa.

Launched in 2009 by the Harvard University Press and the John M. Olin Center for Law, Economics, and Business, the *Journal of Legal Analysis* is fairly unique as a generalist, peer-edited, faculty-edited law review. According to its web site, it "aspires to be broad in coverage, including doctrinal legal analysis and interdisciplinary scholarship." The journal is now published by Oxford University Press.

3330. *Journal of Legal Education.* Formerly (until 1940): *National Journal of Legal Education.* [ISSN: 0022-2208] 1937. q. USD 50 domestic (Free to members). Georgetown University Law Center, Southwestern Law School, 3050 Wilshire Blvd, Los Angeles, CA 90010; http://www.law.georgetown.edu. Illus., index. Sample. Refereed. Vol. ends: Dec. Microform: WSH. *Indexed:* A22, ABS&EES, BRI, CLI, HEA, L14. *Bk. rev.:* 0-4, 500-10,000 words. *Aud.:* Ac, Sa.

The Association of American Law Schools is a membership organization, and this, its professional journal, is distributed to most law professors in the country. Its primary purpose is to foster a rich interchange of ideas and information about legal education and related matters—including, but not limited to, the legal profession, legal theory, and legal scholarship. The *Journal* features general articles; shorter discussions of developments in legal education; an occasional symposium; and from time to time, even a poem or a short story. It is currently edited at Southwestern Law School.

3331. *The Journal of Legal Studies (Chicago).* [ISSN: 0047-2530] 1972. s-a. USD 117 (print & online eds.). Ed(s): Maureen Callahan, Thomas J Miles. University of Chicago Press, 1427 E 60th St, Chicago, IL 60637; subscriptions@press.uchicago.edu; http://www.journals.uchicago.edu. Illus., index, adv. Sample. Refereed. Vol. ends: Jun. Microform: WSH; PQC. Reprint: PSC; WSH. *Indexed:* A22, B01, B02, CLI, EconLit, IBSS, JEL, L14, P02, P61, SSA. *Aud.:* Ac, Sa.

Like other law-related publications from the University of Chicago, this title ranks among the most frequently cited of the legal literature. It provides a forum for basic theoretical, empirical, historical, and comparative research into the operation of legal systems and institutions, relying on contributions from economists, political scientists, sociologists, and other social scientists, as well as legal scholars, for its content. Occasionally, an issue is published in two parts or has a special focus. The number and length of articles are consistent with its companion journal, *The Journal of Law and Economics* (see above in this section).

Journal of Maritime Law and Commerce. See Transportation section.

3332. *Journal of Supreme Court History.* Formerly (until 1990): *Supreme Court Historical Society. Yearbook.* [ISSN: 1059-4329] 1976. 3x/yr. GBP 152. Ed(s): Clare Cushman. Wiley-Blackwell Publishing, Inc., 111 River St, Hoboken, NJ 07030; info@wiley.com; http://onlinelibrary.wiley.com/. Illus., adv. Sample. Refereed. Reprint: PSC. *Indexed:* A01, A22, BRI, CLI, E01, L14, P61, SSA. *Bk. rev.:* 5-7, 500-1,000 words. *Aud.:* Ga.

Established in 1974, the Supreme Court Historical Society is dedicated to the collection and preservation of the history of the Supreme Court of the United States. Its *Journal* reflects this commitment. Initially published as an annual, it expanded to three issues per year in 1999. Articles are brief, historical in nature, and highly illustrated from archival sources. All aspects of the court are discussed, including justices, cases, and themes.

3333. *Journal of the Legal Profession.* [ISSN: 0196-7487] 1976. s-a. USD 24. Ed(s): Cole Richins, Bret Beldt. University of Alabama, School of Law, 101 Paul W Bryant Dr, E, PO Box 870382, Tuscaloosa, AL 35487; http://www.law.ua.edu. Illus., index. Microform: WSH. Reprint: WSH. *Indexed:* A01, A22, BRI, CLI, L14. *Aud.:* Ac, Sa.

This publication was the country's first student-edited journal devoted to the legal profession in general. The *Journal* is intended as a forum for the explanation and exposition of the legal profession's problems, shortcomings, and achievements, as well as a legal ethics and law publication for lawyer and judge. The content is clear, concise, and readable enough to be enjoyed by any segment of the legal community. Each annual volume also contains annotated "compilations" of law review articles about the legal profession and abstracts of selected ethics opinions and cases. (See also *Georgetown Journal of Legal Ethics,* above in this section.) The students at the University of Alabama School of Law also edit the *Alabama Law Review, Alabama Civil Rights and Civil Liberties Law Review,* and *Law and Psychology Review.*

Journal of Transportation Law, Logistics, and Policy. See Transportation section.

3334. *Judicature.* Formerly (until 1966): *American Judicature Society Journal.* [ISSN: 0022-5800] 1917. bi-m. USD 60. Ed(s): Michael Ream. American Judicature Society, 2700 University Ave, Des Moines, IA 50311; http://www.ajs.org. Illus., index, adv. Refereed. Microform: PQC. Reprint: WSH. *Indexed:* A22, BRI, CJPI, CLI, L14, P61, SSA. *Bk. rev.:* 2-3, 500-5,000 words. *Aud.:* Ga, Ac, Sa.

The American Judicature Society has as its purpose the promotion of the effective administration of justice and is open to all persons interested in working toward court improvement. This publication is intended as a forum for fact and opinion relating to the administration of justice and its improvement. The four to eight articles per issue are short, entertaining, and of current interest. The use of graphics, cartoons, and photographs contributes to overall readability.

3335. *Jurimetrics: journal of law, science and technology.* Former titles (until 1978): *Jurimetrics Journal;* (until 1966): *Modern Uses of Logic in Law (MULL).* [ISSN: 0897-1277] 1959. q. Free to members; Non-members, USD 50. Ed(s): Deborah J Pogson. Sandra Day O'Connor College of Law, McAllister & Orange St, P O Box 877906, Tempe, AZ 85287; http://www.law.asu.edu. Illus., index, adv. Circ: 7000. Vol. ends: Summer. Microform: WSH. Reprint: WSH. *Indexed:* A01, A22, BRI, CJPI, CLI, CompR, L14. *Bk. rev.:* 1 per issue. *Aud.:* Ac, Sa.

Co-published by the Section of Science and Technology of the American Bar Association and the Arizona State University College of Law, this journal traces its roots to a previous title called *Modern Uses of Logic in Law* (MULL). It is the oldest journal of law and science in the United States. Articles relate to computer law; law and medicine; the legal reception of scientific evidence; the legal regulation of science or advanced technology; issues relating to new communications technologies; and the use of technology in the administration of justice.

Labor Law Journal. See Labor and Industrial Relations section.

3336. *Law and Contemporary Problems.* [ISSN: 0023-9186] 1933. q. USD 58 domestic; USD 64 foreign. Ed(s): Jeffrey G Mason, Sue Chen. Duke University, School of Law, Science Dr & Toverview Rd, PO Box 90372, Durham, NC 27708; publications@law.duke.edu; http://www.law.duke.edu/. Illus., index, adv. Vol. ends: Sep. Microform: WSH. Reprint: WSH. *Indexed:* A01, A06, A22, B02, BAS, BRI, CJPI, CLI, EconLit, IBSS, JEL, L14, MLA-IB, P02, P61, SSA. *Aud.:* Ac, Sa.

Many journals have symposium issues, but each issue of this journal provides a symposium devoted to a timely legal topic. A special editor for each issue solicits the articles and writes the foreword. It has a distinguished reputation and is frequently cited. "Constitutionality of the Affordable Care Act: Ideas From the Academy" is an example of a recent issue topic. As with other Duke Law School journals, you can find this journal's contents back to volume 1 on the school's web site. URL: www.law.duke.edu/journals/lcp

3337. *Law and History Review.* [ISSN: 0738-2480] 1983. 3x/yr. GBP 129 (print & online eds.). Cambridge University Press, The Edinburgh Bldg, Shaftesbury Rd, Cambridge, CB2 8RU, United Kingdom; journals@cambridge.org; http://journals.cambridge.org. Illus., index, adv. Refereed. Microform: WSH; PQC. Reprint: WSH. *Indexed:* A22, BRI, CLI, L14, MLA-IB, P61, SSA. *Bk. rev.:* 10-15, 1,000-2,000 words. *Aud.:* Ac, Sa.

This is the official publication of the American Society of Legal History, a membership organization dedicated to further research and writing in the fields of social history of law and the history of its legal ideas and institutions. Articles are scholarly and refereed. Its editorial board consists of preeminent scholars throughout the country. As an interdisciplinary journal, it covers the interplay between law and history.

Law and Human Behavior. See Psychology section.

Law & Inequality: a journal of theory and practice. See Civil Liberties/General section.

3338. *Law and Literature.* Formerly (until 2002): *Cardozo Studies in Law and Literature.* [ISSN: 1535-685X] 1989. 3x/yr. USD 248 (print & online eds.). Routledge, 325 Chestnut St, Ste 800, Philadelphia, PA 19106; customerservice@taylorandfrancis.com; http://www.tandfonline.com. Illus., index, adv. Refereed. Vol. ends: Winter. Reprint: PSC; WSH. *Indexed:* A22, AmHI, ArtHuCI, BRI, CLI, E01, L14, MLA-IB, P02. *Aud.:* Ga, Ac.

Edited by the faculty at the Benjamin N. Cardozo School of Law and a board of international scholars, this journal features contributions by practitioners and scholars, poets and playwrights, artists, and technicians of all kinds. The list of noted contributors is impressive, and the content is a delightful diversion from the traditional, often dry law reviews. A somewhat similar journal is the *Yale Journal of Law & the Humanities* (see below).

Law and Philosophy. See Philosophy section.

3339. *Law and Social Inquiry.* Formerly (until 1988): *American Bar Foundation Journal.* [ISSN: 0897-6546] 1976. q. GBP 159 (print & online eds.). Ed(s): Lila M Stromer, Laura Beth Nielsen. Wiley-Blackwell Publishing, Inc., 111 River St, Hoboken, NJ 07030; info@wiley.com; http://onlinelibrary.wiley.com/. Illus. Sample. Refereed. Vol. ends: Fall. Microform: WSH; PQC. Reprint: PSC; WSH. *Indexed:* A01, A22, ABS&EES, BRI, CJPI, CLI, E01, JEL, L14, MLA-IB, P61, SSA. *Bk. rev.:* Number and length vary. *Aud.:* Ac, Sa.

This is a refereed professional journal of the American Bar Foundation, an independent, nonprofit national research institute committed to objective empirical research on law and legal institutions. This was one of the first journals to stress empirical scholarship, which has been increasingly influential in legal scholarship. In addition to lengthy essays, the journal contains critical review essays on books and shorter book notes.

3340. *Law & Society Review.* Formerly (until 1966): *Newsletter.* [ISSN: 0023-9216] 1966. q. GBP 313. Ed(s): David T Johnson, Jonathan Goldberg-Hiller. Wiley-Blackwell Publishing, Inc., 111 River St, Hoboken, NJ 07030; info@wiley.com; http://onlinelibrary.wiley.com/. Illus., index, adv. Sample. Refereed. Vol. ends: Dec. Microform: WSH. Reprint: PSC; WSH. *Indexed:* A01, A22, BAS, BRI, CJPI, CLI, E01, FR, IBSS, L14, P02, P61, PsycInfo, RiskAb, SSA, SWR&A. *Bk. rev.:* 3-4, essay length. *Aud.:* Ac, Sa.

The Law and Society Association is an international group drawn primarily from the legal and social science professions, whose purpose is the stimulation and support of research and teaching on the cultural, economic, political, psychological, and social aspects of law and legal systems. Contributions are drawn from law professors, sociologists, and political scientists.

Law Library Journal. See Library and Information Science section.

3341. *Law Practice: the business of practicing law.* Former titles (until 2004): *Law Practice Management;* (until 1990): *Legal Economics;* Which superseded (in 1975): *Legal Economics News.* [ISSN: 1547-9102] 1975. 6x/yr. Free to members; Non-members, USD 64. Ed(s): Daniel E Pinnington, Joan Hamby Feldman. American Bar Association, Law Practice Management Section, 321 N Clark St, Chicago, IL 60610; lpm@abanet.org; http://www.abanet.org/lpm/about/home.shtml. Illus., index, adv. Sample. Vol. ends: Nov. Microform: WSH. *Indexed:* A01, A22, ABIn, BRI, CLI, L14. *Aud.:* Ac, Sa.

This magazine's purpose is to assist the practicing lawyer in operating and managing the office in an efficient and economical manner. It provides, in an easy-to-read, straightforward style, practical tips and how-to advice on a panoply of topics ranging from how to store files to how to design office space and then plan for the move into it. Increasingly, the articles pertain to law office computer applications.

3342. *Legal Scholarship Network.* irreg. Free. Ed(s): A Mitchell Polinsky, Bernard Black. Social Science Research Network (S S R N), Social Science Electronic Publishing, 2171 Monroe Ave, Ste 3, Rochester, NY 14618; sandy_barnes@ssrn.com; http://www.ssrn.com. *Aud.:* Ga, Ac, Sa.

A division of the Social Science Research Network (SSRN), the *Legal Scholarship Network* (*LSN*) includes articles related to a wide range of legal interests. Articles are free for downloading in many cases. This increasingly popular web-based legal scholarship network includes working papers and accepted articles for publication from law professors and other legal scholars. The *LSN* also includes over 50 subject-specific journals, such as *Wills, Trusts and Estate Law,* or *Family and Children's Law,* which can be accessed and downloaded. The *LSN* remains a favorite of legal scholars.

3343. *Marquette Sports Law Review.* Formerly (until 2000): *Marquette Sports Law Journal (Print).* [ISSN: 1533-6484] 1990. s-a. USD 35 domestic; USD 45 foreign; USD 20 per issue. Ed(s): Alex Porteshawver, Lindsay Caldwell. Marquette University, Sensenbrenner Hall, 1103 W Wisconsin Ave, Milwaukee, WI 53201; law.admission@marquette.edu; http://law.marquette.edu. Illus., index, adv. Vol. ends: Spring. Reprint: WSH. *Indexed:* BRI, CLI, L14, SD. *Bk. rev.:* Occasional, lengthy. *Aud.:* Ac, Sa.

In response to the growing importance of the relationship between sports and the law, Marquette University Law School established the National Sports Law Institute in 1989. The institute's principal purpose is "to promote the development of ethical practices in all phases of amateur and professional sports." This journal, a product of the institute, covers a panoply of legal issues in the sports industry and is aimed at attorneys and sports industry professionals. Because sports are so ingrained in the American tradition, this journal provides coverage of an increasingly important area of specialized legal representation. Sports law is also often covered in entertainment law journals. Since this journal's founding, there have been several other legal journals devoted to sports law or entertainment law in general. Examples include *Vanderbilt Journal of Entertainment and Technology Law, Harvard Journal of Sports & Entertainment Law, Seton Hall Journal of Sports and Entertainment Law, Virginia Sports and Entertainment Law Journal, DePaul Journal of Sports Law and Contemporary Problems,* and *Journal of the Legal Aspect of Sport.*

3344. *Michigan Law Review.* [ISSN: 0026-2234] 1902. 8x/yr. USD 60 domestic; USD 70 foreign; USD 8 per issue. Ed(s): Leah M Litman, Jacqueline D Harrington. Michigan Law Review Association, Hutchins Hall, 625 S State St, Ann Arbor, MI 48109--; michlrev.ed.br@umich.edu; http://www.law.umich.edu/Pages/default.aspx. Illus., index, adv. Vol. ends: Jun. Microform: WSH. Reprint: WSH. *Indexed:* A01, A22, ABIn, ABS&EES, B01, BLI, BRI, CLI, EconLit, JEL, L14, P02. *Bk. rev.:* Occasional, essay length. *Aud.:* Ac, Sa.

This journal is consistently in the top ten of any law journal ranking, and is known for its high-quality legal scholarship. The journal has an annual issue devoted to substantive book reviews that serves as a wonderful library selection tool. This journal is committed to an open-access policy, adopting the Open Access Law Journal Principles of the Open Access Law Program of Science Commons. It has a nonexclusive publishing agreement with authors, and offers the contents on its web site. It also has an online companion called "First Impressions" that publishes "op-ed length articles by academics, judges, and practitioners in an online symposium format." The school also publishes *Michigan Journal of Law Reform, Michigan Journal of Gender & Law, Michigan Journal of International Law, Michigan Telecommunications and Technology Law Review,* and *Michigan Journal of Race & Law.*

3345. *Military Law Review.* [ISSN: 0026-4040] 1958. q. USD 20 domestic; USD 28 foreign. Ed(s): Capt. Joseph D. Wilkinson, II. U.S. Army, Judge Advocate General's Legal Center and School, 600 Masie Rd, Charlottesville, VA 22903; http://www.jagcnet.army.mil/. Illus., index. Sample. Refereed. Microform: MIM; PQC. Reprint: WSH. *Indexed:* A22, ABS&EES, BRI, CLI, L14. *Aud.:* Ac, Sa.

Published at the Judge Advocate General's School, U.S. Army, this journal provides a forum for those interested in military law to share the products of their experience and research. Designed for use by military attorneys in connection with their official duties, it is useful for gaining unique insight into military legal issues. The Library of Congress hosts issues of the journal back to volume 1. URL: www.loc.gov/rr/frd/Military_Law/Military-Law-Review-home.html

3346. *Minnesota Law Review.* [ISSN: 0026-5535] 1917. bi-m. USD 40 domestic; USD 46 foreign; USD 10 per issue. Ed(s): Kyle Hawkins, Hans H Grong. University of Minnesota, Law School, 229 19th Ave S, Minneapolis, MN 55455; law@umn.edu; http://www.law.umn.edu. Illus., index, adv. Vol. ends: Jun. Microform: WSH; PMC. Reprint: WSH. *Indexed:* A01, A22, B02, BLI, BRI, CLI, L14. *Bk. rev.:* Occasional, length varies. *Aud.:* Ac, Sa.

This is another of the frequently cited traditional law reviews that publish articles and student pieces on a myriad of legal topics. Volumes contain articles that represent a wide cross-section of legal thinking that is both provocative and challenging. Also published by this law school are *Constitutional Commentary*; *Law and Inequality: A Journal of Theory and Practice*; *Crime and Justice*; *Minnesota Journal of Law, Science & Technology*; *Minnesota Journal of International Law*; and the *ABA Journal of Labor and Employment Law.*

3347. *The National Black Law Journal.* Formerly (until 1987): *The Black Law Journal.* [ISSN: 0896-0194] 1970. 3x/yr. Ed(s): Jessica Schibler, Michelle Harris. University of California, School of Law, 405 Hilgard Ave, PO Box 951476, Los Angeles, CA 90095; http://www.law.ucla.edu/home/. Illus., index, adv. Vol. ends: No. 3. Microform: WSH; PMC; PQC. Reprint: WSH. *Indexed:* A22, BRI, CLI, IIBP, L14, P02, RiskAb. *Bk. rev.:* 2, 600-2,500 words. *Aud.:* Ac, Sa.

This journal is devoted exclusively to the discussion and analysis of issues related to the African American community. Issues may have a theme; voting rights was the theme of a recent issue. During the history of the journal, students from many schools have contributed to and prepared its issues, so the use of "national" in its title is quite appropriate.

3348. *The National law journal & legal times: the newspaper for the legal profession.* Formerly (until 2010): *The National Law Journal;* Which incorporated (1982-2010): *Legal Times;* Which was formerly (until 1982): *Legal Times of Washington.* [ISSN: 2163-8756] 1978. w. USD 299

combined subscription. Ed(s): David L Brown. A L M, 120 Broadway, 5th Fl, New York, NY 10271; customerservices@incisivemedia.com; http://www.alm.com. Illus., index, adv. Circ: 150000 Paid. Vol. ends: Aug. *Indexed:* A22, ATI, BLI, CLI, Chicano, L14, P02. *Aud.:* Ga, Ac, Sa.

This publication is one of the most often-read national legal newspapers, with its large subscription base and long routing lists in law firm and academic law libraries. It has bureau chiefs in New York, California, Boston, Chicago, and Washington, D.C., and contributors from a host of states. This is a great source for fast-breaking legal developments. It also offers popular supplements, such as national salary surveys and listings of the largest law firms (with billing rates). Its web site includes special content and features for subscribers. In 2009, *The National Law Journal* merged with the *Legal Times,* which covers "law and lobbying in the nation's capital." The *IncisiveMedia* web site is broken down into "National News" (*The National Law Journal*) and "Washington News" (*Legal Times*), with the blog of the *Legal Times* (http://legaltimes.typepad.com/) providing a useful current-awareness service for legal news.

3349. *Negotiation Journal: on the process of dispute settlement.* [ISSN: 0748-4526] 1985. q. GBP 640. Ed(s): Nancy Waters, Michael Wheeler. Wiley-Blackwell Publishing, Inc., 111 River St, Hoboken, NJ 07030; info@wiley.com; http://onlinelibrary.wiley.com/. Adv. Sample. Refereed. Microform: PQC. Reprint: PSC. *Indexed:* A22, ABIn, ABS&EES, B01, BRI, CJPI, E01, IBSS, L14, P61, PsycInfo, RiskAb, SSA. *Aud.:* Ga, Ac, Sa.

Published by the Program on Negotiation (PON) at Harvard Law School, this journal takes a self-professed eclectic, multidisciplinary approach and offers "reports on cutting-edge research, a wide range of case studies, teacher's reports about what does and doesn't work in the negotiations classroom, essays on best practices, and integrative book reviews." Its audience includes lawyers, business executives, family mediators, and "anyone interested in the practice and analysis of negotiation, mediation, and conflict resolution."

Negotiation Journal Labor and Industrial Relations.

3350. *New York University Law Review (New York, 1950).* Former titles (until 1950): *New York University Law Quarterly Review;* (until 1929): *New York University Law Review.* [ISSN: 0028-7881] 1925. bi-m. USD 50 domestic; USD 56 foreign; USD 16 per issue. Ed(s): Helam Gebremariam, Frederick J Lee. New York University School of Law, 110 W Third St, Basement, New York, NY 10012; law.moreinfo@nyu.edu; http://www.law.nyu.edu. Illus., index, adv. Refereed. Vol. ends: Dec. Microform: WSH. Reprint: WSH. *Indexed:* A01, A22, B02, BRI, CLI, L14, MLA-IB, P02. *Aud.:* Ac, Sa.

New York University School of Law, founded in 1835, is one of the oldest law schools in the United States. This student-edited journal provides some of the finest legal scholarship from some of the best legal minds in the country, on just about any legal topic. Likewise, student-written pieces are of high quality. Also published by NYU School of Law are the *Annual Survey of American Law* and *Clinical Law Review* (for the latter, see above in this section), as well as *East European Constitutional Review, International Journal of Constitutional Law, Journal of International Law and Politics, Journal of Law and Liberty, Review of Law & Social Change, Journal of Law and Business, Journal of Legislation and Public Policy, Environmental Law Journal,* and the *Tax Law Review* (for the latter, see below in this section).

News Media and the Law. See Journalism and Writing/Journalism section.

3351. *North Carolina Law Review.* [ISSN: 0029-2524] 1922. bi-m. USD 45 domestic; USD 50 foreign; USD 9.50 per issue domestic. Ed(s): Daniel F E Smith, Jessica A Vance. North Carolina Law Review Association, University of North Carolina, School of Law, Chapel Hill, NC 27599; http://studentorgs.law.unc.edu/. Adv. Refereed. Microform: BHP; WSH. Reprint: WSH. *Indexed:* A22, BRI, CLI, L14. *Bk. rev.:* Occasional, lengthy. *Aud.:* Ac, Sa.

This school's law review has a long history of publishing quality legal scholarship. The format is traditional, with articles, comments, and notes on any type of topic. One issue per year surveys North Carolina and Fourth Circuit law.

Other journals from this school are *First Amendment Law Review, North Carolina Banking Institute Journal, North Carolina Journal of International Law and Commercial Regulation,* and *North Carolina Journal of Law and Technology.*

3352. *Northwestern University Law Review.* Formerly (until 1952): *Illinois Law Review;* (until 1906): *Illinois Law Quarterly;* (until 1921): *University of Illinois Law Bulletin;* (until 1920): *Illinois Law Bulletin.* [ISSN: 0029-3571] 1892. q. USD 50 domestic; USD 60 foreign. Ed(s): Gautam Huded, Leighton Leib. Northwestern University, School of Law, 375 E Chicago Ave, Chicago, IL 60611; http://www.law.northwestern.edu. Illus., index, adv. Refereed. Vol. ends: No. 4. Microform: BHP; WSH; PQC. Reprint: WSH. *Indexed:* A01, A22, B02, BRI, CLI, L14. *Bk. rev.:* Occasional, length varies. *Aud.:* Ac, Sa.

This law review is more than a century old and is well respected. Articles are generally submitted by leading scholars and are varied and thought-provoking. Student comments and notes and lengthy book review essays are also included. The journal also publishes an online companion titled "Colloquy" on its web site (http://colloquy.law.northwestern.edu). Some short essays initially found there are subsequently added to a print edition of the *Law Review.* The prestigious *Journal of Criminal Law & Criminology* (see above in this section), the *Journal of International Law & Business,* the *Northwestern Journal of Technology and Intellectual Property,* the *Journal of Law and Social Policy,* and the *Journal of International Human Rights* are the other review-type publications of this law school.

3353. *Ohio State Journal on Dispute Resolution.* [ISSN: 1046-4344] 1985. q. USD 50 domestic (Members, USD 25). Ed(s): Kevin Mahoney, Keith G DeMaggio. Ohio State University, Moritz College of Law, 55 W 12th Ave, Columbus, OH 43210; moritzlaw@osu.edu; http://moritzlaw.osu.edu. Adv. Microform: WSH. Reprint: WSH. *Indexed:* A01, A22, BRI, CJPI, CLI, L14. *Bk. rev.:* Number and length vary. *Aud.:* Ac, Sa.

A student-initiated, student-run publication, this journal is also the official law journal of the American Bar Association's Section on Dispute Resolution. It is a frequently cited journal in the field of dispute resolution. Its annual "Bibliography Issue," covering articles and books with its own terms and index system, is great for keeping up with literature in the field, and it serves as a useful selection tool.

3354. *The Practical Lawyer.* [ISSN: 0032-6429] 1955. bi-m. USD 65; USD 99 combined subscription (print & online eds.); USD 15 per issue. Ed(s): Mark T Carroll. American Law Institute - American Bar Association, Committee on Continuing Professional Education, 4025 Chestnut St, Philadelphia, PA 19104; custserv@ali-aba.org; http://www.ali-aba.org. Illus., index. Circ: 3500 Paid. Vol. ends: Dec. Microform: WSH; PQC. *Indexed:* A22, ATI, BLI, BRI, CLI, L14. *Aud.:* Ga, Ac, Sa.

A nuts-and-bolts magazine with very practical articles related to the practice of law, including practice checklists for lawyers preparing to cover all salient points. Recent articles include "Seven Questions for Sarbanes-Oxley Whistleblowers to Ask" and "Twenty Reasons People Don't Respect Lawyers the Way They Used To." There is a regular column on writing and style titled "The Grammatical Lawyer" that has been compiled and published as a book. Other subject-specific titles by the same publisher include *The Practical Real Estate Lawyer, The Practical Tax Lawyer,* and *The Practical Litigator.*

3355. *Preview of United States Supreme Court Cases.* [ISSN: 0363-0048] 1963. 8x/yr. USD 155 (Members, USD 105; Non-members, USD 115). American Bar Association, Public Education Division, 321 N Clark, 20.2, Chicago, IL 60654; abapubed@abanet.org; http://www.abanet.org/publiced. Illus. Sample. Circ: 3000. Vol. ends: May. *Indexed:* CJPI. *Aud.:* Ga, Ac, Sa.

More than any other title in this section, this publication serves as a current awareness service. Published by the Division for Public Education of the American Bar Association, it discusses cases that the United States Supreme Court will be deciding soon. Legal professionals with subject expertise present the issues, facts, and an analysis of the case, along with the attorneys for the case and any parties who have filed amicus briefs. The publication's web site provides free copies of merit briefs. This would be a wonderful resource for a public or academic library looking for an interesting current awareness tool for U.S. Supreme Court cases. URL: www.supremecourtpreview.org

3356. *Real Property, Trust and Estate Law Journal.* Formerly (until 2008): *Real Property, Probate and Trust Journal;* Which incorporated: *American Bar Association. Section of Real Property, Probate and Trust Law. Newsletter; American Bar Association. Section of Real Property, Probate, and Trust Law. Proceedings; Probate and Trust Legislation.* [ISSN: 2159-4538] 1966. q. Free to members. American Bar Association, Real Property, Probate and Trust Law Section, 321 N Clark St, Chicago, IL 60654; rpte@americanbar.org; http://www.abanet.org/rpte. Illus., index. Vol. ends: Winter. Microform: WSH. Reprint: WSH. *Indexed:* A01, BRI, CLI, L14. *Bk. rev.:* Occasional, lengthy. *Aud.:* Ac, Sa.

This journal's focus is principally scholarly, and it is edited by students at the University of South Carolina School of Law. Each issue contains four to six heavily researched, substantive articles. Recent articles range from a discussion of the property interests in tissues, cells, and gametes to premarital agreements. Many of the section materials once found in this publication, as well as shorter, more practice-oriented articles, are contained in *Probate & Property,* published by the same ABA section.

3357. *The Scribes Journal of Legal Writing.* [ISSN: 1049-5177] 1990. a. Free to members. Ed(s): Joseph Kimble. American Society of Writers on Legal Subjects, c/o Norman E Plate, Thomas Cooley Law School, PO Box 13038, Lansing, MI 48901; platen@cooley.edu; http://www.scribes.org. Illus. Reprint: WSH. *Indexed:* BRI, CLI, L14. *Bk. rev.:* 5, 1,500-3,000 words. *Aud.:* Ac, Sa.

After years of criticism of lawyers' use of "legalese," this scholarly journal seeks to promote better legal writing within the legal community. Its goals are refreshing. It advocates "lucidity, concision, and felicity of expression" and hopes "to spread the growing scorn for whatever is turgid, obscure, or needlessly dull." Leading legal scholars who are equally good writers and grammarians contribute up to a dozen 6- to 20-page articles in each issue. Student essays are published, and all contributions are first-rate. Those interested in legal writing might also want to take a look at the *Journal of the Association of Legal Writing Directors.*

3358. *Southern California Law Review.* [ISSN: 0038-3910] 1927. bi-m. USD 36 domestic; USD 45 foreign. Ed(s): Jason T Anderson, Stephen G Ng. University of Southern California, Gould School of Law, University Park, Los Angeles, CA 90089; academicsupport@law.usc.edu; http://lawweb.usc.edu. Illus., index, adv. Refereed. Vol. ends: No. 6. Microform: WSH; PMC. Reprint: WSH. *Indexed:* A22, B02, BAS, BRI, CLI, L14, MLA-IB, P61, SSA. *Aud.:* Ac, Sa.

Another well-respected journal from a California law school, this general-interest law review has a traditional format with a couple of lead articles followed by student notes. The journal has an online companion web site called "Postscript" (http://law.usc.edu/students/orgs/lawreview/postscript.cfm), where people can publish responses to articles published in the journal or commentary on significant court decisions or other legal events. University of Southern California law students also publish the *Southern California Interdisciplinary Law Journal* and *Southern California Review of Law and Social Justice.*

3359. *Stanford Law Review.* Formerly (until Nov.1948): *Stanford Intramural Law Review.* [ISSN: 0038-9765] 1948. bi-m. USD 42 domestic; USD 47 foreign; USD 16 per issue. Ed(s): Tim Tatarka, Martine Cicconi. Stanford University, Stanford Law School, Stanford Law School, 559 Nathan Abbott Way, Stanford, CA 94305; communications@law.stanford.edu; http://www.law.stanford.edu/. Illus., index. Refereed. Vol. ends: Jul. Microform: WSH. Reprint: WSH. *Indexed:* A01, A22, ABIn, ATI, BAS, BRI, CLI, L14, P02. *Bk. rev.:* 1-2, 4,000-8,000 words. *Aud.:* Ac, Sa.

A consistently highly ranked publication from a prestigious, competitive law school, this journal could be considered a core source for a basic law journal collection. Its articles cover a broad range of subjects from constitutional law to corporate governance. Occasionally, essays are published in response to an earlier piece in the *Review.* An issue may also contain student notes and book-review essays. Students also edit the *Stanford Environmental Law Journal, Stanford Journal of Civil Rights and Civil Liberties, Stanford Journal of International Law, Stanford Law & Policy Review, Stanford Journal of Law, Business, and Finance,* and *Stanford Technology Law Review.* There are also plans to publish the *Stanford Journal of Animal Law and Policy.*

3360. *Student Lawyer (Chicago).* Former titles (until 1972): *Student Lawyer Journal;* (until 1967): *American Bar Association. Student Lawyer Journal;* (until Sep.1967): *American Law Student Association. Student Lawyer Journal;* (until 1964): *Student Lawyer;* (until 1957): *Student Lawyer Journal;* (until 1955): *Student Lawyer.* [ISSN: 0039-274X] 1952. m. Free to members; Non-members, USD 22. Ed(s): Angela Gwizdala. American Bar Association, Law Student Division, 321 N Clark St, Chicago, IL 60654; abalsd@abanet.org; http://www.americanbar.org/groups/law_students.html. Illus., index, adv. Sample. Vol. ends: May. Microform: WSH. *Indexed:* A01, A22, BRI, CLI, L14, P02. *Aud.:* Ga, Ac, Sa.

Published by the ABA's Law Student Division, this magazine is commonly read by law students. It often contains interesting articles on legal education, social/legal issues, careers, the practice of law, and news of the Law Student Division. Articles in recent issues cover such topics as preparing for the bar exam and loan forgiveness. It provides good insight into issues that affect students and might be a good selection for an academic library with a pre-law program or a public library.

3361. *The Supreme Court Review.* [ISSN: 0081-9557] 1960. a. USD 99 (print & online eds.). Ed(s): Dennis J Hutchinson, David A Strauss. University of Chicago Press, 1427 E 60th St, Chicago, IL 60637; subscriptions@press.uchicago.edu; http://www.journals.uchicago.edu. Illus., index, adv. Refereed. Microform: PMC; PQC. Reprint: WSH. *Indexed:* A01, A22, B02, CLI, L14, P02. *Aud.:* Ac, Sa.

As its web site suggests, since 1960, *The Supreme Court Review* has provided an authoritative survey of the implications of the Court's most significant decisions, with an in-depth annual critique of the Supreme Court and its work. Published by University of Chicago Press, this journal often has an impressive array of authors from a variety of perspectives, including legal academics, judges, political scientists, journalists, historians, economists, policy planners, and sociologists. Its faculty editors from the University of Chicago Law School are very well known and respected. It would be a wonderful selection for any academic or public library that supports patrons who are researching issues related to the Supreme Court. With sponsorship by The Law & Economics Center at the George Mason University School of Law, the University of Chicago Press also publishes *The Supreme Court Economic Review,* a faculty-edited, peer-reviewed series that focuses on economic analysis of Supreme Court cases.

3362. *Tax Law Review.* [ISSN: 0040-0041] 1945. q. Ed(s): Deborah Schenk. New York University School of Law, Tax Law Office, 245 Sullivan St, 4th Fl, New York, NY 10012; law.taxprograms@nyu.edu; http://www.law.nyu.edu. Illus., index, adv. Vol. ends: Summer. Microform: WSH. Reprint: WSH. *Indexed:* A22, ATI, BLI, BRI, CLI, L14, P61, SSA. *Aud.:* Ac, Sa.

This faculty-edited publication of the New York University School of Law is widely regarded as the most prestigious scholarly publication in the field of taxation. The review publishes four issues annually; one is devoted to a discussion of tax policy. Libraries that seek materials on taxation would certainly want to acquire this publication.

3363. *The Tax Lawyer.* Incorporates (1996-2006): *The State and Local Tax Lawyer;* Formerly (until 1967): *American Bar Association. Tax Section. Bulletin.* [ISSN: 0040-005X] 1947. q. Free to members; Non-members, USD 83. Ed(s): Louis A Mezzullo, William H Lyons. Georgetown University Law Center, 600 New Jersey Ave, NW, Washington, DC 20001; http://www.law.georgetown.edu. Illus., index. Refereed. Vol. ends: Summer. Microform: WSH; PQC. Reprint: WSH. *Indexed:* A22, ABIn, ATI, B01, BLI, BRI, CLI, L14. *Aud.:* Ac, Sa.

Published by the American Bar Association's Section of Taxation and students at the Georgetown University Law Center, this journal contains quality articles and notes spanning all issues related to taxation. They also publish an annual "State and Local Tax Edition" of the journal. The ABA Tax Section publishes the Symposium Edition of the *State and Local Tax Lawyer,* in conjunction with the Annual State and Local Tax Symposium that is sponsored by the section and Georgetown University Law Center.

3364. Texas Law Review. [ISSN: 0040-4411] 1922. 7x/yr. USD 47 domestic; USD 55 foreign; USD 15 per issue. Ed(s): Emily B Falconer, Rachael B Novier. University of Texas at Austin, School of Law Publications, 727 E Dean Keeton St, Austin, TX 78705; Publications@law.utexas.edu; http://www.utexas.edu/law/publications/. Illus., index. Refereed. Circ: 900 Controlled. Vol. ends: Jun. Microform: WSH. Reprint: WSH. *Indexed:* A01, A22, ABIn, B01, B02, BRI, CLI, L14, MLA-IB. *Bk. rev.:* Occasional, lengthy. *Aud.:* Ac, Sa.

There is the South, North, East, and West, and then there is Texas. The University of Texas, with its 50,000-member student body and capital-city Austin location, is considered to have one of the finest law schools and law reviews in the nation. Like other student-edited law school publications, this one contains two or three major articles by legal scholars on an array of legal topics; student notes relating to recent legislation or cases; and essay-length book reviews. Its online companion "See Also" offers a forum for responses and critiques of articles in the *Review.* Other publications by University of Texas law students are the *American Journal of Criminal Law; Texas Journal on Civil Liberties & Civil Rights; Texas Hispanic Journal of Law and Policy; The Review of Litigation; Texas Environmental Law Journal; Texas Intellectual Property Law Journal; Texas International Law Journal; Texas Journal of Oil, Gas and Energy Law;* Texas Review of Entertainment and Sports Law; Texas Review of Law & Politics; and *Texas Journal of Women and the Law.*

3365. Tort Trial & Insurance Practice Law Journal. Former titles (until 2003): *Tort & Insurance Law Journal;* (until 1985): *The Forum;* (until 1965): *News-o-gram.* [ISSN: 1543-3234] 1959. q. Free to members; Non-members, USD 50. Ed(s): Richard C Mason, Wendy J Smith. American Bar Association, 321 N Clark St, 20th Fl, Chicago, IL 60654; service@abanet.org; http://www.americanbar.org. Illus., index. Circ: 30000. Vol. ends: Summer. Microform: WSH; PQC. Reprint: WSH. *Indexed:* A01, A22, BRI, CLI, L14, P02. *Aud.:* Ac, Sa.

Because of the myriad of issues associated with tort law and insurance law, the Tort Trial and Insurance Practice section is one of the largest sections of the American Bar Association. This publication mirrors the interests of the section, which spans several general substantive and procedural areas involved in or affecting the law of torts and insurance. An issue will typically contain six or seven articles of approximately 20 pages each, which address such topics as product liability, automotive law, aviation and space law, workers' compensation, media and defamation torts, health and life insurance, medicine, damages, and commercial torts. Once a year, an entire issue is devoted to a survey of tort trial and insurance practice law. Because both torts and insurance cut across all disciplines and impact on our daily lives, this is an especially important publication.

Transportation Law Journal. See Transportation section.

3366. Trial: focus on clients. Formerly: *National Legal Magazine;* Incorporates (1983-2004): *A T L A Advocate;* Which was formerly (until 1983): *A T L A Bar News.* [ISSN: 0041-2538] 1965. m. Members, USD 45; Non-members, USD 89. Ed(s): Jean Hellwege. American Association for Justice, 777 6th St, NW, Ste 200, Washington, DC 20001; membership@justice.org; http://www.justice.org. Illus., index, adv. Sample. Circ: 25692. Vol. ends: Dec. Microform: WSH; PQC. *Indexed:* A22, BRI, CJPI, CLI, L14, P02. *Bk. rev.:* 2-7, 300-1,500 words. *Aud.:* Ga, Ac, Sa.

This magazine is published for members of the American Association of Justice (formerly the Association of Trial Lawyers of America). It provides timely, practical how-to articles on topics relevant to trial lawyers. For example, a recent issue focuses on medical malpratice. A "News and Trends" section provides relevant current awareness, such as recent court cases. There is a fair amount of advertising, including an experts-and-professional-services advertising section.

3367. Trusts & Estates. Formerly (until 1938): *Trust Companies.* [ISSN: 0041-3682] 1904. m. USD 275 domestic; USD 301 foreign. Ed(s): Susan Lipp. Penton Media, Inc., 249 W, 17th St, New York, NY 10011; information@penton.com; http://www.penton.com. Illus., index, adv. Circ: 14597 Paid. Vol. ends: Dec. Microform: CIS; PQC. *Indexed:* A22, ABIn, ATI, B02, BLI, BRI, CLI, L14. *Aud.:* Ga, Ac, Sa.

Planning for one's death during life, dealing with the myriad of issues that arise after death, and capitalizing on the available options to maximize tax benefits during one's lifetime are the main foci of this publication. Prudent tax planning, wise use of trusts, insurance options, and issues involving divorce and separation are examples of the type of coverage. While this title is intended for lawyers, trust officers, and others involved in estate planning and administration, there is sufficient information, presented clearly and concisely, to warrant a far wider readership. As the population ages, this publication will undoubtedly grow in popularity.

3368. U C L A Law Review. Formerly (until 1953): *U C L A Intramural Law Review.* [ISSN: 0041-5650] 1952. bi-m. USD 48 domestic; USD 60 foreign. Ed(s): Seth J Korman, Jonathan J Faria. University of California, School of Law, 1242 Law Bldg, PO Box 951476, Los Angeles, CA 90095; rollera@law.ucla.edu; http://www.law.ucla.edu/home/. Illus., index, adv. Refereed. Vol. ends: Aug. Microform: WSH. Reprint: WSH. *Indexed:* A01, A22, ABIn, B01, B02, BRI, CLI, L14. *Aud.:* Ac, Sa.

Located on the UCLA campus in the foothills of the Santa Monica Mountains, this law school recruits some of the finest students in the country. Its primary journal reflects the same high quality. One to three lead articles on any legal topic, some exceeding 100 pages in length, are written by legal professionals. Student comments frequently examine cutting-edge issues in the law. Student notes on recent cases are rare. UCLA law students also edit *Chicano-Latino Law Review* (see above in this section); *Indigenous Peoples Journal of Law; Culture and Resistance; The Dukeminier Awards: Best Sexual Orientation Law Review Articles; UCLA Pacific Basin Law Journal; UCLA Women's Law Journal; UCLA Asian Pacific American Law Journal; UCLA Journal of International Law and Foreign Affairs; UCLA Journal of Law and Technology; Entertainment Law Review; UCLA Journal of Islamic and Near Eastern Law; National Black Law Journal* (see above in this section); and *UCLA Journal of Environmental Law and Policy.*

3369. University of Chicago Law Review. [ISSN: 0041-9494] 1933. q. USD 45 domestic; USD 48 in Canada & Mexico; USD 51 elsewhere. Ed(s): Garrett Ordower, Eric C Tung. University of Chicago, Law School, 1111 E 60th St, Chicago, IL 60637; bookpage@law.uchicago.edu; http://www.law.uchicago.edu. Illus., index, adv. Refereed. Vol. ends: Fall. Microform: WSH; PMC; PQC. Reprint: WSH. *Indexed:* A01, A22, ABIn, B01, B02, BLI, BRI, CLI, L14, MLA-IB, P02. *Bk. rev.:* 1-2, essay length. *Aud.:* Ac, Sa.

The University of Chicago Law School's curriculum stresses the interdependence of legal and social studies in the training of lawyers. A significant fraction of the faculty represents disciplines other than law, including economics, history, sociology, philosophy, and political science. Certainly the *Review,* which at times reaches more than 1,500 pages, is among the most highly respected and most often cited of all legal periodicals. A representative issue contains a major article or two; student comments; and essay-length book reviews. Students of the law school also edit the *University of Chicago Legal Forum* and the *Chicago Journal of International Law.* The school is also the home of the faculty-edited *Supreme Court Review, Journal of Law and Economics,* and *Journal of Legal Studies* (for these, see above in this section). Students of the law school also edit the *University of Chicago Legal Forum* and the *Chicago Journal of International Law.*

3370. University of Michigan Journal of Law Reform. Former titles (until 1972): *Journal of Law Reform;* (until 1970): *Prospectus.* [ISSN: 0363-602X] 1968. q. USD 35 domestic; USD 40 foreign; USD 15 per issue. Ed(s): William T Wall, Margia K Y Corner. University of

Michigan, Law School, 801 Monroe St, Ann Arbor, MI 48109; michlaw.pr@umich.edu; http://www.law.umich.edu. Illus., index, adv. Microform: WSH; PMC. Reprint: WSH. *Indexed:* A01, A22, CLI, L14, MLA-IB. *Aud.:* Ac, Sa.

This journal seeks to improve the law and its administration by providing a forum for discussion that identifies contemporary issues for reform efforts, proposes concrete means to accomplish change, and evaluates the impact of law reform. Faculty members and other legal professionals contribute the articles; students write the comments and notes.

3371. *University of Pennsylvania. Law Review.* Former titles (until 1945): *University of Pennsylvania. Law Review and American Law Register;* (until 1908): *American Law Register;* (until 1898): *American Law Register and Review;* (until 1892): *American Law Register;* (until 1852): *American Law Journal;* (until 1848): *Pennsylvania Law Journal.* [ISSN: 0041-9907] 1842. bi-m. USD 47 domestic; USD 57 foreign; USD 10 per issue. Ed(s): Christopher Dipompeo, Kindl Shinn. University of Pennsylvania, Law School, 3400 Chestnut St, Philadelphia, PA 19104; reg@law.upenn.edu; http://www.law.upenn.edu/. Illus., index, adv. Refereed. Vol. ends: Jun. Microform: WSH. Reprint: WSH. *Indexed:* A01, A22, B01, B02, BRI, CLI, L14, P02, P61, SSA. *Bk. rev.:* Occasional, essay length. *Aud.:* Ac, Sa.

This is one of the oldest law reviews in the nation, dating from 1886; and if tracked back to its lineal ancestor (the *American Law Register,* which originated in 1852), the *University of Pennsylvania Law Review* has the highest volume number of all existing reviews. It is influential and highly ranked, traditional in format, diverse in the type of subjects discussed, and edited by a student board of editors with first-rate academic credentials. Contributions concentrate mainly on everyday issues such as bankruptcy, constitutional law, intellectual property, and criminal law. With its web site "PENNumbra," the journal was among the first to take advantage of the Internet as a forum for debate and discussion, calling it a project "uniting the public and the legal academy." The web site hosts responses to articles published in the law review, as well as debates between scholars on current controversies. Other journals edited by the law students at the University of Pennsylvania are the *University of Pennsylvania Journal of Business and Employment Law, University of Pennsylvania Journal of Constitutional Law, University of Pennsylvania Journal of Law and Social Change,* and the *University of Pennsylvania Journal of International Law.*

3372. *University of Toronto Law Journal.* [ISSN: 0042-0220] 1935. q. USD 155. Ed(s): David Dyzenhaus. University of Toronto Press, Journals Division, 5201 Dufferin St, Toronto, ON M3H 5T8, Canada; journals@utpress.utoronto.ca; http://www.utpjournals.com. Illus., index, adv. Sample. Refereed. Circ: 432. Vol. ends: Fall. Microform: MML; PQC. Reprint: WSH. *Indexed:* A01, A22, BRI, C37, CBCARef, CLI, E01, L14, P61, SSA. *Bk. rev.:* Occasional, lengthy. *Aud.:* Ac, Sa.

Our neighbor to the north deserves to have some representation in this law listing, and that distinction goes to this highly regarded journal. Edited by members of the prestigious University of Toronto Faculty of Law, it provides a heavy dose of analysis of Canadian law and Canadian legal history. Unlike in the United States, where faculty members prefer to publish anywhere but in their own review, many articles in this publication are by faculty members from the law school. Student pieces are published in a separate journal, the semi-annual *University of Toronto Faculty of Law Review.* Libraries with a special interest in Canadian materials would certainly want to consider either or both of these titles. For libraries that seek materials on the relationship between the United States and Canada, a better choice is the *Canada–United States Law Journal,* published annually by law students at Case Western Reserve University.

3373. *The Urban Lawyer: the national quarterly on state and local government law.* [ISSN: 0042-0905] 1969. q. Free to members; Non-members, USD 69. Ed(s): Erin M Dedrickson, Stephanie L Hill. A B A Publishing, 750 N Lake Shore Dr, Chicago, IL 60611; service@abanet.org; http://www.americanbar.org. Illus., index, adv. Refereed. Circ: 6000. Vol. ends: Fall. Reprint: WSH. *Indexed:* A01, A22, ABS&EES, BRI, CLI, L14, P02. *Bk. rev.:* Occasional. *Aud.:* Ac, Sa.

Local government law is wide-ranging and far-reaching. This publication of the American Bar Association's Section of Urban, State, and Local Government Law has a student editorial board based at the University of Missouri–Kansas City School of Law. Articles run the gamut represented by the section's scope, and cover such issues as gerrymandering, Superfund cleanups, sales tax incentive programs, governmental tort liability, airports, land-use planning and zoning, labor relations, and HUD housing. Each issue contains four or five articles, a section discussing cases and other recent developments, and occasional book reviews.

3374. *Vanderbilt Law Review.* [ISSN: 0042-2533] 1947. bi-m. USD 42 domestic; USD 48 foreign. Ed(s): Ryan T Holt, Andrew R Gould. Vanderbilt University, Law School, 131 21st Ave S, Nashville, TN 37203; http://law.vanderbilt.edu/index.html. Index. Refereed. Microform: WSH; PMC; PQC. Reprint: WSH. *Indexed:* A01, A22, ABIn, ATI, B01, B02, BRI, CLI, L14, MLA-IB. *Bk. rev.:* Occasional, length varies. *Aud.:* Ac, Sa.

The Vanderbilt University School of Law is among the most respected in the nation, and its review enjoys the same reputation. Articles and student notes cover the gamut of legal scholarship, with recent issues addressing nonjudicial precedent, immigration, and prison labor. Other Vanderbilt legal journals are *Vanderbilt Journal of Entertainment and Technology Law* and *Vanderbilt Journal of Transnational Law.*

3375. *Virginia Law Review.* Incorporates (1895-1928): *Virginia Law Register.* [ISSN: 0042-6601] 1913. 8x/yr. USD 54 in US & Canada; USD 65 elsewhere. Ed(s): Paul Belonick, Christi Niehans. Virginia Law Review Association, 580 Massie Rd, Charlottesville, VA 22903. Illus., index, adv. Refereed. Vol. ends: Nov. Microform: WSH. Reprint: WSH. *Indexed:* A01, A22, ABIn, B01, B02, BRI, CLI, L14. *Bk. rev.:* Occasional, essay length. *Aud.:* Ac, Sa.

The University of Virginia School of Law has produced many of the great lawyers of this country. It is an institution rich in tradition, and its *Review* ranks among the best of all those published. With the standard professional articles and student notes and comments, this publication is as widely regarded for the content of the articles as it is for the contributors. It has an online companion called "In Brief." Other journals published by University of Virginia law students are *Virginia Journal of International Law, Virginia Environmental Law Journal, Virginia Law & Business Review, Virginia Journal of Law and Technology, Virginia Sports and Entertainment Law Journal, Journal of Law and Politics, Virginia Journal of Social Policy & the Law,* and *Virginia Tax Review.* URL for "In Brief": http://virginialawreview.org/index.php

3376. *Washington Law Review.* Formerly (until 1962): *Washington Law Review and State Bar Journal;* Which was formed by the 1936 merger of: *Washington Law Review; State Bar Review.* [ISSN: 0043-0617] 1925. q. USD 37.50 domestic; USD 47.50 foreign; USD 12 per issue. Ed(s): David Hancock. University of Washington, School of Law, William H. Gates Hall, PO Box 353020, Seattle, WA 98195; lawadm@uw.edu; http://www.law.washington.edu. Illus. Refereed. Vol. ends: Sep. Microform: WSH. Reprint: WSH. *Indexed:* A01, A22, ABIn, ATI, B02, BRI, CLI, L14, RiskAb. *Bk. rev.:* Occasional, lengthy. *Aud.:* Ac, Sa.

Established in 1899, the University of Washington in Seattle is one of the oldest West Coast law schools. The school has a relatively small but highly diverse student enrollment and an excellent student–faculty ratio. Its law review is traditional in nature, organized around lead articles and student notes and comments, and national in scope. The school also publishes the *Pacific Rim Law & Policy Journal* and the *Shidler Journal of Law, Commerce & Technology.*

3377. *Washington University. Law Review.* Former titles (until 2006): *Washington University. Law Quarterly;* (until 1936): *St. Louis Law Review.* 1915. bi-m. USD 60 domestic; USD 72 foreign; USD 10 per issue domestic. Ed(s): Jason Batts, Justin Cruz. Washington University, School of Law, 1 Brookings Dr, Campus Box 1120, St Louis, MO 63130; registrar@wulaw.wustl.edu; http://law.wustl.edu. Microform: WSH; PMC. Reprint: WSH. *Indexed:* A22, BRI, CLI, L14. *Bk. rev.:* Occasional, length varies. *Aud.:* Ac, Sa.

This review and its law school are known for a long-standing and well-deserved standard of excellence. The facility is outstanding thanks to a significant contribution by Anheuser-Busch. The journal is traditional, with articles, notes, and discussions of recent developments. Other journals prepared by students at this school are *Washington University Journal of Law and Policy* and *Washington University Global Studies Law Review.*

3378. *Wisconsin Law Review.* [ISSN: 0043-650X] 1920. bi-m. USD 36 domestic; USD 40 foreign. Ed(s): Gretchen E Cleveland. University of Wisconsin at Madison, Law School, 975 Bascom Mall, Madison, WI 53706; info@law.wisc.edu; http://www.law.wisc.edu/. Illus., index. Refereed. Vol. ends: No. 6. Microform: WSH; PQC. Reprint: WSH. *Indexed:* A22, B02, BRI, CLI, L14, MLA-IB. *Bk. rev.:* Occasional, length varies. *Aud.:* Ac, Sa.

Started in 1920 with the "hope that a discussion of legal problems, with particular application to state law, will be of service to the bench and the bar and the people of the state, and that a survey of the present condition of Wisconsin law will contribute in some measure to its scientific development," this journal today covers local, state, national, and international topics. Coverage of issues related to Wisconsin includes the recent "Bayh-Dole: Wisconsin Roots and Inspired Public Policy" and the student note "Wisconsin Confidential: The Mystery of the Wisconsin Supreme Court's Decision in Burbank Grease Services v. Sokolowski and its Effect Upon the Uniform Trade Secrets Act, Litigation, and Employee Mobility." The law school also publishes the *Wisconsin Journal of Law, Gender and Society* and the *Wisconsin International Law Journal.*

3379. *Women's Rights Law Reporter.* [ISSN: 0085-8269] 1970. q. USD 50 (Individuals, USD 30; Students, USD 25). Women's Rights Law Reporter, 123 Washington St, Newark, NJ 07102; wrlr@pegasus.rutgers.edu; http://info.rutgers.edu/. Illus., index. Vol. ends: No. 3. Microform: WSH; PMC; PQC. Reprint: WSH. *Indexed:* A22, BRI, CLI, FemPer, L14, WSA. *Bk. rev.:* Occasional, length varies. *Aud.:* Ac, Sa.

The journal and its web site have interesting information about this U.S.-based journal's history. Founded in 1970 by U.S. Supreme Court Justice Ruth Bader Ginsburg and feminist activists, legal workers, and law students, it professes to be the "first legal journal in the country to focus exclusively on women's issues." It was first published independently in New York City, moving to Rutgers in 1972, and becoming formally affiliated with the law school in 1974. Since that time, several other journals that focus on law and gender or feminism have emerged, including *Harvard Journal of Law & Gender* (see above in this section), *Columbia Journal of Gender and the Law* (see above), *Yale Journal of Law and Feminism*, and *Michigan Journal of Gender & Law.* Although some of these other journals are often ranked higher in various law journal–ranking studies, this journal remains a respected, long-standing resource, and it could serve a broad range of audiences.

3380. *Yale Journal of Law & the Humanities.* [ISSN: 1041-6374] 1988. s-a. USD 34 (Individuals, USD 18). Ed(s): Patrick Kabat, Diana Reiter. Yale University, Law School, PO Box 208215, New Haven, CT 06520; cdo.law@yale.edu; http://www.law.yale.edu. Illus., index, adv. Sample. Vol. ends: No. 2. Microform: WSH. Reprint: WSH. *Indexed:* A22, BRI, CLI, L14, MLA-IB, RILM. *Bk. rev.:* Occasional, essay length. *Aud.:* Ga, Ac, Sa.

When this semi-annual publication emerged in 1988, it was refreshing to see a journal that focused on law and liberal arts disciplines such as philosophy, literature, anthropology, fine arts, et al. It is edited by students in both the law school and other graduate departments at Yale. Since its publication, the combination of law and humanities has grown in legal scholarship, influencing the evolution of other journals such as *Law and Literature* (starting in 1989 under the title *Cardozo Studies in Law and Literature*), *Law, Text, Culture* (published in Australia), *Law, Culture and the Humanities,* and *Law and the Humanities* (by Hart Publishing, launched in 2007).

3381. *The Yale Law Journal.* [ISSN: 0044-0094] 1891. 8x/yr. USD 55 domestic; USD 65 foreign; USD 25 per issue. Ed(s): Anthony Vitarelli, Stephanie Hays. Yale Journal Co. Inc., 127 Wall St, PO Box 208215, New Haven, CT 06520; admissions.law@yale.edu; http://

www.law.yale.edu. Illus., index. Vol. ends: Jul. Microform: WSH. Reprint: WSH. *Indexed:* A01, A22, ABIn, B01, B02, BAS, BLI, BRI, CBRI, CLI, Chicano, EconLit, IBSS, JEL, L14, P02, RiskAb. *Bk. rev.:* Occasional, essay length. *Aud.:* Ac, Sa.

One would find the *Yale Law Journal* among the first journals mentioned in any survey or discussion of the most influential law reviews. It also offers articles on its web site, along with an online companion called "Pocket Part" that contains original essays and responses to articles printed in the journal. Other journals edited by Yale law students are *Yale Human Rights & Development Law Journal; Yale Journal of Law and Technology; Yale Law & Policy Review; Yale Journal of Law & the Humanities* (for the latter, see above); *Yale Journal of International Law; Yale Journal of Law & Feminism; Yale Journal of Health Policy Law and Ethics;* and *Yale Journal on Regulation.*

■ LIBRARY AND INFORMATION SCIENCE

See also Archives and Manuscripts; Bibliography; Books and Book Reviews; Printing and Graphic Arts; and Serials sections.

Amy Jackson, Performing & Digital Arts Librarian, University of New Mexico, Albuquerque, NM 87131

Introduction

Access to current information is necessary for professional development of librarians and information professionals. Library administrators and those in charge of collection development should consider library journals an essential part of the collection. Library journals disseminate current research and trends, provide literature and product reviews, and serve as a means of communication between professionals with similar interests. Access to current literature allows library professionals to gain from other libraries' experiences and offer services that meet or exceed user expectations. According to the Association of College & Research Libraries' Statement on Professional Development, "Professional development is an important manifestation of the academic librarian's commitment to personal excellence. It is a necessary response to a rapidly changing environment" (see www.ala.org/ala/mgrps/divs/acrl/publications/whitepapers/acrlstatement.cfm). This statement applies to professionals in all branches of library and information science.

Although traditional publishing models are most common in this discipline, open-access journals are quickly becoming common. In this 2012 edition, 20 percent of all journals included in this section are open access, with more journals embracing this model each year. Librarians should show by example that open access is a growing movement, and, when possible, should publish in open-access journals or self-archive their publications in institutional repositories. This will ensure that more professionals have access to important literature about library and information science while showing other disciplines that open access is beneficial to all.

The following section presents basic titles in the discipline of library and information science, and is not a comprehensive list of all relevant publications. Most journals are devoted to specific topics in librarianship, such as reference, technical services, digital libraries, or management; however, there are some titles that are appropriate for all practicing librarians. Titles should be evaluated for relevance to the individual library's focus of research and/or public services. Local and in-house publications, as well as non-English publications, have been excluded from this list. With a few exceptions, most of the listed titles are published in the United States.

Basic Periodicals

Ems: *Children and Libraries, Library Media Connection, School Library Journal, School Library Media Research, Teacher Librarian;* Hs: *School Library Journal, Young Adult Library Services, Teacher Librarian, Voice of the Youth Advocate;* Ga: *American Libraries, Library Journal;* Ac: *College & Research Libraries, The Journal of Academic Librarianship.*

Basic Abstracts and Indexes

Information Science and Technology Abstracts, Library Literature, LISA: Library and Information Science Abstracts.

3382. *A L C T S Newsletter Online.* Former titles (until 1998): *A L C T S Newsletter (Print);* (until 1990): *R T S D Newsletter.* [ISSN: 1523-018X] 1976. q. Free. Ed(s): Mary Beth Weber. American Library Association, 50 E Huron, Chicago, IL 60611; customerservice@ala.org; http://www.ala.org. *Illus. Aud.:* Ac, Sa.

The primary goal of this open-access newsletter, published by the Association for Library Collections and Technical Services, is to keep members informed of news and activities of the association. Issues contain conference reports, announcements, information about new publications, calendars, and articles that discuss new standards and best practices. Highly recommended for librarians in technical services and members of ALCTS. URL: www.ala.org/ala/mgrps/divs/alcts/resources/ano/index.cfm

3383. *Against the Grain: linking publishers, vendors and librarians.* [ISSN: 1043-2094] 1989. bi-m. USD 50 domestic; USD 60 Canada; USD 85 elsewhere. Ed(s): Katina Strauch. Against the Grain, LLC, 209 Richardson Ave., MSC 98, The Citadel, Charleston, SC 29409; strauchk@earthlink.net. *Illus. Sample. Refereed.* Vol. ends: Dec/Jan. *Indexed:* A22, ISTA, MLA-IB. *Bk. rev.:* 10-20, 100-500 words. *Aud.:* Ga, Ac, Sa.

This bimonthly publication provides information relevant to acquisition and technical services librarians, publishers, vendors, book jobbers, and subscription agents. Each issue contains news, articles, interviews, book reviews, technology issues, legal issues, and current information from the publishing and book selling fields. Recent issues explore trends in health sciences, e-science librarians, and electronic resources. This publication is highly recommended for acquisition librarians, publishers, and booksellers.

American Archivist See Archives and Manuscripts section.

3384. *American Libraries.* Supersedes (in 1970): *A L A Bulletin;* Which was formerly (1907-1939): *American Library Association. Bulletin;* Which incorporated (1924-1930): *Adult Education and the Library;* American Library Association. Bulletin incorporated (1947-1956): *Public Libraries.* [ISSN: 0002-9769] 1970. 10x/yr. USD 45 Free to members. Ed(s): Leonard Kniffel. American Library Association, 50 E Huron, Chicago, IL 60611; customerservice@ala.org; http://www.ala.org. Illus., index, adv. Circ: 58475 Paid. Vol. ends: Jan. Microform: NBI; PMC; PQC. *Indexed:* A01, A06, A22, ABS&EES, ASIP, BEL&L, BRI, C37, CBRI, Chicano, ISTA, MASUSE, MLA-IB, P02, RILM. *Aud.:* Ga, Ac, Sa.

This monthly publication is the official journal of the American Library Association. It reports on the activities, purposes, and goals of the association, as well as broader library-related topics. Regular sections include job postings, national and international library news, continuing education, and information technology. Featured articles cover a broad range of library-related topics and current events. The journal also maintains a strong online presence. This magazine is recommended for all librarians interested in current events, and is highly recommended for all libraries. URL: http://americanlibrariesmagazine.org

3385. *American Society for Information Science and Technology. Bulletin (Online).* [ISSN: 1550-8366] 2001. bi-m. Free. American Society for Information Science & Technology, 1320 Fenwick Ln, Ste 510, Silver Spring, MD 20910; asis@asis.org; http://www.asis.org. *Aud.:* Ga, Ac, Sa.

This open-access publication is the newsmagazine of the American Society for Information Science and Technology. Its primary purpose is to communicate with society members and other information science professionals. In addition to pragmatic, non-research articles, the publication also contains opinion columns and news regarding the members and events of the society. Recent issues discuss museum informatics, knowledge management, and mobile services. This is an important title for information science professionals and other librarians interested in information science. Freely available online. URL: www.asis.org/bulletin.html

3386. *American Society for Information Science and Technology. Journal.* Former titles (until 2001): *American Society for Information Science. Journal;* (until 1970): *American Documentation;* (until 1942): *Journal of Documentary Reproduction.* [ISSN: 1532-2882] 1938. m. GBP 1394. Ed(s): Blaise Cronin, Julie Nash. John Wiley & Sons, Inc., 111 River St, MS 4-02, Hoboken, NJ 07030; info@wiley.com; http://www.wiley.com/WileyCDA/. Illus., index, adv. Refereed. Microform: PQC. Reprint: PSC. *Indexed:* A01, A22, ABIn, ABS&EES, B01, B02, BRI, C&ISA, CerAb, CompLI, CompR, EngInd, ErgAb, FR, ISTA, MLA-IB, RILM, SWR&A. *Bk. rev.:* Number and length vary. *Aud.:* Ac, Sa.

As the scholarly journal of the American Society for Information Science and Technology, this fully refereed journal reports new research in the field of information science and technology. Recent article topics include information retrieval; automatic detection of plagiarism; document dependency in searches; and information-seeking habits of visually disabled searchers. This publication also includes book reviews, calls for papers, best student papers, and brief communications. Highly recommended for information science and technology professionals and library science collections.

3387. *Ariadne.* [ISSN: 1361-3200] 1996. q. Free. U.K. Office for Library and Information Networking, The Library, University of Bath, Bath, BA2 7AY, United Kingdom. Illus. *Indexed:* ISTA. *Bk. rev.:* 4-5, length varies. *Aud.:* Ac, Sa.

Ariadne is an open-access, quarterly magazine published by UKOLN, and its primary focus is digital library initiatives in the United Kingdom and technological developments in related fields. Each issue contains articles, conference reports, and book reviews. Recent articles address digital archiving, social media for researchers, and digital library infrastructure. Highly recommended for professionals interested in digital initiatives in the library, archive, and museum fields. Freely available online. URL: www.ariadne.ac.uk

3388. *Art Documentation.* Formerly (until 1982): *A R L I S - N A Newsletter;* Which incorporated in part (in 1974): *College Art Association of America. Visual Resources Committee. Newsletter;* Which was formerly (19??-1973): *C A A Slides & Photographs Newsletter.* [ISSN: 0730-7187] 1972. s-a. USD 219 (print & online eds.). Ed(s): Judy Dyki. University of Chicago Press, 1427 E 60th St, Chicago, IL 60637; custserv@press.uchicago.edu; http://www.press.uchicago.edu/. Illus., adv. Refereed. Microform: PQC. Reprint: PSC. *Indexed:* A07, A22, A51. *Bk. rev.:* Number and length vary. *Aud.:* Ga, Ac, Sa.

This peer-reviewed publication is the official bulletin of the Art Libraries Society of North America. Articles discuss recent developments in the field of art librarianship and visual resource curatorship, as well as news and events of the society. Recent article topics include digital archives, copyright, and fine art collection management. Each issue includes book reviews, which are also available online. An essential publication for all art libraries and visual resource centers.

3389. *Art Libraries Journal.* Supersedes in part (in 1976): *ARLIS Newsletter.* [ISSN: 0307-4722] 1969. q. Free to members; Non-members, GBP 14. ARLIS - UK & Ireland, The National Art Library, Victoria & Albert Museum, London, SW7 2RL, United Kingdom; arlis@vam.ac.uk; http://www.arlis.org.uk/. Illus., adv. Refereed. Vol. ends: Jan. *Indexed:* A07, A22, A51, API, ISTA. *Bk. rev.:* Number and length vary. *Aud.:* Ac, Sa.

This international journal covers art libraries and visual resource collections around the world. Although most articles are in English, articles written in German, French, and Spanish are also included, accompanied by an English summary. Recent articles cover specific art library collections, the history and future of art libraries, and digitization. Other content includes book reviews and a bibliography of art librarianship. This publication is essential reading for all art librarians and visual resource curators.

Booklist. See Books and Book Reviews section.

3390. *The Bottom Line: managing library finances.* [ISSN: 0888-045X] 1988. q. EUR 1829 combined subscription in Europe (print & online eds.); USD 2189 combined subscription in the Americas (print & online eds.); GBP 1309 combined subscription in the UK & elsewhere (print & online eds.). Ed(s): Sarah Baxter, Bradford Lee Eden. Emerald Group Publishing Ltd., Howard House, Wagon Ln, Bingley, BD16 1WA, United Kingdom; emerald@emeraldinsight.com; http://www.emeraldinsight.com. Sample. Refereed. Reprint: PSC. *Indexed:* A01, A22, ABIn, ATI, C&ISA, CerAb, E01. *Bk. rev.:* Number and length vary. *Aud.:* Ga, Ac, Sa.

Focusing on individuals responsible for financial decisions in libraries, this publication discusses library finances and other broad issues regarding library administration. Recent article topics include the recession, policies and procedures, and crisis management. Issues also include news, opinion columns, and book reviews. Highly recommended for library administrators in all types of libraries.

3391. *Cataloging & Classification Quarterly.* [ISSN: 0163-9374] 1980. 8x/yr. GBP 954 (print & online eds.). Ed(s): Sandra K Roe. Routledge, 325 Chestnut St, Ste 800, Philadelphia, PA 19106; customerservice@taylorandfrancis.com; http://www.tandfonline.com. Illus., adv. Sample. Refereed. Microform: PQC. Reprint: PSC. *Indexed:* A01, A22, C&ISA, CerAb, E01, FR, ISTA, RILM. *Bk. rev.:* Number and length vary. *Aud.:* Ga, Ac, Sa.

This peer-reviewed journal examines all aspects of bibliographic organization from both theoretical and practical points of view. Creation, usability, and findability of records are all examined in the articles included in this publication. Recent articles address cataloging education, RDA, and faceted browsing. This journal is essential reading for all librarians involved in any aspect of cataloging or classification.

3392. *The Charleston Advisor: critical reviews of Web products for information professionals.* [ISSN: 1525-4011] 1999. q. USD 295 (Corporations, USD 495). Ed(s): Rebecca T Lenzini. The Charleston Company, 6180 E Warren Ave, Denver, CO 80222; rlenzini@charlestonco.com; http://www.charlestonco.com. Adv. Sample. Refereed. Circ: 750 Paid. *Indexed:* ISTA. *Aud.:* Ga, Ac, Sa.

The Charleston Advisor is the leading source of reviews for Internet-accessible electronic resources. Each resource reviewed is rated on content, searchability, price, and contract terms, and all reviews are peer reviewed. Readers can browse all products that have been reviewed in the past in the online edition and view ratings assigned to each resource. In addition to formal reviews, each issue of the publication also contains comparative reviews, articles, press releases, editorials, and news. An essential publication for all librarians responsible for purchasing electronic resources.

3393. *Children and Libraries.* Supersedes in part (in 2002): *Journal of Youth Services in Libraries;* Which was formerly (1942-1987): *Top of the News.* [ISSN: 1542-9806] 2003. 3x/yr. Free to members; Non-members, USD 40. Ed(s): Sharon Korbeck. American Library Association, 50 E Huron, Chicago, IL 60611; customerservice@ala.org; http://www.ala.org. Adv. Refereed. Circ: 4538. *Indexed:* A01. *Bk. rev.:* Number and length vary. *Aud.:* Ems, Hs.

Children and Libraries is the official publication of the Association for Library Services to Children, a division of the American Library Association. Articles address all aspects of library services for children, including technology, collection development, cataloging, information literacy, and programming. Issues also include book reviews, association news, and recommended titles. An essential title for libraries that provide services to children.

3394. *Collection Building: dedicated to all aspects of library collection development and maintenance from the practical to the theoretical.* [ISSN: 0160-4953] 1978. q. EUR 1829 combined subscription in Europe (print & online eds.); USD 2189 combined subscription in the Americas (print & online eds.); GBP 1309 combined subscription in the UK & elsewhere (print & online eds.). Ed(s): Kay Ann Cassell. Emerald Group Publishing Ltd., Howard House, Wagon Ln, Bingley, BD16 1WA, United Kingdom; emerald@emeraldinsight.com; http://www.emeraldinsight.com. Sample. Refereed. Reprint: PSC. *Indexed:* A01, A22, C&ISA, CerAb, E01, FR, ISTA, MLA-IB, P02. *Bk. rev.:* Number and length vary. *Aud.:* Ems, Hs, Ga, Ac, Sa.

This publication offers practical and theoretical articles that discuss collection development and management. International in scope, the articles discuss academic, public, and school library collections. Recent articles examine patron-driven acquisition, interdisciplinary collection building, and citation studies. Issues also include library collection news and trends, book reviews, and editorials. Recommended for librarians responsible for collection development.

3395. *Collection Management.* Formerly (until 1977): *De-Acquisitions Librarian.* [ISSN: 0146-2679] 1975. q. GBP 322 (print & online eds.). Ed(s): Karen Fischer. Routledge, 325 Chestnut St, Ste 800, Philadelphia, PA 19106; customerservice@taylorandfrancis.com; http://www.tandfonline.com. Illus., adv. Sample. Refereed. Microform: PQC. Reprint: PSC. *Indexed:* A01, A22, C&ISA, CerAb, E01, FR, ISTA, RILM. *Bk. rev.:* Number and length vary. *Aud.:* Ac, Sa.

This peer-reviewed quarterly publication addresses all issues of collection management, including digital collections, staff training, management, consortial agreements, and assessment. Each issue also includes an extended review section. Recent articles address sustainability, storage of print collections, and data-driven decision making. Recommended for collection managers and library science students.

3396. *College & Research Libraries.* [ISSN: 0010-0870] 1939. bi-m. Free to members; Non-members, USD 75; USD 15 per issue. Ed(s): Joseph J Branin. Association of College and Research Libraries, 50 E Huron St, Chicago, IL 60611; acrl@ala.org; http://www.ala.org/ala/mgrps/divs/acrl/index.cfm. Illus., index, adv. Refereed. Circ: 13950. Vol. ends: Nov. Microform: PQC. *Indexed:* A01, A22, BEL&L, BRI, CBRI, FR, HEA, ISTA, MLA-IB, P02. *Bk. rev.:* 6 per issue; length varies. *Aud.:* Ac, Sa.

A recent open-access journal, *College & Research Libraries* is the scholarly research journal of the Association of College and Research Libraries, a division of the American Library Association. Articles discuss trends and developments that impact academic librarians and research libraries. Recent articles cover library instruction, WorldCat Local, and information-seeking habits of faculty. Articles are supported with tables, figures, and surveys, and each issue includes book reviews. Highly recommended for academic and research libraries. URL: http://crl.acrl.org/

3397. *College & Research Libraries News.* Formerly (until 1967): *A C R L News.* [ISSN: 0099-0086] 1966. 11x/yr. Free to members; Non-members, USD 46; USD 6.50 per issue. Ed(s): David Free. Association of College and Research Libraries, 50 E Huron St, Chicago, IL 60611; acrl@ala.org; http://www.ala.org/ala/mgrps/divs/acrl/index.cfm. Illus., adv. Sample. Circ: 13685. Vol. ends: Dec. *Indexed:* A&ATA, A01, A07, A22, ABS&EES, FR, MLA-IB, P02. *Bk. rev.:* Number and length vary. *Aud.:* Ac, Sa.

The official open-access newsmagazine and publication of record for the Association of College & Research Libraries, this journal reports current news and trends that affect academic and research libraries. Regular columns include "Internet Resources," "Internet Reviews," "Preservation News," "Washington Hotline," "Grants and Acquisitions," "People in the News," and "New Publications." Recent articles address collaboration, mentoring, and training. Highly recommended for academic and research libraries. URL: http://crln.acrl.org

3398. *Communications in Information Literacy.* [ISSN: 1933-5954] 2007. s-a. Free. Ed(s): Christopher V Hollister, Stewart Brower. Communications in Information Literacy, c/o Stewart Brower, University of Oklahoma-Tulsa Library, Tulsa, TX 74135. Refereed. *Aud.:* Ga, Ac, Sa.

This peer-reviewed open-access journal focuses on knowledge, theory, and research of information literacy. Recent articles explore peer-coaching, textbooks, and discipline-specific information literacy skills. An important journal for all information literacy and instruction librarians. Available online. URL: www.comminfolit.org

3399. *D - Lib Magazine: the magazine of digital library research.* [ISSN: 1082-9873] 1995. bi-m. Free. Ed(s): Bonita Wilson. Corporation for National Research Initiatives, 1895 Preston White Dr, Reston, VA 20191; dlib@cnri.reston.va.us; http://www.dlib.org. *Indexed:* ISTA, P61, SSA. *Aud.:* Ac, Sa.

This free online journal is an important publication in the digital library community. A primary goal of the journal is timely exchange of information, and articles are published quickly in order to remain relevant to readers and practitioners. Recent articles examine mobile access to digital collections, rights information registries, and repository protocols. Highly recommended for all librarians involved in digital library activities. URL: www.dlib.org

3400. *D T T P.* Formerly (until 1974): *Documents to the People.* [ISSN: 0091-2085] 1972. q. Free to members; Non-members, USD 35. Ed(s): Andrea Sevetson. American Library Association, 50 E Huron, Chicago, IL 60611; customerservice@ala.org; http://www.ala.org. Illus., adv. Vol. ends: Dec. *Indexed:* A22, P02, P61. *Bk. rev.:* Number and length vary. *Aud.:* Ac, Sa.

This quarterly publication is the official journal of the Government Documents Round Table (GODORT) of the American Library Association. *DttP* covers the news and activities of the roundtable, as well as local, state, national, and international government information and activities. Recent articles discuss patents, the National Archives, and disaster plans. Issues also include book reviews and columns by GODORT officers. An essential publication for government document librarians.

3401. *Evidence Based Library and Information Practice.* [ISSN: 1715-720X] 2006. q. Free. Ed(s): Alison Brettle. University of Alberta, Learning Services, Cameron Library, 5th Floor, Edmonton, AB T6G 2J8, Canada; http://www.ls.ualberta.ca. Refereed. *Indexed:* ISTA. *Aud.:* Ga, Ac, Sa.

Evidence Based Library and Information Practice is an open-access, peer-reviewed journal. Articles and other features provide librarians and library administrators with research that may help inform decision and policy making. Each issue features peer-reviewed articles and some non–peer-reviewed columns. Recent articles discuss library instruction, library design, and reference transactions. Highly recommended for all librarians. Freely available online. URL: http://ejournals.library.ualberta.ca/index.php/EBLIP/index

First Monday. See World Wide Web section.

3402. *Government Information Quarterly: an international journal of information technology management, policies, and practices.* Incorporates (1994-2004): *Journal of Government Information;* Which was formerly (until vol.21, 1994): *Government Publications Review;* Which was formed by the merger of (1980-1981): *Government Publications Review. Part A: Research Articles;* (1980-1981): *Government Publications Review. Part B: Acquisitions Guide to Significant Government Publications at All Levels;* Both of which superseded in part (in 1980): *Government Publications Review.* [ISSN: 0740-624X] 1982. q. EUR 710. Ed(s): John Carlo Bertot. Elsevier Ltd, 32 Jamestown Rd, Camden, London, NW1 7BY, United Kingdom; corporate.sales@elsevier.com; http://www.elsevier.com. Illus., adv. Sample. Refereed. Vol. ends: Oct. Microform: PQC. Reprint: PSC. *Indexed:* A22, B01, ERIC, ISTA, P61, SSA. *Bk. rev.:* Number and length vary. *Aud.:* Ac, Sa.

This peer-reviewed journal presents theoretical and practical articles that explore government information-based resources and services. Each issue contains editorials, articles, and reviews. Recent articles address government information portals, Congress as a publisher, and the use of social media in local governments. This publication is recommended for all government document librarians and library school collections.

3403. *The Indexer.* [ISSN: 0019-4131] 1958. q. GBP 140 (Individuals, GBP 48 (print & online eds.); Free to members). Ed(s): Maureen MacGlashan. Society of Indexers, Woodbourn Business Ctr, 10 Jessell St, Sheffield, S9 3HY, United Kingdom; admin@indexers.org.uk; http://www.indexers.org.uk/. Illus., adv. Refereed. *Indexed:* A22, BRI, BrArAb, CBRI, FR, ISTA, MLA-IB, NumL, SWR&A. *Bk. rev.:* Number and length vary. *Aud.:* Ac, Sa.

Published by the Society of Indexers, this semi-annual peer-reviewed publication informs readers of the trends and developments in the international indexing community. Articles address practical, theoretical, and historical aspects of indexing. Recent article topics address the semantic web, XML indexing, and new technology and indexes. Each issue includes articles that highlight the activities of the Society, reviews of books and electronic resources, and the column "Indexes reviewed," which quotes reviews of indexes from book reviews in other publications. An essential journal for all indexers and librarians interested in the field of indexing.

3404. *Information & Culture.* Former titles (until 2012): *Libraries & the Cultural Record;* (until 2006): *Libraries & Culture;* (until 1988): *The Journal of Library History;* (until 1974): *Journal of Library History, Philosophy, and Comparative Librarianship;* (until 1973): *The Journal of Library History.* [ISSN: 2164-8034] 1966. q. USD 176. Ed(s): William Aspray. University of Texas Press, Journals Division, PO Box 7819, Austin, TX 78713; journals@uts.cc.utexas.edu; http://www.utexas.edu/utpress/journals/journals.html. Illus., index, adv. Refereed. Vol. ends: Nov. Microform: PQC. *Indexed:* A01, A22, ABS&EES, AmHI, ArtHuCI, BRI, CBRI, E01, FR, MLA-IB. *Bk. rev.:* 11-20, 500-1,200 words, signed. *Aud.:* Ac, Sa.

This interdisciplinary journal explores the history of information. The peer-reviewed articles examine the social and cultural context of recorded knowledge and the history of information studies. Recent article topics include collaboration in arts and sciences, the practice of programming, and information-seeking behavior. Highly recommended for library and information science collections and others interested in the history of information and recorded knowledge.

3405. *Information Outlook.* Formed by the merger of (1910-1997): *Special Libraries;* (1980-1997): *SpeciaList.* [ISSN: 1091-0808] 1997. 8x/yr. Free to members; Non-members, USD 160. Ed(s): Stuart Hales. Special Libraries Association, 331 S Patrick St, Alexandria, VA 22314; sla@sla.org; http://www.sla.org. Illus., index, adv. Microform: PQC. *Indexed:* A01, A06, A22, A51, ABIn, B01, B02, BAS, BRI, C&ISA, CBRI, CerAb, FR, I15, ISTA, P02. *Aud.:* Sa.

This is the monthly professional journal of the Special Libraries Association. The practical articles in this publication are directed toward information professionals working in special libraries of all sizes. Recent articles discuss scholarly publishing, politics, and market plans. Case studies are common, and regular features include web site reviews, copyright issues, and news and events of the association. Recommended for all information professionals in special libraries.

3406. *Information Technology and Libraries.* Formerly (until 1982): *Journal of Library Automation;* Which incorporated (1969-1972): *J O L A Technical Communications;* Which was formerly (1968-1969): *Interface.* [ISSN: 0730-9295] 1968. q. Free to members; Non-members, USD 65. American Library Association, 50 E Huron, Chicago, IL 60611; customerservice@ala.org; http://www.ala.org. Illus., index, adv. Refereed. Vol. ends: Mar. Microform: PQC. *Indexed:* A01, A22, ABIn, ABS&EES, B01, B02, BRI, CompLI, CompR, FR, ISTA, MLA-IB, P02, RILM. *Aud.:* Ac, Sa.

This open-access publication is the refereed journal of the Library and Information Technology Association, a division of the American Library Association. Articles address all aspects of information technology relevant to libraries, including digital libraries, online catalogs, software engineering, electronic publishing, and metadata. Each issue includes a "President's Message," editorials, and feature articles. Recent article topics include copyright, research guides, and discovery tools. Highly recommended for all librarians interested in technology and its use in libraries. Freely available online. URL: http://ejournals.bc.edu/ojs/index.php/ital/index

Information Today. See Computers and Information Technology section.

3407. *Issues in Science and Technology Librarianship.* [ISSN: 1092-1206] 1991. q. Free. Ed(s): Andrea L Duda. Association of College and Research Libraries, Science and Technology Section, 50 E Huron St, Chicago, IL 60611; acrl@ala.org; http://www.ala.org/ala/mgrps/divs/acrl/about/sections/sts/sts.cfm. Illus. Refereed. *Indexed:* C&ISA, CerAb, ERIC, ISTA. *Bk. rev.:* 350-500 words; number varies. *Aud.:* Ac, Sa.

This quarterly, open-access, electronic publication from the Science & Technology section of the Association of College & Research Libraries offers materials of interest to science and technology librarians. Each issue contains themed articles, refereed articles, electronic resource reviews, viewpoints, and book reviews. Recent refereed articles have explored citations to Wikipedia, government policy resources, and library video tutorials. Freely available online. URL: www.istl.org/

3408. *The Journal of Academic Librarianship.* [ISSN: 0099-1333] 1975. bi-m. EUR 425. Ed(s): W vanDuinkerken, W Arant-Kaspar. Pergamon, The Blvd, Langford Ln, E Park, Kidlington, OX5 1GB, United Kingdom; JournalsCustomerServiceEMEA@elsevier.com; http://www.elsevier.com. Illus., adv. Sample. Refereed. Microform: PQC. Reprint: PSC. *Indexed:* A01, A22, ABS&EES, B01, BRI, CBRI, ERIC, FR, ISTA, MLA-IB, P02. *Bk. rev.:* Approx. 500 words, number varies. *Aud.:* Ac, Sa.

The Journal of Academic Librarianship, published six times each year, is a refereed journal with international contributions and readership. Contributors present research findings and case studies, analyze policies and procedures, and review books relevant to the library profession. Recent article topics include digital preservation, library web sites, and academic video games. Highly recommended for academic libraries and librarians.

3409. *Journal of Digital Information.* [ISSN: 1368-7506] 1997. irreg. Free. Ed(s): Mark McFarland, Scott Phillips. Texas A & M University Libraries, 5000 TAMU Corner of Spence & Lamar, College Station, TX 77843; ccook@tamu.edu; http://library.tamu.edu. Refereed. *Indexed:* A01, ISTA. *Aud.:* Ac, Sa.

A peer-reviewed, open-access journal, the *Journal of Digital Information* publishes papers about the management of information in the online environment. All articles fit into three main areas: digital libraries, visual interfaces, and information discovery. Recent article topics include recruiting for the institutional repository; XML schemas; and OAI-ORE. Highly recommended for librarians involved in digital projects. Freely available online. URL: http://journals.tdl.org/jodi/index

3410. *Journal of Documentation.* [ISSN: 0022-0418] 1945. bi-m. EUR 1199 combined subscription in Europe (print & online eds.); USD 1369 combined subscription in the Americas (print & online eds.); GBP 869 combined subscription in the UK & elsewhere (print & online eds.). Ed(s): David Bawden. Emerald Group Publishing Ltd., Howard House, Wagon Ln, Bingley, BD16 1WA, United Kingdom; information@emeraldinsight.com; http://www.emeraldinsight.com. Illus., index, adv. Sample. Refereed. Circ: 2000. Reprint: PSC. *Indexed:* A01, A22, ABIn, BAS, BrArAb, C&ISA, CerAb, CompLI, E01, FR, ISTA, MLA-IB, NumL. *Bk. rev.:* Number and length vary. *Aud.:* Ac, Sa.

This peer-reviewed journal focuses on the theories and philosophies of information science. Each issue includes several research articles and book reviews. Recent article topics include professional avatars, classification after Google, knowledge production, and information retrieval. Highly recommended for information science scholars and library science collections.

3411. *Journal of Electronic Resources in Medical Libraries.* [ISSN: 1542-4065] 2004. q. GBP 355 (print & online eds.). Ed(s): C Steven Douglas. Routledge, 325 Chestnut St, Ste 800, Philadelphia, PA 19106; customerservice@taylorandfrancis.com; http://www.tandfonline.com. Adv. Sample. Refereed. Reprint: PSC. *Indexed:* A01, A22, C&ISA, CerAb, E01, FR. *Bk. rev.:* Number and length vary. *Aud.:* Ac, Sa.

This peer-reviewed journal focuses on issues and topics relevant to electronic resource librarians in medical libraries. The topics are designed to complement *Medical Reference Services Quarterly,* which covers the reference and instruction side of electronic resources in libraries. Recent article topics include RDA, evaluating print collections for transition to digital, and mobile computing in the library. Recommended for medical and health science libraries.

3412. *Journal of Electronic Resources Librarianship.* Formerly (until 2008): *The Acquisitions Librarian.* [ISSN: 1941-126X] 1989. q. GBP 422 (print & online eds.). Ed(s): Gary M Pitkin. Routledge, 325 Chestnut St, Ste 800, Philadelphia, PA 19106; customerservice@taylorandfrancis.com; http://www.tandfonline.com. Illus., index, adv. Sample. Refereed. Circ: 345 Paid. Microform: PQC. Reprint: PSC. *Indexed:* A01, A22, C&ISA, CerAb, Chicano, E01, ERIC, FR, ISTA, MLA-IB, RILM. *Bk. rev.:* Number and length vary. *Aud.:* Ga, Ac, Sa.

This quarterly, peer-reviewed publication addresses collection, acquiring, and creating library resources in the digital environment. Each issue includes editorials, "professional communications," scholarly articles, and book reviews. Recent peer-reviewed article topics include ebooks as textbooks, scholarly communications, and ejournal usage reports. Essential reading for all electronic resources librarians.

3413. *Journal of Information Ethics.* [ISSN: 1061-9321] 1992. s-a. USD 120 (Individuals, USD 40). Ed(s): Robert Hauptman. McFarland & Company, Inc., PO Box 611, Jefferson, NC 28640; info@mcfarlandpub.com; http://www.mcfarlandpub.com. Illus., adv. Refereed. *Indexed:* A22, FR, ISTA, MLA-IB, P61, SSA. *Bk. rev.:* Number varies, 800-1,200 words, signed. *Aud.:* Ac, Sa.

This semi-annual publication features articles about ethics and information science. Each issue contains book reviews, web site reviews, and feature articles. Recommended for all library science collections.

3414. *Journal of Information Literacy.* [ISSN: 1750-5968] 2006. s-a. Free. Ed(s): Susie Andretta, Cathie Jackson. Information Literacy, http://www.informationliteracy.org.uk. Refereed. *Bk. rev.:* Number and length vary. *Aud.:* Ga, Ac, Sa.

This semi-annual, peer-reviewed, open-access publication investigates all aspects of information literacy. Articles address practical, technical, and philosophical aspects of information literacy, and recent article topics include online learning, information literacy in the U.K., and information literacy games. Highly recommended for all librarians and teachers of information literacy. Freely available online. URL: http://ojs.lboro.ac.uk/ojs/index.php/JIL/index

3415. *Journal of Library Metadata.* Formerly (until 2008): *Journal of Internet Cataloging.* [ISSN: 1938-6389] 1997. q. GBP 241 (print & online eds.). Ed(s): Jung-ran Park. Routledge, 325 Chestnut St, Ste 800, Philadelphia, PA 19106; customerservice@taylorandfrancis.com; http://www.tandfonline.com. Adv. Sample. Circ: 556 Paid. Microform: PQC. Reprint: PSC. *Indexed:* A01, A22, C&ISA, CerAb, E01, FR, I15, ISTA, MLA-IB, SWR&A. *Aud.:* Ga, Ac, Sa.

This peer-reviewed, quarterly journal examines metadata and all applications of metadata in libraries and information management. Recent articles examine Google Books' metadata, government information management, and digital object metadata. Highly recommended for all metadata librarians and digital library practitioners.

3416. *Journal of Web Librarianship.* [ISSN: 1932-2909] 2007. q. GBP 118 (print & online eds.). Ed(s): Jody Condit Fagan. Taylor & Francis Inc., 325 Chestnut St, Ste 800, Philadelphia, PA 19106; customerservice@taylorandfrancis.com; http://www.tandfonline.com. Sample. Refereed. Reprint: PSC. *Indexed:* A22, C&ISA, CerAb, E01, ERIC. *Bk. rev.:* Number and length vary. *Aud.:* Ga, Ac, Sa.

The Journal of Web Librarianship focuses on the librarianship as practiced on the Internet. Articles address all aspects of online interaction, including user behavior, web interfaces, online project management, and many other related topics. Practical and theoretic topics are examined, and all issues contain peer-reviewed scholarly articles, peer-reviewed practical communications, and reviews. Recent article topics include YouTube as a promotional tool, promoting library collections through Wikipedia, and web analytics. Highly recommended for all librarians.

3417. *Journal of Web Semantics: science, services and agents on the world wide web.* [ISSN: 1570-8268] 2003. 4x/yr. EUR 668. Ed(s): T Finin, S Staab. Elsevier BV, Radarweg 29, PO Box 211, Amsterdam, 1000 AE, Netherlands; JournalsCustomerServiceEMEA@elsevier.com; http://www.elsevier.nl. *Indexed:* EngInd. *Aud.:* Ac, Sa.

The Journal of Web Semantics is an interdisciplinary journal with subjects focused on web technologies, linked data, knowledge organization, databases, human–computer interaction, and other similar fields. The journal publishes research papers, survey papers, ontology papers, and systems papers. Recent topics include mapping life sciences data using RDF, linked data conformance, open government data, and ontology classification. Highly recommended for information scientists and library science collections.

3418. *Knowledge Organization: international journal devoted to concept theory, classification, indexing, and knowledge representation.* Formerly (until 1992): *International Classification.* [ISSN: 0943-7444] 1974. 4x/yr. EUR 198; EUR 229 combined subscription (print & online eds.). Ed(s): Richard Smiraglia. Ergon Verlag, Keesburgstr 11, Wuerzburg, 97074, Germany; service@ergon-verlag.de; http://www.ergon-verlag.de. Illus., adv. Refereed. Circ: 1000 Paid and controlled. Vol. ends: Fall. *Indexed:* A22, FR, ISTA, MLA-IB. *Bk. rev.:* Number and length vary. *Aud.:* Ac, Sa.

This peer-reviewed, quarterly journal is the official journal of the International Society for Knowledge Organization. Each issue contains scholarly articles, reports on conferences, the society's newsletter, book reviews, and letters to the editor. Recent article topics include the semantic web, web-based hierarchical browsing, user tagging, and development of metadata elements. Recommended for library science collections and librarians interested in knowledge organization.

3419. *Knowledge Quest.* Supersedes in part (in 1997): *School Library Media Quarterly;* Which was formerly (1972-1981): *School Media Quarterly;* Which superseded (in 1972): *School Libraries;* Which was formerly (1951-1952): *American Association of School Librarians. Newsletter.* [ISSN: 1094-9046] 1951. 5x/yr. Free to members; Non-members, USD 50; USD 12 per issue. Ed(s): Debbie Abilock, Melissa B Jacobsen. American Library Association, 50 E Huron, Chicago, IL 60611; customerservice@ala.org; http://www.ala.org. Illus., adv. Refereed. Circ: 9052. Vol. ends: Sep. Microform: PQC. *Indexed:* A01, A22, BRI, CBRI, ERIC, P02. *Bk. rev.:* Number and length vary. *Aud.:* Ems, Hs, Ac.

This bimonthly publication from the American Association of School Librarians, a division of the American Library Association, brings information regarding school libraries and library media services to developers of school library centers and services. Each themed issue is shaped by editorial questions, and feature articles address these questions. Recent themes have included coteaching, the solo librarian, and educational gaming. Essential reading for all school library media specialists.

3420. *L O E X Quarterly.* Formerly (until 2004): *L O E X News.* [ISSN: 1547-0172] 1973. q. Members, USD 80 (print & online eds.). Ed(s): Chessa Grasso Hickox, Brad Sietz. Eastern Michigan University Library, 203 Halle Library, Eastern Michigan University, Ypsilanti, MI 48197; loex@emich.edu; http://www.emich.edu/public/loex/loex.html. Circ: 1200. *Bk. rev.:* Number and length vary. *Aud.:* Ac.

This quarterly publication, published by LOEX (Library Orientation Exchange), gathers together articles and research about library instruction and information literacy. Regular columns include "News from the LOEX Office," "Tech Matters," "Book Review," and "Ross' Rave." Recent article topics explore Prezi, mentoring students, cloud storage, and print design. Highly recommended for all teaching librarians.

3421. *Law Library Journal.* Incorporates (1927-1937): *Law Library News.* [ISSN: 0023-9283] 1908. q. Free to members; Non-members, USD 110; USD 27.50 per issue. Ed(s): Janet Sinder. American Association of Law Libraries, 105 W Adams St, Ste 3300, Chicago, IL 60603; orders@aall.org; http://www.aallnet.org. Illus., index, adv. Refereed. Vol. ends: Fall. Microform: PMC. Reprint: WSH. *Indexed:* A22, BRI, CLI, L14, MLA-IB. *Bk. rev.:* Number and length vary. *Aud.:* Ac, Sa.

The official publication of the American Association of Law Libraries, this quarterly journal communicates news and events of the association, as well as articles related to law, legal materials, and librarianship. Issues include book reviews, proceedings and reports of the association, annotated bibliographies, and obituaries. Recent article topics include collaborative digital libraries, non-MARC metadata, and law student information literacy. Essential reading for all law librarians and providers of legal reference services.

3422. *Library & Information Science Research.* Formerly (until 1983): *Library Research.* [ISSN: 0740-8188] 1979. q. EUR 533. Ed(s): Candy Schwartz, Peter Hernon. Pergamon, The Blvd, Langford Ln, E Park, Kidlington, OX5 1GB, United Kingdom; JournalsCustomerServiceEMEA@elsevier.com; http://www.elsevier.com. Illus., adv. Sample. Refereed. Reprint: PSC. *Indexed:* A01, A22, FR, ISTA, RILM. *Bk. rev.:* 4-7; length varies. *Aud.:* Ac, Sa.

This quarterly, refereed journal offers research articles that focus on research in library and information science. Research findings, practical applications, and their significance are presented. Recent articles have explored ethnographic studies of library users, collaboration in the library, and socially-created metadata for images. Highly recommended for all collections that support library and information science programs.

3423. *Library Collections, Acquisitions, and Technical Services.* Formerly (until 1999): *Library Acquisitions: Practice and Theory.* [ISSN: 1464-9055] 1977. q. EUR 404. Ed(s): James R Mouw. Elsevier Ltd, 32 Jamestown Rd, Camden, London, NW1 7BY, United Kingdom; corporate.sales@elsevier.com; http://www.elsevier.com. Illus., adv. Sample. Refereed. Vol. ends: Winter. Microform: PQC. *Indexed:* A01, A22, ABS&EES, C&ISA, CerAb, FR, ISTA. *Bk. rev.:* Number and length vary. *Aud.:* Ac, Sa.

This quarterly publication brings together ideas from diverse specialties within library technical services including collections management, acquisitions, cataloging, and document delivery, as well as publishers and vendors. Articles are based on practical experiences, research reports, and theoretical approaches. Recent article topics include case studies in libraries outside of the U.S., use of the iPad for resource management, and a cost-benefit analysis of shelf-ready purchases. Recommended for all libraries in technical services positions.

3424. *Library Hi Tech.* [ISSN: 0737-8831] 1983. q. EUR 1069 combined subscription in Europe (print & online eds.); USD 1239 combined subscription in the Americas (print & online eds.); GBP 769 combined subscription in the UK & elsewhere (print & online eds.). Ed(s): Dr. Michael Seadle. Emerald Group Publishing Ltd., Howard House, Wagon Ln, Bingley, BD16 1WA, United Kingdom; emerald@emeraldinsight.com; http://www.emeraldinsight.com. Illus., index. Sample. Refereed. Microform: PQC. Reprint: PSC. *Indexed:* A22, ABIn, BRI, C&ISA, CBRI, CerAb, CompLI, E01, ErgAb, FR, I15, ISTA, P02. *Bk. rev.:* Number and length vary. *Aud.:* Ga, Ac, Sa.

Library Hi-Tech is a quarterly, peer-reviewed journal that focuses on all types of technology used in the international library community. The majority of issues focus on specific topics; recent topics include persuasive technology/plagiarism technology, user research and technology, and hardware in libraries. Article formats include case studies, general articles, research papers, technical papers, and conceptual papers. Highly recommended for academic libraries.

3425. *Library Journal.* Former titles (until 1976): *L J (Library Journal);* (until 1974): *Library Journal.* [ISSN: 0363-0277] 1876. 20x/yr. USD 157.99 domestic; USD 199.99 Canada; USD 259.99 elsewhere. Ed(s): Anna Katterjohn. Library Journals, Llc., 160 Varick St, 11th Fl, New York, NY 10013. Illus., index, adv. Sample. Circ: 19510 Paid. Vol. ends:

Dec. Microform: CIS; NBI; RPI; PMC. *Indexed:* A01, A06, A22, ABIn, ABS&EES, ASIP, AmHI, B01, B02, B03, BAS, BRI, C37, C42, CBRI, Chicano, ERIC, GardL, MASUSE, MLA-IB, P02, RILM. *Bk. rev.:* 175-200 words, number varies. *Aud.:* Ga, Ac, Sa.

Library Journal's mission is to be a "one-stop source" for the information needs of all librarians. Each issue contains letters to the editor, opinion pieces, library news, feature articles, interviews, and reviews of books, DVDs, and software. Recommended for all library professionals. The journal also maintains an active web site. URL: www.libraryjournal.com

3426. *Library Leadership & Management.* Former titles (until 2009): *Library Administration and Management;* (until 1987): *L A M A Newsletter;* (until 1979): *L A D Newsletter.* [ISSN: 1945-8851] 1975. q. Free to members; Non-members, USD 85; USD 20 per issue. Ed(s): Lorraine Olley, Eric C Shoaf. American Library Association, 50 E Huron, Chicago, IL 60611; customerservice@ala.org; http://www.ala.org. Illus., adv. Vol. ends: Winter. Microform: PQC. *Indexed:* A22, ABIn, ISTA. *Bk. rev.:* Number and length vary. *Aud.:* Ga, Ac, Sa.

This open-access, peer-reviewed journal is the official publication of the Library Administration and Management Association, a division of the American Library Association. With an audience of library managers at all levels, articles explore issues and methodologies of library management in a practical manner. Articles and columns include case studies, interviews, feature articles, and news of the association. Recent article topics include effectiveness of library leaders and empowerment to promote tolerance. An essential publication for all library administrators and managers.

3427. *Library Management.* Incorporates (1993-1999): *Librarian Career Development.* [ISSN: 0143-5124] 1979. 9x/yr. EUR 14939 combined subscription in Europe (print & online eds.); USD 15939 combined subscription in the Americas (print & online eds.); GBP 10049 combined subscription in the UK & elsewhere (print & online eds.). Ed(s): Steve O'Connor. Emerald Group Publishing Ltd., Howard House, Wagon Ln, Bingley, BD16 1WA, United Kingdom; emerald@emeraldinsight.com; http://www.emeraldinsight.com. Sample. Refereed. Reprint: PSC. *Indexed:* A22, ABIn, C&ISA, CerAb, E01, FR, ISTA. *Bk. rev.:* Number and length vary. *Aud.:* Ga, Ac, Sa.

This peer-reviewed journal seeks to provide international perspectives on library management issues. Articles provide practical implications of management theories through case studies, research papers, and general papers. Recent articles address digital reference in developing countries, LibQUAL surveys, and library education. Highly recommended for library managers.

3428. *Library Media Connection.* Formed by the merger of (1982-2002): *The Book Report;* (1988-2002): *Library Talk.* [ISSN: 1542-4715] 1982. 7x/yr. USD 69. Ed(s): Wendy Medvetz, Gail Dickinson. Linworth Publishing, Inc., PO Box 204, Vandalia, OH 45377; linworth@linworthpublishing.com; http://www.linworth.com. Illus., adv. Vol. ends: May. Microform: PQC. *Indexed:* A01, A22, B01, BRI, CBRI, ERIC, MASUSE, P02. *Bk. rev.:* 25-50 words, number varies. *Aud.:* Ems, Hs.

A professional journal for school library media and technology specialists, *Library Media Connection* provides reviews, professional development, and practical articles for its readers. Recent article topics include political ads, iPads, and backchanneling. Each issue also features evaluations of children's books, multimedia resources, and professional readings. Essential reading for all school library media and technology professionals.

3429. *The Library Quarterly.* [ISSN: 0024-2519] 1931. q. USD 232 (print & online eds.). Ed(s): Paul Jaeger, John Carlo Bertot. University of Chicago Press, 1427 E 60th St, Chicago, IL 60637; subscriptions@press.uchicago.edu; http://www.journals.uchicago.edu. Illus., index, adv. Sample. Refereed. Vol. ends: Oct. Microform: MIM; PMC; PQC. Reprint: PSC. *Indexed:* A01, A22, ABS&EES, B01, BAS, BRI, CBRI, ERIC, FR, MLA-IB, P02, P61, RILM, SSA. *Bk. rev.:* 4-5, 900-1,300 words. *Aud.:* Ac, Sa.

This refereed quarterly journal seeks to inform its readership on research in all aspects of librarianship. Each issue includes book reviews and articles that discuss topics such as digital libraries, diversity in LIS, information literacy training, and information-seeking behavior. Recent article topics include self-publishing, the usability of WorldCat Local, and children's librarians on the radio. Recommended for academic and special libraries.

3430. *Library Resources & Technical Services.* Formerly (until 2004): *New Directions in Technical Services;* Which superseded in part (in 1995): *Library Resources & Technical Services;* Which was formed by the merger of (1950-1957): *Serial Slants;* (1948-1956): *Journal of Cataloging and Classification;* Which was formerly (until 1948): *American Library Association. Division of Cataloging and Classification. Executive Board;* (until 1947): *American Library Association. Division of Cataloging and Classification. Board of Directors. News Notes.* 1957. q. Free to members; Non-members, USD 100. Ed(s): Peggy Johnson. American Library Association, 50 E Huron, Chicago, IL 60611; customerservice@ala.org; http://www.ala.org. Illus., adv. Sample. Refereed. Circ: 5900. Vol. ends: Jan. Microform: PQC. *Indexed:* A01, A22, ABS&EES, BAS, BRI, CBRI, FR, ISTA, P02, RILM. *Bk. rev.:* 4-6; length varies. *Aud.:* Ac, Sa.

This is the official journal of the Association of Library Collections & Technical Services, a division of the American Library Association. Articles in this publication address collection management and development, acquisitions, cataloging and classification, preservation and reformatting, and serials. Articles are subject to a double-blind peer review, and recent topics explore Open Access literature, data mining, and the HathiTrust. A basic publication for all academic library collections.

3431. *Library Review.* [ISSN: 0024-2535] 1927. 9x/yr. EUR 11659 combined subscription in Europe (print & online eds.); USD 13739 combined subscription in the Americas (print & online eds.); GBP 7849 combined subscription in the UK & elsewhere (print & online eds.). Ed(s): Judith Broady-Preston. Emerald Group Publishing Ltd., Howard House, Wagon Ln, Bingley, BD16 1WA, United Kingdom; emerald@emeraldinsight.com; http://www.emeraldinsight.com. Sample. Refereed. Reprint: PSC. *Indexed:* A22, AmHI, BRI, C&ISA, CBRI, CerAb, E01, FR, ISTA, MLA-IB, P02. *Bk. rev.:* 2-6, length varies. *Aud.:* Ga, Ac, Sa.

Library Review provides librarians, educators, and researchers with information from libraries around the world. Articles are written by librarians with diverse backgrounds, and recent topics explore information-seeking behavior, social networking sites, and information literacy assessment. Recent themed issues consider knowledge sharing in emerging economies and open-source software. Each issue also includes reviews of recent library and information science publications. Recommended for all library collections.

3432. *Library Trends.* [ISSN: 0024-2594] 1952. q. USD 155. Ed(s): Cindy Ashwill, Alistair Black. The Johns Hopkins University Press, 2715 N Charles St, Baltimore, MD 21218; http://www.press.jhu.edu. Illus., index, adv. Sample. Refereed. Circ: 1147. Microform: MIM; PQC. Reprint: PSC. *Indexed:* A01, A22, B02, E01, FR, ISTA, MLA-IB, P02, RILM. *Aud.:* Ga, Ac, Sa.

This quarterly publication examines new and emerging trends in the field of library and information science. Each themed issue covers all aspects of a topic and its impact on libraries. Recent issue titles include "Information literacy beyond the academy," "Library design: from past to present," and "Involving users in the co-construction of Digital Knowledge in Libraries, Archives, and Museums." Articles address the impact of the topic on all library departments, including reference, technical services, administration, and systems. Recommended reading for all librarians.

3433. *Medical Library Association. Journal.* Formerly (until 2002): *Medical Library Association. Bulletin.* [ISSN: 1536-5050] 1911. q. Free to members; Non-members, USD 190. Ed(s): Susan S Starr. Medical Library Association, 65 E Wacker Pl, Ste 1900, Chicago, IL 60601; info@mlahq.org; http://www.mlanet.org/publications. Adv. Sample. Refereed. Circ: 4000. *Indexed:* A01, A06, A22, BRI, FR, ISTA, MLA-IB, P02. *Bk. rev.:* Number and length vary. *Aud.:* Sa.

This quarterly, peer-reviewed journal is the official publication of the Medical Library Association. Each issues includes papers, case studies, opinions, and book reviews. Recent articles address information-seeking behaviors, journal impact factors, and subject guides. Essential reading for all medical librarians.

3434. *Medical Reference Services Quarterly.* [ISSN: 0276-3869] 1982. q. GBP 416 (print & online eds.). Ed(s): M Sandra Wood. Routledge, 325 Chestnut St, Ste 800, Philadelphia, PA 19106; customerservice@taylorandfrancis.com; http://www.tandfonline.com. Illus., adv. Sample. Refereed. Microform: PQC. Reprint: PSC. *Indexed:* A01, A22, E01, ISTA. *Bk. rev.:* 8-12, 500-800 words. *Aud.:* Ac, Sa.

Medical Reference Services Quarterly is a peer-reviewed publication for an audience of medical and health sciences librarians who provide reference services in the educational, clinical, and research environments. Articles provide practical information on topics such as postgraduate medical training programs, citation formats, guides to medical information resources, and Internet medical resources. Each issue also includes book reviews and reviews of articles in related publications. Essential for all medical and health sciences reference librarians.

3435. *O C L C Systems & Services: international digital library perspectives.* Formerly (until 1993): *O C L C Micro.* [ISSN: 1065-075X] 1984. q. EUR 1499 combined subscription in Europe (print & online eds.); USD 1829 combined subscription in the Americas (print & online eds.); GBP 1089 combined subscription in the UK & elsewhere (print & online eds.). Ed(s): Bradford Lee Eden. Emerald Group Publishing Ltd., Howard House, Wagon Ln, Bingley, BD16 1WA, United Kingdom; information@emeraldinsight.com; http://www.emeraldinsight.com. Adv. Sample. Refereed. Circ: 2250 Paid. Reprint: PSC. *Indexed:* A01, A22, C&ISA, CerAb, CompLI, E01, I15, ISTA, P02. *Bk. rev.:* Number and length vary. *Aud.:* Ga, Ac, Sa.

This quarterly, peer-reviewed publication covers all aspects of web-based delivery of cultural heritage materials. Article formats include featured articles, case studies, and news and reviews. Recent themed issues examine music information retrieval, open-source ILS and OPAC implementations, and open-source digital tools. Recommended for academic librarians interested in digital projects and services.

3436. *Portal: libraries and the academy.* [ISSN: 1531-2542] 2001. q. USD 198. Ed(s): Jan C Voogd, Sarah M Pritchard. The Johns Hopkins University Press, 2715 N Charles St, Baltimore, MD 21218; http://www.press.jhu.edu. Adv. Sample. Refereed. Circ: 187. Reprint: PSC. *Indexed:* A01, A22, B01, E01, ERIC, ISTA, MLA-IB, P02. *Bk. rev.:* Number and length vary. *Aud.:* Ac.

A quarterly, peer-reviewed journal focusing on new technologies in academic libraries. Recent articles address fair use, social media, and liaison librarians. Recommended for all academic librarians.

3437. *Progressive Librarian: a journal for critical studies and progressive politics in librarianship.* [ISSN: 1052-5726] 1990. s-a. Free. Ed(s): Elaine Harger. Progressive Librarians Guild, Rider University Library, 2083 Lawrenceville Rd, Lawrenceville, NJ 08648; plgwebteam@libr.org; http://libr.org/plg/index.php. *Bk. rev.:* Number and length vary. *Aud.:* Ga.

Progressive Librarian is a peer-reviewed journal about progressive politics in libraries. Recent articles examine the use of space in libraries, GLBT collections, and marketing the library. Recommended for librarians interested in progressive politics and its impact on library services.

3438. *Public Libraries.* Former titles (until 1978): *P L A Newsletter;* (until 1970): *Just Between Ourselves.* [ISSN: 0163-5506] 1962. bi-m. Non-members, USD 65. Ed(s): Kathleen M Hughes. American Library Association, 50 E Huron, Chicago, IL 60611; http://www.ala.org. Illus., index, adv. Circ: 11926. Microform: PQC. *Indexed:* A22, BRI, P02. *Bk. rev.:* Number and length vary. *Aud.:* Ga, Ac, Sa.

This journal is the official publication of the Public Library Association, a division of the American Library Association. Articles and columns examine industry news, association updates, professional development, literature reviews, and ideas and strategies for providing library services to the public. Recent articles explore preserving obituaries, library services to the homeless, and education programs. Essential reading for all public librarians.

3439. *Reference and User Services Quarterly (Online).* [ISSN: 2163-5242] q. USD 65. American Library Association, 50 E Huron, Chicago, IL 60611; ala@ala.org; http://www.ala.org. *Bk. rev.:* 18-25; length varies. *Aud.:* Ga, Ac, Sa.

As the official publication of the Reference and User Services Association of the American Library Association, this journal communicates information regarding user-oriented library services to librarians in special, public, and academic libraries. In addition to reference trends and e-resources, articles also address professional development, literature reviews, and news of the association. Annotated bibliographies are also included. Recent articles examine participatory web design, campus book clubs, and instruction. A basic title for all library collections.

3440. *The Reference Librarian.* [ISSN: 0276-3877] 1981. q. GBP 999 (print & online eds.). Ed(s): Rita M Pellen, William Miller. Routledge, 325 Chestnut St, Ste 800, Philadelphia, PA 19106; customerservice@taylorandfrancis.com; http://www.tandfonline.com. Illus., index, adv. Sample. Refereed. Circ: 636 Paid. Microform: PQC. Reprint: PSC. *Indexed:* A01, A22, C&ISA, CerAb, E01, FR, ISTA. *Aud.:* Ac, Sa.

This semi-annual publication addresses new trends and developments in the field of reference librarianship. Articles are appropriate for professional librarians and graduate students enrolled in reference and user services courses. Recent articles discuss RDA and the reference librarian, text message reference, and library instruction assessment. Recommended reading for all reference librarians.

3441. *Reference Services Review: reference and instructional services for libraries in the digital age.* [ISSN: 0090-7324] 1973. q. EUR 539 combined subscription in Europe (print & online eds.); USD 679 combined subscription in the Americas (print & online eds.); GBP 389 combined subscription in the UK & elsewhere (print & online eds.). Ed(s): Sarah Baxter, Eleanor Mitchell. Emerald Group Publishing Ltd., Howard House, Wagon Ln, Bingley, BD16 1WA, United Kingdom; emerald@emeraldinsight.com; http://www.emeraldinsight.com. Illus., index. Sample. Refereed. Reprint: PSC. *Indexed:* A22, BRI, C&ISA, CBRI, CerAb, E01, FR, ISTA, P02, RILM. *Aud.:* Ac, Sa.

Reference Services Review is a quarterly, peer-reviewed publication that examines all aspects of reference services. Recent themed issues examine mobile services, learning landscapes, and conference reports. Contents include research papers, viewpoints, case studies, and literature reviews. Recent topics cover ebooks, Twitter, and information literacy on Facebook. Recommended for all library collections.

3442. *School Library Journal.* Formerly (until 1961): *Junior Libraries.* [ISSN: 0362-8930] 1954. m. USD 136.99. Ed(s): Rebecca T Miller. Media Source Incorporated, 160 Varick St, 11th Fl, New York, NY 10013; http://www.mediasourceinc.com. Illus., index, adv. Sample. Vol. ends: Aug. Microform: NBI; PQC. *Indexed:* A01, A22, ABIn, ABS&EES, ASIP, B02, BRI, C37, CBRI, Chicano, ERIC, MASUSE, P02. *Bk. rev.:* 50-100 words; number varies. *Aud.:* Ems, Hs, Ga.

This monthly publication contains news, trends, and literature reviews relevant to librarians who provide services for children and young adults. Recent articles discuss collaboration between school and public libraries, access to technology, and encouraging children to read. Each issue also includes book reviews. Essential reading for all young adult and children's librarians.

3443. *School Library Monthly.* Formerly (until 2009): *School Library Media Activities Monthly.* [ISSN: 2166-160X] 1984. 8x/yr. USD 55 domestic; USD 67 foreign. Ed(s): Deborah D Levitov. Libraries Unlimited, Inc., PO Box 291846, Kettering, OH 45429; http://www.abc-clio.com/aboutus/Default.aspx?id=60300. Illus., adv. *Indexed:* A01, A22, ABS&EES, BRI, ERIC, P02. *Bk. rev.:* Number and length vary. *Aud.:* Ems, Hs.

This monthly publication for K–12 school library media specialists addresses collaboration with teachers, current reference sources, technology, and information literacy. Recent articles explore teaching, advocacy, and the instructional role of the school librarian. Issues also review current literature and web sites for children and young adults. Highly recommended for all K–12 school library media specialists.

3444. School Library Research. Former titles (until 2007): *School Library Media Research;* (until 1998): *School Library Media Quarterly (Online);* Which superseded in part (in 1997): *School Library Media Quarterly (Print);* Which was formerly (until 1981): *School Media Quarterly;* Which superseded in part (in 1972): *School Libraries;* Which was formerly (until 1952): *American Association of School Librarians. Newsletter.* [ISSN: 2165-1019] 1951. a. Free. Ed(s): Carol L Tilley, Jean Donham. American Library Association, 50 E Huron, Chicago, IL 60611; customerservice@ala.org; http://www.ala.org. Illus. Refereed. *Indexed:* ERIC. *Aud.:* Ems, Hs.

This open-access journal is a refereed publication of the American Association of School Librarians, a division of the American Library Association. *School Library Media Research* publishes high-quality research papers concerning the management and utilization of school library media programs. Articles emphasize evaluation, teaching methods, and instructional theory. Recent topics cover professional skills development, portrayal of disabilities in young adult graphic novels, and school librarians as health information gatekeepers. A valuable resource for school library media professionals. Available online. URL: www.ala.org/aasl/slr

3445. Science & Technology Libraries. [ISSN: 0194-262X] 1980. q. GBP 481 (print & online eds.). Ed(s): Tony Stankus. Routledge, 325 Chestnut St, Ste 800, Philadelphia, PA 19106. Illus., index, adv. Sample. Refereed. Circ: 538 Paid. Microform: PQC. Reprint: PSC. *Indexed:* A01, A22, C&ISA, CerAb, E01, EngInd, FR, ISTA. *Aud.:* Ac, Sa.

Science & Technology Libraries is a quarterly, peer-reviewed publication with an audience of librarians in science, engineering, clinical investigation, and agriculture. Each issue focuses on original research, and also includes profiles of prominent scientists and reviews of recent developments in the science fields. Recent article topics include citation patterns, collection development, and Libguides. Highly recommended for all science and technology librarians.

3446. The Serials Librarian: the international journal of continuing print & electronic resources. [ISSN: 0361-526X] 1976. q. GBP 810 (print & online eds.). Ed(s): Louise Cole, Andrew Shroyer. Routledge, 325 Chestnut St, Ste 800, Philadelphia, PA 19106; customerservice@taylorandfrancis.com; http://www.tandfonline.com. Illus., adv. Sample. Refereed. Circ: 869 Paid. Vol. ends: No. 4. Microform: PQC. Reprint: PSC. *Indexed:* A01, A22, ABS&EES, C&ISA, CerAb, E01, FR, ISTA, MLA-IB, P02, RILM. *Bk. rev.:* Number and length vary. *Aud.:* Ac, Sa.

This peer-reviewed journal addresses the complex and changing environment of continuing resources management, including preservation, collection development, acquisitions, and cataloging. Recent article topics address RDA, open-access journals, and sustainable scholarship. Highly recommended for all librarians working with continuing resources.

3447. Serials Review. [ISSN: 0098-7913] 1975. 4x/yr. EUR 391. Ed(s): Maria Collins. Elsevier Ltd, The Boulevard, Langford Lane, Oxford, OX5 1GB, United Kingdom; journalscustomerserviceemea@elsevier.com; http://www.elsevier.com. Illus., index, adv. Sample. Refereed. Vol. ends: No. 4. Reprint: PSC. *Indexed:* A01, A22, ABS&EES, B01, BRI, CBRI, ISTA, MLA-IB. *Bk. rev.:* Number and length vary. *Aud.:* Ga, Ac, Sa.

This quarterly, peer-reviewed journal focuses on all issues surrounding serials and their management, from practical and theoretical points of view. Recent article topics include ebook purchasing, classification systems, and discovery layers. Each issue also includes opinion columns, conference reviews, and standards updates. Recommended for all serial and e-resource librarians.

3448. Teacher Librarian: the journal for school library professionals. Formerly (until 1998): *Emergency Librarian.* [ISSN: 1481-1782] 1973. bi-m. except Aug. USD 61 domestic; USD 51 Canada; USD 68 elsewhere. Ed(s): Elizabeth Marcoux, David Loertscher. Scarecrow Press, Inc., 4501 Forbes Blvd, Ste 200, Lanham, MD 20706; custserv@rowman.com; http://www.scarecrowpress.com. Illus., adv. Sample. Refereed. Vol. ends: Jun. Microform: MML; PQC. *Indexed:* A01, A22, BRI, C37, CBRI, CEI, Chicano, ERIC, ISTA, P02. *Bk. rev.:* Number and length vary. *Aud.:* Ems, Hs, Ac.

Published five times a year, *Teacher Librarian* provides information for professional librarians who work with children and young adults. Regular features include reviews of professional literature, Internet resources, and new books for children, as well as articles that discuss information technology and school library management. Highly recommended for school librarians and library media specialists. Available online. URL: www.teacherlibrarian.com/

3449. Technical Services Quarterly: new trends in computers, automation & advanced technologies in the technical operation of libraries & information centers. [ISSN: 0731-7131] 1983. q. GBP 619 (print & online eds.). Ed(s): Gary M Pitkin. Routledge, 325 Chestnut St, Ste 800, Philadelphia, PA 19106; customerservice@taylorandfrancis.com; http:// www.tandfonline.com. Illus., index, adv. Sample. Refereed. Circ: 507 Paid. Reprint: PSC. *Indexed:* A22, C&ISA, CerAb, E01, ISTA, RILM. *Bk. rev.:* Number and length vary. *Aud.:* Ac, Sa.

This peer-reviewed publication provides information, current trends, and research regarding the technical operations of libraries. Each issue includes original articles, technical services reports, reviews of tech services on the web, and book reviews. Recent article topics address collections management, outsourcing acquisitions, and identifying emerging technologies. Highly recommended for all librarians in technical services departments.

3450. Visual Resources: an international journal of documentation. [ISSN: 0197-3762] 1980. q. GBP 654 (print & online eds.). Ed(s): Christine Sundt. Routledge, 4 Park Sq, Milton Park, Abingdon, OX14 4RN, United Kingdom; subscriptions@tandf.co.uk; http:// www.tandfonline.com. Illus., index, adv. Sample. Refereed. Vol. ends: No. 4. Reprint: PSC. *Indexed:* A01, A07, A22, A51, AmHI, BAS, E01. *Bk. rev.:* Number and length vary. *Aud.:* Ac, Sa.

This referred journal examines images, the use of images, and visual literacy. It explores how visual languages are structured, meaning is conveyed, and how images are organized, stored, delivered, and preserved. Although art and architecture are the most common uses of images, other subjects using visual information are also explored. A recent special issue addresses Renaissance Portraiture in Italy. Other articles discuss the use of art in creating national identities, art history research, and the use of digital images in teaching art history. This journal is highly recommended for all information professionals working with visual information.

3451. Voice of Youth Advocates: the library magazine serving those who serve young adults. [ISSN: 0160-4201] 1978. bi-m. USD 57. Ed(s): RoseMary Honnold. E L Kurdyla Publishing LLC, PO Box 958, Bowie, MD 20718-0958. Illus., index, adv. Sample. *Indexed:* A22, BRI, CBRI, MLA-IB. *Bk. rev.:* Number and length vary. *Aud.:* Ems, Hs, Ga.

This bimonthly publication is intended for professionals who provide information services to teenagers. The guiding principles of the journal state that young adults deserve their own targeted library services and collections, free and equal access to information, advocates for their information needs, and participation in decision-making processes. Each issue includes several well-written articles that address various aspects of young adult librarianship, as well as numerous reviews of young adult fiction and reference books. Recent articles explore library services on a tight budget, and library-classroom partnership. Strongly recommended for all librarians who serve young adults. An active web site is maintained. URL: www.voya.com/

3452. Young Adult Library Services. Supersedes in part (in 2002): *Journal of Youth Services in Libraries;* Which was formerly (1942-1987): *Top of the News.* [ISSN: 1541-4302] 2002. q. Non-members, USD 70. Ed(s): Sarah Flowers. American Library Association, 50 E Huron, Chicago, IL 60611; customerservice@ala.org; http://www.ala.org. Adv. Circ: 6624. *Indexed:* A01, BRI, P02. *Aud.:* Ems, Hs, Ga.

Young Adult Library Services is the official publication of the Young Adult Library Services Association (YALSA), a division of the American Library Association. This journal publishes news and articles relevant to providers of teen library services. Recent articles explore teens as advocates, inner-city teens, and summer reading. Other features include bibliographies, association news, and announcements of awards. Essential reading for all professionals who provide library services to young adults.

■ LINGUISTICS

See also Anthropology; Classical Studies; Education; Literature; Psychology; and Sociology and Social Work sections.

Jeff Staiger, Librarian for Romance Languages and Classics, Knight Library, University of Oregon, Eugene, OR; jstaiger@uoregon.edu

Introduction

The articles in linguistic journals are, in the main, written by professionals for professionals. They tend to be technical, some highly so. The generalizations they offer emerge from the close investigation of a restricted phenomenon in the realm of language. Accordingly, one might suppose that their import can be appreciated only by other specialists. Yet we are all users of language, and a brush with scientific investigations of this most uncanny of human endowments will quicken the intellect of any layman who seeks a deeper understanding of our condition.

The journals covered in this section mostly fall into distinct categories that can be outlined as follows:

GENERAL: These journals publish articles on all aspects of linguistics, and are (mostly) ecumenical in the range of approaches they include. Some of the longest-established journals in the field, having come into existence before the development of more recent sub-specialties, are in this category. They thus have an authority based on their function as the publication venues for most important results for the field as a whole. The journals that fall into this category, *Canadian Journal of Linguistics* (1954), *Folia Linguistica* (1967), *Language* (1925), *Lingua* (1947), *Linguistic Inquiry* (1970), and *Linguistics: an interdisciplinary journal of the language sciences* (1963), comprise some of the field's core journals.

FORMALIST: Traditionally, there has been a broad division in linguistics between formalist and historical approaches. *Journal of Phonetics, Journal of Semantics, Morphology,* and *Linguistic Review,* which is devoted to syntax, belong to the former category, as does *Linguistic Analysis,* which publishes analyses devoted to all four basic areas of linguistic research that the others cover separately. *Language Variation and Change* covers the historical side. An important recent subfield that might be classed among the formalist approaches is corpus linguistics, which is the branch of the field that analyzes distinct, bounded *corpora* or field samples of linguistic usage drawn from particular language communities or realms of discourse. Three journals that take this area as their subject, *Corpora, International Journal of Corpus Linguistics,* and the recently founded *Corpus Linguistics and Linguistic Theory,* are reviewed here.

APPLIED (OR PRACTICAL): At the opposite end of the conceptual spectrum from the formalist and theoretical concerns that constitute most linguistic inquiry are the subfields of applied linguistics and pragmatics; covering this area are *Applied Linguistics, The Open Applied Linguistics Journal,* and *Intercultural Pragmatics,* which presents articles that focus on the dynamics of communication between speakers of different languages and/or cultures.

PARTICULAR LANGUAGES: Certain journals are devoted to research into linguistic problems within particular languages. The leading journal for the linguistic scrutiny of English is *Journal of the English Language. English World-Wide* covers the language in its manifestations across the globe. American English is treated in *American Speech: a quarterly of linguistic usage,* while the indigenous languages of the Americas are addressed in *International Journal of American Linguistics.* A well-rounded academic collection should also have *Journal of German Linguistics,* which covers the whole field of Germanic languages, including English up to 1500; and *Probus: International Journal of Latin and Romance Linguistics.* An interesting sub-specialty within this field is covered by *Languages in Contrast,* which publishes studies comparing linguistic phenomena in different languages.

INTERDISCIPLINARY: Interdisciplinary work is a rapidly growing sector of academic research, and most of the journals already mentioned in this introduction will feature work that approaches its topic from the perspective of different disciplines. Certain journals, however, are expressly devoted to publishing studies at the intersection of defined disciplines: *Anthropological Linguistics, Cognitive Linguistics, Language and Education, Language and Literature,* and *Linguistics and Philosophy* are established journals in the field, while several titles new to this edition of *MFL, Laboratory Phonetics, Language Learning and Development,* and *The Mental Lexicon,* represent current interdisciplinary trends in the linguistics, particularly as regards the turn to various domains of empirical research such as cognitive science and neuroscience.

PEDAGOGICAL: Journals in this category address problems in the teaching of language, particularly second languages. *ELT* (or *English Language Teaching*) *Journal, Modern Language Journal, Studies in Second Language Acquisition,* and *T E S O L Quarterly* have such a pragmatic orientation.

Basic Periodicals

Ac: *American Speech, Applied Linguistics, Journal of English Linguistics, Journal of Linguistics, Journal of Phonetics, Language (Washington), Language in Society, Linguistic Inquiry, The Linguistic Review, Linguistics, Modern Language Journal, Natural Language and Linguistic Theory.*

Basic Abstracts and Indexes

Language Teaching, Linguistics Abstracts, Linguistics and Language Behavior Abstracts, MLA International Bibliography, Social Sciences Citation Index, Sociological Abstracts.

American Journal of Philology. See Classical Studies section.

3453. *American Speech: a quarterly of linguistic usage.* [ISSN: 0003-1283] 1925. 5x/yr. USD 226. Ed(s): Charles E Carson, Michael Adams. Duke University Press, 905 W Main St, Ste 18 B, PO Box 90660, Durham, NC 27701; subscriptions@dukepress.edu; http://www.dukepress.edu. Illus., adv. Sample. Refereed. Vol. ends: Winter. Microform: PQC. Reprint: PSC. *Indexed:* A01, A22, AmHI, ArtHuCI, BEL&L, BRI, E01, FR, LT&LA, MLA-IB, P02, P61, RILM, SSA. *Bk. rev.:* 1-2, 2-6 pages. *Aud.:* Ga, Ac.

This journal concentrates primarily on the English Language as it is used in the Western Hemisphere, although it also includes articles on aspects of English in an international context, as well as general linguistic topics. It particularly emphasizes "current usage, dialectology, and the history and structure of English." Recent issues have treated such topics as dialect variation in Washington State and rare regional terms for "corn." The journal includes reviews, and a regular feature, "Among the New Words," in which a recent topic was the political neologism "birther," and similar terms. Subscribers receive the annual hardbound supplement, *Publication of the American Dialectical Society.* In addition to being highly cited, this journal has a wide general appeal, and is therefore recommended for all academic linguistic collections. See also *International Journal of American Linguistics.*

3454. *Anthropological Linguistics.* [ISSN: 0003-5483] 1959. q. USD 184. Ed(s): Douglas R Parks. University of Nebraska Press, 1111 Lincoln Mall, Lincoln, NE 68588; pressmail@unl.edu; http://www.nebraskapress.unl.edu. Illus., index, adv. Refereed. Circ: 800. Microform: PQC. *Indexed:* A01, A22, A47, ABS&EES, AbAn, AmHI, BAS, BEL&L, BRI, E01, FR, IBSS, MLA-IB, P61, RILM, SSA. *Bk. rev.:* 5-12, 2-12 pages. *Aud.:* Ac.

This journal covers a wide array of topics at the intersection of linguistics and anthropology, offering analyses of texts, semantic systems, cultural classifications, onomastics, linguistic prehistory, and more. A recent article illustrating this emphasis is "Ethnobiological Classification in Two Indigenous Languages of the Gran Chaco Region: toba (Guaycuruan) and Maka (Mataco-Mataguayan)." The journal is global in scope, although the majority of its analyses is based on the indigenous languages of the Americas. *Anthropological Linguistics* is published jointly by the Department of Anthropology and the American Indian Research Institute at Indiana University. Institutions whose linguistics programs are complemented by programs in anthropology and Native American studies will be most likely to benefit from a subscription to this journal.

3455. *Applied Linguistics.* [ISSN: 0142-6001] 1980. 5x/yr. EUR 434. Ed(s): Jane Zuengler, Ken Hyland. Oxford University Press, Great Clarendon St, Oxford, OX2 6DP, United Kingdom; enquiry@oup.co.uk; http://www.oxfordjournals.org/. Illus., adv. Sample. Refereed. Reprint: PSC. *Indexed:* A01, A22, E01, ERIC, FR, IBSS, LT&LA, MLA-IB, PsycInfo. *Bk. rev.:* 4-5, 1-3 pages. *Aud.:* Ac.

This journal is devoted to treatments of general issues raised by specific situations in which language is learned and used. Combining theory with the examination of practice, *Applied Linguistics* "is less interested in the ad hoc solution to particular problems and more interested in the handling of problems in a principled way by reference to theoretical studies." The journal's mission statement lists a wide range of studies covered by the journal: "bilingualism and multilingualism; computer-mediated communication; conversation analysis; deaf linguistics; discourse analysis and pragmatics; corpus linguistics; critical discourse analysis; first and additional language learning, teaching, and use; forensic linguistics; language assessment; language planning and policies; languages for special purposes; literacies; multimodal communication; rhetoric and stylistics; and translations." With a view to fostering debate, the journal observes a quicker-than-usual turnaround time for short pieces that appear in its forum section. A highly cited, core journal in the field, *Applied Linguistics* is recommended for all academic libraries.

C L A Journal. See African American section.

3456. *Canadian Journal of Linguistics.* Formerly (until 1961): *Canadian Linguistic Association. Journal.* [ISSN: 0008-4131] 1954. 3x/yr. USD 95. Ed(s): Sarah Cummins. University of Toronto Press, Journals Division, 5201 Dufferin St, Toronto, ON M3H 5T8, Canada; journals@utpress.utoronto.ca; http://www.utpjournals.com. Illus., index. Sample. Refereed. Circ: 618. Vol. ends: Nov. Microform: PQC. *Indexed:* A22, ArtHuCI, BAS, CEI, E01, FR, IBSS, LT&LA, MLA-IB. *Bk. rev.:* 5-15, 1,000 words. *Aud.:* Ac.

The *Canadian Journal of Linguistics / La revue canadienne de linguistique* embraces the full range of general and theoretical issues in linguistics. Published by the Canadian Linguistic Association, it is international in scope while offering a forum for treatment of the languages of Canada, including those of indigenous peoples such as Inuit. There is a discernible emphasis on the formal issues that form the core of traditional areas of linguistic study, such as phonetics, phonology, morphology, syntax, and semantics; but the journal covers the full range of topics in linguistics and also includes articles in the subfields of historical linguistics, sociolinguistics, psycholinguistics, and first and second language acquisition. Articles may be in either English or French, though the former predominates. A supplementary academic purchase.

3457. *Cognitive Linguistics: an interdisciplinary journal of cognitive science.* [ISSN: 0936-5907] 1989. q. EUR 504. Ed(s): Ewa Dabrowska. De Gruyter Mouton, Genthiner Str 13, Berlin, 10785, Germany; mouton@degruyter.de; http://www.degruyter.com. Illus., index, adv. Sample. Refereed. Reprint: PSC. *Indexed:* A01, A22, ArtHuCI, BRI, E01, MLA-IB, PsycInfo. *Bk. rev.:* 0-5, 5-15 pages. *Aud.:* Ac, Sa.

This journal focuses on the mental processes involved in language-use, including such topics as the relationship between language and thought, the experiential background of language-in-use, and the structural characterization of natural language. Examples of articles from a recent issue are "A corpus-based account of the development of English *such* and Dutch *zulk*: Identification, intensification[,] and (inter)subjectification" and "On the interpretation of alienable vs. inalienable possession: A psycholinguistic investigation." Subscribers to the journal receive the *Cognitive Linguistics Bibliography,* which, according to the journal's web site, is updated with 1,000 entries annually, reflecting the diverse range of fields that bear on the study of cognitive linguistics. *CogBib* is also available as a separate online subscription. Membership in the International Cognitive Linguistics Association includes a subscription to the journal. The focused nature of this journal makes it primarily suitable for academic linguistic collections.

3458. *Corpora: corpus-based language learning, language processing and linguistics.* [ISSN: 1749-5032] 2006. s-a. GBP 66.50 (print & online eds.). Ed(s): Tony McEnery. Edinburgh University Press Ltd., 22 George Sq, Edinburgh, EH8 9LF, United Kingdom; journals@eup.ed.ac.uk; http://www.euppublishing.com. Adv. Refereed. *Indexed:* MLA-IB. *Bk. rev.:* 0-2; 3-5 pages. *Aud.:* Ac.

Like the *International Journal of Corpus Linguistics* (see below), this journal is devoted to the study of *corpora,* or bodies or "field samples" of actual linguistics usage, which then are subjected to rigorous study. The web site of *Corpora,* a relatively new journal, stresses its intention of publishing articles "focusing on the many and varied uses of corpora both in linguistics and beyond." Two examples illustrating this interdisciplinary approach are "Love is all around: a corpus-based study of pop lyrics" and "Translator-oriented, corpus-driven technical glossaries: the case of cooking terms." The journal presents analyses of corpora taken from the global range of languages. Considerations of corpus-based theory and methodology are also represented in this journal. Includes reviews. A supplemental purchase for academic libraries.

3459. *Corpus Linguistics and Linguistic Theory.* [ISSN: 1613-7027] 2005. 2x/yr. EUR 213. Ed(s): Stefan Th. Gries. De Gruyter Mouton, Genthiner Str 13, Berlin, 10785, Germany; mouton@degruyter.de; http://www.degruyter.com. Adv. Refereed. Reprint: PSC. *Indexed:* A22, ArtHuCI, BRI, E01, MLA-IB. *Bk. rev.:* Number and length vary. *Aud.:* Ac.

The studies published in this relatively new journal (founded in 2005) publishes "corpus-based research focusing on theoretically relevant issues in all core areas of linguistic research (phonology, morphology, syntax, semantics, [and] pragmatics), or other recognized topic areas." Recent articles that illustrate this orientation are "Scrambling in spoken Dutch: Definiteness versus weight as determinants of word order variation" and "Quotations across the generations: a multivariate analysis of speech and thought introducers across 5 decades of Tyneside speech." A recent special issue addressed the topic of "Corpus Linguistics and sociolinguistic theory," presenting articles that sought to explore the areas of overlap and shared concern between the two fields. The journal also includes squibs, and reviews of books, corpora, and software packages. As corpus linguistics is a major subfield of the discipline, this journal would make a good supplementary purchase for research institutions.

3460. *E L T Journal: an international journal for teachers of English to speakers of other languages.* Former titles (until 1981): *English Language Teaching Journal;* (until 1973): *English Language Teaching.* [ISSN: 0951-0893] 1946. q. EUR 237. Ed(s): Keith Morrow. Oxford University Press, Great Clarendon St, Oxford, OX2 6DP, United Kingdom; enquiry@oup.co.uk; http://www.oxfordjournals.org/. Illus., adv. Sample. Refereed. Microform: PQC. Reprint: PSC. *Indexed:* A01, A22, AmHI, ArtHuCI, BRI, E01, ERIC, LT&LA, MLA-IB. *Bk. rev.:* 2-10, 1-15 pages. *Aud.:* Hs, Ga, Ac.

As the title states, this journal is oriented toward practitioners of English Language Teaching (ELT). Published by the International Association of Teachers of English as a Foreign Language (www.iatefl.org), its stated mission is to unite the concerns of teachers "with insights gained from related academic disciplines such as applied linguistics, education, psychology, and sociology." Recent articles exhibit a corresponding diversity of interest, ranging from a consideration of textbooks to spoken grammar, and from raising sociocultural awareness to evaluating teaching practices. Its authors come from all over the world. In addition to a full slate of research articles, each issue also harbors much other material: there is a "readers respond" section, a "key concepts in ESL" column, book reviews, and a regular feature, "Websites for the Language Teacher," which reviews various sites under different rubrics such as "Business English" or "The Moving Image." Recommended for libraries at institutions with EFL programs. See also *Modern Language Journal, Studies in Second Language Acquisition,* and *TESOL Quarterly.*

3461. *English World-Wide: a journal of varieties of English.* [ISSN: 0172-8865] 1980. 3x/yr. EUR 320 combined subscription (print & online eds.). Ed(s): Edgar W Schneider. John Benjamins Publishing Co., PO Box 36224, Amsterdam, 1020 ME, Netherlands; subscription@benjamins.nl; http://www.benjamins.com. Illus., adv. Sample. Refereed. Circ: 600. *Indexed:* A22, ArtHuCI, BEL&L, FR, IBSS, MLA-IB, P61, RILM, SSA. *Bk. rev.:* 3-5, 1-5 pages. *Aud.:* Ac.

The focus of this journal is on new research into the dialects and social contexts of English-speaking communities of both native and second-language speakers around the world. While it does not focus on issues pertaining to the teaching of English, it aims to provide the background information relevant to that endeavor. Articles in recent issues exhibit approaches ranging from descriptive and empirical to theoretical, and take in English in South Africa, India, Scotland, African-American women's communities, Kenya and the Bahamas. At the same time, the articles are just as likely to focus on larger conceptual issues raised by the study of the variety of global Englishes. The journal also features reviews and review essays. Since the areas covered in this journal are not strictly central to the field of linguistics, it cannot be considered a core journal in the field, although its topics should be of interest to linguistics researchers throughout the English-speaking world.

3462. *Folia Linguistica: acta societatis linguisticae Europaeae.* [ISSN: 0165-4004] 1967. s-a. EUR 303. Ed(s): Teresa Fanego. De Gruyter Mouton, Genthiner Str 13, Berlin, 10785, Germany; mouton@degruyter.de; http://www.degruyter.com. Illus., index, adv. Sample. Refereed. Reprint: SCH. *Indexed:* A01, A22, ABS&EES, ArtHuCI, BAS, E01, FR, LT&LA, MLA-IB, PsycInfo. *Bk. rev.:* 0-1, 1,000 words. *Aud.:* Ac, Sa.

This journal, published by the Societas Linguistica Europaea, treats all "non-historical" areas of general linguistics, as well as "sociological, discoursal, computational, and psychological aspects of language and linguistic theory." This technical–formal approach is illustrated by the recent article, "Causality and causation. A functional approach to causative constructions in Modern Swedish." A recent issue was devoted to the theme of grammatical gender. In addition to scientific articles that feature original research, the journal also contains reviews, conference reports, and bibliographies. Subscribers also receive an annual supplement, *Folia Linguistica Historica.* This journal is an important selection for any large academic linguistics collection.

3463. *Intercultural Pragmatics.* [ISSN: 1612-295X] 2004. q. EUR 229. Ed(s): Istvan Kecskes. De Gruyter Mouton, Genthiner Str 13, Berlin, 10785, Germany; mouton@degruyter.de; http://www.degruyter.com. Adv. Refereed. Reprint: PSC. *Indexed:* A22, ArtHuCI, BRI, E01, MLA-IB. *Bk. rev.:* 2 reviews; 5-9 pages. *Aud.:* Ac, Sa.

This journal presents a broad variety of technical analyses that fall under the rubric "intercultural pragmatics." Pragmatics is a subfield of linguistics that studies how context contributes to meaning. Accordingly, the mission of this journal is "to promote the understanding of intercultural competence by focusing on theoretical and applied pragmatics research that involves more than one language and culture or varieties of one language." Recent articles that exemplify this mission are "Negotiation style, speech accommodation[,] and small talk in Sino-Western business negotiations: A Hong Kong case study" and "Culture-specific concepts of politeness: indirectness and politeness in English,

Hebrew and Korean requests." A recent theme issue offers an array of perspectives on the topic of "negation," united by a general theoretical concern with the contextual use of language. The journal is highly interdisciplinary, and seeks to provide a forum for researchers "who are looking for new tools and methods to investigate human languages and communication." Given the specialized concerns of this journal, it cannot be considered a core purchase in the field, but it is nonetheless a recommended purchase for academic linguistics collections.

3464. *International Journal of American Linguistics.* [ISSN: 0020-7071] 1917. q. USD 357 (print & online eds.). Ed(s): Alma Dean Kolb, Keren Rice. University of Chicago Press, 1427 E 60th St, Chicago, IL 60637; subscriptions@press.uchicago.edu; http://www.journals.uchicago.edu. Illus., index. Sample. Refereed. Vol. ends: Oct. Microform: PMC; PQC. Reprint: PSC. *Indexed:* A01, A22, A47, AmHI, ArtHuCI, BRI, FR, LT&LA, MLA-IB, P02. *Bk. rev.:* 2-5, 2-4 pages. *Aud.:* Ac, Sa.

Founded by the famed anthropologist Franz Boas in 1917, and published in association with "the Society for the Study of the Indigenous Languages of the Americas," this journal is devoted to the study of the indigenous languages of the Americas—North, Central, and South. According to its mission statements, *IJAL* "concentrates on the investigation of the linguistic data and on the presentation of grammatical fragments and other documents relevant to the Amerindian languages." Q'anjob'al, Innu, plains Cree, Itunyoso Trique, and "Natchez Cannibal Speech" are the languages represented in a recent issue. The articles deal with the full range of linguistics issues raised by individual indigenous languages. Representative recent articles are "A Grammar of Mapuche" and "Languages of Pre-Columbian Antilles." As with *Anthropological Linguistics,* this journal will be of particular benefit to academic communities with strong programs in Native American studies and Anthropology. See also *American Speech.*

3465. *International Journal of Corpus Linguistics.* [ISSN: 1384-6655] 1996. 4x/yr. EUR 412 combined subscription (print & online eds.). Ed(s): Michaela Mahlberg. John Benjamins Publishing Co., PO Box 36224, Amsterdam, 1020 ME, Netherlands; subscription@benjamins.nl; http://www.benjamins.com. Illus., index. Sample. Refereed. *Indexed:* A01, A22, ArtHuCI, FR, MLA-IB. *Bk. rev.:* 3-5, 3-15 pages. *Aud.:* Ac, Sa.

Corpus linguistics is the branch of the field that studies samples (*corpora*) of "real-world" language. Such an approach implies the view of languages as a social phenomenon, which can be investigated empirically, on the basis of authentic "spoken texts." Articles tend to be of two sorts: rigorous analyses of specific problems having to do with the use of language, and the conceptual pieces that explore the methodologies appropriate to the carrying out of "corpus linguistics." An example of the former, applied type is "Gei constructions in Mandarin Chinese and bei constructions in Cantonese: a corpus-driven contrastive study." An example of the latter, more methodologically-oriented type is "Meaning in Context: Implementing Intelligent Applications of Language Studies." Other areas of interest represented in recent issues are linguistic description, sociolinguistics, and empirical investigation. A supplementary purchase for academic linguistics collections. See also *Corpora.*

3466. *Journal of English Linguistics.* [ISSN: 0075-4242] 1967. q. USD 666. Ed(s): Robin Queen, Anne Curzan. Sage Publications, Inc., 2455 Teller Rd, Thousand Oaks, CA 91320; info@sagepub.com; http://www.sagepub.com. Illus., index, adv. Sample. Refereed. Vol. ends: Dec. Reprint: PSC. *Indexed:* A01, A22, AmHI, ArtHuCI, E01, FR, MLA-IB. *Bk. rev.:* 1-5, 4-6 pages. *Aud.:* Ac, Sa.

This is the leading journal for the general study of the English language. Embracing an ecumenical range of theoretical perspectives and methodological approaches, the journal variously focuses on the history of English, English grammar, corpus linguistics, sociolinguistics, and dialectology. In keeping with its ambition to serve as the premier journal in its field, it regularly include interviews with leading scholars on their work and trends in the field in general, and a column "on the profession," in which key issues of concern to the members of the profession are discussed. Book reviews and occasional theme issues are also featured. *JEL* also covers such topics as language change, word origins, emerging computer methods and new quantitative methods for the study of English, gender issues in language, and historical and formal studies of Old and Middle English.

3467. *Journal of Germanic Linguistics.* Formerly (until 2001): *American Journal of Germanic Linguistics and Literatures.* [ISSN: 1470-5427] 1989. q. GBP 187. Ed(s): Robert W Murray. Cambridge University Press, The Edinburgh Bldg, Shaftesbury Rd, Cambridge, CB2 8RU, United Kingdom; journals@cambridge.org; http://www.cambridge.org/uk. Illus., index, adv. Sample. Refereed. Circ: 350. Reprint: PSC. *Indexed:* A22, ArtHuCI, E01, MLA-IB. *Bk. rev.:* 1-5, 4-6 pages. *Aud.:* Ac, Sa.

This is the premier journal for the study of the Germanic languages, including English up to 1500, in the English-speaking world (English is the language of most articles, although those in German are also considered). It presents articles that cover a wide range of general topics in linguistics, from formal analyses of phonological, morphological, syntactic, and semantic features of the Germanic languages, to aspects of these languages' historical development. Articles tend to be technical and focused on highly specialized topics, although reflections of a more general nature may appear as well. Each year, the fourth issue is a theme issue, the most recent being "Germanic Languages and Migration in North America." The journal encourages articles that treat general conceptual issues in theoretical issues in the profession, sociolinguistics, and psycholinguistics. Includes one or two substantial book reviews per issue. A recommended purchase for academic collections at large research institutions. Published by the Society for Germanic Linguistics. URL: http://german.lss.wisc.edu/~sgl

3468. *Journal of Linguistics.* [ISSN: 0022-2267] 1965. 3x/yr. GBP 209. Ed(s): Robert D Borsley, Caroline Heycock. Cambridge University Press, The Edinburgh Bldg, Shaftesbury Rd, Cambridge, CB2 8RU, United Kingdom; journals@cambridge.org; http://www.cambridge.org/uk. Illus., index, adv. Sample. Refereed. Circ: 2200. Vol. ends: Nov. Microform: PQC. Reprint: PSC. *Indexed:* A01, A22, AmHI, ArtHuCI, BAS, BRI, E01, FR, IBSS, LT&LA, MLA-IB, P02. *Bk. rev.:* 10-12, 3-6 pages. *Aud.:* Ac, Sa.

Published for the Linguistics Association of Great Britain (www.lagb.org.uk), this journal is strongly oriented toward the theoretical side of linguistics research. The journal favors no particular theoretical approach, but aims to provide a forum for original, cutting-edge contributions to, and discussion of, advances in all branches of theoretical linguistics. All covered in this journal are syntax, morphology, phonology, phonetics, semantics, and pragmatics, as well as historical, sociological, computational, and psychological aspects of language and linguistic theory. In keeping with the journal's status as the premier journal of general theoretical linguistics, some 30 book reviews are included in every issue. The ecumenical scope of this journal makes it a core selection for academic linguistic collections.

3469. *Journal of Phonetics.* [ISSN: 0095-4470] 1973. bi-m. EUR 938. Ed(s): K de Jong. Academic Press, 32 Jamestown Rd, Camden, London, NW1 7BY, United Kingdom; corporate.sales@elsevier.com; http://www.elsevier.com/. Adv. Sample. Refereed. Reprint: PSC. *Indexed:* A01, A22, ArtHuCI, BEL&L, E01, LT&LA, MLA-IB, PsycInfo. *Bk. rev.:* 0-3, length varies. *Aud.:* Ac, Sa.

This is the chief journal for the publication of research dealing with the phonetic aspects of language and communication. Articles are of either an experimental or theoretical nature. The journal also welcomes articles on "technological and/or pathological topics, or papers of an interdisciplinary nature...provided that linguistic-phonetic principles underlie the work reported." Among the topics covered by the journal are: "speech production, acoustics, and perception; phonetic aspects of psycholinguistics; speech synthesis; automatic speech recognition; descriptive phonetics; [and] speech and language." Occasional theme issues are published: the articles in a recent number of the journal variously addressed the topic, "Using the lens of phonetic experience to resolve phonological forms." This is an essential purchase for academic linguistic collections.

3470. *Journal of Semantics.* [ISSN: 0167-5133] 1982. q. EUR 380. Ed(s): Philippe Schlenker. Oxford University Press, Great Clarendon St, Oxford, OX2 6DP, United Kingdom; enquiry@oup.co.uk; http://www.oxfordjournals.org/. Adv. Sample. Refereed. Reprint: PSC. *Indexed:* A01, A22, AmHI, ArtHuCI, BEL&L, E01, FR, IBSS, LT&LA, MLA-IB. *Bk. rev.:* 0-1, length varies. *Aud.:* Ac, Sa.

This journal is concerned with the production of meaning in language usage. International in scope, it publishes analyses that bring philosophical, psychological, and linguistic perspectives to bear on the problem of meaning in natural languages. In keeping with this interdisciplinary flavor, the journal also publishes articles that are informed by the perspectives of research in logic, artificial intelligence, and anthropology. "Concept types," "interadjectival comparison," "expressive modification," and "uninterpretable pronouns" are examples of the highly focused and technical articles that appear in this journal. Notes, discussions, and book reviews are also regularly featured in this journal. The centrality of semantics within the field of linguistics makes this journal a core purchase for all academic libraries.

Journal of Slavic Linguistics. See Slavic Studies section.

3471. *Laboratory Phonology.* [ISSN: 1868-6346] 2010. 2x/yr. EUR 207. Ed(s): Jennifer Cole. Walter de Gruyter GmbH & Co. KG, Genthiner Str 13, Berlin, 10785, Germany; info@degruyter.com; http://www.degruyter.de. *Aud.:* Ac.

This journal, published by the Association of Laboratory Phonology, presents articles that wield empirical and quantitative methods in the study of spoken and signed language. "Spanish Nasal Assimilation Revisited: A cross-dialect electropalatographic study" may serve as a representative title. According to its web site, the journal aims to bring together "a range of disciplinary perspectives including linguistics, psychology, speech & hearing science, communication science, computer science, electrical & computer engineering, and other related fields." The increased prominence given to empirical methods in the field of linguistics makes this a recommended purchase for libraries at research institutions.

3472. *Language and Education.* [ISSN: 0950-0782] 1987. bi-m. GBP 553 (print & online eds.). Ed(s): Viv Edwards. Routledge, 4 Park Sq, Milton Park, Abingdon, OX14 4RN, United Kingdom; subscriptions@tandf.co.uk; http://www.tandfonline.com. Illus., adv. Sample. Refereed. Reprint: PSC. *Indexed:* A01, A22, ArtHuCI, ERIC, LT&LA, MLA-IB, PsycInfo. *Bk. rev.:* 1-4, 2-5 pages, signed. *Aud.:* Ac.

As the title announces, the subject matter of this journal is the role of language in education, particularly in settings around the world. While the teaching of language is a topic covered by the journal, more broadly the journal publishes articles that deal with the implications for the latest research into language for the process of classroom teaching. The journal is practically oriented in that its discussion of language-issues and their impact on teaching bears on one of three aspects of education: curriculum, pedagogy, and/or evaluation. The journal expressly does not cover the teaching of foreign languages, or English as a foreign language. Yet it does cover the role of language in classroom settings around the world: a recent issue featured discussions of language in the educational process in a Greek pre-school, in nineteenth-century Hong Kong, in rural Africa, in a Chinese High School, in a Brazilian High School, and in Singapore. This journal will be a particularly important addition to collections at institutions with strong departments in education, as well as in linguistics.

3473. *Language and Literature.* [ISSN: 0963-9470] 1992. q. USD 985. Ed(s): Paul Simpson, Geoff Hall. Sage Publications Ltd., 1 Oliver's Yard, 55 City Rd, London, EC1Y 1SP, United Kingdom; info@sagepub.co.uk; http://www.uk.sagepub.com. Sample. Refereed. Reprint: PSC. *Indexed:* A01, A22, AmHI, ArtHuCI, E01, MLA-IB, P61, RILM, SSA. *Bk. rev.:* 1-4, 2-5 pages. *Aud.:* Ac.

The province of this journal is stylistics, which is the formal study of features of literary style. The journal has a wide scope, covering not only the stylistic analysis of literature, but also of non-literary texts, the connections between stylistics and other theoretical approaches to literature, and the implications of these issues for the teaching of literature to both native and non-native speakers. A recent special brought stylistic analysis to the issue of pedagogy, with articles on such topics as "A genre and move analysis of written feedback in higher education" and "Personal style and epistemic stance in classroom discussion." The journal provides a "Notes and Comments" section for the discussion of issues of current relevance to the field, as well as between five and ten book reviews per issue. A supplementary purchase for academic library collections, owing to the specialized nature of its focus.

3474. *Language in Society.* [ISSN: 0047-4045] 1972. 5x/yr. GBP 294. Ed(s): Barbara Johnstone. Cambridge University Press, The Edinburgh Bldg, Shaftesbury Rd, Cambridge, CB2 8RU, United Kingdom; journals@cambridge.org; http://www.cambridge.org/uk. Illus., adv. Sample. Refereed. Vol. ends: Dec. Microform: PQC. Reprint: PSC. *Indexed:* A01, A22, AbAn, AmHI, BAS, BEL&L, BRI, CBRI, E01, IBSS, LT&LA, MLA-IB, P02, P61, PsycInfo, RILM, SSA. *Bk. rev.:* 10-15, 2-4 pages; signed. *Aud.:* Ac.

This is the leading journal for the study of sociolinguistics, the discipline that investigates the social aspects of language. The subject matter of the journal is accordingly as diverse as the range of human social situations in which language is employed. Two recent articles, "The voice of others: Identity alterity and gender normativity among gay men in Israel" and "The dynamics of embodied participation and language choice in multilingual meetings." While the core of the journal is the empirical focus on how language is used in social situations, its pieces also maintain a "general theoretical, comparative, or methodological interest to students and scholars in sociolinguistics, linguistic anthropology, and related fields." The journal offers extensive reviews, book notes, and occasional discussion sections on topics of moment as well as theme issues. A core journal, recommended for all academic libraries.

3475. *Language Learning and Development.* [ISSN: 1547-5441] 2005. q. GBP 277 (print & online eds.). Ed(s): Susan Goldin-Meadow. Psychology Press, 325 Chestnut St, Ste 800, Philadelphia, PA 19106; orders@taylorandfrancis.com; http://www.psypress.com. Adv. Sample. Reprint: PSC. *Indexed:* A22, E01, ERIC, MLA-IB, PsycInfo. *Aud.:* Ac.

Published by The Society for Language Development, this widely interdisciplinary journal publishes articles that explore the phenomenon of language learning from a range of current perspectives—linguistic, psychological, cognitive, anthropological, and others—and employ, as stated on the journal's web site, "experimental, observational, ethnographic, comparative, neuro-scientific, and formal methods of investigation." Two recent articles that give an idea of the variety of approaches to be found in the pages of this journal are "When Mommy Comes to the Rescue of Statistics: Infants Combine Top-Down and Bottom-Up Cues to Segment Speech" and "Pragmatic Bootstrapping: A Neural Network Model of Vocabulary Acquisition." Recent issues have also included "commentary" and "response" sections. A recommended purchase for any large research collection.

3476. *Language Variation and Change.* [ISSN: 0954-3945] 1989. 3x/yr. GBP 158. Ed(s): Rena Torres Cacoullos, William Labov. Cambridge University Press, The Edinburgh Bldg, Shaftesbury Rd, Cambridge, CB2 8RU, United Kingdom; journals@cambridge.org; http://www.cambridge.org/uk. Illus., adv. Sample. Refereed. Circ: 800. Microform: PQC. Reprint: PSC. *Indexed:* A22, ArtHuCI, E01, LT&LA, MLA-IB, P61, SSA. *Aud.:* Ac.

This journal is devoted to the sub-branch of linguistics that studies both historical and systemic variation in language usage. The articles consider "actual-speech production (or writing)" and develop general theoretical, conceptual, and methodological considerations out of their analyses of such particular cases. The articles in this journal range widely over language and linguistic situations, and a good portion of them feature quantitative analysis of linguistic features and patterns. This journal would be a supplemental purchase for most academic libraries.

3477. *Language (Washington).* [ISSN: 0097-8507] 1925. q. USD 135 (Individuals, USD 145; Free to members). Ed(s): Greg Carlson. Linguistic Society of America, 1325 18th St, N W, Ste. 211, Washington, DC 20036; lsa@lsadc.org; http://www.lsadc.org. Illus., adv. Sample. Refereed. Vol. ends: Dec. Reprint: PSC. *Indexed:* A01, A22, A47, ABS&EES, AmHI, ArtHuCI, BEL&L, BRI, E01, ERIC, FR, IBSS, LT&LA, MLA-IB, P02. *Bk. rev.:* 5-9, 1-4 pages. *Aud.:* Ac.

Published by the Linguistics Society of America since 1924, this is a leading, authoritative publication in the field. In addition to original research in linguistics, the journal also regularly includes short reports, review articles, book reviews, and book notices. Its special focus is theoretical linguistics, but all aspects of linguistic research are represented here, including historical,

sociological, and pragmatic orientations, among others. At least one author of each article must be a member of the LSA (www.lsadc.org). Highly recommended for academic library collections at all levels.

3478. *Languages in Contrast: international journal for contrastive linguistics.* [ISSN: 1387-6759] 1998. s-a. EUR 197 combined subscription (print & online eds.). Ed(s): Hilde Hasselgaard, Silvia Bernardini. John Benjamins Publishing Co., PO Box 36224, Amsterdam, 1020 ME, Netherlands; subscription@benjamins.nl; http://www.benjamins.com. Refereed. *Indexed:* FR, MLA-IB. *Aud.:* Ac, Sa.

Boundedness and relativity in English and Russian. Puns in English and German. Spanish versus Portuguese subordinate clauses introduced by *para*. These are examples of the sort of comparative studies published in this journal. Articles may concentrate on "any aspect of language" as well as "sociolinguistics and psycholinguistics," and these in turn may be discussed from a wide range of interdisciplinary approaches, including "translation, lexicography, computational linguistics, language teaching, literary and linguistic computing, [and] literary and cultural studies." *Languages in Contrast* also aims to provide a forum for a consideration of the theoretical place of comparative studies within the larger context of linguistics. A recent special issue of this journal explored the relationships between contrastive linguistics and other approaches. The articles in this journal are specialized, yet the subject covered by the journal as a whole is of broad interest. A recommended purchase for academic linguistic collections.

3479. *Lingua.* [ISSN: 0024-3841] 1947. 12x/yr. EUR 1510. Ed(s): J Rooryck. Elsevier BV, Radarweg 29, PO Box 211, Amsterdam, 1000 AE, Netherlands; JournalsCustomerServiceEMEA@elsevier.com; http://www.elsevier.com. Illus., index, adv. Sample. Refereed. Microform: PQC. *Indexed:* A01, A22, AmHI, ArtHuCI, BAS, FR, LT&LA, MLA-IB. *Bk. rev.:* 0-3, 5-10 pages. *Aud.:* Ac, Sa.

This general journal ranges over all topics in the field of linguistics. Yet while the individual pieces may be highly focused and specialized, the editors require that they have "such general theoretical implications as to be of interest to any linguist," regardless of his or her own subfield. In addition to articles that expound original research, *Lingua* publishes review articles of trends in the field, occasional discussions, and critical book reviews. One forum entitled "Lingua Franca" presents debates on current topics in the field; another, "The Decade In," offers surveys of various topics in linguistics for the non-professional. A special section, under the rubric, "Taking up the Gauntlet," presents debates about current topics of moment in the field. Theme issues are also published, the most recent of which was "Tone and Intonation from a Typological Perspective." Essential for academic linguistic collections.

3480. *Linguistic Analysis.* [ISSN: 0098-9053] 1975. 2x/yr. USD 144. Ed(s): Michael K Brame. Linguistic Analysis, PO Box 2418, Vashon, WA 98070; Info@linguisticanlysis.com. Illus., index, adv. Sample. Refereed. Circ: 1000. *Indexed:* A22, ABS&EES, BAS, CompR, LT&LA, MLA-IB. *Aud.:* Ac, Sa.

This highly cited, core linguistics journal is devoted to the strictly formal approach of language. Thus, the articles analyze language as a pure phenomenon in terms of the basic ingredients of phonology, morphology, syntax, and semantics. Recent pieces include "An Algebraic Approach to Japanese Sentence Structure" and "Invisible Endings of English Adjectives and Nouns." Many numbers of the journal are double issues. Recommended for all academic library collections.

3481. *Linguistic Inquiry.* [ISSN: 0024-3892] 1970. q. USD 432 (print & online eds.). Ed(s): Samuel Jay Keyser, Anne Mark. M I T Press, 55 Hayward St, Cambridge, MA 02142; journals-cs@mit.edu; http://mitpress.mit.edu. Illus., adv. Refereed. Microform: PQC. Reprint: SCH. *Indexed:* A22, ABS&EES, ArtHuCI, BAS, E01, FR, LT&LA, MLA-IB. *Aud.:* Ac.

One of the leading journals in the field, *Linguistic Inquiry* presents articles on a variety of topics within the general area of formal linguistics. The articles present cutting-edge research into fundamental properties of language, while at the same time drawing the larger theoretical implications of those investigations. An example of this approeach is the article, "Making a Pronoun:

Fake Indexicals as Windows into the Properties of Pronouns." Each issue of the journal consists of two or three articles of original research and two other sections: "Squibs and Discussions," which presents short treatments of topics of note, and "Remarks and Replies," which allows for more extended commentary on current developments in the field. Essential for academic libraries at institutions with strong linguistics departments.

3482. The Linguistic Review. [ISSN: 0167-6318] 1981. q. EUR 348. Ed(s): Nancy A Ritter, Harry van der Hulst. De Gruyter Mouton, Genthiner Str 13, Berlin, 10785, Germany; mouton@degruyter.de; http://www.degruyter.com. Illus., adv. Sample. Refereed. Reprint: PSC. *Indexed:* A01, A22, ArtHuCI, BAS, BEL&L, E01, FR, LT&LA, MLA-IB, PsycInfo. *Bk. rev.:* 0-1. *Aud.:* Ac.

As the mission statement of this journal declares, this journal is devoted to the field of linguistics known as generative grammar, that is, the view of language as an underlying set of rules that govern the production of correct utterances in the user. Within that general framework, the topics that are addressed by the articles in this journal are the fundamental aspects of general, formal linguistics: syntax, semantics, phonology, and morphology. The journal also publishes "critical discussions of theoretical linguistics as a branch of cognitive psychology." Also included from time to time are letters to the editor, dissertation abstracts, and reviews of important new books on these areas of the field of linguistics. The journal's web site also encourages potential guest-editors to propose theme issues. The material in this journal is highly specialized, but as it is the important organ for an important subfield of the discipline, it is a recommended purchase for academic linguistics collections.

3483. Linguistics: an interdisciplinary journal of the language sciences. [ISSN: 0024-3949] 1963. bi-m. EUR 613. Ed(s): Johan van der Auwera. De Gruyter Mouton, Genthiner Str 13, Berlin, 10785, Germany; mouton@degruyter.de; http://www.degruyter.com. Illus., adv. Sample. Refereed. Microform: SWZ. Reprint: PSC. *Indexed:* A01, A22, AmHI, ArtHuCI, BAS, BRI, E01, FR, LT&LA, MLA-IB, PsycInfo, RILM. *Bk. rev.:* 3-4, 3-7 pages. *Aud.:* Ac.

This journal is devoted to the formal areas of the field of linguistics: semantics, syntax, morphology, and phonology, although its web site invites articles on neighboring disciplines that have interests for linguists across the spectrum of subspecialties. A recent article, "Lexical typology through similarity semantics: Toward a semantic map of motion verbs" is representative of this strictly formalist approach. Theme issues are regularly published; a recent one consists of articles that offer a gamut of perspectives on language acquisition. A core journal in the field.

3484. Linguistics and Philosophy: a journal of natural language syntax, semantics, logic, pragmatics, and processing. [ISSN: 0165-0157] 1977. bi-m. EUR 843 (print & online eds.). Ed(s): Graeme Forbes, Thomas E Zimmermann. Springer Netherlands, Van Godewijckstraat 30, Dordrecht, 3311 GX, Netherlands; http://www.springer.com. Illus., index, adv. Sample. Refereed. Vol. ends: No. 6. Microform: PQC. Reprint: PSC. *Indexed:* A22, AmHI, ArtHuCI, BRI, E01, FR, IPB, LT&LA, MLA-IB. *Bk. rev.:* Number and length vary. *Aud.:* Ac, Sa.

This journal deals with topics that fall into the wide area of overlap between linguistics and philosophy. It is concerned with philosophical theories of meaning and truth and their relation to the fundamental conceptual questions of the study of language, as well as linguistic and psycholinguistic theories of semantic interpretation and related issues. Its other chief interests include "mathematical and logical properties of natural language and general aspects of computational linguistics," as well as "philosophical questions raised by linguistics as a science." Articles, replies, book reviews, and review articles round out the contents of this journal. While *Linguistics and Philosophy* is not a core journal in either discipline, it covers the common ground between them, and is thus a recommended purchase for university linguistics collections.

3485. The Mental Lexicon. [ISSN: 1871-1340] 2005. 3x/yr. EUR 299 combined subscription (print & online eds.). Ed(s): Gary Libben, Gonia Jarema. John Benjamins Publishing Co., PO Box 36224, Amsterdam, 1020 ME, Netherlands; subscription@benjamins.nl; http://www.benjamins.com. Refereed. *Aud.:* Ac.

According to the mission statement on its web site, this relatively new journal (founded in 2006) publishes research "on the issues of representation and processing of words in the mind and brain." It embraces a variety of perspectives spanning the range of today's approaches to linguistic research, from the formal and developmental to the statistical and neurolinguistic. Two recent articles illustrate this journal's interdisciplinary focus: "Interwoven functionality of the brain's action and language systems," which employs neuroimaging, and "Topological spatial representation within and across languages: IN and ON in Mandarin Chinese and English," which relies on a formal/conceptual approach. Covering a new frontier in the science of language and mind, this journal would be an important addition to collections at major research institutions.

3486. Modern Language Journal: devoted to research and discussion about the learning and teaching of foreign and second languages. [ISSN: 0026-7902] 1916. q. GBP 165. Ed(s): Leo van Lier. Wiley-Blackwell Publishing, Inc., 111 River St, Hoboken, NJ 07030; info@wiley.com; http://onlinelibrary.wiley.com/. Illus., index, adv. Sample. Refereed. Vol. ends: Dec. Microform: PMC; PQC. Reprint: PSC. *Indexed:* A01, A22, ABS&EES, BEL&L, BRI, CBRI, Chicano, E01, ERIC, LT&LA, MLA-IB, P02, PsycInfo. *Bk. rev.:* 20-30, 1-2 pages. *Aud.:* Hs, Ga, Ac.

This is the professional organ of the National Federation of Modern Language Teachers Associations, the organization dedicated to fostering the teaching of foreign languages in the United States. It thus publishes quantitative and qualitative articles of immediate concern to members of the profession, such as "Identity and Activism in Heritage Language Education," and "Acquiring Interactional Competence in a Study Abroad Context: Japanese Language Learners' Use of the Interactional Particle ne." The journal also publishes an array of other types of relevant professional material: response articles, editorials, reviews of scholarly books, textbooks, videotapes, and software, as well as professional news consisting of a calendar of events, a listing of relevant articles published in other journals, and an annual survey of doctoral degrees in all areas concerning foreign and second languages. This highly cited, core journal is essential for academic library collections. See also *TESOL Quarterly, ELT Journal,* and *Studies in Second Language Acquisition.*

3487. Morphology. Formerly (until 2006): *Yearbook of Morphology.* [ISSN: 1871-5621] 1988. 2x/yr. EUR 241 (print & online eds.). Ed(s): Adam Albright. Springer Netherlands, Van Godewijckstraat 30, Dordrecht, 3311 GX, Netherlands; http://www.springer.com. Refereed. Reprint: PSC. *Indexed:* A22, BEL&L, BRI, E01, MLA-IB. *Aud.:* Ac.

Morphology is the area of linguistics that is concerned with how words are formed within and across languages. The journal offers articles that deal with every subfield within this area of linguistics, but it is chiefly concerned with the general implications for an understanding of the place of morphology in the human language faculty. The articles engage in the empirical investigation of the morphological properties of a particular language, but then draw out the larger theoretical implications of this study. An example from a recent issue is the article, "Helping a crocodile to learn German plurals: children's online judgment of actual, potential[,] and illegal plural forms." As additional areas of focus, the journal's web page notes the following topics: "the acquisition of morphological knowledge and its role in language processing[,] as well as computational morphology and neurolinguistic approaches to morphology." This is the only journal devoted to this, a central area of study in the field of linguistics, and therefore it is recommended for all academic linguistics collections.

3488. Natural Language and Linguistic Theory. [ISSN: 0167-806X] 1983. q. EUR 1002 (print & online eds.). Ed(s): Marcel den Dikken. Springer Netherlands, Van Godewijckstraat 30, Dordrecht, 3311 GX, Netherlands; http://www.springer.com. Illus., adv. Sample. Refereed. Vol. ends: Nov. Microform: PQC. Reprint: PSC. *Indexed:* A22, AmHI, ArtHuCI, BEL&L, BRI, E01, FR, LT&LA, MLA-IB. *Bk. rev.:* 0-1, 5,000 words. *Aud.:* Ac.

The express intention of this journal is to bridge the gap between the latest developments in linguistic theory and the more concrete, descriptive accounts of particular languages or linguistic corpora. The recent article "Morphological alternations at the intonational phrase edge: The Case of K'ichee" is an example of such a combination. The journal thus facilitates communication among researchers of different theoretical persuasions. In addition to articles that present innovative research, the journal also features surveys of recent theoretical developments "that facilitate accessibility for a graduate student readership"; replies to recent articles; book reviews; and special theme issues. A recommended journal for academic linguistics collections.

3489. *The Open Applied Linguistics Journal.* [ISSN: 1874-9135] 2008. irreg. Ed(s): Dr. C D Qualls. Bentham Open, PO Box 294, Bussum, AG 1400, Netherlands; subscriptions@benthamscience.org; http://www.benthamscience.com. Refereed. *Aud.:* Ac.

A peer-reviewed, open-access journal that first appeared in 2008, *The Open Applied Linguistics Journal* presents original research articles, reviews, and short articles in all areas of applied linguistics. Articles in the first two years' issues have mostly dealt with subjects related to the teaching of foreign languages, giving the journal's offerings a global flavor. A recent article on the "The Content and Language of Newspaper Articles Related to the Official Ban on Smoking in Greece" illustrates the journal's pragmatic orientation.

3490. *Probus: international journal of Latin and Romance linguistics.* [ISSN: 0921-4771] 1989. s-a. EUR 264. Ed(s): W. Leo Wetzels. De Gruyter Mouton, Genthiner Str 13, Berlin, 10785, Germany; mouton@degruyter.de; http://www.degruyter.com. Adv. Refereed. Reprint: PSC. *Indexed:* A01, A22, AmHI, ArtHuCI, E01, MLA-IB. *Aud.:* Ac.

Covering both historical and systematic linguistics of the Romance family of languages, *Probus* concentrates primarily on the central formal disciplines of phonology, morphology, and syntax, as well as language acquisition and sociolinguistics. Typical articles in this journal explore particular linguistic feature of one of the Romance languages at some state of historical development, and then develop the larger theoretical implications for the field of linguistics as a whole. For example, the article "Losing the neuter: The case of the Spanish demonstratives" is illustrative of this method of inquiry. The journal publishes occasional theme issues. This journal would be a good supplemental purchase for academic linguistics collections at large research institutions.

Slavic and East European Journal. See Slavic Studies section.

3491. *Studies in Second Language Acquisition.* [ISSN: 0272-2631] 1977. q. GBP 231. Ed(s): Susan Gass, Albert Valdman. Cambridge University Press, The Edinburgh Bldg, Shaftesbury Rd, Cambridge, CB2 8RU, United Kingdom; journals@cambridge.org; http://www.cambridge.org/uk. Illus., adv. Sample. Refereed. Vol. ends: Dec. Microform: PQC. Reprint: PSC. *Indexed:* A22, BAS, E01, ERIC, LT&LA, MLA-IB, PsycInfo. *Bk. rev.:* 5-12, 1-2 pages. *Aud.:* Ac.

This journal is devoted to the scientific study of all aspects of second and foreign language learning. *Studies in Second Language Acquisition* contains articles of both theoretical and pedagogical bearing, and analyses that are qualitative and quantitative in approach. The journal also harbors a full range of different types of materials, including a "Notes and Discussion" section, review articles, book reviews, book notices, and a feature entitled "State-of-the-Art," which keep readers apprised of trends in the field. This journal is especially recommended for academic collections at institutions at which the teaching of second and foreign languages is a major area of activity. See also *ELT Journal, Modern Language Journal,* and *TESOL Quarterly.*

3492. *T E S O L Quarterly: a journal for teachers of English to speakers of other languages and of standard English as a second dialect.* [ISSN: 0039-8322] 1967. q. USD 410 (print & online eds.) Individuals, USD 70 (print & online eds.). Ed(s): Diane Belcher, Tomiko Chapman. Wiley-Blackwell Publishing, Inc., 111 River St, Hoboken, NJ 07030; info@wiley.com; http://onlinelibrary.wiley.com/. Illus., adv. Sample. Refereed. Vol. ends: Winter. Microform: PQC. Reprint: PSC. *Indexed:* A22, Chicano, ERIC, LT&LA, MLA-IB. *Bk. rev.:* 4-6, 3-5 pages. *Aud.:* Hs, Ac, Sa.

A professional journal for the publication of original research that bridges the theory and practice of ESOL teaching, *TESOL Quarterly* is a premier vehicle for the study of the psychology and sociology of language learning and language teaching, curriculum design, pedagogy, testing and evaluation, professional preparation/standards, language planning, and research methodology. The articles bring together empirical investigation and theoretical perspective. The recent article "Course-Taking Patterns of Latino ESL Students: Mobility and Mainstreaming in Urban Community Colleges in the United States" is typical, in that it brings local inquiry together with broader concerns. Each issue contains not only research articles, but review articles, book reviews, a forum, and brief reports and summaries. The readership of the journal, according to its web site, consists of ESOL teacher educators, teacher learners, researchers, applied linguists, and ESOL teachers. Especially recommended for academic collections at institutions with robust programs for the teaching of English as a second language. See also *ELT Journal, Modern Language Journal,* and *Studies in Second Language Acquisition.*

Visible Language. See Printing and Graphic Arts section.

Yearbook of Morphology. See *Morphology.*

■ LITERARY REVIEWS

See also Fiction; Literature; Little Magazines; and News and Opinion sections.

Mary Beth Clack, Research Librarian, Widener Library, Harvard University, Cambridge, MA 02138; mclack@fas.harvard.edu.

Laura Farwell Blake, Research Librarian, Widener Library, Harvard University, Cambridge, MA 02138; farwell@fas.harvard.edu.

Lynne Kvinnesland, Public Services Librarian, Trexler Library, DeSales University; Lynne.Kvinnesland@desales.edu

Introduction

Online access to the content of literary reviews continues to grow, with some titles moving exclusively to a web format, and others increasing their presence in that medium while continuing to publish print issues as well. Many reviews are now using social media to generate conversation and interaction among an ever-expanding community of readers and writers. Increasingly, audio and video content is available as well, often in the form of author interviews, or podcasts of writers reading from their work. The online format also allows these publications to provide supplemental content between print issues, or, in the case of some of the online-only titles, to update content continuously rather than publish discrete issues at regular intervals. In addition, archival content is often freely available.

Traditional and longstanding print reviews remain strong as well, however, and provide a stable counterpoint to the experimental and ever-changing world of cyber content. Literary reviews in both formats display a growing interest in the work of international writers, providing readers with a wider variety of perspectives, and globalizing the conversation around contemporary literature as well as social and political issues. The work of foreign writers is usually translated into English, but sometimes printed in the original tongue as well. The craft of translation itself is also receiving some attention. The diversity of content and variety of perspectives continue to make literary reviews a source of lively and engaging reading.

Basic Periodicals

Ga, Ac: *The Antioch Review, The Georgia Review, The Harvard Review, Hudson Review, The Iowa Review, Jacket2, The Kenyon Review, The North American Review, The Paris Review, Prairie Schooner, The Sewanee Review, TriQuarterly, Virginia Quarterly Review, The Yale Review.*

Basic Abstracts and Indexes

Annual Bibliography of English Language and Literature (ABELL), Humanities Index, MLA International Bibliography.

3493. Agni. Formerly (until 1988): *Agni Review.* [ISSN: 1046-218X] 1972. 2x/yr. USD 20 domestic; USD 25 Canada; USD 30 elsewhere. Ed(s): Sven Birkerts. Agni Review, Inc., 236 Bay State Rd, Boston, MA 02215-1403. Adv. Circ: 3000. *Indexed:* AmHI, MLA-IB. *Aud.:* Ga, Ac.

Agni publishes fiction, nonfiction, essays, art, and poetry, including translations, by writers and artists from around the world. Interviews and reviews are also included in each issue, with additional content available on the companion web site. The focus is on work that "provokes perceptions and thoughts that help us understand and respond to our age." Content is regularly republished in the Best American, O. Henry Prize, and Pushcart Prize anthologies.

3494. Alaska Quarterly Review: A literary magazine of consequence. [ISSN: 0737-268X] 1982. s-a. USD 18 domestic. Ed(s): Ronald Spatz. University of Alaska at Anchorage, College of Arts and Sciences, 3211 Providence Dr, Anchorage, AK 99508; ayaqr@uaa.alaska.edu; http://www.uaa.alaska.edu/aqr/. Illus. Vol. ends: Fall/Winter. Microform: PQC. *Indexed:* AmHI. *Aud.:* Ga, Ac.

The award-winning *AQR* has been hailed as "one of the nation's best literary magazines" (*Washington Post Book World*). It features traditional and innovative fiction, short plays, poetry, photo essays, and literary nonfiction, with an occasional "Special Feature" such as the photo mosaic published in the 30th anniversary issue (Spring/Summer 2012). *AQR* content is often included in the leading literary anthologies.

3495. anderbo.com. 2005. irreg. Ed(s): Rick Rofihe. Rick Rofihe, Ed. & Pub., 270 Lafayette St, Ste 1412, New York, NY 10012. *Aud.:* Ga, Ac.

Dubbed "a poor man's New Yorker" by editor-in-chief Rick Rofihe, *Anderbo* publishes short fiction (including excerpts from longer works), poetry, and nonfiction (dubbed "fact") by an international selection of writers. Photographic essays and reviews are also included in this online-only literary journal. Content is continuously updated, rather than published in separate issues, and is freely available. *Anderbo* sponsors annual Poetry and Creative Nonfiction contests, and recently added the Self-Published Book Award. A "links & blogs" feature calls attention to additional material on the web that is of interest to *Anderbo* readers.

3496. The Antioch Review (Yellow Springs). [ISSN: 0003-5769] 1941. q. USD 120 (print & online eds.). Ed(s): Robert S Fogarty. Antioch Review, Inc., c/o Muriel Keyes, PO Box 148, Yellow Springs, OH 45387-0148; mkeyes@antioch.edu. Illus., index. Vol. ends: Fall. *Indexed:* A01, A06, A22, ABS&EES, AmHI, ArtHuCI, BAS, BRI, CBRI, MLA-IB, P02, RILM. *Bk. rev.:* 15-30, 300 words. *Aud.:* Ga, Ac.

The *Antioch Review*, "one of the oldest, continuously publishing literary magazines in America," publishes fiction, essays, and poetry by both new and established writers. Notable is its "commitment to the essay as a form." Of additional interest is the "From our Archives" feature, which highlights an early work of a now well-known author. Over the years, works from such authors as Ralph Ellison, Sylvia Plath, Joyce Carol Oates, Daniel Ellsberg, T. C. Boyle, Gordon Lish, and Raymond Carver have been featured. An "All Fiction" issue is also published annually.

3497. Artful Dodge. [ISSN: 0196-691X] 1979. s-a. USD 10 (Individuals, USD 7). Ed(s): Daniel Bourne. Artful Dodge Publications, Department of English, The College of Wooster, Wooster, OH 44691. Illus. *Indexed:* AmHI, MLA-IB. *Bk. rev.:* Number and length vary. *Aud.:* Ga, Ac.

Artful Dodge focuses on contemporary American and international works "with a strong sense of place and cultural landscape." Content includes poetry, fiction, memoirs, interviews, and "graphica." A "Poets as Translators" feature exposes readers to the work of foreign artists, especially those who hail from Eastern Europe and the Third World. Essays on the craft of translation further highlight this area of literary creativity. The web site provides access to selected content from back issues, as well as the full text to all the interviews. URL: www3.wooster.edu/artfuldodge/default.html

3498. Bellevue Literary Review: a journal of humanity and human experience. [ISSN: 1537-5048] 2001. s-a. USD 15. Ed(s): Dr. Danielle Ofri. New York University School of Medicine, 550 First Ave, OBV-A612, New York, NY 10016. *Indexed:* AmHI. *Aud.:* Ga, Ac.

Published by the Department of Medicine at NYU Langone Medical Center, the *Bellevue Literary Review* features previously unpublished fiction, nonfiction, and poetry that provide "creative interpretations" of themes related to illness, health, and healing. Full-text access to selected content from the print publication is provided on the web site, along with interviews with *BLR* contest winners.

3499. Boulevard: journal of contemporary writing. [ISSN: 0885-9337] 1986. 3x/yr. USD 20. Ed(s): Kelly Leavitt. St. Louis University, 6614 Clayton Rd, Box 325, Richmond Heights, MO 63117. Illus., adv. Sample. *Indexed:* AmHI, MLA-IB. *Aud.:* Ga, Ac.

Housed at Saint Louis University, *Boulevard* includes poetry, fiction, and nonfiction by established authors as well as emerging writers. Recent issues included new work by Joyce Carol Oates, Francine Prose, John Updike, and David Guterson. Under the founding editorship of Richard Burgin, *Boulevard* is widely recognized as one of the leading literary journals to which promising young writers will want to consider submitting their work.

3500. Brick: a literary journal. Supersedes (in 1977: *Applegarth's Folly.* [ISSN: 0382-8565] 1973. s-a. CAD 38 for 2 yrs. domestic; USD 38 for 2 yrs. domestic; CAD 41 for 2 yrs. United States. Ed(s): Nadia Szilvassy. Brick, PO Box 609, Toronto, ON M5S 2Y4, Canada. Illus., adv. *Indexed:* BRI, C37, CBCARef, MLA-IB. *Bk. rev.:* Number and length vary. *Aud.:* Ga, Ac.

This journal is based in Toronto, and each issue of *Brick* is a enchanting cornucopia of contemporary writing and visual art. The editors' aim is to bring together "the most invigorating and challenging literary essays, interviews, memoirs, travelogues, belles lettres, and unusual musings we can get our hands on." Selections include the works of a wide array of international writers and artists, and are often accompanied by photographs and delightful illustrations.

3501. Chicago Review. [ISSN: 0009-3696] 1946. q. USD 25 domestic; USD 35 in Central America; USD 55 elsewhere. Ed(s): P Genesius Durica, V Joshua Adams. Chicago Review, 5801 S Kenwood Ave, Chicago, IL 60637; http://humanities.uchicago.edu/humanities/reviews. Illus. Refereed. Microform: PQC. *Indexed:* A01, A22, ABS&EES, AmHI, ArtHuCI, BAS, BRI, MLA-IB, P02, RILM. *Bk. rev.:* 4-9, 2-6 pages; signed. *Aud.:* Ga, Ac.

Now in its 66th year of publication, the *Chicago Review* includes poetry, fiction (both complete and excerpted), essays, reviews, editorial notes, and some photography. An introductory essay is now a part of each issue. Readers will find an international selection of works by both new and well-known authors. Special issues appear regularly, including those devoted to specific national literatures. Most recently, these included issues devoted to new Italian, German, and Polish writing. An online archive is available at the web site.

3502. Colorado Review: a journal of contemporary literature. Former titles (until 1985): *Colorado State Review;* (until 1977): *TransPacific;* (until 1969): *Colorado State Review.* [ISSN: 1046-3348] 1956. 3x/yr. USD 24 domestic; USD 32 Canada; USD 44 elsewhere. Ed(s): Stephanie G'Schwind. Colorado State University, English Department, Colorado State University, Fort Collins, CO 80523; http://www.colostate.edu/Dept/English. Adv. *Indexed:* AmHI, BRI, MLA-IB. *Bk. rev.:* Number and length vary. *Aud.:* Ga, Ac, Sa.

Published by the Center for Literary Publishing at Colorado State University, the *Colorado Review* includes contemporary short fiction, nonfiction, and poetry, and reviews. The web site provides access to selected content from the print publication, as well as an editor's blog that posts additional commentary, author interviews, and podcasts of writers reading from their own works. Home of the annual Nelligan Prize for Short Fiction, and the Colorado Prize for Poetry, the *Colorado Review* is "equally interested in work by both new and established writers."

3503. Conjunctions. [ISSN: 0278-2324] 1982. s-a. USD 40. Ed(s): Micaela Morrissette, Bradford Morrow. Bard College, Publication Department, PO Box 5000, Annandale On Hudson, NY 12504; admission@bard.edu; http://www.bard.edu. *Indexed:* AmHI, MLA-IB, RILM. *Aud.:* Ga, Ac.

Housed at Bard College, *Conjunctions* publishes innovative fiction, poetry, criticism, drama, art, and interviews by "writers and artists whose work challenges accepted forms and modes of expression." Most issues are themed. Recent themes included obsession, kin, voyages, and urban life. Translated work from international artists is also included. Selected content from back issues is available online, often in audio format. An online supplement, *Web Conjunctions* adds new content on a weekly basis.

3504. *The Cortland Review: an online literary magazine in real audio.* [ISSN: 1524-6744] 1997. q. Free. Ed(s): Amy MacLennan, Ginger Murchison. Cortland Review, 527 Third Ave #279, New York, NY 10016. *Bk. rev.:* Number and length vary. *Aud.:* Ga, Ac.

This journal was founded in 1997 and has "twice been distinguished with a Forbes 'Best of the Web' citation." The editors of *The Cortland Review* have chosen an online-only format because it "honors the tradition that poetry is an oral art and allows for a more intimate connection between poet and audience than print alone." Content is available in full text and audio back to 1998. The primary focus is on poetry, but short fiction, essays, interviews, and book reviews appear, as well. Well-known poets are regularly invited to guest-edit issues, which then feature the work of other established poets. Other issues feature the work of new and unpublished writers.

3505. *Critical Quarterly.* [ISSN: 0011-1562] 1959. q. GBP 265. Ed(s): Kate Mellor, Nigella Lawson. Wiley-Blackwell Publishing Ltd., The Atrium, Southern Gate, Chichester, PO19 8SQ, United Kingdom; customer@wiley.com; http://www.wiley.com/. Illus. Sample. Refereed. Vol. ends: Dec. Reprint: PSC. *Indexed:* A01, A22, AmHI, ArtHuCI, BEL&L, BRI, CBRI, E01, MLA-IB, P02, RILM. *Aud.:* Ga, Ac.

Edited by Colin MacCabe at the University of Pittsburgh, each issue of *Critical Quarterly* provides a selection of critical analyses of works in the literary canon alongside poetry and fiction by both established and emerging writers. Special themed issues appear periodically. Recent topics have included "Essentialism in Science and Culture" and "Food." *Critical Quarterly* also has a book series "which aims to bring the most original voices in the humanities to the widest possible audience."

3506. *The Dalhousie Review: a Canadian journal of literature and opinion.* [ISSN: 0011-5827] 1921. 3x/yr. CAD 35.50 (Individuals, CAD 22.50). Ed(s): Anthony Stewart. Dalhousie University Press, Ltd., Dalhousie University, Halifax, NS B3H 4R2, Canada. Illus., index. Refereed. Vol. ends: Winter. Microform: MML. *Indexed:* A01, A22, ABS&EES, AmHI, ArtHuCI, BAS, BEL&L, BRI, C37, CBCARef, CBRI, MLA-IB, P02, RILM. *Bk. rev.:* 2-8, 2-3 pages; signed. *Aud.:* Ga, Ac.

Housed at Dalhousie University in Nova Scotia and in continual operation since its founding in 1921, *The Dalhousie Review* publishes a variety of short fiction, creative nonfiction, and poetry by an international selection of authors, as well as articles in such fields as history, literature, political science, philosophy, sociology, performing arts, and visual culture. Current editor Anthony Stewart has brought the journal into the electronic age, offering online subscriptions, and creating a digital archive of past issues.

3507. *Denver Quarterly.* Formerly (until 1977): *The University of Denver Quarterly.* [ISSN: 0011-8869] 1966. q. USD 29. Ed(s): Laird Hunt. University of Denver, Department of English, 2000 E Ashbury, Denver, CO 80208; kheeps@du.edu; http://www.ud.edu/. Illus., index, adv. Vol. ends: Dec. Microform: PQC. *Indexed:* A22, AmHI, MLA-IB. *Bk. rev.:* 0-3, 3-13 pages; signed. *Aud.:* Ga, Ac.

Based at the University of Denver, the *Denver Quarterly* publishes fiction, essays, interviews, reviews, and poetry, including translations. Under the editorship of Bin Ramke for 17 years, the *Denver Quarterly* will welcome Laird Hunt as the new editor in Fall 2012. An additional point of interest is the cover art, each issue featuring a contemporary and often experimental work by either an American or international artist.

3508. *Fence.* [ISSN: 1097-9980] 1998. s-a. USD 17. Ed(s): Rebecca Wolff. Fence Magazine, Inc., Science Library 320, University at Albany, Albany, NY 12222; fencesubmissions@gmail.com; http://www.fenceportal.org. Adv. *Indexed:* MLA-IB. *Aud.:* Ga, Ac.

Affiliated with the New York State Writers Institute, *Fence* publishes poetry, fiction, art, and criticism. Founded in 1998 by current editor Rebecca Wolff, *Fence* aims "to redefine the terms of accessibility by publishing challenging writing distinguished by idiosyncrasy and intelligence." The web site provides access to selected content from the print edition, as well as supplemental multimedia material (dubbed "Surplus") and book reviews from the "Constant Critic" blog. Fence also sponsors annual book prizes for book-length collections of previously unpublished poetry, and new in 2013 will be the Fence Modern Prize in Prose.

Fiction. See Fiction: General/Mystery and Detective/General section.

3509. *Field: contemporary poetry and poetics.* [ISSN: 0015-0657] 1969. s-a. USD 16 domestic; USD 20 Canada; USD 25 elsewhere. Ed(s): Martha Collins, Linda Slocum. Oberlin College Press, 50 N Professor St, Oberlin, OH 44074; oc.press@oberlin.edu; http://www.oberlin.edu/ocpress/. Microform: PQC. *Indexed:* A22, ABS&EES, AmHI, BEL&L, MLA-IB. *Bk. rev.:* Number and length vary. *Aud.:* Ac, Sa.

Field is subtitled "Contemporary Poetry and Poetics," and each issue contains over 40 poems, accompanied by four or five review-essays. Symposia also appear regularly. The journal was founded in 1969 and is published twice yearly by Oberlin College Press. The editors do not limit selections by style or theme. This journal is included in CLMP's Lit Mag Adoption Program, and teachers can get subscriptions for their students at greatly-reduced rates. *Field* also offers an annual Poetry Prize.

3510. *Fulcrum (Cambridge): an annual of poetry and aesthetics.* [ISSN: 1534-7877] 2002. a. USD 42 (Individuals, USD 17). Ed(s): Philip Nikolayev, Katia Kapovich. Fulcrum Poetry Press, Inc., 138 Larch Rd, Cambridge, MA 02138. Adv. *Aud.:* Ga, Ac.

Hailed by literary editors and reviewers around the world as a "must-read" journal, *Fulcrum* provides a generous (600+ page) selection of poetry, critical and philosophical essays, debates, and art in each massive issue. With a mission to generate "global cross-talk on vital issues among poets, critics, philosophers, artists, psychologists and other humanists," *Fulcrum* publishes the work of writers and artists "from all regions populated by the English language."

3511. *The Georgia Review: poetry, art, fiction, essays, reviews.* [ISSN: 0016-8386] 1947. q. USD 45 combined subscription (print & online eds.). Ed(s): Stephen Corey. University of Georgia, Georgia Review, 285 S Jackson St, The University of Georgia, Athens, GA 30602; http://www.ugd.edu/garev. Illus., index. Sample. Vol. ends: Winter. Microform: PQC. *Indexed:* A01, A22, AmHI, ArtHuCI, BEL&L, BRI, CBRI, MLA-IB, P02, RILM. *Bk. rev.:* 4-11, 1-25 pages; signed. *Aud.:* Ga, Ac.

Founded in 1947, the award-winning *Georgia Review* includes short stories, general-interest essays, poems, reviews, and visual art from a variety of contemporary writers ranging from the unpublished to the Pulitzer-Prize winning. Content in *The Georgia Review* is regularly republished in the annual "best of" anthologies. A five-time recipient of a GAMMA Award for editorial and design excellence, this acclaimed journal is noteworthy as well for the high quality and visual appeal of the print publication. Digital subscriptions are also available.

3512. *The Gettysburg Review.* [ISSN: 0898-4557] 1988. q. USD 12 domestic. Ed(s): Peter Stitt. Gettysburg College, 300 N Washington St, Gettysburg, PA 17325; http://www.gettysburg.edu. Illus., index, adv. Vol. ends: Winter. *Indexed:* A01, A22, AmHI, BRI, MLA-IB, RILM. *Aud.:* Ga, Ac.

Celebrating its 25th anniversary this year (2012), *The Gettysburg Review* is committed to "seeking out and publishing the very best contemporary poetry, fiction, essays, essay-reviews, and art...." The highly selective editorial policy has resulted in a publication renowned for its high literary quality and award-winning editing and design. Many works first published in *The Gettysburg Review* have reappeared in well-known prize anthologies. Selected content is also available online.

3513. The Harvard Review. Incorporates (in 1992): *Harvard Book Review;* Which was formerly: *Erato.* [ISSN: 1077-2901] 1992. s-a. USD 30. Ed(s): Christina Thompson. Harvard University, Lamont Library, Harvard University, Cambridge, MA 02138; http://www.harvard.edu. Illus., adv. *Indexed:* ABS&EES, AmHI, BRI, MLA-IB. *Bk. rev.:* Number and length vary. *Aud.:* Ga, Ac.

This is a major American literary journal; each issue of *The Harvard Review* opens with a thoughtful editorial by editor Christina Thompson, followed by a selection of fiction, essays, poetry, and visual art from an international and eclectic selection of writers and artists. Contributors have included such literary lights as Arthur Miller, Joyce Carol Oates, Seamus Heaney, Jorie Graham, John Updike, John Ashbery, Alice Hoffman, and Gore Vidal, as well as promising new writers. A monthly online supplement, *Harvard Review Online,* publishes book reviews and additional poetry.

3514. The Hudson Review: a magazine of literature and the arts. [ISSN: 0018-702X] 1948. q. USD 44 (Individuals, USD 36). Ed(s): Paula Deitz. Hudson Review, Inc., 684 Park Ave, New York, NY 10021. Illus., index, adv. Circ: 3500. Vol. ends: Winter. Microform: MIM; PQC. *Indexed:* A01, A06, A22, ABS&EES, AmHI, ArtHuCI, BAS, BRI, CBRI, MLA-IB, P02, RILM. *Bk. rev.:* 5-7, 2-11 pages; signed. *Aud.:* Ga, Ac.

Founded in 1948, *The Hudson Review* examines the connections between contemporary literature and American intellectual and cultural life. Fiction, poetry, essays, and literary criticism represent and explore new developments in these areas. The arts—including visual art, theater, dance, film, and music—receive international treatment.

3515. The Iowa Review. [ISSN: 0021-065X] 1970. 3x/yr. USD 25; USD 40. Ed(s): Russell Scott Valentino. University of Iowa, College of Liberal Arts & Scirences, 308 English-Philosophy Bldg, University of Iowa, Iowa City, IA 52242; english@uiowa.edu; http://english.uiowa.edu/. Illus., index, adv. Microform: PQC. *Indexed:* A01, A22, ABS&EES, AmHI, BEL&L, BRI, MLA-IB, RILM. *Bk. rev.:* 2, 2-4 pages; signed. *Aud.:* Ga, Ac.

Housed at the University of Iowa, home of the Writers Workshop as well as the oldest MFA program devoted to literary translation in the United States, *The Iowa Review* publishes the work of Iowa writers as well as a mix of poems, stories, and essays by an international selection of authors. Artwork and interviews are also included. The web site provides access to additional interviews, selected content from the print edition, an archive of book reviews, and the TIR Forum on Literature and Translation.

3516. Jacket 2. Formerly (until 2011): *Jacket.* [ISSN: 2167-2326] 1997. q. Free. University of Pennsylvania, 3451 Walnut St, Philadelphia, PA 19104; http://www.upenn.edu. *Indexed:* MLA-IB. *Aud.:* Ga, Ac, Sa.

In 2011, *Jacket* evolved into *Jacket2,* gaining a new home (University of Pennyslvania) and a new editor (Michael A. Hennessey). This journal has collaborated with PennSound, and thus content has been expanded to include audio recordings of poetry performance, discussion, and criticism. Freely available online and updated continuously, *Jacket2* publishes articles, reviews, interviews, discussions and collaborative responses, archival documents, podcasts, and descriptions of poetry symposia and projects. URL: http://jacket2.org/

3517. Jewish Quarterly. [ISSN: 0449-010X] 1953. q. GBP 166 (print & online eds.). Taylor & Francis, 4 Park Sq, Milton Park, Abingdon, OX14 4RN, United Kingdom; subscriptions@tandf.co.uk; http://www.tandfonline.com. Illus., index, adv. Circ: 3000 Controlled. Microform: PQC. *Indexed:* A22, IJP, MLA-IB, RILM. *Bk. rev.:* Number and length vary. *Aud.:* Ga, Ac.

Based in the United Kingdom, the *Jewish Quarterly* provides readers with a unique blend of essays, fiction, poetry, and satire on topics related to contemporary Jewish culture. The editors seek to challenge and inform, but also to entertain. The online format is very interactive. Readers will also find commentary on art, music, film, history, and Judaism, as well as book reviews.

3518. The Kenyon Review: an international journal of literature, culture, and the arts. [ISSN: 0163-075X] 1939. q. USD 30. Ed(s): Tyler Meier, David H Lynn. The Kenyon Review, Finn House, 102 W. Wiggin St, Kenyon College, Gambier, OH 43022; http://www.kenyon.edu. Illus., index. Refereed. *Indexed:* A01, A06, A22, AmHI, ArtHuCI, BRI, CBRI, MLA-IB, P02, RILM. *Bk. rev.:* 1-2, 7-11 pages; signed. *Aud.:* Ga, Ac.

Founded in 1939, *The Kenyon Review* publishes fiction, nonfiction, drama, and poetry. Content includes international writing in translation. The *KR*'s mission is to publish "the great, highly distinguished authors of our moment—alongside stunning new talents." A very interactive online supplement gives readers access to forums, podcasts, and a daily blog. Cover photography often highlights the work of an international photographer. The *KR* sponsors annual contests for Short Fiction, the Earthworks Prize for Indigenous Poetry, and the Patricia Grodd Poetry Prize for Young Writers (high school sophomores and juniors). It also offers two-year KR Fellowships to "exceptional writers in the early stages of their career."

3519. The Literary Review: an international journal of contemporary writing. [ISSN: 0024-4589] 1957. q. USD 18 domestic; USD 21 foreign. Ed(s): Minna Proctor. Fairleigh Dickinson University, Literary Review, 285 Madison Ave, Madison, NJ 07940; grad@fdu.edu; http://www.fdu.edu/. Refereed. Microform: MIM; PQC. *Indexed:* A01, A22, ABS&EES, AmHI, ArtHuCI, BRI, MASUSE, MLA-IB, P02, RILM. *Bk. rev.:* 4-5. *Aud.:* Ga, Ac.

With each quarterly issue, *The Literary Review* publishes a selection of poetry and fiction loosely related to a theme. Recent themes included "Lives of the Saints," "The Rat's Nest" (collaboration), and "The Rogue Idea." Themes are "suggestive rather than prescriptive." An essay, an interview, and several book reviews are also included in each issue. Submissions from international writers are especially welcome. *TLR* includes an online supplement, TLR Web, where the reader will find additional interviews, book reviews, and announcements of forthcoming events.

3520. Massachusetts Review: a quarterly of literature, the arts and public affairs. [ISSN: 0025-4878] 1959. q. USD 37 (Individuals, USD 27). Ed(s): Aaron Hellem, David Lenson. Massachusetts Review, Inc., South College, University of Massachusetts, Amherst, MA 01003. Illus., index. Refereed. Microform: PQC. *Indexed:* A01, A07, A22, ABS&EES, AmHI, ArtHuCI, BRI, MLA-IB, P02, RILM. *Aud.:* Ga, Ac.

Distinctive in its social engagement with the leading issues of our time, *The Massachusetts Review* publishes a variety of poetry and fiction side-by-side with essays that are often culturally and politically oriented. Special themed issues appear occasionally, and have been devoted to such topics as civil rights, women's rights, and most recently, casualty. The visual arts are also represented. *The Massachusetts Review* sponsors the annual Anne Halley Poetry Prize and the recently-established Jules Chametzky Translation Prize. The work of both established and emerging writers is welcomed, and the editors are particularly interested in the work of international writers.

3521. Michigan Quarterly Review. Supersedes in part (in 1962): *Michigan Alumnus.* [ISSN: 0026-2420] 1894. q. USD 25 domestic; USD 30 foreign; USD 7 newsstand/cover. Ed(s): Vicki Lawrence, Laurence Goldstein. University of Michigan, Law School, 0576 Rackham Bldg, 915 Washington St, Ann Arbor, MI 48109; michlaw.pr@umich.edu; http://www.law.umich.edu. Illus., index. Refereed. Vol. ends: Fall. Microform: PQC. *Indexed:* A07, A22, ABS&EES, AmHI, ArtHuCI, BAS, BEL&L, BRI, CBRI, MLA-IB, P02, RILM. *Bk. rev.:* 1-3, 5-16 pages; signed. *Aud.:* Ga, Ac.

Flagship journal of the University of Michigan, the *Michigan Quarterly Review* is an interdisciplinary journal that combines creative writing with critical essays on literary, cultural, social, and political topics. Aiming for an audience both within and beyond the academy, each issue includes a selection of essays, interviews, memoirs, fiction, poetry, and book reviews. Some issues are themed; past topics have included Bookishness, Motown, and Vietnam. *MQR* publishes work by both established and emerging writers, including essayists and scholars. Readers can access selected content online.

3522. The Minnesota Review: a journal of committed writing; fiction, poetry, essays, reviews. [ISSN: 0026-5667] 1960. s-a. USD 88. Ed(s): Janell Watson. Duke University Press, 905 W Main St, Ste 18 B, PO Box 90660, Durham, NC 27701; subscriptions@dukeupress.edu; http://www.dukeupress.edu. Illus., adv. Microform: PQC. Reprint: PSC. *Indexed:* AmHI, ArtHuCI, BRI, CBRI, MLA-IB, P02. *Bk. rev.:* 7, 6-16 pages; signed. *Aud.:* Ga, Ac.

The Minnesota Review publishes a lively mix of contemporary poetry and short fiction alongside interviews, articles, and review essays that "contextualize, historicize, and assess the intellectual, institutional, and political issues of concern to the critical humanities." Issues frequently include a "Special Focus" section devoted to a topic of interest to humanities scholars. Recent topics included "Global English," "International Cultural Studies," and "Franco-Italian Political Theory."

3523. The Missouri Review. [ISSN: 0191-1961] 1978. q. USD 24. Ed(s): Speer Morgan. University of Missouri at Columbia, 357 McReynolds Hall, Columbia, MO 65211; visitus@missouri.edu; http://www.missouri.edu/. Illus., index, adv. *Indexed:* A22, AmHI, E01, MLA-IB, RILM. *Bk. rev.:* 11-18, 1-5 pages; signed. *Aud.:* Ga, Ac.

Founded in 1978, *The Missouri Review* publishes poetry, fiction, and nonfiction of general interest. Content is often selected for inclusion in leading literary anthologies such as *Best American Short Stories* and *The Pushcart Prize*. Some issues include a "Special Feature" such as a historical document of literary significance, or a previously unpublished work by a well-known author of the past. The web site provides access to a blog, a "Poem of the Week," and podcasts, including interviews and author readings. An annual Editor's Prize is awarded, and unique to this publication, an Audio Contest is held each year.

3524. New Letters: a magazine of writing and art. Former titles (until 1971): *The University Review;* (until 1963): *The University of Kansas City Review.* [ISSN: 0146-4930] 1934. q. USD 30. Ed(s): Robert Stewart. New Letters, 5101 Rockhill Road, Kansas City, MO 64110. Illus., adv. *Indexed:* A22, AmHI, BRI, MLA-IB. *Aud.:* Ga, Ac.

New Letters publishes essays, memoirs, articles, poetry, fiction, interviews, reviews, commentaries, and artwork by both new and established writers and artists. The print quarterly is supplemented by "New Letters on the Air," a nationally-syndicated, award-winning radio show that features weekly interviews with poets and writers. At present, over 1,200 of these programs may be accessed from the *New Letters* web site. A *New Letters* TV show is also available. The magazine also sponsors three annual writing contests, and two summer writing workshops. URL: www.newletters.org

3525. New Millennium Writings. [ISSN: 1086-7678] 1996. a. USD 12 per issue. Ed(s): Don Williams. New Messenger Writing and Publishing, NMW Rm M2, PO Box 2463, Knoxville, TN 37901. Illus. Sample. *Aud.:* Ga.

Founded in 1996, *New Millennium Writings* describes itself as "a journal filled with vibrant imagery, word-craft and pure story-telling talent." Content features the works of winners of the twice-annual *NMW* contests in fiction, short-short fiction, nonfiction, and poetry. The creative work of new writers is complemented by profiles and interviews with established writers. Much of the content is accessible from the web site. URL: www.newmillenniumwritings.com/

3526. The New Renaissance: an international magazine of ideas and opinions, emphasizing literature & the arts. [ISSN: 0028-6575] 1968. s-a. USD 42. Ed(s): Louise T Reynolds. Friends of the New Renaissance, Inc., 26 Heath Rd, 11, Arlington, MA 02474. Illus., index. *Indexed:* AmHI, MLA-IB. *Bk. rev.:* 0-2, 5-7 pages; signed. *Aud.:* Ga, Ac.

The New Renaissance describes itself as "an independent, unsponsored, eclectic literary magazine." Readers will find here a diverse array of genres, including fiction, poetry, art, essays, and book reviews. A political or sociological topic is also presented in the lead article of each issue. Recent topics have included the hidden economics of youth violence, Putin's heritage, and polluted waters in the Bengal Delta. Foreign artists are especially well-represented in this publication, which regularly includes a number of bilingual poems and fiction selections.

3527. News from the Republic of Letters. [ISSN: 1095-1644] 1997. irreg. USD 25 United States; USD 37.50 elsewhere. Ed(s): Keith Botsford. The Republic of Letters, Attn: Keith Botsford, Apartado 29, Cahuita, 70403, Costa Rica; RepublicOfLettersMag@gmail.com; http://mag.trolbooks.com/. Illus. *Indexed:* MLA-IB. *Bk. rev.:* 1-2, length varies. *Aud.:* Ga, Ac.

Published irregularly, *News from the Republic of Letters* is an independent magazine that includes fiction, memoirs, book reviews, and art by an international selection of both new and established authors. Founded in 1997 at Boston University by Saul Bellow and Keith Botsford, it is now edited by the latter from Costa Rica. An online-only format was adopted in 2011, with all content since then freely accessible. Archived content can be accessed at the former web site: www.bu.edu/trl/about.html. Current URL: http://mag.trolbooks.com/articles/

3528. The North American Review. Formerly (until 1821): *The North-American Review and Miscellaneous Journal.* [ISSN: 0029-2397] 1815. 5x/yr. USD 22 domestic; USD 29 Canada; USD 32 elsewhere. Ed(s): Ron Sandvik, Vince Gotera. University of Northern Iowa, 1227 W 27th St, Cedar Falls, IA 50614; http://www.uni.edu. Illus., index, adv. Sample. Refereed. Microform: PMC; PQC. *Indexed:* A01, A22, AmHI, ArtHuCI, BEL&L, BRI, CBRI, MLA-IB, P02, RILM. *Bk. rev.:* 0-1, 3 pages; signed. *Aud.:* Ga, Ac.

This award-winning magazine publishes art, fiction, nonfiction, poetry, and reviews. Nonfiction content emphasizes "environmental and ecological matters, multiculturalism, and exigent issues of gender and class." The *NAR* sponsors an annual poetry prize, as well as a writing festival. The web site provides access to "Literary Roundtable" podcasts, as well as news and events. URL: www.northamericanreview.org/

3529. North Dakota Quarterly. Formerly (until 1956): *University of North Dakota. Quarterly Journal.* [ISSN: 0029-277X] 1911. q. USD 30 (Individuals, USD 25; USD 12 per issue domestic). Ed(s): Kate Sweney, Robert W Lewis. University of North Dakota, Merrifield Hall Rm 110, 276 Centennial Dr Stop 7209, PO Box 7209, Grand Forks, ND 58202; enrollmentservices@mail.und.edu; http://www.und.nodak.edu. Refereed. *Indexed:* A22, ABS&EES, AmHI, MLA-IB, RILM. *Bk. rev.:* 3-8, 2-8 pages; signed. *Aud.:* Ga, Ac.

The *North Dakota Quarterly* publishes a variety of articles, essays, fiction, and poetry by an international array of authors. Book reviews are also included. Themed issues appear regularly, eight of which have been devoted to Hemingway. Access to excerpts from the print content is available online, but *NDQ*'s web presence is otherwise minimal. URL: http://arts-sciences.und.edu/north-dakota-quarterly/

3530. Notre Dame Review. [ISSN: 1082-1864] 1995. s-a. USD 20 (Individuals, USD 15). Ed(s): John Matthias, William O'Rourke. University of Notre Dame, Creative Writing Program, 356 O'Shaughnessy Hall, Notre Dame, IN 46556; creativewriting@nd.edu; http://www.nd.edu/~alcwp/. Illus. *Indexed:* AmHI, MLA-IB. *Bk. rev.:* 13-18, 50-350 words; signed. *Aud.:* Ga, Ac.

The *Notre Dame Review* includes contemporary American and international fiction, poetry, criticism, and art. The editors note that they are "especially interested in work that takes on big issues," using an aesthetic medium to convey a message. The companion web site, called the *ne[re]view*, provides additional content, including audio recordings of authors reading from their works. URL: http://ndreview.nd.edu/

3531. The Paris Review: the international literary quarterly. [ISSN: 0031-2037] 1953. q. USD 40 domestic; USD 45 Canada; USD 55 elsewhere. Ed(s): Caitlin Roper, Philip A Gourevitch. The Paris Review Foundation, Inc., 62 White St, New York, NY 10013. Illus., index. Microform: PQC. *Indexed:* A01, A22, AmHI, ArtHuCI, BEL&L, BRI, MLA-IB, P02, RILM. *Aud.:* Ga, Ac.

Founded in 1953 by American expatriots in Paris but now operating in New York, *The Paris Review* publishes a variety of creative work, including fiction, essays, poetry, and art "portfolios." Eschewing literary criticism in favor of author interviews, both the print journal and the web site provide a wealth of opportunities to either read or listen to writers discussing their life and work. In addition to an audio archive of "Writers at Work" podcasts, the web site offers a blog and a newsletter. URL: www.theparisreview.org

3532. Prairie Schooner. [ISSN: 0032-6682] 1926. q. USD 28 domestic; USD 38 foreign. Ed(s): Hilda Raz. University of Nebraska at Lincoln, 123 Andrews Hall, Lincoln, NE 68588; http://www.unl.edu. Index, adv. Vol. ends: Winter. Microform: PQC. Reprint: PSC. *Indexed:* A01, A22, ABS&EES, AmHI, BRI, CBRI, E01, MLA-IB, P02. *Bk. rev.:* 0-7, 1-8 words; signed. *Aud.:* Ga, Ac.

Prairie Schooner has been publishing the work of beginning, mid-career, and established writers for over 85 years. Now it is under the editorship of Kwame Dawes, and content includes stories, poems, essays, and reviews, including work by Pulitzer Prize winners, Nobel laureates, National Endowment for the Arts recipients, and MacArthur and Guggenheim fellows. Supplementing the print publication is a lively web site where readers will find a blog, featured archival content "From the Vault," and audio recordings ("Air Schooner") of themed discussions—e.g., travel writing, teaching writing, writer workspaces—and authors reading from their works. A new online feature entitled "Fusion" provides a forum for dialog "across geographical spaces and cultures through the sharing of art and writing."

3533. Salmagundi: a quarterly of the humanities & social sciences. [ISSN: 0036-3529] 1965. q. USD 28. Ed(s): Robert Boyers, Peggy Boyers. Skidmore College, 815 North Broadway, Saratoga Springs, NY 12866; http://cms.skidmore.edu. Illus., index, adv. Sample. Refereed. Microform: PQC. *Indexed:* A22, ABS&EES, AmHI, ArtHuCI, BAS, BRI, CBRI, MLA-IB, P02, P61, RILM, SSA. *Bk. rev.:* 0-5, 5-23 pages; signed. *Aud.:* Ga, Ac.

Intended for general readers rather than scholars, *Salmagundi* publishes work in a variety of genres, including essays, reviews, interviews, fiction, poetry, regular columns, polemics, debates, and symposia. Issues often focus on a specific cultural or political theme that "invites argument." An effort is made to provide an array of national and international perspectives. Past topics have included "The Culture of the Museum," "Homosexuality," "Art and Ethics," "The Culture Industry," "Kitsch," and "FemIcons." A blog updates and expands upon content in the print edition.

3534. The Sewanee Review. [ISSN: 0037-3052] 1892. q. USD 53. Ed(s): Leigh Anne Couch, George Core. The Johns Hopkins University Press, 2715 N Charles St, Baltimore, MD 21218; http://www.press.jhu.edu. Illus., index, adv. Sample. Vol. ends: Oct. Microform: PQC. *Indexed:* A01, A06, A22, AmHI, ArtHuCI, BEL&L, BRI, CBRI, E01, MLA-IB, P02, RILM. *Bk. rev.:* 6-10, 2-6 pages; signed. *Aud.:* Ga, Ac.

The Sewanee Review has been continuously published since 1892, and each themed issue includes short fiction, poetry, essays, literary criticism, and reviews. It is committed to a tradition of excellence, and the editor notes that "only erudite work representing depth of knowledge and skill of expression is published here." The work of established writers is predominant, but each issue includes a few promising new authors as well. The Aiken Taylor Prize in Modern American Poetry is awarded each year to a distinguished American poet for the work of a career.

3535. Shenandoah. [ISSN: 0037-3583] 1950. q. USD 25. Ed(s): Lynn Leech, R T Smith. Washington and Lee University, Shenandoah, Mattingly House, 2 Lee Ave, Lexington, VA 24450; http://www.wlu.edu/x6.xml. Illus., index, adv. Vol. ends: Winter. *Indexed:* A22, AmHI, ArtHuCI, BRI, CBRI, MLA-IB. *Bk. rev.:* 0-7, 1-3 pages. *Aud.:* Ga, Ac.

For over 50 years a print quarterly, *Shenandoah* is now a digital magazine of poems, stories, essays, and reviews, published biannually. The complete content of all digital issues is freely available online. Work from *Shenandoah* reappears regularly in the leading anthologies. Prizes for poetry, fiction, and nonfiction published in the journal are awarded annually, and a short-short story contest

was recently added. *Shenandoah*'s mission statement notes that its interest is in "work which has its sources in acutely observed personal experience but which also aims to bear witness to something larger than the individual."

3536. The South Carolina Review. [ISSN: 0038-3163] 1968. s-a. USD 31 (Individuals, USD 26; USD 15 per issue in North America). Clemson University, Department of English, 801 Strode Tower, PO Box 340523, Clemson, SC 29634-0523; http://www.clemson.edu/caah/english/. Illus. *Indexed:* A22, AmHI, BRI, CBRI, MLA-IB, P02. *Bk. rev.:* Number and length vary. *Aud.:* Ga, Ac.

Founded in 1968, *The South Carolina Review* publishes fiction, poetry, interviews, unpublished letters and manuscripts, essays, and reviews by Southern and American writers and scholars. Special themed issues appear occasionally, and have covered such topics as *Virginia Woolf International* and *Ireland in the Arts and Humanities.* An issue devoted to *Locating African American Autobiography* is expected in Spring 2012. The *SCR* web site provides access to selected content from the print edition and a growing archive of digital facsimiles of early volumes.

3537. The Southern Review. [ISSN: 0038-4534] 1935. q. USD 75 (Individuals, USD 40). Ed(s): Cara Blue Adams, Jeanne Leiby. Louisiana State University Press, 3990 W Lakeshore Dr, Louisiana State University, Baton Rouge, LA 70808; http://lsupress.org/. Index, adv. Sample. Vol. ends: Oct. Microform: PQC. *Indexed:* A01, A22, AmHI, BRI, CBRI, MLA-IB, P02, RILM. *Bk. rev.:* 1, 4-6 pages; signed. *Aud.:* Ga, Ac.

The Southern Review publishes poetry, fiction, essays, and visual art. The editors place an emphasis on contemporary writing of a high standard and with clear artistic purpose. Both national and international authors are represented. Visual art is engaging and diverse in style. The web site provides access to supplemental material, including the *TSR* blog, "Lagniappe," and a digital art gallery.

3538. The Southwest Review. Formerly (until 1924): *Texas Review;* Incorporates (1921-1925): *The Reviewer;* Which was formerly (until 19??): *Reviewer of Richmond.* [ISSN: 0038-4712] 1915. q. USD 24; USD 6 per issue. Ed(s): Willard Spiegelman. Southern Methodist University Press, PO Box 750374, Dallas, TX 75275; gshultz@mail.smu.edu; http://www.smu.edu. Illus., index. Sample. Microform: PQC. *Indexed:* A01, A22, AmHI, BEL&L, BRI, CBRI, MLA-IB, P02. *Aud.:* Ga, Ac.

Established in 1915 and now housed at Southern Methodist University, *The Southwest Review* publishes fiction and poetry in both traditional and experimental styles. Each issue also includes approximately four substantive articles on a wide range of topics, including contemporary affairs, history, folklore, fiction, poetry, literary criticism, art, music, and theater. *SWR* editors offer annual awards for the best works of fiction, nonfiction, and poetry published in the review. They also sponsor two annual contests, the Marr Poetry Prize and Meyerson Prize for Fiction.

3539. The Threepenny Review. [ISSN: 0275-1410] 1980. q. USD 25 domestic. Ed(s): Wendy Lesser. Threepenny Review, PO Box 9131, Berkeley, CA 94709; http://www.threepennyreview.com. Adv. *Indexed:* AmHI, BRI, CBRI, MLA-IB. *Bk. rev.:* 0-7. *Aud.:* Ga, Ac.

Based in Berkeley, California, *The Threepenny Review* includes a cosmopolitan array of content including poetry, fiction, memoirs, and symposia. Essay-like book reviews, as well as music, dance, theater, and film reviews, provide readers with a thoughtful and engaging look at the arts. Founding editor Wendy Lesser supplements the print content with regular posts to her blog on the *Threepenny Review* web site. URL: www.threepennyreview.com/index.html

3540. TriQuarterly Online. Formerly (until 2010): *TriQuarterly (Print).* 1964. 3x/yr. Ed(s): Susan Firestone Hahn. Northwestern University Press, 629 Noyes St, Evanston, IL 60208; nupress@northwestern.edu; http://www.nupress.northwestern.edu. Illus., index, adv. Sample. Circ: 5000 Paid. *Indexed:* A22, ABS&EES, AmHI, ArtHuCI, BRI, CBRI, MLA-IB, P02, RILM. *Bk. rev.:* 1, lengthy, signed. *Aud.:* Ga, Ac.

Edited by M.A./M.F.A. graduate students and supervised by faculty at Northwestern University, *TriQuarterly Online* publishes semi-annual issues of fiction, nonfiction, poetry, and drama, supplemented by monthly updates including interviews, book reviews, and essays. *TQO* plans to digitize all print content back to its first issue in 1958. Video essays and a blog also serve "to build a broader dialogue around its contents and broaden the context of new writing in ways that a print-only magazine cannot." URL: http://triquarterly.org/

3541. The Virginia Quarterly Review (Online): a national journal of literature and discussion. [ISSN: 2154-6932] 1925. q. USD 32. Ed(s): Ted Genoways. University of Virginia, 1 West Range, PO Box 400223, Charlottesville, VA 22904; http://www.virginia.edu. Adv. *Bk. rev.:* 90-100, 40-2,000 words; signed. *Aud.:* Ga, Ac.

The Virginia Quarterly Review was established in 1925, and each themed issue contains essays, poetry, and prose by an international selection of authors. Recent topics have included "Northern Africa"; "Emerging Photographers"; "Ruin & Rebirth"; and "Our Threatened Fisheries." Such celebrated writers as H. L. Mencken, Thomas Wolfe, Katherine Anne Porter, Joyce Carol Oates, Robert Penn Warren, Robert Frost, Conrad Aiken, and Marianne Moore have appeared in its pages, alongside new and promising authors. Print subscribers receive access to all *VQR* content from 1975 to the present. URL: www.vqronline.org/

3542. Web del Sol. 1994. m. Free. Ed(s): Mike Neff. Web del Sol Association, 2020 Pennsylvania Ave, NW, Ste 443, Washington, DC 20006. *Aud.:* Ga, Ac.

A collaborative volunteer effort, *Web del Sol* is unaffiliated with any institution. As much a portal as a publication, the web site offers readers "not only literary journals but metazines, blogs, video, music, culture sites, and cinema arts." Of note are a "literary tourism" series that takes readers to "exotic literary locales"; a new series entitled "World Voices" that brings together a collection of chapbooks featuring prose, poetry, visual work, and mixed media by both new and under-recognized writers and artists; and a "Writers on the Job" series of narratives on the non-writing activities of various authors. URL: http://webdelsol.com/

3543. Witness: the modern writer as witness. [ISSN: 0891-1371] 1987. s-a. USD 10 domestic; USD 14 foreign. Ed(s): Amber Withycombe. University of Nevada, Las Vegas, Black Mountain Institute, P O Box 455085, Las Vegas, NV 89154-5085. Illus., adv. Sample. Refereed. Circ: 1500 Paid. *Indexed:* AmHI, MLA-IB. *Aud.:* Ga, Ac.

In accordance with the subtitle, *Witness* includes fiction, nonfiction, poetry, and photography that highlights "the role of the modern writer as witness to his or her times." At present, *Witness* publishes one themed print issue and two general online issues each year. All content from the latter is freely available on the web site. Print issue themes have included such topics as political oppression, religion, the natural world, crime, aging, civil rights, and more. Supplemental online content in the form of photography and video is planned. URL: http://witness.blackmountaininstitute.org/

3544. The Yale Review. Formerly (until 1892): *New Englander and Yale Review.* [ISSN: 0044-0124] 1911. q. GBP 130. Ed(s): Susan Bianconi, J D McClatchy. Wiley-Blackwell Publishing, Inc., 111 River St, Hoboken, NJ 07030; info@wiley.com; http://onlinelibrary.wiley.com/. Illus., index, adv. Sample. Vol. ends: Oct. Microform: PMC; PQC. *Indexed:* A01, A06, A22, ABS&EES, AmHI, ArtHuCI, BAS, BEL&L, BRI, CBRI, E01, MLA-IB, P02, RILM. *Bk. rev.:* 4-5, 6-22 pages; signed. *Aud.:* Ga, Ac.

The nation's oldest literary quarterly, *The Yale Review* has published the work of well-known writers around the world, including Thomas Mann, Henry Adams, Virginia Woolf, George Santayana, Robert Frost, Jose Ortega y Gasset, W. H. Auden, Robert Lowell, Robert Penn Warren, and Katherine Anne Porter, among many others. This journal is committed to new and promising contemporary writers as well, and its content includes a balance of fiction, essays, poetry, and book reviews that "explore the connections between academic disciplines and the broader movements in American society, thought, and culture."

■ LITERATURE

See also Africa; African American; China; Classical Studies; Europe; Fiction; Latin American; Gay, Lesbian, Bisexual, and Transgender; Literary Reviews; Little Magazines; and Theater sections.

Heath Martin, Director of Collections, University of Kentucky Libraries, Lexington, KY 40506; hmartin58@uky.edu.

Heidi Buchanan, Head of Research and Instruction Services, Western Carolina University, Hunter Library, Cullowhee, NC 28723; hbuchanan@wcu.edu

Introduction

In this section, you will find many publications, mostly scholarly and often interdisciplinary, focusing on a number of different literary periods, geographic areas, critical methodologies, and theoretical perspectives. These titles represent the work of criticism, explication, and literary history. Book reviews, review essays, notes, and interviews with authors and literary scholars are sometimes included as well. While the primary audience for these journals is academic, a number of titles are also suitable for public or school libraries.

The intent of this section is to identify core titles for academic libraries, though some selections will also be of interest to public and school libraries. Though a few journals focus on a specific geographic region or time period, most titles are relatively broad in scope, covering a number of different themes, topics, periods, or places. We have not included, most notably, journals devoted to the study of a single author; the number would quickly have overwhelmed the scope of our task.

We have updated this edition to reflect changes, cessations, and new titles. New annotations include brand-new titles and "new to *MFL*" titles. We have excluded a few annotations from the last edition in an effort to streamline well-represented subdisciplines and highlight other areas of study that are important to library collections.

The annotations provide a description of the content and structure of each journal as we experienced them ourselves. In order to provide bases of comparison, a number of characteristics are frequent across all entries, including the types of articles published, any distinct geographic or chronological scope, and the kinds of authors, titles, and topics one is likely to encounter. When relevant, we also describe unique features of a given publication, such as open-access availability or the presence of interviews, special issues or sections, or book reviews. Unless otherwise attributed, all quotations are taken from the respective web sites of the publishers.

Basic Periodicals

Ac: *American Literature, Comparative Literature, Contemporary Literature, Essays in Criticism, Modern Fiction Studies, Nineteenth-Century Literature (Berkeley), P M L A, The Review of Contemporary Fiction, Speculum, Studies in English Literature 1500-1900, Victorian Studies, World Literature Today.*

Basic Abstracts and Indexes

Annual Bibliography of English Language and Literature (ABELL), Arts & Humanities Citation Index, Humanities Index, MLA International Bibliography.

3545. A N Q: A Quarterly Journal of Short Articles, Notes and Reviews. Formerly (until 1988): *American Notes and Queries.* [ISSN: 0895-769X] 1962. q. GBP 148 (print & online eds.). Ed(s): Sandro Jung. Routledge, 325 Chestnut St, Ste 800, Philadelphia, PA 19106; customerservice@taylorandfrancis.com; http://www.tandfonline.com. Index, adv. Refereed. Microform: PQC. Reprint: PSC. *Indexed:* A01, A22, AmHI, ArtHuCI, BRI, CBRI, MLA-IB, P02, RILM. *Bk. rev.:* 1-7, 2-4 pages; signed. *Aud.:* Ac.

This journal targets literary scholars of many stripes by publishing brief, focused research articles on "the literature of the English-speaking world and the language of literature." Maintaining a broad chronological scope, *ANQ* flits with unabashed eclecticism from Old English word studies to twentieth-century source examinations. Essays generally range from 2 to 12 pages, with 10–14 pieces published in each issue. Recent essays include "Reflections in a

Filipino's Eye: Southern Masculinity and the Colonial Subject," "The Judge's Molar: Infanticide and the Meteorite in Cormac McCarthy's *Blood Meridian, or the Evening Redness in the West,*" and "Melancholic Individuality and the Lothian Portrait of Donne." This title is appropriate for academic and large public libraries. (HCM)

3546. *A R I E L.* Formerly (until 1967): *Review of English Literature.* [ISSN: 0004-1327] 1960. q. CAD 80 (Individuals, CAD 30). Ed(s): Pamela McCallum. University of Calgary Press, 2500 University Dr NW, Calgary, AB T2N 1N4, Canada; ucpmail@ucalgary.ca; http://www.uofcpress.com. Illus., index, adv. Refereed. Circ: 650 Paid and free. Vol. ends: Oct. *Indexed:* A01, A22, AmHI, ArtHuCI, BRI, C37, CBCARef, MLA-IB, P02, RILM. *Bk. rev.:* 1-5, 3-5 pages; signed. *Aud.:* Ac.

This journal from the University of Calgary Press publishes scholarly articles about "International English Literature, Postcolonial Literatures, Commonwealth Literature, New Literatures in English, and World Writing in English." Recent issues include studies of Junot Diaz, Indra Sinha, Jhumpa Lahiri, post-9/11 Pakistani writing, feminist poetry, and transnationalism. Book reviews are open access on the journal's web page. The publication's broad scope and good coverage of contemporary authors make it a valuable addition to any academic library. (HB)

3547. *American Imago: psychoanalysis and the human sciences.* [ISSN: 0065-860X] 1939. q. USD 168. Ed(s): Karen Steigman, Louis P Masur. The Johns Hopkins University Press, 2715 N Charles St, Baltimore, MD 21218; http://www.press.jhu.edu. Illus., adv. Sample. Circ: 327. Microform: PMC; PQC. Reprint: PSC. *Indexed:* A01, A22, AmHI, ArtHuCI, BEL&L, BRI, E01, MLA-IB, P02, PsycInfo, RILM. *Bk. rev.:* Yes. *Aud.:* Ac.

This journal, published by Johns Hopkins University Press, examines "Freud's legacy across the humanities, arts, and social sciences." According to the publisher's web site, the journal was founded by Sigmund Freud and Hans Sachs (it began as *Imago* in 1912 and continued as *American Imago* in 1939). The publication is included in this section because it frequently includes literary topics as they relate to psychoanalysis. Each issue contains several lengthy (20–50 pages) scholarly studies from various disciplines. Recent articles include "Freud's Shylock" and "The Novelist's Craft: Reflections on *The Brothers Karamazov.*" Reviews of books relevant to Freud studies are occasionally included. Recommended for academic libraries that support graduate programs. (HB)

3548. *American Literary History.* [ISSN: 0896-7148] 1989. q. EUR 246. Ed(s): Denys Van Renen, Gordon Hutner. Oxford University Press, 2001 Evans Rd, Cary, NC 27513; http://www.oxfordjournals.org. Illus. Sample. Refereed. Vol. ends: Dec. Reprint: PSC. *Indexed:* A01, A22, AmHI, ArtHuCI, BRI, E01, MLA-IB, RILM. *Bk. rev.:* 3-5, 8-16 pages; signed. *Aud.:* Ac.

This journal strives to provide a forum for analyzing and contributing to the diversity of literary inquiry published across disparate sources in American literature. Publishing essays, commentaries, reviews, and critical exchanges, *American Literary History* accepts articles on theoretical and historical issues, as well as those concerned with particular authors and works. A number of essays also analyze the condition and trends of literary scholarship itself. The journal welcomes articles with an interdisciplinary focus, such as the recently published "Transnationalism as Metahistoriography: Washington Irving's Chinese Americas." In fact, the frequency with which essays in this journal cross disciplinary boundaries lends it a strong Americanist flavor that is of potential interest to scholars outside the field of literature. Users of all academic libraries and large public libraries would find value in this publication. (HCM)

3549. *American Literary Realism.* Formerly (until 1999): *American Literary Realism, 1870-1910.* [ISSN: 1540-3084] 1967. 3x/yr. USD 62 (print & online eds.). Ed(s): Cindy Murillo, Gary Scharnhorst. University of Illinois Press, 1325 S Oak St, Champaign, IL 61820; journals@uillinois.edu; http://www.press.uillinois.edu. Illus., index, adv. Refereed. *Indexed:* A22, AmHI, ArtHuCI, BEL&L, BRI, E01, MLA-IB, RILM. *Bk. rev.:* 3-7, 1-2 pages; signed. *Aud.:* Ac.

American Literary Realism publishes critical essays on authors and topics in late nineteenth- and early twentieth-century American literature. Essays average 15–20 pages in length. Each issue also includes between one and four book reviews, as well as occasional pieces contributed to the "Notes and Documents" section. A recent special issue focused on the work of Jack London, while another offered several essays on the work of Willa Cather. Other recent articles include "Religion, Family, and National Belonging in W. D. Howells' *The Undiscovered Country,*" "'Scenes in the History of the Deaf and Dumb': Angeline Fuller's Strategic Sentimentality and the Development of an American Deaf Identity," and "Reading 'Connectedly': Charlotte Perkins Gilman, the Index, and Her Librarian-Father." Recommended for academic libraries. (HCM)

3550. *American Literature.* [ISSN: 0002-9831] 1929. q. USD 366. Ed(s): Emily E Dings, Priscilla B Wald. Duke University Press, 905 W Main St, Ste 18 B, PO Box 90660, Durham, NC 27701; subscriptions@dukepress.edu; http://www.dukepress.edu. Illus., index, adv. Sample. Refereed. Vol. ends: Dec. Microform: MIM; PQC. Reprint: PSC. *Indexed:* A01, A22, AmHI, ArtHuCI, BEL&L, BRI, CBRI, Chicano, E01, MLA-IB, P02, RILM. *Bk. rev.:* 25-40, 1-2 pages; signed. *Aud.:* Ac.

This well-respected quarterly journal, published by Duke University Press in cooperation with the Modern Language Association's American Literature Section, focuses on American authors from colonial to contemporary times. Each issue generally includes six critical essays ranging in length from 25 to 35 pages, 15–30 book reviews, and occasional announcements (updates on conferences, grants, competitions, publishing opportunities) and brief mentions (citations of new editions, anthologies, collections). Special issues are sometimes published, most recently a collection of articles on the theme of "Speculative Fictions." Other recent essays include "Embodied Politics: Antebellum Vegetarianism and the Dietary Economy of *Walden,*" "Marianne Moore's Depression Collectives," and "Enforcement on a Grand Scale: Fugitive Intelligence and the Literary Tactics of Douglass and Melville." *American Literature* is a core title for academic libraries and should be seriously considered for larger public library collections. (HCM)

3551. *Appalachian Journal: a regional studies review.* [ISSN: 0090-3779] 1972. q. USD 48. Ed(s): Sandra L Ballard. Appalachian State University, Center for Appalachian Studies, Belk Library, Appalachian State University, PO Box 32026, Boone, NC 28608; http://www.appjournal.appstate.edu. Illus. Refereed. *Indexed:* A22, ABS&EES, AmHI, ArtHuCI, MLA-IB, RILM. *Bk. rev.:* 5-10, 1-4 pages. *Aud.:* Hs, Ga, Ac.

This interdisciplinary journal features "field research, interviews, and other scholarly studies" on a variety of topics related to the Appalachian mountain region. The journal devotes much attention to Appalachian literature and folklore. Recent issues have featured interviews with novelists, poets, and filmmakers. Each issue features scholarly essays as well, with topics ranging from serpent handling in literature to "white trash stereotypes" in a modern television cartoon. The journal publishes a selection of original poetry by regional authors and relevant book reviews. Longer review essays are often included. A must for any library in the Appalachian region. Also recommended for academic and large public libraries.

3552. *Arizona Quarterly: a journal of American literature, culture and theory.* [ISSN: 0004-1610] 1945. q. USD 50. Ed(s): Edgar A Dryden. University of Arizona, Arizona Board of Regents, 1731 E Second St, Tucson, AZ 85721; pubs@ag.arizona.edu; http://www.ag.arizona.edu/. Illus., index. Refereed. Vol. ends: Winter. Microform: PQC. Reprint: PSC. *Indexed:* A22, AmHI, Chicano, E01, MLA-IB, P02, RILM. *Aud.:* Ac.

This journal "publishes articles offering a variety of scholarly approaches to canonical and non-canonical works of American literature and film." Recent articles, which are 15–30 pages in length, present scholarship on the works of Washington Irving, Harriet Beecher Stowe, Henry James, James Weldon Johnson, Allen Ginsberg, Mary Austin, Abraham Cahan, Helena Viramontes, and Cormac McCarthy. Recommended for large academic libraries. (HB)

3553. Boundary 2: an international journal of literature and culture.
[ISSN: 0190-3659] 1972. 3x/yr. USD 280. Ed(s): Margaret A Havran,
Paul A Bove. Duke University Press, 905 W Main St, Ste 18 B, PO Box
90660, Durham, NC 27701; subscriptions@dukepress.edu; http://
www.dukepress.edu. Illus., index, adv. Sample. Refereed. Vol. ends:
Fall. Reprint: PSC. *Indexed:* A01, A22, ABS&EES, AmHI, ArtHuCI,
BRI, E01, MLA-IB, P02, P61, RILM, SSA. *Bk. rev.:* Number and length
vary. *Aud.:* Ac.

Boundary 2, which expresses commitment "to understanding the present and
approaching the study of national and international culture and politics through
literature and the human sciences," has imposed a more limited editorial filter
than some comparable journals, by eschewing articles that fall within "the
standard professional areas" and publishing only those pieces "that identify and
analyze the tyrannies of thought and action spreading around the world and that
suggest alternatives to these emerging configurations of power." This mission
lends the journal an overtly anti-establishment perspective on the study of
literature. Articles generally number six to nine per issue and run 15–30 pages
in length. Themed issues are common, with a recent example being "China after
Thirty Years of Reform: Critical Reflections." Recent articles include
"Anachronisms of Authority: Authorship, Exchange Value and David Foster
Wallace's *The Pale King,*" "Idolatry, Prohibition, Unrepresentability," and "The
Critic's Byzantine Ploy: Voltairean Confusion in Postsecularist Narratives."
Boundary 2 is recommended for academic libraries. (HCM)

3554. The Cambridge Quarterly. [ISSN: 0008-199X] 1965. q. EUR 297.
Ed(s): Ann Newton. Oxford University Press, Great Clarendon St,
Oxford, OX2 6DP, United Kingdom; enquiry@oup.co.uk; http://
www.oxfordjournals.org/. Illus., index, adv. Sample. Refereed. Reprint:
PSC. *Indexed:* A22, AmHI, ArtHuCI, BEL&L, BRI, E01, MLA-IB. *Bk.
rev.:* 4-7, 4-13 pages. *Aud.:* Ac.

While focusing on literary criticism, *The Cambridge Quarterly* also publishes
articles that address music, cinema, and the visual arts. At times, the journal
attempts to reach an audience beyond academics and speak to a more general
readership. Each issue contains three or four articles and four to seven reviews.
Articles tend to run anywhere from 15 to 30 pages in length. Occasionally, a
special issue is published, with the most recent example being the March 2012
issue devoted to "Cambridge English and China: A Conversation." The journal
covers a wide variety of authors, periods, and geographic frames. Recent essays
include "Penelope Fitzgerald's Beginnings: *The Golden Child* and Fitzgerald's
Anxious Relation to Detective Fiction," "Dialogue and Leisure at the Fin de
Siecle," and "The Peculiar Romanticism of the English Situationists." This title
is suitable for academic and larger public libraries. (HCM)

3555. College Literature. [ISSN: 0093-3139] 1974. q. USD 100 (print or
online ed.); USD 140 combined subscription. Ed(s): Kostas Myrsiades.
West Chester University, 210 East Rosedale Ave, West Chester, PA
19382; http://www.wcupa.edu. Illus., index. Refereed. Vol. ends: Oct.
Indexed: A01, A22, ABS&EES, AmHI, ArtHuCI, BEL&L, BRI, CBRI,
E01, MLA-IB, P02. *Bk. rev.:* 1-5, 2-4 pages. *Aud.:* Ac.

This journal presents "scholarly research across the various periods, intellectual
fields, and geographical locations." The scholarly essays are intended to help
college teachers (and others) keep up in the field of literary scholarship.
Undergraduates may find the material more readable than that of other scholarly
journals. Issues occasionally include articles such as "Doing Shakespeare in a
Kazakhstani College: Teacher Plays Ethnographer," but this journal is focused
on the content of the literary works rather than on providing classroom tips. The
topics in each issue are diverse, and the authors studied range from medieval to
twenty-first century. Issues contain three or four relevant book reviews. This
journal would be valuable for both college instructors and students, and is
recommended for all academic libraries. (HB)

3556. The Comparatist. [ISSN: 0195-7678] 1977. a. USD 50. Ed(s): Zahi
Zalloua. University of North Carolina Press, 116 S Boundary St, Chapel
Hill, NC 27514; uncpress@unc.edu; http://www.uncpress.unc.edu.
Refereed. *Indexed:* A22, ABS&EES, AmHI, BRI, E01, MLA-IB, P02.
Aud.: Ac.

The Comparatist is an annual publication concerned with literature, culture, and
the arts, applying a comparative approach to the study of European and
American texts, as well as "third-world, Afro-Caribbean, and Central European

literary phenomena." In terms of methodology, the journal espouses "a
stimulating interplay of intertextual and comparative methods, of theoretical-
historical analysis, and of critical interpretation." Each issue contains eight to
ten articles that are clustered thematically, along with several reviews. Recently,
issues of *The Comparatist* have included articles such as "Self-Othering in
German Orientalism: The Case of Friedrich Schlegel," "To Risk Immanence/To
Read Schizo-Analytically: Deleuze, Guattari, and the Kleistian War-Machine,"
and "Indo-German Connection, Critical and Hermeneutical, in the First World
War." Recommended for medium-to-large academic libraries.

3557. Comparative Critical Studies. Formed by the merger of (1979-2004):
Comparative Criticism; (1986-2004): *New Comparison;* Which was
formerly (1975-1986): *Comparison.* [ISSN: 1744-1854] 2004. 3x/yr. GBP
81 (print & online eds.). Ed(s): Dr. Maike Oergel, Dr. Glyn Hambrook.
Edinburgh University Press Ltd., 22 George Sq, Edinburgh, EH8 9LF,
United Kingdom; journals@eup.ed.ac.uk; http://www.euppublishing.com.
Adv. Refereed. *Indexed:* A22, AmHI, ArtHuCI, E01, MLA-IB. *Bk. rev.:*
0-9, 2-4 pages. *Aud.:* Ac.

The "house" journal of the British Comparative Literature Association (BCLA)
is published by Edinburgh University Press. The journal emphasizes
"innovative perspectives on the theory and practice of the study of comparative
literature in all its aspects." Some issues focus on a theme such as "Hybrids and
Monsters" or "Xenographies." The journal also publishes winners of the Dryden
Translation Prize, which the BCLA gives for the "best unpublished literary
translations from any language into English" (BCLA web site). The peer-
reviewed articles are generally 14–20 pages long. Some issues contain book
reviews. Best for academic libraries that support graduate programs in
literature. (HB)

3558. Comparative Literature. Incorporates: *A C L A.* [ISSN: 0010-4124]
1949. q. USD 158. Ed(s): George E Rowe. Duke University Press, 905
W Main St, Ste 18 B, PO Box 90660, Durham, NC 27701;
subscriptions@dukepress.edu; http://www.dukepress.edu. Illus., index.
Refereed. Vol. ends: Nov. Microform: PQC. Reprint: PSC. *Indexed:* A01,
A22, ABS&EES, AmHI, ArtHuCI, BAS, BRI, CBRI, MLA-IB, P02,
RILM. *Bk. rev.:* 3-7, 2-5 pages; signed. *Aud.:* Ac.

The "official journal of the American Comparative Literature Association"
dates back to 1949; it is "directed" by the University of Oregon and published
by Duke University Press. The journal "represents a wide-ranging look at the
intersections of national literatures, global literary trends, and theoretical
discourse." The journal accepts different theoretical perspectives and
encourages new scholars to submit their manuscripts. Recent articles
(approximately 20 pages) include "The Multilingual Pleasures of Slavic
Worlds: Sacher-Masoch, Franzos, Freud." A recent special issue focuses on
"original languages." Each issue also features a few thorough and scholarly
book reviews. The content of this journal is not as undergraduate friendly as
others in its field. Recommended for academic libraries that support graduate
programs in literature. (HB)

3559. Comparative Literature Studies. [ISSN: 0010-4132] 1963. q. USD
180 (print & online eds.). Ed(s): Thomas Oliver Beebee. Pennsylvania
State University Press, 820 N University Dr, University Support Bldg 1,
Ste C, University Park, PA 16802; info@psupress.org; http://
www.psupress.org. Illus., index, adv. Refereed. Microform: PQC. Reprint:
PSC. *Indexed:* A01, A22, ABS&EES, AmHI, ArtHuCI, BAS, BEL&L,
BRI, CBRI, E01, FR, MLA-IB, P02. *Bk. rev.:* 4-15, 2-4 pages; signed.
Aud.: Ac.

Critical essays (generally 15–30 pages long) in this journal cross time periods
and cover literature from across the world. The most recent issues are organized
thematically: "Modern Literatures Worldwide," ecocriticism, Chinese
literature, Jorge Amado, and "Comparative Perspectives on the Black Atlantic."
Comparative Literature Studies also publishes a prize-winning paper written by
a graduate student in a comparative literature program. Issues contain a book
review section; many of the reviews relate to the topic of the special issue. The
diverse selection of articles offers something for every literary scholar.
Recommended for all academic libraries. (HB)

3560. *Contemporary Literature.* Formerly (until 1968): *Wisconsin Studies in Contemporary Literature.* [ISSN: 0010-7484] 1959. q. USD 195 (print & online eds.). Ed(s): Thomas Schaub, Rebecca L Walkowitz. University of Wisconsin Press, Journal Division, 1930 Monroe St, 3rd Fl, Madison, WI 53711; journals@uwpress.wisc.edu; http://www.uwpress.org. Illus., index, adv. Refereed. Circ: 2000. Microform: PQC. Reprint: PSC. *Indexed:* A01, A22, ABS&EES, AmHI, ArtHuCI, BEL&L, BRI, E01, MLA-IB, P02, RILM. *Bk. rev.:* 0-3, 5-10 pages; signed. *Aud.:* Ac.

This journal is a premier publication in the scholarship of contemporary literature, engaging the works of established and emerging writers of English-language works and striving to cover "the whole range of critical practices." Articles published, ranging in length from 20 to 30 pages, tend to situate discussion of individual works within relevant cultural, historical, and theoretical contexts. Special issues are sometimes published, with the most recent being "Fiction Since 2000: Postmillennial Commitments" in winter 2012. The journal also recently began making past special issues available in e-book format. Interviews also are an important component of *Contemporary Literature,* with writers such as Arthur Phillips, Caryl Phillips, Nathaniel Mackey, Maurice Scully, and Afaa Michael Weaver interviewed in recent issues. Four to six articles generally are included in each issue, along with two to four book reviews. Recent articles include "Writing Within a Zone of Grace: Eavan Boland, Sacred Space, and the Redemption of Representation," "The Dialogical Avant-Garde: Relational Aesthetics and Time Ecologies in *Only Revolutions* and *TOC*," and "Octavia Butler's Disabled Futures." Suitable for academic and larger public libraries. (HCM)

Critical Inquiry. See Cultural Studies section.

3561. *Criticism: a quarterly for literature and the arts.* [ISSN: 0011-1589] 1959. q. USD 196 (print & online eds.). Ed(s): Renee C Hoogland. Wayne State University Press, The Leonard N Simons Bldg, 4809 Woodward Ave, Detroit, MI 48201; bookorders@wayne.edu ; http://wsupress.wayne.edu/. Illus., index, adv. Refereed. Circ: 300 Paid. Microform: PQC. *Indexed:* A01, A07, A22, ABS&EES, AmHI, ArtHuCI, BRI, CBRI, E01, MLA-IB, P02, RILM. *Bk. rev.:* 0-4, 2-6 pages; signed. *Aud.:* Ac.

Criticism publishes scholarship in literature, music, media, and visual culture. Self-described as a forum for "rigorous theoretical and critical debate as well as formal and methodological self-reflexivity and experimentation," the journal lives up to its interdisciplinary aspirations by situating literature in a variety of critical contexts. Special issues are published on occasion, most recently one focused on Shakespeare and phenomenology. Four to six articles, usually between 20 and 35 pages in length, are included in each issue, as well as a similar number of book reviews. Recent articles include "The Walk-in Closet: Situational Homosexuality and Homosexual Panic in Hellman's *The Children's Hour*," "Ecology and Imagination: Emerson, Thoreau, and the Nature of Metonymy," and "Landscape Culture: Ansel Adams and Mary Austin's *Taos Pueblo*." Recommended for academic and larger public libraries. (HCM)

3562. *Critique (Washington): studies in contemporary fiction.* Formerly (until 1956): *Faulkner Studies.* [ISSN: 0011-1619] 1952. q. GBP 169 (print & online eds.). Ed(s): Geoffrey Green, Larry McCaffery. Routledge, 325 Chestnut St, Ste 800, Philadelphia, PA 19106; customerservice@taylorandfrancis.com; http://www.tandfonline.com. Illus., index, adv. Refereed. Vol. ends: Fall. Reprint: PSC. *Indexed:* A01, A22, AmHI, ArtHuCI, BRI, CBRI, E01, MLA-IB, P02. *Aud.:* Ac.

This influential journal focuses on the study of contemporary fiction and prides itself on the identification and analysis of important and emerging writers from the middle of the twentieth century to the present. The geographic scope is broad, and essays are invited on writers from around the globe. Each issue offers five to eight scholarly essays with lengths between 15 and 25 pages. Recent articles published include "'Psychotic Depression' and Suicide in David Foster Wallace's *Infinite Jest*," "Performing Butler? Rebecca Brown's Literary Supplements to Judith Butler's Theory of Gender Performativity," and "Healing Postmodern America: Plasticity and Renewal in Danielewski's *House of Leaves*." Appropriate for most academic and larger public libraries. (HCM)

3563. *E L H.* [ISSN: 0013-8304] 1934. q. USD 210. Ed(s): Jessica Valdez. The Johns Hopkins University Press, 2715 N Charles St, Baltimore, MD 21218; http://www.press.jhu.edu. Illus., adv. Sample. Refereed. Circ: 999. Vol. ends: Winter. Microform: PQC. Reprint: PSC. *Indexed:* A01, A06, A22, AmHI, ArtHuCI, BEL&L, BRI, E01, MLA-IB, P02, RILM. *Aud.:* Ac.

ELH (the abbreviation is for English Literary History) is published by Johns Hopkins University Press. The journal highlights "superior studies that interpret the conditions affecting major works in English and American literature." Recent articles (around 20–30 pages long) examine authors such Aphra Behn, Laurence Sterne, Charles Chesnutt, Saul Bellow, William Makepeace Thackeray, Benjamin Franklin, and Oscar Wilde. The summer 2013 issue contains essays from the English Institute's 2011 conference at Harvard University; the theme of the year was reading. This core journal is recommended for all academic libraries. (HB)

3564. *Early American Literature.* Formerly (until 1968): *Early American Literature Newsletter.* [ISSN: 0012-8163] 1966. 3x/yr. USD 65. Ed(s): Sandra Gustafson. University of North Carolina Press, 116 S Boundary St, Chapel Hill, NC 27514; uncpress@unc.edu; http://www.uncpress.unc.edu. Illus., index. Sample. Refereed. Circ: 600 Paid and controlled. *Indexed:* A01, A22, AmHI, ArtHuCI, BEL&L, BRI, E01, MASUSE, MLA-IB, P02, RILM. *Bk. rev.:* 3-4, 3-5 pages; signed. *Aud.:* Ac.

Early American Literature, the journal of the Modern Language Association's Division on American Literature to 1800, provides a forum for the examination of American literature from its inception to the early national period (approximately 1830). The publication particularly invites "work treating Native American traditional expressions, colonial Ibero-American literature from North America, colonial American Francophone writings, Dutch colonial, and German American colonial literature[,] as well as writings in English from British America and the U.S." Each issue contains approximately five to seven critical essays ranging from 15 to 35 pages in length, and includes a mix of five to ten book reviews and review essays. It also occasionally publishes primary documents from the period under consideration. Articles published recently include "Legal and Illegal Moneymaking: Colonial American Counterfeiters and the Novelization of Eighteenth-Century Crime Literature," "Reading Less Littorally: Kentucky and the Translocal Imagination in the Atlantic World," and "The Influence of Anne Bradstreet's Innovative Errors." Recommended for academic libraries, particularly those with strong programs in early American literature or American Studies. (HCM)

3565. *Early English Studies.* [ISSN: 2156-0102] 2008. a. Free. University of Texas at Arlington, Department of English, 203 Carlisle Hall, Box 19035, Arlington, TX 76019-0035; atigner@uta.edu; http://www.uta.edu/english/. Refereed. *Bk. rev.:* Number and length vary. *Aud.:* Ac.

Early English Studies is an online journal concerned with the medieval and early modern periods and published by the Department of English at the University of Texas at Arlington. Issues generally are themed, including recent and planned offerings on "Green Thoughts in the Medieval and Early Modern Worlds" and "Shakespeare and the Material World." Each issue includes six or seven articles and an occasion book review. Recent articles include "*The Metamorphosis of Ajax*, Jakes, and Early Modern Sanitation," "Appetite and Ambition: The Influence of Hunger in *Macbeth*," and "Reflections: Spenser, Elizabeth I, and Mirror Literature." Recommended for academic libraries.

3566. *Early Modern Literary Studies: a journal of sixteenth- and seventeenth-century English literature.* [ISSN: 1201-2459] 1995. 3x/yr. Free. Ed(s): Annaliese Connolly, Matthew Steggle. Sheffield Hallam University, Department of English, School of Cultural Studies, c/o Matthew Steggle, City Campus, Howard St, Sheffield, S1 1WB, United Kingdom. Illus. Refereed. Vol. ends: Dec. *Indexed:* AmHI, BRI, C37, CBRI, MLA-IB. *Bk. rev.:* 8-11; signed. *Aud.:* Ac.

Articles in this open-access journal center on "English literature, literary culture, and language during the sixteenth and seventeenth centuries." Recent articles include "Homoerotic Pleasure and Violence in the Drama of Thomas Middleton" and "Learning to Obey in Milton and Homer." The articles are a little clunky to read online; the numbering of paragraphs makes articles easier to cite, but presents a slightly awkward layout for reading. Still, the articles are well-researched, and issues include book and even theater reviews. Academic libraries should consider adding this to their catalogs or research guides. (HB)

3567. *EHumanista: journal of Iberian studies.* [ISSN: 1540-5877] 2001. s-a. Free. Ed(s): Antonio Cortijo-Ocana. University Of California, Santa Barbara, Department of Spanish & Portuguese, Phelps Hall 4206, Santa Barbara, CA 93106; http://www.spanport.ucsb.edu/. Refereed. *Indexed:* MLA-IB. *Bk. rev.:* 6-8; signed. *Aud.:* Ac.

This electronic journal publishes "original research in Spanish and Portuguese Medieval and Early Modern Literatures and Cultures." Two volumes are published each year, each including 10–15 articles and 5–15 reviews and review articles. (Reviews are not included in every volume.) Articles run approximately 15–30 pages in length. The journal accepts articles written in Spanish, Portuguese, English, Catalan, Galician, or Euskera. Articles published in recent volumes include "Cut and Shut: The Hybridity of Cantiga 173" and "Mulheres e bibliografia material: O *Ramalhete de Flores* de D. Mariana de Luna." Academic libraries may wish to facilitate access to this journal. (HCM)

3568. *Eighteenth-Century Fiction.* [ISSN: 0840-6286] 1988. q. USD 165. Ed(s): Eugenia Zuroski, Peter Walmsley. University of Toronto Press, Journals Division, 5201 Dufferin St, Toronto, ON M3H 5T8, Canada; journals@utpress.utoronto.ca; http://www.utpjournals.com. Illus., adv. Sample. Refereed. Circ: 385. *Indexed:* A01, A22, AmHI, ArtHuCI, BRI, C37, CBCARef, E01, MLA-IB. *Bk. rev.:* 10-15, 2-4 pages; signed. *Aud.:* Ac.

This University of Toronto Press journal is "devoted to the critical and historical investigation of literature and culture of the period 1660-1832." Most articles are published in English, though some are in French; corresponding translations are not provided. A recent special issue is entitled, "Exoticism, Cosmopolitanism, and Fiction's Aesthetics of Diversity." The scholarly articles, which tend to be about 20–30 pages long, discuss authors such as The Marquis de Sade, Hannah More, Samuel Richardson, Elizabeth Hamilton, and Daniel Defoe. A large section of each issue is composed of review essays. Suitable for academic libraries that support graduate programs in literature. (HB)

3569. *The Eighteenth-Century Novel.* [ISSN: 1528-3631] 2001. a. USD 194.50 per issue. Ed(s): Albert J Rivero, George Justice. A M S Press, Inc., Brooklyn Navy Yard, 63 Flushing Ave, Bldg 292, Unit #221, Brooklyn, NY 11205; editorial@amspressinc.com; http://www.amspressinc.com. Illus., index. Refereed. *Indexed:* MLA-IB. *Bk. rev.:* 14-17, 2-5 pages each; signed. *Aud.:* Ac.

This publication from AMS Press is released as an annual, and each volume has its own ISBN. The journal provides literary scholarship on "prose fiction of the 'long' eighteenth century, roughly 1660-1830" (http://bengal.missouri.edu/~justiceg/ecn/ECN.html). Recent examples of the 20- to 30-page articles are "Pox Imagery in *Clarissa*" and "Robert Bage's Novel Merchandise: Commercialism, Gender, and Form in Late Eighteenth-Century Fiction." Each volume has an article that discusses tips for using a particular text in the classroom. Volumes contain an index, as well as a lengthy section of book reviews. This publication features a good representation of eighteenth-century authors and themes. Recommended for academic libraries. (HB)

3570. *English Language Notes.* [ISSN: 0013-8282] 1962. s-a. USD 65 (Individuals, USD 40). Ed(s): Karen Jacobs. University of Colorado at Boulder, English Language Notes, Campus Box 226, Boulder, CO 80309; eln2@colorado.edu; http://www.colorado.edu/. Illus., index, adv. Refereed. Vol. ends: Dec. *Indexed:* A01, A22, AmHI, ArtHuCI, BEL&L, BRI, MLA-IB, P02, RILM. *Bk. rev.:* 1-3, 2-3 pages; signed. *Aud.:* Ac.

Each issue of *ELN* is devoted to a special topic in literary and cultural studies, in support of a mission that seeks to reinvigorate the short note format and encourage "interdisciplinary and collaborative work among literary scholarship and fields as disparate as theology, fine arts, history, geography, philosophy, and science." As part of this raison d'etre, two recent issues have focused on "Scriptural Margins: On the Boundaries of Sacred Texts" and "Shape of the I." The number of short articles in each issue can vary widely. Despite the emphasis on shorter notes, many essays run between 10 and 20 pages in length. At times, other content such as poems and interviews is published alongside the critical

essays. The occasional review essay is published as well. The most recent issues of *ELN* have included such articles as "Queer Mormonism: Deuterocanonicity and Discursive Subversion," "Reading Other People Reading Other People's Scripture: The Influence of Religious Polemic on Jewish Biblical Exegesis," and "Family Folktales: Carrie Mae Weems, Allan Sekula, and the Critique of Documentary Photography." This innovative and eclectic publication is recommended for academic libraries. (HCM)

3571. *English Literary Renaissance.* [ISSN: 0013-8312] 1971. 3x/yr. GBP 149. Ed(s): Arthur F Kinney, Kirby Farrell. Wiley-Blackwell Publishing Ltd., The Atrium, Southern Gate, Chichester, PO19 8SQ, United Kingdom; customer@wiley.com; http://www.wiley.com/. Illus., index, adv. Sample. Refereed. Vol. ends: No. 3. *Indexed:* A01, A22, AmHI, ArtHuCI, BEL&L, E01, MLA-IB, P02, RILM. *Aud.:* Ac.

This journal publishes "current criticism and scholarship of Tudor and early Stuart English literature, 1485-1665, including Shakespeare, Spenser, Donne, and Milton." Articles from recent issues include: "Reading through the Fog: Perception, the Passions, and Poetry in Spenser's Bower of Bliss" and "Livery, Liberty, and Legal Fictions." The winter 2013 issue is entitled "Studies in Renaissance Drama." Articles often feature text and illustrations from rare manuscripts, such as broadside ballads and letters. The journal also publishes bibliographic essays that describe "recent studies," which could be on a particular author (Margaret Cavendish) or topic (reading). The word "recent" is misleading—the bibliographic essays generally cover 20 years' worth of scholarship. Recommended for all academic libraries. (HB)

3572. *English Literature in Transition, 1880-1920.* Formerly (until 1963): *English Fiction in Transition, 1880-1920.* [ISSN: 0013-8339] 1957. q. USD 42 (Individuals, USD 30; USD 20 per issue). Ed(s): Robert Langenfeld. E L T Press, English Department, University of North Carolina Greensboro, PO Box 26170, Greensboro, NC 27402; eltpress@gmail.com. Illus., index, adv. Sample. Refereed. Vol. ends: No. 4. Microform: PQC. *Indexed:* A01, A22, AmHI, ArtHuCI, BRI, CBRI, E01, MLA-IB, RILM. *Bk. rev.:* 5-10, 3-5 pages. *Aud.:* Ac.

This journal publishes critical essays "on fiction, poetry, drama, or subjects of cultural interest in the 1880-1920 period of British literature." The focus of the journal is on "less prominent" literary figures of the era or how they relate to major authors. Recent articles include "British Artists and Balzac at the Turn of the Twentieth Century" and "Disease and Degeneration in Marie Corelli's Vendetta." Each issue also includes a substantial section of scholarly review essays. Recommended for academic libraries that support graduate programs in literature. (HB)

3573. *Essays in Criticism.* [ISSN: 0014-0856] 1951. q. EUR 266. Ed(s): Dr. Seamus Perry. Oxford University Press, Great Clarendon St, Oxford, OX2 6DP, United Kingdom; enquiry@oup.co.uk; http://www.oxfordjournals.com/. Illus., adv. Sample. Refereed. Microform: MIM; PQC. Reprint: PSC. *Indexed:* A01, A22, AmHI, ArtHuCI, BEL&L, BRI, E01, MLA-IB, P02. *Bk. rev.:* 3-4, 6-8 pages. *Aud.:* Ac.

This respected British journal of literary criticism "covers the whole field of English Literature from the time of Chaucer to the present day." Each issue of *Essays in Criticism* usually includes two or three scholarly articles and four or five book reviews. Articles generally are 15–20 pages in length. There is also a "Critical Opinion" section, which provides topical discussion of various literary issues. Recent examples from the "Critical Opinion" section are "The Fate of Stupidity" and "The Trouble of an Index." Recent articles include "McGahern, Austen, and the Aesthetics of Good Manners," "Robert Lowell's Afflicted Vision," and "Friendship, Social Class, and Art in Powell and Amis." In the April issue of each volume, the journal publishes the F. W. Bateson Memorial Lecture, an Oxford address named after the journal's founder and delivered by notable scholars in the field. Recommended for all academic and large public libraries. (HCM)

3574. *Exemplaria: a journal of theory in medieval and Renaissance studies.* [ISSN: 1041-2573] 1989. q. GBP 223 (print & online eds.). Ed(s): Patricia Clare Ingham, Noah Guynn. Maney Publishing, Ste 1C, Joseph's Well, Hanover Walk, Leeds, LS3 1AB, United Kingdom; maney@maneypublishing.com; http://maneypublishing.com/. Illus., adv. Sample. Refereed. Reprint: PSC. *Indexed:* A22, AmHI, ArtHuCI, BEL&L, MLA-IB. *Aud.:* Ac.

This journal publishes scholarly essays that address the literature of the Medieval and Renaissance periods and prides itself on the inclusion of "different terminologies and different approaches." Essays are approximately 20 pages in length. Special issues, such as "Premodern Culture and the Material Object," are published on occasion, but not frequently. Articles published in recent issues include "Machaut's Virtual *Voir Dit* and the Moment of Heidegger's Poetry," "Nature's Pharmaceuticals: Sanctioned Desires in Alain de Lille's *De planctu Naturae*," and "Political Animals: Human/Animal Life in *Bisclavret* and *Yonec*." Recommended for academic libraries. (HCM)

3575. The Explicator. [ISSN: 0014-4940] 1942. q. GBP 138 (print & online eds.). Routledge, 325 Chestnut St, Ste 800, Philadelphia, PA 19106; customerservice@taylorandfrancis.com; http://www.tandfonline.com. Illus., index, adv. Refereed. Vol. ends: No. 4. Reprint: PSC. *Indexed:* A01, A22, AmHI, ArtHuCI, E01, MASUSE, MLA-IB, P02, RILM. *Aud.:* Hs, Ac.

This journal features short articles (usually around two to four pages) that are "concise notes on passages of prose or poetry." The journal focuses specifically on literature that is "anthologized and studied in college classrooms." Articles, which are generally two to three pages long, examine an aspect or theme of a particular passage or certain excerpts from a work; for example, technology in Kate Chopin's "The Story of An Hour," Sylvia Plath's use of Chaucer's Wife of Bath, or jazz in a poem by Langston Hughes. *The Explicator,* which has been around since 1942, occupies a special niche in literary research. It covers a wide range of authors and their works, and the journal is a great resource for anyone searching for interpretation of a particular poem or work of fiction. Highly recommended for all academic libraries. High school and public libraries should also consider subscribing to this journal. (HB)

3576. The Global South. [ISSN: 1932-8648] 2007. s-a. Ed(s): Adetayo Alabi. Indiana University Press, 601 N Morton St, Bloomington, IN 47404; journals@indiana.edu; http://iupress.indiana.edu. Adv. Circ: 200. Reprint: PSC. *Indexed:* A22, E01, MLA-IB. *Aud.:* Ac.

This journal focuses on the literature and cultures of "those parts of the world that have experienced the most political, social, and economic upheaval and have suffered the brunt of the greatest challenges facing the world under globalization." Published by Indiana University Press, *The Global South* includes several articles in every issue, ranging in length from 10 to 25 pages. Book reviews are not included. Special issues are the rule, rather than the exception, with recent themes being "Interoceanic Diasporas and the Panama Canal's Centennial" and "States of Freedom: Freedom of States." Articles published in recent issues include "White Supremacy, White Knowledge, and Anti-West Indian Discourse in Panama: Olmedo Alfaro's *El peligro antillano en la America Central*," "Translating African Oral Literature in Global Contexts," and "An Investigation into the Poetic Praxis of Two Tiv Oral Poets." Recommended for academic and larger public libraries. (HCM)

3577. Granta. Formerly (until 1979): *The Granta.* [ISSN: 0017-3231] 1889. q. GBP 36 in Europe; USD 48 United States; USD 56 Canada. Ed(s): John Freeman. Granta Publications Ltd., 12 Addison Ave, London, W11 4QR, United Kingdom. Illus., adv. Microform: PQC. *Indexed:* A01, A22, AmHI, MLA-IB. *Bk. rev.:* Number and length vary. *Aud.:* Ga, Ac.

Granta is an eminent literary journal in the English-speaking world. Published at Cambridge University since 1889, it has published such world-famous authors as E. M. Forster, A. A. Milne, Ted Hughes, Sylvia Plath, Richard Ford, Salman Rushdie, Susan Sontag, John Hawkes, Paul Auster, and Milan Kundera. During the 1970s, *Granta* encountered financial difficulties and was relaunched in its current format in 1979 as a magazine of "new writing" aimed at both writers and a wider audience than the original Cambridge publication. Each issue of this second series of *Granta* is organized around a central theme and contains original fiction, poetry, criticism, opinion, essays, and observations. The web site provides excerpts from the magazine, as well as selected full text and tables of contents for all back issues since 1979. Highly recommended for all academic and public libraries. URL: www.granta.com

The Horn Book Magazine. See Books and Book Reviews section.

3578. J E G P. Former titles (until 1959): *Journal of English and Germanic Philology;* (until 1903): *Journal of Germanic Philology.* [ISSN: 0363-6941] 1897. q. USD 175 (print & online eds.). Ed(s): Marianne Kalinke, Charles D Wright. University of Illinois Press, 1325 S Oak St, Champaign, IL 61820; journals@uillinois.edu; http://www.press.uillinois.edu. Adv. Refereed. Microform: MIM; IDC; PMC; PQC. *Indexed:* A01, A22, AmHI, ArtHuCI, BRI, CBRI, E01, P02. *Bk. rev.:* 6-7, 1-4 pages. *Aud.:* Ac.

JEGP, a premier journal in its field first published in 1897, "focuses on Northern European cultures of the Middle Ages, covering Medieval English, Germanic, and Celtic Studies," as well as links between the medieval and subsequent periods, modern incarnations of "medievalism," and the history of Medieval Studies. Each issue offers three to five scholarly essays that range in length from 20 to 30 pages. Fifteen to 20 book reviews are also included, as well as the occasional review essay. Recent articles include "Black Metaphors in the *King of Tars*," "Enigma Variations: *Hervarar saga*'s Wave-Riddles and Supernatural Women in Old Norse Poetic Tradition," and "The Game of the Courtly Hunt: Chasing and Breaking Deer in Late Medieval English Literature." Recommended for most academic libraries. (HCM)

3579. The Journal of Commonwealth Literature. [ISSN: 0021-9894] 1965. q. USD 791. Ed(s): Susan Watkins, Claire Chambers. Sage Publications Ltd., 1 Oliver's Yard, 55 City Rd, London, EC1Y 1SP, United Kingdom; info@sagepub.co.uk; http://www.uk.sagepub.com. Adv. Sample. Refereed. Reprint: PSC. *Indexed:* A01, A22, AmHI, ArtHuCI, BAS, BEL&L, BRI, E01, MLA-IB, P02. *Aud.:* Ac.

This journal examines postcolonial and Commonwealth literature. Recent articles study literature from Barbados, Guyana, India, Nigeria, Sri Lanka, and St. Lucia. Examples of article titles are "South African literature in the time of AIDS" and "Domesticating the subaltern in the global novel in English." There is a recent special issue on "Postcolonial Print Cultures." The journal's web site also recently featured a "virtual issue" on Salman Rushdie's *The Satanic Verses*; the free online issue presents a selection of articles from previous issues of the journal. Each issue contains book reviews, and the journal features an excellent annual bibliography, which is arranged according to region (e.g., Australia, Canada, The Caribbean, and East and Central Africa). Suitable for academic libraries that support graduate programs in English. (HB)

3580. Journal of Modern Literature. [ISSN: 0022-281X] 1970. q. USD 199.50 (print & online eds.). Ed(s): Laurel Garver, Paula Marantz Cohen. Indiana University Press, 601 N Morton St, Bloomington, IN 47404; journals@indiana.edu; http://iupress.indiana.edu. Illus., index, adv. Sample. Refereed. Circ: 750. Vol. ends: Nov. Microform: PQC. Reprint: PSC. *Indexed:* A01, A22, ABS&EES, AmHI, BRI, E01, MLA-IB, P02, RILM. *Aud.:* Ac.

JML publishes scholarly articles on literature in all languages, and also accepts essays that deal with cultural artifacts and related arts. The chronological scope of the journal is 1900 to the present. The geographic scope is international, with contributors hailing from countries around the world. Content, however, tends to be dominated by studies of English and U.S. authors and works. Special issues are published occasionally. The journal includes approximately 10–15 articles per issue, ranging in length from 8 to 25 pages. Recent issues have included articles such as "Restaging the Disaster: Dos Passos and National Literatures after the Spanish-American War," "Trying It On: Narration and Masking in *The Age of Innocence*," and "Consumerism's Endgame: Violence and Community in J.G. Ballard's Late Fiction." This accessible and respected journal is appropriate for academic and larger public libraries. (HCM)

3581. Journal of Narrative Theory. Formerly (until 1999): *The Journal of Narrative Technique.* [ISSN: 1549-0815] 1971. 3x/yr. USD 35 (Individuals, USD 30; USD 8 per issue). Ed(s): Andrea Kaston Tange, Abby Coykendall. Eastern Michigan University, Department of English Language and Literature, Ypsilanti, MI 48197; JNT@emich.edu; http://www.emich.edu/english. Illus. Sample. Refereed. Microform: PQC. *Indexed:* A22, ABS&EES, AmHI, ArtHuCI, BEL&L, E01, MLA-IB, RILM. *Aud.:* Ac.

This journal "publishes essays addressing the epistemological, global, historical, formal, and political dimensions of narrative from a variety of methodological and theoretical perspectives." Recent articles, which are typically 15–30 pages long, include studies of V. S. Naipaul, Charles Chesnutt, Salman Rushdie, Katherine Mansfield, and Edith Wharton. A special issue examines postcolonial studies as they relate to narrative theory; another recent special issue is entitled "Popular Shakespeares: Modes, Media, Bodies." With articles such as "Ontological Metalepsis and Unnatural Narratology," this journal is best suited for scholars and graduate students with a good grasp of narrative theory. (HB)

3582. *Kritika Kultura.* [ISSN: 1656-152X] 2002. s-a. Free. Ed(s): Maria Luisa Torres Reyes. Ateneo de Manila University, Department of English, Loyola Heights, Quezon City, 1108, Philippines; kritikakultura@admu.edu.ph. *Indexed:* AmHI, ArtHuCI, MLA-IB. *Aud.:* Ac.

This e-journal publishes articles on language and literary/cultural studies that address "issues relevant to the 21st century," and explores the nexus of language, literature, society, and culture. Topics covered by *Kritika Kultura* vary widely and range from the political economy of language to gender and sexuality, to postcolonialism. According to the journal's web site, there also is a desire to focus on "the promising lines of work in Philippine, Asian, Southeast Asian, and Filipino-American studies." Recent issues have included between three and seven articles that range widely in length from 7 to 50 pages. (Review essays sometimes are intermixed with critical essays.) The journal also includes other regular sections, which offer columns, interviews, poetry, and a forum for new scholars. Recent essays include "Women of Will for Nation Building in Pramoedya's Three Early Novels" and "To Conform or Not to Conform, That is the Genderqueer Question: Re-examining the Lesbian Identity in Bernal's *Manila by Night.*" Users of academic libraries may benefit from facilitated access to this title. (HCM)

Literature and Theology. See Religion section.

3583. *M E L U S.* [ISSN: 0163-755X] 1974. q. EUR 110. Ed(s): Martha J Cutter. Oxford University Press, 2001 Evans Rd, Cary, NC 27513. Illus., index, adv. Refereed. Vol. ends: Winter. *Indexed:* A01, A22, ABS&EES, AmHI, ArtHuCI, BRI, Chicano, E01, IIBP, MLA-IB, P02. *Bk. rev.:* 0-7, 2-4 pages; signed. *Aud.:* Ac.

MELUS, published by The Society for the Study of the Multi-Ethnic Literature of the United States, strives to represent "the multi-ethnic scope of American literature past and present," and to explore the "national, international, and transnational contexts of U.S. ethnic literature." Issues tend to be organized thematically, with recent issues focusing on "Media(s) and the Mediation of Ethnic Identity" and "New Perspectives on Puerto Rican, Latina/o, Chicana/o, and Caribbean American Literatures." Each issue contains 8–12 articles and five or more book reviews. Interviews with established and emerging authors also may be included. Some articles published recently are "Shifting Subjectivities: Mestizas, Nepantleras, and Gloria Anzaldua's Legacy," "The Marvelous History of the Dominican Republic in Junot Diaz's *The Brief Wondrous Life of Oscar Wao,*" and "A Revolutionary Romance: Particularity and Universality in Karen Tei Yamashita's *I Hotel.*" This important publication is recommended for all academic and large public libraries. (HCM)

3584. *M L N.* Formerly (until 1962): *Modern Language Notes.* [ISSN: 0026-7910] 1886. 5x/yr. USD 205. The Johns Hopkins University Press, 2715 N Charles St, Baltimore, MD 21218; http://www.press.jhu.edu. Illus., index, adv. Sample. Refereed. Circ: 727. Vol. ends: Dec. Microform: IDC; PMC; PQC. Reprint: PSC. *Indexed:* A01, A22, ABS&EES, AmHI, ArtHuCI, BRI, CBRI, E01, MLA-IB, P02, RILM. *Bk. rev.:* 1-7, 1-3 pages; signed. *Aud.:* Ac.

This long-standing journal, formerly titled *Modern Language Notes,* first was published more than 120 years ago with a focus on contemporary continental criticism. Concerned with critical studies in the modern languages and recent work in comparative literature, *MLN* publishes four issues each year on literature in a single language (one issue each for Italian, Hispanic, German, and French) and devotes the fifth issue of the year to comparative literature. This issue also includes an index to the entire year's volume. Issues contain from 8 to as many as 16 essays that range in length from 8 to 20 pages. Essays often present an interdisciplinary perspective, and sometimes are written in one of the non-English languages under consideration. Five to ten book reviews also are included, as well as occasional notes. Recent articles include "Scenarios of

Colonialism and Culture: Oswald Spengler's Latin America," "L'idea dell'etica dell'artista di Pirandello nella rappresentazione tragica dell'*Enrico IV*," and "The Female Voice in Italian Renaissance Dialogue." Highly recommended for academic libraries, and it should also be considered by larger public libraries. (HCM)

3585. *M L Q: a journal of literary history.* [ISSN: 0026-7929] 1940. q. USD 298. Ed(s): Marshall Brown. Duke University Press, 905 W Main St, Ste 18 B, PO Box 90660, Durham, NC 27701; subscriptions@dukeupress.edu; http://www.dukeupress.edu. Illus., index, adv. Sample. Refereed. Vol. ends: Dec. Microform: MIM; PMC; PQC. Reprint: PSC. *Indexed:* A01, A22, ABS&EES, AmHI, ArtHuCI, BRI, E01, MLA-IB, P02. *Bk. rev.:* 5-6, 3-5 pages; signed. *Aud.:* Ac.

This long-standing journal emphasizes the "broader scope of literary history," and all essays focus on how a topic relates to its place in time. Issues include a range of topics that span time periods, genre, and geography. Articles are typically 20–40 pages long. Recent special issues—"What Counts as World Literature?" and "Peripheral Realisms"—feature studies of world literature and twentieth and twenty-first century writers. Each issue contains several three- to five-page book reviews. The articles are probably best for upper-level undergraduates, graduate students, and scholars. (HB)

3586. *McSweeney's.* 1998. q. USD 55 per issue. Ed(s): Dave Eggers. McSweeney's, 849 Valencia St, San Francisco, CA 94110. *Aud.:* Ga, Ac.

Also known as *McSweeney's Quarterly Concern,* this journal "publishes on a roughly quarterly schedule, and we try to make each issue very different from the last. One issue came in a box, one was Icelandic, and one looks like a pile of mail. In all, we give you groundbreaking fiction and much more." Issues contain fiction by authors such as Roddy Doyle, Ann Beattie, and Joyce Carol Oates, yet the publisher is also "committed to finding new voices...and promoting the work of gifted but underappreciated writers." The archives on the web site include full-text selections from issues dating back to 1998. *McSweeney's* won't be for everyone, but for those liking short fiction pieces, interesting articles, and occasional quarterly surprises with regard to format, this is an obvious choice for large public and academic libraries to consider. URL: http://mcsweeneys.net

3587. *Medium Aevum.* Formerly (until 1932): *Arthuriana.* [ISSN: 0025-8385] 1928. s-a. Ed(s): Corinne Saunders, Sylvia Huot. Society for the Study of Mediaeval Languages and Literature, The Executive Officer, c/o History Faculty, George St, Oxford, OX1 2RL, United Kingdom; ssmll@history.ox.ac.uk; http://mediumaevum.modhist.ox.ac.uk/. Illus., index. Refereed. Vol. ends: No. 2. *Indexed:* A01, A22, AmHI, ArtHuCI, BEL&L, BRI, FR, MLA-IB, P02, RILM. *Bk. rev.:* 16-82, 1-2 pages; signed. *Aud.:* Ac.

This journal, published since its inception in 1932 by The Society for the Study of Medieval Languages and Literature, presents articles in all areas of this field of scholarship. Typically, each issue includes six or seven scholarly essays, 10–20 pages in length. (Occasionally, longer essays and short notes are published, as well.) In addition, 15–30 book reviews and perhaps a review essay are included. Recent article titles include "*The Storie of Asneth*: A Fifteenth-Century Commission and the Mystery of its Epilogue," "Family, Locality, and Nationality: Vernacular Adaptation of the *Expugnatio Hibernica* in Late Medieval Ireland," and "Following in the Footsteps of Christ: Text and Context in the *Vita Mildrethae.*" Appropriate for research libraries and other academic institutions with a strong Medieval Studies program. (HCM)

3588. *Middle Eastern Literatures (Print).* Incorporates (1976-2003): *Edebiyat (Print);* Formerly (until 2002): *Arabic and Middle Eastern Literatures (Print).* [ISSN: 1475-262X] 1998. 3x/yr. GBP 383 (print & online eds.). Ed(s): Wen-Chin Ouyang, Michael C Beard. Routledge, 4 Park Sq, Milton Park, Abingdon, OX14 4RN, United Kingdom; subscriptions@tandf.co.uk; http://www.tandfonline.com. Adv. Sample. Refereed. Reprint: PSC. *Indexed:* A01, A22, AmHI, ArtHuCI, E01, MLA-IB. *Bk. rev.:* Number and length vary. *Aud.:* Ac.

This journal is devoted to the study of "all Middle Eastern literatures," both classical and modern. Submissions are accepted in English, German, or French. *Middle Eastern Literatures* publishes articles "of a cross- and multi-linguistic nature that focus on East-West (and/or East-East) relations," as well as those that examine "the relationship of literature with other arts and media." Three to eight essays, book reviews, and an occasional note are generally included, with special issues sometimes published. Recent essays include "The Propriety of Poetry: Morality and Mysticism in the Nineteenth Century Urdu Religious Lyric," "Fiction and Colonial Identities: Arsene Lupin in Arabic," and "Stoicism or Sufism? Hammer-Purgstall's Persian Meditations." Appropriate for academic libraries.

3589. Modern Fiction Studies. [ISSN: 0026-7724] 1955. q. USD 160. Ed(s): John N Duvall. The Johns Hopkins University Press, 2715 N Charles St, Baltimore, MD 21218; http://www.press.jhu.edu. Illus., adv. Sample. Refereed. Circ: 1352. Vol. ends: Winter. Microform: PQC. Reprint: PSC. *Indexed:* A01, A22, ABS&EES, AmHI, ArtHuCI, BRI, CBRI, E01, MLA-IB, P02, RILM. *Bk. rev.:* 0-40, 1-3 pages; signed. *Aud.:* Ac.

Modern Fiction Studies, or *Mfs,* publishes articles on "all aspects of modern and contemporary fiction," with an openness to theoretical perspectives and equal interest in both canonical and emergent works. A product of the Purdue University English Department and published by the Johns Hopkins University Press, this journal offers two general issues and two special issues each year. The publication is supported by two extensive and distinguished editorial boards. Issues include five to eight scholarly articles that range in length from 20 to 35 pages. General issues also contain approximately 40 book reviews, and occasionally review essays. Recent special issues have focused on "Women's Fiction, New Modernist Studies, and Feminism" and "Modern Fiction and Politics." Articles published in the current and previous volumes include "'Get On or Get Out': Failure and Negative Femininity in Jean Rhys's *Voyage in the Dark,*" "Event, Exceptionalism, and the Imperceptible: The Politics of Nadine Gordimer's *The Pickup,*" and "A Picture of Africa: Frenzy, Counternarrative, Mimesis." The Purdue Department of English also hosts an exemplary comprehensive index of tables of contents and special issue topics for the journal since 1955. Highly recommended for most academic libraries. (HCM)

3590. Modern Language Review. Supersedes in part: *Modern Language Quarterly.* [ISSN: 0026-7937] 1905. q. USD 306 (print & online eds.). Modern Humanities Research Association, 1 Carlton House Terrace, London, SW1Y 5AF, United Kingdom; mail@mhra.org.uk; http:// www.mhra.org.uk. Illus. Refereed. Circ: 1800. Vol. ends: Oct. Reprint: PSC. *Indexed:* A01, A06, A22, AmHI, ArtHuCI, BEL&L, BRI, CBRI, F01, MLA-IB, P02, RILM. *Bk. rev.:* Approx. 125, 1-4 pages; signed. *Aud.:* Ac.

This "flagship" journal of the Modern Humanities Research Association dates back to 1905. The journal publishes scholarly studies "on any aspect of modern and medieval European (including English and Latin American) languages, literatures, and cultures (including cinema)." Recent articles (typically 10–20 pages long) study a variety of genres (French drama, Italian literary magazines, German television). Authors studied in recent issues include Gabriel Garcia Marquez, Peter Ackroyd, Ramon Maria del Valle-Inclan, Bernard Noel, Anna Akhmatova, Gustave Flaubert, and Luigi Pirandello. The wide range of scholarly topics, along with the extensive and diverse book review section, makes *Modern Language Review* a staple for every academic library. (HB)

3591. Modern Philology: critical and historical studies in postclassical literature. [ISSN: 0026-8232] 1903. q. USD 258 (print & online eds.). Ed(s): Jessica K Printz, Richard A Strier. University of Chicago Press, 1427 E 60th St, Chicago, IL 60637; subscriptions@press.uchicago.edu; http://www.journals.uchicago.edu. Illus., index, adv. Sample. Refereed. Vol. ends: May. Microform: IDC; PMC; PQC. Reprint: PSC. *Indexed:* A01, A22, ABS&EES, AmHI, ArtHuCI, BEL&L, BRI, CBRI, MLA-IB, P02. *Bk. rev.:* 10-15, 2-4 pages; signed. *Aud.:* Ac.

This long-standing journal, published since 1903, is concerned generally with literary scholarship, criticism, and history, from the medieval period to the present. The current editor, Richard Strier, strives to "publish literary criticism and scholarship that does its work, whether of appreciation, understanding, or critique, through close attention to the language and details of texts." While *Modern Philology* continues to focus on literatures written in English or European languages, the journal's scope has expanded to include scholarship on non-European language works, including a marked interest in comparative

studies. Issues also include book reviews and review essays, which take part in the publication's expanded geographic scope. A "Notes and Documents" section may contribute research on manuscripts and other archival documents. Special sections sometimes are included. Articles can run from 25 to 40 pages in length. Essays published recently include "Phantom Syllables in the English Alliterative Tradition," "Bloody Records: Manuscripts and Politics in *The Castle of Otranto,*" and "Mantic Alphabets in Medieval Western Manuscripts and Early Printed Books." Highly recommended for most academic libraries. (HCM)

3592. Mosaic (Winnipeg, 1967): a journal for the interdisciplinary study of literature. Formerly (until 1978): *Journal for the Comparative Study of Literature and Ideas.* [ISSN: 0027-1276] 1967. q. CAD 55; CAD 24.95 per issue. Ed(s): Dr. Dawne McCance. University of Manitoba, Tier Bldg, Rm 208, Winnipeg, MB R3T 2N2, Canada; http:// www.umanitoba.ca. Illus., index. Sample. Refereed. Vol. ends: Fall. Microform: PQC. *Indexed:* A01, A22, AmHI, ArtHuCI, BAS, BEL&L, BRI, C37, CBCARef, F01, MLA-IB, P02, RILM. *Aud.:* Ac.

This Canadian (University of Manitoba) journal ties literary topics to other disciplines such as art, history, music, ethics, and film. Topics are wide-ranging and eclectic; the journal allows essays on any "literary works or issues related to any historical period, national culture, ethnic group, genre, or media." Scholarly essays (typically 15–20 pages long) from recent issues include "'Murder Everywhere': Whitman, Lish, and the fate of self-celebration" and "Sherlock Holmes and Game Theory." Special issues from 2011 and 2012 include "Between Poetry and Philosophy" and a "feature issue" highlighting a public address and an essay by Alphonso Lingis, as well as an interview with the philosopher. There is also a two-part special issue, "Freud after Derrida," containing some proceedings from the 2010 conference held at the University of Manitoba. Though popular culture topics often appear, this journal is academic and highly cerebral. Recommended for academic libraries that support graduate programs in the humanities. (HB)

3593. Narrative. [ISSN: 1063-3685] 1993. 3x/yr. USD 95. Ed(s): James Phelan. Ohio State University Press, 180 Pressey Hall, 1070 Carmack Rd, Columbus, OH 43210-1002; info@osupress.org; http:// www.ohiostatepress.org. Refereed. Circ: 1000 Paid. Microform: PQC. *Indexed:* A01, A22, AmHI, ArtHuCI, BRI, E01, MLA-IB, RILM. *Aud.:* Ac.

Narrative, the official journal of The International Society for the Study of Narrative, covers a wide range of scholarship focused on the American, English, and European novel, as well as nonfiction narrative, film, and narrative as performance art. Each issue contains five or six essays in criticism ranging from 10 to 25 pages in length. Occasionally, an editor's column is included. The journal explores literature from several periods, with marked strength in contemporary and twentieth-century fiction. Interdisciplinary studies are not uncommon. In recent issues, *Narrative* has published such essays as "The Chronicle and the Reckoning: A Temporal Paradox in Hawthorne's *Twice-Told Tales,*" "Narrative Temporality and Slowed Scene: The Interaction of Event and Thought Representation in Ian McEwan's Fiction," and "Paratext and Digitized Narrative: Mapping the Field." This journal is relevant to scholars in both literature and film studies and may be of interest to readers outside the academy. Recommended for all academic and medium or large public libraries. (HCM)

3594. New Literary History: a journal of theory and interpretation. [ISSN: 0028-6087] 1969. q. USD 190. Ed(s): Mollie H Washburne, Rita Felski. The Johns Hopkins University Press, 2715 N Charles St, Baltimore, MD 21218; http://www.press.jhu.edu. Illus., index, adv. Sample. Refereed. Circ: 789. Vol. ends: Nov. Microform: PQC. Reprint: PSC. *Indexed:* A01, A22, ABS&EES, AmHI, ArtHuCI, BAS, BEL&L, E01, MLA-IB, P02, P61, RILM, SSA. *Aud.:* Ac.

This formidable journal is focused on "questions of theory, method, interpretation, and literary history" and strives to spark "debate on the relations between literary and cultural texts and present needs." *NLH* is interested especially in scholarship that engages with literary and cultural theory, and pieces that address methodological or theoretical questions of interest to scholars across multiple fields. While the journal no longer organizes each issue under a theme, special issues are published on occasion, including the more recent "A New Europe?" The advisory editors of this publication constitute a virtual "Who's Who" of literature criticism, including but not limited to Helene Cixous, Jonathan Culler, Fredric Jameson, Martha Nussbaum, and Hayden White. Articles published recently include "Cosmopolitanism and Indigenism: The Uses of Cultural Authenticity in an Age of Flows," "Cognition is Recognition: Literary Knowledge and Textual 'Face,'" "Thought in a Strenuous Mood: Pragmatism as a Philosophy of Feeling," and "An Object-Oriented Defense of Poetry." Highly recommended for academic libraries, especially those that support graduate programs in the study of literature. (HCM)

3595. Nineteenth-Century Literature (Berkeley). Former titles (until 1986): *Nineteenth-Century Fiction;* (until 1949): *The Trollopian.* [ISSN: 0891-9356] 1945. q. USD 221 (print & online eds.). Ed(s): Saree Makdisi. University of California Press, Journals Division, 2000 Ctr St, Ste 303, Berkeley, CA 94704; customerservice@ucpressjournals.com; http://www.ucpressjournals.com. Illus., index, adv. Sample. Refereed. Circ: 1446. Vol. ends: Mar. Microform: PQC. Reprint: PSC. *Indexed:* A01, A22, AmHI, ArtHuCI, BRI, CBRI, E01, MLA-IB, P02. *Bk. rev.:* 8-10, 2-4 pages; signed. *Aud.:* Ac.

This elite journal from the University of California Press examines "transatlantic authors and poets, literary characters, and discourses" of the nineteenth century. Each issue contains three or four articles, and approximately ten book reviews. The 20- to 30-page articles exhibit quality literary scholarship. Authors studied in recent issues include George Eliot, Thomas Hardy, Maria Edgeworth, Emily Dickinson, Herman Melville, and Ralph Waldo Emerson. The broad coverage of nineteenth-century topics and authors from both sides of the pond makes this a good selection for all academic libraries. (HB)

3596. Notes and Queries: for readers and writers, collectors and librarians. [ISSN: 0029-3970] 1849. q. EUR 313. Oxford University Press, Great Clarendon St, Oxford, OX2 6DP, United Kingdom; enquiry@oup.co.uk; http://www.oxfordjournals.org/. Adv. Sample. Refereed. Microform: PMC; PQC. Reprint: PSC. *Indexed:* A01, A22, AmHI, ArtHuCI, BEL&L, BRI, BrArAb, E01, MLA-IB, P02, RILM. *Bk. rev.:* 17-30, 1-2 pages; signed. *Aud.:* Ac, Sa.

This unique and well-respected journal, "devoted principally to English language and literature, lexicography, history, and scholarly antiquarianism," has the principal aim of asking and responding to the questions of readers. Articles tend to be brief examinations (no more than a few pages in length) that explore facts and details about language and literature. The journal's scope encompasses work produced from the Medieval period to the early twentieth century. Each issue also includes 10–20 book reviews and sometimes a "Memorabilia" section, offering festschrift or other topical discussion. Recent articles include "A Fugitive Comment on Melville and *The Confidence-Man*," "Agape and Morality: Blake's Caterpillar-Man," "Asyndetic Parataxis in the Old English Poem *The Ruin*," and "Sterne and Warburton Again: Wrestling with a Chimney-Sweep." Most suitable for academic and large public libraries. (HCM)

3597. Novel: A Forum on Fiction. [ISSN: 0029-5132] 1967. 3x/yr. USD 122. Ed(s): Park Honan, Mark Spilka. Duke University Press, 905 W Main St, Ste 18 B, PO Box 90660, Durham, NC 27701; subscriptions@dukeupress.edu; http://www.dukeupress.edu. Illus., index, adv. Sample. Refereed. Circ: 1103. Vol. ends: Spring. Microform: PQC. Reprint: PSC. *Indexed:* A01, A22, ABS&EES, AmHI, ArtHuCI, BRI, MASUSE, MLA-IB, P02. *Bk. rev.:* 6-9, 2-4 pages; signed. *Aud.:* Ac.

This publication seeks to "promote critical discourse on the novel and publish significant work on fiction and related areas of research and theory." Special issues are fairly common, with the most recent example being "The Contemporary Novel: Imagining the Twenty-First Century." Issues generally contain five to nine articles and five to ten book reviews. Articles usually run 15–30 pages in length. Recently published articles include "The Novel as Climate Model: Realism and the Greenhouse Effect in *Bleak House*," "Austen and Translation: National Characters, Translatable Heroines, and the Heroine as Translator," and "Cognitive Investigations: The Problems of Qualia and Style in the Contemporary Neuronovel." Suitable for academic and large public libraries. (HCM)

3598. P M L A. Formerly (until 1888): *Modern Language Association of America. Transactions and Proceedings;* Which was formed by the merger of (1885-1886): *Modern Language Association of America. Transactions;* (1884-1886): *Modern Language Association of America. Proceedings.* [ISSN: 0030-8129] 1886. q. USD 12 per issue. Ed(s): Judy Goulding, Patricia Yaeger. Modern Language Association of America, 26 Broadway, 3rd Fl, New York, NY 10004; execdirector@mla.org; http://www.mla.org. Illus., index, adv. Sample. Refereed. Circ: 32700 Paid and controlled. Vol. ends: Nov. Microform: PQC. Reprint: PSC. *Indexed:* A01, A06, A22, ABS&EES, AmHI, ArtHuCI, MLA-IB, P02, RILM. *Aud.:* Ac.

PMLA, the journal of the Modern Language Association of America, publishes "members' essays judged to be of interest to scholars and teachers of language and literature." A core title in the fields of literature and language studies, this journal publishes six issues a year that offer scholarly essays on language and literature. (The fourth and sixth issues in each volume serve as the annual association directory and annual convention program, respectively.) Content represents a broad spectrum of topics, methods, and theoretical perspectives. Some essays are translated from languages other than English prior to publication. Issues focusing on special topics are sometimes published. The journal also publishes "little-known documentary material" that is deemed appropriate; an editor's column; and letters to the editor. Special topics are covered frequently. The journal's format also employs recurring sections of content, such as "Theories and Methodologies" and "The Changing Profession." Recent essays include "An Image of Europe: Yinka Shonibare's Postcolonial Decadence" and "Homer in a Nutshell: Vergilian Minaturization and the Sublime." This essential title is recommended for all academic and medium-to-large public libraries. (HCM)

3599. Papers on Language and Literature: a journal for scholars and critics of language and literature. Formerly (until 1966): *Papers on English Language & Literature.* [ISSN: 0031-1294] 1965. q. USD 95. Ed(s): Melanie Ethridge, Jack G Voller. Southern Illinois University at Edwardsville, SIUE Campus, Edwardsville, IL 62026; http://www.siue.edu. Illus., index, adv. Refereed. Vol. ends: Fall. Microform: PQC. *Indexed:* A01, A07, A22, ABS&EES, AmHI, ArtHuCI, BEL&L, BRI, MLA-IB, P02, RILM. *Bk. rev.:* 0-3, 4-6 pages; signed. *Aud.:* Ac.

PLL considers itself a generalist journal and publishes scholarship on "literary history, theory, and interpretation, as well as original materials such as letters, journals, and notebooks." The journal's broad scope accommodates all national literatures and periods, although most articles published examine the works of well-known American and English writers. Each issue contains approximately four articles, with an occasional review sometimes included. Articles run 20–30 pages in length. Essays published in recent issues include "The Substance of Fables: Dryden's 'Of the Pythagorean Philosophy,'" "Narratives of Absolutism in Jane Austen's *Mansfield Park*," and "Inscribed Bodies: The Cruel Mirage of Imperialistic Idealism in Kafka's 'Penal Colony.'" Recommended for academic and large public libraries. (HCM)

3600. Postcolonial Text. [ISSN: 1705-9100] 2004. s-a. Free. Postcolonial Text, c/o Ranjini Mendis, Dept of English, Kwantlen University College, Surrey, BC V3W 2M8, Canada. Refereed. *Indexed:* MLA-IB. *Bk. rev.:* 0-5, 3-5 pages. *Aud.:* Ac.

This open-access journal "examines the relationship between postcolonial studies, diaspora studies[,] and such newly emerging fields as transnational cultural and globalization studies." Recent scholarly essays, which are typically around 15 pages long, include studies of literature from Australia, India, Ireland, Guatemala, South Africa, Turkey, and Canada. The 2012 volume featured a special guest issue entitled, "Transnational Inquiries: Representing Postcolonial Violence and Cultures of Struggle," which examined, among other things, the treatment of human rights issues in literature. The journal adds value by publishing interviews with writers, book reviews, and postcolonial poetry and fiction. Articles are easy to view and print. This free peer-reviewed journal is recommended for all academic libraries. (HB)

3601. Postmedieval: a journal of medieval cultural studies. [ISSN: 2040-5960] 2010. q. USD 613. Ed(s): Myra Seaman, Eileen Joy. Palgrave Macmillan Ltd., Houndmills, Basingstoke, RG21 6XS, United Kingdom; orders@palgrave.com; http://www.palgrave.com. Adv. Sample. Refereed. *Indexed:* A22, ArtHuCI, E01, MLA-IB. *Aud.:* Ac.

This peer-reviewed journal from Palgrave Macmillan began in 2010 and has since won a PROSE award from the Association of American Publishers. The aim of this journal is to encourage "present-minded medieval studies in which contemporary events, issues, ideas, problems, objects, and texts serve as triggers for critical investigations of the Middle Ages." The journal is interdisciplinary, but many articles address literature or film and connect contemporary and medieval topics. Issues, or parts of issues, have themes such as "ecomaterialism" or disability and illness. The Spring 2012 issue, "Becoming-Media," was edited by "crowd review," and the articles were posted on a web site (http://postmedievalcrowdreview.wordpress.com) and open to all for comments. It appears that all comments were posted by other scholars. The draft articles remain on the web site, along with the comments. Given the open approach to review, it is a shame the journal itself is not open-access. Though they are relatively short (six to ten pages) and have pithy titles, the essays are very scholarly. This journal is most suitable for graduate students and faculty.

3602. *Qui Parle: critical humanities and social sciences.* Formerly (until 1987): *Ca Parle.* [ISSN: 1041-8385] 1985. s-a. USD 109.20 (print & online eds.). Ed(s): Peter Skafish. University of Nebraska Press, 1111 Lincoln Mall, Lincoln, NE 68588; pressmail@unl.edu; http://www.nebraskapress.unl.edu. Adv. Refereed. Circ: 100. *Indexed:* A22, E01, MLA-IB. *Aud.:* Ac.

Qui Parle strives to publish "provocative interdisciplinary articles covering a range of outstanding theoretical and critical work in the humanities and social sciences." It also "is dedicated to expanding the dialogues that take place between disciplines and that challenge conventional understandings of reading and scholarship in academia." The journal is innovative and formidable, having published such pioneering scholars as Jacques Derrida, Judith Butler, Peggy Kamuf, and Slavoj Zizek. Recent issues have been themed, either in whole or in part, including a recent entire issue concerned with "Higher Education on Its Knees" and a recent "special dossier" on the theme of "Affect Theory." Issues usually contain eight to ten essays that range widely in length from 6 to 60 pages. Recent articles include "Geranium Logic: Intensity and Indifference in Emmanuel Hocquard," "'A Sinister Resonance': Vibration, Sound, and the Birth of Conrad's Marlow," and "Lyric Disaster: Poetic Voice and Its Lacanian Other." Recommended for academic libraries, especially those with graduate programs in the humanities and social sciences. (HCM)

3603. *Religion and Literature.* Formerly (until 1984): *Notre Dame English Journal.* [ISSN: 0888-3769] 1957. 3x/yr. Individuals, USD 25. Ed(s): Craig B Woelfel, Susannah Monta. University of Notre Dame, Department of English, 1146 Flanner Hall, Notre Dame, IN 46556; english.randl.1@nd.edu; http://www.nd.edu. Adv. Refereed. *Indexed:* A01, A22, AmHI, ArtHuCI, C26, FR, MLA-IB, R&TA. *Bk. rev.:* 0-10, 3-6 pages; signed. *Aud.:* Ac.

This journal from Notre Dame publishes scholarly articles regarding "relations between two crucial human concerns: the religious impulse and the literary forms of any era, place, or language." Recent articles (usually 20–30 pages) include "Reading to Live: Miracle and Language" and "Buddhism and Modern Existential Nihilism: Jean-Paul Sartre Meets Nagarjuna." Some issues feature a "Forum" section, which presents shorter essays on a particular topic (e.g., religion in the works of T. S. Eliot). Most issues contain book reviews, which are usually about three pages long. Recommended for academic libraries that support graduate programs in the humanities. (HB)

Research in African Literatures. See Africa section.

3604. *The Review of Contemporary Fiction.* [ISSN: 0276-0045] 1981. q. 3/yr. USD 26 (Individuals, USD 17; USD 8 per issue). Ed(s): Jeremy Davies. University of Illinois, Dalkey Archive Press, 1805 S. Wright St, MC-011, Champaign, IL 61820; contact@dalkeyarchive.com; http://www.dalkeyarchive.com. Illus., index. Vol. ends: Fall. Microform: PQC. *Indexed:* A01, A22, ABS&EES, AmHI, BEL&L, BRI, CBRI, MLA-IB, P02, RILM. *Bk. rev.:* 8-50, 1/2-2 pages; signed. *Aud.:* Ac.

This publication emphasizes "fiction writers whose work resists convention and easy categorization" and highlights "works of foreign writers who may otherwise go unread in the United States, as well as American writers whose work has gone unchampioned in their own country." The journal, which has a refreshingly irreverent feel to it, publishes critical essays, and book reviews.

Interviews with writers are included in some issues. The journal also occasionally includes original literary works. Critical essays are typically 10–20 pages. Recent special issues are devoted to the specific writers including Gert Jonke (Summer 2012) and Robert Coover (Spring 2012). The Fall 2012 issue features contemporary British fiction. Though this is more of a literary review than a traditional academic journal, the topics covered would be useful for any academic curriculum that included contemporary and/or international authors. It is also a valuable resource for readers interested in broadening their options. Recommended for academic libraries. (HB)

3605. *The Review of English Studies: the leading journal of English literature and language.* [ISSN: 0034-6551] 1925. q. EUR 417. Oxford University Press, Great Clarendon St, Oxford, OX2 6DP, United Kingdom; enquiry@oup.co.uk; http://www.oxfordjournals.org/. Illus., index, adv. Sample. Refereed. Microform: PQC. Reprint: PSC. *Indexed:* A01, A22, AmHI, ArtHuCI, BEL&L, BRI, CBRI, E01, MLA-IB, P02. *Bk. rev.:* 7-22, 2-3 pages; signed. *Aud.:* Ac.

This elite journal from Oxford University Press focuses on "historical scholarship" of "English literature and the English language from the earliest period to the present." Recent scholarship includes "War and the Epic Mania in England and France: Milton, Boileau, Prior and English Mock-Heroic," "Money in Jane Austen," "The Making of the Oxford Ben Jonson," and "'The Nietzschean Prophecy Come True': Philip Roth's *The Counterlife* and the Aesthetics of Identity." Each issue also features a large section of two- to three-page reviews. Recommended for academic libraries. (HB)

3606. *Romanticism: the journal of romantic culture and criticism.* [ISSN: 1354-991X] 1995. 3x/yr. GBP 127.50 (print & online eds.). Ed(s): Nicholas Roe. Edinburgh University Press Ltd., 22 George Sq, Edinburgh, EH8 9LF, United Kingdom; journals@eup.ed.ac.uk; http://www.euppublishing.com. Illus. Refereed. *Indexed:* A01, A22, AmHI, ArtHuCI, E01, MLA-IB. *Bk. rev.:* 10-15, 2-4 pages; signed. *Aud.:* Ac.

This journal from Edinburgh University Press features "critical, historical, textual and bibliographical essays" about the Romantic period, which the journal defines as "1750-1850." Recent articles, which are generally 10–15 pages, highlight writers such as William Blake, Robert Burns, Samuel Taylor Coleridge, William Godwin, Percy Shelley, Laurence Sterne, and William Wordsworth. Entire issues are devoted to individual authors (Thomas De Quincey) or topics ("The Wye [River] Valley," "Romantic Wonder"). Issues also contain two- to three-page book reviews. Recommended for academic libraries that serve graduate programs in literature. (HB)

3607. *Romanticism and Victorianism on the Net.* Formerly (until 2007): *Romanticism on the Net.* [ISSN: 1916-1441] 1996. q. Free. Universite de Montreal, Succursale Centre-Ville, P O Box 6128, Montreal, PQ H3C 3J7, Canada. Refereed. *Indexed:* MLA-IB. *Bk. rev.:* 5-15; signed. *Aud.:* Ac.

This open-access journal examines Romantic and Victorian British authors. Recent articles study Leigh Hunt, Charlotte Riddell, Thomas Carlyle, William Blake, and Charles Spurgeon. A recent special issue examines "Romantic Cultures of Print." Issues also contain a substantial section of review essays. Along with the launch of a new web site, the 2011 double issue was posted in June 2013 after "a period of unexpected delay." The new site is sleeker in appearance and is easy to navigate. Academic libraries and public libraries should consider adding this peer-reviewed journal to their catalogs or research guides. URL: http://ravonjournal.org (HB)

3608. *Southern Literary Journal.* [ISSN: 0038-4291] 1968. s-a. USD 47 USD 23.50 per issue domestic. Ed(s): Minrose Gwin, Fred Hobson. University of North Carolina Press, 116 S Boundary St, Chapel Hill, NC 27514; uncpress@unc.edu; http://www.uncpress.unc.edu. Illus., index, adv. Refereed. Circ: 500. Microform: PQC. *Indexed:* A01, A22, AmHI, ArtHuCI, BRI, E01, MLA-IB, P02, RILM. *Bk. rev.:* 3-5, 3-4 pages; signed. *Aud.:* Ac.

Articles in this scholarly journal from the University of North Carolina illuminate "the works of southern writers and the ongoing development of southern culture." The scholarly essays (generally 15–20 pages long) feature studies of authors such as Charles Chesnutt, William Faulkner, Eudora Welty, Flannery O'Connor, Charles Wright, and Natasha Trethewey. Regular issues contain review essays. Recommended for all academic libraries. (HB)

3609. Speculum: a journal of Medieval studies. [ISSN: 0038-7134] 1926. q. GBP 140 (print & online eds.). Ed(s): Ronald G Musto, Eileen Gardiner. Cambridge University Press, The Edinburgh Bldg, Shaftesbury Rd, Cambridge, CB2 8RU, United Kingdom; journals@cambridge.org; http://journals.cambridge.org. Illus., index, adv. Refereed. Vol. ends: Oct. Microform: MIM; PQC. Reprint: PSC. *Indexed:* A01, A06, A07, A22, ABS&EES, AmHI, ArtHuCI, BEL&L, BRI, BrArAb, CBRI, FR, IPB, MLA-IB, NumL, P02, RILM. *Bk. rev.:* 80-90, 2 pages; signed. *Aud.:* Ac.

This multidisciplinary and interdisciplinary journal publishes scholarly essays that deal with the Middle Ages, inclusive of "all disciplines, methodologies, and approaches." The contents of each issue represent this broad scope. For example, two recent issues featured pieces by scholars in Comparative Literature, Art History, Byzantine Studies, Religious Studies, History, and Folkloristics. The journal focuses on Western Europe, although "Arabic, Byzantine, Hebrew, and Slavic studies are also included." Roughly half of each issue is devoted to an enormous number of book reviews and brief notices about publications relevant to Medieval Studies. Recent essays, including copious footnotes to the text, have ranged from 25 to 45 pages in length. While articles are written in English, notes often present material in its original language. Recent articles published in *Speculum* include "Petrarch's War: Florentine Wages and the Black Death," "Boccaccio's Poetic Anthropology: Allegories of History in the *Genealogie deorum gentilium libri*," and "The Place of the Proper Name in the Topographies of the *Paradiso*." While this journal includes much content that does not engage literature directly, those articles that deal with literature are important reading for literary scholars studying the period. Recommended for academic libraries, especially those that support Medieval Studies programs. (HCM)

3610. Studies in American Fiction. [ISSN: 0091-8083] 1973. s-a. USD 70 (print or online ed.). Ed(s): Maria Farland, Duncan Faherty. The Johns Hopkins University Press, 2715 N Charles St, Baltimore, MD 21218; http://www.press.jhu.edu. Illus., adv. Sample. Refereed. Circ: 350. Vol. ends: Fall. Reprint: PSC. *Indexed:* A01, A22, AmHI, ArtHuCI, BEL&L, BRI, E01, MLA-IB, P02. *Bk. rev.:* 2-5, 1-2 pages; signed. *Aud.:* Ac.

Studies in American Fiction publishes scholarship on the prose fiction of the United States from the colonial period to the present. Published by Northeastern University Press since its founding in 1973, the journal suspended publication in fall of 2008. However, The Johns Hopkins University Press is now editing and publishing the journal, with the intent to "maintain its commitment to publishing exciting new work on writers ranging from Susanna Rowson to Toni Morrison, while also emphasizing forms of writing that do not conform to traditional genres and forms." *SAF* now includes approximately six essays in each issue, generally falling in the range of 20–25 pages in length. Recently published articles include "Romantic Revolutions: Love and Violence in Leonora Sansay's *Secret History, or The Horrors of St. Domingo*," "The Gaucho Sells Out: Thomas Pynchon and Argentina," and "The Space that Race Creates: An Interstitial Analysis of Toni Morrison's 'Recitatif.'" Recommended for most academic libraries. (HCM)

3611. Studies in English Literature 1500-1900. [ISSN: 0039-3657] 1961. q. USD 135. Ed(s): Alexander Regier, Joseph Campana. The Johns Hopkins University Press, 2715 N Charles St, Baltimore, MD 21218; http://www.press.jhu.edu. Illus., adv. Sample. Refereed. Circ: 832. Microform: PQC. Reprint: PSC. *Indexed:* A01, A22, AmHI, ArtHuCI, BRI, E01, MASUSE, MLA-IB, P02, RILM. *Aud.:* Ac.

This quarterly journal from Rice University (and published by Johns Hopkins University Press) devotes one issue a year to the following: the "Renaissance non-dramatic literature" (Winter issue), "Tudor-Stuart drama" (Spring), the "the long eighteenth century" (Summer), and the "the nineteenth century" (Fall). Each issue contains eight or nine scholarly essays (typically 20–30 pages long) and concludes with a lengthy review essay of "recent studies" relevant to the issue's literary period. With this journal's wide span of scholarship, each volume provides a great overview of the study of literature. A core title for all academic libraries. (HB)

3612. Studies in Philology. [ISSN: 0039-3738] 1903. q. USD 65. Ed(s): Reid Barbou. University of North Carolina Press, 116 S Boundary St, Chapel Hill, NC 27514; uncpress@unc.edu; http://www.uncpress.unc.edu. Refereed. Circ: 900. Microform: MIM; IDC; PMC; PQC. *Indexed:* A01, A06, A22, AmHI, ArtHuCI, BEL&L, E01, MLA-IB, P02, RILM. *Aud.:* Ac.

This scholarly journal focuses on "British literature before 1900 and articles on relations between British literature and works in the classical, Romance, and Germanic languages." Scholarly studies are typically around 20 pages; the journal does not include book reviews. Recently published articles include "Gold, Land, and Labor: Ideologies of Colonization and Rewriting *The Tempest* in 1622" and "William Wordsworth and Philosophical Necessity." This journal is best suited for academic libraries that support graduate programs in literature. (HB)

3613. Studies in Romanticism. [ISSN: 0039-3762] 1961. q. USD 60 (Individuals, USD 23). Ed(s): Deborah Swedberg, David Wagenknecht. Boston University, Graduate School, 236 Bay State Rd, Boston, MA 02215; http://www.bu.edu/. Illus., index, adv. Refereed. Vol. ends: Winter. Microform: PQC. *Indexed:* A01, A07, A22, AmHI, ArtHuCI, BEL&L, BRI, MLA-IB, P02, RILM. *Bk. rev.:* 4-6, 2-6 pages; signed. *Aud.:* Ac.

Studies in Romanticism publishes scholarly articles on literature, arts, and culture associated with the Romantic movement. The preponderance of essays engages English authors and works, with occasional pieces also addressing other European and U.S. literature. Most issues include six articles, along with three to six book reviews. Articles generally are 15–30 pages in length. Recent essays include "William Rowan Hamilton and the Uses of Poetry for Science," "Contested Bounds: John Clare, John Keats, and the Sonnet," "The Romantic Fragment Poem and the Performance of Form," and "Entailing the Nation: Inheritance and History in Walter Scott's *The Antiquary*." This is a leading journal in the study of Romanticism and is recommended for academic libraries. (HCM)

3614. Studies in the Novel. [ISSN: 0039-3827] 1969. q. USD 45. Ed(s): Jacqueline Foertsch. University of North Texas, English Department, 1155 Union Circle 310680, PO Box 311307, Denton, TX 76203; Holdeman@unt.edu; http://www.engl.unt.edu. Illus., index. Refereed. Vol. ends: No. 4. Microform: PQC. *Indexed:* A01, A22, ABS&EES, AmHI, ArtHuCI, BEL&L, BRI, E01, MLA-IB, P02. *Bk. rev.:* 0-7, 1-2 pages; signed. *Aud.:* Ac.

Studies in the Novel is dedicated to presenting "excellence in criticism of the novel in all periods, by established and emerging novelists worldwide, from all interpretive approaches." In each issue, readers will find five or six essays in criticism, eight to ten book reviews, and an occasional review essay. The journal publishes an occasional special issue, with the most recent being a two-issue focus on the work of David Foster Wallace. Examples of articles published most recently are "The Limitations of Vision and the Power of Folklore in John Dos Passos's *U.S.A.*," "The Formation of Social Class and the Reformation of Ireland: Maria Edgeworth's *Ennui*," and "Allegory and the Critique of Sovereignty: Ismail Kadare's Political Theologies." Recommended for all academic libraries and large public libraries. (HCM)

3615. Studies in Twentieth and Twenty-First Century Literature. Formerly (until 2004): *Studies in Twentieth Century Literature*. [ISSN: 1555-7839] 1976. s-a. Ed(s): Silvia Sauter. Kansas State University, Department of Modern Languages, 104 Eisenhower Hall, Manhattan, KS 66506; mlangs@ksu.edu; http://www.k-state.edu/mlangs/. Illus., index. Refereed. *Indexed:* A22, ABS&EES, AmHI, BRI, MLA-IB. *Bk. rev.:* 0-13, 2-3 pages; signed. *Aud.:* Ac.

This journal, which began publishing in 1976, is devoted to "articles written in English on literature in French, German, Russian[,] and Spanish." Essays often are written with an interdisciplinary perspective, including frequent intersections with theater, history, and aspects of popular culture. Special issues are common, including a recent issue on "Defining Differences: 20th and 21st Century Spanish Poetry." Articles generally run 8–12 pages in length. Recent articles include "Reading Sara Pujol Russell's Poetry of Contemplation and Connection," "In the Heideggerian Tradition: *Acontecimiento* by Concha Garcia," and "'Real' Places in Marguerite Duras's Wartime Paris." Recommended for larger academic libraries. (HCM)

3616. Style (DeKalb). [ISSN: 0039-4238] 1967. q. USD 90 (Individuals, USD 45). Ed(s): John V Knapp. Northern Illinois University, Department of English, Department Office, Dekalb, IL 60115; askEnglish@niu.edu; http://www.engl.niu.edu/index.shtml. Adv. Refereed. Reprint: PSC. *Indexed:* A01, A22, ABS&EES, AmHI, ArtHuCI, BRI, MLA-IB, P02, RILM. *Bk. rev.:* 0-2, 2-3 pages; signed. *Aud.:* Ac.

Style publishes articles "that address questions of style, stylistics, and poetics, including research and theory in discourse analysis, literary and nonliterary genres, narrative, figuration, metrics, and rhetorical analysis." The essays included cover a broad range of fields, including literary criticism and theory, cognitive linguistics, rhetoric and writing studies, computational linguistics, the philosophy of language, and the "new psychologies." Reviews and review essays also may be included. The majority of issues are themed, most recently focusing on "Applied Evolutionary Criticism" and "Literature, Bio-Psychological Reality, and Focalization." Articles range in length from 20 to 35 pages. Among articles published recently are "Homo Oneginensis: Pushkin and Evo-Cognitive Approaches to Literature," "No Ideology Without Psychology: The Emotional Effects of Shakespeare's *Henry V*," and "Ginsberg's Inferno: Dante and 'Howl.'" Recommended for academic libraries. (HCM)

3617. Texas Studies in Literature and Language. Supersedes (in 1959): *Texas Studies in English;* Which was formerly (1911-1957): *University of Texas. Studies in English.* [ISSN: 0040-4691] 1911. q. USD 184. Ed(s): Kurt Heinzelman. University of Texas Press, Journals Division, PO Box 7819, Austin, TX 78713; journals@uts.cc.utexas.edu; http://www.utexas.edu/utpress/journals/journals.html. Illus., index. Refereed. Vol. ends: Winter. Microform: PQC. *Indexed:* A01, A22, ABS&EES, AmHI, ArtHuCI, BEL&L, BRI, E01, FR, MLA-IB, P02, RILM. *Aud.:* Ac.

This journal from the University of Texas Press publishes "substantial essays reflecting a variety of critical approaches and covering all periods of literary history." The journal recently reached its 100th anniversary. Kurt Heinzelman's introduction to the Winter 2012 issue explains that though the journal now includes scholarship from authors around the world, the journal began as a place for the university's faculty to publish their work. In honor of the centennial, he explains, three issues of Volume 54 include University of Texas faculty as editors or contributors. Subjects of the 20- to 40-page articles are broad in scope; authors studied include Joseph Conrad, John Fowles, Ngugi wa Thiong'o, Minnie Bruce Pratt, and Gertrude Stein. The Spring 2013 issue features a thematic section, "Literary Modernism and Melody." Another recent issue includes translations of contemporary Turkish literature. Academic libraries should consider adding this journal to their collection. (HB)

3618. Textual Practice. [ISSN: 0950-236X] 1987. bi-m. GBP 721 (print & online eds.). Ed(s): Peter Boxall. Routledge, 4 Park Sq, Milton Park, Abingdon, OX14 4RN, United Kingdom; subscriptions@tandf.co.uk; http://www.tandfonline.com. Illus., adv. Sample. Refereed. Vol. ends: Winter. Reprint: PSC. *Indexed:* A01, A22, AmHI, ArtHuCI, E01, MLA-IB. *Bk. rev.:* 8-15, 3-7 pages; signed. *Aud.:* Ac.

Textual Practice publishes articles that operate "at the turning points of theory with politics, history, and texts," with emphasis on historically marginalized cultures of ethnicity and sexuality. A recent special issue addressed the topic "Postcolonial Literature and Challenges for the New Millennium." Articles usually run from 20 to 30 pages in length. Recently published essays include "Humans and/as Machines: Beckett and Cultural Cybernetics," "Double-Crossing: Elizabeth Bowen's Ghostly Short Fiction," and "The Poetics of Presentation: Lyn Hejinian's *My Life* Project and the Work of Giorgio Agamben." Reviews and review essays generally are included in each issue. Appropriate for larger academic libraries with strong literature programs. (HCM)

3619. Tulsa Studies in Women's Literature. [ISSN: 0732-7730] 1982. s-a. USD 25 (Individuals, USD 20). Ed(s): Sarah Theobold-Hall, Laura M Stevens. University of Tulsa, 800 S Tucker Dr, Tulsa, OK 74104; news@utulsa.edu; http://www.utulsa.edu. Illus., index, adv. Refereed. Circ: 600. Microform: PQC. *Indexed:* A01, A22, AmHI, ArtHuCI, BRI, CBRI, E01, FemPer, MLA-IB, P02, WSA. *Bk. rev.:* 7-15, 2-3 pages. *Aud.:* Ac.

This scholarly journal publishes "articles, notes, research, and reviews of literary, historicist, and theoretical work by established and emerging scholars in the field of women's literature and feminist theory." The scope is not limited to a geographical or chronological place, and articles discuss all issues dealing with women's literature. Recent issues (as of July 2013, the Fall 2011 issue was the most recent) highlight studies of Al-Khansa', George Eliot, Virginia Woolf, Anne Finch, and Elizabeth Barrett Browning. A recent special issue is entitled "Women and Anglo-American Periodicals." In addition to review essays, there is a section of several book reviews. According to the editor's note in the Spring 2011 issue, the journal plans to include reviews of translations. The journal sometimes includes a unique "Archives" section, which features "bibliographies, descriptions of particular archives, or narratives of archival research." The "Innovations" section has recently featured descriptions of new projects in digital archives or translations. Recommended for academic libraries. (HB)

3620. Twentieth Century Literature. [ISSN: 0041-462X] 1955. q. Ed(s): Lee Zimmerman. Hofstra University, 124 Hofstra University, Hempstead, NY 11549; http://www.hofstra.edu/. Illus., index. Refereed. Vol. ends: No. 4. Microform: MIM; PQC. *Indexed:* A01, A22, AmHI, ArtHuCI, BEL&L, BRI, MASUSE, MLA-IB, P02, RILM. *Bk. rev.:* 3-4, 4-10 pages. *Aud.:* Ac.

As the title suggests, this excellent publication limits its content to studies of literature from the twentieth century. Apart from that constraint, the journal's scope is broad and inclusive. The majority of articles, however, cover American and English writers and works. The editorial board is dominated by distinguished scholars in the field. Each issue typically contains four essays, ranging in length from 20 to 30 pages, followed by three or four book reviews. The journal also publishes the winner of the Andrew J. Kappel Prize in Literary Criticism, awarded each year to "the author (or authors) of a work submitted to the journal during the preceding year that is judged to make the most impressive contribution to our understanding and appreciation of the literature of the twentieth century." Recent articles include "'Fictions Where a Man Could Live': Wordlessness, Utopia, and the Void in Rushdie's *Grimus*," "Letting Moses Go: Hurston and Reed, Disowning Exodus," and "Caretakers/Caregivers: Economies of Affection in Alice Munro." This journal should be considered a core title for academic library collections, and is appropriate for larger public libraries as well. (HCM)

3621. University of Toronto Quarterly: a Canadian journal of the humanities. [ISSN: 0042-0247] 1931. q. USD 200. Ed(s): Victor Li. University of Toronto Press, Journals Division, 5201 Dufferin St, Toronto, ON M3H 5T8, Canada; journals@utpress.utoronto.ca; http://www.utpjournals.com. Adv. Sample. Refereed. Circ: 390. Microform: MML; PQC. *Indexed:* A01, A22, ABS&EES, AmHI, ArtHuCI, BEL&L, BRI, C37, CBCARef, E01, IIPA, MLA-IB, P02, RILM. *Bk. rev.:* Annual review issue. *Aud.:* Ac.

This journal centers on "all areas of the humanities—literature, philosophy, fine arts, music, the history of ideas, [and] cultural studies." Articles are accepted in both English and French (most articles in recent issues are in English). Though this is an interdisciplinary journal, most issues discuss literary topics; for example, recent articles study Shakespeare, Dante, and August Wilson. Articles in the Winter 2012 issue examine the work of Northrup Frye. The Spring 2013 special issue is entitled, "Writing the Foreign in Canadian Literature and Humanitarian Narratives." The annual (bilingual) special issue, "Letters in Canada," reviews a year's work in fiction, poetry, drama, translations, and the humanities. The letters issue includes an index of books reviewed. Recommended for large academic libraries that support relevant programs. (HB)

3622. Victorian Poetry. [ISSN: 0042-5206] 1963. q. USD 100 (Individuals, USD 45). Ed(s): John B Lamb. West Virginia University Press, Victorian Poetry Office, PO Box 6295, Morgantown, WV 26506; press@mail.wvu.edu; http://www.wvu.edu/. Illus., index. Sample. Refereed. Vol. ends: Winter. Microform: PQC. Reprint: PSC. *Indexed:* A01, A07, A22, AmHI, ArtHuCI, BRI, E01, MLA-IB, P02, RILM. *Aud.:* Ac.

This scholarly journal from West Virginia University Press publishes scholarship intended to "further the aesthetic study of the poetry of the Victorian Period in Britain (1830-1914)." Recently, the journal has included studies of Tennyson, Christina Rossetti, Dante Gabriel Rossetti, and Thomas Hardy, as well as an entire issue on Robert Browning. Each year, the journal publishes a "Guide to the Year's Work"—bibliographic essays organized by literary figure (e.g., Matthew Arnold) or broader category (e.g., "The Poets of the Nineties," or the Pre-Raphaelites). The readable articles and inclusive scope make this a good choice for any academic library. (HB)

3623. Victorian Studies: a journal of the humanities, arts and sciences. [ISSN: 0042-5222] 1957. q. USD 199.50 (print & online eds.). Ed(s): Ashley Miller, Ivan Kreilkamp. Indiana University Press, 601 N Morton St, Bloomington, IN 47404; journals@indiana.edu; http://iupress.indiana.edu. Illus., index, adv. Refereed. Circ: 2100. Microform: PQC. Reprint: PSC. *Indexed:* A01, A07, A22, AmHI, ArtHuCI, BAS, BEL&L, BRI, CBRI, E01, MLA-IB, MSN, P02, RILM. *Bk. rev.:* 30-35, 1-3 pages; signed. *Aud.:* Ac.

This journal from Indiana University Press is "devoted to the study of English culture of the Victorian period." Though this journal has an interdisciplinary approach, literature topics are heavily represented. Examples of recent articles include "'The Poet of Science': How Scientists Read Their Tennyson," "George Eliot and the Cosmopolitan Cynic," and "Wild Charges: The Afro-Haitian 'Charge of the Light Brigade'" The Spring 2012 issue contains papers from the North American Victorian Studies Association conference. The substantial book review section in each issue provides a good survey of recent studies in the discipline. Recommended for all academic libraries. (HB)

3624. Western American Literature. [ISSN: 0043-3462] 1966. q. USD 65 (Individuals, USD 25). Ed(s): Melody Graulich. Western Literature Association, Utah State University, English Department, Logan, UT 84322-3200; wal@usu.edu; http://www.usu.edu/westlit/index.htm. Adv. Refereed. Circ: 1200. Microform: PQC. *Indexed:* A22, AmHI, ArtHuCI, BRI, CBRI, Chicano, E01, MLA-IB. *Bk. rev.:* 14-22, 1-2 pages; signed. *Aud.:* Ac, Sa.

Western American Literature publishes literary criticism on any aspect of the literature of the American West, including interdisciplinary pieces with a literary focus. Submission guidelines identify a particular interest in multiculturalism and the "New West." Issues generally contain three scholarly essays (ranging in length from 20 to 35 pages), 14–18 book reviews, and an occasional review essay. Recently published essays include "Shaking Awake the Memory: The Gothic Quest for Place in Sandra Cisneros's *Caramelo*," "'What Manner of Heretic?': Demons in McCarthy and the Question of Agency," and "Critical Regionalism, the US-Mexican War, and Nineteenth-Century American Literary History." This journal's geographic focus allows it a distinctive role within library collections. It should be considered for most academic and larger public libraries. (HCM)

3625. World Literature Today: a literary bimonthly of the University of Oklahoma. Formerly (until 1977): *Books Abroad.* [ISSN: 0196-3570] 1927. bi-m. USD 155 (print & online eds.). Ed(s): Michelle Johnson. University of Oklahoma, 630 Parrington Oval, Ste 110, Norman, OK 73019; ou-pss@ou.edu; http://www.ou.edu/. Illus., index. Refereed. Microform: PQC. Reprint: PSC. *Indexed:* A01, A22, ABS&EES, AmHI, ArtHuCI, BAS, BEL&L, BRI, C37, CBRI, Chicano, MASUSE, MLA-IB, P02, RILM. *Bk. rev.:* 150-250, 1/2-1 page; signed. *Aud.:* Ac.

This bimonthly journal is concerned with contemporary world literature, and it features a variety of content of potential interest to academics and general readers alike. Issues feature essays on writers who work in several languages, original poetry and fiction, interviews, analysis of transnational issues, book reviews, travel writing, author profiles, and a column on children's literature. The journal welcomes interdisciplinary perspectives and, as a result, it features "coverage of the other arts, culture, and politics as [each] intersects with literature." Special sections are frequent, including recent focuses on "The Global South" and jazz poetry. Geoffrey Philp, an award-winning and versatile author of Caribbean literature, and Scottish travel writer, historian, and journalist William Dalrymple are among the people interviewed in the last several months. This extremely accessible title is recommended for both academic and public libraries. (HCM)

■ LITTLE MAGAZINES

See also Alternatives; Literary Reviews; and Literature sections.

Helen Georgas, Reference & Instruction Librarian and Assistant Professor, Brooklyn College of the City University of New York (CUNY)

Introduction

Little magazines have long published alternative work. Voices that would not otherwise be heard are given their place in the hundreds of little magazines being published across the country today. Over the last few years, there has been a veritable explosion of little magazines, many of them extremely promising, all of them committed to publishing exciting new writers alongside well-known ones. Interesting new little magazines such as *The Coffin Factory, The Common, Little Star, PANK,* and *Toad Suck Review* affirm that small press publications and the desire to discover new writers and artists are thriving, perhaps now more than ever.

The titles selected, a mix of newer and more established little magazines, have proven themselves in the quality of their fiction, nonfiction, poetry, and artwork. These journals have consistently produced excellent issues, with many of their stories, poems, and essays being re-published in anthologies such as *Pushcart Prize: Best of the Small Presses, Best American Poetry, Best American Essays, Prize Stories: The O. Henry Awards, Best American Non-Required Reading,* and *Best American Short Stories.* The aim of this list is to ensure that any library purchasing one of the selected little magazines will be adding a valuable title to their collection. Sadly, this list is highly selective, and there are still many other high-quality little magazines that have not been included. In acknowledging that we live in a time in which library budgets are being slashed, the focus here is mainly on U.S. publications, with the exception of a handful of Canadian titles. In addition, journals that are more regional in focus, both in terms of the writing they include and in the audience for which they are intended, have largely been excluded.

Basic Periodicals

Ga: *A Public Space, Glimmer Train, McSweeney's, The Paris Review, Poetry* (Chicago), *Ploughshares, Tin House, Virginia Quarterly Review.* Ac: *A Public Space, Glimmer Train, McSweeney's, The Paris Review, Ploughshares, Poetry* (Chicago), *Tin House, Virginia Quarterly Review.*

Basic Abstracts and Indexes

PIO: Periodicals Index Online, Project Muse, ProQuest Research Library.

Agni. See Literary Reviews section.

Alaska Quarterly Review. See Literary Reviews section.

American Short Fiction. See Fiction: General/Mystery and Detective/General section.

Antioch Review. See Literary Reviews section.

Bellevue Literary Review. See Literary Reviews section.

3626. Black Warrior Review. [ISSN: 0193-6301] 1974. s-a. USD 16; USD 10 per issue. Ed(s): Farren Stanley, Jenny Gropp Hess. Black Warrior Review, PO Box 862936, Tuscaloosa, AL 35486. Adv. *Indexed:* AmHI, BRI, CBRI, MLA-IB. *Bk. rev.:* Number and length vary. *Aud.:* Ga, Ac.

Black Warrior Review publishes poetry, fiction, nonfiction, and art by prize-winning authors alongside up-and-coming ones. Each issue includes a chapbook from a nationally known poet, as well as work (via full-color plates) by a featured artist. Stories and poems that have appeared in *Black Warrior Review* have been reprinted in many of the major anthologies. *Black Warrior Review* is published twice a year by the University of Alabama.

Callaloo. See African American section.

3627. *Cincinnati Review.* [ISSN: 1546-9034] 2004. s-a. USD 30 (Individuals, USD 15). University of Cincinnati, Department of English & Comparative Literature, 248 McMicken Hall, PO Box 210069, Cincinnati, OH 45221-0069; http://www.artsci.uc.edu/english. *Bk. rev.:* 3-4. *Aud.:* Ga, Ac.

Cincinnati Review was founded in 2003 and since then has published stories, poems, nonfiction, and reviews by both established and emerging writers. *Cincinnati Review* has become a highly-regarded literary magazine, and its stories, essays, and poems have been honored in all the "best of" anthologies: *Best American Essays, Best American Poetry,* and *Best American Short Stories.* Recent contributors include Dean Bakopoulos, Angela Ball, and Sarah Shun-Lien Bynum. *Cincinnati Review* is published twice yearly by the University of Cincinnati.

Colorado Review. See Literary Reviews section.

Conjunctions. See Literary Reviews section.

3628. *Cousin Corinne's Reminder.* 2012. s-a. USD 14. Ed(s): Zack Zook, Hannah Zeavin. Cousin Corinne Inc., 161 Court St, Brooklyn, NY 11201. *Aud.:* Ga, Ac.

Cousin Corinne's Reminder is a literary and visual art journal published jointly by Cousin Corinne, an independent publishing group, and Book Court, an independent bookstore located in Brooklyn, New York. This journal is very new, having only published three issues thus far, but what issues they are. Aesthetically, each issue is stunning, with a full-color cover featuring original artwork, along with full-color art spreads (painting, photography, comics) throughout. This title is printed on high-quality paper, and the design of each issue is something to behold. The most recent issue (Issue Number Three) is over 300 pages in length and, along with art and comics, features poetry, short stories, and essays. Contributors, a mix of writers and artists, have included Charles Bock, Arthur Bradford, Simon Dinnerstein, Dean Haspiel, Jhumpa Lahiri, Jocelyn Lee, Emily Raboteau, Emma Straub, and John Wray.

3629. *The Cream City Review.* [ISSN: 0884-3457] 1975. s-a. USD 22; USD 12 per issue. Ed(s): Jay Johnson, Drew Blanchard. University of Wisconsin at Milwaukee, English Department, PO Box 413, Milwaukee, WI 53201; kilkenn3@uwm.edu; http://www4.uwm.edu/letsci/english/. Adv. Refereed. *Indexed:* AmHI, MLA-IB. *Bk. rev.:* 1-3. *Aud.:* Ga, Ac.

The Cream City Review publishes fiction, poetry, creative nonfiction, comics, and full-color artwork that both is energetic and "pushes the boundaries." The magazine also includes reviews of contemporary literature and criticism, as well as author interviews. *Cream City Review* prides itself on featuring the work of both established and previously unpublished writers. Each issue includes a multicolor glossy cover of original artwork, a feature for which the magazine has become known. *Cream City Review* is published twice a year by graduate students at the University of Wisconsin–Milwaukee.

3630. *Ecotone.* [ISSN: 1553-1775] 2005. s-a. USD 39.95 (Individuals, USD 16.95; USD 12.95 per issue). Ed(s): Meredith Fraser, Ben George. University of North Carolina at Wilmington, Department of Creative Writing, 601 S College Rd, Wilmington, NC 28403; registrar@uncw.edu; http://uncw.edu/writers/. Refereed. *Indexed:* MLA-IB. *Aud.:* Ga, Ac.

Ecotone is a semiannual journal that "seeks to reimagine place." Each issue contains work that spans the disciplines, ranging from the literary to the scientific. Since its founding in 2005, *Ecotone* has quickly established a national reputation for publishing high-quality fiction, nonfiction, poetry, and artwork by both well-known and newer writers and artists. Notable recent contributors have included Steve Almond, Gabrielle Bell, Lauren Groff, Ron Rash, and Matthew Vollmer. Many of the issues are themed, and recent themes have included "Remembrance" and "Happiness." Work in *Ecotone* has been reprinted in *Best American Essays, Best American Short Stories, Best American Poetry, Best American Science and Nature Writing, The Pushcart Prize: Best of the Small Presses,* and *The PEN/O. Henry Prize Stories. Ecotone* has been nominated for an Utne Independent Press Award and is published at the University of North Carolina Wilmington.

3631. *Epoch (Ithaca): a magazine of contemporary literature.* [ISSN: 0145-1391] 1947. 3x/yr. USD 11 domestic; USD 15 foreign. Cornell University, English Department, 251 Goldwin Smith Hall, Ithaca, NY 14853; english@cornell.edu; http://www.arts.cornell.edu/english. Microform: PQC. *Indexed:* A22, AmHI, MLA-IB. *Aud.:* Ga, Ac.

EPOCH is published three times a year, in September, January, and May, and includes fiction, poetry, essays, and graphic art. It was founded in 1947, and its reputation is still one of excellence. *EPOCH* publishes both traditional and experimental pieces, including longer-form work. It published the early work of writers such as Don DeLillo and Thomas Pynchon, emphasizing its commitment to featuring exciting new voices. Recent work from *EPOCH* has been reprinted in many of the major annual anthologies: *Best American Short Stories, Best American Poetry, Best American Essays, The Pushcart Prize: Best of the Small Presses,* and *The PEN/O. Henry Prize Stories. EPOCH* is published by Cornell University and staffed by faculty and graduate students.

Fence. See Literary Reviews section.

3632. *Five Points: a journal of literature and art.* [ISSN: 1088-8500] 1996. 3x/yr. USD 20; USD 7 per issue. Ed(s): Megan Sexton, David Bottoms. Georgia State University, Department of English, PO Box 3970, Atlanta, GA 30302; bburmester@gsu.edu; http://english.gsu.edu. Illus. Sample. Refereed. *Indexed:* AmHI, MLA-IB. *Aud.:* Ga, Ac.

Five Points features short stories, poetry, essays, artwork, and interviews, and publishes work by both established and emerging writers. Each issue contains a visual art section, with images reprinted on high-quality color pages and, often, a short statement by the artist. Recent notable contributors include Madison Smartt Bell, Ann Beattie, Robert Bly, Billy Collins, Mark Doty, Lauren Groff, Mary Jo Salter, Melanie Rae Thon, and Chris Verne. Work featured in *Five Points* is regularly re-printed in anthologies such as *Pushcart Prize: Best of the Small Presses.* It is published three times a year by Georgia State University.

Georgia Review. See Literary Reviews section.

Gettysburg Review. See Literary Reviews section.

3633. *Glimmer Train.* [ISSN: 1055-7520] 1991. q. USD 38 domestic; USD 48 in Canada & Mexico; USD 62 elsewhere. Glimmer Train Press, Inc., 4763 SW Maplewood, Box 80430, Portland, OR 97280; http://www.glimmertrain.com. Sample. *Indexed:* AmHI, MLA-IB. *Aud.:* Ga, Ac.

Glimmer Train is a quarterly short story journal founded by two sisters that, since its inception, has risen to great prominence. Each issue features 8–12 stories by "luminaries and fresh new voices" selected from unsolicited submissions. Interviews with writers are also included. Stories published in *Glimmer Train* are regularly featured in Pushcart Prize, PEN/O.Henry, and *Best American Short Stories* anthologies.

3634. *Guernica: a magazine of art and politics.* 2004. irreg. Free. Ed(s): Joel Whitney, Michael Archer. Guernica Magazine, 165 Bennett Ave, 4C, New York, NY 10040. *Aud.:* Ga, Ac.

Guernica is a bimonthly online magazine of art and politics that has risen to national prominence since its founding in 2004. Each issue of *Guernica* features reportage, criticism, first-person narrative, fiction, poetry, visual art, and interviews. It regularly publishes the work of internationally acclaimed writers such as Breyten Breytenbach and Liu Xiaobo, and includes much work in translation. *Guernica* is also committed to publishing younger writers (Porochista Khakpour and Jess Row, for example) and launching new voices. Recent work published in *Guernica* has been included in the *Best American Essays* and *Best of the Net* anthologies.

3635. *Gulf Coast (Houston): a journal of literature and fine arts.* Formerly (until 198?): *Domestic Crude.* [ISSN: 0896-2251] 1987. s-a. USD 16 domestic; USD 26 foreign; USD 10 per issue. Ed(s): Karyna McGlynn, Zachary Martin. University of Houston, Department of English, 205 Roy Cullen Bldg, Houston, TX 77204; http://www.class.uh.edu/english/. Refereed. *Indexed:* AmHI, MLA-IB. *Bk. rev.:* 4-5. *Aud.:* Ga, Ac.

Gulf Coast is a journal of "literature and fine arts" founded by Donald Barthelme and Phillip Lopate in 1983 and published by the University of Houston's English Department in April and October. Each issue features fiction, nonfiction, poetry, interviews, and reviews. *Gulf Coast* is also committed to publishing visual art, and each issue includes the work of two artists via full-color images, along with short introductions. *Gulf Coast* has recently published the work of such writers as Etgar Keret, Josip Novakovich, Sharon Olds, and Kevin Wilson. The work of new voices is also included, such as the poetry of Allyson Paty and Danniel Schoonebeek. Beautifully produced, this is a journal that is as interesting to look at as it is to read.

Harvard Review. See Literary Reviews section.

3636. *Indiana Review.* Formerly (until 1982): *Indiana Writes*. [ISSN: 0738-386X] 1976. s-a. USD 20 (Individuals, USD 17; USD 9 per issue). Ed(s): Nina Mamikunian. Indiana Review, Ballantine Hall 465, Indiana University, Bloomington, IN 47405. Illus. Refereed. Microform: PQC. *Indexed:* AmHI, MLA-IB. *Bk. rev.:* 3-10. *Aud.:* Ga, Ac.

Indiana Review is a biannual literary magazine dedicated primarily to "well-crafted and lively" short stories, poetry, and essays by both emerging and established writers. Each issue features six to ten stories, a wealth of poetry, and one or two nonfiction pieces. There is also a book review section and, on occasion, an insert featuring the work of a particular visual artist (whose work is also featured on the cover). Past and more recent works by contributors to *Indiana Review* have appeared in all the major anthologies, confirming its long-held reputation as a little magazine of excellence. Now in its 35th year of publication, *Indiana Review* is edited and managed by Indiana University graduate students.

Iowa Review. See Literary Reviews section.

3637. *The Malahat Review: essential poetry & fiction.* [ISSN: 0025-1216] 1967. q. CAD 35 domestic; CAD 40 United States; CAD 45 elsewhere. Ed(s): John Barton. The Malahat Review, PO Box 1700, Victoria, BC V8W 2Y2, Canada. Illus., adv. Refereed. *Indexed:* A22, ABS&EES, AmHI, BAS, BEL&L, BRI, C37, CBCARef, MLA-IB. *Bk. rev.:* 5-6. *Aud.:* Ga, Ac.

The focus of *The Malahat Review* is on Canadian and international fiction and poetry, publishing work by established writers right next to work by promising new ones. Each issue of *The Malahat Review* also includes one creative nonfiction piece and book reviews. Over the years, many pieces published in *The Malahat Review* have won Canada's Western Magazine Awards and National Magazine Awards. *The Malahat Review* is published by the University of Victoria, and the cover of each issue features full-color artwork culled from the university's own collection.

3638. *McSweeney's Quarterly Concern.* q. USD 55. Ed(s): Dave Eggers. McSweeney's, 849 Valencia St, San Francisco, CA 94110; custservice@mcsweeneys.net; http://store.mcsweeneys.net/. *Aud.:* Ga, Ac.

McSweeney's Quarterly Concern curiously began as a literary journal that published only works rejected by other magazines. Now it's one of the most unique and important literary journals out there. Founded by Dave Eggers in 1998, *McSweeney's* publishes work by some of the most interesting writers, both new and established, from the United States and abroad. Recent contributors include Jonathan Franzen, Neil Gaiman, Nelly Reifler, Said Sayrafiezadeh, and numerous Egyptian writers who inspired the country's recent uprising. Each issue of the quarterly is completely and imaginatively redesigned. For example, a recent issue was designed to look like a sweaty human head. *McSweeney's* has won multiple National Magazine Awards for fiction, and stories regularly appear in *The Best American Magazine Writing*, the PEN/O. Henry anthologies, and *Best American Short Stories*. *McSweeney's* has also been the recipient of numerous design awards. Other notable publications under the *McSweeney's* umbrella include the excellent *Voice of Witness* series (a series of oral histories), *the Believer* (a monthly magazine of essays, book reviews, and interviews) and *Wholphin* (a quarterly DVD magazine of films).

Michigan Quarterly Review. See Literary Reviews section.

Missouri Review. See Literary Reviews section.

3639. *New England Review.* Former titles (until 1990): *New England Review and Bread Loaf Quarterly;* (until 1982): *New England Review.* [ISSN: 1053-1297] 1978. q. USD 45. Ed(s): Carolyn Kuebler, Stephen Donadio. Middlebury College, Attn: Orders, Middlebury, VT 05753; http://www.middlebury.edu. Microform: PQC. *Indexed:* A01, A22, ABS&EES, AmHI, ArtHuCI, BEL&L, BRI, CBRI, MLA-IB, P02, RILM. *Bk. rev.:* 1. *Aud.:* Ga, Ac.

New England Review (*NER*) prides itself on publishing serious work, and includes both traditional and experimental fiction, poetry, and nonfiction. It also features works in translation, criticism, letters from abroad, and reviews in arts and literature. Recent notable contributors include Mark Doty, Cate Marvin, Carl Phillips, and Christine Sneed. Works from the *NER* are regularly featured in the "best of" anthologies, including Pushcart, PEN/O. Henry, and "Best American." *New England Review* was founded in 1978, and is published four times a year by Middlebury College.

New Letters. See Literary Reviews section.

3640. *Ninth Letter.* [ISSN: 1547-8440] 2004. s-a. USD 21.95; USD 14.95 per issue. University of Illinois at Urbana-Champaign, English Department, 608 S Wright St, Urbana, IL 61801; english@illinois.edu; http://www.english.illinois.edu/. Sample. *Indexed:* AmHI. *Aud.:* Ga, Ac.

Ninth Letter is a semi-annual print journal produced collaboratively by the faculty and students of the Graduate Creative Writing Program and the School of Art & Design at the University of Illinois, Urbana-Champaign. The journal's mission is "to present original literary writing of exceptional quality, illuminated by cutting-edge graphic design." Indeed, every issue is spectacular to both look at and read. In 2005, *Ninth Letter* was named Best New Literary Journal by the Council of Learned Journals, an affiliate of the Modern Language Association. Work published in *Ninth Letter* has been selected for many award anthologies. Recent authors have included Kevin Wilson, Matthew Dickman, and Paisley Rekdal.

3641. *One Story.* 2002. 3 every x wks. USD 21 for 18 issues. Ed(s): Hannah Tinti, Tanya Rey. One Story, 232 3rd St, #A111, Brooklyn, NY 11215. Circ: 7500. *Aud.:* Ga, Ac.

One Story is a unique literary magazine founded in 2002 by Maribeth Batcha and Hannah Tinti. *One Story* publishes a single story every three weeks, in a simply designed but appealing small-format print issue. In keeping with its name and its quest to seek out and publish exciting new writing, *One Story* only publishes any given writer once. Recent notable contributors include Aimee Bender, Stephen O'Connor, Elissa Schappell, and Jim Shepard. *One Story* stories regularly appear in the *Pushcart Prize: Best of the Small Presses* anthologies, and have been cited in *Best American Short Stories* and *Best American Non-Required Reading*.

The Paris Review. See Literary Reviews section.

Ploughshares. See Fiction: General/Mystery and Detective/General section.

3642. *Poetry (Chicago).* [ISSN: 0032-2032] 1912. m. except bimonthly Oct.-Nov. USD 38. Ed(s): Valerie Jean Johnson, Christian Wiman. The Poetry Foundation, 444 N Michigan Ave, Ste 1850, Chicago, IL 60611-4034; mail@poetryfoundation.org; http://www.poetrymagazine.org. Adv. Vol. ends: Oct/Sep. Microform: PMC; PQC. *Indexed:* A01, A22, ASIP, AmHI, ArtHuCI, BRI, CBRI, MASUSE, MLA-IB, P02. *Bk. rev.:* 2-11. *Aud.:* Ga, Ac.

Publishing a new issue every month since its founding in 1912, *Poetry* is one of the most important poetry magazines in the country. In its first year of existence it presented the work of Ezra Pound, William Carlos Williams, and William Butler Yeats. Today, it continues that trend by regularly publishing new work by the most recognized poets. Nonetheless, its primary commitment "is still to discover new voices." In addition to the poetry itself, regular features include a Q&A section (conversations with poets about their work), a "Comment" section (featuring book reviews, essays, and notebooks), and "The View from Here" column, which features artists and professionals from outside the poetry world writing about their experience of poetry. The complete 100-year run of the magazine is available online, as are monthly podcasts with the editors. In 2011, *Poetry* was awarded two National Magazine Awards: for Best Podcast and for General Excellence in Print.

3643. Prairie Fire: a Canadian magazine of new writing. Incorporates: *Writers News Manitoba.* [ISSN: 0821-1124] 1978. q. CAD 30 domestic; CAD 40 United States; CAD 50 elsewhere. Ed(s): Janine Tschuncky, Andris Taskans. Prairie Fire Press, Inc., 423 - 100 Arthur St, Winnipeg, MB R3B 1H3, Canada; prfire@mts.net; http://www.prairiefire.ca/. Adv. Circ: 1400 Paid. *Indexed:* BRI, C37, CBCARef, MLA-IB. *Aud.:* Ga, Ac.

Prairie Fire is a quarterly "Canadian magazine of new writing" that publishes a wide range of poems, short stories, personal essays, and interviews. Work included in *Prairie Fire* may be by a renowned Canadian author like Miriam Toews or Lorna Crozier, or by a new writer being published for the first time. Several pieces published in *Prairie Fire* (fiction, poetry, personal journalism) have won Canada's National Magazine Award.

Prairie Schooner. See Literary Reviews section.

3644. Prism International: contemporary writing from Canada and around the world. [ISSN: 0032-8790] 1959. q. USD 32 (Individuals, USD 25). Ed(s): Kristijanna Grimmelt, Krista Eide. University of British Columbia, Faculty of Arts, Creative Writing Program, E462 1866 Main Mall, Vancouver, BC V6T 1Z1, Canada; prism@interchange.ubc.ca; http://www.arts.ubc.ca/. Adv. Refereed. Circ: 1100 Paid. Microform: MML; PQC. *Indexed:* A22, ABS&EES, AmHI, CBCARef, MLA-IB. *Aud.:* Ga, Ac.

PRISM International is a quarterly magazine that aims to publish "the best in contemporary writing and translation from Canada and around the world." The focus is on fiction and poetry, but *PRISM* also includes, on occasion, creative nonfiction and writing in translation. Several recent stories published in *PRISM* have been selected for inclusion in Canada's *Journey Prize Stories,* one of the country's most prestigious anthologies.

3645. A Public Space. [ISSN: 1558-965X] 2006. q. Ed(s): Anne McPeak. A Public Space Literary Projects, Inc, 323 Dean St, Brooklyn, NY 11217; editors@apublicspace.org. Illus., adv. *Aud.:* Ga, Ac.

Founded by Brigid Hughes, a former editor with *The Paris Review, A Public Space* is a quarterly magazine of literature and culture that has published superlative fiction, nonfiction, and poetry since its inception in 2006. Its aim is "to give voice to the twenty-first century," and it does. *A Public Space* features the work of literary heavyweights (T.C. Boyle, W. G. Sebald, Derek Walcott) alongside new but fast-rising voices (Danielle Evans, Jesmyn Ward). Issues of *A Public Space* also include "If You See Something, Say Something," a series of brief essays or vignettes by various writers; "Illustrated Guide," a visual essay of images or photographs; and, occasionally, "Focus Portfolio," a section that highlights the work of writers from a particular city or region of the world, such as Egypt and Antarctica. Every issue of *A Public Space* is thoughtfully designed, with a full-color photograph by an artist featured on each cover.

Sewanee Review. See Literary Reviews section.

Shenandoah. See Literary Reviews section.

The Southern Review. See Literary Reviews section.

3646. Subtropics. [ISSN: 1559-0704] 2006. 3x/yr. USD 36 (Individuals, USD 21; USD 12.95 per issue). Ed(s): Mark Mitchell, David Leavitt. University of Florida, Department of English, 4008 Turlington Hall, PO Box 117310, Gainesville, FL 32611; http://www.english.ufl.edu/. *Indexed:* AmHI. *Aud.:* Ga, Ac.

The inaugural issue of *Subtropics* came out in 2006, and since then it has been published three times a year by the Department of English at the University of Florida. *Subtropics* seeks to include both established and emerging writers in fiction, poetry, and nonfiction. Most issues include several short stories, one

essay, and an extensive selection of new poems. Several recent pieces published in *Subtropics* have been reprinted in the PEN/O. Henry and Pushcart Prize anthologies. Notable recent contributors include Allegra Goodman, James Lasdun, Edna O' Brien, and G. C. Waldrep.

The Threepenny Review. See Literary Reviews section.

3647. Tin House. [ISSN: 1541-521X] 1999. q. USD 24.95 domestic; USD 12.95 per issue. Ed(s): Win McCormack. Tin House, PO Box 10500, Portland, OR 97296; info@tinhouse.com. Illus., adv. Circ: 12000. *Indexed:* AmHI. *Bk. rev.:* 1-4. *Aud.:* Ga, Ac.

Tin House is a quarterly literary journal of fiction, nonfiction, and poetry based in Brooklyn, New York and Portland, Oregon. Each issue is themed, and recent themes have included "Summer Reading," "Science Fair," "Beauty," "The Ecstatic," and "The Mysterious." *Tin House* is committed to publishing both established and emerging writers and each issue includes a "New Voices" section, featuring the first published piece by both a new fiction writer and a poet. Recent notable contributors include Anne Carson, Amy Hempel, Gary Lutz, Alice Munro, Marilynn Robinson, and the late Adrienne Rich. Within each issue you'll also find interviews, a "Lost & Found" section (short essays about little-known or forgotten older published books or books out of print), and "Readable Feast" (an often humorous food-themed essay followed by a recipe). Since its founding in 1999, *Tin House* has established itself as one of the best literary journals in the country, and its stories, essays, and poems are regularly anthologized in *Pushcart Prizes: Best of the New Presses, Best American Short Stories,* and *The PEN/O. Henry Prize Stories,* among others.

TriQuarterly Online. See Literary Reviews section.

The Virginia Quarterly Review. See Literary Reviews section.

3648. West Branch. [ISSN: 0149-6441] 1977. s-a. USD 16 (Individuals, USD 10). Ed(s): Andrew Ciotola, G C Waldrep. Bucknell University, 701, Moore Ave, Lewisburg, PA 17837; acctrec@bucknell.edu; http://www.bucknell.edu. Illus., adv. Refereed. *Indexed:* AmHI, BRI, MLA-IB. *Bk. rev.:* Number and length vary. *Aud.:* Ga, Ac.

West Branch is a semi-annual magazine of poetry, fiction, essays, and book reviews, and it occasionally includes work in translation. Founded in 1977, *West Branch* is published in the spring and fall of each year at the Stadler Center for Poetry at Bucknell University. *West Branch* also publishes *West Branch Wired,* a quarterly extension of the print magazine. The poetry, fiction, and creative nonfiction included in *West Branch Wired* are distinct from the print publication and therefore original. Book reviews and columns run in both *West Branch Wired* and the print magazine.

3649. Willow Springs: poetry, translations, fiction, essays, artwork. [ISSN: 0739-1277] 1977. s-a. USD 18 domestic; USD 23 foreign. Ed(s): Samuel Ligon. Eastern Washington University, 705 West First Ave, MS-1, Cheney, WA 99004. Adv. *Indexed:* AmHI. *Aud.:* Ga, Ac.

Founded in 1977 and published twice yearly, *Willow Springs* includes fiction, nonfiction, poetry, works in translation, and interviews with contemporary authors (Robert Lopez, Tim O'Brien, and Richard Russo, to name a recent few). For over 30 years, *Willow Springs* has sought out and published the best writing by fresh and established voices. Recent contributors include Erin Belieu, Roxane Gay, and Carl Phillips.

The Yale Review. See Literary Reviews section.

Zoetrope. See Fiction: General/Mystery and Detective/General section.

3650. Zyzzyva: the journal of west coast writers & artists. [ISSN: 8756-5633] 1985. 3x/yr. USD 44 domestic; USD 64 foreign. Ed(s): Howard Junker. Zyzzyva, Inc., PO Box 590069, San Francisco, CA 94159; editor@zyzzyva.org; http://www.zyzzyva.org. Illus., index, adv. Sample. Vol. ends: Winter. *Indexed:* AmHI, MLA-IB. *Aud.:* Ga, Ac.

Zyzzyva publishes fiction, essays, poetry, and visual art produced by West Coast writers and artists. It publishes new voices along with more established writers. Recent contributors include Peter Orner, D.A. Powell, Matthew Dickman, and the late Mexican writer Daniel Sada. The visual art is beautifully rendered in a full-color spread within each issue, and recent artists have included Sandow Birk, Katy Grannan, Julio Cesar Morales, and Owen Smith. The entire magazine was redesigned in 2011, and now features a new cover, color plates, and high-quality paper, thereby acknowledging that each issue is both a physical and intellectual object.

■ MANAGEMENT AND ADMINISTRATION

See also Business; Finance; Labor and Industrial Relations; and Systems sections.

Mary Jane Sobinski-Smith, Head of Information Literacy and Instructional Services, Western New England University

Introduction

Every organization, whether public, private, nonprofit, or governmental, is deeply involved in the important work of management, from organization, planning, and decision-making, to leadership, supply chains, and operations. The selection of management journals and magazines discussed in this section covers a broad spectrum of resources under the umbrella of management, including management science, organization studies, strategic planning and decision-making methods, leadership studies, total quality management, supply chain management, and knowledge management. The selections draw from journals and magazines that provide theoretical, conceptually-based sources, empirical research sources, and review and analytical sources, as well as practical and news sources for academic, research, student, and practitioner audiences.

Basic Periodicals

For academic libraries, a basic collection would include: *Academy of Management Journal; Academy of Management Review; Administrative Science Quarterly; British Journal of Management; Business Strategy Review; Decision Sciences: Information Systems, Operations & Supply Chain Management; International Entrepreneurship and Management Journal; Journal of International Management; Journal of Management; Journal of Management Studies; Journal of Operations Management; Journal of Supply Chain Management; Knowledge Management Research & Practice; Long Range Planning: International Journal of Strategic Management; Management Decision; Management Science; M I T Sloan Management Review; Organization Science; Project Management Journal; Quality Management Journal; Strategic Management Journal.*

For public libraries with more general readers, a basic collection would include: *Academy of Management Perspectives; Business Strategy Review; Ivey Business Journal: Improving the practice of management* (Online); *Interface; Journal of Business Strategy; M I T Sloan Management Review; Organizational Dynamics; S A M Advanced Management Journal; Strategy & Leadership; Strategy + Business.*

Basic Abstracts and Indexes

ABI/INFORM, Business Abstracts Full Text; Business Source Complete.

3651. *A P I C S.* Formerly (until 2005): *A P I C S - The Performance Advantage.* [ISSN: 1946-0384] 1991. bi-m. Free to members. Ed(s): Jennifer Proctor. A P I C S, 8430 West Bryn Mawr Ave, Ste 1000, Chicago, IL 60631-3439; service@apics.org; http://www.apics.org. Illus., index, adv. *Indexed:* A22. *Aud.:* Ga, Ac.

Published and maintained by the Association for Operations Management, *APICS* magazine is available as a digital, open-access (upon registration) publication (as well as a print journal), and is targeted to an audience of busy practitioners in the field of operations management. The publication features short, timely articles written by seasoned, knowledgeable professionals who share successful innovative ideas, along with trends, important changes, events, and news in the field of supply chain and operations management. Topics cover real-world strategies for inventory, materials, production, and supply chain management, planning and scheduling, purchasing, logistics, warehousing, and transportation and logistics. Recommended for academic libraries that support undergraduate business students and public libraries that support busy practitioners. URL: www.apics.org/industry-content-research/publications/apics-magazine

3652. *The Academy of Management Annals.* [ISSN: 1941-6520] 2008. a. GBP 106 (print & online eds.). Ed(s): Royston Greenwood. Routledge, 325 Chestnut St, Ste 800, Philadelphia, PA 19106; customerservice@taylorandfrancis.com; http://www.tandfonline.com. Adv. Sample. Reprint: PSC. *Indexed:* ABIn, B01, PsycInfo. *Aud.:* Ac.

Highly regarded and ranked, *The Academy of Management Annals* provides critical reviews of the research undertaken and written by leaders in management. Its mission is to summarize studies and concepts, identify potential problems, and advance discussions for further research. This annual publication is written for academic scholars in management and allied fields, such as the sociology of organizations and organizational psychology. Highly recommended for all academic libraries. URL: http://aom.org/annals/

3653. *Academy of Management Journal.* Formerly (until 1963): *The Journal of the Academy of Management.* [ISSN: 0001-4273] 1958. bi-m. Ed(s): Michael Malgrande, R Duane Ireland. Academy of Management, 235 Elm Rd, PO Box 3020, Briarcliff Manor, NY 10510; coe-cfp@mailaom.pace.edu; http://www.aomonline.org. Illus., index, adv. Refereed. Vol. ends: Dec. Microform: PQC. *Indexed:* A22, ABIn, B01, B02, BAS, ErgAb, IBSS, PsycInfo. *Bk. rev.:* Number and length vary. *Aud.:* Ac, Sa.

Published by the Academy of Management, the preeminent organization for management and organization scholars, the peer-reviewed, scholarly articles in the highly cited and highly respected *Academy of Management Journal* provide original empirical research that tests, extends, or builds management theory and contributes to management practice. The research presented in these articles is often cited in *The New York Times, The Economist, The Wall Street Journal, The Washington Post, Business Week,* and *Fortune.* All empirical methods—including qualitative, quantitative, field, laboratory, meta-analytic, and combination methods—are included. Written by international scholars and academics, the articles are international and cover a broad spectrum of important management areas. Clearly focused on examining issues with high importance for management theory and practice, the frequently cited and high-impact articles are indispensable reading for management scholars, executive leadership, and graduate business students. This bimonthly journal is an essential title for academic libraries; it is also recommended for corporate libraries interested in cutting-edge awareness, and large public libraries. URL: http://aom.org/amj/

3654. *Academy of Management Learning and Education.* [ISSN: 1537-260X] 2002. q. Ed(s): Michael Malgrande, J Ben Arbaugh. Academy of Management, 235 Elm Rd, PO Box 3020, Briarcliff Manor, NY 10510; coe-cfp@mailaom.pace.edu; http://www.aomonline.org. Refereed. *Indexed:* ABIn, B01, PsycInfo. *Bk. rev.:* 4-5. *Aud.:* Ac, Sa.

Focused on education and the learning process in management, the frequently cited and well respected *Academy of Management Learning & Education* is divided into four sections: "Research & Reviews"; "Essays, Dialogues, & Interviews (EDI)"; "Special Sections"; and "Books & Resource Reviews." The peer-reviewed articles found in the "Research & Reviews" section contain theoretical models and reviews, quantitative and qualitative research, and literature reviews. The "EDI" section contains original essays or critiques of trends or issues in teaching, learning, and management education, dialogues that respond to previously published research, and interviews with academic, business, and thought leaders. Book and resource reviews cover important books and other learning tools. The "Special Contributions" section contains invited papers from prominent scholars and practitioners. A sample of the article topics ranges from group and individual learning behaviors, to leadership development, to social entrepreneurship education. These interdisciplinary articles would be of interest to scholars, academic educators, deans, directors, and administrators as well as policy-makers, practitioners, and consultants involved in management training and development in the public and private sectors. Published quarterly, this title is essential for academic libraries with business programs and for corporate collections interested in training and development. URL: http://aom.org/AMLE/

3655. *The Academy of Management Perspectives.* Former titles (until Feb.2006): *Academy of Management Executive;* (until 1993): *Executive;* (until 1990): *Academy of Management Executive.* [ISSN: 1558-9080] 1987. q. USD 120 (Individuals, USD 80; Corporations, USD 165). Ed(s): Susan Zaid, Garry Bruton. Academy of Management, 235 Elm Rd, PO Box 3020, Briarcliff Manor, NY 10510; http://www.aomonline.org. Illus., adv. Refereed. Circ: 17134. *Indexed:* A22, ABIn, ABS&EES, B01, B02, BRI, IBSS, PsycInfo. *Bk. rev.:* 4-8. *Aud.:* Ac, Sa.

The need to keep abreast of new knowledge in the specialized sub-fields of management is important. The mission of *Academy of Management Perspectives* is to "synthesize and translate theoretical and empirical evidence found in specialized sub-fields of management" for the non-specialist. The well-respected and frequently cited peer-reviewed articles, written by experts in the field, consist of 1) reviews of existing knowledge in the field, 2) integration of theories and empirical evidence to present new ideas with provocative perspectives, and 3) integration of management theory and research with advances in other disciplines. The arrangement of articles within the publication follows two formats: a thematic format in the "Symposium" section and individual articles in the "Articles" section, both with well documented lists of references for further consultation. Articles are written for other academics, executives, consultants, and students, and their language is accessible to non-specialists in the field. Published quarterly, this journal is essential for academic, corporate, and larger public libraries. URL: http://aom.org/amp/

3656. *Academy of Management Review.* Supersedes in part (in 1976): *Academy of Management Journal.* [ISSN: 0363-7425] 1976. q. Ed(s): Amy J Hillman. Academy of Management, 235 Elm Rd, PO Box 3020, Briarcliff Manor, NY 10510; coe-cfp@mailaom.pace.edu; http://www.aomonline.org. Illus., index, adv. Refereed. Vol. ends: Oct. Microform: PQC. *Indexed:* A22, ABIn, B01, B02, BRI, IBSS, PsycInfo. *Bk. rev.:* 4-5, 1,200 words, signed. *Aud.:* Ac, Sa.

The preeminent, highly cited, well-respected *Academy of Management Review* published by the Academy of Management features peer-reviewed, theory-based conceptual papers that advance the understandings of management and organizations. This quarterly publication captures the highest-quality theoretical and conceptual insights in the field of management. Topics in the "Articles" section challenge conventional wisdom of organizations and their roles in society. The "Dialogue" section responds to previously published research. As of April 2013, the *AMR* is reinventing book reviews in the section "Book Reviews: What the Academy is Reading" to include book "essays" that move beyond summaries to a more intellectually and provocative format. Published quarterly, this important journal records the cutting-edge theory of management and organizations, and is essential for all academic libraries and large public libraries. URL: http://aom.org/amr/

3657. *Administrative Science Quarterly.* [ISSN: 0001-8392] 1956. q. USD 280. Ed(s): Gerald F Davis. Sage Publications, Inc., 2455 Teller Rd, Thousand Oaks, CA 91320; info@sagepub.com; http://www.sagepub.com. Illus., index, adv. Sample. Refereed. Vol. ends: Dec. Microform: PQC. Reprint: PSC. *Indexed:* A22, ABIn, B01, B02, BAS, BRI, IBSS, MCR, P02, P61, PsycInfo, SSA, SWR&A. *Bk. rev.:* 10-12, 600-1,200 words, signed. *Aud.:* Ac, Sa.

Published on behalf of the Samuel Curtis Johnson Graduate School of Management at Cornell University, the highly ranked and frequently cited *Administrative Science Quarterly* makes available empirical investigations and theoretical analysis in the social processes of administration. The peer-reviewed research papers seek to "advance the understanding of management, organizations, and organizing" of teams, organizations, government agencies, and markets. Interdisciplinary in nature, the papers incorporate the research from organizational behavior, sociology, psychology, economics, and public policy. The journal publishes new and evolving work from the best dissertations, as well as the work of established scholars. The quarterly publication also provides in-depth book reviews for notable books in the field, as well as a convenient listing of recently published books in the field for current

awareness. Represented in a large number of business, academic, and general indexing and abstracting services, this title is highly recommended for academic libraries and large public libraries. URL: www.sagepub.com/journals/Journal202065

3658. *Asia Pacific Journal of Management.* [ISSN: 0217-4561] 1983. q. EUR 502 (print & online eds.). Ed(s): Michael Carney, Rachel Pinkham. Springer New York LLC, 233 Spring St, New York, NY 10013; service-ny@springer.com; http://www.springer.com/. Adv. Sample. Reprint: PSC. *Indexed:* A22, ABIn, B01, B02, BAS, BRI, E01, PsycInfo. *Aud.:* Ac, Sa.

Asia Pacific Journal of Management is affiliated with the Asia Academy of Management. It publishes research papers written by scholars and researchers on management and organizational research of the Asia Pacific region, including the Pacific Rim countries and mainland Asia. This journal is published quarterly, with one issue each year focused on a single topic, such as the most recently focused-on topic, managing favors in a global economy. The articles address issues such as organizational citizenship behavior, corporate boards and Asian firms, and developing business trust. The articles in this journal will be of interest to scholars, researchers, students, and practitioners. Highly recommended for academic libraries that support business programs. URL: http://link.springer.com/journal/10490

3659. *Associations Now.* Former titles (until 2005): *Association Management;* Which incorporated (in 1963): *A S A E News;* (in 1963): *Here's How;* (until 1956): *American Trade Association Executives. Journal; American Society of Association Executives. Journal.* 1949. m. Free to members; Non-members, USD 60. Ed(s): Lisa Junker, Samantha Whitehorne. American Society of Association Executives, 1575 I St, NW, Washington, DC 20005; editorial@asaecenter.org; http://www.asaenet.org. Illus., index, adv. Circ: 24000 Paid. Vol. ends: Dec. Microform: PQC. *Indexed:* A22, ABIn, ATI, B01, B02, B03, BRI, C42. *Bk. rev.:* Number and length vary. *Aud.:* Sa.

The professional publication of the American Society of Association Executives: The Center for Executive Leadership, *Associations Now* publishes short, timely articles, case studies, interviews, book reviews, and news briefs for executives and professionals managing the work of volunteer associations, individual membership societies, and trade associations. The publication is mailed monthly to members of ASAE. Articles are written either by the editorial staff of *Associations Now* or by experienced association executives. Well-designed graphics enliven the print edition. Recommended for corporate libraries and public libraries with a business collection. URL: www.asaecenter.org/Resources/AnowMagCurrentIssueTOC.cfm?navItemNumber=51803

3660. *British Journal of Management: an international forum advancing theory and research.* [ISSN: 1045-3172] 1990. q. GBP 1072. Ed(s): Mustafa Ozbilgin, Emma Missen. Wiley-Blackwell Publishing Ltd., The Atrium, Southern Gate, Chichester, PO19 8SQ, United Kingdom; customer@wiley.com; http://www.wiley.com/. Adv. Sample. Refereed. Microform: PQC. Reprint: PSC. *Indexed:* A22, ABIn, B01, B02, BRI, E01, ErgAb, IBSS, PsycInfo. *Aud.:* Ac, Sa.

Published in collaboration with the British Academy of Management, the well-respected publication *British Journal of Management* features often-cited, peer-reviewed articles that are of a multi-disciplinary, interdisciplinary, and international nature. Written by scholars from around the globe, articles in the journal are insightful, empirical, and methodological, on topics such as organizational behavior, management development, business ethics, strategic management, operations management, R&D management, and public-sector management. A review of a recent issue reveals timely articles on transformational leadership, team identity, and the composition of high-tech boards. The *British Journal of Management* does not include conceptual and review papers, except for its special issues. Each issue of the quarterly published journal contains seven or eight original articles, about 6,000 words in length, which are targeted to academics and executives interested in cutting-edge, evidence-based management research. Referenced extensively in academic indexing and abstracting services, this publication is highly recommended for academic libraries with a business program. URL: http://onlinelibrary.wiley.com/journal/10.1111/(ISSN)1467-8551

3661. *Business Strategy Review: insight for global business.* [ISSN: 0955-6419] 1990. q. GBP 278. Ed(s): Stuart Crainer. Wiley-Blackwell Publishing Ltd., The Atrium, Southern Gate, Chichester, PO19 8SQ, United Kingdom; customer@wiley.com; http://www.wiley.com/. Adv. Sample. Refereed. Reprint: PSC. *Indexed:* A22, ABIn, B01, B02, BRI, E01, RiskAb. *Bk. rev.:* Number and length vary. *Aud.:* Ac, Sa.

With its finger on the pulse of current international business, *Business Strategy Review,* from the London Business School, publishes articles that analyze and interpret research on strategic management and the broader business environment. International thought leaders from business and academia debate current business issues, as well as leading-edge research and ideas. The research and ideas have both a cross-disciplinary and global focus. Clearly written and easily accessible articles, global case studies, and company profiles discuss original research found in business schools, as well as cutting-edge ideas from business leaders and consultants. A review of recent issues reveals a broad spectrum of timely topics ranging from the impact of mobile technology, to leadership development and Lady Gaga's business strategy. The articles are targeted to executives as well as managers, and are appropriate for undergraduate business students. Published quarterly, this highly engaging and clearly written publication is essential for academic, public, and corporate libraries. URL: http://onlinelibrary.wiley.com/journal/10.1111/(ISSN)1467-8616

3662. *Cross Cultural Management: an international journal.* [ISSN: 1352-7606] 1994. q. EUR 1199 combined subscription in Europe (print & online eds.); USD 1459 combined subscription in the Americas (print & online eds.); GBP 869 combined subscription in the UK & elsewhere (print & online eds.). Ed(s): Simon L Dolan. Emerald Group Publishing Ltd., Howard House, Wagon Ln, Bingley, BD16 1WA, United Kingdom; emerald@emeraldinsight.com; http://www.emeraldinsight.com. Sample. Refereed. Reprint: PSC. *Indexed:* A22, ABIn, B01, E01, PsycInfo, RiskAb. *Aud.:* Ac, Sa.

With the increase in global, multicultural businesses and organizations, research in cross-cultural management is important. The quarterly publication of *Cross Cultural Management: an international journal* features scholarly, peer-reviewed articles on cross-cultural management research. Each issue offers between four and seven lengthy, well documented research articles written by international academics, researchers, senior executives, and consultants that address intracultural, intercultural, and transcultural management issues. Occasional conceptual, viewpoint, and case-study articles are included in some issues. Topics covered include but are not limited to: managing people in organizations, diversity, work values, comparative accounting structures, HRM policies, management theory, entrepreneurial business, teamwork, and organizational life. Academics, researchers, business students, executives, and managers would benefit from the information presented in this journal. Recommended for academic libraries that support a business program and corporate libraries. URL: www.emeraldinsight.com/products/journals/journals.htm?id=ccm

3663. *Decision Sciences: information systems, operations & supply chain management.* [ISSN: 0011-7315] 1970. bi-m. GBP 341. Ed(s): Allyson Haskell, Asoo J Vakharia. Wiley-Blackwell Publishing, Inc., 111 River St, Hoboken, NJ 07030; cs@wiley.com; http://onlinelibrary.wiley.com/. Illus., adv. Sample. Refereed. Vol. ends: Fall. Microform: PQC. Reprint: PSC. *Indexed:* A22, ABIn, B01, B02, E01, IBSS, PsycInfo. *Aud.:* Ac, Sa.

Published for the Decision Sciences Institute, the journal *Decision Sciences* publishes peer-reviewed scholarly research about decision-making within an organization, particularly at the intersection of business functions and organizational boundaries, and between organizations. The journal seeks to impact decision-making theory or practice to enhance managerial understanding. The articles use theoretical, empirical, or analytic research methods to examine decision problems ranging from strategic to operational. A review of the content topics reveals that articles on operations, supply chain management, and information systems are found. Notes on technology and methodology issues are also included. Since 2012, the journal is published bimonthly. Highly recommended for academic libraries that support graduate business programs as well as corporate libraries interested in extending managerial understanding of decisions. URL: http://onlinelibrary.wiley.com/journal/10.1111/(ISSN)1540-5915

3664. *Directors & Boards: thought leadership in governance since 1976.* Incorporates (2004-2008): *Boardroom Briefing.* [ISSN: 0364-9156] 1976. q. USD 325 domestic; USD 350 foreign. Ed(s): James Kristie. Directors & Boards, 1845 Walnut St, 9th Fl, Ste 900, Philadelphia, PA 19103. Illus., index, adv. Circ: 7159. Vol. ends: Summer. Microform: PQC. *Indexed:* A22, ABIn, B01, B02, BLI, BRI, CLI, L14. *Bk. rev.:* 1-2 signed, 500 words each. *Aud.:* Sa.

Written by board chairmen, CEOs, and members of senior management, for board members and for senior management, the quarterly publication *Directors & Boards* publishes short, practical advisories on every aspect of the role of the board in corporate governance. Issues addressed include effective board structure and processes, recruiting the best directors, getting the most value from the board, crisis management, succession planning, and compensation. Each issue contains "Directors Roster," a most comprehensive listing of executives elected each quarter to be new board members. Advisory information useful for directors, board members, and students. Recommended for academic libraries that support a business school and public libraries. URL: www.directorsandboards.com/index.html

3665. *Global Business and Organizational Excellence: a review of research & best practices.* Former titles (until 2006): *Journal of Organizational Excellence;* (until 2000): *National Productivity Review;* Incorporates (19??-2001): *Competitive Intelligence Review;* Which was formerly (until 1990): *Competitive Intelligencer.* [ISSN: 1932-2054] 1981. bi-m. GBP 438. Ed(s): Jane G Bensahel, Isabelle Cohen-DeAngelis. John Wiley & Sons, Inc., 111 River St, MS 4-02, Hoboken, NJ 07030; info@wiley.com; http://www.wiley.com/WileyCDA/. Illus., adv. Vol. ends: Fall. Microform: PQC. Reprint: PSC. *Indexed:* A22, ABIn, B01, B02, BRI. *Bk. rev.:* 8-10, 300-500 words. *Aud.:* Ac, Sa.

Global Business and Organizational Excellence is a bimonthly publication with articles that provides case studies and best practices that investigate organizational excellence in business. Each issue contains an "Articles" section, with six articles between eight and 20 pages in length. The articles combine a synthesis and analysis of scholarly research with experience in the field. Timely topics explore a variety of operational issues, such as leadership, knowledge management, and social media for new business strategies; some articles have a global perspective, such as intercultural management and outsourcing. The articles are written by academics and experienced executives for the practitioner audience. A "Currents" section provides book reviews and articles in brief that summarize important research on organizational issues recently published elsewhere. Recommended for academic libraries with an undergraduate business major, corporate libraries, and public libraries. URL: http://onlinelibrary.wiley.com/journal/10.1002/(ISSN)1932-2062

3666. *Interfaces (Hanover).* Formerly (until 1971): *Institute of Management Sciences. Bulletin.* [ISSN: 0092-2102] 1954. bi-m. USD 466 (print & online eds.). Ed(s): Srinivas Bollapragada. Institute for Operations Research and the Management Sciences (I N F O R M S), 7240 Pky Dr, Ste 300, Hanover, MD 21076; informs@informs.org; http://www.informs.org. Illus., index, adv. Sample. Refereed. *Indexed:* A22, ABIn, B01, B02, BRI, CompR, EconLit, IBSS, LT&LA. *Bk. rev.:* 2-4, signed, essay length. *Aud.:* Ac, Sa.

The journal *Interfaces* is published by The Institute for Operations Research and the Management Sciences (INFORMS), the professional society for operations research, management sciences, and business analytics professionals. *Interfaces,* one of INFORMS's 13 journals, publishes peer-reviewed articles that describe the practical applications of operational research (OR) and management sciences (MS) in organizations and industry worldwide. Each article provides details of the completed applications, along with the results and impact on the organizations, and along with a list of supporting references. Articles cover all areas of OR/MS, including operations management, information systems, finance, marketing, education, quality, and strategy. The accessible articles are written by knowledgeable, experienced OR professional leaders and practitioners in the field, as well as academics. Analysts, engineers, managers, students, and educators would find these articles essential and useful. This bimonthly publication is essential for academic libraries that support business management and engineering studies, as well as corporate libraries. URL: https://www.informs.org/Pubs/Interfaces

3667. *The International Entrepreneurship and Management Journal.*
[ISSN: 1554-7191] 2005. q. EUR 469 (print & online eds.). Ed(s): David
B Audretsch, Domingo Ribeiro. Springer New York LLC, 233 Spring St,
New York, NY 10013; service-ny@springer.com; http://
www.springer.com/. Sample. Refereed. Reprint: PSC. *Indexed:* A22,
ABIn, BRI, E01, EconLit, JEL, PsycInfo. *Aud.:* Ac, Sa.

The highly cited *International Entrepreneurship and Management Journal*
features peer-reviewed articles on entrepreneurship and the management of
entrepreneurial organizations. With articles written by scholars, researchers,
consultants, entrepreneurs, businessmen, managers, and practitioners, the
journal features both conceptual and empirical research papers to advance the
understanding of entrepreneurial organizations and their role in innovation and
the economy. A review of recent issues finds highly relevant topics such as new
venture entry mode and firm performance, sociocultural factors and female
entrepreneurs, and knowledge transfer in corporate venturing activities. With
the growth of the economy tied to new entrepreneurial activities, the articles in
this journal will be of importance to scholars, researchers, students, and
entrepreneurs. The journal is essential for academic libraries that support a
business program and public libraries that encourage and support new business.
URL: www.springer.com/business+%26+management/entrepreneurship/
journal/11365

3668. *The International Journal of Logistics Management.* [ISSN:
0957-4093] 1990. 3x/yr. EUR 499 combined subscription in Europe
(print & online eds.); USD 649 combined subscription in the Americas
(print & online eds.); GBP 349 combined subscription in the UK &
elsewhere (print & online eds.). Ed(s): Katie Spike, Chandra Lalwani.
Emerald Group Publishing Ltd., Howard House, Wagon Ln, Bingley,
BD16 1WA, United Kingdom; emerald@emeraldinsight.com; http://
www.emeraldinsight.com. Illus. Sample. Refereed. Vol. ends: No. 2.
Reprint: PSC. *Indexed:* A22, ABIn, B01, E01. *Aud.:* Ac, Sa.

The *International Journal of Logistics Management* is published three times per
year, and features peer-reviewed, scholarly articles on logistics and supply chain
management. Articles on the managerial applications of the theory or
techniques of logistics or supply chain management are given preference.
Guidelines are posed that provide for "framing, interpreting[,] or implementing
the logistics process in the supply chain." Each issue contains five to eight
detailed and technical articles of 15–20 pages in length. Articles are written by
researchers and practitioners in the field, and academics and executives will find
the information they contain particularly relevant. This title is recommended for
academic libraries with business and engineering programs, and corporate
libraries that are interested in leading-edge logistics information. URL:
www.emeraldinsight.com/products/journals/journals.htm?id=ijlm

3669. *International Journal of Management Reviews.* [ISSN: 1460-8545]
1999. q. USD 101 combined subscription in the Americas (print & online
eds.); EUR 79 combined subscription in Europe (print & online eds.);
GBP 67 combined subscription elsewhere (print & online eds.). Ed(s):
Kamel Mellahi, Oswald Jones. Wiley-Blackwell Publishing Ltd., The
Atrium, Southern Gate, Chichester, PO19 8SQ, United Kingdom;
customer@wiley.com; http://www.wiley.com/. Adv. Sample. Refereed.
Reprint: PSC. *Indexed:* A22, ABIn, B01, E01, PsycInfo. *Aud.:* Ac.

Published on behalf of the British Academy of Management by Wiley, the
International Journal of Management Reviews (IJMR) is the first reviews
journal in the field of business and management. It publishes authoritative
literature surveys and reviews, on all the main management subdisciplines
including HRM; international and strategic management; operations
management; management sciences; information systems and technology
management; accounting and finance; and marketing. This title is published
quarterly, and each issue includes six state-of-the-art literature review articles.
One issue each year has a special topic focus. The reviews will be of particular
interest to academics, researchers, and doctoral students in business and
management. Highly recommended for academic libraries that support business
research. URL: www.wiley.com/WileyCDA/WileyTitle/productCd-IJMR.html

3670. *International Journal of Organizational Analysis.* Former titles
(until 2005): *Organizational Analysis;* (until 2004): *The International
Journal of Organizational Analysis.* [ISSN: 1934-8835] 1993. q. EUR
579 combined subscription in Europe (print & online eds.); USD 659

combined subscription in the Americas (print & online eds.); GBP 419
combined subscription in the UK & elsewhere (print & online eds.).
Ed(s): Peter Stokes. Emerald Group Publishing Ltd., Howard House,
Wagon Ln, Bingley, BD16 1WA, United Kingdom;
emerald@emeraldinsight.com; http://www.emeraldinsight.com. Illus.,
index. Sample. Refereed. Vol. ends: Oct. Reprint: PSC. *Indexed:* A22,
ABIn, B01, E01, PsycInfo. *Bk. rev.:* Number and length vary. *Aud.:* Ga,
Ac, Sa.

The *International Journal of Organizational Analysis* features peer-reviewed,
critical analyses of the theory of organization and its practical impact in
business and society. This title is published quarterly with an occasional special
issue on a focused research topic, and each issue contains six or seven academic
articles that draw from organizational theory, organizational behavior,
organizational development, and organizational learning, as well as strategic
and change management. A review of recent issues finds timely and relevant
articles written by international scholars and researchers; topics include
organizational climate and managerial effectiveness; relationships between
environment, culture, and management control systems; and knowledge-
transfer effectiveness of university–industry alliances. Article types include
research, conceptual, literature reviews, case studies, and book reviews. With
content written for academic scholars, practitioners, and students, this journal is
recommended for academic libraries that support business studies, large public
libraries that support an active business community, and corporate libraries
interested in organizational analysis.

3671. *Ivey Business Journal (Online): improving the practice of*
management. Former titles (until 2002): *Ivey Business Journal (Print);*
(until 1999): *Ivey Business Quarterly;* (until 1997): *Business Quarterly;*
(until 1950): *Quarterly Review of Commerce.* 1933. bi-m. Free. Ed(s):
Stephen Bernhut. Ivey Management Services, 179 John St, Ste 501,
Toronto, ON M5T 1X4, Canada. Illus., adv. Microform: MIM; MML;
PQC. *Indexed:* A22, ABIn, B01, B02, BRI, C37. *Aud.:* Ga, Ac, Sa.

Ivey Business Journal, with its finger on the pulse of contemporary business, is
freely available online. Written by scholars, doctoral students, and practitioners,
the short articles in *Ivey Business Journal* are timely, practical, and accessible.
Topics range from issues such as leadership, strategy, and marketing, to more
recent areas of development and investigation, such as corporate culture,
sustainable business, social media, and entrepreneurship. Examples of recent
relevant articles include "Distributed leadership at Google: Lessons from the
billion-dollar brand" and "Creating competitive advantage using big data." This
is a trade publication, and its primary target audience comprises senior
managers and executives, as well as students. Articles are generally
2,000–2,500 words. Recommended for academic, corporate, and public
libraries. URL: www.iveybusinessjournal.com/#

3672. *Journal of Business Strategy.* Incorporates (1975-1994): *Small
Business Reports;* Incorporates (1989-1994): *Journal of European
Business;* Which incorporated (1990-1991): *Journal of Pricing
Management.* [ISSN: 0275-6668] 1980. bi-m. EUR 579 combined
subscription in Europe (print & online eds.); USD 719 combined
subscription in the Americas (print & online eds.); GBP 419 combined
subscription in the UK & elsewhere (print & online eds.). Ed(s): Nanci
Healy. Emerald Group Publishing Ltd., Howard House, Wagon Ln,
Bingley, BD16 1WA, United Kingdom; emerald@emeraldinsight.com;
http://www.emeraldinsight.com. Illus. Sample. Refereed. Vol. ends: Dec.
Microform: PQC. Reprint: PSC. *Indexed:* A22, ABIn, ABS&EES, Agr,
B01, B02, B03, BRI, C42, E01, RiskAb. *Bk. rev.:* 5-7, mid-length. *Aud.:*
Ac, Sa.

Published on a bimonthly basis, *Journal of Business Strategy* publishes peer-
reviewed articles with a practical perspective. Each issue presents six articles
drawing from a mixture of conceptual papers, research papers, literature
reviews, case studies, and viewpoint articles, which are written by academics,
consultants, policy-makers, and business executives. *Journal of Business
Strategy* explores topics, in unique and innovative ways, such as marketing
strategy, innovation, developments in the global economy, mergers and
acquisition integration, and human resources. Articles are written in an
accessible style, and the audience for *JBS* includes executives, managers,
academics, consultants, and business students, including undergraduates. This
title is referenced in several business indexing and abstracting services. Highly

recommended for academic libraries that support business programs, large public libraries that support the business community, and corporate libraries. URL: www.emeraldinsight.com/products/journals/journals.htm?id=jbs

3673. *Journal of Contingencies and Crisis Management.* [ISSN: 0966-0879] 1993. q. GBP 503. Ed(s): Ira Helsloot. Wiley-Blackwell Publishing Ltd., The Atrium, Southern Gate, Chichester, PO19 8SQ, United Kingdom; customer@wiley.com; http://www.wiley.com/. Adv. Sample. Refereed. Reprint: PSC. *Indexed:* A01, A22, ABIn, B01, E01, H24, P61, PsycInfo, RiskAb, SSA. *Aud.:* Ac, Sa.

Published in collaboration with the European Crisis Management Academy (ECMA), this journal provides scholarly articles on the important topic of crisis management. Interdisciplinary in content, the *Journal of Contingencies and Crisis Management* features peer-reviewed articles on all aspects of contingency planning, scenario analysis, and crisis management, in both corporate and public sectors. It presents analysis and case studies of crisis prevention, crisis planning, recovery, and turnaround management. Authors are drawn from corporations, governmental agencies, think tanks, and influential academics. This journal facilitates the exchange of ideas and best practices between practitioners and academics. URL: http://onlinelibrary.wiley.com/journal/10.1111/(ISSN)1468-5973

3674. *Journal of International Management.* [ISSN: 1075-4253] 1995. q. EUR 887. Ed(s): K A Cahill, M Kotabe. Elsevier Inc., 1600 John F Kennedy Blvd, Philadelphia, PA 19103; JournalCustomerService-usa@elsevier.com; http://www.elsevier.com. Adv. Sample. Refereed. Microform: PQC. *Indexed:* A22, B01, IBSS. *Bk. rev.:* Number and length vary. *Aud.:* Ac, Sa.

The frequently cited *Journal of International Management* publishes peer-reviewed theoretical and empirical research on the theory of global management and the management of global enterprises. The journal also includes literature reviews and critiques on global theory, international management, and educational methodology. Written by international academics and experts, the articles address subdisciplines such as international business strategy; comparative and cross-cultural management; risk management; organizational behavior; and human resource management, among others. Topics from recent issues include (among others) the role of corporate headquarters in multinationals; foreign direct investments; and corporate environmental responsibility. Published quarterly, the journal is designed to serve an audience of academic researchers and educators, as well as business professionals. Each issue has six or seven detailed and technical academic research articles, with occasional book reviews. This journal is essential for academic libraries with international business or graduate business programs, as well as corporate libraries with international interests. URL: www.elsevier.com/locate/intman

3675. *Journal of Management.* [ISSN: 0149-2063] 1975. 7x/yr. USD 865. Ed(s): Deborah E Rupp. Sage Publications, Inc., 2455 Teller Rd, Thousand Oaks, CA 91320; info@sagepub.com; http://www.sagepub.com. Illus., index, adv. Sample. Refereed. Vol. ends: No. 6. Microform: PQC. Reprint: PSC. *Indexed:* A22, ABIn, B01, B02, E01, IBSS, P61, PsycInfo, SSA. *Aud.:* Ga, Ac, Sa.

As the official journal of the Southern Management Association, which is affiliated with the Academy of Management, the preeminent, highly cited *Journal of Management* publishes peer-reviewed scholarly empirical, theoretical, and review articles in the area of management. Its emphasis is on new ideas and perspectives, in pieces written by international scholars. Topic areas covered by the journal include business strategy and policy, entrepreneurship, human resource management, organizational behavior, organizational theory, and research methods. Published bimonthly, each issue contains eight to ten clearly written, detailed, and substantive articles of 25–40 pages. The January and July issues are review issues that provide current scholarly literature reviews and identify theories and ideas important to the future directions of all areas of management. This title is extensively referenced in business indexing and abstracting services. Essential for all academic, large public, and corporate libraries. URL: http://jom.sagepub.com

3676. *Journal of Management Studies.* [ISSN: 0022-2380] 1964. 8x/yr. GBP 1063. Ed(s): Jo Brudenell. Wiley-Blackwell Publishing Ltd., The Atrium, Southern Gate, Chichester, PO19 8SQ, United Kingdom; customer@wiley.com; http://www.wiley.com/. Illus., index, adv. Sample. Refereed. Vol. ends: Nov. Reprint: PSC. *Indexed:* A22, ABIn, B01, B02, BRI, E01, ErgAb, IBSS, PsycInfo. *Aud.:* Ac, Sa.

Published for the Society for the Advancement of Management Studies (U.K.-based), the *Journal of Management Studies* is a well-respected and highly-ranked publication. It celebrates its 50th anniversary in 2013. The journal is multidisciplinary and publishes cutting-edge articles on organization theory and behavior, and strategic and human resource management. Written by international scholars and experienced practitioners, the peer-reviewed, academic articles range from empirical studies and theoretical works to practical applications. The articles are innovative, timely, and relevant. Eight issues are published per year, some with a special thematic focus. Each issue features five to eight substantive, scholarly articles ranging from 20 to 30 pages in length. A review of recent issues reveals topics such as the development of trust among negotiators; outsourcing and knowledge management; theories of organization; and the relationship between corporate social responsibility and financial performance. This title is well represented in indexing and abstracting services for business periodicals. International academics, researchers, students, consultants, executives, and managers would find the information contained in this journal useful. Essential for academic libraries that support business programs and corporate libraries. URL: http://onlinelibrary.wiley.com/journal/10.1111/(ISSN)1467-6486

3677. *Journal of Managerial Issues.* [ISSN: 1045-3695] 1989. q. USD 115 (Individuals, USD 95; USD 190 foreign). Ed(s): Bienvenido S Cortes. Pittsburg State University, Department of Economics, Finance & Banking, 1701 South Broadway, 211 Kelce College of Business, Pittsburg, KS 66762; econ@pittstate.edu; http://www.pittstate.edu/department/economics/. Illus., index. Sample. Refereed. Microform: PQC. *Indexed:* A22, ABIn, B01, B02, P61, PsycInfo, RiskAb, SSA. *Aud.:* Ac.

Published by the Department of Economics, Finance, and Banking at Pittsburg State University, the *Journal of Managerial Issues* features peer-reviewed articles on the theory of organizations and the practice of management. Articles include empirical studies and practical applications, as well as methodological and theoretical developments. The journal disseminates the results of new and original scholarly activity to an audience of university faculty and administrators, business executives, consultants, and governmental managers. The journal was established as a bridge between academic research and practice. The journal is well referenced in business indexing and abstracting services. Recommended for academic libraries. URL: www.pittstate.edu/department/economics/journal-of-managerial-issues/

3678. *Journal of Operations Management.* [ISSN: 0272-6963] 1980. 6x/yr. EUR 843. Ed(s): Morgan L Swink, Kenneth Boyer. Elsevier BV, Radarweg 29, PO Box 211, Amsterdam, 1000 AE, Netherlands; JournalsCustomerServiceEMEA@elsevier.com; http://www.elsevier.nl. Illus., index, adv. Sample. Refereed. Vol. ends: Nov. Microform: PQC. *Indexed:* A22, ABIn, B01, B02, C&ISA, EngInd, RiskAb. *Aud.:* Ac, Sa.

The highly cited *Journal of Operations Management* publishes original, peer-reviewed empirical research that impacts the theory and practice of operations management. This title is published bimonthly in collaboration with the Association for Operations Management (APICS), and its scholarly, peer-reviewed articles focus on the management of operations and supply chain management for both researchers and practitioners. The aims of the journal are to further the generalized theory of operation management and to promote the advancement of the organizational practice of operations management. Topics include operations and information management, project management, quality management, and supply management, to list but a few. Researchers in operations management and operations managers interested in cutting-edge research would be interested in these articles. Highly recommended for academic libraries that support business, industrial engineering, and project management studies and corporate libraries. URL: www.journals.elsevier.com/journal-of-operations-management

3679. *Journal of Product Innovation Management.* [ISSN: 0737-6782] 1984. bi-m. GBP 743. Ed(s): C Anthony Di Benedetto. Wiley-Blackwell Publishing, Inc., 111 River St, Hoboken, NJ 07030; info@wiley.com; http://onlinelibrary.wiley.com/. Illus., index. Sample. Refereed. Vol. ends: Nov. Reprint: PSC. *Indexed:* A22, ABIn, B01, B02, BRI, C&ISA, CerAb, E01, EngInd, RiskAb. *Bk. rev.:* 3-13, 400-1,700 words. *Aud.:* Ac, Sa.

The *Journal of Product Innovation Management* is affiliated with the Product Development and Management Association, the professional organization of corporate practitioners of new-product development. It is an academic journal that publishes peer-reviewed articles on the latest research, theory, and practice in new-product development and service. The journal publishes three types of articles: original theoretical or empirical research articles that are double-blind peer-reviewed; "From Experience" articles, describing new perspectives and techniques to improve new products and services; and "Perspective" articles, which include essays and the application of theory to actual activities. Two book reviews rounds out each issue. Published bimonthly with an additional special issue each year, the journal is of interest to scholars, managers, executives, and new-product professionals. It is extensively referenced in business and engineering indexing and abstracting services. Recommended for academic libraries that support business and industrial engineering studies, and corporate libraries that support new-product development. URL: http://onlinelibrary.wiley.com/journal/10.1111/(ISSN)1540-5885

3680. Journal of Productivity Analysis. [ISSN: 0895-562X] 1988. bi-m. EUR 951 (print & online eds.). Ed(s): Robin C Sickles, Paul W Wilson. Springer New York LLC, 233 Spring St, New York, NY 10013; service-ny@springer.com; http://www.springer.com/. Illus., index, adv. Refereed. Vol. ends: No. 4. Reprint: PSC. *Indexed:* A22, ABIn, B01, C45, E01, EconLit, JEL. *Aud.:* Ac, Sa.

The *Journal of Productivity Analysis* is a bimonthly, peer-reviewed scholarly journal. The scope covers productivity integrated with the research findings from economics, management sciences, operations research, and business and public administration. The journal publishes theoretical and applied research that addresses the measurement, analysis, and improvement of productivity. The empirical research papers apply theory and techniques to the measurement of productivity, and identify the implications for managerial strategies and public policy aimed at enhancing productivity. Articles are written by academics and researchers for other academics, researchers, and students. This title is recommended for academic libraries that support advanced business programs. URL: www.springer.com/economics/microeconomics/journal/11123

3681. Journal of Supply Chain Management: a global review of purchasing and supply. Former titles (until 1999): *International Journal of Purchasing & Materials Management;* (until 1991): *Journal of Purchasing and Materials Management;* (until 1974): *Journal of Purchasing.* [ISSN: 1523-2409] 1965. q. GBP 197. Ed(s): Craig Carter, Lisa Ellram. Wiley-Blackwell Publishing, Inc., 111 River St, Hoboken, NJ 07030; info@wiley.com; http://onlinelibrary.wiley.com/. Illus., index, adv. Sample. Refereed. Vol. ends: Nov (No. 4). Microform: PQC. Reprint: PSC. *Indexed:* A22, ABIn, B01, B02, BRI, E01. *Bk. rev.:* Number and length vary. *Aud.:* Ac, Sa.

The *Journal of Supply Chain Management,* published in collaboration with the Institute for Supply Management, provides frequently cited, peer-reviewed papers on behavioral research that focuses on theory building and empirical methodologies in the field of supply chain management. Scholarly, peer-reviewed articles written by scholars aim to make a strong contribution to supply chain management theory, as well as provide articles of empirical research, with a connection to practical relevance. A review of recent issues reveals specific timely and relevant topics such as the intersection of power, trust, and supplier network size, and humanitarian and disaster relief supply chains. This journal is published quarterly, and each issue provides four or more scholarly articles. Some issues include invited scholarly papers and invited editorials along with essays and papers from other disciplines. One issue per year contains a special-topics forum on a focused topic. Of interest to scholars and supply chain managers, this journal is highly recommended for academic libraries with programs in business management or engineering project management or industrial engineering. URL: http://onlinelibrary.wiley.com/journal/10.1111/(ISSN)1745-493X

3682. Knowledge Management Research & Practice. [ISSN: 1477-8238] 2003. q. USD 591. Ed(s): Giovanni Schiuma. Palgrave Macmillan Ltd., Houndmills, Basingstoke, RG21 6XS, United Kingdom; orders@palgrave.com; http://www.palgrave.com. Adv. Sample. Refereed. Reprint: PSC. *Indexed:* A22, ABIn, E01. *Aud.:* Ac, Sa.

An official publication of the Operational Research Society, this quarterly-produced journal, *Knowledge Management Research & Practice,* publishes articles on all aspects of managing knowledge, organizational learning, intellectual capital, and knowledge economics. The journal includes clearly written, peer-reviewed articles on both theoretical and practical aspects of knowledge management, and especially the relationship between the two. Cross-disciplinary empirical and conceptual articles are included, along with a collection of teaching case studies. Authors include academics as well as practitioners. Highly recommended for academic business libraries, corporate libraries that support managers interested in knowledge management, and large public libraries. URL: www.palgrave-journals.com/kmrp

3683. The Leadership Quarterly: an international journal of political, social and behavioral science. [ISSN: 1048-9843] 1990. bi-m. EUR 692. Ed(s): L Atwater. Pergamon, The Blvd, Langford Ln, E Park, Kidlington, OX5 1GB, United Kingdom; JournalsCustomerServiceEMEA@elsevier.com; http://www.elsevier.com. Adv. Sample. Refereed. Microform: PQC. Reprint: PSC. *Indexed:* A22, ABIn, B01, P61, PsycInfo. *Aud.:* Ac, Sa.

Leadership Quarterly is published in affiliation with the International Leadership Association. This journal brings together a focus of peer-reviewed articles on leadership for an audience of "scholars, consultants, practicing managers, executives[,] and administrators, as well as those numerous university faculty members across the world who teach leadership as a college course." The journal features medium-length research and application articles of eight to 15 pages. It also focuses on yearly reviews of a broad range of leadership topics on cutting-edge areas in special issues. A review of recent issues reveals articles on leader integrity, servant leadership, charisma, and organizational change. This quarterly publication is recommended for academic and corporate libraries. URL: www.journals.elsevier.com/the-leadership-quarterly

3684. Long Range Planning: international journal of strategic management. [ISSN: 0024-6301] 1968. bi-m. EUR 2046. Ed(s): James Robins, Kathleen Low. Pergamon, The Blvd, Langford Ln, E Park, Kidlington, OX5 1GB, United Kingdom; JournalsCustomerServiceEMEA@elsevier.com; http://www.elsevier.com. Illus., adv. Sample. Refereed. Microform: MIM; PQC. *Indexed:* A22, ABIn, B01, B02, BRI, EngInd, PsycInfo, RiskAb. *Bk. rev.:* 4-7, 400-2,000 words. *Aud.:* Ac, Sa.

Long Range Planning is an international journal of the Strategic Planning Society (U.K.-based) in the discipline of strategic management. The journal publishes original research. The empirical and theoretical articles are peer-reviewed, and some may include a review and assessment of the current knowledge in the areas of strategy. Among the areas of work included are corporate strategy and governance, business strategy, strategies for emerging markets, entrepreneurship, innovation, and corporate social responsibility. The "Review Briefs" section rounds out the journal with book and textbook reviews. The scholarly articles are written for academic researchers, students in professional programs, and practicing managers. The journal is published bimonthly, with a combined double-issue on a special focused topic at least once a year. Each issue contains three or four substantive articles. *Long Rang Planning* is recommended for academic libraries that support graduate business studies and corporate libraries interested in cutting-edge research. URL: www.journals.elsevier.com/long-range-planning

3685. M I T Sloan Management Review: MIT's journal of management research and ideas. Former titles (until 1998): *Sloan Management Review;* (until 1970): *Industrial Management Review.* [ISSN: 1532-9194] 1960. q. USD 69 domestic; USD 99 foreign. Massachusetts Institute of Technology, 77 Massachusetts Ave, Cambridge, MA 02139; info@mit.edu; http://mit.edu. Illus., index. Refereed. Vol. ends: Summer. Microform: PQC. *Indexed:* A22, ABIn, B01, B02, BLI, BRI, EconLit, JEL. *Bk. rev.:* 6-12, 200-2,000 words. *Aud.:* Ac, Sa.

The *MIT Sloan Management Review* provides innovative, peer-reviewed articles on the intersection of important, transformative management research and ideas with practice. Two types of accessible articles are found in the magazine. Predominating are articles written by researchers, academic scholars, and thought leaders that analyze and interpret original research for application in the business environment. Rounding out the publication are collaborative "Big Ideas" articles that focus on one significant transformative idea in the business environment, such as sustainability, data and analytics, social business, or digital transformation. Articles from this important publication focus on significant current trends and the impact of current and future innovation that transforms business and society. Executives and top business managers are the primary audience. The publication is also appropriate for undergraduate business students. This quarterly publication is essential for academic libraries that support business programs, and corporate and public libraries. URL: http://sloanreview.mit.edu/

3686. Management Communication Quarterly: an international journal. [ISSN: 0893-3189] 1987. q. Ed(s): James Barker. Sage Publications, Inc., 2455 Teller Rd, Thousand Oaks, CA 91320; info@sagepub.com; http://www.sagepub.com. Illus., adv. Refereed. Vol. ends: May. Reprint: PSC. *Indexed:* A22, ABIn, B01, E01, P02, P61, PsycInfo, RiskAb, SSA. *Bk. rev.:* Number and length vary. *Aud.:* Ac, Sa.

Management Communication Quarterly (MCQ) presents peer-reviewed, conceptual, empirical, and practice-relevant research papers in organizational and management communication. Provocative articles address business communication through the lens of management, organizational studies, organizational behavior and HRM, organizational theory and strategy, critical management studies, leadership, information systems, knowledge and innovation, globalization and international management, corporate communication, and cultural and intercultural studies. In the "Forum" section are found themed essays, commentaries, debates, conference discussions, and book reviews. A recent review of current issues reveals topics that address ideals and identity, corporate social responsibility, use of humor in the workplace, and nonprofit communication, to name a few. Academics, researchers, students, and practitioners will find these articles relevant and useful. This title is extensively referenced in indexing and abstracting services. Recommended for academic libraries that support business studies and corporate libraries. URL: http://mcq.sagepub.com/

3687. Management Decision. Incorporates (1995-2000): *Journal of Management History;* (in 1975): *Management in Action;* Which was formerly (until 1969): *Office Methods and Machines;* Formerly (until 1967): *Scientific Business.* [ISSN: 0025-1747] 1963. 10x/yr. EUR 15299 combined subscription in Europe (print & online eds.); USD 16489 combined subscription in the Americas (print & online eds.); GBP 10299 combined subscription in the UK & elsewhere (print & online eds.). Ed(s): Domingo Ribeiro Soriano. Emerald Group Publishing Ltd., Howard House, Wagon Ln, Bingley, BD16 1WA, United Kingdom; emerald@emeraldinsight.com; http://www.emeraldinsight.com. Illus. Sample. Refereed. Reprint: PSC. *Indexed:* A22, ABIn, B01, B02, BRI, E01, MLA-IB, P02, PsycInfo. *Aud.:* Ac.

The frequently cited, peer-reviewed journal *Management Decision,* with a 50-year history of distinction, presents the research work of international scholars and practitioners in management. The journal covers broad management issues including operations management, financial management, motivation, entrepreneurship, strategic management, and tactics for turning around company crises. A review of recent issues finds articles on the adoption of environment practices as a strategic decision, outsourcing and strategy, and decision models of vertical integration. The title is published ten times per year, and each issue contains between nine and 13 substantive, well-documented research articles on important, relevant topics that keep academics, students, consultants, and executives abreast of the leading ideas and practices in management. Highly recommended for academic libraries that support business programs.

3688. Management Research Review: communication of emergent international management research. Formerly (until 2010): *Management Research News.* [ISSN: 2040-8277] 1978. m. EUR 6259 combined subscription in Europe (print & online eds.); USD 6969 combined subscription in the Americas (print & online eds.); AUD 6099 combined subscription in Australasia (print & online eds.). Ed(s): Joseph Sarkis. Emerald Group Publishing Ltd., Howard House, Wagon Ln, Bingley, BD16 1WA, United Kingdom; information@emeraldinsight.com; http://www.emeraldinsight.com. Sample. Refereed. Circ: 400. *Indexed:* A22, ABIn, B01, E01. *Aud.:* Ac, Sa.

Published monthly, *Management Research Review* has the aim of "rapid publication of the latest research on a broad range of topics in general management." Timely, peer-reviewed research and conceptual papers are written by international scholars, along with experienced practitioners. Each monthly issue contains four to eight lengthy, well-documented articles. A look at recent issues reveals interesting and relevant topics that address sustainability, capital structure theory, green marketing, entrepreneurship, and organizational justice. This title is well represented in business indexing and abstracting sources. Academics, students, consultants, and executives will find the information of interest. Recommended for corporate libraries and academic libraries that support business programs. URL: www.emeraldinsight.com/products/journals/journals.htm?id=mrr

3689. Management Science. Incorporates (1960-1964): *Management Technology.* [ISSN: 0025-1909] 1954. m. USD 1010 (print & online eds.). Ed(s): Stephen C Graves. Institute for Operations Research and the Management Sciences (I N F O R M S), 7240 Pky Dr, Ste 300, Hanover, MD 21076; informs@informs.org; http://www.informs.org. Illus., index, adv. Refereed. Circ: 5000 Paid. Vol. ends: Dec. *Indexed:* A22, ABIn, B01, B02, BRI, C&ISA, CompR, EconLit, EngInd, IBSS, MathR, PsycInfo. *Aud.:* Ac, Sa.

The journal *Management Science* is published by the Institute for Operations Research and the Management Sciences (INFORMS), the professional society for operations research, management sciences, and business analytics professionals. *Management Science,* one of INFORMS's 13 journals, publishes scholarly, peer-reviewed theoretical, computational, and empirical research that focuses on the problems, interests, and concerns of managers. The articles use interdisciplinary tools from fields such as operational research, management sciences, mathematics, statistics, industrial engineering, psychology, sociology, and political science. A wide range of management topics is explored, including business strategy, decision analysis, entrepreneurship, product development, social networks, and supply chains, to name a few. The in-depth, detailed articles with extensive references, written by scholarly, academic authors and practitioners, are important sources for other academics, students, and management executives interested in theory and empirical research. To support the scientific process, *Management Science* encourages (but does not require) the disclosure of data associated with the manuscripts published. Published monthly, *Management Science* is essential for academic libraries that support either business or industrial engineering programs. URL: https://www.informs.org/Pubs/ManSci

3690. Manufacturing and Service Operations Management. [ISSN: 1523-4614] 1999. q. USD 466 (print & online eds.). Ed(s): Frances Moskwa, Stephen C Graves. Institute for Operations Research and the Management Sciences (I N F O R M S), 7240 Pky Dr, Ste 300, Hanover, MD 21076; informs@informs.org; http://www.informs.org. Illus., adv. Refereed. *Indexed:* A22, ABIn, B01, B02, EconLit, EngInd. *Aud.:* Ac, Sa.

Published quarterly by the Institute for Operations Research and the Management Sciences (INFORMS), *Manufacturing & Service Operations Management (M&SOM)* is the premier journal for the operations-management research community. This quarterly journal publishes a wide range of research that focuses on the production and operations management of goods and services, including technology management, productivity and quality management, product development, and cross-functional coordination. Written by academic researchers and practitioners, *M&SOM* publishes articles that help to solve operations management (OM) problems and explore the control, planning, design, and improvement of these OM processes. Other academic researchers and practitioners responsible for operation management would benefit from these articles. Highly recommended for academic libraries that support business and engineering studies, and for corporate libraries interested in the improvement of OM processes. URL: http://msom.journal.informs.org/

3691. Organization: the critical journal of organization, theory and society. [ISSN: 1350-5084] 1994. bi-m. USD 1700. Ed(s): Robyn Thomas, Martin Packer. Sage Publications Ltd., 1 Oliver's Yard, 55 City Rd, London, EC1Y 1SP, United Kingdom; info@sagepub.co.uk; http://www.uk.sagepub.com. Sample. Refereed. Reprint: PSC. *Indexed:* A22, ABIn, B01, E01, IBSS, MLA-IB, P02, P61, SSA. *Bk. rev.:* Number and length vary. *Aud.:* Ac.

Organization studies organizations from a wide range of perspectives and across a broad spectrum of issues. Published bimonthly, it presents peer-reviewed papers and essays that tie together contemporary social problems and the study of organizing. Paul Adler has called this publication "the leading outlet for irreverent thinking that challenges the status quo in both management research and management practice." The articles are theory-oriented, international in scope, provocative, and critical. Each issue contain five to six articles plus and editorials and book reviews. The audience for *Organization* is academic researchers and students. This title is extensively referenced in multiple disciplinary indexing and abstracting sources, including business resources. Academic scholars and students interested in the intersection of organizations, society, and theory will find this journal pertinent. Recommended for academic libraries.

3692. Organization Management Journal. [ISSN: 1541-6518] 2004. q. GBP 214. Ed(s): William P Ferris. Routledge, 325 Chestnut St, Ste 800, Philadelphia, PA 19106; customerservice@taylorandfrancis.com; http://www.tandfonline.com. Adv. Refereed. *Indexed:* A22, ABIn, B01, E01. *Bk. rev.:* Number and length vary. *Aud.:* Ac.

As the official publication of the Eastern Academy of Management, an affiliate of the Academy of Management, the *Organization Management Journal* publishes peer-reviewed articles that intersect theory and practice, address strategies for effective teaching and learning, and "cover the early stages of theoretical thinking on management and organizing." The journal is organized into six distinct sections: "Current Empirical Research," "Emerging Conceptual Scholarship," "Teaching & Learning," "Linking Theory & Practice," "First Person Research," and "Reviews & Research of Note." Each issue provides six or seven peer-reviewed articles on a common theme written by scholars, practitioners, and doctoral students. While the mix of article types is different for each issue, the common theme of the issue is explored through different modes of writing and creating knowledge, including empirical research articles, conceptual articles, analytical essays, case studies, white papers, conference papers, and book reviews. A review of recent issues shows a range of topics including leadership, ethics and values, emergent change, and understanding cultural differences in organizations. "Teaching and Learning," an important section in each issue, provides several articles focused on effective strategies for organizational management teaching. Academic researchers and instructors, as well as business students, will find the articles in this journal relevant. Book reviews related to the topic round out each issue. Published quarterly, *OMJ* is highly recommended for academic libraries that support all business management programs.

3693. Organization Science. [ISSN: 1047-7039] 1990. bi-m. USD 515 (print & online eds.). Ed(s): Daniel Levinthal. Institute for Operations Research and the Management Sciences (I N F O R M S), 7240 Pky Dr, Ste 300, Hanover, MD 21076; informs@informs.org; http://www.informs.org. Illus. Refereed. Vol. ends: Nov/Dec. *Indexed:* A22, ABIn, B01, B02, IBSS, PsycInfo. *Aud.:* Ac.

The journal *Organization Science* is published by the Institute for Operations Research and the Management Sciences (INFORMS), the professional society for operations research, management sciences, and business analytics professionals. *Organization Science,* one of INFORMS's 13 journals, publishes original, theoretical, and empirical research about organizations, including their processes, structures, technologies, identities, capabilities, forms, and performance. The articles, intended to explore new groundbreaking research, are scholarly and peer-reviewed, with extensive reference lists. Presented is research applied to organizations from various disciplines such as artificial intelligence, communication theory, economics, information science, psychology, sociology, strategic management, and systems theory. The journal occasionally publishes essays in the "Perspectives" and "Crossroads" section on new organizational phenomena, redirected lines of research, or debate about current organizations. The articles are written by academics worldwide for students and faculty of business schools. Published bimonthly, this journal is recommended for academic libraries that support business programs.

3694. Organizational Dynamics. [ISSN: 0090-2616] 1972. q. EUR 306. Ed(s): F Luthans. Pergamon, The Blvd, Langford Ln, E Park, Kidlington, OX5 1GB, United Kingdom;

JournalsCustomerServiceEMEA@elsevier.com; http://www.elsevier.com. Illus., adv. Sample. Refereed. Microform: PQC. *Indexed:* A22, ABIn, ASSIA, B01, B02, BRI, E01, PsycInfo. *Bk. rev.:* 2-6, 700-900 words. *Aud.:* Ac, Sa.

The articles featured in *Organizational Dynamics* are written by academics in a lively, lucid, accessible writing style targeted to practicing managers. The analytical articles, in an informal expository style, combine theoretical with practical content, "seeking to illustrate abstract concepts with examples from contemporary organizations." Each article also features a "Selected Bibliography" to document the authors' research process and to emphasize further readings, rather than a formal works-cited "Reference List." An executive summary of each eight- to ten-page article helps busy readers identify relevant information. This journal has focused primarily on organizational behavior and development, and secondarily on HRM and strategic management. Articles in recent issues have covered leadership, teams, goal-setting, career development, organizational change, and organizational design, to name a few. Published quarterly, *Organizational Dynamics* is recommended for corporate libraries and academic libraries that support business programs. URL: www.journals.elsevier.com/organizational-dynamics/

3695. Organizational Research Methods. [ISSN: 1094-4281] 1998. q. USD 1026. Ed(s): Jose M Cortina. Sage Publications, Inc., 2455 Teller Rd, Thousand Oaks, CA 91320; info@sagepub.com; http://www.sagepub.com. Adv. Refereed. Reprint: PSC. *Indexed:* A22, ABIn, B01, C&ISA, CerAb, E01, P61, PsycInfo, RiskAb. *Aud.:* Ac.

Organizational Research Methods (*ORM*), published quarterly, is sponsored by the Research Methods Division of the Academy of Management and the CARMA Global Community: A Research Methods Association for Organizational Scientists, at the Wayne State University School of Business Administration. The journal presents research methodological developments within the organizational sciences. The articles are targeted to an audience that has methodological and statistical training in organizational sciences at the doctoral level. A review of recent articles reveals topics such as "applying neuroeconomics to organizational research" and "Bayesian methods for data analysis in the organizational sciences." Referenced in the psychology and social science indexing and abstracting tools, *ORM* is recommended for academic libraries that support advanced organization and management business and psychology degrees. URL: www.sagepub.com/journals/Journal200894

3696. Production and Operations Management. [ISSN: 1059-1478] 1992. bi-m. GBP 297. Ed(s): Kalyan Singhal. Wiley-Blackwell Publishing, Inc., 111 River St, Hoboken, NJ 07030; info@wiley.com; http://onlinelibrary.wiley.com/. Illus., adv. Sample. Refereed. Reprint: PSC. *Indexed:* A22, ABIn, B01, B02, E01. *Aud.:* Ac, Sa.

Production and Operations Management is published in collaboration with the Productions and Operations Management Society (POMS), an international professional organization dedicated to the improved understanding and practice of production and operations management. This is the main research journal in operations management in manufacturing and services. The double-blind peer-reviewed articles, written by international academic scholars, present research into the management of products and process design, operations, and supply chains. This title is published bimonthly, and each issue includes 9–15 original articles, introduced by two pages of paragraph summaries for each. The articles are of particular interest to practitioners and academic scholars. Recommended for academic libraries that support advanced business and engineering programs and corporate libraries that support production and operations management. URL: http://onlinelibrary.wiley.com/journal/10.1111/(ISSN)1937-5956

3697. Project Management Journal. Formerly (until 1984): *Project Management Quarterly.* [ISSN: 8756-9728] 1970. bi-m. GBP 245. Ed(s): Christophe N Bredillet. John Wiley & Sons, Inc., 111 River St, MS 4-02, Hoboken, NJ 07030; info@wiley.com; http://www.wiley.com/WileyCDA/. Adv. Refereed. Vol. ends: Dec. Reprint: PSC. *Indexed:* A22, ABIn, B01, B02, BRI, RiskAb. *Bk. rev.:* 0-2, 400 words. *Aud.:* Ac, Sa.

The *Project Management Journal* features academic, peer-reviewed articles on the state-of-the-art management techniques, along with research, theories, and applications. As the professional publication of the Project Management Institute, this bimonthly journal provides a balance of content about research, technique, theory, and practice in project, program, and portfolio management. With the "integrative and interdisciplinary nature of these fields," the journal publishes papers that represent the perspectives through the lens of other disciplines, such as organizational behavior and theory, strategic management, sociology, economics, political science, history, information science, systems theory, communication theory, and psychology. Written by academic scholars and professionals, the six to seven academic papers in each issue are of interest to project practitioners, academics, executives, business leaders, and students. Book reviews round out the publication. This title is well represented in business indexing and abstracting services. Highly recommended for academic libraries that support business programs and corporate libraries interested in new developments in project management. URL: http://onlinelibrary.wiley.com/journal/10.1002/(ISSN)1938-9507

3698. *Quality Management Journal.* [ISSN: 1068-6967] 1993. q. Members, USD 50; Non-members, USD 75. Ed(s): Barbara Flynn. American Society for Quality, 600 North Plankinton Ave, P O Box 3005, Milwaukee, WI 53203; help@asq.org; http://www.asq.org. Illus. Refereed. Circ: 14000. Vol. ends: No. 4. *Indexed:* A22, ABIn, B01. *Bk. rev.:* 4-7, 500-1,000 words. *Aud.:* Ac, Sa.

This title is published quarterly by the American Society for Quality (ASQ). The aim of the *Quality Management Journal* is to "link the efforts of academic researchers and quality management practitioners." Each issue contains three to four peer-reviewed articles written by academics and quality management practitioners. Theoretical, empirical, review, and case study articles are featured in the publication on a variety of industries and organizations. The audience for these papers includes quality management practitioners, academic scholars, and students. Essential for academic libraries with business programs and corporate libraries. URL: http://asq.org/pub/qmj/

3699. *Research Technology Management: international journal of research management.* Formerly (until 1988): *Research Management.* [ISSN: 0895-6308] 1958. bi-m. USD 260 (Individuals, USD 115; Institutional members, USD 245). Ed(s): James Euchner, MaryAnn Gobble. Industrial Research Institute, 2200 Clarendon Blvd, Ste 1102, Arlington, VA 22201; http://www.iriweb.org. Illus., index, adv. Refereed. Vol. ends: Nov/Dec. Microform: PQC. *Indexed:* A22, ABIn, ABS&EES, B01, B02, B03, BRI, EngInd, H24, RiskAb. *Bk. rev.:* 4-6, 75-300 words. *Aud.:* Ac, Sa.

Research Technology Management is a bimonthly publication of the Industrial Research Institute (IRI). Each issue includes four peer-reviewed articles written by leading academics, executives, managers, and influential thinkers on the entire spectrum of technological innovation, from research and development through product development and marketing. These accessible articles are the source of best practices and current knowledge on innovation management for leaders of research, development, and engineering. The "Perspectives" section provides short reports on significant international news of the current research-technology scene. Editorials, interviews, and opinion essays round out each issue, as do resources and book reviews on important information resources. Recommended for corporate libraries and academic libraries that support business and engineering programs. URL: www.ingentaconnect.com/content/iri/rtm

3700. *S A M Advanced Management Journal.* Former titles (until 1984): *Advanced Management Journal;* (until 1974): *S A M Advanced Management Journal;* (until 1969): *Advanced Management Journal;* (until 1963): *Advanced Management-Office Executive;* Which was formed by the merger of (1939-1962): *Advanced Management;* Which was formerly (until 1939): *The Society for the Advancement of Management. Journal;* (1951-1962): *Office Executive;* Which was formerly (until 1951): *The N O M A Forum for the Office Executive.* [ISSN: 0749-7075] 1935. q. USD 64. Ed(s): Moustafa H Abdelsamad. Society for Advancement of Management, 6300 Ocean Dr, Corpus Christi, TX 78412; sam@samnational.org; http://islander.tamucc.edu/~cobweb/sam/. Illus., index, adv. Circ: 5000. Microform: PQC. *Indexed:* A22, ABIn, B01, B02, BRI. *Bk. rev.:* Approx. 6; 6-20 pages. *Aud.:* Ac, Sa.

SAM Advanced Management Journal is published quarterly by the Society for Advancement of Management at Texas A&M Corpus Christi. The publication, refereed by an editorial review board, is designed "to provide general managers with knowledge to communicate with specialists without being specialists themselves." Each issue contains five or six articles of medium length, written by academics and business professionals. They cover a variety of management topics, including human resource management and organizational behavior, strategic management, international management, planning, ethics, productivity improvement, time management, health-care management, nonprofit management, sustainability, and computer use in managerial decisions. The articles are accessible and provide contextual information for clarity. The informative articles are well documented for further exploration. This is a recommended source for corporate libraries and academic libraries that support business programs at all levels. URL: www.cob.tamucc.edu/sam/amj/about.htm

3701. *Strategic Management Journal.* [ISSN: 0143-2095] 1980. 13x/yr. GBP 1354. Ed(s): Lois Gast. John Wiley & Sons Ltd., The Atrium, Southern Gate, Chichester, PO19 8SQ, United Kingdom; customer@wiley.com; http://www.wiley.com. Illus., index, adv. Sample. Refereed. Vol. ends: Dec. Microform: PQC. Reprint: PSC. *Indexed:* A22, ABIn, B01, B02, BAS, EngInd, IBSS, PsycInfo, RiskAb. *Aud.:* Ac.

Strategic Management Journal (*SMJ*) is the official publication of the Strategic Management Society, an international organization. *SMJ* features articles that develop theories, test those theories with evidence, and evaluate the methodologies used in strategic management. A review of recent article titles reveals timely and relevant topics, such as corporate governance and environmental performance, foreign IPO markets, and strategies of new venture founders. Written by scholars and researchers, the 15- to 20-page academic, peer-reviewed articles will be of interest to scholars, researchers, students, and practitioners. Highly recommended for academic library with business programs. URL: http://onlinelibrary.wiley.com/journal/10.1002/(ISSN)1097-0266

3702. *Strategy + Business.* [ISSN: 1083-706X] 1995. q. USD 38 domestic; USD 48 foreign. Ed(s): Art Kleiner. Booz & Company, 101 Park Ave, New York, NY 10178. Adv. Circ: 52340 Paid. *Indexed:* A22, C&ISA, CerAb. *Aud.:* Ac, Sa.

Published by the management consulting firm Booz & Company, *Strategy + Business* is a newsmagazine available in print as a quarterly publication, through open access on the web (with new articles added weekly), and through weekly and monthly e-mail newsletters. Lively articles, targeted to executives in business and organizations, address timely issues on strategy, marketing, operations, human capital, and governance. The articles are written by business thought-leaders, including executives, corporate leaders, best-selling business thinkers, academics, researchers, seasoned practitioners from Booz & Company, and journalists. Featured are timely articles, interviews, and commentaries relevant to large-scale corporations. These are written and published from the perspectives of seasoned consultants and practitioners, for an audience of practitioners, potential clients, and students. The content is appropriate for identifying practitioners' perspectives on hot, timely topics for corporate, public, and academic libraries with a business program. URL: www.strategy-business.com

3703. *Strategy & Leadership.* Formerly (until 1996): *Planning Review;* Incorporates (1996-2000): *The Antidote.* [ISSN: 1087-8572] 1972. bi-m. EUR 1939 combined subscription in Europe (print & online eds.); USD 1279 combined subscription in the Americas (print & online eds.); GBP 1399 combined subscription in the UK & elsewhere (print & online eds.). Ed(s): Jo Alexander, Mr. Robert Randall. Emerald Group Publishing Ltd., Howard House, Wagon Ln, Bingley, BD16 1WA, United Kingdom; emerald@emeraldinsight.com; http://www.emeraldinsight.com. Illus. Sample. Refereed. Vol. ends: Nov/Dec. Reprint: PSC. *Indexed:* A01, A22, ABIn, B01, B02, BRI, E01. *Bk. rev.:* Number and length vary. *Aud.:* Ac, Sa.

Strategy & Leadership, a bimonthly publication, features peer-reviewed, medium-length articles of five to ten pages on significant issues and trends in business leadership, strategy, and planning. The articles focus on identifying the successful strategies of innovative companies. Each issue contains five to eight articles and consists of a mix of research-based articles, conceptual papers, general reviews, case studies, interviews, and opinion pieces. The articles are written in a clear and accessible style by a diverse group of well-respected academics, business thought-leaders, seasoned executives, and other professionals in the field. The target audience is executive business leaders and the busy business student. The publication is well referenced in business indexing and abstracting services. *Strategy & Leadership* is highly recommended for academic libraries that support business programs and corporate libraries. URL: www.emeraldinsight.com/journals.htm?issn=1087-8572

■ MARINE SCIENCE AND TECHNOLOGY

General Interest/Marine Biology/Marine Policy/Marine Technology/Ocean Science

Janet G. Webster, Professor/Librarian, Hatfield Marine Science Center, Oregon State University, Newport, OR 97365.

Barbara A. Butler, Professor/Librarian, Oregon Institute of Marine Biology, University of Oregon, Charleston, OR 97420

Introduction

The marine science and technology literature is complicated, interdisciplinary, international, and multifaceted. The job of the librarian used to be researching and purchasing resources related to this complex topic. Now, part of our job is managing access to the field's information in various formats in a cost-effective manner. Many scientific journals are too expensive for the average academic marine science collection. Consequently, we recommend approaching the job of building and maintaining your collection in tandem with those of others, and focus on access to the articles rather than on ownership of the journals.

The titles you choose for your library must reflect the needs of your primary users. "Marine Science and Technology" comprises a broad field with many specialized journals. We have grouped our recommendations into five categories to facilitate your review: general interest, marine biology, marine policy, marine technology, and ocean sciences. While there are few marine science journals in the "general interest" field, they are all free or very reasonably priced. On the other end of the scale, expect to pay upwards of $2000 for titles in the "ocean sciences" subspecialty. The average cost of a subscription in the "marine biology" subspecialty is $1600, and some of these core journals cost upward of $7000 per year.

There is no popular magazine focused strictly on the marine realm. *National Geographic, Scientific American,* and other general science and environmental periodicals are valuable resources for the general public. These, combined with the general-interest titles listed in this section, provide a solid and affordable collection for public and school libraries. Additionally, there are many specialized free trade magazines that are very useful for general collections with interested readers.

For the academic librarian, the task of collection building continues to be challenging as prices rise and electronic options proliferate. Marine science remains highly interdisciplinary and increasingly international. Oceans do not know boundaries, and the animals that live in them range across political barriers. Consequently, awareness of publishing trends worldwide is critical to maintaining a collection that supports international research. Many regional science journals are key components of collections, so be familiar with the relevant ones for your geographic region. Most science journals are in English, but regional titles are usually in the language of the publishing country. There are a number of newly created open-access journals that focus on the marine environment. It is too soon to tell if these will find an audience; however, usage and content needs to be monitored. For many libraries, cooperative collaborative collection development is still the answer.

For the reader of marine science and technology information, the job of identifying information is not simple. One traditional index does not cover the field comprehensively. *Web of Science* provides adequate general access, but is expensive. For the subfield of oceanography, the academic librarian will need access to resources such as *SciFinder Scholar* (*Chemical Abstracts*) or *GeoRef,* depending on the research question. *Biosis* and *Zoological Record* cover the biological aspects well, but have considerable overlap. *Aquatic Science and Fisheries Abstracts* (*ASFA*) historically has been an essential resource for the

applied science of marine and estuarine environments. However, its timeliness and consistency of coverage have diminished in recent years. An alternative is *Fish, Fisheries and Aquatic Biodiversity Worldwide.* Policy and management information remains more difficult to access and requires multiple indexes, with Google Scholar perhaps being one of the better finding guides. For general public and basic academic collections, indexes such as Gale's *GREENR* or EBSCO's *Academic Search Premier* or *GreenFILE* are adequate.

Basic Periodicals

Hs, Ga: *Cousteau Kids, Current, Explorations (La Jolla), Oceanus*; Ac: *Advances in Marine Biology; Deep-Sea Research, Parts 1 and 2; Journal of Experimental Marine Biology and Ecology; Journal of Marine Research; Journal of Physical Oceanography; Limnology and Oceanography; Marine Biology; Marine Ecology–Progress Series; Marine Geology; Marine Mammal Science; Oceanography; Oceanography and Marine Biology; Progress in Oceanography.*

Basic Abstracts and Indexes

ASFA: Aquatic Sciences and Fisheries Abstracts, BIOSIS, National Sea Grant Library Database (http://nsgl.gso.uri.edu), *Web of Science.*

General Interest

3704. *Coastal Services: the magazine that links people, resources and information.* 1998. bi-m. Free. Ed(s): Hanna Goss. National Oceanic and Atmospheric Administration (N O A A), Coastal Services Center, 2234 S Hobson Ave, Charleston, SC 29405; http://www.csc.noaa.gov/index.html. *Aud.:* Hs, Ac, Sa.

This free newsletter provides useful information for resource managers and those interested in coastal issues. Produced by the U.S. National Oceanic and Atmospheric Administration's Coastal Services Center, it highlights projects throughout the country and solutions or strategies to address real issues. The online edition is convenient for its links to other resources. Appropriate for public and academic collections with an audience interested in coastal issues and policy. Available in print or electronically. URL: www.csc.noaa.gov/magazine/

Cousteau Kids. See Children section.

3705. *Current: the journal of marine education.* [ISSN: 0889-5546] 1976. q. Free to members. Ed(s): Lisa Tooker. National Marine Educators Association, 703 E Beach Dr, Ocean Springs, MS 39564; nmea@usm.edu; http://www.marine-ed.org. Illus. Refereed. *Aud.:* Ac, Sa.

The National Marine Educators Association compiles this journal for science teachers. A reasonably-priced membership to NMEA provides readers with well-written, scientifically accurate articles of interest to students and the general reader. Each issue focuses on a single topic (e.g., hydrothermal vents, invasive species), and includes a variety of articles, classroom activities, and supplemental resources. Useful for public and academic collections that serve teachers, homeschoolers, and aquarium volunteers. Available in print only.

3706. *Earth System Monitor.* [ISSN: 1068-2678] 1991. q. Free. U.S. National Oceanographic Data Center, NOAA NESDIS E/OC, SSMC3, 4th Fl, Silver Spring, MD 20910; NODC.Services@noaa.gov; http://www.nodc.noaa.gov/. *Indexed:* OceAb, S25. *Aud.:* Ga, Ac.

National Oceanic and Atmospheric Association research programs, information products, and services are described in this freely available newsletter. Short articles and links to additional information on NOAA environmental data and research programs explain current problems and issues related to the ocean and the atmosphere. Appropriate for general audiences as well as marine scientists. Available in print and electronically. URL: www.nodc.noaa.gov/General/NODCPubs/ESM/esm.html

3707. *Explorations (La Jolla).* Formed by the merger of (19??-1994): *Scripps Institution of Oceanography Associates. Newsletter;* (1983-1994): *Scripps Institution of Oceanography. Annual Report;* Which was formerly (until 1983): *Scripps Institution of Oceanography;* (until 1977): *S I O Scripps Institution of Oceanography;* (until 1976): *Scripps Institution of Oceanography. Annual Report;* (until 197?): *S I O: Scripps Institution of Oceanography;* (until 1971): *Scripps Institution of Oceanography. Annual Report.* [ISSN: 1075-2560] 1983. q. Free. Scripps Institution of Oceanography, Technical Publications Office, 9500 Gilman Dr, Dept 0210, La Jolla, CA 92093; scrippsnews@ucsd.edu; http://www.sio.ucsd.edu/. Illus. *Aud.:* Ems, Hs, Ga.

This e-magazine serves as an outreach tool for UC San Diego's Scripps Institution of Oceanography. The content reflects the breadth of their marine research, both geographically and topically. A special section, "Voyager for Kids," features stories and activities for school-age children. The digital archive is complete for print issues, but the electronic version is not archived. Appropriate for middle school audiences and academic collections with a strong undergraduate marine program. Electronic only. URL: http://explorations.ucsd.edu/Archives/

3708. *Flotsam & Jetsam.* [ISSN: 1948-0997] 1972. q. Individuals, USD 20; Free to members; Students, USD 11. Massachusetts Marine Educators, Inc., c/o Teacher Resource Ctr, New England Aquarium, Boston, MA 02110; mme@massmarineeducators.org; http://www.massmarineeducators.org. *Aud.:* Ga.

Flotsam & Jetsam is an excellent example of a regional marine education publication. Each issue has a theme such as sharks or the intertidal, and then provides a succinct description of the theme, examples of projects, and ideas for conversations. The newsletter also serves as a means of promoting local and national marine education conferences and regional events. It is produced by the Massachusetts Marine Educators Association and comes with the annual membership of $20. The newsletter is free at the Association's web site.

3709. *Mariners Weather Log.* [ISSN: 0025-3367] 1957. 3x/yr. USD 19 domestic; USD 26.60 foreign. National Oceanic and Atmospheric Administration, National Weather Service, 1325 East West Hwy, Silver Spring, MD 20910; http://www.nws.noaa.gov. Illus., index. Vol. ends: Dec. *Indexed:* A22, AmStI, M&GPA, OceAb. *Aud.:* Ga, Sa.

This inexpensive print publication from the National Weather Service (NWS) is also freely available online. Articles address weather forecasting, marine weather phenomena, and news from over 10,000 ships involved in the NWS Voluntary Observing Program. The meteorological content will be of interest to the maritime community, including marine institutions, scientists, and educational and research facilities. This is not a core title, but a nice addition to both public and academic libraries. Available in print and electronically. URL: www.vos.noaa.gov/mwl.shtml

3710. *Oceanography.* [ISSN: 1042-8275] 1988. q. Free to members. Ed(s): Ellen S Kappel. Oceanography Society, 1931, Rockville, MD 20849-1931; anne@ccpo.odu.edu; http://tos.org/. Illus., adv. Refereed. Circ: 2000 Paid. Vol. ends: No. 4. *Indexed:* M&GPA, OceAb. *Bk. rev.:* 2, 1,000 words, signed. *Aud.:* Ga, Ac, Sa.

This title presents a range of research, technological developments, book reviews, and current events of interest to the broad community of scientists and managers involved with ocean science. Written for an informed and knowledgeable audience, it is highly readable, with strong supporting illustrations. Issues frequently focus on a special topic such as ocean modeling or climate change. Selected articles and features are freely available at the Oceanography Society's web site, including a recent issue on marine renewable energy. This is an excellent choice for a college or public library for its general science collection. Available in print and electronically via password. An Open Access white publisher.

3711. *Oceanus: reports on research at the Woods Hole Oceanographic Institution.* Incorporates in 1994: *Woods Hole Oceanographic Institution. Reports on Research.* [ISSN: 0029-8182] 1952. 3x/yr. USD 8. Ed(s): Laurence Lippsett. Woods Hole Oceanographic Institution, 266 Woods Hole Rd, Woods Hole, MA 02543; info@whoi.edu; http://www.whoi.edu. Illus., index, adv. Refereed. Vol. ends: No. 2. Microform: PQC. *Indexed:* A01, A22, BRI, M&GPA, MASUSE, OceAb, P02. *Aud.:* Hs, Ga, Ac, Sa.

The Woods Hole Oceanographic Institution (WHOI), one of the world's premier marine research organizations, resumed publication of this title in 2004, both in print and online. Articles by WHOI scientists and science writers report on current research, expeditions, and marine issues. Topics range from intertidal animals to oceanographic instrumentation. Short news items are interspersed with two- or three-page articles. All are profusely illustrated. The online version has additional features such as video and digital photos. This journal is very affordable, and useful for general public collections as well as for high schools and academic institutions. Available in print or electronically for free. URL: www.oceanusmag.com/

Marine Biology

3712. *Advances in Marine Biology.* [ISSN: 0065-2881] 1963. irreg. Ed(s): David W Sims. Academic Press, 3251 Riverport Ln, Maryland Heights, MO 63043; JournalCustomerService-usa@elsevier.com; http://www.elsevierdirect.com/brochures/academicpress/index.html. Index. Refereed. *Indexed:* A01, A22, OceAb. *Aud.:* Ac.

This publication provides in-depth, timely review articles on a wide range of topics in marine biology, fisheries science, ecology, zoology, and oceanography. One to three volumes are published annually, with some volumes containing three or four review articles on unrelated topics, while others focus on a theme such as aquatic geomicrobiology or biogeography of the oceans. A high-impact journal that is very affordable and essential to both academic and research libraries. Available in print only.

American Fisheries Society. Transactions. See Fish, Fisheries, and Aquaculture section.

3713. *Annual Review of Marine Science.* [ISSN: 1941-1405] 2009. a. USD 246 (print or online ed.). Ed(s): Samuel Gubins, Stephen J Giovannoni. Annual Reviews, PO Box 10139, Palo Alto, CA 94303; service@annualreviews.org; http://www.annualreviews.org. Refereed. *Indexed:* AnBeAb, C45, M&GPA, OceAb. *Aud.:* Ac.

Launched in 2009, this affordable journal features the quality review articles we have come to expect from all *Annual Review* titles. This publication covers a range of emerging marine topics such as ocean physics, biology, chemistry, and geology. The most frequently downloaded articles during the past 12 months focus on hot topics in marine science such as ocean acidification, bioluminesence, and larval dispersal. A good choice for academic libraries that serve marine biology and oceanography programs. Available in print or electronically. An Open Access yellow publisher.

Aquaculture. See Fish, Fisheries, and Aquaculture section.

3714. *Aquatic Botany.* [ISSN: 0304-3770] 1975. 8x/yr. EUR 1905. Ed(s): Jan Vermaat, Dr. G Bowes. Elsevier BV, Radarweg 29, PO Box 211, Amsterdam, 1000 AE, Netherlands; JournalsCustomerServiceEMEA@elsevier.com; http://www.elsevier.nl. Illus., index, adv. Refereed. Vol. ends: No. 4. Microform: PQC. *Indexed:* A01, A22, C45, OceAb, S25. *Bk. rev.:* 1-2, 1,000-3,000 words; signed. *Aud.:* Ac, Sa.

This publication focuses on structure, function, dynamics, and classification of aquatic and marine plant communities. Coverage is split between freshwater and salt/brackish water, with a strong interest in various types of wetlands. While highly specialized, it is recommended for academic collections that support botany and environmental studies. This title is moderately expensive, so consider purchasing a single subscription within your consortium. Available in print or electronically.

3715. *Aquatic Conservation (Online): marine and freshwater ecosystems.* [ISSN: 1099-0755] 1999. 7x/yr. GBP 829. John Wiley & Sons Ltd., 9600 Garsington Rd, Oxford, OX4 2DQ, United Kingdom; customer@wiley.co.uk; http://onlinelibrary.wiley.com/. Refereed. *Bk. rev.:* 3, 500-1,000 words. *Aud.:* Ac, Sa.

Practical management issues and more basic considerations of the biology and ecology of freshwater, brackish, and saltwater environments are examined. Topics are wide-ranging, for example: effect of invasive species on habitats; questions of management and resource use; species distribution; and habitat modeling for conservation ends. Special issues appear annually, usually as supplements, and address issues such as wetlands management. This moderately expensive title is recommended for academic consortia that serve aquatic, conservation, and resource management interests. An open-access "green" title that is available electronically.

3716. *Aquatic Living Resources: international journal devoted to aquatic resources.* Incorporates: *Revue des Travaux de l'Institut des Peches Maritimes;* Formerly (until 1987): *Aquatic Living; I F R E M E R. Revue des Travaux.* [ISSN: 0990-7440] 1928. q. GBP 466 (print & online eds.). E D P Sciences, 17 Ave du Hoggar, Parc d'Activites de Courtaboeuf, Les Ulis, 91944, France; subscribers@edpsciences.org; http://www.edpsciences.org. Illus. Refereed. Circ: 950. *Indexed:* A01, A22, C&ISA, C45, CerAb, IndVet, OceAb, S25. *Aud.:* Ac.

Fisheries science, aquaculture, aquatic botany, and ecology are the primary focus of this title. Coverage is worldwide, with a non–North American bias. Research papers and shorter notes address resource biology as it relates to management and exploitation of those resources. Typically, one of the four issues per volume is dedicated to a special issue, such as an ecosystem approach to fisheries or fish stock assessments; and the full text of many of these special issues is freely available online. Affordable and appropriate for academic collections with a strong marine and fisheries focus. Available in print or electronically. URL: www.alr-journal.org/

3717. *Aquatic Mammals.* [ISSN: 0167-5427] 1972. q. USD 376 (Individuals, USD 158). Ed(s): Jeanette Thomas. Western Illinois University Regional Center, 3561 60th St, Moline, IL 61265. Illus. Refereed. Vol. ends: No. 3. *Indexed:* A01, A22, OceAb. *Bk. rev.:* 1, 1,000 words. *Aud.:* Ac, Sa.

The European Association for Aquatic Mammals, the Alliance of Marine Mammals Parks and Aquariums, and the International Marine Animal Trainers' Association share a strong interest in the husbandry, care, and conservation of aquatic mammals. Articles reflect this interest, covering health issues and human interactions as well as basic life history of various species. They vary in length from brief observations of behavior to in-depth descriptions of diseases. The journal focuses more on medicine and care than *Marine Mammal Science,* another of the few titles that address marine mammals. This inexpensive peer-reviewed journal is appropriate for academic collections that support veterinary schools and marine mammal research. Available in print, on CD, or electronically.

Biological Bulletin. See Zoology section.

3718. *Botanica Marina.* [ISSN: 0006-8055] 1957. bi-m. EUR 1479. Ed(s): A R O Chapman. Walter de Gruyter GmbH & Co. KG, Genthiner Str 13, Berlin, 10785, Germany; info@degruyter.com; http://www.degruyter.de. Illus., index, adv. Sample. Refereed. Circ: 350 Paid. Reprint: PSC. *Indexed:* A01, A22, C45, E01, IndVet, OceAb, RRTA, S25. *Aud.:* Ac, Sa.

This journal is global in scope, but expensive. Covering basic research in marine botany, microbiology, and mycology for scientists at the university level, it includes work on taxonomy and basic biology, as well as on the utilization of marine plants and algae. It differs from *Aquatic Botany,* which focuses on aquatic plant communities. *Botanica Marina* is accredited with the International Association for Plant Taxonomy for the registration of new names of algae and fungi (including fossils). Recommended for consortia that support strong botany or marine plant programs. Available in print and electronically. An Open Access yellow publisher.

3719. *Bulletin of Marine Science: research from the tropical and subtropical waters of the world's oceans.* Formerly (until 1965): *Bulletin of Marine Science of the Gulf and Caribbean.* [ISSN: 0007-4977] 1951. q. USD 695 (print & online eds) Individuals, USD 200 (print & online eds). Ed(s): Su Sponaugle. Rosenstiel School of Marine and Atmospheric

Science, 4600 Rickenbacker Causeway, Miami, FL 33149; bms@rsmas.miami.edu; http://www.rsmas.miami.edu. Refereed. Circ: 1000 Paid. *Indexed:* A01, A22, AnBeAb, C45, IndVet, M&GPA, OceAb, RRTA, S25. *Bk. rev.:* 3, 300 words, signed. *Aud.:* Ac.

A geographic focus on the Gulf of Mexico and Caribbean provides the context for contributions on varied aspects of marine biology. Those involved with research in tropical and subtropical oceans will find this journal useful, as it covers marine science in its broadest sense, including both science and management. Essential to those in tropical and subtropical settings, and useful to academic institutions with a global interest in marine biology. An Open Access white publication, but inexpensive, and available in print and electronically.

Canadian Journal of Fisheries and Aquatic Sciences. See Fish, Fisheries, and Aquaculture section.

3720. *Coral Reefs.* Formerly: *International Society for Reef Studies. Journal.* [ISSN: 0722-4028] 1982. 4x/yr. EUR 1338 (print & online eds.). Ed(s): Barbara E Brown. Springer, Tiergartenstr 17, Heidelberg, 69121, Germany. Adv. Refereed. Microform: PQC. Reprint: PSC. *Indexed:* A22, Agr, BRI, E01, OceAb, S25. *Aud.:* Ac, Sa.

The International Society for Reef Studies produces this journal as a focal point for all aspects of reef-related research. Given the recent focus on coral reefs as indicators of problems in the marine environment, articles cover a wide timeframe and geographic range. One aim of the journal is to emphasize the importance of experimentation, modeling, quantification, and applied science in reef studies. This title is appropriate for academic marine science collections and possibly for environmental studies collections. Moderately expensive, so consider a single purchase within your consortia, especially as accessing the back file incurs an additional cost. Available in print and electronically.

3721. *Deep-Sea Research. Part 2: Topical Studies in Oceanography.* Supersedes in part (in 1993): *Deep-Sea Research. Part A, Oceanographic Research Papers;* Which was formerly (until 1979): *Deep-Sea Research;* (until 1977): *Deep-Sea Research and Oceanographic Abstracts;* (until 1962): *Deep-Sea Research.* [ISSN: 0967-0645] 1993. 14x/yr. EUR 4685. Ed(s): John Milliman. Pergamon, The Blvd, Langford Ln, E Park, Kidlington, OX5 1GB, United Kingdom; JournalsCustomerServiceEMEA@elsevier.com; http://www.elsevier.com. Adv. Sample. Refereed. Microform: PQC. *Indexed:* A01, A22, C&ISA, CerAb, EngInd, M&GPA, OceAb. *Aud.:* Ac, Sa.

Topical issues of this journal include results of international or interdisciplinary projects and collections of conference papers. Recent examples of thematic issues include drifting sea ice and habitats of the Mid-Atlantic Ridge. Issues frequently have non-text supporting materials (numerical data, images, and video), which are made available electronically. Along with its companion journal, *Deep-Sea Research, Part I: Oceanographic Research Papers,* this title is essential for any institution with a marine biology or oceanography program. Due to the expense of this publication, consider a shared purchase within your consortium. Available in print or electronically.

Environmental Biology of Fishes. See Fish, Fisheries, and Aquaculture section.

3722. *Estuaries and Coasts.* Former titles (until 2006): *Estuaries;* (until 1978): *Chesapeake Science;* (until 1960): *Maryland Tidewater News.* [ISSN: 1559-2723] 19??. bi-m. EUR 381 (print & online eds.). Ed(s): Carlos Duarte, J Cloern. Springer New York LLC, 233 Spring St, New York, NY 10013; journals@springer-ny.com; http://www.springer.com. Illus., index, adv. Refereed. Circ: 1800. Vol. ends: No. 4. Microform: MIM; PMC; PQC. Reprint: PSC. *Indexed:* A22, Agr, AnBeAb, C45, E01, IndVet, M&GPA, OceAb, RRTA, S25. *Bk. rev.:* 2, 500 words. *Aud.:* Ac.

Estuaries and Coasts (formerly *Estuaries*) is more limited but also less expensive than *Estuarine, Coastal and Shelf Science.* It contains articles on research relating to physical, chemical, geological, or biological systems of habitats within the ocean/land interface. Recent articles explore the evolution of tidal creeks and wetlands, restoration models, and food resources for sturgeon. Appropriate for academic collections with a near-shore focus or interest in environmental change. Reasonably priced, and available in print and electronically.

3723. Estuarine, Coastal and Shelf Science. Formerly (until 1981): *Estuarine and Coastal Marine Science.* [ISSN: 0272-7714] 1973. 20x/yr. EUR 4245. Ed(s): M Elliott, I Valiela. Academic Press, 32 Jamestown Rd, Camden, London, NW1 7BY, United Kingdom; corporate.sales@elsevier.com; http://www.elsevier.com/. Illus., index, adv. Sample. Refereed. Vol. ends: No. 6. Reprint: PSC. *Indexed:* A01, A22, C&ISA, C45, CerAb, E01, IndVet, M&GPA, OceAb, RRTA, S25. *Aud.:* Ac.

This title provides a focused forum for dealing with the study of estuaries, coastal zones, and continental shelf seas. *Estuarine, Coastal and Shelf Science* is both international and multidisciplinary, and presents research conducted from the upper limits of the tidal zone to the outer edge of the continental shelf. The scope of this journal includes research on the wide range of biological, anthropogenic, physical, and meteorological influences that come to play within estuaries and coasts. This journal is an important part of any marine science collection, but expensive enough that a single copy should be purchased within your consortium. Available in print and electronically.

Fish and Fisheries. See Fish, Fisheries, and Aquaculture section.

Fisheries. See Fish, Fisheries, and Aquaculture section.

Fisheries Management and Ecology. See Fish, Fisheries, and Aquaculture section.

3724. Fisheries Oceanography. [ISSN: 1054-6006] 1992. bi-m. GBP 793. Ed(s): Dr. David Checkley, Jr. Wiley-Blackwell Publishing Ltd., The Atrium, Southern Gate, Chichester, PO19 8SQ, United Kingdom; customer@wiley.com; http://www.wiley.com/. Adv. Sample. Refereed. Microform: PQC. Reprint: PSC. *Indexed:* A01, A22, E01, M&GPA, OceAb. *Aud.:* Ac.

This journal, from the Japanese Society of Fisheries Oceanography, is global in scope and offers a forum for the exchange of information among fisheries scientists worldwide. Typical articles may examine entire food chains, recruitment and abundance of fish species, and dynamics of fish populations. This is a highly ranked journal for a field that has gained repute in the past decade. Moderately expensive, but a core journal for collections that serve a fisheries program. Available in print or electronically. An Open Access yellow publication.

Fisheries Research. See Fish, Fisheries, and Aquaculture section.

Fishery Bulletin. See Fish, Fisheries, and Aquaculture section.

3725. Harmful Algae. [ISSN: 1568-9883] 2002. 6x/yr. EUR 553. Ed(s): Theodore Smayda, Dr. Sandra E Shumway. Elsevier BV, Radarweg 29, PO Box 211, Amsterdam, 1000 AE, Netherlands; JournalsCustomerServiceEMEA@elsevier.com; http://www.elsevier.nl. *Indexed:* A01, C45, FS&TA, IndVet, OceAb, RRTA. *Aud.:* Sa.

This title provides a forum for information on harmful microalgae and cyanobacteria in both fresh and marine waters. It focuses on the life histories, physiology, toxicology, monitoring, and management of blooms, and includes both original research and reviews. This journal is reasonably priced and appropriate for libraries that support research in marine science and botany, as well as those that serve an extensive environmental studies program. Available in print or electronically.

3726. I C E S Journal of Marine Science: journal du conseil. Incorporates (1991-1995): *I C E S Marine Science Symposia;* Which was formerly (1903-1989): *Conseil Permanent International pour l'Exploration de la Mer. Rapport et Proces-Verbaux des Reunions;* Former titles (until 1991): *Conseil International pour l'Exploration de la Mer. Journal;* (until 1968):

Conseil Permanent International pour l'Exploration de la Mer. Journal; (until 1926): *Conseil Permanent International pour l'Exploration de la Mer. Publications de Circonstance.* [ISSN: 1054-3139] 1903. 10x/yr. EUR 1315. Ed(s): Howard I Browman. Oxford University Press, Great Clarendon St, Oxford, OX2 6DP, United Kingdom; enquiry@oup.co.uk; http://www.oxfordjournals.org/. Adv. Sample. Refereed. Reprint: PSC. *Indexed:* A01, A22, C&ISA, C45, CerAb, E01, FS&TA, IndVet, OceAb, RRTA. *Aud.:* Ac.

The International Council for the Exploration of the Sea (ICES) coordinates and promotes applied research in the North Atlantic. Its journal is an outlet for that research, as well as for other information contributing to a broad understanding of all marine systems, their resources, and the effects of human activity on both. Articles address management and conservation issues, biology, ecology, fishing and other human activities, climate change, and changes in technology. Typically, one or two issues of the eight per year are symposium proceedings; ICES offers these as a separate series, but it is more efficient to purchase through the journal subscription. This Open Access yellow journal is moderately priced and an important title for marine science research collections. Available in print and electronically.

Invertebrate Biology. See Zoology section.

3727. The Journal of Cetacean Research and Management. Former titles (until 1999): *International Whaling Commission. Report;* (until 1978): *International Commission on Whaling. Report.* [ISSN: 1561-0713] 1950. 3x/yr. GBP 110 (Individuals, GBP 75; GBP 25 per issue). Ed(s): G P Donovan. International Whaling Commission, The Red House,135 Station Rd, Impington, CB24 9NP, United Kingdom; secretariat@iwc.int; http://www.iwc.int. Refereed. *Indexed:* OceAb. *Aud.:* Ac, Sa.

This title replaces the scientific section of *Reports of the International Whaling Commission* (IWC) and publishes peer-reviewed papers important to the conservation and management of cetaceans. The focus tends toward population abundance and distribution, and the effects of harvest and other human interactions, with occasional notes on unusual sightings or behavior. An annual supplement includes the *Reports of the IWC Scientific Committee,* which contains population trends, discussion of issues and concerns, and management updates. Inexpensive and appropriate for research collections with strong marine mammal programs. Available in print only.

3728. Journal of Experimental Marine Biology and Ecology. [ISSN: 0022-0981] 1967. 28x/yr. EUR 6410. Ed(s): Dr. Sandra E Shumway, S Thrush. Elsevier BV, Radarweg 29, PO Box 211, Amsterdam, 1000 AE, Netherlands; JournalsCustomerServiceEMEA@elsevier.com; http://www.elsevier.nl. Illus., index, adv. Refereed. Vol. ends: No. 2. Microform: PQC. *Indexed:* A01, A22, C45, IndVet, OceAb, RRTA, S25. *Bk. rev.:* 1,000 words; signed. *Aud.:* Ac.

The focus of this journal is laboratory and field experimental study, and its scope includes biochemistry, physiology, behavior, genetics, ecosystems, and ecological modeling. Of interest to marine ecologists, physiologists, and biochemists, this title is appropriate for academic institutions with marine biology, oceanography, and ecology programs. Due to the expense of this publication, libraries will need to purchase it as a consortium. Available in print and electronically.

Journal of Fish Biology. See Fish, Fisheries, and Aquaculture section.

3729. Journal of Marine Animals and Their Ecology. [ISSN: 1911-8929] 2008. q. Free. Ed(s): Dr. Carin Wittnich. Oceanographic Environmental Research Society (O E R S), 12 Burton Ave, Barrie, ON L4N 2R2, Canada; http://www.oers.ca/. *Indexed:* C45, OceAb. *Aud.:* Ac.

This online, open-access journal attempts to fill a niche in marine biology publications—practical science of marine animals. Its potential strength is the focus on practical research and techniques for handling and rehabilitating marine animals, and an interest in the interaction of animals with the human activities in marine environment. It is too early in this journal's life to determine if it will succeed in carving out this niche, but it is worth following its progress in serving academic programs with veterinary interests and marine mammals programs.

3730. *Journal of Marine Biology.* [ISSN: 1687-9481] . USD 395. Hindawi Publishing Corporation, 410 Park Ave, 15th Fl, PMB 287, New York, NY 10022; info@hindawi.com; http://www.hindawi.com. Refereed. *Indexed:* OceAb. *Aud.:* Ac, Sa.

This new open-access journal is global in scope and it publishes original research as well as review articles in all areas of marine biology. Focus and special issues undertaken to date are "Coral Reef Ecosystems" and "Ecosystem-based Management of Pacific Islands." This title is one to watch as it evolves. Freely available online or in print at a modest price.

3731. *Journal of Marine Research.* [ISSN: 0022-2402] 1937. bi-m. USD 160 (print & online eds.) Individuals, USD 60 (print & online eds.). Ed(s): George Veronis. Sears Foundation for Marine Research, c/o Yale University, 210 Whitney Ave, PO Box 208109, New Haven, CT 06520. Illus., index. Refereed. Vol. ends: No. 6. Microform: PMC; PQC. *Indexed:* A01, A22, ApMecR, M&GPA, OceAb, P02. *Aud.:* Ac.

The scope of this journal includes physical, biological, and chemical oceanography, and preference is given to articles that report on a combination or interaction of ecological and physical processes. This publication is global in scope and affordable. Essential to all marine science collections. Available in print and electronically.

Journal of Phycology. See Botany section.

3732. *Journal of Plankton Research.* [ISSN: 0142-7873] 1979. bi-m. EUR 1200. Ed(s): Roger Harris, Lulu Stader. Oxford University Press, Great Clarendon St, Oxford, OX2 6DP, United Kingdom; enquiry@oup.co.uk; http://www.oxfordjournals.org/. Illus., index, adv. Sample. Refereed. Circ: 300. Vol. ends: No. 3. Reprint: PSC. *Indexed:* A01, A22, AnBeAb, C45, E01, IndVet, OceAb, RRTA, S25. *Bk. rev.:* 1, 500 words; signed. *Aud.:* Ac, Sa.

Ecology, physiology, taxonomy, and behavior of plankton are covered in this journal, with a majority of the articles describing marine species. Contributors address these drifting organisms (zooplankton and phytoplankton) with research articles and short communications. Occasional "Horizons" pieces challenge traditional views or review current trends. This is an essential title for biological oceanography research collections, but is moderately expensive, so a single purchase within your consortium is recommended. Available in print and/or electronically. An Open Access yellow publisher.

Journal of Shellfish Research. See Fish, Fisheries, and Aquaculture section.

3733. *Marine and Coastal Fisheries: dynamics, management, and ecosystem science.* [ISSN: 1942-5120] 2008. q. Free. Ed(s): Dan Noakes. American Fisheries Society, 5410 Grosvenor Ln, Ste 110, Bethesda, MD 20814; journals@fisheries.org; http://www.fisheries.org. Refereed. *Aud.:* Ac.

Launched in 2008, this free, peer-reviewed, open-access publication is a welcome addition to the literature of marine biology. From the American Fisheries Society, this journal presents innovative research on marine, coastal, and estuarine fisheries, and its mission is to improve the conservation and sustainability of fishery resources and ecosystems. It is a good choice for all library collections that support a marine biology or fisheries program. An Open Access yellow title that is available electronically.

3734. *Marine & Freshwater Research.* Formerly (until 1995): *Australian Journal of Marine and Freshwater Research.* [ISSN: 1323-1650] 1950. m. USD 2090 combined subscription (print & online eds.); EUR 1745 combined subscription (print & online eds.); GBP 1210 combined subscription (print & online eds.). Ed(s): Max Finlayson. C S I R O Publishing, 150 Oxford St, PO Box 1139, Collingwood, VIC 3066, Australia; publishing@csiro.au; http://www.publish.csiro.au/home.htm. Illus., index, adv. Sample. Refereed. Vol. ends: No. 8. Microform: PQC. *Indexed:* A22, Agr, AnBeAb, C&ISA, C45, CerAb, E01, FS&TA, IndVet, M&GPA, OceAb, RRTA, S25. *Aud.:* Ac, Sa.

This journal includes a broad range of interdisciplinary research in ecology, hydrology, biogeochemistry, and oceanography, with the overarching goal of highlighting the interconnectedness of aquatic environments, processes, and management applications. Specific subjects can include fisheries science, biogeochemistry, physiology, genetics, biogeography, and toxicology. Although published in Australia, this journal is global in scope. It is recommended for academic libraries that support marine or aquatic-based programs, and is moderately priced. Available in print and electronically.

3735. *Marine Biodiversity: international journal of marine science.* Formerly (until 2009): *Senckenbergiana Maritima.* [ISSN: 1867-1616] 1969. 4x/yr. EUR 103 (print & online eds.). Ed(s): Pedro M Arbizu. Springer, Tiergartenstr 17, Heidelberg, 69121, Germany; subscriptions@springer.com; http://www.springer.com. Adv. Refereed. Circ: 650. Reprint: PSC. *Indexed:* A22, E01. *Aud.:* Ac, Sa.

Marine Biodiversity is the newly renamed *Senckenbergiana maritima* and contains short notes, original research, and review articles on all aspects of biodiversity in marine ecosystems. The publisher makes its most frequently downloaded articles available for free from the journal web site. A combined print/electronic subscription is quite affordable, and this title is appropriate for institutions that support either research or a marine biology curriculum.

3736. *Marine Biodiversity Records.* Formerly (until 2008): *Marine and Freshwater Biodiversity.* [ISSN: 1755-2672] 19??. a. Ed(s): Ann L Pulsford. Cambridge University Press, The Edinburgh Bldg, Shaftesbury Rd, Cambridge, CB2 8RU, United Kingdom; journals@cambridge.org; http://www.cambridge.org/uk. Adv. *Indexed:* A01, A22, E01. *Aud.:* Ac, Sa.

This e-only addition to the *Journal of the Marine Biological Association of the United Kingdom* purports to be a rapid, peer-reviewed publication that addresses issues that are somewhat time-sensitive. It focuses on changes in geographical location of marine organisms as well as habitat loss. Articles are short and document new species, new locations for species, and changes in habitat and behavior. This outlet for short reports is welcome; however, the publisher's bundling it with the subscription to the print journal makes it expensive for many. Available electronically only.

3737. *Marine Biological Association of the United Kingdom. Journal.* [ISSN: 0025-3154] 1887. bi-m. GBP 1173. Ed(s): Michael Thorndyke. Cambridge University Press, The Edinburgh Bldg, Shaftesbury Rd, Cambridge, CB2 8RU, United Kingdom; information@cambridge.org; http://www.cambridge.org/uk. Illus., index, adv. Sample. Refereed. Circ: 1600. Vol. ends: No. 4. Microform: BHP; PQC. Reprint: PSC. *Indexed:* A22, AnBeAb, C45, E01, IndVet, OceAb, RRTA. *Aud.:* Ac, Sa.

This journal is international in scope and includes articles on all aspects of marine biology: ecological surveys; population studies of oceanic, coastal, and shore communities; physiology and experimental biology; taxonomy, morphology, and life history of marine animals and plants; and chemical and physical oceanographic work that relates closely to the biological environment. This journal is moderately priced and appropriate for all academic research libraries with a marine biology program. *Marine Biodiversity Records*, a rapid, peer-reviewed new journal, is now bundled with this title. Available in print and electronically.

3738. *Marine Biology: international journal on life in oceans and coastal waters.* [ISSN: 0025-3162] 1967. m. EUR 6367 (print & online eds.). Ed(s): Ulrich Sommer. Springer, Tiergartenstr 17, Heidelberg, 69121, Germany. Illus., adv. Sample. Refereed. Vol. ends: No. 4. Microform: PQC. Reprint: PSC. *Indexed:* A01, A22, Agr, AnBeAb, C45, E01, FS&TA, IndVet, OceAb, P02, RRTA, S25. *Aud.:* Ac, Sa.

This journal is very broad in scope, and includes articles on all aspects of plankton research, biological and biochemical oceanography, environment-organism interrelationships, experimental biology, metabolic rates and routes, biochemical research on marine organisms, biosystem research, energy budgets, dynamics and structures of communities, use of marine resources, anthropogenic influences on marine environments, evolution, modeling, and scientific apparatus and techniques. This is a broadly focused journal essential to every marine science collection, but its high cost may dictate a shared purchase with another institution. Available in print and electronically.

3739. Marine Biology Research. Formed by the merger of (1961-2005): *Sarsia;* (1964-2005): *Ophelia.* [ISSN: 1745-1000] 2005. 10x/yr. GBP 482 (print & online eds.). Ed(s): Franz Uiblein, Tom Fenchel. Taylor & Francis, 4 Park Sq, Milton Park, Abingdon, OX14 4RN, United Kingdom; subscriptions@tandf.co.uk; http://www.tandfonline.com. Adv. Sample. Reprint: PSC. *Indexed:* A01, A22, C45, E01, IndVet, OceAb. *Aud.:* Ac, Sa.

This journal came about as a merger of the long-standing core titles *Sarsia* and *Ophelia.* It aims to provide an international forum for all areas of marine biology and oceanography, including ecology, behavior, taxonomy, environment, and evolution. Articles on applied research that contribute to general biological insight are also included. Affordable and a core title in academic and research institutions with marine biology or oceanography collections. An Open Access yellow publisher.

3740. Marine Biotechnology: an international journal focusing on marine genomics, molecular biology and biotechnology. Formed by the merger of (1930-1999): *Molecular Marine Biology and Biotechnology;* (1993-1999): *Journal of Marine Biotechnology.* [ISSN: 1436-2228] 1998. bi-m. EUR 941 (print & online eds.). Ed(s): J Grant Burgess, Shigetoh Miyachi. Springer New York LLC, 233 Spring St, New York, NY 10013; service-ny@springer.com; http://www.springer.com/. Illus., adv. Sample. Refereed. Vol. ends: No. 4. Reprint: PSC. *Indexed:* A22, ABIn, Agr, BRI, C45, E01, EngInd, FS&TA, IndVet, OceAb. *Aud.:* Ac, Sa.

This title is global in scope, and typical topics include molecular biology, genomics, proteomics, cell biology, biochemistry, and biotechnology. Notably excluded from the journal are articles on genomic or microsatellite sequences or expressed sequence tags, unless this research addresses a larger biological issue. This is a moderately priced but top-ranked journal appropriate for libraries that support marine biology and molecular biology research and advanced undergraduate studies. Available in print and electronically.

3741. Marine Ecology - Progress Series. [ISSN: 0171-8630] 1979. 23x/yr. EUR 4577 combined subscription (print & online eds.). Ed(s): Otto Kinne. Inter-Research, Nordbuente 23, Oldendorf, 21385, Germany; ir@int-res.com; http://www.int-res.com. Illus., index, adv. Refereed. Circ: 1000. Vol. ends: No. 3. *Indexed:* A22, AnBeAb, C45, IndVet, OceAb, RRTA, S25. *Aud.:* Ac, Sa.

This journal features research articles, reviews, and notes on both fundamental and applied topics in marine ecology. The scope includes botany, zoology, ecological aspects of fisheries and aquaculture, resource management, and ecosystem research. Occasional "theme" sections will synthesize information on a topic by a multi-author team. This journal is highly ranked in both the marine biology and oceanography fields; and issues older than five years are freely available on the web. This is a very expensive journal and yet a core title for libraries that support teaching and research in environmental studies and marine biology; therefore, libraries may want to acquire a single copy for their consortium. Available in print and electronically. An Open Access blue publisher.

3742. Marine Environmental Research. Incorporates (in 1991): *Oil and Chemical Pollution;* Which was formerly (until 1986): *Journal of Oil and Petrochemical Pollution.* [ISSN: 0141-1136] 1978. 10x/yr. EUR 2236. Ed(s): F Regoli, I Sokolova. Elsevier Ltd, 32 Jamestown Rd, Camden, London, NW1 7BY, United Kingdom; corporate.sales@elsevier.com; http://www.elsevier.com. Illus., index, adv. Sample. Refereed. Vol. ends: No. 5. Microform: PQC. *Indexed:* A01, A22, AbAn, C&ISA, C45, CerAb, EngInd, ExcerpMed, FS&TA, IndVet, OceAb, RRTA, S25. *Aud.:* Ac, Sa.

This journal focuses on chemical, physical, and biological interactions within the marine realm. Articles examine processes and environmental change with an eye toward understanding systems to facilitate more informed management.

The international scope enhances the sharing of information on marine environmental science. It is moderately expensive, but useful for extensive marine science collections. Available in print and electronically.

Marine Fisheries Review. See Fish, Fisheries, and Aquaculture section.

3743. Marine Mammal Science. [ISSN: 0824-0469] 1985. q. GBP 214 (print & online eds.). Ed(s): Daryl Boness. Wiley-Blackwell Publishing, Inc., 111 River St, Hoboken, NJ 07030; info@wiley.com; http://www.wiley.com/. Illus., adv. Sample. Refereed. Reprint: PSC. *Indexed:* A22, Agr, AnBeAb, C45, E01, IndVet, OceAb, RRTA. *Bk. rev.:* 3, 2,000 words. *Aud.:* Ac, Sa.

Few journals address research on marine mammals even though students, the public, and scientists find them highly interesting. This journal, along with *Journal of Cetacean Research,* is such an outlet. Typical articles address form and function, evolution, systematics, physiology, biochemistry, behavior, population biology, life history, genetics, ecology, and conservation of marine mammals. Articles, review articles, notes, opinions, and letters are all included, and editorial staff screen articles for appropriate experimental procedures involving these often-protected species. This is an inexpensive and a core title for libraries that serve a marine biology major. Available in print and electronically. An Open Access yellow publisher.

3744. Oceanography and Marine Biology: an annual review. [ISSN: 0078-3218] 1963. a. Ed(s): David Hughes, Roger N Hughes. Taylor & Francis, 2 Park Sq, Milton Park, Abingdon, OX14 4RN, United Kingdom; online.sales@tandf.co.uk; http://www.taylorandfrancis.com/books/. *Indexed:* A22, OceAb. *Aud.:* Ac.

These authoritative review articles, including comprehensive reference lists, are appropriate introductory material for students and are also useful for researchers keeping abreast of topics beyond their own field of research. Sample topics from a recent issue include global ecology of kelp, diversity in benthic communities, and effects of climate change on marine life. This is an extremely affordable and essential element in any library that supports marine biology or environmental studies undergraduate education. Starting in 2010, it became available in print or as an e-book.

Reviews in Fish Biology and Fisheries. See Fish, Fisheries, and Aquaculture section.

Marine Policy

3745. Coastal Management: an international journal of marine environment, resources, law and society. Formerly (until 1987): *Coastal Zone Management Journal.* [ISSN: 0892-0753] 1973. bi-m. GBP 811 (print & online eds.). Ed(s): Patrick Christie. Taylor & Francis Inc., 325 Chestnut St, Ste 800, Philadelphia, PA 19106; customerservice@taylorandfrancis.com; http://www.tandfonline.com. Illus., adv. Sample. Refereed. Microform: WSH. Reprint: PSC. *Indexed:* A22, B01, C&ISA, C45, CLI, CerAb, E01, EngInd, IndVet, OceAb, RRTA, S25. *Aud.:* Ac.

This official journal of The Coastal Society focuses on issues relating to the use of coastal environments and resources. Current topics concern coastal tourism, planning and management of seaports and waterfronts, sea level rise, ocean policy and planning, and rise in the sea level. International in scope, this moderately priced publication would be a good addition to any library that supports research in marine policy or law of the sea. Available in print or electronically. An Open Access yellow publisher.

3746. Marine Policy. [ISSN: 0308-597X] 1977. bi-m. EUR 1469. Ed(s): E D Brown. Pergamon, The Blvd, Langford Ln, E Park, Kidlington, OX5 1GB, United Kingdom; JournalsCustomerServiceEMEA@elsevier.com; http://www.elsevier.com. Illus., adv. Sample. Refereed. Microform: PQC. *Indexed:* A22, C&ISA, CerAb, IBSS, OceAb. *Aud.:* Ac, Sa.

The focus of policy formulation and analysis addresses the needs of lawyers, marine resource managers, economists, political scientists, and other social scientists. Recent volumes have an increased focus on fisheries policy, although maritime issues and marine management tools are also covered. Occasionally, issues may contain historical overviews or discussions of emerging trends. This journal is moderately expensive, but a core title for academic collections with a marine policy or management component. Available in print and electronically.

3747. *Ocean & Coastal Management.* Formerly (until 1992): *Ocean and Shoreline Management;* Which was formed by the merger of (1973-1988): *Ocean Management;* (1985-1988): *Journal of Shoreline Management.* [ISSN: 0964-5691] 1988. m. EUR 2141. Ed(s): V de Jonge. Elsevier Ltd, 66 Siward Rd, Bromley, BR2 9JZ, United Kingdom; http://www.elsevier.com. Illus., adv. Sample. Refereed. Vol. ends: No. 44. Microform: PQC. *Indexed:* A22, EngInd, M&GPA, OceAb, S25. *Bk. rev.:* 1-2, 300-600 words. *Aud.:* Ac, Sa.

This multidisciplinary, international journal covers near-shore and coastal environmental issues. Topics include coastal zone management throughout the world, environmental impacts of ocean use, and resolution of multiple-use conflicts. One or two issues of the 12 annually are dedicated to special topics on coastal management. This is a core title for academic collections with marine policy and management aspects, but it is expensive enough to warrant access through a consortial purchase. Available in print and electronically.

3748. *Ocean Development and International Law.* Formerly (until 1973): *Ocean Development and International Law Journal.* [ISSN: 0090-8320] 1973. q. GBP 557 (print & online eds.). Ed(s): Ted L McDorman. Taylor & Francis Inc., 325 Chestnut St, Ste 800, Philadelphia, PA 19106; customerservice@taylorandfrancis.com; http://www.tandfonline.com. Adv. Sample. Refereed. Microform: WSH. Reprint: PSC. *Indexed:* A01, A22, ABS&EES, B01, BRI, C&ISA, C45, CLI, CerAb, E01, IBSS, JEL, L14, OceAb, P02, P61. *Aud.:* Sa.

Less specialized than *Marine Policy,* this journal contains articles on law of the sea; comparative domestic ocean law; shipping, ocean engineering, and marine economics; and marine science that will be of interest to those involved in the management or utilization of ocean resources. It is affordable and appropriate for libraries that support programs in aquaculture, resource management, and environmental law. Available in print and electronically. An Open Access yellow publisher.

3749. *Sea Grant Law & Policy Journal.* [ISSN: 1947-3982] 2008. s-a. Free. Ed(s): Stephanie Showalter. University of Mississippi, National Sea Grant Law Center, 256 Kinard Hall, Wing E, University, MS 38677; http://nsglc.olemiss.edu. *Aud.:* Ac, Sa.

This open-access online journal is relatively new, yet continues a strong Sea Grant tradition of communicating law and policy information on marine issues. One issue publishes selected papers from the National Sea Grant Law Center annual symposium and the other solicits submissions from law students. Articles address a variety of topics from the effect of sea-level rise on coastal community planning to territorial sea policy on marine renewable energy. All are written in a law review style that can be intimidating for the casual reader. *SandBar,* an online quarterly publication from the Center, presents legal and policy information in more of a readable newsletter format. Both are worthy additions to a marine policy collection.

Marine Technology

3750. *Applied Ocean Research.* [ISSN: 0141-1187] 1979. q. EUR 1326. Ed(s): M Kashiwahi. Pergamon, The Blvd, Langford Ln, E Park, Kidlington, OX5 1GB, United Kingdom; JournalsCustomerServiceEMEA@elsevier.com; http://www.elsevier.com. Adv. Refereed. Microform: PQC. *Indexed:* A01, A22, ApMecR, EngInd, M&GPA, OceAb. *Aud.:* Ac, Sa.

Ocean engineering is a very specialized discipline with a limited readership. This title provides solid research articles on topics ranging from mooring systems to wave dynamics. This title is moderately expensive and more so for electronic access, but useful for specialized research collections with engineering interests in the marine environment. Available in print or electronically.

3751. *Coastal Engineering.* [ISSN: 0378-3839] 1977. 12x/yr. EUR 2284. Ed(s): Hans F Burcharth. Elsevier BV, Radarweg 29, PO Box 211, Amsterdam, 1000 AE, Netherlands; JournalsCustomerServiceEMEA@elsevier.com; http://www.elsevier.nl. Refereed. Microform: PQC. *Indexed:* A01, A22, ApMecR, C&ISA, CerAb, EngInd, M&GPA, OceAb. *Aud.:* Ac, Sa.

Another example of a highly specialized title, *Coastal Engineering* is the more expensive sister journal to *Applied Ocean Research.* The focus here is on marine and coastal technology, with particular interest in coastal structures (breakwaters and jetties) and the wave dynamics of this environment. One volume annually is usually devoted to special topics, such as coastal video monitoring systems. Only relevant for specialized research collections with engineering interests in the marine environment. Available in print and electronically.

3752. *I E E E Journal of Oceanic Engineering.* [ISSN: 0364-9059] 1976. q. USD 395; USD 475 combined subscription (print & online eds.). Ed(s): William M Carey. I E E E Oceanic Engineering Society, 3 Park Ave, 17th Fl, New York, NY 10016; http://www.ieeeoes.org. Illus., index, adv. Vol. ends: No. 4. *Indexed:* A22, C&ISA, CerAb, EngInd, M&GPA, OceAb. *Aud.:* Ac, Sa.

The IEEE Oceanic Engineering Society encourages articles and technical communications that apply electrical, electronics, and instrumentation engineering to the marine environment. Topics vary from specific design of new instruments for marine research, such as satellite tags, to investigation of ambient noise. Occasional issues are dedicated to special topics such as sediment acoustic processes. This journal is more important and far more affordable than *Ocean Engineering* to both engineering and oceanographic collections. Available in print and electronically.

3753. *Journal of Marine Science and Technology.* [ISSN: 0948-4280] 1996. q. EUR 217 (print & online eds.). Ed(s): Yoshiaki Kodama. Springer Japan KK, No 2 Funato Bldg, 1-11-11 Kudan-kita, Tokyo, 102-0073, Japan; http://www.springer.jp. Refereed. Reprint: PSC. *Indexed:* A01, A22, Agr, E01, EngInd, OceAb. *Aud.:* Ac, Sa.

This title focuses on issues relating to ocean and marine engineering, and can include articles on naval architecture, hull design, stability modeling, and material strength. It is important to the field, but not terribly relevant to others in marine science. It is inexpensive, but appropriate only for libraries that support marine engineering studies. Available in print and electronically.

3754. *Journal of Waterway, Port, Coastal, and Ocean Engineering.* Former titles (until 1983): *American Society of Civil Engineers. Waterway, Port, Coastal and Ocean Division. Journal;* (until 1977): *American Society of Civil Engineers. Waterways, Harbors, and Coastal Engineering Division. Journal;* (until 1970): *American Society of Civil Engineers. Waterways and Harbors Division. Journal;* (until 1956): *American Society of Civil Engineers. Waterways Division. Journal;* (until 1955): *American Society of Civil Engineers. Proceedings.* [ISSN: 0733-950X] 1873. bi-m. USD 531. Ed(s): Vijay Panchang. American Society of Civil Engineers, 1801 Alexander Bell Dr, Reston, VA 20191; http://www.asce.org. Illus., adv. Refereed. Microform: PQC. *Indexed:* A01, A22, BRI, C&ISA, CerAb, EngInd, H24, M&GPA, OceAb, S25. *Aud.:* Ac, Sa.

This international journal focuses on the applied issues of civil engineering in the aquatic environment, from bridge construction to wave action on breakwaters, to forcing action in open waters. It is sponsored by the American Society of Civil Engineers, and the technical papers, notes, and discussion items address issues of interest globally, while describing local solutions. This journal is essential for engineering collections with an interest in the marine and aquatic environments. Reasonably priced in print and electronically. An Open Access white publisher.

3755. *Marine Geodesy: an international journal of ocean surveys, mapping and sensing.* [ISSN: 0149-0419] 1977. q. GBP 477 (print & online eds.). Ed(s): Rongxing Li. Taylor & Francis Inc., 325 Chestnut St, Ste 800, Philadelphia, PA 19106; customerservice@taylorandfrancis.com; http://www.tandfonline.com. Illus., adv. Sample. Refereed. Vol. ends: No. 4. Reprint: PSC. *Indexed:* A01, A22, E01, M&GPA, OceAb. *Bk. rev.:* 3, 500 words. *Aud.:* Ac, Sa.

This international journal covers the highly specialized science of measuring and monitoring the ocean. Articles describe instrument bias and calibration challenges, boundary datum, and use of remote sensing. This is a relevant yet probably underutilized addition to research collections that support field-based oceanography programs. It is relatively inexpensive. Available in print and electronically. An Open Access yellow publisher.

3756. Marine Georesources & Geotechnology. Formed by the merger of (1975-1993): *Marine Geotechnology;* (1977-1993): *Marine Mining.* [ISSN: 1064-119X] 1993. q. GBP 398 (print & online eds.). Ed(s): John C Wiltshire, Ronald C Chaney. Taylor & Francis Inc., 325 Chestnut St, Ste 800, Philadelphia, PA 19106; customerservice@taylorandfrancis.com; http://www.tandfonline.com. Illus., index, adv. Sample. Refereed. Vol. ends: No. 4. Microform: PQC. Reprint: PSC. *Indexed:* A01, A22, C&ISA, CerAb, E01, EngInd, OceAb, S25. *Aud.:* Ac, Sa.

A companion title to *Marine Geology,* this journal focuses on applied research relating to seafloor sediments and rocks. Topics range from characterizations of dredged materials to restoration of marine macrofauna, to the effect of nodule mining. It is affordable and useful for academic collections with marine engineering and applied geology programs. Available in print and electronically. An Open Access yellow publisher.

3757. Marine Log. Former titles (until 1987): *Marine Engineering - Log;* (until 1979): *Marine Engineering - Log International;* (until 1977): *Marine Engineering - Log;* (until 1956): *Marine Engineering;* (until 1953): *Marine Engineering Shipping and Review;* (until 1935): *Marine Engineering & Shipping Age;* (until 1921): *Marine Engineering;* (until 1920): *International Marine Engineering;* (until 1906): *Marine Engineering.* [ISSN: 0897-0491] 1876. m. USD 92 in North America (print or online ed.) (Free to qualified personnel). Ed(s): John R Snyder. Simmons-Boardman Publishing Corp., 345 Hudson St, New York, NY 10014; http://www.simmonsboardman.com/. Illus., adv. Circ: 27458. Microform: PQC. *Indexed:* A22, ABIn. *Aud.:* Ga, Sa.

The various trade magazines in marine technology have some overlap, but they target slightly different audiences. *Marine Log* is the oldest U.S. trade magazine, starting as *Marine Engineering* in 1876. Today, it broadly covers the business and technology of shipping and the maritime trades from an American perspective. Aimed at maritime business, it has a slick online presence, with topics of articles ranging from policy concerns to greening the industry. Available in print and electronically for free to its target audience.

3758. Marine News. [ISSN: 1087-3864] 19??. m. Free to qualified personnel. Ed(s): Joseph Keefe. Maritime Activity Reports Inc., 118 E 25th St, 2nd Fl, New York, NY 10010; http://www.marinelink.com. Adv. *Aud.:* Ga, Sa.

Maritime Activity Reports publishes two magazines for the maritime industry, *Maritime Reporter and Engineering News* and *Marine News.* The latter targets the shallow-draft workboat audience, including owners, operators, and service providers. As a trade magazine, it includes interviews with industry leaders, short articles on timely topics, and advertisements. It is freely available electronically, making it a useful resource for those that serve a maritime audience.

3759. Marine Pollution Bulletin: the international journal for marine environmental scientists, engineers, administrators, politicians and lawyers. [ISSN: 0025-326X] 1970. 24x/yr. EUR 2132. Ed(s): Charles Sheppard. Elsevier Ltd, 32 Jamestown Rd, Camden, London, NW1 7BY, United Kingdom; corporate.sales@elsevier.com; http://www.elsevier.com. Illus., index, adv. Sample. Refereed. Vol. ends: No. 12. Microform: PQC. *Indexed:* A22, AbAn, C&ISA, C45, CerAb, EngInd, ExcerpMed, FS&TA, IndVet, M&GPA, OceAb, RRTA, S25. *Bk. rev.:* 2, 500 words. *Aud.:* Ac, Sa.

Using a variety of features, this inclusive and rigorous journal documents conditions, effects of human activity, and responses to pollutants in the marine environment. The editorials and invited reviews offer in-depth insight into marine environmental issues and briefer news items cover pollution events around the globe. In addition to the monthly issues, special issues focus on conferences or topics such as water quality in a specific geographic region. This

is a top-ranked journal appropriate for academic and research collections that support environmental science, marine management, and biological oceanography programs. This title is moderately expensive, so consider a single copy within your consortium. Available in print and electronically.

3760. Marine Technology Reporter. [ISSN: 1559-7415] 1994. 9x/yr. Free. Ed(s): Gregory R Trauthwein. New Wave Media, 118 E 18th St 2nd Fl, New York, NY 10010. Adv. Circ: 12825 Controlled. *Aud.:* Ga, Sa.

Marine Technology Reporter competes with *Sea Technology* for the marine techie audience, those buying, installing, and using equipment for marine operations, research, and exploration. Coverage includes salvage, offshore oil and gas, and commercial diving, as well as underwater operations and surveying. The online version uses page-turning technology, or a pdf can be downloaded. While somewhat North American in focus, it provides solid information on global developments in the field at a reasonable (free) price.

3761. Marine Technology Society Journal. Formerly (until 1969): *Journal of Ocean Technology;* Incorporated: *Ocean Soundings.* [ISSN: 0025-3324] 1966. q. USD 124 domestic; USD 140 foreign; USD 435 combined subscription (print & online eds.). Ed(s): Amy Morgante, Brian Bingham. Marine Technology Society, 5565 Sterrett Pl, Ste 108, Columbia, MD 21044; membership@mtsociety.org; http://www.mtsociety.org/shop/. Illus., index, adv. Refereed. Vol. ends: No. 4. *Indexed:* A22, C45, EngInd, M&GPA, OceAb, S25. *Bk. rev.:* 1-3, 500 words. *Aud.:* Ga, Ac, Sa.

This publication addresses all aspects of marine technology—how it works, how to use it in science, how it affects society. Articles are written for a wide audience. Regular issues focus on uses of technology in marine sciences, with articles written by both scientists and industry researchers. Special issues address such topics as acoustic tracking of fish, ocean education, and marine sanctuary management. This is a reasonably priced title for general collections that serve an audience with marine interests, as well as for academic collections that support broad marine programs. Available in print and electronically via password. An Open Access white publisher.

3762. Maritime Reporter and Engineering News. Formerly (until 1962): *Maritime Reporter.* [ISSN: 0025-3448] 1939. m. USD 98 elsewhere (Free to qualified personnel). Ed(s): Greg Trauthwein. Maritime Activity Reports Inc., 118 E 25th St, 2nd Fl, New York, NY 10010; http://www.marinelink.com. Illus., adv. *Aud.:* Ga, Sa.

This publication has a broader scope than its sister magazine, *Marine News.* It is more international, covering all aspects of shipping from design and construction to operations and policy. Available in print and electronically, it provides wide insight into the industry.

3763. Ocean Engineering. [ISSN: 0029-8018] 1968. 18x/yr. EUR 3643. Ed(s): Atilla Incecik, R Cengiz Ertekin. Pergamon, The Blvd, Langford Ln, E Park, Kidlington, OX5 1GB, United Kingdom; JournalsCustomerServiceEMEA@elsevier.com; http://www.elsevier.com. Illus., index, adv. Sample. Refereed. Vol. ends: No. 28. Microform: PQC. *Indexed:* A01, A22, ApMecR, C&ISA, CerAb, EngInd, H24, OceAb, S25. *Aud.:* Ac, Sa.

This highly specialized journal covers marine engineering from ships to structures to instrumentation. It is aimed at engineers, and the coverage of its research articles ranges from offshore engineering to naval architecture. Issues may include review articles as well as short communications on recent field work, instrument modeling, and testing. It is appropriate for specialized marine and engineering collections as interest in marine renewable energy increases, but it is very expensive. Available in print and electronically.

3764. Professional Mariner: journal of the maritime industry. [ISSN: 1066-2774] 1993. 8x/yr. USD 29.95 domestic; USD 39.95 Canada; USD 44.95 elsewhere. Ed(s): John Gormley. Navigator Publishing LLC., 58 Fore St, Portland, ME 04101-4842; http://www.navigatorpublishing.com. Illus. Sample. Circ: 29000. *Indexed:* OceAb. *Aud.:* Sa.

This maritime trade magazine addresses the concerns and interests of the people who work on the water: safety, current news, new and old working vessels, environmental updates, and more. While *Marine Officer* addresses concerns of those who manage vessels, *Professional Mariner* speaks to the people working on a myriad of platforms in various positions. An inexpensive print magazine with a digital version included in the price. Most articles are also available on the magazine's web site.

Remote Sensing of Environment. See Environment and Conservation section.

3765. Sea Technology. Formerly (until 1973): *Undersea Technology and Oceanology International & Offshore Technology;* Which was formed by the merger of (1971-1972): *Oceanology International Offshore Technology;* (1961-1972): *Undersea Technology;* Which was formerly (until 1961): *Underwater Engineering;* (until 1960): *Underwater Engineering News.* [ISSN: 0093-3651] 1972. m. USD 55 domestic (Free to qualified personnel). Ed(s): Lauren Masterson. Compass Publications, Inc. (Arlington), 1501 Wilson Blvd, Ste 1001, Arlington, VA 22209. Illus., index, adv. Vol. ends: No. 12. Microform: PQC. *Indexed:* A22, ApMecR, C&ISA, CerAb, EngInd, H24, M&GPA, OceAb. *Aud.:* Sa.

This monthly trade journal for marine technology and engineering combines short articles on issues and new developments with product reviews and news from the industry and the U.S. government. Articles address such topics as homeland security, toxicity sensors, and remotely operated vehicles. This journal is very inexpensive and appropriate for a general audience with technical and engineering interests. Available in print, and most features are free electronically. URL: www.sea-technology.com/features/index.html

Ocean Science

3766. Continental Shelf Research. [ISSN: 0278-4343] 1982. 20x/yr. EUR 3117. Ed(s): Richard W Sternberg, Michael B Collins. Pergamon, The Blvd, Langford Ln, E Park, Kidlington, OX5 1GB, United Kingdom; JournalsCustomerServiceEMEA@elsevier.com; http://www.elsevier.com. Adv. Sample. Refereed. Microform: PQC. *Indexed:* A01, A22, C&ISA, C45, CerAb, M&GPA, OceAb, RRTA, S25. *Aud.:* Ac, Sa.

This journal focuses on the shallow marine environment that is defined as the coast to the continental shelf break. All aspects of marine science are covered, with an emphasis on processes and innovative techniques applied in this environment. Two to four issues every year address special topics, such as physical oceanographic modeling and harmful algal blooms. This is an expensive but core title for oceanography collections, although it is less important for biologically focused collections. Available in print or electronically.

3767. Deep-Sea Research. Part 1: Oceanographic Research Papers. Supersedes in part (in 1993): *Deep-Sea Research. Part A: Oceanographic Research Papers;* Which was formerly (until 1979): *Deep-Sea Research;* (until 1977): *Deep-Sea Research and Oceanographic Abstracts;* (until 1962): *Deep-Sea Research.* [ISSN: 0967-0637] 1953. m. EUR 3528. Ed(s): M P Bacon. Pergamon, The Blvd, Langford Ln, E Park, Kidlington, OX5 1GB, United Kingdom; JournalsCustomerServiceEMEA@elsevier.com; http://www.elsevier.com. Illus., adv. Sample. Refereed. Microform: PQC. *Indexed:* A01, A22, C&ISA, CerAb, EngInd, M&GPA, OceAb, P02, S25. *Aud.:* Ac, Sa.

This journal focuses on the ocean beyond the continental shelf, including geological, physical, chemical, and biological aspects. It concentrates on research that reports results on theoretical, instrumentation-related, and methodological problems. Along with its companion journal, *Deep-Sea Research, Part 2: Topical Studies in Oceanography,* this title is essential for any institution with a marine biology or oceanography program. Consider a single subscription within your consortium due to the expense of this title. Available in print or electronically.

Dynamics of Atmospheres and Oceans. See Atmospheric Sciences section.

Earth Interactions. See Atmospheric Sciences section.

G3: Geochemistry, Geophysics, Geosystems: an electronic journal of the earth sciences. See Earth Sciences and Geology section.

Geo-Marine Letters: an international journal of marine geology. See Earth Sciences and Geology section.

Geophysical Research Letters. See Earth Sciences and Geology section.

3768. Global and Planetary Change. [ISSN: 0921-8181] 1988. 20x/yr. EUR 2271. Ed(s): T M Cronin, S A P L Cloetingh. Elsevier BV, Radarweg 29, PO Box 211, Amsterdam, 1000 AE, Netherlands; JournalsCustomerServiceEMEA@elsevier.com; http://www.elsevier.nl. Illus., index, adv. Refereed. Vol. ends: No. 6. Microform: PQC. *Indexed:* A01, A22, C&ISA, C45, CerAb, FR, IndVet, M&GPA, OceAb, RRTA, S25. *Aud.:* Ac, Sa.

This journal focuses on the record of change in the earth's history and presents multidisciplinary analysis of recent and future changes. Topics include changes in the chemical composition of the oceans and atmosphere, climate change, sea level variations, human geography, global geophysics and tectonics, global ecology, and biogeography. One or two issues annually focus on a special topic or theme. Relatively expensive, but useful for a wide variety of academic institutions, particularly those with environmental studies and oceanography programs. Available in print and electronically.

3769. Global Biogeochemical Cycles: an international journal of global change. [ISSN: 0886-6236] 1987. q. Wiley-Blackwell Publishing, Inc., 111 River St, Hoboken, NJ 07030; info@wiley.com; http://onlinelibrary.wiley.com/. Illus., adv. Refereed. Vol. ends: No. 4. *Indexed:* A22, Agr, C45, M&GPA, OceAb, S25. *Aud.:* Ac, Sa.

This journal exemplifies the relationship between oceanography and atmospheric science. Articles examine large-scale interactions in the geosphere and biosphere—changes resulting from marine, hydrologic, atmospheric, extraterrestrial, geologic, and human causes over time-scales large and small. This is an essential and affordable part of academic library collections that support oceanography and environmental studies programs. Pricing is relevant to the size of the institution. Available in print and electronically.

Journal of Atmospheric and Oceanic Technology. See Atmospheric Sciences section.

Journal of Geophysical Research: Oceans. See Earth Sciences and Geology section.

3770. Journal of Marine Systems. [ISSN: 0924-7963] 1990. 20x/yr. EUR 3286. Ed(s): E Hofmann, W Fennel. Elsevier BV, Radarweg 29, PO Box 211, Amsterdam, 1000 AE, Netherlands; JournalsCustomerServiceEMEA@elsevier.com; http://www.elsevier.nl. Illus., adv. Refereed. Vol. ends: No. 4. Microform: PQC. *Indexed:* A01, A22, C&ISA, CerAb, EngInd, M&GPA, OceAb. *Aud.:* Ac, Sa.

As implied in its title, this journal examines interdisciplinary, system-driven questions in the marine environment. With its coverage ranging in scale from lagoons to ocean basins, its articles focus on how the marine system shapes the biological, chemical, and physical environment. Coverage is international. It is expensive, but appropriate for research oceanography collections, especially those with a physical emphasis. Available in print and electronically.

3771. Journal of Oceanography. Supersedes in part (in 1992): *Oceanographical Society of Japan. Journal.* [ISSN: 0916-8370] 1941. bi-m. EUR 1199 (print & online eds.). Ed(s): Toshiyuki Hibiya. Springer Netherlands, Van Godewijckstraat 30, Dordrecht, 3311 GX, Netherlands; http://www.springer.com. Illus., adv. Refereed. Reprint: PSC. *Indexed:* A22, Agr, E01, M&GPA, OceAb. *Aud.:* Ac, Sa.

Originally published as the outlet for the Oceanographic Society of Japan, this journal continues to be biased toward basic oceanographic research in the Pacific Basin. Relevant topics include current dynamics, chemical fluxes, and occasional biological phenomena. Moderately expensive, and useful mostly for oceanography collections that support research in the Pacific. Available in print and electronically.

3772. *Journal of Physical Oceanography.* [ISSN: 0022-3670] 1971. m. Non-members, USD 1370 (print & online eds.). Ed(s): Michael Spall. American Meteorological Society, 45 Beacon St, Boston, MA 02108; amspubs@ametsoc.org; http://www.ametsoc.org. Illus., index, adv. Refereed. Vol. ends: No. 12. *Indexed:* A01, A22, ApMecR, CCMJ, E01, EngInd, M&GPA, MSN, MathR, OceAb, S25. *Aud.:* Ac, Sa.

Contributions to this journal relate to the physics of the ocean and the processes that operate at its boundaries. The primary aim of the journal is to promote understanding of the ocean and its role within the earth system. Typical articles address surface phenomena, oceanography (large- and small-scale), circulation, and modeling. An inexpensive, high-impact core journal for all academic libraries that serve an oceanography program. Available in print and electronically.

3773. *Journal of Sea Research.* Formerly (until vol.35, 1996): *Netherlands Journal of Sea Research.* [ISSN: 1385-1101] 1961. 8x/yr. EUR 869. Ed(s): Carlos Heip. Elsevier BV, Radarweg 29, PO Box 211, Amsterdam, 1000 AE, Netherlands; JournalsCustomerServiceEMEA@elsevier.com; http://www.elsevier.nl. Refereed. *Indexed:* A01, A22, C&ISA, C45, CerAb, IndVet, M&GPA, OceAb. *Aud.:* Ac, Sa.

Another of the many titles that examine coastal and shelf ecosystems, this journal has a northern European bias, yet it covers topics of interest to marine biologists and oceanographers everywhere. Affordable and appropriate for research collections in the marine sciences with an international focus. Available in print and electronically.

3774. *Limnology and Oceanography.* [ISSN: 0024-3590] 1956. bi-m. Ed(s): Everett Fee. American Society of Limnology and Oceanography, Inc., 5400 Bosque Blvd, Ste 680, Waco, TX 76710; business@aslo.org; http://www.aslo.org. Illus., index. Refereed. Vol. ends: No. 8. *Indexed:* A01, A22, AnBeAb, BRI, C45, IndVet, M&GPA, RRTA, S25. *Bk. rev.:* 2, 750 words; signed. *Aud.:* Ac, Sa.

This journal is published by the American Society of Limnology and Oceanography, but global in scope. The focus of this journal is aquatic ecosystems, and it includes original research articles on all aspects of limnology and oceanography. This journal is only available as part of a package that also includes the more specialized partner journal *Limnology and Oceanography: Methods* (electronic-only) and the society's *Bulletin.* A top-ranking journal and essential for any academic institution with a marine biology or oceanography program. Available in print and electronically. An Open Access blue journal.

3775. *Limnology and Oceanography: Fluids and Environments.* [ISSN: 2157-3689] 2011. irreg. USD 225. Ed(s): Josef Daniel Ackerman. Duke University Press, 905 W Main St, Ste 18 B, PO Box 90660, Durham, NC 27701; subscriptions@dukeupress.edu; http://www.dukeupress.edu. Adv. *Indexed:* S25. *Aud.:* Ac, Sa.

Limnology and Oceanography: Fluids & Environments is the newest offering from ASLO, but it is published by Duke University Press rather than the Society itself. This unique journal is multidisciplinary in scope, publishing articles relating to physical, biological, chemical, or geological interactions on a variety of scales within aqueous or aquatic environments. Articles range from modeling to theory, but focus on transport mechanisms and phenomena. The publication is online only. There are no issue numbers, and one year is equivalent to one volume for library subscriptions. It is freely available to ASLO members, but selected articles are open to the public as well. While too new to evaluate, it is inexpensive and has the cache of ASLO, so is a safe bet for research-based institutions.

3776. *Limnology and Oceanography: Methods.* [ISSN: 1541-5856] 2003. m. Free. Ed(s): Paul F Kemp, Susana Feng. American Society of Limnology and Oceanography, Inc., 5400 Bosque Blvd, Ste 680, Waco, TX 76710; business@aslo.org; http://www.aslo.org. Refereed. *Indexed:* OceAb, S25. *Aud.:* Ac, Sa.

Developed as a companion to the long-standing *Limnology and Oceanography,* this electronic-only journal is bundled with that as well as with the Society's bulletin. *Methods* provides a mechanism for rapid publication of articles that address problems and solutions in aquatic science methodology. It is becoming more valuable to its audience, and carries the cachet of the American Society of Limnology and Oceanography (now the Association for the Sciences of Limnology and Oceanography). An Open Access blue publication.

3777. *Marine Chemistry.* [ISSN: 0304-4203] 1972. 20x/yr. EUR 2718. Ed(s): Frank J Millero. Elsevier BV, Radarweg 29, PO Box 211, Amsterdam, 1000 AE, Netherlands; JournalsCustomerServiceEMEA@elsevier.com; http://www.elsevier.nl. Illus., adv. Refereed. Vol. ends: No. 4. Microform: PQC. *Indexed:* A01, A22, C&ISA, CerAb, M&GPA, OceAb, S25. *Aud.:* Ac, Sa.

This highly-ranked journal includes original research and occasional reviews that address the dynamics of chemistry of the marine environment. It is an international forum, and will be of interest to marine chemists, chemical oceanographers, and geochemists. This journal is appropriate for academic collections that support a research program in marine chemistry or oceanography, but expensive enough to warrant a single purchase within a consortium. Available in print and electronically.

3778. *Marine Geology.* [ISSN: 0025-3227] 1964. 44x/yr. EUR 4904. Ed(s): John T Wells, G de Lange. Elsevier BV, Radarweg 29, PO Box 211, Amsterdam, 1000 AE, Netherlands; JournalsCustomerServiceEMEA@elsevier.com; http://www.elsevier.nl. Illus., index, adv. Refereed. Vol. ends: No. 4. Microform: PQC. *Indexed:* A01, A22, C&ISA, CerAb, EngInd, M&GPA, OceAb. *Aud.:* Ac, Sa.

Along with *Journal of Geophysical Research,* this top-ranked title contains articles on marine geology, geochemistry, and geophysics. The focus is on the science of marine geology rather than its management or hydrodynamics. Multiple volumes are published annually, with one or two addressing a special topic such as tidal sedimentation or prodelta systems. This is a core, but expensive, title for geologic oceanography collections, so consider a collaborative purchase with partner libraries. Available in print and electronically.

3779. *Marine Geophysical Researches: an international journal for the study of the earth beneath the sea.* [ISSN: 0025-3235] 1970. q. EUR 825 (print & online eds.). Ed(s): Shu-Kun Hsu, Amy E Draut. Springer Netherlands, Van Godewijckstraat 30, Dordrecht, 3311 GX, Netherlands; http://www.springer.com. Illus., adv. Refereed. Microform: PQC. Reprint: PSC. *Indexed:* A01, A22, E01, EngInd, M&GPA, OceAb. *Aud.:* Ac, Sa.

This publication has traditionally dealt with data on the deep ocean basins, but recently has expanded to include the global mid-ocean ridge system and the geophysics of continental margins. Typical articles address techniques and tools for deep-sea-floor imaging and measurement. This affordable publication will be of interest to geologists and oceanographers. Recommended for academic and research libraries that support these types of programs. Available in print and electronically.

3780. *Progress in Oceanography.* [ISSN: 0079-6611] 1963. 16x/yr. EUR 3542. Ed(s): Cisco Werner, Gregory R Lough. Pergamon, The Blvd, Langford Ln, E Park, Kidlington, OX5 1GB, United Kingdom; JournalsCustomerServiceEMEA@elsevier.com; http://www.elsevier.com. Illus., index, adv. Sample. Refereed. Vol. ends: No. 4. Microform: PQC. *Indexed:* A01, A22, ApMecR, C&ISA, CerAb, EngInd, M&GPA, OceAb, S25. *Aud.:* Ac, Sa.

This is essential reading for oceanographers. It includes longer, comprehensive articles that review aspects of oceanography or offer a treatise on a developing aspect of oceanographic research. Some volumes include collections of papers and conference proceedings. This title belongs in libraries that support oceanography programs, and will be of interest to physical and chemical oceanographers as well as marine biologists. Due to the expense of this title, a single copy should be purchased by collaborating libraries. Available in print and electronically.

Tellus. Series A: Dynamic Meteorology and Oceanography. See Atmospheric Sciences section.

■ MARRIAGE AND DIVORCE

Ann Walsh Long, Technical Services/Circulation Services Librarian, Lincoln Memorial University Duncan School of Law, 601 W. Summit Hill Drive, Knoxville, TN 37921; ann.long@lmunet.edu

Introduction

When this reviewer researched magazines for this section, Ulrichsweb Global Serials Directory contained 263 active magazine titles under the subject heading of "matrimony." Of these titles, very few actually deal with the subject of both marriage and divorce. The majority of these titles focus on the bliss of wedding planning. There are numerous online-only journals that are related to divorce and appear to be created as a means for advertising services to a specific geographic area or group (such as services of attorneys or counselors).

A recent U.S. Supreme Court decision will have a big impact on marriage and is likely to spawn new magazine titles. On June 26, 2013, the Supreme Court ruled the Defense of Marriage Act (DOMA) unconstitutional. DOMA was originally signed into law by President Clinton in 1996. The law limited the definition of "marriage" and "spouse" to applying only to legally married heterosexual couples. DOMA barred the federal government from recognizing same-sex marriages that were authorized by state law. The court struck down the federal law because it denied same-sex couples "equal liberty" as guaranteed by the Fifth Amendment. With a new definition of marriage, it will be interesting to see how this section grows over the next few years.

There are many general-interest magazines that discuss marriage and divorce, but those popular titles have not been included due to the breadth of their content.

Basic Periodicals

Divorce Magazine, Journal of Divorce & Remarriage, Marriage & Family Review, Marriage Magazine.

Basic Abstracts and Indexes

Academic Search Complete, Family Studies Abstracts, Periodical Abstracts, ProQuest Central, PsycINFO, Social Sciences Abstracts, Social Work Abstracts, Sociological Abstracts, Studies on Women and Gender Abstracts.

Bride's. See Weddings section.

Contemporary Family Therapy: an international journal. See Family section.

3781. Divorce Magazine. Formerly (until 1998): *Toronto's Divorce Magazine.* [ISSN: 1484-9054] 1996. s-a. CAD 25.99 for 2 yrs. in US & Canada. Ed(s): John Matias. Segue Esprit Inc., 2255B Queen St, E, Ste #1179, Toronto, ON M4E 1G3, Canada; editors@divorcemag.com. Adv. *Indexed:* CBCARef. *Aud.:* Ga.

Divorce Magazine is published annually and aimed at individuals involved in the divorce process. Articles include feature stories; columns that offer tips, advice, and insights for a successful divorce; and an "essential" divorce guide that includes information on working with your divorce lawyer, and an overview of mediation. Recommended for public libraries. URL: www.divorcemag.com/

The Family Journal. See Family section.

Family Law Quarterly. See Law section.

3782. Family Therapy Magazine. Former titles (until 2002): *Family Therapy News;* (until 198?): *American Association for Marriage and Family Therapy Newsletter.* [ISSN: 1538-9448] 1969. bi-m. USD 10 newsstand/cover per issue. Ed(s): Karen Gautney, Michael Bowers. American Association for Marriage and Family Therapy, 112 S Alfred St, Alexandria, VA 22314; http://www.aamft.org. Adv. Circ: 21000. *Aud.:* Ac, Sa.

This bimonthly magazine is produced by the American Association for Marriage and Family Therapy (AAMFT), which is the professional association for the field of marriage and family therapists (MFTs). Aimed at that audience, recent issues discuss courtship and mating, and delve into how technology affects relationships. Future issues will address the new U.S. health-care law and emerging ethical and legal trends for MFTs. Each issue includes a calendar of upcoming professional events. Recommended for academic and special libraries.

Fathering Magazine. See Parenting section.

3783. I N T A M S Review: journal for the study of marriage and spirituality. [ISSN: 1370-6020] 1995. s-a. EUR 50 combined subscription (print & online eds.). Ed(s): T Knieps-Port Le Roi. Peeters Publishers, Bondgenotenlaan 153, Leuven, 3000, Belgium; peeters@peeters-leuven.be; http://www.peeters-leuven.be. Refereed. *Indexed:* A22. *Bk. rev.:* Number and length vary. *Aud.:* Ac, Sa.

The International Academy for Marital Spirituality (INTAMS) is published in the spring and fall and is internationally refereed. This title has an international audience, and contributing authors write in a variety of languages, including English, French, German, Italian, and Spanish. The *INTAMS Review* focuses on "new theological and philosophical trends in the various (ethical, dogmatic, pastoral, exegetical, historical, and juridical) approaches to marriage and the family; relates relevant research findings in the human sciences to the theology of marriage; and traces original approaches to defining and substantiating marital spirituality." In addition to articles, each issue contains several book reviews. Recommended for academic and special libraries.

Journal of Comparative Family Studies. See Family section.

3784. Journal of Divorce & Remarriage: research and clinical studies in family theory, family law, family mediation and family therapy. Formerly (until 1990): *Journal of Divorce.* [ISSN: 1050-2556] 1977. 8x/yr. GBP 1485 (print & online eds.). Ed(s): Craig A Everett. Routledge, 325 Chestnut St, Ste 800, Philadelphia, PA 19106; customerservice@taylorandfrancis.com; http://www.tandfonline.com. Illus., index, adv. Sample. Refereed. Circ: 379 Paid. Vol. ends: No. 4. Microform: PQC. Reprint: PSC. *Indexed:* A01, A22, ASSIA, C42, E01, GW, P02, P61, PsycInfo, SSA, SWR&A. *Bk. rev.:* Number and length vary. *Aud.:* Ac, Sa.

The *Journal of Divorce and Remarriage* covers all aspects of divorce, including pre-divorce marital and family treatment; marital separation and dissolution; children's responses to divorce and separation; single parenting; remarriage; and stepfamilies. The journal is aimed at professionals, such as family therapists, family law lawyers, counselors, and social workers. Three of the most cited articles discussed topics such as reasons for divorce; the factors that contribute to quality co-parenting; and forgiveness of an ex-spouse. Recommended for academic and special libraries.

Journal of Family Issues. See Family section.

Journal of Marital and Family Therapy. See Family section.

Journal of Social and Personal Relationships. See Communication section.

3785. Marriage & Family Review. [ISSN: 0149-4929] 1978. 8x/yr. GBP 1506 (print & online eds.). Ed(s): Walter R Schumm. Routledge, 325 Chestnut St, Ste 800, Philadelphia, PA 19106; customerservice@taylorandfrancis.com; http://www.tandfonline.com. Adv. Sample. Refereed. Circ: 413 Paid. Microform: PQC. Reprint: PSC. *Indexed:* A01, A22, ASSIA, AgeL, Agr, AmHI, BRI, C42, E01, FR, GW, P02, P61, PsycInfo, SSA, SWR&A. *Aud.:* Ac, Sa.

Marriage and Family Review is a peer-reviewed journal that accepts open submissions and research articles on current topics of interest related to family strengths and premarital relationships. Once a year, the "Decade in Review" issue reports on articles published over the past five to 20 years on one area of major research. Three of the most-read articles include: text messaging and connectedness within close interpersonal relationships; the resilience of adult children of divorce: a multiple case study; and parenting styles: the impact on student achievement. Recommended for academic and special libraries.

3786. Marriage (St. Paul). Formerly (until 199?): *Marriage Encounter.* [ISSN: 1063-1054] 1971. q. USD 19.95 domestic; USD 24.95 foreign. Ed(s): Krysta Eryn Kavenaugh. International Marriage Encounter, Inc., PO Box 387, St. Paul, MN -55120-1497. Illus., adv. Circ: 11000 Paid. *Bk. rev.:* Number and length vary. *Aud.:* Ga.

Marriage magazine's mission is "to act as the focal point for the marriage movement[,] serving as a simple[-]to[-]use, but effective guide to support, grow and foster your marriage." The magazine encourages readers to submit their marriage stories on overcoming adversity, or their secrets to a successful marriage, and features a "spotlight couple" in every issue. Columnists include marriage counselors, educators, and ministers. Recommended for public libraries.

3787. The Nest: from the knot. [ISSN: 1933-7981] 2006. s-a. The Knot Inc., 462 Broadway, 6th Fl, New York, NY 10013; salesinfo@theknot.com; http://www.theknot.com. Adv. *Aud.:* Ga.

The Nest provides information to newlyweds on topics such as relationships; home decor; food and recipies; holiday ideas; money; real estate; community; pets; and anniversary ideas. *The Nest* is also available online in a digital format, with an accompanying web site that encourages readers, or "nesties," to follow them on Facebook and Twitter and in blog postings. Recommended for public libraries. URL: www.thenest.com

Sexual and Relationship Therapy. See Sexuality section.

■ MATHEMATICS

General/Research Journals

John J. Meier, Physical and Mathematical Sciences Library, Pennsylvania State University, 201 Davey Lab, University Park, PA 16802; 814-867-2806; FAX: 814-865-2565; meier@psu.edu

Introduction

Mathematicians, as well as students and teachers of mathematics, have both a deep connection to the past and a strong tie to the unfolding future. A mathematical problem can remained unsolved for centuries until proven. Mathematics is at the core of our computational world and can be applied everywhere, from finances to biology to social networks. This dichotomy is reflected in the magazines and journals favored by the discipline for communication and for keeping the record of scholarship. Mathematics is also a field of intense specialization and deep genius. Indeed, the most significant proofs of the past few years could be understood by only a handful of mathematicians and have taken years to confirm.

This section is divided into two subsections of "General" and "Research" to help libraries address the needs of their users, whether students, teachers, or researchers. Public and school libraries should mostly look to periodicals in the "General" category for mathematics presented at an accessible level. Libraries serving teachers of mathematics in K–12 and college, sometimes called K–16, along with those responsible for relevant teacher training, colleges, and

professional development, will most appreciate titles in the "General" category, and some in "Research" that focus on pedagogy and teaching strategies. Most of the "Research" journals will mainly be of interest to academic or special libraries that serve students, faculty, or researchers pursuing pure and applied mathematics. With respect to research journals, only those with broad acceptance parameters were included here, as opposed to the large number of specialized topic journals.

Since the last edition of this book, a number of publications are now available online to libraries by institutional subscription and not simply individual members of an association. The National Council of Teachers of Mathematics (NCTM) (see *Mathematics Teacher*) has partnered with JSTOR (www.jstor.org) through the Current Scholarship Program to offer some of their flagship periodicals online. Many journals are now also available online back to their first volume, either through JSTOR or from their publisher. Only a few publications remain print only, and some mathematicians can still be seen in library periodical browsing areas.

The pre-print repository Arxiv.org is still growing in use by mathematicians and may soon be used to create "overlay journals," which can be created instantly from open-access research articles. *MathSciNet* from the American Mathematical Society (AMS) is still considered the core index for mathematics, but Google and Wikipedia are now basic entry points for the discovery of online journal articles. Beyond this publication, there are a number of resources to support librarians in keeping up with changes in the mathematics literature. The AMS has a portal for librarians (www.ams.org/publications/librarian), and the Special Libraries Association (SLA) has the Physics-Astronomy-Mathematics (PAM) division (http://pam.sla.org/). Some key books are the *Guide to Information Sources in Mathematics and Statistics* by Martha A. Tucker and Nancy D. Anderson, and *Using the Mathematics Literature* by Kristine K. Fowler.

Basic Periodicals

Ems: *Teaching Children Mathematics*; Hs: *Mathematics Teacher*; Ga: *Mathematics Magazine*; Ac: *American Mathematical Monthly, American Mathematical Society. Bulletin. New Series, The Mathematical Intelligencer, S I A M Review*.

Basic Abstracts and Indexes

MathSciNet.

General

Chance. See Statistics section.

3788. Forum of Mathematics, Pi. [ISSN: 2050-5086] 2013. q. Free. Ed(s): Rob Kirby. Cambridge University Press, The Edinburgh Bldg, Shaftesbury Rd, Cambridge, CB2 8RU, United Kingdom; journals@cambridge.org; http://journals.cambridge.org. Refereed. *Aud.:* Ac, Sa.

Forum of Mathematics, Pi and *Forum of Mathematics, Sigma* are recent publications from Cambridge University Press. They are both fully open-access, peer-reviewed journals with editorial boards of the highest standing. *Pi* is intended to be a general mathematics journal accessible to a broad audience of mathematicians. *Sigma* is intended to be a specialist journal with groups of editors working around topical areas such as applied mathematics, computation, topology, and many more. These journals will eventually charge authors for publication of manuscripts in order to develop a sustainable model of journal publishing. URL: http://journals.cambridge.org/action/displayJournal?jid=FMP

3789. The Mathematical Gazette. [ISSN: 0025-5572] 1894. 3x/yr. Free to members; Non-members, GBP 99. Ed(s): Gerry Leversha. The Mathematical Association, 259 London Rd, Leicester, LE2 3BE, United Kingdom; office@m-a.org.uk; http://www.m-a.org.uk. Illus., index, adv. Vol. ends: No. 3. *Indexed:* A22, MathR. *Bk. rev.:* 10-25, 200-1,500 words, signed. *Aud.:* Hs, Ac, Sa.

Mathematical Gazette is published by the United Kingdom's Mathematical Association (www.m-a.org.uk) to cover the teaching and learning of mathematics with a focus on "the 15-20 age range." It includes news and events of the association, but is primarily expository articles, letters, problems, and extensive book reviews. It is useful for teachers of high school students through college undergraduates. A companion publication by the same association is *Mathematics in School,* which is aimed at teachers of students aged 10–18. It has relatively short articles, worksheets for classroom use, occasionally cartoons or fun facts, and a few short, signed book reviews. It is appropriate for middle school and high school libraries, though it is focused on the curriculum of the U.K. Both journals are available online, starting with volume 1 after a five-year embargo on JSTOR (www.jstor.org).

3790. Mathematics Magazine. Incorporates (in 1977): *Delta;* Which was formerly (until 1947): *National Mathematics Magazine;* (until 1934): *Mathematics News Letter.* [ISSN: 0025-570X] 1926. 5x/yr. Ed(s): Walter A Stromquist. Mathematical Association of America, 1529 18th St, NW, Washington, DC 20036; maahq@maa.org; http://www.maa.org. Illus., index, adv. Refereed. Circ: 8400. Microform: PQC. *Indexed:* A01, A22, BRI, CCMJ, MASUSE, MSN, MathR, P02. *Bk. rev.:* 6-8, 300-750 words. *Aud.:* Hs, Ga, Ac, Sa.

Mathematics Magazine is published by the Mathematical Association of America (MAA), which is the "largest professional society that focuses on mathematics accessible at the undergraduate level." Along with *Math Horizons,* this general magazine is intended to introduce advanced mathematical concepts and proofs to students in interesting ways. It uses the history of mathematics, applied mathematics, or visuals to explain difficult concepts. It has a small problems section and several medium-length, unsigned book reviews. Though articles are written by college and university faculty, it is very approachable for undergraduates and advanced high school students. *Mathematics Magazine* and *Math Horizons* are available online through JSTOR, along with other MAA journals (see *The American Mathematical Monthly*). Both are recommended for all academic libraries, and may be of interest to public and high school libraries.

3791. Mathematics Teacher. [ISSN: 0025-5769] 1908. 9x/yr. USD 260 (print & online eds.). Ed(s): Beth Skipper. National Council of Teachers of Mathematics, 1906 Association Dr, Reston, VA 20191; nctm@nctm.org; http://www.nctm.org. Illus., adv. Refereed. *Indexed:* A01, A22, BRI, CBRI, ERIC, MathR, P02. *Bk. rev.:* 5-10, 100-300 words, signed. *Aud.:* Ems, Hs, Ac, Sa.

Mathematics Teacher is the flagship publication of the National Council of Teachers of Mathematics (NCTM) (www.nctm.org). The NCTM is the world's largest organization focused solely on the teaching of mathematics, though the membership is primarily in North America. *Mathematics Teacher* offers activities, lesson ideas, teaching strategies, and problems including a "monthly Calendar" of math problems. Regular columns include teaching with technology or multimedia, math problems with solutions, and a new focus on mathematical modeling from the Common Core State Standards for Mathematics. Each issue has several short, signed book reviews. The audience is primarily high school or college instructors, so it is a core resource for high school libraries and useful both to math and education academic libraries. The NCTM also publishes *Mathematics Teaching in the Middle School* with similar content for middle school educators and *Teaching Children Mathematics* for the pre-K–to–elementary school audience. These also have activities, problems, teaching strategies, and occasionally book reviews. They are best for school libraries and academic libraries that serve education students. All three journals are available online for institutional access through the JSTOR Current Scholarship Program, along with NCTM's research journals (see *Journal for Research in Mathematics Education*). URL: www.nctm.org/publications/mt.aspx

3792. Mathematics Teaching. Incorporates (1985-2005): *Micromath.* [ISSN: 0025-5785] 1955. bi-m. Free to members. Ed(s): Margaret Jones. Association of Teachers of Mathematics, Unit 7 Prime Industrial Park, Shaftesbury St, Derby, DE23 8YB, United Kingdom; admin@atm.org.uk; http://www.atm.org.uk. Illus., adv. Microform: PQC. *Indexed:* A01, A22, ERIC, P02. *Bk. rev.:* Occasional. *Aud.:* Ems, Hs, Sa.

Mathematics Teaching is a publication of the Association of Teachers of Mathematics (ATM), a society in the United Kingdom that was established in 1950 to "encourage the development of mathematics education such that it is more closely related to the needs of the learner." The primary journal of the association has some official reports and conference news, but consists primarily of "reflective, perhaps personal" articles. Indeed, the anecdotes and narratives describe teaching mathematics in the classroom from both a student and teacher perspective, making *Mathematics Teacher* a unique publication. The perspective is strongly British, where a majority of ATM membership is based. There are occasional book reviews, and some articles and extras are available online to ATM members. Some content is open access on the journal's web site, and more is available after signing up for a free account. Recommended for elementary, middle, and high school libraries that are interested in more personal articles. URL: www.atm.org.uk/journal

3793. Pi Mu Epsilon Journal. [ISSN: 0031-952X] 1949. s-a. USD 20 for 2 yrs. domestic; USD 25 for 2 yrs. foreign. Ed(s): Brigitte Servatius. Pi Mu Epsilon, Inc, c/o Leo J Schneider, Department of Mathematics and Computer Science, University Heights, OH 44118; LEO@jcu.edu; http://www.pme-math.org. Illus. Refereed. Microform: PQC. *Indexed:* A22, MathR. *Aud.:* Ac, Sa.

The *Pi Mu Epsilon Journal* is the official publication of the Pi Mu Epsilon National Honorary Mathematics Society (PME) (www.pme-math.org), which is "dedicated to the promotion of mathematics and recognition of students who successfully pursue mathematical understanding." The journal is written for undergraduates and focuses mostly on pure mathematics. Undergraduate authors are preferred, though most seem to be graduate students or faculty. There are short biographies for each author, and a large problem section with open access to upcoming problems in the online "Problem Department." There is a regular "mathacrostic" crossword, as well as art in "From the Right Side" pieces. There are no book reviews. Recommended for academic libraries that serve mathematics majors.

3794. U M A P Journal. [ISSN: 0197-3622] 1980. q. Free to members. Ed(s): Paul Campbell. Consortium for Mathematics and Its Applications, 175 Middlesex Turnpike, Ste 3B, Bedford, MA 01730; info@comap.com; http://www.comap.com. Illus., index, adv. Vol. ends: No. 4. *Indexed:* A22. *Bk. rev.:* 3-10, 250-1,500 words. *Aud.:* Hs, Ac, Sa.

The *UMAP Journal* is published by the Consortium for Mathematics and Its Applications (COMAP) (www.comap.com), which is a "non-profit organization whose mission is to improve mathematics education for students of all ages," founded in 1980. It also publishes *Consortium,* which focuses on teaching activities, and the *International Journal for the History of Mathematics Education,* which is a biannual publication on the past. The *UMAP Journal* "focuses on mathematical modeling and applications of mathematics at the undergraduate level." Written at such a general level, it is also approachable for some high school and public library users, though most authors are college and university professors. It has several medium-length, signed book reviews, and the table of contents is available online, along with article supplements. Recommended for academic libraries, and it may be suitable for some high school and public libraries.

Research Journals

3795. Acta Mathematica. [ISSN: 0001-5962] 1882. q. 2 vols/yr. EUR 449 (print & online eds.). Ed(s): Ari Laptev. Springer Netherlands, Van Godewijckstraat 30, Dordrecht, 3311 GX, Netherlands; http://springerlink.com. Illus., index. Refereed. Vol. ends: No. 2. Reprint: PSC. *Indexed:* A01, A22, ABIn, CCMJ, E01, MSN, MathR. *Aud.:* Ac, Sa.

Acta Mathematica is published by the Royal Swedish Academy of Sciences (www.kva.se/KVA_Root/index_eng.asp). This is an "independent organization whose overall objective is to promote the sciences and strengthen their influence in society." The journal (also known as *Acta Mathematica Djursholm*) is well established and publishes lengthy research articles in all areas of mathematics. With only around 800 pages annually, there are about 12–16 articles, which tend to be of high quality and are frequently cited. There are no book reviews, and it is available online with an archive back to volume 1. Recommended for all academic libraries. URL: www.springerlink.com/content/ 1871-2509

3796. ***American Journal of Mathematics.*** [ISSN: 0002-9327] 1878. bi-m. USD 395. Ed(s): Christopher Sogge. The Johns Hopkins University Press, 2715 N Charles St, Baltimore, MD 21218; http:// www.press.jhu.edu. Illus., index, adv. Sample. Refereed. Circ: 699. Vol. ends: No. 6. Microform: PMC; PQC. Reprint: PSC. *Indexed:* A01, A22, CCMJ, E01, MSN, MathR, P02. *Aud.:* Ac, Sa.

The *American Journal of Mathematics* has been in publication since 1878. It is published by the Johns Hopkins University Press and contains "articles of broad appeal covering the major areas of contemporary mathematics." About 50 articles are published annually, with more than 1,700 pages and no book reviews. The journal is available online through Project Muse with a historic archive at JSTOR (www.jstor.org). Recommended for academic libraries. URL: http://muse.jhu.edu/journals/american_journal_of_mathematics

3797. ***The American Mathematical Monthly.*** [ISSN: 0002-9890] 1894. 10x/yr. USD 464 (print & online eds.). Ed(s): Daniel J Velleman. Mathematical Association of America, 1529 18th St, NW, Washington, DC 20036; maahq@maa.org; http://www.maa.org. Illus., index, adv. Refereed. Circ: 12000. Vol. ends: No. 10. Microform: PQC. *Indexed:* A01, A22, BRI, CCMJ, MSN, MathR, P02. *Bk. rev.:* 1-4, 1,200-2,000 words, signed. *Aud.:* Hs, Ga, Ac, Sa.

The *American Mathematical Monthly* is the most notable research publication of the Mathematics Association of America (MAA). Articles of "broad appeal" are encouraged, as the audience is collegiate-level math students in addition to professional mathematicians. Shorter articles are published as "Notes" along with example math problems and a few long, signed book reviews. Another similar journal from the MAA is *College Mathematics Journal,* which also presents research that may be accessible to undergraduates. It has worked problems in "Classroom Capsules" in addition to problems and book reviews similar to those in the *American Mathematical Monthly.* Both journals are available online through JSTOR along with other MAA journals (see *Mathematics Magazine*), and are recommended for all academic libraries that serve undergraduate mathematics programs. They may also interest some high school or public libraries.

3798. ***American Mathematical Society. Bulletin. New Series.*** Former titles (until 1979): *American Mathematical Society. Bulletin;* (until 1894): *New York Mathematical Society. Bulletin.* [ISSN: 0273-0979] 1891. q. Institutional members, USD 427.20; Individual members, USD 320.40. Ed(s): Susan J Friedlander. American Mathematical Society, 201 Charles St, Providence, RI 02904; cust-serv@ams.org; http://www.ams.org. Adv. Refereed. Microform: PMC; PQC. *Indexed:* A01, A22, BRI, C&ISA, CCMJ, CerAb, MSN, MathR, P02. *Bk. rev.:* 4-8, 3,000-7,000 words, signed. *Aud.:* Ac, Sa.

The *Bulletin (New Series) of the American Mathematical Society,* published since 1891, is the oldest publication of the American Mathematical Society (AMS). The AMS promotes "mathematical research and its uses, strengthens mathematical education, and fosters awareness and appreciation of mathematics and its connections to other disciplines and to everyday life." It publishes a number of significant journals as well as the index of *Mathematical Reviews* (online as MathSciNet). The *Bulletin* publishes articles accessible to most mathematicians, and contains several very lengthy, signed book reviews. It is available free online, including an archive from volume 1 to the present. More advanced research journals from the AMS are *Transactions of the American Mathematical Society* for lengthy articles, *Proceedings of the American Mathematical Society* for shorter articles, and *Journal of the American Mathematical Society,* which is the newest publication. All are recommended as core for academic libraries, available online with an archive through JSTOR. URL: www.ams.org/journals/

3799. ***Annals of Mathematics.*** Formerly (until 1884): *The Analyst.* [ISSN: 0003-486X] 1874. bi-m. USD 485 combined subscription (print & online eds.). Princeton University, Department of Mathematics, Fine Hall, Washington Rd, Princeton, NJ 08544; www@math.princeton.edu; http://www.math.princeton.edu/. Illus., index. Sample. Refereed. Vol. ends: No. 3. Microform: PMC; PQC. *Indexed:* A22, CCMJ, MSN, MathR. *Aud.:* Ac, Sa.

Annals of Mathematics is a university press journal published by Princeton University in cooperation with the Institute of Advanced Study (IAS) (www.ias.edu). "The Institute exists to encourage and support fundamental research in the sciences and humanities," including mathematics. *Annals* is a respected, highly cited journal that publishes in all areas of mathematics. There are 50–60 articles published annually, in over 3,000 pages. There are no book reviews, and current issues are available online. The JSTOR archive has a five-year embargo on content. This is one of a number of journals that allow authors to submit manuscripts through arxiv.org. Highly recommended for academic libraries. URL: www.jstor.org/journals/0003486x.html

Annals of Probability. See Statistics section.

Annals of Statistics. See Statistics section.

Applied Statistics. See *Royal Statistical Society. Journal. Series C. Applied Statistics* in the Statistics section.

3800. ***Cambridge Philosophical Society. Mathematical Proceedings.*** Formerly (until 1975): *Cambridge Philosophical Society. Proceedings. Mathematical and Physical Sciences.* [ISSN: 0305-0041] 1866. bi-m. GBP 586. Ed(s): B J Green. Cambridge University Press, The Edinburgh Bldg, Shaftesbury Rd, Cambridge, CB2 8RU, United Kingdom; journals@cambridge.org; http://www.cambridge.org/uk. Illus., index. Refereed. Vol. ends: No. 3. Microform: PMC; PQC. Reprint: PSC. *Indexed:* A01, A22, ApMecR, CCMJ, E01, MLA-IB, MSN, MathR. *Aud.:* Ac, Sa.

Published by Cambridge University Press, the *Mathematical Proceedings of the Cambridge Philosophical Society* is one of the few renowned mathematics journals that publishes in "the whole range of pure and applied mathematics, theoretical physics[,] and statistics." There are about 50–70 articles published each year, around 1,100 pages. No book reviews are included. The digital archive for the years 1924–96 is available, in addition to current electronic issues, at http://journals.cambridge.org/action/displayJournal?jid=PSP. Appropriate for academic libraries.

3801. ***Canadian Journal of Mathematics.*** [ISSN: 0008-414X] 1949. bi-m. USD 875.50. Ed(s): Nassif Ghoussoub, James B Carrell. University of Toronto Press, Journals Division, 5201 Dufferin St, Toronto, ON M3H 5T8, Canada; journals@utpress.utoronto.ca; http://www.utpjournals.com. Illus., adv. Refereed. Circ: 772. Vol. ends: No. 6. Microform: PQC. *Indexed:* A22, CCMJ, MSN, MathR. *Aud.:* Ac, Sa.

The *Canadian Journal of Mathematics* (also known as *Journal Canadien de Mathematiques*) is one of two research journals published by the Canadian Mathematical Society (CMS). The CMS was originally conceived in June 1945 as the Canadian Mathematical Congress, and works to "share experiences, work on collaborative projects[,] and generally enhance the perception and strengthen the profile of mathematics in Canada." Longer articles (15 pages or more) are published in this journal, and shorter pieces are published in the *Canadian Mathematical Bulletin* (not reviewed here). "Papers must treat new mathematical research" and "be of interest to a significant segment of the mathematical community." Papers are in English and rarely in French. There are about 60 articles published annually, totalling 1,400 pages. It is available online, including an archive from volume 1. Recommended for academic libraries. URL: http://cms.math.ca/cjm/

3802. ***Duke Mathematical Journal.*** [ISSN: 0012-7094] 1935. 15x/yr. USD 2230. Ed(s): Jonathan Wahl. Duke University Press, 905 W Main St, Ste 18 B, PO Box 90660, Durham, NC 27701; subscriptions@dukepress.edu; http://www.dukepress.edu. Illus., index, adv. Sample. Refereed. Vol. ends: No. 3. Microform: MIM; PQC. Reprint: PSC. *Indexed:* A22, CCMJ, MSN, MathR. *Aud.:* Ac, Sa.

An important university press title, *Duke Mathematical Journal (DMJ)* has been published by Duke University Press since 1935. It is one of the more costly of university press titles (compare to *Indiana University Mathematics Journal*). It is focused primarily on pure mathematics and publishes roughly 75–90 articles for about 3,000 pages annually. Volumes 1–100 are available through *DMJ 100* on Project Euclid (http://projecteuclid.org/dmj100). Recommended for academic libraries. URL: http://projecteuclid.org/dmj/

3803. Historia Mathematica. [ISSN: 0315-0860] 1974. q. EUR 550. Ed(s): Niccolo Guicciardini, Thomas Archibald. Academic Press, 3251 Riverport Ln, Maryland Heights, MO 63043; JournalCustomerService-usa@elsevier.com; http://www.elsevierdirect.com/brochures/academicpress/index.html. Illus., adv. Refereed. *Indexed:* A01, A22, ArtHuCI, CCMJ, E01, MSN, MathR. *Bk. rev.:* 6-8, 500-1,500 words, signed; 18-22 pages of 50- to 100-word abstracts. *Aud.:* Ga, Ac, Sa.

Historia Mathematica "publishes historical scholarship on mathematics and its development in all cultures and time periods." It is published by the International Commission on the History of Mathematics (ICHM) (www.unizar.es/ichm). Besides a dozen research articles per year in the 500 pages published, there are 20 or more pages of abstracts from the current literature on the history of mathematics in each issue. There are several medium-length, signed book reviews. It is available online starting at volume 1. Recommended for academic libraries, and it may also be suitable for public libraries for its strong bibliographic focus. URL: www.sciencedirect.com/science/journal/03150860

3804. I M A Journal of Applied Mathematics. Supersedes in part (in 1981): *Institute of Mathematics and Its Applications. Journal.* [ISSN: 0272-4960] 1965. bi-m. EUR 973. Oxford University Press, Great Clarendon St, Oxford, OX2 6DP, United Kingdom; enquiry@oup.co.uk; http://www.oxfordjournals.org/. Illus., adv. Sample. Refereed. Reprint: PSC. *Indexed:* A01, A22, ApMecR, C&ISA, CCMJ, E01, EngInd, MSN, MathR. *Aud.:* Ac, Sa.

The *IMA Journal of Applied Mathematics* is published by the Institute of Mathematics and its Applications (IMA) (www.ima.org.uk). The IMA "exists to support the advancement of mathematical knowledge and its applications and to promote and enhance mathematical culture." The IMA also publishes the *IMA Journal of Numerical Analysis.* The *IMA Journal of Applied Mathematics* focuses on "analytic and numerical treatments of both physical and non-physical applied mathematical problems." Papers that have applications to more than one field are preferred, and occasionally there are surveys "on recent progress in topical fields of mathematics and its applications." There are about 40–60 articles per year, in 900 pages, with no book reviews. It is available online, with a digital archive available back to volume 1. Recommended for academic libraries. URL: http://imamat.oxfordjournals.org

3805. Indiana University Mathematics Journal. Former titles (until 1970): *Journal of Mathematics and Mechanics;* (until 1956): *Journal of Rational Mechanics and Analysis.* [ISSN: 0022-2518] 1952. bi-m. USD 460 (print & online eds.) Individuals, USD 150 (print & online eds.). Ed(s): Michael Larsen. Indiana University, Department of Mathematics, 831 E Third St, Bloomington, IN 47405; http://www.math.indiana.edu/. Illus., index. Refereed. *Indexed:* A22, CCMJ, MSN, MathR. *Aud.:* Ac, Sa.

The *Indiana University Mathematics Journal* is a university press title that publishes research on "both pure and applied mathematics," with an emphasis on "significance, originality, lucidity, and expository concision." Annually, there are 80–100 articles published, for over 2,000 pages. Optional page charges for authors help to keep the subscription price low for libraries. Articles are primarily in English, rarely in French; and there are no book reviews. The journal has quite a long backlog of submissions, but preprints are available on the web site. All issues are available online, with the 1952–94 digital archive that is currently free. Highly recommended for academic libraries. URL: www.iumj.indiana.edu

3806. Inventiones Mathematicae. [ISSN: 0020-9910] 1966. m. EUR 3098 (print & online eds.). Ed(s): H Hofer. Springer, Tiergartenstr 17, Heidelberg, 69121, Germany. Illus., adv. Sample. Refereed. Vol. ends: No. 3. Microform: PQC. Reprint: PSC. *Indexed:* A01, A22, CCMJ, E01, MSN, MathR. *Aud.:* Ac, Sa.

Inventiones Mathematicae (also known simply as *Inventiones*) has been published since 1966 by Springer. It has a strong impact in the area of pure mathematics. Articles are mainly in English, with the rare article in French or German. There are about 60–80 articles per year, for almost 3,000 pages. It is available online, and volumes 1–123 are available free from the Archive Gottingen (http://gdz.sub.uni-goettingen.de). Some current articles are available as open access through an author-pays model. Recommended for academic libraries. URL: www.springerlink.com/content/0020-9910

3807. Journal for Research in Mathematics Education. [ISSN: 0021-8251] 1970. 5x/yr. USD 327 (print & online eds.). Ed(s): Cynthia W Langrall. National Council of Teachers of Mathematics, 1906 Association Dr, Reston, VA 20191; nctm@nctm.org; http://www.nctm.org. Illus., index, adv. Refereed. Vol. ends: Jul. Microform: PQC. *Indexed:* A01, A22, Chicano, ERIC, P02, PsycInfo. *Bk. rev.:* 1-2, 1,500-2,000 words, signed. *Aud.:* Ems, Hs, Ac, Sa.

The National Council of Teachers of Mathematics (NCTM) publishes both general (see *Mathematics Teacher*) and research journals. The *Journal for Research in Mathematics Education* includes original research articles, commentaries on research, brief reports on theoretical topics, discussions of research topics, and a few book reviews that are lengthy and signed. In particular, articles need to go beyond proofs of pure mathematics and have an implication for teaching methods. There may also be official NCTM reports where the focus is often on college education. In partnership with the Association of Mathematics Teacher Educators (AMTE), the NCTM started an online-only journal in 2012, *Mathematics Teacher Educator,* for research manuscripts that address problems in teacher practice, using evidence. This peer-reviewed journal is published twice a year and would best benefit those who educate mathematics teachers. Both journals are available online for institutional access through the JSTOR Current Scholarship Program. They are appropriate for academic education libraries and libraries that support professional development for K-12 teachers. URL: www.nctm.org/publications/jrme.aspx

The Journal of Symbolic Logic. See Philosophy section.

3808. London Mathematical Society. Proceedings. [ISSN: 0024-6115] 1865. m. EUR 1513 (print & online eds.). Ed(s): James Wright, Iain G Gordon. Oxford University Press, Great Clarendon St, Oxford, OX2 6DP, United Kingdom; enquiry@oup.co.uk; http://www.oxfordjournals.org/. Illus., index, adv. Refereed. Vol. ends: No. 3. Microform: PMC; PQC. Reprint: PSC. *Indexed:* A01, A22, ApMecR, CCMJ, E01, MSN, MathR. *Aud.:* Ac, Sa.

The *Proceedings of the London Mathematical Society* is the venue for longer papers published by the London Mathematical Society (LMS) (www.lms.ac.uk). The LMS also publishes medium-length papers in its *Journal* and short research papers in its *Bulletin.* The *Proceedings* has been published since 1865, when the society was founded, and "covers a wide range of mathematical topics" in pure and some applied areas of mathematics. Current issues and an archive are available online. In order to promote access to the most recent research, all articles are open access for the first six months. Recommended for academic libraries along with many of their other journal titles. URL: http://plms.oxfordjournals.org

3809. The Mathematical Intelligencer. [ISSN: 0343-6993] 1977. q. EUR 137 (print & online eds.). Ed(s): Marjorie Senechal. Springer New York LLC, 233 Spring St, New York, NY 10013; service-ny@springer.com; http://www.springer.com/. Illus., index, adv. Refereed. Vol. ends: No. 4. Microform: PQC. Reprint: PSC. *Indexed:* A01, A22, BRI, CCMJ, E01, MASUSE, MLA-IB, MSN, MathR, P02. *Bk. rev.:* 2-5, 1,000-2,000 words, signed. *Aud.:* Hs, Ga, Ac, Sa.

The Mathematical Intelligencer "informs and entertains a broad audience of mathematicians and the wider intellectual community." There are "articles about mathematics, mathematicians, and the history and culture of mathematics," as well as poetry, puzzles, engaging images, and popular esoterica such as stamps. It cultivates a sense of community, but it can also contain controversy. There are a few lengthy, signed book reviews. It is available online, with archives back to volume 1 (1977), and some recent open-access articles. It is appropriate for a broad audience because of its entertaining treatment of mathematics. It should be considered a basic resource for academic libraries, and should be considered for public and high school libraries. URL: www.springerlink.com/content/0343-6993

3810. *S I A M Review.* [ISSN: 0036-1445] 1959. q. Free to members; Non-members, USD 430 (print & online eds.). Ed(s): C T Kelley, Kelly Thomas. Society for Industrial and Applied Mathematics, 3600 Market St, 6th Fl, Philadelphia, PA 19104; siam@siam.org; http://www.epubs.siam.org. Illus., index, adv. Sample. Refereed. Circ: 12909. Vol. ends: No. 4. *Indexed:* A01, A22, ABIn, ApMecR, B01, BRI, C&ISA, CBRI, CCMJ, CompLI, CompR, EngInd, MSN, MathR, P02. *Bk. rev.:* 5-15, 300-1,500 words, signed. *Aud.:* Ga, Ac, Sa.

SIAM Review is the flagship publication of the Society for Industrial and Applied Mathematics (SIAM) that "provides a forum for the exchange of information and ideas among mathematicians, engineers, and scientists." Of the 16 journals published by SIAM, the *Review* offers "articles of broad interest." Each issue has five sections: "Survey and Review," "Problems and Techniques," "SIGEST" (digest of a recent paper from one of SIAM's other journals), "Education," and "Book Reviews," which contains a featured review and several other medium-length, signed reviews. The entire collection of SIAM journals is available online and should be considered a core resource for academic libraries. Archives for these journals are available either from SIAM through its *Locus* collection or from JSTOR. The *Review* is also useful for some public libraries. URL: www.siam.org/journals/

3811. *Studies in Applied Mathematics (Malden).* Formerly (until 1968): *Journal of Mathematics and Physics.* [ISSN: 0022-2526] 1922. 8x/yr. GBP 1216. Ed(s): David Benney. Wiley-Blackwell Publishing, Inc., 111 River St, Hoboken, NJ 07030; info@wiley.com; http://onlinelibrary.wiley.com/. Illus., adv. Sample. Refereed. Vol. ends: No. 3. Microform: PQC. Reprint: PSC. *Indexed:* A01, A22, ABIn, ApMecR, B01, CCMJ, E01, MSN, MathR. *Aud.:* Ac, Sa.

Studies in Applied Mathematics "explores the interplay between mathematics and the applied disciplines." David J. Benney of the Massachusetts Institute of Technology has been the managing editor since 1969. There are about 25–35 articles published each year in roughly 800 pages, with no book reviews. It is available online starting in 1997. Recommended for some academic libraries. URL: http://onlinelibrary.wiley.com/journal/10.1111/(ISSN)1467-9590

■ MEDIA AND AV

See also Communication; Education; Films; and Television, Video, and Radio sections.

Andrea Reed, Media & Digital Services Librarian, Warner Memorial Library, Eastern University, St. Davids, PA 19087-3696; FAX: 610-341-1375; areed@eastern.edu

Introduction

In this digital age, there is hardly a component of life untouched by technology. The "Media and AV" section heavily features publications that focus on the evolving intersection of education and technology. In the past ten years, there have been incredible changes in the role computers play in how people learn. Therefore, it comes as no surprise that publications reviewed in this section primarily address the theoretical and methodical issues in the field of educational technology.

Overall, these journals are rich in research-oriented content, and articles are written geared to professors and researchers of education and instructional technology design. These titles address a wide range of learning environments, from K to 12 to higher education, as well as post-school education. Many are refereed. Common themes throughout the publications include mobile technologies, the online learning environment, performing online assessment and interaction, and the use of interactive learning games. Since this field is becoming increasingly digitized, readers should also consult the other technology-related sections in this volume.

Also included in this section are titles focused on the mass media and audio-visual fields and their educational and cultural impact.

It is worth noting that a few publishers did not send review copies of their titles, and as a result we withdrew those and added in their place a few new journals to this section.

Lastly, the previously reviewed publication *Public Broadcasting Report* is no longer published, and therefore has been removed from this list.

Basic Periodicals

Educational Technology Research & Development, Innovations in Education and Teaching International, International Journal of Instructional Media, Journal of Media Literacy Education, TechTrends.

Basic Abstracts and Indexes

Education Abstracts, ERIC.

3812. *British Journal of Educational Technology.* Formerly (until 19??): *Journal of Eductional Technology.* [ISSN: 0007-1013] 1970. bi-m. GBP 719. Ed(s): Nick Rushby. Wiley-Blackwell Publishing Ltd., The Atrium, Southern Gate, Chichester, PO19 8SQ, United Kingdom; customer@wiley.com; http://www.wiley.com/. Illus., index, adv. Sample. Refereed. Vol. ends: Sep. Microform: PQC. Reprint: PSC. *Indexed:* A01, A22, CompLI, E01, ERIC, EngInd, ErgAb, FR, MLA-IB, P02, PsycInfo. *Bk. rev.:* 10, 150-500 words. *Aud.:* Ac.

One of the many journals that the British Educational Research Association publishes, this title examines the theory, development, application, and current issues relating to educational technology. Each issue contains articles and reviews. This journal's articles are peer-reviewed, are relevant, and are often research studies about worldwide education and technology topics (K–12 and higher education) such as plagiarism, collaborative learning, social technologies, and student/teacher technology perceptions. The featured reviews are related to recently published books, or they are literature reviews on a specific topic. In the rapidly growing age of MOOCs and online learning, this title is a great addition to any academic serials collection.

3813. *Educational Media International.* Former titles (until 1986): *Educational Media International;* (until 1971): *Audio-Visual Media.* [ISSN: 0952-3987] 1967. q. GBP 396 (print & online eds.). Ed(s): Charalambos Vrasidas. Routledge, 4 Park Sq, Milton Park, Abingdon, OX14 4RN, United Kingdom; subscriptions@tandf.co.uk; http://www.tandfonline.com. Illus., adv. Sample. Refereed. Microform: PQC. Reprint: PSC. *Indexed:* A01, A22, E01, ERIC, PsycInfo. *Bk. rev.:* 2-3, 500 words. *Aud.:* Ac.

Published four times a year, *Educational Media International* offers the latest innovations in educational and mass media, including educational technologies and open/distance learning. It examines technology's use in all types of educational environments, from pre-school to professional development practices, as well as lifelong learning situations. Only containing easily read peer-reviewed articles, it seeks to inform and provide a forum for its readers on the challenges and successes relating to educational technologies like blended learning, social media in the classroom, and online course design. Some of the articles are studies while others report on case study findings. Contributors are drawn from academics, educators, and media professionals from around the world. It's worth noting that abstracts of articles published in this journal are available online in multiple languages at http://emi.cardet.org. Recommended for academic library collections.

Educational Technology. See Education/Specific Subjects and Teaching Methods: Technology section.

Educational Technology Research & Development. See Education/ Specific Subjects and Teaching Methods: Technology section.

3814. *Electronic Journal of E-Learning.* [ISSN: 1479-4403] 2003. 3x/yr. Free. Ed(s): Roy Williams. Academic Conferences and Publishing Internatinal Ltd., Curtis Farm, Kidmore End, Nr Reading, RG4 9AY, United Kingdom; info@academic-conferences.org; http://www.academic-conferences.org. *Indexed:* ERIC. *Bk. rev.:* Number and length vary. *Aud.:* Ac.

This open-source e-journal is published by Academic Conferences Limited. It publishes double-blind peer-reviewed papers, empirical research, case studies, action research, theoretical discussions, literature reviews, reports, conference papers, and other work (though, it is light in book reviews). This online journal's aim is to provide a perspective on e-learning practices, theories, and development. Published biannually, the *Electronic Journal of E-Learning* (*EJEL*) additionally offers special issues and, as a result, on average it produces three or four issues each year. Compared to other titles in this Media and AV section, *EJEL* takes a broader perspective of e-learning by its inclusion of technology-focused articles relating to educational gaming, e-safety, grading, and the psychological aspects of an e-learning classroom. Publication content comes from authors worldwide. For academic libraries on a tight budget, this is a great, affordable journal to include in a serials collection.

3815. *Innovations in Education and Teaching International (Print).* Former titles (until 2001): *Innovations in Education and Training International (Print);* (until 1995): *Educational and Training Technology International;* (until 1989): *P L E T. Programmed Learning and Educational Technology;* (until 1984): *Programmed Learning and Educational Technology;* (until 1967): *Programmed Learning;* (until 1964): *Association for Programmed Learning. Bulletin.* [ISSN: 1470-3297] 19??. q. GBP 490 (print & online eds.). Ed(s): Gina Wisker. Routledge, 4 Park Sq, Milton Park, Abingdon, OX14 4RN, United Kingdom; subscriptions@tandf.co.uk; http://www.tandfonline.com. Illus., adv. Sample. Refereed. Vol. ends: Nov. Microform: PQC. Reprint: PSC. *Indexed:* A01, A22, E01, ERIC, FR, PsycInfo. *Bk. rev.:* 1-2, 750-1,000 words. *Aud.:* Ac.

As the official journal of the Staff and Educational Development Association (SEDA), *Innovations in Education and Teaching International* (*IETI*) promotes innovation and best practices in higher education, through staff and educational development. To this end, it publishes articles about research, experience, scholarship, and evaluation pertaining to educational development in higher and post-school education. On average, each issue contains one book review. *IETI* is not as heavily focused on media and technology in education as are other titles reviewed in this section. Rather, it addresses innovative educational technologies and their theories as one aspect within the framework of educational development. The journal's content includes various topics such as pedagogy, blended learning, assessment, student learning support, and technology-supported collaboration. Its contributors are educators from all over the world.

3816. *International Journal of Instructional Media.* [ISSN: 0092-1815] 1973. q. USD 181.20. Ed(s): Phillip J Sleeman. Westwood Press, Inc., ll8 Five Mile River Rd, Darien, CT 06820. Illus., index. Refereed. Vol. ends: No. 4. *Indexed:* A01, A22, BRI, CompLI, ERIC, P02, RILM. *Bk. rev.:* 2-3, 2-21 pages. *Aud.:* Ac.

The aim of the *International Journal of Instructional Media* (*IJIM*) is to examine innovative and current forms of technology used in instruction. It is a refereed journal and acts as an outlet used to share research papers, case studies, and commentary on new strategies and/or research regarding instructional media. It features work from new and experienced authors. General topics addressed include computer technology, distance education technology, interactive technologies and their application, media research and evaluation, and computer-mediated communications. *IJIM* also examines issues and challenges of applying distance-learning strategies and instructional media into the learning process. It is worth noting that it is not hardware-oriented, but rather instructions- and systems-focused. However, *IJIM* does address hardware when examining it as an aspect of instructional media. This journal has an impressive breadth of subjects, covering topics like budgeting for technology, student/teacher perceptions of computer technology in learning environments, and evaluating technologies' tools like screencasting. It is sparse on book reviews. Recommended for academic libraries and institutions that serve the education profession.

3817. *Journal of Educational Technology Systems.* Formerly (until 199?): *Journal of Educational Instrumentation.* [ISSN: 0047-2395] 1972. q. USD 430 (print & online eds.). Ed(s): Thomas T Liao, Lori L Scarlatos. Baywood Publishing Co., Inc., 26 Austin Ave, PO Box 337, Amityville, NY 11701; info@baywood.com; http://www.baywood.com. Illus., index, adv. Sample. Refereed. *Indexed:* A22, C&ISA, CerAb, CompLI, ERIC, I15. *Bk. rev.:* Number and length vary. *Aud.:* Ac.

Published with all levels of education as well as commercial and training organizations in mind, the *Journal of Educational Technology Systems* (*JETS*) is a peer-reviewed publication with a primary interest in applications of technology that enable or improve learning. It contains papers from academia and industry, and addresses topics pertaining to educational systems (hardware and software) that improve or evaluate instruction. There is a special emphasis on papers that address computers and web-based instruction as an important component of the education system. Another area of interest to *JETS* is the design and development of interactive computer-based systems that can be linked to other instructional technologies. It seeks papers that explore techniques that utilize technology and that are curriculum-applied, and/or experimented with, in actual classroom practice. Alternative models of distance learning are also focused on. Each issue includes about six to eight papers, an editorial overview, and book reviews.

3818. *The Journal of Media Literacy: a publication of the National Telemedia Council.* Former titles (until 2006): *Telemedium;* (until 1984): *Better Broadcasts News; Better Broadcasts Newsletter.* [ISSN: 1944-4982] 1953. 3x/yr. USD 80 (Individuals, USD 40). Ed(s): Marieli Rowe. National Telemedia Council, Inc., 1922 University Ave, Madison, WI 53705; ntelemedia@aol.com; http://www.nationaltelemediacouncil.org/. Illus. Sample. *Aud.:* Ems, Hs.

The official publication of the National Telemedia Council, *The Journal of Media Literacy* is published three times a year. This non-refereed periodical produces its issues based on a theme. Each issue contains about 15–20 articles that discuss various media literacy aspects and practices pertaining to the issue's theme. Past issues explored media literacy's role in cultural diversity, K–12 learning in the digital age, and civic engagement. *The Journal of Media Literacy*'s primary readership is K–12 teachers, teacher educators, professors, community activists, and school media professionals. Recommended for K–12 school libraries.

3819. *The Journal of Media Literacy Education.* [ISSN: 2167-8715] 2009. s-a. Free. Ed(s): Renee Hobbs, Vanessa Domine. National Association for Media Literacy Education, Montclair State University, Department of Secondary and Special Education, Montclair, NJ 07043; domine@jmle.org; http://www.namle.net/. Refereed. *Indexed:* ERIC. *Bk. rev.:* 4-6. *Aud.:* Ems, Hs, Ac.

This open-access publication is produced by the National Association for Media Literacy Education (NAMLE) and is generally published twice a year. Its aim is to foster development in media literacy education research, scholarship, and pedagogy for the digestion of scholars, media professions, and educational practitioners. Through its research and scholarship articles, practitioner-focused essays, and reviews, *The Journal of Media Literacy Education* encourages the development and application of media literacy and critical-thinking skills in educating students within the context of the digital age. Content-wise, this journal covers a breadth of educational topics and their relationship to media literacy. Each issue contains five to seven articles/essays and four to six reviews. The reviews examine newly published books in this field as well as curriculum materials and multimedia and online resources. Recommended for K–12 school libraries and academic libraries.

3820. *Media.* [ISSN: 1533-9475] 2000. 4x/yr. USD 48. Ed(s): Joe Mandese. MediaPost Communications, 15 E 32nd St, 7th Fl, New York, NY 10016; feedback@mediapost.com; http://www.mediapost.com. *Aud.:* Ac, Sa.

Media's readership is primarily those working in advertising or media agencies. As a result, the magazine's content is focused toward this specialized field. Its scope centers on the art and science of media buying and planning. Anywhere between 10 and 20 articles, stories, and columns are present in each issue. The content examines all things pertaining to today's media landscape—consumer studies, the art of communication, media trends and current practices, innovators in the field, and the future of media. It specifically looks at trends in television, social media, marketing, web site design, and consumer profiling. Recommended for academic and special libraries.

3821. *Media History Monographs: a online journal of media history.*
[ISSN: 1940-8862] 1997. s-a. Free. Ed(s): David Copeland. Ohio University, E. W. Scripps School of Journalism, 32 Park Place, Athens, OH 45701; hodson@ohio.edu; http://scrippsjschool.org/. Refereed. *Aud.:* Ac.

Only available online, *Media History Monographs* (*MHM*) is a freely available scholarly journal that publishes essays and papers on the history of journalism and mass communication. Submissions that are too long for regular journals but too short to be published as a book are perfect candidates for publication in *MHM*. It is affiliated with the American Journalism Historians Association and sponsored by the School of Communications at Elon University. Generally, the journal is published twice a year, typically featuring one article per issue. Most of the content comes from American institutions of higher education, though a few European colleges and universities are represented. Recommended for academic libraries.

School Library Media Research. See *School Library Research* in Library and Information Science section.

3822. *TechTrends: linking research and practice to improve learning.*
Former titles (until 1985): *Instructional Innovator; Audiovisual Instruction with Instructional Resources; Audiovisual Instruction.* [ISSN: 8756-3894] 1956. bi-m. EUR 116 (print & online eds.). Ed(s): Abbie Brown. Springer New York LLC, 233 Spring St, New York, NY 10013; service-ny@springer.com; http://www.springer.com/. Illus., index, adv. Refereed. Circ: 7000 Paid and free. Vol. ends: Nov. Reprint: PSC. *Indexed:* A01, A22, BRI, E01, ERIC, I15, P02. *Aud.:* Ems, Hs, Ac.

This bimonthly peer-reviewed journal is aimed at professionals within the educational communication and technology field. Produced by the Association for Educational Communications and Technology (AECT), it examines new technologies in education and training that occurs in K–12 schools, colleges and universities, and private industry. *TechTrends* differs from many of the journals reviewed in this section, since each issue is primarily composed of articles on the latest trends and practices and is not as reliant on scholarly research as other titles listed in this section. Therefore, it is a complementary title to include in any academic periodicals collection. General topics of interest to the journal include management of media and programs, and the application of educational technology principles and techniques to instructional programs. Most issues begin with a note from the editor, include AECT news, and include about 10–15 articles, which have a conversational style and are easy to follow.

■ MEDICINE

See also Family Planning; Health and Fitness; Health Care Administration; Health Professions; Nursing; and Public Health sections.

Cynthia J. Vaughn, Preston Medical Library, University of Tennessee Graduate School of Medicine, Knoxville, TN 37920; cvaughn@utmck.edu

Introduction

Medicine is a discipline that changes rapidly, and keeping up with the latest research and evidence is challenging for practicing physicians and those in academic medicine. Medical journal collections offer physicians, medical administrators, residents, students, and the interested public the most current information in the various specialties and subspecialities of medicine. The journals have peer-reviewed information from randomized controlled trials, and reviews of said trials to create new practice guidelines, and potentially change the way conditions are managed and treated.

More and more, the public is looking up information on its own about their health conditions or those of a loved one. Some health sciences and public libraries carry "consumer health" magazines, written for the lay public. In recent years, there has been a push in the medical profession to promote health literacy. Put simply, a very educated person can be functionally illiterate when looking

at a scholarly medical journal. The consumer health magazines strive to write at a level that is easy to understand for the general public. Some journals, such as *JAMA* and *American Family Physician,* offer public-friendly summaries of some of their most pertinent articles.

In this section, journals and magazines have been evaluated for their place in various types of libraries. Naturally, health sciences libraries will have a much broader collection than the journals described here, and some public and academic libraries will have a smaller collection, depending on the population they serve. Most journals and magazines have online content available as well as a print journal, and most are indexed in databases such as MEDLINE and CINAHL.

Basic Periodicals

J A M A: The Journal of the American Medical Association, The Lancet (North American Edition), New England Journal of Medicine.

Basic Abstracts and Indexes

CINAHL, EMBASE, MEDLINE.

3823. *AIDS Patient Care and S T Ds.* Incorporates (1990-1997): *Pediatric AIDS and HIV Infection;* Formerly (until 1996): *AIDS Patient Care.* [ISSN: 1087-2914] 1987. m. USD 1117. Ed(s): Jeffrey Laurence. Mary Ann Liebert, Inc. Publishers, 140 Huguenot St, 3rd Fl, New Rochelle, NY 10801; info@liebertpub.com; http://www.liebertpub.com. Illus., adv. Sample. Refereed. Vol. ends: Dec. Reprint: PSC. *Indexed:* A01, A22, BRI, C45, E01, ExcerpMed, H24, P02, PsycInfo, RiskAb. *Aud.:* Ac, Sa.

This peer-reviewed scholarly journal publishes original articles on HIV/AIDS as well as on other STDs. It has an international scope for its articles, and it also publishes case reports, letters to the editor, and current drug development news. Articles deal with diagnosis, treatment, patient care, epidemiology, education, prevention, policy issues, and psychological issues. This journal is appropriate for all health sciences libraries, as HIV/AIDS is a global concern. Some other academic libraries may consider it as well for their allied health programs.

3824. *American Family Physician.* Formerly (until 1970): *American Family Physician - G P;* Which incorporated (1950-1969): *G P.* [ISSN: 0002-838X] 1950. 24x/yr. USD 204 (Individuals, USD 152; Free to members). Ed(s): Joyce A Merriman, Jay Siwek. American Academy of Family Physicians, PO Box 11210, Shawnee Mission, KS 66207; contactcenter@aafp.org; http://www.aafp.org. Illus., index, adv. Sample. Refereed. Circ: 176286 Paid and controlled. Vol. ends: Dec. Microform: PMC; PQC. *Indexed:* A22, AbAn, B02, BRI, C45, ExcerpMed, IndVet, MCR, P02, RRTA. *Aud.:* Ac, Sa.

Published by the American Academy of Family Physicians, this peer-reviewed, scholarly journal provides several topic reviews per issue. In addition to the reviews, rounding out the journal are practice guidelines, CME opportunities, "Cochrane for Physicians," and editorials. Articles are filled with tables and charts that physicians can easily refer to when needed. The web site offers RSS feeds, e-mail alerts, an "EBM toolkit," and free online access to articles after about one year. Recommended for health sciences libraries especially; some academic and larger public libraries may find it useful as well. URL: www.aafp.org/online/en/home/publications/journals/afp.html

3825. *American Journal of Health Behavior (Online).* [ISSN: 1945-7359] 2009. bi-m. USD 238 (Individuals, USD 128). Ed(s): Elbert D Glover, Penny N Glover. P N G Publications, 2205-K Oak Ridge Rd, #115, Oak Ridge, NC 27310; pglover2@umd.edu; http://www.ajhb.org. Illus. Refereed. *Aud.:* Ac, Sa.

This is the official publication of the American Academy of Health Behavior. All types of health behaviors are analyzed, often within specific populations. Examples are: intention to breastfeed in a low-income population; alcohol use in Latino youth; and self-management in older women. Besides diet, exercise, smoking, and screenings, articles in this journal deal with issues such as health literacy and spirituality. This peer-reviewed, scholarly journal is recommended for any collection of social science materials, as well as health sciences libraries.

3826. *The American Journal of Medicine.* [ISSN: 0002-9343] 1946. m. USD 621. Ed(s): Joseph S Alpert, Pamela J Powers. Excerpta Medica, Inc., 685 US-202, Bridgewater, NJ 08807; excerptamedica@elsevier.com; http://www.excerptamedica.com/. Illus., index, adv. Refereed. Circ: 129128 Paid and controlled. *Indexed:* A01, A22, AbAn, BRI, C45, Chicano, ExcerpMed, H24, P02, RiskAb. *Aud.:* Ac, Sa.

This journal is published by the Association of Professors of Medicine, and its mission is "to lead academic internal medicine, specifically in the education, research, and patient care arenas." Each issue has "Clinical Research Studies," "Images" articles, "Reviews," and "Perspectives." This peer-reviewed, scholarly journal is for both private-practice physicians and those in academic medicine. Recommended for health sciences libraries, especially academic medical libraries.

Autism Spectrum Quarterly. See Disabilities section.

3827. *B E T A.* [ISSN: 1058-708X] 1988. s-a. Free. Ed(s): Reilly O'Neal. San Francisco AIDS Foundation, PO Box 426182, San Francisco, CA 94142; feedback@sfaf.org; http://www.sfaf.org. Sample. *Aud.:* Ac, Sa.

BETA, short for *Bulletin of Experimental Treatments for AIDS,* is a free publication of the San Francisco AIDS Foundation. Note that it is the journal for experimental treatments, so the very latest in trials will be featured. Each issue contains current news, drug information, a "Women and HIV" section, a listing of open clinical trials, and features such as "Aging and HIV" and "HIV and the Recession." English and Spanish versions are available. It is available free online and in print. Recommended for public, academic, and health sciences libraries. URL: http://sfaf.org/hiv-info/hot-topics/beta/

3828. *C A: a cancer journal for clinicians.* [ISSN: 0007-9235] 1950. bi-m. GBP 46. Ed(s): Dr. Otis Webb Brawley, Dr. Ted Gansler. John Wiley & Sons, Inc., 111 River St, MS 4-02, Hoboken, NJ 07030; uscs-wis@wiley.com; http://www.wiley.com/WileyCDA/. Illus., index, adv. Sample. Refereed. Circ: 94500 Controlled. Vol. ends: Nov/Dec. Microform: PQC. Reprint: PSC. *Indexed:* A22, BRI, ExcerpMed, P02. *Aud.:* Ac, Sa.

This peer-reviewed, scholarly journal is published by the American Cancer Society for all physicians, not just oncologists. Each issue has original articles and reviews on various types of cancer, as well as current news and commentary. Because cancer is a disease state that can affect any part of the body, this journal is a valuable supplement to general medical journals. Recommended for all health sciences libraries, and academic libraries with any health programs.

3829. *Coping with Cancer.* Formerly (until 199?): *Coping.* [ISSN: 1544-5488] 1986. bi-m. USD 19 domestic; USD 35 foreign. Media America, Inc., PO Box 682268, Franklin, TN 37068; info@copingmag.com; http://www.copingmag.com. Illus., adv. Sample. Vol. ends: Dec. *Aud.:* Ga, Sa.

According to its web site, this magazine is primarily found in the waiting rooms of doctors' offices. However, it has a place in consumer health collections of health sciences libraries and public libraries. *Coping with Cancer* is filled with upbeat tales of survivorship and "assumes that everyone diagnosed with cancer has a chance to beat the odds." Also of note is that *Coping with Cancer* is not affiliated with any particular treatment center and does not accept advertising in order to remain free of bias. Also, the editorial guidelines state that articles must be written for the lay public, with attention given to short sentences and paragraphs. URL: www.copingmag.com

3830. *Cure.* [ISSN: 1534-7664] 2002. q. USD 100 (Individuals, USD 20; Free to qualified personnel). Cure Media Group, LP., 3102 Oak Lawn Ave, Ste 610, Dallas, TX 75219; subs@healtoday.com. Adv. Circ: 325000. *Aud.:* Ga.

CURE Magazine strives to "make cancer understandable." Each issue is filled with the latest cancer treatment news, various special reports, and inspiration written by cancer survivors. The web site offers additional news, blogs, and an online community. Recommended for public libraries, especially those with a consumer health collection. URL: www.curetoday.com

3831. *Diabetes Care.* Incorporates (in 2000): *Diabetes Reviews.* [ISSN: 0149-5992] 1978. m. USD 750 (print & online eds.) Members, USD 187 (print & online eds.). Ed(s): Vivian Fonseca. American Diabetes Association, 1701 N Beauregard St, Alexandria, VA 22311; mailcall@diabetes.org; http://www.diabetes.org. Illus., adv. Refereed. Circ: 15195. Microform: PQC. *Indexed:* A01, A22, AbAn, Agr, BRI, C45, Chicano, ExcerpMed, RRTA. *Aud.:* Ac, Sa.

Diabetes Care is published by the American Diabetes Association (ADA), and focuses on all types of diabetes research. The original articles are divided into various categories, including "Meta-analysis," "Complications," and "Epidemiology." In addition to original articles, reviews and ADA statements fill out this peer-reviewed, scholarly journal. As diabetes is studied and affects all body systems, *Diabetes Care* is recommended for all health sciences libraries.

3832. *Diabetes Forecast: the healthy living magazine.* Formerly (until 1974): *A D A Forecast.* [ISSN: 0095-8301] 1948. m. USD 28 domestic; USD 68 in Canada & Mexico; USD 98 elsewhere. Ed(s): Andrew Keegan. American Diabetes Association, 377 Industrial Park Rd, Mt. Jackson, VA 22842; mailcall@diabetes.org; http://www.diabetes.org. Illus., adv. Sample. Circ: 445000 Paid. Vol. ends: Dec. *Indexed:* A01, A22, Agr, BRI, P02. *Aud.:* Hs, Ga, Ac, Sa.

Since 1948, the American Diabetes Association has been publishing *Diabetes Forecast* for people with either type 1 or type 2 diabetes. In addition to practical articles, advocacy is a theme that runs throughout the magazine. The magazine is filled with management tips, recipes, and articles about new treatments. This magazine is recommended reading for anyone with diabetes, and is recommended for public libraries and health sciences libraries with a consumer health collection. URL: http://forecast.diabetes.org/

3833. *Diabetes Self-Management.* [ISSN: 0741-6253] 1983. bi-m. USD 9.97. Ed(s): Ingrid Strauch. R.A. Rapaport Publishing, Inc., 150 W 22nd St, Ste 800, New York, NY 10011. Illus. Sample. Vol. ends: Nov/Dec. *Indexed:* A22. *Aud.:* Hs, Ga, Sa.

This magazine features stories on the latest diabetes research, as well as several self-care articles that cover the basics of caring for diabetes. The web site states that this magazine offers "up-to-date, practical 'how-to' information on nutrition, exercise, new drugs, medical advances, self-help, and the many other topics people need to know about to stay healthy." Recommended for public libraries and health sciences libraries with a consumer health collection. URL: www.diabetesselfmanagement.com

3834. *Gender Medicine.* [ISSN: 1550-8579] 2004. q. EUR 303. Ed(s): Marianne J Legato. Excerpta Medica, Inc., 685 US-202, Bridgewater, NJ 08807; excerptamedica@elsevier.com; http://www.excerptamedica.com/. Adv. Sample. Refereed. Circ: 5400. *Indexed:* ExcerpMed. *Aud.:* Ac, Sa.

As the title suggests, this peer-reviewed, scholarly journal focuses on "reports of original scientific investigations that use biological sex and/or gender as a significant variable in the experimental protocol." In addition to original research, the journal has review articles and articles on "Health Policy and Gender Disparities." Recommended for academic libraries, particularly health sciences libraries.

Harvard Men's Health Watch. See Health and Fitness section.

Health Affairs. See Public Health section.

Health Care Management Review. See Health Care Administration section.

3835. *J A M A: The Journal of the American Medical Association.* Formerly (until 1960): *American Medical Association. Journal;* Which superseded (in 1883): *American Medical Association. Transactions.* [ISSN: 0098-7484] 1883. w. 48/yr. USD 966. Ed(s): Howard Bauchner, Stacy L Christiansen. American Medical Association, 330 North Wabash Ave, Ste. 39300, Chicago, IL 60611; mediarelations@jama-archives.org;

http://www.ama-assn.org. Illus., index, adv. Sample. Refereed. Vol. ends: Jun/Dec. Microform: PMC; PQC. *Indexed:* A01, A22, ABS&EES, AgeL, Agr, BRI, C45, Chicano, ExcerpMed, FS&TA, H24, IndVet, MLA-IB, P02, PsycInfo, RILM, RRTA, RiskAb. *Bk. rev.:* Number and length vary. *Aud.:* Ac, Sa.

JAMA is one of the most frequently cited publications in medicine. It is known for having artwork on the cover of each issue, and *JAMA*'s mission is to "promote the science and art of medicine and the betterment of the public health." This peer-reviewed weekly journal publishes original contributions, book reviews, editorials, and correspondence as expected. It also has a "Poetry and Medicine" column for medical poets, as well as a detailed article about the current week's cover art selection. Because many of the published articles are summarized in national news sources, it is an essential journal for all health sciences libraries, and strongly recommended for academic and public libraries.

3836. *The Lancet (North American Edition).* [ISSN: 0099-5355] 1966. w. USD 1682. Ed(s): S Clark, R Horton. The Lancet Publishing Group, 32 Jamestown Rd, London, NW1 7BY, United Kingdom; custserv@lancet.com; http://www.thelancet.com. Illus., index, adv. Sample. Refereed. Vol. ends: Jun/Dec. Microform: PQC. *Indexed:* A01, Agr, B01, ErgAb, P02, RILM. *Bk. rev.:* Number and length vary. *Aud.:* Ac, Sa.

This peer-reviewed British weekly is the "world's leading independent general medical journal." Each issue provides new research articles, commentary, reviews, seminars, and perspectives. Unlike many medical journals, *The Lancet* is completely independent; it is not affiliated with any scientific or medical society. It is one of the "big three" medical journals that are frequently cited in the popular news media, and *The Lancet* is recommended for all health sciences libraries. Academic and public libraries should consider subscribing as well.

3837. *Mayo Clinic Proceedings.* Formerly (until 1964): *Mayo Clinic. Staff Meetings. Proceedings.* [ISSN: 0025-6196] 1926. m. USD 659. Elsevier Inc., 360 Park Ave S, New York, NY 10010; usinfo-f@elsevier.com; http://www.elsevier.com. Illus., adv. Refereed. Circ: 124132 Paid and controlled. Microform: PMC. *Indexed:* A01, A22, AbAn, B02, BRI, C45, ExcerpMed, RRTA. *Aud.:* Ac, Sa.

As the title of this peer-reviewed scholarly journal indicates, *Mayo Clinic Proceedings* is sponsored by the Mayo Clinic. Since 1926, this journal has published "original articles dealing with clinical and laboratory medicine, clinical research, basic science research, and clinical epidemiology." The focus is internal medicine; however, many specialties will benefit from the reviews, images, and original articles. Recommended for all health sciences libraries.

3838. *Medical Care Research and Review.* Former titles (until 1995): *Medical Care Review;* (until 1967): *Public Health Economics and Medical Care Abstracts.* [ISSN: 1077-5587] 1944. bi-m. USD 1103. Ed(s): Gloria Bazzoli. Sage Publications, Inc., 2455 Teller Rd, Thousand Oaks, CA 91320; info@sagepub.com; http://www.sagepub.com. Illus. Sample. Refereed. Vol. ends: Dec. Microform: PQC. Reprint: PSC. *Indexed:* A01, A22, ASSIA, E01, ExcerpMed, MCR, P02, PsycInfo. *Bk. rev.:* 2-3, 200-300 words. *Aud.:* Ac, Sa.

Medical Care Research and Review focuses on the area of medicine known as health services research. Reviews are the heart of this journal; syntheses of previously published literature. Patient safety indicators, nursing homes, technology, health-care plans, screenings, and quality of care are themes that run throughout. These are the types of information that administrators of hospitals, nursing homes, health systems, and insurance companies frequently request. Academic, special, and public libraries with business collections should have this publication.

3839. *N I H Medline Plus: the magazine.* [ISSN: 1935-956X] 2006. q. Free. Ed(s): Selby Bateman, Ginny Gaylor. Vitality Communications, 407 Norwalk St, Greensboro, NC 27407; http://www.vitalitycommunications.com. *Aud.:* Ga, Sa.

A spinoff of the popular MedlinePlus web site (www.medlineplus.gov), this free publication is packed with stories that center on all types of medicine. Many articles are updates from the NIH on research progress on various conditions. Patient stories about overcoming diseases, history of medicine articles, and

seasonal health information are found in this glossy magazine. One of the goals of the MedlinePlus web site is to provide quality information in appropriate reading levels for the lay public, and this magazine strives to do the same. Recommended for public libraries and medical libraries that are open to the public. URL: www.nlm.nih.gov/medlineplus/magazine/

3840. *National Medical Association. Journal.* [ISSN: 0027-9684] 1908. m. USD 280 (Individuals, USD 130; Free to members). Ed(s): Eddie L Hoover. National Medical Association, 1012 Tenth St, NW, Washington, DC 20001; aredd@nmanet.org; http://www.nmanet.org. Illus., index, adv. Sample. Refereed. Vol. ends: Dec. *Indexed:* A22, C45, Chicano, ExcerpMed, MCR, PsycInfo, RRTA. *Aud.:* Ac, Sa.

Called "the nation's leading journal on minority health," this peer-reviewed scholarly journal focuses on issues of minority health, in particular within the African-American population. The journal consists primarily of original reports, and it includes case reports, editorials, correspondence, and relevant recent "InfoPOEMs" (reviews of pertinent clinical trials). Recommended for any health sciences library, particularly those that serve a significant minority population.

3841. *New England Journal of Medicine.* Formerly (until 1928): *Boston Medical and Surgical Journal;* Which was formed by the merger of (1823-1828): *Boston Medical Intelligencer; New England Medical Review and Journal;* Which was formerly: *New-England Journal of Medicine and Surgery.* [ISSN: 0028-4793] 1828. w. USD 765 (print & online eds.) Individuals, USD 159 (print & online eds.). Ed(s): Dr. Jeffrey M Drazen, Gregory D Curfman. Massachusetts Medical Society, 10 Shattuck St, Boston, MA 02115; letter@nejm.org; http://www.massmed.org. Illus., index, adv. Sample. Refereed. Circ: 187127. Vol. ends: Jun/Dec. Microform: PMC; PQC. *Indexed:* A01, A22, AbAn, AgeL, Agr, BRI, C45, Chicano, ExcerpMed, FS&TA, H24, IndVet, MCR, MLA-IB, P02, PsycInfo, RILM, RRTA, RiskAb, SWR&A. *Bk. rev.:* Number and length vary. *Aud.:* Ac, Sa.

Established in 1812, the *New England Journal of Medicine* is one of the most highly regarded peer-reviewed scholarly journals in the medical field. Articles published in the weekly journal frequently become news items on national news programs and publicly discussed. In addition to original articles, the journal contains regular features such as images, book reviews, editorials, and reviews. The web site offers free access to articles after six months, as well as a free table of contents service, e-mail alerts, and RSS feeds. This journal is essential for any type of health sciences library, and highly recommended for academic and public libraries.

3842. *Obstetrics and Gynecology.* [ISSN: 0029-7844] 1952. m. USD 715 (print & online eds.). Ed(s): Dr. James R Scott, Rebecca S Benner. Lippincott Williams & Wilkins, 530 Walnut St, Philadelphia, PA 19106; customerservice@lww.com; http://www.lww.com. Illus., adv. Refereed. Circ: 45629. Vol. ends: No. 97 - No. 98. Microform: PQC. *Indexed:* A01, A22, AbAn, C45, ExcerpMed, IndVet, RRTA. *Aud.:* Ac, Sa.

Known as the "green journal" among Ob/Gyns, this is the official publication of the American College of Obstetricians and Gynecologists (ACOG) and has been published since 1952. Most peer-reviewed articles are original research, but one reason libraries like to keep this journal around is for the frequently-requested ACOG publications. The "Practice Bulletins" and "Committee Opinions" are found at the back of each issue as they are released. In addition, updates on Cochrane articles in the Ob/Gyn field, editorials, and correspondence are published in this monthly journal. Recommended for all health sciences libraries and academic libraries with health-related programs.

3843. *Pediatrics (English Edition).* [ISSN: 0031-4005] 1948. m. USD 648 (print & online eds.). Ed(s): Lewis R First, Alain Douglas Park. American Academy of Pediatrics, 141 NW Pt Blvd, Elk Grove Village, IL 60007; journals@aap.org; http://www.aap.org. Illus., adv. Refereed. Circ: 60000 Paid. *Indexed:* A01, A22, Agr, BRI, C45, Chicano, ExcerpMed, FS&TA, H24, IndVet, P02, PsycInfo, RRTA, RiskAb. *Aud.:* Ac, Sa.

The premier peer-reviewed scholarly journal in the field of pediatrics, this is the official publication of the American Academy of Pediatrics (AAP), and has been published continuously since its founding in 1948. The journal publishes mostly original articles within all areas of pediatrics practice, including but not limited to "nutrition, surgery, dentistry, public health, child health services, human genetics, basic sciences, psychology, psychiatry, education, sociology, and nursing." Issues also contain reviews, AAP statements, historical articles, and commentaries. Recommended for all health sciences libraries and academic libraries with health-related programs.

3844. *Quest (Tucson).* Former titles (until 1994): *M D A Reports;* (until 1992): *M D A Newsmagazine;* (until 1984): *M D A News - Muscular Dystrophy Association;* (until 1975): *Muscular Dystrophy News.* [ISSN: 1087-1578] 1950. q. USD 15 domestic (Free to qualified personnel). Ed(s): Christina Medvescek. Muscular Dystrophy Association, Inc., 3300 E Sunrise Dr, Tucson, AZ 85718; publications@mdausa.org; http://www.mda.org. Illus. Sample. Circ: 130000. Vol. ends: Fall. *Indexed:* BRI. *Bk. rev.:* 1-2, 150 words. *Aud.:* Ga, Sa.

Quest is published by the Muscular Dystrophy Association, and provides "articles on all aspects of living with a neuromuscular disease, and updates on research findings." Reports on clinical trials, celebrity interviews, personal stories, and technology reports fill this glossy magazine. *Quest* is free online and is available at low cost in print format. Recommended for consumer health collections of health sciences libraries and public libraries. URL: http://quest.mda.org/

■ MENOPAUSE/ANDROPAUSE

Miriam Leigh, MLS, Data Specialist, Medford, MA 02155

Introduction

In recent years, our society has become increasingly concerned with the aging process. What does it mean to age, particularly in respect to changes in our bodies brought on by menopause and andropause (a drop in testosterone in older men)? Researchers and journalists are exploring topics such as the effects of menopause on mental functions, traditional and alternative symptom treatments, and changes in relationships as a result of menopause.

The publications listed in this section are scholarly journals, primarily directed toward researchers and physicians, and all are published under the purview of medical societies.

Basic Periodicals

Ac, Sa: *Maturitas.*

Basic Abstracts and Indexes

Current Contents/Clinical Medicine, EMBASE, GenderWatch, MEDLINE, Science Citation Index, ScienceDirect.

The Aging Male. See Geriatrics and Gerontological Studies section.

3845. *Climacteric.* [ISSN: 1369-7137] 1998. bi-m. GBP 365 (print & online eds.). Ed(s): Nick Panay, Anna Fenton. Informa Healthcare, Guardian House, 119 Farringdon Rd, London, EC1R 3DA, United Kingdom; healthcare@informa.com; http://informahealthcare.com/. Illus., index, adv. Refereed. Circ: 725 Paid. Vol. ends: Dec (No. 4). Reprint: PSC. *Indexed:* A01, A22, E01, ExcerpMed, P02. *Aud.:* Ac, Sa.

Climacteric is published six times annually, plus supplementary issues, as the mouthpiece of the International Menopause Society. It offers literature reviews, editorials, letters to the editor, and society meeting details, in addition to peer-reviewed original research articles. Although it claims to report on "all aspects of aging in men and women," *Climacteric*'s subtitle as the "Journal of Adult Women's Health & Medicine" and its primary article focus on women's health concerns belie that statement—there are a mere two articles on andropause since 2005. The content covers "underlying endocrinological changes, treatment of the symptoms of the menopause and other age-related changes, hormone replacement therapies, alternative therapies, effective life-style modifications, non-hormonal midlife changes, and the counselling and education of

perimenopausal and postmenopausal patients." Its articles are largely technical in nature, though there are many that would also appeal to practicing physicians. Recent articles have explored the relationship between physical activity and age at menopause; assessed the efficacy of porcine placental extract in menopausal symptoms; and compared the effects of balance-focused virtual reality games with therapeutic balance classes for older women. Recommended for academic and medical libraries.

3846. *Maturitas.* Incorporates (1994-1998): *European Menopause Journal.* [ISSN: 0378-5122] 1978. 12x/yr. EUR 1972. Ed(s): Margaret Rees. Elsevier Ireland Ltd, Elsevier House, Brookvale Plaza, E. Park, Shannon, Ireland. Refereed. Circ: 453. Microform: PQC. *Indexed:* A01, A22, AbAn, C45, ExcerpMed, IndVet, PsycInfo, RRTA. *Bk. rev.:* Number and length vary. *Aud.:* Ac, Sa.

Maturitas, a peer-reviewed monthly journal, is published as the official journal of the European Menopause and Andropause Society, and is affiliated with Australasian Menopause Society. Thus, it does not merely focus on midlife changes for women, but rather on "all aspects of postreproductive health" for both men and women, "ranging from basic science to health and social care." It is international in scope, and comprises primarily original research articles, although it does also feature book reviews, letters to the editor, review articles, and case studies as appropriate. Articles published fall into the following categories: "Predictors, effects and management of chronic diseases, Sex steroid deficiency in both genders, Epidemiology, health and social care, Therapeutic advances, [and] Complementary and alternative medicines." The journal also publishes notices of conferences and other announcements. In addition, *Maturitas* provides "fast track" publishing, for ground-breaking research that demands rapid dissemination. This technical periodical would be a good fit for an academic or medical research library, although there are a number of more accessible articles that would be of interest to the practicing physician.

3847. *Menopause.* [ISSN: 1072-3714] 1994. m. USD 894 (print & online eds.). Ed(s): Isaac Schiff. Lippincott Williams & Wilkins, 530 Walnut St, Philadelphia, PA 19106; customerservice@lww.com; http://www.lww.com. Illus., adv. Refereed. Circ: 2344 Paid. Microform: PQC. *Indexed:* A22, C45, ExcerpMed, RRTA. *Aud.:* Ac, Sa.

Menopause, launched in 1994, is a peer-reviewed journal geared to providing "a forum for new research, applied basic science, and clinical guidelines on all aspects of menopause." It includes a variety of article formats, including editorials, original research articles, clinical articles, review articles, meeting abstracts, case studies, and letters to the editor. *Menopause* encompasses far more than simply the immediate gynecological aspects of menopause. It explores cancer risk, the effects of menopause on the whole body, treatment trends, cognitive concerns, sleep disorders, alternative therapies, and more. Doctors looking for continuing medical education credits will be pleased to find opportunities offered in selected issues. For subscribers who prefer to read digital versions, the publisher offers an app for iPhone, iPod Touch, and iPad via iTunes. Published for the North American Menopause Society (NAMS), this journal is also used as a forum for NAMS to explore its role in the menopause research community. Because over 60 percent of *Menopause* subscribers have an office-based clinical practice, this publication would be appropriate for academic and research libraries that support practicing physicians and medical researchers.

3848. *Menopause International.* Formerly (until 2007): *British Menopause Society. Journal.* [ISSN: 1754-0453] 1995. q. EUR 558 (print & online eds). Sage Publications Ltd., 1 Oliver's Yard, 55 City Rd, London, EC1Y 1SP, United Kingdom; info@sagepub.co.uk; http://www.uk.sagepub.com. Adv. Sample. Refereed. *Indexed:* A22, E01, ExcerpMed. *Bk. rev.:* Number and length vary. *Aud.:* Ac, Sa.

This readable journal, published quarterly, focuses heavily on subjects that are most relevant to practicing doctors. *Menopause International* is aimed at "all those involved in the study and treatment of menopausal conditions across the world." This journal has a broad scope, and in addition to research articles, it offers editorials, news briefs, practice notes, British Menopause Society reports and meeting proceedings, book reviews, and literature reviews of relevant articles in other journals. Recent topics have included estrogen and cognitive function, alternatives to hormone replacement therapy in women with a history of hormone dependent cancer, estrogen therapy for women with osteoarthritis, and postmenopausal vaginal discomfort. This journal would be most appropriate in a library that supports practicing physicians.

■ MIDDLE EAST

Nada Hussein, Middle Eastern Librarian, Middle Eastern Division, Harvard College Library, Harvard University, Cambridge, MA 02138.

Joshua Parker, Head of Access for Humanities & Social Sciences, Harvard Library, Harvard University, Cambridge, MA 02138

Introduction

The Middle East is a term that covers a variety of cultures, religions, and languages, and it encompasses the history of diverse peoples and places. The journals selected here represent the area generally accepted (by the U.N. and in other usage) to be the area described as "Middle East." For the purposes of this survey of journal publications, the area is assumed to include the Arabian Peninsula, North Africa, Turkey, the Levant, Iraq, and Iran. All of the journals reviewed here are available both online and in print.

Basic Periodicals

British Journal of Middle Eastern Studies, International Journal of Middle East Studies, Middle East Policy, Middle East Report, Middle Eastern Literatures.

Basic Abstracts and Indexes

ATLA Religion Index, Historical Abstracts, Index Islamicus, Index to Jewish Periodicals, PAIS International.

3849. Alo Hayati. [ISSN: 2325-1514] 2005. q. USD 28; USD 8.95 newsstand/cover. Ed(s): Michael D Lloyd. Unique Image, Inc., 19365 Business Center Dr, Bldg 1, Northridge, CA 91324; breathe@uniqueimageinc.com; http://www.uniqueimageinc.com/. Illus., adv. *Aud.:* Ga.

This magazine provides a cultural look at happenings in the Middle East and among its community in the United States. More at home in public than in academic libraries, it opens up a world of Middle Eastern fashion, culture, art, and entertainment. Published quarterly, it looks at life through community living and intercultural exchanges, while it also showcases certain tourist spots in and around the Middle East. Recommended for public libraries.

3850. Azure: ideas for the Jewish nation. [ISSN: 0793-6664] 1996. q. USD 40; ILS 120. Ed(s): Assaf Sagiv, Lorena Avraham. The Shalem Center, 13 Yehoshua Bin-Nun St, PO Box 8787, Jerusalem, 93145, Israel; contact@azure.org.il; http://www.shalem.org.il. Adv. Refereed. *Indexed:* IJP, MLA-IB. *Bk. rev.:* 2-3. *Aud.:* Ga, Ac.

Describing itself as presenting "the best in Jewish thought from Israel and around the world," *Azure* offers a Zionist perspective on Jewish history and culture, the Diaspora, the Middle East, and Israeli politics. A project of the Shalem Center, *Azure* generally reflects the conservative philosophy and priorities of that institution. Each issue includes an essay by editor Assaf Sagiv. Other contributors include Israel's ambassador to the U.S. Michael Oren; Shalem Center Senior Fellow Daniel Gordis; and a range of political leaders and intellectuals. Recent articles include Moshe Koppel's "Judaism as a First Language," in which he argues for an ethics based in a "fluent" understanding of Jewish community values; and an analysis by Uriya Shavit of the recent [pre–Morsi overthrow] Egyptian revolution, which argues that political Islam is incompatible with democratic values. *Azure* also occasionally publishes material that deals with topics in the fields of literature and philosophy deemed to be of interest to Jewish audiences. *Azure* should be considered for collections with a concentration on the contemporary politics of Israel, the Middle East, and Jewish identity.

3851. British Journal of Middle Eastern Studies. Formerly (until 1991): *British Society for Middle Eastern Studies. Bulletin.* [ISSN: 1353-0194] 1974. 4x/yr. GBP 490 (print & online eds.). Ed(s): Ian Netton. Routledge, 4 Park Sq, Milton Park, Abingdon, OX14 4RN, United Kingdom; subscriptions@tandf.co.uk; http://www.tandfonline.com. Adv. Sample. Refereed. Circ: 1000. Reprint: PSC. *Indexed:* A01, A22, A47, ArtHuCI, E01, IBSS, MLA-IB, P02, P61, SSA. *Bk. rev.:* Number and length vary. *Aud.:* Ac.

The *British Journal of Middle Eastern Studies* is an academic, peer-reviewed journal published three times a year for the British Society for Middle Eastern Studies. This journal is available both in print and online. It aims to maintain "a balance between the modern social sciences and the more traditional disciplines associated with Middle Eastern and Islamic studies." Articles cover all aspects of the Middle East "from the end of classical antiquity and the rise of Islam to the present day." It presents articles that primarily focus on cultural, political, and religious history, current and historic. Analysis is often within communities, or between communities and occupying or administering authorities. The articles are well-written and presented with both a scholarly tone and a rich narrative suitable for readers who have at least some college background. Some issues are special issues devoted to particular subjects—for example, "Futuwwa" (volume 40, issue 1 [2013]). Each issue includes a book review section.

3852. International Journal of Middle East Studies. [ISSN: 0020-7438] 1970. q. plus two bulletins. GBP 336. Ed(s): Judith Tucker. Cambridge University Press, The Edinburgh Bldg, Shaftesbury Rd, Cambridge, CB2 8RU, United Kingdom; journals@cambridge.org; http://www.cambridge.org/uk. Illus., adv. Refereed. Vol. ends: Spring. Microform: PQC. Reprint: PSC. *Indexed:* A01, A22, A47, BRI, E01, IBSS, MLA-IB, P02, P61, SSA. *Bk. rev.:* Number and length vary. *Aud.:* Ac.

The *International Journal of Middle East Studies* is published quarterly under the auspices of the Middle East Studies Association of North America and is peer-reviewed. This journal is available both in print and online. The publisher states that the coverage is "history, politics, economics, anthropology, sociology, literature, and cultural studies" of the "Arab world, Iran, Turkey, the Caucasus, Afghanistan, Israel, and Muslim South Asia from the 7th century until the present." A review shows recent articles on politics, economics, culture, and religion that will be mostly of interest to scholars in Middle East Studies, or to college-educated readers researching a specific topic. One example of a recent special issue is "Queer Affects" (volume 45, number 2 [2013]). The "Roundtable" section features essays by scholars on a particular question or topic, submitted prior to publication for discussion by other authors. Each issue of the journal also includes approximately 50 pages of book reviews.

3853. Iranian Studies. [ISSN: 0021-0862] 1967. bi-m. GBP 397 (print & online eds.). Ed(s): Homa Katouzian. Routledge, 4 Park Sq, Milton Park, Abingdon, OX14 4RN, United Kingdom; subscriptions@tandf.co.uk; http://www.tandfonline.com. Illus., index, adv. Sample. Refereed. Reprint: PSC. *Indexed:* A01, A22, AmHI, ArtHuCI, E01, MLA-IB, P61, RILM, SSA. *Bk. rev.:* Number and length vary. *Aud.:* Ac.

Iranian Studies is published six times a year by the International Society for Iranian Studies. This journal is available both in print and online. It is a peer-reviewed, academic journal, featuring articles on "history, literature, culture and society, covering everywhere with a Persian or Iranian legacy, especially Iran, Afghanistan, Central Asia, the Caucasus, and northern India." Some issues are special issues devoted to particular subjects, for example, "Power Interplay Between Iran and Russia from the Mid-Seventeenth to the Early Twenty-First Century " (volume 46, issue 3 [2013]). Issues also include a book review section that addresses books about any aspect of Persian studies. This journal will be most interesting to scholars studying culture, literature, and politics.

3854. Israel Affairs. [ISSN: 1353-7121] 1994. q. GBP 463 (print & online eds.). Ed(s): Efraim Karsh. Routledge, 4 Park Sq, Milton Park, Abingdon, OX14 4RN, United Kingdom; subscriptions@tandf.co.uk; http://www.tandfonline.com. Adv. Sample. Refereed. Reprint: PSC. *Indexed:* A01, A22, E01, IBSS, IJP, P61, RiskAb, SSA. *Bk. rev.:* Occasional. *Aud.:* Ac.

Israel Affairs is a quarterly peer-reviewed journal that covers modern Israeli history, politics, and culture, as well as related topics involving the broader Middle East region. The journal is edited by Efraim Karsh (Middle East and Mediterranean Studies, King's College London), and its board also includes voices such as those of historian Howard Sachar, philosopher and political theorist Michael Walzer, and novelist A.B. Yehoshua. Recent articles include a consideration of the relationship between religion and the Israeli state with regard to the "right to die" debate by Michal Neubauer-Shani; a conservative re-estimation by Karsh of the number of Palestinian refugees displaced by the Israeli War of Independence; and a historical overview of secondary education among Jewish residents during the British Mandate by Nirit Reichel. *Israel Affairs* is recommended for collections that deal with modern Israeli and Middle Eastern history and politics.

3855. Israel Studies. [ISSN: 1084-9513] 1996. 3x/yr. USD 153 (print & online eds.). Ed(s): Natan Aridan, Dr. S Ilan Troen. Indiana University Press, 601 N Morton St, Bloomington, IN 47404. Adv. Refereed. Circ: 500. Reprint: PSC. *Indexed:* A01, A22, BRI, E01, ENW, IBSS, IJP, MLA-IB, P61, SSA. *Bk. rev.:* Occasional. *Aud.:* Ac.

Israel Studies is an academic journal that publishes scholarship related to Israeli history, society, and politics. Published three times a year, the journal is edited by Ilan Troen of Bradeis University. Although primarily focused on modern Israel, *Israel Studies* also publishes material related to events preceding the foundation of the State. Recent offerings have included a special roundtable section examining the relationship between the Israeli state and Diaspora Jews; a special section on Israel and international law; and an analysis by Raanan Rein of Israeli attitudes toward Jewish volunteers in the International Brigades of the Spanish Civil War. Content covers a wide span of modern Israeli society and encompasses a range of political and scholarly perspectives. *Israel Studies* is recommended for collections that deal with modern Israeli and Middle Eastern history, society, and politics.

3856. Israel Studies Review: an interdisciplinary journal. Former titles (until 2011): *Israel Studies Forum;* (until 2001): *Israel Studies Bulletin;* (until 1992): *Association for Israel Studies. Newsletter.* [ISSN: 2159-0370] 198?. s-a. GBP 127 (print & online eds.). Ed(s): Paul L Scham, Yoram Peri. Berghahn Books Inc., 150 Broadway, Ste 812, New York, NY 10038; journals@berghahnbooks.com; http:// www.berghahnbooks.com. Adv. Sample. Refereed. Reprint: PSC. *Indexed:* A01, BRI, MLA-IB, P61, SSA. *Bk. rev.:* 5-8. *Aud.:* Ac.

Israel Studies Review started in 2011 as a continuation of the journal *Israel Studies Forum.* Explicitly interdisciplinary in its approach, the *Review* "explores modern and contemporary Israel from the perspective of the social sciences, history, the humanities, and cultural studies." The journal explicitly seeks to expose and discuss controversy, with each issue prominently featuring a "Forum" section in which scholars of varying perspectives discuss a subject (examples of recent themes are "Is Israeli Democracy in Danger" and "Israeli Immigration/Emigration"). Each issue also features an extensive book review section and at least one review article that discusses a set of related recently published works. Recent articles of interest have included an examination of the portrayal of urban space in early Hebrew cinema by Hiaky Shoham; an investigation by Admeil Kosman of Israeli cultural crisis as a tension between isolationist and universalist theologies; and a look at the sociology of gender in the IDF. *Israel Studies Review* is recommended for collections with materials related to Middle Eastern and Israeli culture, politics, history, and sociology.

3857. The Jerusalem Report. [ISSN: 0792-6049] 1990. bi-w. Ed(s): Eeta Prince-Gibson. Jerusalem Report, PO Box 1805, Jerusalem, 91017, Israel. Illus., adv. *Indexed:* IJP. *Bk. rev.:* 2. *Aud.:* Ga.

Published by the *Jerusalem Post,* the editorially independent *Jerusalem Report* is a biweekly magazine that covers news from "Israel, the Middle East, and the Jewish World." Primarily focused on current affairs, the magazine regularly features articles on Israeli and Palestinian politics, and Israeli foreign relations, culture, and business. Each issue also features book reviews, opinion pieces, and occasional fiction. *The Jerusalem Report* offers a useful perspective on news from Israel and the Middle East, and is recommended for collections that cover international current events.

3858. Jewish Review of Books. [ISSN: 2153-1978] 2010. q. USD 19.95 domestic; USD 29.95 foreign. Ed(s): Abraham Socher. Bee.Ideas, LLC, 745 Fifth Ave, Ste 1400, New York, NY 10151; pgetz@jewishreviewofbooks.com. *Bk. rev.:* Number and length vary. *Aud.:* Ga, Ac.

The *Jewish Review of Books* is a quarterly publication now entering its fourth year. Available both in print and online, the title publishes reviews of books, films, and other works related to Jewish religion, culture, identity, and political life. Each issue also includes original essays on subjects relevant to the Jewish world. Describing itself as "committed to the ideal of the thoughtful essay that illuminates as it entertains," the *Review* is oriented toward an intellectual audience, though not exclusively an academic one. Although not open-access, the *Review* does make several pieces from each issue freely available to the public. The editorial board includes many leading voices in the world of Jewish thought, including Robert Alter, Jon Levenson, Michael Walzer, and Ruth Wisse. Although the balance of the board's membership may appear to some to be weighted slightly to the right of the political spectrum, the *Review* is clearly seeking to publish content that is not limited to a particular political or cultural viewpoint and that will have a wide appeal. Recent reviews have included Adam Kisch on a collection of Rosa Luxemburg's letters; David Biale discussing three works that address secularism and the legacy of the Shabbatean movement; and Alana Cooper on Janet Malcom's Iphigenia in Forest Hills. An occasional feature of particular note is the "Symposiums," which collect brief discussions by several contributors about topics such as the "Thinking About Revolution and Democracy in the Middle East," and the 2011 J14 tent city protests in Tel Aviv. This title is recommended for collections with a focus on Jewish culture and intellectual life, Judaism, Jewish history, and the contemporary politics of the Middle East and Jewish identity.

3859. The Journal of Israeli History: politics, society, culture. Formerly (until 1994): *Studies in Zionism;* Which superseded (in 1982): *Zionism: Studies in the History of the Zionist Movement and of the Jews in Palestine - Ha-Tsiyonut.* [ISSN: 1353-1042] 1980. s-a. GBP 262 (print & online eds.). Ed(s): Derek J Penslar, Anita Shapira. Routledge, 4 Park Sq, Milton Park, Abingdon, OX14 4RN, United Kingdom; subscriptions@tandf.co.uk; http://www.tandfonline.com. Illus., adv. Sample. Refereed. Vol. ends: Fall. Reprint: PSC. *Indexed:* A22, AmHI, ArtHuCI, E01, IJP, MLA-IB, P61, R&TA, SSA. *Bk. rev.:* 3-6. *Aud.:* Ac.

The Journal of Israeli History is a scholarly journal that focuses on modern Israeli history from the period of the British Mandate to the present. Published twice a year, the journal is edited by Anita Shapira of Tel Aviv University and Derek Penslar of the University of Toronto. Recent articles have included an exploration of the relationship between Israeli scholars and politicians, by Moshe Lissak and Uri Cohen; a study of the development of Hebrew identity among Jewish residents of Ottoman Palestine, by Boaz Lev Tov; and a special issue devoted to the kibbutz in Israeli society. *The Journal of Israeli History* is recommended for academic collections with a concentration in Israeli and Middle Eastern history.

3860. Journal of Middle East Women's Studies. [ISSN: 1552-5864] 2005. 3x/yr. USD 139.75 (print & online eds.). Ed(s): Marcia Inhorn. Indiana University Press, 601 N Morton St, Bloomington, IN 47404; journals@indiana.edu; http://iupress.indiana.edu. Adv. Sample. Refereed. Circ: 375. Reprint: PSC. *Indexed:* A01, A22, A47, AmHI, BRI, E01, FemPer, GW, IBSS, MLA-IB, P02, P61, SSA. *Bk. rev.:* Number and length vary. *Aud.:* Ac.

The *Journal of Middle East Women's Studies* is a peer-reviewed, academic journal published by the Association of Middle East Women's Studies. It is published three times a year and is available both in print and online. It aims to "advance the fields of Middle East women's studies, gender studies[,] and Middle East studies through contributions across disciplines in the social sciences and humanities." Issues include book reviews and, sometimes, film reviews. Some issues focus on a single topic—for example, "Emerging Voices in Comparative Literature from the Middle East" (volume 9, issue 2 [2013]). This journal contains well-written articles regarding gender studies, with a strong emphasis on feminist issues. It attempts to bridge gaps between Western feminist scholarship and Middle Eastern perspectives, from a mix of Western and Middle East authors.

3861. *Journal of Palestine Studies.* [ISSN: 0377-919X] 1971. q. USD 252 (print & online eds.). Ed(s): Laurie King, Rashid I Khalidi. University of California Press, Journals Division, 2000 Ctr St, Ste 303, Berkeley, CA 94704; customerservice@ucpressjournals.com; http://www.ucpressjournals.com. Illus., index, adv. Refereed. Circ: 2036. Microform: PQC. Reprint: PSC. *Indexed:* A01, A22, BRI, E01, ENW, IBSS, MLA-IB, P02, P61, SSA. *Bk. rev.:* Number and length vary. *Aud.:* Ac, Sa.

The *Journal of Palestine Studies* is a quarterly, peer-reviewed, academic journal published by the University of California Press on behalf of the Institute for Palestine Studies. This journal is available both in print and online. It is "devoted exclusively to Palestinian affairs and the Arab-Israeli conflict." It includes articles, essays, and book reviews, as well as several special features. A section on Arab views includes a selection of political cartoons from the *al-Hayat* newspaper. Another section titled "Selections from the Press" includes excerpts that are mainly Israeli, but also from some international press sources. "Photos from the Quarter" "aim[s] to convey a sense of the situation on the ground in the occupied territories." The "Quarterly Update on Conflict and Diplomacy" "is a summary of bilateral, multilateral, regional, and international events affecting the Palestinians and the future of the peace process." The "Settlement Monitor" covers settlement activities in the West Bank, the Gaza Strip, the Golan Heights, and East Jerusalem. The "Document and Source Material" section provides reference material that relates to Palestine and the Arab–Israeli conflict. A "Bibliography of Periodical Literature" "lists articles and reviews of books relevant to Palestine and the Arab-Israeli conflict."

3862. *Middle East Journal.* [ISSN: 0026-3141] 1947. q. Individuals, USD 50; Free to members. Ed(s): Adam Mendelson, Michael Collins Dunn. Middle East Institute, 1761 N St, NW, Washington, DC 20036; man-ed@mei.edu; http://www.mei.edu. Illus., adv. Refereed. Vol. ends: Fall. Microform: PQC. *Indexed:* A01, A22, A47, ABIn, ABS&EES, BAS, BRI, CBRI, E01, FR, IBSS, JEL, MLA-IB, P02, P61, SSA. *Bk. rev.:* Number and length vary. *Aud.:* Ga, Ac.

The *Middle East Journal* has been published quarterly by the Middle East Institute since 1947. This journal is available both in print and online. It is a peer-reviewed journal that covers the "post World War II Middle East including Pakistan, the Caucasus, and Central Asia." Articles are written mostly by scholars, and their coverage includes political, social, and economic developments in the Middle East. A chronology section, continuous since 1947, is organized by subject and country and lists events for that quarter. The book review section includes in-depth reviews of books divided by country and subject, as well as annotations of recent publications.

3863. *Middle East Policy.* Formerly (until 1992): *American Arab Affairs.* [ISSN: 1061-1924] 1981. q. GBP 211. Ed(s): Anne Joyce. Wiley-Blackwell Publishing, Inc., 111 River St, Hoboken, NJ 07030; info@wiley.com; http://www.wiley.com/. Illus., index, adv. Sample. Refereed. Vol. ends: Spring/Winter. Reprint: PSC. *Indexed:* A01, A22, ABIn, BRI, CBRI, E01, ENW, IBSS, P02, P61, RiskAb, S25, SSA. *Bk. rev.:* Number and length vary. *Aud.:* Ga, Ac.

Middle East Policy is an academic, peer-reviewed journal published quarterly by the Middle East Policy Council. This journal is available both in print and online. It focuses on the Middle East as it relates to international affairs. It provides a "forum for a wide range of views on U.S. interests in the region and the value of the policies that are supposed to promote them." It would also be interesting to financial and industrial professionals. It includes book and film reviews, and occasionally book excerpts.

3864. *Middle East Quarterly.* [ISSN: 1073-9467] 1994. q. USD 70 (Individuals, USD 50; Students, USD 30). Ed(s): Judy Goodrobb, Efraim Karsh. Middle East Forum, 1500 Walnut St, Ste 1050, Philadelphia, PA 19103-4624; mideastq@aol.com; http://www.meforum.org. Illus., adv. Circ: 2100 Paid. *Indexed:* A01, A22, BRI, CBRI, IBSS, IJP, P61, SSA. *Bk. rev.:* Number varies. *Aud.:* Ga, Ac.

A publication of the Middle East Forum, *Middle East Quarterly* presents reporting, analysis, and policy recommendations intended to help "define and promote American interests in the Middle East." *MEQ* is edited by Efraim Karsh of Kings College London. In addition to university scholars, the editorial board includes representatives from government and influential policy think tanks.

Content covers a wide range of political, economic, and security topics. Individual issues may include sections focused on subjects of particular current interest (examples include "Changes in Turkey," "Israeli Defense," and "The Syrian Uprising"). Content is fully available online at the journal's web site, with the exception of material in the most recently published issue. *Middle East Quarterly* should be considered for inclusion in collections that cover the Middle East and U.S. foreign policy.

3865. *Middle East Report.* Former titles (until 1988): *M E R I P Middle East Report;* (until 1986): *M E R I P Reports;* Which incorporated (1970-1973): *Pakistan Forum.* [ISSN: 0899-2851] 1971. q. USD 150 (Individuals, USD 37). Middle East Research & Information Project, 1500 Massachusetts Ave NW, Ste 119, Washington, DC 20005; http://www.merip.org. Illus., index. Refereed. Microform: PQC. *Indexed:* A22, E01, IBSS, P61, RILM, SSA. *Bk. rev.:* Number and length vary. *Aud.:* Ac.

The *Middle East Report* is a quarterly, academic journal published by the Middle East Research and Information Project. This journal is available both in print and online. It focuses on the "political economy of the contemporary Middle East and popular struggles there." Most issues are thematic, focusing on a topic or region, with articles that address "a broad range of social, political, and cultural issues," and so it will be useful to readers from various disciplines. Issues include a book review section, as well as an "Editor's Picks" section that addresses recent publications relating to the Middle East.

Middle Eastern Literatures. See Literature section.

3866. *Middle Eastern Studies.* [ISSN: 0026-3206] 1964. bi-m. GBP 651 (print & online eds.). Ed(s): Sylvia Kedourie. Routledge, 4 Park Sq, Milton Park, Abingdon, OX14 4RN, United Kingdom; subscriptions@tandf.co.uk; http://www.tandfonline.com. Illus., adv. Sample. Refereed. Microform: PQC. Reprint: PSC. *Indexed:* A01, A22, AbAn, AmHI, BRI, E01, FR, IBSS, MLA-IB, P02, P61, RiskAb, SSA. *Bk. rev.:* Number and length vary. *Aud.:* Ac, Sa.

Middle Eastern Studies is a peer-reviewed, academic journal published six times a year. This journal is available both in print and online. It provides "academic research on the history and politics of the Arabic-speaking countries in the Middle East and North Africa as well as on Turkey, Iran[,] and Israel." Most articles are tightly-focused treatments of individual topics in history or politics within a single state (or even neighborhood), or within narrow timeframes, rather than comparative studies between states or regions, or between historic and contemporary movements. Issues also include book reviews.

3867. *Turkish Studies.* [ISSN: 1468-3849] 2000. q. GBP 303 (print & online eds.). Ed(s): Barry Rubin. Routledge, 4 Park Sq, Milton Park, Abingdon, OX14 4RN, United Kingdom; subscriptions@tandf.co.uk; http://www.tandfonline.com. Adv. Sample. Refereed. Reprint: PSC. *Indexed:* A01, A22, E01, IBSS, P61, SSA. *Bk. rev.:* Number and length vary. *Aud.:* Ac.

Turkish Studies is a quarterly, peer-reviewed journal published by the Global Research in International Affairs Center. This journal is available both in print and online. It features articles on "the history of the Turkish republic from the 1920s to the present, including political, social[,] and intellectual issues; Turkish politics; [g]overnment policies and programs; and Turkish international relations and foreign policy." Some issues focus on a single topic, for example, "The Political Psychology of Turkish Political Behavior" (volume 14, issue 1 [2013]). Most issues include a book review section that addresses books about Turkey.

■ MILITARY

Joseph E. Straw, Head of Instruction, Humanities Bibliographer, Marietta College Library, Marietta, OH 45750; js001@marietta.edu

Introduction

All over the world today, war and the threat of conflict have generated an increased interest in military and national security affairs. Recently for the

United States, concerns about the ongoing War on Terror and the winding down of active wars in Iraq and Afghanistan have placed the role of the military in sharp focus. The available information on this topic in all formats has long reached the point of saturation. In navigating the vast amount of potential material, risks are clearly involved in finding information about either the U.S. or foreign militaries that's superficial or even distorted. Any informed look at military affairs must take into account more nuanced and sophisticated information that makes up only a minority of the available resources.

Knowledge of military and defense periodicals can be an approach to take for increasing the probability of finding information that's reliable and authoritative. These periodicals can often provide an interesting window into this complex and somewhat perplexing world. Periodicals are one of the key ways in which new ideas are communicated to military professionals and civilian policymakers concerned with national defense. Around the world, a wide variety of periodicals report on strategy, tactics, training, logistics, military history, and general defense policy. In the case of the United States, just about every area of the military and national security establishment has a periodical publication that covers its particular niche.

Throughout most of their history, military periodicals served a very limited audience of practitioners and specialists. They were mainly found in special library collections that served military posts and war colleges. In the past few decades, interest in military affairs has peaked among the public and these periodicals can now be found in libraries that serve more general audiences. Academic interest in this area has grown, and university libraries are aggressively acquiring periodicals of this type to supplement collections in international relations, political science, security studies, and history. Public libraries are also seeking to build periodical collections to support real user interests in such topics as unconventional war, defense policy, and military hardware.

With interest in the military increasing in libraries of all types, this section will profile core military periodicals with a particular emphasis on the United States Armed Forces. Selected publications that cover foreign militaries or defense affairs will also be profiled. Two types of periodicals will be included as part of this section: 1) professional military periodicals that focus on problems in contemporary armed forces or current defense policies; and 2) military history periodicals that deal with battles, institutions, and leaders from the past. For all the periodicals that will be listed, titles that are geared to both a general and more specialized academic audience will be covered.

Professional military periodicals have their origin in internal publications of staff and war colleges that were established in Europe and the United States at the end of the nineteenth and beginning of the twentieth centuries. These publications are used to communicate news, ideas, innovations, and doctrine for application in contemporary militaries. Serving officers and defense officials often consult such publications to stay up-to-date and discover what's cutting edge in such disciplines as infantry tactics, intelligence, supply, special operations, and information warfare. The professional military periodical has a long tradition of authorship that comes from serving military personnel or civilian experts active in the defense community. In recent years, the contribution of people outside the defense establishment has increased, as a strong academic and interdisciplinary trend has crept into much of the writing in this area. The interdependency of factors such as culture, geography, religion, politics, and history is increasingly being recognized as impacting the success of potential military missions. Contributions by sociologists, anthropologists, political scientists, and other outside professionals are clearly seen as being of great benefit to military or civilian planners in thinking about future defense contingencies or even about the nature of conflict itself.

Military history periodicals cover the things in the past that deal with war and conflict. Some of the areas of military history would include battles, soldier life, military thought, and leadership. Contributions to military history are made by an eclectic group of people that would include journalists, generals, common soldiers, creative writers, military enthusiasts, genealogists, and trained historians. Military history is popular for the general reading public, but it takes on an added significance because of the important pedagogical role that it plays for many militaries today. By considering history, current operational performance can be improved by appreciating the mistakes of the past and instilling in current leadership an awareness of historical parallels.

Compared to other areas of history, military history retains elements of a very traditional historiography that focuses on detailed battle and biographical narratives. Recently, however, social-history–oriented articles are appearing

more prominently in these periodicals. Several popular magazines regularly publish oral histories that illustrate how soldiers cope with war and military life. A number of academic journals almost exclusively focus on the social context of war. Connecting conflict with social forces like religion, politics, gender, and race is becoming commonplace, as a result linking military history more closely with mainstream methodological approaches in the broader field of history.

Obtaining and providing access to military periodicals provides both challenges and opportunities for libraries. Many periodicals of this type are highly specialized, and knowledge of appropriate titles can easily escape the attention of the uninitiated. Electronic publishing is growing rapidly in this field, but the potential benefits of this format are mitigated by a traditional revenue and distribution model that relies on individual subscriptions, institutional membership, and association dues. Far too many military-oriented titles escape coverage by traditional indexing and abstracting tools, and access to the full-text versions of these periodicals is further complicated by their limited penetration through subscription-based aggregators like JSTOR, ProQuest, and EBSCO.

Despite these problems, the costs of periodicals of this type is not prohibitive and can fall within the budgeting of most libraries. Many of these periodicals are also published by government agencies that are increasingly using free electronic access to disseminate publications, making it easier for libraries to provide access for a broader public. Clearly, careful consideration of the needs of users, and the extent to which these titles will add to or supplement existing resources, must be taken into account by libraries in collecting military periodicals.

Basic Periodicals

Hs: *Aviation History, Soldiers;* Ga: *Air Force Magazine, Armed Forces Journal, Army, Aviation History, Defense Monitor, Leatherneck, Military History, National Guard, Naval History, World War II;* Ac: *The Air & Space Power Journal, AirForces Monthly, Armed Forces and Society, Armed Forces Journal, Army, Defense Monitor, Joint Force Quarterly, Journal of Military History, The Journal of Strategic Studies, Military Review, Naval War College Review, Survival (Abingdon), U S Naval Institute. Proceedings.*

Basic Abstracts and Indexes

Air University Library Index to Military Periodicals.

3868. African Armed Forces: a monthly journal devoted to defence matters. Formerly (until July 1994): *Armed Forces.* 1975. m. ZAR 390 domestic; EUR 190 foreign. Ed(s): S J McIntosh. Africa Conflict & Defense Monitor, PO Box 87561, Houghton, 2041, South Africa. Illus., adv. *Aud.:* Ga, Ac, Sa.

African Armed Forces Journal (*AAFJ*) claims to be a forum for African military professionals to "discuss issues of mutual interest." While this periodical certainly publishes articles about defense matters from across the continent, the principal focus is on the current activities of the South African National Defense Force (SANDF). Supplementing the articles are illustrations and many full-page advertisements that highlight South Africa's native defense industries. One gets the impression that one of the principal audiences for *AAFJ* comprises African militaries that are actively shopping in the arms market. Most of the content is contributed by serving officers in the SANDF and civilian defense experts. *AAFJ* would be most suited to large academic libraries that would collect heavily in African Studies.

3869. The Air & Space Power Journal. Former titles (until 2002): *The Aerospace Power Journal;* (until 1999): *Airpower Journal;* (until 1987): *Air University Review;* (until 1963): *Air University Quarterly Review.* [ISSN: 1555-385X] 1947. q. Ed(s): Col. Michael Pate. U.S. Air Force, Air University, 155 N Twining St, Maxwell, AL 36112. Illus., index. Sample. Refereed. Vol. ends: Winter. Microform: PQC. *Indexed:* A01, A22, ABIn, ABS&EES, BAS, BRI, C&ISA, MLA-IB, P02. *Bk. rev.:* Number varies; 200-500 words. *Aud.:* Ac, Sa.

The Air & Space Power Journal is the official publication of Air University, which serves as the U.S. Air Force's center for professional military education. This journal seeks to present current thinking on issues relating to the employment of air and space forces in the overall framework of national defense. A recent issue contains articles that explore team building, organizational knowledge, and inter-agency cooperation. The articles are heavily researched and are written mostly by senior serving officers, with frequent contributions by leading academics. A real strength of this publication is the large list of book reviews that cover titles related to national defense, air power, foreign relations, and the history of military aviation. This journal has companion international versions that are published in French, Spanish, Portuguese, Arabic, and Chinese. These sister publications are edited by native speakers and provide articles targeted to regions like the Middle East, Latin America, Europe, Africa, and the Caribbean. Since 2011, *The Air & Space Power Journal* has been distributed exclusively online for free and can be used with many standard reading devices that would include the Nook, Kindle, and i-tablet readers. Given the professional and research focus, this publication would be highly recommended for inclusion on the electronic resource pages for large academic libraries.

3870. Air Force Magazine: the force behind the force. Former titles (until 1972): *Air Force and Space Digest;* (until 1959): *Air Force;* (until 1942): *Air Forces News Letter;* (until 1941): *Air Corps News Letter.* [ISSN: 0730-6784] 1927. m. Members, USD 21; Non-members, USD 36. Ed(s): Adam J Hebert, Juliette Kelsey Chagnon. Air Force Association, 1501 Lee Hwy, Arlington, VA 22209; service@afa.org; http://www.afa.org. Illus., adv. Circ: 138295 Paid. Vol. ends: Dec. *Indexed:* A22, ABS&EES, C&ISA, CerAb, P02. *Bk. rev.:* 5, 150-200 words. *Aud.:* Ga, Ac.

Air Force Magazine is one of the most respected and oldest publications dealing with air power in the United States. Published by the Air Force Association, it is geared to serving military personnel and the general public. Print and digital versions of the magazine are made available for free to members of the association. This magazine is a good source of news and current events regarding issues that affect the U.S. Air Force. Feature articles deal with current operations, programs, doctrine, aviation history, and biographical information on key Air Force personnel. A particularly useful annual "Almanac" is published in May, which provides an authoritative statistical overview of the Air Force. Much of the content is drawn from serving officers, freelance journalists, and researchers, many of them affiliated with "think tanks" that deal closely with defense issues. This publication would be of interest to both academic and public libraries.

3871. AirForces Monthly: the world's leading military aviation magazine. [ISSN: 0955-7091] 1988. m. Ed(s): Gary Parsons. Key Publishing Ltd., PO Box 300, Stamford, PE9 1NA, United Kingdom; ann.saundry@keypublishing.com; http://www.keypublishing.com. Illus., adv. *Aud.:* Ga, Ac.

This British publication covers military aviation from an international perspective. Aviation news is divided by region and includes the United Kingdom, Europe, North America, Latin America, Africa, Middle East, Asia/ Pacific, Russia, and Australasia. The feature articles cover technology, conflicts, doctrine, and of course the latest in military aircraft. The articles are by freelance journalists and serving air force officers from around the world. Attractive photographs greatly add to the overall appeal. *AirForces Monthly's* glossy format and international focus make it suitable for purchase by both public and academic libraries.

3872. The American Legion. Former titles (until 1981): *American Legion Magazine;* (until 1937): *The American Legion Monthly;* (until 1926): *The American Legion Weekly.* [ISSN: 0886-1234] 1920. m. Free to members; Non-members, USD 15. American Legion Magazine, 700 N Pennsylvania St, PO Box 1055, Indianapolis, IN 46204; http://www.legion.org. Illus. Vol. ends: Jun/Dec. *Indexed:* A22, BRI, P02. *Aud.:* Ga.

The American Legion is one of the most respected publications that deal with American veterans' affairs. It openly advocates for veterans and their families on issues such as health care, employment, pensions, education, and homelessness. Excellent coverage of current legislation that impacts veterans and currently serving military personnel is provided. One of the other themes of *American Legion* is promotion of "Americanism," patriotism, service, citizenship, and a strong national defense. This would be a good general-interest publication for veterans or any part of the general public interested in issues related to military service. Highly recommended for public library collections.

3873. Armed Forces and Society. [ISSN: 0095-327X] 1972. q. USD 588. Ed(s): Patricia M Shields. Sage Publications, Inc., 2455 Teller Rd, Thousand Oaks, CA 91320; info@sagepub.com; http://www.sagepub.com. Illus., index, adv. Sample. Refereed. Vol. ends: Summer. Microform: PQC. Reprint: PSC. *Indexed:* A01, A22, ABS&EES, BAS, BRI, CBRI, E01, IBSS, P02, P61, RiskAb, SSA. *Bk. rev.:* 5-10, 300-500 words. *Aud.:* Ac.

Armed Forces and Society is one of the premier scholarly journals focusing on the military. Published by the Inter-University Seminar on Armed Forces and Society, it provides an international forum for current topics like military organization, recruitment, family issues, conflict resolution, and defense policy. A recent edition looked at soldier ethics, public support for military interventions, and the role of women soldiers in peacekeeping operations. Most of the articles are written by leading academics, with some contributions by senior military leaders. This publication welcomes contributions from a wide diversity of disciplines and methodological perspectives, with the emphasis mostly in sociology and the behavioral sciences. The strong research orientation of this publication should make it a candidate for academic library collections.

3874. Armed Forces Journal. Former titles (until 2002): *Armed Forces Journal International;* (until 1973): *Armed Forces Journal;* (until 1968): *The Journal of the Armed Forces;* (until 1964): *Army, Navy, Air Force Journal & Register;* Which was formed by the merger of (1950-1962): *Army, Navy, Air Force Journal;* (until 1950): *Army and Navy Journal;* (until 1924): *The American Army and Navy Journal and Gazette of the Regular, National Guard, and Reserve Forces;* (until 1921): *National Service;* Which incorporated (1915-1918): *International Military Digest;* (1961-1962): *Army-Navy-Air Force Register;* Which was formerly (until 1961): *Army-Navy-Air Force Register & Defense Times;* (until 1959): *The Army-Navy-Air Force Register;* (1879-1949): *Army and Navy Register;* Which incorporated (1949-1956): *The R O T C Journal.* [ISSN: 1559-162X] 1863. m. Free to qualified personnel. Ed(s): Tobias Naegele, Linda Monroe. Defense News Media Group, 6883 Commercial Dr, Springfield, VA 22159; custserv@defensenews.com. Illus., adv. Sample. Circ: 23380. Vol. ends: Dec. Microform: PQC. *Indexed:* A01, A22, ABS&EES, BRI. *Aud.:* Ga, Ac.

Armed Forces Journal is a respected American monthly publication geared to senior military officers and civilian defense executives both inside and outside government. Published in some form for nearly 150 years, this periodical is one of the oldest defense publications in the world. Articles are generally short and newsy but provide useful coverage of the defense industry, tactics, strategy, procurement, and public administration. Recent articles explore such topics as department of defense budget reforms, rising military health costs, and officer promotion standards. Senior serving officers provide most of the content, with frequent contributions from civilian defense officials. Despite the orientation to defense insiders, the accessibility of the articles might well appeal to a broader general public with interests in national security. *Armed Forces Journal* is highly recommended to audiences in both academic and public libraries.

3875. Armor. Former titles (until 1950): *Armored Cavalry Journal;* (until 1946): *The Cavalry Journal;* (until 1920): *United States Cavalry Association. Journal.* [ISSN: 0004-2420] 1888. bi-m. Free to qualified personnel. Armor Magazine, Bldg 9230, Room 104, 8150 Marne Road, Fort Benning, GA 31905. Illus., index. *Indexed:* A22, ABS&EES, BRI, P02. *Bk. rev.:* 5-9, 500-1,000 words. *Aud.:* Ac.

This publication is one of the oldest journals dealing with a military specialty in the U.S. armed forces. *Armor* can trace its origins to the *Journal of the United States Cavalry Association,* which first appeared in 1888. The original journal provided a forum for horse cavalry officers who were posted at widely separated frontier posts to exchange ideas about tactics, equipment, and doctrine. As the Army turned in its horses for armored vehicles, *Armor* became the official organ for the U.S. Army Armor Branch. One of the aims of the journal is to connect doctrine with practical operational experience. Articles about equipment, training, and tactics are featured, particularly if they can be connected to the Army's current operational environments. The contributors are exclusively serving officers and enlisted personnel, and many of the articles have a strong training and pedagogical focus. The issues are illustrated with photographs, charts, and high-quality pencil drawings that add to the publication's visual appeal. While aimed at a professional military audience, this journal might be of interest to enthusiasts of armored warfare in the general public, and therefore can be recommended to both public and academic libraries.

3876. *Army.* Former titles (until 1956): *The Army Combat Forces Journal;* Which incorporated (1948-1954): *Antiaircraft Journal;* Which was formerly (until 1948): *The Coast Artillery Journal;* (until 1922): *Journal of the United States Artillery;* The Army Combat Forces Journal was formerly (until 1954): *United States Army Combat Forces Journal;* Which was formed by the merger of (1910-1950): *Infantry Journal;* Which was formerly (1904-1910): *United States Infantry Association. Journal;* (1911-1950): *The Field Artillery Journal.* [ISSN: 0004-2455] 1950. m. USD 33 domestic (Free to members). Ed(s): Mary Blake French, Larry Moffi. Association of the U.S. Army, 2425 Wilson Blvd, Arlington, VA 22201; ausa-info@ausa.org; http://www.ausa.org. Illus., adv. Vol. ends: Dec. *Indexed:* A01, A22, ABS&EES, BRI, P02. *Bk. rev.:* 2-3, 500 words. *Aud.:* Ga, Ac.

A very appealing, glossy, and profusely illustrated publication that provides news and analysis of issues that impact the U.S. Army. Put out by the Association of the U.S. Army, this periodical is free to members of the association. Feature articles deal with recent operational experience, new weapons, logistics, and possible future trends in military science. Most of the articles are written by senior Army officers, with some contributions by civilians in the defense establishment. *Army* is strongly geared to an audience of serving Army officers, but much of the content may be of value to researchers and the general public. This publication can be recommended to users of both academic and public library collections.

3877. *Australian Defence Force Journal: journal of the Australian profession of arms.* Former titles (until 1991): *Defence Force Journal;* (until 1976): *Army Journal;* (until 1968): *Australian Army Journal.* [ISSN: 1320-2545] 1976. 3x/yr. Free. Ed(s): Dr. Bob Ormston. Australia. Department of Defence, PO Box 488, Kensington Park, SA 5068, Australia; FOI@defence.gov.au; http://www.defence.gov.au. Illus., index. Refereed. *Indexed:* RILM. *Bk. rev.:* 6-10, 500-1,000. *Aud.:* Ac, Sa.

Australian Defence Force Journal (*ADFJ*) is the official journal of all the branches of the Australian Defence Forces (ADF). Content focuses on strategy, tactics, logistics, and all facets of national defense. Many articles also look at the broader security contingencies in the Indian Ocean and South Pacific regions. Authors are serving officers in the ADF, academics, and civilian experts from the Department of Defence. This publication is an official Australian government publication, and all issues can be freely accessed off the *ADFJ* web site. The audience for *ADFJ* would primarily be academic, and most large university libraries should consider linking to this publication from their electronic resources pages.

3878. *Aviation History.* Former titles (until 1994): *Aviation;* (until 1993): *Aviation Heritage.* [ISSN: 1076-8858] 1990. bi-m. USD 21.95. Ed(s): Carl von Wodke. Weider History Group, 19300 Promenade Dr, Leesburg, VA 20176-6500; comments@weiderhistorygroup.com; www.historynet.com. Illus., adv. Circ: 49000. *Indexed:* A01, BRI, C37, MASUSE. *Bk. rev.:* 2-5, 500-750 words. *Aud.:* Ga.

Aviation History is a magazine that deals with the history of manned flight. Articles cover all areas of aviation including commercial, high-performance, space flight, and of course military aviation. Recent articles that focus on military aviation include "Myth of the Zero" and "Across the Hypersonic Divide." Biographical pieces on aviation pioneers, military aces, and other famous pilots are often featured. *Aviation History* is profusely illustrated with photographs and aviation art that greatly add to its appeal to general audiences. This publication would best serve users of public libraries.

3879. *Ba-Mahane.* 1948. w. Israel Defense Forces, Military Post, 01025, Israel. Adv. Circ: 70000. *Aud.:* Ga, Ac, Sa.

The Israel Defense Forces, or IDF, are the unified armed forces of the State of Israel, which includes the army, air force, and navy. *Ba-Mahane* is the official weekly publication of the IDF. This publication combines news and analysis on force readiness, tactics, strategy, and general defense issues across the Middle East. With text in Hebrew, this publication would best be suited for specialized academic collections that support programs in Jewish or Middle Eastern studies.

3880. *Blue & Gray Magazine: for those who still hear the guns.* [ISSN: 0741-2207] 1983. bi-m. USD 24.95 domestic; USD 34.95 foreign. Ed(s): David E Roth. Blue & Gray, 522 Norton Road, Columbus, OH 43228. Adv. *Bk. rev.:* 2-6, 250 words. *Aud.:* Ga, Ac.

This publication focuses exclusively on the military history of the American Civil War. The issues are thematic and center on a detailed look at a particular battle. All issues have a unique feature called the "Generals Tour" that provides an easy-chair "staff ride" around the battlefield that's being featured. The tour consists of maps, period and modern photographs, tactical information, and important human-interest stories. This feature is an interesting simulation of the "staff rides" of the early twentieth century, in which the Army War College used Civil War battlefields to teach tactical principles to its senior leaders. Much of this magazine's content is written by public historians who are affiliated with many of the Civil War sites run by the National Park Service. Other articles are written by licensed battlefield guides who are credentialed by the Park Service to give independent tours at Civil War battlefields around the country. Researchers, Civil War buffs, and the general public would find much of interest in this publication, and it can be recommended for both public and academic collections.

3881. *Die Bundeswehr.* [ISSN: 0007-5949] 1956. m. EUR 30. Ed(s): Frank Henning. Deutscher Bundeswehr-Verband e.V, Suedstr 123, Bonn, 53175, Germany; info@dbwv.de; http://www.dbwv.de. Illus., adv. Circ: 179684 Paid and controlled. *Bk. rev.:* Number and length vary. *Aud.:* Ac, Sa.

This German-language publication provides news and analysis of the Bundeswehr, the unified armed forces of the Federal Republic of Germany. *Die Bundeswehr* reports on tactics, strategy, weapons, and general force readiness. Overseas deployments as peacekeepers or in operations as part of the NATO alliance are also given extensive coverage. Published by the German Armed Forces Association, *Die Bundeswehr* also devotes large segments to social issues that impact serving armed forces members and entering recruits. The general tone can be strongly activist, with many articles advising personnel on how to apply for important benefits that come from military service. This publication would best serve large academic libraries that support collections related to NATO or German Studies.

3882. *Canadian Military Journal (Ottawa).* [ISSN: 1492-465X] 2000. q. Free. Ed(s): David Bashow. Minister of National Defence, Department of National Defence, National Defence Headquarters, Ottawa, ON K1A 0K2, Canada; http://www.forces.gc.ca/. *Indexed:* CBCARef. *Bk. rev.:* 6-10, 300-500. *Aud.:* Ac, Sa.

Canadian Military Journal/Revue Militaire Canadienne is the bilingual official publication of the Canadian Armed Forces and the civilian Department of National Defense. This publication gears content to broad issues of interest across the Canadian defense establishment. Contributors are serving officers, academics, and civilian experts. Articles from a recent issue would include "The Many Problems in Military Personnel Law and Policy," "Next Generation Fighter Club: How Shifting Markets will Shape Canada's F-35 Debate," and "The Case for Reactivating the Royal Canadian Army Veterinary Corps." This is an official publication of the Canadian government, and all of the editions have been made available to the public online at no charge. *Canadian Military Journal* is potentially of interest to a wide audience, and should be prominently linked off the web resource pages of large academic and public libraries.

3883. *Civil Wars.* [ISSN: 1369-8249] 1998. q. GBP 324 (print & online eds.). Ed(s): Edward Newman. Routledge, 4 Park Sq, Milton Park, Abingdon, OX14 4RN, United Kingdom; subscriptions@tandf.co.uk; http://www.tandfonline.com. Illus., index, adv. Sample. Refereed. Vol. ends: Winter. Reprint: PSC. *Indexed:* A01, A22, E01, IBSS, P61, RiskAb, SSA. *Aud.:* Ac.

In the post–Cold War era, civil wars have emerged as a dangerous source of international tension and instability. *Civil Wars* is an academic journal that looks at the causes, conduct, and ending of civil wars. This journal invites contributions from scholars across a broad array of disciplines, covering topics such as nation building, ethnic conflict, religious strife, and the politics of intervention. The broad interdisciplinary focus and policy-relevant material make this journal of interest to those in academia, government, and the military. *Civil Wars* can certainly be recommended for most academic library collections.

3884. Defence Journal. [ISSN: 0257-2141] 1975. m. USD 30 in Asia; USD 40 in North America; USD 45 in South America. Ed(s): M Ikram Sehgal. Defence Journal, Defence Housing Society, 16-B 7th Central St., Karachi, 75500, Pakistan. Illus., adv. Circ: 10000. *Indexed:* BAS. *Bk. rev.:* Number and length vary. *Aud.:* Ga, Ac, Sa.

In recent years, Pakistan has emerged as a key ally of the United States in the War on Terror. The Pakistani military plays an important political role in its own country and influences the ongoing war in Afghanistan. *Defence Journal* is a key periodical that reports on the military and defense establishment in Pakistan. This publication combines opinion, news, and analysis on issues that impact Pakistani defense and the broader security of the Central and South Asian regions. Contributors are journalists, academics, military officers, and important policymakers. Appealing to a potentially broad audience, *Defence Journal* would be an important addition to large public and academic libraries.

3885. Defense News. [ISSN: 0884-139X] 1986. w. Mon. USD 169 combined subscription (print & online eds.). Ed(s): Bradley Peniston, Vago Muradian. Defense News Media Group, 6883 Commercial Dr, Springfield, VA 22159; custserv@defensenews.com. Adv. *Indexed:* A22, B03. *Aud.:* Ac, Sa.

Defense News is a trade publication that reports on defense issues from an international perspective. The news section is divided into land, naval, and air warfare sections, and international news is regionally divided with sections for the Americas, Europe, Asia/Pacific Rim, and the Middle East/Africa. The articles focus heavily on the business and procurement side of the defense industry. The pages of this publication have frequent full-color ads for the latest military hardware from around the world. This publication can currently be subscribed to in both a print and online version. Civilian contractors, executives in the defense industry, and military officers concerned with supply would find this publication useful. *Defense News* can be recommended for both academic and large public library collections.

3886. European Security. [ISSN: 0966-2839] 1992. q. GBP 403 (print & online eds.). Ed(s): David J Galbreath. Routledge, 4 Park Sq, Milton Park, Abingdon, OX14 4RN, United Kingdom; subscriptions@tandf.co.uk; http://www.tandfonline.com. Adv. Sample. Refereed. Reprint: PSC. *Indexed:* A01, A22, E01, IBSS, P02, P61, RiskAb, SSA. *Bk. rev.:* Number varies. *Aud.:* Ac.

Is collective security in Europe dependent on economic integration? Does the European Union have global military reach? Can any current European state be considered a world power? *European Security* potentially tackles these questions and others that relate to the defense issues that impact the continent. While having a clear regional focus, this periodical attempts to frame discussions in a global context. Some articles in a recent special issue on the 2008 Russo–Georgian war would include "Georgia: revolution and war," "Reflections on the Rose Revolution," and "The Russo-Georgian war and beyond: towards a European great power concert." Contributors are mainly scholars in political science, international relations, and security affairs. Clearly oriented to an audience of academics and defense experts, this publication is best recommended for academic library collections.

3887. Fortitudine. Formerly (until 19??): *Harumfrodite.* [ISSN: 0362-9910] 1970. q. USD 15 domestic; USD 21 foreign; USD 3.50 per issue domestic. U.S. Marine Corps, History and Museums Division, 3079 Moreell Ave, Quantico, VA 22134; http://hqinet001.hqmc.usmc.mil/HD/. Illus. *Bk. rev.:* 7-10, 75 words. *Aud.:* Ga, Ac, Sa.

Fortitudine is a general military history bulletin that publishes historical articles about the United States Marine Corps, other branches of the U.S. military, and foreign militaries. The purpose is to "educate and train Marines on active duty in the uses of military and Marine Corps history." Issues are generally thematic, covering such topics as counterinsurgency, urban warfare, and historiography.

The most recent issue contains articles on the centennial of Marine aviation. This publication would appeal to active military and civilian audiences with an interest in military history, and is recommended for both public and academic libraries.

3888. Homeland Security Affairs. [ISSN: 1558-643X] 2005. q. Free. Ed(s): Alis Gumbiner. U.S. Naval Postgraduate School, Center for Homeland Defense and Security, I University Circle, Monterey, CA 93943-5001; http://www.chds.us/. Refereed. *Indexed:* RiskAb. *Aud.:* Ac.

Homeland Security Affairs is a scholarly journal that is the official publication of the Naval Postgraduate School Center for Homeland Defense and Security (CHDS). This free online publication provides an active forum for insightful analysis of all dimensions of U.S. homeland security. Articles are contributed by leading academics, policymakers, government officials, military officers, and CHDS faculty. Articles in a recent issue included "The All Needs Approach to Emergency Response," "The Next Meltdown? Responding to a Nuclear Accident in the Developing World," and "Pandemic Vaccine Distribution Policy for the Twenty-First Century." Geared to an audience of scholars and practitioners, *Homeland Security Affairs* would best be linked to from the electronic resource pages of large academic libraries.

3889. I H S Jane's Defence Weekly. Former titles (until 2012): *Jane's Defence Weekly;* (until 1984): *Jane's Defence Review.* [ISSN: 2048-3430] 1980. w. GBP 315 domestic; EUR 390 in Europe; USD 560 elsewhere. Ed(s): Peter Felstead. I H S Jane's, 163 Brighton Rd, Coulsdon, CR5 2YH, United Kingdom; info@janes.co.uk; http://www.janes.com. Illus., adv. Circ: 27543 Paid and controlled. *Indexed:* A22, B03, C&ISA, CerAb, EngInd. *Aud.:* Ga, Ac, Sa.

Jane's Defence Weekly is one of the more respected publications that reports on defense and national security from an international perspective. News and analysis are combined to cover all elements of the contemporary military scene. A large bulk of the news content is divided by region, which includes the Americas, Europe, Asia/Pacific, and Middle East/Africa. "Armed Forces," "Network-Centric Warfare," "Homeland Security," "Business," and "Analysis" are some of the other sections that have regular features. Illustrations and other visual material enhance the text, making the publication glossy and visually appealing in both its print and digital formats. While it certainly strives to be authoritative, this publication's emphasis is often on military technology, and the related specialized terminology may very well baffle readers who come to it without a strong military background. Potentially a core resource for academic libraries, particularly those that support programs in political science or international relations. Some public libraries may also find this publication useful in serving users with an interest in military affairs and technology.

3890. Indian Defence Review. [ISSN: 0970-2512] 1986. 4x/yr. USD 100. Ed(s): Bharat Verma. Lancer Publishers & Distributors, 56 Gautam Nagar, New Delhi, 110 049, India; lancer@ndb.vsnl.net.in; http://www.bharat-rakshak.com. Adv. Refereed. Circ: 4000. *Bk. rev.:* Number varies; 200-500 words. *Aud.:* Ac, Sa.

Indian Defence Review is a respected periodical that deals with national security issues in India. This publication offers news and insightful analysis on the Indian military and broader security affairs for the South Asian region. Contributors are high-ranking military officers, academics, and journalists. The emergence of India as a regional power, its growing problem of domestic terrorism, and its ongoing conflict with Pakistan give this periodical a potentially wide audience. Large public and academic libraries should consider obtaining this publication.

3891. Infantry: a professional bulletin for the U.S. Army infantryman. Former titles (until 1957): *Infantry School Quarterly;* (until 1947): *The Infantry School Mailing List;* (until 1934): *Infantry School. Mailing List.* [ISSN: 0019-9532] 1930. bi-m. U.S. Army Infantry School, PO Box 52005, Ft. Benning, GA 31995; http://www.infantry.army.mil/infantry/index.asp. Microform: PQC. *Indexed:* A22, BRI, P02. *Bk. rev.:* 2 per issue. *Aud.:* Ac, Sa.

Often called the "Queen of Battle," the infantry carries the fight to the enemy. The infantry is the primary way that the Army projects its power and completes its mission of taking and holding ground. *Infantry* is the professional bulletin of the U.S. Army Infantry School at Fort Benning, Georgia. This is one of the older professional publications in the U.S. military, with a publishing history that goes back to 1930. The articles are heavily focused on training and pedagogy, with a strong applicability to current experience. Contributors are overwhelmingly serving officers and senior enlisted personnel. While certainly geared to serving infantrymen, *Infantry* may find an audience among researchers and civilians who want an inside look at military culture. Recommended for academic and larger public library collections.

3892. *International Journal of Intelligence and Counterintelligence.*
[ISSN: 0885-0607] 1986. q. GBP 259 (print & online eds.). Ed(s): Richard R Valcourt. Taylor & Francis Inc., 325 Chestnut St, Ste 800, Philadelphia, PA 19106; customerservice@taylorandfrancis.com; http://www.tandfonline.com. Illus., adv. Sample. Refereed. Reprint: PSC. *Indexed:* A22, E01, P61, RiskAb. *Bk. rev.:* 4 per issue. *Aud.:* Ac, Sa.

Intelligence is the pivot on which military and national security decisions are often made. This scholarly publication serves as a forum for scholars and professionals to exchange ideas on intelligence. Its emphasis is clearly on contemporary experience, but this publication is also a good resource for past and historical uses of intelligence. The articles are interdisciplinary and reflect a wide range of approaches and opinions. This publication would be best for large academic research collections, particularly those that support programs in national security studies or international relations.

3893. *Jiefangjun Huabao.* [ISSN: 0009-3823] 1951. m. USD 144.
Jiefangjun Baoshe, 40 Sanlihe Lu, Ganjiakou, Beijing, 100037, China. Illus. *Aud.:* Ga, Ac, Sa.

The People's Liberation Army (PLA) is the title for the unified armed forces of The People's Republic of China, which consist of the army, navy, air force, strategic missile forces, and militia. The PLA is the largest military force in the world, with 3 million active members and millions more in reserve components. *Jiefangjun Huabao* is a Chinese-language monthly that reports on all branches of the military. Combining news with light analysis, this publication provides an interesting perspective on current Chinese military culture. A major strength of *Jienfangjung Huabao* is the glossy illustrations of personnel and hardware that come with each monthly issue. This is a government publication, and the content still reflects the official Marxism of most Chinese governing institutions. Given the language and area of focus, this publication would be best suited for larger academic libraries, particularly those that have collections that support large Asian Studies programs.

3894. *Joint Force Quarterly.* [ISSN: 1070-0692] 1993. q. USD 20 domestic; USD 28 foreign; USD 15 per issue domestic. Ed(s): Jeffrey D Smotherman, Robert E Henstrand. National Defense University, Fort Lesley J McNair, 300 Fifth Ave. Bldg 62, Washington, DC 20319; ndupress@ndu.edu; http://www.ndu.edu. Illus., index. Sample. *Indexed:* A01, A22, ABS&EES, BRI. *Bk. rev.:* 4, 500 words. *Aud.:* Ac.

Joint Force Quarterly discusses the use of air, land, space, and sea forces in an integrated operational environment. This publication also focuses on the problems and complexities of coalition warfare, interservice coordination, and organizing unified commands. Prepared for the Joint Chiefs of Staff by the Institute for National Strategic Studies, National Defense University, *Joint Force Quarterly* can be regarded as an important official organ for American strategic military doctrine. Recent articles include "Sailing into the 21st Century: Operating Forward, Strengthening Partnerships" and "Building Resiliency into the National Military Strategy." Most of the contributors are high-ranking officers from all branches of the armed services, many of them involved in high-level planning or in leadership positions in unified commands. *Joint Force Quarterly* is an official U.S. government publication, and current and back issues are available free to the public online. This journal would make a useful link from the electronic resources pages of both academic and large public libraries.

3895. *Journal of Military History.* Former titles (until 1989): *Military Affairs;* (until 1941): *American Military Institute. Journal;* (until 1939): *American Military History Foundation. Journal.* [ISSN: 0899-3718] 1937. q. Free to members. Ed(s): Bruce Vandervort. Society for Military

History, George C Marshall Library, Virginia Military Institute, Lexington, VA 24450; http://www.smh-hq.org. Illus., index, adv. Sample. Refereed. Vol. ends: Oct. *Indexed:* A01, A22, ABS&EES, AmHI, ArtHuCI, BAS, BRI, CBRI, E01, MLA-IB, P02. *Bk. rev.:* Number varies; 200-300 words. *Aud.:* Ga, Ac.

This publication is one of the most scholarly and respected titles for general military history. All time periods and geographic areas are examined. At the heart of every issue are detailed and highly researched articles that increasingly use more social-history–based methodologies. Most of the articles are written by historians, with some contributions by academics in other social sciences or humanities fields. One of the strengths of this journal is the 50–60 book reviews that appear in each issue and cover a wide range of military history titles. Copies of the print and electronic versions of the journal are distributed to individuals and organizations for free that are members of the Society of Military History. Many libraries can get complete electronic access through their subscriptions to any of the EBSCOhost databases that index the journal. The academic and research focus of this publication make it far more suitable to audiences served by college and university libraries.

3896. *The Journal of Slavic Military Studies.* Formerly (until 1993): *Journal of Soviet Military Studies.* [ISSN: 1351-8046] 1988. q. GBP 474 (print & online eds.). Ed(s): David M Glantz, Christopher Donnelly. Routledge, 4 Park Sq, Milton Park, Abingdon, OX14 4RN, United Kingdom; subscriptions@tandf.co.uk; http://www.tandfonline.com. Illus., adv. Sample. Refereed. Reprint: PSC. *Indexed:* A01, A22, ABS&EES, E01, IBSS, P02, P61, SSA. *Bk. rev.:* Number varies; 200-600. *Aud.:* Ac.

The Journal of Slavic Military Studies is an academic journal that examines military affairs in Central and Eastern Europe. While it covers security issues for this whole region, the emphasis is clearly on Russia. This journal combines views of the contemporary scene with historical perspectives. Some articles from a recent issue would include "Why and How States Open Frontiers," "Ukraine's Maritime Power in the Black Sea: A Terminal Decline?," and "On the Issue of Using Asphyxiating Gas in the Suppression of the Tambov Uprising." Clearly oriented to a specialized audience, this publication would be best suited to academic library collections.

3897. *The Journal of Strategic Studies.* [ISSN: 0140-2390] 1978. bi-m. GBP 700 (print & online eds.). Ed(s): Joe A Maiolo, Thomas G Mahnken. Routledge, 4 Park Sq, Milton Park, Abingdon, OX14 4RN, United Kingdom; subscriptions@tandf.co.uk; http://www.tandfonline.com. Illus., index, adv. Sample. Refereed. Microform: PQC. Reprint: PSC. *Indexed:* A01, A22, AmHI, BAS, E01, IBSS, P02, P61, SSA. *Bk. rev.:* 3-4, 500 words. *Aud.:* Ac.

The Journal of Strategic Studies is a scholarly publication that seeks to combine theoretical and historical approaches to strategy, defense policy, and the study of warfare. Articles are very heavily researched and are mainly written by academics from a wide range of disciplines and methodological perspectives. Some articles in a recent issue would include "China's Global Equity Oil Investments: Economic and Geopolitical Influence" and "Revisiting J.C. Wylie's Dichotomy of Strategy: The Effects of Sequential and Cumulative Patterns of Operations." The heavy academic and research tone of this journal would make it highly suitable to most academic library collections.

3898. *The Korean Journal of Defense Analysis.* [ISSN: 1016-3271] 1989. q. KRW 35000. Ed(s): Tae-am Ohm. Korea Institute for Defense Analyses, 37 Hoegiro, Dongdaemun-gu, Seoul, 130-871, Korea, Republic of; wklee@kida.re.kr; http://www.kida.re.kr/. Refereed. Reprint: PSC. *Indexed:* BAS, P61, SSA. *Bk. rev.:* Number varies; 300-600 words. *Aud.:* Ac.

This scholarly publication provides analysis of defense issues for the Korean peninsula and the Northeast Asian region. *The Korean Journal of Defense Analysis* pays particular attention to the security and military posture of South Korea (ROK). Much of this treatment looks at South Korea as a regional military power and key geopolitical player for the entire Pacific Rim. Authors are primarily academics with some contributions coming from high-ranking military officers and civilian policymakers. This publication would be best suited to academic libraries, particularly those that support programs in Asian Studies.

3899. *Leatherneck: magazine of the Marines.* Formerly (until 19??): *Quantico Leatherneck.* [ISSN: 0023-981X] 1917. m. Free to members. Ed(s): Walter G Ford. Marine Corps Association, 715 Broadway St, PO Box 1775, Quantico, VA 22134; mca@mca-marines.org; http://www.mca-marines.org. Illus., index, adv. Sample. Circ: 86857 Paid. Vol. ends: Dec. Microform: PQC. *Indexed:* A22. *Bk. rev.:* 5, 200 words. *Aud.:* Ga.

Leatherneck aims to be "the magazine of Marines yesterday, today, and tomorrow." Put out by the Marine Corps Association, this publication is one of the older service publications in the U.S. military with origins going back to 1917. The magazine mostly covers current news of specific interest to Marines, including reports on new weapons, technology, and current conflicts. Articles about general Marine Corps history and personal stories from past wars are also featured. Most of the contributors are serving or retired Marines, both officers and enlisted. Free print and online access to the magazine comes with paid membership in the Marine Corps Association. The general tone and orientation of this publication make it a ideal choice for public library collections of all sizes.

3900. *M H Q: the quarterly journal of military history.* [ISSN: 1040-5992] 1988. q. USD 39.95. Weider History Group, 19300 Promenade Dr, Leesburg, VA 20176-6500; comments@weiderhistorygroup.com; www.historynet.com. Illus., index, adv. Circ: 22000. Vol. ends: Summer. *Indexed:* BRI, MLA-IB. *Bk. rev.:* 2-4, 200-300 words. *Aud.:* Hs, Ga.

MHQ is a highly respected military history publication aimed at a general audience. The articles cover all eras and nations and are very well written and accessible. Some feature articles that appeared in a recent issue include "Rommel's Afrika Korps" and "Ten Minutes at Midway." The contributors are historians, military experts, freelance writers, and the staff of *MHQ*. A column that looks at the origins of military jargon, a book review section, and a regular article on war art are some of the special features of the magazine. This glossy publication is profusely illustrated, which greatly enhances the overall appeal. *MHQ* would be a suitable choice for public library collections of all types.

3901. *Marine Corps Gazette: the professional journal for United States Marines.* [ISSN: 0025-3170] 1916. m. Free to members. Ed(s): John A Keenan. Marine Corps Association, 715 Broadway St, PO Box 1775, Quantico, VA 22134; mca@mca-marines.org; http://www.mca-marines.org. Illus., index, adv. Sample. Circ: 29731. Vol. ends: Dec. Microform: PQC. *Indexed:* A22, BRI, CBRI, P02. *Bk. rev.:* 6, 300-750 words. *Aud.:* Ga, Ac.

Known as "the *Gazette*," this publication is the professional journal for the Marine Corps. Like its news magazine counterpart *Leatherneck*, this is one of the older publications in the military, dating back to 1916. The *Gazette* shares with other professional military publications a desire to link theory and doctrine with practical experience. Articles in a recent issue include "The Officer PME Continuum" and "Building Experts in the Marine Corps." The articles are overwhelmingly written by serving Marine officers, with some contribution from senior enlisted personnel. Published by the Marine Corps Association, the *Gazette* comes free with membership to the association. This publication would have much of interest for audiences in both public and academic libraries.

3902. *Militaergeschichtliche Zeitschrift.* Formerly (until 2000): *Militaergeschichtliche Mitteilungen.* [ISSN: 2193-2336] 1967. s-a. EUR 39.80. Ed(s): Winfried Heinemann, Hans Ehlert. Oldenbourg Wissenschaftsverlag GmbH, Rosenheimer Str 145, Munich, 81671, Germany; orders@oldenbourg.de; http://www.oldenbourg.de. Illus., adv. Refereed. Circ: 1400 Paid and controlled. Reprint: SCH. *Indexed:* ArtHuCI. *Aud.:* Ac, Sa.

This German-language publication is a respected European periodical that deals with general military history. Reflecting a wide range of topics drawn from all periods of history, *Militaergeschichtliche Zeitschrift* seeks to view the changing interaction between conflict, culture, society, and the military. This publication is strongly academic, welcoming a variety of social-history–oriented approaches. Authors are historians or other academics from social science disciplines. The strong research orientation of this publication should make it a candidate for academic library collections that support specialized programs in military history.

3903. *Military: WWII, Korea, Vietnam, Cold War & Today.* Formerly: *Military History Review.* [ISSN: 1046-2511] 1985. m. USD 21 domestic. Ed(s): John Shank. M H R Publishing Corp., 2122 28 St, Sacramento, CA 95818; editor@milmag.com. Illus. Sample. *Bk. rev.:* 8-10, 200-600 words. *Aud.:* Ga.

This publication is unique in that it seeks to use its subscribers as its base of writers. The editors actively invite accounts from former servicemen and women that span all of America's recent wars from World II to the present. The intent seems to be to reverse the trend in writing about military history that makes it an exclusive club for academics, statesman, and high-ranking military officers. The feature articles are mostly firsthand accounts written by active subscribers. Readers can also contribute book reviews and offer opinions in the magazine's regular sections "Sound Off" and "Intercom." It must be noted that the bulk of the editorial content is openly pro-defense and strongly conservative. The firsthand accounts would make this publication attractive to a wide audience, and this journal deserves consideration by public libraries of all sizes.

3904. *Military Collector & Historian.* [ISSN: 0026-3966] 1949. q. Free to members. Company of Military Historians HQ and Museum, PO Box 910, Rutland, MA 01543; cmhhq@aol.com; http://www.military-historians.org. Illus., adv. Microform: PQC. *Indexed:* A22, RILM. *Bk. rev.:* 3-6, 250-750 words. *Aud.:* Ac, Sa.

This is one of the principal periodicals dealing with the history of uniforms, colors, standards, traditions, and weapons of all branches of the United States military. *Military Collector & Historian* also covers the armed forces of other nations that have served in the Western Hemisphere at different times in the past. Published by The Company of Military Historians, this magazine comes with membership and reports on the activities of the organization and provides a forum for members. Contributors are very eclectic and include historians, collectors, archivists, antiquarians, museum people, and members of the military. Beautiful color and black-and-white plates appear in every issue and contribute greatly to the quality and overall appeal of the magazine. Recommended for libraries of all types.

3905. *Military History.* [ISSN: 0889-7328] 1984. bi-m. USD 21.95. Ed(s): Mike Robbins. Weider History Group, 19300 Promenade Dr, Leesburg, VA 20176-6500; comments@weiderhistorygroup.com; www.historynet.com. Adv. Circ: 73500. *Indexed:* A01, A22, BRI, MASUSE, P02. *Bk. rev.:* 3-5, 250-700 words. *Aud.:* Ga.

Military History is one of the most popular publications devoted to general military history. All types of warfare from antiquity to the present day are covered in this publication. Contributors are historians, journalists, military enthusiasts, and freelance writers. The feature articles are very traditional, mostly focusing on great battles or noted people. Recent articles include "American Proconsul: How Douglas MacArthur Shaped Postwar Japan," "War of 1812: Big Night in Baltimore," and "Emory Upton and the Shaping of the U.S. Army." Personality profiles, espionage, weaponry, and firsthand interviews are regular features of the magazine. Frequent and high-quality illustrations grace the pages of *Military History,* making it very attractive to general audiences. This publication would be appropriate for public library collections of all sizes.

3906. *Military Review (English Edition): the professional journal of the United States Army.* Former titles (until 1939): *The Command and General Staff School Quarterly;* (until 1936): *Review of Military Literature;* (until 1933): *Quarterly Review of Military Literature;* (until 1932): *Review of Current Military Literature;* (until 1931): *Review of Current Military Writings;* (until 1925): *Instructor's Summary of Military Articles.* [ISSN: 0026-4148] 1922. bi-m. U.S. Army Combined Arms Center, 294 Grant Ave, Bldg 77, Fort Leavenworth, KS 66027; leav-milrevweb@conus.army.mil; http://usacac.army.mil/CAC2/. Illus., index, adv. Sample. Vol. ends: Dec. Microform: PQC. *Indexed:* A01, A22, ABS&EES, BAS, BRI, P02. *Bk. rev.:* 6-11, 200-300 words. *Aud.:* Ga, Ac.

This publication is the professional journal of the U.S. Army. The purpose of *Military Review* is to provide a forum for exchanging ideas and innovations about doctrine, mostly on the tactical and operational level. The content is mostly geared to the Army's current missions and operational environments. A number of historical articles appear that may have particular lessons for preparedness or current combat operations. Articles are mostly contributed by serving Army officers or credentialed scholars. This title also has substantial book reviews that cover military history or national security titles. The audience is highly geared to field-grade officers that are in many cases commanding troops in active operations. *Military Review* is published in Spanish, Portuguese, and Arabic-language editions. The current and back editions of this journal are now available for free online, and both academic and public libraries should consider linking to this title from their electronic resources pages.

3907. *N A T O Review (Online).* [ISSN: 1608-7569] 1998. q. Free. Ed(s): Christopher Bennett. North Atlantic Treaty Organization (N A T O), Office of Information and Press, Blvd Leopold III, Brussels, 1110, Belgium; natodoc@hq.nato.int; http://www.nato.int. *Aud.:* Ga, Ac, Sa.

NATO Review is the official periodical of the North Atlantic Treaty Organization (NATO). The current incarnation of this publication is an online successor to a print periodical that ceased in 2003. Access to the online version is free, and this version has links to earlier versions of both the online and print editions going back to 1991. *NATO Review* provides both news and analysis on the state of the organization, European security, and the projection of the alliance outside of Europe. Contributors are academics, senior policy makers, alliance officials, and high-ranking military officers from member states. This publication would be a valuable link from the electronic resources pages of large academic and public libraries.

3908. *National Guard.* Former titles (until 1978): *Guardsman;* (until 1975): *National Guardsman.* [ISSN: 0163-3945] 1947. m. Free to members; Non-members, USD 25. Ed(s): Ron Jensen. National Guard Association of the United States, One Massachusetts Ave, NW, Washington, DC 20001; ngaus@ngaus.org; http://www.ngaus.org. Illus., adv. Vol. ends: Dec. Microform: PQC. *Indexed:* A01, A22, P02. *Aud.:* Ga.

National Guard highlights the role that the Guard plays in the overall structure of national defense in the United States. Articles are newsy and often focus on the political and budgetary climate the Guard faces in both Washington and the states. Contributors are journalists, freelance writers, and current members of the Guard. Published by the National Guard Association, this magazine is distributed free for members. Given the role the Guard has played in the wars in both Iraq and Afghanistan, this publication may be on interest to a broader audience, and can be recommended to both public and academic libraries.

3909. *Naval History.* [ISSN: 1042-1920] 1987. bi-m. Free to members; Non-members, USD 35. U S Naval Institute, 291 Wood Rd, Annapolis, MD 21402; customer@usni.org; http://www.usni.org. Illus., adv. *Indexed:* A01, ABS&EES, P02. *Bk. rev.:* 1-2; 250-500 words. *Aud.:* Ga, Ac.

This title deals with the general naval history of the United States and the world. Published by the U.S. Naval Institute, *Naval History* is profusely illustrated and provides high-quality feature articles for a general audience. Many of the articles are oral histories of participants in past conflicts, profiles of historic vessels, and detailed descriptions of important naval actions. Some of the articles in a recent issue covered the War of 1812 at sea, including "The War's Pervasive Naval Dimensions," "America's Frigate Triumphs," and "The Constitution's Great Escape." The articles are written by historians, independent scholars, freelance writers, and both active-duty and retired military. This publication would be a good addition to any public library collection.

3910. *Naval War College Review.* [ISSN: 0028-1484] 1948. q. Free to qualified personnel. Ed(s): Pelham G Boyer. U.S. Naval War College, 686 Cushing Rd, Newport, RI 02841; PAO@usnwc.edu; http://www.nwc.navy.mil. Illus., index. Sample. Microform: BHP; MIM; PQC. *Indexed:* A01, A22, ABS&EES, BAS, BRI, CBRI, P02, P61, SSA. *Bk. rev.:* 20-25, 300-500 words. *Aud.:* Ac.

This title is the official research journal of the U.S. Naval War College. Articles are academic and reflect the interests and mission of the War College as the primary training ground for the Navy's senior leadership. Articles generally focus on current naval affairs, but considerable attention is also given to public-policy issues related to national defense. Contributors are senior naval officers, civilian policy-makers, and leading scholars. Essay-length book reviews generally include naval and general military titles. Beautifully illustrated naval

art and photographs appear on the cover of each issue. In its print form, this publication was long a staple of federal depository collections, and now most issues are available online for free. Most recently (Spring 2012), whole issues of the online versions can now be downloaded to any e-reader that can display pdf files, and such readers would include platforms like Nooks, iPads, Droids, and Kindle devices. *Naval War College Review* should be linked prominently from the electronic resources pages of academic library collections.

3911. *Parameters (Carlisle).* [ISSN: 0031-1723] 1971. q. USD 26 domestic (Free to qualified personnel). Ed(s): Col. Robert H Taylor. U.S. Army, War College, 122 Forbes Ave, Carlisle, PA 17013; carl_atwc-cpa@conus.army.mil. Illus., index. Sample. Refereed. Vol. ends: Winter. Microform: PQC. *Indexed:* A01, A22, ABS&EES, BRI, CBRI, P02, P61, SSA. *Bk. rev.:* 4-13, 500-1,000 words. *Aud.:* Ac.

Parameters is the professional publication of the U.S. Army War College and seeks to encourage reflection on the strategic dimensions of warfare on land. The audience comprises senior army officers and civilian policy-makers from the Department of Defense. Several feature articles appear in each issue. Recent articles include "What not to Learn from Afghanistan" and "Chaos as Strategy." The articles are written by Army officers, leading scholars, and the faculty of the college. The articles are well written and relevant, and are published with the highest standards of documentation and research. Nearly essay-length book reviews will cover 10–15 mostly military titles in each issue. This is clearly an important, core publication, and it should find its way into most academic collections.

3912. *R U S I Journal.* Former titles (until 1972): *Royal United Services Institute for Defence Studies. Journal;* (until 1971): *Royal United Service Institution. Journal;* (until 1860): *United Service Institution. Journal.* [ISSN: 0307-1847] 1857. bi-m. Ed(s): Emma De Angelis. Routledge, 4 Park Sq, Milton Park, Abingdon, OX14 4RN, United Kingdom; subscriptions@tandf.co.uk; http://www.tandfonline.com. Illus., adv. Sample. Vol. ends: Dec. Microform: PQC. Reprint: PSC. *Indexed:* A22, E01, P02. *Bk. rev.:* Number varies. *Aud.:* Ac.

The *RUSI Journal* is the official publication of the Royal United Services Institute and provides an interesting mirror on British thinking on military and security affairs. First published in 1857, this publication is the oldest unified military and defense periodical in the world. Every bimonthly issue contains 10–12 articles on contemporary national defense affairs, and also includes regular features on military history, book reviews, and critiques of the arts. Contributors are high-ranking military officers, currently serving government ministers, academics, and "defence insiders." Despite the journal's high price tag, the articles are of exceptional quality, providing a valuable perspective from a key American ally. The *RUSI Journal* should be strongly considered for academic library collections of all types.

3913. *Revue Defense Nationale.* Former titles (until 2010): *Defense Nationale et Securite Collective;* (until 2005): *Defense Nationale;* (until 1973): *Revue de Defense Nationale.* [ISSN: 2105-7508] 1939. m. EUR 90 domestic; EUR 90 DOM-TOM; EUR 120 in the European Union. Ed(s): Jean Dufourcq. Comite d'Etudes de Defense Nationale, BP 8607, Paris, 75325 Cedex 07, France; cednrevu@worldnet.fr. Circ: 6000. *Indexed:* A22, BAS, IBSS, P61. *Aud.:* Ac, Sa.

Revue Defense Nationale is a French-language periodical that addresses military, strategic, and defense issues as they relate to France. It also publishes articles that deal with broader European security, the NATO alliance, international peacekeeping, and stability in the developing world. Authors are academics, policymakers, defense officials, and military officers. Given the professional and specialized focus, this periodical would be recommended for academic libraries, particularly those that support collections in French or European Studies.

3914. *Russian Military Review.* 2004. m. USD 385. Ed(s): Fyodor Kozanchuk. Rossiiskoe Agentstvo Mezhdunarodnoi Informatsii R I A Novosti, Zubovskii bulv 4, Moscow, 119021, Russian Federation; marketing@rian.ru; http://en.rian.ru. *Aud.:* Ac, Sa.

Russian Military Review is the English-language version of *Rossiiskoe Voennoe Obozrenie,* the official theoretical and analytical magazine of the Ministry of Defense of the Russian Federation. This monthly publication covers all branches of the military and offers an interesting window into the Russian perspective on defense and security. Articles are dense, mostly focusing on very specialized operational topics, and geared to an audience of military practitioners. Authors are high-ranking military officers, academics, and defense officials. While interest in Russian military affairs has waned since the collapse of the Soviet Union in 1991, most large academic collections could still benefit from this publication.

3915. Sea Power. Formerly (until 1971): *Navy;* (until 1958): *Now Hear This.* [ISSN: 0199-1337] 1949. m. USD 58 domestic; USD 145 foreign; USD 5 per issue domestic. Ed(s): Amy Wittman, Richard R Burgess. Navy League of the United States, 2300 Wilson Blvd, Arlington, VA 22201; http://www.navyleague.org. Illus., adv. Microform: PQC. *Indexed:* A01, A22, ABS&EES, BRI, P02. *Aud.:* Ga, Ac.

Sea Power is the voice of the Navy League, a group of citizens that support a vigorous and strong maritime defense for the United States. Articles talk about such topics as technology, satellite reconnaissance, coastal defense, shipping lanes, and port security. In January, an annual almanac issue profiles the mission and organizational structure of the principal maritime services, which would include the Coast Guard, Navy, Marine Corps, and the Merchant Marine. The main audience comprises members of the military and those of the general public who have an interest in maritime security. Recommended for both academic and public library collections.

3916. Small Wars and Insurgencies. Incorporates (1992-2005): *Low Intensity Conflict & Law Enforcement.* [ISSN: 0959-2318] 1990. 5x/yr. GBP 597 (print & online eds.). Ed(s): Paul B Rich, Thomas Mockaitis. Routledge, 4 Park Sq, Milton Park, Abingdon, OX14 4RN, United Kingdom; subscriptions@tandf.co.uk; http://www.tandfonline.com. Adv. Sample. Refereed. Reprint: PSC. *Indexed:* A22, BAS, E01, IBSS, P02, P61, RiskAb, SSA. *Bk. rev.:* Number varies. *Aud.:* Ac.

Terrorism, insurgency, and civil wars are increasingly replacing state-to-state conflict as the face of war in the contemporary world. The U.S. military and militaries around the world are making a difficult transition to respond to this growing contingency. *Small Wars and Insurgencies* is an interesting academic journal that addresses the political, social, and psychological implications of conflict at this level. It is clearly designed as a forum for academics, military professionals, policymakers, and law enforcement officials to air out many of the concerns of preparing and engaging in current or future low-level threats. Many of the issues are thematic, with some recent themes tackling civil/military relations in insurgencies and Russia's war in Georgia. Academic libraries would benefit the most from having this publication, but given the relevance of the topic, many larger public libraries might also consider this journal for their collections.

3917. Soldiers. Former titles (until 1971): *Army Digest;* (until 1966): *Army Information Digest;* (until 1946): *I & E Digest.* [ISSN: 0093-8440] 1946. m. USD 46 domestic; USD 64 foreign; USD 7 per issue domestic. Ed(s): Carrie McLeroy, David Vergun. U.S. Department of the Army, Soldiers Media Center, Box 31, 2511, Arlington, VA 22202; APDFCMP@conus.army.mil; http://www.army.mil. Illus., index. Microform: PQC. *Indexed:* A22, ABS&EES, BAS, BRI, P02. *Aud.:* Ga, Ac, Sa.

Soldiers is the official publication of the U.S. Army. It features reports on recruitment, training, substance abuse, health benefits, and current news about what's happening within the Army community. The content is generally short, and much of it is practical advice for enlisted soldiers for managing their careers or exiting the military. The main audience consists of current soldiers, but the focus is broad enough to appeal to the general public or young people thinking of enlisting in the Army. The last print versions of *Soldiers* appeared at the end of 2011, and currently the magazine is available to the public for free online. This publication would be most appropriately linked from the electronic resources pages in public libraries.

3918. Special Warfare. [ISSN: 1058-0123] 1988. bi-m. Ed(s): Jerry D Steelman. John F. Kennedy Special Warfare Center and School, AOJK-DTD-MP, USAJFKSWCS, Ft. Bragg, NC 28310; steelman@soc.mil; http://www.training.sfahq.com/. *Indexed:* ABS&EES, BRI, P02. *Bk. rev.:* 2; 750-1,000 words. *Aud.:* Ac, Sa.

The Green Berets, Delta Force, and Airborne Rangers are parts of the U.S. Army's special-operations community. The roles of special-ops are broad, with missions that include commando operations, intelligence gathering, reconnaissance, and civil affairs activities. *Special Warfare* is the official publication of this elite segment of the Army. Articles focus on current experience and cover topics like small-unit tactics, training, insertion techniques, equipment, and new weapons systems. Color illustrations, charts, and graphs make this title visually appealing. Much of the content is written by members of the editorial staff and currently serving members of Army special-ops units. Contributions by civilian policy-makers and academic researchers are also encouraged. Clearly, the primary audience would be members of this elite community, but the popular mystique that surrounds special forces would give this title a wider civilian readership. Since 2010, *Special Warfare* has been distributed in an online format only, and both public and academic libraries should consider linking to this publication from their electronic resources pages.

3919. Strategic Balance in the Middle East. 1972. m. USD 800. Ed(s): Pierre Shammas. Arab Press Service, PO Box 23896, Nicosia, Cyprus; apsnews@spidernet.com.cy. *Aud.:* Ac.

This English-language publication from the Arab Press Service (APS) offers intelligence on the military and strategic picture in the Middle East. Military analysis and surveys are provided for the Arab nations, Israel, Iran, Russia, and the United States. APS news reports and updates on defense-related issues in the region are also included as part of the monthly issues. Taken together, the content of this publication gives an important perspective on security questions from an Arab point of view. Given the focus and high cost of subscription, this publication would best support specialized academic libraries that collect heavily in Middle Eastern Studies.

3920. Survival (Abingdon). [ISSN: 0039-6338] 1959. bi-m. GBP 403 (print & online eds.). Ed(s): Jeffrey Mazo, Dana Allin. Routledge, 4 Park Sq, Milton Park, Abingdon, OX14 4RN, United Kingdom; subscriptions@tandf.co.uk; http://www.tandfonline.com. Adv. Sample. Refereed. Microform: PQC. Reprint: PSC. *Indexed:* A01, A22, BAS, BRI, E01, IBSS, P02, P61, SSA. *Bk. rev.:* 1-5 per issue. *Aud.:* Ac.

Published by the International Institute of Strategic Studies, *Survival* provides scholarly discussion of defense and strategic affairs. The focus is on current issues that may potentially be driving conflicts around the world. Content is contributed mainly by leading scholars in the areas of political science, defense studies, history, law, and international relations. The articles are well written, and a peer selection process is used to ensure high standards of documentation and research. This publication is recommended for academic library collections.

3921. U S Naval Institute. Proceedings. Incorporates (1963-1969): *Naval Review;* Formerly (until 1879): *United States Naval Institute. Record.* [ISSN: 0041-798X] 1874. m. Free to members. U S Naval Institute, 291 Wood Rd, Annapolis, MD 21402; customer@usni.org; http://www.usni.org. Illus., index, adv. Circ: 59378. Vol. ends: Dec. Microform: PQC. *Indexed:* A01, A22, ABS&EES, BAS, MLA-IB, P02. *Bk. rev.:* 3, 500-1,000 words. *Aud.:* Ga, Ac.

Another title published by the United States Naval Institute, *Proceedings* focuses on contemporary maritime issues as they relate to the U.S. Navy, Coast Guard, and Marines. With origins going back to 1874, this is one of the oldest periodicals that deals with naval affairs. *Proceedings* provides a rigorous forum for refining doctrine, appraising technology, assessing current practices, and critically debating maritime security. Articles in a recent issue included "Rethinking the Strait of Hormuz," "Russia's World Turned Upside Down," and "30 years after the Falklands War." The articles are contributed by serving military officers, civilian experts, and credentialed scholars. This publication is geared to audiences who are directly involved with national security, or to members of the general public who are interested in naval thinking and practice. Highly recommended to both academic and public library collections.

3922. *Vietnam.* [ISSN: 1046-2902] 1988. bi-m. USD 21.95. Weider History Group, 19300 Promenade Dr, Leesburg, VA 20176-6500; comments@weiderhistorygroup.com; www.historynet.com. Illus., adv. Sample. Circ: 36000. *Indexed:* A22, BRI. *Bk. rev.:* Number varies; 250-600 words. *Aud.:* Ga.

This publication offers interesting articles for a popular audience on the Vietnam War. Content is strongly oriented to the military dimension of the war, and less attention is given to the societal aspects of the conflict. Photographs and profuse illustrations are an attractive part of each issue. Contributors are military historians, veterans, and freelance writers. Aimed at general audiences, this title would be of interest to public library collections of all types.

3923. *War & Society.* [ISSN: 0729-2473] 1983. 3x/yr. GBP 256 (print & online eds.). Ed(s): Jeffrey Grey. Maney Publishing, Ste 1C, Joseph's Well, Hanover Walk, Leeds, LS3 1AB, United Kingdom; maney@maneypublishing.com; http://maneypublishing.com/. Adv. Refereed. Circ: 500. Reprint: PSC. *Indexed:* A22, ArtHuCI, BAS. *Aud.:* Ac.

This respected military-history periodical publishes articles on the social impacts of war and conflict. *War & Society* encourages a broad range of methodological approaches in coming to new and innovative understandings of socially driven topics that are drawn from all periods of military history. Authors are mostly historians, with other contributors coming from social science fields. A recent thematic issue covered the social history of civilians and combatants in twentieth-century wars in Asia. The content of this publication is heavily geared to specialists or members of the general public with more than a casual interest in history. Given the academic thrust of the articles, this periodical would be best suited to academic library collections.

3924. *War in History.* [ISSN: 0968-3445] 1994. q. USD 653. Ed(s): Dennis Showalter, Hew Strachan. Sage Publications Ltd., 1 Oliver's Yard, 55 City Rd, London, EC1Y 1SP, United Kingdom; info@sagepub.co.uk; http://www.uk.sagepub.com. Illus. Sample. Refereed. Reprint: PSC. *Indexed:* A01, A22, AmHI, ArtHuCI, E01. *Bk. rev.:* 15-35 per issue. *Aud.:* Ac.

War in History moves away from the more battle-related and biographical narratives of traditional military history and attempts to put things in a broader context that accounts for political, economic, and social factors. Highly academic and scholarly, this publication looks for innovative approaches that can contribute new interpretations for all periods of warfare. Contributors are overwhelmingly historians, and the articles are all highly documented and researched. Recent articles include "Reappraising Late Medieval Strategy: The Example of the 1415 Agincourt Campaign," "The Kishu Army and the Setting of the Prussian Model in Feudal Japan, 1860-1871," and "Orphans, Converts, and Prostitutes: Social Consequences of War and Persecution in the Ottoman Empire, 1914-1923." An extensive book review section covers 10–35 titles and greatly adds to the utility and scholarly quality of this journal. Highly recommended for academic library collections.

3925. *World War II (Leesburg).* [ISSN: 0898-4204] 1986. bi-m. USD 21.95. Weider History Group, 19300 Promenade Dr, Leesburg, VA 20176-6500; comments@weiderhistorygroup.com; www.historynet.com. Adv. Circ: 102500. *Indexed:* A01, A22, ABS&EES, BRI, C37, MASUSE. *Bk. rev.:* Number and length vary. *Aud.:* Ga.

This publication provides interesting and entertaining articles on the events of World War II. The articles generally detail an important battle or profile a particular individual. Recent articles include "Playing the Odds: Leyte Gulf" and "Field Workhorse: The M2A1 105mm Howitzer." Most of the contributions are made by the editorial staff and freelance authors. Content is overwhelmingly oriented to the military dimension of the conflict, and very limited attention is given to political or social impacts of the war. Photographs, drawings, maps, charts, and other illustrations are liberally spread throughout every issue. Aimed at general audiences, this publication would be of interest for most public library collections.

■ MODEL MAKING

General/Model Railroads/Model Aircraft/Model Automobiles/Model Ships

Hector Escobar, Director of Education & Information Delivery, University of Dayton, 300 College Park Ave., Dayton, OH 45469; escobar@udayton.edu

Introduction

Model making represents unusually broad subject areas that encompass a variety of different genres, formats, specialties, and skill levels. These in turn reflect an equally wide range of interests and abilities found among model enthusiasts. For instance, there are specialty magazines devoted to the construction of model airplanes, model rockets, model railroads, model ships, model cars, and military models, as well as science fiction and fantasy models.

Models run the gamut from static, highly detailed matchstick models to operational radio-controlled flyers and engine-powered locomotives. Models may be realistic commercial replicas, carrying military or historical themes, or they may depict ships and vehicles from a science fiction or fantasy world. A few titles are devoted to radio-controlled enthusiasts for both flying and four-wheeled vehicles.

Models are made of various material types, including wood, plastic, carbon fiber, and metal. Some are assembled from kits, while others are built from scratch. Many models are designed according to scale. Some of these are small enough to fit onto a desktop display stand, while much larger ones are known as "garage models."

In general, this section focuses on the building and collecting of models, and not on the operational aspects of modeling, such as flying, racing, or competing. Additionally, antique and modern doll, miniature, figurine, and toy collecting will not be covered in this section, as they fall outside its scope. Also covered in this section are a couple of titles that focus on retail operation. While the content covered may appeal to only the retail owner, these titles contain information about events and contact information for various model-making equipment and supplies. Finally, many of these titles include helpful tips and best practices for beginners to the advanced modeler. With illustrations and many diagrams, the modeling arena has become a vast network of sharing information to improve one's interest in this wide hobby.

This section is not intended to be an exhaustive or comprehensive list of all the periodicals that touch on modeling as a hobby. Instead, it focuses on mostly what may be recommended for most public libraries to purchase for their collections, taking into account such factors as affordable pricing, electronic availability, and circulation statistics. Most of the magazines listed here are aimed at an adult audience, but some will be suitable for teenagers as well. These publications hopefully serve as a representative cross-section, selected to represent the best of what is commercially available and appealing to a diverse audience of varying skill levels. A few titles now have electronic access, making viewing of articles more readily available.

Basic Periodicals

Ga: *FineScale Modeler, Model Railroader, Model Airplane News, Scale Auto, Seaways' Ships in Scale.*

Basic Abstracts and Indexes

Readers' Guide to Periodical Literature.

General

3926. *FineScale Modeler.* [ISSN: 0277-979X] 1981. 10x/yr. USD 39.95 domestic; USD 47.95 Canada; USD 51.95 elsewhere. Ed(s): Matt Usher. Kalmbach Publishing Co., 21027 Crossroads Circle, Waukesha, WI 53187; customerservice@kalmbach.com; http://www.kalmbach.com. Illus., index, adv. Sample. Vol. ends: Dec. *Indexed:* BRI, IHTDI. *Aud.:* Hs, Ga.

FineScale Modeler targets the serious model builder and is the best known of the plastic scale modeling magazines. All types of plastic scale models are included such as aircraft, military, ships, cars, and figures, with a focus on historically accurate models. Each issue features four or five how-to articles on kit assembly and finishing techniques submitted by experts, as well as reader-submitted photos and tips. Extensive product reviews and directories are also provided. The annual "Great Scale Modeling" issue is a highlight, featuring a selection of the world's best models from various shows. Limited online access to previous articles can be found. URL: www.hobbymerchandiser.com

3927. Hobby Merchandiser. Supersedes in part (in 1982): *Craft, Model and Hobby Industry.* [ISSN: 0744-1738] 1942. m. USD 20 domestic; USD 35 foreign. Ed(s): Jeff Troy. Hobby Publications, Inc., 207 Commercial Ct, PO Box 102, Morganville, NJ 07751; info@hobbymerchandiser.com; http://www.hobbymerchandiser.com. Illus., adv. Circ: 9000. *Aud.:* Ga, Sa.

Hobby Merchandiser covers industry news related to hobby and model merchandising. It features news about radio-controlled and die-cast models, including airplanes, automobiles, and trains. It also covers events and news related to a number of model associations. This publication is strong on advertising and provides good cross-referencing for products.

3928. Model Retailer. [ISSN: 0191-6904] 1971. m. USD 85 (Free to qualified personnel). Ed(s): Hal Miller. Kalmbach Publishing Co., 21027 Crossroads Circle, Waukesha, WI 53187; customerservice@kalmbach.com; http://www.kalmbach.com. Adv. *Bk. rev.:* Number and length vary. *Aud.:* Sa.

Model Retailer is directed toward the business or retail side of model making. This publication includes business news, bylined articles, freelance content, editorials, book reviews, events, videos, press releases, and new product news. For the retail model industry, content includes hobbies such as model railroading, radio-controlled cars, model airplanes, model boats, and tools and accessories.

Model Railroads

3929. Great Model Railroads. [ISSN: 1048-8685] 1991. a. Kalmbach Publishing Co., 21027 Crossroads Circle, Waukesha, WI 53187; customerservice@kalmbach.com; http://www.kalmbach.com. *Aud.:* Hs, Ga.

Great Model Railroads is an annual publication that concentrates on model railroad layouts. It offers step-by-step instructions, photographs, insights, and practical advice. Prior issues are available for purchase on the publisher's web site.

3930. Model Railroad Hobbyist Magazine. [ISSN: 2152-7423] 2009. q. Free. Model Railroad Hobbyist, 515 Willow Ave, Woodburn, OR 97071. *Aud.:* Hs, Ga.

Model Railroad Hobbyist Magazine is one of the (if not the only) digital online publications that are free for anyone to download and view. It is available in pdf format. Publication is now monthly, and the content is extensive. It features a nice layout design and index for both advertisements and related topics. Article entries appear to target practical applications for model railroading, featuring photos and useful design illustrations. This online publication provides very practical details and useful ideas for the intermediate or advanced model railroader. URL: http://model-railroad-hobbyist.com/

3931. Model Railroader. [ISSN: 0026-7341] 1934. m. USD 42.95 domestic; USD 52.95 Canada; USD 62.95 elsewhere. Ed(s): Neil Besougloff. Kalmbach Publishing Co., 21027 Crossroads Circle, Waukesha, WI 53187; customerservice@kalmbach.com; http://www.kalmbach.com. Illus., index, adv. Sample. Vol. ends: Dec. *Indexed:* A22, BRI, C37, CBCARef, CBRI, IHTDI, MASUSE, P02. *Bk. rev.:* 100-400 words. *Aud.:* Hs, Ga.

Model Railroader boasts the highest circulation among model railroad enthusiast magazines and places a focus on creating realistic railroad layouts for operating trains. Regular columns include industry news, event coverage, step-by-step projects, and expert advice. Articles feature outstanding projects, complete with instructions. This attractive, full-color publication includes an advertising index and a directory of retailers by state, as well as buyers' guides and product reviews. *MR* will appeal to a general audience of enthusiasts regardless of skill level. Online subscriptions can be ordered at the web site. URL: http://www.trains.com/mrr/

3932. N M R A Magazine. Former titles (until 2010): *Scale Rails;* (until 2003): *National Model Railroad Association. Bulletin.* [ISSN: 2156-5120] 1935. m. USD 15. National Model Railroad Association, Inc, 4121 Cromwell Rd, Chattanooga, TN 37421; http://www.nmra.org. Illus., adv. Circ: 26000. Microform: PQC. *Indexed:* A22. *Aud.:* Hs, Ga.

NMRA Magazine (formerly *Scale Rails*) is a monthly publication focusing on model trains and railroads. According to the publisher's web site, written submissions, photographs, and drawings of layout designs are highly encouraged and welcomed. Content seems to reflect the membership interests of the National Model Railroad Association. Prior issues are available for purchase on the publisher's web site.

3933. Railroad Model Craftsman. Former titles (19??): *Model Railroad Craftsman;* (until 1949): *Model Craftsman.* [ISSN: 0033-877X] 1933. m. USD 37.95 domestic; USD 50 foreign; USD 4.99 per issue domestic. Ed(s): William Schaumburg. Carstens Publications, Inc., 108 Phil Hardin Rd, Newton, NJ 07860; carstens@carstens-publications.com; http://www.carstens-publications.com. Illus., index, adv. Sample. Vol. ends: May. *Bk. rev.:* 100-400 words. *Aud.:* Hs, Ga.

Railroad Model Craftsman is a leading magazine in the railroad hobby industry geared toward a more advanced skill level than *Model Railroader. RMC* features high-quality articles, photographs, prototype drawings, and critical product reviews, as well as reviews of new books and DVDs on the topic of model railroading. This full-color, glossy magazine includes outstanding projects, how-to articles, and an events calendar.

Model Aircraft

3934. Electric Flight. Formerly (until 2011): *Backyard Flyer.* [ISSN: 2159-0672] 2001. bi-m. USD 32 domestic; USD 37 Canada; USD 42 elsewhere. Ed(s): Debra Cleghorn. Air Age Media, 88 Danbury Rd, Rte 7, Wilton, CT 06897; sales@airage.com; http://www.airage.com. Illus. *Indexed:* MASUSE. *Aud.:* Ems, Hs, Ga.

Electric Flight is a popular magazine aimed at beginning hobbyists and children interested in radio-controlled miniature aircraft. These model airplanes are small and silent enough to be operated in backyards and parks, eliminating the need for liability insurance. The magazine includes tips for proper plane assembly, first-flight success, and troubleshooting. Articles feature product reviews and a buyers' guide to the best ready-to-fly aircraft. Online subscription access can be purchased and viewed online. URL: www.modelairplanenews.com/

3935. Fly R C. [ISSN: 1544-4198] 2003. m. USD 19.95 domestic; USD 29.95 Canada; USD 59.95 elsewhere. Ed(s): Thayer Syme. Maplegate Media Group, 42 Old Ridgebury Rd, Danbury, CT 06810; sales@maplegatemedia.com; http://www.maplegatemedia.com/. *Aud.:* Hs, Ga.

Fly RC is a title devoted to the remote-control flying enthusiast. There are a couple of standing columns about recent conferences and various product reviews. Included in this publication is practical information on how to improve flying and fine-tune equipment. The magazine is divided into sections based on aircraft. For example, there is a section that covers helicopters, as a particular aircraft or engine type. In all, a great publication for information on products and product reviews. Online ordering exists, with access to ordering back issues from the journal's web site.

3936. Flying Models: the model builder's how-to-do-it magazine. [ISSN: 0015-4849] 1927. m. USD 37.95 domestic; USD 50 foreign. Ed(s): Frank Fanelli. Carstens Publications, Inc., 108 Phil Hardin Rd, Newton, NJ 07860; carstens@carstens-publications.com; http://www.carstens-publications.com. Illus., adv. Sample. Vol. ends: Dec. *Aud.:* Hs, Ga.

Flying Models is the oldest U.S. flying-model magazine, and one of the oldest model-making magazines in the world. Unlike some of the newer publications, *FM* devotes space to traditional models as well as to new trends. Contents include columns on new developments in the hobby, model construction, product reviews, and advice for new hobbyists. *Flying Models* also maintains a plans directory service for full-size drawings of projects that have appeared as articles.

3937. Model Airplane News. Former titles (until 1935): *Universal Model Airplane News;* (until 1932): *Model Airplane News and Junior Mechanics; Junior Mechanics and Model Airplane News; Model Airplane News.* [ISSN: 0026-7295] 1929. m. USD 24.95 domestic; USD 30.95 Canada; USD 39.95 elsewhere. Ed(s): Debra Cleghorn. Air Age Media, 88 Danbury Rd, Rte 7, Wilton, CT 06897; sales@airage.com; http://www.airage.com. Illus., adv. Sample. Circ: 61552 Paid. Vol. ends: Dec. Microform: PQC. *Indexed:* A22, BRI, C37, CBCARef, MASUSE, P02. *Aud.:* Hs, Ga.

Model Airplane News is the most popular magazine dedicated to the building and flying of radio-controlled airplanes. Regular content focuses on the construction of planes and engines, flight tests, product reviews, project descriptions, and tips and advice for beginners. Monthly issues feature various themes such as model helicopters or jets. This attractive, full-color title is the model airplane magazine of choice for most public libraries.

3938. Model Aviation. [ISSN: 0744-5059] 1975. m. Individuals, USD 36. Ed(s): Jim Haught. Academy of Model Aeronautics, 5161 E Memorial Dr, Muncie, IN 47302; http://www.modelaircraft.org/Intro.htm. Illus., index, adv. Circ: 170000. Vol. ends: Dec. *Indexed:* IHTDI. *Aud.:* Ga, Sa.

Model Aviation is the official publication of the Academy of Model Aeronautics (AMA). Given its official publication status, issues tend to be highly structured in content. There are roughly 15 regular columns appearing in each issue. Content also includes articles on model airplane construction, reports from national and regional offices, and a calender of events that can be extensive. While the publication supports its membership, it is also highly regarded in the model aviation field.

Model Automobiles

3939. Model Cars Magazine. Formerly (until 1998): *Plastic Fanatic.* [ISSN: 1527-4608] 1985. 9x/yr. USD 34.65 domestic; USD 64.65 foreign. Ed(s): Gregg Hutchings. Golden Bell Press Inc., 2403 Champa St, Denver, CO 80205; print@goldenbellpress.com; http://www.goldenbellpress.com. Illus. Sample. *Bk. rev.:* Number and length vary. *Aud.:* Hs, Ga, Sa.

Model Cars Magazine is dedicated to the building and customizing of static scale models of automobiles. Issues feature reviews of kits and how-to articles, clearly illustrated with step-by-step photographs. The magazine devotes a great deal of space to contests and outstanding modelers and their work. The accompanying web site also sponsors an online forum for readers.

3940. R C Driver. [ISSN: 1544-418X] 2003. m. USD 19.95 domestic; USD 29.95 Canada; USD 59.95 elsewhere. Maplegate Media Group, 42 Old Ridgebury Rd, Danbury, CT 06810; sales@maplegatemedia.com; http://www.maplegatemedia.com/. Adv. *Aud.:* Hs, Ga.

RC Driver is a title geared to those individuals who enjoy remote-controled four-wheeled vehicles. Sections in this publication include a how-to and a product test. Each issue reviews various cars or kits that are available. Includes information that even a novice starting out would find helpful, all the way to an advanced RC car enthusiast. Online ordering exists, with access to ordering back issues from the journal's web site.

3941. Scale Auto. Formerly (until 2002): *Scale Auto Enthusiast.* [ISSN: 1550-5251] 1979. bi-m. USD 27.95 domestic; USD 34.95 foreign. Ed(s): Jim Haught. Kalmbach Publishing Co., 21027 Crossroads Circle, Waukesha, WI 53187; http://www.kalmbach.com. Illus., adv. Sample. Vol. ends: Apr. *Aud.:* Hs, Ga.

Scale Auto is the leading publication on building and collecting static automotive models, including muscle cars, stock cars, street rods, low-riders, and trucks. Regular columns highlight industry news and product and kit reviews, as well as coverage of events. Articles feature readers' outstanding projects, including kit construction, super-detailing, modification, and painting, complete with full-color photographs. If a library can afford only one automotive modeling magazine, this is the one to buy. Online access and subscriptions can be made at the web site. URL: www.scaleautomag.com/

Model Ships

3942. Seaways' Ships in Scale. Formerly (until 1992): *Seaways;* Which incorporated (198?-19??): *Ships in Scale.* [ISSN: 1065-8904] 1990. bi-m. USD 29.95 domestic; USD 34.95 in Canada & Mexico; USD 42.95 elsewhere. Seaways Publishing, Inc., PO Box 525, Niwot, CO 80544; office@seaways.com. Illus., index, adv. Vol. ends: Nov/Dec. *Bk. rev.:* 1, 200-500 words. *Aud.:* Hs, Ga, Sa.

Seaways' Ships in Scale is the only publication of its kind, a specialized workshop and research magazine for ship model builders. Articles feature how-to instructions that cover a wide variety of ship models from all historical eras, spanning a broad range of construction materials, including both wood and steel. The magazine is aimed at readers at all levels of modeling experience, although readers should be aware of the challenging aspects of the hobby. The publication's web site serves as a gateway to nautical research and ship modeling information, and hosts a listserv dedicated to the hobby.

■ MULTICULTURAL STUDIES

Andrea Imre, Electronic Resources Librarian, Morris Library, Southern Illinois University Carbondale, Carbondale, IL 62901; aimre@lib.siu.edu

Introduction

Multicultural studies journals investigate cultural roots, cultural heritage, racial identities, ethnicity, migration, immigration, multiculturalism, and race relations. They promote the understanding of people from different cultures and ethnic backgrounds; investigate the challenges individuals and communities face in multicultural societies; and advocate for diversity. Multicultural scholarly journals are often interdisciplinary, and may focus on history, literature, languages, sociology, education, economy, political science, geology, anthropology, or geography.

This section includes scholarly journals, trade journals, and yearbooks. While some publications are geared toward specific ethnic groups, others appeal to a wider audience and are recommended for all types of libraries. See also the African American, Asian American, Native Americans, and Latino Studies sections to find a wider array of magazines that focus on specific area studies. When selecting journals for academic or public libraries, it is necessary to consider the local community's needs and interests and to build collections that reflect the diversity of the library's clientele.

Basic Periodicals

Ems, Hs: *MultiCultural Review;* Ga, Ac: *Annual Editions: Race & Ethnic Relations;* Ac: *Multicultural Perspectives.*

Basic Abstracts and Indexes

America: History and Life, Ethnic NewsWatch, Historical Abstracts, Humanities International Index, Race Relations Abstracts, Social Sciences Index, Sociological Abstracts, SocINDEX.

3943. Afro-Hispanic Review. [ISSN: 0278-8969] 1982. s-a. USD 60 (Individuals, USD 30). Ed(s): William Luis. Vanderbilt University, Department of Spanish and Portuguese, Station B, PO Box 351617, Nashville, TN 37235; spanish-portuguese@vanderbilt.edu; http://www.vanderbilt.edu/spanport/. Illus., adv. Sample. Refereed. *Indexed:* A01, A22, AmHI, IIBP, MLA-IB, RILM. *Bk. rev.:* Number and length vary. *Aud.:* Ga, Ac.

Published by the Department of Spanish and Portuguese at Vanderbilt University, this bilingual journal includes articles, interviews, testimonies, artwork, poems, and book reviews. The peer-reviewed articles reflect the richness of Afro-Hispanic literature and culture and their influence in the Hispanic world. Recommended for academic and research libraries.

3944. Annual Editions: Multicultural Education. [ISSN: 1092-924X] 1993. a. USD 46.33 per issue. Ed(s): Nancy Gallavan. McGraw-Hill, Contemporary Learning Series, 1221 Ave of the Americas, New York, NY 10020; customer.service@mcgraw-hill.com; http://www.mcgraw-hill.com. Illus. *Aud.:* Ga, Ac.

This publication focuses on multicultural education and provides convenient, inexpensive access to a wide range of current articles previously published in public press magazines, newspapers, and journals. Each volume includes a collection of 35–40 articles grouped into thematic units, along with a list of important Internet references that help further explore article topics. The articles selected for inclusion in recent volumes discussed such topics as the social context of multicultural education; teacher education in multicultural perspective; cultural characteristics; and multicultural curriculum development. Each volume is accompanied by an online *Instructor's Resource Guide* with testing materials. Highly recommended for academic and research libraries.

3945. Annual Editions: Race & Ethnic Relations. [ISSN: 1075-5195] 1991. a. USD 46.33 per issue. Ed(s): John A Kromkowski. McGraw-Hill, Contemporary Learning Series, 1221 Ave of the Americas, New York, NY 10020; customer.service@mcgraw-hill.com; http://www.mhhe.com/cls/. Illus. Refereed. *Aud.:* Ga, Ac.

This collection of public press articles promotes the understanding of racial and ethnic issues in the United States. Editors continuously monitor over 300 periodical sources and regularly update the online version with new content. Each print issue includes around 50 public press articles grouped into units that focus on race, ethnicity, indigenous ethnic groups, immigration, American legal traditions, and cultural pluralism, among others. An annotated list of online resources that support the articles is also included. Highly recommended for academic and research libraries, as well as for general audiences.

3946. E C M I Journal on Ethnopolitics and Minority Issues in Europe. [ISSN: 1617-5247] 2001. s-a. Free. Ed(s): Marc Weller. European Centre for Minority Issues, Schiffbruecke 12, Flensburg, 24939, Germany; info@ecmi.de; http://www.ecmi.de. Refereed. Reprint: WSH. *Indexed:* IBSS, IIBP, P61, SSA. *Aud.:* Ga, Ac.

Edited under the auspices of the European Centre for Minority Issues, this peer-reviewed, open-access journal is devoted to addressing minority issues, minority rights, ethnopolitics, and conflict management in Europe. It provides a forum for scholars and practitioners to investigate such problems as minority policies of the European Union, the social and political status of minorities in Eastern and Western Europe, and the effects of European Union membership on national minority policies. Recommended for academic and research libraries. URL: www.ecmi.de/publications/jemie/

3947. Ethnic and Racial Studies. [ISSN: 0141-9870] 1978. 10x/yr. GBP 767 (print & online eds.). Ed(s): Martin Bulmer. Routledge, 4 Park Sq, Milton Park, Abingdon, OX14 4RN, United Kingdom; subscriptions@tandf.co.uk; http://www.tandfonline.com. Illus., index, adv. Sample. Refereed. Circ: 1550. Vol. ends: Oct. Reprint: PSC. *Indexed:* A01, A22, A47, AbAn, BAS, BRI, C42, CBRI, CJPI, Chicano, E01, FR, IBSS, IIBP, P02, P61, PsycInfo, SSA, SWR&A. *Bk. rev.:* 11-30, 500-1,000 words. *Aud.:* Ac.

This prominent journal, published ten times a year, highlights a variety of interdisciplinary viewpoints on topics related to race, ethnicity, and nationalism. Peer-reviewed research articles, written by a diverse group of international scholars, focus on theory and empirical evidence and discuss sociological, economic, and political issues. The journal also includes review articles and book reviews. Highly recommended for academic and research libraries. Available both in print and online. URL: www.tandf.co.uk/journals/routledge/01419870.asp

3948. Ethnic Studies Review. Formed by the merger of (1978-1996): *Explorations in Ethnic Studies;* (1981-1996): *Explorations in Sights and Sounds.* [ISSN: 1555-1881] 1996. 2x/yr. Free to qualified personnel. Ed(s): Ron Scapp. National Association for Ethnic Studies (NAES), Western Washington University, 516 High St, Bellingham, WA 98225; naes@wwu.edu; http://www.ethnicstudies.org. Refereed. *Indexed:* ABS&EES, BAS, BRI, Chicano, ENW, MLA-IB. *Bk. rev.:* Number and length vary. *Aud.:* Hs, Ac.

Published by the National Association for Ethnic Studies, this journal explores race, ethnicity, and inter-group relations from a variety of cultures around the world. It also seeks to promote activities and scholarship that contribute to the development and understanding of ethnic studies. The journal includes research notes, essays, and book reviews. Recommended for academic libraries and scholarly research centers.

3949. Ethnohistory. [ISSN: 0014-1801] 1954. q. USD 196. Ed(s): Matthew Restall, Michael L Harkin. Duke University Press, 905 W Main St, Ste 18 B, PO Box 90660, Durham, NC 27701; subscriptions@dukeupress.edu; http://www.dukeupress.edu. Illus., adv. Sample. Refereed. Vol. ends: Fall. Microform: PQC. Reprint: PSC. *Indexed:* A01, A22, A47, ABS&EES, AmHI, ArtHuCI, BAS, BRI, BrArAb, Chicano, E01, FR, IBSS, IIBP, MLA-IB, P02, P61, SSA. *Bk. rev.:* 10-15, 800-1,200 words. *Aud.:* Ac.

This scholarly journal looks at "indigenous, diasporic, and minority peoples" through the many centuries, charting the flow of cultures and the history associated therein. While most articles take anthropological and historical approaches, geology, geography, archaeology, literature, and sociology are also well represented. Each issue includes review essays and book reviews. Highly recommended for academic and research libraries. Available both in print and online. URL: http://ethnohistory.dukejournals.org

3950. Identities: global studies in culture and power. Formerly (until 1994): *Ethnic Groups;* Incorporates (1970-1975): *Afro-American Studies.* [ISSN: 1070-289X] 1976. bi-m. GBP 366 (print & online eds.). Ed(s): Claire Alexander. Routledge, 4 Park Sq, Milton Park, Abingdon, OX14 4RN, United Kingdom; subscriptions@tandf.co.uk; http://www.tandfonline.com. Illus., adv. Sample. Refereed. Reprint: PSC. *Indexed:* A01, A22, ABS&EES, AbAn, ArtHuCI, BRI, C45, E01, IBSS, IIBP, MLA-IB, P61, RILM, SD, SSA. *Bk. rev.:* Number and length vary. *Aud.:* Ac.

This journal looks at issues of racial, national, ethnic, and gender identities from an international perspective. Political, social, cultural, and economic boundaries are also explored. The journal deals with global population movements and their effects on our cultural diversity and interactions. Some issues includes book and media reviews. Recommended for academic libraries. Available both in print and online. URL: www.tandf.co.uk/journals/titles/1070289x.asp

3951. Journal of American Ethnic History. [ISSN: 0278-5927] 1981. q. USD 310 (print & online eds.). Ed(s): John J Bukowczyk. University of Illinois Press, 1325 S Oak St, Champaign, IL 61820; journals@uillinois.edu; http://www.press.uillinois.edu. Illus., index, adv. Refereed. Vol. ends: Summer (No. 4). Microform: PQC. *Indexed:* A01, A22, ABS&EES, AmHI, ArtHuCI, BAS, BRI, Chicano, E01, IIBP, P02, P61, RILM, SSA. *Bk. rev.:* Number and length vary. *Aud.:* Ac, Sa.

The official publication of the Immigration History Society, this journal deals with various aspects of immigration and ethnic history in the United States. A large number of articles focus on the history, acculturation, and social interaction of ethnic groups at specific locations in the United States, while others examine national immigration policies. In addition, each issue contains review essays and book reviews. Highly recommended for academic and research libraries. Available both in print and online. URL: www.press.uillinois.edu/journals/jaeh.html

3952. *Journal of Ethnic and Migration Studies.* Former titles (until 1998): *New Community;* (until 1971): *Community.* [ISSN: 1369-183X] 1970. 10x/yr. GBP 1414 (print & online eds.). Ed(s): Jenny Money, Russell King. Routledge, 4 Park Sq, Milton Park, Abingdon, OX14 4RN, United Kingdom; subscriptions@tandf.co.uk; http://www.tandfonline.com. Adv. Sample. Refereed. Reprint: PSC. *Indexed:* A01, A22, AmHI, BRI, E01, IBSS, P61, SSA. *Bk. rev.:* 750-1,000 words, signed. *Aud.:* Ac.

This peer-reviewed journal looks at all forms of migration and includes articles on ethnic conflicts, discrimination, racism, nationalism, citizenship, and policies of integration from an international perspective. Special issues focus on such topics as "Transnational Migration and the Study of Children," "Transnational Parenthood," and "Multicultural East Asia." Each issue includes signed book reviews. Highly recommended for research and academic libraries. Available both in print and online. URL: www.tandf.co.uk/journals/titles/1369183X.asp

3953. *Journal of Intercultural Studies.* Formerly (until 1980): *Ethnic Studies.* [ISSN: 0725-6868] 1977. bi-m. GBP 883 (print & online eds.). Ed(s): Vince Marotta, Fethi Mansouri. Routledge, Level 2, 11 Queens Rd, Melbourne, VIC 3004, Australia; enquiries@tandf.com.au; http://www.routledge.com. Illus. Sample. Refereed. Reprint: PSC. *Indexed:* A01, A22, BRI, E01, IBSS, IIBP, MLA-IB, P61, RILM, SSA. *Bk. rev.:* 15, 400 words. *Aud.:* Ga, Ac.

This international interdisciplinary journal takes a global look at multiculturalism, ethnicity, emerging cultural formations, cultural identity, and intercultural negotiations. Peer-reviewed, theoretically informed articles from the fields of cultural studies, sociology, gender studies, political science, cultural geography, urban studies, and race and ethnic studies are provided. In addition, there are review essays and books reviews. Highly recommended for academic libraries. Available both in print and online. URL: www.tandf.co.uk/journals/titles/07256868.asp

3954. *Migration News.* [ISSN: 1081-9908] 1994. q. USD 30 domestic; USD 50 foreign. University of California, Davis, Department of Agricultural Economics, One Shields Ave, Davis, CA 95616; http://migration.ucdavis.edu. Illus. *Aud.:* Ga, Ac.

Focusing on immigration news of the preceding quarter, this newsletter features articles on international immigration and integration developments. Current policies of various governments and their respective repercussions for migrant families and workers are presented, along with reports on immigration. Topics are grouped into four international geographic regions: "The Americas," "Europe," "Asia," and "Other." Recommended for academic and public libraries. Available both in print and online. URL: http://migration.ucdavis.edu

3955. *Multicultural Education: the magazine of the National Association for Multicultural Education Planning.* [ISSN: 1068-3844] 1993. q. USD 100 (Individuals, USD 50). Ed(s): Alan H Jones, Heather L Hazuka. Caddo Gap Press, 3145 Geary Blvd, PMB 275, San Francisco, CA 94118; info@caddogap.com; http://www.caddogap.com. Illus., adv. Sample. Refereed. Circ: 1000 Paid. Vol. ends: Summer. *Indexed:* BRI, ERIC. *Bk. rev.:* 6-8, length varies. *Aud.:* Ac.

This peer-reviewed journal covers all aspects of multicultural education and includes feature articles; research articles; promising practices; opinion pieces; reviews of books and other multicultural education media; news items; and announcements about organizations, events, conferences, and other multicultural education programs. Recent issues focused on bilingual education; the education of English language learners; diversity; and multiculturalism in teacher education. Recommended for school and academic libraries.

Multicultural Perspectives. See Education/General, K-12 section.

3956. *Patterns of Prejudice.* [ISSN: 0031-322X] 1967. 5x/yr. GBP 711 (print & online eds.). Routledge, 4 Park Sq, Milton Park, Abingdon, OX14 4RN, United Kingdom; subscriptions@tandf.co.uk; http://www.tandfonline.com. Adv. Sample. Refereed. Microform: PQC. Reprint: PSC. *Indexed:* A01, A22, A47, ABS&EES, ArtHuCI, E01, IBSS, IJP, P61, PsycInfo, SSA. *Bk. rev.:* 3-10, 500-1,000. *Aud.:* Ac, Sa.

This peer-reviewed journal provides a forum for exploring the historical roots and contemporary varieties of social exclusion, race, ethnicity, and ethnic conflicts. Articles focus on such issues as asylum, immigration, hate crimes, and citizenship. The journal maintains a global viewpoint, at the same time aiming to scrutinize intolerance and chauvinism in the United States and Europe. Recommended for academic and research libraries. Available both in print and online. URL: www.informaworld.com/openurl?genre=journal&issn=0031-322X

■ MUSIC

General/Popular

See also Music Reviews section.

Sheridan Stormes, Performing and Fine Arts Librarian, Butler University, 4600 Sunset Avenue, Indianapolis, IN 46208; sstormes@butler.edu (General subsection).

Bill Lamb, About.com Top 40 / Pop, http://top40.about.com (Popular subsection)

Introduction

The journals presented in the General subsection of this Music section of this edition of *Magazines for Libraries* reflect a fairly significant reduction in the number of titles presented in previous editions. Greater affordability of and access to computers, and the proliferation of electronic databases in recent years, have dramatically changed the way library users access and utilize magazine and journal articles. Faced with space constraints and few prospects for expanded facilities or remote storage options, libraries of all types are finding it necessary to reduce the size of their print collections.

At the same time, the current economic climate has negatively impacted the world of music and music education. Even major symphony orchestras and opera companies are struggling to survive, and music education programs are being eliminated at many schools. In an effort to demonstrate the importance and power of music, today's music education reflects increasing emphasis on interdisciplinary studies involving such pairings as music and learning, music and culture, and music and medicine.

In recognition of increasing user preference for electronic access and also of the economic and facility-related constraints facing many libraries that house music collections, the editor has sought to select those titles that will be of the greatest value to the majority of music collections. Titles in this list have been chosen based on their scope, quality, cost, perceived stability, regularity, and, to some extent, availability in electronic format. A deliberate effort also has been made to provide a representative selection of reputable open-access (i.e., free, online) journals. In addition, the list includes several titles whose content reflects an interdisciplinary focus. As a general rule, libraries are encouraged to provide access to these titles in electronic format whenever possible. It should be noted, too, that this list seeks to present a core list of music titles that would be appropriate for small- to medium-sized libraries and is not intended to be a comprehensive list for large (i.e., doctorate-granting) institutions.

Those who have followed previous editions will note that many highly reputable titles (e.g., *Fontes Artis Musicae, The Horn Call, ITG Journal,* and *The Saxophone Symposium,* among others) have been deleted. Their elimination is not an indication of diminished quality but rather of the more limited audiences that these titles serve. Libraries that serve larger populations of users with these specific interests are encouraged to include these titles as appropriate.

To the extent that budgets will allow, libraries serving users with music interests and research needs are encouraged to subscribe to the following electronic databases, which include significant full-text coverage of high-quality music magazine and journal publications: Academic Search Premier (EBSCO), JSTOR (especially "Arts & Sciences 3"), and International Index to Music Periodicals—Full Text.

Basic Periodicals

GENERAL. Hs: *American Music Teacher, Choral Journal, Instrumentalist, Music Educators Journal;* Ga: *American Music, Ethnomusicology, The Musical Quarterly, Opera News;* Ac: *American Musicological Society. Journal, Journal of Music Theory, Journal of Research in Music Education.*

POPULAR. Hs, Ga, Ac: *Rolling Stone.*

Basic Abstracts and Indexes

International Index to Music Periodicals, Music Index, RILM Abstracts of Music Literature.

General

3957. *American Music.* [ISSN: 0734-4392] 1983. q. USD 129 (print & online eds.). Ed(s): Neil Lerner. University of Illinois Press, 1325 S Oak St, Champaign, IL 61820; journals@uillinois.edu; http://www.press.uillinois.edu. Illus., adv. Sample. Refereed. Microform: PQC. *Indexed:* A01, A22, ABS&EES, AmHI, ArtHuCI, BRI, CBRI, E01, IIMP, MLA-IB, P02, RILM. *Bk. rev.:* 1-2, 1,000 words, signed. *Aud.:* Ga, Ac, Sa.

American Music is dedicated to all topics relating to music in America, both historical and contemporary. Article content ranges from features on individual performers, composers, publishers, works, and collections, to discussions on American musical institutions, events, and the industry. Genres covered include classical, popular, blues, musical theater, folk, and jazz. Issues generally contain three to six feature-length essays and several reviews of books, recordings, and multimedia. Of interest to both scholars and performers alike, this is a necessary title for academic and public libraries with any focus on American music. Available in both print and online formats.

3958. *American Music Teacher.* Former titles (until 1951): *Music Teachers National Association. Bulletin;* (until 1938): *Advisory Council Bulletin.* [ISSN: 0003-0112] 19??. bi-m. USD 24 (Non-members, USD 30; USD 6 per issue domestic). Ed(s): Marcie Gerrietts Lindsey. Music Teachers National Association, 441 Vine St, Ste 3100, Cincinnati, OH 45202; mtnanet@mtna.org; http://www.mtna.org. Illus., adv. Refereed. Vol. ends: Jun/Jul. *Indexed:* A01, A22, BRI, CBRI, IIMP, P02, RILM. *Bk. rev.:* 5-7, 500 words, signed. *Aud.:* Ac, Sa.

American Music Teacher is the official publication of the Music Teachers National Association (MTNA). Its articles and columns directly address the needs and interests of music educators who are members of MTNA. Each issue features several articles that highlight accomplished individuals, pedagogical methods, or contemporary issues. Also included is a regular section on professional resources; an annual directory of summer program; announcements of competitions, conferences, and workshops; and advertisements for teaching tools, new repertoire, and relevant publications. Particularly useful to music teachers at all levels, it is recommended for academic and large public libraries. Available in both print and online formats.

3959. *American Musicological Society. Journal.* Former titles (until 1948): *American Musicological Society. Bulletin;* (until 1936): *New York Musicological Society. Bulletin.* [ISSN: 0003-0139] 1931. 3x/yr. USD 182 (print & online eds.). Ed(s): Kate van Orden. University of California Press, Journals Division, 2000 Ctr St, Ste 303, Berkeley, CA 94704; customerservice@ucpressjournals.com; http://www.ucpressjournals.com. Illus., index, adv. Refereed. Circ: 4259. Reprint: PSC. *Indexed:* A01, A22, ABS&EES, AmHI, ArtHuCI, BAS, BRI, E01, IIMP, MLA-IB, P02, RILM. *Bk. rev.:* 3-5, 3,000 words, signed. *Aud.:* Ac, Sa.

The *Journal of the American Musicological Society* (*JAMS*) is renowned for its well-documented, refereed articles that focus primarily on western art music, but it also occasionally cover topics related to ethnomusicology, gender studies, and popular music. Articles present scholarship in virtually all fields of historical musicology, including but not limited to historiography, aesthetics,

organology, iconography, performance practice, theory, and criticism. In addition to the extensive articles and book reviews that appear in the print version, subscribers have access to the journal's full text online. Subscribers also receive the *American Musicological Society Newsletter,* published twice a year. Highly recommended for academic libraries; necessary for music libraries that support research programs.

3960. *Choral Journal.* Incorporates (1959-1964): *Texas Choirmaster.* [ISSN: 0009-5028] 1959. m. Aug.-July. USD 45 Free to members. Ed(s): Ron Granger, Carroll Gonzo. American Choral Directors Association, 545 Couch Dr, Oklahoma, OK 73102; http://acda.org. Illus., index. Refereed. Vol. ends: Jul. Microform: PQC. *Indexed:* A01, A22, ABS&EES, IIMP, RILM. *Bk. rev.:* 3-5, 200-500 words, signed. *Aud.:* Hs, Ac, Sa.

Choral Journal is the official publication of the American Choral Directors Association (ACDA), and is relevant for choral directors and educators who work with singers at any level. In addition to providing current news about the association and information on the annual ACDA convention, articles and columns in each issue cover a range of topics, both theoretical and practical in nature, ranging from interviews with leading musicians to feature articles discussing particular pieces (from multiple genres). There are also pedagogical methodologies; educational psychology; and reviews of new music scores, recordings, and books. Some issues focus on a particular topic, such as community choruses or music in the worship service. This publication is available in both print and online formats (URL: http://65.64.86.127/publications/choral_journal). Recommended for academic, public, and high school libraries.

3961. *The Choral Scholar.* [ISSN: 1948-3058] 2009. s-a. Free. Ed(s): Gregory Brown. National Collegiate Choral Organization, c/o Bonnie Borshay Sneed, 100 Campus Dr, Weatherford, OK 73096-3098; the_choral_scholar@ncco-usa.org; http://www.ncco-usa.org. Adv. Refereed. *Bk. rev.:* Number and length vary. *Aud.:* Ac, Sa.

The Choral Scholar: The Online Journal of the National Collegiate Choral Organization is a peer-reviewed journal whose primary focus is music research relating to the study and performance of choral music. The journal accepts submissions from scholars in all music-related disciplines, as well as from scholars outside the field of music whose research relates to choral music. Articles range from approximately 4,000 to 10,000 words in length, and may concern themselves with issues such as choral vocal technique, analyses and/or histories of specific choral works, and discussions of repertoire considerations. Individual issues also may include reviews of books, recordings, and musical scores. Recommended for academic libraries. URL: www.ncco-usa.org/tcs/

3962. *Classical Singer.* Formerly (until Sep. 1998): *New York Opera Newsletter.* [ISSN: 1534-276X] 1987. m. 10/yr. USD 58 domestic; USD 78 Canada; USD 88 elsewhere. Classical Singer Corporation, PO Box 1710, Draper, UT 84020; subscriptions@classicalsinger.com. Adv. Sample. Circ: 3500 Paid and controlled. *Aud.:* Ac, Sa.

Classical Singer Magazine seeks to provide aspiring and active classical vocalists and teachers with practical information relating to care of the voice and development of a professional singing career. Articles are written by singers, voice teachers, doctors, and freelance writers. The publication covers a wide range of topics including (but not limited to) how to prepare for and behave in auditions, how to select repertoire, how to dress, how to care for the voice, how to successfully develop a career, and how to balance a singing career with a family life. Other articles feature interviews with singers and provide information about apprentice programs and vocal competitions. The summer issue contains a "Classical Singer Voice Teacher Directory," "Coach and Accompanist Directory," and "Young Artist Program Directory." The back pages of each issue are devoted to listing auditions and job postings for various operatic, concert, choral, and church/temple positions. Available in both print and online formats. Highly recommended for large public and academic libraries.

3963. *Clavier Companion: a practical magazine on piano teaching.* Formed by ther merger of (1990-2009): *Keyboard Companion;* (1962-2009): *Clavier;* Which was formerly (until 1966): *Piano Teacher.* [ISSN: 2152-4491] 1962. bi-m. USD 29.95 domestic; USD 39.95

Canada; USD 41.95 elsewhere. Ed(s): Peter Jutras, Susan Geffen. Frances Clark Center for Keyboard Pedagogy, PO Box 651, Kingston, NJ 08528; exdir@francesclarkcenter.org; http://www.francesclarkcenter.org. Illus., index, adv. Vol. ends: Dec. *Indexed:* A01, A22, ABS&EES, IIMP, RILM. *Aud.:* Hs, Ac, Sa.

Clavier Companion is the result of the early 2009 merger between *Clavier* and *Keyboard Companion* magazines. Published bimonthly by the Frances Clark Center for Keyboard Pedagogy, it purports to be "the only publication in North America devoted exclusively to the concerns of the piano/keyboard performer and teacher." Geared toward teachers of piano students at all skill levels, it is also of interest to students, performers, and non-specialist music educators. Issues contain practical advice on teaching techniques; recommendations and reviews of new repertoire; and feature articles on successful teachers, performers, and composers. Each issue also includes a freely-reproducible page called "Keyboard Kids' Companion," which contains games and practical tips for engaging young players. Listings of workshops, festivals, camps, and competitions for both teachers and students are presented. A "digital only" subscription also is available (URL: http://www.claviercompanion.com/ subscriptions/digital). Recommended for academic, public, and high school libraries.

3964. Computer Music Journal. [ISSN: 0148-9267] 1977. q. USD 338 (print & online eds.). Ed(s): Keeril Makan, Douglas Keislar. M I T Press, 55 Hayward St, Cambridge, MA 02142; journals-cs@mit.edu; http:// mitpress.mit.edu. Illus., adv. Refereed. Microform: PQC. *Indexed:* A01, A22, ArtHuCI, BRI, C&ISA, CerAb, CompLI, CompR, E01, EngInd, IIMP, P02, RILM. *Bk. rev.:* 2-3, 1,500 words, signed. *Aud.:* Ac, Sa.

Computer Music Journal (*CMJ*) is dedicated to the exploration of digital sound technology and music created with or manipulated by computers. Engineers, computer scientists, composers, performers, and anyone studying or interested in electroacoustic music will find a wide range of relevant topics and current information on both technical and aesthetic issues. Content includes feature articles on technologies, musical analysis, interviews, and reviews of recent events and new publications. Annually a music disc (CD or DVD) accompanies an issue. This journal is also available online. Recommended for academic libraries; highly recommended for those that serve music programs with an emphasis on digital technology.

3965. Council for Research in Music Education. Bulletin. [ISSN: 0010-9894] 1963. q. USD 122 (print & online eds.). University of Illinois Press, 1325 S Oak St, Champaign, IL 61820; journals@uillinois.edu; http://www.press.uillinois.edu. Illus., index, adv. Refereed. Microform: PQC. *Indexed:* A22, ArtHuCI, IIMP, MLA-IB, RILM. *Bk. rev.:* 5-10, 750-1,000 words, signed. *Aud.:* Ac, Sa.

The *Bulletin of the Council for Research in Music Education* is the official publication of the Council for Research in Music Education (CRME). Its articles are scholarly in nature and present research on the effects of various pedagogical techniques and environments on young musicians. Recent issues covered topics such as music faculty workloads, technology-based music classes in high schools in the United States, and music teacher perceptions of issues and problems in urban elementary schools. Relevant to music educators with students at all levels, this publication is recommended for academic and large public libraries. This title also may be subscribed to in electronic format. URL: www.press.uillinois.edu/journals/bcrme.html

3966. Early Music. [ISSN: 0306-1078] 1973. q. EUR 269. Ed(s): Francis Knights. Oxford University Press, Great Clarendon St, Oxford, OX2 6DP, United Kingdom; enquiry@oup.co.uk; http://www.oxfordjournals.org/. Illus., adv. Sample. Refereed. Microform: PQC. Reprint: PSC. *Indexed:* A01, A22, AmHI, ArtHuCI, BRI, E01, IIMP, MLA-IB, P02, RILM. *Bk. rev.:* 2-4, 750-1,000 words, signed. *Aud.:* Ac, Sa.

Early Music looks at all facets of the ever-unfolding study of early music. Among the topics presented include matters of interpretation, notation, iconography, performance practice, period instruments, and both historical and analytical perspectives of specific composers, performers, manuscripts, and performances. In addition to scholarly articles, a typical issue includes reviews of books, new editions of printed music, and recordings, as well as current workshop and festival listings. This journal will be of great use to anyone

interested in early music, and is highly recommended for academic libraries that support historical music programs. Available in both print and online formats. URL: www.oxfordjournals.org/our_journals/earlyj/access_purchase/price_list.html

3967. Early Music History: studies in medieval and early modern music. [ISSN: 0261-1279] 1982. a. GBP 150. Ed(s): Iain Fenlon. Cambridge University Press, The Edinburgh Bldg, Shaftesbury Rd, Cambridge, CB2 8RU, United Kingdom; journals@cambridge.org; http://www.cambridge.org/uk. Illus., adv. Refereed. Circ: 550. Microform: PQC. Reprint: PSC. *Indexed:* A22, AmHI, ArtHuCI, E01, IIMP, RILM. *Bk. rev.:* 2, 2,500 words, signed. *Aud.:* Ac, Sa.

Early Music History presents the scholarship of researchers specializing in European and American music from the early Middle Ages through the end of the seventeenth century. Accepted papers tend to use novel approaches in their methodologies and explore interdisciplinary possibilities. Topics, such as manuscripts and texts, iconography, music within society, and the relationship between words and music, are discussed from both historical and analytic perspectives. Recommended for academic libraries, especially those that support early music studies or musicology. Also available in online format. URL: http://journals.cambridge.org/action/displayJournal?jid=EMH

3968. Eighteenth-Century Music. [ISSN: 1478-5706] 2004. s-a. GBP 117 (print & online eds.). Ed(s): W Dean Sutcliffe. Cambridge University Press, The Edinburgh Bldg, Shaftesbury Rd, Cambridge, CB2 8RU, United Kingdom; journals@cambridge.org; http://www.cambridge.org/uk. Adv. Refereed. Reprint: PSC. *Indexed:* A22, ArtHuCI, E01, IIMP, MLA-IB. *Bk. rev.:* Number and length vary. *Aud.:* Ac, Sa.

Eighteenth-Century Music provides a forum for research and discussion into all aspects of eighteenth-century music (c. 1660–1830). Content focuses on topics ranging from musical analyses of compositions, analyses of performance methods, and critiques to interdisciplinary studies of the music in its cultural and social contexts. Issues include many book, music, and recording reviews, and reports of conferences and related current events. Also available as an online subscription (http://journals.cambridge.org/action/displayJournal?jid=ECM). Recommended for academic collections.

3969. Electronic Musician. Incorporates (1990-2011): *E Q (New York)*; Formerly (until 1985): *Polyphony*. [ISSN: 0884-4720] 1976. m. USD 23.97 domestic; USD 30 Canada; USD 50 elsewhere. Ed(s): Sarah Jones. NewBay Media, LLC, 28 E 28th St, 12th Fl, New York, NY 10016; customerservice@nbmedia.com; http://www.nbmedia.com. Adv. *Indexed:* A01, A22, C37, IIMP. *Aud.:* Ac, Sa.

Published monthly, *Electronic Musician* seeks to cover all aspects of music production, including performance, recording, and technology. Articles feature profiles of influential music-makers, reviews and analyses of the latest recording equipment and applications, and techniques and tips to enhance music production and live performances. In addition, the publication addresses such career-related concerns as promotion, marketing, publishing, and social media. Also available as an online subscription. Recommended for large public and academic libraries, especially those that support programs in electronic music composition and recording industry studies. URL: www.emusician.com

3970. Ethnomusicology. [ISSN: 0014-1836] 1953. 3x/yr. USD 173 (print & online eds.). Ed(s): J Lawrence Witzleben. University of Illinois Press, 1325 S Oak St, Champaign, IL 61820; journals@uillinois.edu; http://www.press.uillinois.edu. Illus., index, adv. Refereed. Vol. ends: Fall. *Indexed:* A01, A22, A47, ABS&EES, AbAn, AmHI, ArtHuCI, BAS, BRI, FR, IBSS, IIBP, IIMP, MLA-IB, P02, RILM. *Bk. rev.:* 6-8, 500-1,000 words, signed. *Aud.:* Ac, Sa.

Published by the Society for Ethnomusicology, this journal presents research and analysis of various subjects from within the large field of ethnomusicology, featuring perspectives from musicology, sociology, cultural anthropology, and others. Some articles look broadly at the very concept of ethnomusicology, while others focus on research done on the music and practices of specific cultures, religions, geographic areas, and so on. Each issue contains substantial reviews of books, recordings, and multimedia. Scholars from a wide variety of fields will find information of relevance. Also available in electronic format (www.press.uillinois.edu/journals/ethno.html). Recommended for academic and large public libraries; essential for those that support research in ethnomusicology.

3971. Gamut. [ISSN: 1938-6990] 2008. s-a. Free. Ed(s): David Carson Berry. University of Tennessee Libraries, Newfound Press, 1015 Volunteer Blvd, Knoxville, TN 37996; http://www.newfoundpress.utk.edu/. Refereed. *Aud.:* Ac, Sa.

Gamut, the online journal of the Music Theory Society of the Mid-Atlantic, is a peer-reviewed publication that seeks submissions covering any aspect of music theory and its cognate disciplines. While submissions that cover music theory-related topics of a traditional nature are welcome, this publication especially encourages submission of articles presenting new theoretical and analytical concepts, including those that might address music theories of non-Western cultures and those related to the music of popular culture (e.g., rock, country, hip hop, etc.). This publication also welcomes submissions from authors outside the field of music whose research may contribute a new perspective to musical understanding. Recommended for academic libraries. URL: http://trace.tennessee.edu/gamut/

3972. The Instrumentalist. [ISSN: 0020-4331] 1946. m. USD 21 domestic; USD 40 foreign. The Instrumentalist Co., 200 Northfield Rd, Northfield, IL 60093; advertising@instrumentalistmagazine.com. Illus., index, adv. Vol. ends: Jul. *Indexed:* A22, IIMP, P02, RILM. *Aud.:* Hs, Ga, Ac, Sa.

This magazine focuses on the interests and needs of band, marching band, and orchestra directors at the primary, secondary, and higher education levels. It offers practical advice and discussions on pedagogy, conducting, repertoire, conducting, and running rehearsals. A typical issue also contains interviews with directors and composers of note, reviews of music scores and audio recordings, and listings of workshops and festivals. Also available as an online subscription. Recommended for academic, public, and high school libraries. URL: www.theinstrumentalist.com/

3973. International Musician. [ISSN: 0020-8051] 1901. m. Free to members; Non-members, USD 39. Ed(s): Antoinette Follett. American Federation of Musicians of the United States and Canada, 120 Walton St., Ste 300, Syracuse, NY 13202; http://www.afm.org. Illus., adv. Circ: 94886 Paid. Vol. ends: Jun. Microform: PQC. *Indexed:* A22, IIMP. *Bk. rev.:* 4, 100 words, unsigned. *Aud.:* Ga, Ac, Sa.

International Musician is the official journal of the American Federation of Musicians. Its content focuses on the interests and concerns of its more than 100,000 American and Canadian members, most of whom are professional musicians and music educators. Presented are union and legislative news, interviews, self-promotion advice, relevant resources for the working musician, and member achievements across the gamut of musical styles. Each issue includes a feature article on an accomplished professional musician or ensemble, and also contains editorials, local chapter news, and classifieds listing auditions, equipment for sale, training opportunities, and stolen-instrument notices. Available through both print and online subscriptions. Recommended for public and academic libraries. URL: www.internationalmusician.org/

3974. Journal of Band Research. [ISSN: 0021-9207] 1964. s-a. USD 15 domestic; USD 20 foreign. Ed(s): Deanna Ernsberger. Journal of Band Research, c/o Dr. John R. Locke, Editor, UNCG School of Music, P O Box 26170, Greensboro, NC 27402-6170; dernsberger@troy.edu. Illus. Circ: 1000 Paid. Microform: PQC. *Indexed:* A01, A22, ArtHuCI, IIMP, RILM. *Aud.:* Ac, Sa.

The official publication of The American Bandmasters Association, the *Journal of Band Research* is a peer-reviewed journal published in the fall and spring of each year. The four or five rather substantial feature articles in each issue are scholarly in nature and cover research that relates to various types of bands and wind ensembles. Among the topics addressed by the articles are repertoire and repertoire analysis, programming considerations, band ensemble histories, pedagogy, and band recruitment. The final pages of each issue provide brief biographies of each of the contributors. Available as a print journal only. Recommended for large public and academic libraries.

3975. Journal of Music Theory. [ISSN: 0022-2909] 1957. s-a. USD 82. Ed(s): Ian Quinn. Duke University Press, 905 W Main St, Ste 18 B, PO Box 90660, Durham, NC 27701; subscriptions@dukeupress.edu; http://www.dukeupress.edu. Illus., index, adv. Sample. Refereed. Vol. ends: Fall. Microform: MIM; PQC. Reprint: PSC. *Indexed:* A01, A22, ArtHuCI, IIMP, RILM. *Bk. rev.:* 2-3, 3-6 pages, signed. *Aud.:* Ac.

Founded in 1957 at the Yale School of Music, the *Journal of Music Theory* publishes peer-reviewed scholarly articles that examine and reexamine theoretical and technical aspects of music compositions, both historical and contemporary. Examples of articles in recent issues include "Transformational Aspects of Arvo Part's Tintinnabuli Music," "Schenker and Schoenberg on the Will of the Tone," and "A. B. Marx's Sonatenform: Coming to Terms with Beethoven's Rhetoric." Each issue also contains several lengthy book reviews. Also available as an online journal (http://jmt.dukejournals.org). Recommended for academic libraries.

3976. Journal of Music Therapy. Supersedes (in 1964): *National Association for Music Therapy. Bulletin.* [ISSN: 0022-2917] 1962. q. EUR 210. Ed(s): Jayne Standley. American Music Therapy Association, 8455 Colesville Rd, Ste 1000, Silver Spring, MD 20910; info@musictherapy.org; http://www.musictherapy.org. Illus., index, adv. Refereed. Vol. ends: Winter. Microform: PQC. *Indexed:* A22, IIMP, PsycInfo, RILM. *Aud.:* Ac, Sa.

The *Journal of Music Therapy,* published by the American Music Therapy Association, presents scholarly articles for music therapists and other professionals, who use music in a therapeutic manner. Submissions undergo an anonymous peer-review. Articles document theoretical and experimental studies on how music affects listeners' physiological, emotional, and mental states. Aspects of music therapy education and problems for students in the field are also considered. Each issue contains from two to five articles of approximately 20–30 pages in length. Articles include abstracts and references. This title also is available online (www.musictherapy.org/). An index appears in the last issue of each volume. Recommended for academic libraries.

3977. The Journal of Musicology: a quarterly review of music history, criticism, analysis, and performance practice. [ISSN: 0277-9269] 1982. q. USD 242 (print & online eds.). Ed(s): Klara Moricz, Daniel R Melamed. University of California Press, Journals Division, 2000 Ctr St, Ste 303, Berkeley, CA 94704; customerservice@ucpressjournals.com; http://www.ucpressjournals.com. Illus., adv. Refereed. Circ: 878. Microform: PQC. Reprint: PSC. *Indexed:* A01, A22, ABS&EES, AmHI, ArtHuCI, BRI, E01, IIMP, MLA-IB, P02, RILM. *Aud.:* Ac, Sa.

The *Journal of Musicology* provides a forum for peer-reviewed articles on topics in all areas of musical scholarship, including history, criticism, theory, analysis, performance, and research. This journal's very accessible and well-documented articles and review essays treat music from a variety of perspectives for scholars, musicians, and other students of music. Each issue contains four to five articles, with abstracts appearing at the end of articles. Also available in online format. Recommended for academic and large public libraries. URL: www.journalofmusicology.org/

3978. Journal of Research in Music Education. [ISSN: 0022-4294] 1953. q. USD 247. Ed(s): Wendy L Sims. Sage Publications, Inc., 2455 Teller Rd, Thousand Oaks, CA 91320; info@sagepub.com; http://www.sagepub.com. Illus., adv. Sample. Refereed. Vol. ends: Winter. Microform: PQC. Reprint: PSC. *Indexed:* A01, A22, ArtHuCI, E01, ERIC, IIMP, MLA-IB, PsycInfo, RILM. *Aud.:* Ac, Sa.

The *Journal of Research in Music Education* (*JRME*), published quarterly for the National Association for Music Education, presents articles on historical, philosophical, descriptive, and experimental research in music education. Articles are critiqued by an editorial committee of scholars and intended for researchers and music teachers in all settings. Each issue contains approximately six articles written by professional educators, and announcements including calls for papers. Articles in recent issues have addressed such topics as the decision-making process in determining whether to maintain or eliminate music in public schools, teaching musical expression, and concerns relating to educating both K–12 teachers and students. Also available as an online subscription. Recommended for academic, high school, and large public libraries. URL: http://jrm.sagepub.com

3979. Journal of Singing. Former titles (until Sep.1995): *N A T S Journal;* (until May1985): *N A T S Bulletin;* (until 1962): *National Association of Teachers of Singing. Bulletin.* [ISSN: 1086-7732] 1944. 5x/yr. USD 60 (Individuals, USD 55; Free to members). Ed(s): Richard Dale Sjoerdsma. National Association of Teachers of Singing (N A T S), 9957 Moorings Dr, Ste 401, Jacksonville, FL 32257; info@nats.org; http://www.nats.org. Illus., index, adv. Refereed. Microform: PQC. *Indexed:* A22, ABS&EES, BRI, IIMP, RILM. *Bk. rev.:* 1-2, 300-500 words, signed. *Aud.:* Ac, Sa.

Published by the National Association of Teachers of Singing (NATS), this journal offers practical information for its members around the world. In addition to information about the organization, each issue contains feature articles on such topics as: the careers of particular singers and singing teachers, pedagogical and vocal techniques, diction, repertoire, medical issues, and music history. The *Journal of Singing* also lists upcoming workshops appropriate for either students or teachers and other relevant events of interest. A section of each publication is devoted to critical reviews of new books, scores, and multimedia items. Of interest to singers, private voice instructors, vocal coaches, and choral conductors, it is recommended for academic and large public libraries.

3980. Medical Problems of Performing Artists. [ISSN: 0885-1158] 1986. q. USD 116 (Individuals, USD 64). Ed(s): Dr. Ralph A Manchester. Science & Medicine, PO Box 313, Narberth, PA 19072. Illus., index, adv. Refereed. Circ: 1000. *Indexed:* A22, ArtHuCI, BRI, ErgAb, ExcerpMed, IIMP, IIPA, RILM. *Bk. rev.:* 1, 250 words, signed. *Aud.:* Ac, Sa.

Medical Problems of Performing Artists publishes peer-reviewed articles that focus on the origins, diagnoses, and treatments of medical problems encountered by performing artists, including muscular and neurological disorders, anxieties, stress, voice and hearing disorders, repetitive stress injuries, and substance abuse. As the official journal of the Performing Arts Medical Association (PAMA), the Dutch Performing Arts Medicine Association (NVDMG), and the Australian Society for Performing Arts Healthcare (ASPAH), this publication serves as a worldwide forum for medical and academic professionals to communicate their research findings and practices. Each issue contains approximately six to eight articles with abstracts, abstracts of relevant articles in other journals, and occasional book reviews. Tables of contents, abstracts, and full text are available for (or from) back issues at www.sciandmed.com/mppa. Recommended for academic and large public libraries.

3981. Music and Arts in Action. [ISSN: 1754-7105] 2008. irreg. Free. University of Exeter, Department of Sociology & Philosophy, Amory Bldg, Rennes Dr, Exeter, EX4 4RJ, United Kingdom. Refereed. *Aud.:* Ga, Ac, Sa.

Music and Arts in Action (MAiA) is a peer-reviewed, online journal that publishes articles that explore issues relating to the interplay of music and arts in society. In an effort to present a broad, inclusive forum for discussion of the issues, this journal includes contributions from not only researchers and educators but also from journalists, art historians, artists, practitioners, cultural professionals, and others. Some issues contain articles that revolve around a specific theme, while others contain articles on a wide variety of topics relating to the interrelations of music, arts, and society. Recent issues have included discussions of Venezuela's national music education program, El Sistema; the use of music in dementia care; and how the dying and mourning engage with the arts. *MAiA*'s articles often include images, sound, and video embedded in the text. A future paper-based edition is planned that will maintain links to online, multimedia enhancements. Recommended for academic and large public libraries. URL: www.musicandartsinaction.net/index.php/maia

3982. Music and Letters. [ISSN: 0027-4224] 1920. q. EUR 267. Ed(s): Sam Barrett, Daniel Grimley. Oxford University Press, Great Clarendon St, Oxford, OX2 6DP, United Kingdom; enquiry@oup.co.uk; http:// www.oxfordjournals.org/. Illus., index, adv. Sample. Refereed. Vol. ends: Nov. Microform: PQC. Reprint: PSC. *Indexed:* A01, A06, A22, AmHI, ArtHuCI, E01, IIMP, MLA-IB, P02, RILM. *Bk. rev.:* 25, 500-1,000 words, signed. *Aud.:* Ac, Sa.

Music and Letters is a refereed journal that publishes articles of any length on aspects of historical, analytical, and critical musicology of any musical period. Article topics can be letters, documents, reminiscences, and other written records that relate to musicians and their compositions, e.g., an examination of contents of an anthology of sixteenth-century sacred vocal music, or a revised view of what caused the disruption of the Dutch premiere of Stockhausen's *Stimmung* in 1969. A typical issue contains three or four articles and a large number of book reviews, as well as occasional music reviews. The journal's web site contains tables of contents back to 1920. Searching capability by author, title, citation, and keyword is provided. Also available as an online subscription (http://ml.oxfordjournals.org/). Recommended for academic libraries.

3983. Music and Politics. [ISSN: 1938-7687] 2007. s-a. Free. Ed(s): Patricia Hall. University of California, Santa Barbara, Music Department, 1315 Music Bldg, Santa Barbara, CA 93106; music@music.ucsb.edu; http://www.music.ucsb.edu/. *Aud.:* Ac, Sa.

Music and Politics is a peer-reviewed, open-access electronic journal published twice a year and hosted by MPublishing, a divison of the University of Michigan Library. First published in 2007, this peer-reviewed publication contains articles exploring the interaction of music and politics. Contributors include both established scholars and graduate students from such fields as ethnomusicology, film studies, musicology, political science, and sociology. All articles are published in English, but individual issues often include translations of relevant articles previously published in foreign language journals. Most issues contain a list of recent books that cover topics related to music and politics. Recommended for academic libraries. URL: http://quod.lib.umich.edu/m/mp/

3984. Music Education Research. [ISSN: 1461-3808] 1999. q. GBP 436 (print & online eds.). Ed(s): Sarah Hennessy. Routledge, 4 Park Sq, Milton Park, Abingdon, OX14 4RN, United Kingdom; subscriptions@tandf.co.uk; http://www.tandfonline.com. Adv. Sample. Refereed. Reprint: PSC. *Indexed:* A01, A22, ArtHuCI, E01, ERIC, RILM. *Bk. rev.:* Number and length vary. *Aud.:* Ac.

An international refereed journal published quarterly, *Music Education Research* provides a "forum for cross-cultural investigations and discussions relating to all areas and levels of music education." The focus of the journal is on research and methodological issues and on the furthering of ideas relating to both practical and theoretical developments in music education for learners of all ages. The articles, written in straightforward, accessible language, address music education concerns from the perspectives of formal and informal teaching and learning, studio and classroom settings, instrumental and vocal studies, musical creativity and development, perceptions and attitudes, implementation of emerging technologies, curriculum design and assessment, and cultural traditions. Annotations precede each of the articles. The journal also includes book reviews. Both print and online subscriptions are available. Recommended for academic libraries that support music education. URL: www.tandfonline.com/loi/cmue20

3985. Music Educators Journal. Former titles (until 1934): *Music Supervisors' Journal;* (until 1915): *Music Supervisors' Bulletin.* [ISSN: 0027-4321] 1914. q. USD 269. Ed(s): Patrick K Freer. Sage Publications, Inc., 2455 Teller Rd, Thousand Oaks, CA 91320; info@sagepub.com; http://www.sagepub.com. Illus., index. Refereed. Circ: 80000. Vol. ends: May. Microform: PQC. Reprint: PSC. *Indexed:* A01, A22, BAS, BRI, CBRI, E01, ERIC, IIMP, MLA-IB, RILM. *Bk. rev.:* 8, 150-200 words, signed. *Aud.:* Ems, Hs, Ga, Ac, Sa.

As a publication of the The National Association for Music Education (MENC), *Music Educators Journal* focuses on the approaches and methods used for teaching music in schools, colleges, community orchestras, and other education environments. Examples of topics addressed in recent issues include reflections on the power of music, improvisation for classically-trained musicians, and curricular reform. Each issue contains six to eight feature articles and several short book, video, and technology reviews. "Samplings" provides abstracts of articles published in other MENC journals. Also available in online format. Recommended for all libraries and music teachers. URL: http://mej.sagepub.com

3986. Music Library Association. Notes. [ISSN: 0027-4380] 1934. q. USD 100 Free to members. Ed(s): James P Cassaro. Music Library Association, 8551 Research Way, Ste 180, Middleton, WI 53562; http://www.musiclibraryassoc.org. Illus., index, adv. Refereed. Vol. ends: Jun. Microform: PQC. *Indexed:* A01, A22, ABS&EES, AmHI, ArtHuCI, BRI, CBRI, E01, IIMP, MLA-IB, P02, RILM. *Bk. rev.:* 40-50, 250-500 words, signed. *Aud.:* Ac, Sa.

Notes, the quarterly journal of the Music Library Association (MLA), publishes articles on contemporary and historical issues in music librarianship, music bibliography, and music publishing. Each issue contains two to four feature articles, but the main body of the journal is an extensive section of signed reviews of books covering a wide range of music-related topics and genres, including publications on music librarianship and research. Issues also contain reviews of scores, sound recordings, digital media, and software; a long list of books recently published; and lists of music and music publishers' catalogs received. Highly recommended for all music librarians and bibliographers.

3987. *Music Perception.* [ISSN: 0730-7829] 1983. 5x/yr. USD 489 (print & online eds.). Ed(s): Christine K Koh, Lola L Cuddy. University of California Press, Journals Division, 2000 Ctr St, Ste 303, Berkeley, CA 94704; customerservice@ucpressjournals.com; http://www.ucpressjournals.com. Illus., index, adv. Refereed. Circ: 640. Vol. ends: Summer. Microform: PQC. Reprint: PSC. *Indexed:* A01, A22, ArtHuCI, BRI, E01, IIMP, PsycInfo, RILM. *Bk. rev.:* 2, 2,000-3,500 words, signed. *Aud.:* Ac, Sa.

Music Perception publishes refereed articles on studies about how music is experienced and interpreted. Contributors include scientists and musicians using critical, methodological, theoretical, and empirical approaches from disciplines such as psychology, neurology, linguistics, acoustics, and artificial intelligence. Topics covered in recent issues include the relationship between musical structures and perceived or felt emotions, the impact of the bass drum on human dance movement, and mental practice in music memorization. Contains some book reviews and announcements of future conferences and meetings. Recommended for academic libraries.

3988. *Music Performance Research.* [ISSN: 1755-9219] 2007. a. Free. Ed(s): Dr. Jane Ginsborg. Royal Northern College of Music, 124 Oxford Rd, Manchester, M13 9RD, United Kingdom; info@rncm.ac.uk; http://www.rncm.ac.uk/. Refereed. *Indexed:* A01. *Aud.:* Ac, Sa.

Music Performance Research is a free online journal that aims "to become part of a broader scientific discussion of music as a model of human behaviour." Articles present theoretical and empirical research on all aspects of the preparation and performance of music, such as the mental, physical, and social aspects of performing. Examples of contents are "The Art of Research in Live Music Performance"; "Contemporary Performance Practice and Tradition"; and "Influence of Strategy on Memorization Efficiency." Recommended for academic libraries. URL: http://mpr-online.net/

3989. *Music Theory Spectrum.* [ISSN: 0195-6167] 1979. s-a. EUR 127. Ed(s): Severine Neff. University of California Press, Journals Division, 2000 Ctr St, Ste 303, Berkeley, CA 94704; customerservice@ucpressjournals.com; http://www.ucpressjournals.com. Adv. Refereed. Circ: 1257. Reprint: PSC. *Indexed:* A01, A22, ArtHuCI, E01, IIMP, RILM. *Bk. rev.:* Number and length vary. *Aud.:* Ac.

The official publication of the Society for Music Theory, *Music Theory Spectrum* publishes well-documented articles on all aspects of music theory, including studies of compositional elements and methods, musical aesthetics, and analyses of compositions of a historical period. Interdisciplinary articles that cover the intersection of music theory with such fields as ethnomusicology, mathematics, musicology, philosophy, psychology, and performance are also included. Issues generally contain four to six articles and extensive book reviews. Some issues also contain research notes, announcements for new books, and sections for reader response. Subscriptions are included with membership in the society. Online access is available (www.ucpressjournals.com/journal.asp?j=mts). Recommended for academic libraries.

3990. *The Musical Quarterly.* [ISSN: 0027-4631] 1915. q. EUR 199. Ed(s): Irene Zedlacher, Leon Botstein. Oxford University Press, 2001 Evans Rd, Cary, NC 27513; http://www.us.oup.com. Illus., index. Sample. Refereed. Vol. ends: Winter. Microform: PMC; PQC. Reprint: PSC. *Indexed:* A01, A22, ABS&EES, AmHI, ArtHuCI, BRI, CBRI, E01, IIMP, MLA-IB, P02, RILM. *Aud.:* Ga, Ac.

The Musical Quarterly, founded in 1915 by Oscar Sonneck, publishes peer-reviewed articles that focus on the contemporary study of music from the perspective of, and in combination with, other scholarly disciplines. Regular sections include "American Musics," "Music and Culture," "Texts and Contents," "The Twentieth Century and Beyond," and "Institutions, Technology, and Economics." Most issues contain four to six feature articles with notes. Issues also may include review essays about new books and recordings and recent performances of note. The web site contains links to tables of contents of issues from 1915 forward, and search functions by author, title, citation, and keyword. Print, online, or package subscription options are available. Recommended for public and academic libraries. URL: http://mq.oxfordjournals.org/

3991. *Musical Times.* Formerly (until 1903): *Musical Times and Singing Class Circular.* [ISSN: 0027-4666] 1844. q. GBP 75. Musical Times Publications Ltd., 7 Brunswick Mews, Hove, BN3 1HD, United Kingdom. Microform: PQC; WMP. *Indexed:* A01, A22, AmHI, ArtHuCI, BRI, IIMP, MLA-IB, RILM. *Bk. rev.:* Number and length vary. *Aud.:* Ga, Ac, Sa.

Begun in 1844 and still published in the United Kingdom, *Musical Times* boasts it is "the world's oldest continuously publishing classical music magazine." Each issue contains several feature articles between 2,000 and 8,000 words in length, often heavily footnoted. These articles are described as covering a "wide variety of subjects pertaining to 'classical' music" that are of potential interest to both scholars and general readers. Article contributors are often university professors, well-published authors, or other experts in their respective fields of writing. Most issues contain at least two lengthy "review-articles" and several book reviews. The "review-articles" are extended essays that provide a detailed analysis of a new publication, and they attempt to place the publication in the context of the author's previous writings. Recommended for large public and academic libraries.

3992. *Nineteenth Century Music.* [ISSN: 0148-2076] 1977. 3x/yr. USD 253 (print & online eds.). Ed(s): Christina Acosta, Lawrence Kramer. University of California Press, Journals Division, 2000 Ctr St, Ste 303, Berkeley, CA 94704; customerservice@ucpressjournals.com; http://www.ucpressjournals.com. Illus., index, adv. Refereed. Vol. ends: Spring. Reprint: PSC. *Indexed:* A01, A22, ABS&EES, AmHI, ArtHuCI, BRI, E01, IIMP, MLA-IB, P02, RILM. *Bk. rev.:* 1, 4,000 words, signed. *Aud.:* Ac, Sa.

Nineteenth Century Music publishes refereed articles on all aspects of western music that was produced during the period from the mid-eighteenth to the mid-twentieth centuries. Topics concern the reciprocal relations between music and society and include composition, analyses, performance, aesthetics, history and historiography, gender studies, and more. Issues contain occasional reviews of books, articles, and performances. Online access is available through JSTOR (www.jstor.org/page/journal/19thcenturymusic/about.html). Recommended for academic libraries.

3993. *Opera News.* [ISSN: 0030-3607] 1936. m. USD 31.95 domestic; USD 71.95 foreign. Ed(s): F. Paul Driscoll. Metropolitan Opera Guild, Inc., 70 Lincoln Center Plaza, New York, NY 10023; http://www.metguild.org/. Illus., index. Circ: 100000 Paid. Vol. ends: Jun/Jun. Microform: PQC. *Indexed:* A01, A22, ABS&EES, AmHI, ArtHuCI, BRI, C37, CBRI, IIMP, IIPA, MASUSE, MLA-IB, P02, RILM. *Bk. rev.:* 1-3, 500 words, signed. *Aud.:* Ga, Ac.

Published by the Metropolitan Opera Guild, *Opera News* provides fans with the latest news and information on the Metropolitan Opera company and opera around the world. Each glossy issue contains approximately three to six feature articles that provide history and analysis of selected works, and profiles of singers, conductors, directors, and composers. A section of the magazine offers information on upcoming Metropolitan Opera broadcasts with lists of cast members, synopses of plots, and references to further information on each opera. Also included in each issue is the latest opera and opera-related news, concert reviews arranged by countries and cities, CD and video reviews, occasional book reviews, and lists of upcoming performances worldwide. Online access to current contents and archives is available with a subscription. Recommended for public and academic libraries.

3994. The Opera Quarterly. [ISSN: 0736-0053] 1983. q. EUR 230. Ed(s): Tami Wysocki-Niimi, David J Levin. Oxford University Press, 2001 Evans Rd, Cary, NC 27513; http://www.us.oup.com. Illus. Sample. Refereed. Vol. ends: Fall. Reprint: PSC. *Indexed:* A01, A22, ABS&EES, AmHI, ArtHuCI, BRI, E01, IIMP, IIPA, MLA-IB, P02, RILM. *Bk. rev.:* 4-5, 1,000-1,500 words, signed. *Aud.:* Ga, Ac.

The Opera Quarterly publishes scholarly articles on opera and opera production, performers, opera history, and analyses of historical and contemporary works, as well as interviews and remembrances of major vocalists. While occasional issues are unthemed, the contents of most issues usually focus on a particularly topic, e.g., opera as a reflection of history, or Mozart's *Die Zauberflöte.* Each issue contains approximately six articles (with illustrations), as well as performance reviews and book, CD, and video reviews. Also listed are books and CDs received. Tables of contents from 1983 to the present are available at the journal's web site. Available in online format. Recommended for large public and academic libraries. URL: http://oq.oxfordjournals.org/

3995. Percussive Notes. Incorporates (in 1983): *Percussive Notes. Research Edition;* Which was formerly (until 1982): *Percussive Notes. Research Edition, Percussionist;* Which superseded in part (in 1980): *Percussionist;* Which incorporated: *Percussionist and Percussive Notes.* [ISSN: 0553-6502] 1961. 6x/yr. Percussive Arts Society, Inc., 701 NW Ferris Ave, Lawton, OK 73507-5442; percarts@pas.org; http://www.pas.org. Illus., adv. Circ: 7000. *Indexed:* A22, IIMP, RILM. *Bk. rev.:* Number and length vary. *Aud.:* Hs, Ga, Ac.

Published six times a year, *Percussive Notes* is the journal of the Percussive Arts Society, the aim of which is "promoting percussion education, research, performance, and appreciation throughout the world." Among the journal's contributors are professors, graduate and doctoral students, performers, composers, and private teachers. Articles focus on percussion instruments, their history, and various aspects of performing on them. Regular headings found in the journal include "Drumset," "Education," "Health and Wellness," "Keyboard," "Symphonic," "Marching," "World," "Technology," "Research," and "Career Development." The journal also includes three regular columns, one of which includes reviews of new books, scores, and recordings. Membership includes online access. Recommended for large public and academic libraries.

3996. Performance Practice Review (Online). Formerly (until 1997): *Performance Practice Review (Print).* [ISSN: 2166-8205] 1988. s-a. Free. Ed(s): Robert Zappulla. Claremont Graduate University, 150 E 10th St, Claremont, CA 91711; http://www.cgu.edu. Refereed. *Indexed:* IIMP, RILM. *Bk. rev.:* Number and length vary. *Aud.:* Ga, Ac, Sa.

Performance Practice Review (PPR), a "blind, peer-reviewed journal devoted to the study of Western musical performance practices," has been published online since 2006 on a continuous basis. (From 1988 to 1997, it was published biannually in print format; all issues of this titles are available from the web site.) Articles are a minimum of 3,000 words and may cover performance practices from any historical period. The online format facilitates the inclusion of audio-visual examples as well as musical examples and illustrations. Articles may appear in languages other than English (including Dutch, French, German, Italian, and Spanish). Many issues include book reviews and correspondence that responds to previously published articles and reviews. Recommended for academic and large public libraries. URL: http://scholarship.claremont.edu/ppr/

3997. Perspectives of New Music. [ISSN: 0031-6016] 1962. s-a. USD 152 (print & online eds.). Ed(s): Benjamin Boretz, Robert Morris. Perspectives of New Music, Inc., 1107 NE 45th St, Ste 424, Seattle, WA 98105. Illus., index, adv. Refereed. Circ: 1350 Paid. Vol. ends: Summer. *Indexed:* A01, A22, ABS&EES, AmHI, BRI, IIMP, MLA-IB, P02, RILM. *Aud.:* Ac, Sa.

Perspectives of New Music publishes articles on musicians and developments in contemporary music and is aimed at composers, performers, and scholars. Articles contain research and analyses of new music theory and composition, sociological and philosophical studies, interviews, reviews, and occasional excerpts from musical scores. Current issues especially explore material on young composers, multimedia art and music, mathematical modeling, collaboration and improvisation, and more "uncharted" territories. Some issues

or parts of issues are devoted to a specific contemporary composer. Issues generally contain seven to nine articles with musical diagrams and notation. Tables of contents of issues back to summer 2006 can be viewed on the journal's web site. Recommended for academic libraries. URL: www.stthomas.edu/rimeonline

3998. R I M E. [ISSN: 1532-8090] 2003. a. Free. Ed(s): Dr. Bruce Gleason. Research and Issues in Music Education, 2115 Summit Ave, LOR 103, St. Paul, MN 55105. Refereed. *Indexed:* ERIC. *Aud.:* Hs, Ac.

RIME (Research and Issues in Music Education) is an online, open-access journal published annually. Its stated purpose is "to provide a forum devoted to thorough research and commentary that energizes, informs, advances, and reforms the practice and pedagogy of music teaching." This privately-funded, peer-reviewed research publication is international in scope. Articles focus on various levels and aspects of music education and are preceded by abstracts. Recent articles address such topics as students' perceptions of teacher turnover in high school bands, curriculum reform in rural China, and assessment in music education. Recommended for academic libraries and some high school libraries. URL: www.stthomas.edu/rimeonline

The Source. See African American section.

3999. The Strad: a monthly journal for professionals and amateurs of all stringed instruments played with the bow. Incorporates (1996-2008): *The Double Bassist.* [ISSN: 0039-2049] 1890. m. GBP 59.95 domestic; EUR 124.95 in Europe; USD 119.95 in US & Canada. Newsquest Media Group, Falmouth Business Park, Bickland Water Rd, Cornwall, TR11 4SZ, United Kingdom; http://www.newsquest.co.uk/. Illus., adv. Sample. Circ: 17000 Paid. Microform: PQC; WMP. *Indexed:* A01, A22, AmHI, ArtHuCI, IIMP, RILM. *Bk. rev.:* 3-5, length varies. *Aud.:* Ac, Sa.

The Strad focuses on all people and things related to the most popular classical string instruments (violin, viola, cello). Topics of articles include profiles of orchestras, ensembles, performers, luthiers; teachers and explication of their methods; instruction on playing technique; a focus on special instruments; etc. Issues also contain book, CD, and concert reviews. This magazine has a well-designed web site that includes job postings, a listing of services and course offerings, reviews, and other relevant, useful information. Issues are available in digital format. Recommended for public and academic libraries. URL: www.thestrad.com

4000. Strings: the magazine for players and makers of bowed instruments. [ISSN: 0888-3106] 1986. 12x/yr. USD 42 domestic; USD 54 Canada; USD 72 elsewhere. String Letter Publishing, 255 West End Ave, San Rafael, CA 94901; http://www.stringletter.com. Adv. Circ: 13957 Paid. *Indexed:* A22, IIMP, RILM. *Bk. rev.:* Number and length vary. *Aud.:* Ac, Sa.

Strings is a magazine devoted to all aspects of stringed instruments played with a bow, including violin, viola, violoncello, and double bass. Articles feature topics such as instrument care and repair, repertoire, performance issues, interviews with players and composers, information about various violin makers, and materials used in creating stringed instruments. Many issues have a special focus (e.g., the double bass, contemporary instruments and bows, buyer's guide, etc.). Issues also provide reviews of books, recordings, and scores. Subscriptions include 24/7 web access to the enhanced, interactive current edition of this publication. The online version provides information about and links to related events, newsletters, an online store, and social media. Of interest to string players, teachers, and stringed instrument makers and repair persons, this title is recommended for academic and public libraries.

4001. Tempo (London, 1939): a quarterly review of modern music. [ISSN: 0040-2982] 1939. q. GBP 95. Ed(s): Calum MacDonald. Cambridge University Press, The Edinburgh Bldg, Shaftesbury Rd, Cambridge, CB2 8RU, United Kingdom; journals@cambridge.org; http://www.cambridge.org/uk. Illus., adv. Reprint: PSC. *Indexed:* A22, AmHI, ArtHuCI, E01, IIMP, RILM. *Bk. rev.:* 2-4, 1,500 words, signed. *Aud.:* Ac, Sa.

Tempo publishes articles on twentieth-century music and contemporary concert music; subjects include profiles of composers and musicians, interviews, aesthetic studies, and historical and analytical studies of composers' works. Articles are international in scope. A typical issue contains four research articles, reviews of books and CDs, and reviews of world premieres. A "News" section lists premieres of new compositions, new books received, and appointments. The journal's web page lists the contents of issues back to winter 1939. Digital copies are available through Cambridge Journals Online (http://journals.cambridge.org/action/displayJournal?jid=TEM). Recommended for academic libraries.

4002. *Voices: a world forum for music therapy.* [ISSN: 1504-1611] 2001. 3x/yr. Free. Uni Health, The Grieg Academy Music Therapy Research Centre, c/o Grieg Academy, Dept of Music, University of Bergen, Bergen, 5015, Norway; http://helse.uni.no/Default.aspx?site=4&lg=2. *Aud.:* Ac, Sa.

Voices: A World Forum for Music Therapy is an online publication of international scope. This journal has two sections: "Original Voices" and "Research Voices." The former includes essays, interviews, perspectives on practice, reports, and stories. The latter (as its name suggests) contains various types of research articles, as well as reviews and theoretical studies. The journal is built around the premise that its free, online access facilitates its purpose as a forum for global exchange of ideas and knowledge relating to the field of music therapy. Recommended for academic, large public, and hospital libraries. URL: www.voices.no

4003. *Women and Music: a journal of gender and culture.* [ISSN: 1090-7505] 1997. a. USD 63. Ed(s): Suzanne G Cusick. University of Nebraska Press, 1111 Lincoln Mall, Lincoln, NE 68588; pressmail@unl.edu; http://www.nebraskapress.unl.edu. Adv. Refereed. *Indexed:* A22, BRI, C42, E01, FemPer, GW, IIMP, MLA-IB, RILM. *Bk. rev.:* 10, essay length, signed. *Aud.:* Ac, Sa.

Women and Music is an annual publication of the International Alliance for Women in Music (IAWM). Articles report on the interrelationships of music, gender, and culture, and their topics are international in scope. The articles analyze cultures, works, and historical periods from the perspective of a variety of disciplines; or they may discuss issues relating to women composers, performers, teachers, etc. This journal contains review essays and book reviews. It is available electronically through Project MUSE (www.nebraskapress.unl.edu/product/Women-and-Music,673171.aspx). Recommended for academic collections.

4004. *The World of Music.* [ISSN: 0043-8774] 1959. 3x/yr. EUR 64 domestic; EUR 78 foreign; EUR 24 newsstand/cover. V W B - Verlag fuer Wissenschaft und Bildung, Postfach 110368, Berlin, 10833, Germany; info@vwb-verlag.com; http://www.vwb-verlag.com. Illus., adv. Refereed. *Indexed:* A22, A47, ArtHuCI, BAS, FR, IBSS, IIMP, MLA-IB, RILM. *Bk. rev.:* 5, 750-1,000 words, signed. *Aud.:* Ac, Sa.

The world of music (new series) is a continuation of the journal *The world of music* as previously edited by Jonathan Stock at the University of Sheffield. The "new series" began in 2009. It is an international, peer-reviewed journal that seeks to publish the results of ethnomusicological research into musical practices and traditions around the world. Although representing a variety of theoretical perspectives and approaches, the articles reflect a shared goal of understanding the musics of the world, their dynamics, their manifold contexts, and their meanings. Each issue focuses on a musical topic or a cultural or geographic region. A typical issue contains six to eight articles and several book and CD reviews. Articles vary in length from five to 20 pages, with notes and bibliographies. Issues include photographs and musical examples. The journal's site also displays abstracts of articles from 1997 to the present, as well as a bibliography arranged alphabetically by author. Recommended for academic libraries.

Popular

Competition from online popular music resources, such as blogs and information provided by online retailers of music, has caused a significant reduction in the past decade in relevant magazines. Primary popular music genres such as rock, jazz, and blues maintain key publications that provide in-

depth information for fans and professionals alike. The publications included here are selected as stable, core resources for those looking for periodicals that provide both quality writing and timely information on the current state of popular music.

4005. *Billboard (New York): the international newsweekly of music, video, and home entertainment.* Formerly: *Billboard Music Week.* [ISSN: 0006-2510] 1894. w. USD 299 combined subscription in US & Canada (print & online eds.); USD 450 combined subscription in Europe (print & online eds.); USD 925 combined subscription Japan (print & online eds.). Prometheus Global Media, 770 Broadway, 7th Fl, New York, NY 10003; http://www.prometheusgm.com. Illus., adv. *Indexed:* A01, A22, ABIn, B01, B02, B03, BRI, C37, C42, CBRI, Chicano, F01, IIMP, IIPA, MASUSE, P02, RILM. *Aud.:* Ga.

Billboard remains the most trusted resource in charting the popularity of music in all forms from pop to country, R&B, Latin, and classical. The coverage of genres is extensive and always growing. In the past year, the publication has extended efforts to chart the impact of social media and Internet streaming on popular music. The publication publishes reviews that focus primarily on describing the songs or albums and their prospects for commercial success. Upcoming trends and artists are documented thoroughly, as well as the latest news affecting the music industry. The publication's web site covers the same material, as well as adding access to voluminous historical archives of music charts from the past. URL: http://Billboard.com

4006. *Down Beat.* [ISSN: 0012-5768] 1934. m. USD 26.99 domestic; USD 37.99 Canada; USD 48.99 foreign. Maher Publications, 102 North Haven Rd, Elmhurst, IL 60126; editor@downbeat.com. Illus., adv. Microform: PQC. *Indexed:* A01, A22, AmHI, ArtHuCI, BRI, CBRI, Chicano, IIMP, MASUSE, P02. *Bk. rev.:* 25-35, 500-1,000 words. *Aud.:* Ga.

This publication is one of the oldest and most respected periodicals in any popular music genre. Coverage centers on jazz, but it also provides extensive material on blues and related music. Readers' polls on the year's best music have been published since the 1930s, and critics' polls since the 1950s. The results of these polls are archived on the publication's web site. Extensive reviews of current music are provided. Profiles of current artists and in-depth interviews help provide an even richer view of the current world of jazz and blues music. A unique feature of the periodical is "The Blindfold Test," in which a current musician is asked to listen to tracks and discuss the relevance of the music heard. This publication is an outstanding introduction to current jazz and blues music for a general audience, as well as being an essential resource for academic audiences.

4007. *JazzTimes: America's jazz magazine.* Supersedes: *Radio Free Jazz.* [ISSN: 0272-572X] 1972. 10x/yr. USD 23.95 domestic; USD 35.95 Canada; USD 59.95 elsewhere. Ed(s): Lee Mergner. Jazz Times Inc., Madavor Media, 85 Quincy Ave, Ste B, Quincy, MA 02169; jtimes@aol.com. Illus., adv. Circ: 100000 Paid. Microform: PQC. *Indexed:* A22, IIMP, RILM. *Bk. rev.:* Number and length vary. *Aud.:* Ga.

This publication provides a very thorough examination of the current state of jazz music for an audience ranging from casual fans to music professionals. Many of the contributors have received awards for being among the best in jazz journalism. The reviews cover not only recorded music, but also books, concerts, audio equipment, and even instruments. Regular columns provide examinations of key artists, interviews, and previews of upcoming events. Extensive directories of record labels, festivals, and artists are provided as a useful reference resource. The publication provides extensive annual critics and readers' polls to give a snapshot of the current state of jazz music. These are archived on the publication's web site. The stylish look of this publication and the quality of the photography included make it very pleasing to read and browse.

4008. *Living Blues: the magazine of the African American blues tradition.* Incorporates: *Living Bluesletter.* [ISSN: 0024-5232] 1970. bi-m. USD 25.95 domestic; USD 31.95 Canada; USD 41.95 elsewhere. Ed(s): Brett Bonner. University of Mississippi, Center for the Study of Southern Culture, Barnard Observatory, Sorority Row and Grove Loop, PO Box 1848, University, MS 38677; cssc@olemiss.edu; http://www.olemiss.edu/depts/south/. Illus., adv. Microform: PQC. *Indexed:* A22, IIBP, IIMP, MLA-IB, RILM. *Aud.:* Ga, Ac.

This publication sets the standard for magazines covering the blues scene. The magazine not only provides in-depth coverage of the music with profiles of artists, reviews of new music, and radio charts, it also helps sponsor events that preserve the blues tradition. The approach and style of the magazine is suitably laid back, to match the music itself. For general to academic audiences, this publication is a first choice for coverage of blues music. URL: www.livingblues.com

4009. *Rolling Stone.* [ISSN: 0035-791X] 1967. 26x/yr. USD 14.97 domestic; USD 38 Canada; USD 65 elsewhere. Ed(s): Eric Bates, Will Dana. Rolling Stone LLC, 1290 Ave. of the Americas, 2nd Fl, New York, NY 10104; letters@rollingstone.com. Illus., adv. Circ: 1469213 Paid. Microform: PQC. *Indexed:* A01, A22, BRI, C37, CBCARef, CBRI, Chicano, F01, IIMP, IIPA, MASUSE, P02, RILM. *Bk. rev.:* Number and length vary. *Aud.:* Ga.

This publication continues to be a cornerstone of popular music criticism and news in the U.S. The periodical's rock leanings are not as prominent as in the past. There have been changes in coverage, as the relative size of rock in the commercial marketplace has shrunk. Politics and movies continue to be areas in which the publication reaches beyond simple coverage of music. Quality feature writing continues to be a hallmark of the magazine. Album reviews graded with a five-star system are influential in the industry. The publication's web site has a very extensive and well-organized archive of material from the past. Subscribers have complete access to all past issues of the publication, while extensive material remains available for free browsing. URL: www.rollingstone.com/

4010. *Sing Out!: folk music - folk songs.* [ISSN: 0037-5624] 1950. q. Free to members; Non-members, USD 30. Ed(s): Mark D Moss. Sing Out Corp., 512 E Fourth St, PO Box 5460, Bethlehem, PA 18015; http://www.singout.org. Illus., adv. *Indexed:* A01, A22, BRI, IIMP, MLA-IB, RILM. *Bk. rev.:* Number and length vary. *Aud.:* Ga.

This magazine is a quarterly publication issued by an organization of the same name that is dedicated to supporting and preserving traditional and contemporary folk music. A centerpiece of the print publication remains complete lead sheets on ten folk songs, accompanied by a CD with performances by the original artists. In addition, the magazine provides articles, news, and reviews. The definition of folk music is broad and ranges from blues to bluegrass, Celtic, and Cajun music. Festivals and awards dedicated to folk music are covered. The web site for the publication provides access to a streaming radio magazine as well as folk music directories. URL: www.singout.org/magazine.html

■ MUSIC REVIEWS

General/Audio Equipment

Erica Lynn Coe, Head, Instruction Services, University of Washington Tacoma Library, 1900 Commerce Street, Tacoma, WA 98402; elcoe@u.washington.edu

Introduction

With the ever-increasing methods to freely access music, consumers are more selective about the music they actually purchase. This section is devoted to magazines published in the United States and the United Kingdom that focus primarily on reviews of music and audio equipment. Because of this focus, the music publications below focus on classical and jazz. For other genres, see the "Music/Popular" section.

In addition, there are several noteworthy web sites. For classical reviews, see *Classical CD Review: a site for the serious collector* (http://classicalcdreview.com), with reviews by well-established reviewers, and *Classical Net* (www.classical.net), with reviews and articles. For jazz, try *Jazzreview* (www.jazzreview.com), and for independent music, try *Pitchfork* (http://pitchfork.com). For equipment reviews, consult *Audio Critic* (www.theaudiocritic.com/plog/) and *SoundStage Network* (www.soundstagenetwork.com).

Basic Periodicals

Ga: *The Absolute Sound, All About Jazz, American Record Guide, Fanfare* (Tenafly), *Gramophone;* Ac: *The Absolute Sound, American Record Guide, Fanfare* (Tenafly), *Gramophone.*

Basic Abstracts and Indexes

International Index to Music Periodicals, Music Index, RILM Abstracts of Music Literature.

General

4011. *All About Jazz.* 1995. d. Ed(s): John Kelman. All About Jazz, 761 Sproul Road, #211, Springfield, PA 19064. Adv. *Bk. rev.:* Number and length vary. *Aud.:* Ga, Ac.

All About Jazz provides reviews, articles, interviews, and news with an international scope. Reviews of new and reissued albums, as well as individual tracks, are added daily. While focusing on music and performance, the conversational-style reviews often begin with a brief background of the artist or group to place the recording in context. Album reviews include track listings, personnel, artist web sites, and internal links to pages about the artist and music label. Reviews can be searched by artist name, album title, record label, and author of review. Additional reviews are provided for live performances, books, and DVD/film. Recommended for both neophytes and serious jazz aficionados. URL: www.allaboutjazz.com

4012. *American Record Guide.* Former titles (until 1944): *Listener's Record Guide;* (until Sep.1944): *The American Music Lover;* (until 1935): *Music Lover's Guide.* [ISSN: 0003-0716] 1932. bi-m. USD 43 domestic; USD 55 Canada; USD 65 in Western Europe. Ed(s): Donald R Vroon. Record Guide Productions, 4412 Braddock St, Cincinnati, OH 45204; subs@americanrecordguide.com. Illus., index, adv. Sample. Vol. ends: Dec. *Indexed:* A01, A22, BRI, C37, CBRI, IIMP, MASUSE, P02. *Bk. rev.:* Number and length vary. *Aud.:* Ga, Ac.

American Record Guide, "America's oldest classical music review magazine," aims to remain free of advertiser influence. This results in a high-quality, robust magazine with few ads and over 150 pages of straightforward, critical recording reviews. The engaging reviews often begin with a history of the composer, performer, or work to place the recording in context, and most end with a recommendation. All aspects of the recording are up for scrutiny, including vocal and instrumental performance, listenability, interpretation of classics, song selection in collections, recording quality, and even CD packaging with regard to liner notes and accompanying texts. Most issues contain an "Overview" article that provides an extensive review of recordings by one composer, or from one area of the repertoire, such as Russian music. The magazine also includes video and live-performance reviews, as well as articles on current events in the classical music world. An annual index is published in the November/December or January/February issue. The web site provides an index to the overviews, current contents, brief biographies of reviewers, and a searchable index for subscribers only. The large number of reviews makes this an excellent magazine for public and academic libraries. URL: www.americanrecordguide.com

4013. *Classics Today: your online guide to classical music.* 1999. d. Free. Ed(s): David Vernier, David Hurwitz. Classics Today. *Aud.:* Ga, Ac.

Classics Today is the "world's first and only classical music DAILY." The easy-to-read reviews usually discuss the composer, performer, and sound quality, and occasionally include comparisons with other albums. A one-to-ten scale is used to rate both the artistic quality and the sound quality, with one being unacceptable, with no redeeming qualities, and ten being superior, with qualities of unusual merit. Reviews can be browsed by composer, orchestra/ensemble, conductor, and soloist. The advanced search options are extensive, including genre, composer, ensemble/orchestra, conductor, soloist, record label, medium, and date range. The site also includes features, discographies, and reviews of books and concerts that are limited to subscribers only at $49 per year. Recommended for both neophytes and classical aficionados. URL: www.classicstoday.com

Down Beat. See Music/Popular section.

4014. Fanfare (Tenafly): the magazine for serious record collectors.
[ISSN: 0148-9364] 1977. bi-m. USD 50 domestic; USD 75 foreign. Ed(s): Joel Flegler. Fanfare, Inc., 17 Lancaster Rd, PO Box 17, Tenafly, NJ 07670. Illus., adv. Sample. Vol. ends: Jul/Aug. *Indexed:* A01, A22, BRI, CBRI, IIMP. *Bk. rev.:* Number and length vary. *Aud.:* Ga, Ac.

Since its inception, *Fanfare* was intended to provide informative reviews without being "stuffy and academic," and this is still the case. Each issue includes over 250 reviews written in an easy-to-read, descriptive, and informal style. The "Classical Recordings" section includes CD and DVD reviews arranged by composer. The "Collections" section is divided into vocal, choral, early music, instrumental, ensemble, orchestral, and miscellaneous. Extensive reviews often cover the background of the composer, artist, or work; performance quality; sound quality; and comparisons with other recordings. Additional review columns include "Jazz" and "Classical Hall of Fame." The magazine also includes articles, interviews, label profiles, and book reviews. The web site includes tables of contents and a sampling of recently published articles and reviews. Subscribers can access full articles and reviews in the archive. With numerous and lengthy reviews, this magazine is highly recommended for public and academic libraries. URL: www.fanfaremag.com

4015. Gramophone. Incorporates (in 1923): *Vox; Radio Critic; Broadcast Review; Cassettes and Cartridges.* [ISSN: 0017-310X] 19??. 13x/yr. GBP 59.80 domestic; GBP 74.80 in Europe; USD 87 United States. Haymarket Publishing Ltd., 174 Hammersmith Rd, London, W6 7JP, United Kingdom; info@haymarket.com; http://www.haymarket.com. Illus., index, adv. Vol. ends: May. *Indexed:* A22, IIMP. *Bk. rev.:* Occasional. *Aud.:* Ga, Ac.

Gramophone, "the world's best classical music reviews," provides articles, news, and reviews from a global perspective. The entertaining, informative, and easy-to-read reviews cover orchestral, chamber, vocal, instrumental, and opera. While the performance and music are the focus of the review, there is often discussion of the performer and history of the works. Issues also include profiles, interviews, news, obituaries, book and DVD reviews, and a small product-review section. The web site includes news, blogs, forums, feature articles, and a festival guide. A digital archive app can be purchased to view the entire contents of every issue back to 1923. Recommended for both neophytes and classical aficionados. URL: www.gramophone.co.uk

JazzTimes. See Music/Popular section.

Sound & Vision. See Television, Video, and Radio section.

Audio Equipment

4016. The Absolute Sound: the high end journal of audio & music.
[ISSN: 0097-1138] 1973. 10x/yr. USD 19.95 domestic; USD 35.95 Canada; USD 54.95 elsewhere. Ed(s): Chris Martens. NextScreen, LLC, 4544 S Lamar Blvd, Bldg G300, Austin, TX 78745; info@avguide.com; http://www.nextscreen.com/. Illus., index, adv. Sample. Circ: 33000. Vol. ends: Dec/Jan. *Aud.:* Ga, Ac.

The Absolute Sound "explores music and the reproduction of music in the home" by providing columns, reports, and reviews of audio equipment and music recordings. Equipment reports are easy to read and include physical attributes, performance quality, comparisons to similar products, and discussion of the testing process and recordings used. A sidebar highlights specifications, manufacturer information, and a list of associated equipment when appropriate. The music review section is divided by genre and covers rock, classical, and jazz, with an average of five reviews in each category. Ratings are provided for music and sonics based on a scale of one to five, with one being poor and five extraordinary. Reviews generally begin with a brief background of the artist, group, or album, followed by discussion of music quality, and wrap up with production quality. Further listening recommendations of albums by other groups are also included. *The Absolute Sound's* online version is part of AVguide.com, which also includes reviews from *Playback, Perfect Vision,* and

Hifi Plus. Reviews, "Buyers' Guides," news, blogs, and forums round out the site. With well-written reviews and extensive content, this magazine and web site are highly recommended for public and academic libraries. URL: www.theabsolutesound.com

Stereophile. See Television, Video, and Radio section.

■ NATIVE AMERICANS

Law/Education

Berlin Loa, Museum/Archives Technician; berlinloa@gmail.com

Introduction

The Native American collection of publications includes scholarly works and popular magazines relating to Native American cultures, law, art, and general interest subjects. The journals included here include those targeted to academic and public library audiences.

Basic Periodicals

Hs: *American Indian Law Review, Native Peoples, Winds of Change;* Ga: *Native Peoples;* Ac: *American Indian Culture and Research Journal, Wicazo Sa Review.*

Basic Abstracts and Indexes

Abstracts in Anthropology, Academic Search Premier, Alternative Press Index, America: History and Life, Anthropological Literature, Ethnic NewsWatch, Historical Abstracts, Project Muse, OmniFile Full Text.

4017. American Indian Culture and Research Journal. Formerly (until 1974): *American Indian Culture Center. Journal.* [ISSN: 0161-6463] 1971. q. Individuals, USD 195 (print & online eds.). Ed(s): Pamela Grieman. University of California, Los Angeles, American Indian Studies Center, 3220 Campbell Hall, PO Box 951548, Los Angeles, CA 90095-1548; sales@aisc.ucla.edu; http://www.books.aisc.ucla.edu. Illus., adv. Refereed. *Indexed:* A01, A22, A47, AmHI, ArtHuCI, BRI, CBRI, ERIC, FR, MLA-IB, P02, P61, RILM, SSA. *Bk. rev.:* 20-21, 400-800 words. *Aud.:* Ac, Sa.

The contents of the *American Indian Culture and Research Journal* represent a spectrum of the Native American experience and cultures. This journal contains articles, book reviews, and features regarding culture, film, arts, rights issues and activism, education, and cultural resource management and research. It invites academic articles, poetry, and commentary; it covers the fields of history, anthropology, geography, sociology, health, law, literature, education, and the arts. Recommended for academic libraries. Specifically recommended for institutions with cultural studies programs, including Native American Studies, anthropology, literature, and interdisciplinary cultural-resource studies.

4018. Etudes Inuit Studies. [ISSN: 0701-1008] 1977. s-a. CAD 225 (print & online eds.) Individuals, CAD 50 (print & online eds.). Ed(s): Murielle Nagy. Inuksiutiit Katimajiit Association, Inc., Universite Laval, 0450 Pavillon Charles de Konink, Quebec, PQ G1V 0A6, Canada; http://www.fss.ulaval.ca/etudes-inuit-studies/. Adv. Refereed. *Indexed:* A47, FR, IBSS, MLA-IB, P61, PdeR, RILM, SSA. *Bk. rev.:* Number and length vary. *Aud.:* Ac, Sa.

Etudes/Inuit/Studies is an academic journal that features articles and research papers, as well as book reviews and dissertation reviews. Issues are thematic and contents relate primarily to traditional and contemporary Inuit ethnology, history, politics, cultures, and Inuit-related global issues. Additionally, issues may include conference call-for-papers, research notes, memorials, and recognition of scholars contributing to Inuit studies. The journal is published semi-annually and is multilingual in English and French, with a limited use of the Inuit language in the form of Inuktitut syllabics. Articles are refereed. This journal is recommended for academic and research libraries—specifically for those serving studies in ethnology, politics, archaeology, linguistics, and history pertaining to indigenous cultures, Native American Studies, and First Nations.

4019. *Indigenous Woman.* [ISSN: 1070-1400] 1991. a. USD 40 (Individuals, USD 25). Ed(s): Pamela Kingsfisher. Indigenous Women's Network, 13621 FM 2769, Austin, TX 78726; almademujer@igc.org; http://www.honorearth.com/iwn/. Illus., adv. Circ: 5000. *Aud.:* Hs, Ga, Ac, Sa.

Indigenous Woman Magazine is a publication of the Indigenous Women's Network. Issues contain articles, essays, and features regarding legal, ethical, health, and cultural concerns of indigenous peoples. Items in this journal are written and published by women activists and artists. Recommended for public and academic libraries, specifically for those with Gender Studies, Women's Studies, or Native American Studies programs.

4020. *Native Peoples.* Incorporates (in 1999): *Native Artists.* [ISSN: 0895-7606] 1987. bi-m. USD 19.95 domestic; USD 28 Canada; USD 40 elsewhere. Ed(s): Daniel Gibson. Media Concepts Group, Inc., 5333 N 7th St, Ste C224, Phoenix, AZ 85014; info@mediaconceptsgroupinc.com; http://www.mediaconceptsgroupinc.com. Illus., index, adv. Vol. ends: Summer (No. 4). *Indexed:* A07, BRI, CBRI, MLA-IB. *Bk. rev.:* 2-3, 650-850 words. *Aud.:* Hs, Ga.

Native Peoples is developed for the general public. The magazine includes a variety of articles, illustrations, and features including film, book and music reviews, art reviews, and traditional foods and recipes, as well as announcements for regional festivals and events. An index of issues and content are available on the web site.

4021. *Whispering Wind: American Indian: past & present.* [ISSN: 0300-6565] 1967. bi-m. USD 23 domestic; USD 39 foreign. Jack Heriard, Ed. & Pub., PO Box 1390, Folsom, LA 70437. Illus., index, adv. Sample. Refereed. Circ: 22120. Vol. ends: No. 6. *Indexed:* A47, BRI, ENW. *Bk. rev.:* 4-6, 300-500 words. *Aud.:* Hs, Ga, Sa.

Whispering Wind is a bimonthly magazine dedicated to the review of Native American material culture, traditions, and arts. The magazine features book and music reviews, articles regarding dance, music, traditional and modern arts, clothing and traditions, and advertisements for craft materials. A calendar of events is available on the web site, and a list of events is included in the print copy. Recommended for public or school libraries.

4022. *Wicazo Sa Review: a journal of Native American studies.* [ISSN: 0749-6427] 1985. s-a. USD 50 (Individuals, USD 20). Ed(s): James Riding In. University of Minnesota Press, Ste 290, 111 Third Ave S, Minneapolis, MN 55401; ump@umn.edu; http://www.upress.umn.edu. Illus., adv. Sample. Refereed. Vol. ends: No. 2. *Indexed:* A01, A22, A47, AmHI, BRI, E01, MLA-IB, RILM. *Bk. rev.:* 1-2, 800 words. *Aud.:* Ac, Sa.

Wicazo Sa Review is a journal developed with the goal of assisting indigenous peoples in intellectual and creative endeavors. Published semi-annually, the journal includes articles, interviews, reviews, and research primarily regarding cultural, religious, legal, and historical issues. The journal also includes book reviews, literature and poetry reviews, and essays. Recommended for academic libraries, this journal is essential to those that offer Native American Studies, but is also recommended for public libraries that serve Native American populations or within regions with an interest in Native American cultures.

4023. *Winds of Change: empowering native Americans through higher education and careers.* [ISSN: 0888-8612] 1986. q. Free to members; Non-members, USD 24. A I S E S Publishing, 4450 Arapahoe Ave, Ste 100, Boulder, CO 80303; info@aises.org; http://www.aises.org. Illus., index, adv. Sample. Vol. ends: Fall. *Bk. rev.:* 2-10, 250-600 words. *Aud.:* Hs, Ga, Ac, Sa.

Winds of Change is a full-color, quarterly magazine focused on career and educational opportunities for Native American and Alaska Native peoples. The journal is primarily business-related and STEM-related ("STEM" means "science, technology, engineering, or mathematics"). It includes contents related to business, universities, health and well-being, and Native cultures from both tribal and non-tribal resources. Issues contain articles related to career development, educational opportunities and strategies, book reviews, and advertisements. The journal also publishes an annual "College Issue" for students and recruiters. Recommended for school, public, and academic libraries.

4024. *Yellow Medicine Review: a journal of indigenous literature, art, and thought.* [ISSN: 1939-4624] 2007. s-a. USD 20 domestic; USD 25 foreign. Ed(s): Ralph Salisbury. Southwest Minnesota State University, 1501 State St, Marshall, MN 56258; http://www.smsu.edu/. *Aud.:* Hs, Ga, Ac, Sa.

Yellow Medicine Review is published as a place for new artists, writers, and scholars to present new work, and is published through the Difficult Dialogues Initiative of Southwest Minnesota State University. The journal invites poetry, essays, art, memoir, drama, and fiction of indigenous perspectives. The journal defines indigenous "universally as representative of all pre-colonial peoples." Subscriptions are available via the journal's web site; single current and past issues are available via the journal web site and on Amazon.

Law

4025. *American Indian Law Review.* [ISSN: 0094-002X] 1973. s-a. USD 30. Ed(s): Mary Huckabee. University of Oklahoma, College of Law, Andrew M Coats Hall, 300 Timberdell Rd, Norman, OK 73019; law@law.ou.edu; http://www.law.ou.edu. Refereed. Microform: WSH; PMC. Reprint: WSH. *Indexed:* BRI, CLI, L14. *Aud.:* Ac, Sa.

American Indian Law Review is a scholarly journal published semi-annually, and features articles and expository essays by legal scholars and practitioners. The *Law Review* also includes commentary from students and editorial board members. Contents of the journal pertain to legislation and legal issues that affect Native Americans and indigenous peoples throughout the U.S. and internationally. Submissions are double-blind peer-reviewed. The journal is recommended for academic libraries and is essential to those that offer studies in Native American cultures and U.S. law. Reprints and subscription information are available on the web site, but full-text articles are only available in print.

4026. *N A R F Legal Review.* Formerly (until 1983): *Native American Rights Fund. Announcements.* [ISSN: 0739-862X] 1972. s-a. Free. Ed(s): Ray Ramirez. Native American Rights Fund, 1506 Broadway, Boulder, CO 80302; pubrequest@narf.org; http://www.narf.org. *Aud.:* Ga, Ac, Sa.

The *Native American Rights Fund Legal Review* provides information on current law topics and updates on NARF cases. The review is free, but contributions are suggested, which would support NARF. Recommended for academic libraries, specifically those with a Native American Studies program and for public libraries that serve Native American populations.

Education

4027. *Financial Aid for Native Americans.* Supersedes in part (in 1999): *Directory of Financial Aids for Minorities.* [ISSN: 1099-9116] 1985. biennial. USD 45 per issue. Ed(s): R David Weber, Gail A Schlachter. Reference Service Press, 5000 Windplay Dr, Ste 4, El Dorado Hills, CA 95762; info@rspfunding.com; http://www.rspfunding.com. *Aud.:* Hs, Ga, Ac.

Financial Aid for Native Americans is a reference list of scholarships, grants, fellowships, and other financial sources for Native American students. The journal is published a part of a series of financial aid guides for minorities. A preview of the current issue is available on the web site. Recommended for public, school, and academic libraries that serve Native American students.

4028. *Journal of American Indian Education.* [ISSN: 0021-8731] 1961. 3x/yr. USD 65 (Individuals, USD 30; USD 8 per issue). Ed(s): Teresa L McCarty, Bryan Brayboy. Arizona State University, Center for Indian Education, c/o Laura Williams, PO Box 871311, Tempe, AZ 85287; http://coe.asu.edu/cie/index.html. Illus., index. Refereed. Vol. ends: Spring (No. 3). Microform: PQC. *Indexed:* A22, AbAn, ERIC, HEA, MLA-IB, P61, SSA. *Bk. rev.:* Number and length vary. *Aud.:* Ac, Sa.

Journal of American Indian Education is published three times per year by the Arizona State University Center for Indian Education. Contents include articles, book reviews, research papers, and field report features related to educational issues and innovations that affect Native American, First Nations, and other indigenous cultures. This journal is recommended for academic and research libraries that support studies in education and Native American cultures.

■ NEWS AND OPINION

See also Alternatives; General Interest; and Newspapers sections.

Emily Krug, Emerging Technologies and Cataloging Librarian, Somerset Community College Learning Commons, Somerset, KY 42501.

Devin Phelps, Collection Development Librarian, Somerset Community College Learning Commons, Somerset, KY 42501

Introduction

Since CNN launched in 1980 to bring television news to America 24 hours a day, the rapidity with which news is distributed has increased exponentially, to the point that today news travels around the world almost instantaneously. The immediate distribution of news is only compounded by online news sources, social media, and the phenomenon of viral stories. In such a culture, weekly or monthly newsmagazines may seem obsolete and unnecessary. However, the need for the quality reporting that these magazines provide still exists. Although these publications are not as timely as a story that appears in a Twitter feed, the social and political commentary that news and opinion magazines provide is vital to creating an informed public capable of thinking critically.

To meet the challenges of the 24-hour news culture, many publications have changed format. *U.S. News and World Report* moved entirely online in late 2010; in the past year, *Newsweek* has followed suit and is now available online and through a tablet subscription. Likewise, the conservative political opinion journal *Human Events* has ceased print in favor of online publication. Even those magazines that remain in print have a well-crafted web site.

Additionally, some newer news and opinion magazines began as online publications, notably *Huffington Post, Slate,* and *TPM.* Furthermore, recent increases in sales of smart phones and tablets have created another electronic niche for publishers to fill. Although many news and opinion magazines have embraced the tablet format, a few stand out as having excellent mobile interfaces. *Newsweek's* tablet version maintains the integrity of this important publication, and *Commentary's* iPad version is exemplary, with its integration of social media sharing and online shopping for reviewed books and films.

In addition to the technological changes in the news and opinion world, the strong partisan atmosphere of today's political culture is impacting newsmagazines. As liberal and conservative schools of thought continue to oppose each other and refuse to find common ground, newsmagazines representing those opinions have, in some cases, embraced a vitriolic means of reporting. As a result, providing unbiased news sources is a difficult but necessary task for libraries.

Developing a balanced collection of news and opinion resources is certainly not a new trial for libraries; however, the mobility of news and the political atmosphere of the twenty-first century present formidable challenges to this enterprise. Whether your library continues to buy print news and opinion magazines or provides access to online and tablet subscriptions, we hope this section will help you develop a collection that encourages your patrons to think critically and engage in public discourse about what happens in the world.

Basic Periodicals

The Nation, National Review, The New Republic, Newsweek (Online), Time.

Basic Abstracts and Indexes

Academic OneFile, Alt-Press Watch, PAIS International.

4029. *The American (Online).* [ISSN: 1932-8125] 2006. bi-m. Ed(s): Nick Schulz, Eleanor Stables. American Enterprise Institute for Public Policy Research, 1150 17th St NW, Washington, DC 20036; http://www.aei.org/. Adv. *Bk. rev.:* 3, length varies; signed. *Aud.:* Ga, Ac.

This is a publication out of the American Enterprise Institute, an influential conservative think tank that has been around since 1943. Coverage includes business, technology, education, culture, book reviews, and current affairs. A number of the articles consist of in-depth reporting. Some of the notable contributors include Norman Ornstein and Jonathan Yardley. There is a punchy feel to the overall aesthetic of this magazine. Recommended for larger public and academic libraries. The web site presents a quick side bar to RSS feeds, as well as a timely blog written by a host of the magazine's contributors. The archive is broken down by topic ("Boardroom," "Public Square," "World Watch") and year, although content only appears to be from 2006 to the present.

4030. *The American Spectator.* Formerly (until 1977): *The Alternative.* [ISSN: 0148-8414] 1967. m. except Jul.-Aug.and Dec.-Jan combined. USD 39; USD 3.90 per issue. The American Spectator, 1611 N Kent St, Ste 901, Arlington, VA 22209; aspc@kable.com. Illus., index, adv. Sample. Circ: 139000 Paid. Vol. ends: Dec. Microform: BHP; PQC. *Indexed:* A01, A22, ABS&EES, ASIP, BRI, C37, CBRI, F01, MASUSE, MLA-IB, P02. *Bk. rev.:* 3-4, 1,500 words; signed. *Aud.:* Ga, Ac.

The American Spectator is a right-leaning newsmagazine that offers articles on political, cultural, and social issues. Recurring authors include Benjamin J. Stein, Grover G. Norquist, and Seth Lipsky. The tone of many of the articles is very informal, contributing to this magazine's quality as one of opinions and editorial pieces rather than true journalism. Left-wing readers will be put off by the magazine's open ridicule of Democrats and liberals. While many conservatives may enjoy this magazine for its lightheartedness, its content leaves it hard to recommend except for the very largest public libraries and large academic libraries whose universities have a political science department.

4031. *Commentary: journal of significant thought and opinion on contemporary issues.* Formerly (until 1945): *Contemporary Jewish Record.* [ISSN: 0010-2601] 1938. m. except Jul./Aug. combined. USD 19.95 domestic; USD 38.95 Canada; USD 44.95 elsewhere. Ed(s): Jonathan S Tobin, John Podhoretz. American Jewish Committee, 165 E 56th St, New York, NY 10022; PR@ajc.org; http://www.ajc.org. Index, adv. Sample. Circ: 27000 Paid. Vol. ends: Jun/Dec. *Indexed:* A01, A06, A22, ABS&EES, AmHI, BAS, BEL&L, BRI, C37, C42, CBRI, IJP, MASUSE, MLA-IB, P02, RILM. *Bk. rev.:* 5, 1,500-2,000 words; signed. *Aud.:* Ga, Ac.

Originally published by the American Jewish Committee starting in 1945, *Commentary* is a moderate-to-conservative news-monthly that touches on timely topics from a Jewish perspective. The magazine includes typical sections such as "Features," "Politics & Ideas," "Culture & Civilization," and reviews. *Commentary* is available in print, but what distinguishes this title from others is its effective use of its tablet versions. Both the Kindle and iPad versions are exemplary tablet editions. Although the Kindle version is more low-tech, the iPad version expertly utilizes enhanced content and images to engage the reader. Of particular note is the inclusion of video clips and excerpts of the films and books reviewed in the magazine. The iPad version also provides sharing options for social media and a place to purchase the books under review in the magazine. The web site for the magazine also allows access to articles; however, most only allow abstract access for non-subscribers. This title would be best suited to academic or public libraries looking to provide a collection of balanced political perspectives.

Commonweal. See Religion section.

4032. *Current (Washington, 1960): required reading recommended by leading opinion makers.* [ISSN: 0011-3131] 1960. 10x/yr. GBP 94. Ed(s): Miriam Aronin. Routledge, 325 Chestnut St, Ste 800, Philadelphia, PA 19106; customerservice@taylorandfrancis.com; http://www.tandfonline.com. Illus., index, adv. Vol. ends: Jan. Reprint: PSC. *Indexed:* A01, A22, ABS&EES, BRI, P02. *Aud.:* Hs, Ga, Ac.

Current, which bills itself as the "finest, most required reading from all available sources for the concerned citizen," is a reprint magazine that gathers the best articles from recently printed journals and consolidates them into one compact source for the reader. Articles are taken from a variety of journals that deal with politics, culture, and current affairs at a national and international level. Since the articles are the best in their fields, they are balanced, researched, and well-written. This journal would be well suited for any academic or large public library. It would also be suitable for the library on a limited budget that could not afford to subscribe to a lot of different journals.

4033. *The Daily Beast.* 2008. Ed(s): Tina Brown. Newsweek Daily Beast Company, 7 Hanover Sq, New York, NY 10004. *Bk. rev.:* Number and length vary. *Aud.:* Ga.

This online newsmagazine was launched in 2008 with the goal of avoiding information overload. Whereas the homepages for publications such as *Time* and *Huffington Post* resemble well-laid out print newspapers, the homepage for *The Daily Beast* inundates the viewer with a jumble of images, video, and headlines. The masthead for the news web site offers the typical news and opinion section options: "Politics," "Business," "Entertainment," "Fashion," "Books," and "Art." The layout within the sections resembles a blog, and each page is updated every few hours. The headlines and writing smack of sarcasm. The one section of the web site that presents the news in a clean and easy to read layout is the *Newsweek* section; the Daily Beast Company purchased *Newsweek* in 2011. Although the content may be appropriate for most audiences, libraries would be better served subscribing only to the *Newsweek* section of the site or choosing another web site such as *Time* or *Huffington Post.*

4034. *Dissent (New York): a quarterly of politics and culture.* [ISSN: 0012-3846] 1954. q. USD 52 (Individuals, USD 25; Students, USD 18). Ed(s): Michael Walzer, Michael Kazin. Foundation for the Study of Independent Social Ideas, Inc., 310 Riverside Dr, Ste 2008, New York, NY 10025. Illus., index, adv. Sample. Vol. ends: Fall (No. 4). Microform: PQC. *Indexed:* A01, A22, ABS&EES, AmHI, BAS, BRI, CBRI, E01, MLA-IB, P02, P61, RILM, SSA, SWR&A. *Bk. rev.:* 5, 2,000 words; signed. *Aud.:* Ga, Ac.

Dissent is a quarterly magazine with a decidedly left-wing bent that is published by the University of Pennsylvania Press. An editorial acknowledged that the lag time between breaking news and the publication of the magazine can lead to mistaken assumptions; however, it also allows the magazine to do particularly in-depth reporting, since the pressure of quick deadlines is absent. Issues often have a theme that a number of writers will touch on, but they also include other original reporting on economics, international and domestic politics, and public policy, as well as book reviews. Unlike many American magazines, *Dissent* goes out of its way to include international politics by including a "Politics Abroad" section in each issue. Articles are written by well-known journalists, academics, and activists, and the editorial board is likewise composed of some of the best-known left-wing intellectuals in the United States. *Dissent* is very up-front about its ideological leanings, and would make a valuable addition to any collection that is looking to add a left-wing perspective to its serials.

The Economist. See Economics section.

Foreign Affairs. See Political Science/International Relations section.

The Guardian. See Newspapers/General section.

4035. *The Huffington Post.* 2005. Free. Ed(s): Arianna Huffington, Jimmy Soni. The Huffington Post Media Group, info@huffingtonpost.com; http://www.huffingtonpost.com/. Adv. *Aud.:* Ga.

Launched in 2005, and acquired for over $300 million by AOL in 2011, Arianna Huffington's *The Huffington Post*—a web publication that aggregates articles as well as produces original content—is a proven online media force. Contributors (or bloggers) include a host of academics, not-for-profit leaders, notable thinkers, and creative types in all industries. Likewise, celebrities from the entertainment world are active contributors of opinion pieces and feature articles—for instance, actor Alec Baldwin, supermodel-turned-maternal-health-activist Christy Turlington, and musician Adam Levine. Sections of *The Huffington Post* that are highlighted from the top page are "News," "Politics,"

"College," "Style," "Entertainment," "Healthy Living," "Local," and "Food." The site's appearance is bold and dense, with a smorgasbord of headlines; it is commonplace for the the leading headline to take up all the opening real estate. The style, however, can appear tabloid-like to a fault—it is easy to turn reading and scanning into a guilty pleasure that blurs the line between serious news and tabloid news (for instance, links often lead to TMZ, *The National Enquirer,* and other tabloid publications). The comments sections are heavily used, and the *Post* is seamless in reposting articles to social networking sites such as Facebook and Twitter.

4036. *Human Events (Online).* . Eagle Publishing, Inc., One Massachusetts Ave, NW, Washington, DC 20001; info@eaglepub.com; http://www.eaglepub.com. *Bk. rev.:* Number and length vary; signed. *Aud.:* Ga, Ac.

Now an entirely online publication, *Human Events* presents the news through a conservative lens. Contributors to the publication include Pat Buchanan, Ann Coulter, Newt Gingrich, and other high-profile conservatives in American politics and news. *Human Events* includes only three main sections: "News & Politics," "Money," and "Health." The rest of the content is included in regular columns and contributed articles, as well as blog posts. The layout and design for this online publication are clean and straightforward, with limited advertisements. The site includes options for RSS and up-to-the-minute news feeds and e-mail lists. This publication is recommended for those libraries that need a conservative viewpoint to round out their collection.

4037. *In These Times.* [ISSN: 0160-5992] 1976. m. USD 24.95 domestic; USD 39.95 Canada; USD 45.95 elsewhere. Ed(s): Joel Bleifuss. Institute for Public Affairs, 2040 N Milwaukee Ave, Chicago, IL 60647. Illus., adv. Vol. ends: Nov. Microform: PQC. *Indexed:* A22, ASIP, Chicano, MLA-IB. *Bk. rev.:* Number and length vary. *Aud.:* Ga, Ac.

In These Times bills itself as a magazine devoted to expanding the range of both independent reporting in and of itself, and also the coverage of issues that are not often given much notice by the mainstream press. Each issue has a number of feature articles with in-depth reporting on international and domestic issues. The tone of the magazine is far-left, and it is unafraid to criticize or even ridicule conservative Republicans and the Tea Party. However, the magazine is not afraid to be critical of the left when writers feel criticism is warranted. Opinion articles are included, as well as a "Culture" section. This latter often looks at a particular issue from a historical perspective. The magazine would be a good addition to a library looking to balance a more conservative magazine. The web page offers full-text coverage of the current issues and at least some full-text coverage of back issues.

4038. *Interview (New York).* Former titles (until 1977): *Andy Warhol's Interview;* (until 1972): *Inter/View.* [ISSN: 0149-8932] 1969. m. USD 9.97 domestic; USD 49.95 Canada; USD 65 elsewhere. Ed(s): Christopher Bollen. Brant Publications, Inc., 575 Broadway, 5th Fl, New York, NY 10012. Illus., adv. Vol. ends: Dec (No. 12). Microform: PQC. *Indexed:* A22, ABS&EES, ASIP, BRI, C37, F01, IIFP, IIPA, MASUSE, P02. *Bk. rev.:* Number and length vary. *Aud.:* Ga, Ac.

The masthead of this eye-catching, oversized, popular-culture–infused monthly, which is heavy with graphics, reads "Andy Warhol's Interview." Founded in 1969 by the artist, it offers a peek into the world of mostly coastal-dwelling notables and emerging hipsters in the entertainment, arts, and fashion worlds. The sections feature fashion spreads, photo essays, promotional blurbs on new products, the latest in makeup and clothing, articles about music and fashion, and, of course, interviews. A number of the interviews are conducted by other high-profile people. Recommended for leisure reading in public libraries and academic libraries, though its readership may be limited. The companion web site offers limited articles and interviews; and access in the archives is only to the covers. A nice feature, however, is a fleshed-out section of videos, with behind-the-scenes clips, on a number of the magazine's subjects.

4039. *Monthly Review.* [ISSN: 0027-0520] 1949. m. Individuals, USD 39; USD 5 per issue. Ed(s): John Bellamy Foster. Monthly Review Foundation, 146 W 29th St, #6W, New York, NY 10001. Illus., index, adv. Refereed. Vol. ends: Dec. Microform: PQC. *Indexed:* A01, A22, ABS&EES, B02, BAS, BRI, MLA-IB, P02, P61, SSA. *Bk. rev.:* Number and length vary; signed. *Aud.:* Ga, Ac.

The Monthly Review: An Independent Socialist Magazine has been a core journal for hard-left scholarship for the last 60+ years (the first issue was produced out of New York City in May 1949). Contributors provide an international perspective on current world issues. These contributors have included Prabhat Patnaik, Elizabeth "Betita" Martinez, and Adrienne Rich. Recommended for some public and academic libraries that are looking to fill out their collections with political discourse from a variety of perspectives. The online site provides deep back-files to subscribers only, although content from the more recent issues is available for free. This site provides users with a nice slice of copy from the print *Monthly Review*.

Mother Jones. See General Interest section.

4040. Ms. [ISSN: 0047-8318] 1972. q. USD 25 domestic; USD 42 Canada; USD 78 elsewhere. Ed(s): Michel Cicero. Liberty Media for Women, L.L.C., 1600 Wilson Blvd, Ste 801, Arlington, VA 22209. Illus., adv. Vol. ends: Nov/Dec. Microform: PQC. *Indexed:* A01, A22, ABS&EES, BEL&L, BRI, C37, C42, CBRI, Chicano, F01, FemPer, GW, MASUSE, MLA-IB, P02, RILM, WSA. *Bk. rev.:* 8, 124-300 words; signed. *Aud.:* Hs, Ga, Ac.

Ms. is perhaps the country's best-known feminist magazine and features articles on culture and politics. It was founded in the 1970s with an explicitly activist tone; today the banner on its web page reads "More than a Magazine—A Movement." Its investigative reporting covers a wide range of women's issues and is international in scope. The magazine also examines issues relating to race, class, labor, environmentalism, and public policy. Each issue also has opinion columns and reviews of films, TV shows, and books. It is recommended for public and academic libraries. The web page offers some free content from the current and back issues. It also has a "Feminist Daily Wire," with news updates on relevant issues. As do an increasing number of magazines across the political spectrum, it also maintains a presence on Facebook and Twitter.

4041. The Nation. [ISSN: 0027-8378] 1865. w. except the second week in Jan.; bi-w. in July & Aug. USD 29.97 domestic; USD 55.97 Canada; USD 88.97 elsewhere. Ed(s): Roane Carey, Katrina Vanden Heuvel. The Nation Company, L.P., 33 Irving Pl, 8th Fl, New York, NY 10003; permissions@thenation.com; http://www.thenation.com. Illus., index, adv. Sample. Vol. ends: Jun/Dec. Microform: PMC; PQC. *Indexed:* A01, A22, ABS&EES, BRI, C37, C42, CBRI, Chicano, F01, MASUSE, MLA-IB, P02. *Bk. rev.:* 4, 1,000 words; signed. *Aud.:* Ga, Ac.

The Nation is an unabashedly left-wing publication and includes numerous editorials and columns, as well as original reporting. The magazine ranges widely over a variety of topics, including politics (foreign and domestic), economics, and book and film reviews. It also frequently publishes cartoons and the humorous short poems of noted New York writer Calvin Trillin. Each issue has a crossword puzzle. Its journalistic hallmark is a breezy irreverence. This will be a valuable addition to any library that seeks to have solid coverage of left-wing political perspectives. *The Nation*'s companion web page offers free access to a selection of articles from the current issue. Subscribers have full access to all material, including the magazine's archives, which date back to 1865. The web page also offers a wide range of blogs, videos, and podcasts.

4042. National Review. [ISSN: 0028-0038] 1955. bi-w. USD 29.50 domestic; USD 41.50 foreign; USD 5 per issue. Ed(s): Rich Lowry. National Review, Inc., 215 Lexington Ave, 4th Fl, New York, NY 10016; nronline@nationalreview.com. Illus., index, adv. Circ: 160000. Vol. ends: No. 25. *Indexed:* A01, A22, ABS&EES, BAS, BRI, C37, C42, CBRI, Chicano, F01, MASUSE, MLA-IB, P02, SWR&A. *Bk. rev.:* 4, 1,000 words; signed. *Aud.:* Ga, Ac.

National Review was founded in 1955 by William F. Buckley. It is widely considered to be the most important American conservative magazine and should be owned by most academic and public libraries. Published weekly, it typically features three to five feature articles and several shorter pieces as well, on politics, public policy, economics, and international affairs. Each issue also has a "Books, Arts and Manners" section, with essays on a variety of cultural issues, in addition to film and book reviews. At least a handful of opinion columns appear weekly, as well. The web page has extensive free content that is essentially independent of the print magazine (though the print magazine is

also available online to subscribers), and it includes a range of blogs, the best known of which is probably the group blog "The Corner." The web page also has two sections called "NRO Radio" and "NRO TV" and includes audio and video RSS feeds.

4043. The New American (Appleton). Formed by the merger of (1958-1985): *American Opinion;* Which was formed by the 1958 merger of: *One Man's Opinion; Hubert Kregeloh Comments;* (1965-1985): *Review of the News;* Which was formerly (until 1965): *Correction, Please;* Review of the News incorporated (1956-1971): *The Dan Smoot Report;* Which was formerly (until 1956): *Dan Smoot Speaks.* [ISSN: 0885-6540] 1985. bi-w. USD 39 domestic; USD 48 Canada; USD 66 elsewhere. Ed(s): Gary Benoit. American Opinion Publishing Inc., PO Box 8040, Appleton, WI 54912. Illus., adv. Sample. Vol. ends: Dec. Microform: PQC. *Indexed:* A01, A22, BRI, MASUSE, MLA-IB, P02. *Bk. rev.:* Number and length vary; signed. *Aud.:* Ga, Ac.

The New American is a right-wing magazine published by the John Birch Society, a fundamentalist Christian organization. Its articles are clearly written to cater to a fiscally and socially conservative audience. While containing references to Christianity, it should not be placed in the category of "Christian magazines," as its subject matter is far more diverse, and many articles do not deal with any matters of faith. The articles are lengthy and well-written, acknowledging an editorial point of view, but approaching the news "honestly, [and] relying on facts and reason to make our case and allowing the chips to fall where they may." This journal is recommended for any reading level, but only if coupled with a more liberal journal to offer multiple points of view and maintain balance. The web page offers full-text articles, but it is not clear to what extent they correspond to the print version of the magazine.

New Criterion. See Art/General section.

4044. New Perspectives Quarterly: a journal of social and political thought. Formerly (until 1986): *Center for the Study of Democratic Institutions. Center Magazine;* (until 1967): *Center for the Study of Democratic Institutions. Center Diary.* [ISSN: 0893-7850] 1963. q. GBP 365. Ed(s): Nathan Gardels. Wiley-Blackwell Publishing, Inc., 111 River St, Hoboken, NJ 07030; info@wiley.com; http://onlinelibrary.wiley.com/. Illus., adv. Sample. Refereed. Vol. ends: No. 5. Microform: PQC. Reprint: PSC. *Indexed:* A01, A22, ABS&EES, B01, BAS, BRI, E01, MASUSE, P02, P61, SSA. *Bk. rev.:* Number and length vary. *Aud.:* Hs, Ga, Ac.

Each issue of this journal, *NPQ*, is organized thematically. Coverage includes domestic and international affairs. Some noteworthy contributors have included Jimmy Carter, Kofi Annan, Paul Samuelson, and Anthony Giddens. In addition, several articles explore the worlds of culture and literature, as well as current thought. Recommended for larger public and academic libraries. *NPQ*'s web presence offers the current issues; however, it is unclear how much of the deep back-file is available on this site. There are few bells and whistles on the site, but the content from the current issue appears to be freely available.

4045. The New Republic: a journal of politics and the arts. [ISSN: 0028-6583] 1914. 20x/yr. USD 34.97; USD 4.95 newsstand/cover. Ed(s): Chris Highes. New Republic, 1400 K St, NW, Ste 1200, Washington, DC 20005. Illus., index, adv. Vol. ends: Jun/Dec. Microform: NBI; PMC; PQC. *Indexed:* A01, A06, A22, ABIn, ABS&EES, B01, BAS, BEL&L, BRI, C37, C42, CBRI, Chicano, F01, MASUSE, MLA-IB, P02, RILM. *Bk. rev.:* Number and length vary. *Aud.:* Ga, Ac.

The New Republic is a well-written, unbiased newsmagazine that "covers politics, culture, and big ideas." Similar to *Time* in its layout, style, and coverage, *The New Republic* offers articles that are thought-provoking, well-researched, and intended for a diverse audience. In addition to the magazine, its web site features multimedia content that is available in a wide variety of formats, including tablets and smartphones. Some full-text articles are available on the web site through keyword searching, but not in a magazine format. While *The New Republic* is forging ahead in the digital age, the print version should be subscribed to by all academic and large public libraries.

4046. *New Statesman.* Formerly (until 1996): *New Statesman & Society;* Which incorporated (1957-1991): *Marxism Today;* Which was formerly (until 1957): *Marxist Quarterly;* (until 1954): *Communist Review;* Which was formed by the merger of (1962-1988): *New Society;* Which incorporated (1979-1985): *Voluntary Action;* Which was formerly (until 1979): *Social Service Quarterly;* (until 1955): *Social Service;* (1957-1988): *New Statesman;* Which was formerly (until 1957): *New Statesman and Nation;* Which was formed by the merger of (1913-1931): *The New Statesman;* (1921-1931): *The Nation and the Athenaeum;* Which incorporated (1930-1934): *The Week-End Review.* [ISSN: 1364-7431] 1988. w. GBP 145 (print & online eds.) Individuals, GBP 87 (print & online eds.). Ed(s): Jason Cowley. New Statesman Ltd., 7th Fl, John Carpenter House, John Carpenter St, Blackfriars, EC4Y 0AN, United Kingdom; comments@newstatesman.co.uk. Illus., index, adv. Vol. ends: Jun/Dec. Microform: PMC; PQC. *Indexed:* A01, A06, A22, ABIn, AmHI, B01, B02, BRI, C37, CBRI, F01, MASUSE, MLA-IB, P02, RILM. *Bk. rev.:* Long and brief reviews in each issue; signed. *Aud.:* Ga, Ac.

New Statesman, one of Britain's most important newsmagazines, should be considered a standard subscription for any public or academic library that serves patrons interested in European politics. It is generally liberal in tone; however, each issue includes in-depth reporting with an overall focus on British politics. International affairs are also covered. Top journalists provide commentary, and an "Arts and Books" section offers reviews of films, radio, and television, as well as general cultural topics. The web page has some of the same content as the print magazine, and also has additional material updated daily. It also has a handful of blogs on current events.

4047. *Newsweek (Online).* [ISSN: 1069-840X] 1993. USD 24.99. Newsweek Daily Beast Company, 7 Hanover Sq, New York, NY 10004. *Bk. rev.:* 2-5, 500-1,300 words; signed. *Aud.:* Hs, Ga, Ac.

In late 2012, the Newsweek/Daily Beast Company announced that this 80-year-old publication would no longer be published in print. Embracing a more mobile news environment, the newsweekly is now available as a paid subscription for Kindle, Apple's Newsstand, Nook, and other e-readers. Limited content is available for free online in the *Newsweek* section of TheDailyBeast.com. The magazine is divided into three main sections with names that keep the "beast" imagery of its parent company: "Features," "NewsBeast," and "Omnivore." "NewsBeast" appears to carry *Newsweek's* politics, economy, and ideas stories, while "Omnivore" could be classified as its entertainment section with stories on sports, television, and literature. The differences between these two sections are not as clear on the e-reader as on the web site. The layout for both the e-reader version and the web site is clean and engaging. The e-reader version succeeds in making the reader feel as if she is flipping through a traditional print magazine while also allowing the magazine editors to include enhanced content for a satisfying and informative experience. This magazine will be best for those libraries that circulate e-readers and tablets, but a subscription for the web site content would not be wasted.

4048. *The Progressive (Madison).* Supersedes (in 1929): *La Follette's Magazine;* Which was formerly (until 1914): *La Follette's Weekly;* (until 1913): *La Follette's Weekly Magazine.* [ISSN: 0033-0736] 1909. m. USD 14.97 domestic (print or online ed.). The Progressive, Inc., 409 E Main St, Madison, WI 53703. Illus., index, adv. Sample. Microform: PQC. *Indexed:* A01, A22, ABS&EES, BAS, BRI, C37, C42, CBRI, Chicano, MASUSE, MLA-IB, P02. *Bk. rev.:* 2, 1,200 words; signed. *Aud.:* Ga, Ac.

The Progressive is one of the country's best-known liberal magazines. Notably, it was a vocal critic of the Bush Administration and of post–September 11th American foreign policy. Billing itself as a champion of "real democracy," however, it is critical of left-wing politicians when the editorial staff deems it necessary. It features writing from such well-known activists as Howard Zinn and Barbara Ehrenreich, and often has long interviews with other prominent intellectuals. It offers in-depth reporting as well as commentary and analysis of political, economic, social, and cultural issues. The magazine also prints poetry and cartoons. The web page offers some material from the current and older print editions, and highlights other key liberal blogs and web pages.

Reason. See Civil Liberties/Political-Economic Rights section.

4049. *Slate.* [ISSN: 1091-2339] 1996. d. Free. Washington Post Co., 204 West Washington St, Lexington, VA 24450; http://www.washpostco.com. Illus., adv. *Indexed:* ABS&EES. *Aud.:* Ga, Ac.

Slate is a free online daily magazine (the site is owned by the Washington Post Company) that covers topics of general interest, with focus on "analysis and commentary about politics, news, and culture." *Slate* has won several awards, including the National Magazine Award for General Excellence Online. Content is categorized into several sections, including "News & Politics," "Arts & Life," "Business & Tech," and "Health & Science." Aside from the categories and links to the daily issues and search feature of the site, it can be a bit difficult to navigate. When full articles are accessed, links to related articles are given. This is a good source of opinion pieces in a variety of subject areas, and should be available in most public and academic libraries. Of note is *Slate's* drive to make its content deliverable to a variety of devices including iPads, Android phones, and Kindles. These apps condense the vastness of the web site into an easily manageable, highly readable format that closely resembles a magazine.

Social Policy. See Labor and Industrial Relations section.

4050. *The Spectator: champagne for the brain.* [ISSN: 0038-6952] 1828. w. GBP 124 in Europe; GBP 116 in US & Canada; GBP 153.19 in Australia & New Zealand. Ed(s): Matthew d'Ancona. The Spectator, 22 Old Queen St, London, SW1H 9HP, United Kingdom; letters@spectator.co.uk; http://www.spectator.co.uk. Illus., index, adv. Circ: 77146. Microform: PMC; PQC. *Indexed:* A06, A22, ABS&EES, B01, BRI, CBRI, MLA-IB, P02. *Bk. rev.:* Number and length vary; signed. *Aud.:* Ga, Ac.

Published in England and often viewed as a more conservative twin to *New Statesman, The Spectator* should be considered by libraries that are interested in European politics and culture. It offers cultural and political commentary, as well as original reporting. Coverage is international in scope, but with a particular emphasis on British politics. The magazine has numerous cartoons with a distinctly British sense of humor. Some of the material is available online, with additional writing on a series of blogs and a discussion forum dubbed "The Coffee House." Subscribers appear to have access to an archive of past issues, as well.

4051. *Talking Points Memo.* 2000. Ed(s): David Kurtz, Josh Marshall. T P M Media LLC, http://talkingpointsmemo.com. Adv. *Aud.:* Ga.

TPM was founded by Josh Marshall in 2000 as a blog focusing on political analysis. The site retains a distinctly left-leaning bias, but it has expanded into a news organization that also engages in original reporting. However, the blog is still featured prominently on the homepage, and it tends to bring attention to domestic political stories that are under-reported in mainstream news outlets. Articles are available via daily e-mail and RSS feeds.

4052. *Tikkun: to heal, repair and transform the world.* [ISSN: 0887-9982] 1986. q. USD 108. Ed(s): Michael Lerner, Alana Yu-lan Price. Duke University Press, 905 W Main St, Ste 18 B, PO Box 90660, Durham, NC 27701; dukepress@duke.edu; http://www.dukeupress.edu. Illus., adv. Sample. Vol. ends: Nov/Dec. Reprint: PSC. *Indexed:* A01, A22, ABS&EES, AmHI, BRI, C37, CBRI, ENW, IJP, P02, RILM. *Bk. rev.:* Number and length vary. *Aud.:* Ga, Ac.

Tikkun (in Hebrew: "to mend, repair, and transform the world"), founded by Michael Lerner, an activist and rabbi, is a voice of the progressive Jewish and interfaith community. While many of its articles are written about subjects of interest to the Jewish community, it goes out of its way to include a variety of faiths and worldviews, so that its left-leaning articles and essays provide a unique viewpoint on global current events. Recurring threads in a number of the issues include the Arab–Israeli conflict, the Jewish world, Zionism, and the Middle East. In addition, space is dedicated to a section on culture that includes books, film, and music reviews, as well as profiles of notable people. Contributors include academics, writers, and thinkers such as Cornel West, Robert Thurman, Harvey Cox, and Marge Piercy. Recommended for academic libraries and public libraries with a strong Jewish or left-leaning patron community.

4053. *Time.* Incorporates (in 1937): *Literary Digest;* Which was formerly (1890-1937): *Digest;* Which incorporated (in 1937): *Review of Reviews;* Which was formerly (until 1935): *Review of Reviews and World's Work;* (until 1932): *Review of Reviews;* (until 1929): *American Review of Reviews;* Literary Digest incorporated (1912-1925): *Current Opinion;* Which was formerly (Jul.1888-Dec.1912): *Current Literature;* Which incorporated: *Current History and Modern Culture;* Current Opinion incorporated: *Democracy.* [ISSN: 0040-781X] 1923. w. USD 30 combined subscription in US & Canada (print & online eds.). Ed(s): John Huey, Richard Stengel. Time Inc., 1271 Ave of the Americas, New York, NY 10020; information@timeinc.com; http://www.timeinc.com. Illus., index, adv. Vol. ends: Jun. *Indexed:* A01, A06, A22, ABIn, AgeL, B01, B02, BEL&L, BLI, BRI, C37, CBRI, Chicano, F01, IIPA, MASUSE, MLA-IB, P02, RILM. *Bk. rev.:* Number and length vary; signed. *Aud.:* Hs, Ga, Ac.

This staple newsweekly remains relevant in the rapidly changing news environment by incorporating text and images in an easily readable layout. Most columns are brief, with longer feature and cover stories on major news events. With sections such as "Briefing" and "The Culture," *Time* covers a variety of news stories touching on politics, religion, arts, and entertainment, to name a few. *Time's* web site layout is reminiscent of the front page of a print newspaper, inviting the reader to virtually flip through the news. The online version provides a searchable database of all issues from 1923 to the present, although some articles are only available to paid subscribers. This newsweekly belongs in all types of libraries and is one of the few remaining print weeklies of its ilk.

4054. *U.S. News & World Report (Online).* Former titles (until 2010): *U.S. News & World Report Digital Edition; U S News.com.* [ISSN: 2169-9283] 1933. w. USD 19.95. U.S. News & World Report, L.P., 1050 Thomas Jefferson St, NW, 4th Fl, Washington, DC 20007. Adv. *Aud.:* Hs, Ga, Ac.

U.S. News & World Report was a longtime standard among print newsmagazines before it ceased publication in 2010. Now it consigns itself to offering its slightly-conservative-to-slightly-liberal news articles through its web site and a variety of platform-based subscriptions. The subjects it covers are extensive and varied. Each is covered under separate headings: "News & Opinion," "Health," "Money," "Education," "Cars," "Travel," and "Law." However, *U.S News & World Report* also limits its coverage by focusing on "service news and information that improves the quality of life of its readers." This includes its well-known rankings that offer information on a multitude of subjects, including cars, colleges, hospitals, etc. Unfortunately, the fact that this magazine tries to cover so many subjects leaves its web site cluttered and disjointed. Although its layout is better than that of some other news web sites, such as *The Daily Beast,* its disjointed design is surpassed by others such as that of *The Huffington Post.* However, its strength lies in its subscription-based digital magazine *U.S. News Weekly,* which is available on a variety of platforms including iPad and Nook, at different subscription rates. This digital magazine not only offers up-to-date news and information not available on its web site, but its easy layout—which is easy to navigate and read—far surpasses its alternative web version.

4055. *The Washington Monthly.* [ISSN: 0043-0633] 1969. 6x/yr. USD 29.95 domestic; USD 39.95 foreign. Ed(s): Paul Glastris. Washington Monthly LLC, 5471 Wisconsin Ave, Ste 300, Chevy Chase, MD 20815. Illus., adv. Sample. Circ: 33000. Vol. ends: Feb. Microform: PQC. *Indexed:* A01, A22, ABIn, ABS&EES, B01, B02, BRI, CBRI, MASUSE, P02. *Bk. rev.:* Number and length vary; signed. *Aud.:* Ga, Ac.

Priding itself on being an "independent voice" that offers "innovative solutions" instead of partisan talking points, *The Washington Monthly* offers lengthy, in-depth articles that cover a wide variety of political subjects, both historical and modern. The magazine has always attracted big names such as James K. Gailbraith, Wesley Clarke, and James Fallows to pen its in-depth essays, and it favors a relatively informal, if still well-researched, approach to journalism. Despite its slightly liberal viewpoint, it should be held by most libraries, as it provides a balanced approach to the day's major issues. The web site offers access to the full text of the previous year's issues, as well as some older articles.

■ NEWSPAPERS

General/Commercial Web News Systems

See also newspapers in other sections (Latin America, Europe, etc.) and check the index for specific titles not included here.

Jim Ronningen, Associate Librarian, Social Sciences, 218 Doe Library, University of California, Berkeley, CA 94720-6000; FAX 510-642-6830; jronning@library.berkeley.edu

Introduction

For newspaper readers in recent years, the possibility of the medium's demise has been a constant hovering dark cloud. The move toward digital news sources has siphoned off advertising revenue. The process began when classified ads were rendered obsolete by web sites such as Craigslist, and the remaining retail ad pages generally lack the campaigns targeted toward the younger demographic. Though the future looks pretty grim, for the present we still have print titles to recommend here.

There's been some good news and some bad news since the publication of our previous edition. After emerging from a near-fatal bankruptcy, the Tribune Company has managed to keep its titles (including the *Chicago Tribune, Los Angeles Times, Baltimore Sun,* and others) on life-support. However, its decision to divide into separate broadcast and publishing companies is regarded as a vote of no confidence for its newsprint business; the move would make it easier to arrange sale or redirection (i.e., no more print) of those titles. The New Orleans *Times-Picayune* had reduced its print run to three days per week, but has returned to a daily appearance after widespread outrage. While such a move can be seen as positive, overall these maneuvers can only erode public confidence.

Industry-wide, the anecdotal evidence of staff layoffs and other cost-cutting is supported by statistics from the American Society of News Editors. The ASNE's annual newsroom census shows that roughly 2,600 full-time professional editorial positions at newspapers were lost in 2012, a 6.4 percent decline from the previous year's count. The reductions in trained, dedicated editorial staff (a category that includes all journalists involved in the production of news content) are a separate and more troubling issue than the death of print. We can adjust to a change in the medium that brings us the news, but the economics of the transition appear to be weakening some news organizations to such a degree that the public's trust in them may be lost.

Basic Periodicals

All libraries should have every local newspaper if possible, larger metropolitan dailies that cover their region, and at least one national newspaper of quality that offers comprehensive, in-depth reporting on national and international events; and they should consider foreign newspapers, because they can broaden horizons. Don't spurn the weekly "alternative" titles because they look scruffy or might offend—they sometimes raise issues and offer viewpoints that can't be found in other more mainstream publications.

Basic Abstracts and Indexes

Depending on a library's budget and focus, the options here may be numerous. Title-specific indexing for the newspaper titles subscribed to is an obvious choice, and they may be available in print or online. The larger scope of an online aggregator that indexes your titles and others may provide article content as well, which is desirable if affordable. Web sites from the news publishers themselves normally offer searchable indexing and article content from recent issues (usually numbered in weeks or months, not years), but sometimes photos and graphics are excluded. Archiving for older articles may also be available through newspapers' web sites but normally involves a fee.

General

4056. *The Atlanta Journal - Constitution.* Formed by the merger of (1868-2001): *Atlanta Journal;* (1868-2001): *Constitution (Atlanta).* [ISSN: 1539-7459] 2001. d. Ed(s): Julia Wallace. Cox Newspapers, Inc., 223 Perimeter Center Pkwy, Atlanta, GA 30346. Circ: 382421. *Indexed:* B02, BRI, NewsAb. *Aud.:* Ga.

The *AJC*, as it's commonly known, is the result of a merger of the *Constitution* and the *Journal* that began in 1982, with separate morning and afternoon deliveries phased out by 2001. The flagship of Cox Enterprises, the seven-day-a-week, mornings-only newspaper is the major regional newspaper for the South. The editorial stance generally leans center to liberal. In response to its revenue slump, it started reducing staff in 2007, and more reductions have occurred through various efficiencies worked out among the Cox titles in the region. The web version adopts the strategy (popular with many news publishers) of presenting not just a news site but a portal to information about many aspects of life in Atlanta. The article archive does not include photos. URL: www.ajc.com

4057. The Baltimore Sun: light for all. Formerly (until 2008): *The Sun.* 1837. d. Ed(s): Anthony Barbieri, Tom Waldron. The Baltimore Sun Company, 501 N Calvert St, PO Box 1377, Baltimore, MD 21278; http://www.baltimoresun.com/. Circ: 321165 Paid. *Indexed:* B02. *Bk. rev.:* Number and length vary. *Aud.:* Ga.

Founded in 1837, *The Baltimore Sun* has a long history of publishing prize-winning journalism, warranting its inclusion here, even thought *The Washington Post* is the dominant title in the region. In recent years, the staff size has been reduced by more than 60 percent, including particularly harsh, abrupt firing of editors and managers in 2009. Currently owned by the Tribune Company, it has emerged from bankruptcy intact but with the likelihood of further cutbacks. The print edition and digital versions continue to demonstrate the publication's dedication to excellent local coverage. URL: www.baltimoresun.com

4058. The Boston Globe. [ISSN: 0743-1791] 1872. d. Ed(s): Matthew V. Storin. New York Times Company, 135 Morrissey Blvd, Boston, MA 02107; letters@nytimes.com; http://www.nytimes.com. Circ: 450538. *Indexed:* B03, C42, NewsAb. *Aud.:* Ga.

The Boston Globe was the most respected newspaper in New England before it joined the New York Times Corporation in 1993, which increased its content resources. However, the decline in newspaper readership and ad revenue in recent years put the *Globe* in jeopardy. The NYT Corp. tried various means of responding to the *Globe*'s annual losses of millions of dollars, including staff reductions and requesting concessions from the unions. Presumably the revenue stream will transition toward subscriptions to digital platforms. An early adopter of a community-oriented web presence, the publication's Boston.com site has been a leader in using multimedia components. Archival material is searchable (but it takes persistence to find the archive).

4059. Chicago Tribune. [ISSN: 1085-6706] 1847. d. Ed(s): Ann Marie Lipinski. Chicago Tribune Newspapers, Inc., 435 N Michigan Ave, Chicago, IL 60611-4041; http://www.chicagotribune.com/. Circ: 600988 Paid. *Indexed:* B02, BRI, NewsAb. *Aud.:* Ga.

The *Tribune* is a principal source for Midwest regional news and the largest-circulation paper in Chicago itself. Chicagoans are lucky to have a choice between the *Tribune* and the more populist voice of the *Sun-Times,* since many large cities are down to one major daily. In 2011, the *Sun-Times* closed a printing plant, laying off hundreds, to have printing done at the *Tribune* plant. The reduction of the *Tribune*'s editorial staff through layoffs and buyouts has been accompanied by a directive to focus on local coverage and the web site, which incorporates elements to facilitate dialog with readers. URL: www.chicagotribune.com

4060. The Christian Science Monitor (Treeless ed., Daily Online). [ISSN: 1540-4617] 2002. d. Ed(s): Marshall Ingwerson, John Yemma. The Christian Science Publishing Society, 210 Massachusetts Ave, Boston, MA 02115; http://www.csmonitor.com. Illus. *Aud.:* Ga.

Started with church funding as an alternative to commercial newspapers, *The Christian Science Monitor* had the means to examine its subjects in depth and did that very well for more than a century. With the growth of web-based publishing, it was decided to abandon the daily print publication in favor of digital efforts, reducing print to a once-a-week appearance. The last daily edition was published on March 27, 2009. The print weekly provides a wrap-up of the week's events, many of them covered in long-form pieces. It avoids sensational subjects, with no parade of celebrities heading off to rehab, so one's

appetite for pop culture will need to be satisfied elsewhere. The web site was an early adopter of "push" features, such as RSS feeds, and is fully engaged with social media. URL: www.csmonitor.com

4061. Financial Times (North American Edition). [ISSN: 0884-6782] 1985. d. Mon.-Sat. USD 348 domestic; CAD 498 Canada; USD 398 combined subscription domestic (print & online eds.). The Financial Times Inc., 1330 Ave of the Americas, New York, NY 10019; circulation@financialtimes.com; http://www.ft.com. Illus., adv. Microform: RPI. *Aud.:* Ga.

Readers looking for a tighter focus on business news than is found in the more all-encompassing *Wall Street Journal* may find they prefer the *Financial Times.* It is exactly what it claims to be, a "world business newspaper," with a global network and bureaus in the money capitals of the world. Noteworthy are the special reports that give lengthier treatment to selected topics and rival those of *The Economist* for depth. Worsening print subscription numbers have forced tightening measures such as layoffs and fewer pages. As did *The Wall Street Journal,* it recognized early that a free, advertising-supported online presence would not be sustainable; its metered paywall model allows a small number of free accesses per month, with full access only by subscription. URL: www.ft.com

4062. The Globe and Mail. Formed by the 1936 merger of: *Globe; Mail and Empire;* Which was formerly (until 1929): *Daily Mail and Empire;* Which was formed by the 1895 merger of: *Empire; Toronto Daily Mail;* Which was formerly (1872-1880): *Mail.* [ISSN: 0319-0714] 1936. d. Mon.-Sat. Globe and Mail Publishing, 444 Front St W, Toronto, ON M5V 2S9, Canada; Newsroom@globeandmail.com; http://www.globeandmail.com. Illus., adv. Sample. Microform: PQC. *Indexed:* B02, B03, BRI, C02, C37, CBCARef, CBRI. *Bk. rev.:* Number and length vary. *Aud.:* Ga.

The Globe and Mail is a nationally distributed, Toronto-based newspaper with the largest national paper circulation in Canada (the *Toronto Star* taking first in total circulation). This results in the macro view are what one expects: Toronto and Canadian regions are covered, but not in depth. Historically, the paper had the resources for excellent provincial, national, and international reportage, but more recently it has had to cut back on staff and is looking for other ways to economize. Politics and business coverage remain particularly thorough, including the "Report on Business" section. Subscription packages offer many options that combine print and digital formats. URL: www.theglobeandmail.com

4063. The Guardian. Former titles (until 1959): *Manchester Guardian;* (until 1828): *Manchester Guardian and British Volunteer;* Which was formed by the merger of (18??-1825): *British Volunteer;* (1821-1825): *Manchester Guardian.* [ISSN: 0261-3077] 1821. d. GBP 1.40 newsstand/cover. Guardian News and Media Ltd., Kings Place, 90 York Way, London, N1 9GU, United Kingdom; userhelp@guardian.co.uk; http://www.guardian.co.uk. Illus., adv. Sample. Microform: PQC. *Indexed:* AmHI, B02, BAS, BRI, NewsAb, RILM. *Bk. rev.:* Number and length vary. *Aud.:* Ga.

The Guardian and the Sunday-only *Observer* provide an opportunity for Americans to get news and opinion that are an alternative to what, in comparison, can seem a homogenous viewpoint from U.S. newspapers. These papers are part of the Guardian Media Group, which is independently financed through the Scott Trust, and they also have relatively little space set aside for advertising, resulting in a truly startling lack of consumerism throughout. The future of these two titles may be relatively bright compared to that of other newspapers, but subscription statistics are trending down according to the Audit Bureau of Circulations. The Guardian Media Group was in the forefront of web publishing; the previously very clean interface now struggles with the typical crowding issues as multiple media sources are incorporated. URL: www.guardian.co.uk

4064. Los Angeles Times. Formerly: *Los Angeles Daily Times.* [ISSN: 0458-3035] 1886. d. Ed(s): Dean Baquet. Los Angeles Times Newspapers, Inc., 202 W 1st St, Los Angeles, CA 90012. Circ: 955211. *Indexed:* BRI, Chicano, MLA-IB, N01, NewsAb. *Bk. rev.:* Number and length vary. *Aud.:* Ga.

When the Tribune Company bought the *Los Angeles Times* in 2000, the newspaper's character continued its path away from the local roots of the Chandler era to a more anonymous corporate personality. A decrease in staff that had been devoted to covering localities within the megalopolis has further reduced its importance to the region. The print publication is still chief among newspapers in Southern California, but further erosion is likely given its precarious financial situation. The web site fully exploits multimedia content, and a variety of digital formats are offered for subscription. URL: www.latimes.com

4065. *The Miami Herald*. [ISSN: 0898-865X] 1910. d. Ed(s): Anders Gyllenhaal, Dave Wilson. The/McClatchy Company, 2100 Q St, Sacramento, CA 95816. Circ: 280496 Paid. *Indexed:* BRI, C42, ENW. *Aud.:* Ga.

The Miami Herald is the principal news source for that very interesting spot where North American, Caribbean, and Latin American cultures come together. It responded to demographic change early on by teaming up with a sister newspaper, *El Nuevo Herald,* for South Florida's large Spanish-speaking population. *El Nuevo* is not just a Spanish translation of the English paper, but a different animal with its own staff and editorial choices. Unfortunately, how their readers and advertisers value them on newsprint is—not so much. Subscriptions and ad revenues have declined steeply. Large-scale layoffs occurred in spring 2009, and there have been further reductions since. The English-language *Herald*'s web site offers standard overall content, plus sections targeting the area's diverse communities; in addition to local coverage, *El Nuevo* adds stories about the countries of origin important to its readership. URLs: www.miamiherald.com, www.elnuevoherald.com

4066. *The New York Times*. Formerly (until 1857): *New-York Daily Times*. [ISSN: 0362-4331] 1851. d. USD 6.05 per week. New York Times Company, 620 8th Ave, New York, NY 10018; letters@nytimes.com. Illus., adv. *Indexed:* A01, Agr, B03, BLI, BRI, C42, CBRI, Chicano, F01, I15, IIMP, IIPA, MLA-IB, N01, NewsAb, P02, RILM. *Bk. rev.:* Number and length vary. *Aud.:* Ga.

If your library can subscribe to only one national newspaper, this is the obvious choice. Through comprehensive coverage of state, national, and international events, and some local coverage added for the different regional editions printed, *The New York Times* simply provides far more quality journalism than a competitor like *USA Today*. The writing and editing are regularly excellent, and rarely does one finish reading an *NYT* article with questions left unanswered. With the high quality of its color printing and the high cost of its subscription, the paper has taken on the feel of a luxury brand. The publisher recognized that free web access wasn't financially sustainable; as of 2011, it began controlling access through a metered paywall, and offered subscription packages for a variety of digital formats in addition to print. Their designers have made progress in the struggle to maximize news content while minimizing visual clutter on computer screens, tablets, and smartphones. URL: www.nytimes.com

4067. *San Francisco Chronicle*. Formerly (until 1869): *Daily Morning Chronicle*. [ISSN: 1932-8672] 1865. d. Ed(s): Narda Zacchino, Kenn Altine. Hearst Corp., The, 959 Eighth Ave., New York, NY 10019. Circ: 512000 Paid. *Indexed:* BRI, Chicano, NewsAb. *Bk. rev.:* Number and length vary. *Aud.:* Ga.

The *San Francisco Chronicle* is owned by the large Hearst chain; at least, that can feel like local roots to readers with knowledge of local history. Like other papers, the *Chronicle* has had to make hard choices to stay afloat. During the last decade, the news operation was downsized by waves of layoffs. In 2009, printing was outsourced to a local plant with newer presses, so mordant humor had it that the paper had become slimmer and better looking. In content, recent emphasis has been on more space for good writers focusing on subjects dear to Bay Area residents—liberal politics, culture, food, and the natural and built environments. Coverage of news important to the city's large LGBT population, such as the legalization of homosexual marriage, has been prominent. The related web site, *SF Gate,* has (like *The Boston Globe*'s Boston.com site) grown into a multimedia-rich source for helpful community information, going beyond the normal scope of a newspaper. URL: www.sfgate.com

4068. *Seattle Times*. [ISSN: 0745-9696] 1896. d. Seattle Times Co., PO Box 70, Seattle, WA 98111. Adv. Circ: 215000 Paid. *Indexed:* B02, RILM. *Aud.:* Ga.

In spring 2009, the *Seattle Times* became the city's only major daily newspaper when the *Post-Intelligencer* went to web-only publishing. The *Times* reduced its workforce and the parent company, The Seattle Times Co., rid itself of some struggling papers in Maine. The following year, the *Times* avoided bankruptcy by getting concessions from its remaining workers and renegotiating its debt with its bankers. That deal created optimism that the print edition would continue to appear at least for the near future. It has a moderate editorial stance in a liberal city, and remains the best option for local and regional Pacific Northwest coverage. The web site, like that of many urban news outlets, incorporates content from "local news partners." It seems to be having success in selling ad space. URL: http://seattletimes.nwsource.com

4069. *Wall Street Journal (Eastern Edition)*. Supersedes (in 1959): *Wall Street Journal;* Which was formerly (until 1930): *The Wall Street News;* (until 1924): *Daily Financial America;* (until 1915): *Financial America;* (until 1910): *The Wall Street Summary*. [ISSN: 0099-9660] 1889. d. Mon.-Sat. Ed(s): Paul E. Steiger, Bill Grueskin. Dow Jones & Company, 1 World Financial Ctr, 200 Liberty St, New York, NY 10281; wsj.service@dowjones.com; http://www.dowjones.com. Illus., adv. Circ: 1857050 Paid. *Indexed:* A01, ABIn, Agr, B01, B02, B03, BLI, BRI, C42, CBRI, Chicano, F01, GardL, MCR, N01, NewsAb, P02. *Aud.:* Ga.

The expansion of the *Wall Street Journal*'s scope from finance to general news is linked to its growth into a mass-circulation national newspaper. Financial data and reportage are still the top priority, of course, but they share space with selected local as well as national and international coverage. Sales figures for print and digital versions combined make it the top-selling news daily in the United States. It apparently has emerged unscathed from the 2011 scandals surrounding its parent company, Rupert Murdoch's News Corporation. In the Internet era, early recognition that its readership would be likely to pay for complete access to the web version has hedged it against the continued atrophy of its paper subscription base. Its web site requires that subscription for current and archival material; non-subscribers get previews of partial content. URL: http://online.wsj.com/public/us

4070. *The Washington Post*. [ISSN: 0190-8286] 1877. d. Ed(s): Steve Coll, Leonard Downie, Jr. Washington Post Co., 1150 15th St, N W, Washington, DC 20071; http://www.washpostco.com. Circ: 732872. *Indexed:* Agr, BRI, IIMP, IIPA, MLA-IB, N01, NewsAb. *Bk. rev.:* Number and length vary. *Aud.:* Ga.

The Washington Post is the preeminent newspaper for analysis of federal politics; post-Watergate, the national spotlight on it has never wavered. It is deservedly known for aggressive investigative reporting, as well as for being a part of the very power structure it reports on, in the sense that there have been close "inside the Beltway" relationships between its reporters and D.C. politicians that outsiders were not privy to. Its opinion pages are, unsurprisingly, very influential. Despite its unique position, the litany of problems plaguing it is just the same as at other major dailies, and the reactions are, too: buyouts, layoffs (a large wave in March 2009), and trimming wherever possible. It claims a higher percentage of households receiving the print edition than any other major market daily, but of course its web site has developed into the multimedia home base typical of major urban dailies. URL: www.washingtonpost.com

Commercial Web News Systems

The market in web news systems changes very rapidly: most news-producing vendors offer some kind of electronic option, with some text available immediately online. News files are often incorporated into other electronic products, too, and recent years have seen small companies engulfed by larger publishers and information aggregators. The good news is that these online infobases give researchers ready access to sources that were previously available to only the most determined and mobile scholars. Some sources offer added value by including news feeds from newswires, but free news sources that are now established on the web are superseding the necessity of incorporating such feeds.

Accessible Archives. Accessible Archives Inc., 697 Sugartown Rd., Malvern, PA 19355. www.accessible.com. Provides full-text primary source materials from eighteenth- and nineteenth-century newspapers and magazines, through databases such as *The Pennsylvania Gazette 1728–1800, The Civil War: A Newspaper Perspective, African American Newspapers: The 19th Century,* and *Godey's Lady's Book.*

Alt-Press Watch. ProQuest, 300 North Zeeb Rd., P.O. Box 1346, Ann Arbor, MI 48106-1346. www.il.proquest.com. The description of this database calls its sources "the alternative and independent press," which may still leave one wondering. Scanning the title list, a mix of newspapers and magazines, is the best method for getting it. Some examples: *The Advocate, Auto-Free Times, Creative Loafing* (in four Southern cities), *Industrial Worker, Miami New Times, SF Weekly,* and *Youth Today.*

Canadian Business & Current Affairs (CBCA). ProQuest Information and Learning, 300 North Zeeb Rd., P.O. Box 1346, Ann Arbor, MI 48106-1346. www.il.proquest.com. Full text for over 300 serials, indexing for over 700, *CBCA* covers *The Globe and Mail* and other major Canadian papers. The successor to *Canadian Index.* A related ProQuest product, *Paper of Record,* is an online historic newspaper archive for Canada, with some source material dating back as far as 1752.

Custom Newspapers. Infotrac/Gale/Thomson, 27500 Drake Rd., Farmington Hills, MI 48331. www.gale.com. This product replaces *British Newspaper Index* and goes well beyond it. Titles can be chosen from an extensive list of British and American papers. The earliest start date, which applies to many entries on the *Custom Newspapers* source list, is January 1996. Allows setting up a customized source list and search parameters, letting users create their own electronic edition.

Ethnic NewsWatch. ProQuest Information and Learning, 300 North Zeeb Rd., P.O. Box 1346, Ann Arbor, MI 48106-1346. www.il.proquest.com. *Ethnic NewsWatch* is a full-text database of over 200 newspapers and magazines "of the ethnic, minority and native press," in English and Spanish. The search interface is available in Spanish as well as English. Sources range from small- to relatively large-circulation publications, with titles like the *New York Amsterdam News,* the *Navajo Times,* the *Armenian Reporter, El Sol de Texas,* and *AsianWeek.*

Factiva. Dow Jones Reuters Business Interactive Ltd., 105 Madison Ave., 10th floor, New York, NY 10016. www.factiva.com. Succeeds *Dow Jones Interactive. Factiva* is a large full-text database with a focus on business research, drawing upon newspapers, newswires, trade journals, newsletters, magazines, and transcripts. A simple company name search can yield a very complete picture of relevant recent events.

FACTS.com. Facts on File News Services, 512 Seventh Ave., 22nd floor, New York, NY 10018. www.facts.com/online-fdc.htm. This five-part reference suite includes the *Facts on File World News Digest,* which features reworked news source material. The format is useful in environments where prepackaged topic searches are appropriate—not the place to go for large databases of verbatim news articles. Other files in the suite are almanacs, selected current issues, or science-oriented.

Global NewsBank. NewsBank Inc., 5020 Tamiami Trail N., Suite 110, Naples, FL 34103. www.newsbank.com. *Global NewsBank* is an online information system that offers grouped, topic-oriented links that are helpful for the less-experienced researcher. The worldwide resources include transcribed broadcasts. Excellent for students researching the varying perspectives on international issues.

Historical Newspapers. ProQuest, 300 North Zeeb Rd., P.O. Box 1346, Ann Arbor, MI 48106-1346. www.proquestcompany.com. *Historical Newspapers Online* contains four major historical resources: *Palmer's Index to the Times,* covering the period from 1790 to 1905 in *The Times; The Official Index to the Times,* which takes the coverage forward from 1906 to 1980; *The Historical Index to the New York Times,* which covers *The New York Times* from 1851 to September 1922; and *Palmer's Full Text Online 1785–1870,* providing access to the full-text articles referenced in *Palmer's Index to the Times.*

LEXIS-NEXIS Academic Universe. Reed Elsevier plc, 25 Victoria St., London SW1H 0EX, U.K. www.lexis-nexis.com. *LexisNexis Academic Universe* is the simplified, user-friendly package derived from the huge Lexis-Nexis database of news text. Full text from almost all major U.S. newspapers is here, with the notable exception being the *Wall Street Journal*'s abstracts only. The database provides news, financial, medical, and legal text from newspapers, broadcasts, wire services, government documents, and other categories. Images

and graphics are not included. Of (probably long-term) interest is the 2003 addition of translated transcripts from *Al-Jazeera.* International resources in Dutch, French, German, Italian, Portuguese, and Spanish are also included.

NewsBank Full-Text Newspapers. NewsBank Libraries can customize a subscription to create a list of local titles. The community-level information can be a valuable resource for public libraries, and is often under the radar screen of other aggregators with a more macro level of coverage.

Newspaper Source. EBSCO Publishing, 10 Estes St., Ipswich, MA 01938. www.epnet.com. The patchwork quilt of full text, indexing, and abstracting in this online source (also available on CD-ROM) can be valuable, but pay close attention to coverage details. *The Christian Science Monitor* is here cover-to-cover back to January 1995, but with other titles, there's partial coverage with too many exceptions to list.

World News Connection. National Technical Information Service, U.S. Department of Commerce, Springfield, VA 22161. http://wnc.fedworld.gov/description.html. Distributed by the National Technical Information Service, U.S. Department of Commerce, *WNC* provides web access to full-text, English translations of current non-U.S. media sources beginning in 1996. This is a derivative of intelligence-gathering efforts begun over 60 years ago, and there are sources here that you won't find transcribed in other full-text databases, such as local radio broadcasts of government statements. This is the online continuation of the *FBIS* and *JPRS* index and content microform systems.

■ NUMISMATICS

David Van de Streek, Library Director, York Campus, Penn State University, Lee R. Glatfelter Library, 1031 Edgecomb Ave., York, PA 17403; SDV1@psu.edu

Introduction

Numismatics is commonly thought of as being coin collecting, but the field is much more expansive, encompassing coins, paper money, tokens, medals, and associated areas. Further, it includes both the collecting of and the study and scholarship of these differing monetary forms. Of these varied areas of numismatics, coin collecting is easily the largest and most popular, one that has felt a swell of collector interest and market activity for the last decade or so. General estimates suggest that within the United States, millions of people are involved in some fashion with numismatics, even if it doesn't go much beyond saving the newest quarter or penny designs.

Even with such wide interest, though, there are only a handful of numismatic publications that broadly address the interests and needs of most collectors. While there are additional other publications available about the field, most are either too narrowly focused or have such limited readership potential that their usefulness for most library collections would be minimal. Of the periodicals listed in this section, five (*Coin World, Coinage, Coins, Numismatist,* and *Numismatic News*) have broad enough coverage that they can be thought of as general numismatic resources, even though a large share of their material is specifically about coins. Each of them contains enough about paper money, tokens, and some of the very specialized areas of numismatics that they will be useful to a wide audience of collectors and perhaps specialists as well.

Librarians looking for one representative numismatic periodical should strongly consider *Coin World,* which has long been highly respected within the field.

Basic Periodicals

Hs: *Coins;* Ga: *Coin World, Coinage, Coins, Numismatist.*

Basic Abstracts and Indexes

Numismatic Literature.

4071. Bank Note Reporter. [ISSN: 0164-0828] 1973. m. USD 39.98; USD 4.99 newsstand/cover. Ed(s): Bob Van Ryzin. F + W Media Inc., 38 E 29th St, 3rd Fl, New York, NY 10016; contact_us@fwmedia.com; http://www.fwmedia.com/. Illus., adv. Circ: 4261 Paid. *Indexed:* NumL. *Bk. rev.:* Occasional, 200-400 words. *Aud.:* Ga, Sa.

Broadly covering the collecting of all forms of paper money and related items, this publication focuses primarily on U.S. currency, while still having representative material on international currency. Its news content often addresses current trends and developments in paper money collecting, as well as the present condition of the marketplace for paper currency. As a pricing and value aid, a standard feature is a lengthy price guide that lists approximate retail prices for most U.S. paper money issues since 1861. Feature material is interesting and informative, is often comprehesive, and is typically well-written. These articles usually center on a specific piece or type of currency, and frequently provide historical background events relating to that currency. This is a solid and reliable resource for collectors of U.S. paper money.

4072. The Celator: journal of ancient and medieval coinage. Incorporates: *Roman Coins and Culture.* [ISSN: 1048-0986] 1987. m. USD 36 domestic; USD 45 Canada; USD 75 elsewhere. Ed(s): Kerry K Wetterstrom. P N P, Inc., PO Box 10607, Lancaster, PA 17605-0607; kerry@celator.com. Illus., adv. Circ: 2550 Paid and free. *Indexed:* NumL. *Bk. rev.:* 1, 150-200 words. *Aud.:* Ac, Sa.

Dedicated to a branch of numismatics commonly called "ancients," this covers all coinage from the earliest known coins of the seventh century B.C.E. through those of the medieval period. It follows a regular format of having two lengthy and well-developed feature articles in each issue, rounded out with columns on such things as general antiquities, Biblical coins, Celtic coins, relevant Internet resources, and opinions. Feature articles are scholarly, well-written, and solidly referenced, and can be so extensive that they are continued in successive issues. Given the historical nature of ancient coins, feature material is usually well steeped in ancient history and mythology. The publication has earned several numismatic literary awards, which speaks to the quality of its features. The audience for this may not be large, but it offers specialty material that is not usually picked up by other numismatic periodicals. Academic institutions with Classics or Ancient History departments should consider.

4073. Coin Prices. [ISSN: 0010-0412] 1967. bi-m. USD 24.98; USD 4.99 newsstand/cover. Ed(s): Bob Van Ryzin. F + W Media Inc., 38 E 29th St, 3rd Fl, New York, NY 10016; contact_us@fwmedia.com; http://www.fwmedia.com/. Illus., adv. Sample. Circ: 20278. *Aud.:* Ga.

Virtually the entire content of this magazine is a price guide for all regularly issued U.S. coins from 1793 to the present, plus all U.S. Mint–issued commemorative and precious metals coins, such as silver and gold American Eagle coins. Prices reflect an average retail cost, approximating what a buyer would pay to acquire a specific coin. Each listed coin has a range of prices that correspond to various quality grades for that coin, from heavily circulated to uncirculated. Mintage figures for each coin are also provided, which can help collectors gauge the relative rarity of a particular coin. Spring issues of the magazine are expanded to include pricing sections for Mexican and Canadian coins, plus U.S. paper money. As an indicator of coin values for frequently changing marketplace conditions, this can be a useful collector tool.

4074. Coin World. Formerly: *Numismatic Scrapbook.* [ISSN: 0010-0447] 1960. w. USD 59.99 combined subscription (print & online eds.); USD 5.99 per issue. Ed(s): Beth Deisher. Amos Publishing, Hobby, PO Box 926, Sidney, OH 45365; http://www.amospress.com. Illus., adv. Sample. Vol. ends: Dec. Microform: PQC. *Indexed:* A22, B01, BRI, NumL. *Bk. rev.:* 1-3, 200-400 words. *Aud.:* Hs, Ga.

This is one of the most highly respected and widely read of all numismatic publications. Issued weekly, it covers a broad range of numismatic interests and topics, effectively mixing current news items with feature material. Regular articles and contributed features are typically written by specialists or acknowledged experts in their field, most of whom are highly regarded within numismatics. Coverage extends to virtually all areas of numismatics, and includes a considerable amount of material that can be very useful for collectors in enhancing their knowledge and collecting skills. Special monthly editions feature an extensive and comprehensive retail price guide for all U.S. coins, as well as sections devoted to paper money and world coins. This is an informative, instructional, and comprehensive publication, with quality features and departments, and it should be a primary resource for most libraries.

4075. Coinage. [ISSN: 0010-0455] 1964. m. USD 29.95 domestic; USD 44.95 foreign; USD 4.99 per issue. Ed(s): Marcy Gibbel, Ed Reiter. Miller Magazines, Inc, 290 Maple Ct, Ste 232, Ventura, CA 93003; http://www.millermags.com. Illus., adv. Sample. Circ: 150000 Paid. Vol. ends: Dec. Microform: PQC. *Indexed:* A22, NumL. *Bk. rev.:* Occasional; 500-600 words. *Aud.:* Ga.

This is a very sound general-interest magazine that covers a wide array of numismatic topics. Feature articles are informative and can be extensive, focusing most often on currently significant numismatic topics. These frequently include historically based content as well as material that addresses collecting techniques or the condition of the coin marketplace. An interesting and sometimes educational regular feature is "Coin Capsule," which highlights the coinage or significant numismatic events of a selected year, and sets these events in the perspective of that year's noteworthy historical, political, and cultural events. The magazine has solid writing, is well produced, and has excellent close-up color photos of coins and paper money. The magazine's general content and broad coverage have potential appeal to both beginning and experienced collectors, and should be strongly considered as an integral part of a basic numismatics collection.

4076. Coins. Former titles (until 1962): *Coin Press Magazine;* (until 196?): *Coin News Magazine.* [ISSN: 0010-0471] 1955. m. USD 39.98; USD 4.99 newsstand/cover. Ed(s): Bob Van Ryzin. F + W Media Inc., 38 E 29th St, 3rd Fl, New York, NY 10016; contact_us@fwmedia.com; http://www.fwmedia.com/. Illus., adv. Circ: 21105 Paid. *Indexed:* A22, NumL. *Bk. rev.:* Occasional, 600-800 words. *Aud.:* Hs, Ga.

This is a general-purpose magazine that has long been popular in the field. It covers most areas of numismatics and has enough breadth that it has potential appeal and usefulness to a variety of collectors. Each issue is usually built around a specific collecting theme, such as silver dollars, and has several feature articles devoted to that topic. It is then rounded out with additional shorter features, news items, and regularly appearing columns. A regular feature, one that makes up over half of each issue, is an extensive price guide to approximate retail values for all regularly issued U.S. coins. This is supplemented periodically by issues that have price guides for other popular numismatic areas, such as paper money or Canadian coins. Because of its general nature, this magazine can be used either as part of a basic collection or as a complement to one.

4077. CoinWeek. Incorporates (1995-2012): *CoinLink.* 2011. m. Ed(s): Scott Purvis. CoinWeek LLC., PO Box 916909, Longwood, FL 32791-6903; news@CoinWeek.com. Adv. *Aud.:* Ga.

This web site is based largely on what was formerly CoinLink.com, and is an impressive source of current and archived information that blankets a very large sector of numismatic interest. It is frequently updated, and its extensive content is predominantly news, commentary, and opinion, centered on current numismatic events, collector tips and advice, and directions and trends within the coin and precious metals marketplace. Information on specialty and niche areas of numismatics is abundant. Also present is a video library of more than 1,000 titles, produced by Cointelevision.com. Many videos are educational and instructive, though access to some of these is through a paid membership. The archival content of the site is substantial, extending back many years, and is keyword-searchable, further enhancing the usefulness and accessibility of the site. This is a very complete and comprehensive resource, potentially useful for almost anyone who has an interest in numismatics.

4078. Numismatic News. Formerly (until 19??): *Numismatic News Weekly.* [ISSN: 0029-604X] 1952. 52x/yr. USD 79.99; USD 2.99 newsstand/cover. Ed(s): Dave Harper. F + W Media Inc., 700 E State St, Iola, WI 54990; contact_us@fwmedia.com; http://www.fwmedia.com/. Illus., adv. Circ: 30275 Paid. *Indexed:* NumL. *Bk. rev.:* Occasional, 100-300 words. *Aud.:* Ga.

Broadly covering the major areas of numismatics, this is primarily a source of current news and events, often with a focus on how these affect collectors or conditions within the coin market. Its regular columns and features are frequently aimed at improving collector knowledge and skills, and are sometimes augmented with longer historically-oriented pieces. Articles may feature lesser-known and less popular areas of collecting, which can serve as good introductions to those fields. Successive issues contain retail price guides that highlight several different areas of the U.S. coin market. As a general numismatics resource, this may serve to supplement a basic collection.

4079. *Numismatist: for collectors of coins, medals, tokens and paper money.* Incorporates (1987-1994): *First Strike;* (1951-1981): *A N A Club Bulletin.* [ISSN: 0029-6090] 1888. m. Free to members (print & online eds.). Ed(s): Barbara Gregory. American Numismatic Association, 818 N Cascade Ave, Colorado Springs, CO 80903; http://www.money.org. Illus., index. Sample. Vol. ends: Dec. *Indexed:* A06, ABS&EES, NumL. *Bk. rev.:* 1-3, 50-200 words. *Aud.:* Ga, Ac.

This is the membership publication of the American Numismatic Association, the premier collecting and leadership society in American numismatics. It is the oldest continuously published magazine in the field and is a wide-ranging resource that combines news and informational articles with comprehensive feature material. Articles and features are consistently well written and are typically interesting and informative, touching on almost any numismatic topic. A continuing editorial focus is providing material that collectors can use to enhance their numismatic knowledge and to sharpen their awareness of key issues in numismatics. This is a very inclusive publication that is potentially interesting to a wide range of collectors, and it should be considered as a part of almost any basic collection.

4080. *Paper Money.* [ISSN: 0031-1162] 1962. bi-m. Free to members. Ed(s): Fred L Reed. Society of Paper Money Collectors, Inc., c/o Frank Clark, PO Box 117060, Carrollton, TX 75011; frank_clark@spmc.org; http://www.spmc.org/. Illus., index. Sample. Vol. ends: Nov/Dec. *Indexed:* NumL. *Bk. rev.:* 1, 250 words. *Aud.:* Ga, Sa.

This is the membership journal of the Society of Paper Money Collectors, and it provides usually lengthy, interesting, and informative articles about all forms of paper money and related fiscal paper. Feature articles are typically historical treatments of specific currency issues or monetary events, with the added perspective of such things as national economic situations or significant bank or banking events. Articles are frequently contributed by acknowledged paper money experts, and are usually well researched and scholarly in approach. Some articles are very extensive, perhaps offering more thoroughness and depth than those in any other numismatic publication. The material is enhanced by high-quality visuals and photography. This should have strong appeal for readers interested in the historical context of paper money, and may also be useful academically for programs in American Studies or American History.

4081. *World Coin News.* [ISSN: 0145-9090] 1973. m. USD 39.99; USD 4.99 newsstand/cover. Ed(s): Maggie Judkins. F + W Media Inc., 38 E 29th St, 3rd Fl, New York, NY 10016; contact_us@fwmedia.com; http://www.fwmedia.com/. Illus., adv. Circ: 3467. *Indexed:* NumL. *Aud.:* Ga.

Dealing exclusively with international coinage, this publication mixes current news articles with feature material on coins and occasionally paper money. Feature material is usually informative, often including the historical or political context of the described coins or monetary events. Article content ranges from current coinage to that of centuries earlier, and can include any money-issuing country or municipality. Some content is aimed at keeping collectors apprised of trends within the coin marketplace, as well as aiding them in developing or refining their collecting knowledge and skills. As a general resource that covers the vast expanse of international coinage, this is a useful periodical that can serve as a nice supplement to core numismatic titles.

■ NURSING

See also Health Care Administration; and Medicine sections.

Lynn McMain, MLIS, M.Ed., Sam Houston State University, Huntsville, TX 77340

Introduction

The discipline of nursing is a constantly adapting and changing profession. The last several decades have seen the rise of multiple specialties within nursing. Forensic Nurses, Certified Registered Nurse Anesthetists, Nurse Practitioners, Home Health Nurses, and Hospice Nurses are but a few of the growing number of nursing specialities. As the discipline has grown and developed specialized areas of practice, so have the number of periodicals that provide support to the discipline grown.

The nursing periodicals selected for inclusion in this section reflect the multifaceted nature of the discipline, and are varied in focus, and in no way do they cover all aspects but reflect a portion of the larger jewel that is nursing. Included are periodicals for basic nursing practice, professional journals, journals for nursing educators, and nursing students, and journals for the highly specialized areas of nursing practice.

Basic Periodicals

Hs: *Imprint (New York);* Ac: *American Journal of Nursing, International Nursing Review;* Sa: *The Nurse Practitioner, Nursing (Year).*

Basic Abstracts and Indexes

CINAHL, ProQuest Nursing and Allied Health Source, Nursing Resource Center, Health Source: Nursing/Academic.

4082. *American Association of Nurse Practitioners. Journal.* Formerly (until 2012): *American Academy of Nurse Practitioners. Journal.* [ISSN: 2327-6886] 1988. m. GBP 306. Ed(s): Charon Pierson. Wiley-Blackwell Publishing, Inc., 111 River St, Hoboken, NJ 07030; info@wiley.com; http://onlinelibrary.wiley.com/. Sample. Refereed. Reprint: PSC. *Indexed:* A01, A22, E01, PsycInfo. *Aud.:* Ac, Sa.

The official publication of the American Academy of Nurse Practitioners (AANP) is a peer-reviewed, professional journal that contains articles of original clinical research, reviews, case studies, professional news, and continuing education credit on an array of topics. The *JAANP* focuses on "serving the needs of nurse practictitioners...who have a major interest in primary, acute[,] and/or long-term health care." Recent articles include "Polymyalgia Rheumatic and Giant-cell Arthritis: An in-depth look at diagnosis and treatment" and "Spontaneous Intracranial Hypotension: A case study." Samples of the tables of contents of all issues, along with a sample copy of the journal, are available online. This journal is recommended for academic libraries with graduate nursing programs, and for large medical libraries. URL: www3.interscience.wiley.com/journal/118489147/home

4083. *American Journal of Nursing.* [ISSN: 0002-936X] 1900. m. USD 425 (print & online eds.). Ed(s): Diana J Mason. Lippincott Williams & Wilkins, 333 7th Ave, 19th Fl, New York, NY 10001; customerservice@lww.com; http://www.lww.com. Illus., index, adv. Sample. Refereed. Vol. ends: Dec. Microform: PMC; PQC. *Indexed:* A01, A22, ASSIA, AgeL, BRI, CBRI, Chicano, MCR, P02, SWR&A. *Aud.:* Ac, Sa.

This very professional journal, simply known as *AJN,* is the official journal of the American Nurses Association (ANA), and is a staple in every medical library and academic library that supports a nursing program. Articles focus on evidence-based clinical practice, continuing education credit opportunities, professional news, and some peer-reviewed original research. Recent topics include "Competence in CPR," "Key Ideas in Nursing's First Century," and "Posterior Reversible Encephalopathy Syndrome: A case study." The journal's web site provides tables of contents of past volumes and free access to several of the current volume's articles, including continuing education credit articles.

This small, readable periodical is of value to every nursing student and practicing registered nurse, and should be in every academic or clinical library that supports nursing programs and nurses. URL: http://journals.lww.com/ajnonline/paages/default.aspx

4084. *Heart & Lung: the journal of acute and critical care.* [ISSN: 0147-9563] 1972. bi-m. USD 525. Ed(s): Dr. Kathleen S Stone. Mosby, Inc., 1600 John F. Kennedy Blvd, Ste 1800, Philadelphia, PA 19103; elspcs@elsevier.com; http://www.us.elsevierhealth.com. Illus., adv. Sample. Refereed. Microform: PQC. *Indexed:* A22, AbAn, E01, ExcerpMed. *Aud.:* Ac, Sa.

The official journal of the American Association of Heart Failure Nurses features scholarly, peer-reviewed articles on acute and critical care of heart and respiratory failure patients. The regularly occurring sections "Care of Patients with Pulmonary Disorders" and "Care of Patients with Cardiovascular Disorders" focus on advances, innovations, and research observations primarily in an acute and critical care nursing environment. Patient education, pharmacotherapy, and infection control are regularly occurring topics of articles. Recent articles discuss mediastinitis and blood transfusion in cardiac surgery, and the relationship between red cell distribution width and right ventricular dysfunction in COPD patients. Tables of contents of current and archived issues are available at the web site. This journal is essential for all critical care nurses, and nursing students studying critical care in undergraduate or graduate courses. This outstanding journal is recommended for all academic libraries that support nursing programs and clinical settings that support critical care. URL: www.heartandlung.org

4085. *Home Healthcare Nurse.* Incorporates (1979-1983): *Nephrology Nurse.* [ISSN: 0884-741X] 1983. 10x/yr. USD 347 (print & online eds.). Ed(s): Tina M Marrelli. Lippincott Williams & Wilkins, Two Commerce Sq, 2001 Market St, Philadelphia, PA 19103; customerservice@lww.com; http://www.lww.com. Illus., adv. Sample. Refereed. Circ: 5125. *Indexed:* A22, AbAn, Chicano. *Bk. rev.:* Number and length vary. *Aud.:* Ac, Sa.

This is the official journal of the Home Heathcare Nurses Association. Peer-reviewed articles focus primarily on the clinical and operational aspects of this nursing specialty, which includes hospice nursing. There are also two or three continuing education (CE) credit articles per issue, with free online access to the current issue's CE articles at the web site. Tables of contents for current and back issues are also available at the web site. Recent articles include "Managing Patients with Bipolar Disorder at Home" and "The Fundamentals of Hospice Compliance[:] What Is It and What are the Implications for the Future? An Overview for Hospice Clinicians" (one of the free CE articles). Regular sections include "Hospice and Palliative Care" and "VNAA's Voice" (Visiting Nurse Associations of America). As the U.S. population ages, the need for this type of nursing publication will increase greatly. Recommended for hospice, home health agencies, libraries that serve clinical practice, and consumer health collections. URL: www.homehealthcarenurseonline.com

4086. *Imprint (New York).* Former titles (until 1968): *N S N A Newsletter;* (until 1965): *National Student Nurses' Association. Newsletter.* [ISSN: 0019-3062] 1954. 5x/yr. USD 36 (Individuals, USD 18; Members, USD 3). Ed(s): Jonathan Buttrick, Alison Faust. National Student Nurses' Association, 45 Main St, Ste 606, Brooklyn, NY 11201; nsna@nsna.org; http://www.nsna.org. Illus., index, adv. Sample. Circ: 51000. Vol. ends: Dec/Jan. *Indexed:* A22. *Aud.:* Hs, Ac.

The official publication of the National Student Nurses Association (NSNA), this title contains focused articles specifically for high school students interested in nursing; nursing or pre-nursing and college students; recent nursing graduates; and nursing and pre-nursing educators. The title is heavy with advertisements, but that can be overlooked when one considers free access online to the current issue and archives at the web site. Regular departments and columns include "Guest Editorials," "NSNA News," and "NSNA: People." Recent articles include "Shaken Baby Syndrome: Where you fit in" and "Student Nurses Spreading the Word to End the R-Word." This periodical is recommended for high school libraries, especially those that support health career vocational programs, and academic libraries that support nursing programs. Additionally, hospitals that provide clinical experience for the students mentioned above should have this title in their library's collection. URL: www.nsna.org/Publications.aspx

4087. *International Nursing Review.* Incorporates (1968-1971): *I C N Calling;* Former titles (until 1954): *International Nursing Bulletin;* (until 1945): *International Nursing Review;* (until 1930): *The I C N.* [ISSN: 0020-8132] 1926. q. GBP 228. Ed(s): Dr. Jane Robinson. Wiley-Blackwell Publishing Ltd., The Atrium, Southern Gate, Chichester, PO19 8SQ, United Kingdom; customer@wiley.com; http://www.wiley.com/. Illus., adv. Sample. Refereed. Vol. ends: Nov/Dec. Microform: PQC. Reprint: PSC. *Indexed:* A01, A22, ASSIA, AbAn, E01, H24, PsycInfo. *Bk. rev.:* Number and length vary. *Aud.:* Ac, Sa.

The official journal of the International Council of Nurses, this journal provides U.S. nurses with a glimpse into the profession worldwide, and into global health issues. There are sections such as "International Perspectives" and "Nursing and Health Policy Perspectives," along with review and peer-reviewed research articles. Articles focus on topics such as the government's impact on nursing, ethics, technology, innovations in practice, and much more. Some of the most recent articles include "Globalization in Nursing: What does it mean for ICN and INR?," "Approaches to Nursing Skills Training in Three Countries," and "Translations and Validation of Two Evidence-Based Nursing Practice Instruments." The table of contents and a sample copy are available online. This title is a nice counterpoint to U.S. nursing titles and is recommended for all academic libraries that support nursing programs, and any other nursing collections. URL: www.wiley.com/bw/journal.asp?ref=0020-8132

4088. *Journal of Professional Nursing.* [ISSN: 8755-7223] 1985. 6x/yr. USD 398. Ed(s): Ellen Olshansky. W.B. Saunders Co., Independence Sq W, Ste 300, The Curtis Center, Philadelphia, PA 19106-3399; hhspcs@wbsaunders.com; http://www.us.elsevierhealth.com. Adv. Refereed. Circ: 2396. *Indexed:* A22, ASSIA, E01, PsycInfo. *Aud.:* Ac, Sa.

This scholarly, peer-reviewed journal is the official publication of the American Association of Colleges of Nursing and aims to address "the practice, research, and policy roles of nurses with baccalaureate and undergraduate degrees, the education and management concerns of the universities in which they are educated, and the settings in which they practice." Examples of recent articles are "Nursing as the Elusive Core of Care in Hospitals," "Course Strategies for Clinical Nurse Leader Development," and "A Teaching Mentorship Program to Facilitate Excellence in Teaching and Learning." There is a web site containing the table of contents of the most current issue, and also lists of the "Most Read," "Most Cited," and "ScienceDirect Top 25" that provide some free access to articles. This is a very valuable resource to all professional nurses, and specifically to the faculty in nursing programs leading to baccalaureate and graduate degrees. Highly recommended for all academic libraries that support baccalaureate and graduate degree nursing programs. URL: www.professionalnursing.org/

4089. *M C N: the American Journal of Maternal Child Nursing.* [ISSN: 0361-929X] 1976. bi-m. USD 317 (print & online eds.). Ed(s): Margaret Comerford Freda. Lippincott Williams & Wilkins, Two Commerce Sq, 2001 Market St, Philadelphia, PA 19103; customerservice@lww.com; http://www.lww.com. Illus., index, adv. Sample. Vol. ends: Nov/Dec. Microform: PQC. *Indexed:* A22, PsycInfo. *Bk. rev.:* Number and length vary. *Aud.:* Ac, Sa.

This scholarly, peer-reviewed journal focuses on the nursing issues of women's health, particularly childbearing women, and prenatal and neonatal infants. Featured are research articles, continuing education credit articles, and ongoing columns. Recent research articles discuss women's perceptions of midlife mothering; and smoking cessation interventions in perinatal partners. The ongoing columns such as "Toward Evidence-based Practice," "Nutrition for the Family," and "Global Health and Nursing" are clinically relevant. The tables of contents for current and previous issues are available online at the web site, but very little is available for free. This journal is indispensable for nurses in maternal/child care, and nursing students studying maternal/child care at either the undergraduate or graduate level. Highly recommended for all academic libraries that support nursing programs, and clinical collections of large institutions with a focus on maternal/child health and care. URL: www.mcnjournal.com

Minority Nurse. See Health Professions section.

4090. *The Nurse Practitioner: the American journal of primary healthcare.* [ISSN: 0361-1817] 1975. m. USD 430 (print & online eds.). Ed(s): Jamesetta A Newland. Lippincott Williams & Wilkins, 323 Norristown Rd, Ste 200, Ambler, PA 19002; customerservice@lww.com; http://www.lww.com. Illus., index, adv. Sample. Refereed. Circ: 20490. Vol. ends: Dec. Microform: PQC. *Indexed:* A01, A22, BRI. *Bk. rev.:* Number and length vary. *Aud.:* Ac, Sa.

Clinical and practical are the focus of this journal, aimed at the clinical nursing specialty of Nurse Practitioners. This useful journal has peer-reviewed feature articles and regularly occurring departments. Among the departments are "This Just In," "Legal File," "Lab Logic," "CE Connection," and "Medication Update." Featured articles in a recent issue are titled "Uncomplicated UTIs in Women" and "Strategies for Success as a Clinical Preceptor." A recent continuing education credit article was titled "Peripheral Neuropathy: Evidence-based treatment of a complex disorder." Limited free access to articles, along with the tables of contents of recent and archival issues, is available at the web site. This journal is a must for all academic libraries that serve graduate nurse practitioner programs, and institutional clinical collections where nurse practitioners are actively practicing. URL: http://journals.lww.com/tnpj/pages/default.aspx

4091. *Nursing Education Perspectives.* Former titles (until 2002): *Nursing and Health Care Perspectives;* (until 1997): *N and H C Perspectives on Community;* (until 1995): *Nursing and Health Care;* (until 1980): *N L N News.* [ISSN: 1536-5026] 1952. bi-m. USD 152 (Members, USD 40; Non-members, USD 90). Ed(s): Joyce Fitzpatrick. National League for Nursing, 61 Broadway, 33rd Fl, New York, NY 10006; generalinfo@nln.org; http://www.nln.org. Illus. Sample. Refereed. *Indexed:* A01, A22, BRI, MCR, MLA-IB. *Bk. rev.:* 0-7, length varies. *Aud.:* Ac, Sa.

The official publication of the National League of Nursing (NLN), this peer-reviewed journal centers on nursing education and educators. There is a section, "Teaching with Technology," that highlights the latest in technological innovations to enhance instruction, especially in clinical simulation and distance learning. Other sections and departments address best practices in education and curriculum; news from the NLN; book reviews; and career opportunities for nursing educators. Current and archival issues, with tables of contents and some free access, are available at the web site; and, of course, a subscription allows for full access to online issues. This is an invaluable resource for nursing educators in all types of nursing programs, from associate degree to baccalaureate to graduate level, and should be in every academic library that supports a nursing program. URL: www.nlnjournal.org/

Nursing Forum. See Health Professions section.

4092. *Nursing Management.* Formerly (until 1981): *Supervisor Nurse;* Incorporates (1994-1999): *Recruitment, Retention & Restructuring Report;* Which was formerly (1988-1994): *Recruitment & Retention Report.* [ISSN: 0744-6314] 1970. m. USD 397 (print & online eds.). Ed(s): Richard Hader. Lippincott Williams & Wilkins, 323 Norristown Rd, Ste 200, Ambler, PA 19002; customerservice@lww.com; http://www.lww.com. Illus., adv. Sample. Circ: 110000 Paid. Vol. ends: Dec. Microform: PQC. *Indexed:* A01, A22, ABIn, B01, BRI. *Bk. rev.:* 0-2, length varies. *Aud.:* Ac, Sa.

This publication focuses on the needs and interests of nurses who are in management or supervisory positions within the profession of nursing. Recently featured articles include increasing data transparency and health-care technologies in the twenty-first century. There are also articles that provide continuing education (CE) credit, and others that address management issues such as leadership, critical thinking, and quality improvement. Regularly occurring departments present articles on "Information Technology," "Evidence-based Nursing," "Team Concepts," and "Regulatory Readiness." Online access provides current and archived tables of contents and limited free access to selected articles. Recommended for all academic libraries that support nursing programs, and all clinical collections that support nurses and nurse managers. URL: www.nursingmanagement.com

Nursing Outlook. See Health Professions section.

4093. *Nursing (Year): the voice and vision of nursing.* Incorporates (1981-1988): *Nursing Life;* (1970-1976): *Nursing Update.* [ISSN: 0360-4039] 1971. m. USD 470 (print & online eds.). Ed(s): Linda Laskowski-Jones, Erika Fedell. Lippincott Williams & Wilkins, 323 Norristown Rd, Ste 200, Ambler, PA 19002; http://www.lww.com. Illus., index. Sample. Refereed. Vol. ends: Dec. Microform: PQC. *Indexed:* A01, A22, B02, BRI, P02. *Bk. rev.:* Number and length vary, some signed. *Aud.:* Ac, Sa.

This magazine is an excellent resource for all nurses that contains practical, hands-on, and how-to articles, as well as continuing education credit articles, updates on the latest techniques, and legal issues. The magazine is available online, and the web site provides access to tables of contents back to 1971, with limited free access to selected articles. Recent featured articles include "Mitochondrial Diseases: Problems in the power plant"; free continuing education credit articles, such as "Is This Patient with Heart Failure a Candidate for Ultrafiltration?"; and "Preventing Central Line-Associated Bloodstream Infections CLABSI." Regularly occurring sections include "Legal Questions," "Drug News," and "Medication Errors," to mention only a few. This long-lasting periodical continues to be a popular resource for practicing nurses, both vocational and registered, across North America. Recommended for all academic libraries that support nursing programs, and all institutional and clinical collections where nurses practice. URL: http://journals.lww.com/nursing/pages/default.aspx

Policy, Politics & Nursing Practice. See Health Professions section.

■ OCCUPATIONS AND CAREERS

See also Education; and Labor and Industrial Relations sections.

Kate Irwin-Smiler, Reference Librarian, Wake Forest University Professional Center Library, Winston-Salem, NC 27106; kate.irwin.jd@gmail.com

Introduction

Most people seeking career or job opportunity information do so only when necessary: when they are in need of a job, when they are dissatisfied with their career or lack thereof, or when a new career or job opportunity presents itself. It is unlikely that library patrons subscribe to career periodicals on a regular basis, and they are likely to rely on a library for access to these publications. Academic researchers, of course, often do not maintain a sufficient collection even of periodicals they subscribe to, so they must rely on their supporting research library.

Periodicals that focus on careers and occupations fall into a few basic categories: job listings, career development, and academic research. While these categories sometimes overlap in a single periodical, most titles are primarily one of these. Both the job listing and career development periodicals often specialize in a subject area or industry; in other cases, they specialize in terms of their projected audience. Many career periodicals are aimed at college students or people considering additional training.

Academic journals publish research in the career development or recruiting processes, with articles authored by career services personnel, psychologists, or education specialists. Such research is not generally directed toward job seekers, but rather toward educators, fellow researchers, or career services personnel.

Particularly in regard to career development publications, some publishers may produce highly specialized periodicals in several overlapping areas. While each title may be appropriate for some audiences, it is unlikely that all titles would be appropriate for any one library, due to duplication and minute variations. Some specialized publications aimed a job seekers offer free or very low-cost subscriptions.

Many career development and most job listing periodicals have accompanying web sites that expand on the material that is already published. Links to advertising employers are common on these pages. In addition, some job listing sites include more information online for each listing, or more listings than are included in the print publication.

National job listing web sites, not associated with any print publications, are plentiful and can be extremely useful to library patrons who are using job listing periodicals. Indeed.com, Monster.com, CareerBuilder.com, and JobBankUSA.com are but a few examples of broadly-based sites that post jobs in many geographical and employment areas. RegionalHelpWanted.com maintains scores of local job-listing sites in the United States and Canada, listing jobs available by city and employment category. Specialized online sites such as HigherEdJobs.com or TheLadders.com provide listings in a particular industry, or those meeting particular criteria. Professional associations often list available jobs on a web site or discussion list, although these listings may be restricted to members of the association.

Basic Periodicals

Hs: *Occupational Outlook Quarterly;* Ga: *Federal Jobs Digest, Insight into Diversity, Occupational Outlook Quarterly;* Ac: *Career Development Quarterly, Occupational Outlook Quarterly;* Sa: *Careers and the Disabled, Career Development International, Journal of Employment Counseling.*

Basic Abstracts and Indexes

ProQuest Research Library, ERIC, PsycINFO.

4094. *African-American Career World: the diversity employment magazine.* 2001. s-a. USD 18 (Free to qualified personnel). Ed(s): James Schneider. Equal Opportunity Publications, Inc., 445 Broad Hollow Rd, Ste 425, Melville, NY 11747; info@eop.com; http://www.eop.com. Adv. Sample. *Bk. rev.:* 3-6. *Aud.:* Ga.

This oversized magazine profiles industries via descriptions of three to four successful African Americans in a variety of related occupations. Practical tips emphasize the importance of workplace diversity and encourage career success; and reviews of general career and occupations books highlight diversity issues. Employer advertisements throughout the magazine are indexed in each issue.

Black Enterprise. See African American section.

4095. *Career Development International.* Formed by the merger of (1989-1996): *International Journal of Career Management;* Which incorporated (1992-1994): *Recruitment Selection and Retention;* (1988-1995): *Executive Development.* [ISSN: 1362-0436] 1996. 7x/yr. EUR 11789 combined subscription in Europe (print & online eds.); USD 13579 combined subscription in the Americas (print & online eds.); GBP 7919 combined subscription in the UK & elsewhere (print & online eds.). Ed(s): Jim M Jawahar. Emerald Group Publishing Ltd., Howard House, Wagon Ln, Bingley, BD16 1WA, United Kingdom; information@emeraldinsight.com; http://www.emeraldinsight.com. Illus. Sample. Refereed. Reprint: PSC. *Indexed:* A22, ABIn, B01, E01, ERIC, PsycInfo. *Aud.:* Ac.

This academic journal publishes peer-reviewed academic manuscripts and less formal "think pieces" that address international aspects of career development. These international aspects may refer to the scope of an article, addressing topics of interest to an international audience, or the content, addressing topics that are inherently international, such as cross-border employment. Highly structured abstracts give a quick overview of research methodology, findings, and practical implications. Topics covered by the articles include careers, policy, recruitment, and organizational strategies.

4096. *The Career Development Quarterly.* Formerly (until 1986): *Vocational Guidance Quarterly.* [ISSN: 0889-4019] 1952. q. GBP 141. Wiley-Blackwell Publishing, Inc., 111 River St, Hoboken, NJ 07030; info@wiley.com; http://blackwellpublishing.com. Illus., index, adv. Sample. Refereed. Vol. ends: Jun. Microform: PQC. Reprint: PSC. *Indexed:* A01, A22, ABIn, ABS&EES, B01, B02, ERIC, HEA, P02, PsycInfo, SWR&A. *Aud.:* Ac, Sa.

This peer-reviewed journal of the National Career Development Association publishes articles that promote the practical application of career development theories. The editorial board is primarily composed of U.S. academics, but the articles demonstrate a commitment to an international perspective on careers; a section titled "Global Vision" now appears, reflecting an "internationalization of the profession." All articles are thoroughly grounded in supporting research, including the "Effective Techniques" (best practices) section. Occasional special sections focus attention on particular disciplines.

4097. *Careers and the Disabled.* Formerly (until 1986): *Careers and the Handicapped.* [ISSN: 1056-277X] 1986. q. Ed(s): James Schneider. Equal Opportunity Publications, Inc., 445 Broad Hollow Rd, Ste 425, Melville, NY 11747; info@eop.com; http://www.eop.com. Illus., adv. Sample. *Indexed:* BRI. *Bk. rev.:* 3-5, 150 words. *Aud.:* Ga, Sa.

This magazine profiles careers, industries, and companies that are friendly to employees with disabilities of various kinds, as well as successful professionals with various disabilities. Job-hunting advice includes suggestions for handling visible and invisible disabilities during the job search process, as well as more generalized concerns. Disabilities discussed include impaired vision, hearing, and mobility, as well as learning and developmental disabilities. A few pages of Braille text are included in each issue. Advertisements for employers are scattered throughout but indexed in each issue; these employers are committed to hiring people with disabilities.

The Chronicle of Higher Education. See Education/Higher Education section.

Entrepreneur. See Business and Finance/Small Business section.

4098. *Federal Jobs Digest.* [ISSN: 0739-1684] 1977. 25x/yr. USD 125. Ed(s): Young S Kim. HYR LLC, PO Box 89, Edgemont, PA 19028. Illus., adv. *Aud.:* Ga, Ac.

This newsletter provides job listings for the federal government. Each issue lists several thousand jobs, organized regionally and listed by General Schedule code and grade level. An index by federal job title and General Schedule code indicates what jobs are listed in each issue, but not how to find the listings, making this publication most useful to someone job hunting in one geographical region. Separate lists include overseas jobs, Veterans Affairs jobs, Senior Executive Service jobs, and Postal Exams. Job listings include the title, grade, closing date for applications, location, term of employment, salary range, contact information, and announcement number. A key to the listings is available to interpret this information, which is presented in a brief format and very small type. Information about the federal resume requirements and application process is also provided. Brief news articles highlight upcoming opportunities in federal agencies. Web sites listing agency job vacancies are listed.

4099. *Hispanic Career World: the diversity employment magazine.* 2001. s-a. USD 18 (Free to qualified personnel). Ed(s): James Schneider. Equal Opportunity Publications, Inc., 445 Broad Hollow Rd, Ste 425, Melville, NY 11747; info@eop.com; http://www.eop.com. Adv. Sample. *Aud.:* Ga.

This oversized magazine provides career and industry profiles that focus on interviews with professionals of Hispanic extraction, discussing their career paths, obstacles they faced and how they overcame them, and their advice for job seekers. Articles about careers and industries highlight diversity initiatives in training and hiring, as well as jobs with an international aspect or where language ability is important, and areas in which there are programs designed to increase Hispanic presence in a field. Notes in the top margin identify the field or industry in each article and make for easy skimming. Columns provide new developments in the employment of Hispanics, including profiles of employers. While the table of contents headings are presented in English and Spanish, content is exclusively English. Advertising employers are indexed in each issue.

4100. *Insight into Diversity.* Formerly (until 2009): *Affirmative Action Register.* [ISSN: 2154-0349] 1974. m. except July. Free. Ed(s): Michael Rainey. Potomac Publishing, Inc, 225 S Meramec Ave Ste 400, St. Louis, MO 63105; http://www.potomacpub.com/. Illus., adv. Sample. Vol. ends: Feb/Aug. *Aud.:* Ga, Ac.

This magazine features brief interviews and employer and industry profiles in each themed issue that address topics of diversity. Diversity is broadly conceived, including religious diversity and paying special attention to veterans. A large percentage of the magazine consists of job listings for professionals in academic settings. Most advertisements are display ads, generally taking up a quarter to a half-page, with full descriptions and application information included. Up-to-date listings are available on the web site, and news updates are available by RSS feed and on Twitter (@INSIGHT_ News). URL: www.insightintodiversity.com

4101. Journal of Career Development. Formerly (until 1984): *Journal of Career Education.* [ISSN: 0894-8453] 1972. bi-m. USD 746. Sage Publications, Inc., 2455 Teller Rd, Thousand Oaks, CA 91320; info@sagepub.com; http://www.sagepub.com. Illus., index, adv. Sample. Refereed. Microform: PQC. Reprint: PSC. *Indexed:* A22, ABIn, ABS&EES, B01, E01, ERIC, HEA, PsycInfo, SWR&A. *Aud.:* Ac, Sa.

This peer-reviewed academic journal provides well-researched scholarly articles that concentrate on theoretical approaches to career counseling and development, techniques, and issues of work–life balance. Research addresses populations that are diverse in terms of ethnicity, national origin, age, and area of professional interest. The board of editors and slate of authors represent international perspectives on career counseling, student services, psychology, sociology, education, and human resources. Tables of contents are available online at the publisher's web site. URL: http://jcd.sagepub.com

4102. Journal of Employment Counseling. [ISSN: 0022-0787] 1965. q. GBP 106. Wiley-Blackwell Publishing, Inc., 111 River St, Hoboken, NJ 07030; info@wiley.com; http://www.wiley.com/. Illus., index, adv. Sample. Refereed. Vol. ends: Dec. Microform: PQC. Reprint: PSC. *Indexed:* A01, A22, ABIn, ASSIA, B01, BRI, ERIC, HEA, PsycInfo, SWR&A. *Bk. rev.:* Number and length vary. *Aud.:* Ac, Sa.

This academic journal publishes peer-reviewed research articles in social science disciplines related to career counseling, such as counseling, education, and psychology. Common topics include career planning, unemployment, work/life balance, job performance, and recruiting, with occasional special issues on one subject area. A new section titled "In the Field" focuses on practical applications and book reviews. This publication should be useful to researchers working in career-related fields and counseling professionals.

Monthly Labor Review. See *Monthly Labor Review Online* in the Labor and Industrial Relations section.

4103. N A C E Journal. Former titles (until 2002): *Journal of Career Planning & Employment;* (until 1985): *Journal of College Placement;* (until 1952): *School and College Placement;* (until 1940): *University Placement Review.* [ISSN: 1542-2046] 1929. q. Free to members; Non-members, USD 70. National Association of Colleges and Employers, 62 Highland Ave, Bethlehem, PA 18017; customer_service@naceweb.org; http://www.naceweb.org. Illus., index. Sample. Vol. ends: May. Microform: PQC. *Indexed:* A01, A22, BRI, CBRI, HEA, P02. *Bk. rev.:* 10-12, 100-250 words. *Aud.:* Ac, Sa.

This journal, published by the National Association of Colleges and Employers, is geared toward career services personnel in colleges and universities, and recruiting personnel with employers. Most of the articles are written by career-services professionals or academics. Many focus on best practices in employer recruiting, operation of a college-based career center (including that involving other college administrators and faculty), and new developments in the field of career advising. Research articles analyze data collected from Association surveys. Association news, including conferences and publications, is included, as well as reviews of career-oriented books and a column on legal issues in hiring.

4104. Occupational Outlook Quarterly. Formerly (until 1958): *The Occupational Outlook.* [ISSN: 0199-4786] 1957. q. Sep.-June. USD 15 domestic; USD 21 foreign; USD 6 per issue domestic. U.S. Department of Labor, Bureau of Labor Statistics, 2 Massachusetts Ave, NE, Rm 2850, Washington, DC 20212; blsdata_staff@bls.gov; http://www.bls.gov. Illus., index. Sample. Vol. ends: Winter. Microform: CIS; NBI; PQC. *Indexed:* A01, A22, ABIn, AmStI, B01, B02, BRI, C37, ERIC, MASUSE, P02, P61, SSA. *Aud.:* Ems, Hs, Ga, Ac.

This publication uses statistics from the federal government to profile and often forecast projected labor markets for careers and industries. Job duties, education background and training, and earnings data are all provided, as well as sources of more information for interested readers. Other occupational trends are also outlined, such as opportunities for telecommuting. Occupational news such as information about reports, scholarships, and other material are reported in brief. The *Occupational Outlook Quarterly* updates the biennial *Occupational Outlook Handbook,* a standard reference work. This duo forms a valuable resource for those researching careers, whether they are students in search of a first career or adults looking for a change. A biennial "Job Outlook in brief" offers projections for hundreds of career fields from the *Occupational Outlook Handbook.* Online access is available, including an index back to 1999. URL: www.bls.gov/opub/ooq/home.htm

Techniques. See Education/Specific Subjects and Teaching Methods: Technology section.

Training. See Management, Administration, and Human Resources section.

Work and Occupations. See Sociology and Social Work/General section.

■ PALEONTOLOGY

See also Biological Sciences; and Earth Sciences sections.

Hilary Kline, Manager of Reformatting Support Services, Preservation and Imaging Department, Harvard College Library, Widener Library, Harvard University, Cambridge, MA 02138; kline@fas.harvard.edu

Introduction

When most people hear the word *paleontology,* they probably think of the skeleton of a dinosaur that they see at the natural history museum. In fact, there is much more to the study of prehistoric life than just dinosaur bones. Fossils are the keys to understanding the history of life on our planet; without them, we would know little of past climate change, and virtually nothing of evolution and extinction.

Not surprisingly, the field of paleontology is closely related to archaeology, but it also has a connection to biology, geology, ecology, and climatology. Due to the overlapping nature of the field, there are many journals from which to choose. Unfortunately, for the general public, the one title that was included in this section in the past ceased publication in December 2012.

Two of the titles included for review are free open-access publications, so there is nothing to lose by taking a look at *Acta Palaeontologica Polonica* and *Palaeontologia Electronica.* Another good web site to look at is the University of Kansas's Paleontological Institute page, http://paleo.ku.edu, which has both an open-access publication and print ones for purchase, as well as some basic paleontology information.

It should also be noted that this reviewer was not able to obtain review copies, since many publishers do not wish to part with even one free issue, so all of the reviews in this section have been done by looking at the online versions of the journals.

Basic Periodicals

Journal of Paleontology, Journal of Vertebrate Paleontology, Lethaia, Palaeontology, Palaeontologia Electronica, Palaios, Paleobiology.

Basic Abstracts and Indexes

BioOne (http://www.bioone.org/), BIOSIS, GeoRef, Zoological Record.

4105. *Acta Palaeontologica Polonica.* [ISSN: 0567-7920] 1956. q. EUR 194 foreign. Ed(s): Zofia Kielan-Jaworowska. Polska Akademia Nauk, Instytut Paleobiologii, ul Twarda 51-55, Warsaw, 00-818, Poland. Illus., adv. Refereed. Circ: 500. *Indexed:* A22. *Bk. rev.:* 0-1, 500-1,200 words. *Aud.:* Ac, Sa.

Acta Palaeontologica Polonica is a quarterly, open-access journal that publishes original research papers from all areas of paleontology, especially those rooted in biologically-oriented paleontology. Areas covered in the journal include fossils, ancient organisms, vertebrates, and evidence of evolution of the biosphere and its ecosystems. Two recent articles include "A new species of saurolophine hadrosaurid dinosaur from the Late Cretaceous of the Pacific coast of North America" and "A new albanerpetontid amphibian from the Barremian (Early Cretaceous) Wessex Formation of the Isle of Wight, southern England." URL: www.app.pan.pl

Cretaceous Research. See Earth Sciences and Geology section.

4106. *International Journal of Paleopathology.* [ISSN: 1879-9817] 2011. q. EUR 278. Ed(s): Jane Buikstra. Elsevier Ltd, The Boulevard, Langford Lane, Oxford, OX5 1GB, United Kingdom; journalscustomerserviceemea@elsevier.com; http://www.elsevier.com. *Aud.:* Ac, Sa.

This relatively new journal focuses on the study and application of methods and techniques for investigating diseases and related conditions from skeletal and soft tissue remains. Research articles, case studies, technical notes, brief communications, reviews and invited commentaries may be included in issues of *International Journal of Paleopathology.* Two recent inclusions are "Dental health in Iron Age Cambodia: Temporal variations with rice agriculture" and "Spina bifida in a pre-Columbian Cuban population: A paleoepidemiological study of genetic and dietary risk factors."

4107. *Journal of Paleontology.* [ISSN: 0022-3360] 1927. bi-m. Ed(s): Richard Lupia, Steve Westrop. Paleontological Society, c/o Roger D. K. Thomas, Secretary, Department of Earth and Environment, PO Box 3003, Lancaster, PA 17604; roger.thomas@fandm.edu; http://www.paleosoc.org/. Illus., index, adv. Refereed. Vol. ends: Nov (No. 6). Microform: PQC. *Indexed:* A01, A22, AbAn, E01, OceAb, P02. *Bk. rev.:* 4, 500 words. *Aud.:* Ac, Sa.

Published by The Paleontological Society, the *Journal of Paleontology* publishes original articles and notes on the systematics, phylogeny, paleoecology, paleogeography, and evolution of fossil organisms. It emphasizes specimen-based research and features high-quality illustrations. All taxonomic groups are treated, including invertebrates, microfossils, plants, vertebrates, and ichnofossils. Recent articles include "Multi-Segmented Arthropods from the Middle Cambrian of British Columbia (Canada)" and "The Ichnotaxonomy of Vertically Oriented, Bivalve-Generated Equilibrichnia."

Journal of Quaternary Science. See Earth Sciences and Geology section.

4108. *Journal of Vertebrate Paleontology.* [ISSN: 0272-4634] 1980. bi-m. GBP 340 (print & online eds.). Ed(s): Mark V H Wilson, Laura Healy. Taylor & Francis Inc., 325 Chestnut St, Ste 800, Philadelphia, PA 19106; customerservice@taylorandfrancis.com; http://www.tandfonline.com. Illus., index, adv. Refereed. Vol. ends: Dec (No. 4). Reprint: PSC. *Indexed:* A01, A22, E01. *Bk. rev.:* 0-4, 1,000-2,000 words. *Aud.:* Ac, Sa.

The Society of Vertebrate Paleontology publishes this quarterly journal, with original peer-reviewed contributions on all aspects of vertebrate paleontology, including evolution, functional morphology, taxonomy, phylogeny, biostratigraphy, paleoecology, and paleobiogeography. The contributions include articles, reviews, interdisciplinary papers, and book reviews. A recent issue contains the two articles "A New Fossil Salamander (Caudata, Proteidae) from the Upper Cretaceous (Maastrichtian) Hell Creek Formation, Montana, U.S.A." and "New Data on the Diversity and Abundance of Small-Bodied Ornithopods (Dinosauria, Ornithischia) from the Belly River Group (Campanian) of Alberta."

4109. *Lethaia: an international journal of palaeontology and stratigraphy.* [ISSN: 0024-1164] 1968. q. GBP 268 (print & online eds.). Ed(s): Peter Doyle. Wiley-Blackwell Publishing Ltd., The Atrium, Southern Gate, Chichester, PO19 8SQ, United Kingdom; customer@wiley.com; http://www.wiley.com/. Illus., index, adv. Sample. Refereed. Vol. ends: No. 4. Microform: PQC. Reprint: PSC. *Indexed:* A01, A22, AbAn, E01. *Bk. rev.:* 1,700 words. *Aud.:* Ac, Sa.

This journal is the formal publication for the International Palaeontological Association (IPA) and the International Commission on Stratigraphy (ICS). It emphasizes new developments and discoveries in paleobiological and biostratigraphical research and is published quarterly. Two recent articles are "Nearly circular, oval and irregular holes in Cretaceous ammonoids from Nigeria" and "The jaw apparatuses of Cretaceous Phylloceratina (Ammonoidea)."

4110. *Palaeontologia Electronica.* [ISSN: 1094-8074] 1998. s-a. Free. Ed(s): P David Polly, Mark Purnell. Coquina Press, PO Box 577, Columbia, CA 95310; coquinapress@mac.com; http://www.coquinapress.com. Refereed. *Bk. rev.:* 0-3, 1,000-1,500 words. *Aud.:* Ac, Sa.

Palaeontologia Electronica is funded by the Palaeontological Association, the Paleontological Society, the Society of Vertebrate Paleontology, and the Western Interior Paleontological Society. It deals with all aspects of paleontology and related biological disciplines. All articles are peer-reviewed and freely available on the web site. Two recent articles include "The oldest fossil record of bandicoots (Marsupialia; Peramelemorphia) from the late Oligocene of Australia" and "Multibody dynamics model of head and neck function in Allosaurus (Dinosauria, Theropoda)." URL: http://palaeo-electronica.org

4111. *Palaeontology.* [ISSN: 0031-0239] 1957. bi-m. GBP 695. Ed(s): S Stouge. Wiley-Blackwell Publishing Ltd., The Atrium, Southern Gate, Chichester, PO19 8SQ, United Kingdom; customer@wiley.com; http://www.wiley.com/. Illus., index, adv. Sample. Refereed. Vol. ends: No. 6. Reprint: PSC. *Indexed:* A01, A22, E01, OceAb, P02. *Aud.:* Ac, Sa.

This journal of the Palaeontological Association has a very broad scope and publishes a variety of papers on paleontological topics, including paleozoology, paleobotany, systematic studies, paleoecology, micropaleontology, paleobiogeography, functional morphology, stratigraphy, taxonomy, taphonomy, paleoenvironmental reconstruction, paleoclimate analysis, and biomineralization studies. Two recent articles are "Atlas of vertebrate decay: a visual and taphonomic guide to fossil interpretation" and "Mass mortality of an asteriid starfish (Forcipulatida, Asteroidea, Echinodermata) from the late Maastrichtian (Late Cretaceous) of Morocco."

4112. *Palaios: emphasizing the impact of life on earth's history.* [ISSN: 0883-1351] 1986. bi-m. Free to members; Non-members, USD 415 (print, online & CD-ROM eds.). Ed(s): Jill M Hardesty, Stephen T Hasiotis. Society for Sedimentary Geology (S E P M), 4111 S Darlington, Ste 100, Tulsa, OK 74135; foundation@sepm.org; http://www.sepm.org. Illus., index, adv. Refereed. Vol. ends: No. 6. *Indexed:* A22, E01, M&GPA. *Bk. rev.:* 1-3, 300-800 words. *Aud.:* Ac, Sa.

This journal is published monthly by the Society for Sedimentary Geology to disseminate information to geologists and biologists who are interested in a broad range of topics, including biogeochemistry, ichnology, paleoclimatology, paleoecology, paleoceanography, sedimentology, stratigraphy, geomicrobiology, paleobiogeochemistry, and astrobiology. The articles published in *Palaios* emphasize the impact of life on Earth's history as recorded in the paleontological and sedimentological records. Two recently published articles include "Diatom Ecology and Microbial Mat Structure and Function in Antarctic Dry Valleys" and "Echinoderm Diversity and Environmental Distribution in the Ordovician of the Builth Inlier, Wales."

4113. *Paleobiology.* [ISSN: 0094-8373] 1975. q. Ed(s): Matthew Carrano, Peter J Wagner. Paleontological Society, Department of Paleobiology, National Museum of Natural History, PO Box 37012, Washington, DC 20013; roger.thomas@fandm.edu; http://www.paleosoc.org/. Illus., index, adv. Refereed. Vol. ends: Fall (No. 4). Microform: PQC. *Indexed:* A22, AbAn, BrArAb, C45, E01. *Bk. rev.:* 1, 1,500-2,000 words. *Aud.:* Ac, Sa.

Paleobiology is published quarterly by The Paleontological Society, with an emphasis on biological or paleobiological processes and patterns, including speciation, extinction, development of individuals and of colonies, natural selection, evolution, and patterns of variation, abundance, and distribution in space and time. Two recent articles are "Cats in the forest: predicting habitat adaptations from humerus morphometry in extant and fossil Felidae (Carnivora)" and "Habitat breadth and geographic range predict diversity dynamics in marine Mesozoic bivalves."

■ PARANORMAL

Christianne Casper, Instruction Coordinator, Broward Community College, South Campus, 7200 Pines Blvd., Pembroke Pines, FL 33024; ccasper@broward.edu.

Cheryl LaGuardia, Research Librarian, Widener Library, Harvard University

Introduction

Paranormal experiences have been reported throughout history and in all cultures, but recently there has been a heightened interest in the subject, due in good part to the myriad television shows (such as *Ghost Hunters, Ghost Adventures, Fact or Faked: Paranormal Files,* and *Paranormal State*) that have appeared over the past ten years. The paranormal includes near-death experiences, visions, astral traveling, ghosts, clairvoyant/psychic perceptions, and other phenomena that are unexplainable through known scientific principles. The journals reviewed here reflect multiple viewpoints, providing as reliable and authoritative information as is presently scientifically possible.

Basic Periodicals

Ac, Sa: *American Society for Psychical Research. Journal; Skeptic; Skeptical Inquirer.*

Basic Abstracts and Indexes

Reader's Guide to Periodical Literature.

4114. American Society for Psychical Research. Journal. Former titles (until 1932): *Psychic Research;* (until 1928): *American Society for Psychical Research. Journal.* [ISSN: 0003-1070] 1907. q. Free to members. American Society for Psychical Research, Inc., 5 W 73rd St, New York, NY 10023; aspr@aspr.com; http://www.aspr.com. Illus., index. Sample. Refereed. Vol. ends: Oct. Microform: PQC. *Indexed:* A22. *Bk. rev.:* 3-4. *Aud.:* Ac, Sa.

The American Society for Psychical Research was founded in 1885 and is the oldest psychic research organization in the United States. Its journal is known for its informative, scholarly coverage of topics including, but not limited to, ESP, precognition, psychokinesis, and psychic healing. The journal includes scholarly reports, research, and field studies that focus on firsthand reports of paranormal phenomena. Issues average about four articles, with tables/graphs, footnotes, and references. Some issues include a correspondence column and a book review section. The society's web site includes sample articles. URL: www.aspr.com

4115. Fortean Times. Formerly (until 1976): *News.* [ISSN: 0308-5899] 1973. m. GBP 39.98 domestic; GBP 47.50 in Europe; GBP 55 elsewhere. Dennis Publishing Ltd., 30 Cleveland St, London, W1T 4JD, United Kingdom; http://www.dennis.co.uk/. Illus., adv. *Bk. rev.:* 7-9. *Aud.:* Ga, Ac, Sa.

Fortean Times was founded to continue the investigative research of Charles Fort (1874–1932), one of the first UFOlogists and a skeptical investigator of the bizarre and unusual. This publication provides news; reviews; research on strange phenomena, psychic experiences, and prodigies; and portents from around the world. While the publication maintains a humorous air, its goal is to provide thought-provoking, educational information. The articles provide resources that usually include recommended readings, web-surfings, and/or

notes. In addition to articles, each issue includes book and media reviews, "Strange Days," and "Forum." The online edition includes the table of contents for the current issue, brief book and media reviews, archives, a community board to share information, breaking news, and exclusive features.

4116. The Journal for Spiritual and Consciousness Studies. Former titles (until 2012): *The Journal of Spirituality and Paranormal Studies;* (until 2006): *The Journal of Religion & Psychical Research;* (until 1981): *Academy of Religion and Psychical Research. Journal.* 197?. q. Free to members. Ed(s): Michael E Tymn, Boyce Batey. Academy of Spirituality and Paranormal Studies, Inc., PO Box 614, Bloomfield, CT 06002; http://www.aspsi.org. Index. Sample. *Indexed:* A01. *Bk. rev.:* 3-5. *Aud.:* Ac, Sa.

This journal was established to provide a forum among clergy, academics, and researchers concerning religion, philosophy, and psychical research. There are about five articles in each issue, some with references. In addition, there are research proposals, abstracts of completed research, views and comments, book reviews, and correspondence. Recommended for religion or parapsychology collections. An index to the publishing organization's journals and some samples of journal articles are available online. URL: www.aspsi.org/pubs/journal_and_newsletter.php

4117. Journal of Parapsychology. [ISSN: 0022-3387] 1937. s-a. Free to members. Ed(s): John A. Palmer. Rhine Research Center, 2741 Campus Walk Ave, Bldg 500, Durham, NC 27705; office@rhine.org; http://www.rhine.org/. Illus., index, adv. Sample. Refereed. Vol. ends: Dec. Microform: PQC. *Indexed:* A01, A22, BRI, CBRI, P02, PsycInfo. *Bk. rev.:* 3-5. *Aud.:* Ac, Sa.

The *Journal of Parapsychology,* founded by J.B. Rhine, was one of the first scholarly parapsychology journals published. Its primary focus is to provide a professional forum for original research reports on experimental parapsychology. In addition to the technical experimental reports, the journal averages six to eight articles and includes surveys of literature, book reviews, and correspondence. Tables of contents for previous issues are available online. URL: www.rhine.org/researchjournal.htm

4118. Skeptic. [ISSN: 1063-9330] 1992. q. USD 30 domestic; USD 40 in Canada & Mexico; USD 50 elsewhere. Ed(s): Michael Shermer. Millenium Press, PO Box 338, Altadena, CA 91001. Illus., adv. Refereed. *Indexed:* A01, ASIP, AmHI, BRI, CBRI, MLA-IB, P02. *Bk. rev.:* 5-7. *Aud.:* Ga, Ac.

Skeptic promotes scientific and critical thinking while investigating claims made on a variety of topics, including pseudoscience, pseudohistory, the paranormal, magic, superstition, fringe claims, and revolutionary science. The features included in every issue are "Articles," "News," "Forum," "Reviews," and "Junior Skeptic." Some issues of *Skeptic* also include movie and audio reviews. The online version provides issues of the "eSkeptic" newsletter, archives, a reading room, forum, "Junior Skeptic," and podcasts.

4119. Skeptical Inquirer: the magazine for science and reason. Formerly (until 1978): *The Zetetic.* [ISSN: 0194-6730] 1976. bi-m. USD 19.95. Ed(s): Benjamin Radford, Kendrick Frazier. Committee for the Scientific Investigation of Claims of the Paranormal, PO Box 703, Buffalo, NY 14226; info@csicop.org; http://www.csicop.org. Illus., index. *Indexed:* A22, BRI, MLA-IB, P02. *Bk. rev.:* 2-4. *Aud.:* Ga, Ac, Sa.

Skeptical Inquirer focuses on what the scientific community knows about claims of the paranormal as opposed to media sensationalism. The journal promotes scientific research, critical thinking, and science education. Standard features include "News and Comment," "Notes on a Strange World," "Science Watch," "Articles," and "Book Reviews," as well as "Investigative Files," "Skeptical Inquiree," "Psychic Vibrations," and "Thinking @ Science." In addition to parapsychology, topics investigated include UFOs, alternative therapy, psychic claims, astrology, skepticism in general, and other paranormal experiences. The online version includes an archive, resources, special articles, and "Skeptical Briefs."

4120. *Society for Psychical Research. Journal.* [ISSN: 0037-9751] 1884. q. Free to members; Non-members, GBP 40. Ed(s): Chris Roe. Society for Psychical Research, 49 Marloes Rd, Kensington, London, W8 6LA, United Kingdom; http://www.spr.ac.uk/. Illus., index, adv. Sample. Vol. ends: Oct. *Indexed:* A01, A22. *Bk. rev.:* Occasional. *Aud.:* Sa.

The journal of the Society for Psychical Research is one of the oldest parapsychological publications. It aims to objectively examine paranormal experiences and reports that appear to be otherwise inexplicable. The journal publishes field and case studies, experimental reports, book reviews, and historical and theoretical papers. All papers are strictly peer reviewed. There are approximately five articles per issue, complete with tables, graphs, and references. The contents of approximately 120 years' worth of journals, proceedings, and abstracts from 2000 are available online to society members only. URL: www.spr.ac.uk/main/page/spr-publications-parapsychology

■ PARENTING

Caroline M. Kent, Director of Research Support and Instruction, Charles E. Shain Library, Connecticut College, New London, CT 06320

Introduction

Are there publications that can actually help a new (or even experienced) parent?! It is certainly the case that new parents are always desperate for information and help, and that there is therefore a market for such publications. This is particularly so in this era when many parenting individuals are separated from the older generations of their families—generations that carry parenting wisdom and experience.

It is also arguable that parenting is now more complicated in this era of dual-career families, single and divorced parents, and alternative families of all sorts. Even those families who are practicing a more traditional family form, with a stay-at-home mom, may find the lack of neighborhoods and extended family daunting. The modern reality is that there aren't too many parents who don't feel that they need all the help they can get!

Parenting magazines really fall neatly into two categories: magazines that are general enough to contain articles of interest to a wide range of families; and magazines that contain articles interesting to particular parents, such as adoptive or single parents. Social computing on the web also is taking a front seat for communities of people (like parents of all sorts) that need fast information and community support.

An increasing number of former magazines, both print and online, are becoming pure blogging sites, and those are not included here. There are moments when I wonder if blogging and web sites will actually, someday, fully replace print journals in this subject area. "Mommy blogging" and, for that matter, "Daddy blogging" provide powerful writing as well as new-product reviewing. Unfortunately, many blogging sites drift off; and an increasing number of more ephemeral parent publications are taking the same route.

Another note on format: This section necessarily must be more tolerant of the newsletter format, since parents often have little time for prolonged reading. There are some very thoughtful newsletters that address a niche need, and these should be evaluated carefully.

There aren't many journals in this section that would appeal to the clientele at most college and university libraries. The exception to that would be any school that has an active child development or family therapeutic program.

In addition to the titles listed here, there are a large number of excellent local parenting magazines (such as *Boston Parents' Paper* and *Black Parenting Today: Information and Resources for Greater Philadelphia Families*). Public libraries should identify such publications for their areas and include them in current collections.

Basic Periodicals

Ga: *American Baby, BabyTalk, FamilyFun, Parent & Child, Parents.*

Basic Abstracts and Indexes

ERIC, PsycINFO, Readers' Guide to Periodical Literature.

4121. *Adoption Today (Online).* Former titles (until 200?): *Adoption Today (Print);* (until 2000): *Chosen Child.* 1998. bi-m. USD 12; USD 2 per issue. Louis & Company Publishing, 541 E Garden Dr, Unit N, Windsor, CO 80550-3150. *Bk. rev.:* 3-4, 50-100 words. *Aud.:* Ga, Sa.

Unlike the softer, more adoptive-parent–oriented *Adoptive Families, Adoption Today* pulls few punches. It more clearly represents all voices in adoption, that is, the voices of adoptees, birth parents, and adoption professionals, as well as those of adoptive parents. The result is an interesting magazine that seeks to illuminate those adoption issues that are often hard to face. A new and very interesting aspect is that the magazine now advertises itself as being "The only magazine dedicated to International and Transracial Adoption." Its articles and editorials are edgy and interesting, often authored by controversial adoption advocates such as Marley Greiner ("The Bastard Nation"). Some recent articles include "What's the Best Therapy for My Traumatized Child?," "The Legacy of Attachment: How Our Own Attachment Histories Impact Our Children," and "Our Tiniest Patients, Ethical Considerations of Embryo Adoption." Any public library that serves a large adoption community should consider its purchase, as well as any academic or special library that serves the needs of social work students or adoption professionals.

4122. *Adoptive Families.* Former titles (until 1994): *Ours (Minneapolis);* (until 1969): *News of Ours.* [ISSN: 1076-1020] 1967. bi-m. USD 24.95 domestic; USD 32.95 Canada; USD 44.95 elsewhere. Ed(s): Susan Caughman. Adoptive Families Magazine, 39 W 37th Str, 15th fl, New York, NY 10018. Illus., adv. Sample. Circ: 25000. *Bk. rev.:* 3-8, 50 words. *Aud.:* Ga, Sa.

This glossy, family-oriented magazine is considered the standard publication by the adoptive family community. The editor, Susan Caughman, has done much to broaden the editorial perspective from the magazine's earlier version: there are now regular columns contributed by birth parents, adoption lawyers, doctors, and adoption experts, such as Lois Melina, etc. The magazine still maintains its family orientation, with pictures of subscribing families and feature articles of general interest. Recent examples of articles include "Our Initiation Into Parenthood" and "Finally Feeling Like Mummy." *Adoptive Families* has a slightly softer, more cheerful take on adoption than the harder *Adoption Today,* but it remains a central and important magazine for the adoption community. American adoption has become less secret and more of a topic for public discussion. For that reason, any public library that serves growing families should consider purchasing this magazine, as should academic or special collections that serve adoption professionals.

4123. *American Baby: for expectant and new parents.* Formerly: *Mothers-to-Be - American Baby.* [ISSN: 0044-7544] 1938. m. Free. Ed(s): Judith Nolte. Meredith Corporation, 125 Park Ave, 25th Fl, New York, NY 10017; http://www.meredith.com. Illus., adv. Sample. Circ: 2000000. *Indexed:* A22, Agr, BRI, P02. *Aud.:* Ga.

There aren't too many American families with young children who don't read or at least receive issues of this magazine. Expectant parents can get it free for several months. It is the oldest and most reliable of the commercial baby-parenting magazines, containing a wide range of short, easy-to-read articles on baby and parent health issues, developmental discussions, baby care, and family issues. In addition to the huge number of advertisements for baby-related products, this magazine also contains discussion and reviews of new products. There are advice columns that cover everything from behavior to health and nutrition. The magazine also has a healthy and well-maintained web site that is updated frequently. All public libraries should invest in this.

4124. *Baby Talk.* Former titles (until 2000): *Parenting's Baby Talk;* (until 1996): *Baby Talk;* (until 1977): *New Baby Talk;* (until 1976): *Baby Talk.* [ISSN: 1529-5389] 1935. m. Free. Ed(s): Megan Padilla, Kim Hays. Bonnier Corp., 460 N Orlando Ave, Ste 200, Winter Park, FL 32789; http://www.bonniercorp.com. Illus., adv. Sample. Circ: 2016872. Vol. ends: Nov. *Indexed:* BRI. *Bk. rev.:* 2-3. *Aud.:* Ga.

Baby Talk, one of the oldest continuing parenting magazines, is targeted to the needs of expectant mothers and parents of newborns. For these readers, it is even free for the asking. Packed with short, informative articles on baby care, health, developmental concerns, family issues, and product discussions, it also has regular columns, many of them based on readers' questions (such as "Wit and Wisdom" and "Ask Dr. Mom"). Some recent titles include "Feeding Fish to Your Baby" and "Get Great After-Baby Sex." Every public library should consider this publication.

4125. Brain, Child: the magazine for thinking mothers. [ISSN: 1528-5170] 2000. q. USD 19.95; USD 5.95 per issue. Ed(s): Jennifer Niesslein, Stephanie Wilkinson. March Press, LLC, PO Box 714, Lexington, VA 24450. Adv. Circ: 36000. Vol. ends: Winter. *Bk. rev.:* 2-4. *Aud.:* Ga, Ac.

How can we resist a journal that says in its mission statement that "motherhood is worthy of literature"? Or that this "isn't your typical magazine. We couldn't cupcake-decorate our way out of a paper bag." This journal is totally irresistible! Each issue contains a mix of intriguing essays, feature articles, humor, fiction, and art—some of which has some powerful names attached, such as Barbara Kingsolver, Perri Klass, Mary Gordon, and Alice Hoffman (all mothers themselves). This isn't a how-to magazine; rather, it is a why-do-we-do-it-at-all magazine. Recent essays include "Indecent Exposure," "The Difference a Mother Makes," and finally "There is No Such Thing as a Perfect Waffle." There's a great humor column ("MotherWit") and a book review section that is thoughtful without taking itself too seriously. Funny, thought-provoking, and full of terrific reads, this magazine should be considered by any college library with a writing program and any public library with the right constituency. And although it helps to be a mother when reading this, it is not necessary!

Child & Family Behavior Therapy. See Family section.

4126. Digital Parenting. [ISSN: 2051-1221] 2010. irreg. Vodafone Group Plc, Vodafone House, The Connection, Newbury, RG14 2FN, United Kingdom; http://www.vodafone.com. Adv. *Aud.:* Ga.

Digital Parenting fits an important niche. In this world of ever-changing technologies, social media, and ever-increasing web content, parents are often at a loss as to how to protect their children, how to teach them to use social media responsibly, and how to evaluate the web-based materials that their children find. This magazine seeks to assist in solving many of those puzzles. It is British, so there are times that the content is geographically irrelevant to American parents. But of the content is interesting, up-to-date, and very useful. Some recent articles include "Spotlight on Digital Spaces," "Real Life, Digital Life, Striking the Right Balance," and "Top Tech for Teens." Any public library should consider this publication, as well as any teacher resource collection.

Exceptional Parent. See Family section.

4127. FamilyFun. [ISSN: 1056-6333] 1991. 10x/yr. USD 10 domestic; USD 22 Canada; USD 30 elsewhere. Ed(s): Jonathan Adolph. Family and Children's Magazine Group, 244 Main St, Northampton, MA 01060. Illus., adv. Circ: 2100000. *Bk. rev.:* 5-6, 75-100 words. *Aud.:* Ga.

Once a Disney property, but now published independently, this publication is still full of, well, fun ideas. The format is nice, with great photographs of kids and their families—all having fun! There are craft activities, rainy-day-fun ideas, traveling-with-the-kids ideas, and party ideas of all kinds, as well as reviews of toys and games, books, and videos. This is actually a wonderful magazine, jam-packed with ideas for even the most creative of parents. It is really the only magazine that has family activities as its total focus; therefore, it is an invaluable addition to any parenting magazine collection. Any public library not located in a retirement home should purchase this. Very highly recommended.

4128. Fathering Magazine: the online magazine for men with families. [ISSN: 1091-5516] 1995. m. Free. Ed(s): John Gill. Fathering Enterprises, Inc., PO Box 231891, Houston, TX 77223. Illus., adv. *Indexed:* BRI. *Aud.:* Ga, Sa.

This substantive online journal is intended for teachers, students, and practitioners, as well as dads themselves. It includes research and practice-based articles on all aspects of fatherhood and males in the role of parent. Issues covered include parenting, father/child relationships, divorce, stepfathers, child

custody, and more. There are copious links, and Twitter feeds. *Fathering Magazine* is a title that academic and research librarians should be aware of and recommend when appropriate. All public libraries should consider it.

4129. Fostering Families Today. [ISSN: 1531-409X] 2001. bi-m. USD 24 domestic; USD 29.50 Canada; USD 5.95 per issue in US & Canada. Ed(s): Richard Fischer. Louis & Company Publishing, 541 E Garden Dr, Unit N, Windsor, CO 80550-3150. *Aud.:* Ga, Sa.

Thank goodness! We have needed this magazine for so long, and finally, here it is. The foster parent community clearly deals with many of the same issues as adoptive parents and people parenting their birth children; but there is a deep range of social, legal, medical, and psychological issues that are particular to their interests. This glossy magazine strives to service those interests, and it includes recent articles such as "Creating a Meaningful Lifebook for your Foster or Adopted Child," "Handling Foster Parent Stress, Loss and Grief," and "A Checklist: Does My Child Need Residential Treatment?" There are also regular columns, such as "Washington Beat" and "Family Talk," which keep an eye on important legislative and medical issues relevant to fostering. Given the number of children in foster care in the United States, any medium-to-large public library should purchase this magazine. In addition, any special or academic library that serves social workers or social work students should consider its purchase.

4130. Gay Parent. [ISSN: 1545-6714] 1998. bi-m. USD 22 domestic; USD 30 foreign. Ed(s): Angeline Acain. Gay Parent, PO Box 750852, Forest Hills, NY 11375. Adv. Sample. *Bk. rev.:* 1, 150 words; signed. *Aud.:* Ga.

With the June 2013 Supreme Court decision concerning gay marriage, journals like this one will become increasingly important as more members of the LGBT community find easier paths to parenting. Beyond its obvious audience, *Gay Parent* is one of the more thoughtful parenting magazines in print. It assumes that its readership is interested in substantive book reviews, extensive interviews, and legislative information. It periodically publishes lists of gay-friendly private schools and camps, and articles on adoption and foster care. Subscribers may elect to get the full text of the magazine online for a reduced subscription rate. This magazine will be well placed in any public library with a parent population interested in diverse family structures.

4131. Gifted Child Today. Former titles (until 1993): *The Gifted Child Today;* (until 1986): *G C T (Gifted, Creative, Talented Children).* [ISSN: 1076-2175] 1978. q. USD 108. Ed(s): Susan K Johnsen. Sage Publications, Inc., 2455 Teller Rd, Thousand Oaks, CA 91320; info@sagepub.com; http://www.sagepub.com. Illus. Sample. Refereed. Reprint: PSC. *Indexed:* A22, BRI, ERIC, RILM. *Bk. rev.:* 3-5, 100 words. *Aud.:* Ga, Sa.

This magazine is intended to support both teachers and parents of gifted children, but is increasingly focused on the former. It is full of articles not only on the educational theory of the teaching of the gifted but also on ideas for both curriculum development and learning plans for home. Recommended for school libraries, academic libraries that support education programs, and large public libraries.

4132. The Informed Parent. 19??. w. Ed(s): John H Samson, Louis P Theriot. Intermag Productions, 23546 Coyote Springs Dr, Diamond Bar, CA 91765. *Aud.:* Ga.

The Informed Parent is published by the Pediatric Medical Center of Long Beach, California. Articles are written by staff and other experts in the fields of education, social work, and psychology. Titles of recent features include "Coping with Academic Stress," "The Child with Enuresis," and "Teens and Eating Disorders." The articles are well written and informative, and a loosely indexed online archive is maintained. Further, the site offers a list of both children's and adult books on health topics that is linked to Amazon.com. This is a clear, well-developed, and recently well-redesigned site that all public libraries that serve families should consider.

4133. Kiwi: growing families the natural and organic way. [ISSN: 1933-2920] 2006. bi-m. USD 11.95; USD 3.99 newsstand/cover domestic; USD 4.99 newsstand/cover Canada. May Media Group, Llc., 152 Madison Ave, Ste 700, New York, NY 10016; info@kiwimagonline.com. Adv. *Bk. rev.:* 3-4, 100-200 words. *Aud.:* Ga.

It is notable that retail grocers such as Whole Foods and Wild Oats feature this journal at their checkout stands! The editors of the magazine state as their mission that *Kiwi* "is dedicated to helping parents raise their children the healthiest way possible." There are columns on food, nutrition, eco-crafts, and book reviews of both adult and children's selections, as well as feature articles. A few recent article titles include "The Nutrition Behavior Connection" and "Freezing 101." Public libraries with environmentally-minded parent groups should consider purchasing this title.

4134. Parent & Child: the learning link between home & school. [ISSN: 1070-0552] 1993. q. USD 0.79. Ed(s): Stephanie Izarek. Scholastic Inc., 557 Broadway, 3rd Fl, New York, NY 10012; http://www.scholastic.com. Adv. *Indexed:* A01. *Bk. rev.:* 3-4, 25 words. *Aud.:* Ga, Sa.

Parent & Child has an interesting life: first, it is a printed magazine that covers learning issues from birth to about six years, happening to be part of Scholastic's larger web presence, which not only includes this magazine's content. But also, it takes the reader further through middle school. Not surprisingly, Scholastic has collected an advisory board for the magazine that includes several national early-childhood experts. The articles are short and informative and are intended to bridge a child's preschool learning experience with its learning life at home. The magazine presents learning and health issues, behavioral and developmental information, and lots of activities for parents to use at home. All public libraries should consider this magazine; also, learning resource centers at schools that train early childhood staff should purchase it.

4135. Parenting Children with Special Needs. [ISSN: 2168-1449] 2010. bi-m. Free. Ed(s): Kendra Mathewson. Parenting Children with Special Needs, Inc., 30905 E Stony Point School Rd, Grain Valley, MO 64029; Sales@pcwsn.com. Adv. Circ: 50000 Free. *Aud.:* Ga.

This is a long-needed publication. As more and more is known about how to raise and educate children with special needs, more and more parents are keeping their children home with them instead of relying on special schools and institutions. This means that there are an ever-increasing number of parents needing resources to help them with their children's issues. This particular publication has the feel of a one-time local newsletter, which is quickly growing into a magazine with national focus. We very much hope it succeeds. For all public libraries with good parenting collections.

4136. Parents. Former titles (until 1993): *Parents' Magazine;* (until 1985): *Parents;* Which incorporated (in 1981): *Parents Home;* Which was formerly (until 19??): *Handy Andy Magazine;* (until 1978): *Parents' Magazine;* (until 1977): *Parents' Magazine and Better Homemaking;* *Parents' & Better Family Living;* (until 1973): *Parents' Magazine and Better Family Living;* (until 1968): *Parents' Magazine & Better Homemaking;* (until 1959): *Parents' Magazine & Family Home Guide;* (until 1953): *Parents' Magazine; Children; Mother's Magazine; Mother's Activities.* [ISSN: 1083-6373] 1926. m. Ed(s): Dana Points. Meredith Corporation, 1716 Locust St, Des Moines, IA 50309; patrick.taylor@meredith.com; http://www.meredith.com. Illus., adv. Circ: 2200000. *Indexed:* A22, BRI, C37, CBRI, IHTDI, P02, PdeR. *Bk. rev.:* 4-5, 50 words. *Aud.:* Ga.

Parents has in many ways become the industry standard for parenting magazines. As with many others, its focus tends to be on early-childhood development and health topics rather than on issues associated with older children. There are many regular columns on child development and health, and on maternal and parental health—which are often focused on readers' questions. Feature articles include many short pieces on family life, home style, fun time, and health and safety, to name just a few departments. Highly recommended for any public library that addresses the needs of families.

4137. Twins: the magazine for multiples. [ISSN: 0890-3077] 1984. q. USD 39.95 combined subscription domestic (print & online eds.); USD 61.95 combined subscription Canada (print & online eds.). Ed(s): Christa D Reed. Business Word, Inc., PO Box 271924, Fort Collins, CO 80527; http://www.businessword.com. Illus., adv. Sample. Vol. ends: Nov/Dec. *Bk. rev.:* 2-3, 50 words. *Aud.:* Ga.

Oh, my. Double the joy—and double the trials of parenthood! Although there probably isn't a parent of twins (or triplets) who would have it any other way, there's no question that there are particular issues, both logistical and psychological, of handling the children of multiple birth. With fertility technologies increasing in use and sophistication, twinning (and beyond!) is much more common than it once was, so a cheerful, helpful magazine like *Twins* is welcome. It contains product reviews, feature articles, developmental discussions, and more. Articles are thoughtful, often highly personal discussions of issues and successes. Recommended for public libraries.

■ PEACE AND CONFLICT STUDIES

Suhasini L. Kumar, Professor Library Administration, Coordinator Information and Research Services, Carlson Library, The University of Toledo, 2801 W. Bancroft St., Toledo, OH 43606; Skumar@utnet.utoledo.edu

Introduction

The earliest intimations of peace and conflict studies emerging as an academic discipline was first discerned at the end of World War I. It was during this time that Woodrow Wilson made his famous Fourteen Points for peacemaking proposal at the Peace of Paris meeting in 1919. This led to the establishment of the League of Nations, which was intended to further the cause for peace but in reality laid the foundations for other types of turmoil. World War II saw the establishment of the U.N. System and the emergence of a forceful peace and conflict studies program.

It was later in the Fifties and Sixties that Peace and Conflict Studies was accepted as an academic discipline that needed to be pursued and established in order to understand the underlying reasons for social conflicts, analyze violent and nonviolent behaviors, study ways to prevent conflict, and find peaceful solutions. This field encompasses a broad spectrum of subjects that may include political science, geography, economics, psychology, sociology, international relations, history, and religious studies, to name a few.

It was also during this period that the International Peace Research Institute was first established in Oslo; this was followed by the forming of the Peace Science Society (International), International Peace Research Association, Peace and Justice Studies Association, and several other peace associations worldwide.

There are presently several organizations, societies, and associations that are committed to peace and strive relentlessly to eliminate war. They believe that it is of vital importance to teach people the basic tenets of peaceful coexistence and are filled with a strong desire to promote a culture of peace. These organizations publish books, journals, and newsletters in order to keep us informed about every aspect of peace and explore every event and incident that might threaten to escalate into a dispute, and provide in-depth analysis of various conditions, and offer possible solutions to these controversial situations.

Peace associations such as the Canadian Peace Research and Education Association, the International Peace Research Association, and the Peace Science Society publish scholarly journals with well-researched articles that include statistical information and empirical tests with results. Journals such as the *Journal of Peace Research, The Journal of Conflict Resolution,* and *Conflict Management and Peace Science* fall into this category. There are also newsletters and grassroots publications that ardently support peace and provide news and articles of interest to all strata of society and encourage readers to voice their opinions freely. *Peace Magazine* is an example of this type of publication.

There has been a remarkable increase in the number of peace journals available on the Internet, and many publishers are also trying to offer access to archival information. There are several journals and newsletters that are available both in print and online. Although a subscription is usually required for Internet access to these publications, some of them, such as the newsletter *Peace Watch,* are free.

The periodicals selected for this section represent a broad array of journals, magazines, and newsletters that are committed to the pursuit of peace. The authors and editors of these publications are international contributors who are passionately involved with peace efforts. These publications have proven to be a valuable source of information to academicians, researchers, peace activists, and other advocates of peace.

Basic Periodicals

Hs: *Arms Control Today, Fellowship, Peace Review;* Ac: *Arms Control Today, Bulletin of the Atomic Scientists, Conflict Management and Peace Science, Journal of Conflict Resolution, Journal of Peace Research, Peace & Change, Peace Review.*

Basic Abstracts and Indexes

Alternative Press Index, Peace Research Abstracts.

4138. Action Report. Former titles: *Peace Action;* (until 1993): *SANE - Freeze News;* (until 1990): *SANE World - Freeze Focus.* 1961. 4x/yr. Peace Action, 1100 Wayne Ave., Ste. 1020, Silver Spring, MD 20910-5643; paprog@igc.apc.org; http://www.webcom.com/peaceact/. Illus. Vol. ends: Winter. Microform: PQC. *Aud.:* Ga.

Action Report is a quarterly publication of Peace Action, one of the largest grassroots peace and justice organizations. This newsletter was formerly known as *Peace Action* and *SANE/Freeze News. Action Report* acts as the official voice of Peace Action, through which the organization communicates important news and issues related to the peace movement to its members and supporters. The latest issue of the newsletter takes an in-depth look at nuclear weapons issues, the occupation of Iraq, and the outcomes of decisions made during the Bush administration. The article "2012 Elections and the Afghanistan War" talks about Peace Action using a petition campaign as political strategy to remind candidate Obama that inaction on ending the war in Afghanistan would endanger the grassroots mobilization that he enjoyed in 2008. This publication encourages supporters to act on important peace and nonviolence-related issues and can be a source of inspiration to both peace activists and educators.

4139. Arms Control Today: the source on nonproliferation and global security. Formerly (until 1974): *A C A Newsletter.* [ISSN: 0196-125X] 1971. 10x/yr. USD 85 (Individuals, USD 65; Free to members). Ed(s): Daniel Horner. Arms Control Association, 1313 L St, NW, Ste 130, Washington, DC 20005; aca@armscontrol.org; http://www.armscontrol.org. Illus., index, adv. Vol. ends: Dec. Microform: PQC. *Indexed:* A22, BRI, P02, P61, SSA. *Bk. rev.:* 1, 800-1,200 words. *Aud.:* Ac.

The Arms Control Association, which publishes this magazine *Arms Control Today,* was founded in 1971 and is dedicated to promoting public understanding and support of arms control. It helps provide policy makers, the press, and the public with authoritative information, analysis, and commentary on arms control proposals, treaties, negotiations, agreements, and other national-security–related issues. This magazine is dedicated to promoting a better understanding of arms control subjects and offers comprehensive data and intelligence on national-security issues. Each issue begins with a "Focus" essay that highlights an important issue related to arms control—a recent article talks about "Nuclear Deterrence in a Changed World." Other feature articles include "Resolving the Ambiguity of Nuclear Weapons Costs." Interviews with important decision makers in the arms control arena are also conducted and well documented. The "News" section has articles such as "P5+1 and Iran Claim Progress in Talks" and "U.S. Plans to Sell Bahrain More Arms." A bibliography with citations to current literature on topics relevant to the subject being discussed is found in each issue. Each issue ends with news briefs. An excellent resource for academic libraries and research centers.

4140. Bulletin of the Atomic Scientists (Online). [ISSN: 1938-3282] 1945. bi-m. USD 242. Ed(s): Mindy Kay Bricker. Sage Publications, Inc., 2455 Teller Rd, Thousand Oaks, CA 91320; info@sagepub.com; http://www.sagepub.com. Adv. Sample. *Bk. rev.:* Number and length vary. *Aud.:* Ga, Ac, Sa.

Published by the Educational Foundation for Nuclear Science, the mission of the *Bulletin of the Atomic Scientists* is to educate citizens about global security concerns, especially the continuing dangers posed by nuclear and other weapons of mass destruction. Founded in 1945 by two atomic scientists, Eugene Rabinowitch and Hyman Goldsmith, this journal has faithfully adhered to its mission. Feature articles cover such topics as missile defense, international weapons trade, analysis of the causes of world conflict, prescriptions for survival, and nuclear weapon statistics. The recent May/June issue of the *Bulletin,* is a themed issue looking at low-level radiation risks. In the article "Lessons from Hiroshima and Nagasaki: The most exposed and most vulnerable," David Richardson, an epidemiologist, examines the quantitative data used in linear non-threshold theory predictions of dose response, resulting primarily from the one-time exposures of Japanese atomic-bomb survivors. Gordon Thompson, in his article "Unmasking the truth: The science and policy of low-dose ionizing radiation," asks experts and professional bodies to acknowledge the implication of the linear non-threshold hypothesis and to refrain from mixing science and policy. The *Bulletin* provides the general public, policy makers, scientists, and journalists with nontechnical, scientifically sound, policy-relevant information about nuclear weapons and other global security issues. Available online.

4141. Conflict Management and Peace Science. Formerly (until 1980): *Journal of Peace Science.* [ISSN: 0738-8942] 1973. 5x/yr. USD 545. Ed(s): Glenn Palmer. Sage Publications Ltd., 1 Oliver's Yard, 55 City Rd, London, EC1Y 1SP, United Kingdom; info@sagepub.co.uk; http://www.uk.sagepub.com. Illus., adv. Sample. Refereed. Vol. ends: No. 2. Reprint: PSC. *Indexed:* A22, E01, EconLit, IBSS, JEL, P61, RiskAb, SSA. *Bk. rev.:* 1, 1,200 words. *Aud.:* Ac.

Conflict Management and Peace Science is a peer-reviewed journal published by the Peace Science Society (International) at Pennsylvania State University. It contains scientific papers on topics such as foreign-policy decision making, international conflict, international mediation, and the effect of international trade on political interactions. The society's main objective is to encourage the exchange of ideas and promote studies on peace analysis using scientific methods. Scholars and an international group of experts who specialize in diverse fields contribute articles to this journal. A current issue includes articles such as "Staying the Course: Assessing the Durability of Peacekeeping Operations" and "Power and Deterrence in Alliance Relationships: The Ally's Decision to Renege." Research articles provide empirical results based on statistical tests. Each issue includes five or six articles, each preceded by an abstract. A list of references provides the researcher with further reading. Primarily written for a scholarly clientele, the journal will be useful in academic and research libraries.

4142. Fellowship. Formerly (until 1935): *The World Tomorrow.* [ISSN: 0014-9810] 1918. q. USD 40 in North America; USD 75 elsewhere; USD 6 per issue. Ed(s): Ethan Vesely-Flad. Fellowship of Reconciliation, 521 N Broadway, PO Box 271, Nyack, NY 10960; for@forusa.org; http://www.forusa.org. Illus., index, adv. Sample. Refereed. Vol. ends: Nov/Dec. Microform: PQC. *Indexed:* A22. *Bk. rev.:* 6, 350 words. *Aud.:* Hs, Ga, Ac.

Fellowship is an important, multi-faith, multicultural magazine committed to justice and peace. It is published by the organization Fellowship of Reconciliation (FOR), and it is one of the longest-running peace journals in the United States. Published since 1935, it follows its predecessor, *The World Tomorrow,* which began in 1918. Committed to active nonviolence as a way of life, *Fellowship* serves FOR's mission and strives for an ideal world of peace. A recent issue contains articles such as "Healing Moral Injury: A Lifelong Journey" and "Money, Usury, and the Economics of Peace." *Fellowship* provides interesting reading with feature articles, interviews, poems, and news briefs. Philosophical and reflective, *Fellowship* is concerned with conflict resolution through the united effort of all peoples. A very useful resource for public and academic libraries.

4143. Global Change, Peace & Security (Print). Former titles (until 2003): *Pacifica Review: Peace, Security & Global Change (Print);* (until 1994): *Interdisciplinary Peace Research (Print).* [ISSN: 1478-1158] 1989. 3x/yr. GBP 465 (print & online eds.). Ed(s): Aran Martin. Routledge, 4 Park Sq, Milton Park, Abingdon, OX14 4RN, United Kingdom; subscriptions@tandf.co.uk; http://www.tandfonline.com. Index, adv. Sample. Refereed. Reprint: PSC. *Indexed:* A22, E01, IBSS, P61, RiskAb, SSA. *Bk. rev.:* Number and length vary. *Aud.:* Ac.

This is a scholarly journal that addresses complex practical and theoretical issues about rapid globalization and its effects. It not only analyzes sources and consequences of conflict, violence, and insecurity, but also the conditions and prospects for conflict transformation, peacekeeping, and peace building. A current special issue concentrates on politics and international relations 20 years after the fall of the U.S.S.R. and shows that the effects of the collapse of the Soviet Union are still prevalent. Articles include "Twenty years after the fall: continuity and change in Russian foreign and security policy," "Understanding order and violence in the post-Soviet space: the Chechen and Russo-Georgia wars," and "Corruption in Post-Soviet Russia." An international journal, it is refereed by specialists in the subject area for originality and factual accuracy. A good resource for academic libraries and research centers.

4144. *International Journal on World Peace.* [ISSN: 0742-3640] 1984. q. USD 35 (Individuals, USD 25). Ed(s): Gordon L Anderson. Professors World Peace Academy, 1925 Oakcrest Ave, Ste 7, Saint Paul, MN 55113; http://www.pwpa.org. Illus., index. Sample. Refereed. Vol. ends: Dec. Microform: PQC. *Indexed:* A01, A22, BRI, C42, P02, P61, SSA, SWR&A. *Bk. rev.:* 6, 150-1,100 words. *Aud.:* Ga, Ac.

International Journal on World Peace is a scholarly publication committed to peace, and it cuts across all disciplines, politics, and philosophies. It is published by the Professors World Peace Academy, and its editorial board consists of scholars from several countries ranging from Australia and the United States to Norway and India. A recent issue provides articles such as "Peace Research in the Digital Age," "Religion Peace and the Post-Secular Public Sphere," and "Non-Proliferation Regimes, Immoral and Risky: A Game-Theoretic Approach." The authors include a diverse group of international scholars. A news section and book reviews follow feature articles. The journal should provide interesting reading to patrons in both public and academic libraries.

4145. *International Peacekeeping.* [ISSN: 1353-3312] 1994. 5x/yr. GBP 497 (print & online eds.). Ed(s): Neil Cooper. Taylor & Francis, 4 Park Sq, Milton Park, Abingdon, OX14 4RN, United Kingdom; http://www.tandfonline.com. Illus., adv. Sample. Refereed. Vol. ends: Winter. Reprint: PSC. *Indexed:* A01, A22, E01, IBSS, P02, P61, RiskAb, SSA. *Bk. rev.:* 4-6. *Aud.:* Ac.

International Peacekeeping fundamentally studies the theory and practice of peacekeeping. It propagates the theory that peacekeeping is primarily a political act. This refereed journal analyzes peacekeeping concepts and operations and presents in-depth research on peace and conflict resolution. It provides debates and articles on sanction enforcements; international policing; and the relationship between peacekeepers, state authorities, rival factions, civilians, and governmental organizations. A recent issue of the journal has an article, "Peacebuilding in UN Peacekeeping Exit Strategies: Organized Hypocrisy and Institutional Reform," which investigates the relationship within the theory of "organized hypocrisy and institutional reform in UN peacekeeping." Another article is entitled, "The UN and Afghanistan: Contentions in Democratization and Statebuilding." The author suggests that instead of trying to achieve a system of governance related to western concepts, the U.N. Assistance Mission in Afghanistan (UNAMA) should try to concentrate its efforts on supporting "a workable political order, regional consensus, and national reconciliation as the necessary foundations for bringing peace and stability to the country." This journal is an important resource for academic and research institutions that promote peace studies, international relations, security and strategic studies, the history of the United Nations, peace research, and conflict resolution.

4146. *International Security.* [ISSN: 0162-2889] 1976. q. USD 265 (print & online eds.). Ed(s): Steven E Miller, Sean M Lynn-Jones. M I T Press, 55 Hayward St, Cambridge, MA 02142; journals-info@mit.edu; http://mitpress.mit.edu. Illus., adv. Refereed. Microform: PQC. *Indexed:* A01, A22, ABS&EES, BAS, BRI, E01, IBSS, P02, P61, RiskAb, SSA. *Aud.:* Ac.

International Security is published by the Belfer Center for Science and International Affairs at Harvard University. It is primarily concerned with international peacekeeping. Scholarly, well-researched articles analyze all aspects of international security and are contributed by experts in the theory and practice of peacekeeping. The publication is committed to "timely analysis" of security issues. It provides information on new developments in the areas of causes and prevention of war; ethnic conflict and peacekeeping; post–Cold War security problems; European, Asian, and regional security; nuclear forces and strategy; arms control and weapons proliferation; and post-Soviet security issues and diplomatic and military history. "Targeting Top Terrorists: How Leadership Decapitation Contributes to Counterterrorism," "Does Decapitation Work? Assessing the Effectiveness of Leadership Targeting in

Counterinsurgency Campaigns," and "Barriers to Bioweapons: Intangible Obstacles to Proliferation" are titles of some interesting articles found in a recent issue. The "Editor's Note" provides an introduction to essays in the journal. This is a valuable resource for academic and research libraries that promote peace and international studies.

4147. *The Journal of Conflict Resolution: research on war and peace between and within nations.* Formerly: *Conflict Resolution.* [ISSN: 0022-0027] 1957. bi-m. USD 1485. Ed(s): Paul Huth. Sage Publications, Inc., 2455 Teller Rd, Thousand Oaks, CA 91320; info@sagepub.com; http://www.sagepub.com. Illus., index, adv. Sample. Refereed. Vol. ends: Dec. Microform: PQC. Reprint: PSC. *Indexed:* A01, A22, ABIn, ABS&EES, B01, BAS, BRI, E01, ERIC, EconLit, IBSS, JEL, P02, P61, PsycInfo, RiskAb, SSA, SWR&A. *Aud.:* Ac.

The scholarly *Journal of Conflict Resolution* focuses on international conflict, but it also provides articles and research reports on intergroup conflicts within and between nations and promotes a better understanding of war and peace. It is the official publication of the Peace Science Society (International). The editorial board members belong to universities and colleges from all over the world. This journal is mainly directed toward academicians and researchers, and is described as "an inter-disciplinary journal of social scientific theory and research on human conflict." The journal usually contains six to eight articles that focus on solid, measurable facts and carefully reasoned arguments. *JCR* provides the latest ideas, approaches, and processes in conflict resolution. It offers theoretical and empirical results that intend to provide a better understanding of military strategy and war. Detailed research projects provide statistics, tables, charts, graphs, and results of case studies. Articles include abstracts and references. Recent articles of interest include "Disaggregating Noncompliance: Abstention versus Predation in the Nuclear Nonproliferation Treaty," "Social Revolution, the State, and War: How Revolutions Affect War-Making Capacity and Interstate War Outcomes," and "When War Hits Home: The Geography of Military Losses and Support for War in Time and Space." This journal is an excellent resource for academic libraries that focus on peace studies. It is also available online.

4148. *Journal of Peace Education.* [ISSN: 1740-0201] 2004. 3x/yr. GBP 292 (print & online eds.). Ed(s): Jeannie Lum. Routledge, 4 Park Sq, Milton Park, Abingdon, OX14 4RN, United Kingdom; subscriptions@tandf.co.uk; http://www.tandfonline.com. Adv. Sample. Refereed. Reprint: PSC. *Indexed:* A01, A22, E01, ERIC. *Bk. rev.:* Number and length vary. *Aud.:* Ga, Ac.

The *Journal of Peace Education* publishes articles that encourage and promote theory, research, and practice in peace education that involve diverse educational, social, and ethnic settings. It is multidisciplinary and intercultural in its vision, and aims at linking theory and research to practice. Sponsored by the Peace Education Commission of the International Peace Research Association, it is "committed to furthering original research on peace education, theory, curriculum[,] and pedagogy." Topics addressed in the journal include conflict resolution, global issues, disarmament, environmental care, ecological sustainability, gender equality, anti-racism, civic responsibility, human rights, cultural diversity, and intercultural understanding. Recent articles include "Analyzing Peace Pedagogies," "Perceptions of Forgiveness among Palestinian Teachers in Israel," and "The Role of TESOL in Educating for Peace." This journal reviews other publications on topics related to peace education. A "Special Features" section provides brief reports and summaries of research and innovations in peace education and readers' comments on current practices, articles, and reviews. This journal is a valuable resource for academic and research libraries that are involved with peace and conflict studies.

4149. *Journal of Peace Research.* [ISSN: 0022-3433] 1964. bi-m. USD 1610. Ed(s): Nils Petter Gleditsch. Sage Publications Ltd., 1 Oliver's Yard, 55 City Rd, London, EC1Y 1SP, United Kingdom; info@sagepub.co.uk; http://www.uk.sagepub.com. Illus., index. Sample. Refereed. Vol. ends: Nov. Microform: PQC. Reprint: PSC. *Indexed:* A01, A22, AmHI, BRI, CBRI, E01, EconLit, IBSS, JEL, P02, P61, RiskAb, SSA, SWR&A. *Bk. rev.:* 15-20, 150-450 words. *Aud.:* Ga, Ac.

The *Journal of Peace Research* is published by the International Peace Research Association. Edited at the Peace Research Institute, it is supported by the Nordic Publishing Board in Social Sciences. It is an interdisciplinary, international quarterly that provides empirical, theoretical, and timely articles on global security and peace. It addresses the causes of violence, methods of conflict resolution, and ways of sustaining peace. A recent article, "Does transnational terrorism reduce foreign direct investment? Business-related versus non-business-related terrorism," proves that when countries execute counterterrorism measures that are projected to lessen the impact of business-related terrorist activities, they are likely to attract more foreign capital which eventually enhances economic development. Authors from over 50 countries have published in this journal. Each issue includes an extensive review section that presents and evaluates leading books in the field of peace research. This journal keeps the reader abreast of the latest developments in the area of peace studies, and it will be appreciated in academic libraries and peace research centers.

4150. *Peace & Change: a journal of peace research.* [ISSN: 0149-0508] 1972. q. GBP 379. Ed(s): Jason Hills, Robbie Leiberman. Wiley-Blackwell Publishing, Inc., 111 River St, Hoboken, NJ 07030; info@wiley.com; http://onlinelibrary.wiley.com/. Illus., index, adv. Sample. Refereed. Vol. ends: Oct. Reprint: PSC. *Indexed:* A01, A22, ABS&EES, E01, P61, RILM, RiskAb, SSA. *Bk. rev.:* 3-4, essay length. *Aud.:* Ga, Ac.

Published on behalf of the Peace History Society and the Peace and Justice Studies Association, this scholarly journal consists of analytical and deductive articles on peace and conflict resolution. It addresses a wide variety of topics concerning nonviolence, peace movements and activists, conflict resolution, race and gender issues, cross-cultural studies, international conflict, and post–Cold War concerns. The journal attempts to transcend national, disciplinary, and other arbitrary boundaries while trying to link peace research, education, and activism. Each issue has four or five feature articles, a review essay, book reviews, and a notes section with short biographical information about each author. Recent articles include "Nonviolent Resistance and Culture," "The Peace Path of the Cleveland Cultural Gardens: Making Place for Cultures of Peace," and "The De-Threatenization of the Other: An Israeli and a Palestinian Case of Understanding the Other's Suffering." This journal would be useful in an academic library or research center.

4151. *Peace and Conflict: journal of peace psychology.* [ISSN: 1078-1919] 1995. q. USD 642 (Individuals, USD 104; Members, USD 67). Ed(s): Susan Opotow. American Psychological Association, Division 48, 750 First St, NE, Washington, DC 20002-4242; division@apa.org; http://www.apa.org/about/division/div48.html. Illus., index, adv. Sample. Refereed. Vol. ends: Dec. Reprint: PSC. *Indexed:* A22, E01, IBSS, P02, P61, PsycInfo, SSA. *Bk. rev.:* 4, 500-600 words. *Aud.:* Ac.

Peace and Conflict: Journal of Peace Psychology is published by the American Psychological Association's Division of Peace Psychology. The journal strives to support the ideals of the division and helps advance psychological knowledge that would build "peace in the world at large and within nations, communities, and families." The journal tries to apply information gathered from various areas in the field of psychology to solving issues relating to peace. It advocates equity, social justice, and protection of the environment, which it considers to be the hallmark of world order and peace. The journal publishes clinical, research-oriented articles, historical work, policy analysis, case studies, essays, interviews, and book reviews. The focus of a recent issue is on the post-conflict experience, as each article examines the violence of the past and the effect it has on the mental and physical health of the individuals and their families. The three articles included in this issue are "Sectarian and Nonsectarian Violence: Mothers' Appraisals of Political Conflict in Northern Ireland," "Who Are the Resilient Children in Conditions of Military Violence? Family- and Child-Related Factors in a Palestinian Community Sample," and "Witnesses to Genocide: Experiences of Witnessing in the Rwandan Gacaca Courts." This journal would be a fine addition to peace research centers and academic libraries.

4152. *Peace, Conflict & Development: an interdisciplinary journal.* [ISSN: 1742-0601] 2002. s-a. Free. Ed(s): Zuhair Bashar. University of Bradford, Department of Peace Studies, Richmond Rd, Bradford, BD7 1DP, United Kingdom; course-enquiries@bradford.ac.uk; http://www.bradford.ac.uk/ssis/peace-studies/. Refereed. *Indexed:* SSA. *Bk. rev.:* Number and length vary. *Aud.:* Ac.

This is an open-access journal that focuses on contemporary issues in peace and conflict studies. The journal is managed and edited by doctoral students at the University of Bradford's Department of Peace Studies, with the support of a part-time paid coordinator and academic staff. Its main purpose is to publish innovative articles on a wide range of topics including human rights issues, democracy, conflict resolution, security, war, and the peace process. The journal consists of academic essays, fieldwork reports from researchers and practitioners, and book reviews. A recent issue includes an essay titled "Volatile Landscapes: The Impact of Explosive Remnants of War on Land Rights in Conflict Affected Countries" and articles such as "Peacebuilding in Complex Social Systems" and "Clash of Perceptions: Hostility Perception and the US-Muslim World Relationship." A good online resource for academic libraries.

4153. *Peace Magazine.* Formerly (until 1985): *Peace Calendar.* [ISSN: 0826-9521] 1985. q. CAD 18.90 domestic; USD 23 United States; CAD 30 elsewhere. Ed(s): Metta Spencer. Canadian Disarmament Information Service (CANDIS), PO Box 248, Toronto, ON M5S 2S7, Canada. Illus., index, adv. Sample. Circ: 2600 Paid. Vol. ends: Nov/Dec. Microform: MML. *Indexed:* A01, ABS&EES, BRI, C37, CBCARef, MASUSE. *Bk. rev.:* 3-4, 250-600 words. *Aud.:* Hs, Ga, Ac.

Peace Magazine is a quarterly that consists of articles, news stories, book and film reviews, letters, and a calendar of events focusing on peace issues. It is published by the Canadian Disarmament Information Service, a group dedicated to educating the public on every aspect of peace. Articles deal with subjects related to the terrible effect that wars have on people, their minds, and the minds of their children. They address human rights abuses, inequity, corrupt governance, and intolerance of diversity. Articles are written by activists, journalists, and scholars. Recent articles include "Building Peace on Jeju Island" and "Five Reasons to Reconsider the F-35s." The "Our Readers Write" section encourages readers to voice their opinions on issues that concern them; readers also offer their comments on articles from previous issues. There is a book review section and a news section that highlights peace issues, as well as a "Peace Crossword." All articles and letters (but not listings and ads) from *Peace Magazine,* from January 1983 to the present, are now available electronically. A good resource for public, high school, and academic libraries.

4154. *Peace Research: the Canadian journal of peace and conflict studies.* [ISSN: 0008-4697] 1969. s-a. Ed(s): John Derksen, Richard McCutcheon. M.V. Naidu, Ed. & Pub., c/o Menno Simons College, 210-520 Portage Ave, Winnipeg, MB R3C 0G2, Canada. Illus., index. Sample. Refereed. Vol. ends: Nov. Microform: MML. *Indexed:* A22, ABS&EES, BRI, C37, CBCARef. *Bk. rev.:* 1-2, 500-1,000 words. *Aud.:* Ga, Ac.

This journal is one of Canada's oldest scholarly journals on peace studies, it focuses on peace education, peace research, and peace movements. Deeply committed to the eradication of violence, armament, and war, it advocates nonviolence, disarmament, and peaceful settlement of disputes. Articles address human rights issues relating to equality, liberty, justice, economic development, environmental protection, cultural advancement, feminism, and humanism. Published under the auspices of the Canadian Peace Research and Education Association (CPREA), the journal concludes with the CPREA newsletter. Academicians and researchers from all over the world contribute articles. Academic libraries and peace research centers will find this journal a useful resource.

4155. *Peace Review: a journal of social justice.* [ISSN: 1040-2659] 1989. q. GBP 517 (print & online eds.). Ed(s): Robert Elias. Routledge, 4 Park Sq, Milton Park, Abingdon, OX14 4RN, United Kingdom; subscriptions@tandf.co.uk; http://www.tandfonline.com. Illus., adv. Sample. Refereed. Reprint: PSC. *Indexed:* A01, A22, E01, MLA-IB, P02, P61, SSA. *Bk. rev.:* 2-3, 1,000-1,500 words. *Aud.:* Ga, Ac.

Peace Review is a multidisciplinary, transnational journal that focuses on research and analysis and is directed toward important issues and controversies that hinder the maintenance of peace. The journal publishes articles related to peace research and may include human rights issues, conflict resolution, protection of the environment, and anything else concerned with peace. The journal's aim is to present the results of this research in short, informative essays. Each issue generally revolves around a particular theme; sometimes essays relating to other topics are also published in the same issue. Recent articles include "Child-Sex Tourism, HIV/AIDS, and Social Justice in India," "Revisiting UN Peacekeeping in Rwanda and Sierra Leone," and "Making Peace With All Creation." Contributors include journalists, political scientists, teachers, activists, theologians, and peace enthusiasts. In addition to articles and other features, there is a separate section on recommended books and videos.

Peace Watch. See Government Periodicals—Federal section.

4156. *Security Dialogue.* Formerly (until 1992): *Bulletin of Peace Proposals.* [ISSN: 0967-0106] 1970. bi-m. USD 1273. Ed(s): J Peter Burgess. Sage Publications Ltd., 1 Oliver's Yard, 55 City Rd, London, EC1Y 1SP, United Kingdom; info@sagepub.co.uk; http://www.uk.sagepub.com. Illus., index, adv. Sample. Refereed. Microform: PQC. Reprint: PSC. *Indexed:* A01, A22, BAS, E01, IBSS, P61, SSA. *Aud.:* Ac.

Security Dialogue provides the most current information on global peace and security. It offers new ideas on important issues concerning peace and security. It intends to provoke thought and reflection through "interregional dialogue" on issues concerning international security. A recent issue contains articles such as "Resilience and human security: The post-interventionist paradigm," "Is securitization a 'negative concept'? Revisiting the normative debate over normal versus extraordinary politics," and "Thinking critically about food security." The journal provides expert coverage of such topics as the role of the United Nations, conflict prevention, mediation, sovereignty, and intervention. This journal would prove to be a very useful resource in academic or research libraries that specialize in peace research.

4157. *Win: through revolutionary nonviolence.* Former titles (until 2007): *The Nonviolent Activist;* (until 1984): *W R L News.* 1945. q. USD 25 (Individuals, USD 15). Ed(s): Francesca Fiorentini. War Resisters League, 339 Lafayette St, New York, NY 10012-2782. Illus., index, adv. Sample. Vol. ends: Nov/Dec. Microform: PQC. *Bk. rev.:* 1-3, 300-500 words. *Aud.:* Ga, Ac.

Win, formerly *The Nonviolent Activist,* is a notable grassroots publication, and it is the official new quarterly magazine of one of the most important American peace organizations, the War Resisters League (WRL). The WRL affirms that all war is a crime against humanity and is determined not to support any kind of war, international or civil, and it strives nonviolently for the removal of all causes of war. *Win* reflects the ideals of the WRL. It publishes articles related to peace and social justice issues. Recent articles of interest are "The Resistance Is Global" and "Rising Up Without Burning Out." There are sections for book reviews, letters, activists' news, and WRL news. A good resource for activists and researchers interested in world peace.

■ PETS

Associations

See also Animal Welfare; Birds; Horses; Sports; and Veterinary Science sections.

Camille McCutcheon, Librarian, Coordinator of Collection Management, University of South Carolina Upstate, 800 University Way, Spartanburg, SC 29303; CMcCutcheon@uscupstate.edu

Introduction

Articles concerning health, wellness, nutrition, care, welfare, behavior, communication, grooming, training, and the human–animal bond, as well as heartwarming stories of actual animals, are commonly featured in many of the magazines in this section.

Most pet magazines, such as *The Bark, Cat Fancy, Reptiles,* and *Tropical Fish Hobbyist,* focus exclusively on either dogs, cats, reptiles, or fish. *Pets Magazine,* however, contains articles on various kinds of pets, including dogs, cats, birds, fish, and rabbits.

One of the leading pet magazine publishers is BowTie Magazines, which publishes such titles as *Aquarium Fish International, Dog Fancy, Cat Fancy,* and *Bird Talk.* BowTie Magazines also produces a line of annual titles such as

Ferrets USA and *Birds USA,* which contain relevant information for new or prospective pet owners. These annual editions are mentioned throughout the section. Two noteworthy annual publications that do not have monthly counterparts are *Rabbits USA* and *Critters USA,* the latter of which provides information on small mammals such as gerbils, rats, mice, guinea pigs, hamsters, and sugar gliders.

During the past several years, there has been an increase in the number of titles that publish articles on natural care, nutrition, and holistic medicine. Periodicals such as *Animal Wellness Magazine* and *The Whole Dog Journal* focus on natural health care. Two of the most popular pet magazines, *Cat Fancy* and *Dog Fancy,* have sections on natural care. *Cat Fancy* has a "Natural Cat" section that appears periodically and has information and articles on natural care. "Natural Dog" is a section that appears quarterly in *Dog Fancy* and has articles on nutrition and health care. BowTie Magazines also produces an annual publication called *Natural Dog,* which is a guide to holistic dog care.

Other publications provide medical information for pet owners. The Cummings School of Veterinary Medicine at Tufts University publishes *Catnip* and *Your Dog,* which are newsletters that provide medical and behavioral information on cats and dogs.

Titles that are part lifestyle magazine, part pet publication, continue to be popular. Many of these magazines, such as *Life+Dog* and *Modern Dog,* contain articles on fashion, beauty, design, and travel, as well as profiles of and interviews with celebrity pet owners.

Although all of the periodicals in this section have a web presence, *Ferrets Magazine* is the only title that is exclusively available online. Most of the publications noted in this section have web sites where visitors can locate subscription information, scan the tables of contents, and view photographs of the covers of the current issues. Other sites are more extensive and allow visitors to read selected articles from current and previous issues, participate in online forums, and pose questions to veterinarians and other pet experts.

Basic Periodicals

Hs: *Cat Fancy, Dog Fancy;* Ga: *AKC Family Dog, Aquarium Fish International, Best Friends, Bird Talk, Cat Fancy, Dog Fancy, I Love Cats, Pets Magazine, Reptiles;* Ac: *Amazonas, Anthrozoos, Coral.*

Basic Abstracts and Indexes

Reader's Guide to Periodical Literature.

4158. *A F A Watchbird.* [ISSN: 0199-543X] 1974. q. Free to members. Ed(s): Mark Moore. American Federation of Aviculture, PO Box 91717, Austin, TX 78709; afaoffice@earthlink.net; http://www.afabirds.org/. Illus., adv. Vol. ends: Nov/Dec. *Aud.:* Hs, Ga, Ac.

AFA Watchbird is the official publication of the American Federation of Aviculture. The AFA is dedicated to "represent[ing] all aspects of aviculture and to educat[ing] the public about keeping and breeding birds in captivity." The magazine's color photography is beautiful. The articles are detailed and informative, and some of them contain a list of references. Contributors include aviculturists, veterinarians, avian scientists, and avian biologists. Featured are profiles of bird species, as well as articles on conservation, bird breeding, the health and welfare of birds, legislative issues that affect aviculture and aviculturists, and the activities of the AFA. The web site for the American Federation of Aviculture contains general information about *AFA Watchbird,* including the table of contents and a photograph of the cover of the current issue. URL: www.afabirds.org

4159. *A K C Family Dog.* [ISSN: 1559-5072] 2003. bi-m. USD 9.95. American Kennel Club, Inc., 260 Madison Ave, New York, NY 10016; ejm@akc.org; http://www.akc.org. Illus., adv. Sample. *Aud.:* Ga.

AKC Family Dog is an informative magazine for owners of purebred dogs and for dog enthusiasts. Each issue contains feature articles, columns, and departments on topics such as health, behavior, training, and grooming. Contributors include veterinarians, professional dog trainers, and authors of books on dogs. The American Kennel Club web site is extensive and includes general information about the magazine, along with the table of contents and a photograph of the cover of the current issue. Information about breeds, breeders, AKC events, and an online store are all available on the web site. Recommended for public library collections. URL: www.akc.org

4160. *Amazonas: freshwater aquariums & tropical discovery.* [ISSN: 2166-3106] 2012. bi-m. USD 29 domestic; USD 41 Canada; USD 49 elsewhere. Ed(s): Hans-Georg Evers, James M Lawrence. Reef to Rainforest Media, Llc., 140 Webster Rd, PO Box 490, Shelburne, VT 05482; http://www.reef2rainforest.com/. Adv. *Aud.:* Ga, Ac, Sa.

Lavishly illustrated, *Amazonas* caters to serious freshwater aquarists and tropical fish enthusiasts. The color photography is beautiful, the layout is very attractive, and the articles are well written. Some of the articles even contain a list of references. Contributors include internationally renowned aquarists and tropical aquatic biology experts. There are feature articles on fishes, invertebrates, aquatic plants, husbandry and breeding, and field trips to tropical locales. The web site for *Amazonas* contains general information about the magazine. Recommended for academic and large public library collections. URL: www.amazonasmagazine.com

4161. *Animal Wellness: for a long, healthy life!* Formerly (until 2001): *Animal.* [ISSN: 1710-1190] 1999. bi-m. CAD 24 domestic; USD 19 United States; USD 80 elsewhere. Redstone Media Group Inc., 164 Hunter St., West, Peterborough, ON K9H 2L2, Canada; http://redstonemediagroup.com/. Adv. *Bk. rev.:* 2; 150-200 words. *Aud.:* Hs, Ga.

The purpose of *Animal Wellness Magazine* is to provide owners of companion animals with the information needed to improve the quality of life for their animals. It is an attractive publication that has many color photographs and well-written and interesting articles. It offers information on holistic and natural alternatives to Western medicine. There are also feature articles on nutrition, health, behavior, and social and activism issues. Contributors include veterinarians who practice holistic veterinary medicine, psychologists, authors of books on holistic and natural medicine for animals, animal behaviorists, professional groomers, and veterinary naturopaths. Regularly featured columns and departments include a dog breed profile, a wellness resource guide, pet products endorsed by *Animal Wellness Magazine,* book reviews that average 150 words in length, and a classified ads section. The web site for the magazine provides additional content. Recommended for large public library collections. URL: www.animalwellnessmagazine.com

4162. *Anthrozoos: a multidisciplinary journal of the interactions of people and animals.* Formerly (until 1987): *Delta Society. Journal.* [ISSN: 0892-7936] 1984, q. USD 491 (print & online eds.). Ed(s): Anthony L. Podberscek. Bloomsbury Publishing plc, 50 Bedford Sq, London, WC1B 3DP, United Kingdom; contact@bloomsbury.com; http://www.bloomsbury.com. Illus., adv. Sample. Refereed. Vol. ends: No. 4. *Indexed:* A01, A22, Agr, BRI, C45, IndVet, P61, PsycInfo, RRTA, SSA. *Bk. rev.:* 1-4; 1,000 to 2,000 words. *Aud.:* Ac.

Anthrozoos is the official journal of the International Society for Anthrozoology. It is a multidisciplinary, refereed journal that would appeal to individuals interested in human–animal interactions. Some of the fields covered include psychology, anthropology, ethology, medicine, zoology, and veterinary medicine. One of the primary components of this publication is the "Reviews and Research Reports" section, which includes research articles on human–animal interactions. There are conference announcements and in-depth book reviews. The web site contains general information about *Anthrozoos,* including the tables of contents of issues dating back to 1987, when the journal was launched. Recommended for academic and large public library collections. URL: www.bergpublishers.com

4163. *The Bark: dog is my co-pilot.* [ISSN: 1535-1734] 1997. bi-m. USD 15 domestic; USD 30 in Canada & Mexico; USD 35 elsewhere. Ed(s): Claudia Kawczynska. The Bark, Inc., 2810 8th St, Berkeley, CA 94710; customerservice@thebark.com. Illus., adv. Sample. Circ: 100000 Paid and controlled. *Bk. rev.:* 7-9; 500 words. *Aud.:* Ga.

The Bark is an upscale and intelligent publication about dog culture. The magazine's motto is "Dog is my co-pilot." The layout is very attractive, and the color photography is impressive. Focusing on the human–canine bond, *The Bark* offers a variety of interesting and well-written articles on behavior, health,

wellness, art, literature, travel, recreation, and social and activism issues. There are also interviews, stories, poetry, and book reviews. *The Bark*'s web site provides additional content. Recommended for large public library collections. URL: www.thebark.com

4164. *Best Friends (Kanab): leading the way toward no more homeless pets.* Formerly (until 1992): *Best Friends Magazine.* [ISSN: 1949-0259] 19??. bi-m. USD 25 donation. Best Friends Animal Society, 5001 Angel Canyon Rd, Kanab, UT 84741; info@bestfriends.org; http://www.bestfriends.org. Illus., adv. Sample. *Bk. rev.:* 3- 5; 100-200 words. *Aud.:* Hs, Ga.

Best Friends is the official magazine of the Best Friends Animal Society, which runs the largest sanctuary in the United States for abused and abandoned animals. It is a perfect magazine for people who love animals. Some of the magazine's features are news and articles about animals and wildlife; stories and special adoptions featured in the "Best Friends Animal Sanctuary"; and information about pet health and behavior. *Best Friends* also contains book reviews that average 100–200 words in length. The web site for *Best Friends* is attractive, is easy to navigate, and provides additional content. Recommended for public library collections. URL: www.bestfriends.org

4165. *Bird Talk: dedicated to better care for pet birds.* Formerly (until 198?): *International Bird Talk;* Incorporates (1978-1995): *Bird World;* (1928-1950): *American Canary Magazine.* [ISSN: 0891-771X] 1982. m. USD 13 domestic; USD 25 foreign. BowTie, Inc., PO Box 6050, Mission Viejo, CA 92690; http://www.bowtieinc.com. Illus., index, adv. Vol. ends: Dec. *Aud.:* Hs, Ga.

Bird Talk is a superb resource for bird owners. This attractive publication contains excellent color photographs and well-written and informative articles on topics ranging from profiles of bird species to bird psychology and health. Contributors include ornithologists, avian behaviorists, avian veterinarians, authors of books on birds, parrot behavior consultants, and bird breeders. Columns include "Causes & Cures," which provides information on avian health and welfare; "Small Birds," which provides information on small bird care and training; "Heart to Heart," which concerns the human–avian experience; and "Parrot Psychology," which provides information on bird behavior. A calendar of avian conventions and seminars, a breeder directory for large and small birds, bird photographs submitted by readers, and a classified ads section are some of the regular features of *Bird Talk*. The annual publication *Birds USA* is a guide to buying and keeping pet birds and would be an excellent resource for new or prospective bird owners. The *Bird Talk* web site is also a terrific resource. It is user-friendly and very attractive. The tables of contents and photographs of the covers of recent issues are featured. Also included are species profiles; tips on behavior, training, grooming, health, and nutrition; a breeder locator; information for young bird lovers; online forums; a photo gallery; and subscription information. URL: www.birdchannel.com

4166. *Cat Fancy.* Supersedes (in 1986): *International Cat Fancy.* [ISSN: 0892-6514] 1965. m. USD 13 domestic; USD 25 foreign. BowTie, Inc., PO Box 6050, Mission Viejo, CA 92690; http://www.bowtieinc.com. Illus., index, adv. Vol. ends: Dec. *Indexed:* A22, BRI. *Bk. rev.:* Number vary; 20-50 words. *Aud.:* Hs, Ga.

Cat Fancy is a terrific resource for cat owners. The articles are informative and practical, with topics ranging from profiles of breeds to features on cat health, behavior, grooming, training, advocacy, and rescue. The magazine has an attractive layout and contains many color photographs. Some of the magazine's contributors are veterinarians. There is a section for young cat fanciers called "Cats for Kids," where kids can submit poetry and artwork. There are also "Ask the Veterinarian" and "Ask the Behaviorist" sections where readers can pose health and behavior questions. Other departments include topics of articles featured in the upcoming issue, a calendar of cat club shows, a breeder directory, a classified ads section, and a gallery of photographs that have been submitted by readers. Some of the issues have brief book reviews. "Natural Cat" is a section that appears periodically in *Cat Fancy* and contains information and articles on natural care. BowTie Magazines also has annual publications about cats. *Kittens USA* is a guide to adopting and caring for kittens, and *Cats USA* is a guide to purebred cats. The *Cat Fancy* web site is very informative and extensive. The table of contents and a photograph of the cover of the current issue are featured. Also included are breed profiles; resources on kittens, behavior, health, nutrition, and adoption; a breeder locator; online forums; a photo gallery; subscription information; classified ads; and a section where visitors can pose questions to veterinarians and other cat experts. URL: www.catchannel.com

4167. *Catnip: the newsletter for caring cat owners.* [ISSN: 1069-6687] 1993. m. USD 20. Ed(s): John Berg, Arden Moore. Tufts University, Cummings School of Veterinary Medicine, 200 Westboro Rd, North Grafton, MA 01536; vetadmissions@tufts.edu; http://www.tufts.edu. Illus., adv. Sample. *Aud.:* Ga.

Catnip is a monthly newsletter published by the Cummings School of Veterinary Medicine at Tufts University. Sixteen pages in length, *Catnip* provides medical and behavioral information and does not accept commercial advertising. This newsletter contains numerous black-and-white photographs. The articles are informative and would be of interest to cat owners. *Catnip* has articles on cat medicine, health, behavior, feline diseases, cat product comparisons, stories of actual cats, cats in the news, and a question-and-answer section. *Catnip*'s web site provides general information about the newsletter. Recommended for large public library collections. URL: www.tuftscatnip.com

4168. *Cesar's Way: secrets from the dog whisperer.* [ISSN: 1949-2790] 2009. bi-m. USD 14.99. Ed(s): Brandusa Niro. I M G Worldwide, 304 Park Ave, 8th Fl, New York, NY 10010; susank.lynch@imgworld.com; http://www.imgworld.com. *Bk. rev.:* Number and length vary. *Aud.:* Ga.

Cesar's Way is a terrific magazine for dog lovers. It contains feature articles, news, photographs submitted by readers, product information, and profiles of shelter dogs that are available for adoption. There are also book reviews that vary in length, as well as advice from veterinarians and Cesar Millan, star of the popular television show *Dog Whisperer*. The *Cesar's Way* web site provides additional content. Recommended for large public library collections. URL: www.cesarsway.com

4169. *Coral: the reef & marine aquarium magazine.* [ISSN: 1556-5769] 2004. bi-m. USD 37. Ed(s): James M Lawrence. Reef and Rainforest Media, 823 Ferry Rd, Charlotte, VT 05445. Circ: 66000. *Aud.:* Ga, Ac, Sa.

Coral caters to serious marine aquarists. The color photography is beautiful, the layout is very attractive, and the articles are well written. Some of the articles even contain a list of references. Topics of recent articles include nano coral farms, dragonets, deep sand beds, and the importance of blue light for the colors of stony corals. "Reef News" and departments such as "Species Spotlight," "Reefkeeping 101," and "Advanced Aquatics" are included in every issue. *Coral*'s web site contains general information about the magazine. Recommended for academic and large public library collections. URL: www.coralmagazineus.com

4170. *Dog Fancy.* Former titles (until 1986): *International Dog Fancy;* (until 198?): *Dog Fancy.* [ISSN: 0892-6522] 1970. m. USD 13 domestic; USD 25 foreign. BowTie, Inc., PO Box 6050, Mission Viejo, CA 92690; http://www.bowtieinc.com. Illus., index, adv. *Indexed:* BRI. *Bk. rev.:* Number and length vary. *Aud.:* Hs, Ga.

Dog Fancy is an excellent publication for dog owners and enthusiasts. The layout is attractive, and the magazine contains many color photographs and informative and well-written articles. Contributors include veterinarians and authors of books on dogs. There are profiles of breeds and feature articles on topics such as nutrition, health and welfare, behavior, and living with dogs. Monthly sections and columns include "Bark Back," which consists of letters to the editor; "Two Words," which contains dog photographs submitted by readers; "Everyday Dog," which offers advice on grooming and cleaning; and "Breed Bites," which has news about various breeds. Other departments include "Healthy Dog," which highlights what's new in veterinary medicine and natural remedies, and "Smart Dog," which has training ideas and success stories submitted by readers. *Dog Fancy* also has a directory of breeders and a classified ads section. "Natural Dog: caring for your whole dog" is a section that appears quarterly in *Dog Fancy* and contains articles on nutrition and health care. BowTie Magazines also has annual publications about dogs. *Puppies USA* is a guide to adopting and caring for puppies; *Dogs USA* is a guide to purebred dogs; and *Natural Dog* is a guide to holistic dog care. The *Dog Fancy* web site

is very informative and extensive. A partial table of contents and a photograph of the cover of the current issue are featured. There are also breed profiles; resources on puppies and dogs; a breeder locator; photo galleries; subscription information; classified ads; and a section where visitors can pose questions to dog experts. URL: www.dogchannel.com

4171. *Dog World: active dogs, active people.* [ISSN: 0012-4893] 1916. m. USD 15 domestic; USD 27 foreign. BowTie, Inc., PO Box 6050, Mission Viejo, CA 92690; http://www.bowtieinc.com. Illus., index, adv. Vol. ends: Dec. Microform: PQC. *Indexed:* A22, MASUSE, P02. *Bk. rev.:* Number and length vary. *Aud.:* Ga, Sa.

Loaded with color photographs and well-written and in-depth articles, *Dog World* is an excellent publication for dog owners, trainers, and breeders. There are feature articles on breeds, shows, health, training, showing, and breeding. *Dog World* even has a monthly profile of rare dog breeds. Contributors include veterinarians, judges, exhibitors, breeders, handlers, and authors of books on dogs. Featured in every issue of *Dog World* are numerous columns such as "Training and Behavior," "Breeder's Notebook," "Conformation Corner," and "Advice from the Natural Vet." Monthly departments include dogs in the news, a directory of breeders, and a classified ads section. The *Dog World* web site is very informative and extensive. A partial table of contents and a photograph of the cover of the current issue are featured. There are also breed profiles; resources on puppies and dogs; a breeder locator; online forums; a photo gallery; subscription information; classified ads; and a section where visitors can pose questions to dog experts. Recommended for large public library collections. URL: www.dogchannel.com

4172. *Ferrets Magazine.* Formerly (until 2007): *Ferrets (Print).* 1997. m. Free. BowTie, Inc., 3 Burroughs, Irvine, CA 92618-2804; http://www.bowtieinc.com. *Aud.:* Hs, Ga.

Ferrets Magazine is a terrific online resource for ferret owners and enthusiasts. The articles are well written and interesting. Features include a table of contents section for the current issue; an "Ask the Doc" section where visitors can pose questions concerning the health of their ferrets; the latest ferret-related news; a calendar of upcoming events; new products for ferrets; ferret FAQs; online forums; contests; a photo gallery; classified ads; and an archive of previously featured articles. There is also an annual publication called *Ferrets USA,* which is an excellent resource for new or prospective ferret owners. URL: www.smallanimalchannel.com

4173. *Fido Friendly: the travel & lifestyle magazine for you & your dog.* [ISSN: 1945-5828] 2001. m. USD 19.95 domestic. Fido Friendly, PO Box 160, Marsing, ID 83639. Illus., adv. Sample. *Bk. rev.:* 2; 200-250 words. *Aud.:* Hs, Ga.

Fido Friendly is an upscale lifestyle magazine for dogs and their owners, and its motto is "Leave no dog behind." This publication has articles on travel, health, wellness, pet nutrition, and fashion, and is also a guide to dog-friendly accommodations in the United States. It provides tips for traveling with dogs and has departments such as "Crate & Garden," "Bowser on a Budget," and "The Doc is In." The web site for *Fido Friendly* provides additional content. Recommended for large public library collections. URL: www.fidofriendly.com

4174. *I Love Cats.* [ISSN: 0899-9570] 1988. bi-m. USD 36 domestic; USD 46 Canada; USD 56 elsewhere. Ed(s): Marcia Cavan, Lisa Allmendinger. I Love Cats Publishing Company, 900 Oaktree Ave, Ste C, South Plainfield, NJ 07080. Illus., adv. Sample. Circ: 15000. *Bk. rev.:* 1-4; 100 words. *Aud.:* Hs, Ga.

I Love Cats is a magazine that contains entertaining and useful information for cat lovers. Article topics range from stories of actual cats to health concerns to how cats communicate. Other regular features generally found in *I Love Cats* include cats in the news, a new product guide, and a gallery of photographs that have been submitted by readers. The *I Love Cats* web site contains general information about the magazine. Recommended for public library collections. URL: www.iluvcats.com

4175. *Life + Dog: modern living with man's best friend.* 2011. m. USD 29.99; USD 34.99 combined subscription (print & online eds.). Ed(s): Ryan Rice, Sharon Castellanos. L + D Publishing, Switchbud Pl, #192-210, The Woodlands, TX 77380; info@lifeanddog.com; http://www.lifeanddog.com/. Illus. *Aud.:* Ga.

Life+Dog is a glossy lifestyle magazine that is committed to "promoting responsible pet ownership and the benefits of spaying and neutering and therefore works with nonprofit groups that have similar goals." It contains profiles of nonprofit groups that work to save the lives of animals and other groups that work in the companion animal product sector. There are articles on health, travel, fashion, and the human–canine bond. In addition to feature articles, there are also interviews with celebrity pet owners, recipes, a new product guide, and a department called "This Month in Dog History." *Life+Dog* has an online presence that is attractive, is easy to navigate, and supplements the magazine. Recommended for large public library collections. URL: www.lifeanddog.com

4176. *Modern Dog: the lifestyle magazine for modern dogs and their companions.* [ISSN: 1703-812X] 2002. q. CAD 18 domestic; USD 15 United States; USD 45 elsewhere. Ed(s): Connie Wilson. Modern Dog, 343 Railway St, Ste 202, Vancouver, BC V6A 1A4, Canada; connie@moderndog.ca. Illus., adv. Sample. Circ: 240000. *Aud.:* Ga.

According to the magazine's web site, "a large part of *Modern Dog*'s mission is to support the efforts of organizations that work tirelessly to assist abused, neglected or homeless dogs." Published in Canada, *Modern Dog* is a glossy publication for dogs and their companions. It contains a breed profile; a guide to new products; dog art; articles on health, behavior, and nutrition; interviews with celebrity pet owners; grooming and training tips; and queries posed by readers to veterinarians and other dog experts. The web site for *Modern Dog* provides additional content. Recommended for large public library collections. URL: www.moderndogmagazine.com

4177. *Our Animals: the award-winning magazine of the San Francisco SPCA.* [ISSN: 0030-6789] 1906. q. USD 25 in US & Canada. Ed(s): Paul M Glassner. San Francisco Society for the Prevention of Cruelty to Animals, 2500 16th St, San Francisco, CA 94103; ouranimals@sfspca.org; http://www.sfspca.org. Illus., adv. Sample. Circ: 20000. Vol. ends: No. 4. *Aud.:* Hs, Ga.

Our Animals is the publication of the San Francisco Society for the Prevention of Cruelty to Animals. Full of color photographs, it contains heartwarming stories about SF SPCA's animals finding "forever" homes, and about some of the special programs sponsored by the organization. The web site contains information about the SF SPCA and its programs, along with general information about the magazine. URL: www.sfspca.org

4178. *Pets Magazine: exploring the human-animal bond.* Former titles (until 1985): *Pets;* (until 1983): *Pets Magazine.* [ISSN: 0831-2621] 1983. bi-m. CAD 24 domestic; USD 30 United States. Ed(s): John Simmons. Simmons Publishing Ltd., 32 Foster Crescent, Whitby, ON L1R 1W1, Canada. Illus., adv. Sample. Circ: 34500. *Indexed:* C37, CBCARef. *Aud.:* Hs, Ga.

The Canadian publication *Pets Magazine* explores the bond between humans and animals. The articles are informative and well written, and the format is very attractive. Many of the contributors are veterinarians. This excellent resource has the latest pet news; information on pet health; and feature articles on caring for puppies, dogs, kittens, cats, birds, fish, ferrets, rabbits, guinea pigs, and older pets. Published bimonthly, *Pets Magazine* has a different theme for each issue. These themes are puppies and kittens, resources for pet owners, preventive health, cat care, dog care, and senior pets. The web site for *Pets Magazine* provides general information about the publication. Visitors can read the complete edition of the current issue and selected back issues online. Recommended for public library collections. URL: www.petsmagazine.ca

4179. *Practical Fishkeeping.* Former titles (until 1978): *P F M: Practical Fishkeeping Monthly;* (until 1976): *Petfish Monthly.* [ISSN: 0262-5806] 19??. 13x/yr. USD 31.98 domestic; USD 55 United States includes Europe; USD 60 elsewhere. Ed(s): Jeremy Gay. H. Bauer Publishing Ltd., Media House, Lynchwood, Peterborough, PE2 6EA, United Kingdom; http://www.bauermedia.co.uk. Illus., adv. *Aud.:* Ga, Sa.

Published in the United Kingdom, *Practical Fishkeeping* is a terrific resource for fishkeeping enthusiasts. The articles are well written and extremely informative. The magazine's layout is very attractive, and it contains lots of color photographs. It has fish news, new product evaluations, and feature articles on topics ranging from marine fish, tropical fish, and marine invertebrates, to fish husbandry, aquatic plants, and aquascaping, to water quality, lighting, and aquarium set-ups. One of the features of *PFK* is a 15-page question-and-answer section where readers can pose questions to a panel of experts. The magazine's web site is attractive, is easy to navigate, and provides additional content. URL: www.practicalfishkeeping.co.uk

4180. *Reptiles: the world's leading reptile magazine.* Incorporates (1988-2000): *The Vivarium.* [ISSN: 1068-1965] 1993. m. USD 14.99 domestic; USD 26.99 foreign. BowTie, Inc., PO Box 6050, Mission Viejo, CA 92690; http://www.animalnetwork.com/. Illus., index, adv. Vol. ends: Dec. *Aud.:* Ga.

Loaded with stunning photographs, *Reptiles* contains feature articles on both reptiles and amphibians. These in-depth articles are well written and informative, and the magazine's layout is very attractive. Some of the departments featured in each issue of *Reptiles* include "The Vet Report," which highlights reptile case histories, medical news, and health advice; "Herp Queries," a question-and-answer section; and "Herp Happenings," a listing of reptile events. Each issue also has a breeder directory and a classified ads section. BowTie Magazines has an annual publication called *Reptiles USA,* which is a guide to buying and caring for reptiles and amphibians. New and prospective owners of reptiles and amphibians would find *Reptiles USA* very informative. The web site for *Reptiles* is extensive and filled with useful information about reptiles and amphibians. It contains the table of contents and a photograph of the cover of the current issue. Other features include the latest reptile news, subscription information, a photo gallery, a breeder locator, species profiles, and online forums. URL: www.reptilechannel.com

4181. *Tropical Fish Hobbyist.* [ISSN: 0041-3259] 1953. m. USD 28 domestic; USD 48 Canada; USD 53 elsewhere. T.F.H. Publications, Inc., One TFH Plaza, Third and Union Aves, Neptune, NJ 07753; info@tfh.com; http://www.tfh.com. Illus., index, adv. Sample. Vol. ends: Aug. *Indexed:* BRI. *Aud.:* Ga, Sa.

Tropical Fish Hobbyist is an excellent resource for the tropical fish enthusiast. The color photography is beautiful, the layout is attractive, and the in-depth articles are well written. Some of the articles even have a list of references. Contributors include biologists; veterinarians; aquarium hobbyists; breeders; freshwater, marine, and reef aquarists; and authors of books on marine aquariums. There are several question-and-answer sections where readers can submit questions and problems related to freshwater and saltwater aquariums. "Adventures in Aquascaping," "Life with Livebearers," a product spotlight section, a calendar of events for aquarium and tropical fish club meetings, and a classified ads section are included in each issue. *TFH*'s web site is informative, is easy to navigate, and provides additional content. Recommended for large public library collections. URL: www.tfhmagazine.com

4182. *Whole Dog Journal: a monthly guide to natural dog care and training.* [ISSN: 1097-5322] 1998. m. USD 39 combined subscription in US & Canada (print & online eds.); USD 48 combined subscription elsewhere (print & online eds.). Ed(s): Nancy Kerns. Belvoir Media Group, LLC, PO Box 5656, Norwalk, CT 06856; customer_service@belvoir.com; http://www.belvoir.com. Illus. Sample. Vol. ends: Dec. *Indexed:* BRI. *Aud.:* Ga, Sa.

Whole Dog Journal offers dog owners "in-depth information on effective holistic healthcare methods and successful nonviolent training." There are feature articles on herbal remedies, adoption, neutering, behavior, training, health, diet, and care, as well as information on complementary therapies such as chiropractic care, massage, acupuncture, and homeopathy. There are also product reviews. *Whole Dog Journal* does not accept commercial advertising and conducts its own tests, reviews, and evaluation of products. The web site is attractive and easy to navigate, and contains general information about magazine content. Recommended for large public library collections. URL: www.whole-dog-journal.com

4183. Your Cat: Britain's best selling cat magazine. [ISSN: 1353-260X] 1994. m. GBP 37.20 domestic; GBP 52.80 in Europe; GBP 63.80 elsewhere. Ed(s): Sue Parslow. Bourne Publishing Group Ltd. (B P G), Roebuck House, 33 Broad St, Stamford, PE9 1RB, United Kingdom; info@bournepublishinggroup.co.uk; http://www.bournepublishinggroup.com/. Illus., adv. Sample. *Bk. rev.:* Number and length vary. *Aud.:* Hs, Ga.

Published in the United Kingdom, *Your Cat* is a terrific resource for cat owners and enthusiasts. The articles are well written and extremely informative. The magazine's layout is very attractive, and it contains many color photographs. Contributors include veterinarians, professional pet groomers, pet behaviorists, counseling psychologists, and authors of books on cats. Topics of articles range from health and welfare, to personality and behavior, to profiles of breeds, to the human–feline bond. One of the features of *Your Cat* is a question-and-answer section where readers pose questions to a panel of experts. Overall topics of these Q&A sections include general cat care, health, behavior, veterinary, and nutrition. Other regular features include fictional stories about cats, cats in the news, a breeder directory, a preview of the upcoming issue of the magazine, cat photographs submitted by readers, book reviews, and a classified ads section. The web site is attractive and easy to navigate, and provides additional content. URL: www.yourcat.co.uk

4184. Your Dog: Britain's best selling dog magazine. [ISSN: 1355-7386] 1994. m. GBP 40.80 domestic; GBP 55.20 in Europe; GBP 69.30 elsewhere. Ed(s): Sarah Wright. Bourne Publishing Group Ltd. (B P G), Roebuck House, 33 Broad St, Stamford, PE9 1RB, United Kingdom; info@bournepublishinggroup.co.uk; http://www.bournepublishinggroup.com/. Illus., adv. Sample. Circ: 31299. *Aud.:* Ga.

Published in the United Kingdom, *Your Dog* is a terrific resource for dog owners and enthusiasts. The articles are well written and extremely informative. The magazine's layout is very attractive, and it contains lots of color photographs. Contributors include veterinarians, breeds experts, show judges, professional groomers, canine behaviorists, animal nutrition specialists, trainers, homeopathic veterinarians, and authors of books on dogs. Topics of articles range from health and welfare, to personality and behavior, to breed profiles, to the human–canine bond. One of the features of *Your Dog* is a question-and-answer section where readers pose questions to a panel of experts. Other regular features include dog news, dog photographs submitted by readers, and a classified ads section. The web site is attractive and easy to navigate, and provides additional content. URL: www.yourdog.co.uk

4185. Your Dog: the newsletter for caring dog owners. [ISSN: 1078-0343] 1994. m. USD 20. Ed(s): John Berg. Tufts University, Cummings School of Veterinary Medicine, 200 Westboro Rd, North Grafton, MA 01536; vetadmissions@tufts.edu; http://www.tufts.edu. Illus., adv. Sample. *Aud.:* Ga.

Your Dog is a monthly newsletter published by the Cummings School of Veterinary Medicine at Tufts University. Sixteen pages in length, *Your Dog* provides medical and behavioral information on canines. The articles are informative and would be of interest to dog owners. *Your Dog* does not accept commercial advertising and conducts its own tests and evaluations of products. This newsletter has articles on canine behavior, medicine, health, nutrition, welfare, training, and grooming. The *Your Dog* web site provides general information about the newsletter. Recommended for large public library collections. URL: www.tuftsyourdog.com

Associations

American Cat Fanciers Association, P.O. Box 1949, Nixa, MO 65714-1949; www.acfacat.com, acfa@aol.com.

American Cichlid Association, 43081 Bond Court, Sterling Heights, MI 48313; www.cichlid.org.

American Federation of Aviculture, P.O. Box 91717, Austin, TX 78709-1717; www.afabirds.org, afaoffice@earthlink.net.

American Fancy Rat and Mouse Association, 9230 64th Street, Riverside, CA 92509-5924; www.afrma.org, rattusratt@yahoo.com.

American Ferret Association, Box 554, Frederick, MD 21705-0554; www.ferret.org, afa@ferret.org.

American Gerbil Society, c/o 2283 Barker Court NE, Albany, OR 97321-9507; agsgerbils.org, libby.hanna@agsgerbils.org.

American Kennel Club, 260 Madison Avenue, New York, NY 10016; www.akc.org.

American Society for the Prevention of Cruelty to Animals, 424 E. 92nd Street, New York, NY 10128-6804; www.aspca.org.

Avicultural Society of America, P.O. Box 5516, Riverside, CA 92517-5516; www.asabirds.org, info@asabirds.org.

Canadian Cat Association, 5045 Orbitor Drive, Building 12, Suite 102, Mississauga, ON L4W 4Y4, Canada; cca-afc.com, office@cca-afc.com.

Canadian Kennel Club, 200 Ronson Drive, Suite 400, Etobicoke, ON, M9W 5Z9, Canada; www.ckc.ca, information@ckc.ca.

Cat Fanciers' Association, 260 East Main Street Alliance, OH 44601; cfainc.org, cfa@cfa.org.

Goldfish Society of America, P.O. Box 551373, Fort Lauderdale, FL 33355; www.goldfishsociety.org, info@goldfishsociety.org.

House Rabbit Society, 148 Broadway, Richmond, CA 94804; rabbit.org, mec@rabbit.org.

Humane Society of the United States, 2100 L Street, NW, Washington, DC 20037; www.humanesociety.org.

■ PHILATELY

Tara Murray, Director of Information Services/Librarian, American Philatelic Research Library, 100 Match Factory Place, Bellefonte, PA 16823

Introduction

Philately is often defined as stamp collecting, but it also encompasses study of the design, production, and use of stamps and related items. It is one of the world's most popular hobbies, and is nearly as old as postage stamps themselves.

The first postage stamp, the Penny Black, was issued by Great Britain in 1840. Other countries soon followed suit, and the first U.S. postage stamps, the 5 cent Franklin and the 10 cent Washington, were issued in 1847.

Literature related to stamp collecting began to appear in the 1860's. The first issue of *The Stamp-Collector's Magazine* was published in England in February 1863, and M. Georges Herpin coined the term "philately" in *Le Collectionneur de Timbres-Poste* in 1864. The American Philatelic Society, the national organization for philatelists in the U.S., was founded in 1886, and the first issue of its journal appeared in 1887.

While some rare stamp errors, such as the famous "upside-down airplane" or Inverted Jenny, are extremely valuable, anyone can start a stamp collection for a small amount of money at a local hobby shop or stamp show, by ordering through advertisements in philatelic magazines, or simply by removing stamps from envelopes received in the mail. Some philatelists don't even collect, choosing to study stamps and postal history without acquiring the items themselves. In some cases, the objects of their study may be available only in museum collections.

In the early days, it was possible to assemble a worldwide collection, but today even the most advanced collectors specialize—by geography, type of material (e.g., postal stationery), or topic (e.g., baseball on stamps).

Philatelists are prolific writers, contributing to magazines and journals published all over the world, covering just about every specialty imaginable. The titles selected for inclusion here are general with broad appeal, and most have worldwide coverage with a focus on U.S., Canadian, or British stamps.

Basic Periodicals

Ga: *American Philatelist, Canadian Philatelist, Gibbons Stamp Monthly, Linn's Stamp News, Mekeel's and Stamps Magazine*; Ac: *Philatelic Literature Review, Postal History Journal.*

4186. *American Philatelist.* [ISSN: 0003-0473] 1887. m. Ed(s): Barbara Boal. American Philatelic Society, Inc., 100 Match Factory Pl, Bellefonte, PA 16823; flsente@stamps.org; http://www.philately.com/philately/aps.htm. Illus., index, adv. Sample. Vol. ends: Dec. *Indexed:* ABS&EES, BRI, CBRI, MLA-IB. *Bk. rev.:* 100-300 words. *Aud.:* Ga, Ac.

The American Philatelist is the official publication of the American Philatelic Society (APS), the leading philatelic organization in the United States. The journal covers worldwide stamps and postal history, as well as news about the hobby and the society in a colorful, attractive format. Articles range from collecting tips ("Have Fun Selling Your Stamps!") to detailed discussions of individual stamp issues ("Celebrating the Penny Black"). Each issue includes a calendar of stamp shows and society events, a list of U.S. new issues, book reviews, and classified ads. Recommended for all general collections.

4187. *Canadian Philatelist.* [ISSN: 0045-5253] 1950. bi-m. Free to members; Non-members, CAD 30. Ed(s): Tony Shaman. Philaprint Ltd., 10 Summerhill Ave, Toronto, ON M4T 1AB, Canada. Illus., index, adv. Vol. ends: Nov/Dec. Microform: MML. *Indexed:* CBCARef. *Bk. rev.:* 5-10, 300-500 words. *Aud.:* Ga, Ac.

The Canadian Philatelist (*Le Philateliste canadien*) is the official publication of the Royal Philatelic Society of Canada. Articles cover worldwide stamps and postal history, with color illustrations. Most articles are in English, but a few are in French, and news items and other short pieces are usually in both languages. Each issue includes society news, an events calendar, a list of philatelic resources on the web, book reviews, and classified ads. The society's web site provides a searchable index of articles and pdf images of issues from 1950 to current, excluding the most recent five years, as well as pdf images of the society's previous journals dating back to 1887. URL: www.rpsc.org/tcp

4188. *Gibbons Stamp Monthly.* Formerly (until 1977): *Stamp Monthly.* [ISSN: 0954-8084] 1890. m. GBP 45 domestic; GBP 85 foreign. Ed(s): Hugh Jefferies. Stanley Gibbons Ltd., 7 Parkside, Christchurch Rd, Ringwood, BH24 3SH, United Kingdom; info@stanleygibbons.co.uk; http://www.stanleygibbons.com. Illus., index, adv. Sample. Vol. ends: May. *Bk. rev.:* 3-5, 300-700 words. *Aud.:* Ga.

Published by the same company that produces Great Britain's most popular stamp catalog, *Gibbons Stamp Monthly* appeals to both the novice collector and the serious philatelist. It includes a section on British stamps and a monthly supplement to the *Stanley Gibbons Catalogue,* as well as articles on stamps from around the world with plentiful color illustrations. Regular features include society and auction house news, a column for the new collector, book reviews, and classified ads.

4189. *Linn's Stamp News.* Formerly: *Linn's Weekly Stamp News.* [ISSN: 0161-6234] 1928. w. USD 59.99 domestic; USD 104.99 Canada; USD 134.99 elsewhere. Ed(s): Michael Baadke. Amos Publishing, Hobby, PO Box 926, Sidney, OH 45365; http://www.amospress.com. Illus., adv. Sample. Circ: 40678 Paid. Vol. ends: Dec. Microform: PQC. *Indexed:* A22. *Bk. rev.:* Occasional. *Aud.:* Ga.

Linn's, as most collectors refer to the weekly stamp newspaper, is one of the most widely read philatelic publications in the world, and essential for those who buy and sell stamps. It covers new issues, the stamp market, auctions, shows, societies, and awards, and includes several pages of classified ads. In 2010, *Scott Stamp Monthly* merged with *Linn's.* As a result, one issue of *Linn's* each month appears in a larger, glossier format and includes content from *Scott Stamp Monthly,* most notably a new issues update to the *Scott Stamp Catalogue,* the most popular stamp catalog in the U.S. Recommended for all general collections.

4190. *Mekeel's and Stamps Magazine.* Formed by the merger of (1891-1995): *Mekeel's Stamp News; Stamp Auction News.* [ISSN: 1095-0443] 1995. w. Stamp News Publishing, Inc., 42 Sentry Way, Merrimack, NH 03054-4407; JD@StampNewsNow.com; http://www.stampnewsnow.com/. Illus., adv. Sample. *Bk. rev.:* Occasional. *Aud.:* Ga.

This weekly newspaper includes news and short articles, as well as numerous display and classified ads. The primary focus is on the U.S., although there is some worldwide coverage. Each issue contains a show calendar, an auction calendar, a list of pictorial postmarks, and U.S. stamp issues. Some issues also contain book reviews and reprints of older articles from other philatelic magazines. The cover and a few illustrations are printed in color.

4191. *Philatelic Literature Review.* [ISSN: 0270-1707] 1942. q. Free to members; Non-members, USD 18. Ed(s): Barbara Boal. American Philatelic Research Library, 100 Match Factory Pl, Bellefonte, PA 16823; plr@stamps.org; http://www.stamps.org. Illus., index, adv. Sample. Vol. ends: Dec. *Indexed:* BRI, CBRI. *Bk. rev.:* 10-20, 100-750 words. *Aud.:* Ac, Sa.

This journal focuses on the literature of philately and is aimed at bibliophiles, researchers, and librarians. It began its life as a publication of the Philatelic Literature Association, and is now the official journal of the American Philatelic Research Library (APRL). Articles discuss the history of philately and research resources and techniques. The journal also includes original bibliographies and indexes on all aspects of philately, in-depth book reviews, news from the APRL and other philatelic libraries, and a literature clearinghouse and dealer directory. A companion blog (http://blog.stamplibrary.org) provides updates and short articles between quarterly issues. Recommended for all collections that support philatelic or postal history research.

4192. *Postal History Journal.* [ISSN: 0032-5341] 1957. 3x/yr. USD 50. Ed(s): Diane F DeBlois, Robert Dalton Harris. Postal History Society, Inc., PO Box 20387, Columbus, OH 43220. Illus., index, adv. Vol. ends: Oct. Microform: PQC. *Indexed:* A22. *Bk. rev.:* 2-5, 500 words. *Aud.:* Ac, Sa.

Published by the Postal History Society, this journal features research articles on all aspects of postal history and the development of communication and transportation systems related to the mail. Articles are thorough and include numerous references and color scans and photographs of the material discussed. Each issue also includes a bibliography of postal history articles in other journals, in-depth book reviews by subject experts, and news for society members. Recommended for all collections that support philatelic or postal history research.

Scott Stamp Monthly. See *Linn's Stamp News.*

4193. *Topical Time.* [ISSN: 0040-9332] 1949. bi-m. USD 25 domestic; USD 33 foreign. Ed(s): Wayne L Youngblood. American Topical Association, Inc., PO Box 8, Carterville, IL 62918; americantopical@msn.com; http://www.americantopicalassn.org. Illus., index, adv. Circ: 3500 Paid. Vol. ends: Nov/Dec. *Bk. rev.:* 3-5, 250 words. *Aud.:* Ga, Sa.

Topical stamp collecting, or collecting based on the subject depicted rather than on geography or type of philatelic material, is very popular. *Topical Time* features articles on a wide variety of topics, with numerous color illustrations. Each issue also includes reviews of books and periodicals, and a list of topical articles in other publications. As the official journal of the American Topical Association, it includes news from the society and its many chapters and study units. The latter help topical collectors connect with others who share their interest (e.g., sports on stamps, or cats on stamps).

■ PHILOSOPHY

Jason A. Pannone, Librarian, Robbins Library, Department of Philosophy, Harvard University, Cambridge MA 02138; FAX: 617-495-2194; pannone@fas.harvard.edu

Introduction

Journals in philosophy have a potential appeal to a wide audience, given the nature of the discipline.

Some of the most prominent philosophy journals, such as *The Journal of Philosophy* and *Philosophical Review,* are general and broad in scope. However, many more are specialized, covering various subdivisions of the discipline (e.g.,

Mind & Language, Philosophy of Science, and *Philosophy and Public Affairs*) or prominent historical eras or figures in the history of philosophy (e.g., *Phronesis, Hume Studies,* and *Kant-Studien*).

Moreover, philosophy intersects with many disciplines, not only the arts and humanities but the social and empirical sciences as well. As a result, philosophy journals have the potential to support scholarship in these areas, whether in the arts, education, law, linguistics, literature, political science, religion, or the social and empirical sciences.

In the subfields of philosophy that touch on the social and empirical sciences, for example, many of the published articles engage with current research and researchers in physics, evolutionary biology, neuroscience, cognitive science, sociology, computer science, and technology, where relevant.

For students of law, politics, and ethics, policy development and discussion will benefit from current philosophical research in the areas of legal theory, political theory, and ethics.

Those interested in literature and the arts may find journals that focus on aesthetics and literary theory useful for their work.

Thus, philosophy journals can be very useful in supporting research across a wide range of disciplines.

Basic Periodicals

Ac: *Analysis, Australasian Journal of Philosophy, Erkenntnis, Ethics, Journal of Philosophy, Journal of the History of Philosophy, Journal of Symbolic Logic, Mind, Monist, Nous, Philosophical Review, Philosophical Studies, Philosophy, Philosophy and Public Affairs, Philosophy of Science, Synthese.*

Basic Abstracts and Indexes

L'Annee Philologique, Arts and Humanities Citation Index, Humanities Index, International Philosophical Bibliography, Philosopher's Index.

4194. *Acta Analytica.* [ISSN: 0353-5150] 1986. q. EUR 280 (print & online eds.). Ed(s): Danilo Suster. Springer Netherlands, Van Godewijckstraat 30, Dordrecht, 3311 GX, Netherlands; http://www.springer.com. Adv. Reprint: PSC. *Indexed:* A01, A22, ArtHuCI, BRI, E01, IPB. *Aud.:* Ac.

Acta Analytica is an English-language Slovenian journal that publishes articles in the analytic tradition on topics such as philosophical logic, metaphysics, epistemology, philosophy of science, and philosophy of mind, with special attention given to cognitive science.

4195. *American Philosophical Quarterly.* [ISSN: 0003-0481] 1964. q. USD 297 (print or online ed.) Individuals, USD 55). Ed(s): Nicholas Rescher, Paul Moser. University of Illinois Press, 1325 S Oak St, Champaign, IL 61820; journals@uillinois.edu; http://www.press.uillinois.edu. Illus., index, adv. Sample. Refereed. *Indexed:* A01, A22, AmHI, ArtHuCI, FR, IBSS, IPB, P02. *Aud.:* Ac.

American Philosophical Quarterly is a general philosophy journal that covers, for example, issues and problems in metaphysics, epistemology, philosophy of mind, ethics, philosophy of language, and action theory. Recent issues have focused on the work of various philosophers such as Quine and Wittgenstein.

4196. *Analysis.* [ISSN: 0003-2638] 1933. q. EUR 181. Ed(s): Michael Clark. Oxford University Press, Great Clarendon St, Oxford, OX2 6DP, United Kingdom; enquiry@oup.co.uk; http://www.oxfordjournals.org. Illus., index. Sample. Refereed. Circ: 1350. Vol. ends: No. 4. Reprint: PSC. *Indexed:* A01, A22, AmHI, ArtHuCI, CCMJ, E01, IPB, MLA-IB, MSN, MathR. *Bk. rev.:* 10-15, 1,000-2,500 words, signed. *Aud.:* Ac.

The short articles in *Analysis* present tightly-argued defenses or critiques of positions on topics of concern in contemporary analytic philosophy, primarily in metaphysics, philosophical logic, philosophy of language, philosophy of mind, epistemology, and ethics. The journal also carries book symposia, critical notices, and overviews of recent work in selected topics in its pages. For collections that support work in contemporary analytic philosophy, this journal is highly recommended.

4197. *Analytic Philosophy.* Formerly (until Jan. 2011): *Philosophical Books.* [ISSN: 2153-9596] 1960. q. GBP 333. Ed(s): David Sosa. Wiley-Blackwell Publishing Ltd., 9600 Garsington Rd, Oxford, OX4 2DQ, United Kingdom; customerservices@blackwellpublishing.com; http://www.wiley.com/. Illus., index, adv. Sample. Refereed. Vol. ends: No. 4. Reprint: PSC. *Indexed:* A01, A22, E01, IPB. *Bk. rev.:* Number and length vary. *Aud.:* Ac.

Formerly known as *Philosophical Books, Analytic Philosophy* publishes reviews of newly published English-language philosophy books and serials in the analytic tradition. For those charged with collection development in philosophy, this journal is a useful source of information. Each issues centers on a featured book: several reviewers provide their criticism, with a response by the author at the end. Additionally, one book is singled out in each issues for a more lengthy review under the heading "Critical Notice," though this will not have a reply from the author. Moreover, under its new title, the journal now includes original research in all areas of philosophy with the book reviews.

4198. *Ancient Philosophy (Print): semi-annual journal devoted to original research in ancient Greek and Roman philosophy and science.* [ISSN: 0740-2007] 1980. s-a. USD 70 (Individuals, USD 32; Students, USD 25). Ed(s): Dr. Ronald Polansky. Duquesne University, Department of Philosophy, 600 Forbes Ave, Pittsburgh, PA 15282; http://www.sites.duq.edu/philosophy/. Illus. Refereed. Vol. ends: No. 2. Reprint: PSC. *Indexed:* A22, AmHI, BRI, IPB. *Bk. rev.:* 15-20, 1,000-2,000 words, signed. *Aud.:* Ac.

This journal focuses a good deal on scholarship on Plato and Aristotle. Nonetheless, other members of the ancient philosophical tradition, such as Parmenides and other Presocratics, Hellenistic philosophers, Neoplatonists such as Porphyry, and medieval commentators on Aristotle are represented and discussed in this journal's pages. The articles and discussions papers tend to be technical and heavily sourced, with footnotes and extensive bibliographies. For collections with a strong emphasis on ancient philosophy, this journal serves as a useful complement to *Phronesis* (below in this section).

4199. *Archiv fuer Geschichte der Philosophie.* [ISSN: 0003-9101] 1976. 3x/yr. EUR 239. Ed(s): Christoph Horn, Wolfgang Bartuschat. Walter de Gruyter GmbH & Co. KG, Genthiner Str 13, Berlin, 10785, Germany; info@degruyter.com; http://www.degruyter.de. Illus., index, adv. Refereed. Circ: 650 Paid. Vol. ends: No. 3. Reprint: SCH. *Indexed:* A22, AmHI, ArtHuCI, E01, FR, IPB, MLA-IB. *Bk. rev.:* 5-10, 500-1,000 words. *Aud.:* Ac.

This journal publishes articles in the history of philosophy, primarily in German, but with English and French also represented. The articles cover examinations of all philosophers from antiquity to the first half of the twentieth century. From time to time, the journal will publish texts of previously unpublished short historical primary texts. The journal also publishes discussion papers and book reviews.

4200. *Aristotelian Society. Proceedings. Supplementary Volume.* [ISSN: 0309-7013] 1918. a. GBP 106. Ed(s): Dr. Mark Eli Kalderon. Aristotelian Society, c/o Rachel Carter, Rm 281 Stewart House, London, WC1B 5DN, United Kingdom; mail@aristoteliansociety.org.uk; http://www.aristoteliansociety.org.uk. Illus., adv. Refereed. Reprint: PSC. *Indexed:* A01, A22, E01. *Aud.:* Ac.

The annual proceedings of the Aristotelian Society contain the papers that are read at the annual joint sessions of the Aristotelian Society and the Mind Association. These are generally published in June as a supplementary volume to the Society's quarterly journal, with the first article being the presidential address. The papers found in this volume are from many of the top philosophers in the English-speaking world, covering all topics and historical figures. Given this, they are generally of the highest quality and scholarship that one can find in contemporary philosophical writing. Selectors are strongly recommended to include this in their collections.

4201. *The Australasian Journal of Logic.* [ISSN: 1448-5052] 2003. a. Free. Australasian Association for Logic, c/o Greg Restall, School of of Philosophy, Anthropology and Social Inquiry, Parkville, VIC 3010, Australia; aal-info@unimelb.edu.au; http://www.cs.otago.ac.nz/staffpriv/hans/aal/index.html. Refereed. *Indexed:* CCMJ, MSN, MathR. *Aud.:* Ac, Sa.

Sponsored by the Australasian Association for Logic, this free online journal publishes articles of interest to those working in logic, both pure logic (i.e., theory) and applied logic (i.e., logic as it relates to mathematics, computer science, linguistics, and philosophy).

4202. *Australasian Journal of Philosophy.* Formerly (until 1947): *Australasian Journal of Psychology and Philosophy.* [ISSN: 0004-8402] 1923. q. GBP 171 (print & online eds.). Ed(s): Stewart Candlish. Routledge, 4 Park Sq, Milton Park, Abingdon, OX14 4RN, United Kingdom; subscriptions@tandf.co.uk; http://www.tandfonline.com. Illus., index, adv. Sample. Refereed. Vol. ends: No. 4. Microform: MIM. Reprint: PSC. *Indexed:* A22, AmHI, ArtHuCI, E01, IPB, MLA-IB. *Bk. rev.:* 5-10, 750-1,000 words, signed. *Aud.:* Ac.

This journal is one of the top-tier analytic philosophy journals. Now in its 90th year of publication by the Australasian Association of Philosophy, the journal publishes articles dealing with contemporary issues in metaphysics, epistemology, philosophy of science, and ethics. While many of the contributors are Australian, others are from other parts of the Anglophone world. In addition to articles, the journal also contains "Discussion Notes," longer "Book Reviews," and shorter "Book Notes." Collections that support work in analytic philosophy will want to have this journal as part of their collection.

Bioethics. See Civil Liberties/Bioethics: Reproductive Rights, Right-to-Life, and Right-to-Die section.

4203. *British Journal for the History of Philosophy.* [ISSN: 0960-8788] 1993. bi-m. GBP 581 (print & online eds.). Ed(s): Michael Beaney. Routledge, 4 Park Sq, Milton Park, Abingdon, OX14 4RN, United Kingdom; subscriptions@tandf.co.uk; http://www.tandfonline.com. Illus., index, adv. Sample. Refereed. Vol. ends: No. 3. Reprint: PSC. *Indexed:* A01, A22, AmHI, ArtHuCI, E01, FR, IPB. *Bk. rev.:* 10-15, 1,500-2,000 words, signed. *Aud.:* Ac.

The articles in this journal emphasize the study of the intellectual, political, and social contexts in which philosophical texts were created. As such, articles will also examine historical topics in the natural and social sciences and theology when they bear on philosophical problems. The focus is mainly on European philosophy from the early modern period through the middle of the twentieth century, though topics in ancient philosophy are also studied from time to time. For those collections with an emphasis on early modern British philosophy and on early modern philosophy in general, this journal is a good resource.

4204. *The British Journal for the Philosophy of Science.* [ISSN: 0007-0882] 1950. q. EUR 233. Ed(s): Steven French, Michela Massimi. Oxford University Press, Great Clarendon St, Oxford, OX2 6DP, United Kingdom; enquiry@oup.co.uk; http://www.oxfordjournals.org/. Illus., index, adv. Sample. Refereed. Vol. ends: No. 4. Reprint: PSC. *Indexed:* A01, A22, AmHI, ArtHuCI, BRI, CCMJ, E01, FR, IPB, MLA-IB, MSN, MathR, P02. *Bk. rev.:* 5-7, 1,000-3,000 words, signed. *Aud.:* Ac.

This journal, the official publication of the British Society for the Philosophy of Science, presents philosophical explorations of all areas of the empirical and social sciences, from methodology to theory to logic and even mathematics. It is a useful complement to the American journal *Philosophy of Science,* given that it often covers areas of research in philosophy of science, such as logic and mathematics, that are less prominent in the American version. This journal is a good core journal to have, given its applicability not only for philosophy but for the sciences as well.

4205. *British Journal of Aesthetics.* [ISSN: 0007-0904] 1960. q. EUR 297. Ed(s): John Hyman, Elisabeth Schellekens. Oxford University Press, Great Clarendon St, Oxford, OX2 6DP, United Kingdom; enquiry@oup.co.uk; http://www.oxfordjournals.org/. Illus., adv. Sample. Refereed. Microform: PQC. Reprint: PSC. *Indexed:* A01, A06, A07, A22, A51, AmHI, ArtHuCI, BEL&L, BRI, E01, FR, IPB, MLA-IB, P02, RILM. *Bk. rev.:* 4-6, 250-1,000 words. *Aud.:* Ac.

This journal offers research into and discussion of philosophical topics in aesthetics, whether in architecture, theater, literature, art, photography, and other types. Moreover, the aesthetic theories of individual philosophers, e.g., Plato, Hume, Kant, Hutcheson, Collingwood, and Scruton, are examined and analyzed. The articles, symposia, and discussions look at aesthetics and aesthetic experiences from a variety of perspectives, including philosophical, psychological, sociological, scientific, historical, critical, and educational perspectives. This is a useful journal for collections that support teaching and theory of the fine arts.

4206. *Canadian Journal of Philosophy.* [ISSN: 0045-5091] 1971. bi-m. GBP 168 (print & online eds.). Taylor & Francis, 4 Park Sq, Milton Park, Abingdon, OX14 4RN, United Kingdom; subscriptions@tandf.co.uk; http://www.tandfonline.com. Illus., index. Refereed. Vol. ends: No. 4. Microform: MML. *Indexed:* A01, A22, AmHI, ArtHuCI, BRI, C37, CBCARef, E01, FR, IBSS, IPB, MLA-IB, MSN, P02. *Bk. rev.:* 2-5, 2,500-5,000 words. *Aud.:* Ac.

Ethics, social and political philosophy, epistemology, and the history of philosophy constitute the core strengths of this leading Canadian journal of philosophy, and it will be a good offering for collections that support research in these areas. Most articles are in English, though there are, from time to time, articles in French. Additionally, a subscription includes an annual thematic supplementary volume with a collection of articles on a single topic.

4207. *Charles S. Peirce Society. Transactions: a quarterly journal in American philosophy.* [ISSN: 0009-1774] 1965. q. USD 113 (print & online eds.). Ed(s): Douglas R Anderson, Scott Pratt. Indiana University Press, 601 N Morton St, Bloomington, IN 47404; journals@indiana.edu; http://iupress.indiana.edu. Adv. Sample. Refereed. Circ: 600. Reprint: PSC. *Indexed:* A01, A22, AmHI, ArtHuCI, BRI, E01, FR, IPB, MLA-IB, MSN. *Bk. rev.:* 2-4, 1,500-2,000 words, signed. *Aud.:* Ac.

This journal is the official publication of the Charles S. Peirce Society. While its general focus is on the study of the work of Charles S. Peirce, readers will often find excellent research on other American philosophers—James, Royce, Mead, and Emerson, for example—and the history of philosophy and intellectual history in the United States, especially in regard to Pragmatism. This journal is recommended for studies in American philosophy and American intellectual history, with applications to related disciplines such as the histories of psychology and sociology.

Criminal Justice Ethics. See Criminology and Law Enforcement section.

4208. *Dialogue: Canadian philosophical review/revue Canadienne de philosophie.* [ISSN: 0012-2173] 1962. q. GBP 118 (print & online eds.). Ed(s): Mathieu Marion, Eric Dayton. Cambridge University Press, The Edinburgh Bldg, Shaftesbury Rd, Cambridge, CB2 8RU, United Kingdom; journals@cambridge.org; http://journals.cambridge.org. Illus., adv. Refereed. Circ: 1200 Paid. *Indexed:* A22, AmHI, ArtHuCI, BRI, C37, CBCARef, CBRI, CCMJ, FR, IPB, MLA-IB, MSN, MathR, P61, RILM, SSA. *Bk. rev.:* 10-15, 500-2,500 words. *Aud.:* Ac.

Dialogue is the official journal of the Canadian Philosophical Association, with the stated editorial goal of fostering dialog between Anglophone and Francophone Canadian philosophers. To this end, the contents of this journal are in French and English, and cover all areas of philosophy from both analytic and Continental perspectives. A single issue may, for example, contain articles on Wittgenstein, Ricoeur, Searle, and analytic discussions of externalism versus internalism. As the discipline of philosophy moves beyond a hard-line analytic/Continental divide, this journal is a good example of how dialog between the two views can occur.

4209. *Diogenes (English Edition).* [ISSN: 0392-1921] 1952. q. USD 702. Ed(s): Maurice Aymard, Luca Maria Scarantino. Sage Publications Ltd., 1 Oliver's Yard, 55 City Rd, London, EC1Y 1SP, United Kingdom; info@sagepub.com; http://www.uk.sagepub.com. Illus., index, adv. Sample. Refereed. Vol. ends: No. 4. Reprint: PSC. *Indexed:* A01, A22, ABS&EES, AmHI, ArtHuCI, BRI, E01, IPB, MLA-IB, P02. *Aud.:* Ga, Ac.

Diogenes is published under the auspices of the International Council for Philosophy and Humanistic Studies with the support of UNESCO, initially in French, with the English-language edition appearing the following year. The perspective of the research in this journal is generally from the social sciences, whether anthropological, sociological, economic, educational, and historical, though the humanities are represented as well, with literature, drama, and political science being prominent. This is a good journal for interdisciplinary collections and programs, and collections that support the social science and humanities fields listed above.

Environmental Ethics. See Environment and Conservation section.

4210. *Erkenntnis: an international journal of analytic philosophy.* [ISSN: 0165-0106] 1930. bi-m. EUR 1159 (print & online eds.). Ed(s): Hans Rott. Springer Netherlands, Van Godewijckstraat 30, Dordrecht, 3311 GX, Netherlands; http://www.springer.com. Illus., index, adv. Sample. Refereed. Vol. ends: No. 3. Microform: PQC. Reprint: PSC. *Indexed:* A22, AmHI, ArtHuCI, BRI, CCMJ, E01, FR, IPB, MSN, MathR. *Bk. rev.:* 1-2, 1,500-2,500 words. *Aud.:* Ac.

Erkenntnis is a long-time top-tier journal in analytic philosophy. Its offerings tend to be highly technical articles that either analyze current systematic issues or present original research in epistemology, philosophical logic, philosophy of mathematics, philosophy of science, ontology and metaphysics, philosophy of mind, and practical philosophy (e.g., philosophy of action, philosophy of law, and ethics). There are occasionally articles in German, but for the most part the journal is in English. There are regular special thematic issues over the course of the year. This journal is best for collections that support graduate-level coursework in philosophy, especially in the fields listed above.

4211. *Essays in Philosophy.* [ISSN: 1526-0569] 2000. s-a. Free. Ed(s): David Boersema. Pacific University, 2043 College Way, Forest Grove, OR 97116; silkroad.pacific@gmail.com. Refereed. *Indexed:* AmHI, MLA-IB. *Bk. rev.:* Number varies, 1,000-4,000 words. *Aud.:* Ac.

This is a free e-journal that publishes issues centered on specific themes that are coordinated by guest editors. The articles are from a variety of philosophical perspectives and styles, with no one system, figure, or style dominating. Recent issues have focused on philosophy of language, philosophy of science, and ethics.

4212. *Ethical Theory and Moral Practice: an international forum.* [ISSN: 1386-2820] 1998. 5x/yr. EUR 483 (print & online eds.). Ed(s): Albert W Musschenga, F R Heeger. Springer Netherlands, Van Godewijckstraat 30, Dordrecht, 3311 GX, Netherlands; http://www.springer.com. Illus., adv. Sample. Refereed. Reprint: PSC. *Indexed:* A01, A22, AmHI, ArtHuCI, BRI, E01, FR, IBSS, IPB, P02. *Bk. rev.:* 2-3, 1,500-3,000 words. *Aud.:* Ac, Sa.

The editorial aim of this journal is to encourage interdisciplinary cooperation between ethics, medicine, economics, psychology, sociology, and law, so as to lessen the divide between theoretical and applied ethics. There is a wide variety of articles offered in this respect, from analyses of Platonic dialogs to contemporary discussions of organ donation, and from a range of philosophical perspectives. Contributions are in French, German, and English. The third number of each volume contains papers presented at the Annual Conference of the British Society for Ethical Theory. For collections with strong holdings in ethics and that support interdisciplinary studies with a strong basis in ethics, this is an important specialized publication.

4213. *Ethics: an international journal of social, political, and legal philosophy.* Former titles (until 1938): *International Journal of Ethics;* (until 1890): *The Ethical Record.* [ISSN: 0014-1704] 1888. q. USD 271 (print & online eds.). Ed(s): Catherine M Galko Campbell, Henry S Richardson. University of Chicago Press, 1427 E 60th St, Chicago, IL 60637; subscriptions@press.uchicago.edu; http://www.journals.uchicago.edu. Illus., adv. Sample. Refereed. Vol. ends: Jul. Microform: MIM; PMC; PQC. Reprint: PSC. *Indexed:* A01, A22, AmHI, ArtHuCI, BRI, CBRI, CLI, FR, IBSS, IPB, L14, MLA-IB, P02, P61, SSA. *Bk. rev.:* 35-45, 250-7,500 words, signed. *Aud.:* Ac.

Ethics is one of the premier philosophy journals in the fields of social and political philosophy and ethics. The discussions found in the articles of this journal range across traditional and contemporary normative theories, metaethics, philosophy of law, public policy issues, religious ethics, normative economics, international law, and social and rational choice theory. The journal

also features theme-centered symposia on various topics or recently published works in ethics and related fields. *Ethics* is a great journal for general collections and for collections that support work in ethics, law, and economics.

4214. *Ethics & Behavior.* [ISSN: 1050-8422] 1991. bi-m. GBP 675 (print & online eds.). Ed(s): Gerald P Koocher. Routledge, 325 Chestnut St, Ste 800, Philadelphia, PA 19106; customerservice@taylorandfrancis.com; http://www.tandfonline.com. Illus., adv. Sample. Refereed. Vol. ends: No. 4. Reprint: PSC. *Indexed:* A01, A22, ABIn, ASSIA, E01, P02, P61, PsycInfo, RiskAb, SSA. *Bk. rev.:* 1-3, 750-1,000 words. *Aud.:* Ac.

The articles in this journal examine ethical and social responsibility in human behavior, ethical dilemmas and professional (mis)conduct in health and human services delivery. The research found in this journal tends to be more empirically-based in nature than the articles found in more theoretically-oriented journals like *Ethics* (see below in this section). The audience of this journal is primarily clinical practitioners in psychology, psychiatry, psychotherapy, and counseling. Nonetheless, *Ethics & Behavior* will be useful in supporting research in applied ethics.

4215. *European Journal of Philosophy.* [ISSN: 0966-8373] 1993. q. GBP 463. Wiley-Blackwell Publishing Ltd., The Atrium, Southern Gate, Chichester, PO19 8SQ, United Kingdom; customer@wiley.com; http://www.wiley.com/. Illus., index, adv. Sample. Refereed. Vol. ends: No. 3. Reprint: PSC. *Indexed:* A01, A22, AmHI, ArtHuCI, E01, IBSS, IPB, P02. *Bk. rev.:* 7-10, 2,000-3,000 words. *Aud.:* Ac.

As a previous annotator wrote, "This journal was founded with the goal of serving as a forum for the exchange of ideas among philosophers working within the various European schools of thought, who tended to be culturally isolated before the political upheavals of the 1990s." The articles are from contributors around the Anglophone philosophical world, and include discussions on topics and figures from both Continental and analytic philosophy, historical and contemporary. The journal also publishes annually the The Mark Sacks Lecture, named in honor of the journal's late founder. Recommended for collections that focus broadly on European philosophy.

4216. *Faith and Philosophy.* [ISSN: 0739-7046] 1984. q. USD 79 (Individuals, USD 45; Free to members). Ed(s): Michael L Peterson, Thomas P Flint. Philosophy Documentation Center, PO Box 7147, Charlottesville, VA 22906; order@pdcnet.org; http://www.pdcnet.org. Illus., index, adv. Refereed. Microform: PQC. *Indexed:* A22, IPB, R&TA. *Bk. rev.:* 3-5, 1,500-3,000 words. *Aud.:* Ac.

Faith and Philosophy offers articles that examine philosophical issues, questions, and foundations from a Christian perspective. Major scholars in philosophy of religion such as Marilyn McCord Adams, Robert Audi, Alvin Plantiga, Elliot Sober, and William Wainwright contribute to this journal. There are also reviews of recent books in the field. For libraries that support work in philosophy of religion and religious studies, the journal's quality and low price make it an attractive addition to these collections.

4217. *History and Philosophy of Logic.* [ISSN: 0144-5340] 1980. q. GBP 597 (print & online eds.). Ed(s): Volker Peckhaus. Taylor & Francis, 4 Park Sq, Milton Park, Abingdon, OX14 4RN, United Kingdom; http://www.tandfonline.com. Illus., adv. Sample. Refereed. Vol. ends: No. 4. Reprint: PSC. *Indexed:* A01, A22, ArtHuCI, CCMJ, E01, IPB, MSN, MathR. *Bk. rev.:* 6-8, 750-1,500 words. *Aud.:* Ac.

The research found in this journal addresses the general history and philosophy of logic, with the exception of very recent work and highly specialized studies in this area of philosophy. All periods of history and all areas of the world are covered. Articles are in French, English, or German, examining the existential and ontological aspects of logic, analyzing the relationship between classical and nonclassical logic, and exploring the application of logic to mathematics, economics, science, and linguistics, for instance. Logicians and logic students looking for current research on major historical figures such as Aristotle, Leibniz, Frege, Russell, Tarski, and Wittgenstein will find this journal to be of great use.

4218. *History of Philosophy Quarterly.* [ISSN: 0740-0675] 1984. q. USD 297 (print or online ed.) Individuals, USD 55). Ed(s): Nicholas Rescher, Jeffrey Tlumak. University of Illinois Press, 1325 S Oak St, Champaign, IL 61820; journals@uillinois.edu; http://www.press.uillinois.edu. Illus., index, adv. Sample. Refereed. Vol. ends: No. 4. *Indexed:* A22, IPB. *Aud.:* Ac.

This journal in the history of philosophy explores major philosophers and historical topics from antiquity to the present, emphasizing the value and relevance of historical studies for contemporary issues. Notable is that the journal also offers Asian philosophers such as Confucius and Zhuangzi. This journal serves as a useful complement to the *Journal of the History of Philosophy,* the definite first choice for most academic libraries.

4219. *Human Studies: a journal for philosophy and the social sciences.* [ISSN: 0163-8548] 1978. q. EUR 632 (print & online eds.). Ed(s): Martin Endress. Springer Netherlands, Van Godewijckstraat 30, Dordrecht, 3311 GX, Netherlands; http://www.springer.com. Illus., index, adv. Sample. Refereed. Vol. ends: No. 4. Microform: PQC. Reprint: PSC. *Indexed:* A01, A22, ABS&EES, BRI, E01, IBSS, IPB, MLA-IB, P61, RILM, SSA. *Bk. rev.:* 1-3, 1,000-3,000 words. *Aud.:* Ac.

This publication is the official journal of the Society for Phenomenology and the Human Sciences. Its articles are generally written from a phenomenological perspective and discuss empirical, methodological, philosophical, and theoretical topics in the social sciences. Thus, there is a definite Continental slant to the journal, with recent articles on, e.g., Foucault and Heidegger. Good for library collections with strong holdings in the social sciences and in Continental philosophy, as well as for interdisciplinary programs.

4220. *Hume Studies.* [ISSN: 0319-7336] 1975. s-a. USD 60 (Individuals, USD 35; Students, USD 25). Ed(s): Corliss Swain. Hume Society, c/o Saul Traiger, Department of Philosophy, Los Angeles, CA 90041; president@humesociety.org; http://www.humesociety.org. Illus. Refereed. Vol. ends: No. 2. Microform: MML. Reprint: PSC. *Indexed:* A22, ArtHuCI, BRI, E01, FR, IPB. *Bk. rev.:* 5-7, 1,000-1,500 words. *Aud.:* Ac.

This journal is the scholarly organ of the Hume Society, devoted to historical, systematic, and bibliographic research on the philosophy of David Hume. Thus, the content of this journal includes the topics of metaphysics, epistemology, philosophy of mind, ethics, political philosophy, and philosophy of religion in light of Hume's oeuvre and thought. It also includes research that analyzes Hume's thought in relation to the ideas of his predecessors and contemporaries. This journal is good for collections that support research in early modern philosophy and British philosophy.

4221. *Husserl Studies.* [ISSN: 0167-9848] 1984. 3x/yr. EUR 461 (print & online eds.). Ed(s): Sonia Rinofner, Steven Crowell. Springer Netherlands, Van Godewijckstraat 30, Dordrecht, 3311 GX, Netherlands; http://www.springer.com. Illus., index, adv. Sample. Refereed. Microform: PQC. Reprint: PSC. *Indexed:* A22, AmHI, ArtHuCI, BRI, E01, FR, IPB. *Bk. rev.:* 1-3, 1,500-3,000 words. *Aud.:* Ac.

Husserl Studies is to scholarship on Edmund Husserl and his work as *Hume Studies* (above) is to scholarship on David Hume and his work. The articles of this journal present historical, systematic, interpretive, and comparative studies on Husserl and the phenomenological movement that he founded. In recent years, the editors have widened the scope of the journal to include other areas of phenomenological research that develop, promote, adapt, and critique Husserlian phenomenology. They are also accepting contributions that relate phenomenology to, e.g., critical theory, analytic philosophy, and hermeneutics. Articles found in this journal are in English and German. A good journal for collections strong in Continental and European philosophy.

Hypatia. See Gender Studies section.

4222. *Idealistic Studies.* [ISSN: 0046-8541] 1971. 3x/yr. USD 64 (Individuals, USD 35). Ed(s): Gary Overvold. Philosophy Documentation Center, PO Box 7147, Charlottesville, VA 22906; order@pdcnet.org; http://www.pdcnet.org. Illus., index, adv. Sample. Refereed. Vol. ends: No. 3. Reprint: PSC. *Indexed:* A01, A22, AmHI, ArtHuCI, FR, IPB, MLA-IB. *Aud.:* Ac.

This journal offers research into idealism, historical and contemporary, both in terms of topics and in terms of figures, such as Berkeley, Hegel, Fichte, Schelling, Bradley, McTaggart, Foucault, Freud, and Wittgenstein. There is also examination of the legacy and influence of idealism in other philosophical movements like phenomenology, neo-Kantianism, Pragmatism, existentialism, and hermeneutics, for example. This journal would be good for general collections.

4223. *Inquiry: an interdisciplinary journal of philosophy.* [ISSN: 0020-174X] 1958. bi-m. GBP 337 (print & online eds.). Ed(s): Herman Cappelen. Routledge, 4 Park Sq, Milton Park, Abingdon, OX14 4RN, United Kingdom; subscriptions@tandf.co.uk; http://www.tandfonline.com. Illus., index, adv. Sample. Refereed. Vol. ends: No. 4. Microform: PQC. Reprint: PSC. *Indexed:* A01, A22, AmHI, ArtHuCI, B01, BAS, BRI, E01, FR, IBSS, IPB, MCR, MLA-IB, P02, P61, SSA, SWR&A. *Bk. rev.:* 1-3, 1,500-3,000 words. *Aud.:* Ac.

Inquiry is an interdisciplinary journal with articles mainly in the areas of metaphysics, epistemology, philosophy of mind, ethics, aesthetics, social and political philosophy, and Continental philosophy. There are often special issues devoted to a single topic with contributions from top scholars around the world. As an interdisciplinary journal, the research often looks at topics from perspectives and figures — e.g., Kierkegaard — that are not as mainstream in contemporary analytic discourse. This journal is a good one to have in all collections.

International Journal for Philosophy of Religion. See Religion section.

4224. *International Journal of Philosophical Studies (Print).* Formerly (until 1993): *Philosophical Studies (Print).* [ISSN: 0967-2559] 1951. 5x/yr. GBP 637 (print & online eds.). Ed(s): Maria Baghramian. Routledge, 4 Park Sq, Milton Park, Abingdon, OX14 4RN, United Kingdom; subscriptions@tandf.co.uk; http://www.tandfonline.com. Illus., adv. Sample. Refereed. Reprint: PSC. *Indexed:* A01, A22, AmHI, ArtHuCI, E01, FR, IBSS, IPB. *Bk. rev.:* 10-15, 2,000-7,500 words. *Aud.:* Ac.

This journal, relaunched in 1993, aims to promote comprehension and dialog between analytic and Continental philosophers on current topics of philosophy. There is also discussion of the history of philosophy and how this discussion can illuminate contemporary debates. Additionally, the journal carries lengthy book reviews; recent reviews have looked at Heidegger, analytic discussions of philosophy of language, and Confucianism. This journal would be good for general collections.

4225. *International Philosophical Quarterly.* [ISSN: 0019-0365] 1961. q. USD 72 (Individuals, USD 37; USD 30 in developing nations). Ed(s): Joseph W Koterski. Philosophy Documentation Center, PO Box 7147, Charlottesville, VA 22906; order@pdcnet.org; http://www.pdcnet.org. Illus., index, adv. Sample. Refereed. Vol. ends: No. 4. Microform: PQC. Reprint: PSC. *Indexed:* A01, A22, ABS&EES, AmHI, ArtHuCI, BAS, BEL&L, BRI, CBRI, FR, IPB, MLA-IB, P02, RILM. *Bk. rev.:* 10-15, 500-1,000 words. *Aud.:* Ac.

This journal is a joint collaboration of Fordham University and the Facultes Universitaires Notre-Dame de la Paix (Namur, Belgium). It serves as an international forum for philosophical discussion between Europe, the United States, and the East, with an orientation in the intercultural tradition of theistic, spiritualist, and personalist humanism. Moreover, there are short book reviews in each issue. This is a good journal for general collections and for collections that support work in East–West intellectual exchanges.

Journal of Aesthetics and Art Criticism. See Cultural Studies section.

4226. *The Journal of Ethics: an international philosophical review.* [ISSN: 1382-4554] 1997. q. EUR 592 (print & online eds.). Ed(s): J Angelo Corlett. Springer Netherlands, Van Godewijckstraat 30, Dordrecht, 3311 GX, Netherlands; http://www.springer.com. Illus., adv. Sample. Refereed. Vol. ends: No. 4. Reprint: PSC. *Indexed:* A01, A22, BRI, E01, FR, IPB. *Bk. rev.:* 1-2, 2,000-3,000 words, signed. *Aud.:* Ac.

This journal, as the title indicates, publishes research that addresses contemporary and historical issues and personages in ethics, moral philosophy, political philosophy, and public affairs. While its primary orientation is philosophical, the journal description notes that its contents will be of value not only to philosophers, but also to other academics and professionals whose work touches on these fields. This journal is an excellent choice for collections with strong holdings in ethics, law and government collections, and medical ethics.

4227. Journal of Ethics & Social Philosophy: journal of moral, political and legal philosophy. [ISSN: 1559-3061] 2005. irreg. Free. Ed(s): Andrei Marmor, Julia Driver. University of Southern California, Gould School of Law, University Park, Los Angeles, CA 90089; academicsupport@law.usc.edu; http://lawweb.usc.edu. Refereed. *Indexed:* AmHI, L14. *Aud.:* Ac.

This free electronic journal is published by the Center for Law and Philosophy at the University of Southern California. It offers articles and shorter discussion notes on topics relevant to contemporary ethical, political, and legal issues, and would be useful for collections that support these areas of study. The contributors are prominent scholars in these sub-fields of philosophy as well as up-and-coming scholars and graduate students.

4228. Journal of Indian Philosophy. [ISSN: 0022-1791] 1970. bi-m. EUR 919 (print & online eds.). Ed(s): Phyllis Granoff. Springer Netherlands, Van Godewijckstraat 30, Dordrecht, 3311 GX, Netherlands; http://www.springer.com. Illus., index, adv. Sample. Refereed. Microform: PQC. Reprint: PSC. *Indexed:* A22, AmHI, ArtHuCI, BAS, BRI, E01, FR, IBSS, IPB, MLA-IB. *Aud.:* Sa.

This is a highly specialized and technical journal for the study of the philosophical and religious traditions of the Indian subcontinent and Tibet, particularly Hinduism, Buddhism, and Jainism. The articles address traditional and contemporary arguments and issues in metaphysics, epistemology, philosophical logic, philosophy of language, philosophy of religion, and ethics. From time to time, special thematic issues coordinated by guest editors are offered. This is a graduate-level journal for collections that support the study of Eastern philosophy and religion.

4229. Journal of Moral Philosophy. [ISSN: 1740-4681] 2004. bi-m. EUR 510. Ed(s): Thom Brooks. Brill, PO Box 9000, Leiden, 2300 PA, Netherlands; cs@brill.nl; http://www.brill.nl. Adv. Refereed. Reprint: PSC. *Indexed:* A01, A22, ArtHuCI, E01, P61, SSA. *Aud.:* Ac.

This journal offers articles, discussions, and review essays on historical and contemporary issues in ethics, political philosophy, and jurisprudence. There is a nice mix of articles from several philosophical perspectives found in the journal's contents. For instance, recent issues have contained articles on analytic, Continental, and Pragmatist themes. The journal publishes one thematic issue annually. It is a good supplement to *Ethics* and *The Journal of Ethics* (see above in this section) for those collections seeking a journal with broader topic offerings in the field of ethics.

4230. Journal of Nietzsche Studies. [ISSN: 0968-8005] 1991. s-a. USD 166 (print & online eds.). Ed(s): Christa Davis Acampora. Pennsylvania State University Press, 820 N University Dr, University Support Bldg 1, Ste C, University Park, PA 16802; info@psupress.org; http://www.psupress.org. Adv. Sample. Refereed. Reprint: PSC. *Indexed:* A01, A22, AmHI, ArtHuCI, E01, MLA-IB. *Bk. rev.:* 5-15, 1,500-2,500 words. *Aud.:* Ac.

The Friedrich Nietzsche Society sponsors this prominent journal of scholarship on all areas of Nietzsche's intellectual project, authored by leading international researchers. Attention is given not only to scholarship and interpretation of Nietzsche, but also to his relevance to contemporary issues. Several reviews of recent works in Nietzsche scholarship are contained in every issue. Nietzsche casts a long shadow over philosophy and German intellectual history. Thus, collections that support philosophy (especially twentieth-century Continental philosophy) and German intellectual history will want to subscribe to it.

4231. Journal of Philosophical Logic. [ISSN: 0022-3611] 1972. bi-m. EUR 895 (print & online eds.). Ed(s): B Fitelson, John Horty. Springer Netherlands, Van Godewijckstraat 30, Dordrecht, 3311 GX, Netherlands; http://www.springer.com. Illus., index, adv. Sample. Refereed. Microform: PQC. Reprint: PSC. *Indexed:* A01, A22, AmHI, ArtHuCI, CCMJ, E01, FR, IPB, MLA-IB, MSN, MathR. *Aud.:* Sa.

This journal is one of the leading journals in all things and topics related to logic. It is published by the Association for Symbolic Logic. In addition to looking at topics in logic, the articles also examine areas of ontology, philosophy of language, philosophy of mathematics, philosophy of science, and epistemology that relate to formal logic. This journal is best for graduate-level collections, especially those that support work in logic and the related fields just listed.

4232. Journal of Philosophy. Formerly (until 1921): *The Journal of Philosophy, Psychology and Scientific Methods.* [ISSN: 0022-362X] 1904. m. USD 100 (Individuals, USD 45; Students, USD 20). Ed(s): John Smylie. Journal of Philosophy, Inc., c/o John Smylie, 1150 Amsterdam Ave, New York, NY 10027. Illus., index, adv. Refereed. Vol. ends: No. 12. Microform: PMC. *Indexed:* A01, A06, A22, AmHI, ArtHuCI, BEL&L, BRI, CBRI, CCMJ, FR, IBSS, IPB, MLA-IB, MSN, MathR, P02. *Bk. rev.:* 1-2, 1,000-3,000 words. *Aud.:* Ac.

This journal has long been a top-tier American philosophy journal, publishing two or three articles per issue (along with one or two book reviews) on topics and problems of interest and relevance to the professional academic philosophy community in the United States. Prominent philosophers from around the United States contribute their work in metaphysics, epistemology, philosophy of mind, philosophy of language, philosophical logic, social and political philosophy, ethics, action theory, and aesthetics to this journal. Definitely a core publication for academic libraries.

Journal of Philosophy of Education. See Education/Comparative Education and International section.

4233. The Journal of Philosophy, Science & Law. [ISSN: 1549-8549] 2001. bi-m. Free. Ed(s): Jason Borenstein. The Journal of Philosophy, Science and Law, c/o Jason Borenstein, School of Public Policy, PO Box 4089, Atlanta, GA 30332-0345; jason.borenstein@pubpolicy.gatech.edu. Refereed. *Bk. rev.:* Number and length vary. *Aud.:* Ac.

The University of Miami Ethics Programs and the Georgia Institute of Technology School of Public Policy co-sponsor this free e-journal. The contributors to this journal examine the moral and legal aspects of scientific evidence; research in science and technology; teaching ethical and legal guidelines within the scientific disciplines; and bioethics from a philosophical perspective. The journal also publishes news items and editorials. A good offering for collections that support ethics and law, especially in connection with the sciences.

4234. Journal of Speculative Philosophy. [ISSN: 0891-625X] 1867. q. USD 182 (print & online eds.). Ed(s): John J Stuhr, Vincent M Colapietro. Pennsylvania State University Press, 820 N University Dr, University Support Bldg 1, Ste C, University Park, PA 16802; info@psupress.org; http://www.psupress.org. Illus., index, adv. Refereed. Vol. ends: No. 4. Microform: PQC. Reprint: PSC. *Indexed:* A01, A22, AmHI, E01, IPB. *Bk. rev.:* 2-10, 750-1,250 words. *Aud.:* Ac.

The original edition of this journal, begun in 1867, was the first American journal devoted to philosophy. Many notable figures in American philosophy during this time, such as James, Dewey, and Peirce, published some of their early work in here. The contents of this journal focus on systematic and interpretive analyses of basic philosophical questions, especially when they are tied to the aims and methodology of Pragmatism. The hope is that the work of this journal promotes a constructive interaction between Continental and American philosophy, rather than present the history of philosophical movements or historical figures. Moreover, the journal does not limit itself to research that is strictly or narrowly philosophical in presentation: articles on art, literature, and religion, for example, are explored from other perspectives. This is a good journal for collections that support American philosophy, American intellectual history, and Continental philosophy programs.

4235. *The Journal of Symbolic Logic.* [ISSN: 0022-4812] 1936. q. Free to members; Non-members, USD 575 (print or online ed.). Association for Symbolic Logic, 124 Raymond Ave, Vassar College, PO Box 742, Poughkeepsie, NY 12604; asl@vassar.edu; http://www.aslonline.org. Illus., index. Refereed. Circ: 2500. Vol. ends: No. 4. Microform: PMC; PQC. *Indexed:* A22, AmHI, BRI, CCMJ, IPB, MLA-IB, MSN, MathR. *Bk. rev.:* 10-15, 1,000-2,000 words. *Aud.:* Sa.

This journal is best for professional logicians and mathematicians interested in highly technical and specialized articles in symbolic and mathematical logic. It should be a core title for graduate-level collections. Sponsored by the Association for Symbolic Logic, this journal also includes a subscription to *The Bulletin of Symbolic Logic.* The contents of this latter journal, a quarterly publication, are of a more general and broader type, and include announcements of new ideas and results in all areas of logic, along with a "Reviews Section."

Journal of the History of Ideas. See Cultural Studies section.

4236. *Journal of the History of Philosophy.* [ISSN: 0022-5053] 1963. q. USD 125. Ed(s): Henry Southgate, Steven Nadler. The Johns Hopkins University Press, 2715 N Charles St, Baltimore, MD 21218; http://www.press.jhu.edu. Illus., index, adv. Sample. Refereed. Circ: 805. Vol. ends: No. 4. Microform: PQC. Reprint: PSC. *Indexed:* A01, A22, AmHI, ArtHuCI, BEL&L, BRI, E01, FR, IBSS, IPB, MLA-IB, P02. *Bk. rev.:* 15-20, 750-1,000 words. *Aud.:* Ac.

This is a core journal for general collections, focusing on the history of Western philosophy. Although the articles focus for the most part on the works and ideas of the major philosophers, readers will, from time to time, find work published on less-mainstream figures (such as the Islamic philosophers Averroes and Ibn Tufayl); lesser-known medieval and Renaissance philosophers like Chatton, Desgabets, and Giles of Rome; and scientists such as Boyle and Newton. Most articles are in English, but work in other languages sometimes appears. Finally, the "Current Scholarship" section provides critical literature reviews on selected historical figures and philosophical topics, a useful feature for scholars exploring current work on certain figures and areas in the history of philosophy.

4237. *The Journal of Value Inquiry.* [ISSN: 0022-5363] 1967. q. EUR 773 (print & online eds.). Ed(s): Thomas Magnell. Springer Netherlands, Van Godewijckstraat 30, Dordrecht, 3311 GX, Netherlands; http://www.springer.com. Illus., index, adv. Sample. Refereed. Vol. ends: Oct/Dec. Microform: PQC. Reprint: PSC. *Indexed:* A22, ABIn, AmHI, ArtHuCI, BRI, E01, FR, IPB, MLA-IB, RILM. *Bk. rev.:* 3-5, 1,000-2,000 words. *Aud.:* Ac.

This prominent journal discusses issues and concerns of axiology, i.e., the study of values and value judgments. Thus, the articles found in its pages focus on the nature, justification, and epistemic status of values. There are likewise studies examining values in the respective contexts of, for example, aesthetics, ethics, law, medicine, politics, science, society, and technology. Good for general collections, and especially for collections that support ethics and related fields.

4238. *Kant Studien: philosophische Zeitschrift der Kant-Gesellschaft.* [ISSN: 0022-8877] 1896. q. EUR 207. Ed(s): Manfred Baum, Thomas M Seebohm. Walter de Gruyter GmbH & Co. KG, Genthiner Str 13, Berlin, 10785, Germany; info@degruyter.com; http://www.degruyter.de. Illus., index, adv. Refereed. Circ: 1000 Paid and controlled. Vol. ends: No. 4. Reprint: SCH. *Indexed:* A22, AmHI, ArtHuCI, BRI, E01, FR, IPB, MLA-IB. *Bk. rev.:* 4-6, 750-1,500 words. *Aud.:* Ac.

As the title indicates, the primary focus of this journal is the thought and works of the Immanuel Kant. With articles in French, German, and English by top scholars, this journal looks not only at Kant's work, but the work of other philosophers and issues that fall broadly within the frame of transcendental philosophy, such as Descartes, Leibniz, Hume, Hegel, and Frege. The fourth issue of the year includes a great bibliography of recent work in Kant. A good journal for a general collection, and for those collections that emphasize early modern thought.

4239. *Law and Philosophy: an international journal for jurisprudence and legal philosophy.* [ISSN: 0167-5249] 1982. bi-m. EUR 923 (print & online eds.). Ed(s): Douglas N Husak. Springer Netherlands, Van Godewijckstraat 30, Dordrecht, 3311 GX, Netherlands; http://

www.springer.com. Illus., index, adv. Sample. Refereed. Microform: WSH; PQC. Reprint: PSC. *Indexed:* A22, BRI, CLI, E01, IBSS, IPB, L14, P61, SSA. *Bk. rev.:* Occasional, 750-1,500 words. *Aud.:* Ac.

This journal is a great source of contemporary philosophical discussions of justice, rights, liberty, punishment, moral and criminal responsibility, legal ethics, legal positivism, and legal reasoning and interpretation. As such, it will be of value to collections that support moral, political and legal philosophy, law, and criminology studies.

Linguistics and Philosophy. See Linguistics section.

4240. *Logique et Analyse.* Formerly (until 1958): *Centre National Belge de Recherches de Logique. Bulletin Interieur.* [ISSN: 0024-5836] 1954. q. Nationaal Centrum voor Navorsingen in de Logica, c/o Jean-Paul van Bendegem, Vrije Universiteit Brussel, Faculteit Letteren en Wijsbegeer, Sectie Wijsbegeerte, Brussels, 1050, Belgium; jpvbende@vub.ac.be. Illus., index. Refereed. Circ: 1000. Vol. ends: Dec. *Indexed:* A01, A22, ArtHuCI, CCMJ, IPB, MLA-IB, MSN, MathR. *Aud.:* Sa.

The Centre National de Recherches de Logique/Nationaal Centrum voor Navorsingen in de Logica publishes this quarterly journal. The contents are in English, French, German, and Dutch. The articles are highly technical, examining philosophical and symbolic logic, philosophy of language, and philosophy of mathematics. Moreover, the journal publishes selected papers from the annual conference of the Dutch-Flemish Association for Analytic Philosophy (Vereniging voor Analytische Filosofie). For graduate-level collections, especially those that support logic.

4241. *Metaphilosophy.* [ISSN: 0026-1068] 1970. q. GBP 481. Ed(s): Armen T Marsoobian, Otto Bohlmann. Wiley-Blackwell Publishing Ltd., The Atrium, Southern Gate, Chichester, PO19 8SQ, United Kingdom; customer@wiley.com; http://www.wiley.com/. Illus., adv. Sample. Refereed. Vol. ends: No. 4. Reprint: PSC. *Indexed:* A01, A22, AmHI, ArtHuCI, E01, FR, IPB, MLA-IB, RILM. *Bk. rev.:* 2-6, 1,000-4,000 words. *Aud.:* Ac.

Metaphilosophy looks at foundational issues in philosophy: its scope, function, and direction, how philosophical methods and arguments are justified, and the relationships and connections between the various branches and persons of philosophy. Readers will also find discussions of the aspects and presuppositions of various philosophical schools, the relationship of philosophy to other academic disciplines, and philosophy's relevance to social and political action. *Metaphilosophy* has long been known to be on the cutting edge of publishing work on new trends in philosophy. A good journal for core collections.

4242. *Midwest Studies in Philosophy.* [ISSN: 0363-6550] 1976. a. GBP 437 (print or online ed.). Ed(s): Howard K Wettstein, Peter A French. Wiley-Blackwell Publishing, Inc., 111 River St, Hoboken, NJ 07030; info@wiley.com; http://www.wiley.com/. Adv. Sample. Reprint: PSC. *Indexed:* A01, A22, AmHI, E01, FR, IPB, RILM. *Aud.:* Ac.

Established in 1976, this journal has become a top-tier philosophy journal, publishing quality articles in an annual volume around a given philosophical area, theme, philosopher, or historical period. Contributors are philosophers at the top of their field or area of expertise. Several articles published in this journal are now considered classical works in contemporary philosophy. Topics and themes for the various issues range widely. Recent issues have looked at ontology, emotions, ethics, early modern philosophy, American philosophy, and film, for example. This should be a core journal for general philosophy collections.

4243. *Mind: a quarterly review of philosophy.* [ISSN: 0026-4423] 1876. q. EUR 214. Ed(s): Thomas Baldwin. Oxford University Press, Great Clarendon St, Oxford, OX2 6DP, United Kingdom; enquiry@oup.co.uk; http://www.oxfordjournals.org/. Illus., index, adv. Sample. Refereed. Vol. ends: No. 4. Microform: PMC; PQC. Reprint: PSC. *Indexed:* A01, A22, AmHI, ArtHuCI, BRI, CCMJ, E01, IPB, MLA-IB, MSN, MathR, P02, P61, SSA. *Bk. rev.:* 30-40, 1,500-2,000 words. *Aud.:* Ac.

Mind is one of the premier British philosophy journals. Many now-classic philosophy articles have appeared in its pages, especially under the editorships of G. K. Stout, G. E. Moore, and Gilbert Ryle. Readers will find articles, discussions, symposia, and critical notices that focus on epistemology, metaphysics, philosophy of language, philosophical logic, and philosophy of mind from an analytic perspective. A core journal for general collections.

4244. The Monist: an international quarterly journal of general philosophical inquiry. [ISSN: 0026-9662] 1888. q. USD 55 (Individuals, USD 35). Ed(s): George Reisch, Dr. Barry Smith. Hegeler Institute, c/o George Reisch, 315 Fifth St, Peru, IL 61354. Illus., index. Refereed. Vol. ends: No. 4. *Indexed:* A01, A22, AmHI, ArtHuCI, BRI, FR, IPB, MLA-IB, P02, P61, RILM, SSA. *Aud.:* Ac.

The six to eight articles that appear in each issue of the *The Monist* address a single topic that has been selected by the journal's editorial board and coordinated by an advisory editor. These topics range from the traditional, e.g., realism and the meaning of life, to the contemporary, e.g., multiculturalism, climate change, and racism under the broad aegis of the topic of ethics, though other areas of philosophy, such as metaphysics, the history of philosophy, and philosophy of language are also represented. Given its low cost and quality, this is a good addition for collections that support all levels of philosophy programs.

4245. Notre Dame Journal of Formal Logic. [ISSN: 0029-4527] 1960. q. USD 278. Ed(s): Peter Cholak, Michael Detlefsen. Duke University Press, 905 W Main St, Ste 18 B, PO Box 90660, Durham, NC 27701; subscriptions@dukeupress.edu; http://www.dukeupress.edu. Illus., index, adv. Sample. Refereed. Vol. ends: No. 4. Reprint: PSC. *Indexed:* A22, ArtHuCI, CCMJ, IPB, MSN, MathR. *Bk. rev.:* Occasional, 500-2,500 words. *Aud.:* Ac, Sa.

This is a good journal for scholars of philosophical and mathematical logic, especially in the areas of the philosophy, history, and foundations of logic and mathematics. Unlike in *The Journal of Symbolic Logic* (discussed above in this section), here there is more emphasis on the philosophy of language and formal semantics for natural languages. For graduate-level collections that support advanced work in logic.

4246. Nous. [ISSN: 0029-4624] 1967. q. GBP 538 (print or online ed.). Ed(s): Ernest Sosa. Wiley-Blackwell Publishing, Inc., 111 River St, Hoboken, NJ 07030; info@wiley.com; http://onlinelibrary.wiley.com/. Illus., index, adv. Sample. Refereed. Vol. ends: No. 4. Microform: PQC. Reprint: PSC. *Indexed:* A01, A22, AmHI, ArtHuCI, CCMJ, E01, FR, IPB, MSN, MathR, P02, P61, RILM. *Bk. rev.:* 2-3, 2,000-4,000 words. *Aud.:* Ac.

Nous is a well-respected philosophy journal that publishes on a variety of topics from an analytic perspective: metaphysics, epistemology, philosophical logic, philosophy of religion, ethics, and the history of philosophy. Additionally, a subscription to this journal includes the two annual supplementary publications, *Philosophical Perspectives* and *Philosophical Issues*. Finally, one recently published book receives a lengthy "Critical Study" in each issue. A top-tier core journal for general collections.

4247. Oxford Studies in Ancient Philosophy. [ISSN: 0265-7651] 1983. s-a. Oxford University Press, Great Clarendon St, Oxford, OX2 6DP, United Kingdom; enquiry@oup.co.uk; http://www.oxfordjournals.org/. Illus. Refereed. *Indexed:* IPB. *Aud.:* Ac.

This journal is a useful complement to *Phronesis* (discussed below in this section) in terms of scholarship in ancient philosophy. The primary focus of the articles in this journal is the work of Plato and Aristotle, but other figures and schools of antiquity are given space as well. The scholarship is more exegesis and critical analysis of primary texts rather than mere exposition. Articles here are somewhat longer than one usually finds in academic journals, given the more in-depth scholarship. There is an *Index Locorum*.in each volume. Good for collections that support classics programs and work in ancient philosophy, though more for advanced scholars.

4248. Pacific Philosophical Quarterly. Formerly (until Jan.1980): *Personalist.* [ISSN: 0279-0750] 1920. q. GBP 293. Ed(s): Indrek Reiland. Wiley-Blackwell Publishing Ltd., The Atrium, Southern Gate, Chichester, PO19 8SQ, United Kingdom; customer@wiley.com; http://www.wiley.com/. Illus., index, adv. Sample. Refereed. Vol. ends: No. 4. Microform: PQC. Reprint: PSC. *Indexed:* A01, A22, AmHI, ArtHuCI, BEL&L, E01, FR, IPB, MLA-IB, P02, RILM. *Aud.:* Ac.

Pacific Philosophical Quarterly is published on behalf of the School of Philosophy, University of Southern California. A solid journal in the analytic tradition, it publishes between four and seven articles per issue, with primary focus on metaphysics, epistemology, philosophy of science, philosophical logic, ethics, and the history of philosophy. From time to time, readers will find special thematic issues published. This is an excellent general analytic philosophy journal for collections that aim for comprehension in contemporary Anglo-American philosophy.

4249. Philosophers' Imprint. [ISSN: 1533-628X] 2001. q. Free. Ed(s): J David Velleman, Stephen Darwall. University of Michigan, Library, 435 S State St, An Arbor, MI 48109; http://www.lib.umich.edu/. Refereed. *Indexed:* ArtHuCI. *Aud.:* Ac.

This free e-journal began as a means of demonstrating that electronic publishing of philosophical scholarship can be of high quality and prestige. Since this time, under the editorship of the philosophy faculty at the University of Michigan, *Philosopher's Imprint* has established itself as one of the higher-quality electronic-only philosophy journals. Many prominent and up-and-coming philosophers publish work in metaphysics, epistemology, perception, logic, and the history of philosophy here. A great journal of value to philosophers and philosophical research.

4250. The Philosophical Forum. [ISSN: 0031-806X] 1942. q. GBP 308. Ed(s): Alan W Grose, Doug Lackey. Wiley-Blackwell Publishing, Inc., 111 River St, Hoboken, NJ 07030; info@wiley.com; http://onlinelibrary.wiley.com/. Illus., index, adv. Sample. Refereed. Vol. ends: No. 4. Reprint: PSC. *Indexed:* A01, A22, AmHI, ArtHuCI, BRI, E01, FR, IPB, MLA-IB, P02, P61, SSA. *Aud.:* Ac.

Philosophical Forum is known for fostering discussion of philosophical issues from diverse approaches and viewpoints, whether these be critical or constructive, speculative or analytic, systematic or historical. Recent issues have ranged from analyses of Rawls and anti-realism to Badiou, Derrida, and Husserl. It is a journal of interest to those curious about looking at philosophical topics and historical figures from perspectives that may be at the fringes or outside of the contemporary mainstream analytic world, especially in the areas of ethics, social and political philosophy, aesthetics, feminist philosophy, and Continental philosophy.

4251. Philosophical Investigations. [ISSN: 0190-0536] 1978. q. GBP 362. Ed(s): H O Mounce. Wiley-Blackwell Publishing Ltd., The Atrium, Southern Gate, Chichester, PO19 8SQ, United Kingdom; customer@wiley.com; http://www.wiley.com/. Illus., index, adv. Sample. Refereed. Vol. ends: No. 4. Reprint: PSC. *Indexed:* A01, A22, AmHI, ArtHuCI, E01, FR, IPB. *Bk. rev.:* 2-6, 1,000-5,000 words. *Aud.:* Ac.

This journal is of most interest to those scholars of Ludwig Wittgenstein, one of the twentieth century's most influential philosophers. Its contents are mostly critical studies of Wittgenstein's work, with the occasional selection from Wittgenstein's unpublished writings and lectures (based on the lecture notes of his students). The slant of the research published in *Philosophical Investigations* generally tends toward the standard tradition of Wittgensteinian exegesis and interpretation. However, readers will find work from scholars sympathetic to the resolute or therapeutic (the so-called New-Wittgenstein) within the journal's pages. Good for collections that support work in twentieth-century analytic philosophy and Wittgenstein scholars.

4252. Philosophical Practice: client counseling, group facilitation, and organizational consulting. [ISSN: 1742-8173] 2005. 3x/yr. USD 180 Free to members. Ed(s): Lauren Tillinghast, Lou Marinoff. American Philosophical Practitioners Association, The City College of New York, 160 Convent Ave, New York, NY 10031; admin@appa.edu; http://www.appa.edu/. Index, adv. Sample. Refereed. *Indexed:* A01, A22, E01. *Bk. rev.:* 3-4, 1,000-1,500 words. *Aud.:* Ac, Sa.

This is the official journal of American Philosophical Practitioners Association (APPA). Founded by Lou Marinoff, the APPA offers counseling and services from a philosophical perspective to a wide array of clients. Thus, the journal's contents examines how the methods and insights of philosophical analysis impact ethical, legal, social, and political issues in client counseling, clinical psychology, group facilitation, organizational consulting, human resources management, social work, psychotherapy, and psychiatry. While philosophical counseling is still a relatively new field, the work being done in this area will be of interest not only to philosophers, but to those working in counseling and human services fields like psychology, sociology, social work, counseling, and so on.

4253. The Philosophical Quarterly. [ISSN: 0031-8094] 1950. q. EUR 320. Ed(s): Sarah Broadie. Wiley-Blackwell Publishing Ltd., The Atrium, Southern Gate, Chichester, PO19 8SQ, United Kingdom; customer@wiley.com; http://www.wiley.com/. Illus., index, adv. Sample. Refereed. Microform: PQC. Reprint: PSC. *Indexed:* A01, A22, AmHI, ArtHuCI, BRI, CCMJ, E01, FR, IPB, MLA-IB, MSN, MathR, P02. *Bk. rev.:* 10-15, 500-3,000 words. *Aud.:* Ac.

This journal is a high-quality U.K. philosophy journal, sponsored by the Scots Philosophical Club and the University of St. Andrews. Most of the work found in this journal centers on epistemology, metaphysics, philosophical logic, philosophy of language, and ethics. Readers will also find discussions of issues raised in the journal and elsewhere, generally in the form of objections, defenses, and replies. The "Critical Reviews" section contains moderate-length book reviews. A core journal for collections that support work in contemporary Anglo-American philosophy and the analytic tradition.

4254. Philosophical Review. [ISSN: 0031-8108] 1892. q. USD 168. Duke University Press, 905 W Main St, Ste 18 B, PO Box 90660, Durham, NC 27701; subscriptions@dukepress.edu; http://www.dukepress.edu. Illus., index, adv. Sample. Refereed. Vol. ends: No. 4. Microform: MIM; PMC; PQC. Reprint: PSC. *Indexed:* A01, A06, A22, AmHI, ArtHuCI, BAS, BRI, CBRI, IPB, MLA-IB, P02. *Bk. rev.:* 4-6, 1,000-2,500 words. *Aud.:* Ac.

The *Philosophical Review* is a top-tier American philosophy journal, famous for its high-quality work in metaphysics, epistemology, philosophy of mind, ethics, the history of philosophy, and other areas of contemporary philosophical interest. It is one of the oldest continuously published philosophy periodicals in the United States. Many distinguished philosophers, especially in the post–World War II era, have published in its pages. A core journal for all collections, especially for those that support philosophy programs at all levels.

4255. Philosophical Studies: an international journal for philosophy in the analytic tradition. [ISSN: 0031-8116] 1950. 15x/yr. EUR 2687 (print & online eds.). Ed(s): Stewart Cohen. Springer Netherlands, Van Godewijckstraat 30, Dordrecht, 3311 GX, Netherlands; http://www.springer.com. Illus., index, adv. Sample. Refereed. Vol. ends: No. 3. Microform: PQC. Reprint: PSC. *Indexed:* A01, A22, AmHI, ArtHuCI, BRI, CCMJ, E01, FR, IPB, MLA-IB, MSN, MathR, P61, SSA. *Aud.:* Ac.

Philosophical Studies is a leading, top-tier journal for analytic philosophy. Its articles generally present tightly-argued original research on contemporary issues and traditional problems explored from new perspectives. Work generally focuses on metaphysics, epistemology, philosophy of mind, philosophical logic, philosophy of science, action theory, and ethics. However, there are occasional forays into historically oriented analyses as well. In addition to publishing original research on a variety of topics, it offers some thematic issues each year, coordinated by guest editors. Readers will also find issues over the course of a year devoted to selected conference papers—for example, from the American Philosophical Association's annual Pacific Division meetings, the Bellingham Summer Philosophy Conference, and the Oberlin Colloquium in Philosophy. Finally, there are regular symposia on recently published books that include critique and analysis followed by replies from the authors. A core journal for collections that support work in contemporary philosophy, given its quality and prominence, in spite of its high cost.

4256. Philosophical Topics. Formerly (until 1981): *Southwestern Journal of Philosophy.* [ISSN: 0276-2080] 1970. s-a. USD 70 (Individuals, USD 45). Ed(s): Edward Minar. University of Arkansas Press, 105 N McIlroy Ave, Fayetteville, AR 72701; http://www.uapress.com. Illus., adv. Refereed. Vol. ends: No. 2. *Indexed:* A22, IPB, MLA-IB. *Aud.:* Ac.

Philosophical Topics has began as a regional Southern journal of philosophy. Now, it is a highly regarded publication of about ten articles per issue, which are exclusively invited papers on a given topic, philosopher, or historical period. The papers are of high quality, written by leading scholars on an international level. A good core journal for collections.

4257. Philosophy. Formerly (until 1931): *Journal of Philosophical Studies.* [ISSN: 0031-8191] 1926. q. plus two supplements. GBP 356 (print & online eds.). Ed(s): Anthony O'Hear. Cambridge University Press, The Edinburgh Bldg, Shaftesbury Rd, Cambridge, CB2 8RU, United Kingdom; journals@cambridge.org; http://www.cambridge.org/uk. Illus., index, adv. Refereed. Circ: 2000. Vol. ends: No. 4. Microform: PQC. Reprint: PSC. *Indexed:* A01, A22, AmHI, ArtHuCI, BAS, BRI, E01, FR, IPB, MLA-IB, MSN, MathR, P02. *Bk. rev.:* 5-7, 1,000-2,500 words. *Aud.:* Ac.

This is the official journal of the Royal Institute of Philosophy (RIP). Its focus and authorship are, for the most part, British. The journal is noted for covering all branches of philosophy without emphasis on any particular philosophical orientation or method. This is a good journal for nonspecialists, since its contents are to be written without unnecessary technical language and preciousness. As a result, there is less of the highly-narrow focus on points of philosophical concern that are only of concern to specialists among the contents, though the work is not thereby of lesser quality. Included in the subscription price for institutional subscribers is the Royal Institute of Philosophy Lecture Series, published as *RIP Supplements*. A good core journal for general collections.

4258. Philosophy and Literature. [ISSN: 0190-0013] 1976. s-a. USD 113. Ed(s): Garry L Hagberg. The Johns Hopkins University Press, 2715 N Charles St, Baltimore, MD 21218; http://www.press.jhu.edu. Illus., index, adv. Sample. Refereed. Circ: 450. Vol. ends: No. 2. Reprint: PSC. *Indexed:* A01, A22, ABS&EES, AmHI, ArtHuCI, BEL&L, BRI, CBRI, E01, FR, IPB, MLA-IB, P02. *Bk. rev.:* 2-4, 750-1,500 words. *Aud.:* Ac.

Bard College sponsors this interdisciplinary journal. Its contents cover a wide variety of topics, sometimes in thematic-arranged issues. For instance, there are philosophical interpretations of American, British, and Continental literature, such as Eliot and Hardy. Other articles provide literary investigations of classic works of philosophy, such as Nietzsche and Montaigne. Still other contributions look at more philosophically-oriented topics such as the aesthetics of literature, the philosophy of language as it pertains to literature, and the literary theory of criticism. Finally, readers will find shorter papers of five to ten pages in the "Notes and Fragments" section. Recommended for both literature and philosophy collections.

4259. Philosophy and Phenomenological Research. [ISSN: 0031-8205] 1940. bi-m. GBP 280 (print & online eds.). Ed(s): Ernest Sosa. Wiley-Blackwell Publishing, Inc., 111 River St, Hoboken, NJ 07030; info@wiley.com; http://onlinelibrary.wiley.com/. Illus., index, adv. Sample. Refereed. Microform: PQC. Reprint: PSC. *Indexed:* A01, A22, ABS&EES, AmHI, ArtHuCI, BRI, E01, IPB, MLA-IB, RILM. *Bk. rev.:* 6-8, 750-1,500 words. *Aud.:* Ac.

Philosophy and Phenomenological Research is another top-tier analytic philosophy journal, and is the official organ of the International Phenomenological Society. The main foci of this journal are metaphysics, epistemology, philosophy of mind, ethics, and issues in the history of philosophy when they have relevance to contemporary problems. However, the journal does publish research in other areas of philosophy. A good core journal for philosophy collections.

4260. Philosophy and Public Affairs. [ISSN: 0048-3915] 1971. q. GBP 145. Ed(s): Krysia Kolodziej, Alan W Patten. Wiley-Blackwell Publishing, Inc., 111 River St, Hoboken, NJ 07030; info@wiley.com; http://onlinelibrary.wiley.com/. Illus., index, adv. Sample. Refereed. Microform: PQC. *Indexed:* A22, AmHI, BRI, CJPI, E01, FR, IBSS, IPB, P02, P61, SSA. *Aud.:* Ac.

Philosophy and Public Affairs is a prominent analytic journal in the areas of contemporary ethical, political, social, legal, and public-policy issues. Many of the top philosophers in Anglo-American political thought publish work in this journal. Topics may ranges from discussions of broad concepts, such as autonomy and punishment to analyses of specific issues such as preemptive war and reparations to reviews of the work of political philosophers like John Rawls and Amartya Sen. Thus, it is a good journal choice for philosophy, law, and political science collections.

4261. *Philosophy and Rhetoric.* [ISSN: 0031-8213] 1968. q. USD 180 (print & online eds.). Ed(s): Gerard A Hauser. Pennsylvania State University Press, 820 N University Dr, University Support Bldg 1, Ste C, University Park, PA 16802; info@psupress.org; http://www.psupress.org. Illus., index, adv. Refereed. Microform: PQC. Reprint: PSC. *Indexed:* A22, AmHI, ArtHuCI, E01, FR, IPB, MLA-IB. *Bk. rev.:* 1-3, 1,500-2,500 words. *Aud.:* Ac.

Rhetoric and philosophy may seem to be, at first, strange bedfellows, given the longstanding tension between the two dating back to the classical era. Nonetheless, the contents of this journal show that there is a great deal of fruitful exchange between the two subjects. Readers will find articles, for instance, researching the relationship between philosophy and rhetoric, including the relationship between formal and informal logic and rhetoric. They will also see work indicating the philosophical aspects of argumentation and argumentation within the discipline of philosophy itself. There are analyses of the nature of rhetoric of historical figures and during historic periods. More anthropological and sociological studies and discussions look at the analysis of rhetoric and human culture and thought and of the psychological and sociological aspects of rhetoric. Recommended for philosophy, English, and speech communication collections.

4262. *Philosophy & Social Criticism: an international, interdisciplinary journal.* Formerly (until 1978): *Cultural Hermeneutics.* [ISSN: 0191-4537] 1973. 10x/yr. USD 2476. Ed(s): David Rasmussen. Sage Publications Ltd., 1 Oliver's Yard, 55 City Rd, London, EC1Y 1SP, United Kingdom; info@sagepub.co.uk; http://www.uk.sagepub.com. Illus., index. Sample. Refereed. Vol. ends: No. 6. Reprint: PSC. *Indexed:* A01, A22, ABS&EES, ArtHuCI, E01, FR, IBSS, IPB, MLA-IB, P61, SSA. *Aud.:* Ac.

This interdisciplinary journal covers a broad range of topics—political philosophy, social theory, ethics, hermeneutics, literary theory, aesthetics, feminism, modernism and postmodernism, neostructuralism and deconstruction, universalism and communitarianism, and more—from a Continental perspective, generally with a political slant. It covers much of the contemporary work that is being done in Continental philosophy. Thus, it will appeal to scholars of Adorno, Arendt, Derrida, Habermas, Foucault, Ricouer, and others. This journal is best for general collections that support programs in philosophy and other disciplines interested in contemporary Continental philosophy.

4263. *Philosophy East and West: a quarterly of comparative philosophy.* [ISSN: 0031-8221] 1951. q. USD 120. Ed(s): Roger T Ames. University of Hawaii Press, 2840 Kolowalu St, Honolulu, HI 96822; uhpjourn@hawaii.edu; http://www.uhpress.hawaii.edu. Illus., index, adv. Sample. Refereed. Circ: 775. Vol. ends: No. 4. Microform: PQC. *Indexed:* A01, A22, AmHI, ArtHuCI, BAS, BRI, E01, IBSS, IPB, MLA-IB, P02, P61, R&TA, RILM, SSA. *Bk. rev.:* 5-7, 500-2,500 words. *Aud.:* Ac.

As the title suggests, *Philosophy East and West* publishes specializes in studies on specific points of and figures in Asian philosophy, as well as offering comparative intercultural articles on the philosophical traditions of East and West. The main focus is on demonstrating the relevance of philosophy for the art, literature, science, and social practice of Asian civilizations. Book reviews cover not only scholarship on philosophy of the Far East, but also philosophy of the Middle and Near East, as well as interactions of Asian philosophers with Western philosophers such as Jacques Derrida and Richard Rorty. Thus, the general scope of this publication is much broader than that of the *Journal of Indian Philosophy*. This journal is of benefit for both philosophy and Asian Studies collections.

4264. *Philosophy Now: a magazine of ideas.* [ISSN: 0961-5970] 1991. bi-m. GBP 24 (print & online eds.). Ed(s): Rick Lewis. Philosophy Now, 43a Jerningham Rd, London, SE14 5NQ, United Kingdom. Illus., adv. *Indexed:* AmHI. *Bk. rev.:* 2-4, 750-1,500 words. *Aud.:* Ga.

This magazine of ideas is very popular in the U.K. Its aim is to make philosophy more accessible to educated laypeople and nonspecialists. Thus, its contents are on a wide variety of general-interest philosophical topics, and written in a non-technical style without footnotes or jargon. Moreover, these articles may include photographs, cartoons, caricatures, and other illustrations and graphics. Readers will also find interviews with practicing philosophers, film and theater reviews, and fiction and poetry. *Philosophy Now* is best for public libraries where *The Humanist, Skeptical Inquirer,* and related publications are popular. It may also have some appeal to academic collections looking for popular magazines that appeal to generalists.

4265. *Philosophy of Science.* Incorporates (1970-1994): *P S A.* [ISSN: 0031-8248] 1934. 5x/yr. USD 278 (print & online eds.). Ed(s): Jeffrey Barrett, Cailin O'Connor. University of Chicago Press, 1427 E 60th St, Chicago, IL 60637; subscriptions@press.uchicago.edu; http://www.journals.uchicago.edu. Illus., index. Sample. Refereed. Vol. ends: Dec. Microform: PMC; PQC. Reprint: PSC. *Indexed:* A01, A22, AmHI, ArtHuCI, BRI, CCMJ, FR, IBSS, IPB, MLA-IB, MSN, MathR, P02. *Bk. rev.:* 4-8, 750-1,000 words. *Aud.:* Ac.

This is a top-tier journal for discussion of issues in the philosophy of science. Topics range: there are examinations of the logic of deductive, nomological, and statistical explanations; the nature of scientific laws and theories; observation; evidence; confirmation; induction; probability; and causality. Moreover, contributors look at philosophical issues in the various branches of the sciences, whether the physical sciences, biological sciences, cognitive sciences, social sciences, and mathematics. Among these are space-time and quantum mechanics; evolution and teleology; decision theory; artificial intelligence; and so forth. The fourth issue of the year (in December) offers the contributed or symposia papers of the biennial meetings of the Philosophy of Science Association. A core journal for all academic libraries.

4266. *Philosophy of the Social Sciences.* [ISSN: 0048-3931] 1971. q. USD 727. Ed(s): Ian C Jarvie. Sage Publications, Inc., 2455 Teller Rd, Thousand Oaks, CA 91320; info@sagepub.com; http://www.sagepub.com. Illus., index. Sample. Refereed. Vol. ends: No. 4. Reprint: PSC. *Indexed:* A01, A22, ArtHuCI, BRI, C37, CBCARef, E01, FR, IBSS, IPB, P02, P61, SSA. *Bk. rev.:* 2-4, 1,500-3,000 words. *Aud.:* Ac.

As its title indicates, this interdisciplinary journal explores the philosophical issues arising in the behavioral and social sciences. Content takes the form of articles, discussions, symposia, review essays, and literature surveys. There is a good mixture of perspectives and schools of thought represented in this journal, with the editorial hope of fostering debate and discussion among the various perspectives and schools. In addition to short book reviews, several books receive extended review essays in each issue. Philosophers (both analytic and Continental) as well as economists, linguists, political scientists, psychologists, and sociologists will benefit from this journal. It serves as a complement to the philosophy of science scholarship found in the journal *Philosophy of Science* (see above in this section).

4267. *Philosophy, Psychiatry & Psychology.* [ISSN: 1071-6076] 1994. q. USD 195. Ed(s): K W M Fulford. The Johns Hopkins University Press, 2715 N Charles St, Baltimore, MD 21218; http://www.press.jhu.edu. Illus., adv. Sample. Refereed. Circ: 270. Vol. ends: No. 4. Reprint: PSC. *Indexed:* A01, A22, CJPI, E01, PsycInfo. *Bk. rev.:* Occasional, 5,000-7,000 words. *Aud.:* Ac.

This journal is sponsored by the Royal Institute of Philosophy and affiliated with the Association for the Advancement of Philosophy and Psychiatry and the Royal College of Psychiatrists Philosophy Group. The work published here examines a number of philosophical issues relevant to psychiatry and abnormal psychology. Additionally, articles address issues in clinical theory and methodology that impact philosophical problems in, for example, metaphysics, epistemology, and ethics. The articles are often followed by commentaries and rejoinders. There are one or two longer feature articles in each issue, with the remainder being shorter ones along the lines of the articles one finds published in *Analysis*(see above in this section). Since this is an interdisciplinary journal, the authors come from a variety of fields, such as general medicine, law, neuroscience, social science, anthropology, nursing, and theology. Other helpful features of this journal are the ongoing bibliography, "Concurrent Contents: Recent and Classic References at the Interface of Philosophy, Psychiatry, and Psychology" and the "Clinical Anecdotes" section. This latter feature presents concise narrative essays that recount actual clinical experiences in psychiatric practice, accompanied by discussions of their underlying philosophical issues. A good journal for interdisciplinary programs and programs that support philosophy of mind, ethics, psychology, and psychiatry programs.

4268. Philosophy Today. [ISSN: 0031-8256] 1957. q. USD 50 domestic; USD 60 Canada; USD 62 Mexico. Ed(s): David Pellauer. DePaul University, Department of Philosophy, 2352 North Clifton Ave, Chicago, IL 60614. Illus., index, adv. Refereed. Vol. ends: No. 4. Microform: PQC. *Indexed:* A01, A22, AmHI, ArtHuCI, FR, IPB, MLA-IB, P02. *Aud.:* Ac.

Philosophy Today publishes work primarily on phenomenology, existentialism, and other philosophical work of interest to scholars working within the Christian tradition. Thus, it has a more Continental than analytic slant, given recent articles on Derrida, Simone de Beauvoir, Hebermas, and Ricoeur. A subscription also includes an annual supplementary issue with selected papers from the annual meeting of the Society for Phenomenology and Existential Philosophy (SPEP). Recommended for collections that support contemporary work in Continental philosophy, philosophy of religion, Christian philosophy, and theology.

4269. Phronesis: a journal for ancient philosophy. [ISSN: 0031-8868] 1956. 4x/yr. EUR 327. Ed(s): Christof Rapp, George Boys-Stones. Brill, PO Box 9000, Leiden, 2300 PA, Netherlands; cs@brill.nl; http://www.brill.nl. Illus., index, adv. Refereed. Reprint: PSC. *Indexed:* A01, A22, AmHI, ArtHuCI, E01, FR, IPB. *Bk. rev.:* 1-2, 1,000-2,000 words. *Aud.:* Ac.

For work in classical Greek and Roman thought, *Phronesis* is the premier journal, though it should be complemented with *Oxford Studies in Ancient Philosophy* for collections that support advanced work in classical studies and thought. Topics range widely, covering logic, metaphysics, epistemology, ethics, political philosophy, philosophy of science, psychology, and medicine. Much of the work centers on Plato and Aristotle, but there are, from time to time, studies of Stoicism, other Hellenistic schools, and late antique philosophy up to the sixth century A.D. The articles may be in English, French, German, or Italian. As noted above, this journal is critical for collections that support classical studies and ancient philosophy, and for general comprehensive collections.

4270. Ratio: an international journal of analytic philosophy. [ISSN: 0034-0006] 1958. q. GBP 472. Ed(s): John G Cottingham. Wiley-Blackwell Publishing Ltd., The Atrium, Southern Gate, Chichester, PO19 8SQ, United Kingdom; customer@wiley.com; http://www.wiley.com/. Illus., adv. Sample. Refereed. Vol. ends: No. 4. Reprint: PSC. *Indexed:* A01, A22, AmHI, ArtHuCI, E01, FR, IPB, MLA-IB, MathR. *Bk. rev.:* 1-2, 1,000-2,500 words. *Aud.:* Ac.

Ratio is a leading analytic philosophy journal, publishing work in contemporary issues in metaphysics, epistemology, philosophical logic, and ethics, with the aim of bridging the English-speaking and German-speaking philosophical divide. In addition to articles, there are often discussions and lengthy book reviews to be found in the contents of each issue. The June issue includes a starred contribution from an internationally prominent philosopher as the lead article. The December issue is a special issue edited by a guest editor. Recent themes of these special issues include "Agents and Their Actions" and "Developing Deontology." A good core journal for general collections and philosophy collections.

4271. The Review of Metaphysics: a philosophical quarterly. [ISSN: 0034-6632] 1947. q. USD 60 (Individuals, USD 40). Ed(s): Kenneth J Rolling, Jude P Dougherty. Philosophy Education Society, Inc., Catholic University of America, Washington, DC 20064; mail@reviewofmetaphysics.com; http://www.reviewofmetaphysics.org. Illus., index, adv. Refereed. Vol. ends: No. 4. Microform: PQC. *Indexed:* A01, A06, A07, A22, ABS&EES, AmHI, ArtHuCI, BRI, CBRI, IPB, MLA-IB, P02, RILM. *Bk. rev.:* 30-35, 500-1,000 words. *Aud.:* Ac.

The Review of Metaphysics is a leading journal in the Catholic Philosophical tradition, though it publishes work on a wide variety of authors from the broader history of philosophy, as well as on people outside of philosophy, such as Charles Darwin and Karol Wojtyla (Blessed John Paul II). Much of the research published in here focuses on metaphysics, philosophy of mind, phenomenology and existentialism, ethics, and the history of philosophy. Useful for scholars in philosophy are the abstracts of articles in current philosophy periodicals, generally written by the authors of these articles, to be found in each issue. Also helpful is the list of doctoral dissertations awarded by North American universities in the last 12 months that is found in the September issue. Best for core academic collections and collections that support work in the Continental and Catholic philosophy traditions.

4272. Review of Philosophy and Psychology. [ISSN: 1878-5158] 2010. q. Ed(s): Paul Egre. Springer Netherlands, Van Godewijckstraat 30, Dordrecht, 3311 GX, Netherlands; http://www.springer.com. Refereed. Reprint: PSC. *Indexed:* PsycInfo. *Aud.:* Ac.

This journal is hosted at the Institut Jean Nicod, a research center of the French Centre National de la Recherche Scientifique. The goal of this journal is to publish research that examines and debates research trends, philosophical underpinnings of cognitive science, psychology, and philosophy of mind, and their intersections. As such, the articles and other contributions delve into many areas of linguistics; cognitive and developmental psychology; cognitive anthropology; ethology; and neuroscience. From time to time, special thematic issues are also published. This is a good journal for collections supporting programs in philosophy of mind, psychology, and cognitive science.

4273. Review of Symbolic Logic. [ISSN: 1755-0203] 2008. q. GBP 517. Ed(s): Jeremy Avigad. Cambridge University Press, The Edinburgh Bldg, Shaftesbury Rd, Cambridge, CB2 8RU, United Kingdom; journals@cambridge.org; http://www.cambridge.org/uk. Adv. Reprint: PSC. *Indexed:* A01, A22, ArtHuCI, E01, MSN. *Aud.:* Ac, Sa.

This journal is the third sponsored by the Association for Symbolic Logic (ASL), along with the *Journal of Symbolic Logic* and *Bulletin of Symbolic Logic*. The stated editorial aim of this journal is to "cultivate research on the borders of logic, philosophy, and the sciences, and to support substantive interactions between these disciplines." Thus, its contents focus on philosophical and nonclassical logics and their applications (e.g., in the fields of computer science, linguistics, game theory and decision theory, formal epistemology, cognitive science, and artificial intelligence); history and philosophy of logic; and philosophy and methodology of mathematics. Recommended for libraries that subscribe to the ASL's other publications and for collections that support advanced work in logic.

4274. Revue Internationale de Philosophie. [ISSN: 0048-8143] 1938. q. EUR 27.83. Universa Press, Rue Hoender 24, Wetteren, 9230, Belgium. Illus., adv. Refereed. Vol. ends: No. 4. Microform: IDC. *Indexed:* A22, ArtHuCI, FR, IPB, MLA-IB, MathR. *Bk. rev.:* 1-5, 500-2,500 words. *Aud.:* Ac.

This Belgian journal focuses each issue on a single philosophical movement, problem, or philosopher. Articles, numbering between six and eight per issue, are in generally in English, French, German, or Italian. Topics of recent issues have included Stanley Cavell, Renaissance theater, Buddhism, Jaako Hintikka, Goethe, and Shakespeare. Contributors to each of these themed issues are often authorities in their respective subjects. A good journal for core collections and collections that support interdisciplinary studies.

4275. Social Epistemology: a journal of knowledge, culture and policy. [ISSN: 0269-1728] 1987. q. GBP 589 (print & online eds.). Ed(s): James H Collier. Routledge, 4 Park Sq, Milton Park, Abingdon, OX14 4RN, United Kingdom; subscriptions@tandf.co.uk; http://www.tandfonline.com. Illus., index, adv. Sample. Refereed. Vol. ends: No. 4. Reprint: PSC. *Indexed:* A01, A22, E01, FR, IBSS, IPB, MLA-IB, P61, SSA. *Aud.:* Ac.

This interdisciplinary journal presents research that examines the field of epistemology: particularly, how knowledge is produced, assessed, and validated, as well as the normative ramifications of such research. Thus, the journal's discussions are an exchange among several scholars, writing critical symposia, open peer commentary reviews, dialectical debates, applications, provocations, and reviews and responses, for example. One issue a year is a special issue devoted to a single topic. Recent special issues have looked at scholarly publishing ("Scientific Publications 2.0. The End of the Scientific Paper?"), the language of experts ("Rhetorics of Expertise"), and the social nature of epistemology in regard to just and injustice practice ("Epistemic Injustice"). The journal is now collaborating with the Society for Social Studies of Science (4S) and the European Association for the Study of Science and Technology (EASST). An excellent choice for philosophy and social science collections, especially those looking at epistemology and the social nature and practice of knowledge.

4276. *Social Philosophy and Policy.* [ISSN: 0265-0525] 1983. s-a. GBP 177. Ed(s): Ellen Frankel Paul, Jeffrey Paul. Cambridge University Press, The Edinburgh Bldg, Shaftesbury Rd, Cambridge, CB2 8RU, United Kingdom; journals@cambridge.org; http://www.cambridge.org/uk. Illus., adv. Refereed. Circ: 1000. Vol. ends: No. 2. Reprint: PSC. *Indexed:* A22, ABS&EES, ArtHuCI, E01, IBSS, IPB, P02, P61, SSA. *Aud.:* Ac.

This is another interdisciplinary journal, but devoted to research in contemporary discussions of matters of social, political, economic, legal, and public policy issues by authors from a variety of viewpoints and disciplines. Contributors are generally at the top of their respective fields. Recent issues have centered on "What Should Constitutions Do?" and "Liberalism and Capitalism." The general orientation of this journal is similar to that of *Philosophy and Public Affairs,* and it would be a good complement to the latter journal for collections that support ethics, moral philosophy, philosophy of law, law, government, economics, and political science programs.

4277. *Sorites: digital journal of analytical philosophy.* [ISSN: 1135-1349] 1995. q. Ed(s): Lorenzo Pena. Spanish Institute for Advanced Studies, Center for Analytic Philosophy, Pinar 25, Madrid, 28006, Spain; http://www.ifs.csic.es/sorites/. Refereed. *Indexed:* CCMJ, MSN, MathR. *Aud.:* Ac.

This English-language philosophy e-journal is headquartered in Spain, with an international board of editorial advisors. The articles discuss issues of metaphysics, ethics, philosophy of language, and logic with the methods and tools of contemporary analytic philosophy. A good journal for collections that support work in contemporary analytic philosophy.

4278. *The Southern Journal of Philosophy.* [ISSN: 0038-4283] 1963. q. GBP 159 (print & online eds.). Ed(s): Stephan Blatti. John Wiley & Sons, Inc., 111 River St, MS 4-02, Hoboken, NJ 07030; info@wiley.com; http://onlinelibrary.wiley.com/. Illus. Refereed. Vol. ends: No. 4. Microform: PQC. Reprint: PSC. *Indexed:* A01, A22, AmHI, ArtHuCI, E01, FR, IPB, MLA-IB. *Aud.:* Ac.

This is a solid general philosophy periodical. Each issue centers on a broad topic, looking at the topic from a variety of perspectives. Included in the subscription is a supplementary volume each year. This supplementary volume publishes the featured papers presented at the annual Spindel Conference held at the University of Memphis. Recent issues have examined what a post-Continental/analytic divide philosophy might look like; Kantian ethics; emotions in the moral psychology of Kant and Hume; and epistemology. A great core journal for philosophy collections of all types.

4279. *Studia Logica: an international journal for symbolic logic.* [ISSN: 0039-3215] 1953. 9x/yr. EUR 1563 (print & online eds.). Ed(s): Jacek Malinowski. Springer Netherlands, Van Godewijckstraat 30, Dordrecht, 3311 GX, Netherlands; http://www.springer.com. Illus., index, adv. Sample. Refereed. Vol. ends: No. 3. Microform: PQC. Reprint: PSC. *Indexed:* A22, ArtHuCI, BRI, CCMJ, E01, IPB, MLA-IB, MSN, MathR. *Bk. rev.:* 1-2, 1,000-1,500 words. *Aud.:* Sa.

This English-language logic journal is sponsored by the Institute of Philosophy and Sociology, Polish Academy of Sciences. As the title suggests, the research found in this journal's pages center on technical issues in symbolic and philosophical logic, with an emphasis on semantics, methodology, and applications of logical systems, particularly when new and important technical results appear. Recommended for graduate-level collections with strong holdings in logic, in conjunction with the other logical journals mentioned in this section.

Studies in History and Philosophy of Modern Physics. See Physics section, *Studies in History and Philosophy of Science Part B: Studies in History and Philosophy of Modern Physics.*

4280. *Studies in History and Philosophy of Science Part A.* [ISSN: 0039-3681] 1970. q. EUR 743. Ed(s): Anjan Chakravartty, Jessica Baron. Pergamon, The Blvd, Langford Ln, E Park, Kidlington, OX5 1GB, United Kingdom; JournalsCustomerServiceEMEA@elsevier.com; http://www.elsevier.com. Illus., adv. Sample. Refereed. Microform: PQC. *Indexed:* A01, A22, AmHI, ArtHuCI, BRI, CCMJ, IBSS, IPB, MLA-IB, MSN, MathR, P02, P61, SSA. *Bk. rev.:* 1-7, 1,500-2,500 words. *Aud.:* Ac.

This valuable journal publishes articles and research examining the sciences (generally understood) from historical, methodological, philosophical, and sociological perspectives. (Modern physics and the biological and biomedical sciences are covered in separate Pergamon publications.) Some of the contributions might look at individual philosophers and scientists from across human history, from the classical age (e.g., Ptolemy) through the early modern period (e.g., Kepler, Newton, Descartes, or Priestly) up through the twentieth century (e.g., Mach and Neurath). Other articles examine philosophical issues and concerns in the history of science. From time to time, guest editors will coordinate special issues and sections. A high-quality journal for collections that focus on the history and philosophy of science.

4281. *Synthese: an international journal for epistemology, methodology and philosophy of science.* [ISSN: 0039-7857] 1936. 18x/yr. EUR 2869 combined subscription (print & online eds.); USD 3000 combined subscription in the Americas (print & online eds.). Ed(s): O Bueno, Vincent F Hendricks. Springer Netherlands, Van Godewijckstraat 30, Dordrecht, 3311 GX, Netherlands; http://www.springer.com. Illus., index, adv. Sample. Refereed. Vol. ends: No. 3. Microform: PQC. Reprint: PSC. *Indexed:* A22, AmHI, ArtHuCI, CCMJ, E01, FR, IPB, MLA-IB, MSN, MathR, RILM. *Aud.:* Ac.

Synthese has long been a top-tier analytic philosophy journal, focusing on the history and philosophy of science, epistemology, mathematical and philosophical logic, philosophy of language, and philosophy of mathematics. Those who contribute articles to this publication include philosophers, mathematicians, scientists, and economists among their numbers. There are several special issues a year, including an annual one dedicated to "Neuroscience and Its Philosophy" that continues the scholarly tradition of the ceased Kluwer journal *Brain and Mind.* Also included in the subscription is a separately edited publication, *Knowledge, Rationality, and Action.* This regular section is of interest to scholars of game theory and artificial intelligence. *Synthese* is a highly technical and very costly journal; nonetheless, given its prominence and quality, it is recommended for graduate-level collections, especially those that support work in analytic philosophy and the areas listed in the first sentence of this description.

4282. *Theory and Decision: an international journal for multidisciplinary advances in decision sciences.* [ISSN: 0040-5833] 1970. 8x/yr. EUR 1275 (print & online eds.). Ed(s): Mohammed Abdellaoui. Springer New York LLC, 233 Spring St, New York, NY 10013; service-ny@springer.com; http://www.springer.com/. Illus., index, adv. Sample. Refereed. Vol. ends: No. 4. Microform: PQC. Reprint: PSC. *Indexed:* A22, ABIn, BRI, C&ISA, CCMJ, CerAb, E01, EconLit, EngInd, IBSS, IPB, JEL, MSN, MathR, P61, PsycInfo, SSA. *Aud.:* Ac.

This interdisciplinary journal publishes highly technical articles on decision-making from researchers in philosophy, economics, management, statistics, operations research, finance, mathematics, psychology, and sociology. The aim is to encourage not only research, but discussion and cross-fertilization of knowledge and scholarship about decision-making in a variety of disciplines. The articles may look at mathematical and computer science models; preference and uncertainty modeling; multicriteria decision-making; social choice, negotiation, and group decision; game theory, gaming, and conflict analysis; rationality, cognitive processes, and interactive decision-making; economics; and methodology and philosophy of the social sciences. Given the technical nature of the work found in this journal, it is best for graduate-level collections that work in these areas of research.

4283. *Utilitas.* Formed by the merger of (1978-1988): *Bentham Newsletter;* (1965-1988): *Mill News Letter.* [ISSN: 0953-8208] 1989. q. GBP 236. Ed(s): Brad Hooker. Cambridge University Press, The Edinburgh Bldg, Shaftesbury Rd, Cambridge, CB2 8RU, United Kingdom; journals@cambridge.org; http://www.cambridge.org/uk. Illus., adv. Sample. Refereed. Vol. ends: No. 3. Reprint: PSC. *Indexed:* A01, A22, ABIn, AmHI, ArtHuCI, E01, IBSS, IPB. *Bk. rev.:* Number and length vary. *Aud.:* Ac.

The International Society for Utilitarian Studies sponsors this journal. The broad focus of the journal's research is utilitarianism, but the research is not merely historical or exegetical analysis of Jeremy Bentham's and John Stuart Mill's work. Rather, the journal's content encompasses all aspects of utilitarian thought, historical (including its opponents) and contemporary, examining utilitarian themes in ethics, politics, economics, jurisprudence, literature, and public policy. Also to be found are symposia on various topics, philosophers, or recently published books. For collections that support work in ethics (both historical and contemporary), political philosophy, and intellectual history, this journal is good.

■ PHOTOGRAPHY

I *Berlin Loa, Museum/Archives Technician; berlinloa@gmail.com*

Introduction

The periodicals selected here are considered basic to any library collection and include those targeted to general audiences, as well as those targeted to more experienced photographers.

Basic Periodicals

Hs: *Popular Photography;* Ga: *Afterimage, Aperture, Popular Photography, Shutterbug;* Ac: *Aperture, Popular Photography.*

Basic Abstracts and Indexes

Academic Search Premier, Reader's Guide to Periodical Literature.

4284. *Afterimage: the journal of media arts and cultural criticism.* [ISSN: 0300-7472] 1972. bi-m. USD 100. Ed(s): Karen vanMeenen. Visual Studies Workshop, 31 Prince St, Rochester, NY 14607; info@vsw.org; http://www.vsw.org/. Illus., index. Sample. Vol. ends: May/Jun. Microform: PQC. *Indexed:* A01, A06, A07, A22, A51, ABIn, AmHI, BRI, CBRI, F01, MLA-IB, P02. *Bk. rev.:* 2-3, 1,500 words. *Aud.:* Hs, Ga, Ac.

Afterimage is a full-color journal that contains articles, book and film reviews, exhibit reviews, and cultural features that cover photography as well as multimedia arts. Issues also include notices regarding exhibits, screenings, events, jobs, and opportunities for freelance work. The web site contains highlights from current issues and a searchable "article archive." Recommended for academic as well as public libraries.

4285. *Aperture.* [ISSN: 0003-6420] 1952. q. USD 40 domestic; USD 65 foreign; USD 18.50 newsstand/cover per issue. Ed(s): Melissa Harris. Aperture Foundation, Inc., 547 W 27th St, 4th Fl, New York, NY 10001; magazine@aperture.org; http://www.aperture.org. Illus., adv. Circ: 664 Controlled. Microform: PQC. *Indexed:* A06, A07, A22, A51, ABS&EES, AmHI, ArtHuCI, BRI, P02. *Aud.:* Hs, Ga, Ac.

Aperture is a full-color publication developed by renowned photographers and writers under the auspices of the Aperture nonprofit foundation for photography. Contents include articles, scholarly essays, exhibit reviews, artist profiles, advertisements, and an extensive display of photography from a wide range of international contributors. The web site offers an index of the current issue, as well as feature images. Back issues are available for purchase directly from the web site. Recommended for academic and public libraries.

4286. *Black & White.* Formerly (until 2012): *B & W + Color;* Which was formed by the merger of (1999-2011): *B & W;* (2009-2011): *Color.* [ISSN: 2168-6688] 2011. bi-m. USD 35 domestic; USD 50 Canada; USD 60 elsewhere. Ross Periodicals, Inc., PO Box 1529, Ross, CA 94957; rosspub@pacbell.net. Adv. Sample. *Bk. rev.:* Number and length vary. *Aud.:* Ga, Ac, Sa.

Black & White + Color is the journal for those with experience or a developed interest in black-and-white photography. Issues contain essays, feature articles, and book reviews. The magazine is known for its extensive display of photographic works submitted by professional and amateur artists in both traditional and digital formats. Special color issues are published periodically. Fee-based back issues and no-fee sample issues are available on the web site. A limited selection of full-text articles are also available on the web site, from back issues. Recommended primarily for academic and public libraries, the journal is also appropriate for school libraries with an arts or humanities focus.

4287. *European Photography.* [ISSN: 0172-7028] 1980. s-a. EUR 72 for 2 yrs. in Europe; EUR 92 for 2 yrs. elsewhere. Ed(s): Andreas Mueller-Pohle. European Photography, Postfach 080227, Berlin, 10002, Germany. Illus., index, adv. Vol. ends: Fall. *Indexed:* A07, A51. *Aud.:* Ga, Ac, Sa.

This international magazine features contemporary digital and traditional photography and visual media. The journal is published bilingually in English/German, and offers in-depth articles, artist profiles, book and exhibit reviews, and technical equipment articles from throughout Europe. Recommended for academic libraries. *European Photography* also publishes the *European Photography Guide*, a sourcebook for photographers, journalists, curators, and collectors who are interested in European photography and visual artists.

4288. *Exposure (Cleveland).* [ISSN: 0098-8863] 1963. s-a. USD 35 (Individuals, USD 15; Free to members). Ed(s): Carla Williams. Society for Photographic Education, 2530 Superior Ave, #403, Cleveland, OH 44114; membership@spenational.org; http://www.spenational.org/. Illus., adv. Refereed. Circ: 2500. *Indexed:* A07, A22, A51. *Bk. rev.:* Number and length vary. *Aud.:* Ac, Sa.

The Society for Photographic Education has published *Exposure* since 1973. The journal is published biannually and includes content on traditional and digital photography as well as related visual media. Issues include scholarly articles, essays, interviews, reviews, and images from a range of contributors that include photographers, writers, critics, students, and educators. *Exposure* seeks to highlight the work of photographers and artists working in visual media. Recommended primarily for academic libraries.

4289. *Nueva Luz: photographic journal.* Incorporates (in 1997): *Critical Mass.* [ISSN: 0887-5855] 1984. 3x/yr. USD 65 (in US and Puerto Rico) Individuals, USD 24 (in US and Puerto Rico). Ed(s): Carla Williams, Miriam Romais. En Foco, Inc, 1738 Hone Ave, Bronx, NY 10461; info@enfoco.org; http://www.enfoco.org. Illus., adv. *Aud.:* Ems, Hs, Ga, Ac, Sa.

Nueva Luz is an award-winning journal published by En Foco, Inc., a nonprofit group dedicated to cultural diversity in the photographic arts. The journal is bilingual (English/Spanish), and features specifically Latino, African, Asian, Pacific Islander, and Native American artists, but it is open to all ethnicities. Issues include artist portfolios, photographic essays, commentary, interviews, and minimal advertising. It also contains notifications regarding grants, exhibits, and awards. Photo features are professionally selected and high-quality, and beautifully represent multicultural American experiences. Highly recommended for any library collection.

4290. *Outdoor Photographer: scenic - travel - wildlife - sports.* [ISSN: 0890-5304] 1985. 11x/yr. USD 14.97 domestic; USD 29.97 foreign; USD 7 per issue. Werner Publishing Corporation, 12121 Wilshire Blvd, 12th Fl, Los Angeles, CA 90025; editors@outdoorphotographer.com; http://www.wernerpublishing.com. Illus. Sample. *Aud.:* Ga.

Outdoor Photographer content is targeted to the outdoor photography enthusiast. Issues include articles, essays, and tips for the travel, sports, plant, and wildlife photographer. Features include product reviews, site tips and recommendations, profiles, and news primarily related to digital photography techniques and equipment. The web site offers limited access to articles, a blog, and multiple links to additional sources. Recommended for public libraries.

4291. *Photo District News.* Supersedes in part (in 198?): *Photo District News;* Which was formerly: *New York Photo District News.* [ISSN: 1045-8158] 1980. m. USD 65 combined subscription domestic (print & online eds.); USD 105 combined subscription Canada (print & online eds.); USD 125 combined subscription elsewhere (print & online eds.). Ed(s): Holly Hughes. Nielsen Business Publications, 770 Broadway, New York, NY 10003; ContactCommunications@nielsen.com; http://www.nielsenbusinessmedia.com. *Indexed:* A22, ABIn, B02, BRI. *Bk. rev.:* Number and length vary. *Aud.:* Ac, Sa.

Photo District News contains product reviews, industry news, interviews, artist portfolios, an events calendar, and essays. Issues are often theme-based and include industry-related content specific to professionals such as intellectual property rights, photography markets, and digital manipulation; there are also reviews of both digital and analog equipment and techniques. The web site offers access to selected feature articles, links to popular photography blogs, and links to additional resources for professional and new photographers. Recommended for academic and public libraries.

4292. *Popular Photography: the image of today.* Former titles (until 2008): *Popular Photography & Imaging;* (until 2003): *Popular Photography;* (until 1955): *Photography;* Popular Photography was incorporated (1949-1989): *Modern Photography;* Which was formerly (until 1950): *Minicam Photography;* (until 1941): *Minicam.* [ISSN: 1944-0510] 1937. m. USD 14 domestic; USD 22 foreign. Ed(s): John Owens, Mason Resnick. Hachette Filipacchi Media U.S., Inc., 1633 Broadway, New York, NY 10019; flyedit@hfmus.com; http://www.hfmus.com. Illus., index, adv. Sample. Circ: 457132 Paid. Vol. ends: Dec. *Indexed:* A&ATA, A01, A07, A22, BRI, C37, CBRI, IHTDI, MASUSE, P02. *Bk. rev.:* Number and length vary. *Aud.:* Hs, Ga, Ac, Sa.

Popular Photography is widely known and popular with photographers of all levels for its buyer's guides, product reviews, tips, and tricks. Content includes illustrated how-to articles, feature images, techniques, and tips for the beginning and experienced photographer, and special-interest sections. Content covers both digital and traditional photography in language accessible to professionals and amateurs. Extensive advertisements also make this journal available for a lighter read. Recommended primarily for public libraries and school libraries, but can be popular for academic libraries as well.

4293. *Shutterbug: tools, techniques & creativity.* Former titles (until 198?): *Shutterbug Ads Photographic News;* (until 19??): *Shutterbug Ads.* [ISSN: 0895-321X] 1971. m. USD 17.95 domestic. Ed(s): Kevin McNutly. Source Interlink Companies, 6420 Wilshire Blvd, 10th Fl, Los Angeles, CA 90048; dheine@sourceinterlink.com; http://www.sourceinterlinkmedia.com. Illus., adv. *Indexed:* IHTDI. *Aud.:* Hs, Ga.

Shutterbug is targeted to both amateur and professional photographers, as well as photo enthusiasts. Issues contains articles, product test reports, equipment reviews, and photographer profiles. The magazine is popular for reviews, a Q&A section, and articles written for the general public; however, the magazine also contains a large number of product and service advertisements. Content addresses both digital and traditional photography and the layout makes it appealing for browsing. Recommended primarily for public libraries.

■ PHYSICS

Kiyomi D. Deards, Assistant Professor, Love Library, University of Nebraska-Lincoln, Lincoln, NE 68506

Introduction

Physicists often regard physics as the central science. Physicists are known for studying the universe, space, time, energy, and matter. The physics of atoms explains chemical interactions and how fast dolphins swim. Physics determines whether a structure will stand or fall, and it explains how hummingbirds and planes fly. Although often regarded as a "hard" science, biophysicists work to cure diseases, increase crop yields, and create exoskeletons to enable people who are paralyzed to walk again.

As our understanding of the world has evolved, physics has become increasingly interdisciplinary and specialized. This specialization has led to several subdisciplines of study such as: acoustics; astrophysics; atmospheric and space physics; biophysics; condensed matter physics; cryogenics; electromagnetism; fluid mechanics and aerodynamics; general relativity; geophysics; gravitation; mechanics; medical physics; nanotechnology; nuclear physics; optics; particles; plasmas; quantum mechanics; solid-state matter; thermodynamics and statistical mechanics; and waves. Researchers tend to concentrate their work within one subdiscipline, leading to highly specialized knowledge and skill sets. This high degree of specialization has led to a small but growing trend, of physicists collaborating with other experts on multidisciplinary projects.

Physics journals consist primarily of original research articles that are focused on a problem unique to a specific subdiscipline. The increase in subdisciplines has led to an increase in the number of highly specialized physics journals. This increase is demonstrated by *Physical Review,* one of the most highly used journals in the field. It was originally published as a single title, until 1969, and is currently distributed as ten separate publications, three of which are open-access journals and only available online. Additionally, the number of physics papers being published has increased significantly in size, with some journals publishing in excess of 500,000 pages per year. The increase in publications can lead to information overload for even the most dedicated researcher, emphasizing the importance of curated collections of journals that are focused on local research interests.

Due to the highly specialized nature of physics, researchers often find it difficult to understand articles published in a separate subdiscipline, often consulting colleagues to check their interpretation of these articles. A thorough understanding of mathematics, at the very least college calculus, is required to understand most research articles published in physics journals. Because of the use of higher-level math in physics research, even journals targeted at a broader scientific audience contain numerous mathematical equations. The understanding of these equations is necessary to comprehend and apply the research being presented.

Specialists often work together on large-scale research projects creating multi-author papers whose publication chronicles and preserves their research for future generations. These articles are most often published in highly specialized journals that are read in depth only by those scientists whose work is contributed to the journals due to the small number of researchers working on related projects. In many cases, most interested individuals have been made privy to the results of a research project before a paper is published. This is in part due to the length of time from submission to publication, ranging anywhere from a few months to well over a year. It is also related to the fact that physicists have long been the leaders in creating and contributing to online preprint archives, allowing individuals to read drafts of accepted and submitted papers long before they are formally printed in a journal. ArXiv.org, primarily hosted by Cornell University, is the largest physics and related fields preprint archive online. INSPIRE, formerly the SPIRES HEP database available through the Stanford Linear Accelerator Center, specializes in articles about high-energy physics. These databases, as is the case with their journal counterparts, present materials according to area of specialization. In addition to journal article preprints, white papers are also included in some preprint archives.

Physics associations in the United States and Europe have long been the premier publishers of high-impact journals. The American Institute of Physics and the Institute of Physics publish *Physical Review* and the *Journal of Physics,* respectively. The *European Physical Journal* and related publications are produced by a collaboration of European professional physics organizations, primarily in English. These three publishers comprise over half of the titles recommended on this list. The major commercial publishers are: Elsevier, Springer, and Taylor & Francis.

Because of the specialized nature and high volume of articles, the cost of physics journals is significantly higher than that for most subject areas. Ignoring the open-access journals, the price range for most physics journals ranges between $1,300 and $10,000+ per year. As the number of papers published per year continues to increase, the price, and number of publications, will rise as well.

Almost all physics journals are published online, as well as in print, with several newer titles being published exclusively online. The *New Journal of Physics, Physical Review Focus, Physical Review Special Topics,* and *Physical Review X* are examples of popular online physics journals.

Many publishers have implemented pay-per-article models to allow individual articles to be published by researchers. The average price for pay-per article ranges from $25 to $50. Libraries are still able to subscribe to these publications and provide unlimited access to their users, but they may be excluded from pay-per-article purchasing, depending on the publisher.

The bulk of the titles listed should only be purchased by libraries that support major research in physics, or related sciences. Given the high costs, and highly specialized nature, of many of the titles, librarians will need to carefully select titles for subscription. Titles that have lower use-rates should be considered for patron-driven acquisition of articles instead of subscriptions. The number of articles used per year, and limits on interlibrary loan set by the each publisher, should be examined to determine the most cost-effective options for each title. Journal packages are often significantly less expensive, especially from nonprofit associations, than purchasing titles individually for those libraries that need to subscribe to multiple physics journals.

While many physics journals are still offered in print, the majority of physics researchers and students access them electronically. Electronic journals are routinely offered at a lower cost, and in the case of institutional subscriptions, they allow multiple, often unlimited, users to access their contents simultaneously. The continued and increasing popularity of ArXiv demonstrates the physics community's commitment and desire for rapid and open dissemination of research results.

Physics Today remains the only physics subscription a public library should subscribe to. Non-researchers are more likely to read *Scientific American* and *Science* to catch the latest physics news in print. More news and informational options written for a general audience are freely available online, allowing libraries to connect patrons to the latest news and trends in physics for free. Titles include: *Physics, Physical Review Focus, Physics News, The Planetary Society Blog,* and *Gallileo's Pendulum.*

As library budgets are in flux, and costs continue to rise, lost-cost and open-access journals and preprint archives will enable libraries to maintain and enhance research collections in physics. Journals that continue to rise in cost may still be relevant, but are likely to see a drop in subscriptions, leading to an eventual drop in citations, as students and researchers lose access to their materials. Libraries that do not support physics research will be less affected by fluctuations in price—creating collections that consist of open-access materials and a single subscription.

Basic Periodicals

Hs: *American Journal of Physics, Physics, Physics Education, The Physics Teacher, Physics Today;* Ga: *Physical Review Focus, Physics, Physics Today;* Ac: *American Journal of Physics, Applied Physics Letters, Journal of Applied Physics, Journal of Physics, Nature Physics, Physical Review, Physics, Physics Letters, Physics Today.*

Basic Abstracts and Indexes

Physics Abstracts.

4294. *A I P Advances.* [ISSN: 2158-3226] 2011. m. Free. American Institute of Physics, 1 Physics Ellipse, College Park, MD 20740; aipinfo@aip.org; http://www.aip.org. Adv. Refereed. *Aud.:* Ac, Sa.

AIP Advances is a open-access, online-only, community-led journal, covering all areas of the applied physical sciences. It publishes original research papers in topics such as superconductors, condensed matter, nanotechnology, quantum mechanics, computational physics, plasma physics, and ultrafast science. To create communication and discussion of the papers published, readers are allowed to comment on any article in a blog-like fashion. Multi-media material is encouraged, and there are video interviews with the executive editors and select authors. As a free, open-access title with creative commons licensing, this journal should become part of any physics research collection.

4295. *Acoustical Society of America. Journal.* [ISSN: 0001-4966] 1929. m. USD 2155 combined subscription domestic (print & online eds.); USD 2315 combined subscription foreign (print & online eds.). Ed(s): Allan D Pierce. Acoustical Society of America, 2 Huntington Quadrangle, Ste 1NO1, Melville, NY 11747; asa@aip.org; http://acousticalsociety.org/. Illus., index, adv. Sample. Refereed. Vol. ends: Jun/Dec. *Indexed:* A01, A22, AnBeAb, ApMecR, EngInd, ErgAb, M&GPA, MLA-IB, MathR, OceAb, RILM. *Bk. rev.:* 1-3 per issue. *Aud.:* Ac, Sa.

Available in print and online. The *Journal of the Acoustical Society of America* is the leading source of theoretical and experimental research results in the broad interdisciplinary subject of sound. It is designed to serve physical scientists, life scientists, engineers, psychologists, physiologists, architects, musicians, and speech communication specialists. Subject coverage includes: linear and nonlinear acoustics; aeroacoustics, underwater sound, and acoustical oceanography; ultrasonics and quantum acoustics; architectural and structural acoustics and vibration; speech, music, and noise; psychology and physiology of hearing; engineering acoustics, sound transducers, and measurements; and bioacoustics, animal bioacoustics, and bioresponse to vibration. In addition to full-length research papers, the *Journal* contains news items of interest to acoustical scientists, book reviews, references to contemporary papers in acoustics, reviews of acoustical patents, and news on the development of standards. The *JASA Express Letters,* section provides rapid dissemination of important new research results and technical information. *JASA Express Letters,* are published online as accepted. *Letters* are included in *Journal* volumes as they are published. In the online version, some articles include multimedia components such as video or sound recordings. As the most comprehensive journal in the world on this branch of physics, this title belongs in every physics collection.

4296. *Acoustics Today.* [ISSN: 1557-0215] 2005. q. Free to members. Ed(s): Dick Stern. Acoustical Society of America, 2 Huntington Quadrangle, Ste 1NO1, Melville, NY 11747; asa@aip.org; http:// acousticalsociety.org/. Adv. Circ: 10000. *Aud.:* Ga, Ac, Sa.

Acoustics Today was created as a means for disseminating interesting research and developments in the study of sound to a wide audience. Authors strive to present their article in a manner that readers will find interesting, understandable (regardless of their own acoustic discipline), and most importantly, worth reading. It contains tutorials, technical articles about and related to acoustics, and articles that expand upon conference presentations. Some articles contain multimedia components, which is very appropriate in a field of study based on sound. In addition, it also provides news of developments in the field, notices of events and meetings and new publications, and the work of the committees of the Acoustical Society of America. *Acoustics Today* is also interested in the business of acoustics and provides free advertising space to anyone in the industry. Although the journal is a benefit to members of the society, it is also freely available to everyone on the web. More than simply a newsletter, this journal belongs in any collection that supports research or study in the field of acoustics.

4297. *Advances in Optics and Photonics.* [ISSN: 1943-8206] 2009. q. USD 519. Ed(s): Bahaa Saleh. Optical Society of America, 2010 Massachusetts Ave, NW, Washington, DC 20036; info@osa.org; http://www.osa.org. Refereed. *Aud.:* Ac, Sa.

Available online only. Published by the Optical Society of America, this journal is designed to provide review articles and tutorials to assist researchers in the field of optics. It also includes peer-reviewed letters to the editor and replies to published review articles and tutorials. It covers fundamental and experimental optics, along with applications of optics and photonics technology, including: fiber optics and optical communications; quantum optics; ultrafast optics; lasers and laser optics; nonlinear optics; and optical devices. All of the articles emphasize multimedia content and applications. To maximize their reach, tutorials feature interactive components such as animation and video. Each article has navigational links and external reference-linking for easy sourcing and enhanced learning. Every article also has an alternative XHTML version available that allows readers to access the MathML code behind each equation. In addition, the journal also links to review articles in recent issues of other journals published by the society. Articles are published as completed and grouped into quarterly issues. Citations and download statistics are available for each article. This journal belongs in all collections that support research in optics.

4298. *Advances in Physics.* [ISSN: 0001-8732] 1952. bi-m. GBP 3331 (print & online eds.). Ed(s): David Sherrington. Taylor & Francis, 4 Park Sq, Milton Park, Abingdon, OX14 4RN, United Kingdom; subscriptions@tandf.co.uk; http://www.tandfonline.com. Illus., adv. Sample. Refereed. Vol. ends: Nov/Dec. Reprint: PSC. *Indexed:* A01, A22, C&ISA, CerAb, E01, EngInd, MathR. *Aud.:* Ac, Sa.

Available in print and online. *Advances in Physics* publishes authoritative critical reviews by experts on topics of interest and importance in condensed matter physics, broadly interpreted, including hard and soft matter; biological and materials physics; the overlap of cold atoms and quantum information with solid-state physics; and statistical and many-body physics and their applications. These reviews present the current state of knowledge within this highly specialized subfield of physics and serve as benchmarks in our knowledge of the physical universe. They are written for readers with a basic knowledge of condensed matter physics who want to learn more about specific research areas within that field. Because of the comprehensiveness of the research, most papers in this journal are very long, often over 100 pages. Most issues consist of a single article that essentially serves as a monograph on the topic under review. One of the key features of each article is its bibliography, which lists all the important past research on the topic under consideration. The "Perspectives" section is occasionally included to present shorter provocative articles that are intended to be controversial and to promote debate. *Annals of Physics, Contemporary Physics,* and *Reports on Progress in Physics* (all below in this section) also publish review articles, but these journals are all aimed at the nonspecialist. *Advances in Physics* is written for the specialized researcher or student of condensed matter, and will only be of marginal value to the nonspecialist or to scientists working in other disciplines.

4299. *American Journal of Physics.* Formerly (until 1940): *American Physics Teacher.* [ISSN: 0002-9505] 1933. m. USD 1077 combined subscription domestic (print & online eds.); USD 1180 combined subscription foreign (print & online eds.). Ed(s): David P Jackson. American Association of Physics Teachers, One Physics Ellipse, College Park, MD 20740; eo@aapt.org; http://www.aapt.org. Illus., index, adv. Sample. Refereed. Circ: 6400. *Indexed:* A01, A22, BRI, CCMJ, MLA-IB, MSN, MathR, P02, RILM. *Bk. rev.:* Number and length vary. *Aud.:* Hs, Ga, Ac.

Available in print and online. While most physics journals serve solely as archives of original research results, the *American Journal of Physics* exists to help teachers do a better job of instructing students about physics. As the official journal of the American Association of Physics Teachers, this title is devoted to the instructional and cultural aspects of the physical sciences. Rather than concentrating on new research results, this journal focuses on methods of teaching physics to students at the university and college level. Articles provide a deeper understanding of physics topics taught at the undergraduate and graduate level; insight into current research in physics and related areas; suggestions for instructional laboratory equipment and demonstrations; insight into and proven suggestions for better teaching methodologies; insight into how college students learn physics; and information on the historical, philosophical, and cultural aspects of physics. In addition to full-length papers, the journal also publishes letters, notes, book reviews, information on laboratory equipment, and editorials. Occasional articles that discuss research in physics education are also included. All libraries that support college physics courses should subscribe to this title.

4300. *Annalen der Physik.* Former titles (until 1799): *Neues Journal der Physik;* (until 1795): *Journal der Physik.* [ISSN: 0003-3804] 1790. 10x/yr. GBP 882. Ed(s): Ulrich Eckern. Wiley - V C H Verlag GmbH & Co. KGaA, Postfach 101161, Weinheim, 69451, Germany; subservice@wiley-vch.de; http://www.wiley-vch.de. Illus., index. Sample. Refereed. Reprint: PSC. *Indexed:* A22, CCMJ, EngInd, MSN, MathR. *Bk. rev.:* Occasional. *Aud.:* Ac, Sa.

Available in print and online. As the oldest continuously published German physics journal, *Annalen der Physik* occupies a historic place in the physics literature. This journal publishes original papers in the areas of experimental, theoretical, applied, and mathematical physics, and related areas. Throughout its long history, it has published some of the most important papers in the field, including the original work of Planck, Roentgen, and Einstein. Unlike many other long-standing journals, this title continues to cover the entire field of physics rather than specializing in a particular subdiscipline. It still publishes peer-reviewed original papers in the areas of experimental, theoretical, applied, and mathematical physics and related areas. In addition to original research papers, and review articles, the journal welcomes "Rapid Research Letters" ("RRLs"). The "Then & Now" section offer a historical perspective on important concepts in physics. Even though it is a German journal, all of the articles are now published in English. Although it has been surpassed in prestige by several other prominent physics journals, such as *Journal of Physics* and the *Physical Review* (see below), *Annalen der Physik* is still an important component of any comprehensive physics collection.

4301. *Annals of Physics.* [ISSN: 0003-4916] 1957. m. EUR 6020. Ed(s): Frank Wilczek. Academic Press, 3251 Riverport Ln, Maryland Heights, MO 63043; JournalCustomerService-usa@elsevier.com; http://www.elsevierdirect.com/brochures/academicpress/index.html. Illus., index, adv. Sample. Refereed. *Indexed:* A01, A22, CCMJ, E01, MSN, MathR. *Aud.:* Ac, Sa.

Available in print and online. Unlike most physics research journals, which publish brief reports of original research aimed at the specialist in the field, *Annals of Physics* presents original work in all areas of basic physics research. The journal publishes papers on topics spanning theory, methodology, and applications. It emphasizes clarity and intelligibility in the articles it publishes, thus making them more accessible to the reader than in many other journals. Researchers familiar with recent developments in the field are provided with sufficient detail and background to follow the arguments and understand their significance. Because of the emphasis on extensive background material, the articles in this journal can be very long, sometimes consisting of 50 or more pages. *Contemporary Physics, Reports on Progress in Physics,* and *Reviews of Modern Physics* (all below in this section) all serve the same general purpose as *Annals of Physics,* and each is useful for a college-level physics collection.

4302. *Applied Optics.* Formed by the merger of (1990-2003): *Applied Optics. Information Processing;* (1995-2003): *Applied Optics. Optical Technology and Biomedical Optics;* (1990-2003): *Applied Optics. Lasers, Photonics, and Environmental Optics;* All of which superseded (1962-1989): *Applied Optics.* [ISSN: 1559-128X] 2004. 36x/yr. USD 5291 (print & online eds.). Ed(s): Joseph N Mait. Optical Society of America, 2010 Massachusetts Ave, NW, Washington, DC 20036; info@osa.org; http://www.osa.org. Illus., index, adv. Refereed. *Indexed:* A22, AbAn, BRI, C&ISA, EngInd, M&GPA, OceAb, PhotoAb. *Aud.:* Ac, Sa.

Available in print and online. Along with the *Journal of the Optical Society of America* and *Optics Letters* (see below), *Applied Optics* is one of the official journals of the Optical Society of America. While the other two titles publish reports of original research, this journal concentrates on the applications of optical principles and methods. As such, it is the most widely read journal in the field of optics. Articles are published online as accepted and gathered in three issues per month. Articles cover a wide variety of topics including: optical testing and instrumentation; lens design; x-ray optics; micro-optics; gradient-index optics; radiometry and detectors; fiber-optic sensors; thin films; optical materials; image-detection devices and systems; Fourier optics; holography; 3-D sensing, processing, and display; optical image processing, restoration, enhancement, and quality measurement; pattern recognition; target detection and recognition; image understanding; machine vision; statistical optics and speckle; optical neural networks; optical data recording and storage; optical signal processing; photonic networks; optical interconnection systems, packaging, and subsystems; optical materials, devices, algorithms, and architectures relevant to these technologies; laser materials and design; nonlinear optics and wavelength conversion; optical and infrared spectroscopy; optoelectronics; integrated optics; fiber-optic technology; laser instrumentation, measurements, and metrology; laser materials processing; atmospheric optics and propagation; lidar and remote sensing; ocean optics and propagation; and atmospheric scattering and meteorological optics. In addition to full-length papers, the journal provides occasional review articles, and notes on equipment and methodologies. This is one of the core journals in the field of optics, and it belongs in any physics or engineering research collection.

4303. *Applied Physics A: materials science & processing.* Former titles: *Applied Physics A: Solids and Surfaces;* Supersedes in part (in 1981): *Applied Physics;* Which superseded: *Zeitschrift fuer Angewandte Physik.*

[ISSN: 0947-8396] 1973. 16x/yr. EUR 5678 (print & online eds.). Ed(s): Michael Stuke. Springer, Tiergartenstr 17, Heidelberg, 69121, Germany. Illus., adv. Refereed. Microform: PQC. Reprint: PSC. *Indexed:* A01, A22, E01, EngInd, PhotoAb. *Aud.:* Ac, Sa.

Available in print and online. *Applied Physics A* is a monthly journal for the rapid publication of experimental and theoretical investigations in applied research. It primarily covers the condensed state, including nanostructured materials and their applications. It publishes full-length articles and short, rapid communications. It also features invited reviews. Many of the issues are devoted to papers on a single topic, often presenting the proceedings of relevant conferences or Festschriften. Th journal jointly sponsors the Julius Springer Prize for Applied Physics, which is awarded annually to a researcher who has made outstanding and innovative contributions to the field of applied physics. For libraries that seek a comprehensive physics collection, this journal will serve as a European complement to the *Journal of Applied Physics* .

4304. Applied Physics B: lasers and optics. Formerly: *Applied Physics. B: Photophysics and Laser Chemistry;* Supersedes in part (in 1981): *Applied Physics.* [ISSN: 0946-2171] 16x/yr. EUR 5269 (print & online eds.). Ed(s): Dieter Meschede. Springer, Tiergartenstr 17, Heidelberg, 69121, Germany. Adv. Refereed. Microform: PQC. Reprint: PSC. *Indexed:* A01, A22, C&ISA, E01, EngInd, PhotoAb. *Aud.:* Ac.

Available in print and online. *Applied Physics B* is a journal for the rapid publication of laser and optical experimental and theoretical research. This research includes the applications of laser radiation in chemistry and biochemistry. The journal publishes both full-length articles and short, rapid communications. Occasional issues present the proceedings of relevant conferences or festschriften. This journal is published in cooperation with the German Physical Society and was originally published under its German title, *Zeitschrift fur Angewandte Physik.* Much of the research reported in this title is still conducted in German universities and research centers. However, all of the papers accepted are published in English. For libraries seeking a comprehensive physics collection, this journal will serve as a European complement to the *Journal of Applied Physics.*

4305. Applied Physics Letters. [ISSN: 0003-6951] 1962. w. Ed(s): Nghi Q Lam. American Institute of Physics, 1 Physics Ellipse, College Park, MD 20740; aipinfo@aip.org; http://www.aip.org. Illus., index, adv. Sample. Refereed. *Indexed:* A01, A22, EngInd, PhotoAb. *Aud.:* Ac, Sa.

Available in print and online. This title serves as the letters section of the *Journal of Applied Physics* (below in this section). It is the most highly cited journal in applied physics. Thus, it provides for the rapid dissemination of key data and physical insights, including new experimental and theoretical findings on the applications of physics to all branches of science, engineering, and technology. Topics covered by this journal include lasers and optics; condensed matter; nanotechnology; plasmas; semiconductors; magnetic devices; applied biophysics; and interdisciplinary research. Because all of the papers accepted are letters, they are extremely brief, with none longer than three printed pages. Content is published online daily, then collected into weekly online and printed issues. In addition to original research results, each issue also includes comments on previously published material. The comments can result in lively debate over the accuracy and interpretation of experimental results. This title is the most heavily cited journal in the field of applied physics. It is one of the core journals in physics and belongs in any physics research collection.

4306. Applied Physics Research. [ISSN: 1916-9639] 2009. s-a. Ed(s): Patrick Mc Nally. Canadian Center of Science and Education, 4915 Bathurst St, Unit 209-309, Toronto, ON M2R 1X9, Canada; info@ccsenet.org; http://www.ccsenet.org. Sample. Refereed. *Indexed:* A01, ABIn, C37. *Aud.:* Ac, Sa.

Available in print and online. *Applied Physics Research* is an open-access journal that publishes original research reports in all areas of physics. Topics covered include physics theory, applied physics, theoretical physics, particle physics and nuclear physics, atomic and molecular physics, plasma physics, condensed-matter physics, acoustics, optics, radiophysics, electromagnetism, thermodynamics, quantum electronics, high-energy physics, and mechanics and engineering. Because the articles are reports of original research, they tend to be highly technical in nature and readable only by other experts in the field. The journal is available in both print and electronic formats. With free open access

to the online version, it is unlikely that many libraries will choose to spend $20.00 plus shipping per issue for the print equivalent. Because it is free open-access title, the online edition of this journal should be included in all physics research collections. URL: www.ccsenet.org/journal/index.php/apr

Biophysical Journal. See Biology/Biochemistry and Biophysics section.

4307. Canadian Journal of Physics. [ISSN: 0008-4204] 1929. m. CAD 1070. Ed(s): Michael Steinitz. N R C Research Press, 1200 Montreal Rd, Bldg M-55, Ottawa, ON K1A 0R6, Canada; pubs@nrc-cnrc.gc.ca; http://pubs.nrc-cnrc.gc.ca. Illus., index, adv. Refereed. Circ: 777. Vol. ends: Dec. Microform: MML; PMC; PQC. *Indexed:* A01, A22, C&ISA, C37, CBCARef, CerAb, E01, EngInd, M&GPA, MathR, PhotoAb. *Aud.:* Ac, Sa.

Available in print and online. As an official publication of the National Research Council of Canada, the *Canadian Journal of Physics* is the premier physics publication emanating from that nation. It covers all branches of physics, including atomic and molecular physics, condensed matter, elementary particles and nuclear physics, gases, fluid dynamics and plasmas, electromagnetism and optics, mathematical physics, and interdisciplinary, classical, and applied physics. Most of the articles are published in English, although French-language articles are also accepted. In addition to full research reports, shorter rapid communications and research notes are also accepted. The journal also occasionally publishes review articles and tutorials that bring together and explain previously published research results. Supplemental data and other accompanying materials are available to subscribers on the journal web site. Although this journal is an official publication of the Canadian government, it is not restricted to Canadian authors and it attracts research reports from around the world. As the major Canadian journal in physics, it should be part of any comprehensive physics research collection.

4308. Chaos: an interdisciplinary journal of nonlinear science. [ISSN: 1054-1500] 1991. q. Ed(s): David K Campbell. American Institute of Physics, 1 Physics Ellipse, College Park, MD 20740; aipinfo@aip.org; http://www.aip.org. Adv. Sample. Refereed. *Indexed:* A01, A22, AbAn, ApMecR, CCMJ, MSN, MathR. *Aud.:* Ac, Sa.

Available in print and online. While most of physics seeks to describe the universe in an orderly fashion, some processes and systems simply do not fit in an orderly model. Chaos theory is a discipline that tries to understand such behaviors. The journal *Chaos* is devoted to research of such nonlinear systems. This journal covers the most recent developments in nonlinear science, including contributions from physics, mathematics, chemistry, biology, engineering, economics, and social sciences, as well as other disciplines in which inherently nonlinear phenomena are of interest and importance. In addition to full-length peer-reviewed articles, it also includes letters, brief reports, and technical reviews. Every other issue is a special-focus issue, which is intended to provide a critical introduction and overview of a particular topic, suitable as an introduction to nonspecialists but also of value to experts in the area. In addition, occasional articles that are aimed at the teaching of chaos theory are provided. This journal covers an interesting and unique subdiscipline of physics, and it belongs in any collection that supports research in this area.

4309. Communications in Mathematical Physics. [ISSN: 0010-3616] 1965. 24x/yr. EUR 5051 (print & online eds.). Ed(s): Horng-Tzer Yau. Springer, Tiergartenstr 17, Heidelberg, 69121, Germany. Illus., index, adv. Sample. Refereed. Microform: PQC. Reprint: PSC. *Indexed:* A01, A22, CCMJ, E01, MSN, MathR. *Aud.:* Ac, Sa.

Available in print and online. The field of physics relies heavily on high-level mathematics as a tool for developing new theories and in explaining experimental results. Whether defining the motion of an apple, exploring the heavens, or analyzing the nature of fundamental particles, physicists always attempt to explain natural phenomena in terms of mathematical functions. *Communications in Mathematical Physics* was developed in order to present physicists with a source for learning new mathematical techniques as well as for presenting new research findings. It also attempts to generate, among mathematicians, an increased awareness of and appreciation for the current problems in physics. All branches of physics are covered, although particular emphasis is placed on statistical physics, quantum theory, string theory, dynamical systems, atomic physics, relativity, and disordered systems. The common thread among all the papers is the strong mathematical approach to the problem. This journal complements the *Journal of Mathematical Physics* (see below) and belongs in comprehensive physics collections.

4310. *Computer Physics Communications.* [ISSN: 0010-4655] 1969. 12x/yr. EUR 7080. Elsevier BV, North-Holland, Postbus 211, Amsterdam, 1000 AE, Netherlands; JournalsCustomerServiceEMEA@elsevier.com; http://www.elsevier.nl/homepage/about/us/regional_sites.htt. Illus., index, adv. Sample. Refereed. *Indexed:* A01, A22, C&ISA, CCMJ, CerAb, CompLI, CompR, EngInd, MSN, MathR. *Aud.:* Ac, Sa.

Available in print and online. *Computer Physics Communications* deals with the applications of computing to physics and physical chemistry. Unlike most scientific research journals, the focus is on the computational techniques rather than the experimental results. Specific topics covered include computational models in physics and physical chemistry; computer programs in physics and physical chemistry; computational models and programs associated with the design, control, and analysis of experiments; numerical methods and algorithms; algebraic computation; the impact of advanced computer architecture and special-purpose computers on computing in the physical sciences; and software topics related to the physical sciences. In addition, subscribers have access to a web site containing a program library of actual computer software that may be used for these purposes. Most of the older programs in the library were written in FORTRAN for mainframe systems, while newer entries tend to be PC-based and run under Windows, UNIX, or Linux. Some are available in other scientific programming languages, including Maple and Mathematica. When new versions of existing programs are developed, announcements are included in this journal. With the program library, researchers are able to duplicate or modify experiments that would be otherwise difficult to conduct. Over 2,200 programs are currently available in the CPC program library. Each issue of the journal is evenly divided between articles and program descriptions. This journal is unique in providing not only original research articles, but also the research tools used in compiling the information.

4311. *Contemporary Physics.* [ISSN: 0010-7514] 1959. bi-m. GBP 943 (print & online eds.). Ed(s): Peter L Knight. Taylor & Francis, 4 Park Sq, Milton Park, Abingdon, OX14 4RN, United Kingdom; http://www.tandfonline.com. Illus., index, adv. Sample. Refereed. Vol. ends: Nov/Dec. Microform: MIM; PMC. Reprint: PSC. *Indexed:* A01, A22, BRI, C&ISA, CerAb, E01, P02, PhotoAb. *Bk. rev.:* 5-15 per issue, varying length. *Aud.:* Ac, Sa.

Available in print and online. *Contemporary Physics* has a unique place in the spectrum of physics journals. Although written primarily for physicists, the articles appearing in this journal have more background material and are more accessible to a wider scientific audience than articles in most physics journals. Each article attempts to explain the essential physical concepts of the topic and to relate those concepts to more familiar aspects of physics that are accessible to a broader range of readers. Because of this emphasis, students and scientists in other scientific disciplines can use this journal to learn about important developments in the field of physics. *Contemporary Physics* is of particular use to undergraduates, teachers and lecturers, and those starting postgraduate studies. A feature of interest to librarians is that in addition to the review articles, the journal publishes dozens of reviews of books in physics and related fields. *Contemporary Physics* is the most readable of all of the physics review journals, and belongs in every college-level physics collection.

4312. *Cryogenics.* [ISSN: 0011-2275] 1960. bi-m. EUR 3040. Ed(s): B Baudouy, H-M Chang. Pergamon, The Blvd, Langford Ln, E Park, Kidlington, OX5 1GB, United Kingdom; JournalsCustomerServiceEMEA@elsevier.com; http://www.elsevier.com. Illus., adv. Sample. Refereed. Microform: PQC. *Indexed:* A01, A22, ApMecR, BrTechI, C&ISA, CEA, CerAb, EngInd. *Bk. rev.:* Number and length vary. *Aud.:* Ac, Sa.

Available in print and online. *Cryogenics* is the world's leading journal that focuses on all aspects of cryoengineering and cryogenics. Papers published in this journal cover a wide variety of subjects in low-temperature engineering and research, including: the applications of superconductivity in magnets, electronics, and other devices; superconductors and their properties; properties of materials; new applications of cryogenic technology; refrigeration and liquefaction technology; thermodynamics; fluid properties and fluid mechanics; heat transfer; thermometry and measurement science; cryogenics in medicine; and cryoelectronics. The majority of the publication consists of full-length research papers, although review articles, research notes, and technical notes are also included. Conference papers are published on an occasional basis, in addition to book reviews, news features, and a calendar of events relevant to the field. As the premier journal for low-temperature studies, this journal belongs in any physics or engineering collection that supports research in this field.

4313. *European Journal of Physics.* [ISSN: 0143-0807] 1980. bi-m. GBP 671 (print & online eds.). Ed(s): J Mostowski. Institute of Physics Publishing Ltd., Temple Circus, Temple Way, Bristol, BS1 6HG, United Kingdom; custserv@iop.org; http://ioppublishing.org. Illus., adv. Sample. Refereed. Vol. ends: Nov. *Indexed:* A01, A22, CCMJ, ERIC, EngInd, M&GPA, MSN, MathR. *Aud.:* Ga, Ac, Sa.

Available in print and online. The primary mission of the *European Journal of Physics* is to assist in maintaining and improving the standard of physics teaching in universities and other institutes of higher education. It publishes articles on topics relating to the fundamentals of physics education; papers on laboratory exercises illustrating novel techniques; original insights into the derivation of results; reports on new developments in physics curricula and the techniques of teaching physics; and papers describing the cultural, historical, and technological aspects of physics. It is a place for teachers, instructors, and professors to exchange their views on teaching physics at university level and share their experiences. Because the papers are intended to aid in the teaching of the subject rather than to present original research results, the editors encourage authors to avoid high-level mathematics, thus making the papers more accessible to a general audience. Although this is a European journal, almost every article published is in English. Full papers and letters are accepted, along with comments on previously published works. Some articles have accompanying multimedia content that is available through the web site. Occasional special issues follow specific themes. In order to reach the widest possible audience in the physics education community, all articles from the current month are provided free for the first 30 days after publication. This title is the European equivalent of the *American Journal of Physics* (above) and is a useful supplement to any college or university physics collection.

4314. *European Physical Journal A. Hadrons and Nuclei.* Incorporates (2004-2006): *Acta Physica Hungarica. B. Quantum Electronics;* (1951-2006): *Acta Physica Hungarica. A. Heavy Ion Physics;* Which was formerly (until 1994): *Acta Physica Hungarica;* (until 1982): *Acta Physica Academiae Scientiarum Hungaricae;* (until 1949): *Hungarica Acta Physica;* Incorporated in part (1903-2000): *Anales de Fisica;* (1855-1999): *Societa Italiana di Fisica. Nuovo Cimento. A. Nuclei, Particles and Fields;* Which was formerly (until 1982): *Societa Italiana di Fisica. Nuovo Cimento A;* (until 1971): *Nuovo Cimento A;* Which superseded in part (in 1965): *Nuovo Cimento;* Former titles (until 1997): *Zeitschrift fuer Physik A. Hadrons and Nuclei;* (until 1991): *Zeitschrift fuer Physik. Section A. Atomic Nuclei;* (until 1986): *Zeitschrift fuer Physik. Section A: Atoms and Nuclei; Zeitschrift fuer Physik.* [ISSN: 1434-6001] 1920. m. EUR 3545 (print & online eds.). Ed(s): N Alamanos, U-G Meissner. Springer, Tiergartenstr 17, Heidelberg, 69121, Germany. Illus., adv. Refereed. Microform: PMC; PQC. Reprint: PSC. *Indexed:* A01, A22, E01, M&GPA, MathR. *Aud.:* Ac, Sa.

Available in print and online. In 1998, the German, French, and Italian Physical Societies decided to merge all of their specialized national physics journals into a single publication. The *European Physical Journal* in all six of its parts is the result of that merger. Over the past decade, national physics societies in over 40 nations have joined in to expand this effort. *Part A* directly replaces the former *Zeitschrift fuer Physik A* and *Il Nuovo Cimento A.* It covers the specialized subfield of high-energy physics relating to hadrons and nuclei, including nuclear structure; nuclear reactions; heavy-ion physics; weak interactions; heavy-ion physics; hypernuclei; radioactive beams; nuclear astrophysics; and related interdisciplinary topics. The common framework of these systems is that they are few- and many-body systems bound by strong interactions. This section is complemented by *Part C,* which emphasizes the elementary aspects of particles and fields. Articles that present experimental results, including methods and instruments, are published in addition to theoretical papers. Full-length research papers, review articles, short research notes, and letters are all included. Although this is a European journal, all of the articles are in English. The *European Physical Journal* is now the premier physics journal published on the continent, and it belongs in all physics research collections.

4315. ***European Physical Journal B. Condensed Matter and Complex Systems.*** Incorporates in part (1903-2000): *Anales de Fisica;* Formed by the merger of (1963-1998): *Journal de Physique I;* Which was formerly (until 1991): *Journal de Physique;* (until 1962): *Jopurnal de Physique et le Radium;* (1963-1998): *Zeitschrift fuer Physik B: Condensed Matter;* Which was formerly (until 1980): *Zeitschrift fuer Physik B (Condensed Matter and Quanta);* (until 1973): *Physik der Kondensierten Materie - Physique de la Matiere Condensee - Physics of Condensed Matter;* (1771-1998): *Societa Italiana di Fisica. Nuovo Cimento D;* Which superseded in part (in 1982): *Nuovo Cimento;* Which was formerly (until 1885): *Il Cimento;* (until 1843): *Miscellanee di Chimica, Fisica e Storia Naturale;* Which superseded in part (in 1843): *Giornale Toscano di Scienze Mediche Fisiche e Naturali;* Which was formerly (until 1840): *Nuovo Giornale dei Letterati;* (until 1822): *Accademia Italiana di Scienze Lettere ed Arti. Giornale Scientifico e Letterario;* (until 1810): *Giornale Pisano di Letteratura, Scienze ed Arti;* (until 1807): *Giornale Pisano dei Letterati;* (until 1806): *Nuovo Giornale dei Letterati;* (until 1820): *Giornale dei Letterati.* [ISSN: 1434-6028] 1998. s-m. EUR 5355 (print & online eds.). Ed(s): Alois Loidl, A Rubio. Springer, Tiergartenstr 17, Heidelberg, 69121, Germany. Illus., index, adv. Refereed. Microform: PMC; PQC. Reprint: PSC. *Indexed:* A01, A22, CCMJ, E01, EngInd, M&GPA, MSN, MathR. *Aud.:* Ac, Sa.

Available in print and online. *Part B* of the *European Physical Journal* concentrates on solid-state physics, condensed matter, and complex systems. Topics covered include: solid state and materials; mesoscopic and nanoscale systems; computational methods; statistical and nonlinear physics; and interdisciplinary physics. The majority of the articles published are full-length research reports, although some colloquia papers are also included. Colloquia papers describe the development of new areas of research or the impact of new and promising experimental or theoretical methods in the field. While not as extensive and complete as reviews in the usual sense, they are intended to suitably introduce new research directions and techniques in their early stages of development, and to a wider audience. All of the articles are published in English. In order to speed publication, many of the articles are published in the *Online First* electronic delivery service before appearing in print. As the official publication of over 40 different European physics societies, this title belongs in any comprehensive physics collection.

4316. ***European Physical Journal C. Particles and Fields.*** Incorporates in part (1903-2000): *Anales de Fisica;* (1855-1999): *Societa Italiana di Fisica. Nuovo Cimento. A. Nuclei, Paticles and Fields;* Which was formerly (until 1982): *Societa Italiana di Fisica. Nuovo Cimento. A;* (until 1971): *Nuovo Cimento A;* Which superseded in part (in 1965): *Nuovo Cimento;* Formerly (until 1997): *Zeitschrift fuer Physik C. Particles and Fields.* [ISSN: 1434-6044] 1979. 20x/yr. EUR 5670 (print & online eds.). Ed(s): I Antoniadis, G Isidori. Springer, Tiergartenstr 17, Heidelberg, 69121, Germany. Illus., index, adv. Sample. Refereed. Microform: PMC; PQC. Reprint: PSC. *Indexed:* A01, A22, CCMJ, E01, MSN, MathR. *Aud.:* Ac, Sa.

Available in print and online. *Part C* of the *European Physical Journal* covers high-energy physics, including both theoretical and experimental research. It emphasizes the elementary aspects of particles and fields and specializes in reporting research results from the world's leading laboratories, including CERN, Fermilab, and KEK. Topics covered include the standard model; quantum chromodynamics; heavy-ion physics; astroparticle physics; hadron and lepton collisions; high-energy nuclear reactions; neutrino physics; high-energy cosmic rays; and dark matter. This section of the journal is the continuation of *Il Nuovo Cimento A* and *Zeitschrift fuer Physik C.* Full-length articles, rapid notes, reviews, notes on new experimental tools and devices, and letters are all included. Occasional issues contain the proceedings of relevant conferences. Although this is a European journal, all of the articles are published in English. This is the premier journal for European research in particle physics, and it belongs in comprehensive physics collections. Also available in an online edition.

4317. ***European Physical Journal D. Atomic, Molecular, Optical and Plasma Physics.*** Incorporates (1951-2007): *Czechoslovak Journal of Physics;* Incorporates in part (1903-2000): *Anales de Fisica;* Formed by the merger of (1991-1998): *Journal de Physique II;* (1986-1998): *Zeitschrift fuer Physik D. Atoms, Molecules and Clusters;* Supersedes in part (1982-1999): *Societa Italiana di Fisica. Nuovo Cimento D;* Which incorporated in part (1855-1965): *Nuovo Cimento;* Which superseded (1843-1847): *Cimento; Miscellanee de Chimica, Fisica e Storia Naturale;* Which superseded in part (in 1843): *Giornale Toscano di Scienze Mediche Fisiche e Naturali;* (until 1840): *Nuovo Giornale dei Letterati;* Which superseded (in 1822): *Accademia Italiana di Scienze Lettere ed Arti. Giornale Scientifico e Letterario;* (until 1809): *Giornale Pisano di Letteratura, Scienze ed Arti;* (until 1807): *Giornale Pisano dei Letterati;* (1802-1806): *Nuovo Giornale dei Letterati;* Which superseded (1771-1796): *Giornale dei Letterati.* [ISSN: 1434-6060] 1998. 15x/yr. EUR 3114 (print & online eds.). Ed(s): K H Becker, V Buzek. Springer, Tiergartenstr 17, Heidelberg, 69121, Germany. Illus., index, adv. Refereed. Reprint: PSC. *Indexed:* A01, A22, CCMJ, E01, MSN, MathR. *Aud.:* Ac, Sa.

Available in print and online. The fourth section of the *European Physical Journal* is devoted to atomic, molecular, plasma, and optical physics. This journal was formed through the combination of three similar journals: *Il Nuovo Cimento D, Journal de Physique,* and *Zeitschrift fuer Physik D.* Topics in this section include atomic physics; molecular physics; chemical physics; atomic and molecular collisions; clusters and nanostructures; plasma physics; laser cooling and quantum gas; nonlinear dynamics; optical physics; quantum optics and quantum information; and ultraintense and ultrashort laser fields. In addition to full-length research articles, the journal publishes occasional colloquia papers that describe the development of new areas of research or the impact of new and promising experimental or theoretical methods in the fields that are within the spectrum of topics covered by the respective journals. Some of the issues present the papers from conferences in the disciplines represented by the journal. All of the papers are published in English, even though they represent the results of European research. Recommended for comprehensive physics collections.

4318. ***European Physical Journal E. Soft Matter.*** Formed by the merger of part of (1998-2000): *European Physical Journal. B. Condensed Matter Physics;* part of (1992-2000): *Anales de Fisica;* Which was formed by the merger of (1903-1992): *Anales de Fisica. Serie A: Fenomenos e Interacciones;* (1903-1992): *Anales de Fisica. Serie B: Aplicaciones, Metodos e Instrumentos;* Both of which superseded in part (in 1981): *Anales de Fisica;* Which was formerly (until 1968): *Real Sociedad Espanola de Fisica y Quimica. Anales. Serie A: Fisica;* Which superseded in part (in 1948): *Anales de Fisica y Quimica;* Which was formerly (until 1941): *Sociedad Espanola de Fisica y Quimica. Anales.* [ISSN: 1292-8941] 2000. m. EUR 2481 (print & online eds.). Ed(s): Frank Juelicher, J-M Di Meglio. Springer, Haber Str 7, Heidelberg, 69126, Germany. Adv. Sample. Refereed. Reprint: PSC. *Indexed:* A01, A22, E01, EngInd. *Aud.:* Ac, Sa.

Available in print and online. The fifth section of the *European Physical Journal* covers the fields of soft matter and biological physics. Soft matter is a term for a large group of condensed, often heterogeneous systems that display a large response to weak external perturbations and that possess properties governed by slow internal dynamics. Biological physics studies the new physics that emerges from novel insights into the properties and behaviors of living systems. The range of topics covered includes: polymers and polyelectrolytes; liquid crystals, liquids, and complex fluids; self-organization and supramolecular assemblies; colloids, nanoparticles, and granular matter; functional materials and nanodevices; interfacial phenomena and nanostructured surfaces; liquids and complex fluids; structure and function of biological matter; biomimetic systems; cellular processes; multicellular systems; and biological networks. Full-length research articles and instructional colloquia papers are both included. As in each of the other sections of this journal, all of the articles are published in English. Recommended only for comprehensive physics collections.

4319. ***European Physical Journal H.*** Formerly (until 2009): *Annales de Physique;* Which superseded in part (in 1914): *Annales de Chimie et de Physique.* [ISSN: 2102-6459] 1816. q. EUR 589 (print & online eds.).

Ed(s): Wolf Beiglboeck. Springer, Tiergartenstr 17, Heidelberg, 69121, Germany; http://www.springer.com. Illus. Refereed. Microform: PMC. *Indexed:* A22, C&ISA, CerAb, MathR. *Aud.:* Ac, Sa.

Available in print and online. Most physics journals publish current research results, but this is not the purpose of this new section of the *European Physical Journal*. This journal focuses on the history of modern physics, presenting papers that discuss how current concepts in the field were identified and developed. The purpose of this title is to provide an awareness and understanding of the historical development of ideas in contemporary physics, and more generally, ideas about how Nature works. The journal specifically encourages contributions that address the history of physics and of physical ideas and concepts; the interplay of physics and mathematics, as well as with the natural sciences; and the history and philosophy of sciences, together with discussions of experimental ideas and designs—inasmuch as they clearly relate, and preferably add, to the understanding of modern physics. In addition, this journal also seeks articles that discuss past mistakes and abandoned ideas in physics, providing a historical perspective on the rise and failure of those concepts. In addition to papers about the history of physics, the journal also reproduces key historical articles from the field, and publishes personal recollections by people who shaped modern physics. This journal belongs in any collection that supports research into the history of physics.

4320. *The European Physical Journal. Special Topics.* Former titles (until 2007): *Journal de Physique IV;* (until 1991): *Journal de Physique. Colloque.* [ISSN: 1951-6355] 1966. 14x/yr. EUR 1964 (print & online eds.). Springer, Tiergartenstr 17, Heidelberg, 69121, Germany; subscriptions@springer.com. Refereed. Reprint: PSC. *Indexed:* A22, C&ISA, CerAb, E01, EngInd. *Aud.:* Ac, Sa.

Available in print and online. The newest section of the *European Physical Journal* publishes topical issues that are collections of review-type articles or extensive, detailed progress reports. Each issue is focused on a specific subject matter of topical interest. The journal scope covers the whole spectrum of pure and applied physics, including related subjects such as materials science, physical biology, physical chemistry, and complex systems. Papers are invited or are the result of specialized workshops or conferences. The journal offers a new feature in the form of *Discussion and Debate* issues. The aim of such topical issues is to provide balanced critical presentation of specific unsolved problems, controversial topics, rival theories, alternative methodologies, and negative results of interest at the cutting edge of scientific and technological development. Formerly published as part IV of the *Journal de Physique*, this title will be a source for highly specialized research in a wide range of fields within physics.

4321. *Europhysics Letters: a letters journal exploring the frontiers of physics.* Formed by the merger of (1974-1986): *Journal de Physique. Lettres;* (1971-1986): *Societa Italiana di Fisica. Lettere al Nuovo Cimento;* Which was formerly (until 1971): *Lettere al Nuovo Cimento.* [ISSN: 0295-5075] 1986. s-m. GBP 2591 (print & online eds.). Ed(s): Graeme Watt, Frederic Burr. E D P Sciences, 17 Ave du Hoggar, Parc d'Activites de Courtaboeuf, Les Ulis, 91944, France; contact@edpsciences.org; http://www.edpsciences.org. Sample. Refereed. *Indexed:* A22, C&ISA, CCMJ, CerAb, MSN, MathR. *Aud.:* Ac, Sa.

Available in print and online. *EPL* serves as the letters-to-the-editor journal for all of the sections of the *European Physical Journal*. It publishes short, rapid communications of important research results. Letters published in *EPL* contain new research results, ideas, concepts, experimental methods, and theoretical treatments of broad interest and importance to one or several sections of the physics community, including those with application potential. Articles are written for the specialist, yet remain understandable to the researchers in other fields. Topics include general physics; physics of elementary particles and fields; nuclear physics; atomic, molecular, and optical physics; classical areas of phenomenology; physics of gases, plasmas, and electrical discharges; condensed matter; cross-disciplinary physics; and related areas of science and technology. For a fee, authors may elect to have their article available as an open-access article. Although the journal is European, all of the articles are published in English. This title belongs in research-level physics collections.

4322. *Foundations of Physics: an international journal devoted to the conceptual bases and fundamental theories of modern physics.* Incorporates (1988-2006): *Foundations of Physics Letters.* [ISSN:

0015-9018] 1970. m. EUR 2488 (print & online eds.). Ed(s): Gerard 't Hooft. Springer New York LLC, 233 Spring St, New York, NY 10013; service-ny@springer.com; http://www.springer.com/. Illus., index, adv. Refereed. Vol. ends: Dec. Microform: PQC. Reprint: PSC. *Indexed:* A01, A22, BRI, CCMJ, E01, MSN, MathR. *Bk. rev.:* Number and length vary. *Aud.:* Ac, Sa.

Available in print and online. One of the major objectives of modern physics research is to develop a single unified theory that can explain all physical properties, effects, and interactions. Ever since Einstein proposed that researchers work toward a single theory of the universe, scientists have approached this problem from a number of angles. *Foundations of Physics* emphasizes the logical, methodological, and philosophical premises of modern physical theories and procedures. Much of the material covers cosmology, quantum mechanics, wave theory, gravitation, general relativity, and gauge theory. The editors also accept contributions in the areas of quantum gravity, quantum information, string theory, M-theory, and brane cosmology. Articles tend to be speculative in nature and often question existing theoretical concepts. This journal is somewhat unusual in the field of physics in that it stresses theory rather than experimental results. Full-length papers and letters to the editor are accepted. Because of its focus on one of the single most important questions in physics today, this title is a useful addition to comprehensive collections in theoretical physics.

4323. *General Relativity and Gravitation.* Formerly (until 1970): *Bulletin on General Relativity and Gravitation.* [ISSN: 0001-7701] 1962. m. EUR 2466 (print & online eds.). Ed(s): H Nicolai, G F R Ellis. Springer New York LLC, 233 Spring St, New York, NY 10013; service-ny@springer.com; http://www.springer.com/. Illus., index, adv. Refereed. Vol. ends: Dec. Microform: PQC. Reprint: PSC. *Indexed:* A01, A22, BRI, CCMJ, E01, M&GPA, MSN, MathR. *Bk. rev.:* Number and length vary. *Aud.:* Ac, Sa.

Available in print and online. Einstein spent much of his professional life working on the theories of gravity and relativity. This journal was developed to continue that research. Coverage includes extensions of general relativity; numerical relativity; astrophysical applications of relativistic gravity; experimental gravitational physics, in particular experimental tests of general relativity; gravitational wave data analysis and phenomenology; theoretical and observational cosmology; quantum field theory in curved space-time; supergravity and gravitational aspects of string theory and its extensions; quantum gravity and cosmology; and the teaching, public understanding, and history of general relativity and gravitation. Although this title primarily publishes research papers on the theoretical and experimental aspects of these areas, it occasionally includes letters, review articles, book reviews, conference programs, historical articles, and news items. Most of the articles are of a highly theoretical nature, which is inherent in the subject matter. As the official publication of the International Society on General Relativity and Gravitation, this journal serves as the premier source for research on and discussion of the two topics in its title. It was founded by some of the most prominent researchers in twentieth-century physics, and it maintains those high standards today. *General Relativity and Gravitation* is an important title in any comprehensive collection on theoretical physics.

4324. *International Journal of Theoretical Physics.* [ISSN: 0020-7748] 1968. m. EUR 2991 (print & online eds.). Ed(s): Heinrich Saller. Springer New York LLC, 233 Spring St, New York, NY 10013; service-ny@springer.com; http://www.springer.com/. Illus., index, adv. Sample. Refereed. Vol. ends: Dec. Microform: PQC. Reprint: PSC. *Indexed:* A01, A22, CCMJ, E01, MSN, MathR. *Aud.:* Ac, Sa.

Available in print and online. One of the major goals of modern physics is to develop a grand unification theory that links all known physical forces. Dedicated to the unification of the latest physics research, the *International Journal of Theoretical Physics* seeks to map the direction of future research that arises from new analytical methods, including the latest progress in the use of computers, and to complement traditional physics research by providing fresh inquiry into quantum measurement theory, relativistic field theory, and other similarly fundamental areas. It covers such topics as quantum theory; space-time structure; quantum communication; cosmology; gravity; space-time; quantum geometry; quantum logic; and topology. Only full-length research papers are accepted. Occasional special issues contain the proceedings of conferences related to unification theory. *Foundations of Physics* (see above) serves a similar objective and contains very similar material. With the continuing search for a grand unification theory, both of these journals will remain important for comprehensive physics collections.

4325. *J C P: Biochemical Physics.* [ISSN: 1931-9223] 2007. m. Ed(s): Marsha I Lester. American Institute of Physics, 1 Physics Ellipse, College Park, MD 20740; aipinfo@aip.org; http://www.aip.org. *Aud.:* Ac, Sa.

Available online only. As interest in biochemical processes has grown, the editors of the *Journal of Chemical Physics* created a spin-off online journal dedicated specifically to biophysics. This title includes the subset of articles from the *Journal of Chemical Physics* that directly deal with or have important implications for biologically-related systems. All articles included in this journal are also published in the *Journal of Chemical Physics,* but those interested only in the biological section may purchase this title separately. Articles appear online on a daily basis and are compiled into monthly issues. Like its parent title, this journal publishes primarily full-length research articles, but it also includes brief communications and letters to the editor. Libraries that specialize in biological research and not physics may wish to purchase only this section of the *Journal of Chemical Physics.*

4326. *Japanese Journal of Applied Physics.* Supersedes (in 2008): *Japanese Journal of Applied Physics: Part 1. Regular Papers & Short Notes;* Which superseded in part (in 1981): *Japanese Journal of Applied Physics.* 1962. m. 15 special issue. GBP 1333 (print & online eds.). Ed(s): Tadashi Shibata, Kazuo Tsutsui. Japan Society of Applied Physics, Yushima Urban Bldg, 7F, 2-31-22 Yushima, Tokyo, 113-0034, Japan; http://www.jsap.or.jp. Illus. Refereed. *Indexed:* A&ATA, C&ISA, EngInd, PhotoAb. *Aud.:* Ac, Sa.

Available in print and online. The *Japanese Journal of Applied Physics* is an international journal, and is the primary publication outlet for Japanese research in all fields of applied physics. The journal publishes articles that deal with the applications of physical principles as well as articles that concern the understanding of physics that have particular applications in mind. Topics covered by this journal include: semiconductors, dielectrics, and organic materials; photonics, quantum electronics, optics, and spectroscopy; spintronics, superconductivity, and strongly correlated materials; device physics; nanoscale science and technology; crystal growth, surfaces, interfaces, thin films, and bulk materials; plasmas, applied atomic and molecular physics, and applied nuclear physics; device processing, fabrication and measurement technologies, and instrumentation; and cross-disciplinary areas. The journal publishes research papers, rapid communications, brief notes, and reviews. Letters are published in the sister journal *Applied Physics Express.* Although the journal is Japanese, all of the articles are published in English. Articles in this journal are free to any registered user for 90 days, after which time a subscription is required to retrieve them. As one of the major journals that cover Japanese research, this title is essential to providing balanced coverage of worldwide physics research.

4327. *Journal of Applied Physics.* Formerly (until 1937): *Physics;* Which incorporated (1929-1932): *Journal of Rheology.* [ISSN: 0021-8979] 1929. 48x/yr. Ed(s): James P Viccaro. American Institute of Physics, 1 Physics Ellipse, College Park, MD 20740; aipinfo@aip.org; http://www.aip.org. Illus., index, adv. Sample. Refereed. *Indexed:* A01, A22, ApMecR, BRI, EngInd, MathR, PhotoAb. *Aud.:* Ac, Sa.

Available in print and online. The *Journal of Applied Physics* is a primary journal for the publication of applications-centered research in optics, photonics, imaging, and sensing. As opposed to most other physics journals, which concentrate on theoretical or experimental advances, this journal specializes in the application of physical concepts to industrial processes and to other scientific disciplines. Its articles emphasize the understanding of the physics underlying modern technology, but distinguished from technology on the one side and pure physics on the other. Topics include lasers, optics, and optoelectronics; plasmas and electrical discharges; structural, mechanical, thermodynamic, and optical properties of condensed matter; electronic structure and transport; magnetism and superconductivity; dielectrics and ferroelectricity; nanoscale science and design; device physics; applied biophysics; and interdisciplinary and general physics. The common thread is that the articles clearly describe the uses and applications of a physical concept

rather than its theoretical foundations. Full papers and brief communications are included in each issue. Some articles include multimedia components to enhance the text. This journal is the single most highly cited archival research journal in the area of applied physics. Letters are published in the sister publication *Applied Physics Letters* (see above). This title belongs in every physics research collection.

4328. *The Journal of Chemical Physics.* [ISSN: 0021-9606] 1933. w. 48/yr. Ed(s): Marsha I Lester. American Institute of Physics, 1 Physics Ellipse, College Park, MD 20740; aipinfo@aip.org; http://www.aip.org. Illus., index, adv. Refereed. Circ: 140000. *Indexed:* A01, A22, ApMecR, CEA, EngInd, MathR. *Aud.:* Ac, Sa.

Available in print and online. The purpose of the *Journal of Chemical Physics* is to bridge the gap between scholarly research journals in physics and chemistry. As the boundary between these two disciplines continues to narrow, there are more and more researchers working on issues related to both fields of study. This journal publishes quantitative research based on physical principles and techniques as applied to chemical systems, covering topics such as spectroscopy, kinetics, statistical mechanics, and quantum mechanics. In addition, newer areas such as polymers, materials, surfaces/interfaces, information theory, and systems of biological relevance are of increasing importance. Most of this journal consists of full-length research reports, although brief communications, letters, and notes are also occasionally included. As the leading journal to focus on the crossover between physics and chemistry, this title belongs in any research collection devoted to either physics or chemistry.

4329. *Journal of Computational Physics.* [ISSN: 0021-9991] 1966. 24x/yr. EUR 8838. Ed(s): G Tryggvason. Academic Press, 3251 Riverport Ln, Maryland Heights, MO 63043; JournalCustomerService-usa@elsevier.com; http://www.elsevierdirect.com/brochures/academicpress/index.html. Illus., index, adv. Refereed. *Indexed:* A01, A22, ApMecR, C&ISA, CCMJ, CerAb, CompR, E01, M&GPA, MSN, MathR. *Aud.:* Ac, Sa.

Available in print and online. The mission of the *Journal of Computational Physics* is to publish material that will assist in the accurate solution of scientific problems by numerical analysis and computational methods. The journal seeks to emphasize methods that cross disciplinary boundaries. Most of the papers deal with the development and application of algorithms for the solution of physical problems. The articles do not contain new research findings, but provide scientists with the methodology for conducting and refining the research process using mathematical processes. Papers dealing solely with hardware or software are excluded; each article must discuss the applications of computing to a physical or mathematical problem. Full-length research reports, short notes, and letters to the editor are all accepted. Occasional theme issues deal with special topics. Supplemental material such as audio, video, animation, images, or data are included in the online version of this journal along with the article. This journal supplements other physics research titles and belongs in comprehensive collections.

4330. *Journal of Magnetism and Magnetic Materials.* [ISSN: 0304-8853] 1975. 24x/yr. EUR 8946. Ed(s): S D Bader. Elsevier BV, North-Holland, Postbus 211, Amsterdam, 1000 AE, Netherlands; JournalsCustomerServiceEMEA@elsevier.com; http://www.elsevier.com. Illus., index, adv. Sample. Refereed. Microform: PQC. *Indexed:* A01, A22, C&ISA, CerAb, EngInd. *Aud.:* Ac, Sa.

Available in print and online. As one of the basic forces of physics, magnetism is a property that has been widely studied for centuries. The *Journal of Magnetism and Magnetic Materials* provides an important forum for the disclosure and discussion of original contributions that cover the whole spectrum of topics, from basic magnetism to the technology and applications of magnetic materials and magnetic recording. The journal encourages greater interaction between the basic and applied subdisciplines of magnetism. Theoretical, experimental, and applied-research papers are all included. The journal also publishes letters to the editor, short communications, and occasional review articles. Some issues contain the proceedings of conferences relating to magnetism or magnetic materials. This journal belongs in any library that supports research in this field.

4331. *Journal of Mathematical Physics.* [ISSN: 0022-2488] 1960. m. Ed(s): Bruno L Z Nachtergaele. American Institute of Physics, 1 Physics Ellipse, College Park, MD 20740; aipinfo@aip.org; http://www.aip.org. Illus., index, adv. Sample. Refereed. Vol. ends: Dec. *Indexed:* A01, A22, CCMJ, MSN, MathR, P02. *Aud.:* Ac, Sa.

Available in print and online. The purpose of this journal is to provide a place for the publication of articles that deal with the application of mathematics to problems in modern physics. It also covers the development of mathematical techniques and research methods and the application of mathematics to physical theories. Specific topics cover the entire range of the field of physics, including classical mechanics, kinetic theory, dynamical systems, quantum mechanics, scattering theory, particles and fields, relativity, gravitation, string theory, statistical mechanics, dynamical systems, and quantum information and computation. New articles are published online every day, then collected into monthly online and print issues. An annual special issue provides in-depth analysis of one specific aspect of mathematical physics. The editors request that the mathematics be presented in such a way as to be understandable by a wide audience within the physics community. Even so, most of the articles will require a graduate-level understanding of mathematics and physics in order to completely comprehend the material. An important addition to any graduate physics collection.

4332. *Journal of Physics A: Mathematical and Theoretical.* Formerly (until 2007): *Journal of Physics A: Mathematical and General;* Which superseded in part (in 1975): *Journal of Physics A: Mathematical Nuclear and General;* Which was formerly (until 1973): *Journal of Physics. A, Physical Society. Proceedings. General;* Which superseded in part (in 1968): *Physical Society. Proceedings;* Which was formed by the merger of (1949-1958): *Physical Society. Proceedings. Section A;* (1949-1958): *Physical Society. Proceedings. Section B;* Both of which superseded in part (in 1949): *Physical Society. Proceedings;* (until 1926): *Physical Society of London. Proceedings;* Physical Society. Proceedings incorporated (1900-1932): *Optical Society. Transactions.* [ISSN: 1751-8113] 1958. 50x/yr. GBP 5196 (print & online eds.). Ed(s): M T Batchelor. Institute of Physics Publishing Ltd., Temple Circus, Temple Way, Bristol, BS1 6HG, United Kingdom; custserv@iop.org; http://ioppublishing.org. Illus. Sample. Refereed. *Indexed:* A01, A22, ApMecR, CCMJ, MSN, MathR. *Aud.:* Ac, Sa.

Available in print and online. As the British counterpart to the *Physical Review* (see below), the *Journal of Physics* is one of the two most prominent collections of physics research journals published anywhere the world. It is also one of the most heavily cited sources in the field, and is highly respected by researchers worldwide. Like the *Physical Review,* this journal is issued in many parts that cover the various subdisciplines of physics. *Part A* covers mathematical and statistical physics. Thus, it is primarily concerned with the mathematical structures that describe fundamental processes of the physical world and on the analytical, computational, and numerical methods for exploring these structures. It is divided into six subsections, covering the fields of: statistical physics; chaotic and complex systems; mathematical physics; quantum mechanics and quantum information theory; field theory and string theory; and fluid and plasma theory. Both full-length research papers and letters to the editor are included, along with short corrections to previously published material. Review articles appear occasionally, and sometimes special issues are devoted to specific topics. This title belongs in every physics research collection.

4333. *Journal of Physics and Chemistry of Solids: an international journal.* Formerly (until 1963): *Physics and Chemistry of Solids.* [ISSN: 0022-3697] 1956. m. EUR 6288. Pergamon, The Blvd, Langford Ln, E Park, Kidlington, OX5 1GB, United Kingdom; JournalsCustomerServiceEMEA@elsevier.com; http://www.elsevier.com. Illus., adv. Sample. Refereed. Microform: MIM; PQC. *Indexed:* A01, A22, ApMecR, C&ISA, EngInd. *Aud.:* Ac, Sa.

Available in print and online. The *Journal of Physics and Chemistry of Solids* publishes original research in condensed-matter physics and materials science. General areas of interest are the electronic, spectroscopic, and structural properties of solids; the statistical mechanics and thermodynamics of condensed systems, including perfect and defect lattices; surfaces, interfaces, thin films, and multilayers; amorphous materials and nanostructures; and layered and low-dimensional structures. Specific topics covered include: the preparation and structural characterization of novel and advanced materials, especially in relation to the measurement and interpretation of their electrical, magnetic, optical, thermal, and mechanical properties; phase transitions, electronic structure, and defect properties; and the application of appropriate experimental and theoretical techniques in these studies. Also covered is the application of appropriate experimental and theoretical techniques used in these studies. From time to time, special issues of the journal are published that contain invited articles devoted to topical or rapidly developing fields. Only full-length articles are accepted, with letters published in the related *Solid State Communications* (see below). For comprehensive physics research collections.

4334. *Journal of Physics B: Atomic, Molecular and Optical Physics.* Incorporates (in 1999): *Journal of Optics B: Quantum and Semiclassical Optics;* Which was formerly (until 1999): *Quantum and Semiclassical Optics;* (until 1995): *Quantum Optics;* Former titles (until 1988): *Journal of Physics B: Atomic and Molecular Physics;* (until 1969): *Journal of Physics B: Physical Society. Proceedings. Atomic and Molecular Physics;* Which superseded in part (in 1968): *Physical Society. Proceedings;* Which was formed by the merger of (1949-1958): *Physical Society. Proceedings. Section A;* (1949-1958): *Physical Society. Proceedings. Section B;* Both of which superseded in part (in 1949): *Physical Society. Proceedings;* Which was formerly (until 1926): *Physical Society of London. Proceedings;* Physical Society. Proceedings incorporated (1900-1932): *Optical Society. Transactions.* [ISSN: 0953-4075] 1958. s-m. GBP 3776 (print & online eds.). Ed(s): Paul Corkum. Institute of Physics Publishing Ltd., Temple Circus, Temple Way, Bristol, BS1 6HG, United Kingdom; custserv@iop.org; http://ioppublishing.org. Illus. Sample. Refereed. *Indexed:* A01, A22, ApMecR, C&ISA, CCMJ, CerAb, EngInd, MSN, MathR. *Aud.:* Ac, Sa.

Available in print and online. As part of the *Journal of Physics* collection of titles, this is one of the most prominent physics journals published worldwide. This section covers atomic physics; molecular and cluster structure, properties, and dynamics; atomic and molecular collisions; cold matter; optical and laser physics; quantum optics, information, and control; ultrafast, high-field, and X-ray physics; and astrophysics and plasma physics. In addition to publishing full-length research reports, the journal also publishes review articles, fast-track communications, and Ph.D. tutorials. The Ph.D. tutorials guide newcomers into rapidly developing fields, and the "Fast Track" papers take the place of the former letters to the editor. This journal is similar in coverage and scope to *Part B* of the *Physical Review* (see below). Occasional special issues are devoted to a single topic. This is one of the most respected journals in the field, and it belongs in every physics research collection.

4335. *Journal of Physics: Condensed Matter.* Formed by the merger of (1971-1989): *Journal of Physics F: Metal Physics;* Which superseded in part (in 1971): *Metal Physics;* (1968-1989): *Journal of Physics C: Solid State Physics;* Which was formerly (until 1968): *Journal of Physics C: Physical Society. Proceedings. Solid State Physics;* Which superseded in part (in 1968): *Physical Society. Proceedings;* Which was formed by the merger of (1949-1958): *Physical Society. Proceedings. Section A;* (1949-1958): *Physical Society. Proceedings. Section B;* Both of which superseded in part (in 1949): *Physical Society. Proceedings;* Which was formerly (until 1926): *Physical Society of London. Proceedings;* Physical Society. Proceedings incorporated (1900-1932): *Optical Society. Transactions.* [ISSN: 0953-8984] 1958. 50x/yr. GBP 7173 (print & online eds.). Ed(s): Jason S Gardner. Institute of Physics Publishing Ltd., Temple Circus, Temple Way, Bristol, BS1 6HG, United Kingdom; custserv@iop.org; http://ioppublishing.org. Illus., adv. Sample. Refereed. *Indexed:* A22, ApMecR, C&ISA, CerAb, EngInd, MathR. *Aud.:* Ac, Sa.

Available in print and online. Another journal in the important *Journal of Physics* collection, this title is devoted to articles on experimental and theoretical studies of the structural, thermal, mechanical, electrical, magnetic, optical, and surface properties of condensed matter. Specific topics include: surface, interface, and atomic-scale science; liquids, soft matter, and biological physics; nanostructures and nanoelectronics; solid structure and lattice dynamics; electronic structure; correlated electrons; superconductors and metals; semiconductors; dielectrics and ferroelectrics; and magnetism and magnetic materials. Most articles are full research papers, although the journal also publishes topical review articles. "Fast Track Communications" takes the place of letters to the editor and publishes short, important research findings. The journal provides free open access to articles that the editors consider to be outstanding. As part of the *Journal of Physics,* this title belongs in all physics research collections.

4336. Journal of Physics: Conference Series (Online). [ISSN: 1742-6596] 2004. a. Institute of Physics Publishing Ltd., Temple Circus, Temple Way, Bristol, BS1 6HG, United Kingdom; custserv@iop.org; http://publishing.iop.org/. *Aud.:* Ac, Sa.

Available online only. This section of the *Journal of Physics* was established as an open-access journal for the publication of the proceedings of conferences, workshops, and institutes on topics throughout the field of physics. Since it is freely available online, it allows for publication within three months of the event and provides long-term archiving of the papers. All papers are printed in pdf format, with accompanying multimedia materials where appropriate. As it has become an established publication outlet, it has recruited more and more conferences to participate. In 2010, the papers from 61 different conferences were published through this journal. Because the papers are presented at meetings for specialists in the field, they are highly specific in content and not for the casual reader. This journal makes conference proceedings available to a worldwide audience at no cost. It belongs in every physics research collection.

4337. Journal of Physics D: Applied Physics. Former titles (until 1970): *British Journal of Applied Physics. Journal of Physics D;* (until 1968): *British Journal of Applied Physics.* [ISSN: 0022-3727] 1950. 50x/yr. GBP 2963 (print & online eds.). Ed(s): Giorgio Margaritondo. Institute of Physics Publishing Ltd., Temple Circus, Temple Way, Bristol, BS1 6HG, United Kingdom; custserv@iop.org; http://ioppublishing.org. Illus. Sample. Refereed. *Indexed:* A01, A22, C&ISA, CerAb, EngInd, PhotoAb. *Aud.:* Ac, Sa.

Available in print and online. The *Journal of Physics D* is concerned with all aspects of applied-physics research. The editors welcome experimental, computational (including simulation and modeling), and theoretical studies of applied physics, and also studies in physics-related areas of biomedical and life sciences. Specific areas of interest include: applied magnetism and magnetic materials; photonics and semiconductor device physics; plasmas and plasma-surface interactions; applied surfaces and interfaces; and the structure and properties of matter. The editors are particularly interested in publishing articles on novel effects and new materials. It publishes full-length research papers; "Fast Track Communications," which are short, timely articles of high impact; and occasional topical reviews. This title is the British equivalent of the *Journal of Applied Physics* (see above), and is an essential component of all physics research collections.

4338. Journal of Physics G: Nuclear and Particle Physics. Formerly (until 1989): *Journal of Physics G: Nuclear Physics;* Which superseded in part (in 1975): *Journal of Physics A: Mathematical Nuclear and General;* Which was formerly (until 1973): *Journal of Physics A: Physical Society. Proceedings. General;* Which superseded in part (in 1968): *Physical Society. Proceedings;* Which was formed by the merger of (1949-1958): *Physical Society. Proceedings. Section A;* (1949-1958): *Physical Society. Proceedings. Section B;* Both of which superseded in part (in 1949): *Physical Society. Proceedings;* Which was formerly (until 1926): *Physical Society of London. Proceedings;* Physical Society. Proceedings incorporated (1900-1932): *Optical Society. Transactions.* [ISSN: 0954-3899] 1989. m. GBP 2221 (print & online eds.). Ed(s): A Schwenk. Institute of Physics Publishing Ltd., Temple Circus, Temple Way, Bristol, BS1 6HG, United Kingdom; custserv@iop.org; http://ioppublishing.org. Illus. Sample. Refereed. Vol. ends: Dec. *Indexed:* A01, A22, MathR. *Aud.:* Ac, Sa.

Available in print and online. As another section of the *Journal of Physics* collection, *Part G* covers theoretical and experimental topics in the physics of elementary particles and fields, intermediate-energy physics, and nuclear physics. The particle astrophysics section includes all aspects of experimental and theoretical research into cosmic rays, nuclear and particle astrophysics, gamma ray astronomy, and neutrino astrophysics and dark matter. Full-length research papers, review articles, and research notes are all included, with full-

length papers predominating. One volume each year consists of the annual *Review of Particle Physics.* This journal is the British equivalent of *Physical Review Sections C* and *D* (see below), and it belongs in any physics research collection.

4339. Journal of Plasma Physics. [ISSN: 0022-3778] 1967. bi-m. GBP 1318. Ed(s): Bengt Eliasson. Cambridge University Press, The Edinburgh Bldg, Shaftesbury Rd, Cambridge, CB2 8RU, United Kingdom; journals@cambridge.org; http://www.cambridge.org/uk. Illus., index, adv. Refereed. Microform: PQC. Reprint: PSC. *Indexed:* A01, A22, ApMecR, E01, EngInd, M&GPA. *Aud.:* Ac, Sa.

Available in print and online. Plasma physics is a branch of physics that has applications in a wide variety of fields, including astrophysics, fluids, and nuclear physics. This specialized journal publishes original-research reports on plasma science in all of these areas. Basic topics include: the fundamental physics of plasmas; ionization; kinetic theory; particle orbits; stochastic dynamics; wave propagation; solitons; stability; shock waves; transport; heating; and diagnostics. Applications include: fusion; laboratory plasmas; communications devices; laser plasmas; technological plasmas; space physics; and astrophysics. Both theoretical and experimental results are presented, along with applications of plasma science in other fields. Full research papers, reviews, and letters to the editor are included. Occasionally special themed issues are published. This journal belongs in specialized and comprehensive physics collections.

4340. Measurement Science and Technology. Former titles (until 1990): *Journal of Physics E: Scientific Instruments;* (until 1970): *Journal of Physics. E, Journal of Scientific Instruments;* (until 1968): *Journal of Scientific Instruments;* (until 1950): *Journal of Scientific Instruments and of Physics in Industry;* (until 1948): *Journal of Scientific Instruments.* [ISSN: 0957-0233] 1922. m. GBP 1403 (print & online eds.). Ed(s): David J S Birch. Institute of Physics Publishing Ltd., Temple Circus, Temple Way, Bristol, BS1 6HG, United Kingdom; custserv@iop.org; http://ioppublishing.org. Illus. Sample. Refereed. Vol. ends: Dec. *Indexed:* A22, ApMecR, BrTechI, C&ISA, CEA, CerAb, EngInd, MLA-IB, PhotoAb. *Aud.:* Ac, Sa.

Available in print and online. Experimental research in physics relies a great deal on specialized equipment and precise instrumentation. This journal is devoted to the theory, practice, and application of measurement in physics, chemistry, engineering, and the environmental and life sciences. Topics of interest include: measurement theory and practical developments; sensors and sensor systems; optical and laser-based techniques; measurement methods for fluids; imaging techniques; spectroscopy; techniques for materials and materials processing evaluation; measurement techniques for biological, medical, and life science applications; instrumentation for environmental and atmospheric measurements; and novel instrumentation. Full-length research papers, rapid communications, review articles, and technical design notes are all included. This title is part of the *Journal of Physics* collection and is the British equivalent of the *Review of Scientific Instruments* (see below). It belongs in any physics research collection.

4341. Nanotechnology. [ISSN: 0957-4484] 1990. 50x/yr. GBP 2827 (print & online eds.). Ed(s): Mark Reed. Institute of Physics Publishing Ltd., Temple Circus, Temple Way, Bristol, BS1 6HG, United Kingdom; custserv@iop.org; http://ioppublishing.org. Sample. Refereed. *Indexed:* A01, A22, C&ISA, CerAb, EngInd. *Aud.:* Ac, Sa.

Available in print and online. Nanotechnology is the study of phenomena in extremely small dimensions, usually on the order of the size of a hydrogen atom. In this journal, nanotechnology is taken to include the ability to individually address, control, and modify structures, materials, and devices with nanometer precision, and the synthesis of such structures into systems. It encompasses the understanding of the fundamental physics, chemistry, biology, and technology of nanometer-scale objects and how such objects can be used in the areas of computation, sensors, nanostructured materials, and nano-biotechnology. *Nanotechnology* is the official publication of the Institute of Physics that is dedicated to this area of research. It publishes papers that present original research in the field, as well as review articles and tutorials. Articles are grouped into seven sections: biology and medicine; electronics and photonics; patterning and nanofabrication; energy at the nanoscale; sensing and actuating; materials (synthesis or self-assembly); and materials (properties, characterization or tools). Some articles have supplemental multimedia files that are available alongside the text in the online version of the journal. A related web site, http://nanotechweb.org, provides links to news, conferences, employment opportunities, and key papers on nanotechnology from other scientific journals. As the premier journal covering this branch of physics, this title belongs in every collection that supports research in the field.

4342. *Nature Physics.* [ISSN: 1745-2473] 2005. m. EUR 3936 in Europe; USD 4958 in the Americas; GBP 2544 in the UK & elsewhere. Ed(s): Alison Wright. Nature Publishing Group, The MacMillan Bldg, 4 Crinan St, London, N1 9XW, United Kingdom; nature@nature.com; http://www.nature.com. Adv. Sample. Refereed. *Indexed:* A01. *Bk. rev.:* 1-3, 500 words. *Aud.:* Ga, Ac, Sa.

Available in print and online. For many years, *Nature* has been one of the two most prestigious science journals published anywhere in the world (the other is *Science*). In order to expand its ability to publish significant research, the editors of *Nature* have created a series of subject-specific spinoff journals that cover the entire range of science and medicine. *Nature Physics* is the title that is devoted to research in physics. The journal content reflects core physics disciplines, but is also open to a broad range of topics whose central theme falls within the bounds of physics. Theoretical physics, particularly where it is pertinent to experiment, also is featured. Research areas covered in the journal include: quantum physics; atomic and molecular physics; statistical physics, thermodynamics, and nonlinear dynamics; condensed-matter physics; fluid dynamics; optical physics; chemical physics; information theory and computation; electronics, photonics, and device physics; nanotechnology; nuclear physics; plasma physics; high-energy particle physics; astrophysics and cosmology; biophysics; and geophysics. The main body of the journal consists of original research papers and letters to the editor. Although the most outstanding findings in the field are still published in the general journal *Nature,* the papers published in *Nature Physics* are still considered to be highly prestigious. In addition to research papers, the journal also contains news from the field, information on conferences and workshops, job ads, and book reviews. Although a derivative of the general journal *Nature,* this title publishes original material and belongs in all physics research collections.

4343. *New Journal of Physics.* [ISSN: 1367-2630] 1998. m. Free. Ed(s): Eberhard Bodenschatz. Institute of Physics Publishing Ltd., Temple Circus, Temple Way, Bristol, BS1 6HG, United Kingdom; custserv@iop.org; http://ioppublishing.org. Illus. Sample. Refereed. *Indexed:* A01, CCMJ, EngInd, MSN, MathR. *Aud.:* Ac, Sa.

Available online only. The *New Journal of Physics* is an open-access publication sponsored by 20 national physics societies around the world. The scope of the journal is the entire range of the field of physics, including experimental, theoretical, and applied research. Research areas covered by the journal include: quantum physics (including quantum information); atomic and molecular physics; optics; condensed matter; surface science; nanoscale science; photonics and device physics; soft matter and polymers; chemical physics; statistical mechanics, thermodynamics, and nonlinear systems; fluid dynamics; plasmas; nuclear physics; high-energy particle physics; cosmology and astrophysics; biological and medical physics; and earth science and geophysics. By publishing only in electronic format, the journal allows for rapid distribution of articles of any length. All articles are subject to the standard peer-review process, but they are not limited by the space and distribution considerations of the print format. Journal coverage extends across the entire range of the discipline of physics, encompassing pure, applied, theoretical, and experimental research, as well as interdisciplinary topics. The journal's online format allows it to be made available to readers at no cost. It is funded by article charges paid by the authors, which is similar to the page charges of print journals. Key articles on hot topics in physics are grouped together to form "Focus" issues. Because of its electronic-only format, many of the articles have accompanying multimedia files. With its no-cost pricing model and the ease of electronic access, this journal should be available in all college libraries. URL: www.iop.org/EJ/journal/1367-2630

4344. *Optical Society of America. Journal A: Optics, Image Science, and Vision.* Formerly (until 1993): *Optical Society of America. Journal A, Optics and Image Science;* Which superseded in part (in 1983): *Optical Society of America. Journal;* Which superseded in part (in 1929): *Optical*

Society of America. Journal. Review of Scientific Instruments; Which was formerly (until 1922): *Optical Society of America. Journal.* [ISSN: 1084-7529] 1984. m. USD 2790 combined subscription (print & online eds.). Ed(s): Franco Gori. Optical Society of America, 2010 Massachusetts Ave, NW, Washington, DC 20036; info@osa.org; http://www.osa.org. Illus., index, adv. Refereed. Vol. ends: Dec. *Indexed:* A22, ApMecR, C&ISA, CCMJ, EngInd, MSN, MathR. *Aud.:* Ac, Sa.

Available in print and online. As one-half of the official journal of the Optical Society of America, this title is the premier publication outlet for research in the field of optics. *Part A* covers classical optics, image science, and vision. Topics include: atmospheric and oceanic optics; diffraction and gratings; Fourier optics and signal processing; geometric optics; holography; image processing; imaging systems; lasers and laser optics; medical optics and biotechnology; optics at surfaces; physical optics; scattering; and vision, color, and visual optics. Only full-length research papers are included. Letters to the editor are published in the sister journal, *Optics Letters* (see below). Articles are published online as they are accepted and collected in monthly volumes. Along with the *Journal of the Optical Society of America B* (below), this title forms the core of the optics literature and belongs in all physics research collections.

4345. *Optical Society of America. Journal B: Optical Physics.* Supersedes in part (in 1983): *Optical Society of America. Journal;* Which superseded in part (in 1929): *Optical Society of America. Journal. Review of Scientific Instruments;* Which was formerly (until 1922): *Optical Society of America. Journal.* [ISSN: 0740-3224] 1984. m. USD 2790 combined subscription (print & online eds.). Ed(s): Grover Swartzlander. Optical Society of America, 2010 Massachusetts Ave, NW, Washington, DC 20036; info@osa.org; http://www.osa.org. Illus., index, adv. Refereed. *Indexed:* A22, ApMecR, C&ISA, CCMJ, EngInd, MSN, MathR, PhotoAb. *Aud.:* Ac, Sa.

Available in print and online. As the second half of the official journal of the Optical Society of America, this title comprises part of the core literature in the field of optics. *Part B* covers research on the fundamentals of the interaction of radiation with matter such as quantum optics, nonlinear optics, and laser physics. It includes such topical areas as atom optics and cold atoms, integrated and fiber optics, metamaterials, nanophotonics, photonic crystals, photorefractive optics and holography, physics of optical materials, spectroscopy, THz optics, ultrafast phenomena, and other related subjects. Like its sister section the *Journal of the Optical Society of America [Part] A,* it only publishes full-length research reports. Letters are published in the related *Optics Letters* (see below). Articles are published online as accepted and collected in monthly volumes. As major journals in one of the most prominent branches of physics, *Part A* and *Part B* belong in all physics research collections.

4346. *Optics Express.* [ISSN: 1094-4087] 1997. bi-w. Free. Ed(s): Andrew Weiner. Optical Society of America, 2010 Massachusetts Ave, NW, Washington, DC 20036; info@osa.org; http://www.osa.org. Refereed. *Indexed:* EngInd. *Aud.:* Ac, Sa.

Available in online. *Optics Express* is an open-access journal. It publishes original, peer-reviewed articles that report new developments of interest to the optics community in all fields of optical science and technology. All subfields of optics are covered, including: atmospheric and oceanic optics; detectors; diffraction and gratings; fiber optics and optical communications; holography; image processing; imaging systems; instrumentation, measurement, and metrology; integrated optics; laser micromachining; lasers and laser optics; medical optics and biotechnology; metamaterials; microscopy; nonlinear optics; optical design and fabrication; optical devices; optical trapping and manipulation; optics at surfaces; optoelectronics; photonic crystal fibers; photonic crystals; physical optics; quantum optics; remote sensing and sensors; scattering; thin films; ultrafast optics; and coherence and statistical optics. Occasional focus issues cover specific topics of interest in the field of optics. Articles related to energy, including photovoltaic cells, are published in a bimonthly supplement titled *Energy Express.* Because it is available to all individuals at no charge, this journal belongs in all physics collections. URL: www.opticsexpress.org

4347. *Optics Letters.* [ISSN: 0146-9592] 1977. s-m. USD 3055 (print & online eds.). Ed(s): Alan E Willner. Optical Society of America, 2010 Massachusetts Ave, NW, Washington, DC 20036; info@osa.org; http://www.osa.org. Illus., index. Refereed. Vol. ends: Jan/Dec. *Indexed:* A22, C&ISA, EngInd, PhotoAb. *Aud.:* Ac, Sa.

Available in print and online. *Optics Letters* serves as the letters-to-the-editor section for both *Applied Optics* and the *Journal of the Optical Society of America* (see above). It covers the latest research in optical science, including: atmospheric and oceanic optics; fiber optics and optical communications; Fourier optics and signal processing; image processing; imaging systems; instrumentation, measurement, and metrology; integrated optics; lasers and laser optics; materials; medical optics and biotechnology; microscopy; nonlinear optics; optical devices; optics at surfaces; physical optics; quantum optics; scattering; spectroscopy; and ultrafast optics. Criteria used in the selection of contributions include newsworthiness to a substantial part of the optics community and the effect of rapid publication on the research of others. All articles are short, usually three pages or less. This is a core journal in the field of optics, and it belongs in any collection that supports research in this field.

4348. *Physical Review A (Atomic, Molecular and Optical Physics).*
Formerly (until 1990): *Physical Review A (General Physics);* Which superseded in part (in 1970): *Physical Review.* [ISSN: 1050-2947] 1893. m. Ed(s): Margaret Malloy, Gordon W.F. Drake. American Physical Society, One Physics Ellipse, College Park, MD 20740; help@aps.org; http://www.aps.org. Illus., index. Refereed. Vol. ends: Jun/Dec. Microform: BHP. *Indexed:* A01, A22, ApMecR, CCMJ, EngInd, MSN, MathR. *Aud.:* Ac, Sa.

Available in print and online. The *Physical Review* collection of journals is the most prestigious set of physics journals published in the world. Along with its British counterpart, the *Journal of Physics* collection (see above), the various components of the *Physical Review* comprise the core research literature of the field. Like many other journals in the sciences, the *Physical Review* has been subdivided into a number of sections that cover specific branches and subdisciplines of physics. *Section A* covers the area of atomic, molecular, optical physics, and related fundamental concepts. Specific subjects found in this title include: quantum mechanics; quantum information theory; atomic and molecular structure and dynamics; collisions and interactions (including interactions with surfaces and solids); clusters (including fullerenes); atomic and molecular processes in external fields; matter waves (including Bose-Einstein condensation); and quantum optics. Full-length articles, brief reports, comments, and short rapid communications are all included. Letters are published in the related *Physical Review Letters* (see below). As in all of the sections of the *Physical Review*, the number of articles and pages published is tremendous, with over 2,500 articles and 20,000 pages per year. However, the refereeing process is highly selective, rejecting over half of all articles submitted. The large number of papers published has led to a paper/page system, instead of consecutively numbered pages. Color images are not published in the print edition, but are included in the web version of appropriate papers. As one section of the most important journal in the field, this title belongs in every physics research collection.

4349. *Physical Review B (Condensed Matter and Materials Physics).*
Former titles (until 1998): *Physical Review B (Condensed Matter);* (until 1978): *Physical Review B (Solid State);* Which superseded in part (in 1970): *Physical Review.* [ISSN: 1098-0121] 1893. 48x/yr. Ed(s): Gene D Sprouse. American Physical Society, One Physics Ellipse, College Park, MD 20740; help@aps.org; http://www.aps.org. Illus., index. Refereed. *Indexed:* A01, A22, ApMecR, MathR, PhotoAb. *Aud.:* Ac, Sa.

Available in print and online. The second section of the *Physical Review* is devoted to condensed matter and materials science. It is published monthly in two sections, B1 and B15. Topics covered in B1 include: structure, phase transitions, ferroelectrics, nonordered systems, liquids, quantum solids, magnetism, and superconductivity. B15 covers: superfluidity, electronic structure, photonic crystals, semiconductors, mesoscopic systems, surfaces, clusters, fullerenes, graphene, and nanoscience. Full-length papers predominate, but short, rapid communications are also accepted. Accompanying color images are included only in the online version of the journal. Letters to the editor are published in the related *Physical Review Letters* (see below). This is the most frequently cited journal in the world devoted to condensed matter physics. Like all sections of the *Physical Review*, this section is not for the casual reader. It publishes close to 50,000 pages each year of primary research results of a highly technical nature. The large number of papers published has led to a paper/page system, instead of consecutively

numbered pages. Along with the *Journal of Physics: Condensed Matter* (see above), *Part B* of the *Physical Review* presents the most important research in the field. Like all of the sections of the *Physical Review*, it belongs in every physics research collection.

4350. *Physical Review C (Nuclear Physics).* Supersedes in part (1893-1969): *Physical Review.* [ISSN: 0556-2813] 1970. m. Ed(s): Gene D Sprouse, Benjamin F. Gibson. American Physical Society, One Physics Ellipse, College Park, MD 20740; help@aps.org; http://www.aps.org. Illus., index. Refereed. Vol. ends: Jun/Dec. Microform: BHP. *Indexed:* A01, A22, ApMecR, MathR. *Aud.:* Ac, Sa.

Available in print and online. *Part C* of the *Physical Review* covers experimental and theoretical research results in all aspects of nuclear physics, including the nucleon–nucleon interaction, few-body systems, nuclear structure, nuclear reactions, relativistic nuclear collisions, hadronic physics and QCD, electroweak interaction, symmetries, and nuclear astrophysics. Both full-length research papers and brief reports are included, along with comments on previously published research. Letters to the editor are published in the separate *Physical Review Letters* (see below). Like all of the sections of the *Physical Review*, this section is the most prestigious journal published in its branch of physics. *Physical Review*, publishes over 1,000 articles per year. The large number of papers published has led to a paper/page system, instead of consecutively numbered pages. Along with the *Journal of Physics G* (see above), this title represents the core literature of nuclear physics and belongs in any physics research collection.

4351. *Physical Review D (Particles, Fields, Gravitation and Cosmology).*
Formerly (until 2004): *Physical Review D (Particles and Fields);* Which superseded in part (in 1970): *Physical Review.* [ISSN: 1550-7998] 1893. s-m. Ed(s): Gene D Sprouse, Erick J. Weinberg. American Physical Society, One Physics Ellipse, College Park, MD 20740; help@aps.org; http://www.aps.org. Illus., index. Refereed. Microform: BHP. *Indexed:* A01, A22, ApMecR, CCMJ, MSN, MathR. *Aud.:* Ac, Sa.

Available in print and online. This section of the *Physical Review* covers particles, field theory, gravitation, and cosmology. The first issue of each month, D1, is devoted to experimental high-energy physics, phenomenologically oriented theory of particles and fields, cosmic-ray physics, electroweak interactions, applications of QCD, and lattice gauge theory. The second issue of the month, D2, covers general relativity, the quantum theory of gravitation, cosmology, particle astrophysics, formal aspects of theory of particles and fields, general and formal development in gauge field theories, and string theory. Issues consist primarily of full-length research reports, and some (short) rapid communications. Review articles also appear on an irregular basis. Letters appear in the related *Physical Review Letters* (see below). Almost 3,000 articles are published per year, filling well over 30,000 pages. As with the other sections of the *Physical Review*, the editors have abandoned sequential page numbering in favor of an article/page system. Along with all the other parts of the journal, *Part D* is the premier journal in the world covering its branch of physics, and it belongs in every physics research library.

4352. *Physical Review E (Statistical, Nonlinear, and Soft Matter Physics).*
Formerly (until 2001): *Physical Review E (Statistical Physics, Plasmas, Fluids, and Related Interdisciplinary Topics);* Which superseded in part (in 1993): *Physical Review A (Atomic, Molecular and Optical Physics);* Which was formerly (until 1990): *Physical Review A (General Physics);* Which superseded in part (in 1970): *Physical Review.* [ISSN: 1539-3755] 1893. m. Ed(s): Margaret Malloy, David Voss. American Physical Society, One Physics Ellipse, College Park, MD 20740; help@aps.org; http://www.aps.org. Illus., index. Refereed. Vol. ends: Jun/Dec. Microform: PQC. *Indexed:* A01, A22, CCMJ, EngInd, MSN, MathR. *Aud.:* Ac, Sa.

Available in print and online. *Physical Review E* is broad and interdisciplinary in scope. It focuses on collective phenomena of many-body systems, with statistical physics and nonlinear dynamics as the central themes of the journal. It publishes recent developments in chaos, granular materials, statistical physics, equilibrium and transport properties of fluids, liquid crystals, biological physics, complex fluids, polymers, chaos, fluid dynamics, plasma physics, films, interfaces, classical physics, computational, and interdisciplinary physics. The journal is very large, with over 20,000 pages published annually. Full articles, brief research reports, and rapid communications of important findings are all accepted, along with comments on previously published material. Letters are published in the related *Physical Review Letters* (see below). As with all other sections of the *Physical Review,* the editors reject over half of all papers submitted. The journal uses an article/page numbering system, instead of page numbering. *Part E,* as one part of the most prestigious physics journal in the world, belongs in any physics research collection.

4353. *Physical Review Letters.* Supersedes in part (in 1958): *Physical Review.* [ISSN: 0031-9007] 1893. w. Ed(s): Gene D Sprouse. American Physical Society, One Physics Ellipse, College Park, MD 20740; help@aps.org; http://www.aps.org. Illus., index. Refereed. *Indexed:* A01, A22, ApMecR, CCMJ, EngInd, MSN, MathR, PhotoAb. *Aud.:* Ac, Sa.

Available in print and online. This title is the letters-to-the-editor section for all parts of the *Physical Review* (see above). It publishes brief reports of important discoveries in any branch of physics. Topical sections are devoted to general physics (including statistical and quantum mechanics); gravitation, and astrophysics; elementary particles and fields; nuclear physics; atomic, molecular, and optical physics; nonlinear dynamics, fluid dynamics, and classical optics; plasma and beam physics; condensed matter; and soft-matter, biological, and interdisciplinary physics. All articles published are very brief, with a maximum length of five pages. Like its parent journal, *Physical Review Letters* is one of the most respected and most cited journals in all of physics. It was one of the very first letters-only journals and maintains the high editorial standards of the *Physical Review.* Even though hundreds of pages are published each week, the editors reject over half of all papers submitted. *Physical Review Letters* is the single most prestigious journal of its kind and belongs in every physics research collection.

4354. *Physical Review Special Topics - Accelerators and Beams.* [ISSN: 1098-4402] 1998. m. Free. Ed(s): Gene D Sprouse, Frank Zimmermann. American Physical Society, One Physics Ellipse, College Park, MD 20740; help@aps.org; http://www.aps.org. Refereed. *Aud.:* Ac, Sa.

Available online only. *Physical Review Special Topics—Accelerators and Beams* is a peer-reviewed, open-access journal distributed without charge to readers and funded by contributions from national, and international, laboratories, and other partners. The articles are published by the American Physical Society under the terms of the Creative Commons Attribution 3.0 License. It covers the full range of accelerator science and technology: subsystem and component technologies; beam dynamics; accelerator applications; and design, operation, and improvement of accelerators used in science and industry. This includes accelerators for high-energy and nuclear physics, synchrotron radiation production, spallation neutron sources, medical therapy, and intense beam applications. Papers may present new research results; review the state of the art of accelerator research or technology; propose new experiments; review active areas of research; or expand upon previously published research. Because of its electronic nature, there is no limit to the number of pages or illustrations that can be included in any given article. Although not as large as other sections of the *Physical Review,* this journal publishes hundreds of articles and thousands of pages each year. Another important feature of the electronic nature of this publication is that most articles are freely available, without restriction, to any reader. In addition to the original research articles, the journal links to relevant papers published in other sections of the *Physical Review* and *Physical Review Letters.* Recommended for any library that supports specialized research in this area. URL: http://prst-ab.aps.org

4355. *Physical Review Special Topics - Physics Education Research.* [ISSN: 1554-9178] s-a. Ed(s): Robert Beichner. American Physical Society, One Physics Ellipse, College Park, MD 20740; http://www.aps.org. Refereed. *Indexed:* ERIC. *Aud.:* Ga, Ac, Sa.

Available online only. *Physical Review Special Topics—Physics Education Research* is a peer-reviewed, open-access journal sponsored by the American Physical Society (APS), the American Association of Physics Teachers (AAPT), and the APS Forum on Education (APS FEd). The articles are published by the American Physical Society under the terms of the Creative Commons Attribution 3.0 License. The journal covers the full range of experimental and theoretical research on the teaching and/or learning of physics. Contents consist

of review articles, replication studies, descriptions of the development and use of new assessment tools, presentation of research techniques, and methodology comparisons/critiques. Because of its high standards and free availability, it is recommended for any college or university that has a physics program.

4356. *Physical Review X.* [ISSN: 2160-3308] 2011. irreg. Free. Ed(s): Jorge Pullin. American Physical Society, One Physics Ellipse, College Park, MD 20740; help@aps.org; http://www.aps.org. Refereed. *Aud.:* Ac, Sa.

Available online only. *Physical Review X* is a peer-reviewed, open-access journal distributed without charge to readers and funded by contributions from national, and international, laboratories, and other partners. The articles are published by the American Physical Society under the terms of the Creative Commons Attribution 3.0 License. It is a highly selective peer-reviewed journal that aims to publish, as timely as possible, exceptional original research papers from all areas of pure, applied, and interdisciplinary physics. *PRX's* mission is to bring innovative and important results to the broad science and engineering communities under its open-access publishing model. Because of its electronic nature, there is no limit to the number of pages or illustrations that can be included in any given article. Another important feature of this publication is that all articles are freely available, without restriction, to any reader. Recommended for any library that supports a physics research program. URL: http://prx.aps.org

4357. *Physical Society of Japan. Journal.* Formerly: *Physico-Mathematical Society of Japan. Proceedings.* [ISSN: 0031-9015] 1946. m. Ed(s): Tsuneya Ando. Institute of Pure and Applied Physics, Toyokaiji Bldg, no.12, 6-9-6 Shinbashi, Minato-ku, Tokyo, 105-0004, Japan; subscription@ipap.jp; http://www.ipap.jp. Illus., index. Refereed. Vol. ends: Dec. *Indexed:* A22, ApMecR, CCMJ, MSN, MathR, PhotoAb. *Aud.:* Ac, Sa.

Available in print and online. This title is the official journal of the Physical Society of Japan, publishing some of the most significant physics research conducted in Japan and Asia. It is devoted to the rapid dissemination of important research results in all fields of physics, from condensed-matter physics to particle physics. All of the subdisciplines of physics are covered, including: elementary particles and fields; nuclear physics; atomic and molecular physics; fluid dynamics; plasma physics; condensed matter; metal, superconductor, semiconductor, magnetic materials, and dielectric materials; physics of nanoscale materials; optics and quantum electronics; physics of complex systems; mathematical physics; chemical physics; biophysics; geophysics; and astrophysics. Despite the broad nature of its scope, this journal publishes more articles on condensed-matter physics than any other topic. Although the journal is published in Japan, all of the articles are written in English, making them accessible to the wider scientific community. Full-length scientific papers, research notes, and letters to the editor are all included. This title is the Japanese equivalent of the other national journals included here, and it belongs in comprehensive physics research collections.

4358. *Physics: spotlighting exceptional research.* Incorporates (1998-2011): *Physical Review Focus.* [ISSN: 1943-2879] 2008. w. Ed(s): David Voss. American Physical Society, One Physics Ellipse, College Park, MD 20740; subs@aps.org; http://www.aps.org. Refereed. *Aud.:* Ac, Sa.

It takes a little audacity to name your publication after the field of study, but *Physics* lives up to that burden. Published online by the American Physical Society, this open-access title highlights key articles from all of the sections of the *Physical Review* (see above). Rather than reproduce or link to the original research paper, *Physics* has the author(s) rewrite the paper to a state where they explain the results of the research to non-specialists in that specific field of research. Thus, the articles in this journal are accessible to a wider audience than that of the original research reports. In addition, the editors ask expert researchers and the article referees to comment on the articles, placing them in another perspective. Three types of papers are included in *Physics:* "Viewpoints" comprises essays that focus on a single *Physical Review* paper or letter and put this work into broader context; "Focus" are written by professional science writers and are intended to be accessible to students and non-experts; and "Synopses" are editor-written distillations of interesting and important papers each week. In addition, selected letters to the editor are included to allow readers a chance to comment on the commentaries and summaries. All subfields within physics are covered. The goal of this journal is to provide a guide to the best research in physics. Given the quality of the source material, *Physics* is able to achieve that goal. This title belongs in any collection serving researchers, and students, in the field of physics.

4359. *Physics Education.* [ISSN: 0031-9120] 1966. bi-m. GBP 336 (print & online eds.). Ed(s): Gary Williams. Institute of Physics Publishing Ltd., Temple Circus, Temple Way, Bristol, BS1 6HG, United Kingdom; custserv@iop.org; http://ioppublishing.org. Illus. Sample. Refereed. Vol. ends: Nov. *Indexed:* A01, A22, ERIC, RILM. *Bk. rev.:* Number and length vary. *Aud.:* Hs, Ga, Ac.

Available in print and online. *Physics Education* is a British journal for teaching physics at the high school and beginning undergraduate college levels. As such, it is one of the few physics journals that can be read by a general audience. The editors seek to provide teachers with a forum for practicing teachers to make an active contribution to: the physics teaching community; knowledge updates in physics, educational research, and relevant wider curriculum developments; and strategies for teaching and classroom management that will engage and motivate students. Research papers are presented on: the teaching and learning of physics; the examining and assessment of physics; new approaches to the general presentation and application of physics in the classroom; and curriculum developments around the world. All of the articles are written for the nonspecialist and avoid much of the higher-level mathematics inherent in most physics research publications. The goals of the journal are to cover the wide range of topics included in the field of physics, to enhance the standards and quality of teaching, to make physics more attractive to students and teachers, to keep teachers up-to-date on new developments in the field, and to provide a forum for the sharing of ideas about teaching physics. Each issue contains articles on new developments in physics, ideas for teaching physical concepts, profiles of prominent scientists, reviews of resources that can be used by physics teachers, news from the field, and even a little humor. Articles in the electronic version are supplemented by multimedia content such as worksheets, spreadsheets, programs, and audio and video clips. This journal is the British equivalent of *The Physics Teacher* (see below), and it is an excellent choice for those libraries that seek to add a general physics journal to their collections.

4360. *Physics Letters. Section A: General, Atomic and Solid State Physics.* Supersedes in part (in 1967): *Physics Letters.* [ISSN: 0375-9601] 1962. 48x/yr. EUR 6955. Ed(s): C R Doering, A R Bishop. Elsevier BV, North-Holland, Postbus 211, Amsterdam, 1000 AE, Netherlands; JournalsCustomerServiceEMEA@elsevier.com; http://www.elsevier.com. Illus., index. Sample. Refereed. Vol. ends: No. 278 - No. 291. Microform: PQC. *Indexed:* A01, A22, C&ISA, CCMJ, CerAb, MSN, MathR. *Aud.:* Ac, Sa.

Available in print and online. *Physics Letters* is a publication outlet for rapid communication of significant, original, and timely research results. Articles tend to be very brief, with longer review articles printed in the related journal *Physics Reports* (see below). *Section A* of this journal is the general physics portion, covering all branches of physics except high-energy nuclear and particle physics. Topics usually included are: condensed matter physics; theoretical physics; nonlinear science; statistical physics; mathematical and computational physics; general and cross-disciplinary physics; atomic, molecular, and cluster physics; plasma and fluid physics; optical physics; biological physics; and nanoscience. Articles are accepted for publication based on the originality of the research, desirability for speedy publication, and the clarity of the presentation. This journal publishes an incredible number of articles, producing around close to 5,000 pages per volume. Along with the *Physical Review Letters* (see above), it is one of the most cited and most prominent letters journals in the field. This title belongs in any physics research collection.

4361. *Physics Letters. Section B: Nuclear, Elementary Particle and High-Energy Physics.* Supersedes in part (in 1967): *Physics Letters.* [ISSN: 0370-2693] 1962. 60x/yr. EUR 3063. Ed(s): M Doser, W D Schlatter. Elsevier BV, North-Holland, Postbus 211, Amsterdam, 1000 AE, Netherlands; JournalsCustomerServiceEMEA@elsevier.com; http://www.elsevier.com. Illus., index. Sample. Refereed. Vol. ends: No. 497 - No. 523. Microform: PQC. *Indexed:* A01, A22, CCMJ, CompR, MSN, MathR. *Aud.:* Ac, Sa.

Available in print and online. *Physics Letters B* is the second part of the *Physics Letters* series. It covers the two areas excluded from *Part A*: nuclear and particle physics. Despite its more limited subject scope, this section is the larger of the two journals, reflecting the vast amount of research published in nuclear and particle physics. There can be as many as 5,000 pages printed in this journal in a single year. Each issue is divided into four sections: astrophysics and cosmology; experiments; phenomenology; and theory. Because of the specialized nature of the field, separate editors are assigned to the areas of experimental nuclear physics, theoretical nuclear physics, experimental high-energy physics, theoretical high-energy physics, and astrophysics. As with most physics research journals, each article must be the result of original research and must not have appeared in print before. This journal is frequently used to determine precedent in scientific discoveries in its fields of interest. Both sections of *Physics Letters* should be a part of any serious physics research collection.

4362. *Physics of Fluids.* Formerly (until 1994): *Physics of Fluids A: Fluid Dynamics;* Which superseded in part (in 1988): *Physics of Fluids.* [ISSN: 1070-6631] 1958. m. Ed(s): L Gary Leal, John Kim. American Institute of Physics, 1 Physics Ellipse, College Park, MD 20740; aipinfo@aip.org; http://www.aip.org. Illus., index, adv. Sample. Refereed. Vol. ends: Dec. *Indexed:* A01, A22, ApMecR, CCMJ, EngInd, M&GPA, MSN, MathR, S25. *Aud.:* Ac, Sa.

Available in print and online. This journal is the official publication of the Division of Fluid Dynamics of the American Physical Society. It is devoted to the publication of original research in the field of gases, liquids, and complex or multiphase fluids. Theoretical, experimental, and computational studies are all included. Specific areas covered include kinetic theory, fluid dynamics, wave phenomena, hypersonic physics, hydrodynamics, compressible fluids, boundary layers, conduction, and chaotic phenomena. Material on plasmas and plasma physics is published in the related *Physics of Plasmas* (see below), which can be purchased in combination with this title at a reduced rate. Full papers, brief reports, and letters are all accepted. Comments on previously published papers are also included, sometimes leading to interesting scientific debate. A few of the articles include multimedia components that contribute to the understanding of the underlying physics discussed in the text. The annual *Gallery of Fluid Motion* presents visual representations of fluid flow and fluid problems. The editors also invite award-winning speakers at the annual conference of the Division of Fluid Dynamics to write expanded papers for the journal. This is the primary journal for research in fluids and belongs in any comprehensive physics collection.

4363. *Physics of Plasmas.* Formerly (until 1994): *Physics of Fluids B: Plasma Physics;* Which superseded in part (in 1989): *Physics of Fluids.* [ISSN: 1070-664X] 1958. m. Ed(s): Ronald C Davidson. American Institute of Physics, 1 Physics Ellipse, College Park, MD 20740; aipinfo@aip.org; http://www.aip.org. Illus., index, adv. Sample. Refereed. Vol. ends: Dec. *Indexed:* A01, A22, CCMJ, EngInd, MSN, MathR. *Aud.:* Ac, Sa.

Available in print and online. As the official publication of the Division of Plasmas of the American Institute of Physics, *Physics of Plasmas* is devoted to original contributions to and reviews of the physics of plasmas, including: equilibria, linear waves, and instabilities; nonlinear behavior (including turbulent and stochastic phenomena and associated transport) and solitons and shock waves; plasma physics of lasers and particle beams and charged-particle acceleration and transport; radiation generation, transport, propagation, and interaction with plasmas; low-temperature plasmas; plasma chemistry and processing; geophysical, planetary, solar, and astrophysical plasmas; plasma confinement by magnetic fields; inertial confinement physics; physics of high-energy density plasmas or matter under extreme conditions; and dusty plasmas. Specific topics covered by this journal include equilibria, waves, nonlinear behavior, lasers, particle beams, radiation, astrophysics, geophysical plasmas, plasma chemistry, physics of dense plasmas, and containment techniques. Articles are published online on a daily basis and are then compiled into online and print monthly issues. This journal formerly was published with *Physics of Fluids*, but the two journals were divided in 1994. Full-length articles, brief reports, and letters to the editor are all included. This journal is the most highly cited publication in this branch of physics, and it belongs in any collection that supports research in this area.

4364. *Physics Reports.* Incorporates (1983-1991): *Computer Physics Reports;* (1972-1975): *Case Studies in Atomic Physics.* [ISSN: 0370-1573] 1971. 90x/yr. EUR 8147. Ed(s): M P Kamionkowsi. Elsevier BV, North-Holland, Postbus 211, Amsterdam, 1000 AE, Netherlands; JournalsCustomerServiceEMEA@elsevier.com; http://www.elsevier.com. Illus., index. Sample. Refereed. Vol. ends: No. 338 - No. 353. Microform: PQC. *Indexed:* A01, A22, CCMJ, MSN, MathR. *Aud.:* Ac, Sa.

Available in print and online. In contrast to its sister publications *Physics Letters A* and *B* (see above), both of which publish large numbers of brief papers that present new research findings, *Physics Reports* publishes lengthy articles designed to provide state-of-the-art reviews that benchmark research throughout the field of physics. Each issue contains a single article, which is usually somewhat longer than a literature review but shorter than a monograph. The published reviews are specialist in nature, but contain enough background and introductory material to be understandable to physicists who are working in other subdisciplines. In addition to identifying significant developments and trends, the extensive literature reviews serve as indexes to the topic being discussed. Subjects can be from any field of physics, and the editorial board consists of specialists in a variety of fields who are able to judge the quality and accuracy of the manuscripts. This title is similar in scope to *Contemporary Physics* (above) and *Reports on Progress in Physics* (below), although *Physics Reports* is written at the highest level of the three. All three of these journals are useful additions to a physics research collection.

4365. *The Physics Teacher.* [ISSN: 0031-921X] 1963. 9x/yr. USD 691 combined subscription domestic; USD 757 combined subscription foreign. Ed(s): Karl Mamola. American Association of Physics Teachers, One Physics Ellipse, College Park, MD 20740; eo@aapt.org; http://www.aapt.org. Illus., index, adv. Sample. Refereed. Circ: 8600. Vol. ends: Dec. *Indexed:* A01, A22, BRI, ERIC, P02. *Bk. rev.:* Number and length vary. *Aud.:* Hs, Ga, Ac.

Available in print and online. *The Physics Teacher* publishes papers on the teaching of physics, and on topics such as contemporary physics, applied physics, and the history of physics—all aimed at the introductory-level teacher. It is the primary journal that supports high school physics teachers. Articles are written for the nonspecialist and present physics principles without the higher-level mathematics that are usually included in physics research journals. Papers cover topics of interest to students and to the general public, often focusing on the applications of physical principles to everyday life. In addition to full articles, the journal also publishes: ideas for new teaching methods; notes on interesting applications and phenomena; information on equipment and apparatus for teaching physics; and editorials, web sites, and book reviews. Every month, the journal publishes several problems for readers to solve, and follows this up in the next issue with solutions and the names of the people who answer correctly. Other features include tips for new teachers, web resources, reviews of YouTube videos that can be used in the classroom, and "Fermi questions," where readers use physics to estimate answer to everyday problems. A few papers and several features in each issue are free to all readers, although a subscription is required to see all content. This journal is similar to its British equivalent, *Physics Education* (see above). *The Physics Teacher* is a very readable journal and one of the few that is approachable by both the specialist and non-scientist. It is one of the few physics journals that should be considered for general library collections.

4366. *Physics Today.* [ISSN: 0031-9228] 1948. m. American Institute of Physics, 1 Physics Ellipse, College Park, MD 20740; aipinfo@aip.org; http://www.aip.org. Illus., index, adv. Sample. Refereed. Circ: 120000. Vol. ends: Dec. *Indexed:* A&ATA, A01, A22, ApMecR, BRI, BrTechI, C&ISA, C37, CBRI, CerAb, EngInd, M&GPA, MASUSE, MSN, P02, RILM. *Bk. rev.:* 7-10. *Aud.:* Hs, Ga, Ac.

Available in print and online. If a library subscribes to just one physics journal, this should be it. *Physics Today* is the only true general-interest physics journal currently being published. It is the flagship publication of the American Institute of Physics and is intended to keep readers informed on new research in physics and its impact on society. In addition to providing full-length articles on interesting areas throughout the discipline of physics, this journal serves as a news source for anyone interested in the field, including scientists, teachers, students, and the general public. Its wide appeal is evidenced by the fact that it is the only physics journal to be indexed in the *Readers' Guide to Periodical Literature.* Articles are written specifically for the nonspecialist and present advanced physical concepts without burdening the reader with advanced mathematics. With color photographs, well-written prose, and timely and engaging subject matter, this is the only physics journal that consistently could be considered for newsstand distribution. Each issue provides feature articles, news of recent discoveries, conference updates, editorials, book reviews, new-product announcements, and obituaries. The daily online version also provides news, editorials, policy and politics updates, the editor's blog, and links to original research in other journals published by the American Institute of Physics. *Physics Today* is essential for any college or university library and should be considered by public and school libraries as well. Unless a library supports a physics research program, this title is the only physics journal that should be included in its journal collection.

4367. *Reports on Progress in Physics.* [ISSN: 0034-4885] 1934. m. GBP 1911 (print & online eds.). Ed(s): Laura H Greene. Institute of Physics Publishing Ltd., Dirac House, Temple Back, Bristol, BS1 6BE, United Kingdom; custserv@iop.org; http://ioppublishing.org. Illus. Sample. Refereed. *Indexed:* A&ATA, A01, A22, ApMecR, CCMJ, MSN, MathR. *Aud.:* Ac, Sa.

Available in print and online. *Reports on Progress in Physics* publishes review articles in all subdisciplines of physics. Articles combine a critical evaluation of the field with a reliable and accessible introduction to the topic, making the articles accessible to a wider scientific community. As with all review journals, its articles tend to be very long, often over 100 pages. Topics include condensed matter and materials; soft matter and biological physics; atomic molecular and optical physics; astrophysics and cosmology; nuclear and particle physics; earth science; and general physics. In addition to full-length review articles, the journal also publishes two types of more speculative articles. The section "Reports on Progress" provides an accurate and well-organized presentation of the present status of research results, even if these results and their interpretation are not in universal accord. "Key Issues Reviews" highlights critical questions in a line of physics research that continues to develop, where important advances are widely acknowledged, but whose ultimate significance and goals have not yet been realized or are in dispute. This journal does not review papers submitted by potential authors; rather, most articles are invited by the editors from distinguished researchers in the field. Researchers may also submit proposals to write review articles. This journal is similar in scope to *Contemporary Physics* and *Physics Reports* (see above). College libraries should subscribe to at least one of these titles, and research libraries will probably wish to get all three.

4368. *Review of Scientific Instruments.* Supersedes in part (in 1930): *Optical Society of America and Review of Scientific Instruments. Journal;* Which was formerly (until 1922): *Optical Society of America. Journal.* [ISSN: 0034-6748] 1917. m. Ed(s): Albert T Macrander. American Institute of Physics, 1 Physics Ellipse, College Park, MD 20740; aipinfo@aip.org; http://www.aip.org. Illus., index, adv. Sample. Refereed. Vol. ends: Dec. *Indexed:* A01, A22, ApMecR, EngInd, MLA-IB, PhotoAb. *Aud.:* Ac, Sa.

Available in print and online. Modern physics research relies heavily on sophisticated instrumentation to make measurements, conduct experiments, analyze data, and test current theories. *Review of Scientific Instruments* is a specialized journal whose role is to evaluate equipment, apparatus, experimental techniques, and mathematical analysis of results. This journal publishes original research articles and literature reviews on instrumentation in physics, chemistry, and the life sciences. The editors interpret the concept of instrumentation very widely and include all of the tools used by the modern scientist. Topics typically covered include optics; atoms and molecules; spectroscopy; particle sources; microscopy; nuclear physics, fusion, and plasmas; condensed matter; chemistry; biology and medicine; electronics and thermometry; and acoustics. In addition to full articles, the journal also provides notes on new instruments and materials, letters to the editor, and occasional conference proceedings from relevant meetings. Online versions of articles may include multimedia components. Because of its focus on instrumentation, many manufacturers also advertise their products in this journal. This title is similar in scope to the British *Measurement Science and Technology* (see above). North American libraries that serve scientific researchers will want to subscribe to *Review of Scientific Instruments,* and comprehensive physics and scientific research libraries will probably need both titles.

4369. *Reviews of Modern Physics.* Formerly (until 1930): *Physical Review, Supplement.* [ISSN: 0034-6861] 1929. q. Ed(s): Gene D Sprouse, Achim Richter. American Physical Society, One Physics Ellipse, College Park, MD 20740; help@aps.org; http://www.aps.org. Illus., index. Refereed. Microform: MIM. *Indexed:* A01, A22, ApMecR, CCMJ, EngInd, MSN, MathR. *Aud.:* Ac, Sa.

Available in print and online. *Reviews of Modern Physics* enhances communication among physicists by publishing comprehensive scholarly reviews and tutorials on significant topics in modern physics. As with *Contemporary Physics, Physics Reports,* and *Reports on Progress in Physics* (see above), the articles do not contain results of original research but collect and synthesize existing research on topics of current interest. Research from any branch or subdiscipline of physics is included, although articles from newly developing fields are given preference. Its review articles offer in-depth treatment of a research area, surveying recent work and providing an introduction that is aimed at physics graduate students and nonspecialists. These reviews also feature bibliographies that are of great value to the specialist. In addition to lengthy review articles, some shorter colloquia articles are also included. The colloquia articles describe recent work of interest to all physicists, especially work at the frontiers of physics, which may have an impact on several different subfields. Each year, *Reviews of Modern Physics* also publishes the Nobel lecture from the Nobel Prize winner in physics. This title is especially useful for helping physics teachers and graduate students keep abreast of recent developments. To enhance this role, the journal also accepts occasional tutorial articles aimed primarily at students or those new to the field. *Reviews of Modern Physics* is the most cited of all physics journals and belongs in most physics research collections.

4370. *Solid State Communications: an international journal.* [ISSN: 0038-1098] 1963. s-m. EUR 6050. Ed(s): A Pinczuk. Pergamon, The Blvd, Langford Ln, E Park, Kidlington, OX5 1GB, United Kingdom; JournalsCustomerServiceEMEA@elsevier.com; http://www.elsevier.com. Illus., adv. Sample. Refereed. Microform: MIM; PQC. *Indexed:* A01, A22, ApMecR, C&ISA, CerAb, EngInd. *Aud.:* Ac, Sa.

This journal serves as the letters section of the *Journal of Physics and Chemistry of Solids* (see above). *Solid State Communications* publishes original experimental and theoretical research on the physical and chemical properties of solids and other condensed systems, and also on their preparation. It also publishes original research on the basic physics of materials science and devices, as well as of state-of-the-art microstructures and nanostructures. The emphasis is on brevity, with papers usually four to five pages in length. A coherent quantitative treatment that emphasizes new physics is expected, rather than a simple accumulation of experimental data. The "Fast-Track" section allows for very rapid publication of short communications on significant developments in condensed-matter science. The goal is to offer the broad condensed-matter community quick and immediate access to publish recently completed papers in research areas that are rapidly evolving and in which there are developments with great potential impact. Like its parent title, *Solid State Communications* belongs in graduate research physics collections.

4371. *Spotlight on Optics: highlighted articles from O S A journals.* 2009. m. Free. Ed(s): Miguel A Alonso. Optical Society of America, 2010 Massachusetts Ave, NW, Washington, DC 20036; info@osa.org; http://www.osa.org. Vol. ends: Dec. *Aud.:* Ac, Sa.

Spotlight on Optics features articles nominated by The Optical Society of America's Topical and Associate Editors to show the breadth and quality of OSA content from the six major technical divisions: "Information Acquisitions, Processing, and Display"; "Light–Matter Interactions"; "Optical Design and Instrumentation"; "Optics in Biology"; "Optoelectronics"; and "Vision and Color." Journal editors identify articles for *Spotlight* that have excellent scientific quality, are representative of the level of work taking place in a specific area, and put other work in perspective. Readers may post comments to the web site, creating the potential for dialogue. In addition to the research paper, each article is summarized in more general terms, making it accessible to those who are not experts in optics. Four types of commentaries are included: "An Explanation" of the content, the foremost purpose being a description of the research that makes it understandable to the nonspecialist; a "Viewpoint" piece that presents a subjective evaluation of the research; an "Application" perspective that connects and/or introduces this work to a discipline other than

its stated category; and/or a "Review/Synopsis" of the research, with perspective points as applicable. This free online journal will serve as a useful tool for researchers, students, and scientists in other fields who are interested in reading about the most significant current research in optics.

4372. *Studies in History and Philosophy of Science Part B: Studies in History and Philosophy of Modern Physics.* [ISSN: 1355-2198] 1995. q. EUR 752. Ed(s): G Sengers, D Dieks. Pergamon, The Blvd, Langford Ln, E Park, Kidlington, OX5 1GB, United Kingdom; JournalsCustomerServiceEMEA@elsevier.com; http://www.elsevier.com. Illus., adv. Sample. Refereed. Microform: PQC. *Indexed:* A01, A22, ArtHuCI, CCMJ, IPB, MSN, MathR. *Bk. rev.:* 0-5; 1,000-2,000 words. *Aud.:* Ac, Sa.

As scientists make new discoveries and develop new theories, they also change the ways in which we understand and approach our world. One result of this has been a rise in the study of the history of science, with particular emphasis on the history of modern physics, including astronomy, chemistry, and other non-biological sciences. This journal focuses on those areas. The primary emphasis is on research from the mid- to late nineteenth century to the present, the period of emergence of the kind of theoretical physics that came to dominate in the twentieth century. In each issue, original articles and review essays are published. About one issue each year is devoted to a special theme, such as quantum field theory or mathematical modeling. Because the focus is on the history of ideas, many of the articles are approachable by a wider audience. This journal belongs in any collection dealing with the history of science.

■ PHYSIOLOGY

See also Biology; Botany; and Zoology sections.

Jim Hodgson, Tracing Supervisor, Circulation Division, The Widener Library of The Harvard College Libraries, Harvard Yard, Cambridge, MA 02138

Introduction

Physiology is the study of the function of the parts of the human body, and other organisms, as compared to studying the structures themselves, which is called anatomy. This section is intended to help guide selection of titles essential to research in physiology at a professional level. According to the Online Computer Library Center, at least 900 institutions subscribe to all of the titles reviewed in this section. All are distinguished by high peer-citation ratings. Many of these, as well as other titles that are perhaps more accessible to laypersons, are published through Highwire.org, an excellent site run by Stanford University, with most content freely available after one year (if not sooner), and with an option to purchase individual current articles. There is also provision for making articles freely available to patients. All of these titles are published by physiological societies that have been in existence since the late 1800s.

Basic Periodicals

American Journal of Physiology (Consolidated), Journal of Applied Physiology, Journal of General Physiology, Physiological Reviews.

Basic Abstracts and Indexes

Biological Abstracts, Biological Abstracts/RRM, Biological and Agricultural Index, Current Contents/Life Sciences.

4373. *American Journal of Physiology (Consolidated).* [ISSN: 0002-9513] 1898. m. USD 5280 domestic; USD 5810 foreign. American Physiological Society, 9650 Rockville Pike, Bethesda, MD 20814; http://www.the-aps.org. Illus., adv. Refereed. Microform: PMC; PQC. *Indexed:* A01, A22, Agr, BRI, C45, IndVet, MLA-IB. *Aud.:* Ac, Sa.

The *American Journal of Physiology (Consolidated)* is published by the American Physiological Society (APS), arguably the preeminent publishing society in this field, and the journal is an important title for medical and biology collections. In addition to the seven titles of which the *AJP (Consolidated)* is composed, two of the other five titles in this edition of *Magazines for Libraries* are also published by the APS. The seven subtitles of the *AJP* are published separately as well as combined, covering the following fields: cell physiology; endocrinology and metabolism; gastrointestinal and liver physiology; heart and circulatory physiology; lung cellular and molecular physiology; regulatory, integrative, and comparative physiology; and renal physiology. The *AJP (Consolidated)* weighs in at around 2,000 pages monthly, and arrives split into two parts. Color diagrams and photos support the text, but it is not lavishly illustrated. It contains very rare ads for equipment or vendors. Editorials that summarize recent developments are at the beginning of each issue, followed by sections corresponding to segments within each field. For example, the issue on "GI and Liver Physiology" has sections titled "Mucosal Biology," "Inflammation/Immunity/Mediators," "Hormones and Signaling," "Neuroregulation and Motility," and "Liver and Biliary Tract." The *American Journal of Physiology (Consolidated)* is available for free online after one year through Highwire.org, and current articles are available for subscribers online.

4374. *Annual Review of Physiology.* [ISSN: 0066-4278] 1939. a. USD 269 (print or online ed.). Ed(s): Samuel Gubins, David Julius. Annual Reviews, PO Box 10139, Palo Alto, CA 94303; service@annualreviews.org; http://www.annualreviews.org. Refereed. Microform: PQC. Reprint: PSC. *Indexed:* A01, A22, Agr, C45, ExcerpMed. *Aud.:* Ac, Sa.

This journal "strives to bring mechanistic and molecular insights to problems concerning physiology of the whole organism." Sections include "'Perspectives' of the Editor"; "Cardiovascular Physiology"; "Cell Physiology"; "Ecological, Evolutionary, and Comparative Physiology"; "Endocrinology"; "Gastrointestinal Physiology"; "Neurophysiology"; "Renal and Electrolyte Physiology"; "Respiratory Physiology"; and a "Special Topic" that provides a focus for a collection of articles. Most of the articles require a strong medical or research background. Articles are available for purchase individually at the publisher's web site. One feature that is not available online is a section titled "Other reviews of interest to physiologists," with recommended article and journal titles, and author information.

4375. *Journal of Applied Physiology.* Former titles (until 1985): *Journal of Applied Physiology: Respiratory, Environmental and Exercise Physiology;* (until 1977): *Journal of Applied Physiology.* [ISSN: 8750-7587] 1948. m. USD 1680 domestic; USD 1780 foreign. Ed(s): Peter Wagner. American Physiological Society, 9650 Rockville Pike, Bethesda, MD 20814; http://www.the-aps.org. Illus., adv. Refereed. Microform: PQC. *Indexed:* A22, AbAn, C45, ErgAb, IndVet, RRTA, SD. *Aud.:* Ac, Sa.

This is another publication of the American Physiological Society, presenting "original papers that deal with diverse areas of research in applied physiology, especially those papers emphasizing adaptive and integrative mechanisms." However, unlike the several publications from this society that are consolidated as research into cellular mechanisms and metabolic pathways, this journal presents cohort studies in mammals, more specifically regarding "gross" physiology of larger-scale systems, and thus is more applicable to sports medicine or surgical procedures, for example. There is an emphasis on the effects of exercise and stress; one recent article is titled "The 10-20-30 training concept improves performance and health profile in moderately trained runners." A "Highlighted Topic" consists of editorials and article reviews that represent various points of view in debated subjects. Another section, "Innovative Methodologies," will appeal to researchers. As with its sibling publications from this society, color diagrams and photos support the text, but this journal is not lavishly illustrated, and it contains very rare ads for equipment or vendors. The *Journal of Applied Physiology* is available for free online after one year through Highwire.org, and current articles are available for subscribers online.

4376. *Journal of General Physiology.* [ISSN: 0022-1295] 1918. m. USD 2260 (print & online eds.). Ed(s): Edward N Pugh. Rockefeller University Press, 1114 First Ave, New York, NY 10021; jgpcopy@rockefeller.edu; http://www.rupress.org. Illus., index, adv. Sample. Refereed. Circ: 546 Paid. Microform: PQC. *Indexed:* A01, A22, P02. *Aud.:* Ac, Sa.

The *Journal of General Physiology* is the official organ of the Society of General Physiologists, which has a mixed membership of botanists and zoologists. Thus some of the articles relate to the physiology of flora as well as fauna, but many are specific to humans or mammals, especially when studied at a cellular level. This is another sizable contender at 400–600 pages per issue, with a few ads in the front and back. The articles are extremely technical and accessible only to highly educated readers, so this journal would be most appropriate for libraries that support biologists, physicians, and physiologists. Current articles are available for subscribers online, and are free after six months through Highwire.org.

4377. *The Journal of Physiology.* [ISSN: 0022-3751] 1878. s-m. plus proceedings 5/yr. GBP 3509. Ed(s): David J Paterson, Carol Huxley. Wiley-Blackwell Publishing Ltd., The Atrium, Southern Gate, Chichester, PO19 8SQ, United Kingdom; customer@wiley.com; http://www.wiley.com/. Illus., index, adv. Sample. Refereed. Microform: PMC; PQC. Reprint: PSC. *Indexed:* A22, C45, E01, ExcerpMed, IndVet, PsycInfo. *Aud.:* Ac, Sa.

This journal is a mix of lighter fare along with original research studies, with no advertisements. The contents of each issue include the following sections: "Perspectives"—providing articles that are like mini-lectures from experts, summarizing recent developments in the field within a historical context; "Journal Club"—articles that review recently published studies, giving context, discussing the study's impact, and presenting new/remaining questions; "Classical Perspectives"—articles that provide a comprehensive review of an historic paradigm, and how it has changed with more recent research; and research studies divided into categories such as neuroscience, cardiovascular, alimentary, skeletal muscle and exercise, and integrative. The first few sections will be interesting to readers who possess at least a little medical background. The research studies would be meaningful only to professionals in the field, graduate students, or interested laypersons researching a specific topic.

4378. *Physiological Reviews.* [ISSN: 0031-9333] 1921. q. USD 625 domestic; USD 660 foreign. Ed(s): Dennis Brown. American Physiological Society, 9650 Rockville Pike, Bethesda, MD 20814; http://www.the-aps.org. Illus., adv. Refereed. Microform: PMC; PQC. *Indexed:* A01, A22, C45, ExcerpMed, IndVet, P02. *Aud.:* Ac, Sa.

Physiological Reviews is another publication from the American Physiological Society; its content is written for "physiologists, neuroscientists, cell biologists, biophysicists, and clinicians with special interest in pathophysiology." Many articles are reviews of the current state of knowledge regarding some molecule or pathway, and they are highly readable if quite technical, with good bibliographies. The publication contains 800-plus glossy pages in each quarterly issue, with very few ads. Current articles are available for subscribers online, and for free after 12 months through Highwire.org.

■ POLITICAL SCIENCE

General and Political Theory/Comparative and American Politics/International Relations

David Lincove, History, Political Science, Public Affairs & Philosophy Librarian, Ohio State University Libraries, Columbus, OH; 614-292-2393; lincove.1@osu.edu

Introduction

This section provides information on selected, core English-language periodicals in political science. These periodicals offer varying approaches to research and contemporary issues that are appropriate for academic, public, or high school libraries. Choices for the list are subjective, and no attempt is made at providing a comprehensive guide to the full range of periodicals on related political topics or ideologies. In particular, this section does not cover core titles that focus on public administration, peace and security studies, and political economy that may be covered in other sections of this volume.

The titles in this section are grouped into "General and Political Theory," "Comparative and American Politics," and "International Relations." The information about each periodical includes the suggested audience, as well as the presence of book reviews and special features.

Basic Periodicals

Hs: *Current History, Foreign Affairs, Foreign Policy, National Journal, The Washington Quarterly, World Affairs;* Ga: *American Political Science Review, Annals of the American Academy of Political and Social Sciences, Current History, CQ Weekly, Foreign Affairs, Foreign Policy, Governance, Governing, International Affairs, International Studies Quarterly, Journal of Democracy, National Journal, Political Communication, PS: Political Science, Presidential Studies Quarterly, The Washington Quarterly, World Affairs;* Ac: *American Political Science Review, American Politics Research, Annals of the American Academy of Political and Social Science, Annual Review of Political Science, British Journal of Political Science, Comparative Political Studies, CQ Weekly, Current History, European Journal of International Relations, European Journal of Political Research, Foreign Affairs, Foreign Policy, Governance, Governing, International Affairs, International Organization, International Studies Quarterly, Journal of Democracy, Journal of Politics, National Journal, Policy Studies Journal, Political Analysis, Political Communication, PS: Political Science, Political Theory, Presidential Studies Quarterly, Publius, Quarterly Journal of Political Science, Review of International Studies, State Politics & Policy Quarterly, Third World Quarterly, The Washington Quarterly, World Affairs, World Politics.*

Basic Abstracts and Indexes

International Political Science Abstracts, PAIS International, Social Sciences Citation Index, Social Sciences Abstracts, Worldwide Political Science Abstracts.

4379. Governing. Incorporates: *Public's Capital;* (1984-1994): *City & State.* [ISSN: 0894-3842] 1987. m. Free to qualified personnel. Ed(s): Christopher Swope, Alan Ehrenhalt. C Q Press, Inc., 2300 N St, NW, Ste 800, Washington, DC 20037; customerservice@cqpress.com; http://www.cqpress.com. Illus., adv. Sample. Circ: 86000 Paid and controlled. Vol. ends: Sep. *Indexed:* A22, BRI, P02. *Aud.:* Ac, Sa.

Governing is intended for persons involved or interested in federal, state, and local governments and politics, and also government interactions with the private sector and the media. It seeks to provide ?intelligence and analysis on management, policy[,] and politics to help guide and inspire innovative leaders across state and local government.? Each issue has feature articles on contemporary issues, such as local bankruptcies, building codes, and prison reform, as well as a section on ?politics and policy? that focuses on issues such as fixing bridges and early voting. Also, this journal has a section called ? problem solver? that focuses on ways of addressing specific government problems, such as understanding debt and data-gathering techniques. Recommended for academic and public libraries.

General and Political Theory

The periodicals in this subsection provide broad coverage of contemporary scholarship in political science, including political philosophy and the theoretical foundations and analytical methodologies that are used in political science research.

4380. American Academy of Political and Social Science. Annals. [ISSN: 0002-7162] 1889. bi-m. USD 1013. Ed(s): Emily Wood. Sage Publications, Inc., 2455 Teller Rd, Thousand Oaks, CA 91320; info@sagepub.com; http://www.sagepub.com. Illus., adv. Sample. Refereed. Vol. ends: Nov. Microform: IDC; PMC; PQC. Reprint: PSC. *Indexed:* A22, ABS&EES, AgeL, BAS, BEL&L, BRI, BrArAb, CBRI, CJPI, Chicano, CompR, E01, EconLit, HEA, IBSS, JEL, MLA-IB, P02, P61, PsycInfo, RILM, RiskAb, SSA. *Bk. rev.:* . *Aud.:* Ga, Ac, Sa.

The *Annals* are published in thematic issues, individually edited with essays that offer multidisciplinary approaches to a wide range of topics in the social sciences. Each issue is designed to "promote the use of the social sciences to inform public opinion and improve public policy." Proposals for thematic issues are reviewed by the editorial review board. The *Annals* publishes on contemporary social issues in the United States and in other regions of the world. Recent thematic issues focus on institutional structures to help urban disadvantaged, validity of surveys and statistics, politics and consumerism, social impact of immigration in American cities, migrant children, gender and race inequality, and adulthood in Asia. Because of the broad social issues covered, the *Annals* will appeal to a wide variety of academics, professionals, and students of the social sciences. Recommended for academic and public libraries.

4381. American Political Science Review: the leading journal of political science research. Incorporates (1904-1914): *American Political Science Association. Proceedings.* [ISSN: 0003-0554] 1906. q. Ed(s): Steven Forde, Marijke Breuning. Cambridge University Press, The Edinburgh Bldg, Shaftesbury Rd, Cambridge, CB2 8RU, United Kingdom; journals@cambridge.org; http://www.cambridge.org. Illus., index, adv. Sample. Refereed. Circ: 16000. Vol. ends: No. 4. Microform: MIM; PMC; PQC. Reprint: PSC. *Indexed:* A01, A22, ABIn, ABS&EES, B01, BAS, BEL&L, BRI, CBRI, Chicano, E01, EconLit, IBSS, JEL, MLA-IB, P02, P61, RiskAb, SSA, SWR&A. *Aud.:* Ac, Sa.

APSR is sponsored by the American Political Science Association and has been published since 1906. It seeks new research in all areas of political science, including political theory, American politics, public policy, public administration, comparative politics, and international relations. Recent articles focus on the politics of genetics (genopolitics), the influence of cell phones on violence in Africa, bias in voter decision-making, transitions to democracy, Aristotle's *Politics,* and ethnic conflict. Recommended for academic and public libraries.

4382. Annual Review of Political Science. [ISSN: 1094-2939] 1986. a. USD 226 (print or online ed.). Ed(s): Samuel Gubins, Margaret Levi. Annual Reviews, PO Box 10139, Palo Alto, CA 94303; service@annualreviews.org; http://www.annualreviews.org. Refereed. Microform: PQC. *Indexed:* A01, A22, B01, IBSS, P61, SSA. *Aud.:* Ac.

Covering all areas of political science, this publication's annual volumes provide comprehensive critical reviews of the literature on broad topics in "political theory and philosophy, international relations, political economy, political behavior, American and comparative politics, public administration and policy, and methodology." The articles provide the historical development of scholarship on a topic, analyze the direction of research in recent years, and propose issues for future work. Recent articles focus on survey research methodology, climate change, behavioral economics, nuclear weapons proliferation, and leadership. Recommended for academic libraries.

4383. British Journal of Political Science. [ISSN: 0007-1234] 1971. q. GBP 328. Ed(s): Shaun Bowler, Kristian Skrede Gleditsch. Cambridge University Press, The Edinburgh Bldg, Shaftesbury Rd, Cambridge, CB2 8RU, United Kingdom; journals@cambridge.org; http://www.cambridge.org/uk. Illus., index. Refereed. Circ: 1350. Vol. ends: Oct. Microform: PQC. Reprint: PSC. *Indexed:* A01, A22, ABIn, B01, BAS, BRI, E01, IBSS, P02, P61, RiskAb, SSA. *Aud.:* Ac.

This journal covers all areas of political science, "including political theory, political behaviour, public policy[,] and international relations," and related disciplines such as "sociology, social psychology, economics[,] and philosophy." Each issue has research articles, and essays under the heading of "Notes and Comments"; and some issues have a review article on the literature of a topic of research. Recent articles are on the election violence, human rights networks, political socialization, comparative authoritarianism, global migration, and coded political texts. Recommended for academic libraries.

4384. European Journal of Political Research. [ISSN: 0304-4130] 1973. bi-m. GBP 649. Ed(s): Richard S Katz, Kris Deschouwer. Wiley-Blackwell Publishing Ltd., 9600 Garsington Rd, Oxford, OX4 2DQ, United Kingdom; customerservices@blackwellpublishing.com; http://www.wiley.com/. Illus., index, adv. Sample. Refereed. Circ: 900. Microform: PQC. Reprint: PSC. *Indexed:* A01, A22, E01, IBSS, P02, P61, RiskAb, SSA. *Aud.:* Ac.

EJPR, published for the European Consortium of Political Research, offers a broad approach to new theoretical and comparative research, particularly on European affairs, that appeals to political scientists and other scholars in the social sciences. The variety of articles in recent issues include bias in agenda setting of the European Council, unions and job security in Western Europe, compulsory voting and party identification, a multinational study of interest group relations with political parties, European integration and electoral democracy, the radical right in Western Europe, and unemployment insurance and monetary policy in 17 OECD nations. A subscription to *EJPR* includes the *European Journal of Political Research Political Data Yearbook,* which was formerly published as a double issue of *EJPR* but now appears separately in print and at the publisher's web site. The yearbook "provides commentary by recognized scholarly experts on election results, national referenda, changes in government, and institutional reforms in all EU member states (plus Australia, Canada, Iceland, Israel, Japan, New Zealand, Norway, Switzerland, and the United States) as well as on the principal issues in national politics during the year." Associated with the yearbook is a free interactive resource (www.politicaldatayearbook.com) with graphic representations of data on each country. Recommended for academic and public libraries.

4385. *The Journal of Politics.* Supersedes (in 1939): *Southern Political Science Association. Annual Session. Proceedings.* [ISSN: 0022-3816] 1933. q. GBP 285 (print & online eds.). Ed(s): William Mishler, Jan E Leighley. Cambridge University Press, The Edinburgh Bldg, Shaftesbury Rd, Cambridge, CB2 8RU, United Kingdom; journals@cambridge.org; http://www.cambridge.org/uk. Illus., index, adv. Refereed. Vol. ends: Nov. Microform: PQC. Reprint: PSC. *Indexed:* A01, A22, ABS&EES, B01, BAS, BRI, CBRI, Chicano, E01, IBSS, MLA-IB, P02, P61, PsycInfo, RiskAb, SSA. *Bk. rev.:* 10 per issue. *Aud.:* Ac.

JOP is published for the Southern Political Science Association. The journal offers "theoretically innovative and methodologically diverse research in all subfields [of political science] including, but not limited to, American politics, comparative politics, formal theory, international relations, methodology, political theory, public administration[,] and public policy." Recent articles were on historical perspectives of U.S. Senate voting on Supreme Court justices, stock market response to left-wing governments, electoral accountability in Argentina, isolationism in foreign policy, and theories of political liberalism. The journal includes book reviews. Recommended for academic libraries.

4386. *P S: Political Science & Politics.* Incorporates (1988-1990): *Political Science Teacher;* Which was formerly (until 1988): *News for Teachers of Political Science;* (until 1978): *D E A News;* Formerly (until 1988): *Political Science;* Which superseded in part (in 1968): *American Political Science Review;* Which incorporated (1904-1906): *American Political Science Association. Proceedings.* [ISSN: 1049-0965] 1904. q. GBP 436 (print & online eds.). Cambridge University Press, The Edinburgh Bldg, Shaftesbury Rd, Cambridge, CB2 8RU, United Kingdom; journals@cambridge.org; http://www.cambridge.org/uk. Illus., index, adv. Refereed. Circ: 16000. Vol. ends: No. 4. Microform: PQC. Reprint: PSC. *Indexed:* A22, ABS&EES, BRI, Chicano, E01, ERIC, P02, P61, RiskAb, SSA, SWR&A. *Aud.:* Ga, Ac, Sa.

PS, published by the American Political Science Association, is the organization's "journal of record for the profession." It is a peer-reviewed journal "focusing on contemporary politics, teaching, and the discipline" that offers a mix of research articles, news about the profession, activities of members, and memorials. Articles range broadly in the field and offer "critical analyses of contemporary political phenomena" for scholars, students, and general readers. Articles may examine social media and politics; using political content on television in teaching; scholarly communication; and election studies. *PS* occasionally offers a thematic symposium, such as "Technology, Data, and Politics." Recommended for academic and public libraries.

4387. *Political Analysis.* Formerly (until 1985): *Political Methodology.* [ISSN: 1047-1987] 1974. q. EUR 487. Ed(s): Christopher Zorn. Oxford University Press, Great Clarendon St, Oxford, OX2 6DP, United Kingdom; enquiry@oup.co.uk; http://www.oxfordjournals.org. Adv. Refereed. Reprint: PSC. *Indexed:* A22, E01, P02, P61, RiskAb, SSA. *Aud.:* Ac.

This journal, published on behalf of the Society for Political Methodology and the Political Methodology Section of the American Political Science Association, is at the forefront of communicating the use of quantitative methodologies in political science research. The research incorporates empirical analysis and seeks to be consistent with the rules and terminology of mathematics, probability, and statistics to offer greater understanding of political and related social phenomena. This analytical approach is applied to issues such as voting and elections, political campaigns, decision making, public policy evaluation, budgets, relations between nations, analysis of political regimes such as democracy, and public support for political parties. Also, there are studies that merge quantitative with qualitative methods that typically do not involve using numerical data in analysis. Recommended for academic libraries.

4388. *Political Theory: an international journal of political philosophy.* [ISSN: 0090-5917] 1973. bi-m. USD 1189. Ed(s): Mary G Dietz. Sage Publications, Inc., 2455 Teller Rd, Thousand Oaks, CA 91320; info@sagepub.com; http://www.sagepub.com. Illus., index. Refereed. Vol. ends: No. 6. Microform: PQC. Reprint: PSC. *Indexed:* A01, A22, ABS&EES, BRI, E01, FR, IBSS, IPB, P02, P61, SSA. *Bk. rev.:* 2-3 review essays; 2-4 shorter reviews. *Aud.:* Ac.

This journal focuses on "political philosophy from every philosophical, ideological and methodological perspective. Articles address historical political thought, modern political theory, normative and analytical philosophy, the history of ideas[,] and critical assessments of current work." Recent articles are on themes such as immigration, morality, inequality, human rights, freedom, ethics, and analyses of ideas from one or more political philosophers such as Kant and Habermas. Issues may have thematic symposium, multi-book review essays, and individual reviews of books. Recommended for academic libraries.

4389. *Quarterly Journal of Political Science.* [ISSN: 1554-0626] 2006. q. USD 440 in the Americas (print or online ed.); EUR 440 elsewhere (print or online eds.); USD 510 combined subscription in the Americas (print & online eds.). Ed(s): Nolan McCarty, Keith Krehbiel. Now Publishers Inc., PO Box 1024, Hanover, MA 02339; sales@nowpublishers.com; http://www.nowpublishers.com. Sample. Refereed. *Indexed:* EconLit, JEL, P61, SSA. *Aud.:* Ac.

Founded in 2005, this relatively new journal emphasizes quality research in "positive political science and contemporary political economy." The journal encourages scientific methodology in political analyses that propose positive hypotheses and test hypotheses with data and rational methods. Articles may also examine previously tested generalizations. The editors believe that no other political science journal is so clearly focused on this type of research, and they endeavor to attract "cutting-edge research on any aspect of private, local, national, comparative, or international politics" that may also involve economics, business, and law. Recent articles have dealt with executive compensation regulation, compulsory voting in Australia, perceptions of government service quality, and legacies of British and French colonialism in Cameroon. Recommended for academic libraries.

Comparative and American Politics

Periodicals in this subsection focus on either research in politics or contemporary policy in the United States, or the subfield of political science known as comparative politics. The latter uses research methodologies of the social sciences and sciences to draw causal inferences about political issues in multiple countries or regions.

4390. *American Journal of Political Science.* Formerly (until 1973): *Midwest Journal of Political Science.* [ISSN: 0092-5853] 1950. q. GBP 474. Ed(s): Rick K Wilson. Wiley-Blackwell Publishing, Inc., 111 River St, Hoboken, NJ 07030; info@wiley.com; http://onlinelibrary.wiley.com/. Illus. Sample. Refereed. Vol. ends: No. 4. Microform: PQC. Reprint: PSC. *Indexed:* A01, A22, ABIn, ABS&EES, B01, BAS, E01, IBSS, P02, P61, RiskAb, SSA. *Aud.:* Ac.

Sponsored by the Midwest Political Science Association, *AJPS* seeks "significant advances in knowledge and understanding of citizenship, governance, and politics, and to the public value of political science research." To a substantial degree, the journal publishes research on American politics, but also prevalent are international, philosophical, and theoretical/quantitative studies. Recent papers focused on political communication networks, the role of election primaries in Ghana, causal inference in political science research, U.S. Supreme Court legitimacy, and the impact of social networks on political behavior. Recommended for academic libraries.

4391. *American Politics Research.* Formerly (until 2001): *American Politics Quarterly.* [ISSN: 1532-673X] 1973. bi-m. USD 1214. Ed(s): Brian J Gaines. Sage Publications, Inc., 2455 Teller Rd, Thousand Oaks, CA 91320; info@sagepub.com; http://www.sagepub.com. Illus., index, adv. Sample. Refereed. Vol. ends: No. 4. Reprint: PSC. *Indexed:* A01, A22, E01, IBSS, P02, P61, RiskAb, SSA. *Aud.:* Ac.

APR is dedicated to the "dissemination of the latest theory, research and analysis in all areas of American politics, including local, state, and national." It offers scholarly articles on a wide variety of topics related to political institutions, leadership, elections, and social influences on politics. Recent articles have covered social pressures on voters, presidential press conferences, media ownership and reporting on election campaigns, legislative professionalism, voting by mail and voter turnout, and the influence of Congressional health-care votes on reelection in 2010. Recommended for academic and public libraries.

4392. *C Q Weekly.* Formerly (until vol.56, no.15, 1998): *Congressional Quarterly Weekly Report.* [ISSN: 1521-5997] 1945. w. 48/yr. Congressional Quarterly, Inc., 1255, 22nd St, N.W., Washington, DC 20037; customerservice@cq.com; http://corporate.cq.com. Illus., index, adv. Sample. Vol. ends: No. 52. *Indexed:* A01, A22, ABS&EES, B01, BLI, BRI, C37, Chicano, MASUSE, P02. *Aud.:* Hs, Ac, Sa.

Each issue of *CQ Weekly* provides current information about activities related to the United States Congress. It includes feature and brief articles on key issues and persons who work in or with the government, the "status of bills in play, behind-the-scenes maneuvering, committee and floor activity, debates, and all roll-call votes." Recent issues had articles on environmental impact of ocean garbage, Chinese telecommunication industry, health care, gun control, hydropower development, violence against women, Afghanistan, legislative process, budget issues, and Congressional committee activities. Recommended for academic, public, and school libraries.

4393. *Comparative Political Studies.* [ISSN: 0010-4140] 1968. m. USD 1615. Ed(s): James A Caporaso. Sage Publications, Inc., 2455 Teller Rd, Thousand Oaks, CA 91320; info@sagepub.com; http://www.sagepub.com. Illus., index, adv. Sample. Refereed. Vol. ends: No. 6. Microform: PQC. Reprint: PSC. *Indexed:* A01, A22, ABS&EES, BAS, BRI, E01, IBSS, P02, P61, RiskAb, SSA. *Bk. rev.:* 2-3 per issue. *Aud.:* Ac.

CPS offers the "timeliest methodology, theory, and research" studies on political issues related to global, multinational, and single-nation perspectives. The journal publishes articles that may contribute to decision making on domestic and foreign policies. Recent issues focus on interest group lobbying in Denmark and Norway, the economy and emerging democracies in Asia, modeling the European party systems, policies on same sex unions in Mexico and Argentina, quantitative and qualitative research methodologies, and the decline of religious voting in Italy. Each issue includes book reviews. Recommended for academic libraries.

4394. *Governance: an international journal of policy, administration, and institutions.* [ISSN: 0952-1895] 1987. q. GBP 602. Ed(s): Alasdair Roberts, Robert Henry Cox. Wiley-Blackwell Publishing, Inc., Commerce Pl, 350 Main St, Malden, MA 02148; info@wiley.com; http://onlinelibrary.wiley.com/. Adv. Refereed. Circ: 567 Paid. Reprint: PSC. *Indexed:* A01, A22, ABIn, B01, E01, IBSS, P61, RiskAb, SSA. *Bk. rev.:* 5-6 per issue. *Aud.:* Ac, Sa.

Governing is intended for persons involved or interested in federal, state, and local governments and politics, and also government interactions with the private sector and the media. It seeks to provide ?intelligence and analysis on management, policy[,] and politics to help guide and inspire innovative leaders across state and local government.? Each issue has feature articles on contemporary issues, such as local bankruptcies, building codes, and prison reform, as well as a section on ?politics and policy? that focuses on issues such as fixing bridges and early voting. Also, this journal has a section called ?

problem solver? that focuses on ways of addressing specific government problems, such as understanding debt and data-gathering techniques. Recommended for academic and public libraries.

4395. *Journal of Democracy.* [ISSN: 1045-5736] 1990. q. USD 155. Ed(s): Brent Kallmer, Larry Diamond. The Johns Hopkins University Press, 2715 N Charles St, Baltimore, MD 21218; http://www.press.jhu.edu. Illus., index, adv. Sample. Refereed. Circ: 1750. Vol. ends: No. 4. Reprint: PSC. *Indexed:* A01, A22, ABS&EES, BRI, E01, IBSS, P02, P61, SSA. *Bk. rev.:* 1+ per issue. *Aud.:* Ac, Sa.

The *Journal of Democracy* web site says that it is the "world's leading publication on the theory and practice of democracy," drawing discussion and debate from academics and activists regarding "problems and prospects of democracy around the world." This includes articles on the "establishment, consolidation[,] and maintenance of democracy" as influenced by politics, culture, and society. Each issue includes articles, book reviews or review essay, a report on recent national election results, and selected primary source documents, such as an excerpt from a national leader's speech or the text of a European Union document. Recommended for academic and public libraries.

4396. *National Journal: the weekly on politics and government.* Former titles (until 1975): *National Journal Reports;* (until 1973): *National Journal.* [ISSN: 0360-4217] 1969. w. Ed(s): Ron Fournier. National Journal Group, Inc., The Watergate 600 New Hampshire Ave, NW, Washington, DC 20037; service@nationaljournal.com; http://www.nationaljournal.com. Illus., index, adv. Circ: 11381 Paid. Vol. ends: No. 52. Microform: PQC. *Indexed:* A01, A22, ABS&EES, AgeL, B02, BAS, BLI, BRI, C37, MASUSE, MCR, P02, SWR&A. *Aud.:* Ga, Ac, Sa.

National Journal provides informative, analytical articles on key issues under consideration by the United States Congress. In addition to brief weekly highlights of congressional activities and the "insider's poll" on issues of the day, there are long and short articles written by *National Journal* reporters on specific topics relating to the economy, politics, lobbying, foreign affairs, health, the federal budget, and national defense. Recent lead articles focus on political aftermath of the Boston marathon bombing; the desirability of running for Congress, climate change, and implementation of the Affordable Care Act. The periodical is directed toward a wide variety of readers who want a tool that explains contemporary issues and conflicts in congressional politics. Recommended for academic, public, and school libraries.

4397. *Policy Studies Journal (Online).* [ISSN: 1541-0072] 1972. q. GBP 1261. Ed(s): Chris Weible, Peter deLeon. Wiley-Blackwell Publishing, Inc., 111 River St, Hoboken, NJ 07030; info@wiley.com; http://www.wiley.com/. Refereed. *Aud.:* Ac, Sa.

PSJ is sponsored by the Public Policy Section of the American Political Science Association and the Policy Studies Organization. It offers "theoretically and empirically grounded research on policy process and policy analysis." The journal seeks articles in which the data are clearly stated and the research advances the literature of the field. Recent articles focus on state gambling policies, vaccination legislation for girls, public assistance in cities, school vouchers, stability of renewable energy policies, and China's policies on urban poverty. *PSJ* also provides the *Public Policy Yearbook* as a supplementary issue with topical literature reviews and a "detailed international listing of policy scholars with contact information, fields of specialization, research references, and individual scholars' statements of current and future research interests." Recommended for academic libraries.

4398. *Political Communication: an international journal.* Formerly (until 1992): *Political Communication and Persuasion.* [ISSN: 1058-4609] 1980. q. GBP 467 (print & online eds.). Ed(s): Shanto Iyenga. Taylor & Francis Inc., 325 Chestnut St, Ste 800, Philadelphia, PA 19106; customerservice@taylorandfrancis.com; http://www.tandfonline.com. Illus., adv. Sample. Refereed. Vol. ends: No. 4. Reprint: PSC. *Indexed:* A01, A22, BRI, E01, IBSS, P02, P61, SSA. *Bk. rev.:* 3-4 per issue. *Aud.:* Ac, Sa.

This journal is sponsored by the Political Communications divisions of the American Political Science Association and the International Communication Association. It seeks "cutting-edge research at the intersection of politics and communication, broadly conceived." Editors call for a broad array of literature on practice, process, and policy. The journal seeks a multidisciplinary audience of scholars and practitioners. Articles are substantially focused on the American scene, with occasional studies on other countries. Recent issues have covered news coverage of early voting in elections, citizens' response to conflicting information, persuasive social communication, and an analysis of America's reputation as represented in popular, international news sources. Book reviews and an occasional topical issue also appear. Recommended for academic and public libraries.

4399. *Presidential Studies Quarterly.* Formerly (until 1974): *Center House Bulletin.* [ISSN: 0360-4918] 1972. q. GBP 295. Ed(s): Carolyn Allen-Bates, George C Edwards, III. Wiley-Blackwell Publishing, Inc., 111 River St, Hoboken, NJ 07030; info@wiley.com; http://onlinelibrary.wiley.com/. Illus., index. Sample. Refereed. Vol. ends: No. 4. Microform: PQC. Reprint: PSC. *Indexed:* A01, A22, ABS&EES, BRI, CBRI, E01, IBSS, P02, P61, RiskAb, SSA. *Bk. rev.:* 10-18 per issue. *Aud.:* Ac, Sa.

PSQ is a journal about the United States presidency from historical and contemporary perspectives on a broad range of topics, such as elections, campaigns, voters, foreign policy, decision making, relations with Congress and federal courts, character and judgment, and managing the government. Scholars and professionals in history, political science, and communications contribute articles for an interdisciplinary journal that appeals to a broad audience of scholars, students, and political professionals. Recent articles focus on counterterrorism policy, signing statements, war powers in the early republic, and the nature of Ronald Reagan's leadership. Issues include book reviews and special feature essays. Recommended for academic and public libraries.

4400. *Publius: the journal of federalism.* [ISSN: 0048-5950] 1971. q. EUR 437. Ed(s): Carol S Weissert. Oxford University Press, Great Clarendon St, Oxford, OX2 6DP, United Kingdom; enquiry@oup.co.uk; http://www.oxfordjournals.org. Illus., index, adv. Sample. Refereed. Vol. ends: No. 4. Microform: PQC. Reprint: PSC. *Indexed:* A01, A22, ABS&EES, BRI, E01, IBSS, P02, P61, SSA. *Bk. rev.:* 0-10 per issue. *Aud.:* Ac, Sa.

Publius is sponsored by the Section on Federalism and Intergovernmental Relations of the American Political Science Association. It focuses on "the latest research from around the world on the theory and practice of federalism; the dynamics of federal systems; intergovernmental relations and administration; regional, state and provincial governance; and comparative federalism." It seeks theoretical and analytical methodologies and articles that illustrate the impact of policy changes on governments. In addition to articles and book reviews, issues may include symposium, literature reviews, and research notes. *Publius* publishes special issues on topics such as health policy, and an annual analysis of "federalism and intergovernmental issues in the preceding year." Recent articles examine U.S. Supreme Court review of state statutes, peace and federalism in India and Nigeria, internal trade policy in Canada, hybrid federalism in health insurance policy, and intergovernmental grants. Recommended for academic libraries.

4401. *State Politics & Policy Quarterly.* [ISSN: 1532-4400] 2000. q. USD 308. Ed(s): Thomas Carsey. Sage Publications, Inc., 2455 Teller Rd, Thousand Oaks, CA 91320; info@sagepub.com; http://www.sagepub.com. Adv. Refereed. Reprint: PSC. *Indexed:* A01, IBSS, P02, P61, SSA. *Aud.:* Ac.

This journal is the official publication of the State Politics and Policy Section of the American Political Science Association. It seeks articles "that develop and test general hypotheses of political behavior and policy making, exploiting the unique advantages of the states." The 50 states each offer variations of politics, economics, and culture that provide laboratories for analysis and comparison in the context of the larger American political system. In a broader sense, the journal branches out into "legislative studies, political methodology, comparative politics, and political psychology." Most issues include research articles and a section called "The Practical Researcher," which focuses on research methodologies such as conducting statistical inferences or the use of a policy database in Pennsylvania. Examples of recent research topics are immigrant social policy in the states, wealth in majority party districts, the Georgia voter ID statute, state policy innovativeness, and gubernatorial budgetary power. Recommended for academic libraries.

International Relations

This subsection has periodicals that focus on a broad field of interests. The research and analysis of contemporary issues in these journals cover international relations theory, relations between nation states, international organizations, multinational corporations, and political economy. These journals my also cover international security and peace studies, but journals dedicated to these subjects are found in the "Peace and Conflict Studies" section of this volume.

4402. *Current History: a journal of contemporary world affairs.* Formed by the merger of (1940-1941): *Current History & Forum;* (1937-1941): *Events;* Incorporates (1940-1941): *Key to Contemporary Affairs;* (1945-1950): *Forum;* Which was formerly (until 1945): *Forum and Column Review;* (until 1943): *Column Review and Editorial Digest;* (until 1939): *Column Review.* [ISSN: 0011-3530] 1914. 9x/yr. USD 38 domestic (print or online ed.); USD 46 foreign; USD 48 combined subscription domestic (print & online eds.). Ed(s): Alan Sorensen. Current History, Inc., 4225 Main St, Philadelphia, PA 19127. Illus., index, adv. Vol. ends: Dec. Microform: NBI; PQC. *Indexed:* A01, A22, ABS&EES, AmHI, BAS, BRI, C37, CBRI, E01, IBSS, MASUSE, MLA-IB, P02, P61. *Bk. rev.:* 1+ essays per issue. *Aud.:* Hs, Ga, Ac, Sa.

This long-running periodical is distinguished by its analyses of contemporary international affairs by contributors who range from academic scholars, government and diplomatic leaders, to politicians with expertise. The journal projects a nonpartisan image with its independent, objective approach to issues. Each issue typically has a thematic focus on important current issues related to the world at large or to a particular country or region. Articles usually examine national politics, foreign relations, economic development, demography, drugs, violence, peace, and international organizations. Each issue includes a book review section and also the "Month in Review," with a chronology of important events organized by region and country. Recommended for academic, public, and school libraries.

4403. *European Journal of International Relations.* [ISSN: 1354-0661] 1995. q. USD 1440. Ed(s): Colin Wight, Lene Hansen. Sage Publications Ltd., 1 Oliver's Yard, 55 City Rd, London, EC1Y 1SP, United Kingdom; info@sagepub.co.uk; http://www.uk.sagepub.com. Illus., index, adv. Sample. Refereed. Vol. ends: No. 4. Reprint: PSC. *Indexed:* A01, A22, ABIn, B01, E01, EconLit, IBSS, JEL, P61, RiskAb, SSA. *Aud.:* Ac.

Published for the European Consortium for Political Research, this journal offers research on all aspects of international relations worldwide. Articles may provide contemporary or historical perspectives. Recent articles examine global warming in the context of global governmentality, an historical perspective to war, masculinity and the concept of liberal peace, the state and urban divide regarding climate change, the U.N. charter, international genocide studies, and third-party intervention in civil wars. Recommended for academic libraries.

4404. *Foreign Affairs.* Former titles (until 1922): *The Journal of International Relations;* (until 1919): *The Journal of Race Development.* [ISSN: 0015-7120] 1910. bi-m. USD 32 domestic; USD 44 Canada; USD 67 elsewhere. Ed(s): Gideon Rose, James F Hoge, Jr. Council on Foreign Relations, Inc., PO Box 420235, Palm Coast, FL 32142; membership@cfr.org; http://www.cfr.org. Illus., index, adv. Vol. ends: No. 6. Microform: WSH; PMC; PQC. Reprint: WSH. *Indexed:* A01, A22, ABIn, ABS&EES, B01, B02, BAS, BRI, C37, CBRI, EconLit, IBSS, JEL, MASUSE, MLA-IB, P02, P61. *Bk. rev.:* 1-3 essays per issue; usually 35-50 short reviews. *Aud.:* Hs, Ga, Ac, Sa.

Foreign Affairs is published by the Council on Foreign Relations, a nonpartisan organization that is "dedicated to improving the understanding of United States foreign policy and international affairs through the free exchange of ideas." The CFR publishes articles that do "not represent any consensus of beliefs" and are written by academics, foreign affairs practitioners, journalists, and other informed writers. The journal covers a broad range of issues in contemporary international affairs from political, historical, legal, and economic perspectives. Articles are enhanced with illustrations and maps, and bimonthly issues include topical essays and usually a large number of book reviews arranged by region of interest. Recommended for academic, public, and school libraries.

4405. *Foreign Policy (Washington): the magazine of global politics, economics and ideas.* [ISSN: 0015-7228] 1971. bi-m. USD 19.95 domestic (print or online ed.). Ed(s): Moises Naim, Susan Glasser. Slate Group, 1899 L St NW Ste 550, Washington, DC 20036; FP@ForeignPolicy.com. Illus., index. Refereed. Circ: 101208. Microform: PQC. *Indexed:* A01, A22, ABIn, ABS&EES, B01, B02, BRI, C37, CLI, IBSS, MASUSE, P02, P61. *Bk. rev.:* 1-3 essays per issue. *Aud.:* Ga, Ac, Sa.

FP is a magazine of contemporary "politics, economics, and ideas" in the context of foreign policy making worldwide. Notable academics, policy makers, and journalists contribute to a resource that is accessible to both specialists and a general audience seeking current information and ideas from a nonpartisan source. Recommended for academic, public, and school libraries.

4406. *International Affairs (London).* Former titles (until 1944): *International Affairs Review Supplement;* (until 1940): *International Affairs;* (until 1931): *Royal Institute of International Affairs. Journal;* (until 1926): *British Institute of International Affairs. Journal.* [ISSN: 0020-5850] 1922. bi-m. GBP 401. Ed(s): Caroline Soper. Wiley-Blackwell Publishing Ltd., The Atrium, Southern Gate, Chichester, PO19 8SQ, United Kingdom; customer@wiley.com; http://www.wiley.com/. Illus., index, adv. Sample. Refereed. Microform: PMC. Reprint: PSC. *Indexed:* A01, A22, AmHI, B01, BAS, BRI, E01, IBSS, P02, P61, RiskAb, SSA. *Bk. rev.:* 1-3 topical review essays; 40+ reviews per issue. *Aud.:* Hs, Ac, Sa.

Published on behalf of Chatham House, the Royal Institute of International Affairs in London, this journal is intended for a broad audience, with an emphasis on scholars and practitioners of international relations. Articles offer "critical thinking on the key issues shaping world economic and political change." Recent issues cover the state system in the middle east after World War I, constitutional change in Egypt, drone warfare, Africa in international affairs, Britain in European defense, an interview with the German foreign minister on problems with the European Community, U.S. defense strategy, and the influence of U.S. presidents and faith-based initiatives on American foreign policy. Each issue includes topic review essays and individual reviews of books organized by topics and regions. Recommended for academic and public libraries.

4407. *International Organization.* [ISSN: 0020-8183] 1947. q. GBP 164. Ed(s): Elana Matthews, Jon Pevehouse. Cambridge University Press, The Edinburgh Bldg, Shaftesbury Rd, Cambridge, CB2 8RU, United Kingdom; journals@cambridge.org; http://www.cambridge.org/uk. Illus., index, adv. Refereed. Circ: 1700. Vol. ends: No. 4. Microform: PQC. Reprint: PSC. *Indexed:* A22, ABIn, ABS&EES, B01, B02, BAS, BRI, CLI, E01, EconLit, IBSS, JEL, L14, P02, P61, PsycInfo, RiskAb, SSA. *Bk. rev.:* 0-1 thematic review of multiple books. *Aud.:* Ac, Sa.

IO is published on behalf of the International Organization Foundation. Its mission is the "improvement of general knowledge or empirical theory" on international affairs. The journal covers "foreign policies, international relations, international and comparative political economy, security policies, environmental disputes and resolutions, regional integration, alliance patterns and war, bargaining and conflict resolution, economic development and adjustment, and international capital movements." Each issue contains a "research note" section that highlights specific topics, and an occasional "review essay" that focuses on developments and future research needs in a particular field of study. Recent articles examine problems of treaty ratification, models of agency in international politics, the role of emotion by decision makers in the Korean War, the logic of child soldiering, and public attitudes toward torture. Recommended for academic libraries.

International Security. See Peace and Conflict Studies section.

4408. *International Studies Quarterly.* Former titles (until 1967): *Background;* (until 1962): *Background on World Politics.* [ISSN: 0020-8833] 1957. q. USD 1737 (print & online eds.). Ed(s): William R Thompson. Wiley-Blackwell Publishing, Inc., 111 River St, Hoboken, NJ

07030; info@wiley.com; http://onlinelibrary.wiley.com/. Illus., index, adv. Sample. Refereed. Circ: 4154 Paid. Vol. ends: No. 4. Microform: PQC. Reprint: PSC. *Indexed:* A01, A22, ABS&EES, AmHI, BAS, BRI, E01, IBSS, P02, P61, RiskAb, SSA. *Aud.:* Ga, Ac, Sa.

The mission of *ISQ*, published for the International Studies Association, is to offer a journal that will appeal to a "broad audience of readers." To judge from the articles published in recent years, the readership may be defined as scholars, writers, and persons in leadership positions who may benefit from studies of contemporary issues and controversies in international politics, societies, and cultures. The journal contains articles with "theoretical, empirical, and normative" approaches, but the editors insist that when statistical studies are deployed, authors must provide sufficient data and explanation to ensure that a broad range of readers may understand or test the data. Recent issues cover the impact of sanctions on global investments; modeling violence and ethnic segregation in Iraq; foreign capital and taxation treaties; state support for non-state armed groups; and democratization after civil war. Recommended for academic and public libraries.

The Journal of Conflict Resolution. See Peace and Conflict Studies section.

4409. *Political Science Quarterly: the journal of public and international affairs.* [ISSN: 0032-3195] 1886. q. GBP 344 (print & online eds.). Ed(s): James Caraley Caraley. Wiley-Blackwell Publishing, Inc., 111 River St, Hoboken, NJ 07030; info@wiley.com. Illus., index, adv. Refereed. Circ: 8000 Paid. Vol. ends: No. 4. Microform: PMC; PQC. *Indexed:* A01, A22, ABIn, ABS&EES, BAS, BRI, CBRI, EconLit, IBSS, JEL, MLA-IB, P02, P61, SSA, SWR&A. *Bk. rev.:* 25-30. *Aud.:* Ga, Ac, Sa.

Published since 1886 by the Academy of Political Science, this is a nonpartisan scholarly journal that covers government, politics, and public policy. Its intended audience is political scientists and general readers interested in politics and foreign affairs. Written by leading scholars, its articles often include a historical perspective on domestic and international topics. Recent topics include the labor market problems in Ireland, Greece, and Portugal; the impact of the economy and partisanship in the 2012 U.S. elections; the future of Islam; America's use of force after the Cold War; and Chinese and Russian responses to 9/11. The book review section is extensive, with approximately 30 reviews in an issue. Recommended for academic and public libraries.

4410. *Review of International Studies.* Formerly (until 1981): *British Journal of International Studies.* [ISSN: 0260-2105] 1975. q. plus one supplement. GBP 385. Cambridge University Press, The Edinburgh Bldg, Shaftesbury Rd, Cambridge, CB2 8RU, United Kingdom; journals@cambridge.org; http://www.cambridge.org/uk. Illus., index, adv. Refereed. Circ: 1700. Vol. ends: No. 4. Reprint: PSC. *Indexed:* A01, A22, ABIn, AmHI, E01, EconLit, IBSS, JEL, P61, RiskAb, SSA. *Aud.:* Ac.

As the official journal of the British International Studies Association, *RIS* is an interdisciplinary periodical that publishes articles related to politics, history, law, and sociology. Recent articles focus on topic such as the American views of Muslim women in the context of conflicting views of Islam, philosophies of the democratic state and war, trade unions and social movements in the European Union, causal factors in foreign policy analysis, and secularism in international relations. Occasionally *RIS* publishes literature reviews, forums, and interviews with important scholars. The last issue (#5) of each volume is a special issue focused on a theme. Recommended for academic libraries.

4411. *Third World Quarterly.* [ISSN: 0143-6597] 1979. 10x/yr. GBP 1446 (print & online eds.). Ed(s): Shahid Qadir. Routledge, 4 Park Sq, Milton Park, Abingdon, OX14 4RN, United Kingdom; subscriptions@tandf.co.uk; http://www.tandfonline.com. Illus., index, adv. Sample. Refereed. Vol. ends: No. 10. Reprint: PSC. *Indexed:* A01, A22, AmHI, B01, BAS, BRI, C45, E01, IBSS, P02, P61, RRTA, SSA. *Bk. rev.:* 0-1 thematic review articles on multiple books. *Aud.:* Ac, Sa.

This interdisciplinary journal offers "analysis of micro-economic and grassroot efforts of development practitioners and planners." The focus is on political, social, and economic structure and policy studies in Asia, Africa, Latin America, and the Middle East. Editors welcome "provocative and exploratory" themes to encourage debate. Issues are often thematically organized, with themes such as responses to aid workers as persons, governance amid inequality and inequity in India and China, and relationships between culture and development. Recent articles examine the responses of rising powers to global governance, humanitarian access denial to distressed populations, and strategies for responding to and defining poverty. Recommended for academic libraries.

4412. The Washington Quarterly. Formerly (until 1978): *The Washington Review of Strategic and International Studies.* [ISSN: 0163-660X] 1978. q. GBP 264 (print & online eds.). Ed(s): Alexander T J Lennon. Routledge, 711 3rd Ave, 8th Fl., New York, NY 10017; customerservice@taylorandfrancis.com; http://www.tandfonline.com. Illus., index, adv. Refereed. Vol. ends: No. 4. Microform: PQC. Reprint: PSC. *Indexed:* A01, A22, ABS&EES, BAS, BRI, E01, IBSS, MASUSE, MLA-IB, P02, P61, SSA. *Aud.:* Hs, Ga, Ac, Sa.

This journal of international affairs, published by the Center for Strategic and International Studies, offers analyses of "global strategic changes and their public policy implications." It seeks an image of nonpartisanship in articles that range across a wide focus of international issues, such as human rights, democratization, diplomacy, energy and environment, foreign aid, economic development, health, contemporary political philosophy, and America's influence and interactions with other nations. Recent issues have articles on nuclear nonproliferation, the rising power of China and India, the Arab uprising, U.S. relations with Iran, and the volunteer military. The editors strive to present an independent, authoritative journal that appeals to academia, corporations, public media, and general readers. Recommended for academic, public, and school libraries.

4413. World Affairs (Washington): a journal of ideas and debate. Former titles (until 1932): *Advocate of Peace Through Justice;* (until 1920): *The Advocate of Peace;* (until 1894): *The American Advocate of Peace and Arbitration;* (until 1892): *American Advocate of Peace;* (until 1847): *Advocate of Peace;* (until 1846): *The Advocate of Peace and Universal Brotherhood; The Advocate of Peace;* (until 1837): *American Advocate of Peace;* Which incorporates (1831-1835): *The Calumet;* Which was formerly (1828-1831): *Harbinger of Peace.* [ISSN: 0043-8200] 1834. bi-m. USD 39. Ed(s): Andrew Ivers. World Affairs Institute, 1319 Eighteenth St, NW, Washington, DC 20036. Illus., index, adv. Refereed. Vol. ends: Summer. Microform: PQC. Reprint: PSC. *Indexed:* A01, A22, ABS&EES, BAS, BRI, MASUSE, P02, P61, SSA. *Bk. rev.:* 1+ essays per issue. *Aud.:* Hs, Ga, Ac.

World Affairs has its origins in the peace literature of the 1830s-1930s and has maintained its present name since 1932. It is now published by the World Affairs Institute, which is dedicated to promoting "public education and awareness on international issues related to war and peace." The journal presents a wide range of perspectives and opinions as it "argues the big ideas behind U.S. foreign policy." Each issue includes essays and a book review written for a wide range of readers. Recent issues have articles on Scotland's bid for independence, pollution in China, censorship in historical analysis, freedom in Burma, and U.S. economic aid to Afghanistan. Recommended for academic, public, and school libraries.

4414. World Politics: a quarterly journal of international relations. [ISSN: 0043-8871] 1948. q. GBP 171. Ed(s): Atul Kohli. Cambridge University Press, The Edinburgh Bldg, Shaftesbury Rd, Cambridge, CB2 8RU, United Kingdom; journals@cambridge.org; http://www.cambridge.org/uk. Illus., index, adv. Refereed. Vol. ends: No. 4. Microform: PQC. *Indexed:* A01, A22, ABS&EES, BRI, CBRI, E01, IBSS, P02, P61, SSA. *Aud.:* Ac.

This journal is published on behalf of the Princeton Institute for International and Regional Studies at Princeton University. Editors seek "analytical/ theoretical articles, review articles, and research notes bearing on problems in international relations and comparative politics." Recent issues have had articles on ethnic politics in Africa, separatist conflicts in the Soviet Union and contemporary Russia, Japan and the Asian Development Bank, and electoral impact on welfare states in Europe. Recommended for academic libraries.

■ POPULATION STUDIES

Mara Rojeski, Public Policy & Data Library, Lauinger Library, Georgetown University, Washington, DC 20057; mr1167@georgetown.edu

Introduction

As a field, population studies pulls from a wide assortment of academic disciplines; the periodicals listed here reflect the interdisciplinarity of the area. All of the publications stress that the articles come from multiple disciplines, including, but not limited to, demography; sociology; public policy; political science; economics; history; statistics; geography; biology; and health. Due to the nature of the area of study, most publications have a global scope of coverage. The titles listed here also reflect the relatively academic and professional nature of the field, with most having target audiences of scholars, professionals, and policy makers. However, a couple titles address topics in population studies for a general audience.

Basic Periodicals

Ga: *Population Bulletin;* Ac: *Demography, European Journal of Population, Population and Development Review, Population Research and Policy Review.*

Basic Abstracts and Indexes

ABI/INFORM, AgeLine, LexisNexis, MEDLINE, PAIS International.

4415. Demography. [ISSN: 0070-3370] 1964. q. EUR 198 (print & online eds.). Ed(s): Stewart Tolnay. Springer New York LLC, 233 Spring St, New York, NY 10013; journals@springer-ny.com; http:// www.springer.com. Illus., adv. Refereed. Vol. ends: No. 4. Reprint: PSC. *Indexed:* A01, A22, ABIn, ABS&EES, AbAn, AgeL, B01, B02, BAS, BRI, C45, Chicano, E01, EconLit, IBSS, JEL, P02, P61, SSA. *Aud.:* Ac.

Published by the Population Association of America (PAA) since 1964, this bimonthly, peer-reviewed publication comes out every February, April, June, August, October, and December. The PAA "is a non-profit, scientific professional organization that promotes research on population issues." Articles in *Demography* present research from multiple disciplines, including the social sciences, geography, history, biology, statistics, epidemiology, and public health. As indicated by the definition on the cover, "n. the statistical study of human populations," the journal features many statistically based, quantitative research articles on population studies. Geographical coverage of this publication is global, covering both the developed and developing world and related population issues. Recent issues included articles on a variety of issues in infant mortality, adult mortality, life expectancy, racial diversity, and immigration policy impacts. Recommended for academic libraries.

Ethnic and Racial Studies. See Multicultural Studies section.

4416. European Journal of Population. Formerly (until 1983): *European Demographic Information Bulletin.* [ISSN: 0168-6577] 1970. q. EUR 715 (print & online eds.). Ed(s): Hill Kulu, Myriam Khlat. Springer Netherlands, Van Godewijckstraat 30, Dordrecht, 3311 GX, Netherlands; http://www.springer.com. Illus., adv. Refereed. Vol. ends: No. 4. Reprint: PSC. *Indexed:* A22, ABIn, BRI, C45, E01, EconLit, IBSS, P61, SSA. *Bk. rev.:* 2-3, 1,000-1,200 words. *Aud.:* Ac.

This quarterly, peer-reviewed publication also goes by its French title *Revue Europeenne de Demographie.* The journal is published under the auspices of the European Association for Population Studies (EAPS). It seeks to improve "understanding of population phenomena, fostering development of theory and method." The *European Journal of Population* covers the intersection of demography and a wide range of social science disciplines and the health sciences. Its stated geographic coverage includes European and non-European countries. This title will occasionally have special, thematic issues. Issues typically have a few research articles and a couple book reviews. Articles in recent issues have covered topics ranging from fertility, cohabitation and marital habits, and childbearing. Despite the stated global scope, recent articles focused on European countries. Recommended for academic libraries.

4417. *International Migration Review: a quarterly studying sociological, demographic, economic, historical, and legislative aspects of human migration movements and ethnic group relations.* Formerly (until 1966): *International Migration Digest;* Which incorporated (in 1973): *International Newsletter on Migration;* Which was formerly (1971-1972): *International Migration Newsletter.* [ISSN: 0197-9183] 1964. q. GBP 242 (print & online eds.). Ed(s): Joseph Chamie. Wiley-Blackwell Publishing, Inc., 111 River St, Hoboken, NJ 07030; info@wiley.com; http://onlinelibrary.wiley.com/. Illus., index, adv. Sample. Refereed. Circ: 1037 Paid. Vol. ends: Winter. Microform: PQC. Reprint: PSC. *Indexed:* A01, A22, A47, ABS&EES, ASSIA, AbAn, BAS, BRI, C45, Chicano, E01, FR, IBSS, P02, P61, SSA, SWR&A. *Bk. rev.:* 3-6; 350-700 words. *Aud.:* Ac.

The Center for Migration Studies of New York (CMS) puts out the *International Migration Review,* which embraces an interdisciplinary approach to the study of population movement. This peer-reviewed publication focuses on the population movement aspect of population studies. Global in scope, it addresses all aspects of the title topic, including socio-demographic, historical, economic, political, legislative, and pastoral dimensions of human mobility. Article topics generally focus on migration, immigration, and refugees. A typical issue will include six to seven research articles and three signed book reviews. Recent issues of the *International Migration Review* included articles on the following topics: illegal immigration; Group Conflict Theory; and migrant domestic work. Recommended for academic and research libraries.

Journal of Ethnic and Migration Studies. See Multicultural Studies section.

Journal of Family History. See Family section.

Perspectives on Sexual and Reproductive Health. See Family Planning section.

4418. *Population and Development Review.* [ISSN: 0098-7921] 1975. q. GBP 164 (print & online eds.). Ed(s): Ethel Churchill, Paul Demeny. Wiley-Blackwell Publishing, Inc., 111 River St, Hoboken, NJ 07030; info@wiley.com; http://onlinelibrary.wiley.com/. Illus. Sample. Refereed. Vol. ends: No. 4. Microform: PQC. Reprint: PSC. *Indexed:* A01, A22, ABS&EES, ASSIA, B02, BAS, BRI, C42, C45, Chicano, E01, EIP, EconLit, IBSS, JEL, P02, P61, SSA. *Bk. rev.:* 10-12. *Aud.:* Ac.

Published by Wiley-Blackwell on behalf of the Population Council, this journal focuses on the relationship between population studies and development. The journal's stated scope is the interplay between population and social, economic, and environmental change, as well as related public policy issues. Geographic coverage includes both the developed and developing world and come from across a variety of academic disciplines. The journal welcomes theoretically focused articles and empirical analysis, but strives to maintain readability by publishing articles that present ideas and insights instead of highly analytical work. Time period coverage of articles spans both current and historical topics. Document types include articles, commentaries, review essays, book reviews, and relevant excerpts from past writings. Recent issues included articles on fertility in the developed world; adult mortality in the developing world; and Alexis de Tocqueville's influence. Recommended for academic and research libraries. URL: www.popcouncil.org/publications/pdr.asp

4419. *Population Bulletin.* [ISSN: 0032-468X] 1945. q. Free to qualified personnel. Ed(s): Marlene Lee. Population Reference Bureau, Inc., 1875 Connecticut Ave, NW, Ste 520, Washington, DC 20009; popref@prb.org; http://www.prb.org. Illus. *Indexed:* A01, A22, ABIn, ABS&EES, BAS, C45, EIP, EconLit, JEL, MASUSE, P02. *Aud.:* Ga, Ac.

This is one of the major publications of the Population Reference Bureau (PBR). Issues of the *Population Bulletin* are highly regarded by academics and professionals alike. The PBR "informs people around the world about population, health, and the environment, and empowers them to use that information to advance the well-being of current and future generations." The journal presents trends in population studies on both a domestic and international level. Topic areas of editions of the *Population Bulletin* are the core themes of the PBR's work: aging; education; environment; gender; health/ nutrition; HIV/AIDS; immigration/migration; income/poverty; marriage/ family; population basics; race/ethnicity; reproductive health; U.S. Census 2010 & ACS; and youth. Written by experts in the field for a general audience, the *Population Bulletins* present their topics in thematic issues with clear text and colorful graphics. Target audiences of the publication include university classes, population professionals, and the media. Themes of recent issues included: "Achieving a Demographic Dividend"; "Household Change in the United States"; and "A Post-Recession Update on U.S. Social and Economic Trends." Highly recommended for academic, research, and public libraries. URL: www.prb.org/Publications/PopulationBulletins.aspx

4420. *Population Research and Policy Review.* [ISSN: 0167-5923] 1980. bi-m. EUR 919 (print & online eds.). Ed(s): Thomas W Pullum. Springer Netherlands, Van Godewijckstraat 30, Dordrecht, 3311 GX, Netherlands; http://www.springer.com. Illus., adv. Refereed. Microform: PQC. Reprint: PSC. *Indexed:* A22, ABIn, Agr, C45, E01, EconLit, IBSS, JEL, P61, RRTA, SSA, SWR&A. *Bk. rev.:* 3, 400-500 words. *Aud.:* Ac.

The flagship journal of the Southern Demographic Association (SDA), this peer-reviewed publication presents interdisciplinary work on population studies, as well as implications for policy and program development of such studies. With a relatively practical focus, the articles in this journal frequently present the related policy issues with demographic research. Subject coverage includes the fields of demography, economics, politics, and health studies. The journal includes work utilizing all methodological approaches, including ethnographic studies, comparative-historical studies, and discourse analysis. Recent issues include articles on mortality in the United States, immigrants in Swedish schools, population aging in Europe, and survival rates of diabetics. Recommended for academic and research libraries.

4421. *Population Review (Online).* [ISSN: 1549-0955] 2003. s-a. Ed(s): Archibald O Haller. Population Review Publications, 3522 2nd fl. rm.2 AL 11B, Lardproa Rd., Klongchang Bangkapi, Bangkok, 10240, Thailand. Refereed. *Bk. rev.:* Number and length vary. *Aud.:* Ac, Sa.

This is a longstanding journal published since 1957. Articles in *Population Review* tend to focus on sociological demography, but may come from an array of social science fields. The journal prioritizes articles that present empirical research in population studies. Content includes international coverage from both the developed and developing world. Content types include original articles and book reviews. A recent issue presented a series of articles on population issues for Southern Europe, mostly Italy and Spain. Issues do not necessarily have such a geographic or thematic focus; other recent articles cover topics such as historical Czech marriage trends and land conflict in Brazil. Recommended for academic and research libraries. URL: http://populationreview.com/

Population, Space and Place (Online). See Geography section.

4422. *Population Studies: a journal of demography.* [ISSN: 0032-4728] 1947. 3x/yr. GBP 203 (print & online eds.). Ed(s): John Simons. Routledge, 4 Park Sq, Milton Park, Abingdon, OX14 4RN, United Kingdom; subscriptions@tandf.co.uk; http://www.tandfonline.com. Illus., adv. Sample. Refereed. Reprint: PSC. *Indexed:* A01, A22, A47, ABIn, AbAn, B01, BAS, BRI, C45, E01, EconLit, IBSS, JEL, P02, P61, SSA. *Bk. rev.:* 4-6; 800-1,200 words. *Aud.:* Ac.

A peer-reviewed journal published since 1947, *Population Studies* has a long history of publishing demography research, and covers all aspects of the field comprehensively: "applications in developed and developing countries; historical and contemporary studies; quantitative and qualitative studies; analytical essays and reviews. The Population Investigation Committee (PIC)[,] based at the London School of Economics (LSE)[,] produces this journal. The subjects of papers range from classical concerns, such as the determinants and consequences of population change, to such topics as family demography and evolutionary and genetic influences on demographic behaviour [*sic*]. Often the Journal's papers have had the effect of extending the boundaries of its field." This title includes articles on a variety of methods and theories of demographic analyses, as well as practical applications of theories and methods. An issue typically includes six or seven research articles, as well as several book reviews. Recent issues addressed topics pertaining to fertility in India, divorce and mortality in Belarus, and migration within and from China. Recommended for academic and research libraries.

4423. ***The Reporter (Washington, D.C.).*** Former titles (until 2003): *The Z P G Reporter;* (until 1979): *Z P G National Reporter.* [ISSN: 2165-0004] 1969. 3x/yr. Free to members. Ed(s): Marian Starkey. Population Connection, 2120 L St, NW, Ste 500, Washington, DC 20037; info@populationconnection.org; http://www.population connection.org. Adv. *Bk. rev.:* 1-2. *Aud.:* Ga.

The Population Connection, formerly known as Zero Population Growth, is an organization that advocates for population stabilization. The organization publishes *The Reporter* quarterly. Geared toward a general audience, the publication reports on population news and demographic trends with approachable language and colorful graphics. Each thematic issue includes a few feature articles on the the theme, book reviews, an "Editor's Note," "Letters to the Editor," "Pop Facts," "In the News," "The President's Circle," "Washington View," "Field & Outreach," "PopEd," a cartoon, and "Editorial Excerpts." *The Reporter* covers global issues, but recent issues have focused on the United States. Themes of recent issues included: the teen birth rate in the United States; "Population Aging and the U.S. Economy"; and "Congressional Report Card." Recommended for all readers. URL: www.populationconnection.org/site/PageServer?pagename=news_publications_reporter

Studies in Family Planning. See Family Planning section.

■ PREGNANCY

Lynn McMain, MLIS, M.Ed., Sam Houston State University, Huntsville, TX 77340

Introduction

Not unlike riding a roller-coaster, pregnancy can be an experience that is exciting, fulfilling, and unsettling all at the same time. A woman's first pregnancy usually finds her with a multitude of questions and seeking as much information as possible about her changing body and the baby she is carrying. Even experienced mothers want access to the latest information about pregnancy. Magazines and journals about women's health, pregnancy, fetal development, and fertility exist to provide health-care professionals as well as consumers with the latest in research and helpful information.

The periodicals in this section fall into three categories: those written for professional health-care providers, such as *ACOG Clinical Review*; those written for a more general consumer audience, such as *Pregnancy*; and those that address the needs of a more specific consumer audience like *Fertility Today*.

Basic Periodicals

The Compleat Mother, Fertility Today, Fit Pregnancy, Midwifery Today, Mothering, Pregnancy, Pregnancy and Newborn.

Basic Abstracts and Indexes

CINAHL, Family Index, MEDLINE.

4424. ***A C O G Clinical Review.*** Supersedes (in 1996): *A C O G Current Journal Review.* [ISSN: 1085-6862] 1987. bi-m. Free to members. Ed(s): Nancy Rowe, Morton A Stenchever. American College of Obstetricians and Gynecologists, PO Box 96920, Washington, DC 20090; publication@acog.org; http://www.acog.org. Sample. Microform: PQC. *Indexed:* C&ISA, CerAb. *Aud.:* Ga, Ac, Sa.

This newsletter is a publication of the American College of Obstetricians and Gynecologists (ACOG). ACOG is a private, nonprofit membership organization of physicians practicing in obstetrics and gynecology (OB/GYN). It advocates

for quality health care for women, high clinical standards, and continuing education for its members; it also promotes patient education. This newsletter accomplishes most of those stated goals by reviewing several of the major journals in the field and then publishing summaries of the articles that feature the latest advancements in the areas of obstetrics, gynecology, infertility, and oncology. Also included in each issue is a review article on a contemporary OB/GYN topic. Published primarily to assist physicians in staying current on the OB/GYN specialty literature, this periodical is also valuable to consumers looking for the latest research in OB/GYN. This small but informative periodical is an excellent resource for all medical libraries and for larger public libraries that support an educated reader population.

4425. ***The Compleat Mother: the magazine of pregnancy, birth and breastfeeding.*** [ISSN: 0829-8564] 1985. q. USD 12 domestic. Ed(s): Jody McLaughlin. Compleat Mother, c/o Jody McLaughlin, P O Box 209, Minot, ND 58702. Illus., index, adv. Vol. ends: Winter. *Bk. rev.:* Number and length vary. *Aud.:* Ga.

This simple and fascinating newsprint periodical is an interesting counterpoint to the mainstream culture and the traditional medicine's view of pregnancy and childbirth. Anecdotal articles are submitted by readers, and range in topic from personal experiences with home childbirth, breastfeeding, and parenting, to disparaging hospital deliveries and labor induction. Circumcision, infant vaccinations, and formula feeding are no-no's, as well. There are guest editorials, recipes, reader forums, humorous cartoons, poems, and book and music reviews. The magazine is freely available online, but the online editorial is from November 2009, so the site may not be frequently updated. This periodical is passionate about pregnancy, midwife-assisted home childbirth, and breast feeding, and there is no doubting the sincerity of the editor and the reader-authors. A magazine recommended for public libraries with clientele that would have an interest, and as a contrast to mainstream print media on pregnancy. URL: www.compleatmother.com

4426. ***Fertility Today.*** [ISSN: 1559-8888] 2005. bi-m. USD 27.80 domestic; USD 34 Canada; USD 42 elsewhere. Fertility Today, PO Box 117, Laurel, MD 20725. Adv. Circ: 2250000. *Bk. rev.:* Number and length vary. *Aud.:* Ga.

A consumer-oriented periodical that contains information specifically on fertility/infertility issues. The magazine is glitzy, with a celebrity photograph on each cover. The magazine's stated mission is to provide "comprehensive and up to date information on all aspects of fertility and infertility;...and to offer hope...." The editors and contributing writers are all well credentialed. Multiple sections cover every aspect of fertility/infertility issues. Examples of sections are "Polycystic Ovarian Syndrome," "Ovarian Function," "Cancer and Fertility," "Male Infertility," "Assisted Reproductive Technologies," "Fertility Drugs," "Donor Egg/Donor Sperm/Donor Embryo/Surrogacy," "Law and Ethics," and many others. The web site provides magazine access to subscribers; however, it also provides a great deal of free information on many of the issues mentioned above, as well as access to fact sheets from the American Society for Reproductive Medicine. Given that there are "approximately 10 million couples in the United States" who are experiencing infertility issues (according to the web site), this magazine meets a sizable need in an intelligent and sensitive manner and is recommended for all public libraries. URL: http://fertilitytoday.org

4427. ***Fit Pregnancy.*** [ISSN: 1079-3615] 1995. bi-m. USD 11.97 domestic; USD 22.97 foreign. Ed(s): Peg Moline. A M I - Weider Publications, 1 Park Ave, 3d Fl, New York, NY 10016; http://www.amilink.com. Illus., adv. *Indexed:* BRI, C37, SD. *Aud.:* Ga.

This is a consumer-oriented magazine for pregnant women and new mothers, but with a fitness and health focus. There are sections on fertility, pregnancy, workouts, labor and delivery, and motherhood and babies. Articles are about pre- and post-natal workouts, food and nutrition, weight loss, celebrity pregnancies, and the "new" mom experiences of celebrities. There are a lot of articles and advertisements about beauty, style, and various products. For the most part, the articles are timely and informative for the intended audience; however, there is a decisive "green" slant to the entire magazine. The web site provides free access to some articles and, of course, the advertising. In a time when so many Americans are overweight, and pregnancy is such a vulnerable time for potentially even more excess weight gain, it is wonderful to have a magazine that encourages fitness and healthy lifestyle choices for mothers-to-be. Recommended for all public libraries. URL: www.fitpregnancy.com

Journal of Midwifery & Women's Health. See Health Professions section.

MCN: the American Journal of Maternal Child Nursing. See Nursing section.

4428. Midwifery Today: the heart and science of birth. Formerly (until 1997): *Midwifery Today and Childbirth Education with International Midwife;* Which was formed by the merger of (1987-1996): *Midwifery Today;* (1995-1996): *International Midwife.* [ISSN: 1551-8892] 1996. q. USD 55 domestic; USD 65 in Canada & Mexico; USD 75 elsewhere. Ed(s): Jan Tritten, Alice Evans. Midwifery Today with International Midwife, PO Box 2672, Eugene, OR 97402; http:// www.midwiferytoday.com. Illus., index, adv. Sample. Circ: 2500. *Indexed:* BRI, C42, FemPer, GW. *Aud.:* Ga.

This periodical is a professional magazine intended for practicing midwives, and states a goal "...to actively promote midwifery everywhere in the world." There is value here for any women who are considering a home delivery with a midwife. Issues often have a theme, and there are regularly occurring departments such as "Vital Topics," "News and Reviews," "Networking," "Tricks of the Trade," and "International Midwifery." Featured articles are written by doulas (women who assist before and after childbirth), practicing midwives, certified professional midwives, certified nurse-midwives, childbirth educators, and physicians. The articles are mostly anecdotal; however, some are well-researched technical pieces with bibliographies, and all are easily readable by laypersons. Recent articles are about personal home-birth experiences, post-date pregnancies, safe breast-milk sharing, and birth services for incarcerated mothers. The magazine is available online with access to past issues and with informative forums, but the latest issue requires a subscription. It is impossible to miss the passion and commitment of these childbirth practitioners. This magazine is recommended for public libraries and is a nice contrast to the mainstream view of childbirth. URL: www.midwiferytoday.com/magazine/

4429. Pregnancy. [ISSN: 1540-8485] 2000. m. USD 10 domestic; USD 15 Canada. Ed(s): Abigail Tuller, Clary Alward. Future U S, Inc., 4000 Shoreline Ct, Ste 400, South San Francisco, CA 94080; http:// www.futureus.com. Adv. Circ: 205000 Paid. *Aud.:* Ga.

This general consumer magazine states it is "the leading monthly magazine for first[-]time moms." There are really informative articles on nutrition, baby and child development, baby and child care, pregnancy and baby products, labor and delivery, and breastfeeding, and a whole department titled "For Dads." There are articles about celebrities and their children, and of course style and fashion, lots of style and fashion. The online site provides a plethora of free articles from the magazine, blogs, and informative videos. Be prepared for all the advertisements, despite that this is a well-rounded and all-around helpful magazine for pregnant women from first-timers to seasoned moms. Highly recommended for all public libraries. URL: www.pregnancymagazine.com/

4430. Pregnancy and Newborn. 2006. m. USD 24 domestic; USD 37.50 Canada; USD 44 elsewhere. Ed(s): Lauren Brockman. Halcyon Media, LLC, 280 Interstate N Cir, Ste 650, Atlanta, GA 30339. Adv. *Aud.:* Ga.

This is a vital and dynamic general consumer magazine for pregnant women and new mothers. There is the obligatory unrealistically gorgeous pregnant model or celebrity on the cover, and articles about pregnancy, childbirth, newborn care, infant development, nutrition, breastfeeding, weight loss, and baby care products and other baby paraphernalia and style and beauty. There is a section titled "Maternity & Baby Gear Reviews," which provides helpful information on baby care products, including suggested prices. The online site provides free access to some articles, several discussion boards, and blogs, with one blog, "Dad's Eye View," singularly for fathers-to-be and new fathers. This monthly publication would be a helpful magazine for any pregnant woman, but is especially helpful to first-time pregnant women and couples. Recommended for public libraries. URL: www.pnmag.com/

■ PRINTING AND GRAPHIC ARTS

Donna B. Smith, Assistant Head of Technical Services, W. Frank Steely Library, Northern Kentucky University, Highland Heights, KY 41099.

Wendy Wood, Head of Cataloging, W. Frank Steely Library, Northern Kentucky University, Highland Heights, KY 41099

Introduction

Communicating the message visually is the job of the graphic designer and the printer. Designers and printers work with innovation and persuasion in order to inform, entertain, and impress visually inundated and discriminating audiences. Clients look to these groups for marketing, technical, and high-impact graphic support. Competition is stiff as customers increasingly demand better service, more innovative products, and faster cycle times. Successful professionals need to be active in the marketing of their skills, as well as identify new markets for their products.

Recent years have witnessed major changes in the graphic design services and printing industries, including the rise of desktop publishing, the Internet, and digital technology. Designers and printers make use of new technology to create images that are more visually active than in the past. The industry has transformed into an imaging business that feeds a variety of media, only one of which is print. It is expected that print will continue in an expanded role that enhances the emerging interactive non-print alternatives. The recent increased use of mobile devices does not yet appear to have accelerated the switch from print to digital information consumption for consumers. And, businesses still maintain an advertising mix of print and digital formats.

As in most industries today, graphic designers and printers must remain current with the latest technology and marketing innovations. Profitability for individual companies depends on decreasing costs via the introduction of new workflow efficiencies and growing new revenue sources. Therefore, the majority of publications recommended here are trade publications that provide necessary and timely information to practitioners, managers, suppliers, and anyone else interested in visual communications. They may cover the entire graphic communications industry or target specific segments, such as gravure printers, paper producers, or screen printers. Most magazines provide practical how-to information, and many profile artists, design studios, and printing firms. Some provide a showcase of leading designs in the industry by sponsoring competitions and displaying the winners in special issues. The trade publications also address the business side of the industry: legal concerns, environmental regulations, economic trends, marketing and sales, and management issues. Scholarly publications focus on the history of printing, the impact of visual phenomena, and new research in the field.

Colorful glossy journals dominate the resources for the graphic designers. Strictly electronic publications are not yet prevalent in this field. Although some publications are available online, these versions complement or coexist with the print issues. Some publishers' web sites do offer additional resources and articles not available in the print versions. The professional organizations tend to provide electronic publications such as newsletters for members. However, these may be delivered via e-mail and are not often archived.

Basic Periodicals

Ga: *Communication Arts, Print;* Ac: *Communication Arts, Design Issues, Print, Printing History, Visible Language;* Sa: *Communication Arts, Graphic Design USA, Print, Printing News, The Seybold Report.*

Basic Abstracts and Indexes

Abstract Bulletin of Paper Science and Technology, Art Index, Design and Applied Arts Index (Online), Engineering Index Monthly, Pirabase (http:// pira.ais.co.uk/), *Scopus.*

4431. C M Y K Magazine. [ISSN: 1935-8229] 1996. q. USD 29 domestic; USD 8.50 newsstand/cover domestic; USD 12.75 newsstand/cover Canada. Ed(s): Curtis Clarkson. C M Y K Magazine, 3001 Bridgeway Blvd, Ste, K (PMB 335), Sausalito, CA 94965; editor@cmykmag.com. Adv. *Aud.:* Ac.

This magazine is particularly useful to university libraries that support graphic design programs. It publishes the best creative work from students at art schools, universities, and programs around the world. Categories include advertising, photography, design, and illustration. Recent graduates and self-taught nonprofessionals are also invited to enter the contests. Special issues feature the works of established artists and designers. Regular issues include articles that target the aspiring professional such as job hunting tips, interviews with professional designers, and spotlights of educational programs. Professionals will find the magazine useful in recruiting new talent.

4432. Communication Arts. Former titles (until 1969): *C A Magazine;* (until 1967): *C A;* (until 1959): *Annual Exhibition of Communication Art.* [ISSN: 0010-3519] 19??. bi-m. Students, USD 39 (print & online eds.); USD 53 combined subscription domestic (print & online eds.). Ed(s): Tad Crawford. Communication Arts, 110 Constitution Dr, Menlo Park, CA 94025. Illus., adv. Circ: 54661 Paid. Vol. ends: Dec. *Indexed:* A01, A06, A07, A22, A51, BRI, F01, P02. *Bk. rev.:* 2, 100-200 words, signed. *Aud.:* Ga, Ac, Sa.

Communication Arts is a high-quality trade publication for commercial artists. Issues serve as juried showcases for leading work in advertising, design, illustration, interactive design, and photography. Included are seven or eight feature articles that may profile design studios and artists or highlight special advertising and design projects. Informative columns cover typography, design trends, advertising, business advice, and new books. Additional features are available online. This title is an important addition to any graphic arts collection. URL: www.commarts.com

4433. Design Issues. [ISSN: 0747-9360] 1984. q. USD 294 (print & online eds.). Ed(s): Stacey Manz Lotz. M I T Press, 55 Hayward St, Cambridge, MA 02142; journals-cs@mit.edu; http://mitpress.mit.edu. Illus., adv. Refereed. Microform: PQC. *Indexed:* A01, A07, A22, A51, AmHI, ArtHuCI, B01, E01, MLA-IB. *Bk. rev.:* Number and length vary. *Aud.:* Ac, Sa.

This scholarly journal focuses on the history, criticism, and theory of design. Regular issues offer six to eight articles on diverse perspectives of past and present design issues. Some issues feature special guest editors. Themed issues present broad topics such as examinations of social influences on the field, design practices in various countries, and the state of design education throughout the world. The journal provides an international forum to explore the various dimensions of design, not only as a professional practice, but also as an economic force and a form of cultural art. This journal is an important addition to academic libraries that support a design program.

4434. Eye (London, 1990). [ISSN: 0960-779X] 1990. q. GBP 68 domestic; GBP 86.74 in Europe; EUR 104 in Europe. Ed(s): John L Walters. Haymarket Publishing Ltd., Studio 6, The Lux Bldg, 2-4 Hoxton Sq, London, N1 6NU, United Kingdom; info@haymarket.com; http://www.haymarket.com. Illus., adv. *Indexed:* A07, A22, A51, BRI. *Bk. rev.:* 10-15, 200-600 words. *Aud.:* Ac, Sa.

Noted for its articles combined with extraordinary visual material, this journal is an important addition to any graphic design collection. It focuses on typography, history, art direction, and graphic design for multimedia, advertising, publishing, and the web. Features include interviews with international designers, overviews of new trends in graphic design, and profiles of design studios. Regular columns provide critiques and book reviews. Article extracts from past issues are available online. URL: www.eyemagazine.com

4435. Flexo: the flexographic technology source. Formerly (until 1984): *Flexographic Technical Journal.* [ISSN: 1051-7324] 1976. m. Ed(s): Chris Bonawandt. Foundation of Flexographic Technical Association, 900 Marconi Ave, Ronkonkoma, NY 11779; memberinfo@flexography.org; http://www.flexography.org. Illus., adv. Sample. Vol. ends: Dec. *Indexed:* A22, EngInd. *Aud.:* Ac, Sa.

Flexo is the official journal of the Flexographic Technical Association, which is devoted to advancing flexographic technology. This relief printing process is especially popular in the packaging and newspaper industries. Although *Flexo* is mainly a trade publication directed toward managers and technicians, its audience includes anyone who is interested in learning more about the technical

aspects of flexography. Articles include such topics as designing packaging, comparing flexo presses, improving color quality, and examining printing techniques. The articles are written by practitioners, so they are informative and practical. Regular columns highlight new products, events, and association news. Issues are archived on the web site.

4436. Graphic Design: U S A. Formerly: *Graphics: U S A;* Incorporates: *Graphics: New York.* [ISSN: 0274-7499] 1965. 10x/yr. Free to qualified personnel. Kaye Publishing Corporation, 89 5th Ave, Ste 901, New York, NY 10003; http://www.gdusa.com. Illus., adv. *Aud.:* Ac, Sa.

This trade publication provides news and information for and about the professional design community, including graphic design firms, corporate and publishing in-house departments, advertising agencies, and nonprofit organizations. Popular features consist of people in the industry to watch, salary surveys, a products and services directory for design professionals, and ideas for the production of annual and corporate reports. Each issue provides news, events, and updates on people in the field. The magazine also sponsors national design competitions in 23 categories from print and packaging to web and interactive design.

4437. Gravure. Former titles (until 1987): *Gravure Bulletin;* (until 1980): *Gravure Technical Association Bulletin.* [ISSN: 0894-4946] 1950. bi-m. Free to members; Non-members, USD 67. Ed(s): Roger Ynosroza. Gravure Association of America, Inc., 75 W Century Rd, Paramus, NJ 07652; gaa@gaa.org; http://www.gaa.org. Illus., adv. Sample. *Indexed:* EngInd. *Aud.:* Ac, Sa.

This is the trade publication of the Gravure Association of America, which promotes the advancement of the gravure printing industry. This title's main focus is on the technological developments in this high-quality, expensive process. Feature articles examine such topics as new products and materials, environmental concerns, training programs, and automation development. The business side of the industry is covered as well, with timely information on industry news and personnel moves, an events calendar, marketing advice, and association news.

4438. How. [ISSN: 0886-0483] 1985. bi-m. USD 40; USD 14.95 newsstand/cover. Ed(s): Sarah Whitman. F + W Media Inc., 10151 Carver Rd, Ste 200, Blue Ash, OH 45242; contact_us@fwmedia.com; http://www.fwmedia.com/. Illus., adv. Circ: 20039 Paid. *Indexed:* A22, A51, EngInd, IHTDI. *Aud.:* Ac, Sa.

This is an instructional trade magazine that addresses the ideas and techniques that graphic design professionals use to create their work. Directed toward practitioners and design firm managers, it provides hands-on advice on making a design studio more profitable and more professional, and increasing its profile. Special issues focus on international design, typography, and creativity, plus there is a business annual. Feature articles may include advice on managing a freelance business, tips for building a design portfolio, details on award-winning design projects, or comparisons of fonts. Regular columns profile design firms, report on new technology, and provide general industry news.

4439. The Imaging Channel: the business and people of managed print. [ISSN: 2153-375X] 2010. bi-m. Free to qualified personnel. 1105 Media Inc., 9121 Oakdale Ave, Ste 101, Chatsworth, CA 91311; info@1105media.com; http://www.1105media.com. Adv. *Aud.:* Sa.

The managed print industry is the focus of this quarterly magazine that brings together vendors, distributors, manufacturers, and resellers to report on the latest trends. In every issue is an online section that covers discussions, blogs, and polls from TheImagingChannel.com. Interviews with prominent industry executives are also featured. Profiles of independent Channel dealers are included, as are accounts of how their corporations are structured to support managed service offerings. An editorial column offers commentary on the latest industry happenings, as well as makes suggestions for transforming recent events into practical applications for dealerships. This magazine also provides case studies, vertical market profiles, and hardware information for managed print industry professionals.

4440. *In-Plant Graphics.* Former titles (until 1996): *In-Plant Reproductions;* (until 1988): *In-Plant Reproductions and Electronic Publishing;* (until 1985): *In-Plant Productions;* (until 1979): *Reproductions Review and Methods; Graphic Arts Supplier News; Reproductions Methods; Reproductions Review.* [ISSN: 1087-2817] 1951. m. Free to qualified personnel. Ed(s): Bob Neubauer. North American Publishing Co., 1500 Spring Garden St., 12th Fl, Philadelphia, PA 19130; magazinecs@napco.com; http://www.napco.com. Illus., adv. Circ: 23600. *Indexed:* A22, ABIn, B03, EngInd. *Aud.:* Sa.

In-plant printing operations include the printing departments in corporations, government agencies, and institutions. This journal targets the special needs of the managers, graphic artists, and technical personnel that work in these shops. Articles offer tips to managers on increasing productivity and controlling costs, profiles of successful in-plant shops, the latest graphic arts equipment and software, industry news, and conference information. Special reports cover a variety of topics, such as analysis of shops in specific industries and tips for expansion into marketing services.

4441. *Ink World: covering the printing inks, coatings and allied industries.* [ISSN: 1093-328X] 1995. m. Individuals, USD 95; Free to qualified personnel. Ed(s): David Savastano. Rodman Publishing, Corp., 70 Hilltop Rd, 3rd Fl, Ramsey, NJ 07446; info@rodpub.com; http://www.rodmanpublishing .com. Adv. Sample. Circ: 5185 Controlled. *Indexed:* B01, B02, B03, EngInd. *Aud.:* Ac, Sa.

This monthly trade magazine provides ink industry professionals with in-depth information on the development, manufacture, and sale of all lithographic, flexographic, gravure, radiation-cured, letterpress and specialty inks, coatings, and allied products. Developments affecting printers and suppliers of ink companies are discussed. Annual features include top North American companies, top international companies, buyers' guides, U.S. ink directory, European ink directory, literature showcase, and a UV/EB corner. *Ink World* offers advertisers the opportunity to sponsor targeted webinars to subscribers, providing them relevant market information. This publication's readership continues to expand, reaching an estimated audience of 20,000.

4442. *PackagePrinting: the package printer's leading resource for business solutions.* Former titles (until 1999): *Package Printing & Converting;* (until 1987): *Package Printing;* (until Mar. 1978): *Package Printing and Diecutting;* Which was formed by the merger of: *Diemaking, Diecutting and Converting; Gravure; Flexography Printing and Converting.* [ISSN: 1536-1039] 1974. m. Free to qualified personnel. Ed(s): Tom Polischuk. North American Publishing Co., 1500 Spring Garden St., 12th Fl, Philadelphia, PA 19130; magazinecs@napco.com; http://www.napco.com. Illus., index, adv. Circ: 24500. Vol. ends: Dec. *Indexed:* A22, ABIn, B03, EngInd. *Aud.:* Sa.

This trade publication targets the industry of container and package design and production. Diemaking/diecutting, tags, labels, and tape, as well as flexible packaging, folding cartons, and corrugated containers are all this industry's focus. Articles included each month discuss innovations in the equipment needed to manufacture these containers and labels. Inks and printing techniques, suppliers, and management issues are also discussed. Also available online.

4443. *Paper360.* Formerly (until 2006): *Solutions;* Which was formed by the merger of (1982-2001): *T A P P I Journal;* Which was formerly (until 1982): *T A P P I;* (until 1949): *Technical Association Papers; Technical Papers and Addresses;* (1997-2001): *P I M A's ... Papermaker.* [ISSN: 1933-3684] 1920. m. Free to members. Ed(s): Cheryl Higley, Jan Bottiglieri. Questex Media Group Inc., 275 Grove St, Bldg 2, Ste 130, Newton, MA 02466; questex@sunbeltfs.com; http://www.questex.com. Illus., index, adv. Sample. Circ: 28679. Vol. ends: Dec. *Indexed:* A&ATA, A22, Agr, B01, C&ISA, CEA, CerAb, EngInd, PhotoAb. *Aud.:* Ac, Sa.

A very comprehensive journal of the paper industry, *Paper360* combines journalistic articles with peer-reviewed papers. Every aspect of paper production is discussed, including finances and industry trends. Its readership is largely members of the Technical Association of the Pulp and Paper Industry, so each issue includes information about the association and its conferences.

4444. *Print.* Incorporates (1911-1950): *Print Collectors' Quarterly;* (1938-1941): *Printing Art;* Which was formerly (until 1938): *Printing Art Quarterly;* (until 1935): *Printed Salesmanship;* (until 1925): *Printing Art.* [ISSN: 0032-8510] 1940. bi-m. USD 57. Ed(s): Sarah Whitman. F + W Media Inc., 10151 Carver Rd, Ste 200, Blue Ash, OH 45242; contact_us@fwmedia.com; http://www.fwmedia.com/. Illus., adv. Circ: 19497 Paid. Vol. ends: No. 6. *Indexed:* A01, A06, A07, A22, A51, ABIn, ABS&EES, B01, BRI, F01, MLA-IB, P02. *Aud.:* Ga, Ac, Sa.

The purpose of this high-quality journal is to provide thorough and wide-ranging coverage of the graphic design field. Directed mainly at practitioners, it provides in-depth articles on pertinent topics. Half of the six issues published each year are devoted to juried showcases of leading work in graphic design. The annual "Regional Design" issue organizes artists' work by geographic region. Highly aware of the development of digital technology, *Print* offers a "Digital Design and Illustration" issue that explores the effects of computers on design. This title is an important addition to any graphic design collection. Also available online.

4445. *Print Solutions Magazine.* Formerly (until 2001): *Form.* [ISSN: 1535-9727] 1962. m. Free to members; Non-members, USD 29. Ed(s): Peter L Colaianni, Kristin Quinn. Print Services & Distribution Association, 433 E Monroe Ave, Alexandria, VA 22301; psda@psda.org; http://www.psda.org. Illus., adv. Circ: 13800. *Aud.:* Sa.

This award-winning magazine addresses issues of importance to professionals involved in printing, document distribution, promotional products, bar coding, security documents, commercial printing, and on-demand printing. Each issue is devoted to a current topic that is central to the printing industry. Some articles are available in podcast format. In every issue there is an industry events calendar, industry news, and a profile of a successful innovator or entrepreneur in the field. A subscription includes the award-winning "Buyer's Guide," an annual 500-page directory of industry sources of supply published in October. The annual Print Solutions Conference and Expo is exclusively focused on the independent print distribution channel. The web site for the magazine includes a career center where employers can search resumes and job seekers can find opportunities. Available online.

4446. *Printing Historical Society. Journal.* Formerly (until 1965): *The Black Art;* Incorporates (1980-2000): *Printing Historical Society. Bulletin;* Which was formerly (until 1980): *Printing Historical Society. Newsletter.* [ISSN: 0079-5321] 1962. a. Free to members. Printing Historical Society, The Secretary, St Bride Institute, Bride Ln, Fleet St, London, EC4Y 8EE, United Kingdom; secretary@printinghistoricalsociety.org.uk; http://www.printinghistoricalsociety.org.uk/. *Bk. rev.:* 6-9, 200-300 words, signed. *Aud.:* Ac, Sa.

This journal is published by the Printing Historical Society. All aspects of printing history and the preservation of equipment and printed materials are examined. Contributors include practitioners and researchers in the printing field. Three to four articles are featured and are scholarly in nature. Shorter articles and book reviews are found in the society's *Bulletin,* which appears as part of the journal. Historically important typefaces that have been revived are also reviewed. The *Bulletin* features society news and a list of antiquarian book catalogs. Both publications are free to society members.

4447. *Printing History.* [ISSN: 0192-9275] 1979. s-a. Free to members. Ed(s): William S Peterson. American Printing History Association, Grand Central Sta, PO Box 4519, New York, NY 10163; publications@printinghistory.org; http://www.printinghistory.org. Illus., adv. Sample. Refereed. Vol. ends: No. 2. *Indexed:* B02, BRI, MLA-IB. *Bk. rev.:* 3, 500-600 words, signed. *Aud.:* Ga, Ac.

This scholarly publication offers five or six research articles on topics that may range from profiles of leaders in the field to fifteenth-century papermaking. Its main focus is on American printing history, but its actual range is much broader and includes international developments that influenced the industry. Contributors are researchers in the field. This journal is only available through membership in the association. It is a useful addition to any printing history collection. Also available on the American Printing History Association's web site.

4448. Printing Impressions. Incorporates (1970-197?): *Printing Management;* Which superseded in part (1958-1970): *Printing Production;* Which was formerly (1930-1958): *Printing Equipment Engineer.* [ISSN: 0032-860X] 1958. 24x/yr. Free to qualified personnel. Ed(s): Mark T Michelson, Erik Cagle. North American Publishing Co., 1500 Spring Garden St., 12th Fl, Philadelphia, PA 19130; magazinecs@napco.com; http://www.napco.com. Illus., adv. Sample. Circ: 80491. *Indexed:* A22, ABIn, EngInd. *Aud.:* Ac, Sa.

This trade publication offers commercial printers, graphic artists, and newspaper publishers up-to-date information in the areas of printing, marketing, finance, and technology. Each issue includes profiles of successful businesses, how-to reports on recent technological advances, management advice, and a calendar of events. New products are reviewed. News about important people in the printing industry is a prominent feature. Also available online.

4449. Printing Industries of America: The Magazine. Formerly (until 2009): *Management Portfolio.* [ISSN: 1947-4164] 1989. m. except July-Aug. combined. Free to membership. Ed(s): Deanna M Gentile. Printing Industries of America, Inc., 200 Deer Run Rd, Sewickley, PA 15143-2600; membership@printing.org; http://www.printing.org. Circ: 10000. *Indexed:* ABIn. *Aud.:* Ac, Sa.

This is the magazine of the Printing Industries of America, a member-supported organization that promotes scientific, technical, and educational advancements in the graphic communications industry. Articles are written by either the association's staff or experts in a particular area. Each issue focuses on a particular theme such as offset technologies, color management, or production processes. Regular features include technology updates, business advice, case studies, interviews, and association news.

4450. Printing News. Former titles (until 1997): *Printing News - East;* (until 1989): *Printing News;* (until 19??): *New York Printing News.* [ISSN: 1556-0163] 1928. w. Free to qualified personnel. Ed(s): Bob Hall, Denise Gustavson. Cygnus Business Media, Inc., 1233 Janesville Ave, PO Box 803, Fort Atkinson, WI 53538; Kathy.Scott@Cygnusb2b.com; http://www.cygnus.com. Illus. Sample. *Indexed:* ABIn, B02. *Aud.:* Sa.

This is the weekly newspaper for printing industry professionals in New York, New Jersey, Connecticut, and Pennsylvania. Each issue includes feature articles, industry and product news, and a calendar of events. Two special issues cover the Graphic Communications exhibit held annually in Philadelphia and the Graph Expo held annually in New York City. This is an important resource for printing and graphics professionals in the eastern states. Also available online.

4451. Publishing Executive. Former titles (until Jan. 2006): *Print Media Magazine;* (until 2000): *Publishing & Production Executive;* (until Nov. 1989): *Publishing Technology.* [ISSN: 1558-9641] 1987. bi-m. USD 29.95 domestic (Free to qualified personnel). Ed(s): Noelle Skodzinski. North American Publishing Co., 1500 Spring Garden St., 12th Fl, Philadelphia, PA 19130; magazinecs@napco.com; http://www.napco.com. Adv. Circ: 16500. *Indexed:* A22, ABIn, B02, C42, EngInd. *Aud.:* Sa.

Available both in print and electronically, *Publishing Executive* is important to top management involved in the magazine publishing industry. Issues focus on best management and manufacturing practices, and "leader profiles" that detail leading publishing companies' strategies for growth. Major issues facing the industry are documented, as are ways to cut costs and reduce time to market. In addition to the magazine, the following resources are also offered: sponsored white pages, an InBox e-newsletter, the annual *Publishing Executive Resource Guide,* an annual Conference and Expo (produced in conjunction with *Book Business Magazine*), podcasts, Gold Ink Awards, and webinars. A "Job Connection" for both seekers and employers is also on the magazine's web site.

4452. Pulp & Paper International. Incorporates (in 2009): *Pulp & Paper;* Which was formerly (until 1947): *Pulp & Paper Industry;* (1927-1944): *Pacific Pulp & Paper Industry;* Pulp & Paper incorporated (1872-1986): *Paper Trade Journal;* (1941-1964): *Paper Mill News;* Which was formerly (1876-1941): *Paper Mill and Wood Pulp News.* [ISSN: 0033-409X] 1876. m. Free to qualified personnel. Ed(s): Graeme Rodden, Mark Rushton. R I S I, Inc., 4 Alfred Cir, Bedford, MA 01730; info@risiinfo.com; http://www.risiinfo.com. Illus., adv. Circ: 15000. *Indexed:* A22, ABIn, B01, B02, B03, C&ISA, EngInd. *Aud.:* Ac, Sa.

This monthly publication is the definitive journal of the paper industry and provides information on all aspects of paper production in Europe, Asia, North America, Latin America, the Middle East, and Africa. There is expanded Chinese coverage, with a quarterly *PPI China Special Edition.* The international editorial staff provides a global perspective to help managers at pulp and paper companies make informed buying decisions and run their operations more efficiently. Articles cover every aspect of the papermaking process. *Pulp & Paper International* is known for its exclusive in-depth market reports, such as the top 100. Each issue includes financial information about the international paper market and worldwide timber supplies. Also available online.

4453. Quaerendo: a journal devoted to manuscripts and printed books. Former titles (until 1971): *Het Boek (Antwerpen);* (until 1912): *Tijdschrift voor Boek- en Bibliotheekwezen.* [ISSN: 0014-9527] 1903. 4x/yr. EUR 276. Ed(s): Lisa Kuitert. Brill, PO Box 9000, Leiden, 2300 PA, Netherlands; cs@brill.nl; http://www.brill.nl. Illus., index, adv. Sample. Refereed. Vol. ends: No. 4. Reprint: PSC. *Indexed:* A01, A22, AmHI, BEL&L, E01, FR, MLA-IB. *Bk. rev.:* Number and length vary. *Aud.:* Ac.

Devoted to the history of printing and books, this peer-reviewed journal presents scholarly articles in English, French, and German. Important manuscripts, collections, and recent discoveries are highlighted. The subjects of codicology and palaeography, printing from around 1500 until present times, humanism, book publishers and libraries, typography, bibliophily, and book binding receive special attention. Book reviews and information about upcoming exhibits and conferences are provided. *Quaerendo* is delightful reading for anyone who loves books. Also available online.

4454. Quick Printing: the information resource for commercial, sign & digital printing. [ISSN: 0191-4588] 1977. m. Free to qualified personnel. Ed(s): Bob Hall, Karen Lowery Hall. Cygnus Business Media, Inc., 3 Huntington Quadrangle, Ste 301 N, Melville, NY 11747; http://www.cygnus.com. Illus., adv. Circ: 43000. *Indexed:* ABIn, B02, EngInd. *Aud.:* Ac, Sa.

This is the oldest and largest monthly magazine for quick printers, small commercial printers, in-plant printers, and copy shop owners and managers. Improved efficiency and increasing sales and profits in the print shop are its focus. Monthly columns by industry experts offer advice and technical knowledge on ways to improve operations. The award-winning editorial staff attends all major industry trade shows, which ensures that the magazine stays abreast of current trends and innovations and provides maximum exposure for the publication.

4455. S G I A Journal. [ISSN: 1546-4431] 1997. bi-m. Free to members. Specialty Graphic Imaging Association, 10015 Main St, Fairfax, VA 22031; sgia@sgia.org; http://www.sgia.org. Adv. *Aud.:* Ac, Sa.

This journal is a publication of the Specialty Graphic Imaging Association and is free to its members. Screen printing, digital printing, embroidery, sublimation, and pad printing are the imaging technologies covered. The journal features new products, production techniques, best business practices, and market trends. Readers are provided with the latest news shaping the industry, including emerging markets, government regulations, and technological developments.

4456. Screen Printing. [ISSN: 0036-9594] 1953. m. Free to qualified personnel. Ed(s): Gail Flower. S T Media Group International, Inc., PO Box 1060, Skokie, IL 60076; customer@stmediagroup.com; http://www.stmediagroup.com. Illus., index, adv. Sample. Vol. ends: Dec. *Indexed:* A&ATA, A22, EngInd, PhotoAb. *Aud.:* Ac, Sa.

This journal reflects its artistic focus by providing readers with clear instructions for a polished end-product. Included also is technical information about screen printing systems, care and maintenance of screen printing equipment, and industry trends. New products are also highlighted. *Screen Printing* is the foremost journal in the screen printing industry. Also available online.

4457. *The Seybold Report.* Formed by the merger of (1982-2001): *Seybold Report on Publishing Systems;* Which was formerly (197?-1982): *Seybold Report;* (1996-2001): *Seybold Report on Internet Publishing;* Which was formerly (until 1996): *Seybold Report on Desktop Publishing; Editing Technology.* [ISSN: 1533-9211] 1971. s-m. USD 499; USD 599 combined subscription (print & online eds.). Ed(s): Molly Joss. Seybold Publications, PO Box 4250, Frederick, MD 21705; http://www.seyboldpublications.com/. Illus., index. Sample. *Indexed:* A01, B01, B02, B03, BRI, CompLI, EngInd, I15. *Aud.:* Ac, Sa.

This international journal is very clearly organized so that the publishing professional can see at a glance the important issues and developments in the electronic prepress industry. Information about new technologies and capabilities is combined with financial reports and discussions about legal implications. Overviews of conference proceedings are provided. This is essential reading for anyone in the publishing industry or anyone selecting a publishing system. Available online.

4458. *Visible Language.* Formerly (until 1971): *Journal of Typographic Research.* [ISSN: 0022-2224] 1967. 3x/yr. Ed(s): Sharon Helmer Poggenpohl. Rhode Island School of Design, Graphic Design Department, 2 College St, Providence, RI 02903; charris@risd.edu; http://gd.risd.edu. Illus., index. Vol. ends: Sep. Microform: PQC. *Indexed:* A07, A22, A51, BAS, ERIC, ErgAb, MLA-IB, P02. *Aud.:* Ac.

This scholarly journal is concerned with written language (as opposed to verbal language) and its impact on humanity and civilization. Literacy is a frequent topic, but there are also many others, including typography, the effect of computer technology on the written word, and semantics. Many issues are devoted to a specific topic. *Visible Language* is important reading for language scholars and researchers.

4459. *Visual Communication.* [ISSN: 1470-3572] 2002. q. USD 865. Sage Publications Ltd., 1 Oliver's Yard, 55 City Rd, London, EC1Y 1SP, United Kingdom; info@sagepub.co.uk; http://www.uk.sagepub.com. Sample. Refereed. Reprint: PSC. *Indexed:* A22, A51, E01, F01, IBSS, MLA-IB, P61, SSA. *Aud.:* Ac.

This scholarly journal appeals to a wide audience in the humanities, social sciences, linguistics, and graphic arts academic communities. Its purpose is to bring together interrelated but diverse disciplines in a discussion of how the visual (in general) impacts these disciplines and society at large. Articles accepted in the journal include academic papers, visual essays, and reflective papers by practitioners on aspects of their work. Works on still and moving images; graphic design and typography; the role of the visual in language, music, sound, and action; and visual phenomena such as fashion, posture, and professional vision are all welcomed in this international forum. Available online and in print.

4460. *The Wide - Format Imaging: premier source for wide and grand format imaging.* Formerly (until 200?): *Modern Reprographics.* [ISSN: 1547-9463] 1993. m. USD 30 domestic (Free to qualified personnel). Ed(s): Denise M Gustavson. Cygnus Business Media, Inc., 3 Huntington Quadrangle, Ste 301 N, Melville, NY 11747; http://www.cygnus.com. Illus., adv. Circ: 17600. *Indexed:* ABIn, B02. *Aud.:* Ac, Sa.

This journal engages its readership through articles by experienced imaging professionals who work in the field. Industry news, trends, products, services, and management issues are all covered. Its intended audience is corporate and senior management focused on wide-format and grand-format imaging. Print-for-pay and in-plant imaging businesses will find pertinent information in this publication. This business and technology monthly maintains its leadership position in wide-format imaging through expert editorial, reader, and industry involvement.

■ PSYCHOLOGY

Jill L. Woolums, M.L.I.S., M.A., University of California, Berkeley, Education Psychology & Social Welfare Library, Berkeley, CA 94720

Introduction

What is psychology? Who are psychologists?

Psychology is a discipline concerned with the behavior, mental functions, personal development, and activities of humans. Psychology is both a science and a social science. Both academic researchers and clinical practitioners call themselves psychologists. Among the sub-areas of psychology are: biological psychology; human development; social psychology; personality; abnormal behavior; learning; motivation and emotion; memory; language, thinking, and intelligence; sensation and perception; stress and health; consciousness; and treatment and therapy.

Both psychiatry and cognitive science closely align with and overlap with psychology. Research in cognitive and brain science has significantly increased in the past decade. Other disciplines have overlapping interest in the various sub-fields of psychology. They include education, medicine, law, government, sociology, social welfare, public health, art, performing arts, communication, literature, sports, biology, business, and industry.

What access is there to journals related to psychology? What is available online or in print? What is free, open-access, or available only through a fee-based subscription?

The primary index to psychological literature is the American Psychological Association's PsycInfo database. PsycInfo is fee-based and available only through subscription. PsycInfo provides a sophisticated search engine to search psychological literature dating from the 1800s to the present. PsycInfo is available through its own PsycNet platform or from several vendors, including ProQuest and EBSCO. Most academic libraries provide SFX technology that links PsycInfo citations directly to the full-text journals for which libraries have paid access.

PubMed is also a primary index of science and medicine-based information on psychology, psychiatry, and cognitive science. PubMed, produced by the National Institute of Health and the National Library of Medicine, is freely searchable online, although most of the full-text content to which it points is fee-based. Other important online resources for research in psychology, psychiatry, and cognitive science include APA's PsycTests, APA's e-book collection, APA's PsycCritiques, APA's PsycTherapy videos, MIT's Cognet (on cognitive and brain science), and PsychiatryOnline's DSM-5.

The journals selected for review in this section lean more heavily toward social and clinical psychology and less toward psychiatry and cognitive science. Psychologists rely primarily on peer-reviewed, scholarly journals for the latest information and research in psychology. Nearly all of the journals listed in this section of *Magazines for Libraries* are scholarly and are available in full text online, through either their own publisher or an aggregating vendor, such as Sage, Elsevier, or the APA. Most journals provide current tables of contents online free of charge, but require a subscription for full-text access.

As the trend toward open access gains momentum, selected issues can be found free online, either permanently or for a limited time. There are a few scholarly journals that are entirely open access, i.e., fully available online in full text and entirely free. Popular press titles, such as *Psychology Today, Discover,* and *Scientific American* are usually available through a multi-subject database, such as EBSCO's Academic Complete, Thomson-Gale's Expanded Academic, or SIRS.

What about archives and repositories?

Archives are increasingly available online. Archives (a.k.a. back files) online are usually only fee-based. Such fees are sometimes negotiable depending on consortia or multiple-subscription purchasing. Large university libraries or regional consortia are working together to archive print back files in programs such as the Western Regional Storage Trust (WEST). Since volumes are increasing and space is decreasing, libraries are increasingly relying on nonprofit digital archives, such as JSTOR, Portico, and Lockss, for online preservation.

Open-access repositories provide search engines and organized links to scholarly publications that make some full-text content freely available on the Internet. Institutional repositories such as the California Digital Library's scholarship (www.escholarship.org/) and Ohio's Knowledge Bank (http://kb.osu.edu/dspace/) link to many pre- and post-print scholarly articles. See also the Directory of Open Access Journals (http://doaj.org), PsycLine (www.psycline.org), PubMed Central (http://pubmedcentral.nih.gov), and the Public Library of Science (http://plos.org) for free scholarly articles. The Digital Public Library of America (http://dp.la/) also promises to become a large archive of materials digitized from major library collections. The HathiTrust (www.hathitrust.org/) archive is now included. The web-searchable Internet Archive has also generously archived substantial amounts of content. The open-access movement extends beyond journal titles, and includes theses, dissertations, reports, conference proceedings, papers-in-process, white papers, and some e-books in all disciplines. Repositories of such content are often found through the web site of the work's sponsoring institution. Directories of such repositories have also arisen on the web. See Opendoar (http://opendoar.org) and CogPrints (http://cogprints.org). CogPrints describes itself as an "electronic archive for self-archived papers" in any area of psychology, neuroscience, linguistics, and many related fields.

Subscription-based online archives are also available, not only from vendors that provide current titles, but also from nonprofit organizations. JSTOR and Portico both emerged as nonprofit archive databases in the last decade. In a 2009 merger, Ithaka joined its database, Portico, with JSTOR. Their combined mission is "to create and maintain a trusted archive of important scholarly journals, and to provide access to these journals as widely as possible." Most large university and college libraries subscribe to JSTOR/Portico to access titles, ranging from three to five years back to the earliest available. Hundreds of titles, including many in psychology, are being made available by major libraries and publishers to create this archive. JSTOR also now provides access to current issues of some titles.

In recent years, new media resources have emerged. Alexander Street Press has created Primary Sources in Counseling and Psychology, 1950 to Present, and Counseling and Therapy in Video, as well as Education in Video. The APA just produced its video archive, PsycTherapy. These new primary materials promise to be archival resources for practicing and research psychologists, by providing transcripts and audio files of therapy sessions, videos, reference works, first-person accounts, diaries, letters, autobiographies, oral histories, and personal memoirs.

What about current trends in psychology?

There are several modern and historical approaches to psychology. Biological, cognitive, behavioral, psychoanalytic, humanistic, and cross-cultural approaches are considered modern. Other historical approaches include structuralism, functionalism, gestalt, behaviorism, and survival. In addition, many sub-fields have evolved, including neuropsychology, personality psychology, experimental psychology, and applied psychology (which involves assessment, intervention, and evaluation). Various perspectives also exist, including universal versus differential, holistic versus analytic, and theoretical versus pragmatic. Neuroscience and cognitive science research are increasing rapidly. Interest in cross-disciplinary research is significantly expanding to address many contemporary issues, such as crime, violence, ethnic tensions, and war-related conditions.

While interest in all approaches and sub-fields continues, the literature of the new millennium definitely reflects a scientific emphasis. Notwithstanding this trend, there remains strong support for research in psychology that has a social science perspective and for studies that reflect humanistic thinking. The American Psychological Association's "Decade of Behavior" demonstrates this support, with its focus on improving health, safety, education, prosperity, and democracy through a better understanding of psychology. There is and will continue to be a significant overlap among psychology and its sub-fields and other fields, such as law, political science, social welfare, public health, biology, language and linguistics, the applied and performing arts, anthropology, and education.

What is there to note about English-based, American, and foreign publications?

The titles selected for inclusion in this edition are primarily English-language based, emerging mostly from the United States. However, many from England and its Commonwealth countries have been added. Some titles draw from an international base of researchers and authors. Library selectors in larger institutions that have budgetary capacity and area studies departments will want to consider non–English-language publications. Academic and clinical libraries will find the titles included to be relevant to their collections. Smaller libraries and institutions will find many titles appropriate for their wider, general audiences, especially to the extent that such titles are available at least partially via open-access repositories or large multi-discipline subscription databases.

The titles selected for this edition are only a portion of all the psychology-related publications identified in *Ulrich's Periodicals Directory*. This selection takes into account current Thomson Reuters' ranking status, as well as rank assigned by ACRL's EBSS Psychology Section. American titles are favored over foreign titles. *Ulrich's* identifies additional titles relevant to specific concerns, such as the arts, ethnic or national issues, philosophical or

transpersonal interests, and assessment and intervention techniques. The present edition of *Magazines for Libraries* includes titles that cover most of the sub-areas of psychology, but since *Ulrich's* identifies over 2,000 psychology-related titles worldwide, selectors may also want to peruse the *Ulrich's* list.

ACRL's Education & Behavioral Science Section core list of psychology journals is another primary source for psychology journal titles. This list was compiled by psychology specialist librarians from major U.S. universities, and is based on a careful analysis of usage and impact metrics. Another useful source is PsycLine, which covers more than 2,000 psychology and social science titles in English, German, French, Dutch, and Spanish. PsycLine (www.psycline.org) is owned and managed by psychologist Dr. Armin Gunther, University of Augsburg, Germany. It is useful to find out about existing journals in the field, contact publishers, and browse tables of contents and abstracts. Although PsycLine searches both publication titles and article titles, full text is generally not available unless a publication has an open-access policy or the researcher has access privileges through a subscribing institution.

Since psychology overlaps with other research areas, other sections of this volume of *Magazines for Libraries* should be consulted, such as "African American"; "Aging"; "Asian American"; "Biology"; "Disabilities"; "Education"; "Family and Marriage"; "Lesbian, Gay, Bisexual, and Transgender"; "Gender Studies"; "Linguistics"; "Medicine and Health"; "Multicultural Studies"; "Parapsychology"; "Parenting"; "Philosophy"; "Political Science"; "Population Studies"; "Religion"; "Sociology"; and "Sports."

Selectors will also want to consult the lists provided by major vendors of psychology journals, including the American Psychological Association (PsycArticles), and the titles aggregated by major publishers that include Sage, Elsevier, Wiley, Springer, Taylor & Francis, Guilford, Alexander Street, and Academic Press.

What about the types of research?

Types of research and articles vary among the journals. The annotations describe each journal's editorial preferences. For each title, information is provided about the journal's purpose, general topic areas, coverage of recent issues, types of articles, and intended audience.

Articles may reflect empirical or experimental research. Papers may demonstrate new theoretical thinking or comparative analyses of theories. Case studies commonly appear. Literature reviews and special book reviews are frequently included. Empirical research bases its findings on direct or indirect observation, either using an instrument or the unaided human senses. These observations are recorded in the form of data that become the basis for discussion and conclusions.

Empirical research usually begins with a hypothesis and follows a process of deductive reasoning. Theoretical papers discuss concepts; propose hypotheses; speculate on, explain, and interpret theories and ideas; criticize other works; summarize and interpret previous research; discuss relationships and implications of prior research and other theories; and argue points of view.

Experimental research occurs under controlled conditions and involves the observation of humans, animals, or computer simulations. Experimental studies usually involve the collection of data as subjects are watched, thereby making the research also empirical. The results of such experiments provide information to form new theories or to create implications for existing theory.

Studies frequently use, as part of their methodology, one or more test, scale, or other measurement instrument. The data gathered from implementing a scale is then evaluated to develop theories or recommendations for further research. PsycInfo, the primary index to psychological literature, provides a tests and measurements field for easy identification of studies based on scales and instruments.

Literature reviews provide overviews and evaluation of published studies. Some reviews provide quantitative analysis, also known as meta-analysis. Literature reviews are important for their summaries, critical assessment, comparative analyses, and historical integration of previous psychological research. Book reviews highlight major current literature in a field. PsycInfo also provides for easy searching with its literature review field. PsycCritiques, another APA resource, searches and provides book reviews.

Case studies are in-depth analyses of certain aspects of a single subject or specific group of subjects. Such aspects may include behaviors, beliefs, emotions, thoughts, or personal histories. These are generally non-experimental, descriptive, empirical studies, typically involving the collection of multiple forms of data about the subject(s).

Basic Periodicals

American Psychologist, Annual Reviews of Psychology, Annual Review in Clinical Psychology, Archives of General Psychiatry, PsycCritiques, Psychological Bulletin, Psychological Review, Psychology Today.

Basic Abstracts and Indexes

Communication Abstracts, Counseling and Therapy Transcripts, Counseling and Therapy in Videos, EBSCO Full-text, ERIC, Linguistics and Language Behavior Abstracts, MIT Cognet, PILOTS, PrimateLit, PsycArticles, Psychiatry Online, PsycInfo, PsycLine, PsycTests, PsycBooks, PsycCritiques, PubMed, Social Sciences Citation Index, Social Services Abstracts, Social Work Abstracts, Sociological Abstracts.

4461. *A P S Observer.* [ISSN: 1050-4672] 1988. 10x/yr. Free to members. Ed(s): Sarah Brookhart, Ann Conkle. Association for Psychological Science, 1133 15th St, NW, Ste 1000, Washington, DC 20005; member@psychologicalscience.org; http://www.psychologicalscience.org. Illus., adv. *Aud.:* Ga, Ac.

APS Observer, free online, is the monthly bulletin of the American Psychological Society. The society is dedicated to the advancement of scientific psychology in research and teaching and to the representation of its interests on a national level to improve human welfare. The *Observer* serves over 15,000 APS members and is available online, with special sections reserved for members only or subscribers. Features include a section written by and for psychology students. Recent issues have presented articles on finding humor in tragedy; financial decision-making and the aging brain; managing large classrooms; discarding negative thoughts; gifted education policy; and feeling comfortable with negative feelings. Students, teachers, and researchers in psychology on all levels will want to find this title in their academic and public libraries.

4462. *Acta Psychologica.* [ISSN: 0001-6918] 1941. 9x/yr. EUR 1422. Ed(s): J Wagemans, B Hommel. Elsevier BV, Radarweg 29, PO Box 211, Amsterdam, 1000 AE, Netherlands; JournalsCustomerServiceEMEA@elsevier.com; http://www.elsevier.com. Illus., index, adv. Sample. Refereed. Microform: PQC. *Indexed:* A01, A22, C&ISA, CerAb, ErgAb, FR, MLA-IB, PsycInfo. *Bk. rev.:* 0-3, 1,000-2,500 words. *Aud.:* Ac, Sa.

This Elsevier journal, also known as *International Journal of Psychonomics,* focuses on empirical studies and evaluative review articles in the area of experimental psychology. Book reviews and articles that increase the theoretical understanding of human capabilities are included. The journal's current topics of concern include human performance, attention, perception, memory, and decision making, and to some extent papers on social processes, development, psychopathology, neuroscience, or computational modeling. Recent issues have discussed topics such as early and late states of working-memory maintenance and long-term memory; the development of organized visual search; how maximizers and satisficers [*sic*] perceive time differently when making decisions; adapting to target error without visual feedback; the effects of healthy aging on mental imagery as revealed by egocentric and allocentric mental spatial transformations; how we get the size of an object from its sound; the impact of social information on executive control, alerting, and orienting; how disgust-, not fear-, evoking images hold our attention; and plagiarism as an illusional sense of authorship. Single-topic supplements are published from time to time. *Acta Psychologica* is a high-impact journal that appears at the top of the list of frequently cited journals in ISI Journal Citation Reports. It is a must for research-oriented academic libraries, especially those that support experimental psychology programs.

4463. *Addiction.* Former titles (until 1993): *British Journal of Addiction;* (until 1980): *British Journal of Addiction to Alcohol and Other Drugs;* (until 1947): *British Journal of Inebriety;* (until 1903): *Society for the Study and Cure of Inebriety. Proceedings.* [ISSN: 0965-2140] 1884. m. GBP 1595. Ed(s): Robert West. Wiley-Blackwell Publishing Ltd., The

Atrium, Southern Gate, Chichester, PO19 8SQ, United Kingdom; customer@wiley.com; http://www.wiley.com/. Illus., adv. Sample. Refereed. Reprint: PSC. *Indexed:* A01, A22, AbAn, C45, CJPI, Chicano, E01, H24, IBSS, P02, P61, PsycInfo, RRTA, RiskAb, SD, SSA. *Bk. rev.:* Number and length vary. *Aud.:* Ac.

Addiction, a peer-reviewed journal from Wiley, publishes international research and provides editorials, commentaries, interviews, and book reviews. Its focus on addiction results in a selection of papers relating to science, clinical practice, and public policy. This title's scope spans human clinical, epidemiological, experimental, policy, and historical research relating to any activity that has addictive potential. Recent issues have addressed: problematic alcohol use in clients recovering from drug dependence; a life-course perspective on economic stress and tobacco smoking; whether 1976–85 birth cohorts are heavier drinkers; population drinking and drunk driving in Norway and Sweden; the relationship between minimum alcohol prices, outlet densities, and alcohol-attributable deaths in British Columbia; random student drug testing as a school-based drug prevention strategy; attention deficit hyperactivity disorder among illicit psychostimulant users; egocentric social network analysis of pathological gambling; and problematic computer game use among adolescents, and younger and older adults. *Addiction* is an important journal for clinical psychology programs.

4464. *Aggressive Behavior.* [ISSN: 0096-140X] 1975. bi-m. GBP 1726. Ed(s): L Rowell Huesmann. John Wiley & Sons, Inc., 111 River St, MS 4-02, Hoboken, NJ 07030; info@wiley.com; http://www.wiley.com/ WileyCDA/. Illus., index, adv. Refereed. Vol. ends: No. 6. Microform: PQC. Reprint: PSC. *Indexed:* A01, A22, ASSIA, AnBeAb, BRI, C45, FR, P61, PsycInfo, RRTA, RiskAb, SSA. *Bk. rev.:* 0-3, 800-1,000 words. *Aud.:* Ac, Sa.

This is the official journal of the International Society for Research on Aggression. The journal focuses on behavioral psychology issues and is of particular interest to researchers in the fields of animal behavior, anthropology, ethology, neuroendocrinology, psychiatry, psychobiology, psychiatry, political science, and sociology. The society seeks through its journal to publish peer-reviewed empirical research on the causes, consequences, and control of violence in human behavior. Recent issues have examined the dynamics of friendships and victimization in adolescence; the influence of individual differences in sensitivity to provocations on provoked aggression; school outcomes of aggressive-disruptive children; the roles of antisocial history and emerging adulthood developmental adaptation in predicting adult antisocial behavior; the effects of rejection sensitivity on reactive and proactive aggressive; how violent videogames stress people out and make them more aggressive; and bullying in classrooms. Libraries that support behavioral programs and researchers in the area of violence will want this title.

4465. *American Academy of Child and Adolescent Psychiatry. Journal.* Formerly (until 1986): *American Academy of Child Psychiatry. Journal.* [ISSN: 0890-8567] 1962. m. USD 677. Ed(s): Dr. Andres Andres Martin. Elsevier BV, Radarweg 29, PO Box 211, Amsterdam, 1000 AE, Netherlands; JournalsCustomerServiceEMEA@elsevier.com; http:// www.elsevier.nl. Illus., index, adv. Refereed. Circ: 7634 Paid. Vol. ends: Nov/Dec. *Indexed:* A01, A22, ASSIA, BRI, ERIC, ExcerpMed, FR, MLA-IB, P02, P61, PsycInfo, RILM, SSA, SWR&A. *Aud.:* Ac, Sa.

This Elsevier title and the official journal of the American Academy of Child and Adolescent Psychiatry focuses on the psychiatric treatment of children and adolescents in accomplishing its purpose to advance research, clinical practice, and theory in child and adolescent psychiatry. Studies represent various viewpoints, including genetic, epidemiological, neurobiological, cognitive, behavioral, psychodynamic, social, cultural, and economic. This journal publishes research about diagnostic reliability and validity, and the effectiveness of psychotherapeutic and psychopharmacological treatment and mental health services. Recent issues have addressed: social outcomes in mid-to later adulthood among individuals diagnosed with autism and average nonverbal IQ as children; identifying prolonged grief reactions in children; being bullied during childhood and the prospective pathways to self-harm in late adolescence; hippocampal shape abnormalities of patients with childhood-onset schizophrenia and their unaffected siblings; white matter microstructure in subjects with attention-deficit-hyperactivity disorder and their siblings; late preterm birth, maternal depression, and the risk of preschool psychiatric disorders; childhood gender nonconformity, bullying victimization, and depressive symptoms across adolescence and early adulthood as evidenced in an 11-year longitudinal study; and reward processing in adolescents with bipolar I disorder. Medical and academic libraries with clinical programs will want to have this title.

4466. American Behavioral Scientist. Formerly (until 1960): *Political Research, Organization and Design.* [ISSN: 0002-7642] 1957. m. USD 2375. Ed(s): Laura Lawrie. Sage Publications, Inc., 2455 Teller Rd, Thousand Oaks, CA 91320; info@sagepub.com; http://www.sagepub.com. Adv. Sample. Refereed. Microform: PQC. Reprint: PSC. *Indexed:* A01, A22, ABIn, B01, BAS, BEL&L, BRI, C45, Chicano, E01, EIP, IBSS, MLA-IB, P02, P61, PsycInfo, RRTA, SSA. *Aud.:* Ac.

American Behavioral Scientist, a Sage peer-reviewed journal, provides in-depth perspectives on contemporary topics throughout the social and behavioral sciences. Each issue offers comprehensive analysis of a single topic, examining its inter-disciplinary aspects. Recent issues have concerned: climategate, public opinion, and the loss of trust; the rise and decline of an open collaboration system and how Wikipedia's reaction to popularity is causing its decline; social margins and precarious work in Vietnam; the impact of treatment on the public safety outcomes of mental health court participants; the effect of partisanship and ideological value on individual recycling and conservation behavior; the polarized American and views on humanity and the sources of hyper-partisanship; moral, ethical, and realist dilemmas of transnational governance of migration; luxury, necessity, and anachronistic workers and whether the U.S. needs unskilled immigrant labor; the effects of opportunity to learn, family socioeconomic status, and friends on the rural math achievement gap in high school; and visual landscapes and the abortion issue. This journal is valuable across the social sciences and many new intersections of cross-disciplinary research.

4467. American Journal of Community Psychology. [ISSN: 0091-0562] 1973. q. EUR 1504 (print & online eds.). Ed(s): Jacob Kraemer Tebes. Springer New York LLC, 233 Spring St, New York, NY 10013; service-ny@springer.com; http://www.springer.com/. Illus., index, adv. Sample. Refereed. Vol. ends: Dec. Microform: PQC. Reprint: PSC. *Indexed:* A01, A22, AbAn, Chicano, E01, FR, H24, P02, P61, PsycInfo, RiskAb, SSA, SWR&A. *Aud.:* Ac, Sa.

This scholarly journal is published in association with the Society for Community Research and Action: the Division of Community Psychology of the American Psychological Association. The journal publishes "quantitative and qualitative research on community psychological interventions at the social, neighborhood, organizational, group, and individual levels." A wide range of topics is covered, including social justice, education, legal environments, public health issues, promotion of emotional health, empowerment of marginal groups, institutional and organizational environments, social problems, well-being and competence, social action and networks, and self-help and mutual aid. The peer-reviewed journal evaluates and features interventions, including collaborative research, advocacy, consulting, training, and planning, and it presents the work of leaders in the field. Recent issues have looked at the impact of participatory research on urban teens; digital animation as a method to disseminate research findings to the community using a community-based participatory approach; factors of empowerment for women in recovery from substance use; individual and contextual effects on perceptions of neighborhood scale; battling discrimination and social isolation among Latino day laborers; evaluating New York City's smoke-free parks and beaches law; the role of community development teams to build infrastructure; enhancing teen pregnancy prevention in local communities using the interactive systems framework; using systems of care to reduce incarceration of youth with serious mental illness; and a mental health needs assessment of urban American Indian youth and families. This is a core journal for libraries that support psychology, social welfare, public health, and social science programs.

4468. American Journal of Drug and Alcohol Abuse. [ISSN: 0095-2990] 1975. bi-m. GBP 1428 (print & online eds.). Ed(s): Byron Adinoff. Informa Healthcare, 52 Vanderbilt Ave, New York, NY 10017; healthcare.enquiries@informa.com; http://www.informahealthcare.com. Illus., adv. Sample. Refereed. Microform: RPI. Reprint: PSC. *Indexed:* A01, A22, ABS&EES, ASSIA, C45, Chicano, E01, ExcerpMed, P02, PsycInfo, RRTA, SD, SWR&A. *Aud.:* Ac.

The *American Journal of Drug and Alcohol Abuse,* on the Informa platform, publishes diverse research examining the neurobiology, pathophysiology, and treatment of addictive disorders. The journal includes articles that concern preclinical through clinical aspects of substance use and addictive disorders. Research topics may include issues related to molecular biology, cellular physiology, human and animal pharmacology of abused drugs, pathophysiology, behavioral pharmacology, neuroimaging, family-genetic studies of assessments, pharmacotherapies, behavioral therapies, and the medicinal use of substances traditionally considered substances of abuse. Recent issues have addressed: probability and predictors of the transition from abuse to dependence on alcohol, cannabis, and cocaine; impulsivity, expectancies, and evaluations of expected outcomes as predictors of alcohol use and related problems; how sleep quality moderates the relation between depression symptoms and problematic cannabis use among medical cannabis users; resisting the urge to smoke and craving during a smoking quit attempt on varenicline; perceptions of HIV risk among methamphetamine users in China; occupation as an independent risk factor for binge drinking; correlates of concurrent energy drink and alcohol use among socially active adults; the relationship between wisdom and abstinence behaviors in women in recovery from substance abuse; and interpersonal guilt in college student pathological gamblers.

4469. American Journal of Orthopsychiatry: interdisciplinary approaches to mental health and social justice. [ISSN: 0002-9432] 1930. q. GBP 267. Ed(s): Gary B Melton, Oscar A Barbarin. John Wiley & Sons, Inc., 111 River St, MS 4-02, Hoboken, NJ 07030; info@wiley.com; http://www.wiley.com/WileyCDA/. Illus., index. Refereed. Vol. ends: Oct. Microform: PQC. Reprint: PSC. *Indexed:* A01, A22, Chicano, E01, ExcerpMed, FR, P02, P61, PsycInfo, RiskAb, SSA, SWR&A. *Aud.:* Ac, Sa.

This journal has a wide scope that includes the areas of public policy and professional practice and "the expansion of knowledge relating to mental health and human development from a multidisciplinary and inter-professional perspective." It publishes research, clinical, theoretical, and policy papers, and focuses on concepts or theories related to major issues that include human rights and social justice. Recent issues have looked at parent–youth discrepancies in ratings of youth victimization and associations with psychological adjustment; self-reported methods of cessation of adult-male child abusers; identifying and addressing mental health risks and problems in primary-care pediatric settings; parental practices and political violence—the protective role of parental warmth and authority-control in Jewish and Arab Israeli children; emerging adults' perspectives on their relationships with mothers with mental illness and the implications for caregiving; deliberate self-harm behavior among Italian young adults; and promoting positive parenting in the context of homelessness. This is an important public policy journal for academic, public health, and social science research libraries.

4470. The American Journal of Psychiatry. Formerly (until 1921): *The American Journal of Insanity.* [ISSN: 0002-953X] 1844. m. Ed(s): Robert Freedman. American Psychiatric Publishing, Inc., 1000 Wilson Blvd, Ste 1825, Arlington, VA 22209; appi@psych.org; http://www.appi.org. Illus., index. Refereed. Vol. ends: Dec. Microform: PMC; PQC. *Indexed:* A01, A22, AbAn, AgeL, BAS, BRI, C45, CBRI, Chicano, ExcerpMed, FR, H24, MCR, MLA-IB, P02, PsycInfo, RILM, RiskAb, SWR&A. *Bk. rev.:* 10-15, 250-1,000 words. *Aud.:* Ac, Sa.

The *American Journal of Psychiatry,* published by the American Psychiatric Association on the Psychiatry Online platform, is a leading international psychiatric journal. Published monthly, it is important for all psychiatrists and other mental health professionals who need to stay current on every aspect of psychiatry. Thomson rates this journal with one of its highest impact factors. This journal publishes the findings of research studies that explore the full spectrum of issues and advances related to mental health diagnoses and treatment. Articles present new developments in diagnosis, treatment, neuroscience, and special patient populations. Included are case studies, book reviews, literature reviews and overviews, brief reports, editorials, narrative introspections, and articles that reflect new empirical research. For an extra fee, the online journal links to audio versions of key articles and quizzes that can be taken to fulfill CME credits for practitioners. The journal also includes association news, letters to the editor, and job announcements. Recent issues have covered: moderators of outcome in late-life depression; transitions in illicit-drug–use status over three years; whether fetal exposure to SSRIs or maternal depression impacts infant growth; genome-wide methylation changes in the brains of suicide completers; prevalence and correlates of prolonged fatigue in a U.S. sample of adolescents; early smoking onset and risk for subsequent nicotine dependence; the effects of pharmacologically induced hypogonadism on mood and behavior in healthy young women; comorbidities and mortality in persons with schizophrenia in a Swedish cohort study; and association between older age and more successful aging and the critical role of resilience and depression. URL: http://ajp.psychiatryonline.org

4471. *The American Journal of Psychoanalysis.* [ISSN: 0002-9548] 1941. q. USD 735. Ed(s): Giselle Galdi. Palgrave Macmillan Ltd., Houndmills, Basingstoke, RG21 6XS, United Kingdom; orders@palgrave.com; http://www.palgrave.com. Index, adv. Sample. Refereed. Microform: PQC. Reprint: PSC. *Indexed:* A01, A22, BRI, E01, FR, MLA-IB, P02, PsycInfo, RILM, SWR&A. *Bk. rev.:* Number and length vary. *Aud.:* Ac, Sa.

The American Journal of Psychoanalysis, a Palgrave MacMillan publication, is an international psychoanalytic quarterly founded in 1941 by Karen Horney. The journal provides an international forum on a range of contemporary clinical and theoretical concepts. Included in the publication are original papers, special issues devoted to a single topic, book reviews, film reviews, reports on the activities of the Association for the Advancement of Psychoanalysis of the Karen Horney Psychoanalytic Center, and comments. Recent issues have covered: dreams, catharsis, and anxiety; the art of living in Otto Rank's will therapy; critical transference in a case of severe epilepsy; empathy deficit in antisocial personal disorder; loss of humanness as the ultimate trauma; destructive women and the men who can't leave them—pathological dependence or pathological omnipotence; psychodynamic, cultural, and clinical aspects of sacrifice; losing the certainty of self; corrective emotional experience remembered; and trauma and the wise baby.

4472. *American Journal of Psychology.* [ISSN: 0002-9556] 1887. q. USD 304 (print & online eds.). University of Illinois Press, 1325 S Oak St, Champaign, IL 61820; journals@uillinois.edu; http://www.press.uillinois.edu. Illus., index, adv. Sample. Refereed. Microform: MIM; PMC; PQC. *Indexed:* A01, A22, ASSIA, BRI, CBRI, ErgAb, FR, MLA-IB, P02, PsycInfo, SSA. *Bk. rev.:* 4-6, 450-3,000 words. *Aud.:* Ac, Sa.

This long-standing journal has published scientific, theoretical, empirical, and experimental research of philosophical and historical significance by leading psychologists since 1887. Topics include conscious and non-conscious processes; memory; senses; rationality; problem-solving and reasoning; intelligence; introspection; brain imaging and neuropathology; and perception of reality. Recent issues have looked at how the need for cognition is related to the rejection but not the acceptance of false memories; assessing change in a personality profile; how musical experience influences statistical learning of a novel language; emotion and mood; how neuropsychological status in older adults influences susceptibility to false memories; the psychology of time; the illusion of fame and how the nonfamous become famous; transference in view of a classical conditioning model; and modality and variability of synesthetic experience. Libraries that support programs in psychology will want this title. URL: www.jstor.org/journals/00029556.html

4473. *American Journal of Psychotherapy.* Incorporates (1992-2001): *The Journal of Psychotherapy Practice and Research.* [ISSN: 0002-9564] 1946. q. USD 147 USD 47 per issue. Ed(s): Bruce J Schwartz. Association for the Advancement of Psychotherapy, Belfer Education Center, 1300 Morris Park Ave, Rm 402, Bronx, NY 10461; info@ajp.org; http://www.ajp.org. Refereed. Microform: RPI. *Indexed:* A01, A22, ASSIA, AbAn, BAS, BRI, Chicano, FR, MLA-IB, P02, PsycInfo, SSA, SWR&A. *Aud.:* Ac.

The *American Journal of Psychotherapy,* on the Ingenta platform, is the official journal of the Association for the Advancement of Psychotherapy. Since 1947, the journal has published an eclectic variety of articles for psychotherapists. Articles include several schools, techniques, and psychological modalities within the larger domain of clinical practice. Broad themes include dynamic, behavioral, spiritual, and experiential aspects of psychotherapy. The Journal

offers varying viewpoints and serves as a conceptual bridge among them. Recent issues have covered: obesity and the role of the mental health practitioner; psychotherapy with a sexually abused teenager; the role of edge-sensing in experimental psychotherapy; healing stress in military families; the psychodynamics of transference; pleasure-seeking and the aspect of longing for an object in perversion; the psychology of religion and spirituality for clinicians; marriage education for clinicians; and an object relations approach to cult membership.

4474. *American Psychologist.* [ISSN: 0003-066X] 1946. 9x/yr. USD 907 (Individuals, USD 310). Ed(s): Dr. Norman B Anderson, Dr. Gary VandenBos. American Psychological Association, 750 First St, NE, Washington, DC 20002; journals@apa.org; http://www.apa.org. Illus., adv. Sample. Refereed. Circ: 98900. Microform: PMC; PQC. Reprint: PSC. *Indexed:* A01, A22, ABS&EES, ASSIA, B01, B02, CJPI, Chicano, ERIC, FR, IBSS, MLA-IB, P02, P61, PsycInfo, SSA, SWR&A. *Aud.:* Ga, Ac, Sa.

This official journal of the American Psychological Association contains articles that cover a broad range of current issues in the science and practice of psychology and psychology's contribution to public policy. Articles cover all aspects of psychology, but generally do not represent empirical studies. Contributions often address national and international policy issues, as well as topics relevant to association policy and activities. Recent issues have covered the following topics: the humanistic psychology–positive psychology divide—contrasts in philosophical foundations; assessment of capacity in an aging society; violent videogames and the Supreme Court; the modern obesity epidemic, ancestral hunter-gatherers, and the sensory/reward control of food intake; the work-home resources model; Asian American mental health; why confessions trump innocence; how major depression can be prevented; and empowering the community to take action for better mental health. The journal includes the APA's archival documents, such as the annual report of the association, council minutes, the presidential address, editorials, reports, ethics information, surveys of the membership, employment data, obituaries, calendars of events, announcements, and selected award addresses. Occasionally, special issues on particular topics are published.

4475. *Annals of General Psychiatry.* Formerly (until 2004): *Annals of General Hospital Psychiatry.* [ISSN: 1744-859X] 2002. irreg. Free. Ed(s): Konstantinos Fountoulakis. BioMed Central Ltd., 236 Gray's Inn Rd, London, WC1X 8HB, United Kingdom; info@biomedcentral.com; http://www.biomedcentral.com. Adv. Refereed. *Indexed:* A01, ExcerpMed, PsycInfo. *Aud.:* Ac, Sa.

This open-access journal, from BioMed Central, seeks to offer support for the fields of psychiatry, neurosciences, and psychological medicine, aiming to publish articles on all aspects of psychiatry. Research articles are the journal's priority, and both basic and clinical neuroscience contributions are encouraged. The journal also seeks to support and follow the principles of evidence-based medicine. Recent topics have included a cross-cultural comparison study of depression assessments conducted in Japan; the Greek version of the MacArthur competence assessment tool for treatment; quality-of-life changes following inpatient and outpatient treatment of obsessive-compulsive disorder; the estimated economic benefits for low-frequency administration of atypical antipsychotics in treatment of schizophrenia; sexual obsessions and suicidal behaviors in patients with mood disorders, panic disorder, and schizophrenia; psychiatric comorbidities in Asperger syndrome and high-functioning autism; and deep transcranial magnetic stimulation for the treatment of auditory hallucinations. Students, practitioners, and researchers in psychiatry will benefit from access to this journal.

4476. *Annual Review of Neuroscience.* [ISSN: 0147-006X] 1978. a. USD 246 (print or online ed.). Ed(s): Samuel Gubins, Steven E Hyman. Annual Reviews, PO Box 10139, Palo Alto, CA 94303; service@annualreviews.org; http://www.annualreviews.org. Refereed. Microform: PQC. Reprint: PSC. *Indexed:* A01, A22, Agr, AnBeAb, C45, ExcerpMed, IndVet, PsycInfo. *Aud.:* Ac.

The *Annual Review of Neuroscience,* in publication since 1978, covers the significant developments in neuroscience, including molecular and cellular neuroscience, neurogenetics, development, plasticity and repair, systems neuroscience, cognitive neuroscience, behavior, and neurobiology of disease.

Occasionally, reviews on the history of neuroscience and ethics appear. Recent issues have addressed: songbirds as a model for basic and applied medical research; the RNA protein interactions in neurons; the neural basis of empathy; the evolution of synapse complexity and diversity; gender development and the human brain; reward, addiction, and withdrawal from nicotine; olfactory maps in the brain; and deep-brain stimulation for psychiatric disorders.

4477. Annual Review of Psychology. [ISSN: 0066-4308] 1950. a. USD 226 (print or online ed.). Ed(s): Samuel Gubins, Susan T Fiske. Annual Reviews, PO Box 10139, Palo Alto, CA 94303; service@annualreviews.org; http://www.annualreviews.org. Illus. Refereed. Microform: PQC. Reprint: PSC. *Indexed:* A01, A22, B01, B02, BAS, FR, MLA-IB, P02, PsycInfo, RILM. *Aud.:* Ga, Ac, Sa.

This highly cited journal is produced by a nonprofit scientific publisher, Annual Reviews. The journal publishes critical reviews of significant, current, primary literature in psychology. The journal covers a wide spectrum of topics, and recent issues contained articles that concern cognitive neuroscience; emotion; judgment and decision-making; adulthood and aging; substance abuse; political ideology and attitude; community psychology; consumer behavior; and research methodology. Each online issue includes abstracts, chapter/title indexes, and extensive bibliographies. Recent issues have addressed the endocannabinoid system and the brain; synesthesia; visual aesthetics and human preference; the role of neuroimaging in detecting consciousness; the social sharing and reshaping of memories; experimental philosophy; fear extinction as a model for translational neuroscience; the evolutionary origins of friendship; the neuroscience of social decision-making; speech perception; a taxonomy of external and internal attention; and the neural bases of social cognition and story comprehension. Research and academic libraries should have this core title.

4478. Anxiety, Stress and Coping. Formerly (until 1992): *Anxiety Research.* [ISSN: 1061-5806] 1988. 6x/yr. GBP 1154 (print & online eds.). Ed(s): Aleksandra Luszczynska, Nazanin Derakhshan. Routledge, 4 Park Sq, Milton Park, Abingdon, OX14 4RN, United Kingdom; subscriptions@tandf.co.uk; http://www.tandfonline.com. Illus., adv. Sample. Refereed. Reprint: PSC. *Indexed:* A01, A22, E01, ErgAb, FR, PsycInfo, SD. *Aud.:* Ac.

Anxiety, Stress and Coping, on the Taylor & Francis platform, is the official journal of the Stress and Anxiety Research Society. This online publication is international in scope and publishes scientific, theoretical, and clinical research. The research must be methodologically sound. Literature reviews; meta-analyses; case studies; and clinical, therapeutic, and educational articles are included. Articles may relate to assessment of anxiety, stress and coping, experimental field studies, and the antecedents and consequences of stress and emoting. Recent issues have addressed: how coping profiles characterize individual flourishing, languishing, and depression; dyadic coping in Latino couples and the validity of the Spanish version of the Dyadic Coping Inventory; attentional bias, distractibility, and short-term memory in anxiety; influences of personal standards and perceived parental expectations on worry for Asian American and White American college students; main and interactive effects of social support in predicting mental health symptoms in men and women following military stressor exposure; the role of meaning-focusing coping in significant loss; and self-compassion and social anxiety disorder. Academic libraries with clinical, medical, or behavioral sciences programs will benefit by having this title.

4479. Applied Psychological Measurement. [ISSN: 0146-6216] 1976. 8x/yr. USD 1065. Ed(s): Mark L Davison. Sage Publications, Inc., 2455 Teller Rd, Thousand Oaks, CA 91320; info@sagepub.com; http://www.sagepub.com. Illus., index, adv. Sample. Refereed. Vol. ends: Dec. Microform: PQC. Reprint: PSC. *Indexed:* A01, A22, B01, CCMJ, E01, ERIC, MSN, MathR, PsycInfo. *Bk. rev.:* 1-2, 500-1,000 words. *Aud.:* Ac, Sa.

The online journal publishes empirical research from educational, organizational, industrial, social, and clinical settings. It presents an international perspective and focuses on current techniques and cutting-edge methodologies to address measurement problems. The journal's contents include empirical articles, brief reports, computer program reviews, book reviews, and announcements. Special issues are regularly published to present

the ideas of leading scholars and to address emerging, significant topics. Topics covered may include item response theory; test equations and linking; reliability theory and methods; measurement of change; algorithmic test construction; validity methodology; computerized adaptive testing; Rasch models; and generalizability theory and methods. Recent issues have addressed: two approaches to estimation of classification accuracy rate under item response theory; optimal test design with rule-based item generation; uncertainties in the item parameter estimates and robust automated test assembly; using logistic approximations of marginal trace lines to develop short assessments; an overview of software for conducting dimensionality assessment in multidimensional models; and data-driven learning of Q-matrix. As one of the top journals in quantitative psychology, *Applied Psychological Measurement* should be included in academic and professional research collections.

4480. Applied Psychophysiology and Biofeedback. Formerly (until 1997): *Biofeedback and Self Regulation.* [ISSN: 1090-0586] 1975. q. EUR 1097 (print & online eds.). Ed(s): Frank Andrasik. Springer New York LLC, 233 Spring St, New York, NY 10013; service-ny@springer.com; http://www.springer.com/. Illus., index, adv. Refereed. Circ: 1950. Vol. ends: Dec. Microform: PQC. Reprint: PSC. *Indexed:* A01, A22, E01, ErgAb, FR, PsycInfo, SD. *Bk. rev.:* Number and length vary. *Aud.:* Ac, Sa.

Applied Psychophysiology and Biofeedback, a Springer title, is the official publication of the Association for Applied Psychophysiology and Biofeedback. This international, interdisciplinary journal studies the interrelationship of physiological systems, cognition, social and environmental parameters, and health. Articles represent scholarly research that contributes to the theory, practice, and evaluation of applied psychophysiology and biofeedback. Other journal sections include evaluative reviews; a clinical forum with case studies; treatment protocols; a discussion forum; innovations in instrumentation; letters to the editor; and book reviews. Recent issues have addressed: the use of paced respiration to alleviate intractable hiccups; developing a performance brain training approach to baseball; how electrodermal activity at acupuncture points differentiates patients with current pain from pain-free controls; the effect of a single session of short-duration heart-rate variability biofeedback on EEG; a heart-rate variability examination of acute physical activity on cognitive function; how electrocardiographic anxiety profiles improve speech anxiety; a self-report and psychophysiological study of the Emotional Movie Database (EMDB); emotional intelligence and electro-dermal activity; and cortisol-awakening response and pain-related fear-avoidance versus endurance in patients six months after lumbar disc surgery. Libraries that support clinical psychology programs will want this title.

4481. Archives of Sexual Behavior. [ISSN: 0004-0002] 1971. bi-m. EUR 1898 (print & online eds.). Ed(s): Allison Owen-Anderson, Kenneth J Zucker. Springer New York LLC, 233 Spring St, New York, NY 10013; service-ny@springer.com; http://www.springer.com/. Illus., adv. Sample. Refereed. Vol. ends: Dec. Reprint: PSC. *Indexed:* A01, A22, AbAn, BRI, C45, Chicano, E01, H24, HEA, P02, P61, PsycInfo, RRTA, RiskAb, SSA. *Bk. rev.:* 3-6, 1,000 words. *Aud.:* Ac, Sa.

This journal from Plenum, on the Springer platform, is the official publication of the International Academy of Sex Research. The journal publishes interdisciplinary work in the field of human sexual behavior. Features include empirical research (both quantitative and qualitative), theoretical reviews and essays, clinical case reports, letters to the editor, and book reviews. Recent issues have addressed: shared social and emotional activities within adolescent romantic and non-romantic sexual relationships; birth order and avuncular tendencies in Samoan men and Fa'afafine; men and women with bisexual identities showing bisexual patterns of sexual attraction to male and female "swimsuit models"; evidence of unwanted sexual experiences in young men from a survey of university students in Chile; how the discovery of penicillin reshaped modern sexuality; relationship commitment, perceived equity, and sexual enjoyment among young adults in the United States; and the use of the theory of planned behavior in heterosexual daters' sexual initiation behaviors. Researchers in sexuality and clinical practitioners in medicine, psychology, or rehabilitation will benefit from this journal.

4482. Behavior Modification. Formerly (until 1977): *Behavior Modification Quarterly.* [ISSN: 0145-4455] 19??. bi-m. USD 1193. Ed(s): Alan S Bellack. Sage Publications, Inc., 2455 Teller Rd, Thousand Oaks, CA

91320; info@sagepub.com; http://www.sagepub.com. Illus., index, adv. Sample. Refereed. Vol. ends: Oct. Reprint: PSC. *Indexed:* A01, A22, E01, ERIC, FR, P02, P61, PsycInfo, SSA. *Bk. rev.:* 0-1, 400 words. *Aud.:* Ac, Sa.

This Sage journal provides innovative research, reports, and reviews on applied behavior modification. Each issue is practically oriented, offering comprehensive coverage. It includes "research and clinical articles, treatment manuals, program descriptions, review articles, assessment and modification techniques, theoretical discussions, group comparison designs, and book and media reviews of significant literature in the field." This journal is also interdisciplinary, with articles on variety of topics. Recent issues have provided articles on: computerized behavioral activation treatment for depression; a pilot study to increase chewing in children with feeding disorders; acceptance and commitment therapy as a treatment for scrupulosity in obsessive-compulsive disorder; the effectiveness of mindfulness-based interventions for supporting people with intellectual disabilities; new methods in exposure therapy; risk recognition and sensation-seeking in revictimization and post-traumatic stress disorder; evidence-based behavioral treatment of dog phobia with young children; advances in trauma conceptualization and treatment; worry as a predictor of fear acquisition in a nonclinical sample; and inclusion of children with autism spectrum disorder in general education. This journal belongs in libraries that support applied psychology disciplines.

4483. *Behavioral and Brain Sciences: an international journal of current research and theory with open peer commentary.* [ISSN: 0140-525X] 1978. bi-m. GBP 820 (print & online eds.). Ed(s): Paul Bloom, Barbara L Finlay. Cambridge University Press, The Edinburgh Bldg, Shaftesbury Rd, Cambridge, CB2 8RU, United Kingdom; journals@cambridge.org; http://www.cambridge.org/uk. Illus., index, adv. Sample. Refereed. Circ: 2100. Vol. ends: Dec. Microform: PQC. Reprint: PSC. *Indexed:* A01, A22, BRI, E01, ExcerpMed, FR, MLA-IB, P02, P61, PsycInfo, SSA. *Bk. rev.:* 0-30, 500-2,000 words. *Aud.:* Ac, Sa.

This Cambridge online publication is an international journal of current scholarly research in psychology, neuroscience, behavioral biology, and cognitive science. In addition to research articles, the journal publishes commentaries on each article. The commentaries are written by specialists within and across these disciplines. Written replies of authors are also included. This format makes the journal a forum for communication and criticism, encouraging both debate and unification across its subject areas. Topics range from behavioral and brain science to molecular neurobiology, artificial intelligence, and the philosophy of the mind. Recent issues have covered: the psycho-historical framework for the science of art appreciation; a cognitive system for revenge and forgiveness; a universal model of reading; the cognitive basis of human tool use; a meta-analysis of the brain basis of emotion; what punishment experiments demonstrate about weak or strong reciprocity; a new framework for non-addictive psychoactive drug use; descriptivism versus normativism in the study of human thinking; and the evolution and psychology of self-deception. This is an important journal for academic and research programs in psychology, philosophy, cognitive science, information science, and broader social sciences.

4484. *Behavioral Neuroscience.* Supersedes in part (in 1983): *Journal of Comparative and Physiological Psychology;* Which was formerly (until 1947): *Journal of Comparative Psychology;* Which was formed by the merger of (1917-1921): *Psychobiology;* (1911-1921): *Journal of Animal Behavior.* [ISSN: 0735-7044] 1921. bi-m. USD 1148 (Individuals, USD 321). Ed(s): Mark S Blumberg. American Psychological Association, 750 First St, NE, Washington, DC 20002; journals@apa.org; http://www.apa.org. Illus., index, adv. Sample. Refereed. Circ: 700. Vol. ends: Jan. Microform: PMC; PQC. Reprint: PSC. *Indexed:* A01, A22, AbAn, Agr, AnBeAb, C45, ExcerpMed, FR, IndVet, P02, PsycInfo. *Aud.:* Ac, Sa.

Behavioral Neuroscience, from the American Psychological Association, publishes empirical and experimental research papers concerned with the biological bases of behavior. The journal includes papers regarding mechanisms by which nervous systems produce and are affected by behavior. Experimental subjects may include human and non-human animals and may address any phase of the lifespan, from early development to senescence. Research may involve brain-imaging techniques in human populations. Studies may use non-

traditional species (including invertebrates) and employ comparative analyses. Articles often reveal manipulation of some aspect of nervous system function, ranging across molecular, cellular, neuroanatomical, neuroendocrinological, neuropharmacological, and neurophysiological levels of analysis. Brief communications and commentaries also appear. Topic areas covered include: learning and memory; molecular and cellular bases of behavior; synaptic plasticity; motivation, homeostasis, and reward; sleep and circadian rhythms; sex and reproduction; human and non-human animal cognition and emotion; decision-making; sensory and motor processing; animal models of psychopathology, addiction, and neurodegenerative disorders; and developmental and lifespan analyses. Recent issues have addressed: the effects of discrimination training on fear generalization gradients and perceptual classification in humans; the paradoxical effects of stress on an executive task on decisions under risk; how pup odor and ultrasonic vocalizations synergistically stimulate maternal attention in mice; the role of central amygdala dopamine in disengagement behavior; social problem-solving, social cognition, and mild cognitive impairment in Parkinson's disease; neocortical synaptic proliferation following forebrain-dependent trace associative learning; depressive behavior and activation of the orexin/hypocretin system; fovea and foveation in Parkinson's disease; the implications of temporal variation in maternal care for the prediction of neurobiological and behavior outcomes in offspring; how moderate stress enhances immediate and delayed retrieval of educationally relevant material in healthy young men; how chronic stress impairs prefrontal cortex-dependent response inhibition and spatial working memory; and explaining neural signals in the human visual cortex with an associative learning model. Academic and special libraries that support scientifically based psychological research will want to include this title. URL: www.apa.org/pubs/journals/bne/index.aspx

4485. *Behaviour Research and Therapy.* Incorporates (1977-1994): *Advances in Behaviour Research and Therapy;* (1979-1992): *Behavioral Assessment.* [ISSN: 0005-7967] 1963. m. EUR 2108. Ed(s): G T Wilson. Elsevier Ltd, 32 Jamestown Rd, Camden, London, NW1 7BY, United Kingdom; corporate.sales@elsevier.com; http://www.elsevier.com. Illus., index, adv. Sample. Refereed. Vol. ends: No. 12. Microform: MIM; PQC. *Indexed:* A01, A22, ASSIA, AbAn, Agr, BRI, ExcerpMed, FR, HEA, MLA-IB, P02, PsycInfo, SWR&A. *Aud.:* Ac, Sa.

This Elsevier online publication is an international, multidisciplinary journal with a focus on cognitive behavior therapy (CBT). The journal's scope includes traditional clinical disorders and behavioral medicine. Topics of interest include experimental analyses of psychopathological processes; empirically supported interventions; behavior change; and evidence-based treatments for clinical practice. Topics that are excluded include measurement, psychometric analyses, and personality assessment. Recent issues have looked at: emotion regulation in broadly defined anorexia nervosa in association with negative affective memory bias; effectiveness, response, and dropout of dialectical behavior therapy for borderline personality disorder in an inpatient setting; Internet-based guided self-help for university students with anxiety, depression, and stress; fear, avoidance, and physiological symptoms during cognitive-behavioral therapy for social anxiety disorder; control and coping in chronic insomnia; sex differences in recovery from PTSD in male and female interpersonal assault survivors; executive function training with game elements as a treatment to enhance self-regulatory abilities for weigh-control in obese children; understanding depressive rumination from a mood-as-input perspective and the effects of stop-rule manipulation; integrating cognitive-bias modification into a standard cognitive behavioral treatment package for social phobia; and suppressing disgust-related thoughts and performance on a subsequent behavioral avoidance and the implications for OCD. This is a journal to be included in collections that support clinical psychology and medical research programs.

4486. *Biological Psychology.* [ISSN: 0301-0511] 1974. 9x/yr. EUR 2103. Ed(s): O V Lipp. Elsevier BV, Radarweg 29, PO Box 211, Amsterdam, 1000 AE, Netherlands; JournalsCustomerServiceEMEA@elsevier.com; http://www.elsevier.com. Adv. Refereed. Microform: PQC. *Indexed:* A01, A22, ErgAb, ExcerpMed, FR, PsycInfo. *Aud.:* Ac.

Biological Psychology, available online via Elsevier Science Direct, publishes articles on the biological aspects of psychology. Empirical articles are the journal's primary focus; however, review, brief notes, meeting announcements, critical commentaries, and technical notes also appear. Topics include electrophysiology, biochemical assessments, psychopathology, and all aspects of psychological functioning. Recent issues have addressed: flexibility as the key for somatic health—from mind wandering to preservative cognitive; worried sleep-monitoring in high and low worriers; the neural oscillations of conflict adaptation in the human frontal region; emotional modulation of pain-related evoked potentials; the psychophysiological correlates of interpersonal cooperation and aggression; how cardiac vagal tone is associated with social engagement and self-regulation; how electrocortical indices of selective attention predict adolescent executive functioning; psychophysiological responses to stress following alcohol intake in social drinkers who are at risk of hazardous drinking; and variability in ratings of trustworthiness across the menstrual cycle. This title is written primarily for an academic audience.

4487. *British Journal of Psychiatry.* Former titles (until 1963): *Journal of Mental Science;* (until 1858): *Asylum Journal of Psychiatry.* [ISSN: 0007-1250] 1853. m. USD 688 (print & online eds.). Ed(s): Peter Tyrer. Royal College of Psychiatrists, 17 Belgrave Sq, London, SW1X 8PG, United Kingdom; rcpsych@rcpsych.ac.uk ; http://www.rcpsych.ac.uk/. Illus., index, adv. Sample. Refereed. Circ: 15800. Vol. ends: No. 6. *Indexed:* A22, ASSIA, AbAn, AgeL, C45, ExcerpMed, FR, PsycInfo, RRTA. *Bk. rev.:* 6-20, 300 words. *Aud.:* Ac, Sa.

The *British Journal of Psychiatry,* a publication of The Royal College of Psychiatrists, is a leading psychiatric journal for mental health professionals. The scope of the journal includes not only peer-reviewed, scholarly research papers, but also literature reviews, commentaries, short reports, book reviews, short reports, and a correspondence column. Periodic supplements provide in-depth coverage of certain topics. Recent issues of the journal have addressed: age differences in treatment response to a collaborative-care intervention for anxiety disorders; characteristics and rates of mental health problems among Indian and White adolescents in two English cities; the structure of paranoia in the general population; changes in capacity to consent over time in patients involved in psychiatric research; the influence of problematic child-teacher relationships on future psychiatric disorder; bright light therapy for symptoms of anxiety and depression in focal epilepsy; joint crisis plans for people with borderline personality disorder; mental health problems in the workplace and changes in employers' knowledge, attitudes, and practices in England, 2006–10; gender differences in mental health expectancies in early life and midlife in six European countries; and the impact of the physical environment of psychiatric wards on the use of seclusion. This journal is important for the collections of libraries that support psychiatrists, clinical psychologists, and all professionals with an interest in mental health.

4488. *British Journal of Psychology.* Formerly (until 1953): *British Journal of Psychology. General Section;* Which superseded in part (in 1920): *British Journal of Psychology.* [ISSN: 0007-1269] 1904. q. GBP 417 (print & online eds.). Ed(s): Peter Mitchell. John Wiley & Sons Ltd., 9600 Garsington Rd, Oxford, OX4 2DQ, United Kingdom; cs-journals@wiley.com; http://www.wiley.com. Illus., index. Sample. Refereed. Vol. ends: Nov. Microform: PQC. Reprint: PSC. *Indexed:* A01, A22, ASSIA, B01, BRI, E01, ErgAb, FR, IBSS, MLA-IB, P02, P61, PsycInfo, SSA. *Bk. rev.:* 0-5, 500-1,000 words. *Aud.:* Ac, Sa.

This international publication is sponsored by The British Psychological Society and is available via the Wiley online library. The journal publishes empirical studies, critical literature reviews, book reviews and critiques, theoretical papers, and other original research to further the understanding of psychology. The scope of articles includes psychological specialties and the interface between them; new theories and methodologies; integrative reviews with meta-analyses; the history of psychology; and interdisciplinary studies related to psychology. Recent issues have considered an examination across race of family expressivity, emotion regulation, and the link to psychopathology; how facial adiposity conveys information about women's health; evidence for a "kinship premium" with respect to altruism in social networks; personality and place; the role of general cognitive ability in moderating the relation of adverse life events to emotional and behavioral problems; how personality and risk-taking propensity predicts mavericism; personality differences in mental imagery and the effects on verbal memory; the effect of background music on the taste of wine; and how reproductive ambition predicts partnered, but not unpartnered, women's preferences for masculine men. This journal is core to general psychology collections.

Canadian Journal of Human Sexuality. See Sexuality section.

4489. *Child Development.* [ISSN: 0009-3920] 1930. bi-m. USD 609 (print or online ed.). Ed(s): Detra N Davis, Jeffrey J Lockman. Wiley-Blackwell Publishing, Inc., 111 River St, Hoboken, NJ 07030; info@wiley.com; http://onlinelibrary.wiley.com/. Illus., index, adv. Sample. Refereed. Circ: 8712 Paid. Vol. ends: Dec. Microform: PQC. Reprint: PSC. *Indexed:* A01, A22, ASSIA, AbAn, Agr, BAS, C45, CBRI, Chicano, E01, ERIC, FR, IBSS, MLA-IB, P02, PsycInfo, RRTA, SSA. *Aud.:* Ac.

Child Development, available online via Wiley InterScience, is published for the Society for Research in Child Development. The journal publishes articles, essays, reviews, and tutorials on topics related to child development. Recent issues have addressed: imitation in infancy and rational or motor resonance; trajectories of the home learning environment across the first five years and their associations with children's vocabulary and literacy skills at prekindergarten; the effects of foster care on young children's language learning; the influence of classroom aggression and classroom climate on aggressive-disruptive behavior; the consequences of minimal group affiliations in children; friendship preferences among German and Turkish preadolescents; Latino adolescents' experiences of discrimination across the first two years of high school and their correlates and influences on educational outcomes; the role of parenting and early intervention on developmental pathways to integrated social skills; and maternal employment, work schedules, and children's body mass index. *Child Development*'s primary audience includes child psychiatrists, clinical psychologists, psychiatric social workers, special education teachers, educational psychologists, and other researchers.

4490. *Clinical Psychology: science and practice.* [ISSN: 0969-5893] 1994. q. GBP 343 (print & online eds.). Ed(s): Philip Kendall. Wiley-Blackwell Publishing, Inc., 111 River St, Hoboken, NJ 07030; info@wiley.com; http://onlinelibrary.wiley.com/. Illus., index. Refereed. Vol. ends: Dec. Reprint: PSC. *Indexed:* A01, A22, E01, PsycInfo. *Bk. rev.:* 1, 1,200-2,000 words. *Aud.:* Ac, Sa.

Clinical Psychology: Science and Practice, available on the Wiley online platform, is a publication of the Society of Clinical Psychology (APA Division 12). It provides scholarly reviews of research, theory, and application in the field of clinical psychology. The journal focuses on innovations. Topics include assessment, intervention, service delivery, and other professional issues. Recent issue reviews have addressed: the presentation and classification of anxiety in autism spectrum disorders; a social-cognitive perspective on posttraumatic stress disorder; the mechanisms underlying sexual violence exposure and psychosocial sequelae; clinical neuroscience of addiction; treating disgust in anxiety disorders; the relationship between physical activity and mood across the perinatal period; and bereavement interventions, end-of-life cancer care, and spousal well-being. Libraries that support clinical psychology programs will want this title.

4491. *Clinical Psychology Review.* [ISSN: 0272-7358] 1981. 8x/yr. EUR 1821. Ed(s): Dr. Alan S Bellack. Pergamon, The Blvd, Langford Ln, E Park, Kidlington, OX5 1GB, United Kingdom; JournalsCustomerServiceEMEA@elsevier.com; http://www.elsevier.com. Illus., adv. Sample. Refereed. Microform: PQC. *Indexed:* A01, A22, AbAn, ExcerpMed, PsycInfo. *Bk. rev.:* 0-4, 300 words. *Aud.:* Ac, Sa.

This Elsevier journal publishes scholarly reviews on issues important to the field of clinical psychology. It seeks to keep clinical psychologists "up-to-date on relevant issues outside of their immediate areas of expertise." Topics include psychopathology, psychotherapy, behavior therapy, behavioral medicine, community mental health, assessment, child development, psychophysiology, learning therapy, and social psychology. Reports of innovative clinical research programs and literature reviews may also appear. Recent issues have covered: efficacy of hypnosis in adults undergoing surgery or medical procedures; the relationship between anorexia nervosa and body dysmorphic disorder; effects of relationship education on maintenance of couple relationship satisfaction; the prevalence of child sexual abuse among adults and youths with bipolar disorder; the associations between parenting, callous-unemotional traits, and antisocial behavior in youth; a consensus definition of pathological videogaming; the impact of incarceration on juvenile offenders; anxiety and oppositional defiant disorder; a systematic review of the effectiveness of sex-offender risk-assessment tools in predicting sexual recidivism of adult male sex offenders; the treatment of internet addiction; sleep disturbance and cognitive deficits in bipolar disorder; and psychotherapy for military-related posttraumatic stress disorder. This is a journal for libraries that support several areas of psychological studies.

4492. Cognition. [ISSN: 0010-0277] 1972. 12x/yr. EUR 2108. Ed(s): Gerry T M Altmann. Elsevier BV, Radarweg 29, PO Box 211, Amsterdam, 1000 AE, Netherlands; JournalsCustomerServiceEMEA@elsevier.com; http://www.elsevier.nl. Illus., index, adv. Sample. Refereed. Vol. ends: Dec. Microform: PQC. *Indexed:* A01, A22, ERIC, ExcerpMed, FR, IBSS, LT&LA, MLA-IB, P61, PsycInfo, RILM, SSA. *Aud.:* Ac.

This Elsevier international journal of cognitive science publishes empirical, theoretical, and experimental research on the mind. Articles may come from the fields of psychology, neuroscience, linguistics, computer science, mathematics, ethology, and philosophy. Topics covered include all aspects of cognition, "ranging from biological and experimental studies to formal analysis." The journal also provides a forum for discussion of the social and political aspects of cognitive science and stress innovation. Special issues are devoted to areas with rapid recent progress, promising new approaches and convergence among disciplines. Recent issues have looked at: how the effect of word predictability on reading time is logarithmic; the power of human gaze on infant learning; the qualitative change in executive control during childhood and adulthood; how spatial language facilitates spatial cognition as evidenced from children who lack language input; the acquisition of abstract words by young infants; vocal imitation of song and speech; sound morality and how irritating and icky noises amplify judgments in divergent moral domains; what children value in artistic creation; how the envisioned physical formidability of terrorists tracks their leaders' failures and successes; and infants' perception of chasing. Libraries that support study in neuroscience, computer science, psychology, and linguistics will want this title.

4493. Cognitive Development. [ISSN: 0885-2014] 1986. 4x/yr. EUR 515. Ed(s): D Kuhn. Elsevier Ltd, 32 Jamestown Rd, Camden, London, NW1 7BY, United Kingdom; corporate.sales@elsevier.com; http://www.elsevier.com. Illus., index, adv. Sample. Refereed. Vol. ends: No. 4. Reprint: PSC. *Indexed:* A01, A22, ERIC, PsycInfo. *Bk. rev.:* 1, 3,000 words. *Aud.:* Ac, Sa.

This Elsevier journal publishes high-quality empirical and theoretical studies that are of current significance to psychological and cognitive researchers. It focuses on perception, memory, language, concepts, thinking, problem solving, metacognition, and social cognition. Moral and social development papers, if they are related to the development of knowledge or thought processes, are also included. Recent issues have addressed: how young children show a dissociation in looking and pointing behavior in falling events; perspective-taking ability in bilingual children and extending advantages in executive control to spatial reasoning; the past, present, and future of computational models of cognitive development; the mechanisms of developmental change in infant categorization; contributions of dynamic systems theory to cognitive development; language and age effects in children's processing of word order; how children's use of semantic organizational strategies is mediated by working memory capacity; age-related changes in cognitive processing of moral and social conventional violations; and children's and adolescents' reasons for socially excluding others. Libraries that support study and research in child development and work in education or psychology will want this journal.

4494. Cognitive Neuropsychology. [ISSN: 0264-3294] 1984. 8x/yr. GBP 1323 (print & online eds.). Ed(s): Brenda Rapp. Routledge, 4 Park Sq, Milton Park, Abingdon, OX14 4RN, United Kingdom; subscriptions@tandf.co.uk; http://www.tandfonline.com. Illus., index, adv. Sample. Refereed. Reprint: PSC. *Indexed:* A01, A22, ASSIA, E01, FR, MLA-IB, PsycInfo, RILM, SSA. *Bk. rev.:* 0-1, 1,500 words. *Aud.:* Ac, Sa.

This Taylor & Francis online publication provides empirical and scholarly articles on cognitive processes from the perspective of neuropsychology. The journal focuses on cognition topics, including perception, attention, planning, language, thinking, memory, and action with respect to any stage of lifespan. Neuroimaging and computational modeling research that is informed by a consideration of neuropsychological phenomena are also covered. Recent issues have looked at: taste and odor-induced taste perception following

unilateral lesions to the anteromedial temporal lobe and the orbitofrontal cortex; preserved morphological processing in semantic dementia; capturing specific abilities as a window into human individuality using the example of face recognition; developmental prosopagnosia in childhood; spatial and temporal attention deficits following brain injury: a neuroanatomical decomposition of the temporal order judgment task; the contribution of stimulus-driven and goal-driven mechanisms to feature-based selection in patients with spatial attention deficits; and selective impairment of grammatical masculine gender processing. This core title is important for students and researchers in cognition, neuropsychology, clinical psychology, and psychiatry.

4495. Cognitive Psychology. [ISSN: 0010-0285] 1970. 8x/yr. EUR 1358. Ed(s): Dr. G D Logan. Academic Press, 3251 Riverport Ln, Maryland Heights, MO 63043; JournalCustomerService-usa@elsevier.com; http://www.elsevierdirect.com/brochures/academicpress/index.html. Illus., adv. Refereed. *Indexed:* A01, A22, ASSIA, B01, E01, ERIC, ErgAb, FR, MLA-IB, P02, PsycInfo, RILM. *Aud.:* Ac.

This Academic Press title, available via Elsevier, publishes empirical, theoretical, and methodological articles as well as tutorial papers and critical reviews. The journal focuses on advances in the study of memory, language processing, perception, problem solving, and thinking. Articles that significantly impact cognitive theory and articles that provide new theoretical advances are specialties of the journal. Research topics include artificial intelligence, developmental psychology, linguistics, neurophysiology, and social psychology. Recent issues have addressed understanding decimal proportions; sortal concepts and pragmatic inference in children's early quantification of objects; the impact of losses on cognitive performance; lack of evidence for bilingual advantage in executive processing; how explanation and prior knowledge interact to guide learning; memorization and recall of very long lists accounted for within the Long-Term Working Memory framework; a rational model of the effects of distributional information on feature learning; and an integrated theory of whole number and fractions development. Researchers and students of psychology, cognition, linguistics, computer and information science, and artificial intelligence will want access to this title.

4496. Cognitive Science: a multidisciplinary journal. Incorporates (in 1984): *Cognition and Brain Theory;* Which was formerly (until 1980): *The S I STM Quarterly Incorporating the Brain Theory Newsletter;* Which was formed by the merger of (1975-1978): *Brain Theory Newsletter;* (1977-1978): *S I S T M Quarterly.* [ISSN: 0364-0213] 1977. 8x/yr. GBP 435. Ed(s): Arthur B Markman, Caroline Verdier. Wiley-Blackwell Publishing, Inc., 111 River St, Hoboken, NJ 07030; info@wiley.com; http://www.wiley.com/. Illus., index. Sample. Refereed. Vol. ends: Oct/Dec. Reprint: PSC. *Indexed:* A01, A22, AbAn, B01, E01, ERIC, ErgAb, FR, MLA-IB, P02, PsycInfo, RILM. *Aud.:* Ac, Sa.

This Wiley journal publishes articles in all areas of cognitive science, focusing on research written for a multidisciplinary audience. Topics addressed include knowledge representation, inference, memory, learning, problem solving, planning, perception, natural language, connectionism, brain theory, motor control, and intentional systems. Recent issues have looked at: young children's trust in overtly misleading advice; essentialist beliefs about bodily transplants in the United States and India; neural computation and the computational theory of cognition; an eye-tracking study of exploitations of spatial constraints in diagrammatic reasoning; interactive team cognition; mapping the structure of semantic memory; how children apply principles of physical ownership to ideas; how young children learn from examples; the role of novelty in early word learning; what difference reveals about similarity; and attentional factors in conceptual congruency. Researchers in cognitive science and the fields of anthropology, education, psychology, philosophy, linguistics, computer science, information science, neuroscience, and robotics will want access to this title.

4497. Cognitive Therapy and Research. [ISSN: 0147-5916] 1977. bi-m. EUR 1405 (print & online eds.). Ed(s): Rick E Ingram. Springer New York LLC, 233 Spring St, New York, NY 10013; service-ny@springer.com; http://www.springer.com/. Illus., index, adv. Sample. Refereed. Vol. ends: Dec. Microform: PQC. Reprint: PSC. *Indexed:* A01, A22, E01, ExcerpMed, FR, PsycInfo. *Aud.:* Ac, Sa.

This Springer online publication is an interdisciplinary journal. It focuses on studies on "the role of cognitive processes in human adaptation and adjustment." The journal's content includes empirical, experimental, and theoretical research; reviews; technical and methodological articles; case studies; and brief reports. Topics span diverse areas of psychology, including clinical, counseling, developmental, experimental, learning, personality, and social psychology. Psychologists and researchers from all of these areas will want this title in their library's collection. Recent issues have addressed: tolerance of negative affective states; automatic evaluative processes in health anxiety and their relations to emotion regulation; the interpretation of ambiguity in individuals with obsessive-compulsive symptoms; motivation and changes in depression; coping, negative cognitive style, and depressive symptoms in the children of depressed parents; the role of beliefs about mood swings in determining outcome in bipolar disorder; and examining the association between thought suppression and eating disorder symptoms in men. Libraries with academic programs in clinical psychology will want to include this title.

4498. *Community Mental Health Journal.* [ISSN: 0010-3853] 1965. bi-m. EUR 1208 (print & online eds.). Ed(s): Jacqueline M Feldman. Springer New York LLC, 233 Spring St, New York, NY 10013; service-ny@springer.com; http://www.springer.com/. Illus., adv. Sample. Refereed. Microform: PQC. Reprint: PSC. *Indexed:* A01, A22, ABIn, ASSIA, AbAn, BRI, Chicano, E01, FR, H24, HEA, P02, P61, PsycInfo, RiskAb, SSA, SWR&A. *Aud.:* Ac.

Community Mental Health Journal, on the Springer platform, focuses on the improvement of public sector services for people who are affected by or at risk of severe mental disorders, serious emotional disturbances, and/or addictions. The journal includes articles about nationally representative epidemiologic projects as well as intervention research that involves benefit-and-risk comparisons between service programs. The areas of behavioral health evaluation and methodology may also appear. Recent issues have addressed: the implementation of a weight loss program for Latino outpatients with severe mental illness; the effects of a complete smoking ban on inpatients at an intermediate to long-term psychiatric facility; epidemiology of problem gambling in a Canadian community; the impact of self-stigma and mutual help programs on the quality of life of people with serious mental illness; how under-served women in a women's health clinic describe their experiences of depressive symptoms and why they have low uptake of psychotherapy; evaluation of a suicide prevention training program for mental health services staff; and therapeutic horseback riding for ACT patients with schizophrenia.

4499. *The Counseling Psychologist.* [ISSN: 0011-0000] 1969. 8x/yr. USD 1120. Ed(s): Nadya A Fouad. Sage Publications, Inc., 2455 Teller Rd, Thousand Oaks, CA 91320; info@sagepub.com; http://www.sagepub.com. Illus., adv. Sample. Refereed. Microform: PQC. Reprint: PSC. *Indexed:* A22, ABS&EES, ASSIA, E01, ERIC, HEA, P02, PsycInfo, SSA. *Aud.:* Ac, Sa.

This Sage online publication is the official journal of the American Psychological Association's Division of Counseling Psychology. The journal publishes scholarly articles that provide comprehensive coverage of research and practice issues in counseling psychology. In-depth issues focus on topics such as counseling HIV-infected clients; counseling lesbian and gay clients; the counseling relationship; multicultural training; victimization; White racial identity; and delayed memory debate. Regular features include a forums section; treatises on current subjects; historical and current topic articles; reviews; and news and highlights of the division's activities. The forum section provides position papers, survey reports, illustrations of assessment and intervention techniques, such as those from the Legacies and Traditions Forum, the Professional Forum, the Scientific Forum, and the International Forum. Recent issues have looked at adult children of gay and lesbian parents with respect to religion and parent–child relationship; African American men's beliefs about mental illness, perceptions of stigma, and help-seeking barriers; a counseling psychology perspective on being a psycho-oncologist; a social cognitive perspective on coping with cancer; effective and ineffective supervision; the complexity of multiple feminist identities; feminism revisited and lessons beyond the privileged lens; acceptance and commitment therapy as a unified model of behavior change; dialectical behavior therapy as emerging approaches to counseling intervention; and narrative, poststructuralism, and social justice in current practices in narrative therapy. Academic and professional libraries that support clinical psychologists will want to have this title.

4500. *Current Psychology: a journal for diverse perspectives on diverse psychological issues.* Formerly (until 1988): *Current Psychological Research and Reviews;* Which was formed by the merger of (1981-1984): *Current Psychological Research;* (1981-1984): *Current Psychological Reviews.* [ISSN: 1046-1310] 1984. q. EUR 503 (print & online eds.). Ed(s): Jeffrey A Schaler. Springer New York LLC, 233 Spring St, New York, NY 10013; service-ny@springer.com; http://www.springer.com. Adv. Sample. Refereed. Reprint: PSC. *Indexed:* A01, A22, ABS&EES, B01, E01, MASUSE, PsycInfo. *Aud.:* Ac, Sa.

The journal *Current Psychology,* on the Springer platform, is an international forum for papers on issues at the cutting edge of psychology. It includes empirical articles from the areas of social psychology; small groups and personality; human development; sensation, perception, and cognition; clinical and abnormal psychology; and methodology and field research. Recent issues have addressed: the intermingling of social and evolutionary psychology influences on hair-color preferences; sex differences in relationships between verbal fluency and personality; rating of intensity of emotions across auditory, visual, and auditory-visual sensory domains; sports participation and loneliness in adolescents and the mediating role of perceived social competence; children's understanding of real vs. pretend emotions; experiences of touch avoidance; identifying cognitive style and cognitive complexity in reflective personality; the effect of high-anxiety situations on conspiracy thinking; the effect of immorally acquiring money on its spending; and assessing vindictiveness and the psychological aspects by a reliability and validity study of the Vengeance Scale in the Italian context. This is an important journal for studies in comparative psychology. URL: www.springer.com/psychology/journal/12144

4501. *Current Research in Social Psychology.* [ISSN: 1088-7423] 1995. irreg. Free. Ed(s): Shane Soboroff, Michael J Lovaglia. University of Iowa, Department of Sociology, 140 Seashore Hall W, Iowa City, IA 52242; sociology@uiowa.edu; http://www.uiowa.edu/~soc/. Illus. Refereed. *Indexed:* ERIC, IBSS, P61, PsycInfo, SSA. *Aud.:* Ac.

This is a publication of the Center for the Study of Group Processes at the University of Iowa. The journal is peer-reviewed and published only in electronic format, with free access to its contents. Articles cover a broad range of social psychology issues and reflect empirical, analytical, and theoretical studies. Recent issues have addressed: laboratory evidence of plea bargaining's innocence problem; the moral identity and group affiliation; threat, prejudice, and stereotyping in the context of Japanese, North Korean, and South Korean intergroup relations; how priming ability-relevant social categories improves intellectual test performance; how ambivalence toward the in-group underlies individual identity management strategies; the relative influence of values and identities on academic dishonesty; mitigating damage following scandals—when the personal becomes political; and self-enhancement through group and individual social judgments. Academic libraries that support programs in social psychology should provide an easily found link in their digital interfaces and catalogs to this accessible scholarly journal.

Death Studies. See Death and Dying section.

4502. *Developmental Psychology.* [ISSN: 0012-1649] 1969. bi-m. USD 907 (Individuals, USD 280). Ed(s): Jacquelynne S Eccles. American Psychological Association, 750 First St, NE, Washington, DC 20002; journals@apa.org; http://www.apa.org. Illus., adv. Sample. Refereed. Circ: 2100. Vol. ends: Dec. Microform: PQC. Reprint: PSC. *Indexed:* A01, A22, ASSIA, C45, CJPI, Chicano, ERIC, FR, IBSS, MLA-IB, P02, PsycInfo, SWR&A. *Aud.:* Ac, Sa.

Developmental Psychology, from the American Psychological Association, publishes empirical studies, scholarly reviews, and methodological articles about human development in all stages. Experimental studies such as ethnographies, field research, and data-set analysis are included. The journal seeks to advance knowledge and theory, and welcomes controversies and studies of new populations. Studies may concern any aspect of development including biological, social, and cultural factors. Articles may address other species insofar as they provide insight with respect to humans. Recent issues have included topics such as social motivations, social withdrawal, and socioemotional functioning in later childhood; the relationship between memory and inductive reasoning; early influences and later outcomes associated with developmental trajectories of Eriksonian fidelity; a couple-level analysis of reaction and adaptation to the birth of a child; the home literacy environment and Latino "head start" children's emergent literacy skills; understanding infants' and children's social learning about foods; selective trust and children's use of intention and outcome of past testimony; the emergence of flexible spatial strategies in young children; the emergence of probabilistic reasoning in very young infants; cultural issues in understanding neurodevelopmental disorders; phase-adequate engagement at post-school transition; and achievement, agency, gender, and socioeconomic background as predictors of postschool choices. Libraries that support departments of psychology, education, sociology, and social welfare will find this title an important addition.

4503. Educational and Psychological Measurement: a bimonthly journal devoted to the development and application of measures of individual differences. [ISSN: 0013-1644] 1941. bi-m. USD 1148. Ed(s): George A Marcoulides. Sage Publications, Inc., 2455 Teller Rd, Thousand Oaks, CA 91320; info@sagepub.com; http://www.sagepub.com. Adv. Sample. Refereed. Microform: PQC. Reprint: PSC. *Indexed:* A01, A22, B01, BRI, CCMJ, Chicano, E01, ERIC, FR, HEA, MLA-IB, MSN, MathR, P02, PsycInfo, RILM. *Aud.:* Ac.

Educational and Psychological Measurement, a Sage journal, publishes articles in the field of measurement. Articles are based on both current data and theoretical issues. Studies concern education, psychology, government, and industry testing. Every issue contains short studies that deal with the validity of tests and scales. Recent issues have addressed: a new method for analyzing content-validity data using multidimensional scaling; the search for value in the case of complex school effects; a Monte Carlo comparison study of the power of the analysis of covariance, simple difference, and residual change scores in testing two-wave data; item selection for the development of parallel forms from an IRT-based seed test using a sampling and classification approach; an analysis of the predictive validity of the General-Decision-making Style Inventory; investigating ESL students' performance on outcomes assessments in higher education; and balancing flexible constraints and measurement precision in computerized adaptive testing. Research, academic, and professional educators and psychologists will rely on this valuable journal. URL: http://epm.sagepub.com/

4504. Educational Psychologist. [ISSN: 0046-1520] 1963. q. GBP 456 (print & online eds.). Ed(s): Clark A Chinn, Gale M Sinatra. Routledge, 325 Chestnut St, Ste 800, Philadelphia, PA 19106; customerservice@taylorandfrancis.com; http://www.tandfonline.com. Illus., adv. Sample. Refereed. Vol. ends: Fall. Microform: PQC. Reprint: PSC. *Indexed:* A01, A22, E01, ERIC, PsycInfo. *Aud.:* Ac, Sa.

This Taylor & Francis publication presents scholarly essays, reviews, critiques, and theoretical and conceptual articles on all aspects of educational psychology. Articles explore both new and accepted practices. Topics range from meta-analyses of teaching effectiveness to historical examination of textbooks. Empirical studies are not included. Recent issues have looked at: a meta-analytic review of learning through case comparisons; team effectiveness and team development in computer-supported collaborative learning; the strength of the relation between performance-approach and performance-avoidance goal orientations; seeing deep structure from the interactions of surface features; teaching the conceptual structure of mathematics; rethinking formalisms in formal education; and what university admissions tests should predict. Educational psychologists, researchers, teachers, administrators, and policy makers will want access to this title.

Educational Psychology Review. See Education/Educational Psychology and Measurement, Special Education, Counseling section.

4505. Environment and Behavior. [ISSN: 0013-9165] 1969. 8x/yr. USD 1337. Ed(s): Barbara Brown. Sage Publications, Inc., 2455 Teller Rd, Thousand Oaks, CA 91320; info@sagepub.com; http://www.sagepub.com. Illus., index, adv. Sample. Refereed. Vol. ends: Nov. Microform: PQC. Reprint: PSC. *Indexed:* A01, A22, ABS&EES, ASSIA, Agr, BRI, C&ISA, CerAb, E01, ERIC, GardL, IBSS, P02, P61, PsycInfo, S25, SSA. *Bk. rev.:* 2, 600 words. *Aud.:* Ac, Sa.

This Sage publication presents current research and theoretical articles that concern the influence of environment on individuals, groups, and institutions. The journal includes feature articles, discussions, and book reviews. Topics covered include values and attitudes of people toward various environments; the effectiveness of environmental designs; transportation issues; recreation issues; interrelationships between human environments and behavior; and planning, policy, and political issues. The journal is interdisciplinary, with articles from specialists in anthropology, architecture, design, education, geography, political science, psychology, sociology, and urban planning. Special supplements are sometimes published to highlight leading scholars and significant issues such as litter control, public participation in evaluation of designs, and museum design. Recent issues have addressed: a cross-cultural study of environmental values and their effect on the environmental behavior of children; an examination of the effect of perceived risk on preparedness behavior; factors influencing homeowner support for protecting local urban trees; linking personal values to energy-efficient behaviors in the home; preference and tranquility for houses of worship; the influence of social class and cultural variables on environmental behaviors; linking lighting appraisals to work behaviors; the presence of a pleasant ambient scent in a fashion store and the moderating role of shopping motivation and affect intensity; and way-finding and spatial reorientation by Nova Scotia deer hunters. This interdisciplinary journal is important for libraries that serve humanities, social sciences, and science undergraduate and graduate programs.

4506. Exceptional Children. Former titles (until 1951): *Journal of Exceptional Children;* (until 1935): *Council Review;* (until 1934): *Council Newsletter.* [ISSN: 0014-4029] 1934. q. USD 196 (print & online eds.) Free to members. Ed(s): Thomas Scruggs, Margo Mastropieri. Council for Exceptional Children, Division on Career Development and Transition, 1110 N Glebe Rd, Ste 300, Ballston Plz Two, Arlington, VA 22201; service@cec.sped.org; http://www.cec.sped.org/. Illus., adv. Refereed. Vol. ends: Summer. Microform: PQC. *Indexed:* A01, A22, BRI, Chicano, ERIC, FR, MLA-IB, P02, SWR&A. *Bk. rev.:* Number and length vary. *Aud.:* Ac.

Exceptional Children is an official journal of The Council for Exceptional Children and is available selectively via EBSCO. The research articles it publishes focus on the education and development of exceptional infants, toddlers, children, youth, and adults. Material includes descriptions of research, research reviews, methodological reviews of the literature, data-based position papers, and policy analyses. *Exceptional Children* publishes quantitative, qualitative, and single-subject design studies. Articles must have implications for research, practice, or policy. Although examinations of interventions appear, descriptions of instructional procedures do not (except as a part of an intervention study or classroom materials, accounts of personal experiences, letters to the editor, book or test reviews, and anecdotal single case studies). Recent issues have addressed: sleep and cognitive functioning in children with disabilities; peer modeling of academic and social behaviors during small-group direct instruction; evidence-based practices and implementation science in special education; predicting eighth-grade algebra placement for students with individualized education programs; the relationship between parent expectations and postschool outcomes of adolescents with disabilities; cost effectiveness of alternative-route special education teacher preparation; the sustainability of school-wide positive behavior interventions and supports; and the effects of a tier 2 supplemental reading intervention for at-risk fourth-grade students.

Family Process. See Family section.

4507. Health Psychology. [ISSN: 0278-6133] 1982. bi-m. USD 536 (Individuals, USD 179). Ed(s): Jackie McBride, Dr. Anne E Kazak. American Psychological Association, 750 First St, NE, Washington, DC 20002; journals@apa.org; http://www.apa.org. Illus., adv. Sample. Refereed. Circ: 4600. Vol. ends: Dec (No. 6). Reprint: PSC. *Indexed:* A22, ASSIA, AbAn, ExcerpMed, FR, FS&TA, H24, PsycInfo, RiskAb, SWR&A. *Bk. rev.:* 0-1, 1,500 words. *Aud.:* Ac, Sa.

This is an APA peer-reviewed, scholarly journal concerning behavioral and physical health. Most articles present empirical, theoretical, or practically-based research. Studies may focus on cross-cultural and interdisciplinary issues. Topics may include the "role of environmental, psychosocial, or socio-cultural factors that may contribute to disease or its prevention; behavioral methods used in the diagnosis, treatment, or rehabilitation of individuals having physical disorders; and techniques that could reduce disease risk by modifying health beliefs, attitudes, or behaviors[,] including decisions about using professional services. Interventions used may be at the individual, group, multicenter, or community level." Recent issues have covered: physical activity and the reduced risk of depression; daily analysis of physical activity and satisfaction with life in emerging adults; changes in health-risk behaviors for males and females from early adolescence through early adulthood; affective science and health and the importance of emotion and emotion regulation; the associations between personality, diet, and body mass index in older people; predicting adult physical illness from infant attachment; racial identification, racial composition, and substance-use vulnerability among African American adolescents and young adults; and insomnia symptoms and well-being. This journal should be in libraries that serve clinical psychology and human performance programs.

4508. *Hispanic Journal of Behavioral Sciences.* [ISSN: 0739-9863] 1979. q. USD 886. Ed(s): Dr. Amado M Padilla. Sage Publications, Inc., 2455 Teller Rd, Thousand Oaks, CA 91320; info@sagepub.com; http://www.sagepub.com. Illus., adv. Sample. Refereed. Vol. ends: Nov. Microform: PQC. Reprint: PSC. *Indexed:* A01, A22, BRI, C45, CJPI, Chicano, E01, ERIC, HEA, P02, P61, PsycInfo, RILM, RiskAb, SSA, SWR&A. *Bk. rev.:* 0-1, 400-800 words. *Aud.:* Ac.

This Sage publication is a multidisciplinary behavioral sciences journal that publishes research and analyses on Hispanic issues. Scholarly articles provide theoretical, empirical, and analytical studies from leading experts in Hispanic Studies. Topics include cultural assimilation, communication barriers, intergroup relations, employment discrimination, substance abuse, AIDS prevention, family dynamics, and minority poverty. Recent issues have presented work on Latina teen suicide and bullying; assessing gender differences in the relationship between negative interaction with the clergy and health among older Mexican Americans; individual, family, and community influences on the migration decision-making among Mexican youth; the relation between maternal and child depression in Mexican American families; the role of family cohesion and family discord in anxiety disorders in Latinos; an ecological perspective on U.S. Latinos' health communication behaviors, access, and outcomes; how Latino economic and citizenship status impact health; the impact of health care and immigration reform on Latino support for President Obama and Congress; and the role of skin color on Hispanic women's perceptions of attractiveness. Researchers and professionals in the fields of psychology, sociology, anthropology, education, linguistics, public health, economics, and political science will find this title important to their work.

4509. *History of Psychology.* [ISSN: 1093-4510] 1998. q. USD 410 (Individuals, USD 110). Ed(s): Wade E Pickren. American Psychological Association, 750 First St, NE, Washington, DC 20002; journals@apa.org; http://www.apa.org. Illus., adv. Refereed. Circ: 600. Vol. ends: Jan. Reprint: PSC. *Indexed:* A22, FR, PsycInfo. *Aud.:* Ga, Ac.

History of Psychology, an APA journal, publishes peer-reviewed articles that concern psychology's past. It addresses the context of psychology's emergence and its ongoing practice. The journal presents scholarly work in related areas, including the history of consciousness and behavior, psychohistory, theory in psychology as it pertains to history, historiography, biography and autobiography, and the teaching of the history of psychology. Libraries that serve students and faculty interested in psychology's history should have this title. Recent articles have looked at such topics as: the archives of Jean Piaget; backlash against American psychology—an indigenous reconstruction of the history of German critical psychology; the vocabulary of Anglophone psychology in the contexts of other subjects; Columbian approaches to psychology in the nineteenth century; Alfred Binet and experimental psychology in the Sorbonne laboratory; tough love: a brief cultural history of the addiction intervention; the Roosevelt years as a crucial milieu for Carl Rogers' innovation; and the first representations of Italian social psychology between 1875 and 1954.

4510. *International Journal of Eating Disorders.* [ISSN: 0276-3478] 1981. 8x/yr. GBP 1609. Ed(s): Dr. Michael Strober. John Wiley & Sons, Inc., 111 River St, MS 4-02, Hoboken, NJ 07030; info@wiley.com; http://

www.wiley.com/WileyCDA/. Adv. Refereed. Reprint: PSC. *Indexed:* A01, A22, AbAn, Agr, BRI, C45, ExcerpMed, FR, FS&TA, H24, P02, PsycInfo, RRTA, RiskAb. *Aud.:* Ac, Sa.

This Wiley journal and official publication of the Academy of Eating Disorders publishes scholarly clinical and theoretical research. Articles concern several aspects of anorexia nervosa, bulimia, obesity, and atypical patterns of eating behavior and body weight regulation. Clinical and nonclinical populations are the subjects of investigation. The journal includes reviews, brief reports, case studies, literature reviews, and forums for addressing psychological, biological, psychodymamic, socio-cultural, epidemiological, or therapeutic issues. Recent issues have looked at avoidant restrictive food-intake disorder; a cost-effectiveness analysis of stepped care treatment for bulimia nervosa; increased emergency department use by adolescents and young adults with eating disorders; the role of state anxiety in the executive function in eating disorders; the role of eating and emotion in binge eating disorder and loss of control eating; an empirical study of diagnostic subtypes with respect to feeding disorders of early childhood; links between psychopathological symptoms and disordered eating behaviors in overweight/obese youths; childbearing and mortality among women with anorexia nervosa; evaluation of appetite-awareness training in the treatment of childhood overweight and obesity; how recovery from anorexia nervosa includes neural compensation for negative body image; and the patient's perspective on preferred therapist characteristics in treatment of anorexia nervosa. Behavioral scientists, psychologists, psychiatrists, neurologists, sociologists, health-care and mental health professionals, neuropsychiatrists, and anthropologists will benefit from access to this title through their libraries.

4511. *International Journal of Group Psychotherapy.* [ISSN: 0020-7284] 1951. q. USD 705 (print & online eds.) Individuals, USD 110 (print & online eds.). Ed(s): Les R Greene. Guilford Publications, Inc., 72 Spring St, 4th Fl, New York, NY 10012; info@guilford.com; http://www.guilford.com. Illus., index, adv. Sample. Refereed. Circ: 3500 Paid. Vol. ends: Oct. *Indexed:* A22, ASSIA, AbAn, BRI, Chicano, E01, FR, P02, P61, PsycInfo, SSA, SWR&A. *Bk. rev.:* 5, 750 words. *Aud.:* Ac, Sa.

This Guilford publication and official journal of the American Group Psychotherapy Association focuses on all aspects of group therapy and treatment, including theory, practice, and research. Recent issues have looked at applying systems-centered theory and methods in organizational contexts; interpersonal and social rhythm group therapy for patients with bipolar disorder; attachment style changes following intensive short-term group psychotherapy; a synthesis of psychodynamic and cognitive-behavioral group treatments in integrating empirically supported therapies for treating personality disorders; passion, containment, and commitment as essential elements of groups across the lifespan in Bruce Springsteen's work; long-term improvement in coping skills following multimodal treatment in war veterans with chronic PTSD; and the development and content of an interpersonal psychotherapy group for postnatal depression. Clinicians, researchers, and mental health administrators will want their libraries to have this leading journal in their field.

4512. *Journal of Abnormal Child Psychology.* [ISSN: 0091-0627] 1973. 8x/yr. EUR 1676 (print & online eds.). Ed(s): John E Lochman. Springer New York LLC, 233 Spring St, New York, NY 10013; service-ny@springer.com; http://www.springer.com/. Illus., adv. Refereed. Vol. ends: Dec. Microform: PQC. Reprint: PSC. *Indexed:* A01, A22, ASSIA, Chicano, E01, ERIC, FR, P02, PsycInfo. *Aud.:* Ac, Sa.

This journal, available on the Springer platform, is the official publication of the International Society for Research in Child and Adolescent Psychopathology. The journal, available online, publishes primarily empirical research on the major childhood disorders. Papers focus on epidemiology, etiology, assessment, treatment, prognosis, follow-up, risk factors, prevention, and the development of child and adolescent disorders. Topics include the major childhood disorders, including disruptive behavior, depression, anxiety, and pervasive developmental disorders. Recent issues have looked at intergenerational continuity in maltreatment; examining the validity of ADHD as a diagnosis for adolescents with intellectual disabilities; sex and age differences in the risk threshold for delinquency; goal internalization and outcome expectancy in adolescent anxiety; transactional relationships among cognitive vulnerabilities, stressors, and depressive symptoms in adolescence; etiological contributions to the covariation between children's perceptions of the inter-parental conflict and child behavioral problems; how early childhood assessments of community pediatric professionals predict autism-spectrum and attention deficit hyperactivity problems; trajectories of social anxiety during adolescence and relations with cognition, social competence, and temperament; and the effects of parenting and deviant peers on early to mid-adolescent conduct problems. This is an important journal for clinical, research, medical, behavioral, and social science libraries. URL: www.springer.com/psychology/child+%26+school+psychology/journal/10802

4513. *Journal of Abnormal Psychology.* Supersedes in part (in 1965): *Journal of Abnormal and Social Psychology;* Which was formerly (until 1925): *Journal of Abnormal Psychology and Social Psychology;* (until 1921): *Journal of Abnormal Psychology.* [ISSN: 0021-843X] 1906. q. USD 574 (Individuals, USD 179). Ed(s): Dr. David Watson. American Psychological Association, 750 First St, NE, Washington, DC 20002; journals@apa.org; http://www.apa.org. Illus., adv. Sample. Refereed. Circ: 2600. Vol. ends: Jan. Microform: PMC; PQC. Reprint: PSC. *Indexed:* A01, A22, ASSIA, AbAn, CJPI, Chicano, ExcerpMed, FR, MLA-IB, P02, PsycInfo, SWR&A. *Aud.:* Ac, Sa.

This journal, from the American Psychological Association, publishes articles on abnormal behavior, its determinants, and its correlates. Articles may be based on empirical and/or experimental research, on case studies, or on theory. Studies dealing with diagnosis or treatment are not included. The journal focuses on several topics, including psychopathology (its etiology, development, and symptomatology); normal processes in abnormal individuals; pathological or atypical behavior of normal persons; disordered emotional behavior or pathology; socio-cultural effects on pathological processes; gender and ethnic issues; and tests of theories. Recent issues have looked at: predictors of first lifetime onset of major depressive disorder in young adulthood; information-seeking bias in social anxiety disorder; sleep and affect coupling in interepisode bipolar disorder; the latent structure of posttraumatic stress disorder distinguishing different models and different populations; eye-contact perception in schizophrenia and the relationship with symptoms and socioemotional functioning; DSM-5 personality traits and DSM-IV personality disorder; shame regulation in personality disorders; interpretation bias in preschool children at risk for anxiety; and gene-environment interplay in the association between pubertal timing and delinquency in adolescent girls. With its theoretical aim, this scholarly journal belongs in academic libraries that support advanced degrees in psychological research. URL: www.apa.org/pubs/journals/abn/index.aspx

4514. *Journal of Anxiety Disorders.* [ISSN: 0887-6185] 1987. 8x/yr. EUR 1105. Ed(s): Deborah Beidel. Pergamon, The Blvd, Langford Ln, E Park, Kidlington, OX5 1GB, United Kingdom; JournalsCustomerServiceEMEA@elsevier.com; http://www.elsevier.com. Illus., adv. Sample. Refereed. Microform: PQC. *Indexed:* A01, A22, ASSIA, ExcerpMed, FR, PsycInfo. *Bk. rev.:* Number and length vary. *Aud.:* Ac, Sa.

This Elsevier online title is an interdisciplinary journal focused on anxiety disorders. Papers address all age groups. Empirical research studies, theoretical and review articles, clinical reports and case studies, and book reviews appear in the journal. Topics include traditional, behavioral, cognitive, and biological assessment; diagnosis and classification; psychosocial and psychopharmacological treatment; genetics; epidemiology; and prevention. Recent issues have looked at: pre-treatment shyness mindset predicts less reduction of social anxiety during exposure therapy; influence of social stress on risk-taking behavior in adolescents; parenting practices, interpretive biases, and anxiety in Latino children; emotion-regulation difficulties as a prospective predictor of posttraumatic stress symptoms following a mass shooting; experiential avoidance and emotion-regulation difficulties in hoarding disorder; concordance of self- and proxy-rated worry and anxiety symptoms in older adults with dementia; disgust, mental contamination, and posttraumatic stress as unique relations following sexual versus non-sexual assault; validating the Flight Anxiety Situations Questionnaire as a clinical identification measure; and ethnoracial differences in anxiety sensitivity. Academic libraries will want this title for their behavioral and social science students and researchers.

4515. *Journal of Applied Behavior Analysis.* [ISSN: 0021-8855] 1968. q. GBP 78 (print & online eds.). Ed(s): Cathleen C Piazza. Wiley-Blackwell Publishing, Inc., 111 River St, Hoboken, NJ 07030; info@wiley.com. Illus., adv. Refereed. *Indexed:* A01, A22, ABIn, B01, BRI, ERIC, FR, MLA-IB, P02, PsycInfo, RILM. *Aud.:* Ac, Sa.

This is a publication of the Society for the Experimental Analysis of Behavior is part of the Wiley Online Library. Tables of contents are available online. The journal publishes research on the application of analyses of behavior to current social issues. Recent issues have addressed research on the functional analysis of problem behavior; comparing the teaching interaction procedure to social stories for people with autism; analysis of variables that affect self-control with aversive events; a computer-based program to teach braille reading to sighted individuals; acquisition of social referencing via discrimination training in infants; generalized instruction following with pictorial prompts; evaluation of strengthening precursors to increase preschooler compliance; disruptive effects of contingent food on high-probability behavior; a comparison of two flash-card methods for improving sight-word reading; and comparison of a stimulus equivalence protocol and traditional lecture for teaching single-subject designs. Access to the behavioral analyses and intervention techniques in this journal is important for students, researchers, and professionals in psychology and social sciences.

4516. *Journal of Applied Psychology.* [ISSN: 0021-9010] 1917. bi-m. USD 836 (Individuals, USD 280). Ed(s): Steve W J Kozlowski. American Psychological Association, 750 First St, NE, Washington, DC 20002; journals@apa.org; http://www.apa.org. Illus., adv. Sample. Refereed. Circ: 2600. Vol. ends: Jan. Microform: PMC; PQC. Reprint: PSC. *Indexed:* A22, ABIn, ASSIA, B01, B02, Chicano, ERIC, ErgAb, FR, IBSS, MLA-IB, P02, PsycInfo, RILM. *Aud.:* Ac, Sa.

This APA journal publishes articles that represent new investigations that seek knowledge in the field of applied psychology. The journal considers research that concerns the psychological and behavioral phenomena of individuals, groups, or organizations in institutional settings such as education, business, government, or health care. Articles are empirical, theoretical, or conceptual, but not clinical, applied experimental, or treatment-based. Topical themes include personnel issues, leadership, job performance and attitudes, addiction, training, organizational design, the impact of technology, and cross-cultural differences. Recent issues have looked at: the impact of furloughs on emotional exhaustion, self-rated performance, and recovery experiences; reciprocal effects of work stressors and counterproductive work behavior; turnover rates and organizational performance; the role of mindfulness in emotion regulation, emotional exhaustion, and job satisfaction; how team personality composition and task conflict interact to improve performance; the importance and outcomes of work-family support policies; employees' behavioral reactions to supervisor aggression; leader identity as an antecedent of the frequency and consistency of transformational, consideration, and abusive leadership behaviors; and how employees pay cognitive costs when customers exhibit verbal aggression. Libraries that support programs in behavioral and organizational psychology will want to have this journal.

4517. *Journal of Behavioral Health Services and Research.* Formerly (until 1998): *Journal of Mental Health Administration.* [ISSN: 1094-3412] 1972. q. EUR 353 (print & online eds.). Ed(s): Bruce Lubotsky Levin. Springer New York LLC, 233 Spring St, New York, NY 10013; service-ny@springer.com; http://www.springer.com/. Illus., adv. Sample. Refereed. Circ: 2000 Paid. Microform: PQC. Reprint: PSC. *Indexed:* A01, A22, ABIn, ASSIA, B01, BRI, CJPI, E01, P02, P61, PsycInfo, SSA, SWR&A. *Bk. rev.:* Number and length vary. *Aud.:* Ac.

The *Journal of Behavioral Health Services & Research,* on the Springer platform, is the official publication of the National Council for Community Behavioral Healthcare and the Association of Behavioral Healthcare Management. It covers the organization, financing, delivery, and outcomes of behavioral health services, as well as provides the results of empirical studies. Issues include overviews of contemporary topics, policy perspectives, commentaries, brief reports, and book reviews, as well as scholarly research studies. Recent issues have addressed: improving implementation of mental health services for trauma in multicultural elementary schools; characteristics and severity of psychological distress after abortion among university students; successful treatment outcomes among urban American Indians/Alaska Natives and the role of social environment; caregiver participation in community-based mental health services for children receiving outpatient care; hospital readmission among Medicaid patients with an index hospital for mental and/or substance-use disorder; mental health communications-skills training for medical assistants in pediatric primary care; common mental health disorders in developing countries with insights from urban Ghana; and quality of communication between primary health care and mental health care.

4518. *Journal of Child Psychology and Psychiatry.* [ISSN: 0021-9630] 1960. m. GBP 582. Ed(s): Edmund Sonuga-Barke. Wiley-Blackwell Publishing Ltd., The Atrium, Southern Gate, Chichester, PO19 8SQ, United Kingdom; customer@wiley.com; http://www.wiley.com/. Illus., index, adv. Sample. Refereed. Vol. ends: Nov. Microform: PQC. Reprint: PSC. *Indexed:* A01, A22, ASSIA, BRI, E01, ERIC, FR, H24, P02, PsycInfo, SSA. *Bk. rev.:* 2-12, 350-2,000 words. *Aud.:* Ac, Sa.

This is a publication of the Association for Child and Adolescent Mental Health, and it is available on the Wiley online platform. The journal is internationally recognized as a leader in the field of child and adolescent psychology and psychiatry. Contents feature empirical research, clinical studies, and reviews. Articles represent both experimental and developmental studies. Special topic issues appear yearly. Recent issues have addressed: attention deficit hyperactivity disorder, tic disorder, and allergy; facial emotional-expression recognition by children at familial risk for depression and high-risk boys' oversensitivity to sadness; the relationship between large cavum septum pellucidum and antisocial behavior, callous-unemotional traits, and psychopathy in adolescents; efficacy of language intervention in the early years; the effects of juvenile court exposure on crime in young adulthood; diagnosis of autism spectrum disorders in two-year-olds; the impact of maternal depression on young children's executive function; the impact of early father–infant interactions on the onset of externalizing behaviors in young children; brain structure abnormalities in adolescent girls with conduct disorder; child and adolescent predictors of male intimate partner violence; and dimensions of oppositional defiant disorder in three-year-old preschoolers. Libraries that support education and behavioral and social science researchers, students, and clinicians will want to have this title. URL: http://onlinelibrary.wiley.com/journal/10.1111/(ISSN)1469-7610

4519. *Journal of Clinical Child and Adolescent Psychology.* Formerly (until 2001): *Journal of Clinical Child Psychology.* [ISSN: 1537-4416] 1972. bi-m. GBP 766 (print & online eds.). Ed(s): Mitchell J Prinstein. Routledge, 325 Chestnut St, Ste 800, Philadelphia, PA 19106; customerservice@taylorandfrancis.com; http://www.tandfonline.com. Illus., index, adv. Sample. Refereed. Vol. ends: Dec. Reprint: PSC. *Indexed:* A01, A22, ASSIA, BRI, E01, ERIC, P02, PsycInfo. *Bk. rev.:* 0-2, 100-200 words. *Aud.:* Ac, Sa.

This is the official publication of the American Psychological Association's Society of Clinical Child and Adolescent Psychology (Division 53), available on the Taylor & Francis platform. The journal publishes empirical research and scholarly articles, including those focusing on theoretical and methodological issues. Topics include assessment and intervention techniques; development and maintenance of clinical child and adolescent problems; cross-cultural and sociodemographic issues; training and professional practice; and child advocacy. Recent issues have addressed: borderline personality features and implicit shame-prone self-concept in middle childhood and early adolescence; potential pathways from stigmatization and externalizing behavior to anger and dating aggression in sexually abused youth; motorsports involvement among adolescents and young adults with childhood ADHD; the reciprocal relationship between alliance and symptom improvement across the treatment of childhood anxiety; perceived barriers to help-seeking among parents of at-risk kindergarteners in rural communities; disentangling the temporal relationship between parental depressive symptoms and early child-behavior problems; and an inventory of callous-unemotional traits in a community sample of preschoolers. Libraries that support clinical psychology, education, and social science research will want to collect this title.

4520. *Journal of Clinical Psychology.* Incorporates (1995-1998): *In Session: Psychotherapy in Practice.* [ISSN: 0021-9762] 1945. m. GBP 602. Ed(s): Beverly E Thorn. John Wiley & Sons, Inc., 111 River St, MS

4-02, Hoboken, NJ 07030; info@wiley.com; http://www.wiley.com/WileyCDA/. Adv. Refereed. Reprint: PSC. *Indexed:* A01, A22, ABS&EES, AbAn, AgeL, Chicano, FR, P02, PsycInfo, SWR&A. *Aud.:* Ac.

Founded in 1945, the *Journal of Clinical Psychology* is devoted to research, assessment, and practice. The journal includes articles on professional issues; single case research; brief reports (including dissertations in brief); notes from the field; and news. Papers focus on psychopathology, psychodiagnostics, the psychotherapeutic process, psychotherapy effectiveness, psychological assessment and treatment matching, clinical outcomes, clinical health psychology, and behavioral medicine. From time to time, the journal publishes "Special Sections," featuring articles related to a single theme. Recent issues have addressed: the influence of family stability on self-control and adjustment; the relationship of self-reported and acute stress to smoking in emerging adult smokers; role reversal and psychosocial adjustment among emerging adults when mother is mentally ill; the impact of shame on the therapeutic alliance and intimate relationships; complex trauma in children and adolescents; clinical decision-making in the treatment of complex PTSD and substance misuse; roles of identity formation and moral identity in college student mental health, health-risk behaviors, and psychological well-being; assessing depression in rural communities; and poverty and mental health practice. This is an important journal for institutions with clinical psychology programs.

4521. *Journal of Cognitive Neuroscience (Online).* [ISSN: 1530-8898] 1989. m. USD 1007. Ed(s): Mark D'Esposito. M I T Press, 55 Hayward St, Cambridge, MA 02142; journals-cs@mit.edu; http://mitpress.mit.edu. Adv. Sample. *Aud.:* Ac.

This is an MIT Press journal published with the Cognitive Neuroscience Institute. The journal seeks to promote communication among researchers in the mind sciences, including neuroscience, neuropsychology, cognitive psychology, neurobiology, linguistics, computer science, and philosophy. Articles selected for publication investigate brain behavior interaction and provide descriptions of brain function and underlying brain events. Recent issues have looked at: spatial frequency tuning reveals interactions between the dorsal and ventral visual systems; how contextual processing of abstract concepts reveals neural representations of nonlinguistic semantic content; how implicit and explicit second-language training recruits common neural mechanisms for syntactic processing; building blocks of visual working memory with respect to objects or Boolean maps; how the biology of linguistic expression impacts neural correlates for spatial language; dopamine D2–receptor modulation of human response-inhibition and error awareness; the representation of audiovisual regularities in the human brain; and neurocognitive buffers of adolescent risk-taking in the context of meaningful family relationships. Students and researchers in neuroscience, cognition, and neuropsychology will want access to this title through their libraries.

4522. *Journal of Comparative Psychology.* Supersedes in part (in 1983): *Journal of Comparative and Physiological Psychology;* Which was formerly (until 1947): *Journal of Comparative Psychology;* Which was formed by the merger of (1917-1921): *Psychobiology;* (1911-1921): *Journal of Animal Behavior.* [ISSN: 0735-7036] 1921. q. USD 384 (Individuals, USD 107). Ed(s): Dr. Gordon M Burghardt. American Psychological Association, 750 First St, NE, Washington, DC 20002; journals@apa.org; http://www.apa.org. Illus., index, adv. Sample. Refereed. Circ: 700. Vol. ends: Feb. Microform: PQC. Reprint: PSC. *Indexed:* A01, A22, AbAn, C45, FR, IndVet, P02, PsycInfo. *Aud.:* Ac.

This American Psychological Association journal publishes comparative research studies on the behavior, cognition, social relationships, and perception of diverse species. Articles may reflect original empirical or theoretical research and be descriptive or experimental. Studies conducted both in the field and in captivity are included. The journal covers several topics, such as behavior genetics, behavioral rhythms, communication, comparative cognition, the behavioral biology of conservation and animal welfare, development, endocrine–behavior interactions, evolutionary psychology, methodology, phylogenetic comparisons, orientation and navigation, sensory and perceptual processes, social behavior, and social cognition. Recent issues have more specifically addressed: turtle vocalizations as the first evidence of portthatching parental care in chelonians; extinction of food-reinforced instrumental behavior in Japanese quail; salmon fishing by bears and the dawn of cooperative predation; effects of overtraining on extinction in newts; choice behavior in pigeons, college students, and preschool children in the Monty Hall dilemma; how wild female African elephants exhibit personality traits of leadership and social integration; inferential reasoning by exclusion in *Homo sapiens* children; characteristics of serial-order learning in common marmosets; outcome-based observational learning in human infants; how imitation, pretend play, and childhood may be essential elements in the evolution of human culture; and explaining both selectivity and fidelity in children's copying behavior with respect to social learning. Libraries that support experimental research should have this title.

4523. *Journal of Consulting and Clinical Psychology.* Formerly (until 1968): *Journal of Consulting Psychology.* [ISSN: 0022-006X] 1937. bi-m. USD 907 (Individuals, USD 280). Ed(s): Arthur M Nezu. American Psychological Association, 750 First St, NE, Washington, DC 20002; journals@apa.org; http://www.apa.org. Illus., index, adv. Sample. Refereed. Circ: 2900. Vol. ends: Jan. Microform: PMC; PQC. Reprint: PSC. *Indexed:* A01, A22, ASSIA, AbAn, Chicano, ERIC, ExcerpMed, FR, MLA-IB, P02, PsycInfo, SWR&A. *Aud.:* Ac, Sa.

This journal, from the American Psychological Association, publishes original research that deals with clinical diagnosis, treatment, and prevention issues. Its primary audience is the community of clinical practitioners who treat humans with mental illness, clinical dysfunction, and behavioral disorders. Articles concern a variety of populations, including medical patients, ethnic groups, and persons with serious mental illness, regardless of place in the human lifespan. Studies of personality assessment; cross-cultural, gender, or sexual orientation issues; and psychosocial issues of health behaviors are covered. The journal publishes case studies, empirical research, and theoretical manuscripts that investigate change or the effectiveness of treatments. Topics covered include epidemiology; the use of psychological services; health-care economics for behavioral disorders; and critical analyses and meta-analyses of treatment approaches. Recent issues have addressed: cultural integration for health research and intervention with respect to religiousness/spirituality, cardiovascular disease, and cancer; treating depressed and anxious smokers in smoking cessation programs; mechanisms in psychosocial interventions for adults living with cancer; the effect of a significant other on client change talk in motivational interviewing; telephone-based physical-activity counseling for major depression in people with multiple sclerosis; the effect of mindfulness-based therapy on symptoms of anxiety and depression in adult cancer patients and survivors; behavioral economic predictors of overweight children's weight loss; the influences of delay and severity of intellectual disability on event memory in children; and maternal depressive symptoms as a predictor of alcohol-use onset and heavy episodic drinking in youths. This is a journal for clinicians and the libraries that support their practice and training.

4524. *Journal of Counseling Psychology.* [ISSN: 0022-0167] 1954. q. USD 415 (Individuals, USD 145). Ed(s): Dr. Brent S Mallinckrodt. American Psychological Association, 750 First St, NE, Washington, DC 20002; journals@apa.org; http://www.apa.org. Illus., index, adv. Sample. Refereed. Circ: 4800. Vol. ends: Dec. Microform: PQC. Reprint: PSC. *Indexed:* A01, A22, ABIn, ASSIA, B01, BRI, CBRI, Chicano, ERIC, FR, HEA, P02, PsycInfo, SWR&A. *Aud.:* Ac, Sa.

This American Psychological Association journal publishes empirical research and theoretical works in the areas of counseling, career development, diversity issues, assessment and measures, and other professional issues. Articles primarily concern clients who have problems with living or who are experiencing developmental crises, rather than those who exhibit severe disturbance, unless the research concerns healthier aspects of the disturbance. Both quantitative and qualitative methods are included. Research that represents an extension of previous studies or that investigates implications for public policy or social action may also appear in the journal. Recent issues have addressed: racial microaggressions and daily well-being among Asian Americans; disentangling the link between "perceiving a calling" and "living a calling"; examining a model of life satisfaction among unemployed adults; a meta-analysis of acculturation/culturation and mental health; reciprocal influence of alliance to the group and outcome in day treatment for eating disorders; differing trajectories among Asian and Latino youth with respect to cultural identity and mental health; experiences of Christian clients in secular

psychotherapy; perfectionism, procrastination, and psychological distress; and the development of the Coping Flexibility Scale. Libraries that support clinical, pastoral, marriage and family, and career counseling programs will want this journal.

4525. *Journal of Cross-Cultural Psychology.* [ISSN: 0022-0221] 1970. 8x/yr. USD 1344. Ed(s): David R Matsumoto. Sage Publications, Inc., 2455 Teller Rd, Thousand Oaks, CA 91320; info@sagepub.com; http://www.sagepub.com. Illus., index, adv. Sample. Refereed. Microform: PQC. Reprint: PSC. *Indexed:* A22, ABS&EES, ASSIA, BAS, BRI, Chicano, E01, IBSS, MLA-IB, P02, P61, PsycInfo, SSA. *Bk. rev.:* 0-5, 300-500 words. *Aud.:* Ac, Sa.

This Sage online journal is published in association with the International Association for Cross-Cultural Psychology and the Center for Cross-Cultural Research, Department of Psychology, Western Washington University. The journal serves as an "interdisciplinary forum for psychologists, sociologists[,] and educators who study how cultural differences in developmental, social[,] and educational experiences affect individual behavior." Articles address a wide range of topics, such as individualism, self-enhancement, acculturation, family values, ethnic group comparisons, and gender differences and personality. Regular features include empirical and theoretical research, reviews, and book reviews. Special thematic issues appear occasionally. Recent issues have looked at: how the experience of extreme hardship predicts religious meaning-making; a cross-cultural comparison of shared parenting, parental effort, and life-history strategy; similarities and differences in implicit personality concepts across ethnocultural groups in South Africa; changes in pronoun use in American books and the rise of individualism from 1960 to 2008; the relationship between life satisfaction and emotional experience in 21 European countries; a study of 70 nations with respect to consanguinity as a major predictor of levels of democracy; machismo and marital satisfaction in Mexican-American couples; self-enhancement and self-protection strategies in China; and how culture, age, and manual dominance affect directionality in drawing side view objects. Libraries that support programs in cross-cultural studies, as well as general psychology and behavioral and social sciences, will want this title.

Journal of Educational Psychology. See Education/Educational Psychology and Measurement, Special Education, Counseling section.

4526. *Journal of Experimental Child Psychology.* [ISSN: 0022-0965] 1964. 12x/yr. EUR 2406. Ed(s): D F Bjorklund, B P Ackerman. Academic Press, 3251 Riverport Ln, Maryland Heights, MO 63043; JournalCustomerService-usa@elsevier.com; http://www.elsevierdirect.com/brochures/academicpress/index.html. Illus., index, adv. Refereed. Vol. ends: Dec. *Indexed:* A01, A22, E01, ERIC, FR, MLA-IB, P02, PsycInfo, RILM. *Aud.:* Ac, Sa.

This is an Academic Press journal, on the Elsevier Science Direct platform, with a focus on child development. It publishes empirical, theoretical, methodological, and analytical studies on child development that span infancy through adolescence and including cognitive, social, and physical aspects. Features include a "Reflections" forum in which scholars discuss issues raised in an initial paper, and a brief notes section. Special-topic supplements appear periodically. Recent research addresses the influence of averageness on children's judgments of facial attractiveness; gender influences on children's selective trust of adult testimony; anger and selective attention to reward and punishment in children; working memory and social functioning in children; young children's fast mapping and generalization of words, facts, and pictograms; investigation of color constancy in 4.5-month-old infants under a strict control of luminance contrast for individual participants; word comprehension and production asymmetries in children and adults; the role of relational memory in thinking about the future early in life; the approximate number system and its relation to early math achievement as evidenced from preschool years; and the development of social learning in interactive and observational contexts. This is an important title for libraries that support students and researchers in psychology and education.

4527. *Journal of Experimental Psychology: Animal Behavior Processes.* Supersedes in part (in 1975): *Journal of Experimental Psychology.* [ISSN: 0097-7403] 1916. q. USD 388 (Individuals, USD 107). Ed(s): Anthony Dickinson. American Psychological Association, 750 First St,

NE, Washington, DC 20002; journals@apa.org; http://www.apa.org. Illus., index, adv. Refereed. Circ: 600. Vol. ends: Dec. Microform: PQC. Reprint: PSC. *Indexed:* A01, A22, AnBeAb, C45, FR, IndVet, P02, PsycInfo. *Aud.:* Ac, Sa.

This American Psychological Association journal publishes articles based on empirical, theoretical, or experimental studies. Any aspect of animal behavior, including associative, non-associative, cognitive, perceptual, and motivational processes, may be the subject of investigation. Relevant specialized reviews and brief communications on novel experiments are also published. Recent issues have looked at: perceptual learning with complex visual stimuli based on location, rather than content, of discriminating features; a further assessment of the Hall-Rodriguez theory of latent inhibition; contextual control of attentional allocation in human discrimination learning; the influence of excitatory and inhibitory landmarks on choice in environments with a distinctive shape; two ways to deepen extinction and the difference between them; how pigeons make errors as a result of interval timing in a visual, but not visual-spatial, midsession reversal task; changes in attention to relevant and irrelevant stimuli during spatial learning; and human sensitivity to the magnitude and probability of a continuous causal relation in a videogame. This journal is particularly appropriate for libraries that support researchers in experimental psychology.

4528. *Journal of Experimental Psychology: Applied.* [ISSN: 1076-898X] 1995. q. USD 388 (Individuals, USD 107). Ed(s): Wendy A Rogers. American Psychological Association, 750 First St, NE, Washington, DC 20002; journals@apa.org; http://www.apa.org. Adv. Sample. Refereed. Circ: 900. Vol. ends: Feb. Reprint: PSC. *Indexed:* A22, ASSIA, B01, ERIC, ErgAb, P61, PsycInfo, SSA. *Aud.:* Ac, Sa.

This APA journal publishes empirical investigations that bridge practically-oriented problems and psychological theory. It also publishes relevant review articles and research studies that concern "models of cognitive processing or behavior in applied situations, including laboratory and field settings." Topics covered may include "applications of perception, attention, decision making, reasoning, information processing, learning, and performance." Studies may have been conducted in industrial, academic, or consumer-oriented settings. Recent issues have looked at: how feedback reduces the metacognitive benefits of tests; implicit approach-avoidance associations for craved-food cues; the influence of affective states on the process of lie detection; extracting the truth from conflicting eyewitness reports; how the effectiveness of test-enhanced learning depends on trait test-anxiety and working-memory capacity; an eye-movement analysis of the spatial contiguity effect in multimedia learning; specificity of postural sway to the demands of a precision task at sea; how humor breaks resistance to influence; and how caffeine enhances real-world language processing as evidenced from a proofreading task. Libraries that support programs in experimental research will find this title important.

4529. *Journal of Experimental Psychology: General.* Supersedes in part (in 1975): *Journal of Experimental Psychology.* [ISSN: 0096-3445] 1916. q. USD 388 (Individuals, USD 107). Ed(s): Dr. Fernanda Ferreira. American Psychological Association, 750 First St, NE, Washington, DC 20002; journals@apa.org; http://www.apa.org. Illus., adv. Sample. Refereed. Circ: 1200. Vol. ends: Feb. Microform: PQC. Reprint: PSC. *Indexed:* A01, A22, ERIC, ErgAb, FR, P02, PsycInfo. *Aud.:* Ac.

This APA journal publishes empirical research that bridges two or more communities of psychology. Such issues may concern combinations of work in applied, animal, learning and memory, and human performance experimental research. The journal also publishes articles on other psychological topics, including social processes, developmental processes, psychopathology, neuroscience, or computational modeling. Recent issues have contained articles concerning: listening to the heart and when false somatic feedback shapes moral behavior; a subjective time-perception account of sexual-cue effects on impatience; the role of first impression in operant learning; how eye movements to audiovisual scenes reveal expectations of a just world; the modular nature of trustworthiness detection; sex differences in the spatial representation of number; the physical burdens of secrecy; fluid movement and creativity; the interplay between nonsymbolic number and its continuous visual properties; stability and change in markets of core numerical competencies; how eye movements reveal sustained implicit processing of others' mental states; the

gendering of numbers; the sensorimotor contributions to implicit memory, familiarity, and recollection; and the effect of mental progression on mood. Appropriate for libraries that support experimental psychology programs.

4530. *Journal of Experimental Psychology: Human Perception and Performance.* Supersedes in part (in 1975): *Journal of Experimental Psychology.* [ISSN: 0096-1523] 1916. bi-m. USD 1148 (Individuals, USD 392). Ed(s): Dr. Glyn W Humphreys. American Psychological Association, 750 First St, NE, Washington, DC 20002; journals@apa.org; http://www.apa.org. Adv. Refereed. Circ: 900. Vol. ends: Jan. Microform: PQC. Reprint: PSC. *Indexed:* A01, A22, ASSIA, B01, ERIC, ErgAb, FR, MLA-IB, P02, PsycInfo, RILM. *Aud.:* Ac, Sa.

This APA journal publishes primarily empirical research on perception, language processing, human action, and related cognitive processes and covers all sensory modalities and motor systems. The journal seeks to increase theoretical understanding of human perception and performance and encourages studies with a neuroscientific perspective. Articles concerning machine and animal studies that reflect on human capabilities may also appear. Nonempirical reports, including theoretical notes, commentary, or criticism on pertinent topics are also published. Recent issues have addressed: matching voice and face identity from static images; collective enumeration; divergent effects of cognitive load on quiet stance and task-linked postural coordination; the hue of shapes; rapid acquisition but slow extinction of an attentional bias in space; variants of independence in the perception of facial identity and expression; how eye movements reveal how task difficulty moulds visual search; the contributions of facial shape, skin texture, and viewing angle in signals of personality and health; an archer's perceived form scales the "hit-ableness" of archery targets; rapid activation of motor responses by illusory contours; and the gradual, practice-dependent, and hierarchically organized top-down control of attention. Researchers concerned with human physical performance will want to find this title in their library's collection.

4531. *Journal of Experimental Psychology: Learning, Memory, and Cognition.* Formerly (until Jan.1982): *Journal of Experimental Psychology: Human Learning and Memory;* Which supersedes in part (in 1975): *Journal of Experimental Psychology.* [ISSN: 0278-7393] 1916. bi-m. USD 1148 (Individuals, USD 392). Ed(s): Randi C Martin. American Psychological Association, 750 First St, NE, Washington, DC 20002; journals@apa.org; http://www.apa.org. Adv. Sample. Refereed. Circ: 1100. Vol. ends: Dec. Microform: PQC. Reprint: PSC. *Indexed:* A01, A22, B01, ERIC, ErgAb, FR, MLA-IB, P02, PsycInfo, RILM. *Aud.:* Ac, Sa.

The *Journal of Experimental Psychology: Learning, Memory, and Cognition* publishes empirical and experimental research on cognition, learning, memory, imagery, concept formation, problem solving, decision making, thinking, reading, and language processing. Specialized reviews and other non-empirical theoretical notes, commentary, or criticism on pertinent topics are also included. Recent issues have included articles on: experimentally evoking nonbelieved memories for childhood events; effects of emotional valence and arousal on recollective and nonrecollective recall; the role of rehearsal on the output order of immediate free recall of short and long lists; the processing advantage and disadvantage for homophones in lexical decision tasks; visual statistical learning based on the perceptual and semantic information of objects; the auditory memory-distortion for spoken prose; and the effects of prior knowledge on incidental category learning. Researchers interested in cognition, organizational psychology, or educational psychology will want to find this title in their library's collection.

4532. *Journal of Experimental Social Psychology.* [ISSN: 0022-1031] 1965. bi-m. EUR 1730. Ed(s): J Cooper. Academic Press, 3251 Riverport Ln, Maryland Heights, MO 63043; JournalCustomerService-usa@elsevier.com; http://www.elsevierdirect.com/brochures/academicpress/index.html. Illus., adv. Sample. Refereed. Vol. ends: Nov. *Indexed:* A01, A22, E01, FR, IBSS, P02, PsycInfo. *Aud.:* Ac.

This Academic Press peer-reviewed, scholarly journal, on the Elsevier platform, publishes empirical research, literature reviews, theoretical analyses, and methodological reports in the field of social behavior. The journal seeks to advance understanding of important social psychological phenomena. Recent issues have looked at: how follower belongingness and leader empathy influences leaders' adherence to procedural fairness rules; competence and warmth as a fundamental distinction in social rejection; asymmetries between victims' need for apologies and perpetrators' willingness to apologize; rumor clustering, consensus, and polarization with respect to dynamic social impact and self-organization of hearsay; the consequences of faking anger in negotiations; the insidious and ironic effects of positive stereotypes; evidence for group-based control and the power of "we"; the role of support-giving schemas in increasing state self-compassion; the ironic effect of financial incentive on empathic accuracy; ingroup rejection and attributions to discrimination; implicit open-mindedness and evidence for and limits on stereotype malleability; and long-term reduction in implicit race bias with a prejudice habit-breaking intervention. Behavioral scientists, sociologists, psychologists, and other social scientists will want access to this title.

4533. The Journal of General Psychology: experimental, physiological, and comparative psychology. [ISSN: 0022-1309] 1927. q. GBP 225 (print & online eds.). Routledge, 325 Chestnut St, Ste 800, Philadelphia, PA 19106; customerservice@taylorandfrancis.com; http://www.tandfonline.com. Adv. Refereed. Reprint: PSC. *Indexed:* A01, A06, A22, ABIn, B01, BRI, Chicano, E01, ErgAb, FR, MLA-IB, P02, P61, PsycInfo, SSA, SWR&A.

The Journal of General Psychology, on the Taylor & Francis platform, is devoted to experimental, physiological, and comparative psychology. Articles emphasize functional relationships, involve a series of integrated studies, or present new theoretical insights. Human and animal studies, mathematical and other theoretical investigations, and technological reports are included. Recent issues have addressed: hemispheric differences in the processing of words learned early versus later in childhood; relations among children's coping strategies and anxiety; the effect of a final exam on long-term retention; the relationship between basic psychological needs satisfaction and aggression in late adolescents; recognition memory for faces and scenes; the relationship between language use and depression and illuminating the importance of self-regulation, self-rumination, and the need for absolute truth; the influence of person traits on lawyer selection among British adults; and the examination of personality characteristics in a Turkish sample and the development of Basic Personality Traits Inventory.

4534. Journal of Humanistic Psychology. [ISSN: 0022-1678] 1961. q. USD 938. Ed(s): Shawn Rubin, Kirk J Schneider. Sage Publications, Inc., 2455 Teller Rd, Thousand Oaks, CA 91320; info@sagepub.com; http://www.sagepub.com. Illus., index, adv. Sample. Refereed. Vol. ends: Fall. Microform: PQC. Reprint: PSC. *Indexed:* A01, A22, ABS&EES, ASSIA, BRI, E01, P02, PsycInfo. *Aud.:* Ac, Sa.

This online Sage publication is the official journal of the Association of Humanistic Psychology. The journal provides an interdisciplinary forum for addressing diverse issues in the areas of personal growth, social problems, interpersonal relations, and philosophical thinking. Founded in 1961 by Abraham Maslow and Anthony Sutich, it maintains close connection with the Saybrook Institute. Topics include authenticity, community, consciousness, creativity, existentialism, holistic health, politics, identity, peace and mediation, self-actualization, self-transcendence, and spiritual development. Features include scholarly articles, experiential reports, analyses, theoretical papers, personal essays, poetry, narratives, news, editorial commentary, and research that emphasizes human scientific methods. The work of notable thinkers such as Rollo May, Carl Rogers, Brewster Smith, Ken Wilber, and James Bugental have appeared in its pages. Special supplements appear periodically with in-depth coverage of topics. Recent issues have covered: "venturing uncertainty" as a means to personal growth and authenticity; female veterans, identity negotiation, and reintegration into society; dialogue bridging personal, community, and social transformation; natural disasters and existential concerns—a test of Tillich's theory of existential anxiety; the enduring allure of synchronicity; peak-experiences among Americans in midlife; a reflection on Montaigne's marvelous invention of writing essays; transcribing and transcending the ego, and the phenomenology of chronic social comparison; the relationship of hardiness and other variables to college performance; and humanistic psychology's impact and accomplishments. Students and researchers of philosophy, religion, psychology, and other social sciences will want access to this title.

Journal of Learning Disabilities. See Education/Educational Psychology and Measurement, Special Education, Counseling section.

4535. Journal of Mathematical Psychology. [ISSN: 0022-2496] 1964. bi-m. EUR 2020. Ed(s): J Myung. Academic Press, 3251 Riverport Ln, Maryland Heights, MO 63043; JournalCustomerService-usa@elsevier.com; http://www.elsevierdirect.com/brochures/academicpress/index.html. Illus., index, adv. Sample. Refereed. Vol. ends: Dec. *Indexed:* A01, A22, CCMJ, CompR, E01, MSN, MathR, PsycInfo, RILM. *Bk. rev.:* 1-5, 100-3,000 words. *Aud.:* Ac.

This Elsevier title is a publication of the Society for Mathematical Psychology. The journal publishes empirical and theoretical articles, monographs and reviews, notes and commentaries, and book reviews in the field of mathematical psychology. Topics covered include fundamental measurement and psychological process models; models for sensation and perception, and learning and memory; neural modeling and networks; neuropsychological theories; psycholinguistics; animal behavior; psychometric theory; problem solving, judgment, and decision making; and motivation. Recent issues have addressed: using logarithmic derivative functions for assessing the risky weighting function for binary gambles; modeling geometric-optical illusions with a variational approach; information-sharing and aggregation models for interacting minds; connections among decisional field-theory models of cognition; a neural computation model for decision-making times; statistical measures for workload capacity analysis; intractability and approximation of optimization theories of cognition; quantum-like generalization of the Bayesian updating scheme for objective and subjective mental uncertainties; a lexicographic semiorder polytope and probabilistic representations of choice; and a probabilistic study of the psychology of inferring conditionals from disjunctions. Libraries that support quantitative and scientific psychology researchers and students will want this title.

4536. The Journal of Mind and Behavior. [ISSN: 0271-0137] 1980. q. USD 158 (Individuals, USD 46; Students, USD 27). Ed(s): Dr. Raymond C Russ. Institute of Mind & Behavior, Village Sta, PO Box 522, New York, NY 10014. Illus., index, adv. Sample. Refereed. *Indexed:* A01, A22, ExcerpMed, MLA-IB, P61, PsycInfo, SSA, SWR&A. *Bk. rev.:* 0-4, 300-2,000 words. *Aud.:* Ac.

This publication of the Institute of Mind and Behavior at the University of Maine is not yet available online; however, its tables of contents are. The journal is interdisciplinary in that it focuses on the relationship of mind and behavior. Contents reflect the publishing of scholarly work that is experimental, theoretical, empirical, or methodological. Subjects of interest include relationships among psychology, philosophy, sociology, and the scientific method; the mind/body problem in social sciences, medicine, and physical science; the philosophical impact of a mind/body epistemology upon psychology and its theories of consciousness; ethical studies of cognition, self-awareness, and higher functions of consciousness in nonhumans; and historical perspectives in psychology. While it seeks experimental research, the journal also recognizes "the need to propagate ideas and speculations as well as the need to form empirical situations for testing them." With its emphasis on theory, this is a core journal for libraries with advanced psychology and social-science programs and research collections. Recent issues have addressed: the equilibration of the self and the sense of sublation—spirituality in thought, music, and meditation; a theory of hemispheric specialization based on cortical columns; a qualitative perspective on deja vu; counterfactuals, belief, and inquiry by thought experiment; and physiological sources, biological functions, and psychological implications of dreaming.

4537. Journal of Occupational and Organizational Psychology. Former titles (until 1992): *Journal of Occupational Psychology;* (until 1975): *Occupational Psychology;* (until 1938): *Human Factors;* (until 1932): *National Institute of Industrial Psychology. Journal.* [ISSN: 0963-1798] 1922. q. GBP 299 (print & online eds.). Ed(s): Jan de Jonge. John Wiley & Sons Ltd., The Atrium, Southern Gate, Chichester, PO19 8SQ, United Kingdom; customer@wiley.com; http://www.wiley.com. Illus., index, adv. Sample. Refereed. Vol. ends: Dec. Reprint: PSC. *Indexed:* A01, A22, ABIn, ASSIA, B01, B02, BRI, E01, ErgAb, FR, H24, IBSS, P02, PsycInfo, SSA. *Bk. rev.:* 3, 500-1,000 words. *Aud.:* Ac, Sa.

This publication of the British Psychological Society, on the Wiley platform, provides empirical and theoretical articles concerning people and organizations at work. Papers address issues in industrial, organizational, vocational, and personnel psychology, and consider behavioral concerns in industrial relations, ergonomics, and industrial sociology. Recent issues have looked at: the underpinnings of a positive climate for diversity; how ruminative thinking exacerbates the negative effects of workplace violence; affective reactions to a pay-system reform and their impact on employee behavior; understanding the mediating role of toxic emotional experiences in the relationship between negative emotions and adverse outcomes; perceived value congruence and team innovation; investigating the effect of collective organizational commitment on unit-level performance and absence; how being in one's chosen job determines pre-training attitudes and training outcomes; the contradictory influence of perception of organizational politics on organizational citizenship behavior; and age-related differences in work motivation. Libraries that support studies in organizational psychology, industrial relations, and business will want this title.

4538. *Journal of Organizational Behavior.* Formerly (until 1988): *Journal of Occupational Behaviour.* [ISSN: 0894-3796] 1980. 8x/yr. GBP 1386. Ed(s): Neal M Ashkanasy, Katherine Wilkinson. John Wiley & Sons Ltd., The Atrium, Southern Gate, Chichester, PO19 8SQ, United Kingdom; customer@wiley.com; http://www.wiley.com. Illus., adv. Sample. Refereed. Microform: PQC. Reprint: PSC. *Indexed:* A22, ABIn, ASSIA, B01, B02, BRI, ErgAb, PsycInfo, RiskAb. *Aud.:* Ac, Sa.

The *Journal of Organizational Behavior,* a Wiley publication, publishes empirical reports and theoretical reviews of research in organizational behavior and about the workplace. Topics include all levels of individual, group, and organization, as well as across levels. Articles may discuss personality, motivation, commitment, career behavior, leadership, politics, goal-setting, change management, decision making, turnover, or absenteeism. Recent issues have addressed: employee silence motives; pay satisfaction and work-family conflict across time; the role of positive affectivity in team effectiveness during crises; the effects of leadership consideration and structure on employee perceptions of justice and counterproductive work behavior; the dark side of organizational citizenship behavior; an empirical analysis of surface acting in intra-organizational relationships; trust in supervisor and individual performance; increasing the effectiveness of workplace interventions in creating pro-environmental behavior change; and high-performer turnover and firm performance and the moderating role of human capital investment and firm reputation. This journal is important for clinical psychologists, human resources managers, and researchers in occupational psychology.

4539. *Journal of Pediatric Psychology.* Formerly: *Pediatric Psychology.* [ISSN: 0146-8693] 1976. 10x/yr. EUR 1119. Ed(s): Grayson N Holmbeck. Oxford University Press, Great Clarendon St, Oxford, OX2 6DP, United Kingdom; enquiry@oup.co.uk; http://www.oxfordjournals.org/. Illus., index, adv. Sample. Refereed. Circ: 2000. Microform: PQC. Reprint: PSC. *Indexed:* A22, E01, FR, PsycInfo, RiskAb, SWR&A. *Bk. rev.:* 5-8, 150-3,000 words. *Aud.:* Ac, Sa.

This Oxford title is the official journal of the Society of Pediatric Psychology, Division 54, of the American Psychological Association. The interdisciplinary journal publishes theoretical papers, empirical research, and professional-practice articles concerning pediatric psychology. Features include analytical reviews, brief reports, and case studies. Articles focus on preventive health and treatment issues, as well as the training of pediatric psychologists. Recent issues have looked at: parenting stress in the Infant Aphasia Treatment Study; trauma reactions in mothers and fathers after their infant's cardiac surgery; body mass index (BMI) differences and psychosocial adjustment among early adolescent girls; the relationship between camp attendance and self-perceptions in children with chronic health conditions; impulse control, diabetes-specific self-efficacy, and diabetes management among emerging adults with type 1 diabetes; how videogame distraction reduces behavioral distress in a preschool-aged child undergoing repeated burn-dressing changes; how stigmatization predicts psychological adjustment and quality of life in children and adolescents with a facial difference; and abdominal pain and health-related quality of life in pediatric inflammatory bowel disease. Clinical child psychologists, medical and health-care professionals who work with children, and researchers pursuing studies related to children's medicine and psychology will want access to this title.

4540. *Journal of Personality.* Formerly (until 1945): *Character and Personality.* [ISSN: 0022-3506] 1932. bi-m. GBP 1056. Ed(s): Howard Tennen. Wiley-Blackwell Publishing, Inc., 111 River St, Hoboken, NJ 07030; info@wiley.com; http://onlinelibrary.wiley.com/. Illus., index. Sample. Refereed. Vol. ends: Dec. Reprint: PSC. *Indexed:* A01, A22, ASSIA, E01, FR, IBSS, MLA-IB, P02, P61, PsycInfo, RiskAb, SSA. *Aud.:* Ac, Sa.

This Wiley online title publishes scientific research on the many aspects and issues in the field of personality. Coverage addresses behavior dynamics; personality development; and cognitive, affective, and interpersonal differences. Empirical, theoretical, and methodological approaches are included. Recent issues have looked at: the experience of authenticity; the interface between empathy and social dominance orientation; how curious people are viewed and how they behave in social situations; age differences in attachment from early adulthood to old age; anxious and angry rejection sensitivity, social withdrawal, and retribution in high- and low-ambiguous situations; a five-factor model framework for understanding childhood personality disorder antecedents; interpersonal development, stability, and change in early adulthood; personality and relationship quality during the transition from high school to early adulthood; and ideological passion, identity threat, and extremism. Academic libraries that support study and research in personality will want this title.

4541. *Journal of Personality and Social Psychology.* Supersedes in part (in 1965): *Journal of Abnormal and Social Psychology;* Which was formerly (until 1925): *The Journal of Abnormal Psychology and Social Psychology;* (until 1921): *The Journal of Abnormal Psychology.* [ISSN: 0022-3514] 1965. m. USD 1696 (Individuals, USD 548). Ed(s): Dr. Charles M Judd, Laura A King. American Psychological Association, 750 First St, NE, Washington, DC 20002; journals@apa.org; http://www.apa.org. Illus., index, adv. Sample. Refereed. Circ: 2300. Vol. ends: Dec. Microform: PQC. Reprint: PSC. *Indexed:* A01, A22, ABIn, ABS&EES, ASSIA, AbAn, B01, B02, BAS, Chicano, FR, HEA, IBSS, MLA-IB, P02, P61, PsycInfo, RILM, SSA, SWR&A. *Aud.:* Ac, Sa.

This APA online journal publishes empirical, specialized theoretical, methodological, and review articles in all areas of personality and social psychology. It has three sections: "Attitudes and Social Cognition," "Interpersonal Relations and Group Processes," and "Personality Processes and Individual Differences." "Attitudes and Social Cognition" focuses on cognition and social behavior and covers such topics as attitudes, attributions, stereotypes, person memory, self-regulation, the origins and consequences of moods and emotions, the effect of cognition on persuasion, communication, prejudice, social development, and cultural trends. "Interpersonal Relations and Group Processes" addresses psychological interaction and covers such topics as interpersonal attraction, communication, emotion, relationship development, social influence, group decision-making and task performance, intergroup relations, aggression, and pro-social behavior. "Personality Processes and Individual Differences" covers all aspects of personality psychology. Topics may include behavior, emotions, coping, health, motivation, personality structure, personality development, personality assessment, interplay of culture and personality, and personality in everyday life. Recent issues have looked at: promoting cooperative behavior through imagined group discussion; a theoretical framework for personality traits related to intellectual achievements; trust and biased memory of transgressions in romantic relationships; the relationship between age, acceptance, and negative affect; the diverging effects of clean versus dirty money on attitudes, values, and interpersonal behavior; the dynamic interplay between perceived true self-knowledge and decision satisfaction; rising income and the subjective well-being of nations; and an examination of the latent structure of gender. This journal is basic to any psychology collection.

4542. *Journal of Personality Assessment.* Former titles (until 1971): *Journal of Projective Techniques and Personality Assessment;* (until 1963): *Journal of Projective Techniques;* (until 1950): *Rorschach Research Exchange and Journal of Projective Techniques;* (until 1947): *Rorschach Research Exchange.* [ISSN: 0022-3891] 1936. bi-m. GBP 508 (print & online eds.). Ed(s): Gregory J Meyer. Routledge, 325 Chestnut St, Ste 800, Philadelphia, PA 19106;

customerservice@taylorandfrancis.com; http://www.tandfonline.com. Illus., index, adv. Sample. Refereed. Vol. ends: Winter. Microform: PQC. Reprint: PSC. *Indexed:* A01, A22, ASSIA, B01, Chicano, E01, FR, H24, P02, PsycInfo, RiskAb, SD. *Aud.:* Ac, Sa.

This Taylor & Francis title is the official publication of the Society for Personality Assessment. The journal publishes articles "dealing with the development, evaluation, refinement, and application of personality assessment methods." Papers may concern the empirical, theoretical, instructional, or professional aspects of using tests, data, or an applied clinical assessment process. The journal seeks to advance the use of personality-assessment methods in clinical, counseling, forensic, and health environments. Articles involve both normal and abnormal subjects. Areas where research is minimal are especially sought by this journal, such as "(a) systematic reviews or meta-analyses that summarize a body of evidence, (b) the effective integration of nomothetic empirical findings with the idiographic requirements of practice in which the assessor reasons through test and extra-test information to make individualized judgments and provide assessment feedback, and (c) the practical value of the clinical assessment process on the individuals receiving services and/or those who refer them for evaluation." Recent issues have addressed: verbal expressive testing with older adults after 25 years; using cognitive interviewing for the semantic enhancement of multilingual versions of personality questionnaires; a social-relations analysis of the interpersonal perception of pathological narcissism; the effects of exposure to Internet information about Rorschach on selected comprehensive system variables; gender differences on the MMPI across American and Korean adult and adolescent normative samples; examining the Interpersonal Reactivity Index (IRI) among early and late adolescents and their mothers; measuring positive and negative affect and physiological hyperarousal among Serbian youth; the IIS-32—a brief Inventory of Interpersonal Strengths; and treatment of a woman diagnosed with metastatic cancer and attachment trauma. In addition to researchers and students taking advanced courses in assessment, those who will find this material useful include professionals in clinical, counseling, forensic, community, cross-cultural, education, and health psychology settings.

4543. *The Journal of Psychology: interdisciplinary and applied.* [ISSN: 0022-3980] 1935. bi-m. GBP 280 (print & online eds.). Routledge, 325 Chestnut St, Ste 800, Philadelphia, PA 19106; customerservice@taylorandfrancis.com; http://www.tandfonline.com. Adv. Refereed. Reprint: PSC. *Indexed:* A01, A06, A22, ABIn, ASSIA, AbAn, B01, Chicano, E01, ErgAb, HEA, IBSS, MLA-IB, P02, P61, PsycInfo, RILM, RiskAb, SD, SSA, SWR&A. *Aud.:* Ac.

The Journal of Psychology is an interdisciplinary journal that publishes empirical research and theoretical articles in all aspects of applied areas of psychology. It includes interdisciplinary research that integrates psychology and other fields (e.g., psychology and law, psychology and consumer behavior, psychology and religion). In addition to publishing manuscripts that have a clearly applied focus, the journal publishes interdisciplinary research that integrates literatures from psychology with other related fields (e.g., occupational health, consumer behavior, law, religion, communication, and political science). The journal encourages critical analysis of all issues. Recent issues have addressed: the effects of material and experiential discretionary purchases on consumer happiness; the role of self-compassion in physical and psychological well-being; achievement goals and emotions; exploring the relationship between identity status development and alcohol consumption among Italian adolescents; a team motivation approach to collective autonomy and absenteeism within work teams; negative affectivity and educational attainment as predictors of newlyweds' problem-solving communication and marital quality; processes through which adolescents believe romantic relationships influence friendship quality; and how company norms affect which traits are preferred in job candidates and may cause employment discrimination.

4544. *Journal of School Psychology.* [ISSN: 0022-4405] 1963. bi-m. EUR 590. Ed(s): R Floyd. Pergamon, The Blvd, Langford Ln, E Park, Kidlington, OX5 1GB, United Kingdom; JournalsCustomerServiceEMEA@elsevier.com; http://www.elsevier.com. Illus., adv. Sample. Refereed. Microform: PQC. *Indexed:* A01, A22, ASSIA, Chicano, ERIC, PsycInfo, SWR&A. *Aud.:* Ac, Sa.

Articles in this Elsevier online journal report on research and practice related to school psychology as both "scientific and an applied specialty." This journal averages seven articles per issue, and its abstracts and tables of contents are available on the publisher's web site. Recent issues have addressed: the upward spiral of adolescents' positive school experiences and happiness; a study of whether preschool special education services make a difference in kindergarten reading and mathematics skills; exit examinations, peer academic climate, and adolescents' developmental outcomes; children with co-occurring academic and behavior problems in the first grade and the distal outcomes in 12th grade; peer and self-reports of victimization and bullying; the role of parenting styles and teacher interactional styles in children's reading and spelling development; academic achievement in African American boys in relation to academic achievement in African American girls; a multilevel investigation of measurement invariance and gender match in teacher-student relationship; and preschool children's development in classic Montessori, supplemental Montessori, and conventional programs. Along with such titles as *School Psychology Review*, this title is desirable for libraries that support programs in school psychology and related courses in education.

Journal of Sex Research. See Sociology and Social Work/General section.

4545. *The Journal of Social Psychology.* Incorporates (1985-2006): *Genetic, Social, and General Psychology Monographs;* Which was formerly (1926-1984): *Genetic Psychology Monographs.* [ISSN: 0022-4545] 1929. bi-m. GBP 258 (print & online eds.). Psychology Press, 325 Chestnut St, Ste 800, Philadelphia, PA 19106; subscriptions@tandf.co.uk; http://www.tandf.co.uk/journals/. Illus. Refereed. Microform: PQC. Reprint: PSC. *Indexed:* A01, A22, ABIn, ABS&EES, ASSIA, AbAn, B01, BAS, BRI, C42, Chicano, E01, FR, HEA, IBSS, MLA-IB, P02, P61, PsycInfo, RILM, SD, SSA, SWR&A. *Aud.:* Ac, Sa.

This Taylor & Francis online journal was founded in 1929 by John Dewey and Carl Murchison. It publishes empirical research in basic and applied social psychology. The core areas of social and organizational psychology, attribution theory, attitudes, social influence, consumer behavior, decision making, groups and teams, stereotypes and discrimination, interpersonal attraction, pro-social behavior, aggression, organizational behavior, leadership, and cross-cultural studies are all reflected in the journal's selection of articles. Recent articles have covered: gender and gender-role differences in self- and other-estimates of multiple intelligences; effects of playing videogames on perceptions of one's humanity; customer emotion regulation in service interactions; portrayals of gender and ethnicity in television advertisements; partner discrepancies in distressed marriages; an investigation of abusive supervision, vicarious abusive supervision, and their joint impacts; cultural stereotypes and personal beliefs about individuals with dwarfism; the impact of the 2008 Mumbai attacks on British and Indian students and the role of revenge, denial, and terrorism distress in restoring just world beliefs; how the voluntariness of apologies affects actual and hypothetical victims' perceptions of the offender; how ego depletion increases risk-taking; and attitudes toward cosmetic surgery patients. An important journal for academic behavioral and social science collections.

4546. *Journal of Youth and Adolescence: a multidisciplinary research publication.* [ISSN: 0047-2891] 1972. m. EUR 1967 (print & online eds.). Ed(s): Roger J R Levesque. Springer New York LLC, 233 Spring St, New York, NY 10013; service-ny@springer.com; http://www.springer.com/. Illus., adv. Refereed. Vol. ends: Dec. Microform: PQC. Reprint: PSC. *Indexed:* A01, A22, ABIn, Agr, BRI, CJPI, Chicano, E01, ERIC, FR, HEA, P02, P61, PsycInfo, RILM, RiskAb, SSA. *Aud.:* Ac, Sa.

This Springer multidisciplinary journal publishes empirical, experimental, and theoretical research and review articles in the fields of psychology, sociology, psychiatry, criminology, and education. The journal focuses especially on papers that address social policies or have policy implications with respect to society's response to youth and adolescence. Recent issues have addressed: how parents' participation in work-based anti-poverty program can enhance their children's future orientation; how the age-crime curve in adolescence and early adulthood is not due to age differences in economic status; associations of neighborhood and family factors with trajectories of physical and social aggression during adolescence; social influences on cyberbullying behaviors among middle and high school students; individual and family predictors of the perpetration of dating violence and victimization in late adolescence; motives for using Facebook, patterns of Facebook activities, and late adolescents' social adjustment to college; adolescent neglect, juvenile delinquency, and the risk of recidivism; thriving in context—findings from the 4-H study of positive youth development; sexual attraction, sexual identity, and psychosocial well-being in a national sample of young women during emerging adulthood; and religiosity profiles of American youth in relation to substance use, violence, and delinquency. Clinical psychologists, social science researchers, educators, and health-care and legal professionals will have interest in this journal.

4547. *Law and Human Behavior.* [ISSN: 0147-7307] 1977. bi-m. EUR 1183 (print & online eds.). Ed(s): Brain L Cutler. Springer New York LLC, 233 Spring St, New York, NY 10013; service-ny@springer.com; http://www.springer.com/. Illus., adv. Refereed. Vol. ends: Dec. Microform: PQC. Reprint: PSC. *Indexed:* A22, ABIn, B01, BRI, C&ISA, CJPI, CLI, CerAb, E01, L14, P61, PsycInfo, RiskAb, SSA. *Aud.:* Ac, Sa.

This APA title, formerly on the Springer platform, is the official journal of the American Psychological Association's Division 41, the American Psychology Law Society. The journal publishes multidisciplinary articles on issues relating to human behavior and the law, the legal system, or legal process. Papers include empirical studies, theoretical research, and reviews. A forum for debate is also featured. Recent issues have addressed: concurrent and predictive validity of psychopathy in a batterers' intervention sample; the influence of multiple interviews on the verbal markets of children's deception; actuarial risk assessment in sexually motivated intimate-partner violence; the reliability of forensic evaluations of legal sanity; the effects of negotiated and delegated apologies in settlement negotiation; myths and realities of female-perpetrated terrorism; how firm, fair, and caring officer–offender relationships protect against supervision failure; an examination of risk factors and sex offense recidivism with respect to failure-to-register laws and public safety; how online solicitation offenders are different from child pornography offenders and lower-risk-contact sexual offenders; and assessing children's competency to take the oath in court and the influence of question type on children's accuracy. Professionals and researchers in criminal justice, law, psychology, sociology, psychiatry, political science, education, communication, and other related social science areas will want access to this title through their libraries.

4548. *Media Psychology.* [ISSN: 1521-3269] 1999. q. GBP 548 (print & online eds.). Ed(s): Rick Busselle, Silvia Knobloch-Westerwick. Routledge, 325 Chestnut St, Ste 800, Philadelphia, PA 19106; customerservice@taylorandfrancis.com; http://www.tandfonline.com. Adv. Sample. Refereed. Reprint: PSC. *Indexed:* A01, A22, ArtHuCI, E01, F01, PsycInfo. *Aud.:* Ac, Sa.

This interdisciplinary, scholarly journal, on the Taylor & Francis platform, publishes research concerning the intersection of psychology and communication media. Empirical studies, theoretical papers, state-of-the-art reviews, and meta-analyses appear regularly in its contents. The effects, uses, and processes of media as they relate to psychology are primary topics. Various forms of communication, including mass media, television, telecommunications, computer networks, personal media, and multi-media are represented in the journal's articles. Recent issues have looked at: effects of Facebook self-presentation on implicit self-esteem and cognitive task performance; videogames, immersion, and cognitive aggression and whether the controller matters; gaming addiction, gaming engagement, and psychological health complaints among Norwegian adolescents; the influence of moral intuitions on decisions in videogames; narrative persuasion, transportation, and the role of need for cognition in online viewing of fantastical films; pessimism and anxiety and the effects of "tween" sitcoms on expectations and feeling about peer relationships in school; gender disparity in videogame usage; and the role of emotional involvement and trait absorption in the formation of spatial presence. Libraries that support research and studies in communication and media, psychology, education, human development, and related social sciences will want this title.

4549. *Memory and Cognition.* Supersedes in part (in 1973): *Psychonomic Science.* [ISSN: 0090-502X] 1964. 8x/yr. EUR 440 (print & online eds.). Ed(s): James Nairne. Springer New York LLC, 233 Spring St, New York,

NY 10013; journals-ny@springer.com; http://www.springer.com. Illus., adv. Refereed. Circ: 1700. Microform: PQC. Reprint: PSC. *Indexed:* A01, A22, ABIn, B01, E01, FR, MLA-IB, P02, PsycInfo, RILM. *Aud.:* Ac.

Memory & Cognition is a publication of the Psychonomic Society, published on the Springer platform. Its coverage is broad, including topics such as human memory, learning, conceptual processes, decision making, skilled performance, computer simulation, information processing, mathematical psychology, developmental psychology, and experimental social psychology. Recent issues have covered research on: how divided attention selectively impairs memory for self-relevant information; the effects of working-memory training in young and old adults; concreteness and word production; discrepancy-plus-search processes in prospective memory retrieval; the effects of sleep on problem solving; cognitive abilities and the production of figurative language; how peripheral vision benefits spatial learning by guiding eye movements; the role of verbal memory in regressions during reading; and how appearance-based interferences bias source memory. Psychology research libraries will want to add this title.

The Milbank Quarterly. See Public Health section.

4550. *Neuropsychology.* [ISSN: 0894-4105] 1987. bi-m. USD 415 (Individuals, USD 167). Ed(s): Stephen M Rao. American Psychological Association, 750 First St, NE, Washington, DC 20002; journals@apa.org; http://www.apa.org. Illus., adv. Refereed. Circ: 3100. Vol. ends: Dec. Reprint: PSC. *Indexed:* A22, AgeL, ExcerpMed, FR, MLA-IB, PsycInfo. *Aud.:* Ac, Sa.

This APA journal publishes research on the brain and human cognitive, emotional, and behavioral functions. Research studies are generally empirical and represent basic research or an integration of basic and applied research. Experimental, cognitive, and behavior studies are included, as well as articles that focus on improving the practice of neuropsychology and increase understanding of neuropsychological functions. This highly rated journal is a primary one in neuropsychology. Recent issues have addressed: working memory in Parkinson's disease; recognition of famous names related to predicting cognitive decline in healthy elders; neuropsychological tests predict progression in Alzheimer's disease in Hispanics; body-mass index and neurocognitive functioning across the adult lifespan; motor laterality as an indicator of speech laterality; using testing to improve learning after severe traumatic brain injury; metamemory in children with autism—exploring "feeling-of-knowing" in episodic and semantic memory; how high-level, but not low-level, motion perception is impaired in patients with schizophrenia; processing speed and executive abilities in children with phenylketonuria; and sleep quality and cognitive function in healthy old age and the moderating role of subclinical depression.

4551. *Organizational Behavior and Human Decision Processes.* Formerly (until 1985): *Organizational Behavior and Human Performance.* [ISSN: 0749-5978] 1966. bi-m. EUR 2882. Ed(s): John M Schaubroeck. Academic Press, 3251 Riverport Ln, Maryland Heights, MO 63043; JournalCustomerService-usa@elsevier.com; http://www.elsevierdirect.com/brochures/academicpress/index.html. Illus., index, adv. Sample. Refereed. *Indexed:* A01, A22, ABIn, ASSIA, B01, E01, ERIC, ErgAb, FR, IBSS, PsycInfo. *Aud.:* Ac, Sa.

This Elsevier title publishes research in organizational psychology and behavior, and human cognition, judgment, and decision making. Features include empirical research, theoretical papers, literature reviews, and methodological articles. Among the topics found in its contents are cognition, perception, attitudes, emotion, well-being, motivation, choice, and performance. Individuals and variations of social groups are the subjects of these studies. Recent issues have looked at: the impact of learning and performance goals on process and performance; anchoring in sequential judgments; the psychological costs of knowledge specialization in groups, and how unique expertise leaves you out of the loop; the role of moral identity in the aftermath of dishonesty; how past decisions affect future choices; the influence of motivated reasoning on saving and spending decisions; encouraging employees to report unethical conduct internally; social dilemmas between individuals and groups; ostracism and prosocial behavior; self–other decision-making and loss aversion; and the effects of kin density within family-owned businesses. Libraries that support programs in organizational and industrial psychology, education, and related social sciences will want to collect this title.

4552. *Perceptual and Motor Skills.* Former titles (until 1952): *Perceptual and Motor Skills Research Exchange; Motor Skills Research Exchange.* [ISSN: 0031-5125] 1949. bi-m. USD 580 domestic; USD 595 foreign; USD 630 combined subscription domestic (print & online eds.). Ed(s): S A Isbell, Carol H Ammons. Ammons Scientific Ltd., PO Box 9229, Missoula, MT 59807; ejournalservices@ammonsscientific.com; http://www.ammonsscientific.com. Illus., index. Sample. Refereed. Circ: 1800. *Indexed:* A01, A22, AbAn, AgeL, BRI, Chicano, ErgAb, HEA, MLA-IB, P02, PsycInfo, RILM, SD. *Bk. rev.:* 2-6, 120 words. *Aud.:* Ac, Sa.

This Ammons Scientific journal is a publication of the Department of Psychology, University of Louisville, although its editorial board is internationally based. The journal publishes experimental or theoretical articles, sometimes controversial, concerning perception or motor skills; methodological papers; and special reviews. Topics covered may relate to anthropology, physical education, physical therapy, orthopedics, sports psychology, consumer perception, music therapy, physics, aesthetics, education, or statistics. Recent issues have looked at: motor and cognitive performance of overweight preschool children; quiet eye-gaze behavior of expert, and near-expert, baseball plate umpires; vertical force and wrist deviation angle in a sample of elderly people using walkers; epileptic-like symptoms and stress conditions in adolescents; assessing separation anxiety in Italian youth using the Separation Anxiety Assessment Scale; sex-related effects in strength training during adolescence; cognitive strategies for goal-keeper responding to soccer penalty kick; and effect of a physical fitness program on physical self-concept and physical fitness elements in primary school students. Libraries that support research and studies in psychology, education, physical education, and physical therapy will want to include this title in their collections.

4553. *Personality and Social Psychology Bulletin.* Formerly (until 1975): *American Psychological Association. Division of Personality and Social Psychology. Proceedings.* [ISSN: 0146-1672] 19??. m. USD 1780. Ed(s): Shinobu Kitayama. Sage Publications, Inc., 2455 Teller Rd, Thousand Oaks, CA 91320; info@sagepub.com; http://www.sagepub.com. Illus. Refereed. Microform: PQC. Reprint: PSC. *Indexed:* A22, ASSIA, Chicano, E01, P02, P61, PsycInfo, RILM, RiskAb, SSA. *Aud.:* Ac, Sa.

This Sage publication is the official publication of the Society for Personality and Social Psychology. The bulletin provides an international forum for research in all areas of personality and social psychology. Articles reflect many schools of thought and new developments in the field. Based primarily on empirical research, papers on a variety of topics appear, including communication, gender and age stereotypes, interpersonal relationships, group psychology, prejudice, and self-consciousness. Special theme issues are periodically published. Themes have included motivational determinants of self-evaluation; autobiographical narratives; publication trends in the field; meta-analysis in personality and social psychology; and principles of psychology. Recent issues have addressed: how mastering goals promotes challenge and success despite social identity threat; concepts of happiness across time and cultures; exclusion as self-protection and the function of subtypes for ingroup members; optimism following a tornado disaster; the situational affordance of anger and shame in the United States and Japan; how self-affirmation underlies Facebook use; psychological and sexual costs of income comparison in marriage; perceived power moderates the effect of stereotype threat on women's math performance; the self-dehumanizing consequences of social ostracism; the differential value of perspective-taking versus empathy in competitive interactions; and cultural variation in the effectiveness of solicited and unsolicited social support. Libraries that support behavioral and social sciences, education, and industrial psychology will want to have this title.

4554. *Professional Psychology: Research and Practice.* Formerly (until 1983): *Professional Psychology.* [ISSN: 0735-7028] 1969. bi-m. USD 480 (Individuals, USD 145). Ed(s): Dr. Michael C Roberts. American Psychological Association, 750 First St, NE, Washington, DC 20002;

journals@apa.org; http://www.apa.org. Illus., index, adv. Sample. Refereed. Circ: 5000. Vol. ends: Jan. Microform: PQC. Reprint: PSC. *Indexed:* A01, A22, ASSIA, Chicano, P02, PsycInfo, RILM. *Aud.:* Ac, Sa.

This APA journal publishes theoretical and empirical articles for the clinician on applied psychology. Scientific and evidence-based articles on assessment, treatment, and practice implications are stressed. The journal includes literature reviews, case studies, standards-based practice articles, public policy research, and general research of interest to clinical psychologists. Current topics include health psychology, community psychology, psychology of women, clinical neuropsychology, family psychology, psychology of ethnicity and culture, and forensic psychology. Brief reports also appear. Recent issues have looked at: the impact of continuing education mandates on participation in continuing professional development activities; psychological factors in college students' attitudes toward seeking professional psychological help; perceived organizational support, motivation, and engagement among police officers; neuroscience applications to practice in child and adolescent psychology; predictors of career satisfaction among practicing psychologists; crisis intervention with children of illegal migrant workers threatened with deportation; and multicultural office design. This is a core journal for clinical psychologists in practice, research, and training, and for the libraries that support them.

4555. *PsycCRITIQUES (Online).* Formerly (until 2005): *Contemporary Psychology: A P A Review of Books (Print).* [ISSN: 1554-0138] 1956. w. Free to members. American Psychological Association, 750 First St, NE, Washington, DC 20002; journals@apa.org; http://www.apa.org. Illus., index, adv. Reprint: PSC. *Indexed:* A22, BRI, CBRI, Chicano. *Bk. rev.:* 50-60, 100-1,500 words. *Aud.:* Ga, Ac, Sa.

This American Psychological Association product is more than a journal. It is a searchable electronic database of book reviews in psychology that was formerly published in print as the journal *Contemporary Psychology: APA Review of Books.* In its new electronic format, *PsycCritiques* provides access to current reviews and back files from 1956 forward. Each weekly release delivers approximately 18,220 reviews of current psychological books. Also included are reviews of popular films and videos from a psychological perspective, comparative reviews, and occasional retrospective reviews. Faculty, librarians, students, and practitioners will benefit by having easy access to this database, in order to identify literature for research, course studies, and collection development, and to stay up-to-date with the latest psychological thinking.

4556. *Psychological Assessment.* Supersedes in part (in 1989): *Journal of Consulting and Clinical Psychology;* Which was formerly (1937-1968): *Journal of Consulting Psychology.* [ISSN: 1040-3590] 1989. q. USD 459 (Individuals, USD 167). Ed(s): Cecil R Reynolds. American Psychological Association, 750 First St, NE, Washington, DC 20002; journals@apa.org; http://www.apa.org. Illus., adv. Sample. Refereed. Circ: 3000. Vol. ends: Feb. Reprint: PSC. *Indexed:* A01, A22, AbAn, ERIC, ExcerpMed, FR, P02, PsycInfo, SWR&A. *Aud.:* Ac, Sa.

This APA online journal publishes empirical research on measurement and evaluation relevant to the practice of clinical psychology. Articles concern such topics as assessment processes and methods; decision-making models; personality; social psychology; biological psychology; validation; application of assessment instruments; assessment of personality; psychopathological symptoms; cognitive and neuropsychological processes; and interpersonal behavior. The journal focuses on diagnosis, evaluation, and effective interventions. Case studies, reviews, and theoretical articles relevant to assessment and clinical settings are included. Recent issues have looked at: mastery of negative affect and a hierarchical model of emotional self-efficacy beliefs; internal structure of the Reflective Functioning Scale; measuring beliefs about suffering and development of the Views of Suffering Scale; evaluating the properties of the Evidence-Based Practice Attitude Scale in health care; how proportionate responses to life events influence clinicians' judgments of psychological abnormality; convergent validity of and bias in maternal reports of child emotion; and The Positivity Scale. This journal is one to make available to clinical psychology researchers, students, and practitioners.

4557. *Psychological Bulletin.* [ISSN: 0033-2909] 1904. bi-m. USD 765 (Individuals, USD 280). Ed(s): Stephen P Hinshaw. American Psychological Association, 750 First St, NE, Washington, DC 20002;

journals@apa.org; http://www.apa.org. Illus., index, adv. Sample. Refereed. Circ: 2200. Vol. ends: Dec. Microform: PMC; PQC. Reprint: PSC. *Indexed:* A01, A22, ABIn, ASSIA, AbAn, B01, B02, ERIC, ErgAb, FR, H24, IBSS, MLA-IB, P02, PsycInfo, SWR&A. *Aud.:* Ac, Sa.

This APA journal publishes integrative reviews, research syntheses, and pertinent expository articles that focus on empirical studies in scientific psychology. Articles summarize conclusions of past research studies that address similar hypotheses. Primary research is included for illustrative purposes. Research syntheses assess the current state of knowledge on a topic, the strengths and weakness of past research, unresolved issues, and directions for future research. Integrative reviews reveal connections between areas of research. Broad topics include the interface of psychological sciences and society and evaluations of programs in applied psychology. Recent issues have provided articles on: distinguishing *how* from *why* the mind wanders; children's recognition of disgust in others; whether evolutionary principles can explain patterns of family violence; how major depressive disorder is associated with broad impairments on neuropsychological measures of executive function; auditory, tactile, and audiotactile information processing following visual deprivation; whether low self-esteem predicts depression and anxiety; sleep, cognition, and behavioral problems in school-age children; whether religious belief promotes prosociality or is not prosocial at all; and gender differences in self-conscious emotional experience. See *Psychological Methods* for methodological articles and *Psychological Review* for original theoretical articles.

4558. *Psychological Inquiry: an international journal of peer commentary and review.* [ISSN: 1047-840X] 1990. q. GBP 566 (print & online eds.). Ed(s): Ronnie Janoff-Bulman. Psychology Press, 325 Chestnut St, Ste 800, Philadelphia, PA 19106; orders@taylorandfrancis.com; http://www.psypress.com. Illus., adv. Sample. Refereed. Vol. ends: No. 4. Reprint: PSC. *Indexed:* A01, A22, B01, E01, P02, P61, PsycInfo, SSA. *Aud.:* Ac, Sa.

This international journal provides a forum for discussion in the fields of social psychology and personality. Articles discuss theoretical and meta-theoretical concerns. Issues are theme-oriented, containing a primary article followed by peer commentaries and the author's response. Recent articles have included cultural neuroscience; finding meaning in the theories of sense-making; scientific utopia—opening scientific communication; how mind perception is the essence of morality; how social projection can solve social dilemmas; reintegrating the study of accuracy into social cognition research; understanding well-being and optimal functioning with the Multilevel Personal in Context Model; and intuition and "thin slice" judgments. Libraries that support psychology programs will want this title for patrons who perform in-depth topical study.

4559. *Psychological Review.* [ISSN: 0033-295X] 1894. q. USD 629 (Individuals, USD 179). Ed(s): John R Anderson. American Psychological Association, 750 First St, NE, Washington, DC 20002; journals@apa.org; http://www.apa.org. Illus., index, adv. Sample. Refereed. Circ: 2100. Vol. ends: Dec. Microform: PMC; PQC. Reprint: PSC. *Indexed:* A01, A22, AbAn, B02, ERIC, ErgAb, FR, IBSS, MLA-IB, P02, P61, PsycInfo, RILM, SSA, SWR&A. *Aud.:* Ac, Sa.

The focus of this APA online journal is scientific psychology. Its articles present both significant contributions that advance theory and systematic evaluations of alternative theories. Literature reviews, articles regarding methodology and research design, and empirical reports are not included. Theoretical notes and commentary on scientific psychology are part of the contents. Notes may be discussions of earlier articles. Comments may apply to theoretical models in a given domain, may be critiques of alternative theories, or may be meta-theoretical commentary on theory testing. Recent issues have looked at: the co-evolution of knowledge and event memory; how rational temporal predictions can underlie apparent failures to delay gratification; why most dieters fail but some succeed, looking at a goal-conflict model of eating behavior; separating the contributions and unwanted cues in psychophysical studies; when group membership gets personal and a theory of identity fusion; models of verbal working-memory capacity; social class, solipsism, and contextualism—how the rich are different from the poor; and behavioral variability of choices versus structural inconsistency of preferences. This is a basic resource for academic psychology collections.

4560. *Psychological Science.* [ISSN: 0956-7976] 1990. 27x/yr. USD 5538. Ed(s): Robert V Kail. Sage Publications, Inc., 2455 Teller Rd, Thousand Oaks, CA 91320; info@sagepub.com; http://www.sagepub.com. Illus., adv. Sample. Refereed. Reprint: PSC. *Indexed:* A01, A22, B01, BRI, E01, ErgAb, HEA, IBSS, P02, P61, PsycInfo, RILM, SD, SSA, SWR&A. *Aud.:* Ac, Sa.

This Sage journal is the official journal of the Association for Psychological Science. It publishes empirical, theoretical, and applied psychology articles, papers concerning psychological issues related to government and public affairs, and reports that summarize recent research developments. Subject areas include brain and behavior, clinical science, cognition, learning and memory, social psychology, and developmental psychology. Recent issues have addressed: how lip movements affect infants' audiovisual speech perception; how attention is spontaneously biased toward regularities; how increasing recognition of happiness in ambiguous facial expressions reduces anger and aggressive behavior; detection of audiovisual speech correspondences without visual awareness; sleep consolidation of interfering auditory memories in starlings; the interpersonal legacy of a positive family climate in adolescence; learning, memory, and synesthesia; how the experience of power and authenticity enhances subjective well-being; and how responses to resource scarcity, as when the economy falters, depends on childhood environments. Libraries that support general and advanced psychology programs will benefit from having this title.

4561. *Psychology & Health.* [ISSN: 0887-0446] 1987. m. GBP 1687 (print & online eds.). Ed(s): Mark Conner, Daryl O'Connor. Routledge, 4 Park Sq, Milton Park, Abingdon, OX14 4RN, United Kingdom; subscriptions@tandf.co.uk; http://www.tandfonline.com. Illus., adv. Sample. Refereed. Reprint: PSC. *Indexed:* A01, A22, C45, E01, PsycInfo, RRTA, SD. *Bk. rev.:* 0-3, 300. *Aud.:* Ac, Sa.

This Taylor & Francis international journal is a publication of the European Health Psychology Society. The journal focuses on the psychological approaches to health and illness. Subjects covered include psychological aspects of physical illness; treatment and recovery; psychosocial factors of physical illnesses; health attitudes; health behavior; preventive health; and health-care systems. The journal publishes empirical research; papers that present new psychological approaches and interventions; reviews; and short reports. Recent issues have looked at: a qualitative study of people with cancer and intimate partners; closing the intention-behavior gap for sunscreen use and sun-protection behaviors; patient and spouse illness beliefs and quality of life in prostate cancer patients; illness perception of migraineurs from the general population; religious involvement and physical and emotional functioning among African Americans—the mediating role of religious support; the effects of (un)employment on young couples' health and life satisfaction; how, when, and why young women use nutrition information on food labels; and the effect of implementation intentions on physical activity among obese older adults. Libraries that serve researchers and students of public health, psychology, and medicine will want to have this title.

4562. *Psychology of Women Quarterly.* [ISSN: 0361-6843] 1976. q. USD 453. Ed(s): Janice D Yoder. Sage Publications, Inc., 2455 Teller Rd, Thousand Oaks, CA 91320; info@sagepub.com; http://www.sagepub.com. Illus., index, adv. Sample. Refereed. Vol. ends: Dec. Microform: PQC. Reprint: PSC. *Indexed:* A01, A22, ABS&EES, ASSIA, BRI, C45, Chicano, E01, ERIC, FemPer, HEA, IBSS, P02, P61, PsycInfo, RILM, RRTA, SSA, SWR&A, WSA. *Bk. rev.:* 4-10, 500-1,000 words. *Aud.:* Ga, Ac, Sa.

This Wiley journal publishes empirical, qualitative, and theoretical articles related to the psychology of women and gender. It also features critical reviews and invited book reviews. A wide range of topics have been covered, including career choice and preparation; mental health and well-being; education; lifespan role development; management and performance variables; violence, harassment, and abuse; sexuality and sexual orientation; social and cognitive processes; ethnic, minority, and cross-cultural issues; and therapeutic concerns. Recent issues have addressed: women's relationship to feminism and the effects of generation and feminist self-labeling; associations between femininity and women's political behavior during midlife; rape, war, and the socialization of masculinity and why our refusal to give up war ensures that rape cannot be eradicated; motivation and physical activity behaviors among older women;

how presenting thin media models affects women's choice of diet or normal snacks; sanctified sexism and religious beliefs and the gender harassment of academic women; gender differences in pay expectations and the roles of job intention and self view; attitudes toward cosmetic surgery in middle-aged women in connection with body image, aging anxiety, and the media; and gender differences in self-reported posttraumatic growth. Libraries that support research and study in psychology, women's and gender studies, and related social sciences will benefit from having this title.

4563. Psychology Today. Incorporates (in 1969): *Careers Today.* [ISSN: 0033-3107] 1967. bi-m. USD 15.97 domestic; USD 23.97 Canada; USD 27.97 elsewhere. Ed(s): Kaja Perina. Sussex Publishers Inc., 115 E 23rd St, 9th Fl, New York, NY 10010. Illus., adv. Sample. Microform: NBI. *Indexed:* A01, A22, ABIn, B01, BRI, C37, CBCARef, CBRI, Chicano, MASUSE, MLA-IB, P02. *Aud.:* Hs, Ga, Ac.

This is a popular psychology magazine that focuses on articles in the areas of relationships, personal growth, work, health, nutrition, parenting, learning, the brain, and social psychology. Recent issues have looked at: successful communication and active empathy; how chimerism—the role of cells from siblings, children, former lovers that have stayed in one's body—affects one's brain; adaptability after a tragic accident; smiles and facial expression in America; creativity and the negative influence of the fear of failure; lies and socially sanctioned ideas about sex; how a person's sense of what is right for him becomes clouded by what other people think is right; dangerous sleep disorders that include sleepwalking and night terrors; and how cooking has changed from being a trade to a form of creativity.

4564. Psychophysiology: an international journal. Formerly: *Psychophysiology Newsletter.* [ISSN: 0048-5772] 1964. bi-m. GBP 528. Ed(s): Dr. Robert F Simons. Wiley-Blackwell Publishing, Inc., 111 River St, Hoboken, NJ 07030; info@wiley.com; http://onlinelibrary.wiley.com/. Illus., index, adv. Sample. Refereed. Vol. ends: Nov. Microform: PQC. Reprint: PSC. *Indexed:* A01, A22, E01, ErgAb, FR, PsycInfo, RILM, SD. *Bk. rev.:* Number and length vary. *Aud.:* Ac, Sa.

This Wiley journal is an international publication of the Society for Psychophysiological Research. As the first journal in its field, it publishes research on the physiological and psychological aspects of brain and behavior. It features empirical, theoretical, and methodological papers, literature reviews, book reviews, brief reports, meeting announcements, and fellowship opportunities. Topics covered include psychiatry, psychology, cognitive science, cognitive and affective neuroscience, social science, health science, behavioral medicine, and biomedical engineering. Recent issues have looked at: separating mismatch negativity (MMN) response from auditory obligatory brain responses in school-aged children; modulated neural processing of Western harmony in fold musicians; how cardiac timing influences memory for words and is modulated by metacognition and interoceptive sensitivity; blood pressure and pain sensitivity in children and adolescents; an electrophysiological study of abstract and concrete word processing; how retrospective attention enhances visual working memory in the young but not the old; and sound-induced perturbations of the brain network in non-REM sleep and network oscillations in wake. Libraries that support researchers in psychophysiology, cognitive science and neuroscience, psychology, psychiatry, and related biological and social sciences will benefit by collecting this title.

Psychotherapy Networker. See Family section.

4565. School Psychology Review. Formerly (until 1980): *School Psychology Digest.* [ISSN: 0279-6015] 1972. q. USD 142. Ed(s): Matthew K Burns. National Association of School Psychologists, 4340 EW Hwy, Ste 402, Bethesda, MD 20814; publications@naspweb.org; http://www.nasponline.org. Illus., adv. Refereed. Vol. ends: No. 4. Microform: PQC. *Indexed:* A01, A22, ERIC, PsycInfo. *Aud.:* Ac, Sa.

This is the official journal of the National Association of School Psychologists. The journal publishes empirical, theoretical, and practice-related studies that apply scientific methods to school psychology. Recent issues have addressed: evaluating school impairment with adolescents using the classroom performance survey; preschoolers' mathematics skills and behavior; a comparison of computer-adaptive and curriculum-based measurement methods of assessment; the impact of context and word type on students' maze-task

accuracy; behavioral competence and academic functioning among early elementary children with externalizing problems; an evaluation of the technical adequacy of three methods for identifying specific learning disabilities based on cognitive discrepancies; and a meta-analysis of school-based bullying prevention programs' effects on intervention behavior in bystanders. Libraries that support programs in general psychology, clinical psychology, child psychology, and education will want to have this title.

4566. Sexual Abuse: a journal of research and treatment. Formerly (until 1995): *Annals of Sex Research.* [ISSN: 1079-0632] 1988. bi-m. USD 1099. Ed(s): Howard Barbaree. Sage Publications, Inc., 2455 Teller Rd, Thousand Oaks, CA 91320; info@sagepub.com; http://www.sagepub.com. Illus., adv. Refereed. *Indexed:* A22, CJPI, E01, P61, PsycInfo, RiskAb, SSA. *Aud.:* Ac, Sa.

This Sage journal is the official publication of the Association for the Treatment of Sexual Abusers. The journal publishes empirical, theoretical, and clinical research, scholarly reviews, and case studies on sexual abuse. With a focus strictly on the causes, consequences, and treatment aspects of sexual abuse, the articles provide significant data for both clinicians and academic researchers. Psychologists, psychiatrists, social workers, therapists, counselors, corrections officers, and allied professionals will benefit from access to this publication. Recent issues have focused on: the (f)utility of post-conviction polygraph testing; the influence of risk and psychopathy on the therapeutic climate in sex offender treatment; how to integrate the Good Lives Model into treatment programs for sexual offending; the psychological profiles of Internet, contact, and mixed Internet/contact sex offenders; life-course persistent offenders and the propensity to commit sexual assault; a test of two typologies of sexual homicide; predicting relapse for Catholic clergy sex offenders using the Static-99; the relationships of perpetrator and victim substance use to the sexual aggression of rapists and child molesters; failure to register as a predictor of sex-offense recidivism; and offender types and criminality dimensions in male juveniles convicted of sexual offenses. Libraries that serve programs in psychology, education, social work, psychiatry, law, and law enforcement will want to have this title.

4567. Women & Therapy: a feminist quarterly. Formerly: *Women - Counseling Therapy and Mental Health Services.* [ISSN: 0270-3149] 1982. q. GBP 794 (print & online eds.). Ed(s): Ellyn Kaschak. Routledge, 325 Chestnut St, Ste 800, Philadelphia, PA 19106; customerservice@taylorandfrancis.com; http://www.tandfonline.com. Illus., adv. Sample. Refereed. Circ: 433 Paid. Vol. ends: No. 4. Microform: PQC. Reprint: PSC. *Indexed:* A01, A22, ABS&EES, BRI, C42, E01, FemPer, GW, HEA, P02, P61, PsycInfo, SSA, SWR&A, WSA. *Bk. rev.:* 0-7, 900 words; signed. *Aud.:* Ac, Sa.

This Taylor & Francis title is a journal that focuses on women and the therapeutic experience. It publishes empirical, theoretical, clinical, and descriptive articles in multiple subject areas. Coverage includes issues that affect women in greater proportion than men; women's roles in society; the special needs of minorities, lesbians, and older and disabled women; the needs of feminist therapists; interventions; alternative treatments; gender differences; therapist attitudes; and the role of media influence. Recent issues have addressed: the healing power of a female bond; competing discourses for older women: agency/leadership vs. disengagement/retirement; representations of older women in popular culture; the older woman as sage and the satisfaction of mentoring; a comprehensive domestic violence intervention for Latinas; fostering a grassroots women's movement through feminist leadership on the Burma–India border; feminist therapy in Bulgaria; and men as allies in feminist pedagogy in the undergraduate psychology curriculum. Libraries that serve therapists; programs that train therapists and clinical psychologists; law and correctional programs; and researchers in women's studies and related social sciences will want to include this title in their collections.

■ PUBLIC HEALTH

Emily C. Bell, Research Librarian, Services for Academic Programs, Harvard College Libraries; emilybell@fas.harvard.edu

Introduction

Public health is the study and practice of health care for entire populations. According to the World Health Organization, the term "refers to all measures to prevent disease, improve health, and prolong life among the population as a whole. Its activities aim to provide conditions in which people can be healthy and focus on entire populations, not on individual patients or diseases."

The field of public health is inter- and multi-disciplinary. Within the medical sciences, fields such as epidemiology; health education and promotion; disease control and prevention; health policy; global health; and maternal and and child health are all part of public health. Law, government, anthropology, and economics have roles in public health as well.

Assessing journals in public health can be tricky. The Thompson/Reuters ISI Impact Factor, commonly used in the sciences, is applicable, but may not tell the whole story. Epidemiology and health policy publications such as the *American Journal of Epidemiology and Health Affairs* usually have high impact factors, because they're widely used in both clinical and public health medicine. The *Journal of Public Health Dentistry*, by comparison, has a much lower impact factor, but it is among the only oral health and hygiene journals that focus on public health. The *Hastings Center Report*, a bioethics journal, represents unique content applicable to a number of disciplines, while *Women's Health Issues*, a publication of George Washington University, is one of the few major journals to focus on women's health.

As is expected in medical publishing today, all the journals listed here have strong online presences. Videos, podcasts, and blogs are common. Most have some level of open-access content, and several are entirely open-access, in keeping with the goal of global health awareness. Many journals have content approved for continuing education credit, and most of those have electronic methods for the reporting of credit completion.

I have not included all the currently published journals applicable to public health; that list is far too long for a section like this. These are, however, carried by the major academic medical libraries, and OCLC reports relatively large holdings numbers. They are among the best in the field.

Basic Periodicals

American Journal of Epidemiology, American Journal of Preventive Medicine, American Journal of Public Health, Bulletin of the World Health Organization, Environmental Health Perspectives, Health Affairs, Medical Care, Milbank Quarterly.

Basic Abstracts and Indexes

CINAHL, MEDLINE.

4568. AIDS Education and Prevention: an interdisciplinary journal.
[ISSN: 0899-9546] 1989. bi-m. USD 545 (print & online eds.) Individuals, USD 95 (print & online eds.). Ed(s): Dr. Francisco S Sy. Guilford Publications, Inc., 72 Spring St, 4th Fl, New York, NY 10012; info@guilford.com; http://www.guilford.com. Adv. Refereed. Circ: 1000 Paid. *Indexed:* A01, A22, AbAn, C45, CJPI, Chicano, E01, ERIC, ExcerpMed, H24, IBSS, P61, PsycInfo, RiskAb, SSA, SWR&A. *Aud.:* Ga, Ac, Sa.

AIDS Education and Prevention presents current research and information on HIV/AIDS from public health, social, and policy perspectives. Articles address risk behavior, health programs and initiatives, and special concerns in specific populations. Supplementary issues provide in-depth exploration of selected topics. This title's interdisciplinary nature means that it belongs in both general academic and health sciences libraries. URL: www.guilford.com/pr/jnai.htm

4569. American Journal of Epidemiology. Formerly (until 1965): *American Journal of Hygiene.* [ISSN: 0002-9262] 1921. s-m. 2 vols./yr. Ed(s): Dr. Moyses Szklo. Oxford University Press, 2001 Evans Rd, Cary, NC 27513; http://www.oxfordjournals.org. Illus. Sample. Refereed. Reprint: PSC. *Indexed:* A01, A22, ABS&EES, AbAn, BAS, BRI, C&ISA, C45, Chicano, E01, ExcerpMed, H24, IndVet, RRTA, RiskAb. *Aud.:* Ac, Sa.

Published on behalf of the Johns Hopkins Bloomberg School of Public Health, in association with The Society for Epidemiologic Research. Issues contain empirical research findings, methodological developments in the field of epidemiological research, and opinion pieces. Recent articles (and subsequent discussion) include such topics as Ramdan prenatal fasting, arsenic exposure and type II diabetes among Southwestern American Indians, and bias in

socioeconomic health disparities. Supplements in recent years have included the abstracts of the North American Congress of Epidemiology, epidemic assistance by the CDC, and annual meetings of the Society for Epidemiologic Research. A one-year subscription includes the highly rated annual *Epidemiologic Reviews,* from the same publisher. URL: http://aje.oxfordjournals.org

4570. American Journal of Health Promotion. Incorporates (1997-2002): *The Art of Health Promotion.* [ISSN: 0890-1171] 1986. bi-m. USD 184 (Individuals, USD 139 (print & online eds.). Ed(s): Michael P O'Donnell, Josie Jay. American Journal of Health Promotion, PO Box 1254, Troy, MI 48099; contact@healthpromotionjournal.com. Illus., adv. Refereed. Vol. ends: No. 6. *Indexed:* A01, A22, ASSIA, AbAn, C45, H24, P61, PsycInfo, RRTA, SD, SSA. *Aud.:* Ac, Sa.

This title aims to address both the science and the art of health promotion, and each issue is divided accordingly. "The Science of Health Promotion" integrates research and practice. "The Art of Health Promotion" is designed to provide practical information to enhance and improve health-promotion programs. The journal aspires to provide a forum for the many diverse disciplines that contribute to health promotion. Articles are concerned with current issues in public health and issues are often centered around a common theme. URL: www.healthpromotionjournal.com/

4571. American Journal of Preventive Medicine. [ISSN: 0749-3797] 1984. 12x/yr. USD 975. Ed(s): Dr. K Patrick. Elsevier Inc., 360 Park Ave S, New York, NY 10010; usinfo-f@elsevier.com; http://www.elsevier.com. Illus., adv. Sample. Refereed. Circ: 3220 Paid. *Indexed:* A01, A22, ASSIA, AbAn, C45, Chicano, ExcerpMed, H24, IndVet, PsycInfo, RRTA, RiskAb, SSA. *Aud.:* Ac, Sa.

The official journal of the American College of Preventive Medicine and the Association of Prevention Teaching and Research, this journal publishes original research articles, reviews, current issues papers, commentary, and correspondence on all aspects of practice, education, policy, and research in preventive medicine and public health. It focuses on the areas of prevention research, teaching, practice, and policy with an emphasis on interventions for the prevention of chronic and acute disease and promotion of community health. While it's focused primarily on original research papers, the publication includes review articles and essays that discuss teaching preventive medicine. URL: www.journals.elsevier.com/american-journal-of-preventive-medicine/

4572. American Journal of Public Health. Supersedes in part (in 1971): *American Journal of Public Health and the Nation's Health;* Which was formed by the merger of (1921-1928): *Nation's Health;* (until 1919): *Interstate Medical Journal;* (until 1899): *Tristate Medical Journal and Practitioner;* Interstate Medical Journal Incorporated (1881-1907): *St. Louis Courier of Medicine;* Which was formerly (1879-1881): *Saint Louis Courier of Medicine and Collateral Sciences;* (1912-1928): *American Journal of Public Health;* Which was formerly (until 1912): *American Public Health Association. Journal;* (until 1911): *American Journal of Public Hygiene;* (until 1907): *American Journal of Public Hygiene and Journal of the Massachusetts Association of Boards of Health;* (until 1904): *Massachusetts Association of Boards of Health. Journal;* American Journal of Public Health Incorporated (1873-1912): *Public Health Papers and Reports.* [ISSN: 0090-0036] 1911. m. USD 356. Ed(s): Mary E Northridge. American Public Health Association, 800 I St, NW, Washington, DC 20001; comments@apha.org; http://www.apha.org. Illus., index, adv. Sample. Refereed. Circ: 28000. Vol. ends: Dec. Microform: PMC; PQC. *Indexed:* A01, A22, ABIn, ABS&EES, AbAn, AgeL, Agr, B01, BRI, C45, Chicano, ErgAb, FS&TA, H24, MCR, P02, PsycInfo, RILM, RRTA, RiskAb, S25, SD, SWR&A. *Bk. rev.:* 3, length varies. *Aud.:* Ga, Ac, Sa.

While not the oldest, the monthly communication of the American Public Health Association is one of the grandaddies of the public health journals. It publishes a wide range of scientific research in public health and posits itself as a forum for diverse viewpoints on major public-health issues and policies. In addition to original research articles, its many pages are typically divided into sections that deal with government and politics and their relationship to public health, topical debates in commentaries and editorials, and relevant historical subjects in public health. It includes an ad section and "job opportunities" section. As of June 1, 2013, only issues published between 1911 and June 1, 2004, are free to the public (previously, a greater portion of the archives was freely available). URL: http://ajph.aphapublications.org/

4573. Annual Review of Public Health. [ISSN: 0163-7525] 1980. a. USD 226 (print or online ed.). Ed(s): Samuel Gubins, Jonathan E Fielding. Annual Reviews, PO Box 10139, Palo Alto, CA 94303; service@annualreviews.org; http://www.annualreviews.org. Refereed. Microform: PQC. Reprint: PSC. Indexed: A01, A22, Agr, C45, ExcerpMed, FS&TA, IndVet, PsycInfo, RRTA. Aud.: Ac, Sa.

This annual volume is essentially a literature review of recent primary research. It purports to synthesize the scientific literature and present it so that professionals may easily stay up-to-date in their area of research. The reviews are written not only with an eye toward summarizing a topic, but also to eliminate errors of fact or perception and stimulate discussion that will lead to new research activity. Each volume contains a "symposium" of articles around a theme, such as health-care inequalities or the developmental origins of adult disease, as well as sections focusing on epidemiology and biostatistics; environmental and occupational health; public-health practice; social environment and behavior; and health services. With one of the highest Thompson/Reuters ISI five-year impact factors in its field, this is probably a must-have journal for any academic or medical library with a specific collection in public health. Its summary format also lends itself to smaller libraries that must limit their title inventory. URL: www.annualreviews.org/journal/publhealth

4574. B M C Public Health. [ISSN: 1471-2458] 2001. irreg. Free. Ed(s): Natalie Paftis. BioMed Central Ltd., 236 Gray's Inn Rd, London, WC1X 8HB, United Kingdom; info@biomedcentral.com; http://www.biomedcentral.com. Adv. Refereed. Indexed: A01, C45, FS&TA, H24, IndVet, RRTA, RiskAb. Aud.: Ac, Sa.

This is an open-access, peer-reviewed journal with articles on all aspects of epidemiology and public health. The journal proposes to publish "work deemed by peer reviewers to be a coherent and sound addition to scientific knowledge." There is special focus on the social determinants of health; the environmental, behavioral, and occupational correlates of health and disease; and the impact of health policies, practices, and community. Article types and topics include original research, case reports, databases, debates, software articles, study protocols, and technical advances. Recent issues covered disease and risk factors in such diverse locations as Canada, Sweden, Syria, Queensland, and Uganda. Online only. Includes data sets and pre-publication versions. URL: www.biomedcentral.com/bmcpublichealth

4575. Emerging Infectious Diseases (Online). [ISSN: 1080-6059] 1995. m. Free. Ed(s): D Peter Drotman. U.S. Department of Health and Human Services, Centers for Disease Control and Prevention, 1600 Clifton Rd, Atlanta, GA 30333; http://www.cdc.gov. Refereed. Bk. rev.: Number and length vary. Aud.: Ac, Sa.

Established to promote the recognition of new and reemerging infectious diseases around the world and improve the understanding of factors involved in disease emergence, prevention, and elimination. This journal aims to rapidly distribute and address the concerns of emerging infectious disease among and on behalf of the U.S. Centers for Disease Control and scientific researchers worldwide. Article types include reviews, research studies, policy and historical reviews, and updates on trends and research. This journal is appropriate for academic research libraries and health sciences libraries. There is a nice "background and goals" page at the web site, which may help selectors to understand the journal's focus and intentions. Open access. URL: www.cdc.gov/ncidod/EID/index.htm

4576. Environmental Health Perspectives. Incorporates (in 2003): E H P Toxicogenomics. [ISSN: 0091-6765] 1972. m. Ed(s): Hugh A Tilson, Rita B Hanson. U.S. Department of Health and Human Services, National Institute of Environmental Health Sciences, PO Box 12233, Research Triangle Park, NC 27709; http://ehp03.niehs.nih.gov/. Illus., adv. Refereed. Vol. ends: Dec (No. 12). Indexed: A01, A22, ABS&EES, AbAn, Agr, BRI, C45, ExcerpMed, FS&TA, H24, IndVet, RRTA, RiskAb, S25. Bk. rev.: Number and length vary. Aud.: Ac, Sa.

Another journal with a high five-year impact factor, this title serves as a forum for discussion of the interrelationships between the environment and human health by publishing high-quality peer-reviewed research and current, credible news of the field. EHP publishes from a wide range of scientific disciplines, and each issue devotes a section specifically to children's environmental health. The web publication is free and offers additional content in the form of podcasts and thematic "collections" that organize previously published content in searchable pdfs. Their "international programs" feature a Chinese edition; archives translated into Chinese, French, and Spanish; and cross-publishing partnerships with Mexican, Spanish, African, and French publications. This is an important journal for health collections. URL: www.ehponline.org

4577. Epidemiologic Reviews. [ISSN: 0193-936X] 1979. a. EUR 74. Ed(s): Michel A. Ibrahim. Oxford University Press, 2001 Evans Rd, Cary, NC 27513; jnlorders@oup-usa.org; http://www.us.oup.com. Refereed. Reprint: PSC. Indexed: A22, C45, E01, ExcerpMed, FS&TA, H24, RRTA. Aud.: Ac, Sa.

Published on behalf of the Johns Hopkins Bloomberg School of Medicine, this title has by far the highest impact factor among Thompson/Reuters ISI public health periodicals. Issues collect review articles around particular themes; recent years' topics have included epidemiologic approaches to aging, violence and injury, and global health, as well as the examination and discussion of the practice of screening for multiple conditions. Libraries that subscribe to American Journal of Epidemiology will receive complimentary issues of this title; libraries without AJE that collect in the area of public health will want to consider this one. URL: http://epirev.oxfordjournals.org/

4578. Hastings Center Report. Incorporates (1973-1974): Hastings Center Studies. [ISSN: 0093-0334] 1971. bi-m. GBP 240. Ed(s): Gregory E Kaebnick. Wiley-Blackwell Publishing, Inc., 111 River St, Hoboken, NJ 07030; info@wiley.com; http://onlinelibrary.wiley.com/. Illus., index. Sample. Refereed. Vol. ends: Nov/Dec. Reprint: PSC. Indexed: A01, A22, ABS&EES, B02, BRI, CBRI, E01, MCR, P02, P61, SSA, SWR&A. Bk. rev.: 2-3. Aud.: Ga, Ac, Sa.

The Hastings Center is a nonprofit, nonpartisan organization focused on bioethics. Article types within this publication include essays, columns on legal and policy developments, case studies of issues in clinical care and institutional administration, caregivers' stories, peer-reviewed scholarly articles, and book reviews. The Center's research projects are periodically published within the Report. Recent issues included the ethical concerns associated with obesity stigma, generating and disseminating sensitive research, and vaccines against smoking. Recommended for all academic libraries. URL: www.thehastingscenter.org/Publications/HCR/Default.aspx

4579. Health Affairs: the policy journal of the health sphere. [ISSN: 0278-2715] 1981. bi-m. USD 525 (print & online eds.). Ed(s): Donald E Metz. Project HOPE, 7500 Old Georgetown Rd, Ste 600, Bethesda, MD 20814-6133; hope@projecthope.org; http://www.projhope.org. Refereed. Microform: PQC. Indexed: A01, A22, ABIn, AbAn, AgeL, B01, C45, E01, ExcerpMed, H24, P02, P61, SSA, SWR&A. Bk. rev.: 2-3. Aud.: Ga, Ac, Sa.

Published by a nonprofit international health education organization, this title is a leading journal in health policy thought and research that proposes to address health-care system change "from the perspectives of all its players." Health topics include access to care, health spending, quality, Medicare, Medicaid, prescription drug coverage and costs, nursing trends, mental health, insurance reform, hospitals, global health, and disparities in health care. Issues are largely thematic, with occasional "variety" issues. Recommended for general academic libraries, as well as libraries with holdings in health and/or medicine. URL: www.healthaffairs.org

4580. Health Policy and Planning: a journal on health in development. [ISSN: 0268-1080] 1986. bi-m. EUR 564. Ed(s): Sara Bennett, Richard Coker. Oxford University Press, Great Clarendon St, Oxford, OX2 6DP, United Kingdom; enquiry@oup.co.uk; http://www.oxfordjournals.org/. Adv. Sample. Refereed. Reprint: PSC. Indexed: A22, ABIn, ASSIA, AbAn, B01, C45, E01, EconLit, FS&TA, H24, IBSS, IndVet, P61, PsycInfo, SSA. Aud.: Ac, Sa.

Published in association with the London School of Hygiene and Tropical Medicine, this title aims to improve the design, implementation, and evaluation of health policies in low- and middle-income countries with relevant research papers, reviews, and debates. In addition to epidemiology, planning, and health economics and policy, this journal delves into social anthropology and social policy. Intended for public health researchers and practitioners, this title is appropriate for large academic and health-science libraries. URL: http://heapol.oxfordjournals.org

Inquiry (Rochester). See Health Care Administration section.

4581. *International Journal of Epidemiology.* [ISSN: 0300-5771] 1972. bi-m. EUR 676. Ed(s): Dr. George Davey Smith, Dr. Shah Ebrahim. Oxford University Press, Great Clarendon St, Oxford, OX2 6DP, United Kingdom; enquiry@oup.co.uk; http://www.oxfordjournals.org/. Illus., adv. Sample. Refereed. Microform: PQC. Reprint: PSC. *Indexed:* A01, A22, AbAn, C45, E01, ExcerpMed, FS&TA, H24, RRTA, RiskAb. *Bk. rev.:* Number and length vary. *Aud.:* Ac, Sa.

This title is intended to encourage communication among those engaged in the research, teaching, and application of epidemiology of both communicable and non-communicable disease. Regular features include cohort and data resource profiles, reprints of relevant recent articles and historic articles of interest, as well as subsections such as global health, epigenetic epidemiology, and theory and methods. Contains original research and commentaries. Recommended for academic health science libraries. URL: http://ije.oxfordjournals.org/

J A M A: The Journal of the American Medical Association. See Medicine section.

4582. *Journal of Community Health: the publication for health promotion and disease prevention.* [ISSN: 0094-5145] 1975. bi-m. EUR 1564 (print & online eds.). Ed(s): Pascal Imperato. Springer New York LLC, 233 Spring St, New York, NY 10013; service-ny@springer.com; http://www.springer.com/. Adv. Sample. Refereed. Microform: PQC. Reprint: PSC. *Indexed:* A01, A22, AbAn, AgeL, Agr, BRI, C45, Chicano, E01, H24, IndVet, MCR, P02, P61, PsycInfo, RRTA, RiskAb, SSA, SWR&A. *Aud.:* Ac, Sa.

This journal provides original articles on community health in the areas of practice, teaching, and research. Coverage of preventive medicine, innovations in the provision of health-care personnel, environmental factors, delivery of health services, and the study of health maintenance and insurance programs. The publication features articles on those projects that make a significant impact on the education of health personnel. Recent topics include mobile mammography screening programs in Kentucky; treatment-seeking behaviors and reproductive morbidity in Delhi; HPV knowledge and beliefs among primarily-minority nursing students on the U.S.–Mexico border; and peer-delivered HIV awareness programs among IV drug users in Thailand. This title is recommended to libraries with collections focused in community health, and to larger health science libraries and public health-oriented institutions. URL: www.springer.com/public+health/journal/10900

4583. *Journal of Epidemiology & Community Health.* Former titles (until 1979): *Epidemiology and Community Health;* (until 1978): *Journal of Epidemiology and Community Health;* (until 1977): *British Journal of Preventive and Social Medicine;* (until 1953): *British Journal of Social Medicine.* [ISSN: 0143-005X] 1947. m. USD 1030 (Individuals, USD 441 (print & online eds.). Ed(s): James R Dunn, Martin Bobak. B M J Group, BMA House, Tavistock Sq, London, WC1H 9JR, United Kingdom; support@bmjgroup.com; http://group.bmj.com. Illus., adv. Sample. Refereed. Microform: PQC. *Indexed:* A01, A22, AbAn, BRI, C45, E01, FS&TA, H24, PsycInfo, RRTA, RiskAb. *Aud.:* Ac, Sa.

The *Journal of Epidemiology & Community Health* presents papers on original research, evidence-based public-health policy and practice, and theory and methods in all areas of epidemiology and community health worldwide. In addition to standard reports, letters, debates, and original research, the journal features glossaries, evidence-based public-health medicine, and research agendas, among other article types. It is the official journal of the Society for Social Medicine. URL: http://jech.bmj.com

4584. *Journal of Occupational and Environmental Medicine.* Formerly (until 1995): *Journal of Occupational Medicine.* [ISSN: 1076-2752] 1959. m. USD 904 (print & online eds.). Ed(s): Marjorie Spraycar, Dr. Paul W Brandt-Rauf. Lippincott Williams & Wilkins, 530 Walnut St, Philadelphia, PA 19106; customerservice@lww.com; http://www.lww.com. Adv. Refereed. Microform: PQC. *Indexed:* A01, A22, AbAn, BRI, C45, ErgAb, ExcerpMed, H24, P02, PsycInfo, RRTA, RiskAb. *Aud.:* Ac, Sa.

The *Journal of Occupational and Environmental Medicine* is the official journal of the American College of Occupational and Environmental Medicine. This is one of a few journals focused on health in the workplace. The chief concern here is environmentally-induced conditions and work-related injuries and illnesses. Thus, it will be of interest to a variety of readers whose work involves these issues. Recent articles have included the impact of comprehensive health programs and their costs; a variety of items on sleep health; pulmonary lung function; arsenic exposure; and several absence and productivity-loss pieces. Populations studied include civil servants, administrative staff, dairy factory workers, truck drivers, law enforcement personnel, and museum employees. Recommended for health science libraries; collections with a focus on current labor concerns will want to consider it as well. URL: www.joem.org

4585. *Journal of Public Health Dentistry.* Former titles (until 1965): *Public Health Dentistry;* (until 1960): *American Association of Public Health Dentists. Bulletin.* [ISSN: 0022-4006] 1941. q. GBP 223 (print & online eds.). Ed(s): Robert J Weyant. Wiley-Blackwell Publishing, Inc., Commerce Pl, 350 Main St, Malden, MA 02148; info@wiley.com; http://onlinelibrary.wiley.com/. Illus., adv. Refereed. Circ: 1470 Paid. Microform: PQC. Reprint: PSC. *Indexed:* A22, C45, Chicano, E01, H24. *Aud.:* Ga, Ac, Sa.

Part of the American Association of Public Health Dentistry's efforts "to improve oral health for all," this title features research articles in such areas as oral epidemiology, dental health services, behavioral sciences, and public health practice. There are also methods articles that report on the development and testing of new approaches to research design, data collection and analysis, or the delivery of public health services; and there are review articles that synthesize previous research in the discipline. It is one of the very few public-health titles devoted to oral health. Recent coverage includes poor oral health as an obstacle to employment; oral health trends among 35- to 44-year-olds in Germany after reunification; mothers' oral health perspectives during pregnancy and early childhood; and editorials on such topics as a possible increase in childhood dental caries and a recent U.N. meeting on the prevention and control of non-communicable diseases and their significance for oral health worldwide. Health science and health policy libraries and institutions with a dental orientation will want to consider because of its unusual focus. URL: www.wiley.com/bw/journal.asp?ref=0022-4006&site=1

4586. *Journal of Public Health Management and Practice.* [ISSN: 1078-4659] 1995. bi-m. USD 380 (print & online eds.). Ed(s): Lloyd F Novick. Lippincott Williams & Wilkins, 530 Walnut St, Philadelphia, PA 19106; customerservice@lww.com; http://www.lww.com. Adv. Refereed. Microform: PQC. *Indexed:* A22, B02, BRI, C45. *Aud.:* Ac, Sa.

The *Journal of Public Health Management and Practice* is a practice-based public health journal. It has offerings in a wide range of population health topics including research to practice; emergency preparedness; bioterrorism; infectious disease surveillance; environmental health; community health assessment, chronic disease prevention and health promotion; and academic-practice linkages. Recent topics have included engaging partners for the national prevention strategy, integrating public health into medical education and clinical care, and new tuberculosis field testing. This title is recommended for all health sciences libraries and for academic libraries that support public health programs. URL: www.jphmp.com

The Lancet. See Medicine section.

4587. *Medical Care.* [ISSN: 0025-7079] 1963. m. USD 1320 (print & online eds.). Ed(s): Jeroan J Allison, Catarina Kiefe. Lippincott Williams & Wilkins, 530 Walnut St, Philadelphia, PA 19106; customerservice@lww.com; http://www.lww.com. Index, adv. Refereed. Microform: PQC. *Indexed:* A22, AgeL, Chicano, ExcerpMed, P02, PsycInfo. *Aud.:* Ac, Sa.

Medical Care is the official publication of the Medical Care Section of the American Public Health Association; it publishes scholarly articles on the research, planning, organization, financing, provision, and evaluation of health-care services. Article types include full-length articles and brief reports that describe current developments in the field, manuscripts on relevant research methods, and review articles. Recent coverage has addressed the NYU Emergency Department Algorithm (EDA); hospital readmissions; and race, ethnicity, and psychiatric diagnoses in the prevalence of multiple chronic medical conditions. Recommended for health-sciences and hospital libraries. URL: www.lww-medicalcare.com

4588. ***The Milbank Quarterly: a journal of public health and health care policy.*** Former titles (until 1986): *Health and Society;* (until 1973): *Milbank Memorial Fund Quarterly;* (until 1934): *Milbank Memorial Fund Quarterly Bulletin.* [ISSN: 0887-378X] 1923. q. GBP 184. Ed(s): Bradford H Gray. Wiley-Blackwell Publishing, Inc., 111 River St, Hoboken, NJ 07030; info@wiley.com; http://onlinelibrary.wiley.com/. Illus., index. Sample. Refereed. Vol. ends: Dec (No. 4). Microform: PQC. Reprint: PSC. *Indexed:* A01, A22, ASSIA, AgeL, B01, B02, BAS, BRI, E01, ExcerpMed, FR, IBSS, MCR, P02, P61, PsycInfo, RiskAb, SSA, SWR&A. *Aud.:* Ac, Sa.

The Milbank Memorial Fund, a foundation committed to the nonpartisan study and communication of health policy issues, publishes this multidisciplinary journal. Original research, policy analysis, and commentary from academics, clinicians, and policy makers are featured. The title's multidisciplinary approach allows in-depth exploration of social origins of health. Topics include the impact of social factors on health, prevention, allocation of health-care resources, legal and ethical issues in health policy, health and health-care administration, and the organization and financing of health care. This well-respected journal offers free online access to institutions in the developing world through HINARI initiative, a WHO program (www.healthinternetwork.org/). The title belongs in libraries with collections in ethics, bioethics, and public health and health sciences. Social science and larger legal/governmental collections may wish to consider as well. URL: http://onlinelibrary.wiley.com/journal/10.1111/%28ISSN%291468-0009

New England Journal of Medicine. See Medicine section.

4589. ***Public Health Ethics.*** [ISSN: 1754-9973] 2008. 3x/yr. EUR 246. Ed(s): Marcel Verweij, Angus Dawson. Oxford University Press, Great Clarendon St, Oxford, OX2 6DP, United Kingdom; enquiry@oup.co.uk; http://www.oxfordjournals.org/. Adv. Sample. Refereed. Reprint: PSC. *Indexed:* A01, ExcerpMed, H24, IBSS. *Aud.:* Ac, Sa.

Known as the first journal to focus specifically on ethical issues in public health policy and practice, this fairly new title is engaged in analysis of moral issues arising in public health and preventive medicine, with theoretical and practical contributions from multiple disciplines. Recent coverage includes Krabbe newborn screening; the HPV virus, vaccination, and social justice; and the ethics of "medical tourism." Recommended for libraries with collections in public health, bioethics, social sciences, as well as larger academic health science libraries. URL: http://phe.oxfordjournals.org

4590. ***Public Health Reports.*** Former titles (until 1974): *Health Services Report;* (until 1973): *H S M H A Health Reports;* (until 1971): *Public Health Reports;* (until 1896): *Abstract of Sanitary Reports;* (until 1890): *Weekly Abstract of Sanitary Reports;* (until 1887): *United States. Marine Hospital Service.;Bulletins of the Public Health;* Public Health Reports incorporated (1945-1951): *Journal of Venereal Disease Information;* Which was formerly (until 1945): *Venereal Disease Information;* (until 1922): *Abstracts from Recent Medical and Public Health Papers;* (1946-1951): *C D C Bulletin.* [ISSN: 0033-3549] 1878. bi-m. USD 158. Association of Schools of Public Health, 1101 15th St, NW, Ste 910, Washington, DC 20005; info@asph.org; http://www.asph.org. Illus., index, adv. Refereed. Vol. ends: Nov/Dec. Microform: CIS; PMC; PQC. *Indexed:* A01, A22, ABS&EES, Agr, AmStI, BRI, C37, C45, Chicano, E01, ExcerpMed, IndVet, P02, P61, RRTA, S25, SSA, SWR&A. *Bk. rev.:* 2, signed. *Aud.:* Hs, Ga, Ac, Sa.

A publication of the Association of Schools of Public Health since 1999, www.publichealthreports began in 1878 as the official journal of the U.S. Health Service. It offers peer-reviewed articles on public health research and practice, along with commentaries and viewpoints. Recent topics have included organ donation and tranplant; hazardous metals in the air after six years of fireworks; and the experiential teaching of epidemiological concepts. The publication has three columns to which faculty and students at member institutions contribute. Articles older than one year are freely available online. URL: www.publichealthreports.org

4591. ***Social Science & Medicine.*** Formed by the merger of (1981-1982): *Social Science and Medicine. Part A: Medical Sociology;* (1981-1982): *Social Science and Medicine. Part E: Medical Psychology;* Which was formerly (until 1981): *Social Science and Medicine. Medical Psychology and Medical Sociology;* (1978-1982): *Social Science and Medicine. Part B: Medical Anthropology;* (1978-1982): *Social Science and Medicine. Part C: Medical Economics;* (1978-1982): *Social Science and Medicine. Part D: Medical Geography;* All of which superseded in part (in 1978): *Social Science & Medicine;* (1981-1982): *Social Science and Medicine. Part F: Medical and Social Ethics;* Which was formerly (until 1981): *Ethics in Science and Medicine;* (until 1975): *Science, Medicine and Man.* [ISSN: 0277-9536] 1982. s-m. EUR 6461. Ed(s): Subra Subramanian, Ichiro Kawachi. Pergamon, The Blvd, Langford Ln, E Park, Kidlington, OX5 1GB, United Kingdom; JournalsCustomerServiceEMEA@elsevier.com; http://www.elsevier.com. Adv. Sample. Refereed. Microform: PQC. *Indexed:* A01, A22, ABS&EES, AbAn, AgeL, BAS, BRI, C45, Chicano, ExcerpMed, H24, IBSS, IndVet, MCR, MLA-IB, P02, P61, PsycInfo, RRTA, RiskAb, SSA. *Aud.:* Ga, Ac, Sa.

This title's focus is the dissemination of social science research on health. Included are original research articles and critical analytical reviews, with commentary and response; special topical issues; and short reports. All are published with an eye toward health information from the interdisciplinary social sciences, and social science information from the health sciences. There is a strong international focus. Recent coverage includes maternal social capital and child health in Indonesia; parents' perceptions of health-care providers' initial discussion of a child's traumatic brain injury; and precursors to overnutrition in Bolivia. Recommended for health and social-sciences collections. URL: www.journals.elsevier.com/social-science-and-medicine/

4592. ***Tobacco Control.*** [ISSN: 0964-4563] 1992. bi-m. USD 763 (Individuals, USD 348 (print & online eds.). Ed(s): Ruth Malone. B M J Group, BMA House, Tavistock Sq, London, WC1H 9JR, United Kingdom; support@bmjgroup.com; http://group.bmj.com. Illus., adv. Sample. Refereed. *Indexed:* A01, A22, AbAn, BRI, C45, H24, PsycInfo, RRTA. *Aud.:* Ac, Sa.

Tobacco Control publishes analysis, reviews, reports, and original research relevant to "efforts to prevent and control the global tobacco epidemic through population level education and policy changes; the ethical dimensions of tobacco control policies; and the activities of the tobacco industry and its allies." Covered topics have been secondhand smoke levels in Scottish bars years after the passage of anti-smoking legislation; French consumers' perception of cigarette packaging; sources and levels of second-hand smoke exposure in hotels and apartment houses; cultural habits of smoking and cigarette exchange in rural China; and a review of tobacco smoking and smoking cessation practices among Chinese physicians. Online content includes PowerPoint presentations and videos. Recommended for libraries that serve public health researchers, practitioners, and educators. URL: http://tobaccocontrol.bmj.com

4593. ***Women's Health Issues.*** [ISSN: 1049-3867] 1991. 6x/yr. USD 503. Ed(s): Dr. Anne Rossier Markus. Elsevier Inc., 360 Park Ave S, New York, NY 10010; JournalCustomerService-usa@elsevier.com; http://www.elsevier.com. Illus., adv. Sample. Refereed. Circ: 700 Paid. Vol. ends: Nov (No. 11). Microform: PQC. *Indexed:* A01, A22, ASSIA, ExcerpMed, P61, PsycInfo, SSA. *Aud.:* Ga, Ac, Sa.

Women's Health Issues is the official journal of the Jacobs Institute of Women's Health at George Washington University. The title aims to promote the improvement of women's health throughout the life cycle, with a focus on U.S. health and health-care policy. The journal does not publish literature reviews, instead presenting original research on a wide range of topics. Recent articles have included the relationship between combat deployment and the reporting of sexual stressors in a female military cohort; policy issues around maternity care and liability; salary differences between male and female physicians' assistants; and contrasting patterns of adverse birth outcomes in U.S. and foreign-born Latinas. Should be of interest to women's studies and women's health collections, hospital libraries, and public health and health-science libraries. URL: www.whijournal.com/home

4594. *World Health Organization. Bulletin.* Incorporates (1980-1988): *World Health Forum;* Formed by the merger of (1937-1947): *League of Nations. Health Organization. Bulletin;* Which was formerly (1932-1936): *Health Organisation of the League of Nations. Quarterly Bulletin;* (1909-1947): *Office International d'Hygiene Publique. Bulletin Mensuel.* [ISSN: 0042-9686] 1947. m. CHF 331; USD 397.20. World Health Organization, Avenue Appia 20, Geneva, 1211, Switzerland; publications@who.int; http://www.who.int. Illus. Sample. Refereed. Microform: CIS; PMC. *Indexed:* A01, A22, ABIn, BAS, BRI, C42, C45, ExcerpMed, H24, IBSS, IndVet, OceAb, P61, RRTA, RiskAb, SSA. *Bk. rev.:* Number and length vary. *Aud.:* Ac, Sa.

"The WHO seeks to publish and disseminate scientifically rigorous public health information of international significance that enables policy-makers, researchers[,] and practitioners to be more effective; it aims to improve health, particularly among disadvantaged populations." This is the mission statement of one of the most cited scholarly journals in public health. This publication has a focus on developing countries, and content is expected to have implications outside the geographic boundaries of any research it describes. Several theme issues are published each year. This title is open access; the web site has Arabic, Chinese, English, French, Russian, and Spanish content for this publication, and provides downloads in multiple eReader formats. URL: www.who.int/bulletin/en

■ REAL ESTATE

See also Architecture; Building and Construction; and Home sections.

Jeffrey Cronin, Information Research Specialist, Harvard Business School, Boston, MA 02163; jcronin@hbs.edu

Introduction

Despite the problems that the U.S. residential real estate market continues to experience, the subject of real estate and every aspect of it—economic, legal, marketing, taxation—is closely followed by many people. The periodical literature that focuses on real estate consists mostly of trade/industry publications and academic journals.

While some provide rather broad coverage of the industry, the majority of them focus on a particular aspect, and their range of topics is as varied as the industry itself. Some may devote their attention to subjects such as real estate development, real estate taxation, property management, or residential real estate. Other periodicals may concentrate on narrower topics such as housing for seniors, hotel/motel real estate, or landlord/tenant relations. Many publications also have a geographic focus, such as *New England Real Estate Journal* or *N.Y. Real Estate Law Reporter.*

The periodicals listed below are representative of the many publications on this subject, and all are appropriate for special or academic libraries that support the study of real estate or are engaged in some activity related to the real estate industry.

Basic Periodicals

Ac, Sa: *Real Estate Economics, Real Estate Forum, Real Estate Review, Realtor Magazine.*

Basic Abstracts and Indexes

ABI/INFORM, Business Periodicals Index, Business Source Complete, Business Source Premier.

4595. *The Appraisal Journal.* Incorporates (in 1992): *The Real Estate Appraiser;* Which was formerly (until 1991): *The Real Estate Appraiser and Analyst;* (until 1978): *The Real Estate Appraiser;* (until 1963): *The Residential Appraiser;* (until 1956): *Society of Real Estate Appraisers. Review;* (until 1936): *Residential Appraisers' Review;* Formerly (until 1939): *American Institute of Real Estate Appraisers of the National Association of Real Estate Boards. Journal.* [ISSN: 0003-7087] 1932. q. USD 100 Free to members; (Non-members, USD 48). Ed(s): Nancy Bannon. Appraisal Institute, 200 W Madison, Ste 1500, Chicago, IL 60606; info@appraisalinstitute.org; http://www.appraisalinstitute.org. Illus., index, adv. Refereed. Circ: 21000. Vol. ends: Oct. *Indexed:* A22, ABIn, ATI, B01, B02, BLI, BRI, H&TI, RiskAb. *Bk. rev.:* 1-3, 500-700 words. *Aud.:* Ac, Sa.

The Appraisal Institute, an international association of professional real estate appraisers, has published the *Appraisal Journal* since it was organized in 1932. This is a leading, peer-reviewed journal written mostly by appraisal professionals. This journal is published quarterly, and each issue provides current news, research articles, and book reviews of interest to institute members, professional appraisers, and others engaged in the real estate industry, such as real estate attorneys and bankers. Articles range from the practical, e.g., "Are Appraisal Reviews a Mainstay of Your Practice or Just a Sideline?," to the academic, e.g., "The Capital and Spatial Markets: Converging or Diverging?" Strongly recommended for special and academic libraries with collections related to real estate and related subjects.

4596. *Building Operating Management: the leading magazine for buildings owners and facility executives.* Formerly (until 1969): *Building Maintenance and Modernization.* [ISSN: 0007-3490] 1954. m. Free. Ed(s): Greg Zimmerman, Brandon Lorenz. Trade Press Publishing Corp., 2100 W Florist Ave, Milwaukee, WI 53209; info@tradepress.com; http://www.tradepress.com. Illus., index, adv. Circ: 73054. Vol. ends: Dec. *Indexed:* A22, ABIn. *Aud.:* Ac, Sa.

Building Operating Management serves as a leading trade publication for building owners and facility executives who are responsible for a minimum of 100,000 square feet. This monthly trade publication provides articles that deal with all aspects, particularly technological, of managing office buildings, schools/universities, hospitals, and other commercial and institutional buildings. In each issue, an in-house editorial staff and contributing editors write feature articles such as "To Get the Best Ceiling Performance, Ask the Right Questions Before You Buy" and "An Inside Look at Fast-Track Construction." Regular sections include an editorial and a product gallery. The publication's web site provides full-text access to the current issue and to archived issues back through 2002. URL: www.facilitiesnet.com

4597. *Commercial Investment Real Estate.* Former titles (until 1999): *Commercial Investment Real Estate Journal;* (until 1986): *Commercial Investment Journal.* [ISSN: 1524-3249] 1982. bi-m. Free to members; Non-members, USD 45. Ed(s): Sara Drummond. C C I M Institute, 430 N Michigan Ave, Ste 800, Chicago, IL 60611; info@ccim.com; http://www.ccim.com. Illus., index, adv. Circ: 20546. *Indexed:* A22, ABIn, B01. *Aud.:* Ac, Sa.

This trade publication is published by the Certified Commercial Investment Member (CCIM) Institute. Articles are well written and contain both data and analysis. Aspects of commercial real estate that most articles touch on are business development, investment trends, market analysis, property development, and technology. Most readers are CCIM members who are recognized specialists in commercial and investment real estate. Cover stories, written by staff writers and other real estate professionals, include "Commercial Property Trend Watch," "New Concepts for Retail Properties," and "Market Forecast and Legislative Update." Each issue also includes the sections "Regional Outlook," "Financing Focus," "Market Trends," and "Buyers Guide."

4598. *Journal of Corporate Real Estate.* [ISSN: 1463-001X] 1998. q. EUR 789 combined subscription in Europe (print & online eds.); USD 929 combined subscription in the Americas (print & online eds.); GBP 569 combined subscription in the UK & elsewhere (print & online eds.).

Ed(s): Dr. Clare Eriksson. Emerald Group Publishing Ltd., Howard House, Wagon Ln, Bingley, BD16 1WA, United Kingdom; emerald@emeraldinsight.com; http://www.emeraldinsight.com. Sample. Refereed. Reprint: PSC. *Indexed:* A22, ABIn, B01, E01. *Aud.:* Ac, Sa.

The *Journal of Corporate Real Estate* is the only peer-reviewed professional journal dedicated to corporate real estate in the world. The purpose of the journal is to be "the leading forum for authoritative, practical guidance not only on current best practice but also the key issues of tomorrow that the corporate real estate executive needs to be aware of." Topics covered include cost control, outsourcing, corporate tenancy, insurance and lease issues, and the cost of capital. Recent articles include "Impact of the Asian financial crisis on corporate real estate acquisitions," "Sale-and-leaseback as a British real estate model," and "Corporate real estate management (CREM) in Estonia." All articles provide clear implications for business practice. Recommended for academic and special libraries.

4599. *Journal of Housing Economics.* [ISSN: 1051-1377] 1991. q. EUR 707. Ed(s): Henry O Pollakowski. Academic Press, 3251 Riverport Ln, Maryland Heights, MO 63043; JournalCustomerService-usa@elsevier.com; http://www.elsevierdirect.com/brochures/academicpress/index.html. Adv. Sample. Refereed. *Indexed:* A01, A22, B01, E01, EconLit, IBSS, JEL. *Aud.:* Ac, Sa.

The *Journal of Housing Economics* provides a focal point for the publication of economic research related to housing. It encourages papers that bring to bear careful analytical technique on important housing-related questions.

4600. *Journal of Housing Research.* [ISSN: 1052-7001] 1990. s-a. Individuals, USD 200 (print or online ed.); Free to members). Ed(s): Shelton Weeks, Leonard V Zumpano. American Real Estate Society, c/o Diane Quarles, Clemson University, PO Box 341323, Clemson, SC 29634; equarle@clemson.edu; http://www.aresnet.org. Illus. Refereed. *Indexed:* A01, A22, ABIn, EconLit, IBSS, JEL, SWR&A. *Aud.:* Ac, Sa.

The *Journal of Housing Research* is a publication of the American Real Estate Society (ARES). It serves as an outlet for theoretical and empirical research on a broad range of housing-related topics including, but not limited to, the economics of the housing markets, residential brokerage, home mortgage finance and mortgage markets, and international housing issues.

4601. *Journal of Property Management: the official publication of the Institute of Real Estate Management.* Incorporates: *Operating Techniques and Products Bulletin;* Former titles (until 1941): *Journal of Certified Property Managers;* (until 1938): *Journal of Real Estate Management.* [ISSN: 0022-3905] 1934. bi-m. USD 62.95 domestic; USD 72.32 Canada; USD 100.99 elsewhere. Institute of Real Estate Management, 430 N Michigan Ave, Chicago, IL 60611; custserv@irem.org; http://www.irem.org. Illus., index, adv. Sample. Circ: 23750 Paid and free. Vol. ends: Nov/Dec. *Indexed:* A22, ABIn, B01, B02, BRI, H&TI, RiskAb. *Aud.:* Ac, Sa.

Published since 1934, this bimonthly trade publication from the Institute of Real Estate Management (IREM) provides comprehensive coverage of the real estate management industry. The typical reader is a manager of a commercial or residential property, and articles give expert insight on trends and all aspects of property management, including operations and marketing. Each issue includes a special report on such topics as "Anchor Tenant Evolution," "Sustainability in Legislation," and "Water World" (focusing on water management). Issues from the latest year are available for free online at the IREM web site, with older issues available for purchase. Recommended for academic and special libraries with a focus on real estate. URL: www.irem.org

4602. *Journal of Real Estate Finance and Economics.* [ISSN: 0895-5638] 1988. 8x/yr. EUR 1479 (print & online eds.). Ed(s): Steven R Grenadier, C F Sirmans. Springer New York LLC, 233 Spring St, New York, NY 10013; service-ny@springer.com; http://www.springer.com/. Illus., adv. Sample. Refereed. Microform: PQC. Reprint: PSC. *Indexed:* A22, ABIn, B01, BLI, E01, EconLit, H&TI, IBSS, JEL. *Aud.:* Ac, Sa.

This is a scholarly, peer-reviewed journal created to publish empirical and theoretical research on real estate using the methodologies of finance and economics. The subject areas include urban economics, housing, and public policy. Examples of published research include "Return Relationships Between Listed Banks and Real Estate Firms: Evidence from Seven Asian Economies," "Price Effects of Non-Traditionally Broker-Marketed Properties," and "Reduced Form Mortgage Pricing as an Alternative to Option-Pricing Models." Most authors are drawn from academia. This journal is best suited for academic or special libraries.

4603. *Journal of Real Estate Literature.* [ISSN: 0927-7544] 1993. s-a. USD 200 (print or online ed.) Free to members. Ed(s): Karl L Gunterman, John F McDonald. American Real Estate Society, Clemson University, 424 Sirrine Hall, PO Box 341323, Clemson, SC 29634; equarle@clemson.edu; http://www.aresnet.org. Illus., index. Sample. Refereed. Microform: PQC. *Indexed:* A22, ABIn, B01, BRI, E01, EconLit, H&TI, IBSS, JEL. *Bk. rev.:* 1-2, 1,000-1,500 words, signed. *Aud.:* Ac, Sa.

The peer-reviewed *Journal of Real Estate Literature* is an official publication of the American Real Estate Society. It publishes research of interest to real estate academics and practitioners. The articles are quite technical, and each issue includes articles with an international focus. The content is rather comprehensive, providing not just articles but dissertations, working papers, and book reviews. Examples of recent articles include "Changes and Modifications in Residential Neighborhoods as a Factor of Housing Pricing: Jerusalem and Haifa as Case Studies," "Harmonization of Investment Valuation Standards in Europe," and "Integrating Real Estate Property Information Data Standards into Financial Business Processes." The web site provides full-text access to all articles back to 1993, with the exception of the most recent issue.

4604. *The Journal of Real Estate Portfolio Management.* [ISSN: 1083-5547] 1995. q. USD 300 (print or online ed.) Free to members. Ed(s): Randy I Anderson, Glenn R Mueller. American Real Estate Society, Clemson University, 424 Sirrine Hall, PO Box 341323, Clemson, SC 29634; equarle@clemson.edu; http://www.aresnet.org. Illus., adv. Refereed. *Indexed:* A22, ABIn, B01, EconLit, H&TI, IBSS, JEL. *Aud.:* Ac, Sa.

This journal is a publication of the American Real Estate Society. It publishes articles that can "be useful to the business decision maker in areas such as development, finance, management, market analysis, marketing and valuation." Articles chosen are technical in nature and are intended to cover business decision-making applications or scholarly real estate research. Recent articles include "Changes in REIT Stock Prices, Trading Volume and Institutional Ownership Resulting from S&P REIT Index Changes," "Risk and Diversification for Regeneration/Urban Renewal Properties: Evidence from the UK," and "Farm Land in a Mixed-Asset Portfolio: A Mean-Semi Variance Approach." The publisher's web site provides free full-text access to all articles back to 1995.

4605. *Journal of Real Estate Practice and Education.* [ISSN: 1521-4842] 1998. a. Individuals, USD 200 (print or online ed.); Free to members). Ed(s): Kenneth H Johnson, William G Hardin, III. American Real Estate Society, c/o Diane Quarles, Clemson University, PO Box 341323, Clemson, SC 29634; equarle@clemson.edu; http://www.aresnet.org. *Indexed:* ABIn, ATI, EconLit, JEL. *Aud.:* Ac, Sa.

The *Journal of Real Estate Practice and Education* is a publication of the American Real Estate Society (ARES). The journal's purpose is to stimulate research in real estate practice and education and to encourage excellence in training and teaching. An ARES goal is to be an essential source of information and ideas regarding the practice and teaching of real estate in areas such as development, finance, management, market analysis, marketing, and valuation.

4606. *Journal of Real Estate Research.* [ISSN: 0896-5803] 1986. bi-m. Free to members. Ed(s): Ko Wang. American Real Estate Society, c/o Diane Quarles, Clemson University, PO Box 341323, Clemson, SC 29634; http://business.fullerton.edu/journal/. Adv. Refereed. Circ: 1200. *Indexed:* A22, ABIn, B01, EconLit, H&TI, IBSS, JEL. *Aud.:* Ac, Sa.

The *Journal of Real Estate Research* is one of several journals published by the American Real Estate Society. It is a peer-reviewed publication with articles quite technical in nature that are intended to be useful to both business decision-makers and those engaged in scholarly real estate research. Recent articles include "Volatility Clustering in U.S. Home Prices," "Leave Vacant or Rent: The Optimal Decision for Absentee Home Sellers," and "A Meta-Analysis of the Effect of Environmental Contamination and Positive Amenities on Residential Real Estate Values." The publisher's web site provides free full-text access to all articles back to 1986.

4607. *National Real Estate Investor.* [ISSN: 0027-9994] 1958. m. plus a. Directory. USD 129 domestic (Free to qualified personnel). Ed(s): David Bodamer. Penton Media, Inc., 6151 Powers Ferry Rd, Ste 200, Atlanta, GA 30339; information@penton.com; http://www.penton.com. Illus., index, adv. Circ: 33708. Vol. ends: Dec. Microform: PQC. *Indexed:* A22, ABIn, B01, B02, BRI, H&TI. *Aud.:* Ac, Sa.

National Real Estate Investor is a well-known and respected trade publication that provides industry news and in-depth reporting to commercial real estate professionals and real estate investors. Readers of the magazine are engaged in a variety of real estate–related disciplines including brokerage, construction, owner/development, finance/investment, property management, corporate real estate, and real estate services. Articles are very informative, and the special reports are particularly good sources of information. These include "NREI's 17th Annual Top Lenders Survey" and "Real Estate Investment Outlook." Full-text articles back to 1995 are available for free on the publication's web site.

4608. *Real Estate Economics.* Former titles (until 1995): *American Real Estate and Urban Economics Association. Journal;* (until 1988): *A R E U A Journal;* (until 1977): *American Real Estate and Urban Economics Association. Journal.* [ISSN: 1080-8620] 1973. q. GBP 406. Ed(s): Crocker H Liu, N Edward Coulson. Wiley-Blackwell Publishing, Inc., 111 River St, Hoboken, NJ 07030; info@wiley.com; http://onlinelibrary.wiley.com/. Illus., index, adv. Sample. Refereed. Vol. ends: Winter. Microform: PQC. *Indexed:* A22, ABIn, B01, B02, BRI, E01, EconLit, H&TI, JEL, RiskAb. *Aud.:* Ac, Sa.

Real Estate Economics is a leading scholarly journal for real estate–related topics published by the American Real Estate and Urban Economics Association. According to the publisher, the focus of this journal is "to facilitate communication among academic researchers and industry professionals and to improve the analysis of real estate decisions." Articles are substantial and quite technical. Examples of recent articles include "A Comparison of Nonparametric Methods to Measure Efficiency in the Savings and Loan Industry," "Tax Rules and the Sale of Leaseback of Corporate Real Estate," and "An Analysis of Resolution Trust Corporation Transactions: Auction Market Process and Pricing." The publisher's web site provides article abstracts back to 2001 and free full-text access from volume one (1973) through 2000.

4609. *Real Estate Finance and Investment: the newsweekly of the commercial property and capital markets.* [ISSN: 1529-6644] 1995. w. EUR 2350 combined subscription in Europe (print & online eds.); GBP 1804 combined subscription United Kingdom (print & online eds.); USD 2825 combined subscription in US & elsewhere (print & online eds.). Ed(s): Samantha Rowan, Steve Murray. Institutional Investor, Inc., 225 Park Ave S, New York, NY 10003; customerservice@iinews.com; http://www.institutionalinvestor.com. Adv. Sample. *Indexed:* ABIn, ATI, B01, B02, B03, BLI, BRI. *Aud.:* Ac, Sa.

Published by Institutional Investor, *Real Estate Finance and Investment* is a weekly trade publication that provides coverage on all aspects of the real estate industry. It promotes itself as "a 'one-stop shopping' news source for senior real estate executives who need to stay on top of breaking news in the commercial property markets, the real estate capital markets, the CMBS market, and pension funds' investment strategies in real estate." Regular features include "Research Roundup," featuring reports from brokerage firm analysts, and "Investment Strategies," where, every week, top real estate executives and investment managers discuss their acquisition and divestiture strategies. Recommended for academic and special libraries with real estate collections.

4610. *Real Estate Forum.* Incorporates (2002-2004): *Real Estate Mid-America.* [ISSN: 0034-0707] 1946. 8x/yr. USD 129.95 domestic; USD 275 foreign. Ed(s): Danielle Douglas, Sule Aygoren Carranza. A L M Real Estate Media Inc., 120 Broadway, Fl 5, New York, NY 10271; http://www.remediainc.com. Illus., adv. Vol. ends: Dec. *Indexed:* ABIn, H&TI, P02. *Aud.:* Ac, Sa.

Published since 1946, *Real Estate Forum* is a well-regarded trade publication that covers the commercial real estate business. Every month it provides up-to-date information on industry news on topics such as capital flows, new financing structures, leasing trends, and alternative investment vehicles. The articles are written by journalists who are well versed in the business and are rich with data including macro- and micro-economic indicators, property performance issues, and demographic trends. Issues feature property-sector and geographic market reports as well as company profiles, interviews with real estate leaders, and reader surveys on various issues impacting the industry. Highly recommended for libraries with commercial real estate collections.

4611. *Real Estate Issues.* [ISSN: 0146-0595] 1976. 3x/yr. USD 48 domestic; USD 15 per issue. Ed(s): Peter C Burley, Carol Scherf. The Counselors of Real Estate, 430 N Michigan Ave, Chicago, IL 60611; info@cre.org. Illus., index, adv. Refereed. Vol. ends: Winter. Microform: PQC. *Indexed:* A22, ABIn, B01, B02, BRI, H&TI. *Aud.:* Ac, Sa.

Since 1976, *Real Estate Issues* has been published by the Counselors of Real Estate, an association of real estate professionals who have distinguished themselves in a variety of real estate–related activities from appraisal to syndication. According to the publisher, this journal is "not an academic-oriented publication, but a commercial real estate journal written for and by practitioners. Its focus, therefore, is on practical applications and applied theory." Articles published represent a broad range of topics in real estate, including tenants-in-common/1031 exchanges, eminent domain, minority interest in real estate, and dispute resolution. Full-text articles back to volume one (1976) are available for free at the publisher's web site.

4612. *Real Estate Law Journal.* [ISSN: 0048-6868] 1972. 4 Base Vol(s) q. USD 584.04 base vol(s).). Thomson West, 610 Opperman Dr, Eagan, MN 55123; west.customer.service@thomson.com; http://west.thomson.com. Microform: PQC. *Indexed:* A22, ABIn, B02, BLI, BRI, CLI, L14. *Aud.:* Ac, Sa.

According to the editor-in-chief, this journal publishes "articles, essays, decisions, or other items of interest to practicing attorneys, investors, academics and other professionals involved in the real estate industry." Recent articles include "Current Status of Property Rights Compensation Statutes," "Zoning Out Adult-Oriented Businesses: An Analysis of the Recent Ninth Circuit Decision in Dream Palace v. County of Maricopa," and "An After-Tax Analysis of Piggy-Backs and PMI: What Should Real Estate Professionals Know?" In each issue, there are also several regular columns, including "Tax Issues," "From the Environment," "Zoning and Land Use Planning," and "From the Courts."

4613. *Real Estate Review.* [ISSN: 0034-0790] 1971. 4 Base Vol(s) q. USD 351.96 base vol(s).). Thomson West, 610 Opperman Dr, Eagan, MN 55123; west.customer.service@thomson.com; http://west.thomson.com. Illus., index, adv. Circ: 7000 Paid. Microform: PQC. *Indexed:* A22, ABIn, ATI, B01, B02, BLI, BRI, CLI. *Aud.:* Ac, Sa.

Real Estate Review provides informed advice on the latest trends and developments in the real estate industry. Articles are written by real estate attorneys and other real estate professionals and cover all aspects of the real estate business. These include advice on dealing with transactions, capital expenditure, risk, agreements, and environmental issues. Topics covered include tax planning, redevelopment, low-income housing, and asset management. Recommended for both academic and special libraries.

4614. *Real Estate Taxation.* Formerly (until 2001): *Journal of Real Estate Taxation.* [ISSN: 1538-3792] 1973. 1 Base Vol(s) q. USD 275; USD 335; USD 435 combined subscription (print & online eds.). Ed(s): Paul D Carman, Robert J Murdich. R I A, PO Box 6159, Carol Stream, IL 60197; ria@thomson.com; http://ria.thomsonreuters.com. Adv. Microform: PQC. *Indexed:* A22, ABIn, ATI, B02, BRI, CLI, L14. *Aud.:* Ac, Sa.

Real Estate Taxation is a journal written by practitioners in the field, with articles and columns that "focus on structuring clients' transactions to better improve after-tax profits." Topics such as REITs, asset protection, intrafamily transactions, and partnerships are covered. In-depth articles that typically run 15–25 pages are authored by attorneys, accountants, and real estate professionals, offering practical information and tax planning ideas. Articles are not theoretical but instead focus on accounting, tax, legal, and finance issues of importance to those engaged in the real estate industry. Recommended for academic and special libraries.

4615. Realtor Magazine. Former titles (until 1998): *Today's Realtor;* (until 1996): *Real Estate Today;* Which incorporated (in 1968): *Realtor Reviews.* [ISSN: 1522-0842] 1968. m. Free to members; Non-members, USD 56. Ed(s): Stacey Moncrieff, Wendy Cole. National Association of Realtors (Chicago), 430 N Michigan Ave, Chicago, IL 60611; narpubs@realtors.org; http://www.realtor.org. Illus., adv. Sample. Microform: PQC. *Indexed:* A22, ABIn, B01, B02, BRI, P02. *Aud.:* Ac, Sa.

Realtor Magazine is the monthly flagship publication of the National Association of Realtors. With both national and regional coverage, it is read by 2.6 million real estate professionals. It is a well-written industry publication that provides practical how-to articles for those engaged in sales and marketing of real estate. It also includes interviews, market data, and news on important legal and legislative developments that impact real estate. The publisher's web site also provides several online tools and tips, plus all of the articles from the print magazine. In addition, there are exclusive online columns and resources, such as an architecture guide. Strongly recommended for all real estate library collections.

■ RELIGION

Stephen Bales, Humanities and Social Sciences Librarian, Evans Library, Texas A & M University, College Station, TX 77843; sbales@library.tamu.edu

Introduction

Humanity's religious impulse has resulted in the development of many different religious traditions, the emergence of vibrant cultural traditions and expressions of faith, and the amassing of huge corpi of spiritually inspired art and literature. Furthermore, the modern age, despite dire predictions of faith's impending demise at the hands of scientific knowledge, has seen both the spread of traditional religions like Christianity, Islam, and Buddhism, and the creation of many new religious movements like Mormonism, Scientology, and pagan revivalism.

This outburst of religious growth has provided fertile ground for traditional academic pursuits such as theology, history, and philosophy of religion. This growth has also seen the intersection of the study of religion and relatively recently emergent social sciences and humanities fields like sociology, psychology, religious studies, women and gender studies, and Asian studies. Furthermore, the study of faith is equally, if not more, popular among laypeople.

Not surprisingly, then, there are many periodical publications—popular and scholarly, partisan and impartial—devoted to exploring all aspects of religion. A search of *UlrichsWeb Global Serials Directory* for the subject heading "Religions and Theology," for example, retrieves a results set of 596 active publications. This profundity of literature may result in cognitive overload and indecision among library selectors, particularly for librarians who are not subject-specialists in the area.

This section presents 79 excellent popular and scholarly periodicals concerned with religion. Selections range from thematically broad and interdisciplinary scholarly journals such as *History of Religions: An International Journal for Comparative Historical Studies* and *Journal of Religion,* to focused publications such as *International Journal of Hindu Studies* and *Zygon: Journal of Religion and Science.* The reader will note that popular publications tend to fall into the latter category, with many magazines catering to a specific type of religious community or practitioner, e.g., *Yoga International, Commonweal,* and *B'nai B'rith Magazine.* All of this diversity and specialization requires that the library selector carefully consider the needs

of her community. But, at the same time, it allows the librarian to more strategically (and cost-effectively) tailor a serials collection for patrons' research or general reading requirements.

Finally, it is worth noting that many of the publications in this section have followed wider publishing trends when providing an electronic presence for their titles. Some scholarly journals, for example the *Japanese Journal of Religious Studies,* have started providing free, open access to current and/or archival copies of their articles. Consumer publications now often give free access to much of their content, as well as additional services such as web-only content like blogs and newsfeeds. URLs have been included with those publication annotations when value-added content or features are found in their web versions.

Basic Periodicals

America, American Academy of Religion. Journal, Church History, The Humanist, Journal of Biblical Literature, Journal of Ecclesiastical History, The Journal of Religion, Journal of Theological Studies, Judaism, Muslim World, Religious Studies Review, Theology Today.

Basic Abstracts and Indexes

ATLA Religion Index, Catholic Periodical and Literature Index, New Testament Abstracts, Old Testament Abstracts.

4616. America: the national catholic weekly. Supersedes in part (in 1909): *The Messenger;* Which was formerly (1866-1902): *The Messenger of the Sacred Heart of Jesus.* [ISSN: 0002-7049] 1909. w. USD 56 domestic. Ed(s): Rev. Matt Malone. America Press Inc., 106 W 56th St, New York, NY 10019; america@americapress.org; http://www.americapress.org. Illus., index, adv. Sample. Circ: 44872 Paid. Vol. ends: Jun/Dec. Microform: PQC. *Indexed:* A01, A22, ABS&EES, AmHI, BAS, BRI, C26, C37, CBRI, Chicano, F01, MASUSE, MLA-IB, P02, RILM. *Bk. rev.:* 2-3, 1,000-1,300 words; signed. *Aud.:* Ga, Ac.

America is a weekly Roman Catholic magazine that has been in publication since 1909. The magazine has a liberal bent that, in recent years, has put it in conflict with Church hierarchy. Recent issues include progressive perspectives on gun and immigration reform, regularly occurring columns, book and film reviews, poetry, and news briefs of interest to Roman Catholics. *America*'s web site provides free access to articles, additional resources like blogs, and an online archive that stretches back to 2000. This consumer magazine is recommended for both public and academic libraries. URL: http://americamagazine.org/

4617. American Academy of Religion. Journal. Former titles (until 1967): *Journal of Bible and Religion;* (until 1937): *National Association of Biblical Instructors. Journal;* Which incorporated in part: *Christian Education;* Which was formerly (until 1919): *American College. Bulletin.* [ISSN: 0002-7189] 1933. q. EUR 222. Ed(s): Amir Hussain. Oxford University Press, 2001 Evans Rd, Cary, NC 27513; http://www.oxfordjournals.org. Illus., index, adv. Sample. Refereed. Circ: 11000 Paid. Vol. ends: Winter. Microform: PQC. Reprint: PSC. *Indexed:* A01, A22, AmHI, ArtHuCI, BAS, BRI, CBRI, E01, FR, MLA-IB, P02, P61, R&TA, RILM, SSA. *Bk. rev.:* 15-20, 900-2,000 words; signed. *Aud.:* Ac.

Beginning its life in 1917 as the *American College Bulletin,* the *Journal of the American Academy of Religion* is the flagship scholarly publication of the American Academy of Religion, an organization that boasts a current membership in excess of 10,000 people. The journal's content covers world religions and phenomena using a variety of theoretical and methodological approaches. One recent issue, for instance, contains articles on Gandhi and feminism, queer religious sects in the New Testament Epistles, and the religious aspects of the sitcom *The Simpsons.* Contains multiple book reviews, as well as occasional reviews of other media such as film. This journal is a must-have for religious studies scholars and deserves a place in any academic library.

4618. American Baptist Quarterly: a Baptist journal of history, theology and ministry. Formerly (until 1982): *Foundations;* Supersedes (in 1958): *Chronicle.* [ISSN: 0745-3698] 1938. q. USD 50 domestic; USD 66 foreign. Ed(s): Deborah Van Broekhoven, Curtin Freeman. American

Baptist Historical Society, 3001 Mercer University Dr, Atlanta, GA 30341; http://abhsarchives.org. Illus., index. Sample. Refereed. Microform: PQC. *Indexed:* A22, FR, R&TA, RILM. *Bk. rev.:* 0-1, 500-1,400 words; signed. *Aud.:* Ga, Ac, Sa.

Published by the American Baptist Historical Society, this scholarly journal presents articles on Baptist history, theology, and culture, with a primary emphasis on the church history. Issues are often thematic, with recent offerings entitled "[Why] Baptist History Matters" and "Baptist History and Preaching." The journal is published quarterly and the number of essays varies per issue, but the topics covered are wide-ranging, including examinations of Baptist Christianity in multiple countries, as well as various interesting topics such as "Star Wars to Shubal Stearns: How to Preach About Baptist History without Hearing Crickets." Recommended for academic libraries, particularly those that support divinity or theological programs.

4619. *American Journal of Theology & Philosophy.* [ISSN: 0194-3448] 1980. 3x/yr. USD 117 (print & online eds.). Ed(s): Michael L Raposa. University of Illinois Press, 1325 S Oak St, Champaign, IL 61820; uipress@uillinois.edu; http://www.press.uillinois.edu. Adv. Refereed. *Indexed:* A22, E01, FR, R&TA. *Bk. rev.:* 1 or more, 150-500; signed. *Aud.:* Ac, Sa.

This prestigious journal is dedicated "to the creative interchange of ideas between theologians and philosophers on some of the most critical intellectual and ethical issues of our time." Each issue contains approximately five academic articles that address topics such as the theological implications of Hegelian dialectic and religion, war, and philosophical pragmatism. The journal's editorial board consists of both distinguished philosophers and theologians, and the scholarship within is rigorously researched, presented, and documented. Two extensive book reviews are usually included. Recommended for most academic libraries.

4620. *Anglican Theological Review.* [ISSN: 0003-3286] 1918. q. USD 65 (Individuals, USD 45; Students, USD 25). Ed(s): Jacqueline B Winter. Anglican Theological Review, Inc., 8765 W Higgins Rd, Ste 650, Chicago, IL 60631. Illus., index, adv. Sample. Refereed. Vol. ends: No. 4. Microform: PQC. *Indexed:* A01, A22, AmHI, FR, MLA-IB, R&TA, RILM. *Bk. rev.:* 25-30, 600-1,400 words; signed. *Aud.:* Ac, Sa.

According to its web site, the *Anglican Theological Review* "has been the unofficial journal of the seminaries of the Episcopal Church in the United States and the Anglican Church of Canada" for over 90 years. This quarterly journal publishes peer-reviewed articles that explore Anglican theology, as well as theology's relationship to a variety of topics such as art and literature. Poetry, review articles, and multiple book reviews are also included in every issue. This journal is recommended for theologians and Christian studies scholars, and is appropriate for academic libraries that support these disciplines. URL: www.anglicantheologicalreview.com

4621. *Ars Disputandi: the online journal for philosophy of religion.* [ISSN: 1566-5399] 2000. irreg. Free. Ed(s): Michael Scott, Maarten Wisse. Igitur, Utrecht Publishing & Archiving Services, Postbus 80105, Utrecht, 3508 TC, Netherlands; info@igitur.uu.nl; http://www.uu.nl/igitur. Index. Refereed. *Indexed:* AmHI. *Bk. rev.:* 5-10, 500-1,000 words; signed. *Aud.:* Ac, Sa.

Ars Disputandi is an online Open Access journal that has published scholarly articles concerning the philosophy of religion since 2001. Articles are added as soon as they are accepted and tackle many different philosophical subjects, including "Religion as Sedition"; the ongoing philosophical debates between atheists and Christianity; and the applications of Schelling and Merleau-Ponty's philosophies to religious questions. Also included are book reviews and short argument papers ("Discussion Notes"). Users may sign up to receive messages when new material becomes available. This journal is useful to philosophy of religion scholars and, because of its high quality and free access, should be linked to the religion and philosophy guides of all public and academic libraries. Note: *Ars Disputandi* also occasionally publishes monographs as part of its "Supplement Series," with information on these supplements available through its web site. URL: www.arsdisputandi.org/

4622. *Baptist History and Heritage.* [ISSN: 0005-5719] 1965. 3x/yr. USD 60 (Individuals, USD 40). Ed(s): Bruce T Gourley. Baptist History & Heritage Society, 6251 Pearl Dr, Manhattan, MT 59741; jackie@baptisthistory.org; http://www.baptisthistory.org. Illus., index. Refereed. Circ: 1000 Paid. Vol. ends: Oct. *Indexed:* A22, BRI, R&TA, RILM. *Bk. rev.:* 3, 250-300 words; signed. *Aud.:* Ga, Ac.

Baptist History and Heritage, published thrice yearly since 1965 by the Baptist History and Heritage Society, collects historiographical investigations of the Baptist Church as an institution and as a cultural touchstone. Each issue contains regular columns by the editor(s) and approximately five historical essays, usually concerning a particular topical theme. Multiple book reviews concerning church history and culture are also included. Both researchers and laypeople will find this resource valuable, whether they are concerned with Baptist history or with the broader histories of religion in (primarily) North America. This journal is recommended for public and academic libraries, especially those that support large communities of Baptists, or programs that focus on Baptist or modern Christian History. URL: www.baptisthistory.org/bhhs/journal.html

The Beltane Papers. See Spirituality and Well-Being section.

4623. *The Bible Today.* [ISSN: 0006-0836] 1962. bi-m. USD 37 domestic; USD 56.70 Canada; USD 54 foreign. Ed(s): Linda M Maloney, Rev. Donald Senior. Liturgical Press, 2950 Saint John's Rd, P O Box 7500, Collegeville, MN 56321-7500; sales@litpress.org; http://www.litpress.org. Illus., index, adv. Sample. Circ: 3659. Vol. ends: Nov. Microform: PQC. *Indexed:* A01, A22. *Bk. rev.:* 35-40, 50-200 words; signed. *Aud.:* Ga, Ac.

The Bible Today is a consumer magazine published on a bimonthly basis by Liturgical Press, and it provides biblical analysis accessible to academics, clergy, and laypeople. Issues are thematic, e.g., "The Prophet Ezekiel" and "Doomsday Predictions," but also include regular features such as the geographically oriented "Exploring the Digital Landscape." Articles are extensively illustrated with photographs and art. Recommended for both public and academic libraries.

Biblical Archaeology Review. See Archaeology section.

4624. *B'nai B'rith Magazine.* Former titles (until 2003): *The B'nai B'rith I J M;* (until 2001): *The B'nai B'rith International Jewish Monthly;* (until 1981): *The National Jewish Monthly;* (until 1939): *B'nai B'rith National Jewish Monthly;* (until 1934): *B'nai B'rith Magazine;* (until 1924): *B'nai B'rith News.* [ISSN: 1549-4799] 1886. q. Free to membership. Ed(s): Eugene L Meyer. B'nai B'rith International, 2020 K St, NW, 7th Fl, Washington, DC 20006; foundation@bnaibrith.org; http://www.bnaibrith.org. Illus., index, adv. Vol. ends: Jun/Jul. *Indexed:* A22, ABS&EES, IJP. *Aud.:* Ga, Ac.

This venerable consumer magazine delivers news and commentary of interest to the Jewish community. Each full-color issue is approximately 70 pages long, and has four or five feature articles, regular columns, and updates concerning B'nai B'rith, the "global voice of the Jewish community." A recent issue displays the diverse range of topics covered by the magazine, including an historical article about prominent Jewish daredevils, a series of Passover recipes, and a piece concerning the modern state of the Yiddish language. Issues from 2009 to the present are available for free on the magazine's web site, as is additional free online content. Recommended for all libraries that serve Jewish communities. URL: www.bnaibrith.org/magazine-archives.html

4625. *Buddhist - Christian Studies.* [ISSN: 0882-0945] 1981. a. USD 50. Ed(s): Wakoh S Hickey. University of Hawaii Press, 2840 Kolowalu St, Honolulu, HI 96822; uhpjourn@hawaii.edu; http://www.uhpress.hawaii.edu. Illus., adv. Sample. Refereed. Circ: 330. *Indexed:* A01, A22, AmHI, BRI, E01, R&TA. *Bk. rev.:* 10-15, 800-1,000; signed. *Aud.:* Ac, Sa.

Buddhism and Christianity have a long history of cultural and ideological contact and exchange. *Buddhist - Christian Studies* is an annually published journal that examines these two world religions in terms of their relationship to each other, their points of convergence, and how they differ. Each issue contains multiple essays grouped thematically, with issues often containing more than one topical grouping, e.g., "The Scholarly Contributions of Rita M. Gross" or "The Boundaries of Knowledge in Buddhism, Christianity and Science." Other regular sections include a "News and Views" section that provides summaries of important events and meetings, and an extensive collection of book reviews. This is an important journal for academic libraries that support programs in comparative religion, particularly when considering the increasing globalization and diversity of the modern world.

4626. *C C A R Journal: the reform Jewish quarterly.* Former titles (until 1991): *Journal of Reform Judaism;* (until 1978): *C C A R Journal.* [ISSN: 1058-8760] 1953. q. USD 100 (Free to members). Ed(s): Hara E Person, Susan E Laemmle. C C A R Press, 355 Lexington Ave,, 18th Fl, New York, NY 10017; CCARpress@ccarnet.org; http://www.ccarnet.org. Illus., adv. Vol. ends: Spring. Microform: PQC. *Indexed:* A22, IJP, R&TA. *Bk. rev.:* 3-4, 800-1,200 words; signed. *Aud.:* Ga, Ac, Sa.

CCAR Journal: The Reform Jewish Quarterly, published by the Central Conference of American Rabbis, is a major academic journal that specializes in Reform Judaism. Issues typically concern a central theme such as "Gender and Judaism in Conversation" and "Inspiration & Opportunity: The Arts and Jewish Life." Occasional issues are dedicated to CCAR symposia. This journal is particularly useful for exploring the cultural aspects of contemporary Judaism, but articles cover a variety of topics of interest to religion scholars and the Reform Jewish community. Each issue also includes original poetry, book reviews, and occasional extended bibliographic review essays. *CCAR* is recommended for both public and academic libraries, and particularly for those libraries that serve Jewish communities.

4627. *Catholic Biblical Quarterly.* [ISSN: 0008-7912] 1939. q. USD 40. Ed(s): Leslie J Hoppe. Catholic Biblical Association of America, 433 Caldwell Hall, The Catholic University of America, Washington, DC 20064; cua-cathbib@cua.edu; http://catholicbiblical.org/. Illus., index, adv. Sample. Refereed. Vol. ends: Oct. *Indexed:* A01, A22, AmHI, ArtHuCI, BRI, C26, FR, MLA-IB, P02, R&TA. *Bk. rev.:* 60-65, 400-1,100 words; signed. *Aud.:* Ac, Sa.

Published by the Catholic Biblical Association, *Catholic Biblical Quarterly* contains scholarly articles concerning the Bible and related literature. Issues contain articles on a variety of Christian topics, including ancient religious cults, biblical history, theology, and human sacrifice in the Bible. Substantial book reviews are included. This journal will be of interest to those studying the Bible from a Catholic perspective, and is recommended for academic libraries that support large Catholic communities and/or programs in or related to Catholic studies.

4628. *The Christian Century: thinking critically. living faithfully.* Incorporates (1918-1934): *The World Tomorrow;* (in 1926): *The Christian Work;* Which was formerly (until 1914): *Christian Work and the Evangelist;* Which superseded in part (in 1909): *The Arena.* [ISSN: 0009-5281] 1886. bi-w. USD 59 combined subscription (print & online eds.). Ed(s): John M Buchanan. Christian Century Foundation, 104 S Michigan Ave, Ste 1100, Chicago, IL 60603; letters@christiancentury.org; http://www.christiancentury.org. Illus., index, adv. Vol. ends: Dec. Microform: NBI; PQC. *Indexed:* A01, A22, ABS&EES, AmHI, BAS, BRI, C37, CBRI, F01, MASUSE, MLA-IB, P02, R&TA, RILM. *Bk. rev.:* 1-3, 1,000-3,000 words; signed. *Aud.:* Ga.

The Christian Century is a long-running ecumenical Christian consumer magazine. Published biweekly, *CC* contains thoughtful, well-written essays by clergy and academics that apply Christian thought to contemporary topics of interest to Christians. Articles, for example, have appeared about Zionism, the death penalty, and gun ownership from a biblical perspective. Also included is a news section, regular opinion columns, and reviews of different types of media. The publication's web site provides some magazine content free of charge, as well as access to blogs and news of interest to the Christian community. Christians, regardless of denomination, will find this magazine a valuable resource for maintaining current awareness. Recommended for public and academic libraries. URL: www.christiancentury.org/

4629. *Christianity and Literature.* Former titles (until 1973): *Conference on Christianity and Literature. Newsletter;* (until 1956): *Christian Teachers of College English. Newsletter.* [ISSN: 0148-3331] 1951. q. Free to members. Ed(s): Jordan Hardman, Maire Mullins. Conference on

Christianity and Literature, Pepperdine University, Humanities Division, 24255 Pacific Coast Hwy, Malibu, CA 90263; tammy.ditmore@pepperdine.edu; http://www.pepperdine.edu/sponsored/ ccl/. Illus., adv. Sample. Refereed. Vol. ends: Summer (No. 4). *Indexed:* A01, A22, ABS&EES, AmHI, BEL&L, MLA-IB, R&TA. *Bk. rev.:* 9-12, 1,200-2,500 words; signed. *Aud.:* Ga, Ac, Sa.

This longstanding, quarterly journal is published by the Conference on Christianity and Literature and is home to scholarship that explores the Christian faith's relationship with literature. Recent essays explore the theological, philosophical, and literary exposition of Christian concepts in the works of a wide variety of authors, including T.S. Elliot, Dominic Mulaisho, and Robert Frost. Each issue contains approximately five literary essays as well as works of original poetry and several book reviews. This journal is useful to both religious studies and English literature scholars, and is recommended for academic libraries. URL: www.pepperdine.edu/sponsored/ccl/journal/

4630. *Christianity Today: a magazine of evangelical conviction.* Incorporates (1997-200?): *Christianity Online;* Which incorporated (1997-1999): *Computing Today.* [ISSN: 0009-5753] 1956. m. USD 24.95 combined subscription domestic (print & online eds.); USD 37.95 combined subscription foreign (print & online eds.). Ed(s): Harold B Smith, Katelyn Beaty. Christianity Today International, 465 Gundersen Dr, Carol Stream, IL 60188; http://www.christianitytoday.com. Illus., index, adv. Circ: 140000. Vol. ends: Dec. Microform: PQC. *Indexed:* A01, A22, ABS&EES, BAS, BRI, C37, CBRI, Chicano, F01, MASUSE, MLA-IB, P02, R&TA, RILM. *Bk. rev.:* 5-6, 600-1,000 words; signed. *Aud.:* Ga.

This monthly newsmagazine is targeted to an evangelical Christian audience. Issues average about 100 pages and contain five or more feature articles as well as brief news reports, opinion pieces, and book and media reviews. The content is written on a variety of topics of interest to evangelicals, with recent features dealing with sex-selective abortion in China, missionary activity in Guatemala, and church involvement in politics. *Christianity Today* maintains a web site with free and subscriber-only content. Many Christians, regardless of denomination, may find this magazine of interest, and it is recommended for both public and academic libraries, regardless of size. URL: www.christianitytoday.com/

4631. *Church History: studies in Christianity and culture.* [ISSN: 0009-6407] 1932. q. GBP 98. Ed(s): Amanda Porterfield, John Corrigan. Cambridge University Press, The Edinburgh Bldg, Shaftesbury Rd, Cambridge, CB2 8RU, United Kingdom; journals@cambridge.org; http://www.cambridge.org/uk. Illus., index, adv. Refereed. Circ: 3400. Vol. ends: Dec. Reprint: PSC. *Indexed:* A01, A22, AmHI, ArtHuCI, BEL&L, BRI, CBRI, E01, FR, MLA-IB, P02, R&TA, RILM. *Bk. rev.:* 30-50, 250-1,200 words; signed. *Aud.:* Ac, Sa.

Offering historical analyses of Christianity as both institution and as culture, the articles in *Church History* cover diverse expressions of Christianity that stretch throughout the religion's temporal existence, various cultural expressions, and geographic reach. Each issue contains approximately five research articles, with recent issues including titles such as "Signs of Salvation: The Evolution of Stigmatic Spirituality Before Francis of Assisi" and "Why do Lutherans Sing? Lutherans, Music, and the Gospel in the First Century of the Reformation." The journal publishes multiple book reviews, in both short and extended formats. Both religion and history scholars will find *Church History* a valuable resource; laypeople interested in the topic will also find reading this journal to be rewarding. Recommended for academic libraries that support the social sciences and humanities.

Commentary. See News and Opinion section.

4632. *Commonweal: a review of religion, politics & culture.* [ISSN: 0010-3330] 1924. 22x/yr. USD 59 combined subscription domestic (print & online eds.); USD 64 combined subscription Canada (print & online eds.); USD 69 combined subscription elsewhere (print & online eds.). Ed(s): Paul Baumann. Commonweal Foundation, 475 Riverside Dr, Rm

405, New York, NY 10115; commonwealads@gmail.com. Illus., index, adv. Microform: MIM; PMC; PQC. *Indexed:* A01, A06, A22, ABS&EES, BAS, BEL&L, BRI, C37, CBRI, F01, MASUSE, MLA-IB, P02, RILM. *Bk. rev.:* 3-4, 900-1,900 words; signed. *Aud.:* Ga.

Commonweal: A Review of Religion, Politics & Culture is a popular, progressive magazine that presents sociocultural issues from a Catholic perspective. The magazine is published 22 times per year, and features incisive articles that address issues of concern to modern Catholics (although members of Christian denominations may also find it of great interest). In addition to the features and news, the magazine also offers opinion pieces by regular, nationally known columnists (e.g., E.J. Dionne Jr.), as well as original poetry. Substantial reviews concerning the latest books, art, and movies are included. Keeping pace with trends in news publishing, *Commonweal* hosts a dynamic web presence; its web page provides access to many free articles and reviews, and full content access is provided to paid subscribers. Recommended for all libraries, public and academic. URL: http://commonwealmagazine.org/

4633. Cross Currents (New York). Incorporates (1983-1990): *Religion and Intellectual Life;* Which was formerly (1976-1983): *The N I C M Journal for Jews and Christians in Higher Education.* [ISSN: 0011-1953] 1950. q. GBP 48 (print & online eds.). Ed(s): Charles Henderson. Wiley-Blackwell Publishing, Inc., 111 River St, Hoboken, NJ 07030; info@wiley.com; http://onlinelibrary.wiley.com/. Illus., index, adv. Sample. Refereed. Circ: 5000. Vol. ends: Winter. Reprint: PSC. *Indexed:* A01, A22, ABS&EES, AmHI, BAS, BRI, E01, FR, MLA-IB, P02, R&TA. *Bk. rev.:* 6-8, 400-2,000 words; signed. *Aud.:* Ac, Sa.

Cross Currents presents articles on multiple religious faiths. Issues center on particular themes, but the individual articles often come from different disciplinary and methodological approaches, such as cultural, political, and theological studies, all aimed at what the journal's editors describe as creating "crosscurrents" through bringing "people across lines of difference." An issue focusing on religion and art, for example, contains complementary articles on modern art, abstract art, art and liberative praxis, and biblical monotheism as biblical history. Typically, one or more bibliographic essays or extended book reviews are included at the end of every issue, and the latter articles are sometimes geared toward the issue's theme. The journal sometimes includes original poetry. Religious studies scholars, particularly those who deal with interfaith dialogue or comparative religion, will find this to be a valuable resource. Highly recommended for any academic library that supports programs in religious studies and/or theology.

4634. Currents in Biblical Research. Formerly (until 2002): *Currents in Research: Biblical Studies.* [ISSN: 1476-993X] 1993. 3x/yr. USD 408. Ed(s): Scot McKnight, Jonathan Klawens. Sage Publications Ltd., 1 Oliver's Yard, 55 City Rd, London, EC1Y 1SP, United Kingdom; info@sagepub.co.uk; http://www.uk.sagepub.com. Adv. Sample. Reprint: PSC. *Indexed:* A01, A22, E01, R&TA. *Aud.:* Ac.

This journal is a forum for biblical research from multiple disciplinary perspectives, including, but not limited to, archaeology, theology, history, and literature. *Currents in Biblical Research* regularly includes in-depth research summaries and bibliographic essays on subjects of interest to scholars in many subject areas. Recent issues summarize the literature in ancient Jewish coinage, recent literature on the Psalms, and warfare in the Old Testament. Highly recommended for academic libraries, regardless of size, that support social science and the humanities.

4635. Dialogue (Salt Lake City): a journal of mormon thought. [ISSN: 0012-2157] 1966. q. USD 50 combined subscription domestic (print & online eds.); USD 70 combined subscription foreign (print & online eds.). Ed(s): Kristine L Haglund. Dialogue Foundation, PO Box 381209, Cambridge, MA 02238; businessoffice@dialoguejournal.com. Illus., adv. Refereed. Microform: PQC. *Indexed:* A01, A22, MLA-IB, RILM. *Bk. rev.:* 2-3, 250-750 words; signed. *Aud.:* Sa.

Dialogue is a quarterly journal "established to express Mormon culture and to examine the relevance of religion to secular life." Issues contain peer-reviewed research articles and essays on LDS religion and culture. Also included are multiple works of fiction, poetry, photography, and in-depth, critical book reviews. Sermon transcripts are also included, and the editors will consider submissions from any denomination. *Dialogue's* web site gives free access to

pdfs of full issues from (currently) 2004 to 2010, and offers access to current issues by paid subscription. This journal lives up to its name, offering insight into modern Mormonism that is accessible to religion scholars, cultural studies scholars, LDS laypeople, and non-Mormons. Recommended for large public libraries and academic libraries that support programs in Mormon studies and comparative religion. URL: https://www.dialoguejournal.com/

4636. Ecclesiology: the journal for ministry, mission and unity. [ISSN: 1744-1366] 2004. 3x/yr. EUR 212. Ed(s): Paul Avis. Brill, PO Box 9000, Leiden, 2300 PA, Netherlands; cs@brill.nl; http://www.brill.nl. Adv. Refereed. Reprint: PSC. *Indexed:* A01, A22, E01, R&TA. *Bk. rev.:* Number and length vary. *Aud.:* Ac, Sa.

Ecclesiology delivers the latest academic research concerning the study of the Christian Church as institutions. Articles consider the doctrines, theologies, and philosophies of a variety of Christian denominations, both Protestant and Catholic. Oftentimes, issues are thematic, with recent issues focusing on Methodist ecclesiology. Multiple book reviews, as well as more in-depth "Article Reviews," outline the latest ecclesiological research publications. Recommended for academic libraries, particularly those that serve theological schools or religious studies programs (this is an excellent resource for comparative Christian research).

4637. The Ecumenical Review. Incorporates (1935-1948): *Christendom;* Which superseded (in 1935): *Christian Union Quarterly.* [ISSN: 0013-0796] 19??. q. GBP 157. Ed(s): Theodore Gill. Wiley-Blackwell Publishing Ltd., The Atrium, Southern Gate, Chichester, PO19 8SQ, United Kingdom; customer@wiley.com; http://www.wiley.com/. Illus., index, adv. Microform: PQC. Reprint: PSC. *Indexed:* A01, A22, AmHI, ArtHuCI, BRI, CBRI, E01, MLA-IB, P02, R&TA, RILM. *Bk. rev.:* 3-5, 800-1,000 words; signed. *Aud.:* Ac, Sa.

As the leading journal devoted specifically to the ecumenical study of Christianity, the World Council of Churches' *Ecumenical Review* presents essays that explore and promote unity among Christians. At the same time, the journal showcases the diverse nature of Christianity. Issues typically contain several articles (about eight or more per issue) related to an overarching theme, e.g., "Gendered Perspective: 'God of Life, Lead us to Justice and Peace'" and "Justice, Peace and Marginalized Communities." One regular feature is the "Ecumenical Chronicle," which provides updates concerning the latest news and events of interest to religion scholars who study ecumenism. In-depth reviews of relevant books are also provided. This journal is accessible to both scholars and general readers, and is recommended for large public libraries, large academic libraries, and those academic libraries that support theology or religious studies programs.

4638. The Empty Vessel: a journal of Daoist philosophy and practice. [ISSN: 1073-7480] 1993. q. USD 24 domestic; USD 28 Canada; USD 40 elsewhere. The Abode of the Eternal Tao, 1991 Garfield St, Eugene, OR 97405; solala@abodetao.com; http://www.abodetao.com. Illus. *Bk. rev.:* Number and length vary. *Aud.:* Ga, Ac, Sa.

The Empty Vessel is one of very few publications dedicated to Daoist philosophy and practice. This quarterly magazine, published by the Abode of the Eternal Dao, provides articles by expert practitioners on such subjects as Feng Shui, Tai Chi, and Chinese Medicine. The articles (approximately five per issue) are geared toward active practice and are accessible to both newcomers and adept practitioners. The magazine also contains a useful directory to Daoist organizations. This thoughtfully written and presented publication fills a notable gap in the literature of religion that is available to Westerners. It should be made available in both public and academic libraries of any size, but will be particularly valuable to those institutions that support comparative religion or Asian studies programs. Highly recommended.

4639. Evangelical Quarterly: an international review of Bible and theology. [ISSN: 0014-3367] 1929. q. USD 111.15 (print or online ed.) Individuals, USD 74.10 (print or online ed.). The Paternoster Press, c/o Aplhagraphics, 6 Angel Row, Nottingham, NG1 6HL, United Kingdom; periodicals@alphagraphics.co.uk; http://www.paternosterperiodicals.com. Illus., index, adv. Microform: PQC. *Indexed:* A01, A22, MLA-IB, R&TA. *Bk. rev.:* 8-20, 800-1,600; signed. *Aud.:* Ac.

Published since 1929, *Evangelical Quarterly: An International Review of Bible and Theology* is currently edited by I. Howard Marshall, a renowned theologian and Emeritus Professor of New Testament Exegesis at the University of Aberdeen, Scotland. The journal collects theological analyses from a Christian Evangelical perspective, and the journal's motto is "In Defence [sic] of the Historic Christian Faith." Articles cover both Old and New Testament theology, with recent issues addressing topics such as the Creation and the concept of atonement in Leviticus. Recommended for academic and seminary libraries that support theology programs. URL: www.biblicalstudies.org.uk

4640. Evangelical Theological Society. Journal. Formerly (until 1969): *E T S Bulletin*. [ISSN: 0360-8808] 1958. q. USD 30 (Free to members). Ed(s): Andreas Kostenberger. Evangelical Theological Society, 2825 Lexington Rd, PO Box 927, Louisville, KY 40280; http://www.etsjets.org. Illus., index, adv. Refereed. Circ: 5000 Vol. ends: Dec. *Indexed:* A22, R&TA, RILM. *Bk. rev.:* 16-20, 600-2,000 words; signed. *Aud.:* Ac, Sa.

The *Journal of the Evangelical Theological Society* (*JETS*) is a scholarly source for theological explorations of the Old and New Testament from Evangelical Christian perspectives. The stated purpose of the *JETS* is "To foster conservative Biblical scholarship by providing a medium for the oral exchange and written expression of thought and research in the general field of the theological disciplines as centered in the Scriptures." Recent articles include rigorous examinations of Saint Paul's creative use of the Old Testament Book of Isaiah in Ephesians, and a portrait of the author of Hebrews as an early Christian community faith leader. This is a leading journal in its disciplinary area, and should be in both theological libraries and large academic libraries. Excluding the last two years of publication, *JETS*'s web site provides free digital access to the journal beginning with 1969. URL: www.etsjets.org/JETS

Feminist Theology. See Gender Studies section.

4641. First Things: a monthly journal of religion and public life. [ISSN: 1047-5141] 1990. 10x/yr. USD 39 domestic; USD 49 Cambodia; USD 57 elsewhere. Ed(s): Lauren Wilson, R R Reno. Institute on Religion and Public Life, 35 E 21st St, 6th Fl, New York, NY 10010; ft@firstthings.com; http://www.firstthings.com. Index, adv. Circ: 30000 Paid. *Indexed:* A01, A22, AmHI, BRI, P02, R&TA, RILM. *Bk. rev.:* 4-5, 250-500 words; signed. *Aud.:* Ga.

Founded by Protestant-turned-Catholic Priest Richard John Neuhaus and published by the Institute on Religion and Public Life, *First Things* is a monthly Christian magazine that examines modern culture and politics from a conservative Christian, and primarily Catholic, frame of reference. Every issue contains opinion pieces, academic essays on hot topics in the news like intelligent design and health care, poetry, and book reviews. Although the writing is academic, it is easily accessible to consumer audiences; because of this, *First Things* is appropriate for both public and academic libraries. The magazine's web site provides free access to selected articles, essays, and blogs, with a paid subscription providing access to additional features. URL: www.firstthings.com/

4642. Harvard Theological Review. [ISSN: 0017-8160] 1908. q. GBP 148. Ed(s): Jon D Levenson. Cambridge University Press, The Edinburgh Bldg, Shaftesbury Rd, Cambridge, CB2 8RU, United Kingdom; journals@cambridge.org; http://www.cambridge.org/uk. Illus., index, adv. Sample. Refereed. Circ: 1600. Vol. ends: Oct. *Indexed:* A01, A22, AmHI, ArtHuCI, BRI, E01, MLA-IB, P02, R&TA. *Bk. rev.:* Number and length vary. *Aud.:* Ac.

Harvard Theological Review has been publishing the highest-quality research in Christian and Jewish theology since 1908. Each issue contains three or more articles on a variety of subjects that deal with the Christian Old and New Testaments, Jewish texts, and related literature such as the Christian apocrypha. Authors use a diverse range of methods such as historiography, literary criticism, theological exegesis, and philosophical analysis. Issues typically include one or more "review articles," which are in-depth book reviews. This journal is a must-have for any serious scholar of biblical theology and deserves a place in all academic libraries that support religious studies or theology programs.

4643. History of Religions. [ISSN: 0018-2710] 1961. q. USD 247 (print & online eds.). Ed(s): Christian K Wedemeyer, Matthew Kapstein. University of Chicago Press, 1427 E 60th St, Chicago, IL 60637; subscriptions@press.uchicago.edu; http://www.journals.uchicago.edu. Illus., index, adv. Sample. Refereed. Vol. ends: May. Reprint: PSC. *Indexed:* A01, A22, A47, AbAn, AmHI, ArtHuCI, BAS, BRI, FR, MLA-IB, P02, R&TA, RILM. *Bk. rev.:* 0-15, 400-1,800 words; signed. *Aud.:* Ac.

This journal is a key scholarly resource for the historical analysis of religion. Issues contain three historical research articles on religions of many different cultures and historical periods, all of which are rigorously researched and heavily documented. Recent issues have included articles about early Japanese origin myths; ritual politeness and feminist censorship in Iran; and health as portrayed in the writing of Ashraf Ali Thanvi. Approximately ten book reviews are included in every issue, as well as occasional extended bibliographic review articles. Historians of religion will find this publication indispensable, and historians that focus on other topics may also find the information concerning various cultures and time periods of great value. This journal is recommended is for academic libraries, particularly those that support either religious studies or history programs.

4644. Horizons (Villanova). Formerly (until 19??): *21st Century Genetics Cooperative*. [ISSN: 0360-9669] 1974. s-a. GBP 80 (print & online eds.). Ed(s): Anthony J Godzieba. Cambridge University Press, 32 Ave of the Americas, New York, NY 10013; information@cambridge.org; http://www.cambridge.org/us/. Illus. Refereed. Microform: PQC. *Indexed:* A22, ArtHuCI, C26. *Bk. rev.:* 25-30, 400-1,600 words; signed. *Aud.:* Ac.

Horizons is a scholarly journal previously published by Villanova University, and then, beginning in 2013, by Cambridge University Press. Every issue is a top-shelf collection of (primarily) Catholic theological essays that cover a wide variety of topics. Recent issues have included examinations of the work of Catholic radicals and an analysis of Thomas Aquinas in terms of eco-theology. Broader pan-Christian theological essays are also included, e.g., "World Christianity: Its Implications for History, Religious Studies, and Theology." The journal also includes occasional bibliographic review essays, symposium reviews, and relevant news reports. Particularly noteworthy are the large number of book reviews included in every issue, with the journal sometimes providing more than 30 at a time. This journal is recommended for seminaries and academic libraries that support religious studies and theology programs.

4645. The Humanist: a magazine of critical inquiry and social concern. Supersedes (in 1941): *The Humanist Bulletin;* Which superseded (in 1938): *The New Humanist;* Incorporates (1965-1969): *The Ethical Forum;* Which was formerly (until 1965): *Ethical Culture Today;* (until 1964): *The Ethical Outlook;* (until 1956): *The Standard;* (until 1914): *Ethical Addresses and Ethical Record;* Which was formed by the merger of (1899-1904): *Ethical Record;* (18??-1904): *Ethical Addresses.* [ISSN: 0018-7399] 1941. bi-m. USD 24.95. Ed(s): Jennifer Bardi. American Humanist Association, 1777 T St, NW, Washington, DC 20009; aha@americanhumanist.org; http://www.americanhumanist.org/index.html. Illus., adv. Sample. Circ: 15000 Paid. Vol. ends: Dec. Microform: PQC. *Indexed:* A01, A22, AmHI, BRI, C37, CBRI, MASUSE, MLA-IB, P02, RILM. *Bk. rev.:* 0-3, 600-1,200 words; signed. *Aud.:* Ga, Ac.

The Humanist is a bimonthly consumer magazine that offers news and commentary from secular humanist perspectives. As such, this is a valuable resource for free-thinkers, atheists, and agnostics, i.e., groups of people who are often restricted to a small number of popular publications related to their perspectives. The magazine contains five to six feature articles that approach important issues in news and culture, as well as regular columns such as "Church & State," "Fierce Humanism," and "Philosophically Speaking." Most articles contain full-color photographs and/or illustrations. Every issue contains reviews for new books and other media. The magazine maintains a well-constructed web site that provides full-text articles from 2007 to the present, as well as a blog and access to a podcast. The *Humanist* is appropriate for both public and academic libraries, large or small. URL: http://thehumanist.org/

4646. International Journal for Philosophy of Religion. [ISSN: 0020-7047] 1970. bi-m. EUR 741 (print & online eds.). Ed(s): Romald L Hall. Springer Netherlands, Van Godewijckstraat 30, Dordrecht, 3311

GX, Netherlands; http://www.springer.com. Illus., index, adv. Refereed. Vol. ends: Jun/Dec. Microform: PQC. Reprint: PSC. *Indexed:* A01, A22, AmHI, ArtHuCI, BRI, E01, FR, IBSS, P02, R&TA. *Bk. rev.:* 0-4, 600-1,000 words; signed. *Aud.:* Ac.

The *International Journal for Philosophy of Religion* is a bimonthly publication that considers religion and religious phenomena from primarily Western philosophical perspectives (e.g., analytical and continental approaches). Although Western, Abrahamic religions appear frequently as the focus of articles, all religions are fair game. Atheism, for instance, was the topic of a recent themed issue. Issues also include reviews of the latest scholarly monographs investigating the juncture of philosophy and faith. This journal is valuable to researchers in philosophy, theology, and religious studies. Recommended for academic libraries.

4647. *The International Journal for the Psychology of Religion.* [ISSN: 1050-8619] 1991. q. GBP 436 (print & online eds.). Ed(s): Raymond F Paloutzian. Routledge, 325 Chestnut St, Ste 800, Philadelphia, PA 19106; customerservice@taylorandfrancis.com; http://www.tandfonline.com. Illus., adv. Sample. Refereed. Vol. ends: No. 4. Reprint: PSC. *Indexed:* A01, A22, ASSIA, ArtHuCI, E01, PsycInfo, R&TA. *Bk. rev.:* 1-2, 500-1,500 words; signed. *Aud.:* Ac, Sa.

Exploring the relationship between religion and the human mind, this journal publishes quantitative and qualitative studies concerning the psychological components of religious behavior and phenomena. Although there are occasionally issues devoted to a specific subject, the range of topics in an issue is often diverse. One recent issue, for example, contained studies about the psychological basis of spiritual transcendence; religion and coping among college students; and religions as a means for making moral decisions. Suitable for religion scholars, social scientists, and neuroscientists. Recommended for academic libraries.

4648. *International Journal of Hindu Studies.* [ISSN: 1022-4556] 1997. 3x/yr. USD 354 (print & online eds.). Ed(s): Sushil Mittal. Springer Netherlands, Van Godewijckstraat 30, Dordrecht, 3311 GX, Netherlands; http://www.springer-sbm.de. Illus., index, adv. Sample. Refereed. Vol. ends: Dec. Reprint: PSC. *Indexed:* A22, AmHI, ArtHuCI, BAS, BRI, E01. *Bk. rev.:* Usually one per issue. *Aud.:* Ac, Sa.

Although there are many fine journals devoted to Asian religious traditions, the *International Journal of Hindu Studies* is one of few devoted exclusively to Hinduism, the world's third-largest religion. Issues contain original research papers that cover the large variety of "Hinduisms" in terms of both religion and culture, in India and in the Indian diaspora. This publication, as a result, is a valuable resource for religious studies scholars as well as philosophy, history, anthropology, Asian studies, and political science researchers. This title is recommended for large academic libraries.

4649. *International Review of Mission.* [ISSN: 0020-8582] 1911. bi-m. GBP 157. Ed(s): Dr. Jooseop Keum. Wiley-Blackwell Publishing Ltd., The Atrium, Southern Gate, Chichester, PO19 8SQ, United Kingdom; customer@wiley.com; http://www.wiley.com/. Illus., index, adv. Vol. ends: Oct. Microform: PQC. Reprint: PSC. *Indexed:* A01, A06, A22, A47, AmHI, BAS, BRI, Chicano, E01, MLA-IB, P02, R&TA. *Bk. rev.:* 0-5, 200-1,000 words; signed. *Aud.:* Ac, Sa.

The *International Review of Mission* has been published by the World Council of Churches since 1911. Articles cover Christian mission work from sociological, theological, philosophical, and other academic perspectives, and they do so, according to the journal editors, in an ecumenical spirit. Recent articles have covered the use of hospitality in mission work; multiculturalism in mission work; and social justice in mission work. As an organ of the WCC, the *International Review of Mission* also includes the latest news, documentation, and commentary concerning that institution's activities. Extended book reviews covering new, mission-related works are included in every issue. Christian studies scholars will find this journal valuable, as will laypeople, working missionaries, and pastors. Recommended for large public libraries as well as academic libraries that support Christian studies, theology, or missionary training programs.

4650. *Interpretation: a journal of bible and theology.* Former titles (until 1947): *The Union Seminary Review;* (until 1913): *Union Seminary Magazine.* [ISSN: 0020-9643] 1889. q. USD 210. Ed(s): Debra Reagan, Samuel E Balentine. Sage Publications Ltd., 1 Oliver's Yard, 55 City Rd, London, EC1Y 1SP, United Kingdom; info@sagepub.co.uk; http://www.uk.sagepub.com. Illus., adv. Refereed. Vol. ends: Oct. Microform: PQC. Reprint: PSC. *Indexed:* A01, A22, AmHI, ArtHuCI, BRI, CBRI, FR, P02, R&TA. *Bk. rev.:* Number and length vary. *Aud.:* Ga, Ac.

This venerable journal has been a publication of Union Presbyterian Seminary since 1885. Issues are often themed around subjects that explore theological questions in relationship to timely issues (e.g., climate change, modern conceptions of the body). Besides theological essays, the journal includes short "Between Text and Sermon" articles that interpret Bible passages from Christian perspectives. Also included are several substantial book reviews (2–3 pages each) and numerous short book reviews (usually about a paragraph each). Professional theologians and biblical scholars, regardless of religious denomination, will make good use of this journal. Recommended for seminary and academic libraries. URL: www.interpretation.org/

4651. *Japanese Journal of Religious Studies.* Formerly (until 1974): *Contemporary Religions in Japan.* [ISSN: 0304-1042] 1960. s-a. JPY 5000 (Individuals, JPY 3500). Ed(s): Paul I Swanson. Nanzan Institute for Religion and Culture, 18 Yamazato-cho, Showa-ku, Nagoya, 466-8673, Japan; nirc@ic.nanzan-u.ac.jp; http://www.nanzan-u.ac.jp/SHUBUNKEN/index.htm. Illus., index, adv. Refereed. Circ: 600. *Indexed:* A22, ArtHuCI, BAS, FR, MLA-IB, R&TA. *Bk. rev.:* 0-15, 1,000-3,000 words; signed. *Aud.:* Ac, Sa.

Although research concerning Japanese religions appears in many different comparative religion journals and in journals devoted to specific Eastern religions in general or particular religions such as Buddhism, the *Japanese Journal of Religious Studies* is solely devoted to that country's religious movements. The journal is an invaluable resource, considering that Japan has long been a hotbed of religious activity, supporting an indigenous religion (Shintoism), imported religions (e.g., Zen Buddhism), and new religious movements (e.g., Soka Gakkai). Issues contain five or more articles, usually covering a variety of topics like "A Blueprint for Buddhist Revolution" and "Spiritual Therapies in Japan," although issues may be thematic, such as the recent "Aftermath: The Impact and Ramifications of the Aum [Shinrikyo] Affair." *JRS* is available in print, but is also Open Access and freely available on the web. This journal is necessity for researchers of Asian religions and new religious movements and is recommended for all academic libraries. URL: http://nirc.nanzan-u.ac.jp/en/publications/jjrs/

Jewish Quarterly. See Literary Reviews section.

4652. *Journal for the Scientific Study of Religion.* [ISSN: 0021-8294] 1961. q. GBP 146. Ed(s): Laura Olson. Wiley-Blackwell Publishing, Inc., 111 River St, Hoboken, NJ 07030; info@wiley.com; http://onlinelibrary.wiley.com/. Illus., index, adv. Sample. Refereed. Vol. ends: Dec. Microform: PQC. Reprint: PSC. *Indexed:* A01, A22, ABS&EES, AmHI, ArtHuCI, BAS, BRI, E01, FR, IBSS, IJP, MLA-IB, P02, P61, PsycInfo, R&TA, SSA. *Bk. rev.:* 4-8, 600-1,500 words; signed. *Aud.:* Ac.

An organ of the Society for the Scientific Study of Religion, the *Journal for the Scientific Study of Religion* includes analyses of religion from social scientific fields such as sociology, psychology, and history. The articles typically adopt, but are not limited to, either quantitative or qualitative empirical approaches. The interdisciplinary nature of the journal, as well as the global scope of its contents, results in a fascinatingly eclectic collection of material, with recent issues including the articles "Factor Analysis of the Mystical Experience Questionnaire: A Study of Experiences Occasioned by the Hallucinogen Psilocybin," "Countervailing Forces: Religiosity and Paranormal Belief in Italy," and "The Gods Are Watching: An Experimental Study of Religion and Traditional Belief in Burkina Faso." This journal will appeal to students and researchers across the social sciences and should be included in academic libraries that support social scientific disciplines.

4653. *Journal for the Study of the Historical Jesus.* [ISSN: 1476-8690] 2003. 3x/yr. EUR 261. Ed(s): Robert L Webb. Brill, PO Box 9000, Leiden, 2300 PA, Netherlands; cs@brill.nl; http://www.brill.nl. Adv. Refereed. Reprint: PSC. *Indexed:* A01, A22, E01. *Bk. rev.:* 4-8, 100-400 words; signed. *Aud.:* Ac.

Articles in the *Journal for the Study of the Historical Jesus* explore the life of Jesus Christ, the lives of his early followers, and the cultures of the time. Besides the in-depth analysis of Jesus himself, other popular subjects are the life of John the Baptist and the everyday life and practices of believers and other contemporaries. *JSHC* also often prints essays about historical Jesus research as a discipline, giving insight into current theory and practice related to the field. This is a valuable journal of historians of the Abrahamic religions, as well as scholars that focus on the history of the ancient Middle East and/or the Mediterranean world. Appropriate for academic libraries that support religious studies or history programs.

4654. *Journal for the Study of the New Testament.* [ISSN: 0142-064X] 1978. 5x/yr. USD 689. Ed(s): Dr. Catrin H Williams. Sage Publications Ltd., 1 Oliver's Yard, 55 City Rd, London, EC1Y 1SP, United Kingdom; info@sagepub.co.uk; http://www.uk.sagepub.com. Illus., index. Sample. Refereed. Vol. ends: Jun. Reprint; PSC. *Indexed:* A01, A22, E01, FR, R&TA, RILM. *Bk. rev.:* 2-7, 300-400 words; signed. *Aud.:* Ac.

The *Journal for the Study of the New Testament* offers scholarly investigations of New Testament books from multiple academic vantage points including, but not limited to, theological and historical. Recent articles include "What does Matthew Say about Divine Recompense? On the Misuse of the Parable of the Workers in the Vineyard (20.1-16)" and "Narrative Space, Angelic Revelation, and the End of Mark's Gospel." The journal is aimed at the professional Bible scholar; it is a highly rigorous publication, with authors presenting many of the studied passages in their original languages. Recommended for large academic libraries as well as those libraries that support theology programs. This journal is complemented well by its sister journal, the *Journal for the Study of the Old Testament.*

4655. *Journal for the Study of the Old Testament.* [ISSN: 0309-0892] 1976. 5x/yr. USD 689. Ed(s): Yvonne Sherwood, John Jarick. Sage Publications Ltd., 1 Oliver's Yard, 55 City Rd, London, EC1Y 1SP, United Kingdom; info@sagepub.co.uk; http://www.uk.sagepub.com. Illus. Sample. Refereed. Vol. ends: No. 5. Reprint: PSC. *Indexed:* A01, A22, E01, FR, MLA-IB, R&TA. *Bk. rev.:* 100-700 words; signed. *Aud.:* Ac.

The *Journal for the Study of the Old Testament* is an outlet for research concerning the books of the Christian Old Testament. The journal published theological, historical, literary analyses of these books, but it also, according to the editors, encourages "submissions from scholars outside the field of Biblical Studies whose work impinges on Bible/Old Testament in provocative ways." Recent articles include "Between the Goat's Arse and the Face of God: Deleuze and Guattari and Marx and the Bible," "Where there is Dirt, is there System: Revisiting Biblical Purity and Constructions," and "The Type-Scene Connection between Genesis 38 and the Joseph Story." Occasionally the journal publishes book list issues that provide short descriptions, organized by subject, of the latest in Old Testament Studies. This journal is recommended for Christian studies and theology scholars, and is appropriate for large academic libraries as well as those libraries that support theology programs. This journal is complemented well by its sister journal, the *Journal for the Study of the New Testament.*

4656. *Journal of Biblical Literature.* Formerly (until 1890): *Society of Biblical Literature and Exegesis. Journal.* [ISSN: 0021-9231] 1881. q. USD 190 (print & online eds.) Members, USD 45). Ed(s): Adele Reinhartz. Society of Biblical Literature, The Luce Ctr, 825 Houston Mill Rd, Atlanta, GA 30329; sblexec@sbl-site.org; http://www.sbl-site.org. Illus., index, adv. Refereed. Circ: 4200. Vol. ends: Winter. Microform: PMC; PQC. *Indexed:* A01, A22, AmHI, ArtHuCI, BRI, CBRI, IJP, MLA-IB, P02, R&TA, RILM. *Bk. rev.:* 20-25, 900-1,500 words; signed. *Aud.:* Ac.

The *Journal of Biblical Literature* is published quarterly by the Society of Biblical Literature. *JBL* boasts a prestigious editorial of internationally recognized scholars, and this is reflected in the high quality of the research articles included in every issue. These articles include textual criticisms and exegeses of New and Old Testament books of the Bible. Bible theologians will find this journal particularly valuable. Recommended for seminary libraries and those academic libraries that support programs in Christian studies or divinity schools.

4657. *Journal of Church and State.* [ISSN: 0021-969X] 1959. q. EUR 155. Ed(s): Patricia Cornett, Jerold Waltman. Oxford University Press, 2001 Evans Rd, Cary, NC 27513; http://www.us.oup.com. Index, adv. Sample. Refereed. Vol. ends: Fall. Microform: WSH; PMC; PQC. Reprint: PSC; WSH. *Indexed:* A01, A22, ABS&EES, AmHI, ArtHuCI, BAS, BRI, CBRI, CLI, IBSS, L14, P02, R&TA. *Bk. rev.:* 35-40, 300-800 words; signed. *Aud.:* Ac, Sa.

The *Journal of Church and State* is published by Oxford University Press on behalf of Baylor University's J.M. Dawson institute of Church-State Studies. *JCS* chronicles the oftentimes problematic relationship between civil government and religion, with essays such as "Conscience and Compromise: Strategies of Dissent in Late Tudor England" and "Protecting Religious Liberty: A Comparative Analysis of the Educational Philosophies of Thomas Jefferson and John Courtney Murray, SJ." Each contains five or essays, along with multiple substantial book reviews. Recommended for academic libraries that support programs in law, sociology, and/or political science.

4658. *Journal of Early Christian Studies.* Formerly (until 1993): *The Second Century;* Incorporates (1972-1993): *Patristics.* [ISSN: 1067-6341] 1981. q. USD 165. Ed(s): David Brakke. The Johns Hopkins University Press, 2715 N Charles St, Baltimore, MD 21218; http://www.press.jhu.edu. Illus., adv. Sample. Refereed. Circ: 1328. Vol. ends: Winter. Reprint: PSC. *Indexed:* A01, A22, AmHI, ArtHuCI, E01, MLA-IB, R&TA. *Bk. rev.:* 10-20, 400-1,000 words; signed. *Aud.:* Ac.

The *Journal of Early Christian Studies* is issued by the North American Patristics Society and collects, according to the editors, "the best of traditional scholarship while showcasing articles that call attention to newer themes and methodologies than those appearing in other patristics journals." Recent articles include critical analysis of period literature, epigraphic studies, and historical research. Although this journal is appropriate for all academic libraries that serve church historians, historians of ancient history will also find it valuable.

4659. *Journal of Ecclesiastical History.* [ISSN: 0022-0469] 1950. q. GBP 362. Ed(s): James Carleton Paget, Diarmaid MacCulloch. Cambridge University Press, The Edinburgh Bldg, Shaftesbury Rd, Cambridge, CB2 8RU, United Kingdom; journals@cambridge.org; http://www.cambridge.org/uk. Illus., adv. Sample. Refereed. Circ: 1900. Vol. ends: Oct. Microform: PQC. Reprint: PSC. *Indexed:* A01, A22, AmHI, ArtHuCI, BRI, BrArAb, E01, FR, MLA-IB, NumL, P02, R&TA. *Bk. rev.:* 60-75, 300-700 words; signed. *Aud.:* Ac.

Published by Cambridge University Press, this quarterly journal is an excellent source for scholarly research on Christian Church history and the history of the Church clergy. Many articles deal with Christianity in Great Britain, but other geographic regions are represented, e.g., South Africa, Continental Europe, and Mesopotamia. The time period covered tends to be early modern to the nineteenth century, but again, there are exceptions, with articles sometimes looking back into the Middle Ages and later. Issues contain multiple book reviews. Recommended for historians and religious studies scholars, particularly those that study the Church in the West. Appropriate for academic libraries.

4660. *Journal of Feminist Studies in Religion.* [ISSN: 8755-4178] 1985. s-a. USD 91.50 (print & online eds.). Ed(s): Elisabeth Schussler Fiorenza, Stephanie May. Indiana University Press, 601 N Morton St, Bloomington, IN 47404; journals@indiana.edu; http://iupress.indiana.edu. Illus., adv. Sample. Refereed. Circ: 950 Paid. Reprint: PSC. *Indexed:* A01, A22, AmHI, ArtHuCI, BRI, E01, FemPer, MLA-IB, P02, R&TA, WSA. *Bk. rev.:* Essay length; signed. *Aud.:* Ac, Sa.

Published by Indiana University Press, the *Journal of Feminist Studies in Religion* examines religious phenomena and history using critical feminist methodologies. In this capacity, *JFSR* serves as an important counterpoint to the large body of religious scholarship that originates out of patriarchal perspectives and power structures. The aims of the editors are normative; they are "committed to rigorous thinking and analysis in the service of the transformation of religious studies as a discipline and the feminist transformation of religious and cultural studies." Recent articles include "More Slave Women, More Lewdness: Freedom and Honor in Rabbinic Constructions of Female Sexuality" and "Appropriation and Assertion of the Female Self: Materials for the Study of the Female Tantric master Laksmi of Uddiyana," demonstrating the publication's wide range and scope. Besides research articles, the journal sometimes presents special sections of essays dedicated to a particular topic (e.g., the work of Mary Daly), shorter opinion pieces, or works of original poetry. This is an important journal for both religious studies and women and gender studies scholars, and should be included in the collection of libraries that support these researchers and their students. URL: www.fsrinc.org/

4661. *Journal of Jewish Studies.* [ISSN: 0022-2097] 1948. s-a. GBP 140 (print & online eds.). Ed(s): Dr. Sacha Stern, Geza Vermes. Oxford Centre for Hebrew and Jewish Studies, Yarnton Manor, Yarnton, OX1 1PY, United Kingdom; enquiries@ochjs.ac.uk; http://www.ochjs.ac.uk. Illus., adv. Sample. Refereed. Vol. ends: Oct. Microform: PQC. Reprint: PSC. *Indexed:* A01, A22, AmHI, ArtHuCI, FR, IBSS, IJP, MLA-IB, R&TA. *Bk. rev.:* 25-30, 400-3,000 words; signed. *Aud.:* Ac, Sa.

The *Journal of Jewish Studies,* published by the Oxford Centre for Hebrew and Jewish Studies, is a long-running international journal that showcases the historical, religious, and cultural depth of Judaism. Recent articles have included "Compulsive Libationers: Non-Jews and Wine in Early Rabbinic Sources," "In Between Cultures: An Anonymous Commentary on the Book of Proverbs from Thirteenth-Century Iberia," and "Zionism and Violence in Albert Einstein's Political Work." Researchers in many different fields will find this to be an important resource, including the fields of religious studies, theology, Judaic studies, and history. Includes multiple book reviews as well as list of books received. Recommended for academic libraries and large public libraries. URL: www.jjs-online.net/index.php

4662. *Journal of Pentecostal Theology.* [ISSN: 0966-7369] 1992. s-a. EUR 232. Ed(s): John Christopher Thomas. Brill, PO Box 9000, Leiden, 2300 PA, Netherlands; cs@brill.nl; http://www.brill.nl. Adv. Reprint: PSC. *Indexed:* A01, A22, E01, R&TA. *Bk. rev.:* Number and length vary. *Aud.:* Ac.

Christian Pentecostalism is a movement that adopts the position that people can have direct, experiential relationships with God. The *Journal of Pentecostal Theology* is an important international organ of scholarly research for facilitating discourse concerning Pentecostal theology. Each issue covers a variety of theological topics and, according to the journal's web site, includes the contributions of non-Pentecostals in the service of ecumenism. Issues typically include an extended critical book review, as well as occasional response articles to previously published essays. This journal is recommended for seminary libraries as well as large academic libraries. URL: www.brill.com/journal-pentecostal-theology

4663. *Journal of Presbyterian History.* Former titles (until 1997): *American Presbyterians;* (until 1985): *Journal of Presbyterian History;* (until 1962): *Presbyterian Historical Society. Journal;* (until 1943): *Presbyterian Historical Society. Department of History. Journal;* (until 1930): *Presbyterian Historical Society. Journal.* [ISSN: 1521-9216] 1901. s-a. Free to members. Ed(s): J Moorhead, Frederick J Heuser. Presbyterian Historical Society, 425 Lombard St, Philadelphia, PA 19147; refdesk@history.pcusa.org; http://www.history.pcusa.org/. Illus., index. Sample. Refereed. Vol. ends: Winter. *Indexed:* A22, ArtHuCI, BAS, BEL&L, FR, R&TA, RILM. *Bk. rev.:* 5-10, 400-600 words; signed. *Aud.:* Ac, Sa.

This longstanding journal has been published since 1901 by the Presbyterian Historical Society. Each biannual issue contains beautifully illustrated historical studies of the Presbyterian church. The journal will appeal to both scholars and interested laypeople who read in Christian studies and other disciplines. One recent issue, for example, is dedicated to the Church's role in the American civil rights movement, and provides a perspective valuable to researchers in American history as well as ethnic studies. Every issue also includes the section "Our Documentary Heritage," which provides thematically related, high-quality reproduction of images (e.g., photographs, booklet covers). The regular section "On Holy Ground" describes the history and architecture of historic Presbyterian church buildings, as well as provides images of the structures. This journal is recommended for public libraries that support Presbyterian communities and academic libraries that support programs in American history and/or religious studies.

4664. *Journal of Psychology and Theology: an evangelical forum for the integration of psychology and theology.* [ISSN: 0091-6471] 1973. q. USD 46 domestic; USD 60 foreign. Ed(s): Todd W Hall. Biola University, Rosemead School of Psychology, 13800 Biola Ave, La Mirada, CA 90639-0001; jpt.subscriptions@biola.edu; http://www.rosemead.edu. Illus., index, adv. Refereed. Vol. ends: Winter. Microform: PQC. *Indexed:* A01, A22, AmHI, ArtHuCI, BRI, MLA-IB, PsycInfo, R&TA. *Bk. rev.:* 4-6, 750-1,000 words; signed. *Aud.:* Ac.

The *Journal of Psychology and Theology* is based at the Rosemead School of Psychology and published by Biola University. Articles explore the intersection of religion and psychology from Evangelical Christian perspectives. The majority of articles published are empirical, quantitative studies that assess the relationships between such things as sexual harassment in Christian academia; psychological attachment and forgiveness; and religious involvement and health rates. The journal includes book reviews as well as critical analyses of the latest relevant articles that concern religion and psychology. Although *JPT* is aimed at the Evangelical community, it will be of interest to psychologists and specialists in the psychology of religion. Appropriate for large academic libraries and libraries affiliated with religious schools that support research in the psychology of religion.

4665. *The Journal of Religion.* Formed by the merger of (1897-1921): *American Journal of Theology;* (1893-1921): *The Biblical World;* Which was formerly (until 1893): *The Old and New Testament Student;* (until 1889): *The Old Testament Student;* (until 1883): *The Hebrew Student.* [ISSN: 0022-4189] 1921. q. USD 232 (print & online eds.). Ed(s): Franklin I Gamwell, Daniel A Arnold. University of Chicago Press, 1427 E 60th St, Chicago, IL 60637; subscriptions@press.uchicago.edu; http://www.journals.uchicago.edu. Illus., index, adv. Sample. Refereed. Vol. ends: Oct. Microform: MIM; PMC; PQC. Reprint: PSC. *Indexed:* A01, A22, AmHI, ArtHuCI, BAS, BEL&L, BRI, CBRI, FR, IPB, MLA-IB, P02, R&TA. *Bk. rev.:* 50-60, 750-1,500 words; signed. *Aud.:* Ac.

The *Journal of Religion* is a top-tier, rigorously academic theological and philosophy of religion journal published by the Divinity School of the University Chicago. Articles tend to focus on the major Abrahamic religions (Judaism, Christianity, and Islam) but not exclusively, with recent essays appearing on subjects such as Buddhism and Roman paganism. Articles also sometimes deal with religion in the broader sense; for example, recent studies have explored the tension between science and religion, post-secularism in modern society, and civic religion in American history. Theologians, religious studies scholars, and philosophers of religion will find this journal essential. Suitable for academic libraries of any size.

4666. *Journal of Religion and Health.* [ISSN: 0022-4197] 1961. q. EUR 988 (print & online eds.). Ed(s): Curtis W Hart. Springer New York LLC, 233 Spring St, New York, NY 10013; service-ny@springer.com; http://www.springer.com/. Illus., index, adv. Refereed. Vol. ends: Winter. Microform: PQC. Reprint: PSC. *Indexed:* A01, A22, ArtHuCI, BRI, E01, IJP, P02, PsycInfo, R&TA. *Bk. rev.:* 15-20, 300-800 words; signed. *Aud.:* Ga, Ac.

The *Journal of Religion and Health* investigates the connection between faith and all manner of health issues, both physical and psychological. Every issue of the quarterly journal contains multiple original research articles—typically ten or more—with recent articles including "Chaplaincy and Mental Health Care in Aotearoa New Zealand: an Exploratory Study" and "Asklepian Dreaming and the Spirit of Transformational Healing: Linking the Placebo Response to Therapeutic Uses of Self." In addition to the original research articles are occasional "Psychological Explorations" or "Philosophical Explorations" in which essayists present everything from philosophical meditations on the juncture of health and ethics, to poetry concerning sexual attraction, the mind, and spirituality. This journal is valuable to those who study religion, health care, or how the two relate. Recommended for academic and medical libraries.

4667. *Journal of Religious Ethics.* [ISSN: 0384-9694] 1973. q. GBP 215 (print & online eds.). Ed(s): Martin Kawka, Akine Kalbian. Wiley-Blackwell Publishing, Inc., 111 River St, Hoboken, NJ 07030; info@wiley.com; http://onlinelibrary.wiley.com/. Illus., adv. Sample. Refereed. Vol. ends: Fall. Microform: PQC. Reprint: PSC. *Indexed:* A01, A22, ABS&EES, AmHI, ArtHuCI, BRI, E01, MLA-IB, P02, R&TA. *Bk. rev.:* Number varies. *Aud.:* Ac, Sa.

The *Journal of Religious Ethics* focuses on ethics in both contemporary and historical religions. All religious traditions are open for consideration. One recent issue, for instance, contains articles concerning ethics and Judaism, Catholicism, Buddhism, and Neo-Confucianism. Occasionally, the journal dedicates issues to topics of perennial or current interest, such as religious perspectives on torture. Although there is not a book review section, the *Journal of Religious Ethics* often provides a lengthy "Book Discussion" that critically examines one or more books on a particular subject or by a particular author. Religion scholars, historians, and philosophers will all find this to be a valuable resource. Appropriate for academic libraries.

The Journal of Religious Thought. See African American section.

4668. Journal of Theological Studies. [ISSN: 0022-5185] 1899. s-a. EUR 400. Ed(s): Graham Gould. Oxford University Press, Great Clarendon St, Oxford, OX2 6DP, United Kingdom; enquiry@oup.co.uk; http://www.oxfordjournals.org/. Illus., index, adv. Sample. Refereed. Vol. ends: Oct. Microform: PQC. Reprint: PSC. *Indexed:* A01, A22, AmHI, ArtHuCI, BRI, E01, FR, MLA-IB, P02, R&TA. *Bk. rev.:* 180-200, 400-2,500 words; signed. *Aud.:* Ac, Sa.

The *Journal of Theological Studies* is a high-quality academic journal published by Oxford University Press and dedicated to cutting-edge Christian theology and biblical interpretation. Articles examine the Old and New Testaments of the Bible, as well as the works of the Church fathers and other later Christian writings. The journal also publishes previously unpublished "ancient and modern texts, inscriptions, and documents." Every issue contains multiple book reviews, as well as a list of books received. This journal is recommended for Christian theologians, but may also be of interest to historians and archaeologists. Recommended for academic libraries.

4669. Literature and Theology. Formerly (until 1987): *National Conference of Literature and Religion. Newsletter.* [ISSN: 0269-1205] 1983. q. EUR 322. Ed(s): Dr. Andrew Hass. Oxford University Press, Great Clarendon St, Oxford, OX2 6DP, United Kingdom; enquiry@oup.co.uk; http://www.oxfordjournals.org/. Illus., adv. Sample. Refereed. Vol. ends: Dec. Reprint: PSC. *Indexed:* A01, A22, AmHI, ArtHuCI, E01, MLA-IB, R&TA, RILM. *Bk. rev.:* 5-10, 400-1,000 words; signed. *Aud.:* Ac, Sa.

Literature and Theology, published by Oxford University Press, provides literary analyses of religious writings as well as the critical analyses of religious motifs and themes in (not necessarily religious) literature. Articles are accepted from a variety of academic perspectives and, although the articles tend toward analysis of Christian and Jewish themes, the journal is not limited solely to these Abrahamic religions. Issues are occasionally organized around themes or the work of particular authors. Book reviews are included, as well as notices and reports of events of interest to academics. This journal will be of interest to both literature and religion scholars and is recommended for academic libraries that support programs in the humanities.

4670. Mennonite Quarterly Review: a quarterly journal devoted to Anabaptist-Mennonite history, thought, life and affairs. Supersedes (in 1927): *Goshen College Record. Review Supplement.* [ISSN: 0025-9373] 1926. q. USD 35 in US & Canada; USD 45 elsewhere. Ed(s): John D Roth. Goshen College, 1700 S Main St, Goshen, IN 46526; info@goshen.edu; http://www.goshen.edu. Illus., index. Sample. Refereed. Vol. ends: Oct. *Indexed:* A22, ABS&EES, BRI, FR, MLA-IB, R&TA, RILM. *Bk. rev.:* 7-12, 100-600 words; signed. *Aud.:* Ac, Sa.

The *Mennonite Quarterly Review* publishes scholarly articles concerning Anabaptist–Mennonite studies. The journal covers a variety of topics using multiple disciplinary approaches, e.g., philosophical considerations of religious ethics, historical accounts of Mennonite persecutions in Holland, and cultural studies of Amish romance novels. Every issue includes lengthy book reviews as well as news and announcements; both news and reviews are particularly valuable considering the specialist nature of the field of study. The journal's web site provides a useful bibliography to Anabaptist materials from the sixteenth century, a biographical dictionary of European church leaders, and tables of contents for volumes from 1997 to the present. Recommended for large academic libraries and those libraries that support programs in comparative Christianity. URL: www.goshen.edu/mqr/

4671. Methodist History. Supersedes in part (in 1962): *World Parish.* [ISSN: 0026-1238] 1948. q. USD 25 domestic; USD 30 Canada; USD 40 elsewhere. Ed(s): Robert J Williams. United Methodist Church, General Commission on Archives & History, 36 Madison Avenue, PO Box 127, Madison, NJ 07940; gcah@gcah.org; http://www.gcah.org. Illus. Refereed. Microform: PQC. *Indexed:* A22, BAS, BRI, FR, MLA-IB, R&TA, RILM. *Bk. rev.:* 1-5, 50-500 words; signed. *Aud.:* Ac, Sa.

Methodist History is the official publication of the General Commission on Archives and History of the United Methodist Church. The journal is available in print as well as free electronically through the journal's web site (which archives issues from the present back to 1962). Issues contain research articles concerning the history of Methodism as an institution, culture, and community. The journal has also published previously unpublished materials, such as unpublished letters by John Wesley. Both laypeople and professional researchers will find *Methodist History* to be worthy of serious attention. The journal is appropriate for both academic and public libraries that support Methodist communities or researchers concerned with the history of Methodism or Protestant Christianity. The link to the journal's web page should be made freely available on both academic and public library subject guides. URL: http://archives.gcah.org/xmlui/handle/10516/30

4672. Methodist Review: a journal of Wesleyan and Methodist studies. [ISSN: 1946-5254] 2009. a. Free. Ed(s): Dr. Rex D Matthews, Dr. Ted A Campbell. The Methodist Review, Inc., 1001 9th Ave, Nashville, TN 37203-4729; rex.matthews@emory.edu. Refereed. *Aud.:* Ga, Ac.

Methodist Review is an online scholarly journal that is available by free registration. The journal is dedicated to scholarship involving the Methodist Church and Methodist culture and welcomes submissions from a variety of different disciplinary perspectives including, per its web site, "biblical, theological, philosophical, historical, and social-scientific." Articles are published as they become available, taking advantage of the immediate nature of the web. Besides the peer-reviewed articles, *Methodist Review* also publishes a *Methodist Review Newsletter* that contains news concerning academic societies and events, recent publications of interest, and open job positions in academia and the Church (all of which is, again, free with registration). Both scholars and laypeople will find this journal valuable. Because it is open access, both public and academic libraries should consider linking the web site to their online subject guides and catalog. URL: https://www.methodistreview.org/index.php/mr/index

4673. Modern Judaism: a journal of Jewish ideas and experience. [ISSN: 0276-1114] 1981. 3x/yr. EUR 194. Ed(s): Dr. Steven T Katz. Oxford University Press, Great Clarendon St, Oxford, OX2 6DP, United Kingdom; enquiry@oup.co.uk; http://www.oxfordjournals.org/. Illus., index, adv. Sample. Refereed. Reprint: PSC. *Indexed:* A22, ABS&EES, AmHI, ArtHuCI, BRI, E01, ENW, IJP, MLA-IB, R&TA, RILM. *Bk. rev.:* 1-3, 2,000-3,000 words. *Aud.:* Ac, Sa.

Modern Judaism is a platform for articles that explore modern—i.e., from the Jewish Enlightenment to the present—Jewish history, religion, and culture. The range of topics explores the breadth and geographic limits of Jewish experience. Recent articles have dealt with the popularization of the Kabbalah, Jewish orthodoxy in America, and references to Christians and Christianity in eighteenth- and nineteenth-century Jewish literature. Also included are lengthy "review essays" and a list of books received. Useful for scholars of any of the Abrahamic religions, and recommended for large public libraries and academic libraries that support religious studies, Jewish studies, or history programs.

4674. Mountain Record: the Zen practitioner's journal. [ISSN: 0896-8942] 1981. q. USD 24 domestic; USD 39 foreign. Dharma Communications, Inc., PO Box 156, Mt. Tremper, NY 12457; mreditor@dharma.net; http://www.dharma.net/dchome.html. Adv. Circ: 5000 Paid. *Bk. rev.:* Number and length vary. *Aud.:* Ga, Ac, Sa.

Dharma Communications' *Mountain Record* is a quarterly consumer magazine aimed at those interested in Zen Buddhism and related religious traditions. Each beautifully illustrated issue contains articles written by notable Buddhists (including, according to the magazine's web site, the Dalai Lama). Issues contain spiritual teaching, art, and poetry, as well as classified ads of interest to practitioners. Appropriate for public libraries that serve Buddhist communities, as well as large academic libraries or those academic libraries that support programs in religious studies or Asian studies.

4675. The Muslim World. Formerly (until 1948): *The Moslem World.* [ISSN: 0027-4909] 1911. q. GBP 203. Ed(s): Yahya M Michot. Wiley-Blackwell Publishing, Inc., 111 River St, Hoboken, NJ 07030; info@wiley.com; http://onlinelibrary.wiley.com/. Illus., index, adv. Sample. Refereed. Vol. ends: Oct. Microform: PQC. Reprint: PSC. *Indexed:* A01, A22, ABS&EES, AmHI, ArtHuCI, BAS, BRI, E01, FR, MASUSE, MLA-IB, P02, P61, R&TA, SSA. *Bk. rev.:* 2-3, 500-2,000 words; signed. *Aud.:* Ac, Sa.

Founded in 1911, *Muslim World* contains articles concerning Muslim faith, culture, and history, and, according to the journal's web site, the "historical and current aspects of Muslim-Christian relations." As such, the journal is both an important resource for studying Islam as religion and a vehicle for interfaith dialogue. Recent articles included "From Crib to Cage: The Theological Calculus of Solitary Confinement" and "Constructing an Identity between Arabism and Islam: The Druzes in Syria." Multiple book reviews are included. This journal will be of interest to scholars in many disciplines, including religious studies, Middle Eastern studies, history, and political science. Highly recommended for all academic libraries. URL: http://onlinelibrary.wiley.com/journal/10.1111/(ISSN)1478-1913

4676. National Catholic Reporter: the independent news source. [ISSN: 0027-8939] 1964. 26x/yr. USD 47.95 combined subscription domestic (print & online eds.); USD 85.95 combined subscription foreign (print & online eds.). Ed(s): Dennis Coday. National Catholic Reporter Publishing Co., 115 E Armour Blvd, Kansas City, MO 64111-1203; ncrsub@ncronline.org; http://ncronline.org. Illus., adv. Sample. Circ: 50000 Paid. Microform: PQC. *Indexed:* A01, A22, BRI, C26, Chicano, P02. *Bk. rev.:* 1-2, 700-1,000 words; signed. *Aud.:* Ga, Ac.

The *National Catholic Reporter* is a large-circulation weekly newspaper that reports news of interest to a Roman Catholic readership from a progressive Catholic perspective. This full-color newspaper maintains high journalistic standards and reports national and world news, as well as opinion pieces and articles devoted to arts and culture. The world wide web has shifted the print news to an online format, and *NCR* is no exception. Though the publication carries on in print format, it has developed a vibrant web presence that offers full-text access to many articles (although the print version contains special sections unavailable online). Recommended for both public and academic libraries, particularly those that serve Roman Catholic populations. URL: http://ncronline.org/

4677. New Oxford Review. Former titles (until 1977): *American Church News;* (until 1959): *A C U News.* [ISSN: 0149-4244] 1940. m. 11/yr. USD 24 domestic; USD 36 elsewhere; USD 38 combined subscription domestic (print & online eds.). Ed(s): Elena M Vree, Pieter Vree. New Oxford Review, Inc., 1069 Kains Ave, Berkeley, CA 94706. Illus. Vol. ends: Dec. Microform: PQC. *Indexed:* A01, A22, MLA-IB. *Bk. rev.:* Number and length vary. *Aud.:* Ga, Ac.

The *New Oxford Review* is a politically right-leaning "orthodox Catholic magazine that explores ideas concerning faith and culture." Articles are accessible to religion scholars and the general public, and they address prominent political and cultural issues, theological questions, and historical events of interest to Catholics. Also included are brief news items and book reviews. *New Oxford's* web site provides access to content as well as an archive that stretches back to 2009. Recommended for public libraries and those academic libraries that support Catholic studies or religious studies programs. URL: www.newoxfordreview.org/index.jsp

The North Star. See African American section.

4678. Religion. [ISSN: 0048-721X] 1971. q. GBP 325 (print & online eds.). Ed(s): Michael Stausberg, Steven Engler. Taylor & Francis, 4 Park Sq, Milton Park, Abingdon, OX14 4RN, United Kingdom; subscriptions@tandf.co.uk; http://www.tandfonline.com. Illus., adv. Sample. Refereed. Vol. ends: Oct. Reprint: PSC. *Indexed:* A01, A22, AmHI, ArtHuCI, BAS, BRI, E01, FR, IBSS, P02. *Bk. rev.:* 7-10, 1,000-1,700 words; signed. *Aud.:* Ac, Sa.

Religion is a cross-disciplinary religious studies journal that covers world religions from many different angles, including historical, philosophical, and social-scientific. The journal regularly publishes thematic issues. One recent issue, for example, has explored the use of textbooks in religious studies, and included articles about textbooks used in teaching the psychology of religion, Judaism, and Western esotericism. The wide variety of topics and methodological approaches gives this journal real interdisciplinary appeal, and it is appropriate for all academic libraries that support the humanities and/or social sciences.

4679. Religion and American Culture: a journal of interpretation. [ISSN: 1052-1151] 1991. s-a. USD 166 (print & online eds.). Ed(s): Thomas J Davis. University of California Press, Journals Division, 2000 Ctr St, Ste 303, Berkeley, CA 94704; customerservice@ucpressjournals.com; http://www.ucpressjournals.com. Illus., adv. Refereed. Circ: 575. Reprint: PSC. *Indexed:* A01, A22, AmHI, ArtHuCI, BRI, E01, MLA-IB, P61, R&TA, SSA. *Aud.:* Ac, Sa.

Religion and American Culture approaches the American religious experience from historical and cultural-studies perspectives. Articles cover religions indigenous to (i.e., Native American), traditionally associated with (e.g., the Baptist Church), and newly created or imported to (e.g., Yoga) North America. This eclectic journal, as a result, weaves many interdisciplinary perspectives, with articles being of value to historians, sociologists, psychologists, philosophers, legal researchers, and religious studies scholars. Laypeople interested in any of these areas will also find this journal accessible. Recommended for most academic libraries, particularly those that support history, American studies, or religious studies programs. Also recommended for larger public libraries.

4680. Religious Studies: an international journal for the philosophy of religion. [ISSN: 0034-4125] 1965. q. GBP 283. Ed(s): Robin Le Poidevin. Cambridge University Press, The Edinburgh Bldg, Shaftesbury Rd, Cambridge, CB2 8RU, United Kingdom; journals@cambridge.org; http://www.cambridge.org/uk. Illus., index, adv. Sample. Refereed. Circ: 1200. Vol. ends: Dec. Microform: PQC. Reprint: PSC. *Indexed:* A22, AmHI, ArtHuCI, BAS, BRI, CBRI, E01, FR, IJP, IPB, MLA-IB, P02, R&TA. *Bk. rev.:* Number and length vary. *Aud.:* Ac, Sa.

Published by Cambridge University Press, *Religious Studies* is a top-flight philosophy of religion journal with an impressive international editorial board. The journal's articles attempt to tackle religious questions using all manner of philosophical frameworks and methodologies. Recent articles include "John Oman on feeling and theology" and "A Conceptualist Argument for Spiritual Substantial Soul." Philosophers, theologians, and religious studies scholars will all find this to be a valuable resource. Recommended for academic libraries.

4681. Religious Studies Review: a quarterly review of publications in the field of religion and related disciplines. [ISSN: 0319-485X] 1975. q. GBP 158 (print & online eds.). Ed(s): Elias Bongmba, David B Gray. Wiley-Blackwell Publishing, Inc., 111 River St, Hoboken, NJ 07030; info@wiley.com; http://onlinelibrary.wiley.com/. Illus., index. Sample. Refereed. Vol. ends: Oct. *Indexed:* A01, A22, AmHI, ArtHuCI, BRI, CBRI, E01, R&TA. *Bk. rev.:* Over 1,000 annually; signed. *Aud.:* Ac, Sa.

Religious Studies Review is an essential publication for both religious studies researchers and library subject specialists that select for religion. Every issue consists of three sections: (1) "Review Essays," (2) "Notes on Recent Publications," and (3) "Personalia" (i.e., review author information and credentials). The review essays are bibliographic essays that cover particular topics of interest to religious studies researchers. The recent "Buddhism, Politics, Modernization, and Globalization in Contemporary Taiwan: A Review Essay," for example, surveys nine recent scholarly books on various aspects of Taiwanese Buddhism. The bulk of each issue, however, is composed of notes on recent publications, with every issue containing about 60 pages of short book reviews organized by subjects including "Psychology of Religion," "Sociology and Anthropology of Religion," "Theology," and "Ethics." Considering its value as a tool for current awareness and collection development, this quarterly journal is recommended for all academic libraries as well as large public libraries.

4682. *Review and Expositor: a quarterly baptist theological journal.* Formerly (until 1906): *The Baptist Review and Expositor.* [ISSN: 0034-6373] 1904. q. USD 275. Ed(s): Mark E Biddle. Review & Expositor, Inc., PO Box 6681, Louisville, KY 40206; Office@rande.org. Illus., index, adv. Vol. ends: Fall. Microform: PQC. *Indexed:* A22, MLA-IB, R&TA, RILM. *Bk. rev.:* 30-50, 300-700 words; signed. *Aud.:* Ga, Sa.

The *Review and Expositor* has provided theological analysis from a Baptist perspective since 1904. Issues are thematically based, collecting articles on topics such as "Prophetic Preaching," "Race: Foundations and Reflections," and "The Letter of James." In addition to the essays addressing the issue theme are "Expository Words," i.e., essays that analyze particular Bible passages. Book reviews and a list of books received are also included. This journal is particularly appropriate for theologians and Bible scholars in the Baptist tradition. Recommended for seminary libraries and those academic libraries that support programs in Bible studies or theology. URL: http://rande.org/

4683. *Scottish Journal of Theology.* [ISSN: 0036-9306] 1948. q. GBP 155. Ed(s): Ian Torrance, Bryan Spinks. Cambridge University Press, The Edinburgh Bldg, Shaftesbury Rd, Cambridge, CB2 8RU, United Kingdom; journals@cambridge.org; http://www.cambridge.org/uk. Illus., index, adv. Sample. Refereed. Circ: 1200. Vol. ends: No. 4. Reprint: PSC. *Indexed:* A22, AmHI, ArtHuCI, BRI, E01, FR, MLA-IB, P02, R&TA, RILM. *Bk. rev.:* 10-15, 500-1,000 words; signed. *Aud.:* Ac, Sa.

Published by Cambridge University Press, this quarterly journal publishes work on "systematic, historical[,] and biblical theology." Every issue usually contains around five research articles, an extended book review with a response by the reviewed work's author, and multiple short book reviews. The journal is recommended for Christian theologians of all stripes, and is appropriate for academic libraries that support programs in Christian studies.

4684. *Shambhala Sun: buddhism culture meditation life.* Formerly (until Apr. 1992): *Vajradhatu Sun.* [ISSN: 1190-7886] 1978. bi-m. CAD 29.95 domestic; USD 19.95 United States; USD 39.95 elsewhere. Ed(s): Melvin McLeod. Shambhala Sun, 1660 Hollis St Ste 701, Halifax, NS B3J 1V7, Canada; magazine@shambhalasun.com. Illus., adv. Circ: 35000 Paid. *Indexed:* CBCARef. *Bk. rev.:* Number and length vary. *Aud.:* Ga.

Shambhala Sun is a bimonthly consumer magazine dedicated to Buddhism and the modern Buddhist practitioner. This glossy magazine contains multiple feature articles on Buddhist culture and practice; recent articles include essays on art, mindfulness training, and healthy living. Articles are written by notable Buddhist teachers, and the magazine often includes interviews with such luminaries as Thich Nhat Hanh. Short "Other Voices" essays are also included that offer Buddhist wisdom and commentary, and every issue includes multiple short book reviews and one longer review article. *Shambhala Sun*'s web site provides a great deal of free content. This magazine is recommended for both public and academic libraries, regardless of size. URL: www.shambhalasun.com/

4685. *Sociology of Religion: a quarterly review.* Former titles (until 1993): *S A. Sociological Analysis;* (until 1973): *Sociological Analysis;* (until 1964): *The American Catholic Sociological Review.* [ISSN: 1069-4404] 1940. q. EUR 124. Ed(s): Scott Schieman. Oxford University Press, 2001 Evans Rd, Cary, NC 27513; http://www.oxfordjournals.org. Illus., index, adv. Refereed. Circ: 1595. Vol. ends: Winter. Microform: PQC. Reprint: PSC. *Indexed:* A01, A22, ABS&EES, ArtHuCI, BRI, Chicano, FR, HEA, IBSS, P02, P61, R&TA, SSA. *Bk. rev.:* 10-12, 600-1,000 words; signed. *Aud.:* Ac.

This publication of the Association for the Sociology of Religion presents sociological examinations of religion and religious phenomena concerning a variety of topics. The included studies are typically empirical, quantitative, and qualitative analyses, with recent articles including surveys of religious practices and attitudes toward premarital sex in Brazil, and Canadian Catholic women's attitudes toward feminism. Because of its scope and interdisciplinary appeal, *Sociology of Religion* is recommended for all academic libraries. URL: http://socrel.oxfordjournals.org/

4686. *Sophia: international journal of philosophy and traditions.* [ISSN: 0038-1527] 1962. 4x/yr. USD 374 (print & online eds.). Ed(s): Purushottama Bilimoria. Springer Netherlands, Van Godewijckstraat 30, Dordrecht, 3311 GX, Netherlands; http://www.springer.com. Adv. Refereed. Microform: PQC. Reprint: PSC. *Indexed:* A22, ArtHuCI, BRI, E01, FR, MLA-IB. *Aud.:* Ac, Sa.

The articles published in *Sophia: International Journal of Philosophy and Traditions* address philosophical questions concerning religion from multiple philosophical and academic disciplinary perspectives. Recent articles have covered a wide range of topics, including environmental ethics as seen through the Mahabharata; the question of evil and the concept of a loving God; and the difference between panentheism and classical theism. Religious studies, theology, and philosophy scholars will all find this journal useful. *Sophia* is recommended for academic libraries that support these types of researchers and their students.

4687. *Studies in World Christianity: the Edinburgh review of theology and religion.* Formerly (until 1995): *Edinburgh Review of Theology and Religion.* [ISSN: 1354-9901] 1995. 3x/yr. GBP 133.50 (print & online eds.). Ed(s): Brian Stanley. Edinburgh University Press Ltd., 22 George Sq, Edinburgh, EH8 9LF, United Kingdom; journals@eup.ed.ac.uk; http://www.euppublishing.com. Illus. Sample. Refereed. Vol. ends: No. 2. *Indexed:* A01, A22, AmHI, ArtHuCI, E01, R&TA, RILM. *Bk. rev.:* 15-20, 250-1,200 words; signed. *Aud.:* Ac.

Studies in World Christianity: The Edinburgh Review of Theology & Religion is a thrice-yearly-published collection of academic essays and book reviews that covers Christianity as a world religion from "historical, theological, and social scientific perspectives." *Studies in World Christianity* investigates religion as a truly global phenomenon; recent issues contain articles about Christianity in places like Burma, Korea, Uganda, Iran, and North America. Each issue has approximately five articles that employ a variety of research methodologies and disciplinary perspectives. This journal is highly recommended for all academic libraries, regardless of size.

4688. *Theological Studies.* [ISSN: 0040-5639] 1940. q. USD 40 (Individuals, USD 30). Theological Studies, Inc., c/o David G. Schultenover, S. J., Ed, Marquette University, 100 Coughlin Hall, PO Box 1881, Milwaukee, WI 53201; http://www.ts.mu.edu/. Illus., index. Sample. Refereed. Vol. ends: Dec. Microform: PQC. *Indexed:* A01, A22, AmHI, ArtHuCI, BRI, C26, CBRI, FR, MLA-IB, P02, R&TA. *Bk. rev.:* Number and length vary. *Aud.:* Ac, Sa.

This journal, published for the Society of Jesus (the Jesuits), collects the latest Catholic theological research. Every issue of *Theological Studies* includes approximately eight peer-reviewed research articles and includes essays on a diverse range of topics such as political theology, virtue ethics, the outcomes of Vatican II, and theology and economics. Multiple book reviews are included, along with shorter notices for recently published books. *TS* offers a dynamic online version of the journal that includes multiple screen-view choices, direct links to social media, and note-taking functionality. This journal is recommended for academic libraries that support theology and religious studies programs. URL: www.ts.mu.edu/

4689. *Theology Today.* [ISSN: 0040-5736] 1944. q. USD 347. Ed(s): Gordon S Mikoski. Sage Publications, Inc., 2455 Teller Rd, Thousand Oaks, CA 91320; info@sagepub.com; http://www.sagepub.com/. Illus., index, adv. Sample. Refereed. Vol. ends: Jan. Microform: MIM; PQC. Reprint: PSC. *Indexed:* A01, A07, A22, AmHI, ArtHuCI, BRI, CBRI, MLA-IB, P02, R&TA, RILM. *Bk. rev.:* 15-30, 200-1,500 words; signed. *Aud.:* Ga, Ac.

Published since 1944, *Theology Today* is an excellent collection of the latest research covering contemporary theological issues. A recent issue on public witnessing of Christian faith, for example, includes articles on praising God online and witnessing in public spaces. Traditional/historical theological questions are also considered, such as interpreting rabbinical scriptures and the history of women at Princeton's Theological Seminary. Multiple short book reviews are also included. All manner of theological researchers will find this journal indispensable, as will religious studies scholars who focus on Christianity. Recommended for seminary libraries and those academic libraries that support religious studies or theology programs.

Tikkun Magazine. See News and Opinion section.

4690. *Tricycle: the Buddhist review.* [ISSN: 1055-484X] 1991. q. Membership, USD 30. Ed(s): James Shaheen. The Tricycle Foundation, 1115 Broadway, Ste 1113, New York, NY 10010; foundation@tricycle.com. Illus., adv. Vol. ends: Summer. *Indexed:* BRI, CBRI. *Bk. rev.:* 4-6, 400-1,000 words; signed. *Aud.:* Ga.

Tricycle: The Buddhist Review is a popular quarterly consumer magazine aimed at Western Buddhist practitioners. Every issue contains news and opinion of interest to Buddhists, featured articles, and regular columns that deal with incorporating Buddhism into daily life, e.g., "Gardening," "Animal Realm," and "Practice." The featured articles are often written by well-known Zen teachers. Recommended for large public libraries and all academic libraries. URL: www.tricycle.com/

4691. *Weavings: a journal of the Christian spiritual life.* [ISSN: 0890-6491] 1986. bi-m. USD 29.35 domestic; USD 97.95 foreign. Ed(s): Dr. Lynne M Deming. The Upper Room Publications, 1908 Grand Ave, PO Box 340004, Nashville, TN 37203; urbooks@upperroom.org; http://www.upperroom.org. Illus. Sample. Circ: 40000 Paid. Vol. ends: Nov/Dec. *Bk. rev.:* 1-2, 600-900 words; signed. *Aud.:* Ga.

Weavings: A Journal of the Christian Spiritual Life is a bimonthly consumer magazine that collects short essays, original fiction, and poetry offering insight into the Christian faith. Issues are organized around a central theme. These themes are typically based on Bible verses, with upcoming issues being built around "Blessed are you who are poor, for yours is the Kingdom of God" (Luke 6:20) and "Where the Spirit of the Lord is, there is freedom" (2 Cor. 3:17). The journal is beautifully illustrated with full-color photographs and art. Anyone seeking literature related to spiritual life will find *Weavings* worth serious consideration. This title is appropriate for both public and academic librarians, and particularly those libraries that serve Christian communities, regardless of denomination. URL: www.weavings.upperroom.org

4692. *Worship.* Formerly (until 1951): *Orate Fratres.* [ISSN: 0043-941X] 1926. bi-m. USD 68.25 USD 39 domestic. Liturgical Press, 2950 Saint John's Rd, P O Box 7500, Collegeville, MN 56321-7500; sales@litpress.org; http://www.litpress.org. Illus., index. Sample. Refereed. Circ: 2604. Vol. ends: Nov. Microform: PQC. *Indexed:* A22, C26, FR, MLA-IB, R&TA, RILM. *Bk. rev.:* 1-10, 500-1,200 words; signed. *Aud.:* Ac, Sa.

Worship is a bimonthly journal published by the monks of Saint John's Abbey and dedicated to "liturgical renewal," with scholarly articles dealing with topics related to public worship. Each issue contains three or four essays dealing with the Roman Rite. Recent articles have included "Martyrs and the Mass: The Interpolation of the Narrative of Institution into the Anaphora" and "Penitential Services: An Invitation to Conversion, A Celebration of Resurrection, A Call to Action." These essays are rigorously researched and heavily documented. Each issue contains multiple book reviews as well as occasional music reviews. A side note: the journal's covers are beautiful, containing high-quality reproductions of Christian art and sculpture. This journal fits well in large academic library collections, as well as collections that focus on religious ritual and practice.

4693. *Yoga International.* Former titles (until 2010): *Yoga Plus Joyful Living;* (until 2006): *Yoga International;* Which superseded (in Jul.1991): *Dawn.* 1991. q. Himalayan International Institute (HII), 952 Bethany Turnpike, Honesdale, PA 18431- 9706; info@himalayaninstitute.org; http://www.himalayaninstitute.org. Illus., adv. Circ: 24500 Controlled. *Bk. rev.:* Number and length vary. *Aud.:* Ga.

After a brief name change a few years ago to *Yoga + Joyful Living,* this popular magazine has returned to its original name, *Yoga International.* This is a full-color, quarterly consumer journal published by the Himalayan Institute. The magazine is an excellent resource for those wishing to live a yogic lifestyle and explore Eastern spirituality. Typically, issues contain three or more feature articles dedicated to Yogic practice or theory. For example, one recent feature, "The Secret Life of Asana," explores the impact of yoga positions on developing

the mind. In addition to the feature articles, every issue contains news reports and regular columns dedicated to lifestyle concerns such as diet, art, books, and music. Appropriate for both public and academic libraries. URL: www.himalayaninstitute.org/yi/

4694. *Zygon: journal of religion and science.* [ISSN: 0591-2385] 1966. q. GBP 254. Ed(s): Willem B Drees. Wiley-Blackwell Publishing, Inc., 111 River St, Hoboken, NJ 07030; info@wiley.com; http://onlinelibrary.wiley.com/. Illus., index, adv. Sample. Refereed. Vol. ends: Dec. Microform: PQC. Reprint: PSC. *Indexed:* A01, A22, AmHI, ArtHuCI, BRI, CBRI, E01, FR, IPB, P02, P61, R&TA, RILM. *Bk. rev.:* 0-5, 1,300-3,000 words; signed. *Aud.:* Ac.

Zygon focuses on the relationship and (often contentious) dialogue between science and religion. The journal has a broad scope, considering the relationships of both the hard sciences and the social sciences to the gamut of world religions, as well as related non-religious positions such as atheism, agnosticism, and secular humanism. *Zygon's* web site reinforces this expansive scholarly perspective, stating that approximately half of the journal's articles are written by scientists and half are written by humanities scholars. Recent articles included "Untangling False Assumptions Regarding Atheism and Health" and "Human Salvation in an Evolutionary World: An Exploration in Christian Naturalism." Although many academic journals across the disciplines publish occasional articles on the juncture of science and religion, *Zygon's* focus makes it important to researchers in many different disciplines, and particularly to religious studies scholars. Recommended for large academic libraries and all academic libraries that support religious studies programs. URL: www.zygonjournal.org/index.htm

■ ROBOTICS

Sharon L. Siegler, Engineering Librarian, Lehigh University Library & Technology Services, Fairchild/Martindale Library, 8A Packer Ave., Bethlehem, PA 18015; FAX: 610-758-6524; sls7@lehigh.edu

Introduction

Most of the new titles in the field of robotics have come from Open Access or small society publishers. The larger publishers have cast a broader net and use such terms as "intelligent systems" or "automatic control" in their robotics titles. Unfortunately, many of the Open Access titles are from very new publishers and may not survive. At the other end of the spectrum, most of the titles from commercial publishers have returned to double-digit–percentage price increases.

Although large-scale manufacturing systems continue to be important applications for the robotics field, medicine (at the nano-scale in particular) now receives a good deal of attention. Adapting robots to biological functions is one thing; using biology to design robots is another. The terms "bionic" or "biomimetics" have crept into the robotic literature, especially at the nano level, because how nature designs systems helps researchers design robots. Tiny flying robots (not drones) can serve as visual inspectors in dangerous or constricted areas, but, like the bumble-bee, they must be designed so that flight is possible and controllable. Yet another avenue of research is human–robot interaction. Robots that talk and understand human speech are common; robots that can interpret human expressions and gestures are the next challenge.

Compiling a good robotics collection, whether in academia or industry, depends on the local research interests. Automobile manufacturers are unlikely to want robotic surgery titles, and cognitive interpretation laboratories have small use for flying robots. However, robots still capture the imagination and magazines such as *Servo* show what can be done with a small budget and determination.

Basic Periodicals

Hs: *Robot Magazine;* Ga: *I E E E Robotics and Automation Magazine;* Ac: *Autonomous Robots, I E E E Transactions on Robotics, International Journal of Robotics Research, Robotics and Computer-Integrated Manufacturing.*

Basic Abstracts and Indexes

Applied Science and Technology Abstracts, Engineering Index, INSPEC.

4695. *A C M Transactions on Interactive Intelligent Systems.* [ISSN: 2160-6455] 2011. q. Free to members; Non-members, USD 160. Ed(s): John Riedl, Anthony Jameson. Association for Computing Machinery, Inc., 2 Penn Plz, Ste 701, New York, NY 10121; acmhelp@acm.org; http://www.acm.org. Refereed. *Aud.:* Ac, Sa.

A new entrant into the robotics/intelligent machine field, the *ACM Transactions on Interactive Intelligent Systems* has published several theme issues on human/robot interaction, accounting for almost a third of the articles in its first few years of existence. Probably the "easy" task is creating robots or service devices that can communicate with humans; the "hard" part is teaching the robots how to understand how humans communicate with them. One recent article discussed body and hand gesture recognition; another described identifying and responding to a learner's emotional state within an interactive tutoring program. Issues are sparse, averaging about five articles each, but these are lengthy (40 pages) and well referenced. This title will appeal to social scientists, as well as computer science/engineering professionals.

4696. *Advanced Robotics.* [ISSN: 0169-1864] 1986. 18x/yr. GBP 2779 (print & online eds.). Ed(s): Fumihito Arai. Taylor & Francis, 4 Park Sq, Milton Park, Abingdon, OX14 4RN, United Kingdom; subscriptions@tandf.co.uk; http://www.tandfonline.com. Illus., adv. Sample. Refereed. Vol. ends: No. 8. Reprint: PSC. *Indexed:* A01, A22, ApMecR, C&ISA, CerAb, E01, EngInd, H24. *Aud.:* Ac, Sa.

Truly an international effort, this is the official journal of the Robotics Society of Japan, but features articles by Russians, Germans, Arabs, Japanese, and others. Robots may be mobile, stationary (manipulators), built for hostile environments, or merely sensors. Theme issues occur regularly, covering such topics as aerial robots (in particular, the small ones used in surveillance), safety and rescue robots, and nano-robots. The treatment is theoretical with a practical emphasis. Now published by Taylor & Francis, the online version takes full advantage of graphical abstracts with excellent color. Although there are 18 issues per year, they average just five, 15-page papers per issue, with a publication delay of at least a year between submission, acceptance, and online publication. The steep annual price increases have not deterred library subscriptions, which have steadily increased, but the journal's ranking in the *Journal Citation Reports'* Robotics category has been just as steadily declining. Recommended for the complete robotics collection.

4697. *Assembly Automation: the international journal of assembly technology and management.* [ISSN: 0144-5154] 1980. q. EUR 11249 combined subscription in Europe (print & online eds.); USD 14009 combined subscription in the Americas (print & online eds.); GBP 7589 combined subscription in the UK & elsewhere (print & online eds.). Ed(s): Clive Loughlin. Emerald Group Publishing Ltd., Howard House, Wagon Ln, Bingley, BD16 1WA, United Kingdom; emerald@emeraldinsight.com; http://www.emeraldinsight.com. Illus. Sample. Refereed. Reprint: PSC. *Indexed:* A22, ABIn, B01, BrTechI, C&ISA, CerAb, E01, EngInd, ErgAb. *Bk. rev.:* 500 words. *Aud.:* Ac, Sa.

Part of a suite of robotics-related titles published by Emerald, *Assembly Automation* features automation in flexible manufacturing processes, some of which involve robots. With a relatively low Impact Factor, it is primarily a practitioner's journal. Application areas include electrical products, clothing, and pharmaceuticals, with a heavy emphasis on process. Each issue is composed of research articles with lengthy reference lists and color illustrations, new-product reviews of a page or less, company news, "mini-features" that describe practical solutions or techniques, media reviews (books, software), patent abstracts, web sites, and editorial commentary. The research articles may be authored by academics, practicing engineers, or journal staff. Most issues are theme oriented, such as rapid prototyping or nano-electronics. The online version utilizes the same access points and features as this journal's sister publication, *Industrial Robot.* This is a very expensive title in the field, to be considered only by industry libraries and those academic institutions with large consulting efforts in manufacturing and robotics.

4698. *Autonomous Robots.* [ISSN: 0929-5593] 1994. bi-m. EUR 1339 (print & online eds.). Ed(s): Gaurav S Sukhatme. Springer New York LLC, 233 Spring St, New York, NY 10013; service-ny@springer.com; http://www.springer.com/. Adv. Refereed. Reprint: PSC. *Indexed:* A22, ApMecR, CompLI, E01, EngInd. *Aud.:* Ac, Sa.

As the title indicates, this journal specializes in papers on robots that are self-sufficient, which is defined as capable of performing in real-world environments. These robots acquire data through sensors, process it, perform their tasks, and are often mobile (legged, tracked, and even finned). Each issue is comprised of a half-dozen lengthy articles of 15 or more pages, often illustrated with color (in the tables and graphs as well as the photos), and numerous references. The authorship is international, from academia and industrial-research laboratories and often with collaboration from both. This journal is strictly serious in content, but there is opportunity for a little wry comment, such as "a humanoid robot that pretends to listen to route guidance from a human." On the more practical side is the issue of "teaching" robots to adapt to new situations, such as the dart-throwing robot that learns tennis. Both pdf and html versions of articles are available, plus there are occasional supplemental videos. The web site supports RSS feeds and RIS export of bibliographic data and several social bookmark sites. Modestly priced for a scholarly technical journal, it is warmly recommended for academic and industrial collections.

4699. *Bioinspiration & Biomimetics: learning from nature.* [ISSN: 1748-3182] 2006. q. GBP 643 (print & online eds.). Ed(s): R Allen. Institute of Physics Publishing Ltd., Temple Circus, Temple Way, Bristol, BS1 6HG, United Kingdom; custserv@iop.org; http://ioppublishing.org. Sample. Refereed. *Aud.:* Ac.

Aptly named, this new title has rapidly become a central figure in robotics research. The scope of the journal is broader than robotics, covering all branches of engineering. The basic concept is to apply systems and designs adapted from nature to technology. Obvious examples are bird flight to aircraft design, but recent articles have discussed adapting woodpecker tree pecking to the design of shock-absorbing systems, and caterpillar movement adapted to a pliable rolling robot. Articles are well-indexed using the PACS (physics and astronomy) index scheme; they also often have full-color illustrations and occasionally have video (wmv). The extensive reference lists include links to full text where available. This journal is a quarterly, and its issues are generally composed of a dozen or so articles, but issues may also include communications (brief articles) and reviews. The lag between submission and publication is swift, often under six months, and this is a RoMEO green journal. Suitable for engineering design programs, as well as those in robotics.

4700. *I E E E - A S M E Transactions on Mechatronics.* [ISSN: 1083-4435] 1996. bi-m. USD 965; USD 1160 combined subscription (print & online eds.). Ed(s): Kok-Meng Lee, Jeffrey F Cichocki. Institute of Electrical and Electronics Engineers, 445 Hoes Ln, Piscataway, NJ 08854; contactcenter@ieee.org; http://www.ieee.org. Illus., index, adv. Vol. ends: No. 4. *Indexed:* A22, ApMecR, C&ISA, CerAb, EngInd. *Aud.:* Ac, Sa.

The term *mechatronics* is defined by the *Transactions* as "the synergetic integration of mechanical engineering with electronic and intelligent computer control in design and manufacture of industrial products and processes." In other words, the field covers a lot of territory, and this title is actually the joint effort of several IEEE societies and ASME divisions. As in the other *IEEE Transactions* (and the *ASME Journals*), papers are highly mathematical, well referenced, and illustrated with color tables and flowcharts rather than with glossies of mobile robots. Papers often deal with control devices or distinct parts of a whole system, rather than an entire device. Recent articles deal with everything from soft materials in minimally invasive surgery to nanorobots handling nanowires, to battery charging for solar-powered robots. This is a highly ranked (per Impact Factor) title with cross-disciplinary activity in robotics, control, and materials research, and will be a good addition to engineering libraries.

4701. *I E E E Robotics and Automation Magazine.* [ISSN: 1070-9932] 1994. q. USD 440; USD 530 combined subscription (print & online eds.). Ed(s): Peter I Corke. Institute of Electrical and Electronics Engineers, 445 Hoes Ln, Piscataway, NJ 08854; contactcenter@ieee.org; http://www.ieee.org. Illus., index. Vol. ends: No. 4. *Indexed:* A22, C&ISA, CerAb, EngInd. *Bk. rev.:* 1, 500 words. *Aud.:* Ga, Ac, Sa.

This magazine, from the IEEE Robotics and Automation Society, publishes the more practical material not suitable for its *Transactions*. Not really a glossy magazine, it is still attractive, with color covers, many features, a nice presentation, and relatively short, well-illustrated articles. Each issue includes several research papers plus short sections on society business, columns (such as "women in engineering"), calls for papers, industry news, and the like. A new feature is the "article voting system" (only available in the online version) where readers can click on an icon to "like" an article. This is an experiment to see what readers prefer and to show how multimedia can be included in the journal. The content level is quite approachable by undergraduates and lay readers and the price is modest (for a professional journal), making this a suitable selection for a large public or small academic library, as well as libraries that serve active robotics research.

4702. *I E E E Transactions on Automatic Control.* Formerly (until 1963): *I R E Transactions on Automatic Control.* [ISSN: 0018-9286] 1956. m. USD 2045; USD 2455 combined subscription (print & online eds.). Ed(s): P J Antsaklis. Institute of Electronics and Electronics Engineers, 445 Hoes Ln, Piscataway, NJ 08854; contactcenter@ieee.org; http://www.ieee.org. Illus., adv. Refereed. *Indexed:* A01, A22, ApMecR, B01, BRI, C&ISA, CCMJ, CerAb, CompLI, EngInd, MSN, MathR. *Bk. rev.:* 1, 500 words. *Aud.:* Ac, Sa.

The *IEEE Transactions on Automatic Control* is a highly mathematical research journal that focuses on algorithms, modeling, data sampling, and their applications. Although a highly ranked journal (by Impact Factor) in automation and control systems, it serves robotics as a source of theory and tools for automation. Thus, it belongs in strong robotics research collections, but is too theoretical for application-centered work. As is usual with the *IEEE Transactions* series, the articles average 10–15 pages, and illustrations are mostly figures, graphs, and equations. Judicious use of color in graphs and figures is now a regular practice, which aids greatly in following the discussions. Special issues on a theme appear often, and a nice feature is the "scanning the issue" page, which has brief descriptions (not the abstracts) that highlight selected articles.

4703. *I E E E Transactions on Automation Science and Engineering.* Supersedes in part (in 2004): *I E E E Transactions on Robotics and Automation;* Which was formerly (until 1989): *I E E E Journal of Robotics and Automation.* [ISSN: 1545-5955] 2004. q. USD 665; USD 800 combined subscription (print & online eds.). Ed(s): Nukala Viswanadham, Jeffrey E Cichocki. Institute of Electrical and Electronics Engineers, 445 Hoes Ln, Piscataway, NJ 08854; contactcenter@ieee.org; http://www.ieee.org. Adv. *Indexed:* A01, B01, C&ISA, CerAb, EngInd. *Aud.:* Ac.

Split off from the *IEEE Transactions on Robotics and Automation* in 2004, *Automation Science and Engineering* is concerned with methods to improve efficiency, productivity, quality, and reliability for both machines and environments. This is more than robotics, although application areas are in biotechnology, manufacturing, construction, and health care, where robot systems are already in use. Thus *Automation* will cite the robotics literature, but it tends to be cited by the manufacturing literature. Issues feature 10- to 15-page articles and five page short papers; often there is an issue theme such as "automation in green engineering." Treatment of topics is highly mathematical, with data and graphs as the predominant illustrations. This title is a supplement for a robotics collection but useful in cross-disciplinary control engineering.

4704. *I E E E Transactions on Robotics.* Supersedes in part (in 2004): *I E E E Transactions on Robotics and Automation;* Which was formerly (until 1989): *I E E E Journal of Robotics and Automation.* [ISSN: 1552-3098] 1985. bi-m. USD 1155; USD 1385 combined subscription (print & online eds.). Ed(s): Seth Hutchison. Institute of Electrical and Electronics Engineers, 445 Hoes Ln, Piscataway, NJ 08854; contactcenter@ieee.org; http://www.ieee.org. Illus., index, adv. Vol. ends: No. 6. *Indexed:* A01, A22, B01, C&ISA, CerAb, EngInd. *Bk. rev.:* 1, 2,000 words. *Aud.:* Ac, Sa.

This title is still "number two"; top ranking (based on Impact Factor) now goes to the *International Journal of Robotics Research,* also reviewed in this section. The emphasis is on mechanical operation (such as grasping or manipulation), sensors, recognition, and mobility, with some attention to large-scale use

problems. A typical issue has several lengthy papers, a few short articles, and announcements. Often, a special topic will be developed over several papers. The treatment is mathematical; even the salamander robot (it walks *and* swims) rates one picture but seven tables and graphs. The lag time from submission to publication now averages less than 12 months (or less than nine, using the date actually posted online). This is a core title for a robotics collection and is useful in any electrical or mechanical engineering program. The IEEE publishes several *Transactions* titles and magazines that cover robotics to varying degrees. One of them, the *IEEE Transactions on Automatic Control* (also reviewed in this section), is a high-impact journal that should be consulted for specific problems in the control of robotic parts.

4705. *Industrial Robot: an international journal.* Incorporates: *Service Robot.* [ISSN: 0143-991X] 1973. bi-m. EUR 13919 combined subscription in Europe (print & online eds.); USD 15179 combined subscription in the Americas (print & online eds.); GBP 9369 combined subscription in the UK & elsewhere (print & online eds.). Ed(s): Clive Loughlin. Emerald Group Publishing Ltd., Howard House, Wagon Ln, Bingley, BD16 1WA, United Kingdom; emerald@emeraldinsight.com; http://www.emeraldinsight.com. Illus. Sample. Refereed. Reprint: PSC. *Indexed:* A22, ABIn, ApMecR, B02, B03, BRI, BrTechI, C&ISA, CerAb, E01, EngInd, H24. *Bk. rev.:* 3, 500 words. *Aud.:* Sa.

Industrial Robot is the oldest magazine in English devoted to robotics. Although robotic applications in any area may be included, the principal interest is in large-scale industries, such as automobiles, construction, shipbuilding, plastics, and the military, with some attention to biomedical applications and "niche" industries, such as space exploration. Each issue is composed of research articles, illustrated new-product reviews of a page or less, company news, "mini-features" that describe practical solutions or techniques, media reviews (books, software), patent abstracts, one-paragraph reviews of useful web sites, and editorial commentary. The research articles may be authored by academics or practicing engineers and recently have become lengthier and more scholarly. Most issues are theme oriented, covering such topics as humanitarian applications or managing robot systems. This journal still has the dubious distinction of being the most expensive journal in the field (with *Assembly Automation* from the same publisher being a close second), so only corporate libraries would normally consider subscriptions. Academic libraries with strong robotics, automation, and industrial/systems engineering programs should discuss an academic discount with the publisher.

4706. *Intelligent Service Robotics.* [ISSN: 1861-2776] 2006. 4x/yr. Ed(s): Junku Yuh. Springer, Tiergartenstr 17, Heidelberg, 69121, Germany; subscriptions@springer.com; http://www.springer.com. Reprint: PSC. *Indexed:* A22, E01, PsycInfo. *Aud.:* Ac, Sa.

A welcome addition to the Springer robotics collection, *Intelligent Service Robotics* features laboratory-scale working robots and the computer programs and tools that support the function and implementation of these "service" robots. Common applications are automated handlers, such as a raw- or cooked-food packaging, pharmaceutical production, and medical therapy. Brace yourself: one of the services mentioned is the "UJI librarian robot." However, librarians have not been automated yet; the robot in question is a stack pager. Recent theme issues included artificial intelligence techniques (robotic self-learning) and marine robots. Articles average 10–15 pages and are well illustrated with color photographs, tables, and diagrams. The treatment is research level but approachable by undergraduates and practitioners. Libraries interested in this title should also see the *Journal of Social Robots* and the *Journal of Field Robotics* also reviewed in this section. An inexpensive title in this field, *Intelligent Service Robotics* will be useful in collections with a strong application emphasis.

4707. *International Journal of Humanoid Robotics.* [ISSN: 0219-8436] 2004. q. SGD 953 (print & online eds.). Ed(s): Ming Xie, Jean-Guy Fontaine. World Scientific Publishing Co. Pte. Ltd., 5 Toh Tuck Link, Singapore, 596224, Singapore; wspc@wspc.com.sg; http://www.worldscientific.com. Adv. Sample. Refereed. *Indexed:* A22, C&ISA, CerAb, E01, EngInd. *Bk. rev.:* Number and length vary. *Aud.:* Ac.

This scholarly journal describes "humanoid robots" as those that work in a human environment. They may not look human, but, as the editors write, they "require the synergetic integration of mechanics, electronics, control, communication, perception, cognition, decision-making, artificial psychology, machine intelligence and many other areas." Articles are lengthy, often over 20 pages, and they usually involve mobility problems, but they also discuss learned behavior and text and visual understanding. Issues are comprised of research papers, review articles, short "dialogues," book reviews, and (of interest to academics) education curriculum development. Recent articles discussed "modeling the human blink," lip reading, and head movements, all useful in human–robot interaction. The time from submission to publication averages six months (shorter to online release). The web site is simple and well organized, and the price is still inexpensive. Recommended for extensive academic collections in robotics.

4708. International Journal of Medical Robotics and Computer Assisted Surgery. [ISSN: 1478-5951] 2004. q. GBP 487. Ed(s): Mehran Anvari. John Wiley & Sons Ltd., The Atrium, Southern Gate, Chichester, PO19 8SQ, United Kingdom; customer@wiley.com; http://www.wiley.com. Adv. Sample. Reprint: PSC. *Indexed:* C&ISA, CerAb, ExcerpMed. *Aud.:* Ac, Sa.

No, R2-D2 will not be operating on your gallbladder in the near future. What is happening, and has been for some time, is the use of robotic manipulators to assist in surgery, operated by surgeons in the "master–slave" mode. The technique is now so widely used that this journal features articles on improvements to the methods and the robots for different types of surgery. Most of the articles are detailed "how-to-do-it" accounts (often describing use of specific instruments), but there is the occasional systems-approach overview and discussion of legal concerns. (It is interesting to note that a conflict of interest statement accompanies each article.) Illustrations are often in color, since this is important to the understanding of the material and, for that matter, to the "computer-assisted" part of the title. The ability to overlay earlier diagnostic images in real-time surgery is one of the boons of this technique. The title is highly specialized, though, and only medical libraries and those institutions with strong biomedical technology and robotics programs will benefit from a subscription. Another title, the *Journal of Robotic Surgery,* is also reviewed in this section and features shorter articles on technique.

4709. International Journal of Robotics and Automation. [ISSN: 0826-8185] 1986. q. Free to members; Non-members, USD 680 (print or online ed.). Ed(s): Dr. M Kamel. ACTA Press, Bldg B6, Ste #101, 2509 Dieppe Ave SW, Calgary, AB T3E 7J9, Canada; journals@actapress.com; http://www.actapress.com. Adv. *Indexed:* A22, ABIn, ApMecR, C&ISA, CerAb, CompLI, EngInd. *Aud.:* Ac.

Although this journal has been publishing since 1986, it has only recently caught the attention of the larger world. Published by a small specialty press, it features succinct, under-ten-page articles by an international range of academic authors. About half of the articles deal with the functions of robots (as opposed to robots as a whole) and are especially concerned with manipulation, spatial recognition, and wireless activity. The other half feature programming issues. There is no sample issue, and no submission/acceptance dates, but the list of references (without links) for each article does aid the researcher in evaluating papers. The subscription price has not increased in the last two years, but the Impact Factor remains low. Thus, this is an optional title for complete robotics collections.

4710. The International Journal of Robotics Research. [ISSN: 0278-3649] 1982. 14x/yr. USD 2317. Ed(s): Jennet Batten, John M Hollerbach. Sage Publications Ltd., 1 Oliver's Yard, 55 City Rd, London, EC1Y 1SP, United Kingdom; info@sagepub.co.uk; http://www.uk.sagepub.com. Illus., index. Sample. Refereed. Vol. ends: Dec. Microform: PQC. Reprint: PSC. *Indexed:* A01, A22, ApMecR, B01, BrTechI, C&ISA, CerAb, CompLI, CompR, E01, EngInd, ErgAb, OceAb, P02. *Aud.:* Ac, Sa.

Billing itself as the first scholarly publication in robotics, it now has the highest Impact Factor in the field. The articles are relatively lengthy (averaging 15–20 pages each), and the treatment is highly mathematical. Recent theme issues covered three-dimensional exploration and physical human–robot interaction (think handshake). Although there is some attention paid to larger systems, most papers consider specific aspects of robot function, such as light-sensing, flexing of manipulators, force sensing, or motion variables. Experimentation is almost always on laboratory-scale equipment, although the intent is application to actual production environments. Multimedia appendixes (datasets, code, models, and simulations) are available as links, as are the reference lists. The publisher's site has a nice interface, with all of the modern conveniences: links to references, alerts for cites or corrections to an article, RSS feeds, social bookmarking, and marking and downloading to a number of citation managers. This is an excellent title with good value for the money for any institution engaged in robotics research.

4711. International Journal of Social Robotics. [ISSN: 1875-4805] 2009. 4x/yr. EUR 468 (print & online eds.). Ed(s): Shuzhi Sam Ge. Springer Netherlands, Van Godewijckstraat 30, Dordrecht, 3311 GX, Netherlands; http://www.springer.com. Refereed. *Aud.:* Ac, Sa.

Still too new to have an Impact Factor, the *International Journal of Social Robotics* can be considered a companion title to another Springer publication, *Intelligent Service Robotics* (also reviewed in this section). Here the problems of social interaction between robots and people are considered, both in the literal face-to-face mode and in the decision processes that the robots must often perform in dealing with human needs and the human environment. Articles that illustrate the point include "EMYS: Emotive head of a social robot" and "Making social robots more attractive: [T]he effects of voice pitch, humor and empathy." Although it is primarily an engineering publication, there is a good deal of psychology present in many articles. Color and black-and-white photos, graphs, and tables abound; the reference lists are extensive. Recommended for complete psychology collections as well as for engineering.

4712. Journal of Automation, Mobile Robotics & Intelligent Systems. [ISSN: 1897-8649] 2007. q. Ed(s): Janusz Kacprzyk. Industrial Research Institute for Automation and Measurements "P I A P", Building 4, Rm 206, Al Jerozolimskie 202, Warsaw, 02-486, Poland. Refereed. *Bk. rev.:* Number and length vary. *Aud.:* Ac, Sa.

A cross between an academic journal and an industry magazine, *JAMRIS,* as it calls itself, is an internationally authored publication from PIAP (Industrial Research Institute for Automation and Measurements), a Polish national research institute. With a long history of both research and manufacturing (PIAP began in 1965), the journal's editors seek papers that contain both theory and practical application. Many of them are highly mathematical and consider circuit design, materials selection, control programming, and hybrid mechanical systems; this journal demands a high level of engineering experience within the field. The research articles are short (five to seven pages), with gray-tone and color illustrations, and extensive references. Although research notes and book reviews are mentioned, none has appeared in recent issues. Beginning with the 2007 issues, the articles appear both as individual papers in a table-of-contents (downloadable pdf) list and as a full, page-by-page issue. Although there is a subscription price, all articles since 2007 are currently free.

4713. Journal of Bionic Engineering. [ISSN: 1672-6529] 2004. q. EUR 715. Ed(s): Da He, He Huang. Kexue Chubanshe, 16 Donghuang Cheng Genbei Jie, Beijing, 100717, China; http://www.sciencep.com/. Sample. Refereed. *Indexed:* C&ISA, CerAb. *Aud.:* Ac, Sa.

Another title in "biomimetics" (using designs and systems in nature to solve engineering problems), this one is from Jilin University in Changchun, China, but is published in English and mounted on ScienceDirect. It is a quarterly averaging over 100 pages per issue, and its authorship includes some researchers outside China, indicating an aim toward international coverage. Articles are short (under 10 pages) but well illustrated, with use of color in graphs and tables as well as in photographs. Unfortunately, the pdf version of an article does not include links to the references, although there is an html version of the references with the abstract. There is also no indication of the lag from submission to publication, although random checks of the reference lists indicate cites to material one or two years old. This title should be compared to *Bioinspiration and Biomimetics* (also reviewed in this section). The *Journal of Bionic Engineering* appears more theoretical in approach than does the *Bioinspiration and Biomimetics;* the former has titles such as "biomimetic control of mechanical systems equipped with musculotendon actuators," while the latter tends to "manipulators inspired by the tongue of the chameleon." Organizations with extensive interest in biomimetics will want both titles, but *Bioinspiration and Biomimetics* may be a better fit for robotics collections.

4714. *Journal of Dynamic Systems, Measurement and Control.* [ISSN: 0022-0434] 1971. bi-m. USD 584 combined subscription domestic (print & online eds.); USD 647 combined subscription foreign (print & online eds.); USD 120 per issue. Ed(s): Karl Hedrick. A S M E International, Two Park Ave, New York, NY 10016; CustomerCare@asme.org; http://www.asme.org. Illus., index. Sample. Refereed. Vol. ends: Dec. Microform: PQC. *Indexed:* A01, A22, ApMecR, BRI, C&ISA, CEA, CerAb, EngInd. *Aud.:* Ac, Sa.

To those outside the field, the *Journal of Dynamic Systems, Measurement and Control* may seem an unlikely title for a top robotics publication. The clues are "control" and "dynamic," because these play a large part in the design and use of robots. Recent articles discuss a robotic bulldozing, friction in robot joints, repetitive motion control (no, not carpal tunnel syndrome for robots), and a rolling robot. As a research journal, it is heavy on mathematics, usually illustrated with tables and graphs but with an occasional photograph, and it has extensive references. The ASME also publishes the *Journal of Mechanisms and Robotics* (also reviewed in this section); robotics is merely a part of the *Dynamic Systems* journal but the major thrust of the *Mechanisms* title. The ASME Digital Library (now mounted by the ASME itself) allows searching across its entire range of publications (journals, conferences, and books), although it is limited to those publications currently digitized. Useful features are the RSS feeds, social bookmarking, choice of pdf or html views, figures as graphs bundled as a "slide set," and a prominently displayed errata link. An excellent interdisciplinary title.

4715. *Journal of Field Robotics.* Formerly (until 2006): *Journal of Robotic Systems.* [ISSN: 1556-4959] 1984. bi-m. GBP 2150. Ed(s): Sanjiv Singh, Sanae Urano Minick. John Wiley & Sons, Inc., 111 River St, MS 4-02, Hoboken, NJ 07030; info@wiley.com; http://www.wiley.com/WileyCDA/. Illus., index, adv. Sample. Refereed. Vol. ends: Dec. Microform: PQC. Reprint: PSC. *Indexed:* A22, ApMecR, C&ISA, CerAb, CompLI, EngInd. *Aud.:* Ac, Sa.

The *Journal of Field Robotics* specializes in robots that work in unstructured environments (the "field"). The journal is at once practical and theoretical: practical because the robots involved are either working models or production floor systems; theoretical because the treatments involve designs or systems that can be used as models or applied in other environments, rather than specific techniques for a specific application. Almost every article features an actual robot rather than a theoretical concept. In fact, the author guidelines include the statement "Results that are limited to simulation will not be sufficient; experimental validation in field or appropriate analogs is necessary." Color and photographs have been added to the usual graphs, computer models, and flowcharts. There are occasional thematic issues, such as multiple collaborative robots, safety and security robots, and the DARPA Grand Challenge. In the DARPA Challenge, robots had to traverse 140 miles of rough terrain, adding yet another meaning to the term *field robot.* Although a quality journal, this is one of the most expensive publications in the robotics area (and issues are slim).

4716. *Journal of Intelligent and Robotic Systems: theory and applications.* Incorporates (in 1994): *Mechatronic Systems Engineering.* [ISSN: 0921-0296] 1988. 16x/yr. EUR 2310 (print & online eds.). Ed(s): Kimon P Valavanis. Springer Netherlands, Van Godewijckstraat 30, Dordrecht, 3311 GX, Netherlands; http://www.springer.com. Illus., index, adv. Sample. Refereed. Vol. ends: No. 4. Microform: PQC. Reprint: PSC. *Indexed:* A22, ApMecR, BRI, C&ISA, CerAb, E01, EngInd, ErgAb, PsycInfo. *Aud.:* Ac.

The mission of this journal is to cover "the whole technical spectrum from the birth of an idea at the conceptual level to a potential product development." Unmanned systems are emphasized and terms "unmanned" or "UAV" often appear in the article titles. Recent work discusses upper-limb robot motion and object perception by mobile robots. Authorship is international, with most researchers from academia, but there is a fair percentage of material with industrial collaboration. The theory is still present and much of the treatment is simulation or modeling, but the practicality shows through, as exemplified by the article on a robot with a deformed foot. The publication lag is relatively short: six months to online, less than a year to the official publication date. The changes in the "look" of the journal planned for 2012 became the "sectioned" article, with tabs for references, related content, and supplementary material, as well as extensive bibliographic details prominently displayed.

4717. *Journal of Intelligent Manufacturing.* [ISSN: 0956-5515] 1990. bi-m. EUR 1567 (print & online eds.). Ed(s): Andrew Kusiak. Springer New York LLC, 233 Spring St, New York, NY 10013; service-ny@springer.com; http://www.springer.com/. Adv. Refereed. Reprint: PSC. *Indexed:* A22, ABIn, ApMecR, E01, EngInd, H24. *Aud.:* Ac, Sa.

From its inception in 1990, the *Journal of Intelligent Manufacturing* has stressed application, with the chief form for years being the use of robots in automated manufacturing. Research articles (designated as "original paper") average 10–15 pages and are often illustrated with color figures, graphs, and tables. Other features are case studies, reviews, methods, and tutorials. In recent years, many issues are centered on a theme, such as design chain management and intelligent distributed production. The articles themselves often are co-authored by academic and industry researchers, continuing the theme of application. With this cross-disciplinary emphasis, this is a good title for robotics, manufacturing, industrial, and/or mechanical engineering collections.

4718. *Journal of Laboratory Automation.* Former titles (until 2011): *The Association for Laboratory Automation. Journal;* (until 1998): *Laboratory Automation News.* [ISSN: 2211-0682] 1997. bi-m. USD 474. Ed(s): Dean Ho. Sage Publications, Inc., 2455 Teller Rd, Thousand Oaks, CA 91320; info@sagepub.com; http://www.sagepub.com/. Adv. Sample. Refereed. Reprint: PSC. *Indexed:* C&ISA, CerAb, EngInd, ExcerpMed. *Aud.:* Ac, Sa.

Also known as *JALA,* this is the journal of the Society for Laboratory Automation and Screening, itself formed by a 2010 merger of the Society for Biomolecular Sciences and the Association for Laboratory Automation. The journal was formerly published by Elsevier but, as of 2011, it is now published by Sage. The laboratories featured in this journal are clinical testing facilities. With much of their work involving sterile environments and/or possibly dangerous substances, robots have come to be standard equipment. Almost every issue has at least one article on specialized robotic systems as used in the laboratory environment. Thus, this is a peer-reviewed title for the practitioner. Issues include columns on news and literature, review articles, "original reports," and technology briefs. Most entries average five pages; reviews may be longer. Articles often feature specific equipment, implementation methods, and operational support (such as "using Evernote as an electronic lab notebook"). Oddly, the html versions of articles include internal and external links, but the pdf versions do not. Although this journal is for the specialized collection, its cross-disciplinary nature may be a plus for some organizations, especially as biomedical robotics has become a thrust in robotics research.

4719. *Journal of Mechanisms and Robotics.* [ISSN: 1942-4302] 2009. q. Feb., May., Aug., & Nov. USD 481 combined subscription domestic (print & online eds.); USD 519 combined subscription foreign (print & online eds.); USD 143 per issue. Ed(s): Michael McCarthy. A S M E International, Two Park Ave, New York, NY 10016; CustomerCare@asme.org; http://www.asme.org. Sample. Refereed. *Aud.:* Ac, Sa.

The ASME journals publish many articles on robotics, but two of them cover the field itself: the *Journal of Mechanisms and Robotics* and the *Journal of Dynamic Systems, Measurement and Control* (also reviewed in this section). Neither journal mentions the other, but occasionally they cite one another. The *Journal of Mechanisms* is the more applied of the two; the *Journal of Dynamic Systems* covers a broad range of topics, of which robotics is just one. The ;Journal of Mechanisms and Robotics is not all robots, however; an illustration of what is meant by mechanisms is "Kinematic Representations of Pop-Up Paper Mechanisms," a discussion of the joint types and actions that make those pop-up books children (and advertisers) love. Most of the other articles are a little dryer in tone, focusing on modeling and mechanics of robot actions and parts. Articles may be "research," "design innovation," or "technical briefs." The online version of the article (whether html or pdf) uses the DOI instead of the page numbers of the corresponding print publication, but does indicate the total pages (e.g., nine pages) so the reader knows if the article is brief or lengthy. Institutions that subscribe to the full set of ASME publications will automatically receive this title, but those who buy only a few will prefer this to the *Journal of Dynamic Systems.*

4720. *Journal of Robotic Surgery.* [ISSN: 1863-2483] 2007. q. EUR 533 (print & online eds.). Ed(s): Vipul R. Patel, S Samavedi. Springer U K, 236 Gray's Inn Rd, Fl 6, London, WC1X 8HB, United Kingdom; derk.haank@springer.com; http://www.springer.com/. Adv. Refereed. Circ: 250. Reprint: PSC. *Indexed:* A22, E01. *Aud.:* Sa.

Robotic surgery is now commonplace, but there are few publications that emphasize the theory and practice of this technique (see the *International Journal of Medical Robotics and Computer Assisted Surgery,* also reviewed in this section). This journal features short (average of five to ten pages) color-illustrated articles, most of which describe in detail the use of robotic instruments and techniques in specific types of surgery. Occasionally, supplementary material (usually videos) accompany the articles. The extensive list of editors is largely peopled with clinicians and medical school faculty. Although low in price, this title is too specialized for any but medical collections or corporations that produce medical instruments.

4721. *Mechanism and Machine Theory.* Formerly (until 1972): *Journal of Mechanisms.* [ISSN: 0094-114X] 1966. m. EUR 3776. Ed(s): A Kecskemethy. Pergamon, The Blvd, Langford Ln, E Park, Kidlington, OX5 1GB, United Kingdom; JournalsCustomerServiceEMEA@elsevier.com; http://www.elsevier.com. Illus., adv. Sample. Refereed. Microform: PQC. *Indexed:* A01, A22, ApMecR, C&ISA, CCMJ, EngInd, MSN, MathR. *Bk. rev.:* 1, 2,000 words. *Aud.:* Ac.

The emphasis here is on theory, with most papers making extensive use of mathematical symbols rather than engineering diagrams. However, the topics generally concern practical applications, such as robot joints, manipulators, and kinematics. This is the official journal of the International Federation for the Theory of Machines and Mechanisms, and the authors reflect the international membership. An occasional non-English paper appears. This title is often cited by the core robotics journals covered in this section. For the academic library with a strong engineering mechanics/manufacturing program, as the treatment is highly mathematical.

4722. *Mechatronics: the science of intelligent machines.* [ISSN: 0957-4158] 1991. 8x/yr. EUR 1692. Ed(s): Maarten Steinbuch. Pergamon, The Blvd, Langford Ln, E Park, Kidlington, OX5 1GB, United Kingdom; JournalsCustomerServiceEMEA@elsevier.com; http://www.elsevier.com. Illus., adv. Sample. Refereed. Microform: PQC. *Indexed:* A01, A22, ApMecR, C&ISA, CerAb, EngInd. *Aud.:* Ac, Sa.

One of the few titles devoted entirely to the emergent hybrid field for which it is named, *Mechatronics* is chiefly interested in papers on the design of machines and systems that include some level of computer-based intelligence. For instance, one special issue featured velocity control of a washing machine, and another discussed motion control of microrobots. Articles are now on the short side (six or seven pages), a change from earlier years. The major application thrust is specific robotic parts, as opposed to a multifunction and/or mobile robot. Examples of this are such phrases as "two-axis arm motion" and "five-bar finger with redundant activators." The delay from submission to publication is often two years. Compare this title with the *IEEE/ASME Transactions on Mechatronics,* which is cheaper and has a higher ISI Impact Factor. This will be a useful addition to a strong mechanical engineering design collection, as well as for robotics.

4723. *Robot Magazine: the latest in hobby, science and consumer robotics.* [ISSN: 1555-1016] 2005. bi-m. USD 24.95 domestic; USD 29.95 Canada; USD 39.95 elsewhere. Ed(s): Tom Atwood. Maplegate Media Group, 42 Old Ridgebury Rd, Danbury, CT 06810; sales@maplegatemedia.com; http://www.maplegatemedia.com/. Adv. Sample. *Aud.:* Hs, Ga.

This is more than a hobby magazine. It functions like a trade publication, with good overview articles of current developments, interviews with practitioners, and news and links. The hobbyist will find schematics and programs; the teacher will find curriculum guides and examples that appeal to students; teenagers will find the competitions and tips on building inexpensive systems. There is even an annual "Robot Buyers Guide." Although this is a print magazine, its web site has sample articles and serves as the forum for readers. Back issues can be viewed online with a member ID and password. This will be an inexpensive addition to a public or school library.

4724. *Robotica.* [ISSN: 0263-5747] 1983. 7x/yr. GBP 959. Ed(s): G S Chirikjian. Cambridge University Press, The Edinburgh Bldg, Shaftesbury Rd, Cambridge, CB2 8RU, United Kingdom; journals@cambridge.org; http://www.cambridge.org/uk. Illus., index, adv. Sample. Refereed. Circ: 600. Vol. ends: No. 6. Reprint: PSC. *Indexed:* A01, A22, BRI, BrTechI, C&ISA, CBRI, CerAb, CompLI, E01, EngInd, ErgAb. *Aud.:* Ac, Sa.

One of the earliest professional journals on robotics, *Robotica* has remained focused on its mission over the years. It is hard to find an article in any issue that does not have *robot* somewhere in the title (although nowadays it may be part of a technical word, such as *microrobots*). Although papers are research-level–quality, there is always attention to working mechanisms rather than just theoretical modeling. Following the usual academic formula, papers are well illustrated and heavily referenced. Acceptance after submission of a paper is swift, but there is a long delay between the posting of the accepted article and the "official" publication in an issue of the journal. Open Access articles (where the authors have paid so that non-subscribers have access) are highlighted in, naturally, green. This is an excellent journal, useful in both industry and academia.

4725. *Robotics and Autonomous Systems.* Formerly (until 1988): *Robotics.* [ISSN: 0921-8890] 1985. 12x/yr. EUR 2094. Ed(s): T Arai, R Grupen. Elsevier BV, North-Holland, Postbus 211, Amsterdam, 1000 AE, Netherlands; JournalsCustomerServiceEMEA@elsevier.com; http://www.elsevier.com. Illus., index, adv. Sample. Refereed. Vol. ends: No. 4. *Indexed:* A01, A22, ApMecR, BRI, C&ISA, CompLI, EngInd, PsycInfo. *Aud.:* Ac, Sa.

Autonomous systems are special cases that may appear like robots, but operate in a specific environment for a specific task. For instance, the "robots" that are used in automobile assembly plants are more likely to be autonomous systems than full-fledged robots. This journal is affiliated with the Intelligent Autonomous Systems Society. The title should be compared with the publication *Robotics and Computer-Integrated Manufacturing,* also published by Elsevier. Both are research journals that feature quality scholarly papers. They are not competitors, though, but two aspects of the same field: large-scale and/or whole machines versus specific aspects or parts of machines. *Robotics and Autonomous Systems* will publish titles such as "A Biomimetic underwater microrobot," while *Robotics and Computer-Integrated Manufacturing* will feature "Improved robotic deburring." Papers average 10–15 pages in length; the lag from submission to publication is usually a few months. There are several thematic issues per year on such topics as "mobiligence" (intelligence for motor function) and autonomous grasping. Heavily cited by other robotics journals, this is good addition to an academic robotics collection.

4726. *Robotics and Computer-Integrated Manufacturing: an international journal of manufacturing, product and process development.* Incorporates (1988-1998): *Computer Integrated Manufacturing Systems;* (1988-1991): *Advanced Manufacturing Engineering.* [ISSN: 0736-5845] 1984. bi-m. EUR 1711. Ed(s): A Sharon. Pergamon, The Blvd, Langford Ln, E Park, Kidlington, OX5 1GB, United Kingdom; JournalsCustomerServiceEMEA@elsevier.com; http://www.elsevier.nl. Illus., adv. Sample. Refereed. Microform: PQC. *Indexed:* A22, B01, C&ISA, CerAb, CompLI, EngInd, ErgAb. *Aud.:* Ac.

This is a research journal with a mission: dissemination of proven research (either in the laboratory or on the shop floor) of manufacturing technologies and systems. This includes robotics, flexible automation, mechatronics, and rapid-response (or agile) manufacturing. A succinct expression of this approach is contained in the title of the recent article "Optimisation of compressed air and electricity consumption in a complex robotic cell." Almost every author is associated with an engineering department of a large university, with research usually funded by a government agency, so that laboratory work predominates. Articles average 10 pages in length but occasionally are up to 20 pages. Illustrations are largely flow charts, line drawings, and screen images, with judicious use of color, and articles are well referenced and current. This journal cites, and is cited by, both robotics and manufacturing journals and is useful for both fields.

4727. *Servo.* [ISSN: 1546-0592] 2003. m. T & L Publications, 430 Princeland Ct, Corona, CA 92879.

Adv. Circ: 8344 Paid. *Aud.:* Ac, Ga.

This little magazine is one of two from a small press. It is designed for the amateur robot enthusiast, but "amateur" does not mean "untrained." The readership is technology-savvy and the articles (and blog posts) reflect this. The magazine covers robot construction, software, circuits, sensors, batteries, and other devices or brainstorms that will further robotics. Much of the magazine comprises regular columns such as "Ask Mr. Roboto," "GeerHead," or "Robytes," but feature articles are solicited (and receive a modest payment) from the membership. The articles are deliberately short and well-illustrated, and the references are likely to be URLs. Author bios are included to verify their expertise. The online version is a literal copy of the print, with links from a table of contents to the page-by-page rendition of the full-color articles and columns. An impediment to online library subscriptions is that a membership login is required to read entire articles and to participate in the blogs, but the paper copy is quite inexpensive. An excellent title for public libraries and two-year colleges.

■ SAFETY

See also Medicine; and Public Health sections.

Christine K. Oka, Library Instruction Specialist, 270 Snell Library, Northeastern University, Boston, MA 02115; c.oka@neu.edu

Introduction

This section, although small, covers the broad spectrum of safety, ranging from big-picture issues such as industrial safety and hygiene, injury and accident research, to specific occupational health and safety training programs and products. Many of these publications are available online and are of interest to a general audience, while others are more specialized titles for special or academic library collections.

During these tough budgetary times, many publishers have chosen not to send samples of print issues for review, or to direct reviewers to "sample issues" on their journal web page. Unfortunately, often these online samples are older; a 2008 issue may not be representative of the publication today.

Alternatively, the Internet supports open access, allowing libraries, and their readers, to connect to online resources, such as the National Safety Council web page at www.nsc.org/pages/home.aspx. This site provides links to news and information on safety at work, at home, and on the road.

Basic Periodicals

Ga: *Industrial Safety and Hygiene News, Professional Safety;* Ac, Sa: *Accident Analysis & Prevention.*

Basic Abstracts and Indexes

Health and Safety Science Abstracts, Risk Abstracts.

4728. Accident Analysis & Prevention. [ISSN: 0001-4575] 1969. bi-m. EUR 2327. Ed(s): K Kim, R Elvik. Elsevier Ltd, The Boulevard, Langford Lane, Oxford, OX5 1GB, United Kingdom; http:// www.elsevier.com. Illus., index, adv. Sample. Refereed. Vol. ends: Oct. Microform: PQC. *Indexed:* A01, A22, B01, C&ISA, CerAb, EngInd, ErgAb, H24, PsycInfo, RiskAb. *Aud.:* Ac, Sa.

Affiliated with the Association for the Advancement of Automotive Medicine (AAAM), *Accident Analysis & Prevention* "provides wide coverage of the general areas relating to accidental injury and damage, such as medical, legal, economic, educational, behavioral, theoretical or empirical aspects of transportation accidents, as well as with accidents at other sites." The journal topics range from human behavior, and environmental and vehicular factors influencing accidents and injury, to "the design, implementation[,] and evaluation of countermeasures to statistical analysis of accident data; [and] policy planning and decision-making in safety." The multidisciplinary scope makes this journal of interest to "regional planners, research scientists, civil engineers, trauma physicians, psychologists, [and] public health planners." Original research articles are international in scope, and examine different

modes of transportation. Recent issues covered include "Safety Riding Program and Motorcycle-Related Injuries in Thailand," "Different Risk Thresholds in Pedestrian Road Crossing Behavior: A Comparison of French and Japanese Approaches," and "Analysis of U.S. Freight-Train Derailment Severity Using Zero-Truncated Negative Binomial Regression and Quantile Regression." Recommended for special and academic libraries.

American Journal of Public Health. See Public Health section.

4729. E H S Today: the magazine of safety, health and loss prevention. Formerly (until 2008): *Occupational Hazards.* [ISSN: 1945-9599] 1938. m. USD 69 domestic (Free to qualified personnel). Ed(s): Sandy Smith. Penton Media, Inc., 1300 E 9th St, Cleveland, OH 44114; information@penton.com; http://www.penton.com. Illus., index, adv. Sample. Circ: 65000 Paid and controlled. Vol. ends: Dec. Microform: PQC. *Indexed:* A22, ABIn, B01, B02, BRI, C42, H24, P02, RiskAb. *Aud.:* Ga, Ac, Sa.

Published since 1938, this trade publication contains "news on industrial safety, occupational health, environmental control, insurance, first aid, medical care, and hazardous material control," and articles looking at risk in the workplace. Updates on EPA, NIOSH, and OSHA compliance requirements, as well as articles about improving safety and industrial hygiene programs, make this a valuable resource for safety, human resources, business, and industry professionals. Recent articles covered a broad range of news and research topics, ranging from an examination of how domestic violence migrates to the workplace in cases of employees killed by their intimate partners, to "Carpal Tunnel Blues," and prevention of falls at construction sites. There also are safety equipment product reviews. The publisher's web site at www.ehstoday.com provides up-to-date information and links to news articles. Recommended for special, academic, and public libraries. The information is jargon-free and accessible to most readers.

4730. Industrial Safety and Hygiene News: news of safety, health and hygiene, environmental, fire, security and emergency protection equipment. Former titles (until 199?): *Chilton's Industrial Safety and Hygiene News;* (until 1982): *Industrial Safety and Hygiene News;* (until 1981): *Industrial Safety Product News;* (until 1978): *Safety Products News.* 1967. m. Free to qualified personnel (print or online ed.). Ed(s): Maureen Brady, Dave Johnson. B N P Media, 2401 W Big Beaver Rd, Ste 700, Troy, MI 48084; portfolio@bnpmedia.com; http:// www.bnpmedia.com. Illus. Sample. Circ: 62000. Microform: PQC. *Indexed:* ABIn, B01, B02, B03, BRI, C&ISA, CerAb, H24. *Aud.:* Ga, Ac, Sa.

This trade journal focuses on news and products related to health and safety in the work environment with the goal of "targeting 71,400 key safety, health[,] and industrial hygiene[–]buying influences at manufacturing facilities of all sizes." Each issue is packed with information on OSHA and EPA regulations, as well as practical safety and health management news for "managers at high-hazard worksites in manufacturing, construction, health facilities, and service industries...." Recent articles reflect disasters from the news, such as "Texas Blast Shows Oversight Gaps," as well as editorials and the reports. In one article, "What OSHA Ought to Get Into," the author considers what OSHA could add to its health promotion and educational topics and how to deliver this information to the workplace in the twenty-first century. Another article begged the question, "Run, Hide or Confront: How Should You Respond to an Active Shooter?" The ISHN web site at http://www.ishn.com/ provides access to current and archived issues as early as January 1990. The site has added value with links to the latest headlines, the "ISHN Blog," "Featured Stories," and an events calendar for safety professionals. Highly recommended.

4731. International Journal of Occupational and Environmental Health. [ISSN: 1077-3525] 1995. q. GBP 277 (print & online eds.). Ed(s): David S Egilman. Maney Publishing, Ste 1C, Joseph's Well, Hanover Walk, Leeds, LS3 1AB, United Kingdom; maney@maneypublishing.com; http://maneypublishing.com/. Illus., index, adv. Refereed. Reprint: PSC. *Indexed:* AbAn, C45, ErgAb, H24, RILM. *Bk. rev.:* Number and length vary. *Aud.:* Ac, Sa.

The *International Journal of Occupational and Environmental Health (IJOEH)* is described as "an authoritative, interdisciplinary resource covering occupational health, environmental health, and consumer health (the aspects of human disease and injury that are determined or influenced by exposure to consumer goods and their components, including pharmaceuticals, food additives, and other purchased products)." The scientific and social scientific research articles in recent issues ranged from a statistical study of "Risk of Injury by Job Assignment Among Federal Wildland Firefighters, United States, 2003-2007" (which gives an eye to identifying injuries by assignment, to develop prevention strategies), to "Social Movements and Risk Perception: Unions, Churches, Pesticides and Bananas in Costa Rica." This latter story had the objective "to understand the social movement, *Foro Emaus*," and how the unions within it became a force for "putting health and environmental risk issues on the political and research agenda." In addition to research, news and editorials are published. After the editorial "Quebec and Canadian Governments End their Historic Support of the Asbestos Industry" appeared in late 2012, it was followed by a spate of research articles, "Why Countries Ban Asbestos: The Roots of Political Will," "Why Countries Ban Asbestos: Some Alternative Thoughts," and "Why Some, But Not All, Countries Have Banned Asbestos." *IJOEH* is read by researchers, practitioners, policy makers, and activists in the fields of occupational, environmental, and consumer health. Its international readership extends across disciplines, including epidemiology, occupational and environmental medicine, sociology, toxicology, and related fields.

4732. *Journal of Safety Research: a safety and health research forum.*
[ISSN: 0022-4375] 1969. bi-m. EUR 1229. Ed(s): Thomas Planek, Kathleen Porretta. Pergamon, The Blvd, Langford Ln, E Park, Kidlington, OX5 1GB, United Kingdom; JournalsCustomerServiceEMEA@elsevier.com; http://www.elsevier.com. Illus., adv. Sample. Refereed. Microform: PQC. *Indexed:* A01, A22, BRI, EngInd, ErgAb, H24, P02, PsycInfo, RiskAb. *Aud.:* Ac, Sa.

Described as "a joint publication of the National Safety Council http://www.nsc.org and Elsevier," the *Journal of Safety Research: A Safety and Health Research Forum* provides for the interdisciplinary "exchange of ideas and data developed through research experience in all areas of safety[,] including traffic, industry, farm, home, school and public." Original research articles in recent issues examined "Health and Lifestyle Risk Factors for Falls in a Large Population-Based Sample of Older People in Australia," to identify different fall-prevention strategies; and "Risk Analysis System for the Transport of Hazardous Materials," to develop "a framework to visualize [the] risk of hazmat transport along a route." Psychosocial studies included "Waiting for Safety: Responses by Young Canadian Workers to Unsafe Work," where younger workers had a wait-and-see attitude "related to their fear of being fired, [their] status as newcomers, supervisor indifference, and feelings of powerlessness." Risk factors for specific occupations were studied in "Disparities in Work-Related Homicide Rates in Selected Retail Industries in the United States, 2003-2008" and "Workplace Violence among Pennsylvania Education Workers: Differences among Occupations." The range of highly-focused research topics contained in each issue of the journal provides something of interest to scholars and safety practitioners. Recommended for academic and special libraries.

4733. *Professional Safety.* Former titles (until 1970): *A S S E Journal;* (until 1969): *American Society of Safety Engineers. Journal.* [ISSN: 0099-0027] 1956. m. USD 51 (Individuals, USD 60). Ed(s): Sue Trebswether. American Society of Safety Engineers, 1800 E Oakton St, Des Plaines, IL 60018; customerservice@asse.org; http://www.asse.org. Illus., index, adv. Sample. Refereed. Circ: 30500 Paid. Vol. ends: Dec. *Indexed:* A01, A22, ABIn, B01, C45, ErgAb. *Bk. rev.:* 2, 150-250 words; signed. *Aud.:* Ga, Ac, Sa.

The ASSE, founded over 100 years ago, is "the oldest professional safety organization," and publishes *Professional Safety,* a peer-reviewed journal with "information on developments in the research and technology of accident prevention, safety management[,] and program development." Safety professionals and the general reader will find articles and departments relevant and accessible. Recent articles covered traditional emergency management in "Preparing for a Crisis" and "Engaging Employees & Companies in Disaster Preparedness." There also were research articles related to newer topics, such as sustainability as a business strategy that supports safety and health initiatives in "Safety & Sustainability," and the safety of construction workers in "Sustainable Buildings." The general reader will find benefit in journal departments such as "Best Practices," with information about "Best Practices to Travel Safely with Jet-Lag-Induced Fatigue," or book reviews, such as "Six Ways to Apply Ergonomics in Design," a free e-book. Recent issues demonstrate the broad spectrum of *Professional Safety* as it covers industry updates and safety product evaluations. Recommended for academic, special, and large public libraries.

■ SCIENCE AND TECHNOLOGY

General/History and Philosophy of Science/Science and Technology Education

Susan M. Braxton, Head Librarian, Prairie Research Institute, University of Illinois at Urbana Champaign, Urbana, IL 61801

Introduction

Ulrich's Global Serials Directory lists 271 new, active, primary editions of journals/magazines under either "sciences: comprehensive works" or "technology: comprehensive works" from 2008 to mid-2012. The vast majority are academic journals, and only 163 of them are offered in print. There is a trend of increasing numbers of new titles per year; the number of new titles was near or well below 50 titles between 2000 and 2008, but for 2009 through 2011, the average number of new titles per year was 71. Similarly, the number of titles reviewed by *Journal Citation Reports* (*JCR*) and categorized as "multidisciplinary sciences" has increased, by about 40 percent from a recent low of 42 in 2008 to 59 in 2010. Only 22 titles are reported by Ulrich's to have ceased publication since 2000.

The most common countries of publication for 2008 to mid-2012 new titles in *Ulrich's* are the United States (64 titles), India (62 titles), United Kingdom (33 titles), and Pakistan (10 titles). The long tail of countries of origin spans the globe, but the regions from which most titles emanate are Asia, North America, and Western Europe (in that order), which combined account for more than 80 percent of the titles.

Titles that include the social sciences in their scope are relatively common. Of the 271 new titles in *Ulrich's* from 2008 to mid-2012, 66 titles (approximately 25 percent) are also indexed with subjects of "social sciences and humanities," "business and economics," "philosophy and religion," or "government, law and public administration."

Of the 271 titles that began publication in 2008 to mid-2012 in *Ulrich's,* 78 (29 percent) are listed as Open Access (OA). An increasing proportion of new titles are OA since 2000, from about 17 percent of 2000 titles, to about 40 percent of the titles beginning publication in 2010. The author-pays model is common. For example, Nature Publishing Group's *Scientific Reports,* reviewed herein, charges a USD 1,350 article-processing charge on acceptance, with articles published under a Creative Commons (http://creativecommons.org/) license. It may soon be possible for institutions to purchase article-processing charge memberships for this and other Nature titles. How this might compare to the average subscription fee is not yet evident. Not included is the *British Journal of Science,* which solicits articles from all science disciplines for rapid publication. However, editorial board members' institutional affiliations were vague and this reviewer was unable to verify them, and as of June 2012 no articles were found in the high-profile A&I services listed on the journal web site (e.g., *Scopus, Compendex,* or *GEOBASE*). Nevertheless this 2011 title, now in its fifth volume, seems to have little trouble attracting authors. In 2009, Jeffery Beall published his first review of OA publishers in *The Charleston Advisor.* In 2010, he posted the first annual list of "Predatory Open Access Publishers" to his blog. The 2012 list was recently issued, and includes a watch list in addition to the publishers designated predatory. Ongoing reviews and news are available from Beall's blog, *Scholarly Open Access* (http://scholarlyoa.com/). While there has been debate on his reviews, Beall's blog provides current awareness of publishers and practices. An excellent resource for information on OA scholarly publishers is the Open Access Scholarly Publishers Association, established in 2008 (http://oaspa.org).

News of note for reviewed titles includes a new publisher for a venerable standard, *Scientific American,* which moved to Nature Publishing Group (NPG) from within parent MacMillan Publishers Ltd. in 2009. NPG increased the price for 2010 from $39.95 to $299 for print and by more than 30 percent for online access. The negative reaction from libraries was covered in *Library Journal* and the *Chronicle of Higher Education,* with groups of libraries (e.g., Oberlin Group, the California Digital Library, and the Committee for Institutional Cooperation) cancelling subscriptions and pushing collectively for better pricing.

A recent development with the potential for long-term transformative impact on scholarly publishing in the sciences comprises data management, sharing, and preservation requirements for federally funded research. Early in 2011, the National Science Foundation began requiring data management plans for all proposals. This followed similar requirements from the National Institutes of Health, and other U.S. federal agencies have implemented similar requirements. Academies and commercial interests have taken notice. New requirements offer opportunities for librarians to promote institutional and disciplinary repositories for data curation. Products for discovery and dissemination of literature has been held up as a model for data management and sharing services. Dryad (http://datadryad.org) is a partnership coordinated by research institutions and involving societies and commercial publishers, which offers a repository for data that support articles published in partner journals. Ironically, at least some disciplinary or extra-institutional solutions are themselves federally funded, and the January 2012 termination of USGS's National Biological Information Infrastructure begs the question of sustainability of data management/curation solutions based on federal support. Joel Hammond of Thompson Reuters suggested that commercial information providers are prepared to provide data management services in his presentation, "From Documents to Data: Challenges in Linking, Aggregating and Citing," made during the August 2010 National Information Standards Organization Webinar, "Show Me the Data: Managing Data Sets for Scholarly Content."

The European Science Foundation's European Reference Index for the Humanities (ERIH) published their 2011 revised lists. A joint editorial published in 2009 in response to the inaugural 2007 lists had protested the ERIH due to potential negative consequences: namely, that the discipline would become less diverse as lower-tier journals would tend to disappear. Signed by editors of more than 50 journals, the editorial criticized the methodology, committee composition, and lack of communication with professional societies and editors in the development of the system. The signatories, among them editors of *Social Studies of Science, Science, Technology and Human Values,* and *British Journal for the History of Science* (all reviewed herein), asked that their titles be removed from the rankings. Records can be found for two of the three titles in the 2011 list.

Science achievement and literacy continues to be an area of focus and concern. The Trends in International Mathematics and Science Study (TIMSS), begun by the International Association for the Evaluation of Educational Achievement in 1995, tracks performance of fourth- and eighth-grade students from participating countries every four years. The 2007 results show the average science score of United States eighth-graders below that of ten other nations (http://nces.ed.gov/timss/table07_3.asp). The 2011 results of TIMSS will be released in 2012. The American Association for the Advancement of Science (AAAS) Project 2061, founded in 1985 to "to help all Americans become literate in science, mathematics, and technology," emphasizes "the connections among ideas in the natural and social sciences, mathematics, and technology." The National Academies formed the Center for Education in 1999 (www7.nationalacademies.org/cfe) for "improvement of mathematics, science, technology and engineering education from the kindergarten through post[-]graduate education." Though emphasis is typically on curriculum and instruction, the role of school and public librarians in science and technology literacy for students and citizens is critical, if implicit. In addition to the titles intended to support science educators, many titles reviewed in this section are appropriate for students and general audiences. Free online content is common, and may include supplementary content not available in the print counterpart. Knowledge of these titles and their web site offerings can help librarians to help patrons, even if subscriptions to the titles themselves are out of reach. Additional current awareness sources are freely available online, among them *ScienceDaily* (www.sciencedaily.com/), a web portal that offers "breaking news about the latest discoveries and hottest research projects."

Reviewed here are 33 titles from 29 publishers, representing general science and technology, history and philosophy of science (including social aspects of science and technology), and science and technology education. Scholarly, popular, and trade/professional titles are covered, and some fall into multiple categories (e.g., *Science*). An attempt was made to assess online publishing

practices that may affect library serials management. In the following annotations, if no mention of Digital Object Identifiers (DOIs) is made, it is because the reviewer did not find evidence of DOIs. COUNTER compliance is reported from the list of compliant vendors on the Project COUNTER web site (www.projectcounter.org/compliantvendors.html) in June 2012.

Basic Periodicals

Ems: *Current Science, Science and Children* (see also titles in Children section); Hs: *Discover, Science News, Scientific American;* Ga: *Discover, Popular Science, Science, Science News, Scientific American, The Scientist;* Ac: *American Scientist, Discover, National Academy of Sciences. Proceedings, Nature, New Scientist, Science, Science News, Scientific American, Technology Review.*

Basic Abstracts and Indexes

Applied Science and Technology Index.

General

4734. Advanced Science Letters. [ISSN: 1936-6612] 2008. q. USD 1180; USD 2080 combined subscription (print & online eds.). Ed(s): Hari Singh Nalwa. American Scientific Publishers, 26650 The Old Rd, Ste 208, Valencia, CA 91381-0751; order@aspbs.com; http://www.aspbs.com. Adv. Refereed. *Aud.:* Ac, Sa.

Advanced Science Letters was launched in 2008, publishing two issues in that year, with publication frequency increasing each year since. Editorial offices are based in California, with a large and international editorial board; honorary editors listed on the board web site are Nobel laureates Douglas Osheroff and Richard Ernst. This journal is multidisciplinary in scope, and covers life, Earth, and physical sciences, and engineering and mathematics. It publishes full research papers, mini-reviews, and rapid communications. Special sections may include news, commentary, features and perspectives, business, conference papers, and more. Institutional online access is available via IngentaConnect. DOIs assigned.

4735. American Scientist. Formerly (until 1942): *Sigma XI Quarterly.* [ISSN: 0003-0996] 1913. bi-m. USD 28 domestic; USD 36 Canada; USD 44 elsewhere. Ed(s): Morgan Ryan, David Schoonmaker. Sigma XI, Scientific Research Society, 3106 East NC Highway 54, PO Box 13975, Research Triangle Park, NC 27709; info@sigmaxi.org; http://www.sigmaxi.org/. Illus., index, adv. Vol. ends: Dec. Microform: PMC; PQC. *Indexed:* A01, A22, AbAn, Agr, AnBeAb, BRI, BrArAb, CBRI, CompR, GardL, M&GPA, MASUSE, MLA-IB, MathR, NumL, P02, RILM, S25. *Bk. rev.:* 12 or more per issue, 250-2,200 words, signed. *Aud.:* Hs, Ga, Ac.

Published by Sigma Xi since 1913, *American Scientist* is a general illustrated magazine on science and technology, with broad disciplinary coverage. Each issue includes three or more feature articles, most invited and written by research scientists. Features are technical but accessible, and include bibliographies. In addition to features, also published are interviews, shorter articles, and brief news accounts. In honor of the centennial of the magazine, special features under the banner of "American Scientist Classic" have been published; an example is a review of the state of behavioral science since the publication of Skinner's seminal 1957 work. Numerous signed critical book reviews are included in each issue. Strongly recommended for academic, public, and high school libraries. Institutional licensing for online access is available, with cost based on institution type and FTE. Book reviews and some features and other content are freely available online. DOIs assigned.

4736. Current Science: a fortnightly journal of research. [ISSN: 0011-3891] 1932. fortn. USD 300 Free to members. Ed(s): P Balaram. Indian Academy of Sciences, C.V. Raman Ave, Sadashivanagar, PO Box 8005, Bangalore, 560 080, India; office@ias.ernet.in; http://www.ias.ac.in. Illus., adv. Refereed. Microform: PQC. *Indexed:* A01, A22, C&ISA, C45, CCMJ, CerAb, FS&TA, H24, IndVet, M&GPA, MSN, MathR, NumL, RRTA, S25. *Bk. rev.:* Number and length vary; signed. *Aud.:* Ac, Sa.

Published by the Current Science Association for the Indian Academy of Science, and founded in 1932, *Current Science* is "intended as a medium for communication and discussion of important issues that concern science and scientific activity." This title covers science and technology broadly, including agriculture, biology, chemistry, Earth sciences, engineering, medicine, and physics. Content includes articles on administration and policy, reviews of research trends, full research articles and rapid communications, research news, and commentary/opinions. Frequent themed special sections are published; recent examples include malaria research, nanomaterials, and climate change. Signed book reviews are published, usually four or five per issue. Supplementary data are accepted for online publication. Freely available online, volume 1 through preprints of accepted articles.

Current Science (Weekly Reader Corp.). See Classroom Magazines/Science section.

4737. *Discover: science, technology and the future.* [ISSN: 0274-7529] 1980. m. USD 19.95 (print or online ed.); USD 29.95 combined subscription (print & online eds.). Kalmbach Publishing Co., 21027 Crossroads Circle, Waukesha, WI 53187; customerservice@kalmbach.com; http://www.kalmbach.com. Illus., adv. Vol. ends: Dec. Microform: PQC. *Indexed:* A01, A22, Agr, BRI, C37, MASUSE, P02. *Aud.:* Hs, Ga, Ac.

A leading popular science magazine, *Discover* offers accessible articles for a lay audience on recent advances in all scientific disciplines. Ten issues per year offer numerous regular sections. "Data" provides multiple brief summaries of recent scientific advances. Other regular features include "Vital Signs"(medicine), "The Brain," and "20 Things You Didn't Know About..." (recent examples include fire, clouds, and fraud). The combined January/February issue lists the top scientific developments of the prior year. Interviews with prominent scientists were published in some 2011 issues, but none were found in the 2012 issues examined. Similarly, book reviews appear to have been dropped. This publication features attractive, compelling photos and illustrations, and tends to offer more coverage of basic research (as opposed to invention and applications) than does *Popular Science*. Recommended for high school, public, and academic libraries. Online access is available through aggregators. Free access to some content from 1992 through the next-to-last issue is available via the publisher site. Blogs, RSS feeds, podcasts, and themed e-newsletters on various topics are available online, in addition to content from the monthly issues.

4738. *Journal of Scientific Exploration.* [ISSN: 0892-3310] 1987. q. Free to members. Ed(s): Kathleen E Erickson. Society for Scientific Exploration, c/o Mark Urban-Lurain, Michigan State University, East Lansing, MI 48824; http://www.scientificexploration.org. Illus., index. Sample. Refereed. Vol. ends: No. 4. *Indexed:* A01, EngInd, M&GPA. *Bk. rev.:* 10-15 per issue, varying length; signed. *Aud.:* Ac, Sa.

The Society for Scientific Exploration is a "professional organization of scientists and scholars who study unusual and unexplained phenomena." The *Journal of Scientific Exploration* publishes material consistent with that description: from "anomalies in well-established disciplines to paradoxical phenomena that seem to belong to no established discipline, as well as philosophical issues about the connections among disciplines." Research articles, commentary, essays, reviews, book and film reviews, and correspondence on previously published material are published. Coverage runs the gamut from extraterrestrials to parapsychology, as well as unconventional examinations of mainstream topics such as climate change. Although clearly outside mainstream scientific literature, it is appropriate for academic library collections, both for its maverick appeal and for social science and historical value. Like the now-defunct *Cryptozoology*, this title is enticing in ways that many traditional journals are not, and has potential as a teaching tool in undergraduate science education. Publisher offers free full text with a two-year embargo.

4739. *Journal of the Royal Society. Interface.* [ISSN: 1742-5689] 2004. m. EUR 3150 (print & online eds.). Ed(s): Leslie Dutton. The Royal Society Publishing, 6-9 Carlton House Terr, London, SW1Y 5AG, United Kingdom; sales@royalsociety.org; http://royalsocietypublishing.org. Sample. Refereed. *Indexed:* A22, AnBeAb, C45, E01, ExcerpMed. *Aud.:* Ac, Sa.

A cross-disciplinary publication for "research at the interface of the physical and life sciences," this journal includes "research applying chemistry, engineering, materials science, mathematics[,] and physics to the biological and medical sciences," as well as "discoveries in the life sciences that allow advances in the physical sciences." This title is published by The Royal Society, the national academy of science of the U.K. and the Commonwealth. Topics include biocomplexity, bioengineering, bioinformatics, biomaterials, biomechanics, bionanoscience, biophysics, chemical biology, computer applications in life science, medical physics, synthetic biology, systems biology, theoretical biology, and tissue engineering. Infrequent themed supplements, titled *Interface Focus,* are published; the most recent example (December 2010) covered translation and commercialization of regenerative medicine. Original research articles, shorter reports of preliminary research, and invited reviews are published. This title ranked fourth of 59 titles in the 2010 Journal Citation Reports Multidisciplinary Sciences category. Recommended for academic and special libraries that support research programs in physical, life sciences, or biomedical sciences. Online access, via Highwire Press, includes accepted articles. Free online access is available to all review articles; there is a one-year embargo on other content. Also, the society offers an author-pays option for open access. DOIs assigned. Publisher is partially COUNTER-compliant.

4740. *N A S A Tech Briefs: engineering solutions for design and manufacturing.* Formerly (until 1976): *N A S A Tech Brief.* [ISSN: 0145-319X] 1963. m. USD 75 domestic includes Puerto Rico (Free to qualified personnel). Ed(s): Ted Selinsky, Linda Bell. Associated Business Publications International, 1466 Broadway, Ste 910, New York, NY 10036; info@abpi.net; http://www.abpi.net. Adv. *Indexed:* A22, C&ISA, CerAb. *Aud.:* Ac, Sa.

A publication of the National Aeronautics and Space Administration's Innovative Partnerships Program, *NASA Tech Briefs* highlights new developments in sensors, electronics, biomed, materials, mechanics, and other areas. This title helps fulfill the legislative mandate from 1958 for NASA to "report to industry any new, commercially-significant technologies developed in the course of their R&D...." The briefs are "exclusive reports of innovations developed by NASA and its industry partners/contractors that can be applied to develop new/improved products and solve engineering or manufacturing problems," and most have an associated "Technical Support Package" or freely available white papers from the companion web site. Regular features are "Who's Who" and "Technologies/Products of the Month." Recommended for academic libraries, including those at community colleges that support engineering and industrial technology or manufacturing programs. Public and high school libraries may also benefit from this free publication.

4741. *The National Academies In Focus.* Former titles (until 2001): *The National Academies News Report;* (until 1999): *National Research Council. News Report.* [ISSN: 1534-8334] 1951. 3x/yr. USD 10 domestic; USD 12 foreign. Ed(s): Valerie Chase. National Academy of Sciences, 500 Fifth St, NW, Washington, DC 20001; news@nas.edu; http://www.nationalacademies.org. Illus. Refereed. Microform: PQC. *Indexed:* A22, ABIn, Agr. *Aud.:* Hs, Ga, Ac, Sa.

The National Academy of Sciences, National Research Council, National Academy of Engineering, and Institute of Medicine—collectively called The National Academies—"serve as independent advisers to the federal government on scientific and technical questions of national importance." *In Focus,* published by the National Academies' Office of News and Public Information, highlights the activities of these bodies. Regular sections are "Education and social issues," "Environment and resources," "Health and safety," and "Engineering and technology." "Spotlight" highlights academy programs, events, or partnerships. New academy publications are listed, but not reviewed. This title facilitates current awareness of science and policy issues with accessibly written articles. Recommended for high school, public, academic, and sci-tech special libraries in the United States. It is freely available online (html and pdf available) back to the first issue (2001), and a back file of the preceding title, *NewsReport,* is available to 1999. Print subscriptions of one to three years are available at a nominal cost. URL: http://infocusmagazine.org

National Academy of Sciences. Proceedings. See Biology/General section.

4742. *Natural History.* Formerly (until 1919): *The American Museum Journal;* Incorporates (in 1960): *Nature Magazine.* [ISSN: 0028-0712] 1900. 10x/yr. USD 22. Ed(s): Peter Brown, Avis Lang. Natural History Magazine, Inc., 36 W 25th St, 5th Fl, New York, NY 10010. Illus., index, adv. Circ: 250000 Paid. Vol. ends: Dec. Microform: PQC. *Indexed:* A01, A06, A22, A47, ABS&EES, AbAn, Agr, BRI, C&ISA, C37, CBRI, CerAb, GardL, MASUSE, MLA-IB, P02, RILM. *Bk. rev.:* 2-3, 500-750 words, signed. *Aud.:* Hs, Ga, Ac.

Natural History is an attractive, accessible magazine that covers nature in the broadest sense, with a mission "to promote understanding and appreciation of the world around us." Long affiliated with the American Museum of Natural History, the publication now has affiliations with nine additional U.S. museums and science centers. Features, two per issue, are written for a general audience by research scientists or professional naturalists about their own work. Feature topics more often than not are life science–related. "Samplings" are short reports on recent research findings. Regular columnists include astrophysicist Neil deGrasse Tyson and plant biologist Robert H. Mohlenbrock. "Bookshelf" offers two to three book reviews each issue. Stunning graphic content includes the work of award-winning photographers. "The Natural Moment" is a photographic feature in each issue. Recommended for high school, public, and academic libraries. Some content from each issue is freely available via the publisher web site, along with supplementary content such as author podcasts and highlights from affiliated museums.

Nature. See Biology/General section.

4743. *Popular Science.* Formerly: *Popular Science Monthly.* [ISSN: 0161-7370] 1872. m. USD 12. Ed(s): Mark Jannot, Cliff Ransom. Bonnier Corp., 2 Park Ave, 9th Fl, New York, NY 10016; http://www.bonniercorp.com. Illus., index, adv. Microform: NBI; PMC; PQC. *Indexed:* A01, A22, ABS&EES, BRI, C37, CBCARef, IHTDI, MASUSE, MLA-IB, P02. *Aud.:* Hs, Ga, Ac.

Popular Science covers the latest scientific and technological developments for a lay audience. The print magazine was founded in 1872; the web site was established in 1999. Emphasis is on applications, inventions, and consumer products and services, although basic research is not excluded. Feature authors usually have some experience or expertise with the feature subject matter, but are not themselves researchers. Regular sections include "How 2.0" with "tips, tricks, hacks[,] and do-it-yourself projects"; and "What's New," which features such content as "gadgets to buy" and appears only in some issues. "FYI" answers questions sent by readers. The January issue profiles the coming year in science, offering projected developments in science and technology, with a graphic month-by-month timeline. The June issue announces the annual Invention Awards bestowed by the magazine; 2012 honorees included an inflatable tourniquet, and a self-contained treatment plant for recirculating shower water to save both water and energy. The December issue offers an "Best of What's New" for the year. Recommended for high school, public, and academic libraries. Institutional online access is available through aggregators. Some content is freely available online, and supplementary online content includes book reviews. The entire archive was digitized in a collaboration with Google in 2009, and an innovative text explorer allows readers to see the frequency of topics and retrieve and read entire issues from the digitized archive. RSS alerts for new content are available.

4744. *R & D Magazine: where innovation begins.* Former titles (until Jul. 1995): *Research & Development;* (until 1984): *Industrial Research and Development;* Which was formed by the merger of (1959-1978): *Industrial Research;* (1950-1978): *Research - Development;* Which was formerly (until 1960): *Industrial Laboratories.* 1978. m. Free to qualified personnel. Ed(s): Paul Livingstone, Lindsay Hock. Advantage Business Media, 100 Enterprise Dr, Ste 600, PO Box 912, Rockaway, NJ 07886; AdvantageCommunications@advantagemedia.com; http://www.advantagebusinessmedia.com. Illus., index. Vol. ends: Dec. Microform: CIS. *Indexed:* A22, ABIn, Agr, B01, B02, B03, BRI, C42, EngInd, P02. *Aud.:* Ac, Sa.

"The high technology journal of applied research and development," this is intended for "lab, R&D and project managers across all industries, government and universities." This title's content is written for a multidisciplinary audience whose work involves physics, chemistry, materials science, biology, and engineering, and meant to be accessible to readers from all disciplines and specialties. Areas of focus are "state-of-the-art scientific and technical advances, how the latest R&D instruments and techniques help researchers work more productively, and important trends in research management, funding, and policy." Issues regularly cover informatics, materials science, microscopy, nanotechnology, photonics, and software, including product reviews. Regular sections include "New to market," which highlights the latest products featuring technological innovations, and "Tools and technology," which covers innovations that facilitate research. The publisher issues the R&D 100 awards (the 50th annual R&D 100 awards celebration will be in 2012), which recognize technologically significant new products, as well as Laboratory, Scientist, Corporation, and Innovator of the Year awards. Recommended for libraries in technical industrial settings, and for academic libraries that support engineering and industrial technology programs. Free print or electronic subscriptions are currently available to qualified applicants. The web site includes supplementary information, including a collection of industry white papers. Recommended for academic and special libraries that serve industrial technology and engineering programs.

4745. *Royal Society of London. Philosophical Transactions A. Mathematical, Physical and Engineering Sciences.* Former titles (until 1996): *Royal Society of London. Philosophical Transactions. Physical Sciences and Engineering;* (until 1990): *Royal Society of London. Philosophical Transactions. Series A. Mathematical and Physical Sciences;* (until 1933): *Royal Society of London. Philosophical Transactions. Series A. Containing Papers of a Mathematical or Physical Character;* (until 1897): *Royal Society of London. Philosophical Transactions A;* Which superseded in part (in 1887): *Royal Society of London. Philosophical Transactions;* Which was formerly (until 1776): *Royal Society of London. Philosophical Transactions;* (until 1682): *Royal Society of London. Philosophical Collections;* (until 1679): *Royal Society of London. Philosophical Transactions.* [ISSN: 1364-503X] 1665. bi-w. EUR 4382 (print & online eds.). Ed(s): Dave Garner. The Royal Society Publishing, 6-9 Carlton House Terr, London, SW1Y 5AG, United Kingdom; sales@royalsociety.org; http://royalsocietypublishing.org. Sample. Refereed. Microform: IDC; PMC. Reprint: PSC. *Indexed:* A01, A22, ApMecR, BrArAb, C45, CCMJ, E01, M&GPA, MSN, MathR, RRTA. *Aud.:* Ac, Sa.

The "[w]orld's longest running scientific journal," *Philosophical Transactions* began in 1665, with sections A (Life Sciences) and B diverging in 1887. Themed issues cover an advancing research frontier in math, physical science, or engineering, and typically contain 12 research articles headed by a general review. global warming, biosensors, and the "dialectic of materials and information" were recent topics covered. Several discussion-meeting issues per year cover the proceedings of Society meetings and are also devoted to a specific topical area. This journal is intended for mathematicians, physicists, engineers, and other physical scientists. The publication frequency increased from monthly to every two weeks in 2008. Online access comes via Highwire Press. A complete back file to 1665 is available. DOIs are assigned; cited references are linked.

4746. *Science.* Incorporates (1915 -1957): *The Scientific Monthly.* [ISSN: 0036-8075] 1880. w. USD 1176. Ed(s): Bruce Alberts, Katrina Lm Kelner. American Association for the Advancement of Science, 1200 New York Ave, NW, Washington, DC 20005; membership@aaas.org; http://www.scienceonline.org. Illus., index, adv. Sample. Refereed. Circ: 131286 Paid. Microform: PMC; PQC. *Indexed:* A&ATA, A01, A06, A22, ABS&EES, AbAn, Agr, AnBeAb, BRI, BrArAb, C&ISA, C45, CBRI, CCMJ, CerAb, CompLI, CompR, EngInd, ExcerpMed, FS&TA, IndVet, M&GPA, MASUSE, MCR, MLA-IB, MSN, MathR, NumL, OceAb, P02, PsycInfo, RILM, RRTA, S25. *Bk. rev.:* 2-3, 2,500 words; signed. *Aud.:* Hs, Ga, Ac, Sa.

Science is a venue for "significant original scientific research, plus reviews and analyses of current research and science policy," published by the American Association for the Advancement of Science. According to the publisher, *Science* has the largest paid circulation of any peer-reviewed general science journal. Full research papers (usually one per issue) and shorter reports (about a dozen per issue) present original research from a full spectrum of disciplines. Editor-commissioned pieces feature "broadly accessible commentary," including "Perspectives," which relates to specific research or reports in the issue. This is a core resource for current awareness; regular sections cover science news, including briefs in "News of the Week" and one-page write-ups in "News and Analysis" and longer pieces in "News Focus." Signed book reviews are published weekly. Frequent thematic special issues are published; recent topics include computational biology, human conflict, and gut microbiota. Ranks second by 2010 Impact Factor of 59 titles in *JCR*'s multidisciplinary sciences category. E-mail alerts and RSS feeds are available for the entire contents, or just portions (e.g., position postings). Substantial supplementary online content includes podcasts, streaming and video. "Science Express"—previews of upcoming articles, which comprise potentially high-demand content—are not included with the basic online license. Strongly recommended for all college, university, and research libraries, as well as for public and high school libraries where budgets allow. DOIs assigned; open URL linking is at the article level; partially COUNTER-compliant.

Science News. See Classroom Magazines/Science section.

4747. Science Progress: a review journal of current scientific advance. Former titles (until 1916): *Science Progress in the Twentieth Century;* (until 1906): *Science Progress.* [ISSN: 0036-8504] 1894. q. GBP 305 (print & online eds.); USD 580 (print & online eds.); EUR 380 (print & online eds.). Ed(s): Michael Abraham, Terence Kemp. Science Reviews 2000 Ltd., PO Box 314, St Albans, AL1 4ZG, United Kingdom; info@sciencereviews2000.co.uk; http://www.sciencereviews2000.co.uk. Illus., index. Refereed. *Indexed:* A22, AbAn, BRI. *Bk. rev.:* Occasional, brief, unsigned. *Aud.:* Ac.

Science Progress is presents reviews intended to inform non-specialists in academia and industry of new developments in science, technology, and medicine. Articles are written on commission by researchers who write about their own area of expertise for those in other disciplines. The "Commentaries" section, introduced in 2011, offers "shorter articles focusing on developments in fields that have undergone major conceptual change in the last 2 to 3 years." Brief, unsigned book reviews and retrospective excerpts from 100-year-old issues have also been added. Topical coverage is wide-ranging, including cell and molecular biology, biomedicine, physics, chemistry, energy, and environmental remediation. Recommended for academic libraries. Online access is offered via IngentaConnect and some aggregator databases. At least some free and open-access content is available on IngentaConnect. DOIs assigned.

4748. Scientific American. Incorporates (1920-1921): *Scientific American Monthly;* Which superseded (in 1920): *Scientific American Supplement;* (1853-1854): *People's Journal.* [ISSN: 0036-8733] 1845. m. USD 24.97 domestic; USD 37 Canada; USD 44 elsewhere. Nature Publishing Group, 75 Varick St, 9th Fl, New York, NY 10013; subscriptions@nature.com; http://www.nature.com. Illus., index. Vol. ends: Dec. Microform: PMC; PQC. *Indexed:* A01, A06, A22, ABIn, ABS&EES, AbAn, Agr, AnBeAb, ApMecR, B01, BAS, BRI, BrArAb, BrTechI, C&ISA, C37, CBCARef, CBRI, CerAb, EngInd, FS&TA, GardL, IHTDI, M&GPA, MASUSE, MCR, MLA-IB, MSN, MathR, NumL, P02, RILM. *Bk. rev.:* Number and length vary. *Aud.:* Hs, Ga, Ac, Sa.

Categorized by major topical area, from animal behavior to space science, eight to ten features per issue offer in-depth, authoritative, accessible, and timely information. These may be authored by researchers or science writers. Brief author profiles and short lists of related research papers are included. The substantial "Advances" section keeps readers current in research news across scientific disciplines. Brief book reviews are published in each issue, along with a list of "notable" books that are not reviews. Special editions are published, and include an annual "World Changing Ideas" issue. Recommended for high school, public, academic, and research libraries. An institutional online license is available; recent acquisition of the title by *Nature* was accompanied by large price increases for institutional license. Content is also available via aggregators. Some content from monthly issues, plus supplementary content, is freely available on the publisher web site. Publisher is partially COUNTER-compliant.

4749. Scientific Reports. [ISSN: 2045-2322] 2011. irreg. Free. Nature Publishing Group, The MacMillan Bldg, 4 Crinan St, London, N1 9XW, United Kingdom; NatureReviews@nature.com; http://www.nature.com. Refereed. *Aud.:* Ac, Sa.

An online-only, open-access title from Nature Publishing Group, *Scientific Reports* offers "original research papers of interest to specialists" across a broad range of scientific disciplines. Emphasis is on rapid review and publication of submissions. Articles are published as they are accepted as numbered papers within the year's volume; currently it is in its second volume. Users can search for articles or browse by date or discipline. This journal follows an author-pays open-access model, and "all expenses, including peer review, production, and online hosting and archiving, are recovered via an article-processing charge (APC)," which is payable on acceptance; the current fee is USD 1,350. Note that *Nature Communications,* launched in 2010 by Nature Publishing Group, has a similar focus, and is also appropriate for academic and special libraries, but is not a wholly open-access title. Articles are then published under a Creative Commons license, and authors may post published pdfs to their web sites and deposit in an institutional repository. DOIs assigned. Publisher is partially COUNTER-compliant.

4750. The Scientist: magazine of the life sciences. [ISSN: 0890-3670] 1986. m. USD 400. Ed(s): Mary Beth Aberlin. LabX Media Group, 478 Bay St, Midland, ON L4R 1K9, Canada; help@labx.com; http://www.labx.com. Illus., adv. *Indexed:* A22, Agr, BRI. *Aud.:* Ac, Sa.

The Scientist offers life scientists "the latest scientific discoveries, trends in research, innovative techniques, new technology, business, and careers," with articles written by both scientists and professional journalists. It targets active researchers, but is accessible to a broader audience, including undergraduates and the general public. Founded by Eugene Garfield, the title was acquired from ScienceNow, Inc., by LabX Media in 2011, which also publishes *LabX* and *Lab Manager Magazine.* In each issue are profiles (of an established researcher, a "scientist to watch," and/or a business); highlights from the literature; a "Notebook" section on research methodologies; coverage of careers and business; and "Foundations," which describes early work of historical significance. The "Lab Tools" column, initiated in January 2006, features cutting-edge developments. Themed supplements appear to have ceased after 2010. Recommended for academic and research libraries. Content from each issue is offered free online, and the web site offers some supplemental multimedia content, and users may subscribe to a daily news update.

Skeptical Inquirer. See Paranormal section.

4751. Technology Review. Former titles (until 1998): *M I T's Technology Review;* (until 1997): *Technology Review.* [ISSN: 1099-274X] 1899. bi-m. m. until 2006. USD 24.95 (print or online ed.). Technology Review, One Main St, 7th Fl, Cambridge, MA 02142. Illus., index. Vol. ends: Nov/Dec. Microform: PQC. *Indexed:* A01, A22, ABIn, ABS&EES, Agr, B01, B02, BRI, C&ISA, C37, CBRI, CerAb, CompLI, EngInd, F01, H24, I15, MASUSE, P02. *Bk. rev.:* Number and length vary; signed. *Aud.:* Hs, Ga, Ac, Sa.

Founded in 1899 and billing itself as the "oldest technology magazine in the world," *Technology Review* "identifies emerging technologies and analyzes their impact for technology leaders." It is produced by an independent media company that is owned by the Massachussets Institute of Technology, but its content is not limited to research and developments of that institution. Feature articles are authored by expert guest contributors and professional writers, and they cover technological developments in all areas, at a level appropriate for a general adult audience. Also published are essays and reviews—of books, products, and trends (e.g., startup energy companies). "From the labs" briefly summarizes recent research findings and their implications. "To market" briefly describes products that are newly available or coming soon. Each issue revisits a feature from a past issue, and addresses advances or absence thereof in that area of research; a recent example was books on tape first covered 51 years ago. The annual "TR10" names ten technologies that "could change the world"; for 2012, named technologies included egg stem cells, solar microgrids, and the Facebook timeline. Highly recommended for academic libraries and libraries that serve adult and young-adult populations. Free individual registration allows access to content on the publisher web site.

History and Philosophy of Science

4752. British Journal for the History of Science. Formerly (until 1962): *British Society for the History of Science. Bulletin.* [ISSN: 0007-0874] 1949. q. GBP 183. Ed(s): John Agar. Cambridge University Press, The

Edinburgh Bldg, Shaftesbury Rd, Cambridge, CB2 8RU, United Kingdom; journals@cambridge.org; http://www.cambridge.org/uk. Illus., adv. Refereed. Vol. ends: Dec. Microform: PQC. Reprint: PSC. *Indexed:* A01, A22, AmHI, ArtHuCI, BRI, CCMJ, E01, FR, IBSS, MLA-IB, MSN, MathR, P02. *Bk. rev.:* Number varies, 2-3 pages, signed. *Aud.:* Ac, Sa.

BJHS publishes "scholarly papers and review articles on all aspects of the history of science," including medicine, technology, and social studies of science. Recent topical coverage is broad, with research articles on crop improvement, invention and inventors, Earth science, and operations research. Themed special issues are published; a recent example was "states of secrecy," which addresses secrecy in corporate- and state-sponsored scientific research. Typically, more than a dozen signed book reviews are in each issue, and these plus an extensive "books received" list offers excellent current awareness of new books in the field. Recommended for academic libraries. Content from the current issue apparently is freely available online. Institutional subscriptions are available, online-only or online-plus-print. A digital archive is available as a separate purchase and covers 1962–96 of *BJHS* and 1949–61 of the preceding title, *Bulletin of the British Society for the History of Science.* DOIs are assigned; cited and citing references are linked. Publisher is partially COUNTER-compliant.

The British Journal for the Philosophy of Science. See Philosophy section.

4753. *Bulletin of Science, Technology & Society.* [ISSN: 0270-4676] 1981. bi-m. Ed(s): Willem H Vanderburg. Sage Publications, Inc., 2455 Teller Rd, Thousand Oaks, CA 91320; info@sagepub.com; http://www.sagepub.com. Illus., index, adv. Sample. Refereed. Vol. ends: No. 6. Microform: MIM; PQC. Reprint: PSC. *Indexed:* A01, A22, C45, E01, ERIC, H24, P61, SSA. *Bk. rev.:* Occasional, length varies. *Aud.:* Ac, Sa.

Bulletin of Science, Technology & Society aims "to provide a means of communication within as wide of a spectrum of the STS community as possible." The intended audience includes researchers, educators, and students in across disciplines, policy makers, and the general public, including journalists. Topics include the place of science and technology in societies, policy issues related to science and technology, technology assessment, the impact of technology upon human values, and public understanding of technology and science. Special thematic issues are published; a forthcoming example is "Commoditization." Issues may include news and correspondence. Recommended for academic libraries. Online access is available with print or alone; a back file can be leased or purchased. Early-view articles are available with online access. Publication appears to lag behind dates on issues; as of June 2012, no 2012 issues have been published. DOIs are assigned; cited and citing references are linked. Publisher is partially COUNTER-compliant.

4754. *Endeavour: a quarterly magazine reviewing the history and philosophy of science in the service of mankind.* [ISSN: 0160-9327] 1942. q. EUR 680. Ed(s): J C Waller. Elsevier Ltd., Trends Journals, 84 Theobald's Rd, London, WC1X 8RR, United Kingdom; JournalsCustomerServiceEMEA@elsevier.com; http://www.elsevier.com. Illus., index, adv. Sample. Refereed. Microform: MIM; PQC. *Indexed:* A&ATA, A01, A22, AbAn, ApMecR, BRI, BrTechI, C&ISA, C45, CCMJ, EngInd, FR, M&GPA, MLA-IB, MSN, MathR, P02. *Bk. rev.:* 20-30 per year, 800-1,000 words, signed. *Aud.:* Ac.

"*Endeavour* publishes brief articles that review the history and philosophy of science," serving as a "critical forum for the inter-disciplinary exploration and evaluation of specific subjects or people that have affected the development of the scientific discipline throughout history." All science disciplines are covered, with a strong focus on life science, technology, and medicine. This title is intended to be accessible to general readers, but is appropriate for historians and practicing scientists. Recent feature articles include Richard Owens' sea serpent investigations, food in space, and AIDS images. Reviews, opinions, and book reviews are also published. A recent themed issue covered polar exploration. Recommended for academic libraries. Online access is available with or without print. There is free access to content from the latest issue (as the sample issue). DOIs assigned. Publisher is partially COUNTER-compliant.

Gender, Technology & Development. See Gender Studies section.

4755. *International Journal of Technoethics.* [ISSN: 1947-3451] 2010. s-a. USD 625 (Individuals, USD 220). Ed(s): Rocci Luppicini. I G I Global, 701 E Chocolate Ave, Ste 200, Hershey, PA 17033; cust@igi-global.com; http://www.igi-global.com. Refereed. *Indexed:* PsycInfo. *Bk. rev.:* 1-2 per year, signed. *Aud.:* Ac, Sa.

An official publication of the Information Resource Management Association, *International Journal of Technoethics* (*IJT*) aims "to evolve technological relationships of humans with a focus on ethical implications for human life, social norms and values, education, work, and ecological impacts." It publishes empirical research, theoretical studies, innovative methodologies, practical applications, case studies, and book reviews. Themed issues are published; recent examples were violence as a technology-mediated phenomenon, and cyborgs and robotics. Published article topics have included biometrics, cyberactivism, surveillance, nuclear waste, piracy, cyberweapons, and nanotechnology. DOIs assigned. Publisher is partially COUNTER-compliant.

4756. *Isis: international review devoted to the history of science and its cultural influences.* [ISSN: 0021-1753] 1913. q. USD 538 (print & online eds.). Ed(s): Bernard Lightman. University of Chicago Press, 1427 E 60th St, Chicago, IL 60637; subscriptions@press.uchicago.edu; http://www.journals.uchicago.edu. Illus., index, adv. Sample. Refereed. Vol. ends: Dec. Microform: PMC; PQC. Reprint: PSC. *Indexed:* A01, A06, A22, ABS&EES, AmHI, ArtHuCI, BRI, CBRI, CCMJ, FR, IBSS, IPB, MLA-IB, MSN, MathR, P02, P61, SSA. *Bk. rev.:* 50 or more, signed. *Aud.:* Ac, Sa.

The official publication of the History of Science Society, *Isis* is the oldest English-language journal in the field. Scholarly articles, research notes, commentary, and reviews on "the history of science, medicine, and technology, and their cultural influences" are published. Book reviews comprise a substantial proportion of the content; 50 or more titles per issue may be covered in signed, critical reviews categorized by historical period. The "Focus" section is "designed to attract readers in all areas of the field by dealing with themes that cut across chronological boundaries" and is also useful in teaching; recent topics include alchemy, scientific instruments, and textbooks. "Focus" content is freely available online. The annual "Current Bibliography" supplement provides a comprehensive, categorized list of books and journals; back issues of the supplement are freely available online. Online access is available via JSTOR, with print or alone; there is supplementary content online, including datasets. All "Focus" sections, and all but the most recent Current Bibliography, are freely available online. DOIs assigned. Publisher is partially COUNTER-compliant.

4757. *Issues in Science and Technology.* [ISSN: 0748-5492] 1984. q. USD 126 (Individuals, USD 48; USD 12 newsstand/cover. Ed(s): Kevin Finneran. University of Texas at Dallas, Cecil and Ida Green Center for the Study of Science and Society, 800 W Campbell Rd, Richardson, TX 75080-3021; http://www.utdallas.edu. Illus., index, adv. Sample. Refereed. Vol. ends: Summer (No. 4). Microform: PQC. *Indexed:* A01, A22, ASIP, AbAn, Agr, BRI, C37, EngInd, H24, M&GPA, MASUSE, MCR, P02, RiskAb, S25. *Bk. rev.:* 2-4 per issue, 2-3 pages, signed. *Aud.:* Hs, Ga, Ac, Sa.

Published jointly by the National Academies and the University of Texas at Dallas, *Issues in Science & Technology* is a "forum for discussion of public policy related to science, engineering, and medicine," including science policy as well as science that informs policy. Intended as a venue for researchers, policy-makers, and industry representatives, this publication is accessible to lay readers and "offers authorities an opportunity to share their insights directly with a broad audience." Topical article clusters are published; recent topics included the energy-climate complex and innovation policy. Contributors are national political figures, administrators at research institutions and federal agencies, and industry leaders, and are selected by the editor based on their expertise. Recent contributors include Ben Bernanke and Jeff Bingaman. Feature articles, legislative updates, an extensive reader forum section, opinion pieces, and two or more signed, critical book reviews per issue. Recommended especially for college and university libraries, but appropriate for public and school libraries as well. Online access (html only) is free; back issues to 1996 can be searched or browsed. Some articles are available online in advance of print. E-mail contents alerts are available.

4758. Science and Engineering Ethics. [ISSN: 1353-3452] 1995. q. EUR 394 (print & online eds.). Ed(s): R Spier, S J Bird. Springer New York LLC, 233 Spring St, New York, NY 10013; journals@springer-ny.com; http://www.springer.com. Illus., adv. Refereed. Reprint: PSC. *Indexed:* A01, A22, AmHI, BRI, E01, FS&TA, IPB, RiskAb. *Bk. rev.:* 1 per year; 700 words; signed. *Aud.:* Ac.

"*Science and Engineering Ethics* is [a] multi-disciplinary journal that explores ethical issues of direct concern to scientists and engineers," including "professional education, standards[,] and ethics in research and practice, extending to the effects of innovation on society at large." It covers both conduct of science and application of new technologies. It is relevant to practicing researchers in the sciences and social sciences, and to science educators. Medicine, agricultural biotechnology, environmental science, science education, intellectual property, and animal and human subjects in research are covered. Original papers, educational forums, reviews, commentary, and occasional book reviews are published. Themed issues are published; recent themes were public engagement and responsible data management. Highly recommended for academic libraries. Institutional online access and back file to volume 1 (1995) are available. Some open-access content is available via Springer's author-pays "Open Choice" option. DOIs assigned; cited references are linked. Publisher is partially COUNTER-compliant.

4759. Science, Technology & Human Values. Former titles (until 1978): *Science, Technology & Human Values. Newsletter;* (until 1976): *Program on Public Conceptions of Science. Newsletter;* Incorporated (in 1988): *Science and Technology Studies;* Which was formerly (until 1986): *4S Review;* (until 1983): *4S. Society for Social Studies of Science;* (until 1976): *SSSS. Newsletter of the Society for Social Studies of Science.* [ISSN: 0162-2439] 1972. bi-m. USD 852. Ed(s): Susan Leigh Star, Geoffrey C Bowker. Sage Publications, Inc., 2455 Teller Rd, Thousand Oaks, CA 91320; info@sagepub.com; http://www.sagepub.com. Illus. Refereed. Reprint: PSC. *Indexed:* A01, A22, B01, BRI, E01, FR, IBSS, P02, P61, RILM, SSA. *Bk. rev.:* 6 per year, signed. *Aud.:* Ac, Sa.

Published by Sage for the Society for Social Studies of Science, *STHV* offers "research, analyses[,] and commentary on the development and dynamics of science and technology, including their relationship to politics, society[,] and culture." Represented disciplines include political science, sociology, environmental studies, anthropology, literature, history, economics, and philosophy. Articles and commentary are published. Occasional special sections may be published; a recent theme was the cause and implications of research policies emphasizing material outputs. Signed book reviews (3,000 words) are published intermittently. The title ranks second by 2010 Impact Factor among 35 journals in *JCR Social Sciences Edition*'s "social issues" category. Recommended for academic and research libraries. Online access and a back file to 1976 are available. DOIs assigned; cited references are linked. Publisher is partially COUNTER-compliant.

4760. Social Studies of Science: an international review of research in the social dimensions of science and technology. Formerly (until 1975): *Science Studies.* [ISSN: 0306-3127] 1971. bi-m. USD 1837. Ed(s): Sergio Sismondo. Sage Publications Ltd., 1 Oliver's Yard, 55 City Rd, London, EC1Y 1SP, United Kingdom; info@sagepub.co.uk; http://www.uk.sagepub.com. Illus., index. Sample. Refereed. Vol. ends: Dec. Reprint: PSC. *Indexed:* A01, A22, ArtHuCI, B01, C45, E01, FR, IBSS, IPB, IndVet, P02, P61, RRTA, SSA. *Bk. rev.:* 1 per year, 3000 words, signed. *Aud.:* Ac.

Social Studies of Science publishes original research on science, technology and medicine, covering political science, sociology, economics, history, philosophy, psychology, social anthropology, law, and education. Research articles and shorter research notes are published, as well as review essays (book reviews) and discussion papers. Special sections are published; recent topics were Thomas Kuhn (marking the 50th anniversary of the publication of *The Structure of Scientific Revolutions*) and ethnomethodological studies of science. This title is ranked second by 2010 Impact Factor of 50 titles in the 2010 *JCR Science Edition*'s history and philosophy of science category, and third of 36 titles in the *JCR Social Science Edition*'s history and philosophy of science category. Recommended for academic libraries. Institutional online access is available with or without print. DOIs assigned; cited references are linked. Publisher is partially COUNTER-compliant.

4761. Technology and Culture. [ISSN: 0040-165X] 1959. q. USD 183. Ed(s): Peter Soppelsa. The Johns Hopkins University Press, 2715 N Charles St, Baltimore, MD 21218; http://www.press.jhu.edu. Illus., index, adv. Sample. Refereed. Circ: 2129. Vol. ends: Oct (No. 4). Microform: PQC. Reprint: PSC. *Indexed:* A&ATA, A01, A22, ABIn, ABS&EES, ArtHuCI, BAS, BRI, BrArAb, CBRI, CompLI, E01, FR, IBSS, JEL, MLA-IB, NumL, P02, P61, RILM, SSA. *Bk. rev.:* Approx. 30 per issue, 500-1,000 words; signed. *Aud.:* Ac.

The quarterly journal of the Society for the History of Technology, *Technology and Culture* is billed as the "preeminent journal for the history of technology." It offers scholarly articles and critical reviews on the history of technology, with broadly interdisciplinary subject coverage. Organizational information, conference reports, memorials and essays are also published. This title is intended for a broad audience of scientists, social scientists, and nonprofessionals. It includes an extensive book review section, with about 30 full, critical reviews per issue. Occasional themed issues may be published. Museum exhibit reviews are also included. Recommended for academic libraries. Some content is freely available on the publisher web site (www.techculture.org). Institutional online access is available via Project MUSE. DOIs assigned. Article-level open URL linking; online platform is partially COUNTER-compliant.

Science and Technology Education

4762. Journal of College Science Teaching. [ISSN: 0047-231X] 1971. bi-m. Free to members. Ed(s): Caroline Barnes. National Science Teachers Association, 1840 Wilson Blvd, Arlington, VA 22201; pubinfo@nsta.org; http://www.nsta.org/. Illus., index, adv. Sample. Refereed. Circ: 6000. Vol. ends: May. Microform: PQC. *Indexed:* A01, A22, BRI, ERIC, P02. *Aud.:* Hs, Ac.

The mission of the NSTA is to "promote excellence and innovation in science teaching and learning for all." The *Journal of College Science Teaching* offers "a forum for the exchange of ideas on and experiences with undergraduate science courses, particularly those for non-science majors." Innovative materials, methods, and evaluation are covered, as are suggestions for improving science instruction and descriptions of disciplinary science teaching with relevance across science disciplines. About six features are published per issue; recent feature topics include undergraduate research collaboratives, integrated STEM instruction, authentic research-based versus cookbook lab courses, and concept maps. Brief synopses from the research literature are offered in "Headline Science." "Case studies" demonstrate the application of the scientific method in a current research area; recent examples were immune response to HIV infection and chemistry of cocaine. Editorials and point of view articles are published. Social networking links include Facebook and Twitter. This title is intended for college-level educators and students of science education, but high school science teachers could also benefit. Recommended for academic libraries, including community college libraries. Although there is an online archive of all articles available to individual members via the NSTA web site, institutional online access is via aggregators.

4763. Journal of Research in Science Teaching. [ISSN: 0022-4308] 1963. 10x/yr. GBP 1051. Ed(s): Joseph Krajcik, Angela Calabrese Barton. John Wiley & Sons, Inc., 111 River St, MS 4-02, Hoboken, NJ 07030; info@wiley.com; http://www.wiley.com/WileyCDA/. Illus., adv. Sample. Refereed. Vol. ends: Dec. Microform: PQC. Reprint: PSC. *Indexed:* A22, ASSIA, ERIC, EngInd, FR, PsycInfo. *Aud.:* Ac.

The *Journal of Research in Science Teaching* "publishes reports for science education researchers and practitioners on issues of science teaching and learning and science education policy," and research "investigations employing qualitative, ethnographic, historical, survey, philosophical, or case study research approaches." This title is published by Wiley on behalf of the National Association for Research in Science Teaching. Position papers, policy perspectives, critical reviews, and comments and criticism are also accepted. Themed issues are published; a recent theme was globalization in education. Recommended for academic libraries. Institutional online access is available. Supplementary information for research articles may be posted online. RSS and e-mail alerts of new content are available. DOIs assigned. Publisher is partially COUNTER-compliant.

Kids Discover. See Children section.

4764. *School Science and Mathematics.* Formerly (until 1905): *School Science.* [ISSN: 0036-6803] 1901. 8x/yr. GBP 167. Ed(s): Shelly Harkness, Carla C Johnson. John Wiley & Sons, Inc., 111 River St, MS 4-02, Hoboken, NJ 07030; info@wiley.com; http://www.wiley.com/WileyCDA/. Illus., index, adv. Sample. Refereed. Vol. ends: May. Microform: PMC; PQC. *Indexed:* A01, A22, BRI, E01, ERIC, MLA-IB, P02. *Aud.:* Ac.

School Science and Mathematics is the journal of the School Science and Mathematics Association. It publishes research papers on "science, mathematics, and connections between science and mathematics for grades K–graduate and teacher education." Areas of focus are assessment, attitudes, beliefs, curriculum, equity, research, translating research into practice, learning theory, alternative conceptions, philosophy and history of science, sociocultural issues, special populations, technology, nontraditional forms of instruction, and science/technology/society. This title typically includes five or six research articles per issue, a letter from the editor, and a "problems section" in which readers can "exchange interesting mathematical problems and solutions." Although the aims-and-scope page of the journal states that research-in-brief and book reviews are regular sections, none were found in 2011–12 issues, and the number of full research articles per issue has increased since the last review. Recommended for academic libraries that support science and mathematics education programs. The first 100 years are available for purchase on CD-ROM. Online access is via Wiley, which is partially COUNTER-compliant; DOIs assigned.

Science and Children. See Classroom Magazines/Teacher and Professional section.

4765. *Science Education.* Incorporates (1973-1976): *A Summary of Research in Science Education;* Formerly (until 1929): *General Science Quarterly.* [ISSN: 0036-8326] 1916. bi-m. GBP 942. Ed(s): John L Rudolph. John Wiley & Sons, Inc., 111 River St, MS 4-02, Hoboken, NJ 07030; info@wiley.com; http://www.wiley.com/WileyCDA/. Illus., adv. Refereed. Vol. ends: Nov. Microform: PQC. Reprint: PSC. *Indexed:* A01, A22, BAS, BRI, ERIC, FR, P02, PsycInfo. *Bk. rev.:* Number and length vary. *Aud.:* Hs, Ac.

Science Education publishes "original articles on the latest issues and trends occurring internationally in science curriculum, instruction, learning, policy[,] and preparation of science teachers[,] with the aim to advance our knowledge of science education theory and practice." Three to five general research articles and two signed, full book reviews are published in each issue. Semi-regular topical sections, including "Issues and Trends," "Learning," "Science Education Policy," and "Science Teacher Education," offer one or more research articles or reviews. "Comments and Criticism" offers a forum for dialogue or differing interpretations of research. The intended audience includes science educators, science education researchers, and administrators, and the focus is on primary and secondary grades. Online access is available via Wiley; a back file to 1916 is available. RSS and e-mail alerts of new content are available. DOIs assigned; cited references are linked. Publisher is partially COUNTER-compliant.

Science Scope. See Classroom Magazines/Teacher and Professional section.

■ SEXUALITY

See also Gay, Lesbian, Bisexual, and Transgender section.

Daniel C. Tsang, Economics, Political Science and Asian American Studies Bibliographer, Langson Library, University of California, P.O. Box 19557, Irvine, CA 92623-9557; 949-824-4978; FAX: 949-824-0605; dtsang@uci.edu

Introduction

Sex, although widely practiced, still appears to be a taboo topic for library shelves. The more scholarly collections may contain such titles as the *Journal of Homosexuality,* the *Journal of Sex Research,* or *Archives of Sexual Behavior,* but for titles that veer beyond academia into more-explicit depictions of the phenomenon, their absence from libraries is quite apparent and, from this reviewer's point of view, this needs to be rectified.

Sexually explicit periodicals, often termed "adult magazines," proliferate in American society; even the corner drugstore may stock a few. DVDs have now largely given place to online versions. These sexual videos are mass-marketed all over the United States (in some states more discreetly than in others), and their publishers and editors proclaim themselves to be advocates of sexual liberation and free speech. They may shock some people, since much of the output appears to arouse and stimulate only certain areas of the body; only a few publications attempt to reach the mind.

The proliferation of erotic videos has also spawned a related publishing trend: what a *New York Times* essayist called meta-porn, or porn-on-porn, with review publications that attempt to document, critique, or promote that scene. The prolific migration of erotic content to the electronic world has made such imagery and text almost ubiquitous and unavoidable, making any web surfer a potential instant critic.

The proliferation of independently produced, noncommercial zines with some erotic content brings a new dimension to the sex scene. There is perhaps more attempt at analysis, deconstruction, and intellectual stimulation in these publications. Like their profit-making and market-oriented contemporaries, these zines also may shock the sexually inhibited.

Taken together, these publications reflect contemporary popular culture and society's obsession with matters sexual. Libraries can ill afford to ignore these publications, even if acquiring even one of them may challenge the hardiest librarian to see how far he or she is willing to uphold the Library Bill of Rights.

If libraries are to better serve their communities, we might consider doing more than letting just the corner drug store, liquor store, or adult bookstore satisfy the public's demand for erotica. Some titles have managed to penetrate library walls, as evidenced by the few catalogued under the subject heading "Erotic Literature—Periodicals." Other more scholarly titles have also managed to enter the hallowed halls of academia, given the HIV/AIDS crisis and the moral panic over often-taboo sexual expressions.

In this supposedly liberated era, patrons are unlikely to heed the advice that used to be found in many card catalogs: "For sex, see librarian," a relic of an era when certain such books were not catalogued or were kept in locked cases. Today, patrons want to find it themselves, often by going online. With even the U.S. Supreme Court endorsing formerly taboo sexual behavior, libraries have no excuse not to collect at least some of this material.

Note, however, that some of the publications or sites reviewed in this section are for adults only.

Basic Periodicals

Hs: *Sex, Etc.;* Ga: *Libido; Penthouse; Playboy; Sex, Etc.;* Ac: *Culture, Health & Sexuality; Libido; Penthouse; Playboy; Sexuality and Culture;* Sa: *Prometheus* (New York).

Basic Abstracts and Indexes

Academic Search Complete, Academic Search Premier, LGBT Life, PsycINFO, Sociological Abstracts, Women's Studies International.

4766. *Adult Video News: the adult entertainment monthly.* [ISSN: 0883-7090] 1982. m. A V N Publications Inc., 9414 Eton Ave, Chatsworth, CA 91311; erik@avn.com. Illus., adv. Sample. Circ: 45000 Paid. *Bk. rev.:* Number and length vary. *Aud.:* Ga, Ac.

The flagship publication of the adult video industry—which rakes in several billion dollars a year—*AVN,* or *Adult Video News,* which was founded with $900 by several college students, is today the bible of the porn industry, akin to what *Billboard* is to the music industry. With thousands of hardcore videos entering the commercial market each year, *AVN* manages to highlight the most marketable, especially to online viewers. There are feature articles on specific new films and videos, and legal advice to porn retailers. But the bulk of the now-free online magazine (with separate print subscription) is devoted to profiles of aspiring adult performers, capsule reviews of new erotic films, videos, and DVDs, as well as reviews of hardware (e.g., vibrators or latex pants). While it is largely heterosexual in its approach, it now has made a big effort to include reviews of gay and bisexual videos, as well as covering gay porn industry news. The magazine is profusely illustrated with explicit color photos and ads from the industry. Many of the news items deal with confrontations with state and church. A serious essay might address zoning laws, while an "Adult Who's Who" section might feature an obituary of a noted anti-censorship lawyer. A "Links" section provides URLs of relevant web sites. Aimed at retailers, it is nonetheless highly recommended for the serious collector. Note that with VOD (video on demand), one can actually view sexually explicit clips online or choose to pay to watch the entire video, gay or straight. Current and back issues are all available for free viewing online or downloadable as pdfs, but one can still subscribe to the hard copy. (DT)

4767. *The Buzz: good vibrations online magazine.* Formerly (until 2013): *Good Vibes Magazine.* 1997. w. Ed(s): Violet Blue. Good Vibrations, 1210 Valencia St, San Francisco, CA 94110. *Aud.:* Ga.

A web-based zine from Good Vibrations, the San Francisco–based bookstore that promotes positive sexual attitudes and literature, has now transformed itself to a blog tied to the bookstore. *GV Weekly,* or *Good Vibes Online Magazine,* as it was formerly known, includes regular contributors such as Carol Queen and the former Pat Califia (now Patrick). A recent feature focused on how to identify fake vibrators. A regular section includes erotic stories. There are also sex education resources. The erotic stories often end up becoming a sex education resource. Highly recommended. URL: http://goodvibesblog.com/ (DT)

4768. *Canadian Journal of Human Sexuality.* Former titles (until 1992): *S I E C C A N Journal;* (until 1986): *Journal - S I E C C A N.* [ISSN: 1188-4517] 1986. q. CAD 70 domestic; USD 90 foreign; CAD 80 combined subscription domestic (print & online eds.). Ed(s): Michael Barrett. University of Toronto Press, Journals Division, 5201 Dufferin St, Toronto, ON M3H 5T8, Canada; journals@utpress.utoronto.ca; http://www.utpjournals.com. Refereed. Circ: 1000. *Indexed:* A01, ASSIA, BRI, C37, C42, CBCARef, ExcerpMed, IBSS, P02, P61, PsycInfo, SSA, SWR&A. *Aud.:* Ac.

The only peer-reviewed, interdisciplinary journal to focus on Canadian sex research and sex education, *CJHS* is published by SIECCAN, the Sex Information and Education Council of Canada. Articles cover such topics as Canadian undergraduates' "Friends With Benefits" relationships; drug use and HIV risk among East Asian and Southeast Asian men who have sex with men in Toronto; Canadian attitudes toward female topless behavior; teen sexual initiation and perception of parental disapproval; sexual compatibility and sexual functioning in intimate relationships; and sexual health education in the schools. Socio-medical aspects of sexuality are addressed. Facilitating scholarly communication, detailed English-language abstracts of each article from 1997 are freely posted online at www.sieccan.org/cjhs_abstracts.html. Selected full-text articles are also posted free online at http://www.sieccan.org/resources.html. Recommended for major collections. (DT)

4769. *Clean Sheets.* 1998. w. Free. Ed(s): Susannah Indigo, Brian Peters. Clean Sheets, c/o Mary Anne Mohanraj, 1658 N. Milwaukee Ave, Chicago, IL 60647; m@mamohanraj.com. *Aud.:* Ga, Ac.

Founded by a "small group of writers who dreamed of an online erotic magazine that didn't take itself too seriously, but still did its best to be fresh, clear and exciting," *Clean Sheets* sees itself as "Good Vibrations [the sex-toy store] meets Salon.com." It seeks to foster a dialog on sexuality, publishing fiction, poetry, and "exotica." Artwork is featured in an archived gallery. Contributors have included David Steinberg. It has even celebrated a "Sex & Politics Month." An article once reviewed the Paris Museum of Erotic Art. It has an "Erotic Tales" section. Its online archive—free to all browsers—preserves all contributions. Overall, a well-designed site that serves up a rather pleasant if not always expected experience. Highly recommended. (DT)

4770. *Culture, Health and Sexuality: an international journal for research, intervention and care.* [ISSN: 1369-1058] 1999. 10x/yr. GBP 934 (print & online eds.). Ed(s): Peter Aggleton. Routledge, 4 Park Sq, Milton Park, Abingdon, OX14 4RN, United Kingdom; subscriptions@tandf.co.uk; http://www.tandfonline.com. Adv. Sample. Refereed. Reprint: PSC. *Indexed:* A01, A22, A47, AbAn, C45, E01, FR, IBSS, P61, PsycInfo, RRTA, SSA. *Aud.:* Ac, Sa.

This is a cutting-edge research journal that invites practitioners of sexuality studies to discuss policy implications and outcomes of applied sex research. Its strong point is its refreshing international coverage, especially from developing countries, reflecting its editorial stance. With a score of 1.553, it garnered one of the highest impact factors for a journal. It covers not just HIV/AIDS research but also other health-related studies. According to the publisher, the focus is not just on methodological concerns but also on empirical and conceptual issues as well. It "offers a forum for debates on policy and practice and adopts a practitioner focus where appropriate." For example, it has researched the issue of how gay men negotiate love and HIV serostatus in actual relationships. A supplement once provided abstracts of papers from a Conference of the International Association for the Study of Sexuality, Culture and Society (IASSCS). Members of IASSCS can subscribe at a reduced rate. For residents from least developed countries, there is also a reduced rate. An excellent source for scholarly debates about international policies related to reproductive and sexual health research and applications in particular. Available in print and online versions. (DT)

4771. *Erotica Readers and Writers Association.* 1998. m. Free. Erotica Readers Association. *Bk. rev.:* Number and length vary. *Aud.:* Ga.

This site, "dedicated to readers and writers of erotica since 1996," "is an international community of women and men interested in the provocative world of erotica and sexual pleasure." It showcases "explicit fiction, poetry, and discussions about sexuality." The site provides "advice, news, current calls for submissions, and market information for authors." For readers, it provides information on books "for all persuasions and desires, book reviews and interviews." For "sensualists," it "highlights recommendations for adult videos [and] sex toy information," as well as providing "a forum for discussions about sexuality." Its online forum encourages sexual frankness: "We hope our open approach to sexuality creates sex-positive ripples around the world." Inside, the "Erotic Mind" section asks readers to "tell us what are you are thinking about when the clothes come off, and love making heats up the sheets." Features have included advice on getting erotic literature published, dealing with literary agents, and overcoming rejection letters. Links are also provided to other erotic literature and movie sites. Readers can sign up for "Erotic Lure," an e-mail notification service of new additions to the site. There is also now a blog intended for adult readers. Highly recommended. URL: http://erotica-readers.com/ERA/index.htm (DT)

4772. *International Journal of Sexual Health.* Formerly (until 2007): *Journal of Psychology & Human Sexuality.* [ISSN: 1931-7611] 1988. q. GBP 669 (print & online eds.). Ed(s): Howard Adler, Eli Coleman. Routledge, 325 Chestnut St, Ste 800, Philadelphia, PA 19106; customerservice@taylorandfrancis.com; http://www.tandfonline.com. Adv. Sample. Refereed. Circ: 251 Paid. Microform: PQC. Reprint: PSC. *Indexed:* A01, A22, C45, E01, GW, HEA, PsycInfo, RiskAb, SWR&A. *Aud.:* Ac, Sa.

As the official journal for the World Association for Sexual Health, this title "promotes sexual health as a state of physical, emotional, mental, and social well-being through a positive approach to sexuality and sexual rights. The journal publishes peer-reviewed scientific papers, editorials, and reviews, using quantitative and qualitative methods, descriptive and critical analysis, instrument development, surveys, and case studies to examine the essential elements of this broad concept. Leading experts from around the world present original work that covers a variety of disciplines, including sexology, biology, medicine, psychology, sociology, anthropology, history, and religion." It "is dedicated to the basic understanding that sexual health is not merely the absence of disease, dysfunction, and infirmity, but also the presence of pleasurable and safe sexual enjoyment and satisfaction, free of coercion, discrimination, and violence. The journal examines sexual attitudes, beliefs, and behaviors, public policies and legislative issues, and a variety of sexual health problems, including the assessment and treatment of sexual dysfunctions and disorders, sexual abuse and violence, and sexually transmitted infections." Edited by prominent transgender studies sexologist Eli Coleman, this journal is a source for path-breaking research studies on a broad range of sexual health issues. Recent issues have covered job satisfaction of female sex workers in Australia; femininity and sexuality among young females; and the role of androphilia in the psychosexual development of boys. The most cited articles include "Gender Differences in Receptivity to Sexual Offers," "DSM-IV-TR and the

Paraphilias," and "Top/Bottom Self-Label, Anal Sex Practices, HIV Risk and Gender Role Identity in Gay Men in New York City." Highly recommended for its international coverage, with a long advisory board membership from across the globe. (DT)

Journal of Homosexuality. See Gay, Lesbian, Bisexual, and Transgender section.

Journal of Sex Research. See Sociology and Social Work/General section.

4773. *Journal of Sexual Medicine: basic research and clinical studies in male and female sexual function and dysfunction.* [ISSN: 1743-6095] 2004. m. GBP 635 (print or online ed.). Ed(s): Dr. Irwin Goldstein. Wiley-Blackwell Publishing Ltd., The Atrium, Southern Gate, Chichester, PO19 8SQ, United Kingdom; customer@wiley.com; http://www.wiley.com/. Adv. Sample. Refereed. Reprint: PSC. *Indexed:* A01, A22, E01, ExcerpMed, PsycInfo. *Aud.:* Ac, Sa.

"Publishing original research in both basic science and clinical investigations, *The Journal of Sexual Medicine* also features review articles, educational papers, editorials highlighting original research, and meeting information. Special topics include symposia proceedings and the official guidelines from the Second International Consultation on Sexual Dysfunctions in Men and Women." The journal is the official publication of the International Society for Sexual Medicine and the International Society for the Study of Women's Sexual Health (ISSWSH). It ranks high among journals in Urology and Nephrology in *ISI Journal Citation Reports.* It offers research in the following fields: biochemistry, endocrinology, gynecology, neurology, pathophysiology, pharmacology, physiology, physiology, psychiatry, psychology, sex therapy, and surgery. Special issues are published occasionally; a recent one contains the ISSWSH proceedings with abstracts of poster sessions and podium presentations. Research articles may cover such topics as premature ejaculation. Literature reviews are provided for specific topics. An editorial gave voice to patient concerns by quoting a woman who managed to overcome sexual pain and make love again. Not aimed at the lay reader. Recommended for medical collections. (DT)

Journal of the History of Sexuality. See History/Interdisciplinary Interests section.

4774. *Libido: the journal of sex and sensibility.* [ISSN: 0899-8272] 1988. q. Ed(s): Jack Hafferkamp, Marianna Beck. Libido, PO Box 146721, Chicago, IL 61614; rune@mcs.com; http://www.sensualsource.com. Illus., adv. Sample. Circ: 10000. *Bk. rev.:* 6, 500-3,000 words. *Aud.:* Ga, Ac.

This well-designed journal, long migrated to the web, continues to offer some of the best writing on sexual politics and erotica. The editors explain: "Printing is very expensive for a small erotic magazine. We can reach more people with more exciting content by publishing on the web." It describes itself as "a journal about sex that's geared to turn on your mind and your body. It's a web site (formerly a magazine) for women and men who read and think." It is "sex-positive, gender-equal, and all-embracing in terms of sexual orientation." It also claims to be "both intellectually demanding as well as stimulating." There is poetry, reader-written fiction, and, most notably, highly artistic photography, some from its annual photography contest. Fiction articles are prominent, and there is a fiction as well as a reviews archive online. Vintage erotica now appears in an exquisitely designed online gallery and art museum, and there is also a book review archive. A sexuality resources section includes a sex quiz to test your sex IQ. Back issues of the print version that lasted from 1988 to 2000 are on sale on the web site. The publishers seem to have focused more on videos recently. An anthology of selected articles from the magazine came out in 1977 in book form: *The Ecstatic Moment: The Best of Libido.* A sign of the times, the site warns of "adult and sexual" content, and notes, "In an effort to prevent inappropriate eyes from viewing the contents herein, we have registered [*Libido*] with the following filtering services," including Net Nanny and Surf Watch. It is explicitly geared for adults. URL: www.libidomag.com (DT)

4775. *Nerve (Online): love, sex, culture.* 1997. m. Free to members; Non-members, USD 35. Ed(s): Peter Smith. Nerve.com, Inc., 520 Broadway, 9th Fl, New York, NY 10012. Illus., adv. *Bk. rev.:* Number and length vary. *Aud.:* Ga.

Nerve, according to its original mission statement, "exists because sex is beautiful and absurd, remarkably fun[,] and reliably trauma-inducing. In short, it is a subject in need of a fearless, intelligent forum for both genders. We believe that women (men too, but especially women) have waited long enough for a smart, honest magazine on sex, with cliche-shattering prose and fiction as well as striking photographs of naked people that capture more than their flesh. You've waited long enough." Now it is a completely a free web site (without its original mission statement), and recent features, divided into "Love & Sex," "Advice," "Entertainment," and "Confession" categories, have covered sex among senior citizens; men going too far; phone apps and privacy; *Star Trek*'s most gay scenes (with video clips); and TV and film reviews. Readers can even post and answer personal ads after signing up for free memberships. Overall, a well-designed and graphically pleasant web site. URL: www.nerve.com (DT)

4776. *Nifty Erotic Stories Archive.* 1992. irreg. Nifty Archive Alliance, PMB 159, 333 Mamaroneck Ave, White Plains, NY 10605; nifty@gaycafe.com; http://www.nifty.org/nifty. *Aud.:* Ga, Ac, Sa.

This online archive of alternative-sexuality erotica—now the granddaddy of such archives—covers fiction involving male–male, female–female, bisexual, bestiality, intergenerational, interracial, and other sexual combinations, including the transgendered. It specifically excludes heterosexual stories. Within each category included, there are even further subcategories (e.g., under "gay male," there are first-time, high school, and adult–youth fiction, among many others). The site contains links to lists of rejected stories, and of removed stories (because of copyright, for instance). Links are also provided to other online repositories of erotic literature, to chat rooms about *Nifty,* and to bookstore and publisher sites. While the site is free, donations are sought to maintain it. There is also lists of authors who are no longer with us. This site warns that it contains sexually explicit text and is for adults. It is an indispensable source for raw, uncensored erotica written by anyone. It remains still the best reader-written erotica for sexual minorities, focusing on gay male reader-written fiction. URL: http://nifty.org (DT)

4777. *Penthouse: the magazine of sex, politics and protest.* [ISSN: 0090-2020] 1969. m. USD 29.95; USD 8.99 per issue. Ed(s): Bob Guccione, Peter Bloch. General Media Communications, Inc., 6800 Broken Sound Pkwy, Ste 100, Boca Raton, FL 33487. Illus., adv. Circ: 980106. *Indexed:* A22, ASIP, BRI. *Aud.:* Ga, Ac.

This long-standing heterosexual erotica magazine continues to be a strong proponent of sexual freedom and free speech. It is decidedly on the side of those who fight state repression. In addition to explicit photography (more private parts showing in the female than the male), the magazine offers strong investigative reportage and analysis of national and international issues by the likes of Joe Conason, Alan Dershowitz, and Nat Hentoff. For more than two decades, until his death in 2001, journalist Tad Szulc's writings graced its pages. Some may dislike how women are depicted in its fiction, news clips, or full-page color layouts, but one cannot dismiss its outstanding contribution by alerting readers to the latest threats to our liberties, such as an article on "Whose Homeland Security?" Regular departments include "Online Humor," "Technomania," "Politics in the Miltary," "Men's Health & Fitness," and "Ribald Rimes." Selected articles and sections are free online. For the intelligent person's collection. URL: http://penthousemagazine.com/ (DT)

Perspectives on Sexual and Reproductive Health. See Family Planning section.

4778. *Playboy (Chicago): entertainment for men.* [ISSN: 0032-1478] 1953. m. USD 29.97 domestic; USD 47.05 Canada; USD 45 elsewhere. Ed(s): Hugh Hefner, Kevin Buckley. Playboy Enterprises, Inc., 680 N Lake Shore Dr, Chicago, IL 60611; http://www.playboy.com. Illus., adv. Sample. Circ: 3150000 Paid. Vol. ends: No. 12. Microform: BHP; PQC. *Indexed:* A22, ASIP, BEL&L, BRI, MLA-IB, P02. *Bk. rev.:* 6-9, 200 words, signed. *Aud.:* Ga, Ac.

America's best-selling men's magazine for over half a century, *Playboy* continues to publish excellent, high-quality fiction and nonfiction, along with its well-regarded "Playboy Interview" with notable subjects, including recently Chinese dissident Ai Weiwei. The "Playmate of the Month" centerfold is still offered. Readers definitely have to wade through pages of color nudes (mainly of women), but if the photographs don't interest a reader, the text offerings are definitely the "meat" of the magazine. Now it also highlights a "DVD of the month" and includes what's available online on its web site. There has also been a "20Q" column, where politicians or other notables are asked 20 questions; it's a shorter and more concise version of the "Playboy Interview." Reviews cover films, music, games, DVDs, and books. Sexual liberation may be commonplace in many regions, and its message of "entertainment for men" may sound dated and limited, but the audience is still there for this magazine. It now boasts multiple international editions from Brazil to Japan. A digital version is also available. (DT)

4779. Scarleteen: sex ed for the real world. 1998. m. Scarleteen, 1752 N W Market St, #524, Seattle, WA 98107. *Aud.:* Hs, Ga.

Originally conceived as a sister web publication to the feminist erotic zine *Scarlet Letters* (now sadly no longer available), *Scarleteens* is aimed at teens and those in their twenties. It offers a clear and frank discussion of sexual matters of interest to teenagers. The web site celebrates sexual pleasure while not ignoring unpleasant issues. In sum, it is a well-balanced site for sexual knowledge and information aimed at young people, providing them with concise data to make informed decisions. Sections fall under the categories "gaydar," bully-free zone, and crisis hotline. This site answers questions such as "He gets oral sex from me: what can I do to get him to give me some?" Surprisingly, while the site naturally promotes sexual health and safety, it also promotes progressive politics. There was even a 2012 voting guide on U.S. presidential candidates' positions and their party planks not just on same-sex marriage, for example, but also on health care and Guantanamo Bay. It is the only site among those reviewed in this section to incorporate so much of the latest social media tools, including "Scaletweets" and Tumblr posts, as well as a Facebook presence. As such, it is cutting-edge aimed at the most tech-savvy youth, providing them with sex-positive material easily digestible. Highly recommended. URL: www.scarleteen.com (DT)

4780. Sex Education: sexuality, society and learning. [ISSN: 1468-1811] 2001. q. GBP 366 (print & online eds.). Ed(s): Michael Reiss. Routledge, 4 Park Sq, Milton Park, Abingdon, OX14 4RN, United Kingdom; subscriptions@tandf.co.uk; http://www.tandfonline.com. Adv. Sample. Refereed. Reprint: PSC. *Indexed:* A01, A22, E01, ERIC, GW, PsycInfo. *Aud.:* Ac, Sa.

This journal focuses on sex education (or lack thereof) within schools and the family as well as society, but its scope is not limited to the United States or Europe. An article in an early issue covered, for example, sex education about AIDS in selected countries in Asia and the Pacific—it delineated the heterosexual bias in some of the government-sponsored programs. Another article more recently argues that sexual pleasure is ignored in evaluating the success of sex education programs in schools. Other articles address the difficulties in teaching sex education to boys; puberty or sex education of primary school students; or the limits of abstinence-only sex education. This journal's editorial board includes members from around the globe. It notes that it "does not assume that sex education takes place only in educational institutions and the family. Contributions are therefore welcomed which, for example, analyse [sic] the impacts of media and other vehicles of culture on sexual behaviour [sic] and attitudes. The journal is accessible: "Medical and epidemiological papers (e.g., of trends in the incidences of sexually transmitted infections) will not be accepted unless their educational implications are discussed adequately." Highly recommended for coverage that is often ignored or politicized. (DT)

4781. Sex, Etc: sex education by teens, for teens! 19??. 3x/yr. USD 15. Network for Family Life Education, Rutgers University, The State University of New Jersey, Piscataway, NJ 08854. *Aud.:* Hs, Ga.

This is both a magazine and a web site. It's a "telling it like it is" national sex education newsletter, edited by teenagers for other teens, which does not mince words nor sugarcoat the topic. Topics cover a range as you might expect, but the language is blunt and explicit, such as in "Sex 4.1.1: Answers to Your Most

Common Questions about Sex," where the query posed, "I'm a 17-year-old guy and I cum too fast. Is that normal?" is answered: "It's okay and normal if you orgasm ("cum") quickly...." Its editorial board is selected each year from youth in New Jersey–area high schools. It aims to reach "millions" of readers. In its eight pages, it manages to stimulate, educate, and address succinctly and accurately the concerns of American youth today. Each magazine contains 20 full-color pages. Lesson plans for teaching with *Sex, Etc.* are included with a subscription. A web site (www.sexetc.org) provides more resources, such as to HIV/AIDS organizations and materials. Newsletter articles are screened by health professionals. The publisher is an established university-based organization that is guided by the following principles: "Young people deserve honest, medically accurate[,] and balanced information about sexuality in schools, homes[,] and communities. Teen-to-teen communication is an effective vehicle for educating about sexual health. Educators and youth-serving professionals need training and support." A highly recommended addition to your collection. (DT)

Sexual Abuse. See Psychology section.

4782. Sexual Addiction & Compulsivity: the journal of treatment and prevention. [ISSN: 1072-0162] 1994. q. GBP 231 (print & online eds.). Ed(s): Charles Samenow. Routledge, 325 Chestnut St, Ste 800, Philadelphia, PA 19106; customerservice@taylorandfrancis.com; http://www.tandfonline.com. Sample. Refereed. Reprint: PSC. *Indexed:* A01, A22, ASSIA, CJPI, E01, P61, PsycInfo, RiskAb, SSA. *Aud.:* Ac, Sa.

This journal of the National Council on Sexual Addiction and Compulsivity focuses on all aspects of sexual addiction, described as a "growth phenomenon." Article topics include addiction among lesbians, seropositive men who have sex with men, ephebophiles, and priests, as well as fraternity males and pornography. A special issue addressed "hypersexual disorder." It offers continuing education material for professionals. Articles seek to provide guidance to working sex therapists for relating to clients. An editorial concedes that "addiction" may not always be the best description to apply to a particular set of behaviors. (DT)

Sexual and Marital Therapy. See *Sexual and Relationship Therapy.*

4783. Sexual and Relationship Therapy. Formerly (until 2000): *Sexual and Marital Therapy.* [ISSN: 1468-1994] 1986. q. GBP 554 (print & online eds.). Ed(s): Dr. Alessandra Iantaffi. Routledge, 4 Park Sq, Milton Park, Abingdon, OX14 4RN, United Kingdom; subscriptions@tandf.co.uk; http://www.tandfonline.com. Illus., index, adv. Sample. Refereed. Vol. ends: Nov. Reprint: PSC. *Indexed:* A01, A22, ASSIA, BAS, E01, P61, PsycInfo, SSA. *Aud.:* Ac, Sa.

With an applied orientation for professionals in psychology, medical, and marriage-counseling fields, this established journal from the British Association for Sexual and Relationship Therapy had earlier changed its title to better embrace its clientele, thus including couples who are not in traditional marriages. Articles give advice to general practitioners about discussing sex life issues with coronary heart patients; and address such issues as sexual boundaries between clinicians and clients; the connection between induced abortion and sexual attitudes; and the impact of sexual assault on one's life. A recent article also discussed exercise-induced orgasm among women. While it deals with sexual crises, the journal also provides hope, for example, in an article on women over 65: "still doing it." It has also published editorials such as one paying tribute to martyred Ugandan gay activist David Kato. Recommended for collections that cater to marriage and relationship counseling. (DT)

4784. Sexual Health (Online). [ISSN: 1449-8987] 2004. bi-m. USD 675; EUR 565; GBP 396. Ed(s): Roy Chan, Christopher Fairley. C S I R O Publishing, 150 Oxford St, PO Box 1139, Collingwood, VIC 3066, Australia; publishing@csiro.au; http://www.publish.csiro.au/home.htm. Refereed. *Aud.:* Ac, Sa.

According to its scope note, "*Sexual Health* publishes original and significant contributions to the fields of sexual health[,] including HIV/AIDS, sexually transmissible infections, issues of sexuality and relevant areas of reproductive health. This journal is directed towards those working in sexual health as clinicians, public health practitioners, or researchers in behavioural, clinical, laboratory, public health[,] or social sciences. The journal publishes peer-reviewed original research, editorials, review articles, topical debates, case reports and critical correspondence." It is the official journal of the International Union against Sexually Transmitted Infections (IUSTI), Asia-Pacific, and the Asia-Oceanian Federation for Sexology. It is also "officially sponsored" by the Australasian Chapter of Sexual Health Medicine of the Royal Australasian College of Physicians and the Sexual Health Society of Queensland. Special issues include one on HIV in Australia, but articles cover sexual practices from Vietnam to Nigeria. A recent article discussed "Condom Use Errors Among Sexually Unfaithful and Consensually Nonmonogamous Individuals." The journal's focus is more on informing practitioners and researchers than on reaching the general public. A key feature is editorial involvement by sexuality professionals in the region, including in Australia, Singapore, Thailand, Indonesia, India, Taiwan, Hong Kong, and China. Its article on the influence of traditional Vietnamese culture on young Vietnamese Australian women's utilization of sexual health services is among its most accessed articles. Highly recommended. (DT)

4785. *Sexual Intelligence.* 200?. m. Free. Ed(s): Marty Klein. Sexual Intelligence, c/o Dr. Marty Klein, 2439 Birch St. #2, Palo Alto, CA 94306; mklein@sexed.org; http://www.sexualintelligence.org. *Aud.:* Ga, Ac.

Sex therapist and marriage counselor Marty Klein steadfastly analyzes current sexuality-related topics in this provocative, blog-like monthly. Topics include "Ten Things Humanists Need to Know About Sex," National Masturbation Day, and "Reagan's Legacy: World AIDS." The pithy newsletter analyzes news on sexuality from a sex-positive perspective, dismissing as faddish and ideological the popular concept of "sexual addiction," calling it a myth. Another brief item: "F-Word a WMD?" (whether the four-letter word is a weapon of mass destruction). Klein brilliantly skewers sex-negativity, while keeping his analysis concise and pointed. Even earlier items, all posted on the web site, are worth re-reading to remind us how precarious sexual liberty remains in the United States. His annual Sexual Intelligence Awards, profiled in the newsletter, honor those who manage to overcome such assaults on personal sexual freedom. Favorite targets are the federal government's crackdown on sex research and the religious right's self-righteousness on moral issues. The blog is located here: http://sexualintelligence.wordpress.com/ (DT)

4786. *Sexualidades.* [ISSN: 1938-6419] 2007. irreg. Free. Ed(s): Eliane Borges Berutti, Maria Mercedes Gomez. City University of New York, Center for Lesbian and Gay Studies, 365 Fifth Ave, Rm 7-115, New York, NY 16016; clags@gc.cuny.edu; http://web.gc.cuny.edu/clags. *Aud.:* Ac, Sa.

This e-journal, which is a working-paper series on Latin American and Caribbean sexualities, aims to reach sexuality practitioners and researchers, especially in areas where Spanish and/or Portuguese are read. The paper is published in three languages, English, Spanish, and Portuguese. The second paper in the series focuses on low-income transvestites. The latest issue (ninth) analyzed masculine identity in the Chilean army. Unfortunately, after the sixth edition (2010), the issues are not available online but can be requested from the publisher, International Research Network, which self-identifies as a "global community of teachers and researchers sharing knowledge about sexualities," funded by the Ford Foundation. Highly recommended for special collections. URL: www.irnweb.org/en/journals/view/sexualidades

4787. *Sexuality and Culture.* [ISSN: 1095-5143] 1997. q. EUR 378 (print & online eds.). Ed(s): Roberto Refinetti. Springer New York LLC, 233 Spring St, New York, NY 10013; service-ny@springer.com; http://www.springer.com. Adv. Sample. Reprint: PSC. *Indexed:* A01, A22, AmHI, BRI, E01, GW, P61, PsycInfo, SSA. *Aud.:* Ga, Ac.

Originally an annual, this journal emerged out of concern about "sexual correctness" (or political correctness involving sexualities), especially in the face of sexual harassment policies in academia. It now covers a broader range of issues, and it plays less of an advocacy role, becoming more research-oriented. The journal states that it "offers an international forum for analysis of ethical, cultural, psychological, social, and political issues related to sexual relationships and sexual behavior. Coverage extends to sexual consent and sexual responsibility; harassment and freedom of speech; privacy; censorship

and pornography; impact of film and literature on sexual relationships; and university and governmental regulation of intimate relationships, such as interracial relationships and student-professor relationships." Its pages critically explore affirmative action and child sexual-abuse research, with covered topics including "sexting" and infidelity in cyberspace. Its editorial board includes some of the big names in sex research, even as it takes on the daunting task of critiquing established norms. Look here for past and current sex debates that are often missing from more mainstream journals. The publisher is no longer Transaction; Springer has been publishing it since 2010. (DT)

4788. *Sexuality Research and Social Policy.* [ISSN: 1553-6610] 2004. q. EUR 209. Ed(s): Jeffrey T Parsons. Springer New York LLC, 233 Spring St, New York, NY 10013; journals-ny@springer.com; http://www.springer.com. Refereed. Reprint: PSC. *Indexed:* A22, C45, E01, GW, RRTA. *Bk. rev.:* 2, 500 words. *Aud.:* Ga, Ac.

This online journal, from the Ford Foundation–funded National Sexuality Resource Center (based at San Francisco State University), boasts an impressively multinational editorial board of major scholars doing sexuality studies and public health. It is a platform that: "Presents state-of-the-art research on sexuality, along with theoretical and methodological discussions; [d]iscusses the implications of new research for worldwide policies on sexual health, sexuality education, and sexual rights; [p]ublishes brief research and conference reports, white papers, and special topical issues; [and] [p]ublishes research from a wide spectrum of disciplines." Topics cover teen sexuality; youth viewing sexually explicit material online; HIV/AIDS; circumcision; marriage denial and mental health and sexual citizenship; and governmental attacks on sexuality research, from across the globe. Also of new interest are research and policy on the transgendered. The style is less dense than usual for academic journals, for the journal is aimed at the non-academic reader as well as the scholar. The policy articles often take an advocacy stance while grounded in empirical research. In 2010, the publisher changed from University of California Press to Springer. Highly recommended for all major collections. (DT)

Studies in Gender and Sexuality. See Gender Studies section.

4789. *Theology and Sexuality.* [ISSN: 1355-8358] 1994. 3x/yr. GBP 246 (print & online eds.). Acumen Publishing Ltd, 4 Saddler St, Durham, DH1 3NP, United Kingdom; enquiries@acumenpublishing.co.uk; http://www.acumenpublishing.co.uk/. Adv. Refereed. *Indexed:* A01, GW, R&TA. *Aud.:* Ac, Sa.

This journal describes itself as "the primary vehicle for those undertaking theological studies of sexuality and gender issues" that also aims to be accessible to counselors. Themes addressed include "deconstructive and reconstructive approaches to traditional Christian (and other traditions) teaching on sexuality, sexuality and violence and oppression, and the ethics of personal relationships." Members of the Centre for the Study of Christianity and Sexuality receive the journal as part of their annual membership. A liberal take on Christian issues relating to sexuality, it was previously (2008 and before) published by Sage, and subsequently by Equinox before migrating to Maney Publishing. One article advocated for why faith communities should support homosexual relationships, while another was on "The Rainbow Connection: Bridging Asian[-]American and Queer Theologies." Recommended. (DT)

■ SLAVIC STUDIES

See also Asia; Europe; and Middle East sections.

Hugh K. Truslow, Librarian for the Davis Center for Russian and Eurasian Studies Collection, Fung Library, Harvard University, 1737 Cambridge St., Cambridge, MA 02138; truslow@fas.harvard.edu

Introduction

The year 2011 saw a host of reappraisals, re-visitations, and re-examinations of the 20-year period since the fall of the Soviet Union, and the changes brought by the events of 1991. The many special issues of the journals in the section that follows, which are dedicated to exploring one or another aspect of the 20-year period, are testament to the many still unanswered questions. The former Soviet sphere of influence has proved stubbornly durable as a framework of inquiry for the diversity of countries that once fell within its bounds.

Yet the familiar phrase "Slavic Studies" all the more frequently, and rightly, carries the insertion of "Eurasian" and "East European" within it, and the still-unfolding changes in the countries of the region continue to invite new approaches and bring to light ever-shifting, expanding geographical connections. In so many ways, it is a region still in progress, a region of rich diversity, complex interrelations, and enduring fascination. Thus, collecting materials for the study of the people, politics, cultures, societies, languages, and histories of these countries will remain an important consideration for libraries of many types. The journals recommended here often cross disciplinary boundaries, spanning the social sciences and humanities, and with the exception of certain titles that primarily deal with Russia, they encompass many if not most countries of the region, as opposed to one country.

Basic Periodicals

Hs: *Moscow News, Russian Life;* Ga: *Current Digest of the Post-Soviet Press, Moscow News;* Ac: *The Russian Review, Slavic Review, Studies in East European Thought.*

Basic Abstracts and Indexes

American Bibliography of Slavic and Eastern European Studies (ABSEES), Historical Abstracts, MLA International Bibliography, PAIS International.

4790. *Anthropology and Archeology of Eurasia: a journal of translations.* Formerly (until 1992): *Soviet Anthropology and Archeology.* [ISSN: 1061-1959] 1962. q. USD 1104 (print & online eds.). Ed(s): Marjorie M Balzer. M.E. Sharpe, Inc., 80 Business Park Dr, Armonk, NY 10504; custserv@mesharpe.com; http://www.mesharpe.com. Illus., index, adv. Sample. Refereed. Vol. ends: Spring (No. 4). Reprint: PSC. *Indexed:* A01, A22, A47, AbAn, BAS, E01, FR, MLA-IB, RILM. *Aud.:* Ac, Sa.

This journal "presents scholarship from Russia, Siberia, the Caucasus, and Central Asia, the vast region that stretches from the Baltic to the Black Sea and from Lake Baikal to the Bering Strait. Each thematic issue, with a substantive introduction to the topic by the editor, features expertly translated and annotated manuscripts, articles, and book excerpts reporting fieldwork from every part of the region and theoretical studies on topics of special interest." The articles include complete citations to the original, and editors' notes, when applicable, and specify the translators. One recent issue featured scholarship that covered the entire 20-year period since the end of the Soviet Union. For academic and special libraries that support programs in anthropology, archaeology, and ethnology—as well as Slavic Studies—this publication is highly recommended. It has particular value for researchers in these disciplines who do not have reading knowledge of Russian.

4791. *Baltic Horizons.* Formerly (until 2004): *Monthly Survey of Baltic and Post-Soviet Politics.* [ISSN: 1736-1834] 1990. q. EUR 3.19 per issue. Euroakadeemia, Mustamae tee 4, Tallinn, 10621, Estonia; euro@euroakadeemia.ee; http://euroakadeemia.ee. Circ: 300. *Aud.:* Ac, Sa.

Based at Euroacademy in Tallinn, Estonia, this multidisciplinary, peer-reviewed journal "publishes original research and review papers in English" on the Baltic states and the region. Each issue is dedicated to one of the following subject areas: translation or interpreting; international relations; environmental science; business management; and art and design. Recommended for academic and special libraries that support programs in Baltic Studies, and for public libraries with user populations interested in Baltic affairs.

4792. *Canadian - American Slavic Studies.* Formerly (until 1972): *Canadian Slavic Studies.* [ISSN: 0090-8290] 1967. q. EUR 167. Ed(s): Charles Schlacks. Brill, PO Box 9000, Leiden, 2300 PA, Netherlands; cs@brill.nl; http://www.brill.nl. Illus., index. Refereed. Vol. ends: Winter (No. 4). Microform: BHP. *Indexed:* A22, ABS&EES, E01, MLA-IB, RILM. *Bk. rev.:* 20-30, 300-1,000 words, signed. *Aud.:* Ac, Sa.

The scope of this peer-reviewed scholarly journal is "Slavic and East European (including Albania, Hungary and Romania) culture, past and present." It publishes articles, documents, translations, and book reviews in English, French, German, Russian, and Ukrainian. While the focus is largely on history and literature, the journal "welcomes contributions in all areas of the humanities and social sciences." It also publishes special topical issues with guest editors. For librarians with collection-development responsibilities, the lists of books received are useful for selecting materials. Recommended as a significant title for academic and research libraries that support Slavic Studies.

4793. *Canadian Slavonic Papers: an interdisciplinary journal devoted to Central and Eastern Europe.* [ISSN: 0008-5006] 1956. q. CAD 65 Free to members. Ed(s): Oleh S Ilnytzkyj. Canadian Association of Slavists, 200 Arts Bldg, Dept of Modern Languages and Cultural Studies, Edmonton, AB T6G 2E6, Canada; http://www.ualberta.ca/~csp/cas/. Illus., index. Refereed. Reprint: PSC. *Indexed:* A01, A22, ABS&EES, BRI, C37, CBCARef, FR, IBSS, MLA-IB, P02. *Bk. rev.:* 35-40, 300-500 words, signed. *Aud.:* Ac, Sa.

From the Canadian Association of Slavists, this interdisciplinary journal serves as "a forum for scholars from a range of disciplines: language and linguistics, literature, history, political science, sociology, economics, anthropology, geography and the arts." One recent issue included a special section called "Twenty Years On: Slavic Studies Since The Collapse Of The Soviet Union." Articles are in English and French. The book reviews and review essays are of high quality, with coverage of materials from Canada and Europe as well, and can be valuable for librarians in collection development. Recommended as a major title for academic and research libraries that support Slavic Studies.

4794. *Communist and Post-Communist Studies.* Former titles (until 1993): *Studies in Comparative Communism;* (until 1968): *Communist Affairs.* [ISSN: 0967-067X] 1962. q. EUR 580. Ed(s): Andrzej Korbonski, Lucy Kerner. Pergamon, The Blvd, Langford Ln, E Park, Kidlington, OX5 1GB, United Kingdom; JournalsCustomerServiceEMEA@elsevier.com; http://www.elsevier.com. Illus., adv. Sample. Refereed. Microform: PQC. *Indexed:* A01, A22, ABS&EES, BAS, BRI, IBSS, MLA-IB, P02, P61, SSA. *Aud.:* Ac, Sa.

This "is an international journal covering all communist and post-communist states and communist movements, including both their domestic policies and their international relations. It is focused on the analysis of historical as well as current developments in the communist and post-communist world, including ideology, economy, and society. It also aims to provide comparative foci on a given subject (e.g., education in China) by inviting comments of a comparative character from scholars specializing in the same subject matter but in different countries (e.g., education in Poland or Romania). In addition to the traditional disciplines of history, political science, economics, and international relations, the editors encourage the submission of articles in less developed fields of social sciences and humanities, such as cultural anthropology, education, geography, religion, and sociology." Most articles published focus on the countries of the former Soviet Union and the Soviet bloc, while countries such as China, Cuba, and North Korea are treated less frequently. Recommended for academic and research libraries; may be of interest to larger public libraries with patrons interested in the politics, economics, and contemporary society of the former Soviet sphere of influence.

4795. *Current Digest of the Russian Press.* Former titles (until 2011): *Current Digest of the Post-Soviet Press;* (until 1992): *Current Digest of the Soviet Press;* Which incorporated (1968-1970): *Current Abstracts of the Soviet Press.* [ISSN: 2159-3612] 1949. w. USD 1889. East View Information Services, 10601 Wayzata Blvd, Minneapolis, MN 55305; info@eastview.com; http://www.eastview.com/. Illus., index. Sample. Vol. ends: No. 52. *Indexed:* A01, A22, BAS, BRI, CDSP, MLA-IB, P02. *Aud.:* Hs, Ga, Ac.

This weekly digest, published since 1949, offers a selection of articles from the Russian-language press translated into English for use in teaching and research. Its mission is "to provide the reader with a broad picture of the news presented to the Russian public," and it "strives to ensure that the articles included reflect multiple perspectives, incorporating articles from a number of independent newspapers with diverse editorial stances." Articles on important events are grouped under the heading "Featured News Stories," with additional items, often shorter, appearing under the sections "The Russian Federation," "Other Post-Soviet States," and "International Affairs." Each article includes a citation to the original publication and an indication of whether the text is complete or has been condensed. This is a valuable compilation source for current events in Russia, and is of particular use for readers without reading knowledge of Russian. Recommended for all libraries, academic or public, with readers interested in the current political scene in Russia.

4796. *Demokratizatsiya: the journal of post-soviet democratization.* [ISSN: 1074-6846] 1992. q. USD 148 (Individuals, USD 60 (print & online eds.). Ed(s): Rachel Adams. Heldref Publications, c/o Taylor & Francis, 325 Chestnut St, Ste 800, Philadelphia, PA 19106; heldref@subscriptionoffice.com; http://www.heldref.org. Adv. Refereed. Reprint: PSC. *Indexed:* A01, ABS&EES, BRI, P61, SSA. *Bk. rev.:* Varies, 500-600 words, signed. *Aud.:* Ac, Sa.

Beginning with perestroika, and covering the Yeltsin era through the current era of "managed democracy" under Putin, this is the leading international journal on democratization in post-Soviet countries. "It focuses on the end of the Soviet Union and the contemporary transformation of its successor states," and aims to be "a tool for building institutions from the ashes of the USSR and communism." In each issue, "scholars from around the world address politics, economics, social issues, legal systems, nationalities, international relations, and human rights. Recent articles have also addressed the post-Soviet countries' continuing struggles against crime and corruption." A recent special issue provided substantive and thought-provoking answers to the question, "Twenty Years Since the Collapse of the USSR: What Have We Learned?" As of the Winter 2012 issue, ownership of the journal was transferred from the World Affairs Institute to the Institute for European, Russian and Eurasian Studies, or IERES, at George Washington University. Recommended highly for academic and research libraries that support the study of the former Soviet Union and the former Soviet bloc.

4797. *East European Jewish Affairs.* Former titles (until 1992): *Soviet Jewish Affairs;* (until 1971): *Bulletin on Soviet and East European Jewish Affairs.* [ISSN: 1350-1674] 19??. 3x/yr. GBP 252 (print & online eds.). Ed(s): Sam Johnson. Routledge, 4 Park Sq, Milton Park, Abingdon, OX14 4RN, United Kingdom; subscriptions@tandf.co.uk; http://www.tandfonline.com. Illus., index, adv. Sample. Refereed. Vol. ends: Winter (No. 2). Microform: PQC. Reprint: PSC. *Indexed:* A22, AmHI, ArtHuCI, E01, FR, IBSS, IJP, MLA-IB, RILM, RiskAb. *Bk. rev.:* 5-10, 300-500 words, signed. *Aud.:* Ac, Sa.

This interdisciplinary journal seeks to provide an "understanding of the position and prospects of Jews in the former Soviet Union and the countries of East-Central Europe. It deals with issues in historical perspective and in the context of general, social, economic, political, and cultural developments in the region. The journal includes analytical, in-depth articles; review articles; archival documents; conference notes; and annotated books." The quality and selection of the articles is excellent, as are the book reviews and the review articles when included. The lists of books received for review are of great value for scholars as well as for collection development librarians. Recommended highly for academic and research libraries, and for larger public libraries with reader populations interested in Jewish affairs of the region.

4798. *East European Politics.* Former titles (until 2011): *Journal of Communist Studies and Transition Politics;* (until 1994): *Journal of Communist Studies;* (until 1985): *Communist Affairs;* (until 1982): *Documents in Communist Affairs.* [ISSN: 2159-9165] 1977. q. GBP 431 (print & online eds.). Routledge, 4 Park Sq, Milton Park, Abingdon, OX14 4RN, United Kingdom; subscriptions@tandf.co.uk; http://www.tandfonline.com. Illus., index. Sample. Refereed. Vol. ends: No. 4. Microform: PQC. Reprint: PSC. *Indexed:* A01, A22, AmHI, E01, IBSS, P61, SSA. *Bk. rev.:* Varies, 500-800 words, signed. *Aud.:* Ac, Sa.

Until last year called *Journal of Communist Studies and Transition Politics,* this "refereed journal publishes articles in the government, politics[,] and international relations of the post-communist space." Geographic coverage is for "the entire post-communist region, including East Central and South Eastern Europe, Russia[,] and all the other countries of the former Soviet Union. The journal publishes original scholarship on political developments in individual countries, together with cross-country comparative analyses and studies of the

relations between post-communist regions and other parts of the world, including internationally based organizations." In addition to a substantial book review section, the journal also publishes thematic special issues, symposium sections, and "review articles devoted to briefer analysis of particular events, political issues[,] and important theoretical and conceptual developments." The journal's new editorial leadership says that "although the journal aims for a relatively broad methodological coverage, including quantitative and qualitative approaches, and comparative or single country studies," it will now "prioritize empirical scholarship." Recommended for academic and special libraries that support Slavic Studies, and for larger public libraries with user populations interested in the topic.

4799. *East European Politics & Societies.* [ISSN: 0888-3254] 1987. q. USD 446. Ed(s): Irena Grudzinska-Gross, Ivo Banac. Sage Publications, Inc., 2455 Teller Rd, Thousand Oaks, CA 91320; info@sagepub.com; http://www.sagepub.com. Illus., adv. Sample. Refereed. Vol. ends: No. 3. Microform: PQC. Reprint: PSC. *Indexed:* A01, A22, ABS&EES, BRI, E01, IBSS, MLA-IB, P02, P61, RiskAb, SSA. *Aud.:* Ac, Sa.

This journal "covers issues in Eastern Europe from social, political, and humanities perspectives. The journal focuses on expanding readers' understanding of past events and current developments in countries from Greece to the Baltics." The publisher writes that the journal "maintains a tradition of imaginative and erudite vision, uniting the cutting-edge social research and political analysis of leading area specialists, historians, sociologists, political scientists[,] and anthropologists from around the world." The coverage is broad and engaging, and the articles are of consistently high quality. Published in association with the American Council of Learned Societies. Recommended for academic and research libraries that support Slavic Studies generally, and in particular those with a focus on East Central European Studies.

4800. *Eastern European Economics.* [ISSN: 0012-8775] 1962. bi-m. USD 1590 (print & online eds.). Ed(s): Josef Brada. M.E. Sharpe, Inc., 80 Business Park Dr, Armonk, NY 10504; custserv@mesharpe.com; http://www.mesharpe.com. Illus., index, adv. Sample. Refereed. Vol. ends: Nov/Dec (No. 6). Reprint: PSC. *Indexed:* A22, ABIn, ABS&EES, B01, E01, EconLit, JEL. *Aud.:* Ac, Sa.

This journal "publishes original research on the newly emerging economies of Central and Eastern Europe, with coverage of the ongoing processes of transition to market economics in different countries, their integration into the broader European and global economies, and the ramifications of the 2008-9 financial crisis." Recent issues have tended to include around five articles, and all feature an introduction by the journal's editor to add "context and expert insights on the articles presented." Themes of recent issues have included "Outward FDI from Post-Transition Economies" and "Development Perspectives on Southeastern Europe." Recommended highly for academic and research libraries that support Slavic Studies as well as the economics and business of the region.

4801. *Eurasian Geography and Economics.* Former titles (until 2002): *Post-Soviet Geography and Economics;* (until 1996): *Post-Soviet Geography;* (until 1992): *Soviet Geography;* (until 19??): *Soviet Geography - Review and Translation.* [ISSN: 1538-7216] 1960. bi-m. GBP 541 (print & online eds.). Taylor & Francis, 4 Park Sq, Milton Park, Abingdon, OX14 4RN, United Kingdom; subscriptions@tandf.co.uk; http://www.tandfonline.com. Illus., index. Refereed. Vol. ends: No. 8. Reprint: PSC. *Indexed:* A01, A22, ABIn, ABS&EES, B01, B02, BAS, BRI, EconLit, FR, JEL, P02. *Aud.:* Ac, Sa.

This journal "features original papers by leading specialists and scholars on salient geographic and economic issues in China, Russia, India, [the] European Union, and other regions within the Eurasian realm. Included in all issues are symposia on topics of worldwide significance, review papers, and empirical research focused on analysis of recent economic and geographic developments." Though the scope of recent issues has focused on China and India as much as on countries within the former Soviet realm, this expansive regional approach—as in a recent group of articles on water issues, for example—will be welcomed by some scholars. Recommended for academic and research libraries with Slavic Studies programs, as well as geography programs and researchers studying in the non-Slavic Eurasian countries. Also recommended for larger public libraries with readers interested in the spatial aspects of Eurasia and its economies.

4802. *Europe - Asia Studies.* Formerly (until 1993): *Soviet Studies.* [ISSN: 0966-8136] 1949. 10x/yr. GBP 1436 (print & online eds.). Ed(s): Terry Cox. Routledge, 4 Park Sq, Milton Park, Abingdon, OX14 4RN, United Kingdom; subscriptions@tandf.co.uk; http://www.tandfonline.com. Illus., index, adv. Sample. Refereed. Vol. ends: Dec (No. 8). Reprint: PSC. *Indexed:* A01, A22, ABIn, ABS&EES, AmHI, B01, B02, BAS, BRI, E01, EconLit, IBSS, JEL, MASUSE, MLA-IB, P02, P61, RiskAb, SSA. *Bk. rev.:* 20-25, 500-1,000 words, signed. *Aud.:* Ac, Sa.

According to the publishers, this title is "the principal academic journal in the world focusing on the history and current political, social[,] and economic affairs of the countries of the former 'communist bloc' of the Soviet Union, Eastern Europe and Asia. At the same time, the journal explores the economic, political[,] and social transformation of these countries and the changing character of their relationships with the rest of Europe and Asia." One recent special issue on "Russia and the World" looked at foreign and security policies under Putin and Medvedev. The journal is published on behalf of the Central and East European Studies program at the School of Social and Political Sciences at the University of Glasgow. In addition to a well-selected array of book reviews, the list of books received will be helpful to collection-development librarians. Recommended highly for academic, research, and special libraries that support research in Slavic Studies.

Folklore. See Folklore section.

4803. *Journal of Baltic Studies.* Formerly (until 1972): *Bulletin of Baltic Studies.* [ISSN: 0162-9778] 1970. q. GBP 340 (print & online eds.). Ed(s): Terry Clark. Routledge, 325 Chestnut St, Ste 800, Philadelphia, PA 19106; customerservice@taylorandfrancis.com; http://www.tandfonline.com. Illus., index, adv. Sample. Refereed. Circ: 1300. Vol. ends: Winter (No. 4). Microform: PQC. Reprint: PSC. *Indexed:* A22, ABS&EES, E01, IBSS, MLA-IB, NumL, RILM. *Bk. rev.:* 5-10, 300-500 words, signed. *Aud.:* Ac, Sa.

This journal is a "peer-reviewed multidisciplinary journal dedicated to advancing knowledge about all aspects of the Baltic Sea Region's political, social, economic, and cultural life, past and present." It is the journal of the Association for the Advancement of Baltic Studies. Most articles are in English. The book reviews and lists of books received may be useful to collection-development librarians with responsibilities for the Baltic region. Recommended for all academic and research libraries with Baltic and Slavic Studies programs, and for those public libraries that have readers interested in Baltic affairs.

4804. *The Journal of Eurasian Studies.* [ISSN: 1879-3665] 2010. s-a. USD 275. Elsevier Inc., 360 Park Ave S, New York, NY 10010; http://www.elsevier.com. *Aud.:* Ac, Sa.

According to the publisher, "Eurasian countries are among the most rapidly and drastically changing places since the collapse of the former Soviet Union. From the year of 1991 on, the demise of the colossus has brought seemingly unlimited and far-flung turmoil among all social spheres on the Eurasian continent." The journal focuses on the following six issues in particular: national identity; political and economic transition; democratization and marketization; migration; energy problems; and international development and ODA (official development assistance). The engaging range of articles and high quality of scholarship in recent issues make good on the editors' claim that the journal "internationalizes local concerns within Eurasian communities and beyond the various Asian civilizations in more cross-regional perspectives." Published on behalf of Hanyang University in Seoul, South Korea, the journal has a distinguished editorial board. Recommended for academic and research libraries with programs that cover the region.

4805. *Journal of Russian and East European Psychology.* Formerly (until 1992): *Soviet Psychology;* Which superseded in part (in 1966): *Soviet Psychology and Psychiatry.* [ISSN: 1061-0405] 1962. bi-m. USD 1422 (print & online eds.). Ed(s): Pentti Hakkarainen. M.E. Sharpe, Inc., 80 Business Park Dr, Armonk, NY 10504; custserv@mesharpe.com; http://www.mesharpe.com. Illus., index, adv. Sample. Refereed. Vol. ends: Nov/Dec (No. 6). Reprint: PSC. *Indexed:* A01, A22, B01, E01, PsycInfo. *Aud.:* Ac, Sa.

This journal "publishes thematic issues with translations of original submissions as well as articles published in scholarly journals on a variety of topics from child development to creativity to memory to post-traumatic stress." Another element of the journal's editorial mission is to publish translated works by preeminent Russian scholars in psychology "in excellent translations with helpful bibliographic information, contributions by peers and proteges," as the publishers write. The articles include complete citations to the original publication and the name of translator. Aimed at specialists in psychology, this journal will be of particular interest those to scholars without Russian-language reading abilities. Recommended for academic and research libraries that support study and research in psychology as well as Slavic Studies.

4806. *Journal of Slavic Linguistics.* [ISSN: 1068-2090] 1993. s-a. USD 60 (Individuals, USD 40; Free to members). Ed(s): Steven Franks, Rosemarie Connolly. Slavica Publishers, Inc., Indiana University, 2611 E 10th St, Bloomington, IN 47408; slavica@indiana.edu; http://www.slavica.com/. Illus. Refereed. Vol. ends: No. 2. *Indexed:* A22, ABS&EES, AmHI, BRI, E01, MLA-IB. *Bk. rev.:* 1-3, 500-1,000 words, signed. *Aud.:* Ac, Sa.

This publication, which is the official journal of the Slavic Linguistics Society (www.utexas.edu/world/sls), "is intended to address issues in description and analysis of Slavic languages of general interest to linguists, regardless of theoretical orientation." It publishes "papers dealing with any aspect of synchronic or diachronic Slavic phonetics, phonology, morphology, syntax, semantics and pragmatics, as long as they raise substantive problems of broad theoretical concern or propose significant descriptive generalization." Special emphasis is placed on "comparative studies and formal analysis." Each issue is about 150 to 200 pages in length. The journal is aimed at specialists in the field and should be acquired by academic and research libraries that support Slavic Studies and general linguistic programs.

4807. *Journal of Southeast European and Black Sea Studies.* [ISSN: 1468-3857] 2001. q. GBP 416 (print & online eds.). Ed(s): Ioannis Armakolas. Routledge, 4 Park Sq, Milton Park, Abingdon, OX14 4RN, United Kingdom; subscriptions@tandf.co.uk; http://www.tandfonline.com. Adv. Sample. Refereed. Reprint: PSC. *Indexed:* A01, A22, AmHI, E01, IBSS, P61, SSA. *Bk. rev.:* Varies; 1,000-1,500 words; signed. *Aud.:* Ac, Sa.

Associated with ELIAMEP, the Hellenic Foundation for European and Foreign Policy, the journal aims "to establish a line of communication with these regions of Europe. Previously isolated from the European mainstream, the Balkan and Black Sea regions are in need of serious comparative study as are the individual countries, no longer 'at the edge' of Europe." In the main, the journal covers "politics, political economy, international relations and modern history; other disciplinary approaches are accepted as appropriate." The journal largely fulfills its claim to provide "a unique opportunity to establish a new paradigm of analysis for the region and one that attempts to break away from the traditional ethnocentric approaches and develop a deeper and more fruitful understanding of the area." Some issues have featured an editorial that examines current issues of the region, which may not reflect the rest of the content of the issue. Issues are often thematic, with both the expansion of the European Union and concerns spanning the whole Black Sea region serving as recurring frameworks. Recommended for academic and research libraries that support Slavic and Balkan Studies programs.

4808. *Lituanus: the lithuanian quarterly journal of arts and sciences.* [ISSN: 0024-5089] 1954. q. USD 30 (Individuals, USD 20). Ed(s): Violeta Kelertas, Arvydas Tamulis. Lituanus Foundation, Inc., 47 W Polk St, Ste 100-300, Chicago, IL 60605. Illus., index. Sample. Refereed. Vol. ends: Winter (No. 4). Microform: PQC. *Indexed:* A22, ABS&EES, MLA-IB, P61, RILM, SSA. *Bk. rev.:* 3-4, 500-1,000 words, signed. *Aud.:* Ac, Sa.

This English language journal is "dedicated to Lithuanian and Baltic art, history, language, literature and related cultural topics." The focus is predominantly Lithuania, though articles on the other Baltic countries and East Central Europe are occasionally featured. The issues general include scholarly research articles as well as poetry, memoirs, essays, and book reviews. The publisher is working to make the back issues of the journal available online, with the full text of issues for 1954, 1963–66, and 1969–2010 currently available. Recommended for any academic and public library with readers interested in Lithuania and the other Baltic states. URL: www.lituanus.org

4809. Moscow News: international weekly. [ISSN: 0027-1306] 1930. s-w. USD 349 foreign. Ed(s): Tim Wall. Moskovskie Novosti, ul Zubovskii bul'var, dom 4, Moscow, 119021, Russian Federation; info@mn.ru. Illus., adv. Circ: 76000. Vol. ends: Jan. Microform: PQC. *Indexed:* BRI, P02. *Aud.:* Hs, Ga, Ac.

This is an English-language general interest newspaper published in Moscow, with some content from its recently relaunched sister Russian-language version, *Moskovskie novosti,* as well as original content. Its coverage includes local and national politics and contemporary events, business and finance, culture, sports, and opinions and editorials. While it is relatively small in its print run compared to other Moscow-based national newspapers, its main value to an American readership is a Russian perspective on current events. Many articles are available free online at the newspaper's site. Recommended for all libraries with patrons interested in international affairs. URL: http://themoscownews.com

4810. Nationalities Papers. [ISSN: 0090-5992] 1972. bi-m. GBP 838 (print & online eds.). Ed(s): Florian Bieber. Routledge, 4 Park Sq, Milton Park, Abingdon, OX14 4RN, United Kingdom; subscriptions@tandf.co.uk; http://www.tandfonline.com. Illus., adv. Sample. Refereed. Reprint: PSC. *Indexed:* A01, A22, ABS&EES, AmHI, E01, IBSS, MLA-IB, P61, RILM, SSA. *Bk. rev.:* 15-25, 500-800 words, signed. *Aud.:* Ac, Sa.

According to the publisher, this "is the leading journal on nationalism, ethnicity, ethnic conflict and national identity in Central Europe, the Balkans, the former Soviet Union, the Caucasus, the Turkic world and Central Eurasia. Furthermore, the journal also publishes contributions on theories of nationalism, comparative studies of nationalism, and trans- and supranational aspects of interethnic relations and national identity. The journal publishes timely, high[-]quality articles from a variety of disciplines, including history, political science, sociology, anthropology, and literature." As the journal of the Association for the Study of Nationalities, it brings "together scholars worldwide working on nationalism and ethnicity, Central and Eastern Europe, the Balkans and Eurasia." The book reviews are of high quality and can assist collection development librarians with selection. Recommended highly for academic and research libraries with programs in Slavic as well as European Studies programs, and also for all libraries where patrons may have an interest in the minorities of the former Soviet space and East Central Europe.

4811. Polish Review. [ISSN: 0032-2970] 1956. q. USD 134 (print & online eds.). Ed(s): Timothy Kearney. University of Illinois Press, English Department, UH 2027 MC 162, University of Illinois at Chicago, Chicago, IL 60607. Illus., index. Refereed. Vol. ends: Dec (No. 4). Microform: PQC. *Indexed:* A22, ABS&EES, AmHI, MLA-IB, RILM. *Bk. rev.:* 4-5, 300-1,000 words, signed. *Aud.:* Ac, Sa.

According to the editors, this publication is a "peer-edited scholarly quarterly, published without pause since 1956 by the Polish Institute of Arts and Sciences of America." The journal publishes "scholarly articles dealing with all aspects of Polish culture, as well as, on occasion, translations of important Polish literature." Articles encompass Polish arts, linguistics, history, sociology, ethnography, and Polish Americana. For collection development librarians, the book reviews, lists of books received, and review articles will be of value. Recommended for academic and research libraries that support Slavic Studies programs, and also for those public libraries with readers interested in Polish history and culture.

4812. Post-Communist Economies. Former titles (until 1999): *Communist Economies and Economic Transformation;* (until 1991): *Communist Economies.* [ISSN: 1463-1377] 1989. q. GBP 758 (print & online eds.). Ed(s): Roger Clarke. Routledge, 4 Park Sq, Milton Park, Abingdon, OX14 4RN, United Kingdom; subscriptions@tandf.co.uk; http://www.tandfonline.com. Illus., adv. Sample. Refereed. Reprint: PSC. *Indexed:* A22, ABIn, B01, BAS, E01, EconLit, IBSS, JEL. *Aud.:* Ac, Sa.

This journal "publishes key research and policy articles in the analysis of post-communist economies. The basic transformation in the past two decades through stabilization, liberalization[,] and privatization has been completed in virtually all of the former communist countries, but despite the dramatic changes that have taken place, the post-communist economies still form a clearly identifiable group, distinguished by the impact of the years of communist rule. Post-communist economies still present distinctive problems that make them a particular focus of research. These countries' economies need further stabilization, liberalization[,] and privatization and have fundamental problems of low efficiency, productivity[,] and income. All still have some distance to go to match the long-established market economies[,] and more attention needs to be devoted to the microeconomic aspects of the post-communist countries' efforts to catch up with the much richer countries of the European Union." There are around eight articles in each issue, and the geographic and subject coverage ranges fairly evenly across the economies of all of the post-communist countries. A recent issue included a special section on "Labor Problems in Post-Communist Economies." Recommended highly for academic and research libraries with programs in Slavic or Central Asian Studies, as well as those with international economics programs.

4813. Post-Soviet Affairs. Formerly (until 1992): *Soviet Economy.* [ISSN: 1060-586X] 1985. 6x/yr. GBP 341 (print & online eds.). Ed(s): George W Breslauer. Bellwether Publishing, Ltd., 8640 Guilford Rd, #200, Columbia, MD 21046; info@bellpub.com; http://www.bellpub.com. Illus., index. Refereed. Vol. ends: Dec (No. 4). Reprint: PSC. *Indexed:* A01, A22, ABIn, ABS&EES, B01, BRI, EconLit, IBSS, JEL, P02, P61, SSA. *Aud.:* Ac, Sa.

This journal "features the work of prominent Western scholars on the republics of the former Soviet Union, providing exclusive, up-to-the-minute analyses of the state of the economy and society, progress toward economic and political reform, and linkages between political and social changes and economic developments." The editorial board of this journal features many prominent scholars in the field of Slavic Studies. The four or so articles in each issue are characterized by high standards of scholarship, with a focus, as the title implies, on the successor states of the former Soviet Union, and in particular on Russia. Recommended highly for any academic and research libraries with programs in Slavic Studies.

4814. Problems of Economic Transition. Formerly (until 1992): *Problems in Economics.* [ISSN: 1061-1991] 1958. m. USD 1644 (print & online eds.). Ed(s): Vladimir M Belenky. M.E. Sharpe, Inc., 80 Business Park Dr, Armonk, NY 10504; custserv@mesharpe.com; http://www.mesharpe.com. Illus., index, adv. Sample. Refereed. Vol. ends: Apr (No. 12). Reprint: PSC. *Indexed:* A22, ABIn, ABS&EES, B01, B02, E01, EconLit, IBSS, JEL. *Aud.:* Ac, Sa.

According to the publisher, this journal "enables English-language readers to follow the principal theoretical and policy issues that constitute the core of post-Soviet economic discourse in various regions of the former USSR. Coverage ranges from the most recent research papers, policy studies, and analytical reports to articles in leading professional journals. Topics covered on an ongoing basis include reform policy; natural resource economics; foreign economic relations and the impact of the global financial crisis on the transition economies; industrial reorganization; labor economics and social policy; and regional economic development." The articles include complete citations to the original publication and the name of translator. Aimed at specialists in psychology, this journal will be of particular interest those to scholars without Russian-language reading abilities. Each issue features a helpful introduction by the editor. Most articles are drawn from the most important Russian economic journals. Recommended for academic and research libraries that support programs in Slavic Studies as well as international economics.

4815. Problems of Post-Communism. Formerly (until Jan.1995): *Problems of Communism.* [ISSN: 1075-8216] 1951. bi-m. USD 378 (print & online eds.). Ed(s): Ann E Robertson, Robert T Huber. M.E. Sharpe, Inc., 80 Business Park Dr, Armonk, NY 10504; custserv@mesharpe.com; http://www.mesharpe.com. Illus., index, adv. Sample. Refereed. Vol. ends: Nov/Dec (No. 6). Microform: PQC. Reprint: PSC. *Indexed:* A01, A22, ABS&EES, BAS, BRI, E01, MLA-IB, P02, P61, SSA. *Aud.:* Ac, Sa.

This journal "features readable analysis, reliable information, and lively debate about the communist and post-communist world. Emphasis is placed on thoughtful but timely research on current economic, political, security, and international issues, as well as historical research that provides a relevant context for understanding current issues. This magazine seeks to serve as a forum for students of communist and post-communist affairs by publishing research of high quality written for a broad-based audience of researchers and policymakers in a compelling and interesting way. We also wish to provide materials for classroom use, as part of a commitment to educate the next generation of scholars in communist and post-communist studies." Each issue includes five or so articles focusing on current issues in the Soviet successor states and those in East Central Europe that were once part of the Soviet bloc. The topic of one recent special issue was "Ideas and Political Communication in the Service of Power in Russia and the Post-Soviet Space"; another revisited an issue of the journal from 20 years ago after the failed August 1991 coup that hastened the fall of the Soviet Union. Recommended for academic and research libraries, and also for large public libraries.

4816. Religion, State and Society. Formerly (until 1992): *Religion in Communist Lands.* [ISSN: 0963-7494] 1973. q. GBP 741 (print & online eds.). Ed(s): Dr. Philip Walters. Routledge, 4 Park Sq, Milton Park, Abingdon, OX14 4RN, United Kingdom; subscriptions@tandf.co.uk; http://www.tandfonline.com. Adv. Sample. Refereed. Microform: PQC. Reprint: PSC. *Indexed:* A01, A22, E01, IBSS, P61, R&TA, SSA. *Bk. rev.:* 3-5, 400-800 words, signed. *Aud.:* Ac, Sa.

According to the publisher, this journal "has a long-established reputation as the leading English-language academic publication focusing on communist and formerly communist countries throughout the world, and the legacy of the encounter between religion and communism." Coverage has since expanded "to include religious developments in countries which have not experienced communist rule, and to treat wider themes in a more systematic way. The journal encourages a comparative approach where appropriate, with the aim of revealing similarities and differences in the historical and current experience of countries, regions and religions, in stability or in transition. The journal will retain its interdisciplinary approach broadly based in the humanities, and continue to cover issues in communist and postcommunist countries, including Central Asia and China." Most issues include a selection of book reviews. Topics of recent special issues have included "Evangelical, Pentecostal and Charismatic Churches in Latin America and Eastern Europe" and "Muslim Young People in Britain and Russia: Intersections of Biography, Faith and History." Recommended for academic and research libraries with Slavic Studies or religious studies programs, and for larger public libraries with reader populations interested in the topic.

4817. Revolutionary Russia. Former titles (until 1988): *Sbornik;* (until 1975): *Study Group on the Russian Revolution. Newsletter.* [ISSN: 0954-6545] 19??. s-a. GBP 268 (print & online eds.). Ed(s): Aaron Retish, Sarah Badcock. Routledge, 4 Park Sq, Milton Park, Abingdon, OX14 4RN, United Kingdom; subscriptions@tandf.co.uk; http://www.tandfonline.com. Adv. Sample. Refereed. Reprint: PSC. *Indexed:* A22, ArtHuCI, E01, P61, SSA. *Bk. rev.:* 10-12, 800-1,000 words, signed. *Aud.:* Ac, Sa.

This is the journal of the Study Group on the Russian Revolution, and according to the publisher, it is "the only English-language journal to concentrate on the revolutionary period of Russian history, from c. 1880-c. 1932." The journal is "interdisciplinary and international in approach, publishing original research, documentary sources, book reviews and review articles in the fields of history, politics, economics, sociology, art history and literary and intellectual history from scholars across the world, including Russia and other countries of the former Soviet Union. Submissions to the editor are welcome from established, young, and independent scholars." Each issue includes three or four scholarly articles and a very high-quality book review section, of great interest both to scholars and for librarians working in collection development. Recommended highly for academic and research libraries with programs in Slavic Studies programs, or history at the advanced level.

4818. Russian Education and Society. Formerly (until 1992): *Soviet Education.* [ISSN: 1060-9393] 1958. m. USD 1620 (print & online eds.). Ed(s): Anthony Jones. M.E. Sharpe, Inc., 80 Business Park Dr, Armonk,

NY 10504; custserv@mesharpe.com; http://www.mesharpe.com. Illus., index, adv. Sample. Refereed. Vol. ends: Dec (No. 12). Reprint: PSC. *Indexed:* A01, A22, ABS&EES, E01, ERIC, FR, MLA-IB, RILM. *Aud.:* Ac, Sa.

This journal features selected "material for translation from the Russian-language professional literature on education and socialization. The materials surveyed cover preschool, primary, secondary, vocational, and higher education; curricula and methods; and socialization issues related to family life, ethnic and religious identity formation, youth culture, addiction[,] and other behavioral and health problems; professional training and employment. The scope of the journal extends beyond Russia proper to provide coverage of all the former Soviet states as well as international educational issues." Each issue includes five to eight articles, each with a complete citation to the original publication source, and the names of translators. Aimed at specialists in education, this journal will be of particular interest those to scholars without Russian-language reading abilities. Recommended for academic and research libraries that support Slavic Studies programs as well as advanced study in education.

4819. Russian History. [ISSN: 0094-288X] 1974. q. EUR 221. Ed(s): Lawrence N Langer. Brill, PO Box 9000, Leiden, 2300 PA, Netherlands; cs@brill.nl; http://www.brill.nl. Illus., index, adv. Sample. Refereed. Vol. ends: Winter (No. 4). Reprint: PSC. *Indexed:* A22, ABS&EES, ArtHuCI, E01, MLA-IB. *Bk. rev.:* 15-20, 500-1,000 words, signed. *Aud.:* Ac, Sa.

This scholarly journal's "mission is the publication of original articles on the history of Russia through the centuries, in the assumption that all past experiences are inter-related." The journal "seeks to discover, analyze, and understand the most interesting experiences and relationships and elucidate their causes and consequences. Contributors to the journal take their stand from different perspectives: intellectual, economic[,] and military history, domestic, social[,] and class relations, relations with non-Russian peoples, nutrition and health, all possible events that had an influence on Russia." Each issue contains a varying number of articles, generally written in English, and occasional review articles. One recent issue included a range of contributions on Russian monasticism; another special issue consisted of a single article by Richard Pipes on nine of the Itinerant group of Russian painters. The journal has an impressive list of prominent scholars on its editorial board. Highly recommended for academic and research libraries that support Slavic Studies programs or advanced study in history.

4820. Russian Life. Former titles (until 1993): *Soviet Life;* (until 1965): *U S S R;* Incorporates (1992-1995): *Russian Travel Monthly;* Which incorporated (19??-1977): *Soviet Panorama.* [ISSN: 1066-999X] 1956. bi-m. USD 36 domestic; USD 48 foreign; USD 9 per issue. Ed(s): Maria Antonova, Paul E Richardson. Russian Life, PO Box 567, Montpelier, VT 05601; sales@rispubs.com. Illus., adv. Sample. Circ: 15000 Paid. Vol. ends: Dec (No. 12). Microform: PQC. *Indexed:* A01, A22, ABIn, ABS&EES, BRI, ENW, P02. *Bk. rev.:* Number and length vary. *Aud.:* Ga, Ac.

Published bimonthly, this "is a colorful, insightful look at life as it is lived in Russia today. Featuring quality journalism, amazing photography[,] and a breadth and depth of coverage no other publication can match, *Russian Life* is a bimonthly trip into the heart of Russian reality, past and present." The editor also notes that the journal is "100 percent independent of the Russian government." Although geared toward the nonspecialist, this journal does an excellent job of providing an overview of current events, with an emphasis on culture. It also provides the Russian perspective on world events. Each issue is richly illustrated with color photographs and includes book reviews. The web site includes articles that are not found in the print edition. Highly recommended for all public, academic, and research libraries. URL: www.rispubs.com

4821. Russian Linguistics: international journal for the study of Russian and other Slavic languages. [ISSN: 0304-3487] 1974. 3x/yr. EUR 726 (print & online eds.). Ed(s): Ulrich Schweier, Roger Comtet. Springer Netherlands, Van Godewijckstraat 30, Dordrecht, 3311 GX, Netherlands; http://www.springer.com. Illus., index, adv. Sample. Refereed. Vol. ends: Nov (No. 3). Microform: PQC. Reprint: PSC. *Indexed:* A22, AmHI, ArtHuCI, BRI, E01, FR, LT&LA, MLA-IB. *Bk. rev.:* Varies, 800-1,500 words, signed. *Aud.:* Ac, Sa.

This journal "is an international forum for all scholars working in the field of Slavic linguistics (Russian and other Slavic languages) and its manifold diversity, ranging from phonetics and phonology to syntax and the linguistic analysis of texts (text grammar), including both diachronic and synchronic problems." The journal "publishes original articles and reviews as well as surveys of current scholarly writings from other periodicals." Coverage includes: "Traditional-structuralist as well as generative-transformational and other modern approaches to questions of synchronic and diachronic grammar; phonetics and phonology, morphology, syntax, pragmatics[,] and semantics of Russian and other Slavic languages (synchronic and diachronic); philological problems of Russian/Old-Russian texts as well as texts in other Slavic languages; grammar of Russian and other Slavic languages in their relation to linguistic universals; history of Russian and other Slavic literary languages; [and] Slavic dialectology." While highly specialized, this is a very high-quality journal and essential for those in the field. Articles are mostly in English with some in Russian. Book reviews are occasionally published. Recommended for academic and research libraries that support programs in Russian linguistics, language, and literature.

4822. *Russian Literature.* [ISSN: 0304-3479] 1973. 8x/yr. EUR 1281. Ed(s): W G Weststeijn. Elsevier BV, North-Holland, Postbus 211, Amsterdam, 1000 AE, Netherlands; JournalsCustomerServiceEMEA@elsevier.com; http://www.elsevier.com. Illus., index. Sample. Refereed. Vol. ends: No. 4 - No. 8. Microform: PQC. *Indexed:* A22, ArtHuCI, MLA-IB. *Aud.:* Ac, Sa.

This journal "combines issues devoted to special topics of Russian literature with contributions on related subjects in Croatian, Serbian, Czech, Slovak and Polish literatures. Moreover, several issues each year contain articles on heterogeneous subjects concerning Russian literature. All methods and viewpoints are welcomed, provided they contribute something new, original or challenging to our understanding of Russian and other Slavic literatures." The journal "regularly publishes special issues devoted to: the historical avant-garde in Russian literature and in the other Slavic literatures; [and] the development of descriptive and theoretical poetics in Russian studies and in studies of other Slavic fields." Most articles in this high-quality, rather specialized journal are published in Russian, and quotations often appear in the vernacular language, even when the main text is in English. Recent thematic issues have looked at "Sources, Practice and Significance" of the Russian avant-garde, and at literary relationships between Finland and Russia. Recommended for academic and research libraries that support Russian language and literature programs.

4823. *Russian Politics and Law.* Formerly (until 1992): *Soviet Law and Government.* [ISSN: 1061-1940] 1962. bi-m. USD 1545 (print & online eds.). Ed(s): Dmitry P Gorenburg. M.E. Sharpe, Inc., 80 Business Park Dr, Armonk, NY 10504; custserv@mesharpe.com; http://www.mesharpe.com. Illus., index, adv. Sample. Refereed. Vol. ends: Nov/Dec (No. 6). Microform: WSH; PMC. Reprint: PSC. *Indexed:* A01, A22, ABS&EES, CLI, E01, IBSS, L14, P61, SSA. *Aud.:* Ac, Sa.

This journal "publishes thematic issues featuring translations of some of the most important political science articles by authors working in the Soviet successor states. Selections are drawn from both print and electronic sources, as well as from previously unpublished work. The materials selected include both articles examining the politics of the region and theoretical works of interest to the field as a whole. Each issue includes a substantive introduction to the theme by the chief editor or a guest editor who is an expert on the issue's theme." As with the other M.E. Sharpe journals of translation, full citations to the original publication source are given, and so are the original end notes and the name of the translator. Scholars in the fields covered who do not have reading knowledge of Russian will find this a very useful source. Recommended for academic and research libraries with programs in Slavic Studies, international politics, and international law.

4824. *The Russian Review: an American quarterly devoted to Russia past and present.* [ISSN: 0036-0341] 1941. q. GBP 215. Ed(s): Eve Levin. Wiley-Blackwell Publishing, Inc., 111 River St, Hoboken, NJ 07030; info@wiley.com; http://onlinelibrary.wiley.com/. Illus., index, adv. Sample. Refereed. Vol. ends: Oct (No. 4). Microform: PQC. Reprint: PSC. *Indexed:* A01, A22, ABS&EES, AmHI, ArtHuCI, BRI, CBRI, E01, IBSS, MLA-IB, P02, P61, RILM, SSA. *Bk. rev.:* 25-40, 300-1,000 words, signed. *Aud.:* Ac, Sa.

The editors of this venerable journal describe its mission as "the presentation of a broad panorama of the Russian scene, both past and present." It contains "articles and book reviews on a variety of aspects of Russia's history, literature, culture, film, fine arts, society, and politics." The journal's scope "includes not only the Russian nationality, but all the peoples of the Russian Empire, Soviet Union, and contemporary Russian Federation. Topics of particular interest at this time include nationality policy, civil society, identity, gender, religion, modern literature and literary figures, and cultural studies." Scholars and collection development librarians will find the extensive book review sections essential for keeping up with a broad range of current scholarship. The lists within the publications received section are also valuable for librarians. Recommended highly as an essential title for any academic or research library with a program in Slavic Studies, and it will also be of interest to larger public libraries with interested user populations.

4825. *Russian Social Science Review.* Formerly (until 1992): *Soviet Review;* Which superseded (in 1960): *Soviet Highlights.* [ISSN: 1061-1428] 1959. bi-m. USD 432 (print & online eds.). Ed(s): Patricia A Kolb. M.E. Sharpe, Inc., 80 Business Park Dr, Armonk, NY 10504; custserv@mesharpe.com; http://www.mesharpe.com. Illus., index, adv. Sample. Refereed. Vol. ends: Nov/Dec (No. 6). Microform: PQC. Reprint: PSC. *Indexed:* A01, A22, ABIn, ABS&EES, BRI, E01, MLA-IB, P02, P61, SSA. *Aud.:* Ac, Sa.

This journal "publishes interdisciplinary thematic issues compiled from M.E. Sharpe's translation series. The articles selected are drawn from a cross-section of Russian-language scholarly publications," including the core journals in economics, history, philosophy, psychology, literature, political science, and sociology, among others in the social sciences. "Recurrent themes include youth culture, women's studies, political trends, national and religious identity, public opinion, and social issues of all kinds." Full citations to the original publication source are given, as are the original end notes and the name of the translator. Scholars in the fields reflected here who do not have reading knowledge of Russian will find it a worthwhile source. Recent issues have examined "Cultural Trends and Values," "Russia's Special Path," and "Youthful Ambitions," about prospects and challenges for the youth in Russia. Recommended for academic and research libraries, and also for larger public libraries with readers interested in Russian scholarly advances in the broad topical coverage.

4826. *Russian Studies in History.* Formerly (until 1992): *Soviet Studies in History.* [ISSN: 1061-1983] 1962. q. USD 1102 (print & online eds.). Ed(s): Christine Ruane, Joseph Bradley. M.E. Sharpe, Inc., 80 Business Park Dr, Armonk, NY 10504; custserv@mesharpe.com; http://www.mesharpe.com. Illus., index, adv. Sample. Refereed. Vol. ends: Spring (No. 4). Reprint: PSC. *Indexed:* A01, A22, ABS&EES, BAS, E01. *Aud.:* Ac, Sa.

This journal "publishes thematic issues featuring translations of scholarly articles selected from diverse Russian sources and introduced by an expert guest editor. Issue topics range over all periods and subfields of Russian and Soviet history[,] as well as more general theoretical and historiographical questions of interest to historians of many specialties." Articles are drawn from the major historical journals, and include the footnotes from the original article and well as complete citations to the original publication. Translators' names are also given. This journal would be of use for students and scholars who do not have a reading knowledge of Russian, and for any historian with even a passing interest in Russia. Recent thematic issues on Tsar Nicholas II and the Khrushchev period contain many insights that would otherwise remain hidden to non-specialist readers. Recommended for all academic and research libraries with programs in Russian and international history.

4827. *Russian Studies in Literature.* Formerly (until 1992): *Soviet Studies in Literature.* [ISSN: 1061-1975] 1964. q. USD 1102 (print & online eds.). Ed(s): John Givens. M.E. Sharpe, Inc., 80 Business Park Dr, Armonk, NY 10504; custserv@mesharpe.com; http://www.mesharpe.com. Illus., index, adv. Sample. Refereed. Vol. ends: Fall (No. 4). Reprint: PSC. *Indexed:* A01, A22, ABS&EES, AmHI, ArtHuCI, BRI, E01, MLA-IB. *Aud.:* Ac, Sa.

This journal "publishes high-quality, annotated translations of Russian literary criticism and scholarship on contemporary works and popular cultural topics as well as the classics. Selections are drawn from the leading literary periodicals," and an "editorial introduction to every issue provides context and insight that will be helpful for English-language readers." Articles include all the footnotes in the original article, as well as complete citations to the original publication source. Translators' names are also given. This journal would be of value to students and scholars without reading knowledge of Russian. Recent thematic issues on "Russian Literature in the First Decade of the Twenty-First Century" and current views and scholarship on Pasternak's *Doctor Zhivago* would be of interest to a broad, non-specialist readership. Recommended for academic and research libraries that support comparative literature programs.

4828. Russian Studies in Philosophy. Formerly (until 1992): *Soviet Studies in Philosophy.* [ISSN: 1061-1967] 1962. q. USD 988 (print & online eds.). Ed(s): Marina F Bykova. M.E. Sharpe, Inc., 80 Business Park Dr, Armonk, NY 10504; custserv@mesharpe.com; http://www.mesharpe.com. Illus., index, adv. Sample. Refereed. Vol. ends: Spring (No. 4). Reprint: PSC. *Indexed:* A01, A22, ABS&EES, AmHI, ArtHuCI, E01, FR, MLA-IB. *Aud.:* Ac, Sa.

This journal "publishes thematic issues featuring selected scholarly papers from conferences and joint research projects as well as from the leading Russian-language journals in philosophy. Thematic coverage ranges over significant theoretical topics as well as topics in the history of philosophy, both European and Russian, including issues focused on institutions, schools, and figures such as Bakhtin, Fedorov, Il'enkov, Leont'ev, Losev, Mamardashvili, Rozanov, Solov'ev, and Zino'yev." Articles include all the footnotes in the original article, as well as complete citations to the original publication source. Translators' names are also given. Besides articles, the journal sometimes includes translated book excerpts. This journal would be of value to students and scholars without reading knowledge of Russian. One recent issue featured conference papers that deal with philosophical content and messages in the works of Dostoevsky, surely an area with broad potential interest. Another looked at philosophical issues in the works of Tolstoy and Chekhov. Recommended for any academic and research libraries that support programs in philosophy.

4829. Sarmatian Review. Formerly (until 1988): *The Houston Sarmatian.* [ISSN: 1059-5872] 1981. 3x/yr. USD 28 (Individuals, USD 21). Ed(s): Ewa M Thompson. Polish Institute of Houston, PO Box 79119, Houston, TX 77279. Illus. Refereed. *Indexed:* ABS&EES, AmHI, BRI, P61, SSA. *Bk. rev.:* Number and length vary. *Aud.:* Ac.

This "is a scholarly journal on the history, culture, and society of Central and Eastern Europe, with strong attention to Poland, the post-Soviet period, and American ethnic issues. Recent issues have covered religion and state, the mass media, higher education, literature, inter-ethnic relations, government and politics." The journal's editors write that they also "specialize in the translation of documents." Issues often include works of poetry as well. The book reviews and lists of books received may be useful for collection development librarians. Also, "an abbreviated web edition appears six to ten weeks after the print edition." The journal's web site includes an archive of issues back to April 1992. Recommended for academic and public libraries with interested user populations. URL: www.ruf.rice.edu/~sarmatia

4830. Slavic & East European Information Resources. [ISSN: 1522-8886] 2000. q. GBP 257 (print & online eds.). Ed(s): Karen Rondestvedt. Routledge, 325 Chestnut St, Ste 800, Philadelphia, PA 19106; customerservice@taylorandfrancis.com; http://www.tandfonline.com. Illus., adv. Sample. Refereed. Reprint: PSC. *Indexed:* A01, A22, ABS&EES, E01, ISTA. *Bk. rev.:* 10-14; 300-1,200 words; signed. *Aud.:* Ac, Sa.

This journal's central purpose "is to serve as a focal point for the international exchange of information in the field of Slavic librarianship. Information includes news of the profession, technical developments, reviews of the literature, original research, indeed everything that touches on the practice of Slavic librarianship in North America, the countries covered[,] and elsewhere in the world." In addition to featured articles there are book reviews, an Internet column, a section called "In Our Libraries," and occasional columns by vendors of Slavic material. Double issues, often thematic, delve into specific topics. The emphasis is on "the current, concrete[,] and practical sides of Slavic librarianship." While the journal's primary audience is professional librarians

with responsibilities for Slavic collections, it is has substantial, and overlooked, potential value for scholars working in the various Slavic Studies disciplines. Recommended highly for academic and research libraries with the relevant kinds of collections.

4831. Slavic and East European Journal. Former titles (until 1957): *A A T S E E L Journal;* (until 1954): *American Association of Teachers of Slavic and East European Languages. Bulletin;* (until 1947): *American Association of Teachers of Slavonic and East European Languages. Bulletin;* (until 1945): *American Association of Teachers of Slavic and East European Languages. News Bulletin.* [ISSN: 0037-6752] 1943. q. USD 80 Free to members. Ed(s): Gerald Janecek. American Association of Teachers of Slavic and East European Languages, c/o Patricia L. Zody, PO Box 569, Beloit, WI 53512; aatseel@sbcglobal.net; http://www.aatseel.org. Illus., index, adv. Refereed. Vol. ends: No. 4. Microform: PQC. *Indexed:* A01, A07, A22, ABS&EES, AmHI, ArtHuCI, BRI, FR, LT&LA, MLA-IB, P02, RILM. *Bk. rev.:* 25-30, 250-500 words, signed. *Aud.:* Ac, Sa.

This journal "publishes research studies in all areas of Slavic languages, literatures, and cultures. Papers on non-Slavic East European subjects of interest to Slavicists may also be considered." The journal is published quarterly by the American Association of Teachers of Slavic and East European Languages, or AATSEEL. "Pedagogical articles report the results of serious research, experimentation, and evaluation." The scope does not include "original fiction or translations of literary works." Articles are well documented and of consistently high quality. The occasional review articles, a first-rate selection of book reviews, and lists of publications received will be useful to scholars and librarians alike. Recommended highly as essential for academic and research libraries that support Slavic Studies programs.

4832. Slavic Review: American quarterly of Russian, Eurasian and East European studies. Former titles (until 1961): *American Slavic and East European Review;* (until 1945): *Slavonic and East European Review. American Series;* (until 1943): *Slavonic Year-Book. American Series;* (until 1940): *The Slavonic and East European Review;* (until 1928): *The Slavonic Review;* (until 1922): *Anglo-Russian Literary Society. Proceedings.* [ISSN: 0037-6779] 1893. q. USD 245 (print & online eds.). Ed(s): Jane T Hedges, Mark D Steinberg. American Association for the Advancement of Slavic Studies, University of Illinois at Urbana-Champaign, 57 E Armory Ave, Champaign, IL 61820; aaass@fas.harvard.edu; http://www.fas.harvard.edu/~aaass. Illus., index, adv. Refereed. Circ: 5000. Vol. ends: Winter (No. 4). *Indexed:* A01, A22, ABS&EES, AmHI, ArtHuCI, BRI, CBRI, IBSS, MLA-IB, P02, P61, RILM, SSA. *Bk. rev.:* 55-60, 300-1,000 words, signed. *Aud.:* Ac, Sa.

This is the membership journal of the Association for Slavic, East European, and Eurasian Studies, or ASEEES (known for many years as AAASS). One of the leading journals in the field, it is "an international interdisciplinary journal devoted to the study of eastern Europe, Russia, the Caucasus, and Central Asia, past and present. The journal publishes articles of original and significant research and interpretation, reviews of scholarly books and films, and topical review essays and discussion forums. Submissions from all disciplines and perspectives are welcomed. A primary purpose of the journal is to encourage dialogue among different scholarly approaches." Articles are, without exception, of the highest quality of scholarship and documentation. The extensive book reviews and lists of publications received by the journal are essential for collection development librarians, and are highly valuable for scholars as well. A special feature of particular interest is the thematically divided annual list of all dissertations in Slavic Studies granted by U.S. institutions. Recommended highly as essential for academic and research libraries, as well as larger public libraries with any degree of interest in Slavic Studies.

4833. Slavonic and East European Review. [ISSN: 0037-6795] 1922. q. USD 403 (print & online eds.). Modern Humanities Research Association, 1 Carlton House Terrace, London, SW1Y 5AF, United Kingdom; mail@mhra.org.uk; http://www.mhra.org.uk. Illus., index. Refereed. Circ: 1000. Vol. ends: Oct (No. 4). Reprint: PSC. *Indexed:* A01, A22, AmHI, ArtHuCI, BRI, FR, IBSS, LT&LA, MLA-IB, P02, P61. *Bk. rev.:* 50-60, 300-750 words, signed. *Aud.:* Ac, Sa.

This is the journal of the School of Slavonic and East European Studies, University College London, and is published by the Modern Humanities Research Association. In existence since 1928, it is one of the premier journals in Slavic Studies, publishing "scholarly articles on all subjects related to Russia, Central and Eastern Europe—languages [and] linguistics, literature, art, cinema, theatre, music, history, politics, social sciences, economics, [and] anthropology—as well as reviews of new books in the field." The lists of publications received will also be of use to both scholars and librarians in collection development. Recommended highly for all academic and research libraries, and for larger public libraries with even a passing interest in Slavic Studies.

4834. *Social Sciences: a quarterly journal of the Russian Academy of Sciences.* [ISSN: 0134-5486] 1970. q. USD 435. East View Information Services, 10601 Wayzata Blvd, Minneapolis, MN 55305; info@eastview.com; http://www.eastview.com/. Index. Refereed. Circ: 130 Paid. *Indexed:* A01, A22, ABIn, ABS&EES, EIP, EconLit, IBSS, JEL, P02, P61, SSA. *Bk. rev.:* 3-5, 100-1,000 words, signed. *Aud.:* Ac, Sa.

This journal "presents the most prominent papers and studies appearing in more than 30 journals of the Russian Academy of Sciences. Covering the most pressing issues of Russia's social and economic development," the journal "includes articles on philosophy, history, economics, politics, sociology, law, philology, psychology, ethnography, archeology, literature and culture." In addition to book reviews grouped by discipline, it also prints listings of the contents from many other periodicals of the Russian Academy of Sciences. Articles indicate the original publication source along with short biographical information on the author. Names of translators are given following the end notes. Scholars and students without a reading knowledge of Russian will find this a valuable title. Recommended for academic and research libraries.

4835. *Sociological Research.* Formerly (until 1992): *Soviet Sociology.* [ISSN: 1061-0154] 1962. bi-m. USD 1458 (print & online eds.). Ed(s): Paul Hodkinson, Rachel Brooks. University of Surrey, Bookshop, University Of Surrey, Guildford, GU2 5XH, United Kingdom. Illus., index, adv. Sample. Refereed. Vol. ends: Nov/Dec (No. 6). Reprint: PSC. *Indexed:* A01, A22, ABS&EES, B01, E01, FR, P61. *Aud.:* Ac, Sa.

This journal "features unabridged translations of articles that have been selected to reflect trends in the sociological literature and to be of value to researchers interested in the region and the study of societies in transition. Materials are drawn from the major Russian-language scholarly journals," as well as from "other relevant sources." Topical coverage is broad, encompassing a range of areas in sociology, and articles are well chosen. Each article includes a complete citation to the original publication and the end notes from the original article, and specifies the name of the translator. For scholars without reading knowledge of Russian, this journal will hold particular interest, but it is of value to a range of scholars working in the field. Recommended for academic and research libraries that support programs in sociology and Slavic Studies.

4836. *Statutes and Decisions: The Laws of the U S S R & Its Successor States.* Formerly (until 1992): *Soviet Statutes and Decisions.* [ISSN: 1061-0014] 1964. bi-m. USD 1590 (print & online eds.). Ed(s): Alexei Trochev. M.E. Sharpe, Inc., 80 Business Park Dr, Armonk, NY 10504; custserv@mesharpe.com; http://www.mesharpe.com. Illus., index, adv. Sample. Refereed. Microform: WSH; PMC. Reprint: PSC. *Indexed:* A01, A22, CLI, E01. *Aud.:* Ac, Sa.

This journal aims to document "the evolving legal regimes of the post-Soviet states." It "publishes thematic series providing comprehensive coverage of a body of law, or of legal or judicial practice, in high-quality translations with expert introductions." The topics of recent series have included police reform in Russia, the Ukrainian Constitutional Court, and Ukrainian judges. Earlier volumes have featured series on the Russian Federation Law on Extremist Activity; professional ethics for attorneys in Russia; legal regulation of NGOs; the Code of the Russian Federation on Administrative Violations; the Procuracy; local government; and antiterrorism legislation in the CIS. The materials chosen are of interest to those scholars and students engaged with "the laws and court decisions of the Russian Federation" at a serious level; for them, it will be highly useful, even indispensable. For those without reading knowledge of Russian who wish to study these areas, it will also be of great

value, despite the specialized and at times technical nature of its contents. Recommended primarily for law libraries, especially those with a comparative international law program, as well as academic and research libraries that support programs in Slavic Studies.

4837. *Studies in East European Thought.* Formerly (until 1992): *Studies in Soviet Thought.* [ISSN: 0925-9392] 1961. q. EUR 548 (print & online eds.). Ed(s): Edward M Swiderski. Springer Netherlands, Van Godewijckstraat 30, Dordrecht, 3311 GX, Netherlands; http://www.springer.com. Illus., index, adv. Sample. Refereed. Vol. ends: Dec (No. 4). Microform: PQC. Reprint: PSC. *Indexed:* A01, A22, ABS&EES, AmHI, ArtHuCI, BAS, BRI, E01, IBSS, IPB, P02, P61, SSA. *Bk. rev.:* Varies, 500-2,000 words, signed. *Aud.:* Ac, Sa.

This journal "provides a forum for Western-language writings on philosophy and philosophers who identify with the history and cultures of East and Central Europe, including Russia, Ukraine, and the Baltic States. The contents include descriptive, critical, comparative, and historical studies of individuals, schools, currents, and institutions whose work and influence are widely regarded in their own environments to be philosophical or provide insight into the socio-cultural conditions of philosophical life in Eastern Europe," says the publisher. Coverage ranges widely, including "concepts of the social, the cultural and the political, following the demise of Marxism-Leninism; foundational questions in metaphysics and epistemology; the standing of 'culture theory' (i.e., Russian 'kul'turologiia'); the reception of Western theories and methods as well as intellectual traditions; the reassessment of 'local' intellectual traditions; ethics, moral theory, theology[,] and religious studies, and much more." The articles are mostly in English but occasionally in German. Issues are often thematic; recent ones have examined the "Origins of Social Theories of Knowledge," and the Polish writer and philosopher Stanislaw Brzozowski. Recommended for academic and research libraries that support programs in Slavic Studies and advanced work in philosophy.

4838. *Transitions Online.* [ISSN: 1214-1615] 1999. m. updated daily. USD 217 public libraries (Individuals, USD 48). Ed(s): Jeremy Druker. Transitions Online, Baranova 33, Prague, 13000, Czech Republic. *Indexed:* A01. *Bk. rev.:* Number and length vary. *Aud.:* Ga, Ac.

This online magazine and web resource "covers political, social, cultural, and economic issues in the former communist countries of Europe and Central Asia," with a "strong network of local contributors, who provide valuable insight into events in the region's 29 countries." The editors say they are "interested in illustrating underlying issues and the process of change in the countries and regions that we cover." The intended audience is "well-informed and intelligent" readers who are not specialists in the field. Besides country-specific pages and country reports, the web site has sections covering: arts and culture; books; conflict and diplomacy; economy and business; education; environment; media; opinion; people; politics; and society. Access to the full online contents, as well as the back file of the current magazine and its predecessors, is by subscription. Articles are also available through Factiva, Academic Search Premier, and Central and Eastern European Online Library (or CEEOL). Recommended for all libraries with patrons interested in the current events and political developments in the countries of the former Soviet bloc. URL: www.tol.org

■ SOCIAL MEDIA

Rebecca S. Feind, Associate Librarian, San Jose State University, One Washington Square, San Jose, CA 95112

Introduction

Social media is a phrase used for communication technology platforms, such as Twitter and Facebook, as well as types of activities, like blogging and commenting. A defining attribute of social media is individual engagement with online communities, but the quality of engagement ranges from the ridiculous to the politically powerful. This section describes two types of publications, academic journals that focus on or include discussion of social media and emphasize theoretical analysis of its use, and a business-oriented publication that offers advice and best practices to companies and organizations.

While some existing communications and media studies journals have broadened their scope to include information communication technologies, new journals to specifically study the emergence of social media on mobile devices have also been created. As many organizations, including libraries, struggle to keep up with the raft of social media applications as well as the implications for engaging in large-scale, unscripted dialogue, a welcome new publication for libraries to acquire is *The Social Media Monthly*.

Basic Periodicals

Ac: *Information, Communication and Society; Journal of Computer-Mediated Communication; New Media & Society; The Social Media Monthly.*

Basic Abstracts and Indexes

Academic Search Premier, Communication Abstracts, Communication & Mass Media Complete.

4839. Continuum: journal of media and cultural studies. [ISSN: 1030-4312] 1987. bi-m. GBP 764 (print & online eds.). Ed(s): Panizza Allmark, Gregory Noble. Routledge, Level 2, 11 Queens Rd, Melbourne, VIC 3004, Australia; enquiries@tandf.com.au; http://www.routledge.com. Adv. Sample. Refereed. Reprint: PSC. *Indexed:* A01, A22, ArtHuCI, E01, F01, IBSS, IIFP, IIMP, MLA-IB. *Aud.:* Ac.

Continuum is affiliated with the Cultural Studies Association of Australasia, and provides readers with insight into how social media is being used and viewed from a global perspective. Articles range from case studies of specific platforms in a particular country to theoretical discussions on the role of individual voices in virtual participation. Articles on social media are included as part of the journal's study of media and culture, examining social media uses as part of journalistic patterns. For libraries that support cross-cultural studies, this journal is an important resource.

4840. Convergence: the international journal of research into new media technologies. [ISSN: 1354-8565] 1995. q. USD 704. Ed(s): Alexis Weedon, Julia Knight. Sage Publications Ltd., 1 Oliver's Yard, 55 City Rd, London, EC1Y 1SP, United Kingdom; info@sagepub.co.uk; http://www.uk.sagepub.com. Adv. Sample. Refereed. Reprint: PSC. *Indexed:* A22, E01, F01, RiskAb. *Bk. rev.:* Number and length vary. *Aud.:* Ac.

The research agenda of *Convergence* makes this journal an important publication in the area of social media. It publishes the results of studies by researchers on social media platforms and activities. While it covers a wide range of media technologies, mobile social media are frequently discussed in this quarterly.

4841. Information, Communication and Society. [ISSN: 1369-118X] 1998. 8x/yr. GBP 907 (print & online eds.). Ed(s): William H Dutton, Brian D Loader. Routledge, 4 Park Sq, Milton Park, Abingdon, OX14 4RN, United Kingdom; subscriptions@tandf.co.uk; http://www.tandfonline.com. Adv. Sample. Refereed. Reprint: PSC. *Indexed:* A01, A22, B01, CompLI, E01, IBSS, P61, PsycInfo, RiskAb, SSA. *Aud.:* Ac.

Social media continues to be part of the journal's scope, with a 2011 Special Issue titled "Networking Democracy?: Social media innovations and participatory politics," and a 2013 Special Issue titled, "Social Media and Election Campaigns: Key Tendencies and Ways Forward." Libraries that support programs that study political communication will find this a valuable resource for its global perspective.

4842. Media, Culture & Society. [ISSN: 0163-4437] 1979. 8x/yr. USD 1939. Sage Publications Ltd., 1 Oliver's Yard, 55 City Rd, London, EC1Y 1SP, United Kingdom; info@sagepub.co.uk; http://www.uk.sagepub.com. Illus. Sample. Refereed. Reprint: PSC. *Indexed:* A01, A22, BRI, E01, F01, IBSS, IIFP, MLA-IB, P02, P61, SSA. *Bk. rev.:* Number and length vary. *Aud.:* Ac.

Media, Culture & Society examines information communication technologies from social-science perspectives. Through in-depth research articles and scholarly commentaries, this journal contextualizes investigations into identity, political agency, and language use manifested in social media platforms and larger media systems. This journal is useful for journalism and mass media studies, as well as broader history and sociology programs.

4843. New Media & Society. [ISSN: 1461-4448] 1999. 8x/yr. USD 2179. Ed(s): Steve Jones, Nicholas Jankowski. Sage Publications Ltd., 1 Oliver's Yard, 55 City Rd, London, EC1Y 1SP, United Kingdom; info@sagepub.co.uk; http://www.uk.sagepub.com. Sample. Refereed. Reprint: PSC. *Indexed:* A01, A22, E01, F01, IBSS, MLA-IB, P61, PsycInfo, RiskAb. *Bk. rev.:* Number and length vary. *Aud.:* Ac.

This journal takes a multidisciplinary approach to its discussion of "global and local dimensions of the relationship between media and social change." It provides in-depth research articles on how people around the world negotiate with, view, and engage in information communication technologies; in particular, it frequently covers social media. Recent special-issue themes include "The state of online campaigning in politics" in February 2013 and "Scholarly publishing and the Internet" in May 2013.

4844. The Social Media Monthly. [ISSN: 2161-847X] 2011. m. USD 34.99 combined subscription (print & online eds.). Ed(s): Robert Fine. Cool Blue Company, LLC, 2100 M St, NW, Ste 170-242, Washington, DC 20037. Adv. *Aud.:* Sa.

Focusing on the strengths and weakness of social media platforms, *The Social Media Monthly* aims to advise businesses, consumers, and organizations on ways to effectively use these tools for increased productivity as well as communications. Articles range from case studies on successful social media programs to legal issues surrounding terms-of-service language and endorsements. The tone of this magazine is upbeat and informative, useful for making sense of the latest buzzwords like "crowdfunding" and "collaborative consumption." This magazine offers practical advice for individuals and organizations looking to stay on top of best practices for using social media.

■ SOCIOLOGY AND SOCIAL WORK

General/Social Work and Social Welfare

See also Criminology and Law Enforcement; Cultural Studies; Ethnic Studies; Family; Law; Marriage and Divorce; and Population Studies sections.

Kathleen D. Rickert, Reference and Instructional Librarian, St. Catherine University, St. Paul, MN 55105

Introduction

The disciplines of sociology and social work are highly interconnected, and therefore the journals for them are treated together in this volume. Consider the definitions of each field: *sociology* may be defined as the study of relationships between individuals and groups, organizations, cultures, society, and others individuals. It is a science that uses a methodological approach to study and explore these relationships and processes, both in historical and postmodern contexts. *Social work,* on the other hand, is a profession dedicated to advancing individual and societal well-being. The scholarship in this field exists to support and inform professional practice, including clinical practice, management, and policymaking.

The journals listed in this section cross interdisciplinary lines, drawing from (and complementing) fields in the social sciences such as anthropology, political science, economics, psychology, and public administration, and well as religion, history, and law.

In preparing this section, each journal's web site and the contents of several recent issues of each title were thoroughly examined. While several essential or "must-have" titles are noted, each library must decide what to carry in consideration of its own budgets, holdings, and research needs (or gaps). An effective way to increase the quantity and quality of a library's holdings in times of flat budgets may be to add open-access (read *free*) journals. Most of them, as noted in this section, are refereed and indexed in major databases.

Basic Periodicals

GENERAL. Ga: *Annual Review of Sociology, Journal of Social Issues, Social Forces, Social Policy, Social Problems;* Ac: *American Journal of Sociology, American Sociological Review, Annual Review of Sociology, British Journal of Sociology, Current Sociology, International Sociology, Journal of Social Issues, Sex Roles, Social Forces, Social Policy, Social Problems, Social Psychology Quarterly, Social Research, Society, The Sociological Review, Sociology.*

SOCIAL WORK AND SOCIAL WELFARE. Ga: *Child Welfare, Children & Schools;* Ac: *Advances in Social Work, The British Journal of Social Work, Child Welfare, Children & Schools, Children and Youth Services Review, Clinical Social Work Journal, Families in Society, International Social Work, Research on Social Work Practice, Social Service Review, Social Work, Social Work with Groups.*

Basic Abstracts and Indexes

ASSIA: Applied Social Sciences Index and Abstracts, Social Sciences Abstracts, Social Sciences Citation Index, Social Sciences Index, Social Services Abstracts, Social Work Abstracts, Sociological Abstracts.

General

4845. *Acta Sociologica.* [ISSN: 0001-6993] 1955. q. USD 558. Ed(s): Lise Kjolsrod, Arne Mastekaasa. Sage Publications Ltd., 1 Oliver's Yard, 55 City Rd, London, EC1Y 1SP, United Kingdom; info@sagepub.co.uk; http://www.uk.sagepub.com. Illus., index, adv. Sample. Refereed. Microform: SWZ; PQC. Reprint: PSC. *Indexed:* A01, A22, B01, BRI, E01, FR, IBSS, MLA-IB, P02, P61, PsycInfo, RILM, RiskAb, SSA. *Bk. rev.:* 0-5, signed. *Aud.:* Ac.

Acta Sociologica, as the official journal of the Nordic Sociological Association, publishes theoretical and empirical papers on a wide range of sociological and cultural studies issues. Although this journal is published in English, the majority of authors are from Scandinavian and other European countries. Content includes full-length articles, review articles, commentaries, and signed book reviews. The 2011 Journal Impact Factor was 1.135; the 2011 ISI Journal Citation Reports ranked it 42 out of 138 in Sociology. Recommended for support of upper-division, graduate, and international sociological research.

Amerasia Journal. See Asian American section.

4846. *American Journal of Sociology.* [ISSN: 0002-9602] 1895. bi-m. USD 488 (print & online eds.). Ed(s): Susan Allan, Andrew Abbott. University of Chicago Press, 1427 E 60th St, Chicago, IL 60637; subscriptions@press.uchicago.edu; http://www.journals.uchicago.edu. Illus., index, adv. Sample. Refereed. Vol. ends: May. Microform: PQC. Reprint: PSC. *Indexed:* A01, A22, A47, ABIn, ABS&EES, AbAn, B01, BAS, BRI, CBRI, CJPI, Chicano, F01, FR, IBSS, MLA-IB, P02, P61, PsycInfo, RILM, SSA, SWR&A. *Bk. rev.:* 20-40, signed. *Aud.:* Ga, Ac, Sa.

AJS was established in 1895 and was the first scholarly sociological journal. Published by the University of Chicago Press, it stands as the core title in the field. The journal boasts cutting-edge work from all aspects of sociology, with emphasis on theory-building, social analysis, and innovative methods. An impressive book review section in each issue presents 20 or more signed reviews of the most prominent works by social scientists. An essential title for all academic libraries, and highly recommended for public libraries and for special libraries involved in social research.

4847. *American Sociological Review.* [ISSN: 0003-1224] 1936. bi-m. USD 392. Sage Publications, Inc., 2455 Teller Rd, Thousand Oaks, CA 91320; info@sagepub.com; http://www.sagepub.com/. Illus., index, adv. Sample. Refereed. Vol. ends: Dec. Microform: MIM; PQC. Reprint: PSC. *Indexed:* A01, A22, ABIn, ABS&EES, AbAn, B01, B02, BAS, BEL&L, BRI, C45, CBRI, Chicano, E01, ERIC, FR, IBSS, MLA-IB, P02, P61, PsycInfo, RILM, RRTA, SSA, SWR&A. *Aud.:* Ga, Ac.

Founded in 1936 by the American Sociological Association, the *ASR* is considered the "flagship" journal of the ASA. The journal today remains true to the association's mission of publishing original research that employs innovative methodology, results in advances in better understanding of social processes, and advances the public good. Articles cover all aspects of sociology, with emphasis on topics of general interest. Book reviews are not published in *ASR.* Essential for all academic libraries, and highly recommended for public libraries and for special libraries involved in social research.

4848. *The American Sociologist.* [ISSN: 0003-1232] 1965. 3x/yr. EUR 368 (print & online eds.). Ed(s): Lawrence T Nichols. Springer New York LLC, 233 Spring St, New York, NY 10013; journals@springer-ny.com; http://www.springer.com. Illus. Sample. Refereed. Vol. ends: Winter. Microform: PQC. Reprint: PSC. *Indexed:* A01, A22, BRI, Chicano, E01, ERIC, FR, IBSS, P61, SSA. *Bk. rev.:* 1-2, length varies. *Aud.:* Ga, Ac.

This journal publishes papers, essays, and commentaries specific to the intellectual, practical, social, and ethical topics that concern sociologists. Research articles explore the ways in which sociological skills and perspectives relate to issues of broad public concern. Topics include applications of sociological methods and knowledge in a variety of settings, making it ideal for someone considering a career in the field. Recommended for academic libraries and for public libraries that support research.

4849. *Annual Review of Sociology.* [ISSN: 0360-0572] 1975. a. USD 226 (print or online ed.). Ed(s): Samuel Gubins, Douglas S Massey. Annual Reviews, PO Box 10139, Palo Alto, CA 94303; service@annualreviews.org; http://www.annualreviews.org. Refereed. Microform: PQC. Reprint: PSC. *Indexed:* A01, A22, ABIn, ABS&EES, B01, B02, BRI, CJPI, FR, IBSS, P02, P61, PsycInfo, SSA. *Aud.:* Ga, Ac, Sa.

Annual Reviews publishes yearly volumes that cover significant developments in physical, life, and social sciences. The *Annual Review of Sociology* includes current research in the discipline as well as major theoretical and methodological developments in the field. Chapters in a typical issue cover social processes, institutions and culture, individuals and society, social policy, demography, urban and rural sociology, and major sociological developments in other areas of the world. Highly recommended for academic libraries that support sociology.

4850. *Archives Europeennes de Sociologie.* [ISSN: 0003-9756] 1960. 3x/yr. GBP 180. Ed(s): Christopher Hann, Steven Lukes. Cambridge University Press, The Edinburgh Bldg, Shaftesbury Rd, Cambridge, CB2 8RU, United Kingdom; journals@cambridge.org; http://www.cambridge.org/uk. Illus., index, adv. Refereed. Circ: 1750. Vol. ends: Nov. Microform: PQC. Reprint: PSC. *Indexed:* A22, ABIn, BAS, E01, FR, IBSS, P61, SSA. *Bk. rev.:* Number and length vary. *Aud.:* Ac.

The focus of this journal is historical and comparative sociology from an international perspective. Special attention is paid to the transition from totalitarianism to democracy and multiple citizenship; authors include well-known and emerging scholars. Some issues include review essays and an extensive list of book reviews. Abstracts are in English, French, and German. Recommended for academic libraries that support doctoral programs in sociology.

Armed Forces and Society. See Military section.

4851. *British Journal of Sociology.* [ISSN: 0007-1315] 1950. q. GBP 363. Ed(s): Nigel Dodd. Wiley-Blackwell Publishing Ltd., The Atrium, Southern Gate, Chichester, PO19 8SQ, United Kingdom; customer@wiley.com; http://www.wiley.com/. Illus., index, adv. Sample. Refereed. Vol. ends: Dec. Microform: WMP. Reprint: PSC. *Indexed:* A01, A22, A47, ABIn, B02, BAS, BRI, CJPI, E01, FR, MLA-IB, P02, P61, PsycInfo, RILM, RiskAb, SSA. *Bk. rev.:* 4-10, signed. *Aud.:* Ac.

Housed at the London School of Economics and Political Science, the *British Journal of Sociology* is a mainstay in presenting sociological thinking, concepts, and research. International in scope, it covers all aspects of the discipline. Recent topics have included generational differences, institutions, social class, higher education, sports, economics, crime, climate change, and identity. Issues may include a debate section. Most issues include an extensive selection of book reviews. Highly recommended for academic libraries.

4852. *Canadian Journal of Sociology (Online).* [ISSN: 1710-1123] irreg. Free. Ed(s): Kevin D Haggerty. University of Toronto Press, Journals Division, 5201 Dufferin St, Toronto, ON M3H 5T8, Canada; journals@utpress.utoronto.ca; http://www.utpress.utoronto.ca. Refereed. *Bk. rev.:* Number and length vary. *Aud.:* Ac.

This is an online, open-access journal published by the Department of Sociology at the University of Alberta. It publishes research and theoretical articles by social scientists on issues in Canada and around the globe. Regular features include review essays, a debate/commentary section, a "Notes on Society" section that addresses topic issues, and a "Notes on the Discipline" section for discussion on the field of sociology. Each issue includes signed book reviews. A good addition to the online collections of academic libraries that support graduate programs in sociology or Canadian studies.

4853. *Canadian Review of Sociology.* Formerly (until 2008): *The Canadian Review of Sociology and Anthropology.* [ISSN: 1755-6171] 1964. q. GBP 155 (print & online eds.). Ed(s): Terry Wotherspoon, Reza Nakhaie. Wiley-Blackwell Publishing, Inc., 111 River St, Hoboken, NJ 07030; info@wiley.com; http://www.wiley.com/. Illus., adv. Sample. Refereed. Vol. ends: Nov. Microform: MIM; PQC. Reprint: PSC. *Indexed:* A01, A22, A47, ABS&EES, BRI, C37, CBCARef, E01, FR, IBSS, MLA-IB, P02, P61, PsycInfo, SSA. *Bk. rev.:* 0-8; signed. *Aud.:* Ac.

Published on behalf of the Canadian Sociological Association, this journal features theoretical and research articles primarily focused on Canada. A recent special issue on security and surveillance looked into the implications for society and evolution of the country's social policies. Abstracts are in both French and English; the article itself is in one or the other. Recommended for academic libraries that support graduate programs in sociology.

4854. *Child Abuse & Neglect: the international journal.* [ISSN: 0145-2134] 1977. m. EUR 2219. Ed(s): G B Melton, D C Bross. Elsevier Ltd, 66 Siward Rd, Bromley, BR2 9JZ, United Kingdom; customerserviceau@elsevier.com; http://www.elsevier.com. Illus., adv. Sample. Refereed. Microform: PQC. *Indexed:* A01, A22, AbAn, BRI, ERIC, ExcerpMed, FR, H24, P02, P61, PsycInfo, RiskAb, SSA, SWR&A. *Aud.:* Ac, Sa.

As the official publication of the International Society for Prevention of Child Abuse and Neglect, this journal covers all aspects of child abuse, with prevention and treatment. This title is multidisciplinary in scope, and contributors' fields that are represented include psychology, social work, medicine, law enforcement and legislation, education, and anthropology. Articles are intended for educators, policymakers, scholars, and professional practitioners. Highly recommended for academic, public, and special libraries that serve these fields, social services, and child-oriented advocacy organizations.

4855. *Child and Youth Care Forum: journal of research and practice in children's services.* Former titles (until 1991): *Child and Youth Care Quarterly;* (until 1987): *Child Care Quarterly.* [ISSN: 1053-1890] 1971. bi-m. EUR 1144 (print & online eds.). Ed(s): Carl F Weems. Springer New York LLC, 233 Spring St, New York, NY 10013; service-ny@springer.com; http://www.springer.com/. Illus., index, adv. Sample. Refereed. Vol. ends: Dec. Microform: PQC. Reprint: PSC. *Indexed:* A01, A22, ASSIA, Agr, BRI, E01, ERIC, P02, P61, PsycInfo, RILM, SSA, SWR&A. *Aud.:* Ga, Ac, Sa.

The intent of this journal is to bridge the "research-to-practice gap" between empirical and theoretical research and children's intervention and services—that is, identifying problems and proposing strategies for interventions and services. Contributors include practitioners, researchers, and clinicians in child psychology, early childhood education, pediatrics, psychiatry,

public policy, social work, and sociology. The 2011 Journal Impact Factor was 1.245. Recommended for academic libraries that support social work programs and libraries used by social services that work with children, youth, and families.

4856. *Child Maltreatment.* [ISSN: 1077-5595] 1996. q. USD 764. Ed(s): Candice Feiring. Sage Publications, Inc., 2455 Teller Rd, Thousand Oaks, CA 91320; info@sagepub.com; http://www.sagepub.com. Illus., index, adv. Sample. Refereed. Vol. ends: Nov. Reprint: PSC. *Indexed:* A01, A22, ASSIA, CJPI, E01, FR, H24, P02, P61, PsycInfo, RiskAb, SSA. *Aud.:* Ac, Sa.

This journal is the official publication of the American Professional Society on the Abuse of Children. It promotes practice and policy perspectives based on sound empirical evidence. Articles are intended to be useful to practitioners and researchers from mental health, child protection, legal and law enforcement, and medicine. The 2011 Journal Impact Factor was 2.77, and ISI Journal Citation Reports ranked it 2 out of 41 in Social Work and 2 out of 38 in Family Studies. Highly recommended for academic libraries that support social work programs and libraries that support social service agencies.

4857. *Children's Legal Rights Journal.* [ISSN: 0278-7210] 1979. q. USD 75 domestic (Members, USD 58; Students, USD 47). Ed(s): Kelley Menzano, Caroline Cannizzaro. Loyola University of Chicago, School of Law, 25 East Pearson St, Chicago, IL 60611; loyolachicagolaw@luc.edu; http://www.luc.edu. Illus. Sample. Refereed. Vol. ends: Fall. Microform: WSH. Reprint: WSH. *Indexed:* A22, BRI, CLI, L14. *Bk. rev.:* 1-2; signed. *Aud.:* Ac, Sa.

This journal is published in association with the National Association of Counsel for Children as a practice resource for professionals in social work, child welfare, juvenile justice and law enforcement, education, health care and mental health, and family law. It covers many aspects of law as it relates to children, such as child abuse, foster care, child custody and adoption, and children's rights. Recent articles have included interviews with practitioners, global perspectives on issues, and reviews of books and films. Recommended for law libraries and academic libraries that support social work and social service programs.

4858. *Chinese Sociological Review.* Formerly (until 2011): *Chinese Sociology and Anthropology.* [ISSN: 2162-0555] 1968. q. USD 1102 (print & online eds.). Ed(s): Xiaogang Wu. M.E. Sharpe, Inc., PO Box 1943, Birmingham, AL 35201; support@metapress.com; http://www.mesharpe.com. Illus., index, adv. Sample. Refereed. Vol. ends: Summer. Reprint: PSC. *Indexed:* A01, A22, A47, BAS, E01, IBSS, MLA-IB, P61, SSA. *Aud.:* Ac.

Intended for an international audience, this "journal of translations" contains articles by sociologists and other social scientists in mainland China, Taiwan, and abroad. Its mission is to advance the understanding of contemporary Chinese society and to provide a forum for Chinese sociologists to contribute to the global discussion of sociology. Recent topics have included religion, gender, migration patterns, education inequality, social stratification, property rights, and social change in China. Recommended for academic libraries that support graduate programs in sociology, anthropology, or Chinese studies.

4859. *Contemporary Sociology: a journal of reviews.* [ISSN: 0094-3061] 1972. bi-m. USD 374. Ed(s): Alan Sica. Sage Publications, Inc., 2455 Teller Rd, Thousand Oaks, CA 91320; info@sagepub.com; http://www.sagepub.com. Illus., index, adv. Sample. Refereed. Vol. ends: Nov. Microform: PQC. Reprint: PSC. *Indexed:* A01, A22, ABIn, ABS&EES, BRI, CBRI, Chicano, E01, P02, P61, SSA. *Bk. rev.:* 50-60; signed. *Aud.:* Ac.

A journal of the American Sociological Association, this title publishes reviews of recent works in sociology and related disciplines. Reviews are extensive (4–12 pages) and include those of individual works, paired essays, and commentaries and responses to reviews. The books reviewed are selected so as to reflect the most important trends and issues in the field. Highly recommended as a collection development tool for academic libraries.

4860. Critical Social Work. [ISSN: 1543-9372] 2000. s-a. Free. Ed(s): Carol F Scott, Brent Angell. University of Windsor, School of Social Work, Winsor, ON N9B 3P4, Canada. *Aud.:* Ac, Sa.

Critical Social Work is a peer-reviewed, open-access journal hosted by the School of Social Work at the University of Winsor (Ontario). International in scope, the journal offers an opportunity to explore concepts of social justice in the field of social work and anti-oppressive practice. Research articles by scholars, practitioners, and graduate students deal with legal, moral, and economic issues faced by individuals, groups, and institutions. Topics are varied, and approaches include various theoretical, methodological, and analytical approaches and practice applications. Recommended for the electronic holdings of academic libraries that support social work programs and for libraries used by social workers and social service professionals.

4861. Critical Sociology. Formerly (until 1988): *Insurgent Sociologist.* [ISSN: 0896-9205] 1969. bi-m. USD 976. Ed(s): Denis Wall, David Fasenfest. Sage Publications Ltd., 1 Oliver's Yard, 55 City Rd, London, EC1Y 1SP, United Kingdom; info@sagepub.co.uk; http://www.uk.sagepub.com. Illus., adv. Sample. Refereed. Microform: PQC. Reprint: PSC. *Indexed:* A01, A22, BAS, CJPI, E01, IBSS, P61, RiskAb, SSA. *Bk. rev.:* 4-6; signed. *Aud.:* Ac.

Reflecting its roots in the Association for Critical Sociology, the goal of this journal is to engage and promote critical or radical social science. Research focuses on work that delves into and seeks to understand race, gender, and class using postmodern, feminist, Marxist, and other radical perspectives. It boasts being one of the few "alternative" journals with widespread recognition and respect among social science scholarship. Extensive review essays further explore contemporary thought and scholarship. Recommended for academic libraries that support sociology and political science programs.

Cultural Sociology. See Cultural Studies.

4862. Current Sociology. [ISSN: 0011-3921] 1952. 7x/yr. USD 1619. Ed(s): Eloisa Martin. Sage Publications Ltd., 1 Oliver's Yard, 55 City Rd, London, EC1Y 1SP, United Kingdom; info@sagepub.co.uk; http://www.uk.sagepub.com. Illus., adv. Sample. Refereed. Reprint: PSC. *Indexed:* A01, A22, BRI, E01, IBSS, P02, P61, RILM, RiskAb, SSA. *Bk. rev.:* Number and length vary. *Aud.:* Ac.

This is the official journal of the International Sociological Association and has been published since 1952. Articles contain original research, theories, methods, concepts, and critical commentary on current debates within the field, as well as those reviewing emergent and challenging issues. This title is international in focus, and issues also include national/regional developments and controversial sociological topics. Occasional special issues or special sections within a single issue. Recommended for academic libraries that support sociology departments and faculty research.

4863. Deviant Behavior: an interdisciplinary journal. [ISSN: 0163-9625] 1979. 8x/yr. GBP 917 (print & online eds.). Ed(s): Clifton D Bryant, Dr. Craig J Forsyth. Taylor & Francis Inc., 325 Chestnut St, Ste 800, Philadelphia, PA 19106; customerservice@taylorandfrancis.com; http://www.tandfonline.com. Illus., adv. Sample. Refereed. Microform: PQC. Reprint: PSC. *Indexed:* A01, A22, CJPI, E01, P61, PsycInfo, RILM, RiskAb, SSA. *Aud.:* Ac.

This journal is international and interdisciplinary, and is the only one that focuses exclusively on social deviance. It publishes theoretical, descriptive, methodological, and applied research on all aspects of deviance, including crime, juvenile delinquency, substance abuse and addiction, sexual behaviors, societal reaction to handicap and disfigurement, mental illness, and socially inappropriate behavior. Recommended for academic libraries that support programs in sociology, psychology, social work, or criminal justice.

4864. Economy and Society. [ISSN: 0308-5147] 1972. q. GBP 410 (print & online eds.). Ed(s): Fran Tonkiss. Routledge, 4 Park Sq, Milton Park, Abingdon, OX14 4RN, United Kingdom; subscriptions@tandf.co.uk; http://www.tandfonline.com. Illus., index, adv. Sample. Refereed. Vol. ends: Nov. Microform: PQC. Reprint: PSC. *Indexed:* A22, ABIn, B01, B02, BAS, BRI, C42, E01, EconLit, FR, IBSS, JEL, P61, SSA. *Aud.:* Ac.

This is an international, interdisciplinary journal of radical theory and politics, published since 1972. It promotes and explores new debates and social thought in areas of sociology, anthropology, political science, legal theory, philosophy, economy, and other related social science areas. Most issues contain an extensive review article; each volume includes one special theme issue. The 2011 Thompson Reuters Journal Impact Factor was 1.70. Recommended for academic libraries that support graduate programs in the social sciences.

Ethnic and Racial Studies. See Multicultural Studies section.

4865. European Journal of Social Theory. [ISSN: 1368-4310] 1998. q. USD 1125. Ed(s): Gerard Delanty. Sage Publications Ltd., 1 Oliver's Yard, 55 City Rd, London, EC1Y 1SP, United Kingdom; info@sagepub.co.uk; http://www.uk.sagepub.com. Illus., index, adv. Sample. Refereed. Vol. ends: Nov. Reprint: PSC. *Indexed:* A01, A22, B01, E01, FR, IBSS, P61, SSA. *Bk. rev.:* 2-4; signed. *Aud.:* Ac.

This journal publishes international and interdisciplinary articles on the broadly-defined topic of social theory. Included are the theoretical traditions within the social sciences, critical social analysis from a variety of perspectives, and debates within the philosophy of social science. Research articles explore the theoretical contexts related to social transformations; also included are viewpoint essays, book reviews, and review essays. The 2011 Thompson Reuters Journal Impact Factor was 1.291, and ISI Journal Citation Reports ranked it 31 out of 138 for Sociology. Recommended for academic libraries that support graduate programs in sociology, political science, and international studies.

4866. European Societies. [ISSN: 1461-6696] 1999. 5x/yr. GBP 656 (print & online eds.). Ed(s): Goran Therborn. Routledge, 4 Park Sq, Milton Park, Abingdon, OX14 4RN, United Kingdom; subscriptions@tandf.co.uk; http://www.tandfonline.com. Adv. Sample. Refereed. Reprint: PSC. *Indexed:* A01, A22, E01, IBSS, P61, SSA. *Bk. rev.:* Number and length vary. *Aud.:* Ac.

European Societies was developed by the European Sociological Association as an international platform for sociological research and discourse on Europe. It covers social theory and analysis on Europe itself, comparative research on Europe, and Europe in international perspective, with themes that reflect recent changes in Europe from cross-disciplinary viewpoints. Recommended for academic libraries that support graduate programs in sociology, economy, political science, or European studies.

4867. European Sociological Review. [ISSN: 0266-7215] 1985. bi-m. . EUR 621. Ed(s): Melinda Mills. Oxford University Press, Great Clarendon St, Oxford, OX2 6DP, United Kingdom; enquiry@oup.co.uk; http://www.oxfordjournals.org/. Illus., adv. Sample. Refereed. Reprint: PSC. *Indexed:* A22, E01, FR, IBSS, P61, RiskAb, SSA. *Bk. rev.:* Number and length vary. *Aud.:* Ac.

This journal contains articles on all aspects of sociology, ranging from shorter research notes to major reports. Topics include all areas of sociology; recent articles have included migration, xenophobia, gender, labor, religion, families, and children. All articles are in English, with a strong emphasis on Western European countries. The 2011 Thompson Reuters Journal Impact Factor was 1.935, and ISI Journal Citation Reports ranked it 11 out of 137 in Sociology. Recommended for academic libraries that support graduate programs in sociology.

4868. Evaluation: the international journal of theory, research and practice. [ISSN: 1356-3890] 1995. q. USD 1112. Ed(s): Elliot Stern. Sage Publications Ltd., 1 Oliver's Yard, 55 City Rd, London, EC1Y 1SP, United Kingdom; info@sagepub.co.uk; http://www.uk.sagepub.com. Illus., index, adv. Sample. Refereed. Vol. ends: Oct. Reprint: PSC. *Indexed:* A01, A22, ASSIA, E01, IBSS, P61, PsycInfo, SSA. *Bk. rev.:* 1-2; signed. *Aud.:* Ac.

This journal is published in association with the Tavistock Institute of Human Relations, which is engaged in evaluation and action research in organizations. *Evaluation* provides an international and interdisciplinary forum for dialogue on evaluation in the social sciences, including the areas of politics, economics, public administration, psychology, sociology, anthropology, health, education, law, and information technology. Includes occasional special issues, book reviews, practice articles, and a section for debate and opinion. Recommended for academic libraries that support programs in sociology, political science, economics, or public administration.

4869. *Evaluation Review: a journal of applied social research.* Formerly (until Feb.1980): *Evaluation Quarterly.* [ISSN: 0193-841X] 1977. bi-m. USD 1125. Ed(s): E Michael Foster. Sage Publications, Inc., 2455 Teller Rd, Thousand Oaks, CA 91320; info@sagepub.com; http://www.sagepub.com. Illus., index, adv. Sample. Refereed. Vol. ends: Dec. Microform: PQC. Reprint: PSC. *Indexed:* A01, A22, AbAn, CLI, E01, ERIC, IBSS, L14, P02, P61, PsycInfo, SSA, SWR&A. *Aud.:* Ac.

Evaluation Review serves as an interdisciplinary forum in the social sciences for the work of researchers, planners, and policy makers. It presents the latest applied evaluation methods in areas such as homelessness, education, domestic violence, education, public health, substance abuse, and criminal justice. In addition to extensive research articles, included are review essays, reports on innovative evaluative applications, and research briefs of ongoing studies. The 2011 Thompson Reuters Journal Impact Factor was 1.196. Recommended for academic libraries that support social work, sociology, criminal justice, or public administration.

4870. *Forum Qualitative Sozialforschung.* [ISSN: 1438-5627] 1999. 3x/yr. Free. Freie Universitaet Berlin, Institut fuer Qualitative Forschung, Habelschwerdter Allee 45, Berlin, 14195, Germany; katja.mruck@fu-berlin.de; http://www.qualitative-forschung.de. Refereed. *Indexed:* IBSS, P61, SSA. *Aud.:* Ac.

This is a multilingual, online, open-access journal that presents qualitative studies on various topics in the social sciences, as well as articles on theory, methods, and application of qualitative research. Features of the journal include review articles, conference reports, and interviews. Articles may be in English, German, or Spanish. Academic libraries that support the social sciences may find this a useful addition to electronic holdings.

4871. *Global Social Policy: an interdisciplinary journal of public policy and social development.* [ISSN: 1468-0181] 2001. 3x/yr. USD 691. Ed(s): Gerard Boychuk, Stephen McBride. Sage Publications Ltd., 1 Oliver's Yard, 55 City Rd, London, EC1Y 1SP, United Kingdom; info@sagepub.co.uk; http://www.uk.sagepub.com. Adv. Sample. Refereed. Reprint: PSC. *Indexed:* A01, A22, E01, EconLit, IBSS, JEL, P61, SSA. *Bk. rev.:* 6-8; signed. *Aud.:* Ac, Sa.

GSP is an international and interdisciplinary journal that exists to advance discourse and understanding of the impact of globalization on social policy, social development, social health and governance, gender, poverty, social welfare, education, and food. Included are scholarly research articles as well as policy-oriented discourse that is intended to advocate for global welfare policies and programs. Recommended for academic libraries that support programs in sociology, economics, social work, public administration, political science, or criminal justice.

4872. *International Journal of Comparative Sociology.* [ISSN: 0020-7152] 1960. bi-m. USD 955. Ed(s): David A Smith. Sage Publications Ltd., 1 Oliver's Yard, 55 City Rd, London, EC1Y 1SP, United Kingdom; info@sagepub.co.uk; http://www.uk.sagepub.com. Illus., adv. Sample. Refereed. Microform: SWZ. Reprint: PSC. *Indexed:* A01, A22, A47, BAS, BRI, Chicano, E01, FR, IBSS, P02, P61, SSA. *Aud.:* Ac.

This journal offers research that is international in scope and comparative in method, with contributions from sociologists worldwide. Articles present competing perspectives; topics are drawn from scholars in sociology other social sciences. Each issue has six to eight signed book reviews. Recommended for academic libraries that support programs in sociology.

4873. *International Sociology.* [ISSN: 0268-5809] 1986. bi-m. USD 1163. Ed(s): Christine Inglis. Sage Publications Ltd., 1 Oliver's Yard, 55 City Rd, London, EC1Y 1SP, United Kingdom; info@sagepub.co.uk; http://www.uk.sagepub.com. Illus., index. Sample. Refereed. Vol. ends: Dec. Reprint: PSC. *Indexed:* A01, A22, ABS&EES, B01, BAS, E01, FR, IBSS, P02, P61, RILM, RiskAb, SSA. *Bk. rev.:* 2-4; signed. *Aud.:* Ac.

This journal was established in 1986 by the International Sociological Association, and as such, it was one of the first publications to invite the research and perspectives of the international community of sociologists. Articles present innovative theory and empirical approaches to key sociological issues, using comparative, quantitative, and qualitative methods. Several issues per year contain extensive (20+) book reviews. Recommended for academic libraries that support graduate programs in sociology.

4874. *Journal of Applied Social Science.* Formed by the merger of (1999-2007): *Sociological Practice;* (1984 2007): *Journal of Applied Sociology.* [ISSN: 1936-7244] 2007. s-a. USD 387. Ed(s): Jammie Price. Sage Publications, Inc., 2455 Teller Rd, Thousand Oaks, CA 91320; info@sagepub.com; http://www.sagepub.com/. Refereed. Reprint: PSC. *Indexed:* ASSIA, SSA. *Bk. rev.:* 0-3. *Aud.:* Ac.

This online publication is the official publication of the Association for Applied and Clinical Sociology, and the amalgamated successor of previously-published journals: the *Journal of Applied Sociology* and the *Journal of Sociological Practice.* It publishes research articles, essays, research reports, teaching notes, and book reviews on topics of interest to sociological practitioners. Articles apply social science theories or method, critically reflect on the application of social science, or improve the teaching of social science. Recommended for academic libraries that support graduate programs in sociology and other social sciences.

4875. *Journal of Children and Media.* [ISSN: 1748-2798] 2007. q. GBP 339 (print & online eds.). Ed(s): Dafna Lemish, Amy Jordan. Routledge, 4 Park Sq, Milton Park, Abingdon, OX14 4RN, United Kingdom; subscriptions@tandf.co.uk; http://www.tandfonline.com. Adv. Sample. Refereed. Reprint: PSC. *Indexed:* A22, E01, PsycInfo. *Bk. rev.:* Number and length vary. *Aud.:* Ac.

The purpose of this journal is to provide a space for the interdisciplinary discussion and examination of the study of the role of media in the lives of children and youth. Written by scholars and professionals from around the globe, research articles focus on the role and effect of media on children, especially in regard to three complementary areas: children as media consumers, portrayals of children in media, and media organizations and productions that are for and by children. Topics of articles are quite varied, including the interaction of children and media, diversity issues, violence, video games, and advertising. Includes occasional reviews of books and other resources. Recommended for academic and public research libraries.

4876. *Journal of Classical Sociology.* [ISSN: 1468-795X] 2001. 3x/yr. USD 1079. Ed(s): Bryan S Turner, Simon Susen. Sage Publications Ltd., 1 Oliver's Yard, 55 City Rd, London, EC1Y 1SP, United Kingdom; info@sagepub.co.uk; http://www.uk.sagepub.com. Sample. Refereed. Reprint: PSC. *Indexed:* A01, A22, E01, FR, IBSS, P61, PsycInfo, SSA. *Bk. rev.:* Number & length vary. *Aud.:* Ac.

Articles in the *Journal of Classical Sociology* focus on the origins of society and the ways in which classical traditions and thought are reflected in contemporary sociological thinking and research. Research areas include concepts, theory, institutions, ideologies, traditions, methods, and values. Many issues are thematic, often focusing on a single topic or theorist; recent special issues have included Georg Simmel and David Frisby, Durkheim, John Holloway, and natural law. Review essays and book reviews are also included. Recommended for academic libraries that support graduate and faculty-research sociology.

Journal of Comparative Family Studies. See Family section.

Journal of Divorce & Remarriage. See Marriage and Divorce section.

4877. *Journal of European Social Policy.* [ISSN: 0958-9287] 1991. 5x/yr. USD 1174. Ed(s): Traute Meyer, Jochen Clasen. Sage Publications Ltd., 1 Oliver's Yard, 55 City Rd, London, EC1Y 1SP, United Kingdom; info@sagepub.co.uk; http://www.uk.sagepub.com. Sample. Refereed. Reprint: PSC. *Indexed:* A01, A22, E01, IBSS, P02, P61, SSA. *Bk. rev.:* 4-6; signed. *Aud.:* Ac.

SOCIOLOGY AND SOCIAL WORK

This interdisciplinary journal features articles on all aspects of social policy in Europe. Research focuses on innovative insights and empirical analysis that addresses policy-making in the E.U. and elsewhere, cross-national comparative studies, and comparisons outside of Europe. Social policy topics have included aging, pensions and social security, poverty and social exclusion, education, work and training, families, health and social services, migration, privatization, and globalization. Other features include reflections on social policy issues, a section called "European Brief" that summarizes trends and legislation in Europe, and book reviews. The 2011 Thompson Reuters Journal Impact Factor for this title was 1.356; the ISI Journal Citation Reports ranked it 7 out of 45 in Public Administration and 9 out of 38 in Social Issues. Recommended for academic libraries that support programs in sociology, public administration, or European studies.

Journal of Family Issues. See Family section.

4878. *Journal of Historical Sociology.* [ISSN: 0952-1909] 1988. q. GBP 483. Ed(s): Yoke-Sum Wong, Derek Sayer. Wiley-Blackwell Publishing Ltd., The Atrium, Southern Gate, Chichester, PO19 8SQ, United Kingdom; customer@wiley.com; http://www.wiley.com/. Adv. Sample. Refereed. Reprint: PSC. *Indexed:* A01, A22, A47, AmHI, BRI, E01, IBSS, P61, PsycInfo, SSA. *Aud.:* Ac.

The focus of this journal is the interdisciplinary exchange of ideas and perspectives with regard to history and social studies. Editors include historians, anthropologists, geographers, and sociologists from the U.S., Canada, and Europe. In addition to scholarly articles, the journal contains review essays and commentary in its "Issues and Agendas" section intended to provoke discussion and debate. Recommended for academic libraries that support programs in the social sciences.

Journal of Homosexuality. See Gay, Lesbian, Bisexual, and Transgender section.

The Journal of Human Resources. See Labor and Industrial Relations section.

4879. *Journal of Leisure Research.* [ISSN: 0022-2216] 1968. q. USD 399 (print & online eds.) Members, USD 52 (print & online eds.); Non-members, USD 66 (print & online eds.). Ed(s): Kimberly J Shinew. National Recreation and Park Association, 22377 Belmont Ridge Rd, Ashburn, VA 20148; customerservice@nrpa.org; http://www.nrpa.org. Illus., index, adv. Refereed. Microform: PQC. Reprint: PSC. *Indexed:* A01, A22, ABIn, ASSIA, Agr, B01, BRI, C45, H&TI, IndVet, P02, P61, PsycInfo, RRTA, SD, SSA. *Bk. rev.:* Number and length vary. *Aud.:* Ac.

This journal is the official publication of the National Recreation and Park Association, and is published in cooperation with the University of Illinois and Sagamore. It contains empirical reports, theoretical and methodological studies, commentaries, and review papers on subjects in sports and leisure studies. Recent articles have focused on outdoor recreation areas, wilderness experiences, sports and other leisure activities, gender, and community management. Recommended for academic libraries that support research in sociology or public administration.

Journal of Marriage and Family. See Family section.

4880. *Journal of Mathematical Sociology.* [ISSN: 0022-250X] 1971. q. GBP 1711 (print & online eds.). Ed(s): Phillip Bonacich. Taylor & Francis Inc., 325 Chestnut St, Ste 800, Philadelphia, PA 19106; customerservice@taylorandfrancis.com; http://www.tandfonline.com. Illus., index. Sample. Refereed. Reprint: PSC. *Indexed:* A01, A22, E01, FR, IBSS, MSN, MathR, P61, SSA. *Bk. rev.:* Occasional. *Aud.:* Ac.

This is an interdisciplinary journal that publishes papers of interest to social and behavioral scientists. It is oriented toward the mathematical understanding of emergent social structures, networks, groups, organizations, and global systems rather than on individual behavior. Also included are reviews of new and developing areas of mathematics and mathematical modeling with applications in sociology. Recommended for academic libraries that support doctoral programs in sociology.

4881. *Journal of Public and Professional Sociology.* [ISSN: 2154-8935] 2005. irreg. Free. Ed(s): Linda Treiber. Kennesaw State University, 1000 Chastain Rd, English Bldg. #27/Ste 220, Kennesaw, GA 30144; http://www.kennesaw.edu/. *Aud.:* Ga, Ac, Sa.

This open-access online publication serves as the official journal of the Georgia Sociological Association. It contains research and theory articles intended to inform public debate about the social, political, and moral issues related to sociological scientific expertise. Preference is shown for articles that are professional, scientifically sound, relevant, readable, and innovative. Also included are debates, papers by students, research and teaching notes, and occasional reviews. Academic libraries with graduate programs in sociology may wish to add this to their electronic holdings.

4882. *Journal of Sex Research.* Incorporates (in 2007): *Annual Review of Sex Research;* Formerly (until 196?): *Advances in Sex Research.* [ISSN: 0022-4499] 1965. 6x/yr. GBP 415 (print & online eds.). Ed(s): Cynthia Graham. Routledge, 325 Chestnut St, Ste 800, Philadelphia, PA 19106; customerservice@taylorandfrancis.com; http://www.tandfonline.com. Illus., adv. Refereed. Vol. ends: Nov. Microform: PQC. Reprint: PSC. *Indexed:* A01, A22, ASSIA, AbAn, BAS, BRI, C42, C45, Chicano, E01, MLA-IB, P02, PsycInfo, SSA, SWR&A. *Bk. rev.:* Occasional. *Aud.:* Ac, Sa.

As the official publication of the Society for the Scientific Study of Sexuality, this journal provides a forum for research and the promotion of an interdisciplinary understanding of contemporary sexual science. Articles include empirical studies, brief reports, theoretical essays, literature reviews, historical article, book reviews, and letters to the editor. The audience includes researchers and practitioners in psychology, sociology, education, psychiatry, communication, and allied health. The 2011 Thompson Reuters Journal Impact Factor was 2.532; ISI Journal Citation Reports ranked it 2 out of 89 in Social Sciences and 26 out of 110 in Clinical Psychology. Recommended for academic and research libraries with programs in the fields listed here.

4883. *Journal of Social Issues.* [ISSN: 0022-4537] 1944. q. GBP 587 (print or online ed.). Ed(s): Sheri R Levy. Wiley-Blackwell Publishing, Inc., 111 River St, Hoboken, NJ 07030; info@wiley.com; http://onlinelibrary.wiley.com/. Illus., adv. Sample. Refereed. Vol. ends: Winter. Microform: PMC; PQC. Reprint: PSC. *Indexed:* A01, A22, BAS, CJPI, Chicano, E01, IBSS, MLA-IB, P02, P61, PsycInfo, RiskAb, SSA, SWR&A. *Aud.:* Ac.

This journal is published for the Society for the Psychological Study of Social Issues. It contains articles that employ behavioral and social scientific theory, empirical evidence, and practice in order to study human and social problems. Each issue focuses on a single topic; recent themes have included genocide, globalization, racism in the U.S., poverty, youth and violence, and career sustainability. The 2011 Thompson Reuters Journal Impact Factor was 1.963; ISI Journal Citation Reports ranked it 5 out of 38 in Social Issues. Recommended for academic and research libraries.

4884. *Journal of Social Work Education.* Formerly (until 1985): *Journal of Education for Social Work.* [ISSN: 1043-7797] 1965. q. GBP 305 (print & online eds.). Ed(s): Susan Robbins. Routledge, 325 Chestnut St, Ste 800, Philadelphia, PA 19106; customerservice@taylorandfrancis.com; http://www.tandfonline.com. Adv. Refereed. Reprint: PSC. *Indexed:* A01, A22, ASSIA, BRI, ERIC, PsycInfo, SSA, SWR&A. *Aud.:* Ac.

As the official publication of the Council on Social Work Education, this journal covers all aspects of education in social work and social welfare. It serves as a forum for the creative exchange of trends, innovations, and problems with respect to social work education at all levels. Its audience includes educators, students, and practitioners. Topics of research articles in recent issues have included professional socialization, financial literacy for social work students, development of professional skills, measuring learning outcomes, field learning, and evidence-based practice. Other features include research notes and teaching notes. Recommended for academic libraries that support programs in social work at all levels.

4885. *Journal of Social Work Practice: psychotherapeutic approaches in health, welfare and the community.* [ISSN: 0265-0533] 1983. q. GBP 782 (print & online eds.). Ed(s): Stephen Briggs, Martin Smith.

Routledge, 4 Park Sq, Milton Park, Abingdon, OX14 4RN, United Kingdom; subscriptions@tandf.co.uk; http://www.tandfonline.com. Adv. Sample. Refereed. Reprint: PSC. *Indexed:* A01, A22, ASSIA, E01, IBSS, P61, PsycInfo, SSA, SWR&A. *Aud.:* Ac, Sa.

This is the journal of the Group for the Advancement of Psychodynamics and Psychotherapy in Social Work. It publishes articles that explore and analyze practice in social welfare and allied health professions from psychodynamic and systemic perspectives. This may include counseling, social care planning, education and training, research, institutional life, management and organization, or policy making. The scope is international and intercultural. Recommended for academic libraries that support graduate social work programs and for libraries used by social work and social service professionals.

4886. *Journal of Social Work Values & Ethics.* [ISSN: 1553-6947] 2004. q. Free. Ed(s): Stephen M Marson, Donna DeAngelis. Association of Social Work Boards, 400 Southridge Pky, Ste B, Culpeper, VA 22701; http://www.aswb.org/. *Indexed:* A01, P61, SSA. *Bk. rev.:* Number and length vary. *Aud.:* Ac, Sa.

This is an open-access, peer-reviewed journal published by the Association of Social Work Boards. It publishes articles that examine ethical and values issues that inform social work practice, research, education, and theory development. Areas studied include models for analyzing and resolving ethical conflicts, discussions of ethical dilemmas, ethical decision-making in social work practice, and examples of good practice with respect to ethical and value considerations. Features also include book reviews. Recommended for the electronic holdings of academic libraries that support social work programs, and for libraries used by social work and social service professionals.

New Statesman. See News and Opinion section.

4887. *Nonprofit and Voluntary Sector Quarterly.* Formerly (until 1989): *Journal of Voluntary Action Research.* [ISSN: 0899-7640] 1972. bi-m. USD 858. Ed(s): Jeffery L Brudney, Lucas Meijs. Sage Publications, Inc., 2455 Teller Rd, Thousand Oaks, CA 91320; info@sagepub.com; http://www.sagepub.com. Illus., index, adv. Sample. Refereed. Vol. ends: Dec. Microform: PQC. Reprint: PSC. *Indexed:* A01, A22, ABIn, ASSIA, C&ISA, CerAb, E01, EconLit, FR, JEL, P61, RiskAb, SSA. *Bk. rev.:* 4-6; signed. *Aud.:* Ga, Ac.

This is an international, interdisciplinary journal that provides research, discussion, and analysis in the nonprofit sector. The focus is on research within nonprofit organization, philanthropy, and volunteerism for an audience of practitioners, administrators, and policymakers. All aspects of the social sciences are represented, including sociology, social work, anthropology, arts and humanities, economics, education, health, history, law, political science, public administration, and urban affairs. Includes book reviews in each issue. Recommended for academic libraries that support programs in sociology or social work and for public research libraries.

4888. *Qualitative Sociology.* [ISSN: 0162-0436] 1978. q. EUR 1194 (print & online eds.). Ed(s): David Smilde. Springer New York LLC, 233 Spring St, New York, NY 10013; service-ny@springer.com; http://www.springer.com/. Illus., index, adv. Sample. Refereed. Microform: PQC. Reprint: PSC. *Indexed:* A01, A22, B01, BRI, E01, FR, IBSS, P61, RILM, SSA, SWR&A. *Bk. rev.:* 6-8; signed. *Aud.:* Ac.

Qualitative Sociology contains articles that employ qualitative research methods in the interpretation and analysis of social life. Articles demonstrate both theoretical and analytical research based on methods such as interviewing, observation, ethnography, and historical and content analysis. A recent issue included articles on rituals of a Jewish Orthodox congregation, public monuments, and youth violence. Recommended for academic libraries that support sociology programs.

4889. *Qualitative Sociology Review.* [ISSN: 1733-8077] 2005. 4x/yr. Free. Ed(s): Krzysztof Tomasz Konecki. Uniwersytet Lodzki, Wydzial Ekonomiczno-Socjologiczny, Instytut Socjologii, Katedra Socjologii Organizacji i Zarzadzania, Rewolucji 1905 Nr 41-43, Lodz, 90-214, Poland. *Indexed:* IBSS, P61, SSA. *Bk. rev.:* Number and length vary. *Aud.:* Ac.

This is an open-access, international scientific journal sponsored by Lodz University, Poland. It publishes empirical, theoretical, and methodological articles applicable to all aspects and specializations within sociology. Topics of recent articles included migration, homeless people, and motherhood and addiction. Book reviews are also included. Recommended for academic libraries that support sociology programs.

4890. *Quality and Quantity: international journal of methodology.* [ISSN: 0033-5177] 1967. 6x/yr. EUR 1848 (print & online eds.). Ed(s): Vittorio Capecchi. Springer Netherlands, Van Godewijckstraat 30, Dordrecht, 3311 GX, Netherlands; http://www.springer.com. Illus., adv. Sample. Refereed. Microform: PQC. Reprint: PSC. *Indexed:* A01, A22, ABIn, E01, FR, IBSS, P61, PsycInfo, SSA. *Aud.:* Ac.

This is an interdisciplinary, international journal that contains articles that correlate disciplines such as mathematics and statistics with sociology, economics, social psychology, and other social sciences. Its coverage includes models, methods, and applications of classifications; qualitative and feminist methodologies; discussions on the general logic of empirical research; and similar topics. Recommended for academic libraries that support doctoral programs in sociology.

4891. *Rural Sociology: devoted to scientific study of rural and community life.* [ISSN: 0036-0112] 1937. q. GBP 217. Ed(s): Alessandro Bonanno. Rural Sociological Society, 104 Gentry Hall, University of Missouri, Columbia, MO 65211; http://www.ruralsociology.org. Illus., index, adv. Refereed. Vol. ends: Winter. Microform: PQC. Reprint: PSC. *Indexed:* A01, A22, ABS&EES, AbAn, Agr, BRI, C45, Chicano, E01, ERIC, FR, IBSS, IndVet, MLA-IB, P02, P61, RRTA, SSA, SWR&A. *Bk. rev.:* 4-6; signed. *Aud.:* Ac.

Rural Sociology is the journal of the Rural Sociological Society. It uses sociological and interdisciplinary approaches to focus on emerging and recurring issues, policy discussions, and changes in local and global systems that affect rural people and places. The scope is international. Specific issues may include community revitalization, rural demography changes, rural poverty, natural resource conflicts, environmental impacts, and food and agricultural production. Recommended for academic libraries that support programs in sociology, agriculture, or environmental studies.

4892. *School Social Work Journal.* [ISSN: 0161-5653] 1976. s-a. USD 60 (Individuals, USD 30). Ed(s): Sandra Kopels, Carol Massat. Lyceum Books, Inc., 5758 S Blackstone Ave, Chicago, IL 60637; lyceum@lyceumbooks.com; http://www.lyceumbooks.com. Refereed. *Indexed:* A22, ERIC, P61, PsycInfo, SSA, SWR&A. *Aud.:* Ac, Sa.

This journal focuses on the improvement of social work practice in the schools. Articles include reports on research, integrative and comprehensive reviews, conceptual and practical positions, effective assessment and intervention methodologies, and model service delivery programs. Topics in a recent issues included youth in foster care, school violence, homeless children, youth with disabilities, evaluating school social work service, mental health interventions, and working with kids with autism. Recommended for academic libraries that support social work programs and special libraries that serve social services.

4893. *Sex Roles: a journal of research.* [ISSN: 0360-0025] 1975. m. EUR 1901 (print & online eds.). Ed(s): Irene Hanson Frieze. Springer New York LLC, 233 Spring St, New York, NY 10013; service-ny@springer.com; http://www.springer.com/. Illus., index, adv. Sample. Refereed. Vol. ends: Jul/Dec. Microform: PQC. Reprint: PSC. *Indexed:* A01, A22, ABS&EES, AbAn, BRI, Chicano, E01, FR, FemPer, HEA, MLA-IB, P02, P61, PsycInfo, RILM, RiskAb, SSA, SWR&A, WSA. *Bk. rev.:* 2-4; signed. *Aud.:* Ac.

Sex Roles publishes interdisciplinary research and review articles in the behavioral sciences from a feminist perspective, primarily focusing on gender issues and perceptions. Topics of recent articles have included gender roles and socialization, gender stereotypes in the family, feminist identity, marriage, patterns of intimacy, women and math education, role models, body image, eating issues, and mothering. Each issue includes extensive reviews of books and often of media that address gender-related topics. As this title is heavily used in undergraduate research, it is essential for academic libraries.

4894. *Smith College Studies in Social Work.* [ISSN: 0037-7317] 1930. q. GBP 197 (print & online eds.). Ed(s): Kathryn Basham, Carolyn Jacobs. Routledge, 325 Chestnut St, Ste 800, Philadelphia, PA 19106; customerservice@taylorandfrancis.com; http://www.tandfonline.com. Refereed. Circ: 2000 Paid. Reprint: PSC. *Indexed:* A01, A22, E01, P61, PsycInfo, SSA, SWR&A. *Bk. rev.:* Number and length vary. *Aud.:* Ac, Sa.

This is a refereed journal intended for social work and social service practitioners. It features articles that advance theoretical understanding of psychological and social functioning, present clinically relevant research, and promote excellence in clinical practice. Issues addressed include mental health, therapeutic process, trauma and recovery, racial and cultural diversity, community and evidence-based practice, and clinical services to specific populations of psychologically and socially vulnerable clients. Some issues include book reviews. Recommended for academic libraries that support social work programs and special libraries that serve social service programs.

4895. *Social Change.* [ISSN: 0049-0857] 1971. q. USD 319. Ed(s): Poornima Joshi, Manoranjan Mohanty. Sage Publications India Pvt. Ltd., B-1/I-1 Mohan Cooperative Industrial Estate Mathura Rd, PO Box 7, New Delhi, 110 044, India; info@sagepub.in; http://www.sagepub.in. Sample. Refereed. Reprint: PSC. *Indexed:* A22, BAS, C45, E01, P61, SSA. *Bk. rev.:* 4-6, signed. *Aud.:* Ac.

Social Change is a multidisciplinary journal that publishes empirical research, analytic reports, theoretical essays, and policy discussions in the field of social change and development. The language is as non-technical as possible, appealing to a wide readership in academia, social movements, NGOs, and policy-making sectors. Features include book reviews and columns that present various perspectives and commentaries. This title is published in India, and many of the articles are written by scholars in that country. Recommended for academic libraries that support sociology programs.

4896. *Social Compass: international review of sociology of religion.* [ISSN: 0037-7686] 1953. q. USD 700. Ed(s): Jean-Pierre Hiernaux. Sage Publications Ltd., 1 Oliver's Yard, 55 City Rd, London, EC1Y 1SP, United Kingdom; info@sagepub.co.uk; http://www.uk.sagepub.com. Illus., index, adv. Sample. Refereed. Vol. ends: Dec. Reprint: PSC. *Indexed:* A01, A22, ArtHuCI, BAS, CJPI, E01, FR, IBSS, MLA-IB, P02, P61, R&TA, SSA. *Bk. rev.:* 1-2; signed. *Aud.:* Ac.

Social Compass is an international journal that provides a forum for research and review articles on the sociology of religion. Each issue features articles on a theme as well as those on any topic of religion in contemporary societies. Articles are published in English or French, with abstracts in both languages. Recommended for academic libraries that support graduate programs in sociology or religious studies.

4897. *Social Forces.* Formerly (until 1925): *The Journal of Social Forces.* [ISSN: 0037-7732] 1922. q. EUR 334. Ed(s): Arne L Kalleberg. Oxford University Press, 198 Madison Ave, New York, NY 10016; custserv.us@oup.com; http://www.oxfordjournals.org. Illus., index. Refereed. Vol. ends: Jun. Microform: MIM; PMC; PQC. Reprint: PSC; WSH. *Indexed:* A01, A22, ABS&EES, AbAn, B01, BAS, BRI, CBRI, Chicano, E01, ERIC, FR, IBSS, MLA-IB, P02, P61, RILM, SSA, SWR&A. *Bk. rev.:* 2-6; signed. *Aud.:* Ac.

Social Forces is published in association with the Department of Sociology at the University of North Carolina, Chapel Hill. Research articles explore all aspects of sociological inquiry and of other social sciences, including psychology, anthropology, political science, history, and economics. Recent issues have included articles on stratification, immigration, family, health, race, civic and political participation, and unemployment. An extensive list of book reviews in previous volumes has been replaced by shorter book review essays. Recommended for academic libraries that support social science programs.

4898. *Social Indicators Research: an international and interdisciplinary journal for quality-of-life measurement.* [ISSN: 0303-8300] 1974. 15x/yr. EUR 2922 (print & online eds.). Ed(s): Alex C Michalos. Springer Netherlands, Van Godewijckstraat 30, Dordrecht, 3311 GX, Netherlands; http://www.springer.com. Illus., index, adv. Sample. Refereed. Vol. ends: Dec. Microform: PQC. Reprint: PSC. *Indexed:* A01, A22, ABIn, Agr, B01, BAS, BRI, C45, E01, ERIC, EconLit, FR, IBSS, P02, P61, PsycInfo, RRTA, RiskAb, SSA, SWR&A. *Bk. rev.:* 2-3; signed. *Aud.:* Ac.

Social Indicators Research is a journal that publishes research on the quality of life. It presents empirical, philosophical, and methodological studies on all aspects of society, such as individual, public, and private organizations, and local, country, national, and international systems. Topics include health, social customs, law enforcement, politics, economics, poverty and welfare, education, science and technology, and the media and arts. Recommended for academic libraries that support graduate programs in the social sciences.

4899. *Social Networks.* [ISSN: 0378-8733] 1979. 4x/yr. EUR 671. Ed(s): P Doreian, M Evertt. Elsevier BV, Radarweg 29, PO Box 211, Amsterdam, 1000 AE, Netherlands; JournalsCustomerServiceEMEA@elsevier.com; http://www.elsevier.com. Illus., index, adv. Sample. Refereed. Microform: PQC. *Indexed:* A22, A47, FR, IBSS, MathR, P61, PsycInfo, SSA. *Bk. rev.:* Number and length vary. *Aud.:* Ac.

Social Networks is an international and interdisciplinary journal that publishes studies of the empirical structure of social relations, structure, and networks. Topics represented include anthropology, sociology, history, social psychology, economics, communication studies, and others in the social sciences. Included are theoretical and substantive papers, critical reviews of major theoretical or methodological approaches, and occasional book reviews. The 2011 Thompson Reuters Journal Impact Factor was 2.931. Recommended for academic libraries that support graduate programs in the social sciences.

Social Policy. See Labor and Industrial Relations section.

4900. *Social Problems.* [ISSN: 0037-7791] 1953. q. USD 304 (print & online eds.). Ed(s): Becky Pettit. University of California Press, Journals Division, 2000 Ctr St, Ste 303, Berkeley, CA 94704; customerservice@ucpressjournals.com; http://www.ucpressjournals.com. Illus., index, adv. Sample. Refereed. Microform: PQC. Reprint: PSC; WSH. *Indexed:* A01, A22, ABIn, ABS&EES, BAS, BRI, CJPI, Chicano, E01, FR, IBSS, P02, P61, PsycInfo, SSA, SWR&A. *Aud.:* Ga, Ac.

As the journal for the Society for the Study of Social Problems, this title focuses on influential sociological findings and theories in an array of areas, such as conflict, crime, juvenile delinquency, drugs, health and mental health, poverty and class, sexual behavior, and aging. As one of the most enduring, widely-read, and respected journals in the social sciences, *Social Problems* is essential for academic and research libraries.

4901. *Social Psychology Quarterly.* Former titles (until 1979): *Social Psychology;* (until 1978): *Sociometry.* [ISSN: 0190-2725] 1937. q. USD 333. Ed(s): Cathryn Johnson, Karen A Hegtvedt. Sage Publications, Inc., 2455 Teller Rd, Thousand Oaks, CA 91320; info@sagepub.com; http://www.sagepub.com. Illus. Refereed. Vol. ends: Dec. Microform: MIM; PQC. Reprint: PSC. *Indexed:* A01, A22, ABS&EES, ASSIA, BRI, Chicano, E01, ERIC, FR, IBSS, MLA-IB, P02, P61, PsycInfo, SSA. *Aud.:* Ac.

Published in association with the American Sociological Association, this journal publishes theoretical and empirical papers that link individuals to each other and to groups, collectivities, and institutions. The journal is interdisciplinary and publishes work by both sociologists and psychologists. The 2011 Thompson Reuters Journal Impact Factor was 1.892; ISI Journal Citation Reports ranked it 15 out of 59 in Psychology, Social. Recommended for academic libraries that support programs in sociology and psychology.

4902. *Social Research: an international quarterly of the social sciences.* [ISSN: 0037-783X] 1934. q. USD 155. Ed(s): Cara Schlesinger, Arien Mack. Social Research, The New School for Social Research, 65 Fifth Ave, Rm 240B, New York, NY 10003. Illus., adv. Refereed. Circ: 3000. Vol. ends: Dec. Microform: PMC; PQC. *Indexed:* A01, A22, ABIn, ABS&EES, B01, B02, BAS, BRI, CBRI, EconLit, FR, IPB, JEL, MLA-IB, P02, P61, SSA. *Aud.:* Ac.

This journal has been published since 1934 by the New School for Social Research, which offers postgraduate degrees in the social sciences. International in scope, the journal features research by scholars, writers, and experts from a variety of disciplines on topics of political, cultural, and economic concern. Most issues are thematic; recent themes have included giving, politics and comedy, Egypt in transition, the future of higher education, and India. Recommended for academic libraries that support programs in sociology and political science.

4903. *Social Science Computer Review.* Former titles (until 1988): *Social Science Microcomputer Review;* (until 1985): *Social Science Micro Review;* Which incorporated (1985 -1986): *Computers and the Social Sciences.* [ISSN: 0894-4393] 1983. bi-m. USD 880. Ed(s): G David Garson, Ronald E Anderson. Sage Publications, Inc., 2455 Teller Rd, Thousand Oaks, CA 91320; info@sagepub.com; http://www.sagepub.com. Illus., index, adv. Sample. Refereed. Vol. ends: Nov. Reprint: PSC. *Indexed:* A01, A22, BRI, C&ISA, CBRI, CerAb, CompLI, CompR, E01, FR, I15, P61, PsycInfo, SSA, SWR&A. *Bk. rev.:* 2-4; signed. *Aud.:* Ac.

This journal serves as the official publication of the Social Science Computing Association. It is an interdisciplinary journal that covers computer applications in social science instruction and research. Topics include artificial intelligence, business, computational social science theory, computer-assisted survey research and qualitative analysis, computer simulation, the social impacts of computing and telecommunications, and software evaluation. Features also include brief updates, Web resources for social scientists, book reviews, and sections that examine certain themes. Recommended for academic libraries that support graduate programs in the social sciences.

The Social Science Journal. See Cultural Studies section.

Social Science Research. See Cultural Studies section.

4904. *Social Work and Christianity.* Formerly (until 1979): *The Paraclete.* [ISSN: 0737-5778] 1974. q. USD 118 Free to members. Ed(s): David Sherwood. North American Association of Christians in Social Work, PO Box 121, Botsford, CT 06404; info@nacsw.org; http://www.nacsw.org. Refereed. *Indexed:* P61, PsycInfo, SSA, SWR&A. *Bk. rev.:* Number and length vary. *Aud.:* Ac, Sa.

This is a refereed journal published by the North American Association of Christians in Social Work (NACSW). Its purpose is to support and encourage social workers in the ethical integration of professional practice and Christian faith. Examples of recent articles include faith-based social services, professional values, youth programs, and the experiences of Christian students in social work education. A recent special issue focused on HIV/AIDS and a Christian social work response. Included are articles reporting on qualitative and quantitative research, shorter articles such as practice or teaching notes, reviews of books regarding Christian social work practice, and descriptions of new publications from the NACSW. While the NACSW asks a subscription fee, all content of the journal is freely available online. Recommended for academic libraries that support social work programs (especially programs offered by Christian schools) and for libraries that support faith-based social services.

4905. *Social Work in Health Care.* [ISSN: 0098-1389] 1975. 10x/yr. GBP 1177 (print & online eds.). Ed(s): Andrew Weissman, Gary Rosenberg. Routledge, 325 Chestnut St, Ste 800, Philadelphia, PA 19106; customerservice@taylorandfrancis.com; http://www.tandfonline.com. Illus., adv. Sample. Refereed. Microform: PQC. Reprint: PSC. *Indexed:* A01, A22, ASSIA, AgeL, Chicano, E01, MCR, P02, P61, PsycInfo, SSA, SWR&A. *Bk. rev.:* Number and length vary. *Aud.:* Ac, Sa.

This journal contains articles on social work theory, practice, and administration for and by professionals working in health-care settings. Themes include research on leadership, clinical practice, management, education, policy, and ethical issues. Issues occasionally include book reviews. Recommended for academic libraries that support social work, health-care, and social service programs.

4906. *Sociation Today.* [ISSN: 1542-6300] 2003. s-a. Free. Ed(s): George H Conklin. North Carolina Sociological Association, c/o Cathy Zimmer, CB 3355, 22 Manning Hall, Chapel Hill, NC 27599; ncsa@list.appstate.edu; http://www.ncsociology.org/. Refereed. *Indexed:* P61, SSA. *Bk. rev.:* Number and length vary. *Aud.:* Ga, Ac, Sa.

Sponsored by the North Carolina Sociological Association, this is a peer-reviewed, open-access online journal. It publishes research articles of core sociological interest (immigration, inequality, urban life, aging, and so on) written by regional and national authors. A recent issue featured the work of student researchers. Recommended for the electronic collections of academic libraries that support sociology programs.

4907. *Sociological Forum: official journal of the Eastern Sociological Society.* [ISSN: 0884-8971] 1986. q. GBP 484 (print & online eds.). Ed(s): Karen A Cerulo. Wiley-Blackwell Publishing, Inc., 111 River St, Hoboken, NJ 07030; info@wiley.com; http://onlinelibrary.wiley.com/. Illus., index, adv. Sample. Refereed. Microform: PQC. Reprint: PSC. *Indexed:* A01, A22, BRI, E01, FR, IBSS, MLA-IB, P61, PsycInfo, RILM, SSA. *Bk. rev.:* 4-6; signed. *Aud.:* Ac.

This title is the published for the Eastern Sociological Society, a nonprofit founded in 1930 to promote excellence in sociological scholarship and instruction. It features empirical articles, as well as those that develop theories, concepts, and methodological strategies. Topics cover all areas of sociology and related fields. Includes book reviews in each issue. Recommended for academic libraries that support programs in sociology.

4908. *Sociological Inquiry.* [ISSN: 0038-0245] 1930. q. GBP 175. Ed(s): Peter B Wood. Wiley-Blackwell Publishing, Inc., 111 River St, Hoboken, NJ 07030; info@wiley.com; http://onlinelibrary.wiley.com/. Illus., index, adv. Sample. Refereed. Microform: PQC. Reprint: PSC. *Indexed:* A01, A22, AbAn, BRI, CJPI, E01, FR, P02, P61, PsycInfo, RILM, RiskAb, SSA. *Bk. rev.:* . *Aud.:* Ac.

Published in one form or another since 1928, this publication is the official journal of Alpha Kappa Delta, the International Sociology Honor Society. As such, it exists to stimulate scholarship among sociology students, and features both theoretical and empirical studies in all aspects of social and cultural life. Recommended for academic libraries that support programs in sociology.

4909. *Sociological Methodology.* [ISSN: 0081-1750] 1969. a. USD 358. Ed(s): Tim Futing Liao. Sage Publications, Inc., 2455 Teller Rd, Thousand Oaks, CA 91320; info@sagepub.com; http://www.sagepub.com/. Adv. Sample. Refereed. Microform: PQC. Reprint: PSC. *Indexed:* A01, A22, ABIn, E01, IBSS, P02, P61, SSA. *Aud.:* Ac.

Sociological Methodology is published on behalf of the American Sociological Association as an annual edited, hardbound volume. It features a diversity of methodological problems faced in the social sciences, including conceptualization, data analysis and collection, measurement, modeling, and research design. From the journal's web site: "The journal provides a forum for engaging the philosophical issues that underpin sociological research design." Recommended for academic libraries that support programs in sociology.

4910. *Sociological Perspectives.* Formerly (until 1983): *Pacific Sociological Review.* [ISSN: 0731-1214] 1957. q. USD 453. Ed(s): Robert O'Brien, James Elliot. University of California Press, Journals Division, 2000 Ctr St, Ste 303, Berkeley, CA 94704; customerservice@ucpressjournals.com; http://www.ucpressjournals.com. Illus., index, adv. Sample. Refereed. Vol. ends: Sep. Microform: PQC. Reprint: PSC. *Indexed:* A01, A22, B01, BAS, BRI, Chicano, E01, IBSS, P02, P61, PsycInfo, RILM, SSA, SWR&A. *Aud.:* Ac.

This journal was founded in 1957 and is published for the Pacific Sociological Association. It contains research about social problems related to economic, political, anthropological, and historical issues. Topics of recent articles have included immigration, criminal justice, race, cultural transmission, community, parenting, suicide rates, gender, mental health, families, work and employment, and societal inequality. Recommended for academic libraries with programs in sociology.

4911. *The Sociological Quarterly.* Formerly (until 1960): *Midwest Sociologist.* [ISSN: 0038-0253] 1960. q. GBP 286. Ed(s): Lisa K Waldner, Betty A Bobratz. Wiley-Blackwell Publishing, Inc., 111 River St, Hoboken, NJ 07030; info@wiley.com; http://onlinelibrary.wiley.com/. Illus., index. Sample. Refereed. Vol. ends: Nov. Microform: WSH. Reprint: PSC. *Indexed:* A01, A22, ABS&EES, B01, BAS, CJPI, Chicano, E01, FR, IBSS, MLA-IB, P02, P61, PsycInfo, RILM, RiskAb, SSA, SWR&A. *Aud.:* Ac.

This journal feature cutting-edge research and theory in all areas of sociology; especially favored are articles that advance the field and appeal to a wide audience. It focuses on theoretically-informed empirical sociology. Features include an occasional special issue or special section; recent special sections included nature and culture, Latinos and skin color, and first-person ethnography. The 2011 Thompson Reuters Journal Impact Factor was 1.143; ISI Journal Citation Reports ranked it 39 out of 138 in Sociology. Recommended for academic libraries with programs in sociology.

Sociological Research. See Slavic Studies section.

4912. *Sociological Research Online.* [ISSN: 1360-7804] 1996. q. USD 1349. Ed(s): Paul Hodkinson, Rachel Brooks. University of Surrey, Department of Sociology, Guildford, GU2 7XH, United Kingdom. Illus. Refereed. *Indexed:* IBSS, P61, SSA. *Bk. rev.:* 3-10; signed. *Aud.:* Ac.

This online-only journal is jointly published by the University of Surrey, the University of Stirling, the British Sociological Association, and Sage, Ltd. Thus, most of its contributors are from the U.K., and its focus is international. It contains theoretical, empirical, and methodological research and debate on current political, cultural, and intellectual topics. The journal features book reviews, "rapid response" articles, letters to the editors, and special topical sections. Recent topics have included modern girlhoods and the Olympics. Recommended for academic libraries that support programs in sociology. URL: www.socresonline.org.uk

4913. *The Sociological Review.* Formerly (until 1908): *Sociological Papers.* [ISSN: 0038-0261] 1904. q. GBP 332 (print & online eds.). Ed(s): Rolland Munro, Beverley Skeggs. Wiley-Blackwell Publishing Ltd., The Atrium, Southern Gate, Chichester, PO19 8SQ, United Kingdom; customer@wiley.com; http://www.wiley.com/. Illus., adv. Sample. Refereed. Vol. ends: Nov. Microform: PQC. Reprint: PSC. *Indexed:* A01, A22, A47, BRI, C45, CBRI, CJPI, E01, FR, IBSS, MLA-IB, P02, P61, PsycInfo, RRTA, RiskAb, SSA. *Bk. rev.:* 10-12; signed. *Aud.:* Ac.

For over 100 years, *The Sociological Review* has published high-quality, innovative research articles geared toward the general sociological reader. The scope covers all aspects of sociology, including criminology, education, gender, medicine, social policy, women's studies, and social organization. Research orientations vary, and may be anthropological, philosophical, analytical, or ethnographic. Includes book reviews, and there are several special issues per year. Supplemental issues are published as monographs. Recommended for academic libraries.

4914. *Sociological Spectrum.* Formed by the merger of (1968-1980): *Sociological Symposium;* (1978-1980): *Sociological Forum.* [ISSN: 0273-2173] 1981. bi-m. GBP 556 (print & online eds.). Ed(s): Brian P Hinote, Kenin D Breault. Taylor & Francis Inc., 325 Chestnut St, Ste 800, Philadelphia, PA 19106; customerservice@taylorandfrancis.com; http://www.tandfonline.com. Illus., index, adv. Sample. Refereed. Vol. ends: Oct/Dec. Reprint: PSC. *Indexed:* A01, A22, ABS&EES, CJPI, E01, IBSS, P61, PsycInfo, RILM, RiskAb, SSA. *Aud.:* Ac.

As the official journal of the Mid-South Sociological Association, this journal publishes theoretical, methodological, quantitative, and qualitative research. Topics cover all areas of sociology, social psychology, anthropology, and political science. Recent articles have been on caregiving, race, gender, work, wages, cyberbullying, health care, and homelessness. Recommended for academic libraries with graduate programs in sociology.

4915. *Sociological Theory.* [ISSN: 0735-2751] 1983. q. USD 363. Ed(s): Neil Gross. Sage Publications, Inc., 2455 Teller Rd, Thousand Oaks, CA 91320; info@sagepub.com; http://www.sagepub.com/. Sample. Refereed. Reprint: PSC. *Indexed:* A01, A22, E01, FR, IBSS, P02, P61, SSA. *Aud.:* Ac.

Published in association with the American Sociological Association, this journal is international and interdisciplinary in scope. It contains research in all areas of theory, metatheory, ethnomethodology, and world systems analysis from authors of varied disciplines and disciplinary orientations. The 2011 Thompson Reuters Journal Impact Factor was 1.583. Recommended for academic libraries that support graduate programs in sociology.

4916. *Sociology.* [ISSN: 0038-0385] 1967. bi-m. USD 914. Ed(s): Karim Murji, Kath Woodward. Sage Publications Ltd., 1 Oliver's Yard, 55 City Rd, London, EC1Y 1SP, United Kingdom; info@sagepub.co.uk; http://www.uk.sagepub.com. Illus., index. Sample. Refereed. Vol. ends: Nov. Microform: PQC. Reprint: PSC. *Indexed:* A01, A22, ABIn, B01, BAS, BRI, C45, E01, FR, IBSS, P02, P61, PsycInfo, RRTA, SSA. *Bk. rev.:* 10-20; signed. *Aud.:* Ac.

This is the "flagship" journal of the British Sociological Association and is the premier sociology journal in the U.K. It contains reports on empirical research, and articles that challenge current concepts or propose innovative conceptual or methodological approaches and solutions to problems. Other features include "Research Notes," which provides brief reports on recent or ongoing studies, and an extensive book review section in each issue. The 2011 Thompson Reuters Journal Impact Factor was 1.352, while the ISI Journal Citation Reports ranked it 29 out of 138 in Sociology. Highly recommended for academic libraries that support sociology programs.

4917. *Sociology of Education.* Formerly (until 1963): *The Journal of Educational Sociology.* [ISSN: 0038-0407] 1927. q. USD 333. Ed(s): David B Bills. Sage Publications, Inc., 2455 Teller Rd, Thousand Oaks, CA 91320; info@sagepub.com; http://www.sagepub.com/. Illus., index. Refereed. Vol. ends: Oct. Microform: PMC; PQC. Reprint: PSC. *Indexed:* A01, A22, ASSIA, Chicano, E01, ERIC, FR, HEA, P02, P61, PsycInfo, SSA. *Aud.:* Ac.

This journal is published in association with the American Sociological Association; it contains studies that examine social institutions, individuals' experiences within these institutions, and how educational processes and social development are affected. The 2011 Thompson Reuters Journal Impact Factor was 1.750; ISI Journal Citation Reports ranked it 16 out of 138 in Sociology and 18 out of 206 in Education and Educational Research. Recommended for academic libraries that support programs in sociology and education.

4918. *Sociology of Health and Illness: a journal of medical sociology.* Incorporates (1995-1999): *Sociology of Health and Illness Monograph Series.* [ISSN: 0141-9889] 1979. bi-m. plus special issue. GBP 572. Ed(s): Clive Seale, Steven P Wainwright. Wiley-Blackwell Publishing Ltd., The Atrium, Southern Gate, Chichester, PO19 8SQ, United Kingdom; customer@wiley.com; http://www.wiley.com/. Illus., index, adv. Sample. Refereed. Vol. ends: Nov. Reprint: PSC. *Indexed:* A01, A22, BRI, C45, E01, FR, IBSS, MCR, P02, P61, PsycInfo, RRTA, SSA. *Bk. rev.:* 8-12; signed. *Aud.:* Ac.

This journal publishes sociological articles that address all aspects of health, illness, medicine, mental health, and health care. International in scope, it includes empirical and theoretical research reports and review articles. Although published bimonthly, it publishes an additional special issue each year on a topic of important and current interest. A recent special issue was on pandemics and emerging infectious diseases. The 2011 Thompson Reuters Journal Impact Factor was 1.885; ISI Journal Citation Reports ranked it 13 out of 138 in Sociology and 8 out of 37 in Social Sciences Biomedical. Recommended for academic libraries that support programs in sociology, health sciences, or social work.

Sociology of Religion. See Religion section.

4919. *Teaching Sociology.* Incorporates (1979-1985): *Teaching Newsletter;* Which was formerly (197?-1979): *On Teaching Undergraduate Sociology Newsletter.* [ISSN: 0092-055X] 1973. q. USD 333. Ed(s): Kathleen S Lowney. Sage Publications, Inc., 2455 Teller Rd, Thousand Oaks, CA 91320; info@sagepub.com; http://www.sagepub.com. Illus. Refereed. Vol. ends: Oct. Reprint: PSC. *Indexed:* A22, ASSIA, E01, ERIC, FR, MLA-IB, P61, RILM, SSA. *Bk. rev.:* 2-6; signed. *Aud.:* Ac.

The content of *Teaching Sociology* is intended to be of interest to sociology professors. It publishes full articles, shorter notes, review essays, and reviews of books, films, and the occasional Web or computer resource. Topics include pedagogical issues, curriculum development, course design, writing in the discipline, online teaching, and teaching strategies. Recommended for academic libraries that support postgraduate programs in sociology or education.

Theory and Decision. See Philosophy section.

4920. *Theory and Society: renewal and critique in social theory.* [ISSN: 0304-2421] 1974. bi-m. EUR 828 (print & online eds.). Ed(s): Janet Gouldner, Karen G Lucas. Springer Netherlands, Van Godewijckstraat 30, Dordrecht, 3311 GX, Netherlands; http://www.springer.com. Illus., index, adv. Sample. Refereed. Vol. ends: Nov. Microform: PQC. Reprint: PSC. *Indexed:* A01, A22, BAS, BRI, E01, FR, IBSS, P61, SSA. *Bk. rev.:* 2-4; signed. *Aud.:* Ac.

This is an international journal that publishes theoretical research articles on social processes and analysis. Topics cover a broad landscape across history, from prehistory to the contemporary; treatment blends theory, methodological critique, criticism, and observation. Recommended for academic libraries that support graduate programs in sociology.

4921. *Theory, Culture & Society: explorations in critical social science.* [ISSN: 0263-2764] 1982. 8x/yr. USD 1767. Ed(s): Mike Featherstone. Sage Publications Ltd., 1 Oliver's Yard, 55 City Rd, London, EC1Y 1SP, United Kingdom; info@sagepub.co.uk; http://www.uk.sagepub.com. Illus., index. Sample. Refereed. Vol. ends: Nov. Reprint: PSC. *Indexed:* A01, A22, A47, ABIn, ArtHuCI, BRI, E01, FR, IBSS, MLA-IB, P61, RILM, SSA. *Bk. rev.:* 1-2; signed. *Aud.:* Ac.

This journal publishes research and review articles in the social and cultural sciences. International and interdisciplinary in scope, articles present cutting-edge developments in social and cultural theory. Features include research articles, commentaries, interviews, review articles, and book reviews. The 2011 Thompson Reuters Journal Impact Factor was 1.770; ISI Journal Citation Reports ranked it 1 out of 35 in Cultural Studies. Recommended for academic libraries that support graduate programs in the social sciences.

Violence Against Women. See Gender Studies section.

4922. *Work and Occupations: an international sociological journal.* Formerly (until 1982): *Sociology of Work and Occupations.* [ISSN: 0730-8884] 1974. q. USD 956. Ed(s): Daniel B Cornfield. Sage Publications, Inc., 2455 Teller Rd, Thousand Oaks, CA 91320; info@sagepub.com; http://www.sagepub.com. Illus., index, adv. Sample. Refereed. Vol. ends: Nov. Microform: PQC. Reprint: PSC. *Indexed:* A01, A22, ABIn, B01, B02, BRI, C&ISA, CerAb, E01, ErgAb, FR, H24, IBSS, P02, P61, PsycInfo, SSA, SWR&A. *Bk. rev.:* 4-6; signed. *Aud.:* Ac.

This journal publishes social science research on the dynamics of the workplace, employment, and society. It is international in scope and includes the interdisciplinary perspectives of sociology, anthropology, education, history, industrial relations, management, and psychology. Topics addressed in recent articles have included job insecurity and inequality, disability accommodations, gender, immigration policy, workplace diversity, globalization, and work and family. Features also include research notes, review essays, and book reviews. Recommended for academic libraries that support graduate programs in sociology or labor relations.

4923. *Youth & Society.* [ISSN: 0044-118X] 1969. q. USD 1002. Ed(s): Mark Zimmerman. Sage Publications, Inc., 2455 Teller Rd, Thousand Oaks, CA 91320; info@sagepub.com; http://www.sagepub.com. Illus., index, adv. Sample. Refereed. Vol. ends: Jun. Microform: PQC. Reprint: PSC. *Indexed:* A01, A22, ABS&EES, ASSIA, Agr, Chicano, E01, ERIC, H24, HEA, P02, P61, PsycInfo, RILM, RiskAb, SSA, SWR&A. *Aud.:* Ac, Sa.

This is an international journal that focuses on issues faced by adolescents and young adults. Subject coverage is interdisciplinary and includes aspects of sociology, psychology, public health, education, social work, criminology, anthropology, and political science. Topics are of interest to researchers, educators, counselors, policy makers, and others who study and work with adolescents. Articles in recent issues have focused on school culture, youth violence, peer pressure, parenting, tobacco and drug use, and suicide. There are occasional special-theme issues or sections. The 2011 Thompson Reuters Journal Impact Factor was 1.816; ISI Journal Citation Reports ranked it 14 out of 138 in Sociology, 11 out of 89 in Social Sciences, Interdisciplinary, and 6 out of 38 in Social Issues. Highly recommended for academic libraries.

Social Work and Social Welfare

4924. *Administration in Social Work.* [ISSN: 0364-3107] 1977. 5x/yr. GBP 822 (print & online eds.). Ed(s): Richard L Edwards. Routledge, 325 Chestnut St, Ste 800, Philadelphia, PA 19106; customerservice@taylorandfrancis.com; http://www.tandfonline.com. Illus., adv. Sample. Refereed. Circ: 972 Paid. Vol. ends: Winter. Microform: PQC. Reprint: PSC. *Indexed:* A01, A22, ABIn, B01, B02, BRI, E01, P02, P61, PsycInfo, SSA, SWR&A. *Bk. rev.:* Number and length vary. *Aud.:* Ac.

This journal is the official publication of the National Network of Social Work Managers. It provides articles on theory, practice, and research for human services administrators, managers, and educators, focusing on social service administration and social policy planning. Key issues include program development, employment and professional practices, budgeting and finances, and assessment and quality control. Recent articles have had international origins, and special thematic issues are also published. Recommended for academic libraries with graduate programs in social work, and for social service agencies.

4925. *Adoption Quarterly: innovations in community and clinical practice, theory and research.* [ISSN: 1092-6755] 1997. q. GBP 355 (print & online eds.). Ed(s): Scott Ryan. Routledge, 325 Chestnut St, Ste 800, Philadelphia, PA 19106; customerservice@taylorandfrancis.com; http://www.tandfonline.com. Sample. Refereed. Circ: 305 Paid. Reprint: PSC. *Indexed:* A01, A22, E01, P61, PsycInfo, SSA, SWR&A. *Bk. rev.:* Number and length vary. *Aud.:* Ac, Sa.

Adoption Quarterly is an international and multidisciplinary journal that examines issues around adoption and foster care from the ethical, financial, legal, policy, and social perspectives. Recent articles also explored adoptive family relationships, infertility and reproductive technologies, and trends in adoption. This title features conceptual and empirical works focusing on race, culture, and social trends in adoption, as well as commentaries, systematic reviews, and signed book and film reviews that will be relevant to adoption practitioners and researchers. Recommended for academic libraries with social work programs and agencies that serve children and families.

4926. *Advances in Social Work (Online).* s-a. Free. Ed(s): William Barton. Indiana University, School of Social Work, 902 W New York St, Indianapolis, IN 46202; iussw@iupui.edu; http://socialwork.iu.edu/. *Aud.:* Ga, Ac.

Advances in Social Work is an online, open-access journal published by the Indiana University School of Social Work. It features original material on social work practice and research, as it addresses issues, challenges, and thought relevant to practitioners and social work educators. Journal topics and discussion encourage the development of innovation in the field, as well as providing a forum for scholarly exchange of research findings and ideas. Recent special issue topics have included global problems and military social work. This journal is an important addition to the online collections of academic libraries that support social work programs and special libraries that serve social services.

4927. *The British Journal of Social Work.* Formed by the merger of (1947-1970): *British Journal of Psychiatric Social Work;* (1939-1970): *Social Work.* [ISSN: 0045-3102] 1971. 8x/yr. EUR 994. Ed(s): John Pinkerton, Jim Campbell. Oxford University Press, Great Clarendon St,

Oxford, OX2 6DP, United Kingdom; enquiry@oup.co.uk; http://www.oxfordjournals.org/. Illus., adv. Sample. Refereed. Microform: PQC. Reprint: PSC. *Indexed:* A22, BRI, E01, IBSS, PsycInfo, RiskAb, SSA, SWR&A. *Bk. rev.:* 7-10, signed. *Aud.:* Ac.

This journal is published by the British Association of Social Workers, and as such, it is the U.K.'s leading social work journal. Covering every aspect of social work, articles include research on various aspects of practice, principles, and theory. Special issues have included death and dying, the political challenges of social work, and practice innovations. The journal's audience includes social work educators, researchers, practitioners, and managers. Issues include signed book reviews. Recommended for academic libraries that support graduate social work programs.

4928. Child and Adolescent Social Work Journal. Former titles (until 1982): *Family and Child Mental Health Journal;* (until 1980): *Issues in Child Mental Health;* (until vol.5, 1977): *Psychosocial Process.* [ISSN: 0738-0151] 1970. bi-m. EUR 1017 (print & online eds.). Ed(s): Thomas K Kenemore. Springer New York LLC, 233 Spring St, New York, NY 10013; service-ny@springer.com; http://www.springer.com/. Illus., adv. Sample. Refereed. Reprint: PSC. *Indexed:* A01, A22, ASSIA, Agr, BRI, E01, P02, PsycInfo, RiskAb, SSA, SWR&A. *Bk. rev.:* 1-3; signed. *Aud.:* Ga, Ac, Sa.

This journal features research focused on clinical social work practice with children, youth, and families. Articles address problems and current issues in social work as drawn from theory, direct practice, research, and social policy. Examples of recent articles include foster care, juvenile justice, mental health in urban youth, and parenting. Recommended for academic libraries that support social work programs and social services that work with children, youth, and families.

4929. Child & Family Social Work. [ISSN: 1356-7500] 1996. q. GBP 485. Ed(s): Susan White. Wiley-Blackwell Publishing Ltd., The Atrium, Southern Gate, Chichester, PO19 8SQ, United Kingdom; customer@wiley.com; http://www.wiley.com/. Adv. Sample. Refereed. Reprint: PSC. *Indexed:* A01, A22, E01, IBSS, P02, P61, PsycInfo, RiskAb, SSA, SWR&A. *Bk. rev.:* 5-8; signed. *Aud.:* Ac, Sa.

Child & Family Social Work publishes original articles by social work practitioners, researchers, policymakers, and administrators. It "is dedicated to advancing the wellbeing and welfare of children and their families throughout the world." It is international in scope; recent articles include orphans in Botswana, adoption in South Africa, and grandparents raising their grandchildren in Australia. The 2011 ISI Journal Citation Reports rank was 14 out of 41 in Social Work and 26 out of 38 in Family Studies. Recommended for academic libraries that support social work programs and other libraries that support social service professionals.

4930. Child Welfare: journal of policy, practice and program. Formerly (until 1948): *Child Welfare League of America. Bulletin.* [ISSN: 0009-4021] 1921. bi-m. Ed(s): Sarah Sallen. Child Welfare League of America, Inc., 2345 Crystal Dr, Ste 250, Arlington, VA 22202; journal@cwla.org; http://www.cwla.org. Illus., index, adv. Sample. Refereed. Vol. ends: Nov/Dec. Microform: PQC. *Indexed:* A01, A22, ABS&EES, AbAn, Agr, BRI, Chicano, ERIC, IBSS, P02, P61, PsycInfo, SSA, SWR&A. *Aud.:* Ac, Sa.

Child Welfare is published by the Child Welfare League of America in order to advocate for the welfare of children and youth who are homeless, abused, disabled, or new to the country. Additional topics include traumatic stress, children's rights, residential care, mental health, adoption, protective services and welfare, and parenting, and public policy. One or two issues per volume are thematic. Highly recommended for academic libraries that support social work programs and those that support child welfare professionals.

4931. Children & Schools: a journal of social work practice. Formerly (until 2000): *Social Work in Education.* [ISSN: 1532-8759] 1978. q. EUR 132. Ed(s): Melissa Jonson-Reid. Oxford University Press, 2001 Evans Rd, Cary, NC 27513; jnlorders@oup-usa.org; http://www.oxfordjournals.org. Illus., index, adv. Circ: 3700 Paid. Vol. ends: Oct. Microform: PQC. *Indexed:* A01, A22, ASSIA, ERIC, P02, P61, PsycInfo, SSA, SWR&A. *Aud.:* Ac, Sa.

Children & Schools is published by the National Association of Social Workers. It publishes research articles and commentary that focus on trends in professional school social work and interdisciplinary practice, program evaluation, policy, and planning. Recent topics have included bullying, trauma and violence, multiculturalism, early intervention, needs assessment, and ADHD. A vital "practice-to-practitioner" resource; highly recommended for academic and special libraries that support social work programs and education.

4932. Children and Youth Services Review: an international multidisciplinary review of the welfare of young people. [ISSN: 0190-7409] 1979. m. EUR 1743. Ed(s): Duncan Lindsey. Pergamon, The Blvd, Langford Ln, E Park, Kidlington, OX5 1GB, United Kingdom; JournalsCustomerServiceEMEA@elsevier.com; http://www.elsevier.com. Illus., adv. Sample. Refereed. Microform: PQC. *Indexed:* A01, A22, BRI, H24, P61, PsycInfo, RiskAb, SSA, SWR&A. *Bk. rev.:* 0-4; signed. *Aud.:* Ac.

This journal publishes articles that present research and policy discussions that assess social service programs and services for children and youth worldwide. Article topics have included interventions, practice, mental health services, residential placement, case management, and other issues that affect children from early childhood to high school. Book reviews are occasionally included. The 2011 Journal Impact Factor was 1.269. Recommended for academic libraries that support social work, child psychology, or social service programs.

4933. Clinical Social Work Journal. [ISSN: 0091-1674] 1973. q. EUR 1061 (print & online eds.). Ed(s): Carol Tosone, Carol Ganzer. Springer New York LLC, 233 Spring St, New York, NY 10013; service-ny@springer.com; http://www.springer.com/. Illus., adv. Sample. Refereed. Vol. ends: Winter. Microform: PQC. Reprint: PSC. *Indexed:* A01, A22, BRI, E01, P02, P61, PsycInfo, RiskAb, SSA, SWR&A. *Bk. rev.:* 1-4; signed. *Aud.:* Ac, Sa.

This journal serves as an international forum for the advancement of clinical knowledge and insight of practitioners, educators, researchers, and policymakers. Founded in 1973, journal presents articles relevant to contemporary clinical practice with individuals, couples, families, and groups. Emphasis is placed on innovations in theoretical and practice- and evidence-based clinical research as well as on interdisciplinary approaches. This title features frequent special-topic issues; there are occasional book reviews. Highly recommended for academic libraries that support social work programs and for public and special libraries that serve social service professionals.

4934. Critical Social Policy: a journal of theory and practice in social welfare. [ISSN: 0261-0183] 1981. q. USD 758. Sage Publications Ltd., 1 Oliver's Yard, 55 City Rd, London, EC1Y 1SP, United Kingdom; info@sagepub.co.uk; http://www.uk.sagepub.com. Illus., adv. Sample. Refereed. Reprint: PSC. *Indexed:* A01, A22, E01, IBSS, P61, PsycInfo, RiskAb, SSA. *Bk. rev.:* 5-6 signed. *Aud.:* Ac, Sa.

This journal seeks to provide an international forum for advocacy, analysis, and debate on social policy on issues of importance to social welfare. Research is presented from socialist, feminist, anti-racist, and radical perspectives, giving voice to inequalities, injustices, and oppressed individuals and communities. Recent special-theme issues focused on housing and on inequality. Commentaries advocate and provoke debate on social policy issues. Each issue contains signed book reviews. Recommended for academic libraries that support social work, sociology, or political science.

4935. Ethics and Social Welfare. [ISSN: 1749-6535] 2007. 4x/yr. GBP 305 (print & online eds.). Ed(s): Derek Clifford. Routledge, 4 Park Sq, Milton Park, Abingdon, OX14 4RN, United Kingdom; subscriptions@tandf.co.uk; http://www.tandfonline.com. Adv. Sample. Refereed. Reprint: PSC. *Indexed:* A22, E01, PsycInfo, SSA. *Bk. rev.:* Number and length vary. *Aud.:* Ac.

This journal publishes critical and reflective articles concerned with ethical issues in social work and social welfare practice and policy. It focuses on social work practice with individuals, families and groups, social care, youth and community work, and other related professional areas. Contributors include academics, field practitioners, voluntary workers, service users, and others of diverse perspectives. Case studies and a section on ethical issues in practice present problems and dilemmas, as well as reflections on ethics, values, and policy. Recommended for academic libraries that support social work programs.

4936. *Families in Society: the journal of contemporary social services.*
Former titles (until Jan.1990): *Social Casework;* (until 1950): *Journal of Social Casework;* (until 1946): *The Family.* [ISSN: 1044-3894] 1920. q. USD 228 (Individuals, USD 67 (print & online eds.); Free to members). Ed(s): Ms. Kirstin E Anderson, Dr. William E Powell. Alliance for Children and Families, 11700 W Lake Park Dr, Milwaukee, WI 53224; http://www.alliance1.org/. Illus., adv. Refereed. Circ: 2100 Paid. Vol. ends: Dec. Microform: PQC. *Indexed:* A01, A22, BRI, C37, CBRI, Chicano, P02, P61, PsycInfo, SSA, SWR&A. *Bk. rev.:* 2-4; signed. *Aud.:* Ac.

Families in Society was founded in 1920 and is published by the Alliance for Children and Families. It is the oldest and one of the most highly regarded professional journals in North America on social work and social services. Its wide-ranging content appeals to practitioners, educators, and others in the human services. Articles focus on major trends and techniques, research, theory, direct-practice issues, and the delivery and management of services. Book reviews (six to eight) are offered in each issue of the online version only. An essential and standard title for academic libraries with programs in sociology and social work.

Family Process. See Family section.

Family Relations. See Family section.

4937. *Health & Social Work.* [ISSN: 0360-7283] 1976. q. EUR 132. Ed(s): Stephen Gorin. Oxford University Press, 2001 Evans Rd, Cary, NC 27513; jnlorders@oup-usa.org; http://www.oxfordjournals.org. Illus., index, adv. Refereed. Circ: 6500 Paid. Vol. ends: Nov. Microform: PQC. Reprint: PSC. *Indexed:* A01, A22, AbAn, AgeL, BRI, Chicano, ERIC, IBSS, P02, P61, PsycInfo, SSA, SWR&A. *Bk. rev.:* 5-6; signed. *Aud.:* Ga, Ac, Sa.

Published by the National Association of Social Workers Press, this journal covers research, policy, specialized services, quality assurance, and other subjects related to the delivery of health-care service. Health-related topics have included aging, clinical work, oncology, substance abuse, depression, maternal health, and a variety of physical, mental health, and social and cultural issues. Special features include articles on practice, social policy and planning, and legislative issues; and there are occasional book reviews on subjects of interest to professionals in this field. Recommended for academic libraries that support social work, nursing, and social service programs.

4938. *International Journal of Child, Youth and Family Studies.* [ISSN: 1920-7298] 2010. irreg. Free. Ed(s): Sibylle Artz. University of Victoria, School of Child and Youth Care, PO Box 1700, Victoria, BC V8W 2Y2, Canada. Refereed. *Aud.:* Ga, Ac, Sa.

This is an open-access, interdisciplinary journal published by the School of Child and Youth Care at the University of Victoria, British Columbia. Articles include practice issues and research regarding services for children, youth, families, and their communities. Although much of the focus is on Canada, the scope includes other countries as well. Academic libraries that support sociology and social work will find this a useful addition to their electronic holdings.

4939. *International Social Work.* Formerly (until 1958): *Social Welfare in South-East-Asia.* [ISSN: 0020-8728] 1959. bi-m. USD 1451. Ed(s): Simon Hackett, Lena Dominelli. Sage Publications Ltd., 1 Oliver's Yard, 55 City Rd, London, EC1Y 1SP, United Kingdom; info@sagepub.co.uk; http://www.uk.sagepub.com. Illus., index. Sample. Refereed. Vol. ends: Oct. Microform: PQC. Reprint: PSC. *Indexed:* A01, A22, BRI, E01, IBSS, P02, PsycInfo, SSA, SWR&A. *Bk. rev.:* 2-4; signed. *Aud.:* Ac, Sa.

This journal is published in association with the International Association of Schools of Social Work, the International Counsel on Social Welfare, and the International Federation of Social Workers. Scholarly research in the journal focuses on issues regarding the delivery of services, the functions of social work

professionals, and the education of social workers. Emphasis is placed on comparative analysis and cross-national research. Recent theme issues have included religion and spirituality, child rights in Africa, and social work in Latin America. Recommended for academic libraries that support social work programs and those that serve social service programs.

4940. *Journal of Family Social Work.* Formerly (until 1995): *Journal of Social Work and Human Sexuality.* [ISSN: 1052-2158] 1981. 5x/yr. GBP 329 (print & online eds.). Ed(s): Pat Conway. Routledge, 325 Chestnut St, Ste 800, Philadelphia, PA 19106; customerservice@taylorandfrancis.com; http://www.tandfonline.com. Adv. Sample. Refereed. Circ: 408 Paid. Microform: PQC. Reprint: PSC. *Indexed:* A01, A22, ASSIA, AbAn, E01, ERIC, P61, RiskAb, SSA, SWR&A. *Bk. rev.:* Number and length vary. *Aud.:* Ac, Sa.

This journal disseminates information related to families through research articles and conceptual, practical, and creative works devoted to practice subjects and ecosystemic theory. The intent is to advance practitioners' abilities to integrate research, policy, theory, and wisdom into their service to families. Approaches include social work, family therapy and studies, sociology, health and mental health, and child welfare. Highly recommended for academic libraries that support social work programs and for public and special libraries that serve social service professionals.

Journal of Gerontological Social Work. See Geriatrics and Gerontological Studies section.

4941. *Journal of Global Social Work Practice.* [ISSN: 1944-6039] 2008. s-a. Free. Ed(s): Jan A Rodgers. Dominican University, Graduate School of Social Work, 7200 W Division St, River Forest, IL 60305; msw@dom.edu; http://www.dom.edu/academics/gssw/index.html. Refereed. *Aud.:* Ac.

This is an open-access journal that publishes articles on all aspects of global social work practice. The journal aims to encourage global networking and scholarly exchanges about practice, skills building, theoretical framework building, tactics, and techniques. Also discussed is the IFSW Code of Ethics as it relates to international social work practice. Writers are scholars, students, and practitioners. Academic libraries with social work programs may add this to their electronic holdings.

4942. *Journal of Immigrant & Refugee Studies.* Formerly (until 2006): *Journal of Immigrant & Refugee Services.* [ISSN: 1556-2948] 2002. q. GBP 395 (print & online eds.). Ed(s): Anna Triandafyllidou. Routledge, 325 Chestnut St, Ste 800, Philadelphia, PA 19106; customerservice@taylorandfrancis.com; http://www.tandfonline.com. Adv. Refereed. Circ: 53 Paid. Reprint: PSC. *Indexed:* A01, A22, C45, E01, IBSS, P61, SSA. *Bk. rev.:* Number and length vary. *Aud.:* Ac.

This journal focuses on the effects of worldwide migration. It is international and interdisciplinary in scope, and issues include immigration policy, the health and mental health of immigrants, sociological and economic implications, business and service programs and implications, and other related topics. Issues have included the effects of the trauma of war, hate crimes, human trafficking, identity, gender roles, assimilation, and many other challenges faced by displaced people. Recommended for academic libraries that support programs in the social sciences.

4943. *Journal of International and Comparative Social Policy.* Former titles (until 2013): *Journal of Comparative Social Welfare;* (until 2006): *New Global Development;* (until 1995): *Journal of International and Comparative Social Welfare.* [ISSN: 2169-9763] 1984. 3x/yr. GBP 298 (print & online eds.). Ed(s): Dr. Kevin Farnsworth, Dr. Zoe Irving. Routledge, 4 Park Sq, Milton Park, Abingdon, OX14 4RN, United Kingdom; subscriptions@tandf.co.uk; http://www.tandfonline.com. Adv. Sample. Refereed. Reprint: PSC. *Indexed:* A22, E01, IBSS, P61, SSA, SWR&A. *Bk. rev.:* Number and length vary. *Aud.:* Ac.

As implied by the title, the articles in this journal are comparative and/or international in scope and focus on national, regional, or global social policies. Themes included are country case studies, policy processes, welfare outcomes, and the provision of services. Issues have included the financial crisis in Europe, income inequality, social work practice, adoption, human trafficking, and aging and the elderly. Recommended for academic libraries that support graduate programs in social work, sociology, political science, international studies, and public administration.

Journal of Marital and Family Therapy. See Family section.

4944. *Journal of Social Service Research.* [ISSN: 0148-8376] 1977. 5x/yr. GBP 788 (print & online eds.). Ed(s): Sophia F Dziegielewski, Barbara Maisevich. Routledge, 325 Chestnut St, Ste 800, Philadelphia, PA 19106; customerservice@taylorandfrancis.com; http://www.tandfonline.com. Illus., adv. Sample. Refereed. Circ: 435 Paid. Microform: PQC. Reprint: PSC. *Indexed:* A01, A22, E01, FR, P02, PsycInfo, RILM, SSA, SWR&A. *Aud.:* Ac.

The focus of this journal is outcomes-based empirical research and practice, and applications to the design, delivery, and management of social services. Different types of methodologies and funded and non-funded research are featured. Contributors are from a variety national and international social service areas, and include researchers, practitioners, policymakers, and administrators. Recommended for academic libraries that support programs in social work and social services.

4945. *Journal of Social Work.* [ISSN: 1468-0173] 2001. bi-m. USD 936. Ed(s): Steven M Shardlow. Sage Publications Ltd., 1 Oliver's Yard, 55 City Rd, London, EC1Y 1SP, United Kingdom; info@sagepub.co.uk; http://www.uk.sagepub.com. Sample. Refereed. Reprint: PSC. *Indexed:* A01, A22, E01, IBSS, P61, PsycInfo, RiskAb, SSA. *Bk. rev.:* 6-8; signed. *Aud.:* Ac.

The *Journal of Social Work* is an international journal that presents and debates key research and ideas in social work. Empirical and theoretical articles analyze and advance theoretical understanding, shape policy, and inform practice. The scope is international and topics reflect the diversity of the social work profession. In addition to longer research articles, the "Critical Forum" section includes shorter commentaries, reports of research in progress, and analysis of current trends. Extensive, signed book reviews are included in each issue. ISI Journal Citation Reports ranked it 11 out of 41 in Social Work. Recommended for academic libraries that support programs in social work.

4946. *Journal of Social Work Practice in the Addictions.* [ISSN: 1533-256X] 2001. q. GBP 307 (print & online eds.). Ed(s): Shulamith Lala Ashenberg Straussner. Routledge, 325 Chestnut St, Ste 800, Philadelphia, PA 19106; customerservice@taylorandfrancis.com; http://www.tandfonline.com. Adv. Sample. Reprint: PSC. *Indexed:* A01, A22, E01, P61, PsycInfo, SSA, SWR&A. *Bk. rev.:* Number and length vary. *Aud.:* Ga, Ac, Sa.

This is a refereed journal intended to inform social work practitioners about the latest developments in the field of addictions. Articles focus on innovative individual, family, and group work, and community practice in the treatment and prevention of substance abuse and other addictions in diverse populations and ages. Journal coverage includes research findings, health care, social policies, and program administration that affects social work practice in addictions. Features include interviews with experts, books reviews, commentaries, and the occasional special-theme issue. Recommended for academic libraries that support graduate social work programs, and public or special libraries that support social services that work with addiction issues.

4947. *Journal of Sociology and Social Welfare.* [ISSN: 0191-5096] 1973. q. USD 80. Ed(s): Frederick MacDonald, Robert D Leighninger. Western Michigan University, School of Social Work, 1903 W Michigan Ave, Kalamazoo, MI 49008; swrk-jssw@wmich.edu; http://www.wmich.edu/hhs/sw/. Illus., index. Refereed. Vol. ends: Dec. Microform: PQC. *Indexed:* A01, A22, BRI, C42, FR, P61, SSA, SWR&A. *Bk. rev.:* 5-7; signed. *Aud.:* Ac, Sa.

This online journal is sponsored and hosted by the School of Social Work, Western Michigan University. Its purpose is the promotion of social welfare through the application of social science, methodology, and technology to problems involving social policy, politics, and social services. It contains research articles on topics such as social change, gender, race, migration, social

inequality, homelessness, social welfare history, cultural diversity, and health and mental health. International issues are also discussed. Each issue contains signed book reviews. One issue per year is thematic; the topic of the most recent was race. Recommended for academic libraries that support social work and sociology programs.

4948. *Professional Social Work.* [ISSN: 1352-3112] 1994. m. GBP 39.50 domestic (Free to members). Ed(s): Joseph Devo. British Association of Social Workers, 16 Kent St, Birmingham, B5 6RD, United Kingdom; info@basw.co.uk; http://www.basw.co.uk. Adv. Circ: 10000 Paid. *Bk. rev.:* Number and length vary. *Aud.:* Ga, Ac.

This magazine for social work practitioners is published by the British Association of Social Workers. It contains news and analysis, feature articles, opinions and letters, brief book reviews, and reports on professional issues in countries of the U.K. The current issue is available to BASW members; past issues are free to the public. Academic or public libraries used by social work programs or social workers may wish to link to this magazine.

4949. *Psychoanalytic Social Work.* Former titles (until 1999): *Journal of Analytic Social Work;* (until 1992): *Journal of Independent Social Work.* [ISSN: 1522-8878] 1987. s-a. GBP 488 (print & online eds.). Ed(s): Jerrold R Brandell. Routledge, 325 Chestnut St, Ste 800, Philadelphia, PA 19106; customerservice@taylorandfrancis.com; http://www.tandfonline.com. Illus., adv. Sample. Refereed. Circ: 164 Paid. Vol. ends: Winter. Reprint: PSC. *Indexed:* A01, A22, E01, P61, PsycInfo, SSA, SWR&A. *Bk. rev.:* 2-4; signed. *Aud.:* Ac, Sa.

This journal focuses exclusively on the important clinical themes and dilemmas that occur in psychoanalytic social work. It provides research articles relevant to practice with individual clients, including case studies; approaches to special populations, minorities, and the underserved; specialized and innovative techniques and methods in a clinical setting; and clinical approaches to psychoanalytic issues. This title provides clinical social workers with contemporary perspectives, theories, clinical methods, and techniques to enhance knowledge of psychoanalytic practice. Recommended for academic libraries that support graduate social work programs, and for special libraries that serve social work professionals.

4950. *Qualitative Social Work: research and practice.* [ISSN: 1473-3250] 2002. bi-m. USD 976. Ed(s): Karen M Staller, Michael Krumer-Nero. Sage Publications Ltd., 1 Oliver's Yard, 55 City Rd, London, EC1Y 1SP, United Kingdom; info@sagepub.co.uk; http://www.uk.sagepub.com. Sample. Reprint: PSC. *Indexed:* A01, A22, E01, P61, PsycInfo, SSA, SWR&A. *Bk. rev.:* 1-2; signed. *Aud.:* Ac.

This journal contains articles that report on qualitative research and evaluation and qualitative approaches to social work practice. It promotes dialogue on the role of critical perspectives within social work, reflective inquiry and practice, emerging applications for research within the field, and the potential of social constructionist and narrative approaches to research and practice. In addition to full-length research articles, regular and special features of the journal include responses to past articles and commentaries on current research and practice; accounts and reflections on the methodology and practice of qualitative social work; a "New Voices" section from practitioners and new researchers; and signed book reviews. Recommended for academic libraries that support social work programs.

4951. *Research on Social Work Practice.* [ISSN: 1049-7315] 1990. bi-m. USD 956. Ed(s): Bruce A Thyer. Sage Publications, Inc., 2455 Teller Rd, Thousand Oaks, CA 91320; info@sagepub.com; http://www.sagepub.com. Illus., index. Sample. Refereed. Vol. ends: Nov. Reprint: PSC. *Indexed:* A01, A22, BRI, E01, ERIC, P02, P61, PsycInfo, RiskAb, SSA, SWR&A. *Bk. rev.:* 2-4; signed. *Aud.:* Ac.

This journal publishes empirical research reporting on assessment methods and evidence-based outcomes of social work practice. Interventions may include behavior analysis and therapy, psychotherapy or counseling, case management, education, supervision, practice with couples, families or small group, organizational management, community practice, and policy evaluation. Features include special issues or sections, systematic reviews, a section on new methods of assessment, and book reviews. The 2011 Thompson Reuters Journal Impact Factor was 1.532; ISI Journal Citation Reports ranked it 5 out of 41 in Social Work. Recommended for academic libraries that support social work programs.

4952. Social Development Issues. Supersedes (in 1977): *Iowa Journal of Social Work.* [ISSN: 0147-1473] 1968. 3x/yr. USD 105 (print & online eds.). Ed(s): Vijayan Pillai. Lyceum Books, Inc., 5758 S Blackstone Ave, Chicago, IL 60637; lyceum@lyceumbooks.com; http://www.lyceumbooks.com. Refereed. *Indexed:* A22, IBSS, P61, PsycInfo, SSA, SWR&A. *Bk. rev.:* Number and length vary. *Aud.:* Ac.

This journal is sponsored by the International Consortium for Social Development. It serves as an interdisciplinary, scholarly forum to promote issues that affect social justice and advancement of social, cultural, political, and economic theories, policy, and practice within a global context. Topics in recent issues have included women's reproductive health, sustainable development, globalization, and relief services for refugees. Each issue contains book reviews. Recommended for academic libraries that support graduate programs in sociology, social work, political science, and international studies.

4953. Social Service Review. [ISSN: 0037-7961] 1927. q. USD 271 (print & online eds.). Ed(s): Susan Lambert, Michael R Sosin. University of Chicago Press, 1427 E 60th St, Chicago, IL 60637; subscriptions@press.uchicago.edu; http://www.journals.uchicago.edu. Illus., index, adv. Sample. Refereed. Microform: MIM; PMC; PQC. Reprint: PSC. *Indexed:* A01, A22, ASSIA, B01, BRI, CBRI, Chicano, EconLit, IBSS, JEL, MCR, P02, P61, PsycInfo, SSA, SWR&A. *Bk. rev.:* 5-7; signed. *Aud.:* Ga, Ac.

Since 1927, this journal has published original research that examines and evaluates social welfare policy, organization, theory, and practice from multicultural and multidisciplinary perspectives. Emphasis is placed on the presentation of long-range solutions to critical problems. Points of view from scholars and practitioners in various disciplines are represented, including social service, social policy, sociology, public administration, history, economics, and political science. Each issue includes critical books reviews. Essential title for academic, public, and special libraries that serve social service professionals.

4954. Social Work. [ISSN: 0037-8046] 1956. q. EUR 137. Ed(s): Elizabeth Pomeroy. Oxford University Press, 2001 Evans Rd, Cary, NC 27513; jnlorders@oup-usa.org; http://www.oxfordjournals.org. Illus., index, adv. Refereed. Circ: 151000 Paid and free. Vol. ends: Nov. Microform: PQC. Reprint: PSC. *Indexed:* A01, A22, AbAn, AgeL, BRI, CBRI, Chicano, ERIC, MASUSE, P02, P61, PsycInfo, SSA, SWR&A. *Bk. rev.:* 1-2; signed. *Aud.:* Ac, Sa.

As the official journal of the National Association of Social Workers, *Social Work* is considered the premier journal of the social work profession. It is dedicated to improving practice and advancing knowledge in the profession and in social welfare, and thus it is widely read by practitioners, social work educators, and students. Articles center on new insights into established practices, as well as trends and techniques within the profession, and examine social problems with an emphasis on social policy and a solution to human problems. An essential, must-have title for academic libraries and others that support social work, nursing, and social services professionals.

4955. Social Work and Society. [ISSN: 1613-8953] 2003. 3x/yr. Free. Ed(s): Fabian Kessl. Di P P - N R W, Juelicher Str 6, Cologne, 50674, Germany; dipp@hbz-nrw.de; http://www.dipp.nrw.de. Refereed. *Indexed:* SSA. *Bk. rev.:* Number and length vary. *Aud.:* Ga, Ac.

Sponsored by the Center for Social Work and Social Policy, this journal is an early pioneer in open-access publishing. This is an international journal that serves as a forum for innovative theories and views about the interrelationships of social work, social policy, government, and the economy. Features include special issues, research articles, essays and debates, historical portraits, and book reviews. Academic libraries that serve social work programs will want to add this to their electronic holdings.

4956. Social Work Education: the international journal. Incorporates (1981-1999): *Issues in Social Work Education.* [ISSN: 0261-5479] 1981. 8x/yr. GBP 1067 (print & online eds.). Ed(s): Imogen Taylor. Routledge, 4 Park Sq, Milton Park, Abingdon, OX14 4RN, United Kingdom; subscriptions@tandf.co.uk; http://www.tandfonline.com. Adv. Sample. Refereed. Reprint: PSC. *Indexed:* A01, A22, ASSIA, E01, FR, PsycInfo, SSA, SWR&A. *Bk. rev.:* Number and length vary. *Aud.:* Ac.

This journal publishes critical and reflective articles concerned with the theory and practice of social work education. Through international coverage and debate, the journal serves as a forum for new and emerging ideas and proposals on all aspects of social work education, training, development, and field work. Themes of recent special issues have included field education and disability studies. Book reviews are also included. An essential title for academic libraries that support social work programs.

4957. Social Work Research. Supersedes in part (in 1994): *Social Work Research and Abstracts;* Which was formerly (until 1977): *Abstracts for Social Workers.* [ISSN: 1070-5309] 1977. q. EUR 132. Ed(s): James Herbert Williams. Oxford University Press, 2001 Evans Rd, Cary, NC 27513; jnlorders@oup-usa.org; http://www.oxfordjournals.org. Illus., index, adv. Refereed. Vol. ends: Dec. Microform: PQC. Reprint: PSC. *Indexed:* A01, A22, AbAn, ERIC, P61, PsycInfo, SSA, SWR&A. *Aud.:* Ac, Sa.

This journal is published on behalf of the National Association of Social Workers. It contains research articles that contribute to and inform social work practice, including review and theoretical articles, evaluation studies, and diverse research pertaining to social work issues and problems. Recent issues have included case management, mental health, poverty, children and families, and challenges to recent immigrants. An essential title for academic libraries that support social work programs and for libraries that serve social work professionals.

4958. Social Work Today. [ISSN: 1540-420X] 2001. bi-m. USD 14.99. Ed(s): Marianne Mallon. Great Valley Publishing Company, Inc., 3801 Schuylkill Rd, Spring City, PA 19475; Sales@gvpub.com; http://www.gvpub.com. Adv. Sample. *Bk. rev.:* Number and length vary. *Aud.:* Ga, Sa.

Social Work Today is a professional development vehicle for social workers to keep abreast of their field. Topics covered are mental health, addictions, children and families, aging, professional practice, and ethics. Recent articles have focused on the needs of returning veterans, child protection work, and legalized gambling. Features include research reviews, government briefs, book and media reviews, and a jobs bank. Print and electronic access are by subscription; however, most features are freely available online. Recommended for libraries that support social work practitioners.

4959. Social Work with Groups: a journal of community and clinical practice. [ISSN: 0160-9513] 1978. q. GBP 692 (print & online eds.). Ed(s): Andrew Malekoff. Routledge, 325 Chestnut St, Ste 800, Philadelphia, PA 19106; customerservice@taylorandfrancis.com; http://www.tandfonline.com. Illus., adv. Refereed. Microform: PQC. Reprint: PSC. *Indexed:* A01, A22, ASSIA, BRI, E01, P02, P61, PsycInfo, SSA, SWR&A. *Bk. rev.:* Number & length vary. *Aud.:* Ac, Sa.

This journal is unique in that it focuses on practice involving small groups and social work professionals in varied roles and settings. Research articles include issues of group work in clinical and community practice; mental health, and rehabilitative and general social service agencies; crisis, youth, health care, and private practice; and all manner of community and human services departments. Recommended for social services agencies and libraries that support social work practitioners.

4960. Society for Social Work and Research. Journal. [ISSN: 1948-822X] 2009. irreg. Free. Ed(s): Mark Fraser. Society for Social Work and Research, 11240 Waples Mill Rd, Ste 200, Fairfax, VA 22030; info@sswr.org; http://www.sswr.org/. Refereed. *Indexed:* PsycInfo. *Aud.:* Ac.

This peer-reviewed, open-access journal is the official publication of the Society for Social Work Research, an organization founded in 1994 to advance social work research. It publishes research reports, systematic reviews, and methodological studies on social problems, programs, and policies. Special emphasis is placed on research examining the effectiveness of social and health services. The journal is intended for practitioners, administrators, educators, and policy makers interested in social and health problems. A worthwhile addition to the electronic holdings in academic, research, and special libraries that support social work and social services programs, education, and practice.

Suicide and Life-Threatening Behavior. See Death and Dying section.

■ SPIRITUALITY AND WELL-BEING

Marilyn Morgan, Manuscript Processing Archivist, Schlesinger Library on the History of Women, Radcliffe Institute, Harvard University.

Cheryl LaGuardia, Research Librarian, Widener Library, Harvard University

Introduction

The periodicals highlighted here share a commonality: they explore untraditional spiritual means of sustaining well-being. Most include instruction in a number of highly varied practices, ranging from mindfulness and guided meditation to astrology and ritual worship, to deepen spirituality and transform life. Those seeking physical, mental, and emotional well-being through spiritual paths beyond the major organized world religions will form the core readership. Periodicals devoted exclusively to Buddhism are located in the "Religion" section; magazines devoted to the physical practice of yoga may be found in the "Health and Fitness" section.

This section provides a representative sampling of periodicals that offer diverse viewpoints, and it focuses primarily on North American publications. One exception, *Kindred Spirit,* produced in the United Kingdom, is included for the broad perspective it provides. The majority of publications address a general readership interested in spiritual practices. A sampling of these periodicals may prove useful to academic libraries with a strong liberal arts mission.

The alternative viewpoint expressed by these periodicals would enhance special-collections libraries that specialize in theology and divinity studies. *Parabola,* in particular, incorporates more scholarly research and is indexed extensively. All academic libraries should consider titles for which students or faculty express interest.

Various titles in this section provide philosophical theories as well as practical approaches (such as guided meditation and mindfulness) that are becoming increasingly studied by public health researchers and physicians, and have generated widespread public interest. Most of the magazines are published by small organizations. Web sites are available for every publication, and many are available as electronic journals.

See the "Religion" section for periodicals that encompass mainstream religious practice, and the "Health and Fitness" section for other magazines that deal with alternative health.

Basic Periodicals

Circle Magazine: Celebrating Nature, Spirit & Magic; EnlightenNext; Kindred Spirit: Bringing you Health and Happiness; Light of Consciousness: Journal of Spiritual Awakening; Parabola: Where Spiritual Traditions Meet; Pilgrimage; Sedona Journal of Emergence; Spirituality & Health: The Soul and Body Connection; Witches & Pagans.

Basic Abstracts and Indexes

Academic Search Premier, ProQuest Research Library, Reader's Guide to Periodical Literature.

4961. Circle Magazine: celebrating nature, spirit & magic. Formerly (until 1999): *Circle Network News.* 1980. 4x/yr. USD 25 domestic; USD 46 in Canada & Mexico; USD 48 elsewhere. Ed(s): Georgette Paxton. Circle Sanctuary, PO Box 9, Barneveld, WI 53507; circle@mhtc.net. Illus., adv. *Bk. rev.:* Number and length vary. *Aud.:* Ga.

Published quarterly by the Circle Sanctuary in Wisconsin, a recognized Shamanic Wiccan church, *Circle Magazine* provides news, views, notices, rituals, meditations, invocations, contacts, herbal formulas, book reviews, magical development exercises, chants, and other material pertaining to Wicca, pantheistic traditions, and Shamanism. Featured articles examine thematic topics such as urban magic and ritual, herbs in urban spaces, herbal properties and use, and ritual cooking. Most articles explore nature spirituality, paganism, magic, and pantheistic traditions. Articles provide instructional advice on practical tasks, such as making healing candles, and provide various tips for herbcraft, magicraft, and ecomagic. Regular features include "Traditions," "Ritual Design and Facilitation," and poems. Written to a general adult audience with an interested in paganism, *Circle Magazine* is recommended for large public libraries or where there is subject interest.

4962. EnlightenNext: the magazine for evolutionaries. Formerly (until 2008): *What is Enlightenment.* [ISSN: 1946-0805] 1991. q. USD 23.95 domestic; USD 31.95 Canada; USD 35.95 elsewhere. Ed(s): Andrew Cohen, Carter Phipps. EnlightenNext, PO Box 2360, Lenox, MA 01240; info@EnlightenNext.org; http://www.enlightennext.org. Illus., adv. Sample. Circ: 75000. *Bk. rev.:* Number and length vary. *Aud.:* Ga, Sa.

Founded and edited by Andrew Cohen, *EnlightenNext* investigates important and challenging questions that face contemporary spiritual seekers. Articles center on evolutionary spirituality. Cohen approaches spiritual inquiry with an activist and western mission for "the ongoing liberation of human potential," along with a sense of collective responsibility for the future. Articles that explore the "narcissism epidemic," Zen, and sufi co-exist with articles on quantum consciousness, noetic science, and evidence of an afterlife. Regular departments include editorial columns, news briefs, letters, and book reviews. The magazine is also available in a digital online edition. A substantial magazine with sophisticated layout, this publication is appropriate for large public libraries or where there is subject interest. URL: http://magazine.enlightennext.org/

4963. Kindred Spirit: bringing you health and happiness. [ISSN: 0955-7067] 1987. bi-m. GBP 21 domestic; GBP 25.50 in North America & Europe; GBP 31.50 elsewhere. Kindred Spirit, Unit 101, The Purfume Factory, 140 Wales Farm Rd, London, W3 6UG, United Kingdom. Adv. *Indexed:* AmHI. *Aud.:* Ga.

Produced in the United Kingdom, *Kindred Spirit* appeals to readers interested in using spirituality to create positive change on the individual, community, and global levels. Substantive articles within each issue cover a range of diverse subjects such as spiritual growth, personal development, complementary therapies, travel, native shamanism, I Ching, and rune reading, as well as environmental and medical approaches like cryotherapy, crystal energies, and metamorphic technique. Web sites related to topics or authors are included with most articles; these expand the content for readers and help to bridge the geographical gap for United States and Canada subscribers. Regular features include letters, news briefs, astrology, travel, yoga, cosmic gardening, and arts and entertainment reviews. Recommended for public libraries where there is interest in alternative spirituality and health practices. Available online. URL: www.kindredspirit.co.uk/

4964. Light of Consciousness: journal of spiritual awakening. Formerly (until vol.1, no.1, 1988): *Truth Consciousness Journal.* [ISSN: 1040-7448] 1988. q. USD 19.95 domestic; USD 27.95 foreign. Ed(s): Sita Stuhlmiller. Truth Consciousness at Desert Ashram, 3403 W Sweetwater Dr, Tucson, AZ 85745-9301. Illus., adv. Circ: 20000. *Bk. rev.:* Number and length vary. *Aud.:* Ga, Sa.

Published quarterly by the nonprofit organization Truth Consciousness, *Light of Consciousness* highlights the unifying principles that underlie divergent faiths and religious practices and explores the intersection of science and spirituality. Issues examine the transformative power of meditation and contain both philosophical theory and practical instruction in myriad types of meditation. Regular features include a "Satsang" (spiritual discourse) written by Swami

Amar Jyoti, the focus of which reflects each issue's theme and content; "Insight," an introduction written by editor Sita Stuhlmiller; and book reviews. Visually striking cover photography as well as abundant photographs and illustrations purposefully enhance the text. Inspirational articles explore ways to deepen spirituality and attain peace of mind, use meditation to retrain the brain for greater happiness, and incorporate mindfulness and the power of prayer in daily life. Experienced practitioners and scholars contribute essays that explore the practice of self-reflection, meditative self-discovery, and spiritual-centeredness. In 2010, the print edition became a greener publication by using 30 percent post-consumer recycled paper, and a digital online edition is newly available. Recommended for public, academic, and subject-related special libraries or where subject interest exists. URL: http://light-of-consciousness.org/

PanGaia. See *Witches & Pagans.*

4965. *Parabola: where spiritual traditions meet.* [ISSN: 0362-1596] 1976. q. USD 39.95 combined subscription domestic (print & online eds.); USD 49.95 combined subscription Canada (print & online eds.); USD 55.95 combined subscription elsewhere (print & online eds.). Ed(s): Jeff Zaleski. Society for the Study of Myth and Tradition, 20 West 20th St, 2nd Fl, New York, NY 10011; info@parabola.org; http:// www.parabola.org. Illus., index, adv. Sample. Circ: 41000 Paid. Vol. ends: Winter. Microform: PQC. *Indexed:* A22, AmHI, ArtHuCI, BRI, CBRI, MLA-IB, P02, R&TA, RILM. *Bk. rev.:* 5-8, 600-1,200 words. *Aud.:* Ga, Ac, Sa.

Published by the Society for the Study of Myth and Tradition, *Parabola* emphasizes common themes in world religions and spiritual traditions, and includes scholarly articles that explore varied spiritual traditions. Thematic issues explore the role of spirit in the larger world. *Parabola* regularly includes articles written by well-known literary or historical figures such as Julia Alvarez or James Joyce. Some issues incorporate first-person reflections, such as instructions from a Buddhist monk on how to cultivate love and compassion. Illustrations are placed artfully, enriching the text and drawing in the reader. Other regular features include "Poetry," "Tangents," "Book Reviews," and "Focus." Many issues include theme-related stories or parables from world traditions. Advertisements are few and consigned to sections at the end of the issue. *Parabola* is also available as an e-journal from its web site. It is recommended for its eclectic and unbiased approach to religious traditions and its coverage of mythology and symbolism. It is for general academic libraries, special libraries with related collections, and public libraries where there is subject interest. URL: www.parabola.org

4966. *Pilgrimage.* [ISSN: 0361-0802] 1972. 3x/yr. USD 22 domestic; USD 32 in Canada & Mexico; USD 40 elsewhere. Ed(s): Maria Melendez. Pilgrimage Press, Inc., PO Box 9110, Pueblo, CO 81008; info@pilgrimagepress.org; http://www.pilgrimagepress.org. Circ: 1000 Paid. Microform: PQC. *Indexed:* A22. *Aud.:* Ga, Ac, Sa.

A small publication living the big questions, *Pilgrimage Magazine: Story, Witness, Spirit, Place* is a literary magazine that features the work of writers and artists whose work explores various spiritual paths. Issues, published three times a year in Colorado, emphasize themes of place, spirit, peace, and justice, in and beyond the Greater Southwest. Articles, essays, poems, and artwork reflect an eclectic community of readers, writers, artists, and naturalists. The magazine's layout, clear typography, undecorated page margins, and lack of advertisements allow the reader to absorb the contents without distraction. The black-and-white publication is physically sized for the hand, while the poetry, essays, and autobiographical stories within each issue aim "to illuminate the world's great wisdom traditions," and offer to transport the reader into new spiritual insights. Maria Melendez, contributing editor for *Latino Poetry Review*, became the editor of *Pilgrimage Magazine* in 2010. While contributing authors are primarily located in the Southwest United States, the publication explores universal themes. Highly recommended for both its literary quality and spiritual centeredness across religious backgrounds, for academic, public, and special libraries where there is subject interest. URL: www.pilgrimagepress.org/

4967. *Sedona Journal of Emergence.* Formerly (until 199?): *Emergence (Sedona).* [ISSN: 1530-3365] 1989. m. Ed(s): Melody O'Ryin Swanson. Light Technology Publishing, PO Box 3870, Flagstaff, AZ 86003. *Bk. rev.:* Number and length vary. *Aud.:* Ga.

Published by Light Technology Publishing, *Sedona* seeks to "provide a forum for those who wish to speak to us from other dimensions and realities." Writings discuss topics such as fifth dimensional awareness, alchemy, planetary interventions, auric fields, and biorelativity. Regular features include "Channeling," "Predictions," "Tools for Conscious Living," "Predictions," and "Features," which vary in topic according to each issue's theme. Text is primarily black-and-white, with photographs of authors and minimal illustration. Advertising is mainly relegated to an end section, and an advertiser index is included. The magazine covers are colorful and imaginative. An e-journal edition is available. Readership is limited by the special nature of the magazine's content, but it is appropriate for public libraries where there is interest. URL: www.sedonajournal.com

4968. *Spirituality & Health: the soul body connection.* [ISSN: 1520-5444] 1998. bi-m. USD 18.95 domestic; USD 28.95 Canada; USD 38.95 elsewhere. Ed(s): Stephen Kiesling. Spirituality & Health Media, 129 1/2 E Front St, Ste B, Traverse City, MI 49684. Adv. Circ: 70000 Paid. *Indexed:* BRI. *Bk. rev.:* Number and length vary. *Aud.:* Ga.

Published bimonthly, *Spirituality and Health* examines the connection between spirituality and personal well-being in its broadest sense. Articles focus on various aspects of spiritual and physical well-being, including Eastern philosophy, meditation, and mainstream religion; nutrition, wellness, yoga, and holistic medicine; creativity, the inner life, social justice, and issues of conscience; and public health, the human body, and the environment. Feature essays often highlight the experience or perspective of a celebrity, such as Susan Sarandon; they also provide practical resources for individual exploration and practice. Focusing on integrating spirituality with everyday life, articles may examine aspects of Buddhism, Christianity, Zen, or other belief systems. Brief articles focus on personal spiritual perspectives, practical life issues, and environmental concerns such as yogic breathing, chakras, allergies, and native plant gardening. Letters of advice columns and news items similarly deal with topics of health and wellness, emphasizing holistic living and spiritual commonality. Numerous thoughtful reviews of books, music, and film are included in each issue. Use of color, paragraph arrangement, and plentiful illustrations give the magazine an enticing popular appeal. Recommended for public libraries, special libraries, and where there is interest. URL: http://spiritualityhealth.com/

What is Enlightenment? See *EnlightenNext.*

4969. *Witches & Pagans.* Formed by the merger of (2002-2009): *NewWitch;* (1997-2009): *PanGaia;* Which was formerly (until 1997): *The Green Man.* [ISSN: 2153-0467] 2009. q. USD 22 domestic; USD 30 Canada; USD 33 elsewhere. B B I Media, Inc., PO Box 687, Forest Grove, OR 97116; editor2@bbimedia.com; http://www.bbimedia.com. Illus., adv. *Bk. rev.:* Number and length vary. *Aud.:* Ga, Ac, Sa.

Published quarterly, *Witches and Pagans* is dedicated to, featuring, and partially written by young or beginning Witches, Wiccans, Neo-Pagans, and other earth-based, ethnic, pre-Christian, shamanic, and magical practitioners. Thematic issues contain substantial content in various literary forms, including fiction, poetry, and experiential writings. Issues regularly feature practical advice, referenced nonfiction, and interviews with practitioners. Artwork enhances the text while advertisements are relegated to pages with shorter articles. Letters, book reviews, and regular columns complete the magazine, which is recommended for public, academic, or special libraries where there is an interest in alternative spirituality. Available in electronic format. URL: www.witchesandpagans.com/

■ SPORTS

General/Extreme Sports/Physical Education, Coaching, and Sports Sciences/Specific Sports

See also Boats and Boating; Environment and Conservation; Fishing; Hiking, Climbing, and Outdoor Recreation; and Hunting and Guns sections.

Betsy Park, Assistant to the Dean, The University of Memphis Libraries, 126 Ned R. McWherter Library, Memphis, TN 38152; ehpark@memphis.edu

Introduction

On Mother's Day 2012, my city watched as the Memphis Grizzlies were defeated by the Los Angeles Clippers in Game 7 of the first round of the NBA play-offs. In the following days, I could read about it in any of the many fan magazines as well as in my local newspaper. There is no lack of information for anyone interested in sports, as there are almost 10,000 sports magazines in circulation. Sports magazines appeal to a broad audience, including fitness enthusiasts, recreational players, athletes, fans, casual spectators, referees, coaches, managers, sports physicians, academic researchers, and others.

As a general rule, these publications have a long lifespan. I am pleasantly surprised by how few cease publication from one edition of *Magazines for Libraries* to another. Many do face fierce competition from other publications and free online sources. Some may have at one time been the big players, but times have changed. In response, many have redesigned their format, changed their focus, and increased their online presence. Almost all now provide digital as well as print editions (indeed several have phased out the print), have mobile editions, and increasingly have a presence on Facebook and Twitter.

In deciding which titles to review, I have attempted to include general sports magazines, those from representative individual sports, and those of interest to researchers, students, physicians, and others. Hopefully the information provided will reaffirm old titles, identify new ones, and help librarians and readers make informed selection decisions.

Basic Periodicals

GENERAL. All levels: *ESPN The Magazine, Sports Illustrated*.

PHYSICAL EDUCATION, COACHING, AND SPORTS SCIENCES. Ems: *Strategies*; Hs: *Coach and Athletic Director; Journal of Physical Education, Recreation and Dance*; Ac: *American Journal of Sports Medicine, British Journal of Sports Medicine, Journal of Teaching in Physical Education, Quest (Champaign), Research Quarterly for Exercise and Sport*.

SPECIFIC SPORTS. All levels: *Baseball America, Bicycling, Golf Magazine, The Hockey News, International Figure Skating, Runner's World, Ski, Soccer America, Tennis, VolleyballUSA*.

Basic Abstracts and Indexes

Academic Search Complete, Academic OneFile, Omnifile Full Text, Physical Education Index, SPORTDiscus.

Climbing. See Hiking, Climbing, and Outdoor Recreation section.

General

4970. *Aethlon: the journal of sport literature*. Formerly (until 1988): *Arete*. [ISSN: 1048-3756] 1983. s-a. Free to members. Ed(s): Joyce Duncan. Sports Literature Association, East Tennessee State University, PO Box 70270, Johnson City, TN 37614; joyced1001@cs.com; http://www.uta.edu/english/sla/. Illus. Refereed. *Indexed*: AmHI, BRI, CBRI, MLA-IB, SD. *Bk. rev.*: 20, 500 to 2,000 words. *Aud.*: Ac.

Since the 1980s, *Aethlon: The Journal of Sport Literature*, "a print journal designed to celebrate the intersection of literature with the world of play, games, and sport," has been published by the Sport Literature Association at East Tennessee State University. It publishes critical articles, poetry, fiction, nonfiction, drama, and book reviews—the only stipulation being that they somehow relate to sports. University professors, novelists, short story writers, poets, and dramatists contribute both serious and humorous entries. Particularly suitable for academic libraries, although public libraries may also want to consider this publication.

4971. *E S P N The Magazine*. [ISSN: 1097-1998] 1998. bi-w. USD 26 domestic; USD 49 Canada; USD 95 elsewhere. Ed(s): Gary Belsky. E S P N The Magazine, Inc., 19 E 34th St, New York, NY 10016. Illus., adv. Sample. *Indexed*: SD. *Aud.*: Hs, Ga, Ac.

Published since 1998, *ESPN the Magazine* is an oversized, showy, general-interest sports tabloid. Each biweekly issue of 100+ pages contains photographs and advertisements. Regular features include double-page spreads of various sporting events, short articles of current interest, profiles of athletes, brief reports of major sports stories, statistics, a question-and-answer section, and a regular column written by ESPN's Stuart Scott. The writing style is informal, sometimes humorous, and it will appeal to 18- to 40-year-old readers. Sports enthusiasts at academic and public libraries will enjoy this publication.

4972. *The International Journal of the History of Sport*. Incorporates (1999-2003): *The European Sports History Review*; Which was formerly (until 1987): *British Journal of Sports History*. [ISSN: 0952-3367] 1984. 18x/yr. GBP 1514 (print & online eds.). Routledge, 4 Park Sq, Milton Park, Abingdon, OX14 4RN, United Kingdom; subscriptions@tandf.co.uk; http://www.tandfonline.com. Illus., index, adv. Sample. Refereed. Microform: PQC. Reprint: PSC. *Indexed*: A22, AmHI, ArtHuCI, C45, E01, IBSS, P61, RRTA, SD, SSA. *Bk. rev.*: 15-20, 800 words. *Aud.*: Ac.

Anthropologists, sociologists, historians, and others interested in the "historical study of sport in its political, cultural, social, educational, economic, spiritual[,] and aesthetic dimensions" will enjoy *The International Journal of the History of Sport*. Each of the 18 annual issues contains 200 or more pages with anywhere from eight to 20 articles. This peer-reviewed journal covers an interesting variety of subjects, and each issue focuses on a particular topic such as sport and the emancipation of European women; colonial sport in Madagascar; or the history of motorsport. As the journal's title implies, articles are written by an international multidisciplinary group of scholars. Most appropriate for academic libraries.

4973. *Sports Illustrated*. [ISSN: 0038-822X] 1954. w. USD 39; USD 0.70 per issue. Ed(s): Christian Stone, John e Huey. Sports Illustrated Group, 135 W 50th St, 4th Fl, New York, NY 10020; http://sportsillustrated.cnn.com/. Illus., index, adv. Microform: PQC. *Indexed*: A01, A22, BRI, C37, CBCARef, CBRI, MASUSE, MLA-IB, P02, SD. *Aud.*: Ems, Hs, Ga, Ac.

As the most popular and influential of the general sports magazines, the award-winning *Sports Illustrated* covers all the popular sports: basketball, baseball, football, golf, racing, wrestling, and others. It includes articles about players, celebrities, teams, sports, and society. Issues are filled with beautiful and interesting photography and well-written articles. Each 70- to 80-page issue contains letters to the editor, one or two longer features, several shorter articles, analysis, commentary and predictions, and insights. The annual swimsuit issue is legendary. The magazine has made the digitized archives of its collection from 1954 on available in the "SI Vault." Recommended for public, high school, and academic libraries. URL: http://vault.sportsillustrated.cnn.com

Sports Illustrated for Kids. See Children section.

Extreme Sports

4974. *Hang Gliding and Paragliding*. Formerly (until 2007): *U S H P A. Aero*; (until 200?): *Hang Gliding & Paragliding*; Which was formed by the Merger of (1970-2003): *Hang Gliding*; (19??-2003): *Paragliding*. [ISSN: 1936-2552] 2003. m. Ed(s): Gil Dodgen. U.S. Hang Gliding Association, Inc., PO Box 1330, Colorado Springs, CO 80933-1330; ushga@shga.org; http://www.ushga.org. *Aud.*: Ga, Sa.

Hang Gliding and Paragliding is the official publication of the U.S. Hang Gliding and Paragliding Association, an affiliate of the National Aeronautic Association. The content is member-driven. The editor "welcomes editorial submissions from our members and readers...looking for well-written articles, photos[,] and quality artwork." The magazine contains entertaining features on free flight, as well as news and information about the association and its activities. Lead articles may include technical details on improving the flight or entertaining articles that speak to the adventure of ultraflight. A consideration for public libraries.

4975. *Ride B M X.* Incorporates (1994-2004): *Transworld B M X;* Which was formerly (until 2001): *Snap B M X.* [ISSN: 1078-0084] 1991. m. USD 18.97 domestic; USD 30.97 Canada; USD 47.97 elsewhere. TransWorld Media, 1421 Edinger Ave, Ste D, Tustin, CA 92780; http://www.transworldmatrix.com/twmatrix/. Illus., adv. Circ: 40476 Paid. *Indexed:* MASUSE. *Aud.:* Hs, Ga.

Bicycle motocross enthusiasts at all levels will enjoy this glossy magazine with its coverage of extreme freestyle BMX riding, including dirt jumping, flatland, ramp, and street riding. The editors have recently increased the number of dramatic action photographs to please readers. Regular features include letters, event coverage, new product reviews, rider interviews, a Q&A section, photo sections, and accounts of BMX trips. There is an annual photo issue. The magazine's web site provides selected full text, graphics, and video. An appropriate purchase for public libraries. URL: www.bmxonline.com

4976. *Surfer.* [ISSN: 0039-6036] 1960. m. USD 14.97 domestic; USD 27.97 Canada; USD 29.97 foreign. Ed(s): Brendon Thomas, Chris Mauro. Source Interlink Companies, 6420 Wilshire Blvd, 10th Fl, Los Angeles, CA 90048; dheine@sourceinterlink.com; http://www.sourceinterlinkmedia.com. Adv. Circ: 106048 Paid. *Indexed:* A22, BRI, SD. *Aud.:* Ga.

One of the oldest in its class and calling itself the "bible of the sport of surfing," *Surfer Magazine* is filled with dramatic adventure photography, informative articles, interviews, coverage of amateur and professional competitions, and travel articles. It covers not only the sport of surfing, but the surfing lifestyle and mindset. Annual issues include an oversized collector's issue, the "Hot 100" (best new surfers), and the "Top 44" (product reviews). The web site provides selected articles, a photograph gallery, video clips, a merchandise catalog, and chat forum. An appropriate selection for public libraries in surfing communities. URL: www.surfermag.com

4977. *Thrasher.* Formerly (until 198?): *Thrasher Skateboard Magazine.* [ISSN: 0889-0692] 1980. m. USD 17.95 domestic; USD 43 Canada; USD 50 elsewhere. Ed(s): Ryan Henry. High Speed Productions, Inc., 1303 Underwood Ave, San Francisco, CA 94124. *Indexed:* BRI. *Aud.:* Hs, Ga.

For 25 years, *Thrasher* has been read and enjoyed by young enthusiasts of skateboarding, its music, and its alternative lifestyle. Like its readers, the magazine is fast-paced with interviews, action photographs, comics, contests, competitions, fashion tips, and insider industry gossip. One column, "The Lunatic Fringe," indicates the general thrust of this publication. Readers can view videos of stunts and competitions and sign up for RSS feeds, a newsletter, and podcasts at the magazine's web site. Available in print and digital editions. An appropriate selection for public libraries. URL: www.thrashermagazine.com/

4978. *Transworld Motocross.* [ISSN: 1533-6212] 2000. m. USD 16.97 domestic; USD 28.97 Canada; USD 45.97 elsewhere. Ed(s): Donn Maeda. TransWorld Media, 1421 Edinger Ave, Ste D, Tustin, CA 92780; http://www.transworldmatrix.com/twmatrix/. Illus., adv. Circ: 125000. *Aud.:* Hs, Ga.

This glossy magazine covers all aspects of motocross, including freestyle, freeriding, and racing. Each issue is packed with photographs of races and stunts, profiles of riders, how-to columns, product reviews (especially for gear and bikes), interviews with riders and coaches, advice on competing, and always a photo gallery. Sometimes it is difficult to distinguish the articles from the advertisements. The writing is informative but conversational. An appropriate selection for public libraries in areas where motorbiking is popular.

4979. *Transworld Skateboarding.* [ISSN: 0748-7401] 1982. m. USD 16.97 domestic; USD 34.97 Canada; USD 74.97 elsewhere. TransWorld Media, 2052 Corte del Nogal Ste B, Carlsbad, CA 92011; http://www.transworldmatrix.com/twmatrix/. Illus., adv. Circ: 93591 Paid. *Indexed:* BRI. *Aud.:* Hs, Ga.

This glossy magazine for the enthusiastic skateboarder contains over 200 pages and is filled with photographs of daring rides, stunts, and flips. The magazine covers all aspects of the sport, except its culture (i.e., music, clothes, lifestyle). A typical issue includes several photo essays, interviews with leading skaters, and product reviews. Regular columns include letters to the editor; short news reports of people, contests, events, and products; how-to tips; profiles of young skaters; travel stories; and interviews with leading skaters. Like other magazines from Transworld, this one will be remembered for its photography and advertisements. The more than 12 million skateboarders will enjoy this magazine at public libraries. URL: www.skateboarding.com/skate/

4980. *Transworld Snowboarding.* [ISSN: 1046-4611] 1986. 9x/yr. USD 16.97 domestic; USD 29.97 Canada; USD 59.97 elsewhere. TransWorld Media, 2052 Corte del Nogal Ste B, Carlsbad, CA 92011; http://www.transworldmatrix.com/twmatrix/. Illus., adv. Circ: 115125. *Indexed:* BRI, SD. *Aud.:* Hs, Ga.

Snowboard enthusiasts and those simply curious about the sport will enjoy this glossy publication. Each over-200-page issue is filled with dramatic, action photographs of amazing stunts and beautiful places. Feature articles are written in a conversational style and highlight the current season, preview upcoming events, examine snow areas, and profile professional snowboarders. Columns include letters to the editor, a question-and-answer section, competitions, instructional tips, product reviews, and the like. The magazine's web site includes several articles, but readers will love the print version for its full-color, dramatic photography. Appropriate for school and public libraries. URL: http://snowboarding.transworld.net

4981. *Transworld Surf.* [ISSN: 1532-9402] 1999. m. USD 14.97 domestic; USD 29.97 Canada; USD 59.97 elsewhere. TransWorld Media, 2052 Corte del Nogal Ste B, Carlsbad, CA 92011; http://www.transworldmatrix.com/twmatrix/. Illus., adv. Circ: 75005. *Indexed:* BRI. *Aud.:* Ga.

The audience for this glossy monthly is the twenty-something male adventure surfer. The publication is filled with action-packed, dramatic photographs, interviews, travel pieces, product reviews, instruction, and advertisements. Departments include an editorial, music reviews, people, competition, epilog and the like. Annual issues include a travel and a photo issue. The publication's website contains news updates, more photos, and links to sites of interest. Suitable for public libraries. URL: http://surf.transworld.net/

4982. *Triathlete.* Formerly (until 1986): *Triathlon.* [ISSN: 0898-3410] 1983. m. USD 34.95 domestic; USD 59.95 combined subscription domestic (print & online eds.). Ed(s): Susan Grant. Triathlon Group North America, 9401 Waples St, Ste 150, San Diego, CA 92121; customerservice@competitorgroup.com. Illus., adv. *Indexed:* SD. *Aud.:* Ga, Ac.

Published since 1986, this glossy magazine follows a regular format with columns and departments. Departments include editorials, letters, and news. There is a large section devoted to training. Other articles focus on fitness, speed, equipment and product reviews (bikes and shoes), techniques, tests, and new developments. Annually the magazine publishes a guide to the top races in North America. Buyers' guides are also regularly published. Appropriate for public libraries.

4983. *UltraRunning.* [ISSN: 0744-3609] 1981. 10x/yr. USD 40 domestic; USD 75 in Canada & Mexico; USD 90 elsewhere. Ed(s): Tia Bodington. UltraRunning Magazine, 5825 W Dry Creek Rd, Healdsburg, CA 95448. Adv. *Indexed:* SD. *Aud.:* Ga.

As the title implies, an ultrarun or ultra marathon is a run that covers distances greater than the 26+ miles of a marathon. Races may be timed (e.g., how far can you run in six hours, 24 hours, etc.) or based on distance (e.g., 50 or 100 kilometers, 50 or 100 miles, etc.), and a single run can last several days. Ultrarun devotees are committed to their sport and will appreciate this magazine, which covers all aspects of ultraruns. Typically the publication contains interviews and profiles of runners, adventure running (e.g., running in the Antarctic), nutrition advice, injury prevention, training, a philosophical look at runners, and information on clubs and feature races. When not running, runners may enjoy this publication at their public library.

4984. *WakeBoarding.* [ISSN: 1079-0136] 1993. 9x/yr. USD 9.97 domestic; USD 18.97 Canada; USD 27.97 elsewhere. Ed(s): Luke Woodling, Kevin Michael. World Publications LLC, 460 N Orlando Ave, Ste 200, Winter Park, FL 32789; info@worldpub.net; http://www.bonniercorp.com. Illus., adv. Sample. Circ: 45823 Paid. *Indexed:* BRI. *Aud.:* Ga.

Wakeboarding, a combination of waterskiing and snowboarding, is well chronicled by *WakeBoarding Magazine.* The 150- to 200-page issues of this glossy publication are filled with detailed instruction, photos, in-depth interviews, the latest product news, tournament updates, and feature articles. The instruction column, called "Higher Learning," indicates that this is not a magazine for the novice. The magazine is published nine times a year. The online version provides links to sites of interest and videos of stunts and runs. Since wakeboarding is growing in popularity, public libraries in appropriate areas might want to consider adding this publication to their collection. URL: www.wakeboardingmag.com/

Physical Education, Coaching, and Sports Sciences

Adapted Physical Activity Quarterly. See Disabilities section.

4985. *American Journal of Sports Medicine.* Formerly (until 1976): *Journal of Sports Medicine.* [ISSN: 0363-5465] 1972. m. USD 867. Ed(s): Dr. Bruce Reider. Sage Publications, Inc., 2455 Teller Rd, Thousand Oaks, CA 91320; info@sagepub.com; http://www.sagepub.com/. Illus., index, adv. Sample. Refereed. Vol. ends: Nov/Dec. Microform: PQC. Reprint: PSC. *Indexed:* A01, A22, AbAn, BRI, C45, E01, H24, P02, RRTA, SD. *Aud.:* Ac, Sa.

The official publication of the American Orthopaedic Society for Sports Medicine is a highly respected monthly peer-reviewed scientific journal. Articles include original research and case studies that examine sports injuries, their treatment and frequency of occurrence, and rehabilitation and training. Issues of 150 pages contain up to 20 articles. Institutional subscriptions may be print-only or print with e-access. The audience for this journal includes orthopaedic surgeons who specialize in sports medicine, physicians, team physicians, athletic trainers, physical therapists, and anyone specializing in sports medicine. Appropriate for academic, medical, and hospital libraries. URL: www.ajsm.org

4986. *Applied Physiology, Nutrition and Metabolism.* Former titles (until 2006): *Canadian Journal of Applied Physiology;* (until 1993): *Canadian Journal of Sport Sciences;* (until 1987): *Canadian Journal of Applied Sport Science.* [ISSN: 1715-5312] 1976. bi-m. CAD 880. Ed(s): Dr. Terry Graham. N R C Research Press, 1200 Montreal Rd, Bldg M-55, Ottawa, ON K1A 0R6, Canada; pubs@nrc-cnrc.gc.ca; http://pubs.nrc-cnrc.gc.ca. Illus., index, adv. Refereed. Circ: 965 Paid and free. Vol. ends: Dec. Microform: MML. *Indexed:* A01, A22, BRI, C45, CBCARef, ErgAb, RRTA, SD. *Bk. rev.:* 2, 350 words. *Aud.:* Ac, Sa.

The bimonthly *Applied Physiology, Nutrition, and Metabolism* formerly the *Canadian Journal of Applied Physiology,* is a peer-reviewed, interdisciplinary publication with articles that apply physiology, nutrition, and metabolism to the study of health, physical activity, and fitness. Issues average over 200 pages. A recent issue included articles entitled "Exercise-induced vasodilation is associated with menopause stage in healthy middle-aged women," "Neuromuscular fatigue recovery following rapid and slow stretch–shortening cycle movements," and "mTORC1 and the regulation of skeletal muscle anabolism and mass." As is appropriate for a Canadian journal, articles may be written in English or French, with abstracts in both languages. This publication will be of interest to exercise physiologists, physical fitness and exercise rehabilitation specialists, public health and health-care professionals, and basic and applied physiologists, nutritionists, and biochemists. The technical language of this journal makes it of primary interest to medical and academic libraries.

4987. *Athletic Business: the leading resource for athletic, fitness & recreation professionals.* Formerly (until 1984): *Athletic Purchasing and Facilities.* [ISSN: 0747-315X] 1977. m. USD 55 in US & Canada includes Mexico; USD 130 elsewhere; USD 8 per issue includes Mexico. Ed(s): Michael Popke, Andrew Cohen. Athletic Business Publications, Inc., 4130 Lien Rd, Madison, WI 53704-3602; http://www.athleticbusiness.com. Illus., index, adv. Circ: 43000. *Indexed:* A22, SD. *Aud.:* Ac, Sa.

Since 1977 the monthly trade journal *Athletic Business* has covered the business of sports and athletics, including equipment, corporate wellness programs, facility planning, marketing, management, and design. An annual *Buyer's Guide* is published in February or March. Copies are distributed free to qualified professionals, including operators and directors of sports, recreation, and fitness facilities. Feature articles are supplemented by columns on sports law, college and high school programs, the recreation industry, profit-making enterprises. The web site features how-to advice and a blog. Suitable for academic libraries at institutions with business sports programs. URL: www.athleticbusiness.com

4988. *British Journal of Sports Medicine.* Formerly (until 1968): *British Association of Sport and Medicine. Bulletin.* [ISSN: 0306-3674] 1965. m. USD 1178 (Individuals, USD 410 (print & online eds.). Ed(s): Karim Khan. B M J Group, BMA House, Tavistock Sq, London, WC1H 9JR, United Kingdom; http://group.bmj.com. Illus., adv. Sample. Refereed. Vol. ends: Dec. Microform: PQC. *Indexed:* A01, A22, AbAn, BRI, C45, E01, ErgAb, H24, RRTA, SD. *Bk. rev.:* Number and length vary. *Aud.:* Ac, Sa.

Since 1965 the official publication of the British Association of Sport and Exercise Medicine has been a well-known and respected journal in the field of sports medicine. Issues contain editorials, peer-reviewed articles, in-depth reviews of issues in sports medicine, and short reports (usually published online only). Authors may elect (for a fee) to have their articles immediately available online. The journal audience is physicians, physiotherapists, exercise scientists, and those involved in public policy. Full-text access is available for issues before 2007 in PubMed Central. Highly recommended for academic libraries with programs in health or sports sciences. URL: http://bjsm.bmj.com

4989. *Clinical Journal of Sport Medicine.* Former titles (until 1991): *Canadian Academy of Sport Medicine Review;* (until 1986): *Canadian Academy of Sport Medicine Newsletter;* (until 1980): *Canadian Academy of Sport Medicine Journal.* [ISSN: 1050-642X] 1972. bi-m. USD 715 (print & online eds.). Ed(s): Willem Meeuwisse, Catherine Leipciger. Lippincott Williams & Wilkins, 530 Walnut St, Philadelphia, PA 19106; customerservice@lww.com; http://www.lww.com. Illus., adv. Refereed. Circ: 1378. Vol. ends: Oct. *Indexed:* A01, A22, AbAn, ExcerpMed, H24, RiskAb, SD. *Aud.:* Ac, Sa.

The *Clinical Journal of Sport Medicine* is a bimonthly, international, refereed journal for clinicians specializing in the practice of sport medicine. It publishes research, reviews, and case reports that concern "diagnostics, therapeutics, and rehabilitation in healthy and physically challenged individuals of all ages and levels of sport and exercise participation." The editorial board includes international physicians and researchers. A typical issue might include articles on brain injury in professional bicycling, violence in amateur hockey, evidence of ulnar neuropathy in triathletes, and hydration strategies for runners. Appropriate for academic and medical libraries.

4990. *Coach and Athletic Director.* Former titles (until 2010): *Successful Coach and Athletic Director;* (until 2009): *Coach and Athletic Director;* (until 1995): *Scholastic Coach and Athletic Director;* (until 1994): *Scholastic Coach;* Which incorporated (1953-1982): *Coach & Athlete;* (1921-1987): *Athletic Journal.* [ISSN: 2159-6573] 1931. m. USD 19.95 domestic; USD 24.95 foreign. Ed(s): Michael Austin. Lessiter Publications, 225 Regency Ct, Ste 200, Brookfield, WI 53045; info@lesspub.com; http://www.lesspub.com/. Illus., index, adv. *Indexed:* A01, A22, BRI, P02, SD. *Bk. rev.:* Number and length vary. *Aud.:* Hs, Ga, Ac.

Published since 1931 as a monthly during the school year with a combined issue in the summer, this is a professional magazine for high school and college-level athletic coaches. News, information, and advice on sports (including baseball, basketball, football, softball, and soccer), strength training, and administrative activities use non-technical language. Issues include equipment reviews and an annual buyer's guide for facilities and equipment. A recent issue contained articles on fundraising, finding focus, and team-building strategies. Appropriate for high school and academic libraries. URL: www.coachad.com/

4991. European Journal of Sport Science. [ISSN: 1746-1391] 2001. bi-m. GBP 676 (print & online eds.). Ed(s): Andrew M Jones. Taylor & Francis, 4 Park Sq, Milton Park, Abingdon, OX14 4RN, United Kingdom; subscriptions@tandf.co.uk; http://www.tandfonline.com. Adv. Sample. Refereed. Reprint: PSC. *Indexed:* A01, A22, C45, E01, ErgAb, PsycInfo, SD. *Aud.:* Ac.

This peer-reviewed journal, the official publication of the European College of Sport Science (ECSS), publishes original research and review articles that cover all the subsets of sport and exercise. For the purposes of this journal, sports are "all forms of human movement that aim to maintain or improve physical and mental well-being, create or improve social relationships, or obtain results in competition at all levels." Articles in each of the six annual issues are divided into an original research section and a review section. The journal may be purchased as online-only or online + print. Free articles available on the journal web site provide readers with the flavor of the publication. Suitable for academic libraries. URL: www.tandf.co.uk/journals/titles/17461391.asp

4992. Gridiron Strategies. [ISSN: 1533-1652] 2001. bi-m. USD 44.95 domestic. Ed(s): Rex Lardner. Gridiron Strategies, PO Box 14007, North Palm Beach, FL 33408; CustomerService@GridironStrategies.com. Adv. *Aud.:* Hs, Ga, Ac.

Published since 2001, *Gridiron Strategies* is a magazine written by football coaches for football coaches at all levels of competition. Each issue offers advice on strategy, play, offense, defense, strength and conditioning, and coaching and management. Occasionally a famous coach may be featured, but the magazine's focus is of the practical how-to kind. The web site provides a glimpse of articles that may be read in their entirety by subscribers. An annual subscription includes six issues plus online access to current and archived issues. Coaches would appreciate reading this publication at a school or public library. URL: www.gridironstrategies.com/

4993. International Journal of Sport Management. [ISSN: 1546-234X] 2000. q. USD 128 domestic; USD 196 Canada; USD 222 elsewhere. Ed(s): William F Stier. American Press, 60 State St, Ste 700, Boston, MA 02109; americanpress@flash.net; http://www.americanpresspublishers.com. Refereed. *Indexed:* SD. *Aud.:* Ac.

This quarterly publication addresses the business of sports and will be of interest to professionals and researchers in the fields of sports and recreation management as well as those in athletic administration. The journal follows a blind-peer-review process, and article submissions are read by members of a review board. A recent (2012) issue included articles on the media coverage of the 2010 Olympics; intercollegiate athletics; an analysis of research methodology in leading sport management journals; and motives and marketing stimuli that affect eSports consumption. Each issue contains approximately 200 pages. Academic libraries at institutions with sport sciences programs will want to consider adding this title.

4994. International Journal of Sport Nutrition & Exercise Metabolism. Formerly (until 2000): *International Journal of Sport Nutrition.* [ISSN: 1526-484X] 1991. bi-m. USD 649 (print & online eds.). Ed(s): Ronald J Maughan. Human Kinetics, Inc., 1607 N Market St, Champaign, IL 61820; info@hkusa.com; http://www.humankinetics.com. Illus., index, adv. Sample. Refereed. Vol. ends: Dec. Reprint: PSC. *Indexed:* A01, A22, Agr, BRI, C45, ExcerpMed, SD. *Aud.:* Ac, Sa.

This is a highly technical, peer-reviewed journal drawing from biochemistry, physiology, psychology, and sport and exercise science as these disciplines relate to the study of sport nutrition and exercise biochemistry. The journal focuses on original research and scholarly reviews, but also includes articles that apply the principles of biochemistry, physiology, and nutrition to sport and exercise. From 1991 to 1999, this journal was the *International Journal of Sport Nutrition.* In 2000, "& Exercise Metabolism" was added to the title to reflect the

interdisciplinary focus of exercise biochemistry and sport nutrition. The publication is covered by all the major indexing services. This bimonthly is appropriate for academic and medical libraries that support programs in sport medicine and sport sciences.

4995. International Journal of Sports Medicine. [ISSN: 0172-4622] 1980. 14x/yr. EUR 1090 EUR 82 per issue. Ed(s): G M Atkinson, H Appell. Georg Thieme Verlag, Ruedigerstr 14, Stuttgart, 70469, Germany; kunden.service@thieme.de; http://www.thieme.de. Illus., adv. Refereed. Circ: 1350 Paid and controlled. *Indexed:* A01, A22, C45, ErgAb, IndVet, RRTA, SD. *Bk. rev.:* 1, 500-750 words. *Aud.:* Ac, Sa.

Each issue of the monthly *International Journal of Sports Medicine* is approximately 80–200 pages, with sections on physiology and biochemistry, clinical sciences, nutrition, behavioral sciences, training and testing, orthopedics and biomechanics, and immunology. Peer-reviewed research articles written in English are highly technical and largely originate outside the United States. The journal publishes letters to the editor, short articles of recent work for rapid dissemination, review articles, and original research. Typical article titles include "Lipid profiles of Judo athletes during Ramadan" and "PC-1 Genotype and IRS response to exercise and training." Appropriate for medical and academic libraries.

4996. International Journal of Sports Physiology and Performance. [ISSN: 1555-0265] 2006. bi-m. USD 649 (print & online eds.). Ed(s): Carl Foster. Human Kinetics, Inc., 1607 N Market St, Champaign, IL 61820; orders@hkusa.com; http://www.humankinetics.com. Adv. Refereed. *Indexed:* ErgAb, SD. *Aud.:* Ac.

As its name implies, this peer-reviewed research journal will be of interest to sport and exercise physiologists, sports-performance researchers, and other sport scientists. The journal emphasizes original research, but also publishes practical articles, invited reviews, technical reports, case studies, and an editorial. The journal covers team sports, individual sports, performance aspects of environmental physiology, applied sports nutrition, strength and conditioning, biomedical science, and applications of sport technology. Typical articles examine the effect of cold water immersion on swimmers' heart rates; hyponatremia in an endurance run; and the effect of heat on hydration of adolescent Judo athletes. Academic libraries will want to consider this title.

4997. International Journal of Sports Science & Coaching. [ISSN: 1747-9541] 2006. bi-m. GBP 267; GBP 284 combined subscription (print & online eds.). Ed(s): Simon Jenkins. Multi-Science Publishing Co. Ltd., 5 Wates Way, Brentwood, CM15 9TB, United Kingdom; info@multi-science.co.uk; http://www.multi-science.co.uk. Sample. Refereed. *Indexed:* C&ISA, C45, CerAb, PsycInfo, SD. *Bk. rev.:* Number and length vary. *Aud.:* Ac.

Begun in 2006, the *International Journal of Sports Science and Coaching* is a relatively new entry into the study of sports science. This peer-reviewed academic journal bridges the fields of coaching and the sports sciences. Articles are written by an international group of academics and researchers who "integrate theory and practice in sports science, promote critical reflection of coaching practice, and evaluate commonly accepted beliefs about coaching effectiveness and performance enhancement." Articles that reflect collaboration between coaches and sports scientists are particularly encouraged. Typical material includes a discussion of overtraining or burnout; error reduction in soccer practice; classifying drills in Australian football; and the development of a coach–athlete relationship questionnaire. The journal's web site provides detailed information and links to article abstracts. A suitable purchase for academic libraries. URL: www.multi-science.co.uk/sports-science&coaching.htm

Journal of Aging and Physical Activity. See Geriatrics and Gerontological Studies section.

4998. Journal of Applied Biomechanics. Formerly (until 1993): *International Journal of Sport Biomechanics.* [ISSN: 1065-8483] 1985. bi-m. USD 649 (print & online eds.). Ed(s): JJ Crisco. Human Kinetics, Inc., 1607 N Market St, Champaign, IL 61820; info@hkusa.com; http://www.humankinetics.com. Illus., index, adv. Refereed. Reprint: PSC. *Indexed:* A22, EngInd, ErgAb, ExcerpMed, SD. *Aud.:* Ac, Sa.

The quarterly publication of the International Society of Biomechanics is a technical journal, devoted to the study of human biomechanics in sport, exercise, and rehabilitation. Articles accepted for publication in this peer-reviewed journal include original research, technical notes, and reviews. Topics of concern relate not only to exercise and sport, but also to modeling, clinical biomechanics, gait and posture, and the relations between the muscles and the skeleton or nervous system. Readers can read about a mathematical model predicting drivers' reaction times; kinetic analysis of ski turns; or the changes in muscle activity when in high heels. Most appropriate for academic and medical libraries.

Journal of Applied Physiology. See Physiology section.

4999. *Journal of Athletic Training.* Former titles (until 1992): *Athletic Training;* (until 1972): *National Athletic Trainers Association. Journal.* [ISSN: 1062-6050] 1956. bi-m. USD 245 (print & online eds.) Individuals, USD 112 (print & online eds.). Ed(s): Christopher D Ingersoll, Leslie Neistadt. National Athletic Trainers Association, Inc., 2952 N Stemmons Fwy, Dallas, TX 75247; membership@nata.org; http://www.nata.org/. Illus., index, adv. Refereed. Vol. ends: Oct/Dec. Microform: PQC. *Indexed:* A01, A22, BRI, E01, P02, PsycInfo, SD. *Bk. rev.:* 4, 350 words. *Aud.:* Ac, Sa.

The official publication of the National Athletic Trainers' Association, the *Journal of Athletic Training* is a quarterly peer-reviewed (acceptance rate 45 percent) journal with the mission of enhancing "communication among professionals interested in the quality of healthcare for the physically active through education and research in prevention, evaluation, management, and rehabilitation of injuries." Each issue of 120–150 pages is generally subdivided into sections: original research, literature reviews, evidence-based practice, and case reports. Editorials, letters, and announcements supplement the articles. Past issues of the journal (with a one-year embargo) are accessible through PubMed Central. A suggested acquisition for academic institutions with sport sciences and physical education programs.

5000. *Journal of Orthopaedic and Sports Physical Therapy.* [ISSN: 0190-6011] 1979. m. USD 480 (print & online eds.) USD 450 domestic). Ed(s): Guy G Simoneau. American Physical Therapy Association, Orthopedic Section, 1111 N Fairfax St, Ste 100, Alexandria, VA 22314; tdeflorian@orthopt.org; http://www.orthopt.org. Illus., index, adv. Refereed. Circ: 23500 Paid. *Indexed:* A22, SD. *Bk. rev.:* 4, 300 words. *Aud.:* Ac, Sa.

The official publication of the Orthopaedic Section and the Sports Physical Therapy Section of the American Physical Therapy Association is a scholarly, peer-reviewed, international journal, of interest to clinicians, patients, faculty, and students. The journal mission is "to publish scientifically rigorous, clinically relevant content for physical therapists and others in the healthcare community to advance musculoskeletal and sports-related practice." Each monthly issue contains research articles, as well as research reports, case reports, invited commentaries, literature reviews, and employment opportunities. Recently musculoskeletal imaging features and online videos have been added. A suggested purchase for medical and academic libraries. URL: http://jospt.org

5001. *Journal of Physical Education, Recreation and Dance.* Former titles (until 1981): *Journal of Physical Education and Recreation;* (until 1975): *Journal of Health, Physical Education, Recreation;* (until 1954): *American Association for Health, Physical Education, Recreation. Journal;* (until 1950): *The Journal of Health and Physical Education;* Which was formed by the merger of (1928-1930): *Pentathlon;* (1896-1930): *American Physical Education Review;* Which was formerly (until 1896): *American Association for the Advancement of Physical Education. Report of the ... Annual Meeting;* (until 1894): *American Association for the Advancement of Physical Education. Annual Meeting. Proceedings;* (until 1886): *Association for the Advancement of Physical Education. Organization. Proceedings.* [ISSN: 0730-3084] 1930. 9x/yr. GBP 168 (print & online eds.). Ed(s): Tom Lawson. Routledge, 325

Chestnut St, Ste 800, Philadelphia, PA 19106; customerservice@taylorandfrancis.com; http://www.tandfonline.com. Illus., index, adv. Refereed. Circ: 12000. Vol. ends: Dec. Microform: PMC; PQC. *Indexed:* A01, A22, BRI, C45, ERIC, IIPA, P02, RILM, RRTA, SD. *Aud.:* Hs, Ga, Ac.

Published nine times a year by the American Alliance for Health, Physical Education, Recreation and Dance (AAHPERD), the *Journal of Physical Education, Recreation, and Dance* has been in continuous publication since 1896. The peer-reviewed articles are directly relevant to educators at all levels and cover a variety of information on health, physical education, recreation, and dance. Issues include editorials, teaching ideas, an analysis of issues of interest to AAHPERD members and listing of job openings. The journal design has recently been modernized and includes numerous color photographs. Recent issues have featured articles on including paralympic sports in a general physical education program; creating a dialog about transgender and intersex athletes; and supervising PETE candidates. Academic libraries are the most appropriate subscribers.

5002. *Journal of Sports Science and Medicine.* [ISSN: 1303-2968] 2002. q. Free. Ed(s): Hakan Gur. Journal of Sports Science and Medicine, c/o Hakan Gur, MD, PhD, Department of Sports Medicine, Bursa, 16059, Turkey; hakan@uludag.edu.tr. Refereed. *Indexed:* A01, BRI, SD. *Bk. rev.:* Number and length vary. *Aud.:* Ac, Sa.

The mission of this free electronic journal is to "to present easy access to the scientific knowledge for sport-conscious individuals using contemporary methods." It publishes research, review articles, case studies, and book reviews in all areas of the sports sciences and medicine. The journal takes advantage of the electronic medium to publish articles more quickly than is possible in print and to encourage discussion among researchers. The editors suggest that authors include multimedia; however, most entries appear to be pdf files. Each quarterly issue may contain 20 or more articles. The journal provides an avenue for open and scholarly communication of research, and the editors should be complemented for their efforts. Of interest to medical and academic libraries. URL: www.jssm.org

5003. *Journal of Strength and Conditioning Research.* Formerly (until 1993): *The Journal of Applied Sport Science Research.* [ISSN: 1064-8011] 1987. 9x/yr. USD 580 (print & online eds.). Ed(s): William J Kraemer. Lippincott Williams & Wilkins, 530 Walnut St, Philadelphia, PA 19106; customerservice@lww.com; http://www.lww.com. Illus., index, adv. Refereed. Circ: 27671. Vol. ends: Dec. *Indexed:* A01, A22, E01, SD. *Bk. rev.:* Number and length vary. *Aud.:* Ac, Sa.

One of two official journals of the National Strength and Conditioning Association, this publication features "original investigations, reviews, symposia, research notes, and technical and methodological reports contributing to the knowledge about strength and conditioning in sport and exercise." The journal's focus is research with practical applications, and articles conclude with a practical applications section. The audience is the end user, including strength and conditioning specialists, coaches, athletic trainers, and athletes. Articles are written in English by an international group of scholars. Recently the number of issues per year was increased from four to 12, greatly reducing the time between acceptance and publication. An appropriate purchase for medical and academic libraries. URL: http://journals.lww.com/nsca-jscr

5004. *Journal of Teaching in Physical Education.* [ISSN: 0273-5024] 1981. q. USD 502 (print & online eds.). Ed(s): Ping Xiang, Pamela Kulinna. Human Kinetics, Inc., 1607 N Market St, Champaign, IL 61820; info@hkusa.com; http://www.humankinetics.com. Illus., index, adv. Sample. Refereed. Vol. ends: Jul. Reprint: PSC. *Indexed:* A22, C45, ERIC, PsycInfo, RRTA, SD. *Aud.:* Ems, Hs, Ac.

This quarterly journal features empirical research and integrative reviews and analyses, descriptive survey studies, summary and review articles, and discussions of current topics of interest to physical education teachers at all levels. Each issue contains six or seven articles of approximately 15–20 pages in length. As a peer-reviewed journal, focusing on research rather than practice, it uses the more technical language of the social sciences, and is most appropriate for academic libraries.

5005. *Motor Control.* [ISSN: 1087-1640] 1997. q. USD 622 (print & online eds.). Ed(s): Mindy Levin. Human Kinetics, Inc., 1607 N Market St, Champaign, IL 61820; info@hkusa.com; http://www.humankinetics.com. Illus., adv. Sample. Refereed. Reprint: PSC. *Indexed:* A22, ErgAb, ExcerpMed, PsycInfo, SD. *Bk. rev.:* Number and length vary. *Aud.:* Ac, Sa.

The official journal of the International Society of Motor Control is a quarterly peer-reviewed publication that provides "multidisciplinary examination of human movement across the lifespan." Editors and authors are academicians from an international list of universities and research institutions, representing a variety of disciplines including kinesiology, neurophysiology, neuroscience, psychology, rehabilitation, and physical medicine. Each issue of approximately 100 pages contains five to ten articles. In addition to original research, the journal occasionally accepts review articles, book reviews, commentaries, and quick communications. Occasionally an entire issue may be devoted to a single topic. Suitable for medical and academic libraries.

Palaestra. See Disabilities section.

5006. *Pediatric Exercise Science.* [ISSN: 0899-8493] 1989. q. USD 502 (print & online eds.). Ed(s): Bareket Falk. Human Kinetics, Inc., 1607 N Market St, Champaign, IL 61820; info@hkusa.com; http://www.humankinetics.com. Illus., adv. Sample. Refereed. Vol. ends: Nov. Reprint: PSC. *Indexed:* A22, RiskAb, SD. *Bk. rev.:* Occasional. *Aud.:* Ac, Sa.

Published since 1989, *Pediatric Exercise Science,* the official publication of the North American Society of Pediatric Exercise Medicine, is a peer-reviewed quarterly that focuses on research on exercise during childhood and adolescence. In addition to original research, the journal publishes review articles, abstracts from other journals, book reviews, and editorials. Since many disciplines contribute to research on exercise, this journal aims to provide a common focus for disseminating this knowledge. The journal's scope is international, and authors include clinicians and academic researchers. Most appropriate for academic and medical libraries.

5007. *Quest (Champaign).* Incorporates (1984-1992): *American Academy of Physical Education Papers;* Which was formerly (1967-1984): *Academy Papers;* (1979-1985): *National Association for Physical Education in Higher Education. Annual Conference. Proceedings;* Which was formerly (until 1979): *N A P E C W / N C P E A M National Conference. Proceedings.* [ISSN: 0033-6297] 1949. q. GBP 229 (print & online eds.). Ed(s): Mike W Metzier. Routledge, 325 Chestnut St, Ste 800, Philadelphia, PA 19106; customerservice@taylorandfrancis.com; http://www.tandfonline.com. Illus. Sample. Refereed. Vol. ends: Nov. Microform: PQC. Reprint: PSC. *Indexed:* A22, C45, ERIC, RRTA, SD. *Bk. rev.:* Number and length vary. *Aud.:* Ac.

Quest is the official publication of the National Association for Kinesiology in Higher Education (formerly, the National Association for Physical Education in Higher Education). Rather than focusing on original research, the editors seek articles that are based on, complement, or review scholarly work related to the profession. Both theoretical and practice-based articles are considered. The journal's audience includes academicians, teachers, and administrators. Articles vary in length from about 10 to 20 pages, and issues may include as few as five or as many as ten articles. Appropriate for colleges or universities with strong physical education programs.

5008. *Research Quarterly for Exercise and Sport.* Incorporates (1965-1974): *Abstracts of Research Papers;* Former titles (until 1980): *American Alliance for Health, Physical Education, Recreation and Dance. Research Quarterly;* (until 1979): *American Alliance for Health, Physical Education, and Recreation. Research Quarterly;* (until 1974): *American Association for Health, Physical Education, and Recreation. Research Quarterly;* (until 1939): *American Association for Health and Physical Education. Research Quarterly;* (until 1937): *American Physical Education Association. Research Quarterly.* [ISSN: 0270-1367] 1930. q. GBP 205 (print & online eds.). Ed(s): Weimo Zhu, Linda Topper.

Routledge, 325 Chestnut St, Ste 800, Philadelphia, PA 19106; customerservice@taylorandfrancis.com; http://www.tandfonline.com. Illus., index, adv. Refereed. Vol. ends: Dec. Microform: PMC; PQC. *Indexed:* A01, A22, BRI, ERIC, ErgAb, P02, RILM, SD. *Aud.:* Ac.

This journal from the American Alliance for Health, Physical Education, Recreation and Dance (AAHPERD) has been published since 1930. Its mission is to "publish refereed research articles on the art and science of human movement, which contribute to the knowledge and development of theory, either as new information, substantiation or contraction of previous findings, or application of new or improved techniques." *RQES* publishes more than 50 articles a year, and includes an annual online supplement with abstracts of presentations from the Research Consortium program at the AAHPERD National Convention. Issues are divided into "Articles" and "Research Notes." The "Articles" section is further subdivided into disciplines: "Epidemology," "Measurement and Evaluation," "Motor Control and Learning," "Pedagogy," and "Psychology," thus ensuring that the reader may quickly focus on a topic of interest. Recommended for academic libraries that support sports and exercise science programs.

Shape. See Health and Fitness section.

5009. *Sociology of Sport Journal.* [ISSN: 0741-1235] 1984. q. USD 502 (print & online eds.). Ed(s): Michael Atkinson. Human Kinetics, Inc., 1607 N Market St, Champaign, IL 61820; info@hkusa.com; http://www.humankinetics.com. Illus., index, adv. Sample. Refereed. Vol. ends: Dec. Reprint: PSC. *Indexed:* A01, A22, BRI, C37, C45, CBCARef, P61, PsycInfo, RILM, RRTA, RiskAb, SD, SSA. *Bk. rev.:* 1, 750 words. *Aud.:* Ac.

The official journal of the North American Society for the Sociology of Sport publishes "original research, framed by social theory, on exercise, sport, physical culture, and the (physically active) body." The journal provides an international perspective and features empirical, theoretical research and position papers using a multidisciplinary approach. Bibliographies, research notes, and short papers on curriculum issues may also be included. Abstracts in English and French precede the articles. The intended readership includes sport sociologists, sport psychologists, and coaches. An appropriate consideration for academic libraries.

5010. *Strategies (Philadelphia): a journal for physical and sport educators.* [ISSN: 0892-4562] 1987. bi-m. GBP 108 (print & online eds.). Ed(s): Tom Lawson. Routledge, 325 Chestnut St, Ste 800, Philadelphia, PA 19106; customerservice@taylorandfrancis.com; http://www.tandfonline.com. Illus., adv. Refereed. *Indexed:* A22, ERIC, P02, SD. *Aud.:* Ems, Hs, Ac.

The official publication of the National Association for Sport and Physical Education, *Strategies* is a peer-reviewed journal published six times a year for physical education teachers and coaches at all levels. The publication seeks practical, how-to articles for sport and physical education educators, particularly articles that "identify a problem and offer concrete, step-by-step solutions, or describe best practices for typical coach or teacher activities or responsibilities." Each 30- to 35-page issue contains 10 to 12 articles. Typical articles include coaches as role models; the physical educator as a language teacher; and strategies to promote physical fitness. Each issue contains a theory into practice column. The journal is written in a conversational tone, using non-technical language, making this professional magazine appropriate for large public and school libraries, as well as academic libraries.

5011. *Strength and Conditioning Journal.* Former titles (until 1999): *Strength and Conditioning;* (until 1994): *N S C A Journal;* (until 1993): *National Strength & Conditioning Association Journal;* (until 1981): *National Strength Coaches Association Journal.* [ISSN: 1524-1602] 1979. bi-m. USD 196 (print & online eds.). Ed(s): T Jeff Chandler. Lippincott Williams & Wilkins, 530 Walnut St, Philadelphia, PA 19106; customerservice@lww.com; http://www.lww.com. Illus., index, adv. Refereed. Circ: 27608. *Indexed:* A22, E01, P02, SD. *Bk. rev.:* 3, 100-250 words. *Aud.:* Ac, Sa.

The professional journal of the National Strength and Conditioning Association (NSCA) publishes peer-reviewed articles with practical information from research studies on "resistance training, sports medicine and science, and issues facing the strength and conditioning professional." Each bimonthly 80-page issue contains approximately five feature articles and several columns. Some articles include supplemental digital content such as links to video files or similar material. In 2012, the journal was planned to be available as an iPad app, which the editors said is one more step toward the future. The target audience is strength coaches, personal trainers, physical therapists, athletic trainers, and other strength and conditioning professionals. Recommended for academic libraries. URL: www.nsca-lift.org

5012. Women in Sport and Physical Activity Journal (Online). Formerly (until 2004): *Women in Sport and Physical Activity Journal (Print).* [ISSN: 1938-1581] 1992. 3x/yr. USD 50 (Members, USD 20; Non-members, USD 30). Ed(s): Chandelle Schulte, Ann T Boyce. National Association for Girls and Women in Sport, 1900 Association Dr, Reston, VA 20191; NAGWS@aahperd.org; http://www.aahperd.org/ nagws. Illus. Refereed. Vol. ends: Fall. *Indexed:* BRI, C42, FemPer, GW, H24, RiskAb, SD. *Bk. rev.:* 4, lengthy. *Aud.:* Ac, Sa.

Published by the National Association for Girls and Women in Sport (NAGWS), this online-only journal contains peer-reviewed research that examines women's involvement in and/or perspectives on sport and physical activity. The journal is published three times a year. Entries include research articles, review essays, creative writing, book reviews, commentaries, letters and responses, and other scholarly writings relative to sport and physical activity, and emphasize a multidisciplinary approach. The audience is "teachers, coaches, researchers, and scholars, particularly in the following fields: physical education, athletics, intramurals, kinesiology, sport science, fitness, exercise and health, and women's studies." This journal is appropriate for academic libraries.

Specific Sports

5013. Amateur Wrestling News. Formerly (until 1957): *Wrestling News and Reports.* [ISSN: 0569-1796] 1955. 12x/yr. USD 35; USD 45 combined subscription (print & online eds.). Ed(s): Ron Good. Amateur Wrestling News, PO Box 54679, Oklahoma City, OK 73154. Illus., adv. *Indexed:* SD. *Aud.:* Hs, Ga.

Since 1956, *Amateur Wrestling News (AWN)*, the "oldest publication covering all areas of amateur wrestling," has covered high school, collegiate, Olympic, women's, freestyle, and Greco-Roman wrestling. In 2012, facing competition from Internet sites, the magazine announced that it would merge with *The Open Mat,* an award-winning web site. The print magazine will shift its focus to one that is feature-focused, with its web presence driven by *The Open Mat.* The demo for the May 2012 issue featured articles on the *AWN* Rookie of the Year, the *AWN* Rookie team and coach, and the 2012 Olympic team bound for London; it also had a long article on the 1948 Olympics, also held in London. Suitable for high school and academic libraries.

5014. American Fencing. [ISSN: 0002-8436] 1949. q. Free to members. United States Fencing Association, Inc., One Olympic Plz, Colorado Springs, CO 80909; info@usfencing.org; http://www.usfencing.org. Illus. Microform: PQC. *Indexed:* A22, SD. *Aud.:* Hs, Ga, Ac.

The official publication of the United States Fencing Association, this magazine reports the news, people, tournaments, rankings, rules, training, techniques, and equipment of the sport of fencing. Published quarterly, it features articles and essays about fencing and issues surrounding the sport. Regular features include player profiles, sports medicine, the psychology of fencing, rules and referees, tournament results, and product reviews. Membership in the Association includes a subscription to the magazine. An excellent resource for high school and academic libraries at institutions with fencing programs.

5015. Baseball America. Formerly (until 1982): *All-America Baseball News.* [ISSN: 0745-5372] 1981. bi-w. USD 92.95. Ed(s): Will Lingo. Baseball America, Inc., 4319 S Alston Ave, Ste 103, Durham, NC 27713. Illus. *Aud.:* Ga, Ac.

This bimonthly newsprint provides comprehensive coverage of baseball from the international, major, minor, collegiate Division I, and high school teams, and both the minor and the major leagues. Articles highlight teams, players, coaches, prospects, leagues, statistics, and averages. The magazine publishes weekly rankings of the top 25 college teams, and draft and season previews. The print publication is updated by the magazine's interactive web site with current information on teams, players, statistics, and news. Recommended for public, high school, and academic libraries. URL: www.baseballamerica.com

5016. Baseball Digest. [ISSN: 0005-609X] 1941. m. USD 23.94 domestic; USD 40 Canada; USD 50 elsewhere. Ed(s): Robert Kuenster. Century Publishing Inc., PO Box 730, Coeur d'Alene, ID 83816; bb@centurysports.net; http://www.centurypublishing.com. Illus., adv. Circ: 225000 Paid and controlled. Vol. ends: Dec. Microform: PQC. *Indexed:* A22, BRI, C37, MASUSE, SD. *Aud.:* Hs, Ga.

Calling itself "a publication for the true baseball fan," *Baseball Digest* is the oldest baseball magazine and the only one devoted entirely to major league play. It features articles, interviews, statistics, charts, and rosters of major league baseball. It highlights major league history and current stars. Special features include a "Fans Speak Out" section, a crossword puzzle, a trivia challenge, and a review of rules, as well as comprehensive batting, pitching, and fielding statistics; previews; and analysis of upcoming prospects. It is published six times a year—with National and American League schedules, directories, and pre-season rosters. The magazine's "Player and Pitcher of the Year" reads like a list of baseball greats. A suitable purchase for high school and public libraries.

5017. Bicycling. Incorporates: (1990-200?): *Mountain Bike;* (1972-1980): *Bike World;* Formerly (until 1968): *American Cycling.* [ISSN: 0006-2073] 1962. 11x/yr. USD 19.98 domestic; CAD 29.96 Canada; USD 45 elsewhere. Ed(s): Peter Flax. Rodale, Inc., 33 E Minor St, Emmaus, PA 18098; http://www.rodaleinc.com. Illus., adv. Microform: NBI; PQC. *Indexed:* A22, ASIP, BRI, C37, IHTDI, MASUSE, P02, SD. *Aud.:* Hs, Ga, Ac.

This is a glossy magazine for the serious cyclist with news, training and nutrition, bike repair, road maps, and other information of interest to cyclists. The magazine publishes an annual *Buyers' Guide.* The web site includes links to bicycling blogs, videos, information on bicycling gear, and the like. Readers may also sign up for a free newsletter. Suitable for public libraries. URL: www.bicycling.com

5018. Black Belt Magazine. Former titles (until 2005): *Karate - Kung Fu Illustrated;* (until 1991): *Karate Illustrated.* [ISSN: 0277-3066] 1961. m. USD 29 domestic; USD 39 Canada; USD 51 elsewhere. Ed(s): Robert Young. Black Belt Communications, Inc., 24900 Anza Dr, Unit E, Valencia, CA 91355. Adv. *Indexed:* BRI, SD. *Aud.:* Ga.

Billed as the "world's leading magazine of self-defense," *Black Belt* covers more than 15 martial arts. Articles examine different martial arts, their philosophy and principles, spiritual and historical aspects, and techniques. Columns repeated in each 150-page issue include a news digest, interviews with famous martial artists, instruction, nutrition, exercise, sports medicine, gear, a directory of martial arts schools, and more. Typical articles include a martial arts travel guide, a guide to training camps, the best gyms in Vegas, and the essentials of combat in Tang Soo Do. The journal is appropriate for high school, public, and academic library collections.

5019. Collegiate Baseball: the voice of amateur baseball. [ISSN: 0530-9751] 1957. 14x/yr. USD 28 domestic; USD 50 foreign. Ed(s): Louis Pavlovich, Jr. Collegiate Baseball Newspaper Inc., c/o Lou Pavlovich, Jr, Ed, Box 50566, Tucson, AZ 85703; cbn@baseballnews.com; http://www.baseballnews.com. Illus., adv. Circ: 7000. Vol. ends: Oct. Microform: PQC. *Indexed:* A22. *Aud.:* Hs, Ac.

Since 1957 this newsprint has featured up-to-date information for those interested in college and high school baseball. It is published twice a month during the season (and monthly June, July, September, and October). This newspaper contains editorials, letters to the editor, baseball news, rules and regulations, tips for training and game improvement, spotlights of outstanding players, and statistics and standings for all college divisions and high school teams. It publishes polls for all the NCCA, NAIA, NJCAA, and California &

Pacific Association divisions, as well as high school divisions. The audience includes high school and college coaches and players. Well-known players and coaches write many of the columns. An appropriate purchase for high school and academic libraries.

5020. *Cross Country Skier.* Formerly (until 1981): *Nordic Skiing.* [ISSN: 0278-9213] 1976. q. USD 14.95. Ed(s): Lou Dzierzak, Ron Bergin. Country Skier, LLC, PO Box 550, Cable, WI 54821. Illus., adv. Sample. Vol. ends: Feb. *Indexed:* A22, BRI, SD. *Aud.:* Ga.

Cross Country Skier: The Journal of Nordic Skiing will appeal to all who practice this sport. It is published three times a year during the season. Regular columns include training and technique, snow conditions, and cross-country skiing destinations. A recent issue featured an article on a famous biathlete, advice to the competitive skier, and a directory of equipment and apparel. A racing section provides advice for the competitive skier on technique, training, and events. The destination section would make almost everyone want to enjoy this sport. Additional information on cross-country skiing is posted at the web site. This would be a good addition for novice and experienced skiers at public libraries. URL: www.crosscountryskier.com/

5021. *Golf Digest.* Formerly (until 1950): *Arrowhead Golf Digest.* [ISSN: 0017-176X] 1950. m. USD 12 domestic; USD 21.97 foreign. Ed(s): Jerry Tarde. The Golf Digest Companies, 20 Westport Rd, Wilton, CT 06897; glscustserv@cdsfulfilment.com. Illus., adv. Microform: PQC. *Indexed:* A22, BRI, C37, MASUSE, P02, SD. *Aud.:* Hs, Ga, Ac.

Belying its title, each monthly issue of *Golf Digest* is a large publication with over 200 pages. It is filled with advice for game improvement and columns on instruction, equipment, courses, and players. Detailed articles are written by and about famous golfers, with time-lapse photographs to analyze swings. Occasional features focus on golf history, golf courses, country clubs, and interviews with major players. With the demise of *Golf for Women*, the magazine has begun to include articles for women golfers and has a "*Golf Digest* woman" link on its web page. This journal is similar to, and a complement to, *Golf Magazine*. A subscription will delight duffers at public and academic libraries. URL: www.golfdigest.com/

5022. *Golf Magazine.* Former titles (until 1991): *Golf;* (until 1986): *Golf Magazine.* [ISSN: 1056-5493] 1959. m. USD 10 domestic; CAD 20 Canada. Time Inc., 1271 Ave of the Americas, New York, NY 10020; information@timeinc.com; http://www.timeinc.com. Illus. Circ: 1400000. Microform: PQC. *Indexed:* A01, A22, BRI, C37, MASUSE, P02, SD. *Aud.:* Hs, Ga, Ac.

The glossy *Golf Magazine* is a popular golf publication with articles on equipment, rules, instruction, courses, events, courses and travel, and interviews with golfers. Regular columns include golf events, questions and answers, rules, and questions for tour players. "Private Lessons" provides tips for better play for the beginning, the experienced, and the senior golfer. The magazine is filled with beautiful photography. Subscribers to the print also receive access to the mobile edition. Although similar to *Golf Digest,* the two publications complement one another. A suitable purchase for public libraries. URL: www.golf.com

5023. *Handball.* Formerly (until 1971): *Ace.* [ISSN: 0046-6778] 1950. bi-m. Free to members. U.S. Handball Association, 2333 N Tucson Blvd, Tucson, AZ 85716; http://ushandball.org. Illus., adv. Microform: PQC. *Indexed:* A22, SD. *Aud.:* Hs, Ga, Ac.

As the official voice of the U.S. Handball Association (USHA), this magazine will interest all recreational handball players as well as members of the association. Each issue contains instructional articles for beginning and advanced players, tournament information and entry forms, tips from the best players, health advice, photographs and stories from major tournaments, and announcements of specials on handball equipment and gear. Handball is an Olympic sport and popular in many areas of the country. Public libraries may want to consider adding this magazine to their collection.

5024. *The Hockey News: the international hockey weekly.* [ISSN: 0018-3016] 1947. 34x/yr. CAD 52.95 domestic. TC Media, 25 Sheppard Ave West, Ste 100, North York, Toronto, ON M2N 6S7, Canada; info@transcontinental.ca; http://www.transcontinental-gtc.com/. Illus., adv. Circ: 110000. Microform: MML. *Indexed:* A22, BRI, C37, CBCARef, SD. *Aud.:* Ga.

Since 1947, *Hockey News* has published information about North American hockey. Published 30 times a year (weekly during the hockey season), it includes six special issues: "Season Opener," "People of Power and Influence," "Future Watch," "Draft Preview," "Season in Review," and the "Yearbook." The magazine, printed on newsprint, is richly illustrated. Typical content includes editorials, opinion pieces, letters to the editor, news in brief, player profiles and interviews, statistics, schedules, rosters, and the like. Each team in the National Hockey League receives in-depth coverage in every issue. Less detail is provided for teams in the minor pro, junior, and collegiate leagues. This title is appropriate for consideration for school and public libraries in areas where hockey is popular. URL: www.thehockeynews.com

5025. *Hockey Player Magazine (Online).* Formerly (until 1998): *Hockey Player Magazine (Print).* 1991. m. Ed(s): Alex Carswell. Hockey Player Magazine L.P. Illus., adv. *Aud.:* Ga.

Published as a print magazine from 1991 to 1997, *Hockey Player Magazine* became an online-only publication in 1998. Aimed at the recreational ice, roller, and street hockey player, the magazine contains interviews, columns, departments, equipment news, drills, and instruction. The more than 500 online articles are fully searchable and/or browsed by section. Typical sections include "Behind the Bench" (coaching), defense, essays and humor, offense, power skating, profiles, and youth. Hockey fans and players will enjoy this magazine. URL: www.hockeyplayer.com

5026. *Inside Pool Magazine.* [ISSN: 1547-3511] 2001. bi-m. USD 19.99 domestic; USD 28 Canada; USD 39 elsewhere. Ed(s): Sally P Timko. Spheragon Publishing, PO Box 972, Kittanning, PA 16201. Adv. *Aud.:* Ga.

Pool and billiard players will enjoy the monthly *Inside Pool,* with its news about the game, instruction from the pros, profiles, and regular columns. It also contains schedules of televised tournaments, product reviews, monthly profiles, tournament results, reports from the International Pool Tour, advertiser directories, and photographs. Suitable for public libraries. URL: http://insidepoolmag.com

5027. *International Figure Skating.* [ISSN: 1070-9568] 1993. bi-m. USD 28. Ed(s): Susan Wessling. Madavor Media, Llc., 85 Quincy Ave, Ste 2, Quincy, MA 02169; info@madavor.com; http://www.madavor.com. Illus., adv. *Indexed:* SD. *Aud.:* Hs, Ga.

International Figure Skating reports the news, business, and personalities of figure skating, covering both U.S. and international competitions. Based in the U.S., the magazine has correspondents in Canada, Germany, France, Hong Kong, and the U.K., making it a truly global publication. The cover story profiles famous competitors such as the award-winning Aliona Savchenko and Robin Szolkowy. The magazine includes beautiful glossy photographs that will appeal to skaters and would-be skaters alike. The magazine is available both in print or online. Suitable for public libraries. URL: www.ifsmagazine.com/

5028. *International Gymnast.* Former titles (until 1986): *International Gymnast Magazine;* (until 1982): *International Gymnast;* (until 1981): *International Gymnast Magazine;* (until 1979): *International Gymnast;* (until 1976): *Gymnast;* Which was formed by the merger of (1966-1971): *Mademoiselle Gymnast;* (1956-1972): *Modern Gymnast;* Incorporates (1975-1980): *Gymnastics World.* [ISSN: 0891-6616] 1972. 10x/yr. USD 30 domestic; USD 40 Canada; USD 50 elsewhere. Paul Ziert & Associates, Inc., 3214 Bart Conner Dr, Norman, OK 73072; orders@intlgymnast.com; http://www.intlgymnast.com. Illus., adv. *Indexed:* A22, P02, SD. *Aud.:* Hs, Ga.

Since 1956, *International Gymnast* has focused on the individuals that compete in the sport. Ten issues of approximately 40 pages in length include biographical profiles and coverage of international events and teams. Articles are lavishly illustrated and supplemented by columns that contain letters, new products, a calendar, a brief fictional series, and a "Kid's Klub"—the last, no doubt, geared to an important segment of the magazine's readership. In 2007 the magazine launched a digital version, becoming both print and electronic. This magazine is appropriate for public and school libraries. URL: www.intlgymnast.com

5029. *Journal of Asian Martial Arts.* [ISSN: 1057-8358] 1992. q. USD 75 (Individuals, USD 32). Via Media Publishing Company, 821 W 24th St, Erie, PA 16502. Illus., index. Sample. Refereed. *Indexed:* SD. *Bk. rev.:* 3, 750-1,200 words. *Aud.:* Ga, Ac.

This quarterly publishes articles of interest to the serious student of the Asian martial arts. Each issue of approximately of 120 pages contains original research, substantial interviews, and book/audiovisual reviews. Articles are reviewed by members of the editorial board. A recent issue contained articles on the health benefits of Taiji and Qigong, changes in the martial artist's right to firearms, and the correlation of physique and body fat to martial arts performance of elite karate and taekwondo athletes. Articles are illustrated with drawings and photographs. Suitable for large public and academic libraries.

5030. *Marathon & Beyond: run longer, better, smarter.* [ISSN: 1088-6672] 1997. bi-m. USD 36.95 domestic; USD 47.65 Canada; USD 54 elsewhere. Ed(s): Richard Benyo. Marathon & Beyond, 206 N Randolph St, Ste 400, Champaign, IL 61820. Adv. *Indexed:* SD. *Aud.:* Ga.

This bimonthly publication caters to marathoners and ultra runners. Its mission is to "provide practical advice on running or preparing to run marathons and ultradistances." Unlike other magazines of this type, *Marathon & Beyond* does not publish race reports, schedules of events, or reviews of apparel and equipment. Instead, it publishes articles written by accomplished runners, coaches, and scientists that focus on the personal side of running, in-depth profiles of marathoners, training information, nutrition, race strategy, running history, and columns on running specifics. Articles are generally longer than in other magazines of this type, and there are no glossy photographs. First-time runners and experienced long-distance runners alike will welcome this magazine. Suitable for public libraries.

5031. *Nine: a journal of baseball history & culture.* [ISSN: 1188-9330] 1992. s-a. USD 88. Ed(s): Trey Strecker. University of Nebraska Press, 1111 Lincoln Mall, Lincoln, NE 68588; pressmail@unl.edu; http://www.nebraskapress.unl.edu. Illus., adv. Refereed. Circ: 250. *Indexed:* A01, A22, BRI, E01, MLA-IB, P02, SD. *Bk. rev.:* Number and length vary. *Aud.:* Ac.

Published since 1992, this academic peer-reviewed journal promotes "the study of all historical aspects of baseball and the cultural implications of the game wherever in the world baseball is played." Issues include articles, essays, book reviews, biographies, oral histories, and short fiction. Recent issues included articles on free agents in the major leagues; fan perceptions of Latino players; English- and Spanish-speaking minor league players' perspectives on community service; and interviews and book reviews. The journal is available from 2000 on in Project MUSE. Suitable for academic libraries.

5032. *Pro Football Weekly.* [ISSN: 0032-9053] 1967. 32x/yr. USD 44.95 for 15 issues; USD 79.95 for 30 issues. Source Interlink Companies, 302 Saunders Rd, Ste 100, Riverwoods, IL 60015; dheine@sourceinterlink.com; http://www.sourceinterlinkmedia.com. Illus., adv. Sample. Circ: 125262. *Aud.:* Ga.

This newsprint publication features news of professional football and includes team rosters and schedules, player profiles, fantasy football, arena football, NFL Europe, player transactions, statistics, team rankings, and opinion pieces. Noted sports columnists write many of the feature columns. This publication provides an insider's view of the sport to attract true football fans, fantasy football players, and handicappers. It is published 30 times per year, weekly during the professional football season. The newspaper is supplemented by selected articles and other material on its web site. In addition, it hosts both a radio and a television show. Suitable for public libraries and avid football fans. URL: www.profootballweekly.com

5033. *The Ring: the bible of boxing.* [ISSN: 0035-5410] 1922. 13x/yr. USD 53.70 domestic; USD 86.70 in Canada & Mexico; USD 143.70 elsewhere. Ed(s): Michael Rosenthal. Sports & Entertainment Publications, LLC, 510 Township Line Rd, Ste 130, Blue Bell, PA 19422; custsrvcsep@sepublications.com. Illus., adv. Circ: 200000. *Indexed:* SD. *Aud.:* Ga.

Calling itself "the Bible of Boxing" and published since 1922, *The Ring* features professional boxing. It has established several prestigious awards, including fighter of the year; fight of the year; round of the year; upset of the year; comeback of the year; knockout of the year; and event of the year. Numerous famous fighters have been featured on its covers: Jack Dempsey, Joe Louis, Sugar Ray Robinson, Rocky Marciano, Muhammad Ali, Manny Pacquiao, Saul Alvarez, and Wladimir Klitschko, to name a few. Since this is an established publication, and given the number of boxing fans in the country, it should be considered for public libraries.

5034. *Runner's World.* Former titles (until 1987): *Rodale's Runner's World;* Which incorporated (1978-1987): *Runner;* (until 1985): *Runner's World;* (until 1970): *Distance Running News.* [ISSN: 0897-1706] 197?. m. USD 24 domestic; CAD 31 Canada; USD 60 elsewhere. Ed(s): David Willey, Charles Butler. Rodale, Inc., 33 E Minor St, Emmaus, PA 18098; info@rodale.com; http://www.rodaleinc.com. Illus., index, adv. Microform: PQC. *Indexed:* A22, BRI, C37, MASUSE, P02, SD. *Aud.:* Ga, Ac.

Serious and recreational runners will enjoy *Runner's World.* Columns and departments include rave runs (great places to run), letters, nutrition, gear, motivational techniques, injury prevention, training advice, product reviews, vacation tips, and racing reports. Issues may be devoted to special topics such as running a marathon or weight-loss. The magazine's web site contains selected articles, links to relevant sites, and an offer for free online newsletters. Suitable for academic and public libraries. URL: www.runnersworld.com

5035. *Ski.* Incorporates: *Ski Life.* [ISSN: 0037-6159] 1936. 7x/yr. USD 10. Ed(s): Kendall Hamilton, Kimberly Beekman. Bonnier Corp., 5720 Flatiron Pky, Boulder, CO 80301; http://www.bonniercorp.com. Illus., adv. Microform: PQC. *Indexed:* A22, BRI, C37, MASUSE, P02, SD. *Aud.:* Ga, Ac.

With its beautiful photography, travel, equipment, and resort information, *Ski* will attract almost all recreational skiers. The 100+-page issues regularly include instruction, tips for injury prevention, training, interviews, and lifestyle articles. Because skiing is seasonal, articles on the more general aspects of outdoor life are included in the off-season. Since 1936, this magazine has been published seven times a year. The magazine's web site contains selected articles, a buyer's guide, snow reports, a calendar of events, a discussion forum, and more. Suitable for public libraries. URL: www.skinet.com/

5036. *Ski Trax: North America's nordic ski magazine.* m. CAD 13 domestic; USD 14 United States; CAD 17 elsewhere. Ski Trax, 260 Spadina Ave, Ste 200, Toronto, ON M5T 2E4 , Canada. Illus. *Aud.:* Ga.

Enthusiasts of Nordic skiing will welcome *Ski Trax,* the official publication of the Ski and Snowboard Association (USSA), the national governing body of Olympic skiing and snowboarding. Covering all forms of Nordic events (skiing, snowshoeing, snowboarding, biathlons, and the like), this Canadian magazine contains beautiful photographs, articles on places to stay, ski and snowshoe equipment and product reviews, competition (Olympic, national, and international), profiles of coaches and athletes, an annual directory of the best in cross-country skiing and snowshoeing, and a buyer's guide. It is published four times during the ski season. Public libraries in ski areas should consider adding this magazine to their collection.

5037. *Soccer America.* Supersedes (in 1972): *Soccer West.* [ISSN: 0163-4070] 1971. m. Free to members. Ed(s): Paul Kennedy. Soccer America Communications LLC, 1140 Broadway, 4th Fl, New York, NY 10001. Illus., adv. Microform: PQC. *Indexed:* A22. *Bk. rev.:* 1, 800 words. *Aud.:* Ga.

Soccer, the number one sport in the world, is growing in popularity in the United States. For about 40 years, this monthly has published news, statistics, scores, reports, and analysis of U.S. and international soccer, including youth, the MLS, and collegiate teams. Players are highlighted in informative articles. A monthly "Tournament Calendar" contains a comprehensive listing of soccer tournaments in the U.S. and abroad. Editorial columns provide insights into the world of soccer. The publication's web site provides access to selected articles, soccer news, and links of interest to the soccer fan. Recommended for public, high school, and academic libraries. URL: www.socceramerica.com

5038. Soccer and Society. [ISSN: 1466-0970] 2000. bi-m. GBP 458 (print & online eds.). Ed(s): Boria Majumdar. Routledge, 4 Park Sq, Milton Park, Abingdon, OX14 4RN, United Kingdom; subscriptions@tandf.co.uk; http://www.tandfonline.com. Index, adv. Sample. Refereed. Reprint: PSC. *Indexed:* A01, A22, C45, E01, RRTA, SD. *Aud.:* Ac.

This international, peer-reviewed journal examines the world's most popular game (called *football* overseas) from an anthropological, cultural, economic, historical, political, and sociological perspective. Issues are theme-based. A recent issue examined the commercialization of football throughout Europe. Past issues have highlighted football in Africa, U.K. football culture, the social and political history of the Everton & Liverpool football clubs (1878–1914), and models of football governance and management. Academic libraries might want to consider this publication for inclusion in their collections.

Sports 'n Spokes. See Disabilities section.

5039. Swimming World Magazine. Formed by the merger of (1965-2005): *Swimming World and Junior Swimmer;* Which was formerly (1961-1965): *Junior Swimmer - Swimming World;* (1960-1961): *Swimming World;* (199?-2005): *Swim Magazine;* Which was formerly (1984-199?): *Swim;* (1997-2005): *Swimming Technique;* Which was formerly (1996-1997): *Technique;* (1964-1996): *Swimming Technique.* 2005. m. USD 29.95. Ed(s): Jason Marsteller. Sports Publications, Inc., PO Box 20337, Sedona, AZ 86341; editorial@swiminfo.com. Illus., adv. Vol. ends: Dec. *Indexed:* A22, MASUSE, SD. *Aud.:* Hs, Ga, Ac.

This monthly merged with *SWIM Magazine, Swimming Technique,* and *Junior Swimmer* in 2005. It publishes news, swim meet results, training advice, technique tips, swimmer bios, and the like. The magazine contains lots of photos and illustrations. A recent issue included an Olympic preview, the top 12 World Masters of 2011, an article on peer coaching, one on poolside safety, and an interview with a swim coach. Since it contains information for all levels of swimmers, this magazine will be of interest to beginning, recreational, and competitive swimmers, as well as parents and coaches. Suitable for high school, public, and academic libraries.

5040. Tennis. [ISSN: 0040-3423] 1965. 10x/yr. USD 15 domestic; USD 35 Canada; USD 50 elsewhere. Ed(s): James Martin, Abigail Lorge. Miller Publishing Group, Miller Sports Group LLC., 79 Madison Ave, 8th Fl, New York, NY 10016. Illus., index, adv. Microform: PQC. *Indexed:* A22, BRI, C37, MASUSE, P02, SD. *Aud.:* Hs, Ga, Ac.

For over 40 years, *Tennis* has delighted the novice and advanced tennis enthusiast. It is filled with excellent photographs. Tennis instruction is supplemented with profiles of players, coverage of major tournaments, equipment and gear reviews, and information on nutrition, health, and fitness for the tennis player. It is the most popular magazine in the sport. Ten issues are published annually. The 100-page issues are devoted to content rather than to advertising, which is unusual among the more popular single-sport magazines. Appropriate for school, public, and academic libraries. URL: www.tennis.com/

5041. Track & Field News: the bible of the sports. [ISSN: 0041-0284] 1948. m. USD 43.95 domestic; USD 55 Canada; USD 69 elsewhere. Ed(s): Sieg Lindstrom, E Garry Hill. Track & Field News, 2570 El Camino Real, Ste 220, Mountain View, CA 94040; business@trackandfieldnews.com; http://www.trackandfieldnews.com. Illus., adv. Microform: PQC. *Indexed:* A22, SD. *Aud.:* Hs, Ga, Ac.

Calling itself the "Bible of the sport since 1948," *Track & Field News* provides detailed information on the sport in high school, college, and professional competition. International coverage includes the European circuit, the Olympics, and world championships. Feature articles are brief and supplemented by schedules of meets, lists of records, editorials, statistics,

letters, and brief biographical notes. It is published 12 times a year and includes the "Annual Edition," which wraps up the whole year with world rankings and Top 40 lists. This magazine is a good choice for the collections of large public libraries and high schools and academic institutions with track and field programs. URL: www.trackandfieldnews.com/

5042. U S A Hockey Magazine. Former titles (until 200?): *American Hockey Magazine;* (until 198?): *American Hockey and Arena; United States Hockey and Arena Biz; Hockey and Arena Biz; U S Hockey Biz.* [ISSN: 1551-6741] 1973. 10x/yr. Free to members. Ed(s): Harry Thompson. U S A Hockey, 1775 Bob Johnson Dr, Colorado Springs, CO 80906; usah@usahockey.org; http://www.usahockey.com. Illus., adv. Circ: 410594 Paid and controlled. *Aud.:* Hs, Ga, Ac.

As the official publication of USA Hockey and USA Hockey Inline, *USA Hockey* covers all aspects of the sport, with stories of interest to fans, players, and coaches alike. Recent issues contained articles on hockey in the U.S., how the Air Force Academy Hockey Team uses technology, and the North American Hockey League. Regular departments feature biographies of new or famous players, tips from the pros, and equipment reviews. Recently the magazine created the USA Hockey Magazine Podcast, which focuses on various topics covered in the print magazine. Often thought of as a Canadian sport, hockey is quickly finding fans in the U.S. Suitable for public libraries.

5043. U S A Today Sports Weekly. Formerly (until 2002): *U S A Today Baseball Weekly.* [ISSN: 1541-5228] 1991. w. USD 44.95; USD 2 newsstand/cover. Ed(s): Monte Lorell. U S A Today, 7950 Jones Branch Dr, McLean, VA 22108; webads@usatoday.com; http://www.usatoday.com. Illus., adv. Circ: 170795. *Indexed:* A22. *Aud.:* Ga.

Although the title sounds as if this were a general sports magazine, it covers baseball and football. Issues include fantasy baseball and football reports; award-winning statistics; analysis; tips and strategies; feature stories of baseball and professional football; and comprehensive major team notes. For the baseball enthusiast, there is the annual All Star preview issue, while football enthusiasts will enjoy the annual NFL preview issue. College teams are included in the Top 25 college baseball rankings and special college baseball reports. This would be a popular addition to public libraries.

5044. VolleyballUSA. Former titles (until 1992): *Inside U S A Volleyball; Volleyball U S A.* 1972. q. USD 10 domestic; USD 24 foreign. U S A Volleyball, 715 S Circle Dr, Colorado Springs, CO 80910; http://www.usavolleyball.org. Illus., adv. *Bk. rev.:* 2, 250 words. *Aud.:* Hs, Ga.

As the official publication of United States Volleyball Association, *Volleyball USA* provides current information on all types of volleyball in the United States, including indoor, park, and beach volleyball, and national, junior, collegiate, and disabled teams. In addition to association activities, this quarterly contains tournament and competition news, as well as articles about players, coaches and coaching, nutrition, and weight training. It also has camp guides. This glossy magazine will appeal to readers in public and high school libraries where volleyball is popular.

5045. The Water Skier: having fun today - building champions for tomorrow. [ISSN: 0049-7002] 1951. 7x/yr. Free to members; Non-members, USD 35. Ed(s): Scott Atkinson. U S A Water Ski, 1251 Holy Cow Rd, Polk City, FL 33868; memberservices@usawaterski.org; http://usawaterski.org. Illus., index, adv. *Aud.:* Ga, Ac.

Since 1952, *The Water Skier,* the official publication of USA Water Ski, has published articles of interest to the athletes and fans of all types of competitive water skiing (including traditional, show, wakeboard, collegiate, kneeboard, barefoot, hydrofoil, racing, and disabled). Each issue is filled with photographs, instructional articles, tournament reports, profiles of teams and athletes, water skiing safety, equipment reviews, and listings of ski camps and schools. An annual issue contains a comprehensive listing of tournaments throughout the nation, including entry-forms and in-depth information on each event. The magazine is published seven times a year. A link to the magazine and selected articles is available from the association's web site. Recommended for public and academic libraries. URL: www.usawaterski.org

5046. *Women's Running.* Former titles (until 2009): *Her Sports + Fitness;* (until 2006): *Her Sports.* [ISSN: 2165-7106] 2004. 10x/yr. USD 19.95 domestic; USD 29.95 Canada; USD 59.95 elsewhere. Ed(s): Jessica Sebor. Wet Dog Media, Inc., 1499 Beach Dr SE, Ste B, St. Petersburg, FL 33701; http://www.wetdogadvertising.com/. Adv. Circ: 4000. *Aud.:* Hs, Ga, Ac.

This glossy bimonthly magazine targets active, athletic women ages 25 to 49. As the only running magazine specifically for women, it covers all aspects of running from beauty tips to nutrition to training. Several columns are written by experts, including physicians, nutritionists, and coaches. Contributors may want to consider submitting articles for a profile section that highlights "a female runner who has overcome a major obstacle or accomplished something incredible through running." A recent issue featured a woman who lost over 100 pounds and took up running. Women sports and fitness enthusiasts will appreciate reading this magazine at their public libraries. URL: www.womensrunning.com/

5047. *Wrestling U S A (Missoula).* Formerly (until 1980): *Scholastic Wrestling News.* [ISSN: 0199-6258] 1964. m. USD 35. Ed(s): Lanny Bryant, Cody Bryant. Wrestling U.S.A. Magazine, c/o Cody Bryant, 109 Apple House Ln, Missoula, MT 59802. Illus. Sample. *Indexed:* SD. *Aud.:* Hs, Ac.

Wrestling USA publishes articles about amateur wrestling at the youth, high school, and college level. Regular features include news, training, injury prevention, sports medicine, nutrition, coaching tips, events and tournaments, and high school and collegiate teams. The audience for this magazine is the wrestler, not the coach, fan, or parent. It is published 12 times a year: twice a month during October, March, and May; once a month during September, November, December, January, February, and April. The journal's web site provides access to a cover gallery and article previews from 1965 to the present. Subscribers have the option of print only, print plus online, or online only. Appropriate for high school and academic libraries with wrestling programs. URL: www.wrestlingusa.com/

■ STATISTICS

Daniel S. Dotson, Mathematical Sciences Librarian and Science Education Specialist, 175 West 18th Ave., The Ohio State University, Columbus, OH 43210; 614-688-0053; dotson.77@osu.edu

Introduction

Statistics seems to be widely used in nearly every field to seek answers, test for relationships, predict outcomes, or simply have a better understanding of what is going on. Most colleges and universities (and even some high schools) have classes devoted to statistics. Some have an entirely separate department devoted to the study of statistics. You might even find programs developed for crossovers between statistics and other areas, such as biostatistics.

It seems as if statistics is used within nearly every discipline and on nearly any topic imaginable. Medical researches examine various factors to determine the likelihood of developing a certain type of cancer. Statistics can be used to determine ways to deal with traffic near a large city. Public schools make wide use of statistics to examine their students and their performance. The use (and sometimes abuse) of statistics in the realm of politics is in the news nearly every day.

This section includes 40 titles, many of which are of use for libraries that serve a college or university with a statistics program or programs that rely heavily on the use of statistics in their research.

In addition to titles that focus purely on statistics and probability within their own subject area, several titles focus on their application in specific science, social science, or interdisciplinary subject areas.

A few titles can trace their origins back as far as the mid-1800s, showing the longevity of the study of statistics. Most of these titles, however, began in the mid- to late 1900s, and a few premiered in the current century. Many have content back to their first volume via JSTOR, Project Euclid, or their publisher's site.

Multiple societies are represented here, including the American Statistical Association, the Royal Statistical Society, the Institute for Mathematical Statistics, the Statistical Society of Australia, the New Zealand Statistical Association, the Statistical Science Association of Canada, and the Statistical Society of Canada.

In addition to the basic abstracts and indexes, several titles may be included in appropriate subject databases for specific science and social science disciplines. Citation indexes *Web of Science* and *Scopus* also cover many of these titles.

Those wishing to view free content are encouraged to check out arXiv.org for preprints/eprints and to look for open-access journals at the *Directory of Open Access Journals.* Some titles in this list provide select open-access content. Several open-access peer-reviewed journals (such as *Journal of Statistical Software, Bayesian Analysis, Electronic Journal of Statistics,* and *Electronic Journal of Probability*) are excellent sources of information.

Basic Periodicals

Ga: *Chance* (New York, 1988), *Statistical Science: a Review Journal;* Ac: *American Statistical Association. Journal (JASA); The American Statistician; Annals of Applied Probability; Annals of Applied Statistics; Annals of Probability; Annals of Statistics; Canadian Journal of Statistics: La Revue Canadienne de Statistique; International Statistical Review; Royal Statistical Society. Journal. Series A: Statistics in Society.*

Basic Abstracts and Indexes

Current Index to Statistics, MathSciNet, Zentralblatt MATH.

5048. *Advances in Applied Probability.* [ISSN: 0001-8678] 1969. q. GBP 200 (print & online eds.) Individuals, GBP 67 (print & online eds.). Ed(s): S Asmussen, L J Nash. Applied Probability Trust, School of Mathematics and Statistics, The University of Sheffield, Sheffield, S3 7RH, United Kingdom; apt@sheffield.ac.uk; http://www.appliedprobability.org. Illus. Refereed. *Indexed:* A22, ABIn, B01, CCMJ, EngInd, MSN, MathR. *Aud.:* Ac, Sa.

Advances in Applied Probability publishes reviews and expository papers on topics in applied probability and related topics of interest. A special section on stochastic geometry and statistical applications are also included. Articles are typically in the 10- to 25-page range, with issues usually around 300 pages. Recent topics include Brownian motions, diffusion processes, time ruin probabilities, asymptotics of Markov kernels, financial series, and a probability model of colon cancer. The last volume of the year contains an index section. This title is hosted at Project Euclid, and it is in JSTOR with a three-year moving wall. Recommended for libraries that serve colleges or universities with a statistics program.

5049. *American Statistical Association. Journal.* Former titles (until 1922): *American Statistical Association. Quarterly Publications;* (until 1912): *American Statistical Association. Publications.* [ISSN: 0162-1459] 1888. q. GBP 439 (print & online eds.). American Statistical Association, 732 N Washington St, Alexandria, VA 22314; asainfo@amstat.org; http://www.amstat.org. Illus., index, adv. Refereed. Circ: 12000. Vol. ends: Dec. Microform: PMC; PQC. Reprint: PSC. *Indexed:* A22, ABIn, B01, B02, BRI, C45, CCMJ, CompR, EconLit, IBSS, IndVet, JEL, MSN, MathR, P02, RRTA. *Bk. rev.:* 10-20, 500-1,000 words. *Aud.:* Ac, Sa.

Journal of the American Statistical Association dates back to 1888 and has published over 500 issues. Articles are typically in the 10- to 25-page range, with issues usually around 400 pages. Issues are divided into sections. "Applications and Case Studies" includes such topics as sea surface temperature modeling, forecasting of presidential elections, metabolites in complex biological mixtures, and rain connectivity. "Theory and Methods" includes such topics as inferential models, analysis of large geostatistical data, a non-stationary time series, and longitudinal observations. Sections for review articles and book reviews are also included. This title is in JSTOR with a five-year moving wall. Recommended for libraries that serve colleges or universities with a statistics program.

5050. The American Statistician. Formerly (until 1947): *American Statistical Association. Bulletin.* [ISSN: 0003-1305] 1947. q. GBP 134 (print & online eds.). Ed(s): John Stufken. American Statistical Association, 732 N Washington St, Alexandria, VA 22314; asainfo@amstat.org; http://www.amstat.org. Illus., adv. Circ: 11500. Vol. ends: Nov. Microform: MIM; PMC; PQC. Reprint: PSC. *Indexed:* A01, A22, ABIn, B01, BRI, C45, CCMJ, JEL, MSN, MathR, P02. *Bk. rev.:* 4-5, 800-1,200 words. *Aud.:* Ac, Sa.

Dating back to 1947, *The American Statistician* is divided into these sections: "Statistical Practice," "General," "Teacher's Corner," "Short Technical Note," "Statistical Computing and Graphics," "Letters to the Editor," and sections dedicated to reviews of books, teaching materials, and software. Most articles tend to be under ten pages, with most issues totaling under 100. The year's final issue contains the volume index. Older issues are in JSTOR with a five-year moving wall. Recent topics have a comparison of Bayesian inference to Rodney Dangerfield, apportioning the U.S. House of Representatives, legal consulting, ten-pin bowling, and analogies for explaining statistical concepts/. Recommended for libraries that serve colleges or universities with a statistics program. Teachers of statistics may find this title of especial use.

5051. Annals of Applied Probability. [ISSN: 1050-5164] 1991. bi-m. USD 435 (print & online eds.). Ed(s): Michael Phelan, Timo Seppalainen. Institute of Mathematical Statistics, PO Box 22718, Beachwood, OH 44122; ims@imstat.org; http://www.imstat.org. Illus., index. Refereed. Vol. ends: Dec. *Indexed:* A22, B01, CCMJ, MSN, MathR. *Aud.:* Ac, Sa.

Annals of Applied Probability publishes applied probability papers, with a special focus on originality and importance. Content is hosted at Project Euclid, with content at JSTOR with a three-year moving wall. Issues are typically around 400 pages, with articles usually in the 20- to 40-page range. Recent topics include many-server queues, exponentially growing cancer cell populations, stochastic reaction networks, multidimensional stochastic integrals, three-dimensional Brownian motion, and the supermarket model. Recommended for libraries that serve colleges or universities with a statistics program.

5052. The Annals of Applied Statistics. [ISSN: 1932-6157] 2007. q. USD 435 (print & online eds.). Ed(s): Bradley Efron. Institute of Mathematical Statistics, PO Box 22718, Beachwood, OH 44122; ims@imstat.org; http://www.imstat.org. Illus. Refereed. *Indexed:* CCMJ, MSN, MathR. *Aud.:* Ac, Sa.

The Annals of Applied Statistics publishes papers on a wide range of applied statistics topics. Content is hosted at Project Euclid, with content in JSTOR with a three-year moving wall. Issues run around 400 pages, with articles typically in the 15- to 40-page range. Recent topics include late preterm birth outcomes, computer code performance tuning, extreme precipitation, traffic flow prediction, protein gels, and cell memory. Recommended for libraries that serve colleges or universities with a statistics program. Some articles may be of interest to those studying statistics within other subject disciplines.

5053. Annals of Probability. Supersedes in part (in 1973): *Annals of Mathematical Statistics.* [ISSN: 0091-1798] 1930. bi-m. USD 435 (print & online eds.); Free to members. Ed(s): Michael Phelan, Ofer Zeitouni. Institute of Mathematical Statistics, PO Box 22718, Beachwood, OH 44122; ims@imstat.org; http://www.imstat.org. Illus. Refereed. *Indexed:* A22, ABIn, CCMJ, MSN, MathR. *Aud.:* Ac, Sa.

Annals of Probability focuses on topics in probability, including applications to various areas of the sciences, with an emphasis on importance, interest, and originality. Content is hosted at Project Euclid and has a three-year moving wall at JSTOR. Articles are typically in the 20- to 50-page range, with issues typically 400–700 pages in length. Recent topics include the Marcus-Lushnikov process, Sinai's walk, supremum of Levy processes, spin glass models, branching Brownian motion, and Stein identities. Recommended for libraries that serve colleges or universities with a statistics program.

5054. Annals of Statistics. Supersedes in part (in 1973): *Annals of Mathematical Statistics.* [ISSN: 0090-5364] 1930. bi-m. USD 450 (print & online eds.); Free to members. Ed(s): Michael Phelan, Runze Li. Institute of Mathematical Statistics, PO Box 22718, Beachwood, OH 44122; ims@imstat.org; http://www.imstat.org. Illus. Refereed. *Indexed:* A22, ABIn, CCMJ, MSN, MathR. *Aud.:* Ac, Sa.

Annals of Statistics publishes high-quality papers on various topics in statistics, with importance and originality emphasized. Hosted at Project Euclid, it also has a three-year moving wall at JSTOR. Issues are typically 300–700 pages, with articles in the 20- to 50-page range. Recent topics include sparse directed acyclic graphs, Ornstein-Uhlenbeck tree models, genomic motif discovery, definition of a confounder, parametric estimation, and quaternary code designs. Recommended for libraries that serve colleges or universities with a statistics program.

5055. Australian & New Zealand Journal of Statistics. Formed by the merger of (1966-1998): *New Zealand Statistician;* (1959-1998): *Australian Journal of Statistics;* Which was formerly (until 1959): *Statistical Society of New South Wales. Bulletin.* [ISSN: 1369-1473] 1998. q. GBP 215. Ed(s): Stephen Haslett. Wiley-Blackwell Publishing Asia, 155 Cremorne St, Richmond, VIC 3121, Australia; melbourne@wiley.com; http://www.wiley.com/. Illus., index, adv. Sample. Refereed. Vol. ends: Dec. Reprint: PSC. *Indexed:* A01, A22, CCMJ, E01, MSN, MathR. *Bk. rev.:* 3-6, 300-1,000 words. *Aud.:* Ac, Sa.

The Australian & New Zealand Journal of Statistics is divided into two main sections. One covers topics in applications (with such recent topics as parasite growth, Old Faithful, and farm survey economic data). The other covers theory and methods (with such recent topics as bivariate orthonormal polynomials, variable selection in linear mixed models, and correspondence analysis). Reviews and historical or general-interest papers are also accepted. Issues end with book reviews and a list of forthcoming papers. Issues typically run around 80–150 pages, with articles in the 10- to 20-page range. Recommended for libraries that serve colleges or universities with a statistics program.

5056. Bernoulli: a journal of mathematical statistics and probability. [ISSN: 1350-7265] 1995. q. USD 480 (print & online eds.). Ed(s): Richard A Davis. International Statistical Institute, PO Box 24070, The Hague, 2490 AB, Netherlands; isi@cbs.nl; http://www.cbs.nl/. Illus. Refereed. Circ: 1500 Paid. *Indexed:* A22, CCMJ, E01, MSN, MathR. *Aud.:* Ac, Sa.

Published by the Bernoulli Society in conjunction with the Institute of Mathematical Statistics, *Bernoulli* publishes papers on theoretical and applied topics in probability and statistics. Content is hosted at Project Euclid, with older content at JSTOR with a five-year moving wall. Issues are typically in the 300- to 500-page range, with articles usually running 10–30 pages. Recent topics include pair-copula constructions, high-dimensional sparse models, Dirichlet measures, discretely observed scalar diffusions, market share dynamics, and species variety. Recommended for libraries that serve colleges or universities with a statistics program.

5057. Biometrical Journal: journal of mathematical methods in biosciences. Formerly (until 1977): *Biometrische Zeitschrift.* [ISSN: 0323-3847] 1959. bi-m. GBP 1311. Ed(s): Leonhard Held, Tim Friede. Wiley - V C H Verlag GmbH & Co. KGaA, Postfach 101161, Weinheim, 69451, Germany; info@wiley-vch.de; http://www.vchgroup.de. Illus., adv. Sample. Refereed. Reprint: PSC. *Indexed:* A22, CCMJ, MSN, MathR. *Bk. rev.:* Occasional, 400-800 words. *Aud.:* Ac, Sa.

Biometrical Journal publishes statistical topics relevant to the life sciences. Case studies, review articles, and letters to the editors are welcome, but purely theoretical statistical papers are not accepted. Issues are typically 100–200 pages, with articles usually in the 10- to 25-page range. Recent topics include estimated biodiversity indices, clinical trial designs, phage display data, outbreak detection, infections disease surveillance data, and multi-environment trials. Recommended for libraries that serve colleges and universities with statistics or medical programs. Biostatistics programs would find this journal highly useful.

5058. Biometrics. Formerly (until 1947): *Biometrics Bulletin.* [ISSN: 0006-341X] 1945. q. GBP 311. Ed(s): Russell B Millar, Geert Verbeke. Wiley-Blackwell Publishing Ltd., The Atrium, Southern Gate, Chichester, PO19 8SQ, United Kingdom; customer@wiley.com; http://www.wiley.com/. Illus., index, adv. Sample. Refereed. Vol. ends: Dec. Microform: BHP; PMC; PQC. Reprint: PSC. *Indexed:* A01, A22, AbAn, Agr, ApMecR, C45, CCMJ, E01, FS&TA, IndVet, MSN, MathR, P02, SD. *Bk. rev.:* 10-20, 200-1,000 words. *Aud.:* Ac, Sa.

Biometrics publishes papers in statistical or mathematical topics in the biosciences. The journal contains four sections: "Biometric Methodology," "Biometric Practice," "Reader Reaction," and "Letters to the Editors." Older issues are in JSTOR with a five-year moving wall. Issues are typically in the 300- to 400-page range, with articles generally in the 5- to 20-page range. Recent topics include population-size trajectories, monitoring medical outcomes, prevalence projects of chronic diseases, neuroimaging, hazards survival, and genomic data. Recommended for libraries that serve colleges or universities with a statistics program. Medical and biology programs may also find it useful, while biostatistics programs will find it highly useful.

5059. Biometrika. [ISSN: 0006-3444] 1901. q. EUR 165. Ed(s): A C Davison. Oxford University Press, Great Clarendon St, Oxford, OX2 6DP, United Kingdom; enquiry@oup.co.uk; http:// www.oxfordjournals.org/. Illus., adv. Sample. Refereed. Microform: PMC; PQC. Reprint: PSC. *Indexed:* A01, A22, ABIn, C45, CCMJ, E01, IndVet, MSN, MathR. *Aud.:* Ac, Sa.

Biometrika publishes papers on original theoretical contributions of value in applications, with papers on bordering fields occasionally accepted. Older issues are in JSTOR with a five-year moving wall. Issues typically range 200–300 pages, with articles in the 10- to 20-page range. Recent topics include gene-environment interactions, weighting in survey analysis, geostatistics, genetical genomics, competing risks, and data visualization. Recommended for libraries that serve colleges or universities with a statistics program. Medical and biology programs will also find it useful, while biostatistics programs will find it highly useful.

5060. Biostatistics. [ISSN: 1465-4644] 2000. q. EUR 674. Ed(s): Geert Molenberghs, Anastasios Tsiatis. Oxford University Press, Great Clarendon St, Oxford, OX2 6DP, United Kingdom; enquiry@oup.co.uk; http://www.oxfordjournals.org/. Illus., adv. Sample. Refereed. Reprint: PSC. *Indexed:* A01, A22, C45, E01, IndVet. *Aud.:* Ac, Sa.

Biostatistics publishes papers on statistical topics related to human health and disease. The year's last issue includes an index. Issues are typically in the 150- to 250-page range, with articles usually ranging 10–20 pages. Select articles may be followed by commentaries or discussion. Recent topics include EEG data, microbiome data, cancer staging, parametric cure models, biomarker-based prognostic models, and HIV vaccine efficacy trials. Recommended for libraries that serve colleges or universities with a statistics program. Medical and biology programs will find it useful, while biostatistics programs will find it highly useful.

5061. Canadian Journal of Statistics. [ISSN: 0319-5724] 1973. q. GBP 190. Ed(s): Jiahua Chen. Wiley-Blackwell Publishing, Inc., 111 River St, Hoboken, NJ 07030; info@wiley.com; http://onlinelibrary.wiley.com/. Illus., index, adv. Refereed. Vol. ends: Dec. Reprint: PSC. *Indexed:* A01, A22, ABIn, C&ISA, CCMJ, CerAb, IBSS, MSN, MathR. *Aud.:* Ac, Sa.

Canadian Journal of Statistics publishes papers that are broad in scope and of interest to many readers. Older issues are in JSTOR with a three-year moving wall. Issues are typically in the 150- to 250-page range, with articles usually 10–40 pages. Recent topics include multivariate panel count data, case-control studies, the Dantzig selector, change-point detection in copulas, estimating optimal dynamic treatment rules, and sequential design for computer experiments. Recommended for libraries that serve colleges or universities with a statistics program.

5062. Chance (New York, 1988). [ISSN: 0933-2480] 1987. q. GBP 74. Ed(s): Sam Behseta. Taylor & Francis Inc., 325 Chestnut St, Ste 800, Philadelphia, PA 19106; customerservice@taylorandfrancis.com; http:// www.taylorandfrancis.com. Illus., index, adv. Refereed. Vol. ends: No. 4. Microform: PQC. Reprint: PSC. *Indexed:* A01, A22, ABIn, BRI, CCMJ, E01, MSN, MathR. *Aud.:* Hs, Ga.

Chance is a magazine meant for anyone interested in statistics, and it covers statistics topics in all science and social sciences areas. It is meant to entertain and inform. Issues are typically under 75 pages, with articles usually under ten (and often under five) pages. Recent topics include how to beat kindergarteners

at Battleship, course evaluations, prediction markets, vehicle safety standards, child mortality in Sierra Leone, and biostatistics education. This title is good for most libraries, including college, university, and high school libraries that serve schools that teach statistics.

5063. Computational Statistics. Formerly (until 1992): *C S Q - Computational Statistics Quarterly.* [ISSN: 0943-4062] 1982. q. EUR 783 (print & online eds.). Ed(s): Friedrich Leisch, J Symanzik. Physica-Verlag GmbH und Co., Postfach 105280, Heidelberg, 69042, Germany; physica@springer.de. Illus. Refereed. Vol. ends: No. 4. Microform: PQC. Reprint: PSC. *Indexed:* A22, ABIn, BRI, CCMJ, E01, MSN, MathR. *Bk. rev.:* 1, 700-800 words. *Aud.:* Ac, Sa.

Computational Statistics publishes papers on applied and methodological research topics in computational statistics. Issues have grown in size over the past few years, with some nearly 500 pages in length. Articles are usually in the 15- to 30-page range. Recent topics include test of misspecification, structured survival models, an Arabic statistics e-learning system, market basket analysis, Boolean network attractors, and identifying important genes in observational studies. Recommended for libraries that serve colleges or universities with a statistics program. Certain computer science programs may also find it of interest.

5064. Computational Statistics & Data Analysis. Incorporates (1975-1991): *Statistical Software Newsletter.* [ISSN: 0167-9473] 1983. 12x/yr. EUR 2778. Ed(s): S P Azen. Elsevier BV, Radarweg 29, PO Box 211, Amsterdam, 1000 AE, Netherlands; JournalsCustomerServiceEMEA@elsevier.com; http://www.elsevier.com. Illus., index, adv. Sample. Refereed. Vol. ends: No. 35 - No. 37. Microform: PQC. *Indexed:* A01, A22, CCMJ, CompR, EngInd, MSN, MathR. *Aud.:* Ac, Sa.

Computational Statistics & Data Analysis is the official journal of the International Association of Statistical Computing. The journal is divided into three sections: "Computational Statistics," "Statistical Methodology for Data Analysis," and "Special Applications." Issue page counts can vary widely, from under 200 to nearly 1,000. Articles are usually in the 5- to 20-page range. Recent topics include inferring sparse network structures, Bayesian computing with INLA, variograms inference, rare event estimation, robust analysis of complex data, and multidimensional data uniformity tests. Libraries that serve colleges and universities with statistics programs will find this title useful. Some computer science programs may also find the title of use.

5065. Econometrica. [ISSN: 0012-9682] 1933. bi-m. GBP 350 (print & online eds.). Ed(s): Geri Mattson, Daron Acemoglu. Wiley-Blackwell Publishing Ltd., The Atrium, Southern Gate, Chichester, PO19 8SQ, United Kingdom; customer@wiley.com; http://www.wiley.com/. Illus., index, adv. Sample. Refereed. Vol. ends: Nov. Microform: PMC; PQC. Reprint: PSC. *Indexed:* A22, ABIn, B01, B02, BAS, C45, CCMJ, E01, EconLit, IBSS, JEL, MSN, MathR, P02, RRTA, RiskAb. *Aud.:* Ac, Sa.

Econometrica publishes papers on all economics topics. The papers often have a statistical bent. In addition to articles, issues may contain announcements, reports, and a list of forthcoming papers. Older issues are in JSTOR with a two-year moving wall. Issues are generally in the 300- to 500-page range. Articles are usually in the 15- to 50-page range, with many articles on the higher end. Recent topics include endogenous peer-group formation, welfare reform, land–price dynamics, language barriers, demand fluctuations, and speculative overpricing in asset markets. This title is recommended for libraries that serve colleges and universities with a statistics program, and it would be of high value to those with business or economics programs that highly emphasize statistical methods.

5066. International Statistical Review. Incorporates (1980-2007): *Short Book Reviews;* Former titles (until 1972): *International Statistical Institute Review (Print);* (until 1933): *Institut International de Statistique. Office Permanent. Bulletin Mensuel.* [ISSN: 0306-7734] 1920. 3x/yr. GBP 255 (print & online eds.). Ed(s): Vijay Nair, Marc Hallin.

Wiley-Blackwell Publishing Ltd., 9600 Garsington Rd, Oxford, OX4 2DQ, United Kingdom; customerservices@blackwellpublishing.com; http://www.wiley.com/. Illus., index, adv. Sample. Refereed. Reprint: PSC. *Indexed:* A01, A22, C45, E01, MathR, PsycInfo. *Bk. rev.:* 10-30 per issue, 100-400 words. *Aud.:* Ac, Sa.

International Statistical Review is the flagship journal of the International Statistical Institute and publishes articles on general-interest topics in probability and statistics. Types of articles published include reviews, expository papers, tutorials, historical topics, interviews, and book reviews. Issues typically have over a dozen short book reviews. Older issues are in JSTOR with a five-year moving wall. Issues are usually in the 100- to 200-page range, with most scholarly articles under 20 pages. Recent topics include dimension reduction, the likelihood theory in finance, clinical trial data analysis, statistical disclosure risk, and statistical research at Bell Labs. This title fits libraries that serve colleges and universities with statistics programs, and would be of interest to those with science or social science programs that emphasize the use of statistics.

5067. *Journal of Computational and Graphical Statistics.* [ISSN: 1061-8600] 1992. q. GBP 230 (print & online eds.). Ed(s): Richard A Levine. American Statistical Association, 732 N Washington St, Alexandria, VA 22314; asainfo@amstat.org; http://www.amstat.org. Adv. Refereed. Circ: 1600. Reprint: PSC. *Indexed:* A01, A22, ABIn, B01, C45, CCMJ, CompLI, MSN, MathR. *Aud.:* Ac, Sa.

Journal of Computational and Graphical Statistics publishes articles on computational and graphical methods in statistics and data analysis. The journal recommends that articles be written for those with expertise in statistics, but not necessarily in computing. The final issue in the volume contains an index. Select content is free online, and some issues contain discussion articles followed by comments and a rejoinder. Papers from conferences also appear in some issues. Select articles may include supplemental information online, such as data sets or software code. Older issues are in JSTOR with a five-year moving wall. Issues typically range 200–300 pages, with articles usually in the 10- to 30-page range. Recent topics include capture-recapture estimation, latent Markov random fields and social networks, real-time streaming analysis, and biological networks. Recommended for libraries that serve colleges and universities with a statistics program.

5068. *Journal of Multivariate Analysis.* [ISSN: 0047-259X] 1971. 10x/yr. EUR 2447. Ed(s): J DeLeeuw. Academic Press, 3251 Riverport Ln, Maryland Heights, MO 63043; JournalCustomerService-usa@elsevier.com; http://www.elsevierdirect.com/brochures/academicpress/index.html. Adv. Sample. Refereed. *Indexed:* A01, A22, ABIn, C45, CCMJ, CompR, E01, MSN, MathR, PsycInfo. *Aud.:* Ac, Sa.

Journal of Multivariate Analysis publishes papers on topics in theoretical methods—and applications to new theoretical methods—in multivariate (and occasionally, univariate) analysis. Issues are generally in the 150- to 350-page range (sometimes going above that), with articles usually numbering 10–25 pages. Recent topics include value-at-risk multivariate extensions, simplified pair copula constructions, nested Archimedean copulas, correlation tests for high-dimensional data, intrinsic dimension identification, and model discrimination designs. Recommended for libraries that serve colleges and universities with a statistics program.

5069. *Journal of Statistical Planning and Inference.* [ISSN: 0378-3758] 1977. 12x/yr. EUR 4056. Ed(s): N Balakrishnan. Elsevier BV, North-Holland, Postbus 211, Amsterdam, 1000 AE, Netherlands; JournalsCustomerServiceEMEA@elsevier.com; http://www.elsevier.com. Illus. Refereed. Microform: PQC. *Indexed:* A01, A22, CCMJ, CompLI, MSN, MathR. *Aud.:* Ac, Sa.

Journal of Statistical Planning and Inference aims to cover how to collect (planning) and analyze (inference) data. It publishes both research and survey articles. Issue size can vary widely, from under 100 to over 600 pages. Articles are generally in the 10- to 20-page length. Recent topics include local quantile regression, measurement error models, sequential dose-finding, experimental epidemics, rare genetic mutations, and risk models. Recommended for libraries that serve colleges and universities with a statistics program.

5070. *Journal of Theoretical Probability.* [ISSN: 0894-9840] 1988. q. EUR 1057 (print & online eds.). Ed(s): James Allen Fill. Springer New York LLC, 233 Spring St, New York, NY 10013; service-ny@springer.com; http://www.springer.com/. Illus., adv. Sample. Refereed. Microform: PQC. Reprint: PSC. *Indexed:* A22, CCMJ, E01, MSN, MathR. *Aud.:* Ac, Sa.

Journal of Theoretical Probability covers topics in all areas of probability theory. Issues typically range 250–400 pages, with articles in the 10- to 30-page range. Recent topics include denumerable birth and death processes, semigroups of distributions, Markov chains with unbounded range, ordering functions of random vectors, non-homogeneous random walks, and super-coalescing Brownian motion. Recommended for libraries that serve colleges and universities with a statistics program.

5071. *Journal of Time Series Analysis.* [ISSN: 0143-9782] 1980. bi-m. GBP 1209. Ed(s): M Priestley. Wiley-Blackwell Publishing Ltd., The Atrium, Southern Gate, Chichester, PO19 8SQ, United Kingdom; customer@wiley.com; http://www.wiley.com/. Illus., adv. Sample. Refereed. Reprint: PSC. *Indexed:* A01, A22, ABIn, CCMJ, E01, IBSS, MSN, MathR, RiskAb. *Bk. rev.:* One per issue, 400-600 words. *Aud.:* Ac, Sa.

Journal of Time Series Analysis publishes papers on both fundamental theory and applications on topics in time series analysis. Short communications on theoretical developments and book reviews are sometimes included. Occasionally, issues are dedicated to a specific topic. Issues range from 100 to 250 pages, with articles usually in the 5- to 20-page range. Recent topics include financial time series data, testing serial dependence in count data, Nicholson blowfly experiments, microrheology, brain signals in a monkey during learning, and multidimensional hormonal systems. Recommended for libraries that serve colleges and universities with a statistics program.

5072. *Lifetime Data Analysis: an international journal devoted to the methods and applications of reliability and survival analysis.* [ISSN: 1380-7870] 1995. q. EUR 736 (print & online eds.). Ed(s): Mei-Ling Ting Lee. Springer New York LLC, 233 Spring St, New York, NY 10013; journals@springer-ny.com; http://www.springer.com. Illus., adv. Refereed. Reprint: PSC. *Indexed:* A22, ABIn, B01, C45, CCMJ, E01, MSN, MathR, RiskAb. *Aud.:* Ac, Sa.

Lifetime Data Analysis is dedicated to statistical methods and applications in lifetime data analysis. It covers a broad range of lifetime data topics in the sciences and social sciences. Issues are typically 100–150 pages, with articles usually in the 10- to 25-page range. Recent topics include hematopoietic cell transplant patients, myocardial infarction, applying competing-risks regression models, randomized clinical trials, multiple sclerosis, and survival estimation. Libraries that serve colleges and universities with statistics or medical programs will find this title of use. Biostatitics programs will find it highly useful.

5073. *Multivariate Behavioral Research.* [ISSN: 0027-3171] 1966. bi-m. GBP 610 (print & online eds.). Ed(s): Joseph Lee Rodgers. Psychology Press, 325 Chestnut St, Ste 800, Philadelphia, PA 19106; orders@taylorandfrancis.com; http://www.psypress.com. Illus., adv. Sample. Refereed. Microform: PQC. Reprint: PSC. *Indexed:* A01, A22, B01, E01, ERIC, PsycInfo. *Aud.:* Ac, Sa.

Multivariate Behavioral Research publishes substantive, methodological, and theoretical papers with a multivariate research angle in all areas of the social sciences. Pedagogical and historical topics are also welcome. Issues may be dedicated to a specific topic. Issues are typically in the 100- to 200-page range, with articles usually 20–35 pages. Recent topics include substance use craving, college athlete academic performance, nicotine dependence, couples' relationship quality and breakup, smoking cessation, and work and stress research. Recommended for libraries that serve colleges or universities with statistics programs, or programs that highly emphasize the use of advanced statistics in behavioral research.

5074. *Probability Theory and Related Fields.* Supersedes: *Zeitschrift fuer Wahrscheinlichkeitstheorie und Verwandte Gebiete.* [ISSN: 0178-8051] 1962. q. EUR 1501 (print & online eds.). Ed(s): A Dembo, G. Ben Arous. Springer, Tiergartenstr 17, Heidelberg, 69121, Germany. Illus., adv. Sample. Refereed. Microform: PQC. Reprint: PSC. *Indexed:* A01, A22, ABIn, B01, CCMJ, E01, MSN, MathR, P02. *Aud.:* Ac, Sa.

Probability Theory and Related Fields publishes in probability theory and its relations to analysis, geometry, and other areas of mathematics or other, applied fields. Survey papers on emerging areas of importance are also published. Combined double issues are typically in the 400- to 500-page range. Article length is typically 20–40 pages. Recent topics include mobile geometric graphs, spin glasses, partial mass problems, fractional Brownian motion, infinite-rate mutually-catalytic branching in infinitely many colonies, and excited Brownian motions. Recommended for libraries that serve colleges and universities with a statistics program.

5075. *Royal Statistical Society. Journal. Series A: Statistics in Society.*
Incorporates in part (1962-2004): *Royal Statistical Society. Journal. Series D: The Statistician;* Which was formerly (1950-1961): *Incorporated Statistician;* Former titles (until 1988): *Royal Statistical Society. Journal. Series A: General;* (until 1948): *Royal Statistical Society. Journal;* (until 1886): *Statistical Society. Journal;* (until 1838): *Statistical Society of London. Proceedings.* [ISSN: 0964-1998] 1834. q. USD 353 (print or online ed.). Ed(s): A Chevalier, S Day. Wiley-Blackwell Publishing Ltd., The Atrium, Southern Gate, Chichester, PO19 8SQ, United Kingdom; customer@wiley.com; http://www.wiley.com/. Illus., adv. Sample. Refereed. Microform: BHP. Reprint: PSC. *Indexed:* A22, ABIn, Agr, ApMecR, B01, C45, CCMJ, E01, EconLit, IBSS, IndVet, JEL, MLA-IB, MSN, MathR, RRTA. *Bk. rev.:* 5-15 per issue, 300-500 words. *Aud.:* Ac, Sa.

Journal of the Royal Statistical Society, Series A (Statistics in Society) publishes papers on statistical topics that are applicable to the real world. Papers should be clearly written, quantitative approaches to topics rather than technically detailed. This journal covers statistics as applied to a wide range of science and social science topics. Welcome are papers on popular or contentious statistical issues, reviews of topics, historical topics, professional issues, biographies, discussions of data collection methods, and ethical issues. Book reviews and obituaries may be found toward the end of an issue. This journal, along with the *Royal Statistical Society Journals Part B* and *Part C,* can trace its origins back to *Journal of the Statistical Society of London,* which began in 1838. Older issues, including its predecessor titles, are in JSTOR with a four-year moving wall. Issues typically range 200–300 pages, with articles generally 15–30 pages. Recent topics include probabilities of bankruptcy, the European carbon market, big charities, gender wage differentials, epidemics in semi-isolated communities, and depression in older age. Highly recommended to libraries that serve colleges and universities with a statistics program, or those with courses in the social sciences and sciences that heavily emphasize statistics.

5076. *Royal Statistical Society. Journal. Series B: Statistical Methodology.*
Former titles (until 1998): *Royal Statistical Society. Journal. Series B: Methodological;* (until 1948): *Royal Statistical Society. Journal. Supplement.* [ISSN: 1369-7412] 1934. 5x/yr. GBP 265. Ed(s): I Van Keilegom, G O Roberts. Wiley-Blackwell Publishing Ltd., The Atrium, Southern Gate, Chichester, PO19 8SQ, United Kingdom; customer@wiley.com; http://www.wiley.com/. Illus., index, adv. Sample. Refereed. Vol. ends: No. 4. Reprint: PSC. *Indexed:* A22, ABIn, Agr, ApMecR, B01, C45, CCMJ, E01, IBSS, MSN, MathR. *Aud.:* Ac, Sa.

Journal of the Royal Statistical Society, Series B (Statistical Methodology) publishes papers on statistical topics that are at the leading edge of methodological development and that are relevant to statistical practice. This journal, along with the *Royal Statistical Society Journals Part A* and *Part C,* can trace its origins back to *Journal of the Statistical Society of London,* which began in 1838. Older issues, including its predecessor titles, are in JSTOR with a four-year moving wall. Issues are generally in the 150- to 250-page range, although longer issues are sometimes published. Articles are typically 15–30 pages, with occasionally much lengthier ones. Some articles may be followed by comments. Recent topics include fast bivariate p-splines, infectious disease data, stability selection, sequential analysis of state space models, sparse segments in ultrahigh dimensional data analysis, and large-scale multiple testing. Highly recommended for libraries that serve colleges and universities with a statistics program.

5077. *Royal Statistical Society. Journal. Series C: Applied Statistics.*
Incorporates in part (in 2004): *Royal Statistical Society. Journal. Series D. The Statistician;* Which was formerly (1950-1961): *Incorporated Statistician.* [ISSN: 0035-9254] 1952. 5x/yr. GBP 265. Ed(s): R Chandler,

M S Ridout. Wiley-Blackwell Publishing Ltd., The Atrium, Southern Gate, Chichester, PO19 8SQ, United Kingdom; customer@wiley.com; http://www.wiley.com/. Illus., index, adv. Sample. Refereed. Vol. ends: No. 4. Reprint: PSC. *Indexed:* A22, ABIn, Agr, B01, BrArAb, C45, CCMJ, E01, IBSS, IndVet, MSN, MathR, RiskAb. *Aud.:* Ac, Sa.

Journal of the Royal Statistical Society, Series C (Applied Statistics) publishes papers that apply statistics to real-life problems in many areas of science and social science. This journal, along with the *Royal Statistical Society Journals Part B* and *Part C,* can trace its origins back to *Journal of the Statistical Society of London,* which began in 1838. Older issues, including its predecessor titles, are in JSTOR with a four-year moving wall. Issues are typically 150–250 pages, with articles generally in the 10- to 25-page range. Recent topics include socioeconomic stratification, newly licensed teenage drivers, exposure to multiple pollutants, forecasting road traffic flows, surgical complications, and radiation effects in spaceborne microelectronics. Recommended for libraries that serve colleges or universities with a statistics program, or those with science or social science programs that emphasize the use of statistics.

5078. *Scandinavian Journal of Statistics: theory and applications.* [ISSN: 0303-6898] 1974. q. GBP 189. Ed(s): Paavo Salminen, Juha Alho. Wiley-Blackwell Publishing Ltd., The Atrium, Southern Gate, Chichester, PO19 8SQ, United Kingdom; customer@wiley.com; http://www.wiley.com/. Illus., index, adv. Sample. Refereed. Vol. ends: Dec. Reprint: PSC. *Indexed:* A01, A22, ABIn, B01, CCMJ, E01, MSN, MathR, PsycInfo. *Aud.:* Ac, Sa.

Scandinavian Journal of Statistics: Theory and Applications publishes significant and innovative original contributions on applied and theoretical topics in statistical methodology. Older issues are in JSTOR with a five-year moving wall. Issues are typically in the 150- to 250-page range, with articles usually 10–25 pages. Recent topics include conditional graphical model collapsibility, exact inference for diffusions, skew-t distributions, multivariate skew-elliptical distribution, current status data, and variance stabilization. Recommended for libraries that serve colleges and universities with a statistics program.

5079. *Statistica Sinica.* [ISSN: 1017-0405] 1991. q. USD 255. Ed(s): P Hall, K-Y Liang. Academia Sinica, Institute of Statistical Science, 128, Sec 2 Yen-chiu-Yuan Rd, Taipei, 115, Taiwan, Republic of China; http://www.stat.sinica.edu.tw/. Illus. Refereed. *Indexed:* A22, CCMJ, MSN, MathR. *Aud.:* Ac, Sa.

Statistica Sinica focuses on articles that promote the principled use of statistics. Issues may be dedicated to a specific topic or may be dedicated to general topics or discussion. Issues are freely available after one year. Issues are typically 300–500 pages, with articles usually 10–30 pages. Recent topics include sliced orthogonal Latin hypercube designs, self-exciting point processes, double Pareto shrinkage, time series with dependent innovations, the Lasso, and self-weighted two-stage samples. Recommended for libraries that serve colleges and universities with a statistics program.

5080. *Statistical Methods in Medical Research.* [ISSN: 0962-2802] 1992. bi-m. USD 1070. Ed(s): Brian Everitt, Anders Skrondal. Sage Publications Ltd., 1 Oliver's Yard, 55 City Rd, London, EC1Y 1SP, United Kingdom; info@sagepub.co.uk; http://www.uk.sagepub.com. Illus. Sample. Refereed. Reprint: PSC. *Indexed:* A01, A22, ASSIA, C45, CCMJ, E01, ExcerpMed, IndVet, MSN, MathR. *Aud.:* Ac, Sa.

Statistical Methods in Medical Research publishes papers on topics in medical statistics and aims to inform medical professionals on the latest available statistical techniques in medicine. Issues are typically in the 60- to 150-page range, with articles usually 10–30 pages. Recent topics include meta-analysis, observational clinical data, patient records from disparate sources, coronary heart disease, Parkinson's disease, and melanoma data. While libraries that serve colleges and universities with a statistics program may find this title useful, biostatistics or medical programs will find this title even more useful.

5081. *Statistical Science.* [ISSN: 0883-4237] 1986. q. USD 247. Ed(s): Michael Phelan, Jon A. Wellner. Institute of Mathematical Statistics, PO Box 22718, Beachwood, OH 44122; ims@imstat.org; http://www.imstat.org. Illus., index, adv. Refereed. Vol. ends: Nov. *Indexed:* A22, CCMJ, MSN, MathR. *Aud.:* Ac, Sa.

Statistical Science: A Review Journal publishes papers on important statistics topics with a wide range of interest, with casual readers being the main target audience. The interview articles contained in most issues are popular among readers. Older issues are in JSTOR with a three-year moving wall. Issues are typically 100–200 pages, with articles usually in the 10- to 30-page range. Recent topics include small area estimation, fractional Brownian motion, species sampling models, linear mixed models, conversations (with such people as Persi Diaconis and David Findley), and sparse estimation. The last issue of the volume contains the yearly index. Recommended for libraries that serve colleges and universities with a statistics programs, or those with programs that emphasize statistical methods in science or social science research.

5082. Statistics: a journal of theoretical and applied statistics. Formerly (until 1985): *Series Statistics;* Which superseded in part (in 1977): *Mathematische Operationsforschung und Statistik.* [ISSN: 0233-1888] 1970. bi-m. GBP 1936 (print & online eds.). Ed(s): Olaf Bunke. Taylor & Francis, 4 Park Sq, Milton Park, Abingdon, OX14 4RN, United Kingdom; subscriptions@tandf.co.uk; http://www.tandfonline.com. Illus., adv. Sample. Refereed. Reprint: PSC. *Indexed:* A01, A22, CCMJ, E01, MSN, MathR. *Aud.:* Ac, Sa.

Statistics: A Journal of Theoretical and Applied Statistics publishes papers on interesting and novel contributions to theoretical and applied statistics. Occasionally, conference proceedings and related announcements are included. Issues are typically 100–200 pages, with most articles in the 5- to 20-page range. Recent topics include calibration of design weights, extended fatigue life distribution, modeling survival data, fundamental tessellation models, ageing patterns, and power-normal distribution. Recommended for libraries that serve colleges and universities with a statistics program.

5083. Statistics and Computing. [ISSN: 0960-3174] 1991. q. EUR 1087 (print & online eds.). Ed(s): Gilles Celeux. Springer New York LLC, 233 Spring St, New York, NY 10013; service-ny@springer.com; http://www.springer.com/. Illus., adv. Sample. Refereed. Reprint: PSC. *Indexed:* A22, BRI, CCMJ, E01, MSN, MathR. *Bk. rev.:* Occasional. *Aud.:* Ac, Sa.

Statistics and Computing covers topics related to the use of statistics in computer science and the use of computers in data analysis. Included are original research reports, authoritative topic reviews, paper discussions, and occasional book or software reviews. Special issues on a topic or relevant conference papers occasionally appear. Issues are usually 100–150 pages, with articles typically in the 10- to 20-page range. Recent topics include frailty models, horizontally partitioned data, semiparametric expectile regression, nonparametric assessment of model adequacy, models for interval censored data, and sampling for occurrence map construction. Recommended for libraries that serve colleges and universities with statistics programs. Some computer science programs may find it of use as well.

5084. Stochastic Processes and Their Applications. [ISSN: 0304-4149] 1973. 12x/yr. EUR 1409. Ed(s): M E Vares. Elsevier BV, North-Holland, Postbus 211, Amsterdam, 1000 AE, Netherlands; JournalsCustomerServiceEMEA@elsevier.com; http://www.elsevier.com. Illus., refereed. Vol. ends: No. 2. Microform: PQC. *Indexed:* A01, A22, C45, CCMJ, EngInd, MSN, MathR. *Aud.:* Ac, Sa.

Stochastic Processes and Their Applications publishes articles on theoretical or applied stochastic processes topics in mathematics, science, and engineering. Issues are in the 200- to 400-page range, with articles typically 10–30 pages. Recent topics include turbulence, Brownian motions, price impact, diffusion, chaos, and polymers. Recommended for libraries that serve colleges and universities with statistics programs.

5085. Technometrics: a journal of statistics for the physical, chemical and engineering sciences. [ISSN: 0040-1706] 1959. q. GBP 126 (print & online eds.). Ed(s): Hugh A Chipman. American Statistical Association, 732 N Washington St, Alexandria, VA 22314; asainfo@amstat.org; http://www.amstat.org. Illus., index. Refereed. Vol. ends: Nov. Microform: PQC. Reprint: PSC. *Indexed:* A01, A22, ABIn, B01, B02, BRI, C&ISA, CCMJ, EngInd, MSN, MathR. *Bk. rev.:* 30-40, 300-2,000 words. *Aud.:* Ac, Sa.

Technometrics publishes papers on statistical methods in the physical and chemical sciences and in engineering. The journal expresses a desire to address issues related to huge data sets in industry. Book reviews are included in some issues, and the year's last issue contains an index. Occasionally, a paper will be followed by comments and a rejoinder. Some papers contain supplementary information online. Older issues are in JSTOR with a five-year moving wall. Issues are generally in the 100- to 150-page range, with articles typically running 10–20 pages. Recent topics include field-failure predictions, particle sieving studies, noisy computer experiments, radiation portal monitoring, robust design experiments, and accelerated life tests. Recommended for libraries that serve colleges and universities with statistics programs, or those with chemical/physical science programs that emphasize advanced statistics.

5086. Test. Formerly (until 1992): *Trabajos de Estadistica;* Which superseded in part (in 1986): *Trabajos de Estadistica e Investigacion Operativa;* Which was formerly (until 1963): *Trabajos de Estadistica.* [ISSN: 1133-0686] 1950. 3x/yr. EUR 327 (print & online eds.). Ed(s): Domingo Morales, Ricardo Cao. Springer, Tiergartenstr 17, Heidelberg, 69121, Germany; subscriptions@springer.com; http://www.springer.com. Illus., adv. Refereed. Circ: 600. Reprint: PSC. *Indexed:* A22, ABIn, CCMJ, E01, EconLit, MSN, MathR. *Aud.:* Ac, Sa.

Test focuses on publishing papers on original contributions to statistics or operations research that have, or may potentially have, potential applications. Issues are typically 150–250 pages, with articles usually running 15–40 pages. Recent topics include copula-graphic estimator, functional data additive models, rank-based tests for doubly-truncated data, censored quantile regression estimator, stochastic ordering nonparametric tests, and copula-based order selection approach to resting independence. Recommended for libraries that serve colleges and universities with a statistics program.

5087. Theory of Probability and Its Applications. [ISSN: 0040-585X] 1956. q. USD 951 (print & online eds.). Ed(s): Yu V Proklorov. Society for Industrial and Applied Mathematics, 3600 Market St, 6th Fl, Philadelphia, PA 19104; siam@siam.org; http://www.siam.org. Illus., adv. Sample. Refereed. Circ: 1171. Vol. ends: Dec. *Indexed:* A01, A22, ABIn, ApMecR, CCMJ, CompR, MSN, MathR. *Aud.:* Ac, Sa.

Theory of Probability and Its Applications is a translation of the Russian *Teoriya Veroyatnostei i ee Primeneniya.* The journal publishes papers on theoretical and applied topics in probability, statistics, and stochastic processes. News items are also included. Issues are typically in the 150- to 200-page range, with articles generally running 5–25 pages. Recent topics include random walk trajectories, SDE approximations, moving particles, sequences of random variables, Becker epidemic Markov processes, and Berry-Esseen Theorem variations. Recommended for libraries that serve colleges and universities with a statistics program.

■ TEENAGERS

See also Children; Comic Books; Humor; Music; and Sports sections.

Amy Sprung, Librarian, Belmont Day School, 55 Day School Lane, Belmont, MA 02478; asprung@belmontday.org, amysprung@gmail.com

Introduction

Since the last edition of *Magazines for Libraries*, we saw *Teen Voices*, a magazine by and for teenage girls and focused on empowerment, and *Hmoob Teen,;ra a magazine* by and for Hmong teens and focused on community, cease publication. While they both will be missed, a refreshing new entry recently came onto the scene. While not a subscription magazine, *Rookie*, which can be found online at http://rookiemag.com, launched in September 2011. Editor-in-Chief Tavi Gevinson began as a tween fashion blogger and went on to create this smart web site, updated multiple times daily, which features content focused on a monthly theme. This online publication has a distinctly cosmopolitan, feminist bent, much like the sorely missed *Sassy,* and is a link worth sharing with teens looking for content beyond what is available in the standard print choices.

TheRookie print yearbook, published by Drawn and Quarterly in 2012, features highlights from web site contributors, a veritable Who's Who in pop culture. A second edition is slated to follow in 2013.

Otherwise, things have stayed fairly consistent since the tumultuous years in the teen magazine industry when key teen offerings folded or were consolidated. *Seventeen* still covers fashion, beauty, dating, and celebrities, and remains the matriarch of the teen mags. *Seventeen* is still offering blogs on its web site for the defunct print magazines *CosmoGirl* and *Teen,* and has a very active presence on a variety of social media as well as an iPad edition. *Teen Vogue* remains a strong print option for teens interested in fashion, and *Justine!* and *Girls' Life* are viable options for younger teen and tween girls. *J-14* remains a popular choice for entertainment news, especially for stars of Disney and Nick fame, but also consider having *People* available in your young adult section.

For the sporty types, there's *ESPN* and *Sports Illustrated.* If your teens are into basketball, *Dime* and *Slam!* are basketball publications written in a teen-friendly way. Consider other niche sports publications like *Transworld Snowboarding* or *Transworld Skateboarding* (or see the Sports section), depending on which sports are popular with the teens you serve.

Mad is a good option for those who crave comedy. If you've got Manga lovers, *Shonen Jump* should do the trick. Lastly, if you have teens who are looking to get published, or just love reading and writing short fiction and poetry, *Cicada* and *Teen Ink* are good bets.

Basic Periodicals

Hs: *Seventeen, Teen Vogue;* Ga: *J-14, People, Sports Illustrated.*

Basic Abstracts and Indexes

Readers' Guide to Periodical Literature.

5088. B M X Plus. [ISSN: 0195-0320] 1978. m. USD 13.99 domestic; USD 23.99 Canada; USD 28.99 elsewhere. Hi-Torque Publications, Inc., 25233 Anza Dr, Valencia, CA 91355; http://www.hi-torque.com. Illus., adv. Sample. *Indexed:* MASUSE, P02. *Aud.:* Ems, Hs.

This niche publication covers everything related to the world of BMX (bicycle moto-cross) and has a devout teen and tween readership, as evidenced by the pages of letters from readers in each issue. It also has lots of full-page color photos of bike stunt action and tips on how to execute these stunts. Additionally, there are reviews of bikes and products, interviews with riders, and tips on bike maintenance. Recommended for public and school libraries that serve teens with an interest in BMX.

Boys' Life: the magazine for all boys. See Children section.

5089. Cicada (Peru). [ISSN: 1097-4008] 1988. bi-m. USD 33.95; USD 44.55 newsstand/cover. Ed(s): Deborah Vetter. ePals Publishing Company, 30 Grove St, Ste C, Peterborough, NH 03458; customerservice@caruspub.com; http://www.cricketmag.com. Illus. *Indexed:* AmHI, MASUSE. *Aud.:* Hs.

This literary magazine, geared toward teenagers 14 and up, is the older-audience version of *Cricket.* It features short fiction, first-person essays, comics, and poetry written by a diverse collection of authors. Contributors include adult authors as well as teens. Occasional illustrations highlight the stories within. In each issue, *Cicada* makes a "Call for Creative Endeavors," encouraging readers to submit original art, photographs, and poetry on a given theme. An online community counterpart to the print publication, "The Slam," allows readers to submit creative works and receive peer feedback. *Cicada* serves as a significantly more polished alternative to *Teen Ink* and will appeal primarily to teenagers who like reading and writing short fiction and poetry. Recommended for public, middle, and high school libraries.

Dance Spirit. See Dance section.

E S P N The Magazine. See Sports/General section.

5090. The Foxfire Magazine. Formerly (until 1992): *Foxfire.* [ISSN: 1084-5321] 1967. s-a. USD 12.95 domestic; USD 24.95 foreign. Foxfire Fund, Inc., PO Box 541, Mountain City, GA 30562; foxfire@foxfire.org; http://www.foxfire.org. Illus., adv. Sample. Microform: PQC. *Indexed:* A22, MLA-IB. *Aud.:* Ems, Hs.

Originally created by high school students in Southern Appalachia in 1966 as a means of capturing and preserving their culture and the lives of senior citizens from their community, *The Foxfire Magazine* is still going strong. In addition to offering profiles of local elders, it is chock-full of photos, recipes, and other tidbits from local history. The students who work on the magazine do a fantastic job of capturing the voice of their subjects with love and humor. It's clear that a lot of work goes into each issue, which starts out with an editorial statement from one of the senior student editors. Highly recommended for area school and public libraries.

5091. Girls' Life. [ISSN: 1078-3326] 1994. bi-m. USD 14.95. Ed(s): Karen Bokram. Girls' Life Acquisitions Corp., 4529 Harford Rd, Baltimore, MD 21214. Illus., adv. *Indexed:* BRI, C37, C42, GW, ICM, MASUSE, P01. *Bk. rev.:* Number and length vary. *Aud.:* Ems, Hs, Ga.

This wholesome teen magazine, geared toward young teenage girls, features your standard array of beauty, fashion, advice, star profiles, and quizzes. Many of the featured starlets, who often grace the cover, tend to be in their teens, and while there's not much sex talk, there is plenty of boy talk. Giveaways include fashion must-haves and beach reads. Issue-oriented features talk about topics like cutting and body image.

5092. J-14: just for teens! [ISSN: 1522-1989] 1999. 10x/yr. USD 14.97 domestic; USD 24.97 foreign; USD 3.39 per issue. Ed(s): Janet Giovanelli. Bauer Publishing Group, 270 Sylvan Ave, Englewood Cliffs, NJ 07632; info@bauerpublishing.com; http://www.bauerpublishing.com. Adv. Circ: 530469 Paid. *Aud.:* Ems, Hs, Ga.

This colorful, glossy teen magazine focuses on younger stars, many of Disney and Nick fame, as well as pop artists and other heartthrobs of the moment. It's just the fix for star-crazy young teens itching for the latest info on their favorite performers. Beauty and fashion tips abound, as well as red carpet dos and don'ts and celebrity befores and afters. *J-14,* also known as *Just for Teens* (get it?), is just one of a multitude of celeb worship choices. You may wish to consider *Tiger Beat, Bop,* or *Twist,* but more than one magazine of this type is probably unnecessary. My local library's copies of *J-14* were falling apart, but it's unclear if that was from poor staple quality or excessive love. Check with your teens to see what they like, and definitely consider *Word Up!* as well, especially if you have teens who are into hip hop. Recommended for public libraries.

5093. Justine Magazine. [ISSN: 1548-8241] 2004. bi-m. USD 17.95 domestic; USD 30 Canada; USD 50 elsewhere. Pinpoint Publishing, 6263 Poplar Ave, Ste 38119, Memphis, TN 38119. *Bk. rev.:* Number and length vary. *Aud.:* Ems, Hs, Ga.

From the pun-filled world of teen magazines comes *Justine,* another wholesome title for young teen girls. With a clean layout, and a slightly less produced feel than some of the bigger-time fashion mags (read: less airbrushed), *Justine* features relatively conservative fashion geared toward younger teens. Book, movie, and music reviews and lots of suggestions for hot products and web sites are staples. "Spark," the magazine's online book club, features contests, giveaways, and reviews of teen reads organized by genre and theme. Another great feature of *Justine* called "Trendsetters" is a substantial section of each issue devoted to profiling young women, typically in their twenties, about the variety of jobs they could pursue in their chosen career fields. This magazine might be a nice addition to your collection because of its up-to-date career information, which can fill holes in your career books for young adults, and its lack of risque content. Recommended for public and school libraries.

Mad. See Humor section.

People. See News and Opinion section.

5094. *Pro Wrestling Illustrated.* [ISSN: 1043-7576] 1979. m. USD 54.20 domestic; USD 87.20 in Canada & Mexico; USD 144.20 elsewhere. Ed(s): Frank Krewda, Jeff Ruoss. Sports & Entertainment Publications, LLC, 510 Township Line Rd, Ste 130, Blue Bell, PA 19422; custsrvcsep@sepublications.com. Illus., adv. Sample. *Aud.:* Hs, Ga.

As the title would imply, this publication is chock-full of images, which doesn't mean that there isn't plenty of commentary to go along with them. It includes lots of gory, blood-splattered, full-color pictures. The content is geared solely toward professional wrestling fans, so if you serve teens who are into this "sport," this title would be a great addition to your collection. Issues contain profiles of wrestlers, commentary on various personalities in that universe, and coverage of recent and historic matches. The writing is similar to that of other sports journalism. Some racy shots of provocatively clothed stars might be a factor to consider, but pick up an issue to take a look before discounting this one. The content is high-interest, and it might be an opportunity to engage literacy in a novel way for teen patrons.

Rolling Stone. See Music/Popular section.

5095. *Seventeen.* Formerly (until 1944): *Stardom.* [ISSN: 0037-301X] 1944. 10x/yr. USD 10; USD 2.99 newsstand/cover. Ed(s): Ann Shoket, Joanna Saltz. Hearst Magazines, 300 W 57th St, 12th Fl, New York, NY 10019; HearstMagazines@hearst.com; http://www.hearst.com. Illus., adv. Sample. Microform: NBI; PQC. *Indexed:* A22, BRI, C37, CBCARef, MASUSE, P02. *Aud.:* Hs, Ga.

Seventeen is geared toward the older end of the teenage spectrum, with a polished look and some mature content. It includes articles on fashion, beauty, health, and everyday teen drama, including the ever popular "Traumarama." The feature articles are varied, and recent issues have addressed topics ranging from how to flirt to getting robbed at gunpoint. There's a fitness section with ideas for exercises, as well as a fitness blog on the *Seventeen* web site. The web site and related social media include a lot of content that is not in the print magazine, as well as blogs for the now-defunct print magazines *CosmoGirl* and *Teen.* The web site also links to "Mis Quince," a web site dealing with all things Quincinera. Although *Seventeen* focuses quite a bit on making your guy, or potential guy, happy, *Seventeen* is still recommended as standard fare that's appealing to a broad audience. They also offer a digital subscription. Recommended for public and high school libraries.

Sex, Etc. See Sexuality section.

Sports Illustrated. See Sports/General section.

5096. *Teen Ink: written by teens.* Formerly (until 2000): *The 21st Century.* [ISSN: 1545-1283] 1989. m. Individuals, USD 35. Young Authors Foundation, PO Box 30, Newton, MA 02461. Adv. *Indexed:* MASUSE. *Bk. rev.:* Number and length vary. *Aud.:* Ems, Hs, Ga.

This magazine, printed on tabloid-sized newsprint, contains a variety of short fiction, poetry, reviews, opinion pieces, sports stories, nonfiction, and art by teens. There is a healthy serving of teen angst and a wide range in quality. Reviews of music, movies, and books (both recent and classics) abound. Submitting to *Teen Ink* is a great option for teens hoping to get published, and if you have teens who contribute, it's a plus to carry the magazine so they can see their work in the library.

5097. *Teen Vogue.* Incorporates (in 2005): *Y M.* [ISSN: 1540-2215] 2000. 10x/yr. USD 10 for 2 yrs. domestic. Ed(s): Amy Astley. Conde Nast Publications, Inc., 4 Times Sq, 6th Fl, New York, NY 10036; magpr@condenast.com; http://www.condenast.com. Adv. Sample. Circ: 1017125 Paid. *Indexed:* BRI. *Aud.:* Hs, Ga, Ac.

Teen Vogue clearly emphasizes fashion, particularly high fashion (read: stuff that's not affordable for many teens), but it also gives a nod to teen street-wear and affordable party dresses. The production value is high, and models are of the impossibly thin sort without much diversity in size, shape, or race. Additionally, there are articles on bedroom decor, celebrity profiles, and profiles of successful young women in the fashion industry. Recommended for public libraries.

Thrasher. See Sports/Extreme Sports section.

Transworld Skateboarding. See Sports/Extreme Sports section.

Transworld Snowboarding. See Sports/Extreme Sports section.

Tu. See Latin America and Spain section.

TV Guide. See General Interest section.

Weekly Shonen Jump. See Anime, Comics, Graphic Novels, and Manga section.

■ TELEVISION, VIDEO, AND RADIO

Home Entertainment

See also Electronics; Films; and Media and AV sections.

Paul M. Worster, Multimedia Librarian, Lamont Library–Harvard Yard, Harvard University, Cambridge, MA 02138; FAX: 617-496-3692; worster@fas.harvard.edu

Introduction

Television, video, and radio have all been greatly affected by the ubiquitous computer and the Internet connection. While the giant screen in the living room can easily be the computer monitor as well, it may also be connected to the Internet directly or controlled by the small-screen mobile devices. Enthusiasts broadcast their radio shows from their car or laptop more easily than ever, and as the media that we use to receive (and create) this content changes, so, too, does the field. Broadcasters, networks, content producers, and aggregator web sites are all experimenting with online distribution models, and so are our library patrons.

As may be expected, almost every title listed also has a significant online presence. Equipment reviews, technical challenges, interactive data models, and buyer's guides may be more easily accessed at the journal's web site. Additionally, commercial broadcasting titles often have extensive online news updates.

This section attempts to address the needs of Communications and Media Studies departments, radio enthusiasts, film buffs, AV geeks, and media makers. Some of the larger areas of coverage include academic studies (of medium or content), video on any screen, home entertainment enjoyment or installations, network broadcasting, and content creation. Some crossover with other sections, especially communications and film, is inescapable.

Those with an interest in broadcasting should check *Broadcast and Cable, Current, Intermedia,* and *Radio Ink.* Academic departments should also consider *Feminist Media Studies, Journal of Broadcasting and Electronic Media, Journal of Radio and Audio Media,* and *Media Report to Women.* For those with an interest in home theater technologies, there's *Sound & Vision, Stereophile, Widescreen Review,* and of course *Home Theater.* Radio hobbyists may want to scan *CQ* and *Monitoring Times.*

Basic Periodicals

CQ or *Monitoring Times, Sound & Vision, Video Watchdog, Videomaker.*

Basic Abstracts and Indexes

Academic Search Premier, Film & Television Literature Index, ProQuest Research Library.

Afterimage. See Photography section.

5098. *Broadcasting & Cable.* Former titles (until 1993): *Broadcasting (Washington);* (until 1957): *Broadcasting Telecasting;* (until 1948): *Broadcasting - The News Magazine of the Fifth Estate;* Incorporated (in 1961): *Television;* (in 1953): *Telecast;* (in 1933): *Broadcast Reporter; Broadcast Advertising.* [ISSN: 1068-6827] 1931. w. USD 199 combined subscription domestic (print & online eds.); USD 249.99 combined subscription Canada (print & online eds.); USD 360.99 combined subscription elsewhere (print & online eds.). Ed(s): Ben Grossman. NewBay Media, LLC, 28 E 28th St, 12th Fl, New York, NY 10016; customerservice@nbmedia.com; http://www.nbmedia.com. Sample. Circ: 35000 Paid and controlled. Vol. ends: Dec. *Indexed:* A22, ABIn, B01, B02, B03, BRI, C42, Chicano, F01, IIPA, P02. *Aud.:* Ac, Sa.

Broadcasting and Cable seeks to reach and inform corporate broadcast staff and the cable TV professional at an accessible level. Article topics include national programming, city stations, new cable channels, advertising clients, industry leaders, and the future of broadcasting. Articles are generally short and plentiful.

5099. *Current (Washington, 1980): the public telecommunications newspaper.* Former titles: *N A E B Letter; National Association of Educational Broadcasters Newsletter.* [ISSN: 0739-991X] 1980. bi-w. USD 70 domestic; USD 82 Canada; USD 132 elsewhere. Ed(s): Steve Behrens. Current Publishing Committee, 6930 Carroll Ave, Ste 350, Takoma Park, MD 20912; mail@getgabriel.com; http://www.current.org. Illus., adv. Sample. Vol. ends: No. 23. *Aud.:* Ac, Sa.

Current reports on public TV and public radio in the United States, including its history, present, and future. It aims to reach station employees, independent producers, local volunteers, and board members. This publication of the National Association of Educational Broadcasters brings together a myriad of public media organizations, including Public Broadcasting Service, National Public Radio, Public Radio International, American Public Media, Public Radio Exchange, and others. Topics include these organizations, their programs, their staff, and topics of their concern (e.g., grants). An events calendar, job listings, and obituaries are also included.

5100. *Digital Video.* Formed by the merger of (1996-2011): *D V;* Which was formerly (1994-1996): *Digital Video Magazine;* (1993-1994): *Desktop Video World;* (1976-2011): *Videography;* Which incorporated (1988-199?): *Corporate Video Decisions.* [ISSN: 2164-0963] 2011. m. USD 29.97 domestic (Free to qualified personnel). Ed(s): Katie Makal, Cristina Clapp. NewBay Media, LLC, 28 E 28th St, 12th Fl, New York, NY 10016; customerservice@nbmedia.com; http://www.nbmedia.com. Illus., adv. *Indexed:* A22, B02, BRI, F01, I15. *Aud.:* Ac, Sa.

Digital Video aims to inform those in the production, post-production, and delivery of video occupations. Gear reviews are plentiful, and written by professionals who are thoroughly familiar with the daily use of the equipment. Also included are case studies and tutorials, thus moving the journal beyond discussion into a kind of continuing education in the field. Columns address "production, post production, lighting[,] and audio, as well as business and legal issues." This one is geared to the professionals, or those aspiring to their ranks.

5101. *Feminist Media Studies.* [ISSN: 1468-0777] 2001. q. GBP 700 (print & online eds.). Ed(s): Lisa McLaughlin, Cynthia Carter. Routledge, 4 Park Sq, Milton Park, Abingdon, OX14 4RN, United Kingdom; subscriptions@tandf.co.uk; http://www.tandfonline.com. Sample. Refereed. Reprint: PSC. *Indexed:* A01, A22, E01, FemPer, GW, IBSS, MLA-IB, P61, SSA. *Bk. rev.:* Number and length vary. *Aud.:* Ac.

Feminist Media Studies provides a transdisciplinary forum for readers pursuing feminist approaches to the field of media and communication studies. The journal examines "historical, philosophical, cultural, social, political, and economic dimensions" of these issues, and analyzes print, film, the arts, and electronic media. Articles are peer-reviewed by the editor and by at least two scholars. For each of five issues per year, expect six or seven article-papers of about 20 pages each, and a more global focus than that of many feminist media journals.

5102. *InterMedia.* Supersedes (in 1973): *I B I Newsletter.* [ISSN: 0309-118X] 1973. bi-m. Free to members. Ed(s): Joanne Grimshaw. International Institute of Communications (IIC), 2 Printers Yard, 90a Broadway, London, SW19 1RD, United Kingdom; enquiries@iicom.org; http://www.iicom.org/. Illus. Vol. ends: No. 6. Microform: PQC. *Indexed:* A22, ABIn, IIFP. *Aud.:* Ac, Sa.

InterMedia is published by the International Institute of Communications, which aims to supply a forum for government, business, and academia to examine and discuss current communications issues. *InterMedia* has global coverage, but often focuses on Europe and the Americas. While it is admirable in its scope, its article quality can vary greatly. Special library rates may be available for those who e-mail editor Joanne Grimshaw at j.grimshaw@iicom.org.

5103. *Journal of Broadcasting and Electronic Media.* Formerly (until 1985): *Journal of Broadcasting.* [ISSN: 0883-8151] 1956. q. GBP 141 (print & online eds.). Ed(s): Zizi Papacharissi. Routledge, 325 Chestnut St, Ste 800, Philadelphia, PA 19106; customerservice@taylorandfrancis.com; http://www.tandfonline.com. Adv. Sample. Refereed. Microform: WSH; PMC; PQC. Reprint: PSC; WSH. *Indexed:* A01, A22, ABS&EES, AmHI, B01, BRI, CLI, CompLI, E01, F01, IIFP, L14, P02, P61, PsycInfo, RILM, RiskAb, SSA. *Aud.:* Ac.

The *Journal of Broadcasting and Electronic Media* is an academic journal that covers the trends in research of electronic media. Article topics include the "historical, technological, economic, legal, policy, cultural, and social dimensions" of electronic media. The journal's articles have expanded from predominantly experimental and survey methods to also include critical, historical, and ethnographical work as well. Recent articles cover gendering issues, social media, and publicness. This is a recommended resource for colleges and universities with communications or media studies departments. Each issue contains six or seven papers of 15–20 pages each. As a sample, an issue's worth of articles is available online.

Journal of Popular Film and Television. See Films section.

5104. *Journal of Radio & Audio Media.* Formerly (until 2008): *Journal of Radio Studies.* [ISSN: 1937-6529] 1992. s-a. GBP 119 (print & online eds.). Ed(s): Joseph R Blaney. Routledge, 325 Chestnut St, Ste 800, Philadelphia, PA 19106; customerservice@taylorandfrancis.com; http://www.tandfonline.com. Adv. Sample. Refereed. Reprint: PSC; WSH. *Indexed:* A22, C45, E01, IIPA, RRTA. *Bk. rev.:* 3. *Aud.:* Ac.

The *Journal of Radio & Audio Media* is a semiannual, peer-reviewed publication that pertains to the history and present of radio, as well as the alternative audio media that complement and challenge radio. Interdisciplinary approaches are the norm for this journal, and it may address "programming, new technology, policy and regulation, [and] rating systems," as well as history, management, propaganda, social effects, sales, podcasting, gender, or international radio. The journal follows the typical Taylor & Francis publishing model (see also *Journal of Broadcasting and Electronic Media* and *Feminist Media Studies*) in that each issue has six or seven peer-reviewed papers that come in at about 15 pages each. Where it departs from the model is that this journal seems more likely to contain book reviews.

5105. *Media Report to Women.* [ISSN: 0145-9651] 1972. q. USD 70 (Individuals, USD 40). Ed(s): Sheila Gibbons. Communication Research Associates, Inc., 11988 Tramway Dr, Cincinnati, OH 45241; http://www.commres.com. Illus., index. Vol. ends: Fall (No. 4). *Indexed:* A01, A22, BRI, F01, FemPer, GW, P02, WSA. *Bk. rev.:* 3-5, 50-90 words. *Aud.:* Hs, Ga, Ac, Sa.

Media Report to Women provides information on several types of media—television, cable, film, radio, newspapers, magazines, newsletters, and the Internet included—and the way in which they depict women and issues of interest to women. Each issue is 24 pages of low-frills, black-and-white, focused research—although the journal now encourages its readers to receive the newsletter as a pdf, as well. Full-length research papers (an average of six pages) are now included in each issue; the sources listed in the bibliography alone may be worth the price of admission. Also included in most issues are field news, leaders, book reviews, and/or movie reviews.

5106. *Q E X: a forum for communications experimenters.* Incorporates (1945-2000): *C Q.* [ISSN: 0886-8093] 1981. bi-m. Members, USD 24; Non-members, USD 36. Ed(s): Larry Wolfgang. American Radio Relay League, Inc., 225 Main St, Newington, CT 06111; hq@arrl.org; http://www.arrl.org. Adv. *Aud.:* Ac, Sa.

"Of, by, and for the radio amateur," *QEX* is an exchange of ideas, reviews, and (most of all) highly technical information among the practitioners of the amateur radio field. Expect five to ten diagrams, schematics, black-and-white photographs, and/or scope readings per article, and at least as many mathematical formulas.

5107. *QST: devoted entirely to amateur radio.* [ISSN: 0033-4812] 1915. m. Free to members. Ed(s): Steve Ford. American Radio Relay League, Inc., 225 Main St, Newington, CT 06111; pubsales@arrl.org; http://www.arrl.org. Illus., adv. Sample. Vol. ends: Dec. Microform: PQC. *Indexed:* A22. *Bk. rev.:* 1, 825 words. *Aud.:* Hs, Ga.

QST is the main publication of the American Radio Relay League (ARRL), the United States' national association for amateur radio. Coming from the official organization, this magazine is slightly more formal and technical than *CQ*, but it is otherwise very similar in layout and content. This information-rich journal features an average of seven technical project articles, eight news sections, an amateur radio classifieds section, and 30 columns per issue. Additionally, a fair amount of attention is paid to contesting, or seeking to make contact with as many other amateur radio operators as possible within specific limitations. ARRL also publishes *NCJ* (*National Contest Journal*), which specializes in contesting, and *QEX*. As with other ARRL publications, sample news and articles can be found at www.arrl.org/periodicals.

5108. *Radio Ink.* Former titles (until 1992): *Pulse fo Radio;* (until 1989): *Pulse of Broadcasting.* [ISSN: 1064-587X] 1986. fortn. USD 147. Ed(s): Brida Connolly, Wendy Bernstein. Streamline Publishing, Inc., 224 Datura St, Ste 1015, W. Palm Beach, FL 33401; comments@radioink.com. Illus., adv. Sample. Vol. ends: No. 26. *Aud.:* Sa.

Radio Ink aims to inform the broadcast radio manager. Articles vary from inspiration to education, with plenty of marketing advice in between. Frequent topics include HD radio, advertising, Internet radio, personnel moves, obituaries, and the future of radio. *Radio Ink* aims to be "easy to read," and even highlights parts of its articles, presumably for the busy station manager. The journal also contains lists of award winners and interviews with leaders in the field; combine this with its annual *Most Powerful People in Radio* issue, and it's somewhat of a *Who's Who* resource for radio.

5109. *Stereophile.* [ISSN: 0585-2544] 1962. m. USD 12.97 domestic; USD 24.97 Canada; USD 36.97 elsewhere. Ed(s): John Atkinson. Source Interlink Companies, 6420 Wilshire Blvd, 10th Fl, Los Angeles, CA 90048; dheine@sourceinterlink.com; http://www.sourceinterlinkmedia.com. Illus., index, adv. Sample. Circ: 74000 Paid. Vol. ends: Dec. *Indexed:* RILM. *Aud.:* Ga, Sa.

Stereophile is for the experienced and professional home-audio fanatic. This highly technical journal consistently features several scientific charts (e.g., frequency response, "THD+N(%) vs. freq," and circuit maps) in its many gear-review articles. The journal was criticized for its emphasis on analog, vinyl, tubes, and other older technology, but has now fully embraced the current technology. One added nicety is that the manufacturers' responses to gear reviews are also printed.

TV Guide. See General Interest section.

5110. *Videomaker: your guide to creating and publishing great video.* [ISSN: 0889-4973] 1986. m. USD 22.50 domestic; USD 32.50 Canada; USD 47.50 elsewhere. Ed(s): Stephen Muratore, Matthew York. York Publishing, 1350 E 9th St, Chico, CA 95928. Illus., index, adv. Sample. Vol. ends: Dec. *Indexed:* BRI, F01, IHTDI. *Aud.:* Hs, Ac, Sa.

Videomaker is for the recently initiated video makers who are looking to understand more and improve on their skills. Whether for cobbling together a presentation, wedding video, green screen effect, or film festival short, *Videomaker* covers useful tips and tricks, as well as some product reviews. The articles are an excellent starting point for those new to editing, software, and production. An article generally contains a very short introduction to six or seven parts of a topic (or software titles, etc.), so the journal is a good place to start, not finish. Recommended for schools with video production departments and for patrons looking to improve their video skills.

Home Entertainment

5111. *Home Theater.* Former titles (until 199?): *CurtCo's Home Theater;* (until 199?): *CurtCo's Home Theater Technology.* [ISSN: 1096-3065] 1994. m. USD 12.97 domestic; USD 25.97 Canada; USD 27.97 elsewhere. Ed(s): Shane Buettner. Source Interlink Companies, 6420 Wilshire Blvd, 10th Fl, Los Angeles, CA 90048; dheine@sourceinterlink.com; http://www.sourceinterlinkmedia.com. Adv. Circ: 100000. *Indexed:* F01. *Aud.:* Ga.

Home Theater aims to be the authoritative source for product reviews and audio-visual news for the committed enthusiast and casual shopper alike. It was the first in the home theater market, and claims to still be the largest monthly in that market. There are some up-and-coming gear reviews across the money spectrum, though predominantly in the high and mid-range; this excludes the casual, less funded shopper to some degree, who may prefer *Consumer Reports*. Article topics include many gear reviews, new technology, home-theater design advice, film formats, and even some film studio news, when it affects the other magazine topics. Half-page blu-ray disc reviews are also included, discussing the basic plot and the AV details of each release, then rating picture, sound, disc extras, and interactivity. Recommended for window shoppers, or the less technical but well-funded enthusiast.

5112. *Sound & Vision: home theater - audio - video - multimedia - movies - music.* Formerly (until 2003): *Stereo Review's Sound and Vision;* Which was formed by the merger of (1978-1999): *Video Magazine;* Which was formerly (until 1987): *Video (New York);* (1960-1999): *Stereo Review;* Which was formerly (until 1968): *HiFi Stereo Review;* Superseded (1959-1989): *High Fidelity;* Which was formerly (until 1959): *High Fidelity & Audiocraft;* Which was formed by the merger of (1957-1958): *Audiocraft for the Hi-Fi Hobbyist;* (1951-1958): *High Fidelity.* [ISSN: 1537-5838] 1999. 8x/yr. USD 12 domestic; USD 22 Canada. Ed(s): Mike Mettler, Mike Mettler. Bonnier Corp., 2 Park Ave, 10th Fl, New York, NY 10016; http://www.bonniercorp.com. Illus., index, adv. Circ: 500000 Paid. Vol. ends: Dec. *Indexed:* A01, A22, BRI, C37, CBRI, F01, I15, IIMP, MASUSE, P02, RILM. *Aud.:* Ga.

Sound & Vision is another magazine in the home theater arena, but one that happens to include car and mobile-device audio and video equipment as well. All of the expected gear reviews, "how to" guides, and component combination and connection advice columns are present, along with music and even videogame reviews. Multiple Q&A departments help address the concerns of those interested in legacy equipment, setup, or new formats. Gear reviews have plenty of pro–consumer-level detail in 500–800 words each. The average price of reviewed gear may be on the rise—expect to pay a minimum of USD 150 for headphones. CD and DVD reviews rate content but also focus on the picture, sound, and extras.

5113. *Video Watchdog: the perfectionist's guide to fantastic video.* [ISSN: 1070-9991] 1990. m. USD 60 domestic; USD 75 foreign; USD 6.50 newsstand/cover per issue. Ed(s): Tim Lucas. Video Watchdog, PO Box 5283, Cincinnati, OH 45205-0283; videowd@aol.com; http://www.cinemaweb.com/videowd. Illus. *Indexed:* F01, IIFP. *Bk. rev.:* Number and length vary. *Aud.:* Hs, Ga.

Video Watchdog is the home video enthusiast's resource, covering both the domestic and imported home video industry. The journal is jam-packed with detailed reviews of recent releases and previously released but lesser-known titles. Reviews include comparisons to other movies, discussion of different versions, and details on the cast, crew, writers, and cinematographers. Thankfully, these reviews manage to remain accessible to the uninitiated, despite being so detailed. *Video Watchdog* is an excellent resource for those who want to look beyond the mainstream. Also included are a few pages of soundtrack and film book reviews.

5114. *Widescreen Review: the essential home theatre resource.* 1993. m. USD 20 domestic; USD 25 in Canada & Mexico; USD 45 elsewhere. Ed(s): Gary Reber. W S R Publishing, PO Box 2587, Temecula, CA 92593. Illus. *Aud.:* Ga.

Widescreen Review refers to the home theater, not the silver screen. Specifically, the journal limits its disc reviews to those available in widescreen Blu-ray format. This publication may be flashy and colorful, but it features many pages of detailed equipment reviews, both of new equipment and what is still a best buy. Additionally, each issue reviews blu-ray titles, both for in-depth technical aspects and for plot and cinematography. Filled with so many equipment reviews, a shelf-ful of this journal could be quite a resource—which is doubly tempting while back issues are available for USD 1.00 each. The editorials and articles aim to modify a reader's home theater setup to be "the best that it can be." The magazine's web site is less crowded than that of its peers, but it seems to link to just as much content. Subscribers can also download a pdf file of each issue, and non-subscribers can peruse a partial sample issue. A separate subscription is available for iPad, iPhone, and iPod.

■ THEATER

Elizabeth McKeigue, Associate University Librarian, Santa Clara University, Santa Clara, CA 95053; emckeigue@scu.edu

Introduction

This section highlights the core scholarly journals and magazines in Theatre and Drama Studies. The majority of titles are appropriate for public as well as for academic library collections. A number of the academic titles cover criticism, performance, dramaturgy, and comparative drama. The popular magazine titles focus mostly on performance reviews.

All of these journals are indexed, in total or in part, in the major indexes in the field, such as the *International Index to the Performing Arts*. Additionally, most of them offer some percentage of their content freely online, and all provide some amount of full-text content through the major online aggregated databases.

Basic Periodicals

Hs: *American Theatre, Dramatics, Theater* (Durham); Ga: *American Theatre, Modern Drama, Stage Directions, Theater* (Durham); Ac: *American Theatre, Canadian Theatre Review, Modern Drama, P A J, Theater* (Durham), *Theatre Journal* (Baltimore).

Basic Abstracts and Indexes

Academic Search Premier, Humanities Index, International Index to the Performing Arts (IIPA), MLA International Bibliography.

5115. American Theatre: the monthly forum for news, features and opinion. Former titles (until 1984): *Theatre Communications;* (until 1979): *Theatre Communications Group Newsletter.* [ISSN: 8750-3255] 1973. 10x/yr. Free to members. Ed(s): Jim O'Quinn, Nicole Estvanik Taylor. Theatre Communications Group, Inc., 520 Eighth Ave, 24th Fl, New York, NY 10018; tcg@tcg.org; http://www.tcg.org. Illus., adv. Sample. Circ: 16500. Vol. ends: Dec. Microform: PQC. *Indexed:* A01, A22, ASIP, AmHI, BRI, C37, CBRI, Chicano, IIPA, MASUSE, MLA-IB, P02. *Bk. rev.:* Number varies, 400-1,200 words. *Aud.:* Ga, Ac.

This well-illustrated publication would appeal to academics as well as those who are interested in the theater. Each issue includes articles, book reviews, and production reviews. They frequently feature the text of new plays in their entirety: for example, Amy Herzog's play *4000 Miles* appeared in the April 2012 issue. The web site of its publisher, Theatre Communications Group, offers the full text of all the feature articles in the current issue. This journal is an important addition to any college or university library, as well as any large public library that addresses the needs of dedicated theatergoers.

5116. Asian Theatre Journal. Supersedes: *Asian Theatre Reports.* [ISSN: 0742-5457] 1984. s-a. USD 120. Ed(s): Kathy Foley. University of Hawaii Press, 2840 Kolowalu St, Honolulu, HI 96822; http://www.uhpress.hawaii.edu. Illus., adv. Sample. Refereed. Circ: 450. Vol. ends: Fall. *Indexed:* A01, A22, AmHI, ArtHuCI, BAS, BRI, E01, IIPA, MLA-IB, RILM. *Bk. rev.:* 4-6, 1,000-1,500 words. *Aud.:* Ac.

This English-language journal focuses on contemporary and historical Asian theater through scholarly articles, original plays, play translations, and reviews. Back issues from its inception through 2005 are in JSTOR, and more current issues (1999 to the present) are available through ProjectMUSE. The journal is elegantly illustrated with both color and black-and-white photographs. Academic research libraries that support drama or East Asian literature programs should seriously consider owning this publication.

5117. Canadian Theatre Review. [ISSN: 0315-0836] 1974. q. USD 145. Ed(s): Laura Levin. University of Toronto Press, Journals Division, 5201 Dufferin St, Toronto, ON M3H 5T8, Canada; journals@utpress.utoronto.ca; http://www.utpjournals.com. Illus., index. Sample. Refereed. Circ: 565. Microform: MML. *Indexed:* A01, A22, AmHI, BAS, BRI, C37, CBCARef, E01, IIPA, MLA-IB, RILM. *Bk. rev.:* 2-4, 800-1,200 words. *Aud.:* Ac.

This journal focuses mainly on contemporary and often avant-garde theater productions in Canada. Each issue is organized around a theme, and included in each issue is at least one complete play related to the issue's theme, articles, and reviews. Recent themes include "Native Theatre," "Actor Training," "Canadian Women Playwrights," and "Scenography." This interesting journal is well illustrated with production photographs. It is strongly recommended for any academic or research collection that focuses on contemporary theater and drama.

5118. Comparative Drama. [ISSN: 0010-4078] 1967. q. USD 40. Ed(s): Eve Salisbury, Anthony Ellis. Western Michigan University, Department of English, Kalamazoo, MI 49008; english-graduate@wmich.edu; http://www.wmich.edu/english. Illus., index. Sample. Refereed. Vol. ends: Winter. Microform: PQC. *Indexed:* A01, A22, ABS&EES, AmHI, ArtHuCI, BAS, BRI, CBRI, E01, IIPA, MLA-IB, P02, RILM. *Aud.:* Ac.

This quarterly journal from Western Michigan University focuses on drama and theater from a literary point of view. Scholarly in nature, it gives equal treatment to various genres (ancient, medieval, Renaissance, and modern) and themes. Its coverage is broad in terms of time period and geography. The web site includes an index of the articles from every issue. Shakespeare is covered so frequently that there is a separate "sub-index" for those articles. The journal's web site also features abstracts of every article since 2000. It is an important scholarly journal for college or university library collections.

5119. CurtainUp: the Internet magazine of theater news, reviews and features. 1996. 3x/w. Free. Ed(s): Elyse Sommer. CurtainUp, PO Box 751133, Forest Hills, NY 11375; esommer@pipeline.com; http://www.curtainup.com. *Aud.:* Ga, Ac, Sa.

This is a great source for reviews and information about current (and recent) theatrical productions. Its richest areas are in the New York and Berkshire productions, reflecting the main editor's location, but there are several well-known contributing editors, so regular reports for productions in Toronto, London, and Washington, D.C., also appear. The site's organization is very navigable and user-friendly. There is also a subscription service through which individual readers will be notified of changes to the site. Despite its text-heavy web site, this is among the best of online-only theater magazines. Any public or academic library with a theater-going clientele should include this on its list of web sites. URL: www.curtainup.com

5120. Dramatics: the magazine for students and teachers of theatre. Formerly (until 1944): *Dramatics-Dramatic Curtain.* [ISSN: 0012-5989] 1929. m. 9/yr. Free to members; Non-members, USD 27. Ed(s): Donald A Corathers. Educational Theatre Association, 2343 Auburn Ave, Cincinnati, OH 45219; info@edta.org; http://www.edta.org. Illus., index, adv. Sample. Circ: 32000. Vol. ends: Dec. Microform: PQC. *Indexed:* A22, AmHI, IIPA. *Aud.:* Hs, Ac.

This is one of the few publications specifically directed at the interests of collegiate drama students. It presents articles that provide practical information on acting, directing, and design that will be of use to drama students and educators. Content ranges from technique articles, such as advice on auditioning from casting directors, to the full text of short plays. In addition, there is a great deal of information on internships, summer employment, collegiate and institute dramatic programs, and auditions. This is a core journal for colleges and universities that support drama programs. Secondary schools with active drama programs should also consider this title.

5121. *The Dramatist: the voice of American theater.* Incorporates (1982-1998): *Dramatists Guild. Newsletter;* Former titles (until 1998): *Dramatists Guild Quarterly;* (until 1964): *Dramatists Bulletin.* [ISSN: 1551-7683] 1960. bi-m. Free to members; Non-members, USD 25. Dramatists Guild, Inc., 1501 Broadway, Ste 701, New York, NY 10036; http://www.dramatistsguild.com. Illus., adv. Sample. Circ: 5752. Vol. ends: Winter. *Indexed:* AmHI, IIPA. *Aud.:* Ac, Sa.

This is the official publication of The Dramatists Guild of America, the professional association of playwrights, composers, and lyricists. It usually contains eight to ten articles; these articles may contain discussions of some aspect of playwriting, interviews with well-known playwrights, the political and social opinions of playwrights as they affect their writings, or discussions of theatrical companies. There is also a "Dramatists Diary," which lists plays in production around the country, newly published plays and recordings, and recently published books by guild members. This title has great value for any library that supports the needs of a playwriting, music, or creative writing program.

5122. *Modern Drama: world drama from 1850 to the present.* [ISSN: 0026-7694] 1958. q. CAD 120. Ed(s): Alan Ackerman. University of Toronto Press, Journals Division, 5201 Dufferin St, Toronto, ON M3H 5T8, Canada; journals@utpress.utoronto.ca; http://www.utpjournals.com. Illus., index, adv. Sample. Refereed. Circ: 1212. Vol. ends: Winter. Microform: MML. *Indexed:* A01, A22, ABS&EES, AmHI, ArtHuCI, BRI, C37, CBCARef, E01, IIPA, MLA-IB, P02, RILM. *Bk. rev.:* 8-12, 500-1,000 words. *Aud.:* Ac.

One of the oldest scholarly modern theater journals, *Modern Drama* has been published quarterly by the University of Toronto since 1958. A recent issue includes insightful, scholarly articles on the work of dramatists such as Shaw, Synge, Brecht, and Pinter. There are also eight to ten extensive and interesting book reviews in each issue, and an annual bibliography in the summer issue. This journal would be well placed in any academic library collection that supports contemporary drama and literature programs.

5123. *N T Q. New Theatre Quarterly.* Formerly (until 1985): *T Q. Theatre Quarterly.* [ISSN: 0266-464X] 1971. q. GBP 166. Ed(s): Maria Shevtsova, Simon Trussler. Cambridge University Press, The Edinburgh Bldg, Shaftesbury Rd, Cambridge, CB2 8RU, United Kingdom; journals@cambridge.org; http://www.cambridge.org/uk. Illus., adv. Sample. Circ: 1000. Vol. ends: Nov. Microform: PQC. Reprint: PSC. *Indexed:* A01, A22, AmHI, ArtHuCI, BRI, E01, IIPA, MLA-IB, P02, RILM. *Bk. rev.:* Number and length vary. *Aud.:* Ac.

This journal addresses issues of modern performance and dramaturgy. It also claims to provide a forum "where prevailing dramatic assumptions can be subjected to vigorous critical questioning." Its prose style is interesting and eye-catching and therefore more widely accessible than that of some academic journals. *NTQ* usually contains eight to ten scholarly articles that are international in coverage. Book reviews are generally shorter than those of other academic journals, but there are a good number of them. Recommended for academic libraries and special libraries that address modern performance issues.

5124. *New York Theatre Guide.* 2003. d. Free. Ed(s): Alan Bird. New York Theatre Guide, 12 E 86th St, New York, NY 10028. Adv. *Aud.:* Ga.

This site provides everything you need to know about the current New York theater scene. Features include the latest casting and upcoming productions news, links to reviews of both Broadway and off-Broadway productions, production plot synopses, seating plans of major theaters, maps of New York, and, of course, links to sites for purchasing tickets. It is similar to *CurtainUp,* but it has a better site design; moreover, a search box at the top makes it easy to search for reviews. URL: www.newyorktheatreguide.com

5125. *P A J: a journal of performance and art.* Formerly (until 1998): *Performing Arts Journal.* [ISSN: 1520-281X] 1976. 3x/yr. USD 144 (print & online eds.). Ed(s): Bonnie Marranca. M I T Press, 55 Hayward St, Cambridge, MA 02142; journals-cs@mit.edu; http://mitpress.mit.edu. Illus., adv. Refereed. *Indexed:* A01, A07, A22, A51, ABS&EES, AmHI, ArtHuCI, BRI, CBRI, E01, F01, IIPA, MLA-IB, P02, RILM. *Bk. rev.:* Occasional. *Aud.:* Ac, Sa.

This journal covers contemporary international performance: dance, theater, and performance art. Each issue contains eight to ten articles, performance reviews, and opinion pieces. Sometimes an issue may have a theme. The journal often contains reviews of new works in theater, dance, film, and opera, and occasionally book reviews. Its illustrations are extensive and fascinating. Issues of *PAJ* from 1996 to the present are available online via ProjectMUSE. The journal's web site includes interesting podcasts to which anyone can subscribe for free. Recommended for academic or research libraries where contemporary and avant-garde performance artistry is studied.

5126. *Playbill On-Line.* 1994. d. Free. TotalTheater, PO Box 62, Hewlett, NY 11557-0062; http://www.playbill.com. Adv. *Aud.:* Ga.

Anyone who has been in an American commercial theater is familiar with the *Playbill* program, which provides the cast, the number of acts, intermissions, and background on the play. The coverage in the web site is not dramatically different, except that it is all in one place, and therefore a very useful tool for planning for visits to New York City. There is some non–New York coverage, including a little international, but that coverage is spotty, and only the New York coverage can be depended on for completeness. There are also feature articles, gossip, a chat room, casting calls, and links to purchase tickets. This web site is a must for New York theatergoers, particularly for the up-to-date schedules. URL: www.playbill.com/index.php

5127. *Plays: the drama magazine for young people.* Incorporates (1937-1942): *One Act Play Magazine and Radio-Drama Review.* [ISSN: 0032-1540] 1940. m. Oct-May; except Jan.-Feb. combined. USD 44. Ed(s): Liz Preston. Plays Magazine, PO Box 600160, Newton, MA 02460; customerservice@playsmagazine.com; http://www.playsmag.com/. Illus., index. Sample. Vol. ends: Dec. Microform: PQC. *Indexed:* A01, A22, BRI, C37, ICM, IIPA, MASUSE, P01. *Bk. rev.:* 10-15, 50-100 words. *Aud.:* Ems, Hs, Ga.

The classic magazine *Plays* continues to provide an essential resource to school drama programs everywhere. It contains between nine and 12 short plays, with subjects ranging from historic to holidays, to skits and comedies, to dramatized classics. Plays are arranged by general grade level, and each contains production notes that include casting and staging suggestions. The plays are not copyright-free, but any current subscriber may produce copies for the cast and produce the play royalty-free. This magazine should be included in the library of any school with a drama program or club. It should also be included in public libraries' children's collections.

5128. *Stage Directions.* [ISSN: 1047-1901] 1988. m. Free. Ed(s): Jacob Coakley. DanceMedia, LLC., 333 7th Ave, New York, NY 10001; http://dancemedia.com. Illus., adv. Sample. *Indexed:* IIPA, MASUSE, P02. *Bk. rev.:* 2-3, 400 words. *Aud.:* Ga, Ac.

This publication addresses the specific technical needs of "regional, academic, and community" theaters, although the best audience would probably be community and small academic theater groups. Each issue has six to ten articles on such technical aspects of performance production as cost-saving ideas, dramatic effects and techniques, and computer control issues. There is also supplier information, articles describing particular theaters and their companies, columns on computers and networked resources, and book reviews. This magazine's online version includes the table of contents for each issue published since 1988 and links to selected articles online. It is a useful resource for any public library with an active community theater or any academic library that supports a drama program.

5129. *T D R.* Former titles (until 1988): *The Drama Review;* (until 1968): *T D R;* (until 1967): *Tulane Drama Review;* (until 1957): *The Carleton Drama Review;* (until 1956): *Carleton Drama Bulletin.* [ISSN: 1054-2043] 1955. q. USD 219 (print & online eds.). Ed(s): Jessica

Pabon, Richard Schechner. M I T Press, 55 Hayward St, Cambridge, MA 02142; journals-cs@mit.edu; http://mitpress.mit.edu. Illus., index, adv. Sample. Microform: PQC. *Indexed:* A01, A22, ABS&EES, AmHI, ArtHuCI, BAS, BRI, CBRI, E01, IIPA, MLA-IB, P02, RILM. *Aud.:* Ac.

MIT Press for the Tisch School at New York University publishes this important publication on theater production, history, and criticism. Each quarterly issue offers articles on a broad range of topics. There are extensive reviews and descriptions of contemporary and often avant-garde performances with photographic illustrations. This journal should be included in any library that addresses the needs of theater studies and/or contemporary performance art.

5130. *Theater (Durham).* Formerly (until 1977): *Yale - Theatre.* [ISSN: 0161-0775] 1968. 3x/yr. USD 168. Ed(s): Ryan Davis, Tanya Dean. Duke University Press, 905 W Main St, Ste 18 B, PO Box 90660, Durham, NC 27701; subscriptions@dukeupress.edu; http://www.dukeupress.edu. Illus., index. Sample. Refereed. Microform: PQC. Reprint: PSC. *Indexed:* A01, A22, AmHI, ArtHuCI, BRI, E01, IIPA, MLA-IB, P02, RILM. *Bk. rev.:* 2-3, 600-1,800 words. *Aud.:* Ac.

Edited and produced by the venerable Yale School of Drama and published by Duke University Press, this title offers articles reflecting the social politics of contemporary theater thinkers, artistic directors, and writers. Each issue contains four to six articles, usually organized around a theme. The editors try to include at least one new "pathbreaking" play per issue, and some issues contain several. The articles are often illustrated with what are sometimes breathtaking production photographs. The Duke University Press site offers free searchable access to its contents and links to the full-text via subscription. This magazine is an invaluable part of any significant academic theater journal collection, and is also recommended for academic libraries and special libraries that address modern performance issues.

5131. *Theatre Journal (Baltimore).* Formerly (until 1979): *Educational Theatre Journal.* [ISSN: 0192-2882] 1949. q. USD 155. Ed(s): Bob Kowkabany, Penny Farfan. The Johns Hopkins University Press, 2715 N Charles St, Baltimore, MD 21218; http://www.press.jhu.edu. Illus., adv. Sample. Refereed. Circ: 2263. Vol. ends: Dec. Microform: PQC. Reprint: PSC. *Indexed:* A01, A22, ABS&EES, AmHI, ArtHuCI, BAS, BRI, CBRI, E01, IIPA, MLA-IB, P02, RILM. *Bk. rev.:* 8-12, 1,000-1,800 words. *Aud.:* Ac.

This scholarly journal features historical studies, production reviews, and theoretical inquiries that analyze dramatic texts and production. Each issue contains approximately six articles, a performance review section, and book reviews. The articles are substantial and refereed. They may cover topics from a social or historical point of view, or they may analyze text. Occasionally, the articles will be organized around a central theme. The performance review section contains reviews of American theater productions, although some foreign productions do appear. Regional theaters and repertory company productions are well covered. This journal is available online from 1996 to the present via ProjectMUSE. College and university libraries with drama or comparative literature programs should seriously consider subscribing to this journal.

5132. *Women & Performance: a journal of feminist theory.* [ISSN: 0740-770X] 1983. 3x/yr. GBP 133 (print & online eds.). Ed(s): Kara Jesella. Routledge, 325 Chestnut St, Ste 800, Philadelphia, PA 19106; customerservice@taylorandfrancis.com; http://www.tandfonline.com. Illus., adv. Sample. Refereed. Circ: 1300 Paid. Reprint: PSC. *Indexed:* A22, E01, F01, FemPer, GW, IIPA, MLA-IB, RILM. *Aud.:* Ac.

Founded in 1983 by graduate students in the Department of Performance Studies at New York University's Tisch School of the Arts, this journal includes essays on performance, dance, film, new media, and the performance of everyday life from interdisciplinary feminist perspectives. The journal offers a section that promises "artists' statements, polemics, review essays, performance texts, manifestoes, feminist and queer takes on current events and debates, and other modes of intellectual production that are too wily to conform to the standard model of academic publishing." Recommended for academic and research libraries.

■ TRANSPORTATION

See also Aeronautics and Space Science; Automobiles and Motorcycles; Marine Science and Technology; Safety; and Travel and Tourism sections.

Mary Kathleen Geary, Public Services Librarian, Transportation Library, Northwestern University Library, 1970 Campus Dr., Evanston, IL 60208-2300; m-geary@northwestern.edu

Introduction

Humans have been pushing, pulling, toting, floating, and flying goods and people from one point to another throughout history. Transportation is as new as the finest jumbo jet and older than the beating of drums. This section vets all the major journals in transportation to provide a basis for a well-rounded collection on this ancient, ever new topic.

Basic Periodicals

Journal of Transport Economics and Policy, Journal of Transportation Engineering, Transportation Journal, Transportation Research. Parts A-F.

Basic Abstracts and Indexes

Compendex, Engineering Index, Transport, TRANweb (at http://tran.library.northwestern.edu/).

5133. *Air Cargo World: international trends and analysis.* Former titles (until 1983): *Air Cargo Magazine;* (until 1976): *Cargo Airlift; Air Transportation.* [ISSN: 0745-5100] 1910. m. USD 58 domestic; USD 78 foreign. Ed(s): Simon Keeble. U B M Aviation, 3025 Highland Pkwy, Ste 200, Downer's Grove, IL 60515; http://www.ubmaviation.com. Illus., index, adv. Circ: 41000 Controlled. Vol. ends: Dec. Microform: PQC. *Indexed:* ABIn, B01, B02. *Bk. rev.:* Occasional. *Aud.:* Sa.

This journal provides coverage of cargo services, carriers, facilities, equipment, and industry trends throughout the world. Regular features include articles, columns surveying news from regions around the world, updates on people in the industry, at-a-glance industry statistical indicators, and upcoming events. The web site will lead to full-text current and archived articles. Suitable for large general collections and special libraries. URL: www.aircargoworld.com

Air Transport World. See Aeronautics and Space Science section.

5134. *Airfinance Journal.* [ISSN: 0143-2257] 1980. 10x/yr. GBP 1015 combined subscription (print & online eds.); USD 1750 combined subscription (print & online eds.); EUR 1295 combined subscription (print & online eds.). Euromoney Institutional Investor Plc., Nestor House, Playhouse Yard, London, EC4V 5EX, United Kingdom; information@euromoneyplc.com; http://www.euromoneyplc.com/. Adv. Sample. Circ: 2830 Paid and controlled. *Indexed:* A22, ABIn, B01, B02, B03, BRI. *Aud.:* Sa.

This trade journal is geared toward both the practitioner and the researcher in the area of air transportation and finance. It includes feature articles, industry news, and important industry statistical tables; its coverage is international. A password is required to access the journal electronically. Appropriate for large, general collections and special collections. URL: www.airfinancejournal.com

5135. *Airline Business: the voice of airline managements.* [ISSN: 0268-7615] 1985. m. Free to qualified personnel. Ed(s): Mark Pilling. Reed Business Information Ltd., Quadrant House, The Quadrant, Sutton, SM2 5AS, United Kingdom; rbi.subscriptions@qss-uk.com; http://www.reedbusiness.co.uk/. Illus., adv. Circ: 22999. Vol. ends: Dec. *Indexed:* A22, ABIn, B01, B02, B03, C&ISA, CerAb, H&TI. *Aud.:* Sa.

This trade journal provides worldwide coverage of business affairs in all aspects of the airline industry. Topics include developments in regions of the world as well as in specific countries, analysis of policy changes, people who impact the industry, and financing issues. Regular features include commentary, news digests, events calendars, and new appointments. Annual features include the

"Airline Business 100" and "Airports Review." The primary audience is airline managers. There is an online version of the current issue. Appropriate for special collections. URL: www.flightglobal.com/ab

5136. Airline Monitor: a review of trends in the airline and commercial jet aircraft industries. 1988. m. USD 1100; USD 1300 combined subscription (print & online eds.). Ed(s): Edmund S Greanslet. E S G Aviation Services, PO Box 1781, Ponte Vedra Beach, FL 32004. *Aud.:* Ac, Sa.

Published by ESG Aviation Services, this periodical is a unique and thorough source of statistical and financial information on the domestic air transportation industry, including forecasting. It is geared toward the professional and the researcher. Each issue includes an executive summary followed by tables of data current within a month. The journal exists only online. A password is required to access the online version. Appropriate for academic or special libraries. URL: www.airlinemonitor.com

5137. Airliners & Airports Magazine: the world's airline magazine. Formerly (until 2011): *Airliners.* [ISSN: 2165-235X] 1988. bi-m. USD 26.95 domestic; USD 29.95 Canada; USD 38.95 (Mexico, Central and South America, Caribbean). Ed(s): Dwayne Darnell. Airliners Publications LLC, 6355 N W 36 St, Ste 600, Miami, FL 33166; subscriptions@airliners.tv . Illus., adv. Vol. ends: Nov/Dec. *Aud.:* Ga.

Targeting the commercial airline enthusiast, this publication offers detailed coverage of international, national, and local airlines, including industry news and events, local special-interest stories, and some statistical information. Airplane modeling and collecting are occasionally featured. The magazine includes color photography and elaborate layouts. Appropriate for general collections.

5138. Airlines International. Former titles (until 1994): *I A T A Review; I A T A News Review.* 1966. bi-m. Free. Ed(s): Graham Newton. Redactive Media Group, 17 Britton St, Clerkenwell, London, EC1M 5TP, United Kingdom; info@redactive.co.uk; http://www.redactive.co.uk. Circ: 8000. *Aud.:* Ga, Sa.

This journal covers the international commercial airline industry, emphasizing airline management, economics, current industry events, and some statistical information. Published for International Aviation Transport Association (IATA) members, this title is aimed at specialists and includes an IATA calendar of events and an "Insight on IATA" section. Appropriate for special collections.

5139. Airport Magazine. [ISSN: 1048-2091] 1989. 7x/yr. USD 50 domestic; USD 100 elsewhere. Ed(s): Barbara Cook. American Association of Airport Executives, 601 Madison St, Ste 400, Alexandria, VA 22314; http://www.aaae.org/. Illus., index, adv. Vol. ends: Nov/Dec. *Aud.:* Sa.

This publication of the American Association of Airport Executives is for specialists, as it addresses airport management, legislation, technology, research reports, economics, and current industry events. It features some statistics as well as requests for proposals. There is an online version. Appropriate for special collections. URL: http://airportmagazine.net

5140. Airport World. Formerly (until 1996): *Airlines International.* [ISSN: 1360-4341] 1995. bi-m. Insight Media Ltd., Sovereign House, 26-30 London Rd, Twickenham, TW1 3RW, United Kingdom. Illus., adv. *Aud.:* Sa.

Published for the Airports Council International, this journal addresses global airport issues. Geared to the practitioner, it covers industry news and events, technology, safety, automation, the environment, legislation, regulation, airport planning and maintenance, management, and finance. Each issue includes feature articles, a calendar of events, airport traffic data and other statistics, project briefs, a section highlighting a specific airport, and a global airport news section. There are annotated tables of contents for current and archived issues online. Appropriate for special collections. URL: www.airport-world.com/

5141. Airports International Magazine. Former titles (until 1971): *Airports International Directory;* (until 1968): *Airports International.* 1968. 9x/yr. GBP 95 (Free to qualified personnel). Ed(s): Tom Allett. Key Publishing Ltd., PO Box 300, Stamford, PE9 1NA, United Kingdom; info@keypublishing.com; http://www.keypublishing.com. Adv. Sample. *Indexed:* B03, BRI. *Aud.:* Sa.

This publication is international in coverage and is geared to the specialist. It addresses current airport trends, news and events, economics, and technology. An annotated table of contents for the current and archived issues is available online. This magazine is appropriate for special collections. URL: www.airportsinternational.co.uk.

5142. American Shipper: ports, transportation and industry. Former titles (until 1991): *American shipper international;* (until 1990): *American Shipper Magazine;* (until 1976): *Florida Journal of Commerce - American Shipper;* (until 1974): *Florida Journal of Commerce.* [ISSN: 1074-8350] 1959. m. USD 120 domestic; USD 365 foreign. Ed(s): Gary Burrows, Christopher Gillis. Howard Publications, 200 W Forsyth St, Ste 1000, Jacksonville, FL 32202; publisher@shippers.com; http://www.howardpub.com. Illus., adv. Vol. ends: Dec. Microform: PQC. *Indexed:* A22, B02, B03, BRI, OceAb. *Aud.:* Sa.

This trade journal targets the practitioner and is international in coverage. Each issue addresses seven subjects of interest: logistics, forwarding, integrated transport, ocean transport, land transport, NVOs, and ports. There are also sections on shippers' case law and corporate appointments. The online version of the current issue of this journal requires a password. Appropriate for special libraries. URL: www.americanshipper.com

Aviation Week and Space Technology. See Aeronautics and Space Science section.

5143. Better Roads. [ISSN: 0006-0208] 1931. m. Free to qualified personnel. Ed(s): John Latta. Randall-Reilly Publishing Company, 3200 Rice Mine Rd NE, Tuscaloosa, AL 35406; http://www.randallpub.com. Illus., adv. Circ: 40000. Vol. ends: Dec. *Indexed:* A22, C&ISA, CerAb, EngInd. *Bk. rev.:* Number and length vary. *Aud.:* Sa.

Published by James Informational Media for specialists in the fields of road construction, maintenance, and repair, this journal includes industry news, government contract information, book and video reviews, product ratings and reviews, a calendar of industry events, and a forum for letters and professional comment, along with technically-rich feature articles. The December issue contains a pull-out calendar of industry events for the entire year. Archived articles, dating back to 1998, can be accessed online. Appropriate for engineering and transportation collections. URL: www.betterroads.com

5144. Bridge Design & Engineering. [ISSN: 1359-7493] 1995. q. GBP 105 combined subscription (print & online eds.); EUR 168 combined subscription (print & online eds.); USD 216 combined subscription (print & online eds.). Ed(s): Helena Russell. Hemming Information Services Ltd., 32 Vauxhall Bridge Rd, London, SW1V 2SS, United Kingdom; info@hgluk.com; http://www.hgluk.com. Illus., adv. *Indexed:* B02, BRI. *Bk. rev.:* 2-4, 150-250 words. *Aud.:* Ac, Sa.

This journal targets the practitioner. It is international in coverage and addresses bridge aesthetics, design, construction, and management. It includes feature articles, industry news, product information, a calendar of events, and listings of conferences and competitions. There is an online version, and the archive of full-text articles extends back to 2003. Appropriate for special libraries. URL: www.bridgeweb.com

5145. Bus Ride. [ISSN: 0192-8902] 1965. m. USD 39 domestic; USD 42 Canada; USD 75 elsewhere. Ed(s): Steve Kane, David Hubbard. Power Trade Media, LLC, 4742 N 24th St, Ste 340, Phoenix, AZ 85016. Illus., adv. Sample. Circ: 16000. Vol. ends: Dec. *Aud.:* Sa.

This journal addresses the passenger bus industries of the United States and Canada and is meant for bus and transit specialists. It includes current industry news and events, legislative and regulatory information, product reviews, feature articles, and a report on the European passenger-bus industry. The current issue of the journal and some archived issues can be accessed online. A password is necessary for the archives. Appropriate for special collections. URL: www.busride.com

5146. Business and Commercial Aviation. Incorporates (in 2004): *A C Flyer;* Formerly (until 1966): *Business and Commercial Aviation.* [ISSN: 1538-7267] 1958. m. USD 54 combined subscription domestic (print & online eds.); USD 62 combined subscription Canada (print & online eds.); USD 79 combined subscription elsewhere (print & online eds.). Ed(s): Frank Jackman. Aviation Week Group, 2 Penn Plz, 25th Fl, New York, NY 10121; buccustserv@cdsfulfillment.com; http://www.aviationweek.com. Illus., adv. Circ: 50720 Paid. Microform: PQC. *Indexed:* A22, ABIn, B01, B02, B03, BRI. *Aud.:* Sa.

This trade journal targets the practitioner and addresses the commercial aviation industry with a decided emphasis on business flying. Its coverage is international. Each issue includes industry news and events, feature articles, statistics, commentary, product reviews, classifieds, a resale marketplace, and a section devoted to the causes of accidents. There is an online version. Appropriate for special libraries. URL: www.AviationWeek.com/bca

5147. Commercial Carrier Journal. Incorporates (in 1999): *Trucking Company;* Former titles (until 1999): *Commercial Carrier Journal for Professional Fleet Managers;* (until 1997): *Chilton's Commercial Carrier Journal for Professional Fleet Managers;* (until 1990): *Commercial Carrier Journal for Professional Fleet Managers;* (until 1989): *Chilton's C C J;* (until 1984): *Chilton's Commercial Carrier Journal;* (until 1982): *Chilton's C C J;* (until 1977): *Commercial Car Journal.* [ISSN: 1533-7502] 1911. m. USD 48 domestic (Free to qualified personnel). Ed(s): Jeff Crissey. Randall-Reilly Publishing Company, 3200 Rice Mine Rd NE, Tuscaloosa, AL 35406; http://www.randallpub.com. Illus., index, adv. Circ: 96500. Vol. ends: Dec. Microform: CIS; PQC. *Indexed:* A22, B01, B03, BRI. *Aud.:* Sa.

One of the important trade journals in the truck fleet–management industry, this publication contains articles on operations, equipment maintenance, management, regulation, and safety. Regular features include road tests of vehicles, industry news, events and editorials, and a classified section. This title annually provides a "Midyear Report" on a themed topic. Also published is the best 250 fleets of the current year. The current month's issue, and archived cover stories, can be accessed online. Appropriate for special libraries. URL: www.ccjdigital.com/magazine/

5148. Community Transportation. Former titles (until 1997): *Community Transportation Reporter;* (until 1987): *Rural Transportation Reporter.* 1983. bi-m. Free to members. Ed(s): Scott Bogren. Community Transportation Association of America, 1341 G St, NW, 10th Fl, Washington, DC 20005; http://web1.ctaa.org/webmodules/webarticles/anmviewer.asp?a=23&z=2. Illus., index, adv. Circ: 15000. Vol. ends: Nov/Dec. *Bk. rev.:* Number and length vary. *Aud.:* Ga, Sa.

Published by the Community Transportation Association of America, this journal addresses all forms of community transportation: bus, rail, and paratransit. Geared toward the specialist, it would be of use to interested community members. It includes current industry news and events, legislation and regulatory matters, available resources, and feature articles. A substantial annual book review section is published in the July/August issue. This journal has gone digital and can be viewed online. URL: www.ctaa.org

5149. Containerisation International. Incorporates (2009-2010): *Reefer International;* Which was formerly (2006-2009): *R Q;* (1994-2010): *Cargo Systems;* Which was formerly (1973-1994): *Cargo Systems International;* (until 1973): *I C H C A Monthly Journal;* Which was formed by the merger of: *International Cargo Handling Coordination; I C H C A Quarterly Journal.* [ISSN: 0010-7379] 1967. m. GBP 845 combined subscription domestic (print & online eds.); EUR 1105 combined subscription in Europe (print & online eds.); USD 1640

combined subscription elsewhere (print & online eds.). Ed(s): Matthew Beddow. Informa Cargo Information, 4th Fl, 119 Farringdon Rd, London EC1R 3DA, EC1R 3DA, United Kingdom; informacargo@informa.com; http://www.informacargo.com. Illus., adv. Circ: 10000. Vol. ends: Dec. *Indexed:* A22. *Aud.:* Sa.

This publication covers the worldwide containerization business, management, and policy issues for a variety of transportation modes, but with an emphasis on shipping and ports. The feature articles cover specific carriers; analysis of some aspect of the industry; issues for carriers, shippers, and terminals; regional coverage; and regulatory analysis. Each issue contains updates on business, the world fleet, charters, shippers, and news on intermodal transport, terminals, information technology, and statistics on key industry indicators. The web site offers late-breaking news; for full content, a password is required. Appropriate for special collections. URL: www.containershipping.com

5150. Fleet Owner. Formerly: *Fleet Owner: Big Fleet Edition;* Superseded in part: *Fleet Owner.* [ISSN: 1070-194X] 1928. m. USD 75 domestic (Free to qualified personnel). Ed(s): Jim Mele, Brian Straight. Penton Media, Inc., 11 River Bend Dr South, PO Box 4949, Stamford, CT 06907-0949; information@penton.com; http://www.pentonmedia.com. Illus., adv. Circ: 105000 Controlled. Vol. ends: Dec. Microform: PQC. *Indexed:* A22, ABIn, B01, B02, B03, BRI. *Aud.:* Sa.

This journal targets the specialist and addresses the public and private sectors of truck fleet management. Coverage includes fleet management industry news and events, equipment, management, information technology, legislation, safety, and product analysis. It devotes significant attention to information technology. The online version of this journal requires a password. Appropriate for special collections. URL: http://fleetowner.com

Flight International. See Aeronautics and Space Science section.

5151. Great Lakes/Seaway Review: the international transportation magazine of midcontinent North America. Former titles: *Great Lakes Seaway Log;* (until 1998): *Seaway Review;* Which incorporated (1968-1977): *Limnos.* 1970. q. USD 32. Ed(s): Janenne Irene Pung. Harbor House Publishers, Inc., 221 Water St, Boyne City, MI 49712; harbor@harborhouse.com; http://www.harborhouse.com. Illus., adv. Vol. ends: Apr/Jun. Microform: PQC. *Indexed:* A22. *Aud.:* Ga, Sa.

This journal addresses commercial shipping and the maritime industries throughout the Great Lakes and St. Lawrence Seaway areas. Coverage includes shipping industry news and events, legislation and regulation, technology, naval architecture and engineering, ports, import/export, fleet data, and feature articles. Each issue highlights a specific port. The "Shipyard Report" section is a unique feature: broken down by marine repair or shipbuilding company, it supplies the name of the vessel, owner, nature of work being done, and anticipated date of completion. The magazine *Great Laker,* devoted to lighthouses, lake boats, and travel and leisure, has been incorporated into the *Great Lakes Seaway Review.* An index to past issues can be accessed online. Appropriate for a large general collection interested in the Great Lakes or a special collection. URL: www.greatlakes-seawayreview.com

5152. I E E E Transactions on Intelligent Transportation Systems. [ISSN: 1524-9050] 2000. q. USD 620; USD 745 combined subscription (print & online eds.). Ed(s): Fei-Yue Wang. Institute of Electrical and Electronics Engineers, 445 Hoes Ln, Piscataway, NJ 08854; contactcenter@ieee.org; http://www.ieee.org. Adv. Refereed. *Indexed:* A22, C&ISA, CerAb, EngInd, H24. *Aud.:* Ac, Sa.

This scholarly publication focuses on the application of information technology to systems across all modes of transportation. Some of the topics it considers include communications, sensors, man/machine interfaces, decision systems, controls, simulation, reliability, and standards. Frequently, issues of the journal focus on a specific subject. This journal exists only online. URL: http://ieeexplore.ieee.org/xpl/mostRecentIssue.jsp?punumber=6979

5153. I H S Fairplay: the source for maritime information and insight. Former titles (until 2011): *Fairplay;* (until 1992): *Fairplay International;* (until 1989): *Fairplay International Shipping Weekly;* (until 1974): *Fairplay International Shipping Journal;* (until 1966): *Fairplay Shipping*

Journal; (until 1962): *Fairplay Weekly Shipping Journal.* [ISSN: 2048-3538] 1883. s-m. GBP 530. I H S Fairplay, Lombard House, 3 Princess Way, Redhill, RH1 1UP, United Kingdom; info@lrfairplay.com; http://www.fairplay-publications.co.uk. Illus., adv. Sample. Vol. ends: Apr/Dec. *Aud.:* Sa.

This journal is devoted to the international shipping industry and covers industry news and events, including shipbuilding and port news, legislation, regulation, safety, labor and management issues, liner operations, ship sales, and cargo information. Feature articles tend to be brief news flashes, except for the cover story. In addition to international coverage, each issue highlights the shipping industry within a specific nation or region. The section on the shipping market includes graphs, tables, and statistics. The online version of the journal requires a password. Appropriate for a large business collection or a transportation collection. URL: www.fairplay.co.uk/ThisWeek.aspx

5154. *I H S Jane's Airport Review: the global airport business magazine.* Formerly (until 2011): *Jane's Airport Review.* [ISSN: 2048-3465] 1988. m. GBP 200 domestic; EUR 245 in Europe; USD 315 elsewhere. Ed(s): Ben Vogel. I H S Jane's, 163 Brighton Rd, Coulsdon, CR5 2YH, United Kingdom; info@janes.co.uk; http://www.ihs.com. Illus. Vol. ends: Nov/Dec. *Indexed:* ABIn, C&ISA, CerAb, EngInd, H24. *Aud.:* Sa.

This journal covers airport business, addressing market intelligence and strategic planning. Its audience is airport management professionals. Coverage is international. Regular features include sections on news, air traffic control, terminal and ground support equipment, and interviews with leading professionals. The journal's online version can be accessed via password. Appropriate for special libraries. URL: www.ihs.com/products/janes/transport/airport-review.aspx

5155. *I T E Journal.* Former titles (until 1978): *Transportation Engineering;* (until 1977): *Traffic Engineering;* (until 1937): *Traffic Digest.* [ISSN: 0162-8178] 1930. m. Free to members; Non-members, USD 65. Ed(s): Newton D Holt. Institute of Transportation Engineers, 1099 14th St, NW Ste 300 W, Washington, DC 20005; ite_staff@ite.org; http://www.ite.org/. Illus., adv. Refereed. Circ: 17367. Vol. ends: Dec. Microform: PQC. *Indexed:* A22, ABIn, C&ISA, CerAb, EngInd, H24. *Bk. rev.:* Occasional, up to 250 words. *Aud.:* Ac, Sa.

Written by and for transportation engineers and planners, this refereed journal thoroughly covers the field of surface transportation. It focuses largely on North America, particularly the United States, but occasionally includes features from other parts of the world. Regular features include news on people, projects, places, and research, as well as resources available; a calendar of events and meetings; and positions available. The web site offers a searchable index back to 1950 and full-text articles back to 1970, but a password is required. Appropriate for special collections. URL: www.ite.org/itejournal/index.asp

5156. *I T S International: advanced technology for traffic management and urban mobility.* Formerly (until 1996): *I T S - Intelligent Transport Systems.* [ISSN: 1463-6344] 1995. bi-m. Free to qualified personnel. Ed(s): Jason Barnes. Route One Publishing Ltd., Horizon House, Azalea Dr, Swanley, BR8 8JR, United Kingdom; media@ropl.com; http://www.routeonepub.com. Illus. Sample. *Aud.:* Sa.

This journal addresses the specialist in the international intelligent transportation systems (ITS) industry. The journal's major areas are traffic management and urban mobility. Its coverage includes ITS industry news and events, technology, product analysis and review, and feature articles on highlighted ITS issues such as telematics, tolling systems, or multi-modal systems. Each issue includes a focus on the ITS industry within a specific geographic area, a current-events section, and a listing of appointments and promotions within the field. Feature articles from the annual buyers' guide, as well as the full-text articles, can be found online. Appropriate for engineering and transportation collections. URL: www.itsinternational.com

5157. *Inbound Logistics: the magazine for demand-driven logistic.* Former titles (until 1990): *Thomas Register's Inbound Logistics;* (until 1985): *Inbound Traffic Guide;* (until 1983): *Thomas Register's Inbound Traffic Guide for Industrial Buyers & Specifiers.* 1981. m. USD 95 in North

America (Free to qualified personnel). Ed(s): Felecia J Stratton. Thomas Publishing Company (New York), Five Penn Plz, New York, NY 10001; contact@thomaspublishing.com; http://www.thomaspublishing.com. Illus., adv. Sample. Circ: 60000. Vol. ends: Dec. *Indexed:* C&ISA, CerAb. *Aud.:* Sa.

Geared to the specialist, this journal addresses the international logistics industry. Coverage includes logistics industry news and events, technology, business management, personnel management, legislation, and feature articles; a strong emphasis is placed on e-commerce and information technology. Special sections address logistics in the Americas, the Pacific community, and the European community. A voluminous supplementary issue, "Logistics Planner," is published in January. Each issue includes a calendar of logistics industry events and a section devoted to evaluating logistics-oriented web sites. Available online. Appropriate for special collections. URL: www.inboundlogistics.com

5158. *International Journal of Automotive Technology and Management.* [ISSN: 1470-9511] 2001. 4x/yr. EUR 494 (print or online eds.). Ed(s): Jean-Jacques Chanaron, Dr. Giuseppe Giulio Calabrese. Inderscience Publishers, PO Box 735, Olney, MK46 5WB, United Kingdom; editorial@inderscience.com; http://www.inderscience.com. Illus. Sample. Refereed. *Indexed:* ABIn, B01, B02, BRI, C&ISA, CerAb, EngInd, ErgAb, RiskAb. *Bk. rev.:* Number and length vary. *Aud.:* Ac, Sa.

This is a refereed scholarly journal targeting the academician. It addresses all aspects of international automotive technology and management, including product development, research, innovative management, e-commerce, supply chain management, reengineering, efficiency, safety, investment and business, and human resources. Each issue contains referenced articles, charts, graphs, statistics, calls for papers, and a complete index. Some issues contain book reviews. Available online, by subscription. Appropriate for large academic libraries or special collections. URL: www.inderscience.com/jhome.php?jcode=IJATM

5159. *International Journal of Logistics: research and applications.* [ISSN: 1367-5567] 1998. bi-m. GBP 686 (print & online eds.). Ed(s): Dr. Tony Whiteing. Taylor & Francis, 4 Park Sq, Milton Park, Abingdon, OX14 4RN, United Kingdom; http://www.tandfonline.com. Illus., adv. Sample. Refereed. Vol. ends: Nov. Reprint: PSC. *Indexed:* A22, B01, C&ISA, CerAb, E01. *Aud.:* Ac, Sa.

This refereed scholarly journal addresses all aspects of the international logistics industry, including intermodal transportation, warehousing, and supply chain management; it is of interest to both the academician and the practitioner. Each issue includes lengthy research articles that have references, graphs, tables, and charts. The journal can be accessed online, from 1990 forward. Appropriate for academic and special collections. URL: www.tandfonline.com/doi/full/10.1080/13675567.2013.809708#.UeWynUqOksg

5160. *International Journal of Transport Economics.* [ISSN: 0303-5247] 1974. 3x/yr. EUR 695 (print & online eds.). Fabrizio Serra Editore, c/o Accademia Editoriale, Via Santa Bibbiana 28, Pisa, 56127, Italy; accademiaeditoriale@accademiaeditoriale.it; http://www.libraweb.net. Illus., index, adv. Refereed. Circ: 1000. Vol. ends: Oct. *Indexed:* A22, JEL. *Bk. rev.:* 7-12, 100-350 words. *Aud.:* Ac, Sa.

This journal, published in Italy but with a worldwide focus, brings together current research in transport economics, uniting theoretical and applied approaches to the subject. Occasional special issues are devoted to a single topic. The editorial board and the authors of the articles come from around the world. The journal is published in English, with some supporting information also included in Italian. In addition to contributed scholarly articles, it features a review article that extends the theoretical discussion to the practical realm. There is a book review section. Available online. Appropriate for special collections. URL: www.libraweb.net/riviste.php?chiave=67

5161. *International Railway Journal.* Former titles (until 2001): *International Railway Journal and Rapid Transit Review;* (until 1979): *International Railway Journal.* [ISSN: 2161-7376] 1960. m. Free. Ed(s): Luther S Miller. Simmons-Boardman Publishing Corp., 345 Hudson St, New York, NY 10014; http://www.simmonsboardman.com/. Illus., index. Sample. Vol. ends: Dec. *Indexed:* ABIn, B02. *Aud.:* Ac, Sa.

This journal covers the international light-track and heavy-track railroad industries; it is the international version of its sister periodicals for North America, *Railway Age* and *Railway Track and Structures*. Each issue is divided between a section on heavy-rail and a section on light-rail, intraurban, and interurban rapid transit. These sections include industry news and events, world market reports, feature articles, a list of conferences and seminars, a product showcase, and a list of relevant web sites. Maps of the referenced rail lines are often included in feature articles. The subscription includes an annual supplement, *World Railway Investment*, which offers financial data and statistics. The journal can be accessed online. Of interest to both the academician and the practitioner, it is appropriate for large academic collections and special collections. URL: www.railjournal.com

5162. *Journal of Advanced Transportation.* Formerly (until vol.12, 1979): *High Speed Ground Transportation Journal.* [ISSN: 0197-6729] 1967. 3x/yr. GBP 381. Ed(s): S Chan Wirasinghe, William H K Lam. John Wiley & Sons, Inc., 111 River St, MS 4-02, Hoboken, NJ 07030; info@wiley.com; http://www.wiley.com/WileyCDA/. Illus., index. Refereed. Circ: 300 Paid. Vol. ends: Winter. Microform: MIM; PQC. *Indexed:* A01, A22, ApMecR, B02, C&ISA, CerAb, EngInd, H24. *Bk. rev.:* Occasional. *Aud.:* Ac, Sa.

This scholarly journal, sponsored by the Advanced Transit Association, covers all modes of transportation. The focus is on the engineering and technology behind the analysis, design, economics, operations, and planning of transportation systems. Although the focus of the journal has broadened over the past several years, the editors maintain a special interest in advanced urban rail-transit systems. Occasionally, issues focus on a special topic and may include review articles that provide an overall survey of an aspect of the field. The web site features a searchable index of issues back to 1990. Appropriate for special collections. Online version accessed via login and password. URL: http://onlinelibrary.wiley.com/journal/10.1002/%28ISSN%292042-3195

5163. *Journal of Air Law and Commerce.* Formerly (until 1939): *The Journal of Air Law.* [ISSN: 0021-8642] 1930. q. USD 43 domestic; USD 50 foreign; USD 16 per issue. Ed(s): Katharine Lavalley, Denise Johnston. Southern Methodist University, S M U Law Review Association, Southern Methodist University, Dedman School of Law, P O Box 750116, Dallas, TX 75275; browning@smu.edu; http://www.smu.edu. Illus., index. Refereed. Vol. ends: Fall. Microform: WSH; PMC; PQC. Reprint: WSH. *Indexed:* A22, BRI, CLI, L14. *Bk. rev.:* Occasional. *Aud.:* Ac, Sa.

This scholarly publication covers the legal and economic aspects of aviation and space. The journal is managed by a student board of editors in association with the *Southern Methodist University Law Review*. The issues include comprehensive articles, a review of current-interest topics, and book reviews. Articles are written by lawyers, economists, government officials, and scholars. List of archived articles available online. Appropriate for special and academic libraries. URL: http://smu.edu/lra/Journals/JALC/Current.asp

5164. *Journal of Air Transport Management: an international journal of research, policy and practice.* [ISSN: 0969-6997] 1994. 8x/yr. EUR 953. Ed(s): K Button. Pergamon, The Blvd, Langford Ln, E Park, Kidlington, OX5 1GB, United Kingdom; JournalsCustomerServiceEMEA@elsevier.com; http://www.elsevier.com. Illus., adv. Sample. Refereed. Microform: PQC. *Indexed:* ErgAb, H&TI, H24, RiskAb. *Bk. rev.:* Occasional; number and length vary. *Aud.:* Ac, Sa.

Published by Elsevier Science, this refereed journal is of interest to both the academician and the practitioner. It addresses theory and application relative to all aspects of the international air transportation industry, including airlines, infrastructure, airports, traffic control, and management. Each issue consists of lengthy research articles that include graphs, tables, statistics, and detailed references. Some issues offer a book review section. The journal has been issued only in electronic format since 2003 and must be accessed online by subscribers. Appropriate for special and academic collections. URL: www.elsevier.com/locate/jairtraman

The Journal of Commerce. See Business and Finance/International section.

5165. *Journal of Maritime Law and Commerce.* [ISSN: 0022-2410] 1969. q. USD 250 (Individuals, USD 215). Ed(s): Edward V Cattell, Jr. Jefferson Law Book Co., 2100 Huntingdon Ave, Baltimore, MD 21211. Illus., index. Refereed. Reprint: WSH. *Indexed:* A01, A22, BRI, CLI, L14, S25. *Bk. rev.:* 1-25, 500-2,500 words, signed. *Aud.:* Ac, Sa.

This scholarly journal is dedicated to coverage of all aspects of admiralty and maritime law. It targets the professional and the academician. Its contents concentrate on topics of current interest, but the editorial board also includes historical or theoretical treatments of the field. Special issues on single topics are often published. Occasionally, it is possible to find case analyses, review articles, and bibliographies. This journal's table of contents is available online. Full text is available online by subscription. Appropriate for special collections. URL: www.jmlc.org

5166. *Journal of Public Transportation.* [ISSN: 1077-291X] 1997. q. Ed(s): Gary L Brosch. University of South Florida, Center for Urban Transportation Research, College of Engineering, 4202 E Fowler Ave, CUT100, Tampa, FL 33620-5375; http://www.cutr.usf.edu/. *Indexed:* H24, RiskAb. *Aud.:* Ac, Sa.

Presenting new case studies and original research, this journal covers public-transportation modes and related policies from all over the world. The journal strives to present papers with innovative solutions; approaches can come from any number of disciplines, including engineering, management, and others. The journal is provided free by the Center for Urban Transportation Research at the University of South Florida. Available online. Appropriate for special collections. URL: www.nctr.usf.edu/jpt/journal.htm

5167. *Journal of Transport Economics and Policy.* [ISSN: 0022-5258] 1967. 3x/yr. GBP 170 (print & online eds.) Individuals, GBP 50 (print & online eds.). Ed(s): Steven A Morrison, D N Starkie. University of Bath, Claverton Down, Bath, BA2 7AY, United Kingdom; education@bath.ac.uk; http://www.bath.ac.uk. Illus. Refereed. Reprint: PSC. *Indexed:* A22, ABIn, AmHI, B01, B02, BAS, BRI, EIP, EconLit, IBSS, JEL. *Bk. rev.:* Occasional, 150-1,500 words, signed. *Aud.:* Ac, Sa.

This scholarly journal focuses on research on economics and policy for intercity and urban transportation. The editorial board, the authors, and the topics they present are international in scope. Occasionally, issues of the journal cover a single topic in depth. Available online to subscribers. Appropriate for special collections. URL: www.bath.ac.uk/e-journals/jtep/online.html

5168. *Journal of Transport Geography: the international journal focusing on transport and spatial change.* [ISSN: 0966-6923] 1993. 8x/yr. EUR 747. Ed(s): Richard Knowles. Pergamon, The Blvd, Langford Ln, E Park, Kidlington, OX5 1GB, United Kingdom; JournalsCustomerServiceEMEA@elsevier.com; http://www.elsevier.com. Illus., adv. Sample. Refereed. Microform: PQC. *Indexed:* A01, A22, B01, H&TI, H24, OceAb, RiskAb. *Bk. rev.:* 1-5, 500-1,500 words, signed. *Aud.:* Ac, Sa.

This scholarly, refereed publication addresses transport geography and spatial change and land use, including transport policies, infrastructure, operations, and transport networks. Each issue features referenced research articles with bibliographies, charts, graphs, and maps; a viewpoint article; and book reviews. The coverage is international and geared toward the professional and the academician. The journal now appears only online through Elsevier ScienceDirect. Appropriate for special collections. URL: www.sciencedirect.com/science/journal/09666923

5169. *Journal of Transportation Engineering.* Formerly (until 1983): *American Society of Civil Engineers. Transportation Engineering Journal;* Which was formed by the merger of (1962-1969): *American Society of Civil Engineers. Aero-Space Transport Division. Journal;* Which was formerly (until 1962): *American Society of Civil Engineers. Air Transport Division. Journal;* (1956-1969): *American Society of Civil Engineers. Highway Division. Journal;* (1957-1969): *American Society of Civil Engineers. Pipeline Division. Journal;* All of which superseded in part (1873-1956): *American Society of Civil Engineers. Proceedings.* [ISSN: 0733-947X] 1969. m. USD 1026. Ed(s): Chris T Hendrickson,

Laurence R Rilett. American Society of Civil Engineers, 1801 Alexander Bell Dr, Reston, VA 20191; http://www.asce.org. Illus., index, adv. Refereed. Vol. ends: Nov/Dec. Microform: PQC. *Indexed:* A01, A22, BRI, C&ISA, CerAb, EngInd, H24, P02, RiskAb. *Aud.:* Ac, Sa.

This scholarly journal is published by the American Society of Civil Engineers and is geared to the academician and the practitioner. It addresses all transportation modalities, and covers the construction and maintenance of roads, bridges, airports, and pipelines; traffic management; business management; technology; and transportation economics. Each issue includes lengthy research articles with diagrams, charts, tables, and detailed references. Current and archived issues can be accessed online. Appropriate for large academic libraries and special collections. URL: http://ascelibrary.org/teo

5170. *Journal of Transportation Law, Logistics and Policy.* Former titles (until 1994): *Transportation Practitioners Journal;* (until 1984): *I C C Practitioners' Journal;* (until 1933): *Practitioners' Journal;* (until 19??): *Association of Practitioners Before the Interstate Commerce Commission;* (until 1931): *I C C Practitioners' Quarterly Bulletin.* [ISSN: 1078-5906] 19??. q. Free to members; Non-members, USD 100. Ed(s): James F Bromley. Association for Transportation Law, Logistics and Policy, c/o Lauren Michalski, PO Box 5407, Annapolis, MD 21403; info@atlp.org; http://www.atlp.org. Illus., index, adv. Vol. ends: Summer. Microform: WSH; PMC. *Indexed:* A22, ABIn, B01, BRI, CLI, L14. *Bk. rev.:* Occasional, 1,200-2,000 words, signed. *Aud.:* Ac, Sa.

Published by the Association for Transportation Law, Logistics, and Policy (ATLLP), this scholarly, peer-reviewed journal includes articles on transportation law, practice, legislation, regulation, history, theory, logistics, economics, and statistics. It is geared to the professional and the academician. Coverage is focused on North America, but occasionally articles on other areas of the world will be included. Every issue includes updates on recent administrative and regulatory developments. Alternate issues contain book reviews and the ATLLP schedule of events. Available online; the archives can be accessed with a password. Appropriate for special libraries. URL: www.atlp.org/journal.html

Journal of Travel Research. See Travel and Tourism/Research section.

5171. *Logistics Management.* Formerly (until Jun.2002): *Logistics Management & Distribution Report;* Which was formed by the merger (1996-1997): *Logistics Management;* Which was formerly (until 1996): *Traffic Management;* (1992-1997): *Distribution;* Which was formerly (until 1992): *Chilton's Distribution;* (until 1986): *Chilton's Distribution for Traffic and Transportation Decision Makers;* (until 1980): *Chilton's Distribution;* (until 1979): *Chilton's Distribution Worldwide;* (until 1977): *Distribution Worldwide;* (until 1972): *Chilton's Distribution Worldwide;* (until 1970): *Distribution Worldwide;* (until 1969): *Distribution Manager;* (until 1967): *Physical Distribution Manager;* (until 1966): *Distribution Age;* (until 1945): *D and W;* (until 1937): *Distribution & Warehousing;* (until 1920): *Transfer & Storage;* (until 1915): *Team Owners Review.* [ISSN: 1540-3890] 1997. m. Plus annual directory. Free to qualified personnel. E H Publishing, Inc., 111 Speen St, Ste 200, PO Box 989, Framingham, MA 01701; info@ehpub.com; http://www.ehpub.com. Illus., adv. Circ: 74060. Microform: PQC. *Indexed:* A22, ABIn, B01, B02, B03, BRI, C42. *Aud.:* Ac, Sa.

This trade journal provides strong coverage in the areas of transportation operations and policy. Although the focus is on the United States, some coverage is provided on export–import and overseas shipments. Feature articles include company case studies, multipart articles, impacts of government policies and actions, economic analysis, new services, and innovative business practices. The journal includes a large array of monthly columns on various aspects of the industry, e.g., acquisitions, express carriers, railroads, air freight, regulation, etc. It also includes news summaries, economic indicators, and product and equipment notices, as well as an annual salary survey. Other regular annual features include polls and buyers' guides. The journal is available online. Appropriate for special collections. URL: www.logisticsmgmt.com

5172. *Low-Fare & Regional Airlines.* Former titles (until 2006): *Regional Airline World;* (until 1998): *Commuter World;* Which incorporated (1993-199?): *Regional Air International;* Which was formerly (until 1993): *Commuter Air International;* (1979-1990): *Commuter Air.* [ISSN:

1753-0598] 1984. 10x/yr. USD 160 Free to qualified personnel. Ed(s): Bernie Baldwin. Shephard Press Ltd., 268 Bath Rd, Slough, SL1 4DX, United Kingdom; info@shephard.co.uk; http://www.shephard.co.uk. Adv. *Aud.:* Sa.

This journal addresses the regional and low-cost airline industry worldwide and is geared to the practitioner. Coverage includes industry news and events, finances, management and mergers, personnel, technology, and training. Each issue includes a significant international news section, feature articles, the profile of a specific airline, and a calendar of events. Archives of recent articles can be found online. Appropriate for special collections. URL: www.LARAnews.net

5173. *Mass Transit: better transit through better management.* [ISSN: 0364-3484] 1974. 8x/yr. USD 59 domestic (Free to qualified personnel). Ed(s): Fred Jandt. Cygnus Business Media, Inc., 1233 Janesville Ave, PO Box 803, Fort Atkinson, WI 53538; http://www.cygnus.com. Illus., adv. Circ: 21206. Vol. ends: Nov/Dec. *Indexed:* A22, ABIn, B02, B03, BRI, EIP. *Aud.:* Sa.

This trade publication addresses mass transit for the management practitioner. The journal's focus is on North America, although there is some international coverage. Feature article topics include management, policy, operations, and equipment. Each issue also includes industry news, legal notes, a forum for transit managers, a calendar of events, and classified ads. Available online. Appropriate for special collections. URL: www.MassTransitmag.com

5174. *Metro Magazine.* Former titles: *Metro (Torrance);* (until 1994): *Metro Magazine;* (until 1985): *Metro;* (until 1974): *Metropolitan.* 1904. 10x/yr. USD 40 domestic; USD 60 in Canada & Mexico; USD 100 elsewhere. Ed(s): Janna Starcic, Alex Roman. Bobit Business Media, 3520 Challenger St, Torrance, CA 90503; order@bobit.com; http://www.bobitbusinessmedia.com. Illus., adv. Circ: 20616 Controlled. Vol. ends: Nov/Dec. *Indexed:* B02, BRI, F01. *Aud.:* Sa.

This journal, covering national and international urban and interurban transportation systems, targets the practitioner. It addresses all major urban transportation issues: bus systems, light rail, motor coaches, intelligent transportation systems, high-speed rail, urban transit management, finance, and legislation. Each issue includes industry news and events, feature articles, editorials, product and innovation showcases, a calendar of events, and an industry personnel section. The last issue of the year includes a tear-out calendar that highlights dates of industry interest. There is an annual "Top 50 Motorcoach Fleets" list. The journal's online version and archived articles can be accessed. Appropriate for special collections. URL: www.metro-magazine.com

5175. *The Motor Ship.* Former titles (until 1957): *The British Motor Ship;* (until 19??): *Motor Ship.* [ISSN: 0027-2000] 1920. m. 11/yr. GBP 133.50 (Free to qualified personnel). Ed(s): Bill Thomson. Mercator Media Ltd., The Old Mill, Lower Quay, Fareham, PO16 0RA, United Kingdom; corporate@mercatormedia.com; http://www.mercatormedia.com. Illus., index, adv. Circ: 7124. Vol. ends: Dec. *Indexed:* A22, B02, B03, BRI, C&ISA, CerAb, EngInd, OceAb. *Aud.:* Sa.

This publication provides news and in-depth coverage of all aspects of the marine industry. The feature articles are often investigative and include coverage of new buildings, in-depth country reviews, descriptions of ships, and exhibition previews. Regular columns cover news on cruise ships, propulsion, and ship repair, as well as equipment, updates on movers and shakers in the industry, and an events calendar. A quarterly supplement covers all aspects of ship repair and usually includes a directory of ship-repair yards. Other supplements cover cargo management, port infrastructure, and cruise ships. The web site offers feature articles from current and back issues, as well as other parts of the magazine; a password is required. Appropriate for special collections. URL: www.motorship.com

5176. *N R H S Bulletin.* Former titles (until 2005): *National Railway Bulletin;* (until 1976): *National Railway Historical Society. Bulletin.* [ISSN: 1940-3615] 1935. 5x/yr. Free to members. Ed(s): Jeffrey S Smith. National Railway Historical Society, 100 N 20th St, Ste 400, Philadelphia, PA 19103; info@nrhs.com; http://www.nrhs.com. Illus. Vol. ends: No. 6. *Bk. rev.:* 5-12, 200-750 words, signed. *Aud.:* Ga, Sa.

Published by the National Railway Historical Society, this journal is targeted to its membership. Rail fans will enjoy the richly illustrated articles on history and current events in the railroad industry. Although many articles focus on passenger transport, there is also historical coverage of freight trains and services. One issue per year is devoted to the activities of the society, with an annual report as well as section-by-section state-of-the-chapter reports. Every issue contains many book reviews, letters to the editor, and a digest of transit news. Appropriate for large general collections and special collections. URL: www.nrhs.com/publications

5177. *Newport's Heavy Duty Trucking: the fleet business authority.*
Former titles (until 1999): *Heavy Duty Trucking;* (until 1968): *Western Trucking and Motor Transportation;* (until 1959): *Western Trucking and Motor Transportation in the West;* (until 195?): *Motor Transportation;* (until 1951): *Motor Transportation of the West;* (until 1949): *Motor Transportation.* 1925. m. USD 65 domestic (Free to qualified personnel). Newport Business Media, 38 Executive Pk, Ste 300, Irvine, CA 92614; info@truckinginfo.com; http://newportbusinessmedia.net. Illus., adv. Circ: 127105. Vol. ends: Dec. *Aud.:* Sa.

This journal is published by Newport Business Media expressly for fleet owners who operate trucks within classes seven and eight (26,000 pounds gross vehicle weight). It covers the heavy trucking fleet industry, and includes industry news and events, legislation, safety, technology, and equipment. Statistics, including tables and graphs, are provided on diesel fuel costs by state; truck sales by manufacturer; and trucking trends. Buyers' guides, offered several times annually, are a significant supplement to the journal. Current issue contents and archived articles are available online. Appropriate for special collections. URL: www.truckinginfo.com

5178. *Overdrive: the voice of the American trucker.* Incorporates (1970-2001): *Owner Operator.* [ISSN: 0030-7394] 1961. m. USD 34.97 domestic (Free to qualified personnel). Ed(s): Jack Roberts, Lucinda Coulter. Randall-Reilly Publishing Company, 3200 Rice Mine Rd NE, Tuscaloosa, AL 35406; http://www.randallpub.com. Illus., adv. Circ: 90000. Vol. ends: Dec. *Indexed:* B01, BRI. *Aud.:* Sa.

This journal addresses the North American trucking industry and targets the truck driver and fleet operator. It covers industry news and events, legislation, safety, technology, product analysis, management, training, and personnel issues. Each issue includes feature articles, a calendar of events, a financial section, an industry-related web site directory, product/equipment reviews, and a job-hunting section. In 2001, this journal took over the publication of content from *Owner Operator.* Recent editions of the journal can be accessed online. Appropriate for special collections. URL: www.OverdriveOnline.com

5179. *Passenger Transport: the source for public transportation news and analysis.* [ISSN: 0364-345X] 1943. bi-w. USD 75 in North America; USD 87 elsewhere. American Public Transportation Association, 1666 K St, NW Ste 1100, Washington, DC 20006; statistics@apta.com; http://www.apta.com. Illus., index, adv. Vol. ends: Dec. *Aud.:* Sa.

This glossy, newspaper-format weekly publication is targeted to North American transit officials who are likely to be members of the American Public Transportation Association (APTA), the magazine's publisher. There is significant coverage of people involved in the industry, providing interviews and much space to news items about the movement of people in the field. In addition to providing current news on the subject, regular features include industry briefs, international news, classifieds, and regular columns. In conjunction with APTA conferences, special issues are published that focus on city-by-city transit operations. The online version of the journal and archived articles can be accessed. Appropriate for special collections. URL: www.apta.com/passengertransport/Pages/LatestIssue.aspx

5180. *Progressive Railroading.* [ISSN: 0033-0817] 1958. m. Free to qualified personnel. Ed(s): Jeff Stagl, Patrick Foran. Trade Press Publishing Corp., 2100 W Florist Ave, Milwaukee, WI 53209; info@tradepress.com; http://www.tradepress.com. Illus., adv. Circ: 25059. Vol. ends: Dec. *Indexed:* A22, C&ISA, CerAb. *Aud.:* Ac, Sa.

As a major U.S. trade journal in the rail industry, this publication focuses on operations and equipment used in freight and passenger services, including urban transit. The feature articles provide profiles of key companies, articles on safety, alliances, and more. Regular features are extensive, including industry and regional news and analysis, statistics, events, commentary, and equipment information. This magazine publishes many annual guides to the industry on the subjects of cars, locomotives, and track, finance, and leasing. The web site includes late-breaking news and some of the feature articles from the current issue of the magazine. Appropriate for special collections. URL: www.ProgressiveRailroading.com

5181. *Public Roads.* [ISSN: 0033-3735] 1918. bi-m. USD 31 domestic; USD 43.40 foreign. U.S. Federal Highway Administration, 1200 New Jersey Ave, SE, Washington, DC 20590; http://www.fhwa.dot.gov. Illus. Microform: CIS; PQC. *Indexed:* A01, A22, AmStI, B02, C&ISA, CerAb, EngInd, P02. *Aud.:* Ga, Sa.

This publication covers federal highway policies, programs, research, and development. While its primary audience is transportation officials, researchers, field technicians, and engineers, the journal's content could also be used by a general audience wishing to stay informed on transportation issues and progress. Each issue includes features on new research, recent publications, news in the industry, and a calendar of events. Full text of articles back to 1993 is available on the web site. Appropriate for large general collections and special collections. URL: www.tfhrc.gov/pubrds/pubrds.htm

5182. *Public Transport International (French Edition).* Supersedes in part (in 1997): *Public Transport International (Multilingual Edition);* Which was formerly (until 1990): *U I T P Revue; International Union of Tramways, Light Railways and Motor Omnibuses. Review.* [ISSN: 1029-1261] 1952. bi-m. Members, TPE 56; Non-members, EUR 74. Ed(s): Heather Allen. International Union of Public Transport, Rue Sainte-Marie 6, Brussels, 1080, Belgium; http://www.uitp.org. Illus., adv. Circ: 3000. Vol. ends: Nov/Dec. *Indexed:* C&ISA, CerAb, EngInd. *Aud.:* Ac, Sa.

Published by the International Association of Public Transport, this journal addresses the international urban and interurban public-transit industry. It should be of interest to both the academician and the practitioner. Each issue consists of research articles on the technological, socioeconomic, or political aspects of public transportation. Statistical graphs and tables enhance the text; however, references are not provided for the research articles. Some references are available on request. Selected archived articles can be accessed online. Appropriate for special collections. URL: www.uitp.org

5183. *Railfan & Railroad.* Formed by the merger of (1974-1979): *Railfan;* (1937-1979): *Railroad Magazine;* Which was formerly (until 1937): *Railroad Stories;* (until 1932): *Railroad Man's magazine.* [ISSN: 0163-7266] 1979. m. USD 37.95 domestic; USD 50 foreign. Ed(s): Steve Barry. Carstens Publications, Inc., 108 Phil Hardin Rd, Newton, NJ 07860; carstens@carstens-publications.com; http://www.carstens-publications.com. Illus., adv. Vol. ends: Dec. *Bk. rev.:* Number and length vary. *Aud.:* Ga, Sa.

This journal addresses railroading and railway history for the United States, Canada, and occasionally Mexico. It is geared to the enthusiast, although a specialist may be interested in the historical information provided. Contents include railroading news and events; feature articles; book, video, and software reviews; preservation information; sections devoted to railway dining, museums, and tour schedules; and product and hobby reviews. A pull-out index for the previous year is published each spring. Text is enhanced with a large color photography section. The tables of contents for the current and forthcoming issues can be accessed online. Appropriate for large general collections and special collections. URL: www.railfan.com

5184. *Railroad History.* Formerly (until 1972): *Railway and Locomotive Historical Society. Bulletin.* [ISSN: 0090-7847] 1921. s-a. Members, USD 7.50; Non-members, USD 12.50. Ed(s): Peter A Hansen. Railway & Locomotive Historical Society, c/o Peter A. Hansen, 15621 W 87th St, PO Box 152, Lenexa, KS 66219; http://www.rlhs.org/. Illus., index. Refereed. *Bk. rev.:* 20-30, up to 1,500 words, signed. *Aud.:* Ac, Sa.

Published by the Railway and Locomotive Historical Society, this journal is geared to the academician and the enthusiast. It addresses the socioeconomic, business, and technological aspects of domestic and international railroad and railway history. It includes feature essays and lengthy research articles with diagrams, maps, and extensive references. The journal has an impressive book review section and a section on articles recommended for reading. Each issue includes information on preservation and on locomotives, a discussion forum, and a photography section. There is a yearly bonus issue devoted to a specific topic. A cumulative index from 1921 forward and the current issue can be accessed online. Appropriate for large general collections and special collections. URL: www.rlhs.org/Publications/History/

5185. Railway Age: serving the railway industry since 1856. Incorporates (1982-1991): *Modern Railroads;* Which was formerly (until 1982): *Modern Railroads - Rail Transit;* (until 1977): *Modern Railroads; Railway Locomotives and Cars;* Former titles (until 1918): *Railway Age Gazette;* (until 1910): *Railroad Age Gazette;* Which was formed by the merger of (1870-1908): *Railroad Gazette;* Which was formerly (until 1870): *Western Railroad Gazette;* (1900-1908): *Railway Age;* Which was formerly (until 1900): *Railway Age and Northwestern Railroads;* Which was formed by the merger of (1876-1891): *Railway Age;* (1887-1891): *Northwestern Railroads.* [ISSN: 0033-8826] 1876. m. Free to qualified personnel. Ed(s): Douglas John Bowen, William C Vantuono. Simmons-Boardman Publishing Corp., 345 Hudson St, New York, NY 10014; http://www.simmonsboardman.com/. Illus., adv. Vol. ends: Dec. Microform: CIS; PQC. *Indexed:* A22, ABIn, B01, B02, BRI, C&ISA, CerAb, EngInd, H24, P02. *Aud.:* Ac, Sa.

As one of the major North American railroad trade journals, *Railway Age* covers all aspects of the railroad industry. The journal addresses both freight and passenger service, encompassing commuter, rapid, and light-rail transit, as well as the equipment and supply industry, management, finance, and operational considerations. Annual special issues are published and can include buyers' guides, planners' guides, or year-end outlooks. Regular features include at-a-glance industry indicators and outlooks, railroader of the year, meeting information, company indexes, professional directories, classifieds, and commentary on a variety of aspects of the industry. The focus of the latter manifestation of the journal is on business rather than technical aspects of the industry. The web site contains late-breaking news as well as selected articles, commentaries, and statistics from the magazine. Appropriate for large general collections and special collections. URL: www.railwayage.com

5186. Railway Gazette International: a journal of management, engineering and operation. Former titles (until 1971): *International Railway Gazette;* (until 19??): *Railway Gazette;* Which incorporated (1880-1935): *Railway Engineer; Railway News; Railway Times; Transport and Railroad Center.* [ISSN: 0373-5346] 1835. m. GBP 99 domestic; EUR 186 in Europe; USD 252 elsewhere. D V V Media UK Ltd., NINE, Sutton Court Rd, Sutton, SM1 4SZ, United Kingdom. Illus., index, adv. *Indexed:* A22, ABIn, B01, B02, BRI, C&ISA, CerAb, EngInd. *Bk. rev.:* Number and length vary. *Aud.:* Sa.

This journal addresses the international rail industry, encompassing heavy and light rail and both freight and passenger services. It is geared to the practitioner and includes industry news and events, technology, legislation, safety, business, finance, management, research, and the socioeconomic and political environments of the rail industry. Each issue contains feature articles, a detailed industry news section, a calendar of events, product reviews, a small book review section, and a section devoted to industry personnel. A different world region is highlighted in each issue. Current articles and an index back to 1996 can be accessed online, by subscribers. Appropriate for special collections. URL: www.railwaygazette.com

5187. Roads & Bridges. Former titles (until 1985): *Roads;* (until 1983): *R U R: Rural and Urban Roads;* Which was formed by the merger of (1954-1963): *Rural Roads;* (1956-1963): *Street Engineering.* [ISSN: 8750-9229] 1963. m. Free. Ed(s): Allen Zeyher. Scranton Gillette Communications, Inc., 3030 W Salt Creek Ln, Ste 201, Arlington Heights, IL 60005; hgillette@sgcmail.com; http://www.scrantongillette.com. Illus., adv. Microform: PQC. *Indexed:* A01, A22, C&ISA, CerAb. *Aud.:* Sa.

Targeting the practitioner, this journal addresses the domestic transportation construction industry. Coverage includes industry news and events, technology, legislation, safety and regulation, construction materials, construction machinery, products, and equipment. Each issue includes feature articles, a legal section, product and equipment reviews, and sections devoted to technical innovations and construction vehicles. Some issues include information on software and online industry resources. Articles from the current issue and archived issues can be accessed online. Appropriate for special collections. URL: www.roadsbridges.com/rb

5188. Supply Chain Management Review. [ISSN: 1521-9747] 1997. 7x/yr. USD 129 combined subscription domestic (print & online eds.); USD 199 combined subscription Canada (print & online eds.); USD 241 combined subscription elsewhere (print & online eds.). E H Publishing, Inc., 111 Speen St, Ste 200, PO Box 989, Framingham, MA 01701; info@ehpub.com; http://www.ehpub.com. Adv. Circ: 12000. Vol. ends: Feb. *Indexed:* ABIn, B01, B02, BRI. *Bk. rev.:* 3-5, 250-750 words. *Aud.:* Ac, Sa.

This journal addresses the international transportation logistics and supply-chain management industries. It targets both the academician and the practitioner. Coverage includes logistics, supply-chain management, procurement, technology, e-commerce, warehousing, management, training, and information flow. Each issue includes both feature articles and research articles with references; a resource section for literature, web sites, and networking; a professional-development section listing events, seminars, workshops, and academic programs; and statistics, charts, and graphs. There is at least one subject-specific supplement issued per year. Current feature articles are available online. Appropriate for large academic collections and special collections. URL: www.scmr.com

5189. T R News. Former titles (until 1983): *Transportation Research News;* (until 1974): *Highway Research News.* [ISSN: 0738-6826] 1963. bi-m. USD 55 domestic; USD 75 foreign. Ed(s): Javy Awan. U.S. National Research Council, Transportation Research Board, The National Academies, 500 Fifth St, NW, Washington, DC 20001; http://www.trb.org. Illus. Circ: 10000. Vol. ends: Nov/Dec. *Indexed:* A22, C&ISA, CerAb, EngInd. *Bk. rev.:* 4-8, up to 150 words. *Aud.:* Ac, Sa.

This publication covers research and innovations in all modes of transportation. Article contributions come from academics and professionals in the industry. The focus is on U.S.-based initiatives and specifically on Transportation Research Board (TRB) activities. In addition to feature articles, each issue contains profiles of academics and professionals, news briefs and TRB highlights, an events calendar, and a listing of new TRB publications with abstracts. The current issue can be accessed online. Appropriate for special collections. URL: http://onlinepubs.trb.org/onlinepubs/trnews/trnews274toc.pdf

5190. Traffic Engineering & Control. Incorporates (1953-1967): *International Road Safety and Traffic Review.* [ISSN: 0041-0683] 1960. m. 11/yr. GBP 110 combined subscription (print & online eds.); USD 220 combined subscription (print & online eds.); EUR 160 combined subscription (print & online eds.). Ed(s): Adrian Tatum. Hemming Information Services Ltd., 32 Vauxhall Bridge Rd, London, SW1V 2SS, United Kingdom; info@hgluk.com; http://www.hemminginfo.co.uk. Illus., index, adv. Vol. ends: Dec. Microform: PQC. *Indexed:* A22, B02, BRI, BrTechI, C&ISA, CerAb, EngInd. *Bk. rev.:* Occasional, up to 750 words. *Aud.:* Ac, Sa.

This British journal primarily covers European countries, with some international coverage. It encompasses industry issues, news, interviews, and current research in traffic engineering. It is targeted at academics, practicing engineers, and students in the field. Regular features also include buyers' guides, classifieds, product news, opinion pieces, and a calendar of events. Annual features include a review of activities of transportation research centers at British universities. A current table of contents and searchable articles can be accessed online. Appropriate for special collections. URL: www.tecmagazine.com

5191. *Traffic Technology International.* [ISSN: 1356-9252] 1994. bi-m. Free. Ed(s): Nick Bradley. U K & International Press, Abinger House, Church St, Dorking, RH4 1DF, United Kingdom; info@ukintpress.com; http://www.ukipme.com. Adv. *Aud.:* Sa.

This journal addresses the issues of traffic safety and traffic control. It is global in breadth and targets the practitioner. Coverage includes industry news and events, intelligent transportation systems, traffic control devices, traffic safety devices, regulation, legislation, traffic systems operations, research, personnel, management, and training. Each issue includes feature articles, a calendar of events, an international news section, a bulletin board that highlights software and innovative technology, statistics, and tables and graphs. The journal includes a yearly supplement titled "Tolltrans" that addresses every aspect of highway tolls. Appropriate for large academic collections and special collections. URL: www.traffictechnologytoday.com

5192. *Trains.* Formerly: *Trains & Travel.* [ISSN: 0041-0934] 1940. m. USD 42.95 domestic; USD 52.95 Canada; USD 57.95 elsewhere. Ed(s): Jim Wrinn. Kalmbach Publishing Co., 21027 Crossroads Circle, Waukesha, WI 53187; customerservice@kalmbach.com; http://www.kalmbach.com. Illus., index, adv. Vol. ends: Dec. *Indexed:* A22, ABIn, BRI, MASUSE, P02. *Bk. rev.:* 3-5, 250-750 words, signed. *Aud.:* Ga, Sa.

This journal addresses both the light and heavy rail industries of North America, with some cursory international news. It is geared to the enthusiast; however, the specialist may find the historical and management articles of interest. Coverage includes industry news and events, tours, rail-related hobbies and memorabilia, railroad personnel, preservation, museums, and some management and policy matters. Each issue includes feature articles, book and video reviews, a calendar of events, tour schedules, and a significant photography section that sponsors a readers' photography contest. There is a yearly pull-out recreational-railroading supplement. Current and archived tables of contents can be accessed online. Appropriate for large public library collections or special collections. URL: www.TrainsMag.com

5193. *Tramways & Urban Transit: international light rail magazine.* Former titles (until 1997): *Light Rail and Modern Tramway;* (until 1992): *Modern Tramway and Light Rail Transit;* (until 1980): *Modern Tramway and Rapid Transit;* (until 1977): *Modern Tramway and Light Railway Review.* [ISSN: 1460-8324] 1938. m. Free to members. Ed(s): Simon Johnston. Light Rail Transit Association, LRTA, c/o 138 Radnor Ave, Welling, DA16 2BY, United Kingdom; office@lrta.org; http://www.lrta.org. Illus., adv. *Indexed:* BrTechI. *Bk. rev.:* Number and length vary. *Aud.:* Sa.

Published by the Light Rail Transit Association, this journal has been in continuous publication since 1938. It addresses the global, light-rail, and urban transport industry and is geared to the practitioner. The journal covers industry news and events, technology, funding, legislation, safety, management, and industry personnel. Each issue includes feature articles; an international tram and light-rail news section; reviews of books, databases, and videos; a calendar of events; obituaries; and a product review section. Color and black-and-white photography enhance the text. The tables of contents, dating back to 1998, can be accessed online. Appropriate for special collections. URL: www.tramnews.net

5194. *Transport Policy.* [ISSN: 0967-070X] 1993. bi-m. EUR 799. Ed(s): R Vickerman. Pergamon, The Blvd, Langford Ln, E Park, Kidlington, OX5 1GB, United Kingdom; JournalsCustomerServiceEMEA@elsevier.com; http://www.elsevier.com. Illus., adv. Sample. Refereed. Microform: PQC. *Indexed:* A01, A22, B01, H24. *Aud.:* Ac, Sa.

This scholarly publication of the World Conference on Transport Research Society covers all modes of transportation, addressing theoretical and practical aspects of transportation policy and administration. It targets the practitioner, government official, and academician. Some issues will focus on a single aspect of transport policy. In addition to scholarly articles, each issue includes a section on the activities of the World Conference on Transport Research Society. The online version is available by subscription through Elsevier. Appropriate for special collections.

5195. *Transport Reviews: a transnational, transdisciplinary journal.* [ISSN: 0144-1647] 1981. bi-m. GBP 951 (print & online eds.). Ed(s): David Banister. Routledge, 4 Park Sq, Milton Park, Abingdon, OX14 4RN, United Kingdom; subscriptions@tandf.co.uk; http://www.tandfonline.com. Illus., index, adv. Sample. Refereed. Vol. ends: Oct/Dec. Reprint: PSC. *Indexed:* A01, A22, B01, C&ISA, CerAb, E01, ErgAb. *Bk. rev.:* 1-3, 350-750 words, signed. *Aud.:* Ac, Sa.

This refereed, scholarly publication covers all modes of transportation and is global in scope. Topics can touch on social, economic, or technological aspects of the field. The content is aimed at both academic and professional audiences. Occasional issues are organized around a specific topic. Current and back issues are available online, through subscription. Appropriate for special collections. URL: www.tandf.co.uk/journals/tf/01441647.html

5196. *Transport Topics: national newspaper of the trucking industry.* Formerly (until 19??): *A T A News Bulletin.* [ISSN: 0041-1558] 1935. w. Mon. USD 109 domestic (Free to members). Ed(s): Bruce Harmon. American Trucking Associations, Inc., 950 N Glebe Rd, Ste 210, Alexandria, VA 22203; orders@trucking.org; http://www.truckline.com. Illus., adv. Circ: 28666 Paid. Microform: PQC. *Indexed:* A22, ABIn. *Aud.:* Ga, Sa.

This glossy, tabloid-format newspaper covers the trucking industry and is published by the American Trucking Associations. It is geared toward the practitioner. It is composed mostly of short articles concerning all aspects of trucking, but especially state and federal regulations, management, policy analysis, finance, operations, equipment, and events. Issues often include special sections on a single topic. Regular features include state news, a weekly business review, fuel prices, products, people news, a calendar of events, job listings, real estate, and equipment. The web site offers late-breaking news and other regular columns, but a password is required. Appropriate for large general collections or special collections. URL: www.transporttopics.com

5197. *Transportation.* [ISSN: 0049-4488] 1972. 5x/yr. EUR 1072 (print & online eds.). Ed(s): Martin G Richards, David T Hartgen. Springer New York LLC, 233 Spring St, New York, NY 10013; service-ny@springer.com; http://www.springer.com/. Illus., index, adv. Refereed. Vol. ends: No. 4. Microform: PQC. Reprint: PSC. *Indexed:* A22, ABIn, C&ISA, C45, CerAb, E01, EconLit, EngInd, H24, IBSS, JEL, RRTA. *Aud.:* Ac, Sa.

This scholarly publication provides research articles that cover all modes of transportation around the world. The audience is policy makers, transportation planners, and operations managers. Most issues contain four articles, but occasional issues contain many more, focused on a topic. After the print edition of 2009, the journal can be accessed through Springerlink, by subscribers. Appropriate for special collections.

5198. *Transportation Journal.* [ISSN: 0041-1612] 1961. q. USD 361 (print & online eds.). Ed(s): Evelyn Thomchick. Pennsylvania State University Press, 820 N University Dr, University Support Bldg 1, Ste C, University Park, PA 16802; info@psupress.org; http://www.psupress.org. Illus., index, adv. Refereed. Microform: PQC. Reprint: PSC. *Indexed:* A01, A22, ABIn, B01, B02, BRI, CLI, H&TI, JEL, P02. *Bk. rev.:* Occasional, 750-1,000 words, signed. *Aud.:* Ac, Sa.

Published by the American Society of Transportation and Logistics, this scholarly journal includes articles on air transport, international transport, logistics/physical distribution/supply-chain management, management information systems and computer applications, motor transport, rail transport, regulation/law, traffic and transport management, transport policy, and water transport. Special-theme issues are published regularly. There are book reviews in some issues. Tables of contents and abstracts for the last year can be found online. Appropriate for special collections. URL: www.astl.org/i4a/pages/index.cfm?pageid=3288

5199. *Transportation Law Journal: industry leader in multi-modal law, economics & policy.* [ISSN: 0049-450X] 1969. 3x/yr. USD 38 domestic; USD 46 foreign; USD 20 per issue domestic. Ed(s): Justin Marks, Jay M Sim. University of Denver, Sturm College of Law, 2255 E Evans Ave, Ste 448, Denver, CO 80208; mlattimer@law.du.edu; http://www.law.du.edu. Illus., index, adv. Refereed. Vol. ends: Spring. Microform: WSH; PMC. Reprint: WSH. *Indexed:* A01, A22, BRI, CLI, L14, P61, SSA. *Aud.:* Ac, Sa.

Published by the University of Denver College of Law, this scholarly journal addresses the international transportation industry and is geared toward the specialist, academician, and transportation law practitioner. It covers transportation law, regulation, and the politico-economic aspects of all transportation modalities. Each issue includes significant research articles with abundant footnotes. The full text of the journal is available on LexisNexis, Westlaw, and Hein Online, current and archived (back to different years, per respective archive). Appropriate for special collections. URL: www.law.du.edu/ index.php/transportation-law-journal/issues

5200. Transportation Management & Engineering. Formerly (until 2001): *I T S World.* [ISSN: 1537-0259] 1996. q. USD 95 foreign (Free to qualified personnel). Scranton Gillette Communications, Inc., 380 E Northwest Hwy, Ste 200, Des Plaines, IL 60016; hgillette@sgcmail.com; http://www.scrantongillette.com. Illus., index, adv. *Indexed:* ABIn. *Aud.:* Sa.

This journal covers the international intelligent transportation systems industry, and it targets the specialist. Coverage includes industry news and events, feature articles, a product portfolio, editorials, and industry highlights. It is a supplement to *Roads and Bridges.* The current issue and archived articles can be found online. Appropriate for special collections. URL: www.roadsbridges.com/traffic-management

5201. Transportation Research. Parts A-F. 46x/yr. EUR 5678. Pergamon, The Blvd, Langford Ln, E Park, Kidlington, OX5 1GB, United Kingdom; http://www.elsevier.com. *Bk. rev.:* Occasional, 600-2,500 words. *Aud.:* Ac, Sa.

Appropriate for special libraries, this six-part set of journals covers the gamut of transportation research occurring around the world. Each part can be purchased separately.

A: Policy & Practice [ISSN: 0965-8564] 10/yr. USD 1,104. Frank A. Haight. Vol. ends: Dec. Focuses on general-interest articles, particularly on planning and policy and their interaction with political, socioeconomic, and environmental systems.

B: Methodological [ISSN: 0191-2615] 10/yr. USD 1,104. Frank A. Haight. Vol. ends: Apr. Concentrates on the creation, analysis, and performance of models for the movement of freight and people.

C: Emerging Technologies [ISSN: 0968-090X] bi-m. USD 736. Stephen G. Ritchie. Vol. ends: Dec. Discusses implications and applications of new technologies in the field of transportation.

D: Transport and Environment [ISSN: 1361-9209] bi-m. USD 736. Kenneth Button. Covers environmental impacts of transportation, policy issues surrounding that impact, and implications for the design and implementation of transportation systems.

E: Logistics and Transportation Review [ISSN: 1366-5545] bi-m. USD 735. W. K. Talley. Vol. ends: Dec. Features articles on logistics including economics, cost, and production functions; capacity; demand; infrastructure; models; and supply chain topics.

F: Traffic Psychology and Behaviour [ISSN: 1369-8478] q. USD 490. J. A. Rothengatter. Focuses on the behavioral and psychological aspects of traffic and transport.

These journals are geared to the academician and the practitioner. Only available online through Elsevier.

5202. Transportation Research Record. Former titles (until 1974): *Highway Research Record;* Which incorporates (1927-1963): *Highway Research Board. Annual Meeting. Proceedings;* Which was formerly (until 1927): *Annual Meeting. Proceedings;* (until 1963): *Highway Research Board. Bulletin.* [ISSN: 0361-1981] 1963. irreg. 50 issues/yr. USD 2300 in North America; USD 2475 out of North America; USD 2980 combined subscription in North America (print & online eds.). U.S. National Research Council, Transportation Research Board, The National Academies, 500 Fifth St, NW, Washington, DC 20001; trbsales@nas.edu; http://www.trb.org. Illus. Refereed. *Indexed:* A22, C&ISA, C45, CerAb, EngInd, H24, RRTA, RiskAb. *Aud.:* Ac, Sa.

Each issue of this publication contains papers on a topic relating to specific transportation modes and subject areas. The papers come from those prepared for presentation at Transportation Research Board (TRB) annual meetings, conferences, and workshops; they cover various aspects of the issue's theme, including technical, social, economic, or operational perspectives. Between 50 and 60 issues are published each year. Authors and topics come from all over the world. The primary emphasis of this journal is on topics relating to the engineering of highways, urban transportation, and traffic safety. Along with other TRB publications, this is an essential series for any transportation collection. Current issues can be found online. Appropriate for large academic collections and special collections. URL: http://trb.metapress.com/home/ main.mpx

5203. Transportation Science. [ISSN: 0041-1655] 1967. q. USD 466 (print & online eds.). Ed(s): Michel Gendreau. Institute for Operations Research and the Management Sciences (I N F O R M S), 7240 Pky Dr, Ste 300, Hanover, MD 21076; informs@informs.org; http://www.informs.org. Illus., index. Refereed. Vol. ends: Nov. *Indexed:* A01, A22, ABIn, B01, B02, C&ISA, CerAb, EngInd, IBSS, MathR. *Bk. rev.:* Occasional, 500-1,500 words. *Aud.:* Ac, Sa.

Published by the Institute for Operations Research and Management Sciences (INFORMS), this refereed, scholarly journal contains articles on all modes of transportation regarding operational management, such as planning and economic and social design. The mission of the journal is to advance the analytical, experimental, and observational tools in the study of transportation. The journal contains research articles, critical-review articles, technical notes, letters to the editor, and book reviews. Annually, dissertation abstracts submitted for the Transportation Science Section Prize are published. Current and passed articles available online, for subscribers. Appropriate for special collections. URL: http://transci.pubs.informs.org

Ward's AutoWorld. See Automobiles and Motorcycles section.

5204. Waterways Journal. [ISSN: 0043-1524] 1887. w. USD 39 domestic; USD 104 in Canada & Mexico. Ed(s): John Shoulberg. Waterways Journal, Inc., 319 N 4th St, Ste 650, St. Louis, MO 63102. Illus. Vol. ends: No. 52. *Bk. rev.:* Occasional, up to 250 words. *Aud.:* Ga, Sa.

This U.S.-focused, tabloid-format publication covers all aspects of inland waterways, water transportation, and ports. Written for anyone with an interest in inland water transportation, including enthusiasts, its articles cover news, historical articles, letters, barge data, and other statistics and news. Annual features include a combined yearbook-and-directory that provides a chronological listing of the year's important news. Current articles and archived summaries dating back to 2003 are available online. Appropriate for large general collections or special collections. URL: www.waterwaysjournal.net

5205. WorkBoat. Incorporates (1954-1959): *Offshore Drilling; Southern Marine Review.* [ISSN: 0043-8014] 1943. m. Free to qualified personnel. Ed(s): David Krapf. Diversified Business Communications, 121 Free St, Portland, ME 04101; custserv@divcom.com; http:// www.divbusiness.com. Illus., adv. Circ: 25563. Vol. ends: Dec. *Indexed:* B02, BRI. *Aud.:* Sa.

A trade magazine for the North American workboat industry, which includes but is not limited to tugboats, barges, salvage vessels, crewboats, utility boats, excursion vessels, freighters, tankers, patrol craft, fire boats, and research vessels. It is geared to the practitioner and covers industry news and events, legislation, regulation, safety, technology, vessel construction and maintenance, marine personnel, equipment, and product news. Each issue includes feature articles, a calendar of events, a classified section, a product showcase, and a section highlighting a specific port. The table of contents for the current issue and the full text of archived articles can be accessed online. Appropriate for special collections. URL: www.bairdmaritime.com

5206. World Highways (London, 1991). Formed by the merger of (1950-1991): *World Highways (Washington, 1950);* (1964-1991): *Routes du Monde.* [ISSN: 0964-4598] 1991. 10x/yr. Free to qualified personnel. Route One Publishing Ltd., Horizon House, Azalea Dr, Swanley, BR8 8JR, United Kingdom; media@ropl.com; http://www.routeonepub.com. Illus., adv. Sample. *Aud.:* Sa.

This journal addresses the international road and highway construction and maintenance industries and targets the practitioner. It covers industry news and events, materials, signage, lighting, equipment, technology, the environment and weather, traffic, and safety. Each issue includes feature articles, a calendar of events, guides to products and services, relevant web sites, and a highlighted construction site. It offers a whole page devoted to highway construction humor. The current issue's table of contents, news briefs, and the full text of feature articles can be accessed online, but a password is required. Appropriate for special collections. URL: www.worldhighways.com/about-us/

■ TRAVEL AND TOURISM

General/Newsletters/Research

See also Canada section.

Sheila Kasperek, Reference Librarian, Mansfield University of Pennsylvania, Mansfield, PA; skaspere@mansfield.edu

Introduction

In a world of travel apps and online services, where the free iPad-only magazine *TRVL* competes with print and online publications, travel and tourism publications serve two different purposes: to inspire readers to dream of their own trips, and to inform researchers and tourism professionals of current trends, theories, and practical advice in promoting, enhancing, and sustaining tourism services.

For public libraries, patrons who are planning their own travel will likely turn to web sources for the details of their trips, but will rely on a general travel and tourism collection to inspire, inform, and excite readers about their world and their travel options.

In academic libraries, students and faculty across departments will use the collection for both personal and professional purposes, not just those studying travel, tourism, and hospitality. Covering topics ranging from sustainability to marketing to development, these publications will meet the needs of students and researchers with a wide variety of interests and needs.

There are quite literally hundreds of magazines and journals that focus on specific types of tourism (e.g., the best places to mountain bike, gamble, drive, or dive) or that focus on a particular country, region, or state, but the small set of periodicals that follows is chosen very carefully to give a solid, broad base to your travel and tourism collection, regardless of country, state, region, or locale. The magazines and journals included are international and multidisciplinary in scope and touch on a wide array of travel and tourism topics.

Basic Periodicals

Ga: *National Geographic Traveler, Travel & Leisure;* Ac: *Annals of Tourism Research, Journal of Sustainable Tourism.*

Basic Abstracts and Indexes

Hospitality and Tourism Index; Hospitality and Tourism Complete; Leisure, Recreation and Tourism Abstracts; Leisure Tourism Database; Readers' Guide to Periodical Literature.

General

Backpacker: the outdoor at your doorsteps. See Hiking, Climbing, and Outdoor Recreation section.

5207. Conde Nast Traveler: truth in travel. Incorporates (1985-1992): *European Travel & Life;* Formerly (until 1987): *Signature.* [ISSN: 0893-9683] 1954. m. USD 10 domestic; USD 18.97 Canada; USD 39.97 elsewhere. Ed(s): Klara Glowczewska. Conde Nast Publications, Inc., 4 Times Sq, 6th Fl, New York, NY 10036; http://www.condenast.com. Illus., index, adv. Sample. Circ: 820217 Paid. Vol. ends: Dec (No. 12). Microform: PQC. *Indexed:* A22, ASIP, BRI, C37, H&TI, P02. *Aud.:* Ga.

Conde Nast Traveler mixes luxury travel destinations and travel advice with beautiful photography in a magazine synonymous with high class. This title is not for the budget-conscious, but in it, readers will find guides to spas, resorts, and exclusive travel destinations, with deals thrown in to appeal to a broader audience. The magazine's web site offers access to some content, additional information on destinations, and links to customer reviews. Recommended for public libraries.

5208. Cruise Travel: the worldwide cruise vacation magazine. [ISSN: 0199-5111] 1979. bi-m. USD 23.94 domestic; USD 40 Canada; USD 50 foreign. World Publishing Co., 990 Grove St, Evanston, IL 60201. Illus., adv. Sample. Circ: 175000 Paid. Vol. ends: May/Jun. *Indexed:* A22, BRI, C37, H&TI. *Aud.:* Ga.

Cruise travel has posted some of the biggest gains in the tourism industry over the last few decades, and *Cruise Travel* is the leading consumer magazine for those choosing to travel the seas. International in scope, it covers all aspects of cruising, with particular focus on highlight ships, ports, and cruises of the month. Because many cruises stop in ports for a limited time, travelers need to make the most of the little time they have. *Cruise Travel* provides one-day itineraries for ports of call specifically to meet this need. Recommended for public libraries.

Explorers Journal. See Geography section.

Fido Friendly. See Pets section.

5209. Lonely Planet Traveller. Formerly (until 2012): *Lonely Planet Magazine.* [ISSN: 2050-635X] 200?. m. GBP 36 domestic; GBP 65 in Europe; GBP 75 elsewhere. Immediate Media Co. Ltd., Media Ctr, 201 Wood Ln, London, W12 7TQ, United Kingdom; enquiries@immediatemedia.co.uk; http://www.immediatemedia.co.uk. Adv. Sample. *Bk. rev.:* Number and length vary. *Aud.:* Ga.

Lonely Planet is known for its thorough and practical travel guides, and this magazine showcases its expertise in the field. Each issue includes a mix of short dispatches, as well as in-depth destination guides that offer options from budget to luxury, and essay-length travel narratives. As well, each issue covers several major destinations in detail, with maps of locations and major tourist sites. Content also includes easy trips in Europe, historical destinations, travel book and TV show reviews, and removable single-theme mini–travel guides to places like the bistros of Paris or the canals of Amsterdam. This magazine reflects the years of experience in providing high-quality travel information, and mixes it with stunning photography and practical travel advice. Recommended for public libraries.

5210. National Geographic Traveler. [ISSN: 0747-0932] 1984. 8x/yr. USD 10 domestic; CAD 34 Canada; USD 36 elsewhere. Ed(s): Keith Bellows. National Geographic Society, PO Box 98199, Washington, DC 20090; askngs@nationalgeographic.com; http://www.nationalgeographic.com/. Illus., index, adv. Sample. Circ: 723657 Paid. Vol. ends: Nov/Dec. *Indexed:* A01, A22, ASIP, BRI, C37, H&TI, MASUSE, P02. *Aud.:* Ga.

Known for its beautiful photographs and its focus on nature and culture, this magazine inspires readers to learn about the world and dream of travel rather than look for the luxury resort with all the bells and whistles. With a mix of short articles and feature-length essays, this title covers all kinds of travel (e.g., sustainable and adventure travel), locales (urban, rural, and wilderness), and budgets. It includes regular features on green travel, travel with kids, two-day city guides, and road trips. Readers will find articles that, according to National Geographic, "inspire narratives that make readers take trips," and they will find "solid service information to help them plan those trips." Recommended for public libraries.

Outside. See Hiking, Climbing, and Outdoor Recreation section.

5211. *Taste & Travel International.* [ISSN: 1925-6841] 2011. q. USD 25. Taste and Travel Publishing International, Inc., 8289 Boland St # 481, Metcalfe, ON K0A 2P0, Canada; info@TasteandTravelInternational.com; http://www.tasteandtravelinternational.com. *Aud.:* Ga.

This food-lover's guide to travel opens up the world of culinary tourism. Each issue covers one U.S. and at least five worldwide destinations in lengthy food-destination articles that are packed with regional recipes. Readers will discover authentic places to eat, and information on local foods, dishes, restaurants, chefs, and growers. In addition, it includes articles on culinary vacations and classes, food tours, and vineyards. Each issue includes the history and use of a different spice, regional cookbook reviews, and dispatches covering a city's culinary highlights. Recommended for public libraries.

5212. *Travel 50 & Beyond.* [ISSN: 1049-6211] 1990. 4x/yr. USD 14. Vacation Publications, Inc., 5851 San Felipe St, Ste 500, Houston, TX 77057; service@Travel50andBeyond.com. Illus., adv. Sample. Vol. ends: Fall (No. 4). *Indexed:* AgeL. *Aud.:* Ga.

As the only magazine written specifically for the 50+ traveler, this magazine covers worldwide travel destinations for those seeking experiences from "soft adventure to slow meanderings." It provides information to those wanting high-quality, enriching travel experiences, and includes information on train, cruise, and RV travel. Articles are written with older travelers in mind, and include the humorous, poignant, and romantic aspects of travel. Recommended for public libraries, and academic libraries with a gerontology collection.

Newsletters

5213. *International Travel News.* [ISSN: 0191-8761] 1976. m. USD 24 domestic; USD 40 Canada; USD 50 Mexico, W. Europe, Japan, New Zealand, or Australia. Ed(s): David Tykol. Martin Publications Inc., 2120 28th St, Sacramento, CA 95818. Illus., adv. Sample. *Indexed:* BRI. *Bk. rev.:* 1, 750 words. *Aud.:* Ga.

Aimed at Americans who travel frequently outside the United States, this newsletter is primarily written by other travelers. With its pieces in the form of reviews, travel tips, first-person travel essays, and travel guides, readers get real travel reports from real travelers. Each issue includes a focus on archaeology and travel alerts, as well as rewarding readers who have met travel challenges and bits of travel humor. The web site complements the print publication with color photos, up-to-date news, and message boards to facilitate communication between readers. Recommended for public libraries.

5214. *Travel Smart.* Incorporates (1981-1982): *Joy of Travel;* Which was formerly (until 1981): *Joyer Travel Report.* [ISSN: 0741-5826] 1976. m. USD 39 domestic; USD 54 in Canada & Mexico; USD 64 elsewhere. Dunnan Communications, Inc., PO Box 397, Dobbs Ferry, NY 10522. Illus., index. Sample. *Aud.:* Ga.

For travelers on a budget, this information-rich and advertising-free newsletter gets right to the heart of the matter. Filled with "Top" lists of restaurants, travel deals, and locales, it is aimed at getting you the most for your travel dollar. Other regular content includes city insider guides, travel tips, gadget information, featured package deals including a "Steal of the Month," and unbiased reviews. Recommended for public libraries.

Research

5215. *Annals of Tourism Research: a social sciences journal.* [ISSN: 0160-7383] 1973. q. EUR 1045. Ed(s): John Tribe. Pergamon, The Blvd, Langford Ln, E Park, Kidlington, OX5 1GB, United Kingdom; JournalsCustomerServiceEMEA@elsevier.com; http://www.elsevier.com. Illus., adv. Sample. Refereed. Vol. ends: Oct. Microform: PQC. *Indexed:* A22, ABS&EES, C45, H&TI, IndVet, P61, PsycInfo, RRTA, RiskAb, SD. *Bk. rev.:* 8, 750 words. *Aud.:* Ac.

With an intended audience of researchers and scholars, this publication focuses on both theoretical and practical applications of research in tourism and related fields. The focus of the publication is the "academic perspective" of the subject,

and its content represents both domestic and international issues. Recommended for academic libraries, especially those with travel, tourism, hospitality, and recreation and leisure collections.

5216. *Current Issues in Tourism.* [ISSN: 1368-3500] 1998. 8x/yr. GBP 725 (print & online eds.). Ed(s): Dr. Rodolfo Baggio, Dr. Noel Scott. Routledge, 4 Park Sq, Milton Park, Abingdon, OX14 4RN, United Kingdom; subscriptions@tandf.co.uk; http://www.tandfonline.com. Adv. Sample. Refereed. Reprint: PSC. *Indexed:* C45, H&TI, IndVet, P61, RRTA, SSA. *Bk. rev.:* 3,000. *Aud.:* Ac.

This peer-reviewed journal, aimed at tourism researchers, is designed to foster discussion of key tourism issues and encourage debate and critique. Covering a wide range of tourism topics, including international issues, this journal contains applied and theoretical articles from a variety of scholarly fields. A recently added "Letters" section allows for recent highly relevant content to be included. The "Reviews" section and the online "CIT Interactive" allow for extended discussion of the topics raised in the journal, which is a unique feature of this title. Recommended for academic libraries, especially those with travel, tourism, hospitality, or recreation and leisure collections.

5217. *International Journal of Tourism Research.* Formerly (until 1999): *Progress in Tourism and Hospitality Research.* [ISSN: 1099-2340] 1995. bi-m. GBP 532. Ed(s): John Fletcher. John Wiley & Sons Ltd., The Atrium, Southern Gate, Chichester, PO19 8SQ, United Kingdom; customer@wiley.com; http://www.wiley.com. Adv. Sample. Refereed. Microform: PQC. Reprint: PSC. *Indexed:* A22, ABIn, B01, C45, H&TI, IndVet, PsycInfo, RRTA, RiskAb. *Bk. rev.:* 5, 1,000 words. *Aud.:* Ac.

A peer-reviewed journal that is dedicated to research in international tourism and related fields of economics, marketing, sociology, and statistics. Not limited merely to research findings, it also focuses on new methodologies in, and approaches to, tourism research as well as new areas of exploration in research. Geared toward researchers, this title is appropriate for academic libraries with a strong research community focused on hospitality, tourism, or travel.

5218. *Journal of Sustainable Tourism.* [ISSN: 0966-9582] 1993. 8x/yr. GBP 650 (print & online eds.). Ed(s): Bill Bramwell, Bernard Lane. Routledge, 4 Park Sq, Milton Park, Abingdon, OX14 4RN, United Kingdom; subscriptions@tandf.co.uk; http://www.tandfonline.com. Illus., adv. Sample. Refereed. Reprint: PSC. *Indexed:* A01, A22, ABIn, B01, C45, H&TI, IndVet, P61, RRTA. *Bk. rev.:* 3, 1,000 words. *Aud.:* Ac.

A critical understanding of the relationship between sustainability and tourism is the focus of this peer-reviewed journal. Containing both theoretical and research articles, it attempts to present an interdisciplinary and holistic view of the interrelated economic, social, cultural, political, and environmental issues of tourism. Recommended for academic libraries, especially those with travel, tourism, and recreation and leisure collections.

5219. *Journal of Travel Research.* Formerly: *Travel Research Bulletin.* [ISSN: 0047-2875] 1962. q. USD 747. Ed(s): Richard R Perdue. Sage Publications, Inc., 2455 Teller Rd, Thousand Oaks, CA 91320; info@sagepub.com; http://www.sagepub.com. Adv. Refereed. Reprint: PSC. *Indexed:* A01, A22, ABIn, ABS&EES, B01, B02, BRI, C&ISA, C45, CerAb, E01, H&TI, PsycInfo, RRTA, RiskAb. *Bk. rev.:* 2, 750 words. *Aud.:* Ac.

This peer-reviewed journal from the Travel and Tourism Research Association focuses on research in travel and tourism customer behavior and decision making, marketing, economics, and management theory, including recent trends and destination development. The articles are multidisciplinary and international in scope, and are designed for scholars and practitioners alike. Recommended for academic libraries with travel, tourism, or hospitality collections.

5220. *Tourism Management: research, policies, practice.* Formerly (until 1982): *International Journal of Tourism Management.* [ISSN: 0261-5177] 1980. bi-m. EUR 1799. Ed(s): Chris Ryan. Pergamon, The Blvd, Langford Ln, E Park, Kidlington, OX5 1GB, United Kingdom; JournalsCustomerServiceEMEA@elsevier.com; http://www.elsevier.com. Illus., adv. Sample. Refereed. Microform: PQC. *Indexed:* A22, C45, H&TI, IndVet, PsycInfo, RRTA, RiskAb. *Aud.:* Ac.

International, national, and regional tourism management, policy, and planning are the focus of this peer-reviewed journal. Containing research articles, case studies, and discussion of current issues, this title takes an interdisciplinary approach to tourism topics that is relevant to both academics and practitioners. Recent articles range from conservation and social responsibility to marketing, to family travel for the disabled. Recommended for collections in hospitality, travel, and tourism.

■ URBAN STUDIES

Alison Larsen, Serials & Web Resources Librarian, Siena College, 515 Loudon Rd., Loudonville, NY 12189; alarsen@siena.edu

Introduction

The landscape of urban studies continues to grow and evolve. Almost all research that falls under the umbrella of urban studies is multi- and interdisciplinary in nature—two keywords that are often associated with the types of articles the included titles are looking for. Urban spaces are the sums of their parts, and research in this area follows suit, trying to cumulatively tell the story of the past while trying to improve the present to positively affect the future. From your local town to the largest cities in the world, everything is a part of the totality that is urban studies.

For this review, a broad topical and geographic approach was taken. Many of the reviewed periodicals are established and well respected, sprinkled in with some newer and somewhat topical periodicals given today's landscape. At present, there is a very large number of periodicals published that can claim some association with urban studies. To try to review a sampling of all the publications that lay some claim would require a book that could rival the current size of *Magazines for Libraries* as a whole. While reading these annotations, you may want to also look to see if there are more specific, local (city, region, state) publications that will add a greater depth and context to your overall picture. A majority of the publications reviewed in this section are scholarly in nature, thus more appropriate for academic libraries. Still, there are some very fine publications appropriate for the general reader. Publications in this section are all written in English (while some article abstracts are also published in other languages). The annotations are written, and recommendations are made, with libraries in the United States as the potential subscribers. When a recommendation is made for an academic library, it is with the assumption that the library is supporting an urban studies program. If a publication is recommended for the general collection, then it is stated in the annotation. Other recommendations are self-explanatory.

Basic Periodicals

Ga: *American City & County, Planning, Urban Land;* Ac: *American Planning Association. Journal, Cities, Environment and Planning A, International Journal of Urban and Regional Research, Journal of Planning Literature, Journal of Urban Affairs, Journal of Urban Design, Planning, Urban Geography, Urban History, Urban Studies.*

Basic Abstracts and Indexes

ABI/INFORM, Avery Index to Architectural Periodicals, Business Source Premier, Ekistic Index of Periodicals, Index to Current Urban Documents, PAIS International, Sociological Abstracts, Urban Studies Abstracts.

5221. American City & County. Formerly (until 1975): *American City;* Incorporates (1924-1991): *American City & County Municipal Index.* [ISSN: 0149-337X] 1909. m. USD 76 domestic (Free to qualified personnel). Ed(s): Lindsay Isaacs. Penton Media, Inc., 6151 Powers Ferry Rd, Ste 200, Atlanta, GA 30339; http://www.penton.com. Illus., index, adv. Microform: PQC. *Indexed:* A01, A22, ABIn, B01, B02, BRI, CBRI, MASUSE, P02. *Bk. rev.:* Number and length vary. *Aud.:* Ga, Ac, Sa.

American City & County is a magazine dedicated to "serving government leaders." Published since 1909, it is one of the core trade titles in this subject area. It is published monthly and contains a variety of feature articles as well as

recurrent topical categories, including its "Municipal Cost Index." The "Index" incorporates the "Construction Cost Index," the "Consumer Price Index," and the "Producer Price Index" to show the "effects of inflation on the cost of providing municipal services." The web site provides much of the content found in recent print issues at no cost. In addition to viewing past issues (about six months' worth), content is also available via subjects (e.g., technology, public safety, sustainability). A subscription includes access to the digital edition and its "Municipal Index," a purchasing guide for government officials of necessary equipment and services. Highly recommended for public or special libraries that serve local government agencies, and for academic libraries. URL: http://americancityandcounty.com

5222. American Planning Association. Journal. Former titles (until 1979): *American Institute of Planners. Journal;* (until 1944): *The Planners' Journal.* [ISSN: 0194-4363] 1935. q. GBP 271 (print & online eds.). Ed(s): Randy Crane. Routledge, 325 Chestnut St, Ste 800, Philadelphia, PA 19106; customerservice@taylorandfrancis.com; http://www.tandfonline.com. Illus., adv. Sample. Refereed. Vol. ends: Oct. Microform: PQC. Reprint: PSC. *Indexed:* A01, A06, A07, A22, ABIn, API, B01, B02, BAS, BRI, E01, EIP, GardL, MCR, MLA-IB, P02, P61, SSA. *Bk. rev.:* 8-10, 500-1,200 words, signed. *Aud.:* Ac, Sa.

The official scholarly journal of the American Planning Association, the *Journal of the American Planning Association* (*JAPA*) publishes original research and analysis on a quarterly basis. The type of research published by *JAPA* includes methodology of planning practice and implementation, policy formation and implementation, and explanations of empirical relationships. This research examines "the historical or contemporary planning experience in domestic or global contexts." Each issue contains an average of five to seven original research articles and a large book review section. A theme issue is published on occasion. Articles focus heavily on North America but do include some international coverage; predominantly in comparative research articles. Members of the American Planning Association (APA) receive a discount on the subscription cost to the journal. APA's trade magazine, *Planning,* is included as a membership benefit and is reviewed in this section. Subscribers can download articles for free from the online archive. Highly regarded in the field, *JAPA* is a core title and is highly recommended for academic libraries.

5223. Better! Cities & Towns. Formerly (until 2012): *New Urban News.* [ISSN: 2165-476X] 1996. 8x/yr. USD 79. New Urban Publications, Inc., PO Box 6515, Ithaca, NY 14851. Illus., adv. Sample. *Bk. rev.:* Number and length vary. *Aud.:* Ga, Ac, Sa.

Previously published as *New Urban News, Better! Cities & Towns* debuted with the January/February 2012 issue and a new tagline of "the decision maker's bridge to stronger, greener communities." The newsletter style publication is devoted to new urbanism (the reaction to urban sprawl and desire to create human-scale communities) and publishes eight times per year. The previous mission had been to create models and workable techniques to help reform the built environment, and the focus has now shifted to implementing the created models and techniques. *Better! Cities & Towns* is available at a reasonable subscription price or is included as a benefit to members of the Congress for the New Urbanism. Subscription costs include online access. Articles are short and easily read by those outside the profession. Issues include book reviews, and the geographic emphasis is predominantly the United States, with some international coverage. For general collections of public and academic libraries.

5224. Built Environment. Former titles (until 1978): *Built Environment Quarterly;* (until 1975): *Built Environment;* (until 1972): *O A P;* (until 1971): *Official Architecture and Planning;* Which incorporated (1955-1970): *Modular Quarterly;* (until 1955): *Official Architect and Planning Review.* [ISSN: 0263-7960] 19??. q. GBP 290 (print & online eds.) Individuals, GBP 114 (print & online eds.). Ed(s): Stephen Marshall, David Banister. Alexandrine Press, 1 The Farthings, Marcham, OX13 6QD, United Kingdom; info@alexandrinepress.co.uk; http://www.alexandrinepress.co.uk. Illus. Sample. Refereed. *Indexed:* A22, API. *Bk. rev.:* 2-4, 500 words. *Aud.:* Ac, Sa.

Built Environment provides an "interdisciplinary and thematic approach" to planning. This journal is published four times a year, and each issue has a specific theme chosen by the editor. A specialist acts as a guest editor to enhance the professionalism, relevance, and academic integrity of the issue and to provide an introductory, overview article about the chosen theme. Recent themes have included "Urban Morphology and Design" and "Informal Urbanism." The article coverage, as are the members of the editorial board, is international. Each issue contains publication reviews, and online subscriptions include access to articles from 2003 to the present. Recommended for academic libraries.

5225. *Canadian Journal of Urban Research.* [ISSN: 1188-3774] 1992. s-a. CAD 70 (Individuals, CAD 45; Students, CAD 25). Ed(s): Marc Vachon. University of Winnipeg, Institute of Urban Studies, 103-520 Portage Ave, Winnipeg, MB R3C 0G2, Canada; ius@uwinnipeg.ca; http://ius.uwinnipeg.ca. Illus. Sample. Refereed. Circ: 125 Paid. *Indexed:* A01, BRI, C37, CBCARef, EIP, P02, P61, SSA. *Bk. rev.:* 4-6, 600-1,000 words, signed. *Aud.:* Ac, Sa.

A scholarly journal published by the Institute of Urban Research at the University of Winnipeg, the *Canadian Journal of Urban Research* publishes original research on urban Canada. Supported by the Social Sciences and Humanities Research Council of Canada (SSHRC), the *Canadian Journal of Urban Research* is published semi-annually. Articles can be published in English or French, with abstracts appearing in both languages. The subject matter of the articles encompasses a broad and interdisciplinary approach to urban research and includes topics such as city planning, urban policy, housing, and health and environment. Each issue contains an average of five book reviews. Annually a supplement, *Canadian Planning and Policy,* is published, illustrating the "scope and diversity of planning theory and practice in Canada." The *Canadian Journal of Urban Research* is an essential title for Canadian academic libraries and large public libraries. It is also recommended for libraries with a comprehensive urban studies collection.

5226. *Cities: the international journal of urban policy and planning.* [ISSN: 0264-2751] 1983. bi-m. EUR 1291. Ed(s): A Modarres. Pergamon, The Blvd, Langford Ln, E Park, Kidlington, OX5 1GB, United Kingdom; JournalsCustomerServiceEMEA@elsevier.com; http://www.elsevier.com. Illus., index, adv. Sample. Refereed. Microform: PQC. *Indexed:* A01, A22, B01, EIP, IBSS, P61, SSA. *Bk. rev.:* 0-3, signed. *Aud.:* Ac.

An international and interdisciplinary journal, *Cities: The International Journal of Urban Policy and Planning* provides a forum for the exchange of ideas between policy makers and planners by analyzing development based on policy, be it effective, ineffective, or even nonexistent. This is truly an all-encompassing journal in that it covers topics in the developed and undeveloped world that include "housing, homelessness, and health; urban management; public-private sector cooperation; Third World development and planning problems; urban regeneration; urban conservation and design; technological innovation and urban planning; urban transportation." *Cities* is published six times a year, and each issue presents four to six original research articles and one to three book reviews. Each issue also features a city profile (recent cities profiled include Sunderland, U.K., and Seoul, South Korea) that details the historical development, the contemporary conditions and problems, and a critique of the current policy and any responses. *Cities* has begun publishing what will be four supplements, each entitled *Current Research on Cities* (*CRoC*), which will ultimately launch as a new, independent journal in 2014. Though expensive, *Cities* is very highly recommended for academic libraries and general academic collections.

5227. *City: analysis of urban trends, culture, theory, policy, action.* Formerly (until 1995): *Regenerating Cities.* [ISSN: 1360-4813] 1992. bi-m. GBP 535 (print & online eds.). Ed(s): Bob Catterall. Routledge, 4 Park Sq, Milton Park, Abingdon, OX14 4RN, United Kingdom; subscriptions@tandf.co.uk; http://www.tandfonline.com. Adv. Sample. Reprint: PSC. *Indexed:* A01, A22, E01, IBSS. *Bk. rev.:* 1-3, signed. *Aud.:* Ac.

City: analysis of urban trends, culture, theory, policy, action "is a journal of provocative, cutting-edge and committed insights into, analysis of, and commentary on the contemporary urban world." Focused on the future of cities, *City* aims to provide a multidisciplinary vantage point to a wide variety of subjects that affect cities, including "information and digital revolutions, war and imperialism, neoliberalism and gentrification, environment and sustainability, resistance and social movements, regeneration, resurgence and

revanchism, race, class and gender, multi-culturalism and post-colonialism." *City* is published six times per year and contains original research articles, sometimes group into themes, recurring sections, and occasionally one to three substantial book reviews. As *City* focuses on the future of cities, it fulfills a valuable role in the totality of the literature on urban areas and is thus highly recommended for academic libraries.

5228. *City & Community.* [ISSN: 1535-6841] q. GBP 308. Ed(s): Anthony M Orum. Wiley-Blackwell Publishing, Inc., Commerce Pl, 350 Main St, Malden, MA 02148; info@wiley.com; http://onlinelibrary.wiley.com/. Refereed. Reprint: PSC. *Indexed:* A01, A22, E01, P02, P61, PsycInfo, RiskAb, SSA. *Bk. rev.:* 3-5, 500-1,200 words, signed. *Aud.:* Ac, Sa.

Published quarterly, *City & Community* (*C&C*) is the journal of the Community and Urban Sociology Section of the American Sociological Association. Looking to "advance urban sociological theory" and "encourage sociological perspectives on urban policy," *C&C* publishes articles that are theoretical as well as qualitative and quantitative case studies. A typical issue includes five research articles and three to five substantial book reviews. The geographic coverage is predominantly of the United States, but *C&C* is looking to increase international coverage, specifically comparative analyses between cities in the United States and those outside. Recent issues have focused on a theme or a geographic region. Articles are published online in advance of the print edition. Highly recommended for academic libraries. *C&C* may also be relevant to academic libraries that support comprehensive sociology programs.

5229. *Community Development Journal: an international forum.* Former titles (until 1966): *Community Development Bulletin;* (until 1951): *Mass Education Bulletin.* [ISSN: 0010-3802] 1949. q. EUR 352. Ed(s): Mick Carpenter. Oxford University Press, Great Clarendon St, Oxford, OX2 6DP, United Kingdom; enquiry@oup.co.uk; http://www.oxfordjournals.org/. Illus., adv. Sample. Refereed. Microform: PQC. Reprint: PSC. *Indexed:* A01, A22, ABIn, ASSIA, BAS, C45, E01, EconLit, IBSS, JEL, MLA-IB, P61, RRTA, RiskAb, SSA, SWR&A. *Bk. rev.:* 5-6, 1,000 words, signed. *Aud.:* Ac.

Published quarterly, *Community Development Journal* "provides an international forum for political, economic and social programmes, which link the activities of people with institutions and government." This scholarly journal covers such topics as community action; village, town, and regional planning; community studies; and rural development. This journal's geographic coverage is international, with a slight emphasis on the United Kingdom. Every article contains an abstract, and each issue includes a handful of book reviews. Beginning in 2012, the journal will be indexed in SSCI and receive its first impact factor. The editors have also created an accompanying web site, *CDJ Plus,* which provides free access to articles that have received some funding from CDJ, Ltd., an organization associated with the journal. *Community Development Journal* is recommended for academic libraries that support a comprehensive urban studies collection.

5230. *Computers, Environment and Urban Systems.* Former titles (until 1980): *Urban Systems;* (until 1977): *Computers and Urban Society.* [ISSN: 0198-9715] 1975. bi-m. EUR 1687. Ed(s): Jean-Claude Thill. Pergamon, The Blvd, Langford Ln, E Park, Kidlington, OX5 1GB, United Kingdom; JournalsCustomerServiceEMEA@elsevier.com; http://www.elsevier.com. Illus., index, adv. Sample. Refereed. Vol. ends: No. 25. Microform: PQC. *Indexed:* A01, A22, C&ISA, CerAb, CompLI, EngInd, S25. *Aud.:* Ac.

A highly technical journal, *Computers, Environment and Urban Systems* publishes "cutting-edge and innovative computer-based research on environmental and urban systems, that privileges the geospatial perspective." One of the aims of the journal is to demonstrate how computer-based research can help explain and enhance the totality of urban and environmental systems. Publishing applied, theoretical, and technical articles, the journal encourages using methodological approaches like geographic information systems (heavy emphasis), geocomputation, and spatial statistical analysis, and applying them to such areas as environmental analysis, modeling and management, emergency response and hazards, land and resource management, infrastructure and facilities management, transportation, business, and service planning. The journal is published six times a year (including two thematic issues) and is international in coverage. Due to its highly technical nature and cost, this journal is recommended for larger academic libraries that support a technological component to their urban studies or planning programs. Information technology programs may find this title relevant as well. For a less technical and costly title, see *Environment and Planning B: Planning & Design*.

Economic Geography. See Geography section.

Environment and Behavior. See Psychology section.

5231. *Environment and Planning A.* Supersedes in part (in 1974): *Environment and Planning.* [ISSN: 0308-518X] 1969. m. USD 2040 combined subscription in the Americas (print & online eds.); GBP 1150 combined subscription elsewhere (print & online eds.). Ed(s): Jamie Peck. Pion Ltd., 207 Brondesbury Park, London, NW2 5JN, United Kingdom; sales@pion.co.uk; http://www.pion.co.uk/. Illus. Refereed. *Indexed:* A01, A22, BRI, EconLit, FR, IBSS, JEL, P02, S25. *Bk. rev.:* Number varies, 500-1,000 words, signed. *Aud.:* Ac.

The flagship journal in the *Environment and Planning* family of journals, *Environment and Planning A* (*EPA*) is peer reviewed and interdisciplinary in nature. Having existed for over 40 years, *EPA* is published monthly, thus allowing it to "maintain its core interests while simultaneously developing new fields of research as they emerge." The core interest is urban and regional research with specific emphasis on their fate. Each issue contains commentaries, book reviews, editorials, a featured graphic, and at least ten articles. Frequently an issue will have a theme and a guest editor. Recent themes include "Researching policy mobilities: reflections on methods" and "Problematic political economy in geographical context." Geographic coverage of the content is international. Online access is included with a subscription. *EPA* is highly recommended for academic libraries. Sociology, philosophy, and multicultural studies programs may also benefit from this journal.

5232. *Environment and Planning B: Planning & Design.* Formerly (until 1983): *Environment & Planning. B;* Which superseded in part (in 1974): *Environment & Planning.* [ISSN: 0265-8135] 1969. bi-m. USD 728 combined subscription in the Americas (print & online eds.); GBP 415 combined subscription elsewhere (print & online eds.). Ed(s): Mike Batty, David O'Sullivan. Pion Ltd., 207 Brondesbury Park, London, NW2 5JN, United Kingdom; sales@pion.co.uk; http://www.pion.co.uk/. Refereed. *Indexed:* A01, A22, IBSS. *Bk. rev.:* 0-5, 500 words, signed. *Aud.:* Ac.

Environment and Planning B (*EPB*) is one of four journals in the *Environment and Planning* family. The focus of *EPB* is addressing problems of the "built environment and the spatial structure of cities and regions." This journal is published six times a year, and each issue publishes between eight and ten research articles, and book reviews range from not being included to numbering upwards of five. Many of the research articles focus on the applicability of computers and computing to planning and design. Issues may contain commentary and/or editorial pieces. Like *Environment and Planning A*, *EPB* occasionally publishes theme issues with guest editors. *EPB* is recommended for academic libraries, especially those with a technology component in the program. Information technology or computer science programs may also find this title useful. For a more technical (and expensive) title, see *Computers, Environment and Urban Systems*.

5233. *Environment and Planning D: Society and Space.* [ISSN: 0263-7758] 1983. bi-m. USD 728 combined subscription in the Americas (print & online eds.); GBP 415 combined subscription elsewhere (print & online eds.). Ed(s): Stuart Elden. Pion Ltd., 207 Brondesbury Park, London, NW2 5JN, United Kingdom; sales@pion.co.uk; http://www.pion.co.uk/. Refereed. *Indexed:* A01, A22, FR, IBSS, MLA-IB. *Bk. rev.:* 0-6, signed. *Aud.:* Ac.

Published six times a year, *Environment and Planning D* (*EPD*) is one of four journals in the *Environment and Planning* family and focuses on the "mutually constitutive relation between the social and the spatial." This is a scholarly journal, and articles are interdisciplinary and international in coverage. Like the other journals in the *Environment and Planning* family, *EPD* does publish thematic issues on occasion, including a guest editor. Recent themes include "The geographies of counterterror culture" and "Areographies." *EPD* issues include articles, book reviews, and a conversation section. The conversation

section is a panel of interdisciplinary scholars who provide their perspective on a given topic, reinforcing the interdisciplinary intent of the journal. With the subscription cost, the journal includes online access to all content. Sociology and philosophy studies programs may also find this title of interest. For academic libraries.

5234. *Environment and Urbanization.* [ISSN: 0956-2478] 1989. s-a. USD 657. Ed(s): Jane Bicknell, David Satterthwaite. Sage Publications Ltd., 1 Oliver's Yard, 55 City Rd, London, EC1Y 1SP, United Kingdom; info@sagepub.co.uk; http://www.uk.sagepub.com. Illus., index, adv. Sample. Refereed. Vol. ends: No. 2. Reprint: PSC. *Indexed:* A22, C&ISA, C45, CerAb, E01, EIP, IBSS, P61, SSA. *Bk. rev.:* Number and length vary. *Aud.:* Ac.

Environment and Urbanization is a scholarly journal focused on the interconnections of urban and environmental issues. Published in association with the International Institute for Environment and Development, the journal focuses on one specific theme per issue. This journal has a geographic emphasis on Asia, Latin America, and Africa, and recent themes include "Health and the City" and "Youth and the City." *Environment and Urbanization* is published twice yearly, and each issue includes between nine and 15 articles all relating to the chosen theme. Issues also contain a "Book Notes" section that details new books on the market. Additionally, a "Summaries of Articles" section is published at the end of each issue with summaries in English, French, and Spanish. Book reviews are included in select issues. This journal is highly recommended for academic libraries, and also highly recommended for those with Environmental Studies and/or Globalization programs.

5235. *European Journal of Spatial Development.* [ISSN: 1650-9544] 2002. irreg. Free. Ed(s): Lukas Smas, Christer Bengs. Nordregio, PO Box 1658, Stockholm, 11186, Sweden; nordregio@nordregio.se; http://www.nordregio.se. Refereed. *Aud.:* Ac.

Published free of charge and in electronic format only, the *European Journal of Spatial Development* (*EJSD*) publishes scholarly articles on just that, spatial development. For *EJSD*, spatial development includes spatial analysis and planning, regional governance, and policy creation. *EJSD* is published by Nordregio, Nordic Centre for Spatial Development, and by OTB Research Institute at Delft University of Technology. As the name of the journal implies, the geographic coverage is predominantly European. *ESJD* does not take the traditional format of a journal, as no volumes or issues exist. Each article is sequentially numbered and published on the web site as a pdf. Each article contains an abstract. While the articles are current, the other categories (editorials, debate, etc.) tend to be outdated. *EJSD* is recommended for academic libraries with a comprehensive urban studies collection. URL: www.nordregio.se/European-Journal-Spatial-Development/

5236. *European Planning Studies.* [ISSN: 0965-4313] 1993. m. GBP 2286 (print & online eds.). Ed(s): Philip Cooke, Louis Albrechts. Routledge, 4 Park Sq, Milton Park, Abingdon, OX14 4RN, United Kingdom; subscriptions@tandf.co.uk; http://www.tandfonline.com. Adv. Sample. Refereed. Reprint: PSC. *Indexed:* A01, A22, ABIn, B01, C45, E01, IBSS, P02, P61, SSA. *Bk. rev.:* Number and length vary. *Aud.:* Ac.

Published in cooperation with the Association of European Schools of Planning (AESOP), an independent group of European planning educators, *European Planning Studies* looks to publish original, scholarly research on "spatial development processes and policies." With an emphasis on "infrastructure, communications, environmental quality, design, cultural, social welfare, recreational, housing, industrial and employment concerns of planning at whatever spatial scale." This journal is published monthly, and each issue includes several original research articles, a "European Briefing" section, a "Research Briefing" section, and a book review. About three issues per volume are special theme issues. The institutional subscription cost is on the higher end, but when one looks at the publication frequency, the cost per article does bring it into comparison with a similar title, *European Urban and Regional Studies*. Recommended for academic libraries that maintain a comprehensive collection or with a European focus in the program.

5237. *European Urban and Regional Studies.* [ISSN: 0969-7764] 1994. q. USD 1015. Ed(s): Diane Perrons, Kathy Wood. Sage Publications Ltd., 1 Oliver's Yard, 55 City Rd, London, EC1Y 1SP, United Kingdom; info@sagepub.co.uk; http://www.uk.sagepub.com. Adv. Sample. Refereed. Reprint: PSC. *Indexed:* A01, A22, B01, C45, E01, IBSS, P02, P61, RRTA, RiskAb, SSA. *Bk. rev.:* Number and length vary. *Aud.:* Ac.

A scholarly journal, *European Urban and Regional Studies* aims to provide a forum for debate between the different processes of urban and regional development. As the name implies, the journal focuses solely on European development but puts this development into a broader global context and makes connections from the local level to the global level. The journal is published quarterly. Each issue contains between six and eight articles, each containing an abstract. Book reviews are sporadic at best. A similar title (with a significantly higher subscription cost), *European Planning Studies,* is published more frequently and may also be an option for those looking for a European-focused publication. Highly recommended for academic libraries that maintain comprehensive collections or with a European focus.

5238. *Forefront (Philadelphia).* 2012. w. USD 17.88. The Next American City, Inc., 1315 Walnut St, Ste 902, Philadelphia, PA 19107; info@americancity.org; http://www.americancity.org. *Aud.:* Ga, Ac, Sa.

Launched in April 2012, *Forefront* is a new publication from the nonprofit organization, Next American City, which is "dedicated to connecting cities and informing the people who work to improve them." Next American City previously published a magazine with the same title, but it ceased that publication for the new, online only *Forefront. Forefront* publishes one article online per week. Access to articles is available via a monthly subscription ($1.49 for an individual) or through a one-time article purchase ($1.99). Subscriptions for companies and/or libraries are available via IP, but it is advised to contact the journal for accurate pricing. *Forefront* focuses on American cities, but some international cities have already been the focus of the weekly article. The APA sponsored the debut article on April 13, 2012, and that is freely available to the public. A daily blog is also available on the site at no charge. The articles are easily read, fresh, and informative to players in the field and the general public. The site is clean and clear, making it a pleasant experience to read articles on the screen. Articles can also be downloaded to e-readers. Though it is very early in its publication life, I highly recommend checking out this site and this new subscription/publication model.

Geo World. See Cartography, GIS, and Imagery section.

5239. *Growth and Change: a journal of urban and regional policy.* [ISSN: 0017-4815] 1970. q. GBP 292. Ed(s): Dan Rickman, Barney Warf. Wiley-Blackwell Publishing, Inc., 111 River St, Hoboken, NJ 07030; info@wiley.com; http://www.wiley.com/. Illus., index, adv. Sample. Refereed. Vol. ends: No. 4. Microform: PQC. Reprint: PSC. *Indexed:* A01, A22, ABIn, Agr, B01, B02, BAS, BRI, C45, E01, EconLit, IBSS, JEL, P02, P61, RRTA, S25, SSA. *Bk. rev.:* Number varies, 1,000-2,000 words, signed. *Aud.:* Ac, Sa.

Published quarterly, *Growth and Change* is a peer-reviewed, international journal with an interdisciplinary approach to urban studies. The journal encourages manuscript submissions from "scholars and professionals in all disciplines and specialties" that take a multidisciplinary approach to the addressed problem(s). Articles in *Growth and Change* do tend to focus more on economic aspects as compared with other disciplines. Most issues contain a "Perspective" piece, intended as a thought and discussion provoker, three to five research articles, and book reviews. Because *Growth and Change* tends to focus on economic issues, it is recommended for academic libraries with a comprehensive urban studies collection. Programs with strong economics programs may also find this title of interest.

5240. *Housing Policy Debate.* [ISSN: 1051-1482] 1990. q. GBP 340 (print & online eds.). Ed(s): Thomas W Sanchez. Routledge, 325 Chestnut St, Ste 800, Philadelphia, PA 19106; customerservice@taylorandfrancis.com; http://www.tandfonline.com. Illus. Refereed. Microform: PQC. Reprint: PSC. *Indexed:* A22, ABIn, ABS&EES, EconLit, IBSS, JEL, RiskAb, SWR&A. *Aud.:* Ga, Ac, Sa.

Housing Policy Debate (HPD) is a scholarly publication dedicated to the study of U.S. housing policy. Topics of research covered include "housing policy, fair housing policy, land use regulations influencing housing affordability, metropolitan development trends, and linkages among housing policy and energy, environmental[,] and transformational policy." Issues of *HPD* include some, if not all, of the following sections: "Forum," "Articles," and "Outlook." The "Forum" section focuses on an issue of current debate. A central article is presented with responding commentary. The "Articles" section presents

original research that has undergone the double-blind, peer-review process. The "Outlook" section presents a current topic and subsequent commentary by the editors or expert guest writers. Thematic issues tend to appear in at least one issue per volume. *HPD* is published quarterly by Taylor & Francis on behalf of the Metropolitan Institute at Virginia Tech. It is recommended for academic libraries and large public libraries that support government agencies. Public Policy and Political Science programs may also find it relevant.

5241. *Housing Studies.* [ISSN: 0267-3037] 1986. 8x/yr. GBP 825 (print & online eds.). Routledge, 4 Park Sq, Milton Park, Abingdon, OX14 4RN, United Kingdom; subscriptions@tandf.co.uk; http://www.tandfonline.com. Illus., index, adv. Sample. Refereed. Reprint: PSC. *Indexed:* A01, A22, ABIn, ASSIA, B01, BAS, E01, EconLit, IBSS, JEL, P02, P61, RiskAb, SSA. *Bk. rev.:* 3-5, 500-2,000 words, signed. *Aud.:* Ac, Sa.

As the title implies, *Housing Studies* publishes on all aspects involved with housing issues. A scholarly journal, it claims to be "the essential international forum for academic debate in the housing field." The journal is published eight times a year and includes original articles and three to five book reviews per issue. Special theme issues are published often, and recent themes include "Social Enterprise, Hybridity, and Housing Organizations" and "Housing Affordability and Market Stability." The geographic coverage is international, with a slight focus toward Europe. *Housing Studies* is interdisciplinary in its approach to the study of urban areas and welcomes articles with a similar approach. Recommended for academic libraries. Public policy programs may also want to consider this title.

5242. *International Journal of Urban and Regional Research.* [ISSN: 0309-1317] 1976. q. GBP 516. Ed(s): Maria Kaika, Julie Ann Boudreau. Wiley-Blackwell Publishing Ltd., 9600 Garsington Rd, Oxford, OX4 2DQ, United Kingdom; customer@wiley.co.uk; http://www.wiley.com/. Illus., index, adv. Sample. Refereed. Vol. ends: Dec. Reprint: PSC. *Indexed:* A01, A22, BAS, BRI, E01, EconLit, FR, IBSS, JEL, P02, P61, RiskAb, SSA. *Bk. rev.:* Number & length vary; signed. *Aud.:* Ac.

Highly regarded in the field of urban studies, the *International Journal of Urban and Regional Research* publishes articles critical of existing policies and theories by "linking theoretical development and empirical research." A scholarly journal, *IJURR* is published six times per year. In addition to an average of six research articles, *IJURR* presents articles in four other sections ("Debates & Developments," "Urban Worlds," "Symposia," and "Book Reviews"). Usually three of the four sections are published in each issue. As the title implies, the journal is international in its coverage of urban and regional studies. Their online presence is worth mentioning, as the site provides free access to "*IJURR* Virtual Issues." These issues are comprised of previously published articles chosen by the editorial board and compiled to create the thematic virtual issue. Additional special features are also provided at no cost. Highly recommended for academic libraries.

5243. *International Planning Studies.* [ISSN: 1356-3475] 1996. q. GBP 454 (print & online eds.). Ed(s): Francesca Sartorio, Shin Lee. Routledge, 4 Park Sq, Milton Park, Abingdon, OX14 4RN, United Kingdom; subscriptions@tandf.co.uk; http://www.tandfonline.com. Illus., index, adv. Sample. Refereed. Reprint: PSC. *Indexed:* A01, A22, ABIn, B01, E01, FR, IBSS, P02. *Bk. rev.:* 3-5, 500 words, signed. *Aud.:* Ac, Sa.

How the impact of challenges arising from the growth of globalization is affecting the study of planning from the urban, regional, national, and international perspective is at the core of *International Planning Studies.* Published quarterly, *IPS* looks to fill the "gap between the more specialist theoretical and empirical journals in planning and urban-regional studies." Issues contain an editorial, four to six original research papers, and a book review section with an average of five reviews. Each article includes an abstract, and the geographic coverage of the articles is international, as is the editorial board. Special theme issues are occasionally presented—most recently, "Rethinking the Metropolis: Reconfiguring the Governance Structures of the 21st Century City-Region." Recommended for academic libraries, and highly recommended for libraries that support planning programs.

5244. *Journal of Architectural and Planning Research.* Former titles (until 1984): *Journal of Architectural Research;* (until 1974): *Architectural Research and Teaching.* [ISSN: 0738-0895] 1970. q. USD 450 (Individuals, USD 130). Ed(s): Andrew D Seidel. Locke Science

Publishing Company, Inc., 28 E Jackson Bldg, 10th Fl L221, Chicago, IL 60604; customercare@lockescience.com. Illus. Sample. Refereed. *Indexed:* A07, A22, ABS&EES, API, AbAn, C&ISA, CerAb, PsycInfo. *Bk. rev.:* 1-3; length varies. *Aud.:* Ac, Sa.

Published quarterly, the *Journal of Architectural and Planning Research* (*JAPR*) aims to keep readers informed on the most up-to-date research in the broad areas of architecture and design, urban planning, and architectural design, interior design, and urban design. A scholarly journal published for scholars and practitioners in the field, it is international in coverage. Each issue contains between five and ten research articles, one or two book reviews, and sometimes a position paper. Making the connection between architecture and urban planning is the source of this journal's uniqueness. *JAPR* is only available in print. Recommended for academic libraries; highly recommended for those libraries that support programs with a city planning or an architecture component. General architecture and planning programs should also consider this title.

5245. *Journal of Planning Education and Research.* [ISSN: 0739-456X] 1981. q. USD 436. Ed(s): Luci Yamamoto, Michael Brooks. Sage Publications, Inc., 2455 Teller Rd, Thousand Oaks, CA 91320; info@sagepub.com; http://www.sagepub.com. Adv. Sample. Refereed. Reprint: PSC. *Indexed:* A22, C&ISA, CerAb, E01, P61, SSA. *Bk. rev.:* 6-8 signed, length varies. *Aud.:* Ac.

The *Journal of Planning Education and Research* is the scholarly journal of the Association of Collegiate Schools of Planning (ACSP). The ACSP is a consortium of universities offering credentials in urban and regional planning that are committed to understanding and improving the versatility of urban and regional development and subsequently to improve education on the subject matter. Published quarterly, the *Journal of Planning Education and Research* includes six to eight articles per issue. Each article contains an abstract. Articles are a mix of case studies, theory, and pedagogy that focuses on the United States, but with increasing inclusion of other countries. Some recent article topics include community development, neighborhood planning, public policy, and land use. Issues also include upwards of eight book reviews. This journal is a core title and highly recommended for academic libraries, specifically those with planning programs.

5246. *Journal of Planning Literature.* Incorporates (1979-1995): *C P L Bibliography.* [ISSN: 0885-4122] 1986. q. USD 1282. Ed(s): Bardia Nikrahei, Jack Nasar. Sage Publications, Inc., 2455 Teller Rd, Thousand Oaks, CA 91320; info@sagepub.com; http://www.sagepub.com. Adv. Sample. Refereed. Microform: PQC. Reprint: PSC. *Indexed:* A01, A22, E01, IBSS, P02, P61, SSA. *Bk. rev.:* Number and length vary. *Aud.:* Ac, Sa.

The *Journal of Planning Literature* is an international, scholarly journal composed of review articles and abstracts that focus on recent publications in the regional planning and design field. Published quarterly, the *JPL* "aims to give the reader an understanding of the state of knowledge of the field for use in research or professional practice." Each issue includes an average of two review articles, a Council of Planning Librarians (CPL) Bibliography, hundreds of abstracts from journal articles and dissertations, and an author and subject index of entries. Three broad subject headings are used to organize the citations: "History/Theory/Administration," "Methodology/Quantitative/Economic/ Qualitative," and "Physical/Environmental." Some issues contain book reviews. The journal is an excellent resource for practitioners, scholars, and students. A core title for urban studies programs, *JPL* is highly recommended for academic libraries and appropriate special libraries.

5247. *Journal of Urban Affairs.* Formed by the merger of (1979-1981): *Urban Affairs Papers;* (1977-1981): *Urban Interest Journal.* [ISSN: 0735-2166] 1976. 5x/yr. GBP 744. Ed(s): Victoria Bassolo. Wiley-Blackwell Publishing, Inc., 111 River St, Hoboken, NJ 07030; info@wiley.com; http://onlinelibrary.wiley.com/. Illus., adv. Sample. Refereed. Microform: PQC. Reprint: PSC. *Indexed:* A01, A22, ABS&EES, BRI, E01, EconLit, FR, IIBP, P02, P61, RiskAb, SSA, SWR&A. *Bk. rev.:* 4-6, 500-1,000 words, signed. *Aud.:* Ga, Ac, Sa.

Published five times a year, the *Journal of Urban Affairs* is the journal of the Urban Affairs Association (UAA), an international organization that "encourages the dissemination of information and research findings about

urbanism and urbanization." The journal is a member benefit. Each issue publishes an average of five articles. The articles are predominantly focused on North America, but international coverage is included. The nature of the articles ranges from theoretical to case studies. Each article contains an abstract, and most are understandable to the average reader. About five book reviews are published per issue. Their web presence includes virtual issues that pull together the most popular (citations and downloads) articles from recent issues. Two have been published to date. Highly recommended for academic libraries and for public libraries in urban settings.

5248. *Journal of Urban Design.* [ISSN: 1357-4809] 1996. q. GBP 561 (print & online eds.). Ed(s): Taner Oc. Routledge, 4 Park Sq, Milton Park, Abingdon, OX14 4RN, United Kingdom; subscriptions@tandf.co.uk; http://www.tandfonline.com. Illus., adv. Sample. Refereed. Reprint: PSC. *Indexed:* A01, A22, API, AmHI, E01, IBSS, P02. *Bk. rev.:* 3-5, 500-1,000 words, signed. *Aud.:* Ac, Sa.

A scholarly journal, the *Journal of Urban Design* publishes articles relating to all aspects of urban design, now considered a core knowledge component of a planning education. Some subject areas within urban design that are covered include urban aesthetics and townscape, sustainable development, preservation and conservation, local and regional identity, and urban regeneration. The journal occasionally publishes special issues. Each issue produces an average of five to seven original articles, highly international in coverage and each containing an abstract, as well as four to six book reviews. The *Journal of Urban Design* is highly recommended for academic libraries. Architecture programs should also find this title relevant.

Journal of Urban History. See History section.

5249. *Journal of Urban Technology.* [ISSN: 1063-0732] 1992. q. GBP 467 (print & online eds.). Ed(s): Maryann Donato, Richard E Hanley. Routledge, 4 Park Sq, Milton Park, Abingdon, OX14 4RN, United Kingdom; subscriptions@tandf.co.uk; http://www.tandfonline.com. Illus., adv. Sample. Refereed. Reprint: PSC. *Indexed:* A01, A22, E01, ERIC. *Bk. rev.:* 2-6, variable length, signed. *Aud.:* Ga, Ac, Sa.

The *Journal of Urban Technology* publishes original research articles that focus on technology and its impact on cities. The journal aims to educate its readers as well as to foster discussion about maximizing the positive impact, and subsequently minimizing the negative impact, that these technologies pose to cities. The journal is scholarly and international in coverage, and publishes four issues per year. Each issue tends to include an editorial, an average of five research articles, and a book review section. Special theme issues are published frequently. Geared for both practitioners and the general public, the understandable articles help foster the sought-after discussion between specialists and non-specialists; thus, this journal separates itself from the other technology-based journals in this section. The journal is recommended for academic libraries and large public libraries. Libraries that support information technology programs may also find it useful.

5250. *Journal of Urbanism: international research on placemaking and urban sustainability.* [ISSN: 1754-9175] 2008. 3x/yr. GBP 350 (print & online eds.). Ed(s): Emily Talen, Matthew Hardy. Routledge, 4 Park Sq, Milton Park, Abingdon, OX14 4RN, United Kingdom; subscriptions@tandf.co.uk; http://www.tandfonline.com. Adv. Sample. Refereed. Reprint: PSC. *Indexed:* A01, A22, E01, IBSS. *Bk. rev.:* 1-2, signed. *Aud.:* Ac.

As the concept of sustainability has become very popular in recent years, it has become important to include a journal that combines this topic with urban studies. The *Journal of Urbanism: International Research on Placemaking and Urban Sustainability* is in its fifth year of publication, and it publishes three issues per year. It aims to look at "human settlement and its relation to the idea of sustainability, social justice, and cultural understanding." International in coverage, this journal presents original research articles, one or two book reviews, and a "Viewpoint" piece from a player in the field in each issue. Articles include present and historic research and analysis. The *Journal of Urbanism* may become a bigger player if the conversation of sustainability remains at the national and international forefront. Recommended for libraries with comprehensive collections.

Landscape and Urban Planning. See Landscape Architecture section.

5251. *Planetizen Newswire.* [ISSN: 1536-0547] 2000. s-w. Free. Urban Insight, Inc., 3700 Wilshire Blvd., Ste 570, Los Angeles, CA 90010; info@urbaninsight.com; http://www.urbaninsight.com. *Bk. rev.:* Number and length vary. *Aud.:* Ga, Ac, Sa.

Published twice weekly via e-mail, *Planetizen Newswire* is a free electronic publication produced and distributed by the Planetizen web site. Planetizen is a public-interest information exchange provided by Urban Insight. The newsletter includes the "latest news, jobs, features and more related to the urban planning, design, and development community." Each newsletter delivers what the publishers consider the top 20–30 news headlines from the previous three or four days, each represented with the title, source, and a brief summary. The title is hyperlinked back to Planetizen, where more of the story is presented. The news stories are pulled predominantly from newspapers and magazines around the United States, thus written with the general public in mind. The newsletter also has an announcement section and links back to the web site, which includes jobs, blogs, educational resources, op-eds, and organizational information. While the subject matter of this newsletter makes it relevant for students, scholars, and practitioners, the general scope enables the newsletter to be utilized by the public. To receive the *Planetizen Newswire,* you must register on the web site. Recommended for the general collection of public and academic libraries. URL: www.planetizen.com/newswire

5252. *Planning.* Former titles (until 1969): *A S P O Newsletter;* (until 1951): *American Society of Planning Officials. Newsletter;* Incorporates (1976-1979): *Practicing Planner;* Which was formerly (until 1976): *Planner's Notebook.* [ISSN: 0001-2610] 1935. 10x/yr. Free to members; Non-members, USD 75. Ed(s): Sylvia Lewis. American Planning Association, 205 N Michigan Ave, Ste 1200, Chicago, IL 60601; customerservice@planning.org; http://www.planning.org. Illus., index, adv. Vol. ends: Dec. Microform: PQC. *Indexed:* A01, A22, ABIn, B01, B02, BRI. *Bk. rev.:* Number and length vary. *Aud.:* Ga, Ac, Sa.

The professional magazine of the American Planning Association (APA), *Planning* is published ten times a year and is a membership benefit. Members of the APA also receive access to the online edition of *Planning.* This journal is geared to those in the field, but the articles are written so that the general public can understand and appreciate the subject matter. Color photos accompany the feature articles, and each issue includes five to seven articles in addition to the recurring sections. Book reviews are included in the Planners Library section and vary in number from issue to issue. Geographic coverage is predominantly the United States and some issues are thematic. With a reasonable subscription price, *Planning* is highly recommended for general academic and public library collections, especially those that support urban planning programs or located in heavily urban areas.

5253. *Planning Perspectives: an international journal of history, planning and the environment.* Incorporates (1988-2006): *Planning History;* Which was formerly (until 1988): *Planning History Bulletin;* (until 1979): *Planning History Group. Newsletter.* [ISSN: 0266-5433] 1986. q. GBP 1057 (print & online eds.). Routledge, 4 Park Sq, Milton Park, Abingdon, OX14 4RN, United Kingdom; subscriptions@tandf.co.uk; http://www.tandfonline.com. Illus., adv. Sample. Refereed. Reprint: PSC. *Indexed:* A01, A22, API, ArtHuCI, B01, E01. *Bk. rev.:* 7-9, 500 words. *Aud.:* Ac.

Planning Perspectives is an interdisciplinary, peer-reviewed journal that publishes articles focused on history, planning, and the environment. Published four times a year, the journal links the "interest of those working in economics, social and political history, historical geography[,] and historical sociology with those in the applied fields of public health, housing construction, architectures[,] and town planning." Each issue contains research articles, an IPHS (International Planning Historical Society) section, and an extensive book review section (about eight per issue). Book reviews are focused on U.K., North American, and European literature, but the articles and IPHS sections are international in coverage. Members of the IPHS receive *Planning Perspectives* as a membership benefit. Because of its interdisciplinary nature, this journal is recommended for academic libraries and for libraries that maintain extensive history collections.

5254. *Planning Practice and Research.* [ISSN: 0269-7459] 1986. 5x/yr. GBP 656 (print & online eds.). Ed(s): Vincent Nadin. Routledge, 4 Park Sq, Milton Park, Abingdon, OX14 4RN, United Kingdom; subscriptions@tandf.co.uk; http://www.tandfonline.com. Illus., adv. Sample. Refereed. Reprint: PSC. *Indexed:* A01, A22, B01, C45, E01, IBSS, RRTA. *Bk. rev.:* Number and length vary. *Aud.:* Ac, Sa.

A scholarly journal published five times a year, *Planning Practice and Research* looks to be the source for "reflective, critical academics, professionals[,] and students who are concerned to keep abreast of and challenge current thinking" in the present field of planning. The journal is committed to creating links between the research, practice, and education of planning, presenting analytical research, and fostering a place of dialogue for these topics. Each issue includes four to six research articles, and theme issues are published. The coverage is international, with an emphasis on European countries. *Planning Practice and Research* can be chosen as a benefit by members of the Regional Studies Association, giving them online access. Recommended for U.S. academic libraries with comprehensive collections.

5255. *Regional Studies.* [ISSN: 0034-3404] 1967. 10x/yr. GBP 1478 (print & online eds.); Free to members. Ed(s): Dr. Arnoud Lagendijk. Routledge, 4 Park Sq, Milton Park, Abingdon, OX14 4RN, United Kingdom; subscriptions@tandf.co.uk; http://www.tandfonline.com. Illus., adv. Sample. Refereed. Microform: PQC. Reprint: PSC. *Indexed:* A22, ABIn, API, B01, B02, BAS, BRI, C45, E01, EconLit, FR, IBSS, JEL, P02, P61, RRTA, RiskAb, SSA. *Bk. rev.:* 1-5, 500-1,000 words, signed. *Aud.:* Ac.

The journal of the Regional Studies Association, this is a scholarly publication with an emphasis on "theoretical development, empirical analysis[,] and policy debate in the multi- and inter-disciplinary field of regional studies." This journal is published ten times a year, and each issue of *Regional Studies* is composed of seven to nine original research articles, one to three book reviews, and occasionally a survey and/or debate section. Each article contains an abstract published in five different languages. The geographic coverage is international, and theme issues are published. Members of the Regional Studies Association receive the journal as a membership benefit. Though broader in geographic coverage than traditional urban studies journals, *Regional Studies* provides an important subnational view that explores the same concepts as those in the more traditional titles. *Regional Studies* is recommended for academic libraries. Geography and Environmental Studies programs may also find this title of interest.

Topos: European landscape magazine. See Landscape Architecture section.

5256. *Town Planning Review.* [ISSN: 0041-0020] 1910. bi-m. GBP 603 (print & online eds.). Liverpool University Press, 4 Cambridge St, Liverpool, L69 7ZU, United Kingdom; lup@liv.ac.uk; http://www.liverpooluniversitypress.co.uk/. Illus., index, adv. Refereed. Vol. ends: Oct. Reprint: PSC. *Indexed:* A06, A07, A22, ABIn, API, AmHI, BAS, BRI, BrArAb, BrTechI, IBSS, NumL, P02, P61, RiskAb, SSA. *Bk. rev.:* 1-3, 1,000-2,000 words, signed. *Aud.:* Ac.

Founded over 100 years ago, *Town Planning Review* reports on any aspect of urban and regional planning in "advanced economies and emerging industrial states." In addition to the roughly six research articles, issues can include "Viewpoints" on a given subject presented by a single contributor; a discussion "Forum" that presents debates on a given topic; conference reports; review papers; and book reviews. The sections included in each issue vary. A scholarly journal, *TPR* is published six times a year, and the articles are heavily focused on European countries. The subscription price includes electronic access to all issues. *TPR* is recommended for academic libraries; even more so for academic libraries in Europe.

5257. *U R I S A Journal.* [ISSN: 1045-8077] 1989. s-a. USD 295. Urban and Regional Information Systems Association, 1460 Renaissance Dr, Ste 305, Park Ridge, IL 60068-1348; info@urisa.org; http://www.urisa.org/. Refereed. Circ: 3800 Paid. *Indexed:* A01, BRI. *Bk. rev.:* Number and length vary. *Aud.:* Ac, Sa.

An open-access journal for over ten years, the *URISA Journal* is the flagship, and official, journal of the Urban and Regional Information Systems Association, the association for GIS professionals. *URISA Journal* publishes two issues per year and is freely available on the Association's web site. The full back file beginning with the first issue in 1989 is freely available on the site as well. Print copies are available as a membership benefit. Libraries and other organizations can subscribe to the print version for a fee. The *URISA Journal* includes "reports of current research; reports and reviews of system applications; and reviews relating to the design, implementation and evaluation of information systems for federal, state, provincial, regional, local and municipal governments." In addition to the scholarly articles, issues can contain software reviews, book reviews, and literature reviews. This journal publishes more articles that deal with the application of technologies, while *Environment and Planning B: Society and Design* and *Computers, Environment and Urban Systems* both focus more on the development of the technology. The *URISA Journal* is recommended for academic libraries and appropriate special libraries. It may also be of interest to information technology programs. URL: www.urisa.org/urisajournal

5258. Urban Affairs Review. Formerly (until 1995): *Urban Affairs Quarterly.* [ISSN: 1078-0874] 1965. bi-m. USD 1152. Ed(s): Jaime Holland Masterson, Michael A Pagano. Sage Publications, Inc., 2455 Teller Rd, Thousand Oaks, CA 91320; info@sagepub.com; http://www.sagepub.com. Illus., index. Sample. Refereed. Vol. ends: Jun. Microform: PQC. Reprint: PSC. *Indexed:* A01, A22, BRI, C&ISA, CerAb, Chicano, E01, EIP, EconLit, IBSS, JEL, P02, P61, RiskAb, SSA, SWR&A. *Bk. rev.:* 1-3, 1,000-1,500 words, signed. *Aud.:* Ac, Sa.

Published bimonthly, *Urban Affairs Review* is a reputable, multidisciplinary scholarly journal in the field of urban studies. Affiliated with the Urban Politics section of the American Political Science Association, the journal publishes original research articles of timely empirical analysis and research on the programs and policies that affect cities. Each issue contains between three and five articles that include an abstract, as well as one to three book reviews. The articles have increased in international coverage since the last review. Articles are published online first then make their way to print. Subscriptions including the electronic component will enable these articles to be viewed. Similar in scope and geographic coverage to the *Journal of Urban Affairs*, *Urban Affairs Review* costs slightly more. A very solid journal in its own right, *Urban Affairs Review* is highly recommended for academic collections. Political science programs may also find this title relevant.

5259. Urban History. Formerly (until 1992): *Urban History Yearbook;* Which superseded (in 1974): *Urban History Newsletter.* [ISSN: 0963-9268] 1963. 3x/yr. GBP 249. Ed(s): Simon Gunn, Rosemary Sweet. Cambridge University Press, The Edinburgh Bldg, Shaftesbury Rd, Cambridge, CB2 8RU, United Kingdom; information@cambridge.org; http://www.cambridge.org/uk. Adv. Sample. Circ: 750. Reprint: PSC. *Indexed:* A22, API, ArtHuCI, BAS, BrArAb, E01, NumL, P61, SSA. *Bk. rev.:* Number varies; lengthy reviews. *Aud.:* Ac.

Now published four times per year, *Urban History* is a scholarly journal that claims to hold a "central place in historical scholarship." Interdisciplinary in its coverage, *Urban History* publishes research articles "covering social, economic, political[,] and cultural aspects of the history of towns and cities." The articles focus predominantly on towns and cities in Europe. In addition to the five to seven articles published, each issue also contains a substantial book review section, as well as an occasional review of a periodical article. The last part of every volume (published in December) features a bibliography of over 1,000 publications from periodicals, monographs, and collections; this is a very valuable tool for scholars and students. An index of cities and towns covered by *Urban History* during the previous year is also included in the December issue. Subscribers have online access to a consolidated bibliography as well. Because of its focus on European cities and towns, *Urban History* is highly recommended for academic libraries that support international and/or comprehensive urban studies programs.

5260. Urban Land. Incorporates (1998-2008): *Multifamily Trends;* Former titles (until 1944): *Urban Land Institute Bulletin;* (until 1942): *Urban Land Institute. News Bulletin.* [ISSN: 0042-0891] 1941. m. Free to members. Ed(s): Kristina Kessler, Karen Schaar. The Urban Land

Institute, 1025 Thomas Jefferson St, NW, Ste 500 W, Washington, DC 20007; customerservice@uli.org; http://www.uli.org. Illus., index, adv. Microform: PQC. *Indexed:* A22, API, RiskAb. *Bk. rev.:* 2-4, 200-300 words, signed. *Aud.:* Ga, Ac, Sa.

Included as a member benefit from the Urban Land Institute (ULI), *Urban Land* is published six times a year and is available to members in print and electronically. Members also have electronic access to the archive going back to 1992. *Urban Land* publishes articles that reflect the mission of the ULI, which is to work together (from landowners to lawyers to librarians) to create and promote best practices in, and sustainability of, community development. *Urban Land* focuses predominantly on North America, with some European and international coverage. The magazine publishes several feature articles and a number of pieces in recurrent segments such as "ULX," which provides ten items on a given topic (preservation, affordable housing), an "Opinion" section, and "Regional Spotlight." Color photographs accompany most of the articles. *Urban Land* includes book reviews. Although written for ULI members, it is understandable and appropriate for the general public as well. Subscriptions are only available through ULI membership, which would seem a little high if the magazine is the only reason for joining. On the whole, an enjoyable publication and recommended for large public libraries as well as academic libraries.

5261. Urban Morphology. [ISSN: 1027-4278] 1997. s-a. GBP 50 (Individuals, GBP 25). Ed(s): Jeremy Whitehand. International Seminar on Urban Form, c/o Dr Michael Barke, Division of Geography, Newcastle upon Tyne, NE1 8ST, United Kingdom; http://www.urbanform.org/. Illus., adv. Refereed. Circ: 500 Paid. *Indexed:* ArtHuCI. *Bk. rev.:* 13-19, signed. *Aud.:* Ac.

Originating in 1997, *Urban Morphology* is the journal of the International Seminar on Urban Form (ISUF). Urban morphology is the study of human settlements and the change these settlements go through over time. Published twice a year in April and October, *Urban Morphology* contains three to five research articles and a book review section. Reports from various meetings and seminars are also included, as well as a "Viewpoints" section that offers shorter opinion pieces on urban morphology topics. The ISUF offers articles from 1997 to 2001 in pdf format freely available on its web site, and 2006–12 articles are available to subscribers at no additional cost beyond the reasonable subscription price. Articles are international in coverage. Membership to the ISUF is the only way to subscribe to this journal. Recommended for academic libraries.

5262. Urban Studies: an international journal for research in urban studies. [ISSN: 0042-0980] 1964. 16x/yr. USD 3793. Ed(s): Kenneth Gibb. Sage Publications Ltd., 1 Oliver's Yard, 55 City Rd, London, EC1Y 1SP, United Kingdom; info@sagepub.co.uk; http://www.uk.sagepub.com. Illus., index, adv. Sample. Refereed. Vol. ends: Dec. Reprint: PSC. *Indexed:* A01, A22, ABIn, API, AmHI, B01, B02, BAS, BRI, E01, EconLit, FR, IBSS, JEL, P02, P61, RiskAb, SSA. *Bk. rev.:* 4-6, 500 words, signed. *Aud.:* Ac.

Published since 1964, *Urban Studies* is one of the core journals recommended to support an Urban Studies program. The journal publishes articles on any urban or regional problem associated with the social sciences. A scholarly journal, *Urban Studies* publishes 16 issues a year. Each issue contains about ten original articles with abstracts and a handful of book reviews. Some issues have a theme and there are no book reviews in these issues. The articles are international in coverage, with a slight bias toward Europe and the Americas. *Urban Studies* is expensive for libraries in either print or electronic format, but it should be noted that this publication produces a high number of articles per issue; the number of issues published per volume is higher than that for most publications in the field. It also may be relevant for environmental studies and/or sociology programs, which also could help justify the cost. A core title, *Urban Studies* is essential for academic libraries.

■ VETERINARY SCIENCE

C. Trenton Boyd, Distinguished Librarian Curator of the Medical and Veterinary Historical Collections, 328 J. Otto Lottes Health Sciences Library, University of Missouri, One Hospital Drive, Columbia, MO 65212; FAX: 573-884-1421; boydt@missouri.edu

Introduction

The titles in this section have been selected for a library that needs to maintain a very basic core collection of veterinary medical periodicals, such as a medical library in a state that has no veterinary library or an academic library that serves a department of veterinary science. The author of this section is the chair of the Serials Committee of the Veterinary Medical Libraries Section of the Medical Library Association (VMLS/MLA), and he would be happy to answer questions about any veterinary-related title. The third edition of the *Basic List of Veterinary Serials* was used in helping select the titles. It was compiled in 2009 by the Veterinary Serials Committee of the Veterinary Medical Libraries Section of the Medical Library Association, and published in 2010 in the *Journal of the Medical Library Association*. It may be accessed at www.ncbi.nlm.nih.gov/pmc/articles/PMC2947140/?tool=pubmed.

However, in an effort to provide more widespread coverage of species and practice management, the author also made some decisions based on his 42+ years of experience as a veterinary medical librarian. The top ten journals on the "Basic List" are 1) *American Veterinary Medical Association. Journal,* 2) *American Journal of Veterinary Research,* 3) *Journal of Veterinary Internal Medicine,* 4) *Veterinary Pathology,* 5) *Veterinary Clinics of North America—Small Animal,* 6) *Equine Veterinary Journal,* 7) *Veterinary Clinics of North America—Equine,* 8) *Veterinary Clinics of North America—Food Animal,* 9) *American Animal Hospital Association. Journal,* and 10) *Veterinary Surgery.*

A collection for a library that serves a college of veterinary medicine will carry a much more extensive list of veterinary titles, as well as many non-veterinary titles. (Many useful treatments and techniques can be extrapolated from human medicine and the biological sciences to veterinary medicine.) Examples of basic science titles are *Nature, Science,* and *New England Journal of Medicine.* Many human medical journals contain comparative and experimental animal studies that are important in the field of veterinary medicine. Some examples of these are *American Journal of Pathology, American Journal of Physiology, Endocrinology, Journal of Bone & Joint Surgery, Reproduction,:ro and Biology of Reproduction.*

One should remember there are several refereed animal science titles that serve as a very important adjunct to veterinary medicine. The studies contained therein are frequently valuable to veterinary researchers and practitioner/clinicians. Examples are *Journal of Animal Science, Animal, Journal of Dairy Science, Animal Frontiers,* and *Poultry Science.* Additionally, one can find breed-specific titles, such as *American Quarter Horse Journal, Thoroughbred Times, The Register* and *German Shepherd Dog Review,* which will often provide articles on the health, care, and breeding of a particular breed. The majority of the journals selected for this list are for the veterinary student, research scientist and/or practicing veterinarian, and the average reader will probably not find them interesting for leisure reading.

There are several indexing services that offer partial coverage of the veterinary literature (see list of basic abstracts and indexes). However, the only index that attempts to be comprehensive in the coverage of veterinary literature (including conference proceedings) is *Index Veterinarius* and its companion publication, *Veterinary Bulletin.* The online version is called *CAB Abstracts.* In many instances, the articles indexed are available in full text either through *CAB Abstracts* or through library subscriptions to the journals.

New titles continue to be started, but the trend of the veterinary specialties to develop their own journals has stabilized. All of the journals reviewed are available to libraries in full-text online versions.

Basic Periodicals

Ga: *D V M;* Ac: *American Animal Hospital Association. Journal, American Journal of Veterinary Research, American Veterinary Medical Association. Journal, Equine Veterinary Journal, Journal of Veterinary Internal Medicine, Veterinary Clinics of North America: Equine Practice, Veterinary Clinics of North America: Exotic Animal Practice, Veterinary Clinics of North America: Food Animal Practice, Veterinary Clinics of North America: Small Animal Practice, The Veterinary Journal, The Veterinary Record.*

Basic Abstracts and Indexes

Biological Abstracts; CAB Abstracts; Index Veterinarius; PUBMED; Scopus; Web of Science.

5263. *American Animal Hospital Association. Journal.* Former titles (until 1968): *American Hospital; American Animal Hospital Association Bulletin.* [ISSN: 0587-2871] 1965. bi-m. Members, USD 39; Non-members, USD 107. Ed(s): Alan H Rebar. American Animal Hospital Association, 12575 W Bayaud Ave, Lakewood, CO 80228; info@aahanet.org; http://www.aahanet.org. Illus., index, adv. Refereed. Vol. ends: Nov/Dec. Microform: PQC. *Indexed:* A22, C45, IndVet. *Aud.:* Ac, Sa.

The American Animal Hospital Association states that the mission of its official and educational journal is "to publish accurate, timely scientific and technical information pertaining to the practice of small animal medicine and surgery." Effective December 10, 2003, with volume 39, number 6, the journal switched to an entirely online format. However, beginning in January 2011, the print format returned as an option to subscribers. The layout editors do a superb job of intermixing color and black-and-white photographs, tables, and text to make the articles pleasing to the eye. The online format provides the added advantage of viewing photographs at three levels of resolution. The arrangement of the articles is by discipline, followed by a separate section for case reports. Articles on case studies, original research, literature reviews, and retrospective studies are accepted. An interesting feature of the online site is a ranked listing of the 50 most-read articles during the past year. Online full text is available from 1998. This august journal of small-animal medicine, now more than 45+ years old, is still required reading for small-animal practitioners and clinicians. It should be in every veterinary science collection. URL: www.jaaha.org

5264. *American Journal of Veterinary Research.* [ISSN: 0002-9645] 1940. m. USD 245 combined subscription domestic (print & online eds.); USD 255 combined subscription foreign (print & online eds.). Ed(s): Dr. Kurt J Matushek. American Veterinary Medical Association, 1931 N Meacham Rd, Ste 100, Schaumburg, IL 60173-4360; llarson@avma.org; http://www.avma.org. Illus., index, adv. Refereed. Circ: 7000 Paid. Vol. ends: Dec. Microform: PMC; PQC. *Indexed:* A01, A22, Agr, C45, ExcerpMed, FS&TA, IndVet. *Aud.:* Ac, Sa.

The research publication of the American Veterinary Medical Association is the *American Journal of Veterinary Research.* It has set high standards by promising "to publish[.] in a timely manner, peer-reviewed reports of the highest-quality research that has a clear potential to enhance the health, welfare, and performance of animals and human . . . [and that the journal] will maintain the highest ethical standards . . . and will foster global interdisciplinary cooperation in veterinary medical research." The illustrative material is largely in black-and-white. An average issue will carry 20 to 30 articles varying in length from 2 to 12 pages. At the front of each issue is a section titled "Veterinary Research News." It reports on the latest happenings in the veterinary research community. An online version has been available since January 2000. Full text is available only to subscribers, but abstracts of the articles are available to everyone. The index to each volume is available only on the web site and is not included in the printed version. This title ranked number 2 on the *Basic List of Veterinary Serials* compiled in 2009 by the Veterinary Serials Committee of the Veterinary Medical Libraries Section of the Medical Library Association (see section introduction for relevant URL.) This basic research journal is highly recommended for libraries that serve graduate programs in the fields of veterinary medicine, animal science, dairy science, and laboratory animals. URL: http://avmajournals.avma.org

5265. *American Veterinary Medical Association. Journal.* Incorporates (1899-1913): *American Veterinary Medical Association. Proceedings;* (1950-1964): *American Veterinary Medical Association. Annual Meeting. Scientific Proceedings;* Which was formerly (until 1956): *American Veterinary Medical Association. Annual Meeting. Proceedings.* [ISSN: 0003-1488] 1877. s-m. USD 210 combined subscription domestic (print & online eds.); USD 230 combined subscription foreign (print & online eds.). Ed(s): Dr. Kurt J Matushek. American Veterinary Medical Association, 1931 N Meacham Rd, Ste 100, Schaumburg, IL 60173-4360; llarson@avma.org; http://www.avma.org. Illus., index, adv. Refereed. Circ: 77100 Paid. Microform: BHP; PQC. *Indexed:* A01, A22, Agr, C45, FS&TA, IndVet, RRTA. *Bk. rev.:* 2-3, 200-400 words. *Aud.:* Ac, Sa.

The *Journal of the American Veterinary Medical Association* is the official publication of the American Veterinary Medical Association (AVMA), which is the largest veterinary association in the United States. Because the journal is sent to members, practically every U.S. veterinarian receives it. It most likely is the most widely distributed veterinary journal in the world. Each issue carries a section on news related to the association and the profession, as well as sections on interpretive summaries of articles, scientific reports, original studies, member obituaries, commentaries, educational opportunities, and classifieds. Additional features that appear frequently are "Legal Briefs," "Pathology in Practice," "What Is Your Diagnosis," "ECG of the Month," and "Special Reports." The signed book reviews are useful to librarians doing book selection in this subject area. The editors certainly achieve the goals of the journal: "to promote the science and art of veterinary medicine and to provide a forum for discussion of ideas important to the profession." An online version became available in 2000. Only subscribers can download the articles, but everyone can read the abstracts of the articles online. The index to each volume appears only on the web site and is not available in the print format. This title is the only journal to achieve a perfect score in the *Basic List of Veterinary Serials* compiled in 2009 by the Veterinary Serials Commitee of the Veterinary Medical Libraries Section of the Medical Library Association (see section introduction for URL). The title should be considered as the first choice for any U.S. veterinary collection. URL: http://avmajournals.avma.org

5266. *Australian Veterinary Journal.* Formerly (until 1927): *Australian Veterinary Association. Journal.* [ISSN: 0005-0423] 1925. m. GBP 356. Ed(s): Anne Jackson. Wiley-Blackwell Publishing Ltd., The Atrium, Southern Gate, Chichester, PO19 8SQ, United Kingdom; customer@wiley.com; http://www.wiley.com/. Illus., index, adv. Sample. Refereed. Vol. ends: Dec. Reprint: PSC. *Indexed:* A22, Agr, C45, E01, FS&TA, IndVet. *Bk. rev.:* 1-3, 300-600 words. *Aud.:* Ac, Sa.

This title, which is the official journal of the Australian Veterinary Association (AVA), is the premier veterinary journal in Australia. For 88 years it has been providing coverage of leading-edge clinical and scientific veterinary research, case reports, reviews, and news, as well as industry issues. Each issue includes 40 pages of six to nine original research articles, one to five short contributions, and occasional case reports, all of which are classified under the general headings of "clinical" and "scientific." Major review articles and signed editorials are frequently included. The journal also has a news section, classifieds, book reviews, and obituaries. Most of the charts, graphs, tables, and photographs are in color. Because this publication is designed to serve the veterinary practitioner as well as the researcher in Australia, one finds articles on domestic and non-domestic animal species that are native to Australia (kangaroos, wallabies, loggerhead turtles, etc.). Academic libraries that serve animal science departments conducting research on sheep and tropical animal production will find this journal useful. It is also a natural selection for veterinary science collections, as the Australian veterinary community produces high-quality research. Full text from volume 1 (1926) is available from Wiley Online Library - http://onlinelibrary.wiley.com/journal/10.1111/%28ISSN%291751-0813 Full text of the "AVA News" section is available free from January 2010. URL: http://www.ava.com.au/public-2

5267. *Avian Diseases.* [ISSN: 0005-2086] 1957. q. USD 275 domestic; USD 300 foreign. Ed(s): Jagdev M Sharma. American Association of Avian Pathologists, Inc., 12627 San Jose Blvd, Ste 202, Jacksonville, FL 32223; aaap@aaap.info; http://www.aaap.info/index.html. Illus., index. Refereed. Vol. ends: Oct/Dec. Microform: WSH; PMC; PQC. *Indexed:* A22, AbAn, Agr, C45, E01, IndVet. *Aud.:* Ac, Sa.

This title, the official publication of the American Association of Avian Pathologists, publishes the results of original research conducted in the specialty of avian diseases from throughout the world. This is done through full research articles, research notes, and case reports. While the emphasis is on birds of commercial importance—for example, chickens, turkeys, ducks, and geese—articles also appear on wild birds and pet species, such as budgerigars, parrots, and cockatiels. It is a substantial journal, containing 20–40 papers per issue, with each article averaging six to ten pages in length. Illustrations are mostly in black-and-white. Intended readership, according to the editors, includes avian students, educators, practitioners, researchers, diagnosticians, pet and wild bird enthusiasts, and poultry specialists. This journal is strongly recommended for avian diagnostic laboratories, avian veterinarians, and libraries that serve poultry and veterinary science programs. Full text is available from volume 1 (1957) through volume 45 (2001) from JSTOR. Full text from 2002 is available to subscribers from the publisher web site. URL: http://www.aaapjournals.info/avdi

5268. *Canadian Journal of Veterinary Research (Online).* [ISSN: 1928-9022] 2010. q. Free. Canadian Veterinary Medical Association, 339 Booth St, Ottawa, ON K1R 7K1, Canada; admin@cvma-acmv.org ; http://canadianveterinarians.net. Adv. Refereed. *Aud.:* Ac, Sa.

This is the research journal of the Canadian Veterinary Medical Association. It covers results of original research in veterinary and comparative medicine. It is the Canadian counterpart to the *American Journal of Veterinary Research*. Papers may be full-length (up to 20 pages) or short communications (up to 10 pages). Occasional review articles (up to 30 pages) of general interest are published. An average issue will have 8–12 full-length papers and one to three short communications. All articles are in English, but the abstracts are in both English and French. All animal species, domestic and non-domestic, are covered. Color photographs are used very sparingly. The target audience is scientists in the fields of veterinary science, animal science, and comparative medicine. This is a journal that should be found in all North American veterinary libraries. PubMed Central has full text,but not complete cover to cover coverage,available from volume 1 up to within the current six months. URL: http://www.ncbi.nlm.nih.gov/pmc/journals/133/

5269. *The Canadian Veterinary Journal.* [ISSN: 0008-5286] 1960. m. Free to members; Non-members, CAD 170. Ed(s): Carlton Gyles, Heather Broughton. Canadian Veterinary Medical Association, 339 Booth St, Ottawa, ON K1R 7K1, Canada; admin@cvma-acmv.org ; http://canadianveterinarians.net. Illus., index, adv. Refereed. Vol. ends: Dec. Microform: PMC; PQC. *Indexed:* A22, Agr, C45, IndVet. *Bk. rev.:* 1-6, 300-700 words. *Aud.:* Ac, Sa.

As the official publication of the Canadian Veterinary Medical Association (CVMA), this journal is considered to be the "voice of veterinary medicine in Canada." In addition to carrying scientific articles, review articles, case reports, and brief communications, each issue also contains a news section about CVMA activities (in both English and French), notices of upcoming meetings, new-product information, book reviews, obituaries, and employment opportunities. There are also frequent columns appearing under headings such as oncology, orthopedics, animal welfare, veterinary practice management, diagnostic ophthalmology, and the art of private veterinary practice. The abstracts of the scientific articles are provided in both English and French. Online text is available from volume 1 up to within the current six months at PubMed Central: http://www.ncbi.nlm.nih.gov/pmc/journals/202/ This title is especially recommended for North American veterinary libraries. URL: http://www.canadianveterinarians.net/publications/canadian-veterinary-journal.aspx

5270. *D V M: the newsmagazine of veterinary medicine.* [ISSN: 0012-7337] 1970. m. USD 40 domestic; USD 87.50 foreign; USD 17 newsstand/cover domestic. Ed(s): James Lewis, Daniel R Verdon. Advanstar Communications, Inc., 6200 Canoga Ave, 2nd Fl, Woodland Hills, CA 91367; info@advanstar.com; http://www.advanstar.com. Illus., adv. Circ: 56000 Controlled. Vol. ends: Dec. Microform: PQC. *Indexed:* A01, A22, BRI. *Aud.:* Ga, Ac, Sa.

Those interested in the latest news pertaining to veterinary medicine go to *DVM Newsmagazine*. Its large physical size makes it stand out from the other veterinary magazines. It reports on all relevant news, trends, and developments, and offers practical and authoritative medical information. Regular columnists write on practice management and marketing. Exclusive features include interviews and editorial roundtable discussions with professional leaders, feature reports on hot topics, and complete coverage of regulatory and legislative activity. There is a monthly "New Products and Services" section and a quarterly "New Product Review" section in which important new products are introduced. Periodically, there is also a special monthly supplement for veterinary students called "Your DVM Career." a business primer for veterinary students." There are occasional educational supplements, "DVM Best Practices" and "DVM In Focus," to provide the clinician with the latest information on selected topics. The journal is interspersed with many color ads. The writing does not employ technical jargon, so clients in a veterinary waiting room would find the articles of interest. The web site provides the very latest breaking news in the field, articles from the current issue, and selected feature articles from the magazine's archives. Issues back to September 2005 are available online at the publisher's web site. Full-text articles from June 2003 are available through EBSCO Academic Search Complete. This is a useful magazine for the waiting room of veterinary clinics, and a necessary acquisition for veterinary libraries. URL: http://veterinarynews.dvm360.com/

5271. *Equine Veterinary Journal.* [ISSN: 0425-1644] 1968. bi-m. GBP 413. John Wiley & Sons, Inc., 111 River St, MS 4-02, Hoboken, NJ 07030; info@wiley.com; http://www.wiley.com/WileyCDA/. Illus., index, adv. Refereed. Vol. ends: Nov. Reprint: PSC. *Indexed:* A22, Agr, C45, E01, IndVet, RRTA. *Aud.:* Ac, Sa.

In 1968, the British Equine Veterinary Association undertook the task to publish its own publication, calling it the *Equine Veterinary Journal.* Its stature has grown so that it is now the most respected international scientific equine journal in the world. *Equine Veterinary Journal* publishes evidence to improve clinical practice or expand scientific knowledge underpinning equine veterinary medicine. The average issue carries 10–14 full-length articles on original research, plus one to three short communications, and case reports on such diverse topics as dermatology, exercise, anatomy, ergonomics, pain therapy, surgery, behavior, reproduction, and racing. The illustrations are predominantly in black-and-white. The journal uses Wiley/Blackwell's Early View system. Once an article is accepted in its final form, it is made available on the web before actual publication. A must for veterinary libraries, equine practitioners, and libraries that serve colleges with equestrian programs or those conducting equine research. Full text is available from volume one. URL: http://onlinelibrary.wiley.com/journal/10.1001/(ISSN)2042-3306/homepage/ProductInformation.html

5272. *Journal of Avian Medicine and Surgery.* Former titles (until 1995): *Association of Avian Veterinarians. Journal;* (until 1989): *A A V Today;* (until 1987): *A.V.A. Newsletter.* [ISSN: 1082-6742] 1980. q. USD 130 domestic (Free to members). Ed(s): James W Carpenter, Patricia Hildenbrand. Association of Avian Veterinarians, P O Box 811720, Boca Raton, FL 33481; aavpublications@aol.com; http://www.aav.org. Illus., index, adv. Refereed. Vol. ends: Dec. *Indexed:* A01, A22, BRI, C45, E01, IndVet. *Bk. rev.:* 1-2, 400-500 words. *Aud.:* Ac, Sa.

The *Journal of Avian Medicine and Surgery* is published quarterly by the Association of Avian Veterinarians (AAV). It is an international journal on the medicine and surgery of captive and wild birds. It publishes original research, clinical reports, review articles, retrospective studies, case reports, editorials, and research briefs. In addition, it has featured sections including "What's Your Diagnosis?," "Selected Abstracts from the Literature," and "Round Table Discussions." There are also book and DVD reviews and a calendar of upcoming meetings. The illustrations are chiefly in black-and-white, with an occasional use of color. An expensive clay-coated paper is used to achieve the highest resolution of photographs. The journal is essential for the avian practitioner and is highly recommended for zoo and veterinary libraries. Full text for volumes 1 through 13 is available from JSTOR. Online full text is available from 2000 through BioOne. URL: www.bioone.org/loi/avms

5273. *Journal of Exotic Pet Medicine.* Formerly (until 2006): *Seminars in Avian and Exotic Pet Medicine.* [ISSN: 1557-5063] 1992. q. USD 430. Ed(s): Mark A Mitchell, Thomas N Tully. W.B. Saunders Co., Elsevier, Health Sciences Division, Order Fulfillment, Maryland Heights, MO 63043; sales.inquiry@elsevier.com; http://www.us.elsevierhealth.com. Illus., index, adv. Refereed. Vol. ends: Dec. *Indexed:* C45, IndVet. *Aud.:* Ac, Sa.

A relatively new trend in the field of veterinary medicine has been the development of specialty practices that treat exotic animals and/or pet birds. Although practitioners have been witnessing an increasing number of cases in this area, there has been a lack of scholarly journals devoted to this specialty. Hence, the practitioner has often had difficulty locating reliable information. *Journal of Exotic Pet Medicine* is one of three journals that are successfully filling the void (see also *Journal of Avian Medicine and Surgery* and *Veterinary Clinics of North America: exotic animal practice*). The publisher says the journal "is the most complete resource for practitioners who treat avian and exotic pets." The journal's format features a subject specialist as a guest editor; and a section of the issue titled "Topics in Medicine and Surgery" is devoted to the editor's specialty. However, there are additional articles in other regularly featured columns, such as "AEMV Forum," "Diagnostic Challenge," "Avian & Exotic News," and "Literature Review." The journal is printed on clay-based

paper and has an easy-to-read format that features excellent black-and-white and color photographs. There are usually eight or nine articles, three to ten pages in length, per issue. The concise, topical, and authoritative reviews address problems faced in daily practice. Recent themes include "Emergency Medicine of Exotic Mammal Herbivores," "Field Techniques in Exotic Animal Medicine" and "Clinical Anesthesia & Analgesia." This journal is a must for the avian practitioner and for any practitioner who handles exotic-animal cases. It is also highly recommended for veterinary and zoo libraries. Full-text articles are available from vol. 15 (2006). http://www.sciencedirect.com/science/journal/15575063 Earlier issues are found under the previous title *Seminars in Avian and Exotic Pet Medicine.* URL: http://www.sciencedirect.com/science/journal/1055937X

5274. *Journal of Feline Medicine and Surgery.* [ISSN: 1098-612X] 1999. m. USD 658. Sage Publications Ltd., 1 Oliver's Yard, 55 City Rd, London, EC1Y 1SP, United Kingdom; info@sagepub.co.uk; http://www.uk.sagepub.com. Illus., adv. Sample. Refereed. Reprint: PSC. *Indexed:* A22, AbAn, Agr, C45, E01, IndVet. *Bk. rev.:* 1, 200-300 words. *Aud.:* Ac, Sa.

The *Journal of Feline Medicine and Surgery* is an international journal, and the official journal of both the International Society of Feline Medicine (ISFM) and the American Association of Feline Practitioners (AAFP) aimed at both practitioners and researchers with an interest in clinical veterinary healthcare of domestic cats. It may be the only scientific, peer-reviewed journal in the world devoted exclusively to feline medicine and surgery. Due to the unique publishing format, the following is quoted directly from the journal: "The journal is published monthly in two formats ? 'Classic' editions (published in February, April, June, August, October and December) containing high quality original papers on all aspects of feline medicine and surgery, including basic research relevant to clinical practice; and dedicated 'Clinical Practice' editions (published in January, March, May, July, September and November) primarily containing commissioned opinioned review articles providing state of the art information for feline clinicians, along with other relevant articles such as case reports." The journal uses a substantial amount of color illustrations. An international news section provides information about feline veterinary meetings, society news, new developments, book reviews, and relevant issues from other publications and meetings. This journal is a must for the feline practitioner and should be considered a basic title for veterinary libraries. Online full text is available from volume 1 (1999). URL: http://jfm.sagepub.com/

5275. *Journal of Small Animal Practice.* [ISSN: 0022-4510] 1960. m. GBP 390. Wiley-Blackwell Publishing Ltd., The Atrium, Southern Gate, Chichester, PO19 8SQ, United Kingdom; customer@wiley.com; http://www.wiley.com/. Illus., index, adv. Sample. Refereed. Vol. ends: Dec. Reprint: PSC. *Indexed:* A22, AbAn, Agr, C45, E01, IndVet, RRTA. *Bk. rev.:* 1, 300-375 words. *Aud.:* Ac, Sa.

This is the official publication of the British Small Animal Veterinary Association (BSAVA) and the World Small Animal Veterinary Association (WSAVA). Like its American counterpart, *Journal of the American Animal Hospital Association,* it is peer-reviewed and published monthly. Its target audience is veterinarians who are primarily engaged in small-animal medicine and surgery. It is international in scope, publishing original clinical research, invited editorials, review articles, commentary, and case histories that cover all aspects of medicine and surgery relating to dogs, cats, and other small mammals. In addition, it publishes topical news of interest, association news, and reports on U.K., signed book reviews, and international veterinary conferences. Printing on clay-based paper enables the publisher to make excellent use of color layouts that increase eye appeal and readability. Full text is available from volume 1 (1960) through Wiley Online Library. Highly recommended for veterinary medical libraries. URL: http://onlinelibrary.wiley.com/journal/10.1111/(ISSN)1748-5827

5276. *Journal of Swine Health and Production.* Former titles (until 2001): *Swine Health and Production;* (until 1993): *American Association of Swine Practitioners. Newsletter.* [ISSN: 1537-209X] 1993. bi-m. Free to members (print & online eds.); Non-members, USD 125). Ed(s): Catherine Dewey. American Association of Swine Veterinarians, 830 26th St, Perry, IA 50220; aasv@aasv.org; http://www.aasv.org. Refereed. Vol. ends: Nov/Dec. *Indexed:* Agr, C45, IndVet. *Aud.:* Ac, Sa.

The *Journal of Swine Health and Production* is the offical journal of the American Association of Swine Veterinarians (AASV). It is the only refereed journal in North America that focuses exclusively on swine health. It accepts for publication manuscripts on original research, case reports, literature reviews, brief communications, production tips, commentary, and diagnostic notes. In addition, it publishes society news and other items of interest to its membership. Two nice features are the calendar of upcoming national and international meetings and the conversion tables. Almost all the illustrative materials, which consist of tables, charts, graphs, and photographs, are in color. This journal is a must for the swine practitioner, veterinary libraries, and any institution that is involved with swine research. The journal is available online to subscribers, as is the complete backfile. URL: www.aasv.org/shap.html

5277. *Journal of Veterinary Internal Medicine.* [ISSN: 0891-6640] 1987. bi-m. GBP 391 (print & online eds.). Ed(s): Kenneth W Hinchcliff, Stephen P Di Bartola. Wiley-Blackwell Publishing, Inc., 111 River St, Hoboken, NJ 07030; info@wiley.com; http://onlinelibrary.wiley.com/. Illus., index. Sample. Refereed. Reprint: PSC. *Indexed:* A01, A22, Agr, C45, E01, IndVet. *Aud.:* Ac, Sa.

This specialty journal is the official publication of the American College of Veterinary Internal Medicine, the largest specialty board within the American Veterinary Medical Association. It is also the official journal of the European College of Veterinary Internal Medicine, the European College of Veterinary Neurology, and the European College of Equine Internal Medicine. The editors particularly seek clinical and research manuscripts in the area of small-animal and large-animal internal medicine. In addition, they accept review articles, brief communications, and case reports. Generally, there are 25–30 articles per issue. The illustrative materials are largely in black-and-white, although the use of color appears to be increasing. Short video clips or animations of 5 MB or less are accepted with manuscripts. A freeze-frame with the URL link is made available in the paper version. It is a well-edited publication, but readership will be limited to those veterinarians, clinicians, and researchers with an interest in internal medicine. The entire backfile is available online. The review articles are free. The journal ranked number 3 on the *Basic List of Veterinary Serials* compiled in 2009 by the Veterinary Serials Committee of the Veterinary Medical Libraries Section of the Medical Library Association (see section introduction for URL). Without a doubt, this title is considered a necessary purchase for veterinary college libraries. Full text is available back to Vol. 1. URL: http://onlinelibrary.wiley.com/journal/10.1111/(ISSN)1939-1676

5278. *Journal of Veterinary Medical Education.* [ISSN: 0748-321X] 1974. q. USD 355. Ed(s): Daryl J Buss. University of Toronto Press, Journals Division, 5201 Dufferin St, Toronto, ON M3H 5T8, Canada; journals@utpress.utoronto.ca; http://www.utpjournals.com. Illus., adv. Refereed. Circ: 3392. Vol. ends: Dec. Microform: PQC. *Indexed:* A22, C45, IndVet, RRTA. *Bk. rev.:* 1-5, 200-350 words. *Aud.:* Ac, Sa.

The official publication of the Association of American Veterinary Medical Colleges, this is the journal to read if you are interested in veterinary medical education, as it is the only one in any language devoted to the subject. It is an internationally distributed journal whose purpose is to provide a forum for the exchange of ideas, research, and discoveries about veterinary medical education. "The journal's areas of focus include: best practices and educational methods in veterinary education; recruitment, training, and mentoring of students at all levels of education, including undergraduate, graduate, veterinary technology, and continuing education; clinical instruction and assessment; institutional policy; and other challenges and issues faced by veterinary educators domestically and internationally." It is a useful journal to monitor for information regarding changes in the profession and how veterinary colleges are reacting to the changes. Most of the issues are theme-specific. Examples of this include "Innovations in Veterinary Medical Education," "40 Years of Service to veterinary medical education," "Veterinary Medical Simulations," and "Primary Health Care Education." Readership will mostly be limited to teaching faculty, veterinary college administrators, members of curriculum committees, and continuing-education personnel. This is a necessary title in veterinary school libraries and should be considered for libraries that support animal technician programs. Full text online is available from volume 28 (2001). URL: http://www.utpjournals.com/jvme/

5279. *Journal of Wildlife Diseases.* Former titles (until 1970): *Wildlife Disease Association. Bulletin;* (until 1965): *Wildlife Disease Association. Newsletter.* [ISSN: 0090-3558] 1965. q. Individual members, USD 95;

Students, USD 40. Ed(s): Elizabeth S Williams. Wildlife Disease Association, Inc., 810 E 10th St, Lawrence, KS 66044; orders@allenpress.com; http://www.wildlifedisease.org. Illus., index, adv. Sample. Refereed. Vol. ends: Oct. *Indexed:* A22, AbAn, Agr, C45, IndVet, RRTA. *Bk. rev.:* 1-5, 500-600 words. *Aud.:* Ac, Sa.

This journal, the official journal of the Wildlife Disease Association, publishes results, from around the globe, of original research and observations that deal with all aspects of infectious, immunologic, parasitic, toxic, nutritional, physiologic, developmental, epizootic, and neoplastic diseases that affect the health and survival of free-living or captive wild animals, including fish. All of the illustrative material is in black-and-white. As one can surmise from the scope of coverage, each issue contains a diverse array of articles, ranging from leptospirosis in fox squirrels to evaluation of bison semen from Yellowstone, to electrolyte depletion in white-nose syndrome bats. An average issue has 17–23 full-length articles, followed by 10–18 short communications. Full-text articles are available from 1965. This is a must acquisition for academic libraries that support game biology/wildlife science and veterinary science programs. URL: http://www.jwildlifedis.org/

5280. *Journal of Zoo and Wildlife Medicine.* Formerly (until 1989): *Journal of Zoo Animal Medicine.* [ISSN: 1042-7260] 1971. q. USD 310. Ed(s): Dr. Teresa Morishita. American Association of Zoo Veterinarians, 581705 White Oak Rd, Yulee, FL 32097; aazvorg@aol.com; http://www.aazv.org. Illus., index, adv. Refereed. Circ: 1200. Vol. ends: Dec. *Indexed:* A22, AbAn, C45, E01, IndVet. *Bk. rev.:* 2-3, 300-500 words. *Aud.:* Ac, Sa.

The American Association of Zoo Veterinarians has as its official publication the *Journal of Zoo and Wildlife Medicine.* It is considered one of the major sources of information in zoological medicine. The emphasis of the journal is to publish original research findings, clinical observations, and case reports in the field of veterinary medicine that deals with captive and free-ranging wild animals, and it has the stated goal "to improve the husbandry, preventive medicine[,] and research required to preserve these animals." It also publishes editorials, review articles, and special reports. A typical issue has 10–12 full-length articles, plus three or four case reports and 10–13 brief communications. The book reviews are exceptionally well written and useful to librarians doing collection development. Abstracts of selected articles that appear elsewhere in the literature are included in each issue. An interesting regular feature, "Clinical Challenge," gives insight into how difficult cases were solved and/or resolved. All of the illustrative material is mostly in black-and-white. This high-quality research publication is a must for zoo and veterinary libraries, and perhaps for libraries that support marine biology programs. Full text back to 2009 can be found on the association website: http://zoowildlifejournal.com/loi/zamd However, full text is also available back to volume 31 (2000) through BioOne. URL: http://www.bioone.org/loi/zamd

5281. *Research in Veterinary Science.* [ISSN: 0034-5288] 1960. bi-m. EUR 999. Ed(s): P Pasquali. Elsevier Ltd, 32 Jamestown Rd, Camden, London, NW1 7BY, United Kingdom; corporate.sales@elsevier.com; http://www.elsevier.com. Illus., index, adv. Sample. Refereed. Vol. ends: Nov. Microform: PMC; PQC. *Indexed:* A01, A22, AbAn, Agr, C45, E01, ExcerpMed, FS&TA, IndVet. *Aud.:* Ac, Sa.

This official publication of the Association of Veterinary Teachers and Research Workers is a well-respected research journal. Accepted for publication are original contributions, review articles, and short communications on the health, welfare, and diseases of all animal species as well as comparative medicine. Articles are grouped by subjects. Color illustrations are used only infrequently. Most issues contain 30–35 articles. Many of the contributors are from outside the United Kingdom, which gives the journal an international flavor. The articles are categorized under specific subject headings. A recommended title for veterinary libraries. Online full text from 1999 is available through ScienceDirect. URL: http://www.sciencedirect.com/science/journal/00345288/95

5282. *Topics in Companion Animal Medicine.* Former titles (until 2008): *Clinical Techniques in Small Animal Practice;* (until 1997): *Seminars in Veterinary Medicine and Surgery: Small Animal.* [ISSN: 1938-9736] 1986. q. USD 416. Ed(s): Dr. Deborah Greco, Fred Sauter. W.B.

Saunders Co., Elsevier, Health Sciences Division, Order Fulfillment, Maryland Heights, MO 63043; sales.inquiry@elsevier.com; http://www.us.elsevierhealth.com. Illus., index, adv. Refereed. Vol. ends: Nov. *Indexed:* A22, Agr, C45, IndVet. *Aud.:* Ac, Sa.

Topics in Companion Animal Medicine fills a unique niche by publishing the most recent advances in companion animal medicine to enhance the practitioner's office practice. Each quarterly issue includes a comprehensive review of the latest developments and techniques regarding an important topic in veterinary medicine, guest edited by a leading expert in the field. The journal also features peer-reviewed original research articles, case reports and review articles; as well as timely editorials addressing issues that affect the companion animal practitioner. There are usually seven to nine articles per issue. The illustrative photographs are in color and black-and-white. Some recent topics include: "Pituitary Disorders," "Calcium Disorders." "Pancreatitis," and "Coagulation Disorders." Online full-text articles are available from volume one (1995). This title is recommended for veterinary science collections. URL: http://www.companimalmed.com/

5283. *Veterinary Clinics of North America: Equine Practice.* Supersedes in part (in 1985): *The Veterinary Clinics of North America. Large Animal Practice;* Which superseded in part (in 1979): *Veterinary Clinics of North America.* [ISSN: 0749-0739] 1971. 3x/yr. USD 436. Ed(s): Reynolds Cowles. W.B. Saunders Co., Elsevier, Health Sciences Division, Order Fulfillment, Maryland Heights, MO 63043; sales.inquiry@elsevier.com; http://www.us.elsevierhealth.com. Illus., index. Refereed. Vol. ends: Dec. *Indexed:* A22, Agr, C45, IndVet, RRTA. *Aud.:* Ac, Sa.

As with the other three titles in the *Veterinary Clinics of North America* series, each issue has a guest editor who is responsible for inviting other experts on the featured topic to contribute papers. Recent topics include topics in equine anesthesia, advances in equine dentistry, equine dermatology and therapeutic farriery. Illustrations include graphs, tables, and photographs. While this is required reading for equine practitioners and a necessary title for veterinary collections, it is also recommended for animal science and equestrian collections. An online version is available from 2002. URL: http://www.elsevier.com/journals/veterinary-clinics-of-north-america-equine-practice/0749-0739

5284. *Veterinary Clinics of North America: Exotic Animal Practice.* [ISSN: 1094-9194] 1998. 3x/yr. USD 410. Ed(s): Laura Wade. W.B. Saunders Co., Elsevier, Health Sciences Division, Order Fulfillment, Maryland Heights, MO 63043; sales.inquiry@elsevier.com; http://www.us.elsevierhealth.com. Illus., index. Refereed. Vol. ends: Sep. *Indexed:* C45, IndVet. *Aud.:* Ac, Sa.

The newest entry in the *Veterinary Clinics of North America* series provides comprehensive, state-of-the-art reviews by experts in the field and practical information on the diagnosis and treatment of conditions affecting exotic animals. The increasing popularity of exotic animals being used as companion animals has created a new specialty in veterinary medicine, which in turn necessitates peer-reviewed scientific literature for the specialist. As with the other titles in this series, each issue is devoted to a single topic and will contain 10–12 articles. Some recent topics include clinical & diagnostic pathology, new & emerging diseases, exotic animal training & learning, and myobacteriosis. The illustrations are about evenly split between color and black-and-white. This title is essential to wildlife, zoo, and exotic-animal specialists and veterinary collections. Access to full online text back to 2002 is available to subscribers. URL: http://www.elsevier.com/journals/veterinary-clinics-of-north-america-exotic-animal-practice/1094-9194

5285. *Veterinary Clinics of North America: Food Animal Practice.* Supersedes in part (in 1985): *The Veterinary Clinics of North America. Large Animal Practice;* Which superseded in part (in 1979): *Veterinary Clinics of North America.* [ISSN: 0749-0720] 1971. 3x/yr. USD 330. Ed(s): Sanjay Kapil, D Scott McVey. W.B. Saunders Co., Elsevier, Health Sciences Division, Order Fulfillment, Maryland Heights, MO 63043; sales.inquiry@elsevier.com; http://www.us.elsevierhealth.com. Illus., index. Refereed. Vol. ends: Nov. *Indexed:* A22, Agr, C45, IndVet. *Aud.:* Ac, Sa.

As with its companion volumes in the *Veterinary Clinics of North America* series, each issue is under the direction of a guest editor who is an authority in his or her speciality. Information is covered on the latest developments in the diagnosis and management of several species (cattle, swine, goats, sheep, llamas, deer, and ratites) that are treated by large-animal practitioners. Recent topics include pain management, metabolic diseases of ruminants, diagnostic pathology, and mastitis in dairy cows. Illustrations are usually in black-and-white, but the use of color has increased. Charts and tables are also used. This title is recommended for veterinary and animal science collections, and should be found on every food animal practitioner's bookshelf. Online access to full text is available from 2002. URL: http://www.elsevier.com/journals/veterinary-clinics-of-north-america-food-animal-practice/0749-0720

5286. *Veterinary Clinics of North America: Small Animal Practice.* Supersedes in part (in 1979): *Veterinary Clinics of North America.* [ISSN: 0195-5616] 1971. bi-m. USD 506. Ed(s): William B Thomas. W.B. Saunders Co., Elsevier, Health Sciences Division, Order Fulfillment, Maryland Heights, MO 63043; sales.inquiry@elsevier.com; http://www.us.elsevierhealth.com. Illus., index. Refereed. Vol. ends: Nov. Microform: MIM; PQC. *Indexed:* A22, Agr, C45, ExcerpMed, IndVet. *Aud.:* Ac, Sa.

Like all titles in the *Veterinary Clinics of North America* series, each hardback volume is devoted to a specific topic, with an expert on the topic serving as a guest editor. The initial title proved so popular that it split into four sections: small-animal practice, equine practice, food-animal practice, and exotic-animal practice. Each issue includes an average of 10–12 articles. Recent issues have featured clinical dermatology, feline diabetes, clinical veterinary dentistry, and emergency medicine. Illustrative material consists of graphs, tables, and photographs. It is a basic title for veterinary medicine collections and for small-animal practitioners. It ranked number 5 in the *Basic List of Veterinary Serials,* compiled in 2009 by the Veterinary Serials Committee of the Veterinary Medical Libraries Section of the Medical Library Association (see section introduction for URL). Full-text coverage is available back to 2000. URL: http://www.elsevier.com/journals/veterinary-clinics-of-north-america-small-animal-practice/0195-5616

5287. *Veterinary Economics: business solutions for practicing veterinarians.* [ISSN: 0042-4862] 1960. m. USD 43 domestic; USD 60 in Canada & Mexico; USD 85 elsewhere. Ed(s): Amanda Bertholf, Kristi Reimer. Advanstar Communications, Inc., 6200 Canoga Ave, 2nd Fl, Woodland Hills, CA 91367; info@advanstar.com; http://www.advanstar.com. Illus., index, adv. Refereed. Vol. ends: Dec. Microform: PQC. *Indexed:* ABIn, ATI, B02, C45, IndVet. *Aud.:* Ac, Sa.

This is a monthly professional trade magazine for practicing veterinarians that provides detailed articles about the business of client and patient care. It provides excellent coverage of all aspects of veterinary practice management, retirement planning, evaluating practices for purchase, personnel issues, partnership arrangement, contracts, client relations, taxes, and other financial matters. It also covers industry issues that impact the veterinary profession, such as the gender shift and changes in vaccine protocols. Its longtime feature on hospital design is very popular with practitioners. The special reports on trends, salaries, and economics in the profession are well respected and often the only source for this type of information. Other veterinary business magazines have come and gone, but this was the first (1960) and it has always remained at the top. A new feature is a removable section featuring a toolkit on a specific topic, i.e., senior care, vaccines, tick control, flea control and dental care. The same insert also appears in another journal, *Veterinary Medicine,* published by the same publisher. Issues are available full-text online back to January 2004. This title is recommended for veterinary libraries, veterinary hospital managers, and practitioners. URL: http://veterinarybusiness.dvm360.com/vetec/issue/issueList.jsp?id=371

5288. *The Veterinary Journal.* Former titles (until 1997): *British Veterinary Journal;* (until 1949): *The Veterinary Journal;* (until 1900): *The Veterinary Journal and Annals of Comparative Pathology.* [ISSN: 1090-0233] 1875. m. EUR 1318. Ed(s): Andrew J Higgins. Elsevier Ltd, 32 Jamestown Rd, Camden, London, NW1 7BY, United Kingdom;

corporate.sales@elsevier.com; http://www.elsevier.com. Illus., index, adv. Sample. Refereed. Vol. ends: Dec. Microform: PMC; PQC. Reprint: PSC. *Indexed:* A01, A22, AbAn, Agr, C45, E01, ExcerpMed, FS&TA, IndVet, RRTA. *Bk. rev.:* 4-6, 300-500 words. *Aud.:* Ac.

Tracing its history back to 1875, the *Veterinary Journal* has the distinction of being the longest-running English-language veterinary journal. It is international in scope and publishes original papers and reviews on all aspects of veterinary science, with particular emphasis on animal health and preventive medicine. It commissions topical reviews and commentaries on features of major importance. Research areas include infectious diseases, applied biochemistry, parasitology, endocrinology, microbiology, immunology, pathology, pharmacology, physiology, molecular biology, immunogenetics, surgery, ophthalmology, dermatology and oncology. Papers are published under three categories: "Guest Editorials," "Commissioned Topical Reviews," and "Original Articles." The journal also publishes book reviews and has a short communications section. The guest editorials are informative and often thought-provoking. The use of photographic materials is minimal, with a greater reliance on charts, tables, and graphs. Collection development librarians will enjoy the signed book reviews. It should be considered a basic title for veterinary science collections. Online full-text coverage, available since 1997, is through ScienceDirect. URL: http://www.sciencedirect.com/science/journal/10900233

5289. Veterinary Medicine. Formerly (until 1985): *Veterinary Medicine - Small Animal Clinician.* [ISSN: 8750-7943] 1905. m. USD 60 domestic; USD 72 in Canada & Mexico; USD 97 elsewhere. Ed(s): Mindy Valcarcel, Margaret Rampey. Advanstar Veterinary Healthcare Communications, 8033 Flint, Lenexa, KS 66214; http://www.vetmedpub.com. Illus., index, adv. Refereed. Circ: 54135 Controlled. Vol. ends: Dec. Microform: PQC. *Indexed:* A01, A22, Agr, B02, BRI, C45, IndVet. *Aud.:* Ac, Sa.

This is a well-respected journal in American veterinary medicine, having begun publication in 1905. It has undergone serious competition in recent years due to specialization within the profession, but it still provides "concise, credible, and essential information on the most common and emerging diagnostic and therapeutic problems seen in companion-animal practice." Therefore, the emphasis is on articles that present a how-to approach to guide practicing veterinarians in selecting better diagnostic and therapeutic strategies; hence, the articles are more clinical than research-oriented. Due to its practical nature, and because the articles are concise, to the point, and well illustrated in color, this journal is popular with practicing veterinarians. Since January 2000, the journal has focused exclusively on companion animals and exotics. Other regularly featured columns is the Journal Scan which reviews the literature and the Idea Exchange where practitioners can submit practical practice tips. Frequently, one to three video clips are linked that can be viewed online. A new feature is a removable section featuring a toolkit on a specific topic, i.e., senior care, vaccines, tick control, flea control and dental care. The same insert also appears in another journal, *Veterinary Economics,* published by the same publisher. There is an online site for full-text articles, but one can't browse an issue by month and date. The online site is only searchable by subject. It is also unknown how far back the archive is maintained. A recommended title for the small-animal practitioner, veterinary science collections, and libraries that serve veterinary technician programs. URL: http://veterinarymedicine.dvm360.com/vetmed/cathome/catHome6.jsp?categoryId=46738

5290. Veterinary Pathology. Formerly (until 1971): *Pathologia Veterinaria.* [ISSN: 0300-9858] 1964. bi-m. USD 350. Ed(s): Carl L Alden, Jill Findlay. Sage Publications, Inc., 2455 Teller Rd, Thousand Oaks, CA 91320; info@sagepub.com; http://www.sagepub.com/. Illus., index, adv. Sample. Refereed. Vol. ends: Nov. Reprint: PSC. *Indexed:* A22, Agr, C45, E01, IndVet. *Bk. rev.:* 1-2, 250-350 words. *Aud.:* Ac, Sa.

Veterinary Pathology is the official publication of the American College of Veterinary Pathologists, providing international coverage in the field of veterinary pathology. The journal publishes manuscripts, reviews, brief communications, book reviews, editorials, and case reports that deal with experimental and natural diseases. It also carries advertisements for employment opportunities and new products. The journal is printed on a clay-based paper, which gives exceptional quality to the photographs; the use of color versus black-and-white is about 50/50. Generally there are 20–25 full-length articles and 12–14 brief communications and case reports. The scope of

coverage includes diseases in domestic animals, laboratory animals, and exotics. Collection development librarians will find the book reviews useful. The journal ranked number 4 on the *Basic List of Veterinary Serials,* compiled in 2009 by the Veterinary Serials Committee of the Veterinary Medical Libraries Serials Section of the Medical Library Association (see section introduction for URL). Online full text is available from volume 1. This is a recommended title for libraries that serve diagnostic laboratories and/or veterinary programs. URL: http://vet.sagepub.com/

5291. The Veterinary Record. [ISSN: 0042-4900] 1888. w. Individuals, USD 681 (print & online eds.). Ed(s): Martin Alder. B M J Group, BMA House, Tavistock Sq, London, WC1H 9JR, United Kingdom; support@bmjgroup.com; http://group.bmj.com. Illus., adv. Sample. Refereed. Vol. ends: Dec. Microform: PQC. *Indexed:* A01, A22, Agr, C45, FS&TA, IndVet, RRTA. *Bk. rev.:* 1-3, 400-750 words. *Aud.:* Ac, Sa.

The weekly *Veterinary Record,* the voice of the British Veterinary Association, has been published weekly since 1888, and is one of the most venerable journals in the field. 2013 is its 125th anniversary - not many journals achieve this mark. It is a newsy journal, providing information about the association and veterinary matters in the United Kingdom, and it serves as a forum for British veterinarians to present their viewpoints. It is also highly respected for the papers it publishes on original research, as well as for its review articles, clinical case histories, short communications, and letters. All aspects of veterinary medicine and surgery are covered. Its classified advertisement section includes an extensive list of veterinary and veterinary-related jobs. Illustrative materials, i.e., charts, tables, and photographs, are generally in color. The book reviews are invaluable to collection development librarians. Online full text is available from 1996. In addition, abstracts are available from 1975, and the tables of contents are available for the years 1950–74. This title should be considered a must for all veterinary science collections. URL: http://veterinaryrecord.bmj.com/

5292. Veterinary Surgery. Incorporates (1974-198?): *Veterinary Anesthesia;* Formerly (until 1978): *Journal of Veterinary Surgery.* [ISSN: 0161-3499] 1978. 8x/yr. GBP 444. Ed(s): Kimberly E Soehnlein, John R Pascoe. Wiley-Blackwell Publishing, Inc., 111 River St, Hoboken, NJ 07030; info@wiley.com; http://onlinelibrary.wiley.com/. Illus., index, adv. Sample. Refereed. Vol. ends: Nov/Dec. Reprint: PSC. *Indexed:* A22, Agr, C45, E01, IndVet, P02, RRTA. *Aud.:* Ac, Sa.

Veterinary Surgery is the official publication of the American College of Veterinary Surgeons and the European College of Veterinary Surgeons. It provides a source of up-to-date coverage of surgical and anesthetic management of animals addressing significant problems in veterinary surgery with relevant case histories and observations, yet places new developments in perspective. Coverage includes, but is not limited to, surgical and anesthetic techniques, management of the surgical patient, diagnostic aims, care of infections, and the history of veterinary surgery. The periodical covers both large and small animals. The illustrations are high-quality black-and-white photographs interspersed with some in color. In addition to carrying clinical and research papers, it publishes invited reviews and scientific abstracts from the association's annual meetings. The web site provides free access to the five most-cited articles in the journal. Recommended for veterinary collections. Full text is available from volume 1 (1971). URL: http://onlinelibrary.wiley.com/journal/10.1111/(ISSN)1532-950X

■ WEDDINGS

Deborah Jackson Weiss, Romance Languages Cataloger, Harvard Law School Library, Cambridge, MA 02138; djweiss@law.harvard.edu

Introduction

With the average cost of a wedding in the U.S. exceeding $27,000, wedding magazines and their accompanying web sites play a pivotal role in educating brides about the myriad of options available to them in planning their special day, but also put at their fingertips an enormous array of products. The magazines reviewed range from basic coverage of affordable goods to a compendium of high-end resources for the bride with the near limitless budget. All cover the standard fare of fashion, jewelry, beauty products, wedding destinations, honeymoon options, registry suggestions, china, and furnishing advertisements. Most are advertisement-heavy, with varying amounts of editorial content; all display gorgeous photography.

Basic Periodicals

Sa: *Bride's, Martha Stewart Weddings, The Knot Weddings.*

Basic Abstracts and Indexes

MAS Ultra: School Edition; Reader's Guide to Periodical Literature.

5293. Bridal Guide: the how to for "I do". [ISSN: 0882-7451] 1982. bi-m. USD 11.97; USD 5.99 newsstand/cover per issue. Ed(s): Diane Forden. R F P Llc., 330 Seventh Ave, 10th Fl, New York, NY 10001-5591; http://www.BridalGuidemag.com. Illus. Sample. Circ: 205000 Paid and controlled. Vol. ends: Dec (No. 6). *Aud.:* Sa.

Bridal Guide takes a traditional approach to wedding resources: displays of dresses, china, and furnishings are interwoven with short features on fashion, registry suggestions, honeymoon destinations, and advice on how to handle sticky relations within the wedding party and with the in-laws. Real-life weddings are portrayed, as well. The products advertised include some high-end gowns and expensive jewelry, but most of the resources are accessible for the budget-conscious bride. Its web site, similarly, is filled with many advice features as well as multiple links for registry suggestions and fashion tips. *Bridal Guide* is more practical than out-of-this-world dreamy, and thus is more useful for the majority of brides than some wedding magazines. URL: www.bridalgown.com

5294. Bride's. Former titles (until 1995): *Bride's and Your New Home;* (until Nov. 1991): *Bride's; Bride's Magazine.* [ISSN: 1084-1628] 1934. bi-m. USD 11.97 domestic; USD 5.99 newsstand/cover. Ed(s): Millie Martini Bratten, Millie Martini Bratten. Conde Nast Publications, Inc., 750 3rd Ave, New York, NY 10017; letters@brides.com; http://www.condenast.com. Illus., adv. Circ: 500000 Paid. Vol. ends: Nov/Dec. *Indexed:* A22, P02. *Aud.:* Sa.

This magazine is best for the bride who wants to read about weddings and honeymoons, rather than just be assaulted by a storm of graphic images and advertisements. It contains more editorial text than most of the other wedding magazines reviewed. Including lots of ideas and advice on the standard topics (fashion, jewelry, beauty, etiquette, honeymoon destinations, and relationships), the magazine includes feature essays that are fairly long and comprehensive. A recent edition contains a profile of a wedding cake baker, a spread on short dresses for dancing, a piece on the "soul-mate fantasy," and a review of a wedding venue. A wedding countdown spelling out standard tasks that are involved in most weddings is included. Visually this magazine includes people of different ethnicities and races, as well as "normal-sized" brides, not just exquisitely thin and ethereal models. The variety and arrangement of text and photographs make *Bride's* easy to browse as well as to read from cover to cover. The web site similarly provides multiple ideas for engagement rings, honeymoon destinations, and dresses galore for all members of the wedding party. Overall, *Bride's* is a basic resource for someone planning a wedding with a good mix of advice and inspiration. URL: www.brides.com

5295. Grace Ormonde Wedding Style. [ISSN: 1554-1185] 1998. s-a. Free to qualified personnel. Ed(s): Yanni Tzoumas, Jessica Latimer. Elegant Publishing, Inc., PO Box 89, Barrington, RI 02806. Adv. *Aud.:* Sa.

Grace Ormonde Wedding Style stands out from the other publications reviewed as a magazine directed to a very upscale audience. For the bride with an unlimited budget, this magazine offers many resources; for others, it provides visually captivating visions for any bride to dream about. A beautifully designed spread of luscious photographs illustrates the standard wedding magazine content: fashion, cakes, honeymoon locales, jewelry, floral design, and registry suggestions. Exquisite runway style bridal dresses and exotic locations for destination weddings are featured. The real-life weddings features are short cameos without the comprehensive coverage given in some of the other wedding magazines. The magazine includes a "Platinum List" of vendors and wedding resources, organized by state. These resources are also available in searchable format on the web site, which also promotes Grace Ormonde's book,

Grace Ormonde Weddings—Being in Love Never Goes Out of Style, which is a compilation of ten years of magazine features. The web site continues the same sumptuous style and open feel of the magazine—in fact, some of the features include page-turning as if one is reading the print version. It includes resources and vendors recommended by Grace Ormonde and gives the bride the opportunity to hire the Grace Ormonde wedding planning team! A sister magazine, *Grace Ormonde Wedding Style New England,* focuses specifically on vendors and products available to the New England bride. Beautiful to look at, this magazine—which styles itself as "The Luxury Wedding Source"—offers less of practical value for most budget-conscious brides, but provides a delicious array of luxury products and decorating ideas as inspiration for all who read it. URL: www.weddingstylemagazine.com

5296. Inside Weddings. [ISSN: 1552-4647] 2003. q. USD 24. Ed(s): Walt Shepard. Inside Weddings, 6420 Wilshire Blvd, Ste 1060, Los Angeles, CA 90048; info@insideweddings.com; http://insideweddings.com/. Illus., adv. Circ: 35000 Paid. *Aud.:* Sa.

Although this magazine includes the standard fare of fashion, beauty, china, jewelry, honeymoon ideas, and registry gifts portrayed primarily through advertisements, *Inside Weddings* distinguishes itself in its organization and focus. Its real-life wedding features include eight to ten couples and it devotes substantial space (six to ten pages) to each wedding experience. Although rich with photographs, it has considerable text that gives a good sense of the real people profiled; extensive detail on the featured weddings is included. There is also a "Runway Report" that exhibits over 400 gowns from over 40 designers, grouped by designer; this format focuses the review of dresses and makes it easier for the reader to compare gowns than if they were spread throughout the issue. One drawback is that this format does not include store and availability information with the dresses, although some of it can be found elsewhere in the magazine. At the end of the issue, there are a few pages of expert advice on various topics, such as etiquette and photography. The tone of the magazine is more editorial than graphic, although there are abundant photographs providing inspiration to the bride. The accompanying web site includes many links to wedding products, including gift ideas, beauty and fashion productions, and other wedding resources. Organized topically (e.g., dresses, hairstyles, shoes, flowers, cakes, bridesmaids' dresses), the web site includes only its recommended vendors, reflecting the magazine's "commitment to limiting advertisers to professionals with whom we've worked, business we've reference[-]checked, or companies we know extremely well by reputation" (Editor's Letter). Archived features on real-life weddings and expert advice from prior issues are included in the web site. Together, the magazine and the web site give a very balanced approach to editorial content and beautiful photography, making the presentation of the material manageable for the reader. URL: www.insideweddings.com

5297. The Knot Weddings Magazine. Formerly: *The Knot Wedding Gowns.* 1999. s-a. USD 9.95 per issue. Ed(s): Carley Roney. The Knot Inc., 462 Broadway, 6th Fl, New York, NY 10013; salesinfo@theknot.com. *Aud.:* Sa.

Formerly known as *The Knot Wedding Gowns, The Knot Weddings Magazine* focuses primarily on wedding dresses, although there are many advertisements for other wedding products. The web site acts as a portal through which these and other wedding-related products can be purchased by clicking on vendor links; it serves as a leading retail vendor of wedding products and accessories. With 750 dresses in a recent issue, *The Knot Weddings Magazine* offers a photographic gallery of inspiration for any bride. The costs of the dresses cover a wide spectrum that gives the most budget-conscious some affordable options. Although practical wedding and couples advice is sprinkled throughout, the sheer mass of material (over 500 pages per issue) makes this magazine a bit hard to read. The content includes the usual wedding magazine fare—fashion, jewelry, china, and furnishings—but it has the feel of a Sears Roebuck catalog, with a little of everything. The honeymoon destinations section gives brief descriptions of the different locales as well as tips on weather and travel logistics, in addition to photographs and brief descriptions of resorts in that area. Further, although bridal gown advertisements are throughout the magazine, there is a specific section, "The Look Book," which includes photographs of wedding gowns arranged alphabetically by designer. Each dress is linked to store information through links to the designer through the magazine's web site (http://theknot.com) and the designer's own web site (referenced on each page), as well as to the store directory in the back of the print magazine, which includes full contact information for each store that carries the dress. Lastly, special issues, including an annual "Best of Weddings" issue, published annually, feature similar vendor information, organized by region of the country, with ratings by real brides in each region who vote for their favorites resources. There are also quarterly regional magazines that provide localized content in terms of shopping resources. Real-life weddings featured in the regional magazines focus on couples specific to each region. Together, *The Knot Wedding* publications and web site provide an extensive and comprehensive one-stop location for a bride's shopping.

5298. *Martha Stewart Weddings.* Formerly (until 1999): *Martha Stewart Living Weddings.* [ISSN: 1534-553X] 1990. q. USD 16 domestic; CAD 24 Canada. Ed(s): Melissa Morgan. Martha Stewart Living Omnimedia LLC, 601 W 26th St, 10th Fl, New York, NY 10001; mstewart@marthastewart.com; http://www.marthastewart.com. Adv. Sample. Circ: 268663 Paid. *Aud.:* Sa.

Martha Stewart Weddings focuses on wedding accoutrements, rather than on the basics of bridal fashion or wedding planning advice. As with other Martha Stewart publications, the emphasis is on food, flowers decor, craft ideas, and other furnishings. A few real-life weddings are spotlighted, but these very short cameos report more about the vendors used than focus on the people involved in the wedding. Although there are various editorial features (e.g., on dresses, makeup, the "Ask Martha" column, jewelry, and registries), the graphic format of multiple photographs with little text makes it hard to distinguish the editorial content from the advertisements. Attention is placed on details such as the flower arrangements and place settings used in wedding events, although there is a fair selection of bridal gowns, jewelry, hair styles, and general fashion portrayed through the advertisements. The magazine's web site, which is a subsection of the *Martha Stewart Living* site, is similarly full of advertisements that provide links to crafts, recipes, wedding planning message boards, and many Martha Stewart products. At over 360 pages, *Martha Stewart Weddings* provides a broad range of resources for the bride who can wade through the display. Meanwhile, a special issue, *Martha Stewart Real Weddings,* purports to focus on real-life weddings. Although a number of couples are profiled in this publication, the format is quite similar to the main magazine, with more space devoted to photographs of places and furnishings than to the details of the couple's lives.

5299. *Wedding Dresses (Online).* [ISSN: 2153-5124] 1991. 3x/yr. Gerard Bedouk Publishing, Inc., 117 W 58th St, Lower Level, New York, NY 10019. Adv. *Aud.:* Sa.

This magazine, reviewed in prior editions, has now ceased to be published in print; its web site (www.weddingdresses.com) remains, providing subscription information, a shopping directory organized by region, and the features previously in the print edition. A new print magazine entitled *Your Engagement 101* has emerged, with a per issue price of $5.99 (along with its web site, www.yourengagement101.com).

■ WORLD WIDE WEB

See also Business; Communications; Computer Science and Automation; Electronics; Engineering and Technology; and Library Periodicals sections.

Sasha Bishop, Librarian, Technical College of the Lowcountry, 921 Ribaut Rd. Beaufort, SC 29902; sbishop@tcl.edu

Introduction

In recent years the study of the World Wide Web has branched into many directions, making this an exciting time to be involved in Web-related collection development and research. Serial publications devoted to the subject of the Web encompass more than discussions of computers and networks. They explore social media, smartphones, cloud computing, and new developments in storage, networking, software, and hardware. While some of the publications reviewed here touch on all of the aforementioned subjects, many have specific focuses and audiences. This chapter includes publications that do some combination of

the following: present research on the technology and applications that power and define the web; examine the intersection of the Web with areas such as business, education, government, entertainment, and the law; review websites and online tools; assist industry professionals in keeping on top of the field and in making purchasing decisions; and report Web-related news and trends. Because the study of the Web touches so many fields and so many library users, there is something here for every type of library, including public libraries serving the general computer user, academic libraries at institutions with programs in computer science and information science, school media centers, and special collections serving Internet researchers and computer industry professionals.

Basic Periodicals

First Monday, I E E E Internet Computing, Internet Research, The Scout Report, Wired.

Basic Abstracts and Indexes

Academic Search Premier, Computer Science Index, INSPEC, Reader's Guide to Periodical Literature, ScienceDirect.

5300. *A C M Transactions on Internet Technology.* [ISSN: 1533-5399] 2001. q. Free to members; Non-members, USD 195. Ed(s): Patrick McDaniel, Roma Simon. Association for Computing Machinery, Inc., 2 Penn Plz, Ste 701, New York, NY 10121; acmhelp@acm.org; http://www.acm.org. Refereed. *Indexed:* ABIn, C&ISA, CerAb, CompR, EngInd. *Aud.:* Ac, Sa.

A publication of the Association for Computing Machinery, *Transactions on Internet Technology* (TOIT) "publishes original research papers in all areas of network and web systems, digital public policy, and other technically oriented issues on the design, use, and services of the Internet." The editorial staff of *TOIT* hail from computer science departments and companies in an array of nations, and represent an equally impressive range of computer-related specialties, including network management, mobile computing, data management, and e-commerce. The articles are highly technical and thoroughly referenced. Contact information for authors is provided, as well as information on the grants, awards, and projects that supported each work. Recent issues feature articles on cloud computing infrastructures, the middleware platform Juno, and XML keyword queries. Recent representative articles include "One-Time Cookies: Preventing Session Hijacking Attacks with Stateless Authentication Tokens" and "Using Priced Options to Solve the Exposure Problem in Sequential Auctions."

Recommended for academic libraries serving computer science and engineering programs, and any collection serving researchers in the field of Internet technology.

5301. *A C M Transactions on the Web.* [ISSN: 1559-1131] 2007. q. Free to members; Non-members, USD 165. Ed(s): Marc Najork. Association for Computing Machinery, Inc., 2 Penn Plz, Ste 701, New York, NY 10121; acmhelp@acm.org; http://www.acm.org. Refereed. *Indexed:* C&ISA, CerAb. *Aud.:* Ac, Sa.

A publication of the Association for Computing Machinery (ACM), *Transactions on the Web* (TWEB) features research on "Web content, applications, use, and related enabling technologies." *TWEB*'s editor-in-chief is principle researcher with Microsoft Research, and its authors and editors represent a variety of nationalities, educational institutions and corporate research facilities. Subjects include web page design and accessibility, search engines, and servers. Articles from recent issues include "Measuring the Visual Complexities of Web Pages," "Cache-Based Query Processing for Search Engines," and "HTML Automatic Table Layout." Web site usability is a frequent topic; the article "Progress on Website Accessibility," for example, addresses steps taken (or not taken) by various websites to render themselves more accessible to users with disabilities.

This publication is recommended for academic libraries serving computer science and Web design programs and for special libraries serving research endeavors related to the Web.

5302. *The CyberSkeptic's Guide to Internet Research.* [ISSN: 1085-2417] 1995. 10x/yr. USD 194.95 (Individuals, USD 132.95). Ed(s): Sheri R Lanza. Information Today, Inc., 143 Old Marlton Pike, Medford, NJ 08055; custserv@infotoday.com; http://www.infotoday.com. Illus. Sample. *Indexed:* I15, ISTA. *Aud.:* Ga, Sa.

The CyberSkeptic's Guide to Internet Research, a print newsletter published by Information Today, Inc., is devoted to the review of various websites and trending Web-related topics. The *Guide* "provides concise, practical information and expresses strong opinions." Though the authors (mainly librarians and specialists in Internet research) certainly express a healthy skepticism, an equal amount of enthusiasm for low-cost or free web resources is evident in the publication. In the lengthiest reviews, major websites are explored in depth. A recent examination of the World Bank's *Open Knowledge Repository*, for example, includes a description of the searches the author attempted and an evaluation of the site's user-friendliness, advanced search features, and availability of metadata. Issues also include a "Specialty Scans" section offering brief reviews of sites in the areas of Business/Finance, International, Legal/Government, News/Media, and Technical/Medical. The "Ready Reference" section takes on hot topics?recent issues covered in this section include digital rights management and free online learning sites like Coursera. Other regular columns include "Knowing Nonprofits" and "Seriously Search Engines."

This publication will be useful to large public libraries and any institution serving information professionals looking to stay on top of Web resources.

5303. *e-Service Journal: a journal of electronic services in the public and private sectors.* [ISSN: 1528-8226] 2001. 3x/yr. USD 180 (print & online eds.). Ed(s): Ramesh Venkataraman. Indiana University Press, 601 N Morton St, Bloomington, IN 47404; journals@indiana.edu; http://iupress.indiana.edu. Illus. Sample. Refereed. Circ: 100. Reprint: PSC. *Indexed:* A22, ABIn, B01, E01. *Aud.:* Ga, Ac, Sa.

Indiana University Press's *e-Service Journal* "publishes research on the design, delivery, and impact of electronic services via a variety of computing applications and communications technologies. It offers both private and public sector perspectives and explores new approaches in e-business and e-government." The publication's editors, advisory board, and contributors hail largely from business and computer science programs. Many *e-Service* articles discuss the progress made and barriers encountered in the adoption of e-services in contexts such as government information systems and large-scale public sector projects. Articles published in the last few years have addressed e-voting, the IRS's e-file system, Internet banking, and biometrics. Representative articles in the Summer, 2012 issue (the most recent issue published at the time of this review) include "A Model for E-voting Systems Evaluation Based on International Standards: Definition and Experimental Validation" and "Increasing the Adoption of E-Procurement Services at the Municipal Level."

This refereed journal is a useful publication for anyone interested in the Web's role in the areas of business and government. Recommended for large public libraries and academic and special libraries serving researchers in business and government.

Educause Review. See Computers and Information Technology/Professional Journals section.

5304. *EFFector Online Newsletter.* Former titles (until 2002): *EFFector;* (until 1997): *EFFector Online;* (until 1991): *E F F News.* 1991. irreg. 1-4/mo. Free. Ed(s): Stanton McCandlish. Electronic Frontier Foundation, 454 Shotwell St., San Francisco, CA 94110; information@eff.org; http://www.eff.org/. *Aud.:* Ga, Ac, Sa.

The title banner on the *EFFector* homepage includes the following definition: "effector: n, Computer Sci. A device for producing a desired change." This online newsletter published by the Electronic Frontier Foundation, an organization that pursues legal cases in the arena of digital rights, makes no secret of its strong advocacy bent. EFF's advisory board is composed of lawyers, digital rights experts, website creators, and computer industry luminaries. *EFFector* covers issues related to surveillance, online privacy and security, and digital free speech. Headlines from the second April, 2013 issue include "Congress Wants to Make CFAA Penalties Worse — We Need to Stop Them," and "Busting Myths from CISPA Supporters." Issues also include news updates from EFF ("Are You a Teenager Who Reads News Online? According

to the Justice Department, You May Be a Criminal"), a section of "Mini-links" to related stories on other websites, and, on occasion, information on EFF legal cases. Not all articles list an author, but those that do link to biographical information. The newsletter is freely available via the EFF website (https://www.eff.org/effector) but may also be sent to users via email if desired. Back issues are also available online.

A valuable source of passionately opinionated news focused on digital rights-related topics, not to mention an extremely entertaining read, this free resource should be of interest to anyone following the uneasy marriage of law and the digital frontier.

eWEEK. See Computers and Information Technology/Popular Titles section.

5305. *First Monday (Chicago).* [ISSN: 1396-0466] 1996. m. Free. Ed(s): Edward J Valauskas, Rishab Aiyer Ghosh. First Monday Editorial Group, c/o Edward Valauskas, Chief Editor, 9480 Lakeview, PO Box 638, Bridgman, MI 49106. Illus. Refereed. Circ: 314559. *Indexed:* BRI, CBRI, MLA-IB, P61, SSA. *Bk. rev.:* 5-10, 500-1,500 words. *Aud.:* Ga, Ac.

Published by the University of Illinois at Chicago University Library, *First Monday*'s editorial board and contributors are a truly international group. "One of the first openly accessible, peer-reviewed journals on the Internet, solely devoted to the Internet," *First Monday* has published articles from over 30 countries during its history and covers a variety of Internet-related topics. The open source movement, social networking, open online courses, and scholarly communication through electronic means are all frequent subjects. While some articles explore technical issues, many focus on the cultural importance of various Internet technologies and trends. Articles often investigate the behavior of Internet users; the intersection of the Internet and media; and how various forms of technology and Web-based applications are used in specific projects and initiatives in education, politics, and research. Recent article titles include "Scientists' Use of Social Media: The Case of Researchers at the University of the Philippines Los Ba?os" and "Assigning Wikipedia Editing: Triangulation toward Understanding University Student Engagement." Online archives of *First Monday* date back to 1996, making it a valuable resource for the history of the Internet. Current and back issues are accessible at http://firstmonday.org/index. This title is enthusiastically recommended for public and academic libraries.

5306. *I E E E Internet Computing.* [ISSN: 1089-7801] 1997. bi-m. USD 1185; USD 1480 combined subscription (print & online eds.). Ed(s): Fred Douglis. Institute of Electrical and Electronics Engineers, 445 Hoes Ln, Piscataway, NJ 08854; contactcenter@ieee.org; http://www.ieee.org. Illus., index, adv. Refereed. Vol. ends: Dec. *Indexed:* A22, C&ISA, CerAb, CompLI, EngInd, I15, RiskAb. *Aud.:* Ac, Sa.

A publication of the Institute of Electrical and Electronics Engineers (IEEE), *IEEE Internet Computing (IC)* "covers all aspects of Internet computing, from programming and standards to security and networking." In the call for papers at the beginning of each issue it is noted that *IC*'s readers are "primarily practicing engineers and academics who are looking for material that introduces new technology and broadens familiarity with current topics" and that "strictly theoretical or mathematical papers" are not the focus of the publication. Guest editors representing a variety of specialties in computing begin each issue with an introduction to that issue?s theme. The Jan/Feb 2013 *IC*, for example, focuses primarily on the problem of sustainability as it relates to information and communications technology, with articles examining the energy consumption of various network architectures and the use of renewable energy sources to power data centers and cellular networks. The columns and departments comprising the rest of each issue take on various trends in technology and the Internet. The editorial calendar at the back of each issue gives a snapshot of upcoming topics, including smart cities, mobile Internet, and identity and privacy in social networks.

IC's editorial musings on the future of the Internet coupled with lengthier articles on current trends in computing technology make for an entertaining and informative read on developments in the field. Useful for both researchers and practitioners in the industry, this publication is recommended for academic libraries serving web design and computer science programs and any library serving industry professionals. In additional to the print edition, users may subscribe to a digital edition at http://www.computer.org/portal/web/computingnow/internetcomputing.

5307. *International Journal of Web Information Systems.* [ISSN: 1744-0084] 2005. q. EUR 539 combined subscription in Europe (print & online eds.); USD 679 combined subscription in the Americas (print & online eds.); GBP 389 combined subscription in the UK & elsewhere (print & online eds.). Ed(s): David Taniar, Dr. Ismail Khalil. Emerald Group Publishing Ltd., Howard House, Wagon Ln, Bingley, BD16 1WA, United Kingdom; emerald@emeraldinsight.com; http://www.emeraldinsight.com. Sample. Refereed. Reprint: PSC. *Indexed:* C&ISA, CerAb. *Aud.:* Ac, Sa.

The mission of the *International Journal of Web Information Systems* (*IJWIS*) is "to be a source for Web Information Systems research and development, and to serve as an outlet for facilitating communication and networking among Web Information Systems researchers and professionals across academics, government, industry, researchers, and students." *IJWIS* boasts an international group of editors, associate editors, and editorial advisory board members who primarily represent university computer science departments. Issues are comprised of both survey papers and regular research papers. Topics range from database security to social media communities to Internet privacy concerns. Recent articles include "A Survey on Cloud-Based Sustainability Governance Systems" and "NoSQL Databases: A Step to Database Scalability in Web Environment." Detailed abstracts describe the purpose, design, findings, and value of the work. Information is also provided on the various grants used to support the work, and author information is included at the end of most of the articles.

This publication is recommended for academic and research libraries with computer science and engineering or computer and information science collections.

5308. *International Journal of Web Services Research: an international source for researchers and engineers in the field of web services.* [ISSN: 1545-7362] 2004. q. USD 625 (Individuals, USD 220). Ed(s): Liang-Jie Zhang. I G I Global, 701 E Chocolate Ave, Ste 200, Hershey, PA 17033; cust@igi-global.com; http://www.igi-global.com. Refereed. *Indexed:* A22, ABIn, C&ISA, CerAb, E01, EngInd. *Aud.:* Ac, Sa.

A publication of the Information Resources Management Association, the *International Journal of Web Services Research* (*IJWSR*) "is designed to be a valuable resource providing leading technologies, development, ideas, and trends to an international readership of researchers and engineers in the field of Web Services." *IJWSR*'s editor-in-chief is Senior Vice President, Chief Scientist, and Director of Research at Kingdee International Software Group, and its editorial review board represents many nations. The publication covers a variety of topics related to the Web, including Web service architecture, security, the mathematical foundations of computing, and quality of Web services. An editorial preface describes the theme of the issue, and author information included at the end of each paper details author interests and current research. A recent issue focusing on services composition, testing, and invocation includes papers entitled "An Optimal and Complete Algorithm for Automatic Web Service Composition" and "A Scalable Multi-Tenant Architecture for Business Process Executions."

This publication is a good fit for academic and research libraries with computer science or web engineering collections.

5309. *Internet Research.* Formerly (until 1993): *Electronic Networking.* [ISSN: 1066-2243] 1991. 5x/yr. EUR 3409 combined subscription in Europe (print & online eds.); USD 3919 combined subscription in the Americas (print & online eds.); GBP 2449 combined subscription in the UK & elsewhere (print & online eds.). Ed(s): Jim Jansen. Emerald Group Publishing Ltd., Howard House, Wagon Ln, Bingley, BD16 1WA, United Kingdom; emerald@emeraldinsight.com; http://www.emeraldinsight.com. Illus., index. Sample. Refereed. Vol. ends: Dec. Reprint: PSC. *Indexed:* A01, A22, ABIn, C&ISA, CerAb, CompLI, E01, I15, ISTA, P02, RiskAb. *Aud.:* Ac, Sa.

The purpose of *Internet Research* is to "describe, assess and foster understanding of the role of wide-area, multi-purpose computer networks, such as the internet." Its editorial board members represent a range of nationalities and institutions, with the majority coming from corporations or schools of business or computer science located in the U.S., the U.K., and China. Articles in this refereed publication are thoroughly referenced, and often focus on a particular type of web page or service, such as blogs, virtual knowledge sharing communities, and social networking sites. User behavior is a frequent topic and is examined in relation to online gaming, e-commerce and advertising outreach, and social bookmarking and knowledge sharing. Recent articles include "The Determinants of Consumer Behavior Towards Email Advertisement," "The Influence of the Components of Storytelling Blogs on Readers' Travel Intentions," and "Public Contributions to Private-Collective Systems: The Case of Social Bookmarking." Article abstracts providing insight into the purpose, practical implications, and value of each paper are included. Author information follows each piece and includes, in most cases, previously published research and contact information. Information about the grants and financial support for each study is also provided. Given the publication's price, *Internet Research* is recommended mainly for large academic libraries and research libraries with a focus on Web design and Internet research.

5310. *Network World.* Formerly (until 1986): *On Communications.* [ISSN: 0887-7661] 1984. w. USD 129 domestic (Free to qualified personnel). Ed(s): John Dix. Network World Inc., 492 Old Connecticut Path, Framingham, MA 01701; editorialinquiry@nww.com. Illus., adv. Sample. Circ: 170075 Controlled. Vol. ends: Dec. *Indexed:* A22, ABIn, B01, B03, BRI, I15. *Bk. rev.:* 3-4, 200 words. *Aud.:* Ga, Sa.

Published by Network World, a company owned by International Data Group (IDG), the trade magazine *Network World* presents news and articles related to the tech industry, "with an editorial focus on delivering news, opinion and analytical tools for key decision makers who architect, deploy and manage business solutions." Recent topics include cloud technology, enterprise social networking, mobile device overload, and the future of Ethernet. Product reviews and advertisements comprise a large part of each issue, making it a good resource for industry professionals in charge of product decisions. Main articles focus on large products, such as authentication services and network management suites, while smaller pieces offer scans of technology useful for specific consumers or purposes (e.g., gadgets for small businesses). *NW* also features interviews with industry movers and shakers. The *NW* website (http://www.networkworld.com/) provides content from the magazine as well as regularly updated and departments.

Although it is primarily aimed at network IT professionals, *NW* will also be helpful to computer-savvy readers wanting to stay abreast of current trends in computing. Recommended for large public libraries and any collection serving IT professionals.

5311. *The Scout Report.* [ISSN: 1092-3861] 1994. w. Free. University of Wisconsin at Madison, Computer Sciences Department, 1210 West Dayton St, Madison, WI 53706; lab@cs.wisc.edu ; http://www.cs.wisc.edu/. *Aud.:* Ems, Hs, Ac.

The Scout Report is a free online publication that "provides a fast, convenient way to stay informed of valuable STEM and humanities resources on the Internet." The signature publication of the Internet Scout Research Group (part of the University of Wisconsin-Madison's College of Letters and Sciences), the *Scout Report* has been highlighting various free online resources and tools since 1994. According to the *Report*'s "About Us" and "Selection Criteria" pages, a team of librarians and subject specialists investigate and annotate each resource based on content, authority, information maintenance, presentation, availability, and cost. Issues include brief reviews of websites in the areas of General Interest or Research and Education, plus two network tools. In the May 31 issue, the site reviews include the National Air and Space Museum's online educational resources (Research and Education); the University of Florida's Herbarium Collections Catalog (General Interest); and the time management tool RescueTime and the opinion-sharing service Thumb (Network Tools). Full *Scout Report* back issues are also accessible through the site, but readers in search of resources for specific subjects will want to take advantage of the searchable archives, where users can perform keyword searches or browse by LOC subject heading to locate previously reviewed sites.

This is a great resource for librarians (particularly those working in academic libraries or K-12 media centers), teachers, and anyone who has trouble staying on top of the many free web resources popping up daily. Recommended for academic and school libraries.

5312. Wired. [ISSN: 1059-1028] 1993. m. USD 14.99. Ed(s): Evan Hansen, Marty Cortinas. Conde Nast Publications Inc., Wired Ventures Ltd., 520 Third St, 3rd Fl, San Francisco, CA 94107; http://www.condenast.com. Illus., adv. Sample. Vol. ends: Dec. *Indexed:* A22, ABS&EES, ASIP, BRI, BrArAb, C&ISA, CerAb, I15, MLA-IB, P02. *Bk. rev.:* 5-8, 100 words. *Aud.:* Hs, Ga.

The Conde Nast publication *Wired* covers not just the Internet but all things digital, delving into pop culture, media, politics, science, business, and technology at large. The reader never knows what eclectic topics they will find between the covers of *Wired*. The April, 2013 issue, for example, focuses largely on new trends in TV-viewing but also features the articles "How Jimmy Wales' Wikipedia Harnessed the Web as a Force for Good," "Book Publishers Scramble to Rewrite Their Future," and "How the Science of Swarms Can Help Us Fight Cancer and Predict the Future." In addition to feature articles *Wired* includes regular columns and departments covering news and trends in technology, entertainment, and more. Much of the content of the magazine is available on the regularly updated *Wired website* at http://www.wired.com/magazine/, and digital editions are available for download to various tablets. This is a glossy, colorful, ad-heavy publication that makes for entertaining reading on a variety of subjects.

Recommended for public library collections as well as high school media centers.

■ ZOOLOGY

General/Entomology/Herpetology/Invertebrates/Mammalogy

See also Biology; Birds; Ecology; Fish, Fisheries, and Aquaculture; and Marine Science and Technology sections.

Reed Lowrie, Science Reference and Cartographic Librarian, Cabot Science Library, Harvard University, 1 Oxford St., Cambridge, MA 02138

Introduction

"In every Animal there is a world of wonders; each is a Microcosme or a world in itself."

—Edward Tyson (1650–1708)

Zoology is the branch of the biological sciences that deals with animals as integrated organisms, from one-cell creatures up through the nonhuman primates. While there is considerable overlap with genetics, molecular and cellular biology, and other branches of the life sciences, the titles in this section all deal with the entire animal and in many cases with the animal's relationship to its environment. Because the animal kingdom is so complex, the discipline has through the years formed smaller divisions to reflect this complexity.

In light of these divisions, this section includes five subdivisions: General, Entomology, Herpetology, Invertebrates, and Mammalogy. Since there are separate sections in this volume for birds and for fish, fisheries, and aquaculture, titles dealing with ornithology and ichthyology have not been included in the zoology section. Please consult those sections for the appropriate journals in those fields.

Most of the listed titles will only be relevant to academic and the largest public libraries, as they are written by and for specialists in the field. However, some of the journals are somewhat less technical, and undergraduates and general readers will find these titles approachable. I have tried to note these titles in their descriptions.

Once again the field's literature has remained fairly stable since the last edition of this volume. Online features continue to evolve and expand for many titles, and most journals are now publishing a significant number of completed articles online well in advance of print publication. The majority of journals are also leveraging the possibilities of online publishing and are including

supplemental material relevant to certain articles (data sets, additional figures and charts, field notes, and the like). These features, as well as the convenience and timeliness of the online versions, make them preferable for all but the most traditional users.

Basic Periodicals

Animal Behaviour, Annual Review of Entomology, Behavioral Ecology, Herpetologica, Integrative and Comparative Biology, The Journal of Experimental Biology, Journal of Experimental Zoology. Part B, Systematic Biology, Mammal Review.

Basic Abstracts and Indexes

Biological Abstracts, Biological Abstracts/RRM, Biological and Agricultural Index, Biology Digest, Current Contents/Life Sciences, Zoological Record.

General

The American Naturalist. See Ecology section.

5313. Animal Behaviour. Former titles (until 1958): *British Journal of Animal Behaviour;* (until 1953): *Bulletin of Animal Behaviour.* [ISSN: 0003-3472] 1938. m. EUR 1644. Ed(s): Kris Bruner, Angela Turner. Elsevier Ltd, 32 Jamestown Rd, Camden, London, NW1 7BY, United Kingdom; corporate.sales@elsevier.com; http://www.elsevier.com. Illus., index, adv. Sample. Refereed. Microform: PMC; PQC. Reprint: PSC. *Indexed:* A01, A22, Agr, AnBeAb, BRI, C45, E01, FR, FS&TA, IndVet, MLA-IB, OceAb, P02, PsycInfo. *Bk. rev.:* Occasional, 500-1,400 words. *Aud.:* Ac, Sa.

Animal Behaviour publishes papers concerning all facets of animal behavior, including that of humans. The journal primarily contains original research papers, and preference is given to those papers that are considered likely to interest the broad readership of the journal and that test explicit hypotheses rather than those that are merely descriptive. In addition, review articles on fundamental issues in behavior are often published. There is a "Commentaries" section, with brief pieces on issues of general importance to the discipline, including methodology, statistics, and ethics. The online edition of the title includes a "Forum" section where critiques of published papers are posted, and a space is provided for exchanges among scholars regarding issues relevant to the study of behavior. A large number of papers are provided online ahead of print publication. Beginning in late 2009, the journal adopted a double-blind peer-review process. This title should be considered nearly essential for academic libraries.

5314. Behavioral Ecology. [ISSN: 1045-2249] 1990. bi-m. EUR 800. Ed(s): Dr. Mark Elgar, Iain Couzin. Oxford University Press, 2001 Evans Rd, Cary, NC 27513; http://www.oxfordjournals.org. Sample. Refereed. Reprint: PSC. *Indexed:* A01, A22, AnBeAb, C45, E01, IndVet, PsycInfo. *Aud.:* Ac, Sa.

This journal covers all aspects of behavioral ecology, including empirical and theoretical work. The complete range of organisms is covered, comprising plants, invertebrates, vertebrates, and humans. *Behavioral Ecology* considers the field broadly, dealing with "the use of ecological and evolutionary processes to explain the occurrence and adaptive significance of behavior patterns," as well as "the use of behavioral processes to predict ecological patterns" and "empirical, comparative analyses relating behavior to the environment in which it occurs." Original articles, review articles, and a forum section with commentaries on recent issues are all included. The official journal of the International Society for Behavioral Ecology, the title has been gaining in prominence and should be considered by academic libraries. Articles are appropriate for undergraduates through specialists. Online material appears in advance of print publication. Lay summaries are provided for each article for the general reader, a feature this reviewer would like to see other journals adopt.

5315. *Behavioral Ecology and Sociobiology.* [ISSN: 0340-5443] 1976. m. EUR 4897 (print & online eds.). Ed(s): Dr. Tatiana Czeschlik. Springer, Tiergartenstr 17, Heidelberg, 69121, Germany. Adv. Refereed. Microform: PQC. Reprint: PSC. *Indexed:* A22, AbAn, Agr, AnBeAb, C45, CJPI, E01, FR, IndVet, OceAb, P02, PsycInfo. *Aud.:* Ac, Sa.

Behavioral Ecology and Sociobiology publishes original research papers and occasional review articles "dealing with quantitative empirical and theoretical studies in the analysis of animal behavior on the level of the individual, population[,] and community. Special emphasis is placed on the proximate mechanisms, ultimate functions[,] and evolution of ecological adaptations of behavior." A "Methods" section was recently added, dealing with statistical procedures and problems. Articles are generally seven to ten pages long, and are appropriate for advanced undergraduates through specialists.

5316. *Biological Bulletin.* Formerly (until 1899): *Zoological Bulletin.* [ISSN: 0006-3185] 1897. bi-m. USD 470 (Individuals, USD 210). Ed(s): James L. Olds, Ms. Carol Schachinger. Marine Biological Laboratory, 7 MBL St, Woods Hole, MA 02543; http://www.mbl.edu. Illus., index, adv. Sample. Refereed. Circ: 1300. Microform: PMC; PQC. *Indexed:* A01, A22, AnBeAb, C45, IndVet, OceAb, P02. *Aud.:* Ac, Sa.

This title publishes experimental research on a wide range of biological topics and organisms. Papers include investigations in the fields of neurobiology and behavior, physiology and biomechanics, ecology and evolution, development and reproduction, cell biology, symbiosis, and systematics. Contents are primarily research papers, but shorter research notes are also included, as well as occasional review articles and symposia. Published by the Marine Biological Laboratory in Woods Hole, Massachusetts, the journal is primarily concerned with marine organisms. Although written for specialists, the articles are accessible to the educated lay reader and generally well written. The online version includes video and data supplements.

5317. *Canadian Journal of Zoology.* Formerly (until 1950): *Canadian Journal of Research. Section D: Zoological Sciences;* Which superseded in part (in 1935): *Canadian Journal of Research.* [ISSN: 0008-4301] 1929. m. CAD 1850. Ed(s): M B Fenton, Dr. Helga Guderley. N R C Research Press, 1200 Montreal Rd, Bldg M-55, Ottawa, ON K1A 0R6, Canada; pubs-cnrc.gc.ca; http://pubs.nrc-cnrc.gc.ca. Illus., index, adv. Refereed. Circ: 1125. Vol. ends: Dec. Microform: MML; PMC; PQC. *Indexed:* A01, A22, Agr, AnBeAb, C37, C45, CBCARef, E01, EngInd, IndVet, MLA-IB, OceAb, S25. *Aud.:* Ac, Sa.

This journal publishes in the general fields of behavior, biochemistry and physiology, developmental biology, ecology, genetics, morphology and ultrastructure, parasitology and pathology, and systematics and evolution. Papers are published in English and French, and include articles reporting on original research as well as shorter notes on research and comments on papers previously published in the journal. In addition, review articles occasionally appear. Articles are required to report on significant new findings of general zoological interest. Coverage is broad, and articles are accessible to undergraduates and educated lay readers as well as to specialists. Published by the National Research Council of Canada, the online version includes supplementary material such as data sets, graphs, and tables.

5318. *Frontiers in Zoology.* [ISSN: 1742-9994] 2004. irreg. Free. Ed(s): Diethard Tautz, Jurgen Heinze. BioMed Central Ltd., 236 Gray's Inn Rd, London, WC1X 8HB, United Kingdom; info@biomedcentral.com; http://www.biomedcentral.com. Adv. Refereed. *Indexed:* A01, AnBeAb. *Bk. rev.:* Number and length vary. *Aud.:* Ac, Sa.

An online-only, open-access title supported by the Deutsche Zoologische Gesellschaft, one of the world's largest and oldest zoological societies, *Frontiers in Zoology* publishes a wide range of article types, including research articles, book reviews, commentaries, debate articles, hypotheses, methodology articles, review articles, and short reports. The journal aims to present zoology as "an integrative discipline encompassing the most diverse aspects of animal life, from the level of the gene to the level of the ecosystem." Taking advantage of the online platform, links are provided for citation searching on Google Scholar, for other articles by the same authors, and for readers to post and read comments on the published articles. Content is specialized, but most papers should be accessible to advanced undergraduates. URL: www.frontiersinzoology.com

5319. *Integrative & Comparative Biology.* Formerly (until 2002): *American Zoologist.* [ISSN: 1540-7063] 1961. bi-m. EUR 680. Ed(s): Harold Heatwole. Oxford University Press, Great Clarendon St, Oxford, OX2 6DP, United Kingdom; enquiry@oup.co.uk; http://www.oxfordjournals.org/. Illus., adv. Sample. Refereed. Microform: PQC. Reprint: PSC. *Indexed:* A01, A22, Agr, AnBeAb, BRI, C45, E01, IndVet, P02. *Bk. rev.:* Number and length vary. *Aud.:* Ac, Sa.

Formerly *American Zoologist,* this is one of the important journals in the study of zoology. Individual issues are generally organized around one or two common themes—for example, "The Biomechanics and Behavior of Gliding Flight"—and contain invited papers. While original papers are sometimes published, the primary content is review articles and synthetic papers of general interest to comparative biologists. The journal's mission is to "integrate the varying disciplines in this broad field, while maintaining the highest scientific quality." The method of publishing subject-based issues makes this title especially useful for undergraduates, even though the primary audience is specialists. An essential purchase for academic libraries.

Journal of Animal Ecology. See Ecology section.

Journal of Animal Science. See Agriculture section.

5320. *The Journal of Experimental Biology.* Formerly (until 1930): *British Journal of Experimental Biology.* [ISSN: 0022-0949] 1923. s-m. USD 3488. Ed(s): Dr. Hans Hoppeler. The Company of Biologists Ltd., 140 Cowley Rd, Cambridge, CB4 0DL, United Kingdom; sales@biologists.com; http://www.biologists.org. Illus., index. Sample. Refereed. *Indexed:* A01, A22, AbAn, AnBeAb, C45, IndVet, P02. *Bk. rev.:* 0-1, 750-1,000 words. *Aud.:* Ac, Sa.

The Journal of Experimental Biology is the leading title in comparative animal physiology. It publishes articles on living organisms from the molecular and subcellular levels to the organism as a whole, and encourages the spread of knowledge and techniques across disciplinary boundaries. In addition to research articles, the journal publishes a section called "Inside JEB" that has short reports on highlighted articles from the journal. There is also an "Outside JEB" section that offers short summaries of subject-appropriate articles from other journals. A commentary section, book reviews, editorials, and historical articles are also included. The online version provides supplementary data, and a forum is sometimes linked to the commentaries. Although published by a nonprofit company, the title is expensive. Nevertheless it should be considered essential for most academic libraries, as the articles have broad disciplinary appeal and are accessible to a wide range of readers.

5321. *Journal of Experimental Zoology. Part B: Molecular and Developmental Evolution.* Supersedes in part (in 2003): *The Journal of Experimental Zoology.* [ISSN: 1552-5007] 1904. bi-m. Ed(s): Gunter P Wagner. John Wiley & Sons, Inc., 111 River St, MS 4-02, Hoboken, NJ 07030; info@wiley.com; http://www.wiley.com/WileyCDA/. Adv. *Indexed:* A22, C45, IndVet. *Aud.:* Ac, Sa.

An influential title in "evo-devo," this expensive journal should be considered by libraries that support such research. Articles "contribute to a causal understanding of the evolution of development and how development influences patterns of molecular and phenotypic evolution." Contents are primarily papers reporting on original research and tend to be more than ten pages long. Review articles, editorials, and commentaries also appear occasionally, and many articles appear online ahead of print publication, some with supplementary material. Only the most advanced undergraduates will find this title accessible, so purchase primarily with graduate students and faculty in mind.

5322. *The Journal of Wildlife Management.* Incorporates (in 2007): *Wildlife Society Bulletin;* Which superseded (in 1973): *Wildlife Society News;* Which was formerly (until 1952): *Wildlife Society Newsletter;* (until 1945): *Wildlife Society. Wartime Newsletter;* (until 1944): *Wildlife Society. Wildlife News.* [ISSN: 0022-541X] 1937. 9x/yr. GBP 669. Ed(s): Frank R Thompson. John Wiley & Sons, Inc., 111 River St, MS 4-02,

Hoboken, NJ 07030; info@wiley.com; http://onlinelibrary.wiley.com/. Illus., index. Refereed. Vol. ends: Oct. Microform: PQC. Reprint: PSC. *Indexed:* A01, A22, Agr, AnBeAb, BRI, C45, E01, IndVet, P02, RRTA, S25. *Bk. rev.:* 2-5, 600-2,500 words. *Aud.:* Ac, Sa.

This journal publishes original research papers on wildlife management issues as well as more general investigations on wildlife biology and ecology. Areas of interest include population studies, conservation, habitat use, nutrition, natural history, and research techniques, among others. Longer research articles as well as shorter research notes, editorials, and book reviews are included. Articles do not appear online prior to print, but supplemental material is added to selected articles online as appropriate. Articles are accessible to undergraduates and are of broad interest in the fields of biology, ecology, and zoology.

5323. Journal of Zoology. Formed by the 1987 merger of: *Journal of Zoology. Series A; Journal of Zoology. Series B;* Which incorporated (1833-1984): *Zoological Society of London. Transactions;* Both A & B superseded in part (in 1984): *Journal of Zoology;* Which was formerly (until 1965): *Zoological Society of London. Proceedings;* Which was formed by the 1944 merger of: *Zoological Society of London. Proceedings. Series A; Zoological Society of London. Proceedings. Series B.* [ISSN: 0952-8369] 1987. m. GBP 1443. Ed(s): Nigel Bennett. Wiley-Blackwell Publishing Ltd., The Atrium, Southern Gate, Chichester, PO19 8SQ, United Kingdom; customer@wiley.com; http://www.wiley.com/. Adv. Sample. Refereed. Reprint: PSC. *Indexed:* A01, A22, AbAn, Agr, AnBeAb, C45, E01, IndVet, OceAb, RRTA. *Aud.:* Ac, Sa.

Interdisciplinary work is the main focus of the *Journal of Zoology*. It primarily publishes original research in the areas of animal behavior, ecology, physiology, anatomy, developmental biology, evolution, systematics, genetics, and genomics, especially papers that focus on the interface between some of these areas. Articles tend to be six to nine pages long, and they should be accessible to most undergraduates. Longer review articles are published periodically. Many articles are published online ahead of their print publication. The journal also offers free semi-annual podcasts related to material published in the journal.

5324. Linnean Society. Zoological Journal: an international journal. Former titles (until 1969): *Linnean Society of London. Zoology Journal;* (until 1965): *Linnean Society. Proceedings. Zoology Journal;* Which superseded in part (in 1957): *Linnean Society of London. Transactions;* Which superseded in part (in 1936): *Linnean Society of London. Zoology. Transactions;* Which superseded in part (in 1875): *Linnean Society. Transactions.* [ISSN: 0024-4082] 1855. m. GBP 1974. Ed(s): Dr. Peter P Hayward. Wiley-Blackwell Publishing Ltd., The Atrium, Southern Gate, Chichester, PO19 8SQ, United Kingdom; customer@wiley.com; http://www.wiley.com/. Illus., adv. Sample. Refereed. Microform: BHP. Reprint: PSC. *Indexed:* A01, A22, AnBeAb, C45, E01, IndVet. *Bk. rev.:* 1. *Aud.:* Ac, Sa.

One of three titles published by the venerable Linnean Society, this journal publishes papers on systematics and evolutionary zoology. Both living and extinct animals are covered. The contents are primarily original research articles that tend to be quite long. Review articles are also occasionally published, and some issues also contain book reviews. The editors stress that they seek papers with a broad appeal to the zoological community. Articles do not appear online ahead of print, but online articles often do include supplementary resources.

5325. Physiological and Biochemical Zoology: ecological and evolutionary approaches. Formerly (until 1999): *Physiological Zoology.* [ISSN: 1522-2152] 1928. bi-m. USD 824 (print & online eds.). Ed(s): Patricia M Schulte, Kathleen M Gilmour. University of Chicago Press, 1427 E 60th St, Chicago, IL 60637; subscriptions@press.uchicago.edu; http://www.journals.uchicago.edu. Illus., index, adv. Sample. Refereed. Microform: PMC; PQC. Reprint: PSC. *Indexed:* A01, A22, AbAn, AnBeAb, C45, IndVet, OceAb. *Aud.:* Ac, Sa.

As is clear from the journal's title, animal physiology and biochemistry are the focus here. Original research is presented, with an emphasis on "studies that investigate the ecological and/or evolutionary aspects of physiological and biochemical mechanisms." Many subdisciplines are covered, including nutrition and digestion, epithelial and membrane transport, temperature

adaptation, locomotion and muscle function, sensory physiology, and many more. Content is mostly research papers, although there are also special collections of invited papers and brief technical comments. Papers are technical and aimed at specialists, but will be accessible to advanced undergraduates.

Systematic Biology. See Biology section.

5326. Zoologica Scripta: an international journal of systematic zoology. Supersedes (in 1971): *Arkiv for Zoologi;* Incorporates (in 1976): *Norwegian Journal of Zoology;* Which was formerly (until 1971): *Nytt Magasin for Zoologi;* Which superseded in part (in 1952): *Nytt Magasin for Naturvidenskapene;* Which was formerly (until 1935): *Magazin for Naturvidenskaberne.* [ISSN: 0300-3256] 1903. bi-m. GBP 1505. Ed(s): Per Sundberg. Wiley-Blackwell Publishing Ltd., The Atrium, Southern Gate, Chichester, PO19 8SQ, United Kingdom; customer@wiley.com; http://www.wiley.com/. Illus., adv. Sample. Refereed. Microform: PQC. Reprint: PSC. *Indexed:* A01, A22, AnBeAb, C45, E01. *Bk. rev.:* Occasional. *Aud.:* Ac, Sa.

A joint publication of the Norwegian Academy of Science and Letters and the Royal Swedish Academy of Sciences, *Zoologica Scripta* is one of the more important titles in systematic zoology. Original theoretical, empirical, and methodological articles are the bulk of the contents, with a scattering of review articles and book reviews and letters. Papers vary greatly in length and tend to be quite sophisticated. While advanced undergraduates may be able to tackle them, the primary audience will be graduate students and researchers. Articles appear online prior to print publication, often with additional supporting information.

Entomology

5327. Annual Review of Entomology. [ISSN: 0066-4170] 1956. a. USD 246 (print or online ed.). Ed(s): Samuel Gubins, May R Berenbaum. Annual Reviews, PO Box 10139, Palo Alto, CA 94303; service@annualreviews.org; http://www.annualreviews.org. Refereed. Microform: PQC. Reprint: PSC. *Indexed:* A01, A22, AbAn, Agr, AnBeAb, C45, IndVet, MLA-IB. *Aud.:* Ac, Sa.

One of the many Annual Reviews titles, this serial is a must for all medium- to large-sized academic libraries and would be considered a good choice by smaller libraries that seek to add some coverage of entomology to their collection. Papers are generally 15-page or longer review articles, covering all (nonsystematic) areas of the subject, including medical and economic entomology. Papers appear online long before the print volume appears, so libraries should consider electronic access.

5328. Bulletin of Entomological Research: containing original and review articles on economic entomology. [ISSN: 0007-4853] 1910. bi-m. GBP 1185. Ed(s): William Symondson. Cambridge University Press, The Edinburgh Bldg, Shaftesbury Rd, Cambridge, CB2 8RU, United Kingdom; journals@cambridge.org; http://www.cambridge.org/uk. Illus., adv. Refereed. Circ: 1700. Microform: BHP. Reprint: PSC. *Indexed:* A01, A22, AbAn, Agr, AnBeAb, C45, E01, IndVet. *Aud.:* Ac, Sa.

A longstanding title focused on applied entomology, this British journal is a leader in the field. Contains mainly original research papers on "insects, mites, ticks or other arthropods of economic importance in agriculture, forestry, stored products, biological control, medicine, animal health and natural resource management." Short communications appear frequently, and review articles occasionally. Articles are written for the specialist, but should be accessible to advanced undergraduates as well. One issue is made available free of charge in its entirety. Libraries that support agricultural, forestry, or applied entomology programs should consider purchasing this journal.

5329. Journal of Insect Physiology. [ISSN: 0022-1910] 1957. m. EUR 3407. Ed(s): D L Denlinger, F Pennacchio. Pergamon, The Blvd, Langford Ln, E Park, Kidlington, OX5 1GB, United Kingdom; JournalsCustomerServiceEMEA@elsevier.com; http://www.elsevier.com. Illus., adv. Sample. Refereed. Microform: MIM; PQC. *Indexed:* A01, A22, Agr, AnBeAb, C45, IndVet. *Aud.:* Ac, Sa.

A publication of the Entomological Society of America, this is the leading title in the physiology of insects and other arthropods. The journal covers "endocrinology, pheromones, neurobiology, physiological pharmacology, nutrition (food selection, digestion and absorption), homeostasis, excretion, reproduction[,] and behavior." Articles are primarily original research, with the occasional review article. Generally one or two special issues are published each year. The online version has a "graphical abstract" and a bullet-point list of highlights in addition to a traditional abstract. Highly technical writing and very specialized subject matter make this title appropriate for graduate students and faculty. A significant number of articles appear online prior to print.

5330. Systematic Entomology. Former titles (until 1976): *Journal of Entomology. Series B. Taxonomy & Systematics;* (until 1975): *Journal of Entomology. Series B. Taxonomy;* (until 1971): *Royal Entomological Society of London. Series B: Taxonomy. Proceedings; Stylops;* Which superseded in part (in 1936): *Royal Entomological Society of London. Proceedings;* Which was formerly (until 1933): *Entomological Society of London. Proceedings.* [ISSN: 0307-6970] 1932. q. GBP 1056. Ed(s): Peter S Cranston, Thomas J Simonsen. Wiley-Blackwell Publishing Ltd., The Atrium, Southern Gate, Chichester, PO19 8SQ, United Kingdom; customer@wiley.com; http://www.wiley.com/. Illus., index, adv. Sample. Refereed. Vol. ends: Oct/Dec. Microform: PQC. Reprint: PSC. *Indexed:* A01, A22, Agr, C45, E01. *Bk. rev.:* 0-3, 500-800 words. *Aud.:* Ac, Sa.

This journal publishes original research on insect taxonomy and systematics, encouraging papers of interest to a wider audience dealing with theoretical, genetic, agricultural, medical, and biodiversity issues. In addition to research articles, included are review articles, editorials, technical comments, and book and software reviews. Substantial "special virtual issues" are published online to coincide with the Entomological Society of America's annual meeting. Articles are very specialized; the primary audience is entomologists, although evolutionary biologists and zoologists will also find the journal useful.

Herpetology

5331. Herpetologica. [ISSN: 0018-0831] 1936. q. Free to members; USD 360 combined subscription domestic (print & online eds.). Ed(s): Daphne N Smith, Brad Moon. Herpetologists League, c/o Allen Press, PO Box 7065, Lawrence, KS 66044; herp@allenpress.com; http://www.herpetologistsleague.org. Illus., index. Refereed. Vol. ends: Dec. Microform: PQC. *Indexed:* A01, A22, AnBeAb, C45, E01, IndVet. *Aud.:* Ac, Sa.

Herpetologica publishes original papers dealing with the biology of amphibians and reptiles. It is one of the two major publications of the Herpetologists League, along with *Herpetological Monographs*. Original research is published, with emphasis given to theoretical or quantitative papers. Articles vary in length, with most being six to ten pages long. Although aimed toward specialists, articles are generally well written, and some will be accessible to undergraduates. One of the leading titles in the field.

5332. Herpetological Journal. Formerly (until 1985): *British Journal of Herpetology.* [ISSN: 0268-0130] 1948. q. Free to members. Ed(s): Eluned Price, Mr. Chris Barratt. British Herpetological Society, 11, Strathmore Pl, Montrose, Angus, DD10 8LQ, United Kingdom; info@thebhs.org; http://www.thebhs.org/. Adv. Refereed. *Indexed:* A22, AnBeAb, C45, IndVet. *Bk. rev.:* Number and length vary. *Aud.:* Ac, Sa.

Published by the British Herpetological Society, *Herpetological Journal* disseminates papers and features on a wide range of reptile and amphibian biology. Experimental, observational, and theoretical studies are published along with occasional reviews and book reviews. Content is appropriate for upper-level undergraduates and above, as well as the interested lay reader. Online content is available from 2005 forward, and a handful of online articles contain electronic appendices.

5333. Herpetological Review. Incorporates (1958-1966): *Ohio Herpetological Society. Newsletter.* [ISSN: 0018-084X] 1967. q. Free to members; Non-members, USD 25. Ed(s): Robert W Hansen. Society for the Study of Amphibians and Reptiles, Publications Secretary, PO Box 58517, Salt Lake City, UT 84158; ssar@herplit.com; http://www.ssarherps.org. Illus., adv. Refereed. *Indexed:* A22. *Bk. rev.:* Number and length vary. *Aud.:* Ac, Sa.

One of two publications of the Society for the Study of Amphibians and Reptiles. Along with the *Journal of Herpetology, Herpetological Review* is a hybrid journal, containing news features, commentaries, obituaries, book reviews, notes on geographic distribution, and "articles and notes of a semi-technical or non-technical nature." The journal is accessible to undergraduates and lay readers. No online version is available.

5334. Journal of Herpetology. Supersedes (in 1968): *Ohio Herpetological Society. Journal;* Which was formerly (until 1959): *Ohio Herpetological Society. Tri-Monthly Report.* [ISSN: 0022-1511] 1958. q. Free to members. Ed(s): Matthew Parris. Society for the Study of Amphibians and Reptiles, Publications Secretary, PO Box 58517, Salt Lake City, UT 84158; ssar@herplit.com; http://www.ssarherps.org. Illus. Refereed. *Indexed:* A01, A22, AnBeAb, C45, E01, IndVet. *Aud.:* Ac, Sa.

This is the scientific journal of the Society for the Study of Amphibians and Reptiles (*Herpetological Review* is the society's news journal). The journal publishes original research on the biology of amphibians and reptiles "with emphasis on behavior, biochemistry, conservation, ecology, evolution, morphology, physiology, and systematics." Articles are usually under ten pages long and are accessible to upper-level undergraduates and above. Recently sections on "Policy" and "Long-Term Perspectives" were added. Many issues contain articles grouped around a particular subtopic, such as herpetological methods, or herpetology in Brazil.

Invertebrates

5335. Invertebrate Biology. Former titles (until 1995): *American Microscopical Society. Transactions;* (until 1895): *American Microscopical Society. Proceedings;* (until 1892): *American Society of Microscopists. Proceedings.* [ISSN: 1077-8306] 1879. q. GBP 184. Ed(s): Bruno Pernet, Patrick D Reynolds. Wiley-Blackwell Publishing, Inc., 111 River St, Hoboken, NJ 07030; info@wiley.com; http://onlinelibrary.wiley.com/. Illus., adv. Sample. Refereed. Microform: PMC. Reprint: PSC. *Indexed:* A01, A22, Agr, AnBeAb, C45, E01, IndVet. *Aud.:* Ac, Sa.

One of the oldest journals in the United States, *Invertebrate Biology* has been published continuously, under various titles, since 1879. The title covers all aspects of invertebrate animals, including morphology and ultrastructure, genetics, phylogenetics and evolution, physiology and ecology, neurobiology, behavior and biomechanics, reproduction and development, and cell and molecular biology. Content is almost entirely original research papers of ten or more pages, and many of the articles have a microscopical component (the journal is published by the American Microscopical Society and the Division of Invertebrate Biology/Society of Integrative Biology). A large number of articles appear online prior to print and a very small number are provided free of charge.

5336. Malacologia. [ISSN: 0076-2997] 1962. irreg. USD 94 (Individuals, USD 71). Institute of Malacology, PO Box 385, Haddonfield, NJ 08033. Refereed. *Indexed:* A22, C45, OceAb. *Aud.:* Ac, Sa.

For libraries providing support for the study of mollusks, *Malacologia* is a title to own. The journal specializes in long papers and monographic treatments covering systematics, population ecology, genetics, molecular genetics, evolution, and phylogenetics. In addition to the long papers, shorter research notes, historical notes, and letters are also included. Issues from 2006 and earlier are freely available at the Biodiversity Heritage Library site.

Mammalogy

5337. American Journal of Primatology. [ISSN: 0275-2565] 1981. m. GBP 2131. Ed(s): Paul A Garber. John Wiley & Sons, Inc., 111 River St, MS 4-02, Hoboken, NJ 07030; info@wiley.com; http://www.wiley.com/WileyCDA/. Illus., adv. Refereed. Microform: PQC. Reprint: PSC. *Indexed:* A01, A22, AbAn, AnBeAb, BRI, C45, FR, IBSS, IndVet, PsycInfo, RRTA. *Bk. rev.:* Number and length vary. *Aud.:* Ac, Sa.

All aspects of primatology are covered in the official journal of the American Society of Primatologists, including "behavioral ecology, conservation, evolutionary biology, life history, demography, paleontology, physiology, endocrinology, genetics, molecular genetics, and psychobiology of the nonhuman primates." Contents are primarily original research articles, but also include review articles, commentaries, brief reports, research articles, and book and media reviews. Special topic-based issues are published several times each year. Articles are appropriate for upper-level undergraduates and above, and should be accessible to the educated lay reader. Articles appear online several months prior to print.

5338. *International Journal of Primatology.* [ISSN: 0164-0291] 1980. bi-m. EUR 1238 (print & online eds.). Ed(s): Joanna M Setchell. Springer New York LLC, 233 Spring St, New York, NY 10013; service-ny@springer.com; http://www.springer.com/. Adv. Refereed. Microform: PQC. Reprint: PSC. *Indexed:* A01, A22, Agr, AnBeAb, BRI, C45, E01, FR, IBSS, IndVet, P02, PsycInfo, RRTA. *Bk. rev.:* Number and length vary. *Aud.:* Ac, Sa.

The official publication of the International Primatological Society, the *International Journal of Primatology* is a "multidisciplinary forum devoted to current research in fundamental primatology." The journal gives special emphasis to articles that report on threatened or endangered species. Articles tend to be long and technical and, while accessible to advanced undergraduates, are most appropriate for graduate students and researchers. Some shorter reports are included, as are a good number of book reviews. Articles appear online in advance of print publication, sometimes with supplemental material.

5339. *Journal of Mammalian Evolution.* [ISSN: 1064-7554] 1993. q. EUR 439 (print & online eds.). Ed(s): John R Wible. Springer New York LLC, 233 Spring St, New York, NY 10013; service-ny@springer.com; http://www.springer.com/. Adv. Sample. Refereed. Microform: PQC. Reprint: PSC. *Indexed:* A01, A22, Agr, BRI, E01. *Bk. rev.:* Number and length vary. *Aud.:* Ac, Sa.

The official journal of the Society for the Study of Mammalian Evolution, the *Journal of Mammalian Evolution* describes itself as "a multidisciplinary forum devoted to studies on the comparative morphology, molecular biology, paleobiology, genetics, developmental and reproductive biology, biogeography, systematics, ethology and ecology, and population dynamics of mammals and the ways these diverse data can be analyzed for the reconstruction of mammalian evolution." Print issues contain a handful of articles each, ranging from a few pages to more than 20. A significant amount of material is initially published online, occasionally with supplemental material. In addition to original articles—based on both laboratory and field studies—the journal publishes the occasional review article, as well as a large number of book reviews.

5340. *Journal of Mammalogy.* [ISSN: 0022-2372] 1919. bi-m. USD 270 (print & online eds.); Free to members. Ed(s): Emily K Mueller, Edward J Heske. American Society of Mammalogists, c/o Dr H Duane Smith, Sec -Treas, Monte L Bean Life Science Museum, Provo, UT 84602; duane@museum,byu.edu; http://www.mammalogy.org. Illus., index. Refereed. Vol. ends: Nov. Microform: PMC; PQC. *Indexed:* A01, A22, Agr, AnBeAb, BRI, C45, E01, FR, IndVet, OceAb, P02, RRTA. *Bk. rev.:* 1-3, 800-2,100 words. *Aud.:* Ac, Sa.

Published by the American Society of Mammalogists, this journal presents original research on all aspects of the biology of mammals, including ecology, genetics, conservation, behavior, and physiology. Terrestrial as well as marine mammals are covered, and articles include reports on newly found species. In addition to research articles, the journal publishes society news, book reviews, and obituaries, and it occasionally groups articles together in a special feature section. A longstanding title, the *Journal of Mammalogy* is attractively priced and useful for undergraduates and general readers as well as specialists.

5341. *Mammal Review.* Formerly (until 1970): *Mammal Society. Bulletin.* [ISSN: 0305-1838] 1970. q. GBP 483. Ed(s): Nancy Jennings. Wiley-Blackwell Publishing Ltd., The Atrium, Southern Gate, Chichester, PO19 8SQ, United Kingdom; customer@wiley.com; http://www.wiley.com/. Adv. Sample. Refereed. Microform: PQC. Reprint: PSC. *Indexed:* A01, A22, Agr, AnBeAb, C45, E01, IndVet, P02, RRTA. *Aud.:* Ac, Sa.

The main publication of The Mammal Society, this British title covers all areas of mammalian biology and ecology. As the title suggests, the contents are mostly review articles, with an emphasis on "current theoretical and applied research on mammals, practical assessments of techniques for studying mammals, and large-scale considerations of the status, conservation[,] and management of animals." Short communications and original research are occasionally published. Articles are long, technical, and most suited to graduate students and above. Articles appear online long before print publication.

Marine Mammal Science. See Marine Science and Technology/Marine Biology section.

TITLE INDEX

The numbers in this index refer to entry numbers in the text, not page numbers. Titles in boldface have been designated basic periodicals in a given subject area.

J

S

SUBJECT INDEX

845